IMPORTANT NOTICES

Martindale-Hubbell® has used its best efforts in collecting and preparing material for inclusion in the **Martindale-Hubbell Law Directory** but cannot warrant that the information herein is complete or accurate, and does not assume, and hereby disclaims, any liability to any person for any loss or damage caused by errors or omissions in the **Martindale-Hubbell Law Directory** whether such errors or omissions result from negligence, accident or any other cause.

Lawyers providing information regarding themselves and their law firms for inclusion in the **Martindale-Hubbell Law Directory** are responsible for both the accuracy of the information submitted and compliance with local law and bar regulations.

The information contained in this Directory, including *Martindale-Hubbell Legal Ability Ratings*, is intended primarily for the use of lawyers and law firms in the practice of their profession. They may not be used without permission from, and acknowledgement of, Martindale-Hubbell in any advertisement or for any commercial, political or other purpose.

Omission of individual lawyer ratings should not be construed as unfavorable since Martindale-Hubbell does not undertake to develop ratings for every lawyer. In addition, certain lawyers have requested their ratings not be published while in other instances, definitive information has yet to be developed.

Some lawyers and law firms are omitted from the **Martindale-Hubbell Law Directory** by request while others are omitted because adequate information is not available.

EXPLANATORY NOTES AND SYMBOLS

"(IBA)" denotes a member of the International Bar Association.

MARTINDALE-HUBBELL® LAW DIRECTORY

—•—

ALPHABETICAL INDEX

—•—

SERVICES, SUPPLIERS, CONSULTANTS INDEX

MARTINDALE-HUBBELL
A Member of LEXIS Publishing™

LEXIS Publishing™
LEXIS®-NEXIS® • MARTINDALE-HUBBELL® • MATTHEW BENDER® • MICHIE™ • SHEPARD'S®

121 Chanlon Road, New Providence, NJ 07974 • Phone: 1-800-526-4902
Email: info@martindale.com • www.martindale.com • www.lawyers.com

Published by Martindale-Hubbell®, a Member of LEXIS® Publishing™

Louis J. Andreozzi, President and Chief Executive Officer
Carol D. Cooper, Publisher, Senior Vice President, Marketing and Product Development
Larry D. Thompson, Senior Vice President, U.S. Sales and Customer Relations
Andrew W. Meyer, Vice President, Administration
Vera Lang, Vice President and Chief Financial Officer
Dean Hollister, Vice President, Database Production
John Roney, Vice President, Chief Information Officer

International Standard Book Number: 1-56160-376-7 (Set)

Printed and bound in the United States of America
by R.R. Donnelley & Sons Company
Chicago, Illinois and Willard, Ohio

ISBN 1-56160-376-7

9 781561 603763

FOREWORD

Welcome to the 2000 edition of the **Martindale-Hubbell® Law Directory**, the world's leading guide to the legal profession. As we enter a new millennium, we look forward to a new century of service to the legal community across the nation and around the globe.

The **Martindale-Hubbell Law Directory** is the only reference to include virtually every attorney and law firm in the U.S. as well as international lawyers and firms. This new edition now covers more than 900,000 lawyers and firms in 170 countries.

This volume – the **Martindale-Hubbell Alphabetical Index** – provides instant access to all United States lawyers and firms in the database alphabetically by name. It is a helpful tool that enables users to locate a listing for attorneys or law firms in the geographically-arranged Lawyer Volumes even if they do not know their location.

These print volumes are part of an integrated legal networking tool spanning multiple media and delivery formats. For researchers who prefer the power and flexibility of electronic access, the 2000 **Law Directory** is also available in a CD-ROM version featuring advanced Folio VIEWS® 4.0 software, on LEXIS®-NEXIS® and lexis.com℠ and via the *Martindale-Hubbell Lawyer Locator* on the Internet.

The past year saw some exciting developments on the technology front. The *Martindale-Hubbell Lawyer Locator* at *www.martindale.com* continues to be the most popular lawyer directory on the Internet, with over 1.8 million searches a month. *www.lawyers.com* – our new Web site targeted at individuals and small businesses – is also garnering praise from media and users alike. This site is also the basis for the AOL Legal Web Center at www.aol.com/webcenters/legal. Usage of these new sites is growing exponentially.

In addition, we offer cost-effective *Lawyer HomePages* for small law firms within the U.S. as well as an entire menu of custom Web site services for larger firms. Last year also saw the expansion of our Web site offerings to include *International Lawyer HomePages* – bilingual Web site kits for our international subscribers.

You'll notice several new features and improvements to the print edition this year. The **Law Directory** now contains more than 392,468 Email addresses and 25,923 Web site addresses – more than any other source. And the **International Law Digest** now covers 80 countries, including a new section for Nigeria.

Martindale-Hubbell has a 132-year history of linking lawyers with clients around the world. The new millennium promises to be even more eventful, with technological developments preparing the way for exciting new ways to connect attorneys with those who need their services. As always, we encourage you to contact us with any ideas or suggestions, and thank you for your support.

Louis J. Andreozzi
President and Chief Executive Officer

MARTINDALE-HUBBELL®/LEXIS®-NEXIS® LEGAL ADVISORY BOARD

The Martindale-Hubbell/LEXIS-NEXIS Legal Advisory Board was formed to ensure that Martindale-Hubbell and LEXIS-NEXIS are responsive to the constantly changing needs of the legal profession. The following lawyers selected from the private, corporate and international sectors of the profession comprise the 1999-2000 Board.

MARTHA W. BARNETT of Holland & Knight, Tallahassee, Florida. Ms. Barnett is a former Chair of the House of Delegates of the American Bar Association, the first woman lawyer to be so honored, and has served on the ABA's Board of Governors. Currently, she is the President-Elect of the American Bar Association, to serve as such from August 1999 to July 2000, and to serve as President from July 2000 to August 2001.

ALLEN E. BRENNECKE of Harrison, Brennecke, Moore, Smaha & McKibben, Marshaltown, Iowa. Mr. Brennecke has served as a Member of the Board of Directors of the National Judicial College, President of the Iowa State Bar Association, a Member of the ABA House of Delegates since 1975 and its Chair, 1984-1986. His prior service to the ABA also includes four years on the Board of Governors and three years as Chair of the IOLTA Commission. He previously served on the Board of Editors of the American Bar Association Journal and served as Chair from 1989 to 1995.

BENJAMIN R. CIVILETTI of Venable, Baetjer, Howard & Civiletti, Washington, D.C. and Baltimore, Maryland. Mr. Civiletti is a former Attorney General of the United States under President Carter, 1979-1981. He is the former Chairman of the ABA Litigation Section and has been a member of the ABA House of Delegates since 1991. He also serves as the ABA Representative to the United Nations. He is the Chairman of Venable. Mr. Civiletti is a Fellow of the American College of Trial Lawyers and the American Law Institute.

DOUGLAS B. HENDERSON is the Founding and Senior Partner of Finnegan, Henderson, Farabow, Garrett & Dunner, Washington, D.C. Mr. Henderson is a Member of the Advisory Council of the United States Court of Federal Claims, and a Member of the Board of the Federal Circuit Bar Association. He was formerly Chairman of the Patent Division and Member of Council of the Section of Intellectual Property Law of the American Bar Association. He was the Founder of the Federal Circuit Bar Association, a co-founder of the U.S. Court of Federal Claims Bar Association, and a co-founder of the ITC Trial Lawyers Association.

THOMAS G. HEINTZMAN, O.C., Q.C., of McCarthy Tétrault, Toronto, Ontario, is a past President of the Canadian Bar Association (1994-1995). He is a member of the International Bar Association and the past Canadian member of the Council. Mr. Heintzman is a Fellow of the International Academy of Trial Lawyers, and the American College of Trial Lawyers and the past Chair of its Canadian Judiciary Committee. He is an Officer of the Order of Canada.

THOMAS J. KLITGAARD, formerly Senior Vice President and General Counsel of Sega of America, Inc., is now a partner with Dillingham & Murphy, San Francisco. He is a former Chairman of the California State Bar's Committee on the Maintenance of Professional Competence. He is a member of the panel of technology arbitrators of the American Arbitration Association in New York and a member of the Advisory Board of the Southwestern Legal Foundation in Dallas. He is currently the chairman of a graduate business management program in Shanghai, China.

RALPH I. LANCASTER, JR. of Pierce Atwood, Portland, Maine is currently serving as Independent Counsel, In Re Herman, by appointment of the Special Division of the D.C. Court of Appeals. He previously served as Counsel for the United States before the International Court of Justice in a case concerning delimitation of the Maritime Boundary in the Gulf of Maine and as Special Master by appointment of the Untied States Supreme Court in State of New Jersey vs. State of Nebraska. Mr. Lancaster began his legal career as a law clerk to the Honorable Edward T. Gignoux. He is a Past-President of the Maine State Bar Association and a former member of the House of Delegates of the American Bar Association. He served as Chair of the Standing Committee on Federal Judiciary of the ABA. He is a Fellow of the American College of Trial Lawyers and served as its President, 1989-1990.

JERALYN E. MERRITT, a sole practitioner from Denver, Colorado, is an author and frequent lecturer on criminal defense. She was selected by Chairman Bill McCollum, House Judiciary Committee, Subcommittee on Crime, to present oral and written congressional testimony on federal marijuana sentencing laws on behalf of the National Association of Criminal Defense Lawyers (NACDL) on March 6, 1996, in Washington, D.C. She served as Chair from 1995-1996 while a judicially appointed member of the Standing Committee on the Criminal Justice Act for the United States District Court for the District of Colorado from 1994-1996. Ms. Merritt is currently a member of the Board of Directors and Chair of the Advisory Board for the National Association of Criminal Defense Lawyers, the Director of the Cyberspace Bar Association and a member of the Board of Governors for the American Board of Criminal Lawyers.

HARRIET E. MIERS, Co-Managing Partner of Locke Liddell & Sapp LLP, has previously served as President and director of the State Bar of Texas as well as President and Chairman of the Board of Directors for the Dallas Bar Association. She is currently a member of the House of Delegates for the American Bar Association and State Delegate for the State of Texas. Ms. Miers also serves as a Trustee of the Southwestern Legal Foundation, a member of the Executive Board for the Southern Methodist University School of Law and Chair of the Texas Lottery Commission.

WILLIAM G. PAUL of Crowe & Dunlevy, Oklahoma City, Oklahoma. Mr. Paul is the former Senior Vice President & General Counsel, Phillips Petroleum Company, Bartlesville, Oklahoma. In February 1998, he was nominated to be President-Elect of the American Bar Association, to serve as such from August 1998 to August 1999, and is now the President to serve as such from August 1999 to July 2000. He has served as President of the Oklahoma State Bar Association, President of the National Conference of Bar Presidents, a Member of the American Bar Association, House of Delegates 1975-1999 and is a Fellow in the American College of Trial Lawyers.

FERNANDO POMBO, Founder and Senior Partner of Gomez-Acebo & Pombo, Madrid, Spain, has contributed to and authored several publications in the field of international business law. Currently, he is the International Bar Association Chairman of SLP. Mr. Pombo has been a visiting professor at the Institute on International Legal Studies in Salzburg, Austria since 1985. He is also a former President of LES International and a member of the Spanish Arbitration Court. He is fluent in Spanish, English, French and German.

WM. REECE SMITH, JR. of Tampa, Florida, is the senior member of Carlton, Fields, Ward, Emmanuel, Smith & Cutler, P.A. A Rhodes Scholar at Oxford University, England, he was later President of The Florida Bar (1972-73), the American Bar Association (1980-81), and the International Bar Association (1988-90). He is a Fellow of the American College of Trial Lawyers and the International Academy of Trial Lawyers and serves on the Council of the American Law Institute. He received the American Bar Association's Gold Medal for "exceptionally distinguished service to the cause of American Jurisprudence."

WALTER H. WHITE, JR. is a Partner of Bryan Cave L.L.P. in London, England. Mr. White previously has served as a Partner of Steptoe & Johnson L.L.P. in Washington, D.C. and as the Managing Director of its Moscow office. Mr. White is a former Commissioner of Securities for the State of Wisconsin 1988-1991. He has served as a member of the ABA House of Delegates, as the Chair of the Section of Individual Rights and Responsibilities and as chair of the Young Lawyers Division. Mr. White has also been a member of the State Bar of Wisconsin Board of Governors, on the Board of the Milwaukee Foundation and is currently a Board member of the Central-Asian-American Enterprise Fund by appointment of President Clinton.

USER'S GUIDE

The Alphabetical Index is an alphabetical listing of all United States firms and attorneys published in the Directory in an edition year. To the right of each listing is the location(s) (city name and standard postal state name abbreviation) where that lawyer or firm can be located in the Practice Profiles Section (the blue pages in each volume). Through the Practice Profiles Section, rating (and firm affiliation when available) can be identified, as well as whether additional information is available in the Professional Biographies Section. Expanded information is available in the Practice Profiles Section for firms and lawyers appearing in boldface type.

Briskin, Boyd E.	Riverside, CA
Briskin, Freedman & Cunilio	**Bryn Mawr, PA**
Briskin, Gerald J. (IBA)	Monroe, MI
Briskin, Jonathan A.	**Bryn Mawr, PA**
	Doylestown, PA
	Philadelphia, PA
Briskin, Joshua M., P.C	Philadelphia, PA
Briskin, Manuel	Department of Defense, Office of the General Counsel, GV
Britain, Timothy E. (IBA)	Concord, NH
	Lancaster, NH

denotes "IBA" member

Lawyers bearing the "GV" notation after their name are government affiliated and their activity is identified instead of city name. To locate these lawyers in the Practice Profiles Section, the government index should be consulted on page 1G of Volume 5. The page number where a particular activity is listed is identified in that index and the available information for a lawyer can be secured under the corresponding activity.

A.A.A.A. Law, P.A. ... Goose Creek, SC
A Able Advocates ... Los Angeles, CA
Malibu, CA
Santa Monica, CA
A Accident Attorney Firm ... Fresno, CA
Los Angeles, CA
Newport Beach, CA
Oakland, CA
Ontario, CA
Riverside, CA
Sacramento, CA
San Bernardino, CA
San Diego, CA
San Francisco, CA
San Jose, CA
A. Chase Law Group, P.C. ... Acton, CA
Agoura Hills, CA
Corona, CA
Covina, CA
Downey, CA
Los Angeles, CA
Pasadena, CA
Riverside, CA
San Bernardino, CA
Sherman Oaks, CA
Van Nuys, CA
A. Dahut & Weiss LLP ... Agoura Hills, CA
Alhambra, CA
Arcadia, CA
Bakersfield, CA
Chino, CA
Compton, CA
Corona, CA
Covina, CA
Downey, CA
Fullerton, CA
Glendale, CA
Hemet, CA
Indio, CA
Lancaster, CA
Long Beach, CA
Los Angeles, CA
Norco, CA
Northridge, CA
Ontario, CA
Orange, CA
Pasadena, CA
Pomona, CA
Riverside, CA
San Bernardino, CA
San Diego, CA
San Francisco, CA
Santa Clarita, CA
Sherman Oaks, CA
Thousand Oaks, CA
Ventura, CA
A. Thomas Kajander, P.C. ... Houston, TX
AAA Law Offices, A Professional Corporation ... Chicago, IL
AAAfordable Law Offices of Kent E. Seton
Los Angeles, CA
Aab, James L. ... Denver, CO
Aab, Raymond J. ... New York, NY
Aabdollah, Valerie ... Philadelphia, PA
Aaberg, Richard E. ... Bloomington, IL
Aaby, Barbara J. ... Beaverton, OR
Aaby, John ... Bellingham, WA
Aaby, Putnam, Albo & Causey, A Professional Services Corporation ... Bellingham, WA
Seattle, WA
Aach, Wendy Mory ... Allentown, PA
Aadalen, David K. ... Topeka, KS
Aaen, Bernhard ... San Bernardino, CA
Aafedt, Eric J. ... Houston, TX
Aafedt, Forde, Gray & Monson, P.A.
Minneapolis, MN
Aafedt, Michael D. ... Minneapolis, MN
Aafedt, Piper Kenney ... St. Paul, MN
Aagaard, Victor F.M. ... San Francisco, CA
Aagard, David T. ... Salt Lake City, UT
Aagard, Vance W. ... Fountain Green, UT
Aaker, Linda L. ... Austin, TX
Aaker, Linda P. ... Minneapolis, MN
Aaker, Mark Andrew ... Cupertino, CA
Aakhus, Mary A. ... Baxter, MN
Aakre, Steven K. ... Fargo, ND
Aal, Ronald ... Denver, CO
Aalberts, Danielle D. ... Adams, MA
Aalberts, Robert J. ... Las Vegas, NV
Aalbregtse, Jan M. ... Seattle, WA
Aalsberg, H. Scott ... East Brunswick, NJ
Aalseth, K. Gene ... Santa Ana, CA
Aalto, Laura A. ... Los Angeles, CA
Aalyson, Craig B. ... Columbus, OH
Aames, George Larue ... Rowland Heights, CA
Aamodt, David A. ... Portland, OR
Aamodt, Jason Bjorn ... Tulsa, OK
Aamodt, Paul R. ... Bemidji, MN
Aamoth, Robert J. ... Washington, DC
Aandal, Donald J. ... Thief River Falls, MN
Aanenson, Pamela Jean ... Moorhead, MN
Aanes, Patricia A. ... Brainerd, MN
Aanestad, Douglas J. ... Ketchum, ID
Aannestad, Anders T. ... Tucson, AZ
Aardal, Dan C. ... Palo Alto, CA
Aardema, Robert Bryan
Grand Rapids, MI
Aardsma, Richard J. ... Oak Forest, IL
Aarestad, Bruce ... Fargo, ND
Aarestad, Dean A. ... Aurora, CO
Aarestad, Joan E. ... Los Angeles, CA
Aarestad Law Office, P.C. ... Aurora, CO
Aarestad, Stacie Sawchak ... Boston, MA
Aarestad, Thomas L. ... Minneapolis, MN
Aaro, Karl P. ... St. Paul, MN
Aaroe, Lyn Paul ... Belvidere, NJ
Aaroe, Paul ... Belvidere, NJ
Aaroe, Paul. M., II ... Belvidere, NJ
Aaron, A. Bradford ... Chicago, IL
Aaron & Aaron ... Columbia, SC
Aaron, Alan ... Midland, TX
Aaron, Alan H. ... Framingham, MA
Aaron, Albert ... Binghamton, NY
Aaron, Albert G. ... Baltimore, MD
Aaron, Allen H. ... Minnetonka, MN
Aaron, Angela D. ... Houston, TX
Aaron, Ann-Marie Cerda
San Antonio, TX
Aaron, Arthur G. ... Wethersfield, CT
Aaron, Arthur M. ... Denver, CO
Aaron, Barry L. ... Brooklyn, NY
Aaron, Benjamin ... Santa Monica, CA
Aaron, Bennett L. ... Philadelphia, PA
Aaron, Brian D ... Hood River, OR
Aaron, Bryant Kenneth ... Newark, NJ
Aaron, Charles M. ... Martinsville, VA
Aaron, Clifford B. ... New York, NY
Aaron, Colin J. ... New York, NY
Aaron, Cynthia G. ... San Diego, CA
Aaron, Dan D. ... Dallas, TX
Aaron, Daniel J. ... New York, NY
Aaron, Dautch, Sternberg & Lawson, LLP
Buffalo, NY
Aaron, David A. ... Redwood City, CA
Aaron, Debra M. ... New York, NY
Aaron, Diane Konigsberg
San Francisco, CA
Aaron, Donald D. ... Columbia, SC
Aaron, Donald W. ... Cold Spring, KY
Aaron, Douglas G. ... Philadelphia, PA
Aaron, Fredric H. ... New York, NY
Aaron, George S. ... Tarzana, CA
Aaron, Gordon K. ... Milwaukee, WI
Aaron, Gordon K. & Associates, S.C.
Milwaukee, WI
Aaron, H. Michael ... Baton Rouge, LA
Aaron, Harvey D. ... Newton, MA
Aaron, Jaculin ... New York, NY
Aaron, James G. ... Ocean Township, NJ
Aaron, James M., Jr. ... Rossville, GA
Aaron, Jeffrey I. ... New York, NY
Aaron, Jerald N. ... Birmingham, MI
Aaron, Jody L. ... Detroit, MI
Southfield, MI
Aaron, Jonathan S. ... Birmingham, MI
Aaron, Joseph D., Jr. ... Crowley, LA
Aaron, Karen S. ... Livingston, NJ
Aaron, Kenneth E. ... Philadelphia, PA
Aaron, Kristine Y. ... San Diego, CA
Aaron, Laura G. ... Richmond, VA
Aaron, Marcus, II ... Pittsburgh, PA
Aaron, Marion Anna ... San Francisco, CA
Aaron, Marjorie Corman ... Cincinnati, OH
Aaron, Mark T. ... Clarion, PA
Aaron, Merik R. ... Hempstead, NY
Aaron, Michael ... Tucson, AZ
Aaron, Mitchell K. ... New York, NY
Aaron, Noelle L. ... San Francisco, CA
Aaron, Philip Irwin ... Syosset, NY
Aaron, Philip W. ... Sebastopol, CA
Aaron & Quirk, A Professional Corporation
San Antonio, TX
Aaron, Richard J. ... Lansing, MI
Aaron, Richard M. ... Fresno, CA
Aaron, Riechert, Carpol & Riffle, A P.C.
Redwood City, CA
Aaron, Robert S. ... San Francisco, CA
Aaron, Roger S. ... New York, NY
Aaron and Rogers, P.C. ... Tucson, AZ
Aaron, Ronald G. ... Columbia, SC
Aaron, Roy H. ... Los Angeles, CA
Aaron, Roy L. ... Knoxville, TN
Aaron, S. Paul ... Greenville, SC
Aaron, Sherry E. ... Kew Gardens, NY
Aaron, Stanley R. ... Baton Rouge, LA
Aaron, Steven Martin ... Kansas City, MO
Aaron, Steven N. ... Lexington, MA
Aaron, Stewart D. ... New York, NY
Aaron, Susan A.
Federal Communications Commission,
Office of the General Counsel, GV
Aaron & Turner ... Baton Rouge, LA
Aaron, Wayne J. ... Dallas, TX
Aaron, Wayne M. ... New York, NY
Aaron, William ... Miami, FL
Aaron, William D., Jr. ... New Orleans, LA
Aaron, William R. ... Baton Rouge, LA
Aaron & Wilson, LLP ... San Francisco, CA
Aaronian, Elaine D. ... Bloomfield Hills, MI
Aaronian, Winifred R. ... Cambridge, MA
Aaronoff, Steven J. ... Los Angeles, CA
Aarons & Aarons, Inc. ... Costa Mesa, CA
Aarons, Harry ... New York, NY
Aarons, Irwin ... Reno, NV
Aarons, Jonas ... Rhinebeck, NY
Aarons, Julius ... Costa Mesa, CA
Aarons Law Firm, P.C. ... Santa Fe, NM
Aarons, Stephen D. ... Santa Fe, NM
Aarons, Vilma M. ... Laguna Hills, CA
Aaronson & Aaronson ... Encino, CA
Aaronson, Arthur ... Encino, CA
Aaronson, Bonnie J. ... Tucson, AZ
Aaronson, Cassiana ... Novato, CA
Aaronson, Daniel L. ... Kenai, AK
Aaronson, Daniel R. ... Fort Lauderdale, FL
Aaronson, David ... New York, NY
Aaronson, David B. ... Cherry Hill, NJ
Philadelphia, PA
Aaronson, David E. ... Washington, DC
Aaronson, Dickerson, Cohn & Lanzone, A Professional Corporation
San Carlos, CA
Aaronson, Donald W. ... Washington, DC
Chicago, IL
Aaronson, Edward D. ... Encino, CA
Aaronson, Edward D., A Law Corporation
Encino, CA
Los Angeles, CA
Aaronson, Eric L. ... New York, NY
Aaronson, Geoffrey S. ... Miami, FL
Aaronson, Harris N. ... Pittsfield, MA
Aaronson, Harris N., and Associates, P.C.
Pittsfield, MA
Aaronson, Jeffrey B. ... Chicago, IL
Aaronson, Jennifer-Kate M. ... Newark, DE
Wilmington, DE
Aaronson, Joel P. ... Pittsburgh, PA
Aaronson, Joel S. ... Sherman Oaks, CA
Aaronson, Judith B. ... Beverly Hills, CA
Aaronson, Lawrence A. ... Philadelphia, PA
Aaronson, Lawrence H. ... Chicago, IL
Aaronson, Lester H. ... New Haven, CT
Aaronson, Marc A. ... New York, NY
Aaronson, Mark J. ... New York, NY
Aaronson, Mark N. ... San Francisco, CA
Aaronson, Maxine ... Dallas, TX
Houston, TX
Aaronson, Michael ... San Carlos, CA
Aaronson, Michael L. ... El Paso, TX
Aaronson, Mitchell ... Encino, CA
Aaronson, Norman F. ... Boulder, CO
Aaronson, Paul D. ... Cherry Hill, NJ
Aaronson Rappaport Feinstein & Deutsch, LLP ... Jersey City, NJ
New York, NY
Aaronson, Russell T., III ... Richmond, VA
Aaronson, Susan Alane ... Los Angeles, CA
Aaronson, Wayne ... Palm Springs, CA
Aaronson, William H. ... New York, NY
Aarseth, Joanne M. ... McLean, VA
Aarvig, Maria K. ... Riverside, CA
Aase, Mark M. ... San Pedro, CA
Aasgaard, Janice A. ... Marion, IA
Aasland, Stacey Tjon ... Fargo, ND
Aasmaa, Allan I.
General Services Administration,
Office of Regional Counsel, GV
Aavang, Heidi J. ... Waukegan, IL
Abacherli, Michael R. ... San Bernardino, CA
Abad, Jessie M. ... Washington, DC
Abad, Leopoldo A. ... New York, NY
Abad, Terence M. ... San Francisco, CA
Abadia-Muñoz, Maressa ... San Juan, PR
Abadie, Brent P. ... Metairie, LA
Abadie, Cecelia Farace ... New Orleans, LA
Abadie, Geraldine P. ... Marrero, LA
Abadie, James F. ... Baton Rouge, LA
Abadie, Lon Ware ... Durango, CO
Abadie, Peter J., Jr. ... Covington, LA
Abadie & Zimsky, L.L.C. ... Durango, CO
Abadin & Jaramillo, A Ptshp. of Prof. Assoc.
Miami, FL
Abadin, Ramon A. ... Miami, FL
Abady, Jonathan S. ... New York, NY
Abady, Samuel A. ... New York, NY
Abady, Samuel A., P.C., Law Offices of
New York, NY
Abagi, Carole ... Los Angeles, CA
Abair, Suzanne D. ... Boston, MA
Abajian, Alan R. ... Los Angeles, CA
Abakporo, I. Eric ... Brooklyn, NY
Abakumov, Georg ... Cleveland, OH
Aballi, Arturo J., Jr. ... Miami, FL
Aballi, Milne, Kalil & Garrigo, P.A.
Miami, FL
Abalona, William L. ... Sacramento, CA
Abalos, Celia Dorantes ... Newark, NJ
Abalos, Richard C. ... Odessa, TX
Abalos, Richard C., P.C. ... Odessa, TX
Abaray, Janet G. ... Cincinnati, OH
Abarbanel, Arthur ... New York, NY
Abarbanel, Jeffrey ... Baltimore, MD
Abarbanel, Stephen J. ... Boston, MA
Abarca, Carlos J. ... Miami, FL
Abarca, Marco A. ... Denver, CO
Abarca, Rosemary ... Bakersfield, CA
Abarca-Schwartz, Ramón J.
San Juan, PR
Abare, Bess C. ... Atlanta, GA
Abare, Edward J., III ... Vero Beach, FL
Abare, Nicholls & Parker, P.C. ... Barre, VT
Stowe, VT
Waterbury, VT
Abare, Terri Reyering ... Cincinnati, OH
Abariotes, Theodore J. ... Denver, CO
Abarr, Maurice L. ... Huntington Beach, CA
Abarr, Maurice L. ... Santa Ana, CA
Abascal, Manuel A. ... Los Angeles, CA
Abascal, Ralph S. ... San Francisco, CA
Abate & Abate LLC ... Stamford, CT
Abate, Alex M. ... Rockford, IL
Abate, Alex M., and Richard M. Butera
Rockford, IL
Abate, Alfred M. ... Cos Cob, CT
Abate, Anthony J. ... Sarasota, FL
Abate, Charles J., Jr. ... Boston, MA
Abate, Charles P. ... Stamford, CT
Abate, Erica B. ... Boston, MA
Abate, Ernest N. ... Stamford, CT
Abate, Jeffrey J. ... Orchard Park, NY
Abate, Joseph C. ... Boston, MA
Abate, Joseph F. ... Phoenix, AZ
Abate, Joseph L. ... Turnersville, NJ
Abate, Joseph P. ... Farmington, CT
Abate, Kathleen ... Fairmont, WV
Abate, Maria Elena ... Fort Lauderdale, FL
Abate, Mark J. ... New York, NY
Abate, Mary M. ... Department of Justice,
Tax Division, GV
Abate, Michael D. ... Utica, MI
Abate, Michele H. ... Boston, MA
Abate, Nino ... Phoenix, AZ
Abate, Samuel J., Jr. ... New York, NY
Abatemarco, David P. ... Bronx, NY
Abatemarco, John M. ... Jersey City, NJ
Abatemarco, Peter V. ... Belvidere, NJ
Abati, Michele ... Arnold, PA
Abatiell, Anthony F. ... Rutland, VT
Abatiell and Valerio ... Rutland, VT
Abato, Anthony A., Jr. ... Baltimore, MD
Abato, Maureen A. ... Brooklyn, NY
Abato, Rubenstein and Abato, P.A.
Baltimore, MD
Abatti, Alice M. ... Seeley, CA
Abaunza, Donald R. ... New Orleans, LA
Abaza, Sharif N. ... Perkasie, PA
Abb, Irving V. M. ... Frederick, MD
Abbamondi, John G. ... Oklahoma City, OK
Abbamonte, David M. ... Trumbull, CT
Abbamonte, John C. ... Roseland, NJ
Abbamonte, John L. ... Wall Township, NJ
Abbamonto, George X. ... Brea, CA
Abbamonto, Szura & Binder ... Cary, IL
Abbanat, Georgeann F. ... Boston, MA
Abbarno, Anthony D. ... Buffalo, NY
Abbarno, Kenneth P. ... Cleveland, OH
Abbarno, McLaughlin & Kedzielawa
Buffalo, NY
Abbas, Bradley J., Law Office of
Scottsdale, AZ
Abbas, Jeffrey L. ... Coudersport, PA
Abbasi, A. Sonny ... Washington, DC
Abbasi, Rana ... Chicago, IL
Abbass, Jobe J. ... Rensselaer, NY
Abbate, Frank B. ... Harrisburg, PA
Abbate, Guy R., Jr. ... Pensacola, FL
Abbate, Joe, Jr. ... Houston, TX
Abbate, John J. ... Melville, NY
Abbate, Julie ... Federal Trade Commission,
Bureau of Consumer Protection, GV
Abbate, Lawrence & Worden, P.C.
Melville, NY
Abbate, Mary-Elizabeth D. ... Setauket, NY
Abbate, Nathaniel, Jr. ... Birmingham, MI
Abbate, Paul J. ... Waldorf, MD
Abbate, Richard S. ... New York, NY
Abbate, Salvatore P. ... Buffalo, NY
Abbate, Thomas A. ... Woodbury, NY
Abbate, Thomas A., P.C. ... Woodbury, NY
Abbati, Rita A. ... Chicago, IL
Abbatt, William G. ... Southfield, MI
Abbe, Chas. Cleveland ... Portland, OR
Abbe, Cyrus Gilbert ... New York, NY
Abbe, Kenneth H. ... Beverly Hills, CA
Abbe, Richard W. ... Santa Barbara, CA
Abbell, Jos. J. ... Chicago, IL
Abbell, Michael ... Washington, DC
Abbenante, Thomas ... Washington, DC
Abbenda, Joseph ... Glen Cove, NY
Abbene, John J. ... San Diego, CA
Abbene, Maris L. ... Boston, MA
Abberbock, Ellen ... Mineola, NY
Abberley, John J. ... New York, NY
Abberley Kooiman LLP ... New York, NY
Abberman, Jay B. ... Far Hills, NJ
Abbes, George W. ... Santa Ana, CA
Abbett, Vance N. ... Opelika, AL
Abbey & Abbey ... Caro, MI
Abbey, Alfred E. ... Nashville, TN
Abbey & Arquilla, P.C. ... Springfield, VA
Abbey, Arthur N. ... New York, NY
Abbey, Carol G. ... Brooklyn, NY
Abbey, David J. ... St. Petersburg, FL
Abbey, David M. ... Baltimore, MD
Abbey, G. Marshall ... Deerfield, IL
Abbey, Gardy & Squitieri, LLP
New York, NY
Abbey, James R. ... Caro, MI
Abbey, Jay M. ... Holbrook, AZ
Abbey, Jeffrey D. ... Chicago, IL
Abbey, Joe B. ... Dallas, TX
Abbey, Michael Hall ...
Overseas Private Investment Corporation,
GV
Abbey, Richard H. ... Washington, DC
Abbey, Richard W. ... Santa Rosa, CA
Abbey, Steven W. ... Elyria, OH
Abbey, Thomas D. ... Caro, MI
Abbey, Thomas G. ... Springfield, VA
Abbey, Walter L., (P.C.) (IBA) **... Dallas, TX**
Abbey, Weitzenberg, Hoffman & Emery, A Professional Corporation
Santa Rosa, CA
Abbey, William S. ... Los Angeles, CA
Abbin, Byrle M. ... Washington, DC
Abbinante, Chris E. ... Chicago, IL
Abbington, Brian A. ... Galveston, TX
Abbitt, A. Lee, Jr. ... La Porte, TX
Abbo, James J. ... Bloomfield Hills, MI
Abbo, Paul ... Troy, MI
Abbo, Peter ... Farmington Hills, MI
Abbo, Victor L., Law Offices of
Boulder, CO
Abbondante, Karen Lee ... Staten Island, NY
Abbondante, Thomas D. ... New York, NY
Abbondola, Victor A. ... New York, NY
Abbondondelo, Mary C. ... Islandia, NY
Abbot, Edward P. ... New York, NY
Abbot, Louisa ... Savannah, GA
Abbot, Murphy and Harvey, P.C.
Louisville, GA
Abbot, R. Taylor, Jr. ... Birmingham, AL
Abbot, Sybil Vogtle ... Birmingham, AL
Abbott and Abbott ... Savannah, GA
Abbott & Abbott ... Brandon, SD
Abbott & Abbott ... Abilene, TX
Abbott, Alden F. ... Department of Commerce,
Office of the General Counsel, GV
Abbott, Angela A., P.A. ... Titusville, FL
Abbott, Anthony ... Escondido, CA
Abbott, Anthony H. ... Savannah, GA

Abbott, Barbara J. .... Henniker, NH
Abbott, Barry A. .... San Francisco, CA
Abbott, Barry L. .... Chattanooga, TN
Abbott, Barry R., Law Office of
New York, NY
Abbott, Bennett A. .... Oklahoma City, OK
Abbott, Beth .... Santa Ana, CA
Abbott, Bob .... Topeka, KS
Abbott, Bren .... Kansas City, MO
Abbott, Bruce A. .... Los Angeles, CA
Abbott, Bryce A. .... Wichita, KS
Abbott & Burlison .... Memphis, TN
Abbott, C. Jeffrey .... Portland, OR
Abbott, C Michael .... Atlanta, GA
Abbott, C. Michael, P.C. .... Atlanta, GA
Marietta, GA
Abbott, C. Richard .... Detroit, MI
Abbott, Caryl H. .... Brandon, SD
Abbott, Catherine .... Chicago, IL
Abbott, Cecilia O'Connor .... Kansas City, MO
Abbott, Charles B. .... Boston, MA
Abbott, Charles "B.B.", II .... Tampa, FL
Abbott, Charles E. .... Memphis, TN
Abbott, Charles F. .... Provo, UT
Abbott, Charles H. .... Auburn, ME
Abbott, Charles W. .... Orlando, FL
Abbott, Chas. A. .... Dallas, TX
Abbott, Claudia Hahn .... Powell, OH
Abbott, Cynthia Photos .... Libertyville, IL
Abbott, Dan S. .... Abilene, TX
Abbott, Daniel L. .... Hollywood, FL
Abbott, David F. .... Chicago, IL
Abbott, David H. .... Boston, MA
Abbott, David L. .... Cincinnati, OH
Abbott, David V. .... Providence, RI
Abbott, David W. .... Sacramento, CA
Abbott, Davis, Rothwell, Mullin & Earle, P.C. .... Portland, OR
Seattle, WA
Abbott, Dennis .... Huntsville, AL
Abbott, Derek C. .... Wilmington, DE
Abbott, Douglas J. .... Los Altos, CA
Abbott, Douglas L. .... Denver, CO
Abbott, Dwayne L. .... Torrance, CA
Abbott, Elaine R. .... Santa Monica, CA
Abbott, Eliot C. .... Miami, FL
Abbott, Elizabeth .... Providence, RI
Abbott, Emily .... Atlantic City, NJ
Abbott, Ethan D. B. .... Honolulu, HI
Abbott, Forrest K. .... Cayce, SC
Abbott, Frank H. .... Philadelphia, PA
Abbott, Frank L. .... Washington, DC
Abbott, Fred E., III .... Houston, TX
Abbott, Fred M. .... Jacksonville, FL
Abbott, Gardner .... South Holland, IL
Abbott, Garry W. .... Bessemer, AL
Abbott, Gary V. .... Portland, OR
Abbott, George .... Temecula, CA
Abbott, George W. .... Minden, NV
Abbott, Glen C. .... Crystal River, FL
Abbott, Glen C. .... Inverness, FL
Abbott, Gregory B. .... Kirkland, WA
Abbott, Gregory L. .... Portland, OR
Abbott, Gregory W. .... Austin, TX
Abbott, Guthrie T., Jr. .... Oxford, MS
Tupelo, MS
Abbott, H. Bruce .... Barrington, NJ
Abbott, H. Clark .... Springfield, MA
Abbott, Harold L. .... Susanville, CA
Abbott, Haskell T., III .... Conway, SC
Abbott, Heidi Wilson .... Richmond, VA
Abbott, Hirschel T., Jr., (P.C.)
New Orleans, LA
Abbott, Ida O. .... Oakland, CA
Abbott, J. Anthony .... Stockton, CA
Abbott, J. Jordan .... Chicago, IL
Abbott, J. Perry .... Arlington, TX
Abbott, Jacinta Titialii .... Philadelphia, PA
Abbott, Jacquelyn M. .... Fort Wayne, IN
Abbott, James A. .... Hazel Park, MI
Abbott, James C. .... McAllen, TX
Abbott, James E. .... New York, NY
Abbott, James L., Jr. .... Canyon, TX
Abbott, James P. .... Baltimore, MD
Abbott, James V. .... Seattle, WA
Abbott, James W. .... Yankton, SD
Abbott, Jana Deines .... Wichita, KS
Abbott, JeAnna Lanza .... Houston, TX
Abbott, Jeffrey H. .... Bloomfield, IN
Abbott, Jeffrey R. .... Media, PA
Philadelphia, PA
Abbott, Jeffrey T. .... Saginaw, MI
Abbott, Jerry B. .... Santa Rosa, CA
Abbott, John E. .... Lansing, MI
Abbott, John L. .... Longmeadow, MA
Abbott, John P. .... Brandon, SD
Abbott, John W. .... Anchorage, AK
Abbott, Jonathan A. .... Boston, MA
Abbott, Jos. P. .... Quincy, MA
Abbott, Judith P. .... Denton, TX
Abbott, Keith E. .... Greeley, CO
Abbott, Kenneth R. .... Jeffersonville, IN
Abbott, Kenneth W. .... Chicago, IL
Abbott, Kerry S. .... Northbrook, IL
Abbott, Kevin C. .... Pittsburgh, PA
Abbott & Kindermann, LLP
Sacramento, CA
Abbott, Larry A. .... Montpelier, VT
Abbott, Laurie K. .... Savannah, GA
Abbott, Lawrence E. .... Lake Charles, LA
New Orleans, LA
Houston, TX
Abbott, Lawrence J. .... Los Angeles, CA
Abbott, Leslie L. .... Los Angeles, CA
Abbott, Louis Lee .... Los Angeles, CA
Abbott, Lysle I. .... Evansville, IN
Abbott, Malvina E.J. .... Chula Vista, CA
Abbott, Marc A. .... Long Beach, NY
Abbott, Marilyn Nowak .... Omaha, NE
Abbott, Mark Bruce .... Los Angeles, CA
Abbott, Mary L. .... Knoxville, TN
Abbott, Mary Nielsen .... Long Beach, CA
Abbott, Matthew .... New York, NY
Abbott, Melanie Beth .... Hamden, CT
Abbott, Michael .... Atlanta, GA
Abbott, Michael A. .... Houston, TX
Abbott, Michael C. .... Florence, SC
Abbott, Michael C. .... Orange, TX
Abbott, Michael H. .... Wise, VA
Abbott, Michael J. .... Los Angeles, CA
Abbott, Michael L. .... Modesto, CA
Abbott, Mitchell E. .... Los Angeles, CA
Abbott, Mullen, Brumsey & Small
Currituck, NC
Elizabeth City, NC
Abbott, Nancy L. .... Marshalls Creek, PA
Abbott, Nancy T. .... Burlington, NJ
Abbott, Natalie Slavens .... Philadelphia, PA
Abbott, Nelson .... Provo, UT
Abbott, Nicholson, Quilter, Esshaki & Youngblood, P.C. .... Ann Arbor, MI
Detroit, MI
Flint, MI
Abbott & Nolen .... Sacramento, CA
Abbott, O. C. .... Elizabeth City, NC
Abbott & Overholt, L.L.P. .... Media, PA
Abbott, Preston H. .... Stamford, CT
Abbott, Ralph F., Jr. .... Springfield, MA
Worcester, MA
Abbott, Randall .... Springfield, IL
Abbott, Raymond T. .... New York, NY
Abbott, Rebecca D. .... Dallas, TX
Abbott, Richard G. .... Kenmore, NY
Abbott, Richard L. .... Wilmington, DE
Abbott, Richard L. .... Princeton, NJ
Abbott, Richd. A. .... Allentown, PA
Abbott, Robert A. .... Bloomfield Hills, MI
Abbott, Robert Bren .... Kansas City, MO
Abbott, Robert H. .... Fort Myers, FL
Abbott, Robert L. .... Dallas, TX
Abbott, Robert P. .... Coppell, TX
Abbott, Rogers, and Associates
Oklahoma City, OK
Abbott, Scott M. .... Las Vegas, NV
Abbott, Sean D. .... Boston, MA
Abbott, Seth A. .... Hamburg, NY
Abbott, Sharon Stoner .... Costa Mesa, CA
Abbott, Simses, Knister & Kuchler, A Professional Law Corporation
Lake Charles, LA
New Orleans, LA
Houston, TX
Abbott, Stanley W. .... Santa Barbara, CA
Abbott, Stanley W., A Professional Corporation
Santa Barbara, CA
Abbott, Stefanie Jones .... Albany, GA
Abbott, Stephen K. .... San Rafael, CA
Abbott, Stephen L. .... Cranford, NJ
Abbott, Steven B. .... Riverside, CA
Abbott, Steven L. .... Sparta, WI
Abbott, Susan L. .... Washington, DC
Abbott, Teddy J. .... Muskogee, OK
Abbott, Theodore S. .... Houston, TX
Abbott, Theron James .... San Francisco, CA
Abbott, Thomas M. .... Los Angeles, CA
Abbott, Thomas P. .... Miami, FL
Abbott, Tills & Knapp, LLP
Hamburg, NY
Abbott, Tony H. .... Indianapolis, IN
Abbott, Victoria E. .... Dallas, TX
Abbott, W. Kirk, Jr. .... Concord, NH
Abbott, W. Rogers, II .... Oklahoma City, OK
Abbott & Walker .... Provo, UT
Abbott, Wendy J. .... Chicago, IL
Abbott, William A. .... Tacoma, WA
Abbott, William A. .... Madison, WI
Abbott, William Cory .... Houston, TX
Abbott, William F. .... San Francisco, CA
San Jose, CA
Abbott, William Lee .... Houston, TX
Abbott, William M. .... Jackson, MI
Abbott, William S. .... Boston, MA
Abbott, William T. .... New Orleans, LA
Abbott, William W. .... Sacramento, CA
Abbott, William W., Jr. .... Gulfport, MS
Abbott & Woo .... San Francisco, CA
San Jose, CA
Abbotts and Abbotts .... Crosswicks, NJ
Abbotts, Alfred .... Trenton, NJ
Abbotts, John .... Crosswicks, NJ
Abboud, Amy L. .... Dallas, TX
Abboud, Anthony L. .... Chicago, IL
Abboud, Jason David .... Omaha, NE
Abboud, Labeeb M. .... New York, NY
Abboud, Ruth Sharon .... Hinckley, OH
Abbruzzese, Marguerite A.
Department of Justice, Tax Division, GV
Abbruzzese, Michael J. .... Jupiter, FL
Abbruzzese, Salvatore J. .... Parsippany, NJ
Abbs, James .... Kendallville, IN
Abbs, Jan P. .... Muncie, IN
Abbs, Nancy J. .... Grosse Pointe, MI
Abbuhl, David W. .... Beachwood, OH
Abbuhl, David W., Co., L.P.A.
Beachwood, OH
Abbuhl, Richard W. .... Phoenix, AZ
Abcarian, Michael V. .... Dallas, TX
Abdala, George S. .... Springfield, MA
Abdalah, Richard K. .... Cupertino, CA
Abdal-Haqq, Irshad
Department of Commerce, Economic Development Administration, GV
Abdal-Khallaq, Hamida .... Irving, TX
Abdalla, David A.
Environmental Protection Agency, Office of Enforcement and Compliance Assurance, GV
Abdalla, Gerald M. .... Mc Comb, MS
Abdalla, Sidney J., Jr. .... Metairie, LA
Abdalla, Tarek F. .... Pittsburgh, PA
Abdallah, Ahmed M. .... Los Angeles, CA
Abdallah, John J. .... Jacksonville, FL
Abdallah, Kathleen M. .... Stockton, CA
Abdallah, Scott A. .... Canton, SD
Abdeen, Eddie J. .... Jackson, MS
Abdelahad, Arthur A. .... Randolph, MA
Abdella & Abdella .... Jamestown, NY
Abdella, Charles A. .... Worcester, MA
Abdella, Ernest .... Gloversville, NY
Abdella, Ernest and George
Gloversville, NY
Abdella, George .... Gloversville, NY
Abdella, H. James .... Jamestown, NY
Abdella, Peter H. .... Rochester, NY
Abdella, Stephen M. .... Jamestown, NY
Abdellah, Hassen I. .... Elizabeth, NJ
Abdel-Malek, Linda .... New York, NY
Abdelmessih, Emad .... Avon, MA
Abdelnour, Diane L. .... Yorktown, VA
Abdelnour, Joseph A. .... Williamsburg, VA
Abdelrahamn, Aiman .... New York, NY
Abdennabi, Iasmine V. .... Chicago, IL
Abdenour, Joseph E. .... Akron, OH
Abderholden, Edward C. .... Chicago, IL
Abdeslam, Ali Ben .... Dearborn, MI
Abdo and Abdo, P.A. .... Minneapolis, MN
Abdo, Bernard .... New York, NY
Abdo, Cy Matthew .... Clinton, MI
Abdo, George E., III .... Jackson, MS
Abdo, James P. .... Phoenix, AZ
Abdo, Kenneth J. .... Minneapolis, MN
Abdo, Nicholas S. .... Syracuse, NY
Abdo, Robert P. .... Minneapolis, MN
Abdo, Stephanie Silk .... Randolph, MA
Abdo-Gomez, Magda .... Miami, FL
Abdollahi, Bita .... San Francisco, CA
Abdollahi, O. Antony .... Mountain View, CA
Abdoney, Emmett .... Tampa, FL
Abdoney, Emmett Christopher .... Tampa, FL
Abdoo, Elizabeth A. .... Dulles, VA
Abdoo, Frederick F. .... New York, NY
Abdou, Tamer M. .... Plainsboro, NJ
Abdow, Thomas R. .... Shutesbury, MA
Abdulaziz & Grossbart .... Los Angeles, CA
Abdulaziz, Sam K., (A Law Corporation)
Los Angeles, CA
Abdul-Karim, Yasmin J. .... Detroit, MI
Abdullah, D'Andrea Sherelle Pendleton
Austin, TX
Abdullah, Mace .... Los Angeles, CA
Abdullah, Raouf M.
Federal Trade Commission, Bureau of Consumer Protection, GV
Abdullah, Robert Karriem .... Harrisburg, PA
Abdullah, Sharif M. .... Charlotte, NC
Abdul-Raheem, Rasul M.
Farmington Hills, MI
Abdul-Rahim, Lila M. .... Oakland, CA
Abdul-Rahim, Walid .... San Francisco, CA
Abdur-Rahman, Aisha H.
Los Angeles, CA
Abdus-Salaam, Sheila .... New York, NY
Abdy, George J. .... Clifton, NJ
Abe, Arnold T. .... Honolulu, HI
Abe, Eric Y. .... Los Angeles, CA
Abe, Fred Y. .... Honolulu, HI
Abe, Kazuhisa .... Hilo, HI
Abe, Michael K. .... Honolulu, HI
Abe, Roger Tamotsu .... Yuba City, CA
Abe, Victor S. .... San Francisco, CA
Abear & Crane .... Farmington Hills, MI
Abear, Julie D. .... Farmington Hills, MI
Abed, Gil .... San Diego, CA
Abed, Salah J. .... Washington, DC
Abed & Savage .... Washington, DC
Abedon, Herbert J. .... East Providence, RI
Abedon, Richard L.
West Palm Beach, FL
Abeel, Timothy J. .... New York, NY
Philadelphia, PA
Abegg, John K.
Federal Election Commission, Offices of the Commissioners, GV
Abegglen, Diane .... Salt Lake City, UT
Abeita, Christopher L. .... isleta, NM
Abel and Abel .... Hayward, CA
Abel, Adam S. .... San Francisco, CA
Abel, Alfred M. .... Philadelphia, PA
Abel, Annie Lou .... Jackson, MS
Abel, Arend J. .... Indianapolis, IN
Abel, Ashley B. .... Greenville, SC
Abel, Band, Russell, Collier, Pitchford & Gordon, Chartered .... Sarasota, FL
Venice, FL
Abel, Bernard .... Bronx, NY
Abel, Brent M. .... San Francisco, CA
Abel, Bruce D. .... Los Angeles, CA
Abel & Brustein-Kampel .... New City, NY
Abel, Christopher A. .... Norfolk, VA
Abel, Clare H. .... Phoenix, AZ
Abel, Daisy C. .... Trenton, NJ
Abel, Daniel G. .... Metairie, LA
Abel, David A. .... Boston, MA
Abel, David B. .... Los Angeles, CA
Abel, David L., II .... Merrillville, IN
Abel, David R. .... Indianapolis, IN
Abel, David V. .... Albany, NY
Abel, Don G. .... Seattle, WA
Abel, Donald W., Jr. .... Palmer, MA
Abel, Douglas S. .... Fairfax, VA
Abel, E. William .... Framingham, MA
Abel, Ed .... Oklahoma City, OK
Abel, Elizabeth .... Hayward, CA
Abel, Elizabeth W. .... Huntsville, AL
Abel, Eric D. .... Hernando, FL
Abel, Eric M. .... Terre Haute, IN
Abel, F. Bruce .... Cincinnati, OH
Abel, F. Bruce .... Columbus, OH
Abel, George G., III .... Newtown Square, PA
Abel, George Gregory .... San Jose, CA
Abel, George H., II .... Indianapolis, IN
Abel, Glenn R. .... San Jose, CA
Abel, Gordon C. .... Council Bluffs, IA
Abel, Gregory C. .... Tacoma, WA
Abel, Gregory D. .... San Luis Obispo, CA
Abel, Gregory M. .... Vancouver, WA
Abel, Harvey J. .... Sarasota, FL
Abel, Ira R. .... New York, NY
Abel, Jack W. .... Cleveland, OH
Abel, Jeannette M. .... Xenia, OH
Abel, Jeffrey S. .... Schenectady, NY
Abel, Jeffrey W. .... Ontario, CA
Abel, Jennifer Jobson .... Clearwater, FL
Abel, John M. .... Philadelphia, PA
Abel, Jonathan C. .... Hollywood, FL
Abel, Juliet L. .... Pittsburgh, PA
Abel, Katrina L. .... Warwick, RI
Abel, Katy Barklow .... Dallas, TX
Abel, Kenneth B. .... Baltimore, MD
Abel, Kevin M. .... St. Louis, MO
Abel, Kevin M. .... Tulsa, OK
Abel, Kim Elizabeth .... Richland, WA
Abel, Laura Klein .... Newark, NJ
Abel, Lawrence W. .... Philadelphia, PA
Abel, L.M. (Maria) .... San Francisco, CA
Abel, Luther D. .... Gadsden, AL
Abel, Mark R. .... Columbus, OH
Abel, Marlene .... Torrance, CA
Abel, Matthew R. .... Livonia, MI
Abel, Matthew R., P.C. .... Livonia, MI
Abel, Meryl .... Rockville, MD
Abel, Michael A. .... Jacksonville, FL
Abel, Michael A. .... Canton, OH
Abel, Michael A. .... Tulsa, OK
Abel, Michael C. .... Los Angeles, CA
Abel, Michael R. .... Greensboro, NC
Abel, Musser, Sokolosky, Mares & Kouri
Oklahoma City, OK
Abel, Paul E. .... Rutherford, NJ
Abel, Robert B., Jr. .... San Francisco, CA
Abel, S. William .... Colusa, CA
Abel, Sally Anne .... Melville, NY
Abel, Sally M. .... Palo Alto, CA
Abel, Saralyn .... Sarasota, FL
Abel, Seth A. .... Philadelphia, PA
Abel, Steven L. .... New City, NY
Abel, Steven W. .... Portland, OR
Abel, Terry R. .... Dallas, TX
Abel, Timothy .... Hayward, CA
Abel, Wanda J. .... Denver, CO
Abel, William T. .... West Palm Beach, FL
Abela, Victor J. .... Detroit, MI
Abelar, Ambar I. .... Long Branch, NJ
Abele, April E. .... San Francisco, CA
Abele, Charles R. .... St. Louis, MO
Abele, David F. .... San Ramon, CA
Abele, Douglas .... Boonville, MO
Abele, George W. .... Los Angeles, CA
Abele, Joseph M. .... Philadelphia, PA
Abele, Joy D. .... Wilsonville, OR
Abele, Leslie G. .... White Plains, NY
Abele, R. Christopher .... Kansas City, MO
Abele & Sanderson, L.L.C. .... St. Louis, MO
Abele, Sanford T. .... Gloucester, MA
Abeles, Charles C. .... Washington, DC
Abeles, Damaris Sargent .... Louisville, KY
Abeles, Daniel C. .... Pittsburgh, PA
Abeles, Jerrold E. .... Los Angeles, CA
Abeles, Richard A. .... Santa Fe, NM
Abeles, Theodore L. .... Newark, NJ
Abelev, Gary .... New York, NY
Abell, Angela M. .... Immokalee, FL
Lehigh Acres, FL
Abell, Anne Marie .... Milwaukee, WI
Abell, Cathleen .... Lawrence, KS
Abell, Charles S. .... Washington, DC
Abell, David J. .... Dallas, TX
Abell, David R. .... Chicago, IL
Winnetka, IL
Abell, Edward C., Jr. .... Lafayette, LA
Abell, Edwin P. .... Campbellsville, KY
Abell, Elaine Durbin .... Lafayette, LA
Abell, Herbert W. .... Sarasota, FL
Abell, Irvin, III .... Louisville, KY
Abell, Jack R. .... Stow, OH
Abell, James H., Jr. .... Bardstown, KY
Abell, Jan M. .... Houston, TX
Abell, Jeffrey M. .... Northridge, CA
Abell, Kathy Donovan .... Charlottesville, VA
Abell, Leslie B. .... Los Angeles, CA
Abell, Matthew D. .... Denver, CO
Abell, Nancy L. .... Los Angeles, CA
Abell, Nelson D., III .... Monroe, LA
Abell, Norman .... New York, NY
Abell, Richard B.
United States Court of Federal Claims, Office of Special Masters, GV
Abell, Richard T. .... Fort Washington, PA
Abell, Rick W. .... Metropolis, IL
Abell, Robert L. .... Lexington, KY
Abell, Rochelle E. .... Tucson, AZ
Abell, T. Scott .... Louisville, KY
Abell, Teresa Thomas .... Atlanta, GA
Columbus, GA
Abell, Theresa A. .... Treasury Department, Internal Revenue Service, GV
Abell, W. Shepherdson .... Chevy Chase, MD
Abell, William F. .... Omaha, NE
Abell, William F., Jr. .... Frederick, MD

Abell, William K. ... **Montgomery, AL**
Abell, Wm. G. ... Louisville, KY
Abella, Gregory J. ... Kansas City, MO
Abella, Jacob M. ... Detroit, MI
Abella-Austriaco, Aurora N. ... Chicago, IL
Abella-Padilla, Celeste ... **San Juan, PR**
Abelle, Patsy ... Randolph, NJ
Abellera, Philip M. ... **Chicago, IL**
Abellera, Ronald E. ... Atlanta, GA
Abelman, Allan D. ... Denver, CO
Abelman, Arthur F. ... **New York, NY**
Abelman, David ... Waltham, MA
Abelman Frayne & Schwab
New York, NY
Abelman, Henry M. ... Atlanta, GA
Abelman, Jerome B. ... **New York, NY**
Abelman, Julianne ... **New York, NY**
Abelman Law Offices ... Denver, CO
Abelman, Lawrence E. ... **New York, NY**
Abelman, Robert C. ... Denver, CO
Abelman, Steven E. ... **Denver, CO**
Abeln, Gregory B. ... **Carlisle, PA**
Abeln Law Offices ... **Carlisle, PA**
Abeln, Maura J. ... Pittsfield, MA
Abeloff, Dianne ... New York, NY
Abeloff, William H. ... Richmond, VA
Abelove, C. Louis ... **Utica, NY**
Abelove, Jason L. ... Woodmere, NY
Abelow & Cassandro, LLP ... **Jericho, NY**
New York, NY
Abelow, Ross M. ... **Jericho, NY**
New York, NY
Abelow, William J. ... New York, NY
Abels, Brian K. ... **Baton Rouge, LA**
Abels, Caroline R. ... Pasadena, CA
Abels, Edward E., Jr. ... **Lakewood, CO**
Abels, F. Daley ... St. Louis, MO
Abels, Jon B. ... **Indianapolis, IN**
Abels, Marcus F. ... **Des Moines, IA**
Abels, Stephen A. ... Brewster, NY
Abels, Tracy ... **Los Angeles, CA**
Abels, Ulma A. ... Los Angeles, CA
Abelsen, James N. ... Duluth, MN
Abelski, Sidney ... Chicago, IL
Abelson, Arnold D. ... Roslyn Heights, NY
Abelson, Arthur R. ... Newton, MA
Abelson, Barry M. ... **Philadelphia, PA**
Abelson, Gary H. ... **Rochester, NY**
Abelson, H. Edward ... **Boston, MA**
Abelson, Howard P. ... Richmond, CA
Abelson, J. James ... Sebastian, FL
Abelson, Jeremy J. ... Wilmington, DE
Abelson, Joanne S. ... San Francisco, CA
Abelson Law Firm, The ... **Washington, DC**
Rockville, MD
Boston, MA
Philadelphia, PA
Pittsburgh, PA
Alexandria, VA
Fairfax, VA
Abelson, Lawrence A. ... Los Angeles, CA
Abelson, Leroy A. ... **Los Angeles, CA**
Abelson, Mark B. ... San Francisco, CA
Abelson, Michael A. ... **Washington, DC**
Boston, MA
Philadelphia, PA
Pittsburgh, PA
Abelson, Michael Bruce ... **Los Angeles, CA**
Abelson, Neil J. ... Port Jefferson, NY
Abelson, Richard H. ... **New City, NY**
Abelson, Richard H. ... **White Plains, NY**
Abelson, Steven J. ... Freehold, NJ
Abend & Jacobson ... Pleasant Hill, CA
Abend, Richard A. ... Utica, NY
Abend, Ronald M. ... Pleasant Hill, CA
Abendroth, Berns & Warner, LLC
Wellesley, MA
Abendroth, Douglas W.
Newport Beach, CA
Abendroth, Gerald W. ... Jonesboro, GA
Abendroth, Mark U. ... Des Moines, IA
Abendroth, Robert V. ... **Milwaukee, WI**
Abendroth and Russell, P.C.
Des Moines, IA
Abendroth, Thomas W. ... **Chicago, IL**
Abendroth, Timm L.
Federal Energy Regulatory Commission, Office of the General Counsel, GV
Abendroth, William C ... **Portland, OR**
Abendroth, William W. ... **Wellesley, MA**
Abendschein, Karl W. ... **Washington, DC**
Abens, Linda C. ... **Chicago, IL**
Abensohn, Adam M. ... New York, NY
Aber, Bruce H. ... New York, NY
Aber, Francine ... Purchase, NY
Aber, Gary W. ... **Wilmington, DE**
Aber, Jeremy M. ... Little Rock, AR
Aber, John E. ... Malone, NY
Aber, M. Joshua ... New York, NY
Aber, Marcy Elizabeth ... **Charleston, WV**
Aber, Nina J. ... New York, NY
Aber, Robert E. ... Washington, DC
Aberant, Kevin E. ... Moorestown, NJ
Aberasturi, John A. ... **Reno, NV**
Aberasturi, John A. ... New York, NY
Aberasturi, Mark G. ... **Greenwich, CT**
Aberbach, Anne-Rachel ... Tempe, AZ
Aberbach, Robert J. ... Fairfax, VA
Aberbook, Donald J. ... **Los Angeles, CA**
Abercrombie, Ann C. ... Overland Park, KS
Abercrombie, Charles D. ... **New York, NY**
Abercrombie, David W., II ... Kissimmee, FL
Abercrombie, Denis K. ... **Houston, TX**
Abercrombie, Gail Martin ... **Tampa, FL**
Abercrombie, Gene R. ... **Sylvania, OH**
Abercrombie, John B. ... **Houston, TX**
Abercrombie & McGowan ... Laurens, SC
Abercrombie, Ralph L. ... Tulsa, OK
Abercrombie, Robert A. ... Idaho Falls, ID
Abercrombie, W. Arthur, Jr.
Baton Rouge, LA
Abere, Kenneth J, Jr ... **Portland, OR**
Aberg, Charles P. ... Dallas, TX
Aberg, Joel L. ... **Eau Claire, WI**
Aberg, Robert K. ... Madison, WI
Aberle & Aberle ... Timber Lake, SD
Aberle, Andrew ... Timber Lake, SD
Aberle, Christopher A. ... Mandeville, LA
Aberle, Derek K. ... **La Jolla, CA**
Aberle, Douglas S. ... **Beverly Hills, CA**
Aberle, Heather L. ... **Raleigh, NC**
Aberle, Richard M. ... Brooklyn, NY
Aberle, Steve ... Timber Lake, SD
Aberle, Timothy J. ... Hickory, NC
Aberly, Jessica R. ... **Albuquerque, NM**
Aberman, Carolyn Gold ... **Chicago, IL**
Aberman, Debbi L. ... **High Point, NC**
Aberman, J. Mitchell ... **Charlotte, NC**
Aberman, Jonathan E. ... **Chicago, IL**
Aberman, Jonathan M. ... **Vienna, VA**
Abern, Steven S. ... **Oakland, CA**
Abernathy, Anna Mandle ... St. Louis, MO
Abernathy, C. Mark ... Longview, TX
Abernathy, Carroll J., (Mr.)
St. Petersburg, FL
Abernathy, Charles F. ... Washington, DC
Abernathy, Conielyn Lowry
Memphis, TN
Abernathy, David A. ... Treasury Department, Internal Revenue Service, GV
Abernathy, David P. ... St. Louis, MO
Abernathy, Deborah L. ... Caldwell, ID
Abernathy, Frank Gregory ... Nashville, TN
Abernathy, G. Wayne ... **Burlington, NC**
Abernathy, G. Wayne ... **Graham, NC**
Abernathy, George F. ... Spartanburg, SC
Abernathy, James A., II ... **Tuscaloosa, AL**
Abernathy, James R., II ... San Francisco, CA
Abernathy, J. E. ... McKinney, TX
Abernathy, Jon C. ... **Indianapolis, IN**
Abernathy, L. Rebecca ... Marietta, GA
Abernathy, Michael J. ... **Chicago, IL**
Abernathy, Michael Kevin
Birmingham, AL
Abernathy, Michael R. ... San Bernardino, CA
Abernathy, Michele L. ... **Los Angeles, CA**
Abernathy, Nancy J. ... **Orlando, FL**
Abernathy, Richard M. ... **McKinney, TX**
Abernathy, Robert S. ... **Oklahoma City, OK**
Abernathy, Roeder, Boyd & Joplin, A Professional Corporation ... **McKinney, TX**
Abernathy, Ronald ... Stockton, CA
Abernathy, Terry J. ... **Cedar Rapids, IA**
Abernathy, Terry, Law Offices of
Selmer, TN
Abernathy, Thomas E., IV ... **Atlanta, GA**
Abernathy, William L., Jr. ... **Nashville, TN**
Abernethy, Andrew H. ... **New York, NY**
Abernethy, Auld & Young, P.C.
Allison Park, PA
Abernethy, Bruce R., Jr. ... Fort Pierce, FL
Abernethy, Bruce R., Jr., P.A.
Fort Pierce, FL
Abernethy, Christopher M. ... Allison Park, PA
Abernethy, Claudia E. ... Denver, CO
Abernethy, David F. ... **Philadelphia, PA**
Abernethy, Deedra ... Fort Walton Beach, FL
Abernethy, Durant S., III ... Silver Spring, MD
Abernethy, J. Carroll, Jr. ... Hickory, NC
Abernethy, James M. ... **Phoenix, AZ**
Abernethy, James W., Jr. ... Jackson, MS
Abernethy, Jesse David ... Hickory, NC
Abernethy, Jonathan S. ... **New York, NY**
Abernethy Law Office, P.C. ... Hobbs, NM
Abernethy, Oswald C. ... Denver, CO
Abernethy, Pamela L. ... Salem, OR
Abernethy, Perry C. ... Hobbs, NM
Abernethy, Phil B. ... **Jackson, MS**
Abernethy, Richard B. ... Gastonia, NC
Abernethy, Rita M. ... Kansas City, MO
Abernethy, Samuel F. ... **New York, NY**
Abernethy, W. Miller, Jr. ... **Charlotte, NC**
Abernethy, William A.
Corpus Christi, TX
Abernethy, William S., Jr. ... **Cincinnati, OH**
Abers, Jeff S. ... **Fort Lauderdale, FL**
Abers, Julia E. ... Thousand Oaks, CA
Aberson, Leslie D. ... **Louisville, KY**
Abert, Karl J. ... Manhattan Beach, CA
Aberth & Champion, Co., LPA
Akron, OH
Aberth, Joel R. ... **Akron, OH**
Aberwald, W. J. ... Houston, TX
Abery-Wetstone, Holly ... Farmington, CT
Abes, Alan H. ... **Cincinnati, OH**
Abes Baumann, A Professional Corporation
Pittsburgh, PA
Abes, Edward Jaffee ... **Pittsburgh, PA**
Abes, Elisa S. ... Cincinnati, OH
Abesada, Peter R. ... Coral Gables, FL
Abeska, Gary E. ... **Farmington Hills, MI**
Abeska, Gary E., P.C., Law Offices of
Detroit, MI
Farmington Hills, MI
Abeska, Timothy J. ... **South Bend, IN**
Abeyta & Blakenship ... Lubbock, TX
Abeyta, Dan David
Federal Communications Commission, Wireless Telecommunications Bureau, GV
Abeyta, David S., Sr. ... Sacaton, AZ
Abeyta, Sean P. ... Lubbock, TX
Abeyta, Terry P. ... **Yakima, WA**
Abeyta-Nelson P.C. ... **Ellensburg, WA**
Sunnyside, WA
Toppenish, WA
Yakima, WA
Abeywardena, Priya ... Pasadena, CA
Abfalter, Kendra M. ... Keokuk, IA
Abiassi, Virginia Hays ... Houston, TX
Abich, Yvette M. ... **Los Angeles, CA**
Abide, Peter C. ... **Biloxi, MS**
Abide, Samera L. ... Baton Rouge, LA
Abi-Esber, George D. ... Salem, MA
Abikoff, Kevin T. ... Washington, DC
Abilheira & Abilheira ... Warren, RI
Abilheira, Becki Anne ... Warren, RI
Abilheira, Elias ... New York, NY
Abilheira, Louis B. ... Warren, RI
Abilheira, Richard B. ... Warren, RI
Abi-Nader, Francis J. ... Sacramento, CA
Abinanti, Abby ... San Francisco, CA
Abinanti, Thomas J. ... White Plains, NY
Abington, Michelle Stevens ... Chicago, IL
Abington, William H. ... Austin, TX
Abiona, Olu O. ... Philadelphia, PA
Abish, Alan S. ... New Hyde Park, NY
Abislaiman-Quilez, Isabel ... **San Juan, PR**
Abitanta, Susan E. ... **Los Angeles, CA**
Abitbol, R. Gordon ... New York, NY
Abiuso, Robert A. ... Rosedale, NY
Abizaid, John G. ... Bedford, MA
Abkin, Joseph D. ... **Santa Barbara, CA**
Ablah, George M. ... Oklahoma City, OK
Ablan, Michael C. ... La Crosse, WI
Ablan, Michael C., S.C. ... La Crosse, WI
Ablan, Paul M. ... St. Paul, MN
Ablard, Charles D. ... **Washington, DC**
Ablard, Gary P. ... Rancho Cucamonga, CA
Ablard, James Edward ... McLean, VA
Able, Bryan C ... Laurens, SC
Able, Frank D. ... Ocala, FL
Able, Levert J. ... Houston, TX
Able, Walter ... Columbus, IN
Able, William F. ... Irmo, SC
Ableman, Adam J. ... New York, NY
Ableman, S. Bernard ... **Wilmington, DE**
Abler, Julius ... Lake Forest, IL
Abler, Lawrence J. ... Issaquah, WA
Ables, Charles R. ... South Pittsburg, TN
Ables, Clifford M., III ... **Sebring, FL**
Ables, Clifford M., III, P.A. ... **Sebring, FL**
Wauchula, FL
Ables, Clinton E. ... Carrollton, TX
Ables, J. Angela ... **Oklahoma City, OK**
Ables, Jackson H., III ... **Jackson, MS**
Ables, Joseph A., Jr. ... Houston, TX
Ables, Kee A. ... **Fort Worth, TX**
Ables, L. Bruce ... **Huntsville, AL**
Ables, Lyn E. ... Madill, OK
Ables, Michael S. ... Chicago, IL
Ables, Stephen B. ... Kerrville, TX
Ables, Wendell P. ... Salt Lake City, UT
Ables, William M., Jr. ... South Pittsburg, TN
Ableser, Gary D. ... Los Angeles, CA
Ablin, Karyn K. ... **Washington, DC**
Ablin, Rachel Beth ... Deerfield, IL
Abling, Madeliene C. ... Orlando, FL
Abloeser, Samuel ... Philadelphia, PA
Ablon, Herman ... **Los Angeles, CA**
Pasadena, CA
Ablon, Janel R. ... **Cerritos, CA**
Ablon, Paul S. ... Los Angeles, CA
Ablondi, Foster, Sobin & Davidow, P.C.
Washington, DC
Ablondi, Italo H. ... **Washington, DC**
Ablondi Law Firm, P.A. ... **Little Rock, AR**
Ablondi, Leslie R. ... **Little Rock, AR**
Abma, Kimberly A. ... Chicago, IL
Abma, Kimberly Anderle, P.C. ... Chicago, IL
Abma, Shane E. ... **Portland, OR**
Abner, Brett P. ... **Jacksonville, FL**
Abner, Eddie Lee ... San Dimas, CA
Abner, L. Pharr ... **Winter Park, FL**
Abner, Roy Lee ... Houston, TX
Abner, Valencia M. ... Miami, FL
Abneri, Michael D. ... **Mineola, NY**
Riverhead, NY
Abney, Benjamin Cade ... Canton, GA
Abney, Benjamin P. ... **Tulsa, OK**
Abney, Bill H. ... Memphis, TN
Abney, David L. ... **Mesa, AZ**
Abney, F. Glenn ... Clarkston, GA
Abney, Fred S. ... Dallas, TX
Abney, James R. ... **Palo Alto, CA**
Portland, OR
Abney, James W., III ... Wilson, NC
Abney, L. Kent ... Austin, TX
Abney, Michael L. ... **Costa Mesa, CA**
Abney, Robert M. ... Des Arc, AR
Abney, Ruben K. ... **Marshall, TX**
Abney, Russell T. ... **Houston, TX**
Abney, Scott A. ... **Birmingham, AL**
Abney, Stephen E. ... Sugar Land, TX
Abney, Steven Russell ... Irving, TX
Abney, T. Robert ... **Memphis, TN**
Abney & Warwick ... **Marshall, TX**
Abney, William A., (P.C.) ... **Marshall, TX**
Abney, William C., Jr. ... Oklahoma City, OK
Abney, William S. ... Chickamauga, GA
Abney, Wilson R. ... Department of Commerce, Office of the General Counsel, GV
Abney, Wm. L., Jr. ... La Fayette, GA
Abnoosian, Margret ... Glendale, CA
Abod, Christopher P. ... Washington, DC
Abod, Curtis P. ... **Rockville, MD**
Falls Church, VA
Abodeely, John E. ... Worcester, MA
Abodeely, Joseph E. ... **Phoenix, AZ**
Abodeely, Michael N., Jr. ... Worcester, MA
Abokhair, John K. ... **Reston, VA**
Abokhair, Paul K. ... Dallas, TX
Abolafia, Eliot ... Portland, CT
Abolafia, Leon ... New York, NY
Abolafia, Morris M. ... Rockville Centre, NY
Aboloff, Steven A. ... **Moorestown, NJ**
Abolofia, Gary M. ... Bellevue, WA
Aboneaaj, Maiser ... **Washington, DC**
Abood, Abood & Rheaume, P.C.
Lansing, MI
Abood, Andrew P. ... Lansing, MI
Abood, Camille S., (Mr.) ... Lansing, MI
Abood, Charles D. ... Sylvania, OH
Abood, Elizabeth M. ... **Rochester Hills, MI**
Abood, Ernest N. ... Canton, OH
Abood, Fredric Joseph ... Lansing, MI
Abood, Fredric S. ... Lansing, MI
Abood, James Christopher ... Lansing, MI
Abood, Mark S. ... Broadview Heights, OH
Abood, Mary M. ... Chicago, IL
Abood, Norman J. ... Jacksonville, FL
Abood, Randolph G. ... New York, NY
Abood, Richard J. ... Lansing, MI
Abood, Richard R. ... Stockton, CA
Abood, Robert G. ... Clearwater, FL
Abood, Teresa S. ... Lansing, MI
Abood, Thomas J. ... Englewood, CO
Abood, Thomas J. ... Minneapolis, MN
Aborjaily, Richard V. ... Norwich, VT
Aborlleile, Christina ... Philadelphia, PA
Aborn, Audrey B. ... Scarsdale, NY
Aborn, Richard A. ... **New York, NY**
Aborn, Richard M. ... New York, NY
Aborn, Sargent L. ... New York, NY
Abouaf, Michael ... San Fernando, CA
Abou-Assaly, Nicolas ... **Cedar Rapids, IA**
Aboud & Aboud, P.C. ... Tucson, AZ
Aboud, Gary A. ... El Paso, TX
Aboud, John ... Tucson, AZ
Aboud, John E. ... Tucson, AZ
Aboud, Michael J. ... Tucson, AZ
Aboud, Robert Allen ... **Philadelphia, PA**
Aboud, Russell M. ... El Paso, TX
Aboud, Shelley L. ... Honaunau, HI
Aboulafia, Beth ... **San Francisco, CA**
Aboulafia, David I. ... New York, NY
Aboulhosn, Omar J. ... **Princeton, WV**
Abourezk, Charles ... Rapid City, SD
Abourezk Law Firm, P.C. ... Rapid City, SD
Abourezk, Michael C. ... Rapid City, SD
Aboussie, Marilyn ... Austin, TX
Aboussleman, Sharon ... Houston, TX
Abouzeid, Mahmoud ... **San Francisco, CA**
Abouzeid, Walid M. ... San Gabriel, CA
Abow, Steven E.
Office of Personnel Management, Merit Systems Division, GV
Abowitz, C. Alexa ... **Cherry Hill, NJ**
Philadelphia, PA
Abowitz, Larry J. ... Iselin, NJ
Abowitz, Milton D. ... **Philadelphia, PA**
Abowitz, Murray E. ... **Oklahoma City, OK**
Abowitz, Rhodes & Dahnke, P.C.
Oklahoma City, OK
Aboyoun, Joseph S. ... **Fairfield, NJ**
Aboyoun, Joseph S. ... **Hackensack, NJ**
Newark, NJ
Abplanalp, Arthur A., Jr. ... **Vail, CO**
Abracen, Michele ... **Los Angeles, CA**
Abracht-Smith, Jennifer ... **Phoenix, AZ**
Abraha, Negussie A. ... **Denver, CO**
Abraham, A. Lee, Jr. ... **Greenwood, MS**
Jackson, MS
Abraham, Aaron N. ... **New York, NY**
Abraham, Adrienne ... Bayside, NY
Abraham, Ajita E. ... **New York, NY**
Abraham, Andrew ... **Phoenix, AZ**
Abraham, Anil K. ... **Washington, DC**
Abraham, Anslyene A. ... Los Angeles, CA
Abraham, Arthur A. ... El Paso, TX
Abraham, Arthur A., P.C. ... El Paso, TX
Abraham & Associates, P.A.
Greenwood, MS
Jackson, MS
Abraham Bauer & Spalding, P.C.
Phillipsburg, NJ
Allentown, PA
Lancaster, PA
Lebanon, PA
Philadelphia, PA
Reading, PA
Abraham, Beril M. ... **Virginia Beach, VA**
Abraham, Beril M., P.C. ... **Norfolk, VA**
Virginia Beach, VA
Abraham, Brian R. ... Logan, WV
Abraham, Charles P. ... **Morristown, NJ**
Abraham, Daniel N. ... **Columbus, OH**
Abraham, David ... **Palo Alto, CA**
Abraham, David ... Coral Gables, FL
Abraham, David T. ... **Jacksonville, FL**
Abraham, Dennis M. ... Philadelphia, PA
Abraham, Diane L. ... **El Segundo, CA**
Abraham, Don ... White Plains, NY
Abraham, Donald L. ... **Chicago, IL**
Abraham, Donald L. ... Watertown, WI
Abraham, Douglas C. ... Livonia, MI
Abraham, E. Spencer ... Washington, DC
Abraham, Eric I. ... **Newark, NJ**
Abraham, Frank, (P.C.) ... **Houston, TX**
Abraham, George D. ... Washington, DC
Abraham, Gerald ... Villanova, PA
Abraham, Grady J. ... **Lafayette, LA**
Abraham, Herbert L. ... Milwaukee, WI
Abraham, Jacob W. ... New York, NY
Abraham, Jake L. ... Port Gibson, MS
Abraham, James E. ... Tucson, AZ
Abraham, James E. ... **Pittsburgh, PA**
Abraham, Jason F. ... **Milwaukee, WI**
Abraham, Jeffrey L. ... **Milwaukee, WI**
Abraham, Jeffrey S. ... New York, NY
Abraham, Jerry R. ... Farmington Hills, MI
Abraham, Jonathan David ... **New York, NY**
Abraham, Joseph ... Buffalo, NY

Abraham, Joseph J. .... Fenton, MI
Abraham, Joseph J., P.C. .... Fenton, MI
Abraham, Joseph (Sib), Jr., Law Offices of El Paso, TX
Abraham, Julie .... New York, NY
Abraham, Karen Miller .... New York, NY
Abraham, Katherine .... Burbank, IL
Abraham, Kenneth A. .... Wheaton, IL
Abraham, Kenneth M. .... Hood River, OR
Abraham, Kenneth R. .... Fern Park, FL
Abraham, Kenneth S. .... Charlottesville, VA
Abraham, Kimberlee C. .... New York, NY
Abraham, Larry J. .... Bethesda, MD
Abraham, Laurie .... Portland, OR
Abraham, Lawrence F. .... Chicago, IL
Abraham, Lois W. .... Palo Alto, CA
Abraham, Lorraine Abelson Hackensack, NJ
Abraham, Louis, III .... Tulsa, OK
Abraham, Lu Ellen .... San Antonio, TX
Abraham, Lynne M. .... Philadelphia, PA
Abraham, Margaret Johnston Leonardtown, MD
Abraham, Marian .... Boston, MA
Provincetown, MA
Abraham, Mark S. .... McLean, VA
Abraham, Marnie E. .... Jeannette, PA
Abraham, Matthew J. .... Fenton, MI
Abraham, Michael A. .... Los Angeles, CA
Abraham, Michael D. .... San Francisco, CA
Abraham, Nicholas A. .... Boston, MA
Abraham, Nina E. .... Philadelphia, PA
Abraham, Parayil K. .... Seattle, WA
Abraham, Patricia A. .... New York, NY
Abraham, Peter E. .... Miami, FL
Abraham, Philip .... Washington, DC
Baltimore, MD
Abraham, Philip F. .... Richmond, VA
Abraham, Philip T. .... Portland, OR
Abraham, Rene S. .... San Bernardino, CA
Abraham, Richard H. .... Sun Lakes, AZ
Abraham, Richard K. .... Baltimore, MD
Abraham, Richard P. .... Philadelphia, PA
Abraham, Rick Joseph .... Columbus, OH
Abraham, Robert .... Daytona Beach, FL
Abraham, Robert J. .... Pittsburgh, PA
Abraham, Robert K. .... Department of Justice, Civil Rights Division, GV
Abraham, Robert L. .... Glenview, IL
Abraham, Robin A. .... Orlando, FL
Abraham & Rose, P.L.C. Farmington Hills, MI
Abraham, Sammuel David .... Lafayette, LA
Abraham & Silver .... New York, NY
Abraham, Stephen Edward .... Irvine, CA
Abraham, Stephen G. .... Worcester, MA
Abraham, Stephen H. .... Washington, DC
Abraham, Steven E. .... Philadelphia, PA
Abraham, Susan .... Los Angeles, CA
Abraham, Teena M. .... Milwaukee, WI
Abraham, Thomas J. .... North Hollywood, CA
Abraham, V. Mary .... New York, NY
Abraham, Vaughn P. .... Harvard, MA
Abraham, Watkins, Nichols Sorrels, Matthews & Friend .... Houston, TX
Abraham, William J. .... Columbus, OH
Abraham, William J., Jr. .... Milwaukee, WI
Abraham-Handy, Constance V. Lake Charles, LA
Abrahami, Rachelle .... New York, NY
Abrahams, Charles L. .... San Diego, CA
Abrahams, Colin P. .... Woodland Hills, CA
Abrahams, Dana L. .... Bloomfield Hills, MI
Abrahams, Daniel B. .... Washington, DC
Abrahams, Denise M. .... Washington, DC
Abrahams, Douglas A. .... Philadelphia, PA
Abrahams, George N. .... New York, NY
Abrahams, Harlan S. .... Denver, CO
Abrahams, Howard A. .... Potomac, MD
Abrahams, Jay M. .... Kew Gardens, NY
Abrahams, Jessica C. .... Washington, DC
Abrahams, Jonathan D. .... Southfield, MI
Abrahams, Karen L. .... Atlanta, GA
Abrahams Kaslow & Cassman Omaha, NE
Abrahams, Krista M. .... New York, NY
Abrahams, L. Vanessa .... New York, NY
Abrahams, Lewis J. .... Westbury, NY
Abrahams, Loewenstein, Bushman & Kauffman, P.C. .... Haddonfield, NJ
Philadelphia, PA
Abrahams, Mark C. .... Sedona, AZ
Abrahams, Milton R. .... Omaha, NE
Abrahams, Mitchell W. .... Hackensack, NJ
Abrahams, Peter .... Los Angeles, CA
Abrahams, Philip S. .... Chicago, IL
Abrahams, Richard K. .... Warren, CT
Abrahams, Richard N. .... Massapequa, NY
Abrahams, Robert M. .... New York, NY
Abrahams, Robert S. .... Baltimore, MD
Abrahams, Seymour J. .... San Jose, CA
Abrahams, Sharon A. .... Simi Valley, CA
Abrahams, Teri .... Gaithersburg, MD
Abrahamsen, Dana Federal Trade Commission, Bureau of Competition, GV
Abrahamsen, Edwin A. .... Scranton, PA
Abrahamsen, Maria B. Bloomfield Hills, MI
Abrahamsen, Mary Ann Conaboy Scranton, PA
Abrahamsen, Moran & Conaboy, P.C. Scranton, PA
Abrahamsen, Richard J. .... Englewood, NJ
Abrahamsen, Robert M. .... Boston, MA
Abrahamsen, Thomas C. .... West Chester, PA
Abrahamson, A. Craig .... Tulsa, OK
Abrahamson, Alan Y. .... Los Angeles, CA
Abrahamson, Bruce H. .... Omaha, NE
Abrahamson, Dale T. .... Stuart, FL
Abrahamson, Daniel N. .... Madison, WI
Abrahamson, Donald R. .... Las Vegas, NV
Abrahamson, Erik G. .... Clearwater, FL
Tampa, FL
Abrahamson, Harold .... Hammond, IN
Abrahamson, Hugh I. .... Omaha, NE
Abrahamson, Jeffery Alan .... Washington, DC
Abrahamson, Joel E. .... Minneapolis, MN
Abrahamson, Jos. L. .... Minneapolis, MN
Abrahamson, Larry R. .... Fort Collins, CO
Abrahamson, Laura Cline Los Angeles, CA
Abrahamson, Maurice F. .... Morton Grove, IL
Abrahamson, Norman G. .... Canton, MA
Abrahamson, Reed & Adley Crown Point, IN
Hammond, IN
Abrahamson, Richard C. .... Victorville, CA
Abrahamson, S., & Associates, S.C. Milwaukee, WI
Abrahamson, Sally N. .... Chicago, IL
Abrahamson, Scott R. .... San Diego, CA
Abrahamson, Sherman S. .... Milwaukee, WI
Abrahamson, Shirley S. .... Madison, WI
Abrahamson & Uiterwyk .... Bradenton, FL
Clearwater, FL
New Port Richey, FL
St. Petersburg, FL
Spring Hill, FL
Tampa, FL
Abrahamson, Vicki Lafer .... Chicago, IL
Abrahamson Vorachek & Mikva Chicago, IL
Abrahamsson, Nili .... Denver, CO
Abrahamzon, Dennis .... Minneapolis, MN
Abram, Dawn M. .... Boston, MA
Abram, Donald E. .... Denver, CO
Abram, Gregory D. .... Hempstead, NY
Abram, James M., (P.A.) .... Jackson, MS
Abram, John .... Pasadena, CA
Abram, Jonathan B. .... Minneapolis, MN
Abram, Jonathan L. .... Washington, DC
Abram, Marian C. .... Trinity, NC
Abram, Michael E. .... New York, NY
Abram, Morris B. .... New York, NY
Abram, Morris B., Jr. .... Los Angeles, CA
Abram, Paul Henry .... Hanford, CA
Abram, Peggy Steif .... Minneapolis, MN
Abram, Prudence Beatty .... New York, NY
Abram, Richard S. .... Atlanta, GA
Abram, Sam L. .... New York, NY
Abram, Steven .... Los Angeles, CA
Abram, Theodore D. .... Klamath Falls, OR
Abram, Thomas G. .... Chicago, IL
Abram, Thomas L. .... Phoenix, AZ
Abram, William H. .... Overland, MO
Abramczyk, Jon E. .... Wilmington, DE
Abramczyk, Lawrence R. Bingham Farms, MI
Abramitis, W. Robert .... Miami, FL
Abramo, John G. .... Wilmington, DE
Abramo, Paul L. .... Newton, NJ
Abramoff, Bonnie M. .... Milwaukee, WI
Abramoff, David B. .... Baltimore, MD
Abramoff, Howard B. .... Cleveland, OH
Abramoff, Milton M. Ocean Township, NJ
Abramoff, Neuberger and Linder, LLP Baltimore, MD
Abramonte, Frank .... Seattle, WA
Abramov, B. Roslyn .... New York, NY
Abramov, Hope K. .... St. Louis, MO
Abramovici, David .... Miami, FL
Abramovici, Simon Alejandro Boynton Beach, FL
Abramovitz, Carole S. .... New York, NY
Abramovitz, Daniel T. .... Trenton, NJ
Abramovitz, David .... New York, NY
Abramovitz, Lawrence A. .... Chicago, IL
Abramovitz & Merriam .... Denver, CO
Abramovitz, Michael J., (P.C.) Denver, CO
Abramovitz, Naomi Gil .... Park Forest, IL
Abramovitz, Paul S. .... San Rafael, CA
Abramovsky, Abraham .... New York, NY
Abramovsky, Deborah .... Hauppauge, NY
Abramow, Denise H. .... Las Vegas, NV
Abramowich, Patrick L. .... Pittsburgh, PA
Abramowitch, Jay N. .... Wyomissing, PA
Abramowitz, Alan A. .... Baltimore, MD
Abramowitz, Alton L. .... New York, NY
Abramowitz, Andrew .... New York, NY
Abramowitz, Andrew D. .... Philadelphia, PA
Abramowitz, Arnold C. .... Melville, NY
Abramowitz, Arnold M. .... Irvington, NJ
Abramowitz, Arthur J. .... Cherry Hill, NJ
Abramowitz, Benj. .... Flushing, NY
Abramowitz, Bennett I. .... Dallas, TX
Abramowitz, Christine Bacon White Plains, NY
Abramowitz, David E. .... Marlborough, MA
Abramowitz, David N. .... New York, NY
Abramowitz, David S. .... Department of State, Office of the Legal Adviser, GV
Abramowitz & Dorian .... Annandale, VA
Abramowitz, Edward W. .... Annandale, VA
Abramowitz, Elkan .... New York, NY
Abramowitz, Fred .... Albuquerque, NM
Abramowitz, George R. .... Washington, DC
Abramowitz, Jed A. .... Philadelphia, PA
Abramowitz, Jeffrey .... Philadelphia, PA
Abramowitz, Joshua L. .... New York, NY
Abramowitz, Laurie .... New York, NY
Abramowitz, Marc L. .... Oakland, CA
Abramowitz, Mark .... New York, NY
Abramowitz, Mildred W. .... Roslyn, NY
Abramowitz, Morton H. .... Niagara Falls, NY
Abramowitz, Nancy S. .... Potomac, MD
Abramowitz, Nathan .... New York, NY
Abramowitz, Philip B. .... Buffalo, NY
Abramowitz, Philip D. .... Encino, CA
Abramowitz & Pomerantz, P.A. Fort Lauderdale, FL
Abramowitz, Richard Fort Lauderdale, FL
Abramowitz, Robert L. .... Philadelphia, PA
Abramowitz, Robin S. .... Melville, NY
Abramowitz, Ronald A. .... New Brunswick, NJ
Abramowitz, Stephan H. .... Brooklyn, NY
Abramowitz, Steven M. .... New York, NY
Abramowitz, Steven N. .... Miami, FL
Abrams, A. David, Jr. .... Beckley, WV
Abrams, Adele L. .... Washington, DC
Abrams, Alan A. .... San Diego, CA
Abrams, Alan M. .... Richland, WA
Abrams, Allan E. .... Leawood, KS
Abrams, Allan E., P.C. .... Leawood, KS
Abrams, Allen W. .... Philadelphia, PA
Abrams, Alma Lutjen .... Princeton, NJ
Abrams, Amy L. .... Northbrook, IL
Abrams, Amy L. .... Albertson, NY
Abrams, Andrew C. .... Washington, DC
Abrams, Andrew C. .... Saddle Brook, NJ
Abrams, Andrew L. .... Charleston, SC
Abrams, Anessa .... Washington, DC
Abrams Anton P.A. .... Boca Raton, FL
Hollywood, FL
Abrams, Arnold B. .... Encino, CA
Abrams, Arnold B. .... Meriden, CT
Abrams, Arthur J. .... Jersey City, NJ
Abrams, Arthur J. .... Central Islip, NY
Abrams, Arthur L. .... Newark, NJ
Abrams, Barbara .... Woodcliff Lake, NJ
Abrams & Barliant, P.C. .... Santa Fe, NM
Abrams, Barry .... Houston, TX
Abrams, Barry S. .... Newark, NJ
Abrams, Belle-Ann .... Danbury, CT
Abrams, Bernard W. .... Birmingham, MI
Abrams, Bertram A. .... New York, NY
Abrams, Beryl A. .... New York, NY
Abrams, Bobby .... Tarzana, CA
Abrams, Bobby, A Law Corp. .... Tarzana, CA
Abrams, Bobby G. .... Wilson, NC
Abrams, Brenda Glaser .... Bala Cynwyd, PA
Abrams, Brenda M. .... Fort Lauderdale, FL
Miami, FL
Abrams, Brian K. .... Northfield, IL
Abrams, Brian Michael .... Bingham Farms, MI
Abrams, Bruce C. .... Chicago, IL
Abrams, Burton M. .... New York, NY
Abrams, Burton R. .... Chicago, IL
Abrams & Byron .... Beckley, WV
Abrams & Chapman .... Chicago, IL
Abrams & Cincotta .... Framingham, MA
Abrams, Clark S. .... New York, NY
Abrams, Clement Onan .... Houston, TX
Abrams, Clifford E. .... Boerne, TX
Abrams, Danal F. .... New York, NY
Abrams, Daniel E. .... Palm Beach Gardens, FL
Abrams, Daniel L. .... New York, NY
Abrams, David .... Millburn, NJ
Abrams, David .... New York, NY
Abrams, David .... Monroeville, PA
Abrams, David A. .... Cherry Hill, NJ
Philadelphia, PA
Abrams, David I. .... Sacramento, CA
Abrams, David J. .... New York, NY
Abrams, David L. .... Jasper, AL
Abrams, David L. .... Washington, DC
Abrams, David N. .... Newark, NJ
Abrams, David R. .... Minneapolis, MN
Abrams, David S. .... Washington, DC
Abrams, Debora L. .... New York, NY
Abrams, Denise .... Oakland, CA
Abrams, Dennis M. .... Bala Cynwyd, PA
Abrams, Donald L. .... Laguna Beach, CA
Abrams, Donald L. .... New York, NY
Abrams, Donald-Bruce .... Boston, MA
Abrams, Donna Elise .... White Plains, NY
Abrams, Douglas B. .... Raleigh, NC
Abrams, Douglas E. .... New York, NY
Abrams, Edward L. .... Lynbrook, NY
Abrams, Elisha Hoffman .... Philadelphia, PA
Abrams, Elizabeth R. .... Los Angeles, CA
Abrams, Ellen .... Harrison, NY
Abrams, Ellen Joyce .... West Palm Beach, FL
Abrams, Elliott .... Walnut Creek, CA
Abrams, Ellis H. .... Atlanta, GA
Abrams Etter & Marks, Professional Association .... Fort Lauderdale, FL
Miami, FL
Abrams, Florence E. .... Albany, NY
Abrams, Floyd .... New York, NY
Abrams, Francine H. .... Encino, CA
Abrams, Frank A. .... Miami, FL
Abrams, Franklin S. .... New York, NY
Abrams, Franklin S. .... Syosset, NY
Abrams, Gail G. .... Little Silver, NJ
Abrams, Gail L. .... New York, NY
Abrams, Garfinkel & Rosen, LLP Los Angeles, CA
New York, NY
Westbury, NY
Abrams, Gary D. .... Chicago, IL
Abrams, Gary D. & Associates, Ltd. Chicago, IL
Abrams, Geoffrey .... New York, NY
Abrams, George S. .... Boston, MA
Abrams, Gerald H. .... Newton, MA
Abrams, Gorelick, Friedman & Jacobson, P.C. .... Livingston, NJ
New York, NY
Abrams, Gregory S. .... Los Angeles, CA
Abrams, Harold E. .... Atlanta, GA
Abrams, Harold R. .... Chicago, IL
Abrams, Harold R., P.C. .... Chicago, IL
Abrams, Harvey A. .... Tallahassee, FL
Abrams, Heidi J. .... Seattle, WA
Abrams, Helene F. .... Phoenix, AZ
Abrams, Henry R. .... Baltimore, MD
Abrams, Herbert .... Skokie, IL
Abrams, Herbert .... Boston, MA
Abrams, Hesha .... Dallas, TX
Abrams, Howard B. .... Detroit, MI
Abrams, Hugh A. .... Chicago, IL
Abrams, Idelle R. .... New York, NY
Abrams, Ira .... Fort Lauderdale, FL
Miami, FL
Abrams, Irwen .... New York, NY
Abrams, Israel .... North Miami Beach, FL
Abrams, Israel, P.A. North Miami Beach, FL
Abrams, Ivan S. .... Fresno, CA
Abrams, J. Theodore .... Birmingham, AL
Abrams, James H. .... San Francisco, CA
Abrams, James H., Jr. .... Summerville, SC
Abrams, James O. .... Sacramento, CA
Abrams, James T. .... Steubenville, OH
Abrams, James Wilson .... Wallingford, CT
Abrams, Jamie C., (Ms.) .... Peekskill, NY
Abrams, Janis .... Pasadena, CA
Abrams, Jason S. .... New York, NY
Abrams, Jed .... New York, NY
Abrams, Jeffrey A. .... Indianapolis, IN
Abrams, Jeffrey H. .... Dallas, TX
Abrams, Jeffrey I. .... Los Angeles, CA
Abrams, Jeffrey L. .... Philadelphia, PA
Abrams, Jennifer S. .... San Francisco, CA
Abrams, Jerald L. .... Eagle Pass, TX
Abrams, Jeri L. .... Roseland, NJ
Abrams, Jerome B. .... Minneapolis, MN
Abrams, Jerrald B. .... Wheeling, IL
Abrams, Jill Allison .... Harrison, NY
Abrams, Jill S. .... New York, NY
Abrams, Jo Ann .... Weston, FL
Abrams, Jon Elliot .... Boston, MA
Abrams, Joseph M. .... Herndon, VA
Abrams, Joshua E. .... Oak Park, CA
Abrams, Joshua L. .... Boston, MA
Abrams, Judd Steven .... Encino, CA
Abrams, Judith .... Los Angeles, CA
Abrams, Karen .... Brooklyn, NY
Abrams, Karen E. .... Parsippany, NJ
Abrams, Karen H. .... Leonardtown, MD
Abrams, Karen Harless .... Youngstown, OH
Abrams, Katherine S. .... Bedminster, NJ
Abrams, Kathryn .... Chicago, IL
Abrams, Kenneth L. .... Phoenix, AZ
Abrams, Kenneth L. .... Hackensack, NJ
Abrams, Kevin G. .... Wilmington, DE
Abrams, Kevin R. .... Batavia, OH
Abrams, Korri E. .... Syosset, NY
Abrams & Lafargue, L.L.C. Shreveport, LA
Abrams, Landau, Ltd. .... Alexandria, VA
Abrams, Laura A. .... Cincinnati, OH
Abrams, Lawrence B., III .... Harrisburg, PA
Abrams, Lawrence I. .... Bethesda, MD
Abrams, Lee N. .... Chicago, IL
Abrams, Lehn E. .... Orlando, FL
Abrams, Leonard O. .... Chicago, IL
Abrams, Leonard O., Law Offices of, A Prof. Corp. .... Chicago, IL
Abrams, Leonard S. .... Philadelphia, PA
Abrams, Linda T. .... Los Angeles, CA
Abrams, Lisa J. .... Merrick, NY
Abrams, Louis M. .... New York, NY
Abrams, Marc .... New York, NY
Abrams, Marc .... Portland, OR
Abrams, Marc B. .... Bethesda, MD
Abrams, Marc L. .... New York, NY
Abrams, Margaret G. .... Chicago, IL
Abrams, Margaret Smith .... Raleigh, NC
Abrams, Marilyn D. .... Oakland, CA
Abrams, Mark .... Glendale, NY
Abrams, Mark E. .... Chicago, IL
Abrams, Mark E. .... New York, NY
Abrams, Marlene R. .... Chicago, IL
Abrams, Martin L. .... El Monte, CA
Abrams, Martin L., A Law Corporation El Monte, CA
Abrams, Marvin .... Pittsburgh, PA
Abrams, Mary DeMarco .... New York, NY
Abrams, Maurice .... Philadelphia, PA
Abrams, Max A. .... Lincolnwood, IL
Abrams & Mazer .... Monroeville, PA
Abrams, Melvyn A. .... Evanston, IL
Abrams, Michael A., II .... Fort Collins, CO
Abrams, Michael Jay .... Kansas City, MO
Abrams, Michael L. .... Hollywood, FL
Abrams, Michael L., Law Offices of Los Angeles, CA
Abrams, Michael L., P.A. .... Hollywood, FL
Abrams, Michael S. .... Santa Monica, CA
Abrams, Michelle J. .... Baltimore, MD
Abrams, Miri C. .... New York, NY
Abrams, Morris M. .... Bethesda, MD
Abrams, Morton .... Boca Raton, FL
Abrams, Murray .... Rego Park, NY
Abrams, Nancy .... Philadelphia, PA
Abrams, Natalie .... New York, NY
Abrams, Neal E. .... Department of Commerce, Patent and Trademark Office, GV
Abrams, Neil .... Falls Church, VA
Abrams, Neil A. .... Somers, NY
Abrams, Nina Dodge .... Farmington Hills, MI
Abrams, Norman .... Los Angeles, CA
Abrams, Norman J. .... New York, NY
Abrams, Norman S. .... Huntington, NY
Abrams, Paul F. .... Santa Fe, NM
Abrams, Paul L. .... Los Angeles, CA
Abrams, Paula L. .... Portland, OR

Abrams, Phillip J. .... Santa Rosa, CA
Abrams, Rachel C. .... New York, NY
Abrams, Reginald W. .... Shreveport, LA
Abrams, Renana B. .... Olathe, KS
Kansas City, MO
Abrams, Richard A. .... Clayton, MO
St. Charles, MO
Abrams, Richard A. .... St. Louis, MO
Abrams, Richard A. .... New York, NY
Abrams, Richard A. .... Youngstown, OH
Abrams, Richard B. Miller .... Boston, MA
Abrams, Richard D. .... Wilmington, DE
Abrams, Richard I. .... Providence, RI
Abrams, Richard J. .... Wilmington, DE
Abrams, Robert .... New York, NY
Abrams, Robert .... New York, NY
Abrams, Robert A. .... Ocean Township, NJ
Toms River, NJ
Abrams, Robert A. .... New York, NY
Abrams, Robert A. .... Pickerington, OH
Abrams, Robert B. .... Pendleton, OR
Abrams, Robert D. .... Framingham, MA
Abrams, Robert G. .... Washington, DC
Abrams, Robert H. .... Detroit, MI
Abrams, Robert J. .... Atlanta, GA
Abrams, Robert, Law Offices of
New Hyde Park, NY
Abrams, Robert Michael .... Falls Church, VA
Abrams, Robert T. .... Newton, MA
Abrams, Roberts, Klickstein & Levy
Boston, MA
Abrams, Robin E. .... New York, NY
Abrams, Robin W. .... Omaha, NE
Abrams, Roger I. .... Newark, NJ
Abrams, Ronald A. .... San Luis Obispo, CA
Abrams, Ronald B. .... Washington, DC
Abrams, Ronald B. .... Philadelphia, PA
Abrams, Ronald L. .... Minnetonka, MN
Abrams, Ronald P. .... Los Angeles, CA
Abrams, Roy C. .... San Mateo, CA
Abrams, Russell S. .... Portland, OR
Abrams, Ruth I. .... Boston, MA
Abrams, Samuel B. .... New York, NY
Abrams, Samuel J. .... Sumter, SC
Abrams, Samuel K. .... Bethesda, MD
Abrams, Sandra Gentner .... Chicago, IL
Abrams, Sarah K. .... Boston, MA
Abrams, Saul M. .... Albany, NY
Abrams & Schenk .... Phoenix, AZ
Abrams Scott & Bickley, L.L.P.
Houston, TX
Abrams, Scott C. .... San Francisco, CA
Abrams, Seth .... Miami, FL
Abrams, Seth M. .... Albany, NY
Abrams, Sharon E. .... Cincinnati, OH
Abrams, Shayna R. .... Nashville, TN
Abrams, Sheri R. .... Fairfax, VA
Abrams, Sherwin D. .... Chicago, IL
Abrams & Smith, A Professional Association
Minneapolis, MN
Abrams & Solomon .... Hackensack, NJ
Abrams, Stanley .... Beverly Hills, CA
Abrams, Stanley D. .... Bethesda, MD
Abrams, Stanton V. .... Newton, MA
Abrams, Stephen E. .... Denver, CO
Abrams, Steven B. .... Farmingdale, NY
Abrams, Steven J. .... Cherry Hill, NJ
Abrams, Steven J. .... New York, NY
Abrams, Steven L. .... Boca Raton, FL
Abrams, Steven R. .... Brooklyn, NY
Abrams, Steven R. .... New York, NY
Abrams, Stuart E. .... New York, NY
Abrams, Sydney .... Willow Grove, PA
Abrams, Theodore C. .... Tucson, AZ
Abrams, Thomas L. .... Fort Lauderdale, FL
Abrams, Thomas L. .... New York, NY
Abrams & Verri .... Providence, RI
Abrams & Walker .... Sumter, SC
Abrams, Walter K. .... South Plainfield, NJ
Abrams, Warren N. .... Dallas, TX
Abrams, Warren N., P.C. .... Dallas, TX
Abrams, West, Storm & Diamond, P.C.
Bethesda, MD
Abrams, William .... Gainesville, FL
Abrams, William F. .... Palo Alto, CA
Abrams, William L. .... Los Angeles, CA
New York, NY
Abrams & Wofsy .... Jersey City, NJ
Abrams, Y. Hillel .... Rockville, MD
Abramschmitt, Dea .... West Palm Beach, FL
Abramsky, Randi Hammer .... Chicago, IL
Abramsohn, Judith E. .... Glendale, AZ
Abramson, Adena R. .... New York, NY
Abramson, Alan B. .... New York, NY
Abramson, Alan Michael .... New York, NY
Abramson, Alana B. .... Pasadena, CA
Abramson, Albert R. .... San Francisco, CA
Abramson, Alfred .... New Orleans, LA
Abramson, Andrew S. .... Jenkintown, PA
Abramson, Andrew S. .... Philadelphia, PA
Abramson, Bradley Scott .... Denver, CO
Abramson, Bruce D. .... Woodland Hills, CA
Abramson, Carl .... Dallas, TX
Abramson, Carol Rose .... New York, NY
Abramson Church & Stave LLP
Salinas, CA
Abramson, Clarence A. .... Scotch Plains, NJ
Abramson, Cyril .... Troy, MI
Abramson, Cyril, P.C. .... Troy, MI
Abramson, Daniel E. .... Sacramento, CA
Abramson, David .... New York, NY
Abramson, David A. .... New Orleans, LA
Abramson, David H. .... Encino, CA
Abramson, David M. .... Columbia, MD
Abramson, David S. .... Saco, ME
Abramson, David S. .... New York, NY
Abramson, David S., Law Offices of
New York, NY
Abramson, Deborah E. .... New York, NY
Abramson, Deborah N. .... Baltimore, MD
Abramson & Denenberg, P.C.
Philadelphia, PA
Abramson, Douglas L. .... Atlanta, GA
Abramson, Edward Joel .... Miami, FL
Abramson, Edward M., (P.C.)
New York, NY
Abramson, Ellen R. .... Hicksville, NY
Abramson, Elliott M. .... Chicago, IL
Abramson, Eric Marshall
San Francisco, CA
Abramson, Floyd H. .... Chicago, IL
Abramson & Fox .... Evergreen, CO
Chicago, IL
Abramson, Frank .... Minneapolis, MN
Abramson, Fredric D. .... Gaithersburg, MD
Abramson & Freedman, L.L.C.
Haddonfield, NJ
Philadelphia, PA
Abramson, Gil A. .... Baltimore, MD
Abramson, Gilbert .... Jenkintown, PA
Abramson, Gilbert B. .... Philadelphia, PA
Abramson, Gilbert L. .... Albany, NY
Abramson, Gillian A. .... Manchester, NH
Abramson, Glen L. .... Philadelphia, PA
Abramson, Gregory S. .... New Orleans, LA
Abramson, Harold A. .... Natick, MA
Abramson, Harold C. .... Dallas, TX
Abramson, Harold I. .... Huntington, NY
Abramson, Harry S. .... New York, NY
Abramson, Harvey P. .... Holland, PA
Abramson, Harvey S. .... North Miami, FL
Abramson, Herbert .... Harrisburg, PA
Abramson, Howard Andrew
Los Angeles, CA
Abramson, Howland W. .... Philadelphia, PA
Abramson, Irving L. .... Radnor, PA
Abramson, Irwin .... Sherman Oaks, CA
Abramson, Jack B. .... New York, NY
Abramson, Jacqueline .... New York, NY
Abramson, James M., Law Offices of
New York, NY
Abramson, Jay B. .... New York, NY
Abramson, Jeffrey B. .... Waltham, MA
Abramson, Jeffrey R. .... Valley Forge, PA
Abramson, Jerry E. .... Louisville, KY
Abramson, Joanna Stark
West Bloomfield, MI
Abramson, Joel E. .... New York, NY
Abramson, Joel F. .... Haddonfield, NJ
Marlton, NJ
Abramson, Joel Marc .... Columbia, MD
Abramson, John M. .... Miami, FL
Abramson, Keith, P.C. .... Bridgeport, CT
Abramson, Keith V. .... Bridgeport, CT
Abramson, Kerry Lee .... Kansas City, MO
Abramson, Kimberly Lieder
New Orleans, LA
Abramson, Laurence C. .... Bethesda, MD
Abramson Law Office, P.A.
North Miami, FL
Abramson, Lawrence D. .... Columbus, OH
Abramson, Lawrence M.
West Palm Beach, FL
Abramson, Lisabeth Hughes .... Louisville, KY
Abramson & Magidson, P.A. .... Miami, FL
Abramson, Marc E. .... Roseville, CA
Abramson, Marc L. .... Boca Raton, FL
Abramson, Mark A. .... Manchester, NH
Nashua, NH
Abramson, Mark C. .... Toledo, OH
Abramson, Mark D. .... Philadelphia, PA
Abramson, Martin .... Washington, DC
Abramson, Martin J., Law Offices
Woodbury, NJ
Abramson, Mary Ann .... Birmingham, MI
Abramson, Mary Ann, P.L.L.C.
Birmingham, MI
Abramson, Mathile W. .... Baton Rouge, LA
Abramson, Michael A. .... Chicago, IL
Abramson, Michelle R. .... Delray Beach, FL
Abramson, Milton E. .... Silver Spring, MD
Abramson, Neil .... New York, NY
Abramson, Neil C. .... New Orleans, LA
Abramson, Neil H. .... New York, NY
Abramson, Norman M. .... Minneapolis, MN
Abramson & O'Connell .... Columbus, OH
Abramson, Paul .... New York, NY
Abramson, Paul H. .... Colorado Springs, CO
Abramson, Phyllis A. .... Natick, MA
Abramson, Raymond R. .... Clarendon, AR
Abramson, Reis, Brown & Dugan
Manchester, NH
Nashua, NH
Abramson, Richard B., Law Office of
Salinas, CA
Abramson, Richard H. .... San Jose, CA
Abramson, Richard J. .... Holland, PA
Abramson, Richard L. .... River Edge, NJ
New York, NY
Abramson, Richard W. .... Hackensack, NJ
Abramson, Robert M. .... Miami, FL
Abramson, Robert M. .... Philadelphia, PA
Abramson, Robert S. .... Baltimore, MD
Abramson, Robert T. .... New York, NY
Abramson, Roberta .... Bridgewater, NJ
Abramson, Ronald .... New York, NY
Abramson, Ronald D. .... Washington, DC
Abramson, Ronald E. .... Washington, DC
Abramson, Ronald M. .... Hackensack, NJ
Abramson, Ronald Marc .... Bethesda, MD
Abramson, Saml. .... Shreveport, LA
Abramson, Sheldon .... Houston, TX
Abramson & Smith, LLP
San Francisco, CA
Abramson, Stanley H. .... Washington, DC
Abramson, Stephanie W. .... New York, NY
Abramson, Steven M., (P.C.)
Washington, DC
Abramson, Stewart Gary .... New York, NY
Abramson, Stuart H. .... Coral Gables, FL
Abramson, Stuart R. .... Waterbury, CT
Abramson, Sumner .... New Bedford, MA
Abramson, Susan H. .... Medina, OH
Abramson, Suzan A. .... Orlando, FL
Abramson, William I. .... Willow, NY
Abramson, William S.
West Palm Beach, FL
Abramson, Young, Brooks and Pefka, P.A.
Palm Beach, FL
West Palm Beach, FL
Abrandt, Jeffrey G. .... New York, NY
White Plains, NY
Abravanel, Allan R. .... Portland, OR
Abravanel, Evelyn Ginsberg
Washington, DC
Abreau, Claudia M. .... Fall River, MA
Abrecht, Mary Ellen .... Washington, DC
Abrego, Everardo .... Weslaco, TX
Abrell, G. William .... San Diego, CA
Abrell, Jennifer J. .... Muncie, IN
Abrell, John .... Springfield, IL
Abrell, Joseph K. .... Miami, FL
Abrell, Mark L. .... Muncie, IN
Abresch, James H. .... Birmingham, MI
Abreu, Alice G. .... Philadelphia, PA
Abreu, Elizabeth I. .... Los Angeles, CA
Abreu, Kelly .... Temecula, CA
Abreu, Luis A. .... Danville, VA
Abreu, Monica L. .... Albany, NY
Abreu, Neal O. .... North Highlands, CA
Abreu, Paul .... Walpole, MA
Abrevaya, Joan R. .... Seattle, WA
Abriel, Evangeline G. .... New Orleans, LA
Abright, Harlan P. .... Graham, TX
Abril, Jorge M. .... Miami, FL
Abril, Jorge M., P.A. .... Coral Gables, FL
Miami, FL
Abril, Michael S. .... Bakersfield, CA
Abrohams, Abe .... Green Bay, WI
Abrohams, Benjamin J. .... Milwaukee, WI
Abrolat, Nancy L. .... Los Angeles, CA
Abrolat & Teren .... Los Angeles, CA
Abromaitis, Michael J. .... Baltimore, MD
Abromovitz, Gary B. .... Phoenix, AZ
Abromovitz, Joseph G. .... Boston, MA
Abromovitz & Leahy, P.C. .... Boston, MA
Abromovitz, Les J. .... Pittsburgh, PA
Abromowitz, David M. .... Boston, MA
Abromowitz, David M. .... Columbus, OH
Abromowitz, Philip S. .... Tucson, AZ
Abroms, Hillard M. .... Columbus, OH
Abroms & Weisz .... Columbus, OH
Abromson, Ellen Jane .... Bethesda, MD
Abromson, Nathan F. .... Mount Pleasant, PA
Abrons, Arnold H. .... Norfolk, VA
Abrons, Fasanaro & Sceviour .... Norfolk, VA
Abrons, Herbert L. .... New York, NY
Abronson, Ellen G. .... Woodland Hills, CA
Abronson, William H. .... Beverly Hills, CA
Abruscato, Larissa L. .... Long Beach, CA
Abrusley, Judi F. .... Oakdale, LA
Abrutyn, Elliott .... Livingston, NJ
Abrutyn, Stephanie S. .... New York, NY
Abruzese, Consilvio & Barclay
Medford, MA
Abruzese, Margaret M. .... Boston, MA
Abruzese, Robert G. .... Medford, MA
Abruzzese, Peter A. .... New York, NY
Abruzzese, Thomas E. .... Boston, MA
Abruzzino, Frank K. .... Clarksburg, WV
Abruzzo, Anthony J. .... Tucson, AZ
Abruzzo, Craig M. .... New York, NY
Abruzzo, Craig T. .... New York, NY
Abruzzo, David N. .... Eaton, OH
Abruzzo, Douglas W. .... Gainesville, FL
Abruzzo, E. Christopher .... Harrisburg, PA
Abruzzo, Joseph F. .... Glendale, NY
Abruzzo, Judith F. .... Brooklyn, NY
Abruzzo, Ludwig J. .... Huntington, NY
Abruzzo, Ted J. .... New York, NY
Abruzzo, Terri A. .... Chicago, IL
Absalom, John H., III .... Bridgeport, NJ
Absalonsen, Vern .... Westville, IN
Abse, David I. .... Edgewater, MD
Absher, Cecilia T. .... Fairfield, CT
Absher, Lynn C. .... Dallas, TX
Houston, TX
Absher, Nelea A. .... Louisville, KY
Absher, Sean B. .... Walnut Creek, CA
Abshez, Allan J. .... Los Angeles, CA
Abshier, James L. .... Sioux City, IA
Abshier, Ken .... Houston, TX
Abshier, Phillip G. .... Owensboro, KY
Abshire and Abshire .... Lexington, KY
Abshire, Arthur A. .... Lexington, KY
Abshire, Arthur E. .... Lexington, KY
Abshire, Ashley H. .... Chandler, AZ
Abshire, Donald L., Jr. .... Louisville, KY
Abshure, A. Heath .... Little Rock, AR
Abston, Willie Terrell .... Jackson, MS
Abt, Claudia M. .... Goshen, NY
Abt, David L. .... Westby, WI
Abt, Gregory D. .... Mission Viejo, CA
Abt, Lawrence L., III .... Cherry Hill, NJ
Abt, Morton S. .... Chicago, IL
Abt, Ralph E. .... Chicago, IL
Abt, Richard J. .... Philadelphia, PA
Abt, Suzanne C. .... Philadelphia, PA
Abtahi, Fereydoon .... Newton, MA
Abts, LaVerne E. .... Hartington, NE
Abuan, Albert A. .... Jacksonville, FL
Abu-Assal, Nabil L. .... Los Angeles, CA
AbuBakr, Harriett .... Atlanta, GA
AbuBakr, Harriett, P.C. .... Atlanta, GA
Abudu, Nancy G. .... New York, NY
Abuhoff, Daniel M. .... New York, NY
Abuhoff, Jack S. .... New York, NY
Abul-Hawa, Kemal M. .... Washington, DC
Abumeri, Mark M. .... San Diego, CA
Aburano, Brian .... Honolulu, HI
Aburano, Patricia C. .... Honolulu, HI
Abuso, Dawn Amber .... New Orleans, LA
Abut, Charles C. .... Fort Lee, NJ
Aby, Elizabeth G. .... Minneapolis, MN
Abyad, Imad D. .... Washington, DC
Abzug, Bella S. .... New York, NY
Abzug, Jesse Laurin .... Purchase, NY
Academic Professional Group
San Juan, PR
Acalin, David T. .... Los Angeles, CA
Acampora, Anthony C. .... Jericho, NY
Acampora, John A. .... East Haven, CT
New Haven, CT
Acampora, Judith W. .... Santa Ynez, CA
Acard, Brian D. .... Poughkeepsie, NY
Acarregui, Richard A., (P.S.) .... Seattle, WA
Acayan, Camille L. .... San Jose, CA
Accardi, Anthony J. .... Livingston, NJ
Accardi, Cristina Rose .... Livingston, NJ
Accardi, James R. .... Huntsville, AL
Accardi, Joseph M. .... Woodbridge, NJ
Accardi, Joseph S. .... Livingston, NJ
Accardi, Kristin T. .... Trenton, NJ
Accardi, Marie A. .... Ocean Township, NJ
Accardo, Edrington & Golden, A Professional Law Corporation .... La Place, LA
Accardo, Francis P. .... New Orleans, LA
Accardo, Joseph F. .... Morristown, NJ
Accardo, Joseph, Jr. .... La Place, LA
Accardo, Perry A. .... Chicago, IL
Accardo, Samuel J., Jr. .... La Place, LA
Access USA Lawyer .... Fort Lauderdale, FL
Miami, FL
Accetta, Anthony T. .... Denver, CO
Accetta & Associates, A Professional Corporation .... Denver, CO
Accetta, Barbara S. .... Newton, MA
Accetta, Joseph Michael .... White Plains, NY
Accetta, Susan Hegquist .... New York, NY
Accetta, Therese Ann .... Los Alamitos, CA
Accettola, Paul E. .... Toledo, OH
Accettura, Michael V. .... Springfield, IL
Accettura, P. Mark .... Farmington Hills, MI
Accettura, Paul G. .... Treasury Department, Internal Revenue Service, GV
Acchiardo, S. Rod .... Baltimore, MD
Acchione, Julius C. .... Little Rock, AR
Acciani, Henry D. .... Cincinnati, OH
Accinelli, Steven A. .... New York, NY
Accinelli, Theodora .... Anchorage, AK
Accisano, Francis C. .... Freehold, NJ
Accomazzo, Eric Paul .... Denver, CO
Accomendo, Robert .... Melville, NY
Accordino, Carmen A. .... Miami, FL
Accornero, Giulio, Jr. .... San Francisco, CA
Accorsi, Anthony A. .... Sebring, FL
Accuardi, F. Anthony Antone .... Portland, OR
Accurso, Allison E. .... Trenton, NJ
Accurso Law Firm, The, A Professional Corporation .... Kansas City, MO
Accurso, Louis C. .... Kansas City, MO
Ace, Heather M. .... San Diego, CA
Ace, Michael .... Tyler, TX
Acebal, Maria Laura .... Washington, DC
Acebo, Denise A. .... Houston, TX
Aceituno, Thomas A. .... Folsom, CA
Acer, John W., Law Offices of
Phoenix, AZ
Acero, Kamala .... New York, NY
Acerra, Anthony .... Woodland Hills, CA
Acerra, Valerie R. .... New York, NY
Aceste, Vincent J. .... White Plains, NY
Aceti, R. Steven .... San Diego, CA
Aceto, Catherine Welsh .... Pittsburgh, PA
Aceto, David M. .... Pittsburgh, PA
Aceto, Gregory J. .... Boston, MA
Aceto, Joseph A. .... New Haven, CT
Aceto, Leslie Paier .... Bridgeport, CT
Aceto, Mark F. .... Mesa, AZ
Aceto, Steven T. .... Asheville, NC
Aceto, Steven T., P.A. .... Asheville, NC
Acevedo, Adrian Gregory .... Dallas, TX
Acevedo, Anthony .... New York, NY
Acevedo, Ariel .... New York, NY
Acevedo, Arthur .... Oak Brook, IL
Acevedo & Baggott .... Detroit, MI
Acevedo, Camille E.
Department of Housing and Urban Development, Office of General Counsel, GV
Acevedo, Carlos .... Fort Lauderdale, FL
Acevedo, Daniel R. .... Blackfoot, ID
Acevedo, Daniel R., P.C. .... Blackfoot, ID
Acevedo, Elsie .... Center Moriches, NY
Acevedo, Enver R. .... New York, NY
Acevedo, Ernesto, Jr. .... San Antonio, TX
Acevedo, Ernesto, Jr., P.C. .... San Antonio, TX
Acevedo, Francisco L. .... San Juan, PR
Acevedo, Gustavo L. .... Laredo, TX
Acevedo, Lisa J. .... Chicago, IL
Acevedo, Lucy .... Los Angeles, CA
Acevedo, Mary J. .... Edison, NJ
Acevedo, Richard .... San Antonio, TX
Acevedo, Ruth B. .... Detroit, MI
Acevedo, William C. .... Oakland, CA
Acevedo-Bengoechea, Luis J.
San Juan, PR
Acevedo Colom, Alberto .... San Juan, PR
Acevedo Lazzarini, Carlos J. .... Aguadilla, PR
Acevedo-Nogueras, Francisco L.
San Juan, PR
Acevedo-Torres, Antonio .... Levittown, PR

Acevedo-Vallejo, Alberto .... **San Juan, PR**
Acevedo-Vargas, Celia Ines .... **San Juan, PR**
Aceves, William J. .... San Diego, CA
Acey, Thomas E., Jr. .... Tampa, FL
Acford, Joanne P. .... **Boston, MA**
Ach, Bernard J. .... Friend, NE
Ach, David Laurence .... Palo Alto, CA
Ach, Howard F. .... Geneva, NE
Ach, Samuel W. .... Chicago, IL
Acha, Patricia D. .... Milwaukee, WI
Achampong, Francis .... **Norfolk, VA**
Achary, Frank J. .... Metairie, LA
Achatz, John .... Boston, MA
Achatz, Werner S. .... **New York, NY**
Acheatel, Roger J. .... San Diego, CA
Achebe, Adeze Matilda .... Houston, TX
Achee, Roland J. .... **Shreveport, LA**
Achelpohl, Steven E. .... **Omaha, NE**
Achen, Norman W. .... Temecula, CA
Achenbach, Benjamin R., Jr. **Washington, DC**
Achenbach, Dale A. .... York, PA
Achenbach, David B. .... Boston, MA
Achenbach, William L. .... St. Charles, IL
Achenbaum, Lisa Jane .... Bronxville, NY
Achenberg, Arden Lynn .... **Charlotte, NC**
Acher and Acher .... Franklin, IN
Acher, Amy L. .... **Redmond, WA**
Acher, David J. .... **Fort Lauderdale, FL**
Acher, James R. .... Franklin, IN
Acheson, Edwin R., Jr. .... **Cincinnati, OH**
Acheson, Eleanor D. .... Department of Justice, Office of Policy Development, GV
Acheson, Jennifer Elizabeth Redwood City, CA
Acheson, John W. S., III .... Bellevue, WA
Acheson, Linda A. .... Greensburg, PA
Pittsburgh, PA
Acheson, Paul M. .... Bellevue, WA
Acheson, Richard M., Jr. .... Los Angeles, CA
Acheson, Ruth M. .... Alamosa, CO
Achey, Charles A., Jr. .... **Lancaster, PA**
Achey, Gustav V. .... Denver, CO
Achille, Ellermeyer & French **Brookville, PA**
Achille, John G. .... **Brookville, PA**
Achiron, Henry J. .... New York, NY
Acho, Ronald G. .... **Livonia, MI**
Achola, George B. .... **Omaha, NE**
Achor, John W. .... Powhatan, AR
Achor, Robert L. .... Naples, FL
Achor, Robert T. .... Los Angeles, CA
Achor, R. W. .... Santa Rosa, CA
Achord, David T. .... **Novato, CA**
Achord, John B. .... Savannah, GA
Achorn, Tracy Skidmore **San Francisco, CA**
Achramowicz, William J. .... Worcester, MA
Achrem, Edward J. .... Las Vegas, NV
Achrem, Edward J., Ltd. .... Las Vegas, NV
Achstein, Agnes D. .... Torrance, CA
Achstetter, Christian J. .... Bethesda, MD
Achtenberg & Achtenberg, P.C. Kansas City, MO
Achtenberg, David .... Kansas City, MO
Achtenberg, Irving .... Kansas City, MO
Achtenberg, Roberta .... San Francisco, CA
Achterberg, Constance M. .... **Salina, KS**
Achterberg & Neustrom .... **Salina, KS**
Achterhof, John B. .... San Francisco, CA
Achterhof, Kristin J. .... **Chicago, IL**
Achterkirchen, David M. .... Santa Clara, CA
Achterman, Gail L. .... **Portland, OR**
Achtert, Jennifer K. .... **San Francisco, CA**
Achurch, Robert W., III .... **Beaufort, SC**
Achziger, John A. .... Grand Junction, CO
Aciman, Carole V. .... **New York, NY**
Acito, Remo J. .... New York, NY
Acito, Richard A. .... Astoria, NY
Aciukewicz, John C. .... Wilkes-Barre, PA
Ackal, Patricia B. .... Lafayette, LA
Ackel, Elena H. .... Los Angeles, CA
Ackell, John .... New York, NY
Ackels & Ackels, L.L.P. .... **Dallas, TX**
Ackels, Carol A. .... **Dallas, TX**
Ackels, Gregory K. .... **Dallas, TX**
Ackels, Henry J. .... **Dallas, TX**
Ackels, Joseph E. .... **Dallas, TX**
Ackels, Lawrence E. .... **Dallas, TX**
Ackels, Lawrence E., Jr. .... **Dallas, TX**
Ackels, Miriam L. .... **Dallas, TX**
Ackelsberg, Irv .... Philadelphia, PA
Ackenbom-Kelly, Beatrice L. Winston-Salem, NC
Ackenhusen, Anne F. .... **Seattle, WA**
Acker, Alan M. .... Coudersport, PA
Acker, Alan S. .... **Columbus, OH**
Acker, Allison-Claire .... **Los Angeles, CA**
Acker, Andrew Y. .... **Oakbrook Terrace, IL**
Acker, Ann E. .... **Chicago, IL**
Acker, Charles H., III .... Silver Spring, MD
Acker, Charles J. .... **Carmel, NY**
Acker, Christi J. .... **Carmel, NY**
Acker, Christopher B. .... Ogdensburg, NY
Acker, Christopher Edward Colorado Springs, CO
Acker, Christopher B., P.C. Ogdensburg, NY
Acker, Danna M., Law Offices of Mandeville, LA
Acker, David B. .... Coudersport, PA
Acker, David S. .... Wheaton, IL
Acker, Dennis R. .... Westminster, CO
Acker, Eric M. .... **San Diego, CA**
Acker Firm .... **Pickens, SC**
Acker, Frederick G. .... **Chicago, IL**
Acker, Frederick W. .... **Columbus, OH**
Acker, George N., IV .... York, PA
Acker, Gerald H. .... **Southfield, MI**
Acker, Jeffrey M. .... Greensboro, NC
Acker, Kathryn S. .... **San Diego, CA**
Acker, Keith W. .... Middletown, CT
Acker, Kenneth D. .... **Pickens, SC**
Acker, Kevin D. .... **Monahans, TX**
Acker, Kevin D. .... **Monahans, TX**
Acker, Kevin D. .... **Pecos, TX**
Acker, Kowalick & Whipple, A Professional Corporation .... **Los Angeles, CA**
Acker & Larsen .... Coudersport, PA
Acker, Laurence C. .... **Chicago, IL**
Acker, Lawrence G. .... **Washington, DC**
Acker, Lawrence J. .... **Bloomfield Hills, MI**
Acker, Lawrence J., P.C. **Bloomfield Hills, MI**
Acker, Leslie C. .... Post, TX
Acker, Maria R. .... **San Diego, CA**
Acker, Michael A. .... **Fort Lauderdale, FL**
Acker, Michael R. .... Philadelphia, PA
Acker, Neal H. .... **Montgomery, AL**
Acker, Paul A. .... **Las Vegas, NV**
Acker, Peter C. .... Hermitage, PA
Acker, Randal B. .... Portland, OR
Acker, Randal B., P.C. .... Portland, OR
Acker, Richard H. .... **San Francisco, CA**
Acker, Robert T. .... Massapequa, NY
Acker, Robert T., P.C. .... Massapequa, NY
Acker, Rodney .... **Dallas, TX**
Acker, Stephen .... **Los Angeles, CA**
Acker, Tanya Nadra Marie **Los Angeles, CA**
Acker & Welmaker, P.A. .... Pickens, SC
Acker, William B. .... **Troy, MI**
Acker, William G. .... Pickens, SC
Acker, William L. .... Evanston, IL
Acker, William M., Jr. .... Birmingham, AL
Acker, William Marsh, III **Birmingham, AL**
Acker, William Wilson .... Pittsburgh, PA
Ackerbaum Cox, Joyce .... **Orlando, FL**
Ackeret, Jerry M. .... **San Rafael, CA**
Ackeret • Sheron, LLP .... **San Rafael, CA**
Ackerhalt, Arthur H. .... Buffalo, NY
Ackerknecht, Richard E. .... **Los Angeles, CA**
Ackerley, Margaret L. .... Washington, DC
Ackerly, Benjamin C. .... **Richmond, VA**
Ackerly, Carla L. .... **New York, NY**
Ackerly, Dana C. .... **New Canaan, CT**
Ackerly, Dana T., II .... **Washington, DC**
Ackerly, John A. .... Stamford, CT
Ackerly, John P., III .... **Richmond, VA**
Ackerly, Judith K. .... San Francisco, CA
Ackerly, Mary M. .... **Litchfield, CT**
Ackerman & Ackerman, P.C. .... **Troy, MI**
Ackerman, Adam Trevor .... Philadelphia, PA
Ackerman, Alan J. .... Philadelphia, PA
Ackerman, Alan Jay .... Washington, DC
Ackerman, Alan L. .... **Pittsburgh, PA**
Ackerman, Alan R. .... Parsippany, NJ
Ackerman, Alan T. .... **Troy, MI**
Ackerman, Alice Boler .... Denver, CO
Ackerman, Allan A. .... **Chicago, IL**
Ackerman, Allan A., P.C. .... **Chicago, IL**
Ackerman, Alvin S. .... **Media, PA**
Ackerman, Andrew S. .... **Philadelphia, PA**
Ackerman, Barry .... Huntingdon Valley, PA
Ackerman, Bruce A. .... New Haven, CT
Ackerman, Bruce A. .... **Minneapolis, MN**
Ackerman, Bruce J. .... **Hackensack, NJ**
Ackerman, Bryce W. .... Miami, FL
Ocala, FL
Ackerman, Catherine .... Ocala, FL
Ackerman, Christina F. .... Charlotte, NC
Ackerman, Clyde O. .... Walterboro, SC
Ackerman, C.O. Ladd, Jr. .... **Charlotte, NC**
Charleston, SC
Ackerman, Corey B. .... **New York, NY**
Ackerman, Daniel J. .... Greensburg, PA
Ackerman, David .... **Chicago, IL**
Ackerman, David B. .... Pensacola, FL
Ackerman, David G. .... Los Alamitos, CA
Ackerman, David J. .... **Media, PA**
Ackerman, David M. .... Library of Congress, Congressional Research Service, GV
Ackerman, David P. **West Palm Beach, FL**
Ackerman, Deborah .... Dallas, TX
Ackerman, Debra L. .... Washington, DC
Ackerman, Denise Ann .... Poughkeepsie, NY
Ackerman, Donald M. .... Mount Holly, NJ
Ackerman, Douglas W. .... Tallahassee, FL
Ackerman, Edgar D. .... **Florham Park, NJ**
Ackerman, Edward B. .... **New York, NY**
Ackerman, F. Stanton .... Albany, NY
Ackerman, Francis Edward .... Augusta, ME
Ackerman, Frank A. .... **Denver, CO**
Ackerman & Gariepy .... Woonsocket, RI
Ackerman, Gary N. .... **Seattle, WA**
Ackerman, Harold A. .... Newark, NJ
Ackerman, Harold J. .... Toluca Lake, CA
Ackerman, Harold T. .... Birmingham, AL
Ackerman, Heidi Joan .... Washington, DC
Ackerman, Howard B. .... Washington, DC
Ackerman, Ivan J. .... Clarksville, IA
Waverly, IA
Ackerman, Jack E., (P.A.) West Palm Beach, FL
Ackerman, James C. .... Fort Lee, NJ
Ackerman, James H., Law Offices of **Long Beach, CA**
Ackerman, James H., Law Offices of **Santa Clarita, CA**
Ackerman, James L. .... Boston, MA
Ackerman, James M. .... **Phoenix, AZ**
Ackerman, James W. .... Springfield, IL
Ackerman, Jeanine M. .... Royal Oak, MI
Ackerman, Jennifer C. .... **Atlanta, GA**
Ackerman, Jerome .... Washington, DC
Ackerman, Jill Robb .... **Omaha, NE**
Ackerman, Joel A. .... New York, NY
Ackerman, Joel G. .... **San Francisco, CA**
Ackerman, John W. .... Waterloo, IA
Ackerman, Jonathan D. .... **Baltimore, MD**
Ackerman, Joni S. .... Beverly Hills, CA
Ackerman, Joseph L., Jr. **West Palm Beach, FL**
Ackerman, Joyce G. .... Merion, PA
Ackerman, Judith A. .... Bronx, NY
Ackerman, Karen .... **San Francisco, CA**
Ackerman, Kenneth D. Department of Agriculture, Farm Service Agency, GV
Ackerman, Kenneth E. .... **Syracuse, NY**
Ackerman, Kenneth J. .... Linwood, NJ
Ackerman and Kevorkian .... San Jose, CA
Ackerman, Kristine A. .... **Chicago, IL**
Ackerman, Lee B. .... **Los Angeles, CA**
Ackerman, Lee B., P.C., Law Offices of **Los Angeles, CA**
Ackerman, Leonard I. .... **East Hampton, NY**
Ackerman, Levine, Cullen & Brickman, LLP **Great Neck, NY**
Mineola, NY
New York, NY
Ackerman, Linda S. .... **Pittsburgh, PA**
Ackerman, Link & Sartory, P.A. **West Palm Beach, FL**
Ackerman, Lyn C. .... Pittsburgh, PA
Ackerman, Marc E. .... **New York, NY**
Ackerman, Marc J. .... **New York, NY**
Ackerman, Marc L. .... **Philadelphia, PA**
Ackerman, Marion S., 3rd .... Houston, TX
Ackerman, Mark S. .... Department of Defense, Defense Legal Services Agency, GV
Ackerman, Maureen Hackett West Palm Beach, FL
Ackerman, Michael A. .... Oceanside, NY
Ackerman, Michael B. .... Los Angeles, CA
Ackerman, Michael G. .... San Jose, CA
Ackerman, Michael J. .... Palo Alto, CA
Ackerman, Michael S. .... **Los Angeles, CA**
Ackerman, Michael S. .... Mountainside, NJ
Ackerman, Mordock & Bowen, A Professional Corporation .... **Fullerton, CA**
Ackerman, Neil H. .... **Westbury, NY**
Ackerman, Nicholas L. .... **Lincoln, NE**
Ackerman, Paul .... Tustin, CA
Ackerman, Paul D. .... **Baltimore, MD**
Ackerman, Paul D. .... **New York, NY**
Ackerman, Paxton H. .... St. Louis, MO
Ackerman, Peter A. .... West Linn, OR
Ackerman, Peter B. .... **Irvine, CA**
Ackerman, Peter B. .... White Plains, NY
Ackerman, Philip .... **Chicago, IL**
Ackerman, Philip C. .... **Buffalo, NY**
Ackerman & Raphan .... Oceanside, NY
Ackerman, Richard C. .... **Fullerton, CA**
Ackerman, Richard D. .... Santa Ana, CA
Ackerman, Richard L. .... **Los Angeles, CA**
Ackerman, Richard P. .... **New York, NY**
Ackerman, Richard R. .... Woonsocket, RI
Ackerman, Richard S. .... Boca Raton, FL
Ackerman, Risden C. .... San Jose, CA
Ackerman, Robert L. .... Springfield, OR
Ackerman, Robert L., P.C. .... Springfield, OR
Ackerman, Robert M. .... Salem, OR
Ackerman, Robert S. .... Encino, CA
Ackerman, Robert W. .... Fredericksburg, VA
Ackerman & Robinson, PC **Pittsburgh, PA**
Ackerman, Samuel I. .... Beechhurst, NY
Ackerman & Savage, L.L.P. .... **Dallas, TX**
Ackerman, Seymour K. .... New York, NY
Ackerman, Stark .... **Portland, OR**
Ackerman, Steve W. .... **Burbank, CA**
Ackerman, Susan K. .... **Portland, OR**
Ackerman, T. David .... **New York, NY**
Ackerman, Terri L. .... **Philadelphia, PA**
Ackerman & Terry, LLC .... **Mineola, NY**
New York, NY
Westbury, NY
Ackerman, Thomas E. .... Flint, MI
Ackerman & Ventura .... Fredericksburg, VA
Ackerman, W. Randall .... **Dallas, TX**
Ackerman, Wachs and Finton, P.C. Albany, NY
Ackerman & Wainwright, L.L.P. **East Hampton, NY**
Ackerman, Wayne A. .... Bentonville, AR
Ackerman, Wendy E. .... **Washington, DC**
Ackerman, William .... Albany, NY
Ackerman, William .... Pittsburgh, PA
Ackerman, William A. .... **Great Neck, NY**
Ackermann, Glenn J. .... Beverly Hills, CA
Ackermann, James E. .... Chicago, IL
Ackermann, Jeffrey .... Lafayette, LA
Ackermann, John R., Jr. .... **Dayton, OH**
Ackermann, Kathleen S. .... Norcross, GA
Ackermann, Nancy .... Albuquerque, NM
Ackermann & Nichele .... Chicago, IL
Ackermann, Noelie A. .... Lincoln, NE
Ackermann, Robert A. .... **Los Angeles, CA**
Ackermann, Robert P. .... Chicago, IL
Ackermann, Thomas W. .... **Roseland, NJ**
Ackermann, Timothy G. .... San Antonio, TX
Ackerson, David E. .... Hibbing, MN
Ackerson, Fred M. .... **Chicago, IL**
Ackerson Group, The, Chartered **Washington, DC**
Ackerson, Jon W. .... Louisville, KY
Ackerson, Karen M. .... Carson, CA
Ackerson, Lori A. .... **Louisville, KY**
Ackerson, Mosley & Yann, P.S.C. **London, KY**
Louisville, KY
Ackerson, Nels .... **Washington, DC**
Ackerson, Richard H. .... Suffern, NY
Ackerson, Robert L. .... **Louisville, KY**
Ackerson, Sarah B. Securities and Exchange Commission, Division of Enforcement, GV
Ackerstein, Joan .... **Boston, MA**
Ackert, David Andrew .... New York, NY
Ackert, Irving S. .... Van Nuys, CA
Ackert, Stanley M., III .... **New York, NY**
Ackert, T.W., P.A. .... **Winter Park, FL**
Ackert, Terence J. .... **Grand Rapids, MI**
Ackert, Terrence William **Winter Park, FL**
Ackil, Ann B. .... Boston, MA
Ackiron, Evan H. .... San Francisco, CA
Ackland, Amber S. .... **Irvine, CA**
Ackland, Thomas B. .... **Los Angeles, CA**
Acklen, Jennifer H. .... **Lexington, KY**
Ackley, David C. .... Priest River, ID
Ackley, David E. .... **Orlando, FL**
Ackley, Ernest L., III .... Belmont, MA
Ackley, Gary L. .... Oklahoma City, OK
Ackley, Gary R. .... Cottage Grove, OR
Ackley, Harry A. .... Woodland, CA
Ackley, Kopecky & Kingery Cedar Rapids, IA
Center Point, IA
Central City, IA
Ackley, Maria T. .... **Norwich, CT**
Ackley, Matthew C. .... Richmond, VA
Ackley, Monica L. .... Dubuque, IA
Ackley, Richd. M. .... Ottumwa, IA
Ackley, Robert O. .... Mundelein, IL
Ackley, Thomas A. .... **San Francisco, CA**
Ackley, Thomas F. .... **Omaha, NE**
Ackley, Thomas J. .... Wauwatosa, WI
Acklie, Duane W. .... Lincoln, NE
Ackman, Carmela .... New York, NY
Ackman, Jacob D. .... Fishers, IN
Ackman, John L., Jr. .... Louisville, KY
Ackman, Lauress V. .... **Minneapolis, MN**
Ackman, Marek & Boyd, Ltd. **Kankakee, IL**
Watseka, IL
Ackman, Milton R., (P.C.) .... **New York, NY**
Ackman, Purcell & Lorenz, P.S.C. Williamstown, KY
Ackman, Richard L. .... **Kankakee, IL**
Ackourey, Mary Anne .... **Atlanta, GA**
Ackourey, Paul P. .... Scranton, PA
Ackourey, Peter P. .... **Princeton, NJ**
Ackre & Dusek .... Grand Forks, ND
Ackre, George M. .... **Cando, ND**
Ackre Law Firm, Ltd. .... **Cando, ND**
Ackre, Robert G. .... **Cando, ND**
Ackre, Shawn D. .... Grand Forks, ND
Ackrich, Robert S. .... Woodland Hills, CA
Aclin, R. Gregory .... **Fort Smith, AR**
Acoba, Darren .... Burlington, WA
Acoba, James D. .... Los Angeles, CA
Acoba, Simeon R., Jr. .... Honolulu, HI
Acocella, Frank X. .... **New York, NY**
Acocella, Giuseppe .... Riverdale, NY
Acocella, Peter R. .... Babylon, NY
Acocella, Peter R., P.C. .... Babylon, NY
Acoff, Valerie L. .... **Birmingham, AL**
Acomb, Dwight L. .... **New Orleans, LA**
Acomb, Frederick A. .... **Detroit, MI**
Acomb, Glenn M. .... Salt Lake City, UT
Acomb, James R. .... Columbus, OH
Acomb, John D. .... **New Orleans, LA**
Acomb, Robert B., III .... **New Orleans, LA**
Acomb, Robert B., Jr. .... **New Orleans, LA**
Acomb, William Ryan .... **New Orleans, LA**
Acord, Karen E. .... Beckley, WV
Acord, R. Clifton, II .... **Tampa, FL**
Acors, Karen Lindemann .... Norfolk, VA
Acosta Abarca & Ramírez LLP **San Juan, PR**
Acosta, Abel .... **Walnut Creek, CA**
Acosta, Alejandro, Jr. .... **El Paso, TX**
Acosta, Annemarie .... Los Angeles, CA
Acosta, Benjamin, Jr., Law Offices **San Juan, PR**
Acosta, Carlos .... **Austin, TX**
Acosta, Daniel .... **Chicago, IL**
Acosta, Daniel G. .... Albuquerque, NM
Acosta, Desmond B. .... **Dallas, TX**
Acosta, Ernesto J. .... Ventura, CA
Acosta, Eugenia E. .... St. Petersburg, FL
Acosta, Federico .... Tustin, CA
Acosta, Fernando Sabido **Santa Monica, CA**
Acosta, Gabriel Eliud .... Walla Walla, WA
Acosta, George L. .... **Chicago, IL**
Wheaton, IL
Acosta, Geraldo G. .... Houston, TX
Acosta, H. Joseph .... **San Antonio, TX**
Acosta, Howard M. .... **St. Petersburg, FL**
Acosta, James D. .... Tampa, FL
Acosta, James P. .... **Dallas, TX**
Acosta, Janis N. .... Dearborn, MI
Acosta, John V. .... **Portland, OR**
Acosta, José L. .... El Paso, TX
Acosta, Julio C. .... **Miami, FL**
Acosta, Karen Lloyd .... Las Cruces, NM
Acosta, Lori A. .... Cleveland, OH
Acosta, Luis Miguel .... Royal Oak, MI
Acosta, Mario L. .... Panorama City, CA
Acosta, Maritoni .... Los Angeles, CA
Acosta, Miriam R. .... Florham Park, NJ
Acosta, Neifor B. .... **Milwaukee, WI**
Acosta, Pablo .... **Miami, FL**
Acosta, Patricia J. .... San Antonio, TX
Acosta, Philip H. .... Los Angeles, CA
Acosta, Philip H., P.C. .... Los Angeles, CA
Acosta, Raymond L. .... San Juan, PR

Acosta, Raymond T. .... Bronx, NY
Acosta, Roger .... Melville, NY
Acosta, Roland H. .... Orlando, FL
Acosta, Rolando R. .... Chicago, IL
Acosta, Ruben .... Detroit, MI
Farmington Hills, MI
Acosta, Ruben E. .... Hartford, CT
Acosta, S. Grace .... Lincoln, NE
Acosta, Sandra R. .... Department of Justice, Criminal Division, GV
Acosta, Sergio Enrique .... Chicago, IL
Acosta, Thomas W., Jr. .... Port Allen, LA
Acosta, Valli Jo .... El Paso, TX
Acosta, Xavier E. .... Las Cruces, NM
Acosta-Grubb, José A. .... San Juan, PR
Acosta-Lewis, Robert A. .... Richmond, VA
Acosta Reboyras, Juan .... San Juan, PR
Acosta-Rivera, Manuel .... San Antonio, TX
Acosta-Rodriguez, Salvador A.
Trujillo Alto, PR
Acott, Richard D. .... Fort Collins, CO
Acquaah, Kwame .... Washington, DC
Acquafredda, Grace A. .... Staten Island, NY
Acquanita, Christopher S. .... Milford, CT
Acquaro, Paul, Jr. .... Coronado, CA
Acquarulo, Adam F. .... New Haven, CT
Acquaviva, Charlotte M. .... Hartford, CT
Acquaviva, Joseph T., Jr.
Oklahoma City, OK
Acquaviva, Paul A. .... New York, NY
Acquesta, Mary .... Los Altos, CA
Acquisto, Stephen P. .... Sacramento, CA
Acquisto, Vincent A. .... Ellicott City, MD
Acree, Angela D. .... Murphysboro, IL
Acree, Ansley N. .... Austin, TX
Acree, Ernest M. .... Dalton, GA
Acree, G. Michael .... Covington, TN
Acree, Glenn E. .... Lexington, KY
Acree, J. Cabell, III .... Memphis, TN
Acree, John W. .... Virginia Beach, VA
Acree Law Office, PSC .... Lexington, KY
Acree, M. Reid, Jr. .... Salisbury, NC
Acree and Owen .... Covington, TN
Acree, Randall S. .... Hahira, GA
Acree, Russell A., III .... Austin, TX
Acree, W. Cleveland, II .... Orlando, FL
Acree, W. Dent .... Atlanta, GA
Acree, William B., Jr. .... Union City, TN
Acres, John Erland .... Birmingham, AL
Acres, Patrick R. .... Moses Lake, WA
Acres & Ramsey .... Birmingham, AL
Acret, James .... Los Angeles, CA
Acrey, James R. .... Cornelia, GA
Acromite, William J. .... Irvine, CA
Acronico, Stephen A. .... Santa Barbara, CA
Action Criminal Defense Center
Dearborn, MI
Detroit, MI
Actkinson, Jeffrey W. .... Farwell, TX
Actkinson, Johnny W. .... Farwell, TX
Acton, David .... Paoli, PA
Acton, Gregory M. .... Albuquerque, NM
Acton, Gregory M., A Professional Corporation
Albuquerque, NM
Acton, James C. .... Danville, IL
Acton, Jean .... Louisville, KY
Acton, John C. .... Framingham, MA
Acton, John F. .... Columbus, OH
Acton, John T. .... Willow Grove, PA
Acton, Jonathan, II .... Glen Burnie, MD
Acton, Kevan J. .... Albany, NY
Acton, Mary Ann C. .... Pittsburgh, PA
Acton, Oakford W., Jr. .... Woodstown, NJ
Acton, Peter M. .... Armonk, NY
Acton & Point .... Woodstown, NJ
Acton, Shannon M. .... Troy, MI
Acton and Snyder .... Danville, IL
Acton, William D., Jr. .... Charlotte, NC
Acuff & Acuff, A Professional Corporation
Cookeville, TN
Acuff, Cathy M. .... Dallas, TX
Acuff, D. Nicholas .... Fort Worth, TX
Acuff, Fred M., Jr. .... Memphis, TN
Acuff, James T., Jr. .... Phoenix, AZ
Acuff, John E. .... Cookeville, TN
Acuff, Jolie Nicole Moreland
Cookeville, TN
Acuff, Katherine L. .... Washington, DC
Acuff, Norman .... New Market, TN
Acuff, W.I. Howell .... Cookeville, TN
Acuña, Edgar B. .... Tucson, AZ
Acuna, Kimberly T. .... Jacksonville, FL
Acuña, Richard M. .... San Marino, CA
Acuña-Sunshine, Geraldine
New York, NY
Acunzo, Mario J. .... Staten Island, NY
Adachi, Benjamin T. .... Los Angeles, CA
Adachi, Glenn M. .... Honolulu, HI
Adachi, Janet K. .... Boston, MA
Adachi, Jeffrey Gordon .... San Francisco, CA
Adago, Richard J. .... New York, NY
Adair, A. Lee .... Laguna Hills, CA
Adair, Alison K. .... Portland, OR
Adair, Andrew B. .... Media, PA
Adair, Bill, Jr. .... Humble, TX
Adair, Bonnie M. .... Malibu, CA
Adair, Cameron .... Atlanta, GA
Adair, Charles H. .... San Diego, CA
Adair, Charles R., Jr. .... Dadeville, AL
Adair, Christine M. .... Philadelphia, PA
Adair, David N., Jr.
Administrative Office Of The United States Courts, GV
Adair, Donald R. .... Rochester, NY
Adair, Edward H. .... London, KY
Adair, Edward H., P.S.C. .... London, KY
Adair, Evan E. .... Erie, PA
Adair, Ginger D. .... Denver, CO
Adair, Heidi Bieberich .... Fort Wayne, IN
Adair, J. Leon .... Decatur, GA
Adair, J. Wallace .... Boca Raton, FL
Adair, James P. .... Port Huron, MI
Adair, James W., III .... Columbus, OH
Adair, Jeffery B. .... Las Vegas, NV
Adair, Jeffrey S. .... Atlanta, GA
Adair, Jocelyn L.
Environmental Protection Agency, Office of Enforcement and Compliance Assurance, GV
Adair, Joe Dean .... Stilwell, OK
Adair, John D. .... Port Huron, MI
Adair, John H. .... Syracuse, NY
Adair, John L. .... Atlanta, GA
Adair, John R. .... San Francisco, CA
Adair, K. Eric .... Los Angeles, CA
Adair, K. Jerome .... New York, NY
Adair, Kendall D. .... Fort Worth, TX
Adair, Lance A. .... Irvine, CA
Adair, Larry L. .... Fort Lauderdale, FL
Adair Law Firm .... Rochester, NY
Williamsville, NY
Adair, Marc A. .... Phoenix, AZ
Adair, Meredith Page .... Raeford, NC
Adair, Morris & Osborn, A Professional Corporation .... Dallas, TX
Adair & Myers, P.L.L.C. .... Houston, TX
Adair, Patrick E. .... Scotts Valley, CA
Adair, Paul C. .... Department of Labor, Office of the Solicitor, GV
Adair, Perry M. .... Miami, FL
Adair, R. Brett .... Birmingham, AL
Adair, Randall F. .... Dallas, TX
Adair, Robin Watt .... Muskogee, OK
Adair, Robt. G. .... Florence, KY
Adair, Ross .... Dryden, NY
Adair, Schuerman & White
Baton Rouge, LA
Brentwood, TN
Knoxville, TN
Memphis, TN
Adair, Sidney A. .... Los Angeles, CA
Adair, Stephen W. .... Fort Wayne, IN
Adair, Susan G. .... Norman, OK
Adair, Tammy R. .... Memphis, TN
Adair, Thomas S. .... Atlanta, GA
Adair, Warren J. .... Radnor, PA
Adair, Wendell H., Jr. .... New York, NY
Adair, William A. .... Conroe, TX
Adair, Wm. B. (Ben) .... Houston, TX
Adalian, David Philip .... Visalia, CA
Adam, Alice .... Houston, TX
Adam, Bruce C. .... Alexandria, VA
Adam, Christopher J. .... Kansas City, MO
Adam, Fred B. .... Castle Rock, CO
Adam, Frederic J. .... San Francisco, CA
Adam, Gerhard K. .... Schenectady, NY
Adam, Gregg McLean .... San Francisco, CA
Adam, Jane .... Los Angeles, CA
Adam, Jerry C. .... Houston, TX
Adam, Joan Elizabeth .... Atchison, KS
Adam, John F., Jr. .... St. Louis, MO
Adam, Joseph N. .... Moline, IL
Adam, Linda Sherrard .... Carlsbad, CA
Adam, Lynn M. .... Atlanta, GA
Adam, Nancy Shapiro
Greenwood Village, CO
Adam, Richard .... New York, NY
Adam, Robert J. .... Houston, TX
Adam, Robert J., P.C., Law Office of
Houston, TX
Adam, Scott M. .... Overland Park, KS
Adam, Serge, Jr. .... Chicago, IL
Adam, Terry J. .... Houston, TX
Adam, Thomas C. .... Pierre, SD
Adam, Vanessa Ploumis .... New Rochelle, NY
Adam, W. Kay Gardner .... Englewood, CO
Adam, Walter J. .... Placerville, CA
Adam, William Kendall .... Houston, TX
Adamany, David W. .... Detroit, MI
Adamaszek, E. Philip .... Detroit, MI
Adamaszek, E. Philip
Mount Clemens, MI
Adamaszek, E. Philip .... Pontiac, MI
Adamaszek, E. Phillip .... Mount Clemens, MI
Adamcik, Albert J. .... The Woodlands, TX
Adamcik, Joe A. .... Lubbock, TX
Adamco, Peter P. .... Incline Village, NV
Zephyr Cove, NV
Adamczyk, Beverly A. .... Parma Heights, OH
Adamczyk, Irene T. .... Indianapolis, IN
Adamczyk, Joanne E. .... Flint, MI
Adamczyk, Kenneth H. .... Detroit, MI
Adamczyk, Robert S. .... Chicago, IL
Adamczyk, Steven .... Tucson, AZ
Adame, Carlos E. .... New Orleans, LA
Adamec, Carl F. W. .... Troy, NY
Adamec, Justene M. .... Pasadena, CA
Adamek, Charles A. .... Los Angeles, CA
Adamek, G. Andy .... Helena, MT
Adamek, J. David .... Toms River, NJ
Adames, Pedro López .... San Juan, PR
Adames Soto, Enrique R. .... San Juan, PR
Adametz, John H., Jr.
North Little Rock, AR
Adami, Debra L. .... Denton, TX
Adami, Frederick W., III .... Brockton, MA
Adami, Georgina R. .... Wichita, KS
Adami, Goldman & Shuffield, Incorporated
San Antonio, TX
Adami, Grant E., III .... San Antonio, TX
Adami, Guy M. .... Croton-On-Hudson, NY
Adami, Guy M., & Nancy C. Adami
Croton-On-Hudson, NY
Adami, John G. "Buster", Jr. .... Alice, TX
Adami, Nancy C. .... Croton-On-Hudson, NY
Adami, Paul E. .... Springfield, IL
Adami, Richard W. .... Dennis, MA
Adamiak, Harold A. .... Worcester, MA
Adamian, Daniel Gregory .... Belmont, MA
Adamian, Martin J. .... Detroit, MI
Adamich, JoLee M. .... Los Angeles, CA
Adamik, James B. .... River Forest, IL
Adamik, James B., P.C. .... River Forest, IL
Adamini, Stephen F. .... Marquette, MI
Adamis, Eleni .... Palo Alto, CA
Adamo and Adamo .... Lansing, MI
Adamo & Cornelius .... Houston, TX
Adamo, Gary M .... Lansing, MI
Adamo, Heather L. .... Lansing, MI
Adamo, Jane M. .... San Francisco, CA
Adamo, John Joseph .... Westerly, RI
Adamo, Joseph .... Vineland, NJ
Adamo, Kenneth R. .... Cleveland, OH
Adamo, Lauren Marie .... Passaic, NJ
Adamo and Newman .... Providence, RI
Westerly, RI
Adamo, Rose Marie .... Boston, MA
Adamo, Salvatore C. .... Belvidere, NJ
Adamo, Samuel D. .... Houston, TX
Adamo, Sonya A. .... Washington, DC
Adamo, Victor T. .... Okemos, MI
Adamo, Vito .... Carnegie, PA
Adamonis, Robert J. .... Seattle, WA
Adamopoulos, Anthony C. .... Salem, MA
Adamowicz, Christine L. .... Garden City, NY
Adamowski, Gilbert L. .... Park Ridge, IL
Adamowski & Newey .... Chicago, IL
Adams, A. Harris .... Marietta, GA
Adams, A. Hope .... Washington, DC
Adams, A. Kemp .... Corpus Christi, TX
Adams, Abby Lynn
Securities and Exchange Commission, Office of the General Counsel, GV
Adams, Adam G., III .... Jacksonville, FL
Adams, Adam T. .... Livingston, NJ
Adams & Adams .... Birmingham, AL
Adams & Adams .... Fort Lauderdale, FL
Adams and Adams .... Fort Lauderdale, FL
Adams & Adams .... Key West, FL
Miami, FL
Adams & Adams .... Fort Valley, GA
Macon, GA
Adams & Adams .... Macon, GA
Adams & Adams .... Louisa, KY
Adams & Adams .... Somerset, KY
Adams & Adams .... Columbia, MD
Adams & Adams .... Palmer, MA
Adams & Adams .... Beaumont, TX
Adams & Adams .... Tacoma, WA
Adams, Adams and Adams
Marshalltown, IA
Adams & Adams, P.C. .... Houston, TX
Adams, Addison K. .... Irvine, CA
Adams, Adrian J. .... Los Angeles, CA
Adams, Adrian W. .... Newhall, CA
Adams, Alan R. .... Des Moines, IA
Adams, Alayne B. .... Memphis, TN
Adams, Albert T. .... Cleveland, OH
Adams, Alberta L. .... New Orleans, LA
Adams & Alexander .... Beverly Hills, CA
Los Angeles, CA
Pasadena, CA
Adams, Alexandre A. .... Cambridge, MA
Adams & Alford, P.C. .... Athens, GA
Adams, Alfred B., III .... Atlanta, GA
Adams, Alfred G. .... Winston-Salem, NC
Adams, Alfred G., Jr. .... Atlanta, GA
Adams, Alfred H. .... Lincoln, NE
Adams, Alfred T., Jr. .... Nashville, TN
Adams, Alice Pinckney .... Charlotte, NC
Adams, Alice Price .... Columbia, SC
Adams, Alison M. .... Santa Barbara, CA
Adams, Allan B. .... Denver, CO
Adams, Allan B. .... Neenah, WI
Adams, Allisan Lee .... Cheshire, CT
Adams, Alton M. .... Toccoa, GA
Adams, Alycen G. .... Atlanta, GA
Adams, Amelia F. .... Louisville, KY
Adams, Amy .... Dallas, TX
Adams, Amy Ayers .... Weatherford, TX
Adams, Amy B. .... New York, NY
Adams, Amy Elizabeth .... Nashville, TN
Adams, Andrea Kay .... Fort Lauderdale, FL
Adams, Andrew Allan .... Houston, TX
Adams, Andrew M. .... Charlotte, NC
Adams, Andrew S. .... Columbus, OH
Adams, Andrew W. .... Houston, TX
Adams, Andy E. .... Fayetteville, AR
Adams, Angela L. .... Santa Fe, NM
Adams, Angela McClendon
St. Petersburg, FL
Adams, Anita L. Clinton .... Cerritos, CA
Adams, Ann E. .... Oklahoma City, OK
Adams, Anna .... New York, NY
Adams, Anthony .... Detroit, MI
Adams, Anthony J., Jr. .... Rochester, NY
Adams, April J. .... Washington, DC
Adams, Arch G. .... San Antonio, TX
Adams, Arlin M. .... Philadelphia, PA
Adams, Arnold .... Washington, DC
Adams, Arthur H. .... Newport, NH
Adams, Ashley D. .... Phoenix, AZ
Adams, Ashley Stone .... Panama City, FL
Adams & Associates .... Oklahoma City, OK
Adams & Associates, P.C. .... New York, NY
Adams, Atiba D. .... New York, NY
Adams, Baker .... Georgetown, MA
Adams, Barbara .... Philadelphia, PA
Adams, Barbara A. .... Chicago, IL
Adams, Barbara L. .... Rochester Hills, MI
Adams, Barbara Paddock .... Hillsboro, IL
Adams, Barbara R. .... San Francisco, CA
Adams, Barfield, Dunaway & Hankinson, LLP .... Thomaston, GA
Adams, Barry L. .... Santa Rosa, CA
Adams, Barton L. .... Tacoma, WA
Adams, Belanger, Atherton & LoStracco, P.C. .... Nacogdoches, TX
Adams, Ben C., Jr. .... Memphis, TN
Adams, Benjamin M. .... New York, NY
Adams, Benjamin M. .... Neenah, WI
Adams & Bennett .... Azle, TX
Denton, TX
Gainesville, TX
Adams, Bernard R. .... Boston, MA
Adams, Bert, III .... Atlanta, GA
Adams, Betty K. .... Nashville, TN
Adams, Betty Smith .... Columbia, MD
Adams, Bettye S. .... Little Rock, AR
Adams, Beverley L. .... Fargo, ND
Adams, Bill W. .... Princeton, KY
Adams, Billy R. .... Dearborn, MI
Adams, Billye L. .... Monroe, LA
Adams, B. J. .... Canoga Park, CA
Adams & Blinn, Counsellors at Law, P.C.
Cambridge, MA
Sterling, MA
Adams, Bonnie .... Columbia, SC
Adams, Bradley A. .... Eden Prairie, MN
Adams, Bradley L. .... Dallas, TX
Adams Braun, LLP .... Atlanta, GA
Marietta, GA
Adams, Brent E. .... Chicago, IL
Adams, Brent T. .... Reno, NV
Adams, Brenton D. .... Dunn, NC
Raleigh, NC
Adams, Bret A. .... Columbus, OH
Adams, Bret A., & Associates Co., L.P.A.
Columbus, OH
Adams, Brian M. .... Las Vegas, NV
Adams, Brian M. .... Westfield, NJ
Adams, Brian R. M. .... Richmond, VA
Adams, Briggs & Briggs
Daytona Beach, FL
Adams, Brigitte L. .... Washington, DC
Adams Broadwell Joseph & Cardozo, A Professional Corporation
San Francisco, CA
South San Francisco, CA
Adams, Brooking, Stepner, Woltermann & Dusing, P.L.L.C. .... Covington, KY
Florence, KY
Newport, KY
Cincinnati, OH
Adams & Brooks .... Folkston, GA
Adams, Bruce A. .... Washington, DC
Adams, Bruce C. .... Pottsville, PA
Adams, Bruce J. .... Rockville Centre, NY
Adams, Bruce L. .... New York, NY
Adams, Bruce N. .... Oxford, AL
Adams, Bruce T. .... Bethesda, MD
Adams, Byron A. .... Newport News, VA
Adams, C. Calvin, Jr. .... Tallulah, LA
Adams, C. Edward .... Gig Harbor, WA
Adams, C. Kelvin .... Bryan, TX
Adams, C. Kent .... Dallas, TX
Adams, C. Michael, Jr. .... Memphis, TN
Adams, C. Murray .... New York, NY
Adams, Candyce S. .... Oklahoma City, OK
Adams, Carl David, Law Offices of
Dallas, TX
Adams, Carl V. .... Yuba City, CA
Adams, Carol J. .... Los Angeles, CA
Adams, Carol L., Law Office of .... Indio, CA
Adams, Carol M. .... Great Neck, NY
Adams, Carol Y. .... Huntington Beach, CA
Adams, Caroline A. .... Tampa, FL
Adams, Carolyn .... Hyden, KY
Lexington, KY
Adams, Carolyn Anderson .... Topeka, KS
Adams, Carolyn Jackson .... Atlanta, GA
Adams, Carolyn L. .... Catasauqua, PA
Adams, Carolyn M. .... Allentown, PA
Adams, Cary M. .... Sacramento, CA
Adams, Catherine .... Cincinnati, OH
Adams, Catherine .... Columbus, OH
Adams, Catherine C. .... Boston, MA
Adams, Catherine McGinty .... Tampa, FL
Adams, Cathryn Ann .... Houston, TX
Adams, Cecelia A. .... Arlington, VA
Adams & Cesario, P.A. .... Bloomington, MN
Adams, Charles A. .... Sun City, AZ
Adams, Charles A., Jr. .... Laurel, MS
Adams, Charles "Andy"
Oklahoma City, OK
Adams, Charles B. .... West Palm Beach, FL
Adams, Charles B. .... Kirksville, MO
Adams, Charles C. .... Hockessin, DE
Adams, Charles C. .... Somerset, KY
Adams, Charles C., Jr. .... Lexington, KY
Adams, Charles Curtis .... Los Angeles, CA
Adams, Charles D. .... Flagstaff, AZ
Adams, Charles E. .... Syracuse, NY
Adams, Charles Ellis .... Richmond, VA
Adams, Charles F. .... San Francisco, CA
Adams, Charles F. .... Macon, GA
Adams, Charles F. .... Portland, OR
Adams, Charles G. .... Helena, MT
Adams, Charles J. .... Bay Shore, NY
Adams, Charles J. .... Waterbury, VT
Adams, Charles L. .... Houston, TX
Adams, Charles P. .... San Juan, PR
Adams, Charles P., Jr. .... Jackson, MS
Adams, Charles R., III .... Fort Valley, GA
Macon, GA
Adams, Charles R., Jr. .... Fort Valley, GA
Macon, GA
Adams, Charles S. .... Boston, MA
Adams, Charles W. .... Tulsa, OK
Adams, Charles W. .... Arlington, TX
Adams, Charlie Lee .... Jacksonville, FL
Adams, Charlotte J. .... Tustin, CA

Adams, Cherie S. ... **Kingsport, TN**
Adams, Chester ... McLean, VA
Adams, Christie G. ... **Texarkana, TX**
Adams, Christina Louise ... **New Bern, NC**
Wilmington, NC
Adams, Christine M. ... **Fresno, CA**
Adams, Christine T. ... **Jacksonville, FL**
Adams, Christopher ... **Houston, TX**
Adams, Christopher David ... **Athens, GA**
Adams, Christopher J. ... **Wheeling, WV**
Adams, Christopher R. ... Hoboken, NJ
Adams, Christopher T., P.C.
Lawrenceville, GA
Adams, Christopher Todd
Lawrenceville, GA
Adams, Christy J. ... **Louisville, KY**
Adams, Christy Malyn ... Hope, AR
Adams, Clark, Jr. ... Columbus, GA
Adams, Clifford C. ... Tallulah, LA
Adams, Clifford L. ... Orlando, FL
Adams, Clifford S. ... Napa, CA
Adams & Coffey, P.C. ... **Beaumont, TX**
Houston, TX
Adams & Coker, P.C. ... Tyler, TX
Adams, Colin L. ... Albuquerque, NM
Adams, Colleen E. ... **Chicago, IL**
Adams, Colleen Lynn
Equal Employment Opportunity Commission,
Office of Legal Counsel, GV
Adams & Commons ... Indianapolis, IN
Adams & Conway ... Middletown, CT
Adams, Coogler, Watson & Merkel, P.A.
West Palm Beach, FL
Adams, Corliss V. ... Washington, DC
Adams, Cornelia C. ... **Lowell, MA**
Adams & Costley, L.L.P. ... **Greensboro, NC**
Winston-Salem, NC
Adams, Craig A. ... **Denver, CO**
Adams, Craig N. ... **Dallas, TX**
Adams, Craig Randall
Corpus Christi, TX
Adams, Craig S. ... Tyler, TX
Adams, Craig S. ... Tacoma, WA
Adams & Cramer ... **Shelbyville, IN**
Adams, Creighton V. ... Detroit, MI
Adams, Cynthia Croft ... **Portland, OR**
Adams, Cynthia Matson ... Indianapolis, IN
Adams, Cynthia Trimboli ... Fort Valley, GA
Adams, D. Annette
Agency for International Development,
Legal Advisers-Overseas, GV
Adams, D. Fenton ... Orange Beach, AL
Adams, D. Nelson ... **New York, NY**
Adams, D. Welborn ... **Greenwood, SC**
Adams, Dale C. ... Concord, CA
Adams, Dale E. ... Little Rock, AR
Adams, Dale E. ... **Fredericksburg, VA**
Adams, Dale S. ... **San Francisco, CA**
Adams, Dale S. ... Ann Arbor, MI
Adams, Daniel A. ... Chicora, PA
Adams, Daniel C. ... **Minneapolis, MN**
Adams, Daniel D. ... Greenwich, CT
Adams, Daniel D., Jr. ... Oklahoma City, OK
Adams, Daniel L. ... **Fort Lauderdale, FL**
Adams, Daniel P. ... **Poughkeepsie, NY**
Adams, Daniel R. ... Chicago, IL
Adams, Danny E. ... **Washington, DC**
Adams, Darrell ... Charlestown, IN
Adams, Darrell K. ... Atlanta, GA
Adams, Darryl A. ... Gaithersburg, MD
Adams, Darryl J. ... **Austin, TX**
Adams, David A. ... Des Moines, IA
Adams, David B ... Sacramento, CA
Adams, David C. ... Lawrence, KS
Adams, David D. ... Nacogdoches, TX
Adams, David E. ... Senatobia, MS
Adams, David G. ... **Washington, DC**
Adams, David G. ... **Dallas, TX**
Adams, David H. ... Pikeville, KY
Adams, David H. ... Norfolk, VA
Adams, David J. ... **Chicago, IL**
Adams, David Lane ... Lewisburg, TN
Adams, David M. ... Noblesville, IN
Adams, David P. ... Baton Rouge, LA
Adams, David P. ... Baton Rouge, LA
Adams, David R. ... Buffalo, NY
Adams, David R. ... Rosemont, PA
Adams, David S. ... Olathe, KS
Adams, David W. ... **Tampa, FL**
Adams, David W. ... **Savannah, GA**
Adams, David W. ... Duluth, MN
Adams, David W., P.C. ... **Griffin, GA**
Adams, David Walter ... **Griffin, GA**
Adams, David Wm. ... Brookline, MA
Adams, Dawn S. ... Milwaukee, WI
Adams, Dayter & Sheehan ... Albany, NY
Adams, Dean A. ... Treasury Department,
Bureau of the Public Debt, GV
Adams, Dean K. ... **Austin, MN**
Adams, DeBast, Helzer, McFarland,
Richardson & Uffelman ... **Beaverton, OR**
Adams, Deborah ... San Francisco, CA
Adams, Deborah G. ... Okemos, MI
Adams, Deborah R.
Colorado Springs, CO
Adams, Deborah S. ... **Cincinnati, OH**
Adams, Dekristie M. ... Davis, CA
Adams, Delphine S. ... **Santa Rosa, CA**
Adams, Denise Lana ... Kansas City, KS
Adams, Derick W. ... Southfield, MI
Adams, Derry Beach
Colorado Springs, CO
Adams, Desiree W. ... **Metairie, LA**
Adams, Diana Goldberg ... New York, NY
Adams, Diana K. ... Santa Cruz, CA
Adams, Diana Y. ... San Diego, CA
Adams, Dick ... Madisonville, KY

Adams, Dirk S. ... **Oakland, CA**
Adams, Dixon G. ... Papillion, NE
Adams, Donald A. ... Albuquerque, NM
Adams, Donald C. ... Irving, TX
Adams, Donald C., Jr. ... **Cincinnati, OH**
Adams, Donald D. ... Hutchinson, KS
Adams, Donald E. ... Drayton Plains, MI
Adams, Donald Edward
Department of Commerce,
Patent and Trademark Office, GV
Adams, Donald G. ... Quincy, IL
Adams, Donald L. ... Indianapolis, IN
Adams, Donald L. ... Burlington, NC
Adams, Donald M., Jr., Law Office of
Camarillo, CA
Los Angeles, CA
Simi Valley, CA
Thousand Oaks, CA
Adams, Donald M., Jr., Law Office of
Ventura, CA
Adams, Donald M., Jr., Law Office of
Westlake Village, CA
Adams, Donnell G., Jr. ... **Carthage, NC**
Pinehurst, NC
Adams, Doris M. ... Danielson, CT
Adams, Dorothy J. ... Eatonton, GA
Adams, Douglas F. ... New York, NY
Adams, Douglas J. ... Silver Spring, MD
Adams, Douglas L., Jr. ... Wichita, KS
Adams, Douglas P. ... **Sacramento, CA**
Adams & DuBay, P.C. ... Paw Paw, MI
Adams, Durand J. ... Bradenton, FL
Adams, E. Alexander ... Columbia, MD
Adams, E. Stanley ... Cincinnati, OH
Adams, E. Wesley ... Silver Spring, MD
Adams, Earl K. ... San Diego, CA
Adams, Earl T. ... Stone Mountain, GA
Adams, Ed LaVance ... Atlanta, GA
Adams & Edens, A Professional Association
Brandon, MS
Adams, Edgar W. ... Oklahoma City, OK
Adams, Edie A. ... New Windsor, NY
Poughkeepsie, NY
Adams, Edmund I. ... Sparta, NC
Adams, Edmund J. ... **Cincinnati, OH**
Adams, Edward B., Jr. ... **Houston, TX**
Adams, Edward L. ... **Los Angeles, CA**
Adams, Edward M., Jr. ... Wilton, CT
Adams, Edward S. ... Indianapolis, IN
Adams, Edward S. ... **Minneapolis, MN**
Adams, Edwin M. ... Washington, DC
Adams, Elaine ... Seattle, WA
Adams, Eldred E., Jr. ... Louisa, KY
Adams, Eleanor Kaplan ... **San Diego, CA**
Adams & Eliason ... **Enfield, CT**
Adams, Elisabeth ... Fort Myers, FL
Adams, Elisabeth, P.A. ... Fort Myers, FL
Adams, Elise M. ... **New York, NY**
Adams, Elizabeth D. ... Brownsville, TX
Adams, Elizabeth M. ... **Nashville, TN**
Adams, Elizabeth Spencer ... Yarmouth, ME
Adams, Ellard & Frankum, P.C.
Clarkesville, GA
Cornelia, GA
Adams, Ellen H. ... Dallas, TX
Adams, Elmer W. ... Tulsa, OK
Adams, Eric F. ... **Huntsville, AL**
Adams, Eric R. ... Batavia, NY
Adams, Eric S. ... **Washington, DC**
Adams, Eric S. ... **Tampa, FL**
Adams, Erik H. ... Sausalito, CA
Adams, Eugene J. ... New City, NY
Adams, Eugene L. ... Fresno, CA
Adams, Evelyn A. ... **Rochester, NY**
Adams, E. W. ... Marshalltown, IA
Adams, E. W., Jr. ... Valley Falls, NY
Adams, F. Edward, III ... Houston, TX
Adams, F. Kirk ... Ridley Park, PA
Adams, F. Louise ... **Atlanta, GA**
Adams, Felix M. ... Bushnell, FL
Adams, Felix M., P.A. ... Bushnell, FL
Adams, Fisher & Evans ... Ripley, WV
Spencer, WV
Adams & Flake ... Universal City, TX
Adams, Floyd P., Jr.,(P.C.) ... Atlanta, GA
Adams & Ford LLP ... Eatonton, GA
Adams, Forrest L. ... Abbeville, AL
Adams, Frances G., II
Department of the Air Force,
Office of the Judge Advocate General, GV
Adams, Francis L. ... Yuba City, CA
Adams, Frank A. ... Beaumont, TX
Adams, Frank B. ... Mason City, IA
Adams, Frank G. ... **Pittsburgh, PA**
Adams, Frank Lester, III ... Tampa, FL
Adams, Frank M., Jr. ... **Chicago, IL**
Adams, Frank R. ... **New York, NY**
Adams, Frank T. ... **Miami, FL**
Adams, Frank T., P.A. ... **Aventura, FL**
Miami, FL
Adams, Franklin C. ... **Riverside, CA**
Adams, Franklin L., Jr. ... **Nashville, NC**
Adams, Fred C. ... **Greensburg, PA**
Uniontown, PA
Adams, Fred M. ... Idaho Falls, ID
Adams, Frederick S., Jr. ... Dallas, TX
Adams, G. Bryan, III ... **Charlotte, NC**
Adams, G. Harris ... Denver, CO
Adams, Gail A. ... Jacksonville, FL
Adams, Gail Patricia ... Wheaton, IL
Adams, Gallinar, Iglesias & Meyer, P.A.
Miami, FL
Adams, Garlan L. ... Indianapolis, IN
Adams, Garth D ... **Des Moines, IA**
Adams, Gary E. ... Princeton, NJ
Adams, Gary L. ... Department of the Navy,
Office of the Judge Advocate General, GV
Adams, Gary S. ... Cleveland, OH

Adams, Gary W. ... Huntington, WV
Adams, Gene ... **Spartanburg, SC**
Adams, Gene D., Jr. ... **Jacksonville, AR**
Adams, Geo. F. ... Tupelo, MS
Adams, Geoffrey C. S. ... San Francisco, CA
Adams, Geoffrey William ... **Raleigh, NC**
Adams, George B. ... Palmer, MA
Adams, George B. ... **New York, NY**
Adams, George C. ... Austin, TX
Adams, George E. ... Dacula, GA
Adams, George F. ... Philadelphia, PA
Adams, George R. ... **Washington, DC**
Bethesda, MD
Chevy Chase, MD
Adams, George R. ... San Antonio, TX
Adams, George W. ... Rossville, GA
Adams, George W., III ... **Milford, CT**
Adams, Georgette ... **New Canaan, CT**
Adams, Gerald R. ... Sacramento, CA
Adams, Gerard G. ... Pasadena, CA
Adams, Gilbert T., III ... **Beaumont, TX**
Adams, Gilbert T., Jr. ... **Beaumont, TX**
Adams, Gilbert T., P.C., Law Offices of
Beaumont, TX
Adams, Gina F. ... **Memphis, TN**
Adams, Gina Marie ... **Baltimore, MD**
Adams, Givens L. ... Oklahoma City, OK
Adams, Glendon Bryan ... Stafford, TX
Adams, Glenn Arthur ... **Orlando, FL**
Adams, Glenn B. ... **New Orleans, LA**
Adams, Glenn B. ... **Fayetteville, NC**
Adams, Glenn C. ... Indianapolis, IN
Adams, Glenn D. ... Oklahoma City, OK
Adams, Gordon G. ... Belton, TX
Adams & Graham, L.L.P. ... **Austin, TX**
Brownsville, TX
Corpus Christi, TX
Edinburg, TX
Falfurrias, TX
Harlingen, TX
Laredo, TX
McAllen, TX
Raymondville, TX
Rio Grande City, TX
Zapata, TX
Adams, Grant ... **Amarillo, TX**
Adams, Greg F. ... **Seattle, WA**
Adams, Gregory A. ... Decatur, GA
Adams, Gregory B. ... Columbia, SC
Adams, Gregory J. ... **Minneapolis, MN**
Adams, Gregory J. ... **Salt Lake City, UT**
Adams, Gregory L. ... Cincinnati, OH
Adams, Gregory P. ... **Cincinnati, OH**
Adams & Grimm, P.A. ... **Jacksonville, FL**
Adams, H. Mark ... **New Orleans, LA**
Adams, Hall, III ... **Chicago, IL**
Adams, Halvor N., III ... Westbury, NY
Adams, Harold E., Jr.
East Greenwich, RI
Adams, Harold G. ... Dallas, TX
Adams, Harold N. ... **Bloomington, IL**
Adams, Harold W. ... Oak Ridge, TN
Adams, Harry B., III ... Universal City, TX
Adams, Hawekotte & Hudson
Pasadena, CA
Adams & Haydon, P.C.
East Greenwich, RI
Providence, RI
Adams, Heather Bell ... **Raleigh, NC**
Adams, Heather Brantley ... Charlotte, NC
Adams, Helen C. ... **Des Moines, IA**
Adams, Hemingway & Wilson, L.L.P.
Macon, GA
Adams, Hendon, Carson, Crow & Saenger,
P.A. ... **Asheville, NC**
Adams, Henry, III ... Rayne, LA
Adams, Henry L. ... Bountiful, UT
Adams, Henry L., Jr. ... Tampa, FL
Adams, Herbert E. ... Gibsonburg, OH
Adams, Herbert, Jr. ... **Atlanta, GA**
Adams, Herman M. ... Las Vegas, NV
Adams, Hill, Reis, Adams, Hall & Schieffelin,
P.A. ... **Orlando, FL**
Adams, Holly A. ... San Bruno, CA
Adams, Holly A. ... Rochester, NY
Adams, Holly D. ... Kennewick, WA
Adams, Holmes S. ... **Jackson, MS**
Adams & Hood, P.C. ... Houston, TX
Adams, Horace W. ... Paw Paw, MI
Adams, Horstmann & Edwards, Professional
Corporation ... Lodi, CA
Adams, Howard Eugene ... Tallahassee, FL
Adams & Huetsch ... Columbia, IL
Adams, J. Allen ... **Raleigh, NC**
Adams, J. Collier ... Presidio, TX
Adams, J. Collier, Jr. ... Morton, TX
Adams, J. Craig ... **Savannah, GA**
Adams, J. Dinsmore, Jr. ... **New York, NY**
Adams, J. Jane ... Asheboro, NC
Adams, J. Keith ... **Salt Lake City, UT**
Adams, J. Kent ... Houston, TX
Adams, J. Patrick ... **Greensboro, NC**
Adams, J. Phillip ... **New York, NY**
Adams, J. Stokes, III ... Harrisburg, PA
Adams, J. W., Jr., A Professional Corporation
Houston, TX
Adams, Jack A. ... **Houston, TX**
Adams, Jack J. ... St. Louis, MO
Adams, James Albert ... Des Moines, IA
Adams, James B. ... Austin, TX
Adams, James Barton, Jr. ... Louisville, KY
Adams, James C. ... **Ann Arbor, MI**
Adams, James C. ... Beach Haven, NJ
Adams, James C., II ... **Greensboro, NC**
Adams, James D. ... Boca Raton, FL
Adams, James D. ... Jackson, MI

Adams, James E.
Department Of Veterans Affairs,
Office of the General Counsel, GV
Adams, James F. ... **Dallas, TX**
Adams, James F. ... **Dallas, TX**
Adams, James G., Jr. ... **Decatur, AL**
Adams, James G., Jr. ... Hopkinsville, KY
Adams, James J. ... **Lafayette, LA**
Adams, James K. ... Yakima, WA
Adams, James L. ... Shreveport, LA
Adams, James M. ... **West Palm Beach, FL**
Adams, James M. ... **Burlington, IA**
Adams, James M., Jr. ... Tampa, FL
Adams, James M., Jr., P.A. ... Tampa, FL
Adams, James R. ... Sacramento, CA
Adams, James R. ... Fort Myers, FL
Adams, James R. ... LaBelle, FL
Adams, James R. ... **Cincinnati, OH**
Adams, James R. ... Quinton, OK
Adams, James R. ... **Lancaster, PA**
Adams, James Samuel ... New York, NY
Adams, James W. ... Anchorage, AK
Adams, James W., Jr. ... **Wickliffe, OH**
Adams, Jan ... **St. Louis, MO**
Adams, Jane Grant ... **Fairfax, VA**
Adams, Jane K. ... **San Diego, CA**
Adams, Janell M. ... **Phoenix, AZ**
Adams, Janet W. ... **Orlando, FL**
Adams, Janis E. ... Rolling Hills, CA
Adams, Janis Leigh ... Pueblo, CO
Adams, Jared H. ... Sudbury, MA
Adams, Jas Jeffrey ... Salem, OR
Adams, Jas. N. ... Waller, TX
Adams, Jasen Dean ... **Washington, DC**
Adams, Jason R. ... **Elk Point, SD**
Adams, Jay P. ... New Orleans, LA
Adams, Jay, (P.A.) ... **Tallahassee, FL**
Adams, Jay W. ... Litchfield, IL
Adams, Jay William, P.C. ... Litchfield, IL
Adams, Jean A. ... Dolton, IL
Adams, Jean Taylor ... **Winston-Salem, NC**
Adams, Jeannette L. ... **Seattle, WA**
Adams, Jeannette L. ... Seattle, WA
Adams, Jeannie A. ... **Richmond, VA**
Adams, Jean-Vierre ... **Detroit, MI**
Adams, Jeffery T. ... **Clinton, MO**
Adams, Jeffory E. ... **Seattle, WA**
Adams, Jeffrey A. ... **League City, TX**
Adams, Jeffrey A. ... Charlottesville, VA
Adams, Jeffrey C. ... **Atlanta, GA**
Adams, Jeffrey L. ... **Walnut Creek, CA**
Adams, Jeffrey M. ... **St. Petersburg, FL**
Adams, Jeffrey M. ... **Oakhurst, NJ**
Adams, Jeffrey M. ... New City, NY
Adams, Jeffrey R. ... **Phoenix, AZ**
Adams, Jeffrey R. ... **Charlottesville, VA**
Adams, Jennifer Collesano
Washington, DC
Adams, Jennifer H. ... **Philadelphia, PA**
Adams, Jennifer Kincaid ... **Louisville, KY**
Adams, Jennifer L. ... Greenwich, CT
Adams, Jennifer L. ... **New York, NY**
Adams, Jennifer Perry ... **Chicago, IL**
Adams, Jennifer T. ... Columbus, GA
Adams, Jerilynn Brantner ... **Fargo, ND**
Adams, Jerome M. ... Mc Keesport, PA
Adams, Jerrold D. ... Roseville, CA
Adams, Jerry L., (P.C.) ... **Galveston, TX**
Adams, Jesse R., III ... **New Orleans, LA**
Adams, Jesse R., Jr. ... **New Orleans, LA**
Adams, Jill E. ... Carbondale, IL
Adams, Jill G. ... **Dallas, TX**
Adams, Jim Alan ... Richmond, TX
Adams, Joan Casilio ... Buffalo, NY
Adams, Joan Frentz ... **Mankato, MN**
Adams, Jo-Ann M. ... Cupertino, CA
Adams, Joann R. ... Rockville Centre, NY
Adams, Jody T. ... **Syracuse, NY**
Adams, Joe G., Jr. ... Asheville, NC
Adams, John A. ... Gaithersburg, MD
Adams, John A. ... **Salt Lake City, UT**
Adams, John A., Jr. ... **King Of Prussia, PA**
Adams, John B. ... Washington, DC
Adams, John B. ... **Chicago, IL**
Oakbrook Terrace, IL
Adams, John B. ... Somerset, KY
Adams, John B., (P.C.) ... Folkston, GA
Adams, John C. ... Coral Gables, FL
Adams, John C. ... Austin, TX
Adams, John C. ... Fairfax, VA
Adams, John C., III ... **Santa Ana, CA**
Adams, John C., P.A. ... Coral Gables, FL
Adams, John D. ... **Enfield, CT**
Adams, John E. ... Bismarck, ND
Adams, John E. ... Cambridge, OH
Adams, John E., Jr. ... Grove Hill, AL
Adams, John E., Jr. ... Trenton, NJ
Adams, John F. ... **Chicago, IL**
Adams, John F. ... Quincy, IL
Adams, John F. ... Westminster, MA
Adams, John F. ... **St. Clair Shores, MI**
Adams, John H. ... Orlando, FL
Adams, John H. ... Lincoln, NE
Adams, John H. ... New York, NY
Adams, John I. ... Des Moines, IA
Adams, John J. ... **Washington, DC**
Adams, John J. ... Fairview Heights, IL
Adams, John J. ... Swedesboro, NJ
Adams, John J. ... Kettering, OH
Adams, John K.
Federal Communications Commission,
Cable Services Bureau, GV
Adams, John L. ... Salt Lake City, UT
Adams, John Lindsey ... **Hopkinsville, KY**
Adams, John M. ... Beverly Hills, CA
Adams, John M. ... Boise, ID
Adams, John M. ... **Columbus, OH**
Adams, John M. ... Pittsburgh, PA

Adams, John M., Jr. ... Columbus, OH
Adams, John N. ... New York, NY
Adams, John O. ... Beverly Hills, CA
Adams, John O., Jr. ... Decatur, GA
Adams, John P. ... Birmingham, AL
Adams, John P. ... Chicago, IL
Adams, John P. ... Canaan, NY
Adams, John P. ... Berkeley Springs, WV
Adams, John Q. ... Orange, CA
Adams, John Q. ... Jackson, MS
Adams, John Q. ... Staten Island, NY
Adams, John Quincy ... New York, NY
Adams, John R. ... Chicago, IL
Adams, John R. ... Lexington, KY
Adams, John R. ... Akron, OH
Adams, John Ross ... Delray Beach, FL
Adams, John Ross, Professional Association
Delray Beach, FL
Adams, John T. ... Reading, PA
Adams, John V. (Jack) ... Sacramento, CA
Adams, John V., Jr. ... Pittsburgh, PA
Adams, John W., Jr. ... Montgomery, AL
Adams and Johnston, A Professional Law Corporation ... New Orleans, LA
Adams, Jon H. ... Poughkeepsie, NY
Adams, Jon K. ... San Francisco, CA
Adams, Jon P. ... Fresno, CA
Adams, Jonathan C. ... Iselin, NJ
Adams, Jonathan Daniel ... Martinez, CA
Adams, Jonathan E. ... Chicago, IL
Adams & Jones, Chartered ... Wichita, KS
Adams & Jordan, P.C. ... Macon, GA
Adams, Jos. W. ... Birmingham, AL
Adams, Joseph A. ... New York, NY
Adams, Joseph Blaise ... Oakland, CA
Adams, Joseph C. ... York, PA
Adams, Joseph C. ... Seattle, WA
Adams, Joseph E. ... Fort Myers, FL
Adams, Joseph G. ... Phoenix, AZ
Adams, Joseph H. ... Nyack, NY
Adams, Joseph J. ... Omaha, NE
Adams, Joseph Lee ... Jackson, MS
Adams, Joseph M. ... Somerdale, NJ
Doylestown, PA
Adams, Joseph S. ... Chicago, IL
Adams, Joseph T. ... Hillsboro, OR
Adams, Joseph W. ... Ozark, AL
Adams, Julia Hylton ... Winchester, KY
Adams, Julia Marie ... Houston, TX
Adams, Julie K. ... Houston, TX
Adams, June Miller ... New York, NY
Adams, J. W., Jr. ... Houston, TX
Adams, K. Marvin ... Fort Worth, TX
Adams, Karen ... Portland, OR
Adams, Karen J. ... Ararat, NC
Adams, Karen Meriwether ... Richmond, VA
Adams, Karen R. ... Dayton, OH
Adams, Katherine L. ... New York, NY
Adams, Kathleen W. ... Naples, FL
Adams, Kathryn A. ... Waukesha, WI
Adams, Kathy E. ... Piedmont, SC
Adams, Kathy J. ... Chicago, IL
Adams, Kathy K. ... Corpus Christi, TX
Adams & Kellas, P.C. ... Winchester, VA
Adams, Kenneth A. ... New York, NY
Adams, Kenneth C. ... Santa Monica, CA
Adams, Kenneth L. ... Washington, DC
Adams, Kent M. ... Beaumont, TX
Houston, TX
Adams, Kerry L. ... Washington, DC
Adams, Kevin ... Southfield, MI
Adams, Kevin M. ... Louisville, KY
Adams, Kif Augustine ... Provo, UT
Adams, Kimberely J. ... Florence, KY
Adams, Kimberley K. ... New York, NY
Adams Kleemeier Hagan Hannah & Fouts
Asheboro, NC
Greensboro, NC
High Point, NC
Winston-Salem, NC
Adams, Kokie E. ... Lynnwood, WA
Adams & Koss ... Brookline, MA
Adams, Kristi E. ... Jackson, MS
Adams, Kristi M. ... Phoenix, AZ
Adams, Kurt W. ... Portland, ME
Adams, L. Clifford, Jr. ... Atlanta, GA
Adams, L. Howard ... New York, NY
Adams, L. Katherine ... Decatur, GA
Adams, L. Money, Jr. ... Dallas, TX
Adams, Larry J., (P.C.) ... Corpus Christi, TX
Adams, Larry L. ... Daytona Beach, FL
Adams, Laura S. ... San Diego, CA
Adams, Laureen Alford ... Athens, GA
Adams, Laurel A. ... Concord, CA
Adams, Lauren ... Bella Vista, AR
Springdale, AR
Adams, Laurence E. ... Weymouth, MA
Adams, Laurence J. ... Lancaster, PA
Adams, Laurie B. ... Washington, DC
Adams, Laurie J. ... West Palm Beach, FL
Adams Law Firm ... Madisonville, KY
Adams Law Firm, L.L.C. ... Toccoa, GA
Adams Law Firm, P.A. ... Charlotte, NC
Adams Law Firm, P.C. ... New City, NY
Adams Law Firm, The ... Asheville, NC
Adams Law Firm, The ... Dallas, TX
Adams Law Offices ... Blue Springs, MO
Kansas City, MO
Adams, Lawrence C. ... Dallas, TX
Adams, Layne M. ... Monroe, LA
Adams, Lee Ann ... Chattanooga, TN
Adams, Lee S. ... Ukiah, CA
Adams, Lee S. ... Washington, DC
Adams, Lee Towne ... Forestville, NY
Adams, Lee W. ... Palmer, MA
Adams, Leland J., Jr. ... Boston, MA
Adams, Lem, III ... Brandon, MS
Adams, Leon, Jr. ... Atlanta, GA
Adams, Leslie Wm. ... Houston, TX
Adams, Lester E., Jr. ... Browning, MO
Adams, Lester I., Jr. ... Louisville, KY
Adams, Lester L. ... Baltimore, MD
Adams, Lester L., P.A. ... Baltimore, MD
Adams, L. H., Jr. ... Atlanta, GA
Adams, Linda B. ... Pass Christian, MS
Adams, Linda L. ... San Bernardino, CA
Adams, Lindsay S. ... New York, NY
Adams, Lloyd, III ... Albany, NY
Adams, Lloyd S., Jr. ... Memphis, TN
Adams, Lori Nelson ... Seattle, WA
Adams, Lorna H. ... Sacramento, CA
Adams, Louis W., Jr. ... Fort Lauderdale, FL
Adams, Lynch & Loftin, P.C.
Bedford, TX
Dallas, TX
Fort Worth, TX
Adams, Lynn Krapcho ... Westfield, NJ
Adams, Lynne C. ... Phoenix, AZ
Adams, M. Elizabeth ... Statesboro, GA
Adams, M. Reed ... Provo, UT
Adams, Marcia E. ... Brooklyn, NY
Adams, Marcia Howe ... Palo Alto, CA
Adams, Margaret I. ... Los Angeles, CA
Adams, Margaret Rae ... Redmond, WA
Adams, Marguerite L. ... New Orleans, LA
Adams, Marina I. ... New York, NY
Adams, Marion Ann ... Springfield, MO
Adams, Marjorie A. ... Roseland, NJ
Adams, Marjorie Sybul ... New York, NY
Adams, Mark ... Brockton, MA
Adams, Mark A. ... Denver, CO
Adams, Mark F. ... San Diego, CA
Adams, Mark H. ... Tacoma, WA
Adams, Mark K. ... Albuquerque, NM
Adams, Mark L. ... Madison, WI
Adams, Mark R. ... Des Moines, IA
Adams, Mark R. ... Southfield, MI
Adams, Mark S. ... Irvine, CA
Adams, Mark Stephen ... Stockton, CA
Adams, Mark W. ... San Jose, CA
Adams, Mark W. ... Glenside, PA
Adams, Mark-David ... Palm Beach, FL
Adams, Marla Tugwell ... Asheville, NC
Adams, Marlene Y. ... San Francisco, CA
Adams, Marshall A. ... Coral Springs, FL
Adams, Marshall D. ... Tacoma, WA
Adams, Marta A. ... Carson City, NV
Adams, Martha C. ... New York, NY
Adams, Martha K. ... Galveston, TX
Adams, Martin B. ... New York, NY
Adams, Martin O. ... Fort Stockton, TX
Adams, Mary E. ... Green Brook, NJ
Adams, Mary Margaret ... Beaumont, TX
Adams, Mary Ryan ... Center Lovell, ME
Adams, Mary T. Lonergan ... Blue Bell, PA
Adams & Mason, Inc. ... Sacramento, CA
Adams, Matthew C. ... Dallas, TX
Adams, Matthew S. ... Bellevue, WA
Adams, Matthew T. ... Washington, DC
Adams, Matthew Wayne
Minneapolis, MN
Adams, McAndrews, Matson & Landsberg, A Prof. Corp. ... Santa Monica, CA
Adams, McCullough & Beard
Raleigh, NC
Adams, Michael A. ... Weirton, WV
Wheeling, WV
Adams, Michael B. ... Rye Brook, NY
Adams, Michael B., Jr. ... Washington, DC
Adams, Michael D. ... San Francisco, CA
Adams, Michael E. ... Redwood City, CA
Adams, Michael G. ... Charlotte, NC
Adams, Michael G. ... Galveston, TX
Adams, Michael J. ... Department of the Army, Office, Chief of Engineers/Headquarters, U.S. Army Corps of Engineers, GV
Adams, Michael J. ... Bloomington, MN
Adams, Michael J. ... San Augustine, TX
Adams, Michael K. ... Detroit, MI
Adams, Michael M. ... Rancho Santa Fe, CA
Adams, Michael P. ... Austin, TX
Adams, Michael R. ... Irvine, CA
Santa Ana, CA
Adams, Michael R. ... Franklin, MI
Adams, Michael R. ... Hauppauge, NY
Adams, Michael W. ... Houston, TX
Adams, Michele V. ... Ashland, MA
Adams, Michelle L. ... Geneva, IL
Adams, Michelle L. ... Houston, TX
Adams, Michelle Victoria ... Newark, NJ
Adams, Mike ... Pittsburgh, PA
Adams, Milbern J. ... San Antonio, TX
Adams, Miles N. ... Cedar Rapids, IA
Adams, Milton W. ... Kansas City, MO
Adams, Milton W., Law Offices of
Kansas City, MO
Adams, Morgan G., Law Offices of
Ringgold, GA
Altamont, TN
Adams, Morgan G., Law Offices of
Chattanooga, TN
Adams, Morgan G., Law Offices of
Cleveland, TN
Jasper, TN
Adams, Myers & Baczkowski
Mc Keesport, PA
Adams, Nancy A. ... Morristown, NJ
Adams, Nancy D. ... Boston, MA
Adams, Nancy Herstek ... Radnor, PA
Adams, Natalie S. ... Seattle, WA
Adams, Nate L., III ... Winchester, VA
Adams, Nathan A., IV
Colorado Springs, CO
Adams, Nathan P., Jr. ... Greenville, MS
Adams, Nathaniel K. ... Coeur d'Alene, ID
Adams, Neal W. ... Bedford, TX
Adams, Neale T. ... Caribou, ME
Adams, Nell ... Blue Springs, MO
Adams, Nicholas ... Olympia, WA
Adams, Non Quincy ... Mobile, AL
Adams, Norma B. ... Somerset, KY
Adams, Norvan E. ... Fairview Heights, IL
Adams • Nye • Sinunu • Walker LLP
San Francisco, CA
San Jose, CA
Walnut Creek, CA
Adams, Oliver L. ... Bentonville, AR
Adams, Ora R., Jr. ... Albuquerque, NM
Adams, Orr, Jr. ... Metairie, LA
Adams, Orren Sheldon ... Boston, MA
Adams, Orval W., Jr. ... Salt Lake City, UT
Adams, Oscar W., III ... Birmingham, AL
Adams & Osteen ... Greensboro, NC
Adams, Owen J. ... Thomaston, GA
Adams, Owens & Jones ... Aurora, NE
Adams, P. Jane ... Alexandria, VA
Adams, P. Thomas, Jr. ... Bremerton, WA
Adams, Patricia Gibbons ... Riverdale, MD
Adams, Patrick F. ... Bay Shore, NY
Adams, Patrick F., P.C. ... Bay Shore, NY
Adams, Patrick J. ... Potomac, MD
Adams, Paul A. ... Towson, MD
Harrisburg, PA
Adams, Paul C. ... New York, NY
Adams, Paul E. ... Albuquerque, NM
Adams, Paul F. ... Fremont, CA
Adams, Paul Lancaster, Jr.
Philadelphia, PA
Adams, Paul, Law Office of ... Brockton, MA
Adams, Paul M. ... West Palm Beach, FL
Adams, Paul S. ... Fort Lauderdale, FL
Adams, Paul S., Jr. ... Dallas, TX
Adams, Paul Stephen ... New Orleans, LA
Adams, Paul-Joseph R. ... Jackson, MI
Adams, Penni Rush ... Springfield, MO
Adams, Perrotta & Williams, P.C.
St. Clair Shores, MI
Adams, Peter ... Houston, TX
Adams, Peter A. ... Roseland, NJ
Adams, Peter C. ... Savannah, GA
Adams, Peter J. ... Worcester, MA
Adams & Peterson, L.L.C.
Gig Harbor, WA
Adams, Phil L. ... Gainesville, TX
Adams, Philip E. ... Department of Defense, Defense Legal Services Agency, GV
Adams, Philip J., Jr. ... Overland Park, KS
Adams, Philip R., A Professional Law Corporation ... Sherman Oaks, CA
Adams, Philip Victor ... Oakland, CA
Adams, Phillip E., Jr. ... Opelika, AL
Adams, P. J. ... Brockton, MA
Adams, Porter & Radigan, Ltd.
McLean, VA
Adams, Portnoy & Berggren, P.A.
Cary, NC
Raleigh, NC
Adams, R. Martin ... Dothan, AL
Adams, R. Scott ... Oklahoma City, OK
Adams, R. Wade ... Miami, FL
Adams, Rachel A. ... Columbus, OH
Adams and Rafferty, Law Offices of
Santa Rosa, CA
Adams, Ralph W. ... Troy, AL
Adams, Randal J. ... Wichita, KS
Tulsa, OK
Adams, Randall E. ... Los Angeles, CA
Adams, Randall J. ... Salem, OR
Adams, Randall R. ... Coeur d'Alene, ID
Adams, Randall R. ... Rocky Mount, NC
Adams, Randolph W.
Fort Lauderdale, FL
Adams, Ray Harris ... San Antonio, TX
Adams, Ray Harris, P.C.
San Antonio, TX
Adams, Rayford K., III ... Greensboro, NC
Adams, Raymond L. ... Deerfield, MA
Adams, Rebecca L. ... Oklahoma City, OK
Adams and Reese LLP ... Mobile, AL
Washington, DC
Baton Rouge, LA
New Orleans, LA
Jackson, MS
Houston, TX
Adams, Reid C., Jr. ... Winston-Salem, NC
Adams, Rhonda Jean ... Sylacauga, AL
Adams & Rice, P.L.C. ... Des Moines, IA
Adams, Richard A. ... Pine Grove, PA
Adams, Richard A. ... Texarkana, TX
Adams, Richard B., Jr. ... Miami, FL
Adams, Richard D. ... Grants Pass, OR
Adams, Richard F. ... Kansas City, MO
Adams, Richard G. ... Middletown, CT
Adams, Richard H., Jr. ... Orlando, FL
Adams, Richard J. ... Miami, FL
Adams, Richard L. ... Montebello, CA
Adams, Richard L. ... Dallas, TX
Adams, Richard M. ... Orlando, FL
Adams, Richard M., Jr. ... Parkersburg, WV
Adams, Richard N. ... Ridgefield, CT
Adams, Richard N. ... Brevard, NC
Adams, Richard N. ... Houston, TX
Adams, Richard Noel ... League City, TX
Adams, Richard T. ... Fairview Heights, IL
Adams, Richard V. W., III ... McLean, VA
Adams, Richd. W. ... San Antonio, TX
Adams, R. L. ... Raleigh, NC
Adams, Robert B. ... Orange, CA
Adams, Robert B. ... Dalton, GA
Adams, Robert B. ... New York, NY
Adams, Robert C. ... Fairfax, VA
Adams, Robert F. ... Mobile, AL
Adams, Robert F. ... Department of Justice, Criminal Division, GV
Adams, Robert F. ... West Chester, PA
Adams, Robert F., Jr. ... Helena, MT
Adams, Robert G. ... Orinda, CA
Adams, Robert H. ... Birmingham, AL
Adams, Robert J. ... Lafayette, LA
Adams, Robert J. ... Berkley, MI
Adams, Robert K. ... Omaha, NE
Adams, Robert K. ... Virginia Beach, VA
Adams, Robert L. ... Albany, NY
Adams, Robert L. ... Houston, TX
Adams, Robert L., Jr. ... Danville, VA
Adams, Robert M. ... Kansas City, MO
Adams, Robert M. ... Las Vegas, NV
Adams, Robert M. ... Hackensack, NJ
Adams, Robert M., III ... Woodbridge, CT
Adams, Robert N. ... Kansas City, MO
Adams, Robert R. ... Miami, FL
Adams, Robert T. ... Kansas City, MO
Adams, Robert T. ... New York, NY
Adams, Robert T. ... Houston, TX
Adams, Robert T. ... Richmond, VA
Adams, Robert W. ... Shelbyville, IN
Adams, Robert W. ... Elk River, MN
Adams, Robert W. ... Hickory, NC
Adams, Robert W. ... Arlington, VA
Adams, Robert W. ("Tad"), III
Louisville, KY
Adams, Rodney C. ... Beaverton, OR
Adams, Rodney D. ... Irving, TX
Adams, Rodney K. ... Richmond, VA
Adams, Roger ... Pasadena, CA
Adams, Roger C. ... Department of Justice, Office of the Pardon Attorney, GV
Adams, Roger M. ... Jonesville, VA
Adams & Romer, Law Offices of
San Francisco, CA
Adams, Ron A., (P.A.) ... Miami, FL
Adams, Ronald F. ... Brunswick, GA
Adams, Ronald L. ... Fort Worth, TX
Adams, Ronald P. ... Mesa, AZ
Adams, Ronald R. ... Des Moines, IA
Adams, Ronald T. ... Portland, OR
Adams, Ronelle W. ... Arlington, VA
Adams, Ross J. ... Atlanta, GA
Adams, Rothstein & Siegel ... Jacksonville, FL
Adams, Roy M. ... New York, NY
Adams, Roy W., Jr. ... Moraga, CA
Adams, Royal D. ... San Antonio, TX
Adams, Royal D., Law Offices of, P.C.
San Antonio, TX
Adams, Russell B., III ... McLean, VA
Adams, Russell J. ... Granville, OH
Adams, Russell J. ... Houston, TX
Adams, Russell W. ... Birmingham, AL
Adams, Ryal & Flippin, Attorneys, P.C.
Humboldt, TN
Adams, Ryan L. ... Sand Springs, OK
Adams, Ryon Frank ... Stafford, TX
Adams, S. Blake ... Philadelphia, PA
Adams, Salisbury ... Wilson, WY
Adams, Sally L. ... Boston, MA
Adams, Sally Paulson ... Riverwoods, IL
Adams, Samuel ... Montgomery, AL
Adams, Samuel ... Boston, MA
Adams, Samuel L. ... Dothan, AL
Adams, Samuel W. ... New York, NY
Adams, Sandra Durloo ... Plantation, FL
Adams, Sandra Kindig ... Tacoma, WA
Adams, Sandra L. ... Long Beach, CA
Adams, Sara Champion ... New York, NY
Adams & Schefter ... Lacey, WA
Adams, Scott ... Morrilton, AR
Adams, Scott C. ... Aloha, OR
Adams, Scott G. ... Boothbay Harbor, ME
Adams, Scott M. ... Concord, NC
Adams, Sharon J. ... Lafayette, CA
Adams, S. M., Jr. ... Nacogdoches, TX
Adams, Smith & Berkman, P.C.
Brewster, NY
Adams, Spivey & Adams ... Clio, AL
Ozark, AL
Adams, Stacy W. ... Decatur, AL
Adams, Stephen ... Boston, MA
Providence, RI
Adams, Stephen E. ... Fayetteville, AR
Adams, Stephen E., Ltd., A Professional Corporation ... Fayetteville, AR
Adams, Stephen F. ... Chatsworth, CA
Adams, Stephen P. ... Louisville, KY
Adams, Stephen T. ... Overland Park, KS
Adams, Stephen T. ... Boston, MA
Adams, Steven B. ... Naperville, IL
Adams, Steven C. ... Clarkesville, GA
Cornelia, GA
Adams, Steven D. ... Hazel Park, MI
Adams, Steven D., P.C. ... Hazel Park, MI
Adams, Steven E. ... Baton Rouge, LA
Adams, Steven G. ... New York, NY
Adams, Steven J. ... Tulsa, OK
Adams, Steven J. ... Reading, PA
Adams, Steven M. ... Minneapolis, MN
Adams, Steven R. ... Cincinnati, OH
Adams, Steven R. ... Richmond, VA
Adams, Steven T. ... Santa Monica, CA
Adams, Stewart C., Jr. ... Lodi, CA
Adams, Stirling ... Orem, UT
Adams, Stuart D. ... Gold River, CA
Adams, Stuart L., Jr. ... Louisville, KY
Adams, Stuart L., Jr., P.S.C., The Law Offices of ... Louisville, KY
Adams & Sullivan ... Papillion, NE
Adams, Susan D. ... Flushing, NY
Adams, Susan Hoffman ... Lansing, MI
Adams, Susan J. ... Chicago, IL
Adams, Susan M. ... Hartford, CT
Adams, Susan P.
Equal Employment Opportunity

Commission,
Office of Legal Counsel, GV
Adams, Susan Strickroot .... Miami, FL
Adams, Suzanne J. .... New York, NY
Adams, Sylvia L. .... Bethesda, MD
Adams, Sylvia R. .... Memphis, TN
Adams, T. Jonathan .... Charlotte, NC
Adams, Tanzie .... Independence, OH
Adams, Tara Harkins .... New York, NY
Adams, Tarquin J. .... Orlando, FL
Adams, Tarquin J., P.A., Law Offices of
Orlando, FL
Adams, Teresa Gaddy .... Fayetteville, AR
Adams, Terry J. .... Phoenix, AZ
Adams, Terry K. .... Ann Arbor, MI
Adams, Thatcher M. .... Bangor, ME
Adams, Thayer R. .... Gwynedd Valley, PA
Adams, Theisen & May .... Ithaca, NY
Adams, Theodore F., III .... Richmond, VA
Adams, Theodore L. .... Columbus, OH
Adams, Theodore M. .... East Hartford, CT
Adams, Theresa M. .... Frederick, MD
Adams, Thomas A. .... Fort Wayne, IN
Adams, Thomas A., III .... Katy, TX
Adams, Thomas A., III, Law Firm of
Katy, TX
Adams, Thomas A., IV .... Dallas, TX
Adams, Thomas B. .... San Mateo, CA
Adams, Thomas C., Jr. .... Lacey, WA
Adams, Thomas D. .... Everett, WA
Adams, Thomas D. .... Seattle, WA
Adams, Thomas F. .... Caribou, ME
Adams, Thomas F., Jr. .... Raleigh, NC
Adams, Thomas F., P.A. .... Caribou, ME
Adams, Thomas H., Jr. .... Lowell, MI
Adams, Thomas J. .... Richmond Hill, NY
Adams, Thomas J., III .... Chicago, IL
Adams, Thomas J., III .... New York, NY
Adams, Thomas Kirke .... Clio, AL
Ozark, AL
Adams, Thomas L. .... Minneapolis, MN
Adams, Thomas L. .... Edison, NJ
Morristown, NJ
Adams, Thomas L., Jr. .... Washington, DC
Adams, Thomas M. .... Los Angeles, CA
Adams, Thomas P. .... New Orleans, LA
Adams, Thomas R.
South San Francisco, CA
Adams, Thomas R., Jr. .... Santa Barbara, CA
Adams, Thomas S. .... Sacramento, CA
Adams, Thomas T. .... Wilton, CT
New York, NY
Adams, Thomas W. .... Cleveland, OH
Adams, Timothy J. .... Las Vegas, NV
Adams, Timothy J. .... Dallas, TX
Adams, Timothy K. .... Macon, GA
Adams, Todd B. .... Lansing, MI
Adams, Todd S. .... Lincoln, NE
Adams, Tom D. .... Columbia, IL
Adams, Tommy M. .... Goldthwaite, TX
Adams, Tonya Connell .... Beaumont, TX
Adams, Tracy Jacqueline .... Key West, FL
Adams, T.V. .... Charlotte, NC
Adams, V. Cyprian, P.A.
Fort Lauderdale, FL
Adams, Van B. .... California, MO
Adams, Venol C. .... Fort Lauderdale, FL
Adams, Victoria Lewis .... Los Angeles, CA
Adams & Vilmos, P.A. .... Orlando, FL
Adams, Virgil L. .... Macon, GA
Adams, Virginia B. .... Lawrence, KS
Adams, Virginia Green .... Raleigh, NC
Adams, Virginia L. .... Dallas, TX
Adams, V. J., III .... Macon, GA
Adams, V. J., Jr. .... Macon, GA
Adams, W. Allen .... Thomaston, GA
Adams, W. Dean .... Everett, WA
Adams, W. Douglas .... Brunswick, GA
Adams, W. Mark .... Sunbury, OH
Adams, W. Michael .... Shreveport, LA
Adams, W. Ron .... Erlanger, KY
Adams, W. Thad, III .... Charlotte, NC
Adams & Walker, P.C. .... Branson, MO
Adams, Wallace B. .... Santa Rosa, CA
Adams, Wallace B., Law Offices of
Santa Rosa, CA
Adams, Walter G. .... Collinsville, IL
Adams, Walter L. .... Chicago, IL
Adams, Walter N. .... Atlanta, GA
Adams, Ware .... Los Angeles, CA
Adams, Warren S., II .... Austin, TX
Adams, Wayne .... Houston, TX
Adams, Wayne A. .... Des Plaines, IL
Adams, Wayne O, III .... Indianapolis, IN
Adams, Wayne T. .... Kennebunk, ME
Adams, Wendy L.
Environmental Protection Agency,
Office of the General Counsel, GV
Adams, Wesley P., Jr. .... Louisville, KY
Adams, Weston .... Columbia, SC
Adams, Weston, III .... Columbia, SC
Adams, Weston, Law Firm .... Columbia, SC
Adams & Whiteaker, P.C. .... Nashville, TN
Adams Whitmore & Jennings, P.L.L.C.
Seattle, WA
Adams, Whitney .... Washington, DC
Adams, Whitney .... McLean, VA
Adams, Wiley S. .... Chicago, IL
Adams & Wilks .... New York, NY
Adams, William .... Rockport, TX
Adams, William A. .... San Diego, CA
Adams, William A. .... Columbus, OH
Adams, William B. .... Dallas, TX
Adams, William C. .... Newport Beach, CA
Adams, William C., III .... Florence, KY
Adams, William E. .... San Jose, CA
Adams, William E. .... Sioux City, IA
Adams, William E. .... Pittsburgh, PA
Adams, William E. .... San Saba, TX
Adams, William E., Jr. .... Fort Lauderdale, FL
Adams, William E., Jr. .... Dallas, TX
Adams, William F. .... Moraga, CA
Adams, William G. .... Newport Beach, CA
Adams, William G. .... Kirkland, WA
Adams, William H. .... Pueblo, CO
Adams, William H. .... Salt Lake City, UT
Adams, William H. (Hal) .... Fort Myers, FL
Adams, William H., III .... Jacksonville, FL
Adams, William J. .... Los Angeles, CA
Adams, William J. .... Palm Desert, CA
Adams, William J. .... Branson, MO
Adams, William J. .... Pittsburgh, PA
Adams, William K. .... Philadelphia, PA
Adams, William K. .... Dallas, TX
Adams, William L. .... Windsor, CA
Adams, William R. .... Westmont, NJ
Adams, William R. .... Cincinnati, OH
Adams, William R., Jr. .... Philadelphia, PA
Adams, William S. .... Miami, FL
Adams, William S., Jr. .... Cleveland, MS
Adams, William W. .... Adams, MA
Adams, Willie C. .... Atlanta, GA
Adams, Wilsie H., Jr. .... Washington, DC
Adams, Woodrow W. .... Oklahoma City, OK
Adams-Choate, Sandra Sue .... Arlington, VA
Adams-Duma, Carl H. .... San Francisco, CA
Adamske, John A. .... San Diego, CA
Adamske, John A., A Professional Corporation
San Diego, CA
Adamske, Mary L. .... San Diego, CA
Adamski & Conti .... Chicago, IL
Adamski, Gregory A. .... Chicago, IL
Adamski, Karl A. .... Easthampton, MA
Adamski, Mary P. .... Hempstead, NY
Adamski, Patricia M. .... Hempstead, NY
Adamski, Robert C. .... Cape Coral, FL
Cape Coral, FL
Adamski, Robert C. .... Fort Myers, FL
Adamski, Steven J. .... San Luis Obispo, CA
Adamski, Tara L. .... Pierre, SD
Adamsky, Edward H .... Tyngsborough, MA
Adamsky, Steven R. .... Fort Lauderdale, FL
Adamson & Adamson .... Laguna Hills, CA
Adamson & Adamson .... Richmond, VA
Adamson, Anastacia Renae
Kansas City, MO
Adamson, Barbara Judith .... Boston, MA
Adamson, Bryan .... Cleveland, OH
Adamson, Bryan .... Dallas, TX
Adamson, Charles A. .... Mankato, MN
Adamson, Charles Z. .... Cleveland, OH
Adamson, Cheryl R.G. .... Kennewick, WA
Adamson, Craig G., (P.C.)
Salt Lake City, UT
Adamson, Dean H. .... Laguna Hills, CA
Adamson, Edwin A. .... Las Vegas, NV
Adamson, Eric Andrew
Department of Transportation,
Office of Hearings, GV
Adamson, Eric E. .... Front Royal, VA
Adamson, Frank .... Atlanta, GA
Adamson, Frank L. .... Greenbrae, CA
Adamson, Grant F. .... Diboll, TX
Adamson, Gregory J. .... Laguna Hills, CA
Adamson, Ingrid Louise .... Mesa, AZ
Adamson, J. Philip .... Tulsa, OK
Adamson, J. Philip, P.C. .... Tulsa, OK
Adamson, James .... Chicago, IL
Adamson, John E., Jr. .... Naples, FL
Adamson, John Robert .... Rusk, TX
Adamson, Kristin .... Tallahassee, FL
Adamson, Larry R. .... Green Valley, AZ
Tucson, AZ
Adamson, LaVilla S. .... Laguna Hills, CA
Adamson Law Office .... Mankato, MN
Adamson, Louise C. .... San Francisco, CA
Adamson, Louise Gurkin .... Richmond, VA
Adamson, Marie N.
General Services Administration,
Office of the General Counsel, GV
Adamson, Oscar C., II .... Minneapolis, MN
Adamson, Paul F. .... Akron, OH
Adamson, Raymond J. .... Augusta, GA
Adamson, Richard C. .... Shelton, WA
Adamson, Richard D. .... Kutztown, PA
Adamson, Richard W., II .... Montrose, CO
Adamson, Robert W. .... Homer, GA
Adamson, Ronald R. .... Farmington, NM
Adamson, Scott E. .... Los Angeles, CA
Adamson, Stephen Michael .... Hawthorne, CA
Adamson, Steven J. .... Corvallis, OR
Adamson, Susan C. .... Los Angeles, CA
Adamson, Terrence B. .... Washington, DC
Adamson, Tracie L. .... Augusta, ME
Adamson, V. Cassel .... Richmond, VA
Adamson, V. Cassel, Jr. .... Richmond, VA
Adamson, William S. .... Parsons, KS
Adamsons, Lara .... New York, NY
Adams-Taylor, Shavaun .... Chicago, IL
Adams-Webb, Lonna Marie .... Okmulgee, OK
Adamucci, Denise .... Philadelphia, PA
Adan, Sheila M. .... Chicago, IL
Adang, Peter J. .... Albuquerque, NM
Adang, Peter J., P.C. .... Albuquerque, NM
Adanick, Perry .... Louisville, KY
Adaniya, Kevin S. .... Honolulu, HI
Adas, Craig W. .... Menlo Park, CA
Adashek, David G. .... Pasadena, CA
Adashek, James L. .... Milwaukee, WI
Adashek, Lawrence D. .... Owings Mills, MD
Adasiewicz, Lori A. .... Sacramento, CA
Adatto, Jeffrey L. .... Vancouver, WA
Adauto, Gilbert C. .... Oakland, CA
Adcock, A. Mark .... Charlotte, NC
Adcock, C. Clinton .... Lafayette, LA
Adcock, Carl A. .... Morrow, GA
Adcock, Charles D. .... Tustin, CA
Adcock, Christina M. .... Mobile, AL
Adcock, Daniel L. .... Lamesa, TX
Adcock, David B. .... Durham, NC
Adcock, Gerald L. .... Omaha, NE
Adcock, Herschel C. .... New Orleans, LA
Adcock, Herschel C., Jr. .... Baton Rouge, LA
Adcock, John S. .... Houston, TX
Adcock, Ken R. .... Jackson, MS
Adcock, Loral Ashton, (P.A.)
Little Rock, AR
Adcock, Louie N., Jr. .... St. Petersburg, FL
Seminole, FL
Adcock, Marcy Enoch .... McMinnville, TN
Adcock, Orie C. .... Scottsbluff, NE
Adcock, Paul J. .... Sanford, NC
Adcock, Ramon M. .... Smithville, TN
Adcock, Robert H. .... Morris, IL
Adcock, Roy D. .... Bedford, WY
Adcock, Shannon Joines .... Greensboro, NC
Adcock, Steven .... Talladega, AL
Adcock, Terry L. .... Riverside, CA
Adcock, William T. .... Baton Rouge, LA
Adcock, William T., A Professional Law Corp.
Baton Rouge, LA
Adcox, C. Barton .... Tuscaloosa, AL
Adcox, Steven R. .... Newport News, VA
Addabbo, Dominic L. .... Forest Hills, NY
Addamo, Sebastian J. .... New York, NY
Addams, James M. .... Chattanooga, TN
Addams, John S. .... San Diego, CA
Addams, Kimberly B. .... Georgetown, KY
Addams, Robert D. .... New York, NY
Addams & Rundle .... Carlisle, PA
Addams, William A. .... Carlisle, PA
Addas, Frank P., Jr. .... Jersey City, NJ
Addas & Potenza .... Jersey City, NJ
Addelman, David R. .... Buffalo, NY
Addelman & Marszalkowski, P.C.
Buffalo, NY
Addelson, Laura S. .... Evanston, IL
Adden, Herbert J., Jr. .... Whittier, CA
Adden, Robert S., Jr. .... Charlotte, NC
Addeo, Annmarie F.
Croton-On-Hudson, NY
Addeo, Anthony J., III .... Farmingdale, NY
Addeo, Kenneth P. .... White Plains, NY
Adderley, Charlotte R. .... Lakeland, FL
Adderly, Leo .... Miami, FL
Addes, Ethan H. .... Englewood, NJ
Addesa, Emil N. .... West Caldwell, NJ
Addesa, Thomas J. .... Columbus, OH
Addess, Arthur .... Miami, FL
Addessi, Aileen C. .... Pittsburgh, PA
Addesso, Jack A. .... Mount Vernon, NY
Addicks, Jeffery Allen .... Houston, TX
Addicks, Mentor C., Jr. .... Minneapolis, MN
Addicks, Sharon Lowman .... Houston, TX
Addicott & Addicott, Professional Association
Hollywood, FL
Addicott, D. Christian .... Seattle, WA
Addicott, Michael L. .... Hollywood, FL
Addicott, Sari T. .... Hollywood, FL
Addiego, Dawn Marie .... Mount Holly, NJ
Addiego, Joseph E., III
San Francisco, CA
Addiego, Shiela T. .... San Francisco, CA
Addington, Charlotte .... San Francisco, CA
Addington, Darrel B. .... Tacoma, WA
Addington, Gregory W.
Department of Justice, GV
Addington, Hannah W. .... Texarkana, TX
Addington, Laurence M. .... New York, NY
Addington, Leonard M. .... Minneapolis, MN
Addington, Michael David .... Olathe, KS
Addington, Steven L. .... Des Moines, IA
Addis, Albert B. .... Royal Oak, MI
Addis, David H. .... Chicago, IL
Addis, David I. .... Chicago, IL
Addis, David W. .... Washington, DC
Addis & Fiorillo, P.C. .... Tucson, AZ
Addis & Imbrunone, P.C. .... Royal Oak, MI
Addis, James D. .... Hackensack, NJ
Addis, Jeremy A. .... Chicago, IL
Addis, Lauane C. .... Chicago, IL
Addis, Margaret M. .... Greenbelt, MD
Addis, Michael .... Tucson, AZ
Addis, Richard B. .... Albuquerque, NM
Addison, Alexandra J. .... Arlington, VA
Addison, Angela M. .... Washington, DC
Addison, Bradford G. .... Indianapolis, IN
Addison, Bradley R. .... Newcastle, WA
Addison, Brian M. .... York, PA
Addison, C. F. .... Salem, OR
Addison, Colborn M. .... Columbus, OH
Addison, Daniel D. .... Raleigh, NC
Addison, Daniel R. .... Washington, DC
Addison, David C. .... Los Angeles, CA
Addison, David C. .... Denver, CO
Addison, David D. .... Richmond, VA
Addison, Eileen M. .... Yorktown, VA
Addison, Emerson J., Jr. .... Southfield, MI
Addison, Frederick W., III .... Dallas, TX
Addison & Funk .... Marietta, OH
Addison, H. Boyd .... Sacramento, CA
Addison, H. Lee, III .... Virginia Beach, VA
Addison, Hyman J. .... Itasca, IL
Addison, Ilene Jones .... Sonoma, CA
Addison, James R., (Co., L.P.A.)
Marietta, OH
Addison, James W. .... Atlanta, GA
Addison, Jas. C. .... Miami, FL
Addison, Jeff M. .... Texarkana, AR
Addison, Joel N. .... Roswell, GA
Addison, John V. .... Wayne, NE
Addison Law Firm, A Professional
Corporation .... Dallas, TX
Addison, Linda Leuchter .... Houston, TX
Addison, Mark .... Lakewood, NJ
Addison, Matthew C. .... Reno, NV
Addison, Max C. .... Lubbock, TX
Addison, Michael C. .... Bartow, FL
Clearwater, FL
St. Petersburg, FL
Addison, Michael C. .... Tampa, FL
Addison, R. Dallas, Jr. .... Dallas, TX
Addison, Randolph D. .... Dallas, TX
Addison, Richard D. .... Columbia, SC
Addison, Richard Daniel .... Columbia, SC
Addison, Robert J. .... Crown Point, IN
Addison, Robert Martin
Winston-Salem, NC
Addison, Robert S. .... Jackson, MS
Addison, Robert S. .... Dallas, TX
Addison, Robert Spruiell, Jr.
Los Angeles, CA
Addison, Roger G. .... Oklahoma City, OK
Addison, Ronald D. .... Dallas, TX
Addison, Shelley C. .... Eureka, CA
Addison, Sidney T. .... Dallas, TX
Addison, Stefan L. .... Oneida, NY
Addiss, Wendy L. .... Washington, DC
Additon, Richard Leslie .... Charlotte, NC
Addleman, Katherine Smith .... Denver, CO
Addlestone, Claire Alison .... Atlanta, GA
Addlestone, David F. .... Washington, DC
Addlestone, Steven I. .... Atlanta, GA
Addleton, David F. .... Atlanta, GA
Addo, Michael K. .... Baltimore, MD
Addonizio, James J. .... Hazlet, NJ
Addonizio, Peter J. .... Freehold, NJ
Addonizio, Peter J., P.C. .... Freehold, NJ
Address, Stuart M. .... Stuart, FL
Adducci, Dorf, Lehner, Mitchell &
Blankenship, P.C. .... Chicago, IL
Adducci, James D. .... Chicago, IL
Adducci, Steven A. .... Washington, DC
Adduce, David S. .... Chicago, IL
Adduci, James J., Jr. .... Lansing, IL
Adduci, Mastriani & Schaumberg, L.L.P.
Washington, DC
Adduci, S. James .... Hull, MA
Adduci, V. James, II .... Washington, DC
Addy, Brian A. .... Pekin, IL
Addy, Charles J. .... Omaha, NE
Addy, David W. .... Jim Thorpe, PA
Addy, John K. .... Billings, MT
Addy, Lawrence E. .... Colorado Springs, CO
Addy, Meredith Martin .... Chicago, IL
Addy, R. Mark .... Cincinnati, OH
Addy, Susan P. .... San Clemente, CA
Addy, Thomas E., Jr. .... Perth Amboy, NJ
Addy, Waltraut Susanne .... Washington, DC
Ade, Brian R. .... Parsippany, NJ
New York, NY
Ade, James L. .... Jacksonville, FL
Adee, Ronald R. .... New York, NY
Adegbile, Debo P. .... New York, NY
Adel, Bryan R. .... Oak Brook, IL
Adel, Garry D. .... Ocala, FL
Adel, Hilary .... Los Angeles, CA
Adel, Nancy P. .... Los Angeles, CA
Adel & Pollack, A Professional Corporation
Los Angeles, CA
Adel, Raymond O. .... St. Paul, MN
Adel, Robert Elliot, II .... Costa Mesa, CA
Adelberg, Arthur W. .... Augusta, ME
Adelberg, R. David .... Towson, MD
Adelberg, Robert M. .... Plainview, NY
Adelberg, Ronald C. .... Springfield, MO
Adelberg, Rudow, Dorf, Hendler & Sameth,
LLC .... Baltimore, MD
Towson, MD
Adele, Leslie G. .... White Plains, NY
Adelekan, Adebola A. .... Lynwood, CA
Adeletti, Christopher Paul .... Springfield, MA
Adelfio, Marco E. .... Washington, DC
Adelhardt, Andrew J., III .... New York, NY
Adelhock, Michael B. .... Little Falls, NJ
Adeli, Andre A. .... Boulder, CO
Adeli, Mani .... Palo Alto, CA
Adeline, Bryan S. .... Tallahassee, FL
Adelizzi, Joseph .... Vista, CA
Adelkoff, Steven J. .... Pittsburgh, PA
Adell, Hirsch .... Los Angeles, CA
Adell, Laura W. .... Los Angeles, CA
Adelli, Thomas .... Syracuse, NY
Adelman, Alvin .... Brooklyn, NY
Adelman, Amy K. .... New York, NY
Adelman, Amy Weinstein .... Atlanta, GA
Adelman, Barbara E. .... Brooklyn, NY
Adelman, Barry A. .... New York, NY
Adelman, Ben .... Pasadena, CA
Adelman, Bette O., P.C., Law Office of
Phoenix, AZ
Adelman, Bette Orovan .... Phoenix, AZ
Adelman, Boyd G. .... Jersey City, NJ
Adelman, Brian .... Westbury, NY
Adelman, Cass Gunther .... New York, NY
Adelman, Charles M. .... New York, NY
Adelman, Charlotte .... Wilmette, IL
Adelman, Daniel J. .... Phoenix, AZ
Adelman, Daniel W. .... New Haven, CT
Adelman, David .... Encino, CA
Adelman, David .... Philadelphia, PA
Adelman, David E. .... Washington, DC
Adelman, David I. .... Atlanta, GA
Adelman, David W. .... Chicago, IL
Adelman, Dean .... Atlanta, GA
Adelman, Edward B. .... San Rafael, CA
Adelman, Edward L. .... St. Louis, MO
Adelman, Elizabeth .... Milwaukee, WI
Adelman, Ernest Z. .... St. Louis, MO
Adelman, Eugene M. .... Wickliffe, OH
Adelman, Frank J. .... San Antonio, TX
Adelman, Fred .... Los Angeles, CA

Adelman, Fred M. .... Santa Monica, CA
Adelman & Gallant .... New Haven, CT
Adelman, Gary P. .... New York, NY
Adelman, Gerard I. .... Meriden, CT
Adelman, Gettleman, Merens, Berish & Carter, Ltd. .... Chicago, IL
Adelman, Gordon P. .... Sacramento, CA
Adelman, Harry .... Chicago, IL
Adelman, Heather Akawie .... New York, NY
Adelman, Herbert .... Arlington, VA
Adelman, Hirsch & Newman, LLP
Bridgeport, CT
Adelman, Howard K. .... Bridgeton, NJ
Adelman, Howard L. .... Chicago, IL
Adelman & Hynes, S.C. .... Milwaukee, WI
Adelman, Jack .... New York, NY
Adelman, Jacob F. .... Delray Beach, FL
Adelman, James W. .... Philadelphia, PA
Adelman, Jeffrey D. .... Detroit, MI
Adelman, Jeffrey S. .... Encino, CA
Adelman, Jeralyn Sue .... Plantation, FL
Adelman, Joel S. .... Detroit, MI
Adelman, Jonathan Myles .... Atlanta, GA
Adelman, Joseph A. .... Van Nuys, CA
Adelman, Kelly G .... Pepper Pike, OH
Adelman, Kurt Alan .... Santa Monica, CA
Adelman, Laurence T. .... Coral Springs, FL
Adelman Lavine Gold and Levin, A Professional Corporation
Philadelphia, PA
Wayne, PA
Adelman, Leslie A. .... Princeton, NJ
Adelman, Leslie J. .... McLean, VA
Adelman, Lester C. .... Sacramento, CA
Adelman, Lisa G. .... San Antonio, TX
Adelman, Lynn S., (Mr.) .... Milwaukee, WI
Adelman, Marc D. .... San Diego, CA
Adelman, Mark A. .... Atlanta, GA
Adelman, Martie S.
Department Of Veterans Affairs, Office of the General Counsel, GV
Adelman, Martin B. .... New York, NY
Adelman, Martin B., P.C. .... New York, NY
Adelman, Martin J. .... Detroit, MI
Adelman, Mary W. .... Bethesda, MD
Adelman, Michael .... Hattiesburg, MS
Adelman, Michael O. .... Florham Park, NJ
Adelman, Michele L. .... Brooklyn, NY
Adelman, Miriam R. .... New York, NY
Adelman, Neil H. .... Chicago, IL
Adelman, Paul I. .... Anchorage, AK
Adelman, Peter .... New York, NY
Adelman, Philip .... Hartsdale, NY
Adelman, Rebecca .... Memphis, TN
Adelman, Richard .... Roslyn, NY
Adelman, Richard B. .... New York, NY
Adelman, Richard M. .... Memphis, TN
Adelman, Robert A. .... Beverly Hills, CA
Adelman, Robert A., A Law Corporation
Beverly Hills, CA
Adelman, Robert B. .... Bridgeport, CT
Adelman, Robert C. .... New York, NY
Adelman, Robert E. .... Cleveland, OH
Adelman, Robert I. .... Kansas City, MO
Adelman, Robert J. .... Beverly Hills, CA
Adelman, Roger M. .... Washington, DC
Adelman, Ronald S. .... Chicago, IL
Adelman, Ronald W. .... New York, NY
Adelman, S. Allan .... Rockville, MD
Adelman, S. Howard .... Davie, FL
Adelman & Schwartz .... Beverly Hills, CA
Adelman, Seymour .... Lawrence, NY
Adelman, Stanley J. .... Chicago, IL
Adelman & Steiner, P.A. .... Hattiesburg, MS
Adelman, Stevan C. .... San Jose, CA
Adelman, Steven A. .... Phoenix, AZ
Adelman, Steven B. .... Los Angeles, CA
Adelman, Steven H. .... Chicago, IL
Adelman, Suzanne Malloy
Washington, DC
Adelman-Adler, Christelle .... St. Louis, MO
Adelman-Pierson, Rachel .... Washington, DC
Adelo, Abdallah S. .... Santa Fe, NM
Adelo, George E. .... Santa Fe, NM
Adels, Elizabeth .... Lake Success, NY
Adelsberg, Howard M., Law Offices of
New York, NY
Adelsberg, Jonathan A. .... Princeton, NJ
New York, NY
Adelsberg, Kenneth E. .... New York, NY
Adelsberger, Donna, & Associates
Marlton, NJ
Glenside, PA
Philadelphia, PA
Adelsberger, Donna L. .... Marlton, NJ
Glenside, PA
Adelsheim, Maurice, Jr. .... Birmingham, MI
Adelsohn, Lisa Olshen .... Jersey City, NJ
Adelsohn, Marc J. .... New York, NY
Adelson, Amy .... New York, NY
Adelson, Darlene .... New York, NY
Adelson, David .... Chestnut Hill, MA
Adelson, David L. .... New City, NY
Adelson, Dawn A. .... New York, NY
Adelson, Dennis A. .... Fairfax, VA
Adelson, Golden, Loria & Simons, P.C.
Boston, MA
Adelson, Henry M. .... Ventura, CA
Adelson, Jack L. .... New York, NY
Adelson, Jonathan S. .... New York, NY
Adelson, Julie Gross .... Washington, DC
Adelson, Kenneth J. .... San Francisco, CA
Adelson, Lawrence S. .... Chicago, IL
Adelson, Lewis B. .... Santa Monica, CA
Adelson, Mark H. .... New York, NY
Adelson, M. B., IV .... Tallahassee, FL
Adelson, Michael .... Los Angeles, CA
Adelson, Nancy R. .... New York, NY
Adelson, Richard G. .... New York, NY
Adelson, Robert A. .... Boston, MA
Adelson, Samuel .... New York, NY
Adelson & Slater, L.L.P. .... New City, NY
Adelson, Stephen M. .... Boston, MA
Adelson, Stuart .... Sherman Oaks, CA
Adelson, Thea J. Nesis .... Los Angeles, CA
Adelson, William J. .... Roseland, NJ
Adelsperger, Douglas R. .... Fort Wayne, IN
Adelstein, Bruce .... Los Angeles, CA
Adelstein, Carol B. .... Cleveland, OH
Adelstein, David .... Burbank, CA
Adelstein, Fern Susan .... Olean, NY
Adelstein, Harvey M. .... Chicago, IL
Adelstein, Howard A. .... Chicago, IL
Adelstein, Jay D. .... Department of Justice, Civil Rights Division, GV
Adelstein, Jon M. .... Doylestown, PA
Trevose, PA
Adelstein and Laustsen .... Doylestown, PA
Trevose, PA
Adelstein, Lindy M. .... Cleveland, OH
Adelstein, Mark .... Immokalee, FL
Adelstein, Richard P. .... Middletown, CT
Adelstein, Robin D. .... Stamford, CT
Adelstein, Sharpe & Serka
Bellingham, WA
Friday Harbor, WA
Mount Vernon, WA
Adelstein, Stanley I. .... Cleveland, OH
Adelstein, Steven P. .... Bellingham, WA
Adelstein, Stuart .... Miami, FL
Adema, Alison Priske .... San Diego, CA
Adema, Rene M. .... Denver, CO
Ademi, Guri .... Milwaukee, WI
Aden, Gareth S. .... Nashville, TN
Aden, Kelly L. .... Los Angeles, CA
Aden, Robin M. .... Sioux Falls, SD
Aden, Steven H. .... Charlottesville, VA
Aden, Susan Jacobs .... Des Moines, IA
Aden, Theodore D. .... Newark, NJ
Adeniji, Lateph A. .... Fort Worth, TX
Adent, Leonard G. .... Waukesha, WI
Ader, David Lincoln .... Chicago, IL
Ader, Jack .... Tamarac, FL
Ader, James S. .... Oakland, CA
Ader, Jerry .... Attica, NY
Ader, Lisa F. .... New York, NY
Ader, Marshall H. .... Miami, FL
Ader, Robert .... Miami, FL
Ader-Duncan, Melisse N. .... Annapolis, MD
Ader-Duncan, Melisse N. .... Rutherford, NJ
Aderhold, H. Randolph, Jr. .... Macon, GA
Aderhold, J. Cullen .... Dallas, TX
Aderhold, James E. .... San Antonio, TX
Aderhold, Kathleen .... Savannah, GA
Aderhold, Mark T. .... Winston-Salem, NC
Aderholt, Ben L. .... Houston, TX
Aderman, Richard E. .... Chicago, IL
Aders, Robert O. .... Washington, DC
Aderson, Frank, Steiner & Blechman, A Professional Corporation .... Butler, PA
Greensburg, PA
Pittsburgh, PA
Washington, PA
Aderson, Sanford M. .... Pittsburgh, PA
Aderton, Jane R. .... Riverside, CA
Ades, Albert .... New York, NY
Ades, Cesare .... Clearwater, FL
Ades, David J. .... Aberdeen, NJ
Ades, Janet .... Hempstead, NY
Ades, Michael L. .... Lexington, KY
Ades, Patricia L. .... Des Moines, IA
Ades, Paul A.
National Labor Relations Board, Office of the General Counsel, GV
Ades, Paul R. .... Lindenhurst, NY
Ades, R. David .... New York, NY
Ades, Rikki L. .... New York, NY
Ades, Robert A., & Associates, P.C.
Washington, DC
Landover, MD
Springfield, VA
Ades, Stephanie A. .... Montvale, NJ
Adesegun, T. N. Nokware
Upper Marlboro, MD
Ades-Pierri, Caroline .... Newark, NJ
Adess, Jason G. .... Chicago, IL
Adess, Melvin S., (P.C.) .... Chicago, IL
Adest, David Ian .... Dallas, TX
Adest, Jeffry .... Great Neck, NY
Adest, Sarena Cheryl .... Brooklyn, NY
Adeszko, Vincent J. .... Sacramento, CA
Adetula, Olubukola .... East Orange, NJ
Adewale-Mendes, Rose .... Houston, TX
Adewusi, Samuel Gbenga .... Washington, DC
Adey, Mark J. .... South Bend, IN
Adeyeye, Valerie Vance
Department of Energy, Office of Hearings and Appeals, GV
Adezio, Paul R. .... Princeton, NJ
Adger, Allen H. .... Aspen, CO
Adger, Henry L. .... Atlanta, GA
Adham, Bita .... Pasadena, CA
Adham, Dina .... Los Angeles, CA
Adickes, Roland .... Sacramento, CA
Adida, David .... Los Angeles, CA
Adie, Julie R. .... Williamsburg, VA
Adikes, Park T. .... Lynbrook, NY
Adikes, Robert K. .... Chicopee, MA
Adili, Niloofar A. .... Vienna, VA
Adili, Ronnie .... Fort Lauderdale, FL
Adilman, Michael .... Savannah, GA
Adilman, Roy .... Atlanta, GA
Adinamis & Adinamis, Attorneys, A Professional Corporation
Indianapolis, IN
Adinamis, Carol M. .... Indianapolis, IN
Adinamis, George P. .... Indianapolis, IN
Adinamis, James D. .... Chicago, IL
Adinamis, Susan L. .... Indianapolis, IN
Adinolfi, David J., II .... Cortland, NY
Adinolfi, Joseph, Jr. .... West Hartford, CT
Adinolfi, O'Brien & Hayes, P.C.
West Hartford, CT
Adio, Seni M. .... Boston, MA
Adipietro, Frank .... Valley Stream, NY
Adipietro, Frank J. .... Brooklyn, NY
Adise, Stephen Z. .... Bethesda, MD
Adiutori, Anthony J. .... Rochester, NY
Adiyia, Fred .... Minneapolis, MN
Adjei-Brenyah, Dennis, Law Offices of
New York, NY
Adjemian, George R. .... Spokane, WA
Adjoua, Hakim B. .... Columbus, OH
Adkerson, Darrell G. .... Dallas, TX
Adkins, Aaron K. .... Houston, TX
Adkins & Adkins .... Catlettsburg, KY
Adkins, Alden S. .... Washington, DC
Adkins, Alissa Anne .... Austin, TX
Adkins, Allan B. .... Manchester, CT
Adkins, Allen Lee .... Lubbock, TX
Adkins, Armand P. .... Hayward, CA
Adkins & Associates, P.C. .... Denver, CO
Adkins, A. Z., Jr. .... Gainesville, FL
Adkins, Barry W. .... Houston, TX
Adkins, Betty T. .... Houston, TX
Adkins, Blaine .... Monroe, LA
Adkins, Brandy A. .... Montgomery, AL
Adkins, Carvan E. .... Fort Worth, TX
Adkins, Charles E. .... West Point, VA
Adkins, Charles J. .... Louisville, KY
Adkins, Charles J. .... Gallipolis, OH
Adkins and Christiansen, A Professional Corporation .... Coalville, UT
Park City, UT
Adkins, Christin V. .... Oklahoma City, OK
Adkins, Crystal J. .... Jacksonville, FL
Adkins, D. Phillip .... Austin, TX
Adkins, Daren L. .... Trenton, MO
Adkins, David E. .... Reno, NV
Adkins, David E. .... Alexandria, VA
Adkins, David J. .... Kansas City, MO
Adkins, David Joe .... Abilene, TX
Adkins, Dennis J. .... Dayton, OH
Adkins, Derrill B. .... Upland, CA
Adkins, E. Dale, III .... Baltimore, MD
Ocean City, MD
Adkins, Edward A. .... Salisbury, MD
Adkins, Edward C. .... Tampa, FL
Adkins, Edward J. .... Denver, CO
Adkins, Edward J. .... Baltimore, MD
Adkins, Elkins & Hunnicutt .... Norton, VA
Adkins, Erika J. .... New York, NY
Adkins, F. Ross .... San Francisco, CA
Adkins, Ferrell .... Elizabethtown, KY
Adkins, Fred .... Ashland, KY
Charleston, WV
Huntington, WV
Adkins, Frederick W. .... Norton, VA
Adkins, Gary William .... Morehead, KY
Adkins, Gwendolyn P. .... Tallahassee, FL
Adkins, Harold J. .... Baton Rouge, LA
Adkins, Henry L., Jr. .... Roanoke, VA
Adkins, Howard W. .... Toledo, OH
Adkins, J. Mark .... Charleston, WV
Adkins, J. Marty .... Norton, VA
Adkins, James A. .... Austin, TX
Adkins, James D. .... Lansing, MI
Adkins, James E. .... Catlettsburg, KY
Adkins, James E. .... St. Louis, MO
Adkins, James E., II .... Catlettsburg, KY
Adkins, James W. .... Georgetown, DE
Adkins, Jason B. .... Boston, MA
Adkins, Jay R. .... Phoenix, AZ
Adkins, Jerry Wayne .... Dallas, TX
Adkins, Jesse T. .... Minden, NE
Adkins, John A. .... Houston, TX
Adkins, John C. .... Melbourne, FL
Adkins, John F. .... Boston, MA
Adkins, John R. .... Circleville, OH
Adkins, John Steven .... Houston, TX
Adkins, Karl .... Charlotte, NC
Adkins, Katherine E. .... Los Angeles, CA
Adkins & Kelston, P.C. .... Boston, MA
Adkins, Lewis W. .... Akron, OH
Adkins, Lisa Ashner .... Kansas City, MO
Adkins, M. Craig .... Oklahoma City, OK
Adkins, M. Douglas .... Dallas, TX
Adkins, Marilyn Biggs .... Denver, CO
Adkins, Maureen C. .... Detroit, MI
Adkins, Michael .... Helena, MT
Adkins, Michael R. .... San Diego, CA
Adkins, Michael S. .... Salisbury, NC
Adkins, Milton R. .... Coral Gables, FL
Adkins, Nanci C. Pugh .... Nashville, TN
Adkins, Paul M. .... Shreveport, LA
Adkins, Philip S. .... Durham, NC
Adkins, Potts & Smethurst, L.L.P.
Cambridge, MD
Easton, MD
Ocean City, MD
Princess Anne, MD
Salisbury, MD
Snow Hill, MD
Adkins, Ralph W. .... Fort Worth, TX
Adkins, Richard W. .... Parkersburg, WV
Adkins, Robb C. .... San Francisco, CA
Adkins, Robert H., (P.C.) .... Boston, MA
Providence, RI
Adkins, Robert M. .... Charleston, WV
Adkins, Robert W. .... Coalville, UT
Park City, UT
Adkins, Roy A. .... Denver, CO
Adkins, Roy A., P.C. .... Denver, CO
Adkins, Roy E. .... Enumclaw, WA
Adkins, Royce .... Haskell, TX
Adkins, Russell A. .... Wheaton, IL
Adkins, Russell L., Jr. .... Marietta, GA
Adkins, Russell W. .... Kingsport, TN
Adkins, S. Douglas .... Huntington, WV
Adkins, Shirlyn A. .... Rochester, MN
Adkins, Stephen W. .... Greensboro, NC
Adkins, Steven E. .... Washington, DC
Adkins, Steven L. .... Corvallis, OR
Adkins, Susan S. .... Wheaton, IL
Adkins, Tamela Lynn .... Atlanta, GA
Adkins, Tammy L. .... Chicago, IL
Adkins, Terrill L. .... Knoxville, TN
Adkins, Terry L. .... Rochester, MN
Adkins, Thurman W. .... Shamrock, TX
Adkins, Tommy J. .... Ruston, LA
Adkins, Truman R. .... Houston, TX
Adkins, W. Michael .... Dothan, AL
Adkins, Ward N., Jr. .... Houston, TX
Adkins and Whitfield .... Marietta, GA
Adkins, William H., II .... Annapolis, MD
Adkins, William H., III .... Easton, MD
Adkins, Winston L. .... Dallas, TX
Adkins & Wondra .... Minden, NE
Adkins, W. T. .... Lexington, KY
Adkins-Blanch, Charles K.
Department of Justice, Executive Office for Immigration Review, GV
Adkins-Hunnewell, Carol J. .... Torrance, CA
Adkinson, Clayton J. M.
De Funiak Springs, FL
Adkinson, Don R. .... Newport Beach, CA
Adkinson, F. Keith .... Washington, DC
Adkinson, Patrick K. .... Dayton, OH
Adkinson, Patrick K., L.L.C. .... Dayton, OH
Adkinson, Theodore H. .... Long Beach, CA
Adkinson, William F., Jr. .... Washington, DC
Adkison, Cynthia .... Bloomfield Hills, MI
Adkison, Cynthia, P.C.
Bloomfield Hills, MI
Adkison, Larry E. .... Chicago, IL
Adkison, Need, Green & Allen
Bloomfield Hills, MI
Detroit, MI
Pontiac, MI
Adkison, Phillip G. .... Bloomfield Hills, MI
Adkison, Ron .... Henderson, TX
Adkison, Thomas L. .... Carbondale, CO
Adkisson, Catherine P. .... Denver, CO
Adkisson, David M. .... San Antonio, TX
Adkisson, Davis W. .... Nashville, TN
Adkisson & Jackson, L.L.P.
San Antonio, TX
Adkisson, Jay David .... Irvine, CA
Adkisson, John C. .... Minneapolis, MN
Adkisson, John D. .... Sacramento, CA
Adkisson, Thomas F. .... San Antonio, TX
Adkisson, William C. .... Conway, AR
Adlam, Andrea L. .... Philadelphia, PA
Adlam, Chartrisse Antoinette .... New York, NY
Adlard, John F. .... Vancouver, WA
Adle, Sheryln Lee .... Farmington Hills, MI
Adler, A. Michael .... Bend, OR
Adler, A. Peter .... New York, NY
Adler, Aaron D. .... Montpelier, VT
Adler, Abraham L. .... Baltimore, MD
Adler, Adena .... Trenton, NJ
Adler & Adler .... Bethesda, MD
Adler and Adler .... Dallas, TX
Adler, Alan M. .... Albany, NY
Adler, Alan R. .... Morristown, NJ
Adler, Alan S. .... Los Angeles, CA
Adler, Allan Robert .... Washington, DC
Adler, Allen P. .... Columbus, OH
Adler, Alyson K. .... New York, NY
Adler, Andrew L. .... Tampa, FL
Adler, Andrew R. .... Walnut Creek, CA
Adler, Anne .... Greenwich, CT
Adler, Anthony A., (A Professional Corporation) (IBA) **.... Los Angeles, CA**
Adler, Arthur B. .... Chicago, IL
Adler, Arthur B., & Associates, Ltd.
Chicago, IL
Adler, Arthur S. .... New York, NY
Adler, Barbara R. .... Chestnut Hill, MA
Adler, Barry .... Oakland, CA
Adler, Barry .... Houston, TX
Adler, Barry B. .... New York, NY
Adler, Barry D. .... Farmington Hills, MI
Adler, Ben .... Beaumont, TX
Adler, Benjamin A. .... Houston, TX
Adler, Benjamin M. .... Baltimore, MD
Adler, Bernard .... New York, NY
Rockville Centre, NY
Adler, Beth S. .... New York, NY
Adler, Bradley T. .... Atlanta, GA
Adler, Brian H. .... Miami, FL
Adler, Brian Scott .... Miami, FL
Adler, Bruce K. .... Morristown, NJ
Adler, Bruce R. .... Fairfield, CT
Adler, Calonita, Ferry & Pavlatos
Garden City, NY
Adler, Carolyn R. .... South San Francisco, CA
Adler, Charles D. .... New York, NY
New York, NY
Adler, Charles F. .... Cleveland, OH
Adler, Charles F., Jr. .... Chicago, IL
Adler & Claraval .... Harrisburg, PA
Adler, Clifford .... New York, NY
Adler & Cohen .... White Plains, NY
Adler, Copertino & Kershaw, LLP
Melville, NY
Tarrytown, NY
Adler, Craig I. .... Harrisburg, PA
Adler, Cynthia Mehler .... Bridgeton, NJ
Adler, Daniel J. .... Joliet, IL

Adler, David B. ...
Department of State, GV
Adler, David B. ... Seattle, WA
Adler, David F. ... Cleveland, OH
Adler, David G. ... Dallas, TX
Adler, David J. ... Newark, NJ
Adler, David J. ... New York, NY
Adler, David J. ... Portland, OR
Adler, David Michael ... Chicago, IL
Adler, David N. ... Kew Gardens, NY
Adler, David W. ... Phoenix, AZ
Adler, Dean S. ... Philadelphia, PA
Adler, Deborah J. ... Dayton, OH
Adler, Debra B. ... Washington, DC
Reston, VA
Adler, Debra B. ... Baltimore, MD
Adler, Derek J. T. ... New York, NY
Adler, Donald D. ... New York, NY
Adler, Donald H. ... Newburyport, MA
Adler, Douglas B. ... Los Angeles, CA
Adler, Douglas Ochs ... Washington, DC
Adler, Edward A. K. ... New York, NY
Adler, Edward O. ... Garden City, NY
Adler, Elizabeth Buchalter
San Francisco, CA
Adler, Elizabeth M. ... Boston, MA
Adler, Ellen D. ... Eugene, OR
Adler, Ellen Kramer ... Harrisburg, PA
Adler, Elliott B. ... Washington, DC
Adler, Emanuel J. ... New York, NY
Adler, Enid H. ... North Wales, PA
Adler, Eric ... Long Beach, CA
Adler, Eric J. ... Monticello, NY
Adler, Eric L. ... New York, NY
Adler, Ericka L. ... Chicago, IL
Lincolnwood, IL
Adler, Ernest E. ... Farmington Hills, MI
Adler, Ernest E. ... Carson City, NV
Adler, Erwin E. ... Los Angeles, CA
Adler, Evelyn ... Sherman Oaks, CA
Adler, Franklin S. ... Woodland Hills, CA
Adler, Frederic R. ... Los Angeles, CA
Adler, Frederick R. ... New York, NY
Adler, Fredk. J. ... Ponte Vedra Beach, FL
Adler, Fredric L. ... New York, NY
Adler, Gary Allyn ... New York, NY
Adler, Gary C. ... Washington, DC
Adler, George J., P.A. ... Orlando, FL
Adler, Gerald ... New York, NY
Adler, Gerald A. ... New York, NY
Adler, Gerald J. ... Sacramento, CA
Adler Giersch, P.S. ... Seattle, WA
Adler, Gilbert ... New York, NY
Adler, Gregg D. ... Hartford, CT
Adler & Gross ... New York, NY
Adler, Hans A. ... Washington, DC
Adler, Harold A. ... Brooklyn, NY
Adler, Harry R. ... Columbia, MD
Adler, Harry R. ... Bridgeton, NJ
Adler, Henry M. ... New York, NY
Adler, Herbert ... White Plains, NY
Adler, Herbert J., Jr. ... New York, NY
Adler, Herman A. ... Toms River, NJ
Adler, Howard B. ... Washington, DC
Adler, Howard B. ... New York, NY
Adler, Howard B. ... New York, NY
Adler, Howard, Jr. ... Washington, DC
Adler, Howard L. ... North Miami Beach, FL
Adler, Ira J. ... East Meadow, NY
Adler, Ira M. ... Freehold, NJ
Adler, Irene Brooks ... Los Angeles, CA
Adler, Irving ... Washington, DC
Adler, Jack I. ... Los Angeles, CA
Adler, Jack P. ... Hunt Valley, MD
Adler, Jacques M. ... San Francisco, CA
Adler, Jacques M., A Professional Corporation ... San Francisco, CA
Adler, James E. ... Los Angeles, CA
Adler, James F. ... Kansas City, MO
Adler, James L. ... Treasury Department, United States Mint, GV
Adler, James L., Jr. ... Phoenix, AZ
Adler, James N., (P.C.) ... Los Angeles, CA
Adler, James R. ... Portland, OR
Adler, Jan Mark ... San Diego, CA
Adler, Jeff S. ... Brooklyn, NY
Adler, Jeffery ... Rockville, MD
Adler, Jeffery Alan ... Lakewood, CO
Adler, Jeffrey D. ... Youngstown, OH
Adler, Jeffrey S. ... Princeton, NJ
Plymouth Meeting, PA
Adler, Jill C. ... Dallas, TX
Adler, Jim S. ... Bedford, TX
Channelview, TX
Dallas, TX
Houston, TX
Adler, Jim S., P.C. ... Bedford, TX
Channelview, TX
Dallas, TX
Houston, TX
Adler, Joan ... Brattleboro, VT
Adler, Joel A. ... New York, NY
Adler, Joel D. ... San Francisco, CA
Adler, Joel D. ... Miami, FL
Adler, John A. ... Laguna Beach, CA
Adler, John A. ... Newark, NJ
Adler, John H., III ... Mount Laurel, NJ
Adler, John S. ... San Diego, CA
Adler, John S., A Prof. Corp., Law Offices of
San Diego, CA
Adler, John W. ... Chicago, IL
Adler, Jonathan S. ... New York, NY
Adler, Jos. ... Bronx, NY
Adler, Jos. I. ... Chicago, IL
Adler, Judith Lowitz ... Southfield, MI
Adler, Karl W. ... Fort Lauderdale, FL
Adler & Karliner ... Brooklyn, NY
Adler, Kathleen J. ... Oklahoma City, OK

Adler, Kenneth ... Melville, NY
Melville, NY
Tarrytown, NY
Adler, Kenneth A. ... New York, NY
Uniondale, NY
Adler, Kenneth, & Associates, P.C.
Hauppauge, NY
Melville, NY
Mineola, NY
Riverhead, NY
Adler, Kenneth I. ... Los Angeles, CA
Los Angeles, CA
Adler, Kenneth P. ... Sandpoint, ID
Adler, Kenneth S. ... Newport Beach, CA
Adler, Kristin E. ... Washington, DC
Adler, Lance S. ... New York, NY
Adler, Lani A. ... New York, NY
Adler, Lawrence ... Van Nuys, CA
Adler, Lawrence H. ... Hartford, CT
Adler, Lee H. ... Ithaca, NY
Adler, Lee R. ... New Orleans, LA
Adler, Leonard ... Englewood, NJ
Adler, Leonard ... New York, NY
Adler, Leonard J. ... Boca Raton, FL
West Palm Beach, FL
Adler, Lesley Collie ... Bethesda, MD
Adler, Leslie ... Great Neck, NY
Adler, Lester B. ... White Plains, NY
Adler, Lewis G. ... Woodbury, NJ
Adler, Linda K. ... Miami, FL
Adler, Linda P. ... Jamaica, NY
Adler, Lorraine J. ... Washington, DC
Adler, Louis J. ... Harrisburg, PA
Adler, Louise DeCarl ... San Diego, CA
Adler, M. Peter ... Washington, DC
Adler, Mady ... Hauppauge, NY
Adler & Manson, L.C. ... Kansas City, MO
Adler, Marc S. ... Philadelphia, PA
Adler, Marcia J. S. ... West Palm Beach, FL
Adler, Marion B. ... Chicago, IL
Adler, Marjorie G. ... Garden City, NY
Adler, Mark ... Boston, MA
Adler, Mark A. ...
Securities and Exchange Commission, GV
Adler, Mark S. ... Warren, NJ
New York, NY
Adler & Marrinan ... San Diego, CA
Adler, Marshall ... Orlando, FL
Adler, Marshall S., P.A. ... Orlando, FL
Adler, Martin M ... New York, NY
Adler, Martin P. ... Dallas, TX
Adler, Mary A. ... Healdsburg, CA
Adler, Mary Kendall
Environmental Protection Agency, Office of Enforcement and Compliance Assurance, GV
Adler, Matthew D. ... Washington, DC
Adler, Matthew H. ... Cherry Hill, NJ
Philadelphia, PA
Adler, Maxine ... Baltimore, MD
Adler, Michael ... Staten Island, NY
Adler, Michael A. ... New York, NY
Adler, Michael B. ... Roslyn Heights, NY
Adler, Michael E. ... New York, NY
Adler, Michael E. ... Philadelphia, PA
Adler, Michael I. ... Los Angeles, CA
Adler, Michael S. ... New York, NY
Adler, Mickal P. ... Metairie, LA
New Orleans, LA
Adler, Mitchell D. ... Hollywood, FL
Adler, Morton S. ... Des Moines, IA
Adler, Murphy & McQuillen ... Chicago, IL
Adler, Nadia C. ... Murray Hill, NJ
Adler, Naomi L. ... Rochester, NY
Adler, Nathan D. ... Baltimore, MD
Adler, Nathan J. ... West Palm Beach, FL
Adler, Noel D. ... Central Islip, NY
Adler, Norman P. ... Richmond, CA
Adler & O'Halloran, P.C. ... Princeton, NJ
Philadelphia, PA
Plymouth Meeting, PA
Adler, Olivia P. ... Washington, DC
Adler, Pamela D. ... Atlanta, GA
Adler, Pamela D., P.C. ... Atlanta, GA
Adler, Patricia M. ... Detroit, MI
Adler, Paul S. ... New York, NY
Adler, Peter W. ... Wellesley, MA
Adler, Philip P. ... Chicago, IL
Adler, Philippe ... New York, NY
Adler, Phillip E., (A P.C.)
Los Angeles, CA
Adler, Phillip I. ... Terre Haute, IN
Adler Pollock & Sheehan P.C.
Boston, MA
Providence, RI
Adler, Rachel B. ... Newark, NJ
Adler, Raymond M. ... Noblesville, IN
Adler, Reid G. ... Washington, DC
Adler, Richard A. ... Los Angeles, CA
Adler, Richard H. ... Seattle, WA
Adler, Richard M. ... San Francisco, CA
Adler, Richard M. ... Northbrook, IL
Adler, Richard W. ... Pinole, CA
Adler, Rita Choit ... Hillsborough, CA
Adler, Rita Nussbaum ... Longwood, FL
Adler, Robert ... Oradell, NJ
Brooklyn, NY
Garden City, NY
Adler, Robert Alvin ... Jersey City, NJ
Adler, Robert C. ... Los Angeles, CA
Adler, Robert E. ... Boca Raton, FL
Adler, Robert J. ... Bethesda, MD
Adler, Robert J. ... New Brunswick, NJ
Adler, Robert L. ... Los Angeles, CA
Adler, Robert M. ... Washington, DC
Adler, Robert R. ... Delray Beach, FL
Adler, Robert S. ... Worcester, MA
Adler, Robert S. ... St. Louis, MO

Adler, Robert S. ... Chapel Hill, NC
Adler, Robert W. ... Washington, DC
Adler, Roger B. ... New York, NY
Adler, Roger B., P.C. ... New York, NY
Adler, Rosen & Peters, P.C. ... Norfolk, VA
Virginia Beach, VA
Adler, Ross G. ... San Jose, CA
Adler, Russell N. ... New York, NY
Adler, Russell S. ... Fort Lauderdale, FL
Adler, S. Beryl ... Norfolk, VA
Virginia Beach, VA
Adler, S. Thomas ... Oklahoma City, OK
Adler, Sandra H. ... Philadelphia, PA
Adler, Sanford M. ... Department of Justice, Antitrust Division, GV
Adler, Sara ... Los Angeles, CA
Adler, Sara R. ... New York, NY
Adler, Scott Z., (P.C.) ... Los Angeles, CA
Adler, Sheldon H. ... Bingham Farms, MI
Adler, Sheldon S. ... New York, NY
Adler, Shira ... Cleveland, OH
Adler, Sidney W. ... Boston, MA
Adler, Spencer E. ... Washington, DC
Adler & Stauffer, A P.C.
Newport Beach, CA
Adler & Stavros ... Warren, NJ
New York, NY
Adler, Stephanie L. ... Rochester, NY
Adler, Stephen D. ... Tarzana, CA
Adler, Stephen I. ... Austin, TX
Adler, Steven ... Sacramento, CA
Adler, Steven ... New York, NY
Adler, Steven A. ... New York, NY
Adler, Steven A. ... St. Johnsbury, VT
Adler, Steven D. ... Portland, OR
Adler, Steven D., P.C. ... Portland, OR
Adler, Steven F. ... New York, NY
Adler, Steven I. ... Hackensack, NJ
Adler, Steven M. ... Westbury, NY
Adler, Stomel & Tucker, P.A. ... Bridgeton, NJ
Adler, Stuart J. ... Garden City, NY
Adler, Stuart J. ... New York, NY
Adler, Sue H. R. ... Albany, NY
Adler, Susan J. ... San Francisco, CA
Adler, Susan Kahn ... Los Angeles, CA
Adler, Terri L. ... New York, NY
Adler, Terry J. ... Grand Blanc, MI
Adler, Theodore A. ... Camp Hill, PA
Adler, Theodore W. ... New York, NY
Adler, Thomas G. ... Dallas, TX
Adler, Timothy J. ... Eau Claire, WI
Adler, Todd E. ... Palo Alto, CA
Adler, Tolar & Adler
Fort Lauderdale, FL
Adler, Tom C., (A P.C.) ... San Diego, CA
Adler, William J. ... Glendale, CA
Adler, William L. ... Harrisburg, PA
Adlerberg, Herbert J. ... New York, NY
Adler-Greene, Laura ... Garden City, NY
Adlerstein, Jo Anne Chernev
Roseland, NJ
Adlerstein, Lee Alan ... New York, NY
Adles, Deborah K. ... Raleigh, NC
Adleson, Hess & Kelly ... Campbell, CA
San Jose, CA
Adleson, Phillip M. ... Campbell, CA
Adlestein, Alan L. ... Wilmington, DE
Adley, Michael C. ... Hammond, IN
Adley, Michael W. ... Lafayette, LA
Adlin, Michael B. ... Washington, DC
Adlman, Monroe ... New York, NY
Adlong, Matthew W. ... Conway, AR
Admire, Duane ... San Diego, CA
Admire, Jack G. ... Coral Gables, FL
Admire, James R. ... Franklin, IN
Admire, John G. ... Coral Gables, FL
Admire, Leslie Quinlan ... Los Angeles, CA
Admire, Robert O. ... Coral Gables, FL
Admur, Nurit ... New York, NY
Adner, Jerome D. ... Buffalo, NY
Adney, John T. ... Washington, DC
Adnopoz, Stephen J. ... New York, NY
Adobbati, Ricardo M. ... Brownsville, TX
Adochio, Robert M. ... New Brunswick, NJ
Adoff and Glinn ... Woodbridge, NJ
New York, NY
Adoff, Leonard H. ... Woodbridge, NJ
New York, NY
Adolf, Derek S. ... Detroit, MI
Adolf, James R. ... New York, NY
Adolf, Peter S. ... New York, NY
Adolfsen, Louis G. ... New York, NY
Adolph, Alison Gail ... New York, NY
Adolph, Angela W. ... Baton Rouge, LA
Adolph & Bintinger, P.S. ... Seattle, WA
Adolph, Jeffrey A. ... Central Islip, NY
Adolph, Mignon Higgins ... Broomfield, CO
Adolph, Robert J. ... Seattle, WA
Adolph, Thomas H. ... Houston, TX
Adolphson, K. Bradford ... Monroe, CT
Adolphus, Elena J. ... New York, NY
Adomanis, Charles J. ... Philadelphia, PA
Adomeit, Peter ... Springfield, MA
Adomitis, Andrew F. ... Pittsburgh, PA
Adomitis, Daniel J. ... Rolling Meadows, IL
Adonailo, Eileen ... Coral Springs, FL
Adondakis, George S. ... Salt Lake City, UT
Adonizio, Anthony C., Jr. ... Harrisburg, PA
Adoor, Craig A. ... St. Louis, MO
Adoradio, Paula Hopping ... New York, NY
Adorante, Anthony P. ... Syracuse, NY
Adorante, Turner & Myers, P.C.
Syracuse, NY
Adornato, Rocco Lawrence ... Blue Bell, PA
Adornetto, Charles J. ... Phoenix, AZ
Adorno, Celeste F. ... Tallahassee, FL
Adorno, Henry N. ... Miami, FL
Adorno, John D. ... Miami, FL

Adorno, Juan E. ... Cleveland, OH
Adorno & Zeder, A Professional Association
Fort Lauderdale, FL
Miami, FL
West Palm Beach, FL
Adoue, Michael F. ... Gretna, LA
Adour, David ... Endicott, NY
Adourian, Edward N., Jr. ... Cherry Hill, NJ
ADR, Inc., Alternative Dispute Resolution
Bentonville, AR
Fort Smith, AR
Little Rock, AR
Adragna, John Michael ... Washington, DC
Adragna, Joseph T. ... Hicksville, NY
Adrain-Piccorelli, Suzanne H.
Lakewood, OH
Adreani, Michael B. ... Los Angeles, CA
Adreon, Alexandra S. ... Clayton, MO
Adriaansen, Robert ... New York, NY
Adrian, Brian Michael ... Pittsburgh, PA
Adrian, David L. ... Quincy, CA
Adrian, Dawn T. (Penni)
Albuquerque, NM
Adrian & Dunn, P.C. ... Quincy, IL
Adrian, James M. ... New York, NY
Adrian, John T.
Department of the Navy, GV
Adrian, Kevin J. ... St. Louis, MO
Adrian, Kristin ... Glendale, CA
Adrian, Lauren J. ... Framingham, MA
Adrian, Marcy J. ... Stamford, CT
Adrian, Matthew G. ... Joplin, MO
Adrian, Matthew T. ... New York, NY
Adrian, Melvin R. ... Hudson, FL
Adrian, Michael J. ... Chicago, IL
Adrian & Pankratz, P.A. ... Newton, KS
Adrian, Phebe K. ... Winchester, VA
Adrian, Robert K. ... Quincy, IL
Adrian, Robert M. ... Atchison, KS
Adrian, Shaun B. ... Erie, PA
Adrian & Sheppard, P.C.
Albuquerque, NM
Adrian, Stephen G. ... Washington, DC
Adrian, Thomas A. ... Newton, KS
Adrian, Tucker Raney ... New Orleans, LA
Adrian & Vondy, P.L.C. ... Winchester, VA
Adriance, Riva Spear
Commodity Futures Trading Commission, Division of Trading and Markets, GV
Adriatico, Marianne F. ... San Diego, CA
Adrine, Herbert A. ... Shaker Heights, OH
Adrine, Ronald B. ... Cleveland, OH
Adrine, Russell T. ... Cleveland, OH
Adrion, Harold L. ... New York, NY
Adrogue, Matías J. ... Fort Worth, TX
Adrogué, Sofia ... Houston, TX
Adshead, Robert L. ... Norristown, PA
Adsit, Andrew S. ... Chicago, IL
Adsit, Boyd D. ... Wheat Ridge, CO
Adsit, Diane M. ... Weedsport, NY
Adsit, Diane Putney ... Meadville, PA
Adsit, Douglas F. ... San Francisco, CA
Adsit, John M. ... Los Angeles, CA
Adsuar, Enrique, Jr. ... San Juan, PR
Adu, Mary Mack ... San Francisco, CA
Adubato, Charles, Jr. ... Freehold, NJ
Adubato & Jaffe ... Bayonne, NJ
Adubato, Michele A. ... Bayonne, NJ
Aduddell, Michael K. ... Conroe, TX
Aduja, Melodie Rebecca ... Kaneohe, HI
Aduja, Peter A. ... Honolulu, HI
Adulewicz, Casimir T. ... Steubenville, OH
Aduma, Kenyetta T. ... Youngstown, OH
Adusei-Poku, Kwadjo ... Maumee, OH
Adusei-Poku, Marilyn A. Specht
Columbus, OH
Advani, Indru S. ... Apple Valley, MN
Advani, Mukesh ... San Francisco, CA
Advani, Suresh T. ... Chicago, IL
Advincula, Cenon S. ... Glendale, CA
Advisory Law Group, A Professional Corporation ... Los Angeles, CA
Newport Beach, CA
Advocate, Jason A. ... New York, NY
Advocate, Michael ... Bradenton Beach, FL
Advocates at Law, Chartered
Washington, DC
Advocates Law Firm, LLC ... Hartford, CT
Advokat, Jeffrey M. ... Morristown, NJ
Adwan, Teresa B. ... Tulsa, OK
Adwar, Gary S. ... Los Angeles, CA
Adwar, Lila P. ... New York, NY
Adwere, Kwame L. ... San Mateo, CA
Adwon, Edward R. ... Houston, TX
Adwon, Nicholas A. ... Tulsa, OK
Ady, Howard P. ...
Department of Defense, GV
Adyanthaya, Anil ... Boston, MA
Adzgery, Ronald W. ... Houston, TX
Aebel, Bruce A. ... Tampa, FL
Aebel, Erin Smith ... Tampa, FL
Aebi & Aebi ... Carson City, NV
Aebi, Ana Colon ... Carson City, NV
Aebi, Fred M. ... Portland, OR
Aebi, John W. ... Carson City, NV
Aebig, Sheena Ramona ... Seattle, WA
Aebker, Jill E. ... Columbus, OH
Aeder, Arthur ... New York, NY
Aeed, Frederick M. ... Phoenix, AZ
Aeilts, Rick Wayne ... Marion, IL
Aelmore, Martin A. ... Greensburg, KS
Aelvoet, David G. ... San Antonio, TX
Aenlle-Rocha, Fernando L.
Los Angeles, CA
Aerenson, Andrew J. ... Wilmington, DE
Aerenson, Benjamin ... New York, NY
Aerhart & Ernzen, P.A. ... Lenexa, KS
Olathe, KS

Aerni, John M. ... New York, NY
Aeschbacher, Steven J. ... Redmond, WA
Aeschliman, Nicholas R. ... Portsmouth, NH
Aeschliman, Nicholas R., Attorney at Law, P.A. ... Portsmouth, NH
Aeschliman, Reed Jay ... Columbus, OH
Aeschliman, Ronald R. ... Chicago, IL
Aex, Peter S. ... San Diego, CA
Afable, Mark V. ... Madison, WI
Afanador, Victor A. ... Cranford, NJ
Afarin, Lisa Marie Barbacci ... Akron, OH
Afendoulis, Stephen P. ... Grand Rapids, MI
Affanato, Michael S. ... Westmont, NJ
Affatati, Michelle M. ... Madison, WI
Affatato, Domenick ... Flushing, NY
Affatato, Florence A. ... Detroit, MI
Affatato, Peter T. ... Hicksville, NY
Affe, George J. ... Herndon, VA
Affe, Robert B. ... Irving, TX
Affeldt, David A. ... Milwaukee, WI
Affeldt, George R. ... Milwaukee, WI
Affeldt, James W. ... Cedar Rapids, IA
Affeldt, John A. ... Milwaukee, WI
Affeldt, John T. ... San Francisco, CA
Affeldt Law Offices, S.C. ... Milwaukee, WI
Affeldt, Lester H. ... Randolph, WI
Affeldt, Steven A. ... Milwaukee, WI
Affeldt, Thomas M. ... Tulsa, OK
Affholter, Eric S. ... Clayton, MO
Affinito, David P. ... Orange, NJ
Affinito and Glerum ... Totowa, NJ
Affinito, Joseph A. ... Totowa, NJ
Affleck, Adam S. ... Salt Lake City, UT
Affleck, John B. ... Providence, RI
Affleck, John H., Jr. ... Athens, GA
Affleck, Thomas, III ... Decatur, GA
Afflerbach, Mary T. ... Allentown, PA
Afflitto, Joseph T. ... Wayne, NJ
Afflitto, Joseph T., Jr. ... Wayne, NJ
Affolter, Dennis C. ... Clayton, MO
Affolter Gannon & Flynn, Ltd. ... Burlington, VT
Affolter, Richard W. ... Burlington, VT
Affonso, Dale ... Las Vegas, NV
Affonso, Sandra Michael ... Stockton, CA
Affron, Jerome S. ... Newburgh, NY
Affronti, Elaine ... San Francisco, CA
Affronti, Francis A. ... Rochester, NY
Affronti, Francis C. ... Rochester, NY
Affronti, Kimberly Ann ... Kew Gardens, NY
Affronti, Lorna R ... Rochester, NY
Affronti, Stefanie ... New York, NY
Affrunti, Sherri A. ... Atlantic City, NJ
Affsa, Daniel F. ... East Weymouth, MA
Affuso, John N. ... Boston, MA
Afilalo, A. Ari ... New York, NY
Aflalo, Lisa J. Chaiklin ... Boca Raton, FL
Afonso, Antonio, Jr. ... Providence, RI
Afonso, Louis A. ... Bridgeport, CT
Aframe & Barnhill, P.A. ... Worcester, MA
Aframe, Barry Z. ... Worcester, MA
Aframe, Carl D. ... Worcester, MA
Aframe, Jay Z. ... Worcester, MA
Afran, Bruce I. ... Princeton, NJ
Afran, Neil H. ... Huntington, NY
Afrasiabi, Peter R. ... Newport Beach, CA
Africa, Joanna G. ... Montebello, CA
Africa, Thomas E. ... Warren, PA
Africano, J. Victor ... Live Oak, FL
Africano, Kenneth W. ... Buffalo, NY
Africk, Allan V. ... Los Angeles, CA
Africk, Jacqueline Glassman ... New York, NY
Africk, Joel J. ... Chicago, IL
Africk, Lance M. ... New Orleans, LA
Africk, Michael B. ... Los Angeles, CA
Afridi & Angell ... Washington, DC; New York, NY
Afriye-Opetubo, Afua ... Bronx, NY
Afrookteh, Richard C. ... Baltimore, MD
Afrow, Allan ... West Roxbury, MA
Afsahi, Parisa M. ... Rockville, MD
Afshar, Carolyn McKinney ... Herndon, VA
Afshari, Koorosh ... San Francisco, CA
Aftab, Parry ... Paramus, NJ; New York, NY
Aftab & Savitt, P.C. ... Paramus, NJ; New York, NY
Aftanas, Richard B. ... New York, NY
Aftergood, G. Greg ... Woodland Hills, CA
Aftergut, Dennis ... San Francisco, CA
Afterman, Jean ... Oxnard, CA
Afton, Amanda E. ... Bloomfield Hills, MI
Afton, John L. ... Palmerton, PA
Afton, Kenneth K. ... Bloomfield Hills, MI
Aftuck, Scott A. ... Boston, MA
Afzal, Leila J. ... Department of Commerce, National Oceanic and Atmospheric Administration, GV
Aga, Tamatane, Jr. ... Olathe, KS
Agacinski, Robert L. ... Detroit, MI
Agajanian, Anita S. ... Boston, MA
Agajanian, Cary J. C. ... Los Angeles, CA
Agajanian & McFall ... Los Angeles, CA
Agajanian, Tim M. ... Los Angeles, CA
Agami, Steven S. ... Bensalem, PA
Agamy, Ida F. ... Department of the Army, U.S. Army Court of Criminal Appeals, GV
Agan, Steven E. ... Elmira, NY
Agapay, Joe M., Jr. ... Los Angeles, CA
Agapay, Levyn & Halling, A Professional Corporation ... Los Angeles, CA; Orange, CA
Agapion, Bill ... Greensboro, NC
Agapion, Stephen ... Cary, NC
Agar, Elizabeth E. ... Cincinnati, OH
Agar, Gary R. ... Accomac, VA
Agar, John ... Washington, DC
Agar, Philip S. ... Larchmont, NY
Agard, Anthony W. ... Brooklyn, NY
Agard, Judith A. ... McLean, VA
Agard, Keoni K. ... Honolulu, HI
Agard, Keoni K., A Law Corporation ... Honolulu, HI
Agarwal, Asheesh ... Chicago, IL
Agarwal, Atulya R. ... Washington, DC
Agarwal, Brij K. ... Canton, OH
Agarwal, Dinesh ... Alexandria, VA
Agarwal, Julie ... Department of Transportation, Maritime Administration, GV
Agarwal, Monty ... San Francisco, CA
Agarwal, Pavan Kumar ... Washington, DC
Agata, Burton C. ... Hempstead, NY
Agata, Seth Hugh ... Hudson, NY
Agate, Augustus C. ... Kew Gardens, NY
Agate, Carol ... Inglewood, CA
Agate, Deborah L. ... Appleton, WI
Agate, James D. ... Oakland, CA
Agate, John T. ... Buffalo, NY
Agate, Kathryn McCarl ... Arlington, VA
Agathen, Alan J. ... Clayton, MO
Agathen, Jean M. ... Chicago, IL
Agathen, Paul ... St. Louis, MO
Agather, Ruth Kelleher ... San Antonio, TX
Agathis, William T. ... Elizabeth, NJ
Agati, Andrew ... Cleveland, OH
Agati, Salvatore C. ... Waterbury, CT
Agatstein, David ... Baltimore, MD
Agatstein, David J. ... Pasadena, CA
Agatston, Andrew H. ... Marietta, GA
Agatston, Roger C. ... Monroe, CT
Agatston, Sari K. ... Miami Beach, FL
Agatston, Warren S. ... New Rochelle, NY
Agawa, Thomas K. ... San Francisco, CA
Agay, Richard D. ... Encino, CA
Agbaje & Associates, P.A. ... Baltimore, MD
Agbaje, Taiwo A. ... Baltimore, MD
Agbakwu, Charles Arinze, Sr. ... Denver, CO
Agbayani, Tony J., Jr. ... Manteca, CA
Agbe-Davies, Christopher Kole ... Atlanta, GA
Agcaoili, Avelino C. ... Daly City, CA
Agcaoili, Paz M. ... Daly City, CA
Agdern, Barry S. ... New York, NY
Agdern, Robert D. ... Chicago, IL
Agee & Agee ... Bartlett, TN
Agee & Agee ... Lebanon, TN
Agee, Alan ... Oklahoma City, OK; Pauls Valley, OK
Agee, Alan M. ... Colorado Springs, CO
Agee, Beverly G. ... San Francisco, CA
Agee, Brett ... Oklahoma City, OK; Pauls Valley, OK
Agee, Carole M. ... Roanoke, VA
Agee, Charles M., Jr. ... Dyersburg, TN
Agee Clymer Mitchell & Laret ... Chillicothe, OH; Circleville, OH; Columbus, OH; Delaware, OH; Portsmouth, OH
Agee, Danielle C. ... Philadelphia, PA
Agee, David C. ... Springfield, MO
Agee, G. Steven ... Roanoke, VA
Agee, Grady W. ... Bartlett, TN
Agee, Jack K. ... Colorado Springs, CO
Agee, John D. ... Kingston, TN
Agee, Jon ... Fort Lauderdale, FL
Agee, Kelly L. ... Hilton Head Island, SC
Agee Law Firm, P.C. ... St. Louis, MO
Agee, Lea Ellen Ridenour ... Clinton, TN
Agee, Lynn A. ... Nashville, TN
Agee, Mark Ian ... Dallas, TX
Agee, Mark L. ... Trenton, TN
Agee, Martha Colvin ... Waco, TX
Agee & Meriwether ... Chickasaw, AL
Agee, Michael L. ... Bartlett, TN
Agee, Robert C. ... White Plains, NY
Agee, Sharon A. ... St. Louis, MO
Agee, Sonia M. ... Bellevue, WA
Agee, Susan R. ... Houston, TX
Agee, Theresa Viani ... Carthage, MO
Agee, Topping & Stuhldreher ... Atlanta, GA
Agee, Vester Neal, Jr. ... Lebanon, TN
Agee, Vester Neal, (P.C.) ... Lebanon, TN
Agee, Wendell S. ... Atlanta, GA
Agee, Wesley F. ... Huntington, WV
Agee, William A. ... Baltimore, MD
Agee, William Henry ... Winchester, TN
Agee, William P. ... Federal Communications Commission, Common Carrier Bureau, GV
Agege, Charles O. ... Los Angeles, CA
Agel, Sally ... Los Angeles, CA
Agel, Saul Lee ... Burlington, VT
Agelasto, Peter A., III ... Virginia Beach, VA
Ageloff, Kenneth M. ... New York, NY
Agemian, Varoujan V. ... Glendale, CA
Agen, Michael J. ... Springfield, MA
Agen, Roger Arne ... San Francisco, CA
Agena, James Y. ... Honolulu, HI
Agena, Joel J. ... Phoenix, AZ
Agena, Keith S. ... Honolulu, HI
Agena, Melvin Y. ... Honolulu, HI
Agenbroad, Aaron L. ... Washington, DC
Agenlian, Murad ... Arlington Heights, IL
Agents, Robert E. ... Wyoming, MI
Ager, Christina M. ... Seattle, WA
Ager, David M. ... Woodinville, WA
Ager, Jacquelyn J. ... Mount Laurel, NJ; Philadelphia, PA
Ager, John P. ... Phoenix, AZ
Ager, Tracey Ann ... Phoenix, AZ
Ager, William Francis, III ... Southfield, MI; El Paso, TX
Ager, Wm. F., Jr. ... Ann Arbor, MI
Agerter, Lawrence E. ... Mantorville, MN
Agerter, Linda L. ... San Francisco, CA
Ages, Abby ... Roseland, NJ
Ages, Daniel L. ... New York, NY
Ageson, Martin ... Los Angeles, CA
Aggarwal, Ashima ... New York, NY
Aggarwal, Reggie K. ... Washington, DC
Aggen, Janeen Jacobs ... Lenexa, KS
Aggen, Thomas J. ... Overland Park, KS
Agger, James H., Sr. ... Bethlehem, PA
Aggers, David F. ... Cleveland, OH
Aggers & Joseph ... Cleveland, OH
Agha, Oliver A. ... Washington, DC
Aghababian, Robert V. ... Waltham, MA
Aghabeg, Dena S. ... Los Angeles, CA
Aghabegian, Alan ... Glendale, CA
Aghai, Mojgan ... Los Angeles, CA
Aghai, Sima G. ... Los Angeles, CA
Aghajanian, Alex P. ... Pasadena, CA
Aghassi, Viveca ... Boston, MA
Aghayan, Alexander ... New York, NY
Aghazarian, Robert V. ... Breckenridge, CO
Aghdami, Farhad ... Richmond, VA
Aghen, Robyn M ... Cherry Hill, NJ
Aghion, Victor ... Chicago, IL
Aghishian, Ara ... Los Angeles, CA
Aghoian, Charles ... Woodland Hills, CA
Aghoian, Fimy Sonia ... Monterey Park, CA
Agi, Louis Eli ... Anchorage, AK
Agid, Paul W. ... Seattle, WA
Agid, Susan R. ... Seattle, WA
Agidius, Paul C. ... Moscow, ID
Agiewich, Eve M. ... Palo Alto, CA
Agin and Agin Co. L.P.A. ... Cleveland, OH
Agin, Bernard I. ... Cleveland, OH
Agin, Bruce D. ... Chicago, IL
Agin, Richard G. ... Chicago, IL
Agin, Sandra K. ... Cleveland, OH
Agin, Stephen L. ... Chicago, IL
Agin, Thomas C. ... Santa Ana, CA
Agin, Warren E. ... Boston, MA
Agin, William S. ... Canton, MS
Agins Haaz & Seidel, L.L.P. ... Philadelphia, PA
Agins, Rand M. ... Roseland, NJ
Agins, Richard C. ... New York, NY
Agins, Richard H. ... Long Beach, CA
Agins, Siegel & Reiner, L.L.P. ... New York, NY
Agins, Stuart J. ... Philadelphia, PA
Agisim, Keith D. ... New York, NY
Agler, Alfred P. ... Columbus, OH
Agler, David M. ... Sherman Oaks, CA
Agler, H. Richard ... Milton, PA
Agler, Jeffery A. ... Berne, IN
Agler, Timothy B. ... Irvine, CA
Agli, Stephanie M. ... Washington, DC; Baltimore, MD
Agliano, John J. ... Tampa, FL
Agliano, Lisa ... Santa Cruz, CA
Agliano, Nat A. ... San Jose, CA
Agliata, Michael ... Miami, FL
Aglietti & Offret ... Anchorage, AK
Aglietti, Terry C. ... Anchorage, AK
Aglion, Marie G. ... Seattle, WA
Aglow, Eric N. ... Woodbridge, NJ
Aglow, Mitchell I. ... Doylestown, PA
Aglubat, Pablo M., Jr., (P.C.) ... Barrigada, GU
Agman, Richard C. ... Spokane, WA
Agmata, Victor, Jr. ... Honolulu, HI; Waipahu, HI
Agmon, Elizabeth S. ... Los Angeles, CA
Agnant, Linda Dickhaus ... West Palm Beach, FL
Agnelli, Kathleen M. ... Hamburg, NJ
Agnelli, Muriel A. ... Denver, CO
Agnellini, Pacifico S. ... Atlantic City, NJ
Agnello & Agnello ... Passaic, NJ
Agnello, Arthur A. ... Rochester, NY
Agnello, Christine L. ... Berea, OH
Agnello, Edward M. ... Passaic, NJ
Agnello, John M. ... Roseland, NJ
Agnello, Mary F. ... Dallas, TX
Agnello, Thomas J., Jr. ... New York, NY
Agnello, Virginia ... Passaic, NJ
Agnello-Raspa, Olga ... Detroit, MI
Agner, John M. ... Goldsboro, NC
Agner, Royce ... Perry, FL
Agnes, Peter W., Jr. ... Boston, MA
Agnes, Philip M. ... Sarasota, FL
Agneshwar, Anand ... New York, NY
Agness, Kent E. ... Indianapolis, IN
Agnetti, John B. ... Fort Lauderdale, FL; Miami, FL; North Miami Beach, FL
Agnew, Ann Elizabeth ... Kansas City, MO
Agnew, Barbara J. ... Northbrook, IL
Agnew & Brusavich ... Los Angeles, CA; Santa Ana, CA; Torrance, CA
Agnew, Catherine H. ... Havertown, PA
Agnew, Christine L. ... Buffalo, NY
Agnew, Dan J. ... Centralia, WA
Agnew, David B. ... Denver, CO
Agnew, David E. ... Burbank, CA
Agnew, David E. ... Pasadena, CA
Agnew, David M. ... Chicago, IL
Agnew, Gary G. ... Chamblee, GA
Agnew, George E. ... Jackson, MS
Agnew, Gerald E., Jr. ... Torrance, CA
Agnew, Harris H. ... Rockford, IL
Agnew, Jeffrey A. ... Ramona, CA
Agnew, Jerome P. ... Duluth, MN
Agnew, Joan T. ... Chicago, IL
Agnew, John A. ... Royal Oak, MI
Agnew, Lee B., Jr. ... Jackson, MS
Agnew, Linda S. ... Garden City, NY
Agnew, Marian K. ... McLean, VA
Agnew, Michael ... Columbus, GA
Agnew, Patrick J. ... Chicago, IL
Agnew, Paul L. ... Abbeville, SC
Agnew, Randy L. ... Fort Worth, TX
Agnew & Reed, PLLC ... Lubbock, TX
Agnew, Richard A. ... Seattle, WA
Agnew, Ronnie L. ... Lubbock, TX
Agnew, Schlam & Bennett, P.C. ... Columbus, GA
Agnew, Timothy P. ... Augusta, ME
Agnew, William A., Jr. ... Lufkin, TX
Agni, Stephen M. ... Anchorage, AK
Agnich, Richard J. ... Dallas, TX
Agniel, Theodore D. ... St. Louis, MO
Agnihotri, Bhishma Kumar ... Baton Rouge, LA
Agnihotri, Shailly P. ... New York, NY
Agnihotri, Varun ... Walnut, CA
Agnitti, Allen H. ... Bronx, NY
Agnoli, Catherine ... Salt Lake City, UT
Agnoli, Robert G. ... Springfield, MA
Agnolutto, Dario J. ... Greenbelt, MD; Waldorf, MD
Agnor, Jeffrey T. ... Columbia, MD
Agnor, Thomas J., Jr. ... Austin, TX
Agnost, Frank P., Jr. ... San Francisco, CA
Agnostak, Harry M. ... New York, NY
Agocs, Christine A. ... New Brunswick, NJ
Agocs, Stephen F. ... Trenton, NJ
Agoes, Patrick M. ... Trenton, NJ
Agoglia, Emmet J. ... Mineola, NY
Agoglia, Michael J. ... San Francisco, CA
Agoglia, Thomas A. ... New York, NY
Agon, Juliana ... Boynton Beach, FL
Agor, Benn R. ... Seattle, WA
Agoritsas, James W. ... Marlborough, MA
Agosta, Anthony A. ... Detroit, MI
Agosta, Mauri A. ... Labadieville, LA
Agosta, Steven P. ... New York, NY
Agosta, Steven S. ... Millbrae, CA
Agosti, Deborah A. ... Carson City, NV
Agosti, Raymond E. ... San Francisco, CA
Agostinelli, Guy J. ... Buffalo, NY
Agostinelli, Michael A. ... Spokane, WA
Agostinelli, Robert J. ... Ottawa, IL
Agostini, Beth Ann ... New York, NY
Agostini, Hector Pedro ... Lowell, MA
Agostini, John A. ... Pittsfield, MA
Agostini, John J. ... Clifton, NJ
Agostini, John J. ... Paterson, NJ
Agostini, Levitsky, Isaacs & Kulesza ... Wilmington, DE
Agostini, Lucy B. ... Verona, NJ
Agostini, Marco M. ... Somerdale, NJ
Agostini, Peter L. ... Totowa, NJ
Agostini & Slattery ... Verona, NJ
Agostino, Aprilanne ... Brooklyn, NY
Agostino, Frank ... Hackensack, NJ
Agostino, Frank J. ... South Bend, IN
Agostino, Peter J. ... South Bend, IN
Agosto, Benny, Jr. ... Houston, TX
Agosto, David A. ... New York, NY
Agosto, Euclides A., Jr. ... Chicago, IL
Agosto, James P. ... Monticello, MN
Agosto, Luis M. ... Denver, CO
Agoston, Angelique B. ... Naples, FL
Agovino, Frank R. ... St. Louis, MO
Agovino, Peter L. ... New Hyde Park, NY
Agozzino, Joseph J., Jr. ... Ridley Park, PA
Agozzino, Leozino ... Cleveland, OH
Agpaoa, Anthony D. ... San Francisco, CA
Agpaoa & Lopez ... San Francisco, CA
Agrait & Oliveras ... San Juan, PR
Agrait, William E. ... Newark, NJ
Agrait-Llado, Francisco R. ... San Juan, PR
Agrait-Oliveras, Francisco ... San Juan, PR
Agrall, Tracy A. ... Fresno, CA
Agran, Abraham ... Chicago, IL
Agran, Joan ... Philadelphia, PA
Agran, Kenneth D. ... Irvine, CA
Agran, Martin S. ... Chicago, IL
Agran, Michael C. ... Los Angeles, CA
Agran, Raymond D. ... Philadelphia, PA
Agranoff, Efrem Z. ... Everett, WA
Agranoff, Gerald N. ... San Antonio, TX
Agranoff, Jay Steven ... Columbus, OH
Agranoff, Michael H. ... Stafford Springs, CT
Agrapidis, Evans C. ... Hackensack, NJ
Agrast, Mark D. ... House of Representatives, Congressional Assistants, GV
Agrawal, Andy ... Mechanicsburg, PA
Agrawal, Jai ... New York, NY
Agrawal, Sanjay ... Nevada, MO
Agrawal, Sanjay ... St. Louis, MO
Agrawal, Swati ... Washington, DC
Agrawal, Swati ... Bethesda, MD
Agraz, Francisco J. ... Houston, TX
Agraz, Francisco J., P.C. ... Houston, TX
Agraz, Rodolfo R. ... Raleigh, NC
Agre, Louis ... Philadelphia, PA
Agre, Ross D. ... New York, NY
Agree, Lena ... Southfield, MI
Agree, Richard A. ... Farmington Hills, MI
Agrella, Raymond F. ... St. Charles, IL
Agrella-Fitzpatrick, Mary ... St. Charles, IL
Agrelo-Perez, Javier A. ... San Juan, PR
Agren, Brenda L. ... Irvine, CA
Agren, Carl F. ... Irvine, CA
Agress, Ellen S. ... New York, NY
Agress, Vivian H. ... New York, NY
Agrest, Jeffrey ... Red Hook, NY
Agresta, Emanuela ... Steubenville, OH
Agresta, Louis N. ... Mineola, NY
Agresta, Paul ... Albany, NY
Agresta, Steven J. ... Washington, DC
Agresti & Agresti ... Erie, PA
Agresti, Charles D. ... Erie, PA

Agresti, David C. ... Erie, PA
Agresti, Ernest N. ... Providence, RI
Agresti, Joseph V. ... Erie, PA
Agresti, Michael A. ... Pittsburgh, PA
Agresti, Thomas J. ... Denver, CO
Agresti, Thomas P. ... Erie, PA
Agresti, Vincent J. ... Newark, NJ
Agresti, Vincent J., A Professional Corporation
Newark, NJ
Agretelis, Demetrios P. ... Oakland, CA
Agri, Orin E. ... New York, NY
Agricola, Algert S., Jr. ... Montgomery, AL
Agricola, Hugh W. ... Gadsden, AL
Agrillo, Susan R. ... Tucson, AZ
Agrimonti, Lisa M. ... St. Paul, MN
Agris, Laurel A. ... Houston, TX
Agris, Myrna S. ... Houston, TX
Agritelley, Ralph J. ... Brooklyn, NY
Agro, Nancy ... Cortez, CO
Agron, Adam J. ... Denver, CO
Agron, Gary A. ... Denver, CO
Agron, Joel Stuart ... San Francisco, CA
Agronick, Lois B. ... Department of Justice, Executive Office for Immigration Review, GV
Agrons, Joshua P. ... Houston, TX
Agrusa, Angela C. ... Los Angeles, CA
Agrusa, Lisa M. ... Orange, CA
Agruso, Joanne Smith ... Smithtown, NY
Agsalud, Lee M. ... Honolulu, HI
Agsten, Melinda A. ... New Haven, CT
Agster, Richard S. ... Tampa, FL
Agthe, Dale R. ... Colorado Springs, CO
Agthe, Scott A. ... El Paso, TX
Agthe, Thilo C. ... New York, NY
Aguado, Joan C. ... San Francisco, CA
Aguayo-Pereles, Joaquin
Department Of Veterans Affairs, Board of Veterans Appeals, GV
Agudelo, Anthony V. ... Richmond, VA
Agudo, Marcelo M. ... Miami, FL
Aguero, Dorothea G. ... Anchorage, AK
Aguggia, Paul M. ... Washington, DC
Aguglia, Richard L. ... Washington, DC
Aguiar, Antone L. ... El Cajon, CA
Aguiar, Antone S., Jr. ... Attleboro, MA
Aguiar, Lauren E. ... New York, NY
Aguiar, Lisa E. ... San Jose, CA
Aguiar, Mark R. ... New York, NY
Aguiar, William Macy ... Chicago, IL
Aguigui, Ignacio C. ... San Francisco, CA
Aguila, Andres Eduardo ... New York, NY
Aguila, Guillermo M. ... Carson, CA
Aguila, Raul J. ... Miami Beach, FL
Aguilar, Anthony C. ... El Paso, TX
Aguilar, Antonio ... Ventura, CA
Aguilar, Armando Y. ... Denver, CO
Aguilar, Arocles ... San Francisco, CA
Aguilar, Catherine ... Santa Fe, NM
Aguilar, Charles E. ... Modesto, CA
Aguilar, Christopher L.
San Francisco, CA
Aguilar, Edmundo ... Sacramento, CA
Aguilar, Esteban A. ... Albuquerque, NM
Aguilar, Evelyn ... Los Angeles, CA
Aguilar, George A. ... Morristown, NJ
Aguilar, Gloria ... Phoenix, AZ
Aguilar, J. Arnold ... Brownsville, TX
Aguilar, Javier ... Austin, TX
Aguilar, Julie A. ... San Francisco, CA
Aguilar, Kathleen ... Modesto, CA
Aguilar Law Offices, P.C.
Albuquerque, NM
Las Cruces, NM
Santa Fe, NM
El Paso, TX
Aguilar, Liza Marie ... Corpus Christi, TX
Aguilar, Louis V. ... Los Angeles, CA
Aguilar, Luis ... Riverside, CA
Aguilar, Luis A. ... Atlanta, GA
Aguilar, M. Elizabeth ... San Francisco, CA
Aguilar, Mabell Y. ... Palo Alto, CA
Aguilar, Michael ... Glendale, CA
Aguilar, Raul V. ... San Francisco, CA
Aguilar, Richard A. ... New Orleans, LA
Aguilar, Robert ... Orange Park, FL
Aguilar, Robert P. ... Campbell, CA
Aguilar, Robert R. ... Visalia, CA
Aguilar, Rodolfo J., Jr. ... Baton Rouge, LA
Aguilar & Sebastinelli, A Professional Law Corporation ... Los Angeles, CA
San Francisco, CA
Aguilar, Valentin G., II ... Los Angeles, CA
Aguilar, Veronica M. ... San Diego, CA
Aguilar, Victoria T. ... Denver, CO
Aguilar-Gueneo, Brenda ... Oakland, CA
Aguilar-Guerrero, Brenda ... Oakland, CA
Aguilar-Guerrero, Leonor M.
San Juan, PR
Aguilera, A. Eric ... Irvine, CA
Aguilera, Benjamin D. ... Phoenix, AZ
Aguilera, Bruce A. ... Las Vegas, NV
Aguilera, Clark ... Denver, CO
Aguilera, Daniel P. ... Los Angeles, CA
Aguilera, Denise ... New Britain, CT
Aguilera, Guido A. ... Miami, FL
Aguilera, Jacqueline M. ... Los Angeles, CA
Aguilera, John D. ... Watsonville, CA
Aguilera, Juan F. ... San Antonio, TX
Aguilera, Lisa ... New York, NY
Aguilera, Victor E. ... Pasadena, CA
Aguillard, H. Kent ... Eunice, LA
Aguillon, Maria G. ... Santa Ana, CA
Aguiló-Vélez, Rafael E. ... San Juan, PR
Agüiluz, Heroico M. ... Los Angeles, CA
Agüiluz, Victor F. ... New Orleans, LA
Aguiñaga, Jesse ... Houston, TX
Aguinaldo, W. Anthony ... Honolulu, HI
Aguirre, Alex ... Harlingen, TX
McAllen, TX
Aguirre, Annette ... Concord, CA
Aguirre, Anthony, Jr. ... Window Rock, AZ
Aguirre, Barbara F. ... San Diego, CA
Aguirre, Bridgett B. ... Fuquay-Varina, NC
Aguirre, Cory Anthony ... Fullerton, CA
Aguirre, Dario ... San Diego, CA
Aguirre, Digna L. ... San Francisco, CA
Aguirre, Frederick P. ... Santa Ana, CA
Aguirre, James H. ... Los Angeles, CA
Aguirre, John ... Phoenix, AZ
Aguirre, John E. ... San Francisco, CA
Aguirre, Julio L. ... San Juan, PR
Aguirre, L. Kim ... Fresno, CA
Aguirre, Linda D. ... San Francisco, CA
Aguirre, Manuel ... Los Angeles, CA
Aguirre, Mary D. ... Stockton, CA
Aguirre & Meyer, A Professional Corporation
San Diego, CA
Albuquerque, NM
Aguirre, Michael J. ... San Diego, CA
Albuquerque, NM
Aguirre, Richard ... Houston, TX
Aguirre, Richard A. ... Belleville, IL
Aguirre, Rodolfo ... Los Angeles, CA
Aguirre, Rodolfo A. ... Pomona, CA
Aguirre, Rudy ... Alhambra, CA
Aguirre, Samuel J. ... San Antonio, TX
Aguirrechu, Lourdes ... San Juan, PR
Agular, Jeffrey T. ... New Orleans, LA
Agule, Charles G. ... Newton, MA
Agulnick, Peter M. ... New York, NY
Agulnick, Ronald M. ... West Chester, PA
Agun, Igbeare Francis ... New York, NY
Aguren, Gary D. ... Houston, TX
Agus, Deborah ... Baltimore, MD
Agus & Partners ... Parlin, NJ
New York, NY
Agus, Stephen A. ... New York, NY
Agusta, Joseph B. ... Chapel Hill, NC
Agusti, Filiberto ... Washington, DC
Agvald, Sandra K. ... Minneapolis, MN
Agvald, Sandra K., & Associates, P.A.
Minneapolis, MN
Agyeman, Dan B. ... Beverly Hills, CA
Agzigian, Harry J., Jr. ... Levittown, PA
Ahalt, Arthur M. ... Upper Marlboro, MD
Ahalt, Ball & Brodeur, P.C. ... Worcester, MA
Ahalt, Barbara A. ... Worcester, MA
Ahalt, Brent M. ... Upper Marlboro, MD
Ahalt, William S. ... Worcester, MA
Ahamed, Meera ... Oakton, VA
Ahamed, Saleemah H. ... New York, NY
Ahari, Leslie S. ... Washington, DC
Ahari, M. Nader ... New York, NY
Aharoni, Daniel J. ... New York, NY
Aharonian, Richard A. ... Fresno, CA
Aharonian, Taline A. ... Los Angeles, CA
Aharonson, Donna F. ... Boston, MA
Ahart, Alan M. ... Los Angeles, CA
Ahart, Edward W. ... Morristown, NJ
New York, NY
Ahart, Gregory J. ... Vienna, VA
Ahders, Ruff ... Odessa, TX
Ahders, Ruff, P.C. ... Odessa, TX
Ahders, William B. ... Midland, TX
Ahearn, Ashley Brown ... Boston, MA
Ahearn, Beth N. ... Falmouth, ME
A'Hearn, Brian A. ... Baldwin, NY
Ahearn, Brian S. ... Birmingham, MI
Detroit, MI
Ahearn, C. Dennis ... Bethesda, MD
Ahearn, Caroline C.
Environmental Protection Agency, Office of Enforcement and Compliance Assurance, GV
Ahearn, Charles H. ... New York, NY
Ahearn, Christopher J. ... Springfield, MA
Ahearn, Dale E. ... Louisville, KY
Ahearn, Daniel W. ... Malden, MA
Ahearn, David C. ... Norwood, MA
Ahearn, Dennis E. ... Fredericksburg, VA
Ahearn, Donald P. ... Hartford, CT
Ahearn, Edward J. ... Ocean Township, NJ
Ahearn, Erin B. ... Englewood, CO
Ahearn, Frank E. ... Green Valley, AZ
Ahearn, Gregory T. ... Framingham, MA
Ahearn, J. Marleen ... Tallahassee, FL
Ahearn, James J. ... Pittsburgh, PA
Ahearn, John E. ... Hartford, CT
Ahearn, John L. ... Phoenix, AZ
Ahearn, Kathy A. ... Albany, NY
Ahearn, Laura B. ... Washington, DC
Ahearn, Marie Penny
General Accounting Office, Office of the General Counsel, GV
Ahearn, Mark G. ... Indianapolis, IN
Ahearn, Matthew J. ... Orlando, FL
Ahearn, Matthew J. ... Florham Park, NJ
Ahearn, Meredith Appel ... Anchorage, AK
Ahearn, Michael H. ... Riverhead, NY
Ahearn, Richard L. ... Buffalo, NY
Ahearn, Robert J. ... Andover, MA
Ahearn, Terrence J. ... Houston, TX
Ahearn, Thomas ... Los Angeles, CA
Ahearn, Timothy J. ... Hudson, NY
Ahearn, Timothy S. ... Fall River, MA
Ahearn, Vincent P., Jr. ... Silver Spring, MD
Ahearne, Jane ... New York, NY
Ahearne, Thomas F. ... Seattle, WA
Aherin, Darrel W. ... Lewiston, ID
Aherin, Rice & Anegon, A Professional Association ... Lewiston, ID
Ahern & Ahern ... Kings Park, NY
Ahern, Albert J., Jr. ... Arlington, VA
Ahern, Andrew G., III ... Wilmington, DE
Ahern, Ann Marie ... Chicago, IL
Ahern, Ann Marie ... Cleveland, OH
Ahern, Anthony E. ... Westport, CT
Ahern, Arch M. ... New York, NY
Ahern, Carol A. ... Chicago, IL
Ahern, Charles F., III ... Boston, MA
Ahern, Christine K. ... Providence, RI
Ahern, Daniel J. ... Madras, OR
Ahern, Dennis P. ... Kings Park, NY
Ahern, Edith Rasmussen ... Chicago, IL
Ahern, Elizabeth A. ... Chelmsford, MA
Ahern, Ellen Therese ... Chicago, IL
Ahern, Frederick L., Jr.
Jacksonville Beach, FL
Ahern, Gregory E. ... Chicago, IL
Ahern, Helen L. ... Cotuit, MA
Ahern & Hyatt, P.A. ... Santa Fe, NM
Ahern, James D. ... Chicago, IL
Ahern, James J. ... Chicago, IL
Skokie, IL
Ahern, Janet M. ... New Orleans, LA
Ahern, Janet Marie ... Wheaton, IL
Ahern, Janice M. ... Santa Fe, NM
Ahern, Jay T. ... Tampa, FL
Ahern, John E. ... Chicago, IL
Ahern, John E., P.C. ... Chicago, IL
Ahern, John W. ... Bethesda, MD
Ahern, Jon M. ... Virginia Beach, VA
Ahern, Joseph A. ... Troy, MI
Ahern, Joseph M. ... Seattle, WA
Ahern, Julie A.M. ... Boston, MA
Ahern, Kathleen E. ... Newton, MA
Ahern & Keck ... Santa Rosa, CA
Ahern, Kevin T. ... Phoenix, AZ
Ahern, Lawrence R., III ... Nashville, TN
Ahern, Leo E. ... New Haven, CT
Ahern & Maloney ... Chicago, IL
Skokie, IL
Ahern, Mary L. ... Chicago, IL
Ahern, Michael J. ... Minneapolis, MN
Ahern, Michael W. ... Santa Rosa, CA
Ahern, Omer C., Jr. ... Charlestown, NH
Ahern, Patrick J. ... Chicago, IL
Ahern, Paul B. ... Minnetonka, MN
Ahern, Paul L. ... Chicago, IL
Ahern, Paul L., Jr. ... Seattle, WA
Ahern, Richard F. ... Department of Energy, Office of the General Counsel, GV
Ahern, Robert P. ... San Jose, CA
Ahern, Stephen F. ... Toledo, OH
Ahern, Stephen H. ... Cambridge, MA
Ahern, Terrance R. ... Cleveland, OH
Ahern, Terrence ... Kansas City, MO
Ahern, Theresa M. ... Kent, WA
Ahern, Thomas D. ... Chicago, IL
Ahern, Thomas J., Jr. ... Boston, MA
Ahern, Veronica M. ... Washington, DC
Ahern, William F., Jr. ... Cambridge, MA
Providence, RI
Ahern, William F., Jr. ... Kings Park, NY
Ahern, William H. ... Castro Valley, CA
Ahern, William J. ... Columbus, OH
Ahern, William R., III ... Irvine, CA
Ahern, Wynne Augherton ... Oakland, CA
Aherne, Brian W., & Associates
Burbank, CA
Aherne, Edith ... San Francisco, CA
Aherne, Paul A. ... San Mateo, CA
Aherne, Rebecca B. ... Emeryville, CA
San Francisco, CA
Aherne, Richard J., Jr. ... Philadelphia, PA
Aheron, Michael J. ... Roanoke, VA
Aheroni, Elliott L. ... Encino, CA
Ahia, C. Emmanuel ... Yardley, PA
Ahl, Kenneth Evert ... Philadelphia, PA
Ahl, Michael S. ... Fort Lee, NJ
Ahl, Stephen L. ... Lincoln, NE
Ahl, Vicki M. ... Minneapolis, MN
Ahl, Vicki M., P.A. ... Minneapolis, MN
Ahlberg, James G. ... Rochelle, IL
Ahlberg, John A.
Department Of Veterans Affairs, Board of Veterans Appeals, GV
Ahlberg, Kurt M. ... Stratford, CT
Ahlberg Law Firm, Ltd. ... St. Paul, MN
Ahlberg, William E. ... St. Paul, MN
Ahlbrand, Mark W. ... Fort Myers, FL
Ahlbrand, Tracy Ames ... Madison, IN
Ahle, Patrick M. ... Fullerton, CA
Ahlemann, Elizabeth Bottorff ... Elkhart, IN
Ahlemeyer, David G. ... Fairbury, IL
Ahlen, Michael J. ... Grand Forks, ND
Ahlen, Vernon H. ... Omaha, NE
Ahler, James ... San Diego, CA
Ahler, James R. ... Merrillville, IN
Ahlers, Amy E. ... Long Beach, CA
Ahlers, Annette M. ... Washington, DC
Ahlers, Christopher D. ... Buffalo, NY
Ahlers, Clarke F. ... Columbia, MD
Ahlers, Cooney, Dorweiler, Haynie, Smith & Allbee, P.C. ... Des Moines, IA
Ahlers, Dennis D. ... St. Paul, MN
Ahlers, Donald B. ... Cincinnati, OH
Ahlers, Edward C. ... Cincinnati, OH
Ahlers, Heinz W. ... Cincinnati, OH
Ahlers, J. Paul ... Des Moines, IA
Ahlers, Jeffrey W. ... Evansville, IN
Ahlers, Jennifer Susan ... Charlotte, NC
Ahlers, John P. ... Seattle, WA
Ahlers, Keith J. ... White Plains, NY
Ahlers, Laurie K. ... Cincinnati, OH
Ahlers, Lorraine ... Weehawken, NJ
Ahlers, Mark F. ... Orlando, FL
Ahlers, Michele D. ... New Orleans, LA
Ahlers, Paul B. ... Fort Dodge, IA
Ahlers, Paul F. ... Des Moines, IA
Ahlers, Susan L. ... Fort Dodge, IA
Ahlersmeyer, David L. ... Warsaw, IN
Ahles, David P. ... Ypsilanti, MI
Ahles, Richard J. ... St. Cloud, MN
Ahles, Rodney V. ... Lebanon, TN
Ahles, Rodney V., P.C. ... Lebanon, TN
Ahlf, Guenther ... Chicago, IL
Des Plaines, IL
Ahlf, Scott K. ... Lacey, WA
Ahlf, Thomas J. ... New York, NY
Ahlfeld, Loretta McGovern
Stony Brook, NY
Ahlfield, Danny L. ... Austin, TX
Ahlgren & Bangma ... Mora, MN
Ahlgren & Blumenfeld, P.C. ... Chicago, IL
Ahlgren, Erik A. ... Minneapolis, MN
Ahlgren, Frederic F. ... Mora, MN
Ahlgren, Gregory J. ... Manchester, NH
Ahlgren, John L. ... Portsmouth, NH
Ahlgren, John P. ... Mora, MN
Ahlgren & Perrault, P.A. ... Portsmouth, NH
Ahlgren, Richard A., (Ltd.) ... Chicago, IL
Ahlgren, Robert D. ... Chicago, IL
Ahlgren & Smith ... Manchester, NH
Ahlgrim, Kimberly L. ... Chicago, IL
Ahlgrim, Robert F., Jr. ... Indianapolis, IN
Ahlheim, Edward C. ... St. Charles, MO
Ahlheim, Stephen Patrick ... St. Charles, MO
Ahlijanian, Martin J. ... Manassas, VA
Ahlm, Karl M. ... Chicago, IL
Ahlquist, Clyde C. ... Roseville, MN
Ahlquist, Daryl D. ... Erie, KS
Ahlquist, John T. ... Clayton, MO
Ahlquist Law Office, P.A. ... Roseville, MN
Ahlquist, Richard D. ... St. Petersburg, FL
Sarasota, FL
Ahlquist, Richard D., & Associates, P.A.
St. Petersburg, FL
Sarasota, FL
Ahlquist, Todd D. ... Worthington, MN
Ahlrichs & Ahlrichs ... Cincinnati, OH
Ahlrichs, Jas. W. ... Cincinnati, OH
Ahlrichs, Susan M. ... Cincinnati, OH
Ahlschwede, Allen J. ... San Angelo, TX
Ahlschwede, Earl D. ... Grand Island, NE
Ahlstrand, William A. ... Boulder, CO
Ahlstrom, Ann Stiehm ... Minneapolis, MN
Ahlstrom, Bert T., Jr. ... Cheyenne, WY
Ahlstrom & Davis, P.A. ... Columbia, MD
Ahlstrom, Douglas J. ... Tooele, UT
Ahlstrom, J. Millard ... Minneapolis, MN
Ahlstrom, Michael J. ... Atlanta, GA
Ahlstrom, Robert D. ... Columbia, MD
Ahlstrom, Robert J. ... Bellerose, NY
Ahlstrom, Robert J., Jr. ... Bellerose, NY
Ahlstrom, Susan, Law Office of
Severna Park, MD
Ahlum, Greg C. ... Charlotte, NC
Ahluwalia, K. S. ... New York, NY
Ahluwalia, Surinder ... Norwood, MA
Ahluwalia, Suvinder S. ... Las Vegas, NV
Ahmad, Aamina ... Stamford, CT
Ahmad, Fataima Z. ... Department of Justice, Environment and Natural Resources Division, GV
Ahmad, Jadwaa ... Detroit, MI
Ahmad, Joseph Y. ... Houston, TX
Ahmad, Kabir ... New York, NY
Ahmad, M. Kamal ... New York, NY
Ahmad, Muneer Iftikhar ... Los Angeles, CA
Ahmad, Nasim ... Houston, TX
Ahmad, Sehar S. ... Pittsburgh, PA
Ahmad & Zavitsanos, P.C. ... Houston, TX
Ahmadi, Afi ... Rutland, VT
Ahmadia & Carey ... Hilo, HI
Ahmadia, Phyllis G. ... Hilo, HI
Ah Mai, Gerald K. F. ... Honolulu, HI
Ahmann, Bridget M. ... Minneapolis, MN
Ahmann, Matthew C. ... Des Moines, IA
Ahmann, Stewart & Nixon, P.C.
Independence, MO
Ahmed, Adel A. ... Iselin, NJ
Ahmed, Atiq R. ... Silver Spring, MD
Ahmed, Farha ... Sugar Land, TX
Ahmed, Farhat T. ... North Potomac, MD
Ahmed, Mona ... Chicago, IL
Ahmed, Naila Townes ... Richmond, VA
Ahmed, Sabbir ... Los Angeles, CA
Ahmed, Syed I. ... Washington, DC
Ahmedani, Zeeshan ... New York, NY
Ahmuty, Demers & McManus
Albertson, NY
Mineola, NY
New York, NY
Riverhead, NY
White Plains, NY
Ahmuty, Steven J., Jr. ... Lake Success, NY
Ahmuty, William R., III ... Albertson, NY
Ahn, Angela C. ... Boston, MA
Ahn, BoBi ... New York, NY
Ahn, Charles ... Los Angeles, CA
Ahn, Cheolhyo ... New York, NY
Ahn, Cindy ... Washington, DC
Ahn, Ellen ... Santa Ana, CA
Ahn, Harry K. ... New York, NY
Ahn, Jonathan ILsong ... Baltimore, MD
Ahn, Joseph Y. ... Oakland, CA
Ahn, Kristopher K. ... Houston, TX
Ahn, Michael ... Pawtucket, RI
Ahn, Nelson Kyunam ... New York, NY
Ahn, Rachel ... New York, NY
Ahn, Saul S. ... New York, NY
Ahn, Sohee ... Seattle, WA
Ahn, Soo-Jeong ... New York, NY
Ahn, Soon Mo ... Northbrook, IL
Ahn, Woodrow ... New York, NY
Ahn, Yoomie L. ... San Francisco, CA
Ahne, Samuel S. H. ... New York, NY
Ahnen, Christi D. ... Washington, DC
Ahner, Charles W., Jr. ... St. Louis, MO
Ahnn, Michelle M. ... Washington, DC

Ahnstedt, Mitchell J. ... Englewood, CO
Aho, Bruce J. ... Bloomington, MN
Aho, Dale P. ... Farmington, MI
Aho, Donald J. ... Chattanooga, TN
Aho, Ellen S. ... Hamden, CT
Aho, Erik C. ... Salem, OR
Aho, Jon J. ... Rochester, NY
Aho, Ronald C. ... Brookings, SD
Aho, Ronald C., P.C., A Professional Corporation ... Brookings, SD
Ahola, Aaron S. ... Boston, MA
Aholt, Douglas F. ... Atlanta, GA
Ahonen, William D. ... Cleveland, OH
Ahr, Arthur J. ... Albuquerque, NM
Ahr, Tracy J. ... Albuquerque, NM
Ahrberg, William W. ... Cushing, OK
Ahrend, George M. ... Spokane, WA
Ahrend, J. Frederick ... Jackson, MS
Ahrend, Kristopher E. ... New York, NY
Ahrendt, Cynthia J. ... Sioux Falls, SD
Ahrendt, Lorraine B. ... Lincolnshire, IL
Ahrendt, Scott ... Rapid City, SD
Ahrendt, Steven G. ... Sioux Falls, SD
Ahrenhoerster, Edwin R. ... Milwaukee, WI
Ahrenholz, Kevin D. ... Waterloo, IA
Ahrenholz, Robert J. ... Denver, CO
Ahrens, Ann M. ... Cary, NC
Ahrens, Burton Joel ... New York, NY
Ahrens, C. Todd ... Hannibal, MO
Ahrens, Carolyn ... Austin, TX
Ahrens, Christopher D. ... Kansas City, MO
Ahrens, Clifford H. ... St. Louis, MO
Ahrens, David G. ... Appleton, WI
Ahrens & DeAngeli, P.L.L.C. ... Boise, ID
Seattle, WA
Ahrens, Douglas W. ... Seattle, WA
Ahrens, Edward D. ... Seattle, WA
Ahrens, Edward P., Jr. ... Miami, FL
Ahrens, Frederick H., Jr. ... Bath, NY
Ahrens, Frederick P. ... Tulsa, OK
Ahrens, Gary A. ... Milwaukee, WI
Ahrens, Glenn D. ... Milwaukee, WI
Ahrens, Gregg S. ... Miami, FL
Ahrens, Gregory F. ... Cincinnati, OH
Ahrens, Jan G. ... Louisville, KY
Ahrens, Jane E.
Board of Governors Of The Federal Reserve System, Division of Consumer and Community Affairs, GV
Ahrens, Jas. R. ... Topeka, KS
Ahrens, Jeffrey H. ... Newark, NJ
Ahrens, John E. ... Honolulu, HI
Ahrens, Karla ... Fort Myers, FL
North Miami, FL
Ahrens, Klay C. ... St. Paul, MN
Ahrens, Leslie C. ... Santa Ana, CA
Ahrens, Matthew G. ... Fairfax, VA
Ahrens, Matthew H. ... Chicago, IL
Ahrens, Michael H. ... San Francisco, CA
Ahrens, Michele Patterson ... Downey, CA
Ahrens, Michelle R. ... Port Angeles, WA
Ahrens, Nichola G. ... Tampa, FL
Ahrens, Philip F. W., III ... Portland, ME
Ahrens, Richard A. ... St. Louis, MO
Ahrens, Robert E. ... Metairie, LA
Ahrens, Robert E. ... St. Louis, MO
Ahrens, Robert E., P.C. ... St. Louis, MO
Ahrens, Robert W. ... Mountain Home, NC
Ahrens, Roy
Federal Deposit Insurance Corporation, Professional Liability Section, GV
Ahrens, Tom W. ... Fond du Lac, WI
Ahrensfeld, Thomas F. ... Pleasantville, NY
Ahrens Weidling, K. Jane ... Kansas City, KS
Ahronheim, Anna M. ... Chicago, IL
Ahronheim, Keith B. ... Merrick, NY
Ahronian, Jeffrey R. ... Fresno, CA
Ahsan, Aziz M. ... Hopewell Junction, NY
Ahsens, Robert J., III ... Jefferson City, MO
Ahsler, Richard R. ... Princeton, NJ
New York, NY
Ahto, Thomas N. ... Chicago, IL
Ah Tye, Kirk T. ... Santa Barbara, CA
Ahuja, Alok ... Kansas City, MO
Ahuja, Mala ... Washington, DC
Ahuna, Joseph P. H., Jr. ... Kaneohe, HI
Ahwesh, Lynn ... Harrisburg, PA
Aiani, Ronald J. ... Warrenton, VA
Aiardo, Anthony P. ... Orange, CT
Aibel, Daniel
Department Of Health And Human Services, Office of the General Counsel, GV
Aibel, Donald J. ... New York, NY
Aibel, Howard J. ... New York, NY
Aibel, James H. ... Newark, NJ
Aibel, Richard E. ... New York, NY
Aicardi, Deborah I. ... Walnut Creek, CA
Aichele, Barbara ... Torrance, CA
Aichele, Stephen S. ... Berwyn, PA
Philadelphia, PA
Aicher, John G. ... Bayside, NY
Aicher, Robert D. ... Chicago, IL
Aicher, Stacey R.B. ... Garden City, NY
Aicher, Thomas P. ... Rutland, VT
Aichroth, Dennis A. ... West Covina, CA
Aicklen, Josh Cole ... Long Beach, CA
Aid, Kenneth ... Lakewood, CA
Aidala, Arthur L. ... Brooklyn, NY
Aidala, Louis R. ... New York, NY
Aidekman, Gary O. ... Madison, NJ
Aidekman, Richard H. ... New York, NY
Aidelson, David B. ... New York, NY
Aidif, Daniel R. ... Orlando, FL
Aidif & Friedberg ... Orlando, FL
Aidikoff & Kesluk ... Los Angeles, CA
Aidikoff, Philip M. ... Beverly Hills, CA
Las Vegas, NV
Aidikoff & Uhl ... Beverly Hills, CA
Los Angeles, CA
Aidinoff, M. Bernard ... New York, NY
Aidlin, Joseph W. ... Los Angeles, CA
Aidlin, Lisa ... Chicago, IL
Aidman, Evan ... Newtown Square, PA
Aidman, Todd Sidney ... Tampa, FL
Aidun, Christopher K. ... New York, NY
Aidun, Debra ... Fairfax, VA
Aiello, Anthony J. ... Chicago, IL
Aiello & Cannick ... Flushing, NY
Aiello, Christopher M. ... Clearwater, FL
Aiello, Diane F. ... Pittsburgh, PA
Aiello, Domenic P. ... Boston, MA
Aiello, Frank J. ... Riverdale, NJ
Aiello, Frank M. ... New York, NY
Aiello, Frank T. ... Southfield, MI
Aiello, Frank V. ... Mount Shasta, CA
Aiello, Jack J. ... West Palm Beach, FL
Aiello, James J. ... Albany, NY
Aiello, John A. ... Middletown, NJ
Aiello, Laurie B. ... West Palm Beach, FL
Aiello Law Firm, The ... Miami, FL
Aiello, Lisa W. ... West Palm Beach, FL
Aiello, Lois Ann ... Bellport, NY
Aiello, Louis F. ... Woodstock, IL
Aiello, Mark A. ... Southfield, MI
Aiello, Mark F. ... Rockford, IL
Aiello, Michael J. ... New York, NY
Aiello, Michelle T. ... Detroit, MI
Aiello, Paul ... Miami, FL
Aiello, Paula ... San Ramon, CA
Aiello, Philip V. ... Valhalla, NY
Aiello, Robert J. ... Flushing, NY
Aiello, Rosalie E. ... Bronx, NY
Aiello, Sally A. ... Fairfield, CT
Aiello, Thomas P. ... Kenosha, WI
Aiello, Vincent F. ... Encinitas, CA
Aiello, Virgil J. ... Boston, MA
Aiello LeBeau, Josephine
Washington, DC
Aiena, Joseph P. ... New York, NY
Aiesi, Donald P. ... Greenville, SC
Aieta & Greco ... New York, NY
Aieta, Mario A. ... New York, NY
Aiezza-Carpinello, Melissa Anne
Delmar, NY
Aiges, Ronald ... New York, NY
Aigler and Paul ... Bellevue, OH
Aigler, Thomas L. ... Bellevue, OH
Aigler, William F. ... Bellevue, OH
Aigner, Henry J. ... Greenbrae, CA
Aijian, Mark M. ... Santa Barbara, CA
Aik, Timothy R ... Milwaukee, WI
Aiken & Aiken, P.C. ... Hyannis, MA
Aiken, Alicia L. ... Rutland, VT
Aiken, Allison E. ... Columbia, SC
Aiken, Ann ... Eugene, OR
Aiken, Archibald M., Jr. ... Leesburg, VA
Aiken, Arthur K. ... Columbia, SC
Aiken, Casey ... Rockville, MD
Aiken, Casey, II ... Rockville, MD
Aiken, Conrad J. ... Boise, ID
Aiken, D'Angelo & Banner ... San Diego, CA
Aiken, Daniel G. ... Lincoln, ME
Aiken, Deborah L. ... Arlington, VA
Aiken, Donald B. ... Dearborn, MI
Aiken, F. Dennis ... San Diego, CA
Aiken & Fine, P.S. ... Seattle, WA
Aiken, Gary P. ... Towson, MD
Aiken, J. Boone, III ... Florence, SC
Aiken, J. David ... Lincoln, NE
Aiken, James E. ... Great Falls, MT
Aiken, James G. ... Camden, NJ
Aiken, James H. ... Atlanta, GA
Aiken, James R. ... Cortez, CO
Aiken, James W. ... Seattle, WA
Aiken, Jane E. ... Salem, OR
Aiken, Jeffrey H ... Delray Beach, FL
Aiken, Jeffrey P. ... Milwaukee, WI
Aiken, Jerome R. ... Yakima, WA
Aiken, Julius B. ... Greenville, SC
Aiken, Kramer & Cummings, Incorporated
Oakland, CA
Aiken, Leighton ... Dallas, TX
Aiken, Leland J. ... Sacramento, CA
Aiken & Lewis ... Springfield, MO
Aiken, Lionel T. ... San Francisco, CA
Aiken, Lorn ... Vancouver, WA
Aiken, Matthew A. ... Birmingham, AL
Aiken, Michael J. ... Woodland Hills, CA
Aiken, Nancy Chaffee ... Wichita, KS
Aiken, Nunn, Elliott & Tyler, P.A.
Florence, SC
Aiken, Paul ... New York, NY
Aiken, Paul C., II ... Rockville, MD
Aiken, Paul R. ... Hyannis, MA
Aiken, Peter D. ... Fort Lauderdale, FL
Aiken, Ray J. ... Delafield, WI
Aiken, Richard L., Jr. ... Glastonbury, CT
Aiken, Rob ... Springfield, MO
Aiken, St. Louis & Siljeg, P.S.
Seattle, WA
Aiken & Scoptur, S.C. ... Milwaukee, WI
Aiken, Shawn K. ... Phoenix, AZ
Aiken, Steven L. ... Hyannis, MA
Aiken, Timothy J. ... Milwaukee, WI
Aiken, Tina M. ... Seattle, WA
Aiken, Tonia D. ... Metairie, LA
Aiken, Vincent J. ... Glendale, CA
Aiken, W. James, Jr. ... Pittsburgh, PA
Aiken, Wallace ... Seattle, WA
Aiken, William P., Jr. ... Chattanooga, TN
Aikenhead, Cipes & Supanich
Los Angeles, CA
Aikenhead, David S. ... Los Angeles, CA
Aikens, Augustus D., Jr. ... Tallahassee, FL
Aikens, David A., Jr. ... Wilkes-Barre, PA
Aikens, L. Harold, Jr.
Department of Transportation, Federal Highway Administration, GV
Aikens, Linda A. ... Silver Spring, MD
Aikens, Robert B. ... Troy, MI
Aikens, William R. ... Troy, MI
Aikin, John D. ... Hereford, TX
Aikin, Leland M., II ... Pocatello, ID
Aikin, Linda L. ... Santa Fe, NM
Aikin, Roger L. ... Oakland, CA
Aikin, Wendy L. ... Winter Park, FL
Aikin, Wendy L., P.A. ... Orlando, FL
Sanford, FL
Winter Park, FL
Aikins, Deborah Churton
Mountain View, CA
Aikins, Douglas B. ... Mountain View, CA
Aikins, Mark R. ... Asbury Park, NJ
Aikman, Donald M. ... Fort Wayne, IN
Aikman, J. Randall ... Indianapolis, IN
Aikman, John D. ... New Windsor, NY
Aikman, John E. ... Brookville, PA
Aikman, Mary M. ... Kilgore, TX
Aikman, Richard E. ... Indianapolis, IN
Aikman, Richard E., Jr. ... Indianapolis, IN
Aikman, William F. ... Boston, MA
Ailara, Carl E., Jr. ... Morristown, NJ
Ailawadhi, Joginder L. ... Poughkeepsie, NY
Ailes, Aleita J. ... London, OH
Springfield, OH
Ailes, Charles M. ... Holland, MI
Ailes, Charles M., P.L.C. ... Holland, MI
Ailes, Stephen ... Washington, DC
Ailes, Thaddeus R. ... Indianapolis, IN
Ailes, William C. ... Canton, OH
Ailin, June ... Los Angeles, CA
Ailor, Ailor & McKinney ... Knoxville, TN
Ailor, Earl S. ... Knoxville, TN
Ailor, William T. ... Knoxville, TN
Ailshie, Lee W. ... Charleston, SC
Ailslieger, Paul E. ... Des Moines, IA
Ailstock, Charles F. ... Charleston, SC
Ailstock, Janet Parker ... Hialeah, FL
Ailsworth, G. Mark ... Newport News, VA
Ailsworth, Timothy S. ... Raleigh, NC
Ailts, Evelyn T. ... Houston, TX
Aiman, Scott A. ... Lancaster, OH
Aiman-Smith, Randall B.
San Francisco, CA
Aimar, Don ... Las Vegas, NV
Aimen, Julie B. ... Chicago, IL
Aimino, Michael A., Jr. ... Woodbury, NJ
Aimola, Nancy A. ... Pacifica, CA
Aimonette, W. Gregory ... Chicago, IL
Aimufua, Iyke E. ... Valley Village, CA
Ain, Jody Michelle ... Long Island City, NY
Ain, Jonathan A. ... New York, NY
Ain, Linda K. ... Lexington, KY
Ain, Louis ... Tamarac, FL
Ain, Michael M. ... Washington, DC
Rockville, MD
Ain, Phyllis M. ... Denver, CO
Ain, Phyllis M., P.C. ... Denver, CO
Ain, Sanford K. ... Washington, DC
Ain, Stuart L. ... Mineola, NY
Ain, Theodore ... Boynton Beach, FL
Aina, Charleen M. ... Honolulu, HI
Ainbinder, Janeann Nolan ... Jericho, NY
Ainbinder, Larry N. ... San Diego, CA
Ainbinder, Michael C. ... Houston, TX
Ainbinder, Michael D. ... Lakewood, CA
Ainbinder, Steven N. ... Boca Raton, FL
Ainger, Dennis R. ... Chicago, IL
Aini, Jack A. ... New York, NY
Ainlay, Charles W. ... Goshen, IN
Ainley, Gary L. ... Medina, OH
Ainley, Joseph H. ... San Jose, CA
Ainley, Matthew G. ... Cerritos, CA
Ainora, Thomas ... Department of Justice, Federal Bureau of Investigation, GV
Ainsa, Francis S. ... El Paso, TX
Ainsa, Francis S., Jr. ... El Paso, TX
Ainsa, Michael F. ... El Paso, TX
Ainsa Partners, LLP ... El Paso, TX
Ainsa, Richard L. ... El Paso, TX
Ainsley, Kenneth T. ... New Bedford, MA
Ainsley, Stuart M. ... Bainbridge Island, WA
Ainslie & Bronson ... Philadelphia, PA
Ainslie, Elizabeth K. ... Philadelphia, PA
Ainslie, Geo. W. ... Binghamton, NY
Ainslie, Ruth W. ... New York, NY
Ainsman, David I. ... Pittsburgh, PA
Ainsman & Levine, P.C. ... Pittsburgh, PA
Ainsworth, Alfred, III ... Deerfield, IL
Ainsworth, Brian E. ... Grand Rapids, MI
Ainsworth, C. Donald ... Chesterfield, MO
Ainsworth, Charles L. ... Houston, TX
Ainsworth, David V. ... Washington, DC
Ainsworth, Diane, & Associates
Chicago, IL
Ainsworth, George, Jr. ... Paoli, PA
Ainsworth, Harry D. ... Portland, OR
Ainsworth, James S. ... Allegan, MI
Ainsworth, J. C., Jr. ... Monticello, MS
Ainsworth, Jeanlaurie ... Sacramento, CA
Ainsworth, Jennifer Parker ... Houston, TX
Ainsworth, Jenny S. ... Charlotte, NC
Ainsworth, John D. ... Jackson, MS
Ainsworth, Kathryn Monahan ... Portland, ME
Ainsworth, Keith R. ... New Haven, CT
Ainsworth, Kevin D. ... Fall River, MA
Ainsworth, Kevin N. ... New York, NY
Ainsworth, Kyle B. ... Jackson, MS
Ainsworth, Louis L. ... St. Paul, MN
Ainsworth, Max M. ... New Orleans, LA
Ainsworth, Price ... Austin, TX
Ainsworth, Rebecca J. ... Pascagoula, MS
Ainsworth, Richard T. ... San Jose, CA
Ainsworth, Scott B. ... Decatur, IN
Ainsworth, Sidney E. ... Ashland, OR
Ainsworth, Sullivan, Tracy, Knauf, Warner & Ruslander, P.C. ... Albany, NY
Saratoga Springs, NY
Ainsworth & Thelin, P.A.
South Portland, ME
Ainsworth, Thomas G. ... South Portland, ME
Ainsworth, Thomas H., III ... Charlotte, NC
Ainsworth, Todd C. ... Salem, OR
Ainsworth-Southerland, Cheryal Kay
Edmond, OK
Aiona, James R., Jr. ... Ewa Beach, HI
Aiona, Tadd C. ... Santa Rosa, CA
Aiosa, Angelo
Department of Housing and Urban Development, Office of General Counsel, GV
Aiosa, Edward J. ... Largo, FL
Aiossa, Anthony J. ... Craftsbury Common, VT
Aiossa, Frederick N. ... Chicago, IL
Aipa, Nathan T. K. ... Honolulu, HI
Airan, David M. ... Chicago, IL
Airasian, Lynn A. ... Washington, DC
Airdo, Michael A. ... Chicago, IL
Aires, Randolf H. ... Washington, DC
Aires, Timothy Carl ... Newport Beach, CA
Airey, W. Jonathan ... Columbus, OH
Airgood, Victoria J. ... Cherry Hill, NJ
Airhart, Edward C. ... Louisville, KY
Airhart, Teddy W., Jr. ... Baton Rouge, LA
Airola & Airola ... San Andreas, CA
Airola, Glenn E. ... Houston, TX
Airola, John Verrios ... Sacramento, CA
Airola, Kenneth D. ... San Andreas, CA
Airola, Leslie J. ... Portola Valley, CA
Airola, Mark J. ... Houston, TX
Airola, Orrin K. ... San Andreas, CA
Airola, Steven J. ... San Andreas, CA
Airone, Thomas J. ... New Haven, CT
Airth, Hal A. ... Live Oak, FL
Airth, Hal Adams, Jr. ... Jacksonville, FL
Airth, W. C., Jr. ... Orlando, FL
Aisen, Judith Rachel ... New York, NY
Aisenberg, Bennett S. ... Denver, CO
Aisenberg, Bennett S., P.C. ... Denver, CO
Aisenberg, David C. ... Boston, MA
Aisenberg, Irwin M. ... Washington, DC
Aisenberg, Michael A. ... Washington, DC
Aisenbrey, John C. ... Kansas City, MO
Aisenson, David J. ... Los Angeles, CA
Aisenson, Tami J. ... New York, NY
Aisenstark, Avery ... Baltimore, MD
Aisenstein, Robert G. ... Henderson, NV
Aiso, David M. ... Los Angeles, CA
Aison, Howard M. ... Fonda, NY
Aissis, John S. ... Hebron, CT
Aist, James S. ... Baltimore, MD
Aist, Jennifer Buran ... Towson, MD
Aita, P. Stephen ... Seattle, WA
Aitcheson, Frank L., III ... Atlanta, GA
Aitcheson, Jessie A. ... Norwich, NY
Aitcheson, Robert D., L.C.
Charles Town, WV
Aitchison, William B. ... Portland, OR
Aitelli, John ... Los Angeles, CA
Aitelli, Peter ... San Francisco, CA
Aites, Donald J. ... Carlsborg, WA
Aitken, Andrew C. ... Washington, DC
Aitken, B. Scott ... Houston, TX
Aitken, Bruce ... Washington, DC
Aitken, Christopher ... Santa Ana, CA
Aitken, Darren O'Leary ... Santa Ana, CA
Aitken, David N. ... La Mesa, CA
Aitken, Elizabeth L. ... San Antonio, TX
Aitken, George A. ... Baltimore, MD
Aitken, H. John ... Olympia, WA
Aitken, Herve H. ... Alexandria, VA
Aitken Irvin Lewin Berlin Vrooman & Cohn, LLP ... Washington, DC
White Plains, NY
Aitken, Janice ... Cleveland, OH
Aitken, Joslyn ... Laguna Beach, CA
Aitken, Margaret A ... Charlotte, NC
Aitken, Melissa E. ... Silver Spring, MD
Aitken, Richard L. ... Washington, DC
Aitken, Robert Andrew ... Dearborn, MI
Aitken, Robert Lee ... Port Washington, NY
Aitken, Ronald W. ... Roseburg, OR
Aitken, Schauble, Patrick, Neill & Ruff
Colfax, WA
Colton, WA
Pullman, WA
St. John, WA
Aitken, Steven D.
Executive Office Of The President, Office of Management and Budget, GV
Aitken, Thomas D. ... Tampa, FL
Aitken, Thomas J., Jr. ... Holden, MA
Aitken, Veronica E. ... Los Angeles, CA
Aitken, William A. ... Somerset, NJ
Aitken, William M. ... Los Angeles, CA
Aitken, Wylie A. ... Santa Ana, CA
Aitken, Wylie A., A Law Corporation, Law Offices of ... Santa Ana, CA
Aitkens & Aitkens, P.C. ... Atlanta, GA
Marietta, GA
Aitkens, Robert G. ... Atlanta, GA
Aitkens, Teresa Thomas ... Atlanta, GA
Aiuvalasit, Anthony G., Jr.
Jersey City, NJ
Aivalikles, William E. ... Nashua, NH
Aivars, Elizabeth Constance ... Jamaica, NY
Aiyer, Nirja S. ... Houston, TX
Aiyetorro, Adjoa A. ... Washington, DC
Aizawa, Motoko ... Washington, DC
Aizenberg, Gabriel ... Chicago, IL
Aizenstein, Neal I. ... Chicago, IL

Aizer, Sharon D. ... The Woodlands, TX
Aizin, Michael ... Brooklyn, NY
Aizley, Arthur H. ... New York, NY
Aizpuru, Natalie Z. ... Edina, MN
Aizpuru, Rebeca ... Houston, TX
Aizpuru-Sutton, Laura I. ... Palo Alto, CA
Aja, Louise Margret ... Stony Brook, NY
Ajah, Jennifer C. E. ... Valley Stream, NY
Ajalat, Charles R., (A Professional Corporation) ... Los Angeles, CA
Ajalat, Christiana M. ... Newport Beach, CA
Ajalat, Gregory M. ... Burbank, CA
Ajalat, Peter B. ... New York, NY
Ajalat, Polley & Ayoob ... Los Angeles, CA
Ajalat, Sol P. ... Burbank, CA
Ajalat, Stephen P. ... Burbank, CA
Ajalet & Ajalet ... Burbank, CA
Ajami, Tarik Fouad ... New York, NY
Ajamie, Thomas R. ... Houston, TX
McAllen, TX
Ajax, Fred W., Jr. ... Atlanta, GA
Ajazi, Dimitri ... Chicago, IL
Ajello, Daniel Michael ... Brooklyn, NY
Ajello, Michael J. ... New Haven, CT
Ajello, Michael V. ... Brooklyn, NY
Ajemian, Charles P. ... Waynesboro, VA
Ajemian, David R. ... Los Angeles, CA
Ajemian, Marianne ... Boston, MA
Ajemian, Robert ... San Francisco, CA
Ajemian, Van Ralph ... Montebello, CA
Ajhar, Maria K. ... Los Angeles, CA
Ajhar, Marsha G. ... New York, NY
Aji, Rajesh A. ... San Francisco, CA
Ajlouny, Jerry J. A. ... San Ramon, CA
Ajlouny, Joseph S. ... Huntington Woods, MI
Ajlouny, Omar P. ... San Jose, CA
Ajlouny, Peter ... Hempstead, NY
Ajlouny, Robert S. ... San Diego, CA
Ajluni, K. Fred ... Royal Oak, MI
Ajluni, Ray D. ... Livonia, MI
Ajluni, Roger D. ... Plymouth, MI
Ajmeri, Sajid ... New York, NY
Ajootian, Charles J. ... Providence, RI
Ajubita, A. Albert ... New Orleans, LA
Ajubita & Associates, L.L.C. ... New Orleans, LA
Ajunwa-Dumas, Grace O. ... San Diego, CA
Aka, Gary T. ... Palo Alto, CA
Akabas & Cohen ... New York, NY
Akabas, Seth A. ... New York, NY
Akachukwu, Mildred A. ... Durham, NC
Akadiri, Adebola T. ... Cincinnati, OH
Akamine, Louise L. ... Honolulu, HI
Akamine, Ryan M. ... Honolulu, HI
Akan, Sally A. ... Philadelphia, PA
Akana, David A. ... Olympia, WA
Akana, Michael P. ... Hayward, CA
Akana & Yee ... Hayward, CA
Akant, Alison Heiserman ... New York, NY
Akaras, Andreas N. ... Washington, DC
Baltimore, MD
New York, NY
Akard & Griffin ... Houston, TX
Akard, John ... Houston, TX
Akard, John C. ... Lubbock, TX
Akard, Stephen J. ... Bloomington, IN
Akashian, Michael C. ... Boston, MA
Akavickas, Gary R. ... Racine, WI
Akawie, Alice L. ... Oakland, CA
Akay & Associates ... San Francisco, CA
Akay, Douglas N. ... San Francisco, CA
Akbar, Kellianne ... Sacramento, CA
Akbar, Raymond ... Los Angeles, CA
Akbari, Nancy ... Jenkintown, PA
Akbari, Reiss & Graff ... Jenkintown, PA
Akbarian, Anahit N. ... Glendale, CA
Akchin, Linda Sarradet ... Baton Rouge, LA
Akdoruk, Jane S. ... Redwood City, CA
Ake, David S. ... Canton, OH
Ake, J. Whitney ... Canton, OH
Ake, John N. ... Philadelphia, PA
Ake, Sherwood ... Canton, OH
Ake, Stephen D. ... Tampa, FL
Aked, Jonathan C. ... Madison, WI
Akeel, Shereef Hadi ... Huntington Woods, MI
Akehurst, F. Ronald P. ... Eden Prairie, MN
Akel, Daniel D. ... Jacksonville, FL
Akel, Edward C. ... Jacksonville, FL
Akel, Jeremy Brahim ... Jacksonville, FL
Akel, Richard L. ... New York, NY
Akemann, Ernest R. ... Chicago, IL
Aken, David H., Jr. ... Sinton, TX
Akens, Lauryn Gayle ... Birmingham, AL
Akens, Susan E. ... Hollywood, CA
Aker, Christopher R. ... San Francisco, CA
Aker, David ... Norwalk, CT
Aker, Gregory R. ... Oakland, CA
Aker, Hazel Marie ... San Diego, CA
Aker, J. Brooke ... Norristown, PA
Aker, James E. ... Sarasota, FL
Akere & Associates ... Dallas, TX
Akere, Labi M. ... Dallas, TX
Akerley, Mary S. ... Kensington, MD
Akerley, Stephen J. ... Palo Alto, CA
Akerly, Bruce W. ... Dallas, TX
Akerman, Nathaniel H. ... New York, NY
Akerman, Senterfitt & Eidson, P.A.
Fort Lauderdale, FL
Jacksonville, FL
Miami, FL
Orlando, FL
Tallahassee, FL
Tampa, FL
West Palm Beach, FL
Akerman, Walter, Jr. ... Atlanta, GA
Akers & Akers, P.C. ... Weatherford, TX
Akers, Alan Kent, Sr. ... Bardstown, KY
Akers & Boswell, P.A. ... Palm Beach, FL
Akers, Brian P. ... Milwaukee, WI
Akers, Brock C. ... Houston, TX
Akers, Byron L., Jr. ... Colorado Springs, CO
Akers & Carleton, LLC ... Denver, CO
Akers, Charles B. ... Weatherford, TX
Akers, Charles David ... Nashville, TN
Akers, Charles O. ... Foster City, CA
Akers, Cynthia S. ... Pittsburgh, PA
Akers, David S. ... Branson, MO
Akers, Deborah R. ... Cleveland, OH
Akers, Dee A. ... Louisville, KY
Akers, Denise Nelson ... Baton Rouge, LA
Akers, Diane L. ... Detroit, MI
Akers, Donald D., Jr. ... New Iberia, LA
Akers, Edwin D., Jr. ... St. Louis, MO
Akers, Eric J. ... Ashland, OH
Akers, George M. ... Montgomery, AL
Akers, George W., (P.S.) ... Seattle, WA
Akers, Georgia L. ... Houston, TX
Akers, Gregory A. ... San Diego, CA
Akers, J. Blaine ... Brazil, IN
Akers, J. Murray ... Greenville, MS
Akers, James E. ... Washington, DC
Akers, James E. ... Charlotte, NC
Akers, James R., II ... Charleston, WV
Akers, Janet Marie ... Bessemer, AL
Akers, Jeremy Ray ... Palm Beach, FL
Akers, John K.H., Jr. ... Denver, CO
Akers, Johnny P. ... Bartlesville, OK
Akers, Joseph H. ... Marietta, GA
Akers, Katrina ... Cleveland, TN
Akers, Lawrence C. ... New York, NY
Akers, Linda A. ... Phoenix, AZ
Akers, Mark L. ... Potosi, MO
Akers, Martha N. ... Weatherford, TX
Akers, Michael A. ... Brandon, MS
Akers, Noel J. ... Houston, TX
Akers & Obert, P.A. ... Brandon, MS
Canton, MS
Jackson, MS
Akers, Ottie C., Law Offices of ... Birmingham, AL
Akers, Patricia L. ... Austin, TX
Akers, Randal ... Kennesaw, GA
Akers, Randal, P.C. ... Kennesaw, GA
Akers, Richard J. ... Portland, OR
Akers, Robert D. ... Fort Worth, TX
Akers, S. Lee ... Chattanooga, TN
Akers, Sharon L. ... Cleveland, OH
Akers, Stephen R. ... Dallas, TX
Akers, Susan M. ... Department of Justice, Environment and Natural Resources Division, GV
Akers, Tammy W. ... Colorado Springs, CO
Akers, Virginia I. ... Auburn, CA
Akers, William, III ... Ormond Beach, FL
Akers, William, III, P.A. ... Ormond Beach, FL
Akers, William J. ... Princeton, WV
Akers, William L. ... Philadelphia, PA
Akers & Wisbar, L.L.C. ... Baton Rouge, LA
Akerson, Michael J. ... Worcester, MA
Akerson, R. Bruce ... St. Petersburg, FL
Akeson, Robert A. ... St. James, NY
Akey Law Offices, S.C. ... Minocqua, WI
Akey, Thomas N. ... Minocqua, WI
Akhlaghi, Haleh ... Irvine, CA
Akhlaghi, Lily ... Santa Ana, CA
Akhtar, Adeel S. ... San Francisco, CA
Akhtar, Sarah M. ... Dallas, TX
Akhtar, Sher M. ... Troy, MI
Akhtar-Gutman, Halima ... Port Washington, NY
Akiba, Lorraine H. ... Honolulu, HI
Akin & Akin, L.L.P. ... Austin, TX
Georgetown, TX
Akin, Brad S. ... San Antonio, TX
Akin, Christopher J. ... Dallas, TX
Akin, Dain C. ... Reynoldsburg, OH
Akin, Danny L. ... Macon, GA
Akin, David Fredrick ... San Diego, CA
Akin, Dawn E. ... Kansas City, MO
Akin, Gail S. ... Jackson, MS
Akin, Gordon R. (Randy) ... Longview, TX
Akin, Gump, Strauss, Hauer & Feld, L.L.P.
Los Angeles, CA
Washington, DC
New York, NY
Philadelphia, PA
Austin, TX
Dallas, TX
Houston, TX
San Antonio, TX
Akin, Henry D. ... Dallas, TX
Akin, Henry D., Jr. ... Dallas, TX
Akin, Jackson G. ... Albuquerque, NM
Akin, John H. ... Austin, TX
Akin, John R. ... Roseville, CA
Akin, Lilian Alexa ... Pittsburgh, PA
Akin, Mary E. ... New Orleans, LA
Akin, Neeley & Mason, L.L.P. ... Longview, TX
Akin, R. Harry ... Austin, TX
Georgetown, TX
Akin, Rick ... Austin, TX
Akin, Roger A. ... Wilmington, DE
Akin, Rosalind Ross ... Murfreesboro, TN
Akin, Sherrille D. ... Columbus, OH
Akin, T. Bryan ... Galveston, TX
Akin & Tate, P.C. ... Cartersville, GA
Rome, GA
Akin, Ted Martin ... Dallas, TX
Akin, Truett Bryan, IV ... Houston, TX
Akin, Wanda M. ... Newark, NJ
Akin, Warren ... Cartersville, GA
Akin & Webster, P.C. ... Macon, GA
Akin, William R. ... Santa Ana, CA
Akin, Wm. Morgan ... Cartersville, GA
Akinaka, Asa M. ... Honolulu, HI
Akinrinade, Nelson A. ... North Lauderdale, FL
Akins, B. Sean ... Ripley, MS
Akins, Brenda Lee ... Iowa City, IA
Akins, Dale E. ... Bluffton, SC
Hilton Head Island, SC
Akins, Darth D. ... Greenville, NC
Akins, David J. ... Orlando, FL
Akins, Dwain ... San Antonio, TX
Akins, Elwyn M. ... Trenton, FL
Akins, Ferris F. (Rick), Jr. ... Round Rock, TX
Akins, Jacqueline S. ... Dallas, TX
Akins, James H., Jr. ... Indianapolis, IN
Akins, Jeffrey R. ... San Antonio, TX
Akins, Jerry W. ... San Francisco, CA
Akins, Jim F. ... Sherwood, AR
Akins, Johnny J. ... Oklahoma City, OK
Akins, Julie McCoy ... Newport Beach, CA
Akins, Kelly ... Dallas, TX
Akins, Kelly D. ... Los Angeles, CA
Akins, Kelly, P.C. ... Dallas, TX
Akins, Leesa D. ... Atlanta, GA
Akins, Leslie Schwaebe ... San Diego, CA
Akins, Linda Sumner ... Orlando, FL
Akins, Martin P. ... St. Louis, MO
Akins, Marty R. ... Marble Falls, TX
Akins, Sarah Brown ... Savannah, GA
Akins, Thomas C. ... Denison, TX
Akins, Waverly F., Law Offices of ... Fuquay-Varina, NC
Akins, William C. ... Decatur, GA
Akinyemi, Wole ... Riverside, CA
Akita, Jerry S. ... Santa Ana, CA
Akita, Kazuyoshi ... Honolulu, HI
Akiyama, Carol Lynn ... Los Angeles, CA
Akiyama, D. Amy ... San Diego, CA
Akiyama, Emmy ... Torrance, CA
Akiyama, Shinya ... New York, NY
Akiyama, Takeo ... New York, NY
Akkashian, Brian M. ... Detroit, MI
Akkashian, Walter ... Waterford, MI
Akl, Maria Luisa ... Pasadena, CA
Akl, Ronda T. ... Syracuse, NY
Aklufi, Daniel R. ... Riverside, CA
Aklufi, Joseph S. ... Riverside, CA
Aklufi, Michael J. ... New York, NY
Aklufi and Wysocki ... Riverside, CA
Akmajian, Peter ... Tucson, AZ
Akman & Associates, P.C. ... Washington, DC
Frederick, MD
Lutherville, MD
Greensburg, PA
Pittsburgh, PA
Akman, Bryan J. ... Lutherville, MD
Akman, Jerome P. ... Washington, DC
Ako, Samuel Mbo ... Houston, TX
Akolt, John P., III ... Brighton, CO
Akolt, John P., Jr. ... Denver, CO
Akong, Englebert Chia ... Minneapolis, MN
Akorli, Godfried R. ... Pittsburgh, PA
Akouri, Robert L. ... Dearborn, MI
Akoury, Sandra J. ... Darien, CT
Akpaffiong, Bassey Otu ... Houston, TX
Akpan, Emmanuel D. ... Washington, DC
Akpodiete, Alexander Osondu ... Miami, FL
Akpodiete Law Group, P.A. ... Miami, FL
Akrawi, Sherry Ann ... Sacramento, CA
Akre, Bryan & Malin, LLP ... Los Angeles, CA
Akre, Charles T. ... Washington, DC
Akre, Kevin M. ... Salem, MA
Akre, M. Jan ... Los Angeles, CA
Akre, Steven H. ... St. Louis, MO
Akridge & Balch, P.C. ... Auburn, AL
Akridge, Constance L. ... Las Vegas, NV
Akridge, J. Edgar, Jr. ... Auburn, AL
Akridge, John W., Jr. ... Atlanta, GA
Akright, James R. ... Bartlesville, OK
Akrivos, Stamos T. ... San Francisco, CA
Akrotirianakis, Joseph N. ... Los Angeles, CA
Aksamit, Gary L. ... Lincoln, NE
Aksamit, Roger D. ... Houston, TX
Aksell, Allan C. ... Winter Park, FL
Akselrad, Abraham M. ... Succasunna, NJ
Akselrad, Harold E. ... New York, NY
Akselrad, Ira ... New York, NY
Aksen, Gerald ... New York, NY
Aksman, Stanislaus ... Washington, DC
Aksomitas, W. Ward ... Juno Beach, FL
Akst & Akst ... New York, NY
Akst, George S. ... New York, NY
Akst, Leslie K. ... New York, NY
Aktansel, Vera ... Norman, OK
Akuetey, Hubert Rich ... New York, NY
Akulian, Linda F. W. ... San Leandro, CA
Akulian, Theodore A. ... Walnut Creek, CA
Akullian, Arthur J. ... Alhambra, CA
Akwari, Anne Micheaux ... Raleigh, NC
Akyereko, Beth-Sherri ... Washington, DC
Al, Marc A. ... Minneapolis, MN
Al Miller and Associates, P.A. ... Jupiter, FL
Alabart, Javier A. ... Fresno, CA
Alabaster, Gary ... San Francisco, CA
Alabaster, Howard I. ... Coral Springs, FL
Alaburda, Lawrence ... Parsippany, NJ
Alacqua, Joseph A. ... Turnersville, NJ
Aladjem, David R.E. ... Sacramento, CA
Alagero, Charles T. ... Waltham, MA
Alagheband, Shouka D. Rezvani ... Portland, OR
Alagood, Charles Gregory ... Little Rock, AR
Alahydoian, Dork H. ... Palo Alto, CA
Alai, Martha Charepoo ... Denver, CO
Alailima, Charles V. ... Pago Pago, TT
Alaimo, Anthony A. ... Brunswick, GA
Alaimo, Carol J. ... Buffalo, NY
Alaimo, Charles B. ... Enfield, CT
Alaimo, Gaetano J. ... Toms River, NJ
Alaimo, James J., Jr. ... Enfield, CT
Alaimo, Marve Ann M. ... Bonita Springs, FL
Alaimo, Michael A. ... Detroit, MI
Alair, Elise Frost ... East Hartford, CT
Alaka, Aïda M. ... Chicago, IL
Alala Mullen Holland & Cooper P.A.
Asheville, NC
Charlotte, NC
Gastonia, NC
Lincolnton, NC
Shelby, NC
Alam, Joel M. ... Detroit, MI
Alam, Navaid ... New York, NY
Alam, Victor N. ... San Francisco, CA
Alami, Iwona Joanna ... Laguna Niguel, CA
Alamia, Jose R. ... Edinburg, TX
Alamia, Richard R. ... Edinburg, TX
Alamia, Salvatore A. ... Central Islip, NY
Alamo, Cristina ... San Juan, PR
Alamuddin, Sari M. ... Chicago, IL
Alan, David Peter ... New York, NY
Alan, Matthew W. A. ... Aiken, SC
Alan, Sondra K. ... Bristol, VA
Aland, Linda S. ... Dallas, TX
Aland, Robert H. ... Chicago, IL
Aland, Ronald Z. ... Dallas, TX
Alandt & Alandt, P.C. ... Port Huron, MI
Alandt, Clarence J. ... Port Huron, MI
Alandt, Gloriette G. ... Port Huron, MI
Alandt, Patrick J. ... Bloomfield Hills, MI
Alani, Douglas D. ... Costa Mesa, CA
Alanis, Juan Felipe ... Edinburg, TX
Alanis, Lavalle, Serrano y Doblado, S.C. ... Roswell, GA
Alaniz & Alaniz ... McAllen, TX
Alaniz, Amy Howell ... McAllen, TX
Alaniz, Anibal Jaime ... McAllen, TX
Alaniz, Anne Margaret ... Santa Ana, CA
Alaniz, Elizabeth A. ... Seattle, WA
Alaniz, Karen Balter ... Houston, TX
Alaniz, Laura M. ... Houston, TX
Alaniz, Oscar ... Rio Hondo, TX
Alaniz, Richard D. ... Houston, TX
Alaniz and Schraeder, L.L.P. ... Houston, TX
Alansky, Frank R. ... West Trenton, NJ
Alanson, Michael W. ... Traverse City, MI
Alapati, Nanda K. ... Washington, DC
Alarcon, Arthur L. ... Los Angeles, CA
Alarcon, Guillermo Gerardo ... Laredo, TX
Alarcon, J. Alberto ... Laredo, TX
Alarcon, Sergio J. ... New Orleans, LA
Alarcon, Terry Q. ... New Orleans, LA
Alarcon-Cigarroa, Graciela ... Laredo, TX
Alarcon-Rios, Irene ... San Antonio, TX
Alarid, Albert J., III ... Albuquerque, NM
Alarid, Alexander A. ... New York, NY
Alarid, Jason M. ... Albuquerque, NM
Alarimo, Lori Ann ... New York, NY
Alario & Associates, P.C. ... Syracuse, NY
Alario, Charles F. ... Brooklyn, NY
Alario, Linda E. ... Syracuse, NY
Alario, Robert F. ... New York, NY
Alaska Law Offices, Inc., A Professional Corporation ... Anchorage, AK
Alatalo, Richard A. ... Redford, MI
Alatis, Andrew J. ... Columbus, OH
Alatorre, Salvador L. ... St. Louis, MO
Alavezos, David LeRoy ... Ukiah, CA
Alavi, Ali ... Monaca, PA
Alavi, Amir H. ... Houston, TX
Alavi, Ladan ... Los Angeles, CA
Alavi, Tania Z. ... Ocala, FL
Alaynick, David C. ... Woodland Hills, CA
Alayon, Richard A. ... Miami, FL
Alayon, Roberto R. ... Tampa, FL
Alayon, Roberto R., P.A. ... Tampa, FL
Al-Azem, Samer ... Houston, TX
Alazraki, Eliot ... Wilmington, DE
Alazraki, Howard S. ... Los Angeles, CA
Alazraki, Marcia D. ... New York, NY
Alba, David A. ... Naples, FL
Alba, David L. ... Freehold, NJ
Alba, Jonathan Leonard ... San Francisco, CA
Alba, Lourdes D. ... Indianapolis, IN
Alba, Russell T. ... Tampa, FL
Alba, Samuel ... Salt Lake City, UT
Alba, Susana ... Portland, OR
Albair, Robert J. ... St. Louis, MO
Albair, Robert J., P.C. ... St. Louis, MO
Albala, Allan ... Los Angeles, CA
Albala, Brent M. ... Plainview, NY
Albala, Jorge C. ... Phoenix, AZ
Albalah, David ... New York, NY
Albamonte, Elena Marie ... Department of Justice, Executive Office for Immigration Review, GV
Alban, Agnes E. ... Larchmont, NY
Alban & Alban ... Columbus, OH
Alban, Arnold J. ... Santa Monica, CA
Alban, Daniel ... Hailey, ID
Alban, David R. ... Columbus, OH
Alban, Glenn F. ... Columbus, OH
Alban, J. Calvin ... Columbus, OH
Alban, Jon K. ... Irvine, CA
Alban, Juan F. ... Miami, FL
Alban, Ludwig ... Brookline, MA
Alban, Marsha ... Brookline, MA
Alban, Richard L. ... Nampa, ID
Alban, Robert D. ... Long Beach, CA
Alban, Robert J. ... Rocky River, OH

Alban, William R. ... Chicago, IL
Albanese, A. J. ... Fairfax, VA
Albanese and Albanese ... Gloversville, NY
Albanese, Albanese & Fiore LLP
Garden City, NY
Albanese, Anthony J. ... New York, NY
Albanese, Benjamin P., Jr. ... Brockton, MA
Albanese, Bobbie F. ... Escondido, CA
Santa Monica, CA
Albanese, Christopher ... New York, NY
Albanese, F. David J. ... Cincinnati, OH
Albanese, Jack B. ... Atlanta, GA
Albanese, Jan A. ... Orlando, FL
Albanese, Jeffrey ... Goshen, NY
Albanese, John S. ... Department of Defense, Defense Legal Services Agency, GV
Albanese, Jonathan O. ... Ithaca, NY
Albanese, Jonathan O. ... Ithaca, NY
Albanese, Joseph ... Toms River, NJ
Albanese, Joseph P. ... New York, NY
Albanese, Joseph R. ... Garden City, NY
Albanese, Kathleen Witherspoon
Wilmette, IL
Albanese, Lee A. ... Newark, NJ
Albanese, Lionel ... Torrance, CA
Albanese, Mario M. ... Gloversville, NY
Albanese, Maryellen Black ... Goshen, NY
Albanese, Michael A. ... Cleveland, OH
Albanese, Michael M. ... Gloversville, NY
Albanese & Mulvey Law Firm ... Ithaca, NY
Albanese, Richard J. ... Powell, WY
Albanese, Sheryl A. ... Chicago, IL
Albanese, Toni J. ... Garden City, NY
Albanese, Vincent A. ... Garden City, NY
Albanese, Vincent M. ... Garden City, NY
Albanesi, Todd E. ... Dallas, TX
Albani, Suzanne B. ... Westport, CT
Albano, Alfred J., Jr. ... Hadley, MA
Albano, Amelia Ann ... Ventura, CA
Albano, Daniel J. ... New York, NY
Albano, Frank ... Elmwood Park, IL
Albano, Jonathan M. ... Boston, MA
Albano, Kenneth J. ... Springfield, MA
Albano, Laurie L. ... Fredonia, NY
Albano, Mark J. ... Springfield, MA
Albano, Matthew P. ... Summit, NJ
Albano, Michael G. ... New York, NY
Albano, Michael S. J. ... Independence, MO
Albano, Nancy ... Boston, MA
Albano, Nicholas, III ... Newark, NJ
Albano, Nicholas, Jr. ... Caldwell, NJ
Albano, Nicole Bearce ... Roseland, NJ
Albano, Patricia Ann ... Commack, NY
Albaral, Robert H. ... Dallas, TX
Albarian, Kathryn A. ... Glendale, CA
Albarrán, Luis R. ... Waukegan, IL
Albarrán, Luis R., P.C., Law Offices of
Waukegan, IL
Albaugh, Roger A. ... Peace Corps, Office of the General Counsel, GV
Albaum, Joseph H. ... Glendale, CA
Albaum, Mel ... Santa Monica, CA
Albaum, Shelley Lewis ... Los Angeles, CA
Albe, Joseph G. ... Metairie, LA
Albear, Frank M. ... West Palm Beach, FL
Albee, Craig W. ... Milwaukee, WI
Albee, David D. ... Chicago, IL
Albee, Pamela D. ... Ossipee, NH
Albee, Pamela R. ... Portland, OR
Albee, Scott B. ... Fort Myers, FL
Albee, Stephen Francis, P.A., Law Offices of
Orlando, FL
Alben, Alexander D. ... Bellevue, WA
Alben, Ellen B. ... Redmond, WA
Albenda, David ... New York, NY
Albenda, Louise S. ... Brooklyn, NY
Albenze, Donald P. ... North Olmsted, OH
Albenze, Nadine A. ... Cincinnati, OH
Alber, Alyson Suter ... Cleveland, OH
Alber, Christine ... Dallas, TX
Alber, John I. ... St. Louis, MO
Alber, Phillip G. ... Troy, MI
Alberdingkthijm, Yvette ... New York, NY
Alberg, James L. ... Washington, DC
Alberg, Mark D. ... Tomahawk, WI
Alberg, Steven C. ... Overland Park, KS
Albergate, Scott P. ... East Hanover, NJ
Alberger, Bill R., (P.C.) ... Washington, DC
Albergotti, Robert D. ... Dallas, TX
Albergotti, Samuel F. ... Anderson, SC
Albergts, Daniel J. ... Brighton, CO
Alberi & Alberi ... Mount Vernon, NY
Alberi, Albert D. ... Virginia Beach, VA
Alberi, Danielle Renee ... Mount Vernon, NY
Alberi, Dante J. ... Mount Vernon, NY
Alberi, Dante S. ... Mount Vernon, NY
Alberich, H. Glenn ... Boston, MA
Alberino, James J. ... Boston, MA
Alberque, Robert J. ... Ridgefield Park, NJ
Albers & Albers ... Columbus, OH
Albers, Bryan L. ... St. Petersburg, FL
Albers, Carla M. ... Colorado Springs, CO
Albers, Carsten ... New York, NY
Albers, Daniel P. ... Chicago, IL
Albers, Daniel T. ... Louisville, KY
Albers, David R. ... Bakersfield, CA
Albers, Dennis L. ... Grangeville, ID
Albers, Dennis M. ... Oakland, CA
Albers, Everett H. ... Des Moines, IA
Albers, Fern B. ... Minneapolis, MN
Albers, Ferris A. ... Longview, WA
Albers, James B. ... Columbus, OH
Albers, James S. ... Columbus, OH
Albers, Joanna A. ... Albia, IA
Albers, John A. ... Cleveland, OH
Albers, John B. ... Columbus, OH
Albers, John D. ... Springfield, IL
Albers, Kelly P. ... Las Cruces, NM
Albers, Larry V. ... Lincoln, NE
Albers, Larry V., P.C. ... Lincoln, NE
Albers, Leonard L. ... Austin, TX
Albers, Michael F. ... Dallas, TX
Albers, Rebecca J. ... Columbus, OH
Albers, Richard L. ... Nashville, TN
Albers, Rick M. ... Austin, TX
Albers, Ronald E. ... San Francisco, CA
Albers, Scott A. ... Great Falls, MT
Albers, Susan D. ... Austin, TX
Albers, Thomas N.
Federal Communications Commission, International Bureau, GV
Albers, Timothy John ... Memphis, TN
Albers, Virginia A. ... Omaha, NE
Albers, Wendy S. ... Los Angeles, CA
Alberse, Kristin R. ... Washington, DC
Alberstadt, Alexandra Kambouris
New York, NY
Alberstadt, Jonathan ... Erie, PA
Alberstadt, J. W., Jr. ... Erie, PA
Alberstadt, Kenneth G. ... New York, NY
Alberstadt, Samuel L. ... Los Angeles, CA
Alberstone, Dale S. ... Los Angeles, CA
Alberstone, Daniel ... Los Angeles, CA
Alberstone & Evangelatos ... Los Angeles, CA
Alberstone, Todd T. ... Los Angeles, CA
Albert, Alan D. ... Norfolk, VA
Albert and Albert ... Elk City, OK
Albert, Alfred G. ... Scottsdale, AZ
Albert, Amy H. ... New York, NY
Albert, Amy P. ... New York, NY
Albert, Andrew S. ... San Diego, CA
Albert, Arthur ... Brooklyn, NY
Albert, Barbara M. ... Louisville, KY
Albert, Barry ... Oklahoma City, OK
Albert, Benjamin S. ... Boston, MA
Albert, Bernard L. ... Pacific Palisades, CA
Albert, Bradley S.
Federal Trade Commission, Bureau of Competition, GV
Albert, Brandon S. ... Bronx, NY
Albert, Brian G. ... New York, NY
Albert, Brian K. ... McLean, VA
Albert, Brian M. ... Pittsburgh, PA
Albert, Bruce A. ... New York, NY
Albert, Bruce H. ... Arcadia, CA
Sherman Oaks, CA
Albert, Burton L. ... Roanoke, VA
Albert, Charles G. ... Chicago, IL
Albert, Charles T. ... Baltimore, MD
Albert, Craig A. ... Dallas, TX
Albert, Craig B. ... Marina Del Rey, CA
Albert, Craig J. ... Newark, NJ
Albert, Craig S. ... Chardon, OH
Albert, Daniel M. ... St. Albans, VT
Albert, David ... Greenwich, CT
Albert, David ... Bethesda, MD
Sterling, VA
Albert, David W. ... South Bend, IN
Albert, Edie R. ... Washington, DC
Albert, Edward H. ... Brooklyn, NY
Albert, Elaine H. ... Los Angeles, CA
Albert, Eli D. ... New York, NY
Albert, Elizabeth A. ... Chicago, IL
Albert, Eric ... Newark, NJ
Albert, Eric M. ... New York, NY
Albert, Eugene ... Tarrytown, NY
Albert, Eugene M. ... Lake Worth, FL
Albert, Eugene W. ... Fremont, CA
Albert, Fred ... Minneapolis, MN
Albert, Fredric I. ... Costa Mesa, CA
Albert, G. Peter, Jr. ... Chicago, IL
Albert, Gabrielle L. ... Los Angeles, CA
Albert, Garett J. ... New York, NY
Albert & Gefen, P.C. ... Bala Cynwyd, PA
Philadelphia, PA
Albert, Gregory W. ... Oklahoma City, OK
Albert, Harold B. ... Albuquerque, NM
Albert, Harold W. ... Bloomfield, CT
Albert, Harvey ... Chestnut Hill, MA
Albert, Haylee Alison ... Orlando, FL
Albert, Jack N. ... Boca Raton, FL
Albert, James A. ... Des Moines, IA
Albert, James J. ... San Diego, CA
Albert, Jed C. ... Melville, NY
Albert, Jeffrey B. ... Philadelphia, PA
Albert, Jeffrey P. ... Dayton, OH
Albert, Jeffrey W. ... Winter Park, FL
Albert, Jennifer A. ... Washington, DC
Albert, Joel B. ... Bala Cynwyd, PA
Albert, Joel M. ... Hackensack, NJ
Albert, John B. ... Oklahoma City, OK
Albert, John C. ... Columbus, OH
Albert, John C. ... Sun Prairie, WI
Albert, John D. ... Salem, OR
Albert, John J. ... Racine, WI
Albert, John R. ... Rockford, IL
Albert, Joseph G. ... Wilkes-Barre, PA
Albert, Joshua J. ... New York, NY
Albert, Jude, Boyd & Simanek, S.C.
Racine, WI
Albert, Judith
Federal Energy Regulatory Commission, Office of the General Counsel, GV
Albert, Judith D. ... New York, NY
Albert, Karl R. ... Fort Worth, TX
Albert, Kenneth M. ... Washington, DC
Albert, Larry J. ... Baltimore, MD
Albert, Lauren S. ... New York, NY
Albert, Lawrence S. ... New York, NY
Albert, Layne J. ... Houston, TX
Albert, Lee ... Philadelphia, PA
Albert, Lee A. ... Buffalo, NY
Albert & Levy, P.C. ... Ewing, NJ
Albert, Lorrie K. ... Pittsburgh, PA
Albert, Lynne Townsend ... Durham, NC
Albert, Marc E. ... Alexandria, VA
Albert, Marc S. ... New York, NY
Albert, Mark A. ... Los Angeles, CA
Albert, Mark S. ... Menlo Park, CA
Chicago, IL
Albert, Mark W. ... Elk City, OK
Albert, Martin J. ... Bridgeport, CT
Stamford, CT
Westport, CT
Albert, Martin W. ... Bronx, NY
Albert, Marvin A. ... Springfield, MA
Albert, Mary C. ... Washington, DC
Albert, Melvin F. ... Concord, MA
Natick, MA
Albert, Michael A. ... Boston, MA
Albert, Michael A. ... Charleston, WV
Albert, Michael R. ... Rock Falls, IL
Albert, Miriam R. ... New York, NY
Albert, Mitchell Edward
Kansas City, MO
Albert, Mitchell J. ... Santa Monica, CA
Albert, Myron ... Sun City Center, FL
Albert, Natalie ... Staten Island, NY
Albert, Neale M. ... New York, NY
Albert, Neely & Kuhlmann, L.L.P.
Fort Worth, TX
Albert, Neil L. ... Columbia, PA
Lancaster, PA
Lititz, PA
Quarryville, PA
Albert, Norman W. ... Cranford, NJ
Albert, Pamela Hutchens
Virginia Beach, VA
Albert, Paul Anthony ... Elk City, OK
Albert, Paul F. ... San Francisco, CA
Albert, Peter J. ... Mayfield Village, OH
Albert, Philip H. ... San Francisco, CA
Albert, Philip J. ... Ewing, NJ
Albert, Phyllis J. ... Philadelphia, PA
Albert, Richard F. ... New York, NY
Albert, Richard H. ... Allentown, PA
Albert, Richard M. ... Los Angeles, CA
Albert, Richard M. ... Pittsburgh, PA
Albert, Robert ... Scottsdale, AZ
Albert, Robert H., Sr. ... Columbus, OH
Albert, Ronald, Jr. ... Miami, FL
Albert, Ronald P. ... San Francisco, CA
Albert, Ronald P. ... Sausalito, CA
Albert, Rory Judd ... New York, NY
Albert, Ross A.
Securities and Exchange Commission, Office of the General Counsel, GV
Albert, Sara M. ... Dallas, TX
Albert, Scott E. ... Mount Joy, PA
Albert, Sheldon L. ... Philadelphia, PA
Albert, Shelley D. ... Hoboken, NJ
Albert, Sheridan ... Boca Raton, FL
Albert, Sidney W. ... Baltimore, MD
Albert, Stacey Stern ... Washington, DC
Albert, Stanley N. ... New York, NY
Albert, Steven W. ... Cleveland, OH
Albert, Stuart J. ... Barrington, IL
Albert, Theodor C. ... Costa Mesa, CA
Albert, Thomas L. ... Washington, DC
Albert, Tweet, Connolly & Hanna
Portland, OR
Salem, OR
Albert, Victor F. ... Oklahoma City, OK
Albert, Ward & Johnson, P.C.
Fairfield, CT
Greenwich, CT
Norwalk, CT
Stamford, CT
Albert, Weiland & Golden
Costa Mesa, CA
Albert, Whitehead & McGaugh, P.C.
Chicago, IL
Albert, William R. ... Boston, MA
Albert, Williard N. ... Knoxville, TN
Albert & Wohlfeil, LLP, Law Offices of
San Diego, CA
Alberta, Mark E. ... Washington, DC
Albertalli, Roy C. ... New York, NY
Albertazzi, Anthony V. ... Bend, OR
Albertazzi, Janice C. ... Woburn, MA
Albertelli, Alyssa ... Washington, DC
Albertelli & Israel, LLP ... Atlanta, GA
Marietta, GA
Albertelli, James E. ... Marietta, GA
Albert-Fritz, Mary M. ... Brighton, IL
Albert-Goldberg, Nancy ... Chicago, IL
Alberti, Carol B. ... Elkhart, IN
Alberti, Charles R. ... Williamstown, MA
Alberti, Daniel E. ... Redwood City, CA
Alberti, David ... Farmington Hills, MI
Alberti, John Curtis ... Akron, OH
Alberti, John Curtis, Co., L.P.A. ... Akron, OH
Alberti, Nancy Kalfayan ... Berkeley, CA
Alberti, Richard A. ... Monaca, PA
Alberti, Rita A. ... Mineola, NY
Alberti, William B. ... San Francisco, CA
Alberti, William T. ... Durham, NC
Albertine, Christine
Rancho Cucamonga, CA
Albertine, Michael O. ... Fort Lauderdale, FL
Albertini, Dana M. ... Washington, DC
Albertini & Darby ... Baltimore, MD
Albertini, Eugene J. ... Newport Beach, CA
Albertini & Gill ... Newport Beach, CA
Albertini, Guy M. ... Baltimore, MD
Albertini, Ross L. ... Erie, KS
Albertins, Peter R. ... Lansing, MI
Alberto, Lisa M. ... Milford, MA
Alberto, Maria H. ... New York, NY
Albertoli, Kerre Baker ... Lake Forest, CA
Alberton, Victoria ... New York, NY
Albertoni, Susan L. ... Merced, CA
Albertorio, Roberto ... Albuquerque, NM
Alberts, Barry S. ... Chicago, IL
Alberts, Celia A. ... Golden, CO
Alberts, Charlene E. ... Annapolis, MD
Alberts, Colin M. ... Washington, DC
Alberts, David W. ... New York, NY
Alberts, Dennis D. ... Troy, MI
Alberts, Harold ... New York, NY
Alberts, Harold ... Corpus Christi, TX
Alberts, Harry M. ... Hempstead, NY
Alberts, Jacqueline ... Princeton Junction, NJ
Alberts, Joel G. ... Minneapolis, MN
Alberts, John ... Palos Heights, IL
Alberts, John A. ... Oklahoma City, OK
Alberts, Joseph R. ... Indianapolis, IN
Alberts, Katherine A. ... Atlanta, GA
Alberts, L. Michael ... Orange, CA
Alberts, Mark R. ... Pittsburgh, PA
Alberts, Melanie Parks ... Rhinelander, WI
Alberts, Murray ... Waquoit, MA
Alberts, Rebecca M. ... New York, NY
Alberts, Reginald E. ... San Bernardino, CA
Alberts, Risa J. ... Baltimore, MD
Alberts, Robert W. ... Los Angeles, CA
Alberts, Ronald K. ... Los Angeles, CA
Alberts, Sam J. ... Washington, DC
Alberts, Thomas E. ... Avon, SD
Alberts, Thomas Gregory ... Miami Beach, FL
Alberts, Vivian A. ... Los Angeles, CA
Alberts, William ... San Antonio, TX
Alberts, William H. ... Austin, TX
Albertsen, Derek B. ... Santa Cruz, CA
Albertsen, Joanne Allar ... Amityville, NY
Albertsen-Murray, Tammy M.
San Francisco, CA
Albertson, Charles E. ... Seattle, WA
Albertson, Dan M. ... Tacoma, WA
Albertson, Fred W. ... Washington, DC
Albertson, Harold S. ... Charleston, WV
Albertson & Hoch ... Fort Worth, TX
Albertson, Howard R. ... Stillwater, MN
Albertson, James B., III ... Kansas City, MO
Albertson, Janet M. ... Hauppauge, NY
Albertson, Jeffrey G. ... Woodbury, NJ
Albertson and Jones ... Charleston, WV
Albertson, Joseph L., Jr.
New Rochelle, NY
Albertson, Mark David ... Seattle, WA
Albertson, Raymond B. ... Fort Worth, TX
Albertson, Scott D. ... Golden, CO
Albertson, Simmons & Albertson
New Rochelle, NY
Albertson, Steven L. ... West Orange, NJ
Albertson, Terry L. ... Washington, DC
Albertson, Thomas B. ... New Rochelle, NY
Albertson, Wanda M. ... Albany, KY
Albertson, Ward & McCaffrey
Woodbury, NJ
Albertson, William G.
Bloomfield Hills, MI
Alberty, Allison L. ... Chicago, IL
Alberty & Deveny ... Edina, MO
Alberty, Gregory Wayne ... Tulsa, OK
Alberty, John K. ... Columbus, OH
Alberty, Steven C. ... Eugene, OR
Alberty, William E. ... Edina, MO
Albery, Robert S. ... Englewood, CO
Albetta, Frank J. ... Santa Fe, NM
Albi, Fred A. ... Denver, CO
Albietz, Judith Kammins
Sacramento, CA
Albietz Law Corporation
Sacramento, CA
Albin, Alan Seth ... Rockville, MD
Albin, Arnold L. ... Palm Harbor, FL
Albin, Arthur M. ... Omaha, NE
Albin, Barbara ... Albuquerque, NM
Albin, Barry G. ... Kansas City, KS
Albin, Barry T. ... Woodbridge, NJ
Albin, David I. ... Stamford, CT
Albin, Gary K. ... Wichita, KS
Albin, John H. ... Lincoln, NE
Albin, Lee M. ... Garden City, NY
Albin, Mark D. ... Norfolk, NE
Albin, Maurice ... Chicago, IL
Albin, Ronald J. ... Norfolk, NE
Albin, Seth Andrew ... St. Louis, MO
Albin, Sheila A.
National Credit Union Administration, Office of General Counsel, GV
Albin, Thomas ... Groton, CT
Albin, William Todd ... Dallas, TX
Albina, Rene B. ... Jacksonville, FL
Albinder, Barbara Z. ... New York, NY
Albinder, Wayne M. ... New York, NY
Albinger, William J., Jr. ... Princeton, NJ
Albinger, William John ... New Haven, CT
Albini, Dianna L. ... San Francisco, CA
Albino, Arlene F. ... Montclair, NJ
Albino, Frank ... Los Angeles, CA
Albino, Robert C. ... Los Angeles, CA
Albin-Riley, Debra J. ... Los Angeles, CA
Albinson, Henry F. ... Roseland, NJ
Albinson & Welle ... Bloomfield, NJ
Albion, Donald L. ... Cape Coral, FL
Albirt, Harry ... New York, NY
Albis, Michael A. ... East Haven, CT
Albiston, Alfred ... Richmond, VA
Albiston, Debra Cooney
Virginia Beach, VA
Albiston, George T. ... Norfolk, VA
Albiston, Lucinda M. ... Knoxville, TN
Albizu, Luis A. Meléndez ... San Juan, PR
Albo, David B. ... Arlington, VA
Springfield, VA
Albo, James V. ... North Miami Beach, FL
Albo, Jeannette E. ... Miami, FL
Albo, Joe A. ... Globe, AZ
Albo, Joseph A. ... Seattle, WA

Albo & Oblon, L.L.P. ... Arlington, VA
Fairfax, VA
Richmond, VA
Springfield, VA
Albom, Barbara S. ... Lake Success, NY
Albom & Braffman ... Orange, CT
Albores, Richard
Environmental Protection Agency, Environmental Appeals Board, GV
Alborg, Thomas E. ... Walnut Creek, CA
Alborg, Veiluva & Cannata LLP
Walnut Creek, CA
Alborz, Mehrdad ... Glendale, CA
Albosta, Charlene Mary
Newport Beach, CA
Alboum, George J. ... Miami Beach, FL
Albov, Michael A. ... Monterey, CA
Albovias, Benjamin C. ... Chicago, IL
Albracht, James A. ... Los Angeles, CA
Albracht, Joselle M. ... Washington, DC
Albracht, S. J. ... Omaha, NE
Albrecht, Adrienne W. ... Kankakee, IL
Albrecht, Alan M. ... Wayzata, MN
Albrecht, Arthur R. ... San Francisco, CA
Albrecht & Barney ... Irvine, CA
Albrecht, Bonnie K. ... Los Angeles, CA
Albrecht, Cathleen Hainer ... Chicago, IL
Albrecht, Cathryn E. ... Chicago, IL
Albrecht, Cheryl ... Portland, OR
Albrecht, David F. ... Vero Beach, FL
Albrecht, David F., P.A. ... Vero Beach, FL
Albrecht, Donald H. ... Irvine, CA
Albrecht, Edmund C., Jr. ... St. Louis, MO
Albrecht, Franklin H. ... St. Louis, MO
Albrecht, Fred I. ... Akron, OH
Albrecht, Gary M. ... Hackensack, NJ
Albrecht, Geoffrey E. ... Columbus, OH
Albrecht, Gerald T. ... Tampa, FL
Albrecht, Gesine ... New York, NY
Albrecht, H. Peter ... Minneapolis, MN
Albrecht, Hugh G. ... Cedar Rapids, IA
Albrecht, James L. ... North Chicago, IL
Albrecht, James R. ... Minneapolis, MN
Albrecht, John J. ... Bellevue, WA
Albrecht, John M. ... Argonne, IL
Albrecht, John P. ... Carson City, NV
Albrecht, John W. ... Minneapolis, MN
Albrecht, Katherine B. ... Birmingham, MI
Albrecht, Kathleen L. ... Seattle, WA
Albrecht, Kelly ... Oroville, CA
Albrecht, Kenneth Allen ... Jackson, MO
Albrecht, Kenneth J. ... Spokane, WA
Albrecht, Kirk T. ... Canton, OH
Albrecht, Kirsten Wonder
Santa Monica, CA
Albrecht, Kristy L. ... Fargo, ND
Albrecht, Lawrence G. ... Milwaukee, WI
Albrecht, Maguire, Heffern & Gregg, P.C.
Buffalo, NY
Albrecht, Mark A. ... Worthington, OH
Albrecht, Martin K. ... Topeka, KS
Albrecht, Melissa M. ... Irvine, CA
Albrecht, Michael R. ... Washington, DC
St. Louis, MO
Albrecht, Nick ... Portland, OR
Albrecht, Peter L. ... Madison, WI
Albrecht, Peter Leffingwell ... Boston, MA
Albrecht, Ralph P. ... Washington, DC
Albrecht, Randall J. ... Jericho, NY
Albrecht, Raymond P. ... Houston, TX
Albrecht, Rebecca A. ... Phoenix, AZ
Albrecht, Richard F. ... Phoenix, AZ
Albrecht, Richard J. ... Irvine, CA
Albrecht, Richard L. ... Bridgeport, CT
Stamford, CT
Westport, CT
Albrecht, Richard R. ... Seattle, WA
Albrecht, Robert A. ... St. Paul, MN
Albrecht, Robert M. ... Hallock, MN
Albrecht, Scott M. ... Garnerville, NY
Albrecht, Scott R. ... Irvine, CA
Albrecht, Shari Feist ... Topeka, KS
Albrecht, Thomas W. ... Chicago, IL
Albrecht, Virginia S. ... Washington, DC
Albrecht, W. Kenneth ... Bridgeport, CT
Albrecht, Warren H., Jr.
Federal Energy Regulatory Commission, Office of the Administrative Law Judges, GV
Albrecht, Wayne D. ... Ellicott City, MD
Albrecht, William E. ... St. Louis, MO
Albrecht, William E., P.C. ... St. Louis, MO
Albrecht, William M., IV
North Conway, NH
Albrecht, William R. ... Belvidere, NJ
Albrecht & Zelman ... Bloomfield, CT
Albrechta and Coble ... Fremont, OH
Perrysburg, OH
Toledo, OH
Albrechta, Joseph F. ... Fremont, OH
Toledo, OH
Albrechta, Mark J. ... Tallahassee, FL
Albrechtson, Albert S., III ... Fresno, CA
Albregts and Albregts ... Las Vegas, NV
Albregts, Daniel J. ... Las Vegas, NV
Albregts, Jeffrey R. ... Las Vegas, NV
Albrektson, Kathleen B. ... Redlands, CA
Albren, Brett A. ... Natick, MA
Albrett, Adam ... San Jose, CA
Albright, Alan D. ... Austin, TX
Albright, Alan M. ... Los Angeles, CA
Albright, Alexandra Wilson ... Austin, TX
Albright, Alfred, Jr. ... Toledo, OH
Albright, Anne Korbel ... Rockville, MD
Albright, Audra A. ... Philadelphia, PA
Albright, Barbara F. ... Baton Rouge, LA
Albright, Benjamin Spence ... Ramseur, NC
Siler City, NC
Albright, Birge ... Cambridge, MA

Albright, Bradley & Albright, PLLC
Charleston, WV
Parkersburg, WV
Albright, Brian W.
Hot Springs National Park, AR
Hot Springs Village, AR
Albright, Brian W., P.A.
Hot Springs National Park, AR
Hot Springs Village, AR
Albright Brown & Goertemiller, LLC
Baltimore, MD
Elkton, MD
Albright, Bruce S.
Department of Housing and Urban Development, Office of General Counsel, GV
Albright, Carl W., Jr. ... Tuscaloosa, AL
Albright, Carole R. ... Greensboro, NC
Albright, Catherine E. ... Los Angeles, CA
Albright, Charles F. ... Huntington, WV
Albright, Charles L., Jr. ... Pittsburgh, PA
Albright, Charles R. ... Baton Rouge, LA
Albright, Christine L. ... Chicago, IL
Albright, Clifton W. ... Los Angeles, CA
Albright, Clyde B. ... Greensboro, NC
Albright, Cynthia H. ... Duluth, MN
Albright, D. Chris ... Las Vegas, NV
Albright, D. Erik ... Greensboro, NC
Albright, David F. ... Baltimore, MD
Albright, David F., Jr. ... Baltimore, MD
Albright, Deborah E. ... Indianapolis, IN
Albright, Dennis D. ... Red Bluff, CA
Albright, Dennis J. ... Houston, TX
Albright, Douglas E. ... Seattle, WA
Albright, G. Mark ... Las Vegas, NV
Albright, G. Vern ... Las Vegas, NV
Albright & Gaffney, Chartered
Anthony, KS
Albright, George F., Jr. ... McLean, VA
Albright, George J., III ... Ocala, FL
Albright, George O. ... Nashville, TN
Albright, H. Kirby ... Lansing, MI
Albright, Harold G. ... Reno, NV
Albright, Harry W., Jr. ... New York, NY
Albright, Jacquelyn E. ... St. Paul, MN
Albright, James E. ... Dallas, TX
Albright, Jeffrey H. ... Albuquerque, NM
Albright, Jere B. ... Humboldt, TN
Albright, J. L. ... London, KY
Kingsport, TN
Albright, Joan Mongada ... Woodbury, NY
Albright, John A. ... Indianapolis, IN
Albright, John J. ... Newmarket, NH
Albright, John M. ... Atlanta, GA
Albright, John M. ... Poplar Bluff, MO
Albright, John S. (IBA) ... New York, NY
Albright, Johnson S., II ... Rochester, NY
Albright, Joseph P. ... Charleston, WV
Parkersburg, WV
Albright, Joseph P., Jr. ... Charleston, WV
Parkersburg, WV
Albright, Justin W. ... Cedar Rapids, IA
Albright, Karen M. ... Raleigh, NC
Albright, Katharine M. ... San Francisco, CA
Albright, Kenneth F. ... Tulsa, OK
Albright, Kent H. ... Norristown, PA
Albright & Kittell, P.C. ... Tillamook, OR
Albright, L. Stephen ... Tarzana, CA
Albright, Linda C. ... North Plainfield, NJ
Albright, Lois A. ... Tillamook, OR
Albright, Lonnie G., III ... Greensboro, NC
Albright, M. Ashley ... Denver, CO
Albright, Mark Aaron
Fort Lauderdale, FL
Albright, Mark P. ... Allentown, PA
Albright, Mary Alison ... Camden, NJ
Albright, Mary M. ... Newark, OH
Albright, Merrilee G. ... Shreveport, LA
Albright, Nathan W. ... Las Vegas, NV
Albright, Paula A. ... Naperville, IL
Albright, Penrose L. ... Arlington, VA
Albright, R. Chris ... Chattanooga, TN
Albright, R. Stuart ... Greensboro, NC
Albright, Ralph N., Jr. ... Washington, DC
Albright & Rhodes, LLC ... Rockville, MD
Albright, Richard S. ... St. Clair Shores, MI
Albright, Robert D. ... Salem, IL
Albright, Robert E. ... Columbus, OH
Albright, Roger ... Dallas, TX
Albright, Ronald D. ... Anthony, KS
Albright & Rusher, A Professional Corporation ... Tulsa, OK
Albright, S. Alan ... Gastonia, NC
Albright & Smith ... Baton Rouge, LA
Albright, Stephen ... New York, NY
Albright, Stoddard, Warnick & Albright, A Professional Corporation ... Las Vegas, NV
Reno, NV
Albright, Sue ... Waterloo, IA
Albright & Sumner ... Gastonia, NC
Albright, Taylor Mead ... New York, NY
Albright, Terrill D. ... Indianapolis, IN
Albright, Thomas A. ... Austin, TX
Albright, Thomas E. ... New York, NY
Albright, Val J. ... Dallas, TX
Albright, W. Douglas ... Greensboro, NC
Albright, W. Joe ... Sulphur, OK
Albright, Warren H. ... Wilsonville, OR
Albright, William H. ... South Bend, IN
Albright, William J. ... Austin, TX
Albright, William J. ... Bountiful, UT
Albright, Yee & Schmit ... Los Angeles, CA
Albright-Jurs, Lisa ... Gastonia, NC
Albright-Jurs, Lisa ... Fremont, OH
Albrightson, Jon B. ... Minneapolis, MN
Albrigo, Mary R. ... Fairfax, VA
Albrinck, Daniel E ... Cincinnati, OH
Albrinck, J. Jeffrey ... Cincinnati, OH

Albrink, Anne Amy ... Santa Fe, NM
Albritton, A. Brian ... Tampa, FL
Albritton, A. Dale ... Macon, GA
Albritton, A. Dallas ... Tampa, FL
Albritton & Albritton ... Dallas, TX
Rockwall, TX
Albritton, Benjamin H. ... Mobile, AL
Albritton, Brian D. ... Bloomfield Hills, MI
Albritton, Douglas A. ... Chicago, IL
Albritton, Eric M. ... Longview, TX
Albritton, Gayle Miller ... Dallas, TX
Rockwall, TX
Albritton, Gregory L. ... Evergreen, AL
Albritton, John A. ... Dallas, TX
Rockwall, TX
Albritton, John N., Jr. ... Montgomery, AL
Albritton, Lawrence E. ... Marathon, FL
Albritton, Linda F. ... Palm Beach Gardens, FL
Albritton, Louis Marshall ... Nashville, TN
Albritton, Paul B. ... San Francisco, CA
Albritton, Richard H., Jr. ... Panama City, FL
Albritton & Sebring ... Tampa, FL
Albritton, Thomas B. ... Andalusia, AL
Albritton, W. Harold, III ... Montgomery, AL
Albritton, William Harold, IV
Andalusia, AL
Albrittons, Clifton, Alverson & Moody, P.C.
Andalusia, AL
Brewton, AL
Elba, AL
Enterprise, AL
Evergreen, AL
Geneva, AL
Greenville, AL
Monroeville, AL
Troy, AL
Albro, Joyce C. ... Treasury Department, Internal Revenue Service, GV
Albro, Thomas E. ... Charlottesville, VA
Albstein, Andrew W. ... New York, NY
Albstein, Iris A. ... New York, NY
Albu and Albu ... Kailua, HI
Albu, George M. ... Columbus, OH
Albu, Kathryn Momi ... Kailua, HI
Albu, Ronald A. ... Kailua, HI
Albu, Thomas P. ... Canton, OH
Albue, Bryan A. ... Phoenix, AZ
Albulov, James M., Jr. ... Detroit, MI
Album, Betsy L. ... Rochester, NY
Album, Gerald J. ... Rochester, NY
Album, Jerald L. ... Metairie, LA
Album, Michael J. ... New York, NY
Album, Stovall, Radecker & Giordano, L.L.C. ... Metairie, LA
New Orleans, LA
Albunio, Vincent A. ... New York, NY
Albuquerque, Debra Boxman
Atlantic City, NJ
Pleasantville, NJ
Albuquerque, Manuela ... Berkeley, CA
Albuquerque, Richard J.
Atlantic City, NJ
Alburn, Cary R., III ... Fort Collins, CO
Laramie, WY
Alburn, Cary R., III P.C.
Fort Collins, CO
Albury, Robert E., Jr. ... Miami, FL
Albus, Glenn L. ... McMinnville, OR
Albus, Kevin P. ... Troy, MI
Albus, Thomas Christian ... St. Louis, MO
Albuseiri, Mikhail ... Holland, MI
Alcabes, Andrea C. ... Salt Lake City, UT
Alcabes, Elisa A. ... New York, NY
Alcabes, Jaime A. ... Oakland, CA
Alcala, Brett A. ... Redwood City, CA
Alcala, Brian V. ... Cincinnati, OH
Alcala, Dick ... San Angelo, TX
Alcala, Elsa R. ... Houston, TX
Alcala, Marcelino ... San Juan, PR
Alcala, Susanna ... El Monte, CA
Alcalde, Luis M. ... Columbus, OH
Alcamo, Michael C. ... New York, NY
Alcantar and Elsesser ... Portland, OR
San Francisco, CA
Alcantar, Michael Peter
San Francisco, CA
Portland, OR
Alcantara Frame & Formby, Attorneys at Law, A Law Corporation ... San Diego, CA
Honolulu, HI
Alcantara, J. David ... Ventnor City, NJ
Alcantara, James W. ... San Diego, CA
Alcantara, Kimberly White ... Chicago, IL
Alcantara, Leonard F. ... Honolulu, HI
Alcantara, Oscar L. ... Chicago, IL
Alcaraz, Sharyn G. ... Los Angeles, CA
Alcaraz Emmanuelli, Mercedes
San Juan, PR
Alcarese, J. Shawn ... Towson, MD
Alcarese, Joseph P. ... Baltimore, MD
Alcaro, Frederick W. ... Kingston, PA
Alcasabas, Allison M. ... New York, NY
Alcauskas, Richard T. ... Davis, CA
Alcazar, Leah A. ... Fresno, CA
Alcazar, Roberto ... Trenton, NJ
Alch, Darren W. ... Houston, TX
Alch, Jeffrey S. ... Eden Prairie, MN
Alch, Thomas S. ... Beverly Hills, CA
Alcheck, Ronit Michelle
San Francisco, CA
Alcocer, Suzanne Wall ... Calhoun, GA
Alcock, J. Lee, Jr. ... Lafayette, LA
Houston, TX
Alcock, James L. ... Houma, LA
Alcock, Jane ... Atlanta, GA
Alcock, Margaret B. ... Santa Fe, NM
Alcock, Mary E. ... New York, NY
Alcock, Meredith G. ... San Diego, CA

Alcock, Richard L. ... Boston, MA
Alcock, Warren J., III ... Sarasota, FL
Alcoke, Amy K. ... Atlanta, GA
Alcorn, Daniel S. ... Galesburg, IL
Alcorn, Daniel S. ... Vienna, VA
Alcorn, Eli G. ... Northport, MI
Alcorn, Elizabeth A. ... New York, NY
Alcorn, Gregory C. ... San Diego, CA
Alcorn, John F. ... Harrisburg, PA
Alcorn, John R., Law Offices of
Irvine, CA
Chicago, IL
Alcorn, John R., Law Offices of
Newport Beach, CA
San Diego, CA
Alcorn, Lana Kay ... Birmingham, AL
Alcorn, Linda E. ... Washington, DC
Alcorn, Mary H. ... St. Paul, MN
Alcorn, Merritt K. ... Madison, IN
Alcorn, Patrick T. ... Louisville, KY
Alcorn, Richard A. ... Phoenix, AZ
Alcorn, Stephen R. ... Grand Prairie, TX
Alcorn, Timothy P. ... Noblesville, IN
Alcorn, Wendell B., Jr. ... Washington, DC
Alcorns, Carl A. ... Las Vegas, NV
Alcorta, Michael A. ... Santa Clara, CA
Alcott, Kenneth J. ... Richmond, VA
Alcott, Lee ... Syracuse, NY
Alcott, Mark D. ... Bowling Green, KY
Alcott, Mark H. ... New York, NY
Alcott, Shawn Rosso ... Bowling Green, KY
Alcott, Stephen B. ... Weymouth, MA
Alcott, Tim E. ... Houston, TX
Alcover-Acosta, César T. ... San Juan, PR
Alcover-Garcia, Jose B. ... San Juan, PR
Alcox, Patrick J. ... Cleveland, OH
Alcozer, Manuel ... Killeen, TX
Alcser, Marc G. ... Newport Beach, CA
Alcumbrac, Marta A. ... Los Angeles, CA
Ald, L. Sterling ... Flushing, NY
Ald, Steven Michael ... Delevan, NY
Aldad, Lior ... New York, NY
Aldana, Benes
Department of Transportation, U. S. Coast Guard, GV
Aldana, Michael ... Milwaukee, WI
Aldana-Pindell, Raquel E. ... Washington, DC
Aldape, Alina A.C.E. ... Campbell, CA
Aldape, Bernardo J., Jr. ... South Houston, TX
Aldarelli, Carla P. ... Ocean Township, NJ
Aldarondo Girald, Godwin ... San Juan, PR
Aldarondo-Girald, Law Offices
San Juan, PR
Aldave, Barbara Bader ... San Antonio, TX
Alday, Cara J. ... Chattanooga, TN
Aldeborgh, Erik H., II ... Boston, MA
Aldeen, D. Douglas ... Urbana, IL
Aldeen, Donald R. ... Champaign, IL
Aldemeyer, Barrett ... Treasury Department, Office of the Comptroller of the Currency, GV
Alden, Alice S. ... Norristown, PA
Alden, Amy L. ... Oklahoma City, OK
Alden, Anne R.
National Labor Relations Board, Office of Board Members, GV
Alden Aronovsky & Sax LLP
San Francisco, CA
Alden, Cameron ... Bay Shore, NY
Alden, Charles F., III
Oklahoma City, OK
Alden & Clem ... Indianapolis, IN
Alden, David B. ... Cleveland, OH
Alden, David M. ... Sunnyvale, CA
Alden, David W. ... San Francisco, CA
Alden, Ellis J. ... Woodside, CA
Alden, Eric M. ... Torrington, WY
Wheatland, WY
Alden, Erick R. ... Columbus, OH
Alden, Jeffrey Michael ... Portland, OR
Alden, John F., III ... Minneapolis, MN
Alden, John R. ... Northbrook, IL
Alden, John T., Jr. ... Indianapolis, IN
Alden, John W. ... Los Angeles, CA
Alden, John W. ... Atlanta, GA
Alden, John W. (Jack), Jr.
Los Angeles, CA
Alden, Jonathan H. ... Tallahassee, FL
Alden, Kristin D. ... Washington, DC
Alden, Leslie ... Los Angeles, CA
Alden, Leslie M. ... Fairfax, VA
Alden, Mary C. ... Glendale, CA
Alden, Michael H. ... St. Petersburg, FL
Alden, Michael P. ... Oakland, CA
Alden, Neil C. ... Phoenix, AZ
Alden, Nick Argaman ... Beverly Hills, CA
Alden, Philip G. ... Minneapolis, MN
Alden, Phyllis ... Cleveland, OH
Alden, Randolph W. ... Beckley, WV
Alden, Richard F. ... Los Angeles, CA
Alden, Richard H. ... Bristol, CT
Alden, Robert C. ... Austin, TX
Alden, Robert F. ... Indianapolis, IN
Alden, Sheri J. ... Boca Raton, FL
Alden, Steven M. ... New York, NY
Alden, Timothy J. ... Glens Falls, NY
Alden, Tricia Troy ... New York, NY
Alden, William D. ... Somerville, NJ
Aldenberg, Deanna Davis ... Waltham, MA
Alder, C. Michael ... Los Angeles, CA
Alder, Catherine A. ... Indianapolis, IN
Alder, Catherine Jane, P.C.
Fort Worth, TX
Alder, Eugene M. ... Aspen, CO
Alder, Jonathan L. ... Pittsburgh, PA
Alder, Matthias ... Palo Alto, CA
Alder, Nancy Furse ... Los Angeles, CA
Alder, Nathan D. ... Salt Lake City, UT

Alder, Steven F. ... Salt Lake City, UT
Alder, Wayne M. ... Boca Raton, FL
Alderdice, Karen ... Paducah, KY
Alderete, David J. ... Albuquerque, NM
Alderete, Eric M. ... Los Angeles, CA
Alderete-Medjo, Cynthia L. ... Seattle, WA
Alderfer, Kenneth D. ... Washington, DC
Alderfer, Mark S. ... Indianapolis, IN
Alderfer, R. Brent ... Littleton, CO
Alderman & Ahlbrand, P.A. ... Fort Myers, FL
Alderman & Alderman ... Hartford, CT
Alderman and Alderman ... Syracuse, NY
Utica, NY
Watertown, NY
Alderman, Amy L. ... Window Rock, AZ
Alderman, Cyna ... New York, NY
Alderman, Daniel S. ... Los Angeles, CA
Alderman, Edward B. ... Syracuse, NY
Alderman, Elliott Carl ... Washington, DC
Alderman, Eric M. ... Syracuse, NY
Alderman, Eric R. ... Armonk, NY
Alderman, Frank C., III ... Fort Myers, FL
Alderman, Heather Higgins ... Chicago, IL
Alderman, Holly Harris ... Chapel Hill, NC
Alderman, Howard L., Jr. ... Towson, MD
Alderman, James E. ... Okeechobee, FL
Alderman, Jody Harper ... Denver, CO
Alderman, John O. ... Minneapolis, MN
Alderman, John R. ... Richmond, VA
Alderman, Jonathan A. ... Macon, GA
Alderman, Judith Levy ... Syracuse, NY
Alderman, Karla H. ... Eugene, OR
Alderman, Kate K. ... Lafayette, CA
Alderman, Kaye M. ... Lufkin, TX
Alderman, Kent B. ... Salt Lake City, UT
Alderman, Larry D. ... Elyria, OH
Alderman, Leigh Ann ... San Francisco, CA
Alderman, Linda Wiesenthal
Hartford, CT
Alderman, Mark L. ... Philadelphia, PA
Alderman, Michael J. ... Tallahassee, FL
Alderman, Myles H., Jr. ... Hartford, CT
Alderman, Richard B. ... Syracuse, NY
Alderman, Richard C. ... Marietta, GA
Alderman, Richard M. ... Houston, TX
Alderman, Robert E., Jr. ... Agua Dulce, CA
Alderman, Robert E., Jr., Prof. Law Corp.
Agua Dulce, CA
Alderman, Robert, Jr. ... Lufkin, TX
Alderman, Robert L. ... Spencer, IA
Alderman, Samuel G., III ... Macon, GA
Alderman, Silvia Morell ... Tallahassee, FL
Alderman, Stephen B. ... West Haven, CT
Alderman, Stephen M. ... Chicago, IL
Alderman, Steven B. ... Syracuse, NY
Alderman, Taddeo & Associates, LLP
Syracuse, NY
Alderman, Theresa J. ... Lansing, MI
Alderman, William F. ... San Francisco, CA
Alderoty, Stuart ... Newark, NJ
Alderson, Alan F. ... Topeka, KS
Alderson, Alderson, Weiler, Conklin, Burghart & Crow, L.L.C. ... Topeka, KS
Alderson, Edwin B., Jr. ... El Dorado, AR
Alderson, Frank R. ... Eugene, OR
Alderson, Gillian Louise ... St. Johns, MI
Alderson, Ira R., Jr. ... San Francisco, CA
Alderson, J. Chris ... Covington, VA
Alderson, John T., Jr. ... Jacksonville, FL
Alderson, Lori E. ... Houston, TX
Alderson, Michael L. ... Richmond, CA
Alderson, Ondov, Leonard, Sween & Rizzi, P.A. ... Austin, MN
Alderson, Richard L. ... Oakland, CA
Alderson, Robert A. ... Cumberland, MD
Alderson, Robert E. ... Jackson, TN
Alderson, Robert E., Jr. ... New York, NY
Alderson, Stanley E., II
Department of Justice, Civil Division, GV
Alderson, Thomas C., III ... Little Rock, AR
Alderson, Thomas G. ... Banner Elk, NC
Alderson, Vettra G. ... Oxford, MS
Alderson, W. David ... Portland, OR
Alderson, W. Robert, Jr. ... Topeka, KS
Alderson, William F., Jr. ... West Bend, WI
Alderton, Donald L. ... Portland, OR
Alderton, Donald L., P.C. ... Portland, OR
Alderton, Scott W. ... Los Angeles, CA
Alderton, Steven M.
General Services Administration, Office of Inspector General, GV
Alderton, William P. ... Salida, CO
Alderucci, Dean ... Stamford, CT
Alderuccio, Mark J. ... Naples, FL
Aldhizer, George R., Jr.
Harrisonburg, VA
Aldi, Gerald R. ... Bellmawr, NJ
Aldige, Hugh D. ... Metairie, LA
Aldinger, Drew ... Philadelphia, PA
Aldinger, Robert R. ... Norfolk, VA
Aldir-Hernandez, Laura ... Punta Gorda, FL
Aldisert, Gregory J. ... Los Angeles, CA
Aldisert, Robert L. ... Portland, OR
Aldisert, Ruggero J. ... Santa Barbara, CA
Aldock, John D. ... Washington, DC
Aldorfer, Amy B. ... Los Angeles, CA
Aldoroty, Lisa S. ... New York, NY
Aldouby, Sharon L. ... Baltimore, MD
Aldous, Alan K. ... Hillsboro, OR
Aldous, Charla G. ... Sherman, TX
Aldous, E. A. ... Freeport, TX
Aldous, Jeffrey N. ... Provo, UT
Aldous, Kathleen ... Salt Lake City, UT
Aldous, Steven E. ... Austin, TX
Aldous, Thomas W., Jr.
Charlottesville, VA
Aldover, Ernesto F. ... Los Angeles, CA
Aldred, Angelica M. ... Milwaukee, WI
Aldred, David B. ... Maitland, FL
Aldred, Jo E. ... Durham, NC
Aldred, Joseph A., Jr. ... Brunswick, ME
Aldred, William L., Jr. ... Clarksville, TN
Aldredge, Kristin C. ... Raleigh, NC
Aldredge, Sawnie R. ... Nashville, TN
Aldrete, Cristobal P. ... United States Senate, Senatorial Assistants, GV
Aldrich & Aldrich ... Westport, CT
Aldrich, Alexander ... Albany, NY
Aldrich, Ann ... Cleveland, OH
Aldrich & Bonnefin, P.L.C. ... Irvine, CA
Aldrich, Brad B. ... Bingham Farms, MI
Aldrich, C. Phillip ... Larned, KS
Aldrich, Charles J. ... Elyria, OH
Aldrich, Christopher R. ... Hempstead, NY
Aldrich, David F. ... Norway, ME
Aldrich, David H. ... Lansing, MI
Aldrich, Dean E. ... Portland, OR
Aldrich, Debra C. ... Wilmington, DE
Aldrich, Don C. ... Minneapolis, MN
Aldrich, Frank C., III ... Riverside, CA
Aldrich, Frederick G.
Grand Junction, CO
Aldrich, George D. ... Beverly, MA
Aldrich, George H. ... Department of State, Foreign Service Officers (Overseas), GV
Aldrich, James F. ... Kansas City, MO
Aldrich, James G. ... Troy, MI
Aldrich, James H. ... San Diego, CA
Aldrich, Janet G. ... Silver Spring, MD
Aldrich, Jennifer J. ... Columbia, SC
Aldrich, Jerome K. ... Angleton, TX
Aldrich, John H. ... Westport, CT
Aldrich, John R. ... Albany, NY
Aldrich, Jose M. ... Miami, FL
Aldrich, Kathryn M. ... Kenosha, WI
Aldrich, Kenneth C. ... Pacific Palisades, CA
Aldrich, Lauri K. ... Chicago, IL
Aldrich, Lawrence J. ... Tucson, AZ
Aldrich, Lovell W. ... Sugar Land, TX
Aldrich, Lovell W., and Associates, A Prof. Legal Corp. ... Sugar Land, TX
Aldrich, Marcy Levine ... Miami, FL
Aldrich, Mark Bradley
Santa Monica, CA
Aldrich, Mark E. ... Irvine, CA
Aldrich, Misty H. ... Columbus, OH
Aldrich, Nancy ... Westport, CT
Aldrich, Nelson, Weight & Esplin
Provo, UT
Aldrich, Peter J. ... North Palm Beach, FL
Aldrich, Peter J., P.A.
North Palm Beach, FL
Aldrich, Ray J. ... Rapid City, SD
Aldrich, Richard K. ... Billings, MT
Aldrich, Richard O. ... Wellesley, MA
Aldrich, Richard S., Jr. ... New York, NY
Aldrich, Robert E., Jr. ... Fort Worth, TX
Aldrich, Robert F. ... Washington, DC
Aldrich, Robert W. ... Department of Labor, Office of the Solicitor, GV
Aldrich, Roland F. ... Mackinac Island, MI
Aldrich, Theodore F. ... Orange, CA
Aldrich, Thomas A. ... Cleveland, OH
Aldrich, Thomas L. ... Deerfield, IL
Aldrich, Thomas P., III
Cleveland Heights, OH
Aldrich, Vaughn N. ... Hogansburg, NY
Aldrich, Virginia ... Boston, MA
Aldrich, Warren E. ... Woodbridge, VA
Aldrich, William C. ... Hartford, CT
Aldrich, William P. ... Yorba Linda, CA
Aldridge, Anna C. ... Washington, DC
Aldridge, Arthur ... Thousand Oaks, CA
Aldridge, Aycock & Actkinson, L.L.P.
Farwell, TX
Aldridge, Bryan W. ... Trophy Club, TX
Aldridge, Bryant T., Jr. ... High Point, NC
Aldridge, Christopher S. ... New York, NY
Aldridge, Dan A., Jr. ... Atlanta, GA
Aldridge, Daniel F. ... Huntsville, AL
Aldridge, David E. ... Frederick, MD
Aldridge, Elizabeth E. ... Richmond, VA
Aldridge, Fred C., Jr. ... Wayne, PA
Aldridge, Gary L. ... Birmingham, AL
Aldridge, George Irvin ... Manteo, NC
Aldridge & Hall ... Kansas City, MO
Aldridge, Ingrid Ortiz ... Memphis, TN
Aldridge, Jim ... Lubbock, TX
Aldridge, John E. ... Jackson, MS
Aldridge, John G. ... Atlanta, GA
Aldridge, John G., Jr. ... Atlanta, GA
Aldridge, John S. ... Austin, TX
Aldridge, Joy ... New York, NY
Aldridge, Katherine May ... Milltown, NJ
Aldridge, Kathryn McCoy ... Savannah, GA
Aldridge, Kris Williams ... Philadelphia, PA
Aldridge Law Firm, P.C. ... Atlanta, GA
Aldridge, Leah S. ... Atlanta, GA
Aldridge, Lyle D. ... Tucson, AZ
Aldridge, Melanie J. ... Fresno, CA
Aldridge, Millard F. ... Kansas City, MO
Aldridge, Pamela P. ... San Diego, CA
Aldridge, Phillip E. ... Miami, FL
Aldridge, R. Scott ... Media, PA
Aldridge, Richard B. ... Philadelphia, PA
Aldridge, Robert G. ... Jacksonville, FL
Aldridge, Robert L. ... Boise, ID
Aldridge, Robert L., Chartered ... Boise, ID
Aldridge, Saunders ... Savannah, GA
Aldridge, Seawell & Khoury
Kill Devil Hills, NC
Manteo, NC
Aldridge, Shayne L. ... Decatur, IL
Aldridge, Steven K. ... Huntsville, AL
Aldridge, Susan L. ... Denver, CO
Aldridge, Susan M. ... Fairfax, VA
Aldridge, Thomas G.
Department of Commerce, Office of the General Counsel, GV
Aldridge, Thomas V., Jr. ... Whiteville, NC
Aldridge, Timothy D. ... Levittown, NY
Aldridge, Vincent C. ... Lutz, FL
Aldridge, W. Joseph ... Memphis, TN
Aldridge, W. Sidney ... Raleigh, NC
Aldridge, William D. ... Englewood, CO
Katy, TX
Aldridge, William F. ... Albuquerque, NM
Aldrine, Fritz J., II ... Dallas, TX
Aldstadt, Stacey Ryn ... San Bernardino, CA
Aldworth, John C. ... Clinton, AR
Marshall, AR
Ale, Eleasalo V. ... Minneapolis, MN
Aleccia, James P. ... Long Beach, CA
Aledort, Alan R. ... Jericho, NY
Aledort, Eric S. ... Burbank, CA
Aledort, Mark R. ... Hempstead, NY
Alef, Arthur ... Pasadena, CA
Alef, Daniel ... Solvang, CA
Alef, Richard J. ... Bingham Farms, MI
Alegi, August P. ... Lanham, MD
White Plains, NY
Alegria, Annabell ... Brownsville, TX
Alegria, Anselmo A. ... Kew Gardens, NY
Alegria, Cesar V., Jr. ... San Francisco, CA
Alegria, David Orlando ... Topeka, KS
Alegria, Jose E. ... San Juan, PR
Alegria, Joseph John, II ... Boise, ID
Aleinikoff, Eugene N. ... Ancram, NY
Aleixo, Margaret ... Taunton, MA
Aleixo & Murray, P.C. ... Taunton, MA
Aleixo, Theodore J., Jr. ... Taunton, MA
Alejandro, Leonel ... Brownsville, TX
Alejandro, Leonel, P.C. ... Brownsville, TX
Alejandro, Mary K. ... Department of Labor, Office of the Solicitor, GV
Alejandro, Nitza I. Quinones
Philadelphia, PA
Alekman, Ryan E. ... Springfield, MA
Alekman, Susan P. ... Boston, MA
Aleksander, Alan ... Santa Barbara, CA
Aleksy, Richard E. ... Chicago, IL
Aleli, John ... Atlantic City, NJ
Pleasantville, NJ
Aleman, Alison Elle ... Sacramento, CA
Alemán, George
National Labor Relations Board, Division of Administrative Law Judges, GV
Aleman, Kerry A. ... Cambridge, MA
Aleman, Narciso L. ... Milwaukee, WI
Aleman, Raymundo ... San Antonio, TX
Aleman, Steven ... Department of Education, Office for Civil Rights, GV
Aleman-Fernandez, Olga ... Miami, FL
Alemany, Joaquin A. ... Miami, FL
Alemany, Joaquin F ... Bronx, NY
Alembik, Aaron I. ... Atlanta, GA
Alembik & Alembik ... Atlanta, GA
Alembik, Fine & Callner, P.A.
Atlanta, GA
Decatur, GA
Lawrenceville, GA
Marietta, GA
Alembik, Gary M. ... Atlanta, GA
Alembik, Judith M. ... Atlanta, GA
Alembik, Julius ... Atlanta, GA
Alembik, Richard S. ... Atlanta, GA
Alembik, Richard S., P.C. ... Atlanta, GA
Alemifar, Nancy J. ... Kansas City, MO
Alen, Joseph S. ... Danvers, MA
Alen, Katherine T. ... Boston, MA
Alena, Jeffery L. ... Kansas City, MO
Alence, Richard C. ... White Plains, NY
Alencewicz, Robert G. ... Florham Park, NJ
Alenick, Suzanne E. ... New York, NY
Alenik & Associates ... Houston, TX
Alenik, Dennis R. ... Houston, TX
Alenstein, Ronald H. ... New York, NY
Alerding, Dennis Charles ... Covington, KY
Alerding, F. Dennis ... Covington, KY
Alerding, Kevin ... Indianapolis, IN
Alerding, Michael J. ... Indianapolis, IN
Alerding, Steven A. ... Washington, DC
Alers, Jorge E. ... Washington, DC
Alers, Miriam S. ... Bronx, NY
Alerte, Frank A. ... New York, NY
Alerte, Karen Green ... Somerville, NJ
Ales, Barney C. ... Las Vegas, NV
Ales, John F. ... Baton Rouge, LA
Alesandro, John A. ... Rockville Centre, NY
Alesevich, Walter C.
United States Postal Service, Law Department, GV
Aleshire, David A. ... Charleston, WV
Aleshire, David J. ... Costa Mesa, CA
Aleshire, Gregory W. ... Springfield, MO
Alesi, Barbara Shaheen ... Melville, NY
Mineola, NY
Alesi, Louis M. ... Hampton Bays, NY
Alesi, Susan E.
Executive Office Of The President, Office of Management and Budget, GV
Alesi, William V. ... Carle Place, NY
Alesia, Brian J. ... Chicago, IL
Alesia, James H. ... Chicago, IL
Alesia, Michael J. ... Chicago, IL
Alesio, A. Michael ... Lincoln, NE
Alesio, Lori Ann ... Tarrytown, NY
Alessandra, Anita M. ... Dallas, TX
Alessandra, M. Nan ... New Orleans, LA
Alessandria, Peter J. ... Beverly Hills, CA
Alessandro & Alessandro, P.C. ... Bronx, NY
Alessandro, Christopher J.
Worcester, MA
Alessandro, Francis M. ... Bronx, NY
Alessandro, Mary Ellen ... Portland, OR
Alessandro, Nicholas R. ... Bronx, NY
Alessandroni, Eugene V. ... Philadelphia, PA
Alessandroni, John B. ... Philadelphia, PA
Alessandroni, Joseph, Jr. ... Philadelphia, PA
Alessandroni, Paul ... Punta Gorda, FL
Alessandroni, Venan J. ... New York, NY
Alessi, Anthony P. ... Marshfield, MA
Alessi, Deborah Jean ... St. Charles, MO
Alessi, Dennis A. ... York, PA
Alessi, Dennis J. ... Livingston, NJ
Alessi, Diane L. ... Salem, OR
Alessi, Donald A. ... Buffalo, NY
Alessi, Holly P. ... Bellaire, OH
Alessi, Joseph H. ... Fairfield, NJ
Alessi, Marcia Ann Bengry
Los Angeles, CA
Alessi, Michelle ... New York, NY
Alessi, Robert A. ... New York, NY
Alessi, Robert J. ... Albany, NY
New York, NY
Alessi, Salvatore A. ... Barrington, NJ
Alessi, Saundra D. ... Baton Rouge, LA
Alessio, George P., Jr. ... Syracuse, NY
Alessio, John Dominick ... San Diego, CA
Alessio, Kirsten L. ... Dallas, TX
Alessio, Lawrence R. ... San Diego, CA
Alessio, Michael F. ... Dallas, TX
Alessio, Peter C. ... Pittsfield, MA
Alesso, Richard A. ... Long Beach, CA
Aletta, John ... East Hartford, CT
Aletto, Mark V. ... Pittsburgh, PA
Alevizatos, Dorothy C. ... New York, NY
Alevizon, Dennis M. ... Santa Ana, CA
Alevizos and Alevizos ... Cambridge, MA
Alevizos, Susan B. ... Cambridge, MA
Alevizos, Theodore G. ... Cambridge, MA
Alevizos, Thomas J. ... Michigan City, IN
Alevy, Stacy S. ... New York, NY
Alewelt, Edward J. ... Springfield, IL
Alex, Andrew R. ... Phoenix, AZ
Alex & Brinkis ... West Covina, CA
Alex, Donald M. ... Corpus Christi, TX
Alex, Glenn C. ... Berkeley, CA
Alex, Howard M. ... Pittsburgh, PA
Alex, Jack ... West Covina, CA
Alex, James G. ... Chicago, IL
Alex, James G. ... Chicago, IL
Alex, John L. ... Chicago, IL
Alex, Ken ... Oakland, CA
Alex, Marie F. ... Sherman Oaks, CA
Alex, Spero M. ... Dayton, OH
Alex, Steven Michael ... LaBelle, FL
Alexa, William E. ... Valparaiso, IN
Alexander, A. Ann ... Dallas, TX
Alexander, A. Minnie ... Minneapolis, MN
Alexander, A. Nicholas ... Dallas, TX
Alexander, Aaron B. ... Charleston, WV
Alexander, Abner ... Winston-Salem, NC
Alexander, Adam H. ... Dallas, TX
Alexander, Adam S. ... Farmington Hills, MI
Alexander, Adrienne B. ... New York, NY
Alexander, A.G. "Alec", III ... Lafayette, LA
Alexander, Alan M., Jr. ... Athens, GA
Alexander, Alex Thomas ... New York, NY
Alexander & Alexander ... Santa Barbara, CA
Alexander & Alexander ... Chicago, IL
Alexander, Alexander & Alexander
Hastings, NE
Alexander, Alexander & Associates
Chicago, IL
Alexander, Alice D. ... Boston, MA
Alexander, Allan L. ... Los Angeles, CA
Alexander, Amanda Grace
Westlake Village, CA
Alexander and Amos ... Lexington, KY
Alexander, Amy P. ... Portland, OR
Alexander, Andrea ... Boston, MA
Alexander, Andrew C. ... Cleveland, OH
Alexander, Andrew N., III ... Greenville, MS
Alexander & Angelas, P.C. ... Southfield, MI
Alexander, Ann ... Newark, NJ
Alexander, Anthony E. ... Los Angeles, CA
Alexander, Anthony J. ... Akron, OH
Alexander, Aponte & Marks ... New York, NY
Alexander, Archibald S. ... Bozeman, MT
Alexander, Arnold W. ... Swampscott, MA
Alexander, Arthur B. ... New York, NY
Alexander, Arthur L. ... Washington, NJ
Alexander, Arthur Lawrence ... New York, NY
Alexander, Arthur Lawrence, P.C.
New York, NY
Alexander, Ash, Schwartz & Cohen, P.C.
New York, NY
Alexander & Associates ... Washington, DC
Alexander & Associates ... Atlanta, GA
Alexander & Associates, Attorneys at Law, P.S.
Seattle, WA
Alexander & Associates, Ltd. ... Chicago, IL
Alexander, Athena E. ... New York, NY
Alexander, Audrey L. ... Palm Desert, CA
Alexander, B. Lynn ... Lincoln, NE
Alexander, Barbara R. ... Augusta, ME
Alexander, Barry D. ... Washington, DC
Alexander, Barry S. ... New York, NY
Alexander & Bartlett ... Clinton, NJ
Flemington, NJ
Somerville, NJ
Alexander, Baucus, Taleff & Paul, P.C.
Great Falls, MT
Alexander, Bearden, Hairston & Marks, LLP
Washington, DC
Silver Spring, MD
Alexander, Benjamin M. ... Boston, MA
Alexander, Beverly Z. ... San Francisco, CA
Alexander, Bevin R., Jr. ... Lynchburg, VA
Alexander, Bill G. ... Odessa, TX

Alexander, Bill G., A Professional Corporation
Odessa, TX
Alexander, Bradley D. .... Westmont, IL
Alexander, Bramwell H. .... Brooklyn, NY
Alexander, Bret Ellen
Bainbridge Island, WA
Alexander, Brian E. .... Chicago, IL
Alexander, Brian J. .... New York, NY
Alexander, Brian L. .... Edina, MN
Alexander, Brooks .... Louisville, KY
Alexander & Brown .... Kannapolis, NC
Alexander, Bruce .... Miami, FL
Alexander, Bruce .... Elyria, OH
Alexander, Bruce Bowman .... Sacramento, CA
Alexander, Bruce E. .... Frederick, MD
Alexander, Bruce G.
West Palm Beach, FL
Alexander, Bud R. .... McHenry, IL
Alexander, C. Edward, II .... Raleigh, NC
Alexander, C. Stephen .... Birmingham, AL
Alexander, C. Stephen, P.C.
Birmingham, AL
Alexander, Carla Jean .... Kearney, NE
Alexander, Carol A. .... Fairfax, VA
Alexander & Catalano, LLP .... Syracuse, NY
Alexander, Catherine H. .... Atlanta, GA
Alexander, Catherine Pape .... Bettendorf, IA
Alexander, Cecily Chester .... Chicago, IL
Alexander, Charles E. .... Chicago, IL
Alexander, Charles J. .... Bethesda, MD
Alexander, Charles J., II
Winston-Salem, NC
Alexander, Charles M. .... Stamford, CT
Alexander, Charles P. .... Rockford, IL
Alexander, Charles R. .... Clarion, PA
Alexander, Chip .... Muncie, IN
Alexander, Choi .... Washington, DC
Alexander, Christine A. .... Albany, NY
Alexander, Christine M. .... San Antonio, TX
Alexander, Christopher M.
San Diego, CA
Alexander, Christopher S. .... Monroe, MI
Alexander, Clark .... Santa Barbara, CA
Alexander & Cleaver, P.A.
Washington, DC
Annapolis, MD
Baltimore, MD
Fort Washington, MD
La Plata, MD
Upper Marlboro, MD
Waldorf, MD
Alexandria, VA
Alexander, Clifford E. .... Roswell, GA
Alexander, Clifford J. .... Washington, DC
Alexander, Clifford L., Jr. .... Washington, DC
Alexander, Constance J. .... Roseland, NJ
Alexander, Constantine .... Boston, MA
Alexander, Corder, Plunk & Baker, P.C.
Athens, AL
Alexander & Crabtree, P.C. .... Denver, CO
Alexander, Craig A. .... Birmingham, AL
Alexander, Craig A. .... Chevy Chase, MD
Alexander, Craig C. .... Newport Beach, CA
Alexander, Craig W. .... West Orange, NJ
Alexander, Cruzan .... North Oaks, MN
Alexander, Cynthia .... Frisco, TX
Sherman, TX
Alexander, Cynthia L.
Department of Justice, Civil Division, GV
Alexander, D. Wilkes .... Brownsville, TX
Alexander, Damien V. .... Washington, DC
Alexander, Daniel .... Palo Alto, CA
Alexander, Daniel J. .... Newport Beach, CA
Alexander, Daniel R. .... Fayetteville, AR
Alexander, Daniel S. .... Chicago, IL
Alexander, Daniel W. .... Fort Collins, CO
Alexander, Darryl F. .... Detroit, MI
Alexander, David E. .... Washington, DC
Alexander, David E. .... Pocatello, ID
Alexander, David E. .... New York, NY
Alexander, David F. .... Mesa, AZ
Alexander, David H. .... Buffalo, NY
Alexander, David J. .... Plano, TX
Alexander, David L. .... Oakland, CA
Alexander, David M. .... Palo Alto, CA
Alexander, David M. .... Saginaw, MI
Alexander, David T. .... San Francisco, CA
Alexander, David W. .... Columbus, OH
Alexander, Dawn .... Washington, DC
Alexander, Deborah L. .... Los Angeles, CA
Alexander, Deborah R. .... Chicago, IL
Alexander, Deborah Rosenberg .... Chicago, IL
Alexander, Deborah T. .... Chicago, IL
Alexander, DeLisa K. .... McLean, VA
Alexander, Dell A. .... Albany, OR
Alexander, Denise M. .... Santa Ana, CA
Alexander, Denise R. .... Sylvan Lake, MI
Alexander, Dennis M. .... Malibu, CA
Alexander, Dennis W. .... Charlotte, NC
Alexander, Dexter Ray .... Homewood, AL
Alexander, Diane .... Short Hills, NJ
Alexander, Dimitry N. .... Davie, FL
Alexander, Dina E. .... San Francisco, CA
Alexander, Donald B.
Department of Housing and Urban Development,
Office of General Counsel, GV
Alexander, Donald C. .... Washington, DC
Alexander, Donald C. .... Kemp, TX
Alexander, Donald G. .... Augusta, ME
Alexander, Donald P. .... Ardmore, PA
Alexander, Donald V. .... Columbus, OH
Alexander, Donn C. .... Las Vegas, NV
Alexander, Donna K. .... Washington, DC
Alexander, Dorothy Y. .... Sayre, OK
Alexander, Douglas C., II .... Salem, OR
Alexander, Douglas W.
Saint Simons Island, GA
Alexander, Douglas W. .... Austin, TX
Alexander, Douglas W., P.C.
Saint Simons Island, GA
Alexander & Duhl, P.A.
West Palm Beach, FL
Alexander, Dwain, II ....
Department of Defense, GV
Alexander, Edward C. .... Great Falls, MT
Alexander, Edward King, Jr.
Lafayette, LA
New Orleans, LA
Alexander, Edward R., Jr. .... Orlando, FL
Alexander, Effie G. .... Pittsburgh, PA
Alexander, Elaine A. .... San Diego, CA
Alexander, Ellen Evans .... Cranston, RI
Alexander, Ellen J. .... Evanston, IL
Alexander, Elliott E. .... Sacramento, CA
Alexander, Elyse L. .... New York, NY
Alexander, Emmet D. .... Chesterfield, VA
Alexander, Emory G. .... San Antonio, TX
Alexander, Eric L. .... Washington, DC
Alexander, Eugene A., III .... Baltimore, MD
Alexander, Eugene M. .... Hastings, NE
Alexander, Eugene R. .... Florham Park, NJ
Alexander, Femino & Lauranzano
Beverly, MA
Boston, MA
Ipswich, MA
Alexander, Fields .... Austin, TX
Alexander, Floodman & Casey, Chartered
Wichita, KS
Alexander, Fred C., Jr. .... McLean, VA
Alexander, Frederick H. .... Wilmington, DE
Alexander, Fritz W., II .... New York, NY
Alexander, G. Tim, III .... Lafayette, LA
Alexander, Gabriel N. .... Bloomfield Hills, MI
Alexander, Gail Elizabeth .... Houston, TX
Alexander, Garbarino, Kifer, Speer & Neely
Clarion, PA
Alexander, Garrison D.B.
San Francisco, CA
Alexander, Gary .... San Francisco, CA
Alexander, Gary L. .... Chicago, IL
Alexander, Gary O. .... San Francisco, CA
Alexander, Gary P. .... New Kensington, PA
Alexander, Gary R. .... Annapolis, MD
Fort Washington, MD
Waldorf, MD
Alexandria, VA
Alexander, Geoffrey DeWitt Lavies
Mobile, AL
Alexander, George .... Detroit, MI
Alexander, George Ivan .... Greenville, TX
Alexander, George J. .... Santa Clara, CA
Alexander, George W. .... Chicago, IL
Alexander, George W. .... Ann Arbor, MI
Alexander, George W., Ltd. .... Chicago, IL
Alexander, Gerald G. .... Orange Park, FL
Alexander, Gerald M.
Department of Justice, Civil Division, GV
Alexander, Gerry L. .... Olympia, WA
Alexander, Gilbert A. .... Denver, CO
Alexander, Glenn C. .... Department of Justice,
Criminal Division, GV
Alexander, Glenn W. .... Cameron, LA
Alexander & Green .... New York, NY
Alexander, Gregory G. .... Toledo, OH
Alexander, Gregory G. .... Philadelphia, PA
Alexander, Grover G. .... Gray, ME
Alexander, H. Heath .... Charlotte, NC
Alexander, H. Scott .... Beaumont, TX
Alexander, Hal .... Taylorville, IL
Alexander & Hanson .... Palo Alto, CA
Alexander, Hawes & Audet .... Oakland, CA
Redwood City, CA
San Francisco, CA
San Jose, CA
Alexander, Henry G., Jr. .... Cincinnati, OH
Alexander, Herald J. A. .... Atlanta, GA
Alexander, Herbert R. .... Mandeville, LA
Alexander, Howard C. .... Montgomery, AL
Alexander, Howard T. .... Denver, CO
Alexander, Hubert W., Jr. .... Jacksonville, AR
Alexander, Hugh .... Denver, CO
Alexander, Hugh C.D. .... San Francisco, CA
Alexander, Ian Robert .... Chicago, IL
Alexander, Ivan, Jr. .... Greenville, TX
Alexander, J. Ben .... Greenville, SC
Alexander, J. Bernard, III
Los Angeles, CA
Alexander, J. Brendon .... Bend, OR
Alexander, J. Graham .... San Francisco, CA
Alexander, J. Lester .... Bessemer, AL
Alexander, J. Michael .... Salem, OR
Alexander, J. Michael .... Dallas, TX
Alexander, J. Nickolas, Jr. .... Orange Park, FL
Alexander, J. Robert .... Twin Falls, ID
Alexander, J. Scott .... Sacramento, CA
Alexander, J. Steve .... Daytona Beach, FL
Alexander, J. Wilson, Jr. .... Asheboro, NC
Alexander, Jack R. .... Stamford, CT
Alexander, James .... Washington, DC
Alexander, James A. .... Walnut Creek, CA
Alexander, James A. .... Washington, DC
Alexander, James A. .... Chicago, IL
Alexander, James A., Jr. .... Jackson, MS
Alexander, James B. .... Covington, GA
Alexander, James B. .... Clarion, PA
Alexander, James C. .... Pickens, SC
Alexander, James C. .... Madison, WI
Alexander, James E. .... Pasadena, CA
Alexander, James E. .... Panama City, FL
Alexander, James, Jr. .... Cleveland, OH
Alexander, James L. .... Chicago, IL
Alexander, James L. .... Syracuse, NY
Alexander, James M. .... Detroit, MI
Alexander, James N. .... Evanston, IL
Alexander, James Patrick
Birmingham, AL
Alexander, James R. .... Dallas, TX
Alexander, James R. Dick .... Lubbock, TX
Alexander, James S. .... Tucson, AZ
Alexander, James S. .... St. Augustine, FL
Alexander, James S. .... St. Paul, MN
Alexander, James W. .... Grand Rapids, MI
Alexander, Jane .... Dresher, PA
Alexander, Jane E. .... New York, NY
Alexander, Jane M. .... Dillsburg, PA
Alexander, Janet Cooper .... Stanford, CA
Alexander, Janet M. .... San Francisco, CA
Alexander, Jason W. .... Portland, OR
Alexander, Jay I. .... Washington, DC
Alexander, Jay L. .... Washington, DC
Alexander, Jay Scott .... Sacramento, CA
Alexander, Jean M. .... Santa Barbara, CA
Alexander, Jeffery M. .... Providence, RI
Alexander, Jeffrey C. .... Houston, TX
Alexander, Jeffrey L. .... West Palm Beach, FL
Alexander, Jeffrey M. .... Santa Monica, CA
Alexander, Jeffrey S. .... Jacksonville, FL
Alexander, Jennifer .... Anchorage, AK
Alexander, Jennifer E. .... Kansas City, MO
Alexander, Jerry .... Omaha, NE
Alexander, Jerry C. .... Dallas, TX
Alexander, Jesse G. .... Staten Island, NY
Alexander, Jessica R. .... Houston, TX
Alexander, Jim M. .... Lexington, KY
Alexander, Jimmy .... Athens, AL
Alexander, J. L. .... Capitola, CA
Alexander, Joan B. .... Williamsville, NY
Alexander, Joan K. .... Waterbury, CT
Alexander, Joel F., III .... Gretna, LA
Alexander, John A. .... Butte, MT
Alexander, John C. .... Mobile, AL
Alexander, John D. .... Great Falls, MT
Alexander, John D. .... Nutley, NJ
Alexander, John E., III .... Irving, TX
Alexander, John Forsyth .... Philadelphia, PA
Alexander, John H. .... Chicago, IL
Alexander, John M. .... Hartford, CT
Alexander, John M. .... St. Augustine, FL
Alexander, John M. .... Cleveland, OH
Alexander, John Marshall .... Oxford, MS
Alexander, John Nickolas, Jr.
Orange Park, FL
Alexander, John P. .... Toledo, OH
Alexander, John R. .... Pacific Palisades, CA
Alexander, John R. .... Billings, MT
Alexander, John R. .... Elmira, NY
Alexander, John R. .... Cashiers, NC
Alexander, John R. .... Seattle, WA
Alexander, John T. .... Glasgow, KY
Alexander, John T. .... Southfield, MI
Alexander, John T. .... Concord, NH
Alexander, John Vincent .... Wilmington, DE
Alexander, John W. .... Connersville, IN
Alexander, John W. .... Morganton, NC
Alexander, John W. .... Winnsboro, TX
Alexander, Johnston & Alexander, P.A.
Cleveland, MS
Alexander, Jon K. .... Tyler, TX
Alexander, Jon T. .... Chicago, IL
Alexander, Joseph .... Minneapolis, MN
Alexander, Joseph B., Jr. .... Atlanta, GA
Alexander, Joseph, Jr. .... Boston, MA
Alexander, Joseph P. .... Cleveland, OH
Alexander, Joseph R. .... New York, NY
Alexander, Joseph R., Jr. .... Houston, TX
Alexander, Joseph S. .... Clearwater, FL
Alexander, Josie A. .... Atlanta, GA
Alexander, Joy L. .... Hamilton, TX
Alexander, Judith M. .... Birmingham, AL
Alexander, Judith M.
Fort Lauderdale, FL
Alexander, Judy, Law Offices of
Capitola, CA
Alexander, Karen A. .... New Bern, NC
Alexander, Karen Elizabeth Torres
New Bedford, MA
Alexander, Karen Levin
West Palm Beach, FL
Alexander, Karl .... Pittsburgh, PA
Alexander, Katherine J. .... Seattle, WA
Alexander, Kathleen D. .... Little Rock, AR
Alexander, Kathleen G. .... North Adams, MA
Alexander, Keith M. .... Southaven, MS
Alexander, Kenneth B. .... Rockville, MD
Alexander, Kenneth D. .... St. Louis, MO
Alexander, Kenneth P. .... Paducah, KY
Alexander, Kent B. .... Atlanta, GA
Alexander, Kern, LLC, International Law
Offices of .... Gainesville, FL
Alexander, Kerry D. .... Saginaw, MI
Alexander, Kevin D. .... Monroe, LA
Alexander, Kevin F. .... Oak Park, IL
Alexander, Kevin T. .... Little Rock, AR
Alexander, Kevin W. .... San Diego, CA
Alexander, Koteles .... Washington, DC
Silver Spring, MD
Alexander, Kurt E. .... Cocoa, FL
Orlando, FL
Alexander, L. Wayne .... Los Angeles, CA
Alexander, Lanny R. .... New York, NY
Alexander, Larry B.
West Palm Beach, FL
Alexander, Larry B. .... Seattle, WA
Alexander, Larry G. .... San Antonio, TX
Alexander, Laura Catching .... Staunton, VA
Alexander, Laural C. .... Boston, MA
Alexander, Lauren G. .... Rockville, MD
Alexander, Lauren G. .... Oxford, MS
Alexander, Laurence B. .... Gainesville, FL
Alexander Law Firm, P.C. .... Atlanta, GA
Alexander Law Off. .... Omaha, NE
Alexander, Lawrence A. .... San Diego, CA
Alexander, Lee A. .... Washington, DC
Alexander, Lee Ann .... Austin, TX
Alexander, Lee S. .... Marietta, GA
Alexander, Leon C. .... Anaheim, CA
Alexander, Leon J. .... Glendale, CA
Alexander, Leonard .... Thousand Oaks, CA
Alexander, Leota Heil .... Dallas, TX
Alexander, Leslie L. .... Boca Raton, FL
Alexander, Linda G. .... Oklahoma City, OK
Alexander, Lisa C. .... Los Angeles, CA
Alexander, Lisa E. .... Emeryville, CA
Alexander, Lois A.
Department Of Health And Human Services,
Social Security Administration, GV
Alexander, Lori B. .... New Haven, CT
Alexander, Louis A. .... Albany, NY
Alexander, Louis M. .... Sugar Land, TX
Alexander, Luke E. .... Russellville, AL
Alexander, M. David, III .... Lakeland, FL
Lake Wales, FL
Winter Haven, FL
Alexander, M. Nicole .... New Orleans, LA
Alexander, Marc D. .... Irvine, CA
Alexander, Marc Wright .... Campbell, CA
Alexander, Marcia .... Orleans, MA
Alexander, Marian S. .... Greenville, MS
Alexander, Marilyn G. .... Decatur, GA
Alexander, Mark .... Grosse Pointe, MI
Alexander, Mark A. .... Dallas, TX
Alexander, Mark D. .... Hartford, CT
Alexander, Mark G. .... Jacksonville, FL
Alexander, Mark H. .... Department of Defense,
Defense Commissary Agency, GV
Alexander, Mark W. .... Gainesville, GA
Alexander, Mark W. .... Livingston, NJ
Alexander, Martin J.
West Palm Beach, FL
Alexander, Martin S. .... Nyack, NY
Alexander, Mary C. .... Los Angeles, CA
Alexander, Mary E. .... San Francisco, CA
Alexander, Mary Elise .... Menlo Park, CA
Alexander, Mary Hood .... Montpelier, VT
Alexander, Mary M. .... Baltimore, MD
Alexander, Mary Margaret .... Gulfport, MS
Alexander, Mary R. .... Long Island City, NY
Alexander, Mary Rose .... Chicago, IL
Alexander, Mary Suffron .... Phoenix, AZ
Alexander, Mason G., Jr. .... Charlotte, NC
Raleigh, NC
Columbia, SC
Alexander, Matthew L. .... Seattle, WA
Alexander, Matthew S. .... Los Angeles, CA
Alexander, Maxine L. .... Greenwood, SC
Alexander, Melissa C. .... Irvine, CA
Alexander, Meredith L. .... Louisville, KY
Alexander, Merton L. .... New York, NY
Alexander, Michael .... Albany, NY
Alexander, Michael .... New York, NY
Alexander, Michael D. .... Malvern, PA
Alexander, Michael J. .... Muncie, IN
Alexander, Michael T. .... Cincinnati, OH
Alexander, Michael W.
Pension Benefit Guaranty Corporation,
Office of the General Counsel, GV
Alexander, Micheal L. .... Little Rock, AR
Alexander, Michelle .... Oakland, CA
Alexander, Michelle .... Columbia, MD
Alexander, Michelle Dawn .... Jackson, MS
Alexander, Miles J. .... Atlanta, GA
Alexander & Miller, P.A. .... Chapel Hill, NC
Alexander, Myron D. .... Menlo Park, CA
Alexander, Nadine M. .... Charlotte, NC
Alexander, Nancy M. .... Louisville, KY
Alexander, Nathaniel .... St. Paul, MN
Alexander, Neil J. .... White Plains, NY
Alexander, Neil (Ken)ton .... Houston, TX
Alexander, Neil M. .... Reno, NV
Alexander, Nelson D. .... Indianapolis, IN
Alexander, Nicholas P. .... Boston, MA
Alexander, Nicholas Z. .... Columbus, OH
Alexander, Nick .... Wheaton, IL
Alexander, Nicole M. .... New Orleans, LA
Alexander, Nina J. .... Newport, IN
Alexander, O. Allen .... Columbia, SC
Alexander, Pamela G. .... Minneapolis, MN
Alexander, Patience Ann .... Charleston, WV
Alexander, Patricia .... Boca Raton, FL
Alexander, Patrick L. .... Nashville, TN
Alexander, Paul .... Palo Alto, CA
Alexander, Paul .... United States Senate,
Committee Legal Personnel, GV
Alexander, Paul M. .... Atlanta, GA
Alexander & Pelli .... Norristown, PA
Philadelphia, PA
Alexander, Penny Jones .... Petal, MS
Alexander, Peter .... Rockford, IL
Alexander, Peter, Ltd. .... Rockford, IL
Alexander, Philip D. .... Greenville, TX
Alexander, Philip H. .... Derby, KS
Alexander, Philip M. .... Washington, DC
Alexander Professional Association
Orlando, FL
Alexander, Quentin .... Cleveland, OH
Alexander, R. Alan .... Mobile, AL
Alexander, R. Lewis .... Elkin, NC
Alexander, R. Lewis, Jr. .... Elkin, NC
Alexander, R. Lin .... Marshall, MO
Alexander, R. Royal .... Lafayette, LA
Shreveport, LA
Alexander, R. Russell .... Charleston, WV
Huntington, WV
Alexander, Rachel Leigh .... Brockton, MA
Alexander, Ralph J. .... East Hartford, CT
Alexander, Ralph J. .... Hartford, CT
Alexander Ralston, Speckhard & Speckhard, L.L.P. .... Greensboro, NC
Alexander, Randall .... Kearney, NE
Superior, NE

Alexander, Randi E. ... Tucson, AZ
Alexander, Raymond C. ... Corpus Christi, TX
Alexander, Raymond G. ... Sunnyside, WA
Alexander, Raymond M., Jr. ... San Francisco, CA
Alexander, Rebecca ... Alexandria, LA
Alexander, Rhonda ... Knoxville, TN
Alexander, Richard ... San Jose, CA
Alexander, Richard E. ... Rochester, NY
Alexander, Richard E. ... Portland, OR
Alexander, Richard G. ... Washington, DC
Alexander, Richard J. ... Point Richmond, CA
Alexander, Richard L. ... Hastings, NE
Alexander, Richard M. ... Washington, DC
Alexander, Richard P. ... Fayetteville, AR
Alexander, Richard R. ... Jacksonville, FL
Alexander, Richard W. ... Austin, TX
Alexander, Richard W., P.C. ... Austin, TX
Alexander, Robert B. ... Houston, TX
Alexander, Robert C. ... San Francisco, CA
Alexander, Robert C. ... Everett, WA
Alexander, Robert D. ... Kew Gardens, NY
Alexander, Robert E. ... Beulah, ND
Alexander, Robert F. ... Houston, TX
Alexander, Robert G. ... Jacksonville, FL
Alexander, Robert H., Jr. ... Oklahoma City, OK
Alexander, Robert H., Jr., Attorneys and Counselors at Law, P.C., The Law Office of ... Oklahoma City, OK
Alexander, Robert H., Jr., Attorneys and Counselor at Law, p.c., The Law Office of ... Tulsa, OK
Alexander, Robert L. ... Clinton, NJ
Alexander, Robert M. ... Glasgow, KY
Alexander, Robert Pierce ... Atlanta, GA
Alexander, Robert S. ... Neenah, WI
Alexander, Robert T. ... Houston, TX
Alexander, Robert W. ... Boston, MA
Alexander, Robt. M. ... Alexandria, VA
Alexander, Rod M. ... Moulton, AL
Alexander, Rodney E. ... Houston, TX
Alexander, Roger L. ... Woodridge, IL
Alexander, Ronald E. ... Columbia, SC
Alexander, Rose McCleary ... Richmond, VA
Alexander, Rosemary Ryan ... Lake Forest, IL
Alexander, Ross ... Milwaukee, WI
Alexander, Ross D. ... Wichita, KS
Alexander, S. Allan ... Oxford, MS
Alexander, Samuel C. ... Department of Justice, Office of Tribal Justice, GV
Alexander, Samuel Kern, III ... Gainesville, FL
Alexander, Sandra J. ... Tulsa, OK
Alexander, Sarira D. ... Washington, DC
Alexander, Scott D. ... Fort Lauderdale, FL
Alexander, Scott Michael ... Chicago, IL
Alexander, Scott Michael, P.C. ... Chicago, IL
Alexander, Scott R. ... Indianapolis, IN
Alexander, Sharon A. ... Dallas, TX
Alexander, Sharon B. ... Hendersonville, NC
Alexander, Sheila A. ... Los Angeles, CA
Alexander, Sherri Turner ... Dallas, TX
Alexander, Sidney B. ... West Palm Beach, FL
Alexander, Simon ... New York, NY
Alexander, Sol ... Miami, FL
Alexander, Stacy L. ... Indianapolis, IN
Alexander, Stanley J. ... Oklahoma City, OK
Alexander & Starken ... Ottumwa, IA
Alexander, Stephanie D. ... Pensacola, FL
Alexander, Stephanie M. ... Palo Alto, CA
Alexander, Stephanie R. ... Seattle, WA
Alexander, Stephen D. ... Los Angeles, CA
Alexander, Stephen D. ... Houston, TX
Alexander, Steven D. ... Shawnee, KS
Alexander, Steven K. ... Torrance, CA
Alexander, Stewart J. ... San Antonio, TX
Alexander, Stuart E. ... Louisville, KY
Alexander, Stuart E., III ... Louisville, KY
Alexander, Sue ... Oakland, CA
Alexander, Susan D. ... Central Islip, NY
Alexander, Susan H. ... Boston, MA
Alexander, Susan J. G. ... Chicago, IL
Alexander, Susan K. ... Hastings, NE
Alexander, Sydenham B., Jr. ... Chapel Hill, NC
Alexander, T. Richard, II ... Glasgow, KY
Alexander, Tena M. ... Treasury Department, Office of the Comptroller of the Currency, GV
Alexander, Thomas C. ... Macon, GA
Alexander, Thomas F. ... Minneapolis, MN
Alexander, Thomas J. ... Beverly, MA
Alexander, Thomas J. ... Kansas City, MO
Alexander, Thomas P. ... Cleveland, OH
Alexander, Thomas Willis Haywood ... Raleigh, NC
Alexander, Timothy P. ... Hillsboro, OR
Alexander, Todd ... Sapulpa, OK
Alexander, Todd ... Tulsa, OK
Alexander, Todd E. ... Washington, DC
Alexander, Tom ... Houston, TX
Alexander, Tom, & Associates ... Houston, TX
Alexander, Tracy D. ... Walnut Creek, CA
Alexander, Troy ... New York, NY
Alexander, Vahn ... Santa Monica, CA
Alexander, Valerie ... Waterford, CT
Alexander, Vance L. ... Birmingham, AL
Alexander, Vance L., P.C. ... Birmingham, AL
Alexander, Vanessa V. ... Chicago, IL
Alexander & Vann, LLP ... Thomasville, GA
Alexander, Victor, Jr. ... Atlanta, GA
Alexander, Vincent ... Jamaica, NY
Alexander, Virgil E. ... Pittsburgh, PA
Alexander, W. Stanley ... Hockessin, DE
Alexander, Warner ... Christiansted, St. Croix, VI
Alexander, Watt D. ... Norwich, VT
Alexander, Wayne K., Jr. ... Decatur, AL
Alexander, Wayne Taichi ... Burbank, CA
Alexander, Wendy A. ... Manassas, VA
Alexander, William A. ... Benton, IL
Alexander, William Bain, Jr. ... Louisville, KY
Alexander, William D. ... Treasury Department, Internal Revenue Service, GV
Alexander, William F. ... Dallas, TX
Alexander, William G. ... Raleigh, NC
Alexander, William H. ... Atlanta, GA
Alexander, William H. ... Chicago, IL
Alexander, William M. ... Laurens, IA
Alexander, William M., Jr. ... Hendersonville, NC
Alexander, William N., II ... Chatham, VA
Alexander, William P., III ... Brentwood, TN
Alexander, William R. ... DeLand, FL
Alexander, Willie M. ... Department of Labor, Office of the Solicitor, GV
Alexander, Wm. B., Jr. ... Cleveland, MS
Alexander, Wm. Larry ... Minneapolis, MN
Alexander & Yong ... Los Angeles, CA
Alexander, Zachary P. ... Philadelphia, PA
Alexander-Best, Mischelle ... Memphis, TN
Alexander-Kelley, Penelope ... Riverside, CA
San Bernardino, CA
Alexander-Krom, Laurie ... Boston, MA
Alexandersen, Kevin C. ... Cleveland, OH
Alexanderson, Alvin ... Portland, OR
Alexanderson, Davis, Rainey & Whitney ... Caldwell, ID
Alexanderson, Robert L. ... Caldwell, ID
Alexander-Taylor, Amy, (A Law Corporation) ... Honolulu, HI
Alexandre, Benita M. ... Albuquerque, NM
Alexandre, Carl ... Department of Justice, Criminal Division, GV
Alexandre, Kelly ... Portland, OR
Alexandria-Cisneros, D. Andreia ... Denver, CO
Alexandrides, Athena Katcheves ... Crownsville, MD
Alexandris, Penelope ... San Francisco, CA
Alexandroff, Alan S. ... New York, NY
Alexandroff, Denis ... Calabasas, CA
Alexandroff, Victor ... Los Angeles, CA
Alexandrov, Metzger & Kalmansson, P.C. ... Fitchburg, MA
Alexandrov, V. Jon ... Fitchburg, MA
Alexant, Susan Weiss ... Weare, NH
Alexas, Ernest A. ... Fort Lauderdale, FL
Alexeeva, Natasha ... New York, NY
Alexiades, Elias A. ... Milford, CT
Alexiades, John ... Chicago, IL
Alexion, Arthur S. ... Glenside, PA
Philadelphia, PA
Alexion and Casper ... Glenside, PA
Philadelphia, PA
Alexion, Gary A. ... Brooklyn, NY
Alexis, Agnes ... Federal Deposit Insurance Corporation, Professional Liability Section, GV
Alexis, Drew L. ... Oakland, CA
Alexis, Geraldine M. ... Chicago, IL
Alexis, GwenY. ... Chester, NJ
Alexis, Hilary I. ... Chicago, IL
Alexis, Paul A. ... Nashville, TN
Alexis, Ralph R., III ... New Orleans, LA
Alexius, Frederick B. ... Alexandria, LA
Alexopoulos, Alex L. ... Birmingham, MI
Alexopoulos, Christ ... Milwaukee, WI
Alexopoulos, Tina ... Atlanta, GA
Alexson, Alaina M. ... San Diego, CA
Santa Barbara, CA
Alexson, Harriet B. ... Los Angeles, CA
Alexson, John M. ... Boulder, CO
Alexson, Timothy L. ... Pittsford, NY
Alexsy, Steven F. ... Columbus, OH
Alexy, Brooke E. ... North Chicago, IL
Alexy, Christopher ... New Haven, CT
Alexy, James A. ... Kitty Hawk, NC
Alexy, Paul E. ... Elm Grove, WI
Aley, Charles R. ... Beaver Falls, PA
Alf, Barbara Pratt ... Omaha, NE
Alfadl, Sarah S. ... Bryn Mawr, PA
Alfafara, Diane M. ... Mount Clemens, MI
Alfafara, Theresa A. ... Detroit, MI
Alfaks, Boulos A. ... New York, NY
Alfandary, Francine L. ... New York, NY
Alfano, Aaron D. ... Tampa, FL
Alfano, Alexander Joseph ... Miami, FL
Alfano, Alphonse M. ... Washington, DC
Alfano, Alyce Lynn ... West Hartford, CT
Alfano, Annette P. ... Somerset, NJ
Alfano, Anthony P. ... Lyndhurst, NJ
Alfano, Anthony V. ... Washington, DC
Alfano & Baroff, Professional Association ... Manchester, NH
Alfano, Charles T. ... Suffield, CT
Alfano, Charles T., Jr. ... Suffield, CT
Alfano, Edward C. ... New York, NY
Alfano & Flynn, LLC ... Hartford, CT
Suffield, CT
Alfano, Frank G. ... Birmingham, AL
Alfano, Gaetan J. ... Haddonfield, NJ
Philadelphia, PA
Alfano, James J. ... Santa Ana, CA
Alfano, Jane D. ... Tempe, AZ
Alfano, John L. ... Rye, NY
Alfano, Joseph E. ... Hammond, IN
Alfano Law Office ... Rye, NY
Alfano, Michael A. ... Philadelphia, PA
Alfano, Michael D. ... Broomall, PA
Alfano, Michael L. ... Portsmouth, NH
Alfano, Michael, Law Offices of ... Portsmouth, NH
Alfano, Paul J. ... Manchester, NH
Alfano, Peter J. ... Roseland, NJ
Alfano, Salvatore F. ... Glendale, NY
Alfano, Salvatore T. ... Bloomfield, NJ
Alfano, Salvatore T., P.A. ... Bloomfield, NJ
Alfano, Sam J., III ... Houston, TX
Alfano, Thomas W. ... New York, NY
Al-Farisi, Omar H. ... New York, NY
Alfaro, Carlos Enrique ... New York, NY
Alfaro, Christine Comer ... St. Louis, MO
Alfaro, Lisa A. ... New York, NY
Alfaro, Martha Mann ... New York, NY
Alfaro, Tito Hugo ... Houston, TX
Alfaro-Delgado, José E. ... San Juan, PR
Alfaro-Navarro & Tozzini-Freire ... New York, NY
Alfassa, David P. ... Chicago, IL
Alfassa, Lynne R. ... Ventura, CA
Alfeld, Louis E. ... Silver Spring, MD
Alfeld, Philip B. ... Godfrey, IL
Alfera, Vincent J. ... Tallmadge, OH
Alfero, Anthony J. ... Harrison, NY
Alfers & Carver, LLC ... Denver, CO
Alfers, Stephen D. ... Denver, CO
Alfert, Arthur S. ... Floral Park, NY
Alfert, David O. ... New York, NY
Alfert, Peter W. ... Walnut Creek, CA
Alfert, Rebecca ... Dallas, TX
Alfert, Robert, Jr. ... Orlando, FL
Alfert & Schwartz ... Floral Park, NY
Alfes, Thomas J. ... Troy, MI
Alfieri, A. J. ... Bradford, PA
Alfieri, Anthony V. ... Bronx, NY
Alfieri, Anthony W. ... Clearwater, FL
Alfieri Frohman & Primoff ... New York, NY
Alfieri, John B. ... New York, NY
Alfieri, Lawrence J. ... New York, NY
Alfieri, Lee P. ... Plymouth, MA
Alfieri, Mark Charles ... Dallas, TX
Alfieri, Michael J. ... New York, NY
Alfieri, Michele D. ... Smethport, PA
Alfieri, Paul M. ... New York, NY
Alfieri, Peter ... Chicago, IL
Alfieri, Ralph A., (Inc., P.S.) ... Seattle, WA
Alfieri, Salvatore ... Matawan, NJ
Alfieri, Victor J., Jr. ... Nanuet, NY
Alfieri, Vincent ... New York, NY
Alfieris, George S. ... Coronado, CA
Alfin, Susan Lisa ... Concord, NH
Alfini, James J. ... De Kalb, IL
Alfino, Anthony P. ... Vero Beach, FL
Alfisi, Jennifer M. ... Englewood, CO
Alfonse, Thomas W. ... New Bedford, MA
Alfonsi, Christina M. ... Salisbury, MD
Alfonsi, Letitia Utley ... Charlotte, NC
Alfonso, Ana M. ... New York, NY
Alfonso, Ana M. ... Milwaukee, WI
Alfonso, Anthony C. ... Orlando, FL
Alfonso, Anthony, Jr. ... Tampa, FL
Alfonso, Arturo R. ... Miami, FL
Alfonso, Arturo R., P.A. ... Miami, FL
Alfonso, Carlos H. ... Millbrae, CA
Alfonso, Dennis J. ... Dade City, FL
Alfonso, Evelyn ... Newark, NJ
Alfonso, Frank A. ... Los Angeles, CA
Alfonso, Gloria M. ... New York, NY
Alfonso, Haydée I. ... San Francisco, CA
Alfonso, Israel L. ... Miami, FL
Alfonso, James C. ... Tampa, FL
Alfonso, Julian L. ... Queens Village, NY
Alfonso, Leticia D. ... Atlanta, GA
Alfonso, Linda G. ... Old Bridge, NJ
Alfonso, Louis ... Woodland Hills, CA
Alfonso, Louis J. ... Boca Raton, FL
Alfonso, Louis J., P.A. ... Boca Raton, FL
Alfonso, Margaret ... Gulfport, MS
Alfonso, Miriam A. ... Miami, FL
Alfonso, Nancy McClain ... Dade City, FL
Zephyrhills, FL
Alfonso & Ohall, P.A. ... Tampa, FL
Alfonso, S. George ... Dallas, TX
Alfonso, Suzette M. ... Tampa, FL
Alfonso, Tracy L. ... Caledonia, MI
Alfonzo, Charles A. ... Berkeley, CA
Alfonzo-Lasso, Inez ... Department of Justice, Office of Justice Programs, GV
Alford, A. Scott ... Houston, TX
Alford, Alan D. ... Cleveland, OH
Alford & Alford ... Slidell, LA
Alford, Allison L. ... Montgomery, AL
Alford, Barber & Mariani ... Clearwater, FL
Alford, Benjamin G. ... New Bern, NC
Alford & Bertrand, Legal Clinic of ... Watertown, MA
Alford, Bill ... Costa Mesa, CA
Alford, Brigid Q. ... Harrisburg, PA
Alford, Bruce A., The Law Office of ... Plano, TX
Alford, C. Douglas ... San Diego, CA
Alford, C. Wayne ... Jacksonville, FL
Alford, Carolyn W. ... Dallas, TX
Alford, Carolyn Zander ... Atlanta, GA
Alford, Cecile C. ... Jackson, MS
Alford, Charles J., Jr. ... Tucker, GA
Alford, Daniel Lee, IV ... Dallas, TX
Alford, David C. ... Waco, TX
Alford, David C., P.C. ... Waco, TX
Alford, Donald S. ... Ridgeland, MS
Alford, Duncan E. ... Rock Hill, SC
Alford, E. Gregory ... San Diego, CA
Alford, Edwin J. ... Nashville, AR
Alford, Eugene C. ... Overland Park, KS
Alford, Fletcher C. ... San Francisco, CA
Alford, Greg ... Dyersburg, TN
Alford, Gregory M. ... Hilton Head Island, SC
Alford, Haile L. ... Wilmington, DE
Alford, Harvey ... Watertown, MA
Alford, Helen Johnson ... Mobile, AL
Alford, Henry S. ... Louisville, KY
Alford, Howard L. ... Jacksonville, FL
Alford, J. Tucker ... Atlanta, GA
Alford, James K. ... Washington, DC
Alford, James W. ... Columbia, SC
Alford, Jeffrey Stephen ... Soquel, CA
Alford, Joe D. ... Orange, TX
Alford, John D. ... Fort Smith, AR
Alford, John G. ... Camp Hill, PA
Alford, John M. ... Tallahassee, FL
Alford, John R. ... Lynchburg, VA
Alford, John R., Jr. ... Lynchburg, VA
Alford & Kalil, P.A. ... Jacksonville, FL
Alford, Laura Jean ... Roanoke Rapids, NC
Alford, Levy (Lee) S. ... York, SC
Alford, Louis ... Mc Comb, MS
Alford, Lydia Jane ... Slidell, LA
Alford, Margaret S. ... Dallas, TX
Alford, Michael R. ... St. Petersburg, FL
Alford, Neill H., Jr. ... Charlottesville, VA
Alford, Nelson R., Jr. ... Chatham, NY
Alford, Oteka, (Mrs.) ... Chickasha, OK
Alford, Peter T. ... La Grange, GA
Alford, Rebecca H. ... Tampa, FL
Alford, Reece B. ... Birmingham, AL
Alford, Richard L. ... Clearwater, FL
Alford, Robertson F. ... Paramus, NJ
Alford, Roger P. ... Washington, DC
Alford, Sondra S. ... Naples, FL
Alford, T. Swayze ... Oxford, MS
Alford, Terry W. ... Spring Hope, NC
Alford, Thomas H. ... Muskogee, OK
Alford, Thomas and Kilgore ... Philadelphia, MS
Alford, Thomas M. ... Augusta, GA
Alford, W. Barry ... Greenville, SC
Alford, W. Vanmeter, Jr. ... Lexington, KY
Alford, Walter C. ... Tucker, GA
Alford, Walter H. ... Cashiers, NC
Alford, William ... Cambridge, MA
Alford, William C. Neil, II ... Slidell, LA
Alford, William James, III ... New York, NY
Alfred, Deirdre Shaughnessy ... San Diego, CA
Alfred, Gary E. ... Houston, TX
Alfred, Jean-Robert ... Christiansted, St. Croix, VI
Alfred, Kathy M. ... Northridge, CA
Alfred, Louis, Jr. ... New Orleans, LA
Alfred, Lynne B. ... Cleveland, OH
Alfred, Michael A. ... Alameda, CA
Alfred, Michael D. ... Tucson, AZ
Alfred, Randall M. ... Houma, LA
Alfred, Randall M., A Professional Law Corporation ... Houma, LA
Alfred, Richard L. ... Boston, MA
Alfred, Samuel D. ... Tucson, AZ
Alfredson, Patricia K. ... Rochester, MN
Alfree, Scott D. ... Grand Rapids, MI
Alfrey, Curtis C. ... Denver, CO
Alfrey, Gladys Solar ... Knoxville, TN
Alfrey, Stephen D. ... Holbrook, AZ
Alfrey, Thomas N. ... Denver, CO
Alfs, John B. ... Detroit, MI
Alfsen-Cleveland, W. L. ... Petaluma, CA
Alfson, David B. ... Dallas, TX
Alfson, Kathryn ... Englewood, CO
Alfton, Robert J. ... Minneapolis, MN
Algar, John P. ... Charleston, SC
Algar, Linda M. ... Estacada, OR
Algarin-Otero, Lynette ... Humacao, PR
Algase, Roger C. ... New York, NY
Algava-Czik, Esta ... New York, NY
Algazi, Jessica ... Santa Monica, CA
Alge, William S., Jr. ... Ada, OH
Findlay, OH
Algeier, Gary C. ... Morristown, NJ
Algeo, Annemarie ... Mount Laurel, NJ
Algeo & Clarke, P.S. ... Spokane, WA
Algeo, Judith A. ... Doylestown, PA
Algeo, Richard P. ... Spokane, WA
Algeo, Thomas S. ... Sellersville, PA
Alger, Andrew & Rohlfs ... New York, NY
Alger, Christopher R. ... Denver, CO
Alger, John R. ... Osterville, MA
Alger, John R., P.C. ... Osterville, MA
Alger, Jonathan R. ... Washington, DC
Alger, Matthew D. ... Fresno, CA
Alger, Melody A. ... Providence, RI
Alger, Mindy Halpern ... Seal Beach, CA
Alger, Richard L., Jr. ... West Branch, MI
Alger, Sarah F. ... Nantucket, MA
Alger, Sarah F., P.C. ... Nantucket, MA
Alger, Stephen A. ... Miami, FL
Alger, Timothy L. ... Los Angeles, CA
Alger, Vernon L. ... Berrien Springs, MI
Alger-Greulich, Gabriele K. ... Fresno, CA
Algert, Kristen A. ... Austin, TX
Algiane, Ken ... Golden, CO
Algie, Glenn E. ... Cincinnati, OH
Algiene, Kenneth ... Englewood, CO
Algiers, Timothy J. ... West Bend, WI
Algios, Louis ... Mineola, NY
Algorri, Ernest P. ... Pasadena, CA
Algorri, Mark S. ... Pasadena, CA
Alhadeff, Abraham ... Atlanta, GA
Alhadeff, Alan ... Seattle, WA
Alhadeff, Barbra ... New York, NY
Alhadeff Cannon Rose Solar & Parks, LLP ... Lafayette, CA
Los Angeles, CA
San Diego, CA
Temecula, CA
Alhadeff, E. Marilyn ... New Orleans, LA
Alhadeff, E. Richard ... Miami, FL
Alhadeff, Jack C. ... Seattle, WA
Alhadeff, Joseph H. ... New York, NY

Alhadeff, Marla F. ... New York, NY
Alhadeff, Samuel C. ... San Diego, CA
Temecula, CA
Alhalel, Garry J. ... Miami, FL
Alhalel, Garry J., P.A. ... Miami, FL
Alhandy, Marlene Amera ... La Habra, CA
Alhart, Donald E. ... Boston, MA
Alhart, Peter B. ... Albany, NY
Alhashimi, Adnan H. ... Houston, TX
al-Hibri, Azizah Y. ... Richmond, VA
Alhilali, Ruth B. ... Farmers Branch, TX
Alholinna, Jody Marie ... Minneapolis, MN
Alholm, Anthony J. ... Chicago, IL
Alholm, Karen L. ... Marquette, MI
Alholm, Monahan, Keefe & Klauke, L.L.C.
Chicago, IL
Alhonte, Marc ... Brooklyn, NY
Ali, Angelo A. ... Miami, FL
Ali, Irene E. ... Bellmawr, NJ
Ali, Jawad I. ... New York, NY
Ali, Jeffer ... Minneapolis, MN
Ali, Karen S. ... Alexandria, VA
Ali, Lucien ... Syracuse, NY
Ali, Na'imah A., (Mrs.) ... Jamaica, NY
Ali, Nasar F. ... Washington, DC
Ali, Pappas & Cox, P.C. ... Syracuse, NY
Ali & Partners ... Washington, DC
Ali, Reema I. ... Washington, DC
Ali, Thomas J. ... Jupiter, FL
Alia, Gino M. ... Kenosha, WI
Alia, Sebastian M. ... Lake Success, NY
Aliaga, Rocio T. ... Hackensack, NJ
Alian, Jack A. ... Reno, NV
Aliano, Aliano & Aliano ... Westbury, NY
Aliano, Charles J. ... Montrose, PA
Aliano, Richard A. ... Westbury, NY
Aliano, Robert J. ... Westbury, NY
Aliazzo, Frank R. ... Ozone Park, NY
Aliber, Stephen D. ... Kansas City, MO
Aliberti, Joseph M., Law Offices of
Anaheim, CA
Aliberti, Luigi R. ... Boston, MA
Alibhai, Jamil N. ... Dallas, TX
Alibrandi, Nancy J. ... North Billerica, MA
Alicandri, Jay R. ... New York, NY
Alicandro, Theonie Jean ... Boston, MA
Alice, Edward A. ... Trenton, MI
Alice, John A. ... Philadelphia, PA
Alice, Ronald W. ... Parsippany, NJ
Alicea, Hector A. ... San Francisco, CA
Alicea & Nagel ... Springfield, MA
Alicea, Teresita ... Springfield, MA
Alick, Nafe S. ... Elkhart, IN
Alidor, Gary P. ... Mobile, AL
Alifano, Gerald A. ... Springfield, MA
Santa Fe, NM
Aliff, Mark T. ... Tallahassee, FL
Aliff, Nancy ... Charleston, WV
Aliff, Rob J. ... Charleston, WV
Alig, David R. ... Overland Park, KS
Alig, Jon ... Covington, KY
Alig & Michaels ... Overland Park, KS
Kansas City, MO
Alig, Paul C. ... Eugene, OR
Alig, Thomas G., Jr. ... Covington, KY
Ali-Jackson, Kamil ... Chadds Ford, PA
Alijamal, C. L. ... Houston, TX
Alikacem, Martha A. ... Richardson, TX
Alikhan, Cheryl A. ... Cleveland, OH
Alikian, Shawn H. ... San Francisco, CA
Alimanestianu, Alexander A. ... New York, NY
Alimaras, Gus N. ... Long Island City, NY
Aliment, Randy J. ... Seattle, WA
Alimonti, Frederick P. ... New York, NY
Alin, David M. ... Chicago, IL
Alio, Jose R. ... Guaynabo, PR
Alio, Ralph V. ... Melville, NY
Alion, Russell Gable, Jr. ... Baltimore, MD
Alioth, Tressa M. ... Omaha, NE
Alioto, John J. ... Chicago, IL
Alioto, Joseph Gerard ... Milwaukee, WI
Oconomowoc, WI
Alioto, Joseph M. ... San Francisco, CA
Alioto, Lawrence ... San Francisco, CA
Alioto, Mario N. ... San Francisco, CA
Aliotta, Michael ... Paramus, NJ
Aliotta, Randi Pincus ... Staten Island, NY
Aliotti, Melissa Blair ... Sacramento, CA
Aliperta, John A. ... Malden, MA
Aliperti, Jamie B. ... Castlewood, VA
Alires, Ellen G. ... Denver, CO
Alires-Trujillo, Ellen G. ... Denver, CO
Alisankus, Thomas J. ... Evansville, WI
Alisbah, Kathryn ... New York, NY
Alison, John R. ... Washington, DC
Alissandratos, Demosthenes J.
Memphis, TN
Alissi, Amy E. ... Hartford, CT
Alissi, James A. ... Hartford, CT
Alissi, John J. ... Hartford, CT
Alito, Rosemary ... Newark, NJ
Alito, Samuel A., Jr. ... Newark, NJ
Alitz, Jeffrey L. ... Boston, MA
Alivernini, John M. ... St. Davids, PA
Alivernini, Matthew F. ... Cinnaminson, NJ
Aliverto, Deborah ... Garden City, NY
Alix, James E. ... Hartford, CT
Alix, Noelle C. ... New York, NY
Alix, Yale & Ristas, LLP ... Hartford, CT
Aljets, Mark D. ... Des Moines, IA
Aljets, Thomas J. ... Carrington, ND
Aljian, Lisa R. ... Hackensack, NJ
Aljian, Thomas ... Newark, NJ
Aljinovic, Daniel A. ... Chicago, IL
Aljinovic, Michele Antonia ... Chicago, IL
Alkafaji, Intissar Ann ... Detroit, MI
Alkalay, Edward Daniel ... Bronx, NY
Alkalay, Peter C. ... New York, NY
Alkana, Eugene S. ... Los Angeles, CA
Alkana, Eugene S. ... Pasadena, CA
Alkas, Peri H. ... Houston, TX
Alkazin, John J. ... San Francisco, CA
Alke, John L. ... Helena, MT
Alkema, Eugene ... Grand Rapids, MI
Alken, Charles Ford ... New York, NY
Alker, Michael B. ... New Orleans, LA
Alker, Susan C. ... Los Angeles, CA
Alkin, Donna M. ... New Brunswick, NJ
New York, NY
Alkire, Beverly J. ... Gladstone, MO
Alkire, Beverly J., P.C. ... Gladstone, MO
Alkire, E. Lael ... Wichita, KS
Alkire, John D. ... Seattle, WA
Alkire, Richard C. ... Cleveland, OH
Alkire, Steven E. ... Boise, ID
Alkon, Mitchell I. ... Bethesda, MD
Alkon, Rhea & Hart
Christiansted, St. Croix, VI
Charlotte Amalie, St. Thomas, VI
Alkon, Thomas
Christiansted, St. Croix, VI
Alkov, Leonard A. ... Los Angeles, CA
All Dade Law Offices ... Miami, FL
All, David C. ... Augusta, KS
All, Matthew D. ... Lawrence, KS
All, William D., II ... Union, SC
Alla, Seshigiri R.
Charlotte Amalie, St. Thomas, VI
Allaband, Carey S. ... New York, NY
Allaben, Elizabeth A.
Department of Agriculture,
Office of the General Counsel, GV
Allaben, John R. ... Grand Rapids, MI
Allaben, Vander Weyden, Timmer & Bandeen ... Grand Rapids, MI
Allaer, Paul (IBA) ... Cincinnati, OH
Allain, Alex P. ... New Orleans, LA
Allain and Allain ... Jeanerette, LA
Allain, J. François ... New Orleans, LA
Allain, Melissa M. ... Fort Lauderdale, FL
Allain, Peter Kevin ... Jeanerette, LA
Allain, Raymond E. ... Jeanerette, LA
Allaire, Stephen O. ... Bristol, CT
Allaman, Melissa Fletcher
Tallahassee, FL
Allamong, Elden ... Keyser, WV
Allamong, James H., Jr. ... Strasburg, VA
Allan, Aaron P. ... Los Angeles, CA
Allan, Albert P. ... Charlotte, NC
Allan, Andrea Lewis ... New York, NY
Allan, Arlene E. ... Salinas, CA
Allan, Arthur R. ... Chicago, IL
Allan, Charles K. ... Naples, FL
Allan, Clark C. ... Pinedale, WY
Allan, Dan, Law Offices of
Anchorage, AK
Allan, Daniel J. ... Philadelphia, PA
Allan, Don W. ... New York, NY
Allan, Douglas W. ... San Francisco, CA
Allan, Douglas W., Law Offices of
San Francisco, CA
Allan, Edgar, III ... Richmond, VA
Allan, Gail L. ... Austin, TX
Allan, Geraldine L. ... Aurora, CO
Allan, Greever P. ... Valley Falls, KS
Allan, Harry T. ... Amherst, MA
Allan, James N. ... Jericho, NY
Allan, Jean ... San Francisco, CA
Allan, Joan H. ... Glendale, CA
Allan, John J. ... St. Louis, MO
Allan, Julia G. ... Cummington, MA
Allan, Karen C. ... Medford, OR
Allan, Laura J. ... San Diego, CA
Allan, Linda R. ... Clearwater, FL
St. Petersburg, FL
Allan, Lionel M. (Lon) ... Monte Sereno, CA
Allan, Lionel M. (Lon) ... San Jose, CA
Allan, Lynn ... Albuquerque, NM
Allan, Marilee J. ... San Francisco, CA
Allan, Mark D. ... Ridgefield, CT
Allan, Michael J. ... Syracuse, NY
Allan, Michael Lee ... Los Angeles, CA
Allan, Peter W. ... Victorville, CA
Allan, Ralph E. ... Beverly Hills, CA
Allan, Rebecca S. ... Phoenix, AZ
Allan, Richard ... Brooklyn, NY
Allan, Richard H. ... Portland, OR
Allan, Richmond F. ... Washington, DC
Allan, Robert C. ... Wichita, KS
Allan, Robert J. ... Camillus, NY
Allan, Robert Olav ... Window Rock, AZ
Allan, Ronald C. ... Akron, OH
Allan, Sabrina E. ... New York, NY
Allan, Sean P. ... Cleveland, OH
Allan, Sher L. ... Panama City, FL
Panama City Beach, FL
Allan & Shipp, P.A. ... Clearwater, FL
St. Petersburg, FL
Allan, Steven H. ... Long Beach, CA
Allan, Susan M. ... Clearwater, FL
Allan, Susan M. ... Arlington, VA
Allan, Tamas R. ... Lincoln, NE
Allan, W. Edward ... Ephrata, WA
Allan, Wallace M. ... Los Angeles, CA
Allanoff, Daniel B. ... New York, NY
Philadelphia, PA
Allan Severns, Piper ... Orlando, FL
Allar, Marcia J. ... Boston, MA
Allard, Andrew Brian ... New York, NY
Allard, Anthony J. ... Oakland, CA
Allard, B. Robert ... San Jose, CA
Allard, Bernard J. ... San Jose, CA
Allard, David W. ... Detroit, MI
Allard, Debra ... Peoria, IL
Allard, Donald R. ... Richardson, TX
Allard, Edward P., III ... San Diego, CA
Allard & Fish, P.C. ... Detroit, MI
Allard, Gail M. (Franco) ... Worcester, MA
Allard, Genevieve M. ... Hackensack, NJ
Allard, Gregory M. ... Hauppauge, NY
Allard, James L., Jr. ... Wilmington, NC
Allard, Jean ... Chicago, IL
Allard, Jon, Jr. ... Belleville, IL
Allard, Mark S. ... Grand Rapids, MI
Allard, Martha B. ... Stamford, CT
Allard, Nicholas W. ... Washington, DC
Allard, Shelton & O'Connor LLP
Claremont, CA
Pomona, CA
Rancho Cucamonga, CA
Allard, Wendy L. ... Pass Christian, MS
Allard, William J. ... Santa Ana, CA
Allard, William J. ... Department of Defense,
Defense Legal Services Agency, GV
Allard-Bernhardt, Victoria R.
Bakersfield, CA
Allardyce, Gordon E. ... Auburn Hills, MI
Allare, John P. ... Middletown, OH
Allaria, Marc V. ... Beverly Hills, CA
Allario, Kimberly D. ... San Diego, CA
Allatin, Frederick A. ... Brooklyn, NY
Allawas, Lia L. ... Viera, FL
Allawas, Meryl Lee ... Titusville, FL
Allaye-Chan, Richard, Jr.
Sacramento, CA
Allayee, Azadeh ... Irvine, CA
Allbaugh, Michael ... Los Angeles, CA
Allbee, Alan D. ... West Union, IA
Allbee, Barclay, Allison, Denning & Person, A Professional Corporation
Muscatine, IA
West Liberty, IA
Wilton, IA
Allbee, Donald G. ... Marshalltown, IA
Allbee, Harvey G. ... Muscatine, IA
West Liberty, IA
Allbee, Harvey G., Jr. ... Muscatine, IA
West Liberty, IA
Allbee, Richard A. ... Hampton, IA
Allbee, Robert G. ... Des Moines, IA
Allbery, Charles F., III ... Dayton, OH
Allbery Cross Fogarty ... Dayton, OH
Allbright, A. Rodney ... Alvin, TX
Allbright, William R. ... Dallas, TX
Allbritain, Nicole C. ... Middletown, OH
Allbritten, Phillip L. ... Tulsa, OK
Allbritton, Anissa A. ... Austin, TX
Allbritton, J. Lee, Jr. ... Houston, TX
Allbritton, Laura R. ... Dallas, TX
Allbritton, Laura R., P.C. ... Dallas, TX
Allbritton, Owen S. ... Clearwater, FL
Allbritton, Steven N. ... College Station, TX
Allbritton, Terry E. ... New Orleans, LA
Allbritton, Wallace E. ... Tallahassee, FL
Allbrooks, Terry ... Albuquerque, NM
Allcock, Edmund Arthur ... Boston, MA
Allcock, John ... San Diego, CA
Allcorn, Linda S. ... Santa Ana, CA
Allcorn, S. Robert ... Montclair, NJ
Allday, Martin L. ... Austin, TX
Allder, Jeff S. ... El Paso, TX
Allderdice and Denman ... Los Angeles, CA
Allderdice, Linda Auerbach
Los Angeles, CA
Allderdice, Michael B. ... Los Angeles, CA
Alldread, Katherine C. ... Flint, MI
Alldredge, Brett R. ... Visalia, CA
Alldredge, Joseph A. ... Panama City, FL
Alldredge, Melvin C. ... Miami, FL
Alldredge, Melvin C., P.A. ... Miami, FL
Alldredge, Ralph C. ... Emeryville, CA
Alldredge, Rufus, Jr. ... Long Beach, MS
Alldredge, Stephen C. ... Tampa, FL
Alldredge, Suzanne ... Birmingham, AL
Alle, James ... Detroit, MI
Alle, James ... Grosse Pointe, MI
Allebach, David L., Jr. ... Pottstown, PA
Allebest, Edward F. ... Laguna Hills, CA
Allecta, Julie ... San Francisco, CA
Allee, Henry E. ... Tomball, TX
Allee, Jacqueline ... Miami, FL
Allee, John S. ... New York, NY
Allee, Rita T. ... Fairbanks, AK
Allee, Rita T., P.C., Law Office of
Fairbanks, AK
Allega, Gerald F. ... Evansville, IN
Allegaert Berger & Vogel LLP
Princeton, NJ
New York, NY
Allegaert, Christopher ... New York, NY
Allegaert, Theodore ... Palo Alto, CA
Allegaert, Winthrop J. ... New York, NY
Allegra, Frances P. ... Miami, FL
Allegra, Francis M. ... Department of Justice,
Tax Division, GV
Allegra, Geraldine ... Red Bank, NJ
Allegra, John ... Jersey City, NJ
Allegra, Nebelkopf & DeConca, P.C.
Hazlet, NJ
Jersey City, NJ
Red Bank, NJ
Allegra, Peter A. ... Red Bank, NJ
Allegra, Theodore ...
Department of State, GV
Allegretti, D. Dennis ... Boston, MA
Allegretti, Daniel W. ... Concord, NH
Allegretti, Frank ... Rye, NY
Allegretti, James L. ... Chicago, IL
Allegretti, Jon A. ... Canonsburg, PA
Allegretti, Joseph G. ... Omaha, NE
Allegretti, Joseph P. ... Hammond, IN
Allegretti, Kimberly S. ... East Troy, WI
Allegretti, Michael J. ... Chatsworth, CA
Allegretti-Devenport, Regina M.
Somers, NY
Allegrini, John ... North Weymouth, MA
Allegro, James T., Jr. ... Fairfield, NJ
Allegro, Joyce Elaine ... San Jose, CA
Allegrone, Charles R. ...
Department of State, GV
Allegrucci, Donald L. ... Topeka, KS
Allelo, John G. ... Baton Rouge, LA
Allely, Craig M.J. ... Denver, CO
Alleman, Brenda B. ... Columbus, OH
Alleman, David J. ... Minnesota City, MN
Alleman, Kristen L. ... Boulder, CO
Alleman, Mark D. ... Portland, OR
Alleman, Thomas B. ... Dallas, TX
Alleman, Thomas M. (Mick) ... Tyler, TX
Allemand, Denise A. ... Larose, LA
Allemand, Denise A., A Law Corporation
Larose, LA
Allemand, Johnny X. ... Thibodaux, LA
Allemann, Melissa D. ... Springfield, MO
Allemann, Richard S. ... Phoenix, AZ
Allemeier, Daniel R. ... Malibu, CA
Allen, A. Clifford ... Oakland, CA
Allen, A. Demarest ... Bloomington, MN
Allen, A. Gillis, II ... Salisbury, MD
Allen, A. Graham ... Jacksonville, FL
Allen, A. Lewis ... Hampton, VA
Allen, A. Patricia ... Des Moines, IA
Allen, Aaron J. ... Lafayette, LA
Allen, Adam Benjamin ... Jacksonville, FL
Allen, Adrianne Kline ... Seattle, WA
Allen, Albert H. ... Beverly Hills, CA
Allen, Alexander T. ... Seattle, WA
Allen, Alfred G., III ... Graham, TX
Jacksboro, TX
Allen, Aliza C. ... Seattle, WA
Allen and Allen ... Baldwin, NY
Allen, Allen & Allen ... Salem, IN
Allen, Allen, Allen & Allen, A Professional Corporation ... Ashland, VA
Chesterfield, VA
Fredericksburg, VA
Mechanicsville, VA
Petersburg, VA
Richmond, VA
Allen, Allen, Boerner & Breeland
Brookhaven, MS
Allen & Allen, P.C. ... Woodstock, VA
Allen, Allen & Roosa ... Midland, TX
Allen, Allen & Tack, P.A. ... Chickasha, OK
Allen, Allison W. ... Lexington, MA
Allen, Alyson B.G. ... Boston, MA
Allen, Ami F. ... Geneva, IL
Allen, Amy M. ... Washington, DC
Allen, Andrea Caryn ... Florham Park, NJ
Allen, Andrew B. ... Dublin, OH
Allen, Andrew C. ... Birmingham, AL
Allen, Andrew Farr ... Lake Geneva, WI
Allen, Andrew M. ... Crested Butte, CO
Allen, Andrew P. ... Chicago, IL
Allen, Andrew S. ... Bettendorf, IA
Allen, Andrews, III ... St. Paul, MN
Allen, Angela ... Hurst, TX
Allen, Anita B. ... Yonkers, NY
Allen, Anita L. ... Washington, DC
Allen, Ann Rose ... Scottsdale, AZ
Allen, Anne B. ... New York, NY
Allen, Annmarie M. ... Framingham, MA
Allen, Anthony D. ... San Rafael, CA
Allen, Anthony M. ... Menlo Park, CA
Allen, April Lynne ... Farmington Hills, MI
Allen, Arch T., III ... Raleigh, NC
Allen, Ashby B. ... Richmond, VA
Allen & Associates, Chartered
Ocean City, MD
Salisbury, MD
Allen, Atkin & Wells, LLC ... St. George, UT
Allen, B. Gordon ... Holdenville, OK
Allen, B. Lawrence ... Willoughby, OH
Allen, B. Richard ... Newport, AR
Allen & Bailey, P.A. ... Bartow, FL
Allen, Barbara Ann ... Charleston, WV
Allen, Barbara H. ... Charleston, WV
Allen, Barbara P. ... Overland Park, KS
Allen & Barber ... Statesboro, GA
Allen, Barnard L. ... Camillus, NY
Allen, Barry L. ... Santa Ana, CA
Allen, Barry M. ... Agoura Hills, CA
Allen, Barry P. ... Plainsboro, NJ
Allen, Ben ... Little Rock, AR
Allen, Ben M. ... Albuquerque, NM
Allen, Ben T. ... Arcata, CA
Allen, Ben U. ... Henderson, NC
Allen, Benjamin ... Augusta, GA
Allen, Benjamin B. ... Alton, IL
Allen, Benjamin M. ... Portland, OR
Allen, Bernard ... Miami, FL
Allen, Bernard A. ... San Clemente, CA
Allen, Bernard A., P.C.
San Clemente, CA
Allen, Bernard L. ... Ogden, UT
Allen, Bernd. ... New York, NY
Allen, Bertram W. ... Highland Beach, FL
Allen, Bertrand E. ... Santa Fe, NM
Allen, Beth A. ... Portland, OR
Allen, Betsy L. ... San Francisco, CA
Allen, Beverly Rice
Department of Education,
Office for Civil Rights, GV
Allen, Bibb ... Birmingham, AL
Allen, Bill ... Willis, TX
Allen, Billy C. ... Houston, TX
Allen & Blackford ... Gaithersburg, MD
Allen, Blair ... Wallkill, NY
Allen, Bob E. ... Millbrook, AL
Allen, Boyd W., Jr. ... Springfield, VA
Allen, Bradford S. ... Barrington, IL

Allen, Bradley E. ... **Des Moines, IA**
Allen, Bradly E. ... Philadelphia, PA
Allen, Brandon T. ... **Houston, TX**
Allen, Brenda ... Portland, OR
Allen, Brenda Dinkins ... Lexington, KY
Allen, Brent H. ... **Washington, DC**
Allen, Brett S. ... San Francisco, CA
Allen, Brian B. ... Chicago, IL
Allen, Brian D. ... **Dayton, OH**
Allen, Brian T. ... **Mesa, AZ**
Allen, Brian T. ... Hartford, CT
Allen, Brinton, Simmons & McCarthy, P.A.
Fernandina Beach, FL
Jacksonville, FL
St. Augustine, FL
Allen, Bruce C. ... Cleveland, OH
Allen, Bruce F. ... **Sacramento, CA**
Allen, Bruce S. ... Feasterville, PA
Allen, Bryan T. ... **Salt Lake City, UT**
Allen, C. Dale ... **Nashville, TN**
Allen, C. David ... Lafayette, LA
Allen, C. Lee ... McLean, VA
Allen, C. Ray ... Midland, TX
Allen, C. Stephen ... **Tampa, FL**
Allen, C. Stephen, P.A. ... **Tampa, FL**
Allen, C. Walter ... Asheville, NC
Allen, Camille T. ... **St. Albans, NY**
Allen, Cannon F. ... **Memphis, TN**
Allen, Carl W. ... San Francisco, CA
Allen, Carla Whitaker ... Cave City, KY
Allen, Carol ... Department of Commerce, Office of the General Counsel, GV
Allen, Carol Kridner ... San Luis Obispo, CA
Allen, Carol Lumb ... **Daytona Beach, FL**
Allen, Carolyn Holtschlag ... Pittsburgh, PA
Allen, Carrie Hill ... **Washington, DC**
Allen, Carter ... **Atlanta, GA**
Allen, Carter R. ... Waynesboro, VA
Allen & Carwile, P.C. ... Waynesboro, VA
Allen, Cassie J. ... Prestonsburg, KY
Allen, Catherine ... Houston, TX
Allen, Catherine S. ... **White Plains, NY**
Allen, Cathleen D. ... **Melville, NY**
Allen, Cathleen H. ... **Grand Island, NE**
Allen, Chad A. ... Owatonna, MN
Allen, Chad M. ... **Dallas, TX**
Allen, Charles A. ... Marshall, TX
Allen, Charles B. ... Bellevue, WA
Allen, Charles C., Jr. ... **St. Louis, MO**
Allen, Charles E., III ... **Louisville, KY**
Allen, Charles I. ... Oklahoma City, OK
Allen, Charles L. ... Mount Pleasant, SC
Allen, Charles L. ... **Salt Lake City, UT**
Allen, Charles L. ... **Richmond, VA**
Allen, Charles M. ... Louisville, KY
Allen, Charles M. ... **Spring House, PA**
Allen, Charles M. ... **Glen Allen, VA**
Allen, Charles M., II ... Montgomery, AL
Allen, Charles P. ... West Helena, AR
Allen, Charles R., Jr. ... Arlington, VA
Allen, Charles R., Jr. ... **Roanoke, VA**
Allen, Charles W. ... Birmingham, AL
Allen, Charles W. ... **Portland, ME**
Allen, Charlotte L. ... **Midland, MI**
Allen, Charlotte L., P.C. ... **Midland, MI**
Allen, Charlton Laramie ... **Wilmington, NC**
Allen, Cheryl C. ... Arroyo Grande, CA
Allen, Christian S. ... Troy, MI
Allen, Christina Hodge ... Richmond, VA
Allen, Christine E. ... **Seattle, WA**
Allen, Christopher ... **Tacoma, WA**
Allen, Christopher A. ... **St. Louis, MO**
Allen, Christopher B., Law Offices of
Houston, TX
Allen, Christopher J. ... Binghamton, NY
Allen, Christopher L. ... Gaithersburg, MD
Allen, Christopher P. ... Blue Bell, PA
Allen, Christopher R.
Department Of Veterans Affairs, Board of Veterans Appeals, GV
Allen, Cindy M. ... **Tyler, TX**
Allen, Clarice A. ... Texarkana, TX
Allen, Claude T. ... Houston, TX
Allen, Claude W., Jr. ... Oxford, NC
Allen, Claudia G. ... **Cincinnati, OH**
Allen, Claudia H. ... **Chicago, IL**
Allen, Clay Morgan ... **Lafayette, LA**
Allen, Clay T. ... Columbia, SC
Allen, Cleo D., (Mr.) ... San Francisco, CA
Allen, Clifton L. ... Upland, CA
Allen, Coleman & Waltermire
Lake Jackson, TX
Allen, Conni L. ... **Oklahoma City, OK**
Allen, Constance J. ... Detroit, MI
Allen, Cooley & Allen ... **Lawrence, KS**
Topeka, KS
Allen, Cooper & Fowler, L.L.P.
Santa Rosa, CA
Allen, Cori M. ... **Palo Alto, CA**
Allen, Courtenay B. ... **San Antonio, TX**
Allen, C. R. (Reg), Jr. ... **Dallas, TX**
Allen, Craig A. ... **Ironton, OH**
Allen, Craig H. ... **Greenville, SC**
Allen, Craig H. ... **Seattle, WA**
Allen, Craig K. ... Bellingham, WA
Allen, Craig R. ... **Chattanooga, TN**
Allen, Cynthia A. ... Parsippany, NJ
Allen, Cynthia J. ... Los Angeles, CA
Allen, Cynthia Rucker ... **Abilene, TX**
Allen, Cynthia Woolen ... **Dallas, TX**
Allen, Cynthia Y. ... **New York, NY**
Allen, Dale C. ... **Knoxville, TN**
Allen, Dale L., Jr. ... **San Francisco, CA**
Allen, Dan G. ... Duncan, OK
Allen, Dane E. ... Oak Creek, WI
Allen, Daniel J. ... Columbus, OH
Allen, Daniel W. ... Chestertown, MD
Allen, Dannette Watson ... Spokane, WA
Allen, Danny E. ... **Spartanburg, SC**
Allen, Danny G. ... Perry, OK
Allen, Darrell M. ... McLean, VA
Allen, Daryl ... **Corpus Christi, TX**
Allen, David ... Sacramento, CA
Allen, David ... Washington, DC
Allen, David ... **Seattle, WA**
Allen, David A. ... Dallas, TX
Allen, David, & Associates ... Sacramento, CA
Allen, David B. ... **Costa Mesa, CA**
Allen, David B. ... Ontario, CA
Lexington, KY
Allen, David B. ... Houma, LA
Allen, David B. ... Columbia, MD
Allen, David C. ... **Los Angeles, CA**
Allen, David C. ... Madras, OR
Allen, David E., Jr. ... Orange, CA
Allen, David F. ... **Orlando, FL**
Allen, David F. ... **Marysville, OH**
Allen, David F., A Professional Association
Orlando, FL
Allen, David F., (P.C.) ... **Chicago, IL**
Allen, David G. ... Miami, FL
Allen, David G. ... **Dallas, TX**
Allen, David J. ... Wheaton, IL
Allen, David J. ... **Indianapolis, IN**
Allen, David J. ... Detroit, MI
Allen, David L. ... **Encino, CA**
Allen, David L. ... Santa Barbara, CA
Allen, David L. ... Visalia, CA
Allen, David L. ... **Lufkin, TX**
Allen, David Lee ... Lawrenceburg, TN
Allen, David M. ... **Chicago, IL**
Allen, David M. ... **Biloxi, MS**
Allen, David M. ... **Albany, NY**
Allen, David Matthew ... **Tampa, FL**
Allen, David Neal ... **Charlotte, NC**
Allen, David P. ... Salem, IN
Allen, David Paul ... Hammond, IN
Allen, David R. ... **Chula Vista, CA**
Allen, David R. ... Louisville, KY
Allen, David R. ... Beaverton, OR
Allen, David S. ... **Los Angeles, CA**
Allen, David S. ... **Rossville, GA**
Allen, David S. ... Chicago, IL
Allen, David S. ... **Indianapolis, IN**
Allen, David V. ... **Cleveland, OH**
Allen, David W. ... Washington, DC
Allen, David W. ... **Baltimore, MD**
Allen, Deana ... **Dallas, TX**
Allen, Deborah Bourne ... Arlington, VA
Allen, Deborah E. ... New Castle, DE
Allen, Deborah Renée ... Memphis, TN
Allen, Debra Brown ... **Boston, MA**
Allen, Debra E. ... Santa Ana, CA
Allen, Debra L. ... Jackson, MS
Allen, Debra Lee ... **Baltimore, MD**
Allen, Deedra M. ... Plant City, FL
Allen, Dell, Frank & Trinkle, P.A.
Tampa, FL
Allen, Dena Pickering ... **Wenatchee, WA**
Allen, Dennis L. ... **Washington, DC**
Allen, Derek J. ... **Greensboro, NC**
Allen, Derick E. ... **St. Louis, MO**
Allen, Dewayne ... Tulsa, OK
Allen, Diana M. ... Tampa, FL
Allen, Diana Semel ... **Raleigh, NC**
Allen, Diane M. ... San Francisco, CA
Allen, Diane M. ... **South San Francisco, CA**
Allen, Diane Wingo ... Houston, TX
Allen, Dick ... Granite City, IL
Allen & Dill, P.A. ... **Orlando, FL**
Winter Park, FL
Allen, Dillis V. ... Elk Grove Village, IL
Allen & Dillon ... **Ironton, OH**
Allen, Don A. ... **Washington, DC**
Allen, Don B. ... **Provo, UT**
Salt Lake City, UT
Allen, Don W. ... Shreveport, LA
Allen, Don Warren ... **Maitland, FL**
Allen, Donald A. ... **Milwaukee, WI**
Allen, Donald B. ... Southampton, NY
Allen, Donald C. ... **Baltimore, MD**
Allen, Donald D. ... **Denver, CO**
Allen, Donald Eaves ... Landenberg, PA
Allen, Donald Ernest ... Seattle, WA
Allen, Donald H. ... Jackson, TN
Allen, Donald L. ... Independence, MO
Allen, Donald M. ... Philadelphia, PA
Allen, Donald R. ... **Washington, DC**
Allen, Donald R. ... Alexandria, VA
Allen, Donielle C. ... Metairie, LA
Allen, Dorene S. ... Midland, MI
Allen, Dori ... New York, NY
Allen, Doris C. ... **Knoxville, TN**
Allen, Douglas ... Port St. Lucie, FL
Allen, Douglas B. ... San Jose, CA
Allen, Douglas B. ... Oklahoma City, OK
Allen, Douglas C. ... **St. Joseph, MI**
Allen, Douglas C. ... Great Falls, MT
Allen, Douglas F., Jr. ... **New York, NY**
Allen, Douglas H. ... Winnfield, LA
Allen, Douglas P. ... Aspen, CO
Allen, Douglas Reese ... Oklahoma City, OK
Allen, Dudley D., (P.A.) ... Jacksonville, FL
Allen, Durelle L., Jr., (P.L.C.) ... Lafayette, LA
Allen, D.V. & Associates
Elk Grove Village, IL
Allen, Dwight L., Jr. ... Washington, DC
Allen, Dwight S. ... Santa Rosa, CA
Allen, Dwight W. ... Wake Forest, NC
Allen, Dyer, Doppelt, Milbrath & Gilchrist
Melbourne, FL
Orlando, FL
Allen and Eakes ... **Anderson, SC**
Allen, Edmund P. ... **Bellevue, WA**
Allen, Edmund T., III ... Paradise Valley, AZ
Allen, Edward J. ... Red Bluff, CA
Allen, Edward L. ... **Fredericksburg, VA**
Allen, Edward M. ... **Denver, CO**
Allen, Edward S. ... **Birmingham, AL**
Allen, Edwin E. ... Eugene, OR
Allen, Edwin V., Jr. ... Kenedy, TX
Allen, Elaine D. ... Albuquerque, NM
Allen, Eleanor S. ... Brooklyn, NY
Allen, Elisabeth M. ... **Miami, FL**
Allen, Elizabeth A. ... **Washington, DC**
Allen, Elizabeth A. ... New York, NY
Allen, Elizabeth E. ... Covington, LA
Allen, Elizabeth L. ... Encinitas, CA
Allen, Elizabeth M. ... **Petersburg, VA**
Allen, Emerson P. ... Richmond, VA
Allen, Eric A. ... **Bartlesville, OK**
Allen, Eric K. ... Bartow, FL
Allen, Eric N. ... **Greenfield, IN**
Allen, Erin M. ... **Austin, TX**
Allen, Ernest M., III ... Burlington, VT
Allen, Ethan ... New York, NY
Allen, Ethan ... Oklahoma City, OK
Allen, Ethel A. ... Fort Worth, TX
Allen, Eugene ... Columbia, LA
Allen, Evelyn ... Circleville, KS
Allen, Everette G., III
Fredericksburg, VA
Richmond, VA
Allen, Everette G., Jr. ... **Richmond, VA**
Allen, F. Acie, Jr. ... Dillwyn, VA
Allen, F. de la Puente ... Salem, OR
Allen, F. Gordon, III ... **Portland, OR**
Allen, F. Hill ... **Raleigh, NC**
Allen, F. Wendall ... **Birmingham, AL**
Allen & Fasman ... **Beverly Hills, CA**
Allen, Fedder, Herendeen & Kowals
South Bend, IN
Allen & Flatt Incorporated
Newport Beach, CA
Allen & Forehand ... **Moultrie, GA**
Allen, Frances ... Hartford, CT
Allen, Frances O. ... Shreveport, LA
Allen, Francis A. ... Gainesville, FL
Allen, Francis C. ... Rockwall, TX
Allen, Francis W. ... **Statesboro, GA**
Allen, Frank A. ... St. George, UT
Allen, Frank C. ... Charleston, SC
Allen, Frank C., Jr. ... New Orleans, LA
Allen, Frank D. ... **Haddonfield, NJ**
Allen, Frank D., Jr. ... **Washington, DC**
Allen, Frank E. ... Plainfield, NJ
Allen, Frank G., Jr. ... Boston, MA
Allen, Frank H., Jr. ... Albuquerque, NM
Allen, Frank T. ... **Winter Park, FL**
Allen, Frank W. ... **Augusta, GA**
Allen, Frank W. ... Conroe, TX
Allen, Franklin G. ... Chicago, IL
Allen, Franklin G. ... Baltimore, MD
Allen, Franklin W. ... Atlanta, GA
Allen, Fred W. ... Huntsville, AL
Allen, Frederic W. ... Montpelier, VT
Allen, Frederick D., Jr. ... Springfield, OR
Allen, Frederick H. ... Hasbrouck Heights, NJ
Allen, Frederick H., III ... **Somerville, NJ**
Allen, Frederick L. ... **Los Angeles, CA**
Allen, Frederick W. ... Peoria, IL
Allen, Frederick W., Ltd. ... Peoria, IL
Allen, G. David, Jr. ... **Chattanooga, TN**
Allen, G. Wesley ... Philadelphia, PA
Allen, G. William, Jr.
Fort Lauderdale, FL
Allen, Gail D. ... **Baltimore, MD**
Allen & Galego ... **Key Biscayne, FL**
Miami, FL
Allen, Gantt & Best ... Columbia, SC
Allen, Garland H. ... Chicago, IL
Allen, Garth H. ... Greeley, CO
Allen, Gary D. ... Salem, OR
Allen, Gary F. ... Ypsilanti, MI
Allen, Gary G. ... **Boise, ID**
Allen, Gary J. ... Walled Lake, MI
Allen, Gary L. ... Bartow, FL
Allen, Gary Mikel ... Irvine, CA
Allen, Gary O. ... Pelham, GA
Allen, Gary R. ... Department of Justice, Tax Division, GV
Allen, Gary S. ... Gladwin, MI
Allen, Gary W. ... Department of Justice, Civil Division, GV
Allen, Gary W. ... Warren, OH
Allen, Gayle H. ... Portland, ME
Allen, Gemma B. ... **Chicago, IL**
Allen, Genelle M. ... Detroit, MI
Allen, George C. ... Seattle, WA
Allen, George E., III ... **Mechanicsville, VA**
Richmond, VA
Allen, George F. ... Sacramento, CA
Allen, George F. ... Naples, FL
Allen, George F. ... **Richmond, VA**
Allen, George G., Jr. ... Lee's Summit, MO
Allen, George H. ... **Santa Barbara, CA**
Allen, George H. ... Waco, TX
Allen, George M. ... Telluride, CO
Allen, George V. ... Lawrence, KS
Allen, George V., Jr. ... Washington, DC
Allen, George W. ... Tustin, CA
Allen, George W. ... Cincinnati, OH
Allen, Gerald F. ... **Schaumburg, IL**
Allen, Gerald G. ... New York, NY
Allen, Gerald R. ... Butte, MT
Allen, Gertrude K. ... Portland, OR
Allen, Gina R. ... Nashville, TN
Allen, Gizella L., (Mrs.) ... Los Angeles, CA
Allen, Glen K. ... **Baltimore, MD**
Allen, Glenn E. ... Madrid, IA
Allen, Glenn K. ... **Jacksonville, FL**
Allen, Glenn K., A Professional Association
Jacksonville, FL
Allen, Glenn L. ... **San Francisco, CA**
Allen, Glenn S. ... Lansing, MI
Allen, Glenna M. ... St. Louis, MO
Allen, Godwin, Morris, Laurenzi & Bloomfield, P.C. ... **Memphis, TN**
Allen & Gooch, A Law Corporation
Lafayette, LA
Allen, Gordon K. ... Piedmont, OK
Allen, Gordon P. ... Vestal, NY
Allen, Gordon T. ... Rocky Hill, CT
Allen, Gove L. ... Mesa, AZ
Allen, Gregory D. ... **Salyersville, KY**
Allen, Gregory D. ... **St. Paul, MN**
Allen, Gregory L. ... **Abilene, TX**
Allen, Gregory W. ... **Houston, TX**
Allen, Gretchen Gibbons ... **Houston, TX**
Allen, Guthrie H., III ... **Paducah, KY**
Allen Guthrie & McHugh
Charleston, WV
Allen, Guy Michael ... **Hackensack, NJ**
Allen, H. Frank ... Tarboro, NC
Allen, H. Rollin ... **Southfield, MI**
Allen, H. Scott ... Augusta, GA
Allen, H. William ... **Little Rock, AR**
Allen, Hansen & Maybrown, P.S.
Seattle, WA
Allen & Harold, P.L.C. ... Washington, DC
Manassas, VA
Stephens City, VA
Allen, Harrison, Williams, McDonell & Swatek ... Lake Geneva, WI
Whitewater, WI
Allen, Harry A. ... Santa Rosa, CA
Allen, Harry B. ... Sarasota, FL
Allen, Harry R. ... **Gulfport, MS**
Allen, Harvey M. ... Austin, TX
Allen, Harvey S. ... Thayer, MO
Allen, Heath L. ... Camp Hill, PA
Harrisburg, PA
Allen, Helen L. ... Danbury, CT
Allen, Henry A. "Gus" ... **Little Rock, AR**
Allen, Henry S., Jr. ... **Chicago, IL**
Allen, Herbert ... Indian Harbour Beach, FL
Allen, Herbert L. ... **Orlando, FL**
Allen, Hervey C. ... Rockport, ME
Allen, Hilary S. ... **Oklahoma City, OK**
Allen & Hodgman ... Cleveland, OH
Allen, Holden & McIntosh Law Offices, L.L.C. ... **Dexter, MO**
Jefferson City, MO
Allen, Hope Celeste Barbian ... **Atlanta, GA**
Allen, Howard A. ... San Diego, CA
Allen, Hugh O. ... Rancho Cordova, CA
Allen, Hunter S., Jr. ... **Atlanta, GA**
Allen, Ian G. ... Sunnyvale, CA
Allen, Ian I. ... **Southfield, MI**
Allen, Ira Lee ... **Austin, TX**
Allen, Irvin McCreary ... Alexandria, VA
Allen, J. Aron ... **Minneapolis, MN**
Allen, J. Christopher ... Lebanon, MO
Allen, J. Dean, Jr. ... Santa Ana, CA
Allen, J. Edward ... **Athens, GA**
Allen, J. Greg ... **Montgomery, AL**
Allen, J. James ... Jacksonville, FL
Allen, J. Larry ... Sheridan, AR
Allen, J. Paul ... **Cincinnati, OH**
Allen, J. Philip ... Rowayton, CT
Allen, J. Wayne ... Irvine, CA
Allen, J. Witty ... **Decatur, AL**
Allen, Jack F. ... **Clayton, MO**
Allen, Jack K. ... Houston, TX
Allen, Jack M. ... Perryton, TX
Allen, Jacqueline ... **New City, NY**
Allen, Jacqueline F. ... Philadelphia, PA
Allen, Jacqueline Lillard ... **Boston, MA**
Allen, Jacqueline W. ... Midland, TX
Allen, Jame D. ... Santa Rosa, CA
Allen, Jamerson C. ... **San Francisco, CA**
Allen, James ... Burbank, CA
Allen, James ... New York, NY
Allen, James A. ... New York, NY
Allen, James Aaron ... **Washington, DC**
Fairfax, VA
Allen, James B. ... Houston, TX
Allen, James C. ... **San Diego, CA**
Allen, James D. ... **San Diego, CA**
Allen, James D. ... Salem, IN
Allen, James D. ... **Lexington, KY**
Allen, James E. ... **Walnut Creek, CA**
Allen, James E. ... Jackson, MS
Allen, James E., Jr. ... **Oakland, CA**
Allen, James F. ... Buffalo, NY
Allen, James F. (IBA) ... **Houston, TX**
Allen, James & Foley, P.C. ... Southgate, MI
Allen, James G. ... Thousand Oaks, CA
Allen, James G. ... Pikeville, KY
Allen, James H. ... Memphis, TN
Allen, James J. ... Department of Defense, Office of the General Counsel, GV
Allen, James J. ... Joliet, IL
Allen, James, Jr. ... Charlotte, NC
Allen, James L. ... Bloomfield Hills, MI
Allen, James M. ... La Jolla, CA
Allen, James M. ... Redwood City, CA
Allen, James M. ... **San Francisco, CA**
Allen, James M. ... Dixon, IL
Allen, James M. ... Palatine, IL
Allen, James M. ... Hamilton, OH
Allen, James Matthew ... **Englewood, CO**
Allen, James P. ... **Detroit, MI**
Allen, James R. ... Prestonsburg, KY
Allen, James R. ... **Columbia, SC**
Allen, James S., Jr. ... Kansas City, MO
Allen, James W. ... **Kansas City, MO**
Allen, Jana L. ... Auburn, CA
Allen, Jane ... Salt Lake City, UT
Allen, Jane Hanner ... **Nashville, TN**
Allen, Janenne ... Columbus, OH
Allen, Janet C. ... Walnut Creek, CA

Allen, Janet Cheryl .... Atlanta, GA
Allen, Jared W. .... Idaho Falls, ID
Allen, Jason W. .... Milwaukee, WI
Allen, Jasper B., Jr. .... Burlington, NC
Allen, Jay D. .... Salem, IN
Allen, Jay M. .... Mesa, AZ
Allen, Jay V. .... Tulsa, OK
Allen, Jean Curry .... Atlanta, GA
Allen, Jefferson K. .... Rindge, NH
Allen, Jefferson M. .... Atlanta, GA
Allen, Jeffrey .... Oakland, CA
Allen, Jeffrey F. .... Newport Beach, CA
Allen, Jeffrey L. .... Wellesley, MA
Allen, Jeffrey P. .... Boston, MA
Allen, Jeffrey R. .... Columbus, OH
Allen, Jeffrey R. .... Richmond, VA
Allen, Jeffrey Roberts .... Fort Worth, TX
Allen, Jeffrey S. .... Alameda, CA
Allen, Jeffrey S. .... Los Angeles, CA
Allen, Jeffrey W. .... Redwood City, CA
Allen, Jennifer C. .... Stuart, FL
Allen, Jennifer Mae .... Ashland, MA
Allen, Jerold .... Haddonfield, NJ
Philadelphia, PA
Allen, Jerome Jay .... Troy, MI
Allen, Jerome Jay, P.C. .... Troy, MI
Allen, Jerry A., Jr. .... Goldsboro, NC
Allen, Jerry B. .... Claremont, CA
Allen, Jerry O. .... Columbus, OH
Allen, Jessie L. .... Hallettsville, TX
Allen, Jimmy E., Jr. .... Pittsburg, KS
Allen, Joan Virginia .... Santa Ana, CA
Allen, Joanna C. .... Seattle, WA
Allen, Joanne Jones .... Richmond, VA
Allen, Joe B. .... Houston, TX
Allen, Joe B., III, (P.C.) .... Dallas, TX
Allen, Joe Bailey .... Longview, TX
Allen, Joe L., Jr. .... Columbia, SC
Allen, Joe Michael .... Sealy, TX
Allen, Joel S. .... Dallas, TX
Allen, Johanna H. .... Rochester Hills, MI
Allen, John A. .... Woodland Hills, CA
Allen, John A. .... Destin, FL
Allen, John A. .... Atlanta, GA
Allen, John B. .... Jackson, CA
Allen, John B., Jr. .... Columbia, SC
Allen, John C. .... Great Falls, MT
Allen, John C. .... Houston, TX
Allen, John C., IV .... Hampton, VA
Allen, John C., Jr. .... Daytona Beach, FL
Allen, John C., P.C. .... Houston, TX
Allen, John Charles .... New Brunswick, NJ
Allen, John D. .... Oswego, NY
Syracuse, NY
Allen, John D., III .... Hackensack, NJ
Allen, John D. S. .... Los Angeles, CA
Allen, John E. .... Chicago, IL
Allen, John F. .... Southfield, MI
Allen, John J. .... Los Angeles, CA
Allen, John J. .... Larchmont, NY
Allen, John L. .... Norwood, MA
Allen, John L. .... Manchester, NH
Allen, John L. .... Albany, NY
Allen, John L. .... Thomasville, NC
Allen, John L. .... Wheeling, WV
Allen, John L., & Associates, P.C., Law Offices of .... Manchester, NH
Allen, John Lawrence .... New York, NY
Allen, John M. .... Pittsburg, CA
Allen, John M. .... Dallas, TX
Allen, John M., Jr. .... New York, NY
Allen, John Marshall .... Charleston, SC
Allen, John Morison .... New York, NY
Allen, John R. .... Farmingdale, NY
Allen, John R. .... Columbus, OH
Allen, John R. .... New Lexington, OH
Allen, John R. .... Providence, RI
Allen, John R. .... Bellevue, WA
Allen, John T. .... Chicago, IL
Allen, John T., Jr. .... St. Petersburg, FL
Allen, John W. .... Kalamazoo, MI
Allen, John W. .... Syracuse, NY
Allen, John W. .... Mansfield, OH
Allen, Johnson, Alexander & Karp, P.A.
Washington, DC
Annapolis, MD
Baltimore, MD
Rockville, MD
Towson, MD
Upper Marlboro, MD
Alexandria, VA
Arlington, VA
Fairfax, VA
Allen Johnson & Lonergan, LLP
Albany, NY
Allen, Jonathan C. .... Beaumont, TX
Allen, Jonathan H. .... Lancaster, TX
Allen, Jordan B. .... Chicago, IL
Allen, José R. .... San Francisco, CA
Allen, Joseph .... Detroit, MI
Allen, Joseph B., III .... Key West, FL
Allen, Joseph B., III, P.A. .... Key West, FL
Allen, Joseph D. .... Santa Barbara, CA
Allen, Joseph D., III .... Wilmington, DE
Allen, Joseph K. .... San Mateo, CA
Allen, Joseph M. .... Vernon, AL
Allen, Joseph M. .... New Lexington, OH
Allen, Joseph M., Jr. .... Mobile, AL
Allen, Joseph W. .... Buffalo, NY
Allen, Joseph W. .... Ithaca, NY
Allen, Joseph W., III .... Worcester, MA
Allen, Josette C. .... Wheaton, IL
Allen, Judith L. .... Marquette, MI
Allen, Julia C.
General Services Administration, Office of Regional Counsel, GV
Allen, Julia D. .... Coffeyville, KS
Allen, Julian H. .... Colorado Springs, CO

Allen, Julie M. .... New York, NY
Allen, Julie O'Donnell .... Chicago, IL
Allen, June H. .... Treasury Department, Office of the Comptroller of the Currency, GV
Allen, Justin T. .... Little Rock, AR
Allen, Kandy Lee .... Cathedral City, CA
Allen, Karen E. .... Tucson, AZ
Allen, Karen M. .... Philadelphia, PA
Allen, Karen Tietjen .... Los Altos, CA
Allen, Karin Middleton .... Atlanta, GA
Allen, Katherine E. .... Greeley, CO
Allen, Katherine Martin
State College, PA
Allen, Katherine Simpson .... Nashville, TN
Allen, Kathleen M. .... Chicago, IL
Allen, Kathleen N. .... Palo Alto, CA
Allen, Kathryn E. .... Austin, TX
Allen, Kathryn J. .... San Francisco, CA
Allen, Kathryn K. .... Clarksburg, WV
Allen, Kathryn L. .... Atlanta, GA
Allen, Kay-Dawn G. .... Greeley, CO
Allen, Keith .... Washington, DC
Allen, Keith F. .... Moultrie, GA
Allen, Keith G. .... Liberty, TX
Allen, Keith T. .... Rockville, MD
Allen, Keith W.
Department Of Veterans Affairs, Board of Veterans Appeals, GV
Allen, Keller W. .... Spokane, WA
Allen, Kelley & Sowell, P.C. .... Tifton, GA
Allen, Kellie Ann .... Philadelphia, PA
Allen, Kelly A. .... Bloomfield Hills, MI
Allen, Kenneth B. .... Philadelphia, PA
Allen, Kenneth E. .... Columbia, SC
Allen, Kenneth J., & Associates
Akron, IN
Indianapolis, IN
Merrillville, IN
Allen. Kenneth J., & Associates
Michigan City, IN
Allen, Kenneth J., & Associates
South Bend, IN
Allen, Kenneth J., & Associates
Valparaiso, IN
Allen, Kenneth L. .... Sonoita, AZ
Allen, Kenneth L. .... Brighton, MA
Allen, Kenneth R. .... Palo Alto, CA
Allen, Kerry J. .... Colorado Springs, CO
Allen, Kevin C. .... Philadelphia, PA
Allen, Kevin D. .... Denver, CO
Allen, Kevin J. .... Dallas, TX
Allen, Kevin P. .... Pittsburgh, PA
Allen and Kimbell, LLP
Santa Barbara, CA
Allen, Kimberly A. .... Houston, TX
Allen, Kimberly Lemons .... Dalhart, TX
Allen, Kirk R. .... Albuquerque, NM
Allen & Knapstad, PLLP .... Butte, MT
Allen, Kopet & Boyd, PLLC
Chattanooga, TN
Jackson, TN
Knoxville, TN
Allen & Korkowski, & Associates
Rantoul, IL
Allen, Kristen R. .... Manchester, NH
Allen, Kristian N. .... Greensboro, NC
Allen, Kristin .... Bingham Farms, MI
Allen, Kristy L. .... Chicago, IL
Allen, L. Gleason .... Wilmington, NC
Allen, L. Lou .... Atlanta, GA
Allen, L. Walker, II .... New Orleans, LA
Allen, La Sonya D. .... Silver Spring, MD
Allen, Lang, Curotto & Peed, P.A.
Orlando, FL
Allen, Laraine R. .... Pittsburgh, PA
Allen, Larry Dean .... Canon City, CO
Allen, Larry H. .... Des Moines, IA
Allen, Larry L. .... Checotah, OK
Allen, Laura B. .... Phoenix, AZ
Allen, Laura H. .... New York, NY
Allen, Laura Henry .... Jacksonville, FL
Allen, Laura Lea .... San Francisco, CA
Allen, Laura Morrison .... White Plains, NY
Allen, Laurie A. .... Los Angeles, CA
Allen Law Firm, A Professional Corporation
Little Rock, AR
Allen Law Office .... Lafayette, LA
Allen, Lawrence .... Encino, CA
Allen, Lawrence J., Jr. .... Everett, WA
Allen, Lawrence K. .... Clearwater, FL
Allen, Lawrence R. .... Redding, CA
Allen, Lawrence S. .... Miami, FL
Allen, Layman E. .... Ann Arbor, MI
Allen, Lee C. .... Little Rock, AR
Allen, Leigh B., III .... Jackson, MS
Allen, Lemuel B., Jr. .... Seguin, TX
Allen, Leon A., Jr. .... New York, NY
Allen, Leonidas A. .... Philadelphia, PA
Allen, Leslie .... Department of Justice, Environment and Natural Resources Division, GV
Allen, Leslie A. .... Atlanta, GA
Allen, Leslie E., III .... Lynchburg, VA
Allen, Leslie M. .... Montgomery, AL
Allen, Lewis B. .... Marietta, GA
Allen, Lexis MacFadden .... Sacramento, CA
Las Vegas, NV
Allen, Lila .... Orange, CA
Allen, Linda A. .... Houston, TX
Allen, Linda Cory .... Chula Vista, CA
Allen, Linda Holland .... Orlando, FL
Allen, Linda R. .... Milaca, MN
Allen and Lippes .... Buffalo, NY
Allen, Lisa J. .... Atlanta, GA
Allen, Lloyd E. .... Salt Lake City, UT
Allen, Loren J. .... Troy, MI

Allen - Lottmann, A Professional Corporation .... Athens, TX
Lindale, TX
Longview, TX
Tyler, TX
Allen, Louis C., Jr. .... Burlington, NC
Allen, Louis F. .... Memphis, TN
Allen, Louise Jacowitz
Fort Lauderdale, FL
Allen, L. P., Jr. .... Belmont, MS
Allen, Luis E. .... Culver City, CA
Allen, L. Walker, II & Associates
New Orleans, LA
Allen, Lyle W. .... Peoria, IL
Allen, Lynn M. .... Phoenix, AZ
Allen, M. Darlene .... Cypress, CA
Allen, M. Lou .... Topeka, KS
Allen, M. Todd .... Dallas, TX
Allen and MacDonald .... Wilmington, NC
Allen, Mahalley Dawn .... Kansas City, MO
Allen and Mahl .... Bettendorf, IA
Allen & Maller, P.A. .... St. Petersburg, FL
Allen, Marcy Karr .... West Palm Beach, FL
Allen, Margaret J. .... Berkeley, CA
Allen, Margaret M. .... Philadelphia, PA
Allen, Maria .... New York, NY
Allen, Marie-Therese .... New York, NY
Allen, Marion DeKalb .... Angleton, TX
Allen, Marion H., Jr. .... Atlanta, GA
Allen, Marjorie F. .... Santa Barbara, CA
Allen, Mark .... New York, NY
Allen, Mark A. .... Treasury Department, Internal Revenue Service, GV
Allen, Mark A. .... Memphis, TN
Allen, Mark C., III .... Long Beach, CA
Allen, Mark C., Jr., (Professional Corporation)
Los Angeles, CA
Allen, Mark E. .... Delavan, IL
Allen, Mark E. .... Liberty, MO
Allen, Mark E. .... Olympia, WA
Allen, Mark H. .... Tulsa, OK
Allen, Mark K. .... Houston, TX
Allen, Mark R. .... Phoenix, AZ
Allen, Mark R.
Federal Election Commission, Office of the General Counsel, GV
Allen, Mark R. .... Memphis, TN
Allen, Mark S. .... Alexandria, VA
Allen, Marnie .... Portland, OR
Allen, Martin .... Des Plaines, IL
Allen, Martin .... Warren, NJ
Allen, Martin S. .... Boston, MA
Allen, Marva A. .... New York, NY
Allen, Mary Ann D. .... Albany, NY
Allen, Mary Dee Perkins .... Cookeville, TN
Allen, Mary Ellen .... Washington, DC
Allen, Mary S. .... Stockton, CA
Allen, Maryellen B. .... Frankfort, KY
Allen, Maryse C. .... Woodbridge, VA
Allen, Mathews & Baker, P.A.
Belle Glade, FL
Allen, Matkins, Leck, Gamble & Mallory LLP .... Irvine, CA
Los Angeles, CA
San Diego, CA
San Francisco, CA
Allen, Matthew F. .... Missoula, MT
Allen, Matthew T. .... Atlanta, GA
Allen, Max J. .... Plymouth, MA
Allen, Meredith Clayton .... Dallas, TX
Allen, Meredith E. .... Oakland, CA
Allen, Merle M., Jr. .... Laie, HI
Allen, Michael .... Liberal, KS
Allen, Michael B. .... San Mateo, CA
Allen, Michael B. .... Chicago, IL
Allen, Michael B., A Prof. Corp.
San Mateo, CA
Allen, Michael C. .... Richmond, VA
Allen, Michael C. .... Charleston, WV
Allen, Michael D. .... Pasadena, CA
Allen, Michael D. .... Wilmington, DE
Allen, Michael D. .... Philadelphia, PA
Allen, Michael D. .... Tyler, TX
Allen, Michael E. .... Tallahassee, FL
Allen, Michael E. .... Indianapolis, IN
Allen, Michael E. .... Indianapolis, IN
Allen, Michael G. .... Pensacola, FL
Allen, Michael G. .... Falls Church, VA
Allen, Michael H. .... Chicago, IL
Allen, Michael H. .... Saginaw, MI
Allen, Michael I. .... New York, NY
Allen, Michael J. .... Greenwich, CT
Allen, Michael J. .... Greensboro, NC
Allen, Michael J. .... Madison, WI
Sun Prairie, WI
Allen, Michael K. .... San Diego, CA
Allen, Michael K. .... Cincinnati, OH
Allen, Michael K. .... Seattle, WA
Allen, Michael L. .... Newark, NJ
Allen, Michael L. .... Salt Lake City, UT
Allen, Michael P. .... Boston, MA
Allen, Michael P. .... Kansas City, MO
Allen, Michael Patrick
Environmental Protection Agency, Office of the General Counsel, GV
Allen, Michael R. .... St. Louis, MO
Allen, Michael S. .... Phoenix, AZ
Allen, Michael S. .... Cary, NC
Allen, Michael Scott .... Chicago, IL
Allen, Michael T. .... Dansville, NY
Allen, Michele Dana .... New Orleans, LA
Allen, Michele E. .... Galveston, TX
Allen, Michele Z. .... San Jose, CA
Allen, Michelle I. .... Uniondale, NY
Allen, Milton P., Jr. .... Lawrence, KS
Allen, Misti R. .... Minneapolis, MN
Allen, Mitchell G. .... Birmingham, AL
Allen, Mitchell S. .... Atlanta, GA

Allen, Mitchell T. .... Springfield, MA
Allen, Monica J. .... St. Louis, MO
Allen & Moore, L.L.P. .... Raleigh, NC
Allen, Morris L. .... Marion, IA
Allen, Morris & Troisi .... New York, NY
Allen, Mullings & Allen, L.L.P.
Santa Ana, CA
Allen, Myrlyn L. .... Tarpon Springs, FL
Allen, Nadine Lovelace .... Cincinnati, OH
Allen, Nat .... Roundup, MT
Allen, Nathan, Jr. .... Dallas, TX
Allen, Neal C. .... Bronx, NY
Allen, Neal R. .... Midland, TX
Allen, Nelson .... Jasper, AL
Allen, Nelson & Bowers .... Elizabethton, TN
Allen, Newton P. .... Memphis, TN
Allen, Noble F. .... New Haven, CT
Allen, Noel L. .... Raleigh, NC
Allen, Noel M. .... Escondido, CA
Allen, Nora K. .... Chicago, IL
Allen, Norman F. J., III
Panama City Beach, FL
Allen, Norman W. .... Petaluma, CA
Allen, Norton & Blue, Professional Association .... Miami, FL
Orlando, FL
Tallahassee, FL
Tampa, FL
Allen, O. Fay, Jr. .... Barre, VT
Allen & O'Brien .... Rochester, NY
Allen, Otis George .... Brooklyn, NY
Allen & Overy .... New York, NY
New York, NY
Allen, P. Blake .... Oklahoma City, OK
Allen, Pace, Jr. .... Tallahassee, FL
Allen, Pamela .... Oakland, CA
Allen, Pamela K. .... Casa Grande, AZ
Allen, Pamela K., P.C. .... Casa Grande, AZ
Allen, Pamela Rhoads .... Savannah, GA
Allen, Patricia J. .... Tampa, FL
Allen, Patricia K. .... West Palm Beach, FL
Allen, Patricia K., P.A.
West Palm Beach, FL
Allen, Patricia M. .... Chicago, IL
Allen, Patricia P. .... Boston, MA
Allen, Patrick D. .... Albuquerque, NM
Allen, Patrick H. .... Washington, DC
Allen, Patrick J. .... Chicago, IL
Allen, Patrick M. .... Winston-Salem, NC
Allen, Patrick W. .... Middletown, OH
Allen, Paul .... Harrisburg, PA
Allen, Paul A. .... San Francisco, CA
Allen, Paul D. .... San Francisco, CA
Allen, Paul E. .... Meadville, PA
Allen, Paul N. .... Philadelphia, PA
Allen, Paul Shearman, & Associates
Washington, DC
Allen, Paula Dohnal .... Bloomington, IL
Allen, Paula L. .... Waco, TX
Allen, Penny L. .... Olympia, WA
Allen, Peter .... San Francisco, CA
Allen, Peter .... New York, NY
Allen, Peter J. .... Houston, TX
Allen, Peter Joseph .... Pleasanton, CA
Allen, Peter L. .... New York, NY
Allen, Peter Q. .... Southfield, MI
Allen, Philip A., III. .... Miami, FL
Allen, Philip A., III, P.A. .... Miami, FL
Allen, Philip C. .... Los Angeles, CA
Allen, Philip Lon .... Columbus, OH
Allen, Philip O. .... Lakeland, FL
Lake Wales, FL
Winter Haven, FL
Allen, Phillip E. .... Louisville, KY
Allen, Phillip S. .... New York, NY
Allen, Phillip W. .... Yanceyville, NC
Allen, Pinney L. .... Atlanta, GA
Allen and Pinnix, P.A. .... Durham, NC
Raleigh, NC
Research Triangle Park, NC
Allen, Polgar, Proietti & Fagalde
Mariposa, CA
Merced, CA
Allen & Price, P.L.C. .... Phoenix, AZ
Scottsdale, AZ
Tucson, AZ
Allen, R. Clayton .... Chesterfield, VA
Richmond, VA
Allen, R. David .... Lebanon, TN
Allen, R. David, P.C. .... Lebanon, TN
Allen, R. Keith .... Coral Gables, FL
Allen, R. Lee .... Springfield, IL
Allen, R. Mark .... Olympia, WA
Allen, R. Michael .... Charlotte, NC
Allen, R. Thomas .... Santa Maria, CA
Allen, Rachel .... Chicago, IL
Allen, Ralph E. .... Tyler, TX
Allen Ramsey & Associates
Middleburg Heights, OH
Allen, Rand L. .... Washington, DC
Allen, Randall B. .... San Francisco, CA
Allen, Randall C. .... Salt Lake City, UT
Allen, Randall C. .... Vienna, VA
Allen, Randall L. .... Atlanta, GA
Allen, Randel V. .... Murray Hill, NJ
Allen, Randy .... Northport, AL
Allen, Randy G. .... Colorado Springs, CO
Allen, Raymond .... Chicago, IL
Allen, Raymond Morgan .... Lafayette, LA
Allen, Rederick W. .... Birmingham, AL
Allen, Renée B. .... Guilford, CT
Allen, Reynold S. .... Cary, NC
Allen, Rhonda M. Cooper .... Chicago, IL
Allen, Richard .... Seabrook, TX
Allen, Richard A. .... Washington, DC
Allen, Richard A. .... Albuquerque, NM
Allen, Richard B. .... Chicago, IL

Allen, Richard B. .... Beaufort, SC
Hilton Head Island, SC
Allen, Richard C. .... **Boston, MA**
Allen, Richard D. .... **Wilmington, DE**
Allen, Richard D. .... **Minneapolis, MN**
Allen, Richard D., Ltd. .... **Minneapolis, MN**
Allen, Richard E. .... **Appling, GA**
Atlanta, GA
Allen, Richard E. .... **Augusta, GA**
Allen, Richard F. .... Montgomery, AL
Allen, Richard F. .....Department of Agriculture, Office of Inspector General, GV
Allen, Richard F. .... **Seattle, WA**
Allen, Richard G. .... **American Fork, UT**
Allen, Richard G. .... **Lehi, UT**
Allen, Richard H. .... **Montgomery, AL**
Allen, Richard H. .... Watsonville, CA
Watsonville, CA
Allen, Richard H. .... **Wilmington, DE**
Allen, Richard H. .... Salem, OR
Allen, Richard H. .... **Memphis, TN**
Allen, Richard H., Jr. .... **Memphis, TN**
Allen, Richard J., Jr. .... Rutherford, NJ
Allen, Richard K. .... **Boston, MA**
Allen, Richard K., Jr. .... **Anderson, SC**
Allen, Richard L. .... Chickasha, OK
Allen, Richard L., Jr. .... **Orlando, FL**
Allen, Richard Lewis .... **Miami, FL**
Allen, Richard M. .... Jackson, MS
Allen, Richard M. .... **New York, NY**
Allen, Richard M. .... Austin, TX
Allen, Richard S., Jr. .... Clare, MI
Allen, Richard W.
Consumer Product Safety Commission, Office of the General Counsel, GV
Allen, Rita .... Baldwin, NY
Allen, Robert A. .... **San Antonio, TX**
Allen, Robert B. .... **Charleston, WV**
Allen, Robert B. (Skip) .... **Houston, TX**
Allen, Robert D. .... **Oklahoma City, OK**
Allen, Robert D. .... **Dallas, TX**
Allen, Robert E. .... Manhattan Beach, CA
Allen, Robert E. .... Denver, CO
Allen, Robert E. .... **Asheville, NC**
Allen, Robert E., Jr. .... Middleboro, MA
Allen, Robert E. B. .... **Phoenix, AZ**
Allen, Robert F., Jr. .... **Newport Beach, CA**
Allen, Robert G. .... **Oakland, CA**
Allen, Robert G.
Federal Communications Commission, Wireless Telecommunications Bureau, GV
Allen, Robert H., Law Offices of
Phoenix, AZ
Allen, Robert J. .... Augusta, ME
Allen, Robert J .... Saginaw, MI
Allen, Robert J. .... Chattaroy, WA
Allen, Robert L. .... Culver City, CA
Allen, Robert L. .... **Portland, OR**
Allen, Robert M. .... San Jose, CA
Allen, Robert M. .... Wellesley, MA
Allen, Robert M. .... **Addison, TX**
Allen, Robert M., Jr. .... Miami, FL
Allen, Robert N., Jr. .... **Key Biscayne, FL**
Miami, FL
Allen, Robert O. .... **Brookhaven, MS**
Allen, Robert Smith .... **St. Louis, MO**
Allen, Robert W. .... **New Haven, CT**
Allen, Robert W. .... **Charlotte, NC**
Allen, Robert Y. .... Cheyenne, WY
Allen, Roberto N. .... **Baltimore, MD**
Allen, Robin E. .... Los Angeles, CA
Allen, Robin W. .... Mesa, AZ
Allen, Robin W., P.C. .... Mesa, AZ
Allen, Rock W. .... Longmont, CO
Allen, Rodney L. .... **Moultrie, GA**
Allen, Roger D. .... **New Orleans, LA**
Allen, Roger D. .... Arlington, TX
Allen, Roger F. .... **Oakland, CA**
Allen, Roger G. .... Kalamazoo, MI
Allen, Roger J. .... **Dallas, TX**
Allen, Roger K. .... Englewood, CO
Allen, Ron .... **Tucson, AZ**
Allen, Ronald C. ....Department of the Army, Office, Chief of Engineers/Headquarters, U.S. Army Corps of Engineers, GV
Allen, Ronald D. .... **Seattle, WA**
Allen, Ronald G. .... Wichita Falls, TX
Allen, Ronald J. .... Chicago, IL
Allen, Ronald J. .... St. Clair, MI
Allen, Ronald J., P.C. .... St. Clair, MI
Allen, Ronald James .... Clifton, NJ
Allen, Ronald L. .... Anniston, AL
Allen, Ronald L. .... Citrus Heights, CA
Allen, Ronald M. .... Quincy, MA
Allen, Ronald R. .... **Evansville, IN**
Allen, Ronald R., Jr. .... **New York, NY**
Allen, Rosalind K.
Federal Communications Commission, Office of Plans and Policy, GV
Allen, Rose M. .... **Kingsport, TN**
Allen, Rose M. .... Hudson, WI
Allen, Rosemary M. .... **Boston, MA**
Allen, Roy Benton, Jr. .... Tifton, GA
Allen, Roy C., III .... Lee's Summit, MO
Allen, Roy Jefferson .... **Clarksdale, MS**
Allen, Russell E. .... Ashland, VA
Allen, Russell G. .... **Newport Beach, CA**
Allen, Russell M. .... **Portland, OR**
Allen, Ryan .... **Orlando, FL**
Allen, S. Michelle .... Denton, TX
Allen & Sala, P.L.C. .... **Phoenix, AZ**
Allen, Sam T., III .... Sapulpa, OK
Allen, Sam T., IV .... Sapulpa, OK
Allen, Samuel M. .... **Covington, KY**
Allen, Samuel N. .... **Houston, TX**
Allen, Samuel S. .... **San Angelo, TX**
Allen, Sandra E. .... Tallahassee, FL
Allen, Sandra L. .... Albany, NY
Allen, Sandra L. .... **Tacoma, WA**
Allen, Sandra Mills
Joint Committees And Commissions, GV
Allen, Sara E. .... Commerce Township, MI
Allen, Sara H. .... Poteau, OK
Allen, Sarah O. ....Federal Trade Commission, Bureau of Competition, GV
Allen, Scot C. .... **St. Louis, MO**
Allen, Scott D. .... **Stephenville, TX**
Allen, Scott D. .... Salt Lake City, UT
Allen, Scott D., Professional Corporation
Stephenville, TX
Allen, Scott E. .... **Raleigh, NC**
Allen, Scott F. .... Gilbert, AZ
Allen, Scott J. .... **San Francisco, CA**
Allen, Scott S. .... **Miami, FL**
Allen, Scott V. .... **Temple, TX**
Waco, TX
Allen, Scottie D., & Associates .... **Dallas, TX**
Allen, Scruggs, Sossaman & Thompson, P.C.
Memphis, TN
Allen, S. E., Jr. .... Hazlehurst, MS
Allen, Sean .... **Sacramento, CA**
Allen, Shannon A. .... **Milwaukee, WI**
Allen, Sharon K. .... Greensboro, NC
Allen, Sheldon T. .... Van Nuys, CA
Allen, Sheridan & Kreitzberg
Portland, OR
Allen, Sherri .... Seattle, WA
Allen, Sherwin E. .... Baldwin, NY
Allen, Shirli C. .... Mission Viejo, CA
Allen, Sidney S. .... New York, NY
Allen, Sink & Hastings, P.L.L.C.
Hampton, VA
Allen, S. J. Hugh .... San Rafael, CA
Allen, Sonya L. .... Topeka, KS
Allen, Stacey H. .... **Galveston, TX**
Allen, Stacy .... **Hartford, CT**
Allen, Stanley C. .... Anniston, AL
Allen, Stanley C. .... **San Antonio, TX**
Allen, Stanley L. .... Madison, NC
Allen, Stein, Durbin & Hunnicutt, A Professional Corporation .... **Palacios, TX**
San Antonio, TX
Allen, Stephanie A. .... Denver, CO
Allen, Stephanie Ann .... Roseville, CA
Allen, Stephanie E. .... Newport Beach, CA
Allen, Stephen B. .... **Tulsa, OK**
Allen, Stephen C.
Agency for International Development, Office of the General Counsel, GV
Allen, Stephen C. .... Chicago, IL
Allen, Stephen E. .... Red Hill, PA
Allen, Stephen F. .... **Rockville, MD**
Allen, Stephen F., P.C. .... **Rockville, MD**
Allen, Stephen G. .... **Lexington, KY**
Allen, Stephen N. .... Lambertville, NJ
Allen, Steve .... Greensboro, NC
Allen, Steve, Law Firm, The
Greensboro, NC
Allen, Steven A. .... **Towson, MD**
Allen, Steven J. .... United States Senate, Senatorial Assistants, GV
Allen, Steven Johnson .... **Jackson, MS**
Allen, Steven K. .... Tahlequah, OK
Allen, Steven M. .... Ellington, CT
Allen, Steven R. .... **Milwaukee, WI**
Allen, Steven W. .... Mesa, AZ
Allen, Steven W., A Professional Corporation
Mesa, AZ
Allen, Stortz, Fox, Susee & Olson
Salem, OR
Allen, Stuart Bradley .... Portland, OR
Allen, Stuart C. .... **Seattle, WA**
Allen, Susan A. .... Austin, TX
Allen, Susan A. .... **Dallas, TX**
Allen, Susan Au .... Washington, DC
Allen, Susan J. .... **Schaumburg, IL**
Allen, Susan J. .... Port Townsend, WA
Allen, Susan W. .... Chicago, IL
Allen, Susan Walker .... Russellville, AR
Allen, T. Eugene, III .... **Columbia, SC**
Allen, T. Scott, Jr. .... **Houston, TX**
Allen, Ted A. .... Edina, MN
Allen, Teddi Lewis .... Tulsa, OK
Allen, Terrell A. .... **Findlay, OH**
Toledo, OH
Allen, Terrence R. .... **Newport Beach, CA**
Allen, Terry C. .... **Jefferson City, MO**
Allen, Terry Jon .... **Costa Mesa, CA**
Allen, Terry L. .... **Merced, CA**
Allen, Terry S. .... Vista, CA
Allen, Tess .... Iselin, NJ
Iselin, NJ
Allen, Thomas A. .... **Philadelphia, PA**
Allen, Thomas Arnon .... Madison, WI
Allen, Thomas B. .... **Middletown, OH**
Allen, Thomas B. .... Cleburne, TX
Allen, Thomas C. .... Fort Wayne, IN
Allen, Thomas D. .... **Chicago, IL**
Allen, Thomas D. .... **Farmington Hills, MI**
Allen, Thomas E. .... **Monroe, LA**
Allen, Thomas E. .... Rocky River, OH
Allen, Thomas F. .... **Cleveland, OH**
Allen, Thomas H. .... **Phoenix, AZ**
Allen, Thomas H. .... Portland, ME
Allen, Thomas J. .... Clarksburg, WV
Allen, Thomas L. .... **Pittsburgh, PA**
Allen, Thomas L. .... Lancaster, TX
Allen, Thomas N. .... Richmond, VA
Allen, Thomas P., III .... Redondo Beach, CA
Allen, Thomas P., III, A Prof. Corp.
Redondo Beach, CA
Allen, Thomas P., Jr. .... Torrance, CA
Allen, Thomas Peter, III .... **Macon, GA**
Allen, Thomas R. .... **Orlando, FL**
Allen, Thomas R. .... **Columbus, OH**
Allen, Thomas S. .... Cleveland, OH
Allen, Thomas W. .... Irvine, CA
Allen, Thomas W. .... **Clarksdale, MS**
Allen, Timothy C. .... Salt Lake City, UT
Allen, Timothy Craig, M.D. .... **Houston, TX**
Allen, Timothy R. .... **Jackson, MI**
Allen, Timothy W. .... Lexington, KY
Allen, Timothy W. .... Rocky Mount, VA
Allen, Todd B. .... **Los Angeles, CA**
Allen, Tom .... Batesville, AR
Allen, Tom P. .... **Houston, TX**
Allen, Toni K. .... **Washington, DC**
Allen, Tracy C. .... **Livermore, CA**
Allen, Tracy J. .... Washington, DC
Allen, Tracy L. .... Tallahassee, FL
Allen, Tracy L. .... **Southfield, MI**
Allen, Trudy B. .... **Yazoo City, MS**
Allen, V. Claire .... Columbia, SC
Allen, Vahrenwald & Johnson, LLC
Fort Collins, CO
Allen, Vanessa L. .... Beltsville, MD
Allen, Vaughn, Cobb & Hood, P.A.
Biloxi, MS
Gulfport, MS
Hattiesburg, MS
Jackson, MS
Allen & Vernon, P.L.C. .... Marion, IA
Allen, Vincent J. .... **Dallas, TX**
Allen, Virginia M. .... Boston, MA
Allen, W. Austin, II .... Warminster, PA
Allen, W. Charlton, & Associates
Atlanta, GA
Allen, W. Coleman, Jr. .... **Richmond, VA**
Allen, W. David .... Washington, DC
Crofton, MD
Rockville, MD
Rockville, MD
Allen, W. David .... Department of the Navy, Office of the Judge Advocate General, GV
Allen, W. Fred, Jr. .... **Kalamazoo, MI**
Allen, W. George .... Fort Lauderdale, FL
Allen, W. Reynolds .... **Tampa, FL**
Allen, W. Riley .... **Orlando, FL**
Allen, W. Riley, P.A. .... **Orlando, FL**
Allen, W. Scott .... Covington, LA
Allen, W. West .... **Las Vegas, NV**
Allen, Walker Mayo, III .... **Princeton, NJ**
Allen, Walt .... Chickasha, OK
Allen, Walter E. .... Linneus, MO
Allen, Walter H., III .... **Dallas, TX**
Allen, Walter L., Jr. .... Montgomery, AL
Allen, Wanda Nell .... **Newport News, VA**
Allen, Warner E. .... Portland, OR
Allen, Warren D. .... Los Angeles, CA
Allen, Waylon L. .... **Austin, TX**
Allen, Wayne E. .... Eugene, OR
Allen, Wayne L. .... Melbourne, FL
Allen, Wayne R. .... Atlanta, GA
Allen, Weathington & Reeves, A Professional Corporation .... **Atlanta, GA**
Allen • Wellman • McNew
Greenfield, IN
Indianapolis, IN
Allen, Wesley C. .... Philadelphia, PA
Allen, Wesley J. .... Miami, FL
Allen, Wilbur C. .... **Chesterfield, VA**
Richmond, VA
Allen, William A. .... Santa Ana, CA
Allen, William A. .... Houston, TX
Allen, William A., Jr. .... **Kinston, NC**
Allen, William B. .... Levittown, PA
Allen, William B. .... **Dallas, TX**
Allen, William B., III .... Woodstock, VA
Allen, William B., Jr. .... Alexandria, LA
Allen, William D. .... Norwalk, CT
Allen, William D. .... Salem, OR
Allen, William D., III .... Dinwiddie, VA
Allen, William F. .... **Washington, DC**
Allen, William F. .... Saginaw, MI
Allen, William G. .... Lexington, KY
Allen, William H. .... Washington, DC
Allen, William J. .... Charlotte, NC
Allen, William L., III .... New Albany, IN
Allen, William L., Jr. .... **Syracuse, NY**
Allen, William Lee .... Jacksonville, FL
Allen, William O. .... **Jackson, MI**
Allen, William P. .... **Phoenix, AZ**
Allen, William P. .... **Middletown, OH**
Allen, William R. .... **Irvine, CA**
Allen, William R. .... Santa Barbara, CA
Allen, William S. .... Overland Park, KS
Allen, William T. .... **New York, NY**
Allen, William V. .... **Denver, CO**
Allen, William W. .... **Lexington, KY**
Allen, William W. .... Laredo, TX
Allen, William W., Jr. .... Bowling Green, KY
Allen, Wm. A. .... Charlotte, NC
Allen, Wm. Timothy, III .... **Shreveport, LA**
Allen, W. R. .... Dallas, TX
Allen, Wynn Dee .... Montgomery, AL
Allen, Yazbeck, O'Halloran & Hanson, P.C.
Portland, OR
Allen, Yurasek & Merklin .... **Marysville, OH**
Allen, Zachary W. .... **Oklahoma City, OK**
Allen, Zoë G. .... **Washington, DC**
Allen-Bass, DeAnna D. .... **Chicago, IL**
Allenberg, Charles H. .... Virginia Beach, VA
Allen-Berry, Lydia .... Frazer, PA
Allenby, Braden R. .... Basking Ridge, NJ
Allenby, Christopher B. .... **San Jose, CA**
Allenby, Leslie L. .... Los Angeles, CA
Allenby, Melissa M. .... **San Diego, CA**
Allenby, Norman R. .... **San Diego, CA**
Allenby, Robert P. .... **San Diego, CA**
Allende & Brea .... **New York, NY**
New York, NY
Allender, Jerry W. .... Cocoa Beach, FL
Titusville, FL
Allender, John R. .... **Houston, TX**
Allender, Kathleen .... Belleville, MI
Allender, Kathleen, P.C. .... Belleville, MI
Allender, William E. .... **Bowling Green, KY**
Allendoerfer, James H. .... Everett, WA
Allendoerfer & Keithly .... Snohomish, WA
Allendorf, Richard C. .... **Minneapolis, MN**
Allen-Garibaldi, Shari .... **Stockton, CA**
Allen-Hill, Glenda S. .... Fresno, CA
Allen-Niesen, Keith A. .... Los Angeles, CA
Allen-Shaw, Janet .... La Jolla, CA
Allenson, Linda R. .... Larchmont, NY
Allenson, Sheryl Cohen .... **Chicago, IL**
Allenstein, Keith E., Jr. .... Lincoln, NE
Allenstein, Myron K. .... Gadsden, AL
Allensworth, Michael R. .... Los Angeles, CA
Allensworth, Robert Bruce .... **Boston, MA**
Allensworth, Susan A. .... Orange, CA
Allensworth, Thomas L.
Wichita Falls, TX
Allensworth, William R. .... **Austin, TX**
Allentharp, Robt. D. .... Austin, TX
Allentoff, Fred .... Baltimore, MD
Allen-Tunsil, Denise L. .... Jacksonville, FL
Allenza, Carol S. .... Flemington, NJ
Aller, Andrew T. K. .... San Diego, CA
Aller, Leeon F., III .... Roseburg, OR
Aller & Morrison, P.C. .... Roseburg, OR
Aller, Rodney G. .... Lakeville, CT
Aller & Rout .... Lakeville, CT
Allera, Edward John .... **Washington, DC**
Allerdice, Robert J. .... Seattle, WA
Allerding, Michael .... Columbus, OH
Allerhand, Joseph S. .... **New York, NY**
Allers, H. Lee, Jr. .... Timonium, MD
Allert, Thomas D. .... **Riverside, CA**
Allerton, Cheryl J. .... **Reading, PA**
Allerton, Martha .... Santa Ana, CA
Allerton, Robert G. .... Canton, OH
Alletag, Gary M. .... **Houston, TX**
Alletzhauser, Eric W. .... **Hartford, CT**
Alleva, Aldo E. .... Brooklyn, NY
Alleva, Allison Cornelius
New Orleans, LA
Alleva, James .... New York, NY
Allevato, John F. .... **Charleston, WV**
Allewalt, Donald L., (P.A.) .... Baltimore, MD
Allewalt & Murphy, P.A. .... Baltimore, MD
Alley and Alley/Ford & Harrison LLP
Miami, FL
Tampa, FL
Alley, B. Joseph, Jr. .... **Atlanta, GA**
Alley, Bradley K. .... Orlando, FL
Alley, C. Todd .... **Tampa, FL**
Alley, Edward B. .... Anderson, IN
Elwood, IN
Alley, Edward R. .... Laurel, MS
Alley, Edwin R. .... Elizabeth, NJ
Alley, Erin McCall .... **Lake Charles, LA**
Alley, Frank R., III .... Eugene, OR
Alley, G. Keith .... **Clinton, TN**
Alley, G. Robin .... **Columbia, SC**
Alley, Gordon T. .... Tucson, AZ
Alley, Goza, Mullen & Minick
Fort Worth, TX
Alley, Harry C. .... Helena, MT
Alley, Hartley David .... Wheat Ridge, CO
Alley & Ingram .... **Boca Grande, FL**
Tampa, FL
Alley, James B., Jr. .... **Santa Fe, NM**
Alley, Jamie S. .... **Charleston, WV**
Alley, Jeffrey S. .... **El Paso, TX**
Alley, John L. .... Chattanooga, TN
Alley, John T., Jr. .... Montgomery, AL
Alley, John-Edward .... **Miami, FL**
Tampa, FL
Alley, Kimberly A. .... **Baltimore, MD**
Alley, L. Murray .... **Birmingham, AL**
Alley, Maass, Rogers & Lindsay, P.A.
Fort Lauderdale, FL
Palm Beach, FL
Alley, Morgan Wade .... **White Stone, VA**
Alley, Nancye Scott .... Richmond, VA
Alley, Paul .... Covington, KY
Alley, Peter .... **Boston, MA**
Alley, Raymond A., Jr. .... **Tampa, FL**
Alley, Raymond A., Jr., P.A. .... **Brandon, FL**
Tampa, FL
Alley, Richard L. .... **Sacramento, CA**
Alley, Ronald D. .... West St. Paul, MN
Alley, Thomas R. .... Kearney, MO
Alley, Travis .... **Fort Worth, TX**
Alley, Wade H., Jr. .... Charlotte, NC
Alley, Walter D. .... Portland, OR
Alley & Waters, P.C. .... Montgomery, AL
Alley, Wayne E. .... Oklahoma City, OK
Alley, William F., Jr. .... **Knoxville, TN**
Alley, William J. .... Old Greenwich, CT
Alley, Zebulon D. .... **Raleigh, NC**
Alley, Zebulon D., P.A. .... **Raleigh, NC**
Allf, Nancy L. .... **Las Vegas, NV**
Allf, Rebecca Jane .... **Cincinnati, OH**
Allford, Ashmore, Ivester, Zellmer & Green
McAlester, OK
Allford, John A. .... **McAlester, OK**
Allford, Michael Glen .... Bakersfield, CA
Allford, Patricia A. .... Holdenville, OK
Allgaier, Rand D. .... Liverpool, NY
Allgair, Clinten J. .... **Annapolis, MD**
Allgeier, Catherine A. .... Erie, PA
Allgeier, George F., Jr. .... Lexington, KY
Allgeyer, David A. .... **Minneapolis, MN**
Allgood, Alfred L. .... Gainesville, GA
Allgood, C. Thomas, Jr. .... Covington, GA
Allgood, Childs, Mehrhof and Millians, P.C.
Augusta, GA
Allgood & Daniel .... **Augusta, GA**
Allgood, Davis B. .... **Baton Rouge, LA**

Allgood, DeForrest Robertson
Columbus, MS
Allgood, Dwight M., Jr. .... Cleveland, OH
Allgood, Joan U. .... Moreland Hills, OH
Allgood, John F. .... Tucker, GA
Allgood, Judson J. .... Cincinnati, OH
Allgood, Marlene Krousel
Baton Rouge, LA
Allgood, Michele Simmons
Little Rock, AR
Allgood & Misemer, P.A.
New Port Richey, FL
Allgood, Robert L. .... Augusta, GA
Allgood, Sam Y., Jr. .... New Port Richey, FL
Allgood, Tara Linette .... Plummer, ID
Allgood, Thomas F., Jr. .... Augusta, GA
Allgood, Thomas F., Sr. .... Augusta, GA
Allgreen, Chris A. .... Malibu, CA
Allhiser, Mary .... Redwood City, CA
Alli, John D. .... Berkley, MI
Alli, Margaret Carroll .... Birmingham, MI
Detroit, MI
Alli, Omotayo Bayonle .... Atlanta, GA
Alli, Richard J., Jr. .... Portland, OR
Alli, Shoms U. .... Lathrup Village, MI
Allias, Steven R. .... New Kensington, PA
Allibon, Robert M. .... Fort Worth, TX
Allie, David C. .... Houston, TX
Allie, John H. .... Indianapolis, IN
Allie, Monica L. .... Chattanooga, TN
Allie, Ronald D. .... Billings, MT
Allie & Thurmond, L.L.P. .... Houston, TX
Alliegro, Alfred S. .... Lindstrom, MN
Alliegro, Alfred V. .... Lindstrom, MN
Alliegro, Robert P. .... Hawthorne, NJ
Alligood, Brian .... Atlanta, GA
Alligood, Randal M., (P.A.) .... Orlando, FL
Alliker, Ephraim Benjamin
Baltimore, MD
Alliman, Peter J. .... Knoxville, TN
Madisonville, TN
Allin, Jon S. .... Sacramento, CA
Allin, Keri A. .... United States Senate,
Office of the Legislative Counsel, GV
Allina, Franz .... New York, NY
Allinder, John K. .... Independence, MO
Allinder, William L. .... Kansas City, MO
Alling, Douglas V. .... Tacoma, WA
Alling, James W. .... Decatur, IL
Alling, Kathleen M. .... Mount Vernon, IL
Alling, Ronald D. .... Stateline, NV
Allinger, Susan A. .... Houston, TX
Allingham, Jane La Gree .... Tulsa, OK
Allingham Law Offices .... Anchorage, AK
Allingham, Lynn M. .... Anchorage, AK
Allingham, Thomas J. .... New Milford, CT
Allingham, Thomas J., II .... Wilmington, DE
Allingham, William J. .... Holmdel, NJ
Allington, Frances F. .... Strongsville, OH
Allington, Thomas B. .... Indianapolis, IN
Allington, Walter F. .... Solana Beach, CA
Allinson, Dale .... East Meadow, NY
Allinson, David S. .... New York, NY
Allinson, Elihu E., III .... Wilmington, DE
Allinson, Scott B. .... Allentown, PA
Allio, M. Greg .... San Francisco, CA
Allio, Remo A. .... Endicott, NY
Allis, Carol S. .... Grand Rapids, MI
Allis & Creveling, P.A. A Professional
Association .... Tulsa, OK
Allis, Daniel F. .... Tulsa, OK
Allis, Nicholas R., Law Offices of
Los Angeles, CA
Allis, Steven W. .... Washington, DC
Allisan, Marla Ruth .... Northampton, MA
Allison, Alexander C. .... Naperville, IL
Allison, Alissa J. .... New Orleans, LA
Allison, Amy E. .... Denver, CO
Allison, Andrew W. .... Philadelphia, PA
Allison, Ann E. .... Tulsa, OK
Allison, Ann Fitzsimons .... Columbia, SC
Allison, Antone L. .... College Park, GA
Allison & Associates .... Austin, TX
Allison, Barney A. .... Los Angeles, CA
Allison & Bassett, L.L.P. .... Austin, TX
Allison, Bradley D. .... Hollidaysburg, PA
Allison, Brett P. .... Pocatello, ID
Allison, C. Frank, Jr. .... Kansas City, KS
Overland Park, KS
Allison, C. Kent .... Virginia Beach, VA
Allison, Charles P., Jr. .... Tuscaloosa, AL
Allison, Christopher F., Jr. .... Dallas, TX
Allison, Clark J. .... Sacramento, CA
San Francisco, CA
Allison, Craig C. .... Sacramento, CA
Allison, Craig Y. .... Palo Alto, CA
Allison, Cynthia Satel .... Corpus Christi, TX
Allison, D. Clifford .... Wichita, KS
Allison, Daniel S. .... Milwaukee, WI
Allison, David K. .... Easley, SC
Allison, David L. .... Alexandria, VA
Allison, Dean B. .... Los Angeles, CA
Allison, Derek W. .... Scotts Valley, CA
Allison, Diane M. .... Westport, CT
Allison, Dick M. .... Austin, TX
Allison, Donald J. .... Amherst, MA
Allison, Donald M. .... Boca Raton, FL
Allison, Donn G. .... De Queen, AR
Allison, Dorothy M. .... Philadelphia, PA
Allison, Douglas A. .... Corpus Christi, TX
Allison, Earl R. .... Morgan Mill, TX
Allison, Evan A. .... Chattanooga, TN
Allison, Ewen .... Washington, DC
Allison, F. Eugene .... Charlotte, NC
Allison, F. Robert .... Salem, MA
Allison Firm, The .... Tulsa, OK
Allison, G. Burgess .... McLean, VA

Allison, Gale Graham .... Tulsa, OK
Knoxville, TN
Allison, Gary R. .... Muscatine, IA
West Liberty, IA
Allison, George, III .... Jersey City, NJ
Allison, George Thomas, III, (P.C.)
Longview, TX
Allison, George V. .... Carson City, NV
Allison, Gordon Y. .... Fayetteville, AR
Allison, Grace .... Chicago, IL
Allison, Guy H. .... Corpus Christi, TX
Allison, Heatherun S.
Board of Governors Of The Federal Reserve
System,
Office of the General Counsel, GV
Allison and Heistand, P.A.
St. Petersburg, FL
Allison, Henry R., III .... Nashville, TN
Allison, Herman L. .... Atlanta, GA
Allison, Howard M. .... Akron, OH
Allison, J. Bradley .... East Palestine, OH
Allison, James E., Jr. .... Houston, TX
Allison, James H. .... Worthington, OH
Allison, James L. .... Philadelphia, PA
Allison, James M. .... Greenville, SC
Allison, James M. .... Woodville, TX
Allison, James M., Jr. .... Douglasville, GA
Allison, James P. .... Austin, TX
Allison, James R. .... Denver, CO
Allison, James S. .... Powell, WY
Allison, James T. .... Memphis, TN
Allison, James W. .... Charlotte, NC
Allison, Jean M. .... Rochester, NY
Allison, Jeffrey A. .... Irvine, CA
Allison, Jerry C. .... Reading, PA
Allison, Jill C. .... Kansas City, MO
Allison, Joan B. .... Seattle, WA
Allison, Joanna George .... Boston, MA
Allison, John D. .... Charlotte, NC
Allison, John David .... Spokane, WA
Allison, John R. .... St. Paul, MN
Allison, John R. .... Austin, TX
Allison, John R., III .... Miami, FL
Allison, John W., Jr. .... Denver, CO
Allison, Jonathan .... Washington, PA
Allison, Joseph .... Yreka, CA
Allison, Julie Wynne .... Hollywood, FL
Allison, JulieAnn .... Fort Lauderdale, FL
Allison, June K. .... Burlington, NC
Allison, Junius L. .... Venice, FL
Allison, Karen L. .... Denver, CO
Allison, Kathy S. .... Milwaukee, WI
Allison, Kaye A. .... Baltimore, MD
Allison, Kenneth D. .... Treasury Department,
Internal Revenue Service, GV
Allison, Kip H., Law Offices of .... Dallas, TX
Allison, Kip H., Law Offices of
Denton, TX
Fort Worth, TX
Allison, Larry W. .... Lampasas, TX
Allison Law Firm, The, Inc. .... Shreveport, LA
Allison, Lawrence E., Jr. .... Jackson, MS
Allison, Lee E. .... New York, NY
Allison, Leigh .... Jackson, TN
Allison, Lenora M. .... Miami, FL
Allison, Lesley A. .... San Diego, CA
Allison, Linda L. .... Muscatine, IA
West Liberty, IA
Allison, Lindsey J. .... Birmingham, AL
Allison, Loren K. .... Fort Wayne, IN
Allison, Lynn D. .... Wichita, KS
Allison, M. Gene .... Helena, MT
Allison, M. Jay .... Dallas, TX
Allison, MacKenzie, Hartman, Soumbeniotis
& Russell, Ltd. .... Carson City, NV
Elko, NV
Gardnerville, NV
Incline Village, NV
Minden, NV
Reno, NV
Allison, Margaret O. .... Chicago, IL
Allison, Margaret S. .... Mobile, AL
Allison, Mark H. .... Little Rock, AR
Allison, Mark T.
Department of the Air Force,
Office of the Judge Advocate General, GV
Allison, Matthew G. .... Chicago, IL
Allison, May, Alvis, Fuhrmeister & Kimbrouzh
Birmingham, AL
Allison, M. D. .... Rockford, IA
Allison, Michael .... Albuquerque, NM
Allison, Michael L. .... Morrilton, AR
Perryville, AR
Allison, Michael R. .... Columbus, OH
Allison, Mike .... Dallas, TX
Allison, Minna Jayakumar .... Pittsburgh, PA
Allison, Noah G. .... Las Vegas, NV
Allison & Nordquist LLP .... Scotts Valley, CA
Allison, Norman R. .... Jacksonville, FL
Allison, Otto M., Jr. .... Anacortes, WA
Allison, Pat East .... Houston, TX
Allison, Paul J. .... Spokane, WA
Allison, Paul K. .... Lancaster, PA
Allison, Paul W. .... Akron, OH
Allison, Paul W. .... Fostoria, OH
Allison, Ray L. .... Columbus, GA
Allison, Richard C. .... Manhasset, NY
Allison, Rinda Y. .... Lisle, IL
Allison, Robert A. .... Chicago, IL
Allison, Robert B. .... Birmingham, AL
Allison, Robert B. .... Kalispell, MT
Allison, Robert B. .... Seattle, WA
Allison, Robert D. .... Chicago, IL
Allison, Robert J. .... Moweaqua, IL
Allison & Robertson, P.A. .... Key West, FL
Miami, FL
Allison, Rodney I. .... Denver, CO
Allison, Rodney, P.C. .... Denver, CO

Allison, Roy L. .... Atlanta, GA
Allison, Russell Q. .... Birmingham, AL
Allison, Scott B. .... Boulder, CO
Allison, Shari Lynn .... Las Cruces, NM
Allison, Slutsky & Kennedy, P.C.
Chicago, IL
Allison, Sondri .... Phoenix, AZ
Allison, Stephen A. .... Chicago, IL
Allison, Stephen J. .... Moweaqua, IL
Allison, Stephen P. .... San Antonio, TX
Allison, Steven D. .... Washington, DC
Allison, Susan .... Los Angeles, CA
Allison, Theodore S. .... Washington, DC
Allison, Thomas D. .... Chicago, IL
Allison, Thomas E. .... Tampa, FL
Allison, Thomas G. .... Seattle, WA
Allison, Thomas H. .... Cleveland, OH
Allison, Thomas M. .... Albuquerque, NM
Allison, Thomas S., Jr. .... Plaistow, NH
Allison, Todd M. .... Wichita, KS
Allison, Tracey .... New York, NY
Allison, W. D. .... Santa Barbara, CA
Allison, William A. .... Bloomington, IL
Allison, William C., V .... Denver, CO
Allison, William P. .... Little Rock, AR
Allison, William P. .... Austin, TX
Allison, William T. .... Shreveport, LA
Allison, William T., Jr. .... Washington, PA
Allison, William V. .... Houston, TX
Allison, W. T., II .... Sulphur Springs, TX
Allison-Browne, Roxie
Department of Commerce,
National Oceanic and Atmospheric
Administration, GV
Allison-Couto, Thomas .... Tampa, FL
Allison-Davis, K. Michele .... New Orleans, LA
Alliss, Rita M. .... Chicago, IL
Allister, Jeffrey W. .... New York, NY
Allister & Naudon .... New York, NY
Alliston, Douglas R. .... Rancho Cordova, CA
Alliston, James R. .... Treasury Department,
Office of the General Counsel, GV
Alliston, Wiley T. .... Fort Worth, TX
Allman, Andy L. .... Hendersonville, TN
Allman, Bruce M. .... Cincinnati, OH
Allman, C. Edwin, III
Winston-Salem, NC
Allman, Christopher J. .... Flint, MI
Allman, Gary W. .... Branson, MO
Allman, Gary W., P.C. .... Branson, MO
Allman, Kim .... Los Angeles, CA
Allman, Lee R. .... Mount Laurel, NJ
Philadelphia, PA
Allman, Lorraine S. .... Venice, CA
Allman, M. Joseph .... Winston-Salem, NC
Allman, M. Kristen .... Tampa, FL
Allman, Nicole Renee .... Charleston, WV
Allman, Peter J. .... New York, NY
Allman, Richard N. .... Bronx, NY
Allman, Robert L., II .... Pittsburgh, PA
Allman, Robert L., The Law Offices of
Denver, CO
Allman, Sara B. .... San Francisco, CA
Allman Spry Leggett & Crumpler, P.A.
Winston-Salem, NC
Allman, Thomas Y. .... Mount Olive, NJ
Allmand, Jessica Brown
Rochester Hills, MI
Allmand, Kevin D. .... San Jose, CA
Allmaras, Jacob H. .... Anchorage, AK
Allmayer, Daniel N. .... Olathe, KS
Kansas City, MO
Allmayer, Daniel N., P.C. .... Olathe, KS
Kansas City, MO
Allmeroth, Marc D. .... Long Beach, CA
Allmon, Wm. T. .... Carrollton, OH
Allmond, Bayard W., III .... Wilmington, DE
Allmond, Charles M., III .... Wilmington, DE
Allmond & Eastburn .... Wilmington, DE
Allner, Cynthia Collins .... Baltimore, MD
Allo, Clifford D. .... Lansing, MI
Allocca & Felder, P.A. .... Miami, FL
Allocca, Frank J. .... Miami, FL
Allocca, John E. .... Brooklyn, NY
Allocca, Joseph J. .... Florham Park, NJ
Allocca, Louis J. .... Vero Beach, FL
Allocca & Pellegrino, P.C. .... Parsippany, NJ
Allocca, Ralph P. .... Parsippany, NJ
Allocca, Vincent .... Flushing, NY
Allocco, Kathryn I. .... Tinley Park, IL
Allocco, Philip T. .... Chatham, NJ
Allon, Eric R. .... Boston, MA
Allonby, Judith .... Providence, RI
Allor, David W. .... Los Angeles, CA
Allor, Elizabeth P. .... San Francisco, CA
Allora, Ralph A. .... Lyndhurst, NJ
Allott, Ann .... Denver, CO
Allott, Ann, A Professional Corporation
Denver, CO
Allott, Gordon L., Jr. .... Denver, CO
Allott, Michelle .... Portland, ME
Allott, Roger H. .... Englewood, CO
Allotta & Farley Co., L.P.A. .... Toledo, OH
Allotta, Joseph J. .... Toledo, OH
Allouise, Patricia A. .... Boston, MA
Alloway, Clifford C. .... Miami, FL
Alloway, John W., III .... The Woodlands, TX
Alloway, Sherry Fowler .... Greensboro, NC
Alloy, Marjorie P. .... McLean, VA
Alloy, Stephen E. .... Palatine, IL
Allphin, Jeri L. .... Provo, UT
Allphin, Michael G. .... Farmington, UT
Allport, Christine A. .... Cleveland, OH
Allport, John R. .... Lopez, WA
Allport, Michael G. .... Portland, OR
Allport, Susan W. .... Rochester, NY
Allport, William W. .... Auburn Hills, MI
Allran, Austin M., II .... Hickory, NC

Allran, William J., III .... Cherryville, NC
Allred, A. Chad .... Seattle, WA
Allred, Aaron R. .... Chicago, IL
Allred, Allen D. .... St. Louis, MO
Allred, Bacon, Halfhill, Landau & Young,
PC .... Fairfax, VA
Allred, Billy J. .... Huntsville, AR
Allred, C. Keith .... Seattle, WA
Allred, Calvin W. .... Willcox, AZ
Allred, Calvin W., P.C. .... Willcox, AZ
Allred, Chris J. .... El Cajon, CA
Allred, Clark B. .... Roosevelt, UT
Vernal, UT
Allred, Daniel M. .... Salt Lake City, UT
Allred, David E. .... Montgomery, AL
Allred, DeWitt T., III .... Gulfport, MS
Allred, Edward William .... Houston, TX
Allred, Forrest C. .... Aberdeen, SD
Allred, Gloria R. .... Los Angeles, CA
Allred, Howard W. .... Tulsa, OK
Allred, J. Franklin .... Salt Lake City, UT
Allred, James C. .... Fairfax, VA
Allred, Jerry T. .... Pensacola, FL
Allred, Joel M. .... Salt Lake City, UT
Allred, Joel M., P.C. .... Salt Lake City, UT
Allred, John T. .... Charlotte, NC
Allred, Jonathan D. .... Aloha, OR
Allred, Kevin S. .... Los Angeles, CA
Allred Law Firm, The .... Jackson, MS
Allred, Maroko & Goldberg
Los Angeles, CA
Allred, Michael S. .... Jackson, MS
Allred, Michael S. .... Tulsa, OK
Allred, Raymond S. .... Tulsa, OK
Allred, Rhonda N. .... Booneville, MS
Allred, Stephen .... Chapel Hill, NC
Allred, Stephen David .... Charlotte, NC
Allred, Steven Wesley .... Salt Lake City, UT
Allred, Susan Creager .... Salt Lake City, UT
Allred, Timothy H. .... Dalton, GA
Allred, Warren D. .... Ogden, UT
Allred, William .... Atlanta, GA
Allred, William F. .... Dallas, TX
Allred, William Wallace .... Collins, MS
Alls, Howard E. .... Savannah, GA
Alls, Howard E., & Associates, P.C.
Savannah, GA
Allsbrook, R. Colby .... New York, NY
Allsep, L. Michael, Jr. .... Clemson, SC
Allshouse, Beth A. .... Athens, OH
Allshouse, David H. .... Horsham, PA
Allshouse, J.D. Bucky, A Professional
Corporation .... Houston, TX
Allshouse, J.D. Bucky .... Houston, TX
Allshouse, Mark W. .... Torrance, CA
Allsop, D. Meredith .... Toledo, OH
Allsop, Gaylen W. .... Mishawaka, IN
Allsop, Theresa H. .... Berlin, CT
Allsopp, Kolka & Wackerly, P.C.
Bay City, MI
Allsopp, William W. .... Bay City, MI
Allston, Allard A., III .... Barnwell, SC
Allston, Douglas K., Jr. .... Greenbelt, MD
Allston, Monica Roche .... Rockville, MD
Allsup, Kathleen H. .... Bridgeport, CT
Westport, CT
Allsup, Michael Lee .... Birmingham, AL
Allswang, David .... San Francisco, CA
Allswang, David B. .... Chicago, IL
Allsworth, Arthur P. .... Phoenix, AZ
Allsworth, Douglas H. .... Phoenix, AZ
Allsworth, E. Scott, (P.C.)
Fort Lauderdale, FL
Allsworth, Emerson, (P.C.)
Fort Lauderdale, FL
Allsworth, Mark E. .... Fort Lauderdale, FL
Alltmont, Jack M. .... New Orleans, LA
Allton, John D. .... Norwalk, OH
Alluis, Louise J. .... Columbus, OH
Allulis, Paul A. .... Washington, DC
Allums, Carol Brittain .... Alpharetta, GA
Allums, David G. .... Houston, TX
Allums, James C., Jr. .... Dallas, TX
Allums, Vicki Elaine .... Washington, DC
Allums, Victor A. .... Atlanta, GA
Allured, John W. .... Irvine, CA
Allwarden, Christopher J.
Manchester, NH
Allweil, Mandel I. .... Saginaw, MI
Allweiss, Allen P., (P.A.) .... St. Petersburg, FL
Allweiss, David .... Baldwin, NY
Allweiss, Michael D., (P.A.)
St. Petersburg, FL
Allweiss, Michael R. .... New Orleans, LA
Allweiss, Stefanie Band .... New Orleans, LA
Allwine, Deborah J. .... Greensburg, PA
Allwood, Joseph C. .... Troy, MO
Allyn, Barbara L. .... Chicago, IL
Allyn, Burton C. "Skip", IV
San Rafael, CA
Allyn & Fortuna .... New York, NY
Allyn, Gail H. .... Morristown, NJ
Allyn, Givens and Bender .... Evansville, IN
Mt. Vernon, IN
Poseyville, IN
Allyn, Glenn B. .... New City, NY
Allyn, James H. .... New York, NY
Allyn, John B. .... Nashville, TN
Allyn, Kathleen P. .... Boise, ID
Allyn, Richard B. .... Minneapolis, MN
Allyn, Russell L. .... Los Angeles, CA
Allyn, William H., Jr. .... Chillicothe, OH
Alm, David W. .... Chicago, IL
Alm, Kenton L. .... Walnut Creek, CA
Alm, Steven W. .... Greensburg, PA
Almaguer, Adrian .... Houston, TX
Almaguer, Alejandro E. .... Columbus, OH
Almaguer, Francisco D. .... New York, NY

Almaguer, Manuel ... Dallas, TX
Almaguer, Pablo J. ... Edinburg, TX
Almaguer, Pamela M. ... Seattle, WA
Almaguer, Sharon ... McAllen, TX
Alman, David A. ... Chicago, IL
Alman, Elliott A. ... Gaithersburg, MD
Alman, Emily A. ... Highland Park, NJ
Alman, Lee J. ... Washington, DC
Alman, Michael J. ... Hollywood, FL
Alman and Michaels ... Highland Park, NJ
Almand, Alan ... Jacksonville, FL
Almand, Bond H. ... Macon, GA
Almand, James F. ... Arlington, VA
Almand, James W. ... Ocean City, MD
Almand, O. Hale, Jr. ... Macon, GA
Almand & Wiggins ... Macon, GA
Almand, William G. ... Little Rock, AR
Alman-MacDonagh, Catherine M. Garfield, NJ
Almansour, Nabeel ... New York, NY
Almanza, Robert R. ... Manhattan, KS
Almanzán, Andrés E. ... El Paso, TX
Almanzar, Quisaira Y. ... Washington, DC
Almanzar, Steven R. ... Las Cruces, NM
Almanzor, Christina ... Trenton, NJ
Almaraz, David Michael ... Los Angeles, CA
Almas, Mark R. ... Farmington, MI
Almas, Scott R. ... Albany, NY
Almase, Vicki L. ... Boiling Springs, SC
Almasi, Louis Z. ... Ocala, FL
Almasian, Michael V., The Law Offices of Massena, NY
Almason, Allison Louise ... Annandale, VA
Almassi, Mina ... San Jose, CA
Almassian, A. Todd ... Grand Rapids, MI
Almasy, John P. ... Struthers, OH
Almasy, Kurt D. ... Pittsburgh, PA
Almaula, Prabodh I. ... Princeton, NJ
Almazan, Armando ... Chicago, IL
Alme, Kurt G. ... Billings, MT
Alme, Sandra M. ... Billings, MT
Almeda, H. Ramie ... Urbana, OH
Almeida, Alan B. ... Walpole, MA
Almeida, E. Julia ... Marengo, IL
Almeida, Jeff A. ... Philadelphia, PA
Almeida, John A. ... Marlton, NJ
Almeida, Joseph A. ... Steubenville, OH
Almeida, Joseph M. ... Newark, NJ
Almeida, Lillian M. ... Providence, RI
Almeida & Livingston ... Newark, NJ
Almeida, Rebeca C. ... Hialeah, FL
Almeida, Victoria M. ... Boston, MA; Providence, RI
Almendras, Annadel A. San Francisco, CA
Almengual, Brian J. ... Tampa, FL
Almengual & Warner, P.A. ... Tampa, FL
Almerico, Kendall A. ... Tampa, FL
Almerico and Mooney ... Tampa, FL
Almeter, Kevin C. ... Los Angeles, CA
Almeyda, Edward R., Law Offices of Homestead, FL
Almgren, Birgit A. ... New Buffalo, MI
Almgren, Hans ... Santa Ana, CA
Almgren, Paula Kahn ... Williamstown, MA
Almirantearena, Evangelina Menlo Park, CA
Almiron, Ronald A. ... Chicago, IL
Almli, Marta B. ... San Diego, CA
Almodovar, George A. ... Mission Hills, CA
Almodovar, Priscilla ... New York, NY
Almodovar-Acevedo, Martin ... San Juan, PR
Almon, Christopher J. ... Providence, RI
Almon, Edward B. ... Denver, CO
Almon, Lorie E. ... New York, NY
Almon, Louis J. ... Flushing, NY
Almon, McAlister, Baccus & Hall, L.L.C. Tuscumbia, AL
Almon, Orville, Jr. ... Nashville, TN
Almon, Patricia K. ... Los Angeles, CA
Almon, Rebecca L. ... Chicago, IL
Almon, Reneau P. ... Birmingham, AL; Montgomery, AL
Almon, S. Brent ... Evansville, IN
Almon, Samuel A. ... New York, NY
Almon, Thomas F., Jr. ... Miami, FL
Almon, William F. ... Yakima, WA
Almond, A. Jallynn ... Baltimore, MD
Almond, Calandra A. ... Atlanta, GA
Almond, Charles L. ... Houston, TX
Almond, Clinton ... Hillsboro, MO
Almond, David R. ... Oklahoma City, OK
Almond & Hamilton, P.A. ... Baltimore, MD
Almond, Harry H., Jr. ... Arlington, VA
Almond, Honi M. ... Los Angeles, CA
Almond, John J. ... Atlanta, GA
Almond, Lincoln C. ... Providence, RI
Almond, Lincoln Douglas ... Providence, RI
Almond, M. Bradley ... Tuscaloosa, AL
Almond, Michael A. ... Charlotte, NC
Almond, Paul S. ... Los Angeles, CA
Almond, Williams & Brady ... Hillsboro, MO
Almonor, Jeanne-Marie ... Minneapolis, MN
Almonrode, Sharon S. ... Southfield, MI
Almonte, Alfred A., Jr. ... Warwick, RI
Almonte, Franklyn C. ... Flushing, NY
Almonte, Peter A. ... Providence, RI
Almonti, Angelo T. ... Allentown, PA
Almony, Suzan Trinh ... Broomfield, CO
Almour, Dorothy J. ... La Mesa, CA
Almquist, Anthony J. ... Clarinda, IA
Almquist, Arthur R. ... Beaumont, TX; Houston, TX
Almquist, Bruce G. ... Plano, TX
Almquist, Calvin B. ... Dallas, TX
Almquist, J. Jeffrey ... Felton, CA
Almquist, Joel D. ... Boston, MA
Almquist, Peggy V. ... Pasadena, CA
Almquist, Robert D. ... Phoenix, AZ
Almquist, Tod F. ... Dallas, TX
Almroth, David D. ... New York, NY
Alms, David E. ... Park Ridge, IL
Almstedt, Kermit W. ... Washington, DC
Almy, Christopher ... Bangor, ME
Almy, Fred H. ... San Bernardino, CA
Almy, H. Marvin ... Greenwood, NE
Almy, Kenneth J. ... Lancaster, PA
Almy, Monique D. ... Baltimore, MD
Almy, Sarah S. ... Louisville, KY
Almy, Scott A. ... Dallas, TX
Almy, Thomas B. ... Washington, DC
Alneida, Daniela F. ... Sacramento, CA
Alnwick, Timothy P. ... New York, NY
Aloe, Barbara P. ... Melville, NY
Aloe, Paul H. ... Iselin, NJ; New York, NY
Alofs, Douglas J. ... Portland, ME
Alofs & Russo, P.A. ... West Palm Beach, FL
Alofs, Todd Cash ... West Palm Beach, FL
Alogna, John A. ... Bethlehem, PA
Aloi, Anthony F. ... Syracuse, NY
Aloi, Frank A. ... Rochester, NY
Aloi, Leonard C. ... Bronx, NY
Aloi, Michael J. ... Fairmont, WV
Aloi, Paul M. ... Rochester, NY
Aloi, Thomas ... Syracuse, NY
Aloia, Frank J. ... Cape Coral, FL
Aloia, Frank J., Jr. ... Fort Myers, FL
Aloia, Gregory V. ... Philadelphia, PA
Aloia, John L. ... Hempstead, NY
Aloise, Denise Ede ... Miami, FL
Aloise, Denise Ede, P.A. ... Miami, FL
Aloise, Louis P. ... Worcester, MA
Aloise, Michael B. ... Long Island City, NY
Aloisi & Aloisi ... Boston, MA; Lynnfield, MA
Aloisi, Andrew ... Boston, MA
Aloisi, James A., Jr. ... Boston, MA
Aloisi, Peter ... Lynnfield, MA
Alonge, Shauna E. ... Washington, DC
Alongi, Allan C. ... Hinsdale, IL
Alongi, Paul A. ... Parsippany, NJ
Alongi, Thomas P. ... Junction City, KS
Aloni, Ruth ... Jacksonville, FL
Alonso, Alfonso E., Jr. ... San Antonio, TX
Alonso, Amber E. ... San Antonio, TX
Alonso, Andrea M. ... New York, NY
Alonso, Andres F. ... New York, NY
Alonso, Antonio E. ... Miami, FL
Alonso, Barbara L. ... Tampa, FL
Alonso, Beth M. ... Oklahoma City, OK
Alonso & Cersonsky, P.C. ... Houston, TX
Alonso, Daniel R. ... New York, NY
Alonso, Eddie López ... San Juan, PR
Alonso, Fernando C. ... Miami, FL
Alonso, J. Alvaro ... Wayne, NJ
Alonso, Jorge E. ... Miami, FL
Alonso, Jorge E., P.A. ... Miami, FL
Alonso, Julio C. ... Miami, FL
Alonso, Julio C., P.A. ... Miami, FL
Alonso, Louis G. ... San Diego, CA
Alonso, Mark J. ... New York, NY
Alonso, Michael G. ... Las Vegas, NV; Reno, NV
Alonso, Monique ... San Francisco, CA
Alonso, Odalys Caridad ... Bronx, NY
Alonso, Rafael Alonso ... San Juan, PR
Alonso, Richard Environmental Protection Agency, Office of Enforcement and Compliance Assurance, GV
Alonso, Yocel ... Houston, TX
Alonso-Alonso, Rafael ... San Juan, PR
Alonso-Poch, Manuel ... Coral Gables, FL
Alonso-Poch, Manuel, P.A. Coral Gables, FL
Alonzi, Catherine L. ... Denver, CO
Alonzi, Christopher H. ... Berkeley, CA
Alonzi, Saverio J. ... Wilmette, IL
Alonzo, Alex ... San Jose, CA
Alonzo, Arlyn ... Irvine, CA
Alonzo, Gary R. ... San Antonio, TX
Alonzo, Gerard J., Jr. ... Geneseo, NY
Alonzo, Gregory M. ... San Jose, CA
Alonzo, Jan Robey ... St. Louis, MO
Alonzo, Reynolds T., Jr. ... Mobile, AL
Alop, Alan A. ... Chicago, IL
Alos, Andres F. ... Hialeah, FL
Alosco, Salvatore C. ... New York, NY
Alost, Wesley S. ... New Orleans, LA
Alowitz, Arthur L. ... Albany, NY
Aloy, Jennifer A. ... Beverly Hills, CA
Alp, Paul ... Washington, DC
Alpar, Charles A. ... Sacramento, CA
Alpaugh, C. Theodore, III New Orleans, LA
Alpaugh, Thomas Spencer Bainbridge Island, WA
Alpaugh, Vivienne A. Bainbridge Island, WA
Alpay, John M. ... Los Angeles, CA
Alper, Adam R. ... San Francisco, CA
Alper, Andrew K. ... Los Angeles, CA
Alper, Bruce R. ... Chicago, IL
Alper, David ... New York, NY
Alper, David M. ... Encino, CA
Alper, Dean A. ... San Francisco, CA
Alper, Ethyl G. ... New York, NY
Alper, Harold ... Union, NJ
Alper, Harold & Alper, P.A. ... Union, NJ
Alper, Harvey M. ... Altamonte Springs, FL
Alper, Jane K. ... Boston, MA
Alper, Jerome M. ... Washington, DC
Alper, Joanne Fogel ... Arlington, VA
Alper, Jodi Lee ... Roseland, NJ
Alper, Jonathan ... Lake Mary, FL
Alper, Joshua M. ... Boston, MA
Alper, Mann & Weisbaum, P.C. Washington, DC; Rockville, MD
Alper, Marilyn Weiss ... Los Angeles, CA
Alper & McCulloch ... San Francisco, CA
Alper, Michael D. ... San Francisco, CA
Alper, Michael F. ... Union, NJ
Alper, Nancy L. Federal Deposit Insurance Corporation, Compliance and Enforcement Section, GV
Alper, Paul E. ... Washington, DC
Alper, Penni A. ... Atlanta, GA
Alper, Ronald E. Securities and Exchange Commission, GV
Alper, Susan C. ... Norfolk, VA
Alper, Ty ... Washington, DC
Alper, Walden & Miller Altamonte Springs, FL
Alper, William A. ... New York, NY
Alperen, Martin J. ... Cruz Bay, St. John, VI
Alperin, Anthony S. ... Los Angeles, CA
Alperin, Barry J. ... New York, NY
Alperin, Howard J. ... Beverly, MA
Alperin, Howard K. ... Santa Monica, CA; Haddonfield, NJ; Philadelphia, PA
Alperin & Hufjay ... Mount Vernon, NY
Alperin, Janice A. ... Washington, DC
Alperin, Jeffrey ... Atlanta, GA
Alperin, Jeffrey Mark ... Chicago, IL
Alperin, Joseph D. ... New York, NY
Alperin, Kenneth A., (P.C.) ... Boston, MA
Alperin, Lewis ... Mount Vernon, NY
Alperin, Mitchell L. ... Beachwood, OH
Alperin, Rebecca Federman ... Boston, MA
Alperin, Scott N. ... Virginia Beach, VA
Alperin, Stuart N. ... New York, NY
Alpern & Alpern ... Pittsburgh, PA
Alpern, Amy R. ... Portland, OR
Alpern, Andrea G. ... Boca Raton, FL
Alpern, Andrew ... New York, NY
Alpern, Charles H. ... Pittsburgh, PA
Alpern, David F. ... Pittsburgh, PA
Alpern, Dwight C. Environmental Protection Agency, Program Office Attorneys, GV
Alpern, Erwin ... Oklahoma City, OK
Alpern, Erwin A. ... Washington, DC
Alpern, Eugene D. ... Los Angeles, CA
Alpern, Howard J. ... Colorado Springs, CO
Alpern, I. Norman ... Beverly Hills, CA
Alpern, Ingrid Yollick ... Treasury Department, Internal Revenue Service, GV
Alpern, Jack N. ... Warren, OH
Alpern, Jack N., Co., L.P.A. ... Warren, OH
Alpern, Jamie P. ... Mineola, NY
Alpern, Jeffrey R. ... Beverly Hills, CA
Alpern, Matthew ... Washington, DC
Alpern, Myers, Stuart, Scheuerman & Levinson ... Colorado Springs, CO
Alpern, Richard K. ... Rockville, MD
Alpern, Richard L. ... New York, NY
Alpern, Stephen E. Merit Systems Protection Board, Office of Appeals Counsel, GV
Alper-Pressman, Wendi ... St. Louis, MO
Alpers, Bobbi M. ... Davenport, IA
Alpers, John, Jr. ... Cabool, MO
Alpers, Steven J. ... Fremont, CA
Alpers, Steven J., A Professional Corporation Fremont, CA
Alperstein, Arnold S. ... New York, NY
Alperstein, Arthur S. ... Baltimore, MD
Alperstein, Brian Scott ... Washington, DC
Alperstein & Covell, P.C. ... Denver, CO
Alperstein & Diener, P.A. ... Baltimore, MD
Alperstein, Donald W. ... Denver, CO
Alperstein, Glenn M. ... Encino, CA
Alperstein, Michael ... New York, NY
Alpert, Alison D. ... San Diego, CA
Alpert and Alpert ... Southfield, MI
Alpert, Andrew David ... Waldorf, MD
Alpert, Anthony Strukl ... Norwalk, CA
Alpert, Arthur F. ... Framingham, MA
Alpert, Barker & Rodems, P.A. Tampa, FL
Alpert & Barr, A Professional Law Corporation ... Encino, CA; Los Angeles, CA
Alpert, Benjamin ... Waltham, MA
Alpert, Brian L., (P.C.) ... Washington, DC
Alpert, Bruce D. ... Mineola, NY
Alpert, Bruce M. ... Needham, MA
Alpert, Bruce S. ... Oroville, CA
Alpert, Butler & Sanders, P.C. West Orange, NJ; New York, NY
Alpert, Caryll S. ... Nashville, TN
Alpert, Charles E. ... Culver City, CA
Alpert, Charles M. ... Framingham, MA
Alpert, Charles S. ... Long Beach, CA
Alpert, Clark E. ... Trenton, NJ; West Orange, NJ; New York, NY
Alpert, Dan J. ... Arlington, VA
Alpert, Daniel Lee Department of Transportation, Federal Railroad Administration, GV
Alpert, David E. ... Somerset, NJ
Alpert, Diane Botwin ... Kansas City, MO
Alpert, Donn S. ... Tucson, AZ
Alpert, Donn S., P.C. ... Tucson, AZ
Alpert and Eastman ... Waltham, MA
Alpert, Eva ... Boston, MA
Alpert, Fredda L. ... New York, NY
Alpert, Gail S. ... Southfield, MI
Alpert, Gerald ... Huntington, NY
Alpert, Gordon M. ... New York, NY
Alpert & Gregorski, LLP ... Manitowoc, WI
Alpert, Harry A. ... Indianapolis, IN
Alpert, Helaine Y. ... Scarsdale, NY
Alpert, Henry A. ... Hewlett, NY
Alpert, Herbert H. ... New York, NY
Alpert, Hollis J. Federal Energy Regulatory Commission, Office of the General Counsel, GV
Alpert, Howard ... Albany, NY
Alpert, Irene S. ... New York, NY
Alpert, Irwin S. ... Lexington, MA
Alpert, Jack ... New York, NY
Alpert, Jane K. ... Stamford, CT
Alpert, Janet D. ... Bronx, NY
Alpert, Jeremy G. ... Memphis, TN
Alpert, Joel L. ... Southfield, MI
Alpert, Jonathan ... Highland, IN
Alpert, Jonathan L. ... Tampa, FL
Alpert & Kaufman ... New York, NY
Alpert, Laurent ... New York, NY
Alpert, Lee Kanon ... Encino, CA
Alpert, Leonard Z. ... Weirton, WV
Alpert & Levy, P.C. ... Trenton, NJ
Alpert, Linda R. ... New York, NY
Alpert, Marc A. ... New York, NY
Alpert, Mark ... New York, NY
Alpert, Mark D. ... Costa Mesa, CA
Alpert, Mark D. ... Boston, MA
Alpert, Martin H. ... Chicago, IL
Alpert, Martin W. ... Boca Raton, FL; New York, NY
Alpert, Merrick R. ... Houston, TX
Alpert, Michael E. ... San Diego, CA
Alpert, Milton ... Pompano Beach, FL
Alpert, Morton ... New York, NY
Alpert, Myron I. ... Highland Beach, FL
Alpert, Nancy R. ... New York, NY
Alpert, Norman ... New York, NY
Alpert, Paul E. ... Towson, MD
Alpert, Paul L. ... New York, NY
Alpert, Paul S. ... Boston, MA
Alpert, Peter A. ... Boston, MA
Alpert, Peter A. ... Boston, MA
Alpert, Peter H., (Professional Corporation) Los Angeles, CA
Alpert, Peter I. ... Las Vegas, NV
Alpert, Peter Mills ... Melville, NY; Mineola, NY
Alpert, Phillip S. ... San Diego, CA
Alpert, Phillip S., A Professional Law Corporation ... San Diego, CA
Alpert, Ralph ... Santa Cruz, CA
Alpert, Randy S. ... Forest Hills, NY
Alpert, Richard B. ... New York, NY
Alpert, Richard B. ... Fort Worth, TX
Alpert, Richard H. ... Concord, MA
Alpert, Robert ... New York, NY
Alpert, Robert A. ... Allentown, PA
Alpert, Robert L. ... Chapel Hill, NC
Alpert, Robert P. ... Atlanta, GA
Alpert, Rochelle D. ... San Francisco, CA
Alpert, Ronald I. ... Santa Monica, CA
Alpert & Savit ... Needham, MA
Alpert, Shara Mervis ... Ellicott City, MD
Alpert, Stanley ... Baltimore, MD
Alpert, Stanley N. ... Brooklyn, NY
Alpert, Stephen H. ... New York, NY
Alpert, Steven ... Manitowoc, WI
Alpert, Steven A. ... Encino, CA
Alpert, Thomas M. ... Boston, MA
Alphen, Paul F. ... Chelmsford, MA
Alpher, David B. ... Gloucester, MA
Alphin, Fred, Jr. ... Raleigh, NC
Alphin, Katharine B. ... Atlanta, GA
Alphin, Oliver W. ... Durham, NC
Alphin, Thomas H., Jr. ... Department of State, Office of the Legal Adviser, GV
Alphonse, Harold T. ... Campbell, CA
Alphonse, Joseph L. ... Metairie, LA
Alphonse, Richard J. ... Princeton, NJ
Alphonso, Gordon R. ... Atlanta, GA
Alphson, Howard C. ... Santa Monica, CA
Alphson, John A., Jr. ... Clive, IA
Alphson, Robert A. ... Grand Forks, ND
Alpi, Donna Lady ... Washington, DC
Alpi, James V. ... Washington, DC
Alpin, Tara ... Los Angeles, CA
Alpizar, Carmen ... Tampa, FL
Alpizar, O. John, P.A. ... Palm Bay, FL
Alpizar, Ville, Torres & Camfield Melbourne, FL; Palm Bay, FL
Alpren, H. Michael ... Portland, ME
Alprin, Brian D. ... Washington, DC
Alprin, Geoffrey M. ... Washington, DC
Alpuche, Maripat ... New York, NY
Alpuche, Paul E., Jr. ... Bethesda, MD
Alquist, Elizabeth A. ... Hartford, CT
Alquist, Mark H. ... Walworth, NY
Alquist, Nancy V. ... Washington, DC; Baltimore, MD
Alred, Charles Bryan ... Tulsa, OK
Alred, Charles Bryan, P.C. ... Tulsa, OK
Alred, Mary T. ... Chicago, IL
Alrich, Samuel G. ... Goochland, VA
Alridge, Carl Spencer, II ... Charlotte, NC
Alroy, Liore Z. ... New York, NY
Alroy, Orna ... New York, NY
Alrutz, Douglas M. ... Memphis, TN
Al-Sabti, Mohammed Salah Washington, DC
Alsace, Juan A. ... Department of State, GV
Alsaif, Suzanne D. ... Claremore, OK
Al-Salam, Ramsey M. ... Seattle, WA
Alsalihi, Linda E. ... Treasury Department, Internal Revenue Service, GV

Alsandor, Cheryl, Law Office of
Houston, TX
Alsante, Cora A. ....Syracuse, NY
Al-Sarraf, Sermid D. ....Los Angeles, CA
Alsberry, Dennis M. ....Fort Lauderdale, FL
Alsbrooks, John H., Jr. ....Birmingham, AL
Alschuler, Albert W. ....Chicago, IL
Alschuler, Alschuler, Alschuler & Alschuler, A Professional Corporation ....Los Angeles, CA
Alschuler, Benjamin P. ....**Aurora, IL**
Alschuler, Edward S. ....Madison, WI
Alschuler, Fred H. ....**Santa Monica, CA**
Alschuler, George A. ....Oakland, CA
Alschuler Grossman Stein & Kahan LLP
Los Angeles, CA
Alschuler, Herbert E ....Los Angeles, CA
Alschuler, Natt D ....Los Angeles, CA
Alschuler, Norman W. ....Northridge, CA
Alschuler, Sam ....Aurora, IL
Alschuler, Walter W. ....Los Angeles, CA
Alsdorf, Robert H. ....Seattle, WA
Alsen, Leanne ....**Philadelphia, PA**
Alsentzer, William J., Jr. ....Phoenix, AZ
Alsfelder, Deborah T. ....Cincinnati, OH
Alsfelder, Nancy S. ....Falls Church, VA
Alsfelder, Robert F., Jr. ....Cincinnati, OH
Alsher, Bennet D. ....**Atlanta, GA**
Alsher, Michael D. ....Harrisburg, PA
Alshouse, Diane R. ....St. Paul, MN
Alshuler, John D. ....Chicago, IL
Alsin, Vicki A. ....Grand Junction, CO
Alsina, Kathleen Hopkins ....**Houston, TX**
Alsina, Ricardo V. ....Miami, FL
Alsip, Renee L. ....Covington, KY
Alsip, Rick G. ....**Louisville, KY**
Alskog, David A. ....**Kirkland, WA**
Alsnauer, Mary Ann ....**Los Angeles, CA**
Alsnauer, William E., Jr. ....**Santa Ana, CA**
Alsobrook, Athena Dulice ....East Orange, NJ
Alsobrook, Elizabeth Renee ....Coleman, FL
Alsobrook, Henry B., Jr.
New Orleans, LA
Alsobrook, John G. ....**Metairie, LA**
Alsobrook, John G. ....**New Orleans, LA**
Alsobrook, Mark A. ....Department of Labor, Office of Secretary, GV
Alsobrooks, Dan M. ....Charlotte, TN
Alsofrom, Daniel D. ....Linwood, NJ
Alson, Andrew C. ....Harrison, NY
Alson, Beth Nancy ....**New York, NY**
Alsop, Barbara H. ....**Burlington, VT**
Alsop, Christine A. ....**St. Louis, MO**
Alsop, Clark H. ....**Riverside, CA**
Alsop, David D. ....**Minneapolis, MN**
Alsop, Donald D. ....St. Paul, MN
Alsop, Douglas W. ....Redwood City, CA
Alsop, Jack ....Webster Springs, WV
Alsop, John ....Norridgewock, ME
Alsop & Mohlar ....Norridgewock, ME
Alsop, Robert A. ....**Minneapolis, MN**
Alsop, Robert A. ....**Salt Lake City, UT**
Alsop, Robert C. ....Westfield, MA
Alsop, Stuart R.
Department of Transportation, Federal Highway Administration, GV
Alsop, Wayne I. ....Redwood City, CA
Al Sowayel, Dina ....Houston, TX
Alspach, Alfred C. ....**Lancaster, PA**
Alspach, David E. ....**Lancaster, PA**
Alspach, Deborah A. ....Marion, OH
Alspach, George D. ....**Lancaster, PA**
Alspach and Ryder ....**Lancaster, PA**
Alspach, Thomas T. ....**Easton, MD**
Alspaugh & Carruthers ....Greensboro, NC
Alspaugh, David W. ....Wheaton, IL
Alspaugh, Donald H. ....**Longmont, CO**
Alspaugh, Donn P. ....Boulder, CO
Alspaugh, Doris Y. ....El Cajon, CA
Alspaugh, George A. ....El Cajon, CA
Alspaugh, George A., Jr. ....El Cajon, CA
Alspaugh, James A. ....Greensboro, NC
Alspaugh, John H. ....**San Diego, CA**
Alspaugh, M. Clay ....**Birmingham, AL**
Alspector, Jacob I. ....Bingham Farms, MI
Alspector, Sosin, Barson, Schafer & Sosin, P.C.
Bingham Farms, MI
Alspector, Susan L. ....North Miami Beach, FL
Alstadt, Lynn J. ....**Pittsburgh, PA**
Alstars, Sandra M. ....**Washington, DC**
Alster, Caliste J. ....Chicago, IL
Alster, Christopher ....Franktown, CO
Alster, Frank G. ....Hackensack, NJ
Alster, Marc G. ....Hackensack, NJ
Alster, Sheldon H. ....**New York, NY**
Alsterda, John B. ....**Chicago, IL**
Alsterda, R. Scott ....**Chicago, IL**
Alston, Alex A., Jr. ....**Jackson, MS**
Alston, Alvin A. ....Baltimore, MD
Alston & Associates ....Louisville, KY
Alston, Benfred B. ....Baltimore, MD
Alston & Bird LLP ....**Washington, DC**
Atlanta, GA
Charlotte, NC
Raleigh, NC
Research Triangle Park, NC
Alston & Byrd ....Baltimore, MD
Alston, Christopher M. ....**Seattle, WA**
Alston, Courtnage, Proctor & Bassetti LLP
Seattle, WA
Alston, Craig E. F. ....Philadelphia, PA
Alston, Darrell W. ....**Lake Charles, LA**
Alston, Elaine B. ....**Santa Ana, CA**
Alston, Elizabeth A. ....**New Orleans, LA**
Alston, Ethel Richardson ....Louisville, KY
Alston, Gerald M. ....**Philadelphia, PA**
Alston, Gerald W. ....**Phoenix, AZ**
Alston, Heather C. ....**Atlanta, GA**

Alston, Hunt, Floyd & Ing, Attorneys at Law, A Law Corporation ....**Honolulu, HI**
Alston, James H., V ....New York, NY
Alston, J. L. ....Atlanta, GA
Alston & Jones ....**Jackson, MS**
Alston, Joseph K. ....**New York, NY**
Alston, Julie A. ....Lufkin, TX
Alston, Kaileen T. ....**Woodbridge, NJ**
Alston, Kären Frasier ....**Durham, NC**
Alston, Karla Renee ....Brooklyn, NY
Alston Law Firm ....**Mandeville, LA**
New Orleans, LA
Alston, Lisa Elaine ....Austin, TX
Alston, M. Edward ....Santa Maria, CA
Alston, Marcus V. ....Boston, MA
Alston, Maureen T. ....**Rochester, NY**
Alston, Michael K. ....**Chattanooga, TN**
Alston, Michael L. ....Department of Justice, Office of Justice Programs, GV
Alston, Nelson G. ....Denver, CO
Alston, Nicole D. ....**San Francisco, CA**
Alston, Paul D. ....**Honolulu, HI**
Alston, Quentin L. R. ....Salt Lake City, UT
Alston, Richard N. ....North Olmsted, OH
Alston, Robert A. ....**Wayne, PA**
Alston, Robinson M. ....**Salt Lake City, UT**
Alston, Rossie David, Jr. ....Springfield, VA
Alston, Sheldon G. ....**Jackson, MS**
Alston, Thaddas L. ....**Seattle, WA**
Alston, Thomas F. ....Campbell, CA
Alston, V. Jeffery ....Louisville, KY
Alston, Vivienne J. ....**Santa Ana, CA**
Alstott, Anne ....New York, NY
Alsup & Alsup ....Clayton, NM
Alsup & Alsup ....Corpus Christi, TX
Alsup, Charles D. ....Clayton, NM
Alsup, Daniel A. ....Salt Lake City, UT
Alsup, Debora Beck ....**Austin, TX**
Alsup, Fisher, Jr. ....Corpus Christi, TX
Alsup, Gary D. ....Clayton, NM
Alsup, J. Alton ....Houston, TX
Alsup, James Devin ....**Midland, TX**
Alsup, James M. ....**Austin, TX**
Alsup, James M. ....**Midland, TX**
Alsup, James R. ....Department of Justice, Criminal Division, GV
Alsup, Joe J. ....Corpus Christi, TX
Alsup, John W., Jr. ....Mount Sterling, IL
Alsup, Lisa Griffin ....Baltimore, MD
Alsup, Richard A. ....San Diego, CA
Alsup, Richard C. ....**Houston, TX**
Alsup, Robert E. ....Estes Park, CO
Alsup, Robert E. ....St. Francis, KS
Alsup, Roger W. ....Brentwood, TN
Alsup, William ....San Francisco, CA
Alsup, William D. ....Corpus Christi, TX
Alt, Charles A. ....**High Point, NC**
Alt, Constance M. ....**Cedar Rapids, IA**
Alt, Danita S. ....Harrisonburg, VA
Alt, Darlene K. ....**Chicago, IL**
Alt, Dennis M. ....**Kansas City, MO**
Alt, Gerald B. ....Bingham Farms, MI
Alt, Helene A. ....Austin, TX
Alt, James D. ....**Minneapolis, MN**
Alt, Jerry P. ....**Des Moines, IA**
Alt, Jill C. ....Department of Commerce, Patent and Trademark Office, GV
Alt, Julane Brooks ....**Chicago, IL**
Alt, Konrad S. ....United States Senate, Committee Legal Personnel, GV
Alt, Randall G. ....**Denver, CO**
Alt, Stanley Aaron ....New York, NY
Alt, Susan B. ....New York, NY
Alt, Trevor L. ....Los Angeles, CA
Alt, William T. ....Chattanooga, TN
Alta, Lina M. ....San Francisco, CA
Altabef, Jennifer Burr ....**Dallas, TX**
Altabef, Peter A. ....Dallas, TX
Altabef, Richard H. ....**New York, NY**
Altaffer, Dabney R. ....Tucson, AZ
Altaffer, Kervyn B., Jr. ....**Dallas, TX**
Altaffer, Michael R. ....Phoenix, AZ
Altaffer, William W. ....Tucson, AZ
Altagen, Robert S. ....Los Angeles, CA
Altamira, Marilyn S. ....**Houston, TX**
Altamirano, Diane Bradford ....Brawley, CA
Altamirano, Victor H. ....Santa Ana, CA
Altamore, A. F. ....Rockford, IL
Altamore, Albert ....Rockford, IL
Altamore, Joan M. ....Roxbury, MA
Altamore, Steven B. ....**New York, NY**
Altamura, Anthony ....**New York, NY**
Altamura, Leonard J. ....Union City, NJ
Altamura, Patrick M. ....**Clinton, NJ**
Altamura, Vincent ....Newark, NJ
Altamuro, Stephen ....Atlantic City, NJ
Altarac, Jill ....**Garden City, NY**
Altaras & Altaras ....Cleburne, TX
Altaras, Karen Williams ....**Fort Worth, TX**
Altaras, Tim ....Cleburne, TX
Altaras, Tommy ....Cleburne, TX
Altarescu, Howard S. ....New York, NY
Altarescu, Louis A.
Department Of Health And Human Services, Office for Civil Rights, GV
Altavilla, Christina ....**Minneapolis, MN**
Altbach, Jeffrey S. ....Liberty, NY
Altchiler, Robert Yael ....New York, NY
Altebrando, Nancy ....Westbury, NY
Altekruse, Clifford F. ....**Atlanta, GA**
Altemose, Jennifer L. ....**Allentown, PA**
Altemose, Mark K. ....Allentown, PA
Altemus, Christine T. ....**Baltimore, MD**
Altemus, Daniel F., Jr. ....Oakland, CA
Altemus, Michele J.
Department Of The Interior, U.S. Fish & Wildlife Service, GV
Altemus, Robert P. ....Hackensack, NJ

Altemus, Stewart C. ....**Redding, CA**
Altemus, Timothy ....**Lanham, MD**
Altemus & Wagner ....**Redding, CA**
Alten, Brett G. ....**New York, NY**
Alten, Eugene Jay ....Philadelphia, PA
Alten, Richard D. ....Ocean City, NJ
Altenbach, James S. ....**Atlanta, GA**
Altenbach, Robert E. ....**Atlanta, GA**
Altenberger, William V. ....Peoria, IL
Altenbernd, Chris W. ....Tampa, FL
Altenborg, John E. ....Lindsborg, KS
Altenburg, Andrew B., Jr.
Cherry Hill, NJ
Altenburg, John D., Jr.
Department of the Army, Office of the Judge Advocate General, GV
Altenburg, John J. ....Los Angeles, CA
Altenburg, Keith M. ....Detroit, MI
Altenburg, Laurie Joan ....Redmond, WA
Altenburger, Scott R. ....Toledo, OH
Altendorf, Linda ....New Smyrna Beach, FL
Alteneder, Katherine R. ....Anchorage, AK
Altenhof, Robert R. ....Kelso, WA
Altenhofen, Craig ....**Junction City, KS**
Altenof, Charles W. ....Stow, MA
Altenpohl, Michelle L. ....**Philadelphia, PA**
Alter, Aaron J. ....**Palo Alto, CA**
Alter, Amos ....**New York, NY**
Alter, Andrew W. ....**New York, NY**
Alter, B. Mitchell ....**Carle Place, NY**
Alter, Beth H. ....**New York, NY**
Alter, Brian R. ....Beaumont, TX
Alter, Bruce A. ....Miami, FL
Alter, Bruce R. ....New York, NY
Alter, Bruce W. ....Department of Labor, Office of the Solicitor, GV
Alter, Bryan J. ....**New York, NY**
Alter, Burton Z. ....**Waterbury, CT**
Alter, Connie Haar ....Miami, FL
Alter, Daniel ....**Fort Lauderdale, FL**
Alter, Daniel Scott ....**Harrison, NY**
Alter, David ....New York, NY
Alter, David S., II ....Martinsburg, WV
Alter, Denise ....**San Francisco, CA**
Alter, Dennis I. ....Beaumont, TX
Alter, Eleanor Breitel ....**New York, NY**
Alter, Gordon D. ....**New York, NY**
Alter, Ilyssa Rothman ....**New City, NY**
Alter, Irving D. ....North Miami Beach, FL
Alter, Irving D. ....**New York, NY**
Alter, Irwin C. ....**Chicago, IL**
Alter, Ivan ....New York, NY
Alter, Janet ....**Cleveland, OH**
Alter, John E. ....Torrance, CA
Alter, Jonathan B. ....**Hartford, CT**
Alter, June M. ....Evanston, IL
Alter, Keith ....Wichita, KS
Alter, Lauren C. ....Stamford, CT
Alter, Laurence F. ....Clayton, MO
Alter, Lisa ....**New York, NY**
Alter Mantel, LLP ....**New York, NY**
Alter, Mark E. ....Mineola, NY
Alter, Marlene L. ....Woodland Hills, CA
Alter, Melvin A. ....Brookline, MA
Alter, Michael ....Lincolnwood, IL
Alter, Michael J. ....**Washington, DC**
Alter, Mitchell E. ....Miami, FL
Alter, Mitchell J. ....Columbus, OH
Alter, Mitchell L. ....Miami, FL
Alter, Nelson T. ....Beaumont, TX
Alter, Paul R. ....**New York, NY**
Alter, Peter Jay ....**Glastonbury, CT**
Alter, Peter M. ....**Detroit, MI**
Alter, Regina M. ....**New York, NY**
Alter, Rhona S. ....Coudersport, PA
Alter, Richard C. ....San Diego, CA
Alter, Robert J. ....**Newark, NJ**
New York, NY
Alter, Ronald A. ....Miami, FL
Alter, Rory S. ....Pasadena, TX
Alter, Scott M. ....**Washington, DC**
Alter and Sherwood, LLC
Glastonbury, CT
Alter, Spencer R. ....Huntington Beach, CA
Alter, Sylvan R. ....San Antonio, TX
Alter, W. Kevin ....Houston, TX
Alter and Weiss ....**Chicago, IL**
Altera, Allan G. ....**Atlanta, GA**
Alterbaum, James ....**Great Neck, NY**
New York, NY
Altergott, Frederick H. ....**Wilmington, DE**
Altergott, John H., Jr. ....Kansas City, MO
Altergott, John H., Jr., P.C.
Kansas City, MO
Alteri, Albert A. ....Utica, NY
Alterman & Associates, P.C. ....Atlanta, GA
Alterman, Barbara E. ....West Palm Beach, FL
Alterman & Boop, P.C. ....New York, NY
Alterman, Cathy Morris ....Atlanta, GA
Alterman, Daniel L. ....New York, NY
Alterman, Dean N. ....**Portland, OR**
Alterman, Edward M. ....**New York, NY**
Alterman, Howard P. ....Pompano Beach, FL
Alterman, Howard P., P.A.
Pompano Beach, FL
Alterman, Irwin ....**Troy, MI**
Alterman, John ....Opa Locka, FL
Alterman, L. Henry ....Dallas, TX
Alterman, Lauren Palik ....Valley Forge, PA
Alterman, Leonard ....Jacksonville, FL
Alterman, Norman L. ....New York, NY
Alterman, Roy A. ....Melbourne, FL
Alterman, Roy A., P.A. ....Melbourne, FL
Alterman, Stanley R. ....San Antonio, TX
Alterman, Stephen A. ....Washington, DC
Alterman, Susan T. ....Seattle, WA
Altermatt, Mark T. ....**Hartford, CT**
Altermatt, Paul B. ....**New Milford, CT**

Alterowitz Law Offices, P.C. ....Missoula, MT
Alterowitz, Michael G. ....Missoula, MT
Alters, Jeremy W. ....**Miami, FL**
Alters, Rachel ....**Miami, FL**
Alterwein, Leonard ....Fort Lauderdale, FL
Alterwitz, Daryl S. ....Las Vegas, NV
Altes, Jack J. ....Little Neck, NY
Altes, Michael A. ....Jacksonville, FL
Altes, Scott L. ....**Phoenix, AZ**
Altesman, Albert ....New York, NY
Altfeder, Nancy ....New York, NY
Altfeld, Clifford B. ....**Tucson, AZ**
Altfeld, Philip Z. ....Baltimore, MD
Altfield, William Ira ....Miami, FL
Altham, James F., Jr. ....Hamden, CT
Althaus, Thomas Edward ....Los Angeles, CA
Althaus, Thomas R. ....**Tucson, AZ**
Althauser, Donald K. ....New Haven, MO
Owensville, MO
Althauser, Lucinda A. ....**St. Louis, MO**
Althauser, T. Charles ....Centralia, WA
Althauser, Thomas J. ....**Baltimore, MD**
Altheim, Abraham S. ....**New York, NY**
Altheimer & Gray ....Washington, DC
Chicago, IL
Springfield, IL
Althen, William I. ....**Washington, DC**
Alther, Dorothy ....Bishop, CA
Altherr, Robert F., Jr. ....**Washington, DC**
Altherr, Ronald L. ....Tucson, AZ
Althoff, Barrie ....Seattle, WA
Althoff, Bernard M. ....**New York, NY**
Althoff, Cheryl A. ....Rochester, NY
Althoff, Gretchen ....**Boston, MA**
Althoff, J. Jay ....Nashua, NH
Althoff, John J. ....Greeley, CO
Althoff, Kelly W. ....Rockford, IL
Althoff, Linda S. ....**Dallas, TX**
Althoff, Margaret A. ....**Fort Collins, CO**
Althoff, William T. ....Des Moines, IA
Altholtz, Howard A. ....**Boston, MA**
Altholtz, Lawrence A. ....**East Meadow, NY**
Altholz, Andrew P. ....Santa Monica, CA
Altholz, Eric D. ....**Portland, ME**
Althouse, Ann ....Madison, WI
Althouse, Charles S. ....**Upland, CA**
Althouse, Dennis L. ....**Pasadena, CA**
Althouse, Kurt ....**Reading, PA**
Althouse & McDonough ....**Upland, CA**
Althouse, Philip D. ....Cleveland, OH
Althouse, Ralph J., Jr. ....**Reading, PA**
Altice, Kristin L. ....Indianapolis, IN
Altice, Robert R., Jr. ....Indianapolis, IN
Altick & Corwin Co., L.P.A. ....**Dayton, OH**
Altier, Christopher ....Ashtabula, OH
Altier, Christopher, Co., L.P.A.
Ashtabula, OH
Altier, Joseph P. ....New York, NY
Altier, Linda A. ....Dallas, TX
Altier, Mark W. ....Wooster, OH
Altier, Mary W. ....Akron, OH
Altier, Michael J. ....**Hoffman Estates, IL**
Altier, Samuel L. ....Ashtabula, OH
Altier, Samuel L., Ltd. ....Ashtabula, OH
Altiere, James N., III ....Toledo, OH
Altieri, David W. ....Sackets Harbor, NY
Altieri, James M. ....**Florham Park, NJ**
Altieri, Jason R. ....**Palo Alto, CA**
Altieri, John L., Jr. ....**New York, NY**
Altieri, John R. ....Hackensack, NJ
Altieri, Kushner, Miuccio & Frind, P.C.
New York, NY
Altieri, Maria R. ....**Bridgeport, CT**
Altieri, Mark P. ....**Lorain, OH**
Altieri, Peter L. ....**Stamford, CT**
New York, NY
Altieri, Richard P. ....New York, NY
Altieri, Thomas J. ....New Rochelle, NY
Altimari, Anthony F. ....Mineola, NY
Altimari, Frank X. ....Uniondale, NY
Altimari, Nicholas S. ....Richmond, VA
Altimari, P. Charles ....**Atlanta, GA**
Altimari, Phillip C. ....Downers Grove, IL
Altimari, Rita Miller ....Cincinnati, OH
Altin, Mortimer ....Boulder, CO
Alting, Carsten ....Atlanta, GA
Altis, Alaina K. ....Lewisville, TX
Altis, Donna J. ....Jefferson City, MO
Altis, Lisa J. ....Monkton, MD
Altizer & Altizer ....Roanoke, VA
Altizer, Bettina C. ....Roanoke, VA
Altizer, David Grant ....**Tazewell, VA**
Altizer, Delano E. ....Wilmington, DE
Altizer, Jack V. ....Roanoke, VA
Altizer, James H., III ....Virginia Beach, VA
Altizer, John W. ....Simi Valley, CA
Altizer, Robert B. ....**Tazewell, VA**
Altizer, Walk & White ....**Tazewell, VA**
Altland, P. Daniel ....**Harrisburg, PA**
Altland, Steven R. ....Muncie, IN
Altmaier, Martin D. ....**Newark, OH**
Altman, Adam P. ....**Charlotte, NC**
Altman, Alan W. ....**New York, NY**
Altman, Alexandra ....New York, NY
Altman, Alison ....**New York, NY**
Altman, Allen D. ....**Atlanta, GA**
Altman & Altman, P.A. ....**Charleston, SC**
Altman, Alvin ....**New York, NY**
Altman, Anthony M. ....Encino, CA
Altman, Arthur D. ....**Boston, MA**
Altman, Arthur L. ....White Plains, NY
Altman, Barbara F. ....Chicago, IL
Altman, Benjamin ....New York, NY
Altman, Beth ....Blue Bell, PA
Altman & Boucher ....Havre, MT
Altman, Brian ....Goldendale, WA
Altman, Carolyn Beth ....Glendale, CA
Altman, Cathy Lilford ....**Dallas, TX**

Altman, Charles J. ....New Rochelle, NY
Altman, Charles S. ....Charleston, SC
Altman, Christine Crull ....Carmel, IN
Altman, Craig A. ....Vineland, NJ
Philadelphia, PA
Altman, Craig A., A Professional Corporation ....Vineland, NJ
Philadelphia, PA
Altman, D. David ....Cincinnati, OH
Altman, Dan ....Pittsburgh, PA
Altman, Daniel B. ....Indianapolis, IN
Altman, Daniel E. ....Newport Beach, CA
Altman, Daniel G. ....Fort Worth, TX
Midlothian, TX
Altman, Daniel R. ....New York, NY
Altman, Daniel T. ....New York, NY
Altman, Dara F. ....Denver, CO
Altman, David ....Nokomis, FL
Altman, David ....Cleveland, OH
Altman, David B. ....Chicago, IL
Altman, David H. ....Hawthorne, NJ
Altman, David J. ....Los Angeles, CA
Altman, David N. ....Smithtown, NY
Altman, D. David Co., A Legal Professional Association ....Cincinnati, OH
Altman, Deborah M. ....Pittsburgh, PA
Altman, Denise L. ....San Francisco, CA
Altman, Doreen R. ....Sacramento, CA
Altman, Douglas B. ....Minneapolis, MN
Altman, Emily M. ....New York, NY
Altman, Eric L. ....New York, NY
Altman, Evan M. ....Atlanta, GA
Altman, Frank D. ....Havre, MT
Altman, Frederick M. ....Albany, NY
Altman, Gary ....Rockville, MD
Altman, Gary ....New York, NY
Altman, Gary David ....Brookline, MA
Altman, Gary N. ....Uniontown, PA
Altman, Gerald ....Boston, MA
Altman & Greer ....Lake Worth, FL
Altman, Harlan C., Jr. ....Wellington, KS
Altman, Harry Jay, II ....Thomasville, GA
Altman, Harry W. ....Chicago, IL
Altman, Helen J. ....Newtonville, NY
Altman, Herbert I. ....New York, NY
Altman, Howard ....Brooklyn, NY
Altman, James ....Minneapolis, MN
Altman, James A. ....Orlando, FL
Altman, James B. ....Washington, DC
Altman, James F. ....Sault Ste. Marie, MI
Altman, James H. ....Austin, TX
Altman, James J. ....New Port Richey, FL
Altman, James M. ....New York, NY
Altman, Jane R. ....Skillman, NJ
Altman, Jared ....New York, NY
Altman, Jason C. ....Mineola, NY
Altman, Jason D. ....Chicago, IL
Altman, Jeffrey A. ....Los Angeles, CA
Altman, Jeffrey P. ....Washington, DC
Altman, Jeffrey S. ....Miami, FL
Altman, Jennifer A. ....New York, NY
Altman, Jennifer G. ....Miami, FL
Altman, Jerry D. ....Monticello, IN
Altman, Jessie Robertson ....Atlanta, GA
Altman, Jill Robyn ....Farmington Hills, MI
Altman, Joan ....Riverside, CA
Altman, John G. ....Hanahan, SC
Altman, John M. ....Seattle, WA
Altman, Jonathan E. ....Los Angeles, CA
Altman, Jonathan F. ....Philadelphia, PA
Altman, Jonathan S. ....Charleston, SC
Altman, Joseph A. ....Bronx, NY
Altman, Joseph P., Jr. ....New York, NY
Altman, Julia G. ....Lincoln, MA
Altman, Keilbach, Lytle, Parlapiano & Ware, P.C. ....Pueblo, CO
Altman, Kenneth M. ....New Orleans, LA
Altman, Kritzer & Levick, Ltd.
Chicago, IL
Schaumburg, IL
Atlanta, GA
New York, NY
Altman, Lane & Lilly ....Thomasville, GA
Altman, Lawrence D. ....Sterling Heights, MI
Altman, Lawrence H. ....New York, NY
Altman, Lawrence J. ....Chesterfield, MO
Altman, Lawrence R. ....Minneapolis, MN
Altman & Legband ....Skillman, NJ
Altman, Leo S. ....Pueblo, CO
Altman, Leslie J. ....Greenvale, NY
Altman, Leslie M. ....Minneapolis, MN
Altman, Lisa A. ....Salt Lake City, UT
Altman, Lisa M. ....Brooklyn, NY
Altman, Louis ....Chicago, IL
Altman, Louis H. ....Los Angeles, CA
Altman, Luci Staller ....New York, NY
Altman, Marylou G. ....Columbus, OH
Altman, Mel ....Merrick, NY
Altman, Melody E. ....Tampa, FL
Altman, Melvin S. ....Hartford, CT
Altman, Melvyn W. ....Springfield, MA
Altman, Michael ....New York, NY
Altman, Michael D. ....South Fallsburg, NY
Altman, Michael H. ....Chicago, IL
Altman, Michael L. ....Boston, MA
Altman, Miriam Goldstein ....Boston, MA
Altman, Morris ....Washington, DC
Altman, Nancy J. ....Irvine, CA
Altman, Nancy J. ....United States Senate, Senatorial Assistants, GV
Altman, Nancy M. ....Frederick, MD
Altman, Nathan ....Jericho, NY
Altman & Nix ....Wichita Falls, TX
Altman, P. Bradley ....Wichita Falls, TX
Altman, Patricia L. ....Sugar Land, TX
Altman, Paul M. ....Wilmington, DE
Altman, Paul S. ....Chicago, IL
Altman, Philip E. ....New York, NY
Altman & Plaine ....Albany, NY
Altman, Ralph ....Arlington, VA
Altman, Raymond F. ....Baltimore, MD
Altman, Rex L. ....Encino, CA
Altman, Richard A. ....New York, NY
Altman, Richard B. ....Houston, TX
Altman, Richard C. ....Darien, CT
Altman, Richard L. ....Hicksville, OH
Altman, Richard M. ....Princeton, NJ
Altman, Robert ....Palatka, FL
Altman, Robert ....Atlanta, GA
Altman, Robert A., Law Offices of ....Washington, DC
Altman, Robert N. ....New Port Richey, FL
Altman, Robert Stephen ....New York, NY
Altman, Robert T. ....Los Angeles, CA
Altman, Ronald E. ....Menlo Park, CA
Altman, Ross J. ....Deerfield, IL
Altman, S. Hayward ....Swainsboro, GA
Altman, Samuel H. ....Charleston, SC
Altman, Sanford R. ....Middletown, NY
Altman & Schoemaker, A Professional Corporation ....Encino, CA
Los Angeles, CA
Altman, Sheryl Faith ....Canton, MA
Altman, Sidney J., & Associates ....Chicago, IL
Altman, Sidney S. ....Chicago, IL
Altman, Stephanie F. ....Chicago, IL
Altman, Stephen D. ....Department of Justice, Civil Division, GV
Altman, Stephen G. ....New Rochelle, NY
Altman, Stephen L. ....Fairfax, VA
Altman, Steven ....Chicago, IL
New York, NY
Philadelphia, PA
Altman, Steven ....Cambridge, MA
Altman, Steven D. ....New Brunswick, NJ
Altman, Steven S. ....Modesto, CA
Altman, Stewart N., (P.C.) ....Massapequa, NY
Altman, Stuart H. ....Miami, FL
Altman, Stuart M. ....Brooklyn, NY
Altman, Susan P. ....Pittsburgh, PA
Altman, Theodore, (P.C.) ....New York, NY
Altman, Thomas P. ....New Port Richey, FL
Altman, Tracey L. ....New York, NY
Altman, Victor A. ....Washington, DC
Altman, William E. ....Bingham Farms, MI
Altman, William K. ....Wichita Falls, TX
Altman, William M. ....Louisville, KY
Altman, Zell H. ....Lake Worth, FL
Altmann, PhillipaL. ....Glendale, CA
Altmann, Steven D. ....Birmingham, AL
Altmann and Vitt ....Washington, DC
Altmark, Richard J. ....Baltimore, MD
Altmark, Rotter, Saff & Hyatt, P.A. ....Baltimore, MD
Altmayer, Jay P. ....Mobile, AL
Altmayer, Jay P., II ....Mobile, AL
Altmayer, Thomas L. ....Los Angeles, CA
Altmeyer, H. Brann ....Wheeling, WV
Altmeyer, Helen Campbell ....Wheeling, WV
Altmeyer, Jocelyn Richards
Virginia Beach, VA
Altmeyer, Thomas H. ....United States Senate, Committee Legal Personnel, GV
Altmiller, John C. ....Washington, DC
Altmiller, John C., Jr. ....McLean, VA
Altner, Sidney ....Edison, NJ
Alto, Gregory F. ....Summit, NJ
Alto, Joseph S. ....Clinton, NJ
Alto, Theresa ....New York, NY
Alto, Vincent R. ....Fort Lauderdale, FL
Altobella, Michelle Ross ....Somerset, KY
Altobelli, Dean M. ....Detroit, MI
Lansing, MI
Altobelli, Maria Spina ....Uniontown, PA
Altom, Gilbert J., Jr. ....Terrell, TX
Altomare, John ....Indianapolis, IN
Altomare, John ....Worcester, MA
Altomare, Joseph E. ....Meadville, PA
Titusville, PA
Altomare, Nicholas ....Worcester, MA
Altomare, Patricia M. ....Worcester, MA
Alton, Ann Leslie ....Minneapolis, MN
Alton, Brian D. ....St. Paul, MN
River Falls, WI
Alton, Charles R. ....Winchester, VA
Alton, David ....Morris Plains, NJ
Alton, Gregg H. ....Palo Alto, CA
Alton, Howard R., III ....Minneapolis, MN
Alton, Jack R. ....Columbus, OH
Alton, Janis K. ....Portland, OR
Alton, Jerald Mark ....St. Louis, MO
Alton, John M. ....Columbus, OH
Alton, Judith Kuhn ....Dallas, TX
Alton, Kelly E. ....Treasury Department, Internal Revenue Service, GV
Alton, Lindsey D. ....Pittsburgh, PA
Alton, Lloyde L., Jr. ....Tacoma, WA
Alton, Mary S. ....St. Paul, MN
Alton, Patricia D. ....Minneapolis, MN
Alton, Stephen R. ....Fort Worth, TX
Alton, Walter G., Jr ....Cherry Plain, NY
New York, NY
Alton, Walter G., Jr., & Assoc., P.C.
Cherry Plain, NY
New York, NY
Altona, Erick R. ....Escondido, CA
Altonaga, Cecilia M. ....Miami, FL
Altone, Edmund Russell ....Albany, NY
Altongy, Alissa J. ....Washington, DC
Altongy, Patrice Anne ....Richmond, VA
Altonian, Scott C. ....Boston, MA
Altoon, Eric ....Los Angeles, CA
Altorelli, John J. ....Hartford, CT
Altounian, Gregory L. ....Fresno, CA
Altree, Heidi ....San Jose, CA
Altree, Nicholas K.D. ....Arlington, VA
Altreuter & Habermehl ....Buffalo, NY
New York, NY
Altreuter, William C. ....Buffalo, NY
New York, NY
Altruda, Paul F. ....Manalapan, NJ
Altscher, Harold ....Baltimore, MD
Altschuh, Gregory W. ....New York, NY
Altschul, Andrew M. ....Portland, OR
Altschul, David E. ....Burbank, CA
Altschul, Fredric W. ....Jersey City, NJ
Altschul & Goldstein ....Mineola, NY
Altschul, James S. ....New York, NY
Altschul, John A. ....Los Angeles, CA
Altschul, Joseph E. ....Fort Lauderdale, FL
Miami, FL
Altschul, Kimberly A. ....New York, NY
Altschul, Landy & Collier, P.A.
Fort Lauderdale, FL
Miami, FL
Weston, FL
Altschul, Lawrence D. ....Boca Raton, FL
Altschul, Leonard ....New York, NY
Altschul, Michael F. ....Washington, DC
Altschul, Stanford M. ....Mineola, NY
Altschule, Joseph ....Visalia, CA
Altschuler & Altschuler ....West Haven, CT
Altschuler, Ashley R. ....New York, NY
Altschuler, Beverly Boli ....San Jose, CA
Altschuler, Daniel S. ....Philadelphia, PA
Altschuler, Debra E. ....New York, NY
Altschuler, Donald L. ....West Haven, CT
Altschuler, Douglas H. ....Santa Barbara, CA
Altschuler, Fredric L. ....New York, NY
Altschuler, Howard Alan ....Haworth, NJ
Altschuler, Irwin P. ....Washington, DC
Altschuler, Janet ....Flagstaff, AZ
Altschuler, Jeffrey I. ....Bayonne, NJ
Altschuler, Jonathan B. ....New York, NY
Altschuler, Jonathan Bobrow, P.C.
New York, NY
Altschuler, Jonathan R. ....Philadelphia, PA
Altschuler, Leland B. ....San Jose, CA
Altschuler, Mark J. ....New York, NY
Altschuler, Milo J. ....Ansonia, CT
Altschuler, Mitchell A. ....Philadelphia, PA
Altschuler, Myron I. ....New York, NY
Altschuler, Richard P. ....West Haven, CT
Altschuler, Steven C. ....Bayonne, NJ
Altschuler, Stuart ....Chicago, IL
Altschuller, William K. ....Albany, NY
Altshul, Jeffrey E. ....Chicago, IL
Altshul, Amy E. ....Phoenix, AZ
Altshuler, Berzon, Nussbaum, Berzon & Rubin ....San Francisco, CA
Altshuler, Bruce J. ....Beverly Hills, CA
Altshuler, Daniel B. ....Los Angeles, CA
Altshuler, David R. ....Santa Monica, CA
Altshuler, Fred H. ....San Francisco, CA
Altshuler, Jack L. ....Beverly, MA
Altshuler, Kenneth P. ....Portland, ME
Altshuler, Leo ....Beverly Hills, CA
Altshuler, Lynn Allyn ....San Francisco, CA
Altshuler, Michael D. ....Oakland, CA
Altshuler, Richard ....Miami, FL
Altshuler, Robert H. ....Paterson, NJ
Altshuler, Robert H. ....Wayne, NJ
Altshuler & Vincent ....Portland, ME
Altsuler, Kent ....Houston, TX
Altsuler, Kimberly J. ....Houston, TX
Altura, Judith B. ....Oakland, CA
Altus, Abraham ....Forest Hills, NY
Altus & Hemming ....Farmington Hills, MI
Altus, Leslie J. ....New York, NY
Altus, Mark ....Farmington Hills, MI
Altwarg, Daniel B. ....Syracuse, NY
Altwarg, Sheldon H. ....Bloomfield, NJ
Altwegg & Anderson ....Logan, IA
Altwegg, Gary J. ....Logan, IA
Altwies, Charles J. ....Akron, OH
Altwies, Julie N. ....Albuquerque, NM
Alu, Sheryl Jones ....Washington, DC
Aluise, Karen A. ....Boston, MA
Aluise, Timothy J. ....Washington, DC
Aluli, Hayden ....Honolulu, HI
Aluli, Yuklin ....Kailua, HI
Alum, Luis A. ....Guttenberg, NJ
Alumbaugh, Joel ....Joplin, MO
Aluni, Sam A. ....Cook, MN
Virginia, MN
Aluotto, Christopher J. ....Cincinnati, OH
Alusheff, Charles P. ....Cleveland, OH
Alushin, Michael S.
Environmental Protection Agency, Office of Enforcement and Compliance Assurance, GV
Alva, Anthony ....Barnstable, MA
Alva, Curtis S. ....Wilmington, DE
Alva, Daniel Paul ....Philadelphia, PA
Alva, Emilio ....Laredo, TX
Alva, Jose L. ....Modesto, CA
Walnut Creek, CA
Alva, Marlene (IBA) ....**New York, NY**
Alva, Susan ....Los Angeles, CA
Alvar, Anna Regina ....Bronx, NY
Alvarado, Abel ....Broomfield, CO
Alvarado, Alfredo J. ....Millburn, NJ
New York, NY
Alvarado, Antonio ....Austin, TX
Alvarado, Bruce J. ....Indianapolis, IN
Alvarado, Cesar A. ....San Francisco, CA
Alvarado, Donald G. ....Los Angeles, CA
Alvarado, Efrain L. ....Bronx, NY
Alvarado, Elizabeth D. ....Houston, TX
Alvarado, Jeanette E. ....Phoenix, AZ
Alvarado, Jess R. ....Los Angeles, CA
Alvarado, Judith T. ....Los Angeles, CA
Alvarado, Karen M. ....Houston, TX
Alvarado, Karene I. ....San Francisco, CA
Alvarado, Kathleen B. ....San Francisco, CA
Alvarado, Kim S. ....Phoenix, AZ
Alvarado, Leo, Jr. ....San Antonio, TX
Alvarado, Linda K. ....Bakersfield, CA
Alvarado, Lisa D. ....Atlanta, GA
Alvarado, Lucila ....McAllen, TX
Alvarado, Manuel ....San Juan, PR
Alvarado, Manuel Corona ....Sacramento, CA
Alvarado, Mario ....San Jose, CA
Alvarado, Michael ....Poulsbo, WA
Alvarado, Michael A. ....Irvine, CA
Alvarado, P. Mauricio ....Houston, TX
Alvarado, Paul H. ....San Francisco, CA
Alvarado, Paul J. ....Valdosta, GA
Alvarado, Raymond G. ....Irvine, CA
Los Angeles, CA
Alvarado, Ricardo R. ....Boca Raton, FL
Alvarado, Richardo ....Midland, TX
Alvarado, Robert V., Jr. ....Culver City, CA
Alvarado, Smith & Sanchez, A Professional Corporation ....Irvine, CA
Los Angeles, CA
Alvarado-Lliteras, Leslie ....San Juan, PR
Alvaré, Helen Michele ....Washington, DC
Alvarenga, Robert F. ....Redlands, CA
Alvarey, Joel R. ....Nyack, NY
Alvarez, Adolfo Al, Law Offices of
McAllen, TX
Pearsall, TX
Alvarez, Alejandro ....Juno Beach, FL
Alvarez, Alex ....Miami, FL
Alvarez, Alexander ....Daytona Beach, FL
Alvarez, Alexander ....Fort Lauderdale, FL
Alvarez, Alicia ....Chicago, IL
Alvarez, Alicia M. ....New York, NY
Alvarez, Amado A. ....Miami, FL
Alvarez, Anita M. ....Chicago, IL
Alvarez, Antonio R. ....Fresno, CA
Alvarez, Ariadna ....San Juan, PR
Alvarez, Armas & Borron ....Coral Gables, FL
Alvarez, Arturo ....Coral Gables, FL
Alvarez & Associates, P.C.
Rio Grande City, TX
Alvarez, Benjamin C. ....Glendale, CA
Alvarez, Benjamin R.
West Palm Beach, FL
Alvarez, Carlos ....Tallahassee, FL
Alvarez, Carlos ....New York, NY
Alvarez, Carlos A. ....San Francisco, CA
Alvarez, Carlos M. ....North Miami Beach, FL
Alvarez, Carmen H.
Cape May Court House, NJ
Alvarez, Carolyn K. ....Orlando, FL
Alvarez, Catalina M. ....Clayton, MO
Alvarez, Cesar L. ....Miami, FL
Alvarez, Christine E. M. ....Denver, CO
Alvarez, Connie M. ....Sacramento, CA
Alvarez, David T. ....Boca Raton, FL
Alvarez, Dax ....Los Angeles, CA
Alvarez, Derek B. ....Tampa, FL
Alvarez, Domingo G., III ....Winter Haven, FL
Alvarez, Donald R. ....Phoenix, AZ
Alvarez, Donald R. ....Redlands, CA
San Bernardino, CA
Alvarez, E. Victoria ....Miami, FL
Alvarez, Edgard ....New York, NY
Alvarez, Edna R.S. ....Los Angeles, CA
Alvarez, Elizabeth ....Glendale, CA
Alvarez, Elsa ....Coral Gables, FL
Alvarez, Elsa, P.A. ....Coral Gables, FL
Alvarez, F. Dennis ....Tampa, FL
Alvarez, Federico C. ....Denver, CO
Alvarez, Francis P. ....Stamford, CT
Alvarez, Francisco ....Kingsville, TX
Alvarez, Frank ....Dallas, TX
Alvarez, Fred L. ....Chicago, IL
Alvarez, Fred W. ....Palo Alto, CA
Alvarez, Fredy M. ....Atlanta, GA
Alvarez, Gabriela A., Law Office of
Cupertino, CA
Alvarez & Garcia-Montes, P.A.
Miami, FL
Alvarez, Gaston Rey ....Coral Gables, FL
Alvarez & Gilbert ....Phoenix, AZ
Alvarez, Graig J. ....Houston, TX
Alvarez, Gregory E. ....Houston, TX
Alvarez, Gregory T. ....Morristown, NJ
Alvarez, Ignacio ....San Juan, PR
Alvarez, Ivette R. ....Livingston, NJ
Alvarez, J. Anthony ....Houston, TX
Alvarez, Jaime J. ....San Jose, CA
Alvarez, Jane C. ....New Orleans, LA
Alvarez, Jesus M. ....Rio Grande City, TX
Alvarez, John A. ....Gilroy, CA
Alvarez, John C. ....Orlando, FL
Alvarez, Jose ....Oakland, CA
Alvarez, Jose Benito ....Orange City, FL
Alvarez, Jose M. ....Sacramento, CA
Alvarez, Juan Lucas ....Miami, FL
Alvarez, Julie Anna ....New York, NY
Alvarez, Karen D. ....Washington, DC
Alvarez, Kira M. ....Department of Commerce, National Oceanic and Atmospheric Administration, GV
Alvarez, Lazaro ....Lake Arrowhead, CA
Alvarez, Liane T. ....Miami, FL
Alvarez, Lina V. ....Phoenix, AZ
Alvarez, Linda Graham ....Palo Alto, CA
Alvarez, Lisa C. ....Morgan Hill, CA
Alvarez, Luis, Jr. ....Charlottesville, VA
Alvarez, Luisa M.
United States Information Agency, Office of the General Counsel, GV
Alvarez, M. Michelle ....Los Angeles, CA
Alvarez, Manny ....Dallas, TX
Alvarez, Manuel J. ....Ocala, FL
Tampa, FL

Alvarez, Manuel J. ....New York, NY
Alvarez, Margarita Prado ....San Jose, CA
Alvarez, Maria F. ....Long Beach, CA
Alvarez, Micaela ....McAllen, TX
Alvarez, Michael U. ....San Francisco, CA
Alvarez, Michelle B. ....Miami, FL
Alvarez, Nestor ....Coral Gables, FL
Alvarez, Nettie L. ....Seattle, WA
Alvarez & Notzon, L.L.P. ....**Alice, TX**
Eagle Pass, TX
Laredo, TX
Rio Grande City, TX
San Antonio, TX
Alvarez, Oscar ....McAllen, TX
Alvarez, P. Raúl, Jr. ....**Winter Park, FL**
Alvarez, Patricia O'Connell ....**Laredo, TX**
San Antonio, TX
Alvarez, Paul ....**Los Angeles, CA**
Alvarez, Pedro A. ....**Miami, FL**
Alvarez, R. John ....Havana, IL
Petersburg, IL
Alvarez, Raquel M. ....**Philadelphia, PA**
Alvarez, Ray J. ....Houston, TX
Alvarez, Richard C. ....**Tampa, FL**
Alvarez, Richard D. ....New Orleans, LA
Alvarez, Richard I. ....**New York, NY**
Alvarez, Robert K. ....**Memphis, TN**
Alvarez, Ronald V. ....West Palm Beach, FL
Alvarez, Sander ....**Los Angeles, CA**
Alvarez, Scott G.
Board of Governors Of The Federal Reserve System, Office of the General Counsel, GV
Alvarez, Stephanie C. ....**Miami, FL**
Alvarez, Tania M. ....San Francisco, CA
Alvarez, Teresa Maria ....**Miami, FL**
Alvarez, Theresa ....San Francisco, CA
Alvarez, Veronica L. ....**Montebello, CA**
Alvarez, Victor M. ....**Miami, FL**
Alvarez, Victoria J. ....Tampa, FL
Alvarez, Walter J., P.C. ....**Crown Point, IN**
Alvarez, Walter J., Prof. Corp.
Crown Point, IN
Alvarez, Wayne David ....Northridge, CA
Alvarez, Yvonne ....Houston, TX
Alvarez-Farre, Emilio J. ....**Miami, FL**
Alvarez-Giay, Mabel ....New York, NY
Alvarez-Glasman, Arnold M.
Montebello, CA
Alvarez-Glasman & Colvin
Baldwin Park, CA
Montebello, CA
Pico-Rivera, CA
Pomona, CA
South El Monte, CA
South Gate, CA
Alvarez-Ibañez, Alfredo ....**San Juan, PR**
Alvarez-Maldonado, José Julián
San Juan, PR
Alvarez-Mena, Sergio O., III ....**Miami, FL**
Alvaro, Ferdinand, Jr. ....**Murray Hill, NJ**
Alvaro, Jay R. ....Cincinnati, OH
Alventosa, Leopoldo ....**Jericho, NY**
Alverio, Daisy M ....Bronx, NY
Alverno, Anthony F.
United States Postal Service, Law Department, GV
Alverson, David S. ....**Los Angeles, CA**
Alverson, J. Bruce ....**Las Vegas, NV**
Reno, NV
Alverson, J. Donice ....New Orleans, LA
Alverson, James G., Jr. ....Santa Ana, CA
Alverson, Luther ....Atlanta, GA
Alverson, Margaret E. ....New York, NY
Alverson, Taylor, Mortensen, Nelson & Sanders ....**Las Vegas, NV**
Reno, NV
Alverson, William B., Jr. ....**Andalusia, AL**
Alverson, William H. ....**Milwaukee, WI**
Alves, Albert ....South Dartmouth, MA
Alves, Anita L. ....Anchorage, AK
Alves, Arlene R. ....**New York, NY**
Alves, David D. ....Sacramento, CA
Alves, Edmund L., Jr. ....**Providence, RI**
Alves, Emanuel ....**Boston, MA**
Alves, James S. ....**Tallahassee, FL**
Alves, Joseph Hodge, III ....**Mobile, AL**
Alves, Judy ....Cincinnati, OH
Alves, Karen E. ....Fort Myers, FL
Alves, Marian ....Tallahassee, FL
Alves, Mary Jane ....**Washington, DC**
Alves, Paget L. ....Plano, TX
Alves, Wallis April ....Aiken, SC
Alves, Warren W. ....Titusville, FL
Alvestad, L. Paul ....**Tacoma, WA**
Alvey & Alvey, P.C. ....Woodbridge, VA
Alvey, Aubrey R. ....Charleston, SC
Alvey, Bevan B. ....Edina, MN
Alvey, Constance Marie ....Kansas City, KS
Alvey, Darryll E. ....Redding, CA
Alvey & Duty ....Owensboro, KY
Alvey, James D. ....Woodbridge, VA
Alvey, Martin L. ....Astoria, OR
Portland, OR
Alvey, Martin L., P.C. ....Astoria, OR
Portland, OR
Alvey, Michael W. ....Owensboro, KY
Alvey, Richard M. ....Woodbridge, VA
Alvey, Thomas W., Jr. ....**Belleville, IL**
Alvi, Mumtaz H. ....New York, NY
Alvidrez, Richard L. ....**Albuquerque, NM**
Alvillar, James R. ....Grand Junction, CO
Alvin, Louis C. ....Pittsburgh, PA
Alvin, William R. ....Miami, FL
Alvine, Giebink & Hill ....Sioux Falls, SD
Alvine, Robert H. ....**Moline, IL**
Alvino, Ernest L., Jr. ....Woodbury, NJ
Alvino, Ginamarie ....**Uniondale, NY**
Alvino, Peter D. ....Trenton, NJ
Alvino, Timothy J. ....**New York, NY**
Alvir, Roberto B. ....Bayside, NY
Alvis, Amy L. ....San Jose, CA
Alvis, Carssow & Ingalls ....**Austin, TX**
Alvis, Jerry S. ....**Raleigh, NC**
Alvis, John W. ....**Austin, TX**
Alvis, K. Rick ....Birmingham, AL
Alvis, LaBella S. ....**Birmingham, AL**
Alvis, Les ....Tupelo, MS
Alvis, Lester, Jr. ....Jackson, MS
Alvis, W. Barry ....Birmingham, AL
Alvis, William T.
United States Postal Service, Law Department, GV
Alvoid, Dennis E. ....**Dallas, TX**
Alvord, Agnes McDermott ....**Hartford, CT**
Alvord, Alan R. ....San Diego, CA
Alvord and Alvord ....**Washington, DC**
Alvord, Bethany J. ....Springfield, MA
Alvord, Chase C. ....**Seattle, WA**
Alvord, Don L. ....Lyons, KS
Alvord, Edward L. ....Lakeport, CA
Alvord & Ewing ....Lakeport, CA
Alvord, James C. ....Fallbrook, CA
Alvord, Marjorie M. ....San Francisco, CA
Alvord, Robert W. ....**Washington, DC**
Alvo-Sadiky, Lea F. ....Philadelphia, PA
Alvy, Norman D. ....New Hyde Park, NY
Alvy, T'Ablante & Agovino
New Hyde Park, NY
Alvy, Vida M. ....Bronx, NY
Alwan, Suzanne V. ....**New York, NY**
Alwang, Melissa S. ....**New York, NY**
Alward, Mitchell J. ....**Emeryville, CA**
San Francisco, CA
Alward, Thomas R. ....Traverse City, MI
Alway & Craig ....Salem, OR
Alway, Richard F. ....Salem, OR
Alwaya, Semha ....**San Francisco, CA**
Alweis, Kenneth M. ....**Syracuse, NY**
Alweiss, Daniel B. ....**Oakland, CA**
Alweiss, Gary S. ....Garden City, NY
Alwin, Kenneth Michael ....Minneapolis, MN
Alwin, Ronald P. ....Chicago, IL
Alwine, Dana J. ....Harrisburg, PA
Alworth, Charles W. ....Tyler, TX
Alworth & Ford ....**San Antonio, TX**
Alworth, Frederick W. ....**Newark, NJ**
Alworth, Jon R. ....**San Antonio, TX**
Alworth, Lance Dwight, Jr.
Securities and Exchange Commission, Office of Compliance Inspections and Examinations, GV
Alworth, Lee G. ....Conroe, TX
Alworth, Thomas J. ....**Florham Park, NJ**
Aly, Amr O. ....**New York, NY**
Aly, Stewart F. ....Department of Defense, Office of the General Counsel, GV
Alyea, Louis F. ....Falls Church, VA
Alyea, Sara B. ....**New York, NY**
Alyholz, Reed I. ....Clark, NJ
Alzamora, John A. ....**Harrisburg, PA**
Ama, Ayodele M., (Ms) ....Brooklyn, NY
Amabile, Anthony R. ....Ho-Ho-Kus, NJ
Amabile, Frank J. ....Staten Island, NY
Amabile, John C. ....**Atlanta, GA**
Amabile, John L. ....**New York, NY**
Amacher, Going, Yetur & Lin ....Downey, CA
Amacher, Janet E. ....**Norristown, PA**
Amacher, Robert P. ....Downey, CA
Amacher, Todd R. ....**Dallas, TX**
Amack, Edward A. ....Mesa, AZ
Amacker, Dawn ....Bogalusa, LA
Amacker, George A., III ....**Cherry Hill, NJ**
Amaddio, Mark D. ....Cleveland, OH
Amaddio, Mark D.,Co., L.P.A.
Cleveland, OH
Amadeo & Amadeo ....San Juan, PR
Amadeo, Jose Enrique ....San Juan, PR
Amadeo, Louis L., Jr. ....Redwood City, CA
Amadeo, Luis R. ....**San Juan, PR**
Amadeo, Mark A.
Pension Benefit Guaranty Corporation, Office of the General Counsel, GV
Amadio, Alfred J. ....**Garden City, NY**
Amadio, Dominic E. ....St. Petersburg, FL
Amadio, K. Gerard ....**Philadelphia, PA**
Amado, Honey Kessler ....**Beverly Hills, CA**
Amado, Ralph A. ....Los Angeles, CA
Amado, Theodore M. ....Walnut Creek, CA
Amador, Alicia ....Los Angeles, CA
Amador, Catherine Anne ....**Fresno, CA**
Amador, Eric A. ....**Fresno, CA**
Amador, Katherine ....Coral Gables, FL
Amador, Michael J. ....**Las Vegas, NV**
Amador, Michael J., Chtd. ....**Las Vegas, NV**
Amador, Richard S. ....**Los Angeles, CA**
Amador, Robert C. ....Highland, CA
Amador, Robert O. ....San Diego, CA
Amador, Rolando A. ....Miami, FL
Amador, Victor ....**Dallas, TX**
Amador, Victor, P.C. A Professional Corporation ....**Dallas, TX**
Fort Worth, TX
Amaducci, Suzanne M. ....**Miami, FL**
Amaguin, Roman F., Jr. ....**Honolulu, HI**
Amai, Jacqueline W.S. ....**Honolulu, HI**
Amala, Carl R. ....Salem, OR
Amalfe, Christine A. ....**Newark, NJ**
Amalfitano, Gerard ....New City, NY
Aman, Aman, & Lozano ....Lincoln, NE
Aman, Andre Blommer ....Lincoln, NE
Aman, David S. ....**Portland, OR**
Aman, Dawn M. ....Aberdeen, SD
Aman, Geo. J. ....Canton, OH
Aman, George M., III ....**Norristown, PA**
Aman, Jeffrey A. ....**Tampa, FL**
Aman, John Franklin ....Lincoln, NE
Aman, John J. ....Buffalo, NY
Aman, Joseph F. ....Webster, NY
Aman & Lins, P.A. ....**Tampa, FL**
Aman, Patricia Capp ....San Diego, CA
Aman, Philip ....**San Diego, CA**
Aman, Richard L. ....San Antonio, TX
Aman, William R. ....Colorado Springs, CO
Amana, Cheryl E. ....Durham, NC
Amanat, F. Franklin ....Brooklyn, NY
Amandes, Christopher B. ....**Houston, TX**
Amandes, Richard B. ....Murphys, CA
Amann, Angela M. Lutz
South St. Paul, MN
Amann, Anne T. ....**New York, NY**
Amann, Bryan L. ....**Canton, MI**
Amann, C. Scott ....White Plains, NY
Amann, Colin B. ....Houston, TX
Amann, Edward J., Jr. ....New York, NY
Amann, Gregory F. ....**Tacoma, WA**
Amann, Jeffrey T. ....San Mateo, CA
Amann, Joseph C. ....Red Bank, NJ
Amann, Leslie Kiefer ....Houston, TX
Amann, Regis J. ....Union City, CA
Amann, T. Gregory ....Ellsworth, WI
Amann, William A. ....Charlotte, NC
Amano, Donald H. ....Hilo, HI
Amano, Lesley ....**Owings Mills, MD**
Amano & Pinao ....Hilo, HI
Amano, Riki May ....Hilo, HI
Amante, Jerome L. ....**Irvine, CA**
Amante & Shaffer, LLP ....**Irvine, CA**
Amantea, Chris M. ....**Los Angeles, CA**
Amantea, Denise M. ....San Francisco, CA
Amantea, Thomas R. ....Bonita, CA
Amantia, Michael A. ....Trenton, NJ
Amaon, Gary P. ....**Houston, TX**
Amar, Dipanwita Deb ....**San Francisco, CA**
Amar, Kavita ....**Los Angeles, CA**
Amar, Pauline ....San Diego, CA
Amar, Vik D. ....San Francisco, CA
Amara, Dirk R. ....Auburn, CA
Amara & Keller ....Auburn, CA
Amara, Sandra R. ....Auburn, CA
Amaral, Alan A. ....Somerset, MA
Amaral, Anthony, Jr. ....**New York, NY**
Amaral, Edward L., Jr. ....Winthrop, MA
Amaral, Edward M. ....**Los Banos, CA**
Palo Alto, CA
Amaral, Joseph L. ....South Bend, IN
Amaral, Mary Ellen ....Louisville, CO
Amaral, Michael C. ....**Boston, MA**
Amaral, Stephen J. ....New Bedford, MA
Amarandos, Anna B. ....**Costa Mesa, CA**
Amarant, John R. ....Danville, CA
Amarant, Ronald A. ....Newtown Square, PA
Amarante, John J. ....Dayton, OH
Amarante, Margaret B. ....Cincinnati, OH
a Marca, Gian-Michele ....**New York, NY**
Amarel, Irene M. ....Skillman, NJ
Amari, John A. ....**Woodbridge, NJ**
Amari, John E. ....**Birmingham, AL**
Amari, Leonard F. ....Chicago, IL
Amari & Locallo ....Chicago, IL
Amari, Lynn C. ....**New York, NY**
Amari, Raymond R.
Broadview Heights, OH
Amari, Richard S. ....**Cocoa, FL**
Amari & Theriac, P.A. ....**Cocoa, FL**
Cocoa Beach, FL
Melbourne, FL
Orlando, FL
Titusville, FL
Amarilio, Joseph Daniel ....Chicago, IL
Amarilios, John A. ....New Canaan, CT
Amaro, Merling Barbara ....Miami, FL
Amaro, Michael L. ....**Long Beach, CA**
Riverside, CA
Amaro, Rami ....**Coeur d'Alene, ID**
Amarosa, Michael ....New York, NY
Amason, Guy H., Jr. ....Fort Myers, FL
Amason, Linda J. ....**Charleston, SC**
Amat, Daniel A. ....**Ocala, FL**
Amata, Doreen West ....**Hartford, CT**
Amata, E. Paul ....**Springfield, MA**
Amata, Timothy W. ....**New York, NY**
Amatangelo, Baisley & Rega ....Donora, PA
Amatangelo, Raymond P. ....Donora, PA
Amatea, Frank C. ....Ocala, FL
Amateau, Susan ....Oakland, CA
Amati, Alan C. ....Chicago, IL
Amato, Alfred L. ....Metuchen, NJ
Garden City, NY
Amato, Allyn J. ....**Herndon, VA**
Amato, Anderson & Nickel, P.A. ....Naples, FL
Amato, Anthony J. ....Cleveland, OH
Amato, Anthony W., Jr. ....Manhasset, NY
Amato & Berger, P.C. ....Metuchen, NJ
Garden City, NY
Amato, Brent L. ....Elgin, IL
Amato, Christopher J. ....Perrysburg, OH
Amato and Creely, A Professional Law Corporation ....Gretna, LA
Amato, Dale A. ....**San Diego, CA**
Amato, Elita C. ....Washington, DC
Amato, Gary A. ....Fort Collins, CO
Amato, Jacob J., III ....**New Orleans, LA**
Amato, Jacob J., Jr. ....Gretna, LA
Amato, James D. ....Pittsburgh, PA
Amato, James G. ....**Lexington, KY**
Amato, John ....**Stamford, CT**
Amato, John, IV ....Baltimore, MD
Amato, John P. ....**New York, NY**
Amato, Jos. J. ....Tuckahoe, NY
Amato, Joseph G. ....Brooklyn, NY
Amato, Leonard M. ....Marina Del Rey, CA
Amato, Lisa A. ....**Portland, OR**
Amato, Louis J. ....Lexington, KY
Amato, Louis X. ....**Naples, FL**
Amato, Louis X., P.A. ....**Naples, FL**
Amato and Margle, P.C. ....**Allentown, PA**
Bethlehem, PA
Harrisburg, PA
Philadelphia, PA
Scranton, PA
Wilkes-Barre, PA
Amato, Michael ....Atlanta, GA
Amato, Michael Dean ....**New Haven, CT**
Amato, Nicholas R. ....Newark, NJ
Amato, Nicholas T. ....**Wellsville, OH**
Amato, Paul ....**Pittsburgh, PA**
Amato, Ronald ....**Bethlehem, PA**
Amato, Salvatore J. ....Albany, NY
Amato, Stephen G. ....**Lexington, KY**
Amato, Susan K. ....**Santa Rosa, CA**
Amato, Susan L. ....**St. Louis, MO**
Amato, Theresa A. ....Elmhurst, IL
Amato, Thomas A. ....Manchester, CT
Amato, Thomas S. ....Cleveland, OH
Amato, Vincent N. ....New York, NY
Amatong, Alberto Q., Jr. ....**Houston, TX**
Amatruda, Christine A. ....**Emeryville, CA**
Amatruda, Matthew S. ....**Washington, DC**
Amattey, William Horatius ....Chicago, IL
Amatucci, Richard D. ....Tulsa, OK
Amatuzio, Kevin F. ....**Denver, CO**
Amaya, Peter L. ....East Quogue, NY
Ambacher, Martin J. ....**Walnut Creek, CA**
Ambalu, Aaron C. ....New York, NY
Ambaras, Robert ....Brooklyn, NY
Ambardar, Meenakshi ....**New York, NY**
Ambarian, Brad E. ....**Anchorage, AK**
Ambash, Joseph W. ....**Boston, MA**
Ambelang, Peter D. ....**Phoenix, AZ**
Ambelang, Richard L. ....Chariton, IA
Ambeliotis, Nicholas M. ....Danvers, MA
Amber, Allen L. ....Clawson, MI
Amber, Cynthia Penn ....Fort Wayne, IN
Amber, Gregg ....Costa Mesa, CA
Amber, Laurie Kaufman ....South Miami, FL
Amberg, Brantley D. ....Hickman, KY
Amberg, Deborah A. ....Duluth, MN
Amberg, Elizabeth Anne ....Berkeley, CA
Amberg, James H. ....Hickman, KY
Amberg, John W. ....**Santa Monica, CA**
Amberg, McNenly, Zuschlag, Firestone and Lee, P.C. ....Southfield, MI
Amberg, Richard J., Jr. ....Waterford, MI
Amberg, Robert R. ....**Long Beach, CA**
Amberg, Stanley L. ....**New York, NY**
Amberg, Steven J. ....Southfield, MI
Amberg, Thomas ....Phoenix, AZ
Amberger, Larry D. ....Cape Elizabeth, ME
Amberly, Vincent M. ....**McLean, VA**
Ambers, David J. ....Chicago, IL
Ambers, David Joseph ....La Porte, IN
Ambers, Deborah Thalia ....
Department of Housing and Urban Development, GV
Amberson, Jon Christian
San Antonio, TX
Amberson, Joseph H., III ....**Dallas, TX**
Amberson, Legrand H., Jr.
Birmingham, AL
Amberson, Thomas B. ....Coeur d'Alene, ID
Ambery, Regina M. ....**New York, NY**
Ambill, David Edward ....**Lancaster, CA**
Ambinder, Gerald E. ....San Francisco, CA
Ambinder, Lloyd ....New York, NY
Ambinder, Loren P. ....**New York, NY**
Ambinder, Rowena Lee ....Boston, MA
Ambinder, Walter J. ....Bloomfield Hills, MI
Amblard, Ronald ....New York, NY
Ambler, Beth S. ....New Canaan, CT
Ambler, Bruce Melville, Jr. ....Baltimore, MD
Ambler, Christian D. ....**Chicago, IL**
Ambler & Conatser ....Bartlesville, OK
Nowata, OK
Ambler, Diane E. ....**Washington, DC**
Ambler, John J., Jr. ....Norfolk, VA
Ambler, John Matthew ....**Dallas, TX**
Ambler, Kevin C. ....**Tampa, FL**
Ambler, Kevin C., P.A., The Law Offices of
Tampa, FL
Ambler, Larry L. ....South Bend, IN
Ambler, Lee G. ....Bellingham, MA
Ambler, Lewis B. ....Bartlesville, OK
Nowata, OK
Ambler, M. Kirby, Jr. ....Denver, CO
Ambler, Michael N. ....White Plains, NY
Ambler, R. Sterling ....**Denver, CO**
Ambler, Read ....San Jose, CA
Ambler, Robert R., Jr. ....**Atlanta, GA**
Ambler, Scott A. ....Bellingham, MA
Ambler, Thomas W. ....**Norfolk, VA**
Ambler, Tracy B. ....**Redding, CT**
Ambler, William N. ....Corpus Christi, TX
Amborn, Candace ....Klamath Falls, OR
Ambos, Paul ....**Newark, NJ**
New York, NY
Amboss, Monica E. ....Thousand Oaks, CA
Ambrecht & Associates
Santa Barbara, CA
Ambrecht, J. Thomas ....Thousand Oaks, CA
Ambrecht, John W. ....**Santa Barbara, CA**
Ambrecht, Michael R. ....**New York, NY**
Ambrette, L. Conrad ....**Darien, CT**
Ambriano, Anthony M. ....**Boston, MA**
Ambriola, Lori M. ....**Cleveland, OH**
Ambro, George R. ....Columbus, OH
Ambro, Richard ....Riverhead, NY
Ambro, Susan D. ....Riverhead, NY
Ambro, Thomas L. ....**Wilmington, DE**
Ambrogi, John L. ....**Chicago, IL**
Ambrogi, Lawrence R. ....Winchester, VA
Ambrogi, Robert J. ....Rockport, MA

Ambrogio & Associates ... Stratford, CT
Ambrogio, Charles S. ... Stratford, CT
Ambrogio, Mary J. ... Hartford, CT
Ambron, Mary T. ... New York, NY
Ambrose, Adam ... Silver Spring, MD
Ambrose, Algird ... North Palm Beach, FL
Ambrose, Anthony H. ... Louisville, KY
Ambrose, Arlen S. ... Englewood, CO
Ambrose Associates ... Bala Cynwyd, PA
Ambrose, Bruce S. ... Raleigh, NC
Ambrose, Casey K. ... Detroit, MI
Ambrose, Charles D. ... Atlanta, GA
Ambrose, Charles D., Law Office of
Atlanta, GA
Ambrose, Chris E. ... Thomasville, GA
Ambrose, Christopher P. ... Detroit, MI
Ambrose, Christopher R. ... Encinitas, CA
Portland, OR
Ambrose & Cohane ... Fairfield, CT
Ambrose, Colleen E. ... Missoula, MT
Ambrose, Craig A. ... Secaucus, NJ
Ambrose, David R. ... Portland, OR
Ambrose, Dean V. ... Los Angeles, CA
Ambrose, Donald E. ... Pittsburgh, PA
Ambrose, Donald R. ... Aberdeen, NJ
Freehold, NJ
Ambrose, Donald R. ... Red Bank, NJ
Ambrose, Donetta W. ... Pittsburgh, PA
Ambrose, Fred J. ... Bala Cynwyd, PA
Ambrose, Friedman & Weichler ... Erie, PA
Ambrose, G. Louis ... Carmichael, CA
Ambrose, Gerald A. ... Chicago, IL
Ambrose Hanlon LLP ... Portland, OR
Ambrose, Harry D., Jr. ... Collingswood, NJ
Ambrose, Harry D., Jr., A Professional Association ... Collingswood, NJ
Ambrose, J. Raymond, Jr.
New Kensington, PA
Ambrose, James F. ... Portland, OR
Ambrose, James T. ... Dayton, OH
Ambrose, James W., II ... Omaha, NE
Ambrose, John J., Jr. ... New Orleans, LA
Ambrose, John P. ... Washington, DC
Ambrose, John Thomas ... Arlington, VA
Ambrose, Joseph D., III ... Fort Worth, TX
Ambrose, Joseph M. ... Bloomington, IL
Ambrose, Joseph P. ... Bridgeport, CT
Ambrose, Katharine Peckham
Greeneville, TN
Ambrose, Kathleen A. ... Washington, DC
Ambrose, Kimberly D. ... Seattle, WA
Ambrose, Langhorne ... Washington, DC
Ambrose, Laurie ... Amherst, NY
Ambrose, Leonard G., III ... Erie, PA
Ambrose, Linda Hinson ... Birmingham, AL
Ambrose, Marcus ... Phoenix, AZ
Ambrose, Mary Louise ... Moorestown, NJ
Ambrose, Michael J. ... Fort Washington, PA
Ambrose, Michael W., Jr.
Washington, DC
Ambrose, Myles J. ... Washington, DC
Ambrose, Nancy Fisher ... Kingston, NY
Ambrose, Neil J. ... New Haven, CT
Ambrose, Noreen M. ... San Francisco, CA
Ambrose, Patricia ... Erie, PA
Ambrose, Patricia Riley ... Washington, DC
Ambrose, Paul J., Jr. ... Sea Isle City, NJ
Ambrose, Paul N., Jr. ... Hackensack, NJ
Ambrose, Peter ... Fairfield, CT
Ambrose, Ray ... Lexington, SC
Ambrose, Richard J. ... Cleveland, OH
Ambrose, Robert F. ... New York, NY
Ambrose, Robert J. ... Chicago, IL
Ambrose, Ronald D. ... Livonia, MI
Ambrose, S. Robert ... Los Angeles, CA
Ambrose, Scott A. ... Phoenix, AZ
Ambrose, Stephen F., Jr. ... Stamford, CT
Ambrose, Suzanne M. ... Sacramento, CA
Ambrose, Thomas A. ... Fairfield, CA
Ambrose, Vincent W. ... Montrose, NY
Ambrose, Wilson, Grimm & Durand
Knoxville, TN
Ambrosi, E. Michael ... Anaheim, CA
Ambrosi, E. Michael, A Professional Corporation ... Anaheim, CA
Ambrosia-Walt, Sharon ... Bellevue, WA
Ambrosier, Bradley E. ... Elkhart, KS
Ambrosini, Paula E. ... Los Angeles, CA
Ambrosini, Peter A. ... Boston, MA
Ambrosino, Helene Cohen
Environmental Protection Agency, Office of Enforcement and Compliance Assurance, GV
Ambrosino, Michael T. ... Washington, DC
Ambrosino, Vincent S. ... New York, NY
Ambrosio, Anthony A. ... Brooklyn, NY
Ambrosio, Anthony P. ... Bloomfield, NJ
Ambrosio, Christina M. ... New York, NY
Ambrosio, Christopher ... Norfolk, VA
Ambrosio, Gabriel M. ... Lyndhurst, NJ
Ambrosio, John J. ... Topeka, KS
Ambrosio, John J., Chartered ... Topeka, KS
Ambrosio, Joseph P. ... Parlin, NJ
Ambrosio, Kyreakakis, DiLorenzo, Moraff & McKenna LLP ... Bloomfield, NJ
Newark, NJ
Ambrosio, Lawrence J. ... Columbus, OH
Ambrosio, Michael P. ... Newark, NJ
Ambrosio, Ralph F. ... Albany, NY
Ambrosio, Thomas ... Bloomfield, NJ
Ambrosius, James W. ... San Francisco, CA
Ambrosius, Paul W. ... New York, NY
Ambrosi-Wertman, Janet L.
Pacific Palisades, CA
Ambrosy, Curtis J. ... Warren, OH
Ambrosy and Fredericka ... Warren, OH
Ambrozaitis, John J. ... Waterbury, CT
Ambrozek, Janet ... San Diego, CA
Ambroziak, Jeffrey Russell
New Haven, CT
Ambroziak, Michael D. ... Chicago, IL
Ambrozy, Rel S. ... Alexandria, VA
Ambruoso, Andrew C. ... New York, NY
Charlotte, NC
Amburgey, Bryce Hale ... St. Petersburg, FL
Frankfort, KY
Amburgey, Larry K. ... Portland, OR
Amburgey & Rubin, P.C. ... Portland, OR
Amburn, Dean W. ... Farmington Hills, MI
Amburn, Elton V., Jr. ... Ingram, TX
Amburn, W. Dale ... Knoxville, TN
Ambutas, Algirdas P. ... Chicago, IL
Ambutas, Vytas P. ... Elk Grove Village, IL
Amchan, Arthur J.
National Labor Relations Board, Division of Administrative Law Judges, GV
Amchin, Jess ... Gwynedd, PA
Amdahl, Douglas K. ... Minneapolis, MN
Amdahl, Jane B. ... Merrillville, IN
Amdahl, Kenneth ... St. Paul, MN
Amdall, Kenneth H. ... Naperville, IL
Amdor, Michael W. ... Omaha, NE
Amdor, Robert J. ... Omaha, NE
Amdor, Wm. B. ... Omaha, NE
Amdur, Boyle, Maggs & McGann, A Professional Corporation ... Eatontown, NJ
Amdur, James A. ... San Francisco, CA
Amdur, Martin B. ... New York, NY
Amdur, Richard A. ... Eatontown, NJ
Amdur, Richard A., Jr. ... Red Bank, NJ
Amdur, Terry J. ... Pasadena, CA
Amdursky, Eric J. ... San Francisco, CA
Amdursky, Pelky, Fennell and Wallen, P.C.
Oswego, NY
Syracuse, NY
Ameche, Steven C. ... Santa Monica, CA
Ameci, Gina M. ... Philadelphia, PA
Amedee, Lee J., III ... Gonzales, LA
Amedee, Patrick M. ... Metairie, LA
Amedee, Roy F., Jr. ... La Place, LA
Ameden, Gary ... Manchester, VT
Amedeo, Douglas A. ... New York, NY
Amedeo, Robert J. ... Evergreen, CO
Ameduri, Anthony L. ... Staten Island, NY
Ameduri Galante & Friscia
Staten Island, NY
Ameduri, Richard A. ... Alton, IL
Ameel, Christopher J. ... Austin, TX
Ameen, Nancy A. ... New York, NY
Ameen, Robert J. ... Pawtucket, RI
Ameen, Verina ... Paramus, NJ
Amega, Francine ... Los Angeles, CA
Amego, Daniel Scott ... Jefferson City, MO
Ameika, Walter S., Jr. ... Charleston, SC
Ameli, Mark Khosrow ... Beverly Hills, CA
Amelio, Anthony M. ... Vero Beach, FL
Amelio, Eugene A. ... Providence, RI
Amelio, Gary Alan ... Pittsburgh, PA
Amelio, Robert J. ... Pittsburgh, PA
Amelkin, Stanley P. ... Woodbury, NY
Amell, Laurie A. ... Washington, DC
Amelung, James J. ... St. Louis, MO
Amelung, Wulff & Willenbrock, P.C.
Belleville, IL
St. Louis, MO
Amemiya, Ronald Y. ... Honolulu, HI
Amen, Charles A. ... St. Louis, MO
Amen, Daniel J. ... Minneapolis, MN
Amen, Henry J., III ... San Antonio, TX
Amen, Jennifer M. ... Omaha, NE
Amen, Jeremy T. ... Los Angeles, CA
Amen, John D. ... Denver, CO
Amen & Keith ... San Francisco, CA
Amen, Randolph J. ... Honolulu, HI
Amen, Steven P. ... Omaha, NE
Amen, Susan K. ... Dallas, TX
Amen, Vicky L. ... Lincoln, NE
Amen, W. Thomas ... San Francisco, CA
Amend, Elizabeth A. ... St. Louis, MO
Amend, Geoffrey B. ... Wichita, KS
Amend, James M., (P.C.) ... Chicago, IL
Amend, Terry L. ... Poteau, OK
Amend, Virginia G.
Colorado Springs, CO
Amenda, Jos. M. ... Darlington, WI
Amendola, Albertina M. ... Newark, NJ
Amendola & Amendola ... Bridgeport, CT
Fairfield, CT
Amendola, Andrew M. ... East Haven, CT
Amendola, Anthony J. ... Burbank, CA
Amendola, Bonnie L. ... Fairfield, CT
Amendola, David O. ... New York, NY
Amendola, Elaine S. ... Fairfield, CT
Amendola, Francis C. ... Buffalo, NY
Amendola, Gary F. ... Rochester, NY
Amendola, Gary I. ... Coeur d'Alene, ID
Amendola, Madelene C. ... Reno, NV
Amendola, Mark A. ... Willoughby Hills, OH
Amendola, Mary ... New York, NY
Amendola, Robert A. ... Sacramento, CA
Amendola, Stephen A. ... Napa, CA
Amendola, Vincent N., Jr. ... Orange, CT
Amendolara, James M. ... Hollywood, CA
Amendolara, Samuel G. ... Youngstown, OH
Amendolare, John J. ... North Quincy, MA
Amendt, Christian J. ... Pomona, CA
Amengual, Randolph ... New York, NY
Ament, Albert John, Jr. ... Wilmington, DE
Ament, Allan B. ... Seattle, WA
Ament & Ament, P.C. ... Falmouth, MA
Ament, Craig C. ... Waterloo, IA
Ament, David S. ... Colorado Springs, CO
Ament, David S. ... Falmouth, MA
Ament, F. Thomas ... Milwaukee, WI
Ament, Gerald ... Los Angeles, CA
Ament, Jacob J. ... Merrill, WI
Ament, Jeremy B. ... New York, NY
Ament, John R. ... Eau Claire, WI
Ament, John S., III ... Jacksonville, TX
Ament, Joseph D. ... Chicago, IL
Ament Law Firm ... Waterloo, IA
Ament Lynch & Carr ... Wilmington, DE
Ament, Marc C. ... Fresno, CA
Ament, Mark S. ... Louisville, KY
Ament, Neil S. ... Buffalo Grove, IL
Ament, Rickey J. ... Wheeling, IL
Ament, Robert H. ... Falmouth, MA
Ament, Susan D'Alonzo ... Wilmington, DE
Ament, Timothy D. ... Waterloo, IA
Ament, W. Robert ... Pittsburgh, PA
Ament, W. William ... Reston, VA
Ament, Wulf & Frokjer ... Merrill, WI
Amenta, Donald Paul ... North Fort Myers, FL
Amento, Carl J. ... Hamden, CT
Amer, A. (John) F. ... Los Angeles, CA
Amer, Andrew S. ... New York, NY
Amer Cunningham Brennan Co., L.P.A.
Akron, OH
Amer, Harry ... White Plains, NY
Amer, Margaret E. ... Chagrin Falls, OH
Amer, Mona S. ... Los Angeles, CA
Amer, Patrick J. ... Cleveland, OH
Amera, Seth D. ... New York, NY
Ameral, Ann Q. ... Modesto, CA
Ameranti-Byrne, Cecilia ... Garden City, NY
Ameri, Christian A. ... San Francisco, CA
Amerian, Richard ... Sherman Oaks, CA
Amerian, Richard, A Prof. Corp.
Sherman Oaks, CA
American Barristers, P.A. ... Maitland, FL
Miami, FL
Orlando, FL
American Center For Law and Justice, The
Mobile, AL
Phoenix, AZ
Washington, DC
New Hope, KY
American Center for Law and Justice, The
Virginia Beach, VA
Americanos, Peter C. ... Indianapolis, IN
Americus, Bruce A. ... Pittsburgh, PA
Americus, David S. ... Chicago, IL
Americus, Parke E. ... Pittsburgh, PA
Americus, Susan A. ... Chicago, IL
Amerikaner, Steven A.
Santa Barbara, CA
Amerine, Amy C. Cress ... Columbus, OH
Amerine, Carol A. ... Honolulu, HI
Amerine, Carrie S. ... El Monte, CA
Amerine, David R. ... Washington, DC
Amerine, Hal D. ... Worthington, OH
Amerine, Janet ... Clearwater, KS
Amerine, Roy R. ... Woodridge, IL
Ameringer, Carl F. ... Oshkosh, WI
Amerling, Andrew B. ... Albany, NY
Amerling & Burns P.A. ... Portland, ME
Amerling, W. John ... Portland, ME
Christiansted, St. Croix, VI
Charlotte Amalie, St. Thomas, VI
Amerman, A. E., Jr. ... Ingram, TX
Amerman, Burt & Jones Co., L.P.A.
Canton, OH
Amerman, J. Derck ... New Brighton, MN
Amernick, Burton A. ... Washington, DC
Amernick, Marvin M. ... Treasury Department, Office of Regulations and Rulings, GV
Amernick, Terri G. ... Richmond, VA
Amero, Brian J. ... Atlanta, GA
Amero, Gerald M. ... Portland, ME
Amerongen, Jan A.T. van, Jr. ... Salem, NJ
Amershadian, John P. ... Buffalo, NY
Amerson, Andrew D. ... Los Angeles, CA
Amerson, J. Mike ... Houston, TX
Amerson, Lucy E. ... Sacramento, CA
Amery, Brian F. ... Florham Park, NJ
New York, NY
Amery, Eric J. ... Painesville, OH
Ames & Ames ... Homer, NY
Ames & Ames ... Onancock, VA
Ames, Arlene E. ... Fort Lauderdale, FL
Ames & Armstrong ... Dayton, OH
Ames, Arthur A. ... Dayton, OH
Ames, Brooks A. ... Springfield, MA
Ames, Bruce S. ... Kailua, HI
Ames, C. Douglas ... Youngstown, OH
Ames, C. Hayden ... San Francisco, CA
Ames, Carter S. ... Houston, TX
Ames, Charles C. ... Boston, MA
Ames, Charles E. ... Dallas, TX
Ames, Christopher N. ... Boston, MA
Ames, Christy ... Louisville, KY
Ames, Craig L. ... Deerfield, IL
Ames, David C. ... San Francisco, CA
Ames, David E. ... Homer, NY
Ames, Dennis K. ... San Diego, CA
Santa Ana, CA
Ames, Dorian D. ... Binghamton, NY
Hallstead, PA
Ames, E. Jay ... Spokane, WA
Ames, E. Kenly ... Boston, MA
Ames, Edward A., III ... Onancock, VA
Ames, George J. ... New York, NY
Ames, Gerald B. ... San Jose, CA
Ames, Harry C., Jr. ... Bethesda, MD
Ames, Henry T. ... Peoria, IL
Ames, Herbert K. ... Bryan, OH
Ames, Howard N. ... Pittsburgh, PA
Ames, Jack B. ... Elko, NV
Ames, James ... Hurst, TX
Ames, James B. ... Boston, MA
Ames, James P. ... Montgomery, TX
Ames, Joanne ... Washington, DC
Ames, John G. ... Orion, IL
Ames, John W. ... Louisville, KY
Ames, Kathleen L. ... New York, NY
Ames, Loretta M. ... Detroit, MI
Ames, Marc L. ... Pluckemin, NJ
Ames, Margery E. ... New York, NY
Ames, Marilyn S. ... Houston, TX
Ames, Mark A. ... Portland, OR
Ames, Mark K. ... Richmond, VA
Ames, Matthew B. ... Atlanta, GA
Ames, Matthew C. ... Washington, DC
Ames, Mervyn L. ... North Miami, FL
Ames, Mitchell S. ... New York, NY
Ames, Morgan P. ... Stamford, CT
Ames, Mortimer P., III ... Montgomery, AL
Ames, Nicole E. ... Silver Spring, MD
Ames, Oliver F., Jr. ... Boston, MA
Ames, Orrin K., III ... Mobile, AL
Ames, Pamela A. ... Washington, DC
Ames, Pamela J., Law Offices of
Waterville, ME
Ames, Rance E. ... Kansas City, MO
Ames, Richard ... Brookline, MA
Ames, Richard C. ... Brunswick, ME
Ames, Richard L. ... Kittanning, PA
Ames, Richard N. ... Fayetteville, NY
Ames, Richard R. ... San Francisco, CA
Ames, Rick L. ... Philadelphia, PA
Ames, Robert ... San Diego, CA
Ames, Robert C. ... Chattanooga, TN
Ames, Robert G. ... Washington, DC
Baltimore, MD
Ames, Robert H. ... Salinas, CA
Ames, Rodney A. ... Kansas City, MO
Ames, Sarah ... Chicago, IL
Ames, Scott K. ... Columbia, SC
Ames, Scott R. ... Santa Monica, CA
Ames, Sharon L. ... Syracuse, NY
Ames, Stanley L. ... Detroit, MI
Ames, Steven C. ... Rockford, IL
Ames, Stuart D. ... Miami, FL
Ames, W. Allen, Jr. ... Richmond, VA
Ames, Walter D. ... Washington, DC
Ames, Wayne B. ... McKinney, TX
Ames, Wesley B. ... La Jolla, CA
Ames, Whitney Pollack ... Palo Alto, CA
Ames, William F. ... Homer, NY
Ames, Wm. Dennis ... Brookville, PA
Ames, Wm. J. ... Virginia Beach, VA
Amesbury & Cogan ... Las Vegas, NV
Amesbury, David C. ... Las Vegas, NV
Amesbury, William H. ... Wilkes-Barre, PA
Ames-Ledbetter, Richard ... Baltimore, MD
Amestoy, Edward A. ... Malta, MT
Amestoy, Jeffrey L. ... Montpelier, VT
Amey, John T. ... Phoenix, AZ
Amezaga, Dorothea B.
Santa Barbara, CA
Amezaga, Michael F. ... Bronx, NY
Amezaga, Rafael M., Jr. ... Santa Barbara, CA
Amgwerd, Jessica M. ... Sacramento, CA
Amhowitz, Harris J. ... New York, NY
Amicizia, Vincent M. ... Smithtown, NY
Amick, Alice G. ... Kansas City, MO
Amick, Blair Walton ... Greenfield, IN
Amick & Breaden ... Greenville, OH
Amick, Brian J., P.C. ... Kansas City, MO
Amick, Brian Joseph ... Kansas City, MO
Kansas City, MO
Amick, Floyd & Porter, P.C.
McKinney, TX
Plano, TX
Amick, Jeffrey L. ... Greenville, OH
Amick, John M. ... Oklahoma City, OK
Amick, Joseph W. ... Kansas City, MO
Amick, Joseph W., P.C. ... Kansas City, MO
Amick, Kimberly M. ... Walnut Creek, CA
Amick Law Office ... Las Vegas, NV
Amick, Michael D. ... Sacramento, CA
Amick, Nancy B. ... Plano, TX
Amick, Richard C. ... Las Vegas, NV
Amick, Robert L. ... Las Vegas, NV
Amick, Steven H. ... Newark, DE
Amick, Thomas D. ... Las Vegas, NV
Amico, Alan J. ... Temecula, CA
Amico, Joseph ... Los Angeles, CA
Amico, Joseph C. ... Brooklyn, NY
Amico, Michael A. ... Buffalo, NY
Amico, Richard P. ... Buffalo, NY
Amico, Suzanne L. ... Rochester, NY
Amico, Thomas J. ... New York, NY
Amicone, Francis A. ... Sterling Heights, MI
Amicucci, Paul G. ... New York, NY
Purchase, NY
Amidan, Todd C. ... Pittsburgh, PA
Amidano, Arthur E. ... Union City, NJ
Amidei, Maurice E. ... Houston, TX
Amideo, William F. ... Atlanta, GA
Amidon, Daniel W. ... Pittsburgh, PA
Amidon, David M. ... Waltham, MA
Amidon, Edwin H., Jr. ... Burlington, VT
Amidon, Lee ... San Bernardino, CA
Amidon, Linda J. ... Orlando, FL
Amidon, Robert B. ... Burbank, CA
Amidon, Robert B., A Law Corporation
Burbank, CA
Amidon, Suzanne G. ... Concord, NH
Amidon, Thomas J. ... Stowe, VT
Amidon, Todd C. ... Washington, DC
Amiel, Paul H. ... Dallas, TX
Amiet, Ralph D. ... Akron, OH
Amigo, Frank ... Plantation, FL
Amigo, Frank, P.A. ... Plantation, FL
Amigone, Nicholas P., III ... Buffalo, NY
Amigone, Sanchez, Mattrey & Marshall, L.L.P. ... Buffalo, NY
Amigoni, Albert R. ... Cleveland, OH
Amii, Jan M.L.Y., (Atty. at Law, A Law Corp.) ... Honolulu, HI
Amil, Alicia Ann ... Roseland, NJ

Amin, Bhupen B. ... Walnut Creek, CA
Amin, Chintan K. ... Atlanta, GA
Amin, Daksha ... Rosemont, IL
Amin & Eschweiler, LLP ... Cleveland, OH
Amin, Himanshu S. ... Cleveland, OH
Amin, Nimish ... New York, NY
Amin, Rakesh M. ... Chicago, IL
Amin, Suraya ... Tarzana, CA
Amini, Bijan ... Washington, DC
New York, NY
Amini, Farzad E. ... Los Angeles, CA
Amini, Gilda ... Chicago, IL
Amini, Gordon C. ... Oklahoma City, OK
Amini, Rex ... Midland, TX
Aminoff, Jeffrey H. ... Newark, NJ
Aminoff, Joseph ... Miami, FL
Amins, Philip D. ... Scarsdale, NY
Amiot, Brooks Ryan ... Baltimore, MD
Amiott, Laura M. ... Eaton, OH
Amir & Associates, P.A. ... Plantation, FL
Amir, Michael M. ... Santa Monica, CA
Amir, Ofer M. ... Plantation, FL
Amira, Kathryn Kerfes ... Los Angeles, CA
Amirahmadi, Mary Gnewuch ... Anoka, MN
Amirante, Sam L. ... Rolling Meadows, IL
Amirata, Paul A. ... New York, NY
Amirata, Ralph Eric ... Newark, NJ
Amirault, Coviello, Rocco & McNamara, A Professional Association ... Cleveland, OH
Amirault, Leo P. ... Cleveland, OH
Amiri, Michael A. ... San Francisco, CA
Amiri, Shabnam ... Phoenix, AZ
Amirian, Ashod N. ... Bradford, MA
Amirkhan, H. Mirza, Jr. ... Dallas, TX
Amirshahi, Ali John ... Richmond, VA
Amis, Freemyer & Davis ... Arlington, TX
Amis, J. Michael ... Dallas, TX
Amis, J. A., Jr. ... Bryan, TX
Amis, L. Randolph ... Burlington, VT
Amis, L. Randolph, P.C. ... Burlington, VT
Amis, R. Thomas ... Washington, DC
Amis, Robert W. ... Plano, TX
Amis, Robert W., PLLC ... Plano, TX
Amis, Steven P. ... Arlington, TX
Amis, Virginia M. ... Oklahoma City, OK
Amitay, Morris J. ... United States Senate, Senatorial Assistants, GV
Amitay, Sharlene Petry ... Washington, DC
Amith, Adina N. ... Baltimore, MD
Amitin, Alan ... Van Nuys, CA
Amiton, Marshall L. ... Portland, OR
Amitrani, Paul D. ... Somerville, NJ
Amjad, Holly M. ... St. Louis, MO
Amkraut, D. M. H. ... Los Angeles, CA
Amladi, Bela P. ... New York, NY
Amlicke, Manfield G. ... Passaic, NJ
Amlicke, Thomas R., (P.C.)
New York, NY
White Plains, NY
Amlie, Claudia Saenz ... Palm Beach, FL
Amlie, Karsten ... West Palm Beach, FL
Amlin, Darrell M. ... Detroit, MI
Amling, Cynthia S. ... Baltimore, MD
Amling, William H. ... Pana, IL
Amlong & Amlong, P.A.
Fort Lauderdale, FL
Amlong, Karen Coolman
Fort Lauderdale, FL
Amlong, William R. ... Fort Lauderdale, FL
Amlung, Cletus E. ... Louisville, KY
Amlung, Jonathon N. ... Ashland, KY
Amlung, Pamela K. ... Cincinnati, OH
Amman, Barbara B. ... Tallahassee, FL
Amman, Frederic C., III ... Monroe, LA
Ammann, Charles Butler ... Tulsa, OK
Ammann, John J. ... Alton, IL
Ammann, Ken L. ... Salem, OR
Ammar, Joseph M. ... Kalamazoo, MI
Ammar, N. A., Jr. ... Roanoke, VA
Ammarell, Laura Lynne ... Lone Tree, CO
Ammarell, Scott William ... Wheaton, IL
Ammeen, James J., Jr. ... Indianapolis, IN
Ammeian, Benjamin V. ... Los Angeles, CA
Ammel, James M. ... Little Rock, AR
Ammendola, Marina E. ... Chicago, IL
Ammer, Karen A. ... San Jose, CA
Ammer, Timothy C. ... Cincinnati, OH
Ammer, William ... Circleville, OH
Ammerman & Ammerman ... Brookville, PA
Clearfield, PA
Ammerman, David S. ... Clearfield, PA
Ammerman, Fredric J. ... Clearfield, PA
Ammerman & Goldberg ... Washington, DC
Ammerman, Harris S. ... Washington, DC
Ammerman, Jim, II ... Gilmer, TX
Marshall, TX
Ammerman, Joseph S. ... Clearfield, PA
Ammerman, Matthew H. ... Houston, TX
Ammermann, Cathryn L. ... Richmond, VA
Ammermann, Pamela S. ... Washington, DC
Ammermann, Todd G. ... Richmond, VA
Ammeson, Charles F. ... St. Joseph, MI
Ammeter, April L. ... Los Angeles, CA
Ammiano, Rochelle ... Alpharetta, GA
Ammirato, Michael ... Mineola, NY
Ammirato, Palumbo, Milam & Baronian, A Professional Law Corporation
Pasadena, CA
Ammirato, Vincent A. ... Pasadena, CA
Ammon, Barry D. ... Oakland, CA
Ammon, Bernice C. ... Columbia, MD
Ammon, D. Reed ... Pensacola, FL
Ammon, Gary D. ... Philadelphia, PA
Ammon, Jeffrey S. ... Grand Rapids, MI
Ammon, Larry L. ... Arcadia, CA
Ammon, R. Theodore ... New York, NY
Ammons, Carlton E. ... Minneapolis, MN
Ammons, Clifford B. ... Jackson, MS
Ammons, Darrel S. ... Longview, WA
Ammons, David ... Los Angeles, CA
Ammons, David P. ... Ventura, CA
Ammons, James B. ... Wichita Falls, TX
Ammons, James F., Jr. ... Fayetteville, NC
Ammons, Jeffrey M. ... Chicago, IL
Ammons, Jeffrey T. ... Goldsboro, NC
Ammons, Jonasue ... Fort Worth, TX
Ammons, Linda L. ... Cleveland, OH
Ammons, Randal G. ... Cleveland, OH
Ammons, Reginald K. S. ... Palo Alto, CA
Ammons, Richard F., Jr. ... Taftsville, VT
Ammons, Robert E. ... Greenbelt, MD
Ammons, Robert E. ... Houston, TX
Ammons, Scott A. ... Washington, DC
Ammons, Thomas M., III
Virginia Beach, VA
Ammons, Timothy M. ... Dillon, SC
Ammons, Todd M. ... Lake Charles, LA
Amo, Douglas A. ... Irvine, CA
Amoako & Anaman ... St. Louis Park, MN
Amoako, Nana ... St. Louis Park, MN
Amodei, Mark E. ... Carson City, NV
Amodeo, Anthony J., Jr. ... Albany, NY
Amodeo, Damian J. ... Poughkeepsie, NY
Amodeo, Jeannette M. ... Marlton, NJ
Amodeo, John A. ... Washington, DC
Amodeo, Mariano B. ... Poughkeepsie, NY
Amodeo, Mary Ann ... New York, NY
Amodeo, Matthew P. ... Albany, NY
Amodeo, Pasquale ... East Hartford, CT
Amodeo, Thomas P. ... Buffalo, NY
Amodeo, Tina Louise ... Las Vegas, NV
Amodeo, Tina Nielsen ... Cherry Hill, NJ
Amodeo-Vickery, Andrea C.
Manchester, NH
Amodio, Dena Tofte ... Albany, NY
Amodio, James A. ... Medina, OH
Amodio, Michael A. ... Hempstead, NY
Amodio, Michael P. ... White Plains, NY
Amodio, Thomas P. ... Anchorage, AK
Amofah, Emmanuel ... Brooklyn, NY
Amole, Roger L., and Associates
Alexandria, VA
Amole, Roger L., Jr. ... Alexandria, VA
Amols, John S. ... Syosset, NY
Amolsch, Christopher B. ... Chattanooga, TN
Amolsch, Regina B. ... Washington, DC
Amon, Carl H., III ... New York, NY
Amon, Carol Bagley ... Brooklyn, NY
Amon, Claudia J. ... Suffern, NY
Amon, Dorian B. ... St. Louis, MO
Amon, Laura ... Missoula, MT
Amon, Simeon S. ... New York, NY
Amon, Thomas G. ... New York, NY
Amona, Wm. K. ... Honolulu, HI
Amonett, Landon P. ... Akron, OH
Amonette, David M. ... Gallatin, TN
Amonette and Stubbs ... Gallatin, TN
Amoni, David ... Atlanta, GA
Amoni, Larry M. ... Aurora, IL
Chicago, IL
Amoon, Henry A. ... Miami, FL
Amor, Ricardo J. ... San Jose, CA
Amor, Roslyn M. ... South Bend, IN
Amore, Frederick P. ... Branford, CT
Amore, Thomas C. ... Brockton, MA
Amorello, Kenneth H. ... New York, NY
Amorello, Robert E. ... Worcester, MA
Amores, Caridad ... Miami Springs, FL
Amores, Constantino S., Jr. ... Charleston, WV
Amoresano, Floyd V., Jr. ... Boston, MA
Amoresano, Guy V. ... Newark, NJ
Amoresano, Patrick X. ... Hackensack, NJ
Amori & Riegel, L.L.C. ... Stroudsburg, PA
Amori, Scott M. ... Stroudsburg, PA
Amoriello, James D. ... Erie, PA
Amorini, Gina M. ... Mineola, NY
Amorino, Lisa ... Irvine, CA
Amorison, Allison L. ... Wilmington, DE
Amorison, John M. ... Mullica Hill, NJ
Amoros, Fayata & Wallace
White Plains, NY
Amorosa, Dominic F. ... Short Hills, NJ
New York, NY
Amorosa, Lisa A. ... Bridgewater, NJ
Amorosana, Holly H. ... Harrison, NY
Amorose, Frederick J. ... Sacramento, CA
Amorosi, Angela R. ... West Palm Beach, FL
Amorosi, Elizabeth C. ... Phoenix, AZ
Amorosi, Mark C.
Securities and Exchange Commission, Division of Investment Management, GV
Amoroso, Albert Anthony ... Corry, PA
Amoroso, Anthony J. ... East Rochester, NY
Amoroso, Camilla ... San Mateo, CA
Amoroso, Frank L. ... Garden City, NY
Amoroso, Gregory J. ... Rome, NY
Amoroso, Henry J. ... Hackensack, NJ
Amoroso, John D. ... Los Angeles, CA
Amoroso, Joseph A., Jr. ... Cambridge, MA
Amoroso, Linda S. ... Pittsburgh, PA
Amoroso, Michael J. ... Plantation, FL
Amoroso, Richard M. ... Phoenix, AZ
Amoroso, Stephen D., Jr. ... New York, NY
Amoroso, Vincent M. ... Boston, MA
Amoruso, Leonard J. ... New York, NY
Amoruso, Michael J. ... Boston, MA
New York, NY
Amory, Daniel ... Portland, ME
Amos, Alan O. ... Chicago, IL
Amos, Alan O., & Associates, P.C.
Chicago, IL
Amos, Charles C. ... Huntington, WV
Amos, Daniel ... Pasadena, CA
Santa Monica, CA
Amos, Dorothy E. ... Baltimore, MD
Amos, Elisha K. ... Arlington, VA
Amos, Elizabeth F. ... Gretna, LA
Amos, Fred B., II ... Wake Forest, NC
Amos, Gary T. ... Virginia Beach, VA
Amos, Gena R. ... Saginaw, MI
Amos, James W. ... Hernando, MS
Amos, Jeffries & Robinson, L.L.P.
Greensboro, NC
Amos, Jerry W. ... Greensboro, NC
Amos, Jessie A. ... Austin, TX
Amos, John D. ... Fairmont, WV
Amos, John R. ... Richmond, VA
Amos, Joseph L., Jr ... Orlando, FL
Amos, Karen ... San Antonio, TX
Amos, Karen D. ... Ellicott City, MD
Amos, Kathleen Swalla ... Galt, CA
Amos, Kirtley B ... Lexington, KY
Amos, Larry C. ... Louisville, KY
Amos, Marc D. ... Columbus, MS
Amos, Mary R. ... Birmingham, AL
Amos, Paul D. ... Memphis, TN
Amos & Porter ... Birmingham, AL
Amos, Rick Olando ... Gulfport, MS
Amos, Robt. A. ... Towson, MD
Amos, Sharon S. ... Princeton, NJ
Amos, T. Dean ... Hickory, NC
Amos, Timothy J. ... Parkersburg, WV
Amos, Timothy L. ... Nashville, TN
Amos, Valex, Jr. ... Lafayette, LA
Amos, Wm. Mark ... Stockbridge, GA
Amoscato, Anthony M. ... Tarzana, CA
Amoscato, Anthony S. ... Nutley, NJ
Amott, Ralph C. ... Provo, UT
Amoury, Robert J. ... Staten Island, NY
Ampansiri, Don, Jr. ... Kingston, NY
Ampil, Janice P. ... Chicago, IL
Ampolsk, Marilyn ... New York, NY
Amponin, Renato L. ... Chicago, IL
Ampulski, Jennifer E. ... Minneapolis, MN
Amram & Hahn, P.C. ... Washington, DC
Amrein, F. Alexander ... Washington, DC
Amrein, Jeffrey J. ... Kansas City, MO
Amrein, Marian ... Department of the Army, U.S. Army Legal Services Agency, GV
Amrein, Robert S. ... Lowell, MA
Amrein, Todd W. ... Kansas City, MO
Amrhein, Christine B. ... Canton, OH
Amrhein, Cynthia R. ... Burnt Hills, NY
Amrhein, Mark J. ... New York, NY
Amrhein, Raymond A. ... Watsonville, CA
Amrhein, Richard J. ... Washington, PA
Amrhein, Ronald D., Jr. ... Sharon, PA
Amrhein, William M. ... Richmond, VA
Amrine, Danny A. ... Tulsa, OK
Amrod, John B. ... Garden City, NY
Southold, NY
Amrod & Van Der Waag ... Southold, NY
Garden City, NY
Amron, Arthur H. ... Greenwich, CT
Amron, Cory M. ... Washington, DC
Amron, Howard C. ... New York, NY
Amron, Robert K. ... Cherry Hill, NJ
Amrose, Dean ... Boston, MA
Amrose, Frederick J. ... Beverly Hills, MI
Amsbary, Joseph R., Jr. ... Atlanta, GA
Amsbary, William S. ... Huntington Beach, CA
Amsbary, William S., II ... Santa Ana, CA
Amsbaugh, Marian ... Santa Maria, CA
Amsbaugh, Richard Michael ... Plymouth, MI
Amsberry, Russell J. G. ... San Antonio, TX
Amsberry & Soefje, LLP ... San Antonio, TX
Amschel, Edward T. ... Hemet, CA
Amschel Law Corporation ... Hemet, CA
Amschel, Peter ... Hemet, CA
Amschler, James R. ... Westport, CT
Amsden, David L. ... Atlanta, GA
Amsden, James L. ... Fort Lauderdale, FL
Amsden, John L. ... Los Angeles, CA
Amsden, Ted T. ... Detroit, MI
Amsden, Timothy L. ... Kansas City, KS
Amsel, Jody B. ... New York, NY
Amsel, Robert G. ... Miami, FL
Amsel, Seena R. ... Purchase, NY
Amsellem, Perry M. ... New York, NY
Amshoff & Amshoff ... Louisville, KY
Amshoff, Theodore H., Jr. ... Louisville, KY
Amsler, Charles L. ... Fort Worth, TX
Amsler, Edward J. ... New York, NY
Amsler, Guy, Jr. ... Little Rock, AR
Amsler, Robert J., Jr. ... St. Louis, MO
Amsler, Susan K. ... Mayville, NY
Amspacher, Catherine L. ... Charlotte, NC
Amspoker, Ross W. ... Lancaster, CA
Amspoker, Todd A. ... Santa Barbara, CA
Amsrouy, Khadija ... New York, NY
Amstadt, Nancy R. ... Cleveland, OH
Amstadter, Victor S. ... Santa Rosa, CA
Amster, Daniel ... Waldwick, NJ
Amster, Douglas H. ... Newark, NJ
Amster, Glenn J. ... Seattle, WA
Amster, Ilene ... New York, NY
Amster, Jayson L. ... Upper Marlboro, MD
Amster, Jerome J. ... Miami, FL
Amster, John A. ... Menlo Park, CA
Amster, Meryl S. ... White Plains, NY
Amster, Morton ... New York, NY
Amster, Morton ... New York, NY
Amster, Richard L. ... Roseland, NJ
Amster & Rosensweig ... Waldwick, NJ
Amster, Rothstein & Ebenstein
New York, NY
Amster, Seymour I ... Van Nuys, CA
Amster, Shari ... Philadelphia, PA
Amster, Sheldon ... New York, NY
Amster, Steven Robert ... Fort Lauderdale, FL
Amster, Susan L. ... Chestnut Hill, MA
Amster, Tracey L. ... New York, NY
Amsterdam, Adam D. ... Roseland, NJ
Amsterdam, Anthony G. ... New York, NY
Amsterdam, Leonard M.
Hewlett Harbor, NY
Amsterdam & Lewinter ... New York, NY
Amsterdam, Mark L. ... New York, NY
Amsterdam, Mary Cusano ... New York, NY
Amsterdam, Michael ... Wilmington, DE
Amsterdam, Paula T. ... New York, NY
Amsterdam, Valerie S. ... New York, NY
Amstutz, C. John ... Youngstown, OH
Amstutz, Charles H. ... Wapato, WA
Amstutz, Eric B. ... Greenville, SC
Amstutz, Harold E. ... Lafayette, IN
Amstutz, Keira A. ... Indianapolis, IN
Amstutz, Walter G. ... Harvey, LA
Amtman, Jeffrey I. ... Englewood, NJ
Amtmanis, Liza ... Los Angeles, CA
Amtsbuechler, Laura ... Farmington Hills, MI
Amtzis, Michael M. ... Staten Island, NY
Amu, Lanre O. ... Chicago, IL
Amundaray, Francisco J. ... San Juan, PR
Amundsen, Amy J. ... Memphis, TN
Amundsen, Dawn ... Tulsa, OK
Amundsen, Edith Delaine ... Appleton, WI
Amundsen, Glen E. ... Chicago, IL
Amundsen, Moore & Torpy
Melbourne, FL
Tallahassee, FL
Amundsen, Paul H. ... Tallahassee, FL
Amundsen, Richard S. ... Akron, OH
Amundsen, Roland J. ... Fountain Valley, CA
Amundson, Anna Tomalino
San Diego, CA
Amundson, Carolyn M.
Treasury Department, Office of the Comptroller of the Currency, GV
Amundson, Donald M. ... Minneapolis, MN
Amundson, Jan S. ... Washington, DC
Amundson, John A. ... Bowman, ND
Amundson, Kim D., (Mr.)
Minneapolis, MN
Amundson, Laura ... Madison, WI
Amundson, Lisa M. ... St. Paul, MN
Amundson, Luther M. ... Minneapolis, MN
Amundson, Margaret Mead ... Plymouth, MN
Amundson, Paul T. ... Houston, TX
Amundson, Roland C. ... St. Paul, MN
Amundson, Ross M. ... Paynesville, MN
Amundson, Steven G. ... San Diego, CA
Amundson, Steven M. ... New York, NY
Amuny, Christy ... Beaumont, TX
Amussen, Carla A. ... Santa Barbara, CA
Amy, Elaine Moore ... Vero Beach, FL
Amy, Jonathan P. ... Columbus, OH
Amy, Marc T. ... Abbeville, LA
Amy, Stacy N. ... Lafayette, LA
Amyot, Gilbert L. ... Kensington, MD
Amyot, J. Raymond
Saratoga Springs, NY
Amyot, John W. ... Watertown, NY
Amy-Román, Carmen I. ... San Juan, PR
Amyx, Carol ... Berkeley, CA
Amyx, Clyde H., II ... Frederick, OK
Amyx, Monty H. ... Santa Barbara, CA
Amyx, Monty H., and Associates
Santa Barbara, CA
Amzel, Viviana ... Los Angeles, CA
An, Dorothy C. ... San Jose, CA
An, Lisa M. ... Chicago, IL
An, Mildred H. ... Washington, DC
An, Richard W. ... New York, NY
An, Sokyoung Kevin ... Chicago, IL
An, Yong J. ... Houston, TX
Anaba, Ozzy ... Forney, TX
Anable, James W. ... Seattle, WA
Anabtawi, Iman J. ... Los Angeles, CA
Anacker, Thomas R. ... Bozeman, MT
Anacker, Thomas R., P.C. ... Bozeman, MT
Anaclerio, Nicholas, Jr. ... Chicago, IL
Anagick, Ella ... Anchorage, AK
Anagnos, Basil C. ... Chicago, IL
Anagnos, Demos P. ... Ventura, CA
Anagnos, George T. ... Ridgewood, NJ
Anagnos, James Constantine ... Baltimore, MD
Anagnos, Joyce ... Boston, MA
Anagnost, Christ A. ... Saginaw, MI
Anagnost & Hall, P.C. ... Saginaw, MI
Anagnost, Peter G. ... Chicago, IL
Anagnost, Themis J. ... Chicago, IL
Anagnost, Tracy A. ... Department of Justice, Tax Division, GV
Anagnost, Yvonne ... Olympia Fields, IL
Anagnostakis, Pat M. ... Atlanta, GA
Anagnosti, Era ... Palo Alto, CA
Anagnostiadis, Demetrios E. ... Bethesda, MD
Anagnostis, Elisha L. ... Miami, FL
Anagnostis, Jack T. ... Philadelphia, PA
Anagnostou, Stephanie A.
Menlo Park, CA
Anahory, Kevin A. ... Brockton, MA
Anaipakos, Demetrios ... Houston, TX
Anaipakos, John ... Houston, TX
Anaman, Richard K. ... St. Louis Park, MN
Anand, Anita Thomas ... Pittsburgh, PA
Anand, Justin S. ... New York, NY
Anand, Mona ... North Chicago, IL
Anand, Nalini P. ... Washington, DC
Anand, Rakesh ... San Francisco, CA
Ananda & Krause, A Professional Law Corporation ... Westlake Village, CA
Ananda, Mohan ... Westlake Village, CA
Anandarangam, Venkatesan P.
Brooklyn, NY
Anania, Bandklayder, Blackwell & Baumgarten, P.A. ... Miami, FL
Anania, Francis A. ... Miami, FL
Anania, Louis A. ... Des Moines, IA
Anania, Michael L. ... New York, NY

Anania, Peter, Jr. ... Charleston, WV
Ananian, Joseph Vaughn ... Saugus, MA
Ananian, R. Michael ... Palo Alto, CA
Anapoell, Steven T. ... Costa Mesa, CA
Anapol, Neil R. ... Claremont, CA
Anapol, Paul R. ... Philadelphia, PA
Anapol, Schwartz, Weiss, Cohan, Feldman and Smalley, P.C. ... Cherry Hill, NJ
Fairless Hills, PA
Media, PA
Philadelphia, PA
Anapol, Schwartz, Weiss, Cohan, Feldman and Smalley, P.C., P.C. ... Reading, PA
Anapol, Thomas R. ... Philadelphia, PA
Anapolsky, Cynthia Dauber ... Brookline, MA
Anapolsky, Louis J. ... Sacramento, CA
Anapolsky, Morris ... Delray Beach, FL
Anas, Demetra E.
Federal Energy Regulatory Commission, Office of the General Counsel, GV
Anasiewicz, James P.
Merit Systems Protection Board, Office of Appeals Counsel, GV
Anasoulis, Christopher J. ... Greenfield, MA
Anastas, Angela Tarrae ... Canton, MA
Anastas, Franklin P. ... Boston, MA
Anastas, George V. ... Boston, MA
Anastas, Maria ... Chicago, IL
Anastas, Terrence J. ... Quincy, IL
Anastas, Walter ... St. Paul, MN
Anastasi, Alfred J. ... Flushing, NY
Anastasi, Anthony J. ... San Jose, CA
Anastasi & Associates, P.A.
Stillwater, MN
Anastasi, David C. ... Stillwater, MN
Anastasi, E. John ... Oxford, MA
Anastasi, John E. ... Oxford, MA
Anastasi, John N. ... Boston, MA
Anastasi, Mark T. ... Bridgeport, CT
Anastasi & Nielsen ... San Jose, CA
Anastasi, Pascal A. ... San Jose, CA
Anastasi, Richard V. ... West New York, NJ
Anastasi, Salvatore ... Philadelphia, PA
Anastasi, Scott J. ... Redondo Beach, CA
Anastasi, William J. ... Hartford, CT
Anastasia, Damon C. ... Los Angeles, CA
Anastasia, Jane K. ... Philadelphia, PA
Anastasia, Marsha L. ... Stamford, CT
Anastasio, A.T. ... South Dennis, MA
Anastasio, Curtis V. ... San Antonio, TX
Anastasio, Louis N., Jr. ... Branchville, NJ
Anastasio, Shala ... Racine, WI
Anastasiou, Elena Pantel ... Indianapolis, IN
Anastasiou, Michael C ... Kew Gardens, NY
Anastasiou, Paula S. ... Chicago, IL
Anastasiou, Van E. ... Fort Lauderdale, FL
Anastassiou, Effie F., Law Office of
Salinas, CA
Anastassiou, Terry ... Redwood City, CA
Anastopoulo, Akim A. ... Charleston, SC
Anastopoulo & Anastopoulo ... Charleston, SC
Anastopoulo, Constance Apostolou
Charleston, SC
Anastopulos, L. Maxwell ... San Diego, CA
Anastor, Peter ... Flint, MI
Anastos, Anna Vedouras ... Cleveland, OH
Anastos, Arthur J. ... Randolph, MA
Anastos, C. George ... Nantucket, MA
Anastos, Chris ... Paterson, NJ
Anastos, James M. ... Fairfax, VA
Anastos, Lisa M. ... New York, NY
Anastos, Peter C. ... Nashua, NH
Anastos, Themis N. ... Morton Grove, IL
Anastos, Theodore ... Cambridge, MA
Anastos, Thomas L. ... Cleveland, OH
Anatale, Stephanie S. ... Trenton, NJ
Anatole, Michael H. ... Calabasas, CA
Anawalt, Howard C. ... Santa Clara, CA
Anawalt, Paul D. ... Palo Alto, CA
Anawaty, William A., Jr. ... Washington, DC
Anaya, Daniel ... Van Nuys, CA
Anaya, G. Antonio ... Cincinnati, OH
Anaya, Kari M. ... Salt Lake City, UT
Anaya Law Firm, The, P.A. ... Santa Fe, NM
Anaya, Rebecca B. ... Dayton, OH
Anaya, Robert J. ... Pleasanton, CA
Anaya, S. James ... Albuquerque, NM
Anaya, Toney ... Santa Fe, NM
Anaya, William B.
House of Representatives, Congressional Assistants, GV
Anaya, William J. ... Chicago, IL
Anbar, Elic Eliahu ... Vista, CA
Anbild, Lisa S. ... Atlanta, GA
Anbinder, Kathryn M. ... Boston, MA
Anbinder, Robert D. ... Baltimore, MD
Anca Marin, Pedro T. ... Utuado, PR
Ancarrow, N. Hopper, Jr. ... Richmond, VA
Ancel & Dunlap, LLP ... Indianapolis, IN
Ancel, Glink, Diamond, Cope & Bush, P.C.
Chicago, IL
Ancel, Jerald I. ... Indianapolis, IN
Ancel, Mark G. ... Los Angeles, CA
Ancel, Nellie R. ... San Jose, CA
Ancel, Richard J. ... New York, NY
Ancel, Sorelle J. ... Indianapolis, IN
Ancel, Steven H. ... Indianapolis, IN
Ancelet, Albert V. ... Carthage, IL
Ancelet, Karen Daniel ... Lafayette, LA
Anchell, Alan Craig ... Fort Lauderdale, FL
Ancheta, Angelo N. ... San Jose, CA
Ancheta, Michele Sherer ... Los Angeles, CA
Anchia, Rafael M. ... Dallas, TX
Anchondo, Daniel ... El Paso, TX
Anchor, Gerald L. ... Paradise Valley, AZ
Anchordoquy, Arnold ... Bakersfield, CA
Anchors, C. LeDon
Fort Walton Beach, FL
Anchors, Foster, McInnis & Keefe, P.A.
Fort Walton Beach, FL
Anchors, Michelle ... Fort Walton Beach, FL
Anciaux, Benjamin R. ... Polson, MT
Ancker, Deanne B. ... Los Angeles, CA
Ancona, Benjamin, Jr. ... West Hartford, CT
Ancona, Elena ... Buffalo, NY
Ancona, Perry L. ... Cincinnati, OH
Ancowitz, Richard B. ... New York, NY
Andalaft, Michael J. ... Ringwood, NJ
Andalman, Elliott D. ... Silver Spring, MD
Andalman & Flynn, P.C. ... Washington, DC
Silver Spring, MD
Andalman, Robert M. ... Chicago, IL
Andaluz Garcia, Adrian ... Caguas, PR
Andara, Kathleen J. ... Costa Mesa, CA
Andary & Andary ... Cheboygan, MI
Sault Ste. Marie, MI
Andary, Anthony E. ... Cheboygan, MI
Sault Ste. Marie, MI
Andary, Carol S. ... Sault Ste. Marie, MI
Andary, Fred J. ... Dayton, OH
Andary, James R. ... Mount Clemens, MI
Andarza, Ivan A. ... Brownsville, TX
Andaya, Athena E. ... Topeka, KS
Andazola, Ronald E. ... Albuquerque, NM
Andeel, Stanley G. ... Wichita, KS
Andeer, Kyle E. ... Birmingham, MI
Andejeski, Ralph E. ... Downers Grove, IL
Andell, Eric ... Houston, TX
Andell, Randolph W. ... Santa Barbara, CA
Andelman, Barbara F. ... Cleveland, OH
Andelman, David R. ... Boston, MA
Andelman, Emily J. ... Pittsburgh, PA
Andelson, Arlen H. ... Los Angeles, CA
Andelson, Bruce D. ... Los Angeles, CA
Andelson, Michael J., (P.C.)
Rancho Mirage, CA
Andelson, Steven J. ... Cerritos, CA
Andenoro, Brian ... Riverside, CA
Ander, Max ... Forest Hills, NY
Andera Law Offices ... Chamberlain, SD
Andera, Leonard E. ... Chamberlain, SD
Anderberg, Erik A. ... Franklin, MA
Anderberg, Judy R., Law Office of
Frisco, TX
Anderberg, Karen L. ... Washington, DC
Anderberg, Robert K. ... New York, NY
Andereck, Eugene E. ... Springfield, MO
Andereck, Evans, Milne, Peace & Baumhoer, L.L.C. ... Jefferson City, MO
Princeton, MO
Springfield, MO
Trenton, MO
Anderegg, J. Philip ... Forest Hills, NY
Anderegg, Marcia H. ... Boston, MA
Anderegg, Michael J. ... Marquette, MI
Anderegg, Robert G. ... Somers, NY
Anderegg, Scott A. ... Minneapolis, MN
Anderegg, Scott M. J. ... Richmond, VA
Anderer, Stephen J. ... Philadelphia, PA
Anderfuren, Jill ... Chicago, IL
Anderholt & Bonnheim, LLP
Indian Wells, CA
Anderholt, J. John ... Indian Wells, CA
Anderholt, L. Brooks ... El Centro, CA
Anderholt & Storey, A P.L.C.
El Centro, CA
Anderl, Julie Ann ... Chippewa Falls, WI
Anderl, Lisa A. ... Seattle, WA
Anderl, Mark A. ... Perth Amboy, NJ
Princeton, NJ
Anderl & Oakley, P.C. ... Perth Amboy, NJ
Princeton, NJ
Anderl, Richard C. ... Omaha, NE
Anderle, Catherine Criswell ... Cleveland, OH
Anderle, Robert D. ... Cleveland, OH
Anderle, Thomas P. ... Santa Barbara, CA
Anderlie, Robert L. ... Troy, MI
Anderlik, Kathryn James ... Park Ridge, IL
Anderlini, Finkelstein & Emerick, A Professional Corporation
San Mateo, CA
Anderlini, P. Terry ... San Mateo, CA
Anderlini, Philip R. ... Kentfield, CA
Anderman & Anderman ... Forest Hills, NY
Anderman, Arthur A. ... Forest Hills, NY
Anderman & Brielmann, L.L.P.
Media, PA
Anderman, Jason Mark ... Roseland, NJ
Anderman, Jody Edward
Baton Rouge, LA
Anderman, Kimberly ... Media, PA
Anderman, Lisa B. ... Forest Hills, NY
Anderman, Marvin ... Old Tappan, NJ
Anderman, Richard A. ... New York, NY
Anderman, Robert P. ... Media, PA
Anderman, Sigmund ... Alamo, CA
Anderman, Virginia ... Albuquerque, NM
Andernacht & Hurd, P.C. ... Plaistow, NH
Anders, Amanda Brantley ... Charlotte, NC
Anders, Andrea ... Columbia, SC
Anders, Boyett & Brady ... Mobile, AL
Anders, Brett D. ... Kansas City, MO
Anders, Brett M. ... Morristown, NJ
Anders, Bruce K. ... Wilkes-Barre, PA
Anders, Christa ... St. Paul, MN
Anders, Claudia ... Atlanta, GA
Anders, Dan R.
Department Of Veterans Affairs, Board of Contract Appeals, GV
Anders, Daniel J. ... Philadelphia, PA
Anders, David L. ... Tinley Park, IL
Anders, Elizabeth Bowe ... Columbia, SC
Anders, Ferrell S. ... Mobile, AL
Anders, Geoffrey T. ... Plymouth Meeting, PA
Anders, Gerald K. ... Annapolis, MD
Anders, J. David ... Houston, TX
Anders, James C. ... Columbia, SC
Anders, James C., & Associates, P.A.
Columbia, SC
Rock Hill, SC
Anders, Jerrold P. ... Philadelphia, PA
Anders, Joel W., P.C. ... Washington, DC
Anders, John C. ... San Francisco, CA
Anders, Jonathan C. ... Raleigh, NC
Anders, Kristin L. ... Pittsburgh, PA
Anders, Laurin Grollman ... New York, NY
Anders, Louis H., Jr. ... Birmingham, AL
Anders, M. Maureen ... Phoenix, AZ
Anders, Marjorie Moser ... Pensacola, FL
Anders, Mark L. ... Denver, CO
Anders, Marshall E. ... Stroudsburg, PA
Anders, Milton H. ... Houston, TX
Anders, Patrick Maxwell ... Burlington, NC
Anders, Paul D. ... Richmond, VA
Anders, Thomas L. ... Centerville, IA
Anders, Wolfram ... Washington, DC
Andersen, Adam A.
South San Francisco, CA
Andersen, Alan R. ... Salt Lake City, UT
Andersen, Alf R. ... Long Beach, CA
Andersen, Anton C. ... Kansas City, KS
Andersen, Arthur A. ... Marlborough, MA
Andersen, Arthur J. ... Harrison, NJ
Andersen, Benjamin O. ... Oakland, CA
Andersen, Berkshire, Lauritsen & Brower
Omaha, NE
Andersen, Bjarne B., Jr. ... Tallahassee, FL
Andersen, Bonnifield & Cottle
Concord, CA
Andersen, Bradley W. ... Portland, OR
Andersen, Brian Paul ... Audubon, IA
Andersen, Buck & Mann LLP
San Diego, CA
Andersen, C. Lars ... Vienna, VA
Andersen, C. Matthew ... Coeur d'Alene, ID
Spokane, WA
Andersen, Candace Jane Kay
Morgan Hill, CA
Andersen, Carolyn A. ... Bellevue, WA
Andersen, Corinne I. ... Bethpage, NY
Andersen, Craig F. ... Concord, CA
Andersen, Craig S. ... Seattle, WA
Andersen, Crossan R. ... Encino, CA
Andersen, Cynthia Lee ... Westfield, MA
Andersen, Dale E. ... Mesa, AZ
Andersen, Daniel D. ... Salt Lake City, UT
Andersen, David C. ... Grand Rapids, MI
Andersen, David G. ... Santa Monica, CA
Andersen, David L. ... Oakland, CA
Andersen, David S. ... Salt Lake City, UT
Andersen, David V. ... Seattle, WA
Andersen, Davidson & Tate, P.C.
Duluth, GA
Lawrenceville, GA
Norcross, GA
Snellville, GA
Andersen, Dianne M. ... Danbury, CT
Andersen, Donald L. ... Minneapolis, MN
Andersen, Donald R. ... Atlanta, GA
Andersen, Donald S. ... Wichita, KS
Andersen, Edward J., Jr. ... Chicago, IL
Andersen, Edward S. ... Chicago, IL
Andersen, Eileen K. ... Wilmington, DE
Andersen, Einar G. ... Portland, ME
Andersen, Elinar G. ... New York, NY
Andersen, Erich D. ... Redmond, WA
Andersen, Ethel D. ... Lawrenceville, GA
Andersen, F. Dayle ... Yakima, WA
Andersen & Ferlazzo, P.C. ... Danbury, CT
Andersen Firm, The, A Professional Corporation ... Key West, FL
Greeneville, TN
Kingsport, TN
Andersen, Francine O'Brien ... Audubon, IA
Andersen, G. Steven
Manhattan Beach, CA
Andersen, Gary Wayne ... Whittier, CA
Andersen, H. Thomas ... Salem, OR
Andersen, H. Verlan ... Provo, UT
Andersen, Hans Ulfson ... Washington, DC
Andersen, Harry G. ... San Juan, PR
Andersen, Henry S. ... Reston, VA
Andersen & Holland ... Midland Park, NJ
Andersen, J. Carter ... Washington, DC
Andersen, J. Vance ... Phoenix, AZ
Andersen, James A. ... Olympia, WA
Andersen, James R. ... Towson, MD
Andersen, Jane L. ... Key West, FL
Greeneville, TN
Andersen, Jeanne M. ... Mount Laurel, NJ
Andersen, Jill A. H. ... Cedar Rapids, IA
Andersen, Joan ... Seattle, WA
Andersen, Joe V. ... Congress, AZ
Andersen, John G. ... San Mateo, CA
Andersen, John M. ... Burlingame, CA
Andersen, Joseph H. ... Minneapolis, MN
Andersen, Judith T. ... Annandale, VA
Andersen, Kara M. ... San Francisco, CA
Andersen, Karen ... Chicago, IL
Andersen, Karen A. ... Seattle, WA
Andersen, Katherine L. ... Waukesha, WI
Andersen, Kay M. ... Oakland, CA
Andersen, Keith H. ... Albuquerque, NM
Andersen & Keleher ... Los Angeles, CA
Manhattan Beach, CA
Andersen, Kirstie D. ... Indianapolis, IN
Andersen, L. David ... Dallas, TX
Andersen, Lage E. ... Burlingame, CA
Andersen, Laura J. ... Pasadena, CA
Andersen Law Offices ... Audubon, IA
Andersen, Lepant & Hotz ... Beatrice, NE
Andersen, Les ... Midland Park, NJ
Andersen, Lynette ... Sacramento, CA
Andersen, M. Steven ... San Diego, CA
Andersen, Mark A. ... Lawrence, KS
Andersen, Mark L. ... Boone, IA
Andersen, Marvin L. ... Annapolis, MD
Andersen, Merrell L. ... Beatrice, NE
Andersen, Mia ... Summit, NJ
Andersen, Michael P. ... Miami, FL
Andersen, Pamela D. ... Annapolis, MD
Andersen, Peter J. ... Belvedere-Tiburon, CA
Andersen, Philip M. ... San Jose, CA
Andersen, R. Lee ... Corona Del Mar, CA
Andersen, R. Lee ... Newport Beach, CA
Andersen, R. Tyler ... San Francisco, CA
Andersen, Randall J. ... Madison, WI
Andersen, Ray H. ... Wausau, WI
Andersen, Richard E. ... New York, NY
Andersen, Richard Lee ... Modesto, CA
Andersen, Robert J. ... Madison, WI
Andersen, Robert L. ... Charlotte, NC
Andersen, Robert L. ... Valley Forge, PA
Andersen, Robert M.
Department of Defense, GV
Andersen, Robert T., Jr. ... Riverside, CA
Andersen, Roger W. ... Toledo, OH
Andersen, S. Ford ... Ordway, CO
Andersen, Scott D.
Executive Office Of The President, Office of the U.S. Trade Representative, GV
Andersen & Smith ... Mesa, AZ
Andersen, Stacey E. ... Baltimore, MD
Andersen, Stacy C. ... Seattle, WA
Andersen, Stanley J. ... Omaha, NE
Andersen, Stephanie Scheier ... Seattle, WA
Andersen, Stephen G. ... Minneapolis, MN
Andersen, Steven B. ... Boise, ID
Andersen, Steven B ... Portland, OR
Andersen, Steven C. ... Vancouver, WA
Andersen, Steven J. ... Miami, FL
Andersen, Susan K. ... Los Angeles, CA
Andersen, Susan K. ... Portland, OR
Andersen, Thomas A. ... Beaverton, OR
Andersen, Thomas B. ... Houston, TX
Andersen, Thomas J. ... Lawrenceville, GA
Andersen, Todd J. ... Cleveland, OH
Andersen, Trudee ... Grand Junction, CO
Andersen, Warren G. ... Detroit, MI
Andersen, Wayne R. ... Chicago, IL
Andersen, Wendy Lynn ... Cincinnati, OH
Andersen, William E. ... Key West, FL
Greeneville, TN
Kingsport, TN
Andersen, William E. ... Trenton, NJ
Andersen, William W., Jr. ... South Bend, IN
Andersen, Wm. R. ... Seattle, WA
Andersen & Zimmer ... Oakland, CA
Anderson, A. Broadus, III (P.C.)
New York, NY
Anderson, A. Eric ... Fort Myers, FL
Naples, FL
Anderson, A. Eric, P.A. ... Fort Myers, FL
Naples, FL
Anderson, A. Evon ... Fort Benton, MT
Anderson, A. James ... Atlanta, GA
Anderson, A. Laurie ... Louisville, KY
Anderson, A. Ray ... Raytown, MO
Anderson, A. Stephen ... Seattle, WA
Anderson, Aaron R. ... Delmar, NY
Anderson, Ablon, Lewis & Gale, LLP
Los Angeles, CA
San Juan Capistrano, CA
Thousand Oaks, CA
Anderson & Ablon, LLP ... Pasadena, CA
Anderson, Acie G., III ... Clarkston, MI
Anderson, Add B., Jr. ... Blue Bell, PA
Anderson, Adele Konkel ... Pueblo, CO
Anderson, Adler, Cohen & Harvey LLP
Boston, MA
Anderson, Adolph N., Jr. ... Providence, RI
Anderson, Adrienne E. ... St. Louis, MO
Anderson, Adrienne L. ... Knoxville, TN
Anderson, Aileen Casanave ... Sunnyvale, CA
Anderson, Aimee B. ... Chicago, IL
Anderson, A. J. ... Harrisonville, MO
Anderson, Alan A. ... Polk City, IA
Anderson, Alan C. ... Kansas City, MO
Anderson, Alan C. ... Fircrest, WA
Anderson, Alan G. ... Xenia, OH
Anderson, Alan J. ... Logan, IA
Anderson, Alan M. ... San Francisco, CA
Anderson, Alan M. ... Minneapolis, MN
Anderson, Alan S. ... Washington, DC
Anderson, Alan W. ... Denver, CO
Anderson, Alan W. ... Amherst, OH
Anderson, Albeon G. ... Rocky Mount, NC
Anderson, Albert E. ... Wheat Ridge, CO
Anderson, Albert E., P.C. ... Wheat Ridge, CO
Anderson, Albert S., Law Offices of
Atlanta, GA
Anderson, Albert S., Law Offices of
Norcross, GA
Anderson, Alden H. ... York, ME
Anderson, Alden, Hayes, Ziogas & Storm, L.L.C. ... Bristol, CT
Anderson, Alexis J. ... Newton, MA
Anderson, Alice ... Chancellor, AL
Anderson, Alicia ... Minneapolis, MN
Anderson, Aline F. ... Indianapolis, IN
Anderson, Alisa E. ... Burbank, CA
Anderson, Alison G. ... Los Angeles, CA
Anderson, Alissa Balotti ... Wilmington, DE
Anderson, Allan C. ... San Jose, CA
Anderson, Allan E. ... Los Angeles, CA
Anderson, Allan M. ... Santa Rosa, CA
Anderson, Allan W., Jr. ... Washington, DC
Anderson, Allen A. ... Oskaloosa, IA
Anderson, Allen E. ... Sacramento, CA
Anderson, Allen G. ... Lansing, MI
Traverse City, MI
Anderson, Allen L. ... Birmingham, AL

Anderson, Allen Lewis ......Birmingham, AL
Anderson, Allen M. ......Elgin, IL
Anderson, Allison Black ......Gordo, AL
Anderson, Alvin L. ......Scottsdale, AZ
Anderson, Alvin P. ......Williamsburg, VA
Anderson, Amanda Lannon
Administrative Office Of The United States Courts, GV
Anderson, Amber L. ......Houston, TX
Anderson, Amy Abdo ......Phoenix, AZ
Tucson, AZ
Anderson, Amy L. ......Chicago, IL
Anderson, Amy Langer ......Pittsburgh, PA
Anderson, Anders A. ......Oceanside, NY
Anderson & Anderson ......Santa Ana, CA
Anderson & Anderson ......Atlanta, GA
Anderson and Anderson ......Tompkinsville, KY
Anderson & Anderson ......Oakland, NE
Tekamah, NE
Anderson and Anderson ......Raleigh, NC
Rocky Mount, NC
Anderson & Anderson ......Ironton, OH
Anderson & Anderson ......Morristown, TN
Anderson & Anderson ......Crosby, TX
Anderson & Anderson ......Lewisburg, WV
Rainelle, WV
Anderson & Anderson, A P.C.
San Francisco, CA
Anderson, Anderson & Bright, P.C.
El Paso, TX
Anderson & Anderson, L.L.P. ......Slidell, LA
Anderson & Anderson, P.A.
Fort Lauderdale, FL
Stuart, FL
Anderson & Anderson, P.C. ......Danville, IL
Anderson & Anderson, P.C.
Bismarck, ND
Mandan, ND
Anderson & Anderson, P.C. ......Monticello, UT
Anderson & Anderson, PLLP ......Missoula, MT
Anderson & Anderson, S.C. ......Kenosha, WI
Anderson, Andrea ......Washington, DC
Anderson, Andrea S. ......Red Lion, PA
Anderson, Andrew E. ......Toledo, OH
Anderson, Andrew J. ......Rochester, NY
Anderson, Andrew R. ......Des Moines, IA
Anderson, Andrew W. ......Miami, FL
Anderson, Andy R. ......Lincolnshire, IL
Anderson, Angela Joan ......Fresno, CA
Anderson, Angela M. ......Fort Myers, FL
Anderson, Angela S.
National Labor Relations Board, Washington, D. C. Resident Office, GV
Anderson, Angelia Sheets ......Daphne, AL
Anderson, Angelique Layton
East Windsor, NJ
Anderson, Angelita M. ......New York, NY
Anderson, Anita J., Law Offices of
San Antonio, TX
Anderson, Ann Gormican
Santa Barbara, CA
Anderson, Ann K. ......New Haven, CT
Anderson, Anne M. ......Southfield, MI
Anderson, Annette L. ......Costa Mesa, CA
Anderson, Ann-Marie ......Phoenix, AZ
Anderson, Anthony A. ......Washington, DC
Anderson, Anthony A. ......Jacksonville, FL
Anderson, Anthony F. ......Roanoke, VA
Anderson, Anthony L., (P.C.) ......St. Louis, MO
Anderson Aquino LLP ......Boston, MA
Anderson, Archie E., Jr. ......San Antonio, TX
Anderson, Arlene D. ......Minneapolis, MN
Anderson, Arlene G. ......Indianapolis, IN
Anderson, Arnold P. ......Hartford, WI
Anderson, Arthur A. ......Lawrence, KS
Anderson, Arthur A. ......New York, NY
Anderson, Arthur A., Jr. ......Severna Park, MD
Anderson, Arthur E. ......Le Sueur, MN
Anderson, Arthur E., II ......Richmond, VA
Anderson, Arthur H., Jr. ......Chicago, IL
Anderson, Arthur I. ......Boston, MA
Anderson, Arthur J. ......Dallas, TX
Anderson, Arthur P. ......Plattsburgh, NY
Burlington, VT
Anderson, Arthur T. ......Phoenix, AZ
Anderson & Artigliere, P.A. ......Lakeland, FL
Anderson, Arvie J. ......Indianapolis, IN
Anderson & Associates, LLC
Kansas City, MO
Anderson & Associates, P.A.
Columbia, SC
Anderson, Audrey Fox ......Honolulu, HI
Newport News, VA
Anderson, Audrey J. ......Washington, DC
Anderson, Audrey L. ......New Brunswick, NJ
Anderson, Audrey L. ......Nashville, TN
Anderson, Augustus S. ......McLean, VA
Anderson, Aukamp & Gingold
Washington, DC
Anderson, Austin ......Metairie, LA
Anderson, Austin G. ......Ann Arbor, MI
Anderson, Autumn L. ......St. Paul, MN
Anderson, B. Davis ......Cushing, OK
Anderson, B. Douglas ......Columbus, OH
Anderson & Bailly ......Fargo, ND
Anderson, Barbara C. ......Milford, CT
Anderson, Barbara D. ......Chapel Hill, NC
Anderson, Barbara F. ......Lexington, KY
Anderson, Barbara J. ......Stockton, CA
Anderson, Barbara J. ......Chicago, IL
Anderson, Barbara McComas ......Dallas, TX
Anderson, Barbara S. ......Alexandria, VA
Anderson, Barrie W. ......Torrance, CA
Anderson, Barry ......Freeport, IL
Anderson, Barry L. ......Atlanta, GA
Anderson, Barry L. ......Maryville, MO
Anderson, Barry M. ......Keokuk, IA
Anderson, Bart R. ......Bellevue, WA
Anderson, Bebe J. ......New York, NY
Anderson, Belina ......Albany, NY
Anderson, Ben L. ......Lincoln, NE
Anderson, Benjamin H. ......Cleveland, OH
Anderson, Benjamin W., II ......Clemson, SC
Anderson & Bennett ......Los Angeles, CA
Anderson, Bennett Boyd, Jr., (A Professional Law Corp.) ......Lafayette, LA
Anderson, Benny G. ......Houston, TX
Anderson, Berndt W. ......Providence, RI
Anderson, Bethany M. ......Milwaukee, WI
Anderson, Betty Jane ......Chicago, IL
Anderson, Beverly K. ......Tucson, AZ
Anderson, Beverly L. ......Spokane, WA
Anderson, Bill, Jr. ......Memphis, TN
Anderson, Billy D. ......Tyler, TX
Anderson & Bolles, Inc. ......King City, CA
Anderson, Bonnie J. ......Modesto, CA
Anderson, Boston F., Jr.
Department of Housing and Urban Development, Office of General Counsel, GV
Anderson, Boyd H., Jr. ......Fort Lauderdale, FL
Anderson, Brad H. ......Billings, MT
Anderson, Bradford ......Seattle, WA
Anderson, Bradford P. ......Sunnyvale, CA
Anderson, Bradley B ......Reno, NV
Anderson, Bradley S. ......Trumbull, CT
Anderson, Bradley W. ......Jackson, MN
Anderson, Bradley W. ......Minneapolis, MN
Anderson, Brainard L. ......Tribune, KS
Anderson, Brent D. ......Denver, CO
Anderson, Brent E. ......Bellevue, WA
Anderson, Brent Eric ......Celina, OH
Anderson, Brent I. ......Wichita, KS
Anderson, Bret Schrotel ......Tampa, FL
Anderson, Brett C. ......Cedar City, UT
Anderson, Brett D. ......Miami, FL
Anderson, Brett D. ......Minneapolis, MN
Anderson, Brett E. ......Elgin, IL
Anderson, Brett I. ......Des Moines, IA
Anderson, Brian C. ......Washington, DC
Anderson, Brian C. ......Madison, WI
Anderson, Brian D. ......Arlington, VA
Anderson, Brian L. ......Madison, WI
Milwaukee, WI
Anderson & Bridges, LLC ......Chattanooga, TN
Anderson, Bridgett C. ......Dallas, TX
Anderson, Brigitte M. ......Three Forks, MT
Anderson & Brocious, P.C. ......Dallas, TX
Anderson, Brody, Levinson, Weiser & Horwitz, P.A. ......Phoenix, AZ
Anderson & Broussard ......Lafayette, LA
Anderson, Bruce ......Warren, AR
Anderson, Bruce ......New York, NY
Anderson, Bruce A. ......Roseville, CA
Anderson, Bruce A. ......Sandpoint, ID
Anderson, Bruce A. ......Knoxville, TN
Anderson, Bruce C. ......Denver, CO
Anderson, Bruce E. ......La Grande, OR
Anderson, Bruce E. ......San Antonio, TX
Anderson, Bruce Garrett ......Louisville, KY
Anderson, Bruce H. ......Eugene, OR
Anderson, Bruce H. S. ......Omaha, NE
Anderson, Bruce L. ......Boone, IA
Anderson, Bruce L. ......Two Harbors, MN
Anderson, Bruce P. ......Tallahassee, FL
Anderson, Bruce P. ......Balsam Lake, WI
Anderson, Bruce R., Jr. ......Jacksonville, FL
Anderson, Bruce V. ......Wagner, SD
Anderson, Bruce W. ......Santa Cruz, CA
Anderson, Bruce W. ......Austin, TX
Anderson, Bryan C. ......Palo Alto, CA
Anderson, Bryan K. ......San Jose, CA
Anderson, Bryan N. ......Duluth, MN
Anderson, Bryan S. ......Chicago, IL
Anderson, Bryce C. ......Clayton, CA
Anderson, Buist M. ......Bloomfield, CT
Anderson & Burgett ......Willmar, MN
Anderson, Burns & Hostnik ......Tacoma, WA
Anderson, Burnside E., III ......New York, NY
Anderson, Burr E. ......Chicago, IL
Anderson, Burton D. ......St. Paul, MN
Anderson, Byrd, Richeson & Flaherty
Baldwin City, KS
Anderson, Byrd, Richeson, Flaherty & Henrichs ......Ottawa, KS
Anderson, Byron E. ......Washington, DC
Anderson, C. Barry ......Radford, VA
Anderson, C. David ......Los Angeles, CA
Anderson, C. Duane ......Ashland, OH
Anderson, C. Floyd ......Leawood, KS
Anderson, C. Grant ......Pittsburgh, PA
Anderson, C. Harper ......Rockford, IL
Anderson, C. Ian ......New York, NY
Anderson, C. Joseph ......Terre Haute, IN
Anderson, C. Lee ......Harrisburg, PA
Anderson, C. Peter ......Pasadena, CA
Anderson, C. Richard ......Woburn, MA
Anderson, C. Richard ......Butte, MT
Anderson, C. Robert ......South Plainfield, NJ
Anderson, C. Robert ......Breckenridge, TX
Anderson, C. Thomas ......Ocean Springs, MS
Anderson, C. Tom ......Prestonsburg, KY
Anderson & Cahill ......Woodbury, NY
Anderson, Calum B. ......Hartford, CT
Anderson, Calvin R. ......Decorah, IA
Anderson, Campbell & Laugesen, A Professional Corporation ......Denver, CO
Anderson, Candace C. ......Wilmington, DE
Anderson, Candice ......Salt Lake City, UT
Anderson, Canyon W. ......Salt Lake City, UT
Anderson, Carl B., Jr. ......McPherson, KS
Anderson, Carl D. ......Norwich, CT
Anderson, Carl E. ......Cleveland, OH
Anderson, Carl E. ......Chattanooga, TN
Anderson, Carl F. ......Milwaukee, WI
Anderson, Carl H., Jr. ......Atlanta, GA
Anderson, Carl M. ......Topeka, KS
Anderson, Carl T. ......Los Angeles, CA
Anderson, Carl W. ......San Francisco, CA
Anderson, Carl W. ......Sandusky, OH
Anderson, Carla Marie ......Texas City, TX
Anderson, Carmen N. ......Milwaukee, WI
Anderson, Carol A. ......Miami, FL
Anderson, Carol Boyles ......Winston-Salem, NC
Anderson, Carol F. ......Los Angeles, CA
Anderson, Carol Jeanne ......Richmond, VA
Anderson, Carol M. ......Fort Lauderdale, FL
Stuart, FL
Anderson, Carole J. ......Davenport, IA
Anderson, Carolyn A. ......San Francisco, CA
Anderson, Carolyn Browne ......Rutland, VT
Anderson, Carolyn Glass ......Minneapolis, MN
Anderson & Carr, L.L.C. ......Abbeville, AL
Montgomery, AL
Anderson, Carrie M. ......Washington, DC
Anderson, Casey ......Washington, DC
Anderson, Catherine E. ......New York, NY
Anderson, Catherine L.O. ......Minneapolis, MN
Anderson, Catherine N. ......Bridgeport, CT
Anderson, Catherine S.
Executive Office Of The President, Office of Administration, GV
Anderson, Cathleen Bang
Inver Grove Heights, MN
Anderson, Cathy ......Ventura, CA
Anderson, Cathy C. ......Deerfield, IL
Anderson, Chad R. ......Milwaukee, WI
Anderson and Chapin, P.C. ......Brush, CO
Anderson, Charles A. ......Green Valley, AZ
Anderson, Charles A. ......Kalamazoo, MI
Anderson, Charles A. ......Reston, VA
Anderson, Charles B. ......New York, NY
Anderson, Charles C. ......New London, CT
Anderson, Charles C., III ......Monticello, FL
Anderson, Charles D. ......Wichita, KS
Anderson, Charles E. ......Los Angeles, CA
Anderson, Charles E. ......Chicago, IL
Anderson, Charles E. ......Albuquerque, NM
Anderson, Charles E. ......Aurora, OH
Anderson, Charles E. ......Harrisburg, PA
Anderson, Charles E. ......San Antonio, TX
Anderson, Charles E., Jr. ......Kankakee, IL
Anderson, Charles H. ......Louisville, KY
Anderson, Charles Hill ......Nashville, TN
Anderson, Charles J. ......Windsor, WI
Anderson, Charles L. ......Montgomery, AL
Anderson, Charles N., Jr. ......Raleigh, NC
Wilmington, NC
Anderson, Charles R. ......Los Angeles, CA
Pasadena, CA
Anderson, Charles R. ......Irving, TX
Anderson, Charles S. ......Highland Park, MI
Anderson, Charles W. ......Boston, MA
Anderson, Charles W. ......Gillette, WY
Anderson, Charles W., III ......Detroit, MI
Anderson, Cheryl Glen ......San Jose, CA
Anderson, Cheryl H. ......Lexington, KY
Anderson, Cheryl L. ......Palatka, FL
Anderson, Cheryl Rae ......San Diego, CA
Anderson, Chester L. ......Peoria, IL
Anderson, Chris C. ......Indianapolis, IN
Anderson, Chris L., (P.C.) ......Phoenix, AZ
Anderson, Christa M. ......San Francisco, CA
Anderson, Christian M. ......Wahpeton, ND
Anderson, Christin A. ......Hingham, MA
Anderson, Christine D.
Mount Clemens, MI
Anderson, Christine D. ......Mount Clemens, MI
Anderson, Christine E. ......Belleville, IL
Anderson, Christine M. ......Dallas, TX
Anderson, Christine P. ......Chicago, IL
Anderson, Christine S. ......Bedford, NH
Anderson, Christopher ......Rochester, NY
Anderson, Christopher D. ......Little Rock, AR
Anderson, Christopher D. ......Seattle, WA
Anderson, Christopher David ......Duluth, MN
Anderson, Christopher H. ......Seattle, WA
Anderson, Christopher J. ......Atlantic Beach, FL
Anderson, Christopher J.
Kansas City, MO
Anderson, Christopher L. ......Richmond, VA
Anderson, Christopher O. ......Phoenix, AZ
Anderson, Christopher P. ......Norwich, CT
Anderson, Cindy L. ......Atlantic Beach, FL
Anderson, C. J. ......Cresco, IA
Anderson, Clare E. ......Missoula, MT
Anderson, Clare G.
Equal Employment Opportunity Commission, Office of Federal Operations, GV
Anderson, Clarence A. ......St. Paul, MN
Anderson, Clark ......Lufkin, TX
Anderson, Claude W., Jr. ......Portsmouth, VA
Anderson, Claudia Smith ......Danville, IL
Anderson & Clayton ......Eugene, OR
Anderson, Clayton M. ......La Mesa, CA
Ontario, CA
Riverside, CA
Temecula, CA
Anderson, Clifford R., III
Santa Barbara, CA
Anderson, Clifford R., Jr. ......Pasadena, CA
Anderson, Clifford S. ......Minneapolis, MN
Anderson, Clifton L. ......Sunnyvale, CA
Anderson, Clifton W. ......Charlottesville, VA
Anderson, Clinton R. ......Morristown, TN
Anderson, Clyde F. ......Minneapolis, MN
Anderson, Coe & King, L.L.P.
Washington, DC
Baltimore, MD
Ocean City, MD
Towson, MD
Anderson, Colette C. ......Elgin, IL
Anderson & Company ......New York, NY
Anderson & Connell ......Bellingham, WA
Anderson, Constance L. ......Madison, WI
Anderson, Corbett L. ......Washington, DC
Anderson, Corby Cochran ......Charlotte, NC
Anderson & Corrie ......Fairfax, VA
Anderson, Cory S. ......Pittsburg, CA
Anderson, Courtland W. ......Ann Arbor, MI
Anderson, Courtney E. ......Austin, TX
Anderson, Craig A. ......Detroit, MI
Anderson, Craig A. ......Sioux Falls, SD
Anderson, Craig B. ......Dallas, TX
Anderson, Craig E. ......Chicago, IL
Anderson, Craig F. ......Boston, MA
Anderson, Craig H. ......Marina Del Rey, CA
Anderson, Craig H. ......Minneapolis, MN
Anderson, Craig K. ......Woodland Hills, CA
Anderson, Craig R. ......Denver, CO
Anderson, Craig R. ......St. Paul, MN
Anderson, Craig W. ......Salt Lake City, UT
Anderson, Creager & Wittstruck, P.C.
Lincoln, NE
Anderson, Croil J. ......Seattle, WA
Anderson, Cromwell A. ......Miami, FL
Anderson & Cunningham, P.C.
Houston, TX
Anderson, Curt B. ......Portland, OR
Anderson, Curtis A. ......Danville, IL
Anderson, Curtis B. ......Ironton, OH
Anderson, Curtis B. ......Dallas, TX
Anderson, Curtis M. ......McLean, VA
Anderson, Curtis S. ......Baltimore, MD
Anderson, Cynthia A. ......Traverse City, MI
Anderson, Cynthia C. ......Shreveport, LA
Anderson, Cynthia H. ......Department of Justice, Office of Information and Privacy, GV
Anderson, Cynthia S. ......El Paso, TX
Anderson, D. Keith ......Wichita, KS
Anderson, D. Michael ......South Bend, IN
Anderson, D. Phillip ......Peoria, IL
Anderson, D. Reed ......Stewartstown, PA
York, PA
Anderson, D. Richard, Jr.
Falls Church, VA
Anderson, Dale A. ......Lansing, IL
Anderson, Dale A., & Associates, Ltd.
Lansing, IL
Anderson, Dale K. ......Toledo, OH
Anderson, Dale L. ......St. Helens, OR
Anderson, Dan R. ......Lodi, CA
Anderson, Dana A. ......Portland, OR
Anderson, Dana K., Jr. ......Long Beach, CA
Anderson, Daniel A. ......Reno, NV
Anderson, Daniel & Coxe
Wilmington, NC
Wrightsville Beach, NC
Anderson, Daniel G. ......Monticello, UT
Anderson, Daniel J. ......Salt Lake City, UT
Anderson, Daniel M. ......Columbus, OH
Anderson, Daniel M. ......Austin, TX
Anderson, Daniel P. ......Waukesha, WI
Anderson, Daniel R. ......Department of Justice, Civil Division, GV
Anderson, Daniel S. ......Des Moines, IA
Anderson, Daniel W. ......Salt Lake City, UT
Anderson, Darla ......Oklahoma City, OK
Anderson, Darla R. ......Santa Barbara, CA
Anderson, Darren W. ......Houston, TX
Anderson, Darryl J. ......Washington, DC
Anderson, Darryl Wade ......Houston, TX
Anderson, David A. ......Wilmington, DE
Anderson, David A. ......Chicago, IL
Anderson, David A. ......Indianapolis, IN
Anderson, David A. ......Boston, MA
Anderson, David A. ......Columbia, SC
Anderson, David A. ......Austin, TX
Anderson, David A. ......Salt Lake City, UT
Anderson, David B. ......Birmingham, AL
Anderson, David B. ......Chicago, IL
Anderson, David B. ......Kansas City, MO
Anderson, David B. ......Bellingham, WA
Anderson, David C. ......San Diego, CA
Anderson, David C. ......San Francisco, CA
Anderson, David C. ......Southfield, MI
Anderson, David C. ......Troy, MI
Anderson, David C. ......Salt Lake City, UT
Anderson, David C. ......Seattle, WA
Anderson, David C., APC, A Professional Corporation ......San Diego, CA
Anderson, David E. ......Rochester, NY
Anderson, David E. ......Richmond, VA
Anderson, David F. ......Magalia, CA
Anderson, David F. ......Miami, FL
Anderson, David F. ......Chicago, IL
Anderson, David F. ......Boston, MA
Anderson, David F. ......Spartanburg, SC
Anderson, David F., P.A. ......Miami, FL
Anderson, David G. ......Lombard, IL
Anderson, David G. ......Omaha, NE
Anderson, David G. ......Albany, NY
Anderson, David G. ......East Aurora, NY
Anderson, David G. ......Eau Claire, WI
Anderson, David H. ......Santa Barbara, CA
Anderson, David H. ......Chicago, IL
Anderson, David H. ......Westford, MA
Anderson, David J. ......Department of Justice, Civil Division, GV
Anderson, David J. ......Jacksonville, FL
Anderson, David J. ......Haddonfield, NJ
Anderson, David J. ......Philadelphia, PA
Anderson, David James ......Lansing, MI
Anderson, David K. ......Augusta, GA
Anderson, David K. ......McLean, VA
Anderson, David Kent ......Houston, TX
Anderson, David L. ......Flagstaff, AZ
Anderson, David L. ......Washington, DC
Anderson, David L. ......New Port Richey, FL
Anderson, David L. ......Bluffton, OH

Anderson, David L., P.A.
New Port Richey, FL
Anderson, David M. .... Tucson, AZ
Anderson, David M. .... Minneapolis, MN
Anderson, David M. .... New York, NY
Anderson, David M. .... Tulsa, OK
Anderson, David P. .... Pittsburgh, PA
Anderson, David R. .... Atmore, AL
Anderson, David R. .... Marysville, CA
Anderson, David R. .... Sacramento, CA
Anderson, David R. .... Washington, DC
Anderson, David R. .... Chicago, IL
Anderson, David R. .... Santa Fe, NM
Anderson, David R. .... Reedsport, OR
Anderson, David S. .... Bloomfield Hills, MI
Anderson, David S. .... Minneapolis, MN
Anderson, David Sabin .... Washington, DC
Anderson, David T.
Department of Housing and Urban Development, Board of Contract Appeals, GV
Anderson, David T. .... Boston, MA
Anderson, David W. .... Concord, CA
Anderson, David W. .... San Francisco, CA
Anderson, David W. .... Bowling Green, KY
Anderson, David W. .... Oregon City, OR
Anderson, David W. .... Houston, TX
Anderson, David W. .... Marlin, TX
Anderson, Davis G., Jr. .... Tampa, FL
Anderson, Dawn Barker .... Iowa City, IA
Anderson, Dawn C. .... Boulder, CO
Anderson, Dayle L. .... Lakewood, CO
Anderson, Dean H. .... Willmar, MN
Anderson, Debora A. .... Des Moines, IA
Anderson, Deborah .... Durango, CO
Anderson, Deborah L. .... Indianapolis, IN
Anderson, Deborah Lynn .... Boston, MA
Anderson, Debra Z. .... Pittsburgh, PA
Anderson, DeLane E., Jr. .... Lynn, MA
Anderson, Delia A. .... Portland, OR
Anderson, Delia M. .... Dade City, FL
Anderson, Denise Howell .... Austin, TX
Anderson, Denise Marie
Kansas City, MO
Anderson, Dennis P. .... Bridgeport, CT
Anderson, Dennis P. .... Kansas City, MO
Anderson, Denton L. .... Pasadena, CA
Riverside, CA
Upland, CA
Anderson, Derby Ferris .... Southport, CT
Anderson, Derek C. .... Portland, OR
Anderson, Derek W. .... Fort Worth, TX
Anderson, Devin J. .... Boston, MA
Anderson, Dexter L. .... Fillmore, UT
Anderson, Diana L. .... Point Pleasant, NJ
Anderson, Diana L. .... Kennewick, WA
Anderson, Diane .... San Bernardino, CA
Anderson, Diane M. .... Chicago, IL
Anderson, Dianne L. .... Media, PA
Anderson & Dittman .... Tigard, OR
Anderson, Dolly E. .... Mission, KS
Anderson, Dominica Cortum
San Francisco, CA
Anderson, Don L. .... Okanogan, WA
Anderson, Donald A. .... Lakeport, CA
Anderson, Donald A. .... Bloomington, MN
Anderson, Donald A. .... Massapequa, NY
Anderson, Donald C. .... St. Petersburg, FL
Anderson, Donald D. .... Jacksonville, FL
Anderson, Donald E. .... Phoenix, AZ
Anderson, Donald E. .... Walnut Creek, CA
Anderson, Donald E., III .... Alexandria, VA
Anderson, Donald J.
East Longmeadow, MA
Anderson, Donald Kenneth, Jr.
St. Louis, MO
Anderson, Donald L. .... Tacoma, WA
Anderson, Donald L., Jr. .... Abilene, TX
Anderson, Donald M. .... Owatonna, MN
Anderson, Donald R. .... Redding, CA
Anderson, Donald R. .... Indianapolis, IN
Anderson, Donald R., A Law Corporation
Redding, CA
Anderson, Donald T. .... Green Valley, AZ
Anderson, Donald T. .... Elgin, IL
Anderson, Donald W. .... Libertyville, IL
Anderson, Donald W., (P.C.)
New Haven, CT
Anderson, Donna .... St. Louis, MO
Anderson, Donna L. .... San Jose, CA
Anderson, Donna L. .... Vernon, CT
Anderson, Donna W. .... San Francisco, CA
Anderson, Donovan & Poole, A Professional Corporation .... San Francisco, CA
Anderson, Donovan W. .... Washington, DC
Anderson & Dorn, Ltd., A Prof. Law Corp.
Reno, NV
Anderson, Dorothy I. .... Walnut Creek, CA
Anderson, Douglas A. .... Alexandria, VA
Anderson, Douglas C.
House of Representatives, Congressional Assistants, GV
Anderson, Douglas C. .... Missoula, MT
Anderson, Douglas D. .... South Bend, IN
Anderson, Douglas E.
Colorado Springs, CO
Anderson, Douglas G. .... Seattle, WA
Anderson, Douglas G., P.S. .... Seattle, WA
Anderson, Douglas K. .... Minneapolis, MN
Anderson, Douglas L. .... Mobile, AL
Anderson, Douglas L. .... Omaha, NE
Anderson, Douglas L. .... Columbus, OH
Anderson, Douglas P. .... Hayden Lake, ID
Anderson, Douglas P. .... Little Falls, MN
Anderson, Douglas R. .... Renton, WA
Anderson, Douglas Scot .... Brookings, OR
Anderson, Douglas W. .... Fort Collins, CO
Anderson, Douglas W. .... Chicago, IL
Anderson, Douglass L. .... Victoria, TX
Anderson, Dreama .... Akron, OH
Anderson, Drew A. .... Portland, ME
Anderson & Drossel .... Berkeley, CA
Anderson, Duane .... Miami, FL
Anderson, Duane C. .... Sioux Falls, SD
Anderson, Duane W. .... San Francisco, CA
Anderson, Dude & Lebel, P.C.
Colorado Springs, CO
Anderson, Dudley N. .... Williamsport, PA
Anderson, E. Clive .... New York, NY
Anderson, E. Jane .... Norfolk, VA
Anderson, E. Karl .... Dallas, TX
Anderson, E. Riley .... Knoxville, TN
Anderson, E. Robert .... Paris, IL
Anderson & Eaton, P.C. .... Rutland, VT
Anderson, Eddie L., Jr. .... Baton Rouge, LA
Anderson, Eddie M. .... Lake City, FL
Anderson, Eddie M., P.A. .... Lake City, FL
Anderson, Edmund N. .... Bedford, TX
Anderson, Edmund P. .... Plainville, CT
Anderson, Edw. N. .... Richmond, IN
Anderson, Edward B. .... Evansville, IN
Anderson, Edward B. .... Roseburg, OR
Anderson, Edward C. .... Minneapolis, MN
Anderson, Edward G. .... Muskegon, MI
Anderson, Edward Lee, II .... Nashville, TN
Anderson, Edward M., Sr. .... Decatur, GA
Anderson, Edward Muir .... Los Angeles, CA
Anderson, Edward R. .... Houston, TX
Anderson, Edward T. .... Chicago, IL
Anderson, Edward V. .... San Francisco, CA
San Jose, CA
Anderson, Edwin .... Boca Raton, FL
Anderson, Edwin A. .... La Follette, TN
Anderson, Edwin C., Jr. .... Santa Rosa, CA
Anderson, Edwin J. .... Mount Vernon, IL
Anderson, Eks Ayn .... Salt Lake City, UT
Anderson, Elaine .... New York, NY
Anderson, Eldon W. .... Seattle, WA
Anderson, Elena A. .... Dallas, TX
Anderson, Elisabeth Olney .... Oakland, CA
Anderson, Elizabeth B. .... Washington, DC
Anderson, Elizabeth C. .... St. Louis, MO
Anderson, Elizabeth Dennis .... Montpelier, VT
Anderson, Elizabeth Hart .... Washington, DC
Anderson, Elizabeth T. .... St. Louis, MO
Anderson, Elizabeth W. .... Springfield, IL
Anderson, Ellen A. .... Rochester, NY
Anderson, Ellen Gates .... Olympia, WA
Anderson, Ellis B. .... Princeton, NJ
Anderson, Ellis Ross .... San Francisco, CA
Anderson, Elma E. .... Kewaunee, WI
Anderson, Elna M. .... Grayslake, IL
Anderson, Emil C., Jr. .... Mission Hills, KS
Anderson, Emily E. .... Denver, CO
Anderson, Emily E., P.C. .... Denver, CO
Anderson, Eric .... Greenwich, CT
Anderson, Eric A. .... Omaha, NE
Anderson, Eric A. .... New York, NY
Anderson, Eric A. .... Leesburg, VA
McLean, VA
Anderson, Eric C. .... Scottsdale, AZ
Anderson, Eric D. .... Chicago, IL
Anderson, Eric G. .... Costa Mesa, CA
Anderson, Eric H. .... Palo Alto, CA
Anderson, Eric K. .... Billings, MT
Anderson, Eric L. .... Newark, OH
Anderson, Eric N. .... Salina, KS
Anderson, Eric N. .... Pittsburgh, PA
Anderson, Eric S. .... Minneapolis, MN
Anderson, Eric S. .... Houston, TX
Anderson, Eric W. .... Atlanta, GA
Anderson, Erik Arthur .... Vancouver, WA
Anderson, Erik C. J. .... Washington, DC
Anderson, Erik R. .... Modesto, CA
Anderson, Erika F .... De Ridder, LA
Anderson, Erin L. .... Ellensburg, WA
Anderson, Erin W.
Department of Transportation, U. S. Coast Guard, GV
Anderson, Ernest L. .... Hayward, CA
Anderson, Ernest M. .... San Francisco, CA
Anderson, Ernest S., (Law Corporation)
Slidell, LA
Anderson, Esperanza .... Department of Justice, Environment and Natural Resources Division, GV
Anderson, Ethel .... New York, NY
Anderson, Eugene E., Jr. .... Haverford, PA
Anderson, Eugene R. .... New York, NY
Anderson, Eugene V. .... Medford, OR
Anderson, Evalyn Ruth .... Charleston, WV
Anderson, Evelyn K. .... Red Wing, MN
Anderson, Everett P. .... Tallahassee, FL
Anderson, F. Andrew .... Boston, MA
Anderson, F. Lawrence, Jr. .... Atlanta, GA
Anderson, Faith L. .... Fort Worth, TX
Anderson, Fayssoux and Chasteen
Greenville, SC
Anderson & Ferdon, P.C. .... Norwich, CT
Anderson Fields & Kahan, Inc.
Seattle, WA
Anderson, Floyd E. .... Waltham, MA
Anderson, Floyd H., Jr. .... Boston, MA
Anderson, Forrest E. .... San Jose, CA
Anderson, Forrest M. .... Cottage Grove, MN
Anderson, Francine .... Chicago, IL
Anderson, Francis A. .... Milpitas, CA
Anderson, Francis H. .... Albany, NY
Anderson, Francis I. .... Greensboro, NC
Anderson, Francis Norman .... Riverhead, NY
Anderson, Frank G., III .... Houston, TX
Anderson, Frank H. .... Washington, DC
Anderson, Frank H., Jr.
Johnson City, TN
Anderson, Frank J. .... Scottsdale, AZ
Anderson, Frank L. .... Riverdale, MD
Anderson, Fred A., III .... Gloster, MS
Anderson, Frederic F. .... Evanston, IL
Anderson, Frederick B.
West Des Moines, IA
Anderson, Frederick D. .... Wilmington, NC
Anderson, Frederick G. .... Dallas, TX
Anderson, Frederick R. .... Washington, DC
Anderson, Frederick S. .... Lansing, MI
Anderson, Frederick W. .... Santa Ana, CA
Anderson, Fugate, Givens & Belisle
Elizabethton, TN
Erwin, TN
Johnson City, TN
Anderson, G. Roderic .... Lincoln, NE
Anderson, G. Ross, Jr. .... Anderson, SC
Anderson, G. Wells .... Concord, NH
Anderson, Gail A. .... Detroit, MI
Anderson, Gail A. .... Lansing, MI
Anderson, Galloway & Lucchese, A Professional Corporation
Walnut Creek, CA
Anderson, Gamble Hartzell, (Ms.)
Florence, SC
Anderson, Gary A. .... Kansas City, MO
Anderson, Gary A. .... Dallas, TX
Anderson, Gary A. .... Madison, WI
Anderson, Gary D.
Department of the Air Force, Office of the Judge Advocate General, GV
Anderson, Gary D. .... New York, NY
Anderson, Gary F. .... Tama, IA
Anderson, Gary H. .... San Francisco, CA
Anderson, Gary J. .... Long Beach, CA
Anderson, Gary K. .... Council Bluffs, IA
Anderson, Gary L. .... Knoxville, TN
Anderson, Gary M. .... Long Beach, CA
Anderson, Gary M. .... Laurel, MD
Anderson, Gary N. .... Logan, UT
Anderson, Gary P., P.C. .... Auburn Hills, MI
Anderson, Gary S. .... San Francisco, CA
Anderson, Gary W. .... Louisville, KY
Anderson, Gayle F. .... San Diego, CA
Anderson, G. D. .... Gainesboro, TN
Anderson, Geddes Dowling, Jr.
Jacksonville, FL
Anderson, Geffrey W. .... Fort Worth, TX
Anderson, Gene F. .... Hays, KS
Anderson, Gene S. .... Seattle, WA
Anderson, Geoffrey P. .... Denver, CO
Anderson, George .... Norfolk, VA
Anderson, George A. .... Aiken, SC
Anderson, George E. .... Modesto, CA
Anderson, George F. .... Cleveland, OH
Anderson, George H. "Dutch", III
Crystal River, FL
Melbourne, FL
Orlando, FL
Anderson, George J. .... Wilmington, DE
Anderson, George L. .... Hermiston, OR
Anderson, George L., P.C.
Hermiston, OR
Anderson, George M. .... Raleigh, NC
Anderson, George P. .... Rothschild, WI
Anderson, Gerald Lee .... Springfield, OH
Anderson, Gerald T. .... Duluth, MN
Anderson, Gerard .... Tucson, AZ
Anderson & Gilbert .... Clayton, MO
St. Louis, MO
Anderson, Gina M. .... Chicago, IL
Anderson, Gina S. .... New York, NY
Anderson, Glen C. .... Medford, OR
Anderson, Glenn .... Winter Haven, FL
Anderson, Glenn M. .... Rockville, MD
Anderson, Glenn R. .... Hollis, ME
Anderson, Gordon A. .... Sun Prairie, WI
Anderson, Gordon J. .... Detroit, MI
Anderson, Grace Darlene .... Escondido, CA
Anderson, Grant B. .... Tacoma, WA
Anderson, Grant D. .... Treasury Department, Internal Revenue Service, GV
Anderson, Grant L. .... Tacoma, WA
Anderson Greenfield & Dougherty Ltd.
Philadelphia, PA
Anderson, Greg I. .... Pasadena, CA
Anderson, Greg. W. .... Edgefield, SC
Anderson, Gregg .... Houston, TX
Anderson, Gregg A. .... Gainesville, FL
Anderson, Gregg I. .... Denver, CO
Anderson, Gregg M. .... San Francisco, CA
Anderson, Gregory A. .... Jacksonville, FL
Anderson, Gregory C. .... El Paso, TX
Anderson, Gregory D. .... San Antonio, TX
Anderson, Gregory J. .... Tucson, AZ
Anderson, Gregory J. .... Irvine, CA
Anderson, Gregory J. .... Aurora, CO
Anderson, Gregory L. .... Los Angeles, CA
Anderson, Gregory L. .... Seattle, WA
Anderson, Gregory N. .... Miami, FL
Anderson, Gregory R. .... Willmar, MN
Anderson, Gregory S. .... Idaho Falls, ID
Anderson, Gregory S. .... Grand Island, NE
Anderson, Gregory T. .... Los Angeles, CA
Anderson, Gregory T. .... Tampa, FL
West Palm Beach, FL
Anderson, Gregory V. .... Fresno, CA
Anderson, Greta Gainer .... St. Albans, NY
Anderson & Gruenewald .... Reno, NV
Anderson & Guill, Attorneys, P.A.
Winston-Salem, NC
Anderson, Gus C. .... Pocatello, ID
Anderson, Guy W., Jr., (P.C.) .... Dallas, TX
Anderson, H. Eugene .... Burlington, IA
Anderson, H. Russell .... Columbus, OH
Anderson, H. Thomas .... Columbia, SC
Anderson, Hal B. .... Fort Lauderdale, FL
Tampa, FL
West Palm Beach, FL
Anderson, Hal W. .... Lincoln, NE
Anderson, Hank .... Wichita Falls, TX
Anderson, Harmon, Quick & Stumpf
Bloomington, IL
Anderson, Harold J. .... Anderson, IN
Anderson, Harold L. .... Bismarck, ND
Anderson, Harry Edwin, III
New Orleans, LA
Anderson, Harry J. .... Towson, MD
Anderson, Harry K., Jr. .... Orlando, FL
Anderson, Harry K., Jr., P.A. .... Orlando, FL
Anderson, Harry P., Jr. .... Richmond, VA
Anderson, Harry S., (P.L.C.)
New Orleans, LA
Anderson, Harvey J., II .... Mountain View, CA
Anderson, Harvey L. .... Philadelphia, PA
Anderson, Heather Case .... Pittsburgh, PA
Anderson, Heather H. .... Washington, DC
Anderson, Heather R. .... Los Angeles, CA
Anderson, Heather Scott .... San Francisco, CA
Anderson, Helen H. .... Provo, UT
Anderson, Henry B. .... New Milford, CT
Anderson, Henry L., Jr.
Wrightsville Beach, NC
Anderson, Henry M., Jr. .... Florence, SC
Anderson, Herbert H. .... Portland, OR
Anderson, Herbert T. .... Auburn, NY
Anderson, Herman J. .... Detroit, MI
Anderson, Herr & Zapala, L.L.P.
San Jose, CA
Anderson, Hiram D., Jr.
Stevens Point, WI
Anderson, H. J. .... Minneapolis, MN
Anderson & Holland .... Salt Lake City, UT
Anderson, Holly B. .... Atlanta, GA
Anderson, Holly T. .... Houston, TX
Anderson, Holmes W. .... Boston, MA
Anderson, Howard A. .... Spokane, WA
Anderson, Howard Gerry .... Jacksonville, FL
Anderson, Howard J. .... Lansing, MI
Anderson, Howard P. .... Halifax, VA
Anderson, Howard P., Jr. .... Richmond, VA
Anderson, Howard T. .... Washington, DC
Anderson & Howell, P.A.
Jacksonville Beach, FL
Anderson, Hugh B. .... Lansing, MI
Anderson, Hugh N. .... Madison, WI
Anderson, Hugo Wm., Jr. .... Santa Ana, CA
Anderson, Hugo Wm., Jr., A P.C.
Santa Ana, CA
Temecula, CA
Anderson Hunter Law Firm, P.S.
Everett, WA
Lynnwood, WA
Anderson, Hurwitz & Harward, P.C.
Scottsdale, AZ
Anderson, Ian .... New York, NY
Anderson, Ingrid S. .... Clearwater, FL
Anderson, Ira T. .... Houston, TX
Anderson, Isaac Abram .... Silverdale, WA
Anderson, Isaac, Jr. .... Fort Myers, FL
Anderson, Isaac L., III .... Mason, OH
Anderson, Isham L. .... Monticello, FL
Anderson, J. Arvid .... Tacoma, WA
Anderson, J. Blaine, Jr. .... Dillon, MT
Anderson, J. Bristow .... Roswell, GA
Anderson, J. Chris .... Toledo, OH
Anderson, J. Craig .... Topeka, KS
Anderson, J. Drew .... Prestonsburg, KY
Anderson, J. Eric .... Gadsden, AL
Anderson, J. Eric .... Greenwich, CT
Anderson, J. Jeffrey .... Jackson, MI
Anderson, J. Jeffrey, & Associates, P.C.
Jackson, MI
Anderson, J. Mark .... Athens, AL
Anderson, J. Mathew .... Mason City, IA
Anderson, J. Michael .... Rainelle, WV
Anderson, J. Patricia .... Gaffney, SC
Anderson, J. Patricia .... Spartanburg, SC
Anderson, J. Peirce .... Blue Bell, PA
Anderson, J. Robert .... Salt Lake City, UT
Anderson, J. Scott .... Atlanta, GA
Anderson, J. Scott .... Middletown, NJ
Anderson, J. Steve, III .... Oklahoma City, OK
Anderson, J. Steven .... Memphis, TN
Anderson, J. Thomas .... Hammond, LA
Anderson, J. Trent .... Chicago, IL
Anderson, J. Wayne .... New Orleans, LA
Anderson, J. William .... Fayetteville, NC
Anderson, Jack .... San Diego, CA
Anderson, Jack F. .... Oakland, CA
Anderson, Jack H. .... Charleston, IL
Anderson, Jack Kent .... Denver, CO
Anderson, Jack R. .... Tulsa, OK
Anderson, Jackson L. .... Clarksburg, WV
Anderson & Jackson, P.C.
Indianapolis, IN
Anderson, Jacqueline A .... San Jose, CA
Anderson, Jacqueline S. .... Fargo, ND
Anderson, Jacqueline Smith
Hartford, CT
Anderson & Jahde, P.C. .... Denver, CO
Anderson, James A. .... Minneapolis, MN
Anderson, James A., III .... Benton, KY
Anderson, James B. .... Rutland, VT
Anderson, James C. .... Toledo, OH
Anderson, James C. .... Cheyenne, WY
Anderson, James Craig .... Chicago, IL
Anderson, James D. .... Golden, CO
Anderson, James D. .... Chicago, IL
Anderson, James E. .... Palo Alto, CA
Anderson, James E. .... Washington, DC
Anderson, James E. .... Washington, DC
Anderson, James E. .... Le Sueur, MN
Anderson, James E. .... Union City, NJ
Anderson, James E. .... Austin, TX
Anderson, James E. .... Austin, TX
Anderson, James E. .... Anacortes, WA
Anderson, James E., Jr. .... Santa Ana, CA

Anderson, James E., P.S. ... Anacortes, WA
Anderson, James Emmett ... Richmond, VA
Anderson, James F. ... Lake Forest, CA
Anderson, James F. ... Spring Lake, NJ
Anderson, James F. ... Malvern, PA
Anderson, James G. ... Aurora, CO
Anderson, James G., III ... Beckley, WV
Anderson, James H. ... Montgomery, AL
Anderson, James H. ... Campbell, CA
Anderson, James H. ... Department of State, Office of the Legal Adviser, GV
Anderson, James H. ... Boston, MA
Anderson, James H. ... Omaha, NE
Anderson, James H. ... Waldport, OR
Anderson, James H. ... Philadelphia, PA
Anderson, James H. ... Dallas, TX
Anderson, James Hurd ... Minneapolis, MN
Anderson, James, Jr. ... Houston, TX
Anderson, James L.
Commodity Futures Trading Commission, Division of Enforcement, GV
Anderson, James L. ... Bloomington, IL
Anderson, James L. ... Chicago, IL
Anderson, James L., Jr. ... Rockport, TX
Anderson, James Lee ... Fort Worth, TX
Anderson, James M. ... Colorado Springs, CO
Anderson, James M. ... Ridgeland, MS
Anderson, James M. ... Philadelphia, PA
Anderson, James M., III ... Atlanta, GA
Anderson, James M., III ... Richmond, VA
Anderson, James M., III, P.C. ... Atlanta, GA
Anderson, James O., Jr. ... Anderson, IN
Anderson, James P. ... Atlanta, GA
Anderson, James P. ... Mt. Vernon, IN
Anderson, James P., III ... Nashville, TN
Anderson, James P., Jr. ... Greenwood, SC
Anderson, James P., Jr. ... Chattanooga, TN
Anderson, James Patrick ... Melbourne, FL
Anderson, James R. ... Kansas City, MO
Anderson, James R. ... Concord, NH
Anderson, James R. ... Concord, NH
Anderson, James R. ... New York, NY
Anderson, James R. ... Sylva, NC
Anderson, James R. ... Richardson, TX
Anderson, James W. ... Tallahassee, FL
Anderson, James W. ... North Canton, OH
Anderson, James W. ... Pierre, SD
Anderson, Jan Rosker ... Hartford, CT
Anderson, Jan Slater ... Tulsa, OK
Anderson, Jan Walls ... Santa Ana, CA
Anderson, Jane ... West Palm Beach, FL
Anderson, Jane F. ... Chicago, IL
Anderson, Janet Buhrow ... St. Louis, MO
Anderson, Janet L. ... Vancouver, WA
Anderson, Janet M. ... Glen Allen, VA
Anderson, Janette ... Phoenix, AZ
Anderson, Janice Pickrell ... Norfolk, VA
Anderson, Jared L. ... Provo, UT
Anderson, Jarrett ... Austin, TX
Anderson, Jarrett S. ... Glendale, CA
Anderson, Jason E. ... Colorado Springs, CO
Anderson, Jason H. ... Newport Beach, CA
Anderson, Jason M. ... Medford, OR
Anderson, Jason, P.C. ... Colorado Springs, CO
Anderson, Jason W. ... Champaign, IL
Anderson, Jay A. ... Des Moines, IA
Anderson, Jay C. ... Plantation, FL
Anderson, Jean C.
Board of Governors Of The Federal Reserve System, Office of the General Counsel, GV
Anderson, Jean C. ... Bangor, ME
Anderson, Jeanine M. ... Denver, CO
Anderson, Jeanne A.
Department Of Veterans Affairs, Office of the General Counsel, GV
Anderson, Jeanne M. ... Stillwater, MN
Anderson, Jeanne M., & Associates, Ltd.
Stillwater, MN
Anderson, Jeanne Weston ... Athens, AL
Anderson, Jed P. ... Houston, TX
Anderson, Jeff A. ... Omaha, NE
Anderson, Jeff M. ... Lexington, SC
Anderson, Jeff W. ... Johnson City, TN
Anderson, Jeffrey C. ... Baltimore, MD
Anderson, Jeffrey C. ... Minneapolis, MN
Anderson, Jeffrey C., Law Offices of
San Antonio, TX
Anderson, Jeffrey K. ... Troy, NY
Anderson, Jeffrey L. ... Sacramento, CA
Anderson, Jeffrey O. ... Dallas, TX
Anderson, Jeffrey P. ... Minneapolis, MN
Anderson, Jeffrey R. ... St. Paul, MN
Anderson, Jeffrey R. ... Bartlesville, OK
Anderson, Jeffrey W. ... Chicago, IL
Anderson, Jeffry D. ... Lakota, ND
Anderson, Jennie L. ... San Francisco, CA
Anderson, Jennifer B. ... Phoenix, AZ
Anderson, Jennifer G. ... Ann Arbor, MI
Anderson, Jennifer K.
Mendota Heights, MN
Anderson, Jennifer K. ... Salt Lake City, UT
Anderson, Jennifer L. ... Miami, FL
Anderson, Jennifer L. ... New Orleans, LA
Anderson, Jennifer S. ... Costa Mesa, CA
Anderson, Jennifer Stine
Minneapolis, MN
Anderson, Jerome ... Bozeman, MT
Anderson, Jerome ... Helena, MT
Anderson, Jerome T. ... Mankato, MN
Anderson, Jerome W. ... Boston, MA
Anderson, Jerry ... Lexington, KY
Anderson, Jerry D. ... Geneva, NE
Anderson, Jerry L. ... Des Moines, IA
Anderson, Jerry S. ... St. Paul, MN
Anderson, Jett B. ... Scottsdale, AZ
Anderson, Jette R. ... Ontario, CA
Anderson, Jill C. ... Chicago, IL
Anderson, Jill K. ... Collegeville, PA
Anderson, Jill Klamm ... Dallas, TX
Anderson, Jill Lynn ... Douglasville, GA
Anderson, Jill M. ... Philadelphia, PA
Anderson, Jill Pride ... Atlanta, GA
Anderson, Jim ... Nevada City, CA
Anderson, JoAnn L. ... Dallas, TX
Anderson, JoAnn M. Webb ... St. Louis, MO
Anderson, Jock O. ... Helena, MT
Anderson, Jodi M. ... Mount Dora, FL
Anderson, Jody N. ... Brogue, PA
Stewartstown, PA
York, PA
Anderson, Joe D. ... Dallas, TX
Anderson, Joe E. ... San Antonio, TX
Anderson, Joe R. ... Austin, TX
Anderson, Joel E. ... Columbia, MO
Anderson, John ... Canon City, CO
Anderson, John ... Mayfield, KY
Anderson, John A. ... Santa Ana, CA
Anderson, John A. ... Birmingham, MI
Anderson, John A. ... Rochester, NY
Anderson, John A. ... Portland, OR
Anderson, John A. ... Salt Lake City, UT
Anderson, John A., III ... Portland, ME
Anderson, John A., Jr. ... Portsmouth, NH
Anderson, John A., Jr. ... Woodbury, NY
Anderson, John A., Sr. ... Woodbury, NY
Anderson, John B. ... Sioux City, IA
Anderson, John B. ... Takoma Park, MD
Anderson, John B. ... Charlotte, NC
Anderson, John B. ... Salt Lake City, UT
Anderson, John Burton ... Salt Lake City, UT
Anderson, John C. ... Huntsville, AL
Anderson, John C. ... Department of the Army, Office of the Assistant Secretary of the Army (Manpower & Reserve Affairs), GV
Anderson, John C. ... Baton Rouge, LA
Metairie, LA
Anderson, John C., IV ... Crown Point, IN
Anderson, John D. ... Brainerd, MN
Anderson, John D. ... St. Louis, MO
Anderson, John E. ... Los Angeles, CA
Anderson, John E. ... Barbourville, KY
Anderson, John Edward ... Nashville, TN
Anderson, John F. ... Orange, CA
Anderson, John F. ... Alexandria, VA
Anderson, John F. ... Winchester, VA
Anderson, John H. ... Phoenix, AZ
Anderson, John H. ... San Clemente, CA
Anderson, John H. ... West Palm Beach, FL
Anderson, John H. ... Chicago, IL
Anderson, John H. ... Evergreen Park, IL
Anderson, John H. ... Hattiesburg, MS
Anderson, John H. ... Jersey City, NJ
Anderson, John H. ... Bellingham, WA
Anderson, John Hunter ... Winston-Salem, NC
Anderson, John Huske, II
Fayetteville, NC
Anderson, John, III ... Olathe, KS
Anderson, John, Jr. ... Overland Park, KS
Anderson, John K. ... Atlanta, GA
Anderson, John K. ... Baltimore, MD
Anderson, John K. (Mike) ... Leesville, LA
Anderson, John L. ... San Francisco, CA
Anderson, John Lyon ... Hillsboro, MO
Anderson, John M. ... Eureka, CA
Anderson, John M. ... Long Beach, CA
Anderson, John M. ... San Francisco, CA
Anderson, John M. ... Denver, CO
Anderson, John M. ... Minneapolis, MN
Anderson, John P. ... Wilmington, DE
Anderson, John P. ... Princeton, WV
Anderson, John P. ... Washburn, WI
Anderson, John R. ... Sacramento, CA
Anderson, John R. ... Pittsburgh, PA
Anderson, John R. ... Chattanooga, TN
Anderson, John R. ... Vernal, UT
Anderson, John S. ... Georgetown, MA
Anderson, John T. ... Long Beach, CA
Anderson, John T. ... Austin, TX
Anderson, John T. ... Salt Lake City, UT
Anderson, John V. ... Houston, TX
Anderson, John W. ... Honolulu, HI
Anderson, John W. ... Albuquerque, NM
Anderson, John W. ... New York, NY
Anderson, John W. ... Salt Lake City, UT
Anderson, John W. ... Richmond, VA
Anderson, John W., II ... Bethel, CT
Anderson, John W., Jr. ... Tulsa, OK
Anderson, John W., Jr., P.C. ... Tulsa, OK
Anderson, Johna G. ... Chicago, IL
Anderson & Johnson ... Marlin, TX
Anderson, Johnson, Lawrence, Butler & Bock ... Clinton, NC
Dunn, NC
Elizabethtown, NC
Fayetteville, NC
Laurinburg, NC
Lumberton, NC
Anderson, Jon ... Burlington, VT
Anderson, Jon A. ... Maryville, TN
Anderson, Jon C. ... Robinson, IL
Anderson, Jon D. ... Costa Mesa, CA
Anderson, Jon D. ... Milwaukee, WI
Anderson, Jon E. ... Madison, WI
Anderson, Jon G. ... Phoenix, AZ
Anderson, Jon H. ... Lakeland, FL
Anderson, Jon L. ... Lufkin, TX
Anderson, Jon M. ... Columbus, OH
Anderson, Jon M. ... Providence, RI
Anderson, Jon T. ... San Francisco, CA
Anderson, Jonathan J. ... Charleston, SC
Anderson, Jonathan M. ... New York, NY
Anderson, Jonathan R. ... Indianapolis, IN
Anderson, Jonathan S.R. ... Rocky Hill, CT
Anderson, Jonathan W.
Grand Rapids, MI
Anderson, Jonette S ... Houston, TX
Anderson, Joni M. ... Indianapolis, IN
Anderson & Jordan ... Columbia, SC
Anderson, Joseph F., Jr. ... Columbia, SC
Anderson, Joseph I. ... Bakersfield, CA
Anderson, Joseph L. ... Kernersville, NC
Anderson, Joseph L., and Associates, P.C.
Greensboro, NC
Kernersville, NC
Winston-Salem, NC
Anderson, Joseph Louis ... Salt Lake City, UT
Anderson, Joseph N. ... Cedartown, GA
Anderson, Joseph P., Jr. (Law Corporation)
Slidell, LA
Anderson, Joseph W. ... North Branch, MN
Anderson, Joy Anna ... Lexington, KY
Anderson, Joyce A. ... Las Cruces, NM
Anderson, Joyce B. ... Miami, FL
Anderson, Joyce Z. ... Dayton, OH
Anderson, Juan M. ... Washington, DC
Anderson, Judith ... Pittsburgh, PA
Anderson, Judith B. ... Walnut Creek, CA
Anderson, Judith D. ... Santa Ana, CA
Anderson, Judith L. ... Los Angeles, CA
Anderson, Judy M. ... Atlanta, GA
Anderson, Julia B. ... Atlanta, GA
Anderson, Julia G. ... Dallas, TX
Anderson, Julia Gille ... Paradise Valley, AZ
Anderson, Julian & Hull ... Boise, ID
Anderson, Juliann ... Riverside, CA
Anderson, Julie A. ... Wenatchee, WA
Anderson, Julie C. ... Houston, TX
Anderson, Julie Evans ... Denver, CO
Anderson, Julie Schlagel ... St. Paul, MN
Anderson, Julie Watson ... Emerald Isle, NC
Anderson, K. Allen ... Beverly Hills, CA
Anderson, K. Michele ... Denver, CO
Anderson, Kane & Tobiason ... Boise, ID
Anderson, Karen E. ... San Francisco, CA
Anderson, Karen Jean ... Charlottesville, VA
Anderson, Karen L. ... Kalamazoo, MI
Anderson, Karen M. ... Rockford, IL
Anderson, Karen P. ... Palo Alto, CA
Anderson, Karen vom Lehn ... Claremont, CA
Anderson, Karin J. ... Edwardsville, KS
Anderson, Karl B. ... Chicago, IL
Anderson, Karl C. ... Rutland, VT
Anderson, Karl M. ... Milwaukee, WI
Anderson, Karl V., Jr. ... Avoca, NY
Anderson & Karrenberg, P.C.
Salt Lake City, UT
Anderson, Katharine P., (Mrs.)
Scottsdale, AZ
Anderson, Katherine I. ... San Jose, CA
Anderson, Katherine Smith ... Dallas, TX
Anderson, Kathleen A. ... Aurora, IL
Anderson, Kathleen E. ... Pensacola, FL
Anderson, Kathleen M. ... Fort Wayne, IN
Anderson, Kathleen Stewart
San Francisco, CA
Anderson, Kathrin K. ... Milwaukee, WI
Anderson, Kathryn Conley
Tompkinsville, KY
Anderson, Kathryn M. ... Scottsdale, AZ
Anderson, Kathryn R. ... Madison, WI
Anderson, Kathryn Yost ... San Diego, CA
Anderson, Kathy Jane ... Orlando, FL
Anderson, Kathy Jane, P.A. ... Orlando, FL
Anderson, Kaye E. ... Waupaca, WI
Anderson, Keirsten G. ... Rock Island, IL
Anderson, Keith ... Denver, CO
Anderson, Keith A. ... Washington, DC
Anderson, Keith B. ... Huron, SD
Anderson, Keith R. ... Washington, DC
Chicago, IL
Anderson, Keith R. ... Easton, MD
Anderson, Keith W. ... Grand Rapids, MN
Anderson, Keith W. ... Lebanon, OH
Anderson, Kell E. ... New York, NY
Anderson, Kelley Heny ... Casper, WY
Anderson, Ken ... Huntsville, TX
Anderson, Kenneth B. ... New York, NY
Anderson, Kenneth C. ... Washington, DC
Anderson, Kenneth D. ... Houston, TX
Anderson, Kenneth E. ... Portland, OR
Anderson, Kenneth G. ... Santa Monica, CA
Anderson, Kenneth G. ... Jacksonville, FL
Anderson, Kenneth H. ... Boston, MA
Anderson, Kenneth L. ... Lewiston, ID
Anderson, Kenneth L. ... Highland, IN
Anderson, Kenneth L. ... Louisville, KY
Anderson, Kenneth M. ... Houston, TX
Anderson, Kenneth M. ... Seattle, WA
Anderson, Kenneth P. ... Plymouth, NH
Anderson, Kenneth V., Jr. ... Paducah, KY
Anderson, Kenneth W. ... Los Angeles, CA
Anderson, Kenneth W., Jr. ... Dallas, TX
Anderson, Kenneth W., Jr. ... San Antonio, TX
Anderson, Kent ... Honolulu, HI
Anderson, Kent A. ... La Grande, OR
Anderson, Kent, & Associates
Eugene, OR
Anderson, Kent D. ... Kingston, NY
Anderson, Kent J. ... Sarasota, FL
Anderson, Kermit B. ... Des Moines, IA
Anderson, Kerri L. ... Santa Ana, CA
Anderson, Kerry J. ... Denver, CO
Anderson, Kerry L. ... Irving, TX
Anderson, Kevin ... Venice, CA
Anderson, Kevin ... Port Orchard, WA
Anderson, Kevin D. ... Chicago, IL
Anderson, Kevin Egan
Salt Lake City, UT
Anderson, Kevin G. ... Portland, ME
Anderson, Kevin J. ... Anchorage, AK
Anderson, Kevin K. ... Harrisonville, MO
Anderson, Kevin L. ... San Jose, CA
Anderson, Kevin L. ... Durham, NC
Anderson, Kevin N. ... Las Vegas, NV
Salt Lake City, UT
Anderson, Kevin R. ... San Luis Obispo, CA
Anderson, Kevin R. ... Salt Lake City, UT
Anderson, Kevin S.
General Services Administration, GV
Anderson, Kevin S. ... Blue Bell, PA
Anderson Kill & Olick ... Chicago, IL
Washington, DC
Newark, NJ
New York, NY
Philadelphia, PA
Anderson, Kim A. ... Minneapolis, MN
Anderson, Kim Anglin ... Washington, DC
Anderson, Kim E. ... Atlanta, GA
Anderson, Kim R. ... San Diego, CA
Anderson, Kimball R. ... Chicago, IL
Anderson, Kimberley R. ... Seattle, WA
Anderson, Kimberly G. ... New Orleans, LA
Anderson, Kimberly Gay ... Torrance, CA
Anderson, Kimberly Price ... St. Paul, MN
Anderson, Kip Arlie ... Denver, CO
Anderson, Kirsten A. ... Palo Alto, CA
Anderson, Kirsten J. ... Albuquerque, NM
Anderson, Kirsten L. ... Los Angeles, CA
Anderson, K.L. ... Fort Pierce, FL
Indianapolis, IN
Anderson, Klein, Peterson, Swan and Bogle
Holdrege, NE
Anderson, Kline, Tyler & Lingo
Columbia, MO
Anderson, Knight S. ... Indianapolis, IN
Anderson, Krehbiel, McCreary & Bryan
Westlake Village, CA
Anderson & Kreiger ... Cambridge, MA
Anderson & Kriger ... La Mesa, CA
Newport Beach, CA
Ontario, CA
Riverside, CA
Temecula, CA
Anderson, Kristen ... Seattle, WA
Anderson, Kristen Ann ... Roseville, MN
Anderson, Kristen Noël ... Minneapolis, MN
Anderson, Kristian ... Des Moines, IA
Anderson, Kristina M. ... Aiken, SC
Anderson, Kristina M.L. ... Chicago, IL
Anderson, Kristine Eastman ... Longmont, CO
Anderson, Kristine Elaine ... Madison, WI
Anderson, Kristine L. ... Chicago, IL
Anderson, Kristopher L. ... Oak Brook, IL
Anderson, Kristy Kay ... Annapolis, MD
Anderson, Kurt D. ... Las Vegas, NV
Anderson, Kurt D. ... Elyria, OH
Anderson, Kurt E. ... Middletown, NJ
Anderson, Kurt M. ... Minneapolis, MN
Anderson, Kurt R. ... Philadelphia, PA
Anderson, Kurt R. ... Brookfield, WI
Anderson, Kyle S. ... Nashville, TN
Anderson, L. Carter ... Montrose, PA
Anderson, L. David ... Dallas, TX
Anderson, L. Errol ... Houston, TX
Anderson, L. Mark, IV ... Charlotte, NC
Anderson, L. Michael ... Tucson, AZ
Anderson, L. Robert ... Monticello, UT
Anderson, L. Sue ... Washington, DC
Anderson, La Verne E. ... Rockford, IL
Anderson, Lance H. ... Menlo Park, CA
Anderson Lang LLP ... New York, NY
Anderson, Lanie ... Farmington Hills, MI
Anderson, Lara L. ... Los Angeles, CA
Anderson, Larry A. ... Crosby, TX
Anderson, Larry B. ... Windsor, CT
Anderson, Larry C. ... Huntington Beach, CA
Anderson, Larry D. ... Department of Defense, Defense Legal Services Agency, GV
Anderson, Larry D. ... Atlanta, GA
Anderson, Larry E. ... Los Gatos, CA
Anderson, Larry J. ... Eugene, OR
Anderson, Larry K. ... Birmingham, AL
Anderson, Lars E. ... McLean, VA
Anderson Larson Hanson & Saunders, P.L.L.P. ... Willmar, MN
Anderson, Laura ... College Park, MD
Anderson, Laura J. ... Bremerton, WA
Anderson, Laura L. ... Melbourne, FL
Anderson, Laura Lee ... Billings, MT
Anderson, Laura Nigris ... Middletown, NJ
Anderson, Laura R. ... Cleveland, OH
Anderson, Lauren ... Louisville, KY
Anderson, Lauren ... New Orleans, LA
Anderson, Lauren W. ... Nashville, TN
Anderson, Laurence A. ... Minneapolis, MN
Anderson Law Center, P.S.C. ... Louisville, KY
Anderson Law Firm, A Professional Law Corporation ... Hammond, LA
Anderson Law Firm, P.A. ... Charleston, SC
Anderson Law Firm, The ... Rochester, NY
Anderson Law Firm, The, P.C. ... Cordova, TN
Anderson Law Office ... Grand Rapids, MN
Anderson Law Office ... Le Sueur, MN
Anderson Law Office ... Austin, TX
Anderson Law Offices ... Creve Coeur, IL
Anderson Law Offices ... Overland Park, KS
Anderson, Lawrence ... Great Falls, MT
Anderson, Lawrence C. ... Binghamton, NY
Anderson, Lawrence E.
Department of Commerce, Patent and Trademark Office, GV
Anderson, Lawrence John ... Rockville, MD
Anderson, Lawrence L. ... Spokane, WA
Anderson, Lawrence M. ... Coon Rapids, MN
Anderson, Lawrence O. ... Phoenix, AZ
Anderson, Lawrence R., Jr.
Baton Rouge, LA
Anderson, Lawrence S. ... Denver, CO
Anderson, Lawrence W., Jr. ... Austin, TX
Anderson, Layne L. ... Dallas, TX
Anderson, Lea E. ... Pittsburgh, PA

Anderson, Lee Berger
North Chevy Chase, MD
Anderson, Lee D. Mitchell, SD
Anderson, Lee D. Nashville, TN
Anderson, Leesa M. Lincoln, NE
Anderson, Leif K. Birmingham, MI
Anderson, Leighton M., Law Offices of
Los Angeles, CA
Anderson, Leighton M., Law Offices of
Santa Fe Springs, CA
Anderson, Leila D. Fort Lauderdale, FL
Anderson, Leland P. Golden, CO
Anderson, Lenal, Jr. Memphis, TN
Anderson, Leo A. Issaquah, WA
Anderson, Leon E., (Mrs.)
San Francisco, CA
Anderson, Leon L. San Jose, CA
Anderson, Leonard G. Richmond, VA
Anderson, Leonard R. Anchorage, AK
Anderson, LeRoy Los Angeles, CA
Anderson, Leslie B. Baldwin, NY
Anderson, Leslie G. Los Angeles, CA
Anderson, Leslie J. Minneapolis, MN
Anderson, Leslie Michael
Securities and Exchange Commission, Office of Freedom of Information and Privacy Act Operations, GV
Anderson, Levine & Lintel, L.L.P.
Dallas, TX
Anderson & Liechty, P.C. Billings, MT
Anderson, Linda Garden City, NY
Anderson, Linda Diane Los Angeles, CA
Anderson, Linda F. Philadelphia, PA
Anderson, Linda G. Livonia, MI
Anderson, Linda M.
Department of Justice, GV
Anderson, Linda M. Media, PA
Anderson, Linda Randle Jackson, MS
Anderson, Linwood Las Vegas, NV
Anderson, Lisa A. Monterey Park, CA
Anderson, Lisa A. Detroit, MI
Anderson, Lisa J. Hamden, CT
Anderson, Lisa K. Bloomfield, CT
Anderson, Lisa K. Farmington Hills, MI
Anderson, Lisa K. Austin, TX
Anderson, Lisa M. Hartford, CT
Anderson, Lisa M. Las Vegas, NV
Anderson, Lisa M. Manchester, NH
Anderson, Lisa M. Cleveland, OH
Anderson, Lise E. Dallas, TX
Anderson, Lloyd Canterbury, CT
Anderson, Lloyd C. Akron, OH
Anderson, Lloyd D. Phoenix, AZ
Anderson, Lloyd V. Stuart, FL
Anderson, L. N. Borger, TX
Anderson, Lois B. Stamford, CT
Anderson, Lorraine M. Nutley, NJ
Anderson, Louis C. Fort Lauderdale, FL
Anderson, Lowell Newport Beach, CA
Anderson, Lowery W. Tompkinsville, KY
Anderson, Luke Charlotte, NC
Anderson, Lula Jackson, OH
Anderson, Luther G. Atlantic City, NJ
Anderson, L. W. Dallas, TX
Anderson, Lydia Constance Frank
Wilmington, DE
Anderson, Lyle R. Monticello, UT
Anderson, Lynn M. Phoenix, AZ
Sun City, AZ
Anderson, Lynn M. Minneapolis, MN
Anderson, Lynne Anne Newark, NJ
Anderson, M. Ann Pilot Mountain, NC
Anderson, M. Anne Honolulu, HI
Anderson, M. Bruce Mercer Island, WA
Anderson, M. Carolina Lawton, OK
Anderson, M. Jean Washington, DC
Anderson, M. Kent Dallas, TX
Anderson, M. Lea
Environmental Protection Agency, Office of the General Counsel, GV
Anderson, M. Lucille Houston, TX
Anderson, M. Suzanne Northville, MI
Anderson, Malcolm Bradenton, FL
Anderson, Malcolm E. Chesterton, IN
Anderson, Marc A. San Francisco, CA
Anderson, Marci B. Leesburg, VA
Anderson, Margaret E. Houston, TX
Anderson, Margaret L. Santa Rosa, CA
Anderson, Margaret M. Chicago, IL
Anderson, Margaret M. Madison, WI
Anderson, Margaret R. Newport Beach, CA
Anderson, Marie V. Clarence, NY
Anderson, Marilyn E.
Federal Deposit Insurance Corporation, Professional Liability Section, GV
Anderson, Mark Pueblo, CO
Anderson, Mark Helena, MT
Anderson, Mark A. Escondido, CA
Anderson, Mark A. Springport, MI
Anderson, Mark A. Albert Lea, MN
Anderson, Mark A. Minneapolis, MN
Anderson, Mark A. Aberdeen, SD
Anderson, Mark Allan Fort Worth, TX
Anderson, Mark B. Cresco, IA
Anderson, Mark B. Tacoma, WA
Anderson, Mark D. Chicago, IL
Anderson, Mark E. Leland, IL
Ottawa, IL
Anderson, Mark E. Minneapolis, MN
Anderson, Mark E. Raleigh, NC
Anderson, Mark F. San Francisco, CA
Anderson, Mark F. Topeka, KS
Anderson, Mark F. Minneapolis, MN
Anderson, Mark F. Philadelphia, PA
Anderson, Mark G. Jefferson City, MO
Anderson, Mark H. Salt Lake City, UT
Anderson, Mark K. Chicago, IL
Anderson, Mark L. Salt Lake City, UT
Anderson, Mark Layton Salt Lake City, UT
Anderson, Mark Lloyd St. Paul, MN
Anderson, Mark M. Northbrook, IL
Anderson, Mark O. Minneapolis, MN
Anderson, Mark P. Hartford, CT
Anderson, Mark R. Las Vegas, NV
Anderson, Mark R. New York, NY
Anderson, Mark S. San Francisco, CA
Anderson, Mark S. Brookfield, IL
Anderson, Mark S. Chicago, IL
Anderson, Mark S. Minneapolis, MN
Anderson, Mark S. Somerville, NJ
Anderson, Mark S. Seattle, WA
Anderson, Mark V. Barrington, IL
Anderson, Marna L. Anoka, MN
Anderson, Martha A. Milwaukee, WI
Anderson, Martha D. Pontiac, MI
Anderson, Martha M. Buffalo, NY
Anderson, Martha O. San Diego, CA
Anderson, Martin San Rafael, CA
Anderson, Martin Honolulu, HI
Anderson, Martin G. Denver, CO
Anderson, Martin L. Sacramento, CA
Anderson, Martin R. Glendale, CA
Anderson, Martin R.
West Des Moines, IA
Anderson, Marty, (Ms.) Columbus, OH
Anderson, Marvin Great Falls, MT
Anderson, Marvin H. Annapolis, MD
Anderson, Marvin J. San Francisco, CA
Anderson, Marvin Keith San Francisco, CA
Anderson, Marvin R. St. Paul, MN
Anderson, Mary Beth West Hartford, CT
Anderson, Mary Cavins
San Francisco, CA
Anderson, Mary Ellen Phoenix, MD
Anderson, Mary F. Philadelphia, PA
Anderson, Mary H. Philadelphia, PA
Anderson, Mary Hoge Richmond, VA
Anderson, Mary Jeanne Baltimore, MD
Anderson, Mary Jo Ventura, CA
Anderson, Mary Jo Wilmington, DE
Anderson, Mary S. San Diego, CA
Anderson, Mary Sue Wausau, WI
Anderson, Mary V. Blue Bell, PA
Anderson, Mary-Margaret Oakland, CA
Anderson, Mason H. Shallotte, NC
Anderson & Mathers Williamsport, PA
Anderson, Matthew A. San Francisco, CA
Anderson, Matthew A. Anoka, MN
Anderson, Matthew L. St. Paul, MN
Anderson, Matthew L.
Salt Lake City, UT
Anderson, Matthew S. Santa Ana, CA
Anderson, Matthew S. Fort Worth, TX
Anderson, Maureen J. Hartford, CT
Anderson, McCoy & Orta, A Professional Corporation Oklahoma City, OK
Anderson, McGlade & Andrews, S.C.
Plymouth, WI
Anderson, McPharlin & Conners LLP
Los Angeles, CA
Riverside, CA
San Diego, CA
Santa Ana, CA
Anderson, Megan L. Minneapolis, MN
Anderson, Melissa Cornelius, NC
Anderson, Melissa A. Des Moines, IA
Anderson, Melissa N. San Antonio, TX
Anderson, Melissa P. Fort Lauderdale, FL
Anderson, Melissa Weets
Cedar Rapids, IA
Anderson, Melody G. Los Angeles, CA
Anderson, Mercedes A. Omaha, NE
Anderson, Merlaine Oklahoma City, OK
Anderson, Merlyn Slayton, MN
Anderson, Merrill
Department Of The Interior, Minerals Management Service, GV
Anderson, Merry C. Washington, DC
Anderson, Michael A. Atlanta, GA
Anderson, Michael A.
Oklahoma City, OK
Anderson, Michael A. Chattanooga, TN
Anderson, Michael Alan Birmingham, AL
Anderson, Michael B. Billings, MT
Anderson, Michael C. Medina, WA
Anderson, Michael D. Los Angeles, CA
Anderson, Michael Dean Boston, MA
Anderson, Michael E. Washington, DC
Anderson, Michael E. Fitchburg, MA
Anderson, Michael F. New York, NY
Anderson, Michael H. Los Angeles, CA
Anderson, Michael H. San Diego, CA
Anderson, Michael J. Palo Alto, CA
Anderson, Michael J. Sacramento, CA
Anderson, Michael J. South Bend, IN
Anderson, Michael J. New York, NY
Anderson, Michael J. Raleigh, NC
Rocky Mount, NC
Anderson, Michael J., P.C. South Bend, IN
Anderson, Michael P. Lima, OH
Anderson, Michael R. Wheaton, IL
Anderson, Michael S. Cleveland, OH
Anderson, Michael S. Salt Lake City, UT
Anderson, Michael S. Madison, WI
Anderson, Michael T. Los Angeles, CA
Anderson, Michael T. San Francisco, CA
Anderson, Michael W. Denver, CO
Cheyenne, WY
Anderson, Michel E. Miami, FL
Anderson, Michele C. Chicago, IL
Anderson, Michele L. Albany, NY
Anderson, Michelle K. Irving, TX
Anderson, Michelle L. Springfield, IL
Anderson, Miles B. Sag Harbor, NY
Anderson, Millard O., Jr. Dallas, TX
Anderson & Miller Springfield, MA
Anderson, Mims & Associates, P.C.
Corpus Christi, TX
Tyler, TX
Anderson, Monica Leo Austin, TX
Anderson, Morgan & Tjaden, P.A.
Sarasota, FL
Anderson, Murphy & Hopkins, L.L.P.
Little Rock, AR
Anderson, Murray E. Overland Park, KS
Anderson, Murray J. Tacoma, WA
Anderson, N. Calhoun, Jr. Savannah, GA
Anderson, N. Calhoun, Jr., P.C.
Savannah, GA
Anderson, Nanci R. Washington, DC
Anderson, Nancy San Antonio, TX
Anderson, Nancy D. Chicago, IL
Anderson, Nancy D. St. Louis, MO
Anderson, Nancy E. Louisville, KY
Anderson, Nancy E. St. Paul, MN
Anderson, Nancy J. Washington, DC
Anderson, Nancy J. Redmond, WA
Anderson, Nancy L. Seattle, WA
Anderson, Nancy Phillips Wheaton, IL
Anderson, Nancy Watkins Seattle, WA
Anderson, Natalie F. Atlanta, GA
Anderson, Natalie Simone
Fort Lauderdale, FL
Anderson, Neal Spring, TX
Anderson, Neal B. Houston, TX
Anderson, Neil D. Dallas, TX
Anderson, Neil O. J. Lake Zurich, IL
Anderson, Neil T. New York, NY
Anderson Nelson Hall Smith, P.A.
Idaho Falls, ID
Anderson & Nelson, P.C. Rock Island, IL
Davenport, IA
Anderson, Nicholas P. Missoula, MT
Anderson & Nichols Terre Haute, IN
Anderson, Nicole A. New York, NY
Anderson, Norbert E. Phoenix, AZ
Anderson & Norine Grantsburg, WI
Siren, WI
Anderson, Norman C. Madison, WI
Anderson, Norman E. Portland, OR
Anderson, Norman E., P.C. Portland, OR
Anderson, Norman G. Fargo, ND
Anderson, Norman Q. Columbus, OH
Anderson & Norton, LLP Aptos, CA
Anderson, O. Wade Austin, TX
Anderson, Odin P. Boston, MA
Anderson, Olen L. Ocean Springs, MS
Anderson, Olivia Vasquez Pasadena, CA
Anderson, Overton S., II Little Rock, AR
Anderson, Owen L. Norman, OK
Anderson, P. Andrew Langley, SC
Anderson, P. Christian
Salt Lake City, UT
Anderson, P. Hunter Cambridge, MN
Anderson, P. Richard, Jr. Covington, KY
Frankfort, KY
Lexington, KY
Louisville, KY
Cincinnati, OH
Nashville, TN
Anderson, Page M. Honolulu, HI
Anderson, Paige S. Washington, DC
Anderson, Pamela H. Fircrest, WA
Anderson, Pamela J. Riverside, CA
Anderson, Pamela J. Washington, DC
Anderson, Pamela J. Wellesley, MA
Anderson, Pamela Kay Ashville, NY
Anderson, Pamela M. Rock Island, IL
Anderson, Pamela S. Tulsa, OK
Anderson, Pamela W. Wheaton, IL
Anderson, Parkulo, Stansbury & Associates, L.C. Beckley, WV
Anderson, Patricia D. Hartford, CT
Anderson, Patricia E. Los Angeles, CA
Anderson, Patricia Fields Miami, FL
St. Petersburg, FL
Anderson, Patrick B. Winfield, WV
Anderson, Patrick J. Athens, AL
Anderson, Patrick J. Sioux Falls, SD
Anderson, Patrick J. Hartford, WI
Anderson, Patrick J., P.C. Sioux Falls, SD
Anderson, Patrick L. Salt Lake City, UT
Anderson, Patrick Michael
Anchorage, AK
Anderson, Patrick N. Alexandria, VA
Anderson, Paul A. Providence, RI
Anderson, Paul A. Stevens Point, WI
Anderson, Paul B. Baltimore, MD
Anderson, Paul B. Seattle, WA
Anderson, Paul C. Oakland, CA
Anderson, Paul D. Minneapolis, MN
Anderson, Paul E. Waco, TX
Anderson, Paul E., Jr. Houston, TX
Anderson, Paul G. Colorado Springs, CO
Anderson, Paul H. Atlanta, GA
Anderson, Paul H. St. Paul, MN
Anderson, Paul H. Richmond, VA
Anderson, Paul H., Jr. Atlanta, GA
Anderson, Paul J. Reno, NV
Anderson, Paul L. Seattle, WA
Anderson, Paul L., P.L.L.C. Seattle, WA
Anderson, Paul M. Dripping Springs, TX
Anderson, Paul S. Chicago, IL
Anderson, Paul W. Minneapolis, MN
Anderson, Paula Haddock Dallas, TX
Anderson, Paula M. New Haven, CT
Anderson, Peder A. Department of Justice, Immigration and Naturalization Service, GV
Anderson, Peer L. Tulsa, OK
Anderson, Peggy J. Denver, CO
Anderson, Pellie J. San Rafael, CA
Anderson, Pelzer & Hart Estherville, IA
Ringsted, IA
Anderson & Pendleton Alexandria, VA
Anderson & Pentland Worcester, MA
Anderson, Percy Los Angeles, CA
Anderson, Perry L. Newtown Square, PA
Anderson, Peter A. Norwich, CT
Anderson, Peter A., Law Offices of
Bangor, ME
Anderson, Peter C. Los Angeles, CA
Anderson, Peter C. Charlotte, NC
Anderson, Peter D. King City, CA
Anderson, Peter D. Manchester, NH
Anderson, Peter F., Jr. Bronx, NY
Anderson, Peter G. Stowe, VT
Anderson, Peter H. Dallas, TX
Anderson, Peter J. Atlanta, GA
Anderson, Peter J., Law Offices of
Santa Monica, CA
Anderson, Peter M. Washington, DC
Anderson, Peter M. Seattle, WA
Anderson, Peter Wolfskill
Los Angeles, CA
Anderson, Philip J. Mount Clemens, MI
Anderson, Philip J. Las Vegas, NV
Anderson, Philip R. Bend, OR
Anderson, Philip S. Little Rock, AR
Anderson, Philip S. Fort Lauderdale, FL
Stuart, FL
Anderson, Philip Scott Asheville, NC
Anderson, Philip W. Oklahoma City, OK
Anderson, Phillip D.
Palm Beach Gardens, FL
Anderson, Phillip R. Kansas City, MO
Anderson, Phillip V. Roanoke, VA
Anderson, Phillipa L.
Department Of Veterans Affairs, Office of the General Counsel, GV
Anderson, Phyllis R.
Environmental Protection Agency, Program Office Attorneys, GV
Anderson & Preuss, A Ptnrshp. incl. Prof. Corps. St. Louis, MO
Anderson & Quinn Washington, DC
Rockville, MD
Upper Marlboro, MD
Anderson, R. Bruce Naples, FL
Anderson, R. Carl Concord, NH
Anderson, R. Christopher
Charleston, WV
Anderson, R. Craig Fairfax, VA
Anderson, R. Jerome Washington, DC
Anderson, R. John Chicago, IL
Anderson, R. Lanier, III Macon, GA
Anderson, R. Lars Atlanta, GA
Anderson, R. Michael Austin, TX
Anderson, R. Nicolas Monroe, LA
Anderson, R. Patrick Enid, OK
Anderson, R. Scott Decatur, AL
Anderson, R. Scott Dallas, TX
Anderson, R. Steven New York, NY
Anderson, R. Valjon Elm Grove, WI
Hartland, WI
Anderson, R. Wayne Oklahoma City, OK
Anderson, Rachel R. Chippewa Falls, WI
Anderson, Rachelle E. Spokane, WA
Anderson, Rae Anne Clarkston, MI
Anderson, Rae L. Sacramento, CA
Anderson, Ralph K., III Columbia, SC
Anderson, Ralph K., Jr. Florence, SC
Anderson, Ralph M., Jr. Tekamah, NE
Anderson, Ralph O. Miami, FL
Anderson, Ralph W. Seattle, WA
Anderson, Randal A., Jr. Springboro, OH
Anderson, Randall K. New York, NY
Anderson, Randy S. Boise, ID
Anderson, Ray D. Brownfield, TX
Anderson, Ray M. Arlington, VA
Anderson, Raymond A. Jamestown, NY
Anderson, Raymond D. Columbus, OH
Anderson, Raymond D. Texarkana, TX
Anderson, Rebecca Bemidji, MN
Anderson, Reed D. Pikeville, KY
Anderson, Reuben V. Jackson, MS
Anderson, Rex C. Davison, MI
Anderson, Rex C., & Associates, P.C.
Davison, MI
Anderson, Reyburn U. Dallas, TX
Anderson, Rhonda M. Philadelphia, PA
Anderson, Richard Camp Verde, AZ
Anderson, Richard A. Traverse City, MI
Anderson, Richard A. Dallas, TX
Anderson, Richard A., P.C.
Traverse City, MI
Anderson, Richard B. Chester, VT
Anderson, Richard Brian Minneapolis, MN
Anderson, Richard C. Osterville, MA
Anderson, Richard C. Kearney, NE
Anderson, Richard C. Valatie, NY
Anderson, Richard C. E. Bristol, RI
Anderson, Richard D.
Ponte Vedra Beach, FL
Anderson, Richard D. Topeka, KS
Anderson, Richard D.
Greenwell Springs, LA
Anderson, Richard D. St. Paul, MN
Anderson, Richard E. Moline, IL
Anderson, Richard E. Merrillville, IN
Anderson, Richard E. New Orleans, LA
Anderson, Richard E. Houston, TX
Anderson, Richard Ernest Dallas, TX
Anderson, Richard F. Rochester, NY
Anderson, Richard F., Jr. Clifton Park, NY
Anderson, Richard G. Upland, CA
Anderson, Richard G. Lexington, VA
Anderson, Richard H. Chicago, IL
Anderson, Richard H. Chicago, IL
Anderson, Richard H. Media, PA
Anderson, Richard J. Springport, MI
Anderson, Richard J. Minneapolis, MN
Anderson, Richard J. New York, NY

Anderson, Richard J., III ......Brookfield, WI
Anderson, Richard J.T. ......Boise, ID
Anderson, Richard K. ......Dallas, TX
Anderson, Richard L. ......Kimberling City, MO
Anderson, Richard L. ......Omaha, NE
Anderson, Richard L. ......Houston, TX
Anderson, Richard Lee ......Charlotte, NC
Anderson, Richard M. ......Marshall, TX
Anderson, Richard P. ......Fargo, ND
Anderson, Richard R. ......Williamsville, NY
Anderson, Richard T. ......Clarinda, IA
Anderson, Richard T., Jr. ......Beaverton, OR
Anderson, Richard T., (P.C.)
Riverside, CA
Anderson, Richard V. ......Lynchburg, VA
Anderson, Richard W. ......Billings, MT
Anderson, Richard W. ......New York, NY
Anderson, Richard W. ......Oklahoma City, OK
Anderson, Richard W. ......Newport, RI
Anderson, Rickie L. ......Barneveld, WI
Anderson, Rob R. ......Charleston, SC
Anderson, Robert ......San Diego, CA
Anderson, Robert A. ......Boise, ID
Anderson, Robert A. ......Indianapolis, IN
Anderson, Robert A. ......Nashville, TN
Anderson, Robert A. ......Longview, TX
Anderson, Robert A. ......San Antonio, TX
Anderson, Robert A., Jr. ......Covington, LA
Anderson, Robert B. ......Palo Alto, CA
Anderson, Robert B. ......Wilmington, DE
Anderson, Robert B. ......Pierre, SD
Anderson, Robert C. ......Aptos, CA
Anderson, Robert C. ......Sacramento, CA
Anderson, Robert C. ......Venice, FL
Anderson, Robert C. ......Marquette, MI
Anderson, Robert C. ......Pontiac, MI
Anderson, Robert C. ......St. Louis, MO
Anderson, Robert C. ......Carson City, NV
Reno, NV
Anderson, Robert C. ......Ironton, OH
Anderson, Robert C. ......Nashville, TN
Anderson, Robert C., P.C. ......Marquette, MI
Anderson, Robert D. ......Phoenix, AZ
Anderson, Robert D. ......Phoenix, AZ
Anderson, Robert D. ......Agoura Hills, CA
Anderson, Robert D. ......Hillsboro, OR
Anderson, Robert E.
Securities and Exchange Commission,
Division of Enforcement, GV
Anderson, Robert E. ......New York, NY
Anderson, Robert E. ......Fairfax, VA
Anderson, Robert E. ......Spokane, WA
Anderson, Robert E., Jr. ......Danvers, MA
Anderson, Robert E., Jr. ......Trenton, NJ
Anderson, Robert F. ......Columbia, SC
Anderson, Robert G. ......Phoenix, AZ
Anderson, Robert G. ......El Cajon, CA
Anderson, Robert G., P.C. ......Phoenix, AZ
Anderson, Robert H. ......Oklahoma City, OK
Anderson, Robert H. ......Roseburg, OR
Anderson, Robert H. ......Burlington, VT
Colchester, VT
Anderson, Robert H., III ......Richmond, VA
Anderson, Robert J. ......La Habra, CA
Anderson, Robert J. ......Wheaton, IL
Anderson, Robert J. ......New York, NY
Anderson, Robert K. ......Wichita, KS
Anderson, Robert K. ......Farmington Hills, MI
Anderson, Robert L. ......Lodi, CA
Anderson, Robert L. ......Santa Rosa, CA
Anderson, Robert L. ......Walnut Creek, CA
Anderson, Robert L. ......Middleboro, MA
Anderson, Robert L. ......Medford, OR
Anderson, Robert L. ......Renton, WA
Anderson, Robert M.
Department of Commerce,
Patent and Trademark Office, GV
Anderson, Robert M. ......Salt Lake City, UT
Anderson, Robert O. ......Riverton, WY
Anderson, Robert P. ......Berkeley, CA
Anderson, Robert P. ......Overland Park, KS
Anderson, Robert P. ......Farmington Hills, MI
Anderson, Robert P., Jr.
New London, CT
Anderson, Robert, P.C. ......Riverton, WY
Anderson, Robert R. ......Scottsdale, AZ
Anderson, Robert R. ......Chicago, IL
Anderson, Robert S. ......Boulder, CO
Anderson, Robert T. ......Tempe, AZ
Anderson, Robert T. ......Lafayette, CA
Anderson, Robert T. ......Melbourne, FL
Anderson, Robert T. ......Orlando, FL
Anderson, Robert T. ......Seattle, WA
Anderson, Robert W. ......Westfield, NJ
Anderson, Roberta D. ......Pittsburgh, PA
Anderson, Roberta M. ......Mason City, IA
Anderson Roberts and Porth ......Burlington, IA
Anderson, Robin A. ......Lake Charles, LA
Anderson, Robin Adams ......Raleigh, NC
Anderson, Robin K. ......Pueblo, CO
Anderson, Rod ......Tampa, FL
Anderson, Roderick B. ......Liberty Corner, NJ
Anderson, Rodney D. ......Minneapolis, MN
Rochester, MN
Anderson, Rodney M. ......Dallas, TX
Anderson, Rodney W. ......Columbus, OH
Anderson, Rodney W. ......Bryan, TX
Anderson, Rodrick E. ......New Orleans, LA
Anderson, Roger D. ......Wilmington, DE
Anderson, Roger D. ......Grand Rapids, MI
Anderson, Roger F. ......Tigard, OR
Anderson, Roger H. ......Columbus, GA
Anderson, Roger H. ......Ludington, MI
Anderson, Roger L. ......New York, NY
Anderson, Roger W. ......Tyler, TX
Anderson, Roland A. ......Chevy Chase, MD
Anderson, Roland C., (P.C.) ......Dallas, TX
Anderson, Rolf L. ......Portland, OR

Anderson, Ronald C. ......Willmar, MN
Anderson, Ronald C. ......Ambler, PA
Anderson, Ronald E. ......Bremerton, WA
Anderson, Ronald L. ......Des Moines, IA
Anderson, Ronald L. ......St. Paul, MN
Anderson, Ronald M. ......Bellevue, WA
Anderson, Ronald M., Law Offices of
Bellevue, WA
Anderson, Ronald P. ......Portland, OR
Anderson, Ronald T.
Steamboat Springs, CO
Anderson, Ronald W. ......Pittsburgh, PA
Anderson, Ronelle ......Minneapolis, MN
Anderson, Ross A. ......Milwaukee, WI
Anderson, Ross T. ......East St. Louis, IL
Anderson, Rossi & Davis ......Boston, MA
Anderson & Rottenberg, P.C.
Hackensack, NJ
New York, NY
Anderson, Roy David ......East St. Louis, IL
Anderson, Roy E. ......Carmel, CA
Anderson, Roy H. ......Springfield, MA
Anderson, Roy I. ......Blair, NE
Anderson, Roy L. ......Los Angeles, CA
Anderson, Roy L. ......Honolulu, HI
Anderson, Roy R. ......Dallas, TX
Anderson, Roy William, Jr. ......Baltimore, MD
Anderson, Rozlyn L. ......New York, NY
Anderson, Rudd & Donahue
Cumberland, MD
Anderson, Rudolph J., Jr. ......Vero Beach, FL
Anderson & Rush, P.A. ......Orlando, FL
Anderson, Russ B. ......Emporia, KS
Anderson, Russell A. ......Crookston, MN
Anderson, Russell C. ......Pontiac, MI
Anderson, Russell D. ......Rockford, IL
Anderson, Russell L. ......Tulsa, OK
Anderson, Russell R. ......El Centro, CA
Anderson, Russell W., Jr. ......Worcester, MA
Anderson, Ruth E. ......Austin, TX
Anderson & Rutherford, L.L.P. ......Raleigh, NC
Anderson, Ryan G. ......San Antonio, TX
Anderson, S. Denise ......Birmingham, AL
Anderson, S. Jane ......Wheeling, WV
Anderson, S. Newton ......Memphis, TN
Anderson St. Denis & Glenn
Fort Lauderdale, FL
Jacksonville, FL
Anderson & Salisbury ......Los Angeles, CA
Pasadena, CA
Anderson, Sally E. ......Madison, WI
Anderson, Sam J. ......Saratoga, CA
Anderson, Sam Jack ......Morristown, TN
Anderson, Sam L., Sr.
Hot Springs National Park, AR
Anderson, Samuel A. ......Crestview, FL
Anderson, Samuel C. ......Waterloo, IA
Anderson, Samuel E.L. ......Jackson, MS
Anderson, Samuel L. ......Bellevue, WA
Anderson, Samuel Paul, Jr. ......Macon, GA
Anderson, Samuel R. ......Chattanooga, TN
Anderson, Sandra J. ......Columbus, OH
Anderson, Sandra Jones ......Los Angeles, CA
Anderson, Sandra McLean ......Boca Raton, FL
Anderson, Sara J. ......Houston, TX
Anderson, Sara Kathryn ......Las Vegas, NV
Anderson, Sarah L. ......Austin, TX
Anderson, Sarah M. ......St. Paul, MN
Anderson, Sarah W. ......Nashville, TN
Anderson, Schmidt & Rivera, P.C.
St. Louis, MO
Anderson & Schneider ......Balsam Lake, WI
Anderson, Scot W. ......Denver, CO
Anderson, Scott ......Berkeley, CA
Anderson, Scott ......Washington, DC
Anderson, Scott ......Sarasota, FL
Anderson, Scott ......Columbia Falls, MT
Anderson, Scott Bradley ......Sioux Falls, SD
Anderson, Scott D. ......Milwaukee, WI
Anderson, Scott H. ......Philadelphia, PA
Anderson, Scott, Jr. ......Champaign, IL
Anderson, Scott L. ......Brooklyn Park, MN
Anderson, Scott L. ......Minneapolis, MN
Anderson, Scott M. ......Round Rock, TX
Anderson, Scott M., (P.A.) ......Greenville, SC
Anderson, Scott R. ......Chicago, IL
Anderson, Scott T. ......Minneapolis, MN
Anderson, Scott W. ......Des Moines, IA
Anderson, Scyld D. ......Columbus, OH
Anderson, Sean ......New York, NY
Anderson, Sean G. ......Merritt Island, FL
Anderson, Sean L. ......Las Vegas, NV
Anderson, Sean M. ......Chicago, IL
Anderson & Sellers, Chartered
Pensacola, FL
Anderson, Seneca B. ......West Falmouth, MA
Anderson, Seth Marshall ......Fort Worth, TX
Anderson, Shane H. ......Minneapolis, MN
Anderson, Shannon, O'Brien, Rice & Bertz
Plover, WI
Stevens Point, WI
Anderson, Shannon Whitcomb ......Naples, FL
Anderson, Sharon K. ......Cordova, TN
Anderson, Sharon L. ......Martinez, CA
Anderson, Sharon M. ......Great Falls, MT
Anderson, Shawn ......New York, NY
Anderson, Sheila M. ......Department of State,
Foreign Service Officers (Overseas), GV
Anderson, Sheri M. ......San Francisco, CA
Anderson, Sherri M. ......Seattle, WA
Anderson, Sherwood L., III ......Bristol, CT
Anderson, Sheryl L. ......Denver, CO
Anderson, Sidney A. ......Walla Walla, WA
Anderson, Sidney L. ......Tulsa, OK
Anderson, Smith, Null, Stofer & Murphree,
L.L.P. ......Victoria, TX
Anderson, Solette Tiscornia ......Richmond, VA
Anderson, Sonna Marie ......Bismarck, ND

Anderson, Stacy Patton ......New Orleans, LA
Anderson, Stanley E., Jr.
Thousand Oaks, CA
Anderson, Stanley E., Jr.
Mount Kisco, NY
Anderson, Stanley H. ......Upland, CA
Anderson, Stanley L. ......Tishomingo, OK
Anderson, Stanley V. ......Santa Barbara, CA
Anderson, Stanton D. ......Washington, DC
Anderson, Stella Miles ......Chattanooga, TN
Anderson, Stephanie ......Portland, ME
Anderson, Stephen ......Atlanta, GA
Anderson, Stephen A. ......Gulfport, MS
Anderson, Stephen Carr ......Boston, MA
Anderson, Stephen D. ......Cambridge, MA
Anderson, Stephen E. ......Irvine, CA
Anderson, Stephen G. ......Worcester, MA
Anderson, Stephen G. ......Knoxville, TN
Anderson, Stephen J. ......New Britain, CT
Anderson, Stephen J. ......Atlanta, GA
Anderson, Stephen J. ......Dallas, TX
Anderson, Stephen Kreisel
Walnut Creek, CA
Anderson, Stephen Lawler ......Memphis, TN
Anderson, Stephen P. ......Santa Maria, CA
Anderson, Stephen R. ......Worcester, MA
Anderson, Stephen S. (Todd), Jr.
Washington, DC
Anderson, Stephen W. ......Phoenix, AZ
Anderson, Stephen W. ......Jackson, CA
Anderson, Steve ......Salem, OR
Anderson, Steve ......Nashville, TN
Anderson, Steven ......Minneapolis, MN
Anderson, Steven A. ......South Pasadena, CA
Anderson, Steven A. ......Tampa, FL
Anderson, Steven A. ......Minneapolis, MN
Princeton, MN
Anderson, Steven A.
New Philadelphia, OH
Anderson, Steven B. ......St. Paul, MN
Anderson, Steven C. ......Iowa City, IA
Anderson, Steven D. ......Burlingame, CA
Anderson, Steven D. ......New Britain, CT
Anderson, Steven E. ......Nashville, TN
Anderson, Steven E. ......El Paso, TX
Anderson, Steven G. ......Northbrook, IL
Anderson, Steven L. ......Pasadena, CA
Anderson, Steven M. ......Los Angeles, CA
Anderson, Steven M. ......Riverside, CA
Anderson, Steven M. ......Wausau, WI
Anderson, Steven P. ......Ladysmith, WI
Anderson, Steven R. ......Denver, CO
Anderson, Steven R. ......Overland Park, KS
Anderson, Steven R. ......Minneapolis, MN
Anderson, Steven R. ......Columbia, SC
Anderson, Steven S. ......Hackensack, NJ
New York, NY
Anderson, Steven S. ......Seattle, WA
Anderson, Steven T. ......Grand Rapids, MI
Anderson, Steven W. ......San Francisco, CA
Anderson & Stevens, P.A.
Jacksonville, FL
Anderson, Storm P. ......San Diego, CA
Anderson & Strickland ......Fayetteville, NC
Anderson, Stuart G., Jr. ......Greenville, SC
Anderson, Stull & Associates, P.L.L.C
Lansing, MI
Anderson & Sulau ......Cincinnati, OH
Anderson & Sullivan ......Blue Bell, PA
Anderson & Sundell ......Maryville, MO
Anderson, Sunya
Department of Labor, GV
Anderson, Susan ......Marietta, GA
Anderson, Susan A. ......Kansas City, MO
Anderson, Susan A. ......Milwaukee, WI
Anderson, Susan Andersen ......Omaha, NE
Anderson, Susan B. ......Montgomery, AL
Anderson, Susan Collins ......Springfield, OH
Anderson, Susan D. ......Framingham, MA
Anderson, Susan E. ......Portland, OR
Anderson, Susan Hoscheit ......Baltimore, MD
Anderson, Susan K. ......St. Paul, MN
Anderson, Susan K. ......New York, NY
Anderson, Susan L. ......Minneapolis, MN
Anderson, Susan L. ......Philadelphia, PA
Anderson, Susan R. ......Alexandria, MN
Anderson, Suuzen Ty ......Spring Valley, CA
Anderson, Suzanne D. ......Portland, OR
Anderson, Sylvester ......Houston, TX
Anderson, Sylvia E. ......Atlanta, GA
Anderson, T. Mark ......Corpus Christi, TX
Anderson, T. Mark, P.C. ......Corpus Christi, TX
Anderson, T. Reid
La Canada Flintridge, CA
Anderson, T. Valfrid ......Marina Del Rey, CA
Anderson, Tami L. ......Claremore, OK
Anderson, Tania S. ......Syracuse, NY
Anderson, Tara D. ......Columbia, SC
Anderson & Tauber, P.C. ......Merrillville, IN
Anderson, Taylor L. ......Santa Barbara, CA
Anderson, Ted M. ......Corpus Christi, TX
Anderson, Terence J. ......Coral Gables, FL
Anderson, Terrell J.
Jacksonville Beach, FL
Anderson, Terry B. ......Boise, ID
Anderson, Terry D. ......Rockford, IL
Anderson, Terry J. ......Hawthorne, CA
Anderson, Terry L. ......Santa Barbara, CA
Anderson, Terry M. ......Omaha, NE
Anderson, Terry R. ......Frankfort, KY
Anderson, Theodore A. ......Brea, CA
Anderson, Theodore C. ......Lake Forest, CA
Anderson, Theodore C., III ......Dallas, TX
Anderson, Theodore W. ......Chicago, IL
Anderson & Thomas ......Chicago, IL
Skokie, IL
Anderson, Thomas ......Grand Island, NE
Anderson, Thomas B. ......Pittsburgh, PA

Anderson, Thomas B., Jr. ......Raleigh, NC
Anderson, Thomas C. ......Pascagoula, MS
Anderson, Thomas D. ......Ashtabula, OH
Anderson, Thomas D. ......Houston, TX
Anderson, Thomas D. ......Burlington, VT
Anderson, Thomas E. ......Washington, DC
Anderson, Thomas E. ......Birmingham, MI
Anderson, Thomas G. ......Argonne, IL
Anderson, Thomas H. ......McMinnville, OR
Anderson, Thomas H. ......Portland, OR
Anderson, Thomas K. ......Atlanta, GA
Anderson, Thomas L. ......Modesto, CA
Anderson, Thomas L. ......Kalamazoo, MI
Anderson, Thomas M. ......Susanville, CA
Anderson, Thomas M. ......Lansing, MI
Anderson, Thomas M. ......El Campo, TX
Anderson, Thomas O. ......New Britain, CT
Anderson, Thomas P. ......Eagle River, AK
Anderson, Thomas P. ......Buies Creek, NC
Anderson, Thomas R. ......Rochester, NY
Anderson, Thomas R. ......Columbus, OH
Anderson, Thomas T. ......Indio, CA
Anderson, Thomas T., P.C. ......Indio, CA
Palm Springs, CA
Anderson, Thomas W. ......Yuma, AZ
Anderson, Thomas W. ......Minneapolis, MN
Anderson, Thomas W.
Pilot Mountain, NC
Anderson, Thomas W. ......Cleveland, OH
Anderson, Thomas W., Jr. ......Kenosha, WI
Anderson, Thomas W., P.C., The Law Office
of ......Yuma, AZ
Anderson, Thomas W., Sr. ......Kenosha, WI
Anderson, Thornton P. ......Edina, MN
Anderson, Thorwald H. ......Minneapolis, MN
Anderson, Tim G. ......Albuquerque, NM
Anderson, Timothy B. ......Harrisburg, PA
Anderson, Timothy B. ......Harrisburg, PA
Anderson, Timothy B. ......St. George, UT
Anderson, Timothy B. ......Appleton, WI
Anderson, Timothy D. ......Kennewick, WA
Anderson, Timothy D. ......Chippewa Falls, WI
Anderson, Timothy G. ......Tampa, FL
Anderson, Timothy G., P.A.
Brooksville, FL
Tampa, FL
Zephyrhills, FL
Anderson, Timothy K.
North Palm Beach, FL
Anderson, Timothy K. ......Pipestone, MN
Anderson, Timothy M. ......Clarion, IA
Forest City, IA
Anderson, Timothy M. ......Garner, IA
Anderson, Timothy R. ......Minneapolis, MN
Anderson, Timothy R. ......St. Louis, MO
Anderson, Timothy W. ......Jefferson City, MO
Anderson, Tobyn J. ......United States Senate,
Senatorial Assistants, GV
Anderson, Todd David ......Norfolk, VA
Anderson, Todd H. ......Grantsburg, WI
Anderson, Todd S. ......Boston, MA
Anderson, Todd W. ......Cedar Rapids, IA
Anderson, Toni-Renee ......Ebensburg, PA
Anderson, Tracey A. ......South Bend, IN
Anderson, Tracy E. ......Kalona, IA
Anderson, Tracy Houff ......Chicago, IL
Anderson, Trent G., Jr. ......Los Angeles, CA
Anderson, Troy Marie ......Reno, NV
Anderson, Troy S. ......Seattle, WA
Anderson, Valerie J. ......New York, NY
Anderson, Velda B. ......Lincoln, NE
Anderson, Veretta L. ......Dallas, TX
Anderson, Vic, Jr. ......Fort Worth, TX
Anderson, Vicki L. ......Indianapolis, IN
Anderson, Victor ......Excelsior, MN
Anderson, Victor Albert, Jr. ......Raleigh, NC
Anderson, Victor, III ......Santa Monica, CA
Anderson, Victor M. ......San Francisco, CA
Anderson, Victoria L. ......Hollywood, CA
Anderson, Vincent P. ......Media, PA
Anderson, Virgil P. ......Sacramento, CA
Anderson, Virgil R. ......Detroit, MI
Anderson, Virgil V., Jr. ......Springfield, MO
Anderson, W. Curtis ......Marietta, GA
Anderson, W. Mack ......Ironton, OH
Anderson, W. Mark ......Montgomery, AL
Anderson, W. Mark, III ......Montgomery, AL
Anderson, W. Mark, III, P.C.
Montgomery, AL
Anderson, W. Richard ......Yanceyville, NC
Anderson, W. Tinley, III ......Atlanta, GA
Anderson, W. William ......York, PA
Anderson, Wade Gunnar ......Atlanta, GA
Anderson, Wade T. ......Minneapolis, MN
Anderson and Walker ......Moscow, ID
Anderson, Walker E. ......Salt Lake City, UT
Anderson, Walker & Reichert, LLP
Macon, GA
Anderson, Wallace B., Jr.
St. Petersburg, FL
Anderson, Wallace Carroll
Olive Branch, MS
Anderson, Walter C., (A Professional
Association) ......Salisbury, MD
Anderson, Walter D. ......Crestview, FL
Anderson, Walter N. ......Manhattan Beach, CA
Anderson, Ward R. ......Eagan, MN
Anderson, Warren H. ......Grand Rapids, MN
Anderson, Warren K., Jr.
Jacksonville Beach, FL
Anderson, Warren M. ......Binghamton, NY
Anderson, Warren R. ......Austin, TX
Anderson, Warrenn C. ......Morris, MN
Anderson, Wayne D. ......Stillwater, MN
Anderson, Wayne J. ......Bismarck, ND
Anderson, Wayne K. ......Houston, TX
Anderson, Wayne Mccallum ......Sausalito, CA
Anderson, Wayne T. ......Fargo, ND

Anderson, Wells H. ....Minneapolis, MN
Anderson, Wendell R. ....Minneapolis, MN
Anderson, Wendy E. ....Washington, DC
Anderson, Wendy L. ....Sacramento, CA
Anderson, Wendy R. ....Orlando, FL
Anderson & Werner ....Des Moines, IA
Anderson & Wichman ....Hays, KS
Anderson, Wilbert C. ....Seattle, WA
Anderson, Wilbert G. ....Phoenix, AZ
Anderson, Wilbur W. ....Jacksonville, FL
Anderson, Will, O'Donnell & Kitzler
Mansfield, OH
Anderson, William A. ....Beverly Hills, CA
Anderson, William A. ......Westlake Village, CA
Anderson, William A., A Professional Law Corporation ....Beverly Hills, CA
Anderson, William A., II ......Washington, DC
Anderson, William B. ....La Jolla, CA
Anderson, William B. ....Chicago, IL
Anderson, William B. ....Kansas City, MO
Anderson, William Brantley ......Shreveport, LA
Anderson, William C. ....Palo Alto, CA
Anderson, William C. ....Plainville, CT
Anderson, William C. ....St. Louis, MO
Anderson, William C. ....Tulsa, OK
Anderson, William C., III ....Chicago, IL
Anderson, William C., Jr. ....Hampton, SC
Anderson, William D. ....Fresno, CA
Anderson, William D. ....Santa Rosa, CA
Anderson, William D. ....Des Moines, IA
Anderson, William D., Jr. ....New York, NY
Anderson, William (Dale), Jr. (P.A.)
Stuart, FL
Anderson, William E. ....Minnetonka, MN
Anderson, William E. ....Jackson, MS
Anderson, William E. ....Asheville, NC
Anderson, William E. ....Belle Fourche, SD
Anderson, William E. ....Lynchburg, VA
Anderson, William E., (A Sole Proprietorship) ....Moscow, ID
Anderson, William E., II ....Atlanta, GA
Anderson, William Eugene ....Raleigh, NC
Anderson, William G. ....Los Angeles, CA
Anderson, William G. ......Englewood Cliffs, NJ
Anderson, William G., Jr. ....St. Louis, MO
Anderson, William G., Jr. ....Charleston, WV
Anderson, William H. ....Los Angeles, CA
Anderson, William H.
Department of the Air Force, Office of the General Counsel, GV
Anderson, William H. ....Batavia, OH
Anderson, William H. ....Cincinnati, OH
Anderson, William H., III ....Macon, GA
Anderson, William J. ....Pagosa Springs, CO
Anderson, William J. ....Cleveland, OH
Anderson, William J., Jr. ......St. Petersburg, FL
Anderson, William K. ....Corpus Christi, TX
Anderson, William L. ....Stockton, CA
Anderson, William L. ....Yreka, CA
Anderson, William L. ....Washington, DC
Anderson, William Lee ....Charlottesville, VA
Anderson, William M. ....Wichita, KS
Anderson, William M., IV ....Creve Coeur, IL
Anderson, William N. ....Atlanta, GA
Anderson, William P. ....Springdale, AR
Anderson, William R. ....Washington, DC
Anderson, William R. ....Belfast, ME
Anderson, William R. ....Las Cruces, NM
Anderson, William Robert, III
Corpus Christi, TX
Anderson, William S. ....New York, NY
Anderson, William T. ....Ojai, CA
Anderson, William W. ....Eagle River, WI
Anderson, William W., Jr. ....Albany, CA
Anderson, Willis D. ....Portland, OR
Anderson, Willis M. ....Roanoke, VA
Anderson, Wilmarth & Van Der Maaten
Decorah, IA
Ossian, IA
Waucoma, IA
Anderson, W. J. ....Idaho Falls, ID
Anderson, Wm. David ....Mesa, AZ
Anderson, Wm. E., Jr. ....Pine Grove, CA
Anderson, Wm. H. ....Pensacola, FL
Anderson, Wm. O. ....Estherville, IA
Anderson, Wm. R., Jr. ....Cleburne, TX
Anderson, Wolfgang R. ....Seattle, WA
Anderson and Wonch, P.C. ....Lansing, MI
Anderson & Woolley, PLLC ......Lexington, KY
Anderson, Worth S. ....Washington, DC
Anderson and Yamada, P.C. ....Portland, OR
Anderson & Young ....Jackson, MS
Anderson, Zane ....Bowman, ND
Anderson & Zangari ....Providence, RI
Anderson, Zebulon D. ....Raleigh, NC
Anderson, Zeigler, Disharoon, Gallagher & Gray, Professional Corporation
Petaluma, CA
Santa Rosa, CA
Anderson-Adams, Leslie Olivia
Tallahassee, FL
Anderson Bachman, Susan M. ....Huron, SD
Anderson-Bedford, Charlotte G.
New York, NY
Anderson-Carson, Dana ....Metairie, LA
Anderson-Duffy, Lillian ....Malone, NY
Anderson-Fohr, Susan A. ....Elm Grove, WI
Anderson-Karakashian, Susan Dale
Waco, TX
Anderson Knote, Arlene
Columbia Falls, MT
Anderson-Moore, Precious ....Atlanta, GA
Andersons, The, Attorneys & Counselors at Law, P.C. ....Dallas, TX
McKinney, TX
Plano, TX
Anderson-Siler, Cheryl ....Fort Collins, CO
Anderson-Speight, Rhonda Lynn
Silver Spring, MD
Anderson-Trahan, Ernestine L.
New Orleans, LA
Anderson-Viken, Marianne Denise
Durbin, ND
Andersson & Andersson, P.C., Law Offices Of
Walnut Creek, CA
Andersson, Brandt ....Walnut Creek, CA
Andersson, Elaine ....San Francisco, CA
Andersson, Gunnar E., (P.C.)
Colorado Springs, CO
Andersson, Joan ....Topanga, CA
Andersson, Mark W. ....Tucker, GA
Andersson, Patricia K. ....Walnut Creek, CA
Andersson, Stephan E. ....Philadelphia, PA
Andersson, Steven A. ....Aurora, IL
Andersson, Timothy L. ....Southfield, MI
Andersson & Vanatta
Colorado Springs, CO
Andersson, W. Paul ....New Orleans, LA
Anderst, Thomas L. ....Sioux Falls, SD
Anderton, D. Chad ....Santa Ana, CA
Anderton, James P. ....Hermitage, MO
Anderton, John M. ....La Porte, IN
Anderton, Kenneth G. ....Vernal, UT
Anderton, Matthew D. ....Clarkston, MI
Anderton, Matthew J. ....Yakima, WA
Anderton, Michael ....Columbus, OH
Anderton, Michael D. ....Kirkland, WA
Anderton, Paul M. ....Annapolis, MD
Anderton, Robert Marion ....Carrollton, TX
Anderton, Robert N. ....Seattle, WA
Anderton, Roland B., Jr. ....Atlanta, GA
Anderton, Sal M. ....West Orange, NJ
Anderton, Stephen R. ....Dallas, TX
Andes, Diane E. ....St. Louis, MO
Andes, Fredric P. ....Chicago, IL
Andes, J. Graham ....Downingtown, PA
Andes, Pamela L. ....Irvine, CA
Andes, Phyllis E. ....Washington, DC
Andes, Robert J. ....Hackensack, NJ
Andes, Ronald L. ....Findlay, OH
Andes, Roy F. ....Royal Oak, MI
Andes, Roy H. ....Missoula, MT
Andes, Samuel L. ....Lemoyne, PA
Andes, William ....Riverhead, NY
Andes, William F., Jr. ....Riverhead, NY
Andes, William S. ....Cincinnati, OH
Andeweg, Robert D. ....Des Moines, IA
Andewelt, Roger B.
United States Court of Federal Claims, GV
Andia, Gilbert J., Jr. ....Greensboro, NC
Andich & Andich ....Rock Island, IL
Andich, David W. ....Rock Island, IL
Andich, Marvin S. ....Rock Island, IL
Andich, Stephen G. ....Rock Island, IL
Anding, George K. "Buzzy", Jr.
Baton Rouge, LA
Anding, Gregory M. ....Baton Rouge, LA
Anding, John E. ....Grand Rapids, MI
Andino, Lucas E. ....New York, NY
Andino, Thomas P., Jr. ....Syracuse, NY
Andion, James L. ....Los Angeles, CA
Andion, Shaw, Adams & Orleans
Los Angeles, CA
Andis, Bruce E. ....Indianapolis, IN
Andjelkovich, Peter, & Associates
Chicago, IL
Andjich, Nancy L. ....Juno Beach, FL
Andler, John ....Bloomfield Hills, MI
Andler, John J. ....Bloomfield Hills, MI
Ando, Nadine Y. ....Honolulu, HI
Ando, Russell H. ....Honolulu, HI
Ando, Tobin K. ....Costa Mesa, CA
Andolina, Janet A. ....New York, NY
Andolina, Lawrence J. ....Rochester, NY
Andolina, Michael B. ....Morristown, NJ
Andolino, Anthony J. ....Hackensack, NJ
Andolsen, Robert R. ....North Ridgeville, OH
Andonian, Jos. K. ....Portage, MI
Andora, Anthony D. ....Elmwood Park, NJ
Andora, Palmisano & Geaney, A Professional Corporation ....Elmwood Park, NJ
Andorka, Frank H. ....Cleveland, OH
Andorka, Gary D. ....Columbus, OH
Andow, Paul ....El Paso, TX
Andra, Lawrence P. ....Wichita, KS
Andracchio, Laura M. ....San Diego, CA
Andrachik, Gary S. ....Cleveland, OH
Andrachik, Roger A. ....Cleveland, OH
Andrachik & Webster ....Cleveland, OH
Andracki, Richard F. ....Pittsburgh, PA
Andrada, J. Randall ....Oakland, CA
Andrade, Adrian S. ....Santa Maria, CA
Andrade, Alvin R. ....Glendale, CA
Andrade, Anita K. ....New York, NY
Andrade, Anthony J. (IBA)
Kansas City, MO
Andrade & Associates ....Irvine, CA
San Diego, CA
Andrade, Branda N. ....San Francisco, CA
Andrade, Charles P., Jr. ....Marstons Mills, MA
Andrade, Eduardo N.T. ....New York, NY
Andrade, John C. ....Dover, DE
Andrade, Judith M. ....Washington, DC
Andrade, Karen J. ....Southampton, MA
Andrade, Kimberly A. ....Laguna Beach, CA
Andrade, Lauren C. ....Sacramento, CA
Andrade, Leo R. ....Greenbrae, CA
Andrade, Maria E. ....San Francisco, CA
Andrade, Nancy C. ....Chicago, IL
Andrade, Peter R. ....Taunton, MA
Andrade, Richard B. ....Irvine, CA
San Diego, CA
Andrade, Richard M. ....New York, NY
Andrade, Sandra Hardgrove ....San Diego, CA
Andrade, Troy E. ....Neptune Beach, FL
Andrade-Kerdman, Sherry L. ....Encino, CA
Andrae, Alicia ....Phoenix, AZ
Andrae, Henry ....Jefferson City, MO
Andras, Joseph C. ....Costa Mesa, CA
Andrascik, Allen ....Rochester, PA
Andraski, Kenneth J. ....Wausau, WI
Andraski, Louis W. ....Detroit, MI
Andrassy, Dana Rountree ....Cleveland, OH
Andre, Blaustein & Green, L.L.P.
Atlanta, GA
Andre, Carroll L., III ....Memphis, TN
Andre, Christopher S. ....Irvine, CA
André, David J. ....Kansas City, MO
Winchester, VA
Andre, Deron J. ....Green Bay, WI
Andre, Ellen Denise ....Franklin, TN
André, Gary Paul ....Los Angeles, CA
Andre, Gregory R. ....Chicago, IL
André, Helen Choi ....McLean, VA
Andre, John J. ....Department of Justice, Civil Division, GV
Andre, John W., Jr. ....Savannah, GA
Andre, Lionel
Securities and Exchange Commission, Division of Enforcement, GV
Andre, Lucy Knight ....Salt Lake City, UT
André , Michael H. ....New York, NY
Andre, Michael J. ....Denver, CO
Andre, Michael J., P.C. ....Denver, CO
Andre, Morris & Buttery, A Professional Law Corporation ....Paso Robles, CA
San Luis Obispo, CA
Santa Maria, CA
Andre, Nicole K. ....Des Plaines, IL
Andre, Patrick F. ....Chicago, IL
André, Paul J. ....Palo Alto, CA
Andre, Peter R. ....San Luis Obispo, CA
Andre, Richard H. ....Atlanta, GA
André, Robert G. ....Seattle, WA
Andre, Robert J., III ....Davis, WV
Andre, Scott ....Tahoe City, CA
Andre, Steven J. ....Carmel, CA
Andre, Susan E. ....Boulder, CO
Andre, Walter W. ....Pierre, SD
Andrea, Alex ....Hudson, WI
Andrea, Frank A., III ....Garden City, NY
Andrea, Janet ....Thousand Oaks, CA
Andrea, Nicholas R. ....Los Angeles, CA
Andrea & Towsky ....Garden City, NY
Andreacchi, Anthony ....Woodcliff Lake, NJ
Andreacchio, Diana ....Philadelphia, PA
Andreades, Lynne ....Holmdel, NJ
Andreadis, Clea T. ....Cambridge, MA
Andreadis, Jenny ....Bayside, NY
Andreadis, Nikos D. ....Astoria, NY
Andreae, Eric C. ....Montgomery, AL
Andreana, Michael J. ....Hartford, CT
Andreani, Carlo ....San Francisco, CA
Andreani, Patricia M. ....Los Angeles, CA
Andreani, Robert P. ....Los Angeles, CA
Andreano, Dominic J. ....Miami, FL
Andreano, Frank P. ....Joliet, IL
Andreano, Richard J., Jr.
Washington, DC
Andreano, Samuel J. ....Joliet, IL
Andreano, Vincent P.
Fort Lauderdale, FL
Andreas, Ann V.B. ....Honolulu, HI
Andreas, Arthur ....San Francisco, CA
Andreas, Bronwyn D. ....New York, NY
Andreas, Christophe E. ....Novato, CA
Andreas, Christopher Eric ....Novato, CA
Andreas, David W. ....Winfield, KS
Andreas, Eric S. ....Washington, DC
Andreas, Frederick W. ....Cleveland, OH
Andreas, Glenn Allen, III ....Chicago, IL
Andreas, Jennifer E. ....Chicago, IL
Andreas, Martin ....Yreka, CA
Andreas and Muret, L.L.P. ....Winfield, KS
Andreas, Stacy M. ....Kansas City, MO
Andreas, Warren D. ....Winfield, KS
Andreasen, Bryon C. ....Champaign, IL
Andreasen, Dean C. ....Salt Lake City, UT
Andreasen, Gustaf R. ....Detroit, MI
Andreasen, James H. ....Kansas City, MO
Andreasen, Janine Marie ....Mankato, MN
Andreasen, John A. ....Omaha, NE
Andreasen, Jon A. ....Des Moines, IA
Andreasen, Steven J. ....Sioux City, IA
Andreasen, Steven W. ....Seattle, WA
Andreasik, Andrew R. ....Chicago, IL
Andreason, Cynthia T. ....Washington, DC
Andreason, J. C. ....Plymouth, CA
Andreason, Kurt M. ....Beaumont, TX
Andreassi, Scott J. ....Kittanning, PA
Andreatta, Lawrence B. ....St. Louis, MO
André de la Porte-Hooykaas, A. Elisabeth
New York, NY
Andree, Gerard J. ....Southfield, MI
Andree, Jamie ....Bloomington, IN
Andree, Mark S. ....Huntington, NY
Andree, Robert G., Jr. ....Spencer, IN
Andreeff, Margaret E. ....Cleveland, OH
Andreeff, Nickolas P. ....Akron, OH
Andreen, James R. ....Minneapolis, MN
Andreen, Kenneth ....San Luis Obispo, CA
Andreen, Patricia Noyes ....Fresno, CA
Andreen, Robert W. ....Pittsburgh, PA
Tarentum, PA
Andreen, William L. ....Tuscaloosa, AL
Andreesen, Joel T. ....Bakersfield, CA
Andreini, John M. ....Hartford, CT
Andreini, Mark J. ....Cleveland, OH
Andreini, Paul H. ....Port Arthur, TX
Andreini, Sandra S. ....St. Paul, MN
Andreini, Susan M. ....Lansing, MI
Andreiuolo, Mary Rose
Franklin Square, NY
Andrekanic, Robert D. ....Belleville, IL
St. Louis, MO
Andrel, Vika ....Austin, TX
Andren, Joyce M. ....Bronx, NY
Andrén, Magnus ....New York, NY
Andreoff, Alexander ....Springfield, OH
Andreoff, Christopher A. ....Detroit, MI
Andreola, Glenn L. ....Philadelphia, PA
Andreola, Kathy A. ....Pennsauken, NJ
Andreoli, Brian E. ....Ridgefield, CT
Andreoli, Christine ....Garden City, NY
Andreoli, Christine L. ....New York, NY
Andreoli, Craig A. ....Garden City, NY
Andreoli, Elizabeth ....Little Rock, AR
Andreoli, Marcia O. ....White Plains, NY
Andreoli, Michael J. ....Lebanon, IN
Andreoli, Peter D. ....Pelham, NY
Andreoli, Peter D., Jr. ....Fairfax, VA
Andreoli, Thomas A. ....Chicago, IL
Andreone, Dennis M. ....Towson, MD
Andreoni, James A. ....Peru, IL
Andreoni, Orlando A. ....Providence, RI
Andreoni, Patricia A. ....Sylmar, CA
Andreopoulos, Lambros L. ....Southfield, MI
Andreos, George P. ....San Diego, CA
Andreos, George P., A Professional Law Corporation ....San Diego, CA
Andreosky, Lori A. ....Haddonfield, NJ
Andreotta, Donald J.
National Aeronautics And Space Administration, GV
Andreotti, Patrick ....Yakima, WA
Andreou, D. Jennifer ....Detroit, MI
Andreou, James ....Chicago, IL
Andreozzi, Beth A. ....New York, NY
Andreozzi, Bradley J. ....Chicago, IL
Andreozzi, Louis J. ....New Providence, NJ
Dayton, OH
Andreozzi, Michael G. ....Bellville, TX
Andreozzi, Randall P. ....Buffalo, NY
Andres, Albert E. ....Dallas, TX
Andres and Andres, A Professional Corporation ....Santa Ana, CA
Andres, Ann Avery ....Santa Ana, CA
Andres & Berger, A Professional Corporation ....Haddonfield, NJ
Medford, NJ
Andres, Charles R. ....New Haven, CT
Andres, David F. ....Milwaukee, WI
Andres, David M. ....Tuscaloosa, AL
Andres, Douglas R. ....Portland, OR
Andres, Eugen Charles ....Santa Ana, CA
Andres, Greg D. ....New York, NY
Andres, James ....West Caldwell, NJ
Andres, John C. ....Norwalk, CT
Andres, Jonathan F. ....St. Louis, MO
Andres, Joseph E. ....Omaha, NE
Andres, Karen G. ....Los Angeles, CA
Andres, Kenneth G., Jr. ....Haddonfield, NJ
Andres, Paula L. ....Kansas City, MO
Andres, Robert C. ....Waterloo, IA
Andres, Robert J. ....Houston, TX
Andres, Robert K. ....Burlington, VT
Andres & Salerno ....Omaha, NE
Andres, Thomas M. ....Napa, CA
Andres, Tyler & Lemley L.L.C.
Tuscaloosa, AL
Andres, Van P. ....Toledo, OH
Andresen, Charles H. ....Duluth, MN
Andresen, Craig W. ....Bloomington, MN
Andresen, Craig W., P.C. ....Bloomington, MN
Andresen, Denise C. ....Chicago, IL
Andresen, Duane C.
Commodity Futures Trading Commission, Division of Trading and Markets, GV
Andresen, Katheryn A. ....Bloomington, MN
Andresen, Malcolm ....New York, NY
Andresen, Ralph ....Fort Gratiot, MI
Andresen, Richard E. ....San Francisco, CA
Andresen, Robt. H. ....Santa Rosa, CA
Andresen, Roni S. ....Walnut Creek, CA
Andresen, Teresa M. ....New York, NY
Andresini, Joseph M. ....Elmwood Park, NJ
Andresino, Michael L. ....Boston, MA
Andress, D. Keith ....Birmingham, AL
Andress, Laura J. ....Fayetteville, AR
Andress, Laurence M., (P.A.) ....Miami, FL
Andress, P. David ....Jackson, MS
Andress, Peter ....Arlington Heights, IL
Andress, Scott E. ....Jackson, MS
Andress, Stephen M. ....Boston, MA
Andretta, Gage ....Roseland, NJ
Andretta, Robert A.
Department of Housing and Urban Development, Office of Administrative Law Judges, GV
Andretti, Carolyn H. ....Indianapolis, IN
Andreu, Robert A. ....St. Augustine, FL
Andreu, Timothy A. ....Tampa, FL
Andreu-Garcia, Jose A. ....San Juan, PR
Andreu-Garcia, Manuel E. ....San Juan, PR
Andréu-Ramírez de Arellano, César A.
San Juan, PR
Andrew, Anne Slaughter ....Washington, DC
Indianapolis, IN
Andrew, Brian L. ....St. Louis, MO
Andrew, Brian M. ....Grand Rapids, MI
Andrew, Carol A. ....Denver, CO
Andrew, Charles H., Jr. ....Vidalia, GA
Andrew, Christine I. ....Waterbury, CT
Andrew, Cindy W. ....Dallas, TX
Andrew, Craig D. ....Columbus, OH
Andrew, David C. ....Detroit, MI
Andrew, David F. ....Honolulu, HI
Andrew, David M. ....Louisville, KY
Andrew, Dean R. ....Olathe, KS
Andrew, Diane Maxine ....Glen Carbon, IL
Andrew, Francis E. ....Nevada City, CA

Andrew, Harold … Paxton, IL
Andrew, Joanne M. … Santa Ana, CA
Andrew, John H. … Washington, DC
Andrew, Joseph J. … Indianapolis, IN
Andrew, Laura Miller … Atlanta, GA
Andrew, Laurie E. … Long Beach, CA
Andrew Law Office, S.C. … Fond du Lac, WI
Andrew Law Offices, LLC … Columbus, OH
Andrew, Leonard D. … White Plains, NY
Andrew, Louis J., Jr. … Fond du Lac, WI
Andrew, Louise C. B. … Millersville, MD
Andrew, Marcia Voorhis … Cincinnati, OH
Andrew, Michael A., Jr. … Trenton, NJ
Andrew, Michael T. … San Diego, CA
Andrew, Michael W., Jr. … Orlando, FL
Andrew, Michelle Reese … Topeka, KS
Andrew, Paul E. … Lawrenceville, GA
Andrew, Paul E., P.C. … Gainesville, GA
Lawrenceville, GA
Andrew, Raymond A. … Northfield, IL
Andrew, Robert R. … Methuen, MA
Andrew, Scott P. … Tampa, FL
Andrew, Shuvabu … Austin, TX
Andrew, Stephanie Savides … San Bruno, CA
Andrew, Stephen L., & Associates
Tulsa, OK
Andrew, Stephen W. … San Francisco, CA
Andrew, Stewart R. … Eastsound, WA
Andrew, Thomas F. … Duluth, MN
Andrew and Threlkeld, P.C. … Lyons, GA
Vidalia, GA
Andrew, Timothy W., Sr. … Duluth, MN
Andrew, Walter M., Jr. … Westport, CT
André-Wells, Linda … Albuquerque, NM
Andrews, A. James … Knoxville, TN
Andrews, Alan … Lincoln City, OR
Andrews, Alan B. … Las Vegas, NV
Andrews, Alan D. … Houston, TX
Andrews, Albert O'B., Jr.
Minneapolis, MN
Andrews, Alexander G., (P.C.)
Farmington Hills, MI
Andrews, Alexander M. … Columbus, OH
Andrews, Alexis … Chicago, IL
Andrews, Alison M. … Albany, NY
Andrews, Alvin L. … Portland, OR
Andrews, Amy H. … Chicago, IL
Andrews, Amy Jo … Pittsburgh, PA
Andrews, Angus G.
De Funiak Springs, FL
Andrews, Ann L. … Lansing, MI
Andrews, Ann-Martha … Phoenix, AZ
Andrews, Anthony P. … Pittsfield, MA
Andrews, Arthur F.
Hilton Head Island, SC
Andrews, Arthur H. … Baton Rouge, LA
Andrews & Associates … Frankfort, KY
Lexington, KY
Andrews, Audrey T. … Dallas, TX
Andrews, Avis R. … Fremont, NE
Andrews, Barbara T. … Boulder, CO
Andrews, Barry S. … El Segundo, CA
Andrews, Barry W. … Cleveland, OH
Andrews, Barschall, II … Columbus, GA
Andrews & Barth, P.C. … Dallas, TX
Andrews, Ben A. … Tallahassee, FL
Andrews, Benjamin J. … Buffalo, NY
Andrews, Bernstein & Maranto, LLP
Buffalo, NY
Andrews, Beth A. … Troy, MI
Andrews, Blake D. … Birmingham, AL
Andrews, Bradford L. … Long Beach, CA
Andrews, Bradley G. … Boise, ID
Andrews, Brandon Scott
Baton Rouge, LA
Andrews, Brian Anthony … New York, NY
Andrews, Briggs W. … Roanoke, VA
Andrews, Bruce H. … Washington, DC
Andrews, Camilla N. … Lake Forest, CA
Andrews, Carl D. … Charleston, WV
Andrews, Catherine Jane … Omaha, NE
Andrews, Cecelia R. … Los Angeles, CA
Andrews, Charles … Syracuse, NY
Andrews, Charles B. … Bloomington, MN
Andrews, Charles B. … Pembroke, VA
Andrews, Charles D. … Nashville, TN
Andrews, Charles E., Jr. … Topeka, KS
Andrews, Charles F. … Columbus, OH
Andrews, Charles Roger … Columbus, OH
Andrews, Charles S. … Washington, DC
Andrews, Charlotte C. … Baton Rouge, LA
Andrews, Charlton E. … San Francisco, CA
Andrews, Cheri D. … Norristown, PA
Andrews, Claire G. … Portland, ME
Andrews, Clark A. … Sterling Heights, MI
Andrews, Clayton D., Jr. … Syracuse, NY
Andrews, Cosgrove & Young, P.C.
New London, CT
Norwich, CT
Andrews, Craig S. … San Diego, CA
Andrews, Curtis L. … Valley Stream, NY
Andrews, Cynthia L. … Oklahoma City, OK
Andrews, Cynthia S. … Bingham Farms, MI
Andrews, Dale C.
Department of Transportation, Office of the General Counsel, GV
Andrews, Dale E. … Flint, MI
Andrews, Dana G. … Tampa, FL
Andrews, Daniel C. … San Antonio, TX
Andrews, Daniel J. … Plymouth, MI
Andrews, Daniel True … Bartow, FL
Andrews, Daniel W. … Austin, TX
Andrews, David Ashley … Floyd's Knobs, IN
Andrews, David E. … Plymouth, WI
Andrews, David J. … Boston, MA
Andrews, David M. … St. Augustine, FL
Andrews, David M. … Frankfort, KY
Lexington, KY

Andrews, David N. … Eugene, OR
Andrews, David P. … Altoona, PA
Andrews, David T. … Cleveland, OH
Andrews, David V. … Jacksonville, FL
Andrews & Davis … De Funiak Springs, FL
Andrews Davis Legg Bixler Milsten & Price, A Professional Corporation
Oklahoma City, OK
Andrews, Dawn O. … Breckenridge, CO
Andrews, Dawn R. … Long Beach, CA
Andrews, Deborah B. … La Palma, CA
Andrews, Deborah K. … Treasury Department, Office of the Comptroller of the Currency, GV
Andrews, Denise A. … Baltimore, MD
Andrews, Denver R., Jr.
Rancho Santa Margarita, CA
Andrews, Don J. … Chicago, IL
Andrews, Donald J., II … Detroit, MI
Andrews, Donna R. … San Francisco, CA
Andrews, Douglas A. … Cleveland, OH
Andrews, Douglas G., Law Offices of
Hinesville, GA
Andrews, Douglas G., Law Offices of
Savannah, GA
Andrews, Douglas W. … Diamond Bar, CA
Los Angeles, CA
Andrews, Doyll H., III … Merrillville, IN
Andrews, Dynda … New York, NY
Andrews, E. Sherrell … New York, NY
Andrews & Eastman, A Ptnship. incl. a Prof. Corp. … Kewanee, IL
Andrews, Edward A. … Garden City, NY
Andrews, Edward S. … New York, NY
Andrews, Edwin A., III … Mount Vernon, NY
Andrews, Elaine M. … Anchorage, AK
Andrews, Elizabeth A. … Washington, DC
Andrews, Elizabeth E. … Tampa, FL
Andrews, Elizabeth Hallock … Augusta, ME
Andrews, Elizabeth M. … San Diego, CA
Andrews, Elizabeth Welch … Cleveland, OH
Andrews, Ellen R. … Barre, VT
Andrews, Eric B. … Hagerstown, MD
Andrews, Eric C. … Kansas City, MO
Andrews, Eric T. … Washington, DC
Andrews, Eugene … Canton, OH
Andrews, Floy E. … Los Angeles, CA
Andrews, Frank … Portland, OR
Andrews, Frank … Dallas, TX
Andrews, Frank L. … Troy, MI
Andrews, Frank M. … Riverton, WY
Andrews, Fred H. … Yakima, WA
Andrews & Galatis … Fort Lauderdale, FL
Andrews, Garland P. … Dallas, TX
Andrews, Gary E. … Olympia, WA
Andrews, George E. … Waldorf, MD
Andrews, George J. … Chicago, IL
Andrews, George J. … Elmhurst, IL
Andrews, George R. … Manakin-Sabot, VA
Andrews, George T. … Salem, MA
Andrews, George W. … Birmingham, AL
Andrews, George W. … St. Paul, MN
Andrews, Gordon C. … New York, NY
Andrews, Gregory A. … Erie, PA
Andrews, Gregory H. … St. Charles, IL
Andrews, H. Dean … Paris, IL
Andrews, H. Dean, Law Offices of
Vicksburg, MS
Andrews, H. Edward, III … Baltimore, MD
Bel Air, MD
Andrews, Hal … Nashville, TN
Andrews, Harley N. … Marquette, MI
Andrews, Harold G. … Oakbrook Terrace, IL
Andrews, Harper … Kewanee, IL
Andrews, Harrell, Mann, Chapman & Coyne, A Professional Corporation
Bloomington, IN
Indianapolis, IN
Andrews, Harry G. … Colton, CA
Andrews, Henry G., Jr. … Rockwall, TX
Andrews & Hensleigh, LLP
Los Angeles, CA
Andrews, Horace A. … St. Petersburg, FL
Andrews & Hudson, P.C. … Knoxville, TN
Andrews, Hunter B. … Hampton, VA
Andrews, Ike F. … Siler City, NC
Andrews, J. David, P.S. … Seattle, WA
Andrews, J. Don, Jr. … Oklahoma City, OK
Andrews, J. Don, Jr., P.C.
Oklahoma City, OK
Andrews, J. Melvin … Eastlake, OH
Andrews, J. Richard … Lakeland, FL
Andrews, J. Robert … Santa Barbara, CA
Andrews, J. Robert … Cincinnati, OH
Andrews, Jackson M., IV
United States Senate, Committee Legal Personnel, GV
Andrews, Jaen … Madison, WI
Andrews, James A. … South Paris, ME
Andrews, James E.
Department of Agriculture, Office of the General Counsel, GV
Andrews, James F. … Stamford, CT
Andrews, James F. … Petersburg, VA
Andrews, James F., Jr. … Pittsburgh, PA
Andrews, James F., Jr. … Houston, TX
Andrews, James H. … Poland, OH
Andrews, James, Jr. … Alexandria, VA
Andrews, James M. … Roseland, NJ
Andrews, James R. … Santa Monica, CA
Andrews, Jana P. … Tampa, FL
Andrews, Jane … Lewiston, ME
Andrews, Jane … Newark, NJ
Andrews, Jas. D. … Rochester, NY
Andrews, Jay B. Schiegg … Ontario, CA
Andrews, Jay R. … Cedar Rapids, IA
Andrews, Jean A. … New York, NY
Andrews, Jeannette M. … Tallahassee, FL

Andrews, Jeffrey A. … Burlington, NC
Andrews, Jeffrey B. … Dallas, TX
Andrews, Jennifer Dean … Madison, WI
Andrews, Jennifer M. … Fort Worth, TX
Andrews, Jennifer S. … Siler City, NC
Andrews, Jerry D. … Dallas, TX
Andrews, Joan M. … Hartford, CT
Andrews, Joan M. … Salt Lake City, UT
Andrews, Joe Scott … Ardmore, OK
Andrews, John … Salem, MA
Andrews, John B. … Concord, NH
Andrews, John C. … San Francisco, CA
Andrews, John C. … Grant City, MO
Andrews, John C. … Oklahoma City, OK
Andrews, John C. … Fort Worth, TX
Andrews, John C. … Bremerton, WA
Andrews, John C., III … Dallas, TX
Andrews, John E. … Los Angeles, CA
Andrews, John F. … Montgomery, AL
Andrews, John H. … Brodhead, WI
Janesville, WI
Andrews, John J., Jr. … Lexington, GA
Andrews, John J., Jr., P.C. … Lexington, GA
Andrews, John J., Law Offices of
Port Jefferson, NY
Andrews, John, P.C., Law Office of
Salem, MA
Andrews, John S. … Greenville, AL
Andrews, John S., (P.A.)
Fort Lauderdale, FL
Andrews, John T., Jr. … New York, NY
Andrews, John W. … Woodbury, NY
Andrews, John W., (P.A.) … Tampa, FL
Andrews & Johnson … Carlisle, PA
Andrews, Jomarie T. … Farmington, CT
Andrews, Jonathan D. … San Diego, CA
Andrews, Jonathan P. … Elkins Park, PA
Andrews, Jonathan W. … Miami, FL
Andrews, Joseph M. … Los Angeles, CA
Andrews, Joyce D. … Los Altos, CA
Andrews, J.R. … Arkadelphia, AR
Andrews, Judith L. … Seattle, WA
Andrews, Julia
Department of Transportation, Office of the General Counsel, GV
Andrews, Karen E. … New York, NY
Andrews, Karen M. … Los Alamitos, CA
Andrews, Karen N. … Carthage, IL
Andrews, Katherine D. … Tallahassee, FL
Andrews, Kathleen I. … Washington, DC
Andrews, Kathleen K. … Ventura, CA
Andrews, Kay … Austin, TX
Andrews, Keith E. … New Orleans, LA
Andrews, Keith G. … Jacksonville, FL
Andrews, Keith L. … Ruskin, FL
Andrews, Kelli A. … Washington, DC
Andrews, Kelly J.
Securities and Exchange Commission, GV
Andrews, Ken … Graham, TX
Andrews, Kenneth E. … Orlando, FL
Andrews, Kenneth L. … Kokomo, IN
Andrews, Kenneth R., Jr. … Falls Church, VA
Andrews, Kristy A. … Tallahassee, FL
Andrews & Kurth L.L.P.
Los Angeles, CA
Washington, DC
New York, NY
Dallas, TX
Houston, TX
Andrews, L. Don … Sioux Falls, SD
Andrews, Lance … St. Petersburg, FL
Andrews, Larry W. … Charleston, WV
Andrews, Laura R. … Edwardsville, IL
Andrews Law Firm … Arkadelphia, AR
Andrews Law Firm, P.C. … Des Moines, IA
Andrews Law Offices … Syracuse, NY
Andrews, Lawrence
Environmental Protection Agency, Program Office Attorneys, GV
Andrews, Lawrence W. … Salem, OR
Andrews, Leo R., Jr. … Arlington, VA
Andrews, Lilian F. B. … New York, NY
Andrews, Linda R. … Department of Justice, Civil Rights Division, GV
Andrews, Lissa H. … Honolulu, HI
Andrews, Lloyd J. … Phoenix, AZ
Andrews, Lois G. … New London, CT
Andrews, Lori B. … Chicago, IL
Andrews, Lorraine Lynn … Macon, GA
Andrews, Lowell L. … Bellaire, TX
Andrews, Luke W. … Atlanta, GA
Andrews, M. Kirsten … Baltimore, MD
Andrews, Manuel … Providence, RI
Andrews, Marc … Claremont, CA
Andrews, Mark D. … Chicago, IL
Andrews, Mark E. … Dallas, TX
Andrews, Mark J. … Washington, DC
Andrews, Mark L. … Sacramento, CA
Andrews, Mark O. … Mount Pleasant, SC
Andrews, Mark W. … Ashtabula, OH
Andrews, Mark W. … San Antonio, TX
Andrews, Mark W. … Madison, WI
Andrews, Mary Jo Blain … Hartford, CT
Andrews, Mary R. … Miami, FL
Andrews, Mary Sigrid
Environmental Protection Agency, Office of Enforcement and Compliance Assurance, GV
Andrews, Melvyn J.
Department of Commerce, Patent and Trademark Office, GV
Andrews, Michael A. … Washington, DC
Andrews, Michael C. … Boston, MA
Andrews, Michael E. … Indianapolis, IN
Andrews, Michael E. … Seattle, WA
Andrews, Michael J.
Croton-On-Hudson, NY
Andrews, Milton D. … Washington, DC

Andrews, Minerva Wilson … McLean, VA
Andrews, Monica A. … Memphis, TN
Andrews, Mote W., III … Columbus, GA
Andrews Myers & Coulter, P.C.
Houston, TX
Andrews, Neil P. … Charlotte, NC
Andrews, Nicholas S. … Royal Oak, MI
Andrews, Nicole G. … Houston, TX
Andrews, Nigel L. … Jamestown, RI
Andrews, Oakley V. … Cleveland, OH
Andrews, Pamela J. … Chicago, IL
Andrews, Pamela M. … Seattle, WA
Andrews, Patrice Smiley … New York, NY
Andrews, Patricia B. … Fort Worth, TX
Andrews, Patricia E. … Providence, RI
Andrews, Paul D. … San Antonio, TX
Andrews, Paul H. … Jamestown, NY
Andrews, Paul J. … Washington, DC
Andrews, Paul J. … Department of Justice, Criminal Division, GV
Andrews, Paul P.
Securities and Exchange Commission, Division of Market Regulation, GV
Andrews, Paula K. … Boston, MA
Providence, RI
Andrews, Paulette G. … Oakland, CA
Andrews, P. C., Jr. … Thomasville, GA
Andrews, Peggy Q. … Chicago, IL
Andrews, Peter B. … Philadelphia, PA
Andrews, Peter J. … New York, NY
Andrews, Peter R. … York, PA
Andrews, Philip M. … Baltimore, MD
Andrews, Philip S. … Tucker, GA
Andrews, Pusateri, Brandt, Shoemaker & Roberson … Lockport, NY
Andrews, R. Craig … Mentor, OH
Andrews, R. Hale, Jr. … Boston, MA
Andrews, Rawle, Jr. … Phoenix, AZ
Andrews, Raymond S., Jr. … Hartford, CT
Andrews, R. C. … Corpus Christi, TX
Andrews, Richard G. … Santa Ana, CA
Andrews, Richard G. … Wilmington, DE
Andrews, Richard L. … Bellevue, WA
Andrews, Richard S. … Chicago, IL
Andrews, Richard W. … Dalton, GA
Andrews, Robert D. … Wrightwood, CA
Andrews, Robert D., Jr. … Ludington, MI
Andrews, Robert E. … Gainesville, GA
Andrews, Robert E. … Georgetown, MA
Andrews, Robert E. … Milwaukee, WI
Andrews, Robert F. … Fort Worth, TX
Andrews, Robert F., P.C. … Fort Worth, TX
Andrews, Robert H. … Wilbraham, MA
Andrews, Robert J. … Cleveland, OH
Andrews, Robert L. … Fort Lauderdale, FL
Andrews, Robert R., Jr. … Minneapolis, MN
Andrews, Robin K. … Detroit, MI
Andrews, Ross P. … Syracuse, NY
Andrews, Roy V. … Milton, FL
Andrews, Russell R. … Choteau, MT
Andrews, S. Mark … Dothan, AL
Andrews, Sally J. … Hampton, VA
Andrews, Sally S. … Houston, TX
Andrews, Schick, Bongar & Starkey, P.A.
La Plata, MD
Leonardtown, MD
Waldorf, MD
Andrews, Scott W. … Huntington, WV
Andrews & Seery … Thomasville, GA
Andrews, Seward L. … Sacramento, CA
Andrews, Shauna L. … Chicago, IL
Andrews, Shauna Rae … Southfield, MI
Andrews, Sonja Fields … Atlanta, GA
Andrews, Stafford E. … Houston, TX
Andrews, Stanley R. … Titusville, FL
Andrews, Stephan F. … Richmond, VA
Andrews, Stephen C. … Atlanta, GA
Andrews, Stephen G. … Midland, MI
Andrews, Stephen H. … Thomasville, GA
Andrews, Stephen K. … Indianapolis, IN
Andrews, Stephen M. … Tallahassee, FL
Andrews, Stephen S. … Houston, TX
Andrews, Steve … Kent, WA
Andrews, Steven N. … Pontiac, MI
Andrews, Steven R. … Tallahassee, FL
Andrews, Steven R. … Rosemont, IL
Andrews, Steven R., P.A. … Tallahassee, FL
Andrews, Stuart M., Jr. … Columbia, SC
Andrews, Sumner R. … Boston, MA
Andrews, Susan A. … Corte Madera, CA
Andrews, Susan Barker … Topeka, KS
Andrews, Susan G. … Richmond, VA
Andrews, Suzanne E. … New York, NY
Andrews, T. Michael … Tucson, AZ
Andrews, Tammy L. … Santa Monica, CA
Andrews, Taylor P. … Carlisle, PA
Andrews, Telly … Chicago, IL
Andrews, Thomas E. … Fountain Valley, CA
Andrews, Thomas H., Jr. & Associates
Muskegon, MI
Andrews, Thomas J. … Chicago, IL
Andrews, Thomas J. … Raleigh, NC
Andrews, Thomas M. … Aransas Pass, TX
Andrews, Thomas N. … Redding, CA
Andrews, Thomas R. … Seattle, WA
Andrews, Thomas T., Jr. … Rockville, MD
Andrews, Thomas W. … Des Moines, IA
Andrews, Thomas W. … Kensington, MD
Andrews, Timothy G. … Canton, OH
Andrews, Todd Alan … Westmont, IL
Andrews, Todd D. … Minneapolis, MN
Andrews, Torin K. … Gaithersburg, MD
Andrews, Torin K., Attorney at Law Chtd.
Gaithersburg, MD
Owings Mills, MD
Manassas, VA
Andrews, Valerie L. … Boston, MA
Andrews, Vernon J. … Lansing, MI

Angelus, George G., Law Offices of, P.L.C.
New Orleans, LA
Angelus, Michael K. ....Framingham, MA
Angenend, Paul D. ....Austin, TX
Anger, Amy Alana ....Troy, MI
Anger, Jordan M. ....New York, NY
Anger, Kristin D. ....Seattle, WA
Anger, Laurie K. ....San Francisco, CA
Anger, Nancy V. ....Phoenix, AZ
Anger, Susan J. ....Winter Park, FL
Anger, William H. ....Phoenix, AZ
Angera, Andrea A., Jr. ....Wyncote, PA
Angeramo, Joseph F. ....Hingham, MA
Angerbauer, David G. ....Bountiful, UT
Angerer, John M. ....Citrus Heights, CA
Angerer, Robert J. ....Tallahassee, FL
Angerhofer, David J., P.C.
Salt Lake City, UT
Angerhofer, Harold J. ....Pasadena, CA
Angerillo, Gidget A. ....St. Louis, MO
Angermann, Russell P. ....Bristol, PA
Angermayer, Stephen B. ....Pittsburg, KS
Angermeier, Curt J. ....Evansville, IN
Angermeier, Gerald G. ....Columbus, IN
Angermeier, James W. ....Evansville, IN
Angermeier, Robert C. ....Milwaukee, WI
Angermeier & Rogers ....Milwaukee, WI
Angermiller, Patrick M. ....Sonora, CA
Angermueller, Hans H. ....New York, NY
Angerosa, John ....Schenectady, NY
Angers, Glenn W. ....Walnut Creek, CA
Angers, W. Thomas ....Lafayette, LA
Angevin, Josephine G. ....Newton, MA
Angevine, Charles E. ....Department of State, Foreign Service Officers (Overseas), GV
Angevine, Earl F. ....Mount Vernon, WA
Angevine, Elizabethanne Miller
Whittier, CA
Angevine, Ernest G., (P.C.) ....Boston, MA
Anggelis, Gordon, Simpson & Roberts
Lexington, KY
Anggelis, John C. ....Lexington, KY
Angier, Thomas D. ....Port Angeles, WA
Angileri, Frank A. ....Southfield, MI
Angileri, Maria Franek ....Southfield, MI
Angino, Richard C. ....Carlisle, PA
Harrisburg, PA
Angino & Rovner, P.C. ....Carlisle, PA
Harrisburg, PA
Angioletti, Thomas J., III
Redwood City, CA
Angiolillo, Bruce D. ....New York, NY
Angiolillo, Carol ....Old Greenwich, CT
Angiolillo, Glenn J. ....Stamford, CT
Angiolillo, Jos. ....Brooklyn, NY
Angiolillo-Bent, Laurie ....Boston, MA
Angione, Frank, Jr. ....Fort Lauderdale, FL
Angione, Howard F. ....Fresh Meadows, NY
Angione, Howard F. ....Jamaica, NY
Angiuli, Gary C. ....Staten Island, NY
Angiuli, Poznansky & Katkin
Staten Island, NY
Angiulo, James P. ....Tucson, AZ
Angiuoni, Guy, Jr. ....Billerica, MA
Angius, Christopher W. ....Portland, OR
Angius, Daniel E. ....Walnut Creek, CA
Angius & Terry LLP ....Sacramento, CA
Walnut Creek, CA
Las Vegas, NV
Reno, NV
Angkatavanich, N Todd ....Short Hills, NJ
New York, NY
Anglade, Luis J. ....San Juan, PR
Angland, Joseph ....New York, NY
Angle, Amy E. ....Atlanta, GA
Angle & Angle ....St. Louis, MO
Angle & Associates, Ltd. ....Scottsdale, AZ
Eagan, MN
Angle, Carlson, Goldrick & Roberts
Santa Barbara, CA
Angle, Clyde P. ....Jefferson City, MO
Angle, David R. ....St. Louis, MO
Angle, Elizabeth G. ....Schenectady, NY
Angle, Jerry L. ....Phoenix, AZ
Angle, John E. ....Chicago, IL
Angle, Keith M. ....Kansas City, MO
Angle, Loren E. ....Cherokee, OK
Angle, Margaret (Margy) S.
Scottsdale, AZ
Angle, Marvin J. ....Jacksonville, TX
Angle, Murphy, Valentino & Campbell, P.C.
York, NE
Angle, Richard L.
Department of Transportation, Federal Aviation Administration, GV
Angle, Robert ....St. Louis, MO
Angle, Robert A. ....Richmond, VA
Angle, Robert B., Jr. ....Ocklawaha, FL
Angle, Robert O. ....Santa Barbara, CA
Angle, Stephen ....Washington, DC
Angle, Stephen W., (Inc.) ....Warrensburg, MO
Angle, Tammi J. ....Springfield, OH
Angle, Timothy R. ....Booneville, MS
Angle, Wallace W. ....York, NE
Anglea & Bannon, A Professional Corporation ....Los Angeles, CA
Pasadena, CA
Anglea, Berneice A. ....Laguna Beach, CA
Anglehart, Donald L. ....Boston, MA
Anglehart, Scott B. ....Binghamton, NY
Anglemire, Kenneth N. ....Santa Fe, NM
Anglen, Randall S. ....Branson, MO
Anglen, Randall S., P.C. ....Branson, MO
Angles, Christopher J. ....Olathe, KS
Angles, Louis ....Excelsior Springs, MO
Angley, Edward T. ....Hingham, MA
Angley, Jeffrey T. ....Boston, MA
Angley, Jeffrey T., P.C. ....Boston, MA

Angley, Patricia L. ....Larchmont, NY
Anglim, Jennifer M. ....New York, NY
Anglim, Thomas D. ....Washington, NC
Anglin, D. Rex ....Shreveport, LA
Anglin, Daniel K. ....Atlanta, GA
Anglin, David O ....Baton Rouge, LA
Anglin, Dean, (P.A.) ....Cranbury, NJ
Anglin & Giaccherini ....Del Mar, CA
Anglin, J. Michael ....Minneapolis, MN
Anglin, John M. ....Los Angeles, CA
Anglin, June Edmondson ....Evergreen, CO
Anglin, L. Gilbert ....Murfreesboro, TN
Anglin, Mary C. ....Hinsdale, IL
Anglin, Michael S. ....New York, NY
Anglin, Michael W. ....Dallas, TX
Anglin, Nancy J. ....Hamilton, TX
Anglin, Patricia E. ....San Francisco, CA
Anglin, Richard D., II ....Dayton, OH
Anglin, Richard L., Jr. ....Del Mar, CA
Anglin, Stephanie L. ....Overland Park, KS
Anglum, Angela C. ....New York, NY
Anglum, Peter K. ....New York, NY
Angnos, Denise Kathleen ....Poway, CA
Angoff, Goldman, Manning, Pyle, Wanger & Hiatt, P.C. ....Boston, MA
Angoff, Saml. E. ....Boston, MA
Angoff, Walter, (P.C.) ....Boston, MA
Angones, Frank R. ....Miami, FL
Angones, Hunter, McClure, Lynch & Williams, P.A. ....Fort Lauderdale, FL
Key West, FL
Miami, FL
Angorn, Richard A. ....Gainesville, FL
Angotti, Alma M. ....Treasury Department, Financial Crimes Enforcement Network, GV
Angotti, Donna L. ....New York, NY
Angotti, Gary L. ....Long Beach, CA
Angotti, John R. ....Morgantown, WV
Angotti, Lynn R. ....Baltimore, MD
Angotti, Matthew T. ....Baltimore, MD
Angotti & Straface, L.C. ....Morgantown, WV
Angotti-Hare, Mary Beth ....Morgantown, WV
Angowitz, Anne S. ....New York, NY
Angowitz, Stuart J., Law Offices of
New York, NY
Angres, Nancy Ford ....Carson City, NV
Angres, Robert J., (Ltd.)
Incline Village, NV
Angres, Robert L.S. ....Napa, CA
Angres, Robert L.S. ....Santa Rosa, CA
Angst, Candace S. ....Glencoe, IL
Angst, Frederick P. ....St. Paul, MN
Angst, Gerald L. ....Chicago, IL
Angst, Gregory Scott ....Baltimore, MD
Angstadt, Edwin C., Jr. ....Doylestown, PA
Angstadt, Eric P. ....Oakland, CA
Walnut Creek, CA
Angstadt, Janet M. ....Chicago, IL
Angstadt, Todd A. ....Oakland, CA
Angstead, Robert K. ....Jefferson City, MO
Angstman, Albert C. ....Kingwood, TX
Angstman, Myron E. ....Bethel, AK
Angstreich, Scott Harris ....Washington, DC
Angstreich, Steven E. ....Cherry Hill, NJ
Philadelphia, PA
Angueira, Alexander ....Miami, FL
Angueira, David P. ....Boston, MA
Anguiano, Aaron Ocon ....Modesto, CA
Anguilla, Carol J. ....Boston, MA
Anguilla, Fausto C. ....Providence, RI
Anguillo, Lisa M. ....Tampa, FL
Angulo, Alfred F., Jr. ....Little Rock, AR
Angulo, Carlos T. ....Washington, DC
Angulo, David S. ....San Antonio, TX
Angulo, Joe ....San Francisco, CA
Angulo, Manuel R. ....New York, NY
Angulo, Peter M. ....Las Vegas, NV
Angulo, Robert P., Jr. ....Richland, WA
Angulo, Veronica A. ....Miami, FL
Angus Associates, P.C. ....Oklahoma City, OK
Angus, Carol N. ....Essex Junction, VT
Angus, G. Peter ....Columbus, OH
Angus, Heather ....Washington, DC
Angus, Henry B. ....Hurst, TX
Angus, James S. ....Department of Justice, Civil Rights Division, GV
Angus, Jane E. ....Lake Oswego, OR
Angus, John Raymond ....McLean, VA
Angus, Joseph ....Oklahoma City, OK
Angus, Julie Madison ....Ottawa, IL
Angus, Kerry D. ....Myrtle Beach, SC
Angus, Leonard M. ....Bainbridge Island, WA
Angus, Michael J. ....Los Angeles, CA
Angus, Robert M. ....Minneapolis, MN
Angus, Roderick H. ....Arlington, VA
Angus, Samuel B. ....Palo Alto, CA
Angus, Stephen Wade ....New York, NY
Angus, Steven M. ....Cardiff-By-The-Sea, CA
Angus, Ted F., Jr. ....San Francisco, CA
Angvire, Leon S., (P.C.) ....Los Angeles, CA
Anh, William Vu Tam ....Los Angeles, CA
Anhalt, Susan Leckrone ....Los Angeles, CA
Anhang, George E. ....Washington, DC
Anhold, Gordon A. ....Cleveland, OH
Anhut, Matthew D. ....Santa Monica, CA
Anhut, William F. ....Ypsilanti, MI
Aniano, Rita ....West Islip, NY
Anible, Bruce Douglas ....Little Rock, AR
Aniboli, Paul J. ....Babylon, NY
Anich, Matthew F. ....Ashland, WI
Anich and Peterson ....Ashland, WI
Anich, Thomas M. ....Ashland, WI
Anicker, John C., Jr. ....West Linn, OR
Anido, Andrea B. ....Miami, FL
Aniekwu, Bobby C. ....Atlanta, GA
Aniel, Jan H. ....Charlotte, NC
Anielak, Eric M. ....Kansas City, MO
Anielski, Jeffrey M. ....San Diego, CA

Anigbogu, Michael C. ....New York, NY
Anigian, Richard D. ....Dallas, TX
Anik & Heiberg ....Westlake Village, CA
Anik, Paul S. ....Westlake Village, CA
Anikeeff, Anthony H.
Department of Justice, Civil Division, GV
Anile, Joseph S., II ....New York, NY
Anillo, Alvaro I. ....Washington, DC
Aninao, Joseph G. ....Columbus, OH
Aninao, V. Antonio ....Houston, TX
Aniol, John Wm. ....Rolling Meadows, IL
Anise, Fady F. ....Jersey City, NJ
Anisko, Barbara ....Cherry Hill, NJ
Blue Bell, PA
Anisman, Antony M. ....New York, NY
Anisman, Beth E. ....New York, NY
Anisman, Debra R. ....New York, NY
Anisman, Sheldon ....Fort Worth, TX
Anito, Lawrence F., Jr. ....Albany, NY
Anjam, S. Naseem ....Oak Brook, IL
Anjanos, Nicholas J. ....Chicago, IL
Anjier, John C. ....New Orleans, LA
Anjozian, Alan ....Newport Beach, CA
Ankabrandt, Gary F. ....Harrisburg, PA
Ankele, Chadney C. ....Monterey, CA
Ankele, M. Jason ....Dallas, TX
Ankeles, Abraham ....Marblehead, MA
Ankeles, David L. ....Peabody, MA
Ankeles, Debra L. ....Peabody, MA
Ankeles, Harmon & Bonfanti ....Peabody, MA
Ankenbrand, George ....Princeton, IN
Ankenbrandt, Brian J. ....Palo Alto, CA
Ankenman, C. Gregg ....Oakland, CA
Ankenman, W. Douglas, Jr. ....Houston, TX
Ankeny, David C. ....New Orleans, LA
Ankeny, Gary ....Farley, IA
Anker, Benjamin R. ....Valhalla, NY
Anker, Daniel E. ....Cleveland Heights, OH
Anker, Daniel J. ....Wilmington, DE
Anker, Hymes & Schreiber, A Law Corporation ....Encino, CA
Los Angeles, CA
Anker, Jacqueline ....Santa Barbara, CA
Anker, Jerry D. ....Washington, DC
Anker, Kenneth B. ....Hauppauge, NY
Anker, Kent K. ....New York, NY
Anker, Kurt R. ....Encino, CA
Anker, Leslie K. ....New York, NY
Anker, Nicole J. ....Hartford, CT
Anker, Philip D. ....Washington, DC
Anker, Robert T. ....New York, NY
Anker, Samuel H. ....Encino, CA
Anker, Stan H. ....Rapid City, SD
Ankerholz, Rian ....Overland Park, KS
Ankerholz, Richd. L. ....Lyons, KS
Ankerholz & Smith ....Overland Park, KS
Ankerman, Darcy W. ....West Hartford, CT
Ankerman and Smith ....West Hartford, CT
Ankerman, William L. ....West Hartford, CT
Ankers, Gary C. ....Troy, MI
Ankers, Norman C. ....Detroit, MI
Ankin, Howard H. ....Chicago, IL
Anklam, James E. ....Washington, DC
Ankley, Tiffany A. ....Kalamazoo, MI
Anklowitz, William ....Lawrenceville, NJ
Ankner, K. Lianne ....Boston, MA
Ankner, Terence K. ....Boston, MA
Ankney, George W., Jr. ....Columbus, OH
Reynoldsburg, OH
Ankney, Gordon L. ....St. Louis, MO
Ankney, R. Joel ....Virginia Beach, VA
Ankrom, Aaron J. ....Edwardsville, IL
Ankuda, Patrick M. ....Springfield, VT
Ankuda, Stephen S. ....Springfield, VT
Ankus, Joseph E. ....Plantation, FL
Anliker, Deron A. ....Kansas City, MO
Anliker, Maureen Ryan ....Kansas City, MO
Anliot, James R. ....Boston, MA
Ann, Sang Hyun ....New York, NY
Annabi, Majed Farid ....Yonkers, NY
Annakin, Joseph W. ....Evansville, IN
Annala, Carey & VanKoten, P.C.
Hood River, OR
Annala, Wayne C. ....Hood River, OR
Annalora, J. Christian ....New York, NY
Annamarie Fortunato, P.C. ....Brooklyn, NY
Annan, Archison Dawson ....Brooklyn, NY
Annan & Assocs. ....Spokane, WA
Annan, Edgar L., IV ....Spokane, WA
Annand, Iathan T. ....San Francisco, CA
Annand, Megan B. ....Medford, OR
Annand, Stephen Darley ....Charleston, WV
Annandale, Melinda J. ....Rocky River, OH
Annarino, Louise ....Athens, OH
Annarumma, Jeanne M. ....New York, NY
Annas, George J. ....Boston, MA
Annas, James L., Jr. ....Greensburg, PA
Annau, Marion ....New York, NY
Annear, Craig B.
Environmental Protection Agency, Office of the General Counsel, GV
Annear, Harold G. ....Fargo, ND
Annecchino, Louis A. ....Bridgeport, CT
Annelin and Gaskin ....The Woodlands, TX
Annelin, James S. ....The Woodlands, TX
Annelin, Thomas W. ....Birmingham, MI
Annen, Edward J., Jr. ....Kalamazoo, MI
Annen, Richard J. ....San Diego, CA
Annenberg, Alfred B. ....Fresh Meadows, NY
Annenberg, Norman ....New York, NY
Annenberg, Ross ....New Haven, CT
Boston, MA
Annenberg, Ted M. ....New York, NY
Anner, Carolyn M. ....Harrisburg, PA
Lancaster, PA
Anner, John Lloyd, III ....Greenwich, CT
Anner-Hughes, Roberta ....Billings, MT
Annes, Andrew J. ....Chicago, IL

Annes, Gary P. ....Chicago, IL
Annes, George Paul ....Chicago, IL
Annes, Michael D. ....Chicago, IL
Annes, Scott M. ....Chicago, IL
Annes, Scott M., Ltd., Law Offices of
Chicago, IL
Annese, Robert J. ....Arlington, MA
Anness, Charles Wm. ....Cincinnati, OH
Anness, Harold L. ....Cincinnati, OH
Annest, James ....Burley, ID
Annett, Debra ....Watonga, OK
Annett, Robert J. ....Cherry Hill, NJ
Annex, Alan I. ....New York, NY
Annibale & Feinman ....Garden City, NY
Annibale, Frederick J., Jr. ....Garden City, NY
Annicelli, John P. ....New York, NY
Annich, Russell W., Jr. ....Princeton, NJ
Annick, Nancy McAniff ....Los Angeles, CA
Annigian, Gregory T. ....Upland, CA
Annin, Timothy E. ....North Brunswick, NJ
Anning, Douglas K. ....Kansas City, MO
Annino, Anthony, III ....Boston, MA
Annino, Calvin W., Jr. ....Springfield, MA
Westfield, MA
Annino, Draper & Moore, P.C.
Springfield, MA
Westfield, MA
Annino, J. Robert, (P.C.) ....Babylon, NY
Annino & Moody, P.C. ....Boston, MA
Annino, Patricia M. ....Boston, MA
Annino, Stephen J. ....Falls Church, VA
Leesburg, VA
Anninos, Artemis ....New York, NY
Anninos, Hector ....San Francisco, CA
Annis, Alan S. ....Rockville, MD
Annis, Allen D. ....Covina, CA
Annis, Annis & Visser ....Comstock Park, MI
Annis, Christopher J. ....Gainesville, FL
Annis, Eugene I. ....Spokane, WA
Annis, Jack M. ....Woodward, OK
Annis, James Jason ....Portsmouth, VA
Annis, Jennifer ....Tulsa, OK
Annis, Kenneth J. ....Washington, DC
Annis, Michael ....Irvine, CA
Annis, Michael B. ....Pasadena, CA
Annis, Michael D. ....Tampa, FL
Annis, Michael N. ....Martinez, GA
Annis, Michael R. ....St. Louis, MO
Annis, Mitchell, Cockey, Edwards & Roehn, P.A. ....Fort Myers, FL
Naples, FL
Tallahassee, FL
Tampa, FL
Annis, Natalie C. ....Tampa, FL
Annis, Richard C., Jr. ....Comstock Park, MI
Annis, Richard J., (P.C.) ....San Diego, CA
Annis, Sara J. ....Santa Ana, CA
Annis, Sharon L. ....Bennington, VT
Annis & Spievak ....San Diego, CA
Annis, Terry ....Trenton, NJ
Annos, James G. ....Warren, OH
Annos, William ....Newark, DE
Wilmington, DE
Annos, William, Esquire, P.A. ....Newark, DE
Wilmington, DE
Annulis, Brian D. ....Chicago, IL
Annunziata, Albert R. ....New Haven, CT
Annunziata, Christopher K. ....Atlanta, GA
Annunziata, Craig R. ....Chicago, IL
Annunziata, Richard S.
Bonita Springs, FL
Annunziata, Rosemarie ....Fairfax, VA
Annunziata, Scott C. ....St. Louis, MO
Annunziato, Carmine J. ....Bronx, NY
Annunziato, Christopher ....Orlando, FL
Annunziato, Edward S. ....New York, NY
Annutto, Joseph M. ....Nashua, NH
Annweiler, Tara B. ....Galveston, TX
Año, Licia M. ....Philadelphia, PA
Anolic, Isaac ....New York, NY
Anolick, Simon B. ....Chicago, IL
Anolieh, Simon B. ....Washington, DC
Anolik, Alexander ....San Francisco, CA
Anolik, Alexander, A Professional Law Corporation ....San Francisco, CA
Anolik, Irving ....New York, NY
Anolik, Sharon A. ....Corte Madera, CA
Anolik, Stuart H. ....Washington, DC
Anomnachi, Gordy N. ....Washington, DC
Anon, Elizabeth ....Miami, FL
Anon, Walter A. ....Hialeah, FL
Anooshian, Ann ....Santa Barbara, CA
Anooshian & Anooshian ....Port Jervis, NY
Anooshian, Ara ....Port Jervis, NY
Anooshian, John Samuel ....Philadelphia, PA
Anooshian, Marianne ....New Hyde Park, NY
Anooshian, Marion K. ....Port Jervis, NY
Anop, Victor M. ....Chicopee, MA
Anos, George J. ....Chicago, IL
Anouge, Christian B., II
St. Petersburg, FL
Anouge, Maureen J. (Whelan)
St. Petersburg, FL
Anouilh, Lisa D. ....Houston, TX
Anoushirvani, Gita ....Los Angeles, CA
Ansa, Anne M. ....Philadelphia, PA
Ansa, O. Daniel ....Philadelphia, PA
Ansaldi, Michael A. ....Newton, MA
Ansanelli, Vincent W., III ....Amityville, NY
Ansani, Al C. ....New Kensington, PA
Ansani, Daniel R. ....Park Ridge, IL
Ansani, David C. ....Chicago, IL
Ansani, Theodore J. ....Park Ridge, IL
Ansara, Victor L. ....Redford, MI
Ansardi, Glenn ....Kenner, LA
Ansardi, Maxwell & Power ....Kenner, LA
New Orleans, LA
Ansari, Hazim H. ....Newport Beach, CA

Ansari, Talat M. ... New York, NY
Ansary, Cyrus A. ... Washington, DC
Ansay, Jean M. ... Port Washington, WI
Ansay, Michael R. ... West Palm Beach, FL
Ansbach, John E. ... Dallas, TX
Ansbacher, Barry B. ... Jacksonville, FL
Ansbacher, Barry B., P.A.
Jacksonville, FL
Ansbacher, Keith H. ... Mount Olive, NJ
Ansbacher, Lawrence ... Jacksonville, FL
Ansbacher, Lewis ... Jacksonville, FL
Ansbacher, Richard I. ... Washington, DC
Ansbacher & Schneider, P.A.
Jacksonville, FL
Ansbacher, Sidney F. ... St. Augustine, FL
Ansberry, Susan W. ... Los Angeles, CA
San Francisco, CA
Ansbro, John ... New York, NY
Ansbro, Shelley D. ... Westmont, IL
Ansbro, Thomas J. ... Fort Lauderdale, FL
Anschell, Jonathan H. ... Los Angeles, CA
Anscher, Roger ... New York, NY
Anschultz, Andrew S. ... Culver City, CA
Anschutz, Everett L., Jr. ... Houston, TX
Anschutz, Kent C. ... Austin, TX
Anscombe, Anthony J. ... Chicago, IL
Ansehl, Robert A. ... New York, NY
Ansel & Associates ... Boston, MA
Ansel & Carl ... Romney, WV
Ansel, Craig A. ... Corpus Christi, TX
Ansel, David J. ... Boston, MA
Ansel, David Philip ... New York, NY
Ansel, Eric L. ... Hollywood, FL
Ansel, Gary D. ... St. Paul, MN
Ansel, Jeffrey R. ... Minneapolis, MN
St. Paul, MN
Ansel, Marc J. ... Champaign, IL
Ansel, Marc J., Ltd., Law Office of
Champaign, IL
Ansel, Paul ... Hollywood, FL
Ansel, Peter J. ... Miami, FL
Ansell, Brian E. ... Ocean Township, NJ
Ansell, Daniel J. ... New York, NY
Ansell, David K. ... Ocean Township, NJ
Ansell, David L. ... Washington, DC
Ansell, David Monroe ... Hurricane, WV
Ansell, Denise ... New London, CT
Ansell, Don Edward ... Upper Marlboro, MD
Ansell, Edward O. ... Claremont, CA
Ansell, Frederick S. ... Arlington, VA
Ansell, Gerald ... Beverly Hills, CA
Ansell, James R. ... Galveston, TX
Ansell, James S. ... Baltimore, MD
Ansell, Karen L. ... Hauppauge, NY
Ansell and Lafferty ... Upper Marlboro, MD
Ansell, Mitchell J. ... Ocean Township, NJ
Ansell Professional Association
Bedford, NH
Ansell, Richard B. ... Ocean Township, NJ
Ansell, Robert I. ... Ocean Township, NJ
Ansell, Robert J. ... Jericho, NY
Ansell, Ruth ... Bedford, NH
Ansell, W. Leigh ... Virginia Beach, VA
Ansell Zaro Grimm & Aaron, A Professional Corporation ... Asbury Park, NJ
Newark, NJ
Ocean Township, NJ
Red Bank, NJ
Anselm, Kevin C. ... Salem, OR
Anselment, Kenneth L., Jr.
Milwaukee, WI
Anselmi, Andrew E. ... Chatham, NJ
Toms River, NJ
Anselmi, John M. ... Rock Springs, WY
Anselmi, Kurt A. ... Bloomfield Hills, MI
Anselmi, Michael A. ... Baltimore, MD
Anselmi & Mierzejewski, P.C.
Bloomfield Hills, MI
Anselmo, Christopher A. ... Cleveland, OH
Anselmo, Frank M., Jr. ... Chicago, IL
Anselmo, Phillip E. ... San Francisco, CA
Anselmo, Robert F. ... San Diego, CA
Anselmo, Ronald P. ... Fort Lauderdale, FL
Anselmo, Scott R. ... Fort Lauderdale, FL
Anselmo, Thomas J. ... Naperville, IL
Anselmo, Victor V. ... Cleveland, OH
Anselmo-Formica, Judith ... Staten Island, NY
Anseman, Norman E., III
New Orleans, LA
Ansems, Gregory Matthew
Minneapolis, MN
Ansert, William S. ... Reno, NV
Anseth, LeRoy P. ... Williston, ND
Anshell, Stewart A. ... Atlanta, GA
Ansher, Irwin ... Treasury Department,
United States Mint, GV
Anshin, Judith Trigueros ... Sacramento, CA
Ansiaux, Robert R. ... Dallas, TX
Ansilio, Lisa P. ... Santa Clara, CA
Ansis, Fredric W. ... Los Angeles, CA
Ansley, Ben W. ... Overland Park, KS
Ansley, Bonneau, Jr. ... Atlanta, GA
Ansley, David W. ... Springfield, MO
Ansley, Frances Lee ... Knoxville, TN
Ansley, James G. ... Kenton, OH
Ansley, James R. ... Raleigh, NC
Ansley, Jeffrey J. ... Fort Worth, TX
Ansley, Robert B., Jr. ... Atlanta, GA
Ansley, Thomas A. ... Birmingham, AL
Ansley, William S. ... Destin, FL
Anslow, Richard I. ... Freehold, NJ
Anslow, Robert E. ... Newport Beach, CA
Ansman, Ann ... Glendale, CA
Ansnes, Terry ... Riverside, CA
Anson, Chad R. ... Austin, TX
Anson, Crystal ... Albuquerque, NM
Anson, Cynthia Ley ... Tucson, AZ
Anson, David ... Tucson, AZ
Anson, Edward J. ... Coeur d'Alene, ID
Anson, George C. ... Dallas, TX
Anson, Jeffrey M. ... Los Angeles, CA
Anson, Mark M. ... St. Louis, MO
Anson, Peter W. ... Minneapolis, MN
Anson, R. Russell ... Greeley, CO
Anson, Robert B. ... Sacramento, CA
Anson, Sharon H. ... New York, NY
Anson, Thomas K. ... Austin, TX
Anson, Todd J. ... San Diego, CA
Ansorge, Howard J. ... Chicago, IL
Ansorge, Mark ... New York, NY
Ansour, M. Michael ... New York, NY
Anspach, Andrew A. ... New York, NY
Anspach & Associates ... Chicago, IL
Anspach, Herbert K. ... Boca Raton, FL
Anspach, Kenneth G. ... Chicago, IL
Anspach, Robert J. ... Bakersfield, CA
Anspach, Robert M. ... Toledo, OH
Anspach & Serraino ... Toledo, OH
Anspach, William ... New York, NY
Anspach, William N., Jr. ... Chicago, IL
Anspaugh, Donald L. ... Columbus, OH
Anspaugh, Rex H. ... Oklahoma City, OK
Anstaett, Elizabeth L. ... Mandeville, LA
Columbus, OH
Anstaett, Nancy S. ... Overland Park, KS
Anstaett, Robt. E. ... Columbus, OH
Anstandig, Louis ... Pittsburgh, PA
Anstandig, Marshall W. ... Phoenix, AZ
San Jose, CA
Anstandig, McDyer, Burdette & Yurcon, P.C.
Pittsburgh, PA
Anstead, Christopher Lee
West Palm Beach, FL
Anstead, Harry L. ... Tallahassee, FL
Anstead, Laura N. ... New York, NY
Anstead, Laura Nell ... Tallahassee, FL
Anstead, Susann ... Tallahassee, FL
Ansted, Barbara J. ... Fremont, OH
Anstess, Lisa Sabon ... Detroit, MI
Anstey, Ernest G. ... Buffalo, NY
Anstey Law Firm, P.C. ... Atlantic, IA
Anstey, Roger J. ... Avon, CT
Anstey, W. Edward ... Atlantic, IA
Anstine, Arthur H. ... Denver, CO
Anstine, Dale E. ... York, PA
Anstine, Dale E., P.C. ... York, PA
Anstine, Glen R., II ... Denver, CO
Anstine, Glen R., P.C. ... Denver, CO
Anstine, Hill, Richards and Simpson
Denver, CO
Anstine, Mary Beth ... York, PA
Anstine & Sparler ... York, PA
Anstine, Timothy M. ... Harrisburg, PA
Anstine, William B., Jr. ... York, PA
Anstoetter, Mark D. ... Kansas City, MO
Ansuini & Pohlman ... Blasdell, NY
Ansuini, Thomas M. ... Blasdell, NY
Answini, Dominick H. ... Philadelphia, PA
Antablin, Drew R. ... Los Angeles, CA
Antal, Stephen J. ... Newark, NJ
Antalek, Melinda B. ... Baltimore, MD
Antalics, Michael E.
Federal Trade Commission,
Bureau of Competition, GV
Antalis, Gregory M. ... Fort Wayne, IN
Delphos, OH
Antalis, John S. ... Lafayette, IN
Antalis, Sylvia M. ... Sandusky, OH
Antanaitis, Cynthia E. ... Hartford, CT
Antanavage, A. Joseph ... Hamburg, PA
Antao, Roger S. ... Fort Lee, NJ
Antar, Sam ... New York, NY
Antar, Solomon E. ... New York, NY
Antaramian & Easton ... Kenosha, WI
Antaramian, Edward R. ... Kenosha, WI
Antas, Craig M. ... Chicago, IL
Antas, Sarah Mahoney ... Wheaton, IL
Antcliff, Christopher A. ... El Paso, TX
Antczak, David John ... Philadelphia, PA
Antczak, Richard S. ... Jenkintown, PA
Antczak, Val R. ... Salt Lake City, UT
Anteau, Ronald W. ... Beverly Hills, CA
Antebi, Paul R. ... Sugar Land, TX
Antee, Kenneth R., Jr. ... Shreveport, LA
Antel, Harry C. ... Cleveland, OH
Antel, Jerome S., III ... Columbia, MO
Antell & Associates ... Boston, MA
Antell, Barbara Brigham ... Cincinnati, OH
Antell, Debrah L. ... Hollywood, FL
Antell, Diane M. ... Boca Raton, FL
Antell, Kenneth S. ... Portland, OR
Antell, Melvin P. ... Springfield, NJ
Antell, Peter ... Boston, MA
Antell, Rhonda Lee ... Portland, OR
Antell, Robert H. ... Rochester, NY
Antell, Stuart ... New York, NY
Anten, Juhli ... Sherman Oaks, CA
Anten, Lewis ... Encino, CA
Antenucci, Megan Manning
Des Moines, IA
Antenucci, Thomas C. ... Abingdon, VA
Anter, Samuel S. ... Las Vegas, NV
Antes, C. W. ... West Union, IA
Antes, Jon W. ... West Union, IA
Antetomaso, Gerard G. ... Webster, NY
Antezana, Alfredo J. ... Rockville, MD
Antheil, David B. ... Los Angeles, CA
Antheil Maslow & MacMinn
Doylestown, PA
Antheil, William L., III ... Doylestown, PA
Anthenelli, James V. ... Salisbury, MD
Anthenelli & Otway ... Ocean City, MD
Princess Anne, MD
Salisbury, MD
Snow Hill, MD
Anthenelli, Victor H. ... Middlesex, NJ
Anthes, Gregory C. ... Washington, DC
Anthes, John A., Jr. ... Richardson, TX
Anthes, Michelle H. ... Grand Rapids, MI
Anthes, Todd M. ... Grand Haven, MI
Anthis, Clinton W. ... Englewood, CO
Anthis, Ernest R., Jr. ... Muskogee, OK
Anthis, Joe M. ... Oklahoma City, OK
Anthis, Joe M., P.C. ... Oklahoma City, OK
Anthofer, Joseph D. ... Omaha, NE
Anthoine, Robert ... New York, NY
Anthoine, Robert N. ... Fishers Island, NY
Antholis, John K. ... Morristown, NJ
Anthoney, Suzanne Nyhan ... Lisle, IL
Anthony, Alfred M. ... Woodbridge, NJ
Anthony, Andrew J. ... Miami, FL
Anthony, Andrew J., P.A.
Coral Gables, FL
Miami, FL
Anthony & Anthony ... St. Peter, MN
Anthony, Anthony & Anthony
Rosemont, PA
Anthony, Arthur E. ... Dallas, TX
Anthony, Aubra H., Jr. ... El Dorado, AR
Anthony, Barbara B. ... Boston, MA
Anthony, Berry & DiRito
Jacksonville, FL
Orange Park, FL
Ponte Vedra Beach, FL
St. Augustine, FL
Anthony, Bert V. ... Los Angeles, CA
Anthony, Beryl F., Jr. ... Washington, DC
Anthony, Betty Jo ... Roanoke, VA
Anthony, Brannon D. ... Birmingham, AL
Anthony, Brian J. ... Tampa, FL
Anthony, Carl ... Columbus, OH
Anthony, Carl A. ... Columbus, OH
Anthony & Carlson, LLP ... Oakland, CA
Anthony, Carol A. ... Boston, MA
Anthony, Carol Crafton ... El Dorado, AR
Anthony, Caroline G. ... Brookline, MA
Anthony, Christine D. ... Boston, MA
Anthony, Christine T. ... Boston, MA
Anthony, Coretta S. ... Tallahassee, FL
Anthony, Cushman D. ... Portland, ME
Anthony, Cynthia S. ... Fort Worth, TX
Anthony, Dana L. ... Doylestown, PA
Philadelphia, PA
Anthony, Daniel B. ... Winston-Salem, NC
Anthony, David Neal ... Norfolk, VA
Anthony, David V. ... Washington, DC
Anthony, Deborah C. ... Atlanta, GA
Anthony, Deborah P. ... Montgomery, AL
Anthony, Don Mike, (P.C.) ... Pasadena, CA
Anthony, Elaine Cash ... Houston, TX
Anthony, Elizabeth Barger
Birmingham, AL
Anthony, Emory, Jr. ... Birmingham, AL
Anthony, Eugene K. ... Fargo, ND
Anthony, Evelyn Tsamtsouris
Burr Ridge, IL
Anthony, Frank S. ... Worcester, MA
Anthony, Fred J. ... Shelton, CT
Anthony, Fred Paul, Jr. ... Atlanta, GA
Anthony, Frederick P. ... Erie, PA
Anthony, Frederick W. ... New York, NY
Anthony, Gary S. ... Mount Clemens, MI
Anthony, Gayle D. ... Port Orange, FL
Anthony, Gene J. ... Eatontown, NJ
Anthony, George N. ... Detroit, MI
Anthony, Greg ... Harrisburg, PA
Anthony, Gregory Jon ... San Diego, CA
Anthony, Harris R. ... Atlanta, GA
Anthony, Howison, Landis & Arn
Portland, ME
Anthony, J. Danford, Jr. ... Hartford, CT
Anthony, J. Michael ... San Rafael, CA
Anthony, J. Michael, P.C. ... San Rafael, CA
Anthony, Jack H. ... Santa Ana, CA
Anthony, Jack M., Jr. ... Dallas, TX
Anthony, Jack M., Law Offices of
Dallas, TX
Anthony, James D. ... Bakersfield, CA
Anthony, James L. ... Corpus Christi, TX
Anthony, James L., P.C. ... Corpus Christi, TX
Anthony, James Marshall ... Las Vegas, NV
Anthony, James T. ... Allentown, PA
Bethlehem, PA
Jim Thorpe, PA
Anthony, Jeffrey D. ... Laramie, WY
Anthony, Joan Caton
Department Of The Interior,
Office of Hearings & Appeals, GV
Anthony, John A. ... Tampa, FL
Anthony, John C. ... York, SC
Anthony, John F. ... Canton, OH
Anthony, John J., Jr. ... Fort Lauderdale, FL
Anthony, John J., Jr., P.A.
Fort Lauderdale, FL
Anthony, John Matthew ... Irving, TX
Anthony, Joseph E. ... Durham, NC
Anthony, Joseph J. ... Franklin, GA
Anthony, Joseph P. ... Kankakee, IL
Anthony, Joseph W. ... Minneapolis, MN
Anthony, Judith Shults ... Brooklyn, NY
Anthony, Julian D. ... Westwood, MA
Anthony, Julie Maria ... Chicago, IL
Anthony, Kenneth C., Jr.
Spartanburg, SC
Anthony, Kevin R. ... Miami, FL
Anthony, L. Clary, Jr. ... Atlanta, TX
Anthony, Laura Greenberg
Columbus, OH
Anthony Law Firm, P.A. ... Gaffney, SC
Greenville, SC
Spartanburg, SC
Union, SC
Anthony, Len S. ... Raleigh, NC
Anthony, Lisa Battalia
Department of Education,
Office of the General Counsel, GV
Anthony, Lisa Elrod ... Spartanburg, SC
Anthony, Lloyd W. ... Stamford, CT
Anthony, Lovick P., Jr. ... Butler, GA
Anthony, Malcolm
Ponte Vedra Beach, FL
Anthony, Marcell Rose (IBA)
Columbus, OH
Anthony, Mark A. ... Dayton, OH
Anthony, Mark P. ... Bay City, MI
Anthony, Marshall W. ... St. Peter, MN
Anthony, Michael B. ... Corpus Christi, TX
Anthony, Michael F. ... Chicago, IL
Anthony, Michael J. ... Columbus, OH
Anthony, Michael P. ... Phoenix, AZ
Anthony, Michele ... New York, NY
Anthony & Murdock ... Salinas, CA
Anthony, Neil P. ... West Palm Beach, FL
Anthony, Nelson S. ... Las Vegas, NV
Anthony, Nicholas A. ... Greenwich, CT
Anthony, Nicholas & Sharpe, LLC
Cheyenne, WY
Laramie, WY
Anthony, Norman L. ... Salinas, CA
Anthony, Pamela M. ... Los Angeles, CA
Anthony, Patricia B. ... Rocky Mount, NC
Anthony, Patricia L. ... Fountain Valley, CA
Anthony, Patricia L., A Prof. Law Corp.
Fountain Valley, CA
Anthony, Paul J. ... Charlestown, MA
Anthony, Phillip J. ... Raleigh, NC
Anthony, Quentin ... Newport, RI
Anthony, Rachel J. ... Ripley, TN
Anthony, Rebecca J. ... Birmingham, AL
Anthony, Richard A. ... Kingston, NY
Anthony, Richard B. ... Rosemont, PA
Anthony, Richard G. ... Bay Village, OH
Anthony, Robert A. ... Arlington, VA
Anthony, Robert E. ... Rosemont, PA
Anthony, Robert J. ... Hartford, CT
Anthony, Robert M. ... Oklahoma City, OK
Anthony, Robert W. ... Orlando, FL
Anthony, Seibert and Dloski
Mount Clemens, MI
Anthony, Sheila F.
Federal Trade Commission,
Offices of Commissioners, GV
Anthony, Shirley Herman ... Hickory, NC
Anthony, Slaton Jay ... Muskogee, OK
Anthony, Stephen C. ... South Holland, IL
Anthony, Stephen J. ... Phoenix, AZ
Anthony, Stephen P. ... Department of Justice,
Criminal Division, GV
Anthony, Steven J. ... Norfolk, VA
Anthony, Steven M. ... Bearden, AR
Anthony, Steven R. ... Oakland, CA
Anthony, Sue E. ... Wake Forest, NC
Anthony, Susan Freeman ... Morristown, NJ
Anthony, Ted M. ... Lafayette, LA
Anthony, Teisha M. ... Department of Defense,
Defense Legal Services Agency, GV
Anthony, Thomas D. ... Atlanta, GA
Anthony, Thomas D. ... Cincinnati, OH
Anthony, Thomas E. ... Brea, CA
Anthony, Thomas H. ... Mount Pleasant, MI
Anthony, Thomas W., Jr. ... Citrus Heights, CA
Anthony, T. J., Jr. ... New York, NY
Anthony, Vicky L. ... St. Louis, MO
Anthony, Victoria M. ... Syracuse, NY
Anthony, Walter Y. ... Media, PA
Anthony, Wanda Hagan ... Tampa, FL
Anthony, Warner H., Jr. ... Atlanta, GA
Anthony, Willard S. "Kwame", II
Washington, DC
Anthony, William D., Jr. ... Chicago, IL
Anthony, William J. ... Morristown, NJ
Anthony, William L., Jr. ... Menlo Park, CA
Anthony, William N. ... Chicago, IL
Anthopolos, Penny Harkleroad
Hartford, CT
Anthou, Emmanuel S. ... McMurray, PA
Anthou, George E. ... Canonsburg, PA
Anti, Dennis R. ... Springfield, MA
Antico, Anthony P. ... Peabody, MA
Antico, Barrett & Burke ... Peabody, MA
Antico, Steven R. ... Hackensack, NJ
Anticouni & Associates
Santa Barbara, CA
Anticouni, Bruce N. ... Santa Barbara, CA
Anticouni, Marilyn D. ... Santa Barbara, CA
Antignani, N. Edwin ... Bridgeport, CT
Antill, Ronald E. ... Palm Beach Gardens, FL
Antilla, Dean Arthur ... Negaunee, MI
Antilla, Paul E. ... Sacramento, CA
Antin, Bernard S. ... Southfield, MI
Antin & Ehrlich ... New York, NY
Antin, Jeffrey S. ... New York, NY
Antin, Karin T. ... New York, NY
Antin, Kenneth H. ... Middletown, CT
Antin Law Firm ... Hammond, LA
Antin, Mark L. ... Parsippany, NJ
Antin, Mary Quealy ... Houston, TX
Antin, Michael ... Los Angeles, CA
Antin, Michael, A Law Corporation
Los Angeles, CA
Antin, Norman B. ... Washington, DC
Antin, Walter, Jr. ... Hammond, LA
Antine, Marc E. ... Taunton, MA
Antinoff, Steven ... Marlton, NJ
Antinone, Ruth A. ... Pittsburgh, PA
Antinori, Joseph G. ... Atlantic City, NJ
Voorhees, NJ
Antinori, Paul, Jr. ... Tampa, FL
Antinori, Paul, Jr. ... Tampa, FL
Boston, MA
Antinoro, Mark D. ... Vinita, OK

Antinozzi, Anthony T. ....Rye, NY
Antioco, Peter M. ....Jamaica, NY
Antion, D. Stephen ....Los Angeles, CA
Antipas, Constantine G. ....Groton, CT
Antipolo, Virginia Cella ....Everett, WA
Antippas, Suzanne B. ....New York, NY
Antisdale, Terri L. ....Pontiac, MI
Antisdel, Tom C. ....Washington, DC
Antista, Robert A. ....San Jose, CA
Atlanta, GA
Antkoviak, Peter, II ....Allegan, MI
Antkowiak, Bruce A. ....Greensburg, PA
Antkowiak, Michael D. ....Edmond, OK
Antler, Adriane M. ....New York, NY
Antler, Helayne ....Encino, CA
Antler & Rainie ....Fort Bragg, CA
Antler, Steven J. ....Fort Bragg, CA
Antley, Christopher R. ....Greenville, SC
Antley, Corinne M. ....Washington, DC
Antley, Kenneth F. ....Atlanta, GA
Antley, Roy ....Houston, TX
Antley-Olander, Tracy ....Seattle, WA
Antman, Gabriel B. ....Chicago, IL
Antoci, John M. ....Los Angeles, CA
Antoff, Carol J. ....King Of Prussia, PA
Antognini, Richard L. ....Sacramento, CA
Antognini-O'Neill, Jennifer ....Middletown, CT
Antognoli, Benito C. R. ....Cleveland, OH
Antognoli, David L. ....Granite City, IL
Antoine, Amy Y. ....Philadelphia, PA
Antoine, Eric J. ....Mission, SD
Antoine, F. J. ....Prairie du Chien, WI
Antoine, Gerald H. ....Port Washington, WI
Antoine, Juliette ....New York, NY
Antoine, Mary Powers ....Sacramento, CA
Antoine, Richard F. ....Sacramento, CA
Antoine, Ronald J. ....Waukesha, WI
Antoine, Virginia M. ....Milwaukee, WI
Antoinetti, Amelia M. ....Newington, CT
Antoinetti, John Jude ....Rocky Hill, CT
Antokol & Coffin ....Schenectady, NY
Antokol, Joan S. ....Nutley, NJ
Antokol, Richard M. ....Schenectady, NY
Antol, Michael S. ....Pittsburgh, PA
Antol, Sara M. ....Cheswick, PA
Antola, A. Victor ....Los Angeles, CA
Antolak, Steven E. ....Minneapolis, MN
Antolik, Christia M. ....San Antonio, TX
Antolik, John T. ....Voorhees, NJ
Antolin, Edwin P. ....San Francisco, CA
Antolin, Joseph A. ....Chicago, IL
Antolin, Stanislav ....Greensboro, NC
Antoline, Michael ....Decatur, IL
Antolinez, Joseph H., Law Office of
Denver, CO
Antolini, Jennifer D. ....New York, NY
Antolino, Dominick A., Jr. ....Cleveland, OH
Antolino, Ralph, Jr. ....Columbus, OH
Antollino, Angelo & Scalesse ....Branford, CT
Antollino, Frank ....Branford, CT
Antollino, Gregory S. ....New York, NY
Antommaria, Phillip ....Valparaiso, IN
Anton, Alexander ....Portsmouth, NH
Anton, Alfred J. ....Miami, FL
Anton, Becky Ferrell ....Tampa, FL
Anton, Bruce ....Dallas, TX
Anton, Charles A. ....Tewksbury, MA
Anton, Christopher P. ....Parsippany, NJ
Anton, David ....Tampa, FL
Anton, David C. ....Berkeley, CA
Anton, Douglas C. ....Hackensack, NJ
Anton, Eduardo ....Miami, FL
Anton, Frederick J. ....New York, NY
Anton, Frederick W., III ....Blue Bell, PA
Anton, Gary J. ....Tallahassee, FL
Anton, James A. ....Orange, CA
Anton, Jennifer L. ....Dallas, TX
Anton, Jim ....Trussville, AL
Anton, John M. ....Oakland, CA
Anton, John N. ....Monterey, CA
Anton, Joseph E. ....Boston, MA
Anton, Joseph E., Inc. ....Boston, MA
Anton, Laurie H. ....Fort Myers, FL
Anton, Martin B. ....Brick, NJ
Anton, Martin J. ....Brick, NJ
Anton, Milton ....Niceville, FL
Anton, Paul J. ....Melrose, MA
Anton, Richard H. ....Austin, TX
Anton, Richard P. ....Pittsburgh, PA
Anton, Ronald D. ....Niagara Falls, NY
Anton, Scott David ....Tampa, FL
Anton, Shickrey ....Tucson, AZ
Anton, William J. ....Tulsa, OK
Antonacci, Peter ....Tallahassee, FL
Antonacci, Raymond J. ....Waterbury, CT
Antonacci, Sherida ....Hartford, CT
Antonacci, Vincent S. ....Needham, MA
Antonakakis, Elizabeth ....New York, NY
Antonakakis, Linda A. ....Paramus, NJ
Antonakakis, Tina F. ....New York, NY
Antonakos, John ....Redwood City, CA
Antonazzo, Nicholas O. ....Johnstown, PA
Antonchuk, Jeffrey T. ....San Francisco, CA
Antoncich, Michael A. ....Carmel, CA
Antone, Christopher C. ....Dallas, TX
Antone, Debra R. ....Chicago, IL
Antone, Michael C. ....Pittsburgh, PA
Antone, N. Peter ....Southfield, MI
Antone, N. Peter, P.C., Law Offices of
Southfield, MI
Antone, Thomas M., IV ....Washington, DC
Antonecchia, Thomas T. ....Katonah, NY
Antonek, Matthew J. ....Tampa, FL
Antonelli, Alfred P. ....Bethlehem, PA
Antonelli, Andrea P. ....Bethesda, MD
Antonelli, Bruce A. ....New York, NY
Antonelli, Christine M. ....Providence, RI
Antonelli, Daniel ....Union, NJ
Antonelli, David A. ....Bloomfield Hills, MI
Antonelli, Dominic M. ....Cleveland, OH
Antonelli, Donald R. ....Arlington, VA
Antonelli, Giuseppe J. ....West Covina, CA
Antonelli, Laura ....Philadelphia, PA
Antonelli, Mark R. ....Miami, FL
Antonelli, Matthew J. ....New York, NY
Antonelli, Patricia ....Providence, RI
Antonelli, Patrick, Jr. ....Cleveland, OH
Antonelli, Ralph L. ....Hempstead, NY
Antonelli, Richard C. ....East Brunswick, NJ
Antonelli, Richard J. ....Pittsburgh, PA
Antonelli, Susan ....Collegeville, PA
Antonelli, Terry, Stout & Kraus, LLP
Washington, DC
Arlington, VA
Antonellis, Anthony J. ....Boston, MA
Antonellis, Carl J., Jr. ....Westfield, MA
Antonellis, Joseph ....Milford, MA
Antonello, Fegers & Cea
Winter Haven, FL
Antonello, Robert J. ....Winter Haven, FL
Antonetti, Luis F. ....San Juan, PR
Antonetti, Marc A. ....Washington, DC
Antonetti, Matthew S. ....Stamford, CT
Antonetti, Vicente J. ....San Juan, PR
Antonetti-Sttuts, Salvador J.
San Juan, PR
Antonetti-Zequeira, Salvador
San Juan, PR
Antongiorgi, Maria ....San Juan, PR
Antongiorgi-Betancourt, Jorge Antonio
San Juan, PR
Antoni, Deborah Anne ....Miami, FL
Antoni, John D. ....Los Angeles, CA
Antonides, Brett L. ....Washington, DC
Antonietti, Edward A. ....Calumet City, IL
Antonietti & Gulotta ....Calumet City, IL
Antonietti, Joan L. ....Spokane, WA
Antonietti, Joan L., P.S. ....Spokane, WA
Antoniewicz, Gary L. ....Madison, WI
Antoniewicz, Michael ....River Edge, NJ
Antonik, Douglas A., Law Office of
Mount Vernon, IL
Antonik, Joan A. ....Gloversville, NY
Antonin, Frances L. ....Jersey City, NJ
Antonini, A. James, II ....Hayward, CA
Antonini and Antonini ....Clinton, IN
Antonini, Henry J. ....Clinton, IN
Antonini, Henry L. ....Clinton, IN
Antonini, Michael J. ....Toledo, OH
Antonini, Richard E. ....Toledo, OH
Antonini, Thomas J. ....Toledo, OH
Antonino & DiMare ....Amherst, MA
Antonino, Joan A. ....Amherst, MA
Antonino, Lauren Slepin ....Atlanta, GA
Antonio Bates Bernard, Professional Corporation ....Denver, CO
Antonio & Coppola Law Firm .....Branford, CT
Antonio, Douglas J. ....Chicago, IL
Antonio & Flynn ....Old Bridge, NJ
Antonio, Ronald L. ....Denver, CO
Antonio, Susan M.N. ....Boston, MA
Antonio, Vernadette ....Santa Clara, CA
Antonio-Ketcham, Leah ......Los Angeles, CA
Antonio-Ketcham, Leah Katherine
Los Angeles, CA
Antonioli, JoJamette ....Missoula, MT
Antonioli, Vincent ....Guthrie, OK
Antonioli and Wade, P.C. ....Missoula, MT
Antonioli, William ....Sunnyvale, CA
Antonioni, Attilio R. ....Leominster, MA
Antonioni, Robert A. ....Leominster, MA
Antoniono, Gregory J. ....Stanton, CA
Antoniono, James R. ....Greensburg, PA
Antoniou, Andreas A. ......Oakbrook Terrace, IL
Antoniou, Christos T. ....Arlington, VA
Antoniou, Goffstein & Antoniou, L.L.C.
St. Louis, MO
Antoniou, Lydia M. ....Chevy Chase, MD
Antoniou, Paul ....Oak Ridge, NJ
Antoniou, Thomas C. ....St. Louis, MO
Antoniou, Vanessa C. ....St. Louis, MO
Antonis, William N. ....South Bend, IN
Antonoff, Douglas S. ....Denver, CO
Antonoff, Rick B. ....New York, NY
Antonoplis, Robert A. ....Burbank, CA
Antonopoulos, John P. ....Lemont, IL
Antonopoulos, Rosemary
San Francisco, CA
Antonovitz, Frank A. ....South Bend, IN
Antonovych, Boris R. ....Chicago, IL
Antonowich, Michael F. ....Atlanta, GA
Antonowicz, John E. ....Woodbury, NY
Antonowicz, Peter W. ....Rome, NY
Antonsen, Gregory G. ....Honolulu, HI
Antonsen, Raymond G. ....Syosset, NY
Antonsen, Lance C. ....Phoenix, AZ
Antonson, Randall A. ....Duncanville, TX
Antonson, Randall A., P.C.
Duncanville, TX
Antonson, Ross S. ....Minneapolis, MN
Antonsson, Gudrun Hanna ....New York, NY
Antonucci, Alan C. ....Wayne, NJ
Antonucci, Anthony L. ....Niles, OH
Antonucci, Cynthia Weiss ....Millburn, NJ
Antonucci, David P. ....Watertown, NY
Antonucci, Francis J. ....Orange, CT
Westport, CT
Antonucci, Frank E. ....Springfield, MA
Antonucci, James A. ....Malden, MA
Antonucci, Marion K. ....Boston, MA
Antonucci, Peter A. ....New York, NY
Antonucci, Theresa Eileen
Los Angeles, CA
Antonucci, Thomas W. ....Washington, DC
Antonucci, Vincent F. ....Staten Island, NY
Antonuk, John E., Jr. ....Hummelstown, PA
Antonvich, Mark S. ....Tucson, AZ
Antony, John Peter ....Highland Heights, KY
Antony, Michael Greg ....Brooklyn, NY
Antoon, Douglas J. ....McLean, VA
Antoon, Edward ....Greenwood, MS
Antoon, John, II ....Daytona Beach, FL
Antoon, Riggs & Brame ....Alexandria, LA
Antoon, Thomas A. ....Alexandria, LA
Antos, Susan C. ....Albany, NY
Antosh, Louis T., Jr. ....Irvine, CA
Antosiak, James G ....Detroit, MI
Antosik, R.J. ....Flint, MI
Antosz, John M. ....Ephrata, WA
Antoszyk, Peter J. ....Boston, MA
Antoun, Elizabeth S. ....Harrisburg, PA
Antoun, Frederic G., Jr. ....Chambersburg, PA
Antoun, James M. ....Erie, PA
Antoun, Nicholas T. ....Boston, MA
Antounian, Suzy M. ....San Francisco, CA
Antracoli, John L. ....San Jose, CA
Antreasian, Alexandra D.
Indianapolis, IN
Antrican, Gary F. ....Covington, TN
Antrim, Alan H. ....Wynnewood, PA
Antrim, Andrew K. ....Bluffton, IN
Antrim, Bill ....Tarzana, CA
Antrim, Bruce C. ....Pacific, MO
Antrim, Donald A. ....Columbus, OH
Antrim, George E., III ....Minneapolis, MN
Antrim, Glenn H. ....Davenport, IA
Antrim, Hugh T. ....Richmond, VA
Antrim, J. Michael ....Noblesville, IN
Antrim, Patrick S. ....Charlotte, NC
Antrim, Stanley E. ....Liberal, KS
Antrim-Berger, Beth E. ....Bradenton, FL
Antrim-Berger, Beth E., P.A. ....Bradenton, FL
Antrim-Raine, Karen R. ....St. Petersburg, FL
Antton & Associates, P.C.
Washington, DC
Antton, D. Lee ....Washington, DC
Antunes, Steven J. ....Jersey City, NJ
Antúnez, Juan Carlos ....Hialeah, FL
Antush, Ronald A. ....Dallas, TX
Antweil, Brian F. ....Houston, TX
Antzis, David S. ....Berwyn, PA
Antzis, Debra G. ....New York, NY
Anugwom, Charles I. ....Houston, TX
Anulewicz, Christopher S. ....Atlanta, GA
Anuskewicz, Roy A., Jr. ....Albuquerque, NM
Anuta, Karl F., Law Offices of
Boulder, CO
Anuta, Karl Gregory ....Portland, OR
Anutta, Lucile Jamison ....Richmond, VA
Anvari, Sepenta E. ....Beverly Hills, CA
Anvaripour & Associates ....Chicago, IL
Anvaripour, Mark A. ....Chicago, IL
Anwah, Christopher ....Washington, DC
Anwar, Hema Rao ....Los Angeles, CA
Anwyl, James T. ....Sacramento, CA
Anwyl, Scoffield, Stepp & Universal
Sacramento, CA
Anwyll, J. Bradford ....Washington, DC
Anyaibe, Valentine C. ....Washington, DC
Anyon, Joan Temko ....San Francisco, CA
Anzai, Irene A. ....Honolulu, HI
Anzaldi, Matthew A. ....Washington, DC
Anzaldi, Ross R. ....Elizabeth, NJ
Anzaldua, Olga A. ....Houston, TX
Anzaldúa, Theresa
Securities and Exchange Commission,
Division of Enforcement, GV
Anzaldúa-Montoya, Ricardo A.
Washington, DC
Anzalone, Filippa Marullo ....Medford, MA
Anzalone & Fiser ....St. Louis, MO
Anzalone, Frank A. ....St. Louis, MO
Anzalone, Giovanni ....Woodbridge, NJ
Anzalone, James R. ....Philadelphia, PA
Anzalone, Joseph E., Jr. ....Amite, LA
Anzalone, Kerry J. ....Metairie, LA
Anzalone Law Offices ....Scranton, PA
Stroudsburg, PA
Wilkes-Barre, PA
Anzalone, Lawrence ....Tampa, FL
Anzalone, Louis J. ....Florham Park, NJ
Anzalone, Mara L. ....New York, NY
Anzalone, Mark ....Waltham, MA
Anzalone, Richard C. ....Monroe, LA
Anzalone, Steven M. ....Washington, DC
Anzalone, Vincent ....Bronx, NY
Anzalone, William F. ....Scranton, PA
Stroudsburg, PA
Wilkes-Barre, PA
Anzalotta, Jodye M. ....New York, NY
Anzano, Paul ....Trenton, NJ
Anzel, Michael B. ....Port Washington, NY
Anzellotti, Sperling, Pazol & Small Co., L.P.A. ....Warren, OH
Youngstown, OH
Anzelmo, August A. ....Chicago Heights, IL
Anzelmo, Donald J. ....Monroe, LA
Anzelmo, James A. ....Chillicothe, OH
Anzelmo, Salvador ....New Orleans, LA
Anzelmo, Thomas P. ....Metairie, LA
Anzelone, Richard J. ....Providence, RI
Anziano, Antonio R. ....San Francisco, CA
Anziano, Mark E. ....Hartford, CT
Anzich, Methodius J. ....Calabash, NC
Anzick, Stanley F. ....Denver, CO
Anzinger, F. William ....Indianapolis, IN
Anzivina, Michael R ....New York, NY
Anzivino, Ralph C. ....Milwaukee, WI
Anzman, Mark C. ....Miamisburg, OH
Anzur, John A. ....San Francisco, CA
Anzúres, Claudia Fitzpatrick ......San Diego, CA
Aoanan, Manuel C. ....Hagåtña, GU
Aoki, George T. ....Honolulu, HI
Aoki, Paul S., (A Law Corporation)
Honolulu, HI
Aoki, Rod S., (Atty. At Law, A Law Corp.)
Honolulu, HI
Aoki, Russell M. ....Seattle, WA
Aoki & Sakamoto ....Seattle, WA
Aoki, Zachary B. ....San Antonio, TX
Aoun, Joseph T. ....Detroit, MI
Aoyama, Randy J. ....Seattle, WA
Apa, Diane ....Philadelphia, PA
Apadula, John C. ....New York, NY
Apaloo, Khymberli S. ....Ontario, CA
Apap, Paul C. ....Bloomfield Hills, MI
Apar, Irving C. ....New York, NY
Aparicio, Ana M. ....Oxnard, CA
Aparicio, Edward G. ....Edinburg, TX
Aparicio, Francisco Javier
Los Angeles, CA
Aparisi, Jaime W. ....Washington, DC
Aparo, Paul J. ....Hartford, CT
Apat, Richard H. ....Kew Gardens, NY
Apatoff, Adam S. ....Washington, DC
Apatoff, David B. ....Washington, DC
Apcel, Edmund J. ....Morton Grove, IL
Apcel, Melissa A. ....Chicago, IL
Apel, Edwin (WIN) V., Jr. ....Boise, ID
Apel & Miller ....Portsmouth, OH
Apel, Pat ....Portsmouth, OH
Apel, Richard T. ....Los Angeles, CA
Apel, Steven R. ....Chicago, IL
Apel, Susan ....South Royalton, VT
Apel, Susan A. ....Pittsburgh, PA
Apeland, Donald C. ....Dallas, TX
Apelbaum, Perry H.
House of Representatives,
Committee Legal Personnel, GV
Apelian, Mark D. ....Calabasas, CA
Apelian, Robert P. ....Lansdowne, PA
Apell & Detrick, P.A. ....Browns Mills, NJ
Apell, Erwin D. ....Browns Mills, NJ
Apell, Jeffrey S. ....Browns Mills, NJ
Apell, Jennifer C. ....Haddonfield, NJ
Apellaniz Storer, Luis ....San Juan, PR
Apelman, Mark ....Denver, CO
Apelt, Michael ....New York, NY
Apelt, Ronald A. ....Cleveland, OH
Apenbrink, Edwin J. ....Las Vegas, NV
Apenes, Mikal J. ....Santa Barbara, CA
Aperans, Gundars ....Charlotte, NC
Apfel, David J. ....Boston, MA
Apfel, Dennis Mark ....Deer Park, NY
Apfel, Dov ....Rockville, MD
Apfel, Gary ....Los Angeles, CA
Apfel, Gary N. ....Orford, NH
Apfel & Greene, P.C. ....Rockville, MD
Apfel, Jerome B. ....Philadelphia, PA
Apfel, Kenneth S. ....Hackensack, NJ
Apfel, Robert J. ....New York, NY
Apfel, Sharon Margolis ....Rockville, MD
Apfel, William A. ....New York, NY
Apfelbaum, Apfelbaum & Apfelbaum
Sunbury, PA
Apfelbaum, Barry ....Orlando, FL
Apfelbaum, Barry, P.A. ....Orlando, FL
Apfelbaum, Jeffrey ....Sunbury, PA
Apfelbaum, Larry A. ....Bloomington, IL
Macomb, IL
Peoria, IL
Quincy, IL
Rushville, IL
Springfield, IL
Apfelbaum, Marc J. ....Stamford, CT
Apfelbaum, Michael Morris ....Sunbury, PA
Apfelbaum, Michael N.
Department of Labor,
Office of the Solicitor, GV
Apfelbaum, Sidney ....Sunbury, PA
Apfelbaum, Stanley ....Roslyn, NY
Apfelberg, Alvin I. ....New York, NY
Apfelberg, Andrew M. ......San Francisco, CA
Apfelberg, Robert S. ....Woodland Hills, CA
Apfeld, Michael B. ....Milwaukee, WI
Apfeldorf, Morton ....Stamford, CT
Apfeldorf, Sharon ....Peapack, NJ
Apffel, Darrell A. ....Galveston, TX
Apffel, E. A. "Trey", III, Law Office of
Texas City, TX
Apffel, Ervin A., Jr. ....Galveston, TX
Apffel, Paul Andrew ....San Rafael, CA
Apffel, Ralph A. ....Galveston, TX
Apffel & Tracey, L.L.P. ....Alvin, TX
Apgar, E. Mary ....Amherst, MA
Apgar, E. Stormy ....Sheridan, WY
Apgar, Harry E., Jr. ....DeLand, FL
Apgar, Howard J. ....Clinton, NJ
Apgar, Jonathan M. ....Roanoke, VA
Apgar, Kenneth E. ....Tampa, FL
Apgar, Kristen R. ....Malden, MA
Apgar, Robert C. ....Tallahassee, FL
Apgar, Robert F. ....Daytona Beach, FL
Apgar, William M. ....San Diego, CA
Apger, William G. ....Oroville, CA
Apicella, Andrew ....Milford, CT
Apicella, Anthony G. ....Branford, CT
Apicella, Anthony G., P.C. ....Branford, CT
Apicella, Denise D. ....New York, NY
Apicella, Douglas J. ....Branford, CT
Apicella, F. M. ....Cleveland, OH
Apicella, Francis J. ....Bronx, NY
Apicella, Joseph A. ....Hoboken, NJ
Apicella, Richard L. ....New York, NY
Apicella, Scott ....New York, NY
Apicella and Trapp ....Cleveland, OH
Apicella, Vincent A. ....New York, NY
Apicelli, Anthony J., Jr. ....Trenton, NJ
Apicelli, Nicholas Caputo ....Toms River, NJ
Apicelli, Samuel W. ....Philadelphia, PA
Apiscopa, Jennifer R. ....New York, NY

Apitz, John F. .... **Minneapolis, MN**
Apjohn, Nelson G. .... **Boston, MA**
Apke, Thomas M. .... Laguna Niguel, CA
Apker, Burton M., P.C. .... Phoenix, AZ
Apker, David B. .... **Phoenix, AZ**
Apker, David B., P.C. .... **Phoenix, AZ**
Apker, John L. .... **Omaha, NE**
Apkin, Benjamin .... North Adams, MA
Apkin, Joan .... Boston, MA
Aplin, Alison .... Staten Island, NY
Aplin, Kenneth L. .... Cincinnati, OH
Aplin, Maureen .... Santa Ana, CA
Aplin, Ronald S. .... **Madison, WI**
Aplin, Scotti C. .... Austin, TX
Aplin, Thomas P. .... **Costa Mesa, CA**
Aplin, Thomas P. .... **Newport Beach, CA**
Aplington, Kaufman, McClintock, Steele & Barry, Ltd. .... La Salle, IL
Apo, Todd K. .... **Honolulu, HI**
Apocotos, T. Gregory .... Dayton, OH
Apodaca, Lawrence .... Monterey Park, CA
Apodaca, Leslie McCarthy **Albuquerque, NM**
Apodaca, Lillian G. .... **Albuquerque, NM**
Apodaca, Patrick V. .... **Albuquerque, NM**
Apodaca, Rudy S. .... Las Cruces, NM
Apodaca, Ted .... Santa Fe, NM
Apoian, H. Gary .... Chesterfield, MO
Apol, David J. .... United States Senate, Committee Legal Personnel, GV
Apol, John P. .... East Lansing, MI
Apoldo, Louis J. .... Philadelphia, PA
Apolinsky, Craig D. .... **Atlanta, GA**
Apolinsky, Harold I. .... **Birmingham, AL**
Apolinsky, Stephen D. .... **Decatur, GA**
Apollo, Kevin M. .... **Philadelphia, PA**
Apolskis, Michael G. .... Indianapolis, IN
Apolzon, Lawrence Eli .... **New York, NY**
Aponick, John J., Jr. .... **Scranton, PA**
Aponik, Kimberly Ann .... Wilmington, DE
Aponte, Alexander .... New Britain, CT
Aponte, Juliska M. .... **Chicago, IL**
Aponte, Kimberly .... Boston, MA
Aponte, Lester F. .... **Los Angeles, CA**
Aponte, Nilda I. .... General Accounting Office, Civil Rights Office, GV
Aponte Colon, Jose B. .... Aibonito, PR
Aponte De Aviles, Ina R. .... San Juan, PR
Aponte-Parsi, Jaime J. .... San Juan, PR
Aponte-Pedraza, Justa .... **San Juan, PR**
Aponte-Pedraza Law Offices **San Juan, PR**
Aponte Perez, Francisco .... San Juan, PR
Aponte-Sanchez, Raul .... Bayamon, PR
Apostle, Basil N. .... Long Island City, NY
Apostle, James A. .... Long Beach, CA
Apostle, James N. .... Dallas, TX
Apostle, John G., II .... Richmond, VA
Apostolakos, Mary J. Department of Justice, Tax Division, GV
Apostolicas, George P. .... Nashua, NH
Apostolico, David M. .... West Chester, PA
Apostolico, James V. .... Wilmington, DE
Apostolides, George P. .... **Chicago, IL**
Apostolidis, Helen .... Hartford, CT
Apostolik, Richard .... Summit, NJ
Apostolos, George M. .... **Casper, WY**
Apostolou, John L. .... Salem, VA
Apostolou, Mark .... **Ocean Township, NJ**
Apotheker, Charles .... Pomona, NY
Apovian, Mark .... Englewood Cliffs, NJ
Apovian, Philip C. .... Englewood Cliffs, NJ
App, Oliver L. .... Rockville, MD
Appe, Stephen C. .... Albany, NY
Appel, Adam L. .... **Atlanta, GA**
Appel, Alan I. .... **New York, NY**
Appel, Albert M. .... **New York, NY**
Appel, Alfred .... **New York, NY**
Appel, Allan F. .... Miami, FL
Appel, Andrea S. .... Sherman Oaks, CA
Appel, Andrew Hooker .... Lancaster, PA
Appel & Appel .... Tustin, CA
Appel & Appel .... Walnut Creek, CA
Appel & Appel, Ltd. .... Lansing, IL
Appel, Barry M. .... Encino, CA
Appel, Brent R. .... **Des Moines, IA**
Appel, Brian E. .... **Bensalem, PA**; **Jenkintown, PA**
Appel, Britta K. .... Tustin, CA
Appel, Carl R. .... Baltimore, MD
Appel, Charles .... Miami, FL
Appel, Charles Paul .... Orange, CA
Appel, Claude W. .... Walsenburg, CO
Appel, David M. .... **New York, NY**
Appel, Deborah K. .... Paducah, KY
Appel, Deborah L. .... Tampa, FL
Appel, Diane S. .... Morganville, NJ
Appel, Elizabeth K. .... **Charleston, WV**
Appel, Eric M. .... West Palm Beach, FL
Appel, Erin Goldwasser .... **Boston, MA**
Appel, Evan .... **Atlanta, GA**
Appel, Evelyn D. .... **White Plains, NY**
Appel, Garry R. .... **Denver, CO**
Appel, Gary A. .... Aventura, FL
Appel, Gary A., P.A., Law Offices of Aventura, FL
Appel, Gary S. .... Santa Ana, CA
Appel, Gila Rosenstock .... St. Louis, MO
Appel & Glueck, P.C. .... **Seattle, WA**
Appel, Grace R. .... **New York, NY**
Appel, Henry G. .... Columbus, OH
Appel, Howard M. .... **Los Angeles, CA**
Appel, Jack I. .... New York, NY
Appel, James R. .... Santa Ana, CA
Appel, James W. .... Ephrata, PA; **Lancaster, PA**
Appel, Janet F. .... Westbury, NY
Appel, Jeffrey .... Southfield, MI
Appel, Jeffrey E. .... Lakeland, FL
Appel, Jeffrey W. .... **Salt Lake City, UT**
Appel, John B., Jr. .... Gretna, LA
Appel, John G., Jr., Law Offices of **San Diego, CA**; San Francisco, CA
Appel, John H. .... **Cincinnati, OH**
Appel, John J., Jr. .... Baltimore, MD
Appel, John W. .... **San Jose, CA**
Appel, Joseph J. .... Walnut Creek, CA
Appel, Joseph M. .... Worcester, MA
Appel, Karen M. .... Waukesha, WI
Appel, Kellie S. .... Atlanta, GA
Appel, Kenneth J. .... New York, NY
Appel, Kenneth M. .... St. Albans, VT
Appel, Kevin R. .... Arlington, VA
Appel, Laurence B. .... Atlanta, GA
Appel, Lawrence John .... Oakland, CA
Appel, Leon .... Jamaica, NY
Appel, Linden G. .... Lansing, KS
Appel, Lisa Levin .... Denver, CO
Appel, Marc A. .... **Phoenix, AZ**
Appel, Marc A. .... Baltimore, MD
Appel, Marie Noel .... **San Francisco, CA**
Appel, Marjory A. .... **Englewood Cliffs, NJ**
Appel, Marlene .... Phoenix, AZ
Appel, Martin S. .... **Los Angeles, CA**
Appel, Michael J. .... Walnut Creek, CA
Appel, Michael S. .... **Boston, MA**
Appel, Nancy J. .... **San Francisco, CA**
Appel, Nancy Susan .... **Washington, DC**
Appel, Patrick C. .... **Houston, TX**
Appel, Peter T. .... Lansing, IL
Appel, R. Jan .... Jackson, MI
Appel, Richard M. .... **New York, NY**
Appel, Richard N .... **Washington, DC**
Appel, Robert S. .... Denver, CO
Appel, Robert S. .... **New York, NY**
Appel, Robin .... Stockton, CA
Appel, Ronald I. .... Tustin, CA
Appel, Ronald M. .... New York, NY
Appel, Samuel .... **Atlanta, GA**
Appel, Sheila P. .... New York, NY
Appel, Sherman P. .... Chicago, IL
Appel, Sheryl L. .... **Palo Alto, CA**
Appel, Stephen R. .... Evansville, IN
Appel, Susan D. .... **Chicago, IL**
Appel, T. Roberts, II .... **Lancaster, PA**
Appel, Thomas A. .... Lansing, IL
Appel, Thomas A. .... Owings Mills, MD
Appel & Warlaumont .... **Salt Lake City, UT**
Appel, Warren H. .... Chicago, IL
Appel, William E. .... Green Bay, WI
Appel, William H. .... Ottumwa, IA
Appel, William M. .... Boston, MA
Appel, William N. .... **Seattle, WA**
Appel & Yost LLP .... Christiana, PA; Ephrata, PA; **Lancaster, PA**; **New Holland, PA**; Quarryville, PA; Strasburg, PA
Appelbaum, Alan .... **New York, NY**
Appelbaum, Amy M. .... Brooklyn, NY
Appelbaum, Ann H. .... New York, NY
Appelbaum, Arlen M. .... New York, NY
Appelbaum & Associates .... **Atlanta, GA**
Appelbaum, Bauman & Appelbaum Liberty, NY
Appelbaum, Beth L. .... **San Francisco, CA**
Appelbaum, Eve A. .... **Atlanta, GA**
Appelbaum, George D. .... Shingle Springs, CA
Appelbaum, Jeffrey R. .... **Cleveland, OH**
Appelbaum, Joel R. .... Liberty, NY
Appelbaum, John S. .... Hillsboro, MO
Appelbaum, Judith C. .... United States Senate, Committee Legal Personnel, GV
Appelbaum, Karen A. Board of Governors Of The Federal Reserve System, Office of the General Counsel, GV
Appelbaum, Kenneth M. .... Kew Gardens, NY
Appelbaum, Larry A. .... Chicago, IL
Appelbaum, Mark Jeffrey .... White Plains, NY
Appelbaum, Martin M. .... New York, NY
Appelbaum, Michael A. .... Scottsdale, AZ
Appelbaum, Michael E. .... **Buffalo, NY**
Appelbaum, Michael W. .... **New York, NY**
Appelbaum, Michael W., P.C. **New York, NY**
Appelbaum, Mitchel .... **Boston, MA**
Appelbaum, Pauline A. .... Houston, TX
Appelbaum, Peter G. .... Albany, NY
Appelbaum, Richard A. .... **Long Beach, CA**
Appelbaum, Scott L. .... **New York, NY**
Appelbaum, Steven .... Chicago, IL
Appelbaum, Theresa A. .... **St. Louis, MO**
Appelbe, Timothy D. .... Pittsburgh, PA
Appelblatt, Gary M. .... **Sacramento, CA**
Appelgate, Dennis D. .... Toledo, IA
Appelhans, Michael Patrick .... **Irvine, CA**
Appelhans, Patricia F. .... Wheaton, IL
Appell, Annette R. .... Chicago, IL
Appell, Barry M. .... **Los Angeles, CA**
Appell, Charles Samuel, III .... Belton, TX
Appell, Dale S. .... Tampa, FL
Appell, David A. .... Blauvelt, NY
Appell, John J. .... **New York, NY**
Appell, Melvin C. .... Encino, CA
Appell, R. Michael .... **Alice, TX**; Beeville, TX
Appellate Resources Group **Santa Monica, CA**
Appellate Services .... Grosse Pointe, MI
Appello, Elizabeth J. .... Oakhurst, NJ
Appellof, Eric J. .... Bridgeport, CT
Appelman, Avery L. E. .... Minneapolis, MN
Appelman, Daniel L. .... **Menlo Park, CA**
Appelman, Harris B. .... **Hartford, CT**
Appelman, Lily D. .... **Denver, CO**
Appelquist, J. A.(Jack) .... Springfield, MO
Appelquist, John F. .... **Springfield, MO**
Appelquist Law Offices .... Mount Vernon, MO; Springfield, MO
Appelquist, Nancy .... Springfield, MO
Appelquist, Susan .... Mount Vernon, MO; Springfield, MO
Appelrouth, Michelle Rose .... **Atlanta, GA**
Appelsmith, Beth M. .... Sacramento, CA
Appelt, Gary N. .... Roseville, CA
Appelt, Howard F., II .... Riverdale, NJ
Appelt, James M. .... **Houston, TX**
Appelt, Sharon Steberl .... Chicago, IL
Appelwick, Marlin J. .... Seattle, WA
Appelwick, Robert A., Jr .... Madison, SD
Appenfelder, Margaret .... **Louisville, KY**
Appenteng, Kofi .... **New York, NY**
Appenzeller, Phil Carl, Jr. .... **Dallas, TX**
Appenzeller, Rebecca H. .... Fairborn, OH
Apperley, Elizabeth A. .... Austin, TX
Apperson, Ann A. .... Daytona Beach, FL
Apperson, Bernard James .... Alexandria, VA
Apperson, Crump & Maxwell, PLC **Memphis, TN**
Apperson, Jeffrey A. .... Louisville, KY
Apperson, Julie Brown .... Louisville, KY
Apperson, Lawson F. .... **Memphis, TN**
Apperson, Rick L. .... **Knoxville, TN**
Apperson, Ron .... Los Angeles, CA
Appert, Robert H. .... San Gabriel, CA
Appert, Robert J. .... St. Paul, MN
Appet & Appet, P.C. .... Fairfield, NJ
Appet, Laurence .... Fairfield, NJ
Appicelli, Frank A. .... **Hartford, CT**
Appl, Patricia J. .... Norman, OK
Applbaum, Edward A. .... San Diego, CA
Applbaum, Marvin L. .... Vista, CA
Apple and Apple, A Professional Corporation **Pittsburgh, PA**
Apple, Dana K. .... Independence, MO
Apple, Eric W. .... Chicago, IL
Apple, Gordon J. .... St. Paul, MN
Apple, Irving D. .... Los Angeles, CA
Apple, J. David .... **Coppell, TX**
Apple, J. David, P.C. .... **Coppell, TX**; **Denton, TX**; **Irving, TX**
Apple, James G. .... Federal Judicial Center, GV
Apple, James R. .... **Pittsburgh, PA**
Apple, K. Bret .... **Salem, OH**
Apple, Lawrence E. .... Cleveland, OH
Apple, Lesley .... Hood River, OR
Apple, Leslie M. .... **Albany, NY**
Apple, Marvin J. .... **Pittsburgh, PA**
Apple, Miles S. .... **Louisville, KY**
Apple, Paul B. .... Seattle, WA
Apple, Paul L. .... **Manchester, NH**
Apple, R. Ted .... **Palo Alto, CA**
Apple, Robert M., & Associates **Las Vegas, NV**
Apple, Sheldon A. .... Lyndhurst, OH
Apple, Thomas N. .... New York, NY
Apple, Walter E. .... Fort Lauderdale, FL
Apple, Willis W. .... **Reidsville, NC**
Appleang, Dennis R. .... Wayne, NJ
Applebaum, Alan C. .... Southfield, MI
Applebaum, Alan J. .... **Boston, MA**
Applebaum, Amy L. .... Los Angeles, CA
Applebaum, Beth E. .... Troy, MI
Applebaum, Charles .... **Edison, NJ**
Applebaum, David A. .... **Elkins Park, PA**
Applebaum, Deborah C. **St. Petersburg, FL**
Applebaum, Doris .... Bensalem, PA
Applebaum, Eric D. .... Springfield, MA
Applebaum, Harvey M. .... **Washington, DC**
Applebaum, Jacob .... Chicago, IL
Applebaum, Jay Norman .... Tarzana, CA
Applebaum, Jerome M. .... El Monte, CA
Applebaum, Jill R. .... Washington, DC
Applebaum, Joel D. .... **Detroit, MI**
Applebaum, Jonah J. .... **New York, NY**
Applebaum, Kenneth J. .... **New York, NY**
Applebaum, L. A. .... Delray Beach, FL
Applebaum Law Firm .... St. Paul, MN
Applebaum, Lee .... **Philadelphia, PA**
Applebaum, Martha L. .... Los Angeles, CA
Applebaum, Paul .... St. Paul, MN
Applebaum, Paul L. .... **Chicago, IL**
Applebaum, Richard B. .... Providence, RI
Applebaum, Robin B. .... **New York, NY**
Applebaum, Ronald M. .... Southfield, MI
Applebaum, Sandra J. .... El Monte, CA
Applebaum, Scott .... **Plainsboro, NJ**
Applebaum, Sol .... Chicago, IL
Applebaum, Stanley A. .... Staten Island, NY
Applebaum, Stanley D. .... Boynton Beach, FL
Applebaum, Stuart A. .... Bedford Park, IL
Applebee, Alan W. .... Jacksonville, IL
Appleberry, Elaine .... New Orleans, LA
Appleberry, J. Mark .... **Louisville, KY**
Appleberry, Lisa R. .... **San Francisco, CA**
Appleberry, Nicole .... **Ann Arbor, MI**
Appleby, Barbara A. .... Portland, ME
Appleby, Bethany L. .... **New Haven, CT**
Appleby, Cornwell G. .... **New York, NY**
Appleby, David C. .... Miami, FL
Appleby, David N. .... Ozark, MO
Appleby, Frank M. .... Vero Beach, FL
Appleby, George W. .... **Des Moines, IA**
Appleby, Gerald H. .... Ogden, UT
Appleby, Kenneth R. .... **Burlington, VT**
Appleby, Linda King .... Fort Lauderdale, FL
Appleby, Nancy J. .... **Albuquerque, NM**
Appleby, Nancy Ofte .... **Dulles, VA**
Appleby, Richard, Law Offices of **New York, NY**
Appleby, Robert A. .... **New York, NY**
Appleby, Ronald C. .... New Brunswick, NJ
Appleby, Teri E. .... Berkeley, CA
Appleby, Theodore .... South River, NJ
Appleby, William Richard .... New York, NY
Applefeld, David B. .... **Baltimore, MD**
Applefeld, Laurie S. .... Baltimore, MD
Appleford, David R. .... **Bloomfield Hills, MI**
Appleford, John W. .... Staunton, VA
Appleford, Robert W. **Bloomfield Hills, MI**
Applegarth, Barbara F. .... **Cincinnati, OH**
Applegarth, Paul V. .... Washington, DC
Applegarth, S. Renee .... **South Bend, IN**
Applegate, A. Bryant .... Orlando, FL
Applegate, Aaron Albert .... Hoboken, NJ
Applegate, Alan M. .... Jeffersonville, IN
Applegate, Amy G. .... **Cincinnati, OH**
Applegate, Bennett P. .... Chicago, IL
Applegate, Carolyn Marie .... Vacaville, CA
Applegate, David L. .... **Chicago, IL**
Applegate, Douglas A. .... **San Francisco, CA**
Applegate, Douglas L. .... Irvine, CA
Applegate, E. Timothy .... Glendale, CA
Applegate, George .... San Francisco, CA
Applegate, James Edward .... Cincinnati, OH
Applegate, James L. .... **Cheyenne, WY**
Applegate, Jarrett T. .... **Springfield, MO**
Applegate, John S. .... Cincinnati, OH
Applegate, J. S. .... **Yakima, WA**
Applegate, K. Edwin .... Bloomington, IN
Applegate, Kelly J. .... **Salt Lake City, UT**
Applegate, Kelly Quigley **San Francisco, CA**
Applegate, Kenneth H. .... Los Angeles, CA
Applegate, Leta L. .... **New York, NY**
Applegate, Mark W. .... **Indianapolis, IN**
Applegate, Mark W., P.C., Law Offices of **Indianapolis, IN**
Applegate, McDonald, Koch & Arnold Bloomington, IN
Applegate, Robert E. .... **Oklahoma City, OK**
Applegate, Robert P. .... San Pedro, CA
Applegate, Robert W. .... Ilion, NY
Applegate, Sandra L. .... Ukiah, CA
Applegate, Sharon B. .... **New York, NY**
Applegate, Steven D. .... Carbondale, IL
Applegate, Susan L. .... Los Angeles, CA
Applegate & Thorne-Thomsen, P.C. Chicago, IL
Applegate Valauskas Rosen & Bernstein **Chicago, IL**; **Boston, MA**
Applegate, Vicki C. .... **Dallas, TX**
Applegate, W. E., III .... **Charleston, SC**
Applegate, William R. .... West Columbia, SC
Applegate-Lockridge, Shirley J. Indianapolis, IN
Appleget, Robert L., Jr. .... **Ocala, FL**
Applehans, Stephen G. .... Waukegan, IL
Appleman, James P. .... Panama City, FL
Appleman, Jeff T. .... **San Francisco, CA**
Appleman, Jolene Weinstein .... Pittsburgh, PA
Appleman, Joseph .... Monsey, NY
Appleman, Lawrence J. .... Cambridge, MA
Appleman, Michael G. .... **Fort Worth, TX**
Appleman, R Gordon .... **Fort Worth, TX**
Appleman, Thomas G. .... **Troy, MI**
Appleman, Wayne R. .... Portland, OR
Applen, David A. .... Santa Rosa, CA
Applequist, Kimberly F. .... **Los Angeles, CA**
Appler, Charles I. .... Dallas, TX
Appler, Thomas L. .... **Fairfax, VA**
Appler, W. Christopher .... St. Louis, MO
Applestein, Allan H. .... South Miami, FL
Applestein & Applestein, P.A. Bethesda, MD
Applestein, David .... Bethesda, MD
Applestein, Donald .... Wallingford, PA
Applestein, William G. .... Bethesda, MD
Appleton, Alan B. .... Frankfort, IN
Appleton, Aldona E., (Mrs.) New Brunswick, NJ
Appleton, Amie S. .... Hartford, CT
Appleton & Appleton, LLC .... **Hartford, CT**
Appleton & Associates .... **New York, NY**
Appleton, Barry .... **New York, NY**
Appleton, Byron Y. .... Los Angeles, CA
Appleton, Candace Scott .... Islandia, NY
Appleton, David Ross .... Phoenix, AZ
Appleton, Douglas S. .... **Palo Alto, CA**
Appleton, Hartley R. .... Daly City, CA
Appleton, Heather .... **Los Angeles, CA**
Appleton, James B. .... Trenton, NJ
Appleton, John H. .... **Scranton, PA**
Appleton, Jon M. .... **Palo Alto, CA**
Appleton, Kretmar, Beatty & Stolze **St. Louis, MO**
Appleton Law Firm .... **Los Angeles, CA**
Appleton, Mark A. .... **Aledo, IL**
Appleton, Mark J. .... Denver, CO
Appleton, Mary Moss .... **Los Angeles, CA**
Appleton & McHugh .... **Aledo, IL**
Appleton, Michael J. .... **Winter Park, FL**
Appleton, Morton W. .... **Hartford, CT**
Appleton, Nancy Coughlin North Miami, FL
Appleton, Pasternak & Pasternak, A Law Corporation .... Los Angeles, CA
Appleton, Peter M. .... **Los Angeles, CA**
Appleton, Peter M. .... **Hartford, CT**
Appleton, Randall E. .... Portsmouth, VA
Appleton, Richard N. .... **San Diego, CA**
Appleton, Robert O., Jr. .... **St. Louis, MO**
Appleton, Susan F. .... St. Louis, MO
Appleton, Thomas R. .... Springfield, IL

Appleton, William ..... Cincinnati, OH
Appleton, William M. ..... Coeur d'Alene, ID
Appletree, Steven R. ..... Farmington, CT
Applewhaite, Eleanor S. ..... New York, NY
Applewhite, Francine L. ..... Boston, MA
Applewhite, Henry J. ..... Aberdeen, MS
Applewhite, Henry J. ..... Tupelo, MS
Applewhite, Kaye ..... Conroe, TX
Applewhite, Sam P., III ..... Phoenix, AZ
Applewhite, Thomas D. ..... Richmond, VA
Appley, Elizabeth J. ..... Atlanta, GA
Appleyard, Jennifer ..... Boston, MA
Appleyard, William T. ..... Malden, MA
Appling, Cathy L. ..... Department of Justice, Executive Office for Immigration Review, GV
Appling, Dana S. ..... Sacramento, CA
Appling, Marvin R. ..... Wichita, KS
Appman, John E. ..... Jamestown, TN
Appold, Kevin U. ..... Apple Valley, MN
Appollina, Mary A. ..... Rahway, NJ
Appolonia, Felix A. ..... West Warwick, RI
Apps, Antonia M. ..... Washington, DC
Apps, Gary E. ..... Kalamazoo, MI
Aprahamian & Aprahamian, A Professional Corporation ..... Costa Mesa, CA
Aprahamian, Constance E. ..... Irvine, CA
Aprahamian & Friend ..... Los Angeles, CA
Aprahamian, Mark H. ..... Los Angeles, CA
Aprahamian, Michael J. ..... Milwaukee, WI
Aprahamian, Michael T. ..... Costa Mesa, CA
Aprahamian, Richard J. ..... Costa Mesa, CA
Aprati, Daniel J. ..... Markham, IL
Aprati, Robert L. ..... Lisle, IL
Aprea, James J. ..... Anchorage, AK
Aprigliano, Ludovico ..... Morristown, NJ
April, Jeffery A. ..... Linwood, NJ
Marmora, NJ
April, Lewis B. ..... Atlantic City, NJ
April, Lori S. ..... Garden City, NY
April, Mary F. ..... Boca Raton, FL
April & Maudsley, P.A. ..... Linwood, NJ
Marmora, NJ
April, Rand S. ..... Los Angeles, CA
April, Randi Doner ..... Newark, NJ
Aprile, Dominic J. ..... Lakewood, NJ
Aprile, Gregory J. ..... Wayne, NJ
Aprill, Susan H. ..... Miami, FL
Aprilliano, Robert E. ..... Detroit, MI
Apruzzese, McDermott, Mastro & Murphy
Camden, NJ
Elizabeth, NJ
Flemington, NJ
Hackensack, NJ
Jersey City, NJ
Liberty Corner, NJ
Morristown, NJ
Newark, NJ
New Brunswick, NJ
Paterson, NJ
Somerville, NJ
Springfield, NJ
Trenton, NJ
Apruzzese, Theresa ..... Boston, MA
Apruzzese, Vincent J. ..... Liberty Corner, NJ
Apsan, Moses ..... Newark, NJ
Apsan, Moses, P.C. ..... Newark, NJ
Apseloff, Stanford ..... Columbus, OH
Apsley, R. Kent ..... Shelbyville, IN
Apt & Apt ..... Iola, KS
Apt, Benjamin L. ..... Cambridge, MA
Apt, Charles H., III ..... Iola, KS
Apt, Chas. H., II ..... Iola, KS
Apt, Frederick G., Jr. ..... Iola, KS
Apt, Gloria Kurman ..... Encino, CA
Apt, William Burt ..... Austin, TX
Aptaker, David ..... Somerville, MA
Aptaker, Edward ..... Washington, DC
Aptaker, Peri Ann ..... Providence, RI
Apte, Stanley H. ..... Miami Beach, FL
Aptekar, Nancy A. ..... San Francisco, CA
Apter, Alan B. ..... San Francisco, CA
Apter, David ..... Northbrook, IL
Apter, Denise ..... West Palm Beach, FL
Apter, George B. ..... Honolulu, HI
Apter, Gregory ..... Chicago, IL
Apter, Julie Pasquariello ..... Buffalo, NY
Apter, Morris ..... West Hartford, CT
Apter, Ronald S. ..... New Haven, CT
Apter, Yale L. ..... Livingston, NJ
Aptheker, Steven B. ..... Melville, NY
Aptowitz, Andrea B ..... Boston, MA
Apuzzo, Jacob ..... Kennebunk, ME
Apuzzo, Jeffery P. ..... Hartford, CT
Apuzzo, Mario ..... Cranbury, NJ
Apuzzo, Mario ..... Jamesburg, NJ
Apuzzo, Mario ..... Monroe Township, NJ
Apuzzo, Nicole Adele ..... New York, NY
Apuzzo, William J. ..... West Palm Beach, FL
New York, NY
Apy, Chester ..... Toms River, NJ
Apy, David C. ..... Newark, NJ
Apy, Patricia E. (IBA) ..... Red Bank, NJ
Aqua, Jocelyn A. ..... Washington, DC
Aqua, Rebecca M. ..... Chicago, IL
Aquadro, Mark S. ..... Jackson, MS
Aquaro, John R. ..... Mineola, NY
New York, NY
White Plains, NY
Aquavia, James ..... Los Angeles, CA
Aquavia, Julie ..... Waukesha, WI
Aqui, Keith A. ..... Treasury Department, Internal Revenue Service, GV
Aquila, Albert B. ..... Mineola, NY
New York, NY
Aquila, Francis J. ..... New York, NY
Aquila, Frank D. ..... Cleveland, OH
Aquila, Julia Spazzarini ..... Huntsville, AL
Aquilante, Jeffrey M. ..... Rockaway Beach, NY
Aquilina, Carey Ance ..... Eatontown, NJ
Aquilina, James M. ..... New York, NY
Aquilina, Vivian M. ..... Rochester, NY
Aquilino, Michael J. ..... Bethesda, MD
Aquilino, Nicholas J. ..... Arlington, VA
Aquilino, Vincent M. ..... Chicago, IL
Aquilino & Welsh, P.C. ..... Arlington, VA
Aquilino, William J. ..... Scranton, PA
Aquilio, Mark ..... Bethel, CT
Aquino, Allison ..... Pasadena, CA
Aquino, Frank J. ..... Owings Mills, MD
Aquino, Jerome P. ..... Alexandria, VA
Aquino, John J. ..... Boston, MA
Aquino, John Thomas ..... Washington, DC
Aquino, Jose A. ..... New York, NY
Aquino, Juan A. ..... San Juan, PR
Aquino, Maite ..... New York, NY
Aquino, Mario J. ..... Virginia Beach, VA
Aquino, Michael N. ..... Newark, NJ
Aquino, Monica A. ..... Washington, DC
Aquino, Norberito J. ..... Chula Vista, CA
Aquino, Paul ..... Pasadena, CA
Aquino, Rhonel T. ..... Pasadena, CA
Araas, John F. ..... Sheridan, WY
Arabasz, Raymond E. ..... Bridgewater, MA
Arabatzis, Constance Elaine
New York, NY
Arabia, Paul ..... Wichita, KS
Arabian, Armand ..... Van Nuys, CA
Arabian, Azneve Anne ..... Glendale, CA
Arabian, Gregory H. ..... Cambridge, MA
Arabian, Robert A. ..... Van Nuys, CA
Arabian, Robert A. ..... Tamarac, FL
Arabo, Jalal Y. ..... Farmington Hills, MI
Aracic, Nicholas ..... Oakland, CA
Araco, Nicholas A., Jr. ..... Wayne, PA
Aractingi, Helene Hayek ..... New York, NY
Arad, Graham N. ..... New York, NY
Arad, Guy ..... New York, NY
Arado, Frank E. ..... Chicago, IL
Arado, John J. ..... Chicago, IL
Arago, Maureen A. ..... Longwood, FL
Aragon, Arthur O. ..... Pasadena, CA
Aragon, Burlington, Weil & Crockett, P.A.
Miami, FL
Aragon, Cynthia A. ..... Albuquerque, NM
Aragon, Ellen ..... West Los Angeles, CA
Aragón, Gus, Jr. ..... Tucson, AZ
Aragon, John A. ..... Santa Fe, NM
Aragón, José L. ..... Alhambra, CA
Aragon, Lauren J. Ridgeway ..... Miami, FL
Aragon, Manny M. ..... Albuquerque, NM
Aragon, Nadeline ..... Houston, TX
Aragon, Rachel M. ..... Sacramento, CA
Aragon, Ray M. ..... Washington, DC
Aragon, Raymond George ..... Chula Vista, CA
Aragon, Rebecca M. ..... Los Angeles, CA
Aragon, Robert A. ..... Gallup, NM
Aragon, Rudolph F. ..... Miami, FL
Aragon, Ted L. ..... Denver, CO
Aragona & Aragona ..... Oxon Hill, MD
Aragona, Christopher ..... Oxon Hill, MD
Aragona, Cristina A. ..... Washington, DC
Aragona, John T. ..... New York, NY
Aragona, Martin ..... Fort Washington, MD
Aragona, Xavier A. ..... Oxon Hill, MD
Araguel, Patrick J., Jr. ..... Columbus, GA
Arai, Toshiyuki ..... Los Angeles, CA
Araiza, Francisca N. ..... Los Angeles, CA
Araiza, Francisco ..... Milwaukee, WI
Araiza, Richard C. ..... Santa Paula, CA
Araiza, Ronald A. ..... Santa Paula, CA
Araiza, William D. ..... Los Angeles, CA
Arak, Ronald M. ..... Encino, CA
Arak, Sydney F. ..... Indianapolis, IN
Arakaki, Gordon M. ..... Honolulu, HI
Arakaki, Joanne Y.Y.L. ..... Oakland, CA
Arakaki, Lisa ..... Los Angeles, CA
Arakaki, Scott C. ..... Honolulu, HI
Arakas, Peter ..... Enfield, CT
Arakawa, David Z. ..... Honolulu, HI
Arakawa, Gregory P. ..... Los Angeles, CA
Arakelian, Agop G. ..... Los Angeles, CA
Arakelian, Charles M. ..... Fairview, NJ
Arakelian, John P. ..... Milwaukee, WI
Arakelian, Robert J. ..... Worcester, MA
Araki, Kenneth T. ..... Rosemead, CA
Araki, Motonori ..... New York, NY
Araki, Shintaro ..... New York, NY
Araki, Wayne N. ..... Olympia, WA
Arakie, Steven D. ..... New York, NY
Aram, Kathleen
Equal Employment Opportunity Commission, Office of Federal Operations, GV
Aram, William ..... Troy, NY
Aramaki, Scott Noboru ..... Pasadena, CA
Arambula, Juan ..... Fresno, CA
Aramburu, J. Richard ..... Seattle, WA
Aramburu, John ..... Treasury Department, Internal Revenue Service, GV
Aramony, Susan ..... Fort Lauderdale, FL
Aramony, William S. ..... Alexandria, VA
Arán Correa & Guarch, P.A.
Coral Gables, FL
Miami, FL
Arán, Fernando S. ..... Miami, FL
Aran, Jeffrey L. ..... Sacramento, CA
Aran, Kelly J. ..... Los Angeles, CA
Aran, Kenneth J. ..... Los Angeles, CA
Aran, Polk & Berke ..... Los Angeles, CA
Arana, Hector G. ..... Nogales, AZ
Arana, Kimberly A. Howard ..... Nogales, AZ
Arana, Michael A. ..... New York, NY
Arana Arana, Israel ..... San Juan, PR
Aranas, Pauline M. ..... Los Angeles, CA
Aranci, Arnold A. ..... Hamden, CT
Arancibia, Jane Carlson ..... Richmond, VA
Arand, A. David ..... Union, MO
Arand, Mary ..... San Jose, CA
Aranda, Amber L.
Environmental Protection Agency, Office of the General Counsel, GV
Aranda, Amy L. ..... Emporia, KS
Aranda, Andres Manuel ..... New York, NY
Aranda & Guttlein ..... New York, NY
Aranda, James C. ..... Lancaster, OH
Aranda, Robert J. ..... Bartow, FL
Arandia, Alexander ..... Forest Hills, NY
Araneda, Jorgelina E. ..... Raleigh, NC
Araneo, Albert E. ..... Farmingville, NY
Araneo, John T. ..... White Plains, NY
Araneta, Louis A. ..... Mesa, AZ
Araneta, Michelle C. ..... Riverside, CA
Arangio, Charles L. ..... Woodbury, NJ
Arangio, Nicole M. ..... Boston, MA
Arangio, Robert L. ..... Philadelphia, PA
Arango, Ana ..... Houston, TX
Arango, Ignacio E. ..... Miami, FL
Arango, Ignacio E., P.A. ..... Miami, FL
Arango, Jacqueline M. ..... Miami, FL
Arango, Joseph A. ..... Chicago, IL
Arango, Julio V. ..... Coral Gables, FL
Aranguren, H. Irene ..... El Monte, CA
Aranguren, William F. ..... Jersey City, NJ
Aranha, Jean Mills ..... Greenwich, CT
Aranki, Frederick C. ..... New York, NY
Aranoff, Howard N. ..... Hicksville, NY
Aranoff, Jennifer S. ..... New York, NY
Aranoff, Mel, (P.C.) ..... Pasadena, CA
Aranoff, Michael S. ..... New York, NY
Aranoff, Ronald J. ..... New York, NY
Aranoff, Shara L.
United States International Trade Commission, Office of the General Counsel, GV
Aranovich, Florencia R. ..... Los Angeles, CA
Aranow, Edward Ross ..... New York, NY
Aranow, Walter A. ..... Springfield, MA
Aranson, Paul ..... Sanford, ME
Arant, Gene W. ..... Santa Barbara, CA
Arant, Gene W. ..... Ventura, CA
Arant, Lucy ..... Los Angeles, CA
Arant, Michael ..... Medford, OR
Arant, Timothy W. ..... Charlotte, NC
Arany, Lawrence C. ..... Indianapolis, IN
Aranyos, John A. ..... Warren, PA
Aranza, Raymond R., (P.C.) ..... Omaha, NE
Arao, John ..... Los Angeles, CA
Araps, Frank T., Law Offices of
North Brunswick, NJ
Arar, Roger M. ..... New York, NY
Arash, Dora ..... Los Angeles, CA
Arasin, Christine J. ..... Philadelphia, PA
Arata, Blake G., (A P.L.C.)
New Orleans, LA
Arata, Blake G., Jr. ..... Metairie, LA
Arata, David J. ..... San Jose, CA
Arata, Don M. ..... Bogalusa, LA
Arata, George S. ..... Modesto, CA
Arata, John W. ..... Washington, DC
Arata, Joseph J. ..... Williston Park, NY
Arata Law Firm, A Professional Association
Fort Wayne, IN
Arata, Michael P. ..... New Orleans, LA
Arata, Patrick J. ..... Fort Wayne, IN
Arata, Raymond J., Jr. ..... San Francisco, CA
Arata, William H. ..... Bogalusa, LA
Aratani, Ann H. ..... Honolulu, HI
Aratani, Dana M. ..... Los Angeles, CA
Araten, Jeffrey B. ..... New York, NY
Araten, Michael ..... Huntingdon Valley, PA
Aratingi, Michael J. ..... Hamburg, NJ
Arato, Alexander G. ..... Los Angeles, CA
Arato, Cynthia S. ..... New York, NY
Araujo, Arlindo B. ..... Newark, NJ
Araujo, Jaeleen Kookesh ..... Washington, DC
Araujo, Jess J., Sr. ..... Santa Ana, CA
Araujo, John L. ..... New York, NY
Araujo, Manuel U. ..... Whittier, CA
Araujo, Mauricio ..... Chicago, IL
Araujo, Michael ..... Flagstaff, AZ
Araujo, Theodore Lyons ..... Syracuse, NY
Arauz, Rodolfo ..... Sunrise, FL
Arax, Brian M. ..... Fresno, CA
Arb, Robert D. ..... St. Louis, MO
Arb, Susan C. ..... Yakima, WA
Arbab, John E.
National Labor Relations Board, Office of the General Counsel, GV
Arbabi, Darius Alexander ..... Framingham, MA
Arbaugh, Anne McClain ..... Batavia, OH
Arbaugh, David R. ..... Mansfield, OH
Arbaugh, Eugene A. ..... Hunt Valley, MD
Arbaugh, Eugene A., Jr. ..... Baltimore, MD
Arbeeny, Kenneth D. ..... New York, NY
Arbeeny, Michele M. ..... New Brunswick, NJ
New York, NY
Arbeiaez, Claudia M. ..... Brooklyn, NY
Arbeit, Michael Adam
Rockville Centre, NY
Arbeit, Robert S. ..... Hauppauge, NY
Arbeiter, Jay D. ..... Metuchen, NJ
Arbeiter, Ronald W. ..... Chester, IL
Arbeiter, Shawn D. ..... Davie, FL
Arbeitman, Glenn A. ..... Plainview, NY
Arbeitman, Laura F. ..... Northampton, MA
Arbel, Rafi R. ..... Chicago, IL
Arbelaez, Claudia M. ..... Brooklyn, NY
Arbelo, Casto F. Rodriguez ..... Brooklyn, NY
Arber, Carol H. ..... New York, NY
Arber, Gary M. ..... Brookline, MA
Arber, Howard B. ..... Hempstead, NY
Arber, Stephen C. ..... Somerville, NJ
Arberg, Charles S.
Federal Judicial Center, GV
Arbery, Hope Reynolds ..... Atlanta, GA
Arbery, W. Christopher ..... Atlanta, GA
Arbes, Carl J. ..... Department of Commerce, Patent and Trademark Office, GV
Arbes, Jake ..... Atlanta, GA
Arbetman, Jeffrey F. ..... Phoenix, AZ
Arbetter, Brian S. ..... Chicago, IL
Arbetter, Charles M. ..... Oak Brook, IL
Arbeznik, Gary D. ..... Cleveland, OH
Arbeznik, Leo J. ..... Cleveland, OH
Arbide, Francisco J. ..... Miami, FL
Arbide, Z. Suzanne ..... Miami, FL
Arbie, Phillip S. ..... Warren, OH
Arbios, Louis T. ..... Stockton, CA
Arbisser, Aton ..... Los Angeles, CA
Arbit, Sheara Avital ..... New York, NY
Arbit, Terry S.
Commodity Futures Trading Commission, Division of Enforcement, GV
Arbitblit, Donald C. ..... San Francisco, CA
Arbiter, Joan S. ..... Massapequa Park, NY
Arbiter, M. V. ..... Hastings-On-Hudson, NY
Arbittier, Aron ..... Philadelphia, PA
Arbittier, Steven A. ..... Philadelphia, PA
Arbogast, Alane A. ..... Casey, IL
Arbogast, Daniel S. ..... Casey, IL
Arbogast, Deborah A. ..... Waukegan, IL
Arbogast, Donald C. ..... Indianapolis, IN
Arbogast, James D. ..... Austin, TX
Arbogast, John R. ..... Department of State, Office of the Legal Adviser, GV
Arbogast Law Offices, P.C. ..... Casey, IL
Arbogast, Nicole L. ..... Rupert, ID
Arbogast, Oliver W., Jr. ..... Tulsa, OK
Arbogast, Thomas D. ..... Pittsburgh, PA
Arboleda, Alexandra M. ..... Phoenix, AZ
Arboleda, Carolos M. ..... Phoenix, AZ
Arboles, Monika M. ..... Beverly Hills, CA
Arboleya, Carlos J., Jr. ..... Coconut Grove, FL
Arbolino, Jennifer P. ..... Chicago, IL
Arbon, Mark T. ..... Syracuse, NY
Arbon, Thomas Wm. ..... Dallas, TX
Arbona-Arbona, Ignacio M.
San Juan, PR
Arborlaw Associates, PLLC ..... Ann Arbor, MI
Arbour & Aycock ..... West Monroe, LA
Arbour, Donald S. ..... Minneapolis, MN
Arbour, G. Thomas ..... Baton Rouge, LA
Arbour, Joseph L. ..... Tonawanda, NY
Arbour, Larry ..... West Monroe, LA
Arbour, Peter W. ..... Houston, TX
Arbuckle, Anne N. ..... Chicago, IL
Arbuckle, Barbara ..... Albuquerque, NM
Arbuckle, Barry L. ..... Wichita, KS
Arbuckle, Brad B. ..... Troy, MI
Arbuckle, Charles Hoover
Reynoldsburg, OH
Arbuckle, Craig ..... Washington, IA
Arbuckle, Douglas H. ..... Lewisburg, WV
Arbuckle, J. Gordon ..... Washington, DC
Arbuckle, Jeffrey D. ..... Wichita, KS
Arbuckle, Jess W. ..... McPherson, KS
Arbuckle, John C. ..... Walnut Creek, CA
Arbuckle, John H. ..... Palo Alto, CA
Arbuckle, Kurt ..... Houston, TX
Arbuckle, Kurt, P.C. ..... Houston, TX
Arbuckle, Nicholas J. ..... Menlo Park, CA
Arbuckle, Sandra J. ..... Louisville, KY
Arbuckle, William I., III
State College, PA
Arbuckle-Higdon, Kathryn D. ..... Topeka, KS
Arbulu, Agustin Victor ..... Southfield, MI
Arbulu, Marcia Nussbaum ..... Birmingham, MI
Arbus, Lee A., Ltd. ..... Northbrook, IL
Arbus, Martin J. ..... Oakhurst, NJ
Arbuthnot, Robert M. ..... San Francisco, CA
Arbuz, Joseph R. ..... Miami Beach, FL
Arca, Emil ..... New York, NY
Arcabascio, Catherine ..... Fort Lauderdale, FL
Arcadi, Ann Marie ..... Dallas, TX
Arcadi, James V. ..... Buffalo, NY
Arcadipane, Angelo V. ..... Washington, DC
Arcaini, Robert Michael ..... Miami, FL
Arcand, C. Wallace ..... Hingham, MA
Arcand, Eugene J., Jr. ..... Boston, MA
Arcand, James H. ..... Beverly, MA
Arcand, Jon J. ..... St. Paul, MN
Arcand, Wendy L. ..... St. Louis Park, MN
Arcangeli, Richard F. ..... Boston, MA
Arcano, Stephen F. ..... New York, NY
Arcara, Richard J. ..... Buffalo, NY
Arcari, Michael A. ..... East Hartford, CT
Arcaro, Anthony R. ..... Wilmington, DE
Arcaro, Harold C., Jr. ..... Providence, RI
Arcaro, Riccardo D. ..... Southfield, MI
Arcaro, Riccardo D., P.C. ..... Southfield, MI
Arcaro, Timothy L. ..... Fort Lauderdale, FL
Arcate, Ronald J. ..... Staten Island, NY
Arce, Alison Kyler ..... Atlanta, GA
Arce, Edward A. ..... Chicago, IL
Arce, Rebecca E. ..... New York, NY
Arce, Robert ..... Kearny, NJ
Arce, Roman ..... Toledo, OH
Arcell, Lawrence A. ..... New Orleans, LA
Arcella, Craig F. ..... New York, NY
Arcella, David J. ..... Floral Park, NY
Arcellana, Juan J. ..... Sacramento, CA
Arceneaux, Adam ..... Indianapolis, IN
Arceneaux, Adriel Graham
New Orleans, LA
Arceneaux, Ann Allen ..... New Orleans, LA
Arceneaux, Charles J. ..... Lake Charles, LA
Arceneaux, Chas. A. ..... New Orleans, LA
Arceneaux, Cherie M. ..... Baton Rouge, LA
Arceneaux, George, III ..... Lafayette, LA
Arceneaux, Glenda J. ..... Houston, TX

Arceneaux, James C., III ... New Orleans, LA
Arceneaux, James S. ... Metairie, LA
Arceneaux, Louis Graham ... New Orleans, LA
Arceneaux, Mary Elizabeth ... Baton Rouge, LA
Arceneaux, Nester P. ... Metairie, LA
Arceneaux, Richard M. ... Jennings, LA
Arceneaux, Robert E. ... New Orleans, LA
Arceneaux, Scott B. ... New Orleans, LA
Arceneaux, Webster J., III ... Charleston, WV
Arceo, Saul ... Junction City, KS
Arch, John G. ... Pittsburgh, PA
Arch, Michael A. ... Seattle, WA
Wenatchee, WA
Arch, Rebekah R. ... Alexandria, VA
Archambault, Brian J. ... Haverhill, MA
Archambault, Dorene A. ... West Springfield, MA
Archambault, Jean Paul ... Clinton, NJ
Archambault, John C. ... Norwich, CT
Archambault, John R. ... Greensboro, NC
Archambault, Louis E. ... Neenah, WI
Archambault, Reed N. ... Santa Ana, CA
Archambault, W. H. ... Charlottesville, VA
Archambeau, Jason R. ... Atlanta, GA
Archambeault, Gerald T. ... Glasgow, MT
Archambualt, William H. ... Charlottesville, VA
Archbald, Malcolm ... Santa Barbara, CA
Archbald & Spray LLP ... San Luis Obispo, CA
Santa Barbara, CA
Santa Maria, CA
Ventura, CA
Archbell, Roy A., Jr. ... Kitty Hawk, NC
Archbell, Roy A., Jr. ... Manteo, NC
Archbold, Carl T. ... Atlanta, GA
Archbold, Carolyn A. ... Wayne, MI
Archbold, Lillian ... Fort Lauderdale, FL
Archbold, Paul I. ... San Francisco, CA
Archbold, Richard M. ... Stockton, CA
Archbold, Steven L. ... Bloomfield, NE
Archbold, Thomas B. ... Minneapolis, MN
Archbold, Timothy J. ... St. Paul, MN
Archbold, William C., Jr. ... Media, PA
Archdeacon, Meghan L. ... Washington, DC
Archer, Alicia L. ... Annapolis, MD
Archer, Amy Alana ... Raleigh, NC
Archer, Ann ... Boston, MA
Archer & Associates ... Houston, TX
Archer & Associates, Ltd. ... Chicago, IL
Archer, Burke O. ... Atlanta, GA
Archer, Christina L. ... Springfield, IL
Archer, Christopher ... St. Louis, MO
Archer, Christopher J. ... Boulder, CO
Archer, Cindy Thomas ... Costa Mesa, CA
Archer, Dan E. ... Perryton, TX
Archer, Daniel F. ... Monterey, CA
Archer, Danna K. ... Houston, TX
Archer, David F. ... Pittsburgh, PA
Archer, David G. ... Cartersville, GA
Archer, David G., P.C. ... Cartersville, GA
Rome, GA
Archer, David T. ... Winston-Salem, NC
Archer, Deborah Nicole ... New York, NY
Archer, Dennis W. ... Detroit, MI
Archer, Diana ... Phoenix, AZ
Archer, Diane ... New York, NY
Archer, Donald D. ... San Francisco, CA
Archer, E. Glenn ... Lubbock, TX
Archer, Earl H., III ... Jacksonville, FL
Archer, Earl T. ... Pasadena, CA
Archer, Edward P. ... Indianapolis, IN
Archer, Eric D. ... Dallas, TX
Archer, Eric F. ... Jamestown, RI
Archer, Eric H. ... Walnut Creek, CA
Archer, Evan C., Jr. ... Rutland, VT
Archer, F. Mather ... Portsmouth, VA
Archer, G. Dennis ... Bellingham, WA
Archer, George F. ... Chicago, IL
Archer, George M. ... Ballwin, MO
Archer, Gerard P. ... Metairie, LA
Archer, Glenn L., Jr. ... United States Court Of Appeals For The Federal Circuit, GV
Archer & Greiner, A Professional Corporation ... Clinton, NJ
Flemington, NJ
Haddonfield, NJ
Princeton, NJ
Philadelphia, PA
Archer, Guy P. D. ... Wailuku, HI
Archer, Hugh N. ... Frankfort, KY
Archer, J. Thomas ... St. Louis, MO
Archer, James G. ... New York, NY
Archer, Jeffery Kevin ... Duncan, OK
Archer, John F. ... Sioux Falls, SD
Archer, John J. ... Princeton, NJ
Archer, John J. ... Nashville, TN
Archer, John T. ... Kansas City, MO
Archer, Joseph F. ... Houston, TX
Archer, Judith A. ... Liberty Corner, NJ
Archer, Julia C. ... Winston-Salem, NC
Archer, Kathleen P. ... Louisville, KY
Archer, Keith H. ... Melville, NY
Archer, Kelley ... Bridgeport, OH
Archer, Kelly Elizabeth ... Denver, CO
Archer, Kenneth D. ... Hartford, CT
Archer, Kenney, Wilson & Cohen ... Dearborn, MI
Detroit, MI
Archer, Laura P. ... Dallas, TX
Archer, Lee A. ... Walnut Creek, CA
Archer, Lee S. ... Lebanon, KY
Archer, Lisa B. ... Dearborn, MI
Archer, Margaret ... Tacoma, WA
Archer, Mark L. ... Charleston, SC
Archer, Mary Ann E. ... Lino Lakes, MN
Archer, Maurice S. ... Omaha, NE
Archer, Maxine L. ... Brooklyn, NY
Archer, McComas, Breslin, McMahon & Chritton, A Professional Corporation ... Ontario, CA
Walnut Creek, CA
Archer, Michael F. ... San Antonio, TX
Archer, Paul ... Murrells Inlet, SC
Archer, Rebecca M. ... San Francisco, CA
Archer, Richard D. ... Chicago, IL
Archer, Richard H., Jr. ... Toms River, NJ
Archer, Richard J. ... San Francisco, CA
Honolulu, HI
Archer, Robert C. ... Naperville, IL
Archer, Robert K. ... Dearborn, MI
Archer, Robert M. ... Mineola, NY
Archer, Ronald E. ... Houtzdale, PA
Archer, Scott P. ... Atlanta, GA
Archer, Shirley Sugimura ... Palo Alto, CA
Archer, Standley & Neill, P.C. ... San Antonio, TX
Archer, Stephen E. ... Eugene, OR
Archer, Stephen R. ... Defiance, OH
Archer, Steven D. ... Los Angeles, CA
Archer, Susan W. ... Newton, MA
Archer, T. Joshua R. ... Atlanta, GA
Archer, Thomas A. ... Harrisburg, PA
Archer, Thomas G. ... Miami, FL
Archer, Thomas J., III ... Austin, TX
Archer, Thomas S. ... Truckee, CA
Archer, Thomas S., P.C., Law Offices of ... Truckee, CA
Archer, Van H., III ... San Antonio, TX
Archer, Victoria L. ... Pittsburgh, PA
Archer, Waldner & Vickery, L.L.P. ... Houston, TX
Archer, Warren J. ... Pittsburgh, PA
Archer & Weed ... Newport Beach, CA
Archer, Wesley C. ... Brewer, ME
Archer, William ... Los Angeles, CA
Archer, William H. ... Mason, MI
Archer, William R., Jr. ... Houston, TX
Archerd, William F. ... Minneapolis, MN
Archer Yanochik, Nancy ... Houston, TX
Archetto, Daniel J. ... Providence, RI
Archetto, John D. ... Providence, RI
Archey, Connell L. ... Baton Rouge, LA
Archey, Michael T. ... Fort Lauderdale, FL
Archey-Crim, Marlene C. ... St. Louis, MO
Archibald, Barbara ... Sacramento, CA
Archibald, C. Murphy ... Charlotte, NC
Archibald, Douglas R. ... Minneapolis, MN
Archibald, Ellen R. ... Charleston, WV
Archibald & Hap ... Brooklyn, NY
Archibald, J. William ... Oklahoma City, OK
Archibald, James E. ... Department of State, GV
Archibald, James F., III ... Birmingham, AL
Archibald, James K. ... Washington, DC
Baltimore, MD
Archibald, James P. ... Houlton, ME
Archibald, Jeanne S. ... Washington, DC
Archibald, Lane R. ... Idaho Falls, ID
Archibald, Margaret E. ... Rockville, MD
Archibald, Martha L. ... Del Mar, CA
Archibald, R. James ... Rigby, ID
Archibald, Randall S. ... West Orange, NJ
Archibald, Richard E. ... Sacramento, CA
Archibald, Richard T. ... Dallas, TX
Archibald, Robert ... Westover, MD
Archibald, Robert D. ... Cleveland, OH
Archibald, Robert E. ... Laurel, MD
Archibald, Roger V. ... Brooklyn, NY
Archibald, William K. ... Petersburg, VA
Archibeque, Steve P. ... Albuquerque, NM
Archie, James E. ... Dallas, TX
Archie, Jennifer C. ... Washington, DC
Archie, John C. ... Kinston, NC
Archie, Joseph Patrick ... Philadelphia, PA
Archie, Michael R. ... Exton, PA
Archie, Peter B. ... Portland, OR
Seattle, WA
Archie, Richard J. ... Kinston, NC
Archie, Robert L., Jr. ... Philadelphia, PA
Archie, Thomas E. ... Washington, NC
Archilla, Daniel R. ... Buffalo, NY
Archinaco, Jason A. ... Pittsburgh, PA
Architect, Robert J. ... Treasury Department, GV
Architzel, Paul M. ... Commodity Futures Trading Commission, Division of Economic Analysis, GV
Archuleta, David A. ... Boulder, CO
Archuleta, David A. ... Albuquerque, NM
Archuleta, Fran Peter ... Reno, NV
Archuleta, Kathleen Sutherland ... Wheat Ridge, CO
Archuleta, Michael E.J. ... Austin, TX
Archuleta, S. Charles ... Albuquerque, NM
Archuleta, Sam ... Albuquerque, NM
Archuleta-Staehlin, Jacquelyn ... Santa Fe, NM
Archuletta, Gilbert M. ... Los Angeles, CA
Arcia, Omar J. ... Miami, FL
Arciaga, Arthur A. ... Strongsville, OH
Arcidiacono, Thomas Claude ... Douglaston, NY
Arciero, Christopher G. ... West Hartford, CT
Arciniega, Jorge ... Los Angeles, CA
Arciola, Weslee S. ... Fort Lauderdale, FL
Arckey & Reha, L.L.C. ... Littleton, CO
Arckey, Thomas J. ... Littleton, CO
Arcobello, Daniel M. ... Bridgeport, CT
Arcodia, Anthony, Jr. ... Troy, NY
Arcodia, Charles A. ... Glenwood Landing, NY
Arcomano, Keith N. ... West Long Branch, NJ
Arcomano, Nicholas ... New York, NY
Arconti, Richard D. ... Danbury, CT
Arcos, Carlos A. ... Houston, TX
Arcos, Martha ... Department Of Health And Human Services, Food & Drug Administration, GV
Arcovio, Robert A. ... Philadelphia, PA
Pittsburgh, PA
Arcudi, John A. ... Bridgeport, CT
Arculeo, Angelo J. ... Pinehurst, NC
Arcuri, Andrew A. ... Deer Park, NY
Arcuri, Frank ... Washington, PA
Arcuri, Frank C. ... York, PA
Arcuri, Mabel E. ... Brooklyn, NY
Arcuri, Michael A. ... Utica, NY
Arcuri, Patricia L. ... Asheville, NC
Arcuri, Shirley C. ... Tampa, FL
Arcuri, Shirley C., P.A. ... Tampa, FL
Arcuri, Tammy L. ... Newton, MA
Arcus & Goldstein ... Albany, NY
Arcus, Ian R. ... Albany, NY
Arczynski, Andrew V. ... Brea, CA
Ard, Barbara A. ... Tampa, FL
Ard, John L. ... Scotch Plains, NJ
Ard, Marlin D. ... Eugene, OR
Ard, Peter C. ... Morristown, NJ
Ard, Samual J. ... Tallahassee, FL
Ard, Shirley & Hartman, P.A. ... Tallahassee, FL
Ard, Thomas M. ... Princeton, NJ
Ard, William Josh ... Lansing, MI
Ardagna, Ned Anthony ... Bonita, CA
Ardam, David M. ... Smithtown, NY
Ardaman, A. Kurt ... Orlando, FL
Ardaman, Mary Jo ... Winter Garden, FL
Ardaugh, John R. ... Joliet, IL
Ardavany, Juanita F. ... Van Nuys, CA
Ardelean, Feini ... New York, NY
Ardelean, Paula Graves ... Jackson, MS
Ardell, Amy, A Professional Corporation ... Santa Monica, CA
Ardell, Nancy Fox ... Chicago, IL
Arden, Alan K. ... Woodbridge, VA
Arden & Arden ... La Quinta, CA
Arden, Charles D. ... Santa Rosa, CA
Arden, Christine M. ... Santa Monica, CA
Arden, Deanna H. ... Brooklyn, NY
New York, NY
Arden, Glenn S. ... New York, NY
Arden, James D. ... New York, NY
Arden, James Ellis ... Van Nuys, CA
Arden, John ... Redlands, CA
Arden, John R. ... Bordentown, NJ
Arden, June L. ... La Quinta, CA
Arden, Lisa ... Bethpage, NY
Arden, Mark Taylor ... Columbia, SC
Arden, Mary H. ... Vancouver, WA
Arden, R. E. ... Bronx, NY
Arden, Samuel R. ... Atlanta, GA
Arden, Sidney H. ... La Quinta, CA
Arden, Suzan ... New York, NY
Arden, Thomas B. ... Miami, FL
Arden, Thomas P. ... Chicago, IL
Arden, Walter R. ... Anchorage, AK
Ardery, Charles W., Jr. ... Indianapolis, IN
Ardery, Donald M. ... Golden Valley, MN
Ardery, Joseph L. ... Louisville, KY
Ardery, Philip P. ... Louisville, KY
Ardery, Samuel R. ... Bloomington, IN
Ardi, Dennis ... Beverly Hills, CA
Ardiff & Morse, P.C. ... Boston, MA
Danvers, MA
Ardiff, Ralph E., Jr. ... Danvers, MA
Ardiff, William B. ... Danvers, MA
Arding, Jon D. ... Berkeley, CA
Ardinger, William F. J. ... Concord, NH
Ardington, Mary Jo ... Fort Wayne, IN
Ardini, Edward R. ... Jefferson City, MO
Ardis, Frank, Jr. ... Mansfield, OH
Ardis & Lehn ... Downey, CA
Ardis, Patrick M. ... Memphis, TN
Ardis, Robert B. ... Mountainside, NJ
Ardis, Robert B. ... Sulphur Springs, TX
Ardis, Stephen B. ... Stockton, CA
Arditi, Abraham A. ... Seattle, WA
Arditi, Ralph ... New York, NY
Ardito, Charles J. ... West Yarmouth, MA
Ardito, John A. ... Mineola, NY
Ardito, Laurie A. ... Hoffman Estates, IL
Ardito, Sweeney, Stusse, Robertson & Dupuy, P.C. ... West Yarmouth, MA
Arditti, David S. ... Dallas, TX
Arditti, Regina B. ... El Paso, TX
Ardizzi, Robert D. ... Spring House, PA
Ardizzone, Barbara Trevisan ... Media, PA
Ardizzone, C. Gary ... Roseville, CA
Ardizzone, C. Gary, A Prof. Corp. ... Roseville, CA
Ardizzone, Leora F. ... Mineola, NY
Ardman, Ross ... Montrose, NY
Ardoin & Daigle ... Eunice, LA
Ardoin, J. Winston ... Eunice, LA
Ardoin, Julie A. ... New Orleans, LA
Ardoin, Michael V. ... Lafayette, LA
Ardoin, Richard A. ... San Francisco, CA
Ardon, Karen ... Newport Beach, CA
Ardoyno, Edward L., Jr. ... New Orleans, LA
Ardoyno, Kenneth S. ... New Orleans, LA
Arduini, Angelo P. ... Erie, PA
Arduini, Darlene W. ... San Jose, CA
Arduini, Lisa A. ... West Orange, NJ
Area, Steven E. ... Tulsa, OK
Areaux, Daniel G. ... Elkhart, IN
South Bend, IN
Areaux, Raymond G. ... New Orleans, LA
Areces, A. Francisco ... Miami, FL
Areces, A. Francisco, P.A. ... Miami, FL
Areces, Barbara ... Miami, FL
Arechaga, Cristina ... Orlando, FL
Areddy, Richard D., Sr. ... Birmingham, MI
Areeda, Michelle E. ... Bingham Farms, MI
Areeda, Phillip E. ... Cambridge, MA
Areen, Judith C. ... Washington, DC
Aregood, Patrick J. ... Wilkes-Barre, PA
Arehart, James E. ... Lexington, KY
Arehart, Timothy J. ... Olathe, KS
Areheart, Henry W. ... Pittsburgh, PA
Areias, Allison V. ... Department of Commerce, National Oceanic and Atmospheric Administration, GV
Areklett, Heather L. ... Cleveland, OH
Arel, Gary G. ... Redding, CA
Arel, Jocelyn M. ... Boston, MA
Arel, Justin G. ... Redding, CA
Arel, Timothy J. ... Manchester, NH
Arellano, Anita C. ... Pacific Grove, CA
Arellano, Barbara Hackman ... Jamaica, NY
Arellano, Joseph Bruce Wm. ... Cruz Bay, St. John, VI
Charlotte Amalie, St. Thomas, VI
Arellano, Joseph C. ... Portland, OR
Arellano, Nancie Potter ... Portland, OR
Arellano, Robert C. ... San Antonio, TX
Arellano, Silvia R. ... Phoenix, AZ
Arellano, Victor M. ... Madison, WI
Arem, Lawrence J. ... Philadelphia, PA
Arem, Phillip ... Union, NJ
Aren, Edward A. ... Oak Park, IL
Arena, Andrew P. ... Milwaukee, WI
Arena, Anthony J. ... Philadelphia, PA
Arena, Anthony M. ... Medford, MA
Arena, Anthony S. ... Tampa, FL
Arena, Augustine A. ... Putnam Valley, NY
Arena, Charles J. ... Blue Bell, PA
Arena, David T. ... Park Ridge, IL
Arena, Gloria V. ... Fort Lee, NJ
Arena, J. Anthony ... Nashville, TN
Arena, John G. ... Dallas, TX
Arena, Jude ... Philadelphia, PA
Arena, Karen A. ... Philadelphia, PA
Arena, Maria A. ... Livingston, NJ
Arena, Mark S. ... Philadelphia, PA
Arena, Nicholas J. ... Boston, MA
Arena, Patrick Michael ... Rochester, NY
Arena, Paul A. ... Durham, NC
Arena, Robert A. ... Providence, RI
Arena, Robert F. ... Salem, MA
Arena, Robert R. ... Ozone Park, NY
Arena, Ronald D. ... New York, NY
Arena, Roxanne ... Media, PA
Arena, Samuel J., Jr. ... Philadelphia, PA
Arena, Sebastian ... Pittsburgh, PA
Arena, Thomas A. ... New York, NY
Arena, Victoria Lani ... Sacramento, CA
Arenander, Norman L. ... De Witt, NY
Arenare, Debra B. ... New York, NY
Arenare, Scott A. ... New York, NY
Arenas, Justo ... San Juan, PR
Arenas, Paul B. ... San Francisco, CA
Arenas, Vivian ... Tampa, FL
Arenberg, Daniel K. ... Cupertino, CA
Greenwood Village, CO
Arenberg, Pamela Morse ... Birmingham, AL
Arenberg, Stanley I. ... Los Angeles, CA
Arenburg, Richard L. ... Atlanta, GA
Arencibia, Julie K. ... Anaheim, CA
Arencibia, Nancy J. ... Teaneck, NJ
Arencibia, Raul A. ... Coral Gables, FL
Arend, Patrice S. ... Detroit, MI
Arend, Ronald L. ... Fort Myers, FL
Arend, Sean K. ... Palo Alto, CA
Arend, Shirley Dean ... Austin, TX
Arend, Stephanie A. ... Tacoma, WA
Arend, Thomas E., Jr. ... Washington, DC
Arend, Tiffany N. ... Tulsa, OK
Arendal, Rita S. ... Treasury Department, Office of the Comptroller of the Currency, GV
Arendall, David R. ... Birmingham, AL
Arendall, Douglas T. ... Birmingham, AL
Arendell, Robert L. ... Boston, MA
Arendes, Jennifer Lee ... St. Louis, MO
Arendes, Michael C., Jr. ... Austin, TX
Arends, Bradley K. ... Albert Lea, MN
Arends and Lee ... Bode, IA
Humboldt, IA
Arends, Marc D. ... Bode, IA
Humboldt, IA
Arends, Norman L. ... Lamar, CO
Arends, Timothy B. ... Minneapolis, MN
Arends-Biddlecome, Mary ... San Diego, CA
Arendsen, Glenn S. ... Livonia, MI
Arendt, Aloysius J. ... Pierre, SD
Arendt, David M. ... New York, NY
Arendt, Jacqueline M. ... Boxborough, MA
Arendt, James Joseph ... Fresno, CA
Arendt, Michelle R. ... Cleveland, OH
Arendt, Patrick J. ... Red Wing, MN
Arendt, Richard J. ... Chicago, IL
Arendt, Ronald A. ... Sacramento, CA
Arendt, Ronald A., A Professional Law Corporation ... Sacramento, CA
Arendt, Sarah Martin ... St. Anthony, MN
Arendt, Thomas ... Phoenix, AZ
Arenella, Nicholas P. ... Newton, MA
Arenella, Peter L. ... Los Angeles, CA
Arenofsky, Raymond ... Mesa, AZ
Arens, David ... New York, NY
Arens, David James ... Dayton, OH
Arens, Herman J. A. C. ... Harpers Ferry, WV
Arens, John Richard ... Houston, TX
Arens, Retha I. ... Gaithersburg, MD
Arens, Richard P. ... Hagåtña, GU

Arens, Russell R. ... Huntington Beach, CA
Arensberg, Charles Covert ... Pittsburgh, PA
Arensberg, Conrad C. M. ... Harrisburg, PA
Arensberg, Cornelius W. ... St. Petersburg, FL
Arensberg, Mark W. ... Overland Park, KS
Arenson, Claire P. ... Austin, TX
Arenson, Gregory K. ... New York, NY
Arenson, Joseph L. ... Chicago, IL
Arenson & Spears ... Austin, TX
Arenson, Walker ... Austin, TX
Arenstein, David ... Glen Allen, VA
Arenstein, G. Gregory ... Tipp City, OH
Arenstein, Hal R. ... Cincinnati, OH
Arenstein, Robert D., Law Offices of
Teaneck, NJ
New York, NY
Arent, Albert E. ... Washington, DC
Arent Fox Kintner Plotkin & Kahn, PLLC
Washington, DC
New York, NY
Arent, Lisa Magee ... Atlanta, GA
Arent, Shereen ...
Architect of the Capitol, GV
Arent, Stephen W. ... Denver, CO
Arenth, Terese L. ... Garden City, NY
Arentson, Robert M., Jr. ... Jackson, MS
Arentz, Paul F. ... Los Angeles, CA
Arentzen, Roger ... New York, NY
Arenwald, Walter P. ... Scarborough, NY
Arenz, A. John ... Dubuque, IA
Arenz, Dale W. ... Waukesha, WI
Arenz, John H. ... Portland, OR
Arenz, Molter, Macy & Riffle, S.C.
Waukesha, WI
Arenz, Thomas J. ... Portland, OR
Arenz, Thomas J. ... Milwaukee, WI
Ares, Aurora A. ... Miami, FL
Ares, Charles E. ... Tucson, AZ
Ares, Dalila Dolly ... San Jose, CA
Aresco, Sharon L. ... Stamford, CT
Aresty & Associates ... Boston, MA
Aresty International Law Offices, P.C.
Boston, MA
Aresty, Jeffrey M. ... Boston, MA
Aresty, Joel M. ... Miami, FL
Aresty, Joel M., P.A. ... Miami, FL
Aresty, Neil E. ... Boston, MA
Aretakis, James ... Detroit, MI
Aretha, Keith M. ... Troy, MI
Aretsky & Aretsky ... Fort Lee, NJ
Hackensack, NJ
Ridgewood, NJ
Aretsky, Dolores L. ... Hackensack, NJ
Aretsky, Eric J. ... Hackensack, NJ
Aretsky, Lynne A. ... Roseland, NJ
Aretz, Adam N. ... Jeannette, PA
Aretz, Edward M. ... Long Island City, NY
Aretz, Tonya M. ... Indianapolis, IN
Arevalo, Edward J. ... Mineola, NY
Arevalo, Jaime ... Chatsworth, CA
Arevalo, Lily Yan ... Santa Ana, CA
Arevalo, Luz A. ... Boston, MA
Arevalo, Maria Lourdes ... Merced, CA
Arey, D. Franklin, III ... Little Rock, AR
Arey, Gary C. ... Dallas, TX
Arey, Margaret B. ... Norfolk, VA
Arey, Patrick K. ... Baltimore, MD
Arey, Stephen E. ... Tazewell, VA
Arey, Stephen E., P.C. ... Tazewell, VA
Arey, Vernon I. ... Waterville, ME
Arey, Willian H. ... Columbus, GA
Arezina, Alexander I. ... Chicago, IL
Arezina, Vladimir I. ... Fairfax, VA
Arfa, Arthur A. ... Chicago, IL
Arfa, Fay ... Los Angeles, CA
Arfa, Fay, A Law Corporation
Beverly Hills, CA
Los Angeles, CA
Santa Ana, CA
Arfa, Harvey Z. ... New York, NY
Arfa, Jack A. ... Chicago, IL
Arfa, Jonathan P. ... New York, NY
White Plains, NY
Arfa, Rachel L. ... New York, NY
Arfaa, Christopher M. ... Philadelphia, PA
Arfaa, Dottie Ferris ... Bel Air, MD
Arfaa, Julia Renee ... Annapolis, MD
Baltimore, MD
Arfaoui, Zoubida ... New York, NY
Arfe, Edward I. ... Bronx, NY
Arffa, Allan J. ... New York, NY
Arffa, Rachel L. ... San Francisco, CA
Arfin, Miriam R. ... San Francisco, CA
Arfin, Sydney ... Los Angeles, CA
Arfine, Leslie K. ... White Plains, NY
Arfine, Stephen ... Suffern, NY
Arflack, Mary Jo ... Tampa, FL
Arfmann, Dennis L. ... Denver, CO
Arfons, W. Chad ... Akron, OH
Argabrite, William C. ... Johnson City, TN
Kingsport, TN
Argall, Michael H. ... Montrose, CO
Arganbright, Warren R. ... Valentine, NE
Arganese, Debra Lynn ... New York, NY
Arganian, David G. ... Seattle, WA
Argazzi, Robert A. ... East Hartford, CT
Argenio, Thomas E. ... Springfield, MA
Argent, Katherine T. ... Kansas City, MO
Argent, Margaret L. ... Millersville, MD
Argenta, Joseph Peter ... Los Angeles, CA
Argenta, Leslie Anne ... Richmond, VA
Argentar, David S. ... Chicago, IL
Argentati, Patricia L. ... Chicago, IL
Wheaton, IL
Argenti, Linda J. ... Nashua, NH
Argentieri, Emmanuel J. ... Cherry Hill, NJ
Argentieri, Judith D. ... Champaign, IL
Argentieri, Kenneth M. ... Pittsburgh, PA
Argentieri, Maureen Cleary
Philadelphia, PA
Argentieri, Paul A. ... Hornell, NY
Argentieri, Robert K. ... East Providence, RI
Argentine, Stephanie L. ... Buffalo, NY
Argentinis, Elénee ... New York, NY
Argento & Associates ... Washington, DC
Argento, Charles J. ... Houston, TX
Argento, Elise Genco ... Staten Island, NY
Argento, Jeanne ... Wilmington, MA
Argento & Klein, Ltd. ... Elgin, IL
Argento, L. John ... Pittsburgh, PA
Argento, Paula A. ... Washington, DC
New York, NY
Argento, Phillip J. ... Pasadena, CA
Argento, Victoria M. ... Rochester, NY
Argento, Vincent C. ... Elgin, IL
Argentos, Deno J. ... Norman, OK
Arger, Harry N. ... Chicago, IL
Argeris, Dana C. ... Asbury Park, NJ
Argeris, George J. ... Cheyenne, WY
Argeros, William G. ... New Orleans, LA
Argetsinger, Cameron R. ... Montour Falls, NY
Argetsinger, J.C. ... Montour Falls, NY
Arghavani, Fay ... Santa Ana, CA
Argianas, Charles G. ... Lombard, IL
Argie, George J. ... Cleveland, OH
Argila, Raymond P. ... New York, NY
Argilagos, Gaspar G. ... Houston, TX
Argilagos, Lillian M. ... Potomac, MD
Argilla, Luke P. ... San Francisco, CA
Argionis, George G. ... Chicago, IL
Argionis, James G. ... Chicago, IL
Argiriou, Arthur ... Forest Hills, NY
Argiriou & Finkel ... Forest Hills, NY
Argiriou, George D. ... Hicksville, NY
Argiriou, Steven L. ... Brooklyn, NY
Argiroff, Anne L. ... Detroit, MI
Argiropoulos, Anthony ... Trenton, NJ
Argiropoulos, Kathleen O. ... Arlington, VA
Argitis, David W. ... Boston, MA
Argo, B. Wayne ... Ocala, FL
Argo, Doyle W. ... Oklahoma City, OK
Argo, George E. ... Vidalia, GA
Argo, J. Knox ... Montgomery, AL
Argo, J. Knox, P.C. ... Montgomery, AL
Argo, Kim M. ... Omaha, NE
Argo, Linda K. ... Oklahoma City, OK
Argo, Wesley B., Jr. ... Charleston, SC
Argoe, G. Lewis, Jr. ... Orangeburg, SC
Argote-Freyre, Caridad ... Farmingdale, NJ
Argrett, Brian Eugene ... Culver City, CA
Argrett, Loretta C. ... Washington, DC
Argue, Douglas W. ... Los Angeles, CA
Argue, John C. ... Los Angeles, CA
Argue, Matthew W. ... San Diego, CA
Argue Pearson Harbison & Myers, LLP
Los Angeles, CA
Salt Lake City, UT
Argue, Sharon ... Fremont, CA
Argue, Wes ... Hamilton, ND
Argue, Wes, P.C. ... Hamilton, ND
Arguedas, Arthur, Jr. ... Santa Fe, NM
Arguedas, Cristina C. ... Oakland, CA
Arguelles, James P. ... San Diego, CA
Arguelles, John A. ... Irvine, CA
Arguello, B. Anthony ... Denver, CO
Arguello, Carlos ... San Diego, CA
Arguello, Christine M. ... Lawrence, KS
Arguello, Larry K. ... Fremont, CA
Arguello, Sue Linda ... Pittsford, NY
Argueta, Silvia R. ... Los Angeles, CA
Argueta, Violetta V. ... New York, NY
Arguimbau, Nicholas C., Law Offices of
San Rafael, CA
Arguin, James J. ... Boston, MA
Arguindegui, Maria Teresa ... Houston, TX
Argus, Gina M. ... Orange, CA
Argyle, Theodore E. ... Boise, ID
Argyle, Wesley C. ... Bountiful, UT
Argyrakis, Evangelos A. ... Orlando, FL
Argyris, George T. ... San Francisco, CA
Argyris, Thomas A. ... Marco, FL
Argyropoulos & Bender ... Astoria, NY
Argyropoulos, Philip ... Astoria, NY
Argyros, Raymond A. ... Dunedin, FL
Arhelger, Robert M. ... El Macero, CA
Ariagno, Constance R. ... Dallas, TX
Ariagno & Kerns, L.L.C. ... Wichita, KS
Ariagno, Stephen T. ... Wichita, KS
Ariail, John H., Jr. ... Arlington, VA
Ariail, Robert M. ... Greenville, SC
Ariale, John M. ... Orlando, FL
Arian, Stephen ... Kentfield, CA
Arianna, Edward A. ... Dallas, TX
Ariano, Anderson, Hardy & Castillo, P.C. A Professional Corporation ... Elgin, IL
Huntley, IL
Ariano, Ann Economou ... Harrisburg, PA
Ariano, Frank V. ... Elgin, IL
Arians, E. Vicki ... Hackensack, NJ
Arias, Cathy L. ... Oakland, CA
Arias, Eduardo J. ... San Juan, PR
Arias, Elizabeth De Paula
Prospect Heights, IL
Arias, Fernando F., Jr. ... Jackson Heights, NY
Arias, Joseph ... San Bernardino, CA
Arias, Juan F. ... St. Louis, MO
Arias, L. Patricia ... Atlanta, GA
Arias, Maria Victoria ... Miami, FL
Arias, Martin ... Bala Cynwyd, PA
Arias, Mike ... Los Angeles, CA
Arias & Ozzello, LLP ... Los Angeles, CA
Arias, Patricia ... Los Angeles, CA
Arias, Patricia Del Pino ... Miami, FL
Arias, Ramon P. ... San Francisco, CA
Arias, Richard M. ... Los Angeles, CA
Arias, Roberto A. ... Jacksonville, FL
Arias, V. Michael ... Boca Raton, FL
Arias, Vincent Michael ... Miami, FL
Arias, Yolanda ... Los Angeles, CA
Arias-Chapleau, Maria G. ... Denver, CO
Arias-Larcada, Antonio A. ... San Juan, PR
Arias-Marxuach, Raúl M. ... San Juan, PR
Ariathurai, Lynnette ... Fremont, CA
Ariatti, Robert J., Jr. ... Pascagoula, MS
Ariav, Alan ... Tucson, AZ
Arico, James S. ... Los Angeles, CA
Arico-Smith, Gina L. ... Moraga, CA
Arida, Paul N. ... New York, NY
Aridas, Thomas G. ... Chicago, IL
Arie, Gil ... Boston, MA
Ariel, Frank Y. ... Los Angeles, CA
Ariens, Michael S. ... San Antonio, TX
Aries, Christopher ... New York, NY
Aries, James M. ... Scarsdale, NY
Aries, Thomas L. ... Chicago, IL
Arietta, David A., Law Offices of
San Francisco, CA
Arietta, David A., Law Offices of
Walnut Creek, CA
Ariey, Janine Y. ... Los Angeles, CA
Arif, Michael S. ... Springfield, VA
Arif, Sehba S. ... San Mateo, CA
Ariizumi, Koichi ... New York, NY
Arik, Talia L. ... Phoenix, AZ
Arima, Adrian ... Palo Alto, CA
Arimilli, V. Lakshmi ... Knoxville, TN
Arimond, Lucy ... St. Paul, MN
Arin, Imanuel B. ... Las Vegas, NV
Arin, Naomi R. ... Boston, MA
Arinaga, Clifford I. ... Honolulu, HI
Arinaga, Esther K. ... Honolulu, HI
Arinder, Betty Burton ... Jackson, MS
Arington, Michele ... Washington, DC
Arington, Steven Brad ... Palo Alto, CA
Ariola, Marcelo, Jr. ... Chicago, IL
Aris, Charles K. ... Dallas, TX
Aris, John L. ... Philadelphia, PA
Aris, Joram J. ... Bronx, NY
Arisman, Mary Ann McCabe
New York, NY
Arismendi, Andres M., Jr. (P.C.)
Houston, TX
Arisohn, Mark S. ... New York, NY
Arisohn, Sharon ... White Plains, NY
Arison, Barbara J. ... Cleveland, OH
Arispe, Ronald D. ... Muscatine, IA
Arista, Isabel ... New York, NY
Arista-Volsky, Maria E. ... Miami, FL
Aristei, J. Clark ... Los Angeles, CA
Aristei, Joan Burns ... Torrance, CA
Aristide, Thomas Dwight ... Bethlehem, PA
Aristondo, Linda E. ... New York, NY
Aristone, Edmund M., Jr.
Fort Lauderdale, FL
Aristova Derkach, Arina E.
New York, NY
Arisumi, Steven K.
Department Of Veterans Affairs, Office of Management, GV
Aritz, Frank J. ... Kingston, PA
Ariyoshi, George R. ... Honolulu, HI
Ariz, Pedro A. ... Miami, FL
Arizaga, Lavora S. ... Houston, TX
Arizmendi, Ruben F. ... San Diego, CA
Arizmendi, Sylvia M. ... San Juan, PR
Arizpe, Sofia ... McAllen, TX
Arjani, Anita B. ... Frazer, PA
Arjomand, Mehran ... Los Angeles, CA
Arjomand, Saiid ... Los Angeles, CA
Ark, John J. ... Rochester, NY
Ark, Samuel J. ... Silver Creek, NY
Arkans, Steven R. ... Philadelphia, PA
Arkawy, Norman M. ... Port Chester, NY
Arkebauer, Evelyn C. ... Chicago, IL
Arkebauer, J. Todd ... Chicago, IL
Arkelian, Edward ... Fresno, CA
Arkelian, Michael G. ... Sacramento, CA
Arkell, Betty Carter ... Denver, CO
Arkell, F. James ... El Paso, TX
Arkell, J. David ... Denver, CO
Arkell, Robert B. ... Longview, WA
Arkell, Thomas J. ... Bloomington, IL
Arkema, Bruce E. ... Richmond, VA
Arkenberg, Franklin W., III ... Milan, IN
Arkenberg, Jerome Stephen ... Fullerton, CA
Arkenberg, Kenneth J. ... Dayton, OH
Arker, Sol ... Woodmere, NY
Arkfeld, JoAnn M. ... Orangevale, CA
Arkfeld, Larry J. ... Yreka, CA
Arkfeld, Michael R. ... Phoenix, AZ
Arkills, Ronald P. ... Spokane, WA
Arkin, Alan ... New York, NY
Arkin, Angela R. ... Greenwood Village, CO
Arkin, Daniel ... Chicago, IL
Arkin, Gail R. ... Fanwood, NJ
Arkin, Gary M. ... Austin, TX
Arkin, Harry L. ... Denver, CO
Arkin, Harry L., & Associates, P.C.
Denver, CO
Arkin, Henry R. ... Chicago, IL
Arkin, J. Gordon ... Orlando, FL
Arkin, L. Jules ... Miami Beach, FL
Arkin, Lisa Ann ... Glen Rock, NJ
Arkin, Marc M. ... New York, NY
Arkin, Matthew D. ... Scarsdale, NY
Arkin, Michael B. ... San Andreas, CA
Arkin, Michael G. ... San Diego, CA
Arkin, Richard A. ... Coral Springs, FL
Arkin, Richard Lance
Department Of Health And Human Services, Food & Drug Administration, GV
Arkin Schaffer & Kaplan LLP
New York, NY
Arkin, Sharon J. ... Claremont, CA
Arkin, Stanley S. ... New York, NY
Arkin, Steven D. ... Treasury Department, Departmental Offices, GV
Arkin, Uri ... Silver Spring, MD
Arkin and Weissman, Law Offices
Culver City, CA
Arkins, Joseph F. ... New York, NY
Arkison, Peter H. ... Bellingham, WA
Arkiss, Earl ... Chicago, IL
Arkley, Butterfield & Swayne ... Arcadia, CA
Arko, Richard D. ... Costa Mesa, CA
Arko, Victor ... Elkhart, IN
Arkoosh, C. Tom ... Gooding, ID
Arkoosh, John C. ... Boise, ID
Arkoosh Law Offices ... Gooding, ID
Arkovich, Christie D. ... Tampa, FL
Arkovitz, Donald ... Nashville, TN
Arkow, Loryn Dunn ... Los Angeles, CA
Arkow, Richard S. ...
Small Business Administration, GV
Arkow, Seth W. ... Canton, OH
Arkules, Bernard C. ... Paradise Valley, AZ
Arkuss, Neil P. ... Boston, MA
Arkwright, George A. ... Arlington, VA
Arky, Barbara Katz ... New York, NY
Arky, M. Elizabeth
Executive Office Of The President, Office of the U.S. Trade Representative, GV
Arlan, Chloe ... Chicago, IL
Arland & Askew ... Colorado Springs, CO
Albuquerque, NM
Arland, Karen L. ... Indianapolis, IN
Arland, William J., III ... Albuquerque, NM
Arlanson, Carl B. ... Hanover, MA
Arlas, Ronald M. ... Kentfield, CA
Arledge, A. Ann ... Tampa, FL
Arledge, A. Jervis ... Rutherfordton, NC
Arledge, Christopher A. ... Hazlehurst, MS
Arledge, Christopher A.
Oklahoma City, OK
Arledge, Christopher W.
Newport Beach, CA
Arledge, David ... Missouri City, TX
Arledge, G. Edward ... San Diego, CA
Arledge, John B. ... Manassas, VA
Arledge, Oglesby, Williams & Martelle, L.L.P. ... Forest City, NC
Arledge, Oglesby, Williams, Martelle, L.L.P.
Rutherfordton, NC
Arledge, Robert, IV ... Baton Rouge, LA
Arledge, Wade ... New Braunfels, TX
Arlen, Gayle A. ... Livingston, NJ
Arlen, Jennifer ... Los Angeles, CA
Arlen, Robert M. ... Delray Beach, FL
Arlen, Robert M., P.A.
Boynton Beach, FL
Delray Beach, FL
Palm Beach, FL
Arleo, Frank P. ... Chatham, NJ
Arlidge, Carleen R. ... San Jose, CA
Arlin, Carol H. ... Redding, CA
Arlin, Jennifer Brewster ... New York, NY
Arlinghaus, Christopher J.
Covington, KY
Arlington, David T. ... Austin, TX
Arlington, Stephen J. ... Albany, NY
Arlook, Martin M. ... San Juan, PR
Arlos, Alma R. ... Pittsfield, MA
Arlotta, Nicholas ... New York, NY
Arlotta, Russel A. ... Upper Marlboro, MD
Arlow, Allan J. ... Chicago, IL
Arlow, Donna P. ... Los Angeles, CA
Arlt, Mary Ann ... Somerset, NJ
Arluck, Neal ... Long Island City, NY
Arluk, Pamela S. ... Washington, DC
Arluna, Steven F. ... Pittsburgh, PA
Arlyn-Pessin, Bree ... Beverly Hills, CA
Armagno, Dana Simaitis ... Chicago, IL
Armagost, John W. ... Los Angeles, CA
Armaly, Samir B. ... Los Angeles, CA
Arman, Harold ... La Canada Flintridge, CA
Arman, R. Keith
Hot Springs National Park, AR
Arman, Sherri R.
Hot Springs National Park, AR
Armand, Donald, Jr. ... Shreveport, LA
Armani, Dorina A. ... Syracuse, NY
Armani, Frank H. ... Camillus, NY
Armani, Harry V., & Associates
Camillus, NY
Armani, Irene R. ... Encino, CA
Armani, Michael F. ... Syracuse, NY
Armanini, Debra Bonifas ... Dayton, OH
Armanini, Joseph S. ... Dayton, OH
Armanino, John L. ... San Francisco, CA
Armanino, Matthew J. ... Pleasanton, CA
Armano, Kwadwo J. ... St. Louis, MO
Armano, Robert D. ... Lawrence, MA
Armao, Joseph J. ... San Francisco, CA
Armao, Joseph P. ... New York, NY
Armas, J. Todd ... Fresno, CA
Armas, Oliver J. ... New York, NY
Armata, Barry F. ... Bristol, CT
Armata, Cheryl P. ... Springfield, MA
Armatas, Nancy A. ... Northbrook, IL
Armatas, Peter N. ... Denver, CO
Armatas, Steven A. ... Canton, OH
Armato, Leonard ... Santa Monica, CA
Armato, Stephen T. ... Boston, MA
Armatti-Epstein, Linda ... Melville, NY
Armaugh, Richard A. ... Houston, TX
Armbrecht, Conrad P. ... Mobile, AL
Armbrecht, Jackson, DeMouy, Crowe, Holmes & Reeves, L.L.C. ... Mobile, AL
Armbrecht, Timothy ... New York, NY
Armbrecht, Wm. H., III ... Mobile, AL
Armbrister, Cyril E. "Ted"
Los Angeles, CA

Armbrust Brown & Davis, L.L.P.
Austin, TX
Armbrust, Carl W. ... Santa Ana, CA
Armbrust, David B. ... Austin, TX
Armbrust, Erica L ... Columbus, OH
Armbrust, Gary E. ... Kansas City, MO
Armbrust, John C. ... Folsom, CA
Armbrust, Joseph W., Jr. ... New York, NY
Armbrust, Lynette S. ... Littleton, CO
Armbrust, Patricia Moriarty
Washington, DC
Armbrust, R. Mark ... Cherry Hill, NJ
Philadelphia, PA
Armbrust, Ronald O. ... Miami, FL
Armbruster, Allan A., Jr. ... Cozad, NE
Armbruster, Charles ... Jersey City, NJ
Armbruster, Charles W., III
Wood River, IL
Armbruster, Clare Cass ... Toledo, OH
Armbruster, Debra A. ... Englewood, CO
Armbruster, Debra A., P.C. ... Denver, CO
Englewood, CO
Armbruster, George J. ... Fort Lauderdale, FL
Armbruster, George J., III ... Lafayette, LA
Armbruster, James J.
Pension Benefit Guaranty Corporation,
Office of the General Counsel, GV
Armbruster, James R. ... Chicago, IL
Armbruster, Jerry S. ... Sarasota, FL
Armbruster & Kelley ... Akron, OH
Armbruster, Kevin R. ... Atlanta, GA
Armbruster, Mark S. ... Los Angeles, CA
Armbruster, Norman W. ... St. Louis, MO
Armbruster, Renee M. ... Sarasota, FL
Armbruster, Robert ... Akron, OH
Armbruster, Ryan P. ... Boise, ID
Armbruster, Theodore W. ... Spokane, WA
Armbruster, Tim ... Tucson, AZ
Armbruster, Todd ... Fort Lauderdale, FL
Armel, Bernard S. ... Chicago, IL
Armel, Larry D. ... Kansas City, MO
Armen, Carol S. ... Narberth, PA
Armen, Christopher T., Law Offices of
Glendale, CA
Armen, David L. ... Woodland Hills, CA
Armen, Margaret Meis
General Accounting Office,
Office of the General Counsel, GV
Armen, Robert N., Jr.
United States Tax Court,
Special Trial Judges, GV
Armenakis & Armenakis ... New York, NY
Armenakis, Diana L. ... New York, NY
Armenakis, James J. ... New York, NY
Armenante, Frank P. ... Allentown, NJ
Armendariz, Albert, Jr. ... El Paso, TX
Armendariz, Albert, Sr. ... El Paso, TX
Armendariz, Richard C. ... Buena Park, CA
Armendariz, Victor P. ... Chicago, IL
Armengau, Javier H. ... Marion, OH
Armenio, Peter J. ... New York, NY
Armenta, Juan Manuel ... Palm Desert, CA
Armenta, M. Cris, Law Offices of
Los Angeles, CA
Armentano, Anthony J. ... Bayside, NY
Armentano, James A. ... Hartford, CT
Armentano, John M. ... Uniondale, NY
Armenteros, Jorge ... San Juan, PR
Armenti, Joseph ... Philadelphia, PA
Armenti, Lorraine M. ... Denver, CO
Armento, Donald F. ... La Mesa, CA
Armentor, Glenn J. ... Lafayette, LA
Armentor, Glenn, Law Corp., The (A Prof. Law Corp.) ... Lafayette, LA
Armentor, L. James ... Lafayette, LA
Armentrout, Ellen Scherer
Washington, DC
Armentrout, James W. ... Winston-Salem, NC
Armentrout, John B. ... Bethesda, MD
Armentrout, Katharine J. ... Baltimore, MD
Armentrout, Kerry D. ... Harrisonburg, VA
Armentrout, Lynn ... New York, NY
Armentrout, Nancy Carol
Sacramento, CA
Armentrout, Randall D.
Cedar Rapids, IA
Armer, Carolyn Gwen ... Phoenix, AZ
Armer, Karolyne N. ... Penfield, NY
Armer, W. Darrell ... Dallas, TX
Armet, Harold R. ... Huntington, NY
Armey, Michael E. ... Warsaw, IN
Armfield, C. Heath, Jr. ... Marietta, GA
Armfield, Edward Albion ... Roanoke, VA
Armgardt, Charles A. ... Albuquerque, NM
Armi, Osa L. ... San Francisco, CA
Armienti & Brooks, P.C. ... New York, NY
Armienti, Michael ... New York, NY
Armiger, David W. ... Monkton, MD
Armijo, Dennis F. ... Albuquerque, NM
Armijo, Jerry A. ... Socorro, NM
Armijo, John L. ... Albuquerque, NM
Armijo, M. Christina ... Las Vegas, NM
Armijo, Margaret P. ... Albuquerque, NM
Armijo, Maria Y. ... Phoenix, AZ
Armijo, Mark S. ... Santa Ana, CA
Armijo, M. L., Jr. ... Las Vegas, NM
Armijo, Rafael G. ... Northridge, CA
Armijo, Roberto C. ... Albuquerque, NM
Armijo, Roberto L. ... Las Vegas, NM
Armington, W. Scott ... Philadelphia, PA
Arminio, John D. ... Arlington, VA
Armintrout, G. William ... Hillsboro, OH
Armiros, Konstantinos ... Chicago, IL
Armistead, Allie Edwards ... Griffin, GA
Armistead, Bruce C. ... Easton, MD
Armistead & Capute, LLP ... Easton, MD
Armistead, David H. ... Atlanta, GA
Armistead, George B. ... Morgantown, WV
Armistead, Hugh H. ... Olive Branch, MS
Armistead, Hunter ... Nashville, TN
Armistead, Ivor Cary, III ... Boston, MA
Armistead, John M. ... Knoxville, TN
Armistead, L. H. (Bill), III ... Nashville, TN
Armistead, Thomas W. ... Houston, TX
Armistead, William G. ... Tupelo, MS
Armitage, Angela J. ... Los Angeles, CA
Armitage & Armitage, P.A.
Lexington Park, MD
Armitage & Buchli, P.C. ... Kansas City, MO
Armitage, Catherine E. ... Buffalo, NY
Armitage, Dale L. ... Bakersfield, CA
Armitage, Daniel R. ... Lexington Park, MD
Armitage, David M. ... Atlanta, GA
Armitage, David T.
Department of Defense, GV
Armitage, Eric R. ... St. Helena, CA
Armitage, Glen N. ... Clifton Park, NY
Armitage, J. Clark ... Washington, DC
Armitage, Julie K. ... Springfield, IL
Armitage, Kelley H., (Mr.)
West Palm Beach, FL
Armitage, Michael L. ... Long Beach, CA
Armitage, Nancy J. ... Boston, MA
Armitage, Paul C. ... Greenville, SC
Armitage, Richard E. ... Kansas City, MO
Armitage, Robert A. ... Washington, DC
Armitage, Scott R. ... Denver, CO
Armitage, Sue Ann Lewis
Lexington Park, MD
Armitage, Terry L. ... Cheyenne, WY
Armitage, Willard T., Jr. ... Alexandria, LA
Armknecht, Richard F., III
Salt Lake City, UT
Armo, Lance E. ... Fresno, CA
Armogida, Harry ... Oxford, OH
Armogida, James A. ... Houston, TX
Armold, Holly S. ... Lancaster, PA
York, PA
Armold, Judith A. ... Baltimore, MD
Armold, Peter M. ... North Palm Beach, FL
Armon, Bruce D. ... Philadelphia, PA
Armon, Edward F. ... University Heights, OH
Armon, Jan ... Philadelphia, PA
Armon, Naftali P. ... New York, NY
Armonda, Albert J. ... Williams Bay, WI
Armor, G. W. ... Laverne, OK
Armor, Vance W. ... Laverne, OK
Armosino, Thomas F., Jr. ... Medford, OR
Armour, Alan I., II ... West Palm Beach, FL
Armour, Carlos O. ... San Diego, CA
Armour & Cielinski, P.C. ... Columbus, GA
Armour, Clyde L., Jr. ... Columbus, GA
Armour, Frank L. ... Newark, NJ
Armour, George P. ... Pasadena, CA
Armour, James L. ... Dallas, TX
Armour, Jonathan W. J.
Minneapolis, MN
St. Paul, MN
Armour, Maya L. ... San Francisco, CA
Armour, Michele M. ... Dedham, MA
Armour, Norman E. ... Hartford, CT
Armour, Randall D. ... Valencia, CA
Armour, Robert Thomas ... Memphis, TN
Armour, Scott A. ... Columbus, OH
Armour, Tom W. ... Colorado Springs, CO
Armour, William D. ... Pittsburgh, PA
Armouti, Veronica Felton
Edwardsville, IL
Armpriester, Jacob A.
Fort Lauderdale, FL
Arms, Abigail ... Washington, DC
Arms, Brewster L. ... Rancho Santa Fe, CA
Arms, Catherine ... Menlo Park, CA
Arms, Geoffrey ... Houston, TX
Arms, Richard F. ... Needham, MA
Armstead, Thaddeus J. ... Cincinnati, OH
Armstead, Timothy Paul ... Charleston, WV
Armstead, Y. Andrea
Department of Transportation,
Federal Aviation Administration, GV
Armstrong, A. Ann ... Auburn, CA
Grass Valley, CA
Armstrong, Aaron M. ... San Francisco, CA
Armstrong, Aileen A.
National Labor Relations Board,
Office of the Inspector General, GV
Armstrong, Alan Leigh
Huntington Beach, CA
Armstrong, Alan W. ... Philadelphia, PA
Armstrong, Allan L. ... Birmingham, AL
Armstrong Allen Prewitt Gentry Johnston & Holmes, PLLC ... Little Rock, AR
Jackson, MS
Jackson, TN
Memphis, TN
Armstrong, Amy M. ... Austin, TX
Armstrong, Anne C. ... Washington, DC
Armstrong, Anthony T. ... Indianapolis, IN
Armstrong, Arleen ... Jenkintown, PA
Armstrong & Armstrong ... Hollywood, CA
Los Angeles, CA
Armstrong & Armstrong ... San Diego, CA
Armstrong & Armstrong ... Ventura, CA
Westlake Village, CA
Armstrong & Armstrong, P.A.
Smithfield, NC
Armstrong, Arthur John ... McLean, VA
Armstrong, Arthur O. ... Los Angeles, CA
Armstrong & Associates ... Monroe, OH
Armstrong & Baggett ... Fayetteville, NC
Armstrong, Barbara A. ... Fort Worth, TX
Armstrong, Barbara B. ... Livonia, MI
Armstrong, Barbara Lee ... Cleveland, OH
Armstrong, Barry J. ... Atlanta, GA
Armstrong, Benjamin A. ... Phoenix, AZ
Tucson, AZ
Armstrong, Benton Tad ... Collinsville, IL
Edwardsville, IL
Armstrong, Beverly ... Boston, MA
Armstrong, Blake E. ... Tyler, TX
Armstrong, Bob ... Austin, TX
Armstrong, Brad L. ... Austin, TX
Armstrong, Bradley D. ... Madison, WI
Armstrong, Bradley J. ... Tucson, AZ
Armstrong, Brenda A.
Department of the Navy, GV
Armstrong, Brenda L. ... Indianapolis, IN
Armstrong, Brent D. ... Clearwater, FL
Armstrong, Brent R. ... Salt Lake City, UT
Armstrong, Brent R., Law Offices, P.C.
Salt Lake City, UT
Armstrong, Brian J. ... Oak Brook, IL
Wheaton, IL
Armstrong, Brian J. ... New York, NY
Armstrong, Brian P. ... Apopka, FL
Armstrong, Bruce A., (A Professional Corporation) ... Santa Monica, CA
Armstrong, Bruce T. ... Cary, IL
Armstrong, C. Torrence ... McLean, VA
Armstrong, Catherine A. ... Boston, MA
Armstrong, Cathy M. ... Wheeling, WV
Armstrong, Cecile A. ... San Juan, PR
Armstrong, Celeste Patton
Birmingham, AL
Armstrong, Cesar A. ... Miami, FL
Armstrong, Cesar A., & Associates, P.A.
Coral Gables, FL
Fort Lauderdale, FL
Miami, FL
West Palm Beach, FL
Armstrong, Charlene Y. ... Creedmoor, NC
Durham, NC
Greensboro, NC
Raleigh, NC
Armstrong, Charles ... Akron, OH
Armstrong, Charles B. ... Fayetteville, NC
Armstrong, Charles E. ... United States Senate,
Office of the Legislative Counsel, GV
Armstrong, Charles G. ... Seattle, WA
Armstrong, Charlotte P. ... New York, NY
Armstrong, Chester ... Ponca City, OK
Armstrong, Chester Lee, III
Winnemucca, NV
Armstrong, Christine M. ... Rochester, MN
Armstrong, Christopher D. ... Rahway, NJ
Armstrong, Christopher J. ... Boston, MA
Armstrong, Christopher D. ... Elizabeth, NJ
Armstrong, Christopher S.
San Francisco, CA
Armstrong, Christopher W. ... Atlanta, GA
Armstrong, Courtney D. ... Los Angeles, CA
Armstrong, Craig R. ... Tulsa, OK
Armstrong, Craig R. ... Portland, OR
Armstrong, Dale E. ... Columbus, OH
Armstrong, Dan L. ... El Paso, TX
Armstrong, Dan L., A Professional Corporation
El Paso, TX
Armstrong, Daniel M.
Federal Communications Commission,
Office of the General Counsel, GV
Armstrong, David B. ... Washington, DC
Armstrong, David D. ... Greenville, SC
Armstrong, David G. ... Delray Beach, FL
Armstrong, David H. ... Tacoma, WA
Armstrong, David J. ... Phoenix, AZ
Armstrong, David J. ... Detroit, MI
Armstrong, David J. ... Pittsburgh, PA
Armstrong, David K. ... Henderson, KY
Armstrong, David L. ... Louisville, KY
Armstrong, David P. ... Detroit, MI
Armstrong, David W. ... Santa Monica, CA
Armstrong, Deborah Ann Baumgartner
Rockville, MD
Armstrong, Deshler D. ... New York, NY
Armstrong, Donald C. ... Cortland, NY
Armstrong, Donald E. ... Louisville, KY
Armstrong, Donald E., Jr. ... Louisville, KY
Armstrong, Donald K. ... Eugene, OR
Armstrong & Donnelly, Ltd. ... Chicago, IL
Armstrong, Donohue, Ceppos & Vaughan, Chartered ... Rockville, MD
Armstrong, Dwight L. ... Irvine, CA
Armstrong, E. Alan ... Atlanta, GA
Armstrong, E. Bruce ... Baltimore, MD
Armstrong, E. Taylor ... Dallas, TX
Armstrong, E. D., III ... Clearwater, FL
Armstrong, Edward A. ... Slidell, LA
Armstrong, Edward L. ... St. Louis, MO
Armstrong, Edward L., P.C.
St. Louis, MO
Armstrong, Edward S., Jr. ... Glynco, GA
Armstrong, Edwin R. ... Chicago, IL
Armstrong, Elizabeth G. ... Boston, MA
Armstrong, Erick L. ... Helena, MT
Armstrong, Ernie B. ... Snyder, TX
Armstrong, F. Dean ... Flossmoor, IL
Armstrong, F. Dean, P.C. ... Flossmoor, IL
Armstrong & Fisch, A.P.L.C.
San Diego, CA
Armstrong, Frank W. ... Gainesville, GA
Armstrong, Frederick S. ... Foxboro, MA
Armstrong, G. Cliff, Jr. ... Bellevue, WA
Armstrong, G. Timothy ... Oklahoma City, OK
Armstrong, Garrison, Law Corporation
San Diego, CA
Armstrong, Garrison R. ... San Diego, CA
Armstrong, Gary A. ... Irving, TX
Armstrong, Gary W. ... Storm Lake, IA
Armstrong, Gavin W. ... Eugene, OR
Armstrong, Gene L. ... Oak Park, IL
Armstrong, Gene L., & Associates, P.C.
Chicago, IL
Oak Park, IL
Wheaton, IL
Armstrong, Gibbons & Gnys, LLP
Bristol, RI
Providence, RI
Armstrong, Gordon G., III ... Mobile, AL
Armstrong, Gordon G., III, A Professional Corporation ... Mobile, AL
Armstrong, Gordon V. ... San Antonio, TX
Armstrong, Grant M. ... San Jose, CA
Armstrong & Green ... Marion, IL
Armstrong, Gregory C. ... Chicago, IL
Armstrong, Gregory T. ... Lancaster, PA
Armstrong & Grove ... Charleston, IL
Mattoon, IL
Armstrong, H. Jere ... Department of Justice,
Executive Office for Immigration Review,
GV
Armstrong, H. Kenneth ... Rockville, MD
Armstrong, H. Lawrence, Jr. ... Enfield, NC
Armstrong, Harry C. ... Edwardsville, IL
Armstrong, Hazen R. ... Saginaw, MI
Armstrong, Herma R. ... Getzville, NY
Armstrong Hirsch Jackoway Tyerman & Wertheimer, A Professional Corporation
Los Angeles, CA
Armstrong, Holly B. ... Sacramento, CA
Armstrong, Howard L. ... San Diego, CA
Armstrong, Howard L., Jr. ... Pocatello, ID
Armstrong, J. Douglas ... Winston-Salem, NC
Armstrong, J. Gaylord ... Austin, TX
Armstrong, J. Michael ... Carlsbad, CA
Armstrong, J. Patrick ... Spartanburg, SC
Armstrong, J. Sinclair ... New York, NY
Armstrong, Jack D. ... Hartford, CT
Armstrong, Jack G. ... Pittsburgh, PA
Armstrong, Jackie D. ... Mason City, IA
Armstrong, Jacqueline K. ... Louisville, KY
Armstrong, James E. ... San Francisco, CA
Armstrong, James E. ... Greenup, KY
Armstrong, James E., III
Washington, DC
Armstrong, James Elwood, IV
Washington, DC
Pittsburgh, PA
Armstrong, James F. ... Buffalo, NY
Rochester, NY
Armstrong, James G. ... Las Vegas, NV
Armstrong, James J. ... Hollywood, CA
Ventura, CA
Westlake Village, CA
Armstrong, James J. ... Trenton, NJ
Armstrong, James L. ... Ada, OK
Armstrong, James L., III, (P.A.)
New York, NY
Armstrong, James L., Jr.
Walnut Creek, CA
Armstrong, James M. ... Dublin, CA
Armstrong, James M. ... Wichita, KS
Armstrong, James P. ... San Diego, CA
Armstrong, James S. ... Jackson, MS
Armstrong, James S. ... Dayton, OH
Armstrong, James S., Jr. ... Los Angeles, CA
Parker, CO
Armstrong, James T. ... Hollywood, FL
Armstrong, James W. ... Scottsdale, AZ
Armstrong, James W., III ... Covington, LA
Armstrong, Jan R. ... Richland, WA
Armstrong, Jane E. ... New Orleans, LA
Armstrong, Jas. J., Jr. ... Trenton, NJ
Armstrong, Jason S. ... Lufkin, TX
Armstrong, Jeanine R. ... St. Louis, MO
Armstrong, Jeanne M. ... Madison, WI
Armstrong, Jeffrey A. ... Morristown, TN
Armstrong, Jeffrey R. ... Troy, NY
Armstrong, Jennifer L. ... Taylorsville, KY
Armstrong, Joan M. B. ... New Orleans, LA
Armstrong, Joan P. ... Boston, MA
Armstrong, Jody H. ... Dayton, OH
Armstrong, Joe E. ... Omaha, NE
Armstrong, Joel D. ... Washington, DC
Armstrong, Joel S. ... Alexandria, VA
Armstrong, Johanna H. ... Rochester Hills, MI
Armstrong, John Andrew
Colorado Springs, CO
Armstrong, John B. ... Cincinnati, OH
Armstrong, John D. ... La Porte, TX
Armstrong, John H. ... Mattoon, IL
Armstrong, John H. ... Indiana, PA
Armstrong, John J., III ... Allentown, PA
Armstrong, John L. ... Miami, FL
Armstrong, John M. ... Cherry Hill, NJ
Philadelphia, PA
Armstrong, John R. ... Irvine, CA
Armstrong, John R.
Cape May Court House, NJ
Armstrong, John T., Jr. ... Hazlehurst, MS
Armstrong, Joseph G. ... Greenville, SC
Armstrong, Joseph G., III ... Pittsburgh, PA
Armstrong, Joseph M. ... Philadelphia, PA
Armstrong, Joshua ... Los Angeles, CA
Armstrong, Julia Anne ... Long Grove, IL
Armstrong, Julia Lacy ... Austin, TX
Armstrong, Kara M. ... Washington, DC
Armstrong, Karl Wesley ... Las Vegas, NV
Armstrong, Katherine A. ... New York, NY
Armstrong, Katherine L.
Federal Trade Commission,
Offices of Commissioners, GV
Armstrong, Kathleen E. ... San Ramon, CA
Armstrong, Kathleen Joy ... Centerville, SD
Armstrong, Kathy L. ... Lenexa, KS
Armstrong, Kay Ellen ... Carson City, NV
Armstrong, Keith C. ... Baton Rouge, LA
Armstrong, Kelli ... Okanogan, WA
Armstrong, Kendra Hazlett ... Memphis, TN
Armstrong, Kenneth ... Mount Shasta, CA
Armstrong, Kenneth E.
St. Petersburg, FL
Armstrong, Kenneth L., Jr. ... West Union, OH

Armstrong, Kenny W. ...Memphis, TN
Armstrong, Kent P. ...Corpus Christi, TX
Armstrong, Kerry M. ...Fort Worth, TX
Armstrong, Klym & Waite, P.S.
Kennewick, WA
Pasco, WA
Richland, WA
Armstrong, Kristen S. ...San Diego, CA
Armstrong, Kyra C.
Securities and Exchange Commission,
Division of Enforcement, GV
Armstrong, L. Lamar, Jr. ...Smithfield, NC
Armstrong, Lance ...Miami, FL
Armstrong, Lance P. ...Staten Island, NY
Armstrong, Lauren D. ...Boston, MA
Armstrong, Laurie J. ...Hollywood, CA
Armstrong, Laurie S. ...Woodland Hills, CA
Armstrong Law Firm ...Greenville, SC
Armstrong Law Offices ...Collinsville, IL
Edwardsville, IL
Armstrong, Lee A. ...New York, NY
Armstrong, Lee Edwin ...Dickinson, ND
Armstrong, Lee F. ...Auburn, AL
Armstrong, Lee P. ...West Winfield, NY
Armstrong, Lester W. ...Cleveland, OH
Armstrong, Linda S. ...Shelbyville, KY
Armstrong, Lisa Hurtado ...Salt Lake City, UT
Armstrong, Louise E. ...Costa Mesa, CA
Armstrong, Lyn K. ...Atlanta, GA
Armstrong, Lyndel K. ...Bloomington, IL
Armstrong, Lynne M. ...San Francisco, CA
Armstrong, Marcia H. ...Smithfield, NC
Armstrong, Margaret T. ...San Diego, CA
Armstrong, Mark F. ...Lexington, KY
Armstrong, Mark F. ...Findlay, OH
Armstrong, Mark L. ...Danville, CA
Armstrong, Mark S. ...Houston, TX
Armstrong, Mark W. ...Mesa, AZ
Armstrong, Mary Frances
Grand Junction, CO
Armstrong, Mary G. H. ...Santa Barbara, CA
Armstrong, Mary Mitchell
Department Of Health And Human Services,
Office of the General Counsel, GV
Armstrong, Mary N. ...Glendale, CA
Armstrong, Matthew H.
East St. Louis, IL
Armstrong, Matthew Hall ...Granite City, IL
Armstrong, Matthew J. ...Wilmington, NC
Armstrong, McCullen & Philpott, P.C.
Eugene, OR
Armstrong & Mejer, P.A.
Coral Gables, FL
Fort Lauderdale, FL
Miami, FL
Palm Beach, FL
Armstrong, Melodee D. ...Dallas, TX
Armstrong, Michael ...Richmond, VA
Armstrong, Michael A. ...Willingboro, NJ
Armstrong, Michael C. ...Wheaton, MD
Armstrong, Michael F. ...San Diego, CA
Armstrong, Michael F. ...New York, NY
Armstrong, Michael L. ...Los Angeles, CA
Armstrong, Michael W. ...Palo Alto, CA
Armstrong, Michelle A. ...Brooklyn, NY
Armstrong, Michelle L.
Fort Lauderdale, FL
Armstrong, Mitchell, Damiani & Zaccagnini
Cleveland, OH
Armstrong, Nancy Guy ...Mc Comb, MS
Armstrong, Norman Alva, Jr.
Federal Trade Commission,
Bureau of Competition, GV
Armstrong, O. R. ...Becker, MN
Armstrong, Orville A. ...Los Angeles, CA
Armstrong, Owen T. ...St. Louis, MO
Armstrong, P. Michael ...Waxahachie, TX
Armstrong, Pamela D. ...Orlando, FL
Armstrong, Patricia ...New York, NY
Armstrong, Patricia ...Harrisburg, PA
Armstrong, Patricia E. ...Berwyn, PA
Armstrong, Paul R. ...Wilmette, IL
Armstrong, Paul W. ...Roseland, NJ
Armstrong, Peter ...Grand Rapids, MI
Armstrong, Philip H. ...Rockville, MD
Armstrong, Phillip D. ...Minot, ND
Armstrong, Phillip M. ...Atlanta, GA
Armstrong, Phyllis I. ...Middlebury, VT
Armstrong, Phyllis S. ...Indianapolis, IN
Armstrong & Prauser ...Columbus, KS
Armstrong, R. Morgan ...Martinsville, VA
Armstrong, R. W., & Associates
Brownsville, TX
Armstrong, Ralph L. ...Bessemer, AL
Armstrong, Ralph L., P.C. ...Bessemer, AL
Armstrong, Ralph R. ...Chattanooga, TN
Armstrong, Rex ...Salem, OR
Armstrong, Richard Charles ...New York, NY
Armstrong, Richard D., Jr., (P.C.)
Boston, MA
Armstrong, Richard E., III
Department of Transportation,
Surface Transportation Board, GV
Armstrong, Richard J.
Salt Lake City, UT
Armstrong, Richard L., & Associates
Plano, TX
Armstrong, Richard V. ...Tulsa, OK
Armstrong, Robert A. ...Milton, WI
Armstrong, Robert A., Jr. ...Inverness, IL
Armstrong, Robert Allen, II ...Alexandria, VA
Armstrong, Robert B. ...Lexington, VA
Armstrong, Robert C. ...Jersey City, NJ
Armstrong, Robert David ...Houston, TX
Armstrong, Robert E. ...Chicago, IL
Armstrong, Robert E. ...Las Vegas, NV
Reno, NV
Armstrong, Robert E., III ...Selma, AL

Armstrong, Robert F. ...Madison, CT
Armstrong, Robert G. ...San Diego, CA
Armstrong, Robert G. ...Roswell, NM
Armstrong, Robert J. ...Albany, NY
Armstrong, Robert L. ...Wilmington, NC
Armstrong, Robert S. ...Ridgeland, SC
Armstrong, Robert W. ...Long Beach, CA
San Diego, CA
Armstrong, Robert W. ...Los Angeles, CA
Armstrong, Robert W. ...Los Angeles, CA
Armstrong, Roger ...Los Angeles, CA
Armstrong, Roger D. ...Elko, NV
Armstrong, Ronald J. ...Ellijay, GA
Armstrong, Ronald W. ...Brownsville, TX
Armstrong, Rosemary S., P.C. ...Atlanta, GA
Armstrong, Rosemary Smith ...Atlanta, GA
Armstrong, Roxanne ...Houston, TX
Armstrong, Roy L. ...Austin, TX
Armstrong, Russell F. ...Daytona Beach, FL
Armstrong, Russell S. ...Evansville, IN
Armstrong, Sallie Bernard ...Reno, NV
Armstrong, Samuel D. ...Fort Myers, FL
Armstrong, Samuel J. ...Truro, MA
Armstrong, Sara G. ...Wayne, PA
Armstrong, Saundra B. ...Oakland, CA
Armstrong, Seth ...Seattle, WA
Armstrong, Seymour ...New York, NY
Armstrong & Shapiro, P.A. ...Foxboro, MA
Armstrong, Sharon Stewart ...Seattle, WA
Armstrong, Shelley W. ...Boise, ID
Armstrong, Sherry A.
Merit Systems Protection Board,
Washington, D.C. Regional Office, GV
Armstrong, Shona L. ...San Francisco, CA
Armstrong & Sparks ...Ellensburg, WA
Armstrong, Stephen A. ...Fairfax, VA
Armstrong, Stephen H. ...Chicago, IL
Armstrong, Stephen L. ...Pasadena, TX
Armstrong, Stephen M. ...Jacksonville, FL
Armstrong, Stephen W. ...Philadelphia, PA
Armstrong, Steven A. ...Kew Gardens, NY
Armstrong, Steven H. ...New York, NY
Armstrong, Steven M. ...Grand Rapids, MI
Armstrong, Steven R. ...Lexington, KY
Armstrong, Sue Taylor ...Ellensburg, WA
Armstrong, Surin & Hettel ...La Salle, IL
Ottawa, IL
Armstrong, Susan C. ...Richmond, VA
Armstrong, Susan S. ...Louisville, KY
Armstrong, Tamara ...Austin, TX
Armstrong Teasdale LLP
Washington, DC
Belleville, IL
Olathe, KS
Jefferson City, MO
Kansas City, MO
St. Louis, MO
Armstrong, Teresa L. ...Roseville, CA
Armstrong, Theodore M. ...Chesterfield, MO
Armstrong, Thomas ...Milwaukee, WI
Armstrong, Thomas C. ...Oakland, CA
Armstrong, Thomas E. ...Austin, TX
Armstrong, Thomas G. ...Stillwater, MN
Armstrong, Thomas H.
General Accounting Office,
Office of the General Counsel, GV
Armstrong, Thomas I. ...Las Vegas, NV
Armstrong, Thomas K. ...McKinleyville, CA
Armstrong, Thomas, Leach & Lampton
Hazlehurst, MS
Armstrong, Thomas M. ...Hartford, CT
Armstrong, Timothy A. ...Wheaton, IL
Armstrong, Timothy B. ...Los Angeles, CA
Armstrong, Timothy J. ...Miami, FL
Armstrong, Timothy J. ...Cleveland, OH
Armstrong, Timothy K. ...Washington, DC
Armstrong, Tom L., & Associates
Oklahoma City, OK
Armstrong, Tom L., & Associates
Tulsa, OK
Armstrong, Tracy A. ...Eatontown, NJ
Armstrong, Victor T. ...Miami, FL
Armstrong, Victoria Davis ...Roswell, NM
Armstrong, Wacy, Jr. ...San Bernardino, CA
Armstrong, Ward L. ...Martinsville, VA
Armstrong, Wayne W. ...Yucca Valley, CA
Armstrong, Wendy R. ...Monroe, OH
Armstrong, Westerman, Hattori, McLeland & Naughton ...Washington, DC
Pittsburgh, PA
Armstrong, Wil ...Houston, TX
Armstrong, William ...Smackover, AR
Armstrong, William A. ...Marion, IL
Armstrong, William B. ...Richmond, VA
Armstrong, William D. ...Lubbock, TX
Armstrong, William E. ...Cleveland, OH
Armstrong, William J. ...San Jose, CA
Armstrong, William J. ...Atlanta, GA
Armstrong, William J., III
Silver Spring, MD
Armstrong, William N. ...Houston, TX
Armstrong, William R., Jr. ...Jackson, MS
Armstrong, William R., Jr., P.A.
Greenville, MS
Jackson, MS
Armstrong, William R., P.A.
Daytona Beach, FL
Armstrong, William T., III
San Antonio, TX
Armstrong, Willie E., Jr.
Treasury Department,
Internal Revenue Service, GV
Armstrong, Wm. David ...Irvine, CA
Armstrong, Wm. G. ...St. Louis, MO
Armstrong de Watlington, Mary E.
Guaynabo, PR
Armstrong-Wright, Debra ...Auburn, AL
Armwood, Karol Smith ...Atlanta, GA

Army & Army, L.L.C. ...Worcester, MA
Army, Lawrence F. ...Worcester, MA
Army, Lawrence F., Jr. ...Worcester, MA
Arn, Cynthia C. ...Portland, ME
Arn, Dwight C. ...Kansas City, MO
Arn, Mullins, Unruh, Kuhn & Wilson, LLP
Wichita, KS
Arn, Thomas D. ...Phoenix, AZ
Arnaboldi, Leo P., III ...New York, NY
Arnaboldi, Luca (IBA) ...New York, NY
Arnaboldi, Nicole Sinek ...New York, NY
Arnal, Leslie Ann ...Sacramento, CA
Arnall, Alan C. ...Pasadena, CA
Arnall, Alvan S. ...Atlanta, GA
Arnall, Christina M. ...Northridge, CA
Arnall Golden & Gregory, LLP
Atlanta, GA
Macon, GA
Arnall, Patrick J. ...St. Louis, MO
Arnall, Walter W. ...Newnan, GA
Arnao, Antonio R. ...St. Petersburg, FL
Arnason, A. Fred ...Grand Forks, ND
Arnason, Charles W.
Marine On St. Croix, MN
Arnason, Joel F. ...Grand Forks, ND
Arnason, John T. ...Minneapolis, MN
Arnason, Jon Yard ...New York, NY
Arnason, Richard E. ...Martinez, CA
Arnaud, Alfred J. ...San Francisco, CA
Arnavas, Donald P. ...Washington, DC
Arnay, James D. ...New York, NY
Arnberger, H. Bennett ...San Francisco, CA
Arnburg, David M. ...Chicago, IL
Arnd, Maurice J. ...Pittsburgh, PA
Arndorfer, Brad L. ...Billings, MT
Arndorfer, Brian J. ...Merrill, WI
Wausau, WI
Arndorfer Law Firm, P.C. ...Billings, MT
Arndt, Amy H. ...Sioux Falls, SD
Arndt & Benton, P.A. ...Minneapolis, MN
North St. Paul, MN
Arndt, Buswell & Thorn, S.C. ...Sparta, WI
Arndt, Christina Bull ...San Diego, CA
Arndt, Christopher J. ...Long Beach, CA
Arndt, Christopher R. ...Red Wing, MN
Arndt, Craig R. ...Los Angeles, CA
Arndt, Cynthia M. ...Minneapolis, MN
Arndt, Dale L. ...Grand Rapids, MI
Arndt, Daniel C. ...Sparta, WI
Arndt, David A. ...Hibbing, MN
Arndt, Duane E. ...Minneapolis, MN
North St. Paul, MN
Arndt, Frank William ...Baltimore, MD
Arndt, James J. ...Arvada, CO
Arndt, Janet Louise ...Topeka, KS
Arndt, John D. ...Doraville, GA
Arndt, Joseph M., III ...Columbia, SC
Arndt, Joseph M., III, P.A. ...Columbia, SC
Arndt, Karen R. ...Albany, NY
Arndt, Kathleen M. ...St. Louis, MO
Arndt, Kimberly A. ...Newark, NJ
Arndt, Melissa Dawn ...Treasury Department,
Internal Revenue Service, GV
Arndt, Randall K. ...Terre Haute, IN
Arndt, Randall S. ...Columbus, OH
Arndt, Richard C. ...Kansas City, MO
Arndt, Roy W. ...Milwaukee, WI
Arndt, Sarah A. Matter ...Red Wing, MN
Arndt, Shannon R Thomas
Fayetteville, NC
Arndt, Trisha J. ...Detroit, MI
Arndt & Van Patten ...Los Angeles, CA
Arndts, John C. ...Grand Rapids, MI
Arne, Courtland D. ...Oakland, CA
Arne, Paul H. ...Atlanta, GA
Arneal, Richard G. ...Orange, CA
Walnut Creek, CA
Arnebeck, Clifford O., Jr. ...Columbus, OH
Arnebergh, Roger ...Van Nuys, CA
Arnedt, Rachel B. ...New Haven, CT
Arneil, James ...Wenatchee, WA
Arneil, Kari Lavelle ...Austin, TX
Arneil, Lurita J. ...Austin, TX
Arneja, Harnam S. ...Washington, DC
Arneke, Gail C. ...Winston-Salem, NC
Arnel, Curt ...Brooklyn, NY
Arnel, Kevin J. ...Wichita, KS
Arnel, Philip L. ...Norwood, MA
Arnell, Donald E. ...Chicago Heights, IL
Arnell, Louis G. ...San Diego, CA
Arnell, Nathan E. ...Newark, NJ
New York, NY
Arnell, Norman M. ...Kansas City, MO
Arnelle, H. Jesse ...Winston-Salem, NC
Arner & Banner, P.C. ...Boyne City, MI
Arner, Barbara J. ...Wyomissing, PA
Arner, Erika Harmon ...Washington, DC
Arner, Frederick B. ...Kensington, MD
Arner, Jessica F. ...Palo Alto, CA
Arner, Leah F. ...Chicago, IL
Arner, Michael R. ...Treasury Department,
Internal Revenue Service, GV
Arner, Raymond G. ...Kalamazoo, MI
Arner, Stephen M. ...Washington, DC
Arner, Timothy D. ...Boyne City, MI
Arnerich, del Valle & Sinatra ...Pasadena, CA
Arnerich, V. G. ...Pasadena, CA
Arnese, Marlene ...San Francisco, CA
Arnesen, Carl A. ...San Diego, CA
Arnesen, Dwight I. ...New York, NY
Arnesen, Mark R ...Santa Ana, CA
Arneson, Bruce A. ...Barstow, CA
Arneson, Bryan J. ...Sioux City, IA
Arneson, Issenhuth & Gienapp
Madison, SD
Arneson, James A. ...Roseburg, OR
Arneson, James A., P.C. ...Roseburg, OR
Arneson, James H. ...Springfield, MO

Arneson, Joan C. ...Newport Beach, CA
Arneson, Joel K.
Federal Energy Regulatory Commission,
Office of the General Counsel, GV
Arneson, John C. ...Dallas, TX
Arneson, John F. ...Syracuse, NY
Arneson, Jon E. ...Sioux Falls, SD
Arneson, Kristin ...Minneapolis, MN
Arneson, Marjorie D. ...Dallas, TX
Arneson, Mark E. ...St. Cloud, MN
Arneson, Paul ...Warrenton, VA
Arneson, Peder G. ...La Crosse, WI
Arneson, Robert P. ...Hayti, SD
Arneson, Ross ...Mankato, MN
Arneson, Ross R. ...Arlington, MN
Arneson, Thomas Stuart ...Minneapolis, MN
Arneson, Timothy J. ...San Francisco, CA
Arneson, William R. ...Madison, SD
Arness, Frank F. ...Chesapeake, VA
Arness, Franklin ...Department Of The Interior,
Office of Hearings & Appeals, GV
Arness, John E., II ...Washington, DC
Arness, John P. ...Washington, DC
Arness, Lawrence W. ...Michigan City, IN
Arnest, Anthony R. ...Aliso Viejo, CA
Arnestt, Carolyn S. ...Louisville, KY
Arnet, William F. ...Columbia, MO
Arnett, Andrew B. ...Indianapolis, IN
Arnett, Angela Jones ...Washington, DC
Arnett & Arnett, P.C. ...Tempe, AZ
Arnett, Bradley C. ...Cincinnati, OH
Arnett, Christopher A. ...Dallas, TX
Arnett, Dale W. ...Winchester, IN
Arnett, Daniel J. ...Chicago, IL
Des Plaines, IL
Arnett, Deborah C. ...Dayton, OH
Arnett, Debra J. ...Paola, KS
Arnett, Donald R. ...Houston, TX
Arnett, Draper & Hagood ...Knoxville, TN
Arnett, Foster D. ...Knoxville, TN
Arnett, George W., III ...Roseland, NJ
Arnett, Henry A. ...Columbus, OH
Arnett, Howard G. ...Bend, OR
Arnett, James Robert, II ...Dallas, TX
Arnett, James Stanley ...Orange, CA
Arnett, John B., Sr. ...Department of Justice,
Antitrust Division, GV
Arnett, John E. ...Fairfax, VA
Arnett, John G. ...Burlington, KY
Covington, KY
Arnett, John G. ...Florence, KY
Arnett, John G. ...Independence, KY
Arnett, John W. ...Ocala, FL
Arnett, M. Michael ...Oklahoma City, OK
Arnett, Mark W. ...Tempe, AZ
Arnett, Martin A. ...Louisville, KY
Arnett, Mary Beth ...Neenah, WI
Arnett, Maxine H. ...Indianapolis, IN
Arnett, Nancy Spratt ...Atlanta, GA
Arnett, Norman ...Rotan, TX
Arnett, Patricia ...Tampa, FL
Arnett, Quick, Coleman & Shaw
Bardstown, KY
Elizabethtown, KY
Hardinsburg, KY
Hodgenville, KY
Leitchfield, KY
Arnett, Richard L. ...Austin, TX
Arnett, Russell E. ...Anchorage, AK
Arnett, Stephen M. ...Morganfield, KY
Arnett, Susan Lynn ...Honolulu, HI
Arnett, Thomas L. ...Detroit, MI
Arnett, Thomas N., Jr. ...Salt Lake City, UT
Arnett, Wayne C. ...Tempe, AZ
Arnett, Wm. Grover ...Salyersville, KY
Arnette, R. Paige ...Austin, TX
Arnette, W. Gregory, Jr. ...Bedford, TX
Arney, Anne Sumpter ...Nashville, TN
Arney, Charles D. ...Cleveland, OK
Arney, Cloyd L. ...Nashville, TN
Arney, D. Todd ...Kansas City, MO
Arney, John ...Weatherford, OK
Arney, John R., Jr. ...Media, PA
Arney, Lance C. ...Houston, TX
Arney, Neil L. ...Denver, CO
Edwards, CO
Vail, CO
Arney, Pat W. ...Coeur d'Alene, ID
Arney, Rex O. ...Casper, WY
Arney, Tracy A. ...Indianapolis, IN
Arnheim, David L. ...Boston, MA
Arnheim, David L., P.C. ...Boston, MA
Arnheim, Ralph L. (Buddy), III
Menlo Park, CA
Arnhem, Erik M. ...Los Angeles, CA
Arnhold, Thomas D. ...Hutchinson, KS
Arnhols, William C. ...Miami, FL
Arnholz, John ...Washington, DC
Arnholz, Sarah H. ...Boston, MA
Arnick, John S. ...Baltimore, MD
Arnier, Jeffery C. ...Fort Worth, TX
Arnieri, Harry J. ...Sheridan, WY
Arning, Diane E. ...Houston, TX
Arning, J. Nicholas ...Knoxville, TN
Arniotes, Steve C. ...Brooklyn, NY
Arnison, Nancy D. ...Minneapolis, MN
Arnn, Edward W. ...Atlanta, GA
Arno, Daniel J. ...North Syracuse, NY
Arno, James A. ...Fort Worth, TX
Arno, Margaret E. ...Gresham, OR
Arno, Thomas R. ...San Diego, CA
Arnoff, Alisa B. ...Chicago, IL
Arnoff, Fred J. ...Cleveland, OH
Arnoff, Harvey A., Law Offices of
Riverhead, NY
Arnoff, James B. ...Larchmont, NY
Arnoff, Laura E. ...North Palm Beach, FL
Arnoff, Norman B. ...New York, NY

Arnone, Anthony G. ... **Detroit, MI**
Arnone, Christopher P. ... Scranton, PA
Arnone, James L. ... **Los Angeles, CA**
Arnone, James R. ... Buffalo, NY
Arnone, John P. ... Freehold, NJ
Arnone Law Offices ... Scranton, PA
Arnone, William J., Jr. ... **Santa Rosa, CA**
Arnopol, Scott D. ... Washington, DC
Arnosky, Steven Alan ... Midland, MI
Arnot, Justin T. ... Minneapolis, MN
Arnot, Melissa D. ... United States Tax Court, GV
Arnot, Philip M. ... Eureka, CA
Arnot, William G. (Bud), III ... Eastland, TX
Arnott, John J. ... Dallas, TX
Arnott, Maria A. ... **New York, NY**
Arnott, Stephen R. ... St. Paul, MN
Arnoult, G. Patrick ... **Memphis, TN**
Arnoux, Matthew C. ... Chicago, IL
Arnovits, Stuart H. ... Baltimore, MD
Arnovitz, Michael S. ... Cleveland, OH
Arnovitz, Theodore M. ... Dayton, OH
Arnow, Arthur E. ... Plainview, NY
Arnow, Arthur E., P.C. ... Plainview, NY
Arnow, Rachel S. ... Philadelphia, PA
Arnowich, Sylvia ... **New York, NY**
Arnowitt, Edwin ... Stuart, FL
Arnowitt, Gerald A. ... Harrisburg, PA
Arnowitt, Kim B. ... Chicago, IL
Arnowitz & Goldberg ... West Roxbury, MA
Arnowitz, Jerrold N. ... West Roxbury, MA
Arnowitz, Martin G. ... **Fort Myers, FL**
Arnowitz, Martin G., P.A. ... **Fort Myers, FL**
Arnowitz, Seth J. ... **Stamford, CT**
Arnquist, Betty ... San Francisco, CA
Arns Law Firm, The ... **San Francisco, CA**
Arns, Robert S. ... **San Francisco, CA**
Arnsbarger, Linda A. ... **Washington, DC**
Arnsdorf, Ralph L. ... **Towson, MD**
Arnson, Gerald I. ... Beachwood, OH
Arnst, Diane L. ... Chattanooga, TN
Arnstein, Albert E. ... Skokie, IL
Arnstein & Lehr ... **Boca Raton, FL**; **West Palm Beach, FL**; **Chicago, IL**; **Hoffman Estates, IL**; **Milwaukee, WI**
Arnstein & Zeller ... Skokie, IL
Arnsten, Pamela ... **New York, NY**
Arnston, P. Scott ... **Huntsville, AL**
Arnts, Donald F. ... Alexandria, VA
Arntsen, Allen A. ... **Madison, WI**
Arntsen, David H. ... **Garden City, NY**
Arntson, Jon M. ... Fargo, ND
Arntson, Peter A. ... **Fairfax, VA**
Arntson & Stewart, P.C. ... Fargo, ND
Arntt, Steven E. ... **Portland, OR**
Arntz, E. Breen ... **Las Vegas, NV**
Arntz, Jill McCarthy ... **Houston, TX**
Arntz, Matthew Ryan ... Dayton, OH
Arntz, W. Charles ... Rockford, IL
Arntzen, Christopher J. ... **Houston, TX**
Arnwine, Barbara Ruth ... **Washington, DC**
Arnwine, Harold G., II ... **Atlanta, GA**
Arnwine, Roger B. ... **Chattanooga, TN**; **Knoxville, TN**
Arnzen, Jeffrey C. ... **Covington, KY**
Arnzen, Mark G. ... **Covington, KY**
Arnzen, Parry & Wentz, P.S.C. ... **Covington, KY**; **Cincinnati, OH**
Aro, Edwin P. ... **Denver, CO**
Aro, Jason B. ... **Palm Springs, CA**
Aro, Kathleen Hatke ... Detroit, MI
Aro, Linda V. ... **New York, NY**
Arobone, Nancy Moore ... Norristown, PA
Arocho, Angelo N. ... Scottsdale, AZ
Arocho, David ... Albany, NY
Aroesty, Karen J. ... St. Louis, MO
Aroesty Law Firm, L.C. ... St. Louis, MO
Aroesty, Steven M. ... **St. Louis, MO**
Arogeti, James ... Atlanta, GA
Arogeti, Jane ... Marietta, GA
Arogeti, Joel S. ... **Atlanta, GA**
Arola, Michael C. ... **Eugene, OR**
Aromando, John J. ... **Portland, ME**
Aromatorio, Jeffrey G. ... **Pittsburgh, PA**
Aron & Associates, P.C. ... Tucson, AZ
Aron, Brad M. ... Weston, CT; Westport, CT
Aron, Carl R. ... **New York, NY**
Aron, Charles J. ... Chicago, IL
Aron, C. M. "Steve" ... **Laramie, WY**
Aron, David E. ... **Washington, DC**
Aron, David J. ... New York, NY
Aron, Donald R. ... Sacramento, CA
Aron, Elise S. ... Chicago, IL
Aron, Harry B. ... Chicago, IL
Aron and Hennig ... **Laramie, WY**
Aron, Jerry E. ... **West Palm Beach, FL**
Aron, Kenneth L. ... Palisades Park, NJ; **New York, NY**
Aron, Leonard V. ... Chicago, IL
Aron, Lester ... **Newark, NJ**
Aron, Louise ... Lakewood, CO
Aron, Marc A. ... **Little Rock, AR**
Aron, Mark G. ... **Richmond, VA**
Aron, Martin W. ... **Short Hills, NJ**
Aron, Murray M. ... Fresno, CA
Aron, Nan ... Washington, DC
Aron, Simon ... **Los Angeles, CA**
Aron, Stewart H. ... Tamarac, FL
Aron, Thomas M. ... Rye, NY
Aronauer, Goldfarb, Sills & Re, LLP ... **New York, NY**
Aronauer, Joseph ... **New York, NY**
Aronberg, David T. ... Boca Raton, FL
Aronberg Goldgehn Davis & Garmisa ... **Chicago, IL**; Schaumburg, IL
Aronberg & Kouser, P.A. ... Cherry Hill, NJ
Aronberg, M. Craig ... Cherry Hill, NJ
Aronberg, Ronald J. ... **Chicago, IL**
Aronchick, Mark A. ... **Philadelphia, PA**
Aronchick, Martin Charles ... White Plains, NY
Aronds, Joseph M. ... Secaucus, NJ
Aronds, Ronald E. ... New Brunswick, NJ
Arone, Douglas E. ... **Newark, NJ**
Arone, Robert L. ... **Boston, MA**
Aroneck, Sherre M. ... Wayland, MA
Aronfeld, Mandel L. ... Springfield, IL
Aronfeld, Spencer M. ... Coral Gables, FL
Aronfeld, Spencer Marc, & Associates, P.A. ... Coral Gables, FL
Arong, Jessica V. ... **Chicago, IL**
Aronian, Lou ... San Francisco, CA
Aronica, Joseph J. ... **Washington, DC**
Aronie, Jonathan S. ... **Washington, DC**
Aronin, Douglas D. ... **New York, NY**
Aronin, Irving S. ... Brooklyn, NY
Aronin, Robert D. ... East Meadow, NY
Aronoff, Amanda S. ... **Philadelphia, PA**
Aronoff, Arthur I. ... Department of Commerce, Office of the General Counsel, GV
Aronoff, Carol R. ... **Wilton, CT**
Aronoff, David ... **Los Angeles, CA**
Aronoff, David L. ... Los Angeles, CA
Aronoff, George N. ... **Cleveland, OH**
Aronoff, James B. ... **Cleveland, OH**
Aronoff, Karen Feibel ... Cleveland, OH
Aronoff, Michael ... Woodbury, NY
Aronoff, Michael A. ... Federal Way, WA
Aronoff, Michael J. ... Philadelphia, PA
Aronoff, Morris ... Los Angeles, CA
Aronoff, Paul S. ... New York, NY
Aronoff, Philip H. ... San Diego, CA
Aronoff, Richard M. ... **Bethesda, MD**
Aronoff, Robert C. ... **Manhattan Beach, CA**
Aronoff, Rosen & Hunt ... **Covington, KY**; **Cincinnati, OH**; Columbus, OH
Aronoff, Stanley J. ... **Cincinnati, OH**; Columbus, OH
Aronoff, Steven K. ... New York, NY
Aronoff, Terry D. ... **Atlanta, GA**
Aronoff, Valerie K. ... Pittsfield, MA
Aronofsky, David J. ... Missoula, MT
Aronov, Freddi Lynn ... Birmingham, AL
Aronov, Mary ... **Memphis, TN**
Aronovitch, Anne E. ... **Morristown, NJ**
Aronovitz, Alfred ... **Miami, FL**
Aronovitz & Associates, P.A. ... **Miami, FL**
Aronovitz, Cory ... **Chicago, IL**
Aronovitz, Sidney M. ... Miami, FL
Aronovitz, Tod ... **Miami, FL**
Aronovsky, Ronald G. ... **San Francisco, CA**
Aronow, David S. ... Detroit, MI
Aronow, Geoffrey F. ... **Washington, DC**
Aronow, Greta L. ... Newport Beach, CA
Aronow, Joseph M. ... New York, NY
Aronow, Marcia B. ... Jenkintown, PA
Aronow, Paul ... East Meadow, NY
Aronow, Richard Avery ... **New York, NY**
Aronow, Shawn J. ... Seattle, WA
Aronow, Stephen A. ... **Houston, TX**
Aronow, Steven L. ... Miami, FL
Aronow, Victor A. ... Tempe, AZ
Aronow, Wm. Fred ... Liberty Lake, WA
Aronowitz, Alan B. ... **Houston, TX**
Aronowitz, Alan E. ... Federal Communications Commission, Mass Media Bureau, GV
Aronowitz, Albert M. ... New York, NY
Aronowitz & Bordelon ... Auburn, CA
Aronowitz, Daniel ... **Washington, DC**
Aronowitz, David S. ... **New York, NY**
Aronowitz, Dennis S. ... Newton, MA
Aronowitz & Ford, LLP ... **Denver, CO**
Aronowitz, Gary D. ... Glen Rock, NJ
Aronowitz, James David ... **Atlanta, GA**
Aronowitz, Judd A. ... **Miami Beach, FL**
Aronowitz, Mark ... **Houston, TX**
Aronowitz, Michelle M. ... Department of Justice, Civil Rights Division, GV
Aronowitz, Paul S. ... Auburn, CA
Aronowitz, Robert J. ... **Denver, CO**
Aronowitz, Susanne M. ... San Francisco, CA
Arons, Alan L. ... **Deerfield Beach, FL**
Arons, Alan S. ... East Brunswick, NJ
Arons, Benjamin ... Wayne, NJ
Arons, David L. ... Norwell, MA
Arons, Donna ... Trenton, NJ
Arons, Howard ... Stamford, CT
Arons, John L. ... **Mount Kisco, NY**
Arons, Jonathan I. ... **San Francisco, CA**
Arons, Lori Friedland ... **New City, NY**
Arons, Mark D. ... **Bridgeport, CT**
Arons, Mitchell S. ... Hackensack, NJ
Arons, Paul S. ... Redding, CA
Arons, Sara Allswede ... **Lansing, MI**
Arons & Solomon, P.A. ... Hackensack, NJ
Aronsen, Rolf V. ... Mason City, IA
Aronsky, Jeffrey A. ... New York, NY
Aronsohn, Alan J. B. ... New York, NY
Aronsohn, Kristine R. ... Los Angeles, CA
Aronsohn Weiner, A Professional Corporation ... **Hackensack, NJ**
Aronson, Adam L. ... New York, NY
Aronson, Alan A. ... Chicago, IL
Aronson, Alan D. ... **Los Angeles, CA**
Aronson, Alan H. ... **Miami, FL**
Aronson, Alan L. ... **New York, NY**
Aronson, Arnold W. ... New Britain, CT
Aronson, Arthur ... New York, NY
Aronson, Brian ... **Los Angeles, CA**
Aronson, Bruce E. ... **New York, NY**
Aronson, Bruce Jay ... Washington, DC
Aronson, Burton ... Plainview, NY
Aronson, Carole ... **Delray Beach, FL**
Aronson, Clifford H. ... **New York, NY**
Aronson, Craig D. ... **Irvine, CA**
Aronson, Craig E. ... Mount Vernon, NY
Aronson, Daniel H. ... **Fort Lauderdale, FL**
Aronson, David ... **New York, NY**
Aronson, David H. ... Vineyard Haven, MA
Aronson, Deborah L. ... Portland, ME
Aronson, Debra E. ... Rockville, MD
Aronson, Elliot R. ... Andover, MA
Aronson, Eric S. ... Quincy, MA
Aronson, Eric S. ... **Newark, NJ**
Aronson, Esther R. ... **Hartford, CT**
Aronson, Fineman and Davis, Co., L.P.A. ... East Liverpool, OH
Aronson, Frank D. ... **Boston, MA**
Aronson, Franklyn Z. ... Pennington, NJ
Aronson, George A. ... East Liverpool, OH
Aronson, Harold ... Skokie, IL
Aronson, Henry M. ... Seattle, WA
Aronson, Howard N. ... **Scarsdale, NY**
Aronson, Irwin W. ... **Harrisburg, PA**
Aronson, Jeffrey A. ... **Westport, CT**; **New York, NY**
Aronson, Jeffrey D. ... **Palo Alto, CA**
Aronson, Jeffrey H. ... New York, NY
Aronson, Joan K. ... Santa Monica, CA
Aronson, Joel S. ... **Washington, DC**
Aronson, Jonathan B. ... **Miami, FL**
Aronson, Joseph G. ... Livingston, NJ
Aronson, Joseph H. ... **Boston, MA**
Aronson, Judith L. ... Albany, NY
Aronson, Kenneth J. ... New York, NY
Aronson, Lee S. ... **Portland, OR**
Aronson, Marian ... New York, NY
Aronson, Mark E. ... **Los Angeles, CA**
Aronson, Mark I. ... **Miami, FL**
Aronson, Mark I. ... New York, NY
Aronson, Martin A. ... **Phoenix, AZ**
Aronson, Martin L. ... **Boston, MA**
Aronson, Mary Hudanish ... Washington, DC
Aronson, Michael R. ... Owings Mills, MD
Aronson, Milton H. ... St. Louis, MO
Aronson, Nancy D. ... Ventura, CA
Aronson, Neil H. ... **Boston, MA**
Aronson, Pamela ... **Washington, DC**
Aronson, Paul J. ... New York, NY
Aronson, Peter ... **Los Angeles, CA**
Aronson, Peter E. ... New York, NY
Aronson, Randall M. ... Waukesha, WI
Aronson, Raymond L. ... New York, NY
Aronson, Reuben J. ... New York, NY
Aronson, Richard B. ... Wellesley, MA
Aronson, Richard J. ... Chicago, IL
Aronson, Richard S. ... Pittsburgh, PA
Aronson, Robert ... **Springfield, MA**
Aronson, Robert ... **Minneapolis, MN**
Aronson, Robert A. ... Venice, CA
Aronson, Robert H. ... Treasury Department, GV
Aronson, Robert H. ... **Chicago, IL**
Aronson, Robert H. ... Seattle, WA
Aronson, Robert M. ... **Los Angeles, CA**
Aronson, Robert W. ... Pleasant Valley, NY
Aronson, Roberta B. ... **Herndon, VA**
Aronson, Robin L. ... **Cherry Hill, NJ**
Aronson, Roger H. ... Denver, CO
Aronson, Roger J. ... **Minneapolis, MN**
Aronson, Saul ... Albany, NY
Aronson, Scott C. ... Santa Monica, CA
Aronson, Seth ... **Los Angeles, CA**
Aronson, S. J. ... Austin, TX
Aronson Smith & Cross ... Chicago, IL
Aronson & Standard ... Denver, CO
Aronson, Stanley P. ... Akron, OH
Aronson, Stephen D. ... Canandaigua, NY
Aronson, Stephen W. ... Farmington, CT
Aronson, Sylvan B. ... Garden Grove, CA
Aronson, Terrence M. ... **Virginia, MN**
Aronson, Tracey E. ... Securities and Exchange Commission, Office of the General Counsel, GV
Aronson, Virginia L. ... **Chicago, IL**
Aronson-Grosse, Lori P. ... Hollywood, FL
Aronsson, Patricia ... Department of the Air Force, Office of the General Counsel, GV
Aronstam, David J. ... **New York, NY**
Aronstam, Kirk L. ... Menlo Park, CA
Aronstam & Suh ... **New York, NY**
Aronstein, James K. ... **Denver, CO**
Aronstein, Joseph S. ... Philadelphia, PA
Aronstein, Joseph S., P.C. ... Philadelphia, PA
Aronstein, Lori F. ... **New York, NY**
Aronstein, Martin J. ... Philadelphia, PA
Aronstein, Moshe G. ... Jamaica, NY
Aronstein, Richard L. ... Great Neck, NY
Aronstein, William B. ... **New York, NY**
Aronwald, Jeffrey B. ... **New York, NY**
Aronwald and Pykett ... White Plains, NY
Aronwald, William I. ... White Plains, NY
Aronzon, Paul S. ... **Los Angeles, CA**
Arora, Rahul ... Jackson, MI
Arosell, Sarah W. ... Bethlehem, PA; **Harrisburg, PA**
Arost, Aimee E. ... **Palo Alto, CA**
Arostegui, Anthony A. ... **Sacramento, CA**
Arostegui, Catherine E. ... Sacramento, CA
Arostegui, H. Tomás ... **Los Angeles, CA**
Arostegui, Roberto R. ... New Orleans, LA
Arouca, Dennis A. ... Philadelphia, PA
Arouesty, Erica S. ... **Los Angeles, CA**
Arouesty, Raymond L. ... Woodland Hills, CA
Arougheti, Gerald ... Jamaica, NY
Arougheti, Paul J. ... Princeton, NJ
Arouh, Jeffrey A. ... **New York, NY**
Arouh, Kimberly ... **San Diego, CA**
Arouh, Lynn Reitze ... Phoenix, AZ
Arouh, Michael B. ... **New York, NY**
Aroustamian, Ara ... Los Angeles, CA
Arovas, Gregory S. ... **New York, NY**
Arovas, Jack ... Boston, MA
Aroz, Raoul ... Los Angeles, CA
Arp, D. Jarrett ... **Washington, DC**
Arp, Julie D. ... **Atlanta, GA**
Arp, Randal R. ... Cheyenne, WY
Arp, Randall C. ... **Golden, CO**
Arpaia, Frank V. ... Bradenton, FL
Arpaia, James A. ... **Chicago, IL**
Arpaia, Kimberly M. ... **Stamford, CT**
Arpajian, Ralph E. ... **New York, NY**
Arpante, James A. ... Pittsfield, MA
Arpen, Tracey I., Jr. ... Jacksonville, FL
Arpert, Douglas E. ... **West Paterson, NJ**
Arpey, John W. ... Saratoga Springs, NY
Arpin, Edmund P. ... Oshkosh, WI
Arpin, Gregory J. ... **Spokane, WA**
Arpin, James B. ... **Washington, DC**
Arpin, Margaret L. ... **Spokane, WA**
Arpin, Patrick A. ... Watertown, WI
Arpino, Arnold A. ... **Commack, NY**
Arps, Chris M. ... Papillion, NE
Arquette, James A. ... Toledo, OH
Arquette, Tammy J. ... **Glenville, NY**
Arquilla, Alfred F. ... Springfield, VA
Arquit, Kevin J. ... **Washington, DC**; **New York, NY**
Arrabito, John T. ... Lynnwood, WA
Arrabito, Serena D. ... **New York, NY**
Arrache, Clark & Potter ... **Bakersfield, CA**
Arraiza, Manuel F. ... Vega Baja, PR
Arraiza Donate, Manlio ... Arecibo, PR
Arrajj, David ... **Las Vegas, NV**
Arrambide, Joseph Carl ... **Houston, TX**
Arrants, Barbara F. ... Nashville, TN
Arrants, George R., Jr. ... **Knoxville, TN**
Arras, Barbara L. ... **New Orleans, LA**
Arras, Christopher E. ... **San Francisco, CA**
Arras, Gene W. ... St. Louis, MO
Arras, Kurt G. ... Tulsa, OK
Arras, Thomas S. ... Clayton, MO
Arrascada, LeRoy ... Reno, NV
Arrascada, LeRoy, Ltd. ... Reno, NV
Arrastia, Javier A. ... Newark, NJ
Arrastia, John, Jr. ... **Miami, FL**; **Tampa, FL**
Arrazolo, Gilbert ... **Albuquerque, NM**
Arre, Patrick J. ... **Secaucus, NJ**
Arreaza, César Enrique ... Houston, TX
Arrechea, Ana M. ... Paterson, NJ
Arredondo, David ... Los Angeles, CA
Arredondo, Lorenzo ... Crown Point, IN
Arredondo & Mendoza ... Los Angeles, CA
Arredondo, Robert D. ... Houston, TX
Arrell, Gregory L. ... New York, NY
Arrensen, David A. ... **Indianapolis, IN**
Arreola, Marissa Weitzner ... **Houston, TX**
Arrett, Jane Head ... Minnetonka, MN
Arrett, Oliver F. ... Minnetonka, MN
Arrett, Richard A. ... Minnetonka, MN
Arri, Luis E. ... **Houston, TX**
Arriaga, Amparito ... **Exton, PA**
Arriaga, Herlinda M. ... Tulsa, OK
Arriandiaga, Marta B. ... **Los Angeles, CA**
Arrick, Bruce ... Miami, FL
Arrick, Kenneth M. ... Cardiff-By-The-Sea, CA
Arrick, Peacock & Hodges ... **Miami, FL**; **Tampa, FL**
Arrick, Ronald M. ... Cedarhurst, NY
Arrick, Susan J. ... **Miami, FL**
Arrieh, Gabrielle M. ... **Dallas, TX**
Arrien, Phillip F., II ... **Dallas, TX**
Arries, Stephanie L. ... Denver, CO
Arries, William G. ... Greeley, CO
Arrieta, Aileen L. ... **Palo Alto, CA**
Arrieta, Darcy Brum ... **San Juan, PR**
Arrieta, Frank J. ... Mohegan Lake, NY
Arrieta, Manuel I. ... **Las Cruces, NM**
Arrieta Diaz, Milagros ... Humacao, PR
Arrigan, Robert F. ... Providence, RI
Arrighi, Patricia C. ... **Norfolk, VA**
Arrigo, Dina M. ... **Chicago, IL**
Arrigo, Frank J., IV ... Woodland Hills, CA
Arrigo, James P. ... Chicago, IL
Arrigo, Kennis A. ... Santa Ana, CA
Arrigo, Maureen J. ... San Diego, CA
Arrigo, Sheryl M. ... Lisle, IL
Arrigoni, Jeffrey R. ... Woodbury, MN
Arrington, Andrew D. ... Birmingham, AL
Arrington, Charlene M. ... **Hackettstown, NJ**; **Morristown, NJ**; **Trenton, NJ**
Arrington, Charles B., Jr. ... Richmond, VA
Arrington, Clark R. ... Canton, MA
Arrington, Claude B. ... Tallahassee, FL
Arrington, Curtis R. ... Cleveland, OH
Arrington, David L. ... **Salt Lake City, UT**
Arrington, Dean ... Austin, TX
Arrington, Diana C. ... Rockville, MD
Arrington, Henry T. ... **New Orleans, LA**
Arrington & Hollowell, P.C. ... **Atlanta, GA**
Arrington, James E., Jr. ... Lebanon, VA
Arrington, Jeffrey L. ... **Los Angeles, CA**
Arrington, Joan K. ... Shaker Heights, OH
Arrington, John E. ... Atlanta, GA
Arrington, John L., Jr. ... **Tulsa, OK**
Arrington, Kathrine D. ... Atlanta, GA
Arrington, Kathryn M. ... Decatur, AL
Arrington Kihle Gaberino & Dunn, A Professional Corporation ... **Tulsa, OK**

Arrington, Lawr. D. ... Hattiesburg, MS
Arrington, Leslie P. ... Washington, DC
Arrington, Marvin, Jr. ... Atlanta, GA
Arrington, Marvin S. ... Atlanta, GA
Arrington, Melinda Bryant ... Hazlehurst, MS
Arrington, Michael W. ... Wilmington, DE
Arrington, Monica Leonette
Montgomery, AL
Arrington, Nathan S. ... San Diego, CA
Arrington, Norbert J. ... Louisville, KY
Arrington, Patrick ... Irvine, CA
Arrington, Patrick Samuel ... Greensboro, AL
Arrington, Paul ... Jacksonville, FL
Arrington, Paul N. ... O'Fallon, MO
Arrington, Robert Lane ... Kingsport, TN
Arrington, Roger W. ... Wilmington, DE
Arrington, Ronald J.
Equal Employment Opportunity Commission, Office of the General Counsel, GV
Arrington, Ronald K. ... Moberly, MO
Arrington, Roy David ... Marlinton, WV
Arrington, Scott J. ... Houston, TX
Arrington, Tamera Storey ... Georgetown, TX
Arrington, Vernell B. ... Greenbelt, MD
Arrington, W. Jewel ... Austin, TX
Arriola, Anita Perez ... Hagåtña, GU
Arriola, Cowan & Arriola ... Hagåtña, GU
Arriola, Elvia Rosales ... Austin, TX
Arriola, Joaquin C. ... Hagåtña, GU
Arriola, Joaquin C., Jr. ... Hagåtña, GU
Arriola, Joseph T. ... Union City, CA
Arriola-Kern, Maria Trinidad
Palo Alto, CA
Arrisgado, Maurice M. ... Honolulu, HI
Arritola, Luis E. ... Miami, FL
Arrivi Silva, Francisco ... San Juan, PR
Arrizabalaga, Markel ... Miami, FL
Arron, Deborah L. ... Seattle, WA
Arron, Todd S. ... Ventura, CA
Arronge, Steven W. ... San Antonio, TX
Arronis, Tina M. ... Chicago, IL
Arrow, Allan H. ... Los Angeles, CA
Arrow, Allen H. ... New York, NY
Arrow, David P. ... Scottsdale, AZ
Arrow, Jane Lauren ... Chicago, IL
Arrow Legal Solutions ... Midvale, UT
Arrow, Paul S. ... Los Angeles, CA
Arrowood, Catharine Biggs ... Raleigh, NC
Arrowood, John S. ... Charlotte, NC
Arrowood, Larry G. ... Brentwood, TN
Arrowood, Lisa G. ... Boston, MA
Arrowood, Lloyd F., Jr. ... Johnson City, TN
Arrowood, Vicki L. ... Milwaukee, WI
Arrowood, William D. ... Concord, NC
Arrowsmith, James A. ... Sandy, UT
Arrowsmith-Sanders, Cathy Jean ... Tulsa, OK
Arroyo, Angel L. ... Lorain, OH
Arroyo, Armando ... Brooklyn, NY
Arroyo & Arroyo, P.A.
Indian Harbour Beach, FL
Arroyo, Blas P. ... Charlotte, NC
Arroyo Copland & Flaherty ... Albany, NY
Arroyo, David J. B. ... Chicago, IL
Arroyo, Enrique ... Indian Harbour Beach, FL
Arroyo, Felipe J. ... Los Angeles, CA
Arroyo, Javier M. ... Rockville, MD
Arroyo, Joseph A. ... Orange, CA
Arroyo, Laurice Z.B. ... Chicago, IL
Arroyo, Luis I. ... Milwaukee, WI
Arroyo, Myrna E. ... Stamford, CT
Arroyo, Nancy M.
Indian Harbour Beach, FL
Arroyo, Richard F. ... Chula Vista, CA
Arroyo, Robert ... New York, NY
Arroyo, Robert E. ... Chicago, IL
Arroyo, Teresa M.
Department of Commerce, Patent and Trademark Office, GV
Arroyo, William H. ... Tucker, GA
Arroyo-Dávila, Mario ... San Juan, PR
Arroyo-Prokop, Maria T. ... San Diego, CA
Arruda, Karl N. ... Canton, MA
Arruda, M. Beth ... Cranston, RI
Arruda, Michael E. ... San Francisco, CA
Arruda, Michelle M. ... Concord, NH
Arruda, Victor ... Randolph, MA
Arruebarrena, Dean M. ... New Orleans, LA
Arruebarrena, Dian T. ... New Orleans, LA
Arruebarrena, James L. ... Metairie, LA
Arruebarrena & McNamara, L.L.P.
Metairie, LA
Arruti, Mark E. ... Sacramento, CA
Arsanjani, Mahnoush H. ... New York, NY
Arschin, Arthur N. ... New York, NY
Arscott, John R. ... New York, NY
Arsen, Helen S. ... Studio City, CA
Arsenakos, Stella ... Brooklyn, NY
Arsenault, Francoise C. ... Silver Spring, MD
Arsenault, Gary J. ... Alexandria, LA
Arsenault, Gary P. ... Virginia Beach, VA
Arsenault, J. Philip ... Andover, MA
Arsenault, James B., Jr. ... Marmora, NJ
Arsenault, John E. ... Glens Falls, NY
Arsenault, Jon E. ... Hartford, CT
Arsenault, Joseph Gerard ... New York, NY
Arsenault, Kenneth G., Jr. ... Largo, FL
Arsenault, Louise M. ... Chicago, IL
Arsenault, Martin J. ... Georgetown, MA
Arsenault & Reardon, P.A. ... Largo, FL
St. Petersburg, FL
Arsenault, Richard J., (Law Corporation)
Alexandria, LA
Arsenault, Robert J. ... Westerly, RI
Arsenault & Saracusa ... Andover, MA
Arsenault, Scott R. ... New York, NY
Arsenault, Walter Martin ... New York, NY
Arseneault & Fassett ... Chatham, NJ
Elizabeth, NJ
Morristown, NJ
Newark, NJ
Paterson, NJ
Roseland, NJ
Arseneault, Jack ... Chatham, NJ
Arseneault, Michael W. ... New York, NY
Arseneault, Wendy Molinari ... Chatham, NJ
Arsenian, Armenoohy ... Newton, MA
Arsenoff, Robert C.
General Accounting Office, Office of the General Counsel, GV
Arsenovich, Milovan ... Buchanan, MI
Arshack, Daniel N. ... New York, NY
Arsham, James M. ... Shaker Heights, OH
Arshawsky, Joseph ... Albuquerque, NM
Arshawsky, Paul ... Oakland, CA
Arshonsky, Richard I. ... Encino, CA
Arshonsky, Richard J. ... Beverly Hills, CA
Arsht, Roxana C. ... Wilmington, DE
Arsht, Samuel J. ... Westlake Village, CA
Arsi, Joseph Wendell ... Gilbert, SC
Arsiotis, Andrew M. ... New York, NY
Arslanian, George S., Jr. ... New York, NY
Arslanian, James L., Law Offices of
Albuquerque, NM
Arslanian, Paul ... Bloomfield Hills, MI
Arst, David G. ... Wichita, KS
Arst & Loyd ... Wichita, KS
Art, Andrew J. ... Columbus, OH
Art, Karen M. ... West Linn, OR
Art, Richard C., Jr. ... Seal Beach, CA
Art, Robert C. ... Salem, OR
Artabane & Belden, P.C. ... Washington, DC
Artabane, Joseph A. ... Washington, DC
Artall, Mark G. ... Lafayette, LA
Artall, Mark G., P.L.C. ... Lafayette, LA
Artan, Anya C. ... Commerce, CA
Artan, Michael H. ... Los Angeles, CA
Artan, Michael H., A Professional Corporation ... Los Angeles, CA
Artau, Edward L. ... Boca Raton, FL
Arteaga, Harold A. ... Miami, FL
Arteaga, Mabél ... New York, NY
Arteaga, Sonia ... Cambridge, MA
Arteficio, Enrico G. ... New York, NY
Artell, Richard E. ... Harrisburg, PA
Arter, Chester H. ... Atlanta, GA
Arter & Hadden LLP ... Irvine, CA
Los Angeles, CA
Sacramento, CA
San Diego, CA
San Francisco, CA
Woodland Hills, CA
Washington, DC
Cleveland, OH
Columbus, OH
Dayton, OH
Austin, TX
Dallas, TX
San Antonio, TX
Arter, John C. A., Jr. ... Marion, OH
Arter, Margaret H. Wade ... Claremont, CA
Arter, Patrick H., Jr. ... Camp Hill, PA
Arter, Theo. ... San Antonio, TX
Arterberry, John D. ... Department of Justice, Criminal Division, GV
Arterberry, Kathryn Ross ... Louisville, KY
Arterburn, David Keith ... Lincoln, NE
Arterian, Hannah Rose ... Tempe, AZ
Arters, Harry M. ... Danielson, CT
Arterton, Janet Bond ... New Haven, CT
Artery, Michael G. ... Delavan, WI
Artesani, Charles J., Jr. ... Boston, MA
Arteta, Derek A. ... Los Angeles, CA
Arth, Christopher G. ... Overland Park, KS
Arth, Dana D. ... Lenexa, KS
Arth, Gerald E. ... Philadelphia, PA
Arth, James L. ... Austin, TX
Arth, Jon S. ... Atlanta, GA
Arth, Mark A. ... Sarasota, FL
St. Paul, MN
Arth, Peter, Jr. ... San Francisco, CA
Arthanari, Lenin ... Phoenix, AZ
Arthaud, Victoria C.
Federal Trade Commission, Administrative Law Judges, GV
Arther, Cathy Homa ... Orlando, FL
Arthofer, Kenneth B. ... Redding, CA
Arthur & Allamong ... Strasburg, VA
Arthur, Andrew R.
Department of Justice, GV
Arthur & Arthur ... Rome, NY
Arthur, Barbara Sims ... Rossville, GA
Arthur, Bonnie K. ... Washington, DC
Arthur, Chapman, Kettering, Smetak & Pikala, P.A. ... Minneapolis, MN
Arthur, Charles R., Jr. ... Reading, MA
Arthur, Charles S. ... Manhattan, KS
Arthur, Charles S. (Terry), III
Manhattan, KS
Arthur, Craig E. ... Santa Ana, CA
Arthur, Daniel J. ... Seattle, WA
Arthur, David J. ... Irvine, CA
Arthur, David J. ... Newport Beach, CA
Arthur, David L. ... Rome, NY
Arthur, Dean P. ... Morrisville, PA
Arthur, Deborah Nelson ... Springfield, VA
Arthur, Donna Melson ... Englewood, CO
Arthur, Douglas C. ... Strasburg, VA
Arthur, Dwight D. ... Farmington, NM
Arthur, Elizabeth E. ... Springfield, IL
Arthur, Ellen ... Baltimore, MD
Arthur, Ellen M. ... Lexington, VA
Arthur, Everett L. ... Rome, NY
Arthur, Frank ... Kent, OH
Arthur, Geoffrey W. ... Columbus, OH
Arthur, Gloria Herron ... Albany, NY
Arthur - Green, LLP ... Manhattan, KS
Arthur, H. Thomas ... Columbia, SC
Arthur, Harry C. ... Houston, TX
Arthur, Harry L. ... Cleveland, OH
Arthur, Hilary Curtis ... Grand Rapids, MI
Arthur, James F., III ... Memphis, TN
Arthur, James K. ... Chicago, IL
Arthur, Jean Christine ... Silver Spring, MD
Arthur, Jeffrey D. ... Sacramento, CA
Arthur, Jennifer L. ... Denver, CO
Arthur, Jennifer M. ... St. Louis, MO
Arthur, Katharine M. ... Los Angeles, CA
Arthur, Kevin F. ... Baltimore, MD
Arthur, L. James ... Denver, CO
Arthur, Lindsay G., Jr. ... Minneapolis, MN
Arthur, Lindsay G., Sr. ... Minneapolis, MN
Arthur, Macon M. ... Pawleys Island, SC
Arthur, Margaret K. ... Marshfield, VT
Arthur, Mark, Jr. ... Russell, KS
Arthur, Megan M. ... Columbia, MD
Arthur, Michael E., P.C. ... Portland, OR
Arthur, O'Neil, Mertz & Bates Co., L.P.A.
Defiance, OH
Toledo, OH
Arthur, Patricia J. ... Steilacoom, WA
Arthur, Patricia J., The Law Offices of
Englewood, CO
Arthur, Pearson & Ramsey, Ltd.
Falls Church, VA
Arthur and Perlmutter ... Denver, CO
Arthur, R. Andrew ... Boston, MA
Arthur, R. Raymond ... Natchitoches, LA
Arthur, R. Raymond, L.L.C.
Natchitoches, LA
Arthur, R. William ... Wytheville, VA
Arthur, Randy L. ... Portland, OR
Arthur, Robert A. ... Tampa, FL
Arthur, Robert A. ... Chesterfield, MO
Arthur, Robert L. ... Washington, IN
Arthur, Robert S., Jr. ... Denver, CO
Arthur, Robert W. ... Titusville, FL
Arthur, Rodney M. ... Defiance, OH
Toledo, OH
Arthur, Ronald A. ... New Berlin, WI
Arthur, Samuel F., III ... Florence, SC
Arthur, Sara H. ... Annapolis, MD
Arthur, Stefanie ... San Francisco, CA
Arthur, Stephen E. ... Indianapolis, IN
Arthur, Thomas S. ... Los Angeles, CA
Arthur, Tom ... Chicago, IL
Arthur, Tracy K. ... Jacksonville, FL
Arthur, Warren S. ... Melville, NY
Mineola, NY
Arthur, William B. ... Ashland, KY
Arthur, William E. ... Columbus, OH
Arthur, Wm. Keith ... Stockton, CA
Arthurs, Douglas P. ... Gastonia, NC
Arthurs & Foltz ... Gastonia, NC
Arthurs, J. Stewart ... Cushing, OK
Arthurs, Judith W. ... Houston, TX
Arthurs, Timothy M. ... Waukegan, IL
Artiano, A. James ... Torrance, CA
Artiano, Guzman & Toomey, LLP
Torrance, CA
Artiano, Ray J. ... San Diego, CA
Articola, Phillip John ... Washington, DC
Artigliere, Leonard J. ... Phillipsburg, NJ
Artigliere, Ralph ... Lakeland, FL
Artigue, Cameron C. ... Phoenix, AZ
Artigue, Mary B. ... Phoenix, AZ
Artigues, Bertrand F. ... New Orleans, LA
Artigues, Ronald J., Jr. ... Waveland, MS
Artille, Russell E. ... Tampa, FL
Artime, Luis M. ... Miami, FL
Artimez, John E., Jr. ... Wheeling, WV
Artimovich, Patricia M. ... Columbia, MD
Artin, Kenneth R. ... Orlando, FL
Artinian, Susan ... Detroit, MI
Artis, Gregory D. ... Atlanta, GA
Artis, Kenneth J. ... Madison, WI
Artis, Larry R. ... Covina, CA
Artis, Michael Anthony ... Orange, NJ
Artis, Paris A. ... Hyattsville, MD
Artley, James A. ... Albuquerque, NM
Artlip, Mark G. ... Houston, TX
Artman, Eric A. ... San Francisco, CA
Artman, John F. ... Binghamton, NY
Artman, Stephen H. ... Lakeland, FL
Artman, Stephen H., P.A. ... Lakeland, FL
Arto, Fred C. ... Kerrville, TX
Artoe, L. Robert ... Chicago, IL
Artrip, Eric James ... Huntsville, AL
Arts, Waltraud A. ... Madison, WI
Artson, Elana Shavit ... Santa Ana, CA
Artura, Richard F. ... Lindenhurst, NY
Arturi, Anthony X. ... Englewood Cliffs, NJ
Arturi, Peter A., II ... Chicopee, MA
Arturo, Peter J. ... Torrance, CA
Artus, Andrew A. ... Oklahoma City, OK
Artus & Choquette, P.C. ... Anchorage, AK
Artus, William D. ... Anchorage, AK
Artusi, Steven L. ... Warsaw, IN
Artusio, Frank J. ... Santa Barbara, CA
Artuso, Angelo J. ... Albuquerque, NM
Artuso, Barbara J. ... Greensburg, PA
Artwick, Frederic J. ... Chicago, IL
Artz, Brian S. ... Columbus, OH
Artz, Charles I., & Associates
Harrisburg, PA
Artz, Cherie Beth ... Washington, DC
Artz, Daniel J. ... Dallas, TX
Artz, Dewhirst & Farlow ... Columbus, OH
Artz, Jerome D. ... Loomis, CA
Artz, John A. ... Southfield, MI
Artz, John C. ... Pittsburgh, PA
Artz, John S. ... Southfield, MI
Artz, Jon Bryant ... Los Angeles, CA
Artz, Kenneth A. ... Traverse City, MI
Artz, Mauri A. ... Gates Mills, OH
Artz, Philip J. ... Binghamton, NY
Artz, William E. ... Arlington, VA
Artz, William E., A Professional Corporation
Washington, DC
Arlington, VA
Artzer, Christopher A. ... Houston, TX
Artzt, Valerie ... New York, NY
Aruffo, Roy Cristofor ... Houston, TX
Arugu, Odiator ... Orlando, FL
Arum, John B. ... Seattle, WA
Arum, Robert ... Garden City, NY
Arumi, Ana Cristina ... Washington, DC
Arundel, Edward M. ... Minneapolis, MN
Arundel, James D. ... Denver, CO
Arundel, Mary C. ... Chicago, IL
Arundell, Robert J.
Hilton Head Island, SC
Aruri, Jamal T. ... Lowell, MA
Arusha, Kerstin ... San Jose, CA
Arusoo, Diane K. ... Troy, MI
Aruti, Ike ... Rosedale, NY
Arvai, Louis A. ... Dearborn, MI
Arvanetes, Evangelo ... Wichita, KS
Arvanites, Peter J. ... Danvers, MA
Arvanitidis, Lori ... Irvine, CA
Arvanitis, Constantine G. ... Springfield, MA
Arvanitis, Geo. W. ... Lawrence, MA
Arvanitis, George N. ... Asbury Park, NJ
Arvanitis, Yvonne D. ... Los Angeles, CA
Arvantely, Thomas P. ... Enfield, CT
Arvesen, Norman D. ... Fergus Falls, MN
Arveson, Donald F. ... Tucson, AZ
Arvey, Howard ... Chicago, IL
Arvey, James T. ... Chicago, IL
Arvidson, Dean C. ... Atlanta, GA
Arvidson, Fred B. ... Anchorage, AK
Arvidson, George A. ... Des Moines, IA
Arvidson, R. Regner ... Hartford, CT
Arvin, Betty R. ... Fort Worth, TX
Arvin, David E. ... Hopkinsville, KY
Arvin, Kay K. ... Wichita, KS
Arvin, Kenneth I. ... Miami, FL
Arvin, L. Christopher ... Pacific Palisades, CA
Arvin, Lester C. ... Wichita, KS
Arvin, Michael F. ... Denver, CO
Arvin, Michael F., PC, Law Offices of
Denver, CO
Arvin, William Miles ... Lexington, KY
Arvin, William Miles ... Nicholasville, KY
Arvin, William Miles, Jr.
Nicholasville, KY
Arvis, Constance C.
Department of State, GV
Arvizu, R. Trey, III ... Roswell, NM
Arvoy, Cristina M. ... White Plains, NY
Arwe, Michael H. ... Boston, MA
Arweiler, John E. ... Huntington, NY
Arwine, Elizabeth ... Frederick, MD
Ary, Richard Earl ... Columbus, OH
Ary, W. Bartlett ... Christiansted, St. Croix, VI
Ary, William R. ... Dayton, OH
Arya, John D. ... Los Angeles, CA
Arye, Kors, Lustig & Sassower, P.C.
New York, NY
Arye, Leonard A. ... New York, NY
Arza-Goderich, Letvia M. ... San Juan, PR
Arzbaecher, William J., III
San Francisco, CA
Arzberger, Kristy B. ... Mason City, IA
Arzino, Richard A. ... San Jose, CA
Arzola, Antonio ... Miami, FL
Arzoomanian, Karekin ... New York, NY
Arzt, Lee Robert ... Richmond, VA
Arzt, Philip K. ... Scottsdale, AZ
Arzt, Robin J. ... Bronx, NY
Arzuaga, Patricia ... Department of Labor, Pension and Welfare Benefits, GV
Asa, Rachel J. ... Oakland, CA
Asaad, Marc Ezzat Naguib ... Charleston, WV
Asack, David M. ... Brockton, MA
Asack, George N. ... Brockton, MA
Asack, George N., Jr. ... Brockton, MA
Asack, Patricia A. ... Rockport, TX
Asad, Samuel C. ... Parma, OH
Asada, Katherine Tanaka ... San Francisco, CA
Asadoorian, Jodi D. ... Bensalem, PA
Asadoorian, Richard O. ... Boston, MA
Asadourian, Amy ... Plattsburgh, NY
Asadourian, Ara ... Plattsburgh, NY
Asadourian Law Firm, P.C.
Plattsburgh, NY
Asahi Law Offices ... New York, NY
Asai, Irene Kiyoko ... Port Orchard, WA
Asai-Sato, Carol Y. ... Honolulu, HI
Asaji, Shogo ... New York, NY
Asakawa, Bill C. ... Sacramento, CA
Asakura, Hidetoshi ... Los Angeles, CA
Asali, James T. ... Philadelphia, PA
Asam, James A. ... Troy, MI
Asamoah, Harvetta M.
Department of Energy, Office of the General Counsel, GV
Asamura, Saskia Tsushima
Los Angeles, CA
Asandrov Law Offices ... Rochester, NY
Asandrov, Louis V. ... Rochester, NY
Asano, Shirley S.
Palos Verdes Peninsula, CA
Asante, Dominic K. ... New York, NY
Asarch, Chad G. ... Denver, CO
Asarch, Joel K. ... Lynbrook, NY
Asarch, Steven J. ... Boca Raton, FL
Asard, Karen E. ... New Haven, CT
Asari, Tatsuo ... Kapaa, HI
Asari, Yoichi J. ... Los Angeles, CA
Asaro, Andrea G. ... San Francisco, CA

Asaro, Bridget ... **New York, NY**
Asaro, Frank L. ... **San Diego, CA**
Asaro, Keagy, Freeland & McKinley **San Diego, CA**
Asaro, Lenny D. ... **Chicago, IL**
Asaro, Leo J. ... **St. Louis, MO**
Asaro & Murray ... San Diego, CA
Asaro, Sharon G. ... San Diego, CA
Asaro, Tricia A. ... **Albany, NY**
Asaro, V. Frank ... San Diego, CA
Asato, Lloyd Y. ... Honolulu, HI
Asato, Mary Jane ... **Southampton, NY**
Asato, Richard T., Jr. ... **Honolulu, HI**
Asatoorian, Albert P. ... **Costa Mesa, CA**
Asay, Bruce S. ... **Cheyenne, WY**
Asay, Bryan L. ... Helena, MT
Asay, D. Scott ... Billings, MT
Asay, Don A. ... Tigard, OR
Asayama, Phyllis C. ... Los Angeles, CA
Asbach, David W. ... Milwaukee, WI
Asbed, Jeffrey E. ... St. Louis, MO
Asbel, Stephen M. ... Media, PA
Asbell, Anne L. ... Atlanta, GA
Asbell, Coleman & Ho, P.A. ... **Naples, FL**
Asbell, John R. ... **Naples, FL**
Asbell, Joseph ... Camden, NJ
Asbell, Max B. ... Warner Robins, GA
Asbell, Michael J. ... Philadelphia, PA
Asbell, Stacy L. ... **Cherry Hill, NJ**
Asbell, William R., Jr. ... **Atlanta, GA**
Asbell, Yale I. ... Philadelphia, PA
Asberry, Brian K. ... **Springfield, MO**
Asberry, Irma Poole ... Riverside, CA
Asbill, Charles C. ... Sacramento, CA
Asbill, David A. ... **Forney, TX**
Asbill, David A. ... **Mesquite, TX**
Asbill, Henry W. ... **Washington, DC**
Asbill, Junkin & Moffitt, Chtd. **Washington, DC**
Asbill, Mary Ann ... Charleston, SC
Asbill, Mary Maclean ... Charlottesville, VA
Asbill, Nancy L. ... **Palo Alto, CA**
Asbill, Richard M. ... **Atlanta, GA**
Asbill, Thrace E., (Mrs.) ... Emory, TX
Asbille, Robert C. ... Chicago, IL
Asbury & Asbury, L.L.P. ... **Abilene, TX**
Asbury, Carol Cobourn West Palm Beach, FL
Asbury, Charles M. ... El Dorado Hills, CA
Asbury, Gordon, III ... **Abilene, TX**
Asbury, Gordon, Jr. ... **Abilene, TX**
Asbury, Jay D. ... Crescent City, FL
Asbury, John L. ... Rockville, IN
Asbury, Kelley R. ... Catlettsburg, KY
Asbury, Kenneth P. ... **Wise, VA**
Asbury, Lee ... Jacksboro, TN
Asbury, Lloyd T. ... Jacksonville, FL
Asbury, Lloyd T., P.A. ... Jacksonville, FL
Asbury, Mark A. **South San Francisco, CA**
Asbury, Mary ... Cincinnati, OH
Asbury, Philip S. ... Philadelphia, PA
Asbury, Robert I. ... Marion, VA
Asby, Phillip ... Washington, DC **New Bern, NC**
Ascalon, Eric J. ... New York, NY
Ascanio, Vanessa N. ... **Bradenton, FL**
Ascarelli, Richard C. ... Washington, DC
Ascari, Fred C. ... Newport Beach, CA
Ascencio, Eduardo J. ... **Los Angeles, CA**
Asch, Andrew Eric ... **Los Angeles, CA**
Asch & Asch ... Clark, NJ
Asch, David A. ... Sacramento, CA
Asch, Glenn B. ... **Boston, MA**
Asch, Harry M. ... Laguna Niguel, CA
Asch, Julius N. ... Clark, NJ
Asch, Karl ... Clark, NJ
Asch, Karl ... Clark, NJ
Asch, Karl, P.A. ... Clark, NJ
Asch, Laurie A. ... New York, NY
Asch, Roger D. ... Clark, NJ
Asch, Roger P. ... Portland, ME
Asch, Sidney H. ... **New York, NY**
Asch, Sunny Charla ... Montrose, CA
Asch, Susan Brodsky ... **Philadelphia, PA**
Aschaffenburg, Janet Hamrick **New Orleans, LA**
Asche, Richard M. ... **New York, NY**
Aschebrock, Henry ... Metairie, LA
Ascheman, Bryon ... St. Paul, MN
Aschen, Michael ... **New York, NY**
Aschenbrener, Daniel F. ... Shawano, WI
Aschenbrener, Steven E. ... Shawano, WI
Aschenbrener, Woods, Lamia & Schmid, S.C. Shawano, WI Wittenberg, WI
Aschenbrenner, Charles F. ... Madison, WI
Aschenbrenner, Constance ... Anchorage, AK
Aschenbrenner, L. A. ... Anchorage, AK
Aschenbrenner Law Offices, Inc. Fairbanks, AK
Aschenbrenner, Lisbeth ... Culver City, CA
Aschenbrenner, Peter J. ... Fairbanks, AK
Aschenbrenner, Richard W. ... Miami, FL
Aschenbrenner, Richelle L. ... **Chicago, IL**
Aschenbrenner, Ted ... Centreville, VA
Ascher, Andrea Paretts ... **New York, NY**
Ascher, David M. ... Cranford, NJ
Ascher and Denton, PLLC ... Tumwater, WA
Ascher, Herbert, Jr. ... New York, NY
Ascher, Irma B. ... New York, NY
Ascher, James M. ... Tumwater, WA
Ascher, Jonathan C. ... **Allentown, PA**
Ascher, Margaret P. ... Washington, DC
Ascher, Mark L. ... Tucson, AZ
Ascher, Michael P. ... Springfield, MA
Ascher, Michael R. ... **Chicago, IL**
Ascher, Michael R. ... **Denville, NJ**
Ascher, Paul B. ... New York, NY
Ascher, Ralph ... Anaheim, CA
Ascher, Richard A. ... San Diego, CA
Ascher, Stephen C. ... **Chicago, IL**
Ascher, Stephen L. ... **New York, NY**
Ascher, Thomas R. ... Jacksonville, FL
Ascher, Wende S. ... **New York, NY**
Ascher, Yvonne A. ... **Monterey, CA**
Ascherman, Herbert S. ... Potomac, MD
Ascherman, Louis T. ... Chicago, IL
Aschettino, Stephen A. ... **New York, NY**
Aschheim, Deborah S. ... **New York, NY**
Aschheim, Robert H. ... Aventura, FL
Aschheim, Robert H., P.A. ... Aventura, FL
Aschinger, Emily C. ... Hillsboro, MO
Aschkenasy, Jacob ... **New York, NY**
Aschkinasi, David ... **Denver, CO**
Aschleman, James A. ... **Indianapolis, IN**
Aschmann & Aschmann ... Alexandria, VA
Aschmann, Charles G., Jr. ... Alexandria, VA
Aschmann, Frank G. ... Alexandria, VA
Aschoff, Carolann M. ... Jersey City, NJ
Aschoff, Carolann M., P.C. ... Jersey City, NJ
Aschoff, Timothy G. ... **Lincoln, NE** **Omaha, NE**
Aschwanden, Charles R. Environmental Protection Agency, Office of Enforcement and Compliance Assurance, GV
Aschwege, Daniel L. ... **Kearney, NE**
Ascierto, Greg L. ... Corona, NY
Asciolla, Gregory S. ... **Washington, DC**
Ascione, Joseph A. ... **Westfield, NJ**
Asciutto, Linda R. ... **Okemos, MI**
Asciutto, Valerie ... New York, NY
Ascolese, Marc R. ... **Austin, TX**
Ascolillo, Victor H. ... Westfield, MA
Asdorian, Kathleen B. ... Washington, DC
Asdourian, Mark V., (P.C.) ... **Irvine, CA**
Asdourian & Polis, LLP ... **Irvine, CA** **Santa Ana, CA**
Asebedo, Anthony ... **Sacramento, CA**
Asedo, Ramon D. ... Oceanside, CA
Asel, Colette M. ... Los Angeles, CA
Asel, Jodie Capshaw ... Columbia, MO
Aseltine, Peter C. ... Trenton, NJ
Aseltine, Ronald G. ... Livermore Falls, ME Wilton, ME
Aseltyne, Patrick A. ... Farmington Hills, MI Lansing, MI
Aseltyne, William J. ... San Francisco, CA
Asen, Barry ... **Parsippany, NJ** **New York, NY**
Asen, Doria Saletsky ... Larchmont, NY
Asen, Michael Ira ... **New York, NY**
Asen, Michael P. ... **Portland, ME**
Asencio, Diego C. ... **West Palm Beach, FL**
Asencio, Diego C., P.A. **West Palm Beach, FL**
Asendorf, J. Alan ... **Tampa, FL**
Asensio, Cheryl O. ... Baltimore, MD
Asensio, Cynthia B. ... **Dallas, TX**
Asensio, M.J., III ... **Columbus, OH**
Asensio, Sharon O. ... Severna Park, MD
Aserkoff, Janet F., Mrs. ... Boston, MA
Aserkoff, Lisa ... Department of Education, Office of the General Counsel, GV
Asfahl, Donald L. ... Louisville, KY
Asgeirsson & Asgeirsson ... Stoneham, MA
Asgeirsson, Jon A. ... Stoneham, MA
Asgeirsson, Kristjan A. ... Stoneham, MA
Ash, A. Gayle ... Houston, TX
Ash, Andrew W. ... **Los Angeles, CA**
Ash, Angela Alexander ... Princeton, WV
Ash, Ann Wenzel ... **Madison, WI**
Ash, Anos, Freedman & Logan, L.L.C. **Chicago, IL**
Ash, Arthur K. ... New York, NY
Ash, Barbara A. ... Philadelphia, PA
Ash, Barry ... **Chicago, IL**
Ash, C. Jeffery ... **Birmingham, AL**
Ash, Cecil Paul ... Mesa, AZ
Ash, Charles R., III ... **Southfield, MI**
Ash, Christopher C. ... **Morristown, NJ**
Ash, Craig O. ... Sisseton, SD
Ash, Dana J. ... **Philadelphia, PA**
Ash, David C. ... Hicksville, NY
Ash, David Edward ... **Houston, TX** **Nacogdoches, TX**
Ash, David H. ... Bowling Green, MO Vandalia, MO
Ash, David M. ... **New York, NY**
Ash, Denise Kirk ... **Lexington, KY**
Ash, Diane S. ... Birmingham, MI
Ash, Don R. ... Murfreesboro, TN
Ash, Edwin W. ... **Tulsa, OK**
Ash, Eric ... **West Palm Beach, FL**
Ash, Ernest M. ... New York, NY
Ash, George W. ... **Detroit, MI**
Ash, Gregory L. ... **Overland Park, KS**
Ash, Herbert L. ... **New York, NY**
Ash, J. David ... **Baltimore, MD**
Ash, J. Russell, Jr. ... Big Lake, TX
Ash, James C., Jr. ... Arlington, TX
Ash, James C., Jr., A Professional Corporation Arlington, TX
Ash, James M. ... **Kansas City, MO**
Ash, Jeffrey H. ... Guttenberg, NJ
Ash, Jonathan G. ... Tarzana, CA Bend, OR
Ash, Joseph ... Van Nuys, CA
Ash, Joseph ... **Chicago, IL**
Ash, Karen Artz ... **New York, NY**
Ash, Katherine Cooney ... **New York, NY**
Ash Law Firm, The ... **Tulsa, OK**
Ash, Lesley Ann ... San Diego, CA
Ash, Linda A. ... **Cincinnati, OH**
Ash, Linda Kathryn ... **Oxnard, CA**
Ash, M. Scott ... **Tulsa, OK**
Ash, Mark A. ... **Raleigh, NC**
Ash, Mark J. ... Houston, TX
Ash, Mary M. ... Redwood City, CA
Ash, Matthew G. ... **Washington, DC**
Ash, Michael ... **Milwaukee, WI**
Ash, Michael S. ... Phoenix, AZ
Ash, Patricia Ann ... West Palm Beach, FL
Ash, Patricia Tighe ... Cincinnati, OH
Ash, Paul G., Jr. ... Galveston, TX
Ash, Paul V. ... Woodland Hills, CA
Ash, Reuel D. ... **Cincinnati, OH**
Ash, Richard A. ... Philadelphia, PA
Ash, Richard J. ... Merrick, NY
Ash, Richard J. ... Wauwatosa, WI
Ash, Robert B. ... El Paso, TX
Ash, Robert L. ... **Washington, DC**
Ash, Robert Michael ... Novato, CA
Ash, Robert W. ... **Virginia Beach, VA**
Ash, Russell K. ... Topeka, KS
Ash, Ruth C. ... Bala Cynwyd, PA
Ash, Sander ... Boston, MA
Ash, Scott A. ... **Princeton, WV**
Ash, Seana McMann ... Bend, OR
Ash, Sharron E. ... **New York, NY**
Ash, Stephen S. ... Phoenix, AZ
Ash, Sylvia G. ... New York, NY
Ash, Thomas M., III ... **New York, NY**
Ash, Walter B. ... **Denver, CO**
Ashack, James T. ... Oak Forest, IL
Ashamalla, Michele ... Los Angeles, CA
Ashanta-Barker, Terrance L. ... **Orlando, FL**
Ashanti, Karl J. ... **Hackensack, NJ**
Ashanti, Keesha Maria ... Albuquerque, NM
Ashar, Linda C. ... **Lorain, OH**
Ashar, Michael Kenneth ... Vermilion, OH
Ashar, Sameer M. ... New York, NY
Ashare, Edward ... Framingham, MA
Ashare, Richard ... Detroit, MI
Ashave, Jennifer ... **Boston, MA**
Ashba, Paul Owen ... **Rochester, MI**
Ashbaugh, Brian W. ... **Pittsburgh, PA**
Ashbaugh, David L. ... **Seattle, WA**
Ashbaugh, Denise L. ... **Seattle, WA**
Ashbaugh, Frank E. ... Wellington, OH
Ashbaugh, Frank E., Co., L.P.A. Wellington, OH
Ashbaugh, J. William ... **Seattle, WA**
Ashbaugh, Judith A. ... **Tulsa, OK**
Ashbaugh, Patricia Nemec San Luis Obispo, CA
Ashbaugh, Ralph W., Jr. ... La Verne, CA
Ashbaugh, Robert L. ... Department of Justice, Office of the Inspector General, GV
Ashbee, G. Wayne ... Mobile, AL
Ashbell, Theodore Shelly ... Chicago, IL
Ashbey, Julia L. ... Red Bank, NJ
Ashbourne, Anica DeNeen ... Columbus, OH
Ashbran, Richard E. ... Pasadena, CA
Ashbridge, Margaret S. ... Fort Wayne, IN
Ashbrook, Charles W. ... Ann Arbor, MI
Ashbrook, L. Michael ... **Monroe, LA**
Ashbrook, Lisa M. ... **Phoenix, AZ**
Ashburn, Christine M. ... Norwell, MA
Ashburn, Daniel ... Atlanta, GA
Ashburn, David C. ... **Tallahassee, FL**
Ashburn, Gene C. ... Novato, CA
Ashburn, James P. ... **Statesville, NC**
Ashburn, Karen P. ... Danville, VA
Ashburn, Mark E. ... **Anchorage, AK**
Ashburn, Mark L. ... Paducah, KY
Ashburn & Mason, A Professional Corporation ... **Anchorage, AK**
Ashburn, Melissa A. ... **Knoxville, TN**
Ashburn, Michael A. ... Wilkesboro, NC
Ashburn, Steven M. ... **San Diego, CA**
Ashburn, William W., III ... Highlands, NC
Ashburne, Michael R. ... Oakland, CA
Ashburner, Heather L. ... Laurel, MD
Ashby, Alan ... Sacramento, CA
Ashby, Anne ... Dallas, TX
Ashby, Anthony L. ... **Las Vegas, NV**
Ashby, Brent K. ... Provo, UT
Ashby, Brian Turner ... **Denver, CO**
Ashby, Christopher L. ... **Houston, TX**
Ashby, Christopher M. ... Scottsdale, AZ
Ashby, Crystal Elizabeth ... **Chicago, IL**
Ashby, Danny S. ... **Dallas, TX**
Ashby, David C. ... **Palo Alto, CA**
Ashby, Douglas K. ... Yuba City, CA
Ashby, Eve Moulding ... Evergreen, CO
Ashby & Geddes ... **Wilmington, DE**
Ashby, Gerald J. ... Grand Junction, CO
Ashby, James B. ... Savannah, GA
Ashby, Jefferson T. ... Presque Isle, ME
Ashby, Jerry W. ... Houston, TX
Ashby, John ... Decatur, GA
Ashby, John A. ... Woodland Hills, CA
Ashby, John C. ... **Los Angeles, CA**
Ashby, John H. ... **Boston, MA**
Ashby, Julie C. ... **San Diego, CA**
Ashby, Kimberly A. ... **Orlando, FL**
Ashby, Lawrence C. ... **Wilmington, DE**
Ashby, Leslie Garcia ... **Houston, TX**
Ashby, Marilyn A. ... Oakland, CA
Ashby, Mark J. ... United States Senate, Senatorial Assistants, GV
Ashby, Matthew J. ... **Atlanta, GA**
Ashby & Metts ... Savannah, GA
Ashby, Michael P. ... **Redding, CA**
Ashby, Ned T. ... Los Altos, CA
Ashby, O'Conor G. ... **Fredericksburg, VA**
Ashby, Philip R. ... **Albuquerque, NM**
Ashby, Randall B. ... **Houston, TX**
Ashby, Richard J., Jr. ... Lancaster, PA
Ashby, Robert C. Department of Transportation, Office of the General Counsel, GV
Ashby, Roger L. ... Roanoke, VA
Ashby, Ronald David ... Media, PA
Ashby, Ronald David, and Associates, P.C. Media, PA
Ashby, Scott T. ... **Phoenix, AZ**
Ashby, Solomon H., Jr. ... **Norfolk, VA**
Ashby, Steven R. ... **Stone Mountain, GA**
Ashby, Steven R., P.C. ... **Snellville, GA** **Stone Mountain, GA**
Ashby & Strich, L.L.C. ... Cranbury, NJ Doylestown, PA
Ashby, Teri H. ... San Francisco, CA
Ashby, Thomas O. ... **Omaha, NE**
Ashby, Tracy E. ... Laurel, MD
Ashby, Wendy J. ... Cranbury, NJ Doylestown, PA
Ashby & Whitmire, P.C. Clear Lake City, TX **Houston, TX**
Ashcraft, Anna B. ... Chicago, IL
Ashcraft & Ashcraft, Ltd. ... **Chicago, IL**
Ashcraft, Brigid Dolan ... **Houston, TX**
Ashcraft, Carole Anne ... Tulsa, OK
Ashcraft, David B. ... **High Point, NC**
Ashcraft, Earl F. ... Irvine, KY
Ashcraft, Ega ... St. Petersburg, FL
Ashcraft, Elizabeth E. ... San Francisco, CA
Ashcraft & Gerel, LLP ... **Washington, DC** **Baltimore, MD** **Landover, MD** **Rockville, MD** **Boston, MA** **Alexandria, VA**
Ashcraft and Heinz LLP ... **Las Vegas, NV**
Ashcraft, Howard W., Jr. **San Francisco, CA**
Ashcraft, John M., III ... Allentown, PA
Ashcraft, Larry C. ... **Mountain Home, ID**
Ashcraft Law Firm, A Professional Corporation ... **Dallas, TX**
Ashcraft, Martha J. ... **Las Vegas, NV**
Ashcraft, Michael P., Jr. ... **Detroit, MI**
Ashcraft, R. Allen, Jr. ... **Houston, TX**
Ashcraft, Raymond R. ... Cincinnati, OH
Ashcraft, Rosalie Department Of The Interior, Office of Hearings & Appeals, GV
Ashcraft, Susan E. ... San Francisco, CA
Ashcraft, Thomas J. ... **Charlotte, NC**
Ashcraft, Timothy L. ... **Tacoma, WA**
Ashcraft, William E. ... **Fort Lauderdale, FL**
Ashcraft, William E., Law Office, P.A. **Fort Lauderdale, FL**
Ashcraft, William O. ... **Dallas, TX**
Ashcroft, John D. ... St. Louis, MO
Ashcroft, Lynn E. ... **Salem, OR**
Ashcroft Wiles, LLP ... **Salem, OR**
Ashdown, Charles C. ... **Cincinnati, OH**
Ashdown, Gerald G. ... Morgantown, WV
Ashdown, Katherine Conklin San Francisco, CA
Ashdown, Philomena Saldanha **Cincinnati, OH**
Ashe, Andrew D. ... **Boston, MA**
Ashe, Anthony Guy ... Pittsburg, CA
Ashe, Barry W., (P.C.) ... **New Orleans, LA**
Ashe, Bernard F. ... Delmar, NY
Ashe, Braxton W. ... **Tuscumbia, AL**
Ashe, Brian T. ... **San Francisco, CA**
Ashe, Carol Grobman ... **Philadelphia, PA**
Ashe, Charles A. ... Albany, NY
Ashe, David Benjamin ... Virginia Beach, VA
Ashe, Deborah L. ... Broadalbin, NY
Ashe, Frank P. ... Quincy, MA
Ashe, Gena L. ... Annapolis Junction, MD
Ashe, Gregory A. Federal Trade Commission, Bureau of Consumer Protection, GV
Ashe, James J. ... Atascadero, CA
Ashe, Jesse B. ... **Charlotte, NC**
Ashe, Lawrence V. ... **Miami, FL**
Ashe, Linda G. ... Pineville, LA
Ashe, Mason P. ... Washington, DC
Ashe, Michael I. ... Virginia Beach, VA
Ashe, Oliver R., Jr. ... **Washington, DC**
Ashe, R. Lawrence, Jr., (P.C.) **Atlanta, GA**
Ashe, Raymond C. ... Loganville, GA
Ashe, Suzanne ... **Birmingham, AL**
Ashe, Tanner, Wright & Kelley, P.C. **Florence, AL** **Tuscumbia, AL**
Ashe, Thomas E. ... **Coral Gables, FL**
Ashe, Thomas E. ... **Fort Lauderdale, FL** **Miami, FL**
Ashe, Timothy J. ... **Chicago, IL**
Ashe, William J. ... Glen Rock, NJ
Ashe, William R. ... Monroe, GA
Ashelman, Robert K., II ... Warren, OH
Ashen, David Anthony General Accounting Office, Office of the General Counsel, GV
Ashen, Deborah S. ... **Chicago, IL**
Ashen, George Thomas ... Englewood, CO
Ashen & Lippman ... **Beverly Hills, CA** Montrose, CA
Ashen, M. Paula ... Englewood, CO
Ashen, Mark M. ... Los Angeles, CA
Ashen, Robert M. ... **Beverly Hills, CA** Montrose, CA
Ashenbrener, Christopher R. ... Spokane, WA
Ashenden, Flynn & Gottlieb ... Atlanta, GA
Ashenden, James F., Jr. ... **Chicago, IL**
Ashenden, John R. ... **Chicago, IL**
Ashenden & Sor ... **Chicago, IL**
Ashenden, Thomas J. ... Atlanta, GA
Ashendorf, H. Wesley ... Houston, TX
Ashendorf, H. Wesley and Associates, P.C. Houston, TX

Ashendorf, Jeffrey S. ... New York, NY
Ashendorf, Sondra ... New York, NY
Ashenfelter, William H. ... Charlotte, NC
Ashenfelter, Barry J. ... Madison, WI
Ashenfelter, Dennis D. ... Albany, OR
Ashenfelter, James H.
Upper Montclair, NJ
Ashenfelter, John W ... Bloomington, IL
Ashenfelter, Mark J. ... Greenwich, CT
Ashenfelter, Richard B., Jr.
King Of Prussia, PA
Ashenhurst, A. Anthony ... Macomb, IL
Asher, Alan ... New York, NY
Asher, Allan F. ... Colorado Springs, CO
Asher, Anthony A. ... Deerfield Beach, FL
Asher, Audrey B. ... Kansas City, KS
Asher, Bill ... Houston, TX
Asher, Carlton R., Jr., Law Offices of
New York, NY
Asher, Charles A. ... South Bend, IN
Asher, David ... Santa Monica, CA
Asher, Donna R. ... Topeka, KS
Asher, Garrett E. ... Nashville, TN
Asher, Gary P. ... New York, NY
Asher, Gerald E. ... Dallas, TX
Asher, Gittler, Greenfield, Cohen & D'Alba, Ltd. ... Chicago, IL
Asher, Jack O'Hair ... Paris, IL
Asher, James D. ... Whitesburg, KY
Asher, James F. ... Miami, FL
Asher, James M. ... New York, NY
Asher, Jane F. ... Paris, IL
Asher, Jill ... San Diego, CA
Asher, Jonathan D. ... Denver, CO
Asher, Joseph M. ... Wilmington, DE
New York, NY
Asher, Joseph S. ... Atlanta, GA
Asher, Kenneth D. ... Cleveland, OH
Asher, Kenneth R. ... New York, NY
Asher, Kullen & Kassab, A Professional Corporation ... Birmingham, MI
Asher, Le Roy L., Jr. ... Detroit, MI
Asher, Linda S. ... Worcester, MA
Asher, Martin J. ... Atchison, KS
Asher, Mary K. ... Los Angeles, CA
Asher, Melvin J. ... Miami, FL
Asher, Michael J. ... San Francisco, CA
Asher, Mitchell F. ... Palatine, IL
Asher, N. Denise ... San Diego, CA
Asher, Narra S., (Mrs.) ... Orinda, CA
Asher, Norman B. ... Boston, MA
Asher, Paula Gavrel ... Houston, TX
Asher, Peter W. ... Brooklyn, NY
Asher, Raymond L. ... Los Angeles, CA
Asher, Raymond L. ... Chicago, IL
Asher, Raymond L., A Professional Corporation ... Los Angeles, CA
Asher, Raymond L., The, Ltd., Law Offices of ... Chicago, IL
Asher, Raymond M. ... Creve Coeur, MO
Asher, Robert H. ... Washington, DC
Asher, Robert M. ... Boston, MA
Asher, Robert S. ... New York, NY
Asher, Robin W. ... Bloomfield Hills, MI
Asher & Rodman, P.C., Law Offices of
Colorado Springs, CO
Asher, Ross ... Houston, TX
Asher, Sabrina Marie
Bloomfield Hills, MI
Asher, Sanford S. ... New York, NY
Asher, Sheila S. ... Austin, TX
Asher, Smith & Isaf ... Danville, IL
Paris, IL
Asher, Steven ... Santa Fe, NM
Asher, Steven A. ... Philadelphia, PA
Asher, Steven D. ... St. Louis, MO
Asher, Steven E. ... Boston, MA
Asher, Teryl Minasian ... Birmingham, MI
Asher, W. Gerard ... Huntington, NY
Asher, William B., Jr. ... Boston, MA
Asherman, Jeanne E. ... Silver Spring, MD
Asheroff, Hyman ... Bayside, NY
Asherson & Klein ... Los Angeles, CA
Asherson, Neville ... Los Angeles, CA
Ashery, Lawrence E. ... Valley Forge, PA
Ashfield, Harry L. ... San Diego, CA
Ashford, Alexander P. ... San Francisco, CA
Ashford, Amanda J. ... Albuquerque, NM
Ashford & Associates, A Professional Corporation ... Detroit, MI
Ashford & Associates, P.A.
Albuquerque, NM
Ashford, Bruce W. ... Alamo, CA
Ashford, C. Anthony ... Hammond, IN
Ashford, Charles W. ... Alameda, CA
Ashford, Clinton R. ... Honolulu, HI
Ashford, D. Leon, (P.C.) ... Birmingham, AL
Ashford, Deborah Taylor ... Washington, DC
Ashford, Dorothy M. ... East Orange, NJ
Ashford, Earl B. ... Southfield, MI
Ashford, Emmiline P., (Mrs.) ... Memphis, TN
Ashford, George E., III ... Dallas, TX
Ashford, George R. ... Detroit, MI
Ashford, George W., Jr. ... Kailua, HI
Ashford, Hartwell T. ... Jackson, MS
Ashford, Hartwell T., P.A. ... Jackson, MS
Ashford, James H. ... Honolulu, HI
Ashford, James L. ... Sacramento, CA
Ashford, Karin K. ... Reading, PA
Ashford, Kenneth R. ... Winston-Salem, NC
Ashford, Linda D. ... Detroit, MI
Ashford, Robert Harold A. ... Syracuse, NY
Ashford, Thomas S. ... Columbus, OH
Ashford & Wriston ... Honolulu, HI
Kailua-Kona, HI
Ashford-Nolan, Cynthia ... Chicago, IL
Ashgriz, Nasser Anthony ... Amherst, NY
Ashin, Jeffery G. ... College Park, MD
Ashin, Robert W. ... Newport Beach, CA
Ashinoff, Reid L. ... New York, NY
Ashkar, Michael P. ... New York, NY
Ashkin, Roberta E. ... New York, NY
Ashkinaze, Alan S. ... Hackensack, NJ
Ashkins, Robert J. ... Bridgeport, CT
Ashkouti, Joseph H. ... Atlanta, GA
Ashleman, I.V. "Renny", II ... Las Vegas, NV
Ashley, Allen P. ... Chicago, IL
Ashley, Alvin M. ... Newport Beach, CA
Ashley, Anita Harold ... Spencer, WV
Ashley, Anjali A. ... Department of Justice, Civil Division, GV
Ashley, Anthony J. ... Chicago, IL
Ashley, Arnold Lars ... Greenville, SC
Ashley, Ashley & Arnold ... Dyersburg, TN
Ashley, Austin S. ... Boston, MA
Ashley, Barbara Ziegler ... Minneapolis, MN
Ashley, Barret ... Dyersburg, TN
Ashley, Bennett ... New York, NY
Ashley, Blake M. ... Tucson, AZ
Ashley, Bonnie M. ... Richmond, VA
Ashley, Brady & Cerniglia ... San Diego, CA
Ashley, Brian Patrick ... Ashland, KY
Ashley, Bruce P. ... Greensboro, NC
Ashley, Calvin ... Wichita Falls, TX
Ashley, Carl ... Milwaukee, WI
Ashley, Carlos C., Jr. ... Llano, TX
Ashley, Carol R. ... Chicago, IL
Ashley, Cedric ... Newark, NJ
Ashley & Charles ... Newark, NJ
Ashley, Christopher L.
National Science Foundation, Office of the General Counsel, GV
Ashley, Clenna Groom ... Nashville, TN
Ashley, Cooper S. ... Minneapolis, MN
Ashley, Daniel J. ... Chicago, IL
Ashley, Daniel J. ... New York, NY
Ashley, Debra Ann ... San Diego, CA
Ashley, Don R. ... Boonville, IN
Ashley, Donald D. ... Washington, DC
Ashley, Edward J. ... Yarmouth, ME
Ashley, Elaine Hedrick ... Greensboro, NC
Ashley, Emery Denny ... Smithfield, NC
Ashley, Evelyn A. ... Atlanta, GA
Ashley, Everett L. ... Tulsa, OK
Ashley, Fred T. ... Irvine, CA
Ashley, Fred T., Law Offices of ... Irvine, CA
Ashley, G. Luke ... Dallas, TX
Ashley, George E. ... Columbia, MO
Ashley & Gibbons ... Columbia, SC
Ashley, Hannula & Halom ... Superior, WI
Ashley, J. Mayo ... Helena, MT
Ashley, James P. ... Minneapolis, MN
Ashley, James W. ... Chicago, IL
Ashley, James W., Jr. ... Chicago, IL
Ashley, Jennifer P. ... Irvine, CA
Ashley, Jimmy D. ... Houston, TX
Ashley, John B. ... New York, NY
Ashley, John W. ... Allentown, PA
Ashley, Katherine D. ... Washington, DC
Ashley, Kevin Austin ... Lake Wales, FL
Ashley, Kim D. ... Oklahoma City, OK
Ashley, Kimberly D. ... Fort Worth, TX
Ashley & Laird, L.C. ... Dallas, TX
Irving, TX
Ashley, Lane J. ... Los Angeles, CA
San Francisco, CA
Ashley, Lawrence G. ... Huntington Woods, MI
Ashley, Lawrence P. ... New York, NY
Ashley, Leo ... Sacramento, CA
Ashley, Linda ... New York, NY
Ashley, Marc A. ... Superior, WI
Ashley, Marc D. ... New York, NY
Ashley, Maria R. ... Clifton Park, NY
Ashley, Mary Gayle Reynolds
Great Falls, VA
Ashley, Mitchel H. ... New York, NY
Ashley, Nancy ... Modesto, CA
Ashley, Nancy R. ... Seattle, WA
Ashley, Neil H. ... Tucson, AZ
Ashley, Odette L. ... Danville, CA
Ashley, Pamela J. ... Houston, TX
Ashley, Patricia Ann ... San Francisco, CA
Ashley, Perry ... New York, NY
Ashley, Philip S. ... Chicago, IL
Ashley, Phillip P. ... Kansas City, KS
Ashley, Pittard & Stewart, L.L.P.
Smithfield, NC
Ashley, Randolph A., Jr. ... Dyersburg, TN
Ashley, Regina C. ... Chicago, IL
St. Louis, MO
Ashley, Richard W. ... Chicago, IL
Ashley, Richard W. ... Zionsville, IN
Ashley, Richard W., III ... Chicago, IL
Ashley, Richd. L. ... Chanute, KS
Ashley, Robert C. ... Columbia, SC
Ashley, Robert D. ... Owosso, MI
Ashley, Robert F. ... Dallas, TX
Ashley, Ronald N. ... Pace, FL
Ashley, Russell C. ... Kansas City, MO
Ashley, Scottie H., Jr. ... Irving, TX
Ashley, Shapard D. ... Montgomery, AL
Ashley, Stephen C. ... Odessa, TX
Ashley, Stephen D. ... Los Angeles, CA
Ashley, Stephen S., Jr. ... Lexington, MS
Ashley, Susan L. ... Horsham, PA
Ashley, Thomas R. ... Newark, NJ
Ashley, W. Seaborn, Jr. ... Athens, GA
Greensboro, GA
Ashley, Wallace, Jr. ... Smithfield, NC
Ashley, Winford C. ... Jackson, MS
Ashley, Wm. Whitley ... San Francisco, CA
Ashley-Farrand, Margalo ... Pasadena, CA
Ashlock, Howard J. ... Irvine, CA
Ashlock, Kenneth R. ... Bolivar, MO
Nixa, MO
Ashlock, Steven ... Everett, WA
Ashman, Charles R. ... Savannah, GA
Ashman, Gary D. ... Chicago, IL
Ashman, Glen E. ... East Point, GA
Ashman & Griffin ... Chicago, IL
New York, NY
Ashman, Harvey A.
Plymouth Meeting, PA
Ashman, Janis ... Falls Church, VA
Ashman, Jay I. ... Burlington, VT
Ashman, Kenneth J. ... Chicago, IL
New York, NY
Ashman, Kristi J. ... Irvine, CA
Ashman & Lin ... Las Vegas, NV
Ashman, Martin C. ... Chicago, IL
Ashman, Owen I. ... Newport News, VA
Ashman, Pamela L. ... Baton Rouge, LA
Ashman, Peter L. ... Las Vegas, NV
Ashman, Phillip ... Costa Mesa, CA
Ashman, Raymond D., Jr. ... Brecksville, OH
Ashman, Vivienne M. ... New York, NY
Ashmann, Warren H. ... Beverly Hills, CA
Ashmanskas, Donald C. ... Portland, OR
Ashmead, Duffield, III ... Philadelphia, PA
Ashmead, Warren L. ... Hamilton, NY
Ashmeade, Winston A. ... San Francisco, CA
Ashmore, Anthony D. ... McAlester, OK
Ashmore, Beattie B. ... Greenville, SC
Ashmore, Dale ... Granite City, IL
Ashmore, Daniel E. ... Rapid City, SD
Ashmore, David A. ... Boise, ID
Ashmore, G. Maurice ... Greenville, SC
Ashmore, Gary M. ... Dallas, TX
Ashmore, J. Kerye ... Paris, TX
Ashmore, Joseph E., Jr. ... Dallas, TX
Ashmore, Joseph E., Jr., P.C. ... Dallas, TX
Ashmore, L. James ... Denton, TX
Lewisville, TX
Ashmore, Louise ... Durham, NC
Ashmore, Margarete P.
Department of the Air Force, Office of the Judge Advocate General, GV
Ashmore & Rabon, P.A. ... Greenville, SC
Spartanburg, SC
Ashmore, Robert W. ... Atlanta, GA
Ashmore, Steven S. ... Oklahoma City, OK
Ashmore, Teresa "Tracy" ... Denver, CO
Ashmos, Curtis R. ... Austin, TX
Ashmus, Keith A. ... Cleveland, OH
Ashnault, Richard Walter ... Ardsley, NY
Ashnault, Wallace F. ... Penfield, NY
Ashner, Harold J.
Pension Benefit Guaranty Corporation, Office of the General Counsel, GV
Ashner, Michael L. ... Jericho, NY
Ashouri, Pardis P. ... Van Nuys, CA
Ashourzadeh, Afshin ... Santa Monica, CA
Ashraf, Saba ... Atlanta, GA
Ashrafi, Victor ... Newark, NJ
Ashton, Anita ... Austin, TX
Ashton, Ann L. ... Houston, TX
Ashton, Ann M. ... Washington, DC
New York, NY
Ashton, Anthony P. ... Baltimore, MD
Ashton, Braunberger & Boud, P.C.
Sandy, UT
Ashton, Bruce L. ... Los Angeles, CA
Ashton, Charles H. ... Dumfries, VA
Ashton, Christopher B. ... Orchard Park, NY
Ashton, Clifford L. ... Salt Lake City, UT
Ashton, Conway A. ... Salt Lake City, UT
Ashton, Craig Fontaine ... Roseville, CA
Ashton, David P. C. ... Miami, FL
Ashton, David W. ... Palmdale, CA
Ashton, Donna ... Cambridge, MA
Ashton, Edward J. ... Birmingham, AL
Ashton, Eric A. ... Glendale, CA
Ashton, Eric Andrew ... Glendale, CA
Ashton, Frank A. ... Jacksonville, FL
Ashton, Gary L. ... Sonora, CA
Ashton, Gwen A. ... New York, NY
Ashton, Harris J. ... Stamford, CT
Ashton, Heidi F. ... Naples, FL
Ashton, Helaine S. ... San Diego, CA
Ashton, Jean G., (Mr.) ... Campbell, CA
Ashton, Joel B. ... Clawson, MI
Plymouth, MI
Ashton, John A. ... Clawson, MI
Plymouth, MI
Ashton, John B. ... New York, NY
Ashton, John F. ... Stamford, CT
Ashton, John P. ... Park City, UT
Salt Lake City, UT
Ashton, Judith ... Boston, MA
Ashton, Juliet C., (Mrs.) ... San Jose, CA
Ashton, Katherine Fleming
Santa Monica, CA
Ashton, Kimberly Dawn ... Topeka, KS
Ashton, M. John ... Salt Lake City, UT
Ashton, Mark A. ... Lawton, OK
Ashton, Mark R. ... Exton, PA
Ashton, Mary Ellen ... Anchorage, AK
Ashton, Michael S. ... Lansing, MI
Ashton, Nina M. ... Palo Alto, CA
Ashton, Norman L. ... Ogden, UT
Ashton, Paul H. ... Salt Lake City, UT
Ashton, Richard I. ... Sandy, UT
Ashton, Richard M.
Board of Governors Of The Federal Reserve System, Office of the General Counsel, GV
Ashton, Richard Wallace ... Worthington, OH
Ashton, Robert E. ... Columbus, OH
Ashton, Robert W. ... New York, NY
Ashton, Robin C. ... Washington, DC
Ashton, Rudolph A. ... Midlothian, VA
Ashton, Rudolph Alexander, III
New Bern, NC
Ashton, Sandra J.
Department Of The Interior, Office of the Solicitor, GV
Ashton, Steven O. ... Clawson, MI
Plymouth, MI
Ashton, Thomas E., III ... Bellingham, WA
Ashton, Thomas G. ... Chester Springs, PA
Ashton, Wisener and Munkacsy, P.C.
Lawton, OK
Ashukian, Stephen P. ... Cranston, RI
Ashwell, J. Gregory ... Warrenton, VA
Ashwell, James B. ... St. Louis, MO
Ashwill, Max C. ... Madison, WI
Ashwin, Mulan de Quetteville
New York, NY
Ashwood, Cynthia Ferrell ... Chandler, OK
Ashwood, Cynthia Ferrell, P.C.
Chandler, OK
Ashworth, Alton W., Jr. ... Dallas, TX
Ashworth, Amy M. ... Manassas, VA
Ashworth, Andrew S. ... Phoenix, AZ
Ashworth & Blanchet ... San Diego, CA
Ashworth, Brent F. ... Provo, UT
Ashworth, Bruce ... Arlington, TX
Ashworth, Bruce ... Fort Worth, TX
Ashworth, C. Taylor ... Phoenix, AZ
Ashworth, Christopher ... San Jose, CA
Ashworth, Clyde R. ... Arlington, TX
Ashworth, David E. ... Worcester, MA
Ashworth, David L. ... Lancaster, PA
Ashworth, Don W. ... Las Vegas, NV
Ashworth, Douglas G. ... Royston, GA
Ashworth, Gail Vaughn ... Nashville, TN
Ashworth, Glen M. ... Kaufman, TX
Ashworth, Harold G. ... Rochester, NY
Ashworth, Hayes & Moran
Laguna Niguel, CA
Ashworth, John L. ... Marion, OH
Ashworth, John P. ... Portland, OR
Ashworth, Kathryn F. ... San Diego, CA
Ashworth, Ken R., and Associates
Solvang, CA
Las Vegas, NV
Mesquite, NV
Ashworth, Mark S. ... Laguna Niguel, CA
Newport Beach, CA
Ashworth, Michael S. ... Clovis, NM
Ashworth & Moran ... Newport Beach, CA
Ashworth, Philip T. ... Redding, CA
Ashworth, Richard B. ... South Pasadena, CA
Ashworth, Richard G. ... New York, NY
Ashworth, Stephen H. ... San Bernardino, CA
Ashworth, Thomas, III ... San Diego, CA
Ashworth, W. Pruitt ... Dallas, TX
Ashworth, Wayne A. ... Salt Lake City, UT
Ashy, Alexander R., II ... Jackson, MS
Ashy, D. Warren ... Lafayette, LA
Ashy, Michael H. ... Tampa, FL
Asia, Benjamin S. ... Seattle, WA
Asiaf, Lisa M. ... Boston, MA
Asiano, Ann Marilynne ... Sacramento, CA
San Francisco, CA
Asiedu, Kwasi A. ... Beverly Hills, CA
Asiedu & Lubega ... Beverly Hills, CA
Asiedu, Reginald ... Bronx, NY
Asiel, E. Nelson ... New York, NY
Asiello, John P. ... Albany, NY
Asif, Lisa A. ... Los Angeles, CA
Asija, S. Pal ... Shelton, CT
Asimakis, Patrice ... Birmingham, MI
Asimos, George, Jr. ... Berwyn, PA
Asimow, Daniel B. ... San Francisco, CA
Asimow, Michael ... Los Angeles, CA
Asimow, Nathan ... Pacific Palisades, CA
Asimus, Debra D. ... Denver, CO
Asin, Steven G.
Administrative Office Of The United States Courts, GV
Asinof, Wesley R. ... Fayetteville, GA
Ask, Andrew C. ... Warren, OH
Ask, Brenda M. ... Beresford, SD
Ask, Mitchell J. ... Minneapolis, MN
Ask, Ronald W. ... Riverside, CA
Ask, Thomas M. ... Roundup, MT
Askanas, Mark S. ... San Francisco, CA
Askanase, David J. ... Houston, TX
Askarieh, Adrian R. ... Los Angeles, CA
Askegaard, Erik J. ... Brainerd, MN
Askegaard, Robinson, Murphy & Schweich, P.A. ... Brainerd, MN
Askenaizer, Michael S. ... Nashua, NH
Askenazy, Lisa J. ... Washington, DC
Asker, Chapp & Clos, P.C. ... Torrance, CA
Troy, MI
Westland, MI
Asker, Paul P. ... Torrance, CA
Westland, MI
Askew, Anthony B. ... Atlanta, GA
Askew & Archbold, A Professional Corporation ... Stockton, CA
Askew, Bryant R. ... Tulsa, OK
Askew, C. King, (P.C.) ... Rome, GA
Askew, David Revels ... Chicago, IL
Askew, Delphine A. ... Washington, DC
Askew, Garland L. ... Raleigh, NC
Askew, Hulett H. ... Atlanta, GA
Askew, J. Scott ... Phoenix, AZ
Askew, James A. ... Stockton, CA
Askew, James A. ... Colorado Springs, CO
Albuquerque, NM
Askew, James H. ... Shreveport, LA
Askew, Jeffrey D. ... Boca Raton, FL
Stuart, FL
West Palm Beach, FL
Askew, Jess, III ... Little Rock, AR
Askew, Julie ... Daytona Beach, FL
Askew, Justin G. ... New York, NY
Askew, Kim Juanita ... Dallas, TX

Askew, Larry Leroy, II ... Lenexa, KS
Askew, Lash S. ... Swainsboro, GA
Askew, Lewis L., Jr. ... McLean, VA
Askew, Logan B. ... Hopkinsville, KY
Askew, Michelle N. ... Chicago, IL
Askew, Middleton L. ... Amarillo, TX
Askew, Rebecca A. ... Denver, CO
Askew, Reubin O'D. ... Orlando, FL
Askew, Roger Allan ... Ahoskie, NC
Rocky Mount, NC
Askew, Stephen J. ... Anoka, MN
Askew, Thomas M. ... Tulsa, OK
Askew, Timothy R., Jr. ... Sanford, FL
Askew, Wallace K. ... Pine Mountain, GA
Askew, Wm. Steven ... Vidalia, GA
Askey, David H. ... Del Mar, CA
Askey, Elizabeth P. ... Treasury Department, Departmental Offices, GV
Askey, Mary E. ... Bronx, NY
Askey, William Hartman ... Williamsport, PA
Askin, A. Bradley ... Bethesda, MD
Askin, David C. ... Houston, TX
Askin, David J. ... Denver, CO
Askin, Denise Basford ... Louisville, KY
Askin, Frank ... Newark, NJ
Askin, Joseph J. ... Baltimore, MD
Askin, Karen G. ... Potomac, MD
Askin, Marilyn K. ... West Orange, NJ
Askin, Otis F. ... Augusta, GA
Askinas, David M. ... Hartford, CT
Askinas, Steven C. ... Bay Shore, NY
Askinosie, M. Shawn ... Springfield, MO
Askinosie, M. Shawn, LLC, Law Offices of
Springfield, MO
Askins, Ansley Brooks ... Atlanta, GA
Askins & Armstrong, P.C. ... La Porte, TX
Askins, Chandler & Askins ... Hemingway, SC
Askins, Donald H. ... Clintwood, VA
Askins, Donald H., Law Office of, P.C.
Clintwood, VA
Askins, Gregory B. ... Hemingway, SC
Askins, Jerome P., III ... Hemingway, SC
Askins, Knox W. ... La Porte, TX
Askins, Marian L. ... Atlanta, GA
Askins, Richard F. ... Bow, NH
Askins, Robert H. ... Abilene, TX
Askins, Terry ... San Antonio, TX
Askintowicz, John W., III
Charles Town, WV
Askoff, Keith G. ... Sunnyvale, CA
Askoff, Richard A. ... Whippany, NJ
Askot, Stuart K. ... Philadelphia, PA
Askot & Weiner LLP ... Philadelphia, PA
Askounis & Borst, P.C. ... Chicago, IL
Askounis, Homer J. ... Chicago, IL
Askounis, Homer J., P.C. ... Chicago, IL
Askounis, Thomas V. ... Chicago, IL
Askow, Irwin J. ... Chicago, IL
Askowitz, Lisa R. ... Miami, FL
Askren, Kenton G. ... Boonville, MO
Askvig, Jonathan K. ... St. Paul, MN
Askwith, Elizabeth L., P.C.
Sault Ste. Marie, MI
Aslan, Benjamin ... New York, NY
Aslan, Kenneth R. ... Los Angeles, CA
Aslan, Shaoul ... Washington, DC
Aslanian, Aida ... Glendale, CA
Aslanian, Antranig, Jr. ... Fort Lee, NJ
Aslanian & Aslanian ... Fort Lauderdale, FL
Aslanian, George H., Jr.
Fort Lauderdale, FL
Aslanian, Richard J. ... Purchase, NY
Aslanian, Victor C. ... Fort Lauderdale, FL
Aslanides, Peter C. ... Newark, NJ
New York, NY
Aslani-Far, Mohammed ... New York, NY
Asleson, Brian J. ... Buffalo, MN
Asleson, Robert E. ... Duluth, MN
Aslin, John F. ... Seattle, WA
Aslinger, Jason R. ... Arcanum, OH
Asma, William N. ... Winter Garden, FL
Asma, William N., P.A. ... Winter Garden, FL
Asmah, Maxine Young ... Covington, KY
Asman, Andrea Doyle ... Waterbury, CT
Asman, Matthew R. ... New York, NY
Asman, Robert J. ... Cleveland, OH
Asman, Sanford J. ... Atlanta, GA
Asmar, Charles M. ... Washington, DC
Asmar, Mark A. ... Hartford, CT
Asmer, Peter F., Jr. ... Charlotte, NC
Asmundson, R. Mark ... Bellingham, WA
Asmundson, T.B. ... Bellingham, WA
Asmundson, Vigfus A. ... Davis, CA
Asmundson, Vigfus A., Inc. ... Davis, CA
Asmundsson, Eric ... New York, NY
Asmus, Clarence F. ... Monroe, WI
Asmus, David F. ... Houston, TX
Asmus, David G. ... St. Louis, MO
Asmus, Douglas R. ... Sterling, CO
Asmus, Grover E., II ... Mobile, AL
Asmus, Robert, Law Offices ... Roseville, CA
Asmus, Robert Law Offices
Sacramento, CA
Asmus, Ryan Wade ... Chicago, IL
Asmus, Scott J. ... Nashua, NH
Asmussen, Beth ... Edina, MN
Asmussen, James R. ... Chicago, IL
Asmussen, Stephen R. ... San Jose, CA
Asmuth, A. William, Jr. ... Milwaukee, WI
Asmuth, Anthony W., III ... Milwaukee, WI
Asnanee, Anjali G. ... New York, NY
Asner, Jonathan M. ... Minneapolis, MN
Asner, Karen M. ... New York, NY
Asner, Scott I. ... Overland Park, KS
Asness, Barry ... New York, NY
Asnip, Matthew M. ... Atlanta, GA
Asnis, Bradley ... Miami, FL
Asnis, Saul ... New York, NY
Asnis, Shoshanah V. ... New York, NY
Asnoe, Jacquelyn M. ... Ilion, NY
Asofsky, Paul H. ... Houston, TX
Asoian, Richard G. ... Andover, MA
Asoklis, Theresa M. ... Southfield, MI
Asonye, Nkwa I. ... Freeport, NY
Aspaas, Jennifer L. ... Seattle, WA
Aspatore, George A. ... Norfolk, VA
Aspaturian, Nancy Lee ... Monterey Park, CA
Aspden, Matthew Mark ... Somerset, MA
Aspegren, Kathryn Yessian
Washington, DC
Aspelin & Bridgman ... San Francisco, CA
Aspelin, John H. ... San Francisco, CA
Aspell, Bradford J. ... Klamath Falls, OR
Aspell, Della-Rose & Richard
Klamath Falls, OR
Aspell, James F. ... Hartford, CT
Aspelmeier, Fisch, Power, Warner & Engberg ... Mediapolis, IA
West Point, IA
Burlington, IA
Aspelmeier, Kenneth A. ... Burlington, IA
Mediapolis, IA
Aspen, Jessica M. ... Chicago, IL
Aspen, Marvin E. ... Chicago, IL
Aspen Ridge Law Offices, P.C.
Cheyenne, WY
Aspengren, Alfred E. ... Chicago, IL
Aspenson, Everett H. ... Los Angeles, CA
Asper, Denise M. ... Walnut Creek, CA
Asper, Linn H. ... Haines, AK
Asper, Maynard W. ... Los Angeles, CA
Asper, Merle W., Jr. ... Santa Ana, CA
Asper, W. Ryan ... Houston, TX
Asperger, Donald P. ... Fresno, CA
Asperger, James R. ... Los Angeles, CA
Asperger, Jeffrey J. ... Chicago, IL
Asperger, Lisa E. ... Fresno, CA
Asperger, Paul ... Fresno, CA
Asperger, Robert E. ... Gold River, CA
Aspero, Benedict V. ... Morristown, NJ
Aspero, Benedict V., Esq., P.C.
Morristown, NJ
Aspero, Nell Sanders, Mrs. ... Memphis, TN
Aspero, Stephen M. ... Hackensack, NJ
Aspessi, Francis P. ... Los Angeles, CA
Aspey, Frederick M. Fritz ... Flagstaff, AZ
Aspey, Watkins & Diesel, P.L.L.C.
Cottonwood, AZ
Flagstaff, AZ
Page, AZ
Sedona, AZ
Asphaug, Rolf G. ... Denver, CO
Asphaug, Scott Erik ... Portland, OR
Aspinall, Alan J. ... Estes Park, CO
Aspinall, Brian E. ... Cincinnati, OH
Aspinall, Michael H. ... Bronx, NY
Aspinall, Owen S. ... Palisade, CO
Aspinwall, Charles S. ... Albuquerque, NM
Aspinwall, David C. ... Englewood, CO
Aspinwall, James H. ... Stratford, CT
Aspinwall, Marie Stadtmueller ... Stratford, CT
Aspinwall, Mark A. ... Pittsburgh, PA
Aspinwall, Marla J. ... Los Angeles, CA
Aspinwall, Ogden & Watson
Colorado Springs, CO
Aspinwall, William A.
Colorado Springs, CO
Aspis, Harold B. ... Purchase, NY
Aspiz, Ira M. ... Long Beach, CA
Aspland, Michael P. ... Queensbury, NY
Asplen, Christopher H. ... Doylestown, PA
Asplund, Bronwyn Hawks ... Franklin, NH
Asplund, Heather L. ... Tustin, CA
Asplund, Mark J. ... Seattle, WA
Asplundh, E. Boyd ... Bryn Athyn, PA
Aspnes, Anthony S. ... Minneapolis, MN
Aspray, Joseph M., Jr. ... Woodbridge, NJ
Asprelli, Ernest J., Jr. ... Woodbridge, CT
Asprinio, Carl J. ... Providence, RI
Asprinio, Steven E. ... Warwick, RI
Aspromonte, Salvatore ... New York, NY
Aspromonte & Switnicki ... Brooklyn, NY
Aspy, Michael A. ... Indianapolis, IN
Aspy, P. Clark ... Austin, TX
Asquino, Cheryl A. ... Atlanta, GA
Asquith, Harry W. ... Knoxville, TN
Asquith, Harry W., Jr. ... Providence, RI
Asquith, Mahoney & Robinson
Providence, RI
Asquith, Marcia E. ... United States Senate, Committee Legal Personnel, GV
Asquith, Patricia K. ... Providence, RI
Assad, David, Jr. ... Philadelphia, PA
Assad, David Michael ... Fall River, MA
Assad, Edward J. ... Macon, GA
Assad, George ... Las Vegas, NV
Assad, Judy B. ... Providence, RI
Assad, Michael J. ... Cupertino, CA
Assad, Roger F. ... Wayne, NJ
Assael, Michael ... New York, NY
Assael-Shafia, Michele ... San Bernardino, CA
Assaf, Eugene F. ... Washington, DC
Assaf, Jane C. ... Albany, NY
Assaf, Michael D. ... Albany, NY
Assaf, Philip D. ... Emeryville, CA
Assaf, R. James ... Boca Raton, FL
Assaf, R. Robyn ... Oklahoma City, OK
Assaf, Ricardo H. ... Philadelphia, PA
Assaf, Timothy P. ... Akron, OH
Assaid, Violet M. ... Clearwater, FL
Assail, Peter D. ... New York, NY
Assail & Yoeli ... New York, NY
Assatourians, Liza C. ... Washington, DC
Assayag, Michele S. ... Irvine, CA
Asseff, Carl F. ... Independence, OH
Asseff, Michael C. ... Independence, OH
Asselin, Thomas H. ... Atlanta, GA
Asselmeier, Pamela J. ... San Francisco, CA
Asselstine, Brett C. ... Great Falls, MT
Asselstine, Brett C., P.C. ... Great Falls, MT
Asselta, Joseph J. ... New York, NY
Asselta, Joseph P. ... New Hyde Park, NY
Asselta, Mark P. ... Camden, NJ
Westmont, NJ
Assendelft, Barbara Ann
Traverse City, MI
Assenza, Frederick J. ... New York, NY
Assenzo, Joseph R. ... Kansas City, MO
Asseo-Guerra, Mary Zelma ... San Juan, PR
Asserson, Brian M. ... Parsippany, NJ
Assessment Counselling Services
Los Angeles, CA
Westlake Village, CA
Assey, James M., Jr. ... Washington, DC
Assigal, Heidi ... Los Angeles, CA
Assini, Charles J., Jr. ... Schenectady, NY
Assini, Frederick W. ... Cleveland, OH
Assini, Jennifer Marindin ... Schenectady, NY
Assini, Vincent ... Rochester, NY
Assink, Anne H. ... Albuquerque, NM
Assiran, Ellis & Devlin ... Taunton, MA
Assiran, Philip J. ... Taunton, MA
Associated Legal Group, L.L.C.
Cheyenne, WY
Assor, Nathan E. ... New York, NY
Assouline, Eric N. ... Miami, FL
Assunto, Alyne ... Houston, TX
Assuras, Dennis M. ... Chino, CA
Ast, David Alan ... Morristown, NJ
Ast, Paul A. ... Wilson, NC
Ast, Robert J. ... Buffalo, NY
Ast, Scott R. ... Overland Park, KS
Asta, Michael J. ... New York, NY
Astabie, Michelle D. ... San Francisco, CA
Astarita, Kathryn Helen ... Austin, TX
Astarita, Mark J. ... New York, NY
Aste, Lauren J. ... New York, NY
Aste, Louis J. ... Somers, NY
Aste, Robert J. ... Livingston, NJ
Asteak, Gary Neil ... Easton, PA
Asteak Law Offices ... Easton, PA
Astengo, David A. ... San Francisco, CA
Aster, Charles E. ... New York, NY
Aster, Dennis C. ... Cleveland, OH
Aster, Francine ... Verona, NJ
Asti, Alison L. ... Baltimore, MD
Asti, Arthur A., Jr. ... Pittsburgh, PA
Asti, Robert ... Miami, FL
Asti, Robert J. ... Madison, MS
Asti, Robert J. ... Cedarburg, WI
Asti, Russell Z. ... Monroe, NC
Astigarraga, José I. ... Miami, FL
Astill, Dennis M. ... Salt Lake City, UT
Astin, Floyd G. ... Salt Lake City, UT
Astin, J. Steve ... Cedartown, GA
Astin, Rainey L. ... Washington, DC
Astin, Ronald T. ... Houston, TX
Astin, Wayne T. ... Riverside, CA
Astiz, Peter M. ... Palo Alto, CA
Astle and Astle ... Kalispell, MT
Astle, Dale L. ... Tulsa, OK
Astle, David L. ... Kalispell, MT
Astle, Donald C. ... Wichita, KS
Astle, Doris J. "Dorie" ... Tulsa, OK
Astle, Jas., Jr. ... Culver City, CA
Astle, Richard W. ... Chicago, IL
Astle, Ruth ... Oakland, CA
Astle, Scott S. ... Pasadena, CA
Astle, Thomas F. ... Westford, MA
Astle, William E. ... Kalispell, MT
Astleford, Jon C. ... Minneapolis, MN
Astleford, Warren L. ... Sacramento, CA
Astley, Stephen R. ... Department of the Navy, Office of the Judge Advocate General, GV
Astnus, Harry-Todd ... Atlanta, GA
Astolfi, Helena Hadeed ... Philadelphia, PA
Aston, David ... Austin, TX
Aston, Derek Charles ... Winchester, VA
Aston, Gary L. ... Elberton, GA
Aston, H. I. ... Tulsa, OK
Aston, Joe, III ... McKinney, TX
Aston, Marcia Allen ... Atlantic City, NJ
Aston, Patricia Ford ... Jackson, MS
Aston, R. Lee ... Elberton, GA
Aston, Scott B. ... Dallas, TX
Astor, George ... Bronx, NY
Astor, Jack ... Jackson Heights, NY
Astor, John Kelly ... Orange, CA
Astor & Minardi ... Northampton, MA
Springfield, MA
Astor, Paul C. ... Bala Cynwyd, PA
Philadelphia, PA
Astor, Peter Cergizan ... Tulsa, OK
Astor & Phillips, A Professional Law Corporation ... Los Angeles, CA
Orange, CA
Astor, Robert H. ... Northampton, MA
Springfield, MA
Astor, Sanford ... Los Angeles, CA
Astor Weiss Kaplan & Rosenblum, LLP
Bala Cynwyd, PA
Philadelphia, PA
Astor, Z. Harry ... Orange, CA
Astore, Marc A. ... Fairfax, VA
Astore, Thomas H. ... Levittown, NY
Astoria, Valinda J. ... San Antonio, TX
Astorina, John A. ... New York, NY
Astorino, Peter B. ... Lancaster, PA
Astrab, Michael K., Law Office of
Cleveland, OH
Astrachan, Gregory B. ... New York, NY
Astrachan, Gunst, Goldman & Thomas, A Professional Corporation ... Baltimore, MD
Astrachan, James B. ... Baltimore, MD
Astrella, Lance ... Denver, CO
Astrella & Rice P.C. ... Denver, CO
Astroth, Frank S. ... Baltimore, MD
Astrove, David M. ... Washington, DC
Astrove, Steven R. ... Boston, MA
Astrue, Michael J. ... Cambridge, MA
Astrup, Odell M. ... Fargo, ND
Astuno, John, Jr. ... Denver, CO
Asturias, Daniel H. ... Merced, CA
Asturias, Elena M. ... San Francisco, CA
Asturias, Thomas ... Houston, TX
Astuto, S. Keith ... Miami, FL
Asuncion, Jason J. ... Wilmington, DE
Aswad & Ingraham ... Binghamton, NY
Aswad, Kristin D. ... New York, NY
Aswad, Richard N. ... Binghamton, NY
Aswell, Harold W. ... Farmerville, LA
Atack, Charlene B. ... Santa Cruz, CA
Atack, Robert B. ... Santa Cruz, CA
Atadika, Agnes C. ... New York, NY
Atadika & Atadika ... New York, NY
Atadika, Michael R. ... New York, NY
Ataide, Randy M. ... Dinuba, CA
Ataie, Neda ... San Diego, CA
Atalig and Chang ... Saipan, TT
Atalig, Pedro M. ... Saipan, TT
Atallah, Albert ... San Diego, CA
Atallah, Laila K. ... Baltimore, MD
Atallah, Stephen S. ... Pittsburgh, PA
Atamian, Jean-Marie L. ... New York, NY
Atanasio, Pamela ... Mineola, NY
Atanasio, Paul ... New York, NY
Atanasoff, Donn A. ... Iron River, MI
Atanga, Jacob A. ... Indianapolis, IN
Atanous, Sargis G. ... Orange, CA
Atarod, Marion Schnerre ... Oak Brook, IL
Atas, Chas. J. ... Annapolis, MD
Atas, Marc J. ... Baltimore, MD
Atasi, Yasmin Islam ... Houston, TX
Atcachunas, Maureen M. ... Woodbridge, NJ
Atcherley, Linda F., Law Offices of
San Diego, CA
Atcherson, Sophia J. ... Chicago, IL
Atcheson, Frank A. ... New York, NY
Atcheson, Fred ... Kolonia, TT
Atcheson, George S., II ... San Diego, CA
Atcheson, Marcia N. ... United States Senate, Committee Legal Personnel, GV
Atcheson, Richard R. ... League City, TX
Atchinson, Brian K. ... Augusta, ME
Atchinson, Joan Koski ... Portland, ME
Atchinson, William K., Jr. ... Oneonta, NY
Atchison, Alan C. ... Department of Commerce, Patent and Trademark Office, GV
Atchison, Alexander R. ... Clayton, NC
Atchison, Ashley C. ... Baton Rouge, LA
Atchison, Barisone & Condotti, A Professional Corporation
Santa Cruz, CA
Atchison, Crosby, Saad & Beebe, P.C.
Mobile, AL
Atchison, Cynthia Jane ... Bethel Park, PA
Atchison, Daryl A. ... Mobile, AL
Atchison, David L. ... Chicago, IL
Atchison, Dawn G. ... St. Paul, MN
Atchison, Derek ... Birmingham, AL
Atchison, Donald ... Bend, OR
Portland, OR
Atchison, Gary E. ... Montgomery, AL
Atchison, James E. ... Mobile, AL
Atchison, J. D. Roy ... Pensacola, FL
Atchison, John G., Jr. ... Lexington, KY
Atchison, John H. ... Sun City, AZ
Atchison, Julie L. ... Columbus, OH
Atchison, Michael Thomas ... Columbiana, AL
Atchison, Michael W. ... Kansas City, MO
Atchison, Michele ... Raleigh, NC
Atchison, Rodney R. ... Santa Cruz, CA
Atchison, Roy C. ... St. Helens, OR
Atchison, Roy Stephen ... St. Helens, OR
Atchison, W. Michael ... Birmingham, AL
Atchley, Charles E., Jr. ... Sevierville, TN
Atchley, Dennis B. ... Carlsbad, CA
Atchley, Elmer H. ... Camino, CA
Atchley, Fielding H., Jr. ... Chattanooga, TN
Atchley, Jason B. ... Dallas, TX
Atchley, Jeffrey L. ... Memphis, TN
Atchley, Mark R. ... Santa Monica, CA
Atchley, Michael L., II ... Dallas, TX
Atchley, Rebecca ... Lubbock, TX
Atchley, Russell C. ... Berryville, AR
Atchley, Russell, Waldrop & Hlavinka, L.L.P. ... Texarkana, AR
Marshall, TX
Texarkana, TX
Atchley, William T., Jr. ... St. Petersburg, FL
Atcitty, Shenan R. ... Washington, DC
Ateljevich, Sava ... San Francisco, CA
Atella, Michael D. ... San Diego, CA
Atelsek, Paul ... Department of Transportation, National Highway Traffic Safety Administration, GV
Aten, Fred G., Jr. ... Rochester, NY
Aten, Keith ... St. Johnsbury, VT
Aten, Noble & Ide ... Holdrege, NE
Atenaide, Anthony ... San Diego, CA
Atencio, Dolores S. ... Denver, CO
Atencio, Harold O. ... Albuquerque, NM
Atencio, Jerry R. ... Denver, CO
Atencio, Vincent R. ... Englewood, CO
Ater, Derrick A. ... Lewiston, ID
Ater, Gene ... Troup, TX
Ater, Jonathan A. ... Portland, OR
Ater, Kenneth B. ... Ironton, OH
Ater, Michael M. ... Chillicothe, OH
Ater Wynne LLP ... Portland, OR
Seattle, WA
Aterno, Anthony ... Austin, TX

Ates & Associates, A Professional Corporation ... Destrehan, LA; New Orleans, LA
Ates, David Charles ... Atlanta, GA
Ates, J. Robert ... Destrehan, LA; New Orleans, LA
Ates, John R. ... Washington, DC
Ateshoglou, Kavourias & Chrysanthem, P.C. New York, NY
Ateshoglou, Steven Demetrios New York, NY
Atha, Jill C. ... Florham Park, NJ
Atha, Kay Ann ... Rome, GA
Atha, N. L. Rafferty ... San Francisco, CA
Atha, Phyllis Ann ... Ozark, AR
Atha, Stephen W. ... Topeka, KS
Athan, Byron D. ... San Ramon, CA
Athan, G. Helen ... Naples, FL
Athan, Lawrence L., Jr. ... Boston, MA
Athanacio, Gayle M. ... San Francisco, CA
Athanail, Nicholas ... New York, NY
Athanas, Constantine ... Boston, MA
Athanas, Josef S. ... Chicago, IL
Athanas, William C. ... Boston, MA
Athanasakos, Elizabeth, Law Offices of Fort Lauderdale, FL
Athanases, Jennifer ... Plymouth, MN
Athanasia, Chris T. ... New York, NY
Athanason, Michael N. ... St. Petersburg, FL
Athanason, Nicholas M. ... St. Petersburg, FL
Athanasoulas, Christian J. ... Boston, MA
Athanasoulis, Emilie F. ... Boston, MA
Athans, Athanasios G. ... Matthews, NC
Athans, Dean M. ... Chicago, IL
Athans, Michael J. ... Atlanta, GA
Athari, Mohammed J. ... Albany, NY
Athari, Susan R. ... Washington, DC
Athas, Ellen M. Executive Office Of The President, Council on Environmental Quality, GV
Athas, Gus J. ... Chicago, IL
Athas, James G. ... Chicago, IL
Athas, Robert L. ... Boston, MA
Athay, D. Gilbert ... Salt Lake City, UT
Athay, Margaret A. ... Washington, DC; Rockville, MD
Athay, Michael C. ... Philadelphia, PA
Athayde, William P. ... Yorktown, VA
Athearn, Forden ... San Francisco, CA
Athen, Scott C. ... Baltimore, MD
Athens, E. John, Jr. ... Fairbanks, AK
Athens, Everett ... Tulsa, OK
Athens, John S. ... Tulsa, OK
Athens, Lisa A. ... Dallas, TX
Athens, Thomas C. ... Fergus Falls, MN
Atherholt, J. Eric ... Berwyn, PA
Atherly, Darst B. ... Eugene, OR
Atherly, Harold E. ... Carmel, IN
Atherton & Allen ... Chula Vista, CA; San Diego, CA
Atherton & Atherton, LLC ... Denver, CO
Atherton, Bruce D. ... Louisville, KY
Atherton, Christian A. ... Oroville, CA
Atherton, Dale R. ... Pasadena, CA
Atherton & Dozier ... Stockton, CA
Atherton, E. Eugene ... Polson, MT
Atherton, E. Eugene, P.C. ... Polson, MT
Atherton, Harper B. ... Washington, DC
Atherton & Huth ... Emporia, KS
Atherton, Jeffrey M. ... Chattanooga, TN
Atherton, Jerry L. ... Tyler, TX
Atherton, John G. ... Emporia, KS
Atherton, Judith S. Hanson Salt Lake City, UT
Atherton, Michael, (A Professional Corporation) Los Altos, CA
Atherton, Rob ... Nacogdoches, TX
Atherton, Robert A. ... Denver, CO
Atherton, Robert C., III ... Palo Alto, CA; New Orleans, LA
Atherton, Rodney C. ... Denver, CO
Atherton, Stephen J. ... Emporia, KS
Atherton, Steven H. ... Barre, VT
Atherton, Susan V. ... Tulsa, OK
Atherton, Thomas M. ... Indianapolis, IN
Atherton, Timothy N. ... Morristown, NJ
Atherton & Willner ... Barre, VT
Athey, Bernard B., Jr. ... Houston, TX
Athey, Carol J. ... Kansas City, MO
Athey, Clifford L., Jr. ... Front Royal, VA
Athey, Eric N. ... Lancaster, PA
Athey, John E. ... Austin, TX
Athey, Julie K. ... Nashville, TN
Athey, Kathie ... Flint, MI
Athey, Kimberly M. ... Front Royal, VA
Athey, Robert J. ... Walnut Creek, CA
Athias-White, Gretchen ... Bowie, MD
Athol, Elizabeth S. ... Pittsburgh, PA
Athy, Andrew, Jr. ... Washington, DC
Athy, Robert K. ... San Diego, CA
Athy, Susan ... Treasury Department, Internal Revenue Service, GV
Atia, Hoda ... Chicago, IL
Atigh, Stephanie A. ... Salinas, CA
Atik, Jeffery Cyril ... Boston, MA
Atikian, Katherine ... Pasadena, CA
Atinsky, Kahn, Sicula & Teper Milwaukee, WI
Atinsky, Lawrence S. ... New York, NY
Atinsky, Philip L. ... Milwaukee, WI
Atkenson, Charmaine E. ... Hinsdale, IL
Atkerson, Dan A. ... Dallas, TX
Atkeson, Helen Clark ... Denver, CO
Atkeson, Tim ... Denver, CO
Atkin, Andrew S. ... Los Angeles, CA
Atkin, Barbara A. ... Washington, DC
Atkin, Blake S. ... Salt Lake City, UT
Atkin, Gary E. ... Salt Lake City, UT
Atkin, Howard ... Fort Myers, FL
Atkin, J. Ralph ... St. George, UT
Atkin, Jack ... New York, NY
Atkin, James B. ... Washington, DC
Atkin, Jean E. ... Toledo, OH
Atkin, Judith E. ... Melbourne, FL
Atkin, Judith E., P.A. ... Melbourne, FL
Atkin & Lilja, P.C. ... Salt Lake City, UT
Atkin, Lori Meredith ... New York, NY
Atkin, Marsha S. ... Salt Lake City, UT
Atkin, Michael W. ... Pasadena, CA
Atkin, Nelson D., II ... Portland, OR
Atkin, Rachel G. ... Columbia, SC
Atkin, Trevor L. ... Las Vegas, NV
Atkins, Aaron Ardene ... Du Quoin, IL
Atkins, Aileen D. ... New York, NY
Atkins, Alden L. ... Washington, DC
Atkins & Atkins ... Louisville, KY
Atkins & Atkins, P.C. ... Tulsa, OK
Atkins, Ben E. ... Baton Rouge, LA
Atkins, Benjamin Z. ... New York, NY
Atkins, Beth Ferebee ... New Bern, NC
Atkins, Bill ... Arlington, TX
Atkins, Billy ... Fairmont, WV; Morgantown, WV
Atkins, Bobbie M. ... Macon, GA
Atkins, Brendan J. ... Detroit, MI
Atkins, Bruce A. ... Houston, TX
Atkins, Bruce L. ... Hackensack, NJ
Atkins, Bruce T. ... St. Louis, MO
Atkins, C. Clyde ... Miami, FL
Atkins, Cathy M. ... Denver, CO
Atkins, Chad ... New York, NY
Atkins, Chad A. ... Denver, CO
Atkins, Charles G. ... Cincinnati, OH
Atkins, Charles N., II ... United States Senate, Senatorial Assistants, GV
Atkins, Christopher G. ... Middletown, OH
Atkins & Cohen ... Norristown, PA; Philadelphia, PA
Atkins & Craven ... Saluda, NC
Atkins, D. Michael ... Charlottesville, VA
Atkins, Dale N. ... New Orleans, LA
Atkins, Dallas Leigh ... Santa Barbara, CA
Atkins, Daniel E. ... Marlette, MI
Atkins, David P. ... Bridgeport, CT
Atkins, Deana E. ... Annville, PA
Atkins, Don W. ... Detroit, MI
Atkins, Donald B. ... Tulsa, OK
Atkins, Douglas M. ... Petersburg, VA
Atkins, E. Paul ... San Francisco, CA
Atkins, Eddy ... Henrietta, TX
Atkins, Edna R. ... Omaha, NE
Atkins, Edward G. ... Charleston, WV
Atkins, E. L. ... Arlington, TX
Atkins, Elizabeth ... New York, NY
Atkins, Erwin L. ... New York, NY
Atkins & Evans ... Los Angeles, CA
Atkins, Frank A., Jr. ... Williamsburg, KY
Atkins, George W., III ... Salem, MA
Atkins, H. Samuel, Jr. ... Thomson, GA
Atkins, Harry M. ... Kittanning, PA
Atkins, Heidi L. ... Eau Claire, WI
Atkins, Hilary P. ... Alexandria, VA
Atkins, Howard B. ... Indianapolis, IN
Atkins, Hugh S. ... Scottsbluff, NE
Atkins, J. Patrick ... Waco, TX
Atkins, Jacqueline T. ... Chicago, IL
Atkins, James A. ... Charleston, SC
Atkins, James H. ... Gastonia, NC
Atkins, James T. ... San Diego, CA
Atkins, Jane S. ... Raleigh, NC
Atkins, Jane S., P.A. ... Cary, NC; Raleigh, NC
Atkins, Jay R. ... River Edge, NJ
Atkins, Jeanne Paquette ... Portland, OR
Atkins, Jerry K. ... Houston, TX
Atkins, Jerry K., & Associates ... Houston, TX
Atkins, Jessica L. ... New York, NY
Atkins, John B. ... Omaha, NE
Atkins, John G. ... Louisville, CO
Atkins, John L. ... Hopkinsville, KY
Atkins, John P. ... Bozeman, MT
Atkins, Jonathan E. ... Los Angeles, CA
Atkins, Joseph B. ... Rome, GA
Atkins, Joseph P., III ... Upper Marlboro, MD
Atkins, Julie A. ... Harlan, KY
Atkins, Julius R. ... Milwaukee, WI
Atkins, Karen E. ... Sarasota, FL
Atkins, Kimberly A. ... Boston, MA
Atkins, Kimberly E. ... Boston, MA
Atkins, Kristine M. ... Boston, MA
Atkins, Kyle C. ... Humboldt, TN
Atkins, L. Scott ... Montgomery, AL
Atkins Law Firm, The ... Thomson, GA
Atkins, Lawrence T. ... Philadelphia, PA
Atkins, Linda White ... Bellevue, WA
Atkins, Linda Y. ... Louisville, KY
Atkins, Lisa J. ... Philadelphia, PA
Atkins, Lisa Karen ... Memphis, TN
Atkins, Loretta L. ... Albuquerque, NM
Atkins, Marion E. ... Inver Grove Heights, MN
Atkins, Mark H. ... Bakersfield, CA
Atkins, Marylin E. ... Detroit, MI
Atkins, Matthew S. ... Birmingham, AL
Atkins, Maureen O. ... Toledo, OH
Atkins, Michael A. ... Seattle, WA
Atkins, Michael B. ... Garden City, NY
Atkins, Michael G. ... Seattle, WA
Atkins, Michael J. ... Ann Arbor, MI
Atkins, Michael J. ... Nashua, NH
Atkins, Michael K. ... Knoxville, TN
Atkins, Michael R. ... Lansing, MI
Atkins, Michael W. ... Springfield, IL
Atkins, Mike ... Odessa, TX
Atkins, Nelson L. ... Los Angeles, CA
Atkins, Norman R. ... Beverly Hills, CA
Atkins & O'Brien LLP ... Scotch Plains, NJ; New York, NY
Atkins, Pamela S. ... Washington, DC
Atkins, Patricia S. ... Los Angeles, CA
Atkins, Paul S. ... Washington, DC
Atkins, Paul S. ... Buffalo, WV
Atkins, Peter Allan ... New York, NY
Atkins, Phyllis Halsey ... Reno, NV
Atkins, R. Blake ... Tulsa, OK
Atkins, Raymond A. ... Washington, DC
Atkins, Raymond M., Jr. ... Towson, MD
Atkins, Regina F. ... Hoffman Estates, IL
Atkins, Richard F. ... Waterbury, CT
Atkins, Riley J. ... Portland, OR
Atkins, Robert A. ... Berkeley, CA
Atkins, Robert A. ... New York, NY
Atkins, Robert E., Jr. ... New York, NY
Atkins, Robert S. ... Chicago, IL
Atkins, Roger B. ... Honolulu, HI
Atkins, Roland J. ... Philadelphia, PA
Atkins, Ronald R. ... New York, NY
Atkins, Ronald W. ... Dallas, TX
Atkins, Ryan B. ... Phoenix, AZ
Atkins, S. Lee ... Saluda, NC
Atkins, Sally H. ... Newark, NJ
Atkins, Sandra G. ... Panama City, FL
Atkins, Sarita T. ... Selma, AL
Atkins, Sean A. ... Washington, DC
Atkins, Stanley J. ... Union City, NJ
Atkins, Stephen Dana ... Vallejo, CA
Atkins, Steven T. ... Spencertown, NY
Atkins, Steven T. ... Clarksville, TN
Atkins & Sussman ... New York, NY
Atkins, Teresa Harris ... Marietta, GA
Atkins, Theresa A. ... Albany, NY
Atkins, Thomas H. ... Louisville, KY
Atkins, Thomas H. ... Lyndhurst, NJ
Atkins, Thomas I. ... Brooklyn, NY
Atkins, Thomas J. ... Tulare, CA
Atkins, Thomas L. ... Chicago, IL
Atkins, Thomas L. ... Lincoln, MA
Atkins, Thomas P. ... Cincinnati, OH
Atkins, Timothy C. ... Berwyn, PA
Atkins, Vickey R. ... Kennesaw, GA; Marietta, GA
Atkins, William P. ... Washington, DC
Atkins, Woodrow W. ... Baton Rouge, LA
Atkinson, Adrienne ... New York, NY
Atkinson, Amanda E. ... Austin, TX
Atkinson, Andelson, Loya, Ruud & Romo, A Professional Corporation ... Cerritos, CA; Los Angeles, CA; Pleasanton, CA; Riverside, CA; Sacramento, CA; San Bernardino, CA; San Diego, CA
Atkinson, Ann J. ... Aurora, CO
Atkinson, Anne S. ... New York, NY
Atkinson & Associates, P.C. ... Conroe, TX
Atkinson & Atkinson ... Chicago, IL; Evanston, IL
Atkinson & Atkinson ... Columbia, MO
Atkinson, Bonnie H ... Hines, IL
Atkinson, Boyd P. ... Cleveland, MS
Atkinson, Brian Thomas ... Charlotte, NC
Atkinson & Burton ... Marietta, OH
Atkinson, C. Ashley ... Mc Comb, MS
Atkinson, Carl W., Jr. ... Troy, NC
Atkinson, Carol Ann ... Jacksonville, FL
Atkinson, Carolyn C. ... Charleston, WV
Atkinson, Charles E. Department of Commerce, Patent and Trademark Office, GV
Atkinson, Charlotte A. ... Columbia, MO
Atkinson, Clifford K. ... Albuquerque, NM
Atkinson, Conway & Gagnon, Inc., A Professional Corporation Anchorage, AK
Atkinson, Dale J. ... Evanston, IL
Atkinson, Daniel R. ... Baton Rouge, LA
Atkinson, Daniel R., Jr. ... Baton Rouge, LA
Atkinson, Darryl E. ... Dallas, TX
Atkinson, David B. ... Stockton, CA
Atkinson, David M. ... Atlanta, GA
Atkinson, David R., Jr. West Palm Beach, FL
Atkinson, David W. ... Denver, CO
Atkinson, Diner, Stone Mankuta & Ploucha, P.A. ... Hollywood, FL
Atkinson, Donald C. ... Santa Clara, CA
Atkinson, Earl H. ... Tucson, AZ
Atkinson, Edward L. ... Perryton, TX
Atkinson, Edward P. ... Boston, MA
Atkinson, Edward S., Jr. San Francisco, CA
Atkinson, Elliott W., Jr. ... Baton Rouge, LA
Atkinson, Eugene T. ... Papillion, NE
Atkinson • Farasyn, L.L.P. Mountain View, CA
Atkinson, Frank B. ... Richmond, VA
Atkinson, Gary R. ... Hartford, CT
Atkinson, George E., III ... Orange, CA
Atkinson, Gervid ... Bloomfield Hills, MI
Atkinson & Gibson, A P.C. ... Whittier, CA
Atkinson, Gilbert ... Austin, TX
Atkinson, Gordon C. ... San Francisco, CA
Atkinson, Gregory T. ... St. Louis, MO
Atkinson, Gwendolyn A. ... Thomasville, GA
Atkinson & Hall ... Dallas, TX
Atkinson, Hamill & Barrowclough, P.C. Phoenix, AZ
Atkinson, Harry E. ... Newport News, VA
Atkinson, Haskins, Nellis, Boudreaux, Holeman, Phipps & Brittingham Oklahoma City, OK; Tulsa, OK
Atkinson, Heather R. ... Woodland Hills, CA
Atkinson, Henry ... Longview, TX
Atkinson, James D., III ... Minneapolis, MN
Atkinson, James P. ... Quincy, MA
Atkinson, James R. ... Holland, OH
Atkinson, Janet E. ... Rockville, MD
Atkinson, J. D. ... Greenup, KY
Atkinson, Jeannie E. ... Santa Ana, CA
Atkinson, Jeff ... Wilmette, IL
Atkinson, Jeffrey E. ... St. Louis, MO
Atkinson, Jerome A. ... New York, NY
Atkinson, Jerry A. ... Evansville, IN
Atkinson, J. F., Jr. ... Fort Smith, AR
Atkinson, John Bond ... Miami, FL
Atkinson, John F. ... Evanston, IL
Atkinson, John H. ... Ann Arbor, MI
Atkinson, John J. ... Denver, CO
Atkinson, John N. ... Sun City Center, FL
Atkinson, Joseph M. ... Phoenix, AZ
Atkinson, Judith R. ... Baton Rouge, LA
Atkinson, June W. ... Santa Monica, CA
Atkinson, Karen L. ... Miami, FL
Atkinson, Kathryn Cameron Washington, DC
Atkinson, Kathy B. ... Alpharetta, GA
Atkinson, Kathy L. ... Anchorage, AK
Atkinson & Kelsey, P.A. Albuquerque, NM; Farmington, NM; Las Cruces, NM; Rio Rancho, NM; Santa Fe, NM
Atkinson, Kenneth R. ... Anchorage, AK
Atkinson, Kirby G. ... Lilburn, GA; Monroe, GA
Atkinson Law Office ... Evansville, IN
Atkinson, Lee Wm. ... Clearwater, FL
Atkinson, Leonard K., Jr. New Haven, CT
Atkinson, Linda M. ... Detroit, MI
Atkinson, Lynn C., (Mr.) ... Lemoore, CA
Atkinson, M. Gary ... Pocatello, ID; Twin Falls, ID
Atkinson, Marilyn R. ... Ann Arbor, MI
Atkinson, Mark A. ... Charleston, WV
Atkinson, Mark T. ... Charlotte, NC
Atkinson, Mark W. ... Los Angeles, CA
Atkinson, M. Gary, P.A. ... Pocatello, ID; Twin Falls, ID
Atkinson, Michael K. ... Washington, DC
Atkinson, Michael L. ... Conroe, TX
Atkinson, Michael P., P.C. ... Tulsa, OK
Atkinson, Myron H., Jr. ... Bismarck, ND
Atkinson, Nancy A. ... Macon, GA
Atkinson, Nolan N., Jr. ... Philadelphia, PA
Atkinson, Paula G. ... Los Angeles, CA
Atkinson, Perry, Atkinson & Balhoff, L.L.C. Baton Rouge, LA
Atkinson, Polly A. ... Denver, CO
Atkinson, Randal B. ... Chicopee, MA
Atkinson, Reilly, IV ... San Francisco, CA
Atkinson, Richard M., II ... Irwindale, CA
Atkinson, Richard W. ... Conway, AR
Atkinson, Rita Brown ... Conway, AR
Atkinson, Robert B. ... Springfield, MA
Atkinson, Robert C. Federal Communications Commission, Common Carrier Bureau, GV
Atkinson, Robert E. ... Whittier, CA
Atkinson, Robert E. ... Minneapolis, MN
Atkinson, Robert L. ... Baton Rouge, LA
Atkinson, Robert L., III ... Baton Rouge, LA
Atkinson, Robert M. ... New York, NY
Atkinson, Robert M. ... Salem, OR
Atkinson, Robert W. ... Gulfport, MS
Atkinson, Ross E. ... Ojai, CA
Atkinson, Russell Dean ... San Jose, CA
Atkinson, S. Earle ... Albany, CA
Atkinson, Sally A. ... Madison, WI
Atkinson, Schalan A. ... Dallas, TX
Atkinson, Scott K. ... Albuquerque, NM
Atkinson, Simone Anne ... Mesa, AZ
Atkinson, Stephen B. ... Binghamton, NY
Atkinson, Stephen L. ... Clarksburg, WV
Atkinson, Stephen M. ... Channing, MI
Atkinson, Steven D. ... Cerritos, CA
Atkinson, Stuart W. ... Newport News, VA
Atkinson & Thal, P.C. ... Albuquerque, NM
Atkinson, Theodore W. ... Washington, DC
Atkinson, Thomas A. ... Eagan, MN
Atkinson, Thomas D. ... Middletown, NJ
Atkinson, Thomas L. ... Utica, NY
Atkinson, Thomas M. ... Tulsa, OK
Atkinson, Thomas R. ... Marietta, OH
Atkinson, Timothy G. ... Denver, CO
Atkinson, Timothy P. ... Tallahassee, FL
Atkinson, Tyrus R., Jr. ... Atlanta, GA
Atkinson, Virginia (Ginger) ... Little Rock, AR
Atkinson, Wade H., Jr. Commodity Futures Trading Commission, Division of Enforcement, GV
Atkinson, William A. ... Columbia, MO
Atkinson, William H. ... Hamilton, AL; Winfield, AL
Atkinson, William M. ... Charlotte, NC
Atkinson, William M., Jr. Panama City, FL
Atkinson, William R. ... Fairfield, CA
Atkinson, William R. ... Atlanta, GA
Atkinson, William T. ... Hamilton, AL; Winfield, AL
Atkinson, William Y., IV ... Woodstock, GA
Atkinson, Wilson C., III ... Hollywood, FL
Atkinson-Loveless, Linnea Johnson Greenport, NY
Atkins-Pattenson, Philip F. San Francisco, CA

Atkisson, John McE.
Department of Transportation,
Surface Transportation Board, GV
Atlas, Alan G. ... Cerritos, CA
Atlas, Alan L. ... San Diego, CA
Atlas, Allan Jay ... Miami, FL
Atlas, Anthony H. ... New York, NY
Atlas, Babette P. ... New York, NY
Atlas, Betty L. ... Mineola, NY
New York, NY
White Plains, NY
Atlas, Clifford R. ... New York, NY
Atlas, Craig M. ... Syracuse, NY
Atlas, David S. ... Chicago, IL
Atlas, David S. ... West Long Branch, NJ
Atlas, David Y. ... New York, NY
Atlas & Hall, L.L.P. ... McAllen, TX
Atlas, Harold S. ... Morristown, NJ
Atlas, Harry I. ... Baltimore, MD
Atlas, Howard J. ... Melville, NY
Atlas, Howard J., P.C., Law Offices of
Melville, NY
Atlas & Hudon ... West Hartford, CT
Atlas, J. Mark ... Willows, CA
Atlas, James ... Indianapolis, IN
Atlas, Jan Douglas ... Fort Lauderdale, FL
Atlas, Jason B. ... Great Neck, NY
Atlas, Jeffrey M. ... New York, NY
Atlas, Joan Gaughan ... Philadelphia, PA
Atlas, Joan L. ... Boston, MA
Atlas, Joel B. ... New York, NY
Atlas, Louis M. ... New York, NY
Atlas & Marantz LLP ... New York, NY
Atlas, Mark ... Fort Lauderdale, FL
Atlas, Martin ... Washington, DC
Atlas, Morris ... McAllen, TX
Atlas, Nancy Friedman ... Houston, TX
Atlas, Neil E. ... West Hartford, CT
Atlas, Pearlman, Trop & Borkson, P.A.
Boca Raton, FL
Fort Lauderdale, FL
Miami, FL
Naples, FL
Atlas, Renee ... Deerfield, IL
Atlas, Richard I. ... Glenview, IL
Atlas, Ruth G., (Mrs.) ... Philadelphia, PA
Atlas, Saml. ... Rochester, NY
Atlas, Scott J. ... Houston, TX
Atlas, Seth J. ... New York, NY
Atlas, Susan A. ... Bedford, MA
Atlas, Vicki S. ... Bethpage, NY
Atlas, Vladimer ... Elmont, NY
Atlas, Warren D. ... Bedford, MA
Atlass, Michael B. ... Minneapolis, MN
Atlass Professional Corporation
Denver, CO
Atlass, Theodore B. ... Denver, CO
Atlee, Elizabeth E. ... Los Angeles, CA
Atlee, Hall & Brookhart, L.L.P.
Carlisle, PA
Gettysburg, PA
Harrisburg, PA
Lancaster, PA
West Chester, PA
York, PA
Atlee, Richard Y. ... Hampton, VA
Atlee, Richard Y., Jr. ... Hampton, VA
Atlee, Steven ... Los Angeles, CA
Atlee, William A., Jr. ... Lancaster, PA
Atlee, William S. ... Tucson, AZ
Atler, Jennifer VanDerbur ... Denver, CO
Atler, Lawrence A. ... Denver, CO
Atleson, James B. ... Amherst, NY
Atleson, Michael W. ... New York, NY
Atmore, Mary J. ... Bloomington, MN
Atmore, Robert V. ... Minneapolis, MN
Atmore, Thomas C. ... St. Paul, MN
Atnally, Edward V. ... New York, NY
Atneosen, Steven T. ... Minneapolis, MN
Atney-Yurdin, Irene P. ... Upton, NY
Atnip, Joseph P. ... Dresden, TN
Atnipp, Douglas C. ... Houston, TX
Aton, Stephen F. ... Springfield, MO
Atonna, Arthur C. ... Phoenix, AZ
Atonna, Arthur C., Ltd. ... Phoenix, AZ
Ator, Jennifer J. ... Miami, FL
Atorthy, Lawrence C.
Farmington Hills, MI
Atria, Nicholas D. ... Columbia, SC
Atriano, Vincent ... Columbus, OH
Atryzek, Suzanne Temple ... Brookline, MA
Atsatt, Cynthia J. ... Minneapolis, MN
Atsaves, Louis G. ... Chicago, IL
Attaguile, Paul ... Armonk, NY
Attai, Robert P. ... Denver, CO
Attal, Charles A., III ... Fairfax, VA
Attala, Edward E. ... Anchorage, AK
San Francisco, CA
Attanasio, Donna M. ... Washington, DC
Attanasio, Edward T. ... Los Angeles, CA
Attanasio, John R. ... Philadelphia, PA
Attanasio, Margaret A. ... Bel Air, MD
Attanasio, Mark L. ... New York, NY
Attanasio, Michael A.
Department of Justice,
Criminal Division, GV
Attanasio, Michael Mel ... Yonkers, NY
Attanasio, Ralph S. ... New York, NY
Attardi, Carolyn Louise ... White Plains, NY
Attardo, Loretta T. ... Salem, MA
Attardo, Pamela J. ... Boston, MA
Attardo, Robert S. ... Rochester, NY
Attarian, Peter J., Jr. ... San Diego, CA
Attas, Sharon ... Fort Lauderdale, FL
Attaway, Charles Lee ... Texarkana, TX
Attaway, Fritz E. ... Washington, DC
Attaway, James A., Jr. ... Quitman, TX
Attaway, James H. ... Los Angeles, CA
Attaway, John A., Jr. ... Lakeland, FL
Attaway, Joseph Paul ... Tempe, AZ
Attaway, Robert J. ... New York, NY
Attaway, Scott K. ... Washington, DC
Baltimore, MD
Attaya, Michael E. ... Boston, MA
Attaya-McCann, Nancy A.S.
Danvers, MA
Attea, Deirdre J. ... Philadelphia, PA
Attea, Frederick G. ... Buffalo, NY
Attea, Frederick G. ... Buffalo, NY
Attea, Paul J. ... Hyannis, MA
Attea, Richard J. ... North Boston, NY
Atteberry, Beverly A. ... Tulsa, OK
Atteberry, Christopher E. ... Kansas City, MO
Atteberry, Robert E. ... Shawnee, KS
Attebery, Jeffery S. ... Santa Maria, CA
Attebery, Rod A. ... Stockton, CA
Attella, Edwin Joseph ... West Boylston, MA
Attenasio, Arthur P. ... Warren, NJ
Attenborough, Bruce W. ... Cincinnati, OH
Attenborough, Roland M.
Los Angeles, CA
Atter, Helen Sofge ... Ponte Vedra Beach, FL
Atter, Michael A. ... Jacksonville, FL
Atterberry, Mark ... Springfield, IL
Atterberry, Michael L. ... Springfield, IL
Atterbury, Alan L. ... Mission Hills, KS
Atterbury, Boudinot P. ... Santa Fe, NM
Atterbury, Goldberger & Richardson, P.A.
West Palm Beach, FL
Atterbury, Jennifer L. ... Kansas City, MO
Atterbury, Joseph R.
West Palm Beach, FL
Atterbury, Kathryn M. ... Oxnard, CA
Atterbury, Lee R. ... Madison, WI
Atterbury, R. Rennie, III ... Peoria, IL
Atterbury & Riley, S.C. ... Madison, WI
Atterbury, S. Ward ... New York, NY
Atterbury, William W., III
Palm Beach, FL
Atterbury, Wm. W., Jr. ... Riviera Beach, FL
Atteridge, Arthur C. ... Salinas, CA
Atterman, Kenneth S. ... San Rafael, CA
Atterman, Kenneth S., A Professional Corporation ... San Francisco, CA
San Rafael, CA
Atterman, Rori N. ... New York, NY
Attermann, Neal H. ... New York, NY
Attermeyer, Dorothy M. ... Chicago, IL
Attey, John W. ... Denver, CO
Attia, Gilles S. ... Sacramento, CA
Attia Law Corporation ... Sacramento, CA
Attiani, John P. ... Norristown, PA
Attiani & Lohr, P.C. ... Norristown, PA
Attias, Amy M. ... Bronx, NY
Attias, Elizabeth Ellen ... Baltimore, MD
Attias, Jack P. ... North Miami, FL
Atticks, John K., III ... Madison, CT
Attie, Maurice J. ... Los Angeles, CA
Attie, Murray S. ... New York, NY
Attili, Frank ... New Hartford, NY
Attilli, Leo P. ... North Providence, RI
Attisani, David A. ... Boston, MA
Attisano, George P. ... New York, NY
Attkiss, Loren Paige ... Chicago, IL
Attkisson, Carolyn S. ... Mill Valley, CA
Attkisson, Eugene D. ... Lexington, KY
Attlesey, Keith A. ... Tustin, CA
Attlesey, Ronit E. ... Irvine, CA
Attmore, Gary G. ... Hartford, CT
Attmore, Robert E. ... Grand Rapids, MI
Attonito, Joseph R. ... Smithtown, NY
Attorneys At Law Smith ... Atlanta, GA
Attorneys for Motorcyclists
Los Angeles, CA
San Francisco, CA
AttorneyVirginia.Com ... Arlington, VA
Fairfax, VA
Leesburg, VA
Manassas, VA
Attorri, Mark D. ... Manchester, NH
Attrep, Gregory M. ... Lafayette, LA
Attridge, Anne Asbill ... Washington, DC
Attridge, Daniel F. ... Washington, DC
Attridge, Ellen Martin ... Columbus, OH
Attridge, J. William ... Olympia, WA
Attridge, James O'Neil
San Francisco, CA
Attridge, Mary Ellen ... San Diego, CA
Attridge, Mary Pavloff ... Dade City, FL
Attridge, Patrick J.
United States District Court For The District
Of Columbia, GV
Attridge, Patrick James ... Rockville, MD
Attridge, R. Byron ... Atlanta, GA
Attridge, Robert W., Jr.
New Port Richey, FL
Attridge, Robert W., Jr., P.A.
New Port Richey, FL
Attruia-Hartwell, Amalia ... San Francisco, CA
Attura, Clare J. ... Greenwich, CT
Attura, Joseph J. ... South Portland, ME
Attwater, William R. ... Sacramento, CA
Attwell, Gwilym J.O. ... Philadelphia, PA
Attwell, J. Evans ... Houston, TX
Attwood, Belinda Dunmire ... Washington, PA
Attwood, Cynthia L. ... Department of Labor,
Office of Secretary, GV
Attwood, Dorothy T.
Federal Communications Commission,
Common Carrier Bureau, GV
Attwood, James A., Jr. ... New York, NY
Attwood, Julia C. ... Salt Lake City, UT
Attwood, Mark R. ... Los Angeles, CA
Atty, Lisa A. ... Los Angeles, CA
Atwal, Manvir K. ... St. Paul, MN
Atwal, Satwant K. ... Seattle, WA
Atwater, Bruce Hall ... Hayward, CA
Atwater, George J. ... Seattle, WA
Atwater, Julian W. ... Rochester, NY
Atwater, Martha Walters
Grand Rapids, MI
Atwater, Michael Edward ... Chester, SC
Columbia, SC
Lancaster, SC
Rock Hill, SC
Atwater, R. Scott ... Buffalo, NY
Atwater, Randolph S. ... Winter Park, CO
Atwater, Randolph S., Attorneys at Law, P.C.
Winter Park, CO
Atwater, Russell H. ... Hamden, CT
Atwater, Schiller & Reeves, L.L.C.
Chester, SC
Columbia, SC
Lancaster, SC
Rock Hill, SC
Atwater, Todd K. ... United States Senate,
Senatorial Assistants, GV
Atwater, Vernon ... Elkhart, IN
Atwater, William Bennett, Jr. ... Siler City, NC
Atwater, William E., III ... Honolulu, HI
Atwell, Anthony ... Dallas, TX
Atwell, Anthony R. ... Irvington, NJ
Atwell, Anthony R., P.A. ... Irvington, NJ
Atwell & Atwell ... Aurora, IL
Atwell, Barbara L. ... White Plains, NY
Atwell, Bruce W. ... Lake Forest, CA
Atwell, Charles E. ... Kansas City, MO
Atwell, Charles H., Jr. ... Aurora, IL
Atwell, Christopher D.
Steamboat Springs, CO
Atwell, D. Cheryl ... Cleveland, OH
Atwell, David ... Ozark, AL
Atwell, Grace Ellen ... Tucson, AZ
Atwell - Hicks, Inc. ... Washington, MI
Atwell, J. Stanley ... Greensboro, NC
Atwell, Jennifer L. ... Dothan, AL
Atwell, Kevin H. ... Fairfield, OH
Atwell, Mary H. ... San Jose, CA
Atwell, Michael N. ... South Lake Tahoe, CA
Atwell, Nelson M. ... San Antonio, TX
Atwell, Ralph H. ... Pensacola, FL
Atwell, Scott J. ... Englewood, CO
Atwell, William E., Jr. ... Stevens Point, WI
Atwill, Daniel K. ... Columbia, MO
Atwill, James H. ... Port Aransas, TX
Atwill, William H., Jr. ... Leesburg, VA
Atwood, A. Rick, Jr. ... Los Angeles, CA
Atwood, Adrienne J. ... Orange, CA
Atwood, B. Jo ... Murfreesboro, TN
Atwood, Barbara A. ... Tucson, AZ
Atwood, Bradford T. ... Hanover, NH
Atwood, Charles F., III ... Miami, FL
Atwood & Cherny ... Boston, MA
Atwood, Daniel C. ... Cincinnati, OH
Atwood, Denise L. ... Phoenix, AZ
Atwood, Elaine S. ... Lawrenceville, NJ
Atwood, Emile ... Stockton, CA
Atwood, F. Eugene, Jr. ... Jacksonville, FL
Atwood, Frederic L. ... Patchogue, NY
Atwood, Hager & Anderson
Bellingham, WA
Atwood, Haiman & Westerberg
Saratoga, CA
Atwood, Hollye Stolz ... St. Louis, MO
Atwood, Jack M. ... Plymouth, MA
Atwood, Jacob M. ... Boston, MA
Atwood, James M. ... Boston, MA
Atwood, James R. ... Washington, DC
Atwood, James W. ... Coeur d'Alene, ID
Atwood, James W. ... Nashville, TN
Atwood, Jeanne M. ... San Francisco, CA
Atwood, John B., III ... Dallas, TX
Atwood, John F. ... Treasury Department,
Office of Regulations and Rulings, GV
Atwood, John R. ... Augusta, ME
Atwood, Kimball S. ... Oakland, CA
Atwood, Malone, Turner & Sabin, A Professional Association
Albuquerque, NM
Roswell, NM
Atwood, Mark W. ... Washington, DC
Atwood, Mary Pat ... Washington, DC
Atwood, Missy K. ... Austin, TX
Atwood & Moore ... Murfreesboro, TN
Atwood, Raymond P., Jr. ... Lincoln, NE
Atwood, R.F. ... Bellingham, WA
Atwood, Richard K. ... Oak Ridge, TN
Atwood, Robert D. ... Logan, UT
Atwood, Ronald W. ... Portland, OR
Atwood, Ronald W., P.C. ... Portland, OR
Atwood, Roy T. ... Dallas, TX
Atwood, S. Maud ... Keene, NH
Atwood, Scott E. ... Atlanta, GA
Atwood, Sherrill A. ... Hilo, HI
Atwood, Stanford H., Jr. ... Saratoga, CA
Atwood, Stanley P. ... Westport, CT
Atwood, Stephen W. ... Lexington, KY
Atwood, Stetson F. ... Chicago, IL
Atwood, Thomas J. ... Richland, WA
Atwood, Thomas K. ... El Cajon, CA
Atwood, William C. ... Eugene, OR
Atz, Douglas J. ... Kendallville, IN
Atz, Thomas E. ... Indianapolis, IN
Atzbach, Geoffrey H. ... Colorado Springs, CO
Atzbach, Ullrich F. ... Englewood, CO
Atzen, Jonathan F. ... Los Angeles, CA
Atzenhoefer, Janet R. ... Columbus, OH
Atzert, Otto A. ... Silver Spring, MD
Au, Alan ... Los Angeles, CA
Au, Beverly ... New York, NY
Au, Derrick M. ... Los Angeles, CA
Au, Elton W.M. ... Honolulu, HI
Au, Kammy Wing-On ... San Francisco, CA
Au, Lance Scott ... Honolulu, HI
Au, Marjorie Chun Yung, (A Law Corporation) ... Honolulu, HI
Au, Paul K. W. ... Honolulu, HI
Au, Richard S. ... Palo Alto, CA
Au, Robyn Ululani ... Honolulu, HI
Au, Ronald G. S. ... Honolulu, HI
Au, Thomas Y. ... Harrisburg, PA
Aubain, Carlos A. ... Hayward, CA
Aube, John R., (Atty. At Law, A Law Corp.)
Honolulu, HI
Aubel, Leo G. ... Chicago, IL
Aubel, Leo J. ... Washington, DC
Auber, Robert P.
Department of Commerce, GV
Auberger, Marcia A. ... Washington, DC
Auberry, Ann ... Milwaukee, WI
Auberry, Evan Kent ... Greensboro, NC
Aubert, Christopher J. ... Covington, LA
New Orleans, LA
Aubert, Garth W. ... Los Angeles, CA
Aubert & Pajares, L.L.C. ... Covington, LA
Metairie, LA
New Orleans, LA
Aubert, Paul D. ... Houston, TX
Aubert, Ronald D. ... Beverly Hills, CA
Aubin, A. Norman ... Cincinnati, OH
Aubin, Kristine ... Chicago, IL
Aubin, Mark J. ... Tampa, FL
Aubin, Richard E. ... Dallas, TX
Aubin, Terry G. ... Pineville, LA
Aubin, Thomas G. ... Fort Lauderdale, FL
Auble, Cathy Abramson ... Denver, CO
Auble, Neil E. ... Boston, MA
Auble, Thomas N. ... Department of the Army,
U.S. Army Court of Criminal Appeals, GV
Aubrey, David J. ... Walters, OK
Aubrey, Donald M. ... Sterling Heights, MI
Aubrey, Joanne E. ... Columbus, OH
Aubrey, Joel W. ... Lexington, KY
Aubrey, John T. ... Manchester, KY
Aubrey, Karen ... Santa Fe, NM
Aubrey, Mitchell ... Detroit, MI
Aubrey, Nile E. ... Tacoma, WA
Aubrey, Sarah K. ... Los Angeles, CA
Aubrey, Steven C. ... Wenatchee, WA
Aubry, Anthony Jerome ... Austin, TX
Aubry, Anthony Jerome ... Irving, TX
Aubry, Donald R. ... Kansas City, MO
Aubry, Geralda M. ... Nashville, TN
Aubry, Jerold E. ... Jacksonville, FL
Aubry, Jude T. ... Toledo, OH
Aubry, Kathleen A. ... Sycamore, OH
Aubry, Lloyd W., Jr. ... San Francisco, CA
Aubry, M. Scott ... Toledo, OH
Aubry, Meyer, Walsh & Pommeranz
Toledo, OH
Aubry, P. Martin ... Perrysburg, OH
Aubuchon, Andre R. ... Fitchburg, MA
Aubuchon, Catherine A. ... Holden, MA
Aubuchon, Daniel C. ... St. Louis, MO
AuBuchon, F. David ... Chicago, IL
Aubuchon, Gregory P. ... St. Louis, MO
Au Buchon, James L. ... Dallas, TX
Aubuchon, Lisa M. ... Phoenix, AZ
Aubuchon, Randolph Y. ... Fitchburg, MA
Aubuchon, Raniere & Lally, P.C.
St. Louis, MO
Aubuchon, Richard T. ... Phoenix, AZ
Auburn, Albert ... Wellesley, MA
Auburn Legal Clinic ... Auburn, CA
Auburn, Stephen T. ... Pittsford, NY
Auburn, Travers T. ... Hartford, CT
Lakeville, CT
West Hartford, CT
Auby, Gregg ... Madison, WI
Auby, Scott N. ... Washington, DC
Aucaigne, Trina A. Solecki ... Middletown, CT
Aucamp, Frederick P. ... Virginia Beach, VA
Aucamp, Stephen J. ... Delray Beach, FL
Aucella, Peter J. ... Lowell, MA
Auch, Stephen E. ... Columbus, OH
Auchard, Paul ... Fresno, CA
Auchard & Stewart, A Professional Corporation ... Fresno, CA
Auchincloss, Andrew S. ... New York, NY
Auchincloss, Edward H. ... New York, NY
Auchincloss, John W. ... Weston, CT
Auchincloss, Louis S. ... New York, NY
Auchincloss, Mary Rogers
West Chester, PA
Auchincloss, Megan Mingey
Washington, DC
Auchincloss, Stuart ... New City, NY
Auchincloss, Thomas M., Jr.
Washington, DC
Auchincloss-Lorr, Katharine A.
Washington, DC
Auchinleck & Dantzig, P.C. ... Newtown, PA
Auchinleck & Dantzig, P.C. ... Perkasie, PA
Auchinleck, James J., Jr. ... Newtown, PA
Perkasie, PA
Auchter, Donald F. ... Glastonbury, CT
Auchter, John R. ... Palmer, MA
Auchter, Paul R. ... Miami, FL
Auchter & Thompson ... Palmer, MA
Auchterlonie, Richard C. ... Houston, TX
Auchterlonie, Thomas S.
Falls Church, VA
Auciello, Dennis Alan ... New Brunswick, NJ
Auciello, Dennis Alan, P.A.
New Brunswick, NJ
Auciello, Ernest W., Jr. ... Cleveland, OH
Auciello, Lucinda Grace ... Pasadena, CA
Auckland, Emily J. ... Phoenix, AZ
Auclair, David B. ... Treasury Department,
Internal Revenue Service, GV
Auclair, Marcella J. ... Department of the Navy,
Office of the Judge Advocate General, GV

Auclair, Robert A. ... Media, PA
Auclair, Suzanne C. ... New York, NY
AuClair-Valdez, Miguel T. ... San Jose, CA
Au Claro, Karen ... Bethpage, NY
Aucoin, Aline L. ... Houston, TX
Aucoin, Barney R. ... Lafayette, LA
Aucoin, Edward J., Jr. ... Waukegan, IL
Aucoin, George C. ... Lakewood, CO
Aucoin, George C., Jr. ... Metairie, LA
New Orleans, LA
Aucoin, Gilbert W. ... Ville Platte, LA
Aucoin, James P. ... Bangor, ME
Aucoin, Jeanne H. ... Los Angeles, CA
Aucoin, Kevin J. ... Providence, RI
Aucoin, Leon A. ... Metairie, LA
Aucoin, Leon A., A Prof. Law Corp., Law Offices of ... Metairie, LA
New Orleans, LA
Aucoin, Lindy Bode ... Greensboro, NC
Aucoin, Paul G. ... Vacherie, LA
Aucoin, Paul M. ... Columbus, OH
Aucoin, Philip S., Jr. ... Lafayette, LA
Aucoin, Preston N. ... Ville Platte, LA
Aucoin, Ralph J. ... Metairie, LA
Aucoin, Samuel R. ... Lafayette, LA
Aucremanne, Joseph F. ... Princeton, WV
Aucremanne, Joseph, Legal Corporation ... Princeton, WV
Aucutt, Ronald D. ... McLean, VA
Aud, Michael E. ... Little Rock, AR
Aude, George Salim ... Miami, FL
Auden, Nichole M. ... Los Angeles, CA
Auderieth, Steven ... New York, NY
Audet, Alphonse J., Jr. ... McLean, VA
Audet, David M. ... Portland, OR
Audet, Gregg M. ... Los Angeles, CA
Audet, Louis A. ... Los Angeles, CA
Audet, Martin H. ... Bloomfield Hills, MI
Audet & O'Reilly ... Los Angeles, CA
Audet, Paul R. ... Stamford, CT
Audet, William M. ... San Jose, CA
Audette, Bazar & Gonzalez, Inc.
East Providence, RI
Providence, RI
Audette, Lucie C. ... Ann Arbor, MI
Audette, Mary Jean ... San Angelo, TX
Audette, Maryann Pretto ... Greenfield, MA
Audette, Robert P. ... Providence, RI
Audette, Rose Marie L. ... Washington, DC
Audick, Mary D. ... Newport Beach, CA
Audie, Lynn L. ... Miami, FL
Audie, Michael F. ... Miami, FL
Audie, Michael F., P.A. ... Miami, FL
Audiffred, James L. ... Saco, ME
Audilet, W. Alexander ... Greensboro, NC
Audilett, Daryl A. ... Tucson, AZ
Audin, Leah L. ... Commerce City, CO
Audino, Joseph F. ... Cherry Hill, NJ
Audino, Richard J. ... New Castle, PA
Audley & Audley ... Berkeley, CA
Audley, David T. B. ... Chicago, IL
Audley, Michael R. ... Berkeley, CA
Audley, R. Richard ... Berkeley, CA
Audley, Sean P. ... Pittsburgh, PA
Audlin, David J., Jr. ... Key West, FL
Audy, Anne M. ... Chicago, IL
Auen, Michael H. ... Madison, WI
Auer, Andrea ... Oakland, CA
Auer, Colleen M. ... Phoenix, AZ
Auer, David B. ... Tulsa, OK
Auer, Douglass B. ... Denver, CO
Auer, George J., Jr. ... White Plains, NY
Auer, Henry E. ... Chicago, IL
Auer, Stephen G. ... Pasadena, CA
Auer, Susan K. ... Juneau, AK
Auerbach, Alan H. ... Chicago, IL
Auerbach, Andrea ... Freehold, NJ
Auerbach, Arthur H. ... Los Angeles, CA
Auerbach & Associates, A Professional Law Corporation ... San Francisco, CA
Auerbach, Barry R. ... Brooklyn, NY
Auerbach, Bernard ... Fairfax, VA
Auerbach, Bethami ... Washington, DC
Auerbach, Boris ... Cincinnati, OH
Auerbach, Carl A. ... Winnetka, IL
Auerbach, Charles S. ... Far Rockaway, NY
Auerbach, David E. ... Media, PA
Auerbach, David L. ... New York, NY
Auerbach, Dennis B. ... Washington, DC
Auerbach, Erich ... Los Angeles, CA
Auerbach, Ernest S. ... San Antonio, TX
Auerbach, Gary L. ... Chicago, IL
Auerbach, Gerald M. ... Department of Justice, United States Marshals Service, GV
Auerbach, Harold B. ... San Francisco, CA
Auerbach, Hillel J. ... Trumbull, CT
Auerbach, Hillel J., P.C. ... Trumbull, CT
Auerbach, Jeffrey I. ... Washington, DC
Auerbach, Jennifer ... Philadelphia, PA
Auerbach, Jonathan ... Philadelphia, PA
Auerbach, Joseph ... Boston, MA
Auerbach, Joseph ... Falls Church, VA
Auerbach, Judith Aaron ... Belmont, MA
Auerbach, Julie A. ... Media, PA
Auerbach, June W.
Department of Housing and Urban Development, Office of General Counsel, GV
Auerbach, Karl ... Santa Cruz, CA
Auerbach, Kenneth ... Uniondale, NY
Auerbach, Kenneth A. ... Patchogue, NY
Auerbach, Kenneth D. ... Washington, DC
Auerbach, Kenneth D. ... Silver Spring, MD
Auerbach, Kenneth D.
Upper Marlboro, MD
Auerbach, Kenneth Reed ... Eatontown, NJ
Auerbach & Kirsch ... New York, NY
Auerbach & Labes ... New York, NY
Auerbach, Lee David ... Hawthorne, NY
Auerbach, Lee L. ... Los Angeles, CA
Auerbach, Leslie S. ... Silver Spring, MD
Auerbach, Madeline Buchanan ... Miami, FL
Auerbach, Marc H. ... Miami, FL
Auerbach, Marshall J. ... Chicago, IL
Auerbach, Marshall J., & Associates, Ltd. ... Chicago, IL
Auerbach, Martin J. ... New York, NY
Auerbach, Melissa J. ... Chicago, IL
Auerbach, Nancy C. ... Coram, NY
Auerbach, Nicole Nehama ... Chicago, IL
Auerbach, Paul ... Merion, PA
Auerbach, Paul A. ... Boston, MA
Auerbach, Paul I. ... Palm Beach Gardens, FL
Auerbach, Philip G. ... Red Bank, NJ
Auerbach, Philip G., A Professional Corporation ... Red Bank, NJ
Auerbach, Philip I. ... Los Angeles, CA
Auerbach & Porter ... Madison, WI
Auerbach, Randy P. ... Washington, DC
Auerbach, Reed D. ... New York, NY
Auerbach, Richard ... New York, NY
Auerbach, Richard A. ... Tucson, AZ
Auerbach, Richard J. ... Madison, WI
Auerbach, Richard M. ... New York, NY
Auerbach, Robert ... Brooklyn, NY
Auerbach, Robert A. ... Coral Springs, FL
Auerbach, Robert A. ... Murray Hill, NJ
Auerbach, Robert A., P.A.
Coral Springs, FL
Auerbach, Ruth Elin ... San Francisco, CA
Auerbach, Sheryl L. ... Philadelphia, PA
Auerbach and Simmons ... Silver Spring, MD
Auerbach, Sue E. ... Treasury Department, Office of the Comptroller of the Currency, GV
Auerbach, Theodore J. ... New York, NY
Auerbach, Valerie T. ... Portland, OR
Auerbach, William ... New York, NY
Auerbacher, John ... New York, NY
Auerbacher, Mark S. ... Miami, FL
Auerbacher, Sharon R. ... Englewood, NJ
Auerbacher, Steven M. ... Boca Raton, FL
Auer de Saram, Jet ... San Francisco, CA
Auerhan, Arnold M. ... Department of Justice, Civil Division, GV
Auerswald, Steven C. ... Department of Justice, Federal Bureau of Investigation, GV
Auerswald, William H., Jr. ... Vail, CO
Aufdenspring, David R. ... Atlanta, GA
Aufdermaur, Jason C. ... Atlanta, GA
Aufderstrasse, David L. ... Evanston, IL
Aufenger, Richard F., III ... Norfolk, VA
Auffant, James R. ... Orlando, FL
Auffant, Jose A. ... Chicago, IL
Auffart, Shentell L. ... Omaha, NE
Auffart, Shentell L., P.C. ... Omaha, NE
Auffenorde, Daco S. ... Huntsville, AL
Auffenorde, Michael E. ... Huntsville, AL
Auffermann, Paul W. ... Waltham, MA
Auffredou, Martin D. ... Glens Falls, NY
Aufhauser, David D. ... Washington, DC
Aufill, Ben B., III ... Dallas, TX
Hillsboro, TX
Aufmann, Arthur W. ... Chicago, IL
Aufmuth, Fox, Weed & LeBlanc, A Professional Corporation ... Palo Alto, CA
Aufmuth, Lawrence A. ... Palo Alto, CA
Aufox, Jerry M. ... Franklin Park, IL
AuFranc, Richard E. ... Port Orford, OR
Aufrecht, David B. ... Chicago, IL
Aufrecht, Michael D. ... Chicago, IL
Aufricht, Jennifer D. ... Dallas, TX
Aufrichtig, Paul S. ... New York, NY
Aufrichtig, Peter D. ... New York, NY
Aufses, Arthur H., III ... New York, NY
Aug, J. Vincent ... Cincinnati, OH
Aug, J. Vincent, Jr. ... Cincinnati, OH
Auge, Craig R. ... Columbus, OH
Auge, Joel L. ... Portland, OR
Augello, Frances C. ... Treasury Department, Office of Thrift Supervision, GV
Augello, Joseph M. ... Wilkes-Barre, PA
Augello, Leonard N. ... Boston, MA
Augello, Pezold & Hirschmann, P.C.
Huntington, NY
Augello, Thomas R. ... Buffalo, NY
Augello, William J. ... Huntington, NY
Augenbaum, Todd H. ... New York, NY
Yorktown Heights, NY
Augenblick, Mark, (P.C.) ... Washington, DC
Augenbraun, David M. ... Philadelphia, PA
Augenbraun, Sara Spielman ... Wilton, CT
Augenstein, Wayne S. ... Westfield, NJ
Augenstern, Frederick D. ... Boston, MA
Auger, Adrien R.
Federal Communications Commission, Common Carrier Bureau, GV
Auger, Barbara D. ... Tallahassee, FL
Auger, Brian A. ... Memphis, TN
Auger, Cheryl ... Southfield, MI
Auger, Denise M. ... Woonsocket, RI
Auger, Diana J. ... Los Altos, CA
Auger, Matthew E. ... New London, CT
Auger, Pierre M. Fisher ... Boston, MA
Augesen, R. C. "Eric" ... Odessa, TX
Aughenbaugh, Donald ... Oregon City, OR
Aughenbaugh, K. Richard ... Akron, OH
Aughtman, Joseph H. Jay
Montgomery, AL
Aughton, Maureen P. ... Naples, FL
Aughtry, C. Dennis ... Columbia, SC
Aughtry, C. Dennis ... Lexington, SC
Aughtry, David D. ... Atlanta, GA
Aughtry, Dewette C. ... Brooklyn, NY
Augsburger, Constance ... Mount Morris, IL
Augsburger, Marcia L. ... Sacramento, CA
Augspurger, Jennifer L. ... Boca Raton, FL
Augspurger, Jennifer L., P.A.
Boca Raton, FL
Augspurger, Karol W. ... Schenectady, NY
Augspurger, Lisa J. ... Orlando, FL
Augspurger, Lynn L. ... Poughkeepsie, NY
Augspurger, Robert B. ... Schenectady, NY
Augspurger, Steven M. ... Des Moines, IA
Augur, Carolyn Elizabeth ... Hartford, CT
Augur, Harrison H. ... Aspen, CO
Augur, Newell A. ... New York, NY
Augur, Wayland B., Jr. ... Torrance, CA
Augusciak, Joseph S. ... Hadlyme, CT
August, Andrew A. ... San Francisco, CA
August, Ann ... San Diego, CA
Santa Monica, CA
August, Brett A. ... Chicago, IL
August, Brian M. ... New York, NY
August, Chas. E. ... Richmond, VA
August, Dave S. ... Milwaukee, WI
August, Diana Lynne ... Santa Cruz, CA
August, Elizabeth A. ... Syracuse, NY
August, Ellen ... New York, NY
August, Gary K. ... Farmington Hills, MI
August, George R. ... Long Beach, CA
August, Gretchen J. ... Minneapolis, MN
August, Herbert M. ... Southfield, MI
August, Howard J. ... New York, NY
August, James E. ... Miamisburg, OH
August, Jerald David
West Palm Beach, FL
August, Joel E., (A Law Corporation)
Wailuku, HI
August, John Michael ... Woodbridge, NJ
August, Jon L. ... Los Angeles, CA
August, Julie A. ... Los Angeles, CA
August, Kenneth S. ... Costa Mesa, CA
August & Kulick ... Avon, CT
August & Kulunas, P.A. ... Palm Beach, FL
West Palm Beach, FL
August & Landay, P.A. ... San Diego, CA
Santa Monica, CA
August, Marshall J. ... Los Angeles, CA
August, Muriel B. ... College Park, GA
August & Pohlig, P.A. ... Coral Gables, FL
Miami, FL
August, Raymond S. ... Pullman, WA
August, Richard Lee ... Los Angeles, CA
August, Robert B. ... Avon, CT
August, Robert E. ... Greenville, SC
August & Simmons ... Cambridge, MA
August, Stephen H. ... Boston, MA
August, Steven J. A. ... Flagstaff, AZ
August, Stuart I. ... Norwood, MA
August, Thomas F. ... Cambridge, MA
August, Thomas R. ... Southfield, MI
August, Victoria Rae ... Towson, MD
Augusta, Lawrence A. ... Sacramento, CA
Auguste, Christopher Stewart
New York, NY
Auguste, Elizabeth Jeanine ... Brooklyn, NY
Auguste, Jean-Robert B. ... Cooper City, FL
Augusti, Mary Jane ... Feeding Hills, MA
Augustidakis, Amy S. ... Houston, TX
Augustin, David R. ... Philadelphia, PA
Augustin, Genevieve E.
Department of Justice, Washington, D.C. District Office, GV
Augustin, Gerianne P. ... New Orleans, LA
Augustin, Margot G. ... New Orleans, LA
Augustin, Pamela S. ... Cherry Hill, NJ
Augustin, Raymond P., Jr. ... Metairie, LA
Augustin, Raymond W. ... Westfield, NJ
Augustine, Algis K. ... Bridgewater, NJ
Augustine, Andrea M. ... Chicago, IL
Augustine, Anthony J., Jr. ... Chicago, IL
Augustine, Cary G. ... Fulton, MO
Augustine, Charles P. ... Waterloo, IA
Augustine, Cynthia H. ... New York, NY
Augustine, David M. ... Pacific Palisades, CA
Augustine, Douglas A. ... San Diego, CA
Augustine, Frederick J. ... Roanoke, VA
Augustine, James K.
Department of Transportation, U. S. Coast Guard, GV
Augustine, Jason M. ... Yardley, PA
Augustine, Jason R. ... Amarillo, TX
Augustine, Jen J. ... Kansas City, KS
Augustine, Jill M. ... Des Moines, IA
Augustine, John C. ... Springfield, MO
Augustine, John C. ... Austin, TX
Augustine, John R., Jr. ... Phoenix, AZ
Augustine, John R., Jr., A Professional Corporation ... Phoenix, AZ
Augustine, Joseph M. ... Buffalo, NY
Augustine, Joseph P. ... New York, NY
Augustine, Leonard J., Jr. ... Palo Alto, CA
Augustine, Lori L. ... Big Rapids, MI
Augustine, Mark E., (P.C.) ... Los Angeles, CA
Augustine, Marla ... Lincoln, NE
Augustine, Mary Jane ... New York, NY
Augustine, Michael R. ... Alhambra, CA
Augustine, Patrick B. ... Alexandria, LA
Augustine, Paul J. ... Boise, ID
Augustine, Peter ... Stony Brook, NY
Augustine, Philip R. ... Maitland, FL
Augustine, Rene I. ... Washington, DC
Augustine, Richard C. ... Santa Ana, CA
Augustine, Robert J. ... Atlanta, GA
Augustine, Rodney A. ... Modesto, CA
Augustine, Sandra J. ... Ocala, FL
Augustine, Scott A. ... Lorain, OH
Augustine, Scott B. ... Bellport, NY
Augustine and Seymour ... Alhambra, CA
Augustine, Sheila M. R. ... Elyria, OH
Augustine, Stacy ... Phoenix, AZ
Augustine & Steuerwald, LLP ... Bellport, NY
Augustine, Susan M. ... Maple Heights, OH
Augustine, Tamara W. ... Hickory, NC
Augustin-Harper, Jewell ... Atlanta, GA
Augustini, Alfred E. ... Los Angeles, CA
Augustini, Hope Hall
Securities and Exchange Commission, Office of the General Counsel, GV
Augustini, Jeff ... Irvine, CA
Augustini, Michael C. ... Washington, DC
Augustini, Rick ... Los Angeles, CA
Newport Beach, CA
Augustini & Wheeler, LLP
Los Angeles, CA
Augustino, Philip A. ... Williamsville, NY
Augustino, Stephanie Jean Smith
Houston, TX
Augustino, Steven A. ... Washington, DC
Augustinos, Theodore P. ... Hartford, CT
Augustinsky, Ronald A. ... Pleasanton, CA
Augusto, Jorge M. ... Harrisburg, PA
Augusto, Maria ... Brooklyn, NY
Augustus, Bruce ... Sun Valley, ID
Augustus, Howard B., Ltd. ... Glenview, IL
Augustus, Nancy ... Albuquerque, NM
Augustus, Sue L. ... Chicago, IL
Augustyn, Ann Sweeney
Department of Energy, Office of Hearings and Appeals, GV
Augustyn, Cynthia L. ... Miami, FL
Augustyn, Frank J. ... Delray Beach, FL
Augustyn, James E. ... Chicago, IL
Augustyn, John M. ... Chicago, IL
Augustyn, Noel J. ...
Administrative Office Of The United States Courts, GV
Augustyn, Thomas P. ... Salem, OR
Augustyn, Timothy J. ... Omaha, NE
Augustynski, Adam J. ... Chicago, IL
Auh, Paul Sein ... Philadelphia, PA
Aukamp, William M. ... Philadelphia, PA
Aukema, Susan E. ... Denver, CO
Aukema, Susan E., P.C. ... Denver, CO
Auker, Jeffrey A. ... Westerville, OH
Aukerman, Bruce D. ... Terre Haute, IN
Aukerman, James V. ... Wakefield, RI
Aukerman, Malcolm H. ... Newport, IN
Aukerman, Russell R. ... Lorain, OH
Aukland, Duncan D. ... Columbus, OH
Aukstik, Dennis J. ... Chicago, IL
Aul, Greta R. ... Lancaster, PA
Aulakh, Urminder S. ... Rockville, MD
Aulbach, Kevie Ann ... Brooklyn, NY
Aulbach, Ronald T. ... Pittsburgh, PA
Aulbert, Donald P. ... Florissant, MO
Auld, Alexei ... New York, NY
Auld, Bruce ... Fort Worth, TX
Auld, Douglas Warren ... Snellville, GA
Auld, Howard S., Jr. ... Allison Park, PA
Auld, James H. ... Ann Arbor, MI
Auld, John H., II ... Allison Park, PA
Auld, Lexa Anne ... Bedford, TX
Auld, Robert M. ... West Coxsackie, NY
Auld & Stephenson, P.C. ... Bedford, TX
Auld, William L. ... Dawsonville, GA
Aulds, Anthony C. ... Thrall, TX
Aulds, Dayle Bebee ... El Campo, TX
Aulds, Jo Ann (Jody) ... Lebanon, TN
Aulenti, Joseph J. ... Stamford, CT
Auler, Ed ... Austin, TX
Auler, Robert I. ... Urbana, IL
Aulet, Jose ... San Juan, PR
Auleta, Vincent Anthony ... Bronx, NY
Auletta, Glenn ... Encino, CA
Auletta, Hedwig Maria ... Buffalo, NY
Auletta, Suzanne Elizabeth ... New York, NY
Aulgur, Robert D. ... Columbia, MO
Aulgur, Robert T., Jr. ... Odessa, DE
Aulgur, William E. ... Eldorado, IL
Aulick, Bruce B. ... Fort Wayne, IN
Aulick, Cecilia ... Coral Gables, FL
Aulick, Dean D., (P.C.) ... Washington, DC
Aulik, Gordon J. ... Pebble Beach, CA
Aulik, Jack ... Sun Prairie, WI
Aulino, Charles M. ... Richmond, VA
Aulisi, Richard T. ... Gloversville, NY
Aull, Roger J., (Law Corporation)
San Gabriel, CA
Aull, Sherman, Worthington, Giorza & Maycock ... Lexington, MO
Aull, William ... Lexington, MO
Aulls, Ernest C., Jr. ... Tavares, FL
Aulls, Morton D. ... Tavares, FL
Aulls, Rice, Croak & Graves ... Tavares, FL
Ault, Charles R. ... Cleveland, OH
Ault, David A. ... Crawfordsville, IN
Ault, David W., (Inc.) ... La Jolla, CA
Ault, Davis & Schonfeld, LLP
San Diego, CA
Santa Ana, CA
Ault, Hugh J. ... Boston, MA
Ault, J. Peter ... Pekin, IL
Ault, James A. ... Lansing, MI
Ault, Jerry E. ... Mansfield, OH
Ault, Kathy ... Oklahoma City, OK
Ault, Kevin W. ... Rushville, IN
Ault, Lynda S. ... Gainesville, FL
Ault, Lynn Baxley ... Birmingham, AL
Ault, Spencer D. ... Leesburg, VA
Ault, Stephen K. ... Boston, MA
Ault, Thomas H. ... San Diego, CA
Ault, Tim Allen ... Toledo, OH
Ault, Wayne T. ... Department of Justice, Environment and Natural Resources Division, GV
Aultman, Charles A. ... Warner Robins, GA
Aultman, Dorrance ... Hattiesburg, MS
Aultman, Dorrance (Dee), Jr.
Gulfport, MS
Aultman, Gretchen L. ... Denver, CO

Aultman, Mark H. ....Columbus, OH
Aultman, Tyner, Ruffin & Yarborough, Ltd., A Professional Law Corporation
New Orleans, LA
Biloxi, MS
Columbia, MS
Gulfport, MS
Hattiesburg, MS
Jackson, MS
Pascagoula, MS
Aulwurm, David S. ....San Francisco, CA
Auman, Eva M. ....Amarillo, TX
Auman, Fred W., III ....Hartsville, SC
Auman, Gary W. ....Dayton, OH
Auman, Robert R. ....Bainbridge, GA
Auman, William D. ....Asheville, NC
Aument, Robert C. ....Oakbrook Terrace, IL
Aumer, John J. ....Los Angeles, CA
Aumer, Robert T. ....Pittsburgh, PA
Aumiller, Robert J. ....Lutherville, MD
Aumoeualogo, Soli S. P. ....Pago Pago, TT
Aun, Andrew A. ....Columbia, SC
Aune, Debra B. ....Owatonna, MN
Aune, Jerilyn K. ....St. Paul, MN
Aune, Richard E., (Inc.) ....Fresno, CA
Aune, Robert E. ....San Francisco, CA
Auner, Thomas Y. ....Springfield, MO
Aungier, Marshall C. ....Albuquerque, NM
Aungier & Wilson, P.C.
Albuquerque, NM
Aungst, Ronald V. ....Valparaiso, IN
Aunon, Jose E. ....Fairfax, VA
Auperin, Donald L. ....Amityville, NY
Auran, John L. ....Phoenix, AZ
Aurand, Aaron L. ....Harrisonville, MO
Aurand, Donna W. ....Fort Collins, CO
Aurand, Mark D. ....Allentown, PA
Aurandt, Thomas A. ....Johnstown, PA
Aurbach, Laurence Jay ....Washington, DC
Aurbach, Phillip S. ....Las Vegas, NV
Aurbach, Robert M. ....Albuquerque, NM
Aure, Kathleen D. ....Oakland, CA
Aurecchione, Barbara A. ....Hackensack, NJ
Aurelius, John E. ....Fort Lauderdale, FL
Aurelius, John E., P.A. ....Fort Lauderdale, FL
Aurelius, William E. ....Cleveland, OH
Aurell, John K. ....Tallahassee, FL
Aurely, Louis, III ....Downingtown, PA
Reading, PA
West Chester, PA
Aurich, Richard W., Jr. ....Houston, TX
Aurichio, Louis J. ....Chicago, IL
Auriemma, A. Gregory
Point Pleasant Beach, NJ
Auriemma, Marianne F.
Hasbrouck Heights, NJ
Aurigema, Robert J. ....New York, NY
Aurigemma, Julia L. ....New Britain, CT
Aurigemma, Mark A. ....Wood Ridge, NJ
Aurilio, Samuel C. ....North Palm Beach, FL
Aurillo, Gerald P. ....Metairie, LA
Aurini, Geoffrey Douglas ....Alexandria, VA
Auritt, Jon J. ....Media, PA
Aurnou, Joel Martin ....White Plains, NY
Auron, Laura M. ....Albert Lea, MN
Auryansen, Adrienne J. ....Jamaica, NY
Aurzada, Keith M. ....Dallas, TX
Aus, Brian M. ....Durham, NC
Ausbeck, Paul J. ....Birmingham, AL
Ausberger, James M. ....Phoenix, AZ
Ausbrook, Perry C. ....Washington, DC
Ausby, Kendra Young ....Baltimore, MD
Ausdemore, John K. ....Phoenix, AZ
Ausdemore, Michelle S. ....Phoenix, AZ
Ausemus, Stanley R. ....Emporia, KS
Ausenhus, Robert A. ....Loveland, CO
Ausenhus, Scott L. ....Denver, CO
Auser, Wallace Van C., III ....Fulton, NY
Ausherman, Larry P. ....Albuquerque, NM
Ausherman, Vernon K.
Grosse Pointe Park, MI
Ausili, James T. ....North Babylon, NY
Ausili, Peter J. ....Hauppauge, NY
Ausilio & Ausilio, P.C. ....Warren, MI
Ausilio, Dean J. ....Warren, MI
Ausilio, Scott K. ....Warren, MI
Auskern, Barry ....Franklin, MA
Auslander, Charles E., III ....Athens, GA
Auslander, Dana ....New York, NY
Auslander, David S. ....Miami, FL
Auslander, Jay Stuart ....New York, NY
Auslander, M. Arthur ....New York, NY
Auslander, Mervin Y. ....Owings Mills, MD
Auslander, Merwin B. ....Chicago, IL
Auslander, Mitchell J. ....New York, NY
Auslander, Rochelle J. ....Fishkill, NY
Auslander, Rose ....New York, NY
Auslander, Sam S. ....Collingdale, PA
Auslander, Sheila E. ....Chicago, IL
Auslander & Thomas ....New York, NY
Ausley & Algert, L.L.P. ....Austin, TX
Ausley, DuBose ....Tallahassee, FL
Ausley, Margaret B. ....Tallahassee, FL
Ausley & McMullen, P.A.
Crawfordville, FL
Monticello, FL
Quincy, FL
Tallahassee, FL
Thomasville, GA
Ausley, Thomas L. ....Austin, TX
Ausley-Flores, Kelly ....Austin, TX
Ausman, Kenny Joe ....Bessemer, AL
Ausman, Keyes & Keyes ....Bessemer, AL
Ausman, Susan W. ....Chicago, IL
Ausmus, Ausmus & Beck ....Centralia, MO
Ausmus, James T. ....Centralia, MO
Ausmus, Joseph A. ....Denver, CO
Ausmus, Mark D. ....Jefferson City, MO
Ausnehmer, John E. ....Boardman, OH
Ausnehmer, Morley, Durkin, Bouffard, Vaughn, Fire & DeLaurentis ....Boardman, OH
Ausness, Richard C. ....Lexington, KY
Auspitz, Charles ....Philadelphia, PA
Auspitz, Jack C. ....New York, NY
Auspitz, James B. ....Beverly Hills, CA
Ausprunk, Karen S. ....Cleveland, OH
Ausrotas, Raymond P. ....Washington, DC
Ausschnitt, Perry ....New York, NY
Aussem, James S. ....Cleveland, OH
Aussenberg, Elyse ....Alpharetta, GA
Aussenberg, Martin H. ....Memphis, TN
Aussenberg, Martin H., P.C. ....Memphis, TN
Aussprung, H. Leon, III ....Wilmington, DE
Aust, Judy Farrington ....Atlanta, GA
Aust, Myron R. ....Pulaski, VA
Aust, Reynold ....New York, NY
Aust, Thomas W. ....New York, NY
Austad, H. Daniel ....Silverdale, WA
Austad, H. Daniel, Inc. P.S. ....Silverdale, WA
Austad, Jana ....Bemidji, MN
Austen, David Craig ....New York, NY
Austen, James H. ....Logansport, IN
Austen, Jon L. ....Charleston, SC
Austen, Karl R. ....Los Angeles, CA
Austenfeld, Frank L. ....Overland Park, KS
Austenfeld, Terri Z. ....Overland Park, KS
Austensen, P. Bruce ....Reisterstown, MD
Auster, Gail I. ....White Plains, NY
Auster, Jay S. ....Ozone Park, NY
Auster, Julie ....Hollis, NY
Auster, Morris Moses ....Albany, NY
Auster, Scott Y. ....New York, NY
Auster, Walter ....New Rochelle, NY
Austerman, Gary M. ....Wichita, KS
Austermann, Richard O. ....Denver, CO
Austermiller, J. Douglas ....Atlanta, IL
Austermiller, Steven M. ....Chicago, IL
Austermuhl, Charles B. ....Woodbury, NJ
Austern, David T. ....Fairfax, VA
Austern, S. Ezra ....Brooklyn, NY
Austero, Wayne J. ....Newport Beach, CA
Austgen, David M. ....Crown Point, IN
Austgen, Peter J. ....Indianapolis, IN
Austgen, Priscilla Howell ....Carmel, IN
Austgen, Reed & Decker, P.C.
Crown Point, IN
Austgen, Terence M. ....Munster, IN
Austiin, Lewis & Rogers, P.S Professional Association ....Columbia, SC
Austill, Austill & Austill ....Mobile, AL
Austill, Evan ....Mobile, AL
Austill, Evan, Jr. ....Mobile, AL
Austill, Jere, Jr. ....Mobile, AL
Austill, William A. ....Birmingham, AL
Austin & Abrams, A Professional Association
Minneapolis, MN
Austin, Alan K. ....Palo Alto, CA
Austin, Alan L. ....Watertown, SD
Austin, Albert J. ....El Cajon, CA
Austin, Alexandra C. ....Dania, FL
Austin, Amy E. C. ....Hampstead, MD
Austin, Amy Leigh ....Beckley, WV
Austin, Andrea Rae ....Sacramento, CA
Austin, Andrew William ....Austin, TX
Austin, Ariane D. ....New York, NY
Austin, Arlene F. ....Naples, FL
Austin, Arthur D., II ....Cleveland, OH
Austin & Austin ....El Cajon, CA
Austin, Boland, Connor & Giorgi
Reading, PA
Austin, Bonnie ....Austin, TX
Austin, Bonnie J. ....Washington, DC
Austin, Bradford L. ....Des Moines, IA
Austin, Brenda Horn ....Fayetteville, AR
Austin, Brent A. ....Edmond, OK
Austin, Brent R. ....Chicago, IL
Austin, Brock J. ....Eden Prairie, MN
Austin, Brooke Davis
Fort Lauderdale, FL
Austin, Bruce D. ....St. Petersburg, FL
Tampa, FL
Austin, Bruce P. ....San Diego, CA
Austin, C. Glenn ....Elizabeth City, NC
Austin, C. Stanley ....Wheaton, IL
Austin, C.W., Jr., P.C. ....Richmond, VA
Austin, Caroline M. ....Philadelphia, PA
Austin, Carolyn ....Garden City, NY
Austin, Cathy Kiselyak ....Chicago, IL
Austin, C. E. ....Bellevue, WA
Austin, Charles W. ....Houston, TX
Austin, Cheryl L. ....Columbus, OH
Austin, Christina A. ....Grand Forks, ND
Austin, Christopher B. ....Milwaukee, WI
Austin, Christopher E. ....New York, NY
Austin, Christopher J. ....Bangor, ME
Austin, Christopher J. ....Boston, MA
Austin, Craig L. ....San Antonio, TX
Austin, C.W., Jr. ....Richmond, VA
Austin, Cynthia B. ....Jacksonville, FL
Austin, Dale ....Oceanside, CA
Austin, Daniel A. ....Meadville, PA
Austin, Daniel W. ....Taylorville, IL
Austin, David Kelley ....Gilford, NH
Austin, David M. ....Bangor, ME
Austin, David T. ....Burlington, VT
Austin, David W. ....Rumford, ME
Austin, Dawn Ide ....Medfield, MA
Austin, DeArmon, Merryman & Hanzel
Mooresville, NC
Austin, Deborah B. ....Bayonne, NJ
Austin, Deborah P. ....Atlanta, GA
Austin, Deidra L. ....Santa Cruz, CA
Austin, Dolores L. ....Kingston, WA
Austin, Donald E. ....South New Berlin, NY
Austin, Donald F., II ....Santa Barbara, CA
Austin, Douglas J. ....Lansing, MI
Austin, Douglas R. ....Port Huron, MI
Austin, Douglas R. ....Superior, MT
Austin, Douglas V. ....Toledo, OH
Austin, Dwight E. ....Watertown, NY
Austin, Earl B. ....Dallas, TX
Austin, Eddie D., Jr. ....Lake Charles, LA
Austin, Edw. J. ....Stoneham, MA
Austin, Edward Scott ....Roanoke, VA
Austin, Elizabeth A. ....Bethesda, MD
Austin, Elizabeth J. ....Bridgeport, CT
Hartford, CT
New Haven, CT
Stamford, CT
Austin, Erika L. ....Philadelphia, PA
Austin, Eugene H. ....Hackensack, NJ
Austin, Eunice Park ....Roanoke, VA
Austin, G. Mitchell ....Baltimore, MD
Austin, G. William ....Atlanta, GA
Austin, Garrett E. ....New York, NY
Austin, Gary L. ....Indianola, MS
Austin, Gary S. ....Fresno, CA
Austin, Gerald Steven ....Rockville, MD
Austin, Greg ....Portland, OR
Austin, H. Gregory ....Denver, CO
Austin, Hadley W. ....Madison, CT
Austin, Harold L. ....Atlanta, GA
Austin, Hayden D. ....Rancho Mirage, CA
Austin, Heather Aley ....Columbus, OH
Austin & Henry ....Pittsburgh, PA
Austin, Herman R. ....Decatur, GA
Austin, Hinderaker, Hopper, Strait & Bratland, LLP ....Watertown, SD
Austin, Howard B. ....Oklahoma City, OK
Austin, J. Brent ....Lexington, KY
Austin, J. Douglas ....Pittsburgh, PA
Austin, J. Douglas ....Watertown, SD
Austin, J. Rudy ....Roanoke, VA
Austin, Jack F. ....Long Beach, CA
Austin, Jacqueline G. ....Greenville, SC
Austin, James E. ....Berkeley, CA
Mountain View, CA
Austin, James K. ....Savannah, GA
Austin, James L., Jr. ....Seattle, WA
Austin, James R. ....Baton Rouge, LA
Austin, James R. ....Dexter, ME
Austin, James R. ....Northville, MI
Austin, James R., Jr. ....Des Moines, IA
Austin, James W., III ....Leucadia, CA
Austin, Jason S. ....Houston, TX
Austin, Jeannette L. ....Alexandria, VA
Austin, Jeffrey B. ....Florence, AL
Austin, Jeffrey D., P.C. ....Portland, OR
Austin, Jeffrey L. ....Columbus, OH
Austin, Jeffrey M. ....Wilmington, DE
Austin, Jeffrey S. ....Kansas City, MO
Austin, Jennifer J. ....Los Angeles, CA
Austin, Jesse H., III ....Atlanta, GA
Austin, Jim J. ....Wewahitchka, FL
Austin, Joann Clark ....South China, ME
Austin, Joe E., Jr. ....Raleigh, NC
Austin, John ....Lake George, NY
Austin, John B. ....Atlanta, GA
Austin, John D., Jr. ....Washington, DC
Rockville, MD
Austin, John L., III ....Seattle, WA
Austin, John, Law Office of
Washington, DC
Rockville, MD
Austin, John P. ....San Francisco, CA
Austin, John R. ....Milwaukee, WI
Austin, John Ronald ....De Kalb, IL
Austin, John Scott ....Raleigh, NC
Austin, John V. ....Washington, DC
Austin, John W. ....Knoxville, TN
Austin, Jones & Morken ....Indianapolis, IN
Austin, Joyce Phillips, (Mrs.)
New York, NY
Austin, Judd A., Jr. ....Dallas, TX
Austin, Julie A. ....Fairfax, VA
Austin, Karen S. ....Dallas, TX
Austin, Katherine Ann ....Nashville, TN
Austin, Kathleen Ann ....Duncanville, TX
Austin, Kathryn Barr ....Oklahoma City, OK
Austin, Keith C. ....Gainesville, FL
Austin, Keith C., Jr. (P.A.)
Palm Beach, FL
Vero Beach, FL
Austin, Kevin C. ....Kirkland, WA
Austin, Kevin L. ....Springfield, MO
Austin, Kyle D. ....Newland, NC
Austin, L. Scott ....Dallas, TX
Austin, L. Thomas ....Dunlap, TN
Austin, Lanae R. ....Anchorage, AK
Austin, Lane O. ....Princeton, WV
Austin, Larry D. ....Memphis, TN
Austin, Larry J. ....Overland Park, KS
Austin, Larry J. ....Alexandria, VA
Austin, Larry L. ....Hattiesburg, MS
Austin, Laura E. ....Marietta, GA
Austin, Lauren ....Marietta, GA
Austin, Lauren A. ....Ithaca, NY
Austin, Lauren S. ....Jacksonville, FL
Austin Law Firm, P.A. ....Hernando, MS
Southaven, MS
Austin Law Firm, The ....Cornelius, NC
Austin Law Offices ....South China, ME
Austin, Lawrence B. ....Jackson, MS
Austin, Leonard B. ....Huntington Station, NY
Austin, Leonard B., P.C.
Huntington Station, NY
Austin, Leroy B. ....Los Angeles, CA
Austin, Ley, Roe & Patsko, P.A.
St. Petersburg, FL
Tampa, FL
Austin, Linda L.T. ....Memphis, TN
Austin, Lynne B. ....Rockford, IL
Austin, Margaret C. ....Chicago, IL
Austin, Mary K. ....Pittsburgh, PA
Austin, Maryland L. ....Corydon, IN
Austin, Maureen T. ....Los Angeles, CA
Austin, Michael ....Mc Comb, MS
Austin, Michael A. ....Hingham, MA
Austin, Michael D. ....Anderson, IN
Austin, Michelle ....Fort Lauderdale, FL
Austin, Mitzi Cockrell ....Gainesville, FL
Austin, Nedra E. ....Los Angeles, CA
Austin, Neil D. ....West Chester, PA
Austin, Nicholas A. ....Cincinnati, OH
Austin, Norman F. ....Oklahoma City, OK
Austin, Ormand R. ....Madison, VA
Austin, Page I. ....Washington, DC
Austin, Patricia Jane ....Hartford, CT
New York, NY
Austin, Paul Thomas ....Marion, IL
Austin, Peirce & Smith, P.C. ....Aspen, CO
Austin, Penny Lee ....Medford, OR
Austin & Pepperman ....Leesburg, FL
Austin, Peter J. ....Flushing, NY
Austin, Philip B. ....Louisville, KY
Austin, Philip H. ....Olympia, WA
Austin, Phillip A. ....Phoenix, AZ
Austin, R. Faye ....San Francisco, CA
Austin, R. Wayne ....Abingdon, VA
Austin, Ralph W. ....Kennebunk, ME
Austin, Randolph G. ....Olathe, KS
Austin, Randy T. ....Salt Lake City, UT
Austin, Raymond D. ....Window Rock, AZ
Austin, Rebecca S. ....Detroit, MI
Austin, Regina ....Philadelphia, PA
Austin, Richard ....Christiansted, St. Croix, VI
Austin, Richard B. ....Miami, FL
Austin, Richard D. ....Windsor, CT
Austin, Richard K. ....Boulder, CO
Austin, Richard L. ....Flint, MI
Austin & Richard Law Firm
Lake Charles, LA
Austin, Richard William ....Chicago, IL
Austin, Robert ....Plant City, FL
Austin, Robert B. ....Chicago, IL
Austin, Robert D., Jr. ....West Newton, PA
Austin, Robert E. ....Oneonta, AL
Austin, Robert E., Jr. ....Leesburg, FL
Austin, Robert G. ....Long Beach, CA
Austin, Robert L. ....Birmingham, AL
Austin, Robert L. ....Santa Ana, CA
Austin, Robert L. ....Anderson, IN
Austin, Robert M., P.A. ....Plant City, FL
Austin, Roger Q., III ....Jacksonville, FL
Austin, Ronald D. ....Aspen, CO
Austin, Ronald R. ....Washington, DC
Austin, Ronald R. ....Jacksonville, FL
Austin, Ronald Ray ....Jacksonville, FL
Austin, Ross Edwin ....Wilmington, DE
Austin, Roy L., Jr. ....Department of Justice, Civil Rights Division, GV
Austin, Russell A. ....Seattle, WA
Austin, Russell D. ....Andrews, TX
Austin, Russell J. ....Sacramento, CA
Austin, Russell P. ....Columbus, OH
Austin, Russell P. ....Houston, TX
Austin, Sally ....Atlanta, GA
Austin, Sara A. ....York, PA
Austin, Scott L. ....Philadelphia, PA
Austin, Scott R. ....Fort Lauderdale, FL
Austin, Shelley W. ....Austin, TX
Austin, Simpson & Walker, PLLC
Memphis, TN
Austin & Sparks, P.C. ....Atlanta, GA
Austin, Spencer E. ....Salt Lake City, UT
Austin, Stanley D. ....Bend, OR
Austin, Stephanie Kay ....Newark, NJ
Austin, Stephen B. ....Bakersfield, CA
Austin, Stephen G. ....New York, NY
Austin, Steve A. ....Hickory, NC
Austin, Steven G. ....Denver, CO
Austin, Steven K. ....Pittsburg, CA
Austin, Stewart G., Jr. ....Memphis, TN
Austin, Stuart Keith ....Hempstead, NY
Austin, Susan A. ....San Francisco, CA
Austin, Susan B. ....Baltimore, MD
Austin, Susan C. ....Dallas, TX
Austin, T. Edward, Jr. ....Jacksonville, FL
Austin, Terri D. ....Parsippany, NJ
Austin, Thaddeus S. ....St. Paul, MN
Austin, Thomas A. ....Kingston, TN
Austin, Thomas C., Jr. ....East Hartford, CT
Austin, Thomas E., Jr. ....Atlanta, GA
Austin, Thomas K. ....Raleigh, NC
Austin, Thomas N. ....Indianapolis, IN
Austin, Thomas P. ....Greenwood, SC
Austin, Tim O. ....San Antonio, TX
Austin, Timothy ....Houston, TX
Austin, Timothy Edward ....Albany, NY
Austin, Timothy L. ....Bellevue, WA
Austin, Tracy Lynne ....New York, NY
Austin, Troy A. ....Fort Worth, TX
Austin, V. Leon ....Austin, TX
Austin, Victor J. ....Las Vegas, NV
Austin, Virginia M. ....Avondale Estates, GA
Austin, Wanyong Lai ....Brooklyn, NY
Austin, Warren G. ....Omaha, NE
Austin, Wayne R. ....Madison, WI
Austin, Wesley L. ....Salt Lake City, UT
Austin, William C. ....Evanston, IL
Austin, William F. ....Lincoln, NE
Austin, William F. ....Columbia, SC
Austin, William H., Jr. ....Hernando, MS
Southaven, MS
Austin, William Joseph, Jr.
New Bern, NC
Austin, William O. ....Cornelius, NC
Mooresville, NC
Austin, William W. ....Effingham, IL
Austinson, Oliver E. ....Ada, MN
Austinson & Remark ....Fertile, MN
Austin-Weeks, Douglas F. ....Austin, TX

Auston, Kirk D. ....Oklahoma City, OK
Austria, Anthony G., Jr. ....Newburgh, NY
Austria, Duane A. ....Lincoln, NE
Austria, Robert L. ....Akron, OH
Austrian, Mark L. ....Washington, DC
Austrian, Sarah G. ....Basking Ridge, NJ
Austrich, Jaime ....Tampa, FL
Ausubel, Marvin V. ....New York, NY
Ausum, James C. ....Seattle, WA
Auten, Anne C. ....Chicago, IL
Auten, Anthony R. ....Columbus, OH
Auten, David C. ....Philadelphia, PA
Auten, Donald R. ....Philadelphia, PA
Auten, Hanford L., III ....Claremont, NH
Auten, Stephen R. ....Chicago, IL
Auten, William L. ....Charlotte, NC
Autenreith, E. Earl ....Beaver, PA
Auth, Dorothy R. ....New York, NY
Auth, John C. ....Chicopee, MA
Auth, Nancy C. ....Portsmouth, VA
Auth, Robert C. ....Anchorage, AK
Auth, Rosemary L. ....Philadelphia, PA
Auth, Thomas J. ....Old Tappan, NJ
Auth, Thomas L., Jr. ....Southfield, MI
Authement, Douglas J. ....Houma, LA
Authement & Larke ....Houma, LA
Authement, Louis G. ....New Orleans, LA
Auther, David C. ....Phoenix, AZ
Auther, William F. ....Phoenix, AZ
Authur, Hurst P. ....Redwood City, CA
Autieri, Katherine ....Philadelphia, PA
Autieri, Robert C. ....North Andover, MA
Autieri, Steven M. ....Greene, RI
Autio, Michael A. ....Vancouver, WA
Autio, Randy M. ....Albuquerque, NM
Autio, William A. ....Silver Springs, FL
Autman & Bredt, P.A. ....Wilmington, DE
Philadelphia, PA
Autman, W. Lee, Jr. ....Wilmington, DE
Auton, Betty S. N. ....San Bernardino, CA
Auton, Linda M.E., Law Office of
Rockland, MA
Auton, Sean D. ....Chicago, IL
Auton, William G. ....Waltham, MA
Autor, Deborah M. ....Department of Justice, Civil Division, GV
Autorino, Ralph J. ....Union, NJ
Autovino, Benjamin ....Brooklyn, NY
Autrey, Autrey & Stewart ....Texarkana, AR
Texarkana, TX
Autrey, D. Kent ....Manchester, NH
Autrey, D. Robert, Jr. ....Marietta, GA
Autrey, D. Robert, Jr., P.C. ....Marietta, GA
Autrey, Evert A. ....New Braunfels, TX
Autrey, Garland E. (Gene) ....Chicago, IL
Autrey, Henry Edward ....St. Louis, MO
Autrey, James K. ....Hermosa Beach, CA
Autrey, Jeff W. ....Austin, TX
Autrey, LeRoy ....Texarkana, AR
Autrey, LeRoy Wren ....Texarkana, AR
Autry, Cecil J. ....Bloomington, IL
Autry, Charles T. ....Atlanta, GA
Autry, David R. ....Atlanta, GA
Autry, Edward T. ....Memphis, TN
Autry & Horton, LLP ....Atlanta, GA
Tucker, GA
Autry, James E. ....Fairfax, VA
Autry, Mary Gustaitis ....Memphis, TN
Autry, Patrick H. ....San Antonio, TX
Autry, Richard R. ....Des Moines, IA
Autry, Stephanie Hutchins ....Raleigh, NC
Autry, Stephen S. ....Coleman, TX
Autry, Thomas A. ....Austin, TX
Autry, Tina L. ....Richmond, VA
Auty, Jon J. ....Hackensack, NJ
Auvil, Gene H. ....Brooksville, FL
Auvil, Gene H., P.A., Law Offices of
Brooksville, FL
Auvil, Jonathan L. ....Dade City, FL
Auvil, Steven M. ....Cleveland, OH
Auvil, Walt ....Parkersburg, WV
Auw, Pierre E. ....Long Beach, CA
Auwarter, Ellen C. ....New York, NY
Auwarter, Franklin P. ....Chicago, IL
Auwarter, Neil F. ....San Diego, CA
Auwbrey, Robert G. ....Novato, CA
Auwers, Linda S. ....Houston, TX
Auwers, Thomas N. ....Chicago, IL
Auwood, James W. ....North Franklin, CT
Auxier, Darrell M. ....Madison, IN
Auxier, James E. ....Portland, OR
Auxier, Jeffrey S. ....Edwards, CO
Auyang, Heather F. ....Chicago, IL
Auyang, Hunter L. ....Palo Alto, CA
Auyeung, Al ....Lake Oswego, OR
Auyeung, Yvette ....New York, NY
Au Young, Gary W.K. ....Honolulu, HI
Auz, Lori Paleschic ....Fort Lauderdale, FL
Avadenka, Edward ....Bloomfield Hills, MI
Avakian, Joyce A. ....Belmont, MA
Avakian, Michael E. ....Washington, DC
North Springfield, VA
Avakoff, Joseph C. ....San Jose, CA
Avalli, Charles J. ....Pittsburgh, PA
Avallon, Joanne M. ....Beverly, MA
Avallone, Ada Manzano ....Miami, FL
Avallone, Albert J. ....New York, NY
Avallone, Anthony F. ....Las Cruces, NM
Avallone, Anthony V. ....Milford, CT
Avallone, Lawrence J. ....Media, PA
Avallone, Lawrence J. ....Philadelphia, PA
Avallone, Louis R. ....Shreveport, LA
Avallone, Mario ....Bronx, NY
Avallone, Martin D. ....Somers, NY
Avallone, Robert J. ....Melville, NY
Avallone, Vincent N. ....Newark, NJ
Avalos, Claudia ....Houston, TX
Avalos, Helen Elaine ....Cottonwood, AZ
Avalos, Patrick K. ....Pueblo, CO
Avans, George L. ....Rancho Mirage, CA
Avansino, Melarkey, Knobel, McMullen & Mulligan ....Reno, NV
Avansino, Raymond C., Jr. ....Reno, NV
Avant, Andrew J. ....Austin, TX
Avant, Anjel K. ....Richardson, TX
Avant, Clarke C. ....Sandersville, GA
Avant, Daniel L. ....Baton Rouge, LA
Avant & Falcon, A Law Corporation
Baton Rouge, LA
Avant, Grady, Jr. ....Grosse Pointe, MI
Avant, Jim F. ....Houston, TX
Avant, John L. ....Baton Rouge, LA
Avant, Yolanda Lanell ....Washington, DC
Avanzado, Melvin N.A. ....Los Angeles, CA
Avanzato, Joseph ....Boston, MA
Providence, RI
Avanzino, Richard H. ....San Francisco, CA
Avard-Hicks, Carol ....Cape Coral, FL
Avayou, Jacques ....New York, NY
Avazian, Arthur ....Los Angeles, CA
Avazian & Avazian ....Los Angeles, CA
Avazian, Eric ....Los Angeles, CA
Avchen, Barney B. ....Hialeah, FL
Avchen, Barney B., P.A. ....Hialeah, FL
Avchen, Patricia A. ....San Diego, CA
Avchen, Terry D. ....Los Angeles, CA
Avdi, Zion ....Denver, CO
Ave, Gregory R. ....Dallas, TX
Ave, Paul E. ....Dallas, TX
Avedisian & Avedisian ....Paducah, KY
Avedisian, Craig ....New York, NY
Avedisian, Haig ....Birmingham, MI
Avedisian, James R. ....Sunnyvale, CA
Avedisian, Michael ....Paducah, KY
Avedissian, Azita ....Glendale, CA
Avedissian, David A. ....Westmont, NJ
Avedissian, Lucy ....Los Angeles, CA
Avedovech, Myer ....Bend, OR
Aveis, Mark ....Los Angeles, CA
Avellan, Liliana ....Miami, FL
Avellaneda, M. Carolina ....Boston, MA
Avellar, Michael J. ....San Antonio, TX
Avellino, John T. ....Greenwich, CT
New York, NY
Avellino, Victor T. ....St. Louis, MO
Avellone, Harvey C. ....St. Louis, MO
Avellone, Richard, P.C. ....St. Louis, MO
Avellone, Richard S. ....St. Louis, MO
Avellone, Ross D. ....Madison, OH
Aven, James S. ....Brockton, MA
Aven, Jonathan M. ....Chicago, IL
Aven, Mauri L. ....Pittsburgh, PA
Avena, Friedman and Klamo, P.A.
Camden, NJ
Avena, Robert A. ....Pawcatuck, CT
Avena, Salvatore J. ....Camden, NJ
Avendaño, Ana L.
National Labor Relations Board, Office of the General Counsel, GV
Aveni, Anthony J. ....Painesville, OH
Aveni, Carl A., II ....Columbus, OH
Aveni, David J. ....Washington, DC
Aveni, Frank ....Cleveland, OH
Aveni, James V. ....Cleveland, OH
Aveni, Jeffrey A. ....Leominster, MA
Avenia, John J. ....Albany, NY
Avent, Jon Paul I. ....Fresno, CA
Avent, Judith A. ....Buffalo, NY
Avent, Roger D. ....Buffalo, NY
Avent, Sydney M. ....Philadelphia, PA
Avent, Thomas W., Jr. (IBA) ....New York, NY
Aventuro, Christopher J.
White Plains, NY
Aver, Raymond H. ....Los Angeles, CA
Avera, Anne Hendrix ....Tallahassee, FL
Avera & Avera, P.A. ....Gainesville, FL
Avera, Fred E. ....Fremont, CA
Avera, Lance F. ....Gainesville, FL
Avera, Mark A. ....Gainesville, FL
Avera, Stephen R. ....Thomasville, GA
Avera, Troy G., Jr. ....Miami, FL
Avera, William N. ....Gainesville, FL
Averbach, Andrew P. ....New York, NY
Averbach, Gertrude M. ....Belmont, MA
Averbach, Howard S. ....Pittsburgh, PA
Averbach, Lori ....Davie, FL
Averbach, Zane S., (A Professional Corporation) ....Los Angeles, CA
Averback, Jonathan ....Boston, MA
Averbeck, Charles W. ....Fond du Lac, WI
Averbeck & Hammer, S.C.
Fond du Lac, WI
Averbeck, Linda R. ....Cincinnati, OH
Averbook, Charles J. ....Boca Raton, FL
Averbook, Daniel Z. ....Miami Beach, FL
Averbook, Daniel Z., P.A. ....Miami Beach, FL
Averbuch, Amy L. ....Chicago, IL
Averbuch, Kelvin L. ....Lake Mary, FL
Averbuck, Clayton C. ....Westlake Village, CA
Averbuck, David S. ....Oakland, CA
Averch, Craig H. ....Dallas, TX
Averell, Barbara S. ....Louisville, KY
Averett, Dana M. ....Chapel Hill, NC
Averett, Steven Elmo ....Provo, UT
Averetta, Darlene ....Los Angeles, CA
Averette & Barton ....Brevard, NC
Averette, H. Paul, Jr. ....Brevard, NC
Averill, Andrew P. ....Bangor, ME
Averill, Craig Edward ....New York, NY
Averill, Edgar W., Jr. ....Whittier, CA
Averill, James D. ....Portland, OR
Averill, Karel L. ....Orlando, FL
Averill, Lawrence H., Jr. ....Little Rock, AR
Averill, Marilyn ....Lakewood, CO
Averill, Martin P. ....New Orleans, LA
Averill & Varn ....Whittier, CA
Averitt, Barry C. ....Jacksonville, FL
Averitt, Christopher A. ....Little Rock, AR
Averitt, Neil W. ....Federal Trade Commission, Bureau of Competition, GV
Averitte, Clinton E. ....Amarillo, TX
Averna, Raymond ....Garden City, NY
Avernas, Harold S. ....Clifton, NJ
Aversa, David E. ....Lake Worth, FL
Aversa, Donna M. ....Tucson, AZ
Aversa, John M. ....Niagara Falls, NY
Aversa, Robyn L. ....Morristown, NJ
Aversa, Thomas J., Jr. ....Pasadena, MD
Towson, MD
Avery, Alan D. ....Denver, CO
Avery, Alfred A., Jr. ....Troy, MI
Avery, Allison Southgate ....Indianapolis, IN
Avery, Aloma H. ....San Diego, CA
Avery, Anne Robinson ....Denver, CO
Avery & Associates ....San Francisco, CA
Avery & Avery ....Ridgefield, NJ
Avery, Barbara ....Worthington, OH
Avery, Bobby K. ....Birmingham, AL
Avery, Boyer & Van Gilder ....Fort Wayne, IN
Avery, Bruce E. ....Rockville, MD
Avery, C. Richard ....Cincinnati, OH
Avery, Cameron S. ....Chicago, IL
Avery, Caroline D. ....Berkeley, CA
Avery, Charles W. ....Inlet, NY
Avery, Christopher E. ....Phoenix, AZ
Avery, Claire Wengrove ....Fort Myers, FL
Avery, Craig C. ....Duluth, GA
Avery & Crone ....Stamford, CT
Avery, Crosswhite & Crosswhite, P.A.
Hickory, NC
Statesville, NC
Avery, Daniel R. ....Boston, MA
Avery, Darrell R. ....Jonesboro, LA
Avery, David E., III ....Montgomery, AL
Avery, David J. ....Fort Wayne, IN
Avery, Deborah Williams ....Picayune, MS
Avery, Dennis L. ....Fort Myers, FL
Avery, Dennis S. ....Borrego Springs, CA
Avery, Diane S. ....Ridgefield, NJ
Avery, Donald G. ....Washington, DC
Avery, Dooley, Post & Avery ....Boston, MA
Avery, Douglas Stuart ....Pasadena, CA
Avery, E. Cordell ....Greenville, NC
Avery, Edward W., Jr. ....New York, NY
Avery, Emerson R. ....Cortland, NY
Avery, Emerson R., Jr. ....Cortland, NY
Avery, Emily ....Nantucket, MA
Avery, Ernest F. ....San Antonio, TX
Avery, G. Randall ....Stamford, CT
Avery, George A. ....Washington, DC
Avery, Gregory J. ....Metairie, LA
Avery, H. George ....Morristown, NJ
Avery, Howard J. ....Brooklyn, NY
Avery, Isaac T., III ....Raleigh, NC
Avery, Isaac T., Jr. ....Statesville, NC
Avery, J. Mark ....Austin, TX
Avery, Jack ....Tamuning, GU
Avery, James A. ....Canandaigua, NY
Avery, James M. ....Boston, MA
Avery, James T., III ....Chestnut Hill, MA
Avery, James W. ....Denver, CO
Parker, CO
Avery, John A. ....Springfield, NJ
Avery, John G. ....Salt Lake City, UT
Avery, John L., Jr. ....Jupiter, FL
Avery, John O. ....Idaho Falls, ID
Avery, John W.
Securities and Exchange Commission, Office of the General Counsel, GV
Avery, Karen K. ....Glenshaw, PA
Avery, Kevin J. ....Washington, DC
Avery, Kevin S. ....Tarzana, CA
Avery, Lane C. ....Chattanooga, TN
Avery, Laura Julius ....Cleveland, OH
Avery Law Firm ....Denver, CO
Parker, CO
Avery, Lee Mara ....San Diego, CA
Avery, Linda Kaye ....Baton Rouge, LA
Avery, Lori L. ....Darien, CT
Avery, Luther J. ....San Francisco, CA
Avery, Marcia Elaine ....Baton Rouge, LA
Avery, Margaret DuBose ....Greensboro, NC
Avery, Mark H. ....Pembroke, MA
Avery, Mark J. ....San Francisco, CA
Avery, Martha J. ....Northbrook, IL
Avery, Martin F., Jr. ....Fort Lauderdale, FL
Avery, Mary Katherine ....Chicago, IL
Avery, Melissa J. ....Indianapolis, IN
Avery, Michelle Leigh ....Department of Justice, Office of Justice Programs, GV
Avery, Patricia I. ....New York, NY
Avery, Phyllis A. ....Royal Oak, MI
Avery, R. Craig ....Comstock Park, MI
Avery, R. Thomas ....St. Louis, MO
Avery, Richard C. ....Morganton, NC
Avery, Richard M., Jr. ....Marion, AL
Avery, Richard W. ....Houston, TX
Avery, Richard W., (P.C.) ....Dallas, TX
Avery, Robert D. ....Lake Village, AR
Avery, Robert Dean ....Chicago, IL
Avery, Robert W. ....Bridgeport, CT
Avery, Robert W. ....Ridgefield, NJ
Avery, Robt. W. ....Rochester, NY
Avery, Roger W. ....Rochester, NY
Avery, Rosemary Boyd ....Washington, DC
Avery, Shannon E. ....Baltimore, MD
Avery, Stephen F. ....Spencer, IA
Avery, Thomas B. ....Memphis, TN
Avery, Wesley H. ....Los Angeles, CA
Avery, Whigham & Winesett, P.A.
Fort Myers, FL
Sanibel, FL
Avery, Willard M. ....Knightstown, IN
Avery, William G. ....Baton Rouge, LA
Avery, William H. ....Atlanta, GA
Avery, William H. ....Dallas, TX
Avery, William H., P.C. ....Dallas, TX
Avery-Peck, Lisa J. ....Boston, MA
Avery-Smith, Ellen ....Orlando, FL
Avesar, Avner Ron ....Coconut Creek, FL
Avesar, Josef ....Encino, CA
Avey, Anthony A. ....Fort Worth, TX
Avey, Bradley D. ....Oklahoma City, OK
Avey & Gertner ....Newport Beach, CA
Avey, Guy R., Jr. ....Martinsburg, WV
Avey, Robert G. ....Lincoln, NE
Avey, Victoria C. ....Newport Beach, CA
Avgerin, Constantine ....Highland Park, IL
Avgerin, Nicholas C. ....Lake Bluff, IL
Avgerinos, Connie S. ....Chicago, IL
Avgerinos, Nick James ....Chicago, IL
Avgeris, George N. ....Hinsdale, IL
Aviation Law Ctr., P.C. ....Williamsburg, VA
Avidan, Bernard M. ....Pacific Palisades, CA
Avidano, Marc A. ....Fort Lauderdale, FL
Avidon, Michael Evan ....New York, NY
Avidon, Richard S. ....Washington, DC
Avidon, Scott ....Brooklyn, NY
Avigad, Joshua ....St. Louis, MO
Avigdor, David ....New Haven, CT
Avigdor, David B. ....Hadley, NY
Avigliano, Dennis J. ....Randolph, NJ
Avigliano, James F. ....Little Falls, NJ
Avignone, Alfred F. ....Bozeman, MT
Avignone, James I. ....Englewood, NJ
Avil, Richard D., Jr. ....Washington, DC
Avil, Simao J. ....San Jose, CA
Ávila, Alcides I. ....Miami, FL
Avila, Andrea C. ....Salinas, CA
Avila, Carlson & Peros, LLP
Los Angeles, CA
Orange, CA
Avila, Daniel ....Indianapolis, IN
Avila, Edward G. ....Providence, RI
Avila, Everett J. ....Sacramento, CA
Avila, Felix ....Los Angeles, CA
Avila, Frederick A. ....New York, NY
Avila, Janine T. ....Toledo, OH
Avila, Jonathan D. ....Los Angeles, CA
Avila, Juan M. ....Boston, MA
Avila, M. Jayne ....Boston, MA
Avila, Manual A. ....Miami, FL
Avila, Mark Steven ....Encino, CA
Avila, Michael F. ....Los Angeles, CA
Orange, CA
Avila, Pablo ....Crystal City, TX
Avila, Richard A. ....Las Vegas, NV
Avila, Richard A., Chtd. ....Las Vegas, NV
Avila, Richard G. ....Palo Alto, CA
Avila, Robert J. ....Phoenix, AZ
Avila, Robert J. ....Albuquerque, NM
Avila, Robert J., P.A. ....Albuquerque, NM
Avila, Simao J. ....Oakland, CA
Avila, William T. ....San Antonio, TX
Avila-Sánchez, Moisés ....San Juan, PR
Avildsen, Eric B. ....Worcester, MA
Aviles, Arturo M. ....Austin, TX
Aviles & Colon Morales LLP
San Juan, PR
Aviles, Deborah A. ....Melville, NY
Avilés, Karen A. ....Denver, CO
Aviles, Kimberly Corbin
Severna Park, MD
Aviles, Luis Anibal ....San Juan, PR
Avilés-López, Orlando ....San Juan, PR
Avilés-Matos, Leticia M. ....San Juan, PR
Aviles Rodriguez, F. Ariel ....San Juan, PR
Aviles-Vega, Lizbet ....San Juan, PR
Avilez, Victoria M. ....Phoenix, AZ
Avilla, Paul S. ....San Jose, CA
Avillion, Deborah Cooksey
Greenwood, AR
Avina, Jeffrey M. ....New York, NY
Avina, Jon Christopher ....Palo Alto, CA
Avini, Avisheh ....New York, NY
Avino, Louis F., Jr. ....Buffalo, NY
Avins, Alfred ....Alexandria, VA
Avioli Law Firm, The, P.C. ....St. Louis, MO
Avioli, Michael F. ....St. Louis, MO
Avirett, James Alfred ....Cumberland, MD
Avirom & Associates, LLP ....Westport, CT
New York, NY
Avirom, Cheryl R. ....Long Beach, CA
Avirom, Cheryl R., A Prof. Corp.
Long Beach, CA
Avirom, Jonathan E. ....Westport, CT
New York, NY
Avis, Alan S. ....Chico, CA
Avis and Avis ....Newport News, VA
Avis & Avis, P.A. ....North Palm Beach, FL
Palm Beach, FL
Avis, Deborah K. ....North Palm Beach, FL
Palm Beach, FL
Avis, Philip L. ....Newport News, VA
Avis, Richard T. ....St. Petersburg, FL
Avis, Walter J., Jr. ....Worcester, MA
Avis, Warren E., Jr. ....North Palm Beach, FL
Palm Beach, FL
Avitabile, Alex S. ....Brooklyn, NY
Avitabile, Alex S., P.C. ....Brooklyn, NY
Avitabile, Gregg S. ....Washington, DC
Avitabile, Louis S. ....Waterbury, CT
Avitabile, Matthew J. ....Ashland, MA
Avitabile, Scott D. ....New York, NY
Aviv, Joseph ....Bloomfield Hills, MI
Aviza, Christian A. ....Boston, MA
Avner & Avner ....Los Angeles, CA
Avner, Correy B. ....Los Angeles, CA
Avner, Janine M. ....Los Angeles, CA
Avner, Judith I. ....Albany, NY
Avnet, James R. ....Baltimore, MD

Avolio & Hanlon, P.C. ... St. Augustine, FL
Lawrenceville, NJ
Ocean City, NJ
Washington Crossing, PA
Avolio, Robert P. ... Lawrenceville, NJ
Washington Crossing, PA
Avots, Ivar E.
Department Of Health And Human Services,
Social Security Administration, GV
Avots, Peter E. ... **Corpus Christi, TX**
Avrach, Stephen J. ... Miami, FL
Avrakotos, Costas A. ... **Washington, DC**
Avram, Gabriel A. ... **Winston-Salem, NC**
Avram, Gerald W. ... Arvada, CO
Avram, M. Andrew ... **Charlotte, NC**
Avram, Randall David ... **Raleigh, NC**
Avramovich, Michael Paul ... Chicago, IL
Avrasina, Olga ... Brooklyn, NY
Avratin, Gary S. ... Dedham, MA
Avratin, Michael S. ... Dedham, MA
Avratin, Okstein & Queler ... Dedham, MA
Avrett, Milton M., III ... **Augusta, GA**
Avrett, Milton M., III, P.C. ... **Augusta, GA**
Aiken, SC
Avrett, Ponder & Withrock ... **Dalton, GA**
Avrigian, Ara R. ... **Philadelphia, PA**
Avrigian, Mason ... **Blue Bell, PA**
Avrigian, Mason, Jr. ... **Blue Bell, PA**
Avril, Gary L. ... **Plainfield, IL**
Avril, John J. ... Clearwater, FL
Avrin & Fletcher ... Jamaica Plain, MA
Avrin, Frances Martha ... Jamaica Plain, MA
Avrith, Charles ... **Los Angeles, CA**
Avritt & Avritt ... Lebanon, KY
Avritt, James L. ... Lebanon, KY
Avritt, James L., Jr. ... Lebanon, KY
Avromov, Steven M. ... Detroit, MI
Avron, Paul A. ... Birmingham, AL
Avruch, Phillip G. ... **Sterling, VA**
Avruch, Steven N. ... Burlington, MA
Avrunin, Adam ... **Atlanta, GA**
Avrunin, Daniel ... Bloomfield Hills, MI
AvRutick, David R. ... New York, NY
Avrutin, Roberta ... Los Angeles, CA
Avrutine, Howard D. ... **New York, NY**
Avrutis, Andrea M. ... Brooklyn, NY
Avrutis, Thomas ... **Sarasota, FL**
Avsec, Mark E. ... **Cleveland, OH**
Avsharian, Paul R. ... Huntington Woods, MI
Avstreih, David ... Mount Vernon, NY
Avtonomoff, Nick V. ... San Francisco, CA
Awad, George C., Jr. ... Owego, NY
Awad, Jason A. ... Las Vegas, NV
Awad, Joseph P. ... Garden City, NY
Awad, Martha J. ... **New York, NY**
Awad, Nadia E. ... **Los Angeles, CA**
Awad, Suzanne ... **San Francisco, CA**
Awad, Thomas C. ... Garden City, NY
Awada, Mark N. ... Bingham Farms, MI
Awadalla, Mark R. ... **Princeton, NJ**
New York, NY
Awadallah, Saleh S. ... Cleveland, OH
Awad-Rashmawi, Reem O. ... Sacramento, CA
Awakuni, Catherine P. ... **Honolulu, HI**
Awakuni, Gay Tokie ... Torrance, CA
Awakuni, Russ S. ... **Honolulu, HI**
Awalt, Charles H. ... Plano, TX
Awalt, Francis G., Jr. ... Chapel Hill, NC
Awalt, Mary Carol Hopkins ... **Conroe, TX**
Awalt, Stephen B. ... Towson, MD
Awbrey, Nolan Edward ... **Birmingham, AL**
Awdey, Tamara ... Stamford, CT
Awe, Elizabeth J. ... **Chicago, IL**
Awerbach, Martin S. ... **Clearwater, FL**
Awerbach, Murphy & Cohn, P.A.
Clearwater, FL
Awerkamp, Donald T. ... **Tucson, AZ**
Awerkamp, E. Scott ... **St. George, UT**
Awerkamp, Gena J. ... **Quincy, IL**
Awerkamp, Mary Lucinda ... Quincy, IL
Awerkamp & McClain ... Quincy, IL
Awh, Grace H. ... **Nashville, TN**
Awick, Darryl L. ... Westmont, IL
Awiszus, Anna Lisa ... **Sacramento, CA**
Awiszus, Martha J. ... **Plymouth, MA**
Awkard, Linda N. ... Washington, DC
Awner, Jonathan L. ... **Miami, FL**
Awoniyi, Bunmi Olaide ... Sacramento, CA
Awrich, Ellen ... Department of Commerce,
Patent and Trademark Office, GV
Awsumb, Anne W. ... Plymouth, MN
Awsumb, R. A., & Associates, PLC
St. Paul, MN
Awsumb, Robert A. ... **St. Paul, MN**
Awtrey & Parker, P.C. ... **Marietta, GA**
Awuah, Abebe K. ... Silver Spring, MD
Ax, Charles J., Jr. ... Middleburg, PA
Ax, Charles J., Jr., P.C. ... Middleburg, PA
Axam & Adams, P.A. ... **Atlanta, GA**
Axam, Tony L. ... **Atlanta, GA**
Axe, Albert R., Jr. ... **Austin, TX**
Axe, Jason K. ... Los Angeles, CA
Axe, John R., and Associates ... **Detroit, MI**
Axe, John R., and Associates
Grosse Pointe Farms, MI
Axe, Judith W. ... Washington, DC
Axe, Kenneth B. ... **Madison, WI**
Axe, Neal S. ... Philadelphia, PA
Axe, Norman G. ... Santa Monica, CA
Axe, Stuart W. ... **Philadelphia, PA**
Axel, Andrea D. ... **Seattle, WA**
Axel, Blair ... **New York, NY**
Axel, Bradford J. ... **Seattle, WA**
Axel, Byron ... Milwaukee, WI
Axel, Douglas A. ... **Los Angeles, CA**
Axel & Goldman ... Milwaukee, WI
Axel, Joan U. ... **Muscatine, IA**
Wilton, IA

Axel, John Clifford ... Baltimore, MD
Axel, Michael A. ... Cleveland, OH
Axel, Neil Edward ... Simpsonville, MD
Axel, Robert B. ... Los Angeles, CA
Axelberg, Tracy ... **Kalispell, MT**
Missoula, MT
Axell, Karla J. ... **Seattle, WA**
Axelman, Bernard ... Cherry Hill, NJ
Axelman, Joseph B. ... Department of Defense,
Armed Services Board of Contract Appeals,
GV
Axelrad, Andrew ... Miami, FL
Axelrad, Bernard ... Los Angeles, CA
Axelrad, Claire A. ... San Francisco, CA
Axelrad, David M. ... **Los Angeles, CA**
Axelrad, Jane A.
Department Of Health And Human Services,
Food & Drug Administration, GV
Axelrad, Jeffrey F. ... Department of Justice,
Civil Division, GV
Axelrad, Jonathan ... **Palo Alto, CA**
Axelrad, Jonathan E. ... **Houston, TX**
Axelrad, Joy ... New York, NY
Axelrad, Lee ... **Sacramento, CA**
Axelrad, Marcy ... Boston, MA
Axelrad, Maurice ... Washington, DC
Axelrad, Michael J. ... **Denver, CO**
Axelrad, Norman D. ... Lincolnwood, IL
Axelrad, Peter F. ... **Washington, DC**
Baltimore, MD
Rockville, MD
Axelrad, Robert A. ... **Houston, TX**
Axelrad, Stephen ... Long Beach, CA
Axelrod & Adler, P.C. ... St. Johnsbury, VT
Axelrod, Alan B. ... San Francisco, CA
Axelrod, Alan D., (P.A.) ... **Miami, FL**
Axelrod, Alan J. ... **Newburgh, NY**
Axelrod, Allan ... Newark, NJ
Axelrod, Andrew R. ... Freeport, NY
Axelrod & Axelrod ... Brooklyn, NY
Axelrod, Barbara R. ... **Philadelphia, PA**
Axelrod, Barry E. ... Encinitas, CA
Axelrod, Brad J. ... **Baton Rouge, LA**
Axelrod, Brett Ashley ... **Las Vegas, NV**
Axelrod, Carl E. ... **Boston, MA**
Axelrod, Charles D. ... **Los Angeles, CA**
Axelrod, Charles F. ... New York, NY
Axelrod, Charles P. ... **New York, NY**
Axelrod, Cornachio, Famighetti & Davis
Mineola, NY
Axelrod, Daniel L. ... Los Angeles, CA
Axelrod, David A. ... **Chicago, IL**
Axelrod, David F. ... **Columbus, OH**
Axelrod, David J. ... Merion, PA
Axelrod, David W. ... **Portland, OR**
Axelrod, Edna Ball ... **South Orange, NJ**
Axelrod, Eugene N. ... Woodbridge, CT
Axelrod, G. Carla ... Los Angeles, CA
Axelrod, Gary E. ... **Chicago, IL**
Axelrod, Gene ... Santa Ana, CA
Axelrod, George ... New York, NY
Axelrod, Goodman, Steiner & Bazelon
Chicago, IL
Axelrod, Janet R. ... Albany, NY
Axelrod, Jay G. ... New York, NY
Axelrod, Jeffrey B. ... Lexington, MA
Axelrod, Jill L. ... **White Plains, NY**
Axelrod, Jon P. ... **Madison, WI**
Axelrod, Jonathan G. ... Washington, DC
Axelrod, Leon ... Brooklyn, NY
Axelrod, Lisa K. ... **Millburn, NJ**
New York, NY
Axelrod, Margaret ... **New York, NY**
Axelrod, Matthew S. ... **Boston, MA**
Axelrod, Michael C. ... **East Meadow, NY**
Axelrod, Michael E. ... **Atlanta, GA**
Axelrod, Michael S. ... **Philadelphia, PA**
Axelrod, Michelle Deirdre ... **Melville, NY**
Axelrod, Peter ... San Rafael, CA
Axelrod, Peter A. ... **New York, NY**
Axelrod, Peter, & Associates, P.C.
New York, NY
Axelrod, Peter B. ... **San Francisco, CA**
Axelrod, Peter D. ... Tucson, AZ
Axelrod, Philip J. ... New York, NY
Axelrod, Renae B. ... Philadelphia, PA
Axelrod, Richard A. ... St. Johnsbury, VT
Axelrod, Robert D. ... **Houston, TX**
Axelrod, Robert J. ... Edison, NJ
Axelrod, Robert J. ... **New York, NY**
Axelrod, Robert M. ... **Meriden, CT**
Axelrod, Robert N. ... **McLean, VA**
Axelrod, Ronald B. ... Los Angeles, CA
Axelrod, Ronald J. ... **Rochester, NY**
Axelrod, Roy D. ... **San Diego, CA**
Axelrod, Ruth E. ... New York, NY
Axelrod, Ruth H. ... Jersey City, NJ
New York, NY
Axelrod, Samuel ... Silver Spring, MD
Axelrod, Sheryl L. ... **Philadelphia, PA**
Axelrod, Shirli M. ... Seattle, WA
Axelrod, Sidney ... Norwich, CT
Axelrod, Sidney H. ... Chicago, IL
Axelrod, Smith & Kirshbaum
Houston, TX
Axelrod, Stephen L. ... Philadelphia, PA
Axelrod, Susan ... New York, NY
Axelrood, Bryan J. ... **Los Angeles, CA**
Axelrood, Larry G. ... Chicago, IL
Axelrood, Paul B. ... Oak Park, IL
Axelroth, Lynn R. ... **Philadelphia, PA**
Axelsen, Eric ... Novato, CA
Axelsen, Thomas C. ... **Phoenix, AZ**
Axelson, Arthur B. ... **Washington, DC**
Axelson, David R. ... Herndon, VA
Axelson, Jeffrey M. ... **Frederick, MD**
Rockville, MD
Axelson, Vincent J. ... **San Diego, CA**

Axen, Charles S. ... Irvine, CA
Axen, Klaus T. ... Tucson, AZ
Axen, Klaus T., P.C. ... Tucson, AZ
Axen, Page Chancellor ... **Tucson, AZ**
Axenfeld, Maurice S. ... Lafayette, NY
Axenfeld, Robert B. ... Liberty Corner, NJ
Axford, David T. ... **Nashville, TN**
Axford, Laurie A. ... **San Diego, CA**
Axford, Robert S. ... Mount Clemens, MI
Axilbund, Melvin T. ... Vienna, VA
Axinn, David ... **New York, NY**
Axinn, David M. ... Hollidaysburg, PA
Axinn, Mark N. ... **New York, NY**
Axinn, Stephen M. ... **New York, NY**
Axinn, Veltrop & Harkrider LLP
Hartford, CT
New York, NY
Axiotis, Ares Demetrius ... Fairfield, CT
New York, NY
Axiotis, George C. ... Brighton, MA
Axler, Andrew M. ... Kew Gardens, NY
Axler, Mitchel B. ... **Phoenix, AZ**
Axley Brynelson, LLP ... **Madison, WI**
Axley, Frederick W. ... **Chicago, IL**
Axley & Hargrove, A Professional
Corporation ... **Dallas, TX**
Axley, Hartman ... Denver, CO
Axley, Robert J. ... **Dallas, TX**
Axley, Thomas G. ... Prince Frederick, MD
Axley, W. Fred ... Memphis, TN
Axley, William R. ... Addison, IL
Axline, Michael ... Eugene, OR
Axman, Michael B. ... **Miami, FL**
Axner, E. Arthur ... Akron, OH
Axner, Gary R. ... Cleveland, OH
Axon, Gary L. ... Ashland, OR
Axselle, Ralph L., Jr. ... **Richmond, VA**
Axt, Michael P. ... Palm Beach Gardens, FL
Axt, Michael S. ... Denver, CO
Axt, Robt. G. ... Milwaukee, WI
Axtell & Briggs ... Spokane, WA
Axtell, Clayton M., III ... **Binghamton, NY**
Axtell, Clayton M., Jr. ... **Binghamton, NY**
Axtell, Jacqueline A. ... **Los Angeles, CA**
Axtell, James H. ... Los Angeles, CA
Axtell, L. Neil ... Spokane, WA
Axtell, Stephen J. ... **Cincinnati, OH**
Axten, Phillips ... Boston, MA
Axtman, Sarah Adam ... Hoover, AL
Axtmann, David G. ... San Diego, CA
Axtmann, David M. ... Highmore, SD
Axtmayer Adsuar Muñiz & Goyco, P.S.C.
San Juan, PR
Axtmayer, José A. ... **San Juan, PR**
Ayabarreno-Segura, Toni Dean
San Diego, CA
Ayabe, Bert I. ... Honolulu, HI
Ayabe, Chong, Nishimoto, Sia & Nakamura
Honolulu, HI
Ayabe, Gail Otsuka ... **Honolulu, HI**
Ayabe, Sidney K., (P.C.) ... **Honolulu, HI**
Ayala, Adan ... Towson, MD
Ayala, David ... San Juan, TX
Ayala, Dolores ... **Chicago, IL**
Ayala, Glenn ... St. Petersburg, FL
Ayala, Jacquelynn A. ... **Milwaukee, WI**
Ayala, Jennifer Shelby ... Miami, FL
Ayala, Joe J. ... Sacramento, CA
Ayala, Julio ... Miami, FL
Ayala, Kevin Lloyd ... Stevensville, MD
Ayala, Ralph ... Los Angeles, CA
Ayala, Raul ... Montebello, CA
Ayala, Renee I. ... Los Angeles, CA
Ayala, W. DeHart, Jr. ... Tampa, FL
Ayali, Noam ... **Washington, DC**
Ayanian, John V. ... **Washington, DC**
Ayarbe, Karen M. ... Reno, NV
Ayars, Barbara ... Atlantic City, NJ
Ayars, Constance M. ... **New York, NY**
Ayars, Patricia A. ... Glastonbury, CT
Ayau, Edward Halealoha ... Honolulu, HI
Ayaub, John J. ... Brighton, MI
Ayaub, John J., P.C. ... Brighton, MI
Ayaub, Joseph J. ... Detroit, MI
Ayayo, Christopher P. ... Costa Mesa, CA
Ayazi, Armand F. ... **Los Angeles, CA**
Aycock, Anne ... Brooklyn, NY
Aycock, C. Ronald ... Raleigh, NC
Aycock, C. Sellers, III ... Dallas, TX
Aycock, Charles B., III ... Nags Head, NC
Aycock, Charles F. ... Farwell, TX
Aycock, Charles L. B. ... Houston, TX
Aycock, Chris ... **Midland, TX**
Aycock, E. Burt, Jr. ... Greenville, NC
Aycock, E. Kenneth, Jr. ... Tuscaloosa, AL
Aycock, E. Kenneth, P.C. ... Tuscaloosa, AL
Aycock, Edmund D. ... Raleigh, NC
Aycock, Ellis L. ... **Morganton, NC**
Aycock, Frank B., III ... Charlotte, NC
Aycock, Geary S. ... West Monroe, LA
Aycock, Gretchen D. ... Fayetteville, NC
Aycock, Horne & Coleman ... **Franklin, LA**
Morgan City, LA
Aycock, J. Bruce ... Corpus Christi, TX
Aycock, James J. ... **San Antonio, TX**
Aycock, John C. ... Austin, TX
Aycock, John Knox ... Memphis, TN
Aycock, Keith B. ... Lawton, OK
Aycock, Leslie K. ... Detroit, MI
Aycock, Lynda R. ... **Jacksonville, FL**
Aycock, Margaret A. ... Clemmons, NC
Aycock, R. Rex ... **Lubbock, TX**
Aycock, Robert A. (Andy) ... **Lubbock, TX**
Aycock, Samuel E. ... **Morganton, NC**
Aycock, Spence & Butler ... Nags Head, NC
Aycock, William P., II ... **Greensboro, NC**
Aycock, William R. ... Lincoln Park, MI

Aycock, William R., & Associates, P.C.
Lincoln Park, MI
Aycock, William W., Jr. ... **Fayetteville, NC**
Aycock, Wm. B. ... Chapel Hill, NC
Ayd, Joseph M. ... Baltimore, MD
Ayd, Patricia M. ... **Denver, CO**
Ayd, Patricia M., P.C. ... **Denver, CO**
Aydell, John Pershing, Jr. ... Baton Rouge, LA
Aydelott & Aydelott ... Mount Kisco, NY
Aydelott, Gordon B. ... Mount Kisco, NY
Aydelott & Hannah, P.A. ... Searcy, AR
Aydelott, Judith A. ... Mount Kisco, NY
Aydelott, Madison P., III ... Searcy, AR
Aydelott, Martin V. ... **Minneapolis, MN**
Aydelotte, Bryan W. ... **Indianapolis, IN**
Aydin, Katherine ... **Washington, DC**
Aydin, Pauline R. ... Akron, OH
Aydlett, Valerie A. ... Norfolk, VA
Aydlette, D. L. (Dirk), III ... **Columbia, SC**
Aydlette, Kim S. ... St. Helena Island, SC
Aye, J. George, Jr. ... Sanger, CA
Aye Law Firm, P.A. ... **Tampa, FL**
Aye, Michael J. ... Sacramento, CA
Aye, Walter Edwards ... **Tampa, FL**
Ayella, Joseph J. ... **Philadelphia, PA**
Ayeni, Anthony O. ... Walnut Creek, CA
Ayeni, McRansom, & Associates
Washington, DC
Ayeni, Shola Rannie ... **Washington, DC**
Ayer, Carey M. ... **Lexington, SC**
Ayer, Donald B. ... **Washington, DC**
Ayer, Eric K. ... Rockport, IN
Ayer, Francis H., Jr. ... Tucson, AZ
Ayer, Gordon C. ... Wells, ME
Ayer, Harold G. ... **San Diego, CA**
Ayer, Harold G., Jr., A Professionl Law
Corporation ... **San Diego, CA**
Ayer, Jack K. ... Conroe, TX
Ayer, Jeffrey D. ... **Washington, DC**
Ayer, John D. ... Davis, CA
Ayer, Katherine J. ... Sherman Oaks, CA
Ayer, M. Frances ... Washington, DC
Ayer, Mitchell E. ... **Houston, TX**
Ayer, Peter R., Jr. ... **Amesbury, MA**
Ayer, Sarah M. ... Rochester, NY
Ayer, Thomas M. ... Oakland, CA
Ayer, Victoria T. ... Washington, DC
Ayer, William C., Jr. ... **Frankfort, KY**
Ayerbe, Paul R. ... **Macon, GA**
Ayers, Aaron Sheldon ... Memphis, TN
Ayers, Andrew J. ... Toledo, OH
Ayers, Arthur W. ... Red Lodge, MT
Ayers & Ayers ... Dallas, TX
Ayers, Bradley J. ... **Minneapolis, MN**
Ayers & Brown, P.C. ... **Phoenix, AZ**
Ayers, Carroll E. ... Wakefield, MA
Ayers, Charles E., Jr. ... Richmond, VA
Ayers, Charles K. ... **Phoenix, AZ**
Ayers, Charles L. ... Gloucester, MA
Ayers, Charles P., Jr. ... Owego, NY
Ayers, Charles W. ... Mt. Vernon, OH
Ayers, Christan L. ... Long Beach, CA
Ayers, Craig M. ... **Minneapolis, MN**
Ayers, Cynthia J. ... Indianapolis, IN
Ayers, D. Randal ... **Raleigh, NC**
Ayers, David L. ... **Jackson, MS**
Ayers, David P. ... **Houston, TX**
Ayers, Deanne C. ... Dallas, TX
Ayers, Dennis R. ... Lexington, NC
Ayers, Donald ... New York, NY
Ayers, Donald F. ... New York, NY
Ayers, E. Kent ... **Joliet, IL**
Ayers, Earl T. ... Las Vegas, NV
Ayers, Elaine ... Bismarck, ND
Ayers, Elizabeth A. ... **Columbus, OH**
Ayers, G. Randall ... **Cincinnati, OH**
Ayers, Gary L. ... **Wichita, KS**
Ayers, Geoffrey James ... Williamsport, PA
Ayers, Glenn E. ... Richmond, VA
Ayers, Grady G. ... Orlando, FL
Ayers, Gregory L. ... Columbus, OH
Ayers, Homer R. ... Goodlettsville, TN
Ayers, Hope M. ... Huntsville, AL
Ayers, Howard T. ... **Houston, TX**
Ayers, James B. ... **Albany, NY**
Ayers, James C. ... Columbus, OH
Ayers, James C., Jr. ... **Birmingham, AL**
Ayers, James E. ... **Crawfordsville, IN**
Ayers, James L. ... **Monticello, IL**
Ayers, James M., II ... New Bern, NC
Ayers, James R. ... Morganton, NC
Ayers, James R., III ... Arlington, VA
Ayers, James T. "Tom", Jr. ... **Littleton, CO**
Ayers, James T., SR ... Aurora, CO
Ayers, James T. "Tom", Jr. ... **Denver, CO**
Ayers, Jay F. ... Seattle, WA
Ayers, John F., III ... **Charlotte, NC**
Ayers, John L. ... Clear Lake, IA
Ayers, Jonathan P. ... Dallas, TX
Ayers, Joseph Michael ... Jacksboro, TN
Ayers, Judson F., Jr. ... Greenwood, SC
Ayers, Kelli A. ... **Boston, MA**
Ayers, Kenneth D. ... **San Francisco, CA**
Ayers, Kimberly C. ... **Washington, DC**
Ayers, Kingdrel N. ... Tallahassee, FL
Ayers, Krista J. ... Atlanta, GA
Ayers, Laura Dierberg ... St. Louis, MO
Ayers, Lila ... **New York, NY**
Ayers, Lisa Lander ... New York, NY
Ayers, Michael S. ... Long Beach, CA
Ayers, Munsey L., Jr. ... **Denver, CO**
Ayers, Paul R. ... Los Angeles, CA
Ayers, Peter J. ... **Austin, TX**
Ayers, Philip ... Wellesley, MA
Ayers, Philip T. ... Hazelwood, MO
Ayers, R. David, Jr. ... Winter Park, FL
Ayers, R. David, Jr., P.A. ... Winter Park, FL
Ayers, R. Glen, Jr. ... **San Antonio, TX**

Ayers, Reginald L. ... **Bowling Green, KY**
Ayers, Robert S. ... Del Mar, CA
Ayers, Ronald M. ... **Roanoke, VA**
Ayers, Ronald S. ... Redding, CA
Ayers, Rosemary G. ... **Hartford, CT**
Ayers, Smithdeal & Bettis, P.C.
Greenwood, SC
Ayers, Stephen M. ... Coeur d'Alene, ID
Ayers, Steven B. ... **Columbus, OH**
Ayers, Stewart L. ... St. Petersburg, FL
Ayers, Timothy B. ... Louisville, KY
Ayers, Vicky W. ... Charlotte, NC
Ayers, W. Patrick ... **Tampa, FL**
Ayers, Walter L. ... Las Vegas, NV
Ayers, Walter N. ... West Mifflin, PA
Ayers, William T. ... San Francisco, CA
Ayers, Yvonne ... Bisbee, AZ
Ayers-Howard, Deanne L. ... Bethesda, MD
Ayervais, Neil E. ... **Denver, CO**
Ayesh Law Offices ... Wichita, KS
Ayesh, Mark G. ... Wichita, KS
Ayesu, Kwame Danso ... Bronx, NY
Ayik, Robert H. ... Marlton, NJ
Aykanian, Sem ... Marlborough, MA
Aylaian, Sidney ... Boston, MA
Ayler, Sylvia ... **Rahway, NJ**
Ayles, Honoria C. ... Boston, MA
Ayles, Richard P. ... **Los Angeles, CA**
Aylesworth, George N. ... Miami, FL
Aylesworth, John M. ... Chicago, IL
Aylesworth, Thomas W. ... **Boston, MA**
Aylett, Lori G. ... **Houston, TX**
Aylett-Hosch, Andrea L. ... **Orlando, FL**
Ayling, Campbell ... Uniondale, NY
Ayling, Corey J. ... **Minneapolis, MN**
Ayling, Robert J. ... Gouverneur, NY
Ayling, Robert W. ... **San Diego, CA**
Ayling, Teresa J. ... **Minneapolis, MN**
Aylman, Carl E. ... New York, NY
Aylmer, Charles L. ... Buzzards Bay, MA
Aylmer, John F. ... Buzzards Bay, MA
Aylmer, John F., Jr. ... Lexington, MA
Aylor, Jeffrey R. ... Florence, KY
Aylor, John H. ... Falls Church, VA
Aylor, Joshua F. ... **Nashville, TN**
Aylor, Robert B. ... Cincinnati, OH
Aylstock, Bryan Frederick ... **Pensacola, FL**
Aylsworth, G. Thomas ... Leland, MI
Aylsworth, Glenn ... Traverse City, MI
Aylsworth, Justin P. ... **Nampa, ID**
Aylsworth, Robert R. ... Boonville, IN
Aylsworth, Tony ... Boonville, IN
Aylsworth, William E. ... **Miami, FL**
Aylward, Arthur T. ... **Richmond, VA**
Aylward, Brian K. ... Danvers, MA
Aylward, Carolyn Ann ... St. Louis, MO
Aylward, David K. ... Washington, DC
Aylward, Edward F. ... Kansas City, MO
Aylward, George V., Jr. ... Kansas City, MO
Aylward, Gretchen P. ... **Buffalo, NY**
Aylward, J. Patrick ... **Wenatchee, WA**
Aylward, James J. ... Ravenna, OH
Aylward, Janice S. ... Tampa, FL
Aylward, Jas. P., Jr. ... Kansas City, MO
Aylward, Jean ... **Washington, DC**
Aylward, Jillian Kindlund ... **Boston, MA**
Aylward, John D. ... Fort Collins, CO
Aylward, John V. ... Watertown, NY
Aylward, Kristen Bates ... Canton, OH
Aylward, Michael F. ... **Boston, MA**
Aylward, Paula A. ... **Houston, TX**
Aylward, Peter G. ... Jamul, CA
Aylward, Robert E. ... Tampa, FL
Aylward, Robert E., P.A. ... Tampa, FL
Aylward, Robert J. ... **Charlotte, NC**
Aylward, Ronald L. ... St. Louis, MO
Aylward, Sean M. ... **Hackensack, NJ**
Aylward, Sharon ... Quincy, MA
Aylward, Timothy M. ... **Kansas City, MO**
Aylward-Bingman, Lynn M. ... San Diego, CA
Aylward-Bingman, Lynn M., A P.C.
San Diego, CA
Aymé, Deborah M. ... **New Orleans, LA**
Aymond, Carol J., Jr. ... Hessmer, LA
Aymond, Charles H. ... Jackson, MI
Aymond, Charles H., P.C. ... Jackson, MI
Aymond, Gregory R. ... Alexandria, LA
Aynes, James P. ... Irvine, CA
Aynes, Patricia C. ... Irvine, CA
Aynes, Richard L. ... Akron, OH
Ayo, Martha L. ... Thibodaux, LA
Ayon, David ... San Antonio, TX
Ayoob, Lawrence D. ... Fort Fairfield, ME
Ayoob, Nancy Ann ... San Francisco, CA
Ayoob, Richard J. ... **Los Angeles, CA**
Ayoob, Thomas H., III ... Pittsburgh, PA
Ayotte, Amy E. ... **Minneapolis, MN**
Ayotte, Marc P. ... Augusta, ME
Ayotte, Mark J. ... **St. Paul, MN**
Ayotte, Michael ... Saco, ME
Ayotte, Neil P. ... **Minneapolis, MN**
Ayotte, Normand A. ... **Pasadena, CA**
Ayotte, Ronald E., Sr. ... Saco, ME
Ayoub, Jane Cronin ... Newton, MA
Ayoub, Joseph S. ... Boston, MA
Ayoub, Joseph S., Jr. ... **Boston, MA**
Ayoub, Paul J. ... **Boston, MA**
Ayoud, Laura M. ... United States Senate,
Office of the Legislative Counsel, GV
Ayre, Albert G. ... Portland, ME
Ayre, J. Randolph ... Salt Lake City, UT
Ayre, Robert J. ... Woodbury, MN
Ayre, Terry P. ... Houston, TX
Ayres, Anne Downs Ovitz ... Baltimore, MD
Ayres, Ayres & Fleming ... **Johnstown, PA**
Ayres, Barbara Lee ... **Towson, MD**
Ayres, Benjamin H. ... **Belleview, FL**
Ayres, Benjamin H. ... Belleview, FL
Ocala, FL
Ayres, Beth S. ... **Fairfax, VA**
Ayres, Caroline Patricia ... Wilmington, DE
Dillwyn, VA
Ayres, Charles W., Jr. ... Glen Burnie, MD
Ayres, Cluster, Curry, McCall & Briggs, P.A.
Ocala, FL
Ayres, David V. ... Leavenworth, KS
Ayres, Glenn R. ... **Minneapolis, MN**
Ayres, Guy R., III ... **Ocean City, MD**
Ayres & Hartnett, P.C. ... **Accomac, VA**
Ayres, Ian ... New Haven, CT
Ayres, James E. ... **Shreveport, LA**
Ayres, James E., Jr. ... Southfield, MI
Ayres, Jeffrey P., (P.C.) ... **Baltimore, MD**
Ayres, Jenkins, Gordy & Almand, P.A.
Berlin, MD
Ocean City, MD
Snow Hill, MD
Ayres, Joe R. ... El Paso, TX
Ayres, John A., Jr. ... Clearfield, PA
Ayres, John H., III ... Baton Rouge, LA
Ayres, John M. R. ... **Johnstown, PA**
Ayres, Kenneth J. ... **Washington, DC**
Ayres, Kimberly A. ... Miami Beach, FL
Ayres, Lane E. ... Minneapolis, MN
Ayres, Laura A. ... **Lebanon, MO**
Ayres, Leland H. ... **Shreveport, LA**
Ayres, Lindsay E. ... Houston, TX
Ayres, Margaret M. ... **Washington, DC**
Ayres, Marguerite J. ... **Philadelphia, PA**
Ayres, Meredith W. ... **East Meadow, NY**
Ayres & Parkey ... **Knoxville, TN**
Ayres, R. Jack, Jr. ... **Addison, TX**
Ayres, R. Jack, Jr., A Prof. Corp., Law Offices of ... **Addison, TX**
Dallas, TX
Ayres, Richard A. ... Jackson, MS
Ayres, Richard E. ... **Washington, DC**
Ayres, Robert E. ... Albion, CA
Ayres, Russell W., III ... Pittsburgh, PA
Ayres, S. Randolph ... Athens, TN
Ayres, Sandra T. ... Montclair, NJ
Trenton, NJ
Ayres, Sharon Lee ... Concord, NH
Ayres, Stephen R. ... Chicago, IL
Ayres, Steven E. ... **Stamford, CT**
Ayres, Susan ... Austin, TX
Ayres, Tamara McDowell ... **Atlanta, GA**
Ayres, Ted D. ... Wichita, KS
Ayres, Timothy M. ... **Johnstown, PA**
Ayres, Warren W. ... **Philadelphia, PA**
Ayres, William C. ... **West Memphis, AR**
Ayres, William D. ... **Redding, CA**
Ayres, William S. ... **Indianapolis, IN**
Ayscough, Brent ... Torrance, CA
Ayscue, Brandon L. ... **Jacksonville, FL**
Ayscue, E. Osborne, Jr. ... **Charlotte, NC**
Ayubo, Cora B. ... Staten Island, NY
Ayvas, Ming K. ... **New York, NY**
Ayvazi, Rafik ... Encino, CA
Ayvazian, Kim E. ... Georgetown, DE
Ayyildiz, Elisabeth ... **Charlottesville, VA**
Ayze, Thomas M. ... Miami, FL
Azad, Enrieta C. ... **San Juan, PR**
Azad, M. H., Law Offices of ... **Webster, TX**
Azad, Susan S. ... **Los Angeles, CA**
Azallion, David J. ... **Dayton, OH**
Azallion, Melissa Green ... **Dayton, OH**
Azama, Michael ... Honolulu, HI
Azan, Warren B. ... Hartford, CT
Azan-Reyes, Marie E.
National Labor Relations Board,
Office of Board Members, GV
Azar, Afsaneh ... Cleveland, OH
Azar, Alex M., II ... **Washington, DC**
Azar & Azar, L.L.C. ... **Montgomery, AL**
Azar, Dana A. ... Atlanta, GA
Azar, David Wm. ... Melbourne, FL
Azar, Denise B. ... Montgomery, AL
Azar, Douglas A. ... Albuquerque, NM
Azar, Edward J. ... **Montgomery, AL**
Azar, Edward P. ... **Newfoundland, NJ**
Azar, Farah F. ... Mission Viejo, CA
Azar, Franklin D. ... Denver, CO
Azar, Franklin D., & Associates ... Denver, CO
Azar, George B. ... **Montgomery, AL**
Azar, Henry A., Jr. ... Department of Justice,
Civil Division, GV
Azar, Joseph R. ... Arlington, VA
Azar, Kathleen Livingston ... Evanston, IL
Azar, Lauren L. ... **Madison, WI**
Azar, Louis E. ... Pawtucket, RI
Azar, Mark ... Fall River, MA
Azar, Michael C. ... Bloomfield Hills, MI
Azar, Michelle L. ... **West Palm Beach, FL**
Azar, Philip H., II ... Houston, TX
Azar, Philip J. ... **Memphis, TN**
Azar, Richard J. ... Atlanta, GA
Azar, Robert Brian ... Omaha, NE
Azar, Rosemary ... Lafayette, LA
Azar, Stephanie McGee ... **Montgomery, AL**
Azar, Thomas J. ... Swansea, MA
Azar, Thomas J., Jr. ... **Montgomery, AL**
Azar, Victor F. ... Hackensack, NJ
Azar, William D. ... **Montgomery, AL**
Azar, William G. ... Anchorage, AK
Azar, William G., P.C. ... Anchorage, AK
Azar, Zack M. ... **Montgomery, AL**
Azarcon, Januario G. ... Vienna, VA
Azaren, Judith Lee ... Willingboro, NJ
Azari, Elizabeth D. ... **Philadelphia, PA**
Azaria, Dale E. ... **South Burlington, VT**
Azaria, Michael ... New York, NY
Azaria, Murray ... New York, NY
Azarian, David P. ... **Rochester, NH**
Azarian, Debra ... Hawthorne, NJ
Azarian, Diane L. ... Cranston, RI
Azarow, Arnold P. ... Garden City, NY
Azarow, Robert C. ... **New York, NY**
Azbill, David Randall ... London, KY
Azcona, James C. ... New Orleans, LA
Azcue, Therese ... Malden, MA
Azcuenaga, Mary L. ... **Washington, DC**
Azcuy-Diaz, Beatriz ... **Miami, FL**
Azel, Juan ... **Miami, FL**
Azemika, Anthony P. ... **Bakersfield, CA**
Azemika & Azemika ... **Bakersfield, CA**
Azemika, Nicholas P. ... **Bakersfield, CA**
Azen, Ruth Ann ... Irving, TX
Azer, Matthew C. ... **Denver, CO**
Azeredo, Ruth Ann G.
Department of Agriculture,
Office of the General Counsel, GV
Azeris, Ivar R. ... **Chicago, IL**
Azevedo, Arthur ... Modesto, CA
Azevedo, Darlene Marie ... Fresno, CA
Azevedo, Eugene M. ... Modesto, CA
Azevedo, Julie M. ... **Los Angeles, CA**
Azevedo, Ken. M. ... Santa Cruz, CA
Azevedo, Paul S. ... San Diego, CA
Aziere, John T. ... Green Bay, WI
Azimi, Bita M. ... **Woodland Hills, CA**
Azine, Sheldon L. ... Minneapolis, MN
Azios, A. D. ... Houston, TX
Aziz, Azam H. ... **New York, NY**
Aziz, Cynthia A. ... Charlotte, NC
Aziz, Mike A. ... Duluth, GA
Aziz, Sadia A. ... San Antonio, TX
Aziz, Yasmin
Environmental Protection Agency,
Office of the General Counsel, GV
Azizi, David ... Beverly Hills, CA
Azizi, Soheila S. ... Rancho Cucamonga, CA
Azkoul, William Marshall
Grand Rapids, MI
Azkoul, William N. ... Grand Rapids, MI
Azlein, Ryan ... **Los Angeles, CA**
Azman, Mark R. ... **St. Cloud, MN**
Azmon, Linda ... New York, NY
Azmy, Baher ... **New York, NY**
Aznavoorian, Vartan ... **New York, NY**
Azoff, Elliot Stephen ... **Cleveland, OH**
Azoff, Robert A. ... Levittown, PA
Azoni, Thomas J. ... **Farmington Hills, MI**
Azorsky, Gary L. ... **Cherry Hill, NJ**
Philadelphia, PA
Azorsky, Morley ... California, PA
Azorsky, Tami Lyn ... **Washington, DC**
Azoulay, Heather L. ... Trenton, NJ
Azoulay, Matthew ... **Cherry Hill, NJ**
Azouri, Farzaneh ... **San Francisco, CA**
Azrael, Edward ... **Towson, MD**
Azrael, Gann & Franz, LLP
Baltimore, MD
Greenbelt, MD
Towson, MD
Azrael, Jonathan A. ... Greenbelt, MD
Towson, MD
Azrael, Julia ... **Los Angeles, CA**
Azrael, Matthew H. ... **Towson, MD**
Azrael, Miriam L. ... **Towson, MD**
Azrak, Fredric F., & Associates
Pompton Plains, NJ
Azran, David A. ... Encino, CA
Azriliant, Evan B. ... **New York, NY**
Azriliant, Janine Robin ... **New York, NY**
Azriliant, S & E, P.C. ... **New York, NY**
Azriliant, Sidney W. ... **New York, NY**
Azrin, David T. ... **Miami, FL**
Azrin, David T., P.A., Law Office of
Miami, FL
Azuewah, Ndukwe ... Landover Hills, MD
Azulay & Azulay, P.C. ... Chicago, IL
Azulay, Ira ... **Menlo Park, CA**
Azulay, J. Daniel ... Chicago, IL
Azulay, Y. Judd ... Chicago, IL
Azulaye, Carole A. ... **Dallas, TX**
Azzam, Randa Samir ... **Fairfax, VA**
Azzara, Michael P. ... Raynham, MA
Azzariti, Michael J. ... **Atlanta, GA**
Azzariti, Steven J. ... **Washington, DC**
Azzarito, Linda F. ... Lynn, MA
Azzarito, Mary A. ... **Boston, MA**
Azzarone, Jason M. ... **Miami, FL**
Azzato, Lisa ... **Atlanta, GA**
Azzato, Lisa A., P.C. ... **Atlanta, GA**
Azzinari, Glenn M. ... **New York, NY**
Azzinaro, Frank C. ... Livingston, NJ
Azznara, Nat J. ... New York, NY
Azzo, Alex G. ... **Houston, TX**
Azzo & Azzo ... **Houston, TX**
Azzo, Judy Morris ... **Houston, TX**
Azzollini, Phillip J. ... **New York, NY**

Baab, Carole Lofness ... Minneapolis, MN
Baab, Craig H. ... Washington, DC
Baab & Denison, L.L.P. ... **Dallas, TX**
Baab, G. William ... **Dallas, TX**
Baach, Martin R. ... **Washington, DC**
Baach, Richard M. ... Fort Wayne, IN
Baach Robinson & Lewis
Washington, DC
Baach, Scott M. ... **Somerville, NJ**
Baack, Arend R. ... **Grand Island, NE**
Baade, David R. ... Costa Mesa, CA
Baade, John A. ... **Tucson, AZ**
Baade, Robin E. ... Tucson, AZ
Baader, Michael J. ... **Baltimore, MD**
Baal, David W. ... Grosse Pointe Farms, MI
Baal, Melissa ... **New York, NY**
Baal & O'Connor ... Chicago, IL
Baal, Robert B. ... Chicago, IL
Baan, Andrew G. ... Aurora, CO
Baar, Joel W. ... **Lansing, MI**
Baar, Lisa P. ... Boston, MA
Baar, Lois A. ... **Salt Lake City, UT**
Baarda, James R. ... **Washington, DC**
Baarlaer, David C ... Cincinnati, OH
Baarlaer, Dennis J. ... **Denver, CO**
Baase, Jeffrey F. ... **Buffalo, NY**
Baaset, Tracey V. ... **Atlanta, GA**
Baasten, Cornelius J. ... Canton, OH
Baatenburg, David L. ... Grand Rapids, MI
Baatrup, Peter ... **Minneapolis, MN**
Baatz, Catherine P. ... **Hartford, CT**
Baay, John E. W., II ... **New Orleans, LA**
Bab, Andrew L. ... **New York, NY**
Bab, Cheryl Milone ... **New York, NY**
Bab, Donald Stuart ... **New York, NY**
Bab, Emily ... **New York, NY**
Bab, Karen M. ... Wilmington, DE
Baba, David K. ... Reno, NV
Baba, Jason N., (A Law Corporation)
Honolulu, HI
Babachanian, Sarkis Jacob ... Glendale, CA
Babajko, Suzanne E. ... **Princeton, NJ**
Babala, John L. ... **Chicago, IL**
Babalis, Perri Ann ... Salt Lake City, UT
Babanikas, Konstantinos J. ... Brockton, MA
Babanoury, Roya Lin ... **New York, NY**
Babaoglu, Rehim ... **Memphis, TN**
Babaran, Naida ... San Diego, CA
Babarik, Dan E. ... Northbrook, IL
Babat, Amy L. ... **East Hanover, NJ**
Babat, Eric M. ... New York, NY
Babat, Michael M. ... Buffalo, NY
Babayi, Robert S. ... **Alexandria, VA**
Babb, Alfred ... Erie, PA
New Castle, PA
Pittsburgh, PA
Wexford, PA
Babb, Amy Barnes ... Raleigh, NC
Babb & Associates, P.C. ... Erie, PA
New Castle, PA
Pittsburgh, PA
Wexford, PA
Babb, Bernard J. ... **New York, NY**
Babb, Brian M. ... **Cincinnati, OH**
Babb, Brian T. ... Knoxville, TN
Babb, Charles K. ... Oklahoma City, OK
Babb, Charles M. ... Austin, TX
Babb, D. Lynn ... **Oklahoma City, OK**
Babb, Dana P. ... **Dallas, TX**
Babb, Daniel J. ... **Atlanta, GA**
Babb, David J., Jr. ... Pontiac, IL
Babb, David R. ... Belvidere, IL
Babb, Deborah L. ... **San Francisco, CA**
Babb, Dennis L. ... **Knoxville, TN**
Babb, Douglas J. ... Fort Worth, TX
Babb, Edward U. ... **Knoxville, TN**
Babb, Everette H., Law Office of
Mauldin, SC
Babb, Frank E. ... **Chicago, IL**
Babb & Harbeson, P.C. ... Austin, TX
Babb, Henry C., Jr. ... Wilson, NC
Babb, Howard H., Jr. ... Tavares, FL
Babb, James D., Jr. ... Anchorage, AK
Babb, James G. ... Key West, FL
Babb, James H. ... United States Senate,
Senatorial Assistants, GV
Babb, John P. ... **Denver, CO**
Babb, Jonathan Porter ... Raleigh, NC
Babb, Joseph S. ... Austin, TX
Babb, Judith S. ... Wakefield, MA
Babb, Kevin J. ... Edwardsville, IL
Babb, Mae Charles ... **Atlanta, GA**
Babb, Margaret J. ... **Washington, DC**
Babb, Melanie Elaine ... Bronx, NY
Babb, Phillip R. ... San Diego, CA
Babb, R. Kenneth ... Winston-Salem, NC
Babb, Ray A. ... Bend, OR
Babb, Ray K., Jr. ... New Castle, OK
Babb, Rhonda E. ... Cocoa, FL
Babb, Richard J. ... Ripley, MS
Babb, Robert F. ... Portsmouth, VA
Babb, Roger Sumner ... Atlanta, GA
Babb, Ronald D. ... Blue Island, IL
Babb, Russell D. ... **Charlotte, NC**
Babb, Sharon Reider ... **Hackensack, NJ**
Babb, Stan D. ... Marietta, GA
Babb, Steven C. ... **Los Angeles, CA**
Babb, Thomas A. ... Laurens, SC
Babb, Timothy ... Lansing, MI
Babb, Warren E., Jr. ... **Seattle, WA**
Babbe, David B. ... **Los Angeles, CA**
Babbin, F. S. ... Southfield, MI
Babbin, Jed L. ... **Washington, DC**
Babbin, Jeffrey R. ... **New Haven, CT**
Babbin, Sharon L. ... **Washington, DC**
Babbington, John M. ... Mokena, IL
Babbish, Byron C. ... **Southfield, MI**
Babbit, Douglas R. ... Sherman Oaks, CA
Babbit, Harold A. ... Austin, TX
Babbit, Harold W. ... **Cleveland, OH**
Babbit, Kevin Walter ... Emporia, KS
Babbits, Dennis A. ... San Francisco, CA
Babbitt, April H. ... Pepperell, MA
Babbitt, Bradford S. ... **Hartford, CT**
Babbitt, Bruce P. ... **Seattle, WA**
Babbitt, Carol Coplan ... Chicago, IL
Babbitt, Craig M. ... **Akron, OH**
Babbitt, David B. ... Lake Havasu City, AZ
Babbitt, Diane C. ... Seattle, WA
Babbitt, Edward J. ... Cincinnati, OH
Babbitt, Edward J., Jr. ... San Diego, CA
Babbitt, Elizabeth S. ... Harrisburg, PA
Babbitt, Ellen M. ... **Chicago, IL**
Babbitt, Floyd ... **Chicago, IL**
Babbitt, Gary D. ... **Boise, ID**
Babbitt, Gerald D. ... Burtonsville, MD
Babbitt, Gerald J. ... **Columbus, OH**

Babbitt, Gregory J. ....Grand Haven, MI
Babbitt, Harriet C. ....Washington, DC
Babbitt, James D. ....Barron, WI
Babbitt, Jerry R. ....Lawton, OK
Babbitt and Johnson, P.A.
West Palm Beach, FL
Babbitt & Melton ....Chicago, IL
Babbitt, Michael J. ....Salem, OR
Babbitt, Michelle S. ....New York, NY
Babbitt, Robert P. ....Chicago, IL
Babbitt, Robin L. ....Indianapolis, IN
Babbitt, Sherryl Smith ....Middletown, RI
Babbitt, Theodore ....West Palm Beach, FL
Babbitt, W. Thomas ....Los Angeles, CA
Babbitz, David R. ....West Haven, CT
Babbitz, James A. ....Louisville, KY
Babbitz, Todd S. ....Chicago, IL
Babbo, Heidi L. ....Chicago, IL
Babbo, Mary I. ....Chicago, IL
Babbo, Thomas J. ....Chicago, IL
Babboni, Michael J ....Bradenton, FL
Brandon, FL
Clearwater, FL
Holly Hill, FL
Lakeland, FL
Port Charlotte, FL
Port Richey, FL
St. Petersburg, FL
Sarasota, FL
Tampa, FL
Babbush, Glenn ....Brooklyn, NY
Babbush, Howard E. ....Brooklyn, NY
Babbush, Randall M. ....Costa Mesa, CA
Babby, Lon S. ....Washington, DC
Babby, Lorna ....Washington, DC
Babchick, Cohen & Shearer, P.C.
Houston, TX
Babchick, Jack, (P.C.) ....Houston, TX
Babchik, Jack ....New York, NY
Babchik & Young, LLP ....New York, NY
Babcock, Anne F. ....Hopkinton, MA
Babcock, Barak J. ....St. Paul, MN
Babcock, Barbara A. ....Palo Alto, CA
Babcock, Bostwick, Scott, Crawley & Price, P.C. ....Salt Lake City, UT
Babcock, Brent R. ....Tawas City, MI
Babcock, Brenton R. ......Newport Beach, CA
Babcock, Bret S. ....Peoria, IL
Babcock, Brian J. ....Salt Lake City, UT
Babcock, Bruce E. ....Salt Lake City, UT
Babcock, Bruce, Jr. ....Sacramento, CA
Babcock, Bruce R. ....Encinitas, CA
Babcock & Cappelli, LLP
Laguna Niguel, CA
Riverside, CA
Babcock, Charles L. ....Dallas, TX
Houston, TX
Babcock, Charles W., Jr. ....Detroit, MI
Babcock, Cliff G. ....Cleveland, OH
Babcock, Colton W., Jr. ....Augusta, ME
Babcock, Courtland T., II
Forked River, NJ
Babcock, Daniel M. ....Batavia, NY
Babcock, David D. ....Lincoln, NE
Babcock, David W. ....Tucson, AZ
Babcock, Edmund P. ....Anoka, MN
Babcock, Ernest J. ....Portland, ME
Babcock, Gary D. ....Salem, OR
Babcock, George H., (A Professional Corporation) ....Santa Ana, CA
Babcock, Gregory T. ....Chesterton, IN
Babcock, Harry N. ....Rocky River, OH
Babcock, Harvey K. ....Farmington Hills, MI
Babcock, James Dorr ....Indianapolis, IN
Babcock, James Dorr, P.C.
Indianapolis, IN
Babcock, James E. ....Joliet, IL
Babcock, James E., Jr. ....Chicago, IL
Babcock, James P. ....St. Clair Shores, MI
Babcock, Jay P. ....New York, NY
Babcock, Jeffery A. ....Houston, TX
Babcock, Jill J. ....Lansing, MI
Babcock, Joel S. ....Denver, CO
Babcock, John A. ....Laguna Niguel, CA
Riverside, CA
Babcock, John J. ....St. Cloud, MN
Babcock, John W. ....Winston-Salem, NC
Babcock, Jolinda J. ....Winston-Salem, NC
Babcock, Julie B. ....Bellevue, WA
Babcock, Katherine M. ....Fairfield, CA
Babcock, Kathleen Marie ....Franklin, MI
Babcock, Keith M. ....Columbia, SC
Babcock, Kenneth W. ....Los Angeles, CA
Babcock, Lewis T. ....Denver, CO
Babcock, Linda S. ....West Bloomfield, MI
Babcock, Mary Elizabeth P. ....Albany, NY
Babcock, Mary Kathleen ....Wichita, KS
Babcock, Matthew D. ....Utica, NY
Babcock, Michael W. ....Seattle, WA
Babcock, Neilson, Mannella, LaFleur & Klint, P.L.L.P. ....Anoka, MN
Coon Rapids, MN
Babcock, Peter G. ....Marietta, GA
Babcock, Reginald L. ....Hartford, CT
Babcock, Richard J. ....Irvine, CA
Babcock, Robert A. ....Kansas City, MO
Babcock, Robert E. ....Lake Oswego, OR
Babcock, Robert F., (P.C.)
Salt Lake City, UT
Babcock, Robert G. ....Milford, CT
Babcock, Robyn A. ....Philadelphia, PA
Babcock, Ronald J. ....Carmichael, CA
Babcock, Sherman F. ....Sun City Center, FL
Babcock, Sherril Nell ....Los Angeles, CA
Babcock, Stanton ....Lafayette, IN
Babcock, Sumner H. ....Boston, MA
Babcock, William A. ....Springfield, OR
Babcock, William G. ....Philadelphia, PA
Babcock, William L., Jr. ....Alexandria, VA
Babcock, William L., Jr., PC
Alexandria, VA
Babcox, Deborah W. ....Smethport, PA
Babecki, Linda M. ....Trenton, NJ
Babel, John P. ....Irvine, CA
Babel, Thomas S. ....Cleveland, OH
Babel, Walter E., Jr. ....Houston, TX
Babener & Associates ....Portland, OR
Babener, Jeffrey A. ....Portland, OR
Baber, Brant ....Washington, DC
Baber, Brett D. ....Bangor, ME
Baber, Bruce ....Paris, IL
Baber, Bruce W. ....Atlanta, GA
Baber, Charles S. ....Tulsa, OK
Baber, Donna H. ....St. Louis, MO
Baber, James A., III ....Richmond, VA
Baber, James G. ....Monmouth, IL
Baber, James Pendleton ......Cumberland, VA
Baber, James R. ....Little Rock, AR
Baber, John L., III ....Houston, TX
Baber, Mark A. ....Jersey City, NJ
Baber, Mary Helen ....Gallup, NM
Baber, Molly K. ....Huntington, WV
Baber, Walter F. ....San Diego, CA
Baber, Wilbur H., Jr. ....Hallettsville, TX
Baber, William H., III ....Oroville, CA
Baber, William R. ....San Diego, CA
Babetch, Daniel I. ....Chicago, IL
Babey, Sandra J. ....Coral Springs, FL
Babi, Kenneth V. ....Garden City, NY
Babiak, Bartholomew G. ....Freehold, NJ
Babiak, Nicholas J. ....Washington, DC
Babiarz, Claudia V. ....Troy, MI
Babiarz, David J. ....Englewood, CO
Babiarz, Francis S. ....Wilmington, DE
Babiarz, John E., Jr. ....Wilmington, DE
Babiarz, Joseph F., Jr. ....Detroit, MI
Babiarz, Richard S. ....Chicago, IL
Babiarz, Timothy S. ....Ocala, FL
Babic, Jacqueline ....South River, NJ
Babic, Michael W. ....Lancaster, PA
Babich, Adam ....Chicago, IL
Babich, Jos. G. ....Sacramento, CA
Babich, Joseph J. ....Sacramento, CA
Babich, Laurie Dahl ....Fort Worth, TX
Babich, Lawrence H. ....Marion, OH
Babich, Leslie ....Des Moines, IA
Babich, McConnell & Renzo, P.C.
Des Moines, IA
Babich, Rory A. ....New York, NY
Babich, Ted B. ....Marion, OH
Babich, Todd E. ....Des Moines, IA
Babich, Walter Peter ....Wayne, PA
Babich, William ....Denver, CO
Babigian, K. Vasken ....Watertown, MA
Babij, Bruce J. ....Timonium, MD
Babikian, Dayna S. ....San Diego, CA
Babikian, M. Michael ....Glendale, CA
Babin & Babin ....Lafayette, LA
Babin, Helen Hairston ....New Orleans, LA
Babin, James L. ....Lake Charles, LA
Babin, Jane Elizabeth ....Plymouth, NH
Babin, John C. ....Brookings, OR
Babin, Joyce Bradley ....Little Rock, AR
Babin, Larry A., Jr. ....Gonzales, LA
Babin, Leopold B. ....Marietta, GA
Babin, Mara L. ....Cleveland, OH
Babin, Miriam H. ....New Bedford, MA
Babin, Norbert C. ....Santa Rosa, CA
Babin, Philip, III ....Beaumont, TX
Babin, Roger O. ....Plymouth, NH
Babin, Seeger, Crow & Manwell, LLP
Santa Rosa, CA
Babin, Stanley P. ....Lafayette, LA
Babin, Troy J. ....Houston, TX
Babin, W. Brian ....Baton Rouge, LA
Babin, Wilbur J. "Bill", Jr.
New Orleans, LA
Babin, William T. ....Lafayette, LA
Babineau, Anne S. ....Woodbridge, NJ
Babineau, Kelly Lynn Katherine
Sacramento, CA
Babineaux, Joel P. ....Lafayette, LA
Babineaux, Mark A. ....Lafayette, LA
Babinec, Gehl P. ....Cincinnati, OH
Babineck, Frank J. ....Houston, TX
Babinecz, Richard W. ....New York, NY
Babington, Brian A. ....Albuquerque, NM
Babington, Carol G. ....Oakland, CA
Babington, Charles J., Jr. ....Cary, NC
Babington, Charles M., III ....St. Louis, MO
Babington, Joseph P. H. ....Mobile, AL
Babington, Margaret M. ....Cleveland, OH
Babington, Thomas K. ....Naperville, IL
Babington, William R., Jr.
Las Cruces, NM
Babinski, Judith A. ....Warren, NJ
Babione, Byron J. ....Syracuse, NY
Babione, Robert C. ....St. Louis, MO
Babirak, Albert & Vangellow, P.C.
Annapolis, MD
Bethesda, MD
Babirak, Albert, Vangellow & Shaheen, P.C.
Washington, DC
Falls Church, VA
Sterling, VA
Babirak, Milton E., Jr. ....Annapolis, MD
Sterling, VA
Babis, Frank E. ....Santa Cruz, CA
Babiskin, Lisa M. ....New York, NY
Babiskin, William A. ....Rensselaer, NY
Babitch & Babitch ....New York, NY
Babitch, Debra Lynn ....New York, NY
Babitch, Lawrence ....New York, NY
Babits, Joseph P. ....Washington, DC
Babitsky, Steven ....Falmouth, MA
Babitt, Bruce H. ....New York, NY
Babitt, Roy ....New York, NY
Babitz, Alisa ....Washington, DC
Babitz, Martyn S. ....Cherry Hill, NJ
Babjak, Betty Ann ....Avenel, NJ
Babka, Brian A. ....Belleville, IL
Babka, Nancy A. ....Portland, OR
Babkow, David P.
Small Business Administration, Office of the General Counsel, GV
Babler, Gregory J. ....St. Paul, MN
Babler, James C. ....Barron, WI
Babler, Wayne E. ....Boynton Beach, FL
Babler, Wayne E., Jr. ....Milwaukee, WI
Bablitch, James M. ....Stevens Point, WI
Bablitch, Stephen E. ....Madison, WI
Bablitch, William A. ....Madison, WI
Babner, David Perry ....Brooklyn, NY
Babner, David W. ....Boston, MA
Babnick, Richard J., Jr. ....New York, NY
Babody, Joseph A. ....Detroit, MI
Babok, Barry S. ....Los Angeles, CA
Babore, Guido A. ....Philadelphia, PA
Babovich, Wayne M. ....Metairie, LA
Babow, Brent A. ....Vallejo, CA
Babowice, James J. ....Waukegan, IL
Babsin, Marc A. ....Berkeley, CA
Babson, David E. ....Gloucester, MA
Babson, David F. ....Greenwich, CT
Babson, Katherine L., Jr. ....Boston, MA
Babson, Marshall B. ....Washington, DC
Babson, Stacey B. ....New York, NY
Babson, Stephen E. ....Portland, OR
Babst, Calland, Clements and Zomnir, A Professional Corporation
Philadelphia, PA
Pittsburgh, PA
Babst, Charles R., Jr. ....Tulsa, OK
Babst, Chester R., III ....Pittsburgh, PA
Babst, James A. ....New Orleans, LA
Babst, Lawrence F. ....Metairie, LA
Babst, Lawrence F., Jr. ....Metairie, LA
Babst, Loretto M. ....Metairie, LA
Babst, Walter M. ....Metairie, LA
Babtkis, Elyse M. ....Beverly Hills, CA
Babush, Richard K. ....Atlanta, GA
Babut, William C. ....Ypsilanti, MI
Babut, William C., P.C. ....Ypsilanti, MI
Bâby, Henry P., Jr. ....Winnetka, IL
Babyak, Gregory Roger ....Washington, DC
Babych, Douglas W. ....Park Ridge, IL
Babycos, Frank Edward, (P.C.)
Bridgeport, CT
Baca, Adrian M. ....Los Angeles, CA
Baca, Anthony ....Boise, ID
Baca, B. Kurt ....Washington, DC
Baca, Billy G. ....Houston, TX
Baca, Carolyn J. ....Las Cruces, NM
Baca, Daniel Ray ....Albuquerque, NM
Baca, David A. ....Albuquerque, NM
Baca, David C. ....Portland, OR
Baca, Elena R. ....Los Angeles, CA
Baca, Frank A. ....Albuquerque, NM
Baca, Frank A., P.A. ....Albuquerque, NM
Baca, Gene ....Albuquerque, NM
Baca, Gerald E. ....Las Vegas, NM
Baca, Gerald M. ....New Orleans, LA
Baca, Henry J. ....Las Cruces, NM
Baca, Jaime ....Miami, FL
Baca, Jaime J. ....Miami, FL
Baca, James ....Cerritos, CA
Baca, Joe A. ....Cheyenne, WY
Baca, José J. ....El Paso, TX
Baca, Joseph F. ....Santa Fe, NM
Baca, Kathleen ....Albuquerque, NM
Baca, Lawrence R. ....Department of Justice, Civil Rights Division, GV
Baca, Marie G. ....Los Angeles, CA
Baca, Patricia ....Fort Worth, TX
Baca, Paula L. ....Richmond, CA
Baca, Philip J. ....Denver, CO
Baca, Robert T. ....Bakersfield, CA
Baca, Rudolfo Lujan
Federal Communications Commission, International Bureau, GV
Baca, Sandra H. ....Durango, CO
Baca, Theresa M. ....Albuquerque, NM
Baca, Walter E. ....Tustin, CA
Bacaj, Faton A. ....Washington, DC
Bacal, Dan ....El Cajon, CA
Bacal, Glenn Spencer ....Phoenix, AZ
Bacal, Katherine A. ....San Diego, CA
Bacal, Michael W. ....Stamford, CT
Bacalakis, Karen M. ....Medford, NY
Bacalis, Athena ....Lakeland, MI
Bacalis, Daniel R. ....Fort Worth, TX
Bacalis, Daniel R. ....Hurst, TX
Bacalis, Jesse R. ....Detroit, MI
Bacall, Charles P. ....Portland, ME
Bacall, Michael ....San Diego, CA
Bacallao, Andrew S. ....Meadville, PA
Bacallao-Perez, Grisell ....Miami, FL
Bacalski, A. Daniel, Jr. (A Professional Corporation) ....San Diego, CA
Bacalski, Byrne & Koska ....San Diego, CA
Bacalzo, Rachel M. ....Phoenix, AZ
Bacardi, Anton E. ....Newark, NJ
Bacarisse, Louis A. ....Austin, TX
Bacas, Florence ....Barnstable, MA
Bacas & Krogmann ....Glens Falls, NY
Bacas, Thomas J. ....Boca Raton, FL
Bacas, William A. ....Glens Falls, NY
Bacastow, Daniel J. ....Chicago, IL
Bacca, Jeffrey Alan ....New Port Richey, FL
Baccarella, Dominic J. ....Tampa, FL
Baccari, Barbara A. ....New Port Richey, FL
Baccari, John A. ....Reading, MA
Baccari, Paul L. ....Boston, MA
Baccari and Trillo, Law Associates
Warwick, RI
Baccash, Michael F. ....Chicago, IL
Bacchetta, Bernard P. ....Boonton, NJ
Bacchetti, Jerome A. ....Moorestown, NJ
Bacchiocchi, Gianluca ....New York, NY
Bacchus, James L. ....Orlando, FL
Bacci, Forrest N. A. ....Portland, OR
Bacci, Guy J. ....North Riverside, IL
Bacci, Leonardo S. ....San Francisco, CA
Bacciarini, Mark V. ....Merced, CA
Baccini, Laurance E. ....Philadelphia, PA
Baccus, Lisa S.
Department of Transportation, Federal Aviation Administration, GV
Baccus, Steve A. ....Tuscumbia, AL
Baccus, Wilbert
Department of Transportation, Federal Highway Administration, GV
Baccus-Lobel, Shirley (IBA) ....**Dallas, TX**
Bacdayan, Karen May ....Brooklyn, NY
Bace, John C. ....Huntington, NY
Bace, Thomas L. ....Toms River, NJ
Bacek, Donald A. ....Atlanta, GA
Bacen & Kaplan, P.A. ....Fort Lauderdale, FL
Bacen, Stephen F. ....Fort Lauderdale, FL
Bacerdo, Ramon Z. ....Los Angeles, CA
Bacetich, Dominic L. ....Everett, WA
Bacetich-Duffy, Inc., Inc., P.S. ....Everett, WA
Bacevice, John P. ....Cleveland, OH
Bacevich, Michael P. ....Cincinnati, OH
Bach, Amy R. ....San Francisco, CA
Bach & Associates ....New York, NY
Bach, Babette Bryan ....Sarasota, FL
Bach, Barry ....Towson, MD
Bach, Beverly J. ....Fairfax, VA
Bach, Burton ....West Covina, CA
Bach, Carver & Dewberry
Alpharetta, GA
Atlanta, GA
Cumming, GA
Roswell, GA
Bach, Charles L., Jr. ....New York, NY
Bach, Daniel P. ....Madison, WI
Bach, David C. ....Baton Rouge, LA
Bach, David R. ....Rockville, MD
Bach, Donald Leo ....Madison, WI
Bach, Elizabeth H.
Department Of Health And Human Services, Office of the General Counsel, GV
Bach, Ellen M. ....Albany, NY
Bach, Eric A. ....Charlotte, NC
Bach, F. Bruce ....Fairfax, VA
Bach, Francis P. ....Harrisburg, PA
Bach, Gilbert ....New York, NY
Bach, James A. ....San Francisco, CA
Bach, John A. ....Milwaukee, WI
Bach, John C. ....Alpharetta, GA
Bach, John E., Jr. ....Goshen, NY
Bach, John V. ....Garden City, NY
Bach, Jonathan Scott ....Towson, MD
Bach, Julian ....Los Angeles, CA
Bach, Katherine M. ....Racine, WI
Bach, Kyle ....San Francisco, CA
Bach, L. Gabriel ....Miami, FL
Bach, Laura R. ....Washington, DC
Bach, Lawrence R. ....Akron, OH
Bach, Lucinda J. ....Washington, DC
Bach, Mary Ann ....Pittsburgh, PA
Bach, Masha ....Miami, FL
Bach, Maxim N. ....Oroville, CA
Bach, Melissa Dailey ....Henderson, KY
Bach, Michael B. ....Cincinnati, OH
Bach, Michael P. ....New York, NY
Bach, Michele ....Sacramento, CA
Bach, Michelle Depew ....Dayton, OH
Bach, Mitchell L. ....Haddonfield, NJ
Philadelphia, PA
Bach, Murray D. ....Jackson Heights, NY
Bach, Paul M. ....Joliet, IL
Bach, Peter Hansen ....Philadelphia, PA
Bach, Richard D. ....Portland, OR
Bach, Richard E. ....Helena, MT
Bach, Richard N. ....Utica, NY
Bach, Robert H. ....Denver, CO
Bach, Robert L. ....Minneapolis, MN
Bach, Robert W. ....Peoria, IL
Bach, Robt. L. ....Indianapolis, IN
Bach, Samuel John ....Henderson, KY
Bach and Savage ....Lexington, KY
Bach, Scott L. ....New York, NY
Bach, Seyun ....Flushing, NY
Bach, Sidney M. ....Metairie, LA
New Orleans, LA
Bach and Small ....San Francisco, CA
Bach, Steve C. ....Mt. Vernon, IN
Bach, Steven A. ....Madison, WI
Bach, Tammi E. ....Lakeland, FL
Bach, Thomas H. ....New York, NY
Bach & Wasserman ....Metairie, LA
New Orleans, LA
Bach, Wayne M. ....Hickory, NC
Bach, William D. ....Lexington, KY
Bach, William S. ....Bloomington, IL
Bach, William S. ....North Bethesda, MD
Bach, Yvonne G. ....Philadelphia, PA
Bacha, James R. ....Columbus, OH
Bachan, Paul W. ....Watsonville, CA
Bachan, Skillicorn, Marinovich & Balian
Watsonville, CA
Bachand, Clifford B. ....Oakland, CA
Bachand, Donald R., III
Bloomfield Hills, MI
Bachand, Edward N. ....Palo Alto, CA
Bachand, Joseph Ryan ....Melbourne, FL
Bachand, Law Office ....Albuquerque, NM
Bachand, Longo & Higgins ....Putnam, CT
Bachand, Louis J. ....La Canada Flintridge, CA

Bacotti, Christopher .... Massapequa, NY
Bacotti, Louis J. .... Brooklyn, NY
Bacow, Mitchell L. .... Boca Raton, FL
Bacso, Robert W. .... Princeton, NJ
Bacso, Susan E. .... Lawrenceville, NJ
Marlton, NJ
Bacus, Joseph A.
Department of Housing and Urban Development, Office of General Counsel, GV
Bacus, Thomas H. .... Wichita Falls, TX
Bacvar, Richard A. .... Pittsburgh, PA
Baczewski, Matthew T.A. .... Sacramento, CA
Baczkowski, Walter F. .... Mc Keesport, PA
Badach, Frank J. .... Boca Raton, FL
Badagliacca, John .... Montclair, NJ
Badagliacca, Vincent J., Jr. .... New York, NY
Purchase, NY
Badain, David I. .... New York, NY
Badal, Cathy M. .... Reading, PA
Badal, John R. .... Reading, PA
Badal, Rachelle .... San Jose, CA
Badal, Robert G. .... Los Angeles, CA
Badalamente, Mark F.
Environmental Protection Agency, Program Office Attorneys, GV
Badami, James A. .... Little Rock, AR
Badami, Joseph H. .... Lincoln, NE
Badami, Maitreya .... San Francisco, CA
Badami, Robert A. .... Newton, NJ
Badami, Sally .... Huntington, NY
Badami, Scott M. .... Washington, DC
Badamo, Laura .... New York, NY
Badanes, Peter L. .... Danbury, CT
Badaracco, Joseph L. .... St. Louis, MO
Badaruddin, Michelle P. .... Atlanta, GA
Badasarian, Jos. Z. .... Cambridge, MA
Badash, Kate Sydney .... San Antonio, TX
Badash, Mark .... Deer Park, NY
Badavas, Christos P. .... New York, NY
Badawi, Suzanne Y. .... Los Angeles, CA
Badcock, Tasca W. .... Columbus, GA
Baddeley, D. Jeffrey .... Waukegan, IL
Baddeley, Jeffrey .... Cleveland, OH
Baddeley, Michael J. .... Petaluma, CA
Badders, Russell A. .... Pensacola, FL
Badders, William A. .... Nacogdoches, TX
Baddin, A. E. .... Duluth, MN
Baddley, David W. .... Fort Lauderdale, FL
Baddley, Thomas E., Jr. .... Birmingham, AL
Baddock, Franz J. .... Baton Rouge, LA
Baddour & Milner, PLLC .... Chapel Hill, NC
Baddour, Mitchell, Jr. .... Dallas, TX
Baddour, Parker & Hine, Professional Corporation .... Goldsboro, NC
Baddour, Philip A., III .... Goldsboro, NC
Baddour, Philip A., Jr. .... Goldsboro, NC
Baddour, Raymond J. .... Palm Springs, CA
Baddour, Richard Allen, Jr. .... Chapel Hill, NC
Bade, Abdullah A. .... Indianapolis, IN
Bade, Annette L. .... Rochester, NY
Bade, Bridget S. .... Phoenix, AZ
Bade, Bruce C. .... Hartford City, IN
Bade, Donna L. .... Chicago, IL
Bade, Lorrie A. .... Denver, CO
Bade, Thomas W. .... Phoenix, AZ
Badeaux, Ellen Cronin .... New Orleans, LA
Badeaux, Reginald T., III .... Metairie, LA
Badeaux, Reginald T., Jr. .... New Orleans, LA
Badeaux, Richard C. .... Covington, LA
Badeaux, Steven B. .... New Orleans, LA
Badeer, Nancy J. .... New York, NY
Badeker, Roger W. .... Alma, KS
Badel, Julie .... Chicago, IL
Badell, Patrick C., P.C. .... Rushville, IN
Baden, Alan P. .... New York, NY
Baden, Allen J. .... San Jose, CA
Baden, Earl W., Jr. .... Bradenton, FL
Baden, Frederick E. .... Napoleon, OH
Baden & Jones Co., L.P.A. .... Hamilton, OH
Baden, Joseph H. .... Blaine, MN
Baden Kramer Huffman & Brodsky, P.C.
Brooklyn, NY
New York, NY
Scarsdale, NY
White Plains, NY
Baden, Naneen K. .... Seattle, WA
Baden, Naomi J. .... Rockville, MD
Baden, Ruth K. .... Newton, MA
Baden, Steven L. .... North Canton, OH
Baden, Victoria L. .... Davie, FL
Baden, Wayne I. .... New York, NY
Badenoch, Bruce M. .... Minneapolis, MN
Badenoch, George E. .... New York, NY
Bader, Angela M. .... Reno, NV
Bader & Associates, P.C. .... Denver, CO
Bader & Bader .... White Plains, NY
Bader, Benedict .... White Plains, NY
Bader, Bertran T., III, P.C. .... Dallas, TX
Bader, Bertran T., III, (P.C.) .... Dallas, TX
Bader, Christine L. .... Skaneateles, NY
Bader, Clare M. .... Manitowoc, WI
Bader & Cooper .... Baltimore, MD
Bader, D. James .... Olympia Fields, IL
Bader, David A. .... Toledo, OH
Bader, David J. .... Sacramento, CA
Bader, David M. .... New York, NY
Bader & Donkel .... Olympia Fields, IL
Bader, Donna .... Laguna Beach, CA
Bader, Eliot M. .... Delray Beach, FL
Jupiter, FL
Margate, FL
West Palm Beach, FL
Bader, Elizabeth Evriah, Law Offices of
San Francisco, CA
Bader, Gail Donnelly .... Alton, IL
Bader, Gerald L., Jr. .... Denver, CO
Bader, Gregory K. .... West Palm Beach, FL
Bader, Gregory V. .... Houston, TX
Bader, Hans .... Washington, DC
Bader, Herbert R. .... Plainview, NY
Bader, Howard D. .... New York, NY
Bader, I. Walton .... White Plains, NY
Bader, J. Lani .... San Francisco, CA
Bader, John Merwin .... Wilmington, DE
Bader, John R. .... Glen Burnie, MD
Bader, Jonathan David .... Los Angeles, CA
Bader, Laura E. .... Chicago, IL
Bader, Lawrence S. .... New York, NY
Bader, Lillian V. .... Bay Shore, NY
Bader, Louis .... New York, NY
Bader, Margo E. .... New York, NY
Bader, Mark S. .... McLean, VA
Bader, Mary Beth Juelke .... Fargo, ND
Bader, Michael H. .... Arlington, VA
Bader, Michael M. .... St. Paul, MN
Bader, Michelle L. .... Rockport, MA
Bader, Nicole E. .... Stockton, CA
Bader, Paul L. .... New Haven, CT
Bader, Richard B.
Federal Election Commission, Office of the General Counsel, GV
Bader, Richard M. .... Baltimore, MD
Bader, Richard W. .... Voorheesville, NY
Bader & Ryan, Ltd. .... Reno, NV
Bader, Seth D. .... New York, NY
Bader & Stillman .... Delray Beach, FL
Jupiter, FL
Margate, FL
West Palm Beach, FL
Bader, Todd A. .... Reno, NV
Bader, Troy A. .... Minneapolis, MN
Bader, Valorie A. .... Santa Rosa, CA
Bader, W. Reece .... Menlo Park, CA
Bader, Warren W. .... Syracuse, NY
Bader, Wendy
Federal Labor Relations Authority, Authority Member Staff, GV
Bader, William A. .... Leesburg, FL
Bader, William A. .... New York, NY
Badera, Peter J. .... Syracuse, NY
Baderian, Steven D. .... White Plains, NY
Bader-Martin, Anne J.F. .... Waltham, MA
Badertscher, David A. .... Houston, TX
Bader-York, Judith .... New York, NY
Badesch, Robert T. .... Chicago, IL
Badey, George J., III .... Marlton, NJ
Philadelphia, PA
Badger, Alston Calhoun, Jr. .... Charleston, SC
Badger, Alvin H. .... Dallas, TX
Badger, Amy E. .... Albuquerque, NM
Badger & Baker .... Carson City, NV
Badger, Calvin Dion .... Long Island City, NY
Badger, Carlos J. .... Modesto, CA
Badger, Daniel B. .... Greenwich, CT
Badger, David C. .... San Antonio, TX
Badger, David H. .... Indianapolis, IN
Badger, David R. .... Charlotte, NC
Badger, David R., P.A. .... Charlotte, NC
Badger, David W. .... Dixon, IL
Badger, Deborah M.
Equal Employment Opportunity Commission, Office of Federal Operations, GV
Badger, Dolan, Parker & Cohen
Boston, MA
Badger, Don .... Santa Rosa, CA
Badger, Dorothy Allen .... Charleston, SC
Badger, Elizabeth D. .... Kansas City, MO
Badger, Francis B. J. .... Scituate, MA
Badger, Frederick J., Jr. .... Bangor, ME
Badger, James B. .... San Diego, CA
Badger, Janet F. .... Columbia, SC
Badger, Jeffrey E. .... Salisbury, MD
Badger, Jimmy L. .... Nashville, TN
Badger, John M. .... Denver, CO
Badger, Kyle C. .... Cleveland, OH
Badger, Leland J. .... Washington, DC
Badger & Levings .... Kansas City, MO
Badger, Michael D. .... Worcester, MA
Badger, P. Bruce .... Salt Lake City, UT
Badger, Peter R. .... Department of Defense, Defense Legal Services Agency, GV
Badger, Raymond L., Jr. .... Carson City, NV
Badger, Richard I., Jr. .... Chicago, IL
Badger, Richard J., Co., L.P.A.
Ravenna, OH
Badger, Robert E. .... Department of Justice, Civil Division, GV
Badger, Robert E., Jr. .... Honolulu, HI
Badger, Robert L. .... Kingston, TN
Badger, Robert W. .... Indianapolis, IN
Badger, Ronald K. .... Wichita, KS
Badger, S. Campbell .... Portland, ME
Badger, Steven J. .... Dallas, TX
Badger, Steven M. .... Indianapolis, IN
Badger, Susan E. .... San Francisco, CA
Badger, Vincent M. .... New York, NY
Badger, W. John .... Topeka, KS
Badger, Warren H. .... Dixon, IL
Badger, William B. .... Canton, OH
Badgerow, J. Nick .... Overland Park, KS
Badgett, Barbara .... Jackson, TN
Badgett, Barbara, P.C. .... Jackson, TN
Badgett, Catherine D. .... Ridgeland, SC
Badgett, J. N., Jr. .... Maryville, TN
Badgett & Phillips .... Winston-Salem, NC
Badgett, Richard G. .... Winston-Salem, NC
Badgett, Robyn Jill Lazenby .... Danbury, NC
Badgewick, Joseph H. .... Poultney, VT
Badgewick, Joseph H. .... Rutland, VT
Badgley, Brad L. .... Belleville, IL
Badgley, Don Paul .... Seattle, WA
Badgley, Jeffrey Scott .... Tampa, FL
Badgley - Mullins .... Kennewick, WA
Seattle, WA
Wenatchee, WA
Yakima, WA
Badgley, Richard B. .... St. Petersburg, FL
Badgley, Robert A. .... Chicago, IL
Badgley, Robert L. .... Bloomfield Hills, MI
Badham, R. Paxton, Jr. .... Raleigh, NC
Badham, Vera C. .... Salt Lake City, UT
Badham, Walker Percy, III
Birmingham, AL
Badiak, Mary L. .... New York, NY
Badiak, Roman .... New York, NY
Badiak Will & Kallen
North Miami Beach, FL
Badiak Will & Ruddy .... New York, NY
Badian, Larry D.
Department of Transportation, Surface Transportation Board, GV
Badian, Samuel M. .... Boca Raton, FL
Badiani, Purvi .... Washington, DC
Badiano, Gerardo .... Palatine, IL
Badie, James W. .... New York, NY
Badillo, Herman .... New York, NY
Badillo, William J. .... Westbury, NY
Badillo-Rodriguez, Roxanna .... Hartford, CT
Bading, Frederick A. .... Atlanta, GA
Badini, Aldo A. .... New York, NY
Baditoi, George .... Southfield, MI
Baditoi, George, P.C. .... Southfield, MI
Badke, Bradford J. .... New York, NY
Badler, Sara L. .... New York, NY
Badley, Basil .... Seattle, WA
Badley, Bruce P. .... Sheridan, WY
Badley & Rasmussen, P.C. .... Sheridan, WY
Badman, Robert A., Jr. .... Morrisville, PA
Badmus, Ann Massey .... Newark, DE
Badmus, Ann Massey, P.A. .... Newark, DE
Badnell, David C. .... Mansfield, OH
Badnell, Kelly L. .... Mansfield, OH
Badner, Robert H. .... Los Angeles, CA
Bado and Bado .... Edmond, OK
Bado, Barbara K. Arentz .... Edmond, OK
Bado, Fred M. .... Hoboken, NJ
Bado, John Terry .... Edmond, OK
Bado, Peter James .... Lakewood, CA
Badolato, Louis .... Staten Island, NY
Badolato, Richard J. .... Roseland, NJ
Badolato, Vincent J. .... Washington, DC
Badon, Kenneth E., (Professional Law Corporation) .... Cameron, LA
Lake Charles, LA
Badon & Ranier .... Cameron, LA
Lake Charles, LA
Badon, Thomas F. .... Liberty, MS
Badonsky, Deborah K. .... Dayton, OH
Badorek-Welch, Stacy .... New Britain, CT
Badoux, Laurent R. G. .... Atlanta, GA
Badovinac, David L. .... Sacramento, CA
Badowski, Banko, Kroll, Kronthal and Baker, A Professional Corporation
Harrisburg, PA
Badowski, Michael M. .... Harrisburg, PA
Badoyannis, Mary .... Stamford, CT
Badrich, Zlatana .... Washington, DC
Badrinath, Asha Lata .... San Francisco, CA
Badrinath, Vikram .... Tucson, AZ
Badrinath, Vikram, P.C. .... Tucson, AZ
Badura, Donna M. .... Newburgh, NY
Badura, Margaret A. .... Omaha, NE
Badura, William S. .... Suffern, NY
Badway, Ernest E. .... Newark, NJ
Badway, Thomas E. .... Providence, RI
Badwey, Louis M. .... New Bedford, MA
Bae, Alice Mira .... Arnold, MD
Bae, Christine M. .... Fort Lee, NJ
New York, NY
Bae, Eun Jin .... New York, NY
Bae, I. Paul .... Los Angeles, CA
Bae, Jade Y. .... New York, NY
Bae, Jennifer M. .... Los Angeles, CA
Bae, John H. .... New York, NY
Bae, Samuel S. .... Chicago, IL
Baecher, Catherine M. .... New York, NY
Baecher, John T. .... New York, NY
Baechle, Daniel A. .... Champaign, IL
Baechle, James J. .... New York, NY
Baechle, Lisa G. .... Cincinnati, OH
Baechle, Michael S. .... Valparaiso, IN
Baechler, Charles A. .... Newport, WA
Baechtold, George H. .... Palm Springs, CA
Baechtold, James W. .... Richmond, KY
Baechtold, Robert L. .... New York, NY
Baechtold, William J. .... Cincinnati, OH
Baeder, Clellon K. .... Huntsville, AL
Baeder, Steven W. .... Salt Lake City, UT
Baehman, Jackson S. .... Roseville, MN
Baehr, Alexander .... Seattle, WA
Baehr, J. Brian .... Cape Girardeau, MO
Baehr, Raymond A. .... Albuquerque, NM
Baehr, Robert N. .... Deltona, FL
Baehr, Roy D., (P.C.) .... Bakersfield, CA
Baehre, Mark A. .... Buffalo, NY
Baehren, James W. .... Toledo, OH
Baek, Laura A. .... Washington, DC
Baele, Veronica Lema .... Chicago, IL
Baen, Catherine L. .... Houston, TX
Baen, Cindy J. .... Northfield, NJ
Baena, Scott L. .... Miami, FL
Baender, Margo .... New York, NY
Baenen, Richard Anthony .... Washington, DC
Baenen, Steven A. .... Columbus, OH
Baenziger, Julie Ann .... Atlanta, GA
Baer, Adrian S. .... Houston, TX
Baer, Andrea Altin .... Boulder, CO
Baer, Andrew .... New York, NY
Baer, Andrew M. .... Philadelphia, PA
Baer, Andrew S.
Board of Governors Of The Federal Reserve System, Office of the General Counsel, GV
Baer, Arbeiter, Ploshnick, Tanenbaum & Weiss .... Elizabeth, NJ
Metuchen, NJ
New Brunswick, NJ
Somerville, NJ
Trenton, NJ
Baer, Arthur A. .... New York, NY
Baer, Arthur D. .... New York, NY
Baer, Arthur J., Jr. .... Charlotte, NC
Baer & Baer .... Owings Mills, MD
Baer & Baer, Attorneys At Law, P.A.
Fayetteville, NC
Baer, Baer & Baer .... Memphis, TN
Baer, Barbara .... New York, NY
Baer, Barbara J. .... Lombard, IL
Baer, Bartley B. .... San Francisco, CA
Baer, Ben K. .... Cordova, TN
Baer, Billy .... Baltimore, MD
Baer, Bruce F. .... Fayetteville, NC
Baer, Charles A. .... Jacksonville, FL
Baer, Christopher J. .... Reynoldsburg, OH
Baer, Cornelia G. .... Ventura, CA
Baer, Curtis H. .... Towson, MD
Baer, Curtis H., P.A. .... Towson, MD
Baer, Daniel P. .... Hackensack, NJ
Baer, David .... Boston, MA
Baer, David G. .... Pomeroy, OH
Baer, David M. .... Metuchen, NJ
Baer, David W. .... San Francisco, CA
Baer, Dennis R. .... Memphis, TN
Baer, Douglas E. .... Spring, TX
Baer, Earl L. .... Citrus Heights, CA
Baer, Edward .... New York, NY
Baer, Edward B. .... Philadelphia, PA
Baer, Edward G. .... New York, NY
Baer, Edwin I. .... Louisville, KY
Baer, Elizabeth E. .... Toledo, OH
Baer, Elizabeth T. .... Atlanta, GA
Baer, Ervin I. .... Fayetteville, NC
Baer, Eva .... New York, NY
Baer, F. Brandon .... New York, NY
Baer, Frank A., III .... Charleston, WV
Baer, Frank W. .... Media, PA
Baer, Frederick K. .... South Bend, IN
Baer, Gary D. .... Oklahoma City, OK
Baer, Gottlieb J. .... Sacramento, CA
Baer, Gregor .... San Francisco, CA
Baer, Gregory A. .... Treasury Department, Office of the General Counsel, GV
Baer, H. Carl, III .... Bemidji, MN
Baer, H. Douglas .... Dallas, TX
Baer, Harold, Jr. .... New York, NY
Baer, Heather V. .... Needham, MA
Baer, Henry .... Dallas, TX
Baer, Henry P. .... New York, NY
Baer, Holly S. .... Englewood, CO
Baer, Isadore B. .... Memphis, TN
Baer, J. Dan, Jr. .... Forest Park, GA
Baer, J.A. Ted, III .... Santa Barbara, CA
Baer, Jacob H. .... Memphis, TN
Baer, James K. .... Los Angeles, CA
Baer, James L. .... Bethesda, MD
Baer, Janet S. .... Chicago, IL
Baer, Jeanmarie Holder .... Wichita Falls, TX
Baer, Jerome I. .... Chicago, IL
Baer, John J. .... Beverly Hills, CA
Baer, John R. F. .... Chicago, IL
Baer, Jonathan T. .... Boston, MA
Baer, Joseph R. .... Manhattan Beach, CA
Baer, Joseph Winslow .... Glencoe, IL
Baer, Judith Lauter .... San Francisco, CA
Baer, Kevin G. .... Department of Commerce, Patent and Trademark Office, GV
Baer, Kimberley K. .... Des Moines, IA
Baer, Kurt D. .... Chicago, IL
Baer, Lance Alan .... Los Angeles, CA
Baer, Larry M. .... Cando, ND
Baer, Larry R. .... Newton, KS
Baer, Laura I. .... Manhattan Beach, CA
Baer, Laura Marie .... Apple Valley, MN
Baer, Lawrence E. .... Memphis, TN
Baer, Lawrence J. .... New York, NY
Baer, Linda Mosse .... Newton, MA
Baer, Linda Pollitt .... Newark, NJ
Baer, Lisa .... Boston, MA
Baer, Lisa E. .... Hanover, NH
Baer, Lori G. .... Atlanta, GA
Baer, Luke .... Broadview, IL
Baer, Madeline .... New York, NY
Baer, Marc B. .... Minneapolis, MN
Baer, Marc H. .... Los Angeles, CA
Baer, Marc H. .... Baltimore, MD
Baer, Mark B. .... Burbank, CA
Baer Marks & Upham LLP
New York, NY
Baer, Martin S. .... Houston, TX
Baer, Max .... Pittsburgh, PA
Baer, Michael A. .... Troy, OH
Baer, Michael S., III .... Baton Rouge, LA
Baer, Miriam J. .... Raleigh, NC
Baer, Molly .... Houston, TX
Baer, Monroe, Jr. .... San Francisco, CA
Baer, Myles S. .... New York, NY
Baer, Noah S. .... Fairfax, VA
Baer, Norman J. .... Minneapolis, MN
Baer, Ora J., II .... Champaign, IL
Baer, Peter E. .... Gresham, OR
Baer, Peter E., P.C. .... Gresham, OR
Baer, Philip A. .... Huntington, WV
Baer, Phillip H. .... Philadelphia, PA
Baer, Phillip H., Ltd. .... Philadelphia, PA
Baer, Richard N. .... Denver, CO
Baer & Rivieccio .... New York, NY
Baer, Robert B. .... Cleveland, OH

Baer, Robert H. ... Brunswick, GA
Baer, Robert L. ... Topeka, KS
Baer, Robert O. ... Lansing, MI
Baer, Robert T. ... San Francisco, CA
Baer, Robin B. ... New York, NY
Baer, Romain, Abramson & Frank
Valley Forge, PA
Baer, Ross A. ... Venice, FL
Baer, Scott ... Swansea, MA
Baer, Shannon M. ... West Palm Beach, FL
Baer, Sibylle ... Portland, OR
Baer, Simmie Ann ... Seattle, WA
Baer, Stephen D. ... Owings Mills, MD
Baer, Stephen I. ... Valley Forge, PA
Baer, Stephen U. ... Charlottesville, VA
Baer, Steven K. ... Chicago, IL
Baer, Steven R. ... Department of Justice, Environment and Natural Resources Division, GV
Baer, Susan I. ... Springfield, NJ
Baer, Susan Taxin, Law Offices of
White Plains, NY
Baer, Teresa D. ... Washington, DC
Baer, Theo. R. ... Milwaukee, WI
Baer, Thomas H. ... New York, NY
Baer, Thomas J. ... Old Tappan, NJ
Baer & Timberlake, P.C.
Oklahoma City, OK
Baer, Timothy M. ... Fenton, MO
Baer, Timothy R. ... Minneapolis, MN
Baer, Tommy P. ... Richmond, VA
Baer, William E., Jr. ... Washington, DC
Baer, William J. ... Federal Trade Commission, Bureau of Competition, GV
Baer, Zenas ... Hawley, MN
Baer, Zenas, & Associates ... Hawley, MN
Baerg, William R. ... Los Angeles, CA
Baerga, Carmen M. ... New York, NY
Baerga-Duprey, Luis ... San Juan, PR
Baerga Santini, Vimael ... San Juan, PR
Baergen, Elizabeth A.
Grosse Pointe Woods, MI
Baermann, William S. ... Madison, WI
Baernstein, Barbara Ellen ... Ontario, CA
Baerson, Steven L. ... Chicago, IL
Baerveldt Bagsby Lee & Green, L.L.C.
St. Charles, MO
Baerveldt, Donald A., Jr. ... St. Charles, MO
Baerwitz, Herbert G. ... Los Angeles, CA
Baerwitz, Stephen ... Los Angeles, CA
Baese, Andrew M. ... St. Paul, MN
Baesel, Cordon T. ... San Diego, CA
Baesel, Stuart O., Jr. ... Atlanta, GA
Baesler, Caroline Boeh ... Lexington, KY
Baesler, Charles R., Jr. ... Lexington, KY
Baesler, Scotty ... Lexington, KY
Baessler, Joseph E. ... Flint, MI
Baetich, Emanuel ... New York, NY
Baetje, Jennifer Anderson ... St. Louis, MO
Baety, Edward L. ... Atlanta, GA
Baetz, B. Shelby ... Houston, TX
Baetz, Hall ... Seattle, WA
Baetz, Paul D. ... Fort Collins, CO
Baetz, S. ... Houston, TX
Baetz, W. Timothy ... Chicago, IL
Baetzhold, James P. ... Washington, DC
Baeurle, Lisa Barons ... New York, NY
Baeurle, Roger M. ... Cold Spring, NY
Baev, Andrei A. ... New York, NY
Baev, Gail M. ... Los Angeles, CA
Baeverstad, Mark W. ... Fort Wayne, IN
Báez, A. Cristiana ... Bayside, NY
Baez, Braulio L. ... Tallahassee, FL
Baez, Humberto Beau, III ... Washington, DC
Baez, Jose Anibal ... New York, NY
Baez, Juan A. ... New York, NY
Baez, Lucia M. ... Orlando, FL
Baez, Lucia M., A Professional Association
Orlando, FL
Baez, Ricardo A. ... Jericho, NY
Baeza, Guillermo E. ... Bethesda, MD
Baeza, Mario L. ... New York, NY
Baeza, Miguel ... Dallas, TX
Baeza & Orendain, P.C. ... Dallas, TX
Baeza, Paula Gutierrez ... Brea, CA
Baeza, Ruben, Jr. ... Torrance, CA
Baez-Dixon, Susan ... Mayaguez, PR
Báez Rivera, Elba Marie ... San Juan, PR
Baez-Rivera, Jose Luis ... San Juan, PR
Bafalon, Lee ... Ventura, CA
Baffa, Cheryl J. ... Philadelphia, PA
Baffa, David S. ... Chicago, IL
Baffa, Frank ... Rolling Hills Estates, CA
Baffa, George R., (P.C.) ... Pasadena, CA
Baffney, Thomas K. ... Walla Walla, WA
Baffo, Carmine J. ... Patchogue, NY
Baffoe-Bonnie, Sandra Akosua
New York, NY
Baffoni, Joseph F. ... Providence, RI
Baffuto, Bartholomew ... Point Pleasant, NJ
Bafundo, Laurence P. ... Cherry Hill, NJ
Bagal, Seymour M. ... Punta Gorda, FL
Bagalay, John E., Jr. ... Boston, MA
Bagan, Grant A. ... Chicago, IL
Baganz, Mark T. ... Delafield, WI
Bagarazzi, James M. ... Greenville, SC
Bagaria, Gail Farrell ... Bowie, MD
Bagasol, William C. ... Honolulu, HI
Bagatell, Dan L. ... Phoenix, AZ
Bagatelos & Fadem ... San Francisco, CA
Bagatelos, Peter A. ... San Francisco, CA
Bagatti, Jude ... South Miami, FL
Bagay, Lisa M. ... Wheeling, WV
Bagazinski, Gerald A ... Livonia, MI
Bagazinski, Gerald A., P.C. ... Livonia, MI
Bagbey, Francis C. ... Raleigh, NC
Bagby, Angela R. ... North Bend, WA
Bagby, Anita Leslie ... Birmingham, AL
Bagby & Associates ... Mount Laurel, NJ
Philadelphia, PA
Bagby, Bagby & Henley, P.C. ... Dallas, GA
Bagby, Benault ... Springfield, IL
Bagby, Brian L. ... Tewksbury, MA
Bagby, Carlton B. ... Columbia, SC
Bagby, Christopher L. ... Arlington, TX
Bagby, Douglas A. ... Beverly Hills, CA
Bagby, Gajdos & Zachary, A Professional Corporation ... Camarillo, CA
Santa Ana, CA
Sherman Oaks, CA
Bagby, George T. ... Dallas, GA
Bagby, Glen S. ... Lexington, KY
Bagby, Ingrid M. ... New York, NY
Bagby, Jefferson C. ... Stafford, VA
Bagby, John S., Jr. ... Mount Laurel, NJ
Philadelphia, PA
Bagby, Joseph T. ... Valencia, CA
Bagby, Judith F. ... Dallas, GA
Bagby, Kelly Riseden ... Landover, MD
Bagby Law Firm, P.C. ... Arlington, TX
Bagby, Max O. ... Kansas City, MO
Bagby, Michael R. ... Camarillo, CA
Santa Ana, CA
Sherman Oaks, CA
Bagby, Philip Anthony ... Van Buren, AR
Bagby, Steve D. ... Weston, WV
Bagby, Thomas R. ... Roanoke, VA
Bagby, Tina M. ... Chicago, IL
Bagby, W. McFarland ... Arlington, TX
Bagby, William R. ... Lexington, KY
Bagchi, Kasturi ... Morristown, NJ
Bagdade, David M. ... Chicago, IL
Bagdady, Bruce M. ... Detroit, MI
Bagdady, Bryan R. ... Elk Grove Village, IL
Bagdady, Bryan R., P.C.
Elk Grove Village, IL
Bagdasarian, Bruce H. ... Boston, MA
Bagdasarian, Gary G. ... Fresno, CA
Bagdasarian, Richard C. ... Boca Raton, FL
Bagdasarian, Robert J. ... New York, NY
Bagdasarian, Ross ... Montecito, CA
Bagdasarian, Sabrina R. ... New York, NY
Bagdis, B. Jay ... Blue Bell, PA
Bagdis, B. Jay, P.C. ... Blue Bell, PA
Bagdoian, Irene H. ... Middleton, MA
Bagdon, Barbara A. ... Phoenix, AZ
Bagdon, Bonnie F. ... Chicago, IL
Bagdorf, Howard ... New York, NY
Bagel, Lee M. ... Dunwoody, GA
Bagelman, Bruce E. ... Dallas, TX
Bageman, James C. ... Portola Valley, CA
Bagen, Gregory W. ... Brewster, NY
Bagerdjian, Haig Shahen
Woodland Hills, CA
Bagert, Bernard J., Jr., (A P.L.C.)
New Orleans, LA
Bagert Law Firm, The, A P.L.C.
New Orleans, LA
Bagert, Suzanne ... New York, NY
Bagg, Harvey M., Jr. ... New York, NY
Bagg, Thomas G. ... Fairfax, VA
Baga, Rajesh ... Cleveland, OH
Baggaley, James H. ... Pacific Palisades, CA
Baggarly & Associates, P.C. ... Marietta, GA
Baggarly, Bruce W., Jr. ... Marietta, GA
Bagge, Douglas M. ... Tampa, FL
Bagge, Michael ... New York, NY
Bagger, Ian G. ... San Francisco, CA
Bagger, Jocelyn P. ... Wethersfield, CT
Bagger, Paula M. ... Boston, MA
Baggerly, Stuart K. ... Bloomington, IN
Baggerman, Peter C. ... Pittsburgh, PA
Baggett, Arthur Guy, Jr. ... Mariposa, CA
Baggett, Barbara S. ... Brick, NJ
Baggett, Beth C. ... Nashville, TN
Baggett, Billy J. ... Eunice, NM
Baggett, Bryce A. ... Oklahoma City, OK
Baggett, Candace S. ... Houston, TX
Baggett, Carl R. ... West Covina, CA
Baggett, Caryn Hutchinson ... Dallas, TX
Baggett, Dawn T. ... Prattville, AL
Baggett, Don A., Law Offices of
El Segundo, CA
Baggett, Donna M. Banik ... Chicago, IL
Baggett, Enid Evans ... Paradise, CA
Baggett, Fred P. ... High Point, NC
Baggett, Fred W. ... Tallahassee, FL
Baggett, G. Laurence, (P.A.)
Daytona Beach, FL
Baggett, Gordon & Deison ... Conroe, TX
Baggett, H. Mark ... Flower Mound, TX
Baggett, J. Mark ... Birmingham, AL
Baggett, J. Michael ... Pittsburgh, PA
Baggett, Joseph E. ... Department of the Navy, Office of the Judge Advocate General, GV
Baggett, Joseph W. ... Gridley, CA
Baggett, K. Robin ... San Luis Obispo, CA
Baggett, Marvin, Jr. ... Albuquerque, NM
Baggett, McCall & Burgess, A Professional Law Corporation ... Lake Charles, LA
Baggett, Patricia Maidt ... Rogers, AR
Baggett, Rebecca M. ... Memphis, TN
Memphis, TN
Baggett, Sara D. ... West Palm Beach, FL
Baggett, Stephen D. ... Greenwood, SC
Baggett, Steven R. ... Dallas, TX
Baggett, Talmage S., Jr. ... Fayetteville, NC
Baggett, W. Mike ... Dallas, TX
Baggett, William B. ... Lake Charles, LA
Baggett, William B., Jr. ... Lake Charles, LA
Baggett, William L., Jr. ... Atlanta, GA
Baggette, John R., Jr. ... Decatur, AL
Baggette, S. Patrick, II ... Independence, MO
Baggette, Wade R. ... Monroe, LA
Baggett-Hayes, Earlene R.
Bloomfield Hills, MI
Baggiano, Catherine M. ... Philadelphia, PA
Baggio, Mark F. ... Chicago, IL
Baggish, Mindy A. ... Los Angeles, CA
Baggish, Stuart H. ... Los Angeles, CA
Baggitt, William C., III
Princeton Junction, NJ
Baggot, Atmore L. ... Apache Junction, AZ
Baggot, Breffni ... Chicago, IL
Baggot, Michael R. ... Chicago, IL
Baggott, Bonnie S. ... Nashville, TN
Baggott Cohorn & Ivey, L.L.P. ... Houston, TX
Baggott, Horace W. ... Dayton, OH
Baggott, Nancy L. ... Detroit, MI
Baggott & Swaim, P.C. ... Houston, TX
Baggott, Terrance P. ... Houston, TX
Baggott, Thomas M. ... Dayton, OH
Baggott, Wm. K. ... Wilmington, DE
Baggott III, Roland W. ... Metairie, LA
New Orleans, LA
Baggs, William E. ... Norfolk, VA
Baghdadi, Aslan ... Washington, DC
Baghdadi, Khaldoun A.
San Francisco, CA
Baghdadi, Mania K.
Federal Communications Commission, Mass Media Bureau, GV
Baghdady, David G. ... Monroe, CT
Baghdady, Raymond G. ... Greenwich, CT
Baghdady, Rolf M. ... Columbia, SC
Baghdady, Rolf M., P.A. ... Columbia, SC
Baghdady, Sami S. ... Worcester, MA
Baghdassarian, Alex R. ... Los Angeles, CA
Baghdassarian, Mark ... New York, NY
Baghdassarian, Stepan W. ... Encino, CA
Baghdoyan, William E. ... Augusta, ME
Bagherzadeh, Ali ... New York, NY
Bagia, Jay, Law Offices of ... Philadelphia, PA
Bagiackas, Peter J. ... South Bend, IN
Bagileo, John R. ... Washington, DC
Bagin, Bruce ... Pittsburgh, PA
Baginski, John ... Pittsburgh, PA
Baginski, Vincent R. ... Pittsburgh, PA
Baglan, Charlie, & Associates
Batesville, MS
Baglanis, Manuel J. ... San Jose, CA
Bagley, Andrew W. ... Washington, DC
Bagley & Bagley, P.C. ... Boston, MA
Bagley, Ben G. ... Midvale, UT
Bagley, Beth Anne ... Worcester, MA
Bagley, Bruce D. ... Harrisburg, PA
Bagley, Charles F., III ... Huntington, WV
Bagley, Charles F., Jr. ... Huntington, WV
Bagley, Charles, IV ... Annapolis, MD
Bagley, Christopher A. ... Coquille, OR
Bagley, Claude T. ... Vicksburg, MS
Bagley, Constance E. ... Palo Alto, CA
Bagley, David W., II (A Professional Corporation) ... San Diego, CA
Bagley, Dennis J. ... Farmington Hills, MI
Bagley, Donald B., III ... Chagrin Falls, OH
Bagley, Edward C. ... Albuquerque, NM
Santa Fe, NM
Bagley, Edward J. ... Webster, MA
Bagley, H. Jim ... Rockford, IL
Bagley, H. Michael ... Atlanta, GA
Bagley, Harold ... Minneapolis, MN
Bagley, Hilary G. ... Sacramento, CA
Bagley, Irvin & Lynett ... Buffalo, NY
Bagley, James A. ... Colorado Springs, CO
Bagley, James J., II ... Beverly Hills, CA
Chicago, IL
Bagley, Jeffrey S. ... Cumming, GA
Bagley, Jessamyn L. ... Chicago, IL
Bagley, John G. ... Springfield, MA
Bagley, John R. ... Pekin, IL
Bagley, Joseph M. ... Blue Bell, PA
Bagley, Joyce E. ... Dallas, TX
Bagley, Judith W. ... Dallas, TX
Bagley, Kelly ... Springfield, IL
Bagley, Kevin M. ... San Diego, CA
Bagley, Laureen F. ... Houma, LA
Longview, TX
Bagley Law Office ... Cheyenne, WY
Bagley, Linda A. ... Menlo Park, CA
Bagley, Lynn Michelle
West Palm Beach, FL
Bagley, Margo A. ... Atlanta, GA
Bagley, Martha R. ... Boston, MA
Bagley, Marvin D. ... Richfield, UT
Bagley, Matthew G. ... Salt Lake City, UT
Bagley, Michael J. ... Eagle Pass, TX
Bagley & Miller ... Pekin, IL
Bagley, Parker H. ... New York, NY
Bagley, Peter F. ... Arlington, TX
Bagley, Philip H. ... Fremont, CA
Bagley, Philip J., III ... Richmond, VA
Bagley, Ralph R. ... Boston, MA
Bagley, Raymond R., Jr. ... Oregon City, OR
Bagley & Rhody, P.C. ... Annapolis, MD
Bagley, Roger B. ... Manchester, CT
Bagley, Roger J. ... New York, NY
Bagley, Shana A. ... Modesto, CA
Bagley, Stuart B. ... Atlanta, GA
Bagley, Taffy ... El Paso, TX
Bagley, Terrence Mitchell ... Richmond, VA
Bagley, Thomas ... Franklin, MA
Bagley, Thomas O. ... Fayetteville, TN
Bagley, William D. ... Cheyenne, WY
Bagley, William F., Jr. ... Greens Farms, CT
Bagley, William T. ... San Francisco, CA
Bagliebter, Gary M. ... Miami, FL
Bagliebter, William M. ... New York, NY
Baglin, George E. ... San Francisco, CA
Baglini, John A. ... Providence, RI
Baglini, Joseph W. ... Providence, RI
Baglino, James ... Kew Gardens, NY
Baglio, Charles J. ... Rochester, NY
Baglio, Jeffrey T. ... San Diego, CA
Baglione, Frank M. ... Boston, MA
Baglione, Jayma C. ... Cincinnati, OH
Baglivi, Patricia ... Hackensack, NJ
Bagn, Karin ... Boulder, CO
Bagnal, Charles W. ... Columbia, SC
Bagnal, Diane Rabon ... Aynor, SC
Bagnall, Kelly Franklin ... Dallas, TX
Bagnall, Mark O. ... Miami, FL
Bagnall, Robert G. ... Washington, DC
Bagnasacco, Barbara ... Salt Lake City, UT
Bagnaschi, Christopher J.
Los Angeles, CA
Bagnato, John J. ... Johnstown, PA
Bagne, Conrad N. ... Anchorage, AK
Bagne, F. R. & Associate ... Birmingham, MI
Bagne, Farideh R. ... Birmingham, MI
Bagne, Stephon B. ... Troy, MI
Bagnell, Brenda Mary ... Wellesley, MA
Bagnell, E. Everett ... Suffolk, VA
Bagnell, James W. ... Boston, MA
Bagnell, Jeffrey S. ... Norwalk, CT
Bagner, Jeffrey ... New York, NY
Bagneris, Dennis R. ... New Orleans, LA
Bagneris, Emile A., III ... Metairie, LA
Bagneris, Michael G. ... New Orleans, LA
Bagneris, Michele Beal ... Los Angeles, CA
Bagneris, Shyri Patterson ... New Orleans, LA
Bagneris, Suzette P. ... New Orleans, LA
Bagni, Bruce N. ... Jacksonville, FL
Bagni, Cheryl A. ... Floral Park, NY
Bagniefski, Jeffrey D. ... Rochester, MN
Bagniefski & Nicholas ... Rochester, MN
Bagno, Anne Warren ... Detroit, MI
Bagnoli, Joseph T. ... St. Paul, MN
Bagoly, Shelley Lynne ... Rockville, MD
Bagot, Drew N., (P.C.) ... Dallas, TX
Bagot, Free & Shearer, P.C. ... Anderson, IN
Bagot, Michael H. ... New Orleans, LA
Bagot, Michael H., Jr. ... New Orleans, LA
Bagshaw, Bradley H. ... Seattle, WA
Bagshaw, James H. ... Gloucester, MA
Bague, Gary A. ... Santa Monica, CA
Baguley, Norman A. ... Lapeer, MI
Bagwell, Andrea Merritt ... Washington, DC
Bagwell, Arthur Neal ... White Castle, LA
Bagwell & Bagwell, P.C. ... Halifax, VA
Bagwell, Benjamin L. ... Gainesville, GA
Bagwell, David A. ... Mobile, AL
Bagwell, Dianne L. ... Eagan, MN
Bagwell, Don P., Jr. ... Halifax, VA
Bagwell, Douglas ... Gulfport, MS
Bagwell, Edward L., III ... Douglas, GA
Bagwell, George H. ... Halifax, VA
Bagwell, H. Glenn, Jr. ... Raleigh, NC
Bagwell & Holt, P.A. ... Chapel Hill, NC
Durham, NC
Bagwell, James L. ... Charlotte, NC
Bagwell, Jennifer C. ... Gainesville, GA
Bagwell, John E., III ... Washington, DC
Bagwell, John L. ... Grundy, VA
Bagwell, John M. ... Montpelier, VT
Bagwell, Lisa E. ... Bradenton, FL
Bagwell, Louis Lee ... Houston, TX
Bagwell, Marvin N. ... White Plains, NY
Bagwell, O. Kenneth, Jr. ... Chapel Hill, NC
Bagwell, Thomas D. ... Richmond, VA
Bagwell, Tracy F. ... Fordyce, AR
Bagwell, Tracy F., P.A. ... Fordyce, AR
Bagwell, William A. ... Gainesville, GA
Bagwell, William P., Jr. ... Richmond, VA
Bagyi, John M. ... Albany, NY
Bah, Mohamed Sadu ... Silver Spring, MD
Bahakel, Alfred ... Birmingham, AL
Bahakel & Bahakel ... Birmingham, AL
Bahakel, Gloria ... Birmingham, AL
Bahakel, Izas ... Birmingham, AL
Bahakel, John ... Birmingham, AL
Bahakel, S. Philip ... Pelham, AL
Bahal, Alka ... Ridgewood, NJ
Baham, Alvin G. ... Gretna, LA
Baham, Amanda L. ... Jackson, MS
Baham, Curtis M., Jr. ... Hammond, LA
Baham, Monique D. ... Covington, LA
Baham, Ronnie W., Jr. ... Houston, TX
Bahan, Cornelius P. ... Irvine, CA
Bahan, Cornelius P., Inc. ... Irvine, CA
Bahan, Della ... Pasadena, CA
Bahan, Della, Law Offices of ... Pasadena, CA
Bahan, Michael W. ... San Antonio, TX
Bahan, Paul J. ... Pasadena, CA
Bahar, Farhad ... Los Angeles, CA
Bahar, Sarvenaz ... Los Angeles, CA
Baharoglu, Selma F. ... Phoenix, AZ
Bahauddin, Anita M. ... Washington, DC
Bahcall, Albert ... Milwaukee, WI
Bahcall, Miriam G. ... Chicago, IL
Bahcall, Stein & Sullivan ... Milwaukee, WI
Bahe-Jachna, Ruth A. ... Chicago, IL
Bahena, Gary K. ... Washington, DC
Bahensky, Damon T. ... Kearney, NE
Baheri, Leila M. ... Washington, DC
Bahin, Charlotte M. ... Washington, DC
Bahl, David R. ... Williamsport, PA
Bahl, Elizabeth M. ... Bloomfield Hills, MI
Bahl, Josephine M. ... Minneapolis, MN
Bahl, Mathew L. ... Orlando, FL
Bahle, Melvin C. ... St. Louis, MO
Bahler, David D. ... Austin, TX
Bahler, Gary M. ... New York, NY
Bahler, Nelson E. ... Stockton, CA
Bahlert, Norman P. ... San Francisco, CA
Bahlinger, Marie-Louise ... Golden, CO
Bahlke, Conrad G. ... New York, NY
Bahlman, William T., Jr. ... Cincinnati, OH
Bahlmann, Gareth Scott ... Houston, TX
Bahlmann, Jerome R. ... Columbus, OH
Bahls, David C. ... Minneapolis, MN
Bahls, Jeffrey F. ... Quakertown, PA

Bahls, Richard J. .... Lapeer, MI
Bahls, Steven C. .... Columbus, OH
Bahn, Allan M. .... New York, NY
Bahn, Cindy L. .... Pittsburgh, PA
Bahn, David S. .... Ithaca, NY
Bahn, Mark R. .... Fenton, MO
Bahn, Peter R. .... Mount Vernon, IL
Bahn, Susan C. .... Brooklyn, NY
Bahn, William S. .... St. Louis, MO
Bahnak, John J., Jr. .... St. Louis, MO
Bahnck, Donna A. .... Margate City, NJ
Bahner, John M., Jr. .... Albemarle, NC
Bahner and Medlin .... Albemarle, NC
Bahner, Robert H. .... Merrillville, IN
Bahner, S. Brent .... Ardmore, OK
Bahner, T. Maxfield .... Chattanooga, TN
Bahnmuller, Arthur S. .... Sumter, SC
Bahnsen, Deborah Nay .... Hilliard, OH
Bahnsen, Jeffery A. .... Orlando, FL
Bahnson, Carl T. .... Altoona, WI
Bahorski, Bieglecki, Dombrowski & Baratta, Professional Corporation
Mount Clemens, MI
Bahorski, Jeffrey A. .... Mount Clemens, MI
Bahorski, Timothy A. .... Mount Clemens, MI
Bahr, Arthur E. .... Hudson Falls, NY
Bahr, Barbara J. .... Department of Defense, Defense Legal Services Agency, GV
Bahr, Byron J. .... Costa Mesa, CA
Bahr, Dave .... Eugene, OR
Bahr, Donald R. .... Tampa, FL
Bahr, Irene F. .... Wheaton, IL
Bahr, Kevin J. .... Atlanta, GA
Bahr, Matthew F. .... Visalia, CA
Bahr, Michael P., (P.C.) .... Littleton, CO
Bahr, Rita T. .... Schaumburg, IL
Bahr, Stephen J. .... Kansas City, MO
Bahr, Susan J. .... Montgomery Village, MD
Bahr, Susan J., PC, Law Offices of
Montgomery Village, MD
Bahr, William J. .... Manhattan, KS
Bahrambeygui, Scheherazade Sherry
San Diego, CA
Bahrampour, Firouzeh Diana .... Baltimore, MD
Bahrawy, Ramsey A. .... North Andover, MA
Bahre, Jared H. .... Canton, CT
Bahre, Maynard C. .... San Carlos, CA
Bahrenburg, John Claude
West Simsbury, CT
Bahret, Robert J. .... Holland, OH
Bahret, William F. .... Indianapolis, IN
Bahri, Ritu .... Jasper, GA
Bahrick, Thomas L. .... San Jose, CA
Bahrie, Ronald M. .... Lansing, MI
Bahrke, Trilla E. .... Tahoe City, CA
Bahrman & Prewitt .... Barbourville, KY
Corbin, KY
London, KY
Pineville, KY
Williamsburg, KY
Bahrman, Thor H. .... Corbin, KY
Bahrmasel, Harry A. .... Chicago, IL
Bahrmasel, Kenneth C. .... Chicago, IL
Bahrmasel, Steven J. .... Chicago, IL
Bahs, Jess A. .... Lansing, MI
Bai, Ari M. .... St. Louis, MO
Bai, J. Benjamin .... Houston, TX
Bai, Pollock and Coyne, P.C.
Bridgeport, CT
Bai, Su Sun .... New York, NY
Baiamonte, Anthony, III .... Manasquan, NJ
Baiamonte, Brynn M .... New Orleans, LA
Baiamonte, Joseph J. .... Baton Rouge, LA
Baiamonte, Josephine M.
Treasury Department, Office of Regulations and Rulings, GV
Baiamonte, Phillip D. .... Albuquerque, NM
Baiamonte, Rosalia .... Garden City, NY
Baiata, Christina Alicia .... Bronx, NY
Baicker-McKee, Steven .... Pittsburgh, PA
Baida, Andrew H. .... Baltimore, MD
Baida, David E. .... New York, NY
Baida, Robert H. .... Fresno, CA
Baidas, Carole A. .... Scranton, PA
Baiden, Dawn L. .... Greenville, SC
Baier, A. Leigh .... Atlanta, GA
Baier, A. Leigh, P.C. .... Atlanta, GA
Baier, Barbara G. .... Baton Rouge, LA
Baier, Carl A. .... Palo Alto, CA
Baier, David D. .... Falls Church, VA
Baier, Donald E. .... Mt. Vernon, IN
Baier, Donald J. .... Phoenix, AZ
Baier, Elizabeth D. .... Mt. Vernon, IN
Baier, George P. .... Pittsburgh, PA
Baier, James S. .... Auburn, NY
Baier, Jay A. .... Chicago, IL
Baier, Jay A., Ltd. .... Chicago, IL
Baier, Kelly R. .... Cedar Rapids, IA
Baier, Kirsten I. .... Miami, FL
Baier, Kirsten I., P.A. .... Miami, FL
Baier, Lowell E. .... Bethesda, MD
Baier, Maripaul S. .... Auburn, CA
Baier, Molly J. .... Berkeley, CA
Baier, Paul R. .... Baton Rouge, LA
Baier, Richard C. .... St. Louis, MO
Baier, Teresa Stromen .... Hudson, WI
Baier, William Borton .... Garden City, NY
Baier, William H. .... Bethesda, MD
Baiers, James E. .... Detroit, MI
Baietto, Brenda A. .... St. Petersburg, FL
Baigent, Julia M. .... Redwood City, CA
Baik, Steven S. .... Palo Alto, CA
Baikauskas, Albert B., Jr. .... Bel Air, MD
Baikovitz, Robin J. .... Miami, FL
Bail, Daryl D. .... Albert Lea, MN
Bail, Lisa A. .... Honolulu, HI
Bail, Richard N. .... Whitman, MA

Bailard, Frederick N.
Woodland Hills, CA
Bailard, Joelle .... Santa Monica, CA
Bailen, Eliot .... New York, NY
Bailen, John R. .... Chicago, IL
Bailen, Mark I. .... Washington, DC
Bailer, Bonnie L. .... Los Angeles, CA
Bailer, Kermit G. .... Detroit, MI
Bailes, Craig & Yon .... Huntington, WV
Bailes, James R. .... Huntington, WV
Bailes, Julian E. .... Natchitoches, LA
Bailes, Katherine J. .... Kansas City, MO
Bailes, Michael S. .... Cincinnati, OH
Bailes, Richard H. .... Raleigh, NC
Bailes, Robert T. .... Phoenix, AZ
Bailes, Zandra Y.
Securities and Exchange Commission, Division of Investment Management, GV
Bailess, Robert R. .... Vicksburg, MS
Bailet, Melvin E. .... Seattle, WA
Bailey, A. Brent .... Albuquerque, NM
Bailey, A. Richard .... Westmont, NJ
Philadelphia, PA
Bailey, A. Robert D. .... Rochester, NY
Bailey, A. William, III .... Bartow, FL
Bailey, Adam Leitman .... New York, NY
Bailey, A. E. Bud .... Tualatin, OR
Bailey, Alex C. .... Department of the Army, Army Materiel Command, GV
Bailey, Allen A. .... Charlotte, NC
Bailey, Allen M. .... Anchorage, AK
Bailey, Amy Haueter .... Flint, MI
Bailey, Andrea L. .... Atlanta, GA
Bailey, Andrea L. .... Richmond, VA
Bailey, Andrew C. .... Boston, MA
Bailey, Andrew G. .... Baltimore, MD
Bailey, Andrew James .... Kansas City, MO
Bailey, Anita Matyi .... Washington, DC
Bailey, Ann K. .... Cincinnati, OH
Bailey, Ann-Dee Piskac .... Houston, TX
Bailey, Anne C. .... San Jose, CA
Bailey, Anthony William .... Chicago, IL
Bailey, Arthur, III .... Santa Fe, NM
Bailey, Arthur L. .... Washington, DC
Bailey, Arthur N., & Associates
Buffalo, NY
Bailey, Arthur N., & Associates
Jamestown, NY
Bailey, Arthur W., Jr. .... Waco, TX
Bailey & Associates .... Warrensburg, MO
Bailey, B. Carlton, Jr. .... Chicago, IL
Bailey, B. Ralph .... Mandeville, LA
Bailey, B. Todd .... Boise, ID
Bailey & Bailey .... Lafayette, LA
Bailey & Bailey .... Jamaica, NY
Bailey and Bailey .... Burnsville, NC
Bailey and Bailey .... Springfield, OH
Bailey and Bailey .... Fairview, OK
Bailey & Bailey .... Carthage, TX
Bailey & Bailey .... Houston, TX
Bailey, Barbara A. .... Phoenix, AZ
Bailey, Barbara A. .... Maywood, IL
Bailey, Barbara Ann .... Champaign, IL
Bailey, Barbara Ann .... Elgin, TX
Bailey, Barbara E. .... Dallas, TX
Bailey, Barbara J. .... Los Angeles, CA
Bailey, Benjamin L. .... Charleston, WV
Bailey, Beverly L., Law Offices of
Chicago, IL
Bailey, Beverly Lynn .... Chicago, IL
Bailey, Bill W., P.C. .... DeSoto, TX
Bailey, Blair S. .... New Bedford, MA
Bailey, Blake .... Tyler, TX
Bailey, Blake Allen, (P.C.) .... Dallas, TX
Bailey & Block .... Panorama City, CA
Bailey, Bobbie .... Kansas City, MO
Bailey, Borlack, Nadelhoffer & Carroll
Chicago, IL
Bailey, Boyd M. .... Madisonville, TX
Bailey, Brad D. .... Georgetown, CO
Bailey, Bradford W. .... Kenton, OH
Bailey, Bradley J. .... Hyannis, MA
Bailey, Brant A. .... St. Petersburg, FL
Bailey, Brenda S. .... Bryan, TX
Bailey, Brent C. .... Houston, TX
Bailey, Brent William .... Dallas, TX
Bailey, Brett H. .... San Francisco, CA
Bailey, Brian D. .... Department of Justice, Tax Division, GV
Bailey, Brian J. .... Dallas, TX
Bailey, Bridget .... Knoxville, TN
Bailey & Brott .... Orange, CA
Bailey & Brown .... Sacramento, CA
Bailey, Bruce A. .... Burlingame, CA
Bailey, Bruce A. .... Warrensburg, MO
Bailey, Bruce Albion, A Professional Law Corporation .... Burlingame, CA
Bailey, Bruce C. .... Chattanooga, TN
Bailey, Bruce E. .... Columbus, OH
Bailey, Bruce R. .... Los Angeles, CA
Bailey, Bruce S. .... San Diego, CA
Bailey, Buck .... Arlington, VA
Bailey, Burck .... Oklahoma City, OK
Bailey & Burke .... Clinton, MA
Bailey, Buxton Reed .... Salisbury, MD
Bailey, C. Kenneth .... Summerville, SC
Bailey, C. Suzanne .... Montgomery, AL
Bailey, C. William .... Seattle, WA
Bailey, Calvert A. .... Detroit, MI
Bailey, Carl D. .... San Francisco, CA
Bailey, Carlton .... Fayetteville, AR
Bailey, Carol N. .... Rockford, IL
Bailey, Charles B. .... North Beach, MD
Bailey, Charles B., Jr. .... Mobile, AL
Bailey, Charles D., III .... Sarasota, FL
Bailey, Charles D., Jr. .... Sarasota, FL
Bailey, Charles E. .... Cooperstown, NY
Bailey, Charles, Jr. .... Houston, TX

Bailey, Charles R. .... Charleston, WV
Bailey, Charles R., Jr. .... Huntingtown, MD
Bailey, Charles S. .... Manassas, VA
Bailey, Charles T. .... Logan, WV
Bailey, Charles W. .... Austin, TX
Bailey, Charles W. .... Austin, TX
Bailey, Charles W., Jr. .... Houston, TX
Bailey, Charlotte Mortson .... Tulsa, OK
Bailey, Cheryl M. .... Rochester, NY
Bailey, Christine L. .... Reno, NV
Bailey, Christopher .... Manhattan, KS
Bailey, Christopher A. .... Jackson, AL
Bailey, Christopher J. .... Miami, FL
Bailey, Christopher J.
Kennett Square, PA
Bailey, Claude F. .... Spokane, WA
Bailey, Clayton E. .... Dallas, TX
Bailey, Clifford K., III .... Jackson, MS
Bailey, Clinton Thomas .... Beverly Hills, CA
Bailey, Clyde Edward, Sr .... Rochester, NY
Bailey, Colette .... Peoria, IL
Bailey & Colley, L.L.P. .... Tyler, TX
Bailey, Courtney H. .... San Diego, CA
Bailey, Craig B. .... Los Angeles, CA
Bailey, Craig D. .... Mount Laurel, NJ
Bailey, Curtis C. .... Huntsville, AL
Bailey, Curtis R. .... Belleville, IL
Bailey, Cynthia Ann .... Fairfax, VA
Bailey, Cynthia L. .... Everett, WA
Bailey, Cynthia V. .... Richmond, VA
Bailey, D. Charles .... Beaverton, OR
Bailey, Dan A. .... Columbus, OH
Bailey, Daniel A. .... Nashville, TN
Bailey, Daniel B. .... Gillette, WY
Bailey, Daniel J., III .... Boston, MA
Bailey, Daniel S. .... Chicago, IL
Bailey, Danny C. .... Atlanta, GA
Bailey, D'Army .... Memphis, TN
Bailey, Daryl W. .... Houston, TX
Bailey, David A. .... Denver, CO
Bailey, David B. .... Cleveland, OH
Bailey, David E. .... Clinton, MO
Bailey, David E., Jr. .... Pensacola, FL
Bailey, David H., Jr. .... St. Peters, MO
Bailey, David J. .... Atlanta, GA
Bailey, David J. .... Midwest City, OK
Bailey, David Kelvin .... Wheat Ridge, CO
Bailey, David R. .... Philadelphia, PA
Bailey, David S. .... Beaverdam, VA
Bailey, David Scott .... Manassas, VA
Bailey, David W., Jr. .... Winston-Salem, NC
Bailey and Davidson, P.C. .... Clarinda, IA
Bailey, Denise Antonelli .... Philadelphia, PA
West Chester, PA
Bailey, Dennis C. .... Juneau, AK
Bailey, Dennis D. .... Fort Lauderdale, FL
Bailey, Dennis L. .... Dayton, OH
Bailey, Dennis R. .... Montgomery, AL
Bailey, Dexter M. .... Evanston, IL
Bailey, Diana Low .... Los Angeles, CA
Bailey, Diane .... St. Petersburg, FL
Bailey, Dianne C. .... New York, NY
Bailey & Dixon, L.L.P. .... Raleigh, NC
Research Triangle Park, NC
Bailey, Don A. .... Louisa, KY
Bailey, Don E. .... San Francisco, CA
Bailey, Donald A. .... Greensburg, PA
Bailey, Donald A. .... Seattle, WA
Bailey, Donald L. .... San Francisco, CA
Bailey, Donna .... St. Paul, MN
Bailey, Donna J. .... Birmingham, AL
Bailey, Douglas K. .... San Francisco, CA
Bailey, Duskin & Peiffle, A Professional Service Corporation .... Arlington, WA
Bailey, Dwight O. .... Flatwoods, KY
Bailey, Dwight O., P.S.C. .... Flatwoods, KY
Bailey & Dwyer, P.L.C. .... Mandeville, LA
Bailey, Earl P. .... St. Charles, IL
Bailey & Eckert, P.A. .... St. Petersburg, FL
Bailey, Edward A. .... New York, NY
Bailey, Edward A. .... Cleveland, OH
Bailey, Edward G. .... New York, NY
Bailey, Edward G. .... Jacksonville, NC
Bailey, Edward G. .... Springfield, OH
Bailey, Edward J. .... Brentwood, TN
Bailey, Edward L. .... Topeka, KS
Bailey, Edward L. .... Spartanburg, SC
Bailey, Edward L. .... Houston, TX
Bailey, Edwin O. .... Washington, DC
Bailey, Edwin Pate .... Raleigh, NC
Bailey, Elizabeth .... Murrysville, PA
Bailey, Elizabeth A. .... Manchester, NH
Bailey, Elizabeth Dee .... West Hartford, CT
Bailey, Elizabeth H. .... Burlingame, CA
Bailey, Elizabeth J. .... Boston, MA
Bailey, Elizabeth Rover .... Boston, MA
Bailey, Emily Jane .... Kansas City, MO
Bailey, Emma M. .... New York, NY
Bailey, Eric .... New York, NY
Bailey, Essel W., Jr. .... Ann Arbor, MI
Bailey, F. Allen, Jr. .... Lexington, KY
Bailey, F. Clay, Jr. .... Nashville, TN
Bailey, F. Hall .... Jackson, MS
Bailey, F. Kenneth, Jr. .... Houston, TX
Bailey, F. Lee .... West Palm Beach, FL
Bailey & Filosa .... New York, NY
Bailey, Fishman, Freeman & Ferrin
West Palm Beach, FL
Bailey, Francis S. .... Columbus, OH
Bailey, Frank A. .... Bridgeport, CT
Bailey, Frank H. .... Mountain Home, AR
Bailey, Frank J. .... Boston, MA
Bailey, Frank R., III .... Santa Rosa, CA
Bailey, Frank W. .... Gadsden, AL
Bailey, Fred K. .... Lafayette, LA
Bailey, Fred K., (A Law Corporation)
Lafayette, LA
Bailey, Frederick D. .... Arlington, VA

Bailey, Frederick J., III .... Portsmouth, NH
Bailey, G. William, Jr. .... Elizabethtown, KY
Bailey & Galyen .... Arlington, TX
Bedford, TX
Fort Worth, TX
Granbury, TX
Grand Prairie, TX
Irving, TX
Bailey, Garcile Elaine .... Highland, MI
Bailey, Garrett D. .... Burnsville, NC
Bailey, Gary C. .... Kingsport, TN
Bailey, Gary Lee .... Springfield, IL
Bailey, Gary W. .... Baton Rouge, LA
Bailey, Gary W. .... Grand Rapids, MI
Bailey, Gene W., II .... Clarksburg, WV
Bailey, Genevieve N. .... Union City, GA
Bailey, George B., Jr. .... Utica, MI
Bailey, George B., Jr., P.C. .... Utica, MI
Bailey, George H. .... Little Rock, AR
Bailey, George H. .... West Palm Beach, FL
Bailey, George J. .... Lafayette, LA
Bailey, George L. .... Marietta, GA
Bailey, George P. .... Memphis, TN
Bailey, George S. .... Columbia, SC
Bailey, Gina .... Atlanta, GA
Bailey and Glasser .... Charleston, WV
Bailey, Glenn B. .... Morehead City, NC
Bailey, Gordon D. .... San Antonio, TX
Bailey, Gordon F., Jr. .... Anniston, AL
Bailey, Gregory A. .... Martinsburg, WV
Bailey, Gregory S. .... Chicago, IL
Bailey, Gregory W. .... Charleston, WV
Bailey & Griffin, P.A. .... Greenville, MS
Bailey, Grover C. .... Atlanta, GA
Bailey, Guy A. .... Grand Canyon, AZ
Bailey, Guy B., Jr. .... Miami, FL
Bailey, Gypsy Cowherd .... Tallahassee, FL
Bailey, H. Deloyd .... Provo, UT
Bailey & Haltom .... Seminole, TX
Bailey, Harald E. .... Huntsville, AL
Bailey, Harold E., Jr. .... Weston, WV
Bailey, Harold G., Jr. .... Washington, DC
Bailey & Harper, P.L. .... Miami, FL
Bailey, Harry B., III .... Tucker, GA
Bailey, Heather McDaniel .... Dallas, TX
Bailey, Helen K. .... Fairfax, VA
Bailey, Henry F., Jr. .... Cheyenne, WY
Bailey, Henry J., III .... Salem, OR
Bailey, Howard W. .... Fresno, CA
Bailey, Hugh Lee, Jr. .... Winona, MS
Bailey, J. Dennis .... Winston-Salem, NC
Bailey, J. Gene .... Longview, TX
Bailey, J. Gene, P.C. .... Longview, TX
Bailey, J. Latease .... Atlanta, GA
Bailey, J. Michael .... Salt Lake City, UT
Bailey, J. Ruffin .... Raleigh, NC
Bailey, J. Todd .... Burnsville, NC
Bailey, J. Wesley, III .... St. Petersburg, FL
Bailey, Jack M., Jr. .... Shreveport, LA
Bailey, Jack M., Jr., Law Offices of
Shreveport, LA
Bailey, Jack Michael .... Chicago, IL
Bailey, Jack R., Law Offices of
Houston, TX
Bailey, Jack S. .... San Francisco, CA
Bailey, Jacqueline E. .... Palm Springs, CA
Bailey, James A. .... Frankfort, KY
Bailey, James C. .... Washington, DC
Bailey, James D. .... Aiken, SC
Bailey, James Dale, Jr. .... Denver, CO
Bailey, James Dennis .... Birmingham, AL
Bailey, James E., III .... Memphis, TN
Bailey, James E., III .... San Antonio, TX
Bailey, James E., Jr. .... Memphis, TN
Bailey, James F. .... Wilmington, DE
Bailey, James Francis .... Indianapolis, IN
Bailey, James G. .... New York, NY
Bailey, James H. .... Washington, DC
Bailey, James J., III .... Baton Rouge, LA
Bailey, James L. .... Bellaire, TX
Bailey, James L., III .... Columbia, TN
Bailey, James M. .... Ponca City, OK
Bailey, James N. .... Baltimore, MD
Bailey, James N. .... Boston, MA
Bailey, James R. .... Bloomfield Hills, MI
Bailey, James Robert .... Austin, TX
Bailey, James S. .... Denver, CO
Bailey, James S. .... Frederick, MD
Bailey, James S., Jr. .... Denver, CO
Bailey, James T. .... Clanton, AL
Bailey, James T. .... New York, NY
Bailey, James W. .... Cambridge, MA
Bailey, Janet Glaeser .... Livingston, MT
Bailey, Jason L. .... Houston, TX
Bailey, Jay E. .... Maplewood, NJ
Bailey, J.C., III .... Arlington, TX
Bedford, TX
Fort Worth, TX
Granbury, TX
Grand Prairie, TX
Irving, TX
Bailey, Jeffrey B. .... Indianapolis, IN
Bailey, Jeffrey S. .... Coral Gables, FL
Bailey, Jennifer Drechsel .... Miami, FL
Bailey, Jimmy C. .... Dallas, TX
Bailey, Jimmy C., & Associates, P.C.
Dallas, TX
Bailey, J. L., Jr. .... Chattanooga, TN
Bailey, Joe D. .... Portland, OR
Bailey, Joe S. .... Auburn, AL
Bailey, Joe W., II .... Houston, TX
Bailey, Joel W. .... Oceanside, CA
Bailey, John A. .... Houston, TX
Bailey, John A., Jr. .... Pocatello, ID
Bailey, John C. .... Orchard Park, NY
Bailey, John D. .... Waukegan, IL
Bailey, John D., Jr. .... St. Augustine, FL
Bailey, John D., Jr. .... Leonardtown, MD

Bailey, John E., (P.C.) ... Houston, TX
Bailey, John H., III ... Nashville, TN
Bailey, John H., Jr. ... Elberton, GA
Bailey, John H., Jr. ... Hawthorne, NJ
Bailey, John Haslam ... Logan, UT
Bailey, John J., III ... Nashville, TN
Bailey, John Kennedy ... Charleston, WV
Bailey, John L. ... Riverside, CA
Bailey, John M. ... Warwick, RI
Bailey, John M. ... Abilene, TX
Bailey, John P. ... Atlanta, GA
Bailey, John Phillip ... Golden, CO
Bailey, John Preston ... Wheeling, WV
Bailey, John R. ... Portageville, MO
Bailey, John R. ... Las Vegas, NV
Bailey, John S., Jr. ... Parkersburg, WV
Bailey, John T. ... Indianapolis, IN
Bailey, John T. ... Fort Worth, TX
Bailey, John W. ... Huntington, IN
Bailey, John W. ... Albany, NY
Bailey, John W. ... Falls Church, VA
Bailey, Jolene K. ... Oakland, CA
Bailey, Jon M. ... Sterling, CO
Bailey, Jon M. ... Indianapolis, IN
Bailey, Jonathan M. ... Dallas, TX
Bailey, Joni Beth ... Marion, IL
Bailey, Joseph J. ... Alexandria, LA
Bailey, Joseph R. ... Panorama City, CA
Bailey, Joseph W., Jr. ... Logansport, LA
Center, TX
Bailey, Joyce T. ... Arlington, VA
Bailey, Judi A. ... Diamond Bar, CA
Bailey, Judith ... Federal Trade Commission, Office of Executive Director, GV
Bailey, Judith M. ... Phoenix, AZ
Bailey, Judy ... Cedar Crest, NM
Bailey, Judy R. ... La Jolla, CA
Bailey, Judy R., A Professional Corporation
La Jolla, CA
Bailey, Julia E. ... Houston, TX
Bailey, Julia K. ... Washington, DC
Bailey, Julia P. ... South Pasadena, CA
Bailey, Julian J. ... Manhasset, NY
Bailey, Julian W. ... Orange, CA
Bailey, Julie Line ... Chicago, IL
Bailey, K. Brock ... Dallas, TX
Bailey, K. Camp ... Whitehouse, TX
Bailey, K. Ronald ... Sandusky, OH
Bailey, K. William ... Wooster, OH
Bailey, Kathleen E. ... Los Angeles, CA
Bailey, Kathleen H. ... Cincinnati, OH
Bailey, Kathy D. ... Washington, DC
Bailey, Kay ... Washington, DC
Bailey, Kelly Ray ... Department of the Army, U.S. Army Legal Services Agency, GV
Bailey, Kenneth L. ... Dayton, OH
Bailey, Kenneth L., Co., L.P.A. ... Dayton, OH
Bailey, Kenneth N., Jr. ... Greeneville, TN
Bailey, Kevin J. ... Treasury Department, Office of the Comptroller of the Currency, GV
Bailey, Kevin Patrick ... Orlando, FL
Bailey, Kevin S. ... Belle Fourche, SD
Bailey, Kirby G. ... Decatur, GA
Bailey, Kirby L. ... Storm Lake, IA
Bailey & Kornblum ... San Francisco, CA
Bailey, Kristen A. ... London, KY
Bailey, Kristine E. ... San Francisco, CA
Bailey, K. Ronald, & Associates Co., L.P.A.
Sandusky, OH
Bailey, Kyle R. ... New Hope, MN
Bailey, Lamont R. ... Jamaica, NY
Bailey, Lance R. ... Socorro, NM
Bailey, Larry A. ... Huntington, WV
Bailey, Larry O. ... Birmingham, AL
Bailey, Laura Schofield ... Baton Rouge, LA
Bailey Law Firm ... Mountain Home, AR
Bailey Law Firm, The ... Roseville, CA
Sacramento, CA
Bailey Law Group ... Washington, DC
Bailey Law Group, The, P.C. ... Boise, ID
Bailey Law Office ... Elizabethtown, KY
Bailey Law Offices ... Norman, OK
Bailey Law Offices ... Milwaukee, WI
Bailey Law Offices, The, P.C. ... Decatur, GA
Bailey, Lawrence B. ... Seattle, WA
Bailey, Lawrence K. ... Rockville, MD
Bailey, Lawrence R. ... Jamaica, NY
Bailey, Lawrence R., Jr. ... New York, NY
Bailey, Lawrence W. ... Dallas, TX
Bailey, Lester D. ... Baltimore, MD
Bailey, Linda ... Jersey City, NJ
Bailey, Linda A. ... Tallahassee, FL
Bailey, Linda L.H. ... Ukiah, CA
Bailey, Linda M. ... Austin, TX
Bailey, Linda V. ... Knoxville, TN
Bailey, Lisa ... Topeka, KS
Bailey, Lisa Carole ... Picayune, MS
Bailey, Lonnie D. ... Greenwood, MS
Bailey, Lori L. ... Boynton Beach, FL
Bailey, Lou Porter ... Houston, TX
Bailey, Louis Davenport ... New York, NY
Bailey, Louise M. ... Chevy Chase, MD
Bailey, Luke D. ... Dallas, TX
Bailey, Lyn Anne ... Philadelphia, PA
Bailey, Lyn R. ... Lancaster, PA
Bailey, Lynn Palmer ... Washington, DC
Bailey, M. Collins ... Batesville, MS
Bailey, Maggi Fields ... Greenville, SC
Bailey, Mari ... Salem, OR
Bailey, Mark ... Seattle, WA
Bailey, Mark A. ... Indianapolis, IN
Bailey, Mark E. ... Trenton, NJ
Bailey, Mark P. ... Boston, MA
Bailey, Mark R. ... Okemos, MI
Bailey, Mark W. ... Newport, KY
Bailey, Martha D. ... New York, NY
Bailey, Martha M. ... Boston, MA
Bailey, Martin B. ... Knoxville, TN
Bailey, Marvin L. ... Detroit, MI
Bailey, Mary Margaret ... Mobile, AL
Bailey, Mary Page ... Wilmington, DE
Bailey, Mary R. ... Fairview, OK
Bailey, Mary Roberts ... Syracuse, NY
Bailey, Maryann George ... San Antonio, TX
Bailey & Marzano ... Los Angeles, CA
Mather, CA
Sacramento, CA
Santa Monica, CA
Bailey, Matthew T. ... Washington, DC
Bailey, Matthew W. ... Baton Rouge, LA
Bailey, Maura Fahy ... Salem, MA
Bailey, Max A. ... Chicago, IL
Bailey, Mel D. ... Dallas, TX
Bailey, Melanie Sue ... Covington, KY
Bailey, Melissa A. ... Washington, DC
Bailey, Melissa Herring
Salt Lake City, UT
Bailey, Michael A. ... Charlotte, NC
Bailey, Michael F. ... Phoenix, AZ
Bailey, Michael G. ... Chicago, IL
Bailey, Michael H. ... Santa Monica, CA
Bailey, Michael J. ... Clinton, MA
Bailey, Michael K. ... Maitland, FL
Bailey, Michael P. ... New York, NY
Bailey, Michael R. ... Hilton Head Island, SC
Bailey, Michael Scott ... Atlanta, GA
Bailey, Michael W. ... Winlock, WA
Bailey, Michele Pirro ... Syracuse, NY
Bailey, Mitchell M. ... New York, NY
Bailey & Myers, P.A. ... Maitland, FL
Orlando, FL
Bailey, Myra L. ... Paradise, CA
Bailey, Nancy H. ... Florence, SC
Bailey, Nancy J. ... Houston, TX
Bailey, Nathan D. ... Pittsburgh, PA
Bailey, Nelson E. ... West Palm Beach, FL
Bailey, Nicholas D. ... Nashville, TN
Bailey, Nora A., Law Office of
Washington, DC
Bailey, Norman G. ... Wichita, KS
Bailey, P. Howard, Jr. ... Seminole, TX
Bailey, Pamela E. ... Wichita, KS
Bailey, Pamela J. ... Billings, MT
Bailey, Pamela S. ... Rock Island, IL
Bailey, Patricia S. ... Los Angeles, CA
Bailey, Patricia Seasor ... Indianapolis, IN
Bailey, Patrick ... Santa Monica, CA
Bailey, Patrick J. ... San Francisco, CA
Bailey, Patrick L. ... Pompano Beach, FL
Bailey, Patterson, Caddell, Hart, Milliken & Bailey, P.A. ... Charlotte, NC
Bailey, Paul ... New York, NY
Bailey, Paul A. ... Lake Orion, MI
Bailey, Paul E. ... Fairfax, VA
Bailey, Paul L. ... DeSoto, TX
Bailey, Peggy J. ... Atlanta, GA
Bailey, Penny L. ... Minneapolis, MN
Bailey, Percival R. ... New York, NY
Bailey, Peter W. ... Erie, PA
Bailey & Peterson, P.C. ... Edwards, CO
Bailey & Peterson, P.C. ... Denver, CO
Vail, CO
Bailey, Philip L. ... Penn Yan, NY
Bailey, R. Bradford ... Boston, MA
Bailey, R. Emmett ... Glenview, IL
Bailey, R. Greg ... St. Louis, MO
Bailey, R. Lindsay ... Norman, OK
Bailey, R. Russell ... Washington, DC
Bailey, Rachel Lane LaVigne ... Jackson, MS
Bailey, Ralph ... Greenville, SC
Bailey, Ralph J. ... Princeton, NJ
Bailey, Ralph, P.A. ... Greenville, SC
Bailey, Richard ... La Mesa, CA
Bailey, Richard A. ... Arlington, WA
Bailey, Richard B. ... Ann Arbor, MI
Bailey, Richard C., Jr. ... Newport, NH
Bailey, Richard M. ... Southington, CT
Bailey, Richard R. ... Oklahoma City, OK
Bailey, Richard S. ... Bloomfield Hills, MI
Bailey, Richard W. ... Worthington, OH
Bailey, Rick D. ... Denver, CO
Bailey, Rick E. ... Wichita, KS
Bailey, Rickey D. ... Manchester, KY
Bailey, Riley, Buch & Harman, L.C.
Wheeling, WV
Bailey, Robert A. ... Department of the Navy, Office of the Judge Advocate General, GV
Bailey, Robert B. ... Dearborn Heights, MI
Bailey, Robert C. ... Chicago, IL
Bailey, Robert C. ... Oklahoma City, OK
Bailey, Robert E. ... San Mateo, CA
Bailey, Robert E. ... New York, NY
Bailey, Robert E. ... Dallas, TX
Bailey, Robert F. ... Wichita, KS
Bailey, Robert G. ... Stamford, CT
Bailey, Robert G. ... Columbia, MO
Bailey, Robert G. ... Houston, TX
Bailey, Robert H. ... Greeneville, TN
Bailey, Robert H., Jr.
New Smyrna Beach, FL
Bailey, Robert L. ... Norman, OK
Bailey, Robert M. ... Chicago, IL
Bailey, Robert M. ... Clinton, MA
Bailey, Robert M. ... Knoxville, TN
Bailey, Robert P. ... Pleasant Hill, CA
Bailey, Robert S. ... West Chicago, IL
Bailey, Robert S. ... Meadville, PA
Bailey, Robert T. R. ... Montgomery, AL
Bailey, Robert W. ... Meridian, MS
Bailey, Roberts & Bailey, P.L.L.C.
Knoxville, TN
Bailey, Roddy ... Chattanooga, TN
Bailey, Roger Paul ... Denver, CO
Bailey, Roger William ... Yakima, WA
Bailey, Ron D. ... Portland, OR
Bailey, Ron D., P.C. ... Portland, OR
Bailey, Ronald E. ... Portland, OR
Bailey, Rose Lea ... Davidson, NC
Bailey and Ross, LLP ... Los Angeles, CA
Bailey & Rossi, P.C. ... Bloomfield Hills, MI
Bailey, Ruben J. ... Marrero, LA
Bailey, Russell J. ... Amarillo, TX
Bailey, Ryburn H. ... Birmingham, AL
Bailey, Samuel, Jr. ... Farmington, CT
Bailey, Samuel, Jr. ... Washington, DC
Bailey, Sandra ... Houston, TX
Bailey, Sarah Ann ... Tucson, AZ
Bailey, Scott A. ... St. Louis, MO
Bailey, Scott J. ... Eastland, TX
Bailey, Shanan Todd ... Sherman, TX
Bailey, Sharon D. ... Towson, MD
Bailey, Shelia A. ... Austin, TX
Bailey, Shere R. ... Glendale, CA
Bailey, Sherwood R., Jr. ... Biloxi, MS
Bailey, Siobhan Spillane ... Hackensack, NJ
Bailey and Slavin ... Worthington, OH
Bailey, Sloan C. ... San Francisco, CA
Bailey, Stephen A. ... Cincinnati, OH
Bailey, Stephen Edward ... Towson, MD
Bailey, Stephen J. ... Sacramento, CA
Bailey, Stephen R. ... Houston, TX
Bailey, Steve C. ... Medina, OH
Bailey, Steven C. ... Placerville, CA
Bailey, Steven G. ... St. Louis, MO
Bailey, Steven P. ... Colorado Springs, CO
Bailey, Steven R. ... Ogden, UT
Salt Lake City, UT
Bailey & Stock ... Cheyenne, WY
Bailey, Susan Broussard ... New Orleans, LA
Bailey, Susan Heller ... Department of Defense, Defense Legal Services Agency, GV
Bailey, Susan Owens ... Fort Lauderdale, FL
Bailey, Susan R. ... Decatur, GA
Bailey, Suzanne ... Chattanooga, TN
Bailey, Suzanne L. ... Charlottesville, VA
Bailey, Suzin C. ... Washington, DC
Bailey, Terry D. ... Carthage, TX
Bailey, Terry R. ... Los Angeles, CA
Bailey, Theo. E., Jr. ... Houston, TX
Bailey, Theodore M. ... San Antonio, TX
Bailey, Thersea H. ... Columbia, SC
Bailey, Thomas A. ... San Antonio, TX
Bailey, Thomas A. ... Milwaukee, WI
Bailey, Thomas C. ... Boston, MA
Bailey, Thomas C. ... Buffalo, NY
Bailey, Thomas Goodall, Jr.
New York, NY
Bailey & Thomas, P.A.
Winston-Salem, NC
Bailey, Thomas W. ... Harrisburg, PA
Bailey, Thurston C. ... Houston, TX
Bailey, Timothy A. ... Klamath Falls, OR
Bailey, Timothy C. ... Charleston, WV
Bailey, Timothy G. ... Minneapolis, MN
Bailey, Timothy L. ... Pompano Beach, FL
Bailey, Todd H. ... Cincinnati, OH
Bailey, Todd M. ... Sacramento, CA
Bailey, Tom H. ... Sacramento, CA
Bailey, Tricia M. ... San Francisco, CA
Bailey, Trimble, Lowe, Sellars & Thomas
Little Rock, AR
Bailey, Troy T. ... Seattle, WA
Bailey & Trumbo, P.A.
Daytona Beach, FL
New Smyrna Beach, FL
Bailey, Ty A. ... Dallas, TX
Bailey, Valerie I. ... New York, NY
Bailey, Vanessa Patrice ... Anahuac, TX
Bailey, Vaughn L. ... Fort Worth, TX
Bailey, Verd R. ... Clarinda, IA
Bailey, Vicki L. ... St. Paul, MN
Bailey, Victor E. ... Fairview, OK
Bailey, Virginia Benton
Ridgefield Park, NJ
Bailey, Vollie C., III ... Spartanburg, SC
Bailey, W. Charles, Jr. ... Baltimore, MD
Frederick, MD
Bailey, W. Douglas ... Fort Worth, TX
Bailey, W. Edward ... New York, NY
Bailey, Walter L., Jr. ... Memphis, TN
Bailey, Walter M., Jr. ... Summerville, SC
Bailey and Wechsler, L.L.C.
West Hartford, CT
Washington, DC
Bailey, Wesley ... Winston-Salem, NC
Bailey, Wesley G., II ... Jonesboro, GA
Bailey & Wetzel, P.A. ... Dover, DE
Georgetown, DE
Wilmington, DE
Bailey, William C. ... Salt Lake City, UT
Bailey, William D. ... San Antonio, TX
Bailey, William D., Jr. ... Wilmington, DE
Bailey, William D., P.C. ... Lake Oswego, OR
Bailey, William David ... Lake Oswego, OR
Bailey, William E. ... Chicago, IL
Bailey, William F. ... Lafayette, LA
Bailey, William G. ... Houston, TX
Bailey, William J. ... Melrose, MA
Bailey, William J. ... Teaneck, NJ
Bailey, William J. ... Albuquerque, NM
Bailey, William J., III
Federal Communications Commission, Common Carrier Bureau, GV
Bailey, William J., Jr. ... Cleveland, OH
Bailey, William J., P.C. ... Melrose, MA
Bailey, William L. ... Cerritos, CA
Bailey, William M. ... Washington, DC
Bailey, William P. ... Calhoun, GA
Bailey, William R. ... Upper Marlboro, MD
Bailey, William R. ... Camden, SC
Bailey, William S. ... Honolulu, HI
Bailey, William S. ... Seattle, WA
Bailey, William Thames, Jr. ... Lucedale, MS
Bailey and Williams ... Dallas, TX
Bailey, Willie L. ... Greenville, MS
Bailey, Wm. J. ... Springfield, MA
Bailey & Womble, P.A. ... Batesville, MS
Bailey, W. T. ... Lucedale, MS
Bailey, Yvonne C. ... Raleigh, NC
Bailey-Graham, Ilse D. ... Kerrville, TX
Bailey-Jones, Bonnie B. ... Riverside, CA
Bailey Jongbloed, Barbara ... New Haven, CT
Bailey-Rihn, Valerie L. ... Madison, WI
Bailey-Wells, Deborah A.
San Francisco, CA
Bailie, David A. ... Champaign, IL
Bailie, Michael W. ... Department of Justice, Executive Office for United States Attorneys, GV
Bailiff, Sarah J. ... Fort Worth, TX
Bailiff, Stephanie A. ... Irvine, CA
Bailin, Deborah M. ... Manchester, NH
Bailin, Devra G. ... Boston, MA
Bailin, Jayne R. ... Boston, MA
Bailin, Lawrence J. ... Tampa, FL
Bailin, Leonard ... New York, NY
Bailin, Marc L. ... New York, NY
Bailin, Marvin K. ... Hartford, SD
Sioux Falls, SD
Bailin, Michael A. ... Philadelphia, PA
Bailin, Richard H. ... Castro Valley, CA
Bailin, Richard H. ... Hayward, CA
Bailin, Roxanne ... Boulder, CO
Bailin & Seplowitz ... New York, NY
Bailine, Larry H. ... Havertown, PA
Bailinson, James P. ... Portland, ME
Bailinson, Morris ... New York, NY
Bailis, David P. ... Atlanta, GA
Bailis, Jacob W. ... Fort Lee, NJ
Bailkin, Marc B. ... Philadelphia, PA
Bailkin, Michael D. ... New York, NY
Baill, Jeffrey M. ... Minneapolis, MN
Baill, Lawrence M. ... Minneapolis, MN
Baillargeon, Elaine L. ... Gilford, NH
Baillargeon, Paul P. ... North Smithfield, RI
Baillargeon, Paul P., Inc.
North Smithfield, RI
Baillie, Charlotte ... Auburn, CA
Baillie, Donald S. ... Cheshire, CT
Baillie, James L. ... Minneapolis, MN
Baillie, John K. ... Pittsburgh, PA
Baillie, Karen E. ... Pittsburgh, PA
Baillie, Mark S. ... New York, NY
Baillie, Philip ... Riverside, CA
Baillie, William L. ... Great Falls, MT
Bailliff, Michael E. ... New York, NY
Baillis, Albert A. ... Ada, OH
Baillon, Austin J. ... St. Paul, MN
Baillon, Frances E. ... St. Paul, MN
Baillon, Paul A. ... St. Paul, MN
Bailly, David H., Jr. ... Minneapolis, MN
Bailly, David R. ... Fargo, ND
Bailly, John J. ... White Plains, NY
Bailly, John P., Jr. ... Albany, NY
Bailly, Richard Allen ... Alexandria, LA
Bailly, Ron ... Mesa, AZ
Bailly, Ron, P.C. ... Mesa, AZ
Bailly, Stephen F. ... Albany, NY
Bailo, Susan G. ... South Lyon, MI
Bailor, Bernard S. ... Washington, DC
Bailor, Martha E. ... Pittsburgh, PA
Bailowitz, Jordan I. ... Baltimore, MD
Bails, Irvin S. ... Pittsburgh, PA
Bailus, Mark B. ... Las Vegas, NV
Baily, Allan F. ... Sarasota, FL
Baily, Ann ... Pittsburgh, PA
Baily & Baily, P.A. ... Sarasota, FL
Baily, Douglas B. ... Anchorage, AK
Baily, Harold E. ... Coupeville, WA
Baily, Jay Edgar ... Sarasota, FL
Baily, John E. ... Waynesburg, PA
Baily, William M. ... Waynesburg, PA
Baim, Darrin S. ... Chicago, IL
Baim, Gunti, Mouser, Robinson, Havner
Pine Bluff, AR
Sheridan, AR
Stuttgart, AR
Baim, Jason ... Los Angeles, CA
Baim, Joseph M. ... Laguna Beach, CA
Baim, Kenneth B. ... Pine Bluff, AR
Baim, Kimberly A. ... Chicago, IL
Baime & Baime ... Chicago, IL
Baime, Barry L. ... Hackensack, NJ
Baime, Colleen E. ... Chicago, IL
Baime, Joseph L. ... Chicago, IL
Baime, Kenneth E. ... Chicago, IL
Baime, Robert A. ... Princeton, NJ
New York, NY
Baime, Stephen G. ... Chicago, IL
Bain, Alan E. ... Schaumburg, IL
Fort Worth, TX
Bain, Alan L. ... New York, NY
Bain, Alton D. ... Lillington, NC
Bain, Angeline Lindley ... Dallas, TX
Bain & Bain, P.C. ... Farmington Hills, MI
Bain, Basil L. ... Naples, FL
Bain, Beverly ... Corona Del Mar, CA
Bain, Bruce D. ... Dallas, TX
Bain, C. Deborah ... West Palm Beach, FL
Bain, C. Mark ... Birmingham, AL
Bain, C. Randall ... Phoenix, AZ
Bain, C. Ridgley ... Lawrenceville, VA
Bain, Cecil W. ... San Antonio, TX
Bain, Cecil W., P.C., Law Offices of
San Antonio, TX
Bain, Cecil W. (Tres), III
San Antonio, TX
Bain, Charles E. ... Brentwood, TN
Bain, Cynthia Ann ... Seattle, WA
Bain, Daniel B. ... Southfield, MI
Bain, David A. ... Atlanta, GA

Bain, David J., Jr. .... Lawrence, MA
Bain, Donald K. .... Denver, CO
Bain, Dorothy L. .... Wausau, WI
Bain, Douglas G. .... Seattle, WA
Bain, Edgar R. .... Lillington, NC
Bain, Edward H., Jr. .... Charlottesville, VA
Bain, Elizabeth R. .... Austin, TX
Bain, Elton John .... Honolulu, HI
Bain, Fenton A. .... Boulder, CO
Bain, Fenton A., P.C. .... Boulder, CO
Bain Files Worthen and Jarrett, A Professional Corporation .... Tyler, TX
Bain, Florence .... Bloomington, IL
Macomb, IL
Peoria, IL
Quincy, IL
Rushville, IL
Springfield, IL
Bain, Gary .... Lincolnwood, IL
Bain, Harold E. .... Orinda, CA
Bain, Howard M. .... Highland Park, IL
Bain, Irwin A. .... Columbus, OH
Bain, James E. .... North Myrtle Beach, SC
Bain, James W. .... Denver, CO
Bain, Jeffrey M. .... Shaker Heights, OH
Bain, Jerry E. .... Tyler, TX
Bain, John Adam .... Department of Justice, Civil Division, GV
Bain, John H. .... Kernersville, NC
Bain, John H. .... Columbus, OH
Bain, John I. .... Farmington Hills, MI
Bain, John N. .... Roseland, NJ
Bain, John W. .... Washington, DC
Bain, Joseph W. .... West Palm Beach, FL
Bain, Judith S. .... Long Beach, CA
Bain, Kenneth E., Jr. .... Floydada, TX
Bain, Lee N. .... Georgetown, TX
Bain, Lisa M. .... Denver, CO
Bain, Marilyn E. .... Vancouver, WA
Bain & McRae .... Lillington, NC
Sanford, NC
Bain, Michael .... New York, NY
Bain, Michael D. .... Boston, MA
Bain, Michael R. .... Indianapolis, IN
Bain, Pamela T. .... Warren, NJ
Bain, Paul D. .... Jacksonville, FL
Tampa, FL
Bain, Peter R. .... New York, NY
Bain, Randolph A. .... Federal Deposit Insurance Corporation, GV
Bain, Rebecca Strief .... Dallas, TX
Bain, Richard M. .... Cleveland, OH
Bain, Robert G. .... Manhattan Beach, CA
Bain, Robert M. .... St. Louis, MO
Bain, Roger K. .... Silver Spring, MD
Bain, Roy C. .... Wilmington, NC
Bain, Stephen A. .... Denver, CO
Bain, Stephen D. .... Houston, TX
Bain, Steven C. .... St. Louis, MO
Bain, Steven E. .... New Orleans, LA
Bain, Susan Rappa .... Alpharetta, GA
Bain, Terry A. .... New York, NY
Bain, Thomas J. .... Newton, NJ
Bain, Troy E. .... Shreveport, LA
Bain, Virgil E., Jr. .... Waco, TX
Bain, William A., Jr. .... Buffalo, NY
Bain, William G. .... Alpharetta, GA
Bain, Wm. D., Jr. .... Spartanburg, SC
Bainbridge, Andrew J. .... Columbus, OH
Bainbridge, David R. .... Toledo, OH
Bainbridge, Ellen A. .... Fort Bragg, CA
Bainbridge, Frank M. .... Birmingham, AL
Bainbridge Group, A Law Corporation .... Irvine, CA
Bainbridge, Harry B. .... Chicago, IL
Schaumburg, IL
Bainbridge, Jack G. .... Flossmoor, IL
Bainbridge, James D. .... Henderson, NV
Bainbridge, James S. .... Philadelphia, PA
Bainbridge, John S. .... Detroit, MI
Bainbridge, John S., Jr. .... Towson, MD
Bainbridge, Mims, Rogers & Smith, LLP .... Birmingham, AL
Bainbridge, Philippa .... New York, NY
Bainbridge, Phillip E. .... Indianapolis, IN
Bainbridge, Robert L. .... Tulsa, OK
Bainbridge, Robt. .... Fort Bragg, CA
Bainbridge, Stephen M. .... Champaign, IL
Bainbridge, Thomas H., Jr. .... Columbus, OH
Bainbridge, William A. .... Phoenix, AZ
Baine, Elizabeth Lea .... Jackson, MS
Baine, James E. .... El Dorado, AR
Baine, John L. .... Sacramento, CA
Baine, Kevin T. .... Washington, DC
Baine, Louis G., III .... Jackson, MS
Baine, Louis G., Jr. .... Ridgeland, MS
Baine, Wade M. .... Gulfport, MS
Baine, William J. .... San Antonio, TX
Bainer, Roland C. .... Corona, CA
Bainer, Todd R. .... Branford, CT
Baines, Cynthia DeBula .... Nashville, TN
Baines, Cyril .... Brooklyn, NY
Baines, Edward J. .... Baltimore, MD
Baines, Matthew R. .... Gresham, OR
Baines, Nicole Lee .... Annapolis, MD
Baines, Robert A. .... San Jose, CA
Bainnson, Susan D. .... New York, NY
Bains, Bradley H. .... Midland, TX
Bains, David P. .... Mobile, AL
Metairie, LA
Bains, Herman H. .... Minneapolis, MN
Bains, Jack E. .... Pasadena, TX
Bains, Jack Martin .... Oneonta, AL
Bains, Jack Martin, Jr. .... Birmingham, AL
Bains, Kay K. .... Birmingham, AL
Bains, Lee E. .... Bessemer, AL
Bains, Lee E., Jr. .... Birmingham, AL
Bains, Ruben S. .... Houston, TX
Bains & Terry .... Bessemer, AL
Bains-Grebner, Marcia .... Eagle River, WI
Bainter, David T. .... Columbus, OH
Bainter, Harlan W. .... Mt. Pleasant, IA
Bainter, Richard K. .... Brighton, CO
Bainter, Seleta .... Mt. Pleasant, IA
Bainter and Thomas .... Mt. Pleasant, IA
Bainton, Denise M. .... Tucson, AZ
Bainton, J. Joseph .... New York, NY
Bainton McCarthy & Siegel, LLC
Stamford, CT
New York, NY
Bainum, Michael C. .... Dedham, MA
Bainum, Rebecca Saybolt .... Boston, MA
Baio, Claudia A. .... Glastonbury, CT
Baio, Dratfield & Associates, Law Offices of .... Glastonbury, CT
Baio, Joseph T. .... New York, NY
Baio, Laurie E. .... Bronx, NY
Baio, Rocky J. .... Oxnard, CA
Baiocchi, Joel C. .... Sacramento, CA
Baiocco, Dana .... Pittsburgh, PA
Baione, John P. .... Forest Hills, NY
Bair & Bair .... Sacramento, CA
Bair, Bair & Garrity, LLP .... Bismarck, ND
Mandan, ND
Bair, Benjamin C. Gilbert .... New York, NY
Bair, Benjamin G. .... Sterling Heights, MI
Bair, Bruce B. .... Mandan, ND
Bair, C. William .... Holland, OH
Bair, Daniel S. .... Anchorage, AK
Bair, Dudley D., Jr. .... New York, NY
Bair, Elizabeth Siso .... Woodbridge, NJ
Bair, Emily Sanford .... Atlanta, GA
Bair, Gary E. .... Baltimore, MD
Bair, Gregory M. .... Dallas, TX
Bair, Hudson T. .... San Francisco, CA
Bair, Jeffrey J. .... Aiken, SC
Bair, Jodi .... Bloomington, MN
Bair, Jodi J. .... Columbus, OH
Bair, Joel E. .... Grand Rapids, MI
Bair, John S. .... Metairie, LA
Bair, Kristie E. .... Albuquerque, NM
Bair, Matthew R. .... San Antonio, TX
Bair, Pamela A. .... Sacramento, CA
Bair, Patrick H. .... Harrisburg, PA
Bair, Peter A. .... Falls Church, VA
Bair, Robert R. .... Baltimore, MD
Bair, Ronald L. .... Houston, TX
Bair, Steven R. .... Sacramento, CA
Bair, Teri L. .... Houston, TX
Bair, Thomas B. .... Mandan, ND
Bair, Todd Richard .... Atlanta, GA
Bair, Wallace C. .... Atlanta, GA
Bair, Warner B., II .... Sun City, AZ
Bair, Warner B., II, P.C. .... Sun City, AZ
Baird, Alison Kaye .... Los Angeles, CA
Baird, Amy L. .... New Orleans, LA
Baird, Andrew J. .... Norcross, GA
Baird, Anna Kaye .... Raleigh, NC
Baird, Anna L. .... Charlotte, NC
Baird, Archibald W. .... Hartford, CT
Baird, Baird, Baird and Jones, P.S.C.
Lexington, KY
Pikeville, KY
Baird, Barbara Beth .... Diamond Bar, CA
Baird, Barbara J. .... Indianapolis, IN
Baird, Becky Dahms .... Coalgate, OK
Baird, Benita S. .... Atlanta, GA
Baird, Boyd C. .... Traverse City, MI
Baird, Brett C. .... Traverse City, MI
Baird, Brian D. .... Buffalo, NY
Baird, Brian D. .... Houston, TX
Baird, Brian D. .... Milwaukee, WI
Baird, Bruce A. .... Washington, DC
Baird, Bruce R., P.C. .... Salt Lake City, UT
Baird, C. Bruce .... Fairfax, VA
Baird, C. Ronald .... Springfield, MO
Baird, Carla J. .... Fort Wayne, IN
Baird, Carolyn G. .... Anderson, SC
Baird, Catharyn A. .... Denver, CO
Baird, Catherine Foster .... Lenexa, KS
Baird, Charles F. .... Houston, TX
Baird, Charles J. .... Pikeville, KY
Baird, Crews, Schiller & Whitaker, P.C.
Belton, TX
Temple, TX
Baird, Dan W. .... Blue Hill, NE
Clay Center, NE
Baird, Dana Carol .... Tallahassee, FL
Baird, Dara Anne Loetzerich
Metairie, LA
Baird, David A. .... Maryville, MO
Baird, David A. .... Batavia, NY
Baird, David W. .... Stockton, CA
Baird, Denise C. .... Boise, ID
Baird, Dennis A. .... Washington, DC
Baird, Donald G. .... Decatur, IL
Baird, Donald W. .... Des Moines, IA
Baird, Duncan H. .... St. Paul, MN
Baird, Edward P. .... Newark, NJ
Baird, Edward R. .... Houston, TX
Baird, Edward R., Jr. .... Norfolk, VA
Baird, Elizabeth H. .... Washington, DC
Baird, Erica Borden .... New York, NY
Baird, Floyd M. .... Temple, TX
Baird, Frederick R., II .... Chicago, IL
Baird, George Ericson, Jr. .... Troy, NY
Baird, Greg R. .... Portland, OR
Baird, Gregory D. .... Clearwater, FL
Baird, Gregory L. .... Portland, OR
Baird & Griess .... Blue Hill, NE
Clay Center, NE
Sutton, NE
Baird, H. Elizabeth .... Charlotte, NC
Baird, Hal D. .... Salt Lake City, UT
Baird Hanson Quinn LLP .... Boulder, CO
Boise, ID
Houston, TX
Baird, Holm, McEachen, Pedersen, Hamann & Strasheim .... Lincoln, NE
Omaha, NE
Baird, Howard .... Pasco, WA
Baird, J. Brian .... Winter Park, FL
Baird, J. Ernest .... Phoenix, AZ
Baird, J. Kenneth .... Longboat Key, FL
Baird, Jack .... Oklahoma City, OK
Baird, James .... Chicago, IL
Baird, James A. .... Bowling Green, OH
Baird, James F. .... West Brookfield, MA
Baird, James R., Jr. .... Los Angeles, CA
Baird, James T. .... Twin Falls, ID
Baird, James Vernon .... Houston, TX
Baird, Jane C. .... Department Of Health And Human Services, GV
Baird, Jason James .... Montgomery, AL
Baird, Jeffrey .... San Diego, CA
Baird, Jeffrey H. .... San Francisco, CA
Baird, Jeffrey S. .... Whittier, CA
Baird, Jeffrey S. .... Amarillo, TX
Baird, Jerry B. .... Tuscaloosa, AL
Baird, Joan J. .... Stamford, CT
Baird, Joël Elaine .... Houston, TX
Baird, John .... Greenville, KY
Baird, John Baird .... Orlando, FL
Baird, John D. .... Norwalk, OH
Baird, John H. .... Pikeville, KY
Baird, John K. .... Crawfordsville, IN
Baird, John Knapp .... Salt Lake City, UT
Baird, John M. .... Nashville, TN
Baird, John P. .... St. Louis, MO
Baird, John R. .... Columbus, OH
Baird, John W. .... Ephrata, WA
Baird, Jonathan .... Chicago, IL
Baird, Jonathan P. .... Claremont, NH
Baird & Jones L.C. .... Salt Lake City, UT
Baird, Joseph H. .... Boise, ID
Baird, Kate F. .... Lenexa, KS
Baird, Kevin .... Beaumont, TX
Baird, Kevin R. .... Philadelphia, PA
Baird, Kristina L. .... Hagåtña, GU
Baird, LaRoy, III .... Bismarck, ND
Baird, LaRoy, P.C. .... Bismarck, ND
Baird, Laura L. .... Okemos, MI
Baird Law Office .... Ephrata, WA
Baird, Leonard H., Jr. .... Clermont, FL
Baird, Lightner & Millsap, A Professional Corporation .... Springfield, MO
Baird, Lisa A. .... Miami, FL
Baird, Lisa A., P.A. .... Homestead, FL
Miami, FL
Baird, Lisa Gioffre .... Purchase, NY
Baird, Lisa M. .... Los Angeles, CA
Baird, Lourdes G. .... Los Angeles, CA
Baird, Mariah .... San Francisco, CA
Baird, Martha M. K. .... Indianapolis, IN
Baird, Mary E. .... Indianapolis, IN
Baird, Matthew K. .... Houston, TX
Baird, Michael D. .... Santa Fe, NM
Baird, Michael S. .... Chicago, IL
Baird, Michele R. .... Plano, TX
Baird, Morton W., II .... San Antonio, TX
Baird, Morton W. II, Law Offices of, P.C. .... San Antonio, TX
Baird, Nancy D. .... Washington, DC
Baird, Orrin .... Washington, DC
Baird, Paige Leslie .... Albuquerque, NM
Baird, Patricia Ann .... Cleveland Heights, OH
Baird, Perry D. .... Casey, IL
Baird, Peter D. .... Phoenix, AZ
Baird, R. Lawrence .... Louisville, KY
Baird, R. Stewart, Jr. .... San Francisco, CA
Baird, Randy L. .... Topeka, KS
Baird, R.B. "Buddy", III .... Rogersville, TN
Baird, Rhonda N. .... Pension Benefit Guaranty Corporation, Office of the General Counsel, GV
Baird, Rita .... Troy, MI
Baird, Rita J. .... Los Angeles, CA
Baird, Robert K. .... Plainview, NE
Baird, Robert S. .... Austin, TX
Baird, Robin B. .... Fort Worth, TX
Baird, Robin E. .... Waco, TX
Baird, Robt. D. .... Clairton, PA
Baird, Ronald L., Office of .... Anchorage, AK
Baird, Ronald R. .... Wheaton, IL
Baird, Russell M. .... Chicago, IL
Baird, S. Carol .... Atlanta, GA
Baird, Sandra L. .... Burlington, VT
Baird, Stanford D. .... Charlotte, NC
Baird, Stephen R. .... Minneapolis, MN
Baird, Steven G. .... Mountain View, CA
Baird, Steven K. .... Miami, FL
Baird, Stokes A., IV .... Munfordville, KY
Baird, Sue A. .... Denver, CO
Baird, Susan E. .... Fort Worth, TX
Baird, Terence A. .... Palmdale, CA
Baird, Thomas .... Temple, TX
Baird, Thomas A. .... Okemos, MI
Baird, Thomas B., Jr. .... Wytheville, VA
Baird, Thomas J. .... North Palm Beach, FL
Baird, Thomas J., P.A.
North Palm Beach, FL
Baird, Thomas K. .... Phoenix, AZ
Baird, Timothy S. .... Richmond, VA
Baird, Victor McEver .... United States Senate, Committee Legal Personnel, GV
Baird, W. Bruce, Jr. .... Louisville, KY
Baird, W. Douglas .... Clearwater, FL
Baird, William Anthony .... Oxnard, CA
Baird, William J., III .... Pikeville, KY
Baird, William R. .... United States Senate, Office of the Legislative Counsel, GV
Baird, William R. .... Akron, OH
Baird, Williams, Davis & Smith
Phoenix, AZ
Baird, Wm. Alan .... Philadelphia, PA
Bairey, Jeffery G. .... San Francisco, CA
Bairey, Katherine Chester .... Orinda, CA
Bairstow, Karen Grout .... Boston, MA
Bairstow, Richard R. .... Waukegan, IL
Bairstow, Steve .... Belleview, FL
Baisch, Charles O. .... Warsaw, NY
Baisch & Coletti .... Portland, OR
Baisch, Jan Thomas .... Portland, OR
Baisch, Kenneth W. .... San Diego, CA
Baisden, Fred R., Jr. .... Salem, OR
Baisden, Larry J. .... Columbus, OH
Baisden, Randell L. .... Fort Lauderdale, FL
Baisden, W. Eric .... Cleveland, OH
Baise, Gary H. .... Washington, DC
Baise, Miller & Freer, P.C.
Washington, DC
Charlottesville, VA
Baisel, Marvin D. .... East Lansing, MI
Baish, Anthony S. .... Milwaukee, WI
Baish, Richard O. .... El Paso, TX
Baisier, Paul M. .... Atlanta, GA
Baisinger, Glen D. .... Albany, OR
Baisley, Barbara B. .... Bronxville, NY
Baisley, Charles W. .... Sarasota, FL
Baisley, James M. .... Lincolnshire, IL
Baisley, John E. .... Riverhead, NY
Baisley, Margaret D. .... New York, NY
Baisley, Paul J. .... Central Islip, NY
Baisley, Paul J., Jr. .... Central Islip, NY
Baither, C. Philip, III .... Toledo, OH
Baitman, David A. .... Chicago, IL
Baitty, Rebecca A. .... Sarasota, FL
Baitty, Rebecca A., P.A. .... Sarasota, FL
Baity, Billy J., Jr. .... Statesville, NC
Baity, G. Scott .... Jacksonville, FL
Baity, Glenn F. .... San Francisco, CA
Baity, John Cooley .... New York, NY
Baity, Patricia A. .... Greenwich, CT
Baity, Stephen James .... Denver, CO
Baiungo, Joseph W. .... Belfast, ME
Baivier, Jeanne E. .... Oshkosh, WI
Baiz, Thomas A., Jr. .... Great Falls, MT
Baizer & Kolar, P.C. .... Highland Park, IL
Baizer, Robert D. .... Oakland, CA
Baizer, Robert S. .... Highland Park, IL
Bajaj, Sunil S. .... New York, NY
Bajaj-Singh, Monica .... New York, NY
Bajak, Curtis W. .... Los Angeles, CA
Bajak, Joseph A. .... Buffalo, NY
Bajalia, M. Mark .... Jacksonville, FL
Bajalia, Michael M. .... Jacksonville, FL
Bajalia, Nick M. .... Valdosta, GA
Bajandas, Ricardo .... Miami, FL
Bajandas, Zadette .... San Juan, PR
Bajefsky, Robert D. .... Washington, DC
Bajefsky, Vicki E. .... Washington, DC
Bajer, Edward R. .... Washington, DC
Bajgrowicz, James J. .... Santa Rosa, CA
Bajko, Robert F. .... Libertyville, IL
Bajo, Pedro F., Jr. .... Tampa, FL
Bajoczky, Anthony L. .... Tallahassee, FL
Bajoczky & Fournier .... Tallahassee, FL
Bajohr, William E. .... Hempstead, NY
Bajorek, Christine Carol .... Cleveland, OH
Bajwa, Sukhwinder K. .... Bellingham, WA
Bak & Bak .... Philadelphia, PA
Bak, Brafford B. .... Aston, PA
Bak, Hyung J. .... New York, NY
Bak, Joseph .... Philadelphia, PA
Bak, Mary E. .... Prospect Heights, IL
Bak, Mary E. .... Spring House, PA
Bak, Mary M. .... Glenview, IL
Bak, Patricia F. .... Fairfax, VA
Bak, Walter E. .... Northampton, MA
Bak, William .... Spring House, PA
Baka, Andrew F. .... Fort Worth, TX
Baka, Gregory .... Saipan, TT
Bakakos, Peter .... Chicago, IL
Bakal, Emilie L. .... New York, NY
Bakal, Scott J. .... Chicago, IL
Bakal, Todd A. .... New York, NY
Bakalar, George Michael .... Boca Raton, FL
Bakalian, Allan B. .... Kirkland, WA
Bakalis, George J. .... Wheaton, IL
Bakalor, Donna Hope .... New York, NY
Bakalor, Richard H. .... New York, NY
Bakaly, Charles G., Jr. .... Los Angeles, CA
Bakaly & Davies .... Los Angeles, CA
Bakanas, Lisa G. .... Hamden, CT
Bakanauskus, Paul .... Jersey City, NJ
Bakar, Gene B. .... San Francisco, CA
Bakari, Adisa P. .... Washington, DC
Bakarich, Gerald S. .... Sacramento, CA
Bakarich, Peter J., Jr. .... Paramus, NJ
Bakas, John W., Jr. .... Tampa, FL
Bakatsas, Nicholas E. .... Marietta, GA
Bak-Boychuk, I. Michael .... Long Beach, CA
Bakeman, Donald V. .... Hot Springs Village, AR
Bakemeier, Robert F. .... Seattle, WA
Baken, Scott T. .... New York, NY
Baker, A. Diane .... Atlanta, GA
Baker, Aaron C. .... St. Louis, MO
Baker, Abigail T. .... Richmond, VA
Baker, Adam J. .... Farmington Hills, MI
Baker, Adam J. .... Gahanna, OH
Baker, Adam J., P.C. .... Farmington Hills, MI
Baker, Adam S. .... Albuquerque, NM
Baker, Adam S. .... Cleveland, OH
Baker, Adele .... Washington, DC
Baker, Adele C. .... Trenton, NJ
Baker, Adrianne W. .... San Diego, CA
Baker, Adrienne M. .... Boston, MA
Baker, Adrienne Marie .... Sandusky, OH

Baker, Alan ... Fargo, ND
Baker, Alan N. ... Chicago, IL
Baker, Alan Robert ... Wethersfield, CT
Baker, Alisa J. ... Mountain View, CA
Baker, Alison W. ... Washington, DC
Baker, Althea R. ... Los Angeles, CA
Baker, Andrea S. ... Baltimore, MD
Baker, Andrew ... Framingham, MA
Baker, Andrew B., Jr. ... Dyer, IN
Baker, Andrew C. ... Charleston, MS
Baker, Andrew H. ... Beverly Hills, CA
Baker, Andrew M. ... Indianapolis, IN
Baker, Andrew M. ... Dallas, TX
Baker, Andrew W. ... House of Representatives, Committee Legal Personnel, GV
Baker, Ann Morris ... Pittsburgh, PA
Baker, Anna N. ... Austin, TX
Baker, Anne C. ... New York, NY
Baker, Anne F. ... Bloomington, MN
Baker, Anne Lamborn ... Topeka, KS
Baker, Annette Lipari ... Mount Clemens, MI
Baker, Annie Kun ... Los Angeles, CA
Baker, Anthony Joseph ... Mooresville, NC
Baker, Anthony V. ... Malibu, CA
Baker, Antoinette E. ... New York, NY
Baker, Arlene C. ... San Juan Capistrano, CA
Baker & Armistead, PLLC
Morgantown, WV
Baker, Art ... Amarillo, TX
Baker, Arthur C. ... Baldwin Park, CA
Baker, Arthur H., III ... Philadelphia, PA
Pittsburgh, PA
Baker, Arthur W., Jr. ... El Centro, CA
Baker, Audrey ... Denver, CO
Baker, Audrey H. ... New York, NY
Baker, Audrey Ivanetic ... San Francisco, CA
Baker & Baker ... Baltimore, MD
Corpus Christi, TX
Baker & Baker, A Professional Corporation
Santa Ana, CA
Baker Baker & Sweterlitsch
Columbus, OH
Baker, Baker, Tait & Manning
Oklahoma City, OK
Baker, Baker & Twomey, P.A.
Baltimore, MD
Towson, MD
Baker, Barbara A. ... Sheridan, WY
Baker, Barry ... Fayetteville, AR
Baker, Barry I. ... Charleston, SC
Baker, Barry K. ... Melbourne, FL
Baker, Barton L. ... Yuma, AZ
Baker, Basil A. ... Ann Arbor, MI
Baker, Ben F. ... Tulsa, OK
Baker, Benjamin A. ... Sherman, TX
Baker, Benjamin E., Jr. ... Birmingham, AL
Baker, Bennett J. ... Chicago, IL
Baker, Bernard R., II ... Toledo, OH
Baker, Bernard R., III
West Palm Beach, FL
Baker, Bethany R. ... Fresno, CA
Baker, Betsy B. ... Minneapolis, MN
Baker, Betty C. ... Reno, NV
Baker, Beverly P. ... Birmingham, AL
Baker, B. J. ... Casper, WY
Baker, Blaise G. ... Columbus, OH
Baker & Blum, L.C. ... Overland Park, KS
Baker and Bodwell, A Professional Corporation
Connersville, IN
Baker, Boldt & Gallerano ... Austin, TX
Dripping Springs, TX
San Marcos, TX
Baker, Bonnie ... Santa Barbara, CA
Baker, Bonnie Ann ... Orange, CA
Riverside, CA
Baker, Bonnie L. ... Stockbridge, GA
Baker, Bonnie Melissa ... New York, NY
Baker, Bonnie S. ... Albany, NY
Baker Botts, L.L.P. ... Washington, DC
New York, NY
Austin, TX
Dallas, TX
Baker Botts L.L.P. ... Houston, TX
Baker & Boyan, P.L.L.C. ... High Point, NC
Baker, Boyd ... Altus, OK
Baker, Brad B. ... Steelville, MO
Baker, Brad N. ... Hermosa Beach, CA
Baker, Bradford S. ... Tulsa, OK
Baker, Bradford S., Inc. ... Tulsa, OK
Baker, Bradley K. ... Columbus, OH
Baker, Bradley O. ... Portland, OR
Baker Brattain, L.L.C. ... Anchorage, AK
Baker, Braverman, Barbadoro & Sutton, P.C. ... Boston, MA
Braintree, MA
Baker, Brenda B. ... Corpus Christi, TX
Baker, Brett R. ... New York, NY
Baker, Brian Alan ... Pasadena, CA
Baker, Brian C. ... Chicago, IL
Baker, Brian C. ... Stephentown, NY
Baker, Brian L. ... Roseland, NJ
Baker, Brian L. ... San Marcos, TX
Baker, Brian M. ... Olympia, WA
Baker, Brian M., Inc. P.C. ... Olympia, WA
Baker, Brian S. ... Martinez, CA
Baker, Brook K. ... Boston, MA
Baker, Brown & Dixon ... Arlington, TX
Austin, TX
Dallas, TX
Houston, TX
Baker, Bruce ... Chicago, IL
Baker, Bruce D. ... Burlington, VT
Baker, Bruce J. ... Rochester, NY
Baker, Bruce Jay ... Chicago, IL
Baker, Bruce S. ... Sacramento, CA
Baker, Bruce W. ... Des Moines, IA
Baker, Bryan W. ... Houston, TX

Baker & Burton, A Prof. Corp.
Hermosa Beach, CA
Baker, Burton H. ... St. Joseph, MI
Baker, Byron N. ... Kansas City, MO
Baker, C. Daniel ... Pittsburgh, PA
Baker, C. Edwin ... Philadelphia, PA
Baker, C. Gaines ... Batesville, MS
Baker, C. Mark ... Houston, TX
Baker, C. Steven ... Chicago, IL
Baker, Cameron ... San Francisco, CA
Baker, Cami R. ... Augusta, KS
Baker, Campbell & Parsons
Nashville, TN
Baker, Carl ... Philadelphia, PA
Baker, Carl D. ... Marshalltown, IA
Baker, Carl F. ... Houston, TX
Baker, Carl L. ... Fort Wayne, IN
Baker, Carl T. ... Glens Falls, NY
Baker, Carla L. ... Colorado Springs, CO
Baker, Carmody C. ... Houston, TX
Baker, Carol Jean ... Fort Worth, TX
Baker, Caroline E. ... Houston, TX
Baker, Carolyn Pierce ... Little Rock, AR
Baker, Carolyn T. ... Salem, OR
Baker, Cazier and McGowan ... Granby, CO
Baker, Celeste A. ... Austin, TX
Baker, Chapman & Cahoon ... Akron, OH
Baker, Charles A. ... Houston, TX
Baker, Charles A., III ... Boston, MA
Baker, Charles C. ... Wilson, WY
Baker, Charles D., (P.A.) ... Alma, AR
Baker, Charles E. ... Broomfield, CO
Baker, Charles E. ... Columbia, SC
Baker, Charles H. ... New York, NY
Baker, Charles Hamilton ... Kennett, MO
Baker, Charles J., III ... Charleston, SC
Baker, Charles P. ... New York, NY
Baker, Charles P., Jr. ... Painesville, OH
Baker, Charles S. ... Austin, TX
Baker, Charles W. ... Little Rock, AR
Baker, Chester S., Jr. ... Williamsburg, VA
Baker, Christine Peirson ... Laguna Hills, CA
Baker, Christopher D. ... San Francisco, CA
Baker, Christopher E. ... Indianapolis, IN
Baker, Christopher E. ... Fort Worth, TX
Baker, Christopher P. ... Detroit, MI
Baker, Christopher R. ... Beverly Hills, CA
Baker, Cindy L. ... Cashion, OK
Baker, Claire Zivley ... Houston, TX
Baker, Clarence K. ... Redlands, CA
Baker, Clarence L. ... Oakland, CA
Baker & Clark ... Syracuse, NY
Baker, Clate J. ... Springfield, MO
Baker, Clell David ... Newport, KY
Baker, Clifton ... Tulsa, OK
Baker, Clifton A. ... Pasadena, CA
Baker, Constance H. ... Baltimore, MD
Baker, Curtis L. ... Mays Landing, NJ
Baker, Cynthia J. ... Little Rock, AR
Baker, Cynthia R. ... Jamaica, NY
Baker, D. Brent ... Mobile, AL
Baker, D. Jansing ... New York, NY
Baker, D. Kenneth ... Darlington, SC
Baker, D. Mark ... Rockville, MD
Baker, D. Stephen ... Department of Justice, Federal Bureau of Investigation, GV
Baker, D. Suzanne ... Biloxi, MS
Baker, Dan N. ... Brea, CA
Baker, Dana S. ... San Francisco, CA
Baker, Dana V. ... Lincoln, NE
Baker, Daniel A. ... Long Beach, CA
Baker, Daniel J. ... East Meadow, NY
Baker, Daniel M. ... Jackson, MS
Baker, Daniel M. ... Moorestown, NJ
Baker, Daniel T. ... Clarksburg, WV
Baker, Daniel W. ... San Francisco, CA
Baker, Daniel W. ... Chicago, IL
Baker & Daniels ... Washington, DC
Elkhart, IN
Fort Wayne, IN
Indianapolis, IN
South Bend, IN
Baker, Darrell E., Jr. ... Memphis, TN
Baker, Darrell J. ... Wilmington, DE
Baker, Darren C. ... Chicago, IL
Baker, Darryl E. (Chip) ... Little Rock, AR
Baker, David A. ... Orlando, FL
Baker, David A. ... Chicago, IL
Baker, David A. ... Skokie, IL
Baker, David A. ... Des Moines, IA
Baker, David A. ... Covington, KY
Baker, David A. ... Rockville, MD
Baker, David A. ... St. Paul, MN
Baker, David E. ... Gary, IN
Baker, David E. ... Richmond, VA
Baker, David F. ... Omaha, NE
Baker, David G. ... Columbus, OH
Baker, David H. ... Washington, DC
Baker, David H. ... Palm Beach, FL
Baker, David Huntt ... Bellaire, TX
Baker, David L. ... Cedar Rapids, IA
Baker, David L. ... Dallas, TX
Baker, David M. ... Southwick, MA
Baker, David M. ... Huntington, WV
Baker, David N. ... Atlanta, GA
Baker, David P. ... York, PA
Baker, David R. ... Birmingham, AL
New York, NY
Baker, David R. ... Scottsdale, AZ
Baker, David R. ... Walnut Creek, CA
Baker, David R. ... League City, TX
Baker, David Rhett ... Orlando, FL
Baker, David Rhett, P.A. ... Orlando, FL
Baker, David S. ... Andalusia, AL
Baker, David S. ... Sun City, AZ
Baker, David S. ... Atlanta, GA
Baker, David S. ... Kansas City, MO
Baker, David W., P.A. ... Georgetown, DE

Baker, Dean W. ... New Haven, CT
Baker, Deanna M. ... San Diego, CA
Baker, Debbie Goronet ... Raeford, NC
Baker, Deborah Whitt ... Memphis, TN
Baker, Debra A. ... Burbank, CA
Baker, Debra E. ... New York, NY
Baker, Debra L. ... Houston, TX
Baker, Debra Ratterman ... Washington, DC
Baker, Delores Woods ... Grayson, KY
Maysville, KY
Baker, Denise A. ... Troy, MI
Baker, Denise J. ... Philadelphia, PA
Baker, Dennis E. ... Denver, CO
Baker, Dennis J. ... Glendale, CA
Baker, Dennis J. ... Marblehead, MA
Baker, Dennis M. ... Batesville, MS
Baker, Derek J. ... Philadelphia, PA
Baker, Diana C. ... Salinas, CA
Baker, Diane Elizabeth ... San Francisco, CA
Baker, Diane S. ... Harrisburg, PA
Baker, Dillard W. ... Houston, TX
Baker, Donald ... Kenilworth, IL
Baker, Donald Gregory ... Gate City, VA
Baker, Donald H., Jr.
Bloomfield Hills, MI
Detroit, MI
Baker, Donald I. ... Washington, DC
Baker, Donald J. ... New Orleans, LA
Baker, Donald J. ... Waco, TX
Baker, Donald L. ... Shreveport, LA
Baker, Donald M. ... House of Representatives, Committee Legal Personnel, GV
Baker, Donald P. ... Los Angeles, CA
Baker, Donald R. ... Bethlehem, PA
Baker, Donald R., P.C. ... Bethlehem, PA
Baker, Donelson, Bearman & Caldwell
Washington, DC
Jackson, MS
Chattanooga, TN
Huntsville, TN
Johnson City, TN
Knoxville, TN
Memphis, TN
Nashville, TN
Baker, Donn F. ... Tahlequah, OK
Baker, Donna E. ... Philadelphia, PA
Baker, Donna M. ... Riverside, CA
Baker, Donna Sue ... Wise, VA
Baker, Dorothy M. ... Portland, OR
Baker, Dorsey L. ... Lubbock, TX
Baker, Douglas A. ... Albuquerque, NM
Baker, Douglas A. ... Columbus, OH
Baker, Douglas M. ... Chattanooga, TN
Baker, Douglas W. ... Titusville, FL
Baker, Drew E. ... Schaumburg, IL
Baker, Drew Penick ... Tuscaloosa, AL
Baker, Duane A. ... El Paso, TX
Baker, Dublikar, Beck, Wiley & Mathews
Canton, OH
New Philadelphia, OH
Wooster, OH
Baker, Duke & Holman ... Pensacola, FL
Baker & Dull ... Osceola, MO
Baker, Durst, Nelson, Benz & Baldwin
Adrian, MI
Baker, Dwight E. ... Blackfoot, ID
Baker, E. Clifford ... Downers Grove, IL
Baker, E. Graham, Jr. ... Nashville, TN
Baker, E. Niles ... Maitland, FL
Baker, Earl E. ... Tustin, CA
Baker, Earl L. ... Inglewood, CA
Baker, Edgar A., Jr. ... Salisbury, MD
Baker, Edward A. ... Merrick, NY
Baker, Edward G. ... La Jolla, CA
Baker, Edward J. ... Lorain, OH
Baker, Edwin B. ... Keysville, VA
Baker, Edwin H. ... El Cerrito, CA
Baker, Edwin H. ... New York, NY
Baker, Edwin W. ... Corpus Christi, TX
Baker, Eileen E. ... Chicago, IL
Baker, Elizabeth ... Palm Springs, CA
Baker, Elizabeth A. ... Orlando, FL
Baker, Elizabeth A. ... New York, NY
Baker, Elizabeth Diane ... Kansas City, MO
Baker, Elizabeth M. ... Snellville, GA
Baker, Elizabeth S. ... Miami, FL
Baker, Elizabeth S., P.A., Law Offices of
Miami, FL
Baker, Ellen C. ... Gloversville, NY
Baker, Ellen L. ... Poughkeepsie, NY
Baker, Elliott R. ... Canton, GA
Baker, Elvera Elaine Sellin
Minneapolis, MN
Baker, Emanuel M. ... West Bloomfield, MI
Baker and Enright ... Chicago, IL
Baker, E. P. ... Washington, DC
Baker, Eric A. ... Fort Wayne, IN
Baker, Eric D. ... Cleveland, OH
Baker, Eric S. ... Bellevue, WA
Baker, Ethel Jo ... Atlanta, GA
Baker, Evan A. ... Aberdeen, NJ
Baker, Evan A. ... Somerville, NJ
Baker, Eve Kathleen ... Los Angeles, CA
Baker, Evelyn M. ... St. Louis, MO
Baker, Francis W. ... San Antonio, TX
Baker, Frank A. ... Marianna, FL
Baker, Frank A., III ... Bethlehem, PA
Baker, Frank C. ... Bloomsburg, PA
Baker, Frank E. ... Olympia, WA
Baker, Frank Lewis, III ... Stamford, CT
Baker, Franklin G. ... Naples, FL
Baker, Fred L. ... Danbury, CT
New Milford, CT
Baker, Frederick C. ... Charleston, SC
Baker, Frederick D. ... San Francisco, CA
Baker, Frederick L. ... Columbus, OH
Baker, Frederick M., Jr. ... Lansing, MI
Baker, Freling E. ... San Diego, CA

Baker & Friedman ... New York, NY
Baker, G. Christopher ... Princeton, NJ
Baker, G. Clair, Jr. ... Hagerstown, MD
Baker, G. Michael ... Springfield, MO
Baker, G. Richard ... Meridian, MS
Baker, Gabriel ... Seattle, WA
Baker, Gail D. ... Rochester, MN
Baker, Gail Diamond ... Davie, FL
Baker, Gale S. ... Long Beach, CA
Baker, Garber, Duffy & Pedersen, P.C.
Hoboken, NJ
Baker, Garland B. ... West Jefferson, NC
Baker, Gary ... Callahan, FL
Baker, Gary B. ... New York, NY
Baker, Gary E. ... Houston, TX
Baker, Gary L. ... Lincoln, NE
Baker, Gary T. ... Nashville, TN
Baker, Gayle M. ... Doylestown, PA
Baker, Gaylord L. ... Adrian, MI
Baker, Geoffrey A. ... Chicago, IL
Baker, Geoffrey L. ... Columbus, OH
Baker, Geoffrey M. ... Boise, ID
Baker, George A. ... Vernon, CT
Baker, George B. ... Treasury Department, Internal Revenue Service, GV
Baker, George D. ... Washington, DC
Baker, George H. ... Paris, IL
Baker, George W. ... New Canaan, CT
Baker, George W. ... Baltimore, MD
Baker, Georgetta J. ... Lombard, IL
Baker, Gerald A. ... Toledo, OH
Baker, Gerald C. ... Lanham, MD
Baker, Gerald E. ... Washington, DC
Baker, Gerald E. ... Manassas, VA
Baker, Gerald E., P.C. ... Manassas, VA
Baker, Gerald F. ... Ridgecrest, CA
Baker, Gerald Harold ... Hoboken, NJ
Baker, Gerald L., Law Offices of
Canton, OH
Baker, G.H. William ... Alexandria, VA
Baker & Gilchrist ... Avon, IN
Indianapolis, IN
Baker, Glen R. ... Department of Justice, Executive Office for Immigration Review, GV
Baker, Glenn A., (Ltd.) ... Deerfield, IL
Baker, Glynna G. ... Denver, CO
Baker, Gordon B., Jr. ... Florence, SC
Baker, Gregg S. ... White Plains, NY
Baker, Gregory L. ... Washington, DC
Baker, Gregory R.
Federal Election Commission, Office of the General Counsel, GV
Baker, Gregory R. ... Joliet, IL
Baker, H. Burton ... Valdosta, GA
Baker, H. Garrett ... Wilmington, DE
Baker, H. Leslie ... San Ramon, CA
Baker, H. Mitchell, III ... Wilmington, NC
Baker, H. Nicholas ... Louisville, KY
Baker, H. Scott ... San Antonio, TX
Baker, Hackenberg & Collins Co., L.P.A.
Painesville, OH
Baker, Hancock & Pollard, A Professional Corporation ... Waco, TX
Baker, Hardesty & Kaffen ... Akron, OH
Baker, Harold A. ... Urbana, IL
Baker, Harold Clement, III
New York, NY
Baker, Harold D'O. ... New York, NY
Baker, Harold E.
Hot Springs National Park, AR
Baker, Harold F. ... Washington, DC
Baker, Harold G., Jr. ... Belleville, IL
Baker & Harris ... Blackfoot, ID
Baker, Harry E. ... Jacksonville, FL
Baker, Hartselle ... Orlando, FL
Baker & Hayes ... Lebanon, NH
Baker, Hayes & Kloess ... Belleville, IL
Baker, Heather C. ... Franklin, NC
Baker, Helen ... Milwaukee, WI
Baker, Herbert F. ... Ocala, FL
Baker, Herbert W., Jr. ... Zanesville, OH
Baker, Herman D. ... Atlanta, GA
Baker, Hines H., Jr. ... Houston, TX
Baker, Holley F. ... Marion, OH
Baker, Hollie L. ... Boston, MA
Baker, Holly ... Federal Election Commission, Office of the General Counsel, GV
Baker, Holly A. ... St. Clair Shores, MI
Baker & Hostetler LLP ... Long Beach, CA
Los Angeles, CA
Denver, CO
Washington, DC
Orlando, FL
Cincinnati, OH
Cleveland, OH
Columbus, OH
Houston, TX
Baker, Howard A. ... New York, NY
Baker, Howard H., Jr. ... Washington, DC
Chattanooga, TN
Huntsville, TN
Knoxville, TN
Nashville, TN
Baker, Howard L. ... New York, NY
Baker, Howard R., Jr. ... Decatur, IL
Baker, Howe E. ... Burlington, KY
Baker, Hugh G., Jr. ... Indianapolis, IN
Baker, J. Brent ... Houston, TX
Baker, J. Karren ... San Francisco, CA
Baker, J. Norman ... Mountain View, CA
Baker, J. Samuel ... Houston, TX
Baker, J. Shane ... Marianna, AR
Baker, Jack R. ... Canton, OH
Baker and Jacobson, A Professional Corporation ... Los Angeles, CA
Baker, James A. ... Ithaca, NY
Baker, James A. ... Cleveland, OH

Baker, James A. ... Rosenberg, TX
Baker, James A., IV ... Washington, DC
Baker, James Addison, III
Washington, DC
Houston, TX
Baker, James C. ... Dallas, TX
Baker, James C., (P.A.) ... Little Rock, AR
Baker, James E. ... Atlanta, GA
Baker, James E. ... South Hadley, MA
Baker, James E. ... Minneapolis, MN
Baker, James E. ... Warrensburg, MO
Baker, James E. ... Locust Valley, NY
Baker, James E. ... Seattle, WA
Baker, James E., Jr. ... Baltimore, MD
Baker, James E. S. ... Chicago, IL
Baker, James F. ... Fayetteville, GA
Baker, James G. ... Overland Park, KS
Baker, James Gordon ... La Grange, GA
Baker, James H. ... Sioux Falls, SD
Baker, James K. ... Birmingham, AL
Baker, James L. ... Mission, KS
Kansas City, MO
Baker, James L. (Jay) ... Dallas, TX
Baker, James L., Jr. ... Marshall, NC
Baker, James M. ... Frankfort, KY
Baker, James M. ... Syracuse, NY
Baker, James M. ... Houston, TX
Baker, James Noel ... Opelika, AL
Baker, James P. ... San Francisco, CA
Baker, James P., Jr. ... West Helena, AR
Baker, James P., Law Offices of
Springfield, IL
Baker, James R. ... Oklahoma City, OK
Baker, James T. ... Norfolk, VA
Baker, James W. ... Huntsville, AL
Baker, James W. ... Santa Ana, CA
Baker, James W. ... Bay City, MI
Baker, Jamie Kreeger ... San Antonio, TX
Baker, Jana ... Dallas, TX
Baker, Jane K. ... San Francisco, CA
Baker, Janet Cecil ... Little Rock, AR
Baker, Janet Davis ... Overland Park, KS
Baker, Janice Marie ... Jacksonville, FL
Baker, Jay C. ... Tulsa, OK
Baker, J. D. ... Osceola, MO
Baker, Jean C. ... Madison, WI
Milwaukee, WI
Baker, Jeanne ... Miami, FL
Baker, Jeffery P. ... Vandalia, OH
Baker, Jeffrey A. ... Des Moines, IA
Baker, Jeffrey C. ... Kansas City, MO
Baker, Jeffrey L. ... Glen Burnie, MD
Baker, Jeffrey L. ... Albuquerque, NM
Baker, Jeffrey L. ... Nashville, TN
Baker, Jeffrey R. ... Wilmington, NC
Baker, Jeffrey S. ... Boston, MA
Baker, Jeffrey S. ... Albany, NY
Baker, Jeffrey T. ... Birmingham, AL
Baker, Jeffrey T. ... West Chester, PA
Baker, Jeffrey W. ... Rochester, NY
Baker, Jenkins, Jones & Daly, P.A.
Ahoskie, NC
Greenville, NC
Rocky Mount, NC
Baker & Jenkins, PLLC ... Alma, AR
Fayetteville, AR
Fort Smith, AR
Jonesboro, AR
Baker, Jennifer LaPorta ... Harrisburg, PA
Baker, Jerry L. ... Los Angeles, CA
Baker, Jesse Raymond ... New Hyde Park, NY
Baker, Jessica M. ... Elkins, WV
Baker, Jill Ann ... Chicago, IL
Baker, Joan M. ... Cincinnati, OH
Baker, Joan P. ... Pierre, SD
Baker, Joel P. ... Tyler, TX
Baker, John ... Los Angeles, CA
Baker, John A. ... Springfield, IL
Baker, John Barry ... Fayetteville, AR
Baker, John C. ... Sioux City, IA
South Sioux City, NE
Baker, John C. ... Surry, VA
Baker, John E. ... Belle Glade, FL
Baker, John E. ... Castine, ME
Baker, John E. ... Traverse City, MI
Baker, John F. ... Needham, MA
Baker, John G. ... El Segundo, CA
Baker, John G. ... Indianapolis, IN
Baker, John H. ... Fresno, CA
Baker, John H. ... Newport Beach, CA
Baker, John H. ... Bonita Springs, FL
Baker, John H., III ... Murfreesboro, TN
Baker, John H., Jr. ... Portland, OR
Baker, John H., (P.C.) ... Arlington, TX
Austin, TX
Dallas, TX
Houston, TX
Baker, John J. ... Wailuku, HI
Baker, John J., Jr. ... Shelbyville, IL
Baker, John K. ... Little Rock, AR
Baker, John K. ... Allentown, PA
Baker, John L., (P.C.) ... Granby, CO
Baker, John M. ... Montgomery, AL
Baker, John M. ... Washington, DC
Baker, John M. ... Minneapolis, MN
Baker, John M. ... Omaha, NE
Baker, John M. ... Cleveland, OH
Baker, John P. ... Alturas, CA
Baker, John P. ... Denver, CO
Baker, John R. ... Birmingham, AL
Baker, John R. ... Tempe, AZ
Baker, John R. ... Des Moines, IA
Baker, John R., Jr. ... Edmond, OK
Baker, John S. ... Irvine, CA
Baker, John S., Jr. ... Washington, DC
Baker, John T. ... Anchorage, AK
Baker, John T. ... Denver, CO
Baker, John W. ... Venice, FL
Baker, John W. ... Mt. Vernon, OH
Baker, John W., Jr. ... Maryville, MO
Baker, John W., Jr. ... Knoxville, TN
Baker, Johnna W. ... Camp Hill, PA
Baker, Johnsen & Sandblom
Humboldt, IA
Baker, Johnston & Wilson, LLP
Birmingham, AL
Baker, Johnston & Wilson LLP
New York, NY
Baker, Jon D. ... Connersville, IN
Baker, Jonas P. ... New Orleans, LA
Baker, Jonathan A.
Department Of Health And Human Services,
Office of the General Counsel, GV
Baker, Jonathan D. ... Palo Alto, CA
Baker, Jonathan D.
United States Court Of Appeals For The
Federal Circuit, GV
Baker, Jonathan S.
Environmental Protection Agency,
Office of the General Counsel, GV
Baker, Joseph C. ... Princeton, KY
Baker, Joseph E. ... Norfolk, VA
Baker, Joseph J. ... Arlington, VA
Baker, Joseph L. ... Covington, KY
Baker, Joseph P. ... Orlando, FL
Baker, Joseph R. ... Jonesboro, GA
Baker, Joseph R., Jr. ... La Jolla, CA
Baker, Joseph W. ... Woodbridge, NJ
Baker, Joshua ... San Francisco, CA
Baker, Josiah ... Chattanooga, TN
Baker, Joy B. ... San Francisco, CA
Baker, Joye Thomas ... Gate City, VA
Baker, Judith E., (P.A.) ... Gaithersburg, MD
Baker, Julie A. ... Boston, MA
Baker, Julie E. ... Prospect Heights, IL
Baker, Julie Hope ... Louisville, KY
Baker, Julie Kay ... Dallas, TX
Baker, June A. ... Washington, DC
Baker, K. Poncho ... Fresno, CA
Baker, Karen Burris ... Covington, KY
Baker, Karen R. ... Clinton, AR
Baker, Katharine K. ... Chicago, IL
Baker, Katherine E. ... Scottsdale, AZ
Baker, Katherine H. ... Alpine, TX
Baker, Katherine Simpson ... Jackson, MS
Baker, Kathryn Benes ... Overland Park, KS
Baker, Keener & Nahra, LLP
Los Angeles, CA
Santa Monica, CA
Baker, Keith Brian ... Skokie, IL
Baker, Keith D. ... Lexington, KY
Baker, Keith L. ... Washington, DC
Baker, Keith M. ... San Antonio, TX
Baker, Keith W. ... Minneapolis, MN
Baker, Kelley ... Lincoln, NE
Baker, Kelley M. ... Austin, TX
Baker, Ken ... Chico, CA
Baker, Kendra S. ... Wilmington, DE
Baker, Kenneth ... Chicago, IL
Baker, Kenneth A. ... Salida, CO
Baker, Kenneth B. ... Cleveland, OH
Baker, Kenneth C. ... Toledo, OH
Baker, Kenneth C. ... Houston, TX
Baker, Kenneth H. ... Louisville, KY
Baker, Kenneth L. ... Washington, PA
Baker, Kent D. ... San Diego, CA
Baker, Kent Steven ... Norwich, CT
Baker, Kevin R. ... San Francisco, CA
Baker, Kevin S. ... San Antonio, TX
Baker, Kimberly D. ... Seattle, WA
Baker, Kinsman & Hollis, P.C.
Chattanooga, TN
Baker, Kraig L. ... Seattle, WA
Baker, Kristine Gerhard ... Little Rock, AR
Baker, Kyle M. ... Bloomington, IN
Baker, Lance A. ... Nashville, TN
Baker, Lance H. ... Boca Raton, FL
Baker, Lancianese, Campbell & Conaty
Washington, DC
Lexington, KY
Charleston, WV
Huntington, WV
Baker, Larry A. ... North Miami Beach, FL
Baker, Larry D. ... Ventura, CA
Baker, Larry M. ... Valencia, CA
Baker, Larry M. ... Denver, CO
Baker, Larry O. ... Elizabethtown, IL
Baker, Larry S. ... Westland, MI
Baker, Laura M. ... Corpus Christi, TX
Baker, Lauralee B. ... Harrisburg, PA
Baker Law Firm ... Albuquerque, NM
Baker Law Firm ... Darlington, SC
Baker Law Firm, P.A. ... Wilmington, NC
Baker Law Firm, P.C. ... Danbury, CT
New Milford, CT
Baker Law Firm, P.C. ... Brandon, MS
Baker Law Firm, The ... Little Rock, AR
Baker, Lawrence A. ... Berkeley, CA
Baker, Lawrence F. ... Seattle, WA
Baker, Lawrence M. ... Charlotte, NC
Baker, Lawrence M. ... Cleveland, OH
Baker, Lee F. ... Evansville, IN
Baker, LeeAnn ... Boston, MA
Baker, Legal Clinic of ... Fargo, ND
Baker, Leland L., Jr. ... Fredericksburg, VA
Baker, Leon C., P.C. ... White Plains, NY
Baker, Leslie K. ... Portland, OR
Baker, Leslie M. ... Reno, NV
Baker, Lesliegh S. ... Aliso Viejo, CA
Baker, Lewis J. ... McLean, VA
Baker, Lillian D. ... Burlington, NJ
Baker, Lincoln A. ... Petersburg, IN
Baker, Linda L. ... Cleveland, OH
Baker, Lindi L. ... Grants Pass, OR
Baker, Linus L. ... Prairie Village, KS
Baker, Lisa Ann ... San Diego, CA
Baker, Lisa M. ... Los Angeles, CA
Baker, Livingston ... Newark, NJ
Baker, Lizbeth L. ... Lexington, KY
Baker, Lloyd G. ... Gig Harbor, WA
Baker, Lloyd H. ... Islip, NY
Baker, Logsdon & Schulte ... Hennessey, OK
Kingfisher, OK
Baker, Lois A. ... Orlando, FL
Baker, Loren L. ... Department of Defense,
Defense Commissary Agency, GV
Baker, Lori L. ... Dallas, TX
Baker, Louis C. ... San Antonio, TX
Baker, Louis R. ... Los Angeles, CA
Baker, Louis W. ... Wilmette, IL
Baker, Louisa L. ... New York, NY
Baker, Lynn D., (Mr.) ... Lakeside, MT
Baker, Lynne M. ... Chicago, IL
Baker, M. Anthony ... Canton, GA
Baker, M. David ... New York, NY
Baker, M. Miller ... Washington, DC
Baker, Madge ... Springvale, ME
Baker, Manock & Jensen, A Professional
Corporation ... Bakersfield, CA
Fresno, CA
Los Angeles, CA
Santa Barbara, CA
Baker, Marc D. ... New York, NY
Baker and Marcus ... Tempe, AZ
Baker, Margaret
Merit Systems Protection Board,
Office of Appeals Counsel, GV
Baker, Margaret P. ... San Francisco, CA
Baker, Marianne M. ... Austin, TX
Baker, Marilyn L. ... Washington, DC
Baker, Marita Alina ... New York, NY
Baker, Marjorie Gilman ... Cranford, NJ
Baker, Marjorie H. ... Minerva, OH
Baker, Mark ... Wichita Falls, TX
Baker, Mark B. ... Austin, TX
Baker, Mark C., Sr. ... Brandon, MS
Baker, Mark D. ... Everett, WA
Baker, Mark E. ... Calabasas, CA
Baker, Mark E. ... Washington, DC
Baker, Mark H. ... San Diego, CA
Baker, Mark M. ... New York, NY
Baker, Mark R. ... New York, NY
Baker, Mark S. ... Central City, KY
Baker, Mark W. ... Farmington Hills, MI
Baker, Martha Cathey
Securities and Exchange Commission,
Division of Investment Management, GV
Baker, Marti A. ... Indianapolis, IN
Baker, Martin ... Cleveland, OH
Baker, Martin R. ... San Jose, CA
Baker, Martin S. ... New York, NY
Baker, Mary E. ... Houston, TX
Baker, Mary Gordon ... Columbia, SC
Baker, Mary Louise ... Muncie, IN
Baker, Mary M. ... Washington, DC
Baker, Maryellen A. ... South Bend, IN
Baker, Matthew I. ... Chicago, IL
Baker, Matthew J. ... Bowling Green, KY
Baker, Maureen F. ... Newark, NJ
Baker, Max A. ... Pleasantville, NJ
Baker & Maxham, A Professional
Corporation ... San Diego, CA
Baker & McKenzie ... Palo Alto, CA
San Diego, CA
San Francisco, CA
Washington, DC
Miami, FL
Chicago, IL
New York, NY
Dallas, TX
Houston, TX
Baker, McReynolds, Byrne, O'Kane, Shea &
Townsend ... Knoxville, TN
Baker, Melanie A. ... Kansas City, MO
Baker, Merlin O. ... Salt Lake City, UT
Baker, Merlin W. ... San Jose, CA
Baker & Meyer ... Portland, OR
Baker, Mia Ahrens ... Los Angeles, CA
Baker, Michael A. ... Houston, TX
Baker, Michael D. ... Lexington, KY
Baker, Michael D. ... Akron, OH
Baker, Michael Duffy ... Philadelphia, PA
Baker, Michael E. ... Kansas City, MO
Baker, Michael H. ... Lexington, KY
Baker, Michael J. ... Costa Mesa, CA
Baker, Michael J. ... San Francisco, CA
Baker, Michael J. ... New Brunswick, NJ
Baker, Michael K. ... Department of Justice,
Environment and Natural Resources
Division, GV
Baker, Michael K. ... Boston, MA
Baker, Michael L. ... Covington, KY
Baker, Michael L. ... Beaumont, TX
Baker, Michael P. ... Kane, PA
Baker, Michael R. ... Columbia, MO
Baker, Michael R. ... Columbus, OH
Baker, Michael S. ... New York, NY
Baker, Michael T. ... Binghamton, NY
Hallstead, PA
Baker, Michael W. ... Fort Lauderdale, FL
Naples, FL
Baker, Michael W. ... Logansport, IN
Baker, Michelle A. Vitt ... Melbourne, FL
Baker, Michelle L. ... Little Rock, AR
Baker & Miller ... Chicago, IL
Baker, Miller & Day ... Lanham, MD
Baker & Miller, PLLC ... Washington, DC
Baker, Mitchell ... Denver, CO
Baker, Mitchell C. ... Portland, OR
Baker, Mitchell J. ... White Plains, NY
Baker, Moses, Jr. ... West Palm Beach, FL
Baker, N. Kent ... Colorado Springs, CO
Baker, Nancy Lynne ... Rochester, NY
Baker, Nannette A. ... St. Louis, MO
Baker, Nathan A. ... Indianapolis, IN
Baker, Neal A. ... Chicago, IL
Baker, Neal D. ... Cincinnati, OH
Baker, Nelson ... New Brunswick, NJ
Baker, Nelson & Williams, LLP
New York, NY
Baker, Neva Rettig ... Muscatine, IA
Baker, Nigel Scott ... Thousand Oaks, CA
Baker, Nikki L. ... Las Vegas, NV
Baker, Norman E. ... Fort Wayne, IN
Baker, Norton ... Lubbock, TX
Baker, Olson, LeCroy & Danielian
Los Angeles, CA
Glendale, CA
Baker, O. N. Mike ... Houston, TX
Baker, Orbison & Bales, A Professional
Association ... Indianapolis, IN
Baker, Oscar W. ... Bay City, MI
Baker O'Sullivan & Bliss PC
Hartford, CT
Wethersfield, CT
Baker, P. Andrew ... Atlanta, GA
Baker, P. Dawn ... White Plains, NY
Baker, Pacious & Hamilton ... Atlanta, GA
Baker, Paige Merrill ... Santa Ana, CA
Baker, Pamela ... Chicago, IL
Baker, Pamela Fennell ... Rochester, NY
Baker, Pamela Jean ... Baton Rouge, LA
Baker, Pamela Johnson ... Boston, MA
Baker, Pamela Zimlin ... Boston, MA
Baker, Patrick C. ... Philadelphia, PA
Baker, Patrick H. ... Houston, TX
Baker, Patrick J. ... Buffalo, NY
Baker, Patrick Shad ... Kingsbury, TX
Baker, Patrick W. ... Durham, NC
Baker, Paul Edward ... Pottsville, PA
Baker, Paul F. ... Dulles, VA
Baker, Paul H. F. ... Lafayette, LA
Baker, Paul K. ... Boston, MA
Baker, Paul M. ... Louisville, KY
Baker, Paula M. ... New York, NY
Baker, Penny G. ... Jefferson City, MO
Baker, Peter Harrison ... Hammondsport, NY
Baker, Peter, Law Office of ... Tampa, FL
Baker, Peter W. ... Philadelphia, PA
Baker, Philip B. ... Lynchburg, VA
Baker, Phillip A. ... Santa Monica, CA
Baker, Phillip Ray ... Memphis, TN
Baker, Pomphylia G. ... Los Angeles, CA
Baker, Providence ... Albany, NY
Baker, R. Allan ... San Juan Capistrano, CA
Baker, R. Brooks ... Agoura Hills, CA
Baker, R.C., & Associates, Ltd.
Minneapolis, MN
Baker, R. Craig ... Dallas, TX
Baker, R. David ... Nashville, TN
Baker, R. Gordon, Jr. ... Walnut Creek, CA
Baker, R. Gordon, Jr., A Professional
Corporation ... Walnut Creek, CA
Baker, R. Jeffrey ... Xenia, OH
Baker, R. Palmer, Jr. ... New York, NY
Baker, R. Perrin ... Erie, PA
Baker, R. Scott ... Carson City, NV
Baker, Rachel Heath ... Kansas City, MO
Baker, Ralph E. ... Las Vegas, NV
Baker, Ralph T. ... Newport News, VA
Baker, Ramona M.Arena ... Pittsburgh, PA
Baker, Randall H. ... Portland, OR
Baker, Randall P. ... Mexico, MO
Baker, Ravenel & Bender, L.L.P.
Columbia, SC
Baker, Raymond E. ... Columbus, NE
Baker, Raymond E., P.C., Law Offices of
Columbus, NE
Baker, Raymond N. ... Hayward, CA
Baker, Raymond N. ... Washington, DC
Baker, Raymond W. ... Dublin, OH
Baker, Reatha A. ... Washington, DC
Baker, Rebecca M. ... Republic, WA
Baker, Reese W. ... Houston, TX
Baker, Reid S. ... Hollywood, FL
Baker, Rex E. ... Avon, IN
Indianapolis, IN
Baker, Rex G., III ... Dripping Springs, TX
Baker, Richard A. ... Cambridge, OH
Baker, Richard B. ... Norfolk, VA
Baker, Richard C. ... Chicago, IL
Baker, Richard C. ... White Plains, NY
Baker, Richard C. ... Austin, TX
Baker, Richard Carnell ... McLean, VA
Baker, Richard Carnell, P.C.
Washington, DC
McLean, VA
Baker, Richard E. ... Southfield, MI
Baker, Richard F. ... Beaumont, TX
Baker, Richard G. ... Liberty, TX
Baker, Richard J. ... Worcester, MA
Baker, Richard J. ... Minneapolis, MN
Baker, Richard J. ... Milwaukee, WI
Baker, Richard L. ... Moorestown, NJ
Baker, Richard M. ... Inglewood, CA
Baker, Richard M. ... St. Petersburg, FL
Baker, Richard R. ... Winter Park, FL
Baker, Richard R., P.A. ... Winter Park, FL
Baker, Richard S. ... St. Louis Park, MN
Baker, Richard S. ... Toledo, OH
Baker, Robert ... Los Angeles, CA
Baker, Robert A., Jr. ... Buffalo, NY
Baker, Robert B. ... Anchorage, AK
Baker, Robert B. ... Boca Raton, FL
Baker, Robert B., Jr. ... Tucker, GA
Baker, Robert C. ... Santa Monica, CA
Baker, Robert C. ... Minneapolis, MN
Baker, Robert C. ... Akron, OH
Baker, Robert C., Jr. ... Washington, DC
Baker, Robert D. ... San Diego, CA
Englewood, CO
Baker, Robert D. ... Mannford, OK

Balamenti, Jas. J. .... Phoenix, AZ
Balamut, George B. .... New York, NY
Balamuth & Balamuth, LLP .... Orinda, CA
Balamuth, Barry .... Orinda, CA
Balamuth, Kelly .... Orinda, CA
Balanay, Denise P. .... Honolulu, HI
Balancia, Victor N. .... New York, NY
Baland, Timothy J. .... Wadena, MN
Balanis, John P. .... Albany, NY
Balanoff, Gilbert L. .... Mineola, NY
Balanoff, M. Jane .... Chicago, IL
Balanoff, Michael J. .... Syracuse, NY
Balanoff, Miriam D. .... Chicago, IL
Balanoff, Robert .... Chicago, IL
Balantzow, Robert S. .... Cleveland, OH
Balaran, Alan .... Washington, DC
Balardi, Vincent A. .... New York, NY
Balarezo, A. Eduardo .... Washington, DC
Balart, L. Etienne .... New Orleans, LA
Balas, David L. .... Lansing, MI
Balas, Elizabeth M. .... Bellingham, WA
Balas, Francis P. .... Chelmsford, MA
Balas, Philip E. .... Palm Beach Gardens, FL
Balasa, Donald A. .... Chicago, IL
Balaschak, Elizabeth K. .... Raynham, MA
Balaschak, Susan F. .... Arlington, TX
Balasco, Sybil Premack .... Houston, TX
Balash, Paul E. .... Cincinnati, OH
Balash, S. R., Jr. .... Santa Barbara, CA
Balash, Steve R., Jr. .... Santa Barbara, CA
Balasiano, Steven .... West Caldwell, NJ
Balasis, Diana L. .... Livingston, NJ
Balaskas, Joanna .... New York, NY
Balassa, Gabor .... Chicago, IL
Balasso, Anthony A. .... Miami, FL
Balassone, Leah J. .... Poughkeepsie, NY
Balasubramani, Krishna .... Portland, OR
Balasubramani, Venkat .... Seattle, WA
Balavage, A. Albert .... Fairfax, VA
Balavage, Michael S. .... Redding, CA
Balavage, Monica M. .... Redding, CA
Balavender, Paul Thomas .... Hartford, CT
Balazs, Erika .... Spokane, WA
Balazs, JoAnn Armenia
North Tonawanda, NY
Balazs, Joseph B. .... Medina, OH
Balazs, Mary Grace .... Cleveland, OH
Balazs, Stephen Robert .... White Plains, NY
Balbach & Fehr, P.C. .... Urbana, IL
Balbach, George J. .... Jackson Heights, NY
Balbach, Jeanine K. ....
Federal Trade Commission, GV
Balbach, S. Byron, Jr. .... Urbana, IL
Balbach, Stanley B. .... Urbana, IL
Balbas & Arrieta .... Humacao, PR
Balbas, Paul W. .... Hollister, CA
Balbas Felices, Vicente .... Humacao, PR
Balber, Eric D. .... New York, NY
Balber Pickard Battistoni Maldonado & Van Der Tuin, PC .... New York, NY
Balber, Scott S. .... New York, NY
Balbick, Robert J. .... Batavia, NY
Balbin, Donna M. .... Los Angeles, CA
Balbirer, Arthur E. .... Westport, CT
Balbirnie, Gregory L. .... West Chester, PA
Balboa, Isabel C. .... Collingswood, NJ
Balboa, Juan R. .... Grand Rapids, MI
Balboni, Albert A. .... Houston, TX
Balboni, Gerardo M., II .... Atlanta, GA
Balboni, Janet R. .... Houston, TX
Balboni, John G. .... Boston, MA
Balboni Law Group LLC .... Atlanta, GA
Balboni, Michael A. L. .... Mineola, NY
Balboni, Neal B. .... Marion, MA
Balcacer, Marilyn .... New York, NY
Balcao, Dale S. .... Stockton, CA
Balcar, Dan E. .... San Antonio, TX
Balcer, David J. .... Jenkintown, PA
Balcerski, William J. .... New York, NY
Balcerzak, Ann M. .... Columbia, MD
Balcerzak, Gail A. .... New York, NY
Balcerzak, Thomas J. .... Columbus, OH
Balch, Bertram, Jr. .... Rolling Hills, CA
Balch & Bingham LLP .... Birmingham, AL
Huntsville, AL
Montgomery, AL
Washington, DC
Balch, Brian C. .... Spokane, WA
Balch, Bruce L. .... Rock Island, IL
Balch, Charles L., III .... Madison, MS
Balch, Christopher D. .... Atlanta, GA
Balch, Jacintha Kraft .... Columbus, OH
Balch, Mary Amanda .... Austin, TX
Balch, Michael J. .... New York, NY
Balch, Peter D. .... Bethesda, MD
Balch, Robert J., Jr. .... Wichita Falls, TX
Balch, Russell C. .... Auburn, AL
Balch, S. Eason .... Birmingham, AL
Balch, S. Eason, Jr. .... Birmingham, AL
Balcher, Alan M. .... Napa, CA
Balchunas, George C. .... Reading, PA
Balchunas, Z. John .... Chicago, IL
Balck, Charles M. .... St. Paul, MN
Balcom, Raymond D. .... Whitinsville, MA
Balcom, Timothy B. .... Auburn, CA
Balcomb & Green, P.C.
Glenwood Springs, CO
Balcomb, Kenneth
Glenwood Springs, CO
Balcomb, Scott M.
Glenwood Springs, CO
Balcombe, Douglas H. .... Kansas City, MO
Balcon, Steven J. .... Southfield, MI
Balconi, Brian Gerard .... San Diego, CA
Balconi-Lamica, Michael J. .... Austin, TX
Dallas, TX
Balcuk, Joseph A. .... Farmingdale, NY
Bald & Bald .... Annapolis, MD

Bald, Douglas R. .... Port Charlotte, FL
Sarasota, FL
Bald, Geoffrey S. .... Birmingham, AL
Bald, Jeffrey T. .... Annapolis, MD
Bald, Kimberly Alario .... Bradenton, FL
Bald, LeRoy .... Annapolis, MD
Bald, Michael P. .... Freeport, IL
Bald, William A. .... Jacksonville, FL
Balda, Janis Bragan .... Claremont, CA
Baldacci, Elizabeth Walsh .... Bangor, ME
Baldacci, Lea K. .... Walnut Creek, CA
Baldacci, Paris R. .... New York, NY
Baldacci, Peter K. .... Bangor, ME
Baldachin, Alan G. .... New York, NY
Baldani, Rowland & Richardson, P.S.C.
Lexington, KY
Baldani, Russell J. .... Lexington, KY
Baldante, John W. .... Cherry Hill, NJ
Philadelphia, PA
Baldante, John W. .... Rahway, NJ
Baldanzi, Stephanie A. .... Baltimore, MD
Baldasare, Lawrence J. .... Pittsburgh, PA
Baldasare, Suzanne E. .... Hartford, CT
Southport, CT
Baldassano, Steven .... Houston, TX
Baldassano, Valli F. .... Philadelphia, PA
Baldassari, Jack D. .... Pleasant Hill, CA
Baldassarre, Jeannette M. .... New York, NY
Baldassarre, Michael .... Salisbury, MA
Baldassin, William R. .... Missoula, MT
Baldassini & Baldassini .... Weymouth, MA
Baldassini, Frank J., Jr. .... Weymouth, MA
Baldassini, James D. .... Weymouth, MA
Baldauf, Craig R. .... Charlotte, NC
Baldauf, David H. .... Buffalo, NY
Baldauf, Donald H. .... Camp Hill, PA
Baldauf, Kent E. .... Pittsburgh, PA
Baldauf, Kent E., Jr. .... Pittsburgh, PA
Baldauf, Laurence C., Jr. .... Ramona, CA
Balder, John M. .... Baltimore, MD
Balder, Linnea M. .... Chicago, IL
Balderama, Olga A. .... Fresno, CA
Balderamos, Joan M.
Fort Lauderdale, FL
Balderman, Earl W. .... Riverside, NJ
Balderrama, Mónica .... Los Angeles, CA
Balderrama, William .... Los Angeles, CA
Balderree, Willis W., Jr. .... Portland, OR
Balderson, Frank L. .... Alliance, NE
Balderson, R. Bruce, Jr. .... Philadelphia, PA
Balderson, William R., Jr.
New Bedford, MA
Balderston, Kathleen M. .... New York, NY
Balderston, Nilda .... Roswell, NM
Balderston, Scott D. .... Washington, DC
Baldi, Angelo C. .... Atlanta, GA
Baldi, Cepparulo & Williams, P.C.
Doylestown, PA
New Hope, PA
Baldi, Joseph A. .... Chicago, IL
Baldi & Marotta .... Paterson, NJ
Baldi, Paul L. .... New York, NY
Baldi, Richard J. .... Paterson, NJ
Baldi, Robert O. .... New Hope, PA
Baldiga, Joseph H. .... Worcester, MA
Baldiga, William R. .... Boston, MA
Balding, Ronald G. .... Virginia Beach, VA
Baldinger, Beth G. .... Princeton, NJ
Baldinger, Bruce E. .... Bridgewater, NJ
Mineola, NY
Baldinger, James B.
North Palm Beach, FL
Baldinger, Joseph A. .... Rockville, MD
Baldinger & Levine, L.L.C. .... Bridgewater, NJ
Mineola, NY
Baldinger, Morris A. .... Garden City, NY
Baldini, Dominic J. .... Los Gatos, CA
Baldini, Laura Flynn .... Hartford, CT
Baldini, Matthew .... Hartford, CT
Baldini, Paul J. .... Sea Isle City, NJ
Baldini, Stephen M. .... New York, NY
Baldino, Frank S. .... Washington, DC
Baldino, Gerald B., Jr. .... Media, PA
Baldino, John J. .... Hackensack, NJ
Baldino, Joseph L. .... Paradise Valley, AZ
Baldino, Thomas J., Jr. .... Red Bank, NJ
Baldo, Francis E., Jr. .... Media, PA
Baldo, Michael .... White Plains, NY
Baldo, Nicholas S. .... Beaumont, TX
Baldo, Russell P. .... Auburn, CA
Baldocchi, Deborah L. .... San Jose, CA
Baldocchi, Jennifer Stivers
Los Angeles, CA
Baldock, Bill .... Alma, KS
Baldock, Bobby R. .... Roswell, NM
Baldock-Bryant, Anita Beth .... Manassas, VA
Baldonado, Arthur .... Los Angeles, CA
Baldonado, Michael A.
Equal Employment Opportunity Commission,
Office of the Chairman, GV
Baldonado, Sandra N. .... Claremont, CA
Baldone, James C., Sr. .... Birmingham, AL
Baldoni, Barbara L. .... Olney, MD
Baldoni, Paul J. .... La Porte, IN
Baldori, Robert L. .... Okemos, MI
Baldovin, Paul A., Jr. .... Delray Beach, FL
Baldowsky, Frederic G. .... Fort Worth, TX
Baldrate, Eugene J. .... Cincinnati, OH
Baldrate, Kelly M. .... Alexandria, VA
Baldree, Charles J. .... Richardson, TX
Baldridge, David M. .... Bingham Farms, MI
Baldridge, George C. .... Joplin, MO
Baldridge, J. Douglas .... Washington, DC
Baldridge, Mary Ellen .... Los Angeles, CA
Baldrige, John E. .... Washington, IA
Balducci, Claudia M. .... Seattle, WA
Balducci, Michael .... Fort Lauderdale, FL

Balducci, Michael A. .... Sunbury, PA
Balducci, Ralph J. .... Syracuse, NY
Balducci, Timothy R. .... Oxford, MS
Tupelo, MS
Balduf, William L. .... Syracuse, NY
Baldwin, A. Elizabeth .... Erie, PA
Baldwin, A. Quillian, Jr. .... La Grange, GA
Baldwin, Aaron M. .... Albany, NY
Baldwin, Alan J. .... Morristown, NJ
Baldwin, Alexander D. .... Washington, DC
Baldwin, Alfrieda .... St. Paul, MN
Baldwin, Allen A. .... Palatka, FL
Baldwin, Allen R. .... Bowling Green, OH
Baldwin, Andrew .... Fort Washakie, WY
Baldwin, Andrew J., Jr. .... Hillsdale, NY
Baldwin, Angelia M. .... Fort Lauderdale, FL
Baldwin, Ann T. .... Bristol, CT
Baldwin, Ardith L. .... Jamestown, NY
Baldwin & Associates .... Fern Park, FL
Baldwin & Baldwin, L.L.P. .... Marshall, TX
Baldwin, Benjamin Harris .... Dublin, GA
Baldwin, Benjamin W. .... Charlotte, NC
Baldwin, Bernard C., III .... Lynchburg, VA
Baldwin, Bernardine M. .... Santa Monica, CA
Baldwin, Bliss A. .... Minneapolis, MN
Baldwin, Brad A. .... Atlanta, GA
Baldwin, Bradley S. .... Dayton, OH
Baldwin, Brent W., P.C. .... St. Louis, MO
Baldwin, Brian Buckner .... Martinsville, IN
Baldwin, Brian M. .... Hartford, CT
Baldwin & Brown, P.C. .... Denver, CO
Baldwin, Bruce .... Dallas, TX
Baldwin, Bruce A. .... Los Angeles, CA
Baldwin, Bruce L. .... Pottstown, PA
Baldwin & Butler, L.L.C. .... Kenai, AK
Baldwin, C. A. "Cab", Jr. .... Houston, TX
Baldwin, Calvin E. .... Farmersville, CA
Baldwin, Carlos Mark .... Jacksonville, NC
Baldwin, Carol A. .... St. Paul, MN
Baldwin, Carolyn W. .... Concord, NH
Baldwin, Chandra S. .... Cincinnati, OH
Baldwin, Charles B. .... Indianapolis, IN
Baldwin, Charles E. .... Lima, OH
Baldwin, Charles Grantham .... Mobile, AL
Baldwin, Charles K. .... Liberty, MO
Baldwin, Charles R. (Rick) .... Kenai, AK
Baldwin, Charles S., IV .... Wilmington, NC
Baldwin, Clarke F. .... Adrian, MI
Baldwin, Conrad C., Jr.
Winston-Salem, NC
Baldwin, Craig R. .... Newark, OH
Baldwin, Cynthia A. .... Pittsburgh, PA
Baldwin, Cyrus S., Jr. .... Houston, TX
Baldwin, D. Suzanne .... Baltimore, MD
Baldwin & Dakich .... Indianapolis, IN
Baldwin, Dania C. .... Houston, TX
Baldwin, Daniel .... New York, NY
Baldwin, Daniel .... New York, NY
Baldwin, Daniel L. .... Marion, KS
Baldwin, David J. .... Wilmington, DE
Baldwin, David J. .... Milwaukee, WI
Baldwin, David Marc .... Baltimore, MD
Baldwin, Dennis R. .... Syracuse, NY
Baldwin, Donald A. .... Newcastle, WY
Baldwin, Douglas .... Montgomery, TX
Baldwin, Douglas C. .... Scottsdale, AZ
Baldwin, Douglas, P.C. .... Montgomery, TX
Baldwin, E. Terry .... Milton, PA
Baldwin, Eberle A. .... Bartlesville, OK
Baldwin, Edward D. .... San Francisco, CA
Baldwin, Edwin S., (P.C.) .... St. Louis, MO
Baldwin, Eileen P. .... Hartford, CT
Baldwin, Eileen T. .... Phoenix, AZ
Baldwin, Elizabeth A. .... Astoria, OR
Baldwin, Elizabeth B. .... San Francisco, CA
Baldwin, Elizabeth J. .... Columbus, OH
Baldwin, Elizabeth N.
North Miami Beach, FL
Baldwin, Elsa S. .... Oakland, CA
Baldwin, Elwood J. .... Philadelphia, PA
Baldwin, Eugene P. .... Madison, GA
Baldwin, Fletcher N., III, P.A.
West Palm Beach, FL
Baldwin, Fletcher N., Jr. .... Pennington, NJ
Baldwin, Francis E. .... San Jose, CA
Baldwin, Frank A. .... Indianapolis, IN
Baldwin, Frank B., III .... Philadelphia, PA
Baldwin, Frank N., Jr. .... Houston, TX
Baldwin, Frederick D. .... Wethersfield, CT
Baldwin & Friedman, P.A.
North Miami Beach, FL
Baldwin, Gaines .... Marshall, TX
Baldwin, Gary R. .... Adrian, MI
Baldwin, Garza, III .... Washington, DC
Baldwin, Garza, Jr. .... Asheville, NC
Baldwin, George C. .... Austin, TX
San Antonio, TX
Baldwin, George W. .... Lake Park, FL
Baldwin, Gerald L. .... Cincinnati, OH
Baldwin, Gerald M. .... Custer, SD
Baldwin, Geraldine F. .... New York, NY
Baldwin, Glen S. .... Wilmington, DE
Baldwin, Glenda Guthrie .... Apple Valley, MN
Baldwin, Gordon Brewster .... Madison, WI
Baldwin, Gordon N. .... Orange, CA
Baldwin, Graham J. .... San Bernardino, CA
Baldwin, Gregory A. .... Miami, FL
Baldwin, Gregory M. .... Chicago, IL
Baldwin, Grover C., Jr. .... Paris, KY
Baldwin & Haspel, L.L.C.
New Orleans, LA
Baldwin, Helen M. .... Denver, CO
Baldwin, Holly M. .... San Francisco, CA
Baldwin, Howard G., Jr. .... Austin, TX
Baldwin, Howard L. .... Tucson, AZ
Baldwin, Irene M. .... Bronx, NY
Baldwin, J. Lee .... Irving, TX
Baldwin, J. Michael .... Houston, TX

Baldwin, James A. .... Pittsburgh, PA
Baldwin, James A., III .... Centreville, MD
Baldwin, James Alan .... Dillon, CO
Baldwin, James E. .... Lebanon, MO
Baldwin, James E. .... Loveland, OH
Baldwin, James F. .... St. Paul, MN
Baldwin, James J. .... Charlotte, NC
Greensboro, NC
Raleigh, NC
Columbia, SC
Greenville, SC
Baldwin, James L. .... Juneau, AK
Baldwin, James L., Jr. .... Plano, TX
Baldwin, James N. .... Albany, NY
Baldwin, James P. .... Battle Creek, MI
Baldwin, James W. .... Los Angeles, CA
Baldwin, Jana V. T. .... Washington, DC
Baldwin, Janette L. .... Denton, TX
Lewisville, TX
Baldwin, Janice C. .... Winston-Salem, NC
Baldwin, Janice K. W. .... Magnolia, TX
Baldwin, Janis E. .... Treasury Department,
Internal Revenue Service, GV
Baldwin, Jeffrey A. .... Indianapolis, IN
Baldwin, Jeffrey K. .... Danville, IN
Baldwin, Jeffrey M. .... Paintsville, KY
Baldwin, John A. .... Fern Park, FL
Baldwin, John B. "Jack" .... Marshall, TX
Baldwin, John C. .... Oakland, CA
Baldwin, John C. .... Baltimore, MD
Baldwin, John C. .... Salt Lake City, UT
Baldwin, John H. .... Indianapolis, IN
Baldwin, John K. .... Del Mar, CA
Baldwin, Joseph L., Jr. .... Depew, NY
Baldwin, Joseph R. .... Greer, SC
Baldwin, Judith Garrett .... Maumelle, AR
Baldwin, June M. .... Los Angeles, CA
Baldwin, Karen L. .... Morristown, NJ
Baldwin, Katherine A. .... Department of Justice,
Civil Rights Division, GV
Baldwin, Kathleen Uebele .... Raleigh, NC
Baldwin, Kathryn H. .... Kensington, MD
Baldwin, Keith Gormley .... Seattle, WA
Baldwin, Keith R. .... Seattle, WA
Baldwin, Kelley Yeager .... Shelbyville, IN
Baldwin, Kenneth A. .... Fresno, CA
Baldwin, Kenneth C. .... Hartford, CT
Baldwin, Kenneth C. .... Johnson City, TN
Baldwin, Kenneth N. .... Blue Springs, MO
Baldwin, Kevin J. .... Washington, DC
Baldwin, Kimberly A. .... Vineland, NJ
Baldwin, Kimberly G. .... Richmond, VA
Baldwin, Kristin L. .... Sayreville, NJ
Baldwin, L. Blake .... Santa Clara, CA
Baldwin, Laury M. .... San Diego, CA
Baldwin Law Office .... Custer, SD
Baldwin, Leland T. .... Tampa, FL
Baldwin, Leonard A. .... Savannah, GA
Baldwin, Linda Luinstra
Salt Lake City, UT
Baldwin, Linda M. .... New York, NY
Baldwin, Lucian E. .... Hartford, CT
Baldwin, Malcolm F. .... Department of State,
Foreign Service Officers (Overseas), GV
Baldwin, Marc M. .... Marlton, NJ
Baldwin, Marcia L. .... Palo Alto, CA
Baldwin, Margaret A. .... Tallahassee, FL
Baldwin, Marian E. .... New York, NY
Baldwin, Mark Carlyle .... Reading, PA
Baldwin, Mark L. .... Kansas City, MO
Baldwin, Mark S. .... Hartford, CT
Baldwin, Mary Coale .... Annapolis, MD
Baldwin, Maureen T. Furlong .... San Jose, CA
Baldwin, Maurice W., Jr. .... Bel Air, MD
Baldwin, Melissa M. .... Houston, TX
Baldwin, Melissa Waller .... Sidney, OH
Baldwin, Merri A. .... San Francisco, CA
Baldwin, Michael .... Tucson, AZ
Baldwin, Michael .... Utica, MI
Baldwin, Michael, PLC, Law Offices of
Tucson, AZ
Baldwin, Michael W. .... Kearney, NE
Baldwin, Milton L. .... Grass Valley, CA
Baldwin, Mindy M. .... Irving, TX
Baldwin, Norman D. .... Fair Oaks, CA
Baldwin, Orval F., II .... Houston, TX
Baldwin, Pamela .... Library of Congress,
Congressional Research Service, GV
Baldwin, Parley R. .... Ogden, UT
Baldwin, Patricia A. .... Port St. Lucie, FL
Baldwin, Patricia Ann .... Danville, IN
Baldwin, Patrick .... Menlo Park, CA
Baldwin, Paula Fisher .... Austin, TX
Baldwin, Philip C. .... Albion, MI
Baldwin, Phillip B. .... Marshall, TX
Baldwin, Phillip B., Jr. .... Marshall, TX
Baldwin, R. Thomas .... Columbus, OH
Baldwin, Ralph H., III .... Tacoma, WA
Baldwin, Ralph H., III, P.S. .... Tacoma, WA
Baldwin, Ralph V., Jr. .... Beaufort, SC
Baldwin, Ray D. .... Williamsburg, KY
Baldwin, Raymond C. .... Baltimore, MD
Baldwin, Raymond D. .... Toledo, OH
Baldwin, Raymond E., Jr. .... Bridgeport, CT
Southport, CT
Baldwin, Raymond G., Jr. .... Trumbull, CT
Baldwin, Regina T. .... New York, NY
Baldwin, Richard J. .... Hauppauge, NY
Baldwin, Richard W. .... New York, NY
Baldwin, Rignal W., Jr. .... Annapolis, MD
Baldwin, Rita Joy .... Schererville, IN
Baldwin, Robert D. .... Pine Grove, CA
Baldwin, Robert D.
Department of Commerce,
Patent and Trademark Office, GV
Baldwin, Robert D. .... Chicago, IL
Baldwin, Robert F., Jr. .... Syracuse, NY
Baldwin, Robert K. .... Bozeman, MT

Baldwin, Robert M. ... Denver, CO
Baldwin, Robert M. ... Monroe, LA
Baldwin, Robert N. ... Richmond, VA
Baldwin, Robert O. ... Salt Lake City, UT
Baldwin, Robert R. ... New York, NY
Baldwin, Robt. D. ... Pine Grove, CA
Baldwin, Rollie R. ... Liberty, MO
Baldwin, Roy J. ... Oakton, VA
Baldwin, S. Francis ... St. Louis, MO
Baldwin, Samuel C.P., Jr.
Lexington Park, MD
Baldwin, Scott ... Marshall, TX
Baldwin, Scott E. ... Newport, OR
Baldwin, Scott, Jr. ... Marshall, TX
Baldwin, Scott M. ... Metamora, IL
Baldwin, Sean P. ... New York, NY
Baldwin, Sharon ... Chicago, IL
Baldwin, Shaun McParland ... Chicago, IL
Baldwin, Shawn K. ... Atlanta, GA
Baldwin, Shirlee Fager ... Hattiesburg, MS
Baldwin, Soma F., (Ms.) ... Santa Maria, CA
Baldwin, Springfield ... St. Louis, MO
Baldwin, Stanley F. ... Virginia Beach, VA
Baldwin, Stephen E. ... Menlo Park, CA
Baldwin, Stephen K. ... Wichita, KS
Baldwin, Steve C. ... Eugene, OR
Baldwin, Steven L. ... Chesapeake, VA
Baldwin, Steven R. ... Zanesville, OH
Baldwin, Summerfield ... New York, NY
Baldwin, Tammy S.G. ... Madison, WI
Baldwin, Thayer ... Westport, CT
Baldwin, Thomas A. ... Cincinnati, OH
Baldwin, Thomas A., Jr. ... Auburn, WA
Baldwin, Thomas D. ... Short Hills, NJ
Baldwin, Thomas K. ... Ardmore, OK
Baldwin, Tiffany L. ... St. Louis, MO
Baldwin, Timothy C. ... New York, NY
Baldwin, Timothy J. ... Houston, TX
Baldwin, Timothy M. ... Denver, IA
Baldwin, Trina M. ... Erie, PA
Baldwin, Van P. ... Berkeley, CA
Baldwin, Verna Sue ... Fort Lauderdale, FL
Baldwin, Vicki M. ... Salt Lake City, UT
Baldwin, W. Andrew ... Dana Point, CA
Baldwin, Wallace D. ... Sarasota, FL
Baldwin, Wayne K. ... Westlake Village, CA
Baldwin, William D.G. ... Cincinnati, OH
Baldwin, William E. ... Pottsville, PA
Baldwin, William F. ... Shreveport, LA
Baldwin, William F. ... Wenatchee, WA
Baldwin, William H. ... Andalusia, AL
Baldwin, William H. ... Bloomfield Hills, MI
Baldwin, William M. ... Oakland, CA
Baldwin, William R., III
Fredericksburg, VA
Richmond, VA
Baldwin, William T. ... Lexington, MA
Baldwin-Sayre, J. Nicholas ... Portland, OR
Baldy, Anderson L., III ... Tampa, FL
Baldy, Richard L. ... Orlando, FL
Baldyga, Donald A. ... New York, NY
Baldyga, Jeffrey R. ... Exton, PA
Baldys, Karl K. ... Williamsport, PA
Baldys, Warren R. ... Williamsport, PA
Bale Anderson Polstein Randall & Hill, Ltd.
Minneapolis, MN
Bale, Ashley M. ... San Francisco, CA
Bale, David G. ... Columbus, OH
Bale, Heather M. ... Glendale, CA
Bale, J. Gary ... Frankfort, KY
Bale, Jeffrey R. ... Houston, TX
Bale, Larry W. ... San Angelo, TX
Bale, Lisa M. ... St. Paul, MN
Bale, Mark Edward ... San Diego, CA
Bale, Richard W. ... Minneapolis, MN
Bale, William G. ... Minneapolis, MN
Baleda, Pauline Stoey ... Sterling Heights, MI
Baledge, Les R. ... Little Rock, AR
Balef, Steven C. ... New York, NY
Balefsky, Lee B. ... Philadelphia, PA
Balega, Peter J. ... San Antonio, TX
Balen, Agatha ... San Francisco, CA
Balen, Alison Clarke ... Apple Valley, MN
Balen, Mike J. ... Mandeville, LA
Balena, William J. ... Elyria, OH
Balenger, Victoria L. ... Portland, OR
Balenson, Brian A. ... Baltimore, MD
Balent, Michael G. ... Philadelphia, PA
Balentine & Balentine, P.C.
Oklahoma City, OK
Balentine, Grady L., Jr. ... Raleigh, NC
Balentine, James Thomas ... Southaven, MS
Balentine, Jerry D. ... Oklahoma City, OK
Balentine, John G. ... Phoenix, AZ
Tucson, AZ
Balentine, Margie ... Oklahoma City, OK
Balentine, Sherri Bozeman ... San Angelo, TX
Baler, Jeffrey L. ... Medfield, MA
Baler, Lawrence A. ... Brockton, MA
Baleria, Paul Richard ... Sacramento, CA
Balerud Law Firm, P.C. ... Minot, ND
Balerud, Lee J. ... Minot, ND
Bales and Alexander ... Muncie, IN
Bales, Bruce B. ... San Rafael, CA
Bales, Candice M. ... Anchorage, AK
Bales, Douglas M. ... Clearwater, FL
Bales, H. Susanne ... Knoxville, TN
Bales, Inezellen ... Indianapolis, IN
Bales, Jack W. ... Henderson, NV
Bales, Jennifer L. ... Boulder, CO
Bales, Jerald K. ... Kansas City, MO
Bales, Jerome V. ... Kansas City, MO
Bales, John Calhoun ... Tampa, FL
Bales, John F., III ... Philadelphia, PA
Bales, John W. ... Cincinnati, OH
Bales, Jolie Ann ... Great Falls, VA
Bales, Katherine Solomon
Chagrin Falls, OH
Bales, Larry ... Austin, TX
Bales, Michael V. ... Los Angeles, CA
Bales, Richard A. ... Houston, TX
Bales, Richard F. ... Oak Brook, IL
Bales, Richard M., Jr. ... Miami, FL
Bales, Richard M., Jr. A Prossional Association ... Miami, FL
Bales, Sara Joan ... Chicago, IL
Bales, Stephen M. ... Cleveland, OH
Bales, Susan ... La Jolla, CA
Bales, Thomas T. ... New York, NY
Bales, Todd M. ... Jenkintown, PA
Bales, W. Scott ... Phoenix, AZ
Bales, Waldo F. ... Jay, OK
Bales, William A., Jr. ... Garden City, NY
Bales, William H., Jr. ... Muncie, IN
Bales-Lange, Kathleen Marie ... Visalia, CA
Balester, Vivian S. ... Cleveland Heights, OH
Balesteri, Joseph W. ... Chicago, IL
Balestracci, Paul N. ... Stockton, CA
Balestreri, Dorigan & Pendleton
San Diego, CA
Balestreri, Thomas A., Jr. ... San Diego, CA
Balestri, John ... Ladd, IL
La Salle, IL
Spring Valley, IL
Balestri, Ray A. ... Addison, TX
Balestri, William P. ... Ottawa, IL
Balestrieri, Joseph C. ... San Jose, CA
Balestrieri, Patrick F. ... White Plains, NY
Balestrini, Lisa A. ... Pittsburgh, PA
Balette, Jacques ... Houston, TX
Balette, Robin T. ... Houston, TX
Baley & Baley, P.A. ... Asheville, NC
Baley, James M., III ... Asheville, NC
Baley, James M., Jr. ... Asheville, NC
Baley, Nancy J. ... East Sandwich, MA
Balfe, Emily C. ... Evanston, IL
Balfe, Joseph D. ... Anchorage, AK
Balfe, Kevin E. ... Melville, NY
Balfe, Michael R. B. ... Boston, MA
Balfe, Michael William ... Pittsburgh, PA
Balfe, Robert Cramer, III ... Bentonville, AR
Balfour, Amy C. ... Richmond, VA
Balfour, Barbara Kyle ... Alpharetta, GA
Balfour, Clark I. ... Portland, OR
Balfour, Daniel T. ... Richmond, VA
Balfour, David K. ... Lafayette, LA
Balfour, Donald B. ... St. Louis, MO
Balfour, Douglas J. ... Pocatello, ID
Balfour MacDonald Olmsted, A Professional Corporation ... Costa Mesa, CA
Newport Beach, CA
Balfour, Michele ... New York, NY
Balfour, Natalie A. ... San Francisco, CA
Balfour, Ralph E. ... Costa Mesa, CA
Balfour, Raymond L. ... Madison, WI
Balfour, Scott R. ... Ada, MI
Balfour, Valeria ... Los Angeles, CA
Balfrey, Steven John ... Fair Oaks, CA
Balfus, Jonathan C. ... Santa Monica, CA
Balgeman, Thomas E. ... Milwaukee, WI
Balgenorth, Charles R. ... Los Angeles, CA
Balgley, Elise M. ... Newark, CA
Balgooyen, Fredric F. ... Muskegon, MI
Balgooyen & Gibbs, P.C. ... Muskegon, MI
Balhoff, Daniel J. ... Baton Rouge, LA
Balhoff, John Thomas, II
New Orleans, LA
Balhoff, Robert A. ... Houston, TX
Balhoff, Thomas E. ... Baton Rouge, LA
Balhuizen, John R. ... Kansas City, MO
Balian, Armine ... Sherman Oaks, CA
Balian, Habib A. ... Los Angeles, CA
Balian, Harry ... Middletown, PA
Balian, John ... Sherman Oaks, CA
Balian, Mary Ann ... Watsonville, CA
Balian, Melinda A. ... Bloomfield Hills, MI
Balian, Michael J. ... Bloomfield Hills, MI
Balian, Michael J. ... Detroit, MI
Balian, Nairie A. ... Pasadena, CA
Balian, Simon Y. ... New York, NY
Balich, James R. ... San Francisco, CA
Balich, Jos. C. ... Summit, IL
Balick, Adam ... Wilmington, DE
Balick & Balick ... Wilmington, DE
Balick, Helen S. ... Wilmington, DE
Balick, Jacob ... Wilmington, DE
Balick, Martin M. ... Minneapolis, MN
Balick, Sanford E. ... New York, NY
Balick, Sidney ... Wilmington, DE
Balick, Steven J. ... Wilmington, DE
Balicki, Jeffrey B. ... Pittsburgh, PA
Balicki, Linda J. ... St. Louis, MO
Balido, Carlos A. ... Dallas, TX
Balikes, John T. ... Miami, FL
Balikes, Thomas N. ... Miami, FL
Balikian, Ara J. ... Boston, MA
Balikian, Phillip B. ... Torrance, CA
Balikov, Henry R. ... Moorestown, NJ
Balikov, Howard A. ... Northfield, IL
Baliles, Gerald L. ... Richmond, VA
Baliles, Janese McGiboney ... Asheville, NC
Balin, Herbert M. ... East Meadow, NY
Balin, Lawrence B. ... Boston, MA
Balin, Paulette F. ... Cleveland, OH
Balin, Robert D. ... New York, NY
Balin, William M. ... San Francisco, CA
Baline, Naomi Goldfield ... Melrose, MA
Balingit, Alberto Y. ... Sacramento, CA
Balingit Winslow, Elyssa ... Chicago, IL
Balinski, Thomas A. ... Ann Arbor, MI
Balinski, Thomas A., P.C. ... Ann Arbor, MI
Balinsky, Brett A. ... Madison, WI
Balint, Andrew J. ... White Plains, NY
Balint, Charles J. ... Baltimore, MD
Balint, David J. ... Seattle, WA
Balint, Francis J., Jr. ... Phoenix, AZ
Balint, Gary L. ... Philadelphia, PA
Balint, Walter F. ... Baltimore, MD
Balio, John P. ... Utica, NY
Balis & Barrett, P.C. ... Boulder, CO
Balis, Barton S. ... Boulder, CO
Balis, Stanley W. ... Washington, DC
Balis, Steven L.
Department of Housing and Urban Development,
Office of General Counsel, GV
Balisle, Linda S. ... Madison, WI
Balisle & Roberson, S.C. ... Madison, WI
Balisok, Russell S. ... Glendale, CA
Balistocky, Susan ... Los Angeles, CA
Balistreri, Charles M. ... Island Park, NY
New York, NY
Balistreri, Jack A. ... San Diego, CA
Balistreri, John A. ... Los Angeles, CA
Balistreri, Joseph J. ... Milwaukee, WI
Balistreri, Karen A. ... Milwaukee, WI
Balistreri, Peter S. ... Milwaukee, WI
Balistreri, Sal C. ... San Francisco, CA
Balistreri, Theodore T. ... Milwaukee, WI
Balistreri, Thomas J. ... Madison, WI
Balisy, Sam S. ... Pasadena, CA
Denver, CO
Balitis, John J., Jr. ... Phoenix, AZ
Baliunas, Kathleen Bowers ... Chicago, IL
Balius, Louis M. ... Auburn Hills, MI
Balivet, Ernest T. ... Danville, VT
Balk, Heidi ... New York, NY
Balk, Hess and Miller ... Toledo, OH
Balk, Jacob L. ... Newark, NJ
Balk, Jay ... St. Louis, MO
Balk, Lance C. ... New York, NY
Balk, Leah M. ... St. Louis, MO
Balk, Louis David ... Newark, NJ
Balk, Mark D. ... Boston, MA
Balk, Oxfeld, Mandell & Cohen, A Professional Corporation ... Elizabeth, NJ
Newark, NJ
Balk, Ronald S. ... Lexington, MA
Balk, Steven E. ... Silvis, IL
Balka & Balka ... Philadelphia, PA
Balka, Jerome R. ... Philadelphia, PA
Balka, Sigmund R. ... New York, NY
Balkan, Adam Mark ... Fort Lauderdale, FL
Balkan, Christina E. ... Seattle, WA
Balkan, Kenneth J. ... Garden City, NY
Balkan, Paul David ... Seattle, WA
Balkan, Peter S. ... Flagstaff, AZ
Balkany, Caron ... Sun City Center, FL
Balke, William B. ... Detroit, MI
Balkema, Philip A. ... Grand Rapids, MI
Balkenbush, Joseph P. ... Oklahoma City, OK
Balkenbush, Robert F. ... Reno, NV
Balkenbush, Stephen C. ... Reno, NV
Balkenbush, Vincent M. ... Denver, CO
Balkin, Barbara Hollis ... Fair Lawn, NJ
Balkin, Bernard L. ... Kansas City, MO
Balkin, Charles R. ... Chicago, IL
Balkin, Diane E. ... Denver, CO
Balkin & Doran, Ltd. ... Chicago, IL
Balkin, Fred A. ... Rockville, MD
Falls Church, VA
Balkin, Jack M. ... Austin, TX
Balkin, Jacqueline L. ... Dallas, TX
Balkin, Jeffrey G. ... Tarzana, CA
Balkin, Jules A. ... Murray Hill, NJ
Balkin, Mark A. ... New Orleans, LA
Balkin, Pauline Cohen ... Westbury, NY
Balkin, Robert F. ... Alexandria, VA
Balkin, Ruth C. ... Hempstead, NY
Balkind, Benjamin H. ... New York, NY
Balkind, Robert L. ... Telluride, CO
Balkins, A. James, III ... Boise, ID
Balkman, Thad H. ... Norman, OK
Balko, George A., III ... Worcester, MA
Balko, John J. ... Chicago, IL
Balko, Timothy E. ... Valparaiso, IN
Balkovic, James R. ... New Cumberland, PA
Balkun, William J. ... Cranston, RI
Ball, A. Edward ... Shreveport, LA
Ball, Allan E. ... Houston, TX
Ball, Allen R. ... Ventura, CA
Ball, Andrea ... Washington, DC
Ball, Andrew D. ... Rockville, MD
Ball, Andrew D., P.C. ... Washington, DC
Rockville, MD
Ball, Angela L. ... Irvine, CA
Ball, Angela M. ... Perry, FL
Ball, Angela M., P.A. ... Perry, FL
Ball, Ann ... Commack, NY
Ball, Annette E. ... Gulfport, MS
Ball & Associates ... Louisville, KY
Ball, Ball, Matthews & Novak, P.A.
Hayneville, AL
Montgomery, AL
Prattville, AL
Selma, AL
Troy, AL
Tuskegee, AL
Union Springs, AL
Wetumpka, AL
Ball & Ball, P.C. ... Alexandria, VA
Ball, Barbara A. ... Albuquerque, NM
Ball, Barbara Bundock
Berkeley Heights, NJ
Ball, Barden & Bell, P.A. ... Asheville, NC
Ball, Barton & Hoffman, A Professional Association ... Monticello, AR
Ball, Braden K., Jr. ... Pensacola, FL
Ball, Brian D. ... Columbus, OH
Ball, Byron T. ... Los Angeles, CA
Ball, C. Lowell ... Atlanta, GA
Ball, C. Steven ... Birmingham, AL
Ball, Carlos A. ... New York, NY
Ball, Carman F. ... Orchard Park, NY
Ball, Carol S. ... Boston, MA
Ball, Carolyn Louise ... Alexandria, VA
Ball, Charles ... Kansas City, KS
Ball, Charles ... Portland, OR
Ball, Charles H. ... Sarasota, FL
Ball, Charles K. ... Manhattan, KS
Ball, Charles Peter ... Worcester, MA
Ball, Chester G. ... Arlington, TX
Ball, Christopher F. ... Dedham, MA
Ball, Christopher R. ... San Francisco, CA
Ball, Colleen D. ... Milwaukee, WI
Ball, Corinne ... New York, NY
Ball, Court E. ... Billings, MT
Ball, Craig D. ... Dallas, TX
Ball, Cynthia L. ... Danville, IN
Ball, Dallas D., (P.A.) ... Pickens, SC
Ball, Damon ... San Antonio, TX
Ball, Dan H. ... St. Louis, MO
Ball, Daniel A. ... Rockville, MD
Ball, Daniel D. ... Louisa, KY
Ball, Daniel R. ... Washington, DC
Ball, Darlene M. ... Fresno, CA
Ball, David ... New Orleans, LA
Ball, David A. ... Bridgeport, CT
Ball, David E. ... Dayton, OH
Ball, David George ... Washington, DC
Ball, David J., Jr. ... Washington, DC
Ball, David N. ... Los Angeles, CA
Ball, David P. ... Danbury, CT
Ball, David R. ... Kokomo, IN
Ball, David T. ... Stroud, OK
Ball, David W. ... Greenville, SC
Ball, Deborah S. ... Forest Hills, NY
Ball, Dennis H. ... Tacoma, WA
Ball, Diana Kay ... Houston, TX
Ball, Dixie Lee, (P.A.) ... Cape Coral, FL
Ball, Donald A. ... Worcester, MA
Ball, Donald J. ... Syracuse, NY
Ball, Doris R. ... Daytona Beach, FL
Ball, Douglas A. ... Batavia, OH
Ball, Dwight N. ... Oxford, MS
Ball, Dwight R. ... Binghamton, NY
Ball, Edmund P. ... Monterey, CA
Ball, E. E. ... Bay Minette, AL
Ball, Eggleston, Bumbleburg, McBride, Walkey & Stapleton, PC ... Lafayette, IN
Ball, E. J. ... Fayetteville, AR
Ball, Eric T. ... Bailey's Crossroads, VA
Ball, Ervin L., Jr. ... Asheville, NC
Ball, F. Keith ... Louisville, MS
Ball & Ferrari, P.C. ... Yonkers, NY
Ball, Forrest F. ... Mars Hill, NC
Ball, Frank J. ... Denver, CO
Ball, Frederick J. ... Highland, IN
Ball, Frederick James ... Cleveland, OH
Ball, Frederick R. ... Chicago, IL
Ball, G. Thomas ... Orlando, FL
Ball, George F. ... Alexandria, VA
Ball, George F., Jr. ... Alexandria, VA
Ball, George W. ... San Francisco, CA
Ball, Gordon ... Knoxville, TN
Ball, Gregory D. ... South Bend, IN
Ball, Harley R. ... Kansas City, MO
Ball & Hase ... Arlington, TX
Ball, Haywood M. ... Jacksonville, FL
Ball, Hilary E. ... Washington, DC
Ball, Homer T., Jr. ... Oakland, CA
Ball, Ian Traquair ... Minneapolis, MN
Ball, J. Aaron ... Wausau, WI
Ball, Jack P. ... Galesburg, IL
Ball, James A. ... Louisville, KY
Ball, James B. ... Phoenix, AZ
Ball, James F. ... Houston, TX
Ball, James H. ... Glendale, CA
Ball, James H. ... Louisville, KY
Ball, James H., Jr. ... New York, NY
Ball, James K. ... Boise, ID
Ball, James L.
Federal Communications Commission,
International Bureau, GV
Ball, James M. ... Columbus, OH
Ball, James M. H. ... Los Angeles, CA
Ball, James T. ... Golden, CO
Ball, James T. ... Chicago, IL
Ball, James V. ... Memphis, TN
Ball, Jane M. ... Ukiah, CA
Ball Janik LLP ... Washington, DC
Bend, OR
Portland, OR
Salem, OR
Ball, Jean Galloway ... Fairfax, VA
Ball, Jeffrey D. ... Klamath Falls, OR
Ball, Jessica R. ... Skokie, IL
Ball, John H. ... New York, NY
Ball, John Patrick ... Morgantown, WV
Ball, John R. ... Sacramento, CA
Ball, John R. ... Sandusky, OH
Ball, John S. ... Jacksonville, FL
Ponte Vedra Beach, FL
Ball, John T. ... San Jose, CA
Ball, John T. ... Natchez, MS
Ball, John W., III ... United States Senate,
Committee Legal Personnel, GV
Ball, Jonathan F. ... Philadelphia, PA
Ball, Jordan M. ... Sidney, NE
Ball, Joseph ... Troy, NY
Ball, Joseph A. ... Los Angeles, CA
Ball, Judith E. ... Glen Rock, NJ
Ball, Judith E. ... Hackensack, NJ
Ball, Karen L. ... Columbus, OH
Ball, Kathy D. ... Idaho City, ID
Ball, Kendra A. ... San Diego, CA
Ball, Kent H. ... Pleasanton, CA
Ball, Kevin M. ... Bloomfield Hills, MI
Ball, Kimberly Gilmore ... Winchester, VA
Ball, Kirk & Holm, P.C. ... Waterloo, IA
Ball & Koons ... Bay Minette, AL
Ball, Larry Glenn ... Oklahoma City, OK

Ball Law Offices .... Bloomfield, IA
Ball, Lawrence E. .... Kingston, NY
Ball, Lawrence T. .... San Francisco, CA
Ball, Leslie H. .... Tustin, CA
Ball, Leslie M. .... Beaumont, TX
Ball, Lisa Dreyer .... Dallas, TX
Ball Livingston, LLP .... Edison, NJ
Nutley, NJ
Brooklyn, NY
Ball, Louis A. .... Newport, KY
Ball, Lynn H. .... San Diego, CA
Ball, Malcolm C. .... Atlanta, GA
Ball, Marci Fuentes .... West Palm Beach, FL
Ball, Margaret T. .... Ithaca, NY
Ball, Mark D. .... Hampton, SC
Ball, Markham .... Washington, DC
Ball, Matthew G. .... Pittsburgh, PA
Ball, McDonough & Artz, P.C.
Binghamton, NY
Ball, Micah D. .... Greenville, NC
Ball, Michael F. .... Fresno, CA
Ball, Michael W. .... Department of Commerce, Patent and Trademark Office, GV
Ball, Michelle A. .... Sacramento, CA
Ball, Milner S. .... Camden, NJ
Ball, Mitzi Grove .... Charleston, SC
Ball & Mourton, Ltd., PLLC
Fayetteville, AR
Siloam Springs, AR
Ball, Murren & Connell .... Harrisburg, PA
Ball, Nancy L. .... Gilmanton, NH
Ball, Noga & Tanoury .... Columbus, OH
Ball, Owen K., Jr. .... Kansas City, MO
Ball, Pao Lin .... Rockville, MD
Ball, Patricia L. .... New York, NY
Ball, Patricia S. .... Schaumburg, IL
Ball, Patrick D. .... Mount Clemens, MI
Ball, Paula Abercrombie .... Atlanta, GA
Ball, Peter E. .... Boston, MA
Ball, Philip L. .... Los Angeles, CA
Ball, Philip W. .... New Haven, CT
Ball, Phillip B. .... Princeton, WV
Ball, R. Brian .... Richmond, VA
Ball, R. Lawrence .... Peoria, IL
Ball, Ralph G., Jr. .... Topeka, KS
Ball, Ralph W. .... Denver, CO
Ball, Raymond E. .... Sacramento, CA
Ball, Raymond E., A Professional Corporation
Sacramento, CA
Ball, Richard A., Jr. .... Montgomery, AL
Ball, Richard D. .... East Lansing, MI
Ball, Richard E., Jr., A Professional Corporation
Escondido, CA
Ball, Richard Edward, Jr. .... Escondido, CA
Ball, Richard T. .... Phoenix, AZ
Ball, Richard W. .... Loveland, CO
Ball, Robert A. .... San Diego, CA
Ball, Robert A., A Professional Corporation
San Diego, CA
Ball, Robert C. .... Stockton, CA
Ball, Robert K., II .... Kansas City, MO
Ball, Robert O., III .... Atlanta, GA
Ball, Robert R. .... Boise, ID
Ball, Robert S. .... Portland, OR
Ball, Robin D. .... Los Angeles, CA
Ball, Ronald A. .... White Plains, NY
Ball, S. Timothy .... New York, NY
Ball, Sabrina Dawn .... Memphis, TN
Ball, Sally W. .... Los Angeles, CA
Ball, Sanborn N. .... Salem, MO
Ball & Sargent, P.C. .... Worcester, MA
Ball, Scharon L. .... Baltimore, MD
Ball, Scott Arthur .... Gainesville, GA
Ball, Scott G. .... Dallas, TX
Ball, Simon N. .... Baton Rouge, LA
Ball, Stephanie A. .... Duluth, MN
Ball, Stephen C. .... Los Angeles, CA
Ball, Stephen M. .... Winston-Salem, NC
Ball, Stephen T. .... Orlando, FL
Ball, Steven F. .... Santa Ana, CA
Ball, Steven L. .... Columbus, OH
Ball, Stuart .... Yonkers, NY
Ball, Stuart S. .... Edison, NJ
Nutley, NJ
Ball, Stuart S. .... New York, NY
Ball, Susan Cresto .... Redding, CA
Ball, T. Armour .... San Antonio, TX
Ball, Teresa Lynn .... Richmond, VA
Ball, Teresa Raney .... Little Rock, AR
Ball, Terrence L. .... Muskogee, OK
Ball, Theodore C. .... Columbus, OH
Ball, Thomas F., III .... Richmond, VA
Ball, Thomas J., Jr. .... McLean, VA
Ball, Vern M. .... Bloomfield, IA
Ball, Wayne S. .... Dallas, TX
Ball and Weed, A Professional Corporation
San Antonio, TX
Ball, Wessley .... Arlington, TX
Ball, Wilbur S., Jr. .... Louisville, KY
Ball, William C. .... Waterloo, IA
Ball, William G. .... Greensburg, PA
Pittsburgh, PA
Ball, William K. .... Monticello, AR
Balla, G. Alan .... Pittsburgh, PA
Ballachey, Michael E. .... Oakland, CA
Ballack, Joyce U. .... Melbourne, FL
Ballack, Karen N. .... Menlo Park, CA
Ballai, Bruce W. .... Omaha, NE
Ballai, Elaine W. .... Trenton, NJ
Ballaine, William G. .... New York, NY
Ballal, Meera J. .... Nashville, TN
Ballan, Harry .... New York, NY
Ballan, Jack .... Fair Lawn, NJ
Ballan, Jonathan A. .... New York, NY
Ballan, Judith Silber .... New York, NY
Ballan, Linda .... Bloomfield, NJ
Ballan, Robert H. .... Norwood, NY

Ballance, Frank C. .... United States Senate, Senatorial Assistants, GV
Ballance, Frank W., Jr. (P.A.)
Warrenton, NC
Ballance, Lori D. .... Carlsbad, CA
Ballance, Michael W. .... Raleigh, NC
Balland, Nicholas A. .... Arlington, VA
Ballanfant, Burt .... Houston, TX
Ballantine, Andrew V.
Ridgefield Park, NJ
Ballantine, Beverly N. .... Littleton, CO
Ballantine, Douglas C. .... Louisville, KY
Ballantine, Frank D. .... Chicago, IL
Ballantine, James P. .... Santa Barbara, CA
Ballantine, John T. .... Louisville, KY
Ballantine, Lisa M. .... Wilmington, NC
Ballantine, Patrick J. .... Wilmington, NC
Ballantyne, Jay R. .... Visalia, CA
Ballantyne, Michele .... Salt Lake City, UT
Ballantyne, Michele S. .... Washington, DC
Ballantyne, R. Curtis .... Los Angeles, CA
Ballantyne, Richard L. .... Melbourne, FL
Ballantyne, Robert B. .... Los Angeles, CA
Ballantyne, Stephen P. .... San Antonio, TX
Ballard, Alice W. .... Philadelphia, PA
Ballard, Ann Eaton .... Houston, TX
Ballard, Augustus S. .... Philadelphia, PA
Ballard & Ballard .... Fayetteville, GA
Ballard, Barbara M. .... Baton Rouge, LA
Ballard, Basil G. .... Natchez, MS
Ballard, Benjamin H., III
San Francisco, CA
Ballard, Benjamin H., III
San Francisco, CA
Ballard, Bill J. .... Watson, OK
Ballard, Bradley M. .... Las Vegas, NV
Ballard, Brent D. .... Cleveland, OH
Ballard, Brian D. .... Tallahassee, FL
Ballard, Brian L. .... Boise, ID
Ballard, Brian P. .... Trenton, NJ
Ballard, Burnie W. .... Cheraw, SC
Ballard, Carol Morris .... Chattanooga, TN
Ballard, Catherine M. .... Columbus, OH
Ballard, Catherine Pulley .... Winchester, VA
Ballard, Charles T. .... Fayetteville, GA
Ballard, Christopher A. .... Lansing, MI
Ballard, Dan, & Associates .... Austin, TX
Ballard, Darlene D. .... Jackson, MS
Ballard, David E. .... Columbus, OH
Ballard, David G. .... Boise, ID
Ballard, David P. .... New York, NY
Ballard, Dennis D. .... Des Moines, IA
Ballard, Desa A. .... West Columbia, SC
Ballard, Diana C. .... New Haven, CT
Ballard, Douglas D. .... Hillsboro, OR
Ballard, Duard D. .... Toledo, OH
Ballard, Edward R. .... Irvine, CA
Ballard, Elizabeth A. .... Tulsa, OK
Ballard, Ernest S., Jr. .... New York, NY
Ballard, Felicia Nigro .... Newark, NJ
Ballard, Fielding E., III .... Shelbyville, KY
Ballard, Francis .... Philadelphia, PA
Ballard, Frank E., Jr. .... Jeffersonville, IN
Ballard, Frederic L. .... Philadelphia, PA
Ballard, Frederic L., Jr. .... Washington, DC
Philadelphia, PA
Ballard, F. V. .... Westerville, OH
Ballard, Gary L. .... Daytona Beach, FL
Ballard, Gaylord B. .... Louisville, KY
Ballard, Glenn A., Jr. .... Houston, TX
Ballard, Greg K. .... Oklahoma City, OK
Ballard, Gregory G. .... New York, NY
Ballard, Ian Matheson, Jr.
Philadelphia, PA
Ballard, J. Larry .... Fullerton, CA
Ballard, Jack D. .... Houston, TX
Ballard, James H. .... Salida, CO
Ballard, James L. .... Sugar Land, TX
Ballard, James M. .... Des Moines, IA
Ballard, James R. .... San Diego, CA
Ballard, Jeffrey S. .... Washington, DC
Ballard, John B., II .... Oklahoma City, OK
Ballard, John B., Jr. .... Atlanta, GA
Ballard, John E. .... St. Marys, WV
Ballard, John F. .... Cleveland, OH
Ballard, John H., III .... Dallas, TX
Ballard, John R. .... Shreveport, LA
Ballard, John S. .... Medina, OH
Ballard, John W. .... Oil City, LA
Ballard, Joseph R. .... Baton Rouge, LA
Ballard, Kelly M. .... Clearwater, FL
Ballard, Kenneth R. .... Oakhurst, CA
Ballard, Kenneth R. .... Universal City, CA
Ballard, Kriston (Kris) T. .... Las Vegas, NV
Ballard, Kyle .... Dallas, TX
Ballard, Lara Ann .... Department of State, Office of the Legal Adviser, GV
Ballard, Laurel R. .... Los Angeles, CA
Ballard, Marcella .... New York, NY
Ballard, Mark J. .... Chicago, IL
Ballard, Mark J. .... Mount Vernon, IL
Ballard, Marsha Talley .... Little Rock, AR
Ballard, Mary Beth .... Cleveland, OH
Ballard, Megan J. .... Madison, WI
Ballard, Melinda Meador .... Raleigh, NC
Ballard, Michael S. .... Birmingham, AL
Ballard, Nancer H. .... Boston, MA
Ballard, Norma Crippen .... Los Angeles, CA
Ballard, Novelle Frances .... Seattle, WA
Ballard, Patricia W. .... Louisville, KY
Ballard, Paul J. .... Baltimore, MD
Ballard, Paul L. .... Alexandria, MN
Ballard, Perri L. .... Fort Thomas, KY
Ballard & Reeves, A Prof. Corp.
Princeton, IN
Ballard, Richard L. .... Knox, IN
Ballard, Richard P. .... Louisville, MS
Ballard, Robert A. .... Overland Park, KS

Ballard, Robert C. .... Charlotte, MI
Ballard, Robert E. .... Cherry Hill, NJ
Harrisburg, PA
King Of Prussia, PA
Ballard, Robert E. .... Houston, TX
Ballard, Robert E., P.C. .... Houston, TX
Ballard, Robert T. .... Greenwood Village, CO
Ballard, Ronald L. .... Phoenix, AZ
Ballard, Ronald M. .... Lake Forest, CA
Ballard, Rosenberg & Golper
Universal City, CA
Ballard, Sandra A. .... Philadelphia, PA
Ballard, Scott L. .... Fayetteville, GA
Ballard, Shalanda Denise
Minneapolis, MN
Ballard, Shawna L. .... Los Angeles, CA
Ballard, Shelley B. .... Charlotte, NC
Ballard, Shiryl R. .... Columbia, SC
Ballard Spahr Andrews & Ingersoll, LLP
Denver, CO
Washington, DC
Baltimore, MD
Camden, NJ
Voorhees, NJ
Philadelphia, PA
Salt Lake City, UT
Ballard, Stephani J. .... Wilmington, DE
Ballard, Stephenson & Waters, P.C.
Covington, GA
Ballard, Steve P. .... Redding, CA
Ballard, Steven .... Columbus, OH
Ballard, Steven E. .... Iowa City, IA
Ballard, Steven G. .... Fullerton, CA
Ballard, Steven H. .... Stockbridge, GA
Ballard, Steven W. .... Tulsa, OK
Ballard, Stewart J.
Department of Commerce, GV
Ballard, Still & Ayres, L.L.P. .... Atlanta, GA
Ballard, Tracey A. .... Newark, NJ
Ballard, Tracey L. .... Dayton, OH
Ballard, Tracy E. .... Washington, DC
Ballard, Victor H. .... Montgomery, AL
Ballard, Wade E. .... Winston-Salem, NC
Spartanburg, SC
Ballard, Wade H., III .... Peterstown, WV
Ballard, Warren M. .... Philadelphia, PA
Ballard, W. D. .... Covington, GA
Ballard, William B., Jr .... Anna, IL
Ballard, William C. .... St. Petersburg, FL
Ballard, William C., Jr. .... Louisville, KY
Ballard, William D., Jr. .... Bryan, TX
Ballard, William H. .... Irving, TX
Ballard, William L. .... Atlanta, GA
Ballard, William L. .... Charleston, WV
Ballard, William W. .... Hernando, MS
Ballard, Wimer, Brockett & Edwards
Fullerton, CA
Ballard de Fabrega, Marlene
Panama Canal Commission, Office of the General Counsel, GV
Ballard Repasky, Wanda .... Lexington, KY
Ballarotto, Jerome A. .... Trenton, NJ
Ballas, Constantinos J. .... Paramus, NJ
Ballas, Haroula K. .... New York, NY
Ballas, Jack .... Inglewood, CA
Ballas, Lena V. .... Hackensack, NJ
Ballas, Sol .... Dallas, TX
Ballas, Stephen B. .... Los Angeles, CA
San Francisco, CA
Ballas, William J. .... Pueblo, CO
Ballas, William J., P.C. .... Pueblo, CO
Ballati, David L. .... San Francisco, CA
Ballati, Deborah S. .... San Francisco, CA
Ballato, Anthony T. .... Massapequa, NY
Ballato, Josie A. .... Department of Commerce, Patent and Trademark Office, GV
Ballato, Lynnette Pisone .... Dayton, OH
Ballato, Michael B. .... Richmond, VA
Ballato, Thomas A. .... Dayton, OH
Ballatore-Williamson, Annette A.
Fresno, CA
Ballay & Braud, P.L.C. .... Belle Chasse, LA
Ballay, Charles J. .... Belle Chasse, LA
Ballay, Kathleen Shea .... Philadelphia, PA
Balleisen, Carolyn K. .... Louisville, KY
Balleisen, Robert N. W. .... Tacoma, WA
Ballejos, Federico R. .... Albuquerque, NM
Ballen, Arthur E. .... Cherry Hill, NJ
Ballen, Frederick R. .... New York, NY
Ballen & Gertel, A Professional Corporation
Cherry Hill, NJ
Ballen, Gertel & DiCintio, A Professional Corporation .... Philadelphia, PA
Ballen, Howard L. .... Passaic, NJ
Ballen, Irving W. .... New York, NY
Ballen, Leigh J. .... Miami, FL
Arlington, VA
Ballen, Michael D. .... Brooklyn, NY
Ballen, Myron R. .... Bridgeport, CT
Ballen, Robert G. .... Washington, DC
Ballen, Samuel D. .... Boca Raton, FL
Ballengee, Ben .... Amarillo, TX
Ballengee, Billie D. .... DeSoto, TX
Ballengee, James M. .... Philadelphia, PA
Ballengee, Jennifer V. .... Kansas City, MO
Ballenger, B. Garrison, Jr. .... Charlotte, NC
Ballenger, Brian J. .... Northwood, OH
Toledo, OH
Ballenger, Christopher J. .... Chantilly, VA
Ballenger, Fedder, Cain & Norton, L.L.P.
Seneca, SC
Walhalla, SC
Ballenger, John M. .... Alexandria, VA
Ballenger, Karen Fowler .... Walhalla, SC
Ballenger, Kathleen A. .... Columbus, OH
Ballenger, Laurie G. .... Washington, DC
Ballenger, Martha Dantzler
Charleston, SC

Ballenger, Matt R. .... Baltimore, MD
Ballenger, Michael .... Florence, SC
Ballenger & Moore Co., L.P.A.
Northwood, OH
Toledo, OH
Ballenger, R. David
Panama Canal Commission, Office of the General Counsel, GV
Ballenger, W. Benjamin .... Summerville, GA
Ballenger, William H. .... Walhalla, SC
Ballenthin, James E. .... Backus, MN
Ballentine, Carol E. .... Philadelphia, PA
Ballentine, Chris .... Orlando, FL
Ballentine, James S. .... Minneapolis, MN
Ballentine, Lisa L. .... Atlanta, GA
Ballentine, Richard O. .... Kansas City, MO
Ballentine, Robert S. .... Houston, TX
Ballentine, Roger S.
Executive Office Of The President, GV
Baller, Charles H. .... New York, NY
Baller, Emily .... New York, NY
Baller Herbst Law Group, The
Washington, DC
Baller, James .... Washington, DC
Baller, James R. .... Chicago, IL
Baller, Margaret L. .... Somerset, NJ
Baller, Morris J. .... Oakland, CA
Baller, Russell H., Jr. .... Albany, NY
Kinderhook, NY
Baller, Wayne D. .... Dayton, OH
Ballerano, James A., Jr. .... Delray Beach, FL
Ballerini, Andrew A. .... Cherry Hill, NJ
Ballerini, Richard M. .... New York, NY
Balles, Nancy J., A Professional Law Corporation .... Concord, CA
Martinez, CA
Pleasanton, CA
Walnut Creek, CA
Balles, Nancy Jane .... Walnut Creek, CA
Ballesteros, Daniel W. .... San Jose, CA
Ballesteros, Deanna L. .... Los Angeles, CA
Ballesteros, Eugenia M. .... New York, NY
Ballesteros, Gary W. .... Milwaukee, WI
Ballesteros, Mary C. .... New York, NY
Balletta, James .... Orlando, FL
Balletta, Vincent R., Jr. .... Brooklyn, NY
Ballew, Craig F. .... Baltimore, MD
Ballew, David W. .... Seattle, WA
Ballew, Gregory D. .... Kansas City, MO
Ballew, James R. .... Claremont, CA
Ballew, Jeffrey L. .... Douglasville, GA
Ballew, John W., Jr. .... Lincoln, NE
Ballew, Kenneth M. .... Nashville, TN
Ballew, Larry A. .... Morganton, NC
Ballew, Lynn K. .... Harrisonville, MO
Ballew, Maston L., III .... Jackson, MS
Ballew, P. Jefferson .... Dallas, TX
Ballew, Patrick H. .... Seattle, WA
Yakima, WA
Ballew, Robert K. .... Blue Ridge, GA
Ballew, Schneider & Covalt .... Lincoln, NE
Ballew, Steven E. .... Washington, DC
Ballew, Walter W., III .... Savannah, GA
Ballew, William V., III .... El Paso, TX
Ballew, William W. .... Susanville, CA
Ballew-Ward, Brenda J. .... Yucaipa, CA
Balli, Jaime .... Harlingen, TX
Balli, Melinda Y. .... McAllen, TX
Ballidis, James E. .... Newport Beach, CA
Ballien, Gloria M. .... Albany, NY
Balliet, John H. .... Louisville, KY
Balliet, Nancy C. M. .... West Chester, PA
Balliet, Susan J. .... Louisville, KY
Balliett, Thomas D. .... New York, NY
Balliette, Andrea Cafiero .... Wildwood, NJ
Balliette, Barbara Whiten .... Austin, TX
Balliette, William M., Jr. .... Wildwood, NJ
Ballif, Philip M. .... Las Vegas, NV
Ballin & Associates .... Boston, MA
Ballin, James A. .... Boston, MA
Ballin, Jeffrey H. .... Las Vegas, NV
Ballin, Marvin E. .... Memphis, TN
Ballin, Robert W. .... Mineola, NY
Ballin, Stacy D. .... Cleveland, OH
Ballin, Steven M. .... Boston, MA
Ballina, Drew R. .... New Orleans, LA
Ballinger, Beverly K. .... Charleston, SC
Ballinger, Dana L. .... San Francisco, CA
Ballinger, J. David .... Chicago, IL
Ballinger, Jeffrey S. .... Riverside, CA
Ballinger, Kristin .... Seattle, WA
Ballinger, Maria Chan .... Oakland, CA
Ballinger, Max D. .... Greensboro, NC
Ballinger, Richard T. .... Wichita, KS
Ballinger, Steven R. .... Fort Lauderdale, FL
Ballinger, William W. .... San Clemente, CA
Ballintine, Daniel J. .... Minneapolis, MN
Balliro, Joseph J., Sr. .... Boston, MA
Balliro, Juliane .... Boston, MA
Ballis, Jon A. .... Chicago, IL
Ballister, Joseph C. .... Pittsford, NY
Ballman, B. George .... Gaithersburg, MD
Ballman, Donald R. .... Hartford, CT
Ballman, Donna M. .... Miami, FL
Ballman, Donna M., P.A. .... Miami, FL
Ballman, Patricia K. .... Milwaukee, WI
Ballmer, Bruce D. .... Los Angeles, CA
Ballmer, Jody A. .... Chicago, IL
Ballmer, Shána L. .... San Diego, CA
Ballner, Patricia Rose .... New York, NY
Ballo, Brian P. .... Irvine, CA
Ballo, Thomas J. .... San Francisco, CA
Balloff, Edward .... Jacksboro, TN
Ballog, Albert P., Jr. .... Tustin, CA
Ballog, Marian E. .... Tustin, CA
Ballon, Ian C. .... Palo Alto, CA
Ballon, Margot E. .... Albuquerque, NM

Ballon Stoll Bader & Nadler, P.C.
Hackensack, NJ
New York, NY
Ballor, Jeanne Wysocki ... Peoria, IL
Ballot, Alissa E. ... West Palm Beach, FL
Ballot, Richard D. ... Morristown, NJ
Ballotta, Karen A. ... Washington, DC
Ballou & Bedell ... York, ME
Ballou, D. Scott ... Minneapolis, MN
Ballou, Daniel J. ... Rock Hill, SC
Ballou, David J. ... York, ME
Ballou, E. Wade, Jr.
House of Representatives,
Office of Legislative Counsel, GV
Ballou, Ellyn C. ... South Freeport, ME
Ballou, Eric E. ... Richmond, VA
Ballou, Ernest W. ... Roanoke, VA
Ballou, Gail M. ... Fairbanks, AK
Ballou, John D. ... Chicago, IL
Ballou, L. Dennis ... Atlanta, GA
Ballou, Martha A. ... Minneapolis, MN
Ballou, Peter G. ... Augusta, ME
Ballou, Raymond L. ... St. Petersburg, FL
Ballou, Raymond L., P.A. ... St. Petersburg, FL
Ballou, Rebecca W. ... Las Vegas, NV
Ballou, Richard D. ... Honesdale, PA
Ballou, Robert A., Jr. ... Toms River, NJ
Ballou, Robert B. ... Los Angeles, CA
Ballou, Robert S. ... Roanoke, VA
Ballou, Sandy M. ... Madison, WI
Ballou, Scott H. ... Cleveland, OH
Ballou, Tom ... Corpus Christi, TX
Ballou, Vicki A. ... Portland, OR
Ballou, Walter A. ... Denver, CO
Ballou, William J. ... Boston, MA
Balloun, J. Eugene ... Overland Park, KS
Ballout, Haitham Edward
Burlingame, CA
Ballout, Haitham Edward
San Francisco, CA
Ballow, Barry ... Fairless Hills, PA
Ballow, Braisted, O'Brien & Rusin, P.C.
Buffalo, NY
Ballow, John E. ... Buffalo, NY
Ballow, R. Brent ... Nashville, TN
Ballow, Rachel C. ... Alexandria, VA
Ballow, Robert L. ... San Diego, CA
Nashville, TN
Ballowe, James E., Jr. ... Washington, DC
Ballsrud, Robert P. ... St. Louis, MO
Ballsun, Kathryn A. ... Los Angeles, CA
Ballsun & Ledbetter, LLP
Los Angeles, CA
Balluff, Karien L. ... Seattle, WA
Ballway, Joseph H., Jr. ... Cleveland, OH
Ballweg, Ernest C. ... Overland Park, KS
Ballweg, Mitchell J. ... Department of Justice,
Tax Division, GV
Balmages, Michael G. ... Tustin, CA
Balman, Sheldon I. ... Novato, CA
Balman, Steven K. ... Tulsa, OK
Balmer, David C. ... Fleetwood, PA
Reading, PA
Balmer, James W. ... Iowa City, IA
Balmer, James W. ... Duluth, MN
Balmer, John R. ... Roswell, GA
Balmer, Joseph E., III ... Dayton, OH
Balmer, Judd J. ... Las Vegas, NV
Balmer, Norman L. ... Danbury, CT
Balmer, Susan A. ... Leesburg, FL
Balmer, Thomas A. ... Portland, OR
Balmer, William J., Jr. ... Clayton, MO
Balmert, F. Daniel ... Cleveland, OH
Balmert, Neil P. ... San Diego, CA
Balmes, Vernon R. ... Mill Valley, CA
Balmforth, Clinton E. ... Salt Lake City, UT
Balmforth, Kathryn Ogden
Salt Lake City, UT
Balmuth, Barry S., P.A.
West Palm Beach, FL
Balmuth, Barry Seth
West Palm Beach, FL
Balmuth, Robert L. ... Irvine, CA
Balmuth, Saul ... Ballston Spa, NY
Balnave, Richard D. ... Charlottesville, VA
Balocco, Joseph M. ... Fort Lauderdale, FL
Balocco, Joseph M., P.A.
Fort Lauderdale, FL
Miami, FL
West Palm Beach, FL
Balodimas, Eugenia ... Boston, MA
Balog, Andrew E. ... Miami, FL
Balog, Douglas A. ... Melbourne, FL
Balog, Eva E. ... San Francisco, CA
Balog, George G. ... Baltimore, MD
Balog, James M. ... Hagerstown, MD
Balog, James P. ... Chicago, IL
Balog, Jason Edward ... Baltimore, MD
Balog, Joseph A. ... Cleveland, OH
Balog, Michael C. ... Dallas, TX
Balog & Rasch ... Newport Beach, CA
Balog, Richard H. ... St. Charles, IL
Balog, Roger P. ... Houston, TX
Balog, Steve A. ... Graham, NC
Balog, Timothy A. ... Newport Beach, CA
Baloga, Mark A. ... Oak Brook, IL
Balogh, Barbara J. ... Waynesboro, VA
Balogh Becker Dingmann, Ltd.
Minneapolis, MN
Balogh, Bryan Oxford ... Birmingham, AL
Balogh, Ethan Atticus ... San Francisco, CA
Balogh, James A. ... Minneapolis, MN
Balogh, James M. ... Phoenix, AZ
Balogh, James M. ... Phoenix, AZ
Tempe, AZ
Balogh, Kristine E. ... Sacramento, CA
Balogh, Merlin J. ... Loveland, OH
Balogh, Paulette J. ... Pittsburgh, PA
Balogh, Robert B. ... Miami Beach, FL
Balogh, Stephen E. ... Rockford, IL
Baloh, Mary E. ... Greensburg, PA
Balok, Joseph J., Jr. ... Elmira, NY
Balok, Linda M. ... San Francisco, CA
Balon, Bruce J. ... Providence, RI
Balon, Michael D. ... Lincoln, RI
Balone, Thomas J. ... Farmington Hills, MI
Balonek, Barry C. ... Rochester, NY
Balonick, Barney H. ... Chicago, IL
Balonick & Bloch ... Chicago, IL
Balonick, Bruce H. ... Chicago, IL
Balonick, Farrel J. ... Chicago, IL
Balonon, Eugene L. ... Wilton, CA
Balotti, R. Franklin ... Wilmington, DE
Balough, Richard C. ... Chicago, IL
Baloun, Leonard E. ... Spokane, WA
Balouris, Chris J. ... Pittsburgh, PA
Balow, Brian R. ... Bloomfield Hills, MI
Balow, Geraldine M. ... Chicago, IL
Baloyra, Patricia M. ... Miami, FL
Balph, Nicolls, Mitsos, Flannery & Clark
New Castle, PA
Balraj, Solomon F. ... Cleveland, OH
Bals, Lee H. ... Portland, ME
Bals, Robert L. ... Lincoln, NE
Balsa, Luis E. Palou ... San Juan, PR
Balsam, Craig I. ... New York, NY
Balsam, Dahlia A. ... New York, NY
Balsam Felber & Goldfield ... New York, NY
White Plains, NY
Balsam, Hugh S. ... Chicago, IL
Balsam, Jerome M. ... New York, NY
Balsam, Jodi S. ... New York, NY
Balsam, Joel ... Lawrence, NY
Balsam, Martin ... New York, NY
Balsam, Nina P. ... St. Louis, MO
Balsam, Richard F. ... White Plains, NY
Balsam, Robert S. ... New York, NY
Balsam, Robin H. ... Tacoma, WA
Balsam, Robin H., P.S. ... Tacoma, WA
Balsam, Robt. C. ... Billings, MT
Balsam, Roderick D. ... Santa Cruz, CA
Balsam, Steven, (P.C.)
Oakland Gardens, NY
Balsam, Yael Sima ... New York, NY
Balsama, Joseph A. ... Media, PA
Balsamo, Andrea I. ... Johnston, RI
Balsamo, Anthony ... New York, NY
Balsamo, Arthur E. ... Cliffside Park, NJ
Balsamo, Dennis J. ... Nipomo, CA
Balsamo, DiStefano & Dixon, P.C.
Washington, DC
Fort Lauderdale, FL
Balsamo, Dolores D. ... Kew Gardens, NY
Balsamo, Joseph S. ... Lake Forest, IL
Balsamo, Mary E. ... Canton, MA
Balsamo, Michael M.
National Labor Relations Board,
Office of the General Counsel, GV
Balsamo, Richard R. ... Chicago, IL
Balsamo, Richard W. ... Washington, DC
Fort Lauderdale, FL
Balsamo, Salvatore ... Charlotte, NC
Balsamo, Stephen ... New York, NY
Balsan, David H. ... Flushing, NY
Balsawer, Pragati (Peggy) K.
Washington, DC
Balseiro-Fernandez, Enrique ... Bethesda, MD
Balser, David L. ... Atlanta, GA
Balser, Donald R. ... Evansville, IN
Balser, Gail A. ... North Attleboro, MA
Balser, John J. ... Wallingford, CT
Balserak, J. Paul ...
Department Of The Interior, GV
Balshone-Jacobs, Lynn ... Columbus, OH
Balsiger & Carney ... Norfolk, NE
Balsiger, Charles W. ... Norfolk, NE
Balsinger, Daniel F. ... Spring, TX
Balsino, Peter M. ... Tucson, AZ
Balske, Dennis N. ... Lake Oswego, OR
Balskus-Kelly, Caryl E. ... Manchester, CT
Balsley, Donald J., Jr. ... Pittsburgh, PA
Balsley, Heidi R. ... Decatur, IL
Balsley, Koonmen & Dahlberg
Loves Park, IL
Balsley, Stephen G. ... Rockford, IL
Balsley, William L. ... Loves Park, IL
Balsley-Cross, Margaret B. ... Chicago, IL
Balson, Bradley P. ... Chicago, IL
Balson Curley & Stein, LLC
Englewood, CO
Balson, Jarod ... Englewood, CO
Balson, Joe ... Houston, TX
Balson, Merry H. ... Denver, CO
Balson, Ronald H. ... Chicago, IL
Balsters and Hinrichs, A Professional
Corporation ... Bethalto, IL
Balsters, Kenneth E. ... Bethalto, IL
Balt, Edith ... Hackensack, NJ
Baltar, Bruce ... Dillingham, AK
Baltaxe & Baltaxe ... Encino, CA
Baltaxe, Bernhard D. ... Sacramento, CA
Baltaxe, George ... Encino, CA
Baltaxe, Michael F. ... Encino, CA
Baltay, Matthew C. ... Boston, MA
Baltayan, Akop ... Sylmar, CA
Baltch, David L. ... Mineola, NY
Baltch, Raymond J. ... Mineola, NY
Balter, David M. ... San Jose, CA
Balter, Diane B. ... Sacramento, CA
Balter, Jerome ... Philadelphia, PA
Balter, Joseph A. ... Baltimore, MD
Balter, Robert S. ... Mount Laurel, NJ
Baltera, Victor N. ... Boston, MA
Balterman, Harry ... Amagansett, NY
Balthasar, William E. ... Kenmore, NY
Balthaser, James H. ... Columbus, OH
Balthazaar, M. C. Tania ... Philadelphia, PA
Balthazard, Mark J. ... Boston, MA
Balthrop, George H. ... Fairfax, VA
Balthrop, James M. ... Springfield, TN
Balthrop, Perry and Noe ... Ashland City, TN
Balthrop, Ricky D. ... Arlington, TX
Balthrop, Sam M. ... Ashland City, TN
Balthrope, Robin Bernice ... Cincinnati, OH
Baltierra, Elizabeth C. ... Washington, MO
Baltimore, Carol Weiss ... Wilkes-Barre, PA
Baltimore, H. Ladon ... Nashville, TN
Baltimore, Jennifer E. ... Universal City, CA
Baltimore, Joseph N. ... Detroit, MI
Baltimore & Reeves ... Nashville, TN
Baltins, Andris A. ... Minneapolis, MN
Baltins, Maris ... Spokane, WA
Balto, David A. ... Federal Trade Commission,
Bureau of Competition, GV
Balton, David ... Department of State,
Office of the Legal Adviser, GV
Balton, Monroe P. ... Lawndale, CA
Baltus, Debra Shamoun ... Allen Park, MI
Baltus, Debra Shamoun ... Troy, MI
Baltz, Christina M. ... New York, NY
Baltz, Frank J., (P.C.) ... McLean, VA
Baltz, Gregory A. ... Far Hills, NJ
Wyncote, PA
Baltz, Murphy, Gottwald, Schmidt &
Mazullo, LLP ... Far Hills, NJ
Wyncote, PA
Baltz, Phillip D. ... Nashville, TN
Baltz, Randolph M. ... Little Rock, AR
Baltz, Raymond E. ... Atlanta, GA
Baltz, Richard E. ... Washington, DC
Baltz, Richard P. ... Hermitage, TN
Baltz, Thomas E. ... Chicago, IL
Baltz, William S. ... Winnetka, IL
Baltzan, Elizabeth ... Washington, DC
Baltzell, Edward Joseph ... Aston, PA
Baltzell, Victor L., Jr. ... Louisville, KY
Baltzer, Timothy D. ... Honolulu, HI
Baluch, Dennis S. ... Providence, RI
Baluch, Gianfrancesco, Mathieu & Szerlag
Providence, RI
Baluda, Marc R. ... Washington, DC
Baluk, Robert R. ... Chicago, IL
Balulescu, Carol D. ... Boston, MA
Balunek, Adelbert A. ... Lorain, OH
Baluss, Jane E. ... Washington, DC
Baluss, Mary E. ... Washington, DC
Balutis, Daniel J. ... Enola, PA
Plymouth, PA
Baluyot, Ray M. ... San Jose, CA
Baly, Margaret M. ... Glen Allen, VA
Baly, Scott D. ... Fresno, CA
Balyeat, Clay W. ... Lima, OH
Balyeat, Doug R. ... Atlanta, GA
Balyeat, H. John ... Missoula, MT
Balyeat, Robert L. ... Lima, OH
Balyeat, Thomas M. ... Toledo, OH
Balyeat, William B. ... Columbus Grove, OH
Lima, OH
Balyk, Thomas P. ... St. Paul, MN
Balzac, Edgar F. ... San Juan, PR
Balzan, Christopher R. ... Ventura, CA
Balzan, Claude A. ... Miami, FL
Balzano, Laura A. ... Brecksville, OH
Balzano, Ronald A. ... New York, NY
Balzarini, Edward J. ... Pittsburgh, PA
Balzarini, Edward J., Jr. ... Pittsburgh, PA
Balzarini, Michael ... Pittsburgh, PA
Balzarini & Watson ... Pittsburgh, PA
Balzer, Charles A. ... North Hampton, OH
Balzer, Cody L. ... Casper, WY
Balzer, Elyse G. Lehman ... Scarsdale, NY
Balzer, John G. ... Boston, MA
Balzer, Nancy J. ... Richmond, VA
Balzer, Roland N. ... St. Louis, MO
Balzli, Mark D. ... Miami Beach, FL
Balzli, Mark D., P.A. ... Miami Beach, FL
Bambace, Peter J. ... Houston, TX
Bambace, Robert S. ... Houston, TX
Bambach, Alistaire ... New York, NY
Bambach, Lee Ann ... Washington, DC
Bambach, Robin Roth ... Denver, CO
Bambara, Joseph J. ... Greenvale, NY
Bamber, Bosch Banasiak ... Hammond, IN
Bamber, Jeffrey V. ... Cincinnati, OH
Bamberg, George W., Jr. ... Houston, TX
Bamberg, John B. ... St. Augustine, FL
Bamberg, Jonathan B. ... St. Augustine, FL
Bamberger & Abshier ... Owensboro, KY
Bamberger, Carolyn M. ... Washington, DC
Bamberger, David H. ... Washington, DC
Bamberger, David H. ... New York, NY
Bamberger, David T. ... Claremont, CA
Bamberger, E. Clinton, Jr. ... Baltimore, MD
Bamberger & Feibleman ... Indianapolis, IN
Bamberger, Foreman, Oswald and Hahn,
LLP ... Boonville, IN
Evansville, IN
Indianapolis, IN
Jasper, IN
Mt. Vernon, IN
Princeton, IN
Bamberger, Gerald J. ... St. Charles, MO
Bamberger, Gerald J., & Associates
St. Charles, MO
Bamberger, Joanne Cronrath
Securities and Exchange Commission,
Division of Enforcement, GV
Bamberger, Joseph F. ... Burlington, KY
Bamberger, Joyce E. ... Anchorage, AK
Bamberger, Joyce E., Law Office of
Anchorage, AK
Bamberger, Kathryn A.N. ... Columbus, OH
Bamberger, Lawrence K.
Monterey Park, CA
Bamberger, Lori E. ... United States Senate,
Committee Legal Personnel, GV
Bamberger, Michael ... Milwaukee, WI
Bamberger, Michael A. ... New York, NY
Bamberger, Phylis S. ... Bronx, NY
Bamberger, Richard H. ... Cleveland, OH
Bamberger, Ronald J. ... Owensboro, KY
Bamberger, S. Karen ... Seattle, WA
Bamberth, Hugo A., Law Offices
La Porte, IN
Bamberth, Hugo A., Law Offices
Michigan City, IN
Bambery, Daniel G. ... Lansing, MI
Bambery, M. Carol ... Lansing, MI
Bambino, Laurence M. ... New York, NY
Bambo, Gregory, & Associates
San Francisco, CA
Bambo, Gregory B., III ... San Francisco, CA
Bambrick & Bambrick, P.C. ... Lemont, IL
Bambrick, Gerard M. ... Floral Park, NY
Bambrick, James ... Lemont, IL
Bambrick, James M. ... Los Angeles, CA
Bambrick, Janice M. ... Santa Monica, CA
Bambrick & Ryan ... Floral Park, NY
Bambrick, Thomas A. ... Lemont, IL
Bambrick, V. Timothy ... Baltimore, MD
Bambrick, W. Lewis ... Trenton, NJ
Bamburg, Harold B. ... St. Louis, MO
Bamburg, Robert E. ... Jacksonville, AR
Bamburowski, Thomas J.
Bowling Green, OH
Bambury, J. James ... New York, NY
Bambury, Joseph A., Jr. ... Charlotte, NC
Bambury, Kevin J. ... Fairport, NY
Bamdas, Robert L. ... Fort Lauderdale, FL
Bame, Jerome M. ... Fountain Valley, CA
Bametzreider, Paul C. ... Lebanon, PA
Bamford, Barbara ... Morristown, NJ
Bamford, David K. ... Durham, NH
Bamford, Harry V. ... San Jose, CA
Bamford, Thos. K. ... Dallas, TX
Bamman, Fred C., III, P.A.
Pompano Beach, FL
Bamman, Fredrick C., III
Pompano Beach, FL
Bamman, H. William ... Toledo, OH
Bamond, Laura M. ... St. Petersburg, FL
Bamonte, Anna M. ... Pittsburgh, PA
Bamonte, David J. ... Briarcliff Manor, NY
Bamonte, John D. ... Mount Pleasant, SC
Bampfield, Gwendolyn J. ... Brooklyn, NY
Bampton, Debra K. ... Morristown, NJ
Bamundo, Steven ... New York, NY
Bamvakais, Michael R. ... St. Louis, MO
Ban, Daniel J. ... Oakland, CA
Ban, Frank N. ... Houston, TX
Ban, J. Peter ... Washington, DC
Ban, Jason ... New York, NY
Ban, Peggy R. ... Houston, TX
Ban, Stephen F. ... Pittsburgh, PA
Ban, William J. ... White Plains, NY
Ban, Woodrow W. ... Avon Lake, OH
Banack, Emerson, Jr. ... San Antonio, TX
Banagan, James E. ... Albany, NY
Banahan, Brian J. ... Wheaton, IL
Banahan, Jas. E. ... Louisville, KY
Banahan, John A. ... Pascagoula, MS
Banahan, Lillian M. ... Wheaton, IL
Banahan, Michael F. ... St. Louis, MO
Banahan, Thomas A. ... Stamford, CT
New York, NY
Banait, Narinder S. ... Milpitas, CA
Banales, J. Manuel ... Corpus Christi, TX
Banar, Elaine D. ... Brooklyn, NY
Banar, Kathleen M. ... Chicago, IL
Banas, C. Leslie ... Detroit, MI
Banas, Edward J. ... Charleston, WV
Banas, Gary A. ... Canton, OH
Banas, J. Michael ... Detroit, MI
Banas, Jos. A., Jr. ... Newport News, VA
Banas, M. Margaret ... Scottsdale, AZ
Banas, Mitchell J., Jr. ... Buffalo, NY
Banas, Richard P. ... Flint, MI
Banas, Theresa M. ... Aurora, IL
Banash, David M. ... Boston, MA
Banash, Richd. M. ... Boston, MA
Banash, Theresa Kelly ... Wellesley, MA
Banashek, Jon N. ... Boulder, CO
Banashek, Matthew ... Santa Monica, CA
Banashek & Strauss, P.C.
Black Hawk, CO
Boulder, CO
Central City, CO
Denver, CO
Estes Park, CO
Nederland, CO
Rollinsville, CO
Banasiak, Joseph ... Hammond, IN
Banasick, Kristin M. ... Bedford, PA
Banasik, Brad Allen ... Lansing, MI
Banasik, Kevin A. ... Chicago, IL
Banaszak, Christopher P. ... Milwaukee, WI
Banaszak, Michael E. ... Milwaukee, WI
Banaszynski, Thomas J. ... Louisville, KY
Banatoski, Lisa L. ... Hartford, CT
Banbury, Brooke W. ... Naples, FL
Traverse City, MI
Banbury, Davis and Erschen, P.C.
Aurora, IL
Banbury, J. Hunter ... Windsor, VT
Banbury, John C. ... Aurora, IL
Banbury, Lana Proctor ... Denver, CO
Banbury, Richard F. ... Hartford, CT
Banche, Nicholas C., A Professional
Corporation ... Oceanside, CA
Banchefsky, Mitchell H. ... Columbus, OH
Banchefsky, Susan Hannon ... Columbus, OH

Banchek, Melvin H., (Co., L.P.A.)
Cleveland, OH
Bancheri, Christine E. .... Philadelphia, PA
Banchero, E. Jeffrey .... San Francisco, CA
Banchero & Lasater .... San Francisco, CA
Banchik, David .... Mount Olive, NJ
Banciella, Ricardo A. .... Miami, FL
Banciu, Louis James .... Dearborn, MI
Bancone, Jon J. .... White Plains, NY
Bancroft, Alexander C. .... New York, NY
Bancroft, Bruce R. .... South Bend, IN
Bancroft, Daniel A. .... Cambridge, MA
Bancroft, David P. .... San Francisco, CA
Bancroft, Don X. .... Pompton Lakes, NJ
Bancroft, Ellen S. .... Irvine, CA
Bancroft, Faye .... Little Rock, AR
Bancroft, G. Ben .... Big Spring, TX
Bancroft, J. Gail .... Washington, DC
Bancroft, James R. .... San Francisco, CA
Bancroft, John K. .... Fairfax, VA
Bancroft, John R. .... San Francisco, CA
Bancroft, John R. .... Kansas City, MO
Bancroft, Kristen .... New York, NY
Bancroft, Laura K. .... Chicago, IL
Cleveland, OH
Bancroft, Margaret A. .... New York, NY
Bancroft, Mark W. .... Lebanon, CT
Bancroft & McAlister, A Professional Corporation .... San Francisco, CA
Walnut Creek, CA
Bancroft, Michael H. .... Seattle, WA
Bancroft, Paul D. .... Tucson, AZ
Incline Village, NV
Bancroft, Paul D., P.C. .... Phoenix, AZ
Tucson, AZ
Incline Village, NV
Las Vegas, NV
Reno, NV
Bancroft, Peter E. .... Baltimore, MD
Bancroft, Peter M. .... Marlborough, MA
Bancroft, Prentice K. .... Richmond, CA
Bancroft, Richard A. .... Point Richmond, CA
Bancroft, Robert H. .... Flint, MI
Bancroft, Steven W. .... Fairfax, VA
Bancroft, Thomas C. .... Worland, WY
Bancroft, Timothy B. .... Boston, MA
Bancroft, Todd A. .... Chicago, IL
Bancroft, Webb E. .... Lincoln, NE
Bancroft, Zachary J. .... Orlando, FL
Bancsi, Pamela Ward .... Cleveland, OH
Banczak, Peggy J. .... Houston, TX
Band, David .... New Orleans, LA
Band, David, A Prof. Law Corp.
New Orleans, LA
Band, David S. .... Sarasota, FL
Band, Erin P. .... Wheaton, MD
Band, Gary A. .... Washington, DC
Band, Gregory S. .... Sarasota, FL
Band, Ian Phillip .... Washington, DC
Band, Jonathan .... Washington, DC
Band, Jordan C. .... Cleveland, OH
Band, Joseph M.
Office of Personnel Management, GV
Band, Jules .... Sunnyside, NY
Band, Michael R. .... Miami, FL
Bandaries, Madro .... New Orleans, LA
Bandas, Christopher A.
Corpus Christi, TX
Bandazian, Christopher A. .... Manchester, NH
Bandazian, Khoren, II .... Hackensack, NJ
Bandeen, Robert W. .... Grand Rapids, MI
Bandeian, John J., Jr. .... Bristol, TN
Bandel, Nicola .... New York, NY
Bandel, Ralph W. .... Cohoes, NY
Bandel, Steven .... New York, NY
Bandell, Leonard J. .... Redding, CA
Bandemer, June E. .... Pittsburgh, PA
Bandemer, Otto H. .... Carlsbad, CA
Bander, Edward J. .... Concord, MA
Bander, Fox-Isicoff & Associates, P.A.
Fort Lauderdale, FL
Miami, FL
Bander, Holly S. .... San Jose, CA
Bander, Mark B. .... Atlanta, GA
Bander, Michael A. .... Miami, FL
Bander, Milton Edward, P.C. .... Bethesda, MD
Bander, Yigal .... Baton Rouge, LA
Bandera, Denis G. .... Houston, TX
Bandes, Bruce S. .... West Sayville, NY
Bandes, Miriam J. .... Buffalo, NY
Bandettini, Jerome P. .... Whitefish Bay, WI
Bandgren, Jimmie B. .... North Hollywood, CA
Bandi, William Robert .... Oklahoma City, OK
Bandier, Martin N. .... New York, NY
Bandiera, Michael P., Jr. .... Los Angeles, CA
Bandiero, Emilio F. .... Eugene, OR
Bandini, Jeffrey A. .... Raleigh, NC
Bandini, Laura E. .... Washington, DC
Bandklayder, Daniel K. .... Miami, FL
Bandler, Alan E. .... New York, NY
Bandler, Brian .... New York, NY
Bandler, Judith M. .... New York, NY
Bandler, Richard V. .... Bronx, NY
Bandler, Steven E. .... Phoenix, AZ
Bandlow, Lincoln D. .... Los Angeles, CA
Bandman, Jeffrey M. .... Jersey City, NJ
Bandman, Randi Dawn
San Francisco, CA
Bando, Lillian F. .... Glendale, CA
Bandon, William E. .... Katonah, NY
Bandon, William E., III .... New York, NY
Bandon, William E., P.C. .... Katonah, NY
Bandonis, Michael J. .... Newport, OR
Bandow, Doug .... Washington, DC
Bandré, David G. .... Jefferson City, MO
Bandré, Michael P. .... Harrisonville, MO
Bands, William L. .... Charleston, WV

Bandstra Law Firm, The, P.C.
Des Moines, IA
Bandstra, Richard A. .... Grand Rapids, MI
Bandstra, Scott L. .... Des Moines, IA
Bandstra, Ted E. .... Miami, FL
Bandt, Christopher R. .... Manitowoc, WI
Banducci, Janice M. .... Bakersfield, CA
Banducci, Thomas A. .... Boise, ID
Banduch, Thelma .... Brownsville, TX
Bandusky, Raymond L. .... Augusta, ME
Bandy & Bandy .... Diamond Bar, CA
Bandy, Dale Ann .... Marietta, GA
Bandy, David R. .... Ponca City, OK
Bandy, Denise E. .... Topeka, KS
Bandy, Frederick E. .... Madera, CA
Bandy, J. M. (Mick), P.C. .... Tyler, TX
Bandy, Jack D. .... North Hills, CA
Bandy, James .... Kansas City, MO
Bandy, James H. .... Belleville, IL
Bandy, J. M. (Mick) .... Tyler, TX
Bandy, Kenneth L. .... Damascus, OH
Bandy, Mark E. .... Cleveland, OH
Bandy, Marshall M., Jr. .... Ringgold, GA
Bandy, Robert L. .... Charleston, WV
Bandy, Robert M. .... Dallas, TX
Longview, TX
Plano, TX
Tyler, TX
Bandy, Robert M., P.C. .... Dallas, TX
Longview, TX
Plano, TX
Tyler, TX
Bandy, Roland T., Jr. .... Dallas, TX
Bandy & Stagg, P.C. .... Ringgold, GA
Bandy, Thomas E. .... Diamond Bar, CA
Bandy, Thomas R., III .... Kingsport, TN
Bandy, Valerie J. .... Diamond Bar, CA
Bandych, Rachel Brody .... Rochester, NY
Bane, Alison J. .... Portland, ME
Bane, Charles A. .... Palm Beach, FL
Bane, David .... Yardley, PA
Bane, David E., Jr. .... Louisville, MS
Bane, George D. .... Los Angeles, CA
Bane, Jeanette D. .... Lakewood, CO
Bane, John Ward .... Hampton, VA
Bane, Keith J. .... Schaumburg, IL
Bane, Kimberly A. .... Philadelphia, PA
Bane, Lee S. .... Dallas, TX
Bane, Mark I. .... New York, NY
Bane, Richard W. .... San Bernardino, CA
Baneman, Roger J. .... New York, NY
Baner, Richard M. .... Eureka, IL
Baner, Sandra M. .... Janesville, WI
Baner, Yvonne .... Woodland Hills, CA
Banerjee, Krishna Gopal
San Francisco, CA
Banerjee, Roy Amit .... Atlanta, GA
Banerji, Sonia T. .... San Francisco, CA
Banes, David G. .... Saipan, TT
Banes, Gay B. .... Mc Keesport, PA
Banez, Barbara P. .... Los Angeles, CA
Banez, Marissa .... New York, NY
Banfi, Gabriel I. .... Seattle, WA
Banfield, Deborah J. .... Livingston, NJ
Banfield, Donna Zils .... Tyngsborough, MA
Banfield, Jaime D. .... Santa Ana, CA
Banfield, Norman C. .... Juneau, AK
Banfield, Phillip L., II .... Lancaster, CA
Banfield, Robert D. .... Vienna, VA
Banfield, William E. .... New York, NY
Banford, Craig R. .... Huntington, WV
Bang, John D. .... Orlando, FL
Bang, Joyce .... Washington, DC
Bang, Jun Suk .... Philadelphia, PA
Bang, Susan C. .... Los Angeles, CA
Bangasser, Hugh F. .... Seattle, WA
Bange, Kristina A. .... York, PA
Bange, Richard Milton, III .... New York, NY
Bangel, Bangel & Bangel, L.L.P.
Norfolk, VA
Portsmouth, VA
Suffolk, VA
Virginia Beach, VA
Bangel, Herbert K. .... Portsmouth, VA
Bangel, Keith H. .... Portsmouth, VA
Bangel, Paul G. .... Bradenton, FL
Bangeman, Norman R. .... Denver, CO
Bangert, Beth G. .... Cupertino, CA
Bangert, Bruce .... Odessa, TX
Bangert, Charles E. .... Arnold, MD
Bangert, David C. .... Milwaukee, WI
Bangert, Jack T. .... Kansas City, MO
Bangert, Lisa A. .... Milwaukee, WI
Bangert, Patricia S. .... Denver, CO
Bangert, Philip A. .... Washington, DC
Bangert, Richard E., II .... Seattle, WA
Bangert, Sharon J. .... Crofton, MD
Bangert-Drowns, Diana K. .... Albany, NY
Bangerter, D. Shane .... Dodge City, KS
Bangerter, J. Christian, Jr. .... Nashville, TN
Bangerter, Steven R. .... Costa Mesa, CA
Banghart, Donald L. .... Lakewood, CO
Banghart, Donald L., P.C. .... Lakewood, CO
Banghart, Laurance E. .... San Diego, CA
Banghart, Steven F. .... Chicago, IL
Bangiola, Nancy M. .... Morristown, NJ
Bangiola, Paul .... Morristown, NJ
Bang-Jensen, Lars .... New York, NY
Bang-Jensen, Nina .... United States Senate, Committee Legal Personnel, GV
Bangle, Raymond, III .... Fairfield, CA
Sacramento, CA
Bangle, Shannon Wade .... Fort Worth, TX
Bangma, Jeffrey D. .... Mora, MN
Bangor, Paul D., Jr. .... Pittsburgh, PA
Bangos, Nicholas B. .... Cocoa, FL
Bang-Robson, Grace E. .... New York, NY
Bangs, Barbara A. .... Santa Clara, CA

Bangs, Frank S., Jr. .... Tucson, AZ
Bangs, Gregory D. .... Overland Park, KS
Bangs, Jonathan .... Portland, ME
Bangs, McCullen, Butler, Foye & Simmons, L.L.P. .... Rapid City, SD
Bangs, Michael L. .... Camp Hill, PA
Bangs, Nelson A. .... Plano, TX
Bangs, Robert H. L. .... Glen Burnie, MD
Bangs, Shaaron A. .... Covina, CA
Bangs, Steven Edmund .... East Lansing, MI
Bangs, Vera Richardson .... Dallas, TX
Bangser Klein Rocca & Blum LLP
New York, NY
Bangser, Lawrence S. .... New York, NY
Bangser, Michael R. .... New York, NY
Bangser, Paul M.
Environmental Protection Agency, Office of the General Counsel, GV
Banham, Elizabeth A. .... San Diego, CA
Bani, Arya .... Los Angeles, CA
Bania, Donald W. .... Trevose, PA
Bania, Joseph Charles .... Hamburg, NY
Bania, Montesano & Winokur, P.C.
Hamburg, NY
Baniadam, Behfar .... San Diego, CA
Baniak, Michael H. .... Evanston, IL
Baniak Nicholas Pine & Gannon
Evanston, IL
Baniassadi, Mohammad .... Chicago, IL
Banich, Catherine .... Atlanta, GA
Banich, William R., P.C. .... La Salle, IL
Banick, G. Michael .... Atlanta, GA
Banick, Lisa A. .... Bozeman, MT
Banick, Richard S. .... Miami, FL
Baniewicz, Evelyn G. .... Chicago, IL
Baniewicz, Joseph P. .... Treasury Department, Internal Revenue Service, GV
Banihashemi, James .... Mechanicsburg, PA
Bani-Jamali, Maryam .... Houston, TX
Banik, Michael K. .... Elkhart, IN
Banik & Renner .... Elkhart, IN
Banik, Stephen J. .... Wellsboro, PA
Banina, Daniel C. .... Peru, IN
Banino, Bartholomew J. .... New York, NY
Banino, Charles G. .... New York, NY
Banis, Denise M. .... Wadsworth, IL
Banis, Lynn .... Windsor Locks, CT
Banish, Jeffery R. .... Atlanta, GA
Banister, Barclay Walden .... Paducah, KY
Banister, D. Ross .... Baton Rouge, LA
Banister, David Gerald .... Gaylord, MI
Banister, Eleanor .... Atlanta, GA
Banister, John H. .... Oakland, CA
Banister, John R. .... Palm Beach, FL
Banister, John R., III .... Austin, TX
Banister, Michael E. .... San Francisco, CA
Banister, Patience O. .... Stonington, CT
Baniszewski, Chris R. .... Phoenix, AZ
Baniszewski, Joseph J. .... Baltimore, MD
Bank, Andrew W. .... New York, NY
Bank, Arnold R. .... Garden City, NY
Bank, Brigeda D. .... Walnut Creek, CA
Bank, Douglas M. .... Garden City, NY
Bank, Edward P. .... New York, NY
Bank, Ellyn I. .... New York, NY
Bank, Ellyn Pildes .... Chicago, IL
Bank, Gladys S. .... Garden City, NY
Bank, Glenn H. .... New York, NY
Bank, H. Randy .... Columbus, OH
Bank, Harold W. .... Washington, DC
Bank, Holden J. .... Boulder, CO
Bank, Ira Eugene .... Los Angeles, CA
Bank, Jason W. .... Bloomfield Hills, MI
Bank, John S. .... Chicago, IL
Bank, Jonathan F. .... Los Angeles, CA
Bank Law Services .... San Francisco, CA
Bank, Lawrence H. .... Closter, NJ
Bank, Leonard S. .... Victorville, CA
Bank, Malvin E. .... Cleveland, OH
Bank, Mark A. .... Birmingham, MI
Bank, Melvin A. .... Philadelphia, PA
Bank, Michael S. .... White Plains, NY
Bank, Richard D. .... Glenside, PA
Bank, Richard K. .... Washington, DC
Bank, Rita M. .... Washington, DC
Bank, Scott A. .... Philadelphia, PA
Bank, Susan Kantor
Federal Deposit Insurance Corporation, Trial Litigation Section, GV
Bank, Walter M. .... San Francisco, CA
Banke, Barbara R. .... Santa Rosa, CA
Banke, Harold R. .... Jonesboro, GA
Banke, Jacqueline S. .... Fort Lauderdale, FL
Banke, John R. .... Murrysville, PA
Banke, John R., II .... Murrysville, PA
Banke, Karlton V. .... Jonesboro, GA
Banke, Kathy M. .... Oakland, CA
Banken, Jos. L. .... Fairmont, WV
Bankendorf, Elliott C. .... Chicago, IL
Bankenstein, Bruce C. .... York, PA
Banker, Alan .... Bellaire, OH
St. Clairsville, OH
Banker, Brooks, Jr. .... New York, NY
Banker, Charles .... Appleton, WI
Banker, Charles A., III .... McAllen, TX
Banker, Charles D. .... Coral Springs, FL
Banker, Christopher R. .... Greenbelt, MD
Banker, David C. .... Tampa, FL
Banker, Elizabeth A. .... Washington, DC
Banker, Felice .... New York, NY
Banker, Hilary C. .... Buffalo, NY
Banker, Jan G. .... Houston, TX
Banker, John A. .... Show Low, AZ
Banker, Marcia A. .... Cincinnati, OH
Banker, Martin H. .... New York, NY
Banker, Megan .... Bellaire, OH
Banker, Paul A. .... Minneapolis, MN
Banker, Robert E. .... Tampa, FL

Banker, Stephen M. .... New York, NY
Banker & White .... Bellaire, OH
St. Clairsville, OH
Bankers, Melodie Hoagland .... Olympia, WA
Bankert & Associates, P.C. .... Fairfax, VA
Bankert, Joseph E. .... Fairfax, VA
Bankert, Pamela B. .... Brewster, MA
Bankert, Robert A. .... New Hartford, NY
Bankes, Paul J., Jr. .... Bellmawr, NJ
Philadelphia, PA
Bankes, Russell G. .... Van Nuys, CA
Bankester, Daniel T. .... Robertsdale, AL
Bankester, Daniel T., P.C.
Bay Minette, AL
Robertsdale, AL
Bankey, Jill A. .... Detroit, MI
Bankey, Marianne .... Liverpool, NY
Bankhead, Corey F. .... Carthage, TX
Bankhead, John R. .... Madisonville, TX
Bankhead Law Firm .... Carthage, TX
Bankhead, Murray M. .... San Diego, CA
Bankhead Nesthus & Scalone LLP
San Diego, CA
Bankhead & Savage .... Jasper, AL
Bankhead, Steven C. .... Dallas, TX
Bankhead, Tom .... Carthage, TX
Bankhead Bellinger, Sherry .... Houston, TX
Bankier, M. Adam .... Boca Raton, FL
Bankler, Scott B. .... San Antonio, TX
Banko, James R. .... New York, NY
Banko, Nicholas .... San Francisco, CA
Banko, Stephen L., Jr. .... Harrisburg, PA
Bankoff, Joseph R. .... Atlanta, GA
Bankowitz, Frank J. .... Orlando, FL
Bankowski, Carolyn A. .... Boston, MA
Bankruptcy Attorney, A, P.C.
Birmingham, AL
Bankruptcy Law Office, A
Los Angeles, CA
Banks, A. Bowdre, Jr. .... New Orleans, LA
Banks, Andrew K. .... Cincinnati, OH
Banks, Antoinette L. .... New York, NY
Banks & Associates, P.C. .... St. Louis, MO
Banks & Banks .... Elizabethton, TN
Banks & Banks, P.C. .... San Antonio, TX
Banks, Barbara G. .... Coral Springs, FL
Banks, Barbara S. .... Lakewood, CO
Banks, Barton M. .... Philadelphia, PA
Banks, Barton R. .... Rapid City, SD
Banks, Brian D. .... Springfield, MA
Banks, Britt D. .... Denver, CO
Banks, Brooksher T. .... North Little Rock, AR
Banks, Bruce J. .... Ridgefield, CT
Banks, Burt E. .... San Francisco, CA
Banks, CaraLyn .... Las Cruces, NM
Banks, Carl J. .... Columbia City, IN
Banks, Carole A. .... Tampa, FL
Banks, Cecily Venable .... Providence, RI
Banks, Charles .... Kingman, KS
Banks, Charles A. .... Little Rock, AR
Banks, Charles G., Jr. .... Mount Kisco, NY
Banks, Christine .... San Francisco, CA
Banks, Cole G. .... Evansville, IN
Banks, Curran & Keefe, LLP
Mount Kisco, NY
White Plains, NY
Yonkers, NY
Banks, Cynthia Marie .... Baltimore, MD
Banks, Dana Diane .... San Angelo, TX
Banks, Daniel B., Jr. .... Huntsville, AL
Banks, Danielle .... Philadelphia, PA
Banks, Darrell R. .... Lansing, MI
Banks, Darrin W. .... Paintsville, KY
Banks, David .... Philadelphia, PA
Banks, David F.E. .... Honolulu, HI
Banks, David S. .... Edmonds, WA
Banks, Diane Hall .... Salt Lake City, UT
Banks, Don H. .... Palm Springs, CA
Banks, Donald B. .... Minneapolis, MN
Banks, Donald J. .... Panama City, FL
Banks, Edison G., II .... Whitesburg, KY
Banks, Edward G., Jr. .... Salisbury, MD
Banks, Emile, & Associates, LLC
Madison, WI
Milwaukee, WI
Banks, Emile H., Jr. .... Milwaukee, WI
Banks, Eric D. .... Detroit, MI
Banks, Eric Kendall .... St. Louis, MO
Banks, Eric N. .... Treasury Department, Office of the Inspector General, GV
Banks, Estill D., II .... Lexington, KY
Banks, F. David .... Louisville, KY
Banks, F. Douglas .... Charlotte, NC
Banks, Fred L., Jr. .... Jackson, MS
Banks, G. Patterson .... Brownsville, TN
Banks, Gary .... Boston, MA
Banks, Gary .... Brighton, MI
Banks, Gary L. .... San Angelo, TX
Banks, Gerald A. .... Dallas, TX
Banks, Gerald W. .... Toledo, OH
Banks, Gilbert A., Jr. .... Forsyth, GA
Banks, Glen P. .... New York, NY
Banks, Gloria J. .... Wilmington, DE
Banks, Gretchen Quattlebaum
Minneapolis, MN
Banks Gruen Shapiro & Gettinger, LLP
Mount Kisco, NY
Peekskill, NY
White Plains, NY
Banks, Halmon L. .... Philadelphia, PA
Banks, Helene R. .... New York, NY
Banks, Holly Godfrey .... Port Orchard, WA
Banks, Howard O. .... Dallas, TX
Banks & Imatani, P.C. .... Lakewood, CO
Banks, J. Donald .... Mobile, AL
Banks, J. Taylor .... Washington, DC
Banks, James C. .... Tallahassee, FL
Banks, James E., Jr. .... Charlotte, NC

Barajas, John C., P.C., The Law Office of … Denver, CO
Barak, Alex T., P.A., Law Offices of … Hollywood, FL
Barak, Alex Tobias … Hollywood, FL
Barak, Deborah … Los Angeles, CA
Barak, Joanne H. … Palisades, NY
Barak, Mark J. … Kirkland, WA
Barak, Ronald S. … Los Angeles, CA
Barak, Terry A. … Glendale, CA
Barak, Uriel … New York, NY
Baraka, Larry W. … Dallas, TX
Barakat, Barbara A. … Boston, MA
Barakat, Myrna A. … New York, NY
Barakat, Susan L. … Troy, NY
Barakatt, James … Modesto, CA
Barakis, Terry Flett … Dallas, TX
Barald, Patricia A. … Washington, DC
Barall, Herbert … Hartford, CT
Barall, Stanley M. … Bloomfield, CT
Barall, Victor … Brooklyn, NY
Baram, Art … Los Angeles, CA
Baram, David A. … Bloomfield, CT
Baram, David G. … Los Angeles, CA
Baram, Michael S. … Boston, MA
Baram-Clothier, Evelyn M. … Philadelphia, PA
Baran, Andrea Gail … Kansas City, MO
Baran, Andrew T. … Detroit, MI
Baran, Artie … San Diego, CA
Baran, Barbara … Chicago, IL
Baran, Dorothy … Phoenix, AZ
Baran, Edward C. … Mansfield, OH
Baran, Fred R. … Holyoke, MA
Baran, Gregory G. … Mansfield, OH
Baran, Heidi L. … Dayton, OH
Baran & Houle Law Offices … Flagstaff, AZ
Baran, Howard A. … Killingworth, CT
Baran, J. Conrad … Flagstaff, AZ
Baran, Jan Witold … Washington, DC
Baran, Jeralyn H. … Chicago, IL
Baran, John M. … Los Angeles, CA
Baran, Lou M. … Vancouver, WA
Baran, Margaret Esola … Seattle, WA
Baran, Mark R. … Atlanta, GA
Baran, Mary Elizabeth … New Haven, CT
Baran, Matthew J. … Palm Desert, CA
Baran, Morris P. … Jenkintown, PA
Baran, Nancy … Newark, NJ
Baran, Piper, Tarkowsky, Fitzgerald & Theis Co., L.P.A. … Cleveland, OH
Columbus, OH
Lima, OH
Mansfield, OH
Toledo, OH
Twinsburg, OH
Baran, Robert J. … Irvine, CA
Baran, Susan D. … Bridgeport, CT
Baran, Tama Vail … Washington, DC
Baran, Todd S. … Portland, OR
Baran, William B. … Chicago, IL
Baranan, Aaron … Atlanta, GA
Baranauskas, Christina M. … Ypsilanti, MI
Barancik, Martin B. … Piscataway, NJ
Barancik, Tia S. … New York, NY
Baranco, Gordon S. … Oakland, CA
Barandes, Gerald … New York, NY
Barandes, Max … New York, NY
Barandes, Robert … New York, NY
Barandiaran, Jocelyn F. L. … New York, NY
Baranello, Dominic J. … Centereach, NY
Baranello, James J. … Cortland, NY
Baraniak, John R., Jr. … Boston, MA
Baranko, George S. … Department of Justice, Antitrust Division, GV
Baranko, Joseph R., Jr. … Hazleton, PA
Baranoff, Adrienne R. … Staten Island, NY
Baranoff, Evan C. … Washington, DC
Baranoff, Susan L. … Las Vegas, NV
Baranov, Michael M. … Los Angeles, CA
Baranov, Robert L. … Tarzana, CA
Baranov, Suzanne P. … Culver City, CA
Baranov & Wittenberg, LLP … Los Angeles, CA
Baranow, David W. … Anchorage, AK
Baranowicz, Michael A. … Garden City, NY
Baranowicz, Peter S. … Sarasota, FL
Baranowski, Carl … Sioux City, IA
Baranowski, Dennis … San Bernardino, CA
Baranowski, Edwin M. … Columbus, OH
Baranowski, Joel M. … Washington, DC
Baranowski, Robert E. … Chicago, IL
Baranowski, Stanley J. … North Olmsted, OH
Baranski, Amy A. … Detroit, MI
Baranski, John J., Jr. … Carlisle, PA
Baransky, Ulana M. … Chicago, IL
Barany, Gizelle A. … Oakland, CA
Baraona, Robert C. … Barberton, OH
Barasa, J. Laurence … Chicago, IL
Barasa and Larkin … Chicago, IL
Barasa, Robert A. … Lake Forest, IL
Barasch, Adam N. … Walnut Creek, CA
Barasch, Amy P. … New York, NY
Barasch, Clarence S. … New York, NY
Barasch, Clarence S., Law Firm of … New York, NY
Barasch, David M. … Harrisburg, PA
Barasch, Elizabeth A. … New York, NY
Barasch, Lionel A. … New York, NY
Barasch, Mal L. … New York, NY
Barasch, Matthew M. … Los Angeles, CA
Barasch & McGarry, P.C. … New York, NY
Barasch, Melvin S. … Woodside, NY
Barasch, Michael … New York, NY
Barasch, Patricia A. … Cherry Hill, NJ
Barasch, Sheldon … New York, NY
Barasch, Spencer C. … Fort Worth, TX
Barasch, Stephen … Alpine, NJ
Barasch, Stuart T. … Los Angeles, CA
Barash, A. Jeffrey … Bay Harbor Islands, FL
Miami Beach, FL
Barash, Anthony H. … Greenville, SC
Barash, Barry M. … Galesburg, IL
Barash, Beth S. … New York, NY
Barash, Cory A. … Kansas City, KS
Barash, Eyal Hanan … Washington, DC
Barash, James Robert … Colorado Springs, CO
Barash, Jonathan Avi … Atlanta, GA
Barash, Julia … Hillsdale, NJ
Barash, Louis J. … New York, NY
Barash, Louisa … Seattle, WA
Barash, Mark D. … Newton, MA
Barash, Martin R. … Los Angeles, CA
Barash, Philip … Forest Hills, NY
Barash, Salli J. … New York, NY
Barash, Shula Roth … Beverly Hills, CA
Barash & Stoerzbach, P.C. … Galesburg, IL
Galva, IL
Barasha, William C. … Arlington Heights, IL
Barassi, Louis W. … Tucson, AZ
Barat, Dorothy A. … Washington, DC
Barat, Scott E. … McLean, VA
Barath, William J. … Columbus, OH
Baratt, Norman J. … Rochester, NY
Baratta, Anthony … Brooklyn, NY
Baratta, Anthony J. … Huntingdon Valley, PA
Baratta, Anthony P. … Huntingdon Valley, PA
Baratta, Bruno … Mineola, NY
Baratta, Cheryl Lynn … Somerville, NJ
Baratta, Christopher R. … Mount Clemens, MI
Baratta & Fenerty, Ltd. … Huntingdon Valley, PA
Baratta & Goldstein … New York, NY
Baratta, Joseph … Chicago, IL
Baratta, Joseph P. … New York, NY
Baratta, P. Michael … Boston, MA
Baratta, Renald S. … Easton, PA
Baratta, Robert M., Jr. … Chicago, IL
Baratta & Russell, P.C. … Huntingdon Valley, PA
Philadelphia, PA
Baratti, David G. … Minneapolis, MN
Baratti, Mark A. … Haddonfield, NJ
Barattini, Bernadette … Harrisburg, PA
Barattini, Patricia Pittman … Covington, LA
Baraty, Cheryl P. … Milwaukee, WI
Baratz, Alan J. … Parsippany, NJ
Baratz, Arnold P. … Indianapolis, IN
Baratz, Lisa Diamond … Hollywood, FL
Barauskas, Andrew L. … St. Petersburg, FL
Baravarian, Yas Yadegar … Beverly Hills, CA
Baray, Camellia … Martinez, CA
Baraz, Marshall J. … Chicago, IL
Barazzutti, Majda … San Francisco, CA
Barb, Donald E. … Columbus, OH
Barba, Arnold … Los Angeles, CA
Barba, Daniel L. … Berkeley, CA
Barba, Derek B. … Miami, FL
Barba, James J. … Albany, NY
Barba, John W. … Morristown, NJ
Barba, Juan J. … Santa Ana, CA
Barba, Kenneth R. … Springfield, MA
Barba, Michael D. … San Bernardino, CA
Barba, Paul J. … Tustin, CA
Barba, Robert A. … Chicago, IL
Barba, Ronald J. … Milford, CT
Barba, Thomas A. … Boca Raton, FL
Barba, Thomas M. … Washington, DC
Barbaccia, Joseph A. … Freeport, NY
Barbadoro, Nicholas … Dedham, MA
Barbadoro, Paul J. … Concord, NH
Barbadoro, Paul N. … Braintree, MA
Barbagallo, Jennifer Hatfield … Shepherdsville, KY
Barbagallo, Ralph A., Jr. … North Andover, MA
Barbagelata, Robert D. … San Francisco, CA
Barbahen, Paul W. … Chicago, IL
Barbakoff, Dean A. … Carle Place, NY
Barbakoff, Lee R. … Chicago, IL
Barbakoff, Marc L. … Miami, FL
Barbakoff Zazove & Glick, Chartered … Chicago, IL
Barbakow, Daniel R. … Los Angeles, CA
Barbakow & Lerner … Los Angeles, CA
Barbalunga, Alfred A. … Pittsfield, MA
Barbalunga, Ermino S., Jr. … Pittsfield, MA
Barbalunga, Patricia A. … Springfield, MA
Barbanel, Alan H. … Los Angeles, CA
San Diego, CA
Barbanel, Debra Spangler … Los Angeles, CA
Barbanel, Gary A. … New York, NY
Barbanel, Geraldine … Long Island City, NY
Barbanel, Jack A. … Princeton, NJ
Barbanel, Roberta J. … Cincinnati, OH
Barbanell, Natalie A. … Los Angeles, CA
Barbano, Peter K. … Paramus, NJ
Barbar, Kimberly Lynn … Fort Lauderdale, FL
Barbar, Thomas J. … Cambridge, MA
Barbara, Jacqueline F. … Shelton, CT
Barbara, Joanne … Garden City, NY
Barbara, Michael … Wichita, KS
Barbara, Michael A. … Topeka, KS
Barbara, Scott M. … Seattle, WA
Barbare, Ronald F. … Greenville, SC
Barbaree, Tracey T. … Atlanta, GA
Barbaresi, George P. … Stamford, CT
Barbarette, Michael … Gainesville, FL
Barbaris, Ernest A. … Glen Rock, NJ
Barbaris, Jennifer … Denville, NJ
Barbarisi, Alexander … Newark, NJ
Barbarisi, Christopher A. … Newark, NJ
Barbarisi, Dennis A. … Fort Walton Beach, FL
Barbarita, Jennifer L. … Bakersfield, CA
Barbarito, Patricia M. … Denville, NJ
Barbaro, Bruno … Sun Valley, CA
Barbaro, Frank P., (A Professional Corporation) … Santa Ana, CA
Barbaro, Louis F. … Brooklyn, NY
Barbaro, Philip, Jr. … Pasadena, CA
Barbaro, Stephen V. … Brooklyn, NY
Barbarosh, Alison M. … Costa Mesa, CA
Barbarosh, Craig A. … Costa Mesa, CA
Barbarosh, Keith S. … Florham Park, NJ
New York, NY
Barbarotto, Nicholas J. … San Francisco, CA
Barbaroux, Paula E. … Grapevine, TX
Barbarowicz, Robert P. … Calabasas, CA
Barbarula, Michael Jon … Norwalk, CT
Barbaruolo, Paula M. … Albany, NY
Barbary, George F. … Dallas, TX
Barbas, Andrew M. … Southfield, MI
Barbas, Charles J. … Boston, MA
Barbas, Rex Martin … Tampa, FL
Barbas, Stephen M. … Lakeland, FL
Palm Harbor, FL
Tampa, FL
Barbas Weed Koenig Nuñez & Wheeley
Lakeland, FL
New Port Richey, FL
Palm Harbor, FL
Tampa, FL
Barbash, Barry P. … Washington, DC
Barbash, David M. … Boston, MA
Barbash, Joseph … New York, NY
Barbat, Edward F. … San Francisco, CA
Barbatano, Salvatore A. … Los Angeles, CA
Chicago, IL
Barbati, Elia, Jr. … Bound Brook, NJ
Barbato, Carl F. … Virginia Beach, VA
Barbato, Daniel M. … Baton Rouge, LA
Lafayette, LA
Barbato, Martin Frank … Verona, NJ
Barbato, Paul M. … Atlanta, GA
Barbatoe, Ronald P. … Victorville, CA
Barbatsuly, George P. … Newark, NJ
Barbazan, Carmen … Denville, NJ
Barbe, David … Spokane, WA
Barbe, J. Kenneth … Casper, WY
Barbe, Laurie Crytser … Morgantown, WV
Barbe Law Office … Spokane, WA
Barbe, R. David … Roanoke, VA
Barbeau, AndréJ. … Concord, NH
Barbeau & Hake … Batavia, OH
Barbeau, James B. … Batavia, OH
Barbeau, Joseph M. … Palo Alto, CA
Barbee, David S. … Youngstown, OH
Barbee, Donald C., Jr. … Tampa, FL
Barbee & Gehrt, L.L.P. … Dallas, TX
Barbee, Gregory P. … Los Angeles, CA
Barbee, Jon R. … Novato, CA
Barbee, Linton E. … Dallas, TX
Barbee, Michael P. … Los Angeles, CA
Barbee, Mills E. … Hernando, MS
Barbee, Peter Ashton … New Orleans, LA
Barbee, Robert D. … Dallas, TX
Barbee, Roger … Bellevue, WA
Barbee, Ronald … Greensboro, NC
Barbee, Rustam A. … Honolulu, HI
Barbee & Stern, L.L.C. … New Orleans, LA
Barbee-Wooten, Daphne E. … Honolulu, HI
Barbella, Rosemarie … Milford, NJ
Barbeosch, William P. … New York, NY
Barber, Albert W., Jr. … Owensboro, KY
Barber, Alison M. … Boston, MA
Barber, Andrew L. … San Francisco, CA
Barber, Ann H. … Encinitas, CA
Barber, Anna Gonzalez … San Antonio, TX
Barber, Anna W. … New York, NY
Barber, Annette M. … Sherman Oaks, CA
Barber, Anthony L. … Lexington, KY
Barber & Associates, P.A. … Greenville, NC
Barber, Barbara L. … Columbus, OH
Barber and Barber, P.C. … Poteau, OK
Barber, Barry D. … Hope, AR
Prescott, AR
Barber & Bartz, A Professional Corporation
Oklahoma City, OK
Tulsa, OK
Barber, Beatrice … Brooklyn, NY
Barber, Belva Brooks … Poteau, OK
Barber, Bernard B. … Berkeley, CA
Barber, Betty … Miami, FL
Barber, Bill … Owensboro, KY
Barber, Bonnie A. … Chicago, IL
Barber, Brian H. … Shreveport, LA
Barber, Bryan M. … San Francisco, CA
Barber, Bryant D. … Phoenix, AZ
Barber, Carl H. … Henderson, TX
Barber, Catherine Ann … Schenectady, NY
Barber, Catherine M. … Fairborn, OH
Barber, Charles F. … Greenwich, CT
Barber, Charles F. … Clearwater, FL
Barber, Charles K. … Washington, DC
Barber, Christian P. … Department of Labor, Office of the Solicitor, GV
Barber, Christopher D. … Fort Lauderdale, FL
Barber, Christopher J. … Chicago, IL
Barber, Christopher K. … East Norriton, PA
Barber, Christy S. … Waco, TX
Barber, Cindy L. … Monticello, NY
Barber, Clark … Salinas, CA
Barber, Claudia, Law Offices of … Laurel, MD
Barber, Clifford M. … Montgomery, NY
Barber, D. Brett … Mishawaka, IN
Barber, D. Linden … Merrillville, IN
Barber, D. Scott … San Diego, CA
Barber, Darin W. … La Habra, CA
Barber, David A. … Hazard, KY
Prestonsburg, KY
Barber, David Bryce … Olive Hill, KY
Barber, David H. … Dillon, CO
Barber, David J. … Boise, ID
Barber, David J. … Watertown, MA
Barber, Diana … Washington, IL
Barber, Diana Strichard … Atlanta, GA
Barber, Diane M. … Franklin Center, PA
Barber, Donald W. … Anaheim, CA
Barber, Duncan E. … Denver, CO
Barber, Earle N., Jr. … Philadelphia, PA
Barber, Elizabeth Cassidy … Boca Raton, FL
Barber, Elmer P. … St. Petersburg, FL
Barber, Emerson, Springer, Zinn & Murray, L.C. … Lawrence, KS
Barber, Florence I. … New York, NY
Barber, Francine M. … Treasury Department, Office of the General Counsel, GV
Barber, Frank D. … Jackson, MS
Barber, Frank D., III … New Orleans, LA
Barber, Frank T. … Scottsdale, AZ
Barber, Frank T., III … Randolph, MA
Barber, Frederick W. … Oceanside, CA
Barber, Gail F. … Homewood, AL
Barber, Gary S. … Hollywood, FL
Barber, Geo. H. … Albany, NY
Barber, George H. … Dallas, TX
Barber & Gorss … Montgomery, NY
Barber, Grayson … Princeton, NJ
Barber, Gretchen B. … San Francisco, CA
Barber, H. Earl … Miami, FL
Barber, Hamilton & Shoulders … Evansville, IN
Barber, Herman L., Jr. … Crown Point, IN
Barber, James C., Law Offices of … Dallas, TX
Barber, James E. … Wauseon, OH
Barber, James M. … Binghamton, NY
Barber, James M. … Charleston, WV
Barber, James P. … San Francisco, CA
Barber, James R., III … Columbia, SC
Barber, James S. … Chicago, IL
Barber, Janice A. … Buffalo, NY
Barber, Jay Michael … Atlanta, GA
Barber, Jay O. … Tampa, FL
Barber, Jeffrey R. … Jackson, MS
Barber, Jennifer L. … Wilmington, DE
Barber, Jeremy W. … Los Angeles, CA
Barber, Jesse C. … Babson Park, FL
Barber, Joanne M. … Seattle, WA
Barber, John C. … Santa Ana, CA
Barber, John C., Jr. … Buffalo, NY
Barber, John Fay … St. Charles, MO
Barber, John J. … Erie, PA
Barber, John L. … Los Angeles, CA
Barber, John L. … Greensboro, NC
Barber, John L., Jr. … Eugene, OR
Barber, John Paul … Newton, MS
Barber, John T. … Lancaster, PA
Barber, Jon H. … St. Petersburg, FL
Barber, Kaper, Stamm & Robinson … Delta, OH
Toledo, OH
Wauseon, OH
Barber, Kathryn M. … Albany, NY
Barber, Keith D. … Indianapolis, IN
Barber, Kevin E. … New York, NY
Barber, Kevin S. … Philadelphia, PA
Barber, Kirk … Temecula, CA
Barber, Kristopher … Dallas, TX
Barber, Laurie E. … San Diego, CA
Barber, Lawrence L., Jr., P.C. … Odessa, TX
Barber, Lewis, Jr. … Oklahoma City, OK
Barber, Lisa Hunn … Newtown Square, PA
Barber, Lynn Eileen … Raleigh, NC
Barber, M. David … Birmingham, AL
Barber, Madeleine G. … Philadelphia, PA
Barber, Mark … Renton, WA
Barber, Mark A. … Marietta, GA
Barber, Mark H. … San Diego, CA
Barber, Mark H. … Akron, OH
Barber, Mark H. … Houston, TX
Barber, Martha Gayle … Charlotte, NC
Barber, McCaskill, Jones & Hale, P.A. … Little Rock, AR
Barber, Michael D. … Atlanta, GA
Barber, Michael J. … Kissimmee, FL
Barber, Michael L. … Greensboro, NC
Barber, Michele L. … Los Angeles, CA
Barber, Monroe Dykes, Jr. … Birmingham, AL
Jacksonville, FL
Atlanta, GA
Barber, Monty C. … Dallas, TX
Barber, Oliver H., Jr. … Louisville, KY
Barber, Paul A. … Colorado Springs, CO
Barber, Paul D. … Kansas City, MO
Barber, Paul D. … Albuquerque, NM
Barber, Peggy Chang … Washington, DC
Barber, Peter E. … Birmingham, AL
Barber, Peter G. … Albany, NY
Barber, Peter K. … Warren, NJ
Barber, Philip G. … New York, NY
Barber, Phillip D. … Nashville, TN
Barber, Phillip M. … Boise, ID
Barber, Ray A. … Orlando, FL
Barber, Raymond P. … Cincinnati, OH
Barber, Rhonda Lee … Jackson, AL
Barber, Richard A. … Binghamton, NY
Barber, Richard D., Jr. … Salem, OR
Barber, Richard D., Sr. … Salem, OR
Barber, Richard E. … Galesburg, IL
Barber, Richard J., Jr. … Rye, NY
Barber, Robert Cushman … Boston, MA
Barber, Robert J. … Surfside Beach, SC
Barber, Robert, Jr. … Tucson, AZ
Barber, Robert K. … Berkeley, CA

Barber, Robert W. ... Chicago, IL
Barber, Robin L. ... Mechanicsburg, PA
Barber, Ron B. ... Tulsa, OK
Barber, Ronald D. ... Pittsburgh, PA
Barber, Rosamond A. ... New York, NY
Barber, Russell V. ... Poteau, OK
Barber, Sally Nan ... Charlotte, NC
Barber, Scott A. ... Garland, TX
Barber, Scott D. ... Elk Grove Village, IL
Barber, Scott W. ... Alexandria, VA
Barber Segatto Hoffee and Hines
Springfield, IL
Barber, Sharpe & Rosenberger
Philadelphia, PA
Barber, Shelley A. ... Houston, TX
Barber, Stacey S. ... Lubbock, TX
Barber, Staci B. ... New York, NY
Barber, Stephan A. ... San Jose, CA
Barber, Stephen H.
Department of Transportation, U. S. Coast Guard, GV
Barber, Stephen J. ... St. Louis, MO
Barber, Stephen M. ... Cromwell, CT
Barber, Stephen Richard ... Marietta, GA
Barber, Steve ... Evansville, IN
Barber, Steven J. ... Los Angeles, CA
Barber, Steven J. ... Hartford, CT
Barber, Steven K. ... Tampa, FL
Barber, Susan L. ... Lake Wales, FL
Barber, Terri A. ... Los Angeles, CA
Barber, Terry K. ... Lincoln, NE
Barber, Thomas R. ... Houston, TX
Barber, Timothy C. ... Greenville, NC
Barber, Timothy G. ... Charlotte, NC
Barber, Timothy N. ... Charleston, WV
Barber, Vaughn J. ... Chicago, IL
Barber, W. Henry, Jr. ... Gainesville, FL
Barber, W. Keith ... Statesboro, GA
Barber, W. Scott ... Columbus, GA
Barber, Wade ... Hillsborough, NC
Barber, Wilfred L. ... Lindsay, OK
Barber, William A., Jr. ... Dallas, TX
Barber, William G. ... Austin, TX
Barber, William G., III ... Austin, TX
Barber, William J. ... Monroe, CT
Barber, William James ... Arvada, CO
Barber, William L. ... Anaheim, CA
Barbera, Annette L. ... Somerset, PA
Barbera, C. Alexandre ... Sacramento, CA
Barbera, Charles F. ... Metairie, LA
Barbera, Clapper, Beener, Rullo & Melvin
Somerset, PA
Barbera, Denise M. ... Baltimore, MD
Barbera, Janine A. ... Miller Place, NY
Barbera, Jerome J., III ... Thibodaux, LA
Barbera, Joanne M. ... Kansas City, MO
Barbera, John J. ... Bronx, NY
Barbera, John J. ... Somerset, PA
Barbera, Joseph J. ... Pelham, NY
Barbera, Melanie R. ... Somerset, PA
Barbera, Nathaniel A. ... Somerset, PA
Barbera, Richard ... Medina, OH
Barbera, Ronald D. ... Brea, CA
Barbera, Thomas A., Jr.
Haddon Township, NJ
Barbera, Vincent J. ... Somerset, PA
Barbera, William T. ... Pelham, NY
Barbercheck, Catherine H. ... Champaign, IL
Barberi, Joseph T. ... Mount Pleasant, MI
Barberi, Joseph T., P.C.
Mount Pleasant, MI
Barberi, Robert O. ... Westport, CT
Barberic, Edward M. ... Washington, DC
Barberich, Kirk A. ... Phoenix, AZ
Barberio, Beatriz C. ... Miami, FL
Barberio, Francis P. ... New Haven, CT
Barberio, Staley & Moquet ... New Haven, CT
Barberio, Stephen J. ... Birmingham, AL
Barberis, Dana M. ... Huntington, NY
Barberis, Patricia F. ... Torrance, CA
Barber-Mingo, Eric R. ... Cambridge, MA
Barbero, Carol L. ... Washington, DC
Barbero, Ignacio ... Dallas, TX
Barbero-Portman, Mary Beth
Oklahoma City, OK
Barberousse, Bob D. ... Santa Fe, NM
Barberousse, Wendy E. ... Baton Rouge, LA
Barbery, Paul S. ... Mooresville, NC
Barbetta, JoAnn K. ... Wayzata, MN
Barbetta, Joseph A. ... Sarasota, FL
Barbian, John W. ... Sun Prairie, WI
Barbian, W. L. (Skip) ... Long Beach, CA
Barbic, Valerie L. ... Rochester, NY
Barbier & Barbier, P.C.
Grosse Pointe Woods, MI
Barbier, Carl J. ... New Orleans, LA
Barbier, Kelly E. ... New Orleans, LA
Barbier, Margaret Louise ... Seattle, WA
Barbier, Ralph W., III ... Columbia, SC
Barbier, Ralph W., Jr.
Grosse Pointe Woods, MI
Barbier, Robert J. ... New Orleans, LA
Barbier, Timothy J. ... Napoleonville, LA
Barbiere, Janet A. ... Brooklyn, NY
Barbiere, Lawrence E. ... Cincinnati, OH
Barbieri, Albert A., Jr. ... Harvard, MA
Barbieri, Albert M. ... Brooklyn, NY
Barbieri, Alexis L. ... Harrisburg, PA
Barbieri and Associates, A Professional Corporation ... Philadelphia, PA
West Chester, PA
Barbieri, Catherine T. ... Philadelphia, PA
Barbieri, Charles E. ... Lansing, MI
Barbieri, Christina J., & Associates
Philadelphia, PA
Barbieri, Daniel M. ... Hartford, CT
Barbieri, Dean E. ... Alamo, CA
Barbieri, Evans J. ... San Luis Obispo, CA
Barbieri, Francis C., Jr. ... Philadelphia, PA
Barbieri, Frank A., Jr. ... Boca Raton, FL
Barbieri, J. Michael ... Wilton, CA
Barbieri, John A. ... New Britain, CT
Barbieri, John V. ... New York, NY
Barbieri, Joseph N. ... Lexington, KY
Barbieri, Joy ... Santa Ana, CA
Barbieri, Karen R. ... Richmond, CA
Barbieri, Laura D. ... New York, NY
Barbieri, Lisa ... New York, NY
Barbieri, Louis L. ... Spokane, WA
Barbieri, Patricia ... Hawthorne, CA
Barbieri, Patricia A. ... Nutley, NJ
Barbieri, Peter R. ... Framingham, MA
Barbieri, Pietro A. ... Philadelphia, PA
West Chester, PA
Barbieri, Robert J. ... San Francisco, CA
Barbieri & Screnci, P.A. ... Boca Raton, FL
Barbieri, Stephen R. ... San Francisco, CA
Barbieri, T. Mark ... Enfield, CT
Barbieri, Victor J. ... Littleton, CO
Barbieri, Victor J., P.C. ... Littleton, CO
Barbieri, Vito C. ... Lenexa, KS
Barbiero, Anthony F. ... Mineola, NY
New York, NY
White Plains, NY
Barbiero, Anthony V. ... East Islip, NY
Barbiero, Michael L. ... Philadelphia, PA
Barbin, Andrew W. ... Harrisburg, PA
Barbin, Bryan E. ... Harrisburg, PA
Barbin, Debra L. ... Anaheim, CA
Barbin, Harry C. ... Rockledge, PA
Barbin, Jeffrey M. ... Baton Rouge, LA
Barbin & O'Connell ... Rockledge, PA
Barbin, Ryther Lynn ... Wailuku, HI
Barbin, William G. ... Johnstown, PA
Barbire, Paul S. ... Rutherford, NJ
Barbis, Elizabeth M. ... Philadelphia, PA
Barbknecht, Joseph A. ... Dallas, TX
Barbo, Michael J. ... Aurora, CO
Barbolla, Patrick A. ... Fort Worth, TX
Barbolla, Patrick A., P.C. ... Fort Worth, TX
Barbone, Louis M. ... Atlantic City, NJ
Barbor, John H. ... Indiana, PA
Barbor & Vaporis, P.C. ... Indiana, PA
Barborak, Virginia M. ... Lisbon, OH
Barbosa, Edward J. ... Kansas City, MO
Barbosa Garcia LLP ... Los Angeles, CA
Barbosa, Henry S., (P.C.)
Los Angeles, CA
Barbosa, Jose Antonio ... Sacramento, CA
Barbosa, Joseph A. ... New York, NY
Barbosa, Manuel ... Rockford, IL
Barbosa, Mary Helene Rodriguez
Seattle, WA
Barbosa, Patricia ... Huntington Beach, CA
Barbosa, Raymond ... Deerfield, IL
Barbose, Stephen L. ... Santa Rosa, CA
Barbot, Heriberto, Jr. ... Blue Bell, PA
Barbour, Alex ... Wyandotte, MI
Barbour, Alex V. ... Chicago, IL
Barbour, Alyssa R. ... Boca Raton, FL
Barbour, Anita M. ... Seattle, WA
Barbour & Barbour, P.A. ... Asheville, NC
Barbour, Blair S. ... Chicago, IL
Barbour, Carroll ... San Antonio, TX
Barbour, David A. ... Dallas, TX
Barbour, David F.
Federal Mine Safety and Health Review Commission, Office of the Administrative Law Judges, GV
Barbour, David M. ... Norwalk, CT
Barbour, David M. ... Detroit, MI
Barbour, Dennis A. ... Roanoke, VA
Barbour, Elaine Agnes ... Orlando, FL
Barbour, Emily S. ... Dallas, TX
Barbour, Frederick S. ... Asheville, NC
Barbour, Geo. J. ... Walnut Creek, CA
Barbour, Grant A. ... Mill Valley, CA
Barbour, Haley ... Yazoo City, MS
Barbour, Hamilton J. ... Plymouth, MI
Barbour, Hubert U., Jr. ... Atlantic City, NJ
Barbour, Jeptha F. ... Jacksonville, FL
Barbour, Jeptha F., IV ... Yazoo City, MS
Barbour, John A. ... Philadelphia, PA
Pittsburgh, PA
Barbour, John B. ... Russellton, PA
Barbour, John K., Jr. ... Towson, MD
Barbour, John S. ... Detroit, MI
Barbour, John T. ... Ada, MI
Barbour, John T., II ... Maple Shade, NJ
Barbour, Joy Elizabeth ... Atlanta, GA
Barbour, Larry G. ... Houston, TX
Barbour, Mark E. ... Cleveland, OH
Barbour, Maura Henry ... Washington, DC
Barbour, Michael J. ... Blacksburg, VA
Pulaski, VA
Barbour, Monica M. ... Detroit, MI
Barbour, Morton M. ... Island Park, NY
Barbour, R. Kevin ... Poplar Bluff, MO
Barbour, Randall S. ... Winfield, KS
Barbour, Robert G. ... McLean, VA
Barbour, Sasha Edward ... Los Angeles, CA
Barbour, Scott A. ... Albany, NY
Barbour, Sondra Kay ... Los Angeles, CA
Barbour, Stephen E. ... Fort Dodge, IA
Barbour, Susan ... New York, NY
Barbour, Susan Strayhorn ... Asheville, NC
Barbour, Thomas C.
Department of Commerce, Office of the General Counsel, GV
Barbour, Wiley J. ... Yazoo City, MS
Barbour, William E. ... Stockton, CA
Barbour, William G. ... Greensboro, NC
Barbour, William H. ... Yazoo City, MS
Barbour, William H., Jr. ... Jackson, MS
Barbour, Zverina & Buchanan, P.A.
La Plata, MD
Barboza, Philomena A. ... Fall River, MA
Barbrack, Christopher R. ... Princeton, NJ
Barbrack, Joanne H. ... White Plains, NY
Barbre, Steve V. ... New Orleans, LA
Barbrow, Janella L. ... Des Plaines, IL
Barbulescu, Ruxandra ... Washington, DC
Barbur, Peter T. ... New York, NY
Barbuti, Thomas C. ... Baltimore, MD
Barbuto, Richard J ... Mineola, NY
Barby, David W. ... Costa Mesa, CA
Barcal, John J. ... La Habra Heights, CA
Barcan, Reina ... Wilton, CT
Barcan, Stephen E. ... Woodbridge, NJ
Barce, J. Edward ... Fowler, IN
Kentland, IN
Barce, John C. ... Fort Wayne, IN
Barce, John W. ... Fowler, IN
Kentland, IN
Barce, Judson G. ... Fowler, IN
Kentland, IN
Barce & Ryan ... Fowler, IN
Kentland, IN
Barcella, E. Lawrence, Jr.
Washington, DC
Barcellona, Katrina Teresa ... Lakeland, FL
Barcellona, William J. ... Sacramento, CA
Barcelo, John J., III ... Ithaca, NY
Barceló, Reynaldo C. ... San Jose, CA
Barcelona, James D. ... Ann Arbor, MI
Barcelona, John H. ... Hinsdale, IL
Barcelona, John H., Ltd. ... Hinsdale, IL
Barcelona, Laurie A. ... New Orleans, LA
Barcena, Gustavo A. ... Los Angeles, CA
Barch, Ronald A. ... Rockford, IL
Barcham, Deborah S. ... Garden City, NY
Barchas, Rudolf D. ... Boise, ID
Barchas, Samuel I. ... Sonoita, AZ
Barcher, Ann C. ... Poughkeepsie, NY
Barchet, Cynthia ... Columbia, MO
Barchi, David P. ... Warwick, RI
Barchie, Paul F. ... Providence, RI
Barchiesi, John Eric ... Pittsburgh, PA
Barchman, Virginia D. ... Des Moines, IA
Barclay, A. Hayes ... Chicago, IL
Wheaton, IL
Barclay, Albert C., Jr. ... Kingston, NJ
Barclay, Alyson Schlinger ... Fort Mitchell, KY
Barclay, Alyson Schlinger ... St. Louis, MO
Barclay, Andrew W. ... Los Angeles, CA
Barclay, Bernays Thomas ... New York, NY
Barclay, Bert W. ... Orlando, FL
Barclay, Bruce J. ... Santa Clara, CA
Barclay & Bub, P.C. ... Fairfax, VA
Barclay, Byron K. ... Houston, TX
Barclay, Christopher M. ... St. Louis, MO
Barclay, Craig D. ... Columbus, OH
Barclay & Damisch, Ltd. ... Chicago, IL
Wheaton, IL
Barclay, David A. ... Fort Lauderdale, FL
Barclay, David C. ... Annapolis, MD
Barclay, David J. ... Chicago, IL
Barclay, David L. ... Salt Lake City, UT
Barclay, David M. ... Cherry Hill, NJ
Barclay, Elizabeth C. ... Fairfax, VA
Barclay, Francis W. ... Alturas, CA
Barclay, George N.
General Services Administration, Office of the General Counsel, GV
Barclay & Goering, P.C. ... Phoenix, AZ
Barclay, H. Douglas ... Syracuse, NY
Barclay, James ... Monterey Park, CA
Barclay, James M. ... Tallahassee, FL
Barclay, Jeffrey D. ... Chicago, IL
Barclay, Jerry Sanford ... Huntsville, AL
Barclay, John A. ... Newport Beach, CA
Barclay, John Williams ... Hartford, CT
Barclay, Jon Neil ... Denver, CO
Barclay Law Corporation
Newport Beach, CA
Barclay, Lester L. ... Chicago, IL
Barclay, Linda J. ... Salt Lake City, UT
Barclay, Michael ... Palo Alto, CA
Barclay, Mike ... Alpine, TX
Barclay, Pamela G. ... St. Paul, MN
Barclay, Ralph K., Jr. ... Greensburg, PA
Uniontown, PA
Barclay, Robert A. ... Alturas, CA
Barclay, Robert C., III ... Portsmouth, VA
Barclay, Robert C., IV ... Portsmouth, VA
Barclay, Robin M. ... Medford, MA
Barclay, Stephanie ... San Francisco, CA
Barclay, Steven C. ... Phoenix, AZ
Barclay, Steven W. ... Mercer Island, WA
Barclay, William A. ... Syracuse, NY
Barcley, Robert D. ... St. Petersburg, FL
Barclift, Robert P. ... Fort Myers, FL
Barclift, William C. ... Birmingham, AL
Barclift, Zeanta Jill ... St. Louis Park, MN
Barco and Barco ... Meadville, PA
Barco, Carroll S. ... Orlando, FL
Barco, Susan E. ... Durham, NC
Barco, Yolanda G. ... Meadville, PA
Barcott & Christopherson
Mount Vernon, WA
Barcott, Joseph N. ... Mount Vernon, WA
Barcott, Michael A. ... Seattle, WA
Barcroft, Michael W. ... Greenville, SC
Barcus, Ben F., The Law Offices of
Tacoma, WA
Barcus, E. Mark ... Tulsa, OK
Barcus, Heidi Anne ... Knoxville, TN
Barcus, J. Hans ... College Station, TX
Barcus, Robert David ... Decatur, GA
Barcus, Steven L. ... Altamonte Springs, FL
Barczak, Kenneth P. ... New Berlin, WI
Barczak, Ronald J. ... Minneapolis, MN
Bard, Amy ... Weehawken, NJ
Bard, Barbara H. ... Santa Rosa, CA
Bard & Bard, Ltd. ... Minneapolis, MN
Bard, Dean F. ... Mandan, ND
Bard, Edmund F. ... Houston, TX
Bard, Ernest K. ... Tampa, FL
Bard, Howard M. ... Washington, DC
Bard, Howard M. ... Minneapolis, MN
Bard, Jeffrey ... Lake Success, NY
Bard, Joel B. ... Boston, MA
Bard, Lawrence R. ... Washington, DC
Bard, Michael ... Hampstead, NC
Bard, Nancy A. ... Washington, DC
Bard, Nicole Govan ... Flint, MI
Bard, Norman ... New York, NY
Bard, Norman R. ... La Mesa, CA
Bard, Robert E. ... Scottsdale, AZ
Bard, Robert J. ... Northport, NY
Bard, Robert L. ... Hartford, CT
Bard, Stephen A. ... Minneapolis, MN
Bard, Stephen H. ... Stamford, CT
Bard, Stuart F. ... Bismarck, ND
Bard, Terry J. ... Holdenville, OK
Bard, Walter Eliot ... New York, NY
Bard, Williem J. ... Walnut Creek, CA
Bardach, Gail T. Z. ... Carmel, IN
Bardach, Richard B. ... Cincinnati, OH
Bardach, Robert A. ... Cincinnati, OH
Bardach, Sheldon G. ... Los Angeles, CA
Bardack, Lester S. ... Brooklyn, NY
Bardack, Marc H. ... Atlanta, GA
Bardack, Neil R. ... San Francisco, CA
Bardack, Paul Roitman
Department of Housing and Urban Development, GV
Bardacke, Julie M. ... Palo Alto, CA
Bardacke, Paul ... Albuquerque, NM
Bardacos, Jacquette M. ... San Diego, CA
Bardak, Tina M. ... Buffalo, NY
Bardakjy, Eugene ... Miami, FL
Bardales, Norman R. ... Endwell, NY
Bardales, Oscar, II ... Long Beach, CA
Bardanis, Emanuel N. ... Worcester, MA
Bardash, James T. ... Columbus, OH
Bardawil, Rima Catherine
North Miami Beach, FL
Barde, Knut W. ... Porterville, CA
Bardee, Joan Delise
Department of Education, Office of the General Counsel, GV
Bardee, Michael A. ... Washington, DC
Bardeen, Bette ... Seal Beach, CA
Bardell, Alan W. ... Oklahoma City, OK
Bardell, Craig A. ... Huntsville, AL
Bardell, Kathleen Field ... Chicago, IL
Bardell, Michael J. ... Downers Grove, IL
Bardell, Scott Allen ... St. Paul, MN
Bardelli, Edward J. ... Grand Rapids, MI
Bardelli, John F. ... Bethlehem, CT
Bardellini, Keith B. ... Los Angeles, CA
Bardellini, Lee P. ... San Ramon, CA
Bardellini, Perry E. ... Colfax, CA
Bardellini, Straw & Cavin
San Ramon, CA
Barden, Anne ... Philadelphia, PA
Barden, Barbara K. ... Cincinnati, OH
Barden, J. Gentry ... Nashville, TN
Barden, James E. ... San Francisco, CA
Barden, James J. ... Laverock, PA
Barden, James W. ... San Diego, CA
Barden, Larry A. ... Chicago, IL
Barden, Maureen ... Philadelphia, PA
Barden, Paul Garrett ... Rochester, NY
Barden, Stephen L., III ... Asheville, NC
Bardenstein, Cathy Jayne ... Rochester, NY
Bardenwerper, Fred L. ... Milwaukee, WI
Bardenwerper & Lobb, PLLC
Louisville, KY
Bardenwerper, Walter W. ... Bethesda, MD
Bardenwerper, William B. ... Louisville, KY
Bardes, Paul M. ... Indianapolis, IN
Bardet, Gordon P. ... South San Francisco, CA
Bardet, John J. ... Dana Point, CA
Bardet, Susan J. ... South San Francisco, CA
Bardey, Robert ... New York, NY
Bardfeld, Bennett I. ... Vineland, NJ
Bardfeld, J.D. Skip, P.A.
North Miami Beach, FL
Bardfeld, J.D. Skip ... North Miami Beach, FL
Bardfeld, Laurence M. ... Fort Lauderdale, FL
Bardfeld, Lawrence R. ... Jenkintown, PA
Bardgett, Christine ... Mahwah, NJ
Bardgett, John E. ... Jefferson City, MO
St. Louis, MO
Bardi, Henry J. ... Tampa, FL
Bardi, Richard C. ... Boston, MA
Bardige, Stephen I. ... Cambridge, MA
Bardill, Amy J. ... Atlanta, GA
Bardill, Mark D. ... Richlands, NC
Bardin, David J. ... Washington, DC
Bardin, Ian A. ... Playa Del Rey, CA
Bardin, Richard A. ... Los Angeles, CA
Bardine, Richard S. ... Boston, MA
Bardis, Elias D. ... Sacramento, CA
Bardmesser, George S. ... Washington, DC
Bardo, Thomas F. ... Washington, DC
Bardole, Scott ... Austin, TX
Bardonille, Harold ... Washington, DC
Bardonnet, Francois ... New York, NY
Bardorf & Bardorf ... Newport, RI
Bardorf, Brian G. ... Newport, RI
Bardorf, Mark B. ... Newport, RI
Bardos, Claire Sophia ... San Leandro, CA
Bardos, Paul R.
United States International Trade Commission, Office of the General Counsel, GV
Bardos, Richard B. ... Ellicott City, MD
Bardot, Heather Kathleen ... Fairfax, VA
Bardouille & Fugate ... Lynn, MA

Bardouille, Joseph F. .... Lynn, MA
Bardowell, L. Scott .... Richmond, VA
Bardowell, Lloyd Scott .... Richmond, VA
Bardrick, Michael L. .... Oklahoma City, OK
Bardsley & Carlos, LLP .... San Diego, CA
Bardsley, Catherine S. .... Washington, DC
Bardsley, David A. .... Tustin, CA
Bardsley, Francis J. .... San Diego, CA
Bardsley, John L. .... Cortland, NY
Bardsley, Philip G. .... Seattle, WA
Bardsley, Steven G. .... Cherry Hill, NJ
Harrisburg, PA
King Of Prussia, PA
Bardugo, Judy S. .... Los Angeles, CA
Bardunias, Helaina .... Kansas City, MO
Bardusch, William E., Jr. .... Morristown, NJ
Barduson, Scott L. .... Pipestone, MN
Bardwell, Clayton T. .... Delmar, NY
Bardwell, Elizabeth .... Tuba City, AZ
Bardwell, Marjorie R. .... Chicago, IL
Bardwell, Paul A. .... Napa, CA
Bardwell, Robert E., Jr. .... Columbus, OH
Bardwell, Sam B. .... Titusville, FL
Bardwil, Richard B. .... Encino, CA
Bardwil, Robert S. .... Sacramento, CA
Bardwil, Steven C. .... Burbank, CA
Bare, Douglas R. .... York, PA
Bare, Garth K. .... Raytown, MO
Bare, Glen E. .... Dublin, OH
Bare, Ira D. .... Clio, MI
Bare, Joseph E., Jr. .... San Francisco, CA
Bare, Paul I. .... Traverse City, MI
Bare, Samuel L., III .... Miami, FL
Bare, Tracy Victoria .... Cambridge, MA
Barea Fernandez, Jose G. .... San Juan, PR
Bareck, Philip .... Chicago, IL
Barecki, Thaddeus C. .... Hart, MI
Bared, Pablo R. .... Coral Gables, FL
Barefield & Barefield .... Hattiesburg, MS
Barefield, Bruce W. .... Minneapolis, KS
Barefield, Karen .... Minneapolis, KS
Barefield, Michael Clayton .... Jackson, MS
Barefield, Myla D. .... Chicago, IL
Barefield, Robert B. .... Minneapolis, KS
Barefield, Stone D. .... Hattiesburg, MS
Barefoot, Bert B., Jr. .... Oklahoma City, OK
Barefoot, Charles R., Jr. .... Perrysburg, OH
Barefoot, D. Caldwell, Jr. .... Raleigh, NC
Barefoot, Daniel W. .... Lincolnton, NC
Barefoot, David C. .... Wilmington, NC
Barefoot, J. C., Jr. .... Greensboro, NC
Barefoot, Jeffrey C. .... Perrysburg, OH
Barefoot, N. Vinson .... Fairview, OK
Barefoot, Napoleon B. .... Wilmington, NC
Barefoot, Robin Miele .... Chapel Hill, NC
Barefoot, Thomas N., Law Offices of
Raleigh, NC
Barefoot, Walter H. .... Florence, SC
Barefoot & White .... Greensboro, NC
Bareford, Harold S., Jr. .... Carle Place, NY
Bareford, John M., Sr. .... Saluda, VA
Bareford, John M., Sr., P.C. .... Saluda, VA
Bareford, Wm. T. .... Saluda, VA
Barela, A. Dino .... Dallas, TX
Barela, Cynthia J. .... Amarillo, TX
Barella, Derek G. .... Chicago, IL
Barelli, John P. .... Phoenix, AZ
Barelman, Laura Leigh Knox .... Wayne, NE
Baren, Charles H. .... Beverly Hills, CA
Baren, Daniel H. .... Costa Mesa, CA
Barenbaum, Jerrod L. .... Rockford, IL
Barenberg, Mark .... New York, NY
Barenblat, Irving .... San Antonio, TX
Barenblat, Martin .... Dallas, TX
Barengo, Robert R. .... Reno, NV
Barenholtz, Arda .... Huntington Woods, MI
Barenholtz, Brett .... Marina Del Rey, CA
Barenholtz, Celia Goldwag .... New York, NY
Barenholtz, Paul K. .... New York, NY
Barenie, Paul .... Chicago, IL
Barens, Arthur H. .... Los Angeles, CA
Barens, Arthur H., A P.C. .... Los Angeles, CA
Barense, William D. .... Ann Arbor, MI
Barensfeld, David E. .... Ellwood City, PA
Barentine, Joseph P., III .... Dallas, TX
Barentzen, Steven K. .... New York, NY
Barer, Arnold J., Law Offices of .... Seattle, WA
Barer, Daniel P. .... Los Angeles, CA
Barer, Harris A. .... New York, NY
Barer, Harvey S. .... Garden City, NY
Barer, Michael G. .... Great Falls, MT
Barer, Scott I. .... Beverly Hills, CA
Barer, Stanley H. .... Seattle, WA
Bares, Allen R. .... Lafayette, LA
Bares, Barbara H. .... Washington, DC
Bares, Jacqueline C. .... Washington, DC
Bares, James .... Minneapolis, MN
Bares, Wendell J. .... Lafayette, LA
Barest, Richard .... Lakeland, FL
Baretta, Edward C. .... Pasadena, CA
Baretz, Anne F. .... Morristown, NJ
Baretz, Marc I. .... West Memphis, AR
Baretz, Spencer Z. .... New York, NY
Barewin, Howard J. .... Kansas City, MO
Barewin, Robert D. .... Springfield, IL
Barey, Michael B. .... Detroit, MI
Barezky, Bonny S. .... Chicago, IL
Barezky, Lawrence R. .... Chicago, IL
Barfield, Allan .... Jackson, WY
Barfield, Daniel A. .... Evansville, IN
Barfield, Danny R. .... Pasadena, TX
Barfield, David A. .... Jackson, MS
Barfield, David H. .... Houston, TX
Barfield, Donna S. .... West Palm Beach, FL
Barfield, Douglas A., Jr. .... Lancaster, SC
Barfield, Edward T. .... Tallahassee, FL
Barfield, Gilbert A. .... Dallas, TX
Barfield, Glenn A. .... Goldsboro, NC
Barfield, H. Lee, II .... Nashville, TN
Barfield, Issac R. .... Washington, DC
Barfield, James E. .... Las Vegas, NV
Barfield, James E. .... Columbia, SC
Barfield, James E. .... Lexington, SC
Barfield & Jenkins, P.A. .... Fayetteville, NC
Barfield, Jennifer L. .... Boston, MA
Barfield, Jiles M. .... Dublin, GA
Vidalia, GA
Barfield, Jon E. .... Livonia, MI
Barfield, J.P. .... Nashville, TN
Barfield, K. Douglas, Jr. .... Fayetteville, NC
Barfield, Kate S. .... Department of the Army, U.S. Army Legal Services Agency, GV
Barfield, Kenneth E. .... Rome, GA
Barfield, Lowry .... Miami, FL
Barfield, Mindy G. .... Lexington, KY
Barfield, Norma C. .... Livonia, MI
Barfield, Norman J. .... Spring, TX
Barfield, Patricia L. .... Marksville, LA
Barfield, Prescott .... Covington, LA
Barfield, Rhonda Cagle .... Austin, TX
Barfield, Rhonda L. .... New Boston, TX
Barfield, Richard A. .... Orlando, FL
Barfield, Ronald .... Thomaston, GA
Barfield, S. Todd .... Kansas City, MO
Barfield, Thomas A., Jr. .... Baton Rouge, LA
Barfield, Virgil H. .... Houston, TX
Barfield, W. Brooks, Jr. .... Amarillo, TX
Barfield, W. Lowry, Jr. .... Houston, TX
Barfield, Walter L. .... Augusta, GA
Barfield, Wayne B. .... Amarillo, TX
Barfield, Wayne B., P.C., Law Offices of
Amarillo, TX
Barfield, William B. .... Atlanta, GA
Barfield, William E.
Altamonte Springs, FL
Barford, Burns F., Jr. .... Valatie, NY
Barford, George .... Tampa, FL
Barg, David L. .... Encino, CA
Barg, David L., A Professional Corporation
Encino, CA
Barg, Irwin M., (P.C.) .... Houston, TX
Barg, John F. .... San Francisco, CA
Barg, Jonathan V. .... Portland, OR
Barg, Michael F. .... Eden Prairie, MN
Barg, Stanley A. .... West Conshohocken, PA
Barg, Stanley M. .... Washington, DC
Barg, Steven .... Fort Lauderdale, FL
Barga & Barga .... Tiffin, OH
Barga, John T. .... Tiffin, OH
Barga, Rita Bobowick .... Tiffin, OH
Bargainer, David K. .... Houston, TX
Bargamian, C. David .... Detroit, MI
Barganier, Judy H. .... Montgomery, AL
Bargar, Hillary Markman .... Bridgeport, CT
Bargar, Mark L., (P.C.) .... Jamestown, NY
Bargas, Albert A. .... New Orleans, LA
Barge, Gregory A. .... San Francisco, CA
Barge, J. Stephen .... Pittsburgh, PA
Barge, Kathleen E. .... Vienna, VA
Barge, René L. .... Tustin, CA
Barge, Richmond Mason .... Atlanta, GA
Barge, Robert M. .... Providence, RI
Bargell, Cynthia L. .... Denver, CO
Bargeon, Herbert A., Jr. .... Palm Beach, FL
Barger, Bill Dale .... Manhattan Beach, CA
Barger, Brian D. .... Charlotte, NC
Barger, Brian P. .... Toledo, OH
Barger, Carol M. .... Dallas, TX
Barger, Charles G., Jr. .... Melbourne, FL
Barger, Coleen Miller .... Little Rock, AR
Barger, Darrell L. .... Corpus Christi, TX
Barger, David G. .... Alexandria, VA
Barger, Erwin D., Jr. .... Atlanta, GA
Barger, G. Andrew .... Memphis, TN
Barger, Gary .... Purcell, OK
Barger, Glenn E. .... Portland, OR
Barger, Glenn T. .... Los Angeles, CA
Barger, Hermansen, McKibben & Villarreal, L.L.P. .... Corpus Christi, TX
Barger, Howard D. .... Holyoke, MA
Barger, J. Max .... Chesapeake, VA
Barger, Jennifer L. .... Oklahoma City, OK
Barger, Jill Stanton .... Gainesville, FL
Barger, John L. .... Mattoon, IL
Barger, John Mark .... Hazard, KY
Barger, Judith M. .... Washington, DC
Barger, Kathleen C. .... Vienna, VA
Barger, Martin M. .... Red Bank, NJ
Whiting, NJ
Barger, Richard L. .... Hartford, CT
Barger, Richards D. .... Los Angeles, CA
Barger, Robert W. .... Short Hills, NJ
Barger, Ron K. .... Irving, TX
Barger, Rosanne K. .... Omaha, NE
Barger, Susan K. .... Albuquerque, NM
Barger, Thomas J. .... San Mateo, CA
Barger, Thomas M., III .... Bloomington, IL
Barger, Thomas S. .... East Lansing, MI
Barger & Wolen .... Los Angeles, CA
Newport Beach, CA
San Francisco, CA
New York, NY
Bargeron, David Louis .... Philadelphia, PA
Bargeron, H. Brannen .... Louisville, GA
Bargeron, Robin Neal .... Macon, GA
Bargeron, William W. .... Atlanta, GA
Bargetto, Richard A. .... San Francisco, CA
Bargfrede, James A. .... Houston, TX
Bargher, Craig M. .... Chicago, IL
Barghols, Steven L. .... Oklahoma City, OK
Bargiel, Charles S. .... Santa Barbara, CA
Bargiel, Paul J. .... Chicago, IL
Bargiel, Paul J., P.C. .... Chicago, IL
Bargione, Christopher .... Chicago, IL
Barglind, Mary Brouillette
Iron Mountain, MI
Bargman, Phillip E. .... El Paso, TX
Bargmann, Peter L. .... Dallas, TX
Bargmann, Peter L., P.C. .... Dallas, TX
Bargnesi, Julie M. .... Buffalo, NY
Bargo, Sarah L. .... Marietta, GA
Bargren, Paul .... Milwaukee, WI
Barham, Adkins & Tatum .... Ruston, LA
Barham & Arceneaux, A Professional Law Corporation .... New Orleans, LA
Barham, Charles C. .... Ruston, LA
Barham, Charles D., Jr. .... Raleigh, NC
Barham, Clint A. .... Dallas, TX
Barham, Dover, Bennett, Miller, Sherwood & Stone .... Valdosta, GA
Barham, E. Thomas, Jr. .... Los Alamitos, CA
Barham, Kevin .... Paris, AR
Barham, Mack E. .... New Orleans, LA
Barham & Ostrow .... Los Alamitos, CA
Barham, Philip D. .... San Diego, CA
Barham, Richard G. .... Shreveport, LA
Barham, Stephen D. .... Chattanooga, TN
Barham, Tammy L. .... Jackson, MS
Barham, Thomas W. .... Arlington, VA
Barham, Thomas W. A. .... Reston, VA
Barham & Warner, L.L.C.
Shreveport, LA
Barham, William W. .... Atlanta, GA
Barhight, G. Scott .... Towson, MD
Barhorst, Christopher .... Kansas City, MO
Bari, Frank .... New York, NY
Baria, David W. .... Jackson, MS
Baria, Holaday & Johnson, PLLC
Jackson, MS
Baria, J. Murry, Jr. .... Davis, CA
Barial, Ellen V. .... San Francisco, CA
Barian, Dicran B. .... North Chatham, MA
Barian, Harold .... Brookfield, WI
Baribault & Barry .... Baldwin, NY
Baribault, Mark .... Baldwin, NY
Baribault, Richard .... Baldwin, NY
Baribeau, Donald L. .... Little Rock, AR
Baribeault, Raymond L., Jr.
New London, CT
Baric, David A. .... Carlisle, PA
Baric, Drago C. .... San Pedro, CA
Baric, John .... Boca Raton, FL
Woods Cross, UT
Baric, Susan E. .... San Pedro, CA
Barice, Carole Joy .... Orlando, FL
Baricevic, John .... Belleville, IL
Barich, Anthony M. .... St. Cloud, MN
Barich, Joseph M. .... Chicago, IL
Barid, Richard .... Savannah, GA
Barielle, Bruce D. .... Metairie, LA
Baril, Christian J. .... Carbondale, IL
Baril, David C. .... New Orleans, LA
Baril, John P. .... Detroit, MI
Baril, Karen L. .... Minneapolis, MN
Baril, Mary Dalton .... Richmond, VA
Baril, Stephen E. .... Richmond, VA
Barile, Joseph G. .... New York, NY
Barile, Leo F., Jr. .... Brattleboro, VT
Barile, Mary Ann .... East Haven, CT
Barilich, Susan .... Dallas, TX
Barill, Michael W. .... Morgantown, WV
Barilla, Frank F. .... Santa Ana, CA
Barillari, Edward R. .... Basking Ridge, NJ
Barillas, Teressa M. .... New York, NY
Barilovich, Miriam J. .... Dearborn, MI
Barina, Bobby D. .... Killeen, TX
Barina, John .... Belton, TX
Barinaga, Nash J. .... Milwaukie, OR
Barinaga-Burch, Saidy M.
Coral Gables, FL
Ann Arbor, MI
Barineau & Barineau .... Birmingham, AL
Barineau, Leslie R. .... Birmingham, AL
Barineau, Richard C. .... Birmingham, AL
Barineau, Shelley Torian .... Houston, TX
Baring, Ben A., Jr. .... Houston, TX
Baringer, Dale R. .... Baton Rouge, LA
Baringer, Randal S. .... Cleveland, OH
Baringer, Sandra K. .... Fulton, MO
Barinholtz, Alan .... Chicago, IL
Barinholtz, Alec M. .... Irvine, CA
Barinholtz, Mark H. .... Chicago, IL
Barini-García, Lisa, (Chrtd)
Twin Falls, ID
Barinstein, Dimitri .... New York, NY
Barir, Abraham .... Corona, NY
Baris, Allan H. .... Bozeman, MT
Baris, Carrie Beth Lesser
West Palm Beach, FL
Baris, David H. .... Washington, DC
Bethesda, MD
Baris, E. Barbara .... Palm City, FL
Baris, Irl B. .... St. Louis, MO
Baris, Jay G. .... New York, NY
Baris, Jon M. .... St. Louis, MO
Barisano, Andrea S. .... Lowell, MA
Barisano, Arthur M., Jr. .... Melrose, MA
Bariscillo, George A., Jr.
Asbury Park, NJ
Barish, Charles I. .... Cave Creek, AZ
Barish, David M. .... Chicago, IL
Barish, Herbert M. .... Glendale, CA
Barish, Jordana .... New York, NY
Barish, Kenneth M. .... Beverly Hills, CA
Barish, Kenneth Robert .... New York, NY
Barish, Leon J. .... Austin, TX
Barish, Marion Giliberti .... Boston, MA
Barish, Marvin I. .... Philadelphia, PA
Barish, Marvin I., Law Offices, A Prof. Corp.
Cherry Hill, NJ
Philadelphia, PA
Barish, Miriam Benton .... Cherry Hill, NJ
Philadelphia, PA
Barish, Raymond S. .... Mount Prospect, IL
Barish, Rhoda S. .... Rockville, MD
Barish, Stacey E. .... Philadelphia, PA
Barish, Wendi Dawn .... Philadelphia, PA
Barish, William .... Sterling Heights, MI
Barishman, Heidi Block .... Albany, NY
Barish-Straus, Sarah .... Parsippany, NJ
Bariso, Peter F., Jr. .... Secaucus, NJ
Barison, Gregory R. .... Boston, MA
Barisone, John G. .... Santa Cruz, CA
Barisone, Susan Atchison .... Santa Cruz, CA
Barisonek & Dooley .... Cranford, NJ
Barisonek, Lawrence J. .... Cranford, NJ
Barisonek, Walter R. .... Elizabeth, NJ
Barisrothstein, Randy Sue .... Great Neck, NY
Barist, Jeffrey .... New York, NY
Baritot, Rebecca H. .... Orchard Park, NY
Baritz, Neil S. .... Boca Raton, FL
New York, NY
Baritz, Stanley E. .... Rockville, MD
Bark, Christina M. .... Reno, NV
Bark, Thomas W. .... New York, NY
Barkacs, Craig B. .... San Diego, CA
Barkacs, Linda L. .... San Diego, CA
Barkai, John L. .... Honolulu, HI
Barkal, Richard J. .... Chicago, IL
Barkalow, C. Thomas .... Freehold, NJ
Barkalow, Jimmy R. .... St. Louis, MO
Barkan, Alan L. .... Woodland Hills, CA
Barkan & Barkan Co., L.P.A.
Columbus, OH
Barkan, David M. .... Menlo Park, CA
Barkan, Irving .... Columbus, OH
Barkan, Irwin W. .... Fort Myers, FL
Barkan, Joy Charlotte
North Miami Beach, FL
Barkan, Kim A. .... Metairie, LA
Barkan, Kim A., PLC .... Metairie, LA
Barkan, Lee A. .... New York, NY
Barkan, Leonard .... Fairless Hills, PA
Barkan, Lisa A. .... Baltimore, MD
Barkan, Mel P. .... New York, NY
Barkan, Neal J. .... Columbus, OH
Barkan & Neff .... Tampa, FL
New Orleans, LA
Columbus, OH
Barkan, Paul A. .... New York, NY
Barkan, Randall I. .... Palo Alto, CA
Barkan and Robon .... Toledo, OH
Barkan, Sheldon L. .... Van Nuys, CA
Barkan, Steven L. .... New York, NY
Barkan, Steven L., P.C. .... New York, NY
Barkan, Steven M. .... Madison, WI
Barkan, William .... New York, NY
Barkan, William A. .... Columbus, OH
Barkan, William I. .... Toledo, OH
Barkas, Christopher .... Tallahassee, FL
Barkas, Harold Peter .... Miami, FL
Barkasy, Richard A. .... Cherry Hill, NJ
Philadelphia, PA
Barkate, Joseph G., Jr. .... Dallas, TX
Barkats & Associates, Chartered, Attorneys and Counselors at Law .... Washington, DC
Barkats, Pierre-Philippe .... Washington, DC
Barkau, Brad .... Nashville, IL
Barkdoll, Tamara .... Denver, CO
Barkdull, Denise Y. .... Indianapolis, IN
Barkdull, Jayne Regester
West Palm Beach, FL
Barkdull, Jeffrey S. .... Spokane, WA
Barkdull, Thomas H., III
West Palm Beach, FL
Barkdull, Thomas H., Jr. .... Miami, FL
Barke, Brian M. .... Wheaton, MD
Barke-Cain, Janet L. .... Minneapolis, MN
Barkel, Edwin A. .... Toledo, OH
Barkeley, James N. .... Anchorage, AK
Barkelo, D. Edgar .... Cape Coral, FL
Barkemeyer, Donald T. .... Santa Ana, CA
Barken & Bakewell, LLP .... St. Louis, MO
Barken, Bernard A. .... St. Louis, MO
Barken, Marlene Ellen .... Ithaca, NY
Barkenbus, Lora Aylin .... Nashville, TN
Barkenquast, David L. .... Toledo, OH
Barker, A. Lisa .... Mineral, VA
Barker, A. Michael .... Linwood, NJ
Barker, A. Michael, P.C. .... Linwood, NJ
Barker, Abraham F. .... Nashville, TN
Barker, Albert P. .... Boise, ID
Barker, Alex J. .... Bremerton, WA
Barker, Alexander D.
West Palm Beach, FL
Barker, Amanda C. .... Glen Cove, NY
Barker, Andrew M. .... Noblesville, IN
Barker, Ann B. .... Owatonna, MN
Barker, Ann Mallett .... Houma, LA
Barker, Ann S. .... Anaheim, CA
Barker, Anthony J. .... Portland, OR
Barker, April Rockstead .... Green Bay, WI
Barker, Barbara .... Tacoma, WA
Barker, Barbara B. .... Roswell, GA
Barker & Barker .... San Antonio, TX
Barker, B. K. .... Johnson City, TN
Barker, Bo .... Bellevue, WA
Barker, Bo, P.S. .... Bellevue, WA
Barker, Boudreaux, Lamy and Foley, A Law Corporation .... Baton Rouge, LA
Houma, LA
New Orleans, LA
Thibodaux, LA
Barker, Brian L. .... St. Petersburg, FL
Barker, Brown, Busby, Chrisman & Thomas, A Professional Corporation
Las Vegas, NV
Barker, Bruce J. .... New York, NY
Barker, Bruce T. .... Greeley, CO
Barker and Bynon .... Birmingham, AL
Barker, C. Brooks, II .... San Antonio, TX

Barker, Calvin A., Jr. ... Dallas, TX
Pottsboro, TX
Barker, Carol M. ... Salem, OR
Barker, Carolyn Howe ... San Antonio, TX
Barker, Carolyn M. ... Boston, MA
Barker, Charles A. ... Central Valley, NY
Barker, Charles E. ... Indianapolis, IN
Barker, Charles F. ... Los Angeles, CA
Barker, Charles L. ... Evanston, IL
Barker, Charles S. P. ... New York, NY
Barker, Charles T., (P.A.) ... Boca Raton, FL
Barker, Charles V. ... Bolivar, MO
Barker, Charles W., Jr. ... Hobart, OK
Barker, Chris A. ... Tampa, FL
Barker, Christine A. ... New Haven, CT
Barker, Christopher B. ... Boston, MA
Barker, Christopher L. ... Albany, NY
Barker, Clayton L. ... Kansas City, MO
Barker, Clayton Robert, III ... Atlanta, GA
Barker, Constance H. ... Sacramento, CA
Barker, Constance Smith
Montgomery, AL
Barker, Constance T. ... Troutman, NC
Barker, Cynthia ... Jersey City, NJ
Barker, D. Gregory ... Houston, TX
Barker, D. Ray ... Moscow, ID
Barker, Dan T., Jr. ... Greensboro, NC
Barker, Daniel A. ... Mesa, AZ
Barker, Daniel D. ... Madison, WI
Barker, Daniel T. ... Raleigh, NC
Barker, Darin B. ... Grand Forks, ND
Barker, David E. ... Irvine, CA
Barker, David J. ... Indianapolis, IN
Barker, David L. ... Salt Lake City, UT
Barker, David P. ... Orlando, FL
Barker, Derek M. ... Chicago, IL
Barker, Dianne ... Tahlequah, OK
Barker, Douglas A. ... Charleston, SC
Barker, Douglas H. ... San Diego, CA
Barker, Douglas J. ... Vancouver, WA
Barker, E. Elliott (Skip) ... Selma, AL
Barker, E. Gerry ... Jeffersonville, IN
Barker, Earl M., Jr., (P.A.)
Jacksonville, FL
Barker, Edward, & Associates
Corpus Christi, TX
Barker, Edward L. ... Leavenworth, KS
Barker, Edward, (P.C.) ... Simi Valley, CA
Barker, Eileen Evans ... Larkspur, CA
Barker, Elizabeth Kaye ... Martinez, CA
Barker, Epstein & Loscocco ... Boston, MA
Barker, Eric H. ... Orlando, FL
Barker, Ernest E. ... Lomita, CA
Barker, E. T. ... Syracuse, NY
Barker, F. Edward ... Corpus Christi, TX
Barker Firm, The, P.C. ... Dallas, TX
Pottsboro, TX
Barker, Frank P., III ... Kansas City, MO
Barker, Fredk. ... Redmond, WA
Barker & Frick, P.C. ... Colorado Springs, CO
Barker, Gregory K. ... Wichita, KS
Barker, Gregory Samuel ... Jefferson City, MO
Barker, Harold E. ... Lakeland, FL
Barker & Hellen ... Anchorage, AK
Barker, Herbert E., Jr. ... Palo Alto, CA
Barker, Hugh, Jr. ... Salt Lake City, UT
Barker, J. Emery ... Tucson, AZ
Barker, J. John ... Seattle, WA
Barker, J. Madison ... Little Rock, AR
Barker, Jack ... Pinetop, AZ
Barker, Jack E. ... Denver, CO
Barker, Jack L. ... Hillsdale, MI
Barker, Jack L., P.C. ... Hillsdale, MI
Barker, Jack, P.C. ... Pinetop, AZ
Barker, Jack W. ... El Dorado, AR
Barker, James A., Jr. ... Washington, DC
Barker, James E. ... Avon, OH
Barker, James H. ... Houston, TX
Barker, James H., III ... Washington, DC
Barker, James L., Jr. ... Salt Lake City, UT
Barker, James M.
Federal Deposit Insurance Corporation, GV
Barker, James M. ... Las Vegas, NV
Barker, James M., Jr. ... Hamburg, AR
Barker, James P. ... Williamsport, PA
Barker, James T. ... Coronado, CA
Barker, Jane E. ... Bloomington, IN
Barker, Jaryn Iris ... San Francisco, CA
Barker, Jason C. ... Troy, MI
Barker, Jeff J. ... Colorado Springs, CO
Barker, Jeffrey A. ... Los Angeles, CA
Barker, Jeffrey C. ... Wenatchee, WA
Barker, Jeffrey H. ... Tallahassee, FL
Barker, Jerry D. ... Galveston, TX
Barker, Jill M. ... Washington, DC
Barker, Joanne E. ... Saratoga Springs, NY
Barker, Joe F. ... Houston, TX
Barker, John ... Short Hills, NJ
Barker, John A. ... Madera, CA
Madera, CA
Barker, John A. ... Houston, TX
Barker, John A., & Associates, A Prof. Law Corp. ... Alturas, CA
Fresno, CA
Jackson, CA
Madera, CA
Weaverville, CA
Barker, John C. ... Boston, MA
Barker, John D. ... Fort Lauderdale, FL
Barker, John R. ... Montgomery, AL
Barker, John R. ... Tulsa, OK
Barker, John R. ... Portland, OR
Barker, John W. ... Lake Success, NY
Barker, Jon R. ... Woodland Hills, CA
Barker, Jonathan H.
General Accounting Office, Office of the General Counsel, GV
Barker, Joseph A. ... Detroit, MI
Barker, Joseph B. ... Martinsville, IN
Barker, Joseph N. ... Nashville, TN
Barker, Joseph R. ... Hilton Head Island, SC
Barker, Joseph V. ... Raleigh, NC
Barker, Judy Broadstreet ... Union City, TN
Barker, Julie L. ... Los Angeles, CA
Barker, Kathleen H. ... Torrance, CA
Barker, Kathryn S. ... Milwaukee, WI
Barker, Keith L. ... Santa Barbara, CA
Barker, Kenneth E. ... Belle Fourche, SD
Rapid City, SD
Barker, Kenneth R. ... Morgantown, IN
Barker, Kent M. ... Nashua, NH
Barker, Kermit E., Jr. ... Anchorage, AK
Barker, Kim M. ... Chicago, IL
Barker & Lain, A Professional Corporation
Galveston, TX
Barker, Larry D. ... Columbus, OH
Barker, Larry O. ... San Diego, CA
Barker, Laura L. ... Akron, OH
Barker Law Firm ... Portland, OR
Barker Law Office ... South Jordan, UT
Barker Law Office, LTD. ... Owatonna, MN
Barker, Lawrence R. ... Napa, CA
Barker, Lee Ann ... De Ridder, LA
Lafayette, LA
Barker, Leroy J. ... Anchorage, AK
Barker, Linda Daves ... Los Angeles, CA
Barker, Lori A. ... Troy, MI
Barker, Lori J. ... Chico, CA
Barker, Lorin C. ... Salt Lake City, UT
Barker, Lydia E. ... Redding, CA
Barker, Lynn Penix ... Seattle, WA
Barker, M. Paul ... Palo Alto, CA
Barker, M. Ridgway ... Stamford, CT
Barker, M. Theresa ... Baltimore, MD
Barker, Margaret ... Albuquerque, NM
Barker, Margaret, P.C. ... Albuquerque, NM
Barker, Marilyn D.
Securities and Exchange Commission, Division of Enforcement, GV
Barker, Mark E. ... Phoenix, AZ
Barker, Mary A. Becker ... Worcester, MA
Barker, McNeal, Wiese & Holt
Iowa Falls, IA
Barker, Melody A. ... Walnut Creek, CA
Barker, Michael D. ... Corvallis, OR
Barker, Michael H. ... Savannah, GA
Barker, Michael J. ... New York, NY
Barker, Milton E., Jr. ... Birmingham, AL
Barker, Mitchell R. ... South Jordan, UT
Barker, Neil J. ... Pasadena, CA
Barker, Neil J., A Professional Corporation
Pasadena, CA
Barker, Norman A. ... Washington, DC
Barker, Norman B. ... Los Angeles, CA
Barker, Pamela E. ... Milwaukee, WI
Barker, Patricia J. ... Chicago, IL
Barker, Paul ... San Antonio, TX
Barker, Paul D. ... Chevy Chase, MD
Barker, Paul D., Jr. ... Baltimore, MD
Barker, Peggy Murphy ... Covington, KY
Barker, R. Blaine ... New York, NY
Barker, R. Scott ... Fort Myers, FL
Barker, Randy M. ... Holton, KS
Barker & Reininga ... Indianapolis, IN
Barker, Rex A. ... Lansing, MI
Barker, Richard William ... Midland, MI
Barker, Robert A. ... Albany, NY
Barker, Robert E. ... Savannah, GA
Barker, Robert G. ... Indianapolis, IN
Barker, Robert James ... West Somerville, MA
Barker, Robert S. ... Pittsburgh, PA
Barker, Robert T. ... Niskayuna, NY
Barker, Robert W., Law Offices of
Auburn, CA
Barker, Rodney M. ... Boston, MA
Barker, Roger A. ... Orlando, FL
Barker & Romney, A Professional Corporation
Pasadena, CA
Barker, Ronald C. ... Salt Lake City, UT
Barker, Ronald K. ... Kansas City, MO
Barker, Ronald K., P.C. ... Kansas City, MO
Barker, Rosina B. ... Washington, DC
Barker, S. Keith ... Richmond, VA
Barker, S. Keith, P.C. ... Richmond, VA
Barker, S. Price ... Shreveport, LA
Barker, Sabrina L. ... Indialantic, FL
Barker, Sally E. ... St. Louis, MO
Barker, Samuel H. ... Ogden, UT
Barker, Sandra S. ... Jacksonville, FL
Barker, Sarah Evans ... Indianapolis, IN
Barker & Schwindt, A.P.C.
Kansas City, MO
Barker, Scott N. ... Cincinnati, OH
Barker, Scott S. ... Denver, CO
Barker, Sissie Lee ... Rancho Cucamonga, CA
Barker, Stephen G. ... Hazard, KY
Barker, Stephen L. ... Lexington, KY
Barker, Stephen L. ... Philadelphia, PA
Barker, Stevan W. ... San Antonio, TX
Barker, Steven Andrew
San Juan Capistrano, CA
Barker, Suzanne M. ... Albuquerque, NM
Barker, T. Darren ... Santa Ana, CA
Barker, Terrence G. ... Rochester, NY
Barker, Terri D ... Martinez, CA
Barker, Terry J. ... Tulsa, OK
Barker, Thomas R. ... Burlington, MA
Barker Thomas & Walters, A Professional Law Corporation ... San Diego, CA
Barker, Timothy S. ... Los Angeles, CA
Barker, Vicky L. ... Santa Monica, CA
Barker, W. Brek ... Clayton, GA
Barker, Wendell J. ... Ottawa, KS
Barker, William B. ... Topeka, KS
Barker, William Cory ... Birmingham, AL
Barker, William G. ... Los Angeles, CA
Barker, William J. ... Tacoma, WA
Barker, William J., Jr. ... Philadelphia, PA
Barker, William (Mickey) ... Chattanooga, TN
Barker, William R. ... Orlando, FL
Barker, William S. ... Las Vegas, NV
Barker, William T. ... Chicago, IL
Barker, William W. ... Washington, DC
Barker-Jones, Angela ... Tahlequah, OK
Barkes, Larry A. ... Goshen, IN
Barkes, Raymond P. ... Los Angeles, CA
Barket, Bruce A. ... Mineola, NY
Barket, George E. ... Miami, FL
Barket, Mark A. ... Pottsville, PA
Barkett, Bruce D. ... Vero Beach, FL
Barkett, Eric C. ... Vero Beach, FL
Barkett, Gumpert & Reiner ... Sacramento, CA
Barkett, John M. ... Miami, FL
Barkett, Joseph J. ... Sacramento, CA
Barkett, Lawrence A. ... Vero Beach, FL
Barkett, Lawrence A., P.A. ... Vero Beach, FL
Barkett, Lisa Ann ... La Jolla, CA
Barkett, Melissa L. ... Denver, CO
Barkett, Michael J., Jr. ... Stockton, CA
Barkett, Michael L. ... Oklahoma City, OK
Barkett, Phillip J., Jr. ... Sikeston, MO
Barkett, Rosemary ... Miami, FL
Barkewitz, Thomas A. ... Seattle, WA
Barkey, Brett D. ... Treasury Department, Office of Foreign Assets Control, GV
Barkey, Brian M. ... Flint, MI
Barkey, Walter J. ... Flint, MI
Barkhausen, David N. ... Lake Bluff, IL
Barkholz, Amy Jan ... Lansing, MI
Barkhordari, Farzad ... Palo Alto, CA
Barkhorn, Jonathan H. ... Livingston, NJ
Barkhorn, Karin J. ... New York, NY
Barkhurst, Paul D. ... San Antonio, TX
Barkhurst, William J. ... Coronado, CA
Barki, Dan ... San Francisco, CA
Barkidjija, John M. ... Chicago, IL
Barkin, Albert ... Washington, DC
Barkin, Allen J. ... Union, NJ
Barkin, Daniel J. ... Roseland, NJ
Barkin, David R. ... Escondido, CA
Barkin, Eugene N. ... Tamarac, FL
Barkin, Gary M. ... Culver City, CA
Barkin, James L. ... Atlanta, GA
Barkin, Marshall H. ... Daytona Beach, FL
Barkin, Marvin E. ... Tampa, FL
Barkin, Pamela L. ... Washington, DC
Barkin, Richard B. ... Boca Raton, FL
Barkin, Richard B. ... Fort Lauderdale, FL
Barkin, Ronald S. ... Berkeley, CA
Barkin, Samuel L. ... New York, NY
Barkin, Thomas G. ... Salem, OR
Barking, Judy D. ... Ogden, UT
Barkis, Marvin W. ... Louisburg, KS
Barklage, Barklage, Brett, Ohlms & Martin, P.C. ... St. Charles, MO
Barklage, Daniel K. ... St. Charles, MO
Barklage, Thomas John ... St. Charles, MO
Barkley, Alice Suet Yee
San Francisco, CA
Barkley, Alison ... Evanston, IL
Barkley, Barbara A. ... Irvine, CA
Barkley, Brian E. ... Rockville, MD
Barkley, C. Michael ... Tulsa, OK
Barkley, Dean M. ... Loretto, MN
Barkley & DeMier, P.C. ... Tulsa, OK
Barkley, Harold J., III ... Aberdeen, MS
Barkley, Harold J., Jr. ... Jackson, MS
Barkley, Jack R. ... Taylor, TX
Barkley, James H.
Occupational Safety and Health Review Commission, Administrative Law Judges, GV
Barkley, James H. ... Houston, TX
Barkley, James M. ... Indianapolis, IN
Barkley, James N. ... Houston, TX
Barkley, James W. ... Charlottesville, VA
Barkley, Jane ... Plano, TX
Barkley, Jane S. ... Greensboro, NC
Barkley, Jean M. ... Tucson, AZ
Barkley, John L. ... Lodi, CA
Barkley, John P. ... Raleigh, NC
Barkley & Kennedy, Chartered
Rockville, MD
Barkley, Larry J. ... Rome, GA
Barkley, Mary F. ... Houston, TX
Barkley, Michael James ... Manteca, CA
Barkley, N. Buckner, Jr. ... Marrero, LA
Barkley, Richard P. ... Denver, CO
Barkley, Robert D. ... Houston, TX
Barkley, Robert E., Jr. ... New Orleans, LA
Barkley, Sara J. ... Denver, CO
Barkley, Shannon F. ... Pittsburgh, PA
Barkley, Stephen M. ... Tucson, AZ
Barkley, Steven C. ... Beaumont, TX
Barkley, Thierry V. ... Reno, NV
Barkley & Thompson, L.C.
New Orleans, LA
Barkley, W. Benjamin ... Atlanta, GA
Barkley, Willard T. ... Raleigh, NC
Barkley, William G. ... Charlottesville, VA
Barklind, Sharla Marie ... Washington, DC
Barklow, James P., Jr. ... Dallas, TX
Barklow, James Paul, Jr., A Professional Corporation ... Dallas, TX
Barkman, Francis E. ... Morehead City, NC
Barkman, Frederick S. ... Bellevue, WA
Barkman, Jon A. ... Somerset, PA
Barkman, Patrick G. ... Cleburne, TX
Barkmeier, Jerald T. ... Omaha, NE
Barkoff, Rupert M. ... Atlanta, GA
Barkofske, Francis L. ... St. Louis, MO
Barkofske, Peter J. ... St. Louis, MO
Bar-Kokhba, Yuval D. ... New York, NY
Barkon, Gil ... New York, NY
Barkoot, Michael G. ... Cleveland Heights, OH
Barkow, Anthony S. ... Department of Justice, Office of the Attorney General, GV
Barkow, Michael ... New York, NY
Barkow, Rachel E. ... Washington, DC
Barkowitz, Donald B. ... Sullivan's Island, SC
Barkowsky-Starkins, Lesa A.
New York, NY
Barks, Daniel D. ... Arlington, VA
Barks, James A. ... Sanford, FL
Barks & Kell ... Hermann, MO
Barks, P. Dennis ... Hermann, MO
Barks, Shannon K. ... Overland Park, KS
Barksdale, Antoinette
Department of Housing and Urban Development, Office of General Counsel, GV
Barksdale, Bill ... Okmulgee, OK
Barksdale, Bonita Carol ... Dallas, TX
Barksdale, Charles B. ... Laurel, MD
Barksdale, Danelle Dykes ... Tampa, FL
Barksdale, Gracy M. ... Atlanta, GA
Barksdale, H. Gregory ... Wilmington, DE
Barksdale, Henry R. ... Milton, FL
Barksdale, J. Gordon ... Conyers, GA
Barksdale, James H., Jr. ... Austin, TX
Barksdale, Jerry R. ... Athens, AL
Barksdale, John H. W. ... Okmulgee, OK
Barksdale, John R. ... Casper, WY
Barksdale, Kathleen K. ... West Chester, PA
Barksdale, Leonard Nye ... Missouri City, TX
Barksdale, Michael Eric ... Bradenton, FL
Barksdale, O. David ... Jacksonville, FL
Barksdale, Patricia D. ... Jacksonville, FL
Barksdale, Rhesa H. ... Jackson, MS
Barksdale, Richard V. ... Riverside, CA
Barksdale, Robinson & Wiemer, A Professional Corporation ... Okmulgee, OK
Barksdale, Sonya G. M. ... Garden City, NY
Barksdale, Suzanne Southard
Alpharetta, GA
Barksdale, Wales F. ... Conyers, GA
Barksdale, Wales F., P.C. ... Atlanta, GA
Conyers, GA
Barkshire, Mary Ann ... Bellevue, WA
Barkstrom, John E. ... Denver, CO
Barkume, Anthony R. ... New York, NY
Barkus, A. Neal ... Washington, DC
Barkus, David A. ... Miami, FL
Barkus, Frederick G. ... Charleston, WV
Barkus, Lori I. ... Miami, FL
Barkus, Michael M. ... Lorain, OH
Barkus, Paul A. ... Butler, PA
Barkus, Ramune E. ... Glendale, CA
Ontario, CA
Barkus, Tamara L. ... Havre, MT
Barkwill, Brooks K.
New Martinsville, WV
Barkworth, Helena F. ... Birmingham, AL
Barkyoumb, William E. ... Lansing, MI
Barlaam, Raymond R. ... Ossining, NY
Barlament, John L. ... Milwaukee, WI
Barland, Thomas H. ... Eau Claire, WI
Barlar, J. Daniel, Jr. ... Mobile, AL
Barlas, Elaine M. ... Englewood Cliffs, NJ
Barlas, Ned E. ... Philadelphia, PA
Barlay, Andrew E. ... Kirkland, WA
Barlean, Kelly J. ... Everett, WA
Barlett, Carl E. ... Williamsport, PA
Barlett, Jeanne M. ... Naperville, IL
Barletta, Joseph F. ... San Francisco, CA
Barletta, Robert T. ... Orlando, FL
Barletta, Thomas P. ... Washington, DC
Bar-Lev, Joshua ... San Francisco, CA
Bar-Levav, Doron M. ... New York, NY
Barley, Christopher E. ... Columbus, OH
Barley, Donald L. ... Brady, TX
Barley, James F. ... Howell, MI
Barley, John A. ... Tallahassee, FL
Barley, John A., & Associates, P.A.
Tallahassee, FL
Barley, Michele ... Loretto, MN
Barley, Reginald M. ... Richmond, VA
Barley, Snyder, Senft & Cohen, LLC
Birdsboro, PA
Chambersburg, PA
Hamburg, PA
Hanover, PA
Harrisburg, PA
Lancaster, PA
Morgantown, PA
Oley, PA
Reading, PA
York, PA
Barley, Steven F. ... Baltimore, MD
Barley, Suzanne Michele ... Glencoe, MN
Barley-McBride, Mary ... Columbus, OH
Barlia, Carol ... Irvington, NY
Barlia, Neal S. ... New York, NY
Barliant, Donald E. ... Chicago, IL
Barliant, Jared M. ... Santa Fe, NM
Barliant, Ronald ... Chicago, IL
Barliant, Samuel ... Yorkville, IL
Barlin, Wayne A. ... Miami, FL
Barline, John D. ... Tacoma, WA
Barlock, Edward S. ... Denver, CO
Barlock, Joseph A. ... Pittsburgh, PA
Barloga, Scott B. ... Clayton, GA
Barloon, Joseph L. ... Washington, DC
Barlow, A. Wellington ... Jacksonville, FL
Barlow, A. Wellington, Esq., P.A.
Jacksonville, FL
Barlow, Aaron A. ... Chicago, IL
Barlow, Alan ... Oklahoma City, OK
Barlow, Alex ... Dallas, TX
Barlow, Andre ... Washington, DC
Barlow, Angela Marie ... Culpeper, VA
Barlow, Annette ... Palo Alto, CA

Barlow, Anthony M. ..... **Cincinnati, OH**
Barlow & Barlow ..... Bardstown, KY
Barlow, Boce W., Jr. ..... Hartford, CT
Barlow & Bohne ..... **Melbourne, FL**
Barlow, Brian R. ..... Blue Bell, PA
Barlow, Cathy A. ..... Philadelphia, PA
Barlow, Charles H. ..... Spirit Lake, IA
Barlow, Chuck D. ..... Jackson, MS
Barlow, Cynthia M. ..... **Hartford, CT**
Barlow, David A. ..... **Shreveport, LA**
Barlow, David B. ..... **Chicago, IL**
Barlow, David Matthew ..... Arlington, MA
Barlow, David S. ..... Seattle, WA
Barlow, Dennis A. ..... Burbank, CA
Barlow & Derby ..... **Detroit, MI**
Troy, MI
Barlow, Diane M. ..... **Austin, TX**
Barlow, Diane M. ..... Dallas, TX
Barlow, Donald E. ..... Austin, TX
Barlow, Douglas M. ..... Beaumont, TX
Barlow, Edward L. ..... New York, NY
Barlow, Elizabeth T.
Department of Commerce, Office of the Inspector General, GV
Barlow, F. Rendol ..... **Middlebury, VT**
Barlow, Francis J. ..... Boston, MA
Barlow & Garsek, A Professional Corporation ..... **Fort Worth, TX**
Barlow, George W., III ..... **Harrisonburg, VA**
Barlow, H. William ..... Salem, OR
Barlow and Hardtner L.C.
Shreveport, LA
Barlow, Harry E. ..... Springfield, VA
Barlow, Herbert B., Jr. ..... **Providence, RI**
Barlow, J. Benjamin ..... **Fort Worth, TX**
Barlow, J. Clifton, Jr. ..... Atlanta, GA
Barlow, James B. ..... **Fort Worth, TX**
Barlow, James E. ..... San Antonio, TX
Barlow, James L. ..... Paoli, PA
Barlow, James W. ..... Tulsa, OK
Barlow, Jeff D. ..... **Sacramento, CA**
Barlow, Jeffrey N. ..... Salem, OR
Barlow, Jodi S. ..... Greensboro, NC
Barlow, Joe Dee, (P.C.) ..... **Houston, TX**
Barlow, John A. ..... **Longview, WA**
Barlow, John C. ..... Chicago, IL
Barlow, John Charles ..... **Moorpark, CA**
Barlow, John L. ..... **Corvallis, OR**
Barlow, John R., II ..... **Greensboro, NC**
Barlow, Josephs & Holmes, Ltd.
Providence, RI
Barlow, Joyce Krutick ..... Newark, NJ
Barlow, June Babiracki ..... Los Angeles, CA
Barlow, Kathleen T. ..... Washington, DC
Barlow, Kenneth A., Jr. ..... Orlando, FL
Barlow, Kimberly Hall ..... Brea, CA
Barlow & Kinney, P.A. ..... **Albuquerque, NM**
Santa Fe, NM
Barlow, Kobata & Denis ..... **Los Angeles, CA**
Chicago, IL
Barlow, Leo H. ..... Salt Lake City, UT
Barlow & Lewis ..... Hartford, CT
Barlow, M. Glenn ..... Pascagoula, MS
Barlow, Mahlon H. ..... **Tampa, FL**
Barlow, Malcolm F. ..... **Manchester, CT**
Barlow, Marjorie De Santo ..... Scranton, PA
Barlow, Melinda H. ..... Arlington, TX
Barlow, Milton A., Jr. ..... Chevy Chase, MD
Barlow, Milton M. ..... Prairie Village, KS
Barlow, Myron Paul ..... **Washington, DC**
Barlow, Nan ..... Savannah, TN
Barlow, Nancy Diane ..... Sunland, CA
Barlow, Patricia M. ..... San Francisco, CA
Barlow, Paul ..... Brooklyn, NY
Barlow, Peter H. ..... **Salt Lake City, UT**
Barlow, Peter M. ..... **Boston, MA**
Barlow, R. Michael ..... Santa Fe, NM
Barlow, Richard A. ..... Fort Pierce, FL
Barlow, Richard J. S., Jr. ..... Trenton, NJ
Barlow, Richard K. ..... **Albuquerque, NM**
Barlow, Richard S. ..... Bardstown, KY
Barlow & Riddick, P.C. ..... Smithfield, VA
Barlow, Robert D. ..... Atlanta, GA
Barlow, Robert D., Jr. ..... Phoenix, AZ
Barlow, Robert J. ..... Fredericksburg, VA
Barlow, Robert L., II ..... **Madison, IN**
Barlow, Ross J. ..... Sioux City, IA
Barlow, Russell L. ..... **Oakland, CA**
Barlow, Sarah (Sally) W.
Albuquerque, NM
Barlow, Scott Patrick ..... San Francisco, CA
Barlow, Sharla Adams ..... **Atlanta, GA**
Barlow, Stacey A. ..... New Brunswick, NJ
Barlow, Stephen O. ..... Lutz, FL
Barlow, T. Mitchell, Jr. ..... **Melbourne, FL**
Barlow, Terry J. ..... Weatherford, TX
Barlow, Thomas ..... Perth Amboy, NJ
Barlow, Thomas J. ..... **Bordentown, NJ**
Barlow, Thomas Kennedy ..... **Columbia, SC**
Barlow, Thomas W. H. ..... **Troy, MI**
Barlow Todd Jordan & Jones, L.L.P.
Houston, TX
Barlow, W. Lonnie ..... Cochran, GA
Barlow, William H. ..... **Los Angeles, CA**
Barlow, William K. ..... Smithfield, VA
Barlupo, Joseph J., Law Office of
Stockton, CA
Barmack, Peter M. ..... **Ontario, CA**
Barmak, David ..... **Washington, DC**
Barmak, Mark ..... North Chicago, IL
Barmakian, Deanna M. ..... Cambridge, MA
Barmakian, Gail M. ..... **Edgartown, MA**
Barman, Howard M. ..... **Trenton, NJ**
Barmann, Bernard C., Jr.
Los Angeles, CA
Barmann, Bernard C., Sr. ..... Bakersfield, CA
Barmann, Glen R. ..... **Kankakee, IL**
Barmann, Kramer & Bohlen, P.C.
Kankakee, IL
Barmasse, Michael E. ..... Westlake Village, CA
Barmat, Marc P. ..... **Boca Raton, FL**
Barmby, Angela C. ..... **Dallas, TX**
Barmeier, William G. ..... Santa Clara, CA
Barmen, Stewart B. ..... **Pittsburgh, PA**
Barmettler, Joseph J. ..... **Omaha, NE**
Barmettler, Michael A. ..... San Diego, CA
Barmeyer, John R. ..... **Atlanta, GA**
Barmeyer, Patricia T. ..... **Atlanta, GA**
Barna, Alexander, Jr. ..... Foster City, CA
Barna, Allen A.
Federal Communications Commission, Common Carrier Bureau, GV
Barna & Barna ..... Donora, PA
Barna, Elizabeth M. ..... New York, NY
Barna, Florence M. ..... Brooklyn, NY
Barna, Guzy & Steffen, Ltd.
Minneapolis, MN
Barna, James Francis ..... **Memphis, TN**
Barna, Keith L. ..... Bessemer, MI
Barna, Kenneth M. ..... **Boston, MA**
Barna, Nicholas A. ..... Forest City, PA
Honesdale, PA
Barna, Paul N., Jr. ..... Donora, PA
Barna, Stephanie A. ..... Charlottesville, VA
Barna, Steven M. ..... **New York, NY**
Barna, Terence J. ..... **York, PA**
Barnaba, Charlene Stewart
Cherry Hill, NJ
Philadelphia, PA
Barnaba, John A. ..... Syracuse, NY
Barnaba & Marconi, LLP ..... Trenton, NJ
Barnaba, Mario L. ..... Trenton, NJ
Barnabas & Driscoll, L.L.P.
Silver Spring, MD
Barnabas, Eric L. ..... Silver Spring, MD
Barnabei, Arnold A. ..... Harrisburg, PA
Barnabei, Laura M. ..... **New York, NY**
Barnabeo, Susan P. ..... **New York, NY**
Barnaby, Gerald P. ..... St. Paul, MN
Barnaby, Howard B. ..... **New York, NY**
Barnaby, Michael J. ..... **Old Greenwich, CT**
White Plains, NY
Barnaby, Robert A., II ..... **Atlanta, GA**
Barnaby, William E. ..... Sacramento, CA
Bar-Nadav, Ron ..... Hackensack, NJ
Barnako, Frank R. ..... Washington, DC
Barnard, Allen D. ..... **Minneapolis, MN**
Barnard, Amii Larkin ..... Novato, CA
Barnard, Andrew Carey ..... Miami, FL
Barnard, B. Thomas ..... Solvang, CA
Barnard, Bettye ..... Inglewood, CA
Barnard, Brian D. ..... **Fort Worth, TX**
Barnard, Brian M. ..... Salt Lake City, UT
Barnard, Bruce ..... Mountain View, WY
Barnard, Bruce J. ..... **Washington, DC**
Barnard, Charles M. ..... Wichita Falls, TX
Barnard, Christopher S. ..... Charlotte, NC
Barnard, Clifford J. ..... **Boulder, CO**
Barnard, Dale E. ..... Avon Lake, OH
Barnard, David B. ..... **Indianapolis, IN**
Barnard, David M. ..... New York, NY
Barnard, David R. ..... **Kansas City, MO**
Barnard, Deborah ..... Bennington, VT
Barnard, Deborah E. ..... **Boston, MA**
Barnard, Delbert James ..... **Seattle, WA**
Barnard, Douglas C. ..... High Point, NC
Barnard, Eaton G. ..... Mobile, AL
Barnard, Foreman & McCollam, Ltd.
Chicago, IL
Barnard, G. Kenneth ..... Wooster, OH
Barnard, Gary W. ..... **Amarillo, TX**
Barnard, Geoffrey W.
Charlotte Amalie, St. Thomas, VI
Barnard, George S. ..... Pompano Beach, FL
Barnard, Gilbert F. ..... Darlington, WI
Barnard, Glen A. ..... Harlingen, TX
Barnard, Greg A. ..... Norman, OK
Barnard, Gregg P. ..... **Reno, NV**
Barnard, Hollinger F. ..... **Birmingham, AL**
Barnard, J. Deems ..... Timonium, MD
Barnard, John ..... Walnut Creek, CA
Barnard, John H. ..... Riverside, CA
Barnard, Jonathan H. ..... **Quincy, IL**
Barnard, Kathleen P ..... **Seattle, WA**
Barnard, Kathryn A. ..... Mountain View, CA
Barnard, Kevin F. ..... **New York, NY**
Barnard, Larry L. ..... **Fort Wayne, IN**
Barnard, Laura C. ..... Kirtland, OH
Barnard Law Office ..... Darlington, WI
Barnard, Lisa M. ..... Buffalo, NY
Barnard, M. Scott ..... **Dallas, TX**
Barnard, Mary Ann ..... Honolulu, HI
Barnard, Maureen F. ..... **Indianapolis, IN**
Barnard, Melissa Pagni ..... **Las Vegas, NV**
Reno, NV
Barnard Mezzanotte & Pinnie ..... **Media, PA**
Philadelphia, PA
Barnard, Morton John ..... Chicago, IL
Barnard, Nancy Bramlett
Jacksonville, FL
Barnard, Nathan E. ..... **Oklahoma City, OK**
Barnard, Patrice P. ..... **Chicago, IL**
Barnard, Paul ..... Bushnell, FL
Barnard, Paul W. ..... **New York, NY**
Barnard & Pauly, P.S., A Prof. Srvcs. Corp.
Seattle, WA
Barnard, R. Kenneth ..... Babylon, NY
Barnard, Ralph R. ..... **Ithaca, NY**
Barnard, Randy ..... **Bellevue, WA**
Barnard, Remsen C. ..... Walnut Creek, CA
Barnard, Richard E. ..... Los Angeles, CA
Barnard, Robert C. ..... **Washington, DC**
Barnard, Robert J., Jr. ..... Kalamazoo, MI
Barnard, Robert N. ..... **Chicago, IL**
Barnard, Robert T. ..... **New York, NY**
Barnard, Robt. M. ..... Fresno, CA
Barnard, Ronald L. ..... Chicago, IL
Barnard, S. Charles ..... Huntsville, AL
Barnard, Smith and Burness, P.C.
Kalamazoo, MI
Barnard, Stephan C. ..... Princess Anne, MD
Barnard, Stephen Paul ..... Tucson, AZ
Barnard, Stephen Paul, P.C. ..... Tucson, AZ
Barnard, Steven M. ..... **Miami, FL**
Barnard, Susan M. ..... **Boston, MA**
Barnard, Thomas A. ..... **Indianapolis, IN**
Barnard, Thomas H. ..... **Cleveland, OH**
Barnard, Timothy B. ..... **Media, PA**
Barnard, Weakley E. ..... Nashville, TN
Barnard, William C. ..... **Indianapolis, IN**
Barnard, William M. ..... **Washington, DC**
Barnard, Woodburn & Sears, L.L.P.
Amarillo, TX
Barnarr, Peter J. ..... West Long Branch, NJ
Barnas, Michael C. ..... **Schenectady, NY**
Barnas, Michael J. J. ..... New York, NY
Barnatt, Theresa Ann ..... **Lake Charles, LA**
Barnavon, Erez ..... New York, NY
Barnby and Curto, P.A. ..... **Maitland, FL**
Barnby, Linda J. ..... **Maitland, FL**
Barndollar, Livia D. ..... New Canaan, CT
Barndt, Lisa A. ..... Auburn, NY
Barndt, Richard O. ..... San Diego, CA
Barnebey, Lauren R. ..... San Antonio, TX
Barnebey, Mark P. ..... Bradenton, FL
Barneck, Matthew C. ..... **Salt Lake City, UT**
Barnecut, John C. ..... San Francisco, CA
Barnell, Thomas M. ..... Baldwinsville, NY
Barner, Christian L. ..... **Kennebunk, ME**
Barner, Donald ..... Eastlake, OH
Barner, Donald A. ..... Santa Ana, CA
Barner, Freeman W., Jr.
North Palm Beach, FL
Barner, Juanita Jackson ..... Houston, TX
Barner, Kevin M. ..... **Washington, DC**
Barner, Sharon R. ..... **Chicago, IL**
Barner, Theodore E. ..... Roswell, GA
Barnes, A. Elizabeth ..... Raleigh, NC
Barnes, A. Parker, Jr. ..... **Beaufort, SC**
Barnes, A. Parker, Jr., P.A. & Associates
Beaufort, SC
Hilton Head Island, SC
Barnes, A. D. (Del), Jr. ..... Kenner, LA
Barnes, Alan ..... Lincoln, RI
Barnes, Alan R. ..... **Sacramento, CA**
Barnes, Albert D. ..... Point Pleasant Beach, NJ
Barnes, Alexander H. ..... **Durham, NC**
Barnes, Alford, Stork & Johnson, L.L.P.
Columbia, SC
Barnes, Alison Patrucco
United States Senate, Committee Legal Personnel, GV
Barnes, Allen ..... Nashville, TN
Barnes, Allen Jackson ..... **Columbia, SC**
Barnes, Allison M. ..... Broomall, PA
Barnes, Andrew M. ..... **Milwaukee, WI**
Barnes, Angel ..... Orange, CA
Barnes, Angela E.L. ..... **Chicago, IL**
Barnes, Anne Elizabeth ..... Decatur, GA
Barnes, Antonia J. ..... Coral Gables, FL
Barnes & Associates, P.C. ..... Austin, TX
Barnes, Attison L., III ..... **Washington, DC**
Barnes, B. Don ..... Edmond, OK
Barnes, Barbara A. ..... **Norristown, PA**
Barnes & Barnes ..... **Santa Barbara, CA**
Barnes and Barnes ..... Bloomfield Hills, MI
Barnes & Barnes ..... **Morristown, NJ**
Barnes & Barnes ..... Santa Fe, NM
Barnes & Barnes ..... Ossining, NY
Barnes & Barnes, A Professional Corporation ..... **Chatham, NJ**
Newark, NJ
Barnes, Barnes & Cohen, P.A.
Jacksonville, FL
Barnes, Barry M. ..... **Houston, TX**
Barnes & Batzli, P.C. ..... **Chesterfield, VA**
Glen Allen, VA
Richmond, VA
Barnes, Beamer H. ..... Lexington, NC
Barnes Bednorz, P.C. ..... **Austin, TX**
Barnes, Belinda S. ..... **Columbus, OH**
Barnes, Benjamin A. ..... **Northampton, MA**
Barnes, Benjamin A., P.C.
Greenfield, MA
Northampton, MA
Springfield, MA
Barnes, Bennie W. ..... Olympia, WA
Barnes, Blake L. ..... **Seattle, WA**
Barnes, Bonnie ..... Middlebury, VT
Barnes, Braswell & Haithcock, P.A.
Goldsboro, NC
Barnes, Bray B. ..... Red Bank, NJ
Barnes, Brent E. ..... **Los Angeles, CA**
Barnes, Brent O. ..... San Diego, CA
Barnes, Brian A. ..... Middlebury, CT
Barnes, Brigit S. ..... Sacramento, CA
Barnes, Brigit S., & Associates, Inc.
Sacramento, CA
Barnes, Brooke E. ..... Waterville, ME
Barnes, Broom, Dallas & McLeod, PLLC
Jackson, MS
Barnes, Brown and Oesterreicher, S.C.
Eau Claire, WI
Barnes, Bruce A. ..... Lakewood, CO
Barnes, Bruce E. ..... Honolulu, HI
Barnes, Bruce E. ..... Jericho, NY
Barnes, Bruce W. ..... St. Petersburg, FL
Barnes, Candace J. ..... St. Joseph, MO
Barnes, Carl A. ..... Tulsa, OK
Barnes, Carl F. ..... **Waltham, MA**
Barnes, Carolyn ..... **Austin, TX**
Barnes, Catharine S. ..... Mill Valley, CA
Barnes, Catherine Allen ..... **Charlotte, NC**
Barnes, Cecilia Suzette ..... Memphis, TN
Barnes, Chalmers H. ..... Jacksonville, FL
Barnes, Chaplin B. ..... **Westerly, RI**
Barnes, Chaplin B., Inc. ..... **Stonington, CT**
Westerly, RI
Barnes, Charles H. ..... Clanton, AL
Barnes, Charles T. ..... Duluth, MN
Barnes, Cheryl D. ..... **Washington, DC**
Barnes, Christopher ..... Philadelphia, PA
Barnes, Christopher A. ..... Seal Beach, CA
Barnes, Christopher G. ..... Stamford, CT
Barnes, Christopher Lee ..... **Dallas, TX**
Barnes, Christopher W. ..... Houston, TX
Barnes, Clarence E. ..... **Newport, KY**
Barnes, Claudine S. ..... Tulsa, OK
Barnes, Clemens H. ..... **Seattle, WA**
Barnes, Clifford E. ..... **Washington, DC**
Barnes, Clifford H. ..... Fort Pierce, FL
Barnes, Craig S. ..... **Los Angeles, CA**
Barnes, Craig S. ..... Santa Fe, NM
Barnes, Crosby, FitzGerald & Zeman LLP
Irvine, CA
Barnes, Curtis O. ..... **Irvine, CA**
Barnes, Curtis R. ..... Galatia, IL
Barnes, Cynthia Lynn ..... Denver, CO
Barnes, D. Alexander ..... **Malvern, PA**
Barnes, Dale C. ..... Morristown, TN
Barnes, Dale E., Jr. ..... **San Francisco, CA**
Barnes, Dana L. ..... **Portland, OR**
Barnes, Daniel D. ..... **New York, NY**
Barnes, Daryl C.
Christiansted, St. Croix, VI
Barnes, David ..... Birmingham, AL
Barnes, David A. ..... Minneapolis, MN
Barnes, David E. ..... **Detroit, MI**
Barnes, David G. ..... Bloomfield Hills, MI
Barnes, David H. ..... **Manchester, NH**
Barnes, David K. ..... **Louisville, KY**
Barnes, David K., Jr. ..... Detroit, MI
Barnes, David L. ..... St. Clairsville, OH
Barnes, David M. ..... **Raleigh, NC**
Barnes, David R. ..... Oklahoma City, OK
Barnes, David R. ..... Racine, WI
Barnes, David S. ..... **Winston-Salem, NC**
Barnes, Dean L.
Charlotte Amalie, St. Thomas, VI
Barnes, Debora E. ..... Chicago, IL
Barnes, Deborah Browers ..... **Tulsa, OK**
Barnes, Deborah Hawkins ..... Coronado, CA
Barnes, Dennis M. ..... **Detroit, MI**
Barnes, Dennis N. ..... **Washington, DC**
Barnes, Don ..... Oklahoma City, OK
Barnes, Don K. ..... Little Rock, AR
Barnes, Donald ..... Sedalia, MO
Barnes, Donald H. ..... Buzzards Bay, MA
Barnes, Donald M. ..... **Washington, DC**
Barnes, Donna M. ..... **Tupelo, MS**
Barnes, Douglas A. ..... **Dallas, TX**
Barnes, Douglas D. ..... Los Angeles, CA
Barnes, Douglas D. ..... Denver, CO
Barnes, Douglas P. ..... **Campbell, CA**
San Luis Obispo, CA
Barnes, Douglas P. ..... **San Jose, CA**
Barnes, Douglas W. ..... **Fort Lauderdale, FL**
Miami, FL
Barnes, E. Carole ..... **Oklahoma City, OK**
Barnes, E. Gregory ..... **San Diego, CA**
Barnes, Earl A. ..... Long Beach, CA
Barnes, Earl J. ..... **Chicago, IL**
Barnes, Earl J., II ..... **Chicago, IL**
Barnes, Edgar L. ..... Nags Head, NC
Barnes, Edgar R. ..... Lancaster, PA
Barnes, Edw. J., Jr. ..... Bethesda, MD
Barnes, Edward D. ..... **Chesterfield, VA**
Barnes, Edwin C. ..... **Salt Lake City, UT**
Barnes, Eleanor C. ..... Missouri City, TX
Barnes, Elisa ..... New York, NY
Barnes, Elizabeth A. ..... New York, NY
Barnes, Elizabeth M.
South San Francisco, CA
Barnes, Eric D. ..... **Clearwater, FL**
Barnes, Eugene Albert, IV ..... Mesa, AZ
Barnes, Eva, (Mrs.) ..... Fort Worth, TX
Barnes, F. Smith ..... **Oklahoma City, OK**
Barnes, F. Smith, P.C.
Oklahoma City, OK
Barnes & Farrell ..... Laguna Hills, CA
Barnes, Forrest W. ..... Houlton, ME
Barnes, Francis M., III ..... St. Louis, MO
Barnes, Frederick A., Jr. ..... Westminster, CA
Barnes, Frederick C. ..... Orlando, FL
Barnes, G. Lynn ..... Norcross, GA
Barnes, Garret T. ..... **Bradenton, FL**
Barnes, Gary A. ..... **Atlanta, GA**
Barnes, Gary D. ..... **Kansas City, MO**
Barnes, Gary H. ..... **Burlington, VT**
Barnes, Geoffrey K. ..... **Cleveland, OH**
Barnes, George L. ..... **Philadelphia, PA**
West Chester, PA
Barnes, Gerald H. ..... Tulsa, OK
Barnes, Glenn Daniel ..... Wayne, PA
Barnes, Gloria J. ..... Carlsbad, NM
Barnes, Grant, Law Offices of
Los Angeles, CA
Barnes & Green, P.L.L.C.
New Orleans, LA
Hattiesburg, MS
Jackson, MS
Barnes, Gregory ..... Middlebury, CT
Barnes, Gregory L. ..... Jefferson City, MO
Barnes, Grimes & Bunce ..... Lexington, NC
Barnes, H. Robert ..... Covina, CA
Barnes, Harris H. (Trip), III ..... **Jackson, MS**
Barnes, Harry F. ..... El Dorado, AR
Barnes, Haywood A. ..... **Livingston, NJ**
Barnes, Helen Onebane ..... **Lafayette, LA**
Barnes, Henson P. ..... **Goldsboro, NC**
Barnes, Herbert M. ..... Woodbridge, NJ

Barnes, Herbert W., Jr. .... Houma, LA
Barnes, Herschiel S. .... Cookeville, TN
Barnes, Hershell L., Jr. .... Dallas, TX
Barnes & Hilyer .... Clanton, AL
Barnes, Hubert B. .... Dresher, PA
Barnes, Ira A. .... Jensen Beach, FL
Barnes, Iraline G. .... Washington, DC
Barnes, Irwin N. .... Boston, MA
Barnes, J. Alan .... Dallas, TX
Barnes, James A. .... Columbus, OH
Barnes, James B. .... Houston, TX
Barnes, James C., Jr. .... Bloomfield Hills, MI
Barnes, James G. .... Chicago, IL
Barnes, James G. .... Haddonfield, NJ
Barnes, James H. .... Encino, CA
Barnes, James H. .... Richmond, VA
Barnes, James I., III .... Carson City, NV
Barnes, James J. .... Santa Rosa, CA
Barnes, James J. .... Pittsburgh, PA
Barnes, James K., Jr. .... Delaware, OH
Barnes, James M. .... Dalton, GA
Barnes, James M., Jr. .... Marion, AL
Barnes, James M., P.C. .... Dalton, GA
Barnes, James R. .... Pensacola, FL
Barnes, Jane S. .... Pittsburgh, PA
Barnes, Janet Callahan
Farmington Hills, MI
Barnes, Jason T. .... Dallas, TX
Barnes, Jefferson T. .... Chatham, NJ
Barnes, Jeffrey A. .... Baltimore, MD
Barnes, Jeffrey D. .... Charlotte, NC
Barnes, Jeffrey M. .... New York, NY
Barnes, Jeffrey P. .... Atlantic City, NJ
Pleasantville, NJ
Barnes, Jennifer Gibert .... Dallas, TX
Barnes, Jennifer R. .... Phoenix, AZ
Barnes, Jennifer R., P.C. .... Phoenix, AZ
Barnes, Jenny Corotis .... Springfield, OH
Barnes, Jerry F. .... Westminster, MD
Barnes, Jimmie R. "Sam" .... Jackson, NC
Nashville, NC
Rocky Mount, NC
Barnes, Jimmie R. "Sam"
Roanoke Rapids, NC
Barnes, Joan M. .... Bloomfield Hills, MI
Barnes, John Adam .... Seattle, WA
Barnes, John E. .... Cincinnati, OH
Barnes, John G., Jr. .... Santa Barbara, CA
Barnes, John L. .... Three Rivers, MI
Barnes, John M. .... Chicago, IL
Barnes, John M., Jr. .... Sarasota, FL
Barnes, John P. .... New Brunswick, NJ
Barnes, John R. .... Grand Rapids, MI
Lansing, MI
Barnes, John W. .... San Francisco, CA
Barnes, Jonathan B. .... Bakersfield, CA
Barnes, Joseph B. .... Milford, CT
Barnes, Joseph J. .... Pittsburgh, PA
Barnes, Judy Ann .... Las Vegas, NV
Barnes, Julian A. .... New York, NY
Barnes, Julie R. .... San Diego, CA
Barnes, Kaci L. .... Chicago, IL
Barnes, Karen Kay .... Oak Brook, IL
Barnes, Karen S. .... Bakersfield, CA
Barnes, Kathleen Olden .... McLean, VA
Barnes, Kathryn G. .... Pontiac, MI
Barnes, Kelly A. .... Media, PA
Barnes, Kennedy .... Dallas, TX
Barnes, Kenneth J. .... Concord, NH
Barnes, Kenneth Logan, Jr. .... San Pedro, CA
Barnes, Kenneth M. .... Lancaster, OH
Barnes, Kenneth N. .... Raleigh, NC
Barnes, Kenton R. .... Portland, OR
Barnes, Kevin D. .... Cleveland, OH
Barnes, Kevin R. .... Cincinnati, OH
Barnes, Kristen .... Chicago, IL
Barnes, L. Frederick .... Minneapolis, MN
Barnes, La Ronda D. .... Fort Lauderdale, FL
Barnes, Larry D. .... Longwood, FL
Barnes & Lassiter, P.C. .... Mesa, AZ
Barnes Law Firm .... Houston, TX
Barnes Law Group, P.C. .... New York, NY
Barnes Law Office .... Houlton, ME
Barnes Law Office, P.C. .... Three Rivers, MI
Barnes, Lawson .... Syracuse, NY
Barnes, Leo L. .... Austin, TX
Barnes, Lillie M. .... San Diego, CA
Barnes, Linda L. .... New York, NY
Barnes, Lindsay R., Jr. .... Charlottesville, VA
Barnes, Lisa Graivier .... St. Louis, MO
Barnes, Louis J. .... Chicago, IL
Barnes, Lowry N. .... Littlestown, PA
Barnes, LuAnn L. .... Ankeny, IA
Barnes, Lyle Joseph .... Kaysville, UT
Barnes, Macasline D., Jr. .... Roanoke, VA
Barnes, Malcolm D. H. .... Urbana, IL
Barnes, Marcia .... Little Rock, AR
Barnes, Margaret E. .... Lewisville, TX
Barnes, Margaret V. .... Santa Barbara, CA
Barnes, Marilyn Hartsfield .... Houston, TX
Barnes, Mark .... United States Senate,
Senatorial Assistants, GV
Barnes, Mark .... New York, NY
Barnes, Mark A. .... Moline, IL
Barnes, Mark B. .... Indianapolis, IN
Barnes, Mark J.
Department Of Health And Human Services, GV
Barnes, Mark S. .... Waterville, NY
Barnes, Mark S. .... Toledo, OH
Barnes, Mark T. .... Denver, CO
Barnes, Mary A. .... Harrisonburg, VA
Barnes, Mary Elizabeth .... Detroit, MI
Barnes, Mary K. .... Los Angeles, CA
Barnes, Matthew W. .... Birmingham, AL
Barnes, Maxwell N. .... Chicago, IL
Barnes, McGhee & Pryce .... Los Angeles, CA
Barnes, Melissa Stapleton
Indianapolis, IN
Barnes, Melody C. .... United States Senate,
Committee Legal Personnel, GV
Barnes, Melvin L., Jr. .... Washington, DC
Barnes, Michael A. .... San Francisco, CA
Barnes, Michael D. .... Little Rock, AR
Barnes, Michael D. .... Washington, DC
Barnes, Michael David .... Lafayette, IN
Barnes, Michael F. .... St. Louis, MO
Barnes, Michael P. .... South Bend, IN
Barnes, Michael P. .... New York, NY
Barnes, Michael R. .... Key West, FL
Barnes, Michael R. .... Hattiesburg, MS
Barnes, Michael W. .... Alamo, CA
Barnes, Michael W. .... Santa Monica, CA
Barnes, Michelle Elizabeth .... Denver, CO
Barnes, Minor .... Cedar Rapids, IA
Barnes Morris & Yorn, A Professional
Corporation .... Los Angeles, CA
Santa Monica, CA
Barnes, Mortimer P. .... Greenwich, CT
Barnes, Nan C. .... Simsbury, CT
Barnes, Natasha L. .... Austin, TX
Barnes, Nathanael G. .... Dallas, TX
Barnes, Ned M. .... Carolina Beach, NC
Barnes, Ned M. .... Spokane, WA
Barnes, Nelsonna Potts .... Wichita, KS
Barnes, Nicholas P. .... Lakebay, WA
Barnes, Obren V. .... Washington, DC
Barnes, Opal M. .... Houston, TX
Barnes, Oscar P., III .... Monroe, LA
Barnes, Page R. .... Oakland, CA
Barnes, Pamela .... Los Angeles, CA
Barnes, Patricia A. .... Silver Spring, MD
Barnes, Patricia T. .... Austin, TX
Barnes, Patrick L. .... Arcadia, CA
Barnes, Patrick R. .... Topeka, KS
Barnes, Paul E. .... Jackson, MS
Barnes, Paul M. .... Milwaukee, WI
Barnes, Peter .... Washington, DC
Barnes, Peter A. .... Fairfield, CT
Barnes, Peter J., III .... Woodbridge, NJ
Barnes, Philip B. .... Towson, MD
Barnes, Philip G. .... Akron, OH
Barnes, R. Don, Jr. .... Nashville, TN
Barnes and Radney, P.C.
Alexander City, AL
Barnes, Randall O. .... Jefferson City, MO
Barnes, Rebecca K. .... Phoenix, AZ
Barnes, Reginald W. .... United States Senate,
Committee Legal Personnel, GV
Barnes, Renard E. .... New York, NY
Barnes, Richard E. .... Norcross, GA
Barnes, Richard E. .... Albany, NY
Barnes, Richard J. .... Buffalo, NY
Barnes, Richard J. .... Lake Ariel, PA
Barnes, Richard L. .... New York, NY
Barnes, Richard L. .... Tulsa, OK
Barnes, Richard M. .... Baltimore, MD
Barnes, Richard M. .... New York, NY
Barnes, Richard W., Jr. .... Knoxville, TN
Barnes, Richardson & Colburn
Washington, DC
Chicago, IL
New York, NY
Barnes, Robert .... Los Angeles, CA
Barnes, Robert .... Oakland, CA
Barnes, Robert A. .... Atlanta, GA
Barnes, Robert A., Jr. .... Lacon, IL
Barnes, Robert B. .... Frankfort, KY
Barnes, Robert Bryan .... Columbia, SC
Barnes, Robert C. .... Los Angeles, CA
Barnes, Robert C. .... Duluth, MN
Barnes, Robert D. .... Hinsdale, IL
Barnes, Robert D. .... Philadelphia, PA
Barnes, Robert F. .... Hidalgo, TX
Barnes, Robert L., Jr. .... Clearwater, FL
Barnes, Robert M. .... Jacksonville, FL
Barnes, Robert M. .... Kansas City, MO
Barnes, Robert M. .... Pittsburgh, PA
Barnes, Robert N. .... Oklahoma City, OK
Barnes, Robert O. .... Walnut Creek, CA
Barnes, Robert R. .... San Diego, CA
Barnes, Robert Samuel .... Irvine, CA
Barnes, Robert W. .... Lexington, MI
Barnes, Robert W., (Professional
Corporation) .... Los Angeles, CA
Barnes, Roderick R. .... Baltimore, MD
Barnes, Ronald Merrill .... Tulsa, OK
Barnes, Ronald S. .... Revere, MA
Barnes, Rowland W. .... College Park, GA
Barnes, Roy .... Hempstead, NY
Barnes, Roy L. .... Houston, TX
Barnes, Rudolph C., Jr. .... Prosperity, SC
Barnes, Russell S. .... Libby, MT
Barnes, S. Mark .... Salt Lake City, UT
Barnes, Samuel Stephen .... Poteau, OK
Barnes, Sandra P. .... Blaine, MN
Barnes, Scott M. .... Cleveland, OH
Barnes, Scott Y. .... Charleston, SC
Barnes, Shannon Murphy .... Lawrence, MA
Barnes, Sharon L. .... Rancho Cucamonga, CA
Barnes, Sherry T. .... Augusta, GA
Barnes, Smith, Lewis & McCutcheon, P.C.
Oklahoma City, OK
Barnes, Stephen A. .... Clearwater, FL
Tampa, FL
Tampa, FL
Barnes, Stephen D. .... Beverly Hills, CA
Barnes, Stephen E. .... Buffalo, NY
Barnes, Stephen G. .... Laguna Hills, CA
Barnes, Stephen G. .... Eugene, OR
Barnes, Stephen P. .... Washington, DC
Barnes, Steven .... Hanford, CA
Barnes, Steven F. .... Santa Barbara, CA
Barnes, Steven J. .... New York, NY
Barnes, Steven R. .... La Junta, CO
Barnes, Steven W. .... Chula Vista, CA
Barnes, Susan .... West Des Moines, IA
Barnes, Susan E. .... Orlando, FL
Barnes, Susan E. .... Minneapolis, MN
Barnes, Susan E., P.A. .... Orlando, FL
Barnes, Susan Graham .... Wheat Ridge, CO
Barnes, Susan L. .... Seattle, WA
Barnes, T. Ellis, III .... St. Louis, MO
Barnes, T. Larry .... Denver, CO
Barnes, Tahereh K. .... Long Beach, CA
Barnes, Tamara .... New York, NY
Barnes, Teveia R. .... San Francisco, CA
Barnes, Thad M. .... Louisville, KY
Barnes, Theodore D. .... Independence, MO
Barnes, Therese S. .... Atlanta, GA
Barnes, Thomas A., Jr.
Colorado Springs, CO
Barnes, Thomas E. .... Columbus, OH
Barnes, Thomas E. .... Evanston, WY
Barnes, Thomas G. .... Ossining, NY
Barnes, Thomas H. .... Ossining, NY
Barnes, Thomas H. .... Rapid City, SD
Barnes, Thomas J. .... Grand Rapids, MI
Barnes, Thomas J. .... Buffalo, NY
Barnes, Thomas R. .... San Bernardino, CA
Barnes, Thomas R. .... Toccoa, GA
Barnes & Thornburg .... Washington, DC
Chicago, IL
Elkhart, IN
Fort Wayne, IN
Indianapolis, IN
South Bend, IN
Barnes, Timothy H. .... Mesa, AZ
Barnes, Timothy H. .... Haverhill, MA
Barnes, Timothy L. .... Chatham, NJ
Barnes, Tom R., II .... Topeka, KS
Barnes, Trent L. .... Long Beach, CA
Barnes, Truman D. .... Owensboro, KY
Barnes & Turner .... Houston, TX
Barnes, Valerie K. .... Charlevoix, MI
Barnes, W. Bradley .... San Antonio, TX
Barnes, W. Faison .... Charlotte, NC
Barnes, W. Jeffrey .... Fort Lauderdale, FL
Barnes, W. Joey .... Raleigh, NC
Barnes, W. Newton .... Dallas, TX
Barnes, W. Peter .... West Chester, PA
Barnes, W. Scears, Jr. .... Alexander City, AL
Barnes, W. Stuart .... Akron, OH
Barnes & Wadford, P.A. .... Weaverville, NC
Barnes Walker, Chartered .... Bradenton, FL
Barnes, Wallace .... Bristol, CT
Barnes, Wallace E., III .... Berkeley, CA
Barnes, Wallace R. .... Columbus, OH
Barnes, Walter A. .... Milwaukie, OR
Portland, OR
Barnes, Walter S. .... Cedar Crest, NM
Barnes, Walton J. .... Greenwell Springs, LA
Barnes, Walton J., II .... Baton Rouge, LA
Barnes, Walton J., II, A Professional Law
Corporation .... Baton Rouge, LA
Barnes, Wayne R. .... Amarillo, TX
Barnes, William A., Jr. .... Weaverville, NC
Barnes, William B. .... Fairfield, CT
Barnes, William C., Jr. .... Florence, SC
Barnes, William C. C. .... Towson, MD
Barnes, William Curtis, Jr. .... Santa Ana, CA
Barnes, William E. .... Sacramento, CA
Barnes, William E., Jr. .... Livonia, MI
Barnes, William Ferguson, III
West Palm Beach, FL
Barnes, William G. .... Phoenix, AZ
Barnes, William H. .... Austin, TX
Barnes, William H. .... Kenosha, WI
Barnes, William J. .... Woodbridge, NJ
Barnes, William J. .... Greenville, SC
Barnes, William J. G. .... Newport News, VA
Barnes, William M. .... Philadelphia, PA
Barnes, William N. .... Orlando, FL
Barnes, William O., Jr. .... Chatham, NJ
Barnes, William S. .... Cambridge, MA
Barnes, William S. .... Santa Fe, NM
Barnes, William Y., III .... Marietta, GA
Barnes, Willie R. .... Los Angeles, CA
Barnes, Wilson K. .... Lutherville, MD
Barnes, Winsome Y. .... Edison, NJ
Barnes, W. R. .... Odessa, TX
Barnes, W. T. .... Ottumwa, IA
Barnes, Yvonne Y. .... Philadelphia, PA
Barnes-Brown, Peter N. .... Waltham, MA
Barnes-Hulsey, Donrua .... Memphis, TN
Barnes-Pannell, Johnine P.
Washington, DC
Barnes-Pirko, Theresa .... Richmond, VA
Barness, Daniel I. .... Manhattan Beach, CA
New York, NY
Barness, Jordan G.
Manhattan Beach, CA
New York, NY
Barnes Velez, Fernando .... Ponce, PR
Barnet, Christopher A. .... Dallas, TX
Barnet, Elna K. .... Department of Agriculture,
Animal and Plant Health Inspection Service,
GV
Barnet, Howard J., Jr. .... New York, NY
Barnet, Irwin G. .... Los Angeles, CA
Barnet, Lionel .... Miami, FL
Barnet, Lionel, P.A. .... Miami, FL
Barnet, Robert L. .... Muncie, IN
Barnet, Sandy Wald .... San Francisco, CA
Barnett, Alexa B. .... Rockville, MD
Barnett, Alexander E. .... Washington, DC
Barnett, Alice Kupler .... Dallas, TX
Barnett & Allison .... Albuquerque, NM
Barnett, Amanda Wood .... Alexandria, LA
Barnett, Amy S. .... New York, NY
Barnett, Ana T. .... Miami, FL
Barnett, Ann .... Gainesville, FL
Barnett, Anne Love .... Wilmington, DE
Barnett, Arthur J. .... New York, NY
Barnett & Associates .... Greenwich, CT
Stamford, CT
Barnett & Associates, P.A. .... Miami, FL
Barnett & Associates, P.A. .... Tampa, FL
Barnett, Ayesha Mazhar .... New York, NY
Barnett, Barbra .... Los Angeles, CA
Barnett, Barclay & Springmann, P.A.
Kissimmee, FL
Orlando, FL
Sanford, FL
Barnett & Barnard, P.A.
Fort Lauderdale, FL
Miami, FL
Barnett & Barnett .... Santa Monica, CA
Barnett and Barnett, P.C. .... Cherry Hill, NJ
Havertown, PA
Barnett, Barney K. .... Chandler, OK
Barnett, Barry C. .... Dallas, TX
Barnett, Barry H. .... Albuquerque, NM
Barnett, Barry M. .... Alexandria, LA
Barnett, Belinda A. .... Department of Justice,
Antitrust Division, GV
Barnett, Benjamin R. .... Washington, DC
Barnett, Berrett, King & Southam, L.L.C.
Aurora, CO
Barnett, Bolt, Kirkwood & Long, P.A.
Tampa, FL
Barnett, Bonnie Allyn .... Philadelphia, PA
Barnett, Bruce E. .... Eugene, OR
Barnett, Bruce M. .... Stockton, CA
Barnett, Bruce W. .... Albuquerque, NM
Barnett, Bugg & Lee .... Evergreen, AL
Monroeville, AL
Barnett, Burt .... Downey, CA
Barnett, Byron E. .... San Antonio, TX
Barnett, C. Sue .... New York, NY
Barnett, Carol .... Mountain View, CA
Barnett, Carol C. .... St. Joseph, MO
Barnett, Carol Hee .... Rush, NY
Barnett, Charles Dawson
West Palm Beach, FL
Barnett, Charles E. .... Greenwich, CT
Greenwich, CT
Barnett, Charles E. .... Charleston, WV
Barnett, Charles F., Jr. .... Roanoke, VA
Barnett, Charles F., Jr., A Professional
Corporation .... Roanoke, VA
Barnett, Charles G. .... Dallas, TX
Barnett, Charles H. .... Jackson, TN
Barnett, Charles J., P.C. .... Levittown, NY
Barnett, Charles Jeffrey .... Memphis, TN
Barnett, Corol Sue .... New York, NY
Barnett & Craddock, L.L.P. .... Houston, TX
Barnett, Craig S. .... Fort Lauderdale, FL
Barnett, Cynthia Faye .... Boston, MA
Barnett, Cynthia Mitchell .... Nashville, TN
Barnett, Cynthia Singleton
Springfield, OH
Barnett, D. Sean .... Washington, DC
Barnett, Dana Jones .... Sapulpa, OK
Barnett, David A. .... Brooklyn, NY
Barnett, David A. .... Frederick, OK
Barnett, David C. .... Urbana, OH
Barnett, David L. .... Mobile, AL
Barnett, David L. .... New Orleans, LA
Barnett, David L. .... Battle Creek, MI
Barnett, David S. .... Minneapolis, MN
Barnett, Deborah J. .... New York, NY
Barnett, Denise E. .... Jacksonville, FL
Barnett, Devitt D. .... Seattle, WA
Barnett, Don M. .... Austin, TX
Barnett, Donald .... Los Angeles, CA
Barnett, Donald J. .... Carson, CA
Barnett, E. William .... Houston, TX
Barnett, Edgar F. .... Houston, TX
Barnett, Edwin B. .... Cherry Hill, NJ
Havertown, PA
Barnett, Elizabeth M. .... Jamaica, NY
Barnett, Ellen A. .... Miami, FL
Barnett, Emily S. .... New York, NY
Barnett, Erwin M. .... Miami Beach, FL
Barnett, Eugene J. .... Columbia, SC
Barnett, Frederic J. .... Stow, MA
Barnett, Fritz .... Houston, TX
Barnett, Garry D. .... Mankato, MN
Barnett, Gary .... New York, NY
Barnett, Gary, (A Professional Corporation)
Los Angeles, CA
Barnett, George C., Jr. .... Evansville, IN
Barnett, George D. .... Houston, TX
Barnett, George H. .... Los Altos Hills, CA
Barnett, George L. .... Brewster, NY
Barnett, George L., P.C. .... Brewster, NY
Barnett, George M. .... Guntersville, AL
Barnett, Glynn D. .... Ann Arbor, MI
Barnett, Gordon J., Jr. .... Ann Arbor, MI
Barnett, Gordon J., Jr., P.C.
Ann Arbor, MI
Barnett, Gregory G. .... New York, NY
Barnett, H. John .... Terre Haute, IN
Barnett, Hanes, O'Neal, Duffee & Garfield,
LLC .... Birmingham, AL
Barnett, Harvey J. .... Chicago, IL
Barnett, Harvey J., & Associates, P.C.
Chicago, IL
Barnett, Henry C., Jr. .... Montgomery, AL
Barnett, Henry S. .... Atlanta, GA
Barnett, Hollis H., (P.S.) .... Puyallup, WA
Barnett, Howard John .... Terre Haute, IN
Barnett, Hugh .... Springfield, OH
Barnett, Iris S. .... Washington, DC
Barnett, J. Rex .... Fort Worth, TX
Barnett, Jacalyn F. .... New York, NY
Barnett, Jacqueline C. .... York, PA
Barnett, James A., Jr. .... Tupelo, MS
Barnett, James D. .... Miami, FL
Barnett, James E. .... Los Angeles, CA

Barnett, James E., Jr. ....Charlotte, NC
Barnett, James H. ....Providence, RI
Barnett, James J. ....Foster City, CA
Barnett, James J. ....Santa Ana, CA
Barnett, James K. ....Anchorage, AK
Barnett, James L. ....Vicksburg, MS
Barnett, James L. ....Salt Lake City, UT
Barnett, James M. ....Merced, CA
Barnett, James M. ....Kansas City, KS
Overland Park, KS
Barnett, James P., Jr. ....Houston, TX
Barnett, James R. ....Sunnyvale, CA
Barnett, James R. ....Washington, DC
Barnett, James R. ....Des Moines, IA
Barnett, James R. ....Oklahoma City, OK
Barnett, James William ....Danville, KY
Barnett, Jana R. ....Wyomissing, PA
Barnett, Jeffery T. ....Lexington, KY
Barnett, Jeffrey A. ....San Diego, CA
San Jose, CA
Barnett, Jeffrey A., A Professional Corporation ....San Jose, CA
Barnett, Jerome E. ....New York, NY
Barnett, Jerrold H. ....New Haven, CT
Barnett, John B., III ....Monroeville, AL
Barnett, John D., Law Office of
Orange, CA
Barnett, John Douglas ....Columbia, SC
Barnett, John E. ....Boscobel, WI
Barnett, John H., III ....Jackson, MS
Barnett, John V., Jr. ....Indianapolis, IN
Barnett, John W. ....New Haven, CT
Barnett, John W. ....Cahokia, IL
Barnett, John William ....Aurora, CO
Barnett, Joseph P. ....Aberdeen, SD
Barnett, Jules D. ....Santa Monica, CA
Barnett, Karen A. ....Tampa, FL
Barnett, Kathleen ....Arlington, TX
Barnett, Kathleen E. ....Santa Ana, CA
Barnett, Kathleen Virginia ....Rolla, MO
Barnett, Kathryn ....Nashville, TN
Barnett, Kathryn P. ....Kansas City, KS
Overland Park, KS
Barnett, Keith R. ....Boston, MA
Barnett, Keith S. ....New York, NY
Barnett, Kenneth J. ....Summersville, WV
Barnett, Kenneth R. ....Stuart, FL
Barnett, Kevin L. ....Charlotte, NC
Barnett, Kim L. ....New York, NY
Barnett, L. Kenneth ....Fort Lauderdale, FL
Barnett, Lance E. ....New York, NY
Barnett, Larry D. ....Wilmington, DE
Barnett Law Firm, The, Chartered
Kansas City, KS
Overland Park, KS
Barnett Law Offices ....Terre Haute, IN
Barnett, Lawrence R. ....Los Angeles, CA
Barnett, Ledeen G. ....Long Beach, CA
Barnett, Lee R. ....Wakarusa, KS
Barnett, Lena S. ....Bethesda, MD
Chevy Chase, MD
Olney, MD
Potomac, MD
Rockville, MD
Barnett, Lena S. ....Silver Spring, MD
Barnett, Leslie Ann ....Los Angeles, CA
Barnett, Leslie J. ....Tampa, FL
Barnett, Lisa E. ....San Francisco, CA
Barnett, Lisa H. ....Naples, FL
Barnett, Lisa M. ....Washington, DC
Barnett, Lorraine K. ....Piscataway, NJ
Barnett, Louis E. ....San Antonio, TX
Barnett, Lynn D. ....St. Louis, MO
Barnett, Marc M. ....Palos Hills, IL
Barnett, Mark A. ....Department of Commerce, Office of the General Counsel, GV
Barnett, Mark Edward ....Brockton, MA
Barnett, Mark W. ....Pierre, SD
Barnett, Martha W. ....Tallahassee, FL
Barnett, Matthew E. ....Roslyn, NY
Barnett, Matthew S. ....New York, NY
Barnett • Mattice ....Fairfield, CA
Vacaville, CA
Barnett, Maurice S. ....Macon, GA
Barnett, Megan A. ....Washington, DC
Barnett, Michael ....Tampa, FL
Barnett, Michael H. ....New York, NY
Barnett, Michael J. ....Myrtle Beach, SC
Barnett, Michael, P.A. ....Tampa, FL
Barnett, Mickey D. ....Albuquerque, NM
Barnett, Mickey D., P.A. ....Albuquerque, NM
Barnett, Mitchell W. ....North Plainfield, NJ
Barnett, Monty L. ....Denver, CO
Cheyenne, WY
Barnett, Nancy G. ....Houston, TX
Barnett, Neal J. ....Bloomfield Hills, MI
Barnett, Neal J., P.C.
Bloomfield Hills, MI
Barnett, Ned, Law Offices of ....Houston, TX
Barnett, Newell C. ....Berkeley, CA
Barnett, Norman C. ....Georgetown, DE
Lewes, DE
Barnett, Pamelia ....Houston, TX
Barnett, Patricia J. ....Puyallup, WA
Barnett, Paul M. ....Christiansburg, VA
Barnett, Paul T. ....Sioux Falls, SD
Barnett, Paul W. ....Cumberland, MD
Barnett, Paul W. ....Arlington, VA
Barnett, Paula Winner ....Los Angeles, CA
Barnett, Peter P. ....Havertown, PA
Barnett, Philip ....Los Angeles, CA
Barnett, Philip S. ....Juneau, AK
Barnett, Philip S. ....San Mateo, CA
Barnett, Preston B. ....Atlanta, GA
Barnett, Quayla D. ....Canoga Park, CA
Barnett, R. Joseph ....Palm Beach, FL
Barnett, Randal L. ....Marrero, LA
Barnett, Randell E. ....High Point, NC

Barnett, Randy E. ....Boston, MA
Barnett, Richard A. ....Hollywood, FL
Barnett, Richard A., P.A.
Fort Lauderdale, FL
Hollywood, FL
Barnett, Richard J. ....Hoffman Estates, IL
Barnett, Richard L. ....Irvine, CA
Barnett, Richard M. ....San Diego, CA
Barnett, Richard S. ....Covington, KY
Barnett, Rita Fournier ....Costa Mesa, CA
Barnett, Robert ....San Rafael, CA
Barnett, Robert A. ....New Orleans, LA
Barnett, Robert B. ....Washington, DC
Barnett, Robert B., Jr. ....Columbus, OH
Barnett, Robert C. ....Birmingham, AL
Barnett, Robert D. ....Santa Monica, CA
Barnett, Robert E. ....Fairfield, CA
Barnett, Robert E., III ....Louisville, KY
Barnett, Robert Eugene ....Washington, DC
Barnett, Robert G. ....Jackson, MS
Barnett, Robert L. ....Birmingham, AL
Barnett, Robert L. ....Myrtle Beach, SC
Barnett, Robert P. ....Wilmington, DE
Barnett, Robert P. ....Miami, FL
Barnett, Robert S. ....New York, NY
Barnett, Robert S. ....Philadelphia, PA
Barnett, Robt. C. ....Houston, TX
Barnett, Rohan O. ....New York, NY
Barnett, Ross Forrest ....Des Moines, IA
Barnett, Ross R., Jr. ....Jackson, MS
Barnett & Rubin, A Professional Corporation
Irvine, CA
Barnett, Sallie ....Corona, CA
Barnett, Sarah E. ....Washington, DC
Barnett, Saul H. ....Aspen, CO
Barnett, Scott B. ....Chicago, IL
Barnett, Scott F. ....Brandon, FL
Tampa, FL
Barnett, Scott F., Chartered ....Brandon, FL
Tampa, FL
Barnett, Sean M. ....Fairfax, VA
Barnett, Selina D. ....Atlanta, GA
Barnett, Sharon L. ....Pensacola, FL
Barnett, Sheli L. ....Dallas, TX
Barnett, Shelley R.Z. ....Oakbrook Terrace, IL
Barnett & Sivon, P.C. ....Washington, DC
Barnett, Stanley E. ....Charleston, SC
Barnett, Stephanie B. ....Houston, TX
Barnett, Stephen G. ....Dallas, TX
Barnett, Stephen M. ....Richmond, VA
Barnett, Stephen R. ....Berkeley, CA
Barnett, Stephen R. ....Burlingame, CA
Barnett, Stephen R. ....Mesquite, TX
Barnett, Steve ....Roseland, NJ
Barnett, Steve M. ....Northbrook, IL
Barnett, Steven D. ....Louisville, CO
Barnett, Steven R. ....New York, NY
Barnett, Stuart S. ....Beverly Hills, CA
Barnett, Stuart S., A Law Corporation
Beverly Hills, CA
Barnett, Susan J. ....McKinney, TX
Barnett, Susan Kay ....Oakland, CA
Barnett, Suzanne B. ....New York, NY
Barnett, Suzanne M. ....Seattle, WA
Barnett, Tanya ....Olympia, WA
Seattle, WA
Barnett, Terry J. ....Tacoma, WA
Barnett, Theodore R. ....Stowe, VT
Barnett, Theresa A. ....Chicago, IL
Barnett, Thomas C., Jr. ....Pierre, SD
Barnett, Thomas David Hunter
Georgetown, DE
Barnett, Thomas I. ....Palo Alto, CA
Barnett, Thomas J. ....Portland, OR
Barnett, Thomas O. ....Washington, DC
Barnett, Timothy M. ....Minneapolis, MN
St. Paul, MN
Barnett, Tracy G. ....Chicago, IL
Barnett, Vanessa A. ....New York, NY
Barnett, W. Todd ....Houston, TX
Barnett, Walter L. ....Birmingham, AL
Barnett, Wayne ....Boston, MA
Barnett, Wendell ....Dallas, TX
Barnett, William ....New York, NY
Barnett, William A. ....Chicago, IL
Barnett, William A. ....Cleveland, OH
Barnett, William B. ....Sherman Oaks, CA
Barnett, William B. ....Orlando, FL
Barnett, William M. ....New Orleans, LA
Barnett, William N. ....Riverside, CA
Barnett, William R. ....Jackson, MS
Barnett, William S. ....Cadillac, MI
Barnett, William T., Jr. ....Raleigh, NC
Barnett & Wright, P.A. ....Conway, SC
Myrtle Beach, SC
Barnette, C. Kevin ....Washington, DC
Barnette, C. Michael ....Port Orange, FL
Barnette, Carolyn Reid ....Winston-Salem, NC
Barnette, Charles Decker ....Texarkana, AR
Barnette, Christopher K. ....San Diego, CA
Barnette, Curtis H. ....Bethlehem, PA
Barnette, Cynthia Wegley ....Charleston, WV
Barnette, David Allen ....Charleston, WV
Barnette, Evans Taylor ....Columbia, SC
Barnette, H. Vance, III ....Raleigh, NC
Barnette, Henry V., Jr. ....Raleigh, NC
Barnette, Kenneth E. ....Baton Rouge, LA
Barnette, William P. ....New Orleans, LA
Barnett-Luvera, Lita ....Seattle, WA
Barney, Albert W., Jr. ....St. Johnsbury, VT
Barney, Brett S. ....Denver, CO
Barney, Brian J. ....Rochester, NY
Barney, Carey S. ....Chicago, IL
Barney, Carter, Johnson & Baker, P.C.
Lincoln, NE
Barney, Charlotte L. ....Bridgewater, NJ
Barney, Colleen ....Irvine, CA
Barney, Dale E. ....Newark, NJ

Barney, Donald F., Jr. ....Cleveland, OH
Barney, G. Lant, Jr. ....Auburn, CA
Barney, Gary A. ....Lander, WY
Barney, Grossman, Dubow & Marcus
Ithaca, NY
Barney, Isabel ....Dania, FL
Barney, James O. ....Concord, NH
Barney, Jane H. ....Baton Rouge, LA
Barney, Jane Taubner ....Waltham, MA
Barney, Jay Verl ....Sandy, UT
Barney, John Andrew ....Nashville, TN
Barney, John B. ....Portland, ME
Barney, John C. ....Ithaca, NY
Barney, John R., Jr. ....Indianapolis, IN
Barney, Jonathan A. ....Newport Beach, CA
Barney, Justin F. ....Salt Lake City, UT
Barney, Keri ....Minneapolis, MN
Barney, Kevin L. ....Chicago, IL
Barney, Louie L. ....Pittsburg, KS
Barney, Manny I. ....Las Vegas, NV
Barney, Mark T. ....Oxnard, CA
Barney, Mary V. ....Lynchburg, VA
Barney, Melanie Jacobs ....Easton, MD
Barney, Michael E. ....Virginia Beach, VA
Barney, Michael J. ....Southfield, MI
Barney, Michele D. ....Los Angeles, CA
Barney, Patrick E.
Steamboat Springs, CO
Barney, Philip C., Jr. ....Palo Alto, CA
Barney, R. Daren ....St. George, UT
Barney, Richard A. ....Johnstown, NY
Barney, Richard M., Jr. ....Seattle, WA
Barney, Robert S. ....Bloomfield, MO
Barney, Sarah J. ....Los Angeles, CA
Barney, Scott C. ....Baton Rouge, LA
New Orleans, LA
Barney, Sidney ....Petersburg, VA
Barney, Steven L. ....Petoskey, MI
Barney, Thomas L. ....Richmond, VA
Barney, Thomas L., P.C. ....Richmond, VA
Barney, Thomas M. ....Buffalo, NY
Barney, William E. ....Corry, PA
Barney, William H., III ....Dayton, OH
Barngrover, Mary Ann ....San Francisco, CA
Barnhard, David W. ....Bronx, NY
Barnhard, Dean T. ....Indianapolis, IN
Barnhard, Elizabeth M. ....Parsippany, NJ
Barnhardt, Hubert J., III ....Norcross, GA
Barnhardt, John J., III ....Charlotte, NC
Barnhardt, John M. ....Mooresville, NC
Barnhardt, W. Doak ....Charlotte, NC
Barnhardt, Zeb E., Jr. ....Winston-Salem, NC
Barnhart, Arthur G. ....Bethesda, MD
Barnhart, Brent A. ....Sacramento, CA
Barnhart, Bruce A. ....Grand Rapids, MI
Barnhart, Bruce C. ....Omaha, NE
Barnhart, Carl ....Fort Worth, TX
Barnhart, Charles R. ....Albuquerque, NM
Barnhart, Constance R.
Fort Lauderdale, FL
Barnhart, Daniel R. ....Portland, OR
Barnhart, David B. ....Columbus, OH
Barnhart, Dennis G. ....Carson City, NV
Barnhart, Esther R. ....Rockland, ME
Barnhart, F. Gregory
West Palm Beach, FL
Barnhart, Frank A. ....Bloomington, IN
Barnhart, Fred P., (Inc., P.S.) ....Bellevue, WA
Barnhart, Gary E. ....Canton, IL
Barnhart, Gene ....Canton, OH
Barnhart, George Don-Lynn ....Sykesville, MD
Barnhart, H. Mack ....Gainesville, TX
Barnhart, Jacqueline Mary ....Akron, OH
Barnhart, James F. ....Dayton, OH
Barnhart, John G. ....Tulsa, OK
Barnhart, John N. ....Houston, TX
Barnhart, Joyce A. ....Birmingham, MI
Barnhart, Katherine L.
Bloomfield Hills, MI
Barnhart, Katherine L., P.C.
Bloomfield Hills, MI
Barnhart, Keith E. ....Attica, IN
Barnhart, Melissa S. ....Yorkville, IL
Barnhart & O'Connor, Law Office of
Attica, IN
Barnhart, Philip N. ....Eugene, OR
Barnhart, Ralph C. ....Fayetteville, AR
Barnhart, Richard A. ....Columbus, OH
Barnhart, Robert Guy ....Ferndale, MI
Barnhart, Robert J.
Equal Employment Opportunity Commission, GV
Barnhart, Robert W. ....Warm Springs, AR
Barnhart, Steven D. ....Atlanta, GA
Barnhart, Steven D., & Associates, P.C.
Atlanta, GA
Barnhart, Sturgeon & Spencer
Bloomington, IN
Barnhart, Thomas M., II ....Dayton, OH
Barnhart, Timothy V., (P.C.) ....St. Louis, MO
Barnhart, W. Randolph ....Englewood, CO
Barnhart y Chavez, Sandy
Rio Rancho, NM
Barnhill, Allison R. ....Charlotte, NC
Barnhill, Ann H. ....Greenville, NC
Barnhill, Brian R. ....Salt Lake City, UT
Barnhill, Charles, Jr. ....Madison, WI
Barnhill, Curtis G. ....Kansas City, KS
Barnhill, D. Stan ....Roanoke, VA
Barnhill, David H. ....Plant City, FL
Barnhill, Donald E. ....San Antonio, TX
Barnhill, Edward D., Jr. ....Columbia, SC
Barnhill, G. Michael ....Charlotte, NC
Barnhill, George E. ....Waycross, GA
Barnhill & Goodman, P.C.
West Des Moines, IA
Barnhill, H. Grady, Jr.
Winston-Salem, NC

Barnhill, Helen Gwyn ....Boulder, CO
Barnhill, James B. ....Little Rock, AR
Barnhill, James H. ....Worcester, MA
Barnhill, Jimmy H. ....Winston-Salem, NC
Barnhill, Kathryn Schweiker
West Des Moines, IA
Barnhill, Kenneth E. ....Golden, CO
Barnhill, Kenneth M. ....Havelock, NC
Barnhill, Leander D. ....Department of Justice, Executive Office for United States Trustees, GV
Barnhill, Maurice V., Jr. ....Wilmington, NC
Barnhill McKasson & Klein LLP
Long Beach, CA
Barnhill, Norris V. ....Spokane, WA
Barnhill, Robert E., III ....Lubbock, TX
Barnhill, Shannon L. ....Birmingham, AL
Barnhill, Stephen D. ....Lexington, NC
Barnhill, Steven M. ....Long Beach, CA
Barnhill, Tebbie M. ....Houston, TX
Barnhill, William W. ....Goliad, TX
Barnhisel, Peter L. ....Corvallis, OR
Barnhizer, Daniel D. ....Washington, DC
Barnhizer, David R. ....Cleveland, OH
Barnholtz, Drew R. ....St. Louis, MO
Barnhorst, Brian A. ....San Diego, CA
Barnhorst, Howard J., II ....San Diego, CA
Barnhorst, Marnie Wright ....San Diego, CA
Barnhorst Schreiner & Goonan, A Professional Corporation ....San Diego, CA
Barnhouse, Amy N. ....Portland, OR
Barnhouse, James W. ....Cleveland, OH
Barnhouse, Jas. R. ....New Philadelphia, OH
Barnhouse, Kenneth J. ....Dallas, TX
Barnhouse, Randolph H. ....Gallup, NM
Barnhouse, Robert B., Law Offices of
Baltimore, MD
Barnhouse, Thomas T. ....Richardson, TX
Barnhurst, Marie T. ....Philadelphia, PA
Barni, Thomas A. ....Cleveland, OH
Barni, Thomas J. ....Oakland, CA
Barnica, Rick J. ....St. Paul, NE
Barnich, John Paul ....Houston, TX
Barnich, Terrence L. ....Chicago, IL
Barnick, Terry R. ....Adel, GA
Barnick, Terry R., P.C. ....Adel, GA
Barnickol, Karl ....Chicago, IL
Barnickol, Karl R. ....St. Louis, MO
Barnicle, John F. ....Brunswick, ME
Barnicle, Terrence M. ....Chicago, IL
Barnico, Thomas A. ....Boston, MA
Barnier, David J. ....San Diego, CA
Barnier, Gregory J. ....Rapid City, SD
Barnitt, Patrick John ....Glendora, CA
Barnitz, Colin D. ....Arlington, VA
Barnitz, David W. ....Columbus, OH
Barnoff, Michelle Stine ....Uniontown, OH
Barnoski, John C. ....Haddonfield, NJ
Barnosky, Eugene R. ....Melville, NY
Barnosky, John J. ....Uniondale, NY
Barnosky, Joseph J. ....Cedaredge, CO
Barnouw, Benjamin ....Los Angeles, CA
Barnouw, Faye Chen
Commodity Futures Trading Commission, Division of Enforcement, GV
Barnovitz, David M. ....Fort Lauderdale, FL
Barnow, Ben ....Chicago, IL
Barnow and Goldberg, P.C. ....Chicago, IL
Barnowski, Daniel D. ....Washington, DC
Barns, James B. ....Portland, ME
Barns, Laura J. ....Los Angeles, CA
Barns, Lee M. ....Seattle, WA
Barns, Paul D., Jr. ....Miami, FL
Barns, Stephen W. ....Granville, OH
Barnsback, Michael E. ....Alexandria, VA
Barnstead, Richard A. ....New York, NY
Barnstead, Steven W. ....Elmira, NY
Barnston, Jack D. ....New Haven, CT
Barnstorf & Barnstorf ....Baltimore, MD
Barnstorf, George, Jr. ....Baltimore, MD
Barnstorf, Gloria Brozik ....Baltimore, MD
Barntsen, Gregory G. ....Council Bluffs, IA
Barnum, Anna Maria ....Akron, OH
Barnum, Carol Lee ....Columbus, OH
Barnum, Cathy C., P.C. ....Norman, OK
Barnum, Cathy Clinton ....Norman, OK
Barnum, Charles E., III ....Crosby, MN
Barnum, Christopher A. ....Morgantown, WV
Barnum, Darold P. ....El Paso, TX
Barnum, Eric L. ....Los Angeles, CA
Barnum, Evelyn A. ....Killingworth, CT
Barnum, Gary R. ....Portland, OR
Barnum, James A. ....St. Paul, MN
Barnum, Jeanne Schubert
Haddonfield, NJ
Philadelphia, PA
Barnum, June L., (Miss) ....San Francisco, CA
Barnum, Kenneth P. ....San Jose, CA
Barnum, Randal M., Law Offices of
Benicia, CA
Walnut Creek, CA
Barnum, Robert C., Jr. ....Greenwich, CT
Barnum, Samuel F., Law & Mediation Offices of ....San Francisco, CA
Barnum, Samuel F., Law & Mediation Offices of ....San Rafael, CA
Barnum, William F., Law Offices of
Eureka, CA
Barnwell, Charles Brison, Jr.
Orangeburg, SC
Barnwell, Charles F. ....Atlanta, GA
Barnwell, Diette K. ....Livonia, MI
Barnwell, Francis T. ....Portland, OR
Barnwell, Frank L. P. ....Charleston, SC
Barnwell, John G. ....Raleigh, NC
Barnwell, Jon M. ....Greenwood, MS
Barnwell, Joseph W., Jr. ....Memphis, TN
Barnwell, Judy A. ....Orange, CA

Barnwell, Siva ... Houston, TX
Barnwell, Stephen ... Skyland, NC
Barnwell & Stevenson ... Charleston, SC
Barnwell, W. Bartlett ... Dalton, GA
Barnwell Whaley Patterson & Helms, LLC
Charleston, SC
Baro, Angelo J. ... Reading, PA
Barocas, Lawrence A. ... New York, NY
Barocas, Michael P. ... New York, NY
Barocas, Morris L. ... Stamford, CT
Barocchi, Lindy F. ... Cupertino, CA
Barod, Raenu ... New York, NY
Baroff, David L. ... Lilburn, GA
Baroff, Martin J. ... Manchester, NH
Baroff, Roy J. ... Raleigh, NC
Barofsky, Neil M. ... New York, NY
Barokas, Larry L. ... Seattle, WA
Barokas & Martin ... Anchorage, AK
Barokas, Martin, Ahlers & Tomlinson
Seattle, WA
Barol, Daniel H. ... Philadelphia, PA
Barol, Edward N. ... Philadelphia, PA
Barol, Martin S. ... Philadelphia, PA
Barolak, Robert R. ... Riverside, CT
Baroldi, Anthony C. ... Santa Ana, CA
Baron, A. Frank ... Sioux City, IA
Baron, Adolph E. ... Southfield, MI
Baron, Alan I. ... Washington, DC
Baron, Allan L. ... Andover, MA
Baron, Allison M. ... New York, NY
Baron, Andrea J. ... New York, NY
Baron, Andrew B. ... Orlando, FL
Baron, Andrew M. ... Rahway, NJ
Baron, Arthur ... Orlando, FL
Baron, Arthur G. ... Indianapolis, IN
Baron, Barbara R. ... Palm Springs, CA
Baron & Baron ... Emerson, NJ
Baron, Bette ... North Miami, FL
Baron, Bruce ... Brooklyn, NY
Baron, Bruce ... Philadelphia, PA
Baron & Budd, A Professional Corporation
Glen Carbon, IL
Baton Rouge, LA
New York, NY
Cleveland, OH
Monroe, OH
Dallas, TX
Baron, Carol M. ... Phoenix, AZ
Baron, Charlene S. ... Carlsbad, CA
Baron, Charles B. ... St. Louis, MO
Baron, Charles B. ... New York, NY
Baron, Charles Hillel ... Newton, MA
Baron, Charles J. ... Brooklyn, NY
Baron, Charles M.
North Miami Beach, FL
Baron & Cliff ... Miami, FL
Baron, Collin P. ... Bridgeport, CT
Baron, David A. ... Washington, DC
Baron, David F. ... Miami, FL
Baron, David J. ... Sarasota, FL
Baron, David J. ... Forest Hills, NY
Baron, David L. ... Palm Springs, CA
Baron, David R. ... Boston, MA
Baron, David S. ... Tucson, AZ
Baron, Dennis J. ... Kankakee, IL
Baron, Diane M. ... Chicago, IL
Baron, Donna L. ... Framingham, MA
Baron, Douglas M. ... St. Louis, MO
Baron, Edmund M. ... New Hyde Park, NY
Baron, Edwin W. ... Alexandria, VA
Baron, Eric G. ... Irvine, CA
Baron, Evan H. ... Weston, FL
Baron, Frederick D. ... Palo Alto, CA
Baron, Frederick M. ... Cleveland, OH
Dallas, TX
Baron, Gabriela ... New York, NY
Baron, George C. ... New York, NY
Baron, Helayne L. ... New York, NY
Baron, Herbert ... Malden, MA
Baron, Ivan M. ... Roseland, NJ
Baron, Jack P. ... Florham Park, NJ
Baron, Jason R. ... Department of Justice,
Civil Division, GV
Baron, Jean S. ... Baltimore, MD
Baron, Jeffrey I. ... Voorhees, NJ
Baron, Jill A. ... Boca Raton, FL
Baron, John F. ... Charlotte, NC
Baron, Joseph M. ... Lincolnwood, IL
Baron, Joseph M. ... Sundance, WY
Baron, Joseph N. ... Lakeland, FL
Baron, Joyce L. ... La Jolla, CA
Baron, Jules M. ... New York, NY
Baron, Keith Douglas ... Tamarac, FL
Baron, Keith Douglas, P.A. ... Tamarac, FL
Baron, Kerry S. ... West Palm Beach, FL
Baron, Larry ... Sherman Oaks, CA
Baron, Lawrence ... Portland, OR
Baron, Lawrence, Attorney at Law, P.C.
Portland, OR
Baron, Lee ... Quincy, MA
Baron, Lester Alan ... New York, NY
Baron, Lewis R. ... Chicago, IL
Baron, LLoyd A. ... Coral Springs, FL
Baron, Lloyd A., P.A., Law Offices of
Coral Springs, FL
Baron, Lucien ... Ringwood, NJ
Baron, Lucien, P.C. ... Ringwood, NJ
Baron, Marcy R. ... Hastings-On-Hudson, NY
Baron, Mark ... Richmond, VA
Baron, Mark A. ... Staten Island, NY
Baron, Mark E. ... Parsippany, NJ
Baron, Martin L. ... Mineola, NY
Baron, Martin L. ... Scarsdale, NY
Baron, Melvyn D. ... Albuquerque, NM
Baron, Melvyn D., P.C. ... Albuquerque, NM
Baron, Mitchell N. ... New York, NY
Baron, Pamela Stanton ... Austin, TX
Baron, Paul Ellis ... San Francisco, CA
Baron, Philip B. ... Waukegan, IL
Baron, Phyllis Joan ... Washington, DC
Baron, Randall J. ... San Diego, CA
Baron, Richard ... Miami, FL
Baron, Richard D. ... St. Louis, MO
Baron, Richard M. ... New York, NY
Baron, Richard S. ... Detroit, MI
Baron, Robert A. ... Roseburg, OR
Baron, Robert D. ... Oklahoma City, OK
Baron, Robert H. ... New York, NY
Baron, Robert J. ... Joliet, IL
Baron, Robert J. ... Emerson, NJ
Baron, Robert P. ... Manhasset, NY
New York, NY
Baron, Robert R., Jr. ... Philadelphia, PA
Baron, Rochelle M. ... Hollywood, FL
Baron, Roger ... Davis, CA
Baron, Roger F. ... Brigham City, UT
Baron, Roger M. ... Vermillion, SD
Baron, Ronald J. ... Syosset, NY
Baron, Ronald L. ... Mineola, NY
Baron, Russell Z. ... Cleveland, OH
Baron, Sandra S. ... New York, NY
Baron, Sandy David ... Greenbelt, MD
Rockville, MD
Baron, Sar, Goodwin, Gill & Lohr
Sioux City, IA
Baron, Sarah J. Kusiak ... Boston, MA
Baron & Schantz, P.A.
Fort Lauderdale, FL
Weston, FL
Baron, Scott Bryan ... Baltimore, MD
Baron, Scott D. ... Roseland, NJ
Baron, Scott Jeffrey ... Howard Beach, NY
Baron, Sidney S. ... Raleigh, NC
Baron, Solomon N., (P.C.) ... Denver, CO
Baron, Stephen A. ... Los Angeles, CA
Baron, Stephen G. ... Medfield, MA
Baron, Stephen M. ... Santa Monica, CA
Baron, Steven J. ... Stamford, CT
Baron, Steven J. ... Parsippany, NJ
Baron, Steven L. ... Chicago, IL
Baron, Steven T. ... Dallas, TX
Baron, Stuart Jay ... Los Alamitos, CA
Baron, Ted ... New York, NY
Baron, Theodore ... Merrick, NY
Baron, Tracy Anbinder ... New York, NY
Baron and Vesel, P.C. ... Mineola, NY
Baron, Walter R. ... Chicago, IL
Baron, William ... Roslyn, NY
Baron, William F. ... Seattle, WA
Baron, William H. ... Port Jefferson, NY
Baron, William J. ... San Francisco, CA
Baronas, Ann M. ... Toledo, OH
Baronas, Mark W. ... Hartford, CT
Baron-Baer, Nancy K. ... Philadelphia, PA
Baronci, Anthony ... New York, NY
Barondes, Anita ... Washington, DC
Barondes, Royce de R. ... Baton Rouge, LA
Barondess, Mark A. ... Vienna, VA
Barone, Albert B., Jr. ... New Orleans, LA
Barone, Andrew J. ... Maumee, OH
Barone, Anthony G.
Securities and Exchange Commission,
Division of Corporation Finance, GV
Barone, Anthony J., Jr. ... Buffalo, NY
Barone, Anthony M. ... Monroe, NY
Barone, Bonye W. ... Higganum, CT
Barone, Carl P. ... Fishkill, NY
Barone, Carolyn R. ... Warwick, RI
Barone, Donald M. ... Hackensack, NJ
Barone, Ernest G. ... North Providence, RI
Barone, Frank P. ... Marlton, NJ
Barone, Gardiner S. ... Chester, NY
Barone, Gregory ... Rochester, NY
Barone, Guy T. ... Toledo, OH
Barone, James P. ... Newport Beach, CA
Barone, James P. ... St. Paul, MN
Barone, James P., A Professional Law
Corporation ... Newport Beach, CA
Barone, Janice G. ... Rector, PA
Barone, Jocelyn B.
Commodity Futures Trading Commission,
Division of Trading and Markets, GV
Barone, John A. ... Bronx, NY
Barone, John J. ... Toledo, OH
Barone, John S. ... Weirton, WV
Barone, Joseph ... Plymouth, MI
Barone, Joseph J. ... Columbus, OH
Barone, Judy Godnick ... Rutland, VT
Barone, Kenneth F. ... Buffalo, NY
Barone Law Offices, P.L.C. ... Plymouth, MI
Barone, Lawrence F. ... Harrisburg, PA
Barone, Linda M. ... Philadelphia, PA
Barone, Mackay & Toal ... Tuxedo, NY
Barone, Michael ... Washington, DC
Barone, Michael A. ... Staten Island, NY
Barone, Michael F. ... Orchard Park, NY
Barone, Michael P. ... Chicago, IL
Barone, Michele Hope ... Philadelphia, PA
Barone, Monica M. ... Atlanta, GA
Barone, Nathaniel L., Jr. ... Coral Gables, FL
Barone, Nathaniel La Duca, II
Jamestown, NY
Barone, Nicholas P. ... Harrison, NY
Barone, Nikki Lynne ... Charleston, WV
Barone, Patricia S. ... Warren, MI
Barone, Patrick T. ... Bloomfield Hills, MI
Pontiac, MI
Barone, Ralph G. ... Weirton, WV
Barone, Richard Guy ... Los Angeles, CA
Barone, Richard S. ... San Mateo, CA
Barone, Rita F. ... Bedminster, NJ
Barone, Robert D. ... Buffalo, NY
Barone, Russell S. ... Chicago, IL
Barone, Salvatore ... New York, NY
Barone, Susan J. ... West Orange, NJ
Barone, Susan L. ... East Meadow, NY
Barone, Theodore A. ... Quincy, MA
Barone, Toni Ann ... Staten Island, NY
Barone, Victor A. ... Charleston, WV
Barone, Vincent M. ... Rochester, NY
Barone-Jay, Debra A. ... Phoenix, AZ
Baron-Evans, Amy ... Boston, MA
Baroni, Heather L. ... Kansas City, MO
Baroni, John ... Kansas City, MO
Baroni, Lisa A. ... New York, NY
Baroni, Michael Lucien ... New York, NY
Baroni, Roland A., Jr. ... Cross River, NY
White Plains, NY
Baroni, William E., Jr. ... Trenton, NJ
Baronian, Jacqueline ... New York, NY
Baronian Law Firm ... Pasadena, CA
Baronian, Robert H. ... Pasadena, CA
Baronian, Samuel, Jr. ... Richmond, VA
Baronio, Michael V. ... Secaucus, NJ
Baronoff, Steven A. ... New York, NY
Baronoff, Susan J. ... Boston, MA
Baronsky, Kenneth J. ... Los Angeles, CA
Baronsky, Robert ... Seattle, WA
Baronti, Lynn L. ... Rye, NY
Baronzzi, Joseph J. ... Lisbon, OH
Baronzzi, Thomas Mark ... Lisbon, OH
Baroody, David S. ... Marion, SC
Baroody, John M. ... Geneva, NY
Baroody, Neal C. ... Baltimore, MD
Baroody, Theodore G. ... Houston, TX
Barooshian, Jon S. ... Boston, MA
Baros, Eunice Tall ... West Palm Beach, FL
Baroska, Ralph ... West Trenton, NJ
Barouch-Waldman, Janie ... New York, NY
Barouh, Albert ... Beverly Hills, CA
Barouh, Evan R. ... New York, NY
Barouh, Sol ... Los Angeles, CA
Baroumand, Cynthia ... Menlo Park, CA
Barousse & Craton ... Abbeville, LA
Crowley, LA
Jennings, LA
Kaplan, LA
Barousse, Homer Ed, Jr. ... Crowley, LA
Barovick, Andrew J. ... Kew Gardens, NY
Barovick, Julie ... Manhasset, NY
Barovick, Richard L.
Palm Beach Gardens, FL
Barovick, Stuart M. ... Jersey City, NJ
Barovsky, Kenneth ... Palo Alto, CA
Baroway & Dawson, P.C. ... Denver, CO
Englewood, CO
Baroway, E. Scott ... Englewood, CO
Baroway, Richard ... Portland, OR
Baroway, Robert S. ... Philadelphia, PA
Barowich, Cynthia A. ... Pittsburgh, PA
Barozzini, James R. ... Pittsburgh, PA
Barquet, Roy J. ... Miami, FL
Barquin, John H. ... Houston, TX
Barquin, William K. ... Portland, OR
Barquist, Charles S. ... Los Angeles, CA
Barquist, Janis Levart ... Los Angeles, CA
Barr, Adam E. ... Charleston, SC
Barr, Adam R. ... Arlington Heights, IL
Barr, Alan M. ... Baltimore, MD
Barr, Alan R. ... Dallas, TX
Barr, Albert J. ... Stamford, CT
Barr, Albert S., III ... Baltimore, MD
Barr, Alfred K. ... Atlanta, GA
Barr, Anhut & Associates, Professional
Corporation ... Ypsilanti, MI
Barr, Anne M. ... Washington, DC
Barr & Associates ... New York, NY
Stowe, VT
Barr & Barr ... Decatur, IL
Barr, Benson J. ... Southfield, MI
Barr, Beverly M. ... Iselin, NJ
New York, NY
Barr, Billy R. ... Tampa, FL
Barr, Brenda J. ... League City, TX
Barr, Bruce W. ... Los Angeles, CA
Barr, Burt, & Associates, L.L.P.
Dallas, TX
Barr & Canada, L.L.C. ... Clark, NJ
Barr, Candace J. ... Minneapolis, MN
Barr, Capers G., III ... Charleston, SC
Barr, Capers G., IV ... Charleston, SC
Barr, Cary B. ... Bloomington, IL
Barr, Catherine ... Boston, MA
Barr, Charles F. ... Stamford, CT
Barr, Charles H. ... Milwaukee, WI
Barr, Charles J. ... Detroit, MI
Barr, Cheryl L. ... San Diego, CA
Barr, Christopher J. ... Washington, DC
Barr, Christopher M. ... Cherry Hill, NJ
Philadelphia, PA
Barr, Christopher P. ... Norristown, PA
Barr, Colin E. ... Los Angeles, CA
Barr, Craig A. ... Pittsburgh, PA
Barr, Culver K. ... Rochester, NY
Barr, Cynthia M. ... Boston, MA
Barr, D. Daniel ... Chicago, IL
Barr, Dale C. ... Seattle, WA
Barr, Daniel C. ... Phoenix, AZ
Barr, David Eric ... Glen Dale, WV
Barr, David K. ... New York, NY
Barr, David R. ... Matteson, IL
Barr, Diane E. ... Philadelphia, PA
Barr, Douglas A. ... Albuquerque, NM
Barr, Douglas N. ... Cleveland, OH
Barr, Dugan ... Redding, CA
Barr, Dugan, & Associates ... Redding, CA
Barr, Duncan ... San Francisco, CA
Barr, Duncan G. ... Minneapolis, MN
Barr, Edward J.
Department of State, GV
Barr, Eleanor Oths ... Glendale, CA
Barr, Eric James ... Middletown, OH
Barr, Forrest N. ... Phoenix, AZ
Barr, Frank F. ... Pennington, NJ
Barr, Franklin J. ... Larchmont, NY
Barr, Gary L. ... Encino, CA
Barr, Gary W. ... Lexington, KY
Barr, Gary W. ... Ogden, UT
Barr, George R., Jr. ... Harrisburg, PA
Barr, George S. ... Blairstown, IA
Barr, Gerald M. ... Allentown, PA
Barr, Gloria Piliero ... Morris Plains, NJ
Barr, Gonzalo ... Coral Gables, FL
Barr, H. David ... Kansas City, MO
Barr, Hardie R. ... Houston, TX
Barr, Harry E. ... Fort Walton Beach, FL
Barr, Harry Kyle ... New York, NY
Barr, Harvey S. ... New York, NY
Spring Valley, NY
White Plains, NY
Barr, Henry G. ... Pittsburgh, PA
Barr, Howard J. ... Washington, DC
Barr, J. Dustin ... Pittsburgh, PA
Barr, J. McFerran, II ... Louisville, KY
Barr, J. Robert ... Chicago, IL
Barr, Jack C. ... Keyser, WV
Barr, James H., III ... Louisville, KY
Barr, James N. ... Santa Ana, CA
Barr, James P. ... Chicago, IL
Barr, Jamison Jon ... Springfield, MA
Barr, Jeannine Southwick ... Houston, TX
Barr, Jeffrey A. ... New York, NY
Barr, Jerry M. ... Noblesville, IN
Barr, Jill L. ... Sacramento, CA
Barr, Jim ... Houston, TX
Barr, Jimmy D. ... Panama City, FL
Barr, Joel W. ... Norman, OK
Barr, John ... Coronado, CA
Lake Bluff, IL
Barr, John ... Decatur, IL
Barr, John A. ... Augusta, ME
Barr, John H., Jr. ... Houston, TX
Barr, John Holman ... Dallas, TX
Barr, John J. ... Willow Grove, PA
Barr, John L., Jr. ... Chevy Chase, MD
Barr, John M. ... Ypsilanti, MI
Barr, John R. ... College Park, MD
Barr, John S. ... Richmond, VA
Barr, Jonathan R.
Securities and Exchange Commission,
Division of Enforcement, GV
Barr, Jon-Henry ... Clark, NJ
Barr, Joseph J. ... Wood River, IL
Barr, Joseph J., Jr. ... San Diego, CA
Barr, Joseph J., Jr., A Professional
Corporation ... San Diego, CA
Barr, Julie D. ... Decatur, IL
Barr, June Hatton ... Mitchellville, MD
Barr, Kaaren Lynn ... Seattle, WA
Barr, Karen Dove ... Savannah, GA
Barr, Karen L. ... Washington, DC
Barr, Katherine N. ... Birmingham, AL
Barr, Keith W. ... Coral Springs, FL
Barr, Kelly J. ... Phoenix, AZ
Barr, Kenneth ... New York, NY
Barr, Kenneth Charles ... Lake Forest, IL
Barr, Kenneth J. ... Atlanta, GA
Barr, Kenneth R. ... Redlands, CA
Barr, Kenneth S. ... Washington, DC
Barr, Kim J. ... Seattle, WA
Barr, Kimberly A. ... Alexandria, VA
Barr, Kirsten L. ... Charleston, SC
Barr & LaCava ... Stamford, CT
Barr, Lawrence J. ... Ashland, OR
Barr, Leslie S. ... Garden City, NY
Barr, Lewis D. ... San Francisco, CA
Barr, Lewis M. ... Department of Justice,
Environment and Natural Resources
Division, GV
Barr, Lewis T. ... Cleveland, OH
Barr, Linda Hoelzle ... Butler, PA
Barr, Linda S. ... Pollock Pines, CA
Barr, Loren L. ... Pleasant Hill, CA
Barr, Louis B. ... Baltimore, MD
Barr, Louise M. ... Charleston, WV
Barr, Lynne B. ... Boston, MA
Barr, Margaret Rebecca ... Barbourville, KY
Barr, Marion R. Hylan ... Augusta, ME
Barr, Martin ... Hastings-On-Hudson, NY
Barr, Martin P. ... Chicago, IL
Barr, Mary Jo ... San Diego, CA
Barr, Mary R. ... Wayne, PA
Barr, Matthew F. ... Atlanta, GA
Barr, Matthew S. ... New York, NY
Barr & McGogney ... Allentown, PA
Barr, Michael B. ... Washington, DC
Barr, Michael H. ... New York, NY
Barr, Michael R. ... San Francisco, CA
Barr, Michael S. ... Hermitage, PA
Barr, Michele C. ... Roseville, CA
Barr, Murman, Tonelli, Herzfeld & Rubin
New Port Richey, FL
Tampa, FL
Barr, Myer Bernard ... Palm Beach, FL
Barr, Nancy M. ... Hermosa Beach, CA
Barr, Norman W. ... San Angelo, TX
Barr, O. O., Jr. ... Chagrin Falls, OH
Barr, P. Douglas ... Lexington, KY
Barr, Patricia A. ... Bennington, VT
Barr, Peer & Camens ... Washington, DC
Barr, Peter R. ... Topeka, KS
Barr, Philip B., Jr. ... Providence, RI
Barr, R. Gerald ... Traverse City, MI
Barr, Raymond H. ... Buffalo, NY
Barr, Richard A. ... Troy, MI
Barr, Richard J. ... Clinton, MI
Barr, Richard J., Jr. ... Chicago, IL
Barr, Robbie M. ... Louisville, CO
Barr, Robert D. ... Cleveland, OH
Barr, Robert J. ... Philadelphia, PA
Barr, Robert J. ... Georgetown, TX
Barr, Robert L., Jr. ... Marietta, GA

Barr, Robert W. .... Troy, AL
Barr & Rosenbaum, L.L.P.
Hackensack, NJ
Goshen, NY
New City, NY
New York, NY
Spring Valley, NY
White Plains, NY
Barr, Russell D. .... New York, NY
Stowe, VT
Barr, Scott C. .... **Kaukauna, WI**
Barr & Shaffer .... Hermitage, PA
Barr, Sharon .... Anchorage, AK
Barr, Sharon P. .... **Philadelphia, PA**
Barr, Sheryl N. .... **Oklahoma City, OK**
Barr, Stanley G., Jr. .... **Norfolk, VA**
Barr Sternberg Moss Lawrence & Silver, P.C.
Bennington, VT
Barr, Steven J. .... Colorado Springs, CO
Barr, Steven R. .... **New York, NY**
Barr, Stuart G. .... Denver, CO
Barr, Suzanne A. .... **Washington, DC**
Barr, Sylvia Ann .... St. Petersburg, FL
Barr, Tamra ....Hot Springs National Park, AR
Barr, Terrence A. .... Bloomfield Hills, MI
Barr, Thomas D. .... **New York, NY**
Barr, Thomas H. .... **Georgetown, SC**
Barr, Thomas, IV .... **New York, NY**
Barr, Thomas M. .... Nashville, IN
Barr, Thomas V. .... Warren, MI
Barr, Thos., III .... New Orleans, LA
Barr, Todd D. .... **Independence, MO**
Barr, Unger and McIntosh, L.L.C.
Charleston, SC
Edisto Island, SC
Walterboro, SC
Barr, W. Ewell .... Danville, VA
Barr, Warner, Lloyd and Henifin
Savannah, GA
Barr, Wayne Raymond .... New York, NY
Barr, William Andrew .... **Dallas, TX**
Barr, William G. .... Omaha, NE
Barr, William H. .... Westwego, LA
Barr, William J. .... Kingstree, SC
Barr, William L., Jr. .... Chicago, IL
Barr, William M. .... **Ormond Beach, FL**
Barr, William P. .... Washington, DC
Barr, William S. .... **Charleston, SC**
Barr, William T., Jr. .... Dallas, TX
Barra, Daryl M. .... Loudonville, NY
Barra, David A. .... Essex Junction, VT
Montpelier, VT
Barra, Dominic .... Clifton, NJ
Barra, Donna Marie .... Dix Hills, NY
Barra, John A. .... Peoria, IL
Barra, Joseph A. .... **Boston, MA**
Barra, Michael C. .... Dallas, TX
Barra, Raymond P. .... Taylorville, IL
Barra, Richard K.
Palm Beach Gardens, FL
Barra & Salz .... New York, NY
Barra, Vincent J. .... New York, NY
Barra, Walter D. .... Canton, IL
Barrabee, Libby L. .... Westlake Village, CA
Barrabee, Lorraine A. .... San Francisco, CA
Barrabee, Steven D. .... **San Francisco, CA**
Denver, CO
Barracano, Nicole C. .... Hamilton Square, NJ
Barracato, Louis J. .... Washington, DC
Barracca, Mark P. .... New York, NY
Barracca, Peter S. .... Ardsley, NY
Barrack, Craig S. .... New York, NY
Barrack, David L. .... **New York, NY**
White Plains, NY
Barrack, David M. .... San Diego, CA
Barrack, Donald J. .... **Princeton, NJ**
Barrack, Irving .... Oak Ridge, TN
Barrack, Jeffrey Alan .... **Philadelphia, PA**
Barrack, Keith D. .... **Morristown, NJ**
Barrack, Leonard, (P.C.) .... **Philadelphia, PA**
Barrack, Luise A. .... **New York, NY**
Barrack, Malcolm E. .... **Santa Rosa, CA**
Barrack, Martin J. .... Folsom, CA
Folsom, CA
Barrack, Robert M. .... **Hartford, CT**
Barrack, Rodos & Bacine .... **San Diego, CA**
Boston, MA
Haddonfield, NJ
Philadelphia, PA
Barrack, Shyleur .... New York, NY
Barraco, Anthony M. .... Highland, NY
Barraco, Joseph J. .... Trenton, NJ
Barrad, Catherine M. .... Long Beach, CA
Makawao, HI
Barradale, David E. .... **Bedford, NH**
Barragan, Jennifer R. .... **San Francisco, CA**
Barragan, Michael A. .... **Dallas, TX**
Barragar, Anne L. .... **Portland, OR**
Barragar, Harvey C. .... **Portland, OR**
Barragate, Brett P. .... **Cleveland, OH**
Barragate, Phillip C. .... Cleveland, OH
Barragree, Jack .... Oklahoma City, OK
Barragree, Jack, P.C. .... Oklahoma City, OK
Barral, Roland .... New York, NY
Barrall, James D. C. .... **Los Angeles, CA**
Barrall, Scott R. .... Fairfield, CA
Barram, Stephen H. .... Portland, OR
Barran, John R. .... **Huntsville, AL**
Barran Liebman LLP .... **Portland, OR**
Barran, Linda M. .... **Washington, DC**
Barran, Paula A. .... **Portland, OR**
Barranco, A. J., Jr. .... Miami, FL
Barranco, David C. .... Corpus Christi, TX
Barranco, Elizabeth A. .... El Cajon, CA
Barranco, Kimberly Smalkin .... Towson, MD
Barranco, Michael S. .... **Towson, MD**
Barranco, Summer M. .... Fort Lauderdale, FL
Barranger, Christi A. White .... Richmond, VA

Barranger, Garic Kenneth .... **Covington, LA**
Barrans, David J.
Department Of Veterans Affairs, Office of the General Counsel, GV
Barrante, William T. .... Watertown, CT
Barrantes, Barbara T. .... **New York, NY**
Barrar, Jeffrey D. .... Vancouver, WA
Barras & Bunkley, L.L.P. .... **Amarillo, TX**
Barras, Leslie E. .... Austin, TX
Barras, Margaret W. .... Dallas, TX
Barras, Richard A. .... **Amarillo, TX**
Barrash, Kip David .... Denver, CO
Barrasso, Judy Y., (P.C.)
New Orleans, LA
Barrasso, Nedio E. .... North Andover, MA
Barrasso, Robert L. .... Tucson, AZ
Barrat, David T. .... Acton, MA
Barrat, Elliott S. .... Cleveland, OH
Barrat, Robert E. .... Martinsburg, WV
Barrato, Christopher Charles .... New York, NY
Barratt, Kalisa B. .... **Milwaukee, WI**
Barratt-Brown, Elizabeth .... Washington, DC
Barratt-Green, Alison Alberta .... Modesto, CA
Barravecchio, Robert R. .... **New York, NY**
Barraza, Horacio .... **Escondido, CA**
Barraza, Maria Linda .... Wheaton, IL
Barrazotto, Mary E. .... **Louisville, KY**
Barre, Bart A. .... Mountainside, NJ
Barre, Bart Christopher .... **Washington, DC**
Barre, George D. (Denny)
Corpus Christi, TX
Barré, Kenneth Marc, Jr. .... Atlanta, GA
Barre, M. Beaumont .... **Columbia, SC**
Barré, Michael R. .... Metairie, LA
Austin, TX
Barre, Sandra C. .... Manasquan, NJ
Barre, Steven C. .... **Iselin, NJ**
Barreca, Christopher A. .... **Stamford, CT**
Barreca, Hugo .... Brooklyn, NY
Barreca, Joseph A. .... Harahan, LA
Barreca, Joseph A. .... Seattle, WA
Barreca, Kevin G. .... **New Orleans, LA**
Barreca, Marc L. .... **Seattle, WA**
Barr-Efird, Linda K. .... **Columbia, SC**
Barreira, Brian E. .... **Plymouth, MA**
Barreiro, Alyssa M. .... **Binghamton, NY**
Barreiro, Darren C. .... **Woodbridge, NJ**
Barreiro, Jose Agustin .... Tampa, FL
Barreiro, Mauricio E. .... **Baltimore, MD**
Barreiro, Valerie .... Los Angeles, CA
Barrell, Charles D. .... **Culpeper, VA**
Barrella, Vincent R. .... New York, NY
Barren, Michael J. .... Cincinnati, OH
Barrentine, Glen P. .... Charlotte, NC
Barrentine, Kyle C. .... **Birmingham, AL**
Barré-Quick, Lisa .... **Liberty Corner, NJ**
Barrer, Robert A. .... **Syracuse, NY**
Barrera, Alfred C. .... Avondale, LA
Barrera, Armando G. .... Alice, TX
Barrera, Brenda N. .... San Diego, CA
Barrera, Carl J. .... New York, NY
Barrera, Daniel P. .... Alexandria, VA
Barrera, Enrique .... San Antonio, TX
Barrera, Eric I. .... **Corpus Christi, TX**
Barrera, Frances M. .... Fort Lauderdale, FL
Barrera, Horacio L. .... **Brownsville, TX**
Barrera, John R. .... Middlebury, VT
Barrera, Lise Anne .... **Detroit, MI**
Barrera, Manuel, Jr. .... Houston, TX
Barrera, Marcus C. .... McAllen, TX
Barrera, Mario A. .... **San Antonio, TX**
Barrera, Martha Frances
Fort Lauderdale, FL
Barrera, Michael .... **Kansas City, MO**
Barrera, Patricio T.D. .... Los Angeles, CA
Barrera, Randall .... Corpus Christi, TX
Barrera, Ricardo M. .... Denver, CO
Barrera, Robert J., (P.C.) .... San Antonio, TX
Barrera, Roy R., Jr. .... San Antonio, TX
Barrera, Roy R., Sr., (P.C.) .... San Antonio, TX
Barrera, Ruben R. .... **San Antonio, TX**
Barrera, Teresa R. .... **Los Angeles, CA**
Barrera & Tijerina, P.C. .... McAllen, TX
Barrera, Victor T. .... Long Beach, CA
Barreras, Bryan L. .... New York, NY
Barrero, Nestor .... Universal City, CA
Barres, David L. .... New York, NY
Barres, Susan G. .... New York, NY
Barrese, Irene V. .... **San Francisco, CA**
Barrese, Joseph A. .... Boston, MA
Barrese, Rocco S. .... **Uniondale, NY**
Barresi, Diane V. .... Hauppauge, NY
Barret, Albert R. .... San Diego, CA
Barret, Haynes, May, Carter and Roark, P.S.C. .... **Hazard, KY**
Barret, Kendall S. .... **Lexington, KY**
Barret, Maxwell P., Jr. .... **Lexington, KY**
Barreto, Antonio, Jr. .... Culver City, CA
Barreto, Julie Kai .... Gilroy, CA
Barreto, Luis E. .... **Miami, FL**
Barreto, Luis E., P.A. .... **Miami, FL**
Barreto, Margarita .... **Miami, FL**
Barreto, Rafael A. .... **New York, NY**
Barreto-Morehouse, Margaret A.
Los Angeles, CA
Barreto-Solá, Rafael E. .... **San Juan, PR**
Barreto Tercilla, Margarita .... Miami, FL
Barrett, A. Colin .... Tuscaloosa, AL
Barrett, Alan M. .... Commack, NY
Barrett, Alex R. .... Mililani Town, HI
Barrett, Alicen M. .... Dunedin, FL
Barrett, Aline Cole .... Dunlap, IL
Barrett, Allen M. .... St. Petersburg, FL
Barrett, Alvin R. .... San Francisco, CA
Barrett, Andrew L. .... **Boston, MA**
Barrett, Anita Fisher .... New York, NY
Barrett, Arthur Scott, Jr. .... Burlington, VT
Barrett & Associates .... **Cambridge, MA**

Barrett & Associates, P.C. .... Norridge, IL
Barrett, Barbara .... Guerneville, CA
Barrett, Barbara Anne .... Olympia Fields, IL
Barrett, Barbara G. .... **Des Moines, IA**
Barrett, Barbara McConnell .... Phoenix, AZ
Barrett, Barbara S. .... **Evansville, IN**
Barrett, Barbara S. .... **St. Louis, MO**
Barrett & Barrett .... Dunedin, FL
Barrett & Barrett .... Wichita, KS
Barrett and Barrett .... Newark, NY
Barrett & Barrett, P.C. .... **Boston, MA**
Barrett, Benjamin F., Jr. .... **Lorain, OH**
Barrett, Benjamin F., Sr. .... **Lorain, OH**
Barrett, Brett Aaron .... Irvine, CA
Barrett, Brian G. .... New York, NY
Barrett, Brian P. .... **Indianapolis, IN**
Barrett, Brian P. .... Peabody, MA
Barrett, Bridget M. .... **San Francisco, CA**
Barrett, Bruce A. .... Meadville, PA
Barrett, Bruce B. .... Missoula, MT
Barrett, Bruce E. .... **Westmont, NJ**
Barrett, Bryan E. .... Laredo, TX
Barrett Burke Wilson Castle Daffin & Frappier, L.L.P. .... **Addison, TX**
Dallas, TX
Houston, TX
Barrett, C. Butler .... **Emporia, VA**
Barrett, C. Daniel .... **Winston-Salem, NC**
Barrett, C. Francis .... **Cincinnati, OH**
Barrett, C. Stephen, III .... **Newark, NJ**
Barrett, C. Stephen, III, A Professional Corporation .... **Newark, NJ**
Barrett, C. William .... **Boston, MA**
Barrett, Carole F. .... **San Francisco, CA**
Barrett, Carrie G. .... **Birmingham, MI**
Barrett, Chafin, & Lowry
Huntington, WV
Barrett, Chapman & Ruta, P.A.
Orlando, FL
Barrett, Charles A. .... **Sacramento, CA**
Barrett, Charles E. .... **Tallahassee, FL**
Barrett, Charles E. .... Itasca, IL
Barrett, Charles E. .... Peabody, MA
Barrett, Charles Foose .... **New York, NY**
Barrett, Charles M. .... **Fresno, CA**
Madera, CA
Barrett, Charles R. .... Battle Mountain, NV
Barrett, Charles V., III .... Tampa, FL
Barrett, Charles W., Jr. .... **Boston, MA**
Barrett, Chauncey L. .... Mount Laurel, NJ
Barrett, Christie Newman .... Columbia, SC
Barrett, Clark A. .... **San Mateo, CA**
Barrett, Clifton T. .... Winston-Salem, NC
Barrett, Cynthia A. .... Fargo, ND
Barrett, Cynthia L. .... Portland, OR
Barrett & Daines .... Logan, UT
Barrett, Dan S. .... Commerce Township, MI
Barrett, Daniel G. .... Newark, NY
Barrett, Daniel J. .... Athens, PA
Barrett, Daniel P. .... Portland, ME
Barrett, Daniel R., Law Offices of
Fort Worth, TX
Barrett, David A. .... **Washington, DC**
Barrett, David A. .... Tallahassee, FL
Barrett, David A. .... **New York, NY**
Barrett, David B. V. .... Hilton Head Island, SC
Barrett, David C., Jr. .... Washington, DC
Barrett, David E. .... Cleveland, GA
Barrett, David F. .... Joplin, MO
Barrett, David I. .... New York, NY
Barrett, David J. .... Albany, NY
Barrett, David Judson .... **New York, NY**
Barrett, David K. .... Los Angeles, CA
Barrett, David L. .... Bonham, TX
Barrett, David M. .... **Washington, DC**
Barrett, David M. .... Atlanta, GA
Barrett, David O. .... Indianapolis, IN
Barrett, David P. .... **Brookville, IN**
Barrett, David W. .... **Elkhart, IN**
Barrett & Davis .... Akron, OH
Barrett & Deacon, A Professional Association
Batesville, AR
Blytheville, AR
Forrest City, AR
Helena, AR
Jonesboro, AR
Little Rock, AR
West Memphis, AR
Barrett, Deatrice M. .... Darlington, SC
Barrett, Denise .... Baltimore, MD
Barrett, Dennis Michael .... **Birmingham, AL**
Barrett, Dennis T. .... **Syracuse, NY**
Barrett, Derek E. .... **New York, NY**
Barrett, Diane S. .... **Denver, CO**
Barrett, Dirk K., Jr. .... New York, NY
Barrett, D. Michael, & Associates, P.C.
Birmingham, AL
Barrett, Donal B. .... **Cambridge, MA**
Barrett, Donald C. .... Irondequoit, NY
Barrett, Donald F. .... Naperville, IL
Barrett, Donald P. .... Missoula, MT
Barrett, Donald R., Jr. .... Franklin, TN
Barrett and Dratler .... Meadville, PA
Barrett, Dwayne W. .... **Nashville, TN**
Barrett, E. Chandler .... Carrollton, GA
Barrett, E. Clifford, III .... Treasury Department, Office of the Comptroller of the Currency, GV
Barrett, E. Thorpe .... Henderson, NV
Barrett, Edmont T. .... Long Beach, CA
Barrett, Edward J. .... Highland Park, IL
Barrett, Edward J. .... Arlington, MA
Barrett, Edward L., Jr. .... Davis, CA
Barrett, Edward M. .... Ponte Vedra Beach, FL
Barrett, Eleanor Edie .... Los Angeles, CA
Barrett, Eleanor Weston .... Newport News, VA
Barrett, Elizabeth .... Boston, MA
Barrett, Fay N. .... Gulfport, MS

Barrett, Frances M. .... Boston, MA
Barrett, Frank J. .... **Omaha, NE**
Barrett, Gabriel J. .... Evergreen Park, IL
Barrett, Gayle L. .... **Oklahoma City, OK**
Barrett, George E. .... Baltimore, MD
Barrett, George E. .... **Nashville, TN**
Barrett, George R. .... Raleigh, NC
Barrett, Gerald .... Phoenix, AZ
Barrett, Gerald R. .... Pittsford, NY
Barrett Gilman & Ziker .... **Seattle, WA**
Barrett, Glenn T. .... **Washington, DC**
Barrett, Grainger R. .... Chapel Hill, NC
Barrett Gravante Carpinello & Stern LLP
Fort Lauderdale, FL
Albany, NY
New York, NY
Barrett, Gregory E. .... Rockford, IL
Barrett, Gwendolynn Wamble
Greenville, SC
Barrett, Harper, Woll, Raatz & Stenson, A Professional Corporation .... Placerville, CA
Sacramento, CA
Barrett, Harvey Gene .... Baxter Springs, KS
Barrett, Helen M. .... Norridge, IL
Barrett, Henry R., III .... Holly Springs, NC
Barrett, Howard F., Jr. .... Belfast, ME
Barrett, Hugh C. .... **New York, NY**
Barrett, Ian R. .... **Los Angeles, CA**
Barrett, J. Alexander S. .... **Greensboro, NC**
Barrett, J. Tutt .... **Opelika, AL**
Barrett, Jaleh F. .... Department of Justice, Foreign Claims Settlement Commission of the United States, GV
Barrett, James .... **Louisville, KY**
Barrett, James .... Walla Walla, WA
Barrett, James A. .... Asheville, NC
Barrett, James E. .... Cheyenne, WY
Barrett, James H. .... **Miami, FL**
Barrett, James H. .... Cheyenne, WY
Barrett, James J. .... Boston, MA
Barrett, James J., III .... Keene, NH
Barrett, James M. .... **Mountain View, CA**
Barrett, James M., III .... **Fort Wayne, IN**
Barrett, James P. .... New York, NY
Barrett, James R. .... **Washington, DC**
Barrett, James R. .... Owings Mills, MD
Barrett, James T. .... **Boston, MA**
Barrett, Jane F. .... **Washington, DC**
Barrett, Jane H. .... **Los Angeles, CA**
Barrett, Jane N. .... New York, NY
Barrett, Jas. N., Jr. .... Newton, MA
Barrett, Jean deSales .... **Montclair, NJ**
Barrett, Jeannie A. .... Santa Maria, CA
Barrett, Jennifer A. .... **Chicago, IL**
Barrett, Jennifer Jackson .... New York, NY
Barrett, Jennifer K. .... **Denver, CO**
Barrett, Jeremiah F. .... Hingham, MA
Barrett, Jodi G. .... **West Palm Beach, FL**
Barrett, Joe C. .... Jonesboro, AR
Barrett, John .... **Austin, TX**
Barrett, John Adams .... **Houston, TX**
Barrett, John B. .... Wichita, KS
Barrett, John B. .... Townsend Center, MA
Barrett, John D., Jr. .... **Los Angeles, CA**
Barrett, John E. .... West Springfield, MA
Barrett, John E., P.C., The Law Offices of
West Springfield, MA
Barrett, John F. .... **Philadelphia, PA**
Barrett, John H. .... **San Diego, CA**
Barrett, John H., III .... Boulder, CO
Barrett, John J. .... **New York, NY**
Barrett, John J., III .... **Boston, MA**
Barrett, John J., Jr. .... **Philadelphia, PA**
Barrett, John "Jack" .... Omaha, NE
Barrett, John M. .... Webster, NY
Barrett, John Q. .... Jamaica, NY
Barrett, John R. .... Miami, FL
Charlottesville, VA
Barrett, John R. .... Akron, OH
Barrett, John T. .... **Boston, MA**
Barrett, John W. .... **Boise, ID**
Barrett, John W. .... Reno, NV
Barrett, John W. (Don) .... **Lexington, MS**
Barrett, John W., Jr. .... Newark, NY
Barrett, Johnston & Parsley
Nashville, TN
Barrett, Jonathan A. .... **Charlotte, NC**
Barrett, Joseph B. .... **Deerfield, IL**
Barrett, Joseph E. .... New York, NY
Barrett, Joseph L. .... Lutherville, MD
Barrett, Joseph Martin .... Los Angeles, CA
Barrett, Joshua I. .... **Charleston, WV**
Barrett, Joshua M. .... **Portland, OR**
Barrett, Judson B. .... **Oakhurst, NJ**
Barrett, Judy Garcia .... Washington, DC
Barrett, Judy Segerstrom .... **Riverside, CA**
Barrett, Junior Alphonso .... Orlando, FL
Barrett, Karen Moore .... **Pittsburgh, PA**
Barrett, Katherine M. .... **St. Louis, MO**
Barrett, Kathleen B. .... Worley, ID
Barrett, Kathryn A. .... Bethlehem, PA
Barrett, Kathryn E. .... **San Jose, CA**
Barrett, Kenneth R. .... **Houston, TX**
Barrett, Kenneth R. .... **Salt Lake City, UT**
Barrett, Kenneth W. .... Washington, DC
Barrett, Kevin N. .... **Dallas, TX**
Barrett, Kevin W. .... **New York, NY**
Barrett, Laurene M. .... Omaha, NE
Barrett Law Office, P.A. .... **Lexington, MS**
Barrett Law Offices .... Denver, CO
Barrett Law Offices, P.C. .... **Evansville, IN**
Barrett, Lawrence E. .... Omaha, NE
Barrett, Lee E. .... Department of Commerce, Patent and Trademark Office, GV
Barrett, Leo J. .... Oldsmar, FL
Barrett & Letteney, Ltd. .... Elkhorn, WI
Barrett, Linda F. .... Houston, TX
Barrett, Linda G. .... Buras, LA

Barrett, Lionel R., Jr. ... Nashville, TN
Barrett, Lisa Edwards ... Lexington, MS
Barrett, Lydia JoAnn ... Norman, OK
Barrett, M. Colleen ... Seattle, WA
Barrett, Malcolm M. ... Belvedere-Tiburon, CA
Barrett, Manuel L. ... Morristown, NJ
Barrett, Marianne F. ... Quincy, MA
Barrett, Marianne L. ... San Francisco, CA
Barrett, Marilyn ... Los Angeles, CA
Barrett, Mark H. ... Norman, OK
Barrett, Mark J. ... Columbus, OH
Barrett, Mark W. ... Boston, MA
Barrett, Mary C. ... Olympia, WA
Barrett, Mary Jane ... Philadelphia, PA
Barrett, Mary W. ... Princeton, NJ
Barrett, Mary-Alice ... Morristown, NJ
New York, NY
Barrett, Matthew H. ... Lorain, OH
Barrett, Matthew J. ... Notre Dame, IN
Barrett, Matthew P. ... Scranton, PA
Barrett, Maura A. ... Poughkeepsie, NY
Barrett & McNagny ... Fort Wayne, IN
Warsaw, IN
Barrett, Meaghan ... Boston, MA
Barrett, Melissa L. ... Baltimore, MD
Barrett, Michael ... Washington, DC
Barrett, Michael A. ... Seattle, WA
Barrett, Michael B. ... Palos Heights, IL
Barrett, Michael C. ... Annville, PA
Barrett, Michael C. ... Memphis, TN
Nashville, TN
Addison, TX
Houston, TX
Barrett, Michael C. ... Austin, TX
Barrett, Michael D. ... Minneapolis, MN
Barrett, Michael F. ... Cherry Hill, NJ
Philadelphia, PA
Barrett, Michael J. ... Woodbridge, NJ
Barrett, Michael J. ... Fredericksburg, VA
Barrett, Michael L. ... Department of Justice, Civil Rights Division, GV
Barrett, Michael P. ... Chicago, IL
Barrett, Michael R. ... Cincinnati, OH
Barrett, Michael S. ... Cerritos, CA
Barrett, Michael T. ... Princeton, NJ
Barrett, Michael T. ... White Plains, NY
Barrett, Michael T. ... Salem, OR
Barrett, Michelle A. ... Laredo, TX
Barrett, Michelle R. ... San Francisco, CA
Barrett, Michelle T. ... Chicago, IL
Barrett, Monica C. ... New Brunswick, NJ
Barrett, Moody ... Temple, TX
Barrett, Nelda K. ... Long Beach, CA
Barrett, Nelson R. ... Buffalo, NY
Liberty Hill, TX
Barrett, Nicholas ... East Providence, RI
Barrett, P.A. ... Baraboo, WI
Barrett, Pat M., Jr. ... Lexington, MS
Barrett, Patricia D. ... Rancho Cucamonga, CA
Barrett, Patrick J. ... Palo Alto, CA
Barrett, Patrick J. ... Omaha, NE
Barrett, Patrick J. ... Tarrytown, NY
Barrett, Patrick J., III ... Canton, PA
Barrett, Patrick M. ... Detroit, MI
Barrett, Patrick M., III ... Lexington, MS
Barrett, Patrick T. ... Reading, PA
Barrett, Paul ... Elkhorn, WI
Barrett, Paul A. ... Fairbanks, AK
Barrett, Paul A. ... Scranton, PA
Barrett, Paul A., (P.S.) ... Seattle, WA
Barrett, Paul L. ... Addison, TX
Barrett, Paul M. ... Boston, MA
Barrett, Paul W. ... Xenia, OH
Barrett, Peter ... Chicago, IL
Barrett, Peter C. ... West Haven, CT
Barrett, Peter H. ... Biloxi, MS
Barrett, Peter J. ... Washington, DC
Barrett, Peter J. ... New York, NY
Barrett, Peter J., Jr. ... Boston, MA
Barrett, Peter M. ... Dallas, TX
Barrett, Philip Dale ... Kirksville, MO
Barrett, Phillip H. ... Columbus, OH
Barrett, Polly N. ... Las Vegas, NV
Barrett, R. John ... Norfolk, VA
Barrett, R. Michael, II ... Kennesaw, GA
Barrett, R. Vinson, Jr. ... Tallahassee, FL
Barrett, Raymond S. ... Watertown, MA
Barrett, Rebecca Ralph ... St. Davids, PA
Barrett, Richard ... Learned, MS
Barrett, Richard A., Jr. ... Wheaton, IL
Barrett, Richard J. ... Cheyenne, WY
Barrett, Richard Lee ... Orlando, FL
Barrett, Richard R. (Dick) ... Lexington, MS
Barrett, Richard W. ... Dallas, TX
Barrett, Robert ... Denver, CO
Barrett, Robert C. ... Portola Valley, CA
Barrett, Robert C. ... Orlando, FL
Barrett, Robert C., Jr. ... Baton Rouge, LA
Barrett, Robert E. ... Foxboro, MA
Barrett, Robert F. ... Houston, TX
Barrett, Robert J. ... Albuquerque, NM
Barrett, Robert M. ... Marina Del Rey, CA
Barrett, Robert M. ... Chicago, IL
Barrett, Robert M. ... Spartanburg, SC
Barrett, Robin R. ... Fairbanks, AK
Barrett, Roger L. ... Minneapolis, MN
Barrett, Roger Spooner ... Winnetka, IL
Barrett, Roger T. ... Denver, CO
Barrett, Roger W. ... Chicago, IL
Barrett, Ronald A. ... Columbia, SC
Barrett, Ronald D. ... Oakhurst, NJ
Barrett, Ronald E. ... Vienna, VA
Barrett, Rosanne M. ... Cherry Hill, NJ
Barrett, Ross, Rothstein & Tufo, P.C.
Commack, NY
Barrett, Roy L. ... Waco, TX
Barrett, Russel N. ... Wichita, KS
Barrett, Russell D. ... Tijeras, NM
Barrett, S. Katherine ... Lexington, MS
Barrett, Sandra J. ... Asheville, NC
Barrett & Schuler ... Washington, DC
Barrett, Scott N. ... Kenton, OH
Barrett, Scott T. ... Chicago, IL
Barrett, Shannon M. ... Chicago, IL
Barrett, Sharon Tracey ... Asheville, NC
Barrett, Sidney R., Jr. ... Atlanta, GA
Barrett, St. John ... Washington, DC
Barrett, Stephen M. ... Bozeman, MT
Barrett, Steven B. ... Lansdale, PA
Barrett, Steven D. ... Boston, MA
Barrett, Steven F. ... Dallas, TX
Barrett, Steven L. ... Bronx, NY
Barrett, Steven R. ... Denver, CO
Barrett, Steven R. ... Chattanooga, TN
Barrett & Sullivan ... Arlington, MA
Barrett, Susan ... St. Paul, MN
Columbus, OH
Barrett, Susan D. ... Augusta, GA
Aiken, SC
Barrett, Susan Forest ... Boston, MA
Barrett, Tammy D. ... Tulsa, OK
Barrett, Tamra ... Little Rock, AR
Barrett, Ted A. ... Dunedin, FL
Barrett, Terry R. ... Oklahoma City, OK
Barrett, Theresa A. ... Springfield, MA
Barrett, Thomas A. ... San Francisco, CA
Barrett, Thomas G. ... New York, NY
Barrett, Thomas H., II ... Newark, OH
Barrett, Thomas J. ... Minneapolis, MN
Barrett, Thomas J. ... River Edge, NJ
Barrett, Thomas J., Jr. ... Denver, CO
Barrett, Thomas M. ... Holyoke, MA
Barrett, Thomas M. ... Milwaukee, WI
Barrett, Thomas M. ... Wauwatosa, WI
Barrett, Thomas S. ... Quincy, MA
Barrett, Thomas S. ... Harrisburg, PA
Barrett, Timothy G. ... Louisville, KY
Barrett, Timothy R. ... Chesterfield, MO
Barrett, Tod J. ... Oklahoma City, OK
Barrett, Todd C. ... Kansas City, MO
Barrett, Tora A. ... Newark, NJ
Barrett, Traci Lynn ... Annandale, VA
Barrett, Tracy A. ... San Francisco, CA
Barrett, Twomey, Broom, Hughes & Wesley
Carbondale, IL
Barrett, Veronica A. ... Boston, MA
Barrett, W. Hale ... Augusta, GA
Aiken, SC
Barrett, W. Scott ... Logan, UT
Barrett, W. Thomas, III ... Lake Charles, LA
Barrett, W. Troy ... Carbondale, IL
Barrett & Weber, A Legal Professional Association ... Cincinnati, OH
Barrett & Wilhelm ... Brookville, IN
Barrett, William ... West Trenton, NJ
Barrett, William A. ... Oakland, CA
Barrett, William A. ... Washington, DC
Barrett, William A. ... Chapel Hill, NC
Barrett, William A. ... Dallas, TX
Barrett, William C. ... Ithaca, NY
Barrett, William G. ... Newark, NJ
Barrett, William H. ... Washington, DC
Barrett, William Henry ... Chicago, IL
Barrett, William J. ... Chicago, IL
Barrett, William J. ... Smithtown, NY
Barrett, William L. D. ... New York, NY
Barrett, William P. ... Raleigh, NC
Barrett, William P. ... Reading, PA
Barrett, William S. ... West Orange, NJ
Barrett, William Thomas
Winston-Salem, NC
Barrett, William W. ... Salt Lake City, UT
Barrett, William Wallace ... Franklin, IN
Barretta, Samuel N. ... Farmington Hills, MI
Barrett-Anderson, Elizabeth ... Hagåtña, GU
Barrett Bonner, Elizabeth A.
Bloomfield Hills, MI
Barrette, Michael R. ... Yuba City, CA
Barrette, Michelle M. ... St. Paul, MN
Barrette, Thomas L., Jr. ... Boston, MA
Barrett-Kitchen, Heidi J. ... Nashua, NH
Barrett-Mena, Lynn M. ... Fort Lauderdale, FL
Barretto, James D. ... Cambridge, MA
Barrett Park, Kathryn ... New York, NY
Barri, Joseph P. ... Boston, MA
Barria, Claudia A. ... New York, NY
Barriage, John Beckerich ... San Diego, CA
Barricella, Susan J. ... Irvine, CA
Barricelli, David D. ... Boston, MA
Providence, RI
Barrick, Aaron W. ... Castle Rock, CO
Barrick, Andrew J. ... Department of Justice, Civil Rights Division, GV
Barrick & Deinlein, PLC
Charlottesville, VA
Barrick, Duane S. ... Harrisburg, PA
Barrick, Gary W. ... Lakeland, FL
Barrick, Gerald R. ... San Francisco, CA
Barrick, Gregory N. ... Salt Lake City, UT
Barrick, Harold W. ... Sedalia, MO
Barrick, J. Stephen ... Houston, TX
Barrick Law Office ... Des Moines, IA
Barrick, Neil A. ... Des Moines, IA
Barrick, Richard Hamilton
Charlottesville, VA
Barrick, Ronald R. ... Austin, TX
Barrick, Ronald R., & Associates, P.C.
Austin, TX
Barrick, Samuel W. ... Frederick, MD
Barrick, Switzer, Long, Balsley & Van Evera
Rockford, IL
Barrick, William H. ... Naples, FL
Rockford, IL
Barrick, William M. ... Nashville, TN
Barrickman, Allred & Young, LLC
Atlanta, GA
Barrickman, Uhel O. ... Glasgow, KY
Barrickman, W. Bruce ... Atlanta, GA
Barrie, Annmarie ... Neptune, NJ
Barrie, Catherine J. ... Jefferson City, MO
Barrie, David S. ... Maumee, OH
Barrie, Frank W. ... Troy, NY
Barrie, G. Christopher ... Sacramento, CA
Barrie, John P. ... Washington, DC
Barrie, Julie A. ... Washington, DC
Barrie, Martin D. ... Houston, TX
Barrie, Martin D., P.C. ... Houston, TX
Barrie, Robert M. ... Ann Arbor, MI
Barrie, Stephanie L.H. ... Gresham, OR
Barrie, Timothy J ... Ann Arbor, MI
Barrie, Walter L. ... Portland, OR
Barrie, William J. ... Westport, CT
Barrientes, Sally ... Racine, WI
Barrientos, René R. ... Eagle Pass, TX
San Antonio, TX
Barrientos, Sandra Isabel
Los Angeles, CA
Barrier, C. David ... Kansas City, MO
Barrier, Joseph L. ... Charlotte, NC
Barrier, Mary L. ... Kansas City, MO
Barrier, Richard G. ... Beverly Hills, CA
Barrier, Sybil R. ... Portland, OR
Barrier, W. Christopher ... Little Rock, AR
Barriere, Brent B. ... New Orleans, LA
Barriere, James J. ... Albany, NY
Barrieu, J. Jorge ... New York, NY
Barriffe, Eugene, Jr. ... New Orleans, LA
Barrile, J. Craig ... Deer Park, WA
Barrineau, Thomas B., Jr. ... Winnsboro, SC
Barringer, Allen C. ... Washington, DC
Barringer, Arlene S. ... Denver, CO
Barringer & Barringer, L.L.P. ... Cary, NC
Barringer, Bart W. ... Modesto, CA
Barringer, Brent D. ... Cary, NC
Barringer, Greg R. ... New Haven, CT
Barringer, Henry A. ... Tazewell, VA
Barringer, James A. ... San Francisco, CA
Barringer, Janet R. ... Boston, MA
Barringer, Jody M. ... New York, NY
Barringer, John P. ... Charlotte, NC
Barringer, John W., Jr. ... Nashville, TN
Barringer, J. W. (Jay) ... Princeton, WV
Barringer & Lawrence LLP
San Francisco, CA
Barringer, Leland D. ... Detroit, MI
Barringer, Marilyn Dyda
Oklahoma City, OK
Barringer, Paul J., III ... Washington, DC
Barringer, Stanley P., Jr. ... Evansville, IN
Barringer, Steven G. ... Las Vegas, NV
Barringer, Tamara ... Cary, NC
Barringer, William H. ... Washington, DC
Barrington, Belinda K.
Agency for International Development, Legal Advisers-Overseas, GV
Barrington, Betty G. ... Los Angeles, CA
Barrington, Brian R. ... Somersworth, NH
Barrington, Carl A., Jr. ... Fayetteville, NC
Barrington, Deborah Douglas
Chillicothe, OH
Barrington, Gordon F. ... Milwaukee, WI
Barrington, James E. ... Chillicothe, OH
Barrington, John ... Wooster, OH
Barrington and Jones Law Firm, The, P.A.
Fayetteville, NC
Barrington, Martin J. ... New York, NY
Barrington, Robert S., Sr.
San Francisco, CA
Barrington, Scott L. ... Minneapolis, MN
Barrington, Wanji J. ... Bridgewater, NJ
Barrio, Diane C. ... Los Angeles, CA
Barrio, Jon A. ... Studio City, CA
Barrios, Margarita ... Seattle, WA
Barriola, Mirari M. ... Houston, TX
Barrios, Bettye A. ... New Orleans, LA
Barrios, Dawn M. ... New Orleans, LA
Barrios, E. Gregg ... New Orleans, LA
Barrios, Gerardo R. ... New Orleans, LA
Barrios, J. Victor ... Tallahassee, FL
Barrios, James A. ... Lakeland, FL
Barrios, Jarrett Tomás ... Boston, MA
Barrios, Joseph L. ... Birmingham, AL
Alexandria, VA
Barrios, Karl S. ... New York, NY
Barrios, Kingsdorf & Casteix, L.L.P.
New Orleans, LA
Barrios, Mary E. Heck ... Denham Springs, LA
Barrios, Robert L. ... Houma, LA
Barrios, Steven L. ... Department of Justice, Office of Intelligence Policy and Review, GV
Barrios-Amy, Rossell ... San Juan, PR
Barrios-Castellanos, Aida ... San Juan, PR
Barris, Audrey ... Palo Alto, CA
Barris, Donald E. ... Detroit, MI
Barris, Oliver R., III ... Eufaula, OK
Barris, R. Gerald ... Springfield, IL
Barris, Sott, Denn & Driker, P.L.L.C.
Detroit, MI
Barris, Theo. ... Windham, ME
Barris, William G. ... Detroit, MI
Barrish, Arnold D. ... Wheat Ridge, CO
Barrish, Arnold D., P.C. ... Wheat Ridge, CO
Barrish, Daniel C. ... Abington, PA
Barrish, David W. ... Philadelphia, PA
Barrish, Jonathan E. ... Chicago, IL
Barrish, Kenneth J. ... Chicago, IL
Barrish, Mark D. ... Palo Alto, CA
Barrison, Daniel J. ... Pennsauken, NJ
Barrison, Earl ... New York, NY
Barrison, Harvey ... New York, NY
Barrison, Steven M. ... New York, NY
Barrisons, The ... New York, NY
Barritt, David S. ... Chicago, IL
Barritt, Douglas A. ... Irvine, CA
Barritt, Joslyn J. ... Lorton, VA
Barritt, Keith A. ... Washington, DC
Barrix, Jason S. ... Grand Rapids, MI
Barro, Gregory J. ... Shreveport, LA
Barro, Gregory J., PLC ... Shreveport, LA
Barrocas, Sol ... Garden City, NY
Barroll, J. Leeds, IV ... Pasadena, CA
Barroll, Katherine B. ... Sumter, SC
Barroll, R. Stewart ... Chestertown, MD
Barron, Adler & Anderson, L.L.P.
Austin, TX
Barron, Alexis ... Philadelphia, PA
Barron, Almand James ... Columbia, SC
Barron, Ann C. ... Belleville, IL
Barron, Anthony J. ... San Francisco, CA
Barron, Barbara J. ... Beaumont, TX
Barron, Barbara M. ... Austin, TX
Barron & Barron ... Bryan, TX
Barron, Barron & Tucker, P.A.
Little Rock, AR
Barron & Berry, L.L.P. ... Greensboro, NC
Barron, Billy R. ... Trenton, TN
Barron, Bradford D. ... Tulsa, OK
Barron, Bradley C. ... Santa Fe, NM
Barron, Carol Ann ... Chattanooga, TN
Dayton, TN
Barron, Carol Dunn ... West Palm Beach, FL
Barron, Carol Dunn, P.A.
West Palm Beach, FL
Barron, Colette J. ... Austin, TX
Barron, Dan D. ... Oxnard, CA
Barron, Daniel B. ... Charlevoix, MI
Barron, David A. ... Omaha, NE
Barron, David L. ... Las Vegas, NV
Barron, David L. ... Houston, TX
Barron, David M. ... Lewistown, PA
Barron, David S. ... Anderson, TX
Barron, David W. ... Oakland, CA
Barron, David W. ... Lewistown, PA
Barron, Dempsey J. ... Panama City, FL
Barron, Dennis J. ... Cincinnati, OH
Barron, Donald R. ... Atlanta, GA
Barron, Edward ... Chicago, IL
Barron, Esther S. ... Chicago, IL
Barron, Francis B. ... Denver, CO
Barron, Francis P. ... New York, NY
Barron, Fraser ... Washington, DC
Barron, G. Robert ... Shalimar, FL
Barron, Garlan Leah ... College Park, GA
Barron, George A. ... Tarrytown, NY
Barron, George B. ... Orange, TX
Barron, George J. ... Oakland, CA
Walnut Creek, CA
Barron, George L. ... College Park, GA
Barron, Gerald V. ... San Francisco, CA
Barron and Golski ... Charlevoix, MI
Barron, Gordon A. ... South Miami, FL
Barron, Harold S. ... Blue Bell, PA
Barron, Howard R. ... Chicago, IL
Barron, James G. ... New York, NY
Barron, James H. ... Boston, MA
Barron, James L., III, P.A. ... Orlando, FL
Barron, James Ivy, III ... Orlando, FL
Barron, James P. ... Boston, MA
Barron, James R. ... Columbia City, IN
Barron, Jarrod A. ... Flat Rock, MI
Barron, Jarrod, PLLC ... Flat Rock, MI
Barron, Jeffrey S. ... Los Angeles, CA
Barron, Jennifer L. ... Chicago, IL
Barron, Jerome A. ... Washington, DC
Barron, Jillian ... Bellevue, WA
Barron, JoAnne ... Ann Arbor, MI
Barron, John C. ... Toledo, OH
Barron, John H., III ... Scottsdale, AZ
Barron, John H. C., Jr. ... Washington, DC
Barron, John M., Jr. ... Bryan, TX
Barron, John S. ... Jackson, MS
Barron, John W., Jr. ... Little Rock, AR
Barron, Johnny W. ... Stockton, CA
Barron, Johnson & Rial ... Trenton, TN
Barron, Joseph C. ... Huntington Beach, CA
Barron, Joseph M. ... Des Moines, IA
Barron, Julio R. ... St. Paul, MN
Barron, Katharyn A. ... Lansing, MI
Barron, Kathleen C. ... Wasilla, AK
Barron, Kathleen L. ... Washington, DC
Barron, Kathryn R. ... Seattle, WA
Barron, Kevin L. ... Bar Harbor, ME
Barron, Kevin W. ... Erie, PA
Barron, Larry R. ... Philadelphia, PA
Barron, Laurie A. ... New York, NY
Barron, Lee W. ... Alton, IL
Barron, Lyle A. ... Edgewater, CO
Barron, Melvin M. ... Concord, MA
Barron, Michael ... New York, NY
Barron, Michael J. ... Milwaukee, WI
Barron, Michael K. ... Boston, MA
Barron, Michael M. ... Austin, TX
Barron, Michael O'N. ... St. Louis, MO
Barron, Michael S. ... New York, NY
Barron, Michael S. ... Cincinnati, OH
Barron, M. P. ... Audubon, IA
Barron, Myra H. ... Rockville, MD
Barron, Nancy ... San Francisco, CA
Barron & Newburger, P.C. ... Austin, TX
Barron, Norman A. ... Wilmington, DE
Barron, Norman I. ... Cincinnati, OH
Barron, Orendain, Malany & Flanagan
McAllen, TX
Barron, Patrice M. ... Houston, TX
Barron, Paul ... New Orleans, LA
Barron, Peck & Bennie Co., A Legal Professional Association ... Cincinnati, OH
Barron, Peter M. ... Northbrook, IL
Barron, Randall S. ... Concord, MA

Barron, Redding, Hughes, Fite, Bassett, Fensom & Sanborn, P.A. Panama City, FL
Barron, Regina L. .... **Montgomery, AL**
Barron, Richard .... Visalia, CA
Barron, Richard J. ...... **West Palm Beach, FL**
Barron, Richard J., P.A. West Palm Beach, FL
Barron, Richard M. .... Whitesboro, TX
Barron, Richard Morley .... Flint, MI
Barron, Rick .... Coquille, OR
Barron, Rick T. .... Santa Barbara, CA
Barron, Robert F. "Ted", II Evansville, IN
Barron, Robert H. .... Philadelphia, PA
Barron, Robert W. .... **Fort Lauderdale, FL**
Barron, Ronald G. .... Las Vegas, NV
Barron, Ronald G., Chtd., A Prof. Law Corp. Las Vegas, NV
Barron, Rupert F. .... **Washington, DC**
Barron, Russell J. .... **Milwaukee, WI**
Barron, Russell R. .... **McAllen, TX**
Barron, Sally F. .... Memphis, TN
Barron, Scott V. .... Orleans, MA
Barron, Sharon B. .... **Hammond, LA**
Barron & Stadfeld, P.C. .... **Boston, MA** Hyannis, MA
Barron, Stephen C. .... East Hartford, CT
Barron, Stephen D. .... Quincy, FL
Barron, Steven B. .... **Odessa, TX**
Barron, Susan S. .... Odessa, TX
Barron, Suzan M. .... **Boston, MA**
Barron & Swenson, PLLC .... **Havre, MT**
Barron, Thea Rossi .... Falls Church, VA
Barron, Thomas C. .... Dallas, TX
Barron, Thomas C., P.C. .... Dallas, TX
Barron, Thomas L. .... **Little Rock, AR**
Barron, Thomas M. .... Quincy, MA
Barron, Thomas M. .... **Marlton, NJ**
Barron, Thomas W. .... Newnan, GA
Barron, Timothy J. .... **Chicago, IL**
Barron, Todd Louis .... Riverview, MI
Barron, Van H. .... **Havre, MT**
Barron, Vance, Jr. .... **Greensboro, NC**
Barron, Vikki L. .... **Oakland, CA**
Barron, William B. .... Houston, TX
Barron, William G., III .... New York, NY
Barron, William J. .... **Haverhill, MA**
Barron, William M. .... **New York, NY**
Barron, W. S., Jr. .... **Dallas, TX**
Barron & Zimmerman .... Lewistown, PA
Barronian, Barbara .... Tacoma, WA
Barrons, James M. .... **Phoenix, AZ**
Barrood, George .... New Brunswick, NJ
Barrood, Phillip K. .... North Brunswick, NJ
Barros, A. Richard .... **Dover, DE**
Barros, Antonio M., Jr. .... **Washington, DC**
Barros, D. Benjamin .... **New York, NY**
Barros, J. Darrel .... **Washington, DC**
Barros, McNamara, Scanlon, Malkiewicz & Taylor, Professional Association Dover, DE
Barros, Sonia Gupta .... **Chicago, IL**
Barrott, Tyrie Alan .... **Idaho Falls, ID**
Barrow, A. Elliott, Jr. .... Surfside Beach, SC
Barrow, Allen E., Jr. .... **Tulsa, OK**
Barrow, Arthur E. .... Palm Beach, FL
Barrow, Barbara A. .... **Middletown, RI**
Barrow & Barrow .... Flagstaff, AZ
Barrow, Blake W. .... El Paso, TX
Barrow, Brian P. .... **Costa Mesa, CA**
Barrow, C. Dennis, Jr. .... **Houston, TX**
Barrow, Carla M. .... **Miami, FL**
Barrow, Charles K. .... **Waco, TX**
Barrow, Charles W. .... **Savannah, GA**
Barrow, Charles W. .... San Antonio, TX
Barrow, Clisby Hall .... **Nashville, TN**
Barrow, Craig S. .... Toledo, OH
Barrow, David W. .... Flagstaff, AZ
Barrow, David W., III .... West Bend, WI
Barrow, Elizabeth Addison Morristown, NJ
Barrow, Ernest E., II .... Gretna, LA
Barrow Gaddis Griffith & Grimm, A Professional Association ... **Bartlesville, OK** Tulsa, OK
Barrow, Geoffrey A. .... **Washington, DC**
Barrow, H. Spencer .... Raleigh, NC
Barrow, H. Spencer, P.A. .... Raleigh, NC
Barrow, Hal A., & Associates Southampton, PA
Barrow, Hoyett L., Jr. .... **Martinsville, VA**
Barrow, Irene F. .... Flagstaff, AZ
Barrow, James .... **Tampa, FL**
Barrow, James .... Athens, GA
Barrow, James H. .... **San Antonio, TX**
Barrow, James J. .... New Philadelphia, OH
Barrow, James R. .... New Iberia, LA
Barrow, Jas. H. .... Clayton, MO
Barrow, Jesse E., III .... Atlanta, GA
Barrow, John D. .... Corpus Christi, TX
Barrow, John J. .... **Athens, GA**
Barrow, John J. .... Kernersville, NC
Barrow, Joseph H. .... **Savannah, GA**
Barrow, Kenneth S. .... **Houston, TX**
Barrow, Lansen C. .... New Orleans, LA
Barrow, Laura G. .... **Fort Myers, FL**
Barrow, Laura Lee .... West Palm Beach, FL
Barrow, Lew S. .... Columbus, GA
Barrow, Lynda K. .... Tallahassee, FL
Barrow, M. Pope, Jr. House of Representatives, Office of Legislative Counsel, GV
Barrow, Mark Steven .... **Columbia, SC**
Barrow, Marvin L. .... Nevada, MO
Barrow, Michael E. .... Houston, TX
Barrow, M. W. (Bill) .... Freeport, TX
Barrow, Nigle B., Jr. .... **Raleigh, NC**
Barrow, Patricia M. .... Roseland, NJ
Barrow, Peter H. .... **Chicago, IL**
Barrow, Quinn M. .... **Los Angeles, CA**
Barrow, R. Derek .... Media, PA
Barrow, Randy L. .... **Sacramento, CA**
Barrow, Sims & Lee, A Professional Corporation .... **Savannah, GA**
Barrow, Susan R. .... **Kirksville, MO**
Barrow, Timothy D., Law Offices of Lebanon, NJ
Barroway, Andrew .... Bala Cynwyd, PA
Barroway, Kenneth Lee .... Bala Cynwyd, PA
Barrow-Bosshart, Jenette A. New York, NY
Barrowclough, Patrick R. .... **Phoenix, AZ**
Barrowman, Fred W. .... **Tulsa, OK**
Barrows, Bradley E. .... York, NE
Barrows, Dana R. .... Springfield, MA
Barrows, David S. .... Portland, OR
Barrows, Gayla K. .... Medford, OR
Barrows, Joseph H. .... Versailles, KY
Barrows, Keith .... **Williamsport, PA**
Barrows, Kevin R. .... Montclair, NJ
Barrows Law Firm, The Williamsport, PA
Barrows, Marjie D. .... San Francisco, CA
Barrows, Michael J. .... Boston, MA
Barrows, Richard G. .... **Elko, NV**
Barrows, Robert L. .... **Minneapolis, MN**
Barrows, Robert L. .... **San Antonio, TX**
Barrows, Ronald T. .... Grosse Pointe, MI
Barrows, Suzanne S. .... San Antonio, TX
Barrows, Ted .... Columbus, OH
Barrows, Thomas I. .... **Dover, DE**
Barrows, Warren E. .... **New York, NY**
Barrows, William E. .... Olympia Fields, IL
Barrows, Wm. W. .... Seattle, WA
Barr Quinlin, Diane .... **Pittsburgh, PA**
Barrs, Williamson, Stolberg, Townsend and Gonzalez, P.A. .... **Tampa, FL**
Barrueta, Anthony A. .... **Oakland, CA**
Barrus, Alfred E. .... Burley, ID
Barrus, John E. .... Roseville, CA
Barry, Alan & Associates .... Danbury, CT
Barry, Alan Gerard .... Torrance, CA
Barry, Alan Gerard, P.C. .... Torrance, CA
Barry, Alan L. .... **Chicago, IL**
Barry, Alan M. .... Danbury, CT
Barry, Alison Edith Department Of The Interior, Office of the Solicitor, GV
Barry, Alison J. .... **San Diego, CA**
Barry, Ann M. .... **Milwaukee, WI**
Barry, Anthony Scott .... **Topeka, KS**
Barry & Associates .... Los Angeles, CA San Francisco, CA
Barry and Associates, P.C. .... St. Louis, MO
Barry, Barbara A. .... Sacramento, CA
Barry & Basey .... Hartford City, IN
Barry, Ben T. .... **Fort Smith, AR**
Barry, Brendan A. .... **Fort Lauderdale, FL**
Barry, Brian .... Los Angeles, CA
Barry, Brian P. .... Lowell, MA
Barry, Bruce C. .... Junction City, KS
Barry, Carol F. .... **Los Angeles, CA**
Barry, Carol M. .... Bala Cynwyd, PA
Barry, Carroll A. .... **Chicago, IL** Orland Park, IL
Barry, Chester T. ...... Department of Commerce, Patent and Trademark Office, GV
Barry, Christine M. .... Utica, NY
Barry, Christopher J. .... **Seattle, WA**
Barry, Christopher P. "Hawk" San Diego, CA
Barry, Clifford N. .... Beverly Hills, CA
Barry, Coleen A. .... **New York, NY**
Barry, Colleen M. .... Henderson, NV
Barry, Craig W., Jr. .... **Greenfield, MA**
Barry, Cynthia S. .... Bradenton, FL
Barry, Daniel .... Concord, MA
Barry, Daniel E., Jr. .... Buffalo, NY
Barry, Daniel J. .... **San Francisco, CA**
Barry, Daniel J. .... New York, NY
Barry, Daniel J. .... **New York, NY**
Barry, Daniel J., IV .... Philadelphia, PA
Barry, Daniel R. .... Minneapolis, MN
Barry, David .... Los Angeles, CA San Francisco, CA
Barry, David A. .... **Boston, MA**
Barry, David E. .... **Portland, ME**
Barry, David E. .... **New York, NY**
Barry, David F. .... Marblehead, MA
Barry, David J., III .... **Woburn, MA**
Barry, David J., III, Barry Law Office Woburn, MA
Barry, David L. .... Tulsa, OK
Barry, David M. .... Hartford, CT
Barry, David M. .... **Haddonfield, NJ** Philadelphia, PA
Barry, David M. .... Rochester, NY
Barry, David M., Jr. .... **Manchester, CT**
Barry, David P. .... Cambridge, MA
Barry, David R., Jr. .... **Chicago, IL**
Barry, Denis A. .... New Orleans, LA
Barry, Dennis J. .... Racine, WI
Barry, Dennis M. .... **Washington, DC**
Barry, Dennis R. .... Baldwin, NY
Barry, Desmond T., Jr. .... **New York, NY**
Barry, Dianne K. .... San Francisco, CA
Barry, Dianne M. .... Haverhill, MA
Barry, Donald D. .... **Topeka, KS**
Barry, Douglas A. .... **Richmond, VA**
Barry & Doyle .... Pittsfield, MA
Barry, Edmund D. .... Allentown, PA
Barry, Edward F., Jr. .... Boston, MA
Barry, Edward J. .... **Springfield, MA**
Barry, Edwin W. .... Fayetteville, NY
Barry, Eleanor A. .... Department of Justice, Office of Attorney Personnel Management, GV
Barry, Elizabeth .... **San Francisco, CA**
Barry, Elizabeth A. .... Raleigh, NC
Barry, Elizabeth J. .... Anchorage, AK
Barry, Ellen M. .... San Francisco, CA
Barry, Everett G., Jr. .... **San Diego, CA**
Barry, F. Dean .... Jackson, TN
Barry & Fasulo, P.C. .... Pittsburgh, PA
Barry & Feit .... Toledo, OH
Barry, Francis J. .... Daytona Beach, FL
Barry, Francis J. .... Niskayuna, NY
Barry, Francis J., Jr. .... **New Orleans, LA**
Barry, Frederick G., Jr. .... Milton, MA
Barry, George C. .... **New York, NY**
Barry, George R. .... **Cleveland, OH**
Barry, Gerald L., Jr. .... San Diego, CA
Barry, Gordon R. .... Toledo, OH
Barry, Grace Heggelund .... Baton Rouge, LA
Barry, Gregory M. .... Pittsfield, MA
Barry, Hamlet J., III .... Denver, CO
Barry & Harris .... **San Diego, CA**
Barry, Harvey & Later, P.C. Hartford, CT Wethersfield, CT
Barry, Haywood C. .... Lebanon, TN
Barry, Hugh Eric .... Warwick, RI
Barry, J. Kirby .... Houston, TX
Barry, J. Richard .... **Meridian, MS**
Barry, James A. Department of Transportation, Federal Aviation Administration, GV
Barry, James C. .... **West Palm Beach, FL**
Barry, James C. .... Commack, NY
Barry, James E., Jr. .... Stratford, CT
Barry, James J. .... **Cambridge, MA**
Barry, James J. .... Brick, NJ
Barry, James J. .... Ellenville, NY
Barry, James J., Jr. .... Concord, NH
Barry, James M. .... Jupiter, FL
Barry, James Maurice .... New York, NY
Barry, James P. .... Atlantic, IA
Barry, James R. .... San Jose, CA
Barry, James R. .... **Chicago, IL**
Barry, James T., Jr. .... St. Louis, MO
Barry, James T., Jr. .... Milwaukee, WI
Barry, James W. .... Westford, MA
Barry, Jane E. .... Portland, CT
Barry, Janice Leigh Gonzales New Orleans, LA
Barry, Jean E. .... Phoenix, AZ
Barry, Jeffery W. .... Chapel Hill, NC
Barry, Jeffrey D. .... Sherman Oaks, CA
Barry, Jennifer F. .... **Westfield, NJ**
Barry, Jeremiah B. .... Denver, CO
Barry, John A., Jr. .... Pittsfield, MA
Barry, John D. .... **Chattanooga, TN**
Barry, John E. .... **Washington, DC**
Barry, John E. .... **Tulsa, OK**
Barry, John F. .... Kansas City, MO
Barry, John F., Jr. .... New York, NY
Barry, John G., III .... **Jacksonville, FL**
Barry, John Geoffrey ...... **Newport Beach, CA** San Diego, CA
Barry, John J. .... **Greeley, CO**
Barry, John J. .... Convent Station, NJ
Barry, John J. .... Lawrenceville, NJ
Barry, John J. .... **Newark, NJ**
Barry, John J. .... Long Island City, NY
Barry, John K. .... Annapolis, MD
Barry, John O., Jr. .... McKinney, TX
Barry, John P. .... Denver, CO
Barry, John P. .... Washington, DC
Barry, John P. .... **Somerset, NJ**
Barry, John Samuel .... **Los Angeles, CA**
Barry, Joseph M. .... **New York, NY**
Barry, Joseph W., III .... Syracuse, NY
Barry, Julie A. .... Treasury Department, Internal Revenue Service, GV
Barry, Justin .... Brooklyn, NY
Barry, Karen Theresa .... Boston, MA
Barry, Kathleen .... Portland, ME
Barry, Kathleen E. .... **Columbia, MD**
Barry, Kenneth A. .... Richmond, VA
Barry, Kent M. .... Salt Lake City, UT
Barry, Kevin E. .... **Los Angeles, CA**
Barry, Kevin G. .... Mundelein, IL
Barry, Kevin J. .... **Melville, NY**
Barry, Kevin J. .... White Plains, NY
Barry, Kevin J. .... Chantilly, VA
Barry, Kevin M. .... **Boston, MA**
Barry, Kevin M. .... New York, NY
Barry, Kevin R. .... **Washington, DC**
Barry, Kevin R. .... Elgin, IL
Barry, Kirk M. .... Los Angeles, CA
Barry, Kristin Marie .... White Plains, NY
Barry and Krueger .... Beverly Hills, CA
Barry, Kyle C. .... **Chicago, IL**
Barry, Lance Leonard Department of Commerce, Patent and Trademark Office, GV
Barry, Laurel L. .... **San Diego, CA**
Barry Law Office, Ltd., The Maplewood, MN Roseville, MN
Barry Law Offices, L.L.C. .... **Topeka, KS**
Barry, Learned D. .... Williamsburg, VA
Barry, Lee .... Trenton, NJ
Barry, Lee W., III .... Minneapolis, MN
Barry, Leslie P. .... **Laurel, MS**
Barry, Lisa J. .... Meriden, CT
Barry, Lynda A. .... **Hartford, CT**
Barry, Lynne M. .... **New York, NY**
Barry, M. Peter .... **Wethersfield, CT**
Barry, Margaret A. .... **Philadelphia, PA**
Barry, Maria B. .... **Charlotte, NC**
Barry, Mark L. .... Scottsdale, AZ
Barry, Mary Jo .... **New York, NY**
Barry, Mary R. .... **Chicago, IL**
Barry, Mary Snyder .... **Fairfax, VA**
Barry, Maryanne Trump .... Newark, NJ
Barry, Maurice J., Jr. .... Bloomington, IL Eureka, IL
Barry, McTiernan & Moore Jersey City, NJ New York, NY White Plains, NY
Barry, Michael B. .... **New York, NY**
Barry, Michael D. .... **Redwood City, CA**
Barry, Michael E. .... **Chicago, IL**
Barry, Michael F. .... **Phoenix, AZ**
Barry, Michael J. .... **San Diego, CA**
Barry, Michael J. .... Framingham, MA
Barry, Michael J. .... Lynn, MA
Barry, Michael J. .... **Philadelphia, PA**
Barry, Michael MacAdam .... Washington, DC Indianapolis, IN
Barry, Michael P. .... **Wethersfield, CT**
Barry, Michael P. .... Atlanta, GA
Barry, Michael S. .... **New York, NY**
Barry, Michaela M. .... Great Falls, VA
Barry, Nancy J. .... White Plains, NY
Barry, Neil E. .... Weehawken, NJ
Barry, Nelson C. .... **Emeryville, CA** San Francisco, CA
Barry, Nelson C., III .... San Francisco, CA
Barry, Norman J., Jr. .... **Chicago, IL**
Barry, Patricia A. .... Des Moines, IA
Barry, Patricia J. .... Santa Monica, CA
Barry, Patrick .... Department of Justice, Environment and Natural Resources Division, GV
Barry, Patrick .... Chicago, IL
Barry, Patrick A. .... **Fort Lauderdale, FL**
Barry, Patrick A. .... La Salle, IL
Barry, Patrick C. .... **Providence, RI**
Barry, Patrick G. .... **Pittsburgh, PA**
Barry, Patrick J. .... **San Diego, CA**
Barry, Paul David .... Wilbraham, MA
Barry, Peter F. .... Maplewood, MN Roseville, MN
Barry, Peter H. .... **Springfield, MA**
Barry, Peter W. .... Newport, RI
Barry, R. Finley .... **Monroe, WI**
Barry, R. Michael .... **Atlanta, GA**
Barry, Ralph J. .... **Palo Alto, CA**
Barry, Ralph J., Jr. .... Ormond Beach, FL
Barry & Randolph, LLP .... **Sacramento, CA**
Barry, Raymond Charles Bingham Farms, MI
Barry, Rhonda Hammer Rockville Centre, NY
Barry, Richard C., Jr. .... **Worcester, MA**
Barry, Richard E. .... **Chicago, IL**
Barry, Richard F. .... **San Rafael, CA**
Barry, Richard F., III .... Norfolk, VA
Barry, Richard H. .... **Nashville, TN**
Barry, Richard J. .... **Spencer, IA**
Barry, Richard P. .... Jacksonville, FL
Barry, Richard P. .... Jacksonville, FL
Barry, Richard P .... Long Grove, IL
Barry, Richard, and Sharon Mah San Rafael, CA
Barry, Rick .... St. Louis, MO
Barry, Rick, P.C., Law Offices of St. Louis, MO
Barry, Robert .... New Hartford, NY
Barry, Robert A. J. .... **Boston, MA**
Barry, Robert B. .... Westwood, MA
Barry, Robert E. .... **Auburn, NY**
Barry, Robert H., Jr. .... Chelmsford, MA
Barry, Robert J. .... Southbury, CT
Barry, Robert J. .... Lincoln, IL
Barry, Robert J. .... Hartford City, IN
Barry, Robert J. .... **Norfolk, VA**
Barry, Robert P. .... New York, NY
Barry, Robert S., Jr. .... **Los Angeles, CA**
Barry, Roy A. .... Franklin Square, NY
Barry, Sean P. .... Santa Rosa, CA
Barry, Searle J. .... Gladwyne, PA
Barry, Sheila M. .... Boston, MA
Barry, Stephen .... Glendale, CA
Barry, Stephen .... New York, NY
Barry, Stephen A. .... Los Angeles, CA
Barry, Stephen W. .... Wildwood, NJ
Barry, Steven M. .... Encino, CA
Barry, Steven M. .... **Wallingford, CT**
Barry, Susan .... Raleigh, NC
Barry, Susan L. .... St. Paul, MN
Barry, Susan L. .... New York, NY
Barry, Thomas G., Jr. .... Eden Prairie, MN
Barry, Thomas H. .... Miami, FL
Barry, Thomas J. Department of Transportation, Surface Transportation Board, GV
Barry, Thomas J. .... Yorktown, TX
Barry, Thomas R. .... Glendale, CA
Barry, Thomas S. .... Pittsburgh, PA
Barry, Thomas T. .... Hillsborough, NH
Barry, Thomas W. .... Barrington, RI
Barry, Thomasin Tate .... Lincoln, NE
Barry, Timothy A. .... **Salem, OH**
Barry, Tobias G. .... **Chicago, IL** Des Plaines, IL
Barry, Todd D. .... Southfield, MI
Barry, Travis J. .... Silver Spring, MD
Barry, Virginia .... **Houston, TX**
Barry, W. Timothy .... Pittsburgh, PA
Barry, Walker & Walker .... Lexington, TN
Barry, Willard .... Cleveland, OH
Barry, William B. .... Pittsfield, MA
Barry, William C. .... **Sacramento, CA**
Barry, William F. .... Boston, MA

Barry, William Francis, IV
Treasury Department, Internal Revenue Service, GV
Barry, William G. ... Purcell, OK
Barry, William H., III ... Nashua, NH
Barry, William J. ... Lewiston, ME
Barry, William L. ... Lexington, TN
Barry, William P. ... Los Angeles, CA
Barry, William P ... Washington, DC
Barry-Austin, Clarence ... East Orange, NJ
Barrydavid, Lawrence ... Tulsa, OK
Barrymore, Carroll ... Santa Barbara, CA
Barrymore, Marshall ... Port Huron, MI
Barrymore, T. Jay ... Herndon, VA
Bars, Michael A. ... Vernon, CT
Bars, Michael L. ... Waterford, MI
Barsa, Michael R. ... Los Angeles, CA
Barsade, Jonathan ... Dallas, TX
Barsalou & Associates, P.C. ... Houston, TX
Barsalou, W. Austin ... Houston, TX
Barsam, Charles ... Newport Beach, CA
Barsamian, Anthony J. ... Wellesley, MA
Barsamian, Armon ... Pollock Pines, CA
Barsamian, Bonnie A. ... New York, NY
Barsamian, J. Albert ... Albany, NY
Barsamian, Ronald H. ... Fresno, CA
Barsamian, Saqui & Moody, A Professional Corporation ... Fresno, CA
Barsamian, Steven P. ... Philadelphia, PA
Barsamian, Walter ... Newport Beach, CA
Barsamian, Y. Gladys ... Plymouth, MI
Barsanti, Benito G. ... Wakefield, MA
Barsanti, John R., Jr., (P.C.)
St. Louis, MO
Barsanti, Joseph ... Fairfax, VA
Barsch, Karen L. ... Denver, CO
Barschall, Anne E. ... Tarrytown, NY
Barse, J. Joseph ... Washington, DC
Barse, Lawrence P. ... New York, NY
Barse, Stephen D. ... Vineland, NJ
Barse, Thomas M. ... Frederick, MD
Barsell, John E., Jr. ... Orinda, CA
Barsetti, Mary Jo ... Phoenix, AZ
Barsevick, Louis C. ... Oak Forest, IL
Barsh, Gregory S. ... Wayne, PA
Barsh, Harry E., Jr. ... Washington, DC
Barsh, Kerri L. ... Miami, FL
Barsh, Wendy Jo ... Encino, CA
Barshak, Danielle J. ... Greenfield, MA
Barshak, Edward J. ... Boston, MA
Barshak, Joel B. ... Boston, MA
Barshay, Catherine D. ... Atlanta, GA
Barshay, Clifford A. ... Atlanta, GA
Barshay, Herman D. ... Ocean Township, NJ
Barshay, Ilene H. ... Huntington, NY
Barshay, Lawrence N. ... New York, NY
Barshay, Melissa A. ... New York, NY
Barshay, Nathan ... Watchung, NJ
Barshay, Robert H. ... Rockville, MD
Barshay, Scott A. ... New York, NY
Barshay, Scott R. ... San Francisco, CA
Barshop, Bruce B. ... San Antonio, TX
Barshop, Steven M. ... Los Angeles, CA
Barshov, Steven ... New York, NY
New York, NY
Barshter, Nancy E. ... Miami, FL
Barsi, Michael J. ... Aptos, CA
Barski, Katherine A. ...
Department of Justice, GV
Barski-McCracken, Gail K. ... Dearborn, MI
Barsky and Associates, P.C.
Birmingham, MI
Barsky, Daniel J. ... New York, NY
Barsky, David A. ... Washington, DC
Barsky, Dennis ... New York, NY
Barsky, Gail M. ... Media, PA
Barsky, Ira P. ... Forest Hills, TN
Barsky, Janet B. ... East Meadow, NY
Barsky, J. L. ... Worcester, MA
Barsky, Laurence E. ... Westbury, NY
Barsky, Leona L. ... New York, NY
Barsky, Louis ... Boston, MA
Barsky, Michael J. ... Bronx, NY
Barsky, Robert M. ... Beverly Hills, CA
Barsky, Seth H. ... Birmingham, MI
Barsky, Seth M. ... Department of Justice, Environment and Natural Resources Division, GV
Barsky, Simon ... Encino, CA
Barsky, Wayne M. ... Los Angeles, CA
Barsman, Marvin J. ... Cincinnati, OH
Barsness, Chad Jerome ... Englewood, CO
Barsness, George P. ... Washington, DC
Barsness, Hopp & Flesch, LLC
Englewood, CO
Barsness, Jennifer J. ... Denver, CO
Barsness, John G. ... Madison, WI
Barsocchini, Robert J. ... Lake Oswego, OR
Barsom, Valerie ... Boston, MA
Barson, Alan D. ... New York, NY
Barson, Charles A. ... Bingham Farms, MI
Barson, James R. ... Bingham Farms, MI
Barson, James W. ... Pittsburgh, PA
Barson, Leon R. ... Philadelphia, PA
Barson, Marc S. ... Santa Monica, CA
Barson, Nora M. ... Orange, CA
Barson, Ray J. ... Princeton, NJ
Barson, Stephen P. ... Philadelphia, PA
Barsook, Bruce A. ... Los Angeles, CA
Barsotti, Brian ... Ketchum, ID
Barsotti, David ... Denver, CO
Barsotti, Mario H. ... Oakland, CA
Barsotti, Richard A. ... Danville, CA
Barsotti, Rik ... Chico, CA
Barsotti, Roberta A. ... Philadelphia, PA
Barsotti, Todd B. ... Fresno, CA
Barst & Mukamal LLP ... New York, NY
Barstein, Rodney E. ... Birmingham, AL
Barstis, Leonard ... Boca Raton, FL
Barston, John J. ... Westwood, MA
Barstow, Erik T. ... Manchester, NH
Barstow, James H. ... Fresno, CA
Barstow, Jeffrey G. ... Menominee, MI
Barstow, Jonathan P. ... Menominee, MI
Barstow, Rachelle M. ... New York, NY
Barstow & Selsor, P.C. ... Menominee, MI
Barstow, Steven George ... Menominee, MI
Barsumian, Todd C. ... Evansville, IN
Barsy, Janet Zoe ... Department of Energy, Office of the General Counsel, GV
Barsy, Joseph & Lichtenstein ... Chicago, IL
Chicago Heights, IL
Barszcz, Michael V., M.D. ... Orlando, FL
Barszcz, Stephen V. ... Tampa, FL
Bart, Albert J. ... Nashville, TN
Bart, Andrew H. ... New York, NY
Bart, Andrew I. ... New York, NY
Bart, Clifford S. ... Melville, NY
Bart, David A. ... Kew Gardens, NY
Bart, Hollis A. ... New York, NY
Bart, Jacob ... New York, NY
Bart, Jonathan J. ... Philadelphia, PA
Bart, Jos. L., Jr. ... Houston, TX
Bart, Margo A. ... Houston, TX
Bart, Michael D. ... Wilkes-Barre, PA
Bart, Morris, III ... Gulfport, MS
Bart, Morris, P.L.C. ... Gulfport, MS
Bart, Randall K. ... Savannah, GA
Bart & Schwartz ... Melville, NY
Bart, Susan T. ... Chicago, IL
Bart, William L. ... San Jose, CA
Barta, Brian ... Santa Rosa, CA
Barta, Christopher ... Santa Rosa, CA
Barta, Faye C. ... Montrose, CA
Barta, James J. ... St. Louis, MO
Barta, Kent & Sheahon, Chartered
Salina, KS
Barta, Loren M. ... Burnsville, MN
Barta, M. Virginia ... Newark, NJ
Barta, Marc W. ... Fort Worth, TX
Barta, Martin W. ... Canon City, CO
Barta, Michael J. ... Washington, DC
Barta, Richard J. ... Racine, WI
Barta, Robert M., (P.C.) ... Los Angeles, CA
Barta, Ronald D. ... Salina, KS
Barta, Steven Tom ... Honolulu, HI
Barta, Theresa J., Law Offices of
Newport Beach, CA
Bartage, Gordon O. ... Shreveport, LA
Bartalini, C. Richard ... Alameda, CA
Bartash, Ronald P. ... Cherry Hill, NJ
Philadelphia, PA
Bartasi, Thomas A. ... San Jose, CA
Bartazar-Suazo, Mireya ... Manati, PR
Barteau, Betty ... Indianapolis, IN
Barteau, William V. ... Speedway, IN
Bartee, Patricia Diane ... Houston, TX
Bartee, Sidney Travis ... Hoover, AL
McKinney, TX
Bartee, William F., Jr. ... Atlanta, GA
Bartee, Yolanda Molock ... Arlington, TX
Bartee, Yolanda Molock, P.L.L.C., Law Office of, The ... Fort Worth, TX
Arlington, TX
Bartek, Dennis J. ... Akron, OH
Bartek, Diann M. ... San Antonio, TX
Bartek, James E. ... Grand Rapids, MI
Bartek, Mark J. ... Milford, CT
Bartel & Bartel ... Fair Lawn, NJ
Bartel, Charles H. ... Hackensack, NJ
Bartel, Clyde O. ... Allentown, PA
Bartel, David B. ... Milwaukee, WI
Bartel, Deborah Stavile ... New York, NY
Bartel Eng Linn & Schroder
Sacramento, CA
Bartel, Gertrude C. ... Baltimore, MD
Bartel, Harry E. ... Fort Worth, TX
Bartel, Jeffrey S. ... Miami, FL
Bartel, Keith P. ... Burlingame, CA
Bartel, L. Jay ... Lincoln, NE
Bartel, Martin R. ... Latrobe, PA
Bartel, Marvin I. ... Costa Mesa, CA
Bartel, Paul W., II ... New York, NY
Bartel, Peter W., Jr. ... Baltimore, MD
Bartel, Raymond P. ... Des Plaines, IL
Bartel, Robert J. ... Milwaukee, WI
Bartel, Scott E. ... Sacramento, CA
Bartel, Stanley Jay ... Miami, FL
Bartel, Stanley Jay, P.A. ... Miami, FL
Bartel, Thomas A. ... Green Bay, WI
Bartel, Willard E. ... Cleveland, OH
Bartel, William P. ... Fair Lawn, NJ
Barteld, Allen ... Portland, OR
Bartell, Angela B. ... Madison, WI
Bartell, Anthony ... Newark, NJ
Bartell, Carey L. ... Chicago, IL
Bartell, Cynthia R. ... Minneapolis, MN
Bartell, Daniel E. ... Little Rock, AR
Bartell, Denis P. ... Madison, WI
Bartell, Jason S. ... Washington, DC
Bartell, Jeffrey B. ... Madison, WI
Bartell, Kelley T. ... Uvalde, TX
Bartell, Kerry T. ... Buffalo Grove, IL
Bartell, Kim David ... Fort Morgan, CO
Bartell, Kristin N. ... Seattle, WA
Bartell, Laurence A. ... Cleveland, OH
Bartell, Lawson Scott ... San Francisco, CA
Bartell, Lewis A. ... Garden City, NY
Bartell, Michael D. ... San Diego, CA
Bartell, Norman ... Grass Valley, CA
Bartell, Randy S. ... Santa Fe, NM
Bartell, Stephen G. ... Department of Justice, Environment and Natural Resources Division, GV
Bartell, Steven R. ... Orange, CA
Bartell, Thomas E. ... Simsbury, CT
Bartell, Thomas M., Jr. ... Milwaukee, WI
Bartell, Tracy M. ... San Bernardino, CA
Bartelli, Jan R. ... New York, NY
Bartells, Jacqueline ... Berkeley, CA
Bartelmay, Janet L. ... Washington, DC
Bartelmie, Stanley L. ... San Jose, CA
Bartels, Aaron E. ... Santa Fe, NM
Bartels, Anthony W. ... Jonesboro, AR
Bartels, Bradley C. ... Westminster, CO
Bartels, Brenda L. ... Scottsbluff, NE
Bartels, Diane J. ... Wilmington, DE
Bartels, Donald L. ... Palo Alto, CA
San Francisco, CA
Bartels Farrell Law Offices
Milwaukee, WI
Bartels & Feureisen, LLP ... New York, NY
White Plains, NY
Bartels, Gregory B. ... Marietta, GA
Bartels, Helen F. ... York, PA
Bartels, James E. ... Portland, OR
Bartels, Jeffrey K. ... Wilmington, DE
Bartels, John G. ... Naples, FL
Bartels, John R., Jr. ... White Plains, NY
Bartels, Laura Victoria Kline ... Fillmore, CA
Bartels, Mark A. ... De Pere, WI
Bartels, Millard ... Hartford, CT
Bartels, N. Shannon ... Lima, OH
Bartels, Patrick J. ... North Brunswick, NJ
Bartels, Philip H. ... Greenwich, CT
Bartels, Robert ... Dobbs Ferry, NY
Bartels, Robert D. ... Tempe, AZ
Bartels, Robert L. ... Hamilton, OH
Bartels, Sidney A. ... Gresham, OR
Bartels, Steven S. ... Kansas City, MO
Bartels, Todd H. ... St. Joseph, MO
Bartels, Victoria Lennox ... New Orleans, LA
Bartelsmeyer, David L. ... Herrin, IL
Bartelsmeyer, Frederick W.
St. Louis, MO
Bartelstein-Foster, Terri Lynn
Highland Park, IL
Bartelstone, Steven D. ... Hartford, CT
Bartelstone, Ted H. ... Miami, FL
Bartelt, Alice M. ... Salem, OR
Bartelt, Christen E. ... Baltimore, MD
Bartelt, Glenn ... Maquoketa, IA
Bartelt, Jeffrey Wm. ... Waukesha, WI
Bartelt Law Offices, S.C. ... Middleton, WI
Bartelt, Louis F., Jr. ... Valparaiso, IN
Bartelt, Richard C. ... Chicago, IL
Bartelt, Robert L., Jr. ... Milwaukee, WI
Bartelt, Steven S. ... Milwaukee, WI
Bartelt, Virginia M. ... Middleton, WI
Barteluce, Frank J. ... Rochelle Park, NJ
Bartemes, Amy Straker ... Columbus, OH
Barten, Bruce P. ... St. Paul, MN
Barten, JoAnn L. ... Marshalltown, IA
Bartenetti, Philip W. ... Los Angeles, CA
Bartenfield, John David ... Greensboro, NC
Bartenhagen, Erik P. ... Boston, MA
Bartenstein, Edward H. ... Louisville, KY
Bartenstein, Fred, Jr. ... Mendham, NJ
Bartenstein, John C. ... Boston, MA
Barter, Catherine L. ... Houston, TX
Barter, John J. ... Boston, MA
Barter, William E. ... Shrewsbury, NJ
Bartfeld, Arnold L. ... New York, NY
Bartfeld, Bernard A. ... El Sobrante, CA
Bartfeld, Daniel D. ... New York, NY
Bartfeld, Peter M. ... New York, NY
Bartfield, Ira ... New York, NY
Bartgis, Earl W., Jr. ... Frederick, MD
Barth, Alan J. ... North Dartmouth, MA
Barth, Barry J. ... Randolph, MA
Barth, Bruce B. ... Hartford, CT
Barth, Christopher R. ... Chicago, IL
Barth, Colleen M. ... Cicero, NY
Barth, David A. ... Hilliard, OH
Barth, David E. ... Jackson, MI
Barth, David L. ... Cincinnati, OH
Barth, Dean P. ... Houston, TX
Barth, Diann V. ... Springfield, MO
Barth, Donald S. ... Somerville, NJ
Barth, Douglas K. ... Pittsburgh, PA
Barth, Eivind H., Jr. ... Cherry Hill, NJ
Barth, Elizabeth H. ... Bodega Bay, CA
Barth, Francis ... Chicago, IL
Barth, Gerald T. ... Syracuse, NY
Barth, Giselle M. ... Los Angeles, CA
Barth, J. Edward ... Oklahoma City, OK
Barth, J. Nicholas ... Charleston, WV
Barth, James C. ... Destin, FL
Barth, Janice ... Bernardsville, NJ
Barth, Jeffrey L. ... Kirkland, WA
Barth, Jennifer S. ... Barnstable, MA
Barth, John H. ... Pardeeville, WI
Barth, John McLain ... Harrisburg, PA
Barth, Jon F. ... Richboro, PA
Barth, Karen A. ... Los Angeles, CA
Barth, Karl ... Seattle, WA
Barth, Kevin M. ... Florence, SC
Barth, Lawrence ... Philadelphia, PA
Barth, Lawrence C. ... Los Angeles, CA
Barth, Marianne ... San Diego, CA
Barth, Marilyn L. ... Los Angeles, CA
Barth, Mark D. ... Orlando, FL
Barth, Mark H. ... New York, NY
Barth, Max M. ... Arlington Heights, IL
Barth, Michael A. ... Palos Verdes Estates, CA
Barth, Michael A. ... Bridgeview, IL
Barth, Michael A., A Prof. Corp.
Palos Verdes Estates, CA
Barth, Michael G. ... Sacramento, CA
Barth, Michael L. ... Phoenix, AZ
Barth, Patrick H. ... New York, NY
Barth, Peter H. ... Salt Lake City, UT
Barth, Philip C., III ... Buffalo, NY
Barth, Raymond J. ... Syracuse, NY
Barth, Richard S. ... New York, NY
Barth, Richard T. ... Cherry Hill, NJ
Barth, Robert E., Jr. ... Cherry Hill, NJ
Barth, Robert R. ... Minneapolis, MN
Barth, Roger V. ... Washington, DC
Barth, Stanley K. ... Dallas, TX
Barth, Steven J. ... San Jose, CA
Barth, Steven R. ... Milwaukee, WI
Barth, Stuart I. ... Los Angeles, CA
Barth, Sullivan & Behr ... Buffalo, NY
Barth, Thomas William ... Sacramento, CA
Barth, Thompson & George
Charleston, WV
Barth, William A. ... Louisville, KY
Barth, William K. ... Los Angeles, CA
Barth, William M. ... McAllen, TX
Bartha, Karen B. ... Kalamazoo, MI
Barthel, Carol ... Department of Justice, Tax Division, GV
Barthel, Casey A. ... Hobbs, NM
Barthel, Donald R. ... Sacramento, CA
Barthel, Edward P.
Grosse Pointe Woods, MI
Barthel, Lynell M. ... Cambridge, MN
Barthel, Nicholas P. ... Santa Cruz, CA
Barthel, Philip H. ... Hingham, MA
Barthel, Sheila E. ... Denver, CO
Barthel, Tara Klena ... Northfield, IL
Bartheld, Richard H. ... Yakima, WA
Bartheld, Thomas M. ... McAlester, OK
Barthelemy, Michael J. ... Shiprock, NM
Barthell, William E. ... Milpitas, CA
Barthelmess, Craig R. ... San Diego, CA
Barthet, Patrick C. ... Islamorada, FL
Miami, FL
Barthet, Patrick C., A Professional Association ... Islamorada, FL
Miami, FL
Barthmare, Dennis A. ... Hempstead, NY
Barthol, Britta ... Cleveland, OH
Barthold, Aubin K. ... San Francisco, CA
Barthold, Gaele McLaughlin, (Mrs.)
Philadelphia, PA
Barthold, Walter ... New York, NY
Bartholdi, Charles R. ... St. Paul, MN
Bartholdi, Joseph J. ... Ocala, FL
Bartholdt, William E., Jr. ... Seattle, WA
Bartholetti, Victor M. ... Los Angeles, CA
Bartholf, Daniel R. ... Monroe, WI
Bartholf, David A. ... Jacksonville, FL
Bartholic, Clarence L. ... Littleton, CO
Bartholic, Mark A. ... Pittsburgh, PA
Bartholic, Mary E. R. ... Hartford, CT
Bartholic, Robert L. ... Littleton, CO
Bartholomae, William R. ... Syracuse, NY
Bartholomaus, Carl G. ... Wilmington, DE
Bartholomee, Richard G. ... Pikesville, MD
Bartholomew, Anthony K. ... Keaau, HI
Bartholomew, Barry ... Glendale, CA
Bartholomew, Catherine L.
New Orleans, LA
Bartholomew, Charles L.
Upper Sandusky, OH
Bartholomew, Christina G. ... Dallas, TX
Bartholomew, Clare M.
Kennett Square, PA
Bartholomew, Constance O'Brien
Bremerton, WA
Bartholomew, Darin E. ... Falls Church, VA
Bartholomew, David L. ... Chicago, IL
Bartholomew, David M. ... Long Beach, CA
Bartholomew, Donald E. ... Redding, CA
Bartholomew, Edward M., Jr.
Queensbury, NY
Bartholomew & Greenhill ... Shawano, WI
Bartholomew, Greg ... Seattle, WA
Bartholomew, H. Bruce ... Lake Placid, NY
Bartholomew, Hal D. ... Sacramento, CA
Bartholomew, Harold S. ... Metairie, LA
Bartholomew, Harold S., Jr. ... Metairie, LA
Bartholomew, James A. ... Allentown, PA
Bartholomew, Jeffrey ... Denver, CO
Bartholomew, John G. ... Hudson, WI
Bartholomew, John Joseph ... Pittsburgh, PA
Bartholomew, John S. (Jack) ... Shawano, WI
Bartholomew, Joseph A. ... Belleville, IL
Bartholomew, Judith K. ... Louisville, KY
Bartholomew, Julie C. ... Somerville, TN
Bartholomew, Julius R. ... Louisville, KY
Bartholomew, Kenneth C. ... Concord, NH
Bartholomew Law Offices ... Metairie, LA
Bartholomew, Lee H. ... Denver, CO
Bartholomew, Mary Elizebeth
New York, NY
Bartholomew, Matthew L. ... Pasadena, CA
Bartholomew, Milton S. ... Columbus, OH
Bartholomew, P. Raymond ... Hermitage, PA
Bartholomew, Paul L., III ... Media, PA
Bartholomew, Peter D. ... Harper Woods, MI
Bartholomew, Richard E. ... Tustin, CA
Bartholomew, Richard L. ... Olympia, WA
Bartholomew, Samuel W., Jr.
Nashville, TN
Bartholomew, Steven R. ... New York, NY
Bartholomew, Susan H. ... New Haven, CT
Bartholomew, Walter L., Jr.
Philadelphia, PA
Bartholomew, Wasznicky & Molinaro LLP
Sacramento, CA
Bartholomew, Wm. J. ... Memphis, TN
Bartholomew, Wynn E. ... Salt Lake City, UT
Bartholomew-Cook, Allan ... Sarasota, FL
Bartholomot, Henri D. ... Washington, DC
Bartholomy, Erin P. ... Chicago, IL
Bartholow, Molly W. ... Dallas, TX
Bartholow, Steven A. ... Chicago, IL
Bartholow, Theodore O., Jr. ... Dallas, TX
Bartholow, T.O.(Toby), Jr. ... Dallas, TX

Barthrop, John A., Jr.
Newport Beach, CA
Barthwell, Jack C., III
House of Representatives, Committee on District of Columbia, GV
Bartick, David H. ... San Diego, CA
Bartie, Jared F. ... New York, NY
Bartifay, Glenn R. ... Pittsburgh, PA
Bartilson, Laurie Neiger ... Los Angeles, CA
Bartilson, William R., Sr. ... Akron, OH
Bartimole, Todd Welles ... Cleveland, OH
Bartimus, Frickleton & Presley, A Professional Corporation
Jefferson City, MO
Kansas City, MO
Bartimus, James R. ... Kansas City, MO
Bartin, Cindy L. ... St. Augustine, FL
Bartindale, Margaret ... Lansing, MI
Bartine, Edwin W., II ... Marshalltown, IA
Bartine, William D. ... Des Moines, IA
Bartingale, Kari H. ... St. Paul, MN
Bartinik, Gianacoplos, Bates, Brown & Grater, P.C. ... Groton, CT
Bartinik, Lori Nader ... Groton, CT
Bartinik, Peter J., Jr. ... Groton, CT
Bartinik, Peter J., Sr. ... Groton, CT
Bartirome, Anthony D. ... Sarasota, FL
Bartirome, Anthony D., P.A. ... Sarasota, FL
Bartiromo, Anthony P. ... Pittsburgh, PA
Bartiromo, Margaret A. ... Fairfield, CT
Bartish, Michael R. ... Cincinnati, OH
Bartizal, Joyce B. ... Chicago, IL
Bartke, Diana L. ... Laramie, WY
Bartke, Richard H. ... Richmond, CA
Bartkiewicz, Byron M. ... Roseville, CA
Bartkiewicz, Kronick & Shanahan
Sacramento, CA
Bartkiewicz, Paul M. ... Sacramento, CA
Bartko, Andrea M. ... Pittsburgh, PA
Bartko, Gregory ... Atlanta, GA
Bartko, John J. ... San Francisco, CA
Bartko, Michael D. ... Pittsburgh, PA
Bartko, Zankel, Tarrant & Miller, Professional Corporation
San Francisco, CA
Bartkowiak, John B., Jr. ... Towson, MD
Bartkowiak, Patricia J. ... Harrisburg, PA
Bartkowicz, Ronald F. ... Chicago, IL
Bartkowski, Julie A. ... Hastings, MN
Bartkowski, Matthew M. ... Wilmington, DE
Bartkowski, Susan F. ... Albany, NY
Bartkowski, Thaddeus J. ... Villanova, PA
Bartkus, James N. ... Denver, CO
Bartkus, Mary E. ... Whitehouse Station, NJ
Bartkus, Robert E. ... Morristown, NJ
Bartkus, Robert E., A Professional Corporation ... Morristown, NJ
Bartl, James F. ... Eau Claire, WI
Bartl, Richard A. ... Alexandria, VA
Bartl, Timothy J. ... Washington, DC
Bartle, Allison Noreen ... St. Louis, MO
Bartle, Christopher H. ... New York, NY
Bartle, Emery W. ... Minneapolis, MN
Bartle, Frank R. ... Lansdale, PA
Bartle, Harvey, III ... Philadelphia, PA
Bartle, James A. D. ... Topeka, KS
Bartle, John Dixon ... Richfield Springs, NY
Bartle, Matthew V. ... Kansas City, MO
Bartle, McGrane, Duffy & Jones
Albany, NY
Saratoga Springs, NY
Schenectady, NY
Troy, NY
Bartle, Paul Baker ... Norristown, PA
Bartle, Robert F. ... Lincoln, NE
Bartle, William H. ... Sandusky, OH
Bartleman, Allen ... San Bernardino, CA
Bartler, John C. ... Wheaton, IL
Bartles, Denise A. ... Faucett, MO
Bartles, William P. ... Forest Park, GA
Jackson, GA
Bartleson, J. Andrew ... Coral Gables, FL
Bartleson, Kathleen N. ... Seattle, WA
Bartlett, Alex ... Jefferson City, MO
Bartlett, Alison M. ... Springfield, MA
Bartlett, Amy C. ... Glens Falls, NY
Bartlett, Anderson G., III ... St. Helena, CA
Bartlett, Ann R. ... Clinton, NJ
Bartlett, Anthony T. ... Timonium, MD
Bartlett, Arthur K. ... Buffalo, NY
Bartlett, Arthur L. ... Boston, MA
Bartlett, Barbara Ann ... Tulsa, OK
Bartlett, Baron L. ... Jacksonville, FL
Ponte Vedra Beach, FL
Bartlett & Barry ... Greenfield, MA
Bartlett and Bartlett ... Walden, NY
Bartlett, Bartlett & Ziegler, P.C.
New York, NY
Bartlett, Beecher A., Jr. ... Knoxville, TN
Bartlett, Bennett S. ... Houston, TX
Bartlett, Bradley A. ... Escondido, CA
Bartlett, Bradley E. ... San Antonio, TX
Bartlett, Brent ... Louisville, CO
Bartlett, Brian C. ... Toms River, NJ
Bartlett, Bruce R. ... St. Louis, MO
Bartlett, Carl J., Jr. ... Montgomery, AL
Bartlett, Carol J. ... Houston, TX
Bartlett, Catherine A. ... Minneapolis, MN
Bartlett, Chandler O. ... Beverly Hills, CA
Bartlett, Charles J. ... Washington, DC
Bartlett, Charles J. ... Sarasota, FL
Bartlett, Clifford A., Jr. ... Mineola, NY
New York, NY
White Plains, NY
Bartlett, Cody B. ... Wolcott, NY
Bartlett, Cynthia ... Indianapolis, IN
Bartlett, D. Brook ... Kansas City, MO
Bartlett, Dane A. ... Paducah, KY
Bartlett, Daniel, Jr. ... St. Louis, MO
Bartlett, David C. ... Tucson, AZ
Bartlett, David E. ... Boulder, CO
Bartlett, David F. ... Chicago, IL
Bartlett, Dennis J. ... Denver, CO
Bartlett, Edward F. ... Butte, MT
Bartlett, Edward J., Jr. ... Boston, MA
Bartlett, Elizabeth J. ... Milwaukee, WI
Bartlett, Eric E. ... Kansas City, MO
Bartlett, Ernest J. ... Pasadena, CA
Bartlett, Ernestine Conner
Tarrytown, NY
Bartlett, F. Thomas ... Parker, AZ
Bartlett, Frederick B.H. ... Washington, DC
Bartlett, Gail A. ... Houston, TX
Bartlett, George M. ... Rancho Santa Fe, CA
Bartlett, George R., III ... Cobleskill, NY
Bartlett, George R., Jr. ... Walden, NY
Bartlett, Gilbert A. ... Williamsburg, VA
Bartlett, Gregory M. ... Covington, KY
Bartlett, Hackett, Feinberg P.C.
Boston, MA
Bartlett, Heekin & Smith, P.A.
Jacksonville, FL
Ponte Vedra Beach, FL
Bartlett, Howard R. ... Seattle, WA
Bartlett, James ... Chicago, IL
Bartlett, James B. ... York, ME
Bartlett, James B., P.A. ... York, ME
Bartlett, James C. ... Kalispell, MT
Bartlett, James E., III ... Melbourne, FL
Bartlett, James P. ... Phoenix, AZ
Bartlett, James P., Jr. ... Monroe, MI
Bartlett, James S. ... Des Moines, IA
Bartlett, James W., III ... Baltimore, MD
Bartlett, James W., Jr. ... Houston, TX
Bartlett, Jason R. ... Phoenix, AZ
Bartlett, Jay J. ... Tampa, FL
Bartlett, Jeffrey W. ... Northfield, IL
Bartlett, Jennifer L. ... Anaheim, CA
Bartlett, Jerry F. ... Athens, AL
Bartlett, Johanna Viglucci ... Rochester, NY
Bartlett, John A. ... Fullerton, CA
Bartlett, John A. ... Louisville, KY
Bartlett, John F. ... Darien, CT
Bartlett, John L. ... Washington, DC
Bartlett, John S. ... Carson City, NV
Bartlett, John S., Jr. ... Albany, NY
Bartlett, John W. ... Albany, NY
Bartlett, Joseph D. ... Lafayette, IN
Bartlett, Joseph P. ... Los Angeles, CA
Bartlett, Joseph T., Jr. ... Greenfield, MA
Bartlett, Joseph W. ... New York, NY
Bartlett, Katharine T. ... Durham, NC
Bartlett, Katherine T. ... Durham, NC
Bartlett, Keeler & Cohn ... Bridgeport, CT
Bartlett, Keith T. ... Columbus, OH
Bartlett, Kenneth G. ... New Haven, CT
Bartlett, Kevin S. ... Washington, DC
Bartlett Kirch & Lievers ... Escondido, CA
San Diego, CA
Bartlett, Larry D. ... Iowa City, IA
Bartlett, Laurence H. ... Daytona Beach, FL
Bartlett, Laurie A. ... Emeryville, CA
Bartlett Law Offices ... Wolcott, NY
Bartlett Law Offices, P.C.
New Haven, CT
Bartlett, Lawrence J. ... San Diego, CA
Bartlett & Leader-Picone, LLP
Oakland, CA
San Francisco, CA
Bartlett, Linda G. ... New York, NY
Bartlett, Lynn Peter ... Anchorage, AK
Bartlett, Lynne E. ... Evanston, IL
Bartlett, M. Leigh, (P.C.) ... Dallas, TX
Bartlett, Marshall P. ... Florham Park, NJ
Bartlett, Marvin Lewis, Jr. ... Columbia, SC
Bartlett, Marylen Tremaine ... Columbia, MD
Bartlett, Maurine R. ... New York, NY
Bartlett, McDonough, Bastone & Monaghan, LLP ... Mineola, NY
New York, NY
White Plains, NY
Bartlett, Michael J. ... Anaheim, CA
Bartlett, Michael J. ... Lake Forest, CA
Bartlett, Michael J ... Boise, ID
Bartlett, Molly ... Duxbury, MA
Bartlett, Nancy L. ... Austin, TX
Bartlett, Nancy R. ... Atlanta, GA
Bartlett, Paul A. ... Malden, MA
Bartlett, Paul B. ... Tucson, AZ
Bartlett, Paul, Jr. ... San Antonio, TX
Bartlett, Peter, Law Offices of
Anchorage, AK
Bartlett, Phillip W. ... Reno, NV
Bartlett, Pontiff, Stewart & Rhodes, P.C.
Glens Falls, NY
Bartlett, Randall D. ... New York, NY
Bartlett, Randolph A., P.C.
Lake Havasu City, AZ
Bartlett, Richard J. ... Norwalk, CT
Bartlett, Richard J. ... Glens Falls, NY
Bartlett, Richard S. ... Vernon, CT
Bartlett, Rick E. ... Jeffersonville, IN
Bartlett, Robert A. ... Atlanta, GA
Bartlett, Robert B. ... Visalia, CA
Bartlett, Robert P., Jr. ... Dayton, OH
Bartlett, Robert S. ... Oakland, CA
Bartlett, Robert W., II ... Hailey, ID
Bartlett, Robyn J. ... Boston, MA
Bartlett, Rodney J. ... Indianapolis, IN
Bartlett, Roger A. ... Austin, TX
Bartlett, Roger A. ... Clarksburg, WV
Bartlett, Ronald H. ... Columbia, MO
Bartlett, Rosemary V. ... Des Moines, IA
Bartlett, Roy M., Jr. ... Palo Alto, CA
Bartlett, Roy R. ... Topeka, KS
Bartlett & Sabol ... Lafayette, IN
Bartlett, Sara Elizabeth ... Chicago, IL
Bartlett & Spruiell ... Canton, TX
Bartlett, Stephen L. ... Omaha, NE
Bartlett, Terry A. ... Santa Barbara, CA
Bartlett, Thomas Lee ... Houston, TX
Bartlett, Tom B., Jr. ... Marlin, TX
Bartlett, Trace A. ... Phoenix, AZ
Bartlett & Weigle Co., L.P.A.
Covington, KY
Cincinnati, OH
Bartlett, Wendy Martin ... Gillette, WY
Bartlett, William A. ... Bozeman, MT
Bartlett, William H. ... St. Petersburg, FL
Bartlett, William T. ... Cincinnati, OH
Bartlett-McMahon, Gerry ... Kalamazoo, MI
Bartlett-Svehla, Dorothy ... Chicago, IL
Bartley, Albert L., Jr. ... Richardson, TX
Bartley, Ava E. ... Portland, OR
Bartley, Brian J. ... Wilmington, DE
Bartley, Daniel J. ... Boston, MA
Bartley, Daniel R. ... Novato, CA
Bartley & Dean ... Louisville, KY
Middletown, KY
Bartley, Deborah Turpin ... St. Louis, MO
Bartley, Goffstein, Bollato and Lange, LLC
St. Louis, MO
Bartley, Gregory C. ... Kearny, NJ
Bartley, H. Michael ... Cooper, TX
Bartley, Jacquelyn Lee ... Columbia, SC
Bartley, James M. ... Las Vegas, NV
Bartley, James P. ... Chicago, IL
Bartley, Jane J. ... Kansas City, MO
Bartley, Jean ... Iowa City, IA
Bartley, John P. ... Columbus, OH
Bartley, John W. ... Oklahoma City, OK
Bartley, Joseph F., Jr. ... Peoria, IL
Bartley, Keene W. ... Nashville, TN
Bartley, Keith ... Pikeville, KY
Prestonsburg, KY
Bartley, Kevin R. ... Odessa, TX
Bartley, Kevin R., P.C. ... Odessa, TX
Bartley, Marina E. Paige ... Waltham, MA
Bartley, Matthew B. ... Purchase, NY
Bartley, Michael Todd ... Jackson, MS
Bartley, Myles K. ... New York, NY
Bartley, Patricia Ann ... Pikeville, KY
Bartley, Richard E. ... Houston, TX
Bartley, Rickey L. ... Pikeville, KY
Bartley, Roberta Dunn ... Boca Raton, FL
Bartley, Roberta Dunn, P.A.
Boca Raton, FL
Bartley, Sherry P. ... Little Rock, AR
Bartley, Steven C. ... New York, NY
Bartley, Timothy M. ... New York, NY
Bartley, Tom ... Brenham, TX
Bartley, Valerie Smith ... Hindman, KY
Bartley, William E., Jr. ... Louisville, KY
Middletown, KY
Bartley, William H. ... St. Louis, MO
Bartling & Hinkle, P.C. ... Lincoln, NE
Bartling, Stephen V. ... Lincoln, NE
Bartling, William H. ... Dearborn, MI
Bartlit Beck Herman Palenchar & Scott
Denver, CO
Chicago, IL
Bartlit, Fred H., Jr., (P.C.) ... Denver, CO
Chicago, IL
Bartlit, Jennifer R. ... Cedar Crest, NM
Bartlo & Hettler ... Corfu, NY
Kenmore, NY
Bartlo, Noel E. ... Corfu, NY
Kenmore, NY
Bartlo, Sam D. ... Akron, OH
Bartlow, Elizabeth A. ... Lancaster, PA
Bartlow, Robert T. ... Spruce Pine, NC
Bartman, Christi S. ... Toledo, OH
Bartman, Douglas V. ... Cleveland, OH
Bartman, Eugene A. ... Appleton, WI
Bartman, Thomas F. ... Beverly Hills, CA
Bartman, Thomas R. ... Washington, DC
Bartmann, William R. ... Tulsa, OK
Bartmess, Duchess ... Oklahoma City, OK
Bartmess, Geary, III ... Houston, TX
Bartmon, Frederic G. ... Amherst, MA
Bartmon, Joy Anne ... Boca Raton, FL
Bartner, Douglas P. ... New York, NY
Bartner, Elayne F. ... Department of Energy, Office of the General Counsel, GV
Bartness, Becky Ann ... Phoenix, AZ
Bartnicki, Audrey L. ... Chicago, IL
Bartnik, Casimir J. ... Skokie, IL
Bartnik, Keith Blair ... Elkridge, MD
Bartnik, Keith Blair, P.A. ... Elkridge, MD
Bartnik, Michael W. ... Auburn Hills, MI
Bartnof, Howard M. ... Los Angeles, CA
Bartnoff, Judith ... Washington, DC
Barto, Carl M. ... Laredo, TX
Barto, Carl M., Law Office of ... Laredo, TX
San Antonio, TX
Barto, Charles O., Jr. ... Harrisburg, PA
Barto, Jan E. ... Granbury, TX
Barto, John W. ... Concord, NH
Barto, Karin F. ... West Bloomfield, MI
Barto, Lowell A. ... Stillwater, OK
Barto, Lowell A., A Professional Corporation
Stillwater, OK
Barto, Maria Lilia Cavazos ... Laredo, TX
Barto, Morris L. ... Stamford, CT
Barto and Puffer, Professional Association
Concord, NH
Barto, Raymond ... Hackensack, NJ
Barto, Timothy D. ... Washington, DC
Barto, Vincent A. ... Findlay, OH
Bartok, Michael F. ... Charlotte, NC
Bartok, Richard E. ... Westfield, NJ
Bartol, Ernest T. ... Mineola, NY
Bartol, Joseph P. ... Madison, WI
Bartol, Kyle F. ... Alexandria, VA
Fairfax, VA
Bartol, Michael C. ... Indianapolis, IN
Bartol, William E. ... Hartford, CT
Bartolacci, Joseph C. ... Pittsburgh, PA
Bartolacci, Mike W. ... St. Louis, MO
Bartolacci, Paul R. ... Philadelphia, PA
Bartolain, Paul L. ... Gurnee, IL
Bartoldus, Dennis L. ... Newport, OR
Bartolett, C. Stephen ... Margate City, NJ
Bartolett & Kline ... Margate City, NJ
Bartoletta, Dominic M. ... Spokane, WA
Bartoletta, Frank V. ... Spokane, WA
Bartoletti, Karen J. ... Austin, TX
Bartoli, Christopher M. ... Newark, NJ
Bartoli, Maureen T. ... Roseland, NJ
Bartoli-Cain, Michele ... Washington, DC
Bartolini, Anthony L. ... Philadelphia, PA
Bartolini, David A. ... Philadelphia, PA
Bartolini, James D. ... Hartford, CT
Bartolino, Jeffrey A. ... West Trenton, NJ
Bartolino, Jeffrey D. ... Tucson, AZ
Bartolino, Peter C. ... New York, NY
Bartolo, Elizabeth M. ... New York, NY
Bartolo, Marlene B. ... Stamford, CT
Bartolome, Benigno E., Jr.
Washington, DC
Bartolomea, Laura A. ... Calabasas, CA
Simi Valley, CA
Bartolomei, Edward A. ... San Antonio, TX
Bartolomei, Gregory A. ... Phoenix, AZ
Bartolomei, Matthew P. ... Orlando, FL
Bartolomei & Victor, P.C. ... Phoenix, AZ
Bartolomeo, Albert A. ... Philadelphia, PA
Bartolomeo, Paul J., Jr. ... Cherry Hill, NJ
Philadelphia, PA
Bartolomucci, H. Christopher
Washington, DC
Bartolone, Diane A. ... Staten Island, NY
Bartolone, Frank S. ... Boca Raton, FL
Bartolone, Megan W. ... Chicago, IL
Bartoloni & Abbott, P.C. ... Portland, OR
Bartoloni, Andrea ... Portland, OR
Bartolotta, Bruce A. ... Finleyville, PA
Bartolotta, Frank J. ... New York, NY
Bartolotta, Leo ... San Diego, CA
Bartolotta, Mark J. ... Painesville, OH
Bartolotta, Vincent J., Jr., (P.C.)
San Diego, CA
Bartolotto, James G. ... Ann Arbor, MI
New York, NY
Bartolozzi, James J. ... Cleveland, OH
Barton, Adrian Lee ... Irvine, CA
Barton, Alan F. ... Colorado Springs, CO
Barton, Alan J. ... Los Angeles, CA
Barton, Allan D. ... St. Louis, MO
Barton, Amanda A. ... Jackson, MS
Barton, Amy L. ... New York, NY
Barton, Ansley B. ... Atlanta, GA
Barton, Anthony B. ... Melville, NY
Mineola, NY
Barton, Ardy V. ... Santa Barbara, CA
Barton, Arthur M. ... Groton, CT
Barton, B. Hanford ... Martinez, GA
Barton, Babette B. ... Berkeley, CA
Barton, Barbara ... Hauppauge, NY
Barton, Barbara George ... Columbia, SC
Barton, Ben M. ... Dallas, TX
Barton, Benton J. ... Denver, CO
Barton, Bernard A., Jr. ... Tampa, FL
Barton, Bill W. ... Austin, TX
Barton, Brandon J. ... Oklahoma City, OK
Barton, Breck, & Associates, P.A.
Rexburg, ID
Barton, Breck H. ... Rexburg, ID
Barton, Brenda L. ... Phoenix, AZ
Barton, Brenda S. ... Los Angeles, CA
Barton, Bruce ... Van Nuys, CA
Barton, Bruce ... Brooklyn, NY
Barton, Bruce A. ... Jackson, MI
Barton, Bruce A., P.C. ... Jackson, MI
Barton, Bruce Alan ... Phoenix, AZ
Barton, C. Brett ... Columbia, MO
Barton, C. Bruce ... Layton, UT
Barton, C. Christy ... Des Moines, IA
Columbia, MO
Barton, C. Park, Jr. ... Tuscaloosa, AL
Barton, Carl W. ... Salt Lake City, UT
Barton, Carlyle, Jr. ... Baltimore, MD
Barton, Carol Elizabeth ... Austin, TX
Barton, Carol F. ... Walpole, MA
Barton, Charley W. ... Arnett, OK
Barton, Christina ... Seattle, WA
Barton, Christopher ... York, SC
Barton, Christopher A. ... Elmira, NY
Barton, Christopher P. ... Philadelphia, PA
Barton & Cipolla ... Agoura Hills, CA
Barton, Clayton James ... Austin, TX
Barton, Constance Melinda ... Sacramento, CA
Barton, Craig A. ... Chicopee, MA
Barton, Cynthia A. ... San Antonio, TX
Barton, D. James ... Trenton, MI
Barton, Daniel L. ... Palo Alto, CA
Barton, Daryl L. ... Ypsilanti, MI
Barton, David A. ... Omaha, NE
Barton, David F. ... San Antonio, TX
Barton, David H. ... Santa Barbara, CA
Barton, David J. ... Los Angeles, CA
Barton, David J. ... Arnold, MO
Barton, David M. ... Gunnison, CO
Barton, David M., P.C. ... Gunnison, CO
Barton, David P. ... Santa Fe, NM
Barton, David T. ... Phoenix, AZ
Barton, David W. ... Cheboygan, MI
Barton, Denise C. ... Monessen, PA
Barton, Denise Marie ... Boston, MA
Barton, Donald A. ... Los Angeles, CA
Barton, Donald H. ... Brevard, NC

Bash, David A. ....Phoenix, AZ
Bash, Eric J.
Federal Communications Commission, Mass Media Bureau, GV
Bash, Gary M. ....Novelty, OH
Bash, James F. ....Indianapolis, IN
Bash, Jeremy B. ....Washington, DC
Bash, Joshua D. ....Miami, FL
Bash, Michael B. Rodning
Minneapolis, MN
Bash, Ross S. ....Delmont, PA
Bash, Roy ....Kansas City, MO
Basha, Leigh-Alexandra ....Vienna, VA
Basha, Richard E. ....Miami, FL
Basha, Richard E., P.A. ....Miami, FL
Basha, Steven L. ....Treasury Department, U.S. Customs Service, GV
Basha, Steven M. ....Woodland, CA
Bashaar, John Robert ....Baltimore, MD
Basham, Carey E. ....Houston, TX
Basham, Catherine E. ....Fresno, CA
Basham, Christine Affleck ....Towson, MD
Basham, David W. ....Tucson, AZ
Basham, Edward A., III ....Easton, MD
Basham, Eldon L. ....Marietta, GA
Basham, Gary R. ....Sacramento, CA
Basham, George V., III ....Austin, TX
Basham, J. Andrew ....Norfolk, VA
Basham, Jack C., Jr. ....Atlanta, GA
Basham, James G.
Federal Deposit Insurance Corporation, Regulation and Legislation Section, GV
Basham, Jonathan G. ....Bend, OR
Basham, Larry D. ....Cleveland, TN
Basham, Linda Kaplan ....Sacramento, CA
Basham, Lynn A. ....Narberth, PA
Basham, Marshall D. ....Ponca City, OK
Basham, Roy C. ....Fort Worth, TX
Basham, Susan M. ....Boston, MA
Basham, Thomas S. ....Timonium, MD
Bashant, Cynthia A. ....San Diego, CA
Bashant, June P. ....San Francisco, CA
Bashar, John P. ....Stratford, CT
Bashar, Naghmeh ....San Diego, CA
Bashara, Charles L. ....Norfolk, VA
Bashara, Charles V. ....Norfolk, VA
Bashara, George N., Jr. ....Detroit, MI
Bashara & Hubbard ....Norfolk, VA
Bashaw, Catharine M. ....Tulsa, OK
Bashaw, Catherine F. ....East Hartford, CT
Bashaw, Donna R. ....Laguna Hills, CA
Bashaw, John R. ....New Haven, CT
Bashaw, Keith J. ....Monmouth Junction, NJ
Bashaw, Steven B. ....Oakbrook Terrace, IL
Bashaw, Walter R., II ....Pittsburgh, PA
Basheer, B. William ....McLean, VA
Bashein & Bashein Co., L.P.A.
Ashtabula, OH
Cleveland, OH
Bashein, Richard W. ....Cleveland, OH
Bashein, W. Craig ....Cleveland, OH
Basher, Dawn M. ....Newton, MA
Bashey, Rehman H. ....Seattle, WA
Bashford, Janet ....Yorktown Heights, NY
Bashford, Martha S. ....New York, NY
Bashian, James V. ....New York, NY
Bashinelli, Stephen P. ....New York, NY
Bashinsky, Major ....Birmingham, AL
Bashir, Layli Miller ....Washington, DC
Bashir, Talat M. ....St. Louis, MO
Bashline, J. D. ....Houston, TX
Bashline, Terry L. M. ....Pittsburgh, PA
Bashlow, William ....New York, NY
Bashman, Howard J. ....Cherry Hill, NJ
Philadelphia, PA
Bashner, Richard S. ....New York, NY
Bashner, Robert ....Port Washington, NY
Bashoff, Kenneth H. ....Radnor, PA
Bashor, Chris ....St. Paul, MN
Bashor, Ewing C. ....Pittsburgh, PA
Bashor, Gary B. ....Longview, WA
Bashor, Valerie A. ....Missoula, MT
Bashore, Lionel E. ....Troy, MI
Bashore, Sandra K. ....Van Wert, OH
Bashore Smith, J. Brooke ....Pittsburgh, PA
Bashour, George A. ....Grindstone, PA
Bashshur, Ramona ....Ann Arbor, MI
Bashuk, Jeffrey A. ....Atlanta, GA
Bashwiner, John M. ....Cedar Grove, NJ
New York, NY
Bashwiner, Steven L., (P.C.) ....Chicago, IL
Bashwiner and Woods, P.C.
Cedar Grove, NJ
New York, NY
Bashyam, Murali ....Raleigh, NC
Bashyam & Spiro, LLP ....Raleigh, NC
Basi, Bartholomew A. ....Marion, IL
Basial, Patrick J. ....Pittsburgh, PA
Basic, Anne Marie ....Portland, OR
Basich, Anthony M. ....Los Angeles, CA
Basich, Mary Luppi ....Santa Monica, CA
Basie & Fritz, A Ptnrshp. of Professional Corps. ....San Diego, CA
Basie, Ramon ....Shaker Heights, OH
Basie, Robert H. ....San Diego, CA
Basil, Autumn ....Cleveland, OH
Basil, Beth L. ....Cincinnati, OH
Basil, Brian A. ....Columbus, OH
Basil, Danny J. ....Glasgow, KY
Basil, David A. ....Cleveland, OH
Basil, David Augustus ....Carrollton, GA
Basil, Deborah A. ....Independence, OH
Basil, Erik R. ....San Diego, CA
Basil, Erika Kim Nietenhoefer ....Dallas, TX
Basil, Mark A. ....Cincinnati, OH
Basil, Michael W. ....Chicago, IL
Basil, Michelle L. ....Boston, MA
Basil, Robert J. ....Somerset, NJ
Basil, Thomas A., Jr. ....Saginaw, MI
Basil, William C. ....Washington, DC
Basile, Andrée G. ....Houma, LA
Basile, Andrew R. ....Troy, MI
Basile, Andrew R. ....Warren, OH
Basile, Andrew R., Jr. ....San Francisco, CA
Chicago, IL
Basile, Christopher M. ....New York, NY
Basile, Deborah A. ....Springfield, MA
Basile, Edward M. ....Washington, DC
Basile, Francis G. ....Vineland, NJ
Basile, J. Jude ....Solana Beach, CA
Basile, James F. ....Washington, DC
Basile, Joseph J., Jr.
East Longmeadow, MA
Basile, Joseph J., Jr. ....Springfield, MA
Basile, Joseph P. ....Chicago, IL
Basile, Juliet K. ....Brookfield, WI
Basile, Karl A. ....San Antonio, TX
Basile, Katherine M. ....San Francisco, CA
Basile, Lena A. ....Pasadena, CA
Basile, Marjory G. ....Detroit, MI
Basile, Mark Glenn ....Chicago, IL
Basile, Mary E. ....Boston, MA
Basile, Michael ....Miami, FL
Basile, Michael D. ....Washington, DC
Basile, Michael E. ....Schenectady, NY
Basile, Michael J. ....Charleston, WV
Basile, Nancy ....Satellite Beach, FL
Basile, Paul L., Jr. ....Los Angeles, CA
Basile, Peter J. ....Baltimore, MD
Basile, Richard S. ....Greenbelt, MD
Basile, Richard Simon ....Jefferson City, MO
Basile, Rose A. ....Cliffside Park, NJ
Basile, Rudolph J. ....Laguna Beach, CA
Basile, Salvatore ....Santa Cruz, CA
Basile, Salvatore A. ....Las Vegas, NV
Basile, Salvatore J. ....Andover, MA
Basile, Savino J. ....Springfield, MA
Basile & Testa, A Professional Corporation
Vineland, NJ
Basile, Thomas E. ....New York, NY
Basile, Vincent W. ....Hackensack, NJ
Basile, William B. ....Glencoe, IL
Basile Edwards, Zipporah Marie
Charlotte, NC
Basile-Janowski, Susan ....Syracuse, NY
Basileo, Steven ....Los Angeles, CA
Basilevsky, Peter A. ....New York, NY
Basilica, Anthony R. ....New London, CT
Basilico, Brent F. ....Santa Cruz, CA
Basilico, Lori A. ....Providence, RI
Basilone, John E. ....Portsmouth, VA
Basin, James W. ....San Mateo, CA
Basinait, Charles J. ....Fort Myers, FL
Basine, Robert B. ....Glastonbury, CT
Basinger, A. Marshall, II ....Charlotte, NC
Basinger & Associates, P.C. ....Scottsdale, AZ
Basinger, John A. ....Houston, TX
Basinger, Kyle G. ....Dallas, TX
Basinger, L. Kim ....Austin, TX
Basinger, Malcolm D. ....Lima, OH
Basinger, Randall ....Ottawa, OH
Basinger, Richard L. ....Scottsdale, AZ
Basinger, Russell A. ....Midland, PA
Basinger, Stephen P. ....Fort Thomas, KY
Basinger, Susan E. ....San Diego, CA
Basinger, William K. ....Lansing, MI
Basinski, Anthony J. ....Pittsburgh, PA
Basinski, Basinski & Basinski ....Chicago, IL
Basinski, David A. ....Elyria, OH
Basinski, David A., Jr. ....Akron, OH
Basinski, Erwin J. ....San Francisco, CA
Basinski, Stanley E. ....Chicago, IL
Basist, Wayne S. ....Pasadena, CA
Basista, Joseph J. ....Newport Beach, CA
Basista, Michael ....Monterey, CA
Basista, Pryor & Balloff ....Jacksboro, TN
Basista, Terry M. ....Jacksboro, TN
Baska, James L. ....Overland Park, KS
Baskauskas, Edward L. ....Martinez, CA
Baskervill, Charles T. ....Petersburg, VA
Baskervill, Pamela Shell ....Petersburg, VA
Baskerville, Anastasia ....Sacramento, CA
Baskerville, Angela N. ....Lubbock, TX
Baskerville, J. Victor ....Huntsville, AL
Baskerville, Lisa C. ....Washington, DC
Baskerville, Michael S. ....Vernon, TX
Baskerville, Ramona L. ....Minneapolis, MN
Baskerville, Richard W. ....Des Moines, IA
Baskerville, Robert A. ....Seattle, WA
Baskes, Daniel L. ....Chicago, IL
Baskes, Roger S. ....Chicago, IL
Baskett, John M., III ....Los Angeles, CA
Baskett, Richard M. ....Missoula, MT
Baskett, Robert T. ....Dallas, TX
Baskett, W. Paul ....Los Angeles, CA
Baskett, William D., III ....Cincinnati, OH
Baskette & Baskette ....Nashville, TN
Baskette, James Richard ....Stockton, CA
Baskette, Margaret Lee
Department of Justice, Civil Division, GV
Baskette, Roger D., Jr. ....Nashville, TN
Baskette, Roger D., Sr. ....Nashville, TN
Baskette, William L., Jr. ....San Antonio, TX
Baskey, Gerald L. ....West Seneca, NY
Baskies, Jeffrey A. ....Fort Lauderdale, FL
Baskin, Alan S. ....Phoenix, AZ
Baskin, Barrett R. ....San Francisco, CA
Baskin, Barry ....Walnut Creek, CA
Baskin & Baskin ....Chicago, IL
Baskin & Baskin, P.C. ....Marietta, GA
Baskin, Bennett & Komkov, L.L.P.
Austin, TX
Baskin, Bruce Lee ....Dublin, OH
Baskin, Carol R. ....San Antonio, TX
Baskin, Carol S. ....Marietta, GA
Baskin, David Green ....Santa Cruz, CA
Baskin and Feldstein, P.C.
Farmington Hills, MI
Baskin, Gary A. ....Norfolk, VA
Baskin & Grant ....Santa Cruz, CA
Baskin, H. H., Jr., P.A. ....Clearwater, FL
Baskin, Hamden H., III ....Clearwater, FL
Baskin, Hamden H., III, P.A.
Clearwater, FL
Baskin, Harris P., Jr. ....Marietta, GA
Baskin, Henry ....Farmington Hills, MI
Baskin, H. H., Jr. ....Clearwater, FL
Baskin, Isadore ....Chicago, IL
Baskin, Jackson & Hansbarger
Arlington, VA
Fairfax, VA
Falls Church, VA
Baskin, James D. ....San Antonio, TX
Baskin, James D., III ....Austin, TX
Baskin, James H. ....Tucker, GA
Baskin, James M. ....Joliet, IL
Baskin, Jeremy ....Treasury Department, Office of Regulations and Rulings, GV
Baskin, Jonathan D. ....Alexandria, VA
Baskin, Karen M. ....Pittsburgh, PA
Baskin, Lawrence A. ....San Rafael, CA
Baskin, Leslie Beth ....Philadelphia, PA
Baskin, Lisa Watts ....Salt Lake City, UT
Baskin, Louis ....Chicago, IL
Baskin, Maurice ....Washington, DC
Baskin, Michael O. ....Denver, CO
Baskin, Mona L. ....Buffalo, NY
Baskin, Nancy A. ....Boise, ID
Baskin, Pat M. ....Midland, TX
Baskin, Peter J. ....New York, NY
Baskin, Peter M. ....Arlington, VA
Baskin, Philip ....Camp Hill, PA
Baskin, Rae ....Whitestown, IN
Baskin, Richard J., Law Offices of
Oakland, CA
Baskin, Robert M. ....Ventura, CA
Baskin, Roy Howard, III ....Dallas, TX
Baskin, Sarah C. ....Hartford, CT
Baskin, Scott D., (P.C.)
Newport Beach, CA
Baskin, Server, Berke, Weinstein & Spiro
Chicago, IL
Baskin, Seymour ....Pittsburgh, PA
Baskin, Sheldon E. ....Cleveland, OH
Baskin, Sheldon L. ....Chicago, IL
Baskin, Sherry E. ....West Conshohocken, PA
Baskin, Stephen E. ....Cleveland, OH
Baskin, Steven A. ....Willowbrook, IL
Baskin, Stuart J. ....New York, NY
Baskin, Susan Daicoff ....Jacksonville, FL
Baskin, Thomas P., III ....Boise, ID
Baskin, Todd M. ....New York, NY
Baskin, William A. ....Southaven, MS
Baskin, William C., III ....Hartford, CT
Baskin, William C., Jr. ....New Haven, CT
Baskin, William M. ....Falls Church, VA
Baskin, William M., Jr. ....Falls Church, VA
Baskin, William P., III ....Bishopville, SC
Baskind, David Harris ....Cranford, NJ
Baskind, Larry A. ....El Paso, TX
Baskind, Samaniego & Hosford, P.C.
El Paso, TX
Baskind, Stephen L., (P.C.) ....Dallas, TX
Baskins, Ann O. ....Palo Alto, CA
Baskins, Charles W. ....North Platte, NE
Baskins, Lori Jeanette ....Kansas City, MO
Baskins & Roeder ....North Platte, NE
Baskowitz, Eve ....Chicago, IL
Baskowsky, Paul W. ....Philadelphia, PA
Basl, Edwin T. ....Reno, NV
Basler, Christian O. ....Upper Nyack, NY
Basler, David K. ....Des Moines, IA
Basler, Pamela T. ....Barrow, AK
Basler, Stanley L. ....Oklahoma City, OK
Basler, Todd E. ....Sheboygan, WI
Basloe and Basloe, P.C. ....Herkimer, NY
Basloe, Evalyn G. ....Herkimer, NY
Basloe, Joseph S. ....Herkimer, NY
Basloe, Steven M. ....New York, NY
Basmadjian, Karine ....Glendale, CA
Basmaji, Dorothy Hanigan
Birmingham, MI
Basmajian, Richard J. ....Sherman Oaks, CA
Basner, David ....Ukiah, CA
Basner, Elliot R. ....New York, NY
Basner, Norman ....Jamaica, NY
Basner, Thomas C. ....Saginaw, MI
Basnett & Easterwood ....St. Clairsville, OH
Basnett, Jeffrey M. ....Columbus, OH
Basnett, Patricia Moreland ....Tulsa, OK
Basney, William C. ....Jacksonville, FL
Basnight, Cassell D. ....Chesapeake, VA
Basnight, Daniel F. ....Charlotte, NC
Basnight, Kord H. ....Department of Justice, Drug Enforcement Administration, GV
Basnight, W. Brantley, III
Virginia Beach, VA
Basnight, Wright, Kinser, Telfeyan & Leftwich, P.C. ....Chesapeake, VA
Basofin, Michael S. ....Northbrook, IL
Basola, Joseph W. ....Decatur, IL
Sandoval, IL
Basom, Dara Katherine ....Larned, KS
Basombrio, Juan C. ....Costa Mesa, CA
Bason, Ernest F.
Charlotte Amalie, St. Thomas, VI
Bason, George F. ....Raleigh, NC
Bason, George Francis, Jr. ....Washington, DC
Chevy Chase, MD
Bason, George R., Jr. ....New York, NY
Bason, Neil W. ....San Francisco, CA
Bason, Wm. A. ....Raleigh, NC
Basora, Federico L. ....San Juan, PR
Basov, Daniel ....New York, NY
Basque, James F. ....Orlando, FL
Basquill, Timothy M.
West Palm Beach, FL
Basquill Ruf, Maureen ....New York, NY
Basquin, Philip W. ....Glendale, CA
Basrai, Sarbjit S. ....Yuba City, CA
Basralian, Joseph L. ....Hackensack, NJ
Basri, Nancy S. ....New York, NY
Bass, Adam Joel ....Los Angeles, CA
Bass, Allen B. ....Jackson, MI
Bass, Alvin S. ....Nevada City, CA
Bass, Alyse Sue ....Department of Justice, Civil Rights Division, GV
Bass, Anthony Bernard ....Chicago, IL
Bass, Arnold F. ....Murray Hill, NJ
Bass & Associates, P.C. ....Phoenix, AZ
Tucson, AZ
Atlanta, GA
Bass & Bass ....Lake Charles, LA
Bass and Bass ....Carthage, TN
Bass, Bass & Nelson, A Professional Corporation ....El Reno, OK
Oklahoma City, OK
Bass, Benjamin J. ....Chicago, IL
Bass, Berry & Sims PLC ....Knoxville, TN
Memphis, TN
Nashville, TN
Bass, Beverly A. ....Longview, TX
Bass, Bill ....Houston, TX
Bass, Brian David ....Bohemia, NY
Bass, Bryant & Fanney ....Raleigh, NC
Bass & Carlson, P.A. ....Buffalo, MN
Minneapolis, MN
Bass, Carol-Ann Feldman
Westborough, MA
Bass, Carole M. ....New York, NY
Bass, Cary C., Jr. ....Port Arthur, TX
Bass, Charles M., Jr. ....New Orleans, LA
Bass, Charles T. ....Decatur, GA
Bass, Charles W. ....Atlanta, GA
Bass & Chernoff, P.A. ....Naples, FL
Bass, Christopher Martin
Treasury Department, Internal Revenue Service, GV
Bass, Clarence R. ....Albuquerque, NM
Bass, Clifford I. ....New York, NY
Bass, Courtenay L., Ms. ....Dallas, TX
Bass, Cynthia B. ....Philadelphia, PA
Bass, Dale E. ....Springfield, MA
Bass, Daniel A. ....San Antonio, TX
Bass, Daniel B. ....Fort Lauderdale, FL
Bass, David ....Carthage, TN
Bass, David A. ....Chicago, IL
Bass, David Dewey
Charlotte Amalie, St. Thomas, VI
Bass, David E.
National Transportation Safety Board, Office of the General Counsel, GV
Bass, David I. ....Sacramento, CA
Bass, David I. ....White Plains, NY
Bass, David M. ....Los Angeles, CA
Bass, David M. ....Hackensack, NJ
Bass, David S. ....Brooklyn, NY
Bass, Deborah ....Beverly Hills, CA
Bass, Deborah ....New York, NY
Bass, Diane C. ....Laguna Beach, CA
Bass, Doherty & Finks, P.C. ....Boston, MA
Bass, Dondra Suzanne ....Orlando, FL
St. Petersburg, FL
Bass, Donna ....Crawfordville, FL
Bass, Donna Kempler ....Glencoe, IL
Bass, E. Warner ....Nashville, TN
Bass, Edward F. ....Lake Charles, LA
Bass, Ellen Marie ....Oxnard, CA
Bass, Ellen S. ....Morristown, NJ
Bass, Emily M. ....New York, NY
Bass, Eugene L. ....Redwood City, CA
Bass, Frank H., Jr. ....The Woodlands, TX
Bass, Franklin F. ....New York, NY
Bass, Franklin L., (P.C.) ....New York, NY
Bass, Fredric K. ....New York, NY
Bass, G. Allen ....Boston, MA
Bass, Gary F. ....Seattle, WA
Bass, Gary Howard ....Fort Myers, FL
Bass, Geoffrey A. ....New York, NY
Bass, Gerald ....Encino, CA
Bass, Gerald, A Law Corporation
Encino, CA
Bass, Gerald L. ....Raleigh, NC
Bass, Gerald L. ....Milwaukee, WI
Bass, Gilbert S. ....Boston, MA
Bass, Gill Ellen ....Montclair, NJ
Bass, Glenn S. ....Atlanta, GA
Bass, H. Gary ....Baltimore, MD
Bass, Harris D. ....Los Angeles, CA
Bass, Harry M. ....Independence, KS
Bass, Harvey B. ....Chicago, IL
Bass, Herbert ....Cincinnati, OH
Bass, Herbert ....Philadelphia, PA
Bass, Hilarie ....Miami, FL
Bass, Howard I. ....Northfield, IL
Bass, Howard I. ....Minneapolis, MN
Bass, Hugh D., Jr. ....Howey-In-The Hills, FL
Bass, I. Scott ....Washington, DC
Bass, Iris M. ....Fort Lauderdale, FL
Bass, J. Alan ....Union, SC
Bass, J. Michael ....Valdosta, GA
Bass, J. Stewart ....Fort Worth, TX
Bass, James A., III ....Graham, NC
Bass, James C. ....El Reno, OK
Oklahoma City, OK
Bass, James D. ....Bloomington, IL
Bass, James D. ....St. Louis, MO
Bass, James D. ....Tulsa, OK
Bass, James L. ....Carthage, TN
Bass, James M. ....Santa Barbara, CA
Bass, James Martin ....Fredericksburg, VA
Bass, James O. ....Nashville, TN

Bass, James O., Jr. Nashville, TN
Bass, James R. San Antonio, TX
Bass, James R., Inc., Law Offices of San Antonio, TX
Bass, Jason B Carle Place, NY
Bass, Jean Reba Brooklyn, NY
Bass, Jeffrey M. Cookeville, TN
Bass, Jeffrey S. Miami, FL
Bass, Jessica R. Los Angeles, CA
Bass, Jo Omaha, NE
Bass, John A. El Reno, OK
Oklahoma City, OK
Bass, John R., II Portland, ME
Bass, John W. "Bill", Sr. Cairo, GA
Bass, Joleen B. Upland, CA
Bass, Jonathan R. San Francisco, CA
Bass, Judith A. Fort Lauderdale, FL
Bass, Judith B. New York, NY
Bass, Julia McCarley Union, SC
Bass, Justin H. San Francisco, CA
Bass, Kathleen Salas Palo Alto, CA
Bass, Kathryn Oklahoma City, OK
Bass, Kathryn C. Stuart, FL
Bass, Kathryn J. Miami, FL
Bass, Kenneth C., III Washington, DC
McLean, VA
Bass, Kenneth N. Washington, DC
Bass, Kenneth R. Greensburg, IN
Bass, Lance W. Seattle, WA
Bass, Larry W. Houston, TX
Bass, Laura K.
Occupational Safety and Health Review Commission, Office of the General Counsel, GV
Bass Law Firm, P.A. Union, SC
Bass Law Office Chicago, IL
Bass, Lawrence Denver, CO
Bass, Lawrence D. New York, NY
Bass, Lawrence I. West Palm Beach, FL
Bass, Lawrence I. Philadelphia, PA
Bass, Lawrence M., (P.C.) Houston, TX
Bass, Leon D. Columbus, OH
Bass, Leon, Jr. Rosemead, CA
Bass, Lewis Mountain View, CA
Bass, Linda G. Milledgeville, GA
Bass, Lori Robin Miami, FL
Bass, Louis D. Buffalo, MN
Minneapolis, MN
Bass, Marcy A. Atlanta, GA
Bass, Mark K. New York, NY
Bass, Martha A. Quincy, FL
Bass & Martin Dallas, TX
Bass, Mary E. Slay Seabrook, TX
Bass, Mary P. New York, NY
Bass & McKenna Houston, TX
Bass, Melanie Merkle Birmingham, AL
Bass, Melinda Aikins White Plains, NY
Bass, Meredith A., Jr. Hazlehurst, MS
Bass, Michael Newark, NJ
Bass, Michael A. Boston, MA
Bass, Michael G., (P.A.) Miami, FL
Bass, Michael R. Fort Lauderdale, FL
Bass, Milford G., Jr. Birmingham, AL
Bass, Milton A. New York, NY
Bass & Moglowsky, S.C. Milwaukee, WI
Bass, Ogden, Jr. Freeport, TX
Bass, Paige S. Oklahoma City, OK
Bass, Patricia A. Jackson, MS
Bass, Patricia A. Houston, TX
Bass, Patricia D. Miami, FL
Bass, Patricia W. Macon, GA
Bass, Patti H. Tucson, AZ
Atlanta, GA
Bass, Paul H. Miami, FL
Bass, Paul M., III Dallas, TX
Bass, Perkins Manchester, NH
Peterborough, NH
Bass, Perry N. Houston, TX
Bass, Peter B. Ocean Township, NJ
Bass, Peter E. Department of State, Bureau of Economic and Business Affairs, GV
Bass, Philip B. Mill Valley, CA
Bass, Philip B. San Francisco, CA
Bass, Randall Newark, NJ
Bass, Ray Austin, TX
Bass, Raymond L., Jr. Naples, FL
Bass, Regina Keelan Kansas City, MO
Bass, Renée F. Chicago, IL
Bass, Renée F., Ltd. Chicago, IL
Bass, Richard I., & Associates, Ltd.
Chicago, IL
Bass, Richard Ivan Chicago, IL
Bass, Richard S. Oak Brook, IL
Bass, Robert A. Tallahassee, FL
Bass, Robert C., Jr. Austin, TX
Bass, Robert D. Encino, CA
Bass, Robert H. Jackson, MS
Bass, Robert M., Jr. Houston, TX
Bass, Robert N. Phoenix, AZ
Bass, Robert P., Jr. Concord, NH
Bass, Robert P., Jr. Philadelphia, PA
Bass, Robert T. Austin, TX
Bass, Ronald A. San Francisco, CA
Bass, Ronald J. Los Angeles, CA
Bass, Ross F., Jr. Jackson, MS
Bass, Roy Byrn, Jr. Lubbock, TX
Bass & Rubinowitz Carle Place, NY
Bass, Sally Forbes Portland, OR
Bass, Samuel E. Newark, NJ
Bass, Sandra Stephenson Tulsa, OK
Bass, Shirley A. Portland, OR
Bass, Sidney Rochester, NY
Bass, Sigmund Bohemia, NY
Bass, Stacy Waldman Westport, CT
Bass, Stanley A. Long Island City, NY
Bass, Stephen Chace Long Beach, CA
Bass, Stephen D. Albuquerque, NM
Bass, Stephen E. Phoenix, AZ
Bass, Stephen G. Danville, VA
Bass, Steven B. Treasury Department, Internal Revenue Service, GV
Bass, Steven R. Marysville, CA
Bass, Susan Duvier Nashville, TN
Bass, Susan Perkoff Washington, DC
Bass, Suzanne Jacksonville, FL
Bass, T. Langston, Jr. Savannah, GA
Bass, Thomas J. Philadelphia, PA
Bass, Thomas L. Macon, GA
Bass, Timothy A. Springfield, IL
Bass, Timothy C. McLean, VA
Bass, Timothy S.T. New York, NY
Bass, Ursula Washington, DC
Bass, Victor Boston, MA
Bass, William H., III Richmond, VA
Bass, William K. Chicago, IL
Bass, William M. Denver, CO
Bass, William M. Lafayette, LA
Bass, Yale P. Chicago, IL
Bassage, James D. Bishop, CA
Bassak, Andrew A. San Francisco, CA
Bassaline, Peter M. West Palm Beach, FL
Bassan, Aaron D. Roseland, NJ
Bassan, Gabriel San Francisco, CA
Bassan, Lou Ann San Francisco, CA
Bassan, Maurice M. Baltimore, MD
Bassani, Carolyn New York, NY
Bassano, Carletta M. Machias, ME
Bassano, John J. New York, NY
Bassano, Peter N. New York, NY
Bassat, Rhonda L. New York, NY
Basse, Ariel San Francisco, CA
Basse, Eric S. Saipan, TT
Basse, Jewel Kolling San Francisco, CA
Basseches, Mark T. New York, NY
Basseches, Robert T. Washington, DC
Bassein, Laura Helena, MT
Bassel, Dabney D. Fort Worth, TX
Bassel, Elizabeth D. H. Evanston, IL
Bassel, Irene A. Orlando, FL
Bassel, Pamela Arnold Fort Worth, TX
Bassel, Raymond B. Hillsboro, OR
Bassel, Robert N. Southfield, MI
Bassel, Rodney A. Lawton, OK
Bassen, Ned H. New York, NY
Basser, Stephen R. San Diego, CA
Bassett, Barton W.S. Palo Alto, CA
Bassett, Benton Cleveland, OH
Bassett, Brian R. Boston, MA
Bassett, Brooke San Francisco, CA
Bassett, Charles Phoenix, AZ
Bassett, Christin L. Philadelphia, PA
Bassett & Copple, LLP Roswell, NM
Bassett, Craig J. Morgan Hill, CA
Bassett, Daniel Bartlesville, OK
Bassett, David B. Boston, MA
Bassett, Edward C., Jr. Worcester, MA
Bassett, Edwin F. New York, NY
Bassett, Frances C. Albuquerque, NM
Bassett, Glen A. Tampa, FL
Bassett, J. Thomas Syracuse, NY
Bassett, Jack M. Farmington, CT
Bassett, James P. Concord, NH
Bassett, Jane A. Ann Arbor, MI
Bassett, Janene P. Los Angeles, CA
Bassett, Jeffrey C. Panama City, FL
Bassett, Jeffrey M. Opelousas, LA
Bassett, Jennifer Ross New York, NY
Bassett, John Milwaukie, OR
Bassett, John W. San Francisco, CA
Bassett, John W., Jr. Roswell, NM
Bassett, Jonathan D. New York, NY
Bassett, Julia L. Atlanta, GA
Bassett, Kedric A. Las Vegas, NV
Bassett, Kenneth B. Cincinnati, OH
Bassett Law Firm Fayetteville, AR
Bassett Law Office, P.C. Wood River, IL
Bassett, Lisa M. Tallahassee, FL
Bassett, M. Scott Indianapolis, IN
Bassett, Merle C. Wood River, IL
Bassett, Michael H. Dallas, TX
Bassett, Michael L. Santa Ana, CA
Bassett, Michael R. New York, NY
Bassett, Neal W. Phoenix, AZ
Bassett, Paul R. San Diego, CA
Bassett, Peter Q. Atlanta, GA
Bassett, Ralph W., Jr. Milton, WV
Bassett, Randall C. Los Angeles, CA
Bassett, Robert A. Denver, CO
Bassett, Robert A. Danbury, CT
Bassett, Robert J. Belleville, IL
Bassett, Roland L. Galveston, TX
Bassett, Samuel E. Austin, TX
Bassett, Schuyler H. Los Angeles, CA
Bassett, Scott Troy, MI
Bassett, Stephen Jay Cleveland, OH
Bassett, Stephen S. Woodinville, WA
Bassett, Stocker & Boyce Bartlesville, OK
Bassett, Thomas A. Southfield, MI
Bassett, Thomas T. Spokane, WA
Bassett, Tiffany A. Palo Alto, CA
Bassett, Tod C. Fayetteville, AR
Bassett, W. Bruce New York, NY
Bassett, W. George Seattle, WA
Bassett, W. Randall Atlanta, GA
Bassett, W. Sartis Oak Grove, LA
Bassett, William H. Sunnyvale, CA
Bassett, William, Jr. Fort Lauderdale, FL
Bassett, William R. Atlanta, GA
Bassett, William W. San Francisco, CA
Bassett, Woodson W., III Fayetteville, AR
Bassett, Woodson W., Jr. Fayetteville, AR
Bassetti, Andrew B. Seattle, WA
Bassetti, Edward R. Florham Park, NJ
New York, NY
Bassetti, Kay New York, NY
Bassetti, Richelle Gerow Mercer Island, WA
Bassett-Stanford, Mary Concord, MA
Bassewitz, Marc D. Chicago, IL
Bassewitz, Suzanne Marie Mineola, NY
Bassey, Patricia Langan Bethesda, MD
Bassey, Ronald D. Southfield, MI
Bassey and Selesko, P.C. Detroit, MI
Southfield, MI
Bassford, Charles A., Jr. Edina, MN
Bassford, Charles H., IV Fort Wayne, IN
Bassford & Hanvik, P.A. Edina, MN
Bassford, Lockhart, Truesdell & Briggs, P.A. Minneapolis, MN
Bassford, R. Andrew Charlottesville, VA
Bassford, Rita I. San Bernardino, CA
Bass-Frazier, D. A. Mobile, AL
Bassham, David M. Pasadena, CA
Bassham, Eve B. Largo, FL
Bassham, Solveig K. Los Angeles, CA
Bassham, Terry El Paso, TX
Bassi, Bradley M. Charleroi, PA
Washington, PA
Bassi, Kathleen C. Springfield, IL
Bassi, Keith A. Charleroi, PA
Washington, PA
Bassi, Linda J. Denver, CO
Bassi, Marte J. San Francisco, CA
Bassi, McCune & Vreeland, P.C. Charleroi, PA
Washington, PA
Bassi, Melvin B. Charleroi, PA
Washington, PA
Bassi, Michael B. San Francisco, CA
Bassias, George Astoria, NY
Bassichis, Jodie L. Hollywood, FL
Bassick, Edgar W., III Bridgeport, CT
Bassick, Gayle T. North Haven, CT
Bassik, Barry S. Great Neck, NY
Bassil, Janice Boston, MA
Bassin, Alana Minneapolis, MN
Bassin, Elisabeth A. New York, NY
Bassin, Jeffrey L. Cincinnati, OH
Bassin, Michael Robert Los Angeles, CA
Bassin, Michael Robert, A Professional Corporation Encino, CA
Los Angeles, CA
Bassin, Richard H. Union, NJ
Bassin, Scott I. San Francisco, CA
Bassin, Steven Jay New York, NY
Bassin, Stuart J. Department of Justice, Tax Division, GV
Bassing, Peter J. San Rafael, CA
Bassinger, Delos P. Boynton Beach, FL
Bassinger, Lori A. Boston, MA
Bassinger, Todd F. Minneapolis, MN
Bassingthwaighte, Joan Seattle, WA
Bassinson, D. Scott Albany, NY
Bassios, Photios F. San Francisco, CA
Bassiouni, M. Cherif Chicago, IL
Bassis, Barry T. Lake Success, NY
Bassitt, Janet L.H. Roselle, IL
Bassler, Harry W. Atlanta, GA
Bassler, Richard E., Jr. Ridgewood, NJ
Bassler, Sara L. El Granada, CA
Bassler, Thomas B. Cincinnati, OH
Bassler, Thomas G. San Antonio, TX
Bassler, William August Winchester, VA
Bassler, William G. Newark, NJ
Bassman, Mitchell & Alfano, Chartered Washington, DC
Bassman, Robert S. Washington, DC
Bassmann, G. Raymond Claremore, OK
Basso, Andrea F. Rochester, NY
Basso & Basso Okemos, MI
Basso and Burke, L.L.P. Poughkeepsie, NY
Basso, Gary S. Bronx, NY
Basso, Jessica L. Providence, RI
Basso, John J. Poughkeepsie, NY
Basso, Kathleen A. New York, NY
Basso, Krupp & Myers, P.C. St. Louis, MO
Basso, Louis G., Jr. Bloomfield Hills, MI
Basso, Louis J. St. Louis, MO
Basso, Paul D. Westminster, CO
Basso, Robert H. Syracuse, NY
Basso, Ronald Pittsburgh, PA
Basso, Ronald M. Lansing, MI
Basso, Sara Jane Angeli Okemos, MI
Bassock, Irene E. Boston, MA
Bassoff, Joel M. New York, NY
Bassoff, Scott Z. Bethpage, NY
Basson, Martin E. Fort Lauderdale, FL
Bassoni, Deno A. San Francisco, CA
Bassow, Judith Steinberg Wheat Ridge, CO
Bassuk, Gregory D. New York, NY
Bassuk, Irving Jamaica, NY
Bassuk, Jennifer M. New York, NY
Bassuk, Lawrence J. Dallas, TX
Bast, Carol M. Winter Park, FL
Bast, Cynthia L. Austin, TX
Bast, Jeffrey Miami, FL
Bast, Kenneth L. Mattoon, IL
Bast, Michael M. Fresh Meadows, NY
Bast, Robert L. Ambler, PA
Basta, Donald K. Chicago, IL
Basta, Iris H. Helena, MT
Basta, James E. Chicago, IL
Basta, Joseph C. Detroit, MI
Basta, Paul M. New York, NY
Basta, Stephanie Oratz New York, NY
Bastas, Peggy M. Chicago, IL
Bastawros, Vivian L. Brooklyn, NY
Bastedo, Wayne W. Paramus, NJ
Bastek, John A. Cleveland, OH
Bastemeyer, Norman G. Des Moines, IA
Basten, Elizabeth Jolliffe Detroit, MI
Basten, Jonathan A. Mount Pleasant, SC
Bastiaans, David M. Virginia Beach, VA
Bastiaans-Chamovitz, Mary-ann Sewickley, PA
Bastiaanse, Gerard C. Irvine, CA
Santa Rosa, CA
Bastiampillai, Harisha J. McLean, VA
Bastian & Brooks New Orleans, LA
Bastian, Constance A. Orangevale, CA
Bastian, David T. Gig Harbor, WA
Bastian & Dini Los Angeles, CA
Bastian, Frank W. Milwaukee, WI
Bastian, G. Tommy Addison, TX
Bastian, Gary Maplewood, MN
Bastian, Gregory A. Sacramento, CA
Bastian, Herman L., Jr. New Orleans, LA
Bastian, Holly M. Washington, DC
Bastian, James Charles, Jr. Irvine, CA
Bastian, John W. Belle Fourche, SD
Bastian, Julie M.
Department of State, GV
Bastian, Justin Lee Palo Alto, CA
Bastian, Katherine F. Philadelphia, PA
Bastian, Kenneth R. Owego, NY
Bastian, Kevin L. San Francisco, CA
Bastian, Nelsonja N. Albuquerque, NM
Bastian, Philip N. Everett, WA
Bastian, Ralph W., Jr. San Francisco, CA
Bastian, Raphael M. Department of Justice, Antitrust Division, GV
Bastian, Robert Lawrence Los Angeles, CA
Bastian, Stanley A. Wenatchee, WA
Bastian, Ted A., Jr. Yreka, CA
Bastian, Thomas M. Rosemont, IL
Bastian & Wynne New Orleans, LA
Bastian-Dalton, Dolores
San Francisco, CA
Bastianelli, Adrian L., III
Washington, DC
Bastianelli, Brown & Kelley, Chartered
Washington, DC
Bastianelli, David Kenosha, WI
Bastianoni, Lebert D. Elmhurst, IL
Bastible, Denis J. Syracuse, NY
Bastible, Francis X. Huntington Station, NY
Bastible, Kieran X. New York, NY
Bastien, C. Thomas Denver, CO
Bastien, Christopher P. Charleston, WV
Bastien, James A. Austin, TX
Bastien & Martin, L.C. Charleston, WV
Bastien, Robert E. Du Quoin, IL
Bastien, Robert E. Galveston, TX
Bastier, Ellen L. San Francisco, CA
Bastin, Thomas B. Fort Lauderdale, FL
Bastine, Paul A. Spokane, WA
Bastine, Ronique J. Houston, TX
Bastine, Volly C., Jr. Houston, TX
Basting, Ellen K. Milwaukee, WI
Basting, Thomas J., Jr. Minneapolis, MN
Basting, Thomas J., Sr. Janesville, WI
Baston, Valerie D. Fort Worth, TX
Bastone Associates Boston, MA
Bastone, Christine Garden City, NY
Bastone, Christine Cooley
Fort Lauderdale, FL
Bastone, Frank, Jr. Mineola, NY
New York, NY
White Plains, NY
Bastone, Lawrence D. Boston, MA
Bastow, Edward C. (Ned), Jr.
Oklahoma City, OK
Bastow, Thomas F. Washington, DC
Bastress, Robert M., Jr. Morgantown, WV
Bastress, Susan B. Washington, DC
Basu, Krisna M. Boston, MA
Basu, Ranu Washington, DC
Basu, Shantanu Palo Alto, CA
Basuk, Philomena White Plains, NY
Basulto, Vincent New York, NY
Basurto, Mark A. Atlanta, GA
Baswell, Camie Michelle Richardson, TX
Basye, George Sacramento, CA
Basye & Golden San Mateo, CA
Baszler, Alvin E., Jr. Lansing, MI
Bata, Linda E. Grand Forks, ND
Bata, Rudolph A., Jr. Murphy, NC
Bata, Rudolph A., Jr., P.A. Murphy, NC
Batacan, Peter A. Washington, DC
Bataille, Christian N. Fairbanks, AK
Bataille, Tianne Chicago, IL
Bataille-Ferry, Valerie G. Norwich, CT
Bataillon, Joseph F. Omaha, NE
Bataillon, Peter C. Omaha, NE
Batal, Susan E. Rocky River, OH
Batalon, Carrie L. Bloomington, IN
Batalucco, Michael J. Detroit, MI
Batarse, Ray I. Los Alamitos, CA
Batarseh, George J. Miami, FL
Batastini, Lyn A. Mobile, AL
Batavia, Andrew I. Miami Beach, FL
Batch, Nicholas C. Springfield, MI
Batcha, Francis E. Freehold, NJ
Batche, Steve B. Houston, TX
Batchelder, Alice M. Medina, OH
Batchelder, Anne E. Orleans, MA
Batchelder, David W., Jr. Miami, FL
Batchelder, Drake M.
Fort Lauderdale, FL
Batchelder, Gerald F. Fremont, CA
Batchelder, Gerald F., A Prof. Corp.
Fremont, CA
Batchelder, Hadley San Diego, CA
Batchelder, Harry C., Jr. New York, NY
New York, NY
Batchelder, James R. Cupertino, CA
Batchelder, James T. Canton, OH
Batchelder, John T. H.
Westfield Center, OH
Batchelder, Mark Wayland Fort Worth, TX
Batchelder, Richard D., Jr. Boston, MA

Batchelder, Robert B. ... Omaha, NE
Batchelder, Samuel L., Jr. ... Boston, MA
Batchelder, Valerie ... Springfield, MO
Batchelder, William F. ... Concord, NH
Batchelder, William G., Jr. ... Medina, OH
Batchelder, Wm. G., III ... Akron, OH
Batcheler, Colleen ... Cleveland, OH
Batcheler, George C. ... Birmingham, AL
Batcheler, Wayne E. ... New York, NY
Batcheller, Diane ... Livermore, CA
Batcheller, Osmer D.
Fort Lauderdale, FL
Batcheller, Stephanie J. ... Albany, NY
Batchelor & Associates, P.C. ... Juneau, AK
Batchelor & Batchelor ... Van Buren, AR
Batchelor, Bruce A. ... Beverly Hills, CA
Batchelor, Colleen J. ... Bryan, TX
Batchelor, Danny ... Houston, TX
Batchelor, Dean R. ... Farmington, MI
Batchelor, Douglas D., Jr. ... Augusta, GA
Aiken, SC
Batchelor, Edward A., III
St. Clair Shores, MI
Batchelor, Fines F., Jr. ... Van Buren, AR
Batchelor, James D. "Dan"
Oklahoma City, OK
Batchelor, James K. ... Orange, CA
Batchelor, James K., A Professional Corporation ... Orange, CA
Batchelor, James R., Jr. ... Williamston, NC
Batchelor, James W. ... Grand Rapids, MI
Batchelor, Jeffrey M. ... Portland, OR
Batchelor, Jeffrey M., Law Offices of, A Prof. Corp. ... Portland, OR
Batchelor, LeRoy E. ... Kilmarnock, VA
Batchelor, Leslie V. ... Department of Justice, Office of the Attorney General, GV
Batchelor, Patrick C. ... Corsicana, TX
Batchelor and Powers, Professional Corporation
Oklahoma City, OK
Batchelor, Robert J. ... Coshocton, OH
Batchelor, Ronnie K. ... Lawrenceville, GA
Batchelor, Sonya ... Sherman, TX
Batchelor, Suzanne M. ... West Hartford, CT
Batchelor, Tom G. ... Juneau, AK
Batchelor, William C. ... Washington, DC
Batchelor, William F.
Rancho Cucamonga, CA
Batchelor, W. T., II ... Wilmington, NC
Batcher, Karen A. ... Escondido, CA
Batcher, Richard M. ... Moline, IL
Batchik, Michael ... Novi, MI
Batdorf, David J. ... Shillington, PA
Batdorf, Jonathan B. ... Shillington, PA
Batdorf, Timothy D. ... Detroit, MI
Bate, Andrew H. ... Miami, FL
Bate, Bettina A. ... Los Angeles, CA
Bate, Charles T. ... Shelbyville, IN
Bate, David H. ... Los Angeles, CA
Bate, David S. ... Montclair, NJ
Bate, Ellen D. Olian ... Brooklyn, NY
Bate, Harrold & Bate, Prof. Corp.
Shelbyville, IN
Bate, Herman E. ... Lufkin, TX
Bate, Jeffrey S. ... Shelbyville, IN
Bate, Michael H. ... Phoenix, AZ
Bate & Peterson, LLP ... Los Angeles, CA
Bate, Richard H. ... Denver, CO
Bate, Richard H. ... Randolph, NJ
Bate, Richard L. ... Sherman Oaks, CA
Bate, S. John ... Staten Island, NY
Bate, S. John, P.C. ... Staten Island, NY
Bate, William J. ... Clifton, NJ
Bateh, Abraham I. ... Jacksonville, FL
Bateh & Clark, Law Offices of
Jacksonville, FL
Bateh, George Z. ... Jacksonville, FL
Batek, Jerry Lee ... Kingsville, TX
Batelli, Neil C. ... Paterson, NJ
Bateman, Alexander G., Jr. ... Mineola, NY
Bateman, Anthony G. ... Philadelphia, PA
Bateman, Bateman & Darnell, P.C.
Clarksville, TN
Bateman, Charles B. ... Ipswich, MA
Bateman, Charles B. ... Duluth, MN
Bateman, Charles L. ... Burlington, NC
Bateman, Christine U. ... Tupelo, MS
Bateman, Christopher "Kip" ... Warren, NJ
Bateman, Courtney R. ... Washington, DC
Bateman, David A. ... Olympia, WA
Bateman, David A. ... Seattle, WA
Bateman, David L. ... Baton Rouge, LA
Bateman, David P. ... Churchville, PA
Bateman, Frank C., III ... New York, NY
Bateman, Fred W. ... Newport News, VA
Bateman, Frederick L., Jr.
Tallahassee, FL
Bateman, Fritz ... Port Charlotte, FL
Bateman, Gibson & Childers
Memphis, TN
Bateman, Glenn A. ... New York, NY
Bateman, Goodwin & Gardner, A Professional Corporation ... Westlake Village, CA
Bateman, Grace A. ... Washington, DC
Bateman, Hal M. ... Lubbock, TX
Bateman, Herbert Harvell
Newport News, VA
Bateman, John J. ... Philadelphia, PA
Bateman, John W. ... Washington, DC
Bateman, Keith T. ... Schaumburg, IL
Bateman, Kenneth ... Santa Fe, NM
Bateman, Kim S. ... Pontiac, MI
Bateman, M. Ben ... Amarillo, TX
Bateman, M. Stuart ... Newport News, VA
Bateman, Marc A. ... Seattle, WA
Bateman, Marguerite Cameron
Washington, DC
Bateman, Mark R. ... Los Angeles, CA
Bateman, Marlon H. ... Westlake Village, CA
Bateman, Mary Ellen ... Tallahassee, FL
Bateman, Maureen Scannell ... Boston, MA
Bateman, Michael R. ... Lakewood, NJ
Bateman, Michele E. ... Charleston, SC
Bateman, Nancy J. ... Westfield, NJ
Bateman, North & Gardner
Salt Lake City, UT
Bateman, Oertel & Koonts
Burlington, NC
Bateman, Paul E. ... Chicago, IL
Bateman, Peter R. ... Albuquerque, NM
Bateman, Philip L. ... Decatur, IL
Bateman, Randall B. ... Portland, OR
Bateman, Randall B. ... Salt Lake City, UT
Bateman, Reid B. ... Baton Rouge, LA
Bateman, Reid B., A P.L.C.
Baton Rouge, LA
Bateman, Robert H. ... Houston, TX
Bateman, Robert S. ... Houston, TX
Bateman, Robert T. ... Clarksville, TN
Bateman, Sylvia L. ... Chicago, IL
Bateman, Thomas G., Jr. ... Houston, TX
Bateman, Thomas H., III ... Tallahassee, FL
Bateman, Thomas N. ... Clarksville, TN
Bateman, Thomas R. ... Boston, MA
Bateman, Tracy A. ... New York, NY
Bateman, Tyler J. ... Edwardsville, IL
Bateman, Valerie L. ... Raleigh, NC
Bateman, Wallace H., Jr. ... Doylestown, PA
Bateman, William C., Jr. ... Memphis, TN
Batenhorst, Gary R. ... Omaha, NE
Bates, Alben F., Jr. ... Elmhurst, IL
Bates, Albert ... Summertown, TN
Bates, Albert, Jr. IV ... Pittsburgh, PA
Bates, Allen E. ... Atlanta, GA
Bates, Alton ... Baton Rouge, LA
Bates, Amy C. ... Antioch, IL
Bates, Amy Pierson ... Fremont, CA
Bates, Andre Y. ... Los Angeles, CA
Bates, Andrea E. ... Menlo Park, CA
Bates, Andrew ... Eugene, OR
Bates, Arthur V. ... Brooklyn, NY
Bates, Barbara J. ... Chicago, IL
Bates & Baum ... Atlanta, GA
Bates, Bert H. ... Cleveland, TN
Bates, Betsy J. ... Houston, TX
Bates, Betty Bartels ... Dayton, OH
Bates, Beverly B. ... Atlanta, GA
Bates, Blaine F. ... Las Vegas, NV
Bates, Bradford L. ... Washington, DC
Bates, Brenda G. ... Atlanta, GA
Bates, Brent A. ... Edwardsville, IL
Bates, Brian A. ... Chicago, IL
Bates, Brian E. ... Denver, CO
Bates, Brian K. ... Houston, TX
Bates, C. Valentine ... Gainesville, FL
Bates, Candice V. ... New Orleans, LA
Bates, Carl E. ... Arlington, VA
Bates, Carolyn ... Philadelphia, PA
Bates, Carolyn A. ... St. Paul, MN
Bates & Casey ... Fort Worth, TX
Bates, Charles ... Seattle, WA
Bates, Charles D. ... Portland, OR
Bates, Charles T. ... New York, NY
Bates, Christopher A. ... Louisville, KY
Bates, Claude H. ... Evansville, IN
Bates, C. W. ... Birmingham, AL
Bates, Cynthia J. ... Blue Bell, PA
Bates, Daniel B. ... Waterford, MI
Bates, Daniel L. ... Fort Worth, TX
Bates, David ... Houston, TX
Bates, David A. ... South Lake Tahoe, CA
Bates, David F. ... Salem, OR
Bates, David G. ... West Palm Beach, FL
Bates, David L. ... Colusa, CA
Bates, David L. ... Green Bay, WI
Bates, David Smith
Rolling Hills Estates, CA
Bates, David T. ... Carmel, CA
Bates, Douglas B. ... Jeffersonville, IN
Bates, Douglas F. ... Salt Lake City, UT
Bates, Douglas J. ... St. Louis, MO
Bates, Douglas L. ... Plantation, FL
Bates, Douglas M. ... Dothan, AL
Bates, Douglas MacArthur, Jr. ... Tampa, FL
Bates, Douglas P. ... Auburn, NY
Bates, Douglas Thompson, III
Centerville, TN
Bates, E. Charles ... Defiance, OH
Bates, E. William, II ... New York, NY
Bates, Earl E. "Ernie", Jr.
Fort Worth, TX
Bates, Earle S. ... Washington, DC
Bates, Ebonette ... New York, NY
Bates, Edward E., Jr. ... Atlanta, GA
Bates, Edwin R. ... Chicago, IL
Lake Forest, IL
Bates, Elizabeth A. ... Wheaton, IL
Bates, Elizabeth Lewis ... Stamford, CT
Bates, Elizabeth Puller
Department of Justice, Executive Office for Immigration Review, GV
Bates, Eric M. ... New York, NY
Bates, Fred E. ... Ventura, CA
Bates, Frederick N. ... Glenview, IL
Bates, Fredrick H. ... Chicago, IL
Bates, G. Del ... Cleveland, OH
Bates, G. Ronald, Jr. ... Leavenworth, KS
Bates, Gary L. ... Jackson, MS
Bates, Geneva Rich ... Uniontown, OH
Bates, George D. ... Rockford, IL
Bates, Gerald A. ... Fort Worth, TX
Bates, Gerald A., P.C. ... Fort Worth, TX
Bates, Gregory G. ... Kenosha, WI
Bates, Gregory S. ... Overland Park, KS
Bates, H. Richard ... Orlando, FL
Bates, H. Scott ... Orlando, FL
Bates, Harold M. ... Roanoke, VA
Bates, Harry S. ... San Antonio, TX
Bates, Henry G. ... Elmhurst, IL
Bates, J. Harold ... Nacogdoches, TX
Bates, J. Raymond, Jr. ... Dalton, GA
Bates, Jack B. ... Frankfort, KY
Bates, James ... Hindman, KY
Bates, James A. ... Santa Ana, CA
Bates, James C. ... Baton Rouge, LA
Lafayette, LA
Bates, James C. ... Broadview Heights, OH
Bates, James D. ... Toledo, OH
Bates, James V. ... Bristol, VA
Bates, James W. ... Glendale, CA
Bates, Jason G. ... Pittsburgh, PA
Bates, Jay F. ... Rigby, ID
Bates, Jeanne M. ... Albuquerque, NM
Bates, Jeffrey B. ... Lufkin, TX
Bates, Jeffrey C. ... Boston, MA
Bates, Jeffrey P. ... Philadelphia, PA
Bates, Jeffrey P. ... Lufkin, TX
Bates, Jeffrey R. ... Los Angeles, CA
Bates, Jeffrey W. ... Springfield, MO
Bates, Joan M. ... Elk Grove, CA
Bates, John B. ... Birmingham, AL
Bates, John B. ... San Francisco, CA
Bates, John D. ... Washington, DC
Bates, John F. ... Salt Lake City, UT
Bates, John H. ... Columbus, OH
Bates, John L. ... Waco, TX
Bates, John Roddy ... Midwest City, OK
Bates, John W. ... Dallas, TX
Bates, John W., III ... Richmond, VA
Bates, Jonathan J. ... Dallas, TX
Bates, Joseph Henry (Hank)
Little Rock, AR
Bates, Joshua A. ... Seattle, WA
Bates, Julia R. ... Toledo, OH
Bates, Julie E. ... Oklahoma City, OK
Bates, Kelehear, Starr & Cherof, P.C.
Dalton, GA
Bates, Kendall O. ... Fresno, CA
Bates, Kenneth H. ... Bakersfield, CA
Bates, Kevin W. ... Salt Lake City, UT
Bates, Krista P. ... Addison, TX
Bates, Laren D. ... Riverdale, GA
Bates, Larry D. ... Dundee, NY
Bates, Laurel A. ... Dallas, TX
Bates Law Firm ... Las Cruces, NM
Bates, Lawrence F. ... Washington, DC
Bates, Lawrence W., Jr. ... Willimantic, CT
Bates & Lee, P.C. ... Houston, TX
Bates, Lester L., Jr. ... Columbia, SC
Bates, Lloyd O., Jr. ... Las Cruces, NM
Bates, Lyle J. ... Farmington, MI
Bates, M. Susan ... Indianapolis, IN
Bates, Mark A. ... Sacramento, CA
Bates, Mark A. ... Schererville, IN
Bates, Mark R. ... St. Louis, MO
Bates, Marlon L. ... Salt Lake City, UT
Bates, Martin W. ... Salt Lake City, UT
Bates, Marvin J., Jr. ... Dunwoody, GA
Bates, Mary Elizabeth Stricklin
Huntingdon, TN
Bates, Mary Ellen ... Birmingham, AL
Bates, Mathew E. ... Greensboro, NC
Bates, Mathew E., P.A. ... Greensboro, NC
Bates, Maurice J. ... Dallas, TX
Bates Meckler Bulger & Tilson
Chicago, IL
Bates, Michael S.
Department of Transportation, Office of the General Counsel, GV
Bates, Michael T. ... Indianapolis, IN
Bates, Michael T. ... Brentwood, TN
Bates, Nathania
Christiansted, St. Croix, VI
Bates, Nedra J. ... Phoenix, AZ
Bates, Nikola J. ... Lake Forest, CA
Bates, Norman D. ... Sudbury, MA
Bates, Nuala A. ... San Ramon, CA
Bates, Owen J. ... Palo Alto, CA
Bates, Paul A., Law Offices of
Lawrenceburg, TN
Bates, Paul D. ... Tucson, AZ
Bates, Philip A. ... Pensacola, FL
Bates, R. Alan ... Janesville, WI
Bates, Rebecca Gayle ... Shelbyville, KY
Bates, Reed R. ... Birmingham, AL
Bates, Richard G., Jr. ... Concord, CA
Bates, Richard K. ... Danville, IL
Bates, Richard N. ... Redding, CA
Bates, Richard W. ... Orlando, FL
Bates, Robert ... Washington, IA
Bates, Robert B. ... Athens, GA
Bates, Robert B. ... Silver Spring, MD
Bates, Robert C. ... Phoenix, AZ
Bates, Robert C. ... Annapolis, MD
Bates, Robert C. ... Kansas City, MO
Bates, Robert D. ... Houston, TX
Bates, Robert J., Jr. ... Chicago, IL
Bates, Robert K. ... New Hempstead, NY
Bates, Robert L. ... Great Bend, KS
Bates, Robert L., P.A. ... Great Bend, KS
Bates, Robert W. ... San Luis Obispo, CA
Bates, Robin Burrell ... Fort Washington, MD
Bates & Robinson, P.A. ... Cleveland, TN
Bates, Roger L. ... Birmingham, AL
Bates, Roy D. ... Columbia, SC
Bates, Russell H. ... Arlington, VA
Bates, Russell T. ... Los Angeles, CA
Bates, Sarah F. ... Boulder, CO
Bates, Scott W. ... Jackson, MS
Bates, Stephen ... Washington, DC
Bates, Stephen L. ... Williamstown, KY
Bates, Stephen R. A. ... Washington, DC
Bates, Susan Johnson ... San Jose, CA
Bates, Terry B. ... Los Angeles, CA
Bates, Thomas H. ... Hattiesburg, MS
Bates, Thomas M. ... West Palm Beach, FL
Bates, Timothy ... Laconia, NH
Bates, Timothy C. ... Hazard, KY
Bates, Timothy D. ... Groton, CT
Bates, Timothy J. ... Chelsea, OK
Bates, Traci E. ... San Diego, CA
Bates, Veronica M. ... Dallas, TX
Bates, W. Carter, III ... Macon, GA
Bates, W. Daniel, Jr. ... Eugene, OR
Bates, Walter A. ... Cleveland, OH
Bates, Walter William ... Birmingham, AL
Bates, William B. ... Washington, DC
Bates, William B. ... Lincoln, IL
Springfield, IL
Bates, William D. ... Alpine, TX
Bates, William F. ... Riverhead, NY
Bates, William F. ... Southampton, NY
Bates, William F. ... Toledo, OH
Bates, William H. ... Kansas City, MO
Bates, William, III ... San Francisco, CA
Bates, William J. ... Charleston, SC
Bates, William N. ... Nashville, TN
Bates, William P. ... Schenectady, NY
Bates, William R. ... Kalamazoo, MI
Bates, Winnie ... Round Rock, TX
Bates, Wm. Buford ... Nashville, TN
Bates, Yolanda R. ... Detroit, MI
Bates-Crouch, Karen A. ... Omaha, NE
Bateski & Morgenthal, P.C. ... Savannah, GA
Bateski, Thomas R. ... Savannah, GA
Batesky, Richard P., Jr. ... Indianapolis, IN
Indianapolis, IN
Bateson, Amy ... Dearborn, MI
Bates-Rickel, Nancy ... Fort Gratiot, MI
Batey, Douglas L. ... Seattle, WA
Batey, L. Nicole ... Houston, TX
Batey, Lisa M. ... Department of Justice, Immigration and Naturalization Service, GV
Batey, Scott P. ... Southfield, MI
Batey, Tracey L. ... Birmingham, MI
Batey & Yochim, P.L.L.C. ... Southfield, MI
Bath, Bradley P. ... Houston, TX
Bath, Candace V. ... South Windsor, CT
Bath, Daniel G. ... Newport Beach, CA
Bath, David E. ... Loveland, CO
Bath & Edmonds, P.A.
Overland Park, KS
Kansas City, MO
Bath, Kenneth L. ... Canton, IL
Bath, Lynne Diane ... Bainbridge Island, WA
Bath, Patricia Ann ... San Antonio, TX
Bath, Robert M. ... Lexington, KY
Bath, Ronald J. ... Reno, NV
Bath, Russell F., Jr. ... Worcester, MA
Bath, Thomas J., Jr. ... Overland Park, KS
Bath, Turner & Barber ... Henderson, TX
Bathalter, Robert E. ... Alexandria, KY
Bathalter and Woeste ... Alexandria, KY
Falmouth, KY
Bathas, Nicholas P. ... Naperville, IL
Bathe, David H. ... Department of Justice, Executive Office for Immigration Review, GV
Bathelt, Edmund M. ... Kenosha, WI
Bather, Helen D. ... Brea, CA
Bathersfield, Nizanna
Environmental Protection Agency, Office of Administrative Law Judges, GV
Batherson, John G. ... Bangor, ME
Bathgate, Lawrence E., II ... Lakewood, NJ
Bathgate, Wegener & Wolf, P.C.
Lakewood, NJ
Bathon, Ann C. ... Hanover, PA
Bathon, Daniel H. ... Elkton, MD
Bathon, Eastridge & Bathon, P.A.
Elkton, MD
Bathon, John T. ... Towson, MD
Bathon, Matthew G. ... Elkton, MD
Bathory, Joseph P. ... Cambridge, MD
Bathum, Rick ... Enumclaw, WA
Bathum, Rick, Inc., P.S. ... Enumclaw, WA
Bathurst, Camille ... Louisville, KY
Batia, Melissa D. ... Biloxi, MS
Batie, Fatima ... Shakopee, MN
Batine, Rafael ... Atlanta, GA
Batipps, Joyce Stanley ... Washington, DC
Batis, Edward J., Jr. ... San Antonio, TX
Batista, Alberto Victor, Law Offices of
Miami, FL
Batista, Bruce P. ... Cleveland, OH
Batista, Daniel P. ... Lorain, OH
Batista, David O. ... Miami, FL
Batista, Duane R. ... Boston, MA
Batista, Edward B. ... Orange, CA
Batista, Gregory J. ... New York, NY
Batista, Jorge L. ... New York, NY
Batista, Laureano F ... Key Biscayne, FL
Batista, Paul A. ... New York, NY
Batista, Paul A., A Professional Corporation
New York, NY
Batista, Paul J. ... Caldwell, TX
Batista, Roy H. ... Canton, OH
Batista, Victor R. ... Kew Gardens, NY
Batista Jimenez, Diana ... San Juan, PR
Batiste, Alvin, Jr. ... Plaquemine, LA
Batiza, Paul M., (P.C.) ... Metairie, LA
Batjer, Cameron M. ... Chevy Chase, MD
Batjer, Robert D. ... Abilene, TX
Batjer & Wagstaff, P.C. ... Abilene, TX
Batka, Catherine M. ... Beavercreek, OH
Batke, Gary S. ... Columbus, OH
Batkin, Mark R. ... Sacramento, CA
Batla, Raymond J., Jr. (IBA)
Washington, DC
Batla, Walter J. ... Austin, TX
Batlan, Felice J. ... Greenwich, CT

Batler, Michael D. ... Chicago, IL
Lincolnwood, IL
Batley, Lionel G., Jr.
General Services Administration, Office of Regional Counsel, GV
Batliner, Jennifer J. ... Middletown, OH
Batliner, Jennifer L. ... Santa Ana, CA
Batliner, Ronald, Jr. ... Virginia Beach, VA
Batlle, Carlos A., (P.A.) ... Miami, FL
Batlle-Barasorda, Diana M. ... San Juan, PR
Batman, Cynthia P. ... Northbrook, IL
Batman, David R. ... Wilmington, DE
Batman, Donald V. ... Cedar Glen, CA
Batman, Jean L. ... San Francisco, CA
Batmasian, James H. ... Boca Raton, FL
Batoff, Arthur D. ... Wynnewood, PA
Batoff, Helaine B. ... New York, NY
Batoff, Jeffrey S. ... Philadelphia, PA
Batoff, Jerald S. ... Philadelphia, PA
Batoff, Steven I. ... Baltimore, MD
Batoff, Steven I., P.A. ... Baltimore, MD
Batog, Deborah E. ... Milford, MA
Batoon, John R. ... El Paso, TX
Bator & Berlin ... Birmingham, MI
Bator, Chris ... Cleveland, OH
Bator, Christine V. ... Princeton, NJ
Bator, Christopher F. ... Boston, MA
Bator, Gregory J. ... Birmingham, MI
Bator, John E. ... Indianapolis, IN
Bator, Thomas E. ... Boston, MA
Batow, David P. ... Tulsa, OK
Batross, Martin E. ... Columbus, OH
Batrus, William J. ... Boca Raton, FL
Batsakis, Theodore J. ... Long Beach, CA
Batsche, David A. ... Mason, OH
Batsche, David K. ... Mason, OH
Batsche & Peters ... Mason, OH
Batsel, C. Guy ... Englewood, FL
Port Charlotte, FL
Batsel, McKinley, Ittersagen, Gunderson & Berntsson, P.A. ... Boca Grande, FL
Englewood, FL
Fort Myers, FL
Port Charlotte, FL
Venice, FL
Batsel, Robert W. ... Ocala, FL
Batsell, Carol L. ... Minneapolis, MN
Batsell, Marjory Colvin ... Brownsville, TX
Batsell, Samuel C., III
Pension Benefit Guaranty Corporation, Office of the General Counsel, GV
Batsevitsky, Jessica S. ... Boston, MA
Batsides, Demetrios C. ... Newark, NJ
Batson, Buren T. (Ted), Jr. ... Durant, MS
Batson, C. A. Blake ... Arkadelphia, AR
Batson, David C.
Environmental Protection Agency, Office of Enforcement and Compliance Assurance, GV
Batson, David W. ... Decatur, TX
Stephenville, TX
Batson, F. Blair ... Portland, OR
Batson, Frederick A. ... Eugene, OR
Batson, Gordon R. ... Brewton, AL
Batson, James A. ... New York, NY
Batson, John P. ... Augusta, GA
Batson, John T., Jr. ... Knoxville, TN
Batson, Joseph D. ... Houston, TX
Batson, Martha Murnane ... Minneapolis, MN
Batson, Maureen Murphy ... Cincinnati, OH
Batson, Nolan, Brice, Harvey & Williamson, PLLC ... Clarksville, TN
Batson, R. Neal ... Atlanta, GA
Batson, Richard H. ... Clarksville, TN
Batson, Richard H., II ... Nashville, TN
Batson, Richard H., II, P.C., A Prof. Corporation ... Nashville, TN
Batson, Robert C. ... Albany, NY
Batson, Robert D. ... Denver, CO
Batson, Robert J., Jr. ... Chattanooga, TN
Batson, Ron ... Long Beach, CA
Batson, Sharon L. ... Plainfield, NJ
Batson, Susan Crockett ... Pensacola, FL
Batson, Thad D. ... Kansas City, MO
Batson, Thomas F. ... Greenville, SC
Batson, Tracey M. ... Beaumont, TX
Batson, Wanda J. (Wallace)
Sylacauga, AL
Batson, Wm. C., Jr. ... Poplar Bluff, MO
Batt, Charles M. ... Bridgeport, CT
Batt, David V. ... New Orleans, LA
Batt, Dean C. ... Marion, KS
Batt, Douglas Alexander ... Stoughton, MA
Batt, Gerald J. ... Vineland, NJ
Batt, Halpern & Weinraub ... Philadelphia, PA
Batt, Howard C. ... Clearwater, FL
Batt, Howard C., P.A. ... Clearwater, FL
Batt, John F. ... North Tonawanda, NY
Batt, John Paul ... Cleveland, OH
Batt, Kevin D. ... Boston, MA
Batt, Lawrence I., (P.C.) ... Omaha, NE
Batt, Marc E. ... Philadelphia, PA
Batt, Mary D. ... Madison, WI
Batt, Raymond W. ... Shirley, NY
Batt, Raymond Warren, Jr. ... Dallas, TX
Batt, Richard R. ... Palo Alto, CA
Batt, Robert R. ... Philadelphia, PA
Batt, Roger ... Wichita, KS
Batt, Stephen C. ... New Plymouth, ID
Batt, Tony ... Sherman, TX
Batt & Wiech ... North Tonawanda, NY
Batt, William J. ... Boise, ID
Batta, Ravi ... Miami, FL
Battaglia, Alan E. ... San Antonio, TX
Battaglia, Anthony J. ... San Diego, CA
Battaglia, Anthony S. ... St. Petersburg, FL
Battaglia, Anthony T. ... Garden City, NY
Battaglia, Brian P. ... St. Petersburg, FL
Battaglia, Carol S. ... San Diego, CA
Battaglia, Christopher J. ... New York, NY
Battaglia, David Alan ... Los Angeles, CA
Battaglia, Donald C. ... Chicago, IL
Battaglia, Erica Lewis ... Chicago, IL
Battaglia, Frederick S. ... Durham, NC
Battaglia, Jack M. ... Rochester, NY
Battaglia, John J. ... New York, NY
Battaglia, John T. ... Norfolk, VA
Battaglia, Joseph G., Jr.
Staten Island, NY
Battaglia, Laurie H. ... Columbia, MD
Battaglia, Lisa R. ... Cleveland, OH
Battaglia, Lisa R. ... Cleveland, OH
Battaglia, Lynne A. ... Baltimore, MD
Battaglia, Mark E. ... Benson, AZ
Battaglia, Michael C. ... Buffalo, NY
Battaglia, Nancy ... Buffalo, NY
Battaglia, Paul A. ... Buffalo, NY
Battaglia, Paul J. ... Seattle, WA
Battaglia, Peter J. ... Buffalo, NY
Eden, NY
Battaglia, Philip J. ... Clifton, NJ
Battaglia, Philip M. ... Los Angeles, CA
Battaglia, Raymond W. ... San Antonio, TX
Battaglia, Richard A. ... Beaumont, TX
Battaglia, Richard J. ... Chicago, IL
Battaglia, Ricky ... Montgomery, AL
Battaglia, Ross, Dicus & Wein, A Professional Association
St. Petersburg, FL
Tampa, FL
Battaglia, S. Paul ... Syracuse, NY
Battaglia, Sandro Attilio ... New York, NY
Battaglia, Terry J. ... Bloomington, MN
Battaglia, Thomas A. ... Berkeley Heights, NJ
Battaglia, Thomas V., Jr. ... Stratford, CT
Battaglia, Timothy J. ... Houston, TX
Battaglia, Victor F. ... Wilmington, DE
Battaglia, Victor F., Jr. ... Wilmington, DE
Battaglia, William P. ... Winter Park, FL
Battaglia, William P., P.A.
Winter Park, FL
Battagline, Richard F. ... Akron, OH
Battaglini, K. B. ... Houston, TX
Battaglini, R. A. ... Endicott, NY
Battaglino, Joseph M. ... San Diego, CA
Battaile, Frank W. ... Costa Mesa, CA
Battaile, John F., III ... Tucson, AZ
Battalia, Dolores A. ... Larchmont, NY
Battalora, Linda A. ... Lakewood, CO
Battan, David M.
Commodity Futures Trading Commission, Division of Trading and Markets, GV
Battan, Linda J. ... Chicago, IL
Battan, Lisa E. ... Boulder, CO
Battan, Paul ... Olympia, WA
Battan, Shirley W. ... Olympia, WA
Battani, Adam V. ... Atlanta, GA
Battani, Joseph A., JR. ... Toledo, OH
Battani, Marianne ... Detroit, MI
Battard, Frank P. ... New Orleans, LA
Battat, David A. ... New York, NY
Battcher, Donald S. ... Hamilton, OH
Batte, Gregory H. ... Shreveport, LA
Batte, John F., Jr. ... Richmond, VA
Batte, Leslie Katherine ... Lima, OH
Batteen, Dennis J. ... Aberdeen, SD
Batteese, Tyler E. ... Tampa, FL
Batteh, Kevin K. ... Richmond, VA
Battel, Nancy M. ... San Jose, CA
Battelle, Anthony E. ... Boston, MA
Battelstein, Nancy ... Los Angeles, CA
Batten, David H. ... Raleigh, NC
Batten, Edward R., Jr. ... Houston, TX
Batten, Fred W. ... Detroit, MI
Batten, J. William ... Waterville, ME
Batten, Jack Bruce ... Chicago, IL
Batten, John E., III ... Nichols, SC
Batten, John E., III, P.A. ... Nichols, SC
Batten, John E., IV ... West Columbia, SC
Batten, Mark W. ... Boston, MA
Batten, Melissa C. ... Charlotte, NC
Batten, Nicole S. ... Dallas, TX
Batten, Peter R. ... New York, NY
Batten, Phillip R. ... North Wilkesboro, NC
Batten, Timothy C. ... Atlanta, GA
Batten, W. Russell ... Thomasville, NC
Battenberg, Steve R. ... Milwaukee, WI
Battenfeld, John S. ... Los Angeles, CA
Batter, Anne G. ... Washington, DC
Batter, John F., III ... Boston, MA
Batterman, Albert R. ... Glendive, MT
Batterman, Daniel D. ... New York, NY
Batterman, Jamie D. ... New York, NY
Batterman, Jon S.
Securities and Exchange Commission, Division of Enforcement, GV
Batterman, L. Robert ... New York, NY
Batterman, Scott I. ... Honolulu, HI
Batterman, Thomas W. ... Wausau, WI
Battern, Timothy H. ... Ellisville, MO
St. Louis, MO
Battersby, Francis J. ... Oakland, NJ
Battersby, Gregory J. ... Stamford, CT
Mamaroneck, NY
Battersby, Julie A. ... Christiansburg, VA
Battersby, Leigh Anne ... Chattanooga, TN
Battersby, Marguerite P. ... Redlands, CA
San Bernardino, CA
Battersby, Michael L. ... Farmington Hills, MI
Battersby and Tiernan ... Oakland, NJ
Battersby, Wayne Hobbs ... Palm Springs, CA
Battershall, Jeffrey S. ... Grand Rapids, MI
Battershell, John J. ... McCook, NE
Battershell, Rick V. ... Elk Grove, CA
Batterson, Bruce M. ... Minneapolis, MN
Batterson, Donald E. ... Chicago, IL
Batterson, James R. ... Overland Park, KS
Batterson, Richard E. ... Tallahassee, FL
Batterton, Clinton R. ... Washington, DC
Battey, Colden R., Jr. ... Beaufort, SC
Battey, David R. ... Alexandria, MN
Battey, Jonathan C. ... Monterey, CA
Battey, Richard H. ... Rapid City, SD
Battey, Robert A.
Department of Commerce, GV
Battey, Robert W. ... Denver, CO
Battey, Russell H. ... Redfield, SD
Battey, Wendella Ault ... Rocky Hill, CT
Battiato, David A. ... Lincoln, NE
Battiato, John ... Great Neck, NY
Battilega, Carrie ... San Diego, CA
Battin, Ann Harding ... Pinole, CA
Battin, Robert Craig ... Maumee, OH
Battin, Robert W. ... Santa Ana, CA
Battino, Morris R. ... Washington, DC
Battipaglia, Joseph A. ... Philadelphia, PA
Battis, Kenneth R. ... Overland Park, KS
Battis, Mark E. ... Minneapolis, MN
Battis, Richard J. ... Eagan, MN
Battise, Arnold S. ... Dallas, TX
Battist, Gerald E. ... Alexandria, VA
Battista, Andrew M. ... Towson, MD
Battista, Andrew M., P.A. ... Towson, MD
Battista, Anthony ... New York, NY
Battista, Archer B. ... Springfield, MA
Battista & Battista, Co., L.P.A.
Minerva, OH
Battista, Clark E. ... Minerva, OH
Battista, Donato J. ... Jersey City, NJ
Battista, Felicia C. ... Washington, DC
Battista, Frederick A. ... Phoenix, AZ
Battista, Gerard E ... Marshfield, MA
Battista, Julie R. ... Cherry Hill, NJ
Philadelphia, PA
Battista, Leo F. ... Greenwich, CT
Battista, Louis R. ... Fort Lauderdale, FL
Battista, Mark E. ... Falmouth, ME
Battista, Michaela Leigh ... Los Angeles, CA
Battista, Paul J. ... Miami, FL
Battista, Peter L., Jr. ... Lake Toxaway, NC
Battista, Rita Lawton ... Brooksville, FL
Battista, Robert B. ... Brooksville, FL
Battista, Robert J. ... Detroit, MI
Battista, Rudolph E. ... Minerva, OH
Battista, Thomas M. ... Chicago, IL
Battista, Vincent J. ... Mineola, NY
Battiste, Kathy ... Staten Island, NY
Battiste, Leilani F. ... San Francisco, CA
Battiste, Luther J., III ... Columbia, SC
Battiste, Lynda S. ... Albany, NY
Battiste, Paula Fitz ... Albany, NY
Battisti, Alan S. ... Bethlehem, PA
Battisti, Charles A. ... Coral Gables, FL
Battisti, Charles W. ... Coral Gables, FL
Battisti, Eugene F., Jr. ... Columbus, OH
Battisti, Gino F. ... St. Louis, MO
Battisti, James J., Jr. ... Catskill, NY
Battisti, Linda Maria ... Columbus, OH
Battisti, Renee N. ... Philadelphia, PA
Battistini, Linda S. ... Philadelphia, PA
Battistoni, Geraldine ... Westbrook, CT
Battistoni, Gary R. ... Philadelphia, PA
Battistoni, Jeffrey S. ... Poughkeepsie, NY
Battistoni, Lori V. ... Ponte Vedra Beach, FL
Battistoni, Thomas P. ... New York, NY
Battitori, Edward J. ... Baxter Springs, KS
Battle, Anne Glann ... Escondido, CA
Battle, Arthur J. ... Dearborn, MI
Battle, Carl W. ... Kenilworth, NJ
Battle, Carmen J. ... Fayetteville, NC
Battle, Colleen P. ... Cleveland, OH
Battle, Dorothy F. ... Deerfield, IL
Battle & Edenfield, P.A. ... Brandon, FL
Battle, Elizabeth L. ... New York, NY
Battle, F. Gordon ... Hillsborough, NC
Battle Fowler LLP ... Los Angeles, CA
New York, NY
Battle, Frank J. ... Austin, TX
Battle, Frank V., Jr. ... Chicago, IL
Battle, G. Thomas ... Charleston, WV
Battle, George E., III ... Charlotte, NC
Battle, H. Dill, III ... Charleston, WV
Battle, Hyman L., Jr. ... New York, NY
Battle, Jackson B. ... Austin, TX
Battle, John F. ... Wayne, NJ
Battle, John S., Jr. ... Richmond, VA
Battle, Joseph F., Jr. ... Media, PA
Battle, Joseph L. ... Huntsville, AL
Battle, Kelly Michelle ... Houston, TX
Battle, Kenneth ... Chicago, IL
Battle, LaVeeda Morgan ... Birmingham, AL
Battle, Leo A. ... Paradise, CA
Battle, Leslie A.E. ... Warwick, RI
Battle, Maxwell G., Jr. ... Kalispell, MT
Battle, Michael A. ... Treasury Department, Bureau of Engraving and Printing, GV
Battle, Michael A. ... New York, NY
Battle, Michael W. ... Conway, SC
Battle, Michele L. ... Atlanta, GA
Battle, Robert E. ... Arlington, VA
Battle, Robert Eugene ... Birmingham, AL
Battle, Thomas P. ... The Woodlands, TX
Battle, Timothy J. ... Alexandria, VA
Battle & Vaught, P.A. ... Conway, SC
Myrtle Beach, SC
Battle, W. Cullen ... Salt Lake City, UT
Battle, W. Michael ... Los Angeles, CA
Battle, William C. ... Charlottesville, VA
Battle, Winslow, Scott & Wiley, P.A.
Roanoke Rapids, NC
Rocky Mount, NC
Battles, Ann M. ... Santa Barbara, CA
Battles, Anthony Ross ... Minneapolis, MN
Battles, Bungeroth & McBurney, Professional Corporation ... North Conway, NH
Battles, Charles S., Jr. ... Los Angeles, CA
Battles, Emmett L. ... Tampa, FL
Battles, Hayden R. ... Cullman, AL
Battles, John G. ... Flint, MI
Battles, John M. ... Dayton, OH
Battles, Michaele S. ... McLean, VA
Battles, Philip M., III ... Washington, DC
Battles, Richard G. ... Santa Barbara, CA
Battles, Robert A. ... Exeter, NH
Battles, William R. ... North Conway, NH
Battleson, Mark D. ... Atlanta, GA
Battle-Turner, Bettye ... St. Louis, MO
Battmer, Robert Andrew ... Mission Hills, KS
Battocchi, Raymond D. ... McLean, VA
Battocchi, Ronald S.
National Transportation Safety Board, GV
Battoglia, Robert L. ... Chicago, IL
Batton, Darnell A. ... Louisburg, NC
Batton, David J., & Associates, Law Office of
Norman, OK
Batton & Guin ... Louisburg, NC
Batton, Patricia A. ... Houston, TX
Batton, Robert ... Jacksonville, AR
Batton, Timothy J. ... Lansing, MI
Batton, William C. ... Timonium, MD
Battreall, Roger E. ... Minneapolis, MN
Batts, Alicia J. ... Federal Trade Commission, Offices of Commissioners, GV
Batts, Batts & Bell, L.L.P.
Rocky Mount, NC
Batts, Bruce J. ... Hartford, CT
Batts, Charles D. ... Santa Fe, NM
Batts, Christy F. ... Nashville, TN
Batts, Clay Kevin ... Nashville, TN
Batts, Deborah A. ... New York, NY
Batts, Edward H. ... Palo Alto, CA
Batts, Edwin H., III ... Knoxville, TN
Batts, Jeff. D. ... Rocky Mount, NC
Batts, Jeffrey A. ... Rocky Mount, NC
Batts, Jerry L. ... Athens, AL
Batts, Jerry T., Jr. ... Norfolk, VA
Batts, L. Lisa ... Stuart, FL
Batts, Linda S. ... Scottsdale, AZ
Batts, Michael S. ... Rocky Mount, NC
Batts, Robert H. ... Webster Groves, MO
Batts, William M., III ... Hampton, VA
Battson, Bradford L. ... San Francisco, CA
Battuello, Kathryn M. ... Seattle, WA
Batty, Brett W. ... St. Louis, MO
Batty, David L. ... Charlotte, NC
Batty, E. Jerome ... Boston, MA
Providence, RI
Batty, Judith N. ... Fairfax, VA
Batty, Lyn Morton ... Charlotte, NC
Batty, Marci ... Salt Lake City, UT
Batty, Ronald H. ... Minneapolis, MN
Batty & Stein ... Boston, MA
Batty, Walter S., Jr. ... Philadelphia, PA
Batty, William N., Jr. ... Boston, MA
Baturin & Baturin ... Harrisburg, PA
Baturin, Floyd M. ... Harrisburg, PA
Baturin, Harry M. ... Harrisburg, PA
Baturin, Madelaine ... Harrisburg, PA
Batuski, Shellie F. ... Orono, ME
Baty, Amy Bakker ... Grand Haven, MI
Baty, Bruce E. ... Kansas City, MO
Baty, Cecelia Glacy ... Kansas City, MO
Baty, Corliss C. ... Maquoketa, IA
Baty, David R. ... Point Reyes Station, CA
Baty, Donald F., Jr. ... Detroit, MI
Baty, J. Alan ... Birmingham, AL
Baty, John W. ... Ames, IA
Baty, Lee M. ... Kansas City, MO
Baty, Michael W. ... Durango, CO
Baty & Tabor ... Maquoketa, IA
Batz, Sherry E. ... St. Louis, MO
Batzar & Weinberg, A Professional Corporation ... West Palm Beach, FL
Mineola, NY
Rockville Centre, NY
Edison, NJ
Merion, PA
Batzel, Ellen L. ... Fletcher, NC
Batzer, David ... Bel Air, MD
Batzkovich, Chad B. ... Van Nuys, CA
Batzli, Brian H. ... Minneapolis, MN
Batzli, Sarah J. ... Minneapolis, MN
Batzli, Terrence R. ... Chesterfield, VA
Glen Allen, VA
Bau, Ignatius ... San Francisco, CA
Bau, Lawrence ... Chicago, IL
Bauarschi, Lorette ... Houston, TX
Baubie, Cynthia Candler
Grosse Pointe Farms, MI
Baubie, Tracey L. ... Minneapolis, MN
Baubles, Juliana V. ... New York, NY
Bauccio, Carrie A. ... Long Beach, CA
Bauch, Daniel J. ... Torrance, CA
Bauch, J. Stuart, III ... Atlanta, GA
Bauch, Jared O. ... Traer, IA
Bauch, Jim Davis ... Los Angeles, CA
Bauch, John S. ... Traer, IA
Bauch Law Office ... Traer, IA
Bauch, Linda V. ... Nashville, TN
Bauch, Paul M. ... Chicago, IL
Bauch, Philip Brian ... New York, NY
Bauch, Reva S. C. ... Chicago, IL
Bauch, Richard H. ... Newark, NJ
Bauch, Susan Labanowski ... Houston, TX
Bauch, Walter G. ... St. Paul, MN
Bauchan Law Offices, P.C.
Houghton Lake, MI
Bauchan, Michael L. ... Houghton Lake, MI
Bauche, Edward O. ... Sacramento, CA
Bauchner, Joyce Ellyn ... New York, NY
Bauchner, Lawrence ... Bridgeport, CT

Bauchner, Robert J. .... New York, NY
Bauchner, Stuart E. .... New York, NY
Bauckham, John H. .... Kalamazoo, MI
Bauckham, Sparks, Rolfe, Lohrstorfer & Thall, P.C. .... Kalamazoo, MI
Baucom, Claytor, Benton, Morgan & Wood, P.A. .... Charlotte, NC
Baucom, Jerome V. .... Washington, NJ
Baucom, Lloyd F. .... Charlotte, NC
Baucom, Marsha .... Santa Ana, CA
Baucom, Sidney G. .... Salt Lake City, UT
Baucum, Charles E. .... Memphis, TN
Baucum, Don Michael .... San Antonio, TX
Baucum, Elizabeth R. Tyndall
Kansas City, MO
Baucum, Laura B. .... San Antonio, TX
Baucum, Scott B. .... St. Louis, MO
Baucum Steed Barker .... San Antonio, TX
Baucus, Max S. .... Helena, MT
Baude, Patrick L. .... Bloomington, IN
Baudendistel, Karen A. .... St. Louis, MO
Bauder, Steven W. .... North Bend, OR
Bauders, Jerry A. .... Wooster, OH
Baudhuin, James R. .... DeSoto, TX
Baudhuin, Michael D. .... Washington, DC
Baudier, Jeffrey .... Lafayette, LA
New Iberia, LA
Baudier, Julian G., Jr. .... New Orleans, LA
Baudin & Baudin .... Dundee, IL
Baudin, Stanley P. .... Plaquemine, LA
Baudin, W. Randal .... Dundee, IL
West Dundee, IL
Baudin, W. Randal, II .... Dundee, IL
Baudino, James L. .... Dallas, TX
Baudino Law Firm, P.C. .... Des Moines, IA
Baudino, Potter & Maas .... Farmington, IL
Baudino, Robert J., Jr. .... Des Moines, IA
Baudler, Amy R. .... St. Paul, MN
Baudler, Baudler, Maus & Blahnik
Austin, MN
Spring Valley, MN
Baudler, Bryan J. .... Austin, MN
Baudler, David E. .... San Francisco, CA
Baudler, Ellen Jo .... Minneapolis, MN
Baudler, Mark B. .... Palo Alto, CA
Baudler, Richard C. .... Austin, MN
Baudler, Thomas C. .... Austin, MN
Spring Valley, MN
Baudouin, Beverly Klundt
New Orleans, LA
Baudouin, Robert I. .... New Orleans, LA
Baudouin, Waldo J. .... Metairie, LA
Baudry, Alain Marc .... Minneapolis, MN
Bauducco, Paul C. .... Encino, CA
Bauduit, Harold S. .... Estes Park, CO
Baue, Vicki J. .... Chicago, IL
Bauer, Albin, II .... Toledo, OH
Bauer, Alison .... New York, NY
Bauer, Anderson & Gravel
Burlington, VT
Colchester, VT
North Hero, VT
Bauer, Andrew C., Jr. .... Nashua, NH
Bauer, Ann E. .... St. Louis, MO
Bauer, Annelise C. .... San Francisco, CA
Bauer, Arthur .... Bismarck, ND
Bauer, Arthur R. .... Dallas, TX
Bauer & Bauer .... Los Angeles, CA
Bauer, Benjamin W. .... Tucson, AZ
Bauer, Bernard K. .... Findlay, OH
Bauer, Bernard K., Co., L.P.A.
Findlay, OH
Bauer, Bradford P. .... Milwaukee, WI
Bauer, Brian F. .... Saginaw, MI
Bauer, Brian Matthew .... Los Angeles, CA
Bauer, Bruce I. .... Chicago, IL
Bauer, Bruce P. .... Watertown, SD
Bauer, Bruce R. .... Milwaukee, WI
Bauer, Bruce T. .... Irvine, CA
Bauer, Carl T. .... St. Louis, MO
Bauer, Carl W. .... Lafayette, LA
Bauer, Carla A. .... Baltimore, MD
Bauer, Catherine Ellen .... Los Angeles, CA
Bauer, Charles A. .... Huntington Beach, CA
Bauer, Charles B. .... Boise, ID
Bauer, Charles P. .... Concord, NH
Bauer, Charles W. .... New Britain, CT
Bauer, Christina Cramer .... Brush, CO
Bauer, Christopher J.T. .... Greenville, IL
Vandalia, IL
Bauer, Christy Lynn .... Dublin, OH
Bauer, Clarissa K. .... Orange, TX
Bauer, Constance L. .... Chicago, IL
Bauer, Crider & Pellegrino
Clearwater, FL
St. Petersburg, FL
Tampa, FL
Bauer, Crystal Sharp .... Merrillville, IN
Bauer, Cynthia M. .... Milwaukee, WI
Bauer, David E. .... Bloomington, IL
Bauer, David E. .... Augusta, ME
Bauer, David O. .... Toledo, OH
Bauer, Deborah A. .... Refugio, TX
Bauer & Deitch, P.C. .... Atlanta, GA
Bauer, Dennis D. .... Santa Ana, CA
Bauer, Diana C. .... Fort Wayne, IN
Bauer, Dona Fay .... Long Beach, CA
Bauer, Donald B. .... West Chester, PA
Bauer, Donald R. .... Alta Loma, CA
Bauer, Douglas F. .... New York, NY
Bauer, Drew J. .... Pittsburgh, PA
Bauer, Duffy & Ireland .... Terre Haute, IN
Bauer, Edith A. .... San Diego, CA
Bauer, Elizabeth V. .... Plainwell, MI
Bauer, Erick L. .... Dover, OH
Bauer, Francis X. .... Sulphur Springs, TX
Bauer, Fred D. .... Cleveland, OH
Bauer, Fred L .... Great Neck, NY

Bauer, Frederick T. .... Terre Haute, IN
Bauer & French .... Boise, ID
Bauer, G. Brendan .... St. Paul, MN
Bauer, G. Michael .... Austin, TX
Bauer, Gene M. .... Canton, MA
Bauer, George A., III .... New York, NY
Bauer, George E. .... Holland, MI
Bauer, Ginger G. .... Torrance, CA
Bauer, Gregory A. .... Cleveland, OH
Bauer, Gregory L. .... Great Bend, KS
Bauer, H. Clifford .... Cincinnati, OH
Bauer, H. Dan .... Oak Brook, IL
Bauer, H. Stephen .... Portland, OR
Bauer, Harris, Clinkenbeard & Nava, LLP
San Luis Obispo, CA
Santa Barbara, CA
Ventura, CA
Bauer, Heidi L. .... Littleton, CO
Bauer, Helen G. .... Clayton, MO
Bauer, Henry L. .... Portland, OR
Bauer, Henry L., & Associates, A Prof. Corp.
Portland, OR
Bauer, Henry R. .... Troy, NY
Bauer, Henry R., Jr. .... Atlanta, GA
Bauer, Holly M. .... San Francisco, CA
Bauer, Howard Gibbs, Jr. .... Houston, TX
Bauer, J. Albert .... Breckenridge, CO
Bauer, J. Albert, P.C. .... Breckenridge, CO
Bauer, Jacob R. .... Onancock, VA
Bauer, Jacqueline M. .... Pittsburgh, PA
Bauer, James G. .... Elmhurst, IL
Bauer, James G., P.C. .... Elmhurst, IL
Bauer, James H. .... Seattle, WA
Bauer, James L. .... New Orleans, LA
Bauer, James M. .... Atlanta, GA
Bauer, James P. .... Cleveland, OH
Bauer, Jane .... Tustin, CA
Bauer, Janine G. .... New York, NY
Bauer, Jawn J. .... Bloomington, IN
Bauer, Jeffrey M. .... Kansas City, MO
Bauer, Jeffry M. .... Grosse Pointe, MI
Bauer, Jeffry M., P.C. .... Grosse Pointe, MI
Bauer, Jennifer A. .... Bloomington, IN
Bauer, Jerome .... Mineola, NY
Bauer, Jilaine Hummel .... Chicago, IL
Bauer, Jill W. .... Garden City, NY
Bauer, John A. .... New York, NY
Bauer, John C. .... Cincinnati, OH
Bauer, John G. .... Seattle, WA
Bauer, John L. .... Huntington, NY
Bauer, John R. .... Boston, MA
Bauer, John R. .... Dallas, TX
Bauer, John T. .... Mineola, NY
New York, NY
Bauer, Jon .... Hartford, CT
Bauer, Jonathan O. .... Newark, NJ
Bauer, Jos. L. .... Charlotte, MI
Bauer, Joseph M. .... Des Moines, IA
Bauer, Joseph N. .... Oshkosh, WI
Bauer, Joseph P. .... Notre Dame, IN
Bauer, Joseph P. .... Burlington, VT
North Hero, VT
Bauer, Joseph W. .... Wickliffe, OH
Bauer, Julie A. .... Chicago, IL
Bauer, Karen .... Mamaroneck, NY
Bauer, Katharine P. .... Olympia, WA
Bauer, Keith J. .... Salem, OR
Bauer, Kirk T. .... DeLand, FL
Bauer, Kirsten E. .... Philadelphia, PA
Bauer, Kristin .... Houston, TX
Bauer, Kurt S. .... Holland, MI
Bauer, Lane D. .... Kansas City, MO
Bauer, Larry M. .... St. Louis, MO
Bauer, Larry S. .... Franklin Park, IL
Bauer, Laura A. .... New York, NY
Bauer, Laurie M. .... Mobridge, SD
Bauer, Laverne M. Sagmaster
Los Angeles, CA
Bauer, Lawrence A. .... New York, NY
Bauer, Lawrence M. .... Elgin, IL
Bauer, Lee Anthony .... Washington, DC
Bauer, Leigh Ann .... Anchorage, AK
Bauer, Leigh W. .... Philadelphia, PA
Bauer, Linda Ayn .... Fairbury, NE
Bauer, Lisa N. .... Los Angeles, CA
Bauer, Lori D. .... New York, NY
Bauer, Louise .... Chicago, IL
Bauer, Mark .... Great Falls, MT
Bauer, Mark D. .... Chicago, IL
Bauer, Martin R. .... Beverly Hills, CA
Bauer, Martin W. .... Wichita, KS
Bauer, Marvin A. .... Santa Barbara, CA
Bauer, Mary Ann .... Warren, NJ
Bauer, Matthew W. .... Hackettstown, NJ
Morristown, NJ
Trenton, NJ
Bauer, Michael J. .... Troy, MI
Bauer, Michael J. .... New York, NY
Bauer, Michael J. .... Sheboygan, WI
Bauer, Michael R. .... Toppenish, WA
Bauer, Miriam .... Chicago, IL
Bauer, Morelli & Heyd Co., L.P.A.
Cincinnati, OH
Bauer, Morris S. .... Roseland, NJ
Bauer, Moynihan & Johnson .... Seattle, WA
Bauer, Nancy D. .... Bakersfield, CA
Bauer, Neal W. .... Detroit, MI
Bauer, Nicholas .... Cincinnati, OH
Bauer, Nicole M. .... Freeport, IL
Bauer, Patricia S. .... Bloomfield, CT
Bauer, Patrick B. .... Iowa City, IA
Bauer, Paul A., III .... Pottstown, PA
Bauer, Paul C. .... Boston, MA
Bauer, Paul D. .... Milwaukee, WI
Bauer, Paula K. .... San Francisco, CA
Las Vegas, NV
Reno, NV
Bauer, Peter A. .... Oakbrook Terrace, IL

Bauer, Peter T. .... Garden City, NY
Bauer, Philip E. .... Minneapolis, MN
Bauer, Philip W. .... Long Beach, CA
Bauer, Pike, Pike & Johnson, Chtd.
Great Bend, KS
Bauer, R. Glenn .... New York, NY
Bauer, R. Kenneth .... Walnut Creek, CA
Bauer, Ralph A.
Department of the Air Force,
Office of the Judge Advocate General, GV
Bauer, Ralph A. .... Sidney, OH
Bauer, Ralph Henry .... Arlington, TX
Bauer, Raymond W. .... Roselle, NJ
Bauer, Richard J., Jr., Esq. .... Santa Ana, CA
Bauer, Richard M.W. .... Boston, MA
Bauer, Richard P. .... Washington, DC
Bauer, Richard W. .... Los Angeles, CA
Bauer, Robert A. .... Toms River, NJ
Bauer, Robert B. .... Apple Valley, MN
Bauer, Robert C. .... Loveland, OH
Bauer, Robert F. .... Washington, DC
Bauer, Robert G. .... Patchogue, NY
Bauer, Robert G. .... Allentown, PA
Philadelphia, PA
Reading, PA
Bauer, Robert M. .... Arlington, VA
Bauer, Robert O., Jr. .... Clearwater, FL
Bauer, Robert R. .... Phoenix, AZ
Bauer, Roger C. .... Alpena, MI
Bauer, Roger J. .... Buford, GA
Bauer, Roger J., P.C. .... Buford, GA
Bauer, Roger R. .... Warren, OH
Bauer, Ronald G. .... Chicago, IL
Bauer, Ronald L. .... Santa Ana, CA
Bauer, S. Meade .... Austin, TX
Bauer, Samuel C. .... Beaufort, SC
Bauer, Sandra L. .... Irvine, CA
Bauer & Schaffer, LLP .... Mineola, NY
Bauer and Schltz, A Prof. Corp.
Chula Vista, CA
Bauer, Schulte, Hahn, Swanson & Brown
Burlington, IA
Bauer, Scott N. .... The Woodlands, TX
Bauer, Scott R. .... Denver, CO
Bauer, Serge .... Washington, DC
Bauer, Serge, P.C. .... Washington, DC
Bauer, Shawn Dennis .... Indianapolis, IN
Bauer, Sherwood, Jr. .... Stuart, FL
Bauer, Sherylee F. .... New York, NY
Bauer, Stanley L. .... Los Angeles, CA
Bauer, Stephen Eugene .... Battle Creek, MI
Bauer, Stephen H. .... West Bend, WI
Bauer, Stephen R. .... Washington, DC
Bauer, Stephen W. .... St. Paul, MN
Bauer, Steven D. .... Sacramento, CA
Bauer, Steven Frederick .... Pasadena, CA
Bauer, Steven M. .... San Francisco, CA
Bauer, Steven M. .... Schaumburg, IL
Bauer, Steven M. .... Boston, MA
Bauer, Susan Affleck .... Bel Air, MD
Bauer, Susan Ann Thorning .... Troy, MI
Bauer, Susan R. .... Palatine, IL
Bauer, Tamar A. .... New York, NY
Bauer, Thomas A. .... Atlanta, GA
Bauer, Thomas E. .... St. Louis, MO
Bauer, Thomas E., & Associates
Plymouth, MN
Bauer, Torrey J. .... Warsaw, IN
Bauer, Tracey S. .... Roseland, NJ
Bauer, Tracy E. .... Chicago, IL
Bauer & Twohey, P.A. .... Stuart, FL
Bauer, Vincent E. .... New York, NY
Bauer, Wendy Shields .... Champaign, IL
Bauer, William .... Burlington, IA
Bauer, William D. .... Oakdale, MN
Bauer, William F. .... Madison, WI
Bauer, William F., III .... Towson, MD
Bauer, William G. .... Rochester, NY
Bauer, William J. .... Chicago, IL
Bauer, William M. .... Malvern, PA
Bauer, William M. .... Bellevue, WA
Bauer, William R. .... Arlington, VA
Bauer, William R., P.A., Law Offices of
Columbia, SC
Bauer, William Rudolph .... Columbia, SC
Bauer-Alvarez, Hermann D.
San Juan, PR
Bauercamper, John J. .... Waukon, IA
Bauereiss, Arthur E. .... Lufkin, TX
Bauerfeld, Richard J. .... New York, NY
Bauerle, George J., III .... Westerly, RI
Bauerle, James F. .... Pittsburgh, PA
Bauerle, Kurtis T. .... Orlando, FL
Bauerle, Michael C. .... Philadelphia, PA
Bauerle, Richard C. .... Ottumwa, IA
Bauerlein, Elizabeth L. .... St. Petersburg, FL
Bauerly, Craig R. .... Le Mars, IA
Bauerly, Hemmingson, Trotzig & Bauerly, P.L.C. .... Le Mars, IA
Bauerly, Richard A. .... Le Mars, IA
Bauermeister, Don C. .... Anchorage, AK
Bauermeister, Herman O. .... Charlotte, NC
Bauermeister, Jorge .... San Juan, PR
Bauermeister, Scot .... Estherville, IA
Bauermeister-Baldrich, Arturo
San Juan, PR
Bauermeister-Schlott, Linda .... Santa Ana, CA
Bauernfeind, Barbara A. .... Midland, TX
Bauernschmidt, Charles J. .... Cleveland, OH
Bauernschmidt, George W., Jr.
Severna Park, MD
Bauernschmidt, Karen H. .... Cleveland, OH
Bauerschmidt, Robert A. .... Chicago, IL
Bauersfeld, Burton, Hendricks & Vanderhoof, L.L.C. .... Washington, DC
Bethesda, MD
Bauersfeld, Carl F. .... Bethesda, MD
Bauersfeld, John D. .... Woodland Hills, CA

Baugh, Adrienne L. .... Dallas, TX
Baugh, Arthur M. .... Richmond, VA
Baugh, Bradford .... Los Altos, CA
Baugh, Brian C. .... Lexington, KY
Baugh, Brian W. .... Rosemont, IL
Baugh, Charles S. .... Boston, MA
Baugh, David A. .... Chicago, IL
Baugh, David P. .... Richmond, VA
Baugh, Edmund L., Jr. .... Cleveland, TN
Baugh, G. Todd .... Billings, MT
Baugh, George Lee, III .... Fullerton, CA
Baugh & Goodley .... Los Altos, CA
Baugh, Hale .... Cocoa, FL
Baugh, Hoyt L., Jr. .... Rainsville, AL
Baugh, J. Thomas .... Knoxville, TN
Baugh, James R. .... Boise, ID
Baugh, Jerry P. .... Evansville, IN
Baugh, John C. .... Knoxville, TN
Baugh, John G. .... Albuquerque, NM
Baugh, Joseph D., Jr. .... Franklin, TN
Baugh, Madeleine T. .... Lexington, KY
Baugh, Mark A. .... Nashville, TN
Baugh, Paul D. .... Bloomington, IN
Baugh, Richard A. .... Harrisonburg, VA
Baugh, Richard J. .... St. Louis, MO
Baugh, Robert R. .... Birmingham, AL
Baugh, Russell B. .... Kalamazoo, MI
Baugh, Russell L. .... Clarklake, MI
Baugh, Scott R. .... Pasadena, CA
Baugh & Whitmire .... Rainsville, AL
Baugham, Lucille Hino .... Pasadena, CA
Baughan, Edward W. .... Culver City, CA
Baughan, Nancy H. .... Atlanta, GA
Baughan, Scott M. .... Rockledge, FL
Charlotte Amalie, St. Thomas, VI
Baugher, Chris Gregory .... Atlanta, GA
Baugher, Donald E., Jr. .... La Porte, IN
Baugher, Earl H., Jr. .... Albuquerque, NM
Baugher, Mettler & Shelton
Palm Beach, FL
Baugher, Peter V. .... Chicago, IL
Baugher, Roi E., II .... Naples, FL
Baughman, Alan K. .... Linton, IN
Baughman & Associates Co., L.P.A.
Cleveland, OH
Baughman, Beverly A. .... Treasury Department,
Internal Revenue Service, GV
Baughman, Beverly G. .... Kansas City, MO
New York, NY
Baughman, Brent R. .... Louisville, KY
Baughman, Bruce A. .... Baytown, TX
Baughman, Deborah L. .... Detroit, MI
Baughman, Frank J. .... Amarillo, TX
Baughman, Gary D. .... Redlands, CA
Baughman, Harry W. .... Osterville, MA
Baughman, J. Steven .... Washington, DC
Baughman, Jan Allen .... New Lexington, OH
Baughman, John B. .... Frankfort, KY
Baughman, John F. .... New York, NY
Baughman, Jon A. .... Philadelphia, PA
Baughman, Jonathan D. .... Shreveport, LA
Baughman, Lance V. .... Kansas City, MO
Baughman, Lisa B. .... Marlton, NJ
Baughman, M. Wade .... St. Louis, MO
Baughman, Margaret L. .... Morgantown, WV
Baughman, Michael E. .... Philadelphia, PA
Baughman, Michael J. .... Chicago, IL
Baughman, Michael J. .... Jackson, MI
Baughman, Michael J. .... Erie, PA
Baughman, Michael J., Jr. .... Lansing, MI
Baughman, Norman B., Jr. .... Huntsville, AL
Baughman, R. Patrick .... Cleveland, OH
Baughman, Scott E. .... Columbus, OH
Baughman, Steve .... Dallas, TX
Baughman, Steven G. .... Humble, TX
Baughman, Timothy A. .... Detroit, MI
Baughman, William G. .... York, PA
Baughman, William H., Jr.
Cleveland, OH
Baughn, Darrell .... Jackson, MS
Bauguess, Susan Smith .... Thousand Oaks, CA
Bauhof & Dorsey, LLP .... Westminster, MD
Bauhof, James F. .... Kalamazoo, MI
Bauhof, William Bradley
Westminster, MD
Bauhofer, Donald N. .... Bend, OR
Bauhs, Donald J. .... Kenosha, WI
Bauhs, Donald J., S.C. .... Kenosha, WI
Baukert, Joseph J. .... Burr Ridge, IL
Baukman, Deborah Shea .... Shreveport, LA
Bauknecht, Bradford L. .... Oshkosh, WI
Bauknecht, John W. .... Hillsdale, NJ
Bauknight, Charles F. .... Atlanta, GA
Bauknight, Clarence William, III .... Union, NJ
Bauknight, Stacey M. .... New York, NY
Bauknight, Suzanne Hefner
Knoxville, TN
Bauknight, William C. .... Ivy, VA
Baukol, Marcus M., II .... Los Angeles, CA
Baulch, Terry Alvin .... Ada, OK
Baulch, Trent A. .... Oklahoma City, OK
Bauld, William A. .... San Mateo, CA
Bauleke, Howard P.
House of Representatives,
Congressional Assistants, GV
Baulig, Laurie T. .... Alexandria, VA
Baulsier, Carolyn M. .... San Francisco, CA
Baum, Alan .... Santa Monica, CA
Baum, Alan R. .... Encino, CA
Baum, Alan S. .... Pittsburgh, PA
Baum, Alissa .... Washington, DC
Baum, Allen R.
Research Triangle Park, NC
Baum, Allyson Hope .... Norcross, GA
Baum, Alvin H., Jr. .... San Francisco, CA
Baum, Amy Elizabeth .... Evansville, IN
Baum, Andrew .... Los Angeles, CA
Baum, Andrew .... New York, NY

Baum, Andrew C.
Federal Deposit Insurance Corporation, Liquidation Branch, GV
Baum, Ann T. ... Boston, MA
Baum, Arnold ... Pelham, NY
Baum & Associates ... Bloomfield Hills, MI
Detroit, MI
Baum, Bernard M. ... Chicago, IL
Baum & Blake ... San Francisco, CA
Baum, Brandon D. ... Palo Alto, CA
Baum, Brenda G. ... St. Louis, MO
Baum, Bruce S. ... San Jose, CA
Baum, Cari S. ... Santa Ana, CA
Baum, Charles C. ... Baltimore, MD
Baum, Charles M. ... Chicago, IL
Baum, Christopher F. ... Wilmington, DE
Baum, Cindy R. ... Lewistown, IL
Baum, Claude A. ... New York, NY
Baum, David B. ... San Francisco, CA
Baum, David C. ... La Grande, OR
Baum, David E. ... Norcross, GA
Baum, David E. ... Rochester, NY
Baum, David H. ... Washington, DC
Baum, David H., The Law Offices of
Encino, CA
Baum, David J. ... Washington, DC
Baum, David M. ... Chicago, IL
Baum, David N. ... Chicago, IL
Baum, David P. ... Melbourne, FL
Baum, David R. ... New York, NY
Baum, Deborah Brand ... Washington, DC
Baum, Donald H. ... Palo Alto, CA
Baum, E. Harris ... Philadelphia, PA
Baum, E. Richard ... Upper Saddle River, NJ
Baum, Edwin L. ... West Hartford, CT
Baum, Edwin M. ... New York, NY
Baum, Elisabeth Hansen ... Menlo Park, CA
Baum, Elizabeth M. ... Palo Alto, CA
Baum, Elizabeth, P.C. ... Newton, MA
Baum, Elizabeth R. ... Poughkeepsie, NY
Baum, Elizabeth Robin ... Latham, NY
Baum, Elona ... South San Francisco, CA
Baum, Eric I. ... Culver City, CA
Baum, Etengoff & Buckley ... Vancouver, WA
Baum, Francis J., (P.C.) ... Riverside, CA
Baum, Gary M. ... Morgan Hill, CA
Baum, Gary S. ... Encinitas, CA
Baum, George F., Jr. ... Corsicana, TX
Baum, Gordon L. ... St. Louis, MO
Baum, Harvey B. ... New York, NY
Baum, Hedlund, Aristei, Guilford & Downey, A Professional Corporation
Los Angeles, CA
Washington, DC
Baum, Holly ... Buffalo, NY
Baum, Howard J. ... Bronx, NY
Baum, Irving S. ... San Francisco, CA
Baum, J. Rodney ... Baton Rouge, LA
Baum, Jack ... Brooklyn, NY
Baum, Jack L. ... Tarzana, CA
Baum, Jack Louis, A Professional Law Corporation ... Tarzana, CA
Baum, James L. ... Columbus, OH
Baum, James R. ... Providence, RI
Baum, James S. ... Berkeley, CA
Baum, Jay S. ... Staten Island, NY
Baum, Jeanne A. ... Philadelphia, PA
Baum, Jeffrey C. ... El Reno, OK
Oklahoma City, OK
Baum, John B. ... Farmington Hills, MI
Baum, John C. ... San Francisco, CA
Baum, John E. ... Baltimore, MD
Baum, John F. ... San Francisco, CA
Baum, John M., (Inc., P.C.)
Oklahoma City, OK
Baum, John P. ... West Des Moines, IA
Baum, John V. ... Maitland, FL
Baum, John V., P.A. ... Maitland, FL
Orlando, FL
Baum, Jonathan K. ... Chicago, IL
Baum, Jonathan N. ... Greenwich, CT
Baum, Joseph E. ... Columbia, MD
Baum, Joseph H.
Department of Transportation, U. S. Coast Guard, GV
Baum, Joseph T. ... Albany, NY
Baum, Jost J. ... Santa Clara, CA
Baum, Julian M. ... San Anselmo, CA
Baum, Kathleen Strasser ... New York, NY
Baum, Kenneth L. ... Hackensack, NJ
Baum, Kevin J. ... Philadelphia, PA
Baum, Leonard ... Hempstead, NY
Baum, Leonard P. ... Beverly Hills, CA
Baum, Leonard S. ... New York, NY
Baum, Lester V. ... Dallas, TX
Baum, Marc Lewis ... New York, NY
Baum, Mark F. ... Vancouver, WA
Baum, Marsha L. ... Albuquerque, NM
Baum, Martin S. ... Bloomfield Hills, MI
Baum, Marvin R. ... Buffalo, NY
Baum, Marvin R., P.C. ... Buffalo, NY
Baum, Mary Jo ... Chalfont, PA
Baum & McGahren ... Atlanta, GA
Norcross, GA
Baum, Melinda G. ... Orlando, FL
Baum, Michael A. ... Modena, NY
Baum, Michael C. ... Beverly Hills, CA
Baum, Michael E. ... Bloomfield Hills, MI
Baum, Michael L. ... Los Angeles, CA
Baum, Michael Lawrence ... Dallas, TX
Baum, Miles A. ... New York, NY
Baum, Monica S. ... San Francisco, CA
Baum, Morton I. ... Monticello, NY
Baum, Myron C. ... Washington, DC
Baum, Nathan Lee ... Denver, CO
Baum, Norman ... Alexandria, VA
Baum, Norman, Law Firm of
Alexandria, VA
Baum, Peter A. ... Chittenango, NY
Baum, Peter J. ... Farmingdale, NY
Baum, Raymond N. ... Pittsburgh, PA
Baum, Raymond S. ... La Grande, OR
Baum, Redfield T. ... Phoenix, AZ
Baum, Renee ... San Jose, CA
Baum, Richard A. ... Bellingham, WA
Baum, Richard L. ... Portland, OR
Baum, Richard M. ... Cuyahoga Falls, OH
Baum, Richard S. ... Redwood City, CA
Baum, Richard S. ... Monticello, NY
Baum, Richard T. ... Los Angeles, CA
Baum, Richard W. ... Chicago, IL
Baum, Robert B. ... Jericho, NY
Baum, Robert B. ... Houston, TX
Baum, Robert E. ... Williston Park, NY
Baum, Robert H. ... Oak Brook, IL
Baum, Robert L. ... Hackensack, NJ
Baum, Robert M. ... New York, NY
Baum, Robert M. ... Smithtown, NY
Baum, Robin A.
Nuclear Regulatory Commission, Office of the General Counsel, GV
Baum, Ron L. ... Fort Lauderdale, FL
Baum, Ron L., P.A., Law Office of
Fort Lauderdale, FL
Baum, Royce, Jr. ... Beverly Hills, MI
Baum, Ruffolo & Marzal, Ltd. ... Chicago, IL
Baum & Shores, A Professional Association
Oklahoma City, OK
Baum, Sigman, Auerbach, Pierson & Neuman, Ltd. ... Chicago, IL
Baum, Simeon H. ... New York, NY
Baum, Sol ... Kansas City, MO
Baum, Stanley D. ... New York, NY
Baum, Stanley M. ... Atlanta, GA
Baum, Stephen ... New York, NY
Baum, Stephen ... New York, NY
Baum, Steven J. ... Buffalo, NY
Baum, Theodore M. B. ... New York, NY
Rochester, NY
Baum, Victor J. ... Bloomfield Hills, MI
Baum, Victoria Short ... Lake Oswego, OR
Baum, Walter J. ... New York, NY
Baum, Warren Bruce ... North Billerica, MA
Baum, Wendy S. ... Chicago, IL
Baum, William J., Jr. ... Denver, CO
Bauman, Amy E. ... Kansas City, MO
Bauman, Barry H. ... Washington, DC
Bauman & Bauman, P.C. ... Canton, MA
Bauman, Bernadette M. ... Arvada, CO
Bauman, Bert ... New York, NY
Bauman, Brian D. ... New York, NY
Bauman, Bryan W. ... Miami, FL
Bauman, C. Davis ... Duluth, GA
Bauman, C. Davis, P.C. ... Clayton, GA
Duluth, GA
Bauman, Carl J. D. ... Anchorage, AK
Bauman, Christopher P.
Albuquerque, NM
Bauman, David F. ... Florham Park, NJ
Bauman, Del Louis ... Norman, OK
Bauman, Dena R. ... Washington, DC
Bauman, Donald S. ... Bethlehem, PA
Bauman, Douglas W. ... Wausau, WI
Bauman & Dow, P.C. ... Albuquerque, NM
Santa Fe, NM
Bauman, Drew J. ... Maplewood, NJ
Bauman, Elven K. ... Belton, MO
Bauman, Ethan L. ... Baltimore, MD
Bauman, Francis E. ... Louisville, KY
Bauman, Frederick C. ... Phoenix, AZ
Bauman, G. Duncan ... St. Louis, MO
Bauman, Gus ... Washington, DC
Bauman, Harold J. ... Liberty, NY
Bauman, H. C. "Chuck", III ... Tyler, TX
Bauman, Henry J.
United States Postal Service, Postal Inspection Service, GV
Bauman, James E. ... Milwaukee, WI
Bauman, James W. ... Clearwater, FL
Bauman, Janet E. ... Chicago, IL
Bauman, Jay ... New York, NY
Bauman, Jeanine Bennett ... Ukiah, CA
Bauman, Jeffrey ... Wendell, MA
Bauman, Jeffrey D. ... Washington, DC
Bauman, Jerome A. ... Plantation, FL
Bauman, Jerome A., P.A. ... Plantation, FL
Bauman, Joan S. ... Los Angeles, CA
Bauman, Joan S. ... Sherman Oaks, CA
Bauman, John A. ... Pacific Palisades, CA
Bauman, John D. ... Belleville, IL
Bauman, John H. ... New York, NY
Bauman, Jon M. ... Boise, ID
Bauman, Jonathan Hague
Los Angeles, CA
Bauman, Karen Ann ... Bridgewater, NJ
Bauman Katz & Grill LLP
New York, NY
Bauman, Kelly A. ... White Plains, NY
Bauman, Kenneth ... Toledo, OH
Bauman, Kim R. ... High Point, NC
Bauman & Kunkis, P.C. ... New York, NY
Bauman, Larry M. ... Lexington, KY
Bauman Law Offices ... San Diego, CA
Bauman, LeRoy ... Appleton, WI
Bauman, Lori Irish ... Portland, OR
Bauman, Louis W. ... Scarsdale, NY
Bauman, Marion C. ... Norman, OK
Bauman, Mark C. ... Phoenix, AZ
Bauman, Mark D. ... Belleville, IL
Bauman, Mark S. ... New York, NY
Bauman, Martin M., (P.C.) ... St. Joseph, MO
Bauman, Mary P. ... New Brighton, MN
Bauman, Mary V. ... Grand Rapids, MI
Bauman, Maureen G. ... Tinton Falls, NJ
Bauman, Michael A. ... New York, NY
Bauman, Michelle Abend
Universal City, CA
Bauman, Peter B. ... Franklin, MA
Bauman, R. Anthony ... San Diego, CA
Bauman, Randall Allen ... St. Joseph, MO
Bauman, Renata K. ... Denver, CO
Bauman, Richard E. ... New York, NY
Bauman, Richard G. ... Warren, OH
Bauman, Richard K. ... San Francisco, CA
Bauman, Robert A. ... Washington, DC
Bauman, Robert A. ... Tampa, FL
Bauman, Robert D. ... Appleton, WI
Bauman, Robert F. ... Swanton, OH
Bauman, Robert J. ... Milwaukee, WI
Bauman, Robert L. ... Lafayette, IN
Bauman, Ruth M. ... Brookfield, WI
Bauman, Scott H. ... Encino, CA
Bauman, Sharon B. ... Los Angeles, CA
Bauman, Stephen ... New York, NY
Bauman, Stephen A. ... Los Angeles, CA
Bauman, Steve ... Little Rock, AR
Bauman, Steven B., (P.A.)
Fort Walton Beach, FL
Bauman, Steven C. ... Hartford, CT
Bauman, Steven E. ... Canton, MA
Bauman, Sumner ... Canton, MA
Bauman, Susan J. M. ... Madison, WI
Bauman, Tiffany L. ... New York, NY
Bauman, Timothy R. ... Syracuse, NY
Bauman, Todd A. ... Portland, OR
Baumann, Alison G. ... Pittsburgh, PA
Baumann, Catherine Lashar ... Derry, NH
Baumann, Charles E. ... Houston, TX
Baumann, Christopher J. ... Spearfish, SD
Baumann, Craig E. ... Alexandria, VA
Baumann, Craig W. ... Woodbury, MN
Baumann, David N. ... Washington, DC
Baumann, Donald J., (P.C.) ... Scottsdale, AZ
Baumann, Douglas J. ... Staten Island, NY
Baumann, Ellen McPhillips
New York, NY
Baumann, Eugenia Tremaine
Oklahoma City, OK
Baumann, Frederick J. ... Denver, CO
Baumann, Gary F. ... Fort Lauderdale, FL
Baumann, Gary S. ... Roseland, NJ
Baumann, Gwen A. ... Plano, TX
Baumann, Helen B. ... Redwood City, CA
Baumann, Henry L. ... Washington, DC
Baumann, Herbert J., Jr. ... Tampa, FL
Baumann, James E. ... El Paso, TX
Baumann, Jane T. ... Oradell, NJ
Baumann, Jeffrey L. ... Lansing, MI
Baumann, John M. ... Louisville, KY
Baumann, John R. ... Palo Alto, CA
Baumann, John S. ... Woodland Hills, CA
Baumann, Joseph P., Jr. ... Newark, NJ
Baumann, Julian H., Jr. ... Wilmington, DE
Baumann, Kelly, Paytas & Bernstein, P.A.
Phoenix, AZ
Scottsdale, AZ
Baumann, L. Peter ... Englewood, NJ
Baumann, Ladd A. ... Hagåtña, GU
Baumann, Larry R. ... North Platte, NE
Baumann, Lester H. ... Bay Shore, NY
Baumann, Linda A. ... Washington, DC
Baumann, Mark Eric ... Minneapolis, MN
Baumann, Mary A. ... St. Louis, MO
Baumann, Merrill J., Jr. ... Portland, OR
Baumann, Michael C. ... Kingsville, MD
Baumann, Michael E. ... Los Angeles, CA
Baumann, Phillip A. ... Sun City Center, FL
Tampa, FL
Baumann, Richard G. ... Los Angeles, CA
Baumann, Riecke ... Houston, TX
Baumann, Robert E., Jr. ... Hempstead, NY
Baumann, Robert L. ... Phoenix, AZ
Baumann, Roland T., II ... Lansing, MI
Baumann, Thomas C. ... Pittsburgh, PA
Baumann, Thomas R. ... Phoenix, AZ
Baumann, Timothy R. ... Chicago, IL
Baumann, Valerie J. ... Newark, NJ
Baumann & Wrubel ... Oradell, NJ
Baumann-Gonzalez, Brena ... Houston, TX
Baumbach, Charles R. ... Mill Valley, CA
Baumbach, Devon R. ... Madison, WI
Baumbach, James W. ... Philadelphia, PA
Baumbach, Larry L. ... Chico, CA
Baumbaugh, Kimberly Cornell
Santa Rosa, CA
Baumberg, Robert B. ... Wellesley, MA
Baumberger, Charles H. ... Miami, FL
Baumberger, David L. ... Wilmington, DE
Baumberger, Ernest M. ... Sacramento, CA
Baumberger, Michael P. ... Lenoir, NC
Baumberger, Peter S. ... Miami, FL
Baumblatt, Stanley ... New York, NY
Baumbusch, Peter L. ... Washington, DC
Baume, Hal L. ... Princeton, NJ
New York, NY
Baumeister, Anastasia ... Glendale, CA
Baumeister, Arthur G., Jr. ... Buffalo, NY
Baumeister, Bryan H. ... Seal Beach, CA
Baumeister, H. Bruce ... Beverly Hills, CA
Baumeister, Kirk ... King Of Prussia, PA
Baumeister, Michel F. ... Morristown, NJ
New York, NY
Baumeister, Michelle L. ... Lima, OH
Baumeister, Monica B.
Department of Justice, Executive Office for Immigration Review, GV
Baumeister, Richard M. ... Wilmington, DE
Baumeister & Samuels, P.C.
Morristown, NJ
New York, NY
Baumeister, William R. ... North St. Paul, MN
Baumeister, York, Davis & Hunter
Beverly Hills, CA
Baumel, Jeffrey A. ... Newark, NJ
Baumel, Michael J. ... Chicago, IL
Baumel, Susan K. ... Boca Raton, FL
Baumer, Bradford & Walters, Professional Association ... Jacksonville, FL
Baumer, Catherine R. ... Washington, DC
Baumer, Charles B. ... Los Angeles, CA
Baumer, David J. ... Seattle, WA
Baumer, David L. ... Raleigh, NC
Baumer, Edward F. ... Los Angeles, CA
Baumer, Erwin H. ... Atlanta, GA
Baumer, Kristen M. ... Metairie, LA
Baumer, Marguerite Ratelle ... Edina, MN
Baumer & McHaney ... Austin, TX
Baumer, Michael V. ... Austin, TX
Baumer, Robert J. ... San Diego, CA
Baumer, Steven M. ... St. Louis, MO
Baumer, Thomas M. ... Jacksonville, FL
Baumert, Cummings and Hiatt
Ponca City, OK
Baumert, John E. ... Mesa, AZ
Baumert, L. Enloe ... Ponca City, OK
Baumert, William A. ... Hartford, CT
Baumfield, Richard ... New York, NY
Baumgaertner, Martin W. ... Chicago, IL
Baumgaertner, Peter A. ... Jacksonville, FL
Baumgaertner, William G., (A Professional Corporation) ... Santa Monica, CA
Baumgardner, Allen M. ... Waynesboro, PA
Baumgardner, Astrid R. ... New York, NY
Baumgardner, Carolyn T. ... Alexandria, VA
Baumgardner, Douglas K. ... Warrenton, VA
Baumgardner, Douglas K.
Washington, VA
Baumgardner, Fred J. ... Louisville, KY
Baumgardner, Gretchen F. ... Seattle, WA
Baumgardner, John E., Jr. ... New York, NY
Baumgardner, Karl L. ... Amarillo, TX
Dallas, TX
Baumgardner, Kevin C. ... Seattle, WA
Baumgardner, Lorraine R.
Cleveland, OH
Baumgardner, Russell H. ... Las Vegas, NV
Baumgardner, Theodore R. ... Orlando, FL
Baumgardner, Walter L., Jr.
St. Clair Shores, MI
Baumgardner, Woodrow A. ... Alexandria, VA
Baumgarner, Marsha M. ... Washington, DC
Baumgart, Bradley J. ... Kansas City, MO
Baumgart, Deborah ... Los Angeles, CA
Baumgart, Debra Andrea ... Cleveland, OH
Baumgart, Elliot M. ... Montclair, NJ
Baumgart, Fran ... Chicago, IL
Baumgart, Richard A. ... Cleveland, OH
Baumgarten, Allan ... St. Louis Park, MN
Baumgarten, Alyssa M. ... Miami, FL
Baumgarten, Barry S. ... Houston, TX
Baumgarten, Elizabeth M. ... Atlanta, GA
Baumgarten, J. Peter ... Treasury Department, Internal Revenue Service, GV
Baumgarten, Jon A. ... Washington, DC
Baumgarten, Joseph ... New York, NY
Baumgarten, Kenneth R. ... Petersburg, IL
Baumgarten, Lara S. ... Culver City, CA
Baumgarten, Marc T. ... Columbus, OH
Baumgarten, Mark A. ... Roseland, NJ
Baumgarten, Maurice J. ... Miami, FL
Baumgarten, Michael D. ... New York, NY
Baumgarten, Neil S. ... Wayne, NJ
Baumgarten, Paul A. ... New York, NY
Baumgarten, Robert C. ... San Diego, CA
Baumgarten, Ronald N. ... Los Angeles, CA
Baumgarten, Ronald N., A Professional Corporation ... Los Angeles, CA
Baumgarth, John R. ... Duluth, MN
Baumgartner, Adrianne Landry
Covington, LA
Baumgartner & Beitler ... Berne, IN
Baumgartner, Brian M. ... Blaine, MN
Baumgartner, Brigitte ... Bethesda, MD
Baumgartner, Bruce O. ... Cleveland, OH
Baumgartner, Charles E. ... Elyria, OH
Baumgartner & Ciocco ... Oak Harbor, OH
Rocky River, OH
Baumgartner, David N. ... Berne, IN
Baumgartner, David O. ... Phillipsburg, KS
Baumgartner, Edmund T. ... New York, NY
Baumgartner, Elsebeth M. ... Oak Harbor, OH
Rocky River, OH
Baumgartner, Frederick L. ... Indianapolis, IN
Baumgartner, Gregory S. ... Houston, TX
Baumgartner, Harry M. ... Mount Olive, NJ
Baumgartner, Howard E. ... Berne, IN
Baumgartner, James H., Jr., (P.C.)
Dallas, TX
Baumgartner, James M. ... Portland, OR
Baumgartner, James W. ... Garden Grove, CA
Baumgartner, John C. ... Grayslake, IL
Baumgartner, Joseph E., Jr. ... Baltimore, MD
Baumgartner, Kenneth C. ... Rockville, MD
Baumgartner, Kenneth R., S.C.
Kenosha, WI
Baumgartner, Kenneth R., (S.C.)
Kenosha, WI
Baumgartner, Kris R. ... St. Louis, MO
Baumgartner, Lawrence A.
Mount Clemens, MI
Baumgartner, Lawrence A., P.C.
Mount Clemens, MI
Baumgartner, Margaret ... Madison, WI
Baumgartner, Margaret W.
San Francisco, CA
Baumgartner, Michael J. ... Roscommon, MI
Baumgartner, Michele A. ... Richmond, VA
Baumgartner, Morgan ... Reno, NV

Baumgartner, Nelson & Price, P.S. **Vancouver, WA**
Baumgartner & O'Toole ... Amherst, OH
Elyria, OH
Lorain, OH
Baumgartner, Pam M. ... Madison, WI
Baumgartner, Randolph P.
Abita Springs, LA
Baumgartner, Robert B. ... Fairfax, VA
Baumgartner, Robert B., & Associates, P.L.C. ... Fairfax, VA
Baumgartner, Robert P. ... Baton Rouge, LA
Baumgartner, William H., Jr. ... Chicago, IL
Baumgartner, William M., Jr.
Moorestown, NJ
Baumgartner, William V. ... Vancouver, WA
Baumgartner-Novak, Patti ... Findlay, OH
Baumgold, Sharon ... Los Angeles, CA
Baumgras, Erica M. ... Charleston, WV
Baumhart, Julia Turner ... Birmingham, MI
Detroit, MI
Baumhoer, Patrick ... Jefferson City, MO
Baumkel, Mark S. ... Bloomfield Hills, MI
Baumler, Sally A. ... Chicago, IL
Baumoel, James L. ... Dallas, TX
Baumoel, Lynn R. ... Canton, OH
Baumohl, Harry A. ... Towson, MD
Baumohl, Harry A., P.A. ... Towson, MD
Baumohl, Steven L. ... Springfield, MA
Baumol, Robert S. ... Teaneck, NJ
Baumrin, Bernard H. ... New York, NY
Baumstark, Bartholomew J. ... St. Louis, MO
Baumstark, Eric C. ... Grand Ledge, MI
Baumstein, Douglas ... New York, NY
Baumunk, John M. ... Brazil, IN
Baumwald, Sandra M. ... Athens, GA
Baumwell, Howard E. ... Columbus, OH
Baumwohl, David S.
Mammoth Lakes, CA
Baumwohl, David S., A Prof. Corp., Law Offices of ... Mammoth Lakes, CA
Baun, Diane M. ... Roanoke, VA
Baun, Gary W. ... Birmingham, MI
Baun, Mark A. ... Detroit, MI
Grosse Pointe Farms, MI
Harbor Springs, MI
Baunach, Christi G. ... Cincinnati, OH
Baunach, Phyllis Jo ... Department of Justice, Civil Division, GV
Baur, Byron A. ... Erie, PA
Baur, Darin Daniel ... Chicago, IL
Baur, Donald C. ... Washington, DC
Baur, Maureen E. ... Mission Viejo, CA
Baur, Mindy ... Dallas, TX
Baur, Susan Irene ... Kelso, WA
Baur, Susan Renee ... New York, NY
Baur, Thomas ... Miami, FL
Naples, FL
Baur, Woodbridge, Reus & Klein, P.A.
Miami, FL
Naples, FL
Baurecht, Erika S. ... Brookfield, WI
Baurkot, Daniel J ... Basking Ridge, NJ
Baurkot, George M. ... Easton, PA
Baurley, Marion E. ... Washington, DC
Baurnes, Gregory J. ... Munhall, PA
Bauroth, Robert C. ... Fort Lauderdale, FL
Baus, George V. ... Pass Christian, MS
Baus, Hammond & Daly, L.L.P.
New Orleans, LA
Baus, Jeanette ... Cincinnati, OH
Baus, John V. ... New Orleans, LA
Baus, John V., Jr. ... New Orleans, LA
Baus, M. Walker ... New Orleans, LA
Baus, Mark D. ... Mequon, WI
Milwaukee, WI
Racine, WI
Bausano, Melissa Weiss ... New York, NY
Bausano, Vincent ... San Francisco, CA
Bausch, F. Jesse ... Pottsville, PA
Bausch, Jacqueline F ... New York, NY
Bausch, James M. ... Lincoln, NE
Omaha, NE
Bausch, John A. ... Topeka, KS
Bausch, Russell K. ... Titusville, FL
Bausch, Trenten P. ... Omaha, NE
Bauscher, Lonny D. ... Wenatchee, WA
Bauser, Michael A. ... Washington, DC
Bausha, Catherine P. ... Amherst, NH
Bausher, Daniel E. P. ... Reading, PA
Bausher, Richard A. ... Reading, PA
Bauske, Donn C. ... Seaside, OR
Bauske, Eiler and Settles ... Seaside, OR
Bausman, Steven M. ... Fall River, MA
Bausman, William C. ... Baltimore, MD
Bauso, Philip A. ... Cherry Hill, NJ
Baustert, Jeffrey D. ... Dallas, TX
Baustian, Teresa M. ... Des Moines, IA
Bauta, Juan P., II ... Miami, FL
Bautch, Sheryl A. ... Urbana, IL
Baute, Mark D. ... Los Angeles, CA
Bautista, A. Marquez ... Mission Viejo, CA
San Francisco, CA
Bautista, Antonio M. ... San Francisco, CA
Bautista, Antonio M., A Professional Law Corporation ... San Francisco, CA
Bautista, David F. ... Elizabethton, TN
Bautista, Eric J. ... Tustin, CA
Bautista, Henrico T. ... Los Angeles, CA
Bautista, Jennifer L. ... San Jose, CA
Bautista, John V. ... Menlo Park, CA
Bautista, Leo A. ... Los Angeles, CA
Bautista, Leopoldo A. ... Los Angeles, CA
Bautista, Maribeth B. ... San Francisco, CA
Bautista, Marilyn Marcello
San Francisco, CA
Bautista, Rummel Mor ... Los Angeles, CA
Bautz, Michael W. ... New York, NY

Bautz, Peter J. ... Springfield, MA
Bauz, N. Thane ... Menlo Park, CA
Bauzá & Dávila ... San Juan, PR
Bauzá-Figueroa, Arline V. ... San Juan, PR
Bauzá-Higuera, Ramón E. ... San Juan, PR
Bauza-Santos, Antonio ... San Juan, PR
Bava, Gordon M., (P.C.) ... Los Angeles, CA
Bava, Rosa ... Southfield, MI
Bavagnoli, Robert J. ... Totowa, NJ
Bavand, Marisa M. ... Seattle, WA
Bavaro, Hugh Peter ... Fallbrook, CA
Bavaro, Joe Nick ... Glendale, CA
Bavaro, Ralph J. ... Syosset, NY
Bavasi, Robert J. ... Everett, WA
Bavati, Miriam ... Trenton, NJ
Bave, William H., Jr. ... White Plains, NY
Bavely, E. Hanlin ... Cincinnati, OH
Bavender, Ann ... Washington, DC
Arlington, VA
Bave-Planell, Patricia ... White Plains, NY
Baver & Bookwalter, Co., L.P.A.
Miamisburg, OH
Baverman, Alan J. ... Atlanta, GA
Baverman, Alan J., P.C. ... Atlanta, GA
Marietta, GA
Baverman, Elida ... Atlanta, GA
Bavero, Ronald J. ... White Plains, NY
Bavetta, Pellegrino P. ... Larchmont, NY
Bavignoli, Ronald ... Hackensack, NJ
Bavinger, William F., III ... Washington, DC
Bavitz, Christopher T. ... New York, NY
Bavly, Harry D. ... Miami, FL
Bavnick, Stewart ... Los Angeles, CA
Bavol, Bush & Sisco, P.L.L.C. ... Tampa, FL
Bavol, Charles D. ... Tampa, FL
Bavoso, Matthew A. ... Harrison, NY
White Plains, NY
Bavoso & Plotsky ... Port Jervis, NY
Bavoso, William D. ... Port Jervis, NY
Bavouset, James S., IV ... Houston, TX
Bavousett, Steve A. ... Houston, TX
Bavuso Peel, Margaret ... Bedminster, NJ
Bawden, Caroline K. ... Riverdale, IA
Bawden, Daniel D. ... Houston, TX
Bawden, Eric D. ... Salt Lake City, UT
Bawden, Marc R. ... Las Vegas, NV
Bawden, Ralph E. ... Farmersville, IL
Bawden, Ralph E., Ltd. ... Farmersville, IL
Bawden, Richard E. ... Redlands, CA
Bawden, Richard E., A Prof. Law Corp.
Redlands, CA
Baweja, Sandeep ... Seattle, WA
Bawel, Paul F. ... Princeton, NJ
Bawnik, Tammy S. ... Weehawken, NJ
Bawolek, Valerie A. ... Chicago, IL
Bawtinhimer, Stacey B. ... New Bern, NC
Bax, David M. ... Independence, MO
Bax, Douglas W. ... Chicago, IL
Bax, Gary D. ... Erie, PA
Bax, Joe G. ... Houston, TX
Bax, John W. ... Los Angeles, CA
Bax, Richard C. ... Houston, TX
Bax, Timothy G. ... Niagara Falls, NY
Baxa, Diane Wemple ... Beverly Hills, CA
Baxa, Edmund T., Jr. ... Orlando, FL
Baxa, Philip C. ... Richmond, VA
Baxam, Deanna Lynne ... Alexandria, VA
Baxendale, J. Richard ... Seattle, WA
Baxendale, Scott E. ... Chicago, IL
Baxer, Robert A. ... Newark, NJ
Baxley, Andrew P.
Department of Commerce, Patent and Trademark Office, GV
Baxley, Bristol A. ... Friendswood, TX
Baxley, C. William ... Atlanta, GA
Baxley, Charles B. ... Lugoff, SC
Baxley, Charles E. ... New York, NY
Baxley, Dillard, Dauphin & McKnight
Birmingham, AL
Baxley, Douglas W. ... Calabash, NC
Shallotte, NC
Baxley, Harold H., Jr. ... Chattanooga, TN
Baxley, Harold H., Jr. ... Cleveland, TN
Baxley, James F. ... Morristown, NJ
Baxley, Jean Male ... Washington, DC
Baxley, Johnnie W., III ... Charleston, SC
Baxley, Kent, & Associates ... Mobile, AL
Baxley, Matthew W. ... New York, NY
Baxley & Mautino ... San Diego, CA
Baxley, Milton H., II ... Gainesville, FL
Baxley, Nancy L. ... Birmingham, AL
Baxley, Neil H. ... San Diego, CA
Baxley, Philip Gary ... Baltimore, MD
Baxley, Pratt & Wells, P.A. ... Elgin, SC
Lugoff, SC
Ridgeway, SC
Baxley, Robert C. ... San Diego, CA
Baxley, Stephen Andrew ... New York, NY
Baxley, Stephen R. ... Houston, TX
Baxley, Thomas H. ... Blakely, GA
Baxley & Trest ... Calabash, NC
Shallotte, NC
Baxley, Wade H. ... Dothan, AL
Baxley, William J. ... Birmingham, AL
Baxmeier, Cheryl L. ... Monroeville, PA
Baxt, Leonard J. ... Washington, DC
Baxter, Albert J., II ... Houston, TX
Baxter, Allin P. ... Washington, DC
Baxter, Andrew T. ... Syracuse, NY
Baxter, Angela L. ... San Diego, CA
Baxter, Ann E. ... Madison, WI
Baxter, Arthur R., Jr. ... Indianapolis, IN
Baxter, B. Hunt, Jr. ... New Bern, NC
Baxter Baker Sidle & Conn, P.A.
Baltimore, MD
Baxter, Barbara S. ... Huntingdon, PA
Baxter, Barnee C. ... Augusta, GA

Baxter Bruce Brand & Douglas, P.C.
Juneau, AK
Baxter, Catherine A. ... Pittsburgh, PA
Baxter, Charles L. ... Oklahoma City, OK
Baxter, Charles T. ... Louisville, KY
Baxter, Christopher L. ... Moorestown, NJ
Baxter, Christopher L., A Professional Corporation ... Moorestown, NJ
Baxter, Colleen Rae ... Anchorage, AK
Baxter, D. Berry ... La Grange, KY
Baxter, D. Mark ... Macon, GA
Baxter, Daniel L. ... Sacramento, CA
Baxter, David B. ... Dallas, TX
Baxter, David B., P.C. ... Dallas, TX
Baxter, David K. ... Cross Lanes, WV
Baxter, David R. ... Detroit, MI
Baxter, Douglas A. ... Provo, UT
Baxter, Douglas C. ... Columbia, SC
Myrtle Beach, SC
Baxter, Edward H. ... Washington, DC
Baxter, Edward L. ... Philadelphia, PA
Baxter, Elinor E. ... Sarasota, FL
Baxter, Felix von ...
Department of Justice, GV
Baxter, Floyd V. ... Valencia, CA
Baxter, Fred E., Jr. ... Pittsburgh, PA
Baxter, Fred J. ... Juneau, AK
Baxter, Gary D. ... Department of Defense, Defense Legal Services Agency, GV
Baxter, Gary M. ... Glenview, IL
Baxter, George G., III ... New York, NY
Baxter, George T. ... Ridgewood, NJ
Baxter, Gerald L. ... Columbus, GA
Baxter, Glenn N., LLC ... Tuscaloosa, AL
Baxter, Graeme ... Washington, DC
Baxter, Gregory L. ... Baker City, OR
Baxter, Gregory S. ... Shrewsbury, NJ
Baxter, Harvey ... Miami, FL
Baxter, Harvey E. ... Gainesville, FL
Baxter, Howard H. ... Cleveland, OH
Baxter, J. Lamont ... Oklahoma City, OK
Baxter, J. Shelton ... Greenbrae, CA
Baxter, Jack A., Jr. ... Fort Lauderdale, FL
Baxter, Jack A., Sr. ... Fort Lauderdale, FL
Baxter, James A. ... Clearwater, FL
Baxter, James A. ... Milwaukee, WI
Baxter, James C. ... San Antonio, TX
Baxter, James H., III ... Milwaukee, WI
Baxter, James R. ... Victorville, CA
Baxter, James T., III ... Huntsville, AL
Baxter, James W. ... Memphis, TN
Baxter, Janet C. ... Grand Rapids, MI
Baxter, Jean L. ... Glendale, AZ
Baxter, Jeffery D. ... Dallas, TX
Baxter, Jeffrey C. ... Atlanta, GA
Baxter, Jeffrey L. ... Miami, FL
Baxter, Jensen, Payne, Young & Smith
Benton, AR
Hot Springs National Park, AR
Little Rock, AR
Malvern, AR
Sheridan, AR
Baxter, Jerry W. ... Atlanta, GA
Baxter, John A. ... Platteville, WI
Baxter, John B. ... Indianapolis, IN
Baxter, Joseph G. ... Santa Rosa, CA
Baxter, K. Ellen ... Hailey, ID
Baxter, Katc D. ... Point Reyes Station, CA
Baxter, Kathleen R. Mulligan ... Albany, NY
Baxter, Kay Barnes ... New Orleans, LA
Baxter, Keith M. ... Milwaukee, WI
Baxter, Kelley M. ... Frisco, TX
Baxter, Kenneth D. ... Miami, FL
Baxter, Keven F. ... Irvine, CA
San Francisco, CA
Baxter, Kevin J. ... Sandusky, OH
Baxter, Kimberley S. ... Washington, DC
Baxter, Kimberly K. ... Minneapolis, MN
Baxter and Kipphan ... Huntingdon, PA
Baxter, Lance S. ... Plano, TX
Baxter, Laura A. ... House of Representatives, Committee Legal Personnel, GV
Baxter, Lawrence G. ... Winston-Salem, NC
Baxter, Lawrence W. ... Ottawa, IL
Baxter, Leslie A. ... Pleasanton, CA
Baxter, Linda K. ... St. Louis, MO
Baxter, Linda M.
Christiansted, St. Croix, VI
Baxter, Loran F. ... Sierra Vista, AZ
Baxter, M. Michael ... Minneapolis, MN
Baxter, Maithri C. ... Kearney, NE
Baxter, Margaret C. ... Des Plaines, IL
Baxter, Marjorie ... Simi Valley, CA
Baxter, Mark D. ... Fort Lauderdale, FL
Baxter, Martha Post ... Columbus, OH
Baxter, Marvin R. ... Sacramento, CA
Baxter, Mary Patricia Dunkin ... Towson, MD
Baxter, Mary Ruth M. ... Conway, SC
Baxter, Matthew D. ... Philadelphia, PA
Baxter, Melba S. ... Longview, TX
Baxter, Michael J. ... Baltimore, MD
Baxter, Michael St. Patrick
Washington, DC
Baxter, Michael W. ... Jackson, MS
Baxter, Milton D. ... Warwick, RI
Baxter, Murray B. ... Aiken, SC
Baxter, Nancy S. ... Tarzana, CA
Baxter, Norman T., Jr. ... Oberlin, OH
Baxter, O'Meara & Samuelsen, S.C.
Milwaukee, WI
Baxter, Rachel Grossman ... Detroit, MI
Baxter, Ralph H., Jr. ... San Francisco, CA
Baxter, Randolph ... Cleveland, OH
Baxter, Raoul J. ... Cincinnati, OH
Baxter, Ray, (P.A.) ... Benton, AR
Baxter, Raymond E. ... Boston, MA
Baxter, Richard D. ... Winter Park, FL
Baxter, Richard J. ... Hartford, CT

Baxter, Richard S. ... Southampton, NY
Baxter, Robert A. ... Mount Laurel, NJ
Baxter, Robert C. ... New York, NY
Baxter, Robert C., Jr. ... Elon College, NC
Baxter, Robert H. ... Nashville, TN
Baxter, Robert J., Jr. ... Chalmette, LA
Baxter, Robert P., Jr. ... Dallas, TX
Baxter, Robert P., Jr., Law Offices of P.C.
Dallas, TX
Baxter, Robert T. ... Thompson Falls, MT
Baxter, Rodd M. ... New York, NY
Baxter, Rodney W. ... El Paso, TX
Baxter, Ronald H. ... Topeka, KS
Baxter, Rosanne C. ... Armonk, NY
Baxter, Ruth H. ... Carrollton, KY
Baxter, Sam F. ... Dallas, TX
Marshall, TX
Baxter, Samuel R. ... Little Rock, AR
Baxter, Shannon C. ... Atlanta, GA
Baxter & Smith, P.C. ... New York, NY
Baxter, Stephen G. ... Arlington, VA
Baxter, Strohauer & Mannion, P.A.
Clearwater, FL
Baxter, Terrence J. ... Coshocton, OH
Baxter, Thomas ... Chatom, AL
Baxter, Thomas A., (P.C.)
Washington, DC
Baxter, Thomas C. ... St. Paul, MN
Baxter, Thomas C., Jr. ... New York, NY
Baxter, Thomas E. ... Columbus, OH
Baxter, Thomas K. ... Baltimore, MD
Baxter, Thomas W. ... Los Angeles, CA
Baxter, Timothy A. ... Atlanta, GA
Baxter, Timothy C. ... Prairie du Chien, WI
Baxter, Timothy E. ... Bloomfield Hills, MI
Baxter, Timothy E., & Associates, P.C., Law Offices of ... Bloomfield Hills, MI
Grand Rapids, MI
Baxter, Todd W. ... Fresno, CA
Baxter, Victoria G. ... Rowlett, TX
Baxter, Vincent N. ... San Jose, CA
Baxter, W. Thomas, (P.A.)
Little Rock, AR
Baxter, William A. ... Jacksonville, FL
Baxter, William H., II ... Richmond, VA
Baxter, William K. ... Milwaukee, WI
Baxter-Jones, Melinda ... Newport, OR
Bay Area Traffic Defender ... San Jose, CA
Bay, Christine A. ... Chicago, IL
Bay, Don R. ... Pacific Palisades, CA
Bay & Falcinelli ... Rockville, MD
Bay, Franklin R. ... Houston, TX
Bay, James S. ... Los Angeles, CA
Bay, Jeffrey S. ... Kansas City, MO
Bay, John A. ... Columbus, OH
Bay, Jonathan A. ... Springfield, MO
Bay Justice Associates, P.C. ... Bay City, MI
Bay, Kathleen A. ... Rockville, MD
Bay, Kathleen Ford ... Austin, TX
Bay, Kevin A. ... Seattle, WA
Bay, Laurie C. ... Kensington, MD
Bay, Mark W. ... Minneapolis, MN
Bay, Monica M. ... New York, NY
Bay, R. Dale ... Nashville, TN
Bay, Robert H. ... Portland, OR
Bay, Susan M. ... Brookfield, WI
Bay Venture Counsel, LLP ... Oakland, CA
Palo Alto, CA
Bay, Walter D. ... Rochester, NY
Bay, William R. ... St. Louis, MO
Bayar, Charles H. ... New York, NY
Bayard, Alton E., III ... Baton Rouge, LA
Bayard, Anna C. ... Brooklyn, NY
Bayard, Eugene H. ... Georgetown, DE
Bayard Firm, The ... Dover, DE
Newark, DE
Wilmington, DE
Bayard, Forrest S. ... Chicago, IL
Bayard, James A., Jr. ... Wilmington, DE
Bayard, Judith L. ... San Diego, CA
Bayard, Lynn B. ... New York, NY
Bayard, Michael J. ... Los Angeles, CA
Bayard, Richard H. ... Wilmington, DE
Bayard De Volo, Tony ... Chicago, IL
Bayaz, Marcie K. ... Denver, CO
Bayazitoglu, Ozgur K. ... Houston, TX
Baybayan, Ronald A. ... Des Moines, IA
Baybick, Alan B. ... Cinnaminson, NJ
Bayda, I. Michael ... New York, NY
Baydaline, Rod A. ... Sacramento, CA
Baydar, James B. ... Great Neck, NY
Baydin, Lynda Diane ... Morristown, NJ
Baydo, Richard A. ... Tacoma, WA
Baydoun, Nader ... Nashville, TN
Baydoun & Reese, P.A. ... Nashville, TN
Baye, Kenneth E. ... Atlanta, GA
Baye, Sheila Shuster ... Alpharetta, GA
Bayer, Aaron Seth ... Hartford, CT
Bayer, Andrea ... Burlington, VT
Bayer, Andrew ... Teaneck, NJ
Bayer, Arthur J., Jr. ... Carson City, NV
Bayer & August, LLP ... San Francisco, CA
Bayer, Barry D. ... Homewood, IL
Bayer, Bennett E. ... Lexington, KY
Bayer, Brandy A. ... Atlanta, GA
Bayer, Carey & McGee, A Professional Corporation ... Denver, CO
Bayer, Charles M. ... Detroit, MI
Bayer, Cyril D. ... Coon Rapids, MN
Bayer, Dennis K. ... Daytona Beach, FL
Flagler Beach, FL
Maitland, FL
Bayer, Donald F. ... Kansas City, MO
Bayer, Douglas I. ... Wilton, CT
Bayer, Duane K. ... Tampa, FL
Bayer, Edward A. ... Akron, OH
Bayer, Elmer V. A. ... St. Louis, MO
Bayer, Frank J. ... Hudson, OH

Bayer, Gary G. ... Menlo Park, CA
Bayer, Harold C. ... Livonia, NY
Bayer, Harvey ... Mount Vernon, NY
Bayer, Jacob W., Jr. ... Kansas City, MO
Bayer, James T. ... Denver, CO
Bayer, Janet C. ... Frederick, MD
Bayer, Janet S. ... Livingston, NJ
Bayer, Jas. W. ... Chicago, IL
Bayer, Jerger and Ardis, Co., L.P.A.
Mansfield, OH
Bayer, Judith H. ... Monterey Park, CA
Bayer, Karl ... Austin, TX
Bayer, Karl ... Austin, TX
Bayer, Kenneth H. ... Westlake Village, CA
Bayer, Kenneth S. ... Fresno, CA
San Jose, CA
Bayer & LaDue ... Coon Rapids, MN
Bayer, Leon D. ... Long Beach, CA
Los Angeles, CA
Woodland Hills, CA
Bayer, Louis H. ... Birmingham, AL
Bayer, Mark A. ... Washington, DC
Bayer, Mark W. ... Dallas, TX
Bayer, Michael B. ... La Jolla, CA
Bayer, Michelle D. ... Bloomfield Hills, MI
Bayer, Nathan J. ... Washington, DC
Bayer & Neal, PLLC ... Flagler Beach, FL
Bayer, Neil ... Miami, FL
Bayer, Nicole ... Chicago, IL
Bayer, Pamela J. ... Holcomb, NY
Bayer, Peter Brandon ... Miami, FL
Bayer, Richard A. ... Santa Monica, CA
Bayer, Richard S. ... San Diego, CA
Bayer, Richard T. ... Roseland, NJ
Bayer, Richard W. ... Toledo, OH
Bayer, Robert J. ... Ventura, CA
Bayer, Ronald J. ... Philadelphia, PA
Bayer, Ronald M. ... New York, NY
Bayer, Ronda P. ... Minneapolis, MN
Bayer, Shelley A. ... Agoura Hills, CA
Bayer, Stephen Davison ... Philadelphia, PA
Bayer, Theodore F. ... San Francisco, CA
Bayer, Theodore R. ... Miami, FL
Bayer, Thomas P. ... Chicago, IL
Bayer, Walter J., II ... Princeton, NJ
Bayer, William H. ... Lehighton, PA
Bayerd, Susan J. ... San Jose, CA
Bayern, Arthur H. ... San Antonio, TX
Bayern & Aycock ... San Antonio, TX
Bayern, Douglas C. ... Portland, OR
Bayers, William F. ... Chestnut Hill, MA
Bayert, Nicole D. ... Department of Defense, Office of the General Counsel, GV
Bayert, William K. ... Department of the Army, Office, Chief of Engineers/Headquarters, U.S. Army Corps of Engineers, GV
Bayes, James R. W. ... Washington, DC
Bayes, Robert E. ... Katy, TX
Bayford, Anthony ... Toledo, OH
Bayger, Frank R. ... Buffalo, NY
Bayh, Birch ... Washington, DC
Bayh, Evan ... Indianapolis, IN
Bayha, Betsy E. ... Mountain View, CA
Bayham, Alan P., Jr. ... Phoenix, AZ
Bayham, Alan P., Jr., P.C. ... Phoenix, AZ
Bayham, Thomas M. ... Tucson, AZ
Bayham-Lesselyong, Jane ... Phoenix, AZ
Bayhan, Holly S. ... Wheeling, WV
Bayhe, W. George ... Baton Rouge, LA
Bayko Gibson Carnegie Hagan Schoonmaker & Meyer LLP ... Chicago, IL
Houston, TX
Bayko, Tom ... Chicago, IL
Houston, TX
Baylaender, Richard F. ... Chicago, IL
Baylard, David L. ... Union, MO
Bayle, Shirley D. ... Boston, MA
Bayle, Suzanne Ecuyer ... New Orleans, LA
Baylen, Kenneth B. ... Covington, KY
Bayler, H. Carroll ... Louisville, IL
Bayler, R. Mason, Jr. ... Richmond, VA
Bayles, Alan P. ... Washington, DC
Bayles, Calvin D. ... La Crescenta, CA
Bayles, David A. ... Wichita, KS
Bayles, Deborah L. ... Denver, CO
Bayles, Donald H., Jr. ... Flagstaff, AZ
Bayles, J. Wendell ... Topeka, KS
Bayles, James E., Jr. ... Chicago, IL
Bayles, James M. ... Stuart, FL
Bayles, Mark A. ... St. Louis, MO
Bayles, Norman E. ... Washington, DC
Bayles, Thomas James ... St. George, UT
Bayles, W. Mark ... Toms River, NJ
Bayles-Fightmaster, Louise ... Windsor, CA
Bayless, Bobbie G. ... Houston, TX
Bayless, David B. ... San Francisco, CA
Bayless, Franklin D. ... Cheyenne, WY
Bayless, Gregory W. ... Gold River, CA
Bayless, H. Jeffrey ... Denver, CO
Bayless, James L., Jr. ... McLean, VA
Bayless, John D. ... Oregon City, OR
Bayless, Kathryn Reed ... Princeton, WV
Bayless, Kim L. ... Rocky Mount, NC
Bayless, Mark A. ... Valrico, FL
Bayless, Mark E. ... Laguna Beach, CA
Bayless, Mark E., Inc. ... Laguna Beach, CA
Bayless & McFadden L.L.P.
Pineville, WV
Princeton, WV
Welch, WV
Bayless & Murphy ... Portland, OR
Bayless, Philip D. ... Woodland Hills, CA
Bayless, Regan L. ... San Francisco, CA
Bayless, Richard James ... San Diego, CA
Bayless, Richard V. ... Portland, OR
Bayless, Rodney H. ... Merrillville, IN
Bayless, Samuel H. ... San Antonio, TX
Bayless & Slater Law Firm, P.C.
Cheyenne, WY
Bayless & Stokes ... Houston, TX
Bayless, Thomas A. ... Riverside, CA
Bayless, Thomas R. ... Lakeland, FL
Bayless, Vicki G. ... Portland, OR
Bayley, Christopher H. ... Phoenix, AZ
Bayley, Christopher T., (P.S.) ... Seattle, WA
Bayley, Edgar B. ... Carlisle, PA
Bayley, Francis ... Panama City, FL
Bayley, Frank S. ... San Francisco, CA
Bayley, Guy R. ... Los Angeles, CA
Bayliff, Bradford W. ... Austin, TX
Bayliff, Claudia J. ... Longmont, CO
Bayliff, Edgar W. ... Kokomo, IN
Bayliff, Harrigan, Cord & Maugans, P.C.
Kokomo, IN
Baylin, Lee ... Baltimore, MD
Baylin, Victoria A. ... Washington, DC
Baylinson, Christopher M.
Atlantic City, NJ
Baylinson, Judith E. ... Carmel, IN
Baylinson, Kudysh & Greenberg
Washington, DC
Baltimore, MD
Burtonsville, MD
Baylinson, Richd. N. ... Baltimore, MD
Baylinson, Roy ... Northfield, NJ
Baylis, Carl Emmett ... Worcester, MA
Baylis, Owen E. ... Saratoga, CA
Baylis, Thomas S. ... Garden City, NY
Bayliss, Anthony Shawn D. ... Nitro, WV
Bayliss, Delmara Faye ... Leesburg, VA
Bayliss, Hudson & Merritt
Chapel Hill, NC
Bayliss, J. Fred ... College Station, TX
Bayliss, Jack B., Jr. ... Greensboro, NC
Bayliss, Joseph August ... St. Petersburg, FL
Bayliss, Kenneth H. ... St. Cloud, MN
Bayliss, William D. ... Richmond, VA
Bayliss, William H. ... Chapel Hill, NC
Bayliss, W. M. F. ... Goochland, VA
Baylog, Richard L. ... Miami, FL
Baylor, David A. ... San Francisco, CA
Baylor, Diane E. ... San Jose, CA
Baylor, Evnen, Curtiss, Grimit & Witt
Lincoln, NE
Baylor, Gail S., P.C. ... Decatur, GA
Baylor, Gail Scotton ... Decatur, GA
Baylor, Gregory S. ... Washington, DC
Baylor, John R. ... Lincoln, NE
Baylor, Lewis M. ... Department of Justice, Environment and Natural Resources Division, GV
Baylor, Peter Nils ... Boston, MA
Baylor, Robert Edward ... Boston, MA
Baylor, Ronald E. ... Kalamazoo, MI
Baylor, Ross G. ... West Palm Beach, FL
Baylor, Walter R. ... Arlington, VA
Baylson, Michael M. ... Philadelphia, PA
Bayly, Brenda A. ... Fort Myers, FL
Bayly, Brenda A., & Associates, P.A.
Fort Myers, FL
Bayly, Chas. B., Jr. ... New York, NY
Bayly, John H., Jr. ... Washington, DC
Bayly, M. Douglas ... Kaysville, UT
Bayly, Susan L. ... College Park, MD
Bayly, W. Brian ... Department of Justice, Drug Enforcement Administration, GV
Bayman, Andrew T. ... Atlanta, GA
Bayman, William M. ... Dallas, TX
Bayme, Helene Asher ... Brooklyn, NY
Baymiller, Carroll ... Peoria, IL
Baymiller, Douglas A. ... Huntsville, AL
Baymiller, Roger B. ... Los Angeles, CA
Baynard, Brian C. ... Raleigh, NC
Baynard, Ernest C., III ... Washington, DC
Baynard, Mary Kay ... Charlotte, NC
Baynard, McLeod and Lang, P.A.
St. Petersburg, FL
Baynard, Paul R. ... Charlotte, NC
Baynard, Robert E. ... Albany, GA
Baynard, Stephen C. ... Wilmington, NC
Baynard, Walter L. ... St. Petersburg, FL
Bayne, Andrew J. ... Edison, NJ
Bayne, Bernadette F. ... Brooklyn, NY
Bayne, Carroll S., Jr. ... New York, NY
Bayne, David F. ... New York, NY
Bayne, Donald S. ... San Antonio, TX
Bayne, Duncan A. ... Seattle, WA
Bayne, Harry G. ... Dallas, TX
Bayne, Holly M. ... Washington, DC
Bayne, James J. ... Del Rio, TX
Bayne, John M., Jr. ... El Segundo, CA
Bayne, Karin A. ... Fort Lauderdale, FL
Bayne, Michael C. ... Fort Lauderdale, FL
Bayne, Shawn M. ... Fort Lauderdale, FL
Bayne, Sheila ... Los Angeles, CA
Bayne, Snell & Krause ... San Antonio, TX
Bayne, Thomas Maitlen ... Spokane, WA
Bayne, William E. ... Pomona, KS
Baynes, Brendan F. ... Albany, NY
Baynes, Bridget ... Santa Ana Heights, CA
Baynes, Gerald T. ... Mt. Sterling, OH
Baynes, James M. ... Los Angeles, CA
Baynes, Kathleen McCaffrey ... Albany, NY
Baynes, Keith A. ... Elkton, MD
Baynes, Leonard M.
Federal Communications Commission, Office of the General Counsel, GV
Baynes, Robert G. ... Greensboro, NC
Baynes, Thomas E., Jr. ... Tampa, FL
Bayneum, JoAnn ... Atlanta, GA
Baynham, Best & Reginelli, L.L.C.
Metairie, LA
New Orleans, LA
Baynham, Robert J. ... Seattle, WA
Baynham, T. Patrick ... Metairie, LA
Baynham, Thomas E., III ... Griffin, GA
Baynham, Thomas J., Jr. ... Tyler, TX
Baynham, Timothy P. ... Winston-Salem, NC
Baynton, Thomas B. ... Grand Rapids, MI
Bayo, Edwin A. ... Tallahassee, FL
Bayoneto, M. Victoria ... New York, NY
Bayonet-Tartak, Vanessa ... San Juan, PR
Bayorgeon, James T. ... Appleton, WI
Bayó-Santiago, Arline L. ... Rochester, NY
Bayot, Ronald G. ... Center Line, MI
Bayouth, Frank E. ... Houston, TX
Bayr, Frank A. ... Newport Beach, CA
Bayrd, Jodi Lynne ... New York, NY
Bayrock, David ... New York, NY
Bayroff, Adam B. ... New York, NY
Bayrón, Carlos E. ... Mayaguez, PR
Bays, A. Bernard, (A Law Corporation)
Honolulu, HI
Bays, David D. ... San Jose, CA
Bays, David M. ... Houston, TX
Bays, Deaver, Hiatt, Lung & Rose
Honolulu, HI
Kamuela, HI
Bays, Donald W. ... Marquette, MI
Bays, Donna J. ... Indianapolis, IN
Bays and Gerhardt, P.C. ... Sierra Vista, AZ
Bays, Gregory C. ... Chicago, IL
Bays, James C. ... Fairlawn, OH
Bays, Kirsten Crouse ... Charleston, IL
Bays, Larry L. ... Alva, OK
Bays, Michael S. ... Los Gatos, CA
Bays, P. Randall ... Sierra Vista, AZ
Bays, Ray, & Associates
Oklahoma City, OK
Bays, Rebecca A. ... Atlanta, GA
Bays, Richard V. ... Houston, TX
Bays, Robert L. ... Parkersburg, WV
Bays, Stephen D. ... San Jose, CA
Bayse, James H. ... Sacramento, CA
Baysinger, Brian R.
Securities and Exchange Commission, Division of Market Regulation, GV
Baysinger, Eric J. ... Palo Alto, CA
Baysinger, Hugh A. ... Oklahoma City, OK
Baysinger, Julia B. ... Locust Grove, VA
Baysinger, Marcy Gentry
Albuquerque, NM
Baysinger, Robert I. ... Stockton, CA
Baysinger-Cordes, Christina Marie
Huntington, WV
Bayster, Raymond J. ... Chicago, IL
Bayt, Phillip Everett ... Mulberry, FL
Bayt, Phillip L. ... Indianapolis, IN
Bayt, Robert L. ... Indianapolis, IN
Baytosh, Michael J. ... Sacramento, CA
Bayuk & Associates ... San Diego, CA
Bayuk, Christopher W. ... San Diego, CA
Bayuk, Michael J. ... Anchorage, AK
Bayus, Brian E. ... Reston, VA
Bayus, Deborah Fiumera ... Carlsbad, CA
Bayus, Elaine R. ... San Francisco, CA
Bayus, Richard M., II ... Atlanta, GA
Bayz, Panagiotis C. ... Washington, DC
Bazac-Baker, Susan S. ... Beverly Hills, CA
Bazak, Henry V. ... Arlington, VA
Bazaman, Harvey ... Galveston, TX
Bazan, Elizabeth B. ... Library of Congress, Congressional Research Service, GV
Bazan, John F. ... Irvine, CA
Bazan, Joseph R. ... Buffalo, MN
Bazan, Nicolas M. ... Houston, TX
Bazan, Nicolas M., P.C. ... Houston, TX
Bazan, Priscilla ... San Diego, CA
Bazany, Michael Andrew, Jr.
Philadelphia, PA
Bazar, David N. ... Providence, RI
Bazar, Gerald M. ... Los Angeles, CA
Bazar, Jason S. ... Atlanta, GA
Bazar, Peter ... East Greenwich, RI
Bazarian, Charlene S. ... Reading, MA
Bazarian, Edward J. ... Flushing, NY
Bazarian, Laurie Golding ... Stoneham, MA
Bazarian, Stephen C. ... Newton, MA
Bazarko, Volodymyr O. ... Parma, OH
Bazarsky, Barrie E. ... Melville, NY
Bazarsky, David G. ... Portsmouth, RI
Bazata, Christine Marie ... New Haven, CT
Baze, Lineas Lewis ... Jackson, MI
Baze, Mark Edward ... Oakland, CA
Bazel, Barry K. ... Corpus Christi, TX
Bazel, Lawrence S. ... San Francisco, CA
Bazeley, Alison Faye ... Cincinnati, OH
Bazeley, Judith J. ... San Diego, CA
Bazelides, Paul P. ... Houston, TX
Bazell, Haskell ... Cincinnati, OH
Bazell, Michael P. ... San Francisco, CA
Bazelon, Edward G. ... Chicago, IL
Bazelon Less & Feldman, P.C.
Marlton, NJ
Philadelphia, PA
Bazelon, Richard L. ... Philadelphia, PA
Bazemore, Jarrod B. ... Gadsden, AL
Bazemore, Lisa ... Philadelphia, PA
Bazemore, Thomas E., III
Birmingham, AL
Bazerman & Drangel, P.C. ... New York, NY
Bazerman, Steven H. ... New York, NY
Bazes, Elena Biegel ... Los Angeles, CA
Bazhdari, Mergim ... Lake Success, NY
Baziak, David J. ... Santa Ana, CA
Baziak, Lisa L. ... Santa Ana, CA
Baziak & Martin ... Santa Ana, CA
Bazianos, Konstandenos S. ... Lombard, IL
Bazianos, William S. ... Chicago, IL
Bazil, Paul J. ... Washington, DC
Bazil, Rhonda J. ... Aspen, CO
Bazil, Steven J. ... West Chester, PA
Bazil, Wendy Nevett
General Services Administration, Office of the General Counsel, GV
Bazile, Harvey J. ... Somerville, MA
Bazile, Leo ... Oakland, CA
Bazinsky, Stephen W.
Fort Lauderdale, FL
Naples, FL
Bazis, Jeanette M. ... Minneapolis, MN
Bazler, Frank E. ... Troy, OH
Bazley, Frederick A. ... Indianapolis, IN
Bazluke, Francine T. ... Burlington, VT
Bazoukas, Nicholas C. ... Worcester, MA
Bazrod, Lawrence N. ... Wayne, PA
Bazrod, Mark S. ... Wayne, PA
Bazydlo, Charles T. ... Newburgh, NY
Bazydlo, Gary J. ... Bloomfield Hills, MI
Bazyler, Michael J. ... Costa Mesa, CA
Bazyluk, Taras A. ...
Department of State, GV
Bazzana, Ernest R. ... Detroit, MI
Bazzani, Robert W. ... Union City, NJ
Bazzani, Scott W. ... Union City, NJ
Bazzano, Mary Ann P.
Kennett Square, PA
Bazzel, Frank B. ... Atlanta, GA
Bazzell, Erica Loren ... Ardmore, PA
Bazzell, Gregory K. ... Murray, KY
Bazzelle, Suchada Phillips
Salt Lake City, UT
Bazzi, Kari L. ... Anchorage, AK
Bazzle, Carr & Gasperson, P.A.
Hendersonville, NC
Bazzle, Ervin W. ... Hendersonville, NC
Bazzle, J. Parker ... Charleston, WV
Bazzo, Michael L. ... Riverside, CA
Bazzoli, Aaron J. ... Weiser, ID
Bazzone, Tara E. ... Memphis, TN
Bazzurro, John T. ... Red Bank, NJ
BBLP Beiten Burkhardt Mittl & Wegener
New York, NY
New York, NY
BDL MacLean PLLC ... Seattle, WA
Bea, Carlos ... San Francisco, CA
Bea, David ... Chicago, IL
Beaber, Rex J. ... Los Angeles, CA
Beabout, J. Steven ... Atlanta, GA
Beach & Ager ... Southfield, MI
El Paso, TX
Beach, Alexsis C. ... San Francisco, CA
Beach, Ann V. ... Sharon, MA
Beach, Arthur O. ... Albuquerque, NM
Beach, Audrey King ... Allentown, PA
Beach, Barbara P. ... Alexandria, VA
Beach, Benjamin ... Lenoir, NC
Beach, Bruce W. ... San Diego, CA
Beach, Burcke, Helfers, Mittleman and Stewart, L.L.C. ... St. Louis, MO
Beach, C. G. ... Westfield Center, OH
Beach, Charles A. ... Irving, TX
Beach, Charles R. ... Denver, CO
Beach, Chester Paul, Jr. ... East Hartford, CT
Beach, Clifford L., Jr. ... Knoxville, TN
Beach, Clifford R., Jr. ... Glens Falls, NY
Beach, Danielle L. C. ... Washington, DC
Beach, David B. ... Richmond, VA
Beach, David F. ... San Francisco, CA
Beach, David F. ... Santa Rosa, CA
Beach, David F., A Prof. Corp., Law Offices of ... Santa Rosa, CA
Beach, David J. ... Hammond, IN
Beach, David Kenneth ... Tampa, FL
Beach, David R. ... Junction City, OR
Beach, Donald F. ... Falls Church, VA
Beach, Douglas C.
Charlotte Amalie, St. Thomas, VI
Beach, Douglas R. ... St. Louis, MO
Beach, Duane J. ... Greenville, MI
Beach, Edwin F. ... Ventura, CA
Beach, Eugene H., Jr. ... Southfield, MI
El Paso, TX
Beach, Gene L. ... Marshalltown, IA
Beach, Geoffrey K. ... Washington, DC
Beach, George R. ... San Mateo, CA
Beach, Harris L., Jr. ... Walterboro, SC
Beach, Harry A. ... Allegan, MI
Beach, Harry C. ... Wellesley, MA
Beach, James D. ... St. Petersburg, FL
Beach, James D., P.A. ... St. Petersburg, FL
Beach, James G., III ... Venice, FL
Beach, James G., Jr. ... Venice, FL
Beach, James M. ... New York, NY
Beach, James R., Jr. ... Roswell, GA
Beach, Jennifer L. ... Baltimore, MD
Beach, Joel D. ... Philadelphia, PA
Beach, John A. ... Bonita Springs, FL
Albany, NY
Beach, John F. ... Columbia, SC
Beach, Joseph Francis ... Baltimore, MD
Beach, Joseph K. ... Tuscaloosa, AL
Beach, Julie A. ... Crawfordsville, IN
Beach, Karen F. ... Rockville, MD
Beach, Kimberly Galvin ... Albany, NY
Beach, Ladson H., Jr. ... Orangeburg, SC
Beach Law Firm, P.A. ... Columbia, SC
Beach Law Offices ... Lenoir, NC
Beach, Linda M. ... Palo Alto, CA
Beach, Luckett & Ross ... Jackson, MS
Beach, Marshall ... Palm Desert, CA
Beach, Mary Catherine ... Grand Rapids, MI
Beach, Michael D. ... Minneapolis, MN
Beach, Morrison H. ... Hartford, CT
Beach, N. Douglas, Jr. ... Lenoir, NC
Beach, Neil D. ... Lenoir, NC
Beach, Otis W. ... Fort Collins, CO
Beach, Paige K. ... Houston, TX
Beach, Paul B. ... Los Angeles, CA
Beach, Paul L. ... Kennebunk, ME

Beach, Peter T. ... **Concord, NH**
Manchester, NH
Beach, Procter, McCarthy & Slaughter, LLP
Santa Barbara, CA
Ventura, CA
Beach, R. Scott ... **Stamford, CT**
Beach, Robert B., Jr. (P.A.)
Little Rock, AR
Beach, Robert E. ... St. Petersburg, FL
Beach, Robert E., III ... Spokane, WA
Beach, Robert E., Jr. ... Hartford, CT
Beach, Robert S. ... San Francisco, CA
Beach, Robert W. ... Seattle, WA
Beach, Shanda K. ... **Irvine, CA**
Beach, Stephen C. ... Linden, NJ
Beach, Stephen Holbrook ... Darien, CT
Beach, Stephen L., III ... Jackson, MS
Beach, T. Andrew ... **Fort Worth, TX**
Beach, T. Christopher ... Augusta, ME
Beach, Thomas C., III ... **Baltimore, MD**
Columbia, MD
Beach, Thomas E. ... **Ventura, CA**
Beach, William B. ... **Detroit, MI**
Beach, William O. ... Clarksville, TN
Beach, William V. ... **Toledo, OH**
Beacham, Andrea J. ... Evanston, IL
Beacham, Deanna M. ... Newark, NJ
Beacham, Donald W. ... Lancaster, CA
Beacham, G. Rand ... St. George, UT
Beacham, Horace E., Jr. ... Palm Beach, FL
Beacham, Jeffrey B. ... Roseland, NJ
Beacham, Robert J. ... Belle Mead, NJ
Beachboard, James P. ... **Little Rock, AR**
Beachboard, Joseph Lyle
Hermosa Beach, CA
Beachem, N. Gregory ... St. Louis, MO
Beacher, Ronald S. ... **New York, NY**
Beachler, Edwin H. ... **Pittsburgh, PA**
Beachler, Jinx Statler ... Columbus, OH
Beachley, Charles E., III ... Lewisville, TX
Beachley, Donald E. ... Hagerstown, MD
Beachman, Robert G. ... Rochester, NY
Beachum, P. B., Jr. ... Charlotte, NC
Beachy, Robert M. ... **Kansas City, MO**
Beacock, Kathy A. ... Cincinnati, OH
Beacom, David J. ... Denver, CO
Beacom, Edward A., IV ... Wilmington, DE
Beacom, Guy B. ... Wilbraham, MA
Beacom, Paul Q. ... Westminster, CO
Beacom, Richard A., Jr. ... Greenville, TX
Beacom, S. Mark ... Butler, PA
Beada, Richard J. ... Santa Monica, CA
Beadie, David M. ... **Minneapolis, MN**
Beadie, Thomas N. ... Fort Wayne, IN
Beadie, William M. ... **Minneapolis, MN**
Beadle, Burket & Sweet, P.L.C. ... **Troy, MI**
Beadle, Christine ... Oklahoma City, OK
Beadle, James P. ... **Palm Bay, FL**
Beadle, Peter W. ... **New York, NY**
Beadle, Steven R. ... Maywood, IL
Beadle, Thomas ... Detroit, MI
Beadle, Thomas L. ... **Troy, MI**
Beadle, William T. ... Springfield, MO
Beadles, Cydney ... Corrales, NM
Beadles, Dudley ... **Fort Worth, TX**
Beadles, Gary ... Pauls Valley, OK
Beadles, James C. ... **Washington, DC**
Beadles, John F. ... **Fort Worth, TX**
Beadles, Johnson & Biscone, A Professional Association ... Oklahoma City, OK
Beadles, Newman & Lawler, A Professional Corporation ... **Fort Worth, TX**
Beadles, Richard T., Jr. ... Oklahoma City, OK
Beadles, Steven H., Law Offices of
Dallas, TX
Beadleston, Thomas Scott
Newport Beach, CA
Beadling, Keir J. ... **Boston, MA**
Beadling, Paige ... **Atlanta, GA**
Beagan, Robert J. ... **Vienna, VA**
Beagan, Thomas J., Jr. ... Media, PA
Beagen, Thomas P. ... Detroit, MI
Beaghan, John Joseph ... St. Charles, IL
Beagle, C. Alan ... **Portland, ME**
Beagle, Pearce & Ridge, LLC
Portland, ME
Beagle, Peter F. J. ... Columbus, OH
Beagle, Raymond F., Jr. ... **Kansas City, MO**
Beaglehole, John ... **New York, NY**
Beagles, Cynthia C. ... **Newark, NJ**
Beagles, Vance L. ... **Dallas, TX**
Beagley, Roxy Rae ... Greenville, SC
Beahm, Franklin D. ... **New Orleans, LA**
Beahm, Gary A., (A Professional Corporation)
San Antonio, TX
Beahm and Green ... **New Orleans, LA**
Beahn, John M. ... **Washington, DC**
Beahn, Maureen Byrne ... **Washington, DC**
Beaird, A. Michael ... Charlottesville, VA
Beaird, David Jeffrey ... Gadsden, AL
Beaird, Hugh ... Jasper, AL
Beaird, J. Ralph ... **Athens, GA**
Beaird, James Robert ... Jasper, AL
Beaird, Nanette K. ... **Austin, TX**
Beaird, Robert ... Independence, MO
Beaird & Sullivan ... Jasper, AL
Beakes, O. C. ... Jacksonville, FL
Beakley, Robert P. ... Somers Point, NJ
Beal, Albert R. ... New York, NY
Beal, Andrew M. ... **Atlanta, GA**
Beal, Armanda D. ... **Bangor, ME**
Beal, Arthur C., Jr. ... Tallahassee, FL
Beal, Beverly T. ... Lenoir, NC
Beal, Bruce C. ... Canton, IL
Beal, Bruce Leonard ... Pasadena, CA
Beal, Burton C. ... New York, NY
Beal, Carol Ann ... Jericho, NY
Beal, Charles E., II ... **Lexington, KY**
Beal, Charles S. ... **Providence, RI**
Beal, Christopher L. ... Winston-Salem, NC
Beal, Cristine A. ... New Orleans, LA
Beal, David A. ... Richmond Heights, OH
Beal, David B. ... **Newark, NJ**
Beal, David O. ... Oklahoma City, OK
Beal, George ... **Rapid City, SD**
Beal, George M., II ... **Seattle, WA**
Beal, Gerald H. ... Tucson, AZ
Beal, Glen G. ... Kansas City, MO
Lee's Summit, MO
Beal, Gregory J. ... Ogallala, NE
Beal, Gregory J., & Associates, P.C.
Ogallala, NE
Beal, Holly C. ... **Orange, CA**
Beal, Ira F. ... New York, NY
Beal, James C. ... Los Angeles, CA
Beal, James E. ... Northridge, CA
Beal, James E. ... Jonesboro, LA
Beal, John ... Chicago, IL
Beal, John A. ... Andover, MA
Beal, John R. ... New Orleans, LA
Beal, Jon G. ... Missoula, MT
Beal, Jonathan S. R. ... Portland, ME
Beal, Katharina E. ... **Kansas City, MO**
Beal, Kenneth I. ... Forest Hills, NY
Beal, Kenneth L. ... Las Cruces, NM
Beal, Kermit M. ... Lawrence, KS
Beal, Kevin J. ... **Portland, ME**
Beal, Larry E. ... Logan, OH
Beal Law Offices ... **Rapid City, SD**
Beal, Leonard L. ... Lakewood, CO
Beal, Marion L. ... **Monmouth, IL**
Beal, Matt E. ... **Orlando, FL**
Beal, Melvin W. ... Oakland, CA
Beal, Michael D. ... **Mount Airy, NC**
Beal, Michael F. ... Naples, FL
Beal, Michael McNulty ... **Columbia, SC**
Beal, Norman E. ... **Kansas City, MO**
Beal, Pratt and Pratt ... **Monmouth, IL**
Oquawka, IL
Beal, Richard L. ... Department of Justice, Environment and Natural Resources Division, GV
Beal, Richard M. ... **Modesto, CA**
Beal, Richard T., Jr. ... **Seattle, WA**
Beal, Robbie T. ... **Franklin, TN**
Beal, Robert C. ... **Fort Worth, TX**
Beal, Robert F. ... Los Angeles, CA
Beal, Robert J. ... Rangeley, ME
Beal, Robert L. ... **Tucson, AZ**
Beal, Robert W. ... Chickasha, OK
Beal, Ron D. ... **Kansas City, MO**
Beal, Scott D. ... Gulfport, MS
Beal, Shane E. ... Marion, IN
Beal, Thaddeus R., Jr. ... Essex, MA
Beal, Thomas D. ... **Columbus, OH**
Beal, W. Ashby, Jr. ... **Washington, DC**
Beale, Balfour, Davidson & Etherington, P.C.
Chesterfield, VA
Richmond, VA
Beale, David A. ... **Delray Beach, FL**
New York, NY
Beale, David A., P.A. ... **Boca Raton, FL**
Delray Beach, FL
New York, NY
Beale, David F. ... Houston, TX
Beale, David F., P.C. ... Houston, TX
Beale, David S. ... Atlanta, GA
Beale, David S., P.C. ... Atlanta, GA
Beale, David W. ... Colorado Springs, CO
Beale, Hammond A. ... Columbia, SC
Beale, Hammond A., P.A. ... Columbia, SC
Beale, Howard Leo, II ... **Memphis, TN**
Beale & Humphrey, P.S.C.
Jeffersonville, IN
Lexington, KY
Louisville, KY
Beale, J. Burkhardt ... Richmond, VA
Woodbridge, VA
Beale, J. Burkhardt, P.C. ... Richmond, VA
Beale, J. Kyle ... **Marshall, TX**
Beale, J. Vaughan ... Franklin, VA
Beale, John C.
Environmental Protection Agency, Program Office Attorneys, GV
Beale, Joseph H. ... Fairfax, VA
Beale, Linda M. ... **New York, NY**
Beale, Lindy Julian ... Montgomery, AL
Beale, Lisa Mihalick ... **Atlanta, GA**
Beale, Louis C., Jr. ... Weirton, WV
Beale, Louise R. ... Rochester, NY
Beale, Meagan J. ... San Diego, CA
Beale, Melinda Julian ... Montgomery, AL
Beale, Michael A. ... Phoenix, AZ
Beale, Michael J. ... **Midland, MI**
Beale & Micheaels, P.C. ... Phoenix, AZ
Beale, R. Daniel ... **Atlanta, GA**
Beale, Richard C. ... **Norfolk, VA**
Beale, Robert J. ... **Louisville, KY**
Beale, Robert L. ... **Tacoma, WA**
Beale, Robert V. ... Newport News, VA
Beale, Sam T. ... **Richmond, VA**
Beale, Sara Sun ... Durham, NC
Beale, Stephen P. ... **Auburn, ME**
Beale, Susan M. ... Detroit, MI
Beale, Thomas A. ... Midland, MI
Beale, Thomas J. ... **Detroit, MI**
Beale, Walter M., Jr. ... **Birmingham, AL**
Beale, William A. ... Towson, MD
Bealer, Natalie P. ... Englewood, CO
Beales, James A., Jr. ... Elizabeth City, NC
Beales, Walter R., III ... **Boydton, VA**
Bealke, Charles F. ... Kirkwood, MO
Beall, Alex ... Tyler, TX
Beall, Augustus, III ... Cincinnati, OH
Beall & Biehler, P.A. ... **Albuquerque, NM**
Beall, Bradley S. ... Department of Defense, Defense Legal Services Agency, GV
Beall & Burkhardt ... Santa Barbara, CA
Beall, Catherine A. ... **Los Angeles, CA**
Santa Ana, CA
Beall, Charles ... Austin, TX
Beall, Charles E. ... Palm Beach, FL
Beall, Charles F., Jr. ... **Pensacola, FL**
Beall, Christopher P. ... **Denver, CO**
Beall, Clarence W., III ... Westminster, MD
Beall, Colleen Parent ... Santa Barbara, CA
Beall, Garth E. ... **Greenbelt, MD**
Beall, George ... **Baltimore, MD**
Beall, George G. ... San Diego, CA
Beall, Ingrid L. ... Chicago, IL
Beall, James A. ... **Washington, DC**
Portland, OR
Salem, OR
Beall, James E. ... **Troy, MI**
Beall, James S. ... Philadelphia, PA
Beall, James W. ... Carlsbad, CA
Beall, Jill M. ... Little Rock, AR
Beall, John A., IV ... Jonesboro, GA
Beall, John J., Jr. ... Richmond, VA
Beall, John M. ... **Ontario, CA**
Walnut Creek, CA
Beall, John Ninian ... Burke, VA
Beall, John P. ... Houston, TX
Beall, Judith M. ... **Los Angeles, CA**
Beall, Kelly A. ... **Lake Forest, CA**
Beall, Kenneth S., Jr.
West Palm Beach, FL
Beall, Kenneth W. ... **Lansing, MI**
Beall, Kirke M. ... Pensacola, FL
Beall, Kyle B. ... **Baton Rouge, LA**
Beall, L. Anthony ... **Los Angeles, CA**
Beall, Larry D. ... **Albuquerque, NM**
Beall, Larry E. ... Mobile, AL
Beall Law Office ... Alexandria, VA
Beall, Mark H. ... Dallas, TX
Beall, Rebecca S. ... Baltimore, MD
Beall, Robert D. ... Leavenworth, KS
Beall, Robert S. ... **Costa Mesa, CA**
Beall, S. Dick ... Atlanta, GA
Beall, Scott Thomas ... **Memphis, TN**
Beall, Tab ... Tyler, TX
Beall, Theodore J. ... Santa Ana, CA
Beall, Thomas E., Jr. ... Alexandria, VA
Beall, Webber W., Jr. ... **Dallas, TX**
Beall, William C. ... Santa Barbara, CA
Bealle, J. Rufus ... Tuscaloosa, AL
Beall-Templin, Diane ... Escondido, CA
Beals, Bruce M. ... **San Diego, CA**
Beals, D. Kent ... **Atlanta, GA**
Beals, David A. ... **Columbus, OH**
Beals & DiFiore ... Providence, RI
Beals, Douglas W. ... **Marshalltown, IA**
Beals, G. Chandler ... Providence, RI
Beals, George W. ... Portland, ME
Beals Hubbard, P.L.C.
Farmington Hills, MI
Beals, John P. ... **Manchester, NH**
Beals, John T. ... Pharr, TX
Beals, Judith E. ... Boston, MA
Beals, Justin Edward ... Miami, FL
Beals, Kim A. ... Pacific Grove, CA
Beals, Kim A. ... Pacific Grove, CA
Beals, Michael J. ... **Farmington Hills, MI**
Beals & Quinn ... Portland, ME
Beals, Stanley ... Garden City, NY
Beals, W. Russell, Jr. ... Birmingham, AL
Beam, Brobeck & West ... **Los Angeles, CA**
Santa Ana, CA
Beam, Byron J. ... **Santa Ana, CA**
Beam, Clarence Arlen ... Lincoln, NE
Beam, Craig K. ... **San Diego, CA**
Beam, Dayn T. ... Huntsville, AL
Beam, Diane Verderaime ... Huntsville, AL
Beam, Donald C. ... **Hayesville, NC**
Beam, Douglas R. ... Melbourne, FL
Beam, Elizabeth Ward ... Enid, OK
Beam, Gregory B. ... **Irvine, CA**
Beam & Hummel ... Glendale, CA
Beam, J. Robert ... **Zanesville, OH**
Beam, Jack, & Associates ... **Denver, CO**
Beam, James C. ... Arlington, TX
Beam, James R. ... **Albuquerque, NM**
Beam, James R. ... **Philadelphia, PA**
Beam, James R., P.C. ... **Albuquerque, NM**
Beam, Jeff Robert ... **Zanesville, OH**
Beam, Joe B. ... Tyler, TX
Beam, John A., III ... Nashville, TN
Beam, John W., Jr. ... Savannah, GA
Beam, Karin P. ... **Santa Rosa, CA**
Beam, Lori A. ... **Kansas City, MO**
Beam, Margaret R.
Hot Springs National Park, AR
Beam, Martha B. ... Kinston, NC
Beam, Michael E. ... **New Port Richey, FL**
Beam, Michael S., III ... Smithfield, NC
Beam, Patrick L. ... Corpus Christi, TX
Beam, Richard J., Jr. ... Norcross, GA
Beam, Robert Charles ... Blue Bell, PA
Beam, Robert T. ... Naples, FL
Beam, Stephen D. ... **Weatherford, OK**
Beam, Susan ... Glendale, CA
Beam, Thomas L. ... **Denver, CO**
Beam Warden & Mittledorf, PLLC
Nashville, TN
Beam, William A., Jr. ... **St. Petersburg, FL**
Beaman, Andrew V. ... **Honolulu, HI**
Beaman, Colleen B. ... **Milwaukee, WI**
Beaman, Duncan F. ... **Troy, MI**
Beaman, Grafton G. ... Elizabeth City, NC
Beaman, James C. ... Honolulu, HI
Beaman, James R., (P.C.) ... Tucson, AZ
Beaman, James T. ... **Marion, IN**
Beaman & King, P.A. ... Wilson, NC
Beaman, Larry G. ... Irvine, CA
Beaman, Mark T. ... **Austin, TX**
Beaumont, TX
Beaman, Marvin L., Jr. ... Winter Park, FL
Beaman, Marvin L., Jr., P.A.
Winter Park, FL
Beaman, Nathaniel, III ... Norfolk, VA
Beaman, Nathaniel, IV ... Norfolk, VA
Beaman, Patricia A. ... Los Angeles, CA
Beaman, Peter H. ... **Pittsburgh, PA**
Pittsburgh, PA
Beaman, Ralph P. ... Homewood, IL
Beaman, Richard E. ... Flushing, NY
Beaman, Robert L. ... Baltimore, MD
Beaman, Stephen L. ... Wilson, NC
Beaman, Walter H. ... Jupiter, FL
Beaman, William C. ... Cheyenne, WY
Beame, Andrew P. ... **New York, NY**
Beamer, Dirk A. ... **Farmington Hills, MI**
Beamer, George N., Jr. ... Mishawaka, IN
Beamer, Henry G., III ... Pittsburgh, PA
Beamer, Jack G. ... **Kansas City, MO**
Beamer, John E. ... Des Moines, IA
Beamer, John T. ... Riverdale, MD
Beamer, Kathryn M.
West Palm Beach, FL
Beamer, Kathryn M., P.A.
West Palm Beach, FL
Beamer, Lauth & Steinley, LLP
San Diego, CA
Beamer, Norman H. ... **Palo Alto, CA**
Beamer, Robert W. ... Port Charlotte, FL
Beamer, Rufus W., Jr. ... Knoxville, TN
Beamer, Slagg & Thompson, L.L.C.
Kansas City, MO
Beamer, Stephanie J. ... **Fort Worth, TX**
Beamer, William D. ... Fort Lauderdale, FL
Beamer, William E. ... **San Diego, CA**
Beamguard, Nathan D. ... Winston-Salem, NC
Beamish, Cynthia L. ... Coral Gables, FL
Beamish, Thomas J. ... Milwaukee, WI
Beamon, Arthur L.
Federal Deposit Insurance Corporation, Compliance and Enforcement Section, GV
Beamon, Charles A.
Federal Energy Regulatory Commission, Office of the General Counsel, GV
Beamon, Earl A., II ... **Sherman Oaks, CA**
Beamon, Shanuah Y. ... Boston, MA
Beamon, Tina Clark ... **New Haven, CT**
Beam-Rucker, Mildred D. ... **Orlando, FL**
Beams, Bradly D. ... Three Rivers, MI
Beams, Glen J. ... **Fort Wayne, IN**
Beams, John M. ... Fort Wayne, IN
Beams, Mark ... **Fairfield, CT**
Beams, Virginia Callery ... Miami, FL
Beamud, Cristina ... Cambridge, MA
Beam-Ward, Mark ... Overland Park, KS
Beam-Winter, Nancy ... Philadelphia, PA
Bean, A. Jeffrey ... **Bloomfield Hills, MI**
Bean, Amy Stout ... Orange, TX
Bean, Andrew J. ... Detroit, MI
Bean, Andrew J., P.C. ... Detroit, MI
Bean, Angela M. ... San Francisco, CA
Bean, Arthur E., Jr. ... Bedford, NH
Bean, Barbara H. ... New York, NY
Bean & Bean ... **Moorefield, WV**
Bean and Bean, P.A. ... **Spartanburg, SC**
Bean, Bourne, (P.C.) ... **St. Louis, MO**
Bean, Brenton S. ... **Atlanta, GA**
Bean, Brett J. ... **Lansing, MI**
Bean, C. Christopher ... Edenton, NC
Bean, Charles F. ... Coeur d'Alene, ID
Bean, Charles F., & Associates
Coeur d'Alene, ID
Bean, Charles H. ... **St. Clairsville, OH**
Bean, Charles H. ... Martinsburg, WV
Bean, Charles R. ... South Portland, ME
Bean, Charles R., P.A. ... South Portland, ME
Bean, Christopher V. ... Jaffrey, NH
Bean, Daniel K. ... **Jacksonville, FL**
Bean, David E. ... Layton, UT
Bean, Dennis W. ... Silverton, OR
Bean, Diane Reimer ...
Department of State, GV
Bean, Donald ... Haverford, PA
Philadelphia, PA
Bean, Donald, Jr. ... **Washington, DC**
Bean, Edward D. ... Boston, MA
Bean, Edwin T., Jr. ... **Buffalo, NY**
Bean, Elise J. ... Arlington, VA
Bean, Eric A. ... **Bloomfield Hills, MI**
Bean, Felix H., III ... Memphis, TN
Bean, Frank M. ... Houston, TX
Bean, Frank W. ... Atlanta, GA
Bean & Gentry ... **Olympia, WA**
Bean, Gregory R. ... Akron, OH
Bean, Gregory V. ... **Portland, OR**
Bean, Howard Carlisle ... **Spartanburg, SC**
Bean, J. Coleman ... **Washington, DC**
Bean, J. David ... Skippack, PA
Bean, J. Michael ... Irving, TX
Bean, James A. ... Crossville, TN
Bean, James H. ... **Portland, OR**
Bean, James L. ... **Falls Church, VA**
Bean, James Roy, III ... Perry, FL
Bean, James W. ...
Department of State, GV
Bean, Jerry ... Lafayette, IN
Bean, Jill Curfman ... **Prescott, AZ**
Bean, John N. ... **Memphis, TN**
Bean, John W. ... **Geneseo, IL**
Bean, Joseph M. ... Layton, UT
Bean, Joseph W. ... Chicago, IL
Bean, K. Roger ... Layton, UT
Bean, Kauffman & Snyder ... Buffalo, NY
Bean, Kenneth W. ... **Belleville, IL**
St. Louis, MO

Bean, Kinney & Korman, A Professional Corporation ... Arlington, VA
Bean, Larry L. ... Dallas, TX
Bean, Lori A. ... Washington, DC
Bean & Manning ... Houston, TX
Bean, Margaret E. ... Hagåtña, GU
Bean, Mark W. ... Columbus, OH
Bean, Martha B. "Molly" ... Austin, TX
Bean, Martha Lee ... Plano, TX
Bean, Michael D. ... Maryland Heights, MO
Bean and Novack ... Columbus, OH
Bean, Oscar M. ... Moorefield, WV
Bean, Ralph J., Jr. ... Clarksburg, WV
Fairmont, WV
Bean, Richard C. ... Westwood, MA
Bean, Richard G. ... Roswell, NM
Bean, Richard G., P.A. ... Roswell, NM
Bean, Robert ... Garland, TX
Bean, Robert L. ... Fullerton, CA
Bean, Rodney L. ... Morgantown, WV
Bean, Roger J. ... Tullahoma, TN
Bean, Ronald H. ... White River Junction, VT
Bean, Russell J. ... Chattanooga, TN
Bean, Russell K ... Englewood, CO
Bean, Sandra Kay ... Pleasanton, CA
Bean & Smedley, A Professional Corporation
Layton, UT
Bean, Stephen H. ... Chicago, IL
Bean, Stephen J. ... Olympia, WA
Bean, Tedd E. ... Grand Blanc, MI
Bean, Thomas F. ... Willoughby Hills, OH
Bean, Thomas L. ... Crossville, TN
Bean, Thomas O. ... Boston, MA
Bean, Wiley E. ... Grand Ledge, MI
Bean, William A. ... Downers Grove, IL
Bean, William H. ... Moorefield, WV
Bean, William K. ... Arlington, VA
Bean, William S., IV ... Spartanburg, SC
Bean, Woodrow, & Associates
El Paso, TX
Horizon City, TX
Bean, Woodrow W., II & Associates
Horizon City, TX
Bean, Woodrow W., III ... El Paso, TX
Beanblossom, David A. ... Kingsport, TN
Beanblossom, H. Mark ... Collierville, TN
Beane & Beane ... Washington, DC
Beane, Becky A. ... Raleigh, NC
Beane, C. Ernest ... Rock Island, IL
Beane, Catherine Vanchiere ... Washington, DC
Beane, Christian L. ... Clifton, NJ
Beane, Darrell M. ... Richmond, IN
Beane, David R. ... Reading, PA
Beane, Dorothea A. ... St. Petersburg, FL
Beane, Edward F. ... Rye, NY
White Plains, NY
Beane, Eric S. ... Los Angeles, CA
Beane, Frank L. ... Massillon, OH
Beane, Gregory S. ... Hamilton, OH
Beane, James W., Jr. ... Washington, DC
Beane, Jerry L., (P.C.) ... Dallas, TX
Beane, John C. ... Atlanta, GA
Beane, Kenneth M. ... Maitland, FL
Beane, Norman P., Jr. ... Boston, MA
Beane, Stephen W. ... Boise, ID
Beane, Thomas O. ... Manassas, VA
Beanland, Kenneth ... San Antonio, TX
Beanland, William G. ... Vicksburg, MS
Beans, Charles R. ... Atlanta, GA
Beans, William W. ... Chicago, IL
Beanum, John O. ... Los Angeles, CA
Bear, Antanavage & Moyer ... Hamburg, PA
Bear, Audrey S. ... Sarasota, FL
Bear, Dinah
Executive Office Of The President, Council on Environmental Quality, GV
Bear, Henry L. ... Downey, CA
Bear, James B. ... Newport Beach, CA
Bear, Jeffrey L. ... Beverly Hills, CA
Bear, Julie E. ... Plattsmouth, NE
Bear, Kristen D. ... Englewood, CO
Bear, Kristin A. ... Dallas, TX
Houston, TX
Bear, Kristin K. ... Los Angeles, CA
Bear, Larry A. ... Mahwah, NJ
Bear Law Firm, The, P.A. ... Bear, DE
Wilmington, DE
Bear, R. Solomon ... Hamburg, PA
Bear, Robert H. ... Rockville, MD
Bear, Roger D. ... Orlando, FL
Bear, Roger D., P.A. ... Orlando, FL
Bear, Steven F. ... Eugene, OR
Bear, Stuart ... Bridgeport, CT
Bear, Stuart C. ... Minneapolis, MN
Bear, Thomas O. ... Foley, AL
Bear, Thomas O., P.C. ... Foley, AL
Bear, William ... Houston, TX
Bearak, Corey B. ... Jamaica, NY
Bearby, Scott A. ... Hammond, IN
Beard, Alexander N. ... Dallas, TX
Beard, Barbara Lee ... Big Bear Lake, CA
Beard & Beard ... Guntersville, AL
Beard and Beard ... Alexandria, LA
Beard, Ben A. ... Bloomington, IN
Beard, Benjamin Weston ... Pensacola, FL
Beard, Brian K. ... Menlo Park, CA
Austin, TX
Beard, Brooks M. ... San Francisco, CA
Beard, Bruce E. ... Dallas, TX
Beard, Bruce R. ... West Brookfield, MA
Beard, C. Richard ... Clayton, MO
Beard, Carl P. ... Altoona, PA
Beard, Charles Adams ... Jacksonville, FL
Beard, Charles J. ... Boston, MA
Beard, Charles P. ... Cedar Rapids, IA
Beard, Christopher L. ... Annapolis, MD
Beard, Cindy A. ... Phoenix, AZ
Beard, Cindy York ... Wilmington, NC
Beard, Collen A. ... Atlanta, GA
Beard, Craig M. ... Memphis, TN
Beard, D. Benjamin ... Moscow, ID
Beard, Daniel J. ... Jacksonville, IL
Beard, David S. ... Irvine, CA
Beard, Deborah Bigham ... Stuart, FL
Beard, Deena L. ... Albuquerque, NM
Beard, DeLawrence ... Rockville, MD
Beard, Diana L. ... Lexington, KY
Beard, Don L. ... Houston, TX
Beard, Don L., P.C. ... Houston, TX
Beard, Don R. ... Baton Rouge, LA
Lafayette, LA
Beard, E. Keith ... Hutchinson, KS
Beard, Ellen Graves ... Waverly, AL
Beard, Ellen L. ... Department of Labor, Office of the Solicitor, GV
Beard, Elliott M. ... New York, NY
Beard, Gayle Norman ... Baton Rouge, LA
Beard, Gerald A. ... Greenville, SC
Beard, Glenda R. ... Irving, TX
Beard, Glenn A. ... Albuquerque, NM
Beard, Grady L. ... Columbia, SC
Beard, Greg ... Booneville, MS
Beard, Greg E., P.A. ... Booneville, MS
Beard, Heather S.
Office Of Special Counsel, GV
Beard, J. Mitchell ... Henderson, TX
Beard, J. William ... La Mesa, CA
Beard, Jack M. ... Department of Defense, Office of the General Counsel, GV
Beard, James L. ... Chicago, IL
Beard, James M. ... Seattle, WA
Beard, James W., Jr. ... Houston, TX
Beard, Jeffrey J. ... Milwaukee, WI
Beard, Jennifer K. ... Seattle, WA
Beard, Jes ... Chattanooga, TN
Beard, J.M. Scott, Jr. ... Birmingham, AL
Beard, John B. ... Jackson, MS
Beard, John Clayton ... Corsicana, TX
Dallas, TX
Beard, John E. ... Boston, MA
Beard, John E., III ... Pittsburgh, PA
Beard, John G. ... Birmingham, AL
Beard, John L. ... Minneapolis, MN
Beard, John Q. ... Cary, NC
Beard, John R. ... Anchorage, AK
Beard, John W. ... Chattanooga, TN
Beard, Joseph J. ... Boston, MA
Beard, Journey L. ... Fort Lauderdale, FL
Beard, Kathleen Lewis ... Atlanta, GA
Beard, Kelly Jean ... Atlanta, GA
Beard, Kevin L. ... Baltimore, MD
Beard & Kultgen ... Waco, TX
Beard, L. Antoinette ... Lafayette, LA
Beard, Laura L. ... Phoenix, AZ
Beard, Lisa D. ... Nashville, TN
Beard, Lonnie R. ... Fayetteville, AR
Beard, Louis H. ... Beaumont, TX
Beard, M. Frank ... Waco, TX
Beard, M. Stephen ... Waco, TX
Beard, Mark G. ... Seattle, WA
Beard & Medler, L.L.C. ... St. Louis, MO
Beard, Michael Blaine ... Laurel, MD
Beard, Michael J. ... Tulsa, OK
Beard, Michael K. ... Birmingham, AL
Beard, N. Beaumont ... Pittsburgh, PA
Beard, Nadia R. Totino ... Worcester, MA
Beard, Orville S. ... Covington, TN
Beard, Pat ... Waco, TX
Beard, Paul ... Chicago, IL
Beard, Philip E. ... Pittsburgh, PA
Beard, Philip E., II ... Pittsburgh, PA
Beard, Phillip L. ... Xenia, OH
Beard, R. Edward ... Medfield, MA
Beard, R. William, Jr. ... Houston, TX
Beard, Ralph ... San Antonio, TX
Beard, Ralph A. ... Youngstown, OH
Beard, Randy H. ... Guntersville, AL
Beard, Richard A. ... San Jose, CA
Beard, Richard T. ... Salt Lake City, UT
Beard, Robert Davis ... Aurora, CO
Beard, Robert F. ... Culpeper, VA
Beard, Robert L. ... Marietta, GA
Beard, Robert L. ... Reinbeck, IA
Beard, Rodney A. ... Pine Grove Mills, PA
Beard, Ronald ... Greensburg, IN
Beard, Ronald E. ... Seattle, WA
Beard, Ronald Glen ... Alexandria, LA
Beard, Ronald S. ... Irvine, CA
Los Angeles, CA
Beard, Roy C. ... Metairie, LA
Beard, Roy L. ... Shreveport, LA
Beard, R. T., III ... Little Rock, AR
Beard, Russell C. (Rusty) ... Abilene, TX
Beard St. Clair Gaffney McNamara PA
Idaho Falls, ID
Beard, Sarah H. ... Portland, ME
Beard, Steven L. ... Marietta, GA
Beard, Steven L., P.C. ... Atlanta, GA
Canton, GA
Marietta, GA
Beard, Susan F. ... Department of Energy, Office of the General Counsel, GV
Beard & Sutherland ... Shreveport, LA
Beard & Sweet ... Reinbeck, IA
Beard, T. Alexander ... Charleston, SC
Beard, T. Alexander ... Columbia, SC
Mount Pleasant, SC
Beard, Terrence A. ... Antioch, CA
Beard, Timothy R. ... St. Louis, MO
Beard, Vicki Lee ... Yorktown, VA
Beard, W. Cameron ... New York, NY
Beard, W. Gregory ... Alexandria, LA
Beard, W. Robinson ... Louisville, KY
Beard, Will ... Guntersville, AL
Beard, William D. ... Dallas, TX
Beard, William D., P.C. ... Dallas, TX
Beard, William J. ... Hyannis, MA
Beard, William S. ... Dundalk, MD
Beard, William T. ... Marietta, GA
Beard, Winston V. ... Idaho Falls, ID
Beardall and Blankner, P.A. ... Orlando, FL
Beardall, William H. ... Orlando, FL
Beardall, William H. ... Weslaco, TX
Beardell, Lori Yanisko ... Philadelphia, PA
Beardell, Louis W., Jr. ... Valley Forge, PA
Bearden, Bennett L. ... Tuscaloosa, AL
Bearden, Breckenridge & Gidlow
St. Louis, MO
Bearden, Carey D. ... Mandeville, LA
Bearden, D. Lynn ... Calhoun, GA
Bearden, David ... Tampa, FL
Bearden, David M., Jr. ... Houston, TX
Bearden, Diana Joseph ... Dallas, TX
Bearden, Eric ... Bowling Green, KY
Bearden, Frank L. ... Portland, OR
Bearden, Jas. C. ... Lubbock, TX
Bearden, Jim Sharon ... Orange, TX
Bearden, Judith ... Yellville, AR
Bearden, Lane ... Calhoun, GA
Bearden Law Firm ... Blytheville, AR
Jonesboro, AR
Bearden Law Firm ... Calhoun, GA
Cartersville, GA
Bearden, Margaret F. ... El Cajon, CA
Bearden, Mary Ann ... Eugene, OR
Bearden, Mary M. ... Houston, TX
Bearden, Mike ... Blytheville, AR
Bearden, Nolanda H. ... Birmingham, AL
Bearden, Ralph H., Jr. (P.A.) ... Arcadia, FL
Bearden, Richard A. ... Birmingham, AL
Bearden, Stan K. ... Tulsa, OK
Bearden, Thomas G. ... St. Louis, MO
Bearden, W. E., Jr. ... Columbus, MS
Bearden & Weinstein ... Eugene, OR
Beardmore, Thomas C. ... Houston, TX
Beardmore, W. Harvey ... Annapolis, MD
Beardslee, G. William ... Greeley, CO
Beardslee, Paul K. ... Marshall, MI
Beardslee, Robert L. ... Birmingham, MI
Birmingham, MI
Beardslee, William Quinn ... Greeley, CO
Beardsley, Alan J. ... Sherman Oaks, CA
Beardsley, Alberta ... Kittanning, PA
Beardsley, Alvin W. ... Big Bear Lake, CA
Beardsley, Anthony W. ... Ellsworth, ME
Beardsley & Associates ... La Jolla, CA
Beardsley, C. Samuel ... Nedrow, NY
Beardsley, Craig N. ... Bakersfield, CA
Beardsley, Dale A. ... Jacksonville, FL
Beardsley, Donna G.
Pension Benefit Guaranty Corporation, Other Lawyers in Staff or Executive Positions, GV
Beardsley, Erica S. ... McLean, VA
Beardsley, James M. ... Buffalo, NY
Beardsley, Jed Steven ... Atlanta, GA
Beardsley, Joe E., II ... Clinton, IN
Beardsley, Kate C. ... Washington, DC
Beardsley, Laura E. ... Dover, NH
Beardsley, Marilyn K. ... Pleasanton, CA
Beardsley, Mary Ellen ... Anchorage, AK
Beardsley Muela, LLP ... Austin, TX
Beardsley, Nancy A. ... Blue Springs, MO
Beardsley, Nancy T. ... La Jolla, CA
Beardsley, Peter ... Austin, TX
Beardsley, Ruth ... New Haven, CT
Beardsley, Stephen J. ... New Albany, IN
Beardsley, Steven C. ... Rapid City, SD
Beardsley, Walter C. ... San Antonio, TX
Beardsworth, Helen Sweeny
San Francisco, CA
Beardsworth, John Jennings, Jr.
Richmond, VA
Beare, Robin E. ... Carmel, CA
Bearer, Robert Lee ... Tulsa, OK
Bearfield & McClellan ... Johnson City, TN
Bearfield, Rick J. ... Johnson City, TN
Bearg, Martin L. ... West Orange, NJ
New York, NY
Beargie, Amy E. ... Washington, DC
Beariault, Mark D. ... Palo Alto, CA
Bearinger, James I. ... Beulah, MI
Bearley, Kevin L. ... Englewood, CO
Bearman, Anne W. ... Pacific Palisades, CA
Bearman, David L. ... Memphis, TN
Bearman, Edward M. ... Memphis, TN
Bearman, Irving ... New York, NY
Bearman, Leo, Jr. ... Memphis, TN
Bearman, Morton R. ... St. Louis, MO
Bearman, Robert M. ... Denver, CO
Bearman, Samuel ... New York, NY
Bearman, Samuel W. ... Pensacola, FL
Bearman, Stephen J. ... Memphis, TN
Bearmon, Lee ... Minneapolis, MN
Bearmon, Samuel ... Minneapolis, MN
Bearns, Stuyvesant K. ... Lakeville, CT
Bearnson, Brad H. ... Logan, UT
Bearnson & Peck, L.L.C. ... Logan, UT
Bearor, Edmond J. ... Bangor, ME
Bearrows, Thomas R. ... Chicago, IL
Bearse, Aurora R. ... New York, NY
Bearse, Edward W. ... Anoka, MN
Bearse, Michael S. ... Washington, DC
Providence, RI
Bearse, Michael S., P.C. ... Providence, RI
Bearse, Thomas T. ... Southfield, MI
Beart, Robert W. ... Glenview, IL
Bearup, George Frederick
Traverse City, MI
Bearup, Scot A. ... Memphis, TN
Beary, Donna Ruth ... Des Moines, IA
Beary, Marie A. ... Jamaica, NY
Beary, Patrick ... Jamaica, NY
Beary, Roberta ... Washington, DC
Beary, W. Christopher ... New Orleans, LA
Beary Quinn, Sheila ... Chicago, IL
Beaser, Lawrence J. ... Philadelphia, PA
Beasey, Dale W. ... Las Vegas, NV
Beasley, Adrionne D. ... Oakland, CA
Beasley, Alice M. ... Oakland, CA
Beasley, Allen, Crow, Methvin Portis & Miles, P.C. ... Hayneville, AL
Beasley, Allen, Crow, Methvin, Portis & Miles, P.C. ... Montgomery, AL
Beasley, Allen, Crow, Methvin Portis & Miles, P.C. ... Prattville, AL
Selma, AL
Troy, AL
Tuskegee, AL
Union Springs, AL
Wetumpka, AL
Beasley, Allen W. ... Norfolk, VA
Beasley, Arch A., Jr. ... Dallas, TX
Beasley, Barry K. ... Tulsa, OK
Beasley & Beasley ... Greenwood, SC
Beasley, B. R. ... Tulsa, OK
Beasley, Bradley K. ... Tulsa, OK
Beasley, Brandon W. ... Austin, TX
Beasley, Bruce D. ... Fort Worth, TX
Beasley, Byron H. ... Laurinburg, NC
Beasley, Casey & Erbstein
Mount Laurel, NJ
Philadelphia, PA
Beasley, Cecil A., Jr. ... Washington, DC
Beasley, Cecilee Russell ... Birmingham, AL
Beasley, Charles A. ... Fort Smith, AR
Beasley, Daniel F. ... Huntsville, AL
Beasley, David E. ... Cleveland, OH
Beasley, David J. ... Kissimmee, FL
Orlando, FL
Beasley, David M. ... Columbia, SC
Beasley, Donna M. ... Washington, DC
Beasley, Dorothy Toth ... Atlanta, GA
Beasley, Douglas A. ... Asheboro, NC
Beasley, Edward D. ... Bedford, NH
Concord, NH
Keene, NH
Nashua, NH
Portsmouth, NH
Beasley, Eric P. ... Dallas, TX
Beasley & Ferber ... Keene, NH
Bedford, NH
Concord, NH
Nashua, NH
Portsmouth, NH
Beasley, Gary D. ... Murfreesboro, TN
Beasley, George M., III ... Annapolis, MD
Beasley, George W. ... Denver, CO
Beasley Gilkison Retherford Buckles & Clark, LLP ... Muncie, IN
Beasley, Heather C. ... Portland, OR
Beasley, James C., Jr. ... Memphis, TN
Beasley, James D. ... Tallahassee, FL
Beasley, James E. ... Philadelphia, PA
Beasley, James E., Jr. ... Philadelphia, PA
Beasley, James G. ... Wichita, KS
Beasley, James S., The Law Offices of
Reno, NV
Beasley, James W., Jr.
West Palm Beach, FL
Beasley, Jean M. ... Los Angeles, CA
Beasley, Jere Locke ... Montgomery, AL
Beasley, Jesse B. ... Cincinnati, OH
Beasley, Jill M. ... Ann Arbor, MI
Beasley, John ... Greenwood, SC
Beasley, John B. ... Muncie, IN
Beasley, John E. ... Iowa City, IA
Beasley, John F. ... Atlanta, GA
Beasley, John F., Jr. ... Athens, GA
Decatur, GA
Beasley, John H. ... Dayton, OH
Beasley, John R. ... Fort Smith, AR
Waldron, AR
Beasley, John S., II ... Nashville, TN
Beasley, John W. ... Beeville, TX
Beasley, John W., Jr. ... Brandon, VT
Beasley, Joseph W. ... Miami, FL
Beasley, Joseph W., P.A. ... Miami, FL
Beasley, Judith Evelyn ... Nashville, TN
Beasley, Julia Anne ... Montgomery, AL
Beasley, Kathleen McIntosh ... Dallas, TX
Beasley, Keith R. ... Mount Clemens, MI
Beasley, Leacock & Hauser, P.A.
Palm Beach, FL
West Palm Beach, FL
Beasley, Lynn M.
Environmental Protection Agency, Program Office Attorneys, GV
Beasley, Mark V. ... Irving, TX
Beasley, Michael W. ... Vienna, VA
Beasley, Michele E. ... Washington, DC
Beasley & Moore ... Beeville, TX
Beasley, Murray W. ... Tuscumbia, AL
Beasley, Nancy Rumble ... Atlanta, GA
Beasley, Norma Lea ... Dallas, TX
Beasley, Oscar H. ... Santa Ana, CA
Beasley, Patrick R. ... Redding, CA
Beasley, Paul T. ... The Dalles, OR
Beasley, Paula L. ... Dallas, TX
Beasley, Rebecca O. ... Dallas, TX
Beasley, Rex G. ... Council Grove, KS
Beasley, Robert ... Pensacola, FL
Beasley, Robert B., Jr. ... Richmond, VA
Beasley, Robert C. ... Albany, IN
Beasley, Robert C. ... Houston, TX
Beasley, Robert J. ... Garland, TX
Beasley, Robert S. ... Baltimore, MD
Beasley, Sheryl M. ... Los Angeles, CA
Beasley, Stacy Williamson ... Houston, TX
Beasley, Stephen B. ... Shreveport, LA
Beasley, Steven C. ... Des Moines, IA
Beasley, Susan E. ... Columbia, MD

Beasley, T. Tarry, II ....Memphis, TN
Beasley, Tena Gaston ....Chicago, IL
Beasley, Teresa M. ....Cleveland, OH
Beasley, Thomas S. ....Beeville, TX
Beasley and Tims ....Dallas, TX
Beasley, Vicky L. ....Washington, DC
Beasley, W. Wallace ....Austin, TX
Beasley, Walter V. ....Chamblee, GA
Beasley, William, Jr. ....Mineola, NY
Beasley, William L., III ....Scotland Neck, NC
Beasley, William M. ....Tupelo, MS
Beasley, William R. ....Bingham Farms, MI
Beasley-Carlisle, Lois René ....Birmingham, AL
Beaslin, John C., (P.C.) ....Vernal, UT
Beason, Candace Joan ....Los Angeles, CA
Beason, Curtis E. ....Davenport, IA
Beason, Eddie ....Russellville, AL
Beason, Elizabeth Anne ....Huntsville, AL
Beason, Elizabeth Lopes ....
Department of Labor, GV
Beason, George Milton, Jr. ....Huntsville, AL
Beason, Joseph D. ....Long Beach, CA
Beason, Michael A. ....Indianapolis, IN
Beason, Robert A. ....Durham, NC
Beason, Ryan A. ....Houston, TX
Nacogdoches, TX
Beason, Thomas M. ....Tallahassee, FL
Beason, Timothy Bryan ....Alexandria, VA
Beason, W. Douglas ....Tallahassee, FL
Beastrom, Timothy A. ....Minneapolis, MN
Beat, Kenneth S. ....Dallas, TX
Beathard & Beathard ....London, OH
Beathard, Maurice E. ....London, OH
Beathard, Steven P. ....London, OH
Beatie and Osborn LLP ....New York, NY
Beatie, Russel H., Jr. ....New York, NY
Beatley, Chris ....Alexandria, VA
Beatley, James R., Jr. ....Columbus, OH
Beatley, M. Kathleen ....New York, NY
Beatley, Patricia G.
Department of Housing and Urban Development,
Office of General Counsel, GV
Beatman, Lillian E. P. ....Kensington, CT
Beatman, Matthew K. ....Bridgeport, CT
Beato, Andrew Michael ....Washington, DC
Beato, Donna M. ....New York, NY
Beaton, Brenda Ann ....Cambridge, MA
Beaton, Brigette J. ....Washington, DC
Beaton, Christina Neslund
Englewood, CO
Beaton, Donald B. ....Marine City, MI
Beaton, Glenn K. ....Denver, CO
Beaton, H. Daniel, Jr. ....Lansing, MI
Beaton & Hart, P.C. ....Virginia Beach, VA
Beaton, James D., Jr. ....Mason, OH
Beaton, Jeffrey J. ....Virginia Beach, VA
Beaton, John B. ....Virginia Beach, VA
Beaton, Joseph G., Jr. ....Minneapolis, MN
Beaton, Julie R. ....Irvine, CA
Beaton, Kevin J. ....Boise, ID
Beaton, Neal N. ....New York, NY
Beaton, Peter ....West Nyack, NY
Beaton, Robert Paul ....Marine City, MI
Beaton, Roy H., Jr. ....Evergreen, CO
Beaton, Stephen J. ....Orange, CA
Beaton, Timothy J. ....Boulder, CO
Beaton, Timothy J. ....Fargo, ND
Beatrice, Mark A. ....Youngstown, OH
Beatrice, Michael R. ....Hartsdale, NY
Beatt, Bruce H. ....Windsor Locks, CT
Beattey, James L. ....Indianapolis, IN
Beattie, Amy S. ....Des Moines, IA
Beattie, Bret R. ....Los Angeles, CA
Beattie, Brian F. ....Glenwood, IA
Beattie, C. Robert, III ....Minneapolis, MN
Beattie & Chadwick ....Glenwood Springs, CO
Beattie, Chester Sanford, Jr. ....Austin, TX
Beattie, Chester V., III ....Pittsburgh, PA
Beattie, Donald G. ....Pleasant Hill, IA
Beattie, Douglas B. ....Orlando, FL
Beattie, Ellen M. ....Urbana, IL
Beattie, Franklin D. ....Aiken, SC
Beattie, Franklin D., P.A. ....Aiken, SC
Beattie, Gregory L. ....Oakland, CA
Beattie, Ingrid A. ....Boston, MA
Beattie, James M., Jr. ....Loves Park, IL
Beattie, James R. ....Montvale, NJ
Beattie, Jay W. ....Portland, OR
Beattie, John R. ....Minneapolis, MN
Beattie, Lauralyn Elizabeth ....Memphis, TN
Beattie Law Firm, P.C. ....Pleasant Hill, IA
Beattie, Lisa C. ....Washington, DC
Beattie, Lynn F. ....Baltimore, MD
Beattie, Mary Beth ....Rockville, MD
Beattie, Michael Jackson ....Alexandria, VA
Beattie & Murray ....Brielle, NJ
Beattie, Nancy L. ....San Diego, CA
Beattie, Nina M. ....New York, NY
Beattie Padovano, LLC ....Hackensack, NJ
Montvale, NJ
Beattie, Patricia A. ....
Department of Labor, GV
Beattie, Paul H. ....Chicago, IL
Beattie, Paul J. ....Ashland, MA
Beattie, Paula V. ....Providence, RI
Beattie, Richard I. ....New York, NY
Beattie, Robert J. ....Denver, CO
Beattie, Robert T., Jr. ....Silverdale, WA
Beattie, Robert W. ....Brielle, NJ
Beattie, Robin L., Law Offices of
Englewood, CO
Beattie Russell, Inc., P.S. ....Silverdale, WA
Beattie, Samuel W. ....West Chester, PA
Beattie, Scott G. ....Stockton, CA
Beattie, Steven M. ....Glenwood Springs, CO
Beattie, Thomas H. ....Auburn, CA
Beatty & Associates ....Ontario, CA

Beatty, Bryan Elliot ....Raleigh, NC
Beatty, Burton P. ....Boca Raton, FL
Beatty, Charles H. ....Kearney, NE
Beatty, Charles H. M., Jr. ....Silver Spring, MD
Beatty, Conny Davinroy ....St. Louis, MO
Beatty, Cramp, Kauffman & Lincke
Media, PA
Beatty, Dan ....San Carlos, CA
Beatty, David D. ....Raleigh, NC
Beatty, David F. ....Sacramento, CA
Beatty, David L. ....Lewisville, AR
Beatty, Dennis E. ....Marion, IA
Beatty, Donald C. ....Long Grove, IL
Beatty, Dora L. ....Hialeah, FL
Beatty, Edward F., Jr. ....Philadelphia, PA
Beatty, Eric P. ....Ontario, CA
Beatty, Eugene A. ....Birmingham, AL
Beatty, Evan J. ....St. Louis, MO
Beatty, Francesca Bernhardt
St. Petersburg, FL
Beatty, Gary D. ....Tallahassee, FL
Beatty, George W. ....Washington, DC
Beatty, Gresham & Colerick, LLP
Colorado Springs, CO
Beatty, H. Edward ....Cedar Rapids, IA
Beatty, Haradon ....Denver, CO
Beatty, Harry Clark ....New York, NY
Beatty, Heather C. ....Los Angeles, CA
Beatty, Holly Christine ....Troy, MI
Beatty, J. Guy, Jr. ....Atlanta, GA
Chattanooga, TN
Beatty, J. Robert ....Dallas, TX
Beatty, Jacquelyn A. ....Seattle, WA
Beatty, James D. ....Fort Collins, CO
Beatty, James D. ....West Des Moines, IA
Beatty, James D., P.C. ....Fort Collins, CO
Beatty, James F. ....Indianapolis, IN
Beatty, James W. ....Indianapolis, IN
Beatty, John C. ....Fort Worth, TX
Beatty, John F. ....New York, NY
Beatty, John R. ....Aspen, CO
Beatty, John R. A. ....Wilmington, NC
Beatty, John W. ....Cincinnati, OH
Beatty, John W. ....Erie, PA
Beatty, Joseph R. ....Greensboro, NC
Beatty, Kenneth M. ....Fairlawn, OH
Beatty, Kevin L. ....Duluth, MN
Beatty, Kimberly A. ....Helena, MT
Beatty, Kirk D. ....Newport Beach, CA
Beatty, Krista Kearns ....Blue Bell, PA
Beatty, L. Douglas ....Colorado Springs, CO
Beatty, Lewis B., Jr. ....Media, PA
Beatty, Marion L. ....Decorah, IA
Beatty, Mark D. ....Fort Worth, TX
Beatty, Mark R. ....Seattle, WA
Beatty, Matthew R. ....Austin, TX
Beatty, Michael L. ....Denver, CO
Beatty, Michael L., P.C. & Associates
Denver, CO
Beatty, Nancy A. ....New Haven, CT
Beatty, Nora Blair Burgess ....Wallingford, PA
Beatty, Otto, III ....Columbus, OH
Beatty, Paul F. ....Boston, MA
Beatty, Paul S. ....Long Branch, NJ
Beatty, R. Patrick ....Stuart, FL
Beatty, Rex B. ....San Diego, CA
Beatty, Richard H. ....Cleveland, OH
Beatty, Richard J. ....Guilford, CT
Beatty, Richard L. ....Shelby, MT
Beatty, Richard L. ....Shelby, MT
Beatty, Richard S. ....Washington, DC
Beatty, Richd. H. ....Des Moines, IA
Beatty, Robert G. ....Miami, FL
Beatty, Robert H., Jr.
Federal Mine Safety and Health Review Commission,
Office of the Commissioners, GV
Beatty, Samuel Alston ....Tuscaloosa, AL
Beatty, Samuel T. ....Waterloo, IA
Beatty, Sean D. ....Long Beach, CA
Beatty, Sean P. ....San Francisco, CA
Beatty, Steven G., Law Offices of ....Flint, MI
Beatty, Thomas D. ....Las Vegas, NV
Beatty, Thomas G. ....Walnut Creek, CA
Beatty, Vicki L. ....Pittsburgh, PA
Beatty, William G. ....Chicago, IL
Beatty, William H. ....Spokane, WA
Beatty, William L. ....East St. Louis, IL
Beatty, William S. ....Edwardsville, IL
Beatty-Walters, Robert H. ....Portland, OR
Beatus, Brian J. ....Palo Alto, CA
Beatus, Bruce A. ....Chicago, IL
Beatus, Laurie P. ....New York, NY
Beaty, Albert B. ....Eden Prairie, MN
Beaty, Carolyne S. ....Chattanooga, TN
Beaty, Charles H. ....Gallatin, TN
Beaty, Daniel H. ....Albany, NY
Beaty, Dennis M. ....Sacramento, CA
Beaty, Douglas R. ....Memphis, TN
Beaty, Draeger & Locke, P.C.
Anchorage, AK
Beaty, Dyann W. ....Tampa, FL
Beaty, Elizabeth W.
Federal Communications Commission,
Office of Legislative and Intergovernmental Affairs, GV
Beaty, Geoffrey A. ....Oakland, CA
Beaty, James A., Jr. ....Winston-Salem, NC
Beaty, Jennifer L. ....Milwaukee, WI
Beaty, John B. ....Washington, DC
Beaty, Kyle B. ....Irving, TX
Beaty, Louis A. ....Houston, TX
Beaty, M. Stephanie ....New Brunswick, NJ
Beaty, Mary Ann ....Dallas, TX
Beaty, Patrick T. ....Harrisburg, PA
Beaty, Robert E., III ....Bellingham, WA
Beaty, Robert T. ....Oneida, TN
Beaty, Roger H. ....Anchorage, AK

Beaty, Rufus F. ....Charlotte, NC
Beaty, Scarlett A. ....Knoxville, TN
Beaty, Shari Suzuki ....Upper Marlboro, MD
Beaty, William E. ....Venice, FL
Beaty, Wilma E. ....Rochester, NY
Beaty-Gullage, Michelle A. ....Metairie, LA
New Orleans, LA
Beau, John F. ....La Habra Heights, CA
Beaube, Elizabeth G. ....Birmingham, AL
Beaubein, Andrea Kemp ....Los Angeles, CA
Beaubien, James P. ....Los Angeles, CA
Beaubien, Mark H., Jr. ....Barrington Hills, IL
Beaubien, Mark J. ....Chicago, IL
Beauchaine, Amy L. ....Englewood, CO
Beauchamp & Associates, L.L.C.
Albany, GA
Beauchamp and Beauchamp ....Miami, OK
Beauchamp & Beauchamp, Law Offices of
Chiefland, FL
Beauchamp, Bobb A., III ....Chicago, IL
Beauchamp, Craig J. ....Albuquerque, NM
Beauchamp, Cynthia L. ....Detroit, MI
Beauchamp, David G. ....Phoenix, AZ
Beauchamp, Dianne K. ....Salisbury, MD
Beauchamp, Douglas C. ....Phoenix, AZ
Beauchamp, E. William ....Notre Dame, IN
Beauchamp, Edward E. ....Washington, DC
Beauchamp, Emmette W. ....Houston, TX
Beauchamp, Gary F. ....The Woodlands, TX
Beauchamp, Gary J. ....La Place, LA
Beauchamp, Geoffrey L. ....Blue Bell, PA
Beauchamp, Glenn ....Miami, OK
Beauchamp, Gregory V., (P.A.)
Chiefland, FL
Beauchamp, J. Frank, III
Deerfield Beach, FL
Stuart, FL
Beauchamp, J. Patrick ....New Orleans, LA
Beauchamp, James H. ....Tulsa, OK
Beauchamp, James H., P.C. ....Tulsa, OK
Beauchamp, John Henry "Buck"
Albany, GA
Beauchamp, John R. ....Escanaba, MI
Beauchamp, John S. ....San Antonio, TX
Beauchamp, Kelly, Whipple, Zick & Keyes, P.L.L.C. ....Port Huron, MI
Beauchamp, Kelly, Whipple, Zick & Keyes P.L.L.C. ....Sandusky, MI
Beauchamp, L. Keith ....Phoenix, AZ
Beauchamp, Lawrence A., Jr.
San Antonio, TX
Beauchamp, Melvin L. ....Carson City, NV
Beauchamp, Mynette D.
Newport Beach, CA
Beauchamp, Norman D. ....Port Huron, MI
Beauchamp, R. Luther ....Chiefland, FL
Beauchamp, Richard A. ....Fort Lauderdale, FL
Beauchamp, Robert B.
Newport Beach, CA
Beauchamp, Robert M. ....Albany, GA
Beauchamp, Robert S. ....Atlanta, GA
Beauchamp, Tom L., Jr. ....Dallas, TX
Beauchamp, Tracy H. ....Birmingham, AL
Beauchamp, Tracy Staidl ....Chicago, IL
Beauchamp, W.O. (Brett), III ....Chiefland, FL
Beauchamp, Woodrow O., Jr. ....Bronson, FL
Beauchemin, Joseph A. ....West Hartford, CT
Beauchemin, Keith J. ....Farmington Hills, MI
Beauchemin, Philip E. ....Lansdowne, PA
Beauchemin, Richard R. ....Baltimore, MD
Beauchene, Gloria S. ....Atlanta, GA
Beauchene, Mark A. ....Fargo, ND
Beauchesne, Diane L.
West Palm Beach, FL
Beauchesne, Laura Rice ....New York, NY
Beauchesne, M. Elaine ....Hampton, NH
Beauchesne, Philip T. ....Boston, MA
Beauchesne, Robert Donald ....Lewiston, ME
Beauchesne, Roger M. ....Modesto, CA
Beauclair & Cook ....Bismarck, ND
Beauclair, Leo J. ....Bismarck, ND
Beaudet, David R. ....Los Angeles, CA
Beaudet, Ellen J. ....San Jose, CA
Beaudet, Geo. A. ....Woonsocket, RI
Beaudet, Teresa A. ....Los Angeles, CA
Beaudet, Thomas J. ....Palmdale, CA
Beaudette, Daniel Raymond
Belchertown, MA
Beaudette, Edward G. ....Anaconda, MT
Beaudette, Jesse B. ....Butte, MT
Beaudikofer, Eric ....El Centro, CA
Beaudin, Bruce D. ....Washington, DC
Beaudin, Kelly Anne ....Philadelphia, PA
Beaudine, Michael J. ....Orlando, FL
Beaudoen, Russell R. ....Birmingham, MI
Beaudoin, Cariann E. ....Chicago, IL
Beaudoin, David D. ....Omaha, NE
Beaudoin, Denise George ....Dedham, MA
Beaudoin, Roland ....Portland, ME
Beaudoin, Stephen M.
King Of Prussia, PA
Beaudoin, Susan E. ....Albany, NY
Beaudoin, Thomas A. ....Boston, MA
Beaudoin, Wayne E. ....Los Angeles, CA
Beaudouin, Mark T. ....Dedham, MA
Beaudreau, Albert J. ....Orland Park, IL
Beaudreau, Robert H. ....Boston, MA
Beaudreau, Tommy P. ....Washington, DC
Beaudreault, Lindi L.
Securities and Exchange Commission,
Division of Enforcement, GV
Beaudrot, Beverly Hall ....Atlanta, GA
Beaudrot, Charles R., Jr. ....Atlanta, GA
Beaudry, Andrea T. ....Boston, MA
Beaudry Bentler & Associates, LLP
Irvine, CA
Santa Monica, CA
Beaudry, Catherine M. ....Puyallup, WA

Beaudry, David D. ....Saginaw, MI
Beaudry, Donald A. ....Springfield, MA
Beaudry, G. Ward, (P.C.) ....Dallas, TX
Beaudry, Gary M. ....Williston, ND
Beaudry Law Office ....Williston, ND
Beaudry, Lee J. ....Tucson, AZ
Beaudry & Manson, P.C. ....Springfield, MA
Beaudry, Richard P. ....Bellevue, WA
Beaudry, Robert V. ....Santa Monica, CA
Beaudry, Terry G. ....Joliet, IL
Beauduy, John A. ....Dallas, TX
Beaufait, Christopher B. ....Omaha, NE
Beaufait, Mark S. ....Seattle, WA
Beaufait, Teresa A. ....Omaha, NE
Beaufort, Galen P. ....Kansas City, MO
Beaugard, Elizabeth C. ....Coatesville, PA
Beaulaurier, James M., Law Office of
Seattle, WA
Beaulier, Maury D. ....Bloomington, MN
Beaulieu, Carol K. ....Fridley, MN
Beaulieu, Donna J. ....Montevallo, AL
Beaulieu, Eugene W. ....Bangor, ME
Beaulieu, Gerard J. ....New Bedford, MA
Beaulieu, Giovanna M. ....Tarrytown, NY
Beaulieu, Lara Aileen ....Burlington, KY
Beaulieu, Lisa Anne ....Boston, MA
Beaulieu, Paul R. ....Boston, MA
Beaulieu, Robert N. ....Orlando, FL
Beaulieu, Walter J. ....Seagoville, TX
Beauman, Bryan H. ....Lexington, KY
Beaumier, Albert J. ....Springfield, MA
Beaumier, Robert G., Jr. ....Spokane, WA
Beaumont, Anne E. ....Armonk, NY
Beaumont, Garrett ....San Diego, CA
Beaumont, John H. ....Albany, NY
Beaumont, Judi E. ....Tulsa, OK
Beaumont, Lynn Allen ....Doylestown, OH
Rittman, OH
Beaumont, Meaghan McGrath
Washington, DC
Beaumont, Philip D. ....Washington, DC
New York, NY
Beaumont, Susan Linehan
Framingham, MA
Beaumont, Thomas M.
Department of Agriculture,
Office of Civil Rights Enforcement, GV
Beaumont, William E. ....Arlington, VA
Beaumont, William F. ....Alliance, OH
Beaupain, Dean A. ....Millinocket, ME
Beaupied, Aleta M. ....San Francisco, CA
Beaupre, Dean A. ....Oakland, CA
Beaupre, Jack R. ....Bourbonnais, IL
Beaupre, Laurier W. ....Boston, MA
Beauregard, André M. ....Rehoboth Beach, DE
Beauregard & Burke ....New Bedford, MA
Beauregard, George N. ....Holyoke, MA
Beauregard, Mark A. ....Holyoke, MA
Beauregard, Michael R. ....Schaumburg, IL
Beauregard, Patricia R. ....New Haven, CT
Beauregard, Philip H. M. ....Washington, DC
Beauregard, Philip N. ....New Bedford, MA
Beauregard, Robert L. ....Washington, DC
Beauregard, Rosemary Betts
Georgetown, DE
Beauregard, Stephanie A. ....Cincinnati, OH
Beauregard, Todd D. ....Lowell, MA
Beaurivage, Anne G. ....Wichita, KS
Beausang, Michael F., Jr.
King Of Prussia, PA
Beausay, T. Jeffery ....Columbus, OH
Beausejour, Bruce P. ....Boston, MA
Beausey, Karen D. ....San Francisco, CA
Beaushaw, Danetta Lyn ....Houston, TX
Beausoleil, James L. ....Philadelphia, PA
Beausoleil, Roxanne ....Sparks, MD
Beausoleil, William J. ....New York, NY
Beautyman Associates, P.C.
Flourtown, PA
Philadelphia, PA
Beautyman, Michael J. ....Flourtown, PA
Beauvais, David J. ....Berkeley, CA
Beauvais, J. Robert ....Ruidoso, NM
Beauvais, Lisa M. ....West Springfield, MA
Beauvais, Philip H., III ....Flint, MI
Beauvais, Steven L. ....Savannah, GA
Beauzay, Victor H. ....San Jose, CA
Beavan, Bonnie J. ....Baltimore, MD
Beaven, Alan Anthony ....San Francisco, CA
Beaver, Becky ....Austin, TX
Beaver, Chester E. ....Austin, TX
Beaver, Clarance E. ....Department of Labor,
Pension and Welfare Benefits, GV
Beaver, Clayton J., Jr. ....Glendale, CA
Beaver, Clayton J., Jr., Law Offices of
Glendale, CA
Beaver, Clinton D. ....Cheyenne, WY
Beaver, Daniel P. ....San Francisco, CA
Beaver, David A. ....Albemarle, NC
Beaver, David H. ....Cincinnati, OH
Beaver, David N. ....Sacramento, CA
Beaver, David W. ....De Soto, KS
Beaver, Donald W. ....Lakewood, CO
Beaver, Evelyn M. ....Orangevale, CA
Beaver, Fred E. ....Des Moines, IA
Beaver, Gary L. ....Greensboro, NC
Beaver, Gary L. ....Wayne, PA
Beaver, H. Dennis ....Bakersfield, CA
Beaver, H. Gerald ....Fayetteville, NC
Beaver Holt Richardson Sternlicht Burge & Glazier, P.A. ....Fayetteville, NC
Beaver, James L. ....Auburn, CA
Beaver, James R. ....Rensselaer, IN
Beaver, Jeffrey A. ....Seattle, WA
Beaver, Jerome M. ....Ottumwa, IA
Beaver, Joel D. ....Philadelphia, PA
Beaver, John A. ....Phoenix, AZ
Beaver, John A., Jr. ....Phoenix, AZ

Beck, Merritt M., III ... Centralia, MO
Beck, Michael & Beck, P.C.
Indianapolis, IN
Beck, Michael D. ... Indianapolis, IN
Beck, Michael D., (A.P.C.) ... New York, NY
Beck, Michael H. ... Seattle, WA
Beck, Michael J. ...
Judicial Panel On Multidistrict Litigation, GV
Beck, Monte ... Bozeman, MT
Beck, Monty C. ... Franklin, NC
Beck, Morris S. ... Beaumont, TX
Beck, Nancy J. ... Phoenix, AZ
Beck, Nancy M. ... Chicago, IL
Beck, Nathan ... Jersey City, NJ
Beck, Neil ... Houston, TX
Beck, Noel F. ... Bloomfield Hills, MI
Beck, Norman K. ... Chicago, IL
Beck, Owen & Murray ... Griffin, GA
Beck, Pamela E. ... Gallatin, TN
Beck, Pamela P. ... Kearney, NE
Beck, Patricia E. ... Fair Oaks, CA
Beck, Paul A. ... Los Angeles, CA
Beck, Paul A., & Associates
Pittsburgh, PA
Beck, Paul E., Jr. ... Philadelphia, PA
Beck, Paul J. ... Los Angeles, CA
Beck, Paula K. ... Minneapolis, MN
Beck, Peter K. ... Minneapolis, MN
Beck, Peter O. ... Royal Oak, MI
Beck, Philip D. ... New York, NY
Beck, Philip E. ... Atlanta, GA
Beck, Philip S. ... Denver, CO
Chicago, IL
Beck, Phyllis M., (Mrs.) ... Creighton, NE
Beck, Phyllis W. ... Bala Cynwyd, PA
Beck, R. Jerry ... Kingsport, TN
Beck, R. Stewart ... Newark, OH
Beck, Ralph S. ... Batavia, IL
Beck, Ray M. ... Salt Lake City, UT
Beck, Raymond D. ... Cincinnati, OH
Beck, Raymond E., Sr. ... Westminster, MD
Beck, Raymond M. ... Bangor, ME
Beck, Reagan ... Washington, DC
Beck, Redden & Secrest ... Houston, TX
Beck, Richard Alfred ... Evanston, IL
Beck, Richard C. E. ... New York, NY
Beck, Richard E. ... Freehold, NJ
Beck, Richard M. ... Wilmington, DE
Philadelphia, PA
Beck, Richard M. ... Wilmington, DE
Beck, Richard P. ... Wilmington, DE
Beck, Robert C. ... Kalamazoo, MI
Beck, Robert C. ... Hopkins, MN
Beck, Robert C. ... Cherry Hill, NJ
Beck, Robert Christopher ... Wheaton, IL
Beck, Robert D. ... Fort Payne, AL
Beck, Robert D. ... Washington, PA
Beck, Robert E. ... Carbondale, IL
Beck, Robert G. ... Belleville, NJ
Beck, Robert H. ... White Plains, NY
Beck, Robert I. ... Houston, TX
Beck, Robert K. ... Milwaukee, WI
Beck, Robert L. ... Rochester, NY
Beck, Robert L., Jr. ... Alexandria, LA
Beck, Robert M. ... Norman, OK
Beck, Robert M., Jr. ... Lexington, KY
Beck, Robert O. ... Clayton, NM
Beck, Robert P. ... Kent, OH
Beck, Robert S. ... Laguna Hills, CA
Beck, Robert W. ... Torrance, CA
Beck, Rodney J. ... Gladstone, OR
Beck, Rodney J., P.C. ... Gladstone, OR
Beck, Roger Q ... Houston, TX
Beck, Rolla Earl, III ... Helena, AL
Beck, Ronald ... Long Beach, CA
Beck, Rudy D. ... St. Charles, MO
Beck, Russell ... Boston, MA
Beck, S. Garrett ... Petoskey, MI
Beck, Sandra L. ... Santa Rosa, CA
Beck, Sanford E. ... Oak Ridge, NJ
Beck, Scott H. ... Denver, CO
Beck, Sherilyn K. ... Minneapolis, MN
Beck, Sidney F., Jr. ... Olive Branch, MS
Beck, Stanley G. ... Monroeville, PA
Beck, Stanley H. ... Hallandale Beach, FL
Beck, Stanton Phillip ... Seattle, WA
Beck, Stephanie G. ... Binghamton, NY
Beck, Stephen A. ... Washington, DC
Beck, Stephen R. ... Modesto, CA
Beck, Steven G. ... Arkadelphia, AR
Beck, Steven N. ... Minneapolis, MN
Beck, Steven R. ... Denver, CO
Beck, Stuart E. ... Philadelphia, PA
Beck, Stuart E., P.C. ... Philadelphia, PA
Beck, Sue A. ... Erie, PA
Beck, Susana S. ... Department of Defense,
Defense Legal Services Agency, GV
Beck, T. Phillips ... Parsippany, NJ
Beck & Taylor ... Honolulu, HI
Beck, Teresa A. ... Jackson, MS
Beck, Teresa M. ... San Diego, CA
Beck, Terry E. ... Topeka, KS
Beck, Thelton D. ... Prescott, AZ
Beck, Thomas A. ... Wilmington, DE
Beck, Thomas A. ... Mount Vernon, NY
Beck, Thomas Basil ... San Antonio, TX
Beck, Thomas E. ... Los Angeles, CA
Beck, Thomas H. ... New York, NY
Beck, Thomas J. ... Detroit, MI
Beck, Thomas M. ... Washington, DC
Beck, Thomas P. ... Pasadena, CA
Beck Tiemeyer & Zerr, P.C.
St. Charles, MO
Beck, Todd A. ... Marlton, NJ
Beck & Tysver ... Hopkins, MN
Beck, Valerie S. ... Chicago, IL
Beck, Vaughn P. ... Ipswich, SD
Beck, Vincent J. ... Centereach, NY
Beck, W. Ralph ... Bowling Green, KY
Beck, Walter L. ... Brooklyn, NY
Beck, Walter P. ... Cincinnati, OH
Beck, Warren P. ... San Diego, CA
Beck, Wendy Lynn ... Fort Lauderdale, FL
Beck, Werner Peter ... Charleston, SC
Beck, William E., II ... Kokomo, IN
Beck, William G. ... Kansas City, MO
Beck, William G. ... Sioux Falls, SD
Beck, William H., Jr. ... New Orleans, LA
Beck, William J., III ... Clearwater, FL
Beck, William M., Jr. ... Fort Payne, AL
Beck, William P. ... Tallahassee, FL
Beck, William R. ... Nichols, SC
Beck, Winnie B. ... Dallas, TX
Becka, Daniel J. ... Boca Raton, FL
Beckcom, Curt ... Austin, TX
Beckcom, Doneane E. ... Beaumont, TX
Beck-Dudley, Caryn Lee ... Logan, UT
Beckel, Allan J. ... Cold Spring, MN
Beckel, Carl L. ... Ventura, CA
Beckel, Daniel D. ... Chicago, IL
Beckel, Nadine T. ... Kaneohe, HI
Keizer, OR
Beckelman, Marsha Merrill
Cedar Rapids, IA
Beckelman, Steven A. ... Newark, NJ
Beckeman, Jenifer C. ... Farmington Hills, MI
Beckemeier, August E. ... St. Louis, MO
Beckemeier, G. N., Jr. ... St. Louis, MO
Beckemeier, R. Lynn ... St. Louis, MO
Beckenhauer, Charles D. ... Waco, TX
Beckenhauer, Kenneth H. ... West Point, NE
Beckenhauer, Paul W. ... West Point, NE
Beckenstein, Lawrence A. ... Garden City, NY
Becker, Adam H. ... Wakefield, MA
Becker, Alan C. ... Woodbury, NY
Becker, Alan I. ... Chicago, IL
Becker, Alan S. ... Clearwater, FL
Fort Lauderdale, FL
Fort Myers, FL
Maitland, FL
Miami, FL
Naples, FL
St. Petersburg, FL
Sarasota, FL
West Palm Beach, FL
Becker, Alan W. ... Indianapolis, IN
Becker, Alfred ... Las Vegas, NV
Becker, Alfred G. ... Glenview, IL
Becker, Alice J. ... Bellevue, WA
Becker, Alison L. ... Tampa, FL
Becker, Alvin G. ... Springfield, IL
Becker, Alvin R. ... Chicago, IL
Becker, Amy Christine ... Bloomington, MN
Becker, Andrea J. ... Nashville, TN
Becker, Andrew E. ... Middletown, CT
Becker, Andrew I. ... Virginia Beach, VA
Becker, Andrew Nathan ... Port Orchard, WA
Becker, Ann C. ... Milwaukee, WI
Becker, Anne C. ... Minneapolis, MN
Becker, Arnold ... Nanuet, NY
Becker, Arthur J., Jr. ... York, PA
Becker, Arthur W., 3rd ... Las Vegas, NV
Becker, Arto C. ... Los Angeles, CA
Becker & Associates, P.C. ... Granite City, IL
Becker, Avrohom ... New York, NY
Becker, Barbara J. ... Milwaukee, WI
Becker, Barbara L. ... New York, NY
Becker, Barry ... Phoenix, AZ
Becker, Barry, P.C. ... Phoenix, AZ
Becker, Bartley L. ... Los Angeles, CA
Becker & Becker ... Albany, NY
Becker & Becker, P.A. ... Wilmington, DE
Becker, Ben H. ... Millburn, NJ
Becker, Benton L., Law Offices of
Miami, FL
Becker, Beth S. ... Old Greenwich, CT
Becker, Bobbie F. ... Lansing, IL
Becker, Brad H. ... Tustin, CA
Becker, Brad R. ... New York, NY
Becker, Brandon ... Washington, DC
Becker, Brian L. ... Glendale, CA
Becker, Brian S. ... Hartford, CT
Becker, Bruce ... New York, NY
Becker, Bruce A. ... Glenview, IL
Becker, Bruce D. ... Chicago, IL
Becker, Bruce E. ... Sac City, IA
Becker, Bruce E. ... Livingston, MT
Becker, Bruce H. ... Atlanta, GA
Becker, Bruce O. ... Vestal, NY
Becker, Bruce R. ... Peoria, IL
Becker, Buddy J. ... Lakewood, CO
Becker, Carl A. ... Dallas, TX
Becker, Carl F., Jr. ... Stamford, NY
Becker, Carl G. ... Pontiac, MI
Becker, Carl H. ... Red Bud, IL
Becker, Carl H. ... Brooklyn, NY
Becker, Carl J. ... Indianapolis, IN
Becker, Carl W. ... St. Louis, MO
Becker, Caryn ... San Francisco, CA
Becker, Cecily A. ... Portland, OR
Becker, Charles A., Jr. ... Ridgewood, NJ
Becker, Charles C. ... Seattle, WA
Becker, Charles F. ... Des Moines, IA
Becker, Charles H. ... Minneapolis, MN
Becker, Charles H. ... Pittsburgh, PA
Becker, Charles L. ... Raleigh, NC
Becker, Cheryl L. ... North Chicago, IL
Becker, Christine L. ... Johnstown, NY
Becker, Christopher ... Steubenville, OH
Becker, Cindy L. ... Austin, TX
Becker, Claudia M. ... Jenkintown, PA
Becker, Craig A. ... Palo Alto, CA
Becker, Cynthia D. ... Walnut Creek, CA
Becker, Cynthia J. ... Atlanta, GA
Becker, Dana J. ... New York, NY
Becker, Daniel C. ... Roseland, NJ
Becker, Daniel D.
Hot Springs National Park, AR
Becker, Daniel F. ... Washington, DC
Becker, Daniel J. S.
Mendota Heights, MN
Becker, Daniel M. ... Palo Alto, CA
Becker, Daniel P. ... Reading, PA
Becker, Daniel S. ... New York, NY
Becker, Darby M.R. ... Washington, DC
Becker, David ... New York, NY
Becker, David A. ... Washington, DC
Becker, David C. ... Cameron Park, CA
Becker, David H. ... New York, NY
Becker, David J. ... Department of Justice,
Civil Rights Division, GV
Becker, David J. ... Madison, WI
Becker, David L. ... New York, NY
Becker, David M. ... Denver, CO
Becker, David M. ... Overland Park, KS
Becker, David M. ... St. Louis, MO
Becker, David S. ... Bradenton, FL
Becker, Dean H. ... West Valley City, UT
Becker, Deborah Swinford ... New York, NY
Becker, Dennis A. ... Cincinnati, OH
Becker, Dennis C. ... Fort Wayne, IN
Becker, Diane R. ... Raleigh, NC
Becker, Donald D. ... Albuquerque, NM
Becker, Donald D., J.D., P.A., Law Offices of
Albuquerque, NM
Becker, Donald J. ... Vienna, VA
Becker, Donald Lee ... Belmont, MA
Becker, Donald M. ... Chicago, IL
Becker, Donald R. ... Newburgh, NY
Becker, Donald R. ... Linton, ND
Becker, Donald W. ... New York, NY
Becker, Donald W. ... Madison, WI
Becker, Donna C. ... Washington, DC
Becker, Donna E. ... Chicago, IL
Becker, Donna E. ... Frederick, MD
Becker, Donna L. ... Santa Cruz, CA
Becker, Doreen H. ... Dover, DE
Wilmington, DE
Becker, Douglas J. ... Denver, CO
Becker, Douglas M. ... Austin, TX
Becker, Douglas P. ... Seattle, WA
Becker, Douglas W. ... Louisville, KY
Becker, Douglas W. ... San Antonio, TX
Becker, E. David ... Hawthorne, NJ
Becker, Eddie B. ... Dallas, TX
Becker, Edw. R. ... Philadelphia, PA
Becker, Edward A. ... San Jose, CA
Becker, Edward A. ... Concord, MA
Becker, Edward G. ... Irvine, CA
Becker, Edward R. ... Lansing, MI
Becker, Eileen Reynolds ... New Haven, CT
Becker, Eldon H. ... Havana, IL
Petersburg, IL
Becker, Elizabeth Stockman
Washington, DC
Becker, Ellen D. Bennett ... Albany, NY
Becker, Ellen Hoffman ... Jacksonville, FL
Becker, Ellen Shanahan ... Buffalo, NY
Becker, Ellie B. ... New York, NY
Becker, Emanuel ... Mountain View, CA
Becker, Eric F. ... Newport Beach, CA
Becker, Eric L. ... Beaver Dam, WI
Becker, Erick J. ... Santa Ana, CA
Becker, Eugene B. ... Flint, MI
Becker, Eugene J. ... Chicago, IL
Becker, Evelyn ... Washington, DC
Becker, F. H. ... Des Moines, IA
Becker & Fortune LLP ... Norcross, GA
Becker, Frances R. ... Rapid City, SD
Becker, Frank G. ... Southfield, MI
Becker, Frank J. ... Louisville, KY
Becker, Frank T. ... Lexington, KY
Becker, Fred M. ... Calumet City, IL
Becker, Fred R. ... Boston, MA
Becker, Frederic K. ... Woodbridge, NJ
Becker, Frederick R. ... Houston, TX
Becker, Frederick W. ... Silver Spring, MD
Becker, Fredrick A. ... New York, NY
Becker, French & DeMatthew ... Racine, WI
Becker, Gail D. ... Hauppauge, NY
Becker, Gary E. ... Louisville, KY
Becker, Gary E. ... Cincinnati, OH
Becker, Gary G., (P.C.) ... New York, NY
Becker, Gary M. ... Hartford, CT
Becker, Gary W. ... Minneapolis, MN
Becker, George ... New York, NY
Becker, George W. ... New Orleans, LA
Becker, Georgeann ... Denver, CO
Becker, Gerald A. ... Berkeley, CA
Becker & Gibson, P.L.C.
Sterling Heights, MI
Becker, Glenn Ian ... Chicago, IL
Becker, Glynn, Melamed & Muffly LLP
New York, NY
Becker, Gordon A. ... Troy, MI
Becker, Gordon P. ... Mayfield Heights, OH
Becker, Gregory A. ... Granite City, IL
Becker, Gregory Ian ... Los Angeles, CA
Becker & Gurian ... Highland Park, IL
Becker, Hall & Flaum ... Los Angeles, CA
Newport Beach, CA
Becker, Henry P. ... Schaumburg, IL
Becker, Heywood E. ... Frenchtown, NJ
Becker & Hickey, S.C. ... Milwaukee, WI
Becker, Hicks, Irving & Hadeed, P.C.
Washington, DC
Springfield, VA
Becker, Hildreth & Gossard, P.A.
Coffeyville, KS
Becker, Howard A. ... Atlanta, GA
Becker, Howard A. ... New York, NY
Becker, Howard A., P.C. ... Atlanta, GA
Becker, Howard Benson ... Rolla, MO
Becker, Howard Mark ... San Luis Obispo, CA
Santa Maria, CA
Becker, Irvin ... Torrance, CA
Becker, Isabel L. ... New City, NY
Becker, Jack ... New York, NY
Becker, Jacqueline M. ...
Department of Energy, GV
Becker, James A., Jr. ... Jackson, MS
Becker, James C. ... Columbus, OH
Becker, James E. ... Salt Lake City, UT
Becker, James G. ... San Francisco, CA
Becker, James J. ... New York, NY
Becker, James M. ... Philadelphia, PA
Becker, James M., Jr. ... Mt. Pleasant, IA
Becker, James Pahl ... Rehoboth Beach, DE
Becker, James R. ... Sioux Falls, SD
Becker, James R. ... Falls Church, VA
Becker, James R., Jr. ... Memphis, TN
Becker, James W. ... Mercer Island, WA
Becker, James Y. ... Columbia, SC
Becker, Jane ... Santa Cruz, CA
Becker, Janice M. ... Coralville, IA
Becker, Jay Seth ... Middletown, NJ
Becker, Jeffrey A. ... Chicago, IL
Becker, Jeffrey H. ... New York, NY
Becker, Jeffrey J. ... Chicago, IL
Becker, Jeffrey M. ... Dallas, TX
Becker, Jeffrey R. ... Jacksonville, FL
Becker, Jeffry Stanton ... Phoenix, AZ
Becker, Jennifer A. ... San Francisco, CA
Becker, Jerome M. ... New York, NY
Becker, Jerrold L. ... Knoxville, TN
Becker, Joan M. ... Columbia, MD
Becker, Joanna Maxwell ... Washington, DC
Becker, John A. ... Racine, WI
Becker, John C. ... Del Mar, CA
Becker, John C. ... Camp Hill, PA
Becker, John F. ... Pittsburgh, PA
Becker, John H. ... Boston, MA
Becker, John L. ... Brookfield, WI
Becker, John R. ... Scottsdale, AZ
Becker, John R. ... Dubuque, IA
Becker, John W. ... Akron, OH
Becker, Jon D. ... Virginia Beach, VA
Becker, Jon D. ... Madison, WI
Becker, Jon S. (IBA) ... Thousand Oaks, CA
Becker, Jonathan ... Madison, WI
Becker, Jonathan C. ... Lawrence, KS
Becker, Jonathan C., P.A. ... Lawrence, KS
Becker, Jonathan E. ... Philadelphia, PA
Becker, Jonathan L. ... Mill Valley, CA
Becker, Jonathan S. ... New York, NY
Becker, Jonathan S. ... New York, NY
Becker, Jordan D. ... New York, NY
Becker, Jordan M. ... Sunnyvale, CA
Becker, Jos. H. & Norman ... Chicago, IL
Becker, Jos. P. ... Milwaukee, WI
Becker, Joseph D. ... New York, NY
Becker, Joseph D. ... La Crosse, WI
Becker, Joseph F. ... Wayne, NJ
Becker, Joseph J. ... St. Louis, MO
Becker, Joshua ... Phoenix, AZ
Becker, Joyce K. ... Stevenson, MD
Becker, Judith M. ... Norcross, GA
Becker, Judith M. ... Lake Success, NY
Becker, Julia Going ... Norristown, PA
Becker, Julie C. ... Washington, DC
Becker, Julie J. ... Minneapolis, MN
Becker & Kaplan LLC ... Chicago, IL
Becker, Karen McCabe ... Glendale, CA
Becker, Karl M. ... Hilton Head Island, SC
Becker, Katherine B. ... Milton, FL
Becker, Katherine L. ... Washington, DC
Becker, Kathleen C. ...
Department Of The Interior, GV
Becker, Kenneth B. ... New York, NY
Becker, Kenneth Don ... Haleiwa, HI
Becker, Kimberley Ste. Marie
Minneapolis, MN
Becker, Kurt ... Bellevue, WA
Becker, Larry A. ... Toledo, OH
Becker, Larry Beach ... San Francisco, CA
Becker, Larry E. ... Springfield, VA
Becker, Laura Gold ... West Hartford, CT
Becker, Lauren J. ... San Diego, CA
Becker, Lauren L. ... Atlanta, GA
Becker, Laurence P. ... Chicago, IL
Becker, Laurie A. ... Columbia, SC
Becker, Laurie J. ... New York, NY
Becker Law Office ... San Francisco, CA
Becker Law Office ... Mt. Pleasant, IA
Becker Law Office ... Lexington, KY
Louisville, KY
Becker, Lawrence E. ... Albany, NY
Becker, Lawrence F. ... Smithtown, NY
Becker, Lawrence G. ... San Francisco, CA
Becker, Lawrence G. ... Cincinnati, OH
Becker, Lawson E. ... Grand Rapids, MI
Becker, Leonard H. ... Washington, DC
Becker, Leslie ... Albuquerque, NM
Becker, Leslie ... Rio Rancho, NM
Becker, Leslie Anne ... Boston, MA
Becker, Lewis ... Villanova, PA
Becker, Lewis M. ... Palo Alto, CA
Becker, Linda ... Rye Brook, NY
Becker, Lisa R. Bouterse ... Kenosha, WI
Becker, Loftus E., Jr. ... Washington, DC
Becker, Lori Brooks ... Morehead City, NC
Becker, Louis A. ... Ellicott City, MD
Becker, Lucille J. ... Milford, CT
Becker, Mabel L. ... Dayton, OH
Becker, Madeline M. ... Boston, MA
Becker, Marc A. ... Los Angeles, CA
Becker, Marc J. ... New York, NY
Becker, Marcella Z. ... Syracuse, NY
Becker, Marianne ... Waukesha, WI
Becker, Mark B. ... Westfield, NJ
New York, NY

Becker, Mark D. ... Scottsdale, AZ
Becker, Mark D. ... Indianapolis, IN
Becker, Mark E. ... Tallahassee, FL
Becker, Mark J. ... St. Louis, MO
Becker, Mark L. ... Portland, OR
Becker, Mark S. ... San Jose, CA
Becker, Martin Alan ... Baltimore, MD
Becker, Martin L. ... Lynbrook, NY
Becker, Mary E. ... Chicago, IL
Becker, Mary Kay ... Seattle, WA
Becker, Mathis ... Sun City, AZ
Becker, Matthew J. ... Hartford, CT
Becker, Matthew P. ... Chicago, IL
Becker, Max J. ... Skokie, IL
Becker Meisel, LLC ... Millburn, NJ
Becker, Merritt S. ... Washington, DC
Becker, Michael A. ... Irvine, CA
Becker, Michael A. ... St. Louis, MO
Becker, Michael A. ... New York, NY
Becker, Michael A. ... Dallas, TX
Becker, Michael D. ... Cherry Hill, NJ
Philadelphia, PA
Becker, Michael F. ... Cleveland, OH
Becker, Michael L. ... Los Angeles, CA
Becker, Michael R. ... Stamford, CT
Becker, Michael R. ... Columbus, OH
Becker, Michael S. ... Washington, DC
Becker, Michael S. ... Helena, MT
Becker, Michael W. ... Springfield, IL
Becker, Millard M. ... Portland, OR
Becker, Millard W. H., Jr.
Mount Clemens, MI
Becker & Mishkind Co., L.P.A.
Cleveland, OH
Becker, Morrie N. ... Philadelphia, PA
Becker, Mortimer ... New York, NY
Becker, N. Mark, (P.A.) ... Jacksonville, FL
Becker, Nance F. ... San Francisco, CA
Becker, Nancy A. ... Las Vegas, NV
Becker, Nelson J. ... Logansport, IN
Becker, Norman ... Chicago, IL
Becker, Ornah R. ... Los Angeles, CA
Becker, Otto F. ... San Francisco, CA
Becker, Patricia A. ... Austin, TX
Becker, Paul ... Jersey City, NJ
Becker, Paul A. ... Prescott, AZ
Becker, Paul A. ... Middletown, OH
Becker, Paul L. ... Spring Valley, NY
Becker, Paul S. ... Kansas City, MO
Becker, Paula M. ... Chicago, IL
Becker, Perry J. ... Bowie, MD
Becker, Peter E. ... Bellmore, NY
Becker, Peter J. ... Costa Mesa, CA
Becker, Peter W. ... Milwaukee, WI
Becker, Phillip M. ... Gooding, ID
Becker & Poliakoff, P.A. ... Clearwater, FL
Fort Lauderdale, FL
Fort Myers, FL
Fort Walton Beach, FL
Maitland, FL
Miami, FL
Naples, FL
St. Petersburg, FL
Sarasota, FL
Tampa, FL
West Palm Beach, FL
Becker, Ranald ... Detroit, MI
Becker, Randall G. ... Coon Rapids, MN
Becker, Raymond L. ... Wilmington, DE
Becker, Rebecca M. ... Daytona Beach, FL
Becker, Rebecca M. ... Ormond Beach, FL
Becker, Reed, Tilton & Hastings
Cincinnati, OH
Becker, Regis W. ... Pittsburgh, PA
Becker, Reuben J. ... Mill Valley, CA
Becker, Reynold E. ... Schaumburg, IL
Becker, Richard A. ... Seattle, WA
Becker, Richard C. ... New York, NY
Becker, Richard D. ... Wilmington, DE
Becker, Richard K.A. ... McLean, VA
Becker, Richard L. ... Coffeyville, KS
Becker, Richard L. ... Overland Park, KS
Becker, Richard L. ... Lafayette, LA
Becker, Richard O. ... Glenview, IL
Becker, Richard S. ... Washington, DC
Becker, Richard T. ... West Bend, WI
Becker, Rita McGuire ... Muncie, IN
Becker, Robert A. ... New York, NY
Becker, Robert B. ... Peoria, IL
Becker, Robert C., Jr. ... Genoa, IL
Becker, Robert D. ... San Francisco, CA
Becker, Robert D. ... New York, NY
Becker, Robert D., (P.C.) ... New York, NY
Becker, Robert E. ... Belleville, IL
Becker, Robert E. ... Scarsdale, NY
Becker, Robert F. ... Cathedral City, CA
Becker, Robert G. ... San Francisco, CA
Becker, Robert H. ... Washington, DC
Becker, Robert J. ... Meridian, ID
Becker, Robert J. ... Chicago, IL
Becker, Robert J. ... Baltimore, MD
Becker, Robert J. ... Omaha, NE
Becker, Robert L. ... New York, NY
Becker, Robert L. ... Newark, OH
Becker, Robert L., Jr. ... Pittsburgh, PA
Becker, Robert M. ... Evansville, IN
Becker, Robert M. ... Roselle, NJ
Warren, NJ
Becker, Robert P., Jr. ... Woodbury, NJ
Becker, Robert S. ... Washington, DC
Becker, Robert W. ... St. Cloud, MN
Becker, Robert W. ... Albuquerque, NM
Becker, Robert W., & Associates
Tijeras, NM
Becker, Robin A. ... Baltimore, MD
Becker, Roderick W. ... Lenexa, KS
Becker, Roger P. ... Memphis, TN

Becker Ross Stone DeStefano & Klein
New York, NY
Becker, Rudolf B., III ... Bloomfield Hills, MI
Becker, Rudolph ... Milwaukee, WI
Becker & Runkle ... Cameron Park, CA
Becker, Russell R. ... Morganton, NC
Becker, Ruth ... Hewlett, NY
Becker, Ruth Linn ... Marathon, FL
Becker, Samuel H. ... Philadelphia, PA
Becker & Schapiro, P.C. ... Vestal, NY
Becker, Scott ... Chicago, IL
Becker, Scott A. ... Minneapolis, MN
Becker, Scott C. ... Buffalo, NY
Becker, Scott E. ... Chicago, IL
Becker, Scott E. ... Pleasantville, NJ
Becker, Scott E. ... Pittsburgh, PA
Becker, Scott M. ... Washington, DC
Becker, Sean M. ... Boston, MA
Becker & Silverman ... Lansing, IL
Becker, Sonja Ann ... Denver, CO
Becker, Stanley A. ... San Diego, CA
Becker, Stephan E. ... Washington, DC
Becker, Stephen A. ... Washington, DC
Becker, Stephen A. ... King Of Prussia, PA
Becker, Stephen C. ... San Francisco, CA
Becker, Stephen L. ... Lima, OH
Becker, Steven A. ... San Bernardino, CA
Becker, Steven A., A Professional Law Corporation ... San Bernardino, CA
Becker, Steven B. ... Kansas City, MO
Becker, Steven C. ... Milwaukee, WI
Becker, Steven H. ... Roseland, NJ
Becker, Steven H. ... New York, NY
Becker, Steven R. ... Washington, DC
Becker, Steven R. ... Hutchinson, KS
Becker, Steven R. ... New York, NY
Becker Stowe & Bieber LLC ... Denver, CO
Becker, Susan J. ... Cleveland, OH
Becker, Susan R. ... Philadelphia, PA
Becker, Susan T. ... Newark, NJ
Becker, Suzanne Stephens ... San Antonio, TX
Becker, Suzette Toledano ... New Orleans, LA
Becker, Sylvia M. ... Washington, DC
Becker, T. Todd ... Cedar Rapids, IA
Becker, Theodore M. ... Chicago, IL
Becker, Thomas B. ... Kansas City, MO
Becker, Thomas J. ... Eureka, CA
Becker, Thomas S. ... Avon, CT
Becker, Thomas W. ... Scarsdale, NY
Becker, Thomforde, Brown, Knight & Hester, P.C. ... Knoxville, TN
Becker, Timothy J. ... Minneapolis, MN
Becker, Timothy J. ... Kansas City, MO
Becker, Timothy J. ... Rapid City, SD
Becker, Todd A. ... Madison, WI
Becker, Todd B. ... Long Beach, CA
Torrance, CA
Becker, Todd M. ... Seattle, WA
Becker & Van Cleef, P.C. ... Southfield, MI
Becker, Victor ... Dallas, TX
Becker, Wallace ... Lincoln, NE
Becker, Walter F., Jr. ... New Orleans, LA
Becker, Wayne B. ... New York, NY
Becker, Wesley N. ... Chicago, IL
Becker, William Alan ... Manassas, VA
Becker, William B. ... Oxford, MD
Becker, William C. ... Akron, OH
Becker, William C. ... Columbus, OH
Becker, William D. ... Universal City, CA
Becker, William F. X. ... Rockville, MD
Becker, William G. ... Danville, CA
Becker, William G., Jr. ... Morristown, NJ
Becker, William J. ... Edwardsville, IL
Becker, William L. ... Chicago, IL
Becker, William W. ... Washington, DC
Becker, William W. ... Pocatello, ID
Becker, William W., Chartered, Law Offices of ... Washington, DC
Becker-Celik, Astrid C.
San Francisco, CA
Becker-Gosselin, Alison ... Cheswick, PA
Beckerich, Donald L. ... Indianapolis, IN
Beckering, Jane M. ... Grand Rapids, MI
Beckering, Raymond E., III
Grand Rapids, MI
Becker-Johnson, Polly ... Seattle, WA
Beckerle, Robert A. ... Mobile, AL
Beckerleg, Derk W. ... Farmington Hills, MI
Beckerleg, Ronda R. ... Phoenix, AZ
Beckerleg, William H. ... San Juan, PR
Beckerlegge, Bernard R. ... Boston, MA
Becker-Lewke, Laura V. ... Stamford, CT
Beckerman & Beckerman, LLP
Rochester, NY
Beckerman, Bryan Michael ... Troy, MI
Beckerman, Dale L. ... Prairie Village, KS
Kansas City, MO
Beckerman, David M. ... Boca Raton, FL
Beckerman, David M. ... South Orange, NJ
Beckerman, Eric J. ... New York, NY
Beckerman, Gerald ... Rochester, NY
Beckerman, Jason ... Washington, DC
Beckerman, Jay H. ... Phoenixville, PA
Beckerman, Jay L. ... Santa Barbara, CA
Beckerman, Jeffrey S. ... South Orange, NJ
Beckerman, John S. ... New York, NY
Beckerman, Kathryn D. ... Seattle, WA
Beckerman, Lisa G. ... New York, NY
Beckerman, Marc D. ... Sacramento, CA
Beckerman, Miriam ... Oviedo, FL
Beckerman, Murray ... New York, NY
Beckerman, Peter C. ... Minneapolis, MN
Beckerman, Peter M. ... Sidney, ME
Beckerman, Ray ... New York, NY
Beckerman, Robert B. ... Seattle, WA
Beckerman, Steven M. ... Rochester, NY
Beckerman, Stuart J. ... New York, NY
Beckerman, Warren S. ... New City, NY

Beckermann, Michael J. ... St. Louis, MO
Beckerman-Rodau, Andrew ... Ada, OH
Beckers, J. Randall ... Washington, DC
Beckert, Anne M. ... Chicago, IL
Beckert, Halle Hahn ... Cleveland, OH
Beckert, James A. ... Tulsa, OK
Beckert, Karin Moore ... Boonville, NY
Beckert, Michael F. ... New York, NY
Beckert, Paul R. ... Doylestown, PA
Beckert, Paul R., Jr. ... Langhorne, PA
Beckert, Paul R., Jr., P.C. ... Langhorne, PA
Beckert, Sherry Redding ... Bartlesville, OK
Beckert, William F., Jr. ... Hartford, CT
Beckert-Franz, Janice K. ... Pittsburgh, PA
Beckes, Katherine F. ... Denver, CO
Becket, Alane A. ... Malvern, PA
Becket & Lee LLP ... Malvern, PA
Philadelphia, PA
Becket, Milton ... Malvern, PA
Becket, Thomas L. ... Los Angeles, CA
Becket, William J. ... Malvern, PA
Beckett, Alice T. ... Charleston, SC
Beckett, Amy Louise ... Springfield, MO
Beckett & Anderson ... Phoenix, AZ
Beckett & Associates ... Avon, CT
Glastonbury, CT
Hartford, CT
Beckett, Belinda D. ... Loomis, CA
Beckett, Bruce H. ... Columbia, MO
Beckett, Burford & James ... Huntington, WV
Beckett, Candace H. ... Annapolis, MD
Beckett, Carolyn M. ... Austin, TX
Beckett, Chad S. ... Urbana, IL
Beckett, David B. ... Lawrenceville, NJ
Beckett, David I. ... Miami, FL
Beckett, Deirdre Crowe ... New York, NY
Beckett, Donald L. ... Columbus, OH
Beckett, Glenn Frank ... Pasadena, CA
Beckett, Guy W. ... Seattle, WA
Beckett & Hensley, L.C. ... Kansas City, KS
Kansas City, MO
Beckett, J. Steven ... Urbana, IL
Beckett, J. Thomas ... Salt Lake City, UT
Beckett, James B. ... Grand Rapids, MI
Beckett, James H. ... Louisville, KY
Beckett, Jennifer ... Oakland, CA
Beckett, Joanne M. ... Las Vegas, NV
Beckett, Joseph K., Jr. ... Bakersfield, CA
Beckett, Kathy G. ... Charleston, WV
Beckett Law Firm, The ... Kansas City, MO
Beckett, Leroy M., III ... Houston, TX
Beckett, Lewis W. ... Norman, OK
Beckett, Marian L. ... Manassas, VA
Beckett, Mark D. ... New York, NY
Beckett, Mayree ... Nine Mile Falls, WA
Beckett, Riley M. ... Carson City, NV
Beckett, Robert ... Phoenix, AZ
Beckett, Steven K. ... San Bernardino, CA
Beckett, Susan K. ... New York, NY
Beckett, Suzann L. ... Avon, CT
Glastonbury, CT
Hartford, CT
Beckett, Theodore C. ... Kansas City, MO
Beckett, Theodore C., III
Kansas City, MO
Beckett, Thomas Ashton ... Carrboro, NC
Beckett & Webber, P.C. ... Champaign, IL
Monticello, IL
Urbana, IL
Beckett, William A. ... Orlando, FL
Beckett, William A. ... Eugene, OR
Beckett, William A. ... Huntington, WV
Beckett, William H. M. ... Exeter, NH
Beckett, William W. ... Washington, DC
Beckett, William W. ... Washington, DC
Beckett & Yott, Ltd. ... Carson City, NV
Reno, NV
Beckey, Scott A. ... Spartanburg, SC
Beckford, Ernesto R. ... Dulles, VA
Beckford, Joseph G. ... Menlo Park, CA
Beckham & Beckham, P.A.
Fort Lauderdale, FL
Miami, FL
North Miami Beach, FL
Beckham, Benjamin F., III
Birmingham, AL
Beckham, Blake L. ... Dallas, TX
Beckham, Charles A., Jr. ... El Paso, TX
Beckham, David B. ... Albany, OR
Beckham, Diane Burch ... Dallas, TX
Beckham, Eugene G.
North Miami Beach, FL
Beckham, Glenn F. ... Greenwood, MS
Beckham, James K., Law Offices of
Miami, FL
Beckham, John D. ... Jackson, MS
Beckham, John L. ... Abilene, TX
Beckham, Jonathan A. ... Washington, DC
Beckham, Joseph C. ... Tallahassee, FL
Beckham, Kevin G. ... Jacksonville, AR
Beckham, Kimberly Shannon Riley
Austin, TX
Beckham, Nullie Potitong
Redwood City, CA
Beckham, Pamela
North Miami Beach, FL
Beckham, Rector & Eargle, P.C.
Fort Worth, TX
Beckham, Robert J. ... Jacksonville, FL
Beckham, Robert J., Jr.
North Miami Beach, FL
Beckham, Robert P. ... Los Angeles, CA
Beckham, Sonja S. ... Nashville, NC
Beckham, Stephen R. ... Chattanooga, TN
Beckham & Thomas, Limited Liability Partnership ... Dallas, TX
Beckham, Walter H., III ... Atlanta, GA
Beckham, Walter H., Jr. ... Miami, FL

Beckham, Walter H., P.C. ... Atlanta, GA
Beckhard, Daniel C. ... Department of Justice, Environment and Natural Resources Division, GV
Beckhart & Associates ... Pasadena, CA
Beckhart, Leslie Kent ... Pasadena, CA
Beckhoff, Harry ... Albuquerque, NM
Beckhorn, Duane W. ... Falls Church, VA
Beckhorn, Kirk D. ... McLean, VA
Becking, Frank P. ... Palo Alto, CA
Becking, Mary Anne ... Palo Alto, CA
Beckington, Jeffrey S. ... Washington, DC
Beckington, Mark R. ... Newport Beach, CA
Beckish & Morrow, P.C. ... Mobile, AL
Beckish, Richard M., Jr. ... Mobile, AL
Beckius, Michael A. ... San Francisco, CA
Beckjord, Walter E. ... Cincinnati, OH
Beckker, Bernard ... Los Angeles, CA
Beckler, Andrew J. ... New York, NY
Beckler, Howard E. ... Los Angeles, CA
Beckler, Judith T. ... Naples, FL
Beckler, Michael D. ... Harrisonburg, VA
Beckler, Richard W. ... Washington, DC
Beckler, Theresa Ann ... Metairie, LA
Ponchatoula, LA
Beckles, Alphonso ... Huntsville, AL
Beckles, Gale E. ... New York, NY
Beckles, Grafton Edgar, II ... Newark, NJ
Beckles, Linda Joyce
Department of the Army, Office, Chief of Engineers/Headquarters, U.S. Army Corps of Engineers, GV
Beckles, Robert O. ... Dallas, TX
Beckley, Catherine C. ... Washington, DC
Beckley, Charles O., II ... Harrisburg, PA
Beckley, Dennis L. ... Hazelwood, MO
Beckley, Elizabeth S. ... Harrisburg, PA
Beckley, Frances Ruml ... Harrisburg, PA
Beckley, Frederic A. ... Philadelphia, PA
Beckley, James E. ... Wheaton, IL
Beckley, James E., & Associates, P.C.
Wheaton, IL
Beckley, James F. ... Albuquerque, NM
Beckley, James F., P.A. ... Albuquerque, NM
Beckley, John G. ... Columbus, OH
Beckley, John K. ... Costa Mesa, CA
Beckley, John W. ... Hunt Valley, MD
Beckley, Kelly R. ... Eugene, OR
Beckley, Lisa C. ... Overland Park, KS
Beckley & Longtin, P.C. ... Eugene, OR
Beckley & Madden ... Harrisburg, PA
Beckley, Singleton, Jemison, Cobeaga & List, Chartered, A Professional Law Corporation ... Las Vegas, NV
Reno, NV
Beckley, Thomas A. ... Harrisburg, PA
Beckley, Thomas S. ... Harrisburg, PA
Beckloff, Mitchell L. ... Los Angeles, CA
Becklund, Osborne ... San Jose, CA
Beckman, Allen J. ... Philadelphia, PA
Beckman, Andrea S. ... Las Vegas, NV
Beckman, Ann R. ... Charleston, WV
Beckman, Anne ... New York, NY
Beckman, Barbara R. ... Philadelphia, PA
Beckman, Bradley T. ... Blue Bell, PA
Philadelphia, PA
Beckman, Bruce A. ... Los Angeles, CA
Beckman, Caroline Bell ... St. Paul, MN
Beckman, Charles T. ... Dixon, IL
Beckman, Daniel A. ... Minneapolis, MN
Beckman, Darryl S. ... Cherry Hill, NJ
Beckman, David D. ... Burlington, IA
Beckman, David L., Jr. ... Louisville, KY
Beckman, David L., Sr. ... Louisville, KY
Beckman, David S. ... Los Angeles, CA
Beckman, Davis, Smith & Ruddy LLP
Los Angeles, CA
Beckman, Donald ... Philadelphia, PA
Beckman, Douglas G. ... Portland, OR
Beckman, Frederick A. ... Fort Wayne, IN
Beckman, Gail McKnight ... Atlanta, GA
Beckman, Gene W. ... La Habra Heights, CA
Beckman, Gerald H. ... Corpus Christi, TX
Beckman, Harold T. ... Council Bluffs, IA
Beckman, Henry P. ... Chicago, IL
Beckman, Hester R. ... Philadelphia, PA
Beckman and Hirsch ... Burlington, IA
Beckman, James A. ... Treasury Department, Bureau of Alcohol, Tobacco and Firearms, GV
Beckman, James Robert ... Brea, CA
Beckman, Jill M. ... Ada, MI
Beckman, Joanne Caldwell
Signal Mountain, TN
Beckman, Joel G. ... Boston, MA
Beckman, Joel J. ... Whittier, CA
Beckman, Joel S. ... New York, NY
Beckman, John A. ... Brookfield, WI
Beckman, John B. ... Washington, DC
Baltimore, MD
Beckman, John D. ... Golden, CO
Beckman, John W. ... Westfield, NY
Beckman, Joseph P. ... Helena, MT
Beckman, Joseph S. ... Plantation, FL
Beckman, Karen H. ... Irvine, CA
Orange, CA
Beckman, Kelly & Smith
Crown Point, IN
East Chicago, IN
Elkhart, IN
Gary, IN
Hammond, IN
Michigan City, IN
South Bend, IN
Valparaiso, IN
Beckman, Kenneth C. ... Chattanooga, TN
Beckman Law Office, P.C. ... Golden, CO
Wheat Ridge, CO

Beckman, Lawrence J. ......**Council Bluffs, IA**
Beckman Lawson, LLP ....**Fort Wayne, IN**
Syracuse, IN
Warsaw, IN
Beckman, Lisa Pam ....Randolph, MA
Beckman, Louis E., III ....Dallas, TX
Beckman, Marc S. ....**Syracuse, NY**
Beckman, Maria D.
Environmental Protection Agency, Office of the General Counsel, GV
Beckman, Marlene D. .....Department of Justice, Office of Justice Programs, GV
Beckman, Marvin E. ....Chicago, IL
Beckman, Michael ....**New York, NY**
Beckman, Michael L. ....Fort Myers, FL
Beckman, Millman & Sanders, LLP
New York, NY
Beckman, Paul A. ....Davenport, IA
Beckman, Paul C. ....**Cincinnati, OH**
Beckman, Paul E. ....Carmichael, CA
Beckman, Paul LePage, Jr. .....Montgomery, AL
Beckman, Peter W. ....Bakersfield, CA
Beckman, Regina Rapier ....Bardstown, KY
Beckman, Richard L. ....**San Francisco, CA**
Beckman, Robert M. ....**Washington, DC**
Beckman, Ronald J. ....Philadelphia, PA
Beckman, Roslyn J. ....**Minneapolis, MN**
Beckman, Scott H. ....Willow Springs, IL
Beckman, Sheila ....**New York, NY**
Beckman, Sherie Potts ....**Houston, TX**
Beckman, Stacy Solochek ....**Columbus, OH**
Beckman, Steven C. ....Meadville, PA
Beckman, Sydney A. ....Fort Worth, TX
Beckman, T. Scott ....Baltimore, MD
Beckman, Victor R. ....Cupertino, CA
Beckman, Vincent H. ....**Cincinnati, OH**
Beckman, Vincent H., III ....Chicago, IL
Beckman, Weil, Shepardson and Faller, LLC
Cincinnati, OH
Beckmann, Bruce H. ....**New York, NY**
Beckmann, Bryan W. ....Pasadena, CA
Beckmann, Deborah E. ....New York, NY
Beckmann, Deborah R. ....Mineola, NY
Beckmann, John S. ....**Austin, MN**
Beckmann, Leo G., Jr. ....**Savannah, GA**
Beckmann & Lewis ....**Savannah, GA**
Beckmann, Luhr G. C., Jr. .....**Savannah, GA**
Beckmann, Natalie M. ....**Seattle, WA**
Beckmann & Pinson, P.C. ....**Savannah, GA**
Beckmann & Quirk, A Professional Corporation
San Antonio, TX
Beckmann, Richard J. ....**Dayton, OH**
Beckmann, Robert R. ....Anamosa, IA
Beckmann, Thomas L., (P.C.)
Longmont, CO
Beckmire, Garrity & Vogt ....Freeport, IL
Becknell, Heigle & Wallace ....**Metairie, LA**
New Orleans, LA
Becknell, J. William, II ....**Metairie, LA**
Beckner, Achziger, McInnis, Palo & Junge, L.L.C. ....Grand Junction, CO
Beckner, Brian F. ....**Osceola, NE**
Polk, NE
Beckner, Clinton F. ....**Washington, DC**
Beckner, Dean M. ....Flora, IN
Beckner, Donald L. ....Greenwell Springs, LA
Beckner, Holly S. ....Van Nuys, CA
Beckner, James E. ....Morristown, TN
Beckner, James L. ....**Covington, KY**
Frankfort, KY
Lexington, KY
Louisville, KY
Cincinnati, OH
Nashville, TN
Beckner, Larry B. ....Grand Junction, CO
Beckner, Nancy M. ....**Washington, DC**
Beckner, R. Bruce ....**Washington, DC**
Beckner, Terry R. ....London, KY
Beckoff, Alan ....New York, NY
Beckon, Brian J. ....Napa, CA
Beck-Richart, Susan L. ....Kansas City, MO
Becks & Becks ....**Daytona Beach, FL**
Becks, Berrien H., Jr. .....**Daytona Beach, FL**
Becks, Berrien H., Sr. .....**Daytona Beach, FL**
Becks, Harold G. ....**Los Angeles, CA**
Beckstead, John A. ....**Salt Lake City, UT**
Beckstead, Kathleen ....Salisbury, MD
Beckstead, Scott ....Waldport, OR
Becksted, Dennis P. ....Suisun City, CA
Beckstedt, Carl A., III
Christiansted, St. Croix, VI
Beckstein, Frank W., III ....**Boston, MA**
Beckstrand, Armour T. ....Rockford, IL
Beckstrand, Peggy ....Los Angeles, CA
Beckstrand, Shelley M. ....Owego, NY
Beckstrand, Shelley M., P.C. ....Owego, NY
Beckstrom, Bradley R. ....Boise, ID
Beckstrom, Charles G. ....**Jamestown, NY**
Beckstrom, Charles G. ....**Erie, PA**
Beckstrom, James C. ....Fargo, ND
Beckstrom, John H. ....Chicago, IL
Beckstrom & Plumb ....**Jamestown, NY**
Mayville, NY
Beckstrom, Ronald L. ....Valdosta, GA
Beckstrom, Sean C. ....**Cleveland, OH**
Beckstrom, Spencer S. ....**Pasadena, CA**
Beckwith, Brian B. ....Woodside, CA
Beckwith, Carl C. ....Englewood, NJ
Beckwith, Cynthia ....**Encino, CA**
Beckwith, Daniel J. ....Fremont, NE
Beckwith, David E. ....**Milwaukee, WI**
Beckwith, David M. ....**San Diego, CA**
Beckwith, David M. ....**Bethlehem, PA**
Beckwith, Dirk H. ....**Detroit, MI**
Beckwith, Donald L. ....Augusta, ME
Beckwith, Douglas C. ....Los Angeles, CA
Beckwith, Edward Jay ....**Washington, DC**
Beckwith, Frank L. ....Arvada, CO
Beckwith, Geo. L. ....Laguna Beach, CA
Beckwith, George Perry, Jr.
Fort Lauderdale, FL
Beckwith, Grant D. ....Boston, MA
Beckwith, Gregory ....**Fairfax, VA**
Beckwith, Irving H. ....Plymouth, MA
Beckwith, James E. ....New York, NY
Beckwith, James Payne, Jr. ....Durham, NC
Beckwith, Kevin L., Law Offices of
Phoenix, AZ
Beckwith, Lewis D. ....**Indianapolis, IN**
Beckwith, Marta ....**Palo Alto, CA**
Beckwith, Martha ....Anchorage, AK
Beckwith, Michael S., P.C. ....**Houston, TX**
Beckwith, Michael Stone ....**Houston, TX**
Beckwith, Michael V. ....Oxnard, CA
Beckwith, Paul F. ....**Boston, MA**
Beckwith, Raymond W. ....Trumbull, CT
Beckwith, Richard ....**Rock Springs, WY**
Beckwith, Sandra S. ....Cincinnati, OH
Beckwith, Scolnick & Wolf, LLP
Englewood, NJ
Beckwith, Stephen McKinley
Santa Rosa, CA
Beckwith, Tara ....**Louisville, KY**
Beckwith, Van H. ....**Dallas, TX**
Beckworth, Bradley E. ....**Daingerfield, TX**
Beckworth & Carrigan, L.L.P. ....Houston, TX
Beckworth, Elmer C., Jr. ....Rusk, TX
Beckworth, John B. ....Houston, TX
Beckworth, Marthanda J. ....**Tulsa, OK**
Beckworth, Melissa L. ....**Houston, TX**
Becnel, Andrew P. ....**Houston, TX**
Becnel, Charles S. ....Vacherie, LA
Becnel, Christopher A. ....Brentwood, CA
Becnel, Daniel E., Jr. ....Reserve, LA
Becnel, Daniel Elmore, III ....La Place, LA
Becnel, Debra Jean ....Lafayette, LA
Becnel, Landry & Becnel ....Reserve, LA
Becnel, Larry C. ....**New Orleans, LA**
Becnel, Mary Hotard ....Reserve, LA
Becnel, Philip A., III ....New Orleans, LA
Becnel, Renée E. ....New York, NY
Becnel, Robert M., The Law Offices of
La Place, LA
Becnel & Weimer ....Lafayette, LA
Becque, Motier ....Orange, CT
Becraft, Barbara A. ....Americus, GA
Becraft, Charles D., Jr. ....Corning, NY
Becraft, Charles E. ....St. Joseph, MO
Becraft, Lowell H., Jr. ....Huntsville, AL
Becsey, David ....**Indianapolis, IN**
Becton, Bernard A. ....St. Louis, MO
Becton, Charles L. ....**Raleigh, NC**
Becton, Henry P., Jr. ....Boston, MA
Becton, Kelly R. ....**Oklahoma City, OK**
Becton, M. Ross, Jr. ....Savannah, GA
Becvar, Scott S. ....Chicago, IL
Becz, Frank, Jr. ....Florida, NY
Becz, John J. ....Rutherford, NJ
Bedal, Richard W. ....Santa Cruz, CA
Bedall, Thomas G. ....Cincinnati, OH
Bedar, James E. ....**Boston, MA**
Bedard, Benjamin Lawrence
West Palm Beach, FL
Bedard, Biron ....**Concord, NH**
Bedard, Douglas P. ....Los Angeles, CA
Bedard, Gregory O. ....**Walnut Creek, CA**
Bedard, John H., Jr. ....**Atlanta, GA**
Bedard, Michael ....Concord, NH
Bedard, Patrick S. ....Eliot, ME
Bedard, Peter J. ....**Chicago, IL**
Bedard, Ronald H. ....Columbus, GA
Bedard, Theodora L. ....Dallas, TX
Bedarff, Dirk M. ....**Covington, KY**
Louisville, KY
Bedaska, John ....Williamsville, NY
Beddard, Dennis Lee ....Sacramento, CA
Beddingfield, Ann S. ....**New York, NY**
Beddingfield, Elwyn Gary, Jr. ....Augusta, GA
Beddoe, M. Bart ....Las Vegas, NV
Beddoe, Matthew W. ....Klamath Falls, OR
Beddoe, Suzanne A. ....**New York, NY**
Beddow, Bruce P. ....Washington, DC
Beddow, Charles W. ....Chesterfield, VA
Beddow, David T. ....**Washington, DC**
Beddow, Earl ....St. Paul, MN
Beddow, Erben & Bowen, P.A.
Birmingham, AL
Beddow, Jack W. ....Washington, DC
Beddow, John W. ....**Charlotte, NC**
Beddow, Kenneth R. ....**Mansfield, OH**
Beddow, Marley & Associates
Chesterfield, VA
Beddow, Richard H., Jr.
National Labor Relations Board, Division of Administrative Law Judges, GV
Beddow, Roderick, Jr. ....Birmingham, AL
Bede, Carolyn M. ....Mountaintop, PA
Bedecarre, Albert P. ....**Palo Alto, CA**
Bedel, John J. ....Omaha, NE
Bedell, Arthur W. ....Southwest Harbor, ME
Bedell, Benjamin B. ....**New City, NY**
Bedell, Catherine ....Tallahassee, FL
Bedell, Christopher J. ....**New York, NY**
Bedell, Cynthia Cloud ....Tampa, FL
Bedell, Daniel J. ....Portland, OR
Bedell, Deborah Luth ....Cary, NC
Bedell, Dennis P. ....**Washington, DC**
Bedell, Dittmar, DeVault, Pillans & Coxe, Professional Association ...**Jacksonville, FL**
Bedell, Donald W. ....Morristown, NJ
Bedell, Donald W., Jr. ....Colts Neck, NJ
Bedell, Elizabeth ....**Springfield, NJ**
Bedell, Frank M. ....**Orlando, FL**
Bedell, George R. ....**Dallas, TX**
Bedell, Gregory A. ....**Chicago, IL**
Bedell, Janet M. ....Arlington, VA
Bedell, Kathryn ....York, ME
Bedell, Kevin B. ....**Washington, DC**
Bedell, Laureen F. ....**New York, NY**
Bedell, Lloyd C. ....Agoura Hills, CA
Bedell, Mary Lynn ....**Oak Brook, IL**
Bedell, Reginald H. ....San Francisco, CA
Bedell, Richard J., Jr. ....**Cleveland, OH**
Bedell, Richard S. ....Gaithersburg, MD
Bedell, Robert P. ....Washington, DC
Bedell, Stephen P. ....**Chicago, IL**
Bedell, Susanna E. ....**Poughkeepsie, NY**
Bedell, Thomas A. ....Clarksburg, WV
Bedell, Walter H. ....Waterford, MI
Bedells, David J. ....**Beulah, MI**
Bedenis, Kay F. ....Farmington Hills, MI
Bedenko, Alan Joseph ....Brookline, MA
Bedenkop, Barry T. ....Syracuse, NY
Beder, Edward J., Jr. ....**Washington, DC**
Bederka, Anne C. ....**New York, NY**
Bederman, Andrew E. ....Silver Spring, MD
Bederman, David J. ....Atlanta, GA
Bederman, Henriet T. ....Mendocino, CA
Bederman, Steve M. ....**New York, NY**
Bedesi, Nan Kishor ....Jamaica, NY
Bedesky, Michael J. ....**Edwardsville, IL**
Bedevia, Fernando L. ....Holland, MI
Bedford, Barry K. ....**Annandale, VA**
Bedford, Carol Archer ....San Diego, CA
Bedford, Daniel R. ....**San Francisco, CA**
Bedford, Gordon R. ....Palos Park, IL
Bedford, L. A., Jr. ....Dallas, TX
Bedford, Lyman D. ....**San Francisco, CA**
Bedford, Nancy E. ....Atlanta, GA
Bedford, Nathaniel F. ....Boonton, NJ
New York, NY
Bedford, Roger H. ....**Russellville, AL**
Bedford, Roger H., Jr. ....Russellville, AL
Bedford, Rogers & Bowling, P.C.
Russellville, AL
Bedford, Stanley G. ....Caldwell, NJ
Bedford, Susan L. ....**New York, NY**
Bedford, T. Jackson, Jr. ....Atlanta, GA
Bedgood, David A. ....Montgomery, AL
Bedgood, Robert Carl ....Victoria, TX
Bedi, Ben H. ....**Palo Alto, CA**
Bedi, Harpreet Kaur ....San Jose, CA
Bedi, John E. ....Virginia Beach, VA
Bedient, Elizabeth J. ....Denver, CO
Bedient, Steve L. ....El Dorado, CA
Bedig, Laurel A. ....**Washington, DC**
Bedigian, Kimberly A. ....Livonia, MI
Bedinger, Daniel E. ....Houston, TX
Bedinger, Frank C., III ....**Atlanta, GA**
Bedingfield, Christine J. ....**Savannah, GA**
Bedingfield, H. Winston ....Augusta, GA
Bedingfield, Jeffrey T. ....**Greeley, CO**
Bedingfield, M. Dolores ....Tulsa, OK
Bedingfield, William Walter ....Barnwell, SC
Bedke, Kathryn L. ....**New York, NY**
Bedke, Michael A. ....**Tampa, FL**
Bedlivy, Dawn V. ....Department of Defense, Defense Legal Services Agency, GV
Bedman, William L. ....**Houston, TX**
Bednar, Andrew T. ....New York, NY
Bednar, Anna M. ....**Omaha, NE**
Bednar, David G. ....Flagstaff, AZ
Bednar, Emil J., (P.C.) ....Houston, TX
Bednar, Gerald ....Wickliffe, OH
Bednar, James D. ....Oklahoma City, OK
Bednar, Jane E. ....Pacific Grove, CA
Bednar, Joseph P., Jr. ....Jefferson City, MO
Bednar, Kenneth L.
West Palm Beach, FL
Bednar, Mark A. ....**Pensacola, FL**
Bednar, Mark A., P.A. ....**Pensacola, FL**
Bednar, Mary E. ....New York, NY
Bednar, Michael A. ....Garfield Heights, OH
Bednar, Michael C. ....Steubenville, OH
Bednar & Mock, A Professional Association
Atchison, KS
Bednar, Richard A.
United States Court Of Veterans Appeals, GV
Bednar, Richard J. ....**Washington, DC**
Bednar, Robert J. ....Atchison, KS
Bednar, Stephen J. ....Tulsa, OK
Bednar, Steven C. ....**Salt Lake City, UT**
Bednar, William C., Jr. ....Austin, TX
Bednarczuk, Robert ....Lebanon, OH
Bednarczyk, Stanley J. ....Pawtucket, RI
Bednarek, Michael D. ....**Washington, DC**
Bednarek, Michael J. ....Philadelphia, PA
Bednarek, Theodore J. ....Joliet, IL
Bednarski, Laura F. ....**Minneapolis, MN**
Bednarski, Marilyn E. ....Los Angeles, CA
Bednarz, Bernard F. ....Salem, OR
Bednarz, Edward L. ....**Washington, DC**
Bednarz, Gregory M. ....Amarillo, TX
Bednarz, Joe, Law Offices ....Nashville, TN
Bednarz, John A., Jr. ....Wilkes-Barre, PA
Bednarz, Ruth J. ....**New York, NY**
Bednarz, Sharon M. ....Buffalo, NY
Bednash, Michael D. ....**Wilmington, DE**
Bedno, Jane Higgins ....Philadelphia, PA
Bedno, Rebecca A. ....**New York, NY**
Bednorz, Dana R. ....San Antonio, TX
Bedolis, Audrey Hirsch ....**New York, NY**
Bedolla, Kevin C. ....San Jose, CA
Bedor, Shirley A. ....Andover, MA
Bedore, Carrie Raymond ....**Milwaukee, WI**
Bedore, James M. ....**Milwaukee, WI**
Bedore, Jess C., III ....**Roseville, CA**
Bedore, Karen E. ....**Los Angeles, CA**
Bedore, Robert A. ....**Chicago, IL**
Bedortha, James J. ....**Pittsburgh, PA**
Bedosky, John R. ....Minneapolis, MN
Bedoya, Consuelo E. ....Glenview, IL
Bedoyan, Hagop T. ....**Fresno, CA**
Bedoyan Law Offices ....**Fresno, CA**
Bedrava, E. William ....Oak Brook, IL
Bedrava, Lyman and Van Epps
Oak Brook, IL
Bedree, Kathleen Kernan ....Cincinnati, OH
Bedree, Melvin A. ....**Cincinnati, OH**
Bedrick, Barry R.
General Accounting Office, Office of the General Counsel, GV
Bedrick, Benjamin N. .....Department of Justice, Office of Information and Privacy, GV
Bedrick, Leon I. ....North Miami Beach, FL
Bedrick, Melvin L. ....**New York, NY**
Bedrick, Richard E. ....Charlotte, NC
Bedrick, Stephen B. ....Oakland, CA
Bedrock, Martin ....Knox, IN
Bedrock, Neale R. ....New York, NY
Bedrosian, Gary P. ....Fresno, CA
Bedrosian, George J. ....Detroit, MI
Bedrosian, John C. ....Los Angeles, CA
Bedrosian, Melanie M. ....Boston, MA
Bedrossian, B. John ....Hatfield, PA
Bedrossian, Sylvia ....Tarzana, CA
Bedrossian, Victoria ....Los Angeles, CA
Bedsaul, Michael R. ....Galax, VA
Bedsole, Billy C. ....Mobile, AL
Bedsole, Charles, P.C. ....Dallas, TX
Bedsole and Conner ....St. Augustine, FL
Bedsole, E. Charles ....Dallas, TX
Bedsole, James Edwin ....St. Augustine, FL
Bedsole, T. Massey ....**Mobile, AL**
Bedsole, Thomas F. ....**Indianapolis, IN**
Bedsole, Travis M., Jr. ....Mobile, AL
Bedsworth, George A. ....Winston-Salem, NC
Bedsworth, William W., II ....Santa Ana, CA
Bedunah, Donald A. ....Littleton, CO
Bedward, Kathryn S. ....**Chicago, IL**
Bedward, Royce R. ....**Chicago, IL**
Bedwell, E. M. ....Durant, OK
Bedwell, Marsha A. ....Sacramento, CA
Bedwell, Robert R. ....**Birmingham, AL**
Bedwick, Joseph C. ....**Philadelphia, PA**
Bedzow, Korn, Brown, Miller & Zemel, P.A.
Aventura, FL
Miami, FL
North Miami Beach, FL
Bedzow, Michael ....**Aventura, FL**
Bee, C. Michael ....**Charleston, WV**
Bee, Eisman & Ready ....**Mineola, NY**
New York, NY
Bee, Fred A. ....Harrodsburg, KY
Bee, James J. ....Philadelphia, PA
Bee, John H. ....**Boston, MA**
Bee, John M. ....New Orleans, LA
Bee, Peter A. ....**Mineola, NY**
New York, NY
Bee, Richard E. ....Costa Mesa, CA
Beebe, Arnold T. ....Blackfoot, ID
Beebe, Bion J. ....St. Paul, MN
Beebe, Colleen ....St. Paul, MN
Beebe, David C. ....Northampton, MA
Beebe, David K. ....Columbus, OH
Beebe, Donald G. ....**Mobile, AL**
Beebe, Donald R. ....**Norwich, CT**
Beebe, Jack E. ....McPherson, KS
Beebe, Jed Q. ....Santa Maria, CA
Beebe, John W.(Jack) ....Sacramento, CA
Beebe, Keith Allen ....Kingston, WA
Beebe, Linda Garrett ....Lakewood, OH
Beebe, Lydia I. ....**San Francisco, CA**
Beebe, Marcus G., Jr. ....Portland, ME
Beebe, Marcus P., III ....Wilton, CT
Beebe, Mark A. ....American Falls, ID
Beebe, Mark R. ....**New Orleans, LA**
Beebe, Michael G. ....Branford, CT
Beebe, Mike ....**Searcy, AR**
Beebe and O'Neil ....**Norwich, CT**
Beebe, Raymond L. ....Toledo, OH
Beebe, Raymond M. ....Forest City, IA
Beebe, Raymond N. ....Linwood, NJ
Beebe, Richard W. ....Sioux City, IA
Beebe, Robert L. ....Clifton Park, NY
Beebe, Roger L. ....**Houston, TX**
Beebe, Timothy R. ....Enid, OK
Beebe, Tod V. ....**Los Angeles, CA**
Beebe, Waldo F. ....Muncie, IN
Beebe, Walter H. ....**New York, NY**
Beebee, M. Dawn ....San Diego, CA
Beeber, Jessie F. ....**New York, NY**
Beeber, Paul S. ....Hicksville, NY
Beebe-Snell, Cheryl ....**St. Louis, MO**
Beebout, Kathleen J. ....**Des Moines, IA**
Beeby, David Emerson ....**San Francisco, CA**
Beeby, Gwendolyn C. ....Kailua-Kona, HI
Beeby, Jim D. ....Kailua-Kona, HI
Beeby, Kenneth J. ....Middleboro, MA
Beeby, Richard D. ....Tulsa, OK
Beech, Amy J. ....**New York, NY**
Beech, Andrew A. ....Wellsville, OH
Beech, Beth E. ....Angola, IN
Beech, Dennis W. ....**Huntington Beach, CA**
Palmdale, CA
Beech, Douglas M. ....Ankeny, IA
Beech & Dove ....Kinston, NC
Beech Edwards & Percival
Oklahoma City, OK
Beech, Harvey E. ....Kinston, NC
Beech, Jack W. ....Hurst, TX
Beech, Johnny G. ....Oklahoma City, OK
Beech, Jonathan Casey ....Lemont, PA
Beech, Joseph, III ....**Cincinnati, OH**
Beech, Kristen L. ....**Philadelphia, PA**
Beech, Milton J. ....Malverne, NY
Beech Street Law Offices ....Casper, WY
Beecham, Roger E. ....**Dallas, TX**
Beechen, Paul D. ....Los Angeles, CA
Beechen, Paul D., Inc. ....Los Angeles, CA
Beecher, Bryce H. ....**Denver, CO**

Beggs, Michael M. .... Phoenix, AZ
Beggs, Paul F. .... Bay City, MI
Beggs, Robert J. .... Columbus, OH
Beggs, Robert L. .... Coatesville, PA
Beggs, Samuel G. .... Harrisburg, IL
Beggs, Tracy C. .... Chicago, IL
Beggs & Trerice, P.L.C. .... Bay City, MI
Beggs & Vecchio .... Fort Lauderdale, FL
Beggs, William F. .... Fort Lauderdale, FL
Beggs, William J. .... Bloomington, IN
Beggs & Woodruff .... Dallas, TX
Irving, TX
Beggy, Daniel J. .... Pittsburgh, PA
Beghè, Renato
United States Tax Court, GV
Beghin, Barbara J. .... Stamford, CT
Beghtol, DeEtte Wald .... Milwaukie, OR
Begian, Daniel R. .... St. Louis, MO
Begich, Paul M. .... Woodbury, MN
Begier, Harry P., Jr. .... Philadelphia, PA
Begin, Eric J. .... Tulsa, OK
Begin, James S. .... Columbus, OH
Begin, Laurence C. .... Bloomfield Hills, MI
Begland, Michael J. .... Richmond, VA
Begland, Rob R. .... Smithfield, VA
Beglane, Mark J. .... Springfield, MA
Begle, Brian J. .... Houston, TX
Begle, Howell E., Jr. .... Washington, DC
Begleiter, Ellen Mindy .... New York, NY
Begleiter, Lori B. .... New York, NY
Begleiter, Martin D. .... Des Moines, IA
Begleiter, Robert L. .... New York, NY
Begleiter, Ronni F. .... Des Moines, IA
Begler, Ann Lee .... Pittsburgh, PA
Begler, Jay H. .... San Francisco, CA
New York, NY
Begler • Kowall .... Pittsburgh, PA
Begley, Ann M. .... Washington, DC
Begley, Begley & Fendrick, P.C.
Moorestown, NJ
Begley, Brad .... Minneapolis, MN
Begley, Brent .... Reno, NV
Begley, Carlin & Mandio .... Bristol, PA
Doylestown, PA
Langhorne, PA
Begley, Charles M., Jr. .... Mansfield, MA
Begley, Clare Maria .... Morristown, NJ
Begley, Dennis F. .... Washington, DC
Begley, Ellen M. .... Bedford, MA
Begley, Ernest Edward, II
Bowling Green, KY
Nashville, TN
Begley, Gerald F., Jr. .... Springfield, MA
Begley, James M. .... New York, NY
Begley, John A., Jr. .... Colts Neck, NJ
Begley, John C. .... Bolinas, CA
Begley, J. T. .... Knoxville, TN
Begley, Kathleen Burg .... Minneapolis, MN
Begley, Kevin .... Audubon, NJ
Begley Law Offices, P.A. .... Minneapolis, MN
Begley, Louis .... New York, NY
Begley, McCloskey & Gaskill, A Professional Corporation .... Moorestown, NJ
Begley, Michelle M. .... Springfield, MA
Begley, Robert J. .... Mill Valley, CA
Begley, Samuel E. .... London, KY
Begley, Samuel L. .... Jackson, MS
Begley, Sara A. .... Philadelphia, PA
Begley, Steven H. .... Jackson, MS
Begley, Theresa .... New York, NY
Begley, Thomas D., III .... Moorestown, NJ
Begley, Thomas D., Jr. .... Moorestown, NJ
Begley, Thomas J. .... La Jolla, CA
Begley, Walter P. .... Chicago, IL
Begley, William E. .... Holyoke, MA
Begley, William F. .... Tempe, AZ
Begley, William J. .... Moorestown, NJ
Begley, William J. .... Pittsburgh, PA
Begley, Wm. Michael
Black Mountain, NC
Begley, Wm. Michael, P.A.
Black Mountain, NC
Beglin, Brian D. .... New York, NY
Beglin, Edward W., Jr. .... Elizabeth, NJ
Beglin, Philip J. .... Burlingame, CA
Begnaud, Darrel .... Athens, GA
Begnaud, Mark A. .... Natchitoches, LA
Begner, Cory G. .... Atlanta, GA
BeGole, George L. .... Corunna, MI
BeGole, Lamont C. .... Novi, MI
Begos & Horgan, LLP .... Westport, CT
Bronxville, NY
Begos, Patrick W. .... Westport, CT
Begos, Walter A. .... New York, NY
Begotka, Robert A. .... Alexandria, VA
Begoun, Michael J. .... New Orleans, LA
Begovich, Michael .... San Diego, CA
Bégué, Yvette .... Wheaton, IL
Beguelin, Mark Andrew .... Reno, NV
Beguiristain, Maria J. .... Miami, FL
Begun, Andrew S. .... Westlake Village, CA
Begun, Armand G. .... Cambridge, OH
Begun, Darryn .... Danville, CA
Begun, Eric G. .... Philadelphia, PA
Begun, Frederic Carey .... San Jose, CA
Begun, Jason Douglas .... Stamford, CT
Begun, Kenneth M .... San Ramon, CA
Begun, Tammy .... Washington, DC
Begy, Fred C., III .... Chicago, IL
Beh, James C. .... Washington, DC
Beh, Thomas M. .... New Orleans, LA
Beh, Walter, II .... Honolulu, HI
Beha, James A., II .... New York, NY
Beha, Ralph W. .... Minneapolis, MN
Beha, William H. .... Alexandria, VA
Behal, Robert J. .... Columbus, OH
Behan, Austin C. .... Winston-Salem, NC
Behan, Christopher J. .... Middletown, RI
Behan, Edmund J. .... New York, NY
Behan, James .... Grand Prairie, TX
Behan, James D. .... San Jose, CA
Behan, John W. .... Dobbs Ferry, NY
Behan, Kathleen A. .... Washington, DC
Behan, Mary Jean .... Winston-Salem, NC
Behan, Michael R. .... Okemos, MI
Behan, Raymond R. .... Okemos, MI
Behan, Suzanne M. .... Lake Success, NY
Behan, W. Dale .... Baton Rouge, LA
New Orleans, LA
Behan, Wendy M. .... San Diego, CA
Behan, William A. .... Arlington, VA
Behan, William A., Jr. .... Somers, NY
Behar, Aaron .... Fort Lauderdale, FL
Behar, Adam S. T. .... Jersey City, NJ
Behar, Ann G. .... Princeton, NJ
Behar, Brian S. .... Boca Raton, FL
Miami, FL
Behar, Gutt & Glazer, P.A.
Boca Raton, FL
Miami, FL
Behar, Howard D. .... Los Angeles, CA
Behar, Howard R. .... Coral Gables, FL
Behar, Jeffrey S. .... Long Beach, CA
Behar, Joseph .... Simi Valley, CA
Behar, Judith G. .... Greensboro, NC
Behar & Kalman .... Boston, MA
Behar, Kenneth A. .... Boston, MA
Behar, Larry J. .... Fort Lauderdale, FL
Behar, Larry J., P.A.
Fort Lauderdale, FL
Behar, Leon I. .... New York, NY
Behar, Leon I., & Associates, P.C.
New York, NY
Behar, Lori R. .... Santa Monica, CA
Behar, Robert .... Miami, FL
Behar, Samuel .... Albuquerque, NM
Behar, Samuel, P.A. .... Albuquerque, NM
Behar, Saul A. .... Philadelphia, PA
Behar, Stephen M. .... Islip, NY
Behar, Steven Anthony .... New York, NY
Behare, William A. .... Mc Keesport, PA
Beharry, Daniel P. .... Westport, CT
Behaylo, Michelle K.
Department of Commerce, Office of the General Counsel, GV
Behbehani, Zohreh S., (Ms.)
Overland Park, KS
Behdjet, Andrei F.B. .... San Francisco, CA
Beheler, Richard M. .... Kansas City, MO
Behenna, Lorraine M. .... Squantum, MA
Behenna, Thomas E. .... Boston, MA
Behenna, Vicki Zemp .... Oklahoma City, OK
Behensky, Larkin Helen .... Peekskill, NY
Behers, Carol A. .... Pittsburgh, PA
Behesnilian, Daniel V. .... Beverly Hills, CA
Behiel, Arthur J. .... Pleasanton, CA
Behinfar, David J. .... Wheaton, IL
Behjatnia, Russell Farzin .... Tarzana, CA
Behl, Catherine M. .... Wilmington, DE
Behl & Lueders, Ltd. .... Columbus, WI
Behle, Donald A. .... Lincoln, IL
Behle, Roger N., Jr. .... Costa Mesa, CA
Behle, Sheila M. .... Yorba Linda, CA
Behlen, Robert A., Jr. .... Cincinnati, OH
Behler Buzbee & Associates, P.C.
Conroe, TX
Behler, Charles F. .... Grand Rapids, MI
Behler, William H., Jr. .... Conroe, TX
Behles, Daniel J. .... Albuquerque, NM
Behles, J. D., & Associates, P.C.
Albuquerque, NM
Behles, Jennie Deden .... Albuquerque, NM
Behling, Christopher B.
Albuquerque, NM
Behling, David Paul .... Honolulu, HI
Behling, Geo. A., Jr. .... Oak Lawn, IL
Behling, Mary H. .... Cambridge, WI
Behling, Paul L. .... New Haven, CT
Behling, Raymond F. .... Tallahassee, FL
Behling, Richard W. .... Tulsa, OK
Behling, Robert J. .... Pittsburgh, PA
Behlke, William M. .... Wooster, OH
Behm, Arthur G. .... Detroit, MI
Behm, Christopher K. .... Raleigh, NC
Behm, Douglas F. .... Phoenix, AZ
Behm, Frances Kay .... Flint, MI
Behm, Karen Streacker .... Tiffin, OH
Behm, Lisa L. .... Milwaukee, WI
Behm, Margaret L. .... Nashville, TN
Behm, Mark J. .... Wausa, NE
Behm, Mary M. .... Albuquerque, NM
Behm, Michael J. .... Flint, MI
Behm, Mitchell L. .... Bethesda, MD
Behm, Paul B. .... Laguna Hills, CA
Behm, R. Jeffrey .... Burlington, VT
Behm, R. Scott .... Palo Alto, CA
Behm, Richard J. .... Flint, MI
Behm, Roland J. .... Washington, DC
Behm, Scott .... Redmond, WA
Behm, Thomas R. .... Grand Rapids, MI
Behman, Miriam .... San Jose, CA
Behman, Scott R. .... Burlington, MA
Behmer, Brian L. .... San Diego, CA
Behmke, Jay M. .... Healdsburg, CA
Behn, Barry H. .... Guttenberg, NJ
Behn, Kathleen McNichol
Birmingham, MI
Behn, Martin I. .... Chicago, IL
Behn, Michael I. .... Chicago, IL
Behn, Richard E. .... Fullerton, CA
Behn, Victor D. .... Glen Rock, NJ
Behnam, Esther M. .... Newport Beach, CA
Behnam, Saman .... Long Beach, CA
Behne, M. J. (Jerry) .... Richardson, TX
Behnen, Nicole Cress .... St. Louis, MO
Behney, Thomas A. .... Lebanon, PA
Behnfeldt, Carla J. .... Philadelphia, PA
Behnia, Hatef .... Los Angeles, CA
Behning, Lawrence E. .... Charlotte, NC
Behnke, Darrell W. .... Madison, WI
Behnke, David W. .... Woodbridge, CT
Behnke, Dawn D. .... Springfield, IL
Behnke, Debra K. .... Tampa, FL
Behnke, Elizabeth M. .... Phoenix, AZ
Behnke, James M. .... Boston, MA
Behnke, Janet W. .... Ocala, FL
Behnke, Jerry A. .... Indio, CA
Behnke, John A. .... Ukiah, CA
Behnke, Lance W. .... Seattle, WA
Behnke, Mark L. .... Willoughby, OH
Behnke, Michelle A. .... Madison, WI
Behnke, Peter R. .... Chicago, IL
Behnken, R. Randolph .... Leitchfield, KY
Behot, Joseph F., Jr. .... Hackensack, NJ
Behounek, Kathleen Nicol .... Minneapolis, MN
Behr and Abramson .... Los Angeles, CA
Behr & Adams .... Edison, NJ
Morristown, NJ
Behr, Anthony R. .... St. Louis, MO
Behr, Barbara E. .... Bloomsburg, PA
Behr, Deborah E. .... Juneau, AK
Behr, Douglas J. .... Washington, DC
Behr, Joel, (A P.C.) .... Los Angeles, CA
Behr, John R., Jr. .... Pensacola, FL
Behr, Laurence D. .... Buffalo, NY
Behr, Mantovani, McCarter & Potter, P.C.
St. Louis, MO
Behr, Matthew Jeffrey .... Atlantic City, NJ
Behr, Mitchel T. .... Iowa City, IA
Behr, Omri M. .... Edison, NJ
Behr, Ralph S. .... Fort Lauderdale, FL
Behr, Richard J. .... St. Louis, MO
Behr, Richard M. .... Key Largo, FL
Behr, Saul D. .... New York, NY
Behr, Warren C. .... Waukegan, IL
Behr, William H. .... New York, NY
Behr, William Morris .... North Bergen, NJ
Behravesh, Ann E. .... Lexington, MA
Behre, John W., Jr. .... New York, NY
Behre, Kirby D. .... Washington, DC
Behren, Robert A. .... New York, NY
Behren, Roy D. .... New York, NY
Behren, Scott M. .... Fort Lauderdale, FL
Behrenbrinker, James R.
Minneapolis, MN
Behrend, Andrew F. .... Anchorage, AK
Behrend, Beth A. .... New York, NY
Behrend, Clarence O. .... West Bend, WI
Behrend & Ernsberger .... Pittsburgh, PA
Behrend, Kenneth R. .... Pittsburgh, PA
Behrend, Kenneth W. .... Pittsburgh, PA
Behrends, F. Louis .... Peoria, IL
Behrends & Gentry .... Peoria, IL
Behrends, Samuel, IV .... Washington, DC
Behrends, Stephen L. .... Eugene, OR
Behrendt, Allan D. .... West Bloomfield, MI
Behrendt, Charlotte L. .... New York, NY
Behrendt, Daniel E. .... Yarmouth Port, MA
Behrendt, Debra E. .... St. Louis, MO
Behrendt, Harry M. .... Maumee, OH
Behrendt, J. Adam .... Detroit, MI
Behrendt, James D. .... West Bloomfield, MI
Behrendt, John T. .... New York, NY
Behrendt, Judy Esther .... Napa, CA
Behrendt, Lawrence B. .... Los Angeles, CA
Behrendt, Louise A. .... Minneapolis, MN
Behrendt, Michael J. .... Findlay, OH
Behrendt & Montello .... St. Louis, MO
Behrendt, Raymond J. .... Chicago, IL
Behrendt, Stephen A. .... Beverly Hills, CA
Behrenfeld, Craig E. .... Tampa, FL
Behrenfeld, William H. .... Sarasota, FL
Behrens, Albert P., Jr., (P.C.)
Petaluma, CA
Behrens, Barbara L. .... St. Louis, MO
Behrens, Brian C. .... St. Louis, MO
Behrens, Bruce A. .... Sacramento, CA
Behrens, Carl R., P.C., Law Offices of
Warner Robins, GA
Behrens, Christopher R.
Port Washington, WI
Behrens, Cinda Sue .... Santa Ana, CA
Behrens, Curtiss K. .... De Kalb, IL
Behrens, Daniel E. .... Marysville, OH
Behrens, David P. .... Pittsburgh, PA
Behrens, Eric G. .... Austin, TX
Behrens, Eric K. .... Oakland, CA
Behrens, George J. .... Chicago, IL
Behrens, James W. .... Madison, WI
Behrens, Jeanne McLean .... Minot, ND
Behrens, Jerome M. .... Fresno, CA
Behrens, Julie A. .... Newport Beach, CA
Behrens, Kay S. .... San Antonio, TX
Behrens, Kersten .... New York, NY
Behrens, Lawrence H. .... Rutland, VT
Behrens, Loew & Cullen .... Melville, NY
Behrens, Mark A. .... Washington, DC
Behrens, Nelson & Knudson
Petaluma, CA
Behrens, R. Thaddeus .... Sacramento, CA
Behrens, Richard J. .... Van Nuys, CA
Behrens, Robert K. .... Hanford, CA
Behrens, Robert S. .... Burlington, VT
Behrens, Russell G., (P.C.)
Costa Mesa, CA
Sacramento, CA
Behrens & Snyder .... Hanford, CA
Behrens, Taylor, Gee, Wheeler & Rainey
Oklahoma City, OK
Behrens, Theresa A. .... East Hartford, CT
Behrens, Tony K. .... Phoenix, AZ
Behrens, Verland E. (Buddy)
Oklahoma City, OK
Behrens, William F. .... Phoenix, AZ
Behring, David E. .... Danville, CA
Behringer, Alan W. .... Wilmington, DE
Behringer & Behringer .... Southampton, NY
Behringer, John W. .... Washington, DC
Behringer, Kenneth C. .... Phoenix, AZ
Behringer, Michael P. .... New York, NY
Behringer, Samuel J., Jr.
Grosse Pointe Farms, MI
Behringer, Thomas E., III .... Southampton, NY
Behringer, Thomas E., Jr. .... Southampton, NY
Behrins, Bruce G. .... Staten Island, NY
Behrle, Clare Radovich .... St. Louis, MO
Behrle, F. Keenan .... Los Angeles, CA
Behrle, Sandra Gale .... New York, NY
Behrman, Bradley G. .... Seattle, WA
Behrman, C. Thomas, Law Offices of
Houston, TX
Behrman, Hillary A. .... Seattle, WA
Behrman, Kenneth .... Atlanta, GA
Behrman, Leslie A. .... Indianapolis, IN
Behrman, Robert A. .... Greeley, CO
Behrmann, James J. .... Houston, TX
Behrmann, Jodie L. .... Denver, CO
Behrmann, John V. .... Jersey City, NJ
Behrmann, Linda K. .... St. Louis, MO
Behrmann, Randall M. .... East Lansing, MI
Behrnd-Klodt, Menzi L. .... Madison, WI
Behrndt, Kevin B. .... St. Louis, MO
Behrns, Michaelle L. .... Omaha, NE
Behroozi, Mitra .... New York, NY
Behrstock, Victor .... Los Angeles, CA
Behuniak, Julie Barland .... New York, NY
Behuniak, Peter P. .... Kingsport, TN
Behuniak, Thomas E. .... Seymour, CT
Behymer, Cheryl L. .... Columbia, SC
Behymer, Lucy West .... Boston, MA
Behymer, Lynn A. .... Carlsbad, CA
Behzadi, Ken K. .... Los Angeles, CA
Beich, Fritz P. .... Houston, TX
Beicke, Robert W. .... White Plains, NY
Beidelman, Larry P. .... Birmingham, MI
Beiderbecke, Edward J. .... Williamson, NY
Beides, Jeffrey M. .... Jersey City, NJ
Beidler, Craig W. .... Marion, OH
Beidler, David Dennis .... Roanoke, VA
Beidler, John N. .... New Brunswick, NJ
Beidler, Marsha W. .... Princeton, NJ
Beidner, Elyse D. .... Hackensack, NJ
Beier, Bart M. .... Pittsburgh, PA
Beier, Bryan .... Washington, DC
Beier, Carol A. .... Wichita, KS
Beier, Carol Weiss .... New York, NY
Beier, David L. .... Woodside, NY
Beier, David W. .... Washington, DC
Beier, Dean G. .... Bloomfield Hills, MI
Beier, Douglas R. .... Morristown, TN
Beier Howlett, Professional Corporation
Birmingham, MI
Bloomfield Hills, MI
Detroit, MI
Pontiac, MI
Beier, Jason T. .... Madison, WI
Beier, Linda J. .... Phoenix, AZ
Beier, Martin D. .... Denver, CO
Beier, Norman S. .... New York, NY
Beier, Ronald Edwin, II .... Troy, MI
Beier, Vicky J. Maine .... Perry, OK
Beier, William B. .... St. Clair, MI
Beierle, Edward R. .... Pasadena, CA
Beierle, Thomas R. .... Denver, CO
Beiermeister, Kathleen L. .... Atlanta, GA
Beiers, John C. .... Redwood City, CA
Beiersdorf, Oliver K .... New York, NY
Beierwaltes, Mark G. .... Chicago, IL
Beigel, Herbert .... Chicago, IL
Beigelman, Mark L. .... New York, NY
Beighey-Giorgiades, Dawn .... Miami, FL
Beighle, Donald J. .... Deer Lodge, MT
Beighle, Randall P. .... Seattle, WA
Beighley, Adam Scott .... Boca Raton, FL
Beighley, George C. .... Columbia, SC
Beighley & Myrick, P.A. .... Boca Raton, FL
Beighley, Ruthanne .... Hermitage, PA
Beight, Thomas L. .... Gaithersburg, MD
Beightol, Scott C. .... Milwaukee, WI
Beighton, Robert F. .... Milwaukee, WI
Beihl, Bruce A. .... Sun City Center, FL
Beihl, Frederick .... Kansas City, MO
Beihl, Gregory W. .... Chicago, IL
Beihl, John P. .... St. Joseph, MO
Beihoff, Jeffrey J. .... Naples, FL
Beihoffer, Denise Boklach .... Chicago, IL
Beik, Stephen W. .... Orlando, FL
Beil, Elizabeth A. .... New York, NY
Beil, Eugene L. .... Hudson, FL
Beil, Gregory M. .... Atlanta, GA
Beil & Hay, P.A. .... Hudson, FL
Beil, Jacob .... Columbus, GA
Beil, Margaret E. .... Hudson, FL
Beil, Marshall .... New York, NY
Beil, Maureen M. .... New York, NY
Beil, William D. .... Kansas City, MO
Beilenson, Anthony C. .... Woodland Hills, CA
Beilenson, Norton Y. .... St. Louis, MO
Beiler, Benjamin .... Chicago, IL
Beilewech, Michael, Jr. .... Buffalo, NY
Beilewech, Peter W. .... Kissimmee, FL
Beiley, Richard A. .... Miami, FL
Beiley, Stanley A. .... Miami, FL
Beiley, Steven L. .... Miami, FL
Beilfuss, Robert P. .... Chicago, IL
Beilicke, Susanne .... San Francisco, CA
Beilin, David M. .... Miami, FL
Beilin, Nancy B. .... Fort Lauderdale, FL
Beilin, Richard H. .... Morris Plains, NJ
Beilin, Robyn A. .... Newport Beach, CA
Beilinson, Marc A. .... Los Angeles, CA
Beilis & Pols, P.C. .... New York, NY

Beilis, Shlomo A. ... New York, NY
Beilke, Jared Wesley ... Los Angeles, CA
Beilke, Michele Jane ... Los Angeles, CA
Beilke, Stephen C. ... Madison, WI
Beilke, Steven J. ... St. Paul, MN
Beilly, Orrin R. ... West Palm Beach, FL
Beilly, Orrin R., P.A.
West Palm Beach, FL
Beilly, Roxanne K. ... Fort Lauderdale, FL
Beilly, Stewart L. ... New York, NY
Beilock, Ellen J. ... San Francisco, CA
Beilock, Steven Alan, Law Offices of
San Francisco, CA
Beilstein, James R. ... Allison Park, PA
Beilstein, Robert W. ... Pittsburgh, PA
Beilue, Renée ... Houston, TX
Beilue & Stewart ... Houston, TX
Beimdiek, Beverly A. ... St. Louis, MO
Beimdiek, Donald U., (P.C.) ... Belleville, IL
St. Louis, MO
Beimdiek, Stephen L. ... St. Louis, MO
Beimers, Thomas W. ... Washington, DC
Beimesch, B. B. ... Covington, KY
Beimfohr, Douglas A. ... Princeton, NJ
New York, NY
Beimfohr, Edward G. ... Bonita Springs, FL
Iselin, NJ
New York, NY
Beimford & Gleason, P.C. ... Denver, CO
Beimford, James H. ... Denver, CO
Beimford, Louis A. ... Hamilton, OH
Beims, H. Scott ... Atwood, KS
Beims, Leslie ... Atwood, KS
Bein, Abraham C. ... Briarcliff Manor, NY
Bein, Joan C. ... Yonkers, NY
Bein, Marie E. ... Bellevue, WA
Bein, Richard H. ... El Cajon, CA
Bein, Robert J. ... Harrisburg, PA
Bein, William S. ... Beachwood, OH
Beinart, Melvin ... New York, NY
Beine & Benz ... Tipton, IA
Beine, David R. ... Kewaskum, WI
Beine, Lee W. ... Tipton, IA
Beinecke, Candace Krugman
New York, NY
Beinecke, Frederick W., II ... New York, NY
Beinecke, William S. ... New York, NY
Beineke, Susan A. ... Lexington, MA
Beineke, Susan A. & Associates, P.C.
Lexington, MA
Beiner, Stephen F. ... Boca Raton, FL
New York, NY
Beinert, Thaniel J. ... Brooklyn, NY
Beinfest, Elliot C. ... Ventnor City, NJ
Beinfield, Robert H. ... Newark, NJ
New York, NY
Beinhauer, Charles W. ... Buffalo, NY
Beinhaur & Curcillo ... Harrisburg, PA
Huntingdon Valley, PA
Beinhaur, John Randell ... Harrisburg, PA
Huntingdon Valley, PA
Beinin, William J. ... New York, NY
Beinke, Allen Penn, Jr. ... Austin, TX
Dallas, TX
Beinkemper, James A., Sr. ... Pittsburgh, PA
Beinlich, Jeffrey C. ... Green Bay, WI
Beinlich Law Offices, S.C. ... Green Bay, WI
Beinner, Wendy S. ... Burlington, VT
Beins, Axelrod & Kraft ... Washington, DC
Beins, Hugh J. ... Washington, DC
Beins, J. Christian ... Cleveland, OH
Beins, John J. ... Rockville, MD
Beinstein, Debra ... Chicago, IL
Beiriger, Tracey Diane ... Alcoa Center, PA
Beirne, Alice ... Rochelle Park, NJ
Beirne, Eidin J. ... Albany, NY
Beirne, James P. ... United States Senate,
Committee Legal Personnel, GV
Beirne, John P. ... Woodbridge, NJ
Beirne, John P. ... New City, NY
Beirne, K. Ruppert ... Richmond, VA
Beirne, Kathleen Walsh ... Houston, TX
Beirne, Martin D. ... Houston, TX
Beirne, Maureen T. ... Athens, PA
Beirne, Maynard & Parsons, L.L.P.
Houston, TX
Beirne, Michael T. ... Chicago, IL
Beirne, Patrick J. ... Cincinnati, OH
Beirne, Thomas R. ... White Plains, NY
Beirne & Wirthlin, Co., L.P.A.
Cincinnati, OH
Beirute, James Daniel ... Tulsa, OK
Beis, Edward B. ... St. Louis, MO
Beischer, Boles & Beischer ... Durham, NC
Beischer, David Dietrich ... Durham, NC
Beischer, George D. ... Durham, NC
Beisel, Bradley N. ... Minneapolis, MN
Beisel, James R., Jr. ... Cortez, CO
Beisel, John K. ... Kingston, NY
Beisenstein, Brian P. ... Appleton, WI
Beisenstein, Joseph J. ... Appleton, WI
Beiser, Jonathan S. ... Rockville, MD
Beiser, Joshua E. ... Boston, MA
Beiser, Julie B. ... Metairie, LA
Beiser, Robert S. ... Chicago, IL
Beiser, Stephen P. ... New Orleans, LA
Beisheim, George, Jr. ... White Plains, NY
Beisheim, John C. ... Rochester, NY
Beisheim, Sarah D. ... Rochester, NY
Beisher, Brian N. ... Sheridan, WY
Beisler, Anthony J., III, (P.A.)
Fort Lauderdale, FL
Beisler, Anthony J., (P.A.)
Fort Lauderdale, FL
Beisler and Beisler ... Fort Lauderdale, FL
West Palm Beach, FL
Beisler, Daniel Paul, Jr. ... Mc Keesport, PA
Beisler, Walter E. ... West Palm Beach, FL

Beisman, James J., Jr. ... Kansas City, MO
Beisman, Mickey ... Los Angeles, CA
Beisner, Amelia L. ... Tallahassee, FL
Beisner, John D. ... Fullerton, CA
Beisner, John H. ... Washington, DC
Beisner, John R. ... Mission Viejo, CA
Beisner, Ralph A. ... Poughkeepsie, NY
Beissner, John H. ... New York, NY
Beisssel, Kelly M. ... Seattle, WA
Beistline, Ralph R. ... Fairbanks, AK
Beiswanger, Gary L. ... Billings, MT
Beiswanger, William J.
North Palm Beach, FL
Beiswenger, Allan ... Soldotna, AK
Beiswenger, John G. ... Burlington, VT
Beiswenger, Scott T.
Inver Grove Heights, MN
Beit, Georgia Z. ... Boston, MA
Beit, Harvey ... Newburyport, MA
Beitch, Bernard D. ... Hollywood, FL
Cherry Hill, NJ
Philadelphia, PA
Beitchman, Lee B. ... Atlanta, GA
Beitel, Annette S. ... San Francisco, CA
Beitel, Bernard ... New York, NY
Beitel, Gordon ... San Antonio, TX
Beitel, Herbert M. ... Cape May, NJ
Beitel, Jay G. ... San Antonio, TX
Beitel, Randy V. ... Seattle, WA
Beitel, Remsen H., III ... Tulsa, OK
Beitel, Richard C.
Department of Transportation,
Federal Aviation Administration, GV
Beiter, John C. ... Nashville, TN
Beiter, Kevin M. ... San Antonio, TX
Beiter, Nancy R.
Department of Transportation,
Surface Transportation Board, GV
Beiter, Sean P. ... Buffalo, NY
Beiter, Sean T. ... San Antonio, TX
Beithon, Patricia A. ... Minnetonka, MN
Beiting, Mary Ann ... Dayton, OH
Beiting, Michael R. ... Akron, OH
Beitler, Albert M. ... New York, NY
Beitler, James E., Jr. ... Berne, IN
Beitler, Laura M. ... Dallas, TX
Beitler Law Firm, P.A. ... Albuquerque, NM
Beitler, Richard I. ... New York, NY
Beitler, Rick ... Albuquerque, NM
Beitler, Robert B. ... Tallahassee, FL
Beitlich, Paul D. ... Sarasota, FL
Beitling, S. Richard ... Lee's Summit, MO
Beitman, Ronald S. ... Falmouth, MA
Beitner, Elliot I. ... Southfield, MI
Beitner, Elliot I., P.C. ... Southfield, MI
Beitner, Leo D. ... Brooklyn, NY
Beitner, Marie C. ... Bingham Farms, MI
Beitner, Norman H. ... Detroit, MI
Beitner, Seymour ... Brighton, MI
Beito, Kristena K. ... Twin Falls, ID
Beitsch, Leslie M. ... Tallahassee, FL
Beitsch, Sheryl Ann ... Fairfax, VA
Beitz, Daniel K. ... Royal Oak, MI
Beitz, James A. ... Minneapolis, MN
Beitz, Toni A. ... Minneapolis, MN
Beitzel, David E. ... Troy, OH
Beizer, Arnold L. ... Hartford, CT
Beizer, David B. ... West Hartford, CT
Beizer, Lance K. ... San Jose, CA
Beizer, Richard L. ... Washington, DC
Beizer, Robert A. ... Washington, DC
Beizer & Weintraub ... West Hartford, CT
Bejar, Benjamin ... Boston, MA
Bejar, Jan J., (Mr.) ... San Diego, CA
Bejar, Jan Joseph, A Professional Law
Corporation ... San Diego, CA
Bejarano, Dario, Jr. ... Santa Maria, CA
Bejarano, Manuel ... El Paso, TX
Bejarano, Manuel, P.C. ... El Paso, TX
Bejerano, Margarita ... New York, NY
Bejger, Roman A. ... New York, NY
Bejin, Gigette Marie ... Southfield, MI
Bejin, Thomas E. ... Troy, MI
Bejnar, Thaddeus P. ... Santa Fe, NM
Bejoian, Laurie J. ... Watertown, MA
Bejsiuk, Peter S. ... Mount Laurel, NJ
Bejsovec, Roy R. ... Brooklyn, NY
Bekavac, Daniel F. ... Clairton, PA
Bekavac, Nancy Y. ... Hanover, NH
Beke, David A. ... New York, NY
Bekele, Daniel ... New York, NY
Bekelja, Joseph S. ... Philadelphia, PA
Bekelnitzky, Seymour G. ... New York, NY
Bekemeyer, Dennis L. ... Los Angeles, CA
Beker, Harry ... Treasury Department,
Internal Revenue Service, GV
Beker, Semion Alon ... Los Angeles, CA
Bekerman, Matthew D. ... Houston, TX
Bekes, Gregory E. ... Salem, IN
Bekhor, Carolyn A. ... Covina, CA
Bekins, Kate ... Walnut Creek, CA
Bekkedahl, Bruce O. ... Sun City, AZ
Billings, MT
Bekken, Dean E. ... San Diego, CA
Bekken, James M. ... New Rockford, ND
Bekken, Martha Elizabeth ... San Diego, CA
Bekken, Robert J. ... Newport Beach, CA
Bekker, Peter H. F. ... New York, NY
Bekkevold, Ralph B. ... Miami, FL
Bekman, Paul D. ... Baltimore, MD
Bekman, Svetlana V. ... Chicago, IL
Beko, Thomas Peter ... Reno, NV
Bekoff, Ronald Jay ... Mineola, NY
Bekolay, Kelly P. ... Bloomfield Hills, MI
Bekritsky, Bruce R. ... Mineola, NY
Bel, Gary L. ... Scarsdale, NY
Belafsky, Betty M. ... Haddonfield, NJ
Belaga, Debra S. ... San Francisco, CA

Belaga, Julianne N. ... Atlanta, GA
Belair & Evans LLP ... Mineola, NY
New York, NY
Belair, Raymond W. ... New York, NY
Belair, Robert R., (P.C.) ... Washington, DC
Belair, Wayne L. ... Lawrence, MA
Belak, Colleen R. ... Denver, CO
Belak, John P. ... Pittsburgh, PA
Belan, Edward J. ... Kansas City, KS
Belancio, Michael L. ... Kansas City, MO
Belancio, Philip A. ... New Orleans, LA
Beland, Lynn M. ... Boston, MA
Beland, Mark J. ... Attleboro, MA
Belanger, Amy E. ... New York, NY
Belanger, Andrew J., Jr.
Clinton Township, MI
Belanger, Brian S. ... Pittsburgh, PA
Belanger, Christina M. ... Vienna, VA
Belanger, Debra A. ... Santa Monica, CA
Belanger, Edmund J. ... Duluth, MN
Belanger, Elizabeth A. ... Port Huron, MI
Belanger, Elizabeth L. ... Boston, MA
Belanger, James H. ... Boston, MA
Belanger, James J. ... Phoenix, AZ
Belanger, James L. ... Darlington, WI
Belanger, James R. ... Philadelphia, PA
Belanger, Jeanne M. ... Boston, MA
Belanger, John ... Detroit, MI
Belanger, Lawrence H. ... Louisville, KY
Belanger, Madalyn Johns ... Rockville, MD
Belanger, Mark L. ... Cambridge, MA
Belanger, Matthew F. ... Rochester, NY
Belanger, Michael ... Oklahoma City, OK
Belanger, Norman R. ... South Portland, ME
Belanger, Paul H. ... Lincoln Park, MI
Belanger & Plimpton ... Fallon, NV
Lovelock, NV
Belanger, Richard M. ... Washington, DC
Belanger, Robert E. ... Stuart, FL
Belanger, Roland W. ... Lovelock, NV
Belanger, Shawnda L. ... Phoenix, AZ
Belanger, Susan V. ... Cleveland, OH
Belanger, Terri A. ... Treasury Department,
Departmental Offices, GV
Belanger, Thomas L. ... Nacogdoches, TX
Belanger, Timothy E. ... Livonia, MI
Belanger, Todd H. ... Indianapolis, IN
Belanger, William C. ... San Luis Obispo, CA
Belanger, William C. ... Livonia, MI
Belanger, William D. ... Washington, DC
Belanger-McNair, Michele M. ... Fresno, CA
Belani, Jagdish G. ... Saratoga, CA
Belanoff, Erik J. ... New York, NY
Belanoff, Sidney ... Mount Kisco, NY
Belansky, Nathan I. ... Falls Church, VA
Belardi, Avelina S. ... Sterling, VA
Belardi, Gene P. ... Arlington, VA
Belardinelli, Richard A. ... Fresno, CA
Belardo, John P. ... Somerville, NJ
Belas, Richard S. ... Washington, DC
Belasco, David A. ... Culver City, CA
Belasco, David A. ... South Orange, NJ
Belasco, Leslie A. ... Philadelphia, PA
Belasco, Louis J., Jr. ... Wildwood, NJ
Belasco, Steven R. ... New York, NY
Belash, John W. ... New York, NY
Belash, Judith G. ... New York, NY
Belasic, Mark A. ... Cleveland, OH
Belasky, Alisa J. ... Oyster Bay, NY
Belasky, Bryan ... New York, NY
Belatti, John L. ... Seattle, WA
Belatti, Michaela M. ... Omaha, NE
Belaustegui, Thomas L. ... Reno, NV
Belaustegui-Traficanti, Merri Lynn
Reno, NV
Belaval, Graciela J. ... San Juan, PR
Belay, Stephen J. ... Decorah, IA
Belazis, Paul T. ... Toledo, OH
Belbel, Caesar J. ... Cambridge, MA
Belber, Timothy J. ... Summit, NJ
Belbruno, Diana Rousseau ... Hartford, CT
Belbusti, John M. ... New York, NY
Belcamino, Beverly A. ... Stamford, CT
Belcamino, Gregory R. ... New York, NY
Belcaster, John F. ... Chicago, IL
Belcastro, Brannon B. ... Jacksonville, FL
Belcastro, Christina M. ... Elmwood Park, IL
Belcastro, J. Matthew ... Jacksonville, FL
Belcastro, Jacquelyne ... Chicago, IL
Belch, Paul T. ... Indianapolis, IN
Belche, George R. ... Lawrenceville, GA
Belcher, Beatrice Lilly ... Brooklyn, NY
Belcher, Bobby S., Jr. ... Norton, VA
Belcher, Carl W. ... Washington, DC
Belcher, Claudia M. ... Emeryville, CA
Belcher, Dana F. ... Wurtsboro, NY
Belcher, David E. ... Baltimore, MD
Belcher, David M. ... Boston, MA
Belcher, Dennis I. ... Richmond, VA
Belcher, Don J. ... San Diego, CA
Belcher, Emma ... Dulles, VA
Belcher, Fred H., Jr. ... Baton Rouge, LA
Belcher, Fred L. ... Nashville, GA
Belcher, George K. ... Montpelier, VT
Belcher, Gordon F. ... New York, NY
Belcher, Henzie & Biegenzahn, A
Professional Corporation
Los Angeles, CA
Belcher, James F. ... Evansville, IN
Belcher, James R., (P.C.) ... Cheyenne, WY
Belcher, Jesse C. ... Greenville, SC
Belcher, John A. ... Los Angeles, CA
Belcher, John C. ... Bellingham, WA
Belcher, John Christopher ... Oxon Hill, MD
Belcher, John S. ... Golden, CO
Belcher, John W. ... San Bernardino, CA
Belcher, Julianna B. ... Marietta, GA
Belcher, Julie ... Marietta, GA

Belcher, Lawrence A. ... Richmond, VA
Belcher, Mark D. ... Washington, DC
Belcher, Martha M. ... Pasadena, CA
Belcher, Michael L. ... Cleveland, OH
Belcher, Milton E. ... Montgomery, AL
Belcher, Nathaniel L. ... Durham, NC
Belcher, Page, Jr. ... Enid, OK
Belcher, Pakchar & Sams ... Atlanta, GA
Belcher, Pat E., II ... Atlanta, GA
Belcher, Paul E. ... Akron, OH
Belcher & Prendergast ... Baton Rouge, LA
Belcher, Reginald Wayne ... Columbia, SC
Belcher, Sarah Lewis ... Syracuse, NY
Belcher, Scott F. ... Washington, DC
Belcher, Swanson, Lackey, Doran, Lewis &
Robertson, P.L.L.C. ... Bellingham, WA
Belcher, Thomas J. ... Bloomington, IN
Belcher, Timothy D. ... Elkhorn City, KY
Belcher, Timothy L. ... Augusta, ME
Belcher, William Fletcher ... Clearwater, FL
Belcher, William Fletcher
St. Petersburg, FL
Belcher, William Gus, II ... Fort Myers, FL
Belcher, William T. ... Clarksburg, WV
Belchic, Albert M. ... Houston, TX
Belcove, Ira J. ... Chicago, IL
Belcuore, Alfred F. ... Chevy Chase, MD
Belcuore, Fred ... Chatham, NJ
Belczak, Michael R. ... North Tonawanda, NY
Belczak, Thomas J. ... Chicago, IL
Beld, Todd Daniel, The Law Office of
Santa Ana, CA
Belda, Rosemarie ... Los Angeles, CA
Beldecos, Anthony J. ... Narberth, PA
Beldecos, Ariadne ... Pittsburgh, PA
Belden, Abbey, Weitzenberg & Kelly
Santa Rosa, CA
Belden, Belden, Persin & Johnston
Greensburg, PA
Belden, Elizabeth C. ... Norcross, GA
Belden, H. Reginald, Jr. ... Greensburg, PA
Belden, Lisabeth R. ... Seattle, WA
Belden, Lois L. ... Stillwater, OK
Belden, Roy S. ... Washington, DC
Belden, Stephen F. ... Canton, OH
Belden, T. Scott ... Bakersfield, CA
Belden, Thomas G. ... Cleveland, OH
Belden, W. Neil ... Washington, DC
Belden, Willard N., Jr. ... Niagara Falls, NY
Belden, William L. ... Indio, CA
Beldin, Barry E. ... Indianapolis, IN
Belding, Bruce W. ... San Francisco, CA
Belding, David E. ... Columbia, SC
Belding, David R. ... Reno, NV
Belding, Harris & Petroni, Ltd. ... Reno, NV
Beldner, James A. ... New York, NY
Beldock, Allen ... Kew Gardens, NY
Beldock, Howard N. ... New York, NY
Beldock Levine & Hoffman LLP
New York, NY
Beldock, Myron ... New York, NY
Beldock, Ovid R. ... Brighton, CO
Beldock, Steven H. ... New City, NY
Beldon, Harry P. ... Millington, NJ
Beldon, Jonathan A.
Department of the Air Force,
Office of the Judge Advocate General, GV
Beldy, Michael D. ... Clarksburg, WV
Belefant & Beller ... New York, NY
Belefant, Martin S. ... New York, NY
Belefant, Peter Thal ... New York, NY
Belefonte, Carmen P. ... Media, PA
Belej, Marko J. ... New York, NY
Belenchia, Thomas Alexander
Spartanburg, SC
Belendiuk, Arthur V. ... Washington, DC
Belenker, Esther ... Department of Commerce,
Patent and Trademark Office, GV
Belenky, Charles Mark ... Los Angeles, CA
Belenky, Erik ... Atlanta, GA
Belenson, Allen G. ... King Of Prussia, PA
BeLer, C. Peter ... Baltimore, MD
Beles, Craig C. ... Seattle, WA
Beles Group, The ... Seattle, WA
Beles, Robert J. ... Oakland, CA
Beless, James W. ... Salt Lake City, UT
Beless, Rosemary J. ... Salt Lake City, UT
Beletic, Anne Turner ... Dallas, TX
Beletsis, Daphne A. ... Santa Rosa, CA
Beletsky, Barry P. ... New Haven, CT
Beletsky, Madge S. ... Los Angeles, CA
Belevetz, Timothy D.
Securities and Exchange Commission,
Division of Enforcement, GV
Belevich, Joanne T. ... Albertson, NY
Belew, Amanda M. ... Knoxville, TN
Belew & Bell ... Batesville, AR
Belew, Christina H. ... New Orleans, LA
Belew, David O., Jr. ... Fort Worth, TX
Belew, John M. ... Batesville, AR
Belfance, Kathryn A. ... Akron, OH
Belfatto, Thomas A. ... Mount Holly, NJ
Belfer, Ira M. ... New York, NY
Belfer, Robert A. ... New York, NY
Belferman, John M. ... United States Senate,
Committee Legal Personnel, GV
Belfield, George M. ... Los Angeles, CA
Belfield, Maria H. ... Dallas, TX
Belfiglio, Jeff ... Bellevue, WA
Belfiglio, Loretta M. ... Paoli, PA
Belfiglio, Victoria L. ... Cleveland, OH
Belfiglio-Finnegan, Lorraine
West Chester, PA
Belfon, Ronald W.
Charlotte Amalie, St. Thomas, VI
Belfonte, Michael J. ... Kansas City, MO
Belford, Aileen Hirschman
New Bedford, MA

Belford, Craig R. ... St. Charles, IL
Belford, John L., IV ... Central Islip, NY
Belford, John L., Jr. ... St. James, NY
Belford, Kevin B. ... Washington, DC
Belford, Lloyd Earl ... Fall River, MA
Belford, Richard ... New Haven, CT
Belford, Richard D. ... New York, NY
Belford, Scott L. ... Joliet, IL
Belford & Stone ... Fall River, MA
Belford, Willis A., Jr. ... Colorado Springs, CO
Belford, Wm. W. ... Milton, PA
Belfort, David E. ... Somerville, MA
Belfort, Robert ... New York, NY
Belforti, Ernest A. ... Dudley, MA
Belfour, Gregory W. ... Lake Charles, LA
Belfry, K. Scott ... Cloquet, MN
Belfry Law Office, Chtd. ... Cloquet, MN
Belgam, Neal C. ... Wilmington, DE
Belgard, Susan ... San Francisco, CA
Belger, Amy M. ... Newark, NJ
Belger, David Charles ... Woodbridge, NJ
Belger, Kathryn Weathers
Department of Transportation,
Federal Highway Administration, GV
Belger, Laurie, (Mr.) ... Redondo Beach, CA
Belger & Norris ... Redondo Beach, CA
Belgiorno, Michael T. ... Pittsford, NY
Belgrad, Herbert J. ... Baltimore, MD
Belgrad, Marshall J. ... Skokie, IL
Belgrade, Mary N. ... Deerfield, IL
Belgrade, Neale Susan ... Hartford, CT
Belgrade and O'Donnell, A Professional Corporation ... Chicago, IL
Belgrade, Steven B. ... Chicago, IL
Belgrave, Carl C. ... Newark, NJ
Belgrave, Dolores J. ... Philadelphia, PA
Belgrove, Angela M. ... San Francisco, CA
Belgum, Karl D. ... San Francisco, CA
Belgum, Stephen L. ... Glendora, CA
Belhasen, Charles K. ... Paintsville, KY
Belian, Julia ... San Francisco, CA
Belice, Jason J. ... San Diego, CA
Belice, John A. ... San Diego, CA
Belik, Barbara Irene ... Portland, ME
Belilos, Elliot ... Washington, DC
Belilove, Morris E. ... Houston, TX
Belilove, Saul ... Oakland, CA
Belilove, Steve R. ... Los Angeles, CA
Belin, Alletta d'Andelot ... Santa Fe, NM
Belin, Carl A., Jr. ... Clearfield, PA
Belin, Daniel N. ... Los Angeles, CA
Belin, Dorrance R. ... Scranton, PA
Belin, James M. ... Naples, FL
Belin, Kim C. ... Mount Laurel, NJ
Belin & Kubista ... Clearfield, PA
Belin Lamson McCormick Zumbach Flynn, A Professional Corporation
Des Moines, IA
Belin, Matthew F. ... New Orleans, LA
Belin, Melvin S.
Department of Housing and Urban Development,
Office of General Counsel, GV
Belin, Oscar F. ... Wichita, KS
Belin Rawlings & Badal LLP
Los Angeles, CA
Belin, Richard d'A. ... Boston, MA
Beling, John D. ... Boston, MA
Belinkie, Alfred R., & Associates
Bridgeport, CT
Belinkie, Diane ... Bridgeport, CT
Belinkie, Harris J. ... Washington, DC
Belinkie, Milton H. ... Bridgeport, CT
Belinkoff, Dena R. ... Oakland, CA
Belinky, Debra Manson ... Columbus, OH
Belinky, Mark A. ... Youngstown, OH
Belinowiz, Patricia E. ... Ludlow, VT
Belinski, Michael T. ... Cranbury, NJ
Belinsky, Ilene B. ... Brockton, MA
Belinsky, Judith O. ... San Diego, CA
Belinsky, Nancy ... San Antonio, TX
Belisario, Diana L. ... Wilkes-Barre, PA
Belisario, Martin ... Philadelphia, PA
Belisle, Brian G. ... Minneapolis, MN
Belisle, Christopher P. ... New York, NY
Belisle, J. Merritt ... Austin, TX
Belisle, John M. ... Worcester, MA
Belisle, Joseph A., III ... Miami, FL
Belisle, Timothy S. ... Johnson City, TN
Belisle, Wayne T. ... St. Paul, MN
Belisonzi, Jon J. ... Philadelphia, PA
Belissary, Christine E. ... Florence, SC
Belitsis, Michael ... Jericho, NY
Belitsky, Eugene V. ... Menlo Park, CA
Belitsos, George ... Fort Lauderdale, FL
Belitz, Paul E. ... Denver, CO
Belitz, Shari E. ... New York, NY
Belitz, Sloane S. ... Liberty Corner, NJ
Belitzky, Joseph ... Tallahassee, FL
Beliveau, Albert J., Jr. ... Portland, ME
Beliveau, Cheryl LePrine ... Manchester, NH
Beliveau, David M. ... Manchester, NH
Beliveau & Fradette ... Manchester, NH
Beliveau, John B. ... Lewiston, ME
Beliveau, John T. ... Austin, TX
Beliveau, Mark E. ... Hampton, NH
Beliveau, Severin M. ... Augusta, ME
Beliveau, Thomas W. ... Worcester, MA
Belk, Bates M. ... El Paso, TX
Belk, Claudia W. ... Charlotte, NC
Belk, Cobb, Infinger & Goldstein, P.A.
Charleston, SC
Belk, Eric M. ... Springfield, MO
Belk, Eric M., P.C. ... Springfield, MO
Belk, Eric S. ... Baltimore, MD
Belk, Fred M., Jr. ... Holly Springs, MS
Belk, Gene C. ... Sumter, SC
Belk, Harry C. ... Charleston, SC
Belk, J. Dixon ... Dalton, GA
Belk, James S. ... Anderson, SC
Belk, John T. ... San Juan, PR
Belk, John W. ... Houston, TX
Belk, Michael E. ... Tarrytown, NY
Belk, Rita Marie ... Endicott, NY
Belk, Robert C. ... El Paso, TX
Belk, W. Dean ... Indianola, MS
Belkadi, Hamida ... Hartsdale, NY
Belk-Arce, James W. ... San Juan, PR
Belke, Becky J. ... Los Angeles, CA
Belke, Brad L. ... Butte, MT
Belke, Marianne Morris ... Milwaukee, WI
Belke, Paul G. ... Milwaukee, WI
Belker, Norman L. ... Louisville, KY
Belker, Norman L. "Nick" ... Louisville, KY
Belkin, Alan ... General Accounting Office,
Office of the General Counsel, GV
Belkin, Bernard ... Morristown, NJ
Belkin, Billick & Harrold
Beachwood, OH
Cleveland, OH
Belkin Burden Wenig & Goldman, LLP
Westport, CT
New York, NY
Belkin, Charles L. ... Sacramento, CA
Belkin, David H. ... Rockville, MD
Belkin, Elizabeth H. ... Chicago, IL
Belkin, Gary G. ... Chicago, IL
Belkin, Harvey ... Danbury, CT
Belkin, Howard H. ... New Britain, CT
Belkin, Janet E. ... New York, NY
Belkin, Jeffrey ... Washington, DC
Belkin, Jeffrey A. ... Cleveland, OH
Belkin, John D. ... Omaha, NE
Belkin, Leonard ... Washington, DC
Belkin, M. Randolph ... Poughkeepsie, NY
Belkin, Matt Randolph ... White Plains, NY
Belkin, Richard ... Pittsburgh, PA
Belkin, Scott Ross ... Los Angeles, CA
Belkin, Sherwin ... New York, NY
Belkin, Susan S. ... Scarsdale, NY
Belknap, Ann B. Hook ... Bensalem, PA
Belknap, Ann Dudley ... Greenwich, CT
Belknap, Christie C. ... New York, NY
Belknap, Dana Stagg ... Phoenix, AZ
Belknap, Douglas A. ... Phoenix, AZ
Belknap, Hobart D., Jr. ... Rosemead, CA
Belknap, Jerry P. ... Indianapolis, IN
Belknap, Jonathan T. ... Fraser, CO
Belknap, Keith L., Jr. ... Chicago, IL
Belknap, Robert H. ... New Orleans, LA
Belknap, Thomas H. ... Boston, MA
Belknap, Thomas H., Jr. ... New York, NY
Belknap, Wendell L. ... Oregon City, OR
Belko, John M. ... Moorestown, NJ
Belko, Kristin ... Santa Ana, CA
Belkowitz, David F. ... Richmond, VA
Belkowitz, Harold G. ... Washington, DC
Belkowitz, Nancy M. ... Manlius, NY
Belkowski, Anthony J. ... Florham Park, NJ
New York, NY
Bell, A. Fleming, II ... Chapel Hill, NC
Bell, A. Gary, Jr. ... Littleton, CO
Steamboat Springs, CO
Bell, Aaron J. ... Portland, OR
Bell, Adam W. ... Portland, OR
Bell, Adubato & Ligham ... East Orange, NJ
Bell, Aileen ... New Haven, CT
Bell, Alan D. ... Fort Lee, NJ
Montclair, NJ
Bell, Alan J. ... Stayton, OR
Bell, Alan M. ... Chicago, IL
Bell, Alan W. ... Salt Lake City, UT
Bell, Albert J. ... Columbus, OH
Bell, Albert L. ... Columbus, OH
Bell, Albert R. ... Glencoe, IL
Bell, Albert R., Jr. ... New Bern, NC
Raleigh, NC
Bell, Alexander W. ... Lynchburg, VA
Bell, Alexander W., Law Office of
Lynchburg, VA
Bell, Alfred B. ... Greensburg, PA
Bell, Alfred R. ... West Palm Beach, FL
Bell, Alison J. ... Burlington, VT
Bell, Allan C. ... Newark, NJ
Bell, Allan H. ... North Kansas City, MO
Bell, Allen A., Jr. ... Paris, IL
Bell, Allen Eli ... Austin, TX
Bell, Allen M. ... Tenafly, NJ
Bell, Allison C. ... New Orleans, LA
Bell, Alvin E., III ... Phoenix, AZ
Bell, Alvin York ... Chattanooga, TN
Bell, Amanda F. ... Houston, TX
Bell, Amy Clifton ... West Helena, AR
Bell, Angelia D. ... Jackson, MS
Bell, Anker M. ... Columbus, OH
Bell & Ankley ... Kalamazoo, MI
Bell, Ann M. ... Houston, TX
Bell, Anne Middleton Nancy ... Sumter, SC
Bell, Anthony E. ... Los Angeles, CA
Bell, Anthony E. ... Washington, DC
Bell, Arthur Watson ... Searcy, AR
Bell, Asa L., Jr. ... Raleigh, NC
Bell & Associates ... Charleston, WV
Bell & Associates, P.A. ... Cabot, AR
Bell & Associates, P.A. ... Jackson, MS
Madison, MS
Bell and Associates, P.C. ... Cleveland, TN
Bell, Barbara E. ... Great Falls, MT
Bell, Barbara J. ... Fremont, CA
Bell, Barrett S. ... Palmetto, FL
Bell, Barry G. ... Jefferson Valley, NY
Bell, Barry L. ... San Diego, CA
Bell, Barry R. ... Dallas, TX
Bell & Bell ... Fort Lauderdale, FL
Bell & Bell ... Indianapolis, IN
Bell and Bell ... Steelville, MO
Bell and Bell ... Salt Lake City, UT
Bell, Benjamin H., Jr. ... Summerville, SC
Bell, Bernard P. ... Washington, DC
Bell, Bertram ... Akron, OH
Bell, Beverly J. ... Melville, NY
Bell, Blake A. ... New York, NY
Bell, Bonnie A. ... Denver, CO
Bell, Boyd & Lloyd ... Washington, DC
Chicago, IL
Deerfield, IL
Bell, Brandon E. ... Chicago, IL
Bell, Braxton H. ... Rocky Mount, NC
Bell, Brehm T. ... Bay St. Louis, MS
Bell, Brenda J. ... Manhattan, KS
Bell, Brent C. ... Orlando, FL
Bell, Brian M. ... Castle Rock, CO
Bell, Brian W. ... Chicago, IL
Bell, Brigitte Schmidt ... Lake Forest, IL
Bell, Brigitte Schmidt, P.C. ... Chicago, IL
Lake Forest, IL
Bell and Browne, P.A. ... Asheboro, NC
Bell, Bruce A. ... Albany, NY
Bell, Bruce A. ... Philadelphia, PA
Bell, Bruce E. ... Chicago, IL
Bell, Bruce M. ... Fremont, CA
Bell, Bruce R. ... Everett, WA
Bell, C. Raymond ... Alton, IL
Bell, C. Robert ... Wichita, KS
Bell, Candace Lynn ... Buffalo, NY
Bell, Carl A. ... Wichita, KS
Bell, Carl E. ... Mount Airy, NC
Bell, Carmela Leone ... Baltimore, MD
Bell, Carol J. ... St. Cloud, MN
Bell, Carole A. ... San Francisco, CA
Bell, Caroline K. ... Atlanta, GA
Bell, Carolyn Pierce ... Los Angeles, CA
Bell, Carolyn R. ... Palm Beach Gardens, FL
Bell, Catherine Lee ... Houston, TX
Bell, Cathleen G. ... Tampa, FL
Bell, Cathy A. ... New York, NY
Bell, Charles A. ... Fort Lauderdale, FL
Bell, Charles C. ... Pittsburgh, PA
Bell, Charles D. ... Wellsburg, WV
Bell, Charles E. ... San Diego, CA
Bell, Charles F. ... Los Angeles, CA
Bell, Charles G. ... Dallas, TX
Bell, Charles H., Jr. ... Sacramento, CA
Bell, Charles K. ... San Diego, CA
Bell, Charles L., Jr. ... Washington, PA
Bell, Charles M. ... Ellicott City, MD
Bell, Charles M., A Professional Association
Ellicott City, MD
Bell, Charles N. ... Dallas, TX
Bell, Charles T. ... Washington, DC
Bell, Charles T., Jr. ... Atlanta, GA
Bell, Charles W. ... Bethany Beach, DE
Bell, Charles W. ... Savannah, GA
Bell, Charles W., & Associates, P.C.
Savannah, GA
Bell, Charlotte R. ... Falls Church, VA
Bell, Cheri A. ... Palo Alto, CA
Bell, Cheryl A. ... Chicago, IL
Bell, Cheryl L. ... Tustin, CA
Bell, Cheryl Takacs ... Detroit, MI
Bell, Christopher D. ... Portland, OR
Bell, Christopher D. ... McLean, VA
Bell, Christopher G. ... Minneapolis, MN
Bell, Christopher J. ... La Place, LA
Bell, Christopher K. ... Austin, TX
Bell, Christopher L. ... Washington, DC
Bell, Clarence D., Jr. ... Media, PA
Bell, Clarence D., Sr. ... Media, PA
Bell, Clark R. ... Asheboro, NC
Bell, Colin F. ... New York, NY
Bell, Colleen Larkin ... Salt Lake City, UT
Bell, Craig A. ... Grand Rapids, MI
Bell, Craig D. ... Richmond, VA
Bell, Craig H. ... Los Angeles, CA
Bell, Craig M. ... Philadelphia, PA
Bell, Crayton L. ... New York, NY
Bell, Curtis A. ... Des Moines, IA
Bell, Curtis H. ... Elberton, GA
Bell, Curtis J. ... Kalamazoo, MI
Bell, D. Andrew ... Phoenix, AZ
Bell, D. Craig ... Midvale, UT
Bell, Dale W. ... Emporia, KS
Bell, Damon L. ... Rockville, MD
Bell, Daniel C. ... Clearfield, PA
Bell, Daniel L. ... Pasadena, CA
Bell, Daniel L. ... Akron, OH
Bell, Daniel L., II ... Alexandria, VA
Bell, Daniel L., Jr. ... Vero Beach, FL
Bell, Daniel S. ... East Orange, NJ
Bell, Daniel Scott ... Kansas City, MO
Bell, Daniel W. ... Santa Ana, CA
Bell, Darren R. ... Waco, TX
Bell, Darryl S. ... Milwaukee, WI
Bell, Daryl L. ... Bountiful, UT
Bell, David ... Dallas, TX
Bell, David A. ... Palo Alto, CA
Bell, David A. ... Louisville, KY
Bell, David A. ... Lynnfield, MA
Bell, David A. ... Cleveland, OH
Bell, David B. ... Augusta, GA
Bell, David D. ... Evansville, IN
Bell, David I. ... Glendale, CA
Bell, David L. ... Los Angeles, CA
Bell, David L. ... Chicago, IL
Bell, David M. ... Phoenix, AZ
Bell, David O. ... Oxford, MS
Bell, David, P.C. ... Dallas, TX
Bell, David S. ... Baton Rouge, LA
Bell, David S. ... Kansas City, MO
Bell, David T. ... Ann Arbor, MI
Bell, Davis & Pitt, P.A.
Winston-Salem, NC
Bell, Dean B. ... Hilton Head Island, SC
Bell, Deon Woods ... Washington, DC
Bell, Dexter L. ... United States Senate,
Committee Legal Personnel, GV
Bell & Dickey ... Berlin, PA
Bell, Don F. ... Oklahoma City, OK
Bell, Donald C. ... Phoenix, AZ
Bell, Donald G. ... Vincennes, IN
Bell, Donald J. ... New London, IA
Bell, Donald L. ... Tallahassee, FL
Bell, Donald L., II ... Alexandria, VA
Bell, Douglas J. ... Cleveland, OH
Bell, Douglas L. ... Everett, WA
Bell, Douglas McCall ... Berlin, PA
Bell, Douglas R. ... Fort Lauderdale, FL
Bell, Douglas S. ... Tallahassee, FL
Bell, Drucilla E. ... Seminole, FL
Bell, Drucilla E., P.A. ... Seminole, FL
Bell, Duane R. ... Bridgeton, NJ
Bell, Earnest C.S. ... Ventura, CA
Bell, Edward C. ... Alameda, CA
Bell, Edward C. ... Coral Gables, FL
Bell, Edward J. ... Arlington, VA
Bell, Edward J., III ... Norge, VA
Bell, Edward, Jr. ... Altavista, VA
Bell, Edward M. ... Berkeley, CA
Bell, Edwin G. ... Fort Worth, TX
Bell, Eileen L. ... Chicago, IL
Bell, Eleanor Lorraine ... Washington, DC
Bell, Ellen F. ... Cleveland Heights, OH
Bell, Eric E. ... Cleveland, OH
Bell, Erica ... New York, NY
Bell, Ernest L. ... Keene, NH
Bell, Eugene G. ... Tulsa, OK
Bell, Everett ... Houston, TX
Bell, Everett A. ... Cleveland, OH
Bell, F. Cortez, III ... Clearfield, PA
Bell, F. Cortez, Jr. ... Clearfield, PA
Bell, F. Daniel, III ... Raleigh, NC
Bell & Falk, P.A. ... Keene, NH
Bell, Faria & Bell, A Professional Corporation
Fremont, CA
Bell, Felicia G. ... Miami, FL
Bell, Francis D. ... Valley Stream, NY
Bell, Francis L., Jr. ... Lancaster, SC
Bell, Frank ... San Mateo, CA
Bell, Frank L. ... Pensacola, FL
Bell, Frank M., Jr. ... Winston-Salem, NC
Bell, Frank T. ... Colquitt, GA
Bell, Fred E. ... Lansing, MI
Bell, Fred F., Sr. ... Huntsville, AL
Bell, G. Ross ... Birmingham, AL
Bell, G. Thompson, III ... Reading, PA
Bell, Garland O., Jr. ... Pasadena, CA
Bell, Gary M. ... New York, NY
Bell, Gary T. ... Merrillville, IN
Bell, Gene E. ... Birmingham, AL
Bell, George J. ... Champaign, IL
Bell, George M., II ... Winston-Salem, NC
Bell, George T. ... Harrisburg, PA
Bell, Gerald L. ... Murray, KY
Bell, Gierhart & Moore, S.C.
Madison, WI
Bell, Glendon G. ... Woodbury, NJ
Bell, Glenn W., Jr. ... Baltimore, MD
Bell, Gregory A. ... New York, NY
Bell, Gregory D. ... Hutchinson, KS
Bell, Gregory S. ... Fort Collins, CO
Bell, Gregory S. ... Peoria, IL
Bell, Gregory V. ... Chicago, IL
Bell, Griffin B. ... Atlanta, GA
Bell, Griffin B., Jr. ... Atlanta, GA
Bell and Griffith, L.C. ... Princeton, WV
Bell, H. Clark ... Kingston, NY
Bell, H. Gene ... Knoxville, TN
Bell, Haney H., III ... Greensboro, NC
Bell, Harold E. ... Norfolk, VA
Bell, Harry F., Jr. ... Charleston, WV
Bell, Harvey L. ... Cabot, AR
Bell, Helen M. ... Moreland Hills, OH
Bell, Henry Denmark ... Franklin, TN
Bell, Herbert J. ... Downers Grove, IL
Bell, Herbert J., Ltd. ... Downers Grove, IL
Bell, H. F. ... Chesterfield, SC
Bell, Hilton S., (P.C.) ... New Orleans, LA
Bell, Hiram C., Jr. ... Jacksonville, NC
Bell, Howard E. ... New York, NY
Bell, Howard H. ... Oakland, CA
Bell, Howard H. ... Washington, DC
Bell, Hubert J., Jr. ... Atlanta, GA
Bell, Hubert, Jr., Law Office of
Austin, TX
Bell, Hugh H. ... Madison, WI
Bell, Hugh M. ... Fort Lauderdale, FL
Bell, Ida May Peterson ... Long Beach, CA
Bell & Ingram, P.S. ... Everett, WA
Seattle, WA
Bell, Ira ... Chicago, IL
Bell, Irving ... Cleveland, OH
Bell, J. Carlton ... North Myrtle Beach, SC
Bell, J. Edward, III ... Florence, SC
Sumter, SC
Bell, J. Michael ... Houston, TX
Bell, J. Mitchell ... Dallas, TX
Bell, J. Richard ... Salt Lake City, UT
Bell, J. Scott ... Denver, CO
Bell, Jack C. ... Gainesville, GA
Bell, Jacque Benson ... Salt Lake City, UT
Bell, Jacqueline E. ... Seattle, WA
Bell & James ... Augusta, GA
Bell, James A. ... St. George, SC
Summerville, SC
Bell, James A., Attorney at Law, P.A.
Orangeburg, SC
St. George, SC
Summerville, SC
Bell, James A. H., P.C., Law Offices of
Knoxville, TN
Bell, James A., IV ... Philadelphia, PA
Bell, James A. H. ... Knoxville, TN

Bell, James D. ... **Madison, MS**
Bell, James D. ... Brockport, NY
Bell, James E. R. ... Frankfort, KY
Bell, James F. ... Washington, DC
Bell, James F. ... Holmes Beach, FL
Bell, James G. ... Bellingham, WA
Bell, James H. ... **New York, NY**
Bell, James H., (P.C.) ... Kansas City, MO
Bell, James L. ... **Charleston, SC**
Columbia, SC
Bell, James M. ... **Fresno, CA**
Bell, James M. ... Cranford, NJ
Bell, James O. ... Santa Fe, NM
Bell, James O., P.A. ... Santa Fe, NM
Bell, James R. ... **St. Paul, MN**
Bell, James R. ... Cincinnati, OH
Bell, James R. ... **Austin, TX**
Dallas, TX
Bell, James R. ... **Casper, WY**
Bell, James S. ... Woodland Hills, CA
Bell, James W. ... Knoxville, TN
Bell, Jamey ... Hartford, CT
Bell, Jane A. ... **Boston, MA**
Bell, Janet Goldstein ... Scarsdale, NY
Bell, Janet L. ... **Cincinnati, OH**
Bell, Janette M. ... Painesville, OH
Bell, Jason B. ... **Bowling Green, KY**
Elizabethtown, KY
Bell, Jason S. ... **Atlanta, GA**
Bell, Jay B. ... **Salt Lake City, UT**
Bell, Jaynelle K. ... Hayward, CA
Bell, J. C. ... Hattiesburg, MS
Bell, Jeffrey A. ... Little Rock, AR
Bell, Jeffrey H. ... Brigham City, UT
Bell, Jeffrey M. ... Fort Lauderdale, FL
Bell, Jeffrey S. ... North Kansas City, MO
Bell, Jeffrey S. ... **Bridgewater, NJ**
Bell, Jeffrey T. ... Los Angeles, CA
Bell, Jeffrey W. ... **Atlanta, GA**
Bell, Jeffrey W. ... Chicago, IL
Bell, Jennifer ... San Francisco, CA
Bell, Jennifer A. ... Whippany, NJ
Bell, Jeremy S. ... **New York, NY**
Bell, Jerrold M. ... **Dallas, TX**
Bell, Jerry A., Jr. ... **Houston, TX**
Bell, Jerry D. ... Overland Park, KS
Bell, Jesse C. ... **Anchorage, AK**
Bell, Joe D., (P.A.) ... **Little Rock, AR**
Bell, Joe Warner ... Groveton, TX
Bell, Joel ... McLean, VA
Bell, Joel M. ... Chicago, IL
Bell, John A. ... **Keene, NH**
Bell, John A. ... Newport, TN
Bell, John Ashley ... Cincinnati, OH
Bell, John C. ... Birmingham, AL
Bell, John C. ... Mobile, AL
Bell, John C., Jr. ... **Augusta, GA**
Bell, John D. ... **Corpus Christi, TX**
Bell, John D. ... **Dallas, TX**
Bell, John E. ... St. Louis, MO
Bell, John F. ... Washington, PA
Bell, John F., Jr. ... Arlington, TX
Bell, John G. ... St. Paul, MN
Bell, John G. ... Hamilton, MT
Bell, John L. ... Rock Island, IL
Bell, John L. ... Plattsburgh, NY
Bell, John R. ... Sacramento, CA
Bell, John S. ... Redwood City, CA
Bell, John S. ... Front Royal, VA
Bell, John Sammons ... Atlanta, GA
Bell, John T. ... **Rockville, MD**
Bell, John U., III ... **Columbia, SC**
Bell, John V. ... Oceanside, CA
Bell, John W. ... Atlanta, GA
Bell, John W. ... **Chicago, IL**
Bell, John W. ... St. Louis Park, MN
Bell, John W. ... San Antonio, TX
Bell, John W. ... Burke, VA
Bell, Jonathan ... **Boston, MA**
Providence, RI
Bell, Jonathan R. ... **New York, NY**
Bell Jones Quinlisk & Palmer
Chicago, IL
Bell, Jordan ... Chicago, IL
Bell, Joseph ... New York, NY
Bell, Joseph ... **Philadelphia, PA**
Bell, Joseph C. ... **Washington, DC**
Bell, Joseph E., II ... Leonardtown, MD
Bell, Joseph E., Jr. ... **Philadelphia, PA**
Bell, Joseph J. ... Grass Valley, CA
Bell, Joseph J., Jr. ... Boonton, NJ
Bell, Joseph Luther, Jr. ... Rocky Mount, NC
Bell, Joseph W. ... **San Francisco, CA**
Bell, Joshua C. ... Cairo, GA
Bell, Judith V.C. ... Manchester, NH
Bell, Judy B. ... Anchorage, AK
Bell, Jules ... Glenside, PA
Bell, Julia Renell ... Lansing, MI
Bell, Julie Ann ... **Palo Alto, CA**
Bell, Julie L. ... **Raleigh, NC**
Bell, Julie S. ... Redmond, WA
Bell, Karen ... Richmond, VA
Bell, Karen Z. ... Larchmont, NY
Bell, Karla H. ... **Austin, TX**
Bell, Kathleen Rust ... Fairfax, VA
Bell, Keith A. ... **Houston, TX**
Bell, Keith E. ... Department of Labor,
Office of the Solicitor, GV
Bell, Keith E. ... Sharon, PA
Bell, Keith W. ... Anchorage, AK
Bell, Kenneth A. ... Spokane, WA
Bell, Kenneth B. ... Milton, FL
Bell, Kenneth G. ... **Las Vegas, NV**
Bell, Kenneth R. ... Wichita, KS
Bell, Kenneth S. ... Hamilton, MT
Bell, Kevin ... Baltimore, MD
Bell, Kevin H. ... **Washington, DC**
Bell, Kevin H. ... Houston, TX
Bell, Kevin K. ... **Columbia, SC**
Bell, Kevin M. ... **Washington, DC**
Bell, Kim A. ... **Wichita, KS**
Bell, Kimber K. ... Northridge, CA
Bell, L. Graeme, III ... **Washington, DC**
Bell, Laertes T. ... Chicago, IL
Bell, Langdon D. ... **Columbus, OH**
Bell, Laura Jean A. ... New Bern, NC
Bell, Laurie J. ... Walnut Creek, CA
Bell Law Firm ... **Jacksonville, NC**
Bell Law Firm, The, P.A. ... **Magnolia, AR**
Bell Law Firm, The, P.A. ... **Charleston, SC**
Columbia, SC
Bell Law Office ... Mt. Pleasant, IA
Bell, Lawrence C. ... Hackensack, NJ
Bell, Lawrence M. ... **New York, NY**
Bell, Lawrence M. ... **Cleveland, OH**
Bell, Lawrence T. ... **St. Paul, MN**
Bell, Lee J. ... **Canton, OH**
Bell, Leeper & Roper, P.A. ... **Orlando, FL**
Bell, Leon & Ramirez, P.L.C.
Davenport, IA
Bell, Leonard M. ... **Phoenix, AZ**
Bell, Leslie E. ... Atlanta, GA
Bell, Lewis W. ... **Jackson, MS**
Bell, Linda Marie ... Las Vegas, NV
Bell, Lindsey G. ... Burkesville, KY
Bell, Lisa C. ... Charlotte, NC
Bell and Liss, LLC ... Silver Spring, MD
Bell, Lloyd N. ... **Atlanta, GA**
Bell, Lois A. ... Winchester, IL
Bell, Loren P. ... **Salem, OR**
Bell, Louis ... **Philadelphia, PA**
Bell, Louis I., (A Professional Corporation)
Beverly Hills, CA
Bell, Louis Michael ... Chicago, IL
Bell, Lynn E. ... **Pittsburgh, PA**
Bell, M. Doug ... **Coffeyville, KS**
Bell, M. Ramsay ... Darien, CT
Bell, M. Walter ... Indianapolis, IN
Bell, Magdalena ... Bethesda, MD
Bell & Mann ... Winchester, IL
Bell, Marc N. ... Miami, FL
Bell, Marcella A. ... **Los Angeles, CA**
Bell, Marcia R. ... San Francisco, CA
Bell, Margaret G. ... West Unity, OH
Bell, Marie W. ... Mount Holly, NJ
Bell, Mark E. ... **Indianapolis, IN**
Bell, Mark Fitzgerald ... Salt Lake City, UT
Bell, Mark Forrest ... **Denver, CO**
Bell, Mark W. ... Nashville, TN
Bell, Marla R. ... **Kansas City, MO**
Bell & Marra, PLLC ... **Great Falls, MT**
Bell, Marshall A.
Charlotte Amalie, St. Thomas, VI
Bell, Marshall A., and Associates, P.C.
Charlotte Amalie, St. Thomas, VI
Bell, Martin A. ... New York, NY
Bell, Martin L. ... Baton Rouge, LA
Bell, Mary E. ... Pittsburgh, PA
Bell, Mary Hockwalt ... Akron, OH
Bell, Mary Therese
Department Of Veterans Affairs,
Office of the General Counsel, GV
Bell, Maureen A. ... **Orlando, FL**
Bell, Maurice H., Jr. ... Richmond, VA
Bell, Maurice H., Jr., P.C. ... Richmond, VA
Bell, Maurice S. ... Montgomery, AL
Bell, McMullen & Cross ... Wellsburg, WV
Bell & McRight, P.C. ... Birmingham, AL
Bell, Melissa Y. ... **Jacksonville, FL**
Bell, Michael ... Schertz, TX
Bell, Michael A. ... **Riverside, CA**
Bell, Michael A. ... **Washington, DC**
Bell, Michael A. ... **Washington, DC**
Bell, Michael A. ... Lewiston, ME
Bell, Michael A. ... Flat Rock, MI
Bell, Michael C. ... **Oklahoma City, OK**
Bell, Michael D. ... **Washington, DC**
Bell, Michael F. ... **Los Angeles, CA**
Bell, Michael J. ... **Tucson, AZ**
Bell, Michael J. ... **Washington, DC**
Bell, Michael J. ... New Orleans, LA
Bell, Michael K. ... **Houston, TX**
Bell, Michael L. ... **Birmingham, AL**
Bell, Michael L. ... **Pittsburgh, PA**
Bell, Michael M. ... **Orlando, FL**
Bell, Michael P. ... Silver Spring, MD
Bell, Michael S. ... Florence, SC
Bell, Mildred B. ... Macon, GA
Bell, M'Lou Patton ... Austin, TX
Bell, M'Lou Patton ... **Austin, TX**
Bell, Morris R. ... Oklahoma City, OK
Bell, Murphy W. ... Baton Rouge, LA
Bell, Murray W. ... Davenport, IA
Bell, Myrlen L. ... Medicine Lodge, KS
Bell, N. Melina ... **Boston, MA**
Dedham, MA
Bell, Nadine N. ... Los Angeles, CA
Bell, Nancy E.
Federal Election Commission,
Office of the General Counsel, GV
Bell, Nathan D. ... **Skowhegan, ME**
Bell, Nicole ... Norman, OK
Bell, Nunnally & Martin, LLP ... **Dallas, TX**
Bell, O. Nile ... Potomac, MD
Bell, O'Connor, Flegenheimer and Leong
Seattle, WA
Bell & O'Connor, P.C. ... **Phoenix, AZ**
Bell, Orr, Ayers & Moore, P.S.C.
Bowling Green, KY
Bell, Orrock & Watase, LLP
Riverside, CA
Bell & Ort, P.C. ... New London, IA
Bell, Pamela Cole ... Seminole, FL
Bell, Pamela Cole, P.A. ... Seminole, FL
Bell, Patricia G. ... **Los Angeles, CA**
Bell, Patricia Holmes ... Brooklyn, NY
Bell, Patrick B., (Mrs.) ... Richmond, VA
Bell, Patrick J. ... Annapolis, MD
Bell, Paul A., II ... **Indiana, PA**
Bell, Paul B. ... **Charlotte, NC**
Bell, Paul B., Jr. ... Concord, NC
Bell, Paul E. ... San Diego, CA
Bell, Paul L. ... Steelville, MO
Bell, Paul M. ... Redding, CA
Bell, Paul N. ... **Boston, MA**
Bell, Peggy H. ... Greeneville, TN
Bell, Penny P. ... Conroe, TX
Bell, Pensyl & Levine ... **Chicago, IL**
Bell, Peter A. ... Punta Gorda, FL
Bell, Peter G. ... Chicago, IL
Bell, Philip M. ... Pittsburgh, PA
Bell & Pollock, P.C. ... Littleton, CO
Steamboat Springs, CO
Bell, R. Christopher ... **Houston, TX**
Bell, R. Locke ... Gastonia, NC
Bell, R. Ripley, Jr. ... **Albany, GA**
Bell, R. Terry ... **Dallas, TX**
Bell, Ralph Gavin ... New York, NY
Bell, Randall S. ... **Santa Fe, NM**
Bell, Randall Theron ... Columbia, SC
Bell, Ranlet S. ... **Winston-Salem, NC**
Bell, Rebecca ... Princeton, WV
Bell, Rebecca Ann ... Knoxville, TN
Bell, Rebekah E. ... Oak Ridge, TN
Bell, Reginald J. ... **Atlanta, GA**
Bell, Rehder & Rose ... **Bethesda, MD**
Gaithersburg, MD
Potomac, MD
Rockville, MD
Bell, René F. ... Houston, TX
Bell, Rex, & Associates ... **Las Vegas, NV**
Bell, Richard ... Atlanta, GA
Bell, Richard A. ... Norman, OK
Bell, Richard A. ... **Clearfield, PA**
Bell, Richard A., P.C. ... Norman, OK
Bell, Richard C. ... Charleston, SC
Bell, Richard G. ... **Los Altos, CA**
Bell, Richard G. ... **New Haven, CT**
Bell, Richard G. ... Winston-Salem, NC
Bell, Richard J. ... Mt. Pleasant, IA
Bell, Richard M. ... **Minneapolis, MN**
Bell, Richard N. ... **Indianapolis, IN**
Bell, Richard P. ... Galveston, TX
Bell, Richard W. ... **Birmingham, AL**
Bell, Richard W. ... **Atlanta, GA**
Bell, Richardson, Smith & Callahan, P.A.
Athens, AL
Decatur, AL
Guntersville, AL
Hartselle, AL
Huntsville, AL
Scottsboro, AL
Bell, Robbie Hancock ... Nashville, TN
Bell, Robert ... Norman, OK
Bell, Robert A. ... Columbus, OH
Bell, Robert B. ... **Washington, DC**
Bell, Robert B. ... Atlanta, GA
Bell, Robert B. ... Orange, VA
Bell, Robert C. ... **St. Paul, MN**
Bell, Robert C. ... Reno, NV
Bell, Robert C., Jr. ... New Canaan, CT
Bell, Robert C., Jr. ... New York, NY
Bell, Robert D. ... Pensacola, FL
Bell, Robert E. ... Edna, TX
Bell, Robert Holmes ... Grand Rapids, MI
Bell, Robert J. ... **San Diego, CA**
Bell, Robert, Jr. ... **Chicago, IL**
Bell, Robert L. ... Washington, DC
Bell, Robert L., Jr. ... Melrose, MA
Bell, Robert Lamar ... Miami, FL
Bell, Robert M. ... Baltimore, MD
Bell, Robert M. ... Langley, SC
Bell, Robert McKim ... Los Angeles, CA
Bell, Robert P. ... Beaverton, OR
Bell, Robert P. ... Alexandria, VA
Bell, Robert Platt & Assocs., P.C.
Alexandria, VA
Bell, Robert R. ... **Amarillo, TX**
Bell, Robert S. ... Indiana, PA
Bell, Robert S., Jr. ... **Windsor, CT**
Bell, Robert S., Jr. ... Chicago, IL
Bell, Robert T. ... **Missoula, MT**
Bell, Robert W. ... **Sacramento, CA**
Bell, Robert W., Jr. ... **San Diego, CA**
Bell, Robert Y. ... Santa Rosa, CA
Bell, Roberta S. ... **New York, NY**
Bell, Robin Olinger ... Dayton, OH
Bell, Rodland G. ... Portland, OR
Bell, Rodney H. ... **Miami, FL**
Bell, Rodney W. ... **Irvine, CA**
Bell, Ronald ... Colorado Springs, CO
Bell, Ronald A. ... Albuquerque, NM
Bell, Ronald A. ... **Cincinnati, OH**
Bell, Ronald A., & Associates, P.C.
Albuquerque, NM
Bell, Ronald I. ... Chelmsford, MA
Bell, Ronald P. ... Sequim, WA
Bell, Ronald P., P.S. ... Sequim, WA
Bell, Ronald Scott ... Cupertino, CA
Bell, Ronald Wayne ... Evansville, IN
Bell, Ronny J. ... **Magnolia, AR**
Bell, Rosalyn B. ... Silver Spring, MD
Bell, Rosenberg & Hughes LLP
Oakland, CA
San Francisco, CA
Bell, Roy J., III ... Honolulu, HI
Bell, Roy L. ... Odessa, TX
Bell, Roy Morrow ... **Irvine, CA**
San Diego, CA
Bell, Royer & Sanders Co., L.P.A.
Columbus, OH
Bell, Ruby Carpio ... Decatur, GA
Bell, Ryniker & Letourneau, P.C.
Houston, TX
Bell, Sam H. ... Akron, OH
Bell, Samuel K. ... Mount Prospect, IL
Bell, Samuel P., III ... **Tallahassee, FL**
Bell, Sandra F. ... Columbus, OH
Bell, Sandra Gethers ... Treasury Department,
Office of Regulations and Rulings, GV
Bell, Sandra K. ... Pompano Beach, FL
Bell, Sanford A. ... **New York, NY**
Bell, Sarah H. ... **Lee, MA**
Bell, Schuster, Wheeler & Hiers, P.A.
Pensacola, FL
Bell, Scott A. ... **Wellesley, MA**
Bell, Scott T. ... **Seattle, WA**
Bell, Sean W. ... Lancaster, SC
Bell Seltzer Intellectual Property Law Group
Charlotte, NC
Raleigh, NC
Research Triangle Park, NC
Bell, Seth K. ... **Dallas, TX**
Bell, Sharon ... White Plains, NY
Bell, Sharon A. ... Beverly Hills, CA
Bell, Sharon J. ... **Tulsa, OK**
Bell, Sharon Joyce ... Knoxville, TN
Bell, Shawn K. ... **Lewiston, ME**
Bell, Sheila Trice ... **Washington, DC**
Bell, Sherry ... Phoenix, AZ
Bell, Sidney H. ... Welch, WV
Bell, Silberblatt & Wood ... **Clearfield, PA**
Bell, Stanley J. ... **San Diego, CA**
San Francisco, CA
Bell, Stanley J., A Professional Corporation
San Diego, CA
San Francisco, CA
Bell, Stanley M. "Jack" ... **Little Rock, AR**
Bell, Stephen A. ... **Houston, TX**
Bell, Stephen B. ... **Chicago, IL**
Bell, Stephen D. ... **Denver, CO**
Bell, Stephen E. ... **Kansas City, MO**
Bell, Stephen G. ... **St. Louis, MO**
Bell, Stephen K. ... Wheaton, IL
Bell, Stephen M. ... Plantation, FL
Bell, Stephen P., Jr. ... Department of the Army,
U.S. Army Legal Services Agency, GV
Bell, Stephen R. ... **Washington, DC**
Bell, Steve ... **Batesville, AR**
Bell, Steve F. ... Coeur d'Alene, ID
Bell, Steven D. ... **Cleveland, OH**
Bell, Steven J. ... **San Francisco, CA**
Bell, Steven K. ... New Bern, NC
Bell, Steven Lynn ... **Roswell, NM**
Bell, Steven M. ... Orlando, FL
Bell, Steven Scott ... **Seattle, WA**
Bell, Stewart L. ... Las Vegas, NV
Bell, Surasky & Anderson, P.A. ... Langley, SC
Bell, Susan E. ... Steelville, MO
Bell, Susan J. ... Reston, VA
Bell, Susan L. ... Fort Worth, TX
Bell, Susan R. ... **Cincinnati, OH**
Bell, Suzanne L. ... Los Angeles, CA
Bell, Suzanne Y. ... **Palo Alto, CA**
Bell, T. Bruce ... **Lexington, KY**
Bell, T. Knox ... **San Diego, CA**
Bell, Tamara M. ... **Tipp City, OH**
Bell, Tara E. ... **New Orleans, LA**
Bell, Taylor Mcadam ... Fremont, CA
Bell, Terry A. ... Belle Chasse, LA
Bell, Terry L. ... **Upper Marlboro, MD**
Bell, Theodore K. ... **Palo Alto, CA**
Bell, Theodore M. ... **Los Angeles, CA**
Bell, Thomas A. ... **Philadelphia, PA**
Bell, Thomas C. ... **Denver, CO**
Bell, Thomas C. ... **Seattle, WA**
Bell, Thomas F. ... Alpharetta, GA
Bell, Thomas G. ... Las Vegas, NV
Bell, Thomas G., & Associates
Las Vegas, NV
Bell, Thomas G., Jr. ... **Staunton, VA**
Bell, Thomas H. ... **New York, NY**
Bell, Thomas L. ... **St. Louis, MO**
Bell, Thomas L. ... Johnstown, NY
Bell, Thomas M. ... **Jacksonville, FL**
Bell, Thomas M., P.A. ... **Jacksonville, FL**
Bell, Thomas N. ... **Sacramento, CA**
Bell, Thomas P. ... Pembroke Pines, FL
Bell, Thomas R., Jr. ... **Asheville, NC**
Bell, Thomas Reuben ... **Sylacauga, AL**
Bell, Thomas W. ... Sarasota, FL
Bell, Thomas W., Jr. ... Rocklin, CA
Bell, Thomas W., Jr. ... Memphis, TN
Bell, Tindal & Freeland, P.A.
Lancaster, SC
Bell, Tom W. ... Orange, CA
Bell, Troy Nathan ... New Orleans, LA
Bell, Turner & Hobbs ... **Chattanooga, TN**
Bell, Turney, Coogan & Richards, L.L.P.
Austin, TX
Bell, V. Parker ... Escondido, CA
Bell, Valerie A. ... Seattle, WA
Bell, Valerie D. ... New York, NY
Bell, Venetia D. ... **Baltimore, MD**
Bell, Vicki A. ... Huntsville, AL
Bell, Victor A., Jr. ... Atlanta, GA
Bell, Vida Ivy ... **Newport, TN**
Bell, Virginia Ann ... **Minneapolis, MN**
Bell, W. Douglas ... Groton, MA
Bell, W. Kevin ... **Scottsdale, AZ**
Bell, Walter G. ... Winter Haven, FL
Bell, Walter H. ... Stayton, OR
Bell, Walter W. ... **Chicago, IL**
Bell, Wayne L. ... Bristol, VA
Bell, Wayne S. ... Los Angeles, CA
Bell, Wendell A. ... Fort Worth, TX
Bell, William A. ... Tallahassee, FL
Bell, William A., II ... Detroit, MI
Bell, William C. ... **Ridgeland, MS**
Bell, William C. ... Newport News, VA
Bell, William C., Jr. ... **Jackson, TN**
Bell, William D., Sr. ... Cincinnati, OH

Bell, William D., Sr. Law Offices
Cincinnati, OH
Bell, William E. .... New York, NY
Bell, William G. .... Miami, FL
Bell, William G., III .... Savannah, GA
Bell, William H. .... Greeneville, TN
Bell, William H., Jr.
Federal Communications Commission, International Bureau, GV
Bell, William J. F. .... Fairless Hills, PA
Bell, William K. .... Huntsville, AL
Bell, William R. .... Charlotte, NC
Bell, William W. .... West Palm Beach, FL
Bell, William W. .... Rochester, NY
Bell, William W. .... Brownwood, TX
Bell, William W. .... Houston, TX
Bell, William W., Jr. .... Dalton, GA
Bell, William W., Jr. .... Willis, TX
Bell and Young, Ltd. A Professional Corporation .... Las Vegas, NV
Bella, Christine L. .... New York, NY
Bella, Daniel L. .... Dyer, IN
Bella, Johna M. .... Toledo, OH
Bella, Peter A. .... Cambridge, MA
Bella, Ronald T. .... Cincinnati, OH
Bellac, Patricia .... Boulder, CO
Bellace, Janice R. .... Philadelphia, PA
Bellach, Francine A. .... Santa Monica, CA
Bellack, David E. .... Aspen, CO
Bellack, George R.
Federal Trade Commission, Bureau of Competition, GV
Bellacosa, Joseph W. .... Albany, NY
Bellacosa, Peter A. .... New York, NY
Bellafatto, Ralph J. .... Easton, PA
Bellafiore, Cynthia R. .... Saunderstown, RI
Bellafronto, Eric C. .... San Jose, CA
Bellafronto, Maria .... San Jose, CA
Bellagamba, Robert A. .... Menlo Park, CA
Pleasanton, CA
Bellah, C. Richard .... Glendale, AZ
Bellah & Harrian .... Glendale, AZ
Bellah, Kenneth D. .... Chicago, IL
Bellah, Melanie .... Berkeley, CA
Bellah-Maguire, Jennifer .... Los Angeles, CA
Bellair, Gary M. .... Lubbock, TX
Bellairs, Chester K. .... Melville, NY
Bellairs, Dean, Cooley, Siler, Moulton and Smith .... Flint, MI
Bellairs, Keith .... Minneapolis, MN
Bellairs, Robert H. .... Flint, MI
Bellak, Jill M. .... Philadelphia, PA
Bellak, Richard C. .... Tallahassee, FL
Bell-Alexander, Darlene Y. .... Perrine, FL
Bellamak, Ferris W. .... Scottsdale, AZ
Bellamy & Bellamy, Attorneys at Law, P.C.
Marshall, MO
Bellamy, Brian D. .... Thomasville, GA
Bellamy, Calvin E. .... Hammond, IN
Bellamy, Carol .... New York, NY
Bellamy, Earle D., II .... Golden, CO
Bellamy, Elizabeth H. .... Los Angeles, CA
Bellamy, Everett .... Washington, DC
Bellamy, Frederick B. .... Detroit, MI
Bellamy, Frederick R. .... Washington, DC
Bellamy, Fredric D. .... Phoenix, AZ
Bellamy, G. Scott .... Conway, SC
Myrtle Beach, SC
Bellamy, Glenn D. .... Cincinnati, OH
Bellamy, Henry N. .... Shreveport, LA
Bellamy, Howell V., Jr. .... Myrtle Beach, SC
Bellamy, James Tuthill .... Marshall, MO
Bellamy, John A. A. .... Bristol, TN
Bellamy, John W. .... West Palm Beach, FL
Bellamy, Lael Elizabeth .... Alpharetta, GA
Bellamy Law Firm, The, P.C.
Washington, DC
Bellamy, Lorenzo M. .... Washington, DC
Bellamy, Michael J. .... Phenix City, AL
Bellamy, Page .... Marshall, MO
Bellamy, Penelope I. .... New Haven, CT
Bellamy, Rutenberg, Copeland, Epps, Gravely & Bowers, P.A.
Myrtle Beach, SC
Bellamy, Sherry F. .... Washington, DC
Bellamy, Timothy J. .... Burbank, CA
Bellamy, Werten F.W., Jr.
Cambridge, MA
Bellamy, William M., Jr. .... Stamford, CT
Bellamy, William T., Jr. .... Marshall, MO
Bellan, John A., Jr. .... Jackson, MS
Bellanca, Angela M. .... Los Angeles, CA
Bellanca, Anthony J. .... Detroit, MI
Harper Woods, MI
Bellanca, Beattie and DeLisle, P.C.
Detroit, MI
Harper Woods, MI
Bellanca, James V., Jr. .... Detroit, MI
Bellanca, Louis C., & Associates
Tustin, CA
Belland, Eugene R. .... Fairbanks, AK
Belland, Mark E. .... Cherry Hill, NJ
Northfield, NJ
Belland, Stanton P. .... Los Angeles, CA
Belland, Stanton P., P.C. .... Los Angeles, CA
Bellande, Louis E., Jr. .... Chicago, IL
Bellandi, James A. .... Arden Hills, MN
Bellani, Kenneth E. .... Roseland, NJ
Bellantone, Gregory D. .... Garden City, NY
Bellantoni, Diane C. .... Hartford, CT
Bellantoni, George S. .... White Plains, NY
Bellar & Bellar .... Carthage, TN
Bellar, J. Branden .... Carthage, TN
Bellar, Jack O. .... Carthage, TN
Bellar, Lila G. .... Charlotte, NC
Bellar, Melvin L. .... Baton Rouge, LA
Bellar, Ralph E., Jr. .... Kansas City, MO
Bellard, Joseph C. .... Garden City, NY

Bellard, Roland J. .... Friendswood, TX
Bellard, William T. .... Brooklyn, NY
Bellard, William T. .... Garden City, NY
Bellardo, Brian D. .... San Francisco, CA
Bellas, George S. .... Park Ridge, IL
Bellas, Leslie Beth .... Department of Justice, Environment and Natural Resources Division, GV
Bellas, Michael C. .... New York, NY
Bellas, Peter W. .... Miami, FL
Bellas & Wachowski .... Chicago, IL
Des Plaines, IL
Park Ridge, IL
Schaumburg, IL
Bellaschi, John J. .... McLean, VA
Bellatti & Barton .... Springfield, IL
Bellatti, Fay, Bellatti & Beard .... Ashland, IL
Jacksonville, IL
Bellatti, John E. .... Ashland, IL
Jacksonville, IL
Bellatti, Lawrence L. .... Houston, TX
Bellatti, Mary-Ann A. .... Houston, TX
Bellatti, Robert M. .... Springfield, IL
Bellatti, Walter R. .... Jacksonville, IL
Bellavance, Russell C. .... Philadelphia, PA
Bellaver, John S. .... Detroit, MI
Bellavia, Christopher J. .... Pittsburgh, PA
Bellavia, John R., Jr. .... Lincoln, NE
Bellavia & Kassel, P.C. .... Mineola, NY
Bellavia, Leonard Anthony .... Mineola, NY
Bellavia, Timothy C. .... Rochester, NY
Bellavita, Giuseppe E. .... Manchester, NH
Bellcourt, W. Lawrence .... Cobleskill, NY
Belle, Manuel .... Indianapolis, IN
Belle, Michael John .... Sarasota, FL
Venice, FL
Belle, Stephen E. .... Orlando, FL
Belle, Stephen E., P.A. .... Orlando, FL
Belle, Wanda Y. .... Houston, TX
Belleau, Ashley L. .... New Orleans, LA
Belleau, James E. .... Auburn, ME
Belleau, Laura C. .... Tucson, AZ
Belleci, Gerald A. .... Pittsburg, CA
Bellefeuille, Alan J. .... Fairhaven, MA
Bellefleur, Robert (Bob) .... Madawaska, ME
Bellefontaine, Edgar J. .... Boston, MA
Bellefontaine, John F. .... Jeanerette, LA
Bellegarde, Paul A. .... Rockville, MD
McLean, VA
Bellehumeur, Cathy .... Bannockburn, IL
Belle Isle, Kevin E. .... Decatur, GA
Belleman, Pamela Smith .... Richmond, VA
Bellemere, Fred, III .... Kansas City, MO
Bellemere, Julia VanWalleghem
Lawrence, KS
Bellenghi, Julian B. .... Irvine, CA
Bellenot, Ronald K. .... Monroe, CT
Belleperche, Thomas W. .... Fort Wayne, IN
Beller, Alan L. .... New York, NY
Beller, Amy B. .... New York, NY
Beller, Amy T. .... New York, NY
Beller, Barry .... New York, NY
Beller, Bernard .... Chicago, IL
Beller, Beth .... New York, NY
Beller, Charles R., III .... Christiansburg, VA
Beller, Christopher C. .... Bridgewater, NJ
Beller, Daniel J. .... New York, NY
Beller, David E. .... Baltimore, MD
Beller, David L. .... Seattle, WA
Beller, Eric I.B., P.C., Law Offices of
Hartford, CT
New Haven, CT
Beller, Eric I. B. .... New Haven, CT
Beller, Gary A. .... New York, NY
Beller, Herbert N. .... Washington, DC
Beller, Iris L. .... New York, NY
Beller, James L., Jr.
Pension Benefit Guaranty Corporation, Office of the General Counsel, GV
Beller, Jeffrey A.
Department of State, GV
Beller, Jenna D. .... Dallas, TX
Beller, Joseph .... Bala Cynwyd, PA
Beller, Kathryn .... New York, NY
Beller, Lauren Gruber .... Bridgeport, CT
Beller, Linda M. .... Floral Park, NY
Beller, Margaret A. .... Washington, DC
Beller, Michael C. .... The Woodlands, TX
Beller, Neil J. .... Las Vegas, NV
Beller, Norman J. .... Lorain, OH
Beller, Rebeccah L. .... St. Augustine, FL
Beller, Richard D. .... Los Angeles, CA
Beller, Samuel F. .... Ash Flat, AR
Beller, Scott M., & Associates .... Chicago, IL
Beller & Spence, P.C. .... Christiansburg, VA
Beller, Sylvia G. .... Las Vegas, NV
Beller, Tom E. .... Houston, TX
Belles Graham Proudfoot & Wilson
Lihue, HI
Belles, Michael J. .... Lihue, HI
Belles, Thomas A. .... Washington, DC
Bellet, Ellen .... New York, NY
Bellet, Ellen Beth .... Miami, FL
Bellet, Francine Beth .... Sunnyvale, CA
Bellet, Lisbeth M. P. .... Sacramento, CA
Bellet, Sally J. .... Philadelphia, PA
Belletier, Anthony P., Jr. .... Syracuse, NY
Belletier, Linda Gehron .... Syracuse, NY
Belletsky, Marc R. .... Greenwich, CT
Bellettiere, Joseph A. .... Philadelphia, PA
Belletto, Sarah Rashed .... San Rafael, CA
Belleville, Mark L. .... Cleveland, OH
Belleville, Philip F. .... Los Angeles, CA
Bellew, Joseph J. .... Philadelphia, PA
Bellew, Joseph M. .... Baltimore, MD
Bellew, Sandra C. .... Treasury Department, Office of the General Counsel, GV
Bellew, Sean J. .... Philadelphia, PA

Bellezza, Mary Ann .... New Haven, CT
Bellgowan, Robert B., Jr. .... St. Johns, MI
Belli, Dennis C. .... Columbus, OH
Belli, John M. .... Philadelphia, PA
Belli, Peter F. .... West Sacramento, CA
Belli, Richard C., Jr. .... Camden, NJ
Westmont, NJ
Belli, Sandra .... Warren, NJ
Belli, Simon, II .... Trenton, NJ
Belli, Weil & Grozbean, P.C.
Rockville, MD
Belli, William J. .... Reno, NV
Belli, William J., Ltd., Law Offices of
Reno, NV
Bellia, Anthony J., Jr. .... Washington, DC
Bellia, Salvatore .... Vallejo, CA
Bellich, Tricia G. .... Crown Point, IN
Bellido, Juan Carlos .... Philadelphia, PA
Bellido, Nelson C. .... Miami, FL
Bellifemine, Susan Sangillo .... Newark, NJ
Bellile, Kenneth W. .... Highland Park, IL
Bellin, Bruce G.
Environmental Protection Agency, Office of Enforcement and Compliance Assurance, GV
Bellin, Eugene M. .... New York, NY
Bellin, Joseph L. .... Encino, CA
Bellin, Mark S. .... Shrewsbury, NJ
Bellin, Robert E. .... Milwaukee, WI
Belling, Christopher J. .... Buffalo, NY
Belling, David D. .... Hays, KS
Belling, David L. .... Janesville, WI
Bellinger & Associates .... Easton, MD
Bellinger, Catherine H. .... Baltimore, MD
Bellinger & DeWolf .... Dallas, TX
Bellinger, Edgar T. .... Easton, MD
Bellinger, Glen A. .... Dallas, TX
Bellinger, Glenn .... Santa Maria, CA
Bellinger, H. M. .... Houston, TX
Bellinger, Janis Harris .... San Diego, CA
Bellinger, John B., III .... Washington, DC
Bellinger, John (Jack) N. .... Dallas, TX
Bellinger, Joseph J., Jr. .... Baltimore, MD
Bellinger, Michael G. .... New York, NY
Bellinger, Scott P. .... Dublin, OH
Bellinger-Honig, Charlene .... Miami, FL
Bellingham, Bruce .... Philadelphia, PA
Bellingham, Collins & Loyd, P.C.
Oklahoma City, OK
Bellingham, James H.
Oklahoma City, OK
Bellingham, William H. .... Billings, MT
Bellinghiere, Frank R. .... Westlake Village, CA
Jackson, WY
Bellinghieri, Joseph A. .... West Chester, PA
Bellings, David B. .... Greenbrae, CA
Bellington, Janice E. .... Champaign, IL
Bellini, Christopher J. .... Washington, DC
Bellini, Elma A. .... Rochester, NY
Bellino, Anthony S. .... Astoria, NY
Bellino, John Anthony .... Wilkes-Barre, PA
Bellino, Joseph A., III .... Dallas, TX
Bellino, Joseph A., III, P.C., Law Offices of
Dallas, TX
Bellino, Lisa M. .... Philadelphia, PA
Bellino, Vito V. .... West End, NJ
Bellino, William S. .... Danvers, MA
Bellinson, James Lee .... Southfield, MI
Belliotti, Raymond A. .... Fredonia, NY
Bellis, Arnold M. .... Minneapolis, MN
Bellis, Barbara N. .... New Haven, CT
Bellis, Carole H. .... Palo Alto, CA
Bellis, Frank A., Jr. .... Atlantic City, NJ
Bellis, Hook & Nigut, L.L.P.
West Des Moines, IA
Bellis, James R. .... Phoenix, AZ
Bellis, Jeffrey W. .... Beaverton, OR
Bellis, Kenneth M. .... San Clemente, CA
Bellis, M. Douglas
House of Representatives, Office of Legislative Counsel, GV
Bellis, M. Kathryn .... Houston, TX
Bellis, Marvin P. .... Hartford, CT
Bellis, Rachel A. .... Denver, CO
Bellis, Scott S. .... West Des Moines, IA
Bellis, Stephen R. .... New Haven, CT
Bellisario, Domenic A. .... Pittsburgh, PA
Bellisario, Paul .... Lisle, IL
Belliston, Carl J. .... Provo, UT
Bellitto, Rick R. .... Fairfield, CT
Bellitto, Robert B. .... Fairfield, CT
Belliveau, Allan R. .... St. Louis, MO
Belliveau, James D. .... Pittsburgh, PA
Belliveau, James J. .... Providence, RI
Belliveau, James T. .... Waltham, MA
Belliveau, Janet L. .... Pittsburgh, PA
Belliveau, Kathrin Pagonis .... Pawtucket, RI
Belliveau & St. Sauvier .... Providence, RI
Bellizia, Prosper A. .... Newark, NJ
Bellizzi, Angela .... New York, NY
Bellman, Alan N. .... Toledo, OH
Bellman, Amy B. .... Chicago, IL
Bellman, Daniel A. .... Columbus, OH
Bellman, Harold .... Tamarac, FL
Bellman, Howard S. .... Madison, WI
Bellman, Kathryn A. .... Lincoln, NE
Bellman, Richard F. .... New York, NY
Bellman, Steven I. .... Norwood, NJ
Bellmann, Thomas R. .... Kansas City, MO
Bellmann, Thomas R., P.C.
Kansas City, MO
Bell-Moss, Katherine E. .... Austin, TX
Bello, Angelo A. .... Hackensack, NJ
Bello, Christopher R. .... Stamford, CT
Bello, Clare M. .... Pittsburgh, PA
Bello, Elizabeth A. .... Miami, FL
Bello, Harry M. .... New Bedford, MA
Bello, Herbert L. .... Boston, MA

Bello, Herbert L. .... Wellesley, MA
Bello, James A. .... Worcester, MA
Bello, John J., Jr. .... White Plains, NY
Bello, John R., Jr. .... Tampa, FL
Bello, Jonathan H. .... New York, NY
Bello, Juan A. .... Vero Beach, FL
Bello, Judith Hippler .... Washington, DC
Bello, Kenneth M. .... Boston, MA
Bello, Lapine & Cassone .... Stamford, CT
Bello, Leonard M. .... Wareham, MA
Bello, Lori L. .... Fairfield, NJ
Bello, Luis .... Elizabeth, NJ
Bello, Mariellen .... King Of Prussia, PA
Bello & Matheson, P.A. .... Vero Beach, FL
Bello, Robert S. .... Stamford, CT
Bello, Salvatore F., Jr. .... King Of Prussia, PA
Bello, Sol D. .... San Jose, CA
Bello, Susan A. .... Providence, RI
Bello, Thomas F. .... Staten Island, NY
Bello-Acevedo, Felix .... San Juan, PR
Bello-Billini, Angel M. .... Orlando, FL
Bellobuono, Michael C. .... Hartford, CT
Bellocchi, Luke P. .... Department of State, Bureau of Consular Affairs, GV
Bellock, Charles J. .... Oak Brook, IL
Bellocq, Jeanne A. .... Jacksonville, FL
Bellof, Carolyn R. .... Tavares, FL
Bellofatto, Anthony R. .... Mineola, NY
Belloff, Neil S. .... New York, NY
Belloff, Paul F. .... Garden City, NY
Bellomo, Deborah A. .... Potsdam, NY
Bellomo, Lawrence P. .... Irvine, CA
Bellomo, Salvatore .... Paterson, NJ
Bello-Monaco, Deborah A.
South Plainfield, NJ
Bellomy, Christopher M. .... Arlington, VA
Bellomy, Grace Surgvy .... Boerne, TX
Bellon, Carol Barry .... Austin, TX
Bellon, Christine P. .... Boston, MA
Bellon, David G. .... Oceanside, CA
San Diego, CA
Bellon, Gabriel .... Miami, FL
Bellon, Joseph P. .... Port Washington, NY
Bellon & Lisiecki .... San Diego, CA
Bellone, Anthony Joseph .... Encino, CA
Bellone, Robert M. .... Bronx, NY
Bellone, Thomas G. .... Stoneham, MA
Bellonger, Brenda J. .... Lakewood, CO
Belloni, Marc E. .... New Orleans, LA
Belloni, Robt. C. .... Portland, OR
Bellotti, Berenice B. .... San Juan, PR
Bellotti, Francis X. .... Boston, MA
Bellotti, Laura A. .... Hartford, CT
Bellotti, Peter V. .... Cambridge, MA
Bellotti, Stephen M. .... Washington, DC
Bellovin, Barry L. .... Tucson, AZ
Bellovin, Marshall B. .... New York, NY
Bellovin, Marvin J. .... Uniondale, NY
Bellows, Anne B. .... Carrollton, TX
Bellows and Bellows, A Prof. Corp.
Los Angeles, CA
Chicago, IL
Bellows, Beverly .... Santa Clara, CA
Bellows, Carl D. .... New York, NY
Bellows, Carole Kamin .... Chicago, IL
Bellows, Christopher Noel .... Miami, FL
Bellows, George F. .... Buffalo, NY
Bellows, Jay W. .... Skokie, IL
Bellows, Joel J. .... Los Angeles, CA
Chicago, IL
Bellows, John B., Jr. .... St. Paul, MN
Bellows, Laurel G. .... Los Angeles, CA
Chicago, IL
Bellows, Lori B. .... Irving, TX
Bellows, Marcia C. .... Chicago, IL
Bellows, Randy I. .... Alexandria, VA
Bellows, Richard Charles .... Gainesville, GA
Bellows, Roger L. .... Costa Mesa, CA
Bellows, Scott .... Portland, OR
Bellows, Shael .... Rosemont, IL
Bellows, Timothy W. .... Dallas, TX
Bell-Pearson, Ramona M. .... Rockville, MD
Bellsey, Jonathan K. .... San Francisco, CA
Bellsey, Lisa .... White Plains, NY
Bellsey, Peter M. .... New York, NY
Belluardo, Robyn A. .... Toms River, NJ
Bellucci, Anthony F. .... Flushing, NY
Bellucci, Bruno, III .... Northfield, NJ
Bellucci, Bruno, III, P.C. .... Northfield, NJ
Bellucci, Doreen R. .... Costa Mesa, CA
Bellucci, Gina G. .... Trenton, NJ
Bellucci, Joyce A. .... Santa Maria, CA
Bellucci, Michael J. .... New York, NY
Bellucci, Vincent A. .... Bay Minette, AL
Belluco, Hanora .... New York, NY
Belluomini, Emilio V., Jr. .... Dallas, TX
Belluomini, Sandra L. .... Redwood City, CA
Bellury, Reginald L. .... Milledgeville, GA
Bellus, Melinda .... New York, NY
Bellus, Stewart J. .... Roslyn, NY
Belluscio, John A. .... Rochester, NY
Belluscio, Robert F. .... Flushing, NY
Bellush, John R., Jr. .... Morristown, NJ
Bellus-Lewis, Caryn .... Miami, FL
Belluzzi, Michele L. .... San Diego, CA
Bellwin, Janna H. J. .... New York, NY
Bellwin, John A. .... Carmel, NY
Bellwoar, Andrew J. .... Exton, PA
Bellwoar, Harry J. J., III
Haddon Township, NJ
Philadelphia, PA
Bellwoar, Jennifer A. .... Exton, PA
Bellwoar, Robert G. .... Philadelphia, PA
Belly, Armando T. .... New York, NY
Belman, Bruce .... Louisville, KY
Belman, Fred .... Tucson, AZ
Belman, Murray J. .... Washington, DC
Belman, P. Dennis .... Columbia, MD

Bench, Rebecca L. ....Orlando, FL
Bench, Russell W. ....Salt Lake City, UT
Bench, Stuart T. ....Indianapolis, IN
Benchetrit, Serge ....New York, NY
Benchik, Edward P. ....South Bend, IN
Benchoff & Benchoff ....Nacogdoches, TX
Benchoff, E. McAlister ....Nacogdoches, TX
Benchoff, Michael E. ....Phoenix, AZ
Benchoff, Michael E., Ltd. ....Phoenix, AZ
Bencik, Deborah L. ....Chicago, IL
Bencin, Patricia DiRosa ....Mentor, OH
Bencini, Robert L. ....Buffalo, NY
Bencivenga, Daniel ....Philadelphia, PA
Bencivenga, John W. ....Tampa, FL
Bencivengo, Cathy A. ....San Diego, CA
Bencivengo, Mary L. ....Solon, OH
Bencivenni, Michael R. ....Cleveland, OH
Benck, David M. ....Birmingham, AL
Benck, Ernest A., Jr. ....Fresno, CA
Benckart, Judith Corcoran
Bloomington, IN
Benckendorf & Benckendorf, P.C.
Peoria, IL
Benckendorf, David A. ....Peoria, IL
Benckendorf, Glenn E. ....Peoria, IL
Benckendorf, James W. ....Peoria, IL
Benckenstein, Norvell & Nathan, L.L.P.
Beaumont, TX
Houston, TX
Benckenstein & Oxford, L.L.P.
Beaumont, TX
Houston, TX
Benco, Fred P. ....Honolulu, HI
Bencoe, Lori McCamey ....Albuquerque, NM
Bencomo & Associates ....New Orleans, LA
Bencomo, Raul R. ....New Orleans, LA
Bencowitz, Lynn M. ....Beaumont, TX
Bencze, Nola R. ....Lawrenceville, NJ
Marlton, NJ
Bencze, Stephan ....Los Angeles, CA
Bend, Richard H. ....St. Paul, MN
Bend, Richard H., P.A. ....St. Paul, MN
Benda, Elizabeth L. ....New York, NY
Benda, Gail A. ....Ionia, MI
Benda, George ....Ferndale, MI
Benda, Gerald A. ....Atlanta, GA
Benda, James B. ....Des Moines, IA
Benda, Jonathan C. ....Baton Rouge, LA
Benda, Matthew L. ....Albert Lea, MN
Benda, Stephen ....Palo Alto, CA
Benda, Thomas I. ....Boston, MA
Benda, Thomas J. ....Wheaton, IL
Bendalin, Ronald ....Dallas, TX
Bendalin, Sherman R. ....Phoenix, AZ
Bendalin, Sherman R., P.C. ....Phoenix, AZ
Bendall, James M. ....Atlanta, GA
Schenectady, NY
Bendall, James W. ....Atlanta, GA
Schenectady, NY
Bendall, Jennifer L. ....Washington, DC
Bendall & Mednick ....Atlanta, GA
Schenectady, NY
Bendall, Richard C. ....Jupiter, FL
Bendall, Robert W. ....Manassas, VA
Bendall, Sloane E. ....Daytona Beach, FL
Bendall, Theodore L. ....Huntington, IN
Roanoke, IN
Warren, IN
Bendana, Alicia M. ....New Orleans, LA
Bendana, Carlton & Sharp
New Orleans, LA
Bendana, David P. ....New Orleans, LA
Bendana, Orlando G. ....New Orleans, LA
Bendau, James M. ....Beachwood, OH
Ben-David, Deborah R.
Department of Agriculture,
Office of the General Counsel, GV
Ben-David, Neeli ....Atlanta, GA
Bendavid-Arbiv, Susanne M.
Woodland Hills, CA
Bendeck, Juan D. ....Miami, FL
Bendeck, Odette Marie
West Palm Beach, FL
Bendel, David ....Minneapolis, MN
Bendel, Michael J. ....Albany, NY
Bendel, Randy E. ....Woodland Hills, CA
Bendell, Adam S. ....Los Angeles, CA
Bendell, James M. ....Port Townsend, WA
Bendell, Kelly J. ....Los Angeles, CA
Bendell, Michael, P.A. ....Boca Raton, FL
Bendell, Michael S. ....Boca Raton, FL
Bendell, Spencer E. ....Los Angeles, CA
Bendelow & Darling, P.C. ....Denver, CO
Steamboat Springs, CO
Telluride, CO
Bendelow, Edward M. ....Denver, CO
Bender, Alan H. ....Chicago, IL
Bender, Alan Ronald ....Bellevue, WA
Bender, Albert C. ....San Jose, CA
Bender, Albert E., Jr. ....Atlanta, GA
Bender and Anderson, P.C. ....Hamden, CT
Bender, Andrew E., Law Office of
Memphis, TN
Bender, Ann Marie ....San Francisco, CA
Bender, Ann W. ....Palo Alto, CA
Bender, Anthony J. ....Holland, OH
Bender, Ariadne A. ....New York, NY
Bender, Arlene L. ....Boston, MA
Bender, Audrey I. ....New York, NY
Bender, Barbara J. ....Alamo, CA
Sacramento, CA
Bender & Bender ....Wisconsin Rapids, WI
Bender, Bender & Chandler, P.A.
Miami, FL
Bender, Betsy Hall ....Austin, TX
Bender, Brian A. ....New York, NY
Bender, Bruce M. ....Rockville, MD
Bender, Calvin G. ....Roeland Park, KS

Bender, Carole L. ....Los Angeles, CA
Bender, Charles ....Pennsauken, NJ
Bender, Charles W. ....Los Angeles, CA
Bender, Cheryl ....Fortuna, CA
Bender, Christine W. ....Los Angeles, CA
Bender, Clarence ....La Mesa, CA
Bender, Dale O. ....Madison, WI
Bender, Daniel Jason ....New York, NY
Bender, David ....New York, NY
Bender, David B. ....Washington C. H., OH
Bender, David P., Jr. ....Los Angeles, CA
Bender, Debra K. ....Orchard Park, NY
Bender, Dennis F. ....Waterloo, NY
Bender, Diane L. ....Evansville, IN
Bender, Diane L. (Wolf) ....Evansville, IN
Bender, Douglas A. ....Austin, TX
Bender, Earl O. ....Los Angeles, CA
Bender, Earl O., A Professional Corporation
Los Angeles, CA
Bender, Ellen M. ....Los Angeles, CA
Bender, Elliott B. ....Richmond, VA
Bender, Eric D. ....Blue Ash, OH
Bender, Eric J. ....New York, NY
Bender, Frank C. ....Philadelphia, PA
Bender & Frankel ....New York, NY
Bender, Gary C. ....Media, PA
Bender, Gary L. ....East Lansing, MI
Bender, George A. ....White Plains, NY
Bender, George C. ....Miami, FL
Bender, Gerald C. ....Chicago, IL
Bender, Gerald C. ....New York, NY
Bender, Gretchen Ann ....Wilmington, DE
Bender, Harold J. ....Charlotte, NC
Bender, Harold J. ....Erie, PA
Bender, Harry K. ....Miami, FL
Bender, Helen Hadjiyannakis
New York, NY
Bender, Howard A. ....New York, NY
Bender, J. David ....Covington, KY
Bender, J. Timothy ....Cleveland, OH
Bender, Jack C. ....Lexington, KY
Bender, Jack J. ....Houston, TX
Bender, Jack S., III ....Halstead, KS
Bender, James J. ....Minneapolis, MN
Bender, Jay R. ....Birmingham, AL
Bender, Jean H. ....Sioux Falls, SD
Bender, Jeanne Matthews ....Billings, MT
Bender, Jennifer C. ....New York, NY
Bender Jenson Silverstein & Castrataro, LLP ....New York, NY
White Plains, NY
Bender, Jerome D. ....New York, NY
Bender, Jerry Jay ....Columbia, SC
Bender, Joel C. ....White Plains, NY
Bender, John A., Jr. ....Seattle, WA
Bender, John F. ....Columbus, OH
Bender, John P. ....Trenton, NJ
Bender, John T. ....Pittsburgh, PA
Bender, John Thomas ....Mobile, AL
Bender, Jonathan ....Washington, DC
Bender, Jonathan K. ....New York, NY
Bender, Jonathan L. ....Paramus, NJ
Bender, Joseph E. ....Chicago, IL
Bender, Joseph E., Jr.
Department of Justice, GV
Bender, Jules ....Plainview, NY
Bender, Karl ....Tecumseh, MI
Bender, Kathleen M. ....New York, NY
Bender, Kathryn Christian ....Washington, DC
Bender & Katz LLP ....New York, NY
Bender, Kenneth R. ....Los Angeles, CA
Bender, Kristen A. ....Rockville, MD
Bender, Laurie ....Portland, OR
Bender Law Firm, The, P.A.
Minneapolis, MN
Bender Law Firm, The, P.C. ....St. Louis, MO
Bender Law Office ....Raleigh, NC
Bender, Lawrence ....Bismarck, ND
Bender, Lee S. ....Philadelphia, PA
Bender, Leslie ....Syracuse, NY
Bender, Leslie C. ....Baltimore, MD
Bender, Leslie K. ....Oak Brook, IL
Bender, Levi & Buss, S.C. ....Watertown, WI
Bender, Marc D. ....San Mateo, CA
Bender, Marc Lee ....Los Angeles, CA
Bender, Marie Meyer ....Los Angeles, CA
Bender, Mark C. ....Orlando, FL
Bender, Mark E. ....Huntington, NY
Bender, Mark L. ....Columbia, SC
Bender, Martin ....Concord, NH
Bender, Martin ....Mount Kisco, NY
Bender, Martin R. ....Laguna Hills, CA
Bender, Martin R., A Law Corporation
Laguna Hills, CA
Bender, Martin S. ....New York, NY
Bender, Mary K. ....Chardon, OH
Bender, Mary K., Co., L.P.A.
Chardon, OH
Bender, Michael A. ....Detroit, MI
Bender, Michael A. ....Madison, WI
Bender, Michael C. ....Crosby, MN
Bender, Michael J., Jr. ....Lima, OH
Bender, Michael L. ....Denver, CO
Bender, Michael Seth ....Astoria, NY
Bender, Noah Scott ....Miami, FL
Bender, Paul ....Tempe, AZ
Bender, Paul A. ....Buffalo, NY
Bender, Paul E. ....Peoria, IL
Bender, Paul F. ....Marion, NY
Bender, Peter Gabriel ....St. Louis, MO
Bender, Peter J. ....Mount Clemens, MI
Bender, Raymond G., Jr. ....Washington, DC
Bender, Raymond P. ....San Pedro, CA
Bender, Rebecca E. ....Minneapolis, MN
Bender, Richard D. ....Springfield, MO
Bender, Richard E. ....Wisconsin Rapids, WI
Bender, Richard J. ....Sacramento, CA
Bender, Richard S. ....St. Louis, MO

Bender, Risa ....New York, NY
Bender, Rita L. ....Seattle, WA
Bender, Robert A. ....Watertown, WI
Bender, Robert H. ....Gladstone, MO
Bender, Robert J. ....Salem, MA
Bender, Robert P. ....Wisconsin Rapids, WI
Bender, Roberta ....New York, NY
Bender, Robyn R. ....Washington, DC
Akron, OH
Bender, Rodd W. ....Bala Cynwyd, PA
Bender, Ron ....Los Angeles, CA
Bender, Ronald A. ....Missoula, MT
Bender, Ronald M. ....Hamden, CT
Bender, S. Michael ....Gulfport, FL
Bender, Sidney ....New York, NY
Bender, Stanley C., Law Offices of
Portsmouth, OH
Bender, Steffany K. ....Hanover, NH
Bender, Steven A. ....White Plains, NY
Bender, Steven K. ....Atlanta, GA
Bender, Susan A. ....Oakland, CA
Bender, Susan A. ....Honolulu, HI
Bender, Susan G. ....Charlottesville, VA
Bender, Susan K. ....Washington, DC
Bender, Susan L. ....New York, NY
Bender, Susan Walker ....Bethesda, MD
Bender, Theresa M. ....Tallahassee, FL
Bender, Thomas J., Jr. ....Philadelphia, PA
Bender, Thomas R. ....Providence, RI
Bender, Thomas V. ....Kansas City, MO
Bender, Thomas V. ....Neenah, WI
Bender & Thompson ....Mount Clemens, MI
Bender, Timothy J. ....Indianapolis, IN
Bender, Victoria ....Raleigh, NC
Bender, Wayne F. ....Rolling Meadows, IL
Bender, Wayne L. ....San Francisco, CA
San Jose, CA
Bender, William ....Mt. Vernon, IN
Poseyville, IN
Bender, William J. ....Seattle, WA
Bender-Kelner, Nancy S.
Minneapolis, MN
Benderly, Danielle ....Portland, OR
Bendernagel, Anne E. ....New Orleans, LA
Bendernagel, James F., Jr.
Washington, DC
Benderson, Eric S.
Small Business Administration,
Office of the General Counsel, GV
Benderson, Judith K. ....Department of Justice,
Executive Office for United States Attorneys,
GV
Bendes, Barry J. ....Livingston, NJ
New York, NY
Bendes, Charles N. ....Oakland, CA
Bendesky, Larry ....Philadelphia, PA
Bendesky, Lori E. ....Bala Cynwyd, PA
Bendet, Edward R. ....Honolulu, HI
Bendet, Fidell, Sakai & Lee, Attorneys at Law, A Law Corporation ....Honolulu, HI
Bendetowies, Barry S.
Fort Lauderdale, FL
Bendetson, Constance Novick ....Lowell, MA
Bendett, Adam L. ....Farmington, CT
Bendezu, Antonio E. ....Lincoln, NE
Bendfeldt, Sandra K. ....Greenwich, CT
Bendheim, Alice L. ....Phoenix, AZ
Bendheim, Alice L., P.C. ....Phoenix, AZ
Bendich, Judith E. ....Seattle, WA
Bendich, Stobaugh & Strong ....Seattle, WA
Bendicksen, Perry E., III
Albuquerque, NM
Bendickson, Gerald L. ....Chula Vista, CA
Bendig, Brian C. ....Chicago, IL
Bendig, Charles H. ....Columbus, OH
Bendik, David L. ....Kew Gardens, NY
Bendik, Edward ....Hempstead, NY
Bendiksen, Bruce ....New Bedford, MA
Bendiks-Perna, Sohni Y. ....Raleigh, NC
Bendin, Timothy H. ....Atlanta, GA
Bendinelli, Marc ....Westminster, CO
Bendinger, Gary F. ....Salt Lake City, UT
Bendish, Bruce P. ....White Plains, NY
Bendit, Jeffrey ....Brazoria, TX
Bendit, Richard A. ....Philadelphia, PA
Bendit Weinstock, A Professional Corporation ....Morristown, NJ
Newark, NJ
West Orange, NJ
Bendix, Bruce A. ....Uniondale, NY
Bendix, Ernst L. ....New York, NY
Bendix, Gary L. ....Manitowoc, WI
Bendix, Richard M., Jr. ....Chicago, IL
Bendix, William J. ....Brooklyn, NY
Bendixsen, Kurt C. ....Hermiston, OR
Bendler, Karen E. ....Seattle, WA
Bendlin, Gregory J. ....Orlando, FL
Bendo, Gerald M. ....Dallas, TX
Bendo, Marc Constantine ....Philadelphia, PA
Bendo, Marcia E. ....Plano, TX
Bendoff, David M. ....Chicago, IL
Bendon, Sandra L. ....Palm Desert, CA
Bendon, William M. ....Philadelphia, PA
Bendor, Catherine A. ....Department of Justice,
Civil Rights Division, GV
Bendor, Judith A. ....Kingston, WA
Bendorf, Linda M. ....Iowa City, IA
Bendorf, Peter ....Beresford, SD
Bendos, E. George ....Baltimore, MD
Ben-Dov, David J. ....Chicago, IL
Ben-Dov, Elana ....New York, NY
Bendremer, Fredric J. ....Weston, MA
Bendrick, John A. ....Menlo Park, CA
Bendt, Daniel Ray ....Seabrook, MD
Bendure, Mark R. ....Detroit, MI
Bendure, Randall S. ....Tiffin, OH
Bendure & Thomas ....Detroit, MI
Bendush, David C. ....Rahway, NJ

Bendy, Donald N. ....Eagle Lake, TX
Bendy, Donald N., P.C. ....Eagle Lake, TX
Bendy, Marie C. ....San Francisco, CA
Bendycki, Mary Lynn ....Winter Park, FL
Toledo, OH
Bendza, Shirley A. ....Hartford, CT
Benecke, Louis W. ....Kansas City, MO
Benecki, Edward ....Lawrenceville, IL
Benedek, Ann Lowry ....Chicago, IL
Benedek & Benedek ....Oak Park, IL
Benedek, George ....Oak Park, IL
Benedek, John Douglas ....Los Angeles, CA
Benedek, M. Lawrence ....New York, NY
Benedek, Melinda ....Los Angeles, CA
Benedek, Peter ....Beverly Hills, CA
Benedek, Richard S. ....Ann Arbor, MI
Benedek, Zsuzsanna E. ....Harrisburg, PA
Benedetti & Dee ....Wray, CO
Benedetti, Francis A. ....Wray, CO
Benedetti, Gino J. ....Philadelphia, PA
Benedetti, Joseph B. ....Richmond, VA
Benedetti, Joseph C. ....East Rutherford, NJ
Benedetti, Joseph C. ....New York, NY
Benedetti, Paul C. ....Boulder, CO
Benedetti, Richard H. ....Tacoma, WA
Benedetti, Roland ....Staten Island, NY
Benedetti, Thomas J. ....Florham Park, NJ
Benedetto, Annette C. ....Boston, MA
Benedetto, Arthur E. ....Jackson, MI
Benedetto & Bishop, P.C. ....Jackson, MI
Benedetto, Conrad ....Philadelphia, PA
Benedetto, Leonard L., Jr. ....River Ridge, LA
Benedetto, Marcello A. ....Miami, FL
Benedetto, Mary Rourke ....Detroit, MI
Benedetto, Michael A., Jr. ....Oak Brook, IL
Benedetto, Michael V.
Ocean Township, NJ
Benedetto, Terrianne ....Philadelphia, PA
Benedick, Thomas F. ....O'Fallon, IL
Benedict, Alex L. ....Huntington Beach, CA
Benedict and Altman ....New Brunswick, NJ
Somerville, NJ
Benedict, Anthony J. ....Pearl River, NY
Benedict, Anthony M. ....Indianapolis, IN
Benedict, Anthony W. ....Bartlesville, OK
Benedict, Benjamin D. ....Phoenix, AZ
Benedict, Betsy McCoy ....Tampa, FL
Benedict, Charles C. ....Atlanta, GA
Benedict, Coleman J. ....Pittsburgh, PA
Benedict, Cynthia Michelle
San Antonio, TX
Benedict & Depuy ....Stamford, CT
Benedict, George ....San Diego, CA
Benedict, George R. ....Greeley, CO
Benedict, Ginsberg, Sommerfield & Weiss, P.C.
New York, NY
Benedict, Gregory B. ....Bryan, OH
Benedict, Heather M. ....New York, NY
Benedict, James E. ....Portland, OR
Benedict, James N. ....New York, NY
Benedict, Jan Paul ....Lansing, MI
Benedict, Jay L. ....Fayetteville, PA
Benedict, Jeffrey L. ....Merrill, WI
Benedict, Jeril R. ....Houston, TX
Benedict, Jerry L. ....Austin, TX
Benedict, John ....Santa Monica, CA
Las Vegas, NV
Benedict, John E. ....Bethesda, MD
Benedict, Jonathan C. ....Orange, CT
Benedict, Joseph J. ....New Brunswick, NJ
Benedict, Judith C. ....Greenwich, CT
Benedict, Kathleen D. Spong
Olympia, WA
Benedict, Kerry T. ....San Antonio, TX
Benedict, Kevin W. ....Raleigh, NC
Benedict, Lauren L. ....Macon, GA
Benedict, Lee H. ....Baltimore, MD
Benedict, Lillian E. ....Philadelphia, PA
Benedict, Linda Stephens ....Pittsburgh, PA
Benedict, Louis M. ....Pittsburgh, PA
Benedict, Lucius C. ....Barberton, OH
Benedict, Mark R. ....Newport Beach, CA
Benedict, Mark T. ....Kansas City, MO
Benedict, Mary Hope M. ....Bath, NY
Benedict, Mary L. ....Grand Rapids, MI
Benedict, Mary L., P.C. ....Grand Rapids, MI
Benedict, Meredith Anne ....Boston, MA
Benedict, Milner ....Cheverly, MD
Benedict, Miranda ....Augusta, ME
Benedict, Mollie F. ....Los Angeles, CA
Benedict, Peter B. ....Stamford, CT
Benedict, Philippe ....New York, NY
Benedict, Ralph R., Jr. ....Armonk, NY
Benedict, Richard L. ....Traverse City, MI
Benedict, Robert L. ....Barberton, OH
Benedict, Rodman W. ....New York, NY
Benedict, Ronald D. ....Independence, MO
Benedict, Ronald L. ....Cincinnati, OH
Benedict, Scott N. ....Washington, DC
Benedict, Shelton L. ....Tulsa, OK
Benedict, Thane, IV ....New York, NY
Benedict, Thomas C. ....Atlanta, GA
Benedict, Thomas L. ....Honolulu, HI
Benedicto, Patrick D. ....San Jose, CA
Benediktson, Caroline B. ....Tulsa, OK
Benedon, Douglas G. ....Los Angeles, CA
Benedon & Serlin ....Los Angeles, CA
Woodland Hills, CA
Benedosso, Anthony N. ....Milford, CT
Beneduce, Eugene J.
Westhampton Beach, NY
Benedum, Ben T. ....Norman, OK
Benedum, Benedum & Walkley
Norman, OK
Benefiel, Farrer & Glista ....Kalamazoo, MI
Benefiel, John R. ....Birmingham, MI
Benefiel, Philip B. ....Lawrenceville, IL
Benefiel, William L. ....Kalamazoo, MI

Benefield, Catherine Marie ... Duncan, OK
Benefield, Christine F. Kelly ... Jackson, MS
Benefield, C.J., Law ffices Of ... Lakeland, FL
Benefield, David L. ... Duncan, OK
Benefield, Harold G. ... Jonesboro, GA
Benefield, James D., Jr. ... Sea Island, GA
Benefield, James Dewey, III Brunswick, GA
Benefield, J. L. ... Houston, TX
Benefield & Scarlett, L.L.P. Brunswick, GA
Benefield, Steven A. ... Birmingham, AL
Benegas, David F. ... Chicago, IL
Benejam, Aldo A. General Accounting Office, Office of the General Counsel, GV
Beneke, Ann E. ... Laurens, IA
Beneke, Arnold W. ... Glencoe, MN
Beneke, Bruce A. ... St. Paul, MN
Beneke, Candyce T. ... Houston, TX
Beneke, Darlene Duggan ... Orlando, FL
Beneke, Donald A. ... Pocahontas, IA
Beneke, Geo. F. ... Wheeling, WV
Beneke, Paul G. ... Eugene, OR
Beneke, Ron ... Tulsa, OK
Beneke, Stephen G., (P.A.) ... Clearwater, FL
Beneke, Suzanne Stern ... Buffalo, NY
Beneke, William S. ... Princeton, IL
Benelli, Patricia G. ... Chester, VT
Benely, Susan J. ... New York, NY
Beneman, David R. ... Portland, ME
Benenati, Margaret A. ... Hollywood, FL
Benenati, Michael P. ... New York, NY
Benenfeld, Bruce J. ... Plantation, FL
Benenson, Herbert ... Bayside, NY
Benenson, Jay R. ... Millburn, NJ
Benenson, Jennifer K. ... Fort Lee, NJ
Benenson & Kates ... San Francisco, CA New York, NY
Benenson, Mark K. ... New York, NY
Benenson, Richard B. ... Washington, DC
Benenson & Scher, A Professional Corporation Millburn, NJ
Benenson, Steven P. ... Morristown, NJ
Benenson-Bagdan, Laura N. ... Sparta, NJ
Benerofe, Steven J. ... Palo Alto, CA
Benes, Edgar A. ... Boca Raton, FL
Benes, Edward D. ... Los Angeles, CA
Benes, Lois K. ... Palo Alto, CA
Benes, Nicholas E. ... New York, NY
Benes, Richard H. ... San Diego, CA
Benesch & Fermoile ... Reno, NV
Benesch, Friedlander, Coplan & Aronoff LLP ... Cincinnati, OH Cleveland, OH Columbus, OH
Benesch, George ... Anchorage, AK
Benesch, George N. ... Reno, NV
Benesch, Katherine ... Princeton, NJ
Benesch, Valli ... San Francisco, CA
Benesch, Wayne C. ... Yuma, AZ
Benesh, Kathleen B. ... Rochester, NY
Benesh, William Stephen ... Houston, TX
Benet, Dominique ... New York, NY
Benetar Bernstein Schair & Stein New York, NY
Benetatos, George G., Law Office of San Francisco, CA
Benett, Edward J. ... Portland, OR
Benett, Susan L. ... San Jose, CA
Benetti, Timothy C. ... San Francisco, CA
Benevenia, Eugene V. ... Franklin Square, NY
Benevenia, Mark ... Englewood Cliffs, NJ
Beneventano, Guy P. ... Harrisburg, PA
Beneventano, Thomas M. ... New York, NY
Beneventi, Arthur L. ... Garden City, NY
Beneventi, Robert L. ... Granger, IA
Benevento, Anthony ... Totowa, NJ
Benevento, Bryon J. ... Salt Lake City, UT
Benevento, Frank A., II ... New York, NY
Benevento, Sam ... Las Vegas, NV
Benevich, Aaron ... Seattle, WA
Benevides, Diane ... Orange, CT
Beneville, Edward S., III ... Westminster, CA
Beneville, Susan P. ... Oakland, CA
Beneze, N. Lee ... Springfield, IL
Benezette, Jon E. ... Daytona Beach, FL
Benezra, Audrey G. ... Seattle, WA
Benezra, Gerald C. ... Los Angeles, CA
Benezra, Jerry E. ... Melrose, MA
Ben-Ezra, Marc A. ... Miami, FL
Ben-Ezra, Marc A., P.A. Fort Lauderdale, FL Miami, FL
Benezra, Marc L. ... Los Angeles, CA
Benezra, Meyer ... New York, NY
Ben-Ezra, Seth ... Jericho, NY
Benezra, Seth J. ... Boulder, CO Lakewood, CO
Benfer and Bausch, P.A. ... Topeka, KS
Benfer, James E. ... Topeka, KS
Benfer, James E., III ... Topeka, KS
Benfer, Linda Dorsey ... Lawrenceville, NJ
Benfield, Ann K. ... Louisville, KY
Benfield, David A. ... Boston, MA
Benfield, Linda E. ... Milwaukee, WI
Benfield, Marion W., Jr. ... Wake Forest, NC
Benfield, Mary T. ... Seattle, WA
Benfield, Peter B. ... Boston, MA
Benfield, Robert E. ... Los Angeles, CA
Benfield, Robert H., Jr. ... Atlanta, GA
Benforado, David J. ... Sun Prairie, WI
Benford, Elizabeth ... San Francisco, CA
Benford, Gary A. ... Dallas, TX
Benford, Harry C., III ... Evanston, IL
Benford, John Y. ... Orlando, FL
Benford, Lee F., II ... Ravenswood, WV
Benford, Norman J. ... Miami, FL
Bengart & Bengart ... Tonawanda, NY
Bengart, Joseph S. ... Tonawanda, NY
Bengart, Steven B. ... Tonawanda, NY
Benge, Donna H. ... Wharton, TX
Benge, Douglas G. ... London, KY
Benge, G. Jack, Jr. ... Sacramento, CA
Benge, John H., Jr. ... Wilmington, DE
Benge, John J. ... Kansas City, MO
Benge Law Firm ... Kansas City, MO
Benge, Malcolm L. ... Washington, DC
Benge, Mary E. Federal Energy Regulatory Commission, Office of the Commissioners, GV
Benge, William L. ... Moab, UT
Bengel, Lauralyn G. ... Chicago, IL
Bengels, Dennis A. ... Garden City, NY
Benger, Daniel E. ... Downey, CA
Bengier, John E. ... Orlando, FL
Bengoa, Esteban R. ... San Juan, PR
Bengoechea, Shane O. ... Boise, ID
Bengs, David M. ... La Porte, IN
Bengs, Tina M. ... Valparaiso, IN
Bengston, Eric J. ... Hartford, CT
Bengston, Gary L. ... Danville, VA
Bengston, Gary L., P.C. ... Danville, VA
Bengston, Noreen G. ... Madison, WI
Bengtson, Avery K. ... Austin, TX
Bengtson, Bradley P. ... Austin, TX
Bengtson, Brian ... Grand Rapids, MN
Bengtson, C. Russell ... Providence, RI
Bengtson, David A. ... Middletown, CT
Bengtson, David E. ... Wichita, KS
Bengtson, Gary C. ... Ypsilanti, MI
Bengtson, Greg A. ... Salina, KS
Bengtson, John D. ... Oakland, CA
Bengtson, John H. ... Moscow, ID
Bengtson, Karl W. ... Lafayette, LA
Bengtson, Larry E. ... Junction City, KS
Bengtson, L. O. ... Lindsborg, KS Salina, KS
Bengtson, Michael L. ... Austin, TX
Bengtson, Thomas A. ... Lansing, MI
Bengtsson, W. Patrick ... San Francisco, CA
Benguerel, Yvette F. ... Department of Justice, Antitrust Division, GV
Benham, Caroline M. ... Colorado Springs, CO
Benham, Eric V. ... San Diego, CA
Benham, Frank L., III ... Shelby, OH
Benham, Gibson Sean ... Casper, WY
Benham, Harry K., III ... Winchester, VA
Benham, J. Randall ... Minneapolis, MN
Benham, James, (P.C.) ... Phoenix, AZ
Benham, John H., III Charlotte Amalie, St. Thomas, VI
Benham, Lewis G. ... Louisville, KY
Benham, Lezlie A. ... Phoenix, AZ
Benham, Melinda S. ... Memphis, TN
Benham, Paul B., III (P.A.) Little Rock, AR
Benham, Robert ... Atlanta, GA
Benham, Robert D. ... Kansas City, KS
Benham, Robert L., Jr. ... Allen Park, MI
Benham, Samuel B. ... Las Vegas, NV
Benham, Stephen M. ... Washington, DC
Benham, Susan Merrill ... Bakersfield, CA
Benham, Tom B. ... Atlanta, GA
Benham, Tom B., P.C. ... Atlanta, GA
Benham, Toni M. ... Raleigh, NC
Benham, William T. ... Chicago, IL
Benhart, Coralyn M. ... Pittsburgh, PA
Benhart, Kenneth D. ... Des Moines, IA
Ben-Horin, Giora ... Phoenix, AZ
Ben-Horin, Michael K. ... Phoenix, AZ
Ben-Hur, Michelle ... Santa Ana, CA
Benice Group, The, A Professional Corporation Irvine, CA
Benice, J. Lee Department Of Health And Human Services, Social Security Administration, GV
Benice, Jeffrey S. ... Irvine, CA
Benick, Howard A. ... New York, NY
Beniek, Brenda ... St. Paul, MN
Benien Law Offices, Chartered Kansas City, KS
Benien, Ruth M. ... Kansas City, KS
Benigno, Anthony M. ... Greenville, NY
Benigno, Thomas D. ... Malverne, NY
Benigsohn, William L. ... Parker, CO
Benik, Gregory L. ... Providence, RI
Benik, Tina C. ... Lincoln, RI
Benimowitz, Michael K. ... New York, NY
Benin, Sara A. ... Memphis, TN
Beninati, Francis A. ... Chicago, IL
Beninati, John Frank ... New York, NY
Beninato, Frank P., Jr. ... Elizabeth, NJ
Benincasa, Gabriel A. ... New York, NY
Bening, Bradley A. ... San Jose, CA
Beninger, David M. ... Seattle, WA
Beninson, Gary S. ... Lakewood, NJ
Benintendi, Christopher A. Cincinnati, OH
Benion, Robert Eugene ... Milton, PA
Benis, Christopher T. ... La Conner, WA Seattle, WA
Benis, Stuart A. ... Columbus, OH
Benisatto, Salvatore E. ... Jericho, NY
Benisatto, Salvatore E., P.C. ... Jericho, NY
Benisch, Joanne E. ... New York, NY
Benisch, Robert G. ... New York, NY
Benisch, Stephen B. ... Clark, NJ
Benischeck, Robert J. Fort Washington, PA
Benischek, LeeAnn M. ... Cedar Rapids, IA
Benish, Kathryn Godfrey ... Chicago, IL
Benish, William S. ... New York, NY
Benison, A. Richard ... Albuquerque, NM
Ben-Isvy, Lisa H. ... Chicago, IL
Ben-Isvy, Michael L. ... Chicago, IL
Benit, Keith M. ... Metairie, LA
Benites, Roberto ... Woodbridge, NJ
Benitez, Alberto Manuel ... Chicago, IL
Benitez, Brigida ... Washington, DC
Benitez & Butcher, P.A. ... Orlando, FL
Benitez, Gus R. ... Orlando, FL
Benitez, Hugo E. ... Miami, FL
Benitez, John R. ... Denver, CO
Benitez, Juan Carlos ... Washington, DC
Benitez, Kristi Payne ... New York, NY
Benitez, Leonel R. ... Coral Gables, FL
Benitez, Leslie A. ... Austin, TX
Benitez, Peter J. ... Bronx, NY
Benitez Professional Corporation Attorneys, The ... Denver, CO
Benitez, Ray A., III ... New Orleans, LA
Benitez, Roger T. ... El Centro, CA
Benitez, Rosemarie ... Sacramento, CA
Benitez, Wilfredo ... Newark, NJ
Benítez-Colón, Gilberto Félix San Juan, PR
Benitez de Alegria, Yolanda ... San Juan, PR
Benitez Gautier, Jorge ... San Juan, PR
Benitez-Herrmann, Leyda L. Coral Gables, FL
Benitez-Mier, Jose Francisco San Juan, PR
Benítez Quiñones, Vionette ... San Juan, PR
Benito, Daniel A. ... Miami, FL
Benito, Gerald C. ... Redding, CA
Benito, Michael L. ... Tampa, FL
Benitz, Thomas ... Middlesex, NJ
Ben-Jacob, Michael ... New York, NY
Benjamin & Aaronson, P.A. Fort Lauderdale, FL Miami, FL
Benjamin, A. C., Jr. ... New Orleans, LA
Benjamin, Adam L. ... Boston, MA
Benjamin, Adelaide Wisdom New Orleans, LA
Benjamin, Alan G. ... Los Angeles, CA
Benjamin, Amos ... Miami, FL
Benjamin, Amy J. ... New York, NY
Benjamin, Andrew L. ... Seattle, WA
Benjamin, Anglia ... San Francisco, CA
Benjamin, Anita ... San Francisco, CA
Benjamin, Anthony M. ... New York, NY
Benjamin & Associates, P.C. ... Denver, CO
Benjamin, Barry M. ... New York, NY
Benjamin, Ben E. ... Washington, DC
Benjamin & Benson ... Cambridge, MA
Benjamin, Brent D. ... Charleston, WV
Benjamin, Brian R. ... Lewiston, ID
Benjamin, Bruce D. ... Los Angeles, CA
Benjamin, Charles J., Jr. ... Newark, NJ
Benjamin, Charles M. ... Topeka, KS
Benjamin, Christopher M. ... Austin, TX
Benjamin, Dana E. ... Jackson, OH
Benjamin, Daniel A. ... Stamford, CT
Benjamin, David E. ... New York, NY
Benjamin, David M. ... Aurora, OH
Benjamin, David P. ... San Antonio, TX
Benjamin, David R. ... San Francisco, CA
Benjamin, Deborah Binder ... Atlanta, GA
Benjamin, Denise M. Small Business Administration, Office of the General Counsel, GV
Benjamin, Dennis ... Boise, ID
Benjamin & DesPortes, P.C. Richmond, VA
Benjamin, Donald A. ... Rockville Centre, NY
Benjamin, Donald E. ... Glendale, CA
Benjamin, Edward A. ... Boston, MA
Benjamin, Edward B., Jr. New Orleans, LA
Benjamin, Edward R., Jr. ... Portland, ME
Benjamin, Evan ... New York, NY
Benjamin, Frank S. ... Atlanta, GA
Benjamin, Fred I. ... Chicago, IL
Benjamin, Frederick B. ... Southfield, MI
Benjamin, Gary A. ... Detroit, MI
Benjamin, Gary A., Law Offices, P.C. Detroit, MI
Benjamin, Gary H. ... Spokane, WA
Benjamin, Gerald ... Southfield, MI
Benjamin, Gerianne Kelly ... Memphis, TN
Benjamin & Gold, P.C. ... Stamford, CT
Benjamin, Goodwin E. ... New York, NY
Benjamin, Harold H. ... Santa Monica, CA
Benjamin, Harvey E. ... New York, NY
Benjamin, Heather A. ... Wilmington, DE
Benjamin, Hollis W. ... Peoria, IL
Benjamin, Howard ... New York, NY
Benjamin, Irwin ... Harrisburg, PA
Benjamin, Ivan S. ... Weston, FL
Benjamin, Ivan S., P.A. ... Weston, FL
Benjamin, J. K., & Associates Ltd. Chicago, IL
Benjamin, J. Kevin ... Chicago, IL
Benjamin, Jack C. ... New Orleans, LA
Benjamin, Jack C., Jr. ... New Orleans, LA
Benjamin, James G. ... Denver, CO
Benjamin, James J., Jr. ... New York, NY
Benjamin, James S. ... Fort Lauderdale, FL
Benjamin, James W. ... Kansas City, MO
Benjamin, Jeff ... Summit, NJ
Benjamin, Jeffrey S. ... Miami, FL
Benjamin, Jerry ... St. Petersburg, FL
Benjamin, Jill Marie ... Upper Marlboro, MD
Benjamin, Jodi Gordon ... Paoli, PA
Benjamin, John A. ... Cincinnati, OH
Benjamin, Jon L. ... San Francisco, CA
Benjamin, Joyce Holmes ... Salem, OR
Benjamin, Julian R. ... Miami, FL
Benjamin, Karen B. ... Bloomfield Hills, MI
Benjamin, Kathleen D. ... Oakland, CA
Benjamin, Kelly S. ... Stevens Point, WI
Benjamin, Kenneth B. ... New York, NY
Benjamin, Kimberly J. ... Kansas City, MO
Benjamin, Lawrence M. ... Chicago, IL
Benjamin, Lawrence S. ... Beachwood, OH
Benjamin, Linda Hope ... Los Angeles, CA
Benjamin, Lloyd S. ... New Orleans, LA
Benjamin, Louis ... West Hempstead, NY
Benjamin, Louis H. ... New York, NY
Benjamin, Marc A. ... Chicago, IL
Benjamin, Marc A. ... Northbrook, IL
Benjamin, Marilyn Talman Sleepy Hollow, NY
Benjamin, Mark E. ... West Lafayette, IN
Benjamin, Mark W. ... Cambridge, MN
Benjamin, Marvin I. ... Pearl River, NY
Benjamin, Michael D. ... Philadelphia, PA
Benjamin, Michael D., P.C. Philadelphia, PA
Benjamin, Michael J. ... Hollywood, FL
Benjamin, Michael S. Needham Heights, MA
Benjamin, Michelle M. ... Winchester, TN
Benjamin, Milton J., Jr. ... Dedham, MA
Benjamin, Mitchell D. ... Atlanta, GA
Benjamin, Moshe ... New York, NY
Benjamin, Nancy Berg ... Houston, TX
Benjamin, Pamela ... White Plains, NY
Benjamin & Perrey, P.S. ... Spokane, WA
Benjamin, Peter ... Springfield, MA
Benjamin, Peter L. ... Merrillville, IN
Benjamin, Philip B. ... Framingham, MA
Benjamin, R. Scott ... San Diego, CA
Benjamin, R. Scott, A.P.C. ... San Diego, CA
Benjamin, Rhonda M. ... Ridgewood, NJ
Benjamin, Richard Scott ... San Diego, CA
Benjamin, Ricky C. ... Englewood, CO
Benjamin, Robert D. ... Pasadena, CA
Benjamin, Robert D. ... St. Louis, MO
Benjamin, Robert K. ... New York, NY
Benjamin, Robert M. ... Minneapolis, MN
Benjamin, Robert N. ... Glendale, CA
Benjamin, Robert N., A Prof. Corp. Glendale, CA
Benjamin, Robert V. ... Columbus, OH
Benjamin, Robert W. ... Sarasota, FL
Benjamin, Robert W. ... New York, NY
Benjamin, Roberta ... Philadelphia, PA
Benjamin, Roberta F. ... Cambridge, MA
Benjamin, Rochelle K. ... New York, NY
Benjamin, Roger S. ... Indianapolis, IN
Benjamin, Ross P. ... Boston, MA
Benjamin, Saul T. ... Sacramento, CA
Benjamin, Scott ... Hempstead, NY
Benjamin, Scott D. ... Rancho Santa Fe, CA
Benjamin, Seward I. ... Delray Beach, FL
Benjamin, Stephen ... New York, NY
Benjamin, Stephen Keith ... Raleigh, NC
Benjamin, Steven D. ... Richmond, VA
Benjamin & Sutton ... San Diego, CA
Benjamin, Thomas B. ... Portland, ME
Benjamin, Thomas J. Central Intelligence Agency, Office of the General Counsel, GV
Benjamin, Thomas M. ... New Orleans, LA
Benjamin, Virginia D. ... Cleveland, OH
Benjamin, W. Mente ... New Orleans, LA
Benjamin, Walter G. ... Orlando, FL
Benjamin, Walter M. ... Tulsa, OK
Benjamin, Wayne L. ... Albany, NY
Benjamin, Wayne R. ... Reston, VA
Benjamin, Weill & Mazer San Francisco, CA
Benjamin, Wendy L. ... Sacramento, CA
Benjamin, William C. ... Boston, MA
Benjamin, William E. ... Boulder, CO
Benjamin, William M. ... San Diego, CA
Benjamin, William P. ... Greensboro, NC
Benjamin, Willis B. ... Idaho Falls, ID
Benjamin, Yocum & Heather White Oak, OH **Covington, KY Cincinnati, OH**
Benjamini, Dean ... Indio, CA
Benjamini, Emily A. ... Indio, CA
Benjes, Richard A. ... Hutchinson, KS
Benjet, Brian H. ... Washington, DC
Benjoya, Marc F. ... Waukegan, IL
Benka, Richard W. ... Boston, MA
Benkard, James W. B. ... New York, NY
Benke, Patricia D. ... San Diego, CA
Benke, Steven C. ... San Antonio, TX
Benkel, Max ... Atlanta, GA
Benkel, Max, P.C. ... Atlanta, GA
Benkenstein, Teresa A. ... Austin, TX
Benker, G. Scott ... Visalia, CA
Benkert, Joseph P. ... Littleton, CO
Benkert, Linc M. ... Tampa, FL
Benkert, Paul J., Jr. ... Upper Marlboro, MD
Benkert, Robt. R. ... Penn Valley, CA
Benkert, Ronald G. ... Anchorage, AK
Benkert, Ronald J. ... Cincinnati, OH
Benkert, William J., Jr. ... Greenville, OH
Benkin, Isaac D. ... Washington, DC
Benko, George E. ... Croswell, MI
Benko, Istvan ... Los Angeles, CA
Benko, John E. ... Detroit, MI
Benko, Roger W. ... South Bend, IN
Benkoski, Elaine M. ... Dedham, MA
Benkov, Judith L. ... Briarcliff Manor, NY
Benkowitz, Michael Ian ... Kansas City, MO
Benkwith and Heard ... Montgomery, AL
Benkwith, Karl B., Jr. ... Montgomery, AL
Benline, Edward M. ... Houston, TX
Benman & Collins ... Tucson, AZ Los Angeles, CA
Benman, William J., Jr. ... Los Angeles, CA
Ben-Meir, David Heskel ... Los Angeles, CA
Ben-Meir, Izhak ... Harrison, NY
Ben-Meyer, Saul ... New York, NY

Ben-Moshe, Ron ... Atlanta, GA
Ben-Moshe, Sony ... San Diego, CA
Benn, Alex H. ... San Jose, CA
Benn, Anna Goodwin ... Houston, TX
Benn, D. Randall ... Washington, DC
Benn, Edwin H. ... Glencoe, IL
Benn, Herbert P. ... West Palm Beach, FL
Benn, Herman T. ... Suffolk, VA
Benn, John E. ... Houston, TX
Benn, John R. ... Sheffield, AL
Benn, Joshua J. ... College Station, TX
Benn, Lesley A. ... Chicago, IL
Benn, Marvin N. ... Chicago, IL
Benn, Merrick J. ... Baltimore, MD
Benn, Niles S. ... York, PA
Benn, Phyliss A. ... La Porte, IN
Benn and Robinson ... York, PA
Benn, Ted M. ... Dallas, TX
Benna, Robert H. ... Washington, DC
Bennack, Donald Lloyd ... Plano, TX
Bennack & Lowden L.L.P. ... Dallas, TX
Plano, TX
Bennack & Malone, L.L.P. ... San Antonio, TX
Bennack, Shelley A. ... San Antonio, TX
Bennani & Hamel, LLP.
Pawleys Island, SC
Bennani, Teresa L. ... Pawleys Island, SC
Bennardini, Charles J.
West Palm Beach, FL
Bennardo, Frank J. ... Boca Raton, FL
Bennardo, Jack A. ... Merrick, NY
Bennardo, Ronald L. ... Forked River, NJ
Bennazar, Bufete, CSP ... San Juan, PR
Bennazar-Zequeira, A. J. ... San Juan, PR
Benne, Christopher P. ... Chicago, IL
Benne, Max B. ... Mound City, MO
Benneche, Thomas G. ... Hartford, CT
Benneche, Thomas G. ... Simsbury, CT
Bennekin, Maricia Danielle
Montgomery, AL
Benner, Adria ... Washington, DC
Benner & Associates, P.C. ... Portland, OR
Benner, Barbara A. ... Coto De Caza, CA
Benner and Bilicki ... Washington, DC
Detroit, MI
Farmington Hills, MI
Livonia, MI
Benner, Brian J., (P.C.) ... Washington, DC
Farmington Hills, MI
Livonia, MI
Benner, C. Jonathan ... Washington, DC
Benner, Charles A. ... Milwaukee, WI
Benner, David J. ... San Diego, CA
Benner, Deborah ... Philadelphia, PA
Benner, Eric J. ... Noblesville, IN
Benner, Francis W. ... Milford, CT
Benner, George E., Jr. ... Meeker, CO
Benner, H. Charles ... Leola, PA
Benner, Kathleen A. ... St. Charles, IL
Benner, Michael B. ... New York, NY
Benner, Peter W. ... Hartford, CT
Benner, R. David ... Knoxville, TN
Benner, Ray R. ... Portland, OR
Benner, Richard ... White Salmon, WA
Benner, Robert G. ... Rochester, MN
Benner, Susan Carol ... Washington, DC
Benner, Thomas D. ... Brewster, WA
Benner, Tracy M. ... Roanoke, VA
Benner, W. Lloyd ... Phoenix, AZ
Benner, W. Lloyd, Ltd. ... Phoenix, AZ
Benner and Wild ... Doylestown, PA
Benner, William E. ... Doylestown, PA
Benner, Wm. E., Jr. ... Lancaster, PA
Benner-Leon, Wendy ... Tallahassee, FL
Benners, Fred H. ... Dallas, TX
Benners, Wm. H., III ... Dallas, TX
Bennes, Cindy Kaplan ... Buffalo, NY
Bennet, Caressa Davison ... Washington, DC
Bennet, Helen B. ... Chester, CT
Bennet, John S. ... Essex, CT
Bennet, Jos. C., Jr. ... Fairfax, VA
Bennet, Michael R. ... Washington, DC
Bennethum, David John ... Philadelphia, PA
Bennett, A. Laurel ... Sacramento, CA
Bennett, A. Mark, III ... Little Rock, AR
Bennett, A. Stuart ... Lexington, KY
Bennett, Adrienne H. ... Omaha, NE
Bennett, Alan C. ... Grand Rapids, MI
Bennett, Alan K. ... Rockville, MD
Bennett, Alan R. ... Washington, DC
Bennett, Alexander E. ... Washington, DC
Bennett, Alfred H., Law Offices of
Houston, TX
Bennett, Alice J. ... North Hollywood, CA
Bennett, Alice M. ... Treasury Department, Internal Revenue Service, GV
Bennett, Allan J. ... New York, NY
Bennett, Allan P. ... Jackson, MS
Bennett, Allen F. ... Springfield, IL
Bennett, Allen M. ... Southfield, MI
Bennett, Andrea L. ... Philadelphia, PA
Bennett, Andrea N. ... Arden Hills, MN
Bennett, Andrea R. ... Atlanta, GA
Bennett, Andrew F., Jr. ... Cleveland, TN
Bennett, Andrew Jack, Jr. ... Baton Rouge, LA
Bennett, Andy D. ... Nashville, TN
Bennett, Angela Kostis ... Mount Clemens, MI
Bennett, Angela L. ... Saipan, TT
Bennett, Angela M. ... Kansas City, MO
Bennett, Anna K. ... Boston, MA
Bennett, Anne A. ... Chicago, IL
Bennett, Anne M. ... New York, NY
Bennett, Anthony E. ... Syosset, NY
Bennett, Antoinette ... Warren, NJ
Bennett, Arnold J. ... Dunwoody, GA
Bennett, Arthur T. ... Memphis, TN
Bennett & Associates ... Atlanta, GA

Bennett, Ayervais & Bertrand, P.C.
New York, NY
Bennett, B. Michael ... Dallas, TX
Bennett, Barbara ... Washington, DC
Bennett, Barbara L. ... Providence, RI
Bennett, Barry ... Portland, OR
Bennett, Barry ... Port Arthur, TX
Bennett, Barry J. ... Fresno, CA
Bennett, Barry M. ... Chicago, IL
Bennett, Barry R. ... Selma, AL
Bennett, Barry W. ... Winter Haven, FL
Bennett, B. C., Jr. ... Marksville, LA
Bennett & Bennett ... Los Angeles, CA
Tustin, CA
Bennett & Bennett ... Eaton, OH
Bennett & Bennett ... Lima, OH
Bennett & Bennett ... Edmonds, WA
Bennett and Bennett ... Portage, WI
Bennett Bennett and Troiano, P.A.
Portland, ME
Bennett, Bessye W. ... Bloomfield, CT
Bennett, Beswick, McConkey & Marquardt, L.L.P. ... Havelock, NC
Morehead City, NC
Bennett, Bianca C. ... Falls Church, VA
Bennett Bigelow & Leedom, P.S.
Seattle, WA
Bennett, Bob E. ... Ada, OK
Bennett, Boehning & Clary ... Lafayette, IN
Bennett, Bowman, Triplett & Vittitow
Louisville, KY
Owensboro, KY
Bennett, Brandon E. ... Houston, TX
Bennett, Brian ... Kingsville, MD
Bennett, Brian C. ... Milford, NE
Bennett, Brian E. ... Wayne, PA
Bennett, Brian P. ... Minneapolis, MN
Bennett, Brian W. ... Winter Park, FL
Bennett, Bricklin & Saltzburg LLP
Haddon Heights, NJ
Doylestown, PA
Lancaster, PA
Norristown, PA
Philadelphia, PA
West Chester, PA
Bennett, Bruce ... Los Angeles, CA
Bennett, Bruce C. ... Amite, LA
Bennett, Bruce C. ... New York, NY
Bennett, Bruce P.
Christiansted, St. Croix, VI
Bennett, Bruce W. ... Tampa, FL
Bennett, Bruce W. ... Warren, OH
Bennett, Bryant M. ... Oakland, CA
Bennett, Bryce H., Jr. ... Indianapolis, IN
Bennett, Burton H. ... Portland, OR
Bennett, Burton H., P.C. ... Portland, OR
Bennett, Byron ... Philadelphia, PA
Bennett, C. Stephen ... Ridgeland, SC
Bennett, Calvin ... Huntsville, TX
Bennett, Calvin B., III ... Raleigh, NC
Bennett, Calvin, Jr. ... Dallas, TX
Bennett, Camille ... Washington, DC
Bennett, Camille E. ... Chicago, IL
Bennett, Candice L. ... Indianola, IA
Bennett, Carl M. ... Phoenix, AZ
Bennett, Carlton F. ... Virginia Beach, VA
Bennett, Carmichael & Kennedy, L.L.P.
Phoenix, AZ
Scottsdale, AZ
Bennett, Carol J. ... Department of Justice, Civil Division, GV
Bennett, Carter M. ... San Francisco, CA
Bennett, Catherine Adams ... Los Angeles, CA
Bennett, Catherine E. ... Bakersfield, CA
Bennett, Catherine M. ... Troy, NY
Bennett, Charles A. ... Los Angeles, CA
Bennett, Charles A. ... Rolla, MO
Bennett, Charles A. ... New York, NY
Bennett, Charles A. ... Bellefontaine, OH
Bennett, Charles B. ... Jacksonville, FL
Bennett, Charles C. ... Kenosha, WI
Bennett, Charles D., Jr. ... Roanoke, VA
Bennett, Charles E. ... Jacksonville, FL
Bennett, Charles E. ... Attleboro, MA
Bennett, Charles F. ... Chanute, KS
Bennett, Charles F. ... Pittsburgh, PA
Bennett, Charles J. ... Long Beach, CA
Bennett, Charles Kirby ... Lebanon, OH
Bennett, Charles L. ... Washington, DC
Bennett, Charles M. ... Salt Lake City, UT
Bennett, Charles P. ... Manchester, CT
Bennett, Charles R., Jr. ... Boston, MA
Bennett, Charles W. ... Matthews, NC
Bennett, Charles W., Jr. ... Houston, TX
Bennett, Charlotte S. ... Wilkesboro, NC
Bennett, Chas. F. ... Albuquerque, NM
Bennett, Cheryll A. ... Dayton, OH
Bennett, Christina ... Jericho, NY
Bennett, Christina L. ... Morristown, NJ
Bennett, Christopher A. ... Atlanta, GA
Bennett, Christopher L. ... Washington, DC
Bennett, Christopher M. ... New York, NY
Bennett, Clarence E. ... Nashville, TN
Bennett, Clarence J. ... Springfield, MA
Bennett, Claudia N. ... Tulsa, OK
Bennett, Clifford D. ... Gaithersburg, MD
Bennett, Clyde, II ... Cincinnati, OH
Bennett, Craig E. ... Smithfield, RI
Bennett, Craig R. ... Austin, TX
Bennett, Crimmins, Ostrander & Yung
Fort Dodge, IA
Bennett, D. Scott ... Chattanooga, TN
Bennett, Dale E. ... Overland Park, KS
Bennett, Dale L. ... Streator, IL
Bennett, Daniel D. ... St. Louis, MO
Bennett, Daniel P. ... Wilmington, DE
Bennett, Danielle ... Raleigh, NC
Bennett, David ... Worcester, MA

Bennett, David A. ... Seattle, WA
Bennett, David B. ... Cambridge, OH
Bennett, David E. ... Chicago, IL
Bennett, David E. ... Cary, NC
Bennett, David F., Law Offices of
Danbury, CT
Bennett, David F., Law Offices of
New Milford, CT
Bennett, David G. ... Allentown, PA
Bennett, David H. ... Portage, WI
Bennett, David J. ... Birmingham, MI
Bennett, David L.
Department of Transportation, Federal Aviation Administration, GV
Bennett, David L. ... Holden, MA
Bennett, David M. ... Chicago, IL
Bennett, David M. ... Dallas, TX
Bennett, David R. ... Chicago, IL
Bennett, David R. ... Beach Haven, NJ
Bennett, David T. ... Minneapolis, MN
Bennett, Daylene A. ... McCook, NE
Bennett, Dean S. ... Las Vegas, NV
Bennett, Dean T. ... Somerville, NJ
Bennett, Deborah ... Boston, MA
Bennett, Deborah P. ... Redwood City, CA
Bennett, Dennis A. ... Skokie, IL
Bennett, Derrick G. ... Panama City, FL
Panama City Beach, FL
Bennett, Dianna Dawn ... Sheridan, WY
Bennett, Dianne ... Buffalo, NY
Bennett & Dillon, L.L.P. ... Topeka, KS
Bennett Doherty, P.C. ... Livingston, NJ
Bennett & Doherty, P.C. ... Doylestown, PA
Bennett, Don P. ... Dothan, AL
Bennett, Donald P. ... Indianapolis, IN
Bennett, Donald R. ... Little Rock, AR
Bennett, Donald S. ... Tampa, FL
Bennett, Donald S. ... Fostoria, OH
Bennett, Donald Y. ... Sarasota, FL
Bennett, Donn ... Belle Fourche, SD
Bennett, Donna D. ... Indianapolis, IN
Bennett, Doris M. ... Sterling, MA
Bennett, Dorsett C., II ... Roswell, NM
Bennett, Douglas A. ... Atlanta, GA
Bennett, Douglas J. ... Athens, OH
Bennett & Dowcett ... Boston, MA
Bennett, Duane E. ... Oceanside, CA
Bennett, Dunn, Arnold, Ellwood & Neal, L.L.P. ... Houston, TX
Bennett, Dwayne A. ... Charlotte, NC
Bennett, Dyke D. ... Dallas, TX
Bennett, Dyke D., P.C. ... Dallas, TX
Bennett, E. Alan ... Waco, TX
Bennett, E. Kontz, Jr. ... Waycross, GA
Bennett, E. Todd ... Annapolis, MD
Bennett, Ealy A. ... West Hartford, CT
Bennett, Earl M. ... Princeton, NJ
Bennett, Earl W. ... Marengo, OH
Bennett, Earle ... Jacksonville, FL
Bennett, Edmund C. ... Barrington, RI
Newport, RI
Bennett, Edmund C. ... Providence, RI
Bennett, Edward A. ... Lexington, MA
Bennett, Edward F. ... Merrick, NY
Bennett, Edward G. R. ... Charleston, SC
Bennett, Edward H., Jr. ... Marblehead, MA
Bennett, Edward J. ... Washington, DC
Bennett, Edward J. ... White Plains, NY
Bennett, Edward T. ... Temecula, CA
Bennett, Elizabeth A. ... Kalamazoo, MI
Bennett, Elizabeth L. ... Wayne, PA
Bennett, Eric D. ... Los Angeles, CA
Bennett, Eric H. ... Parsippany, NJ
Bennett, Ernest D., III ... Nashville, TN
Bennett, Eugene J. ... Oakland, CA
Bennett, Eugene L. ... Chicago, IL
Bennett, (Eve) Kyla ... Boston, MA
Bennett, Everett R., Jr. ... Tulsa, OK
Bennett, F. Ray ... Los Angeles, CA
Bennett, F. Vernon ... Orlando, FL
Bennett & Fairshter, LLP
Los Angeles, CA
Pasadena, CA
Bennett, Faith H. ... Westfield, NJ
Bennett, Feeney, Clark & Yee
San Francisco, CA
Bennett & Forts, P.C. ... Holden, MA
Bennett, Francis B. ... San Diego, CA
Bennett, Francis B., II ... San Diego, CA
Bennett, Frank B. ... Minneapolis, MN
Bennett, Frank H. ... Clyde, OH
Bennett, Franklin O., Jr.
Highlands Ranch, CO
Bennett, Franklin S., Jr. ... Youngstown, OH
Bennett, Fred G. ... Los Angeles, CA
Bennett, Fred P. ... Melville, NY
Bennett, Fred T. ... Dallas, TX
Bennett, Fred Warren ... Baltimore, MD
Greenbelt, MD
Bennett, Frederick R. ... Los Angeles, CA
Bennett, Fredric B. ... New York, NY
Bennett, Gail Pabarue ... Detroit, MI
Bennett, Gary B. ... Denton, TX
Fort Worth, TX
Sherman, TX
Bennett, Gary C. ... Elyria, OH
Bennett, Gary D. ... Kearny, NJ
Bennett, Gary Lee ... Lyons, NY
Bennett, Gary O. ... New York, NY
Bennett, Gary R. ... Fremont, CA
Bennett, Gary R., A Prof. Corp.
Fremont, CA
Bennett, Gemma Morrison ... Los Alamos, NM
Bennett, Geoffrey C. ... Boca Raton, FL
Bennett, George D. ... Brea, CA
Bennett, George H., Jr. ... Dublin, OH
Bennett, George M. ... Seattle, WA
Bennett, George O. ... Chicago, IL

Bennett, George T. ... San Diego, CA
Bennett, George T. ... Helena, MT
Bennett, Gerald T. ... Gainesville, FL
Bennett, Gerald W. ... Colorado Springs, CO
Bennett, Golden R. ... Twin Falls, ID
Bennett, Gordon R. ... Helena, MT
Bennett, Gray W. ... Eaton, OH
Bennett, Gregory C. ... Portland, OR
Bennett, Gregory E. ... Asheville, NC
Bennett, Gus J. ... Atlanta, GA
Bennett & Guthrie, P.L.L.C.
Winston-Salem, NC
Bennett, H. Eugene ... Lansing, MI
Bennett, H. Kennard ... Indianapolis, IN
Bennett & Hall, L.L.P. ... Fort Worth, TX
Bennett, Harold K. ... Asheville, NC
Bennett, Hartman & Reynolds ... Portland, OR
Bennett, Heather Galligan ... Albany, NY
Bennett, Henry G., Jr. ... Danville, VA
Bennett, Herbert B. ... Princeton, NJ
Bennett, Herbert R. ... Fort Dodge, IA
Bennett, Herd L. ... Eaton, OH
Bennett, Hillel M. ... New York, NY
Bennett and Hollaway
Colorado Springs, CO
Bennett, Howard H. ... Naples, FL
Bennett, Hugh C., Jr. ... High Point, NC
Bennett, Hunter M., Jr. ... Weston, WV
Bennett, Ira R. ... New York, NY
Bennett, J. Bradley ... Washington, DC
Bennett, J. Bruce ... Austin, TX
Bennett, J. David ... Portland, OR
Bennett, J. Gary ... Brockton, MA
Bennett, J. Goodwin ... Stamford, CT
Bennett, J. Julian ... Winter Haven, FL
Bennett, J. William ... Cannon Beach, OR
Bennett, J. William,, P.C.
Cannon Beach, OR
Bennett, Jack ... Spokane, WA
Bennett, Jack A. ... Camdenton, MO
Bennett, Jackie M., Jr. ... Indianapolis, IN
Bennett, Jacqueline C. ... Gaithersburg, MD
Bennett, Jacqueline D. ... Atlanta, GA
Bennett, Jacqueline E. ... Washington, DC
Bennett, James A. ... Mattoon, IL
Bennett, James A. ... Gallipolis, OH
Bennett, James Bruce ... El Dorado, AR
Bennett, James D. ... Rockville Centre, NY
Bennett, James D. ... Troy, OH
Bennett, James D. ... Austin, TX
Bennett, James Dever ... Malvern, PA
Media, PA
Bennett, James E. ... Cedar Rapids, IA
Bennett, James E., Jr. ... Youngstown, OH
Bennett, James F.
Supreme Court Of The United States, GV
St. Louis, MO
Bennett, James Gordon ... Fort Worth, TX
Bennett, James H. ... New Canaan, CT
Bennett, James J. ... Seattle, WA
Bennett, James L. ... West Des Moines, IA
Bennett, James M. ... Trenton, NJ
Bennett, James M. ... Dickinson, TX
Bennett, James P. ... San Francisco, CA
Bennett, James P. ... St. Petersburg, FL
Bennett, James P. ... Baltimore, MD
Bennett, James P. ... Lake Oswego, OR
Bennett, James R. ... Panacea, FL
Bennett, James R. ... New York, NY
Bennett, James T. ... Chico, CA
Bennett, James W. ... Buffalo, NY
Bennett, Jamie M. ... Baltimore, MD
Bennett, Jane F. ... South Bend, IN
Bennett, Jane F. ... Baltimore, MD
Bennett, Jay C. ... Oxford, OH
Bennett, Jay D. ... Atlanta, GA
Bennett, Jay L. ... Minneapolis, MN
Bennett, Jean B. ... Montclair, NJ
Bennett, Jeanne M. ... San Francisco, CA
Bennett, Jeffrey ... Portland, ME
Bennett, Jeffrey A. ... Livingston, NJ
Doylestown, PA
Bennett, Jeffrey Gene ... Ventura, CA
Bennett, Jeffrey J. ... Portland, OR
Bennett, Jeffrey R. ... Washington, DC
Bennett, Jeffrey S. ... Portland, OR
Bennett, Jeffrey T. ... Indianapolis, IN
Bennett, Jeffrey W. ... New Orleans, LA
Bennett, Jennifer ... Yankton, SD
Bennett, Jennifer A. ... Cleveland, OH
Bennett, Jennifer E. ... Charlotte, NC
Bennett, Jesse J., Jr. ... Winter Haven, FL
Bennett, Jim ... Addison, TX
Bennett, Jim L. ... Tallahassee, FL
Bennett, Jim T., Jr. ... Valdosta, GA
Bennett, Jo ... Philadelphia, PA
Bennett, Joel B. ... Austin, TX
Bennett, Joel F. ... Juneau, AK
Bennett, Joel I., (P.C.) ... Los Angeles, CA
Bennett, Joel P. ... Washington, DC
Bennett, Joel R. ... Pasadena, CA
Bennett, John A. ... Portland, OR
Bennett, John B. ... Chattanooga, TN
Bennett, John C. ... Hempstead, NY
Bennett, John C. ... Culpeper, VA
Bennett, John C., Jr. ... Princeton, NJ
Philadelphia, PA
Bennett, John D. ... Rockville Centre, NY
Bennett, John D. M. ... Kansas City, MO
Bennett, John E. ... Garden City, NY
Bennett, John F. ... Colorado Springs, CO
Bennett, John F. ... Orlando, FL
Bennett, John H. ... Raleigh, NC
Bennett, John H., Jr. ... Houston, TX
Bennett, John Henry, Jr. ... Charleston, SC
Bennett, John I. ... Grove City, OH
Bennett, John J. ... Ansonia, CT
Bennett, John J. ... Southampton, NY

Bennion, David J., The Law Offices of
San Jose, CA
Bennion, David M. ....**Salt Lake City, UT**
Bennion, Irving H. ....Spokane, WA
Bennion, Kimberly A. ....San Francisco, CA
Bennion, Molly McLellan ....Seattle, WA
Bennion, Sydney B. ....Los Angeles, CA
Bennis, Donald F. ....Virginia Beach, VA
Bennis, Randy M. ....Fort Lauderdale, FL
Bennison, Alice M. ....Pasadena, CA
Bennison, John Charles ....Washington, DC
Bennison, Robert M. ....**Atlanta, GA**
Bennitt & Bufford, L.L.C. ....Birmingham, AL
Bennitt, Jeffrey W. ....Birmingham, AL
Benno, Edward L. ....Grayslake, IL
Bennon, Lois A. ....Houston, TX
Bennou, Jamila N. N. ....Durham, NC
Benns, Norris E., Jr. ....Pittsburgh, PA
Beno, Donna H. ....Green Bay, WI
Beno, Robert M. ....Montgomery, AL
Benodin, Ellen C. ....Chicago, IL
Benoff, Edward ....Philadelphia, PA
Benoff, Stephan ....Los Angeles, CA
Benoff, Todd ....**Los Angeles, CA**
Benoist & Benoist, L.C. ....Baton Rouge, LA
Benoist, John G. ....**Austin, TX**
Fort Worth, TX
Houston, TX
Benoist, Paul Howard ....Baton Rouge, LA
Benoist, Virginia Gerace ....Baton Rouge, LA
Benoit, Alexander, Sinclair, Harwood & High, L.L.P. ....**Hailey, ID**
Ketchum, ID
Twin Falls, ID
Benoit, Andrea Lynne ....Boston, MA
Benoit, Anne Frances ....New Orleans, LA
Benoit, C. Denise ....**Salinas, CA**
Benoit, David A. ....**Atlanta, GA**
Benoit, Deborah ....**St. Louis, MO**
Benoit, George W. ....Pearl River, NY
Benoit, Gregory A. ....Waterford, CT
Benoit, Henri A, II ....Portland, ME
Benoit, James R. ....Santa Rosa, CA
Benoit, Joel A. ....**Springfield, IL**
Benoit, John E. ....Arlington, VA
Benoit, John W., Jr. ....Rangeley, ME
Benoit, L. Jean ....**Detroit, MI**
Benoit Law Corporation ....**Los Angeles, CA**
Benoit, Luc P. ....**Los Angeles, CA**
Benoit, Michael ....Pacific Grove, CA
Benoit, Michael A. ....**Crofton, MD**
Benoit, Michael W. ....Bloomfield Hills, MI
Benoit, Normand G. ....**Boston, MA**
Providence, RI
Benoit, Paul A. ....Burlington, VT
Benoit, Paul F. ....Worcester, MA
Benoit, Philippe ....Washington, DC
Benoit, Richard A. ....New Bedford, MA
Benoit, Suzanne D. ....Worcester, MA
Benoit, Timothy P. ....**Portland, ME**
Benoit, Wilfred J., Jr. ....**Boston, MA**
Benoliel, D. Jeffry ....Conshohocken, PA
Benoliel, Joel ....Kirkland, WA
Benolken, Ann L. ....San Marcos, TX
Benor, David E. ....Rockville, MD
Benos, Cummings, Mann & Valenti, A Legal Professional Association ....**Cleveland, OH**
Benos, Wayne F. ....**Cleveland, OH**
Benos, William J. ....**Richmond, VA**
Benouis, Catherine McBride ....Austin, TX
Benouis, Kemal I. ....Austin, TX
Benoun, Jack ....Fremont, CA
Benovitz, Stanley V. ....Louisville, KY
Benowich, Leonard A. ....**New York, NY**
White Plains, NY
Benowitz, Howard A ....**Washington, DC**
Benowitz, Jerrold ....Shoreham, NY
Benowitz, J. R. ....San Diego, CA
Benowitz, Martin A. ....San Marcos, CA
Benowitz, Martin A. ....San Marcos, CA
Benowitz, Mitchell J.
United States Postal Service, Mid-Atlantic Office, GV
Benowitz, Robert B. ....Norristown, PA
Benowitz, Robert J. ....**New York, NY**
Benowitz, Saul L. ....Boston, MA
Benoy, Jean A., (Mr.) ....Forest City, NC
Benrubi, Gabriel M. ....**San Diego, CA**
Benrubi, Richard M.
West Palm Beach, FL
Benrubi, Robert A. ....**Glen Cove, NY**
Benrud, Brent P. ....**Denver, CO**
Bens, Rory G. ....**San Jose, CA**
Bensal, Nancy B. ....Bronx, NY
Bensaras, Debbie Zacharia ....Brooklyn, NY
Bensch, Harold P. ....Jamestown, ND
Bensch, Jennifer A. ....**Los Angeles, CA**
Benschar, Tal S. ....Newark, NJ
Bense, Denise Brinker ....**Philadelphia, PA**
Bensel, Charles E. ....Ridgewood, NJ
Bensel, Francis P. ....**New York, NY**
Bensel, Lore ....Madras, OR
Bensen, Eric E. ....**New York, NY**
Bensen, Eric Lee ....Orlando, FL
Bensen, Eric Lee, P.A. ....Orlando, FL
Bensen, Katharine L. ....**Chicago, IL**
Benser, Frank L. ....**Bowling Green, VA**
Bensfield, James A. ....**Washington, DC**
Benshoof, Bruce L. ....**Baltimore, MD**
Benshoof, Janet L. ....New York, NY
Benshoof, Paul T. ....Bemidji, MN
Benshoof, Ward L. ....**Los Angeles, CA**
Bens-Hower, Vivian ....San Rafael, CA
Bensi, Lauren J. ....Houston, TX
Bensi, Phillip R. ....East Meadow, NY
Bensick, J. Christopher ....San Francisco, CA
Bensignor, Laurence E. ....Washington, DC
Bensing, Daniel E. ....Department of Justice, Civil Division, GV
Bensing, Robert ....Atlanta, GA
Bensing, Robert C. ....Northbrook, IL
Bensinger, Alex L. ....Stroudsburg, PA
Bensinger, Carl J. ....**Louisville, KY**
Bensinger, Charles N., III ....**Chicago, IL**
Bensinger, Cotant, Menkes & Aardema, P.C.
Gaylord, MI
Grand Rapids, MI
Marquette, MI
Bensinger, Ethan E. ....**Chicago, IL**
Bensinger, Grayson, Ritt & Gee, L.L.P.
Los Angeles, CA
Pasadena, CA
Bensinger, Kerry R. ....**Pasadena, CA**
Bensinger, Miriam B.
North Miami Beach, FL
Bensinger, Patrick E. ....**Memphis, TN**
Bensinger, Peter B., Jr. ....**Denver, CO**
Chicago, IL
Bensinger, Richard G. ....**Gaylord, MI**
Bensinger, Sarah R. ....Chicago, IL
Bensinger and Weekes, P.A.
Stroudsburg, PA
Benske, John A., II ....Madison, WI
Bensky, Eric A. ....**Washington, DC**
Bensky, Janice N. ....**Madison, WI**
Bensky, Lawrence ....**Madison, WI**
Bensley, Norman C. ....**Washington, DC**
Bensley, William Charles
Philadelphia, PA
Bensman, Daniel A. ....**Sidney, OH**
Bensman, Janet Lynn ....Buffalo, NY
Bensman, Morey R. ....Milwaukee, WI
Benso, John C. ....Pawleys Island, SC
Benson, A. Swain ....Bottineau, ND
Benson, Alexander H. ....**Southfield, MI**
Benson, Alicia M. ....**Cary, NC**
Benson, Allan ....Bottineau, ND
Benson, Allison K. ....Seal Beach, CA
Benson, Amy L. ....**Denver, CO**
Benson, Andrew L. ....Amesbury, MA
Benson, Anna H. ....**Pensacola, FL**
Benson, AnnDrea M. ....Minneapolis, MN
Benson & Annett ....Watonga, OK
Benson, Annette J. ....**Bloomfield Hills, MI**
Benson, Arthur A., II ....**Kansas City, MO**
Benson, Arthur A. II & Associates
Overland Park, KS
Kansas City, MO
Benson, Arthur C. ....Minneapolis, MN
Benson, A. S. ....Bottineau, ND
Benson, B. Brooks ....**Utica, NY**
Benson, Barbara ....**Phoenix, AZ**
Benson, Barbara S. ....**San Francisco, CA**
Benson, Barbara S. ....**Lubbock, TX**
Benson, Barry F. ....Department of Justice, Civil Division, GV
Benson, Barry M. ....**Belle Mead, NJ**
Cranford, NJ
Benson, Barry M. ....**Princeton, NJ**
Benson and Benson ....**Lubbock, TX**
Benson Bertoldo & Baker, Chartered
Las Vegas, NV
Benson, Betty J. ....Douglasville, GA
Benson & Binder, Professional Mediators, Inc
St. Petersburg, FL
Benson, Bonnie M. ....Dover, DE
Benson, Bradford L. ....**Frederick, OK**
Benson, Bradley K. ....**Denver, CO**
Benson, Brenda K. ....**Santa Monica, CA**
Benson, Bruce F. ....Tustin, CA
Benson, Bruce H. ....Seattle, WA
Benson, Bruce W. ....Carson City, NV
Benson, C. Michael ....Auburn, AL
Benson, C. Tama ....**Boston, MA**
Benson, Carl J. ....Canton, OH
Benson, Carol Ford ....Running Springs, CA
Benson, Carolyn R. ....Fulton, MS
Benson, Carrie L. ....Minneapolis, MN
Benson & Case, LLP ....**Denver, CO**
Benson, Charles E. ....**Lubbock, TX**
Benson, Charles H. ....Hartford, CT
Benson, Christina C. ....**Washington, DC**
Benson, Christine M. ....**Tulsa, OK**
Benson, Christine M. ....**Brookfield, WI**
Benson, Christine Renee ....**Jacksonville, FL**
Benson, Christopher A. ....**Charlotte, NC**
Benson, Christopher A. ....Federal Way, WA
Benson, Christopher R. ....**Houston, TX**
Benson, Clifford C. ....**Seattle, WA**
Benson, Craig B. ....Nashville, TN
Benson, Craig H. ....Atlanta, GA
Benson, Craig R. ....**Mineola, NY**
New York, NY
Benson, Craig T. ....**Angola, IN**
Benson, Curt A. ....Grand Rapids, MI
Benson, Curt A., P.C., Law Offices of
Grand Rapids, MI
Benson, Cynthia C. ....**Denver, CO**
Benson, Cyrus, III ....**New York, NY**
Benson, Daniel A. ....St. Cloud, MN
Benson, Daniel H. ....Lubbock, TX
Benson, Daniel R. ....**New York, NY**
Benson, David J. ....Ada, OH
Benson, David M. ....Washington, DC
Benson, David O. ....Douglasville, GA
Benson, David Vance ....**Rock Hill, SC**
Benson, David W. ....Ames, IA
Benson, Dawn G. ....**Albany, GA**
Benson, Deborah H. ....Norwich, CT
Benson, Deborah L. ....**Boston, MA**
Providence, RI
Benson, Dee V. ....Salt Lake City, UT
Benson, Dena Elliott
Kingshill, St. Thomas, VI
Benson, Dennis H. ....Cadillac, MI
Benson, Devin "Buck" ....**San Antonio, TX**
Benson, Diana C. ....Murfreesboro, TN
Benson, Don M. ....**Canton, OH**
Benson, Donald H. ....Fort Lauderdale, FL
North Miami, FL
Benson, Donald L. ....**Alva, OK**
Benson, Donald W. ....**Atlanta, GA**
Benson, Douglas W. ....Newport Beach, CA
San Diego, CA
Benson, Earl B., Jr. ....**Atlanta, GA**
Benson, Edmund J. ....**Lexington, KY**
Benson, Edward O. ....Brookhaven, MS
Benson, Edward S. ....**New York, NY**
Benson, Elizabeth S. ....New York, NY
Benson, Ellen V. ....**Boston, MA**
Benson, Emery B. ....Minneapolis, MN
Benson, Eric R. ....Burlington, VT
Benson, Erol R. ....Ogden, UT
Benson, Eugene B. ....Boston, MA
Benson, Eva N. ....Angwin, CA
Benson, Floyd L. ....Ottawa, IL
Benson, Franklin M., Jr. ....**Baltimore, MD**
Benson, Fred O. ....Portland, OR
Benson, Frederick B. ....Destin, FL
Benson, Frederick R. ....Charlotte, NC
Benson, Fredric ....**Springfield, IL**
Benson, G. Douglas ....Huntsville, AL
Benson, Gail S. ....Detroit, MI
Benson, Gary A. ....Jacksonville, FL
Benson, Gary J. ....**Denver, CO**
Benson, Gary S. ....Chicago, IL
Benson, George J. ....Budd Lake, NJ
Benson, George W. ....**Chicago, IL**
Benson, George W. ....**Siren, WI**
Benson, Gerrit W. ....Virginia Beach, VA
Benson, Glenn S. ....**Washington, DC**
Benson, Gregg C. ....**Groton, CT**
Benson & Guest, LLP ....**St. Louis, MO**
Benson, H. Bixler ....Fort Wayne, IN
Benson, Harry J. ....Oklahoma City, OK
Benson, Heidi A. ....**Macomb, IL**
Benson, Henry N., Jr. ....St. Peter, MN
Benson, Herbert W. ....Tifton, GA
Benson, Howard R. ....Oakland, CA
Benson, Ingram T. ....Arlington, VA
Benson, Ingram T., Ltd. ....Arlington, VA
Benson, J. Clay, Jr. ....Montgomery, AL
Benson, J. Jeffrey ....Chillicothe, OH
Benson, J. Marvin ....Vancouver, WA
Benson, J. Michael ....Clayton, MO
Benson, J. Todd ....**Shreveport, LA**
Benson, James B. ....**Roseland, NJ**
Benson, James C. ....**Duncan, OK**
Benson, James D. ....**Poughkeepsie, NY**
Benson, James M., Jr. ....Houston, TX
Benson, James R., Jr. ....**Denver, CO**
Benson, Jay, P.C. ....**Kirksville, MO**
Benson, Jeffrey A. ....**Raleigh, NC**
Benson, Jeffrey L. ....West Dundee, IL
Benson, Jeffrey L. ....Findlay, OH
Benson, Jeffrey R. ....**Minneapolis, MN**
Benson, Jennifer M. ....**Houston, TX**
Benson, Jerome L. ....**Ayer, MA**
Benson, Jerome L. ....**Devens, MA**
Benson, Jerome T. ....San Francisco, CA
Benson, Jerry Earl ....Watonga, OK
Benson, Joe ....**Fayetteville, AR**
Benson, Joel ....**Denver, CO**
Benson, Joel W. ....**Chicago, IL**
Benson, John ....Whitehall, OH
Benson, John A. ....Barrington, IL
Benson, John A. ....Idabel, OK
Benson, John D. ....**Philadelphia, PA**
Benson, John Douglas ....Plantation, FL
Benson, John E. ....San Francisco, CA
Benson, John G. ....Minneapolis, MN
Benson, John P. ....Framingham, MA
Benson, John R. ....Brawley, CA
Benson, John S. ....Colorado Springs, CO
Benson, John Stewart ....Doylestown, PA
Benson, John W. ....Atlanta, GA
Benson, Jon ....**Cambridge, MA**
Benson, Jon Douglas, Law Offices of
Reno, NV
Benson, Jonathan P. ....**Portland, OR**
Benson, Joseph L., Chrtd. ....Las Vegas, NV
Benson, Joseph W. ....**Wilmington, DE**
Benson, Joseph W., P.A. ....**Wilmington, DE**
Benson, Judith R. ....Cedar Falls, IA
Benson, Kara L. ....**Minneapolis, MN**
Benson, Karen Augeri ....Somerset, MA
Benson, Karen D. ....Denver, CO
Benson, Katie Trettin ....**Milwaukee, WI**
Benson, Katrina Irene ....West Branch, MI
Benson, Kay T. Trettin ....Milwaukee, WI
Benson, Keith ....New York, NY
Benson, Kelly E. ....Walnut Creek, CA
Benson, Kenneth R. ....Clark, NJ
Benson, Kenneth V. ....Sheboygan, WI
Benson, Kristen M. ....**Chicago, IL**
Benson, Kurt R. ....**Pawtucket, RI**
Benson Law Firm, P.A. ....Jonesboro, AR
Benson Law Office ....Bottineau, ND
Benson Law Office ....**Siren, WI**
Benson, Lawrence K., Jr. ....New Orleans, LA
Benson, Lee H. ....San Fernando, CA
Benson, Leonard H. ....Huntington, NY
Benson, Lewis D. ....Owosso, MI
Benson, Linda D. ....Tallassee, AL
Benson, Lorrie B. ....Lincoln, NE
Benson, Loyd L. ....**Frederick, OK**
Benson, Lynda Frazier ....Seattle, WA
Benson, M. Robert ....Fort Wayne, IN
Benson, Mair & Gosselin ....**Batavia, IL**
Benson, Manuela Bernardi
Minneapolis, MN
Benson, Marc R. ....Palo Alto, CA
Benson, Mark E. ....**Los Angeles, CA**
Benson & Marshall, L.L.P.
Greensboro, NC
Benson, Matthew H. ....**Manchester, NH**
Benson, Matthew L. ....**Houston, TX**
Benson, Maurice A. ....San Diego, CA
Benson, M. C. ....Brooklyn, NY
Benson & Merchlewitz ....Winona, MN
Benson, Michael A. ....Buffalo, NY
Benson, Michael E. ....Vineland, NJ
Benson, Michael E. ....**Columbus, OH**
Benson, Michael T.
Department Of Health And Human Services, Food & Drug Administration, GV
Benson, Michele S. ....San Francisco, CA
Benson, Mildred I. ....Manassas, VA
Benson, Molly R. ....Findlay, OH
Benson, Morrie ....Winter Park, FL
Benson, Moyle & Mucci, L.L.P.
Fort Lauderdale, FL
Miami, FL
Benson, Nat B., Jr. ....Mount Pleasant, SC
Benson, Nick ....**Walton, KY**
Benson, Olivia S. ....Miami, FL
Benson, Osa A. ....**Atlanta, GA**
Benson, Page W. ....El Dorado, KS
Benson, Pamela C. ....Department of Defense, Defense Legal Services Agency, GV
Benson, Pantello, Morris, James & Logan
Fort Wayne, IN
Benson, Patricia H., (A Professional Corporation) ....**Los Angeles, CA**
Benson, Paul ....Fargo, ND
Benson, Paul E. ....**Milwaukee, WI**
Benson, Paul F. ....Carrollton, OH
Benson, Peter J. ....**Rock Island, IL**
Davenport, IA
Benson, Philip F. ....**San Antonio, TX**
Benson, Phillips & Hoffman, P.C.
Tifton, GA
Benson, Quinn E. ....Kalamazoo, MI
Benson, Ralph R. ....Calabasas, CA
Benson, Ralph V. ....Bountiful, UT
Benson, Ralph W. ....San Francisco, CA
Benson, Randall D ....**Salt Lake City, UT**
Benson, Reed D. ....Portland, OR
Benson, Reed L. ....Midvale, UT
Benson, Richard A. ....Garden City, NY
Benson, Richard R., Jr. ....Wooster, OH
Benson, Robert A. ....**Salisbury, MD**
Benson, Robert A. ....Grand Rapids, MI
Benson, Robert A. ....**Greensboro, NC**
Benson, Robert D., Jr. ....Washington, DC
Benson, Robert E. ....**Denver, CO**
Benson, Robert E. ....Boston, MA
Benson, Robert F., Jr. ....Boston, MA
Benson, Robert H. ....Rockville, MD
Benson, Robert J. ....**Palo Alto, CA**
Benson, Robert J. ....Chittenango, NY
Benson, Robert N. ....Dallas, TX
Benson, Robert P., Jr. ....Louisville, KY
Benson, Robert R. ....Preston, MN
Benson, Robert S.
Environmental Protection Agency, Program Office Attorneys, GV
Benson, Robert W. ....Los Angeles, CA
Benson, Robert W. ....Atlanta, GA
Benson, Robinson & Wood, P.L.C.
Fayetteville, AR
Benson, Rodney E. ....Redding, CA
Benson, Roger A. ....Kankakee, IL
Benson, Roger C. ....St. Petersburg, FL
Benson, Roger L. ....Ada, OK
Benson, Ronald W. ....Winona, MN
Benson, Ruth ....**Los Angeles, CA**
Benson, S. King ....Jonesboro, AR
Benson, Samuel ....Fort Lauderdale, FL
Benson, Samuel J., Jr. ....Floral Park, NY
Benson, Samuel R. ....Colorado Springs, CO
Benson, Sandra Rae ....Oakland, CA
Benson, Sandy S. ....**Murfreesboro, TN**
Benson, Sandy S., & Associates, P.C., Law Offices of ....**Murfreesboro, TN**
Benson and Schultz, P.S.C. ....**Walton, KY**
Benson, Scott A. ....**Minneapolis, MN**
Benson, Scott M. ....Brookfield, WI
Benson, Seymour ....Sanford, FL
Benson, Stacy I. ....Maplewood, NJ
Benson, Stephanie L. ....New York, NY
Benson, Stephen Aron ....**Scottsdale, AZ**
Benson, Stephen Daniel
Colorado Springs, CO
Benson, Stephen E. ....**Chico, CA**
Paradise, CA
Benson, Steven E. ....Portland, OR
Benson, Steven I. ....Hollywood, CA
Benson, Steven P. ....**Washington, DC**
Benson, Stuart E. ....**Washington, DC**
Benson, Stuart W., III ....**Pittsburgh, PA**
Benson, Susan C. ....Carmichael, CA
Benson, Susan M. ....**Sherman Oaks, CA**
Benson, Tara L. ....**Philadelphia, PA**
Benson, Thomas H. ....Atlanta, GA
Benson, Thomas L., III ....**St. Louis, MO**
Benson, Thomas M. ....**Springfield, MO**
Benson, Thomas Quentin ....**Denver, CO**
Benson, Todd R. ....**Washington, DC**
Benson, Tom ....Dallas, TX
Benson, Tracey G. ....**Bellefonte, PA**
State College, PA
Benson, Tyler D. ....**Kansas City, MO**
Benson, W. Robert ....Cockeysville, MD
Benson, W. Rogers, Jr. ....**New York, NY**
Benson, W. Todd ....Richmond, VA
Benson, Walter F. ....**New York, NY**
Benson, William B. ....**Columbus, OH**
Benson, William C. ....Chicago, IL
Benson, William H. ....**Fort Lauderdale, FL**
Benson, William H., III ....Birmingham, AL

Beratta, Jeanine M. ... Boston, MA
Berbary, George A. ... Buffalo, NY
Berberena, Angel ... San Juan, PR
Berberi, Victoria
Securities and Exchange Commission, Division of Market Regulation, GV
Berberian, Ara ... Southfield, MI
Berberian, Aram ... El Segundo, CA
Berberian, Edward S., Jr. ... San Rafael, CA
Berberian, Everett H. ... San Mateo, CA
Berberian, H. Nicholas ... Chicago, IL
Berberian, Judy L. ... West Orange, NJ
Berberian, Linda J. ... Santa Ana, CA
Berberian, Raymond P. ... Harrington Park, NJ
Kew Gardens, NY
Berberian & Sagatelyan, Inc.
Foster City, CA
Berberich, Joseph E. ... Los Angeles, CA
Berberich, L. Michael ... San Diego, CA
Berberich, William J., Jr. ... Kansas City, MO
Berberick, Frederick C., Jr. ... Norwich, CT
Berberick, Murphy, Devine & Whitty, P.C.
Norwich, CT
Berbert, Laurence H. ... Bethesda, MD
Berbig-Rus, D. Kathleen ... Parkton, MD
Berbit, Warren E. ... Mahwah, NJ
Suffern, NY
Berbusse, Jacquelyn Rohrer ... Whittier, CA
Berc, Harold T. ... Chicago, IL
Berc, Harold T., P.C. ... Chicago, IL
Bercaw, David G. ... Fayetteville, AR
Bercaw, James D. ... New Orleans, LA
Bercaw, Marshall K., Jr. ... Freer, TX
Berceau, David J. ... Salt Lake City, UT
Berceau, David J., P.C. ... Salt Lake City, UT
Berch, Mark F. ... Stoughton, MA
Berch, Michael A. ... Tempe, AZ
Berch, Michael C. ... Pleasanton, CA
Berch, Paul ... Brattleboro, VT
Berch, Rebecca White ... Tempe, AZ
Berchan, Robert ... Oxnard, CA
Berchelmann, David A., Jr. ... Austin, TX
Berchelmann, William G. ... San Antonio, TX
Berchem, Jonathan David ... Milford, CT
Berchem, Kerry E. ... New York, NY
Berchem, Moses & Devlin, A Professional Corporation ... Hartford, CT
Milford, CT
New Haven, CT
Berchem, Robert L. ... Milford, CT
Berchenko, Jeffrey A. ... San Francisco, CA
Bercher, Derek Joseph ... Ventura, CA
Berchild, John D., Jr. ... Los Angeles, CA
Berchin, Eugene C. ... Beverly Hills, CA
Berchin, Jerome J. ... Los Angeles, CA
Berchou, Michael J. ... Buffalo, NY
Berchtold, James E. ... Las Vegas, NV
Bercier, Jennifer Jones ... Cameron, LA
Bercier, Michael H. ... Cameron, LA
Bercik, Bernard J., Jr. ... Pittsburgh, PA
Bercik, Karrie L. ... San Francisco, CA
Bercik, P William ... Monroeville, PA
Bercik & Roberts ... San Francisco, CA
Bercik, Steven J. ... Elizabeth, NJ
Berck, David M. ... Nashville, TN
Berck, Margaret W. ... Boston, MA
Berckholtz, Pablo ... New York, NY
Bercot, David W. ... Tyler, TX
Bercovich, Larry S. ... San Ramon, CA
Bercovich, W. Bruce ... San Francisco, CA
Bercovici, Martin W. ... Washington, DC
Bercovitch, Stephen ... New York, NY
Bercow, Jeffrey ... Miami, FL
Bercow, Paul M ... Somers, NY
Bercow & Radell, P.A. ... Miami, FL
Bercu, Steve ... Austin, TX
Bercun, Stacy E. ... Miami, FL
Bercury, Dennis E. ... West Haven, CT
Bercury & McCarthy ... West Haven, CT
Bercuson, David ... Miami, FL
Bercuson, David, P.A. ... Miami, FL
Berdahl, Sarah Helen ... Raleigh, NC
Berdan, Kristin M. ... Boulder, CO
Berdan, Margaret Bliss ... Schoharie, NY
Berdan, Mary Ann ... Lansing, MI
Berdan, Scott A. ... Denver, CO
Berde, Michael L. ... Minneapolis, MN
Berdelle, Denise L. ... Chicago, IL
Berdelle, James J. ... Chicago, IL
Wheaton, IL
Berdelle, John E. ... Venice, FL
Berdelle, Richard L., Jr. ... Chicago, IL
Berden, Tammi M. ... Atlanta, GA
Berdge, Patrick S. ... San Francisco, CA
Berding, Tyler P. ... Alamo, CA
San Francisco, CA
Berding & Weil, LLP ... Alamo, CA
Oakland, CA
Sacramento, CA
San Francisco, CA
San Jose, CA
Walnut Creek, CA
Berdit, Avery Brian ... Baltimore, MD
Berdo, Robert H. ... Washington, DC
Berdo, Robert H., Jr. ... Washington, DC
Berdon, Allan J. ... New York, NY
Berdon, Peter A ... New Haven, CT
Berdon, Robert I. ... Hartford, CT
Berdon, Young & Margolis, P.C.
New Haven, CT
Berdut, Caridad ... Treasury Department, Office of Regulations and Rulings, GV
Berdy, Christopher S. ... Birmingham, AL
Bereano, Bruce C. ... Annapolis, MD
Berebitsky, Michael J. ... Toledo, OH
Bereche, Alfred C. ... Hicksville, NY
Berecz, Deborah L. ... St. Joseph, MI
Berecz & Klawiter, P.L.C. ... St. Joseph, MI
Berecz, Lisa M. ... Rochester, MI
Bereday, Thaddeus ... Cleveland, OH
Beredo, Mathew B. ... Cleveland, OH
Bereiter, John B. ... Auburn, WA
Berejian, Silva ... Glendale, CA
Berejka, Marc ... Washington, DC
Berelson, Gertrude ... Little Neck, NY
Berelson, Irving P. ... New York, NY
Berelson, Stuart E. ... New York, NY
Bereman, Robert G. ... Visalia, CA
Beren, Daniel E. ... Harrisburg, PA
Beren, Gary ... Phoenix, AZ
Beren, Nancy T. ... Houston, TX
Berena, John P. ... Strongsville, OH
Berena, John P., Co., L.P.A.
Strongsville, OH
Berenato, Elizabeth D. ... Burlington, NJ
Berenato, Joseph W., III ... Bethesda, MD
Berenbaum, Blake ... Philadelphia, PA
Berenbaum, Joseph ... Denver, CO
Berenbaum, Mark H. ... Philadelphia, PA
Berenbaum, Mark H., P.C. ... Philadelphia, PA
Berenbaum, Sheryl L. ... Detroit, MI
Berenbaum, Stanford P. ... Detroit, MI
Berenbaum, Weinshienk & Eason, P.C.
Denver, CO
Berenblatt, Ron S. ... New York, NY
Berenbroick, Kathleen M. ... Fort Lee, NJ
Berenbroick, Robert C. ... Paramus, NJ
Berend, Robert W. ... New York, NY
Berendsen, James R. ... Columbus, OH
Berendt, Emily P. ... Woodstock, IL
Berendt, Gerald E. ... Chicago, IL
Berendt, Robert T. ... St. Louis, MO
Berenfeld, Kathryn L. ... San Mateo, CA
Berengarten, Robert ... New York, NY
Berenger, Lori A. ... Cleveland, OH
Berenholtz, Gary L. ... New York, NY
Berenholz, Jeffrey S. ... Cleveland, OH
Berenknopf, Sandra G. ... Philadelphia, PA
Berens, Barbara Podlucky
Minneapolis, MN
Berens & Berens ... Lancaster, OH
Berens, Brian F. ... Chicago, IL
Berens, Daniel J. ... De Kalb, IL
Berens, Donald P., Jr. ... Albany, NY
Berens, Eileen M. ... Phoenix, AZ
Berens, Jeffrey A. ... Denver, CO
Berens, Kelvin C. ... Omaha, NE
Berens, Lisa B. ... Chicago, IL
Berens, Mark H. ... Chicago, IL
Berens, Matthew R. ... Phoenix, AZ
Berens, Michael ... Minneapolis, MN
Berens, Paul H. ... Cape Girardeau, MO
Berens, Philip E. ... Philadelphia, PA
Berens, Randall S. ... Lancaster, OH
Berens, Raymond M. ... Chicago, IL
Berens, Richard D. ... Fairmont, MN
Berens, Richard E. ... Lancaster, OH
Berens, Robert J. ... Phoenix, AZ
Berens, Robert J. ... New Ulm, MN
Berens, Rodenberg & O'Connor, Chartered
New Ulm, MN
Berens & Tate, P.C. ... Omaha, NE
Berens Thomson & Berens, PLC
Phoenix, AZ
Berens, William J. ... Minneapolis, MN
Berenson, Aimee Robin ... Washington, DC
Berenson, Barbara Fischbein
Cambridge, MA
Berenson, Benjamin ... Lauderhill, FL
Berenson, Bradford A. ... Washington, DC
Berenson, David A. ... Staunton, VA
Berenson, D.S. ... Washington, DC
McLean, VA
Berenson, E. Tyler ... New York, NY
Berenson & Gashin ... Boston, MA
Berenson, Harris E. ... Johnston, RI
Berenson, Harris Troy ... New York, NY
Berenson, Harvey S. ... New York, NY
Berenson, Irving M. ... Kenosha, WI
Berenson, Jamie L. ... Pasadena, CA
Berenson, Jerome N. ... Philadelphia, PA
Berenson, Lawrence I. ... Chestnut Hill, MA
Berenson, Mark ... New York, NY
Berenson, Marvin L. ... New York, NY
Berenson, Michael ... Washington, DC
Berenson, Michael A. ... New Orleans, LA
Berenson, Mitchell ... Santa Monica, CA
Berenson, Nancy B. ... Philadelphia, PA
Berenson, Rachel ... Mankato, MN
Berenson, Renee L. ... Redwood City, CA
Berenson, Robert B. ... Cummington, MA
Berenson, Stanley B. ... Boston, MA
Berenson, Steve ... Boston, MA
Berenson, William K. ... Fort Worth, TX
Berenson, William K., P.C., Law Offices of
Fort Worth, TX
Berenson, William M. ... Washington, DC
Berenstain, Ronald L. ... Seattle, WA
Berenstein, Craig S. ... Sioux City, IA
Berenstein, Greg L. ... Chicago, IL
Berenstein, Joyce L. ... Burlingame, CA
Berenstein, Marvin S. ... Sioux City, IA
Berenstein, Moore, Berenstein, Heffernan & Moeller, L.L.P. ... Sioux City, IA
Berenstein, Sidney ... Burlingame, CA
Berent, James M. ... Chicago, IL
Berent, Larry D. ... Washington, DC
Berenter, Sandra L. ... Boise, ID
Berenter, Steven W. ... Boise, ID
Berenthal, James L. ... Miami, FL
New York, NY
Berenthal & Rodriguez, P.A. ... Miami, FL
New York, NY
Bereny, Joshua B. ... Beverly Hills, CA
Berenz, Frank P. ... Montvale, NJ
Berenzweig, Jack C. ... Chicago, IL
Berenzweig, Seth C. ... Arlington, VA
Beres, Edmund A. ... Fairfax, VA
Beres, James L. ... Eldora, IA
Beres, Joel T. ... Louisville, KY
Beres, Linda S. ... Los Angeles, CA
Beres, Martin J. ... St. Clair Shores, MI
Beres, Steven A. ... Macedonia, OH
Beres, Steven D. ... Stuart, FL
Beres, Vincent J. ... Milwaukee, WI
Beres, William J. ... La Crosse, WI
Beresen, Elliot ... Framingham, MA
Beresford, Booth, Demaray & Trompeter, Inc., P.S. ... Seattle, WA
Beresford, Charles E. ... Houston, TX
Beresford, Douglas L. ... Washington, DC
Beresford, H. Richard ... Ithaca, NY
Beresford, Linda C. ... San Diego, CA
Beresford, Lori M. ... Washington, DC
Beresford, Lynne Greene
Department of Commerce, Patent and Trademark Office, GV
Beresford, Richard R. ... Seattle, WA
Beresford, Robert ... Los Gatos, CA
Beresford, Scott F. ... Tryon, NC
Beresford, William ... Seattle, WA
Beresh, Ray P. ... Novi, MI
Beresin, Marta Ilene ... Washington, DC
Hughesville, MD
Beresko, Alfred R. ... Shreveport, LA
Beresky, Timothy J. ... San Luis Obispo, CA
Beresoff, Alex J. ... Lombard, IL
Beresovski, Catherine M. ... Washington, DC
Berestecki, Philip P. ... Lexington, MA
Berestka, Ronald F., Jr.
San Francisco, CA
Bereston, Clara M. M. ... Annapolis, MD
Bereston, Michael H. ... Annapolis, MD
Bereston, Michael H., P.A.
Annapolis, MD
Berestov, Julie L.
Federal Maritime Commission, Bureau of Enforcement, GV
Berets, Keith J. ... Chicago, IL
Beretta, Frank ... Rochester, NY
Beretta, George A.
Charlotte Amalie, St. Thomas, VI
Beretta, Richard R., Jr. ... Boston, MA
Providence, RI
Beretta, Victor J. ... Providence, RI
Bereveskos, Spiro ... Indianapolis, IN
Berexa, Daniel P. ... Nashville, TN
Berey, Michael J. ... New York, NY
Berey, Michael W. ... Baltimore, MD
Rockville, MD
Berey, Michael W., P.A. ... Baltimore, MD
Rockville, MD
Bereyso, Mark J. ... Chicago, IL
Berez, Ann Weinthal ... Pittsburgh, PA
Berezansky, Vladimir ... Washington, DC
Berezin, Alec ... Painesville, OH
Berezin, Eric P. ... Atlanta, GA
Berezin, Harold S. ... Atlanta, GA
Berezin, James P. ... Needham, MA
Berezin, Joshua Salter ... Walnut Creek, CA
Berezin, Laura A. ... Palo Alto, CA
Berezin, Lawrence M. ... Newark, NJ
Berezin, Robert S. ... New York, NY
Berezin, Sidney ... Hackensack, NJ
Bereznak, Bradley J. ... Sunnyvale, CA
Berezniak, Philip W. ... New Castle, PA
Bereznoff, Gregory M. ... Southfield, MI
Berezny, Jeffrey John ... Springfield, NJ
Berezofsky, Esther E. ... Cherry Hill, NJ
Berezovsky, Bonnie Lorber ... St. Paul, MN
Berfield, Caitlin Doyle
Vineyard Haven, MA
Berfield, Frank Kendo ... Piedmont, CA
Berfield, Morton L. ... Washington, DC
Berfolette, Kathleen B. ... Harrisburg, PA
Berfond, Melvin B. ... New York, NY
Berg, Aagot ... Newton, MA
Berg, Adriane G. ... New York, NY
Berg, Alan ... Woodland Hills, CA
Berg, Alan ... New York, NY
Berg, Alan N. ... Apopka, FL
Berg, Albert ... Woodland Hills, CA
Berg, Alexis M. ... Carmel, IN
Berg, Alyson A. ... Fresno, CA
Berg, Amy P. ... New York, NY
Berg, Andrew G. ... Washington, DC
Berg, Andrew N. ... New York, NY
Berg, Andrew S. ... St. Louis, MO
Berg & Androphy ... New York, NY
Houston, TX
Berg, Ann M. ... St. Paul, MN
Berg, Anne Kathryn ... Chicago, IL
Berg, Anthony K. ... St. Paul, MN
Berg, Arthur P. ... New York, NY
Berg, Arthur Paul ... Glendale, CA
Berg, Arthur Paul, P.C. ... Glendale, CA
Berg & Associates ... Jacksonville, FL
Berg, Barbara L. ... Sacramento, CA
Berg, Barry S. ... West Palm Beach, FL
Berg, Ben E., Jr. ... Bozeman, MT
Berg and Berg, L.L.P. ... Hidden Hills, CA
Los Angeles, CA
Berg, Bernard A. ... Cathedral City, CA
Berg, Bertram H. ... Cincinnati, OH
Berg Borgmann Traeger Wilson & Wolk, LLC ... St. Louis, MO
Berg, Braden L. ... Palo Alto, CA
Berg, Bradley J. ... Seattle, WA
Berg, Bradley W. ... Fargo, ND
Berg, Bryant K. ... New York, NY
Berg, Burton F. ... Worcester, MA
Berg, Carol M. ... Atlanta, GA
Berg, Cecil Eugene ... Onalaska, TX
Berg, Charles E. ... Plymouth, MA
Berg, Charles L. ... Miami, FL
Berg, Cheryl Dyer ... San Francisco, CA
Berg, Cheryl Robbins, Law Offices of
Tacoma, WA
Berg, Connie Bogard ... Milwaukee, WI
Berg, Corii D. ... Culver City, CA
Berg, Craig A.
Merit Systems Protection Board, Office of Appeals Counsel, GV
Berg, Curtis H. ... Green Valley, AZ
Berg, David A. ... Washington, DC
Berg, David H., (P.C.) ... Houston, TX
Berg, David J. ... Boston, MA
Berg, David S. ... New York, NY
Berg, David T. ... Miami, FL
Berg, Deborah S. ... Seattle, WA
Berg, Denise S. ... Los Angeles, CA
Berg, Dennis A. ... Chicago, IL
Berg, Donald A. ... Philadelphia, PA
Berg, Donald A., Associates, P.C.
Philadelphia, PA
Berg, Donald L., II ... Key Biscayne, FL
Berg, Donna ... Mercer Island, WA
Berg, Doran, (Ms.) ... Stockton, CA
Berg, Doug ... Dallas, OR
Berg, Douglas J. ... Edina, MN
Berg & Douglass ... Venice, FL
Berg and Duffy, LLP ... Garden City, NY
Berg, Earl E. ... Phoenix, AZ
Berg, Edward B. ... West Point, PA
Berg, Elizabeth C. ... Chicago, IL
Berg, Emil D. ... Detroit, MI
Berg, Emil R. ... Ontario, OR
Berg, Eric ... Los Angeles, CA
Berg, Eric ... Chicago, IL
Berg, Eric Alan ... Redding, CA
Berg, Eric E.
Federal Housing Finance Board, Office of General Counsel, GV
Berg, Eric L. ... Longmeadow, MA
Berg, Eric L. ... New York, NY
Berg, Eric R. ... Bloomington, MN
Berg, Eric V. ... San Francisco, CA
Berg, Ettelman & Berg, P.A. ... Miami, FL
Berg, Evan B. ... Boston, MA
Berg, F. Steven ... Buffalo, NY
Berg, Fred J. ... New York, NY
Berg, Freddie J. ... New York, NY
Berg, Frederick A., Jr. ... Detroit, MI
Berg, Gabriel A. ... New York, NY
Berg, Gale D. ... Port Washington, NY
Berg, Gary D. ... Boulder, CO
Berg, Gary M. ... Wayzata, MN
Berg, Geoffrey A. ... Houston, TX
Berg, George A. ... Whitehall, PA
Berg, George V., Jr. ... Boulder, CO
Berg, Gerald B. ... Springfield, MA
Berg, Gershon S. ... Skokie, IL
Berg, Gracia M. ... Washington, DC
Berg, Harold ... Skokie, IL
Berg & Howe ... Spencer, IA
Berg, Ira S. ... Roseland, NJ
Berg, Irving L. ... San Francisco, CA
Berg, Irwin M. ... New York, NY
Berg, J. Frederick, Jr. ... New York, NY
Berg, J. Harold ... Pasadena, CA
Berg, Jack ... White Plains, NY
Berg, James A. ... Tumwater, WA
Berg, James L. ... Palo Alto, CA
Berg, James M. ... San Francisco, CA
Berg, James S. ... Yakima, WA
Berg, Jamie K. ... San Diego, CA
Berg, Jan Barteau ... Indianapolis, IN
Berg, Jean Scholl ... Chicago, IL
Berg, Jeffrey A. ... Indianapolis, IN
Berg, Jeffrey A. ... Minneapolis, MN
Berg, Jeffrey B. ... Atlanta, GA
Berg, Jeffrey Christian ... Treasury Department, Community Development Financial Institutions, GV
Berg, Jeffrey John ... Lexington, NC
Berg, Jeffrey P. ... Los Angeles, CA
Berg, Jeffrey P. ... Cedar Rapids, IA
Berg, Jennifer K. ... San Francisco, CA
Berg, Jerome S. ... Lexington, MA
Berg, Jerry L. ... Wichita, KS
Berg, Jerry L., P.A., Law Offices of
Wichita, KS
Berg, Jesse ... San Francisco, CA
Berg, Joan T. ... Chicago, IL
Berg, Joel D. ... Harvard, IL
Berg, John Anton ... Chicago, IL
Berg, John E. ... Detroit, MI
Berg, John E. ... Minneapolis, MN
Berg, John G. ... Minneapolis, MN
Berg, John G. ... Minneapolis, MN
Berg, John L. ... Cincinnati, OH
Berg, John N. ... Medford, OR
Berg, John R. ... Columbus, OH
Berg & Jones, P.C. ... Abilene, TX
Berg, Joseph E., III ... San Ramon, CA
Berg, Julius H. ... St. Louis, MO
Berg, Karen E. ... Federal Trade Commission, Bureau of Competition, GV
Berg, Karl A., Jr. ... Colorado Springs, CO
Berg, Karna A. ... St. Paul, MN
Berg, Kathleen L. ... Omaha, NE
Berg, Kelly R. ... Denver, CO
Berg, Kenneth F. ... Chicago, IL
Berg, Kenneth G. ... Worcester, MA
Berg, Kenneth R. ... Milwaukee, WI
Berg, Kevin A. ... St. Paul, MN
Berg, Kim P. ... White Plains, NY
Berg, Kristina K. ... Chicago, IL
Berg & Laipson ... Worcester, MA
Berg, Larry J. ... Minneapolis, MN
Berg, Lars ... Fort Worth, TX
Berg, Laurel Beth ... La Crescent, MN

Berg, Laurence A. ... Southfield, MI
Berg Law Office ... Syracuse, NY
Berg, Lawrence B. ... Cherry Hill, NJ
Berg, Leon W. ... Towson, MD
Berg, Leon W., P.A. ... Towson, MD
Berg, Leonard F. ... Wood River, IL
Berg, Leslie Klein ... Denver, CO
Berg, Lester O. ... Abilene, TX
Berg, Lilly, Andriolo & Tollefsen, A Professional Corporation ... Bozeman, MT
Berg, Linda Breslau ... Washington, DC
Berg, Linda R. ... Concord, CA
Berg, Lisa ... Miami, FL
Berg, Lisa A. ... Minneapolis, MN
Berg, Lonette Lamb ... Woodstock, AL
Berg, Lori Nelson ... Corona Del Mar, CA
Berg, Lowell A. ... Brick, NJ
Berg, Madelaine R. ... New York, NY
Berg, Marc M. ... Golden Valley, MN
Berg, Marcy Anne ... Buffalo, NY
Berg, Mark A. ... Auburn, CA
Berg, Mark E. ... Urbana, IL
Berg, Mark E. ... New York, NY
Berg, Mark Stephen ... Houston, TX
Berg, Martin D. ... Miami, FL
Berg, Martin D., P.A. ... Miami, FL
Berg, Mary Christianson ... Devils Lake, ND
Berg, Maureen Kane ... Birmingham, AL
Berg, Maxine R. ... Wilton, CT
Berg, McMurry & Culley, P.C. ... Boulder, CO
Berg, Michael ... Los Angeles, CA
Berg, Michael A. ... New York, NY
Berg, Michael D. ... Denver, CO
Berg, Michael D. ... Washington, DC
Berg, Michael E. ... Chicago, IL
Berg, Michael N. ... San Francisco, CA
Berg, Michael S. ... San Diego, CA
Berg, Michelle S. ... Newport Beach, CA
Berg, Mitchell L. ... New York, NY
Berg, Nancy S. ... Bellingham, WA
Berg, Nancy Zalusky ... Minneapolis, MN
Berg, Naomi B. ... West Orange, NJ
Berg, Nelson W. ... Hopkins, MN
Berg, Otto E. ... Fresno, CA
Berg & Parker LLP ... San Francisco, CA
Berg, Patrick R. ... Portland, OR
Berg, Paul E. ... Palm Harbor, FL
Berg, Paul M. ... Westport, CT
Berg, Paul Richard ... Vero Beach, FL
Berg, Paula ... Flushing, NY
Berg, Pearl G. ... Louisville, KY
Berg, Perry A. ... Waseca, MN
Berg, Peter Van Dyk, Jr. ... Monroe, CT
Berg, Philip ... Spring Valley, NY
Berg, Philip C. ... New York, NY
Berg, Philip J. ... Lafayette Hill, PA
Berg, Philip J. ... Philadelphia, PA
Berg, Rebecca L. ... Jacksonville, FL
Berg, Redge O. ... Spencer, IA
Berg, Richard ... Los Angeles, CA
Berg, Richard G. ... Los Angeles, CA
Berg, Richard P. ... Los Angeles, CA
Berg, Richard W. ... Trenton, NJ
Berg, Robert ... San Francisco, CA
Berg, Robert A. ... Corpus Christi, TX
Berg, Robert E. ... Summit, NJ
Berg, Robert J. ... Palatine, IL
Berg, Robert J. ... Fort Lee, NJ
Berg, Robert M. ... Janesville, WI
Berg, Robert N. ... San Francisco, CA
Berg, Robert N. ... Atlanta, GA
Berg, Robeson & Connor, P.C. ... Springfield, IL
Berg, Roger E. ... New York, NY
Berg, Ronald J. ... Virginia Beach, VA
Berg, Ronald S. ... Hidden Hills, CA
Berg, Ronald W. ... Colorado Springs, CO
Berg, Roy A. ... Spokane, WA
Berg, Royal F. ... Chicago, IL
Berg, Russell E. ... River Falls, WI
Berg, Scott M. ... Phoenix, AZ
Berg, Sharon Ann ... Lutherville, MD
Berg, Sidney ... Iselin, NJ
Berg, Skip, (P.A.) ... Venice, FL
Berg, Stacey R. ... Hollywood, FL
Berg, Stefan D. ... Syracuse, NY
Berg, Stephen C. ... Kalispell, MT
Berg, Stephen J. ... Department of the Army, U.S. Army Legal Services Agency, GV
Berg, Steven G. ... New Haven, CT
Berg, Steven J. ... Solvang, CA
Berg, Steven M. ... New York, NY
Berg, Steven R. ... Louisville, KY
Berg, Steven W. ... Springfield, IL
Berg, Stuart W. ... New York, NY
Berg, Susan Marie ... Boston, MA
Berg, Ted Martin ... Wilmington, DE
Berg, Terrence G. ... Detroit, MI
Berg, Thomas C. ... Birmingham, AL
Berg, Thomas C. ... Chicago, IL
Berg, Thomas E. ... Colorado Springs, CO
Berg, Thomas J. ... Des Moines, IA
Berg, Thomas K. ... Minneapolis, MN
Berg, Thomas S. ... Houston, TX
Berg, Timothy ... Phoenix, AZ
Berg, Tomme, (Ms.) ... White Plains, NY
Berg, Victor D. ... Tampa, FL
Berg, Walter H., Jr. ... Brandon, FL
Berg, Ward T. ... New Smyrna Beach, FL
Berg, Ward Toulmin, P.A. ... New Smyrna Beach, FL
Berg, Wendell H. ... Chicago, IL
Berg, Wendy M. ... Northampton, MA
Berg, Weston L. ... Stanton, ND
Berg & Wheeler, P.A. ... Brandon, FL
Berg, William A. ... Portland, OR
Berg, William G. ... Chicago, IL
Berg, William J. ... Atlanta, GA
Berg, William L. ... Alameda, CA
Berg, William L., Law Office of ... Alameda, CA
Berg, William W. ... Department Of Veterans Affairs, Board of Veterans Appeals, GV
Berga, Christopher G. ... Miami, FL
Bergacker, Jane W. ... Palm Beach, FL
Bergadano Zichello & McIntyre, LLP ... New York, NY
Bergal, Mark G. ... New Lenox, IL
Bergamasco, Claudio B. ... Chatham, NJ
Bergamini, Laura M. ... New York, NY
Bergamini, Mary T. ... Enfield, CT
Bergamini, Ronald S. ... Hasbrouck Heights, NJ
Bergamo, Charles ... Prompton, PA
Bergamo, Mark L. ... New Haven, CT
Bergan, DeLila S. ... Hastings, MN
Bergan, Edmund P., Jr. ... New York, NY
Bergan, Faye ... Helena, MT
Bergan, Gary C. ... Issaquah, WA
Bergan, Marsha A. ... Iowa City, IA
Bergan, Michael F. ... Albany, NY
Bergan, Nancy A. ... New York, NY
Bergan, Philip J. ... New York, NY
Bergan, Raymond W. ... Washington, DC
Bergan, Robert K. ... Auburn, NY
Bergan, Timothy N. ... United States International Trade Commission, Office of the Commissioners, GV
Bergan, T. J. ... Marinette, WI
Bergan & Weyer ... Iowa City, IA
Bergan, William L. ... Syracuse, NY
Bergant, Paul R. ... Rogers, AR
Bergdahl, Crane ... Pasco, WA
Bergdahl, Lars H. ... Los Angeles, CA
Bergdahl, Thomas W. ... New York, NY
Bergdoll, David S. ... Bartow, FL
Bergdoll, John C. ... New Whiteland, IN
Bergdoll, John G. ... York, PA
Bergdolt, E. Erich ... Mobile, AL
Bergdolt, Marian Hill ... Raleigh, NC
Bergdolt, Robert H. ... Raleigh, NC
Berge, Amy B. ... Louisville, KY
Berge, B. C. ... Garner, IA
Berge, Bradford C. ... Santa Fe, NM
Berge, Carol J. ... Santa Clara, CA
Berge, Daniel James ... Glendale, CA
Berge, David J. ... Detroit, MI
Berge, James E. ... Saratoga, CA
Berge, John A. ... Bend, OR
Berge, Jonathan M. ... Los Angeles, CA
Berge, Leanne ... Brookline, MA
Berge, Matthew Q. ... Boston, MA
Berge, Peter H. ... Hastings, MN
Berge, Vanessa Mullins ... Frankfort, KY
Berge, William G., P.C. ... Denver, CO
Berge, Woodrow L. ... Arlington, VA
Bergeisen, Michael D. ... San Francisco, CA
Bergel, Rhonda L. ... Boston, MA
Bergel, Steven I. ... Chelmsford, MA
Bergel, Victoria S. ... Hoffman Estates, IL
Bergelson, Vera ... New York, NY
Bergeman Law Office, P.C. ... Fleetwood, PA
Bergeman, Richard H. ... Fleetwood, PA
Bergemann, Susan C. ... Los Angeles, CA
Bergen, Amy Lewis ... Tampa, FL
Bergen, Arthur R. ... New Boston, NH
Bergen & Associates ... Waco, TX
Bergen, Barbara Hart ... Los Angeles, CA
Bergen, Bruce H. ... Elizabeth, NJ
Bergen, Bruce W. ... Kennebunk, ME
Bergen, Carter J. ... St. Paul, MN
Bergen, Charles S. ... Chicago, IL
Bergen, Cletus W., II ... Savannah, GA
Bergen, Cletus W., II J.D., P.C. ... Savannah, GA
Bergen, Curtis M. ... Phoenix, AZ
Bergen, Douglas R. ... Waco, TX
Bergen, Elizabeth M. ... Buffalo, NY
Bergen, Francis J. ... Carlinville, IL
Bergen, Frederick S. ... Savannah, GA
Bergen, Grace J. ... Sacramento, CA
Bergen, Grady K. ... Dallas, TX
Bergen, G. S. Peter ... Kinderhook, NY
Bergen, James M. ... New York, NY
Bergen, Jens-Peter W. ... Kennebunk, ME
Bergen, John A. ... Santa Ana, CA
Bergen, John P. ... Staunton, IL
Bergen, Joseph B. ... Savannah, GA
Bergen, Joseph B., and Frederick S. Bergen ... Savannah, GA
Bergen, Joseph R. ... Williamsville, NY
Bergen, Kenneth W. ... Boston, MA
Bergen, Lee ... Albuquerque, NM
Bergen, Lowell W. ... Salem, OR
Bergen & Parkinson, LLC ... Kennebunk, ME
Bergen, Richard C. ... Los Angeles, CA
Bergen, Robert ... New York, NY
Bergen, Robert C. ... Orange, CA
Bergen, Robert L. ... Spring Valley, CA
Bergen, Robin M. ... Washington, DC
Bergen, Seymour, (P.C.) ... Palo Alto, CA
Bergen, Stephen P. ... San Diego, CA
Bergen, Thomas W. ... Lancaster, PA
Bergen, Van ... Dayton, OH
Bergen, William A. ... Auburn, CA
Bergen, William B., Jr. ... Timonium, MD
Bergendahl, Howard W. ... Wadsworth, TX
Bergendahl, John E. ... Miami, FL
Bergener, John E. ... Los Angeles, CA
Bergener, Karin Carter ... Memphis, TN
Bergenfeld, William Z. ... Valley Stream, NY
Bergenfield, Glenn A. ... Princeton, NJ
Bergenholtz, Stephen R. ... Arlington, VA
Bergenn, James W. ... Hartford, CT
Bergenthal, Katherine M. ... Minneapolis, MN
Berger, A. Alan ... San Jose, CA
Berger, A. Fred ... Davenport, IA
Berger, Aaron D. ... Burbank, CA
Berger, Abraham ... Brooklyn, NY
Berger, Adam J. ... Seattle, WA
Berger, Aimee P. ... New York, NY
Berger, Alan M. ... New York, NY
Berger, Albert A. ... Southfield, MI
Berger, Aldon M. ... Philadelphia, PA
Berger, Alexander B. ... Washington, DC
Berger, Allan ... New Orleans, LA
Berger, Allan ... Circleville, OH
Berger, Allan J. ... Philadelphia, PA
Berger, Allison M. ... Cherry Hill, NJ
Berger, Allison M. ... Princeton, NJ
Berger, Amy F. ... Washington, DC
Berger, Andrea Gilbert ... Nashville, TN
Berger, Andrea J. ... New York, NY
Berger, Andrea S. ... Boulder, CO
Berger, Andrea Y. ... Los Angeles, CA
Berger, Andrew ... New York, NY
Berger, Andrew L. ... New York, NY
Berger, Andrew R. ... Cincinnati, OH
Berger, Andy P. ... Reading, PA
Berger, Anne L. ... Woburn, MA
Berger, Arlene ... Los Angeles, CA
Berger, Arnold A. ... Billings, MT
Berger, Arthur B. ... Salt Lake City, UT
Berger, Arthur Joel ... Miami, FL
Berger & Associates ... New York, NY
Berger, Barry A. ... Collegeville, PA
Berger, Barry E. ... Palm Harbor, FL
Berger, Barry N. ... New York, NY
Berger, Barry S. ... New York, NY
Berger, Barry S. ... Houston, TX
Berger, Benjamin J. ... Wilmington, DE
Berger & Berger ... Dunwoody, GA
Berger and Berger ... Evansville, IN
Berger & Berger ... Buffalo, NY; Rochester, NY
Berger, Bernard ... New York, NY
Berger, Beth Ann ... Chicago, IL
Berger, Beth M. ... Milwaukee, WI
Berger, Betsy G. ... Lincoln, NE
Berger, Bill C. ... Denver, CO
Berger Boardman & LaForge ... St. Joseph, MI
Berger & Bornstein ... Morristown, NJ
Berger, Bradley Ian ... New York, NY
Berger, Brian C. ... Crown Point, IN
Berger, Brian S. ... St. Joseph, MI
Berger, Bruce ... Palo Alto, CA
Berger, Bruce ... Atlanta, GA
Berger, Bruce J. ... Fresno, CA
Berger, Bruce J. ... Washington, DC
Berger, Bruce W. ... Raleigh, NC
Berger, Burman Aaron ... Rockville, MD
Berger, C. Jaye ... New York, NY
Berger, C. William ... Boca Raton, FL
Berger, Calvin M. ... Albany, NY
Berger, Carey P. ... Lawrence, KS
Berger, Carl W. ... Andover, MA
Berger, Carol V. ... Denver, CO
Berger, Carolyn ... Wilmington, DE
Berger, Carolyn Chabrow ... Dulles, VA
Berger, Carrie L. ... Chicago, IL
Berger, Cary J. A. ... Irvine, CA
Berger, Catherine J. ... Oak Lawn, IL
Berger, Charles L. ... Evansville, IN
Berger, Charles M. ... Charlotte, NC
Berger, Charles W. ... Harlan, KY; Pineville, KY
Berger, Charney K. ... Atlanta, GA
Berger, Christopher J. ... West Sacramento, CA
Berger, Corey S. ... St. Louis, MO
Berger, Curtis J. ... New York, NY
Berger, Cynthia C. ... Pittsburgh, PA
Berger, Cynthia L. ... Anchorage, AK
Berger, Dan ... Springfield, MA
Berger, Daniel ... Philadelphia, PA
Berger, Daniel E. ... Toms River, NJ
Berger, Daniel L. ... New York, NY
Berger, Daniel M. ... Pittsburgh, PA
Berger, Daniel O. ... Cincinnati, OH
Berger, Darren S. ... New York, NY
Berger, Darrin H. ... Huntington, NY
Berger, Darryl D. ... New Orleans, LA
Berger, David ... West Palm Beach, FL; Philadelphia, PA
Berger, David A. ... New York, NY
Berger, David A. ... New York, NY
Berger, David B. ... San Diego, CA
Berger, David F. ... Ashland, OR
Berger, David J. ... Palo Alto, CA
Berger, David J. ... Miami, FL
Berger, David M. ... Los Angeles, CA
Berger, David M. ... New York, NY
Berger, David S. ... Miami, FL
Berger Davis & Singerman ... Fort Lauderdale, FL; Miami, FL; Tallahassee, FL
Berger, Deborah L. ... San Diego, CA
Berger & DePaul ... Chicago, IL
Berger, Diane L. ... Omaha, NE
Berger, Dina R. ... Westport, CT
Berger, Dirk S. ... Pottsville, PA
Berger, Donald I. ... Los Angeles, CA
Berger, Donald J. ... South Bend, IN
Berger, Donna D. ... Fort Lauderdale, FL
Berger, Douglas L. ... Washington, DC
Berger & DuCharme, LLP ... Clifton Park, NY
Berger, Edmund J. ... Harrisburg, PA
Berger, Edward A. ... Newark, NJ
Berger, Edward B. ... Tucson, AZ
Berger, Edward L. ... New York, NY
Berger, Edward L. ... Philadelphia, PA
Berger, Edward S. ... Chicago, IL
Berger, Elaine R. ... New York, NY
Berger, Eli ... New York, NY
Berger, Emil ... Elk Grove, CA
Berger, Emily E. ... Brooklyn, NY
Berger, Ennid P. ... Glen Cove, NY
Berger, Ephraim D. ... New York, NY
Berger, Eric ... Washington, DC
Berger, Eric D. ... New York, NY
Berger, Eric H. ... Metuchen, NJ; Garden City, NY
Berger, Eric L. ... Plantation, FL
Berger, Erik W. ... Jacksonville, FL
Berger, Everett W. ... New York, NY
Berger, Ezra S. ... Massapequa, NY
Berger & Fink ... Towson, MD
Berger & Forstall, A P.L.C. ... New Orleans, LA
Berger, Frances C., Law Offices of ... New York, NY
Berger, Frederick J. ... St. Louis, MO
Berger, Friedman & Christiana, PLLC ... Ellenville, NY
Berger, Gary A. ... Towson, MD
Berger, Gary C. ... Detroit, MI
Berger, Gary D., Law Offices of ... San Francisco, CA
Berger, George ... New York, NY
Berger, George J. ... San Diego, CA
Berger, Glenn J. ... Washington, DC
Berger, Glenn L. ... Altavista, VA
Berger, Gordon L. ... Aurora, CO
Berger, Gordon M. ... Marietta, GA
Berger, Gordon M., P.C. ... Atlanta, GA; Canton, GA; Marietta, GA
Berger, Gregory W. ... Denver, CO
Berger, H. Tony ... Miami, FL
Berger, Hal ... Charlotte, NC
Berger, Harold ... Philadelphia, PA
Berger, Harold D. ... Garden City, NY
Berger, Harold J. ... Evanston, IL
Berger, Harold P. ... Rutland, VT
Berger, Harvey C. ... San Diego, CA
Berger, Helaine L. ... Chicago, IL
Berger, Helen C. ... Sacramento, CA
Berger, Henry R. ... Washington, DC
Berger, Henry T. ... New York, NY
Berger & Hopkins ... San Jose, CA
Berger, Howard ... New Rochelle, NY
Berger, Howard C. ... Floresville, TX
Berger, Howard E. ... Buffalo, NY
Berger, Howard J. ... New York, NY
Berger, Howard M. ... Andover, MA
Berger and Hyde, P.C. ... Andover, MA
Berger, I. Joseph ... Cleveland, OH
Berger, Ira M. ... New York, NY
Berger, Irene C. ... Charleston, WV
Berger, Irving ... Long Beach, CA
Berger and Ivarinen, P.S. ... Mount Vernon, WA
Berger, J. Clayton ... Santa Fe, NM
Berger, J. John ... Andover, MA
Berger, Jack H. ... Port St. Lucie, FL
Berger, Jack L. ... Memphis, TN
Berger, James E. ... Kansas City, MO
Berger, James E. ... New York, NY
Berger, James L. ... Fort Lauderdale, FL
Berger, James R. ... Harrisburg, PA
Berger, James S. ... St. Ann, MO
Berger, Jana M. ... Flint, MI
Berger, Jeanne S. ... Inglewood, CA
Berger, Jeffrey A. ... Southfield, MI
Berger, Jeffrey L. ... Washington, DC
Berger, Jeffrey L., P.C. ... Washington, DC
Berger, Jeffrey S. ... New York, NY
Berger, Jeffrey Scot ... Hilton Head Island, SC
Berger, Jenifer ... Baltimore, MD
Berger, Jerold E. ... Topeka, KS
Berger, Jerold F. ... Los Angeles, CA
Berger, Jerome ... New York, NY
Berger, Jerry S., (A P.C.) ... Beverly Hills, CA
Berger, Jo Ellen ... Albany, NY
Berger, Joan F. ... New York, NY
Berger, Jodie ... San Francisco, CA
Berger, Joel ... Boca Raton, FL
Berger, Joel ... New York, NY
Berger, Joel ... New York, NY
Berger, Joel P. ... Bayside, NY
Berger, John A. ... Florence, KY
Berger, John J. ... Norwalk, CT
Berger, John L. ... Roseland, NJ
Berger, John R. ... Angola, IN
Berger, John Torrey, Jr. ... St. Louis, MO
Berger, John W. ... Tarzana, CA
Berger, John W. ... Crestline, OH
Berger, Jonathan ... Los Angeles, CA
Berger, Jonathan ... New York, NY
Berger, Jonathan D. ... Philadelphia, PA
Berger, Jonathan T. ... Englewood Cliffs, NJ
Berger, Joseph ... Milwaukee, WI
Berger, Joseph C. ... Clifton Park, NY
Berger, Joseph S. ... Palo Alto, CA
Berger, Joshua L. ... Pittsburgh, PA
Berger, Joshua S. ... Cleveland, OH
Berger, Kahn, Shafton, Moss, Figler, Simon & Gladstone ... Bend, OR; Irvine, CA; Los Angeles, CA; Novato, CA; San Diego, CA; Woodland Hills, CA
Berger, Karen Joyce ... New York, NY
Berger, Kathryn E. ... Bellingham, WA
Berger & Kaye LLP ... New York, NY
Berger, Kenneth D. ... Oconomowoc, WI

Berger, Kenneth P. ... St. Louis, MO
Berger, Kevin J. ... Kansas City, MO
Berger & Kramer ... New York, NY
Berger & Lagnese, LLC ... Pittsburgh, PA
Berger, Laura ... Carmel Valley, CA
Berger, Laura D. ... Federal Trade Commission, Bureau of Consumer Protection, GV
Berger, Lauren ... San Jose, CA
Berger Law Firm, P.C. ... Billings, MT
Berger Law Firm, P.C. ... Pittsburgh, PA
Berger Law Firm, The ... Atlanta, GA
Berger, Lawrence ... Lincoln, NE
Berger, Lawrence ... Garden City, NY
Berger, Lawrence D. ... Camden, NJ
Voorhees, NJ
Philadelphia, PA
Berger, Lawrence H. ... Philadelphia, PA
Berger, Lawrence J. ... New York, NY
Berger, Lawrence J., P.C. ... New York, NY
Berger, Lawrence R., III ... Philadelphia, PA
Berger, Lawrence S. ... Morristown, NJ
Berger, Lee E. ... New York, NY
Berger, Lee M. ... Buzzards Bay, MA
Berger, Leland R. ... Portland, OR
Berger, Leon H. ... North Hollywood, CA
Berger, Leonard ... West Palm Beach, FL
Berger, Leonard B. ... San Francisco, CA
Berger, Leslie Howard ... Pembroke Pines, FL
Berger, Leslie W. ... Fort Lee, NJ
Berger, Lindsay ... Los Angeles, CA
Berger, Lisa J. ... Columbus, OH
Berger, Lori A. ... Woodbridge, NJ
Berger, Louis H. ... Los Angeles, CA
Berger, Marc ... Pasadena, CA
Berger, Marc A. ... New York, NY
Berger, Marc S. ... Washington, DC
Berger, Marcus E. ... Los Angeles, CA
Berger, Margaret A. ... Brooklyn, NY
Berger, Marilyn J. ... Tacoma, WA
Berger, Marjorie J. ... Hartford, CT
Berger, Mark ... Kansas City, MO
Berger, Mark Evan ... Riverdale, NJ
Berger, Mark H. ... New York, NY
Berger, Mark J. ... Calabasas, CA
Berger & Markir, P.C. ... Buzzards Bay, MA
Berger, Marshall C. ... New York, NY
Berger, Marshall K., Jr. ... New Britain, CT
Berger, Martin A. ... Austin, TX
Berger, Martin A., Law Offices Of, P.C. ... Austin, TX
Berger, Martin I. ... Miami, FL
Berger, Martin M. ... New York, NY
Berger, Mary J. ... Fernandina Beach, FL
Berger, Matthew G. ... New London, CT
Berger, Matthew I. ... Santa Cruz, CA
Berger, Max W. ... New York, NY
Berger, Melissa F. ... New York, NY
Berger, Melvin G. ... Washington, DC
Berger, Michael ... Deerfield, IL
Berger, Michael B. ... Miami, FL
Berger, Michael B. ... Buffalo, NY
Rochester, NY
Berger, Michael D. ... Los Angeles, CA
Berger, Michael F. ... Great Neck, NY
Berger, Michael G. ... New York, NY
Berger, Michael H. ... Denver, CO
Berger, Michael J. ... Encino, CA
Berger, Michael J. ... New York, NY
Berger, Michael J., A Professional Law Corporation ... Encino, CA
Berger, Michael J., (P.C.) ... Chicago, IL
Lake Forest, IL
Berger, Michael Jay ... Beverly Hills, CA
Berger, Michael L. ... Athens, GA
Berger, Michael, Law Offices of
Mammoth Lakes, CA
Monterey, CA
Berger, Michael, Law Offices of
Monterey, CA
Berger, Michael M. ... Santa Monica, CA
Berger, Michael P. ... Smyrna, TN
Berger, Michael R. ... Oakland, CA
Berger, Michael S. ... Haddonfield, NJ
Berger, Michelle L. ... New Hope, MN
Berger, Milton ... Brooklyn, NY
Berger, Miriam, (Miss) ... Brooklyn, NY
Berger, Mitchell H. ... West Orange, NJ
Berger, Mitchell M. ... Waterbury, CT
Berger, Mitchell R. ... Washington, DC
Berger, Mitchell S. ... Cherry Hill, NJ
Philadelphia, PA
Berger, Mitchell W. ... Fort Lauderdale, FL
Berger, Moise E. ... San Diego, CA
Berger & Montague, P.C.
Philadelphia, PA
Berger, Morris M. ... Pittsburgh, PA
Berger, Natasha R. ... Houston, TX
Berger, Nathalie ... Chatham, NJ
Berger, Nathan M. ... Commerce City, CO
Berger, Neal R. ... Milwaukee, WI
Berger, Neil ... New York, NY
Berger, Neil H. ... Calabasas, CA
Berger, Newmark & Fenchel P.C.
Chicago, IL
Palatine, IL
Berger, Norman B. ... Chicago, IL
Berger, Norman M. ... Philadelphia, PA
Berger & Norton, A Law Corporation
Los Angeles, CA
Santa Monica, CA
Berger, Patricia A. ... Harrisburg, PA
Berger, Paul ... New York, NY
Berger, Paul F. ... Charlotte, MI
Berger & Paul, LLP ... Westport, CT
Berger, Paul S. ... Los Angeles, CA
Berger, Paul S. ... Washington, DC
Berger, Paul S. ... Miami, FL
Berger, Paula Kaplan ... Chicago, IL

Berger, Penny J. L. ... Lincoln, NE
Berger, Peter L. ... Ellenville, NY
Berger, Peter L. ... New York, NY
Berger, Philip B. ... Miami, FL
Berger, Philip B., P.A. ... Miami, FL
Berger, Philip E. ... Eden, NC
Berger, Philip M. ... Chicago, IL
Berger, Phillip D. ... Cherry Hill, NJ
Narberth, PA
Berger, Phyllis S. ... Stockton, CA
Berger, Randall K. ... New York, NY
Berger, Randi C. ... New York, NY
Berger, Raphael ... Brooklyn, NY
Berger, Renee E. ... Philadelphia, PA
Berger, Richard E. ... St. Paul, MN
Berger, Richard G. ... Baltimore, MD
Berger, Richard G. ... Hackensack, NJ
Berger, Richard G. ... Buffalo, NY
Niagara Falls, NY
Berger, Richard H. ... Encino, CA
Berger, Richard H., A Law Corporation
Encino, CA
Berger, Richard K. ... Milford, MA
Berger, Richard K. ... Dallas, TX
Berger, Richard L. ... Glendale, CA
Berger, Richard S. ... Los Angeles, CA
Berger, Richard S. ... Neptune, NJ
Berger, Ricki H. ... New City, NY
Berger, Ritchie E. ... Burlington, VT
Berger, Robert ... Philadelphia, PA
Berger, Robert A. ... Washington, DC
Berger, Robert B. ... Enfield, CT
Berger, Robert D. ... Overland Park, KS
Berger, Robert F. ... Virginia, MN
Berger, Robert G. ... Highland, IN
Berger, Robert G. ... Sheridan, WY
Berger, Robert Glenn ... Washington, DC
Berger, Robert I. ... Chicago, IL
Berger, Robert M. ... Woodland Hills, CA
Berger, Robert M. ... Chicago, IL
Berger, Robert N. ... Dayton, OH
Berger, Robert O. ... Boston, MA
Berger, Robert S. ... Denver, CO
Berger, Robert W. ... Ravenna, OH
Berger, Robert Z. ... San Francisco, CA
San Jose, CA
Berger, Roberta E. ... Phoenix, AZ
Berger, Rolf H. ... Salt Lake City, UT
Berger, Ronald ... Rockville, MD
Berger, Ronald C. ... Syracuse, NY
Berger & Rozan ... Houston, TX
Berger, Russell A. ... Treasury Department, Office of Regulations and Rulings, GV
Berger, S. Joshua ... Saipan, TT
Berger, Sally ... Orinda, CA
Berger, Samuel ... New York, NY
Berger, Samuel E. ... New York, NY
Berger, Samuel S. ... Trenton, NJ
Berger, Sanford David ... Washington, DC
Berger, Sanford J. ... Cleveland, OH
Berger & Santy, P.C. ... Enfield, CT
Berger, Sarah J. ... Brooklyn, NY
Berger, Scott A. ... New York, NY
Berger, Scott M. ... North Woodmere, NY
Berger, Scott S. ... Media, PA
Berger, Scott S., A Professional Corporation
Media, PA
Berger, Seymour ... Detroit, MI
Berger, Seymour ... Southfield, MI
Berger, Seymour ... Brooklyn, NY
Berger, Sheldon P., (Professional Corporation) ... Los Angeles, CA
Berger, Shirley, (Mr.) ... Bangor, ME
Berger, Sid L. ... Houston, TX
Berger, Sidney R. ... Chicago, IL
Berger, Stacey ... Columbia, MD
Berger, Stanley L. ... Farmington Hills, MI
Berger, Stephen D. ... Louisville, KY
Berger, Stephen L. ... Chicago, IL
Berger, Stephen W. ... Newport Beach, CA
Berger Stern & Webb, LLP
New York, NY
Berger, Steven A. ... Davenport, IA
Berger, Steven A. ... New York, NY
Berger, Steven A. ... Philadelphia, PA
Berger, Steven B. ... Cleveland, OH
Berger, Steven B. ... Bala Cynwyd, PA
Berger, Steven B., P.C. ... Bala Cynwyd, PA
Berger, Steven M. ... Millersville, MD
Berger, Steven N. ... Phoenix, AZ
Berger, Steven R. ... Miami, FL
Berger, Steven R. ... New York, NY
Berger, Stewart J. ... Philadelphia, PA
Berger, Stewart J., P.C. ... Philadelphia, PA
Berger, Stuart R. ... Baltimore, MD
Berger, Susan C. ... Newark, NJ
Berger, Susan Ward ... Beverly Hills, CA
Berger, Susan Ward ... Long Beach, CA
Berger, Suzanne M. ... New York, NY
Berger, Terrence B. ... Hackensack, NJ
Berger, Theodore ... Chicago, IL
Berger, Thomas A. ... West Palm Beach, FL
Berger, Thomas C. ... Washington, DC
Berger, Thomas Kass ... Leesburg, VA
Berger, Thomas Kass ... Reston, VA
Berger & Thornhill ... Altavista, VA
Berger, Timothy A. ... Media, PA
Berger, Todd E. ... St. Petersburg, FL
Berger, Vada ... Little Rock, AR
Berger, Vincent G., Jr. ... Babylon, NY
Berger, Vincent G., Jr., P.C. ... Babylon, NY
Berger, Vivian O. ... New York, NY
Berger, Walter Moreau ... Houston, TX
Berger, Warren M. ... Commack, NY
Berger, Wendy M. ... Hackensack, NJ
Berger, Wendy W. ... St. Augustine, FL
Berger, William ... Fort Lauderdale, FL
Berger, William C. ... Denver, CO

Berger, William E. ... Lewistown, MT
Berger, William H. ... Dunwoody, GA
Buffalo, NY
Rochester, NY
Berger, William M. ... Pittsburgh, PA
Berger & Zavesky Co., L.P.A.
Cleveland, OH
Bergerbest, Nathan S. ... Boston, MA
Bergere, C. Wendell, Jr. ... San Jose, CA
Bergere, Douglas K. ... Woodbridge, VA
Bergère, Timothy J. ... Philadelphia, PA
Bergerman, George M. ... New City, NY
Bergermann, Vera, Law Office of
Cape Coral, FL
Bergermann, Vera, Law Office of
Fort Myers, FL
Bergeron, Allen J., Jr. ... Baton Rouge, LA
Bergeron, Amy E. ... Atlanta, GA
Bergeron, Arthur P. ... Marlborough, MA
Bergeron, Ashley S. ... New Orleans, LA
Bergeron, Brenda M. ... Hartford, CT
Bergeron, David W. ... Houston, TX
Bergeron, Diane K. ... Fort Lauderdale, FL
Bergeron, Hanson, Bornstein & Carlson, Professional Association ... Berlin, NH
Bergeron, Janice Serbalik
Mechanicville, NY
Bergeron, Jean ... Columbia, SC
Bergeron, Jennifer Lynne ... Hood River, OR
Bergeron, John J. ... Burlington, VT
Bergeron, Joseph E. ... San Mateo, CA
Bergeron, Kathryn T. ... Atlanta, GA
Bergeron, Keith J. ... New Orleans, LA
Bergeron, Kirk A. ... Baton Rouge, LA
Bergeron, Luby Joseph ... Cottonwood, AZ
Bergeron, Maurice A. ... Framingham, MA
Bergeron, Melvin J. ... Houston, TX
Bergeron, Mike ... Framingham, MA
Bergeron, Mitchell P. ... Sulphur, LA
Bergeron, Paradis & Fitzpatrick, LLP
Burlington, VT
Essex Junction, VT
Bergeron, Philip O. ... New Orleans, LA
Bergeron, Renee J. ... Minneapolis, MN
Bergeron, Richard G.
Department Of Health And Human Services, Office of the General Counsel, GV
Bergeron, Robert J. ... New Orleans, LA
Bergeron, Ronald M. ... Standish, MI
Bergersen, Leonard L. ... Peace Dale, RI
Bergersen, Lisa M. ... Milwaukee, WI
Bergerson, Eric E. ... Potomac, MD
Bergerson, J. Steven ... Lisle, IL
Bergerson, John M. ... Los Angeles, CA
Bergerson, Michael S. ... Michigan City, IN
Bergerson, Stephen R. ... Minneapolis, MN
Bergert & Bergert ... Washington, DC
Arlington, VA
Fairfax, VA
Bergert, Frederick L. ... Arlington, VA
Bergert, Shirley J. ... Willimantic, CT
Bergert, Thomas F. ... Arlington, VA
Bergert, Todd A. ... Canton, OH
Bergerud, Marshall T. ... Killdeer, ND
Berges, Ronald A. ... Los Angeles, CA
Bergesen, B. E., III ... Berkeley, CA
Bergesen and Clark ... Troy, MI
Bergesen, James E. ... Troy, MI
Bergeson & Campbell, P.C.
Washington, DC
Bergeson, Daniel J. ... San Jose, CA
Bergeson, Donna Potts ... Atlanta, GA
Bergeson & Eliopoulos, LLP
Menlo Park, CA
Palo Alto, CA
San Jose, CA
Bergeson, George W. ... Des Moines, IA
Bergeson, Jan M. ... Salt Lake City, UT
Bergeson, Karla K. ... Stamford, CT
Bergeson, Lynn L. ... Washington, DC
Bergeson, Mark E. ... Atlanta, GA
Bergeson, Michael O. ... Annapolis, MD
Bergeson, Patricia T. ... Chicago, IL
Bergeson, Rebecca Ann
Salt Lake City, UT
Bergeson, Steven L. ... Jordon, MN
Bergetz, Carl T. ... Chicago, IL
Bergevin, Brian J. ... Buffalo, NY
Bergez, Craig M. ... Houston, TX
Bergez, Raymond J. ... Oakland, CA
Bergfalk, Jerrold F. ... Minneapolis, MN
Bergfeld, Elliot W., Jr. ... St. Louis, MO
Bergfeld, Julius A. ... Tyler, TX
Bergfeld, Julius L., Jr. ... Tyler, TX
Bergfeld, Michael M. ... Pasadena, CA
Berggreen, Leo J. ... Baton Rouge, LA
Berggreen, Raymond G.
Pacific Palisades, CA
Berggren, Arthur T. ... Santa Monica, CA
Berggren, Elizabeth M. ... Seattle, WA
Berggren, Grant V. ... Madison, WI
Berggren, Kurt ... Ann Arbor, MI
Berggren, Kurt, P.C. ... Ann Arbor, MI
Berggren, Lesley W. ... Marietta, GA
Berggren, Lydia R. ... Salt Lake City, UT
Berggren, Mark A. ... Chicago, IL
Berggren, Paul V. ... Wayzata, MN
Berggren, Sonja G. ... Long Beach, CA
Berggren, Thomas ... Salt Lake City, UT
Berggren, William G. ... Raleigh, NC
Bergh, Alton E. ... Marcell, MN
Bergh, Garth Nicholas ... Spokane, WA
Bergh, John E. ... Salem, NJ
Bergh, Marcus B., Jr. ... Nashville, TN
Bergh, R. Andrew ... Seattle, WA
Bergh, Steven L. ... Santa Ana, CA
Bergh, Thomas H. ... Southfield, MI
Bergh, Thomas R. ... Boulder, CO

Berghahn, Marcus J. ... Madison, WI
Berghammer, Joseph J. ... Chicago, IL
Berghaus, V. Hummel, IV ... Concord, NH
Berghausen, Andrew A. ... Sidney, OH
Berghausen, Diana ... Monterey, CA
Berghel, Robert J., (P.C.) ... Atlanta, GA
Berghoff, Ethan A. ... Chicago, IL
Berghoff, John C. ... Chicago, IL
Berghoff, John C., Jr. ... Chicago, IL
Berghoff, Paul H. ... Chicago, IL
Berghoff, Robert A. ... Chicago, IL
Berghold, Eric J. ... Fairfax, VA
Bergholm, Edward, Jr. ... Miami, FL
Bergholt, John W. ... Walnut Creek, CA
Bergholtz, Norbert F. ... Philadelphia, PA
Bergholtz, Richard S. ... Mount Dora, FL
Bergholtz, Richard S., P.A.
Mount Dora, FL
Orlando, FL
Bergholz, Warren E., Jr. ... Aiken, SC
Berghouse, Jack D. ... Menlo Park, CA
Bergida, Robert ... Bronx, NY
Bergin, Anthony P. ... Waterbury, CT
Bergin, Brian M. ... Phoenix, AZ
Bergin, Charles K., Jr. ... Springfield, MA
Bergin, Christopher J.
Oklahoma City, OK
Bergin, Daniel H. ... Phoenix, AZ
Bergin, Daniel T. ... Phoenix, AZ
Bergin, Dawn M. ... Phoenix, AZ
Bergin, Debra A. ... Malden, MA
Bergin, Denis P. ... Boston, MA
Bergin, Edward H. ... New Orleans, LA
Bergin, Eugene W. ... Rochester, NY
Bergin, James M. ... New York, NY
Bergin, Jeffrey T. ... Phoenix, AZ
Bergin, John G. ... Bryan, TX
Bergin, John M. ... New York, NY
Bergin, John P. ... Chicago, IL
Bergin, John T. ... Lanham, MD
Bergin, John W. ... Ilion, NY
Bergin, Kirsten K. ... Chicago, IL
Bergin, Leo P., III ... Reno, NV
Bergin, M. Eileen ... Toms River, NJ
Bergin, Mark P. ... Natick, MA
Bergin, Michael A. ... Indianapolis, IN
Bergin, Patrick T. ... Gulfport, MS
Bergin, Robert E. ... Fresno, CA
Bergin, Robert J. ... East Rochester, NY
Bergin, Robert T., Jr.
West Palm Beach, FL
Bergin, Robert T., Jr., P.A.
West Palm Beach, FL
Bergin, Roderick J. ... Chicago, IL
Bergin, Russell F., Jr. ... Orlando, FL
Bergin, Scott D. ... Poughkeepsie, NY
Bergin, Timothy W. ... Washington, DC
Bergins, Paul B. ... White Plains, NY
Bergkamp, James L., Jr. ... Adel, IA
Bergknoff, Eric J. ... Miami, FL
Bergkuist, David F. ... Treasury Department, Internal Revenue Service, GV
Bergkvist, Carl M. ... Long Beach, CA
Bergland, David P. ... Costa Mesa, CA
Bergland, John H. ... Eugene, OR
Bergland, Kathleen E. ... Baker City, OR
Bergland, Kerri Ann ... Renton, WA
Berglas, Chaim Howard ... Brooklyn, NY
Berglas, David ... New York, NY
Berglas, Esther C. ... Boston, MA
Berglas, Lawrence A. ... White Plains, NY
Berglass, Steven ... New Haven, CT
Bergle, Beth A. ... Dallas, TX
Bergles, Susan B. ... Portland, OR
Berglund, Brian ... St. Louis, MO
Berglund, Daniel C. ... Duluth, MN
Berglund, David W., (A Professional Corporation) ... Woodland Hills, CA
Berglund, James A. ... Chicago, IL
Berglund, James B. ... Oroville, CA
Berglund, James L. ... Salina, KS
Berglund, John E. ... Denver, CO
Berglund, John F. ... Roseville, MN
Berglund, John J. ... Anoka, MN
Berglund, John R. ... Redding, CA
Berglund & Johnson ... Newport Beach, CA
Woodland Hills, CA
Berglund, Keith W. ... Los Angeles, CA
Atlanta, GA
Berglund, L. James, II ... Dallas, TX
Berglund, Marie E. ... Santa Monica, CA
Berglund, Richard W. ... Des Moines, IA
Berglund, Scott V. ... West Palm Beach, FL
Berglund, Thomas C. ... Aledo, IL
Berglund, Timothy P. ... Milwaukee, WI
Berglund & Varco ... Anoka, MN
Berglund-Meiners, Carla S.
West Des Moines, IA
Bergman, Alan M. ... Los Angeles, CA
Bergman, Alan R. ... Oakland, CA
Bergman, Alan S. ... New York, NY
Bergman, Alisa M. ... Washington, DC
Bergman, Allison L. ... Kansas City, MO
Bergman, Allison Layton
Kansas City, MO
Bergman, Andrea ... Newark, NJ
Bergman, Andrew A. ... Dallas, TX
Bergman, Andrew D. ... Decatur, AL
Bergman, Andrew S. ... Columbus, OH
Bergman, Arlene ... New York, NY
Bergman, Arthur ... Hackensack, NJ
Bergman, Aviva ... Beverly Hills, CA
Bergman, Barbara E. ... Albuquerque, NM
Bergman & Barrett ... New Brunswick, NJ
Princeton, NJ
Somerville, NJ
Trenton, NJ
Bergman, Ben Z. ... Los Angeles, CA

Bergman, Bennett J. ... Providence, RI
Bergman, Beth S. ... Los Angeles, CA
Bergman & Bird ... Dallas, TX
Bergman, Bruce E. ... Hartford, CT
Bergman, Bruce E. ... Des Moines, IA
Bergman, Bruce J. ... East Meadow, NY
Bergman, Charles S. ... Detroit, MI
Bergman, Dale S., (P.A.) ... Miami, FL
Bergman, Daniel A., Law Offices of Woodland Hills, CA
Bergman, Daniel C. ... Costa Mesa, CA
Bergman, David B. ... Washington, DC
Bergman, David K. ... New York, NY
Bergman, Donald R. ... New Rochelle, NY
Bergman, Edward "Trey", III, P.C., Law Office of ... Houston, TX
Bergman, Edward J. ... Washington, DC **Princeton, NJ**
Bergman, Edward "Trey" ... Houston, TX
Bergman, Erik A. ... Stamford, CT
Bergman, Ernest ... New Brunswick, NJ
Bergman, G. Merle ... Los Angeles, CA
Bergman, Gary D. ... Smyrna, GA
Bergman, Gibbs & Lassman ... Seattle, WA
Bergman, Glenn A. ... St. Paul, MN
Bergman, Gregory M. ... Los Angeles, CA
Bergman, Harold E. ... Tamarac, FL
Bergman, Horowitz & Reynolds, P.C. New Haven, CT New York, NY
Bergman, Howard J. ... St. Paul, MN
Bergman, Ilene R. ... Albany, NY
Bergman, Ira S. ... New York, NY
Bergman, Irving T. ... Oceanside, NY
Bergman and Jacobs, P.A. ... Miami, FL
Bergman, Jacque L. ... Sugar Land, TX
Bergman, James J. ... Houston, TX
Bergman, James N. ... Sterling, IL
Bergman, Jed I. ... New York, NY
Bergman, Jeffrey H. ... Chicago, IL
Bergman, Joel I. ... East Orange, NJ
Bergman, John ... New York, NY
Bergman, John M. ... Escanaba, MI Menominee, MI
Bergman, Jonathan D. ... Denver, CO
Bergman, Joyce Wilson ... Decatur, GA
Bergman, Julian M. ... Oceanside, NY
Bergman, Kathleen M. ... Phoenix, AZ
Bergman, Keith ... Tulsa, OK
Bergman, Keith S. ... Spokane, WA
Bergman, Kenneth I. ... Alpharetta, GA
Bergman, Klaus ... New York, NY
Bergman, Kristine Marie Ocean Township, NJ
Bergman, Leo H. ... Woodland Hills, CA
Bergman, Lloyd O. ... Minneapolis, MN
Bergman, Marc A. ... White Plains, NY
Bergman, Marcy J. ... San Francisco, CA
Bergman, Mark A. ... Covington, KY
Bergman, Mark S. ... New York, NY
Bergman, Marleen M. ... Bellaire, TX
Bergman, Martin ... Boynton Beach, FL
Bergman, Marvin H. ... Forest Hills, NY
Bergman, Matthew P. ... Seattle, WA
Bergman, Matthew Steven Washington, DC
Bergman, Max ... Washington, DC
Bergman, Melissa R. ... Detroit, MI
Bergman, Melvin G. ... Beltsville, MD
Bergman, Melvyn H. ... New Rochelle, NY
Bergman, Michael ... Washington, DC
Bergman, Michael, (P.C.) Beverly Hills, CA
Bergman, Michelle Duncan New York, NY
Bergman, Michelle F. ... Atlanta, GA
Bergman, Morris A. ... Worcester, MA
Bergman, Neil L. ... Northbrook, IL
Bergman, Nicholas J. ... New York, NY
Bergman, Norma W. ... Norcross, GA
Bergman, Paul B. ... Los Angeles, CA
Bergman, Paul B. ... New York, NY
Bergman, Paul B., P.C. ... New York, NY
Bergman, Peter A. ... Houston, TX
Bergman, Peter H. ... Palo Alto, CA
Bergman, Richard H. ... Miami, FL
Bergman, Robert D. ... Los Angeles, CA
Bergman, Robert D. ... Columbus, OH
Bergman, Robert I. ... New York, NY
Bergman, Robert J. ... Nevada City, CA
Bergman, Robert L. ... Berkeley, CA
Bergman, Robin L. ... Chicago, IL
Bergman, Ronald A. ... Seattle, WA
Bergman, Ronald B. ... New Carrollton, MD Rockville, MD
Bergman, Ronald J. ... Greensburg, PA
Bergman, Sally G. ... San Francisco, CA
Bergman, Stanley L., Jr. ... Atlantic City, NJ
Bergman, Stanley N. ... New Haven, CT New York, NY
Bergman, Stein & Bird LLP ... Dallas, TX
Bergman, Stephanie Philips Philadelphia, PA
Bergman, Street & Ulmen ... Minneapolis, MN
Bergman, Suellen W. ... Atlanta, GA
Bergman, Susan P. ... Laguna Beach, CA
Bergman, Thomas H. ... Cincinnati, OH
Bergman, Victor A. ... Kansas City, KS Overland Park, KS Kansas City, MO
Bergman, Wedner & Dacey, Inc. Los Angeles, CA
Bergman, Willard, Jr. ... Morristown, NJ
Bergman, William A. ... Cedar Rapids, IA
Bergman, William E. ... Minot, ND
Bergman Fong, Nicole V.F. ... New York, NY
Bergmanis, Erik A. ... Camdenton, MO
Bergmanis, Erik M. ... St. Paul, MN
Bergmanis, Imanta M. ... Washington, DC
Bergmanis & McDuffey ... Camdenton, MO
Bergmann, Carl A. ... Hackensack, NJ
Bergmann, Charles E., P.A. ... Tampa, FL
Bergmann, Charles Ed ... Tampa, FL
Bergmann, Cynthia A. ... Chicago, IL
Bergmann, Daryl J. ... Bloomington, MN
Bergmann, Donna M. ... Dayton, OH
Bergmann, Dorothy D. ... St. Petersburg, FL
Bergmann, Edward W. ... Chicago, IL
Bergmann, Edwin G. ... Staten Island, NY
Bergmann, Elizabeth B. ... Chicago, IL
Bergmann, Henry F. ... Carlyle, IL
Bergmann, Jason ... San Francisco, CA
Bergmann, John G. ... Seattle, WA
Bergmann, Joyce M. ... Boulder, CO
Bergmann, Kathy Gail ... Remsenburg, NY
Bergmann, L. James ... Sunriver, OR
Bergmann, L. Patrick ... West New York, NJ
Bergmann, Larry E. Securities and Exchange Commission, Division of Market Regulation, GV
Bergmann, Mary ... New York, NY
Bergmann, Matthew F. ... Chicago, IL
Bergmann, Michael J. ... Cincinnati, OH
Bergmann, Michael J., LLC Cincinnati, OH
Bergmann, Michael R. ... Washington, DC
Bergmann, Nancy A. ... East Greenbush, NY
Bergmann, Paul T. ... Chicago, IL
Bergmann, Peter G. ... New York, NY
Bergmann, Roger A. ... Reno, NV
Bergmann, Roy W. ... Webster Groves, MO
Bergmann, Sandra ... Mountain View, CA
Bergmann, Scott K. Federal Communications Commission, Common Carrier Bureau, GV
Bergmann, William C. Department of Justice, Civil Division, GV
Bergmark, Martha ... Washington, DC
Bergmark, Rett D.B. ... Novato, CA
Bergmeyer, John H. ... Lincoln, NE
Bergna, Louis P. ... Saratoga, CA
Bergner, Alfred P. ... Washington, DC
Bergner, Amy B. ... Washington, DC
Bergner & Bergner ... Morristown, NJ
Bergner, Diane Amy Palm Beach Gardens, FL
Bergner, Eric P. ... New York, NY
Bergner, Isidore ... Washington, DC
Bergner, Jane C. ... Washington, DC
Bergner, John F. ... Dallas, TX
Bergner, L. Frank, Jr. ... Aurora, CO
Bergner, L. Frank, Jr. & Associates, P.C. Aurora, CO
Bergner, Michael ... San Diego, CA San Diego, CA
Bergner, Michael J. ... Boca Raton, FL
Bergner, Peter Gregg ... Garden City, NY
Bergner, Richard F. ... Houston, TX
Bergner, Walter B. ... Morristown, NJ
Bergner, William J. ... Oklahoma City, OK
Bergo, Scott F. ... Bingham Farms, MI
Bergoffen, Charles R. ... New York, NY
Bergoffen, Marc B. ... Washington, DC
Bergoffen, Martin J. ... Asheville, NC
Bergold, Francis J. ... Bronxville, NY
Bergold, Laurel R. Federal Communications Commission, Office of the General Counsel, GV
Bergonzoni, Virginia ... Quincy, MA
Bergounous, Dexter N. ... Sacramento, CA
Bergovoy, Richard R. ... New York, NY
Bergquist, Alison E. ... Brea, CA
Bergquist, Darin P. ... Pierre, SD
Bergquist, David E. ... San Diego, CA
Bergquist, David R. ... Atlanta, GA
Bergquist, Edward W. ... Minneapolis, MN
Bergquist, Eric N. ... Lincoln, NE
Bergquist, Gary A. ... Seattle, WA
Bergquist, Gary Kirby ... St. Louis Park, MN
Bergquist, Harold John ... Larimore, ND
Bergquist, Joel R. ... Menlo Park, CA
Bergquist, John M. ... Birmingham, AL
Bergquist, Kenneth G. ... Boise, ID
Bergquist, Kenneth P. ... Department of Defense, GV
Bergquist, Kenneth R. ... Walnut Creek, CA
Bergquist, Michael J. ... Santa Barbara, CA
Bergquist, Rebecca Turnipseed Huntsville, AL
Bergquist, Robert A. ... Washington, DC
Bergquist, Robert G. ... Seattle, WA
Bergquist & Rossi ... Niles, IL
Bergquist, Roy H. ... Niles, IL
Bergquist, Stephen A. Department Of Veterans Affairs, Office of the General Counsel, GV
Bergreen, Adele G. ... New York, NY
Bergreen, Bernard D. ... New York, NY
Bergreen, Bernard D., P.C., Law Offices of New York, NY
Bergreen, Karen ... White Plains, NY
Bergren, Christine E. ... Santa Monica, CA
Bergren, Colleen D. ... Papillion, NE
Bergren, Holly ... Chicago, IL
Bergren, Laurie ... Cedar Rapids, IA
Bergrin, Irving S. ... Cleveland, OH
Bergrin, Paul Wayne ... Newark, NJ
Bergs, Robert A. ... Sarasota, FL
Bergs, Scott J. ... Minneapolis, MN
Bergs, William F. ... Cranbury, NJ
Bergschneider, Gaye Ann ... Danville, IL
Bergsgaard, Donna M. ... St. Paul, MN
Bergsma & Herald ... Saipan, TT
Bergsma, Joel J. ... San Diego, CA
Bergsman, Marc A. ... Washington, DC
Bergsman, Peter D. ... Novato, CA
Bergsmark & Associates ... Sylvania, OH Toledo, OH
Bergsmark, Edwin M. ... Sylvania, OH
Bergson, Howard M. ... Commack, NY
Bergson, Robert J. ... New York, NY
Bergstedt, Anders S. ... Seattle, WA
Bergstedt, Carl G. ... Weston, MA
Bergstedt, Carlyn Bettinger Lake Charles, LA
Bergstedt, J. Gregory ... Lake Charles, LA
Bergstedt, John E. ... Lake Charles, LA
Bergstedt Law Firm, The Lake Charles, LA
Bergstedt & Mount ... Lake Charles, LA
Bergstedt, Scott J. ... Pullman, WA
Bergstedt, Spencer ... Seattle, WA
Bergstedt, Thomas M. ... Lake Charles, LA
Bergstein, Alan A. ... Hempstead, NY
Bergstein, Barbara ... Sherman Oaks, CA
Bergstein, Daniel G. ... New York, NY
Bergstein, Jack L. ... Monessen, PA
Bergstein, Jeruchom ... Brooklyn, NY
Bergstein, Martin I. ... Great Neck, NY
Bergstein, Melvyn H. ... Roseland, NJ
Bergstein, Scott J. ... Wexford, PA
Bergstein, Sherman ... Minneapolis, MN
Bergstein, Sheryl ... Garden City, NY
Bergstein, Stephen ... Goshen, NY
Bergstein, Steven A. ... Allentown, PA
Bergsten, Alfred J. ... Minneapolis, MN
Bergsten & Bergsten ... Minneapolis, MN
Bergsten, Robert H. ... Santa Ana, CA
Bergsten, Robert T. ... Pasadena, CA
Bergsten, William P. ... Tacoma, WA
Bergstresser and Associates, P.C., Law Offices ... Boston, MA
Bergstresser, Clyde D. ... Boston, MA
Bergstrom, A. Duane ... Orlando, FL
Bergstrom, Alan Lee ... Virginia Beach, VA
Bergstrom, Barbara ... San Francisco, CA
Bergstrom, Barry C. ... Lansing, IL
Bergstrom, Brian D. ... Cedar Rapids, IA
Bergstrom Carlson & Soldo, P.L.L.P. St. Paul, MN
Bergstrom, Charles E. ... Orange, CA
Bergstrom, Chris A. ... East Lansing, MI
Bergstrom, Edward H. ... New Port Richey, FL
Bergstrom, Eldon W., Jr. ... Northbrook, IL
Bergstrom, Eric D. ... Oakland, CA
Bergstrom, Erik ... Phoenix, AZ
Bergstrom & Feldman ... Oakland, CA
Bergstrom, Gary R. ... Traverse City, MI
Bergstrom, Jeffrey R. ... Denver, CO
Bergstrom, John C. ... Champaign, IL
Bergstrom, John R. ... Janesville, WI
Bergstrom, Julia Lance ... Irvine, CA
Bergstrom, Kathryn Jean Minneapolis, MN
Bergstrom & Kotwicki, PLC Traverse City, MI
Bergstrom, Kristin M. ... Milwaukee, WI
Bergstrom, Luke J. ... Palo Alto, CA
Bergstrom, Nancy L. ... Menasha, WI
Bergstrom, Paul W. ... St. Paul, MN
Bergstrom, Peter D. ... St. Paul, MN
Bergstrom, Quinn & Oole, P.C. Grand Rapids, MI
Bergstrom, Randy L. ... Des Moines, IA
Bergstrom, Richard J. ... San Diego, CA
Bergstrom, Richard J. ... Victorville, CA
Bergstrom, Robert B., Jr. North Palm Beach, FL
Bergstrom, Robert L. ... Bellevue, WA
Bergstrom, Robert Q. ... Clovis, CA
Bergstrom, Robert W. ... Carefree, AZ Chicago, IL
Bergstrom, Robert W. ... Phoenix, AZ
Bergstrom, Robert W. ... Seattle, WA
Bergstrom, Sara Stewart ... Fullerton, CA
Bergstrom, Scott A. Department Of The Interior, Office of the Solicitor, GV
Bergstrom, Thomas A. ... Malvern, PA
Bergstrom, Thomas A. ... Philadelphia, PA
Bergstrom, Tod J. ... Seattle, WA
Berg Susich, Laura ... Boston, MA
Bergtholdt, Edward W. ... Spokane, WA
Bergtholdt, Hazel ... Rancho Cordova, CA
Bergtraum, Howard M. ... New York, NY
Bergtraum, Judith E. ... New York, NY
Bergum, Lester N., Jr. ... Frankfort, IN
Bergum, William R.A. ... Milwaukee, WI
Bergus, Linda S. ... Glendale, CA
Berguson, Douglas A. ... Harrisburg, PA
Bergwall, Todd A. ... Dallas, TX
Bergwerk, Ronald L. ... Jacksonville, FL
Berg-Wilion, Elayne C. ... Glendale, CA
Berhalter, Christopher M. Martins Ferry, OH St. Clairsville, OH
Berhalter, W. Anton ... Spokane, WA
Berhenke, Frederick T. ... Denver, CO
Berhold, Jeffrey L. ... Atlanta, GA
Berholtz, Randy J. ... La Jolla, CA
Beri, Sandip K. ... Chicago, IL
Berich and Berich ... Red Bank, NJ
Berich, Watson P. ... Red Bank, NJ
Berick, Daniel G. ... Cleveland, OH
Berick, James H. ... Cleveland, OH
Berick, Joseph G. ... Painesville, OH
Berick, Joshua J.G. ... New York, NY
Berick, Pearlman & Mills, A Legal Professional Association ... Cleveland, OH
Berid, Maxa S. ... Lowell, MA
Berigan, Patrick T. ... Waukesha, WI
Berin, Jeffrey F. ... West Palm Beach, FL
Berin, Jeffrey F., P.A. ... West Palm Beach, FL
Berinato, Thomas ... Kew Gardens, NY
Beringer, Barbara H. ... Reading, PA Temple, PA
Beringer, Barry C. ... House of Representatives, Committee on Science, GV
Beringer, Benjamin P. ... Chicago, IL
Beringer, Robert D. ... Omaha, NE
Beringer, S. Ashlie ... New York, NY
Beringer, William E. ... Atlanta, GA
Beringhaus, Beth Niehaus ... Cincinnati, OH
Beringhaus, Kerry ... Phoenix, AZ
Berinhout, Neal S. ... Atlanta, GA
Berins, Bernard H. ... New Orleans, LA
Berins, Leonard M. ... New Orleans, LA
Berio, Isabel M. ... Miami, FL
Berish, Audrey A. ... Chicago, IL
Berish, Brad A. ... Chicago, IL
Berish, William M. ... Indianapolis, IN
Beritán, Juan C. ... New York, NY
Berizzi, Steven S. ... Hartford, CT
Berjikian, Vicken Ohannes ... Glendale, CA
Berk, Alan K. ... Greensburg, PA
Berk, Arthur J. ... Miami, FL
Berk & Associates, P.C. ... Scottsdale, AZ
Berk, Avram D. ... Appleton, WI Green Bay, WI
Berk, Barbara M. ... New York, NY
Berk, Benjamin ... San Francisco, CA
Berk & Berk ... New York, NY
Berk, Bernard ... Royal Palm Beach, FL
Berk, Blair ... Los Angeles, CA
Berk, Brian D. ... New York, NY
Berk, Charles E. ... Ocala, FL
Berk, Daniel G. ... West Bloomfield, MI
Berk, Daniel I. ... New York, NY
Berk, David R. ... Pittsburgh, PA
Berk, Davida K. ... Chicago, IL
Berk, Deborah A. ... Newark, NJ
Berk, Deborah K. ... Scituate, MA
Berk, Donald J. ... Brooklyn, NY
Berk, Ellen R. ... Laguna Niguel, CA
Berk, Errol ... Ventura, CA
Berk, Errol, Law Offices of, A Prof. Corp. Ventura, CA
Berk, Frank ... South Royalton, VT
Berk, Gabriel ... Philadelphia, PA
Berk, Gail A. ... Ashland, OR
Berk, Gene ... Sacramento, CA
Berk, Gerald A. ... Cleveland, OH
Berk, Greg ... Newport Beach, CA
Berk, Harold R. ... Philadelphia, PA
Berk, I. B. ... San Diego, CA
Berk, Jeffrey L. ... Santa Rosa, CA
Berk, Jerry S. ... Sherman Oaks, CA
Berk, Jon Stephen ... Hartford, CT
Berk, Joseph ... Baltimore, MD
Berk, Karen A. ... Palo Alto, CA
Berk, Keith H. ... Chicago, IL
Berk, Kent S. ... Scottsdale, AZ
Berk, Lauren ... Northbrook, IL
Berk, Laurence ... Philadelphia, PA
Berk, Lon A. ... Washington, DC
Berk, Madeleine Randi ... Brooklyn, NY
Berk, Marnie ... New York, NY
Berk, Matthew B. ... Boston, MA
Berk, Michael ... Chicago, IL
Berk, Michael D. ... Los Angeles, CA
Berk, Michelle Coopersmith Lafayette Hill, PA
Berk, Nancy D. ... Englewood, CO
Berk, Norman M. ... Birmingham, AL
Berk, Peter T. ... Chicago, IL
Berk, Rafael H. ... Nashville, TN Houston, TX
Berk, Robert E ... New York, NY
Berk, Robert J. ... Cleveland, OH
Berk, Robert J., Co., L.P.A. ... Cleveland, OH
Berk, Robert R. ... Phoenix, AZ
Berk, Romy E. ... New York, NY
Berk, Stefanie E. ... Toledo, OH
Berk, Steven ... Philadelphia, PA
Berk, Steven N. ... Washington, DC
Berk, Steven R. ... Department of Commerce, Patent and Trademark Office, GV
Berk, Tobi S. ... New York, NY
Berk, Todd M. ... Philadelphia, PA
Berk, Tony B. ... White Plains, NY
Berk, Whitehead & Cassol, P.C. Greensburg, PA
Berk, William S. ... Miami, FL
Berk, Wm. S. ... New York, NY
Berka, Becky ... Costa Mesa, CA
Berka, Christopher P. ... Palo Alto, CA
Berka, Jerry G., Jr. ... Bay Shore, NY
Berka, Richard J. ... Jamaica, NY
Berkal, Barry D. ... Salem, MA
Berkal, David J. ... Southfield, MI
Berkal, Leonard A. ... Salem, MA
Berkal, Stelman, Davern & Shribman Salem, MA
Berkani, Sheri L. ... Kenosha, WI
Berkau, Thomas S. ... Smithfield, NC
Berkbigler, Dennis L. ... Effingham, IL
Berkbigler, Jeffrey S. ... Carbondale, IL
Berk-Cohen, Diana J. ... Brooklyn, NY
Berke, Albert I. ... Brooklyn, NY
Berke, Alice K. ... Albany, NY
Berke, Allan J. ... New York, NY
Berke, Barry H. ... New York, NY
Berke, Benitta ... Chicago, IL
Berke & Berke ... New York, NY
Berke, Berke & Berke ... Chattanooga, TN
Berke, Beth ... Culver City, CA
Berke, Bill B. ... Cape Coral, FL
Berke & Bolner, A Professional Law Corporation ... Metairie, LA New Orleans, LA
Berke, Charles ... Chicago, IL

Berke, Daniel R., Law Offices of
Long Beach, CA
Berke, Dena ... New York, NY
Berke, Elliott Stanton ... Washington, DC
Berke, Florence M. ... Boston, MA
Berke, Gordon A. ... Walnut Creek, CA
Berke, Gregory S. ... Trevose, PA
Berke, Harry ... Chattanooga, TN
Berke, Howard B. ... New York, NY
Berke, Jason R. ... New York, NY
Berke, Jay S. ... New York, NY
Berke, Jean A. ... Boston, MA
Berke, Jeff ... Los Angeles, CA
Berke, Jeffrey R. ... New York, NY
Berke, Jennifer ... Philadelphia, PA
Berke, John D. ... Boston, MA
Berke, Kenneth J. ... Los Angeles, CA
Berke, Kenneth J. ... Metairie, LA
Berke, Kent R. ... Houston, TX
Berke, Lori V. ... Phoenix, AZ
Tucson, AZ
Berke, Marvin B. ... Chattanooga, TN
Berke, Mary Ellen ... Encino, CA
Berke, Matthew David ... Sherman Oaks, CA
Berke, Michael A. ... Miami, FL
Berke, Michael A. ... Chicago, IL
Berke, Nathan L. ... Jamaica, NY
Berke, Perry M. ... Chicago, IL
Berke, Rachel ... Dallas, TX
Berke, Ralph L. ... Chicago, IL
Berke, Robert, Law Offices of
Santa Monica, CA
Berke, Robyn H. ... New Haven, CT
Berke, Ronald J. ... Chattanooga, TN
Berke, Sidney W. ... Albany, NY
Berke, Stephen P. ... Palo Alto, CA
Berke, Tricia M. ... Redwood City, CA
Berkebile, Daniel C. ... Ashland, KY
Berke-Dreyfuss, Elizabeth ... Oakland, CA
Berkel, John W. ... Houston, TX
Berkel, John W., P.C. ... Houston, TX
Berkel, Michele Lynne ... Edwardsville, IL
Berkel, Suzanne ... Austin, TX
Berkelbach, George W., III ... Philadelphia, PA
Berkelbach, George W., III, Ltd., A Professional Corp. ... Philadelphia, PA
Berkeley, Abiona V. ... Philadelphia, PA
Berkeley, Alan J. ... Washington, DC
Berkeley, Archie C. ... Richmond, VA
Berkeley, Archie C., Jr. ... Richmond, VA
Berkeley, Arthur Eliot ... Charlotte, NC
Berkeley & DeGaetani ... Richmond, VA
Berkeley, Gilbert C. ... Walnut Creek, CA
Berkeley, Jerome S. ... Cleveland Heights, OH
Berkeley, Jill B. ... Chicago, IL
Berkeley, Lawrence M. ... Livingston, NJ
Berkeley, Leonard H. ... Parsippany, NJ
Berkeley, Marvin J. ... Garden City, NY
Berkeley, Norborne, Jr. ... New York, NY
Berkeley, Rhodes & Schwartz ... Oakland, CA
Berkeley, Richard M. ... Baltimore, MD
Berkeley, Steven M. ... New York, NY
Berkeley-Hill, Michael ... New York, NY
Berkelhamer, Lester ... White Plains, NY
Berkelhammer, Jonathan A.
Greensboro, NC
Berkelhammer, Robert B. ... Providence, RI
Berkell, Gerald S., (P.A.) ... North Miami, FL
Berkemann, Rosemary L. ... Trenton, IL
Berkemeier, Francis X. ... Jackson, MI
Berkemeyer, Donald ... Reston, VA
Berkemeyer, Thomas G. ... Columbus, OH
Berken & Associates ... Denver, CO
Berken, Michael H. ... Green Bay, WI
Berken, Sidney R. ... Jericho, NY
Berken, Stephen E. ... Denver, CO
Berkenblit, Howard E. ... Boston, MA
Berkenfeld, Steven L. ... New York, NY
Berkenkotter, Maria E. ... Denver, CO
Berkenpas, Barbara E. ... Irene, SD
Berkens, Michael H. ... Seminole, FL
Berkenstadt, Eugene R. ... San Diego, CA
Berkenstadt, James A. ... Sun Prairie, WI
Berkenstock, H. Roy, Jr. ... Memphis, TN
Berkenwald, Carl ... Seattle, WA
Berkenwald, Elaine S. ... South Orange, NJ
Berker, Linda S. ... Davison, MI
Berkery, Gerald P. ... Syracuse, NY
Berkery, John P. ... New York, NY
Berkery, Karen Bernard ... Detroit, MI
Berkery, Rosemary T. ... New York, NY
Berkes, Robert H. ... Los Angeles, CA
Berkett, Barry W. ... Santa Fe Springs, CA
Berkett, Marian Mayer ... New Orleans, LA
Berke-Weiss, Laurie ... New York, NY
Berke-Weiss & Pechman LLP
New York, NY
Berkey, David L. ... New York, NY
Berkey, Dennis A. ... Los Angeles, CA
Berkey, Jeffrey L. ... Somerset, PA
Berkey, Jon H. ... Bloomfield Hills, MI
Berkey, Jon H., P.C. ... Birmingham, MI
Bloomfield Hills, MI
Detroit, MI
Berkey, Judson O. ... Washington, DC
Berkey, Kendall ... Cathedral City, CA
Berkey, Michael F. ... Baltimore, MD
Berkey, Mitchell S. ... New York, NY
Berkey, Richard F., Jr. ... Turnersville, NJ
Berkey, Todd ... Pittsburgh, PA
Berkheiser, Mary E. ... Phoenix, AZ
Berki, Ronald Z. ... San Jose, CA
Berkin, Edward ... Boston, MA
Berkin, Geoffrey A. ... Los Angeles, CA
Berkin, Jeffrey J. ... Department of Justice, Federal Bureau of Investigation, GV
Berkin, Laurie R. ... Calhoun, GA
Berkland & Brown ... Emmetsburg, IA
Berkland, Gary L. ... Belmond, IA
Berkland, Randall C. ... Mankato, MN
Berkland, Roger A. ... Emmetsburg, IA
Berklas, James P., Jr. ... Los Angeles, CA
Berklee, Betty A. ... Hollywood, FL
Berkley, Alyse G. ... Encino, CA
Berkley, Andrea G. ... New York, NY
Berkley, Benjamin H. ... Fullerton, CA
Berkley, Bill D. ... Downs, KS
Berkley, Burton
Department Of Health And Human Services, Social Security Administration, GV
Berkley & Crane ... Streamwood, IL
Berkley, Daniel T. ... San Francisco, CA
Berkley, Drayton D. ... Hattiesburg, MS
Berkley, E. Carolan ... Philadelphia, PA
Berkley, Frederic I. ... Las Vegas, NV
Berkley, Gordon, Levine, Goldstein & Garfinkel, LLP ... Las Vegas, NV
Berkley, Harold P. (Mike), Jr. ... Dallas, TX
Berkley, Herbert R. ... New York, NY
Berkley, Kent M. ... Bennington, KS
Berkley, Kiera ... Los Angeles, CA
Berkley, Kimberly A. ... Bakersfield, CA
Berkley, Lonni E. ... Chicago, IL
Berkley, Mark A. ... Tescott, KS
Berkley, Mark M. ... Hialeah, FL
Berkley, Marta W.
Federal Deposit Insurance Corporation, Appellate Litigation Section, GV
Berkley, Michael P. ... Pomona, NY
Berkley, Michael Q. ... Orlando, FL
Berkley, Peter L. ... Morristown, NJ
Berkley, Raymond F. ... Hutchinson, KS
Berkley, Richard G. ... New York, NY
Berkley, Robert C. ... Lynchburg, VA
Berkley, Samuel I. ... Streamwood, IL
Berkley, Stuart ... Los Angeles, CA
Berkley, Thomas L. ... Oakland, CA
Berkley, Thomas S. ... Portsmouth, VA
Berkley, Waverley Lee, III ... Norfolk, VA
Berkline, Kelly R., (Mr.)
Palos Verdes Estates, CA
Berkman, Allen H. ... Pittsburgh, PA
Berkman, Allen M. ... Boca Raton, FL
Berkman, Andrew S. ... New York, NY
Berkman, Barry ... New York, NY
Berkman Bottger & Rodd ... New York, NY
Berkman, Brenda ... Brooklyn, NY
Berkman, Carol ... New York, NY
Berkman, Charles S. ... La Jolla, CA
Berkman, David ... Miami, FL
Berkman, David L. ... Tucson, AZ
Berkman, Eileen J. ... New York, NY
Berkman, Elissa D. ... New York, NY
Berkman, Ellen Fels ... Washington, DC
Berkman, Eric Thomas ... Boston, MA
Berkman, Gordon, Murray & DeVan
Cleveland, OH
Berkman, Henoch, Peterson & Peddy, P.C.
Garden City, NY
Melville, NY
Mineola, NY
New York, NY
Berkman, Howard I. ... New York, NY
Berkman, Isidoro ... San Francisco, CA
Berkman, James S. ... Fort Washington, PA
Berkman, Jason M. ... Miami Beach, FL
Berkman, Jason M., P.A. ... Miami Beach, FL
Berkman, Jeffrey W. ... New York, NY
Berkman, Jerome ... Stamford, CT
Berkman, Jordan W. ... Brewster, NY
Berkman, Judy F. ... Glenside, PA
Berkman, Kenneth S. ... Garden City, NY
Berkman, Larry G. ... San Antonio, TX
Berkman, Leonard B. ... Norwich, CT
Berkman, Marcy ... Palo Alto, CA
Berkman, Michael G. ... Glenview, IL
Berkman, Myles P. ... Pittsburgh, PA
Berkman, Richard L. ... Boston, MA
Berkman, Richard L. ... Philadelphia, PA
Berkman, Stephen I. ... San Francisco, CA
Berkman, William R. ... Sausalito, CA
Berkner, Michal ... New York, NY
Berko, Daniel ... San Francisco, CA
Berko, John M. ... Basking Ridge, NJ
Berko, Otto H. ... Boca Raton, FL
Berko, Paul R. ... Mineola, NY
Berko, Steven R. ... Bronx, NY
Berkoben, L. Scott ... Westwood, NJ
Berkoff, Adam ... Chicago, IL
Berkoff, David C. ... Missoula, MT
Berkoff, Gail J. ... New York, NY
Berkoff, Leslie A. ... Garden City, NY
Berkoff, Mark A. ... Chicago, IL
Berkoff, Marshall R. ... Milwaukee, WI
Berkon, Frederick D. ... New York, NY
Berkos, Christy S. ... Cicero, IL
Berkos, Daniel M. ... Mauston, WI
Berkos, Michael J. ... Berwyn, IL
Berkouits, Markus I. ... Greenwich, CT
Berkovich, Alexander ... New York, NY
Berkovich, Edward A. ... Salt Lake City, UT
Berkovich and McMenamin ... New York, NY
Berkovitch, Boris S. ... Vero Beach, FL
Berkovits, Leslie Wolffe ... Scarsdale, NY
Berkovitz, Dan M. ... United States Senate, Committee Legal Personnel, GV
Berkovitz, David A. ... Westlake Village, CA
Berkovitz and Schilit ... Encino, CA
Westlake Village, CA
Berkovsky, Robert A. ... Treasury Department, Internal Revenue Service, GV
Berkow, Bert ... Brooklyn, NY
Berkow, Bonnie Reid ... New York, NY
Berkow, George ... Norcross, GA
Berkow, Gordon ... Woodbridge, NJ
Berkow, Josanna ... Martinez, CA
Berkow, Larry M. ... Washington, DC
Berkow, Max ... New York, NY
Berkow, Michael ... Coachella, CA
Berkowe, Kathleen Hawkins
New York, NY
Berkowe, Kathleen Hawkins, P.C.
New York, NY
Berkower, Howard M. ... New York, NY
Berkowitch, Michael ... New York, NY
Berkowitz, Abraham ... Jamaica, NY
Berkowitz, Abraham L. ... Jamaica, NY
Berkowitz, Adam C. ... New York, NY
Berkowitz, Alan D. ... Philadelphia, PA
Berkowitz, Alan E. ... Baltimore, MD
Berkowitz, Alan R. ... San Francisco, CA
Berkowitz, Alan S. ... New York, NY
Berkowitz, Albert ... Granville, NY
Berkowitz, Alene ... Wilmington, DE
Berkowitz, Angela ... Tulsa, OK
Berkowitz, Arlene M. ... Whitestone, NY
Berkowitz & Associates ... Beverly Hills, CA
Los Angeles, CA
Berkowitz & Associates ... Tampa, FL
Berkowitz & Balbirer, P.C. ... Westport, CT
Berkowitz, Barbara Lee
Beverly Hills, CA
Berkowitz, Bernard J. ... Montville, NJ
Berkowitz, Bernard S. ... West Orange, NJ
Berkowitz, Brian D. ... Tallahassee, FL
Berkowitz, Chaim S. ... New York, NY
Berkowitz & Cook ... Kansas City, KS
Kansas City, MO
Berkowitz & Currie ... Somerville, MA
Berkowitz, David A. ... Kings Park, NY
Berkowitz, David H. ... New York, NY
Berkowitz, David J. ... Lawrence, KS
Berkowitz, David S. ... Fairfield, CT
Berkowitz, Deborah Tellerman
Miami, FL
Berkowitz, Diane L. ... Chicago, IL
Berkowitz, Edward C. ... Washington, DC
Berkowitz, Edward H. ... Palo Alto, CA
Berkowitz, Ellen ... Los Angeles, CA
Berkowitz, Ellen C. ... Huntington, NY
Berkowitz, Elliot S. ... Los Angeles, CA
Berkowitz, Elliot S., A Professional Corporation
Los Angeles, CA
Berkowitz, Emily M. ... New York, NY
Berkowitz, Eric D. ... Los Angeles, CA
Berkowitz, Eric S. ... New York, NY
Berkowitz, Eugene J. ... Kew Gardens, NY
Berkowitz, Feldmiller, Stanton, Brandt, Williams & Stueve LLP
Prairie Village, KS
Berkowitz, Feldmiller, Stanton, Brandt, Williams & Stueve, LLP
Kansas City, MO
Berkowitz, Felice ... Fairfax, VA
Berkowitz Firm, The, P.C. ... Denver, CO
Berkowitz, Gail ... Kansas City, MO
Berkowitz, Gary ... Providence, RI
Berkowitz, Gerald S. ... Lancaster, PA
Malvern, PA
Berkowitz, Gerald Z. ... Wilmington, DE
Berkowitz, Gordon M. ... Stoughton, MA
Berkowitz, H. David ... New York, NY
Berkowitz, H. Steven ... Toms River, NJ
Berkowitz, Hannah ... New York, NY
Berkowitz, Harold D., (A P.C.)
Los Angeles, CA
Berkowitz, Herbert ... Anchorage, AK
Berkowitz, Herbert M. ... Tampa, FL
Berkowitz, Hyman S. ... Sharon, MA
Berkowitz, Ian M. ... Washington, DC
Berkowitz, Ira M. ... St. Louis, MO
Berkowitz, Janice ... Albertson, NY
Berkowitz, Jeffrey ... Beverly Hills, CA
Berkowitz, Jeffrey ... Kenilworth, NJ
Berkowitz, Jeffrey A. ... Washington, DC
Berkowitz, Jeffrey I. ... Chicago, IL
Berkowitz, Jeffrey L. ... Miami, FL
Berkowitz, Jeffrey L., P.A. ... Miami, FL
Berkowitz, Jeffrey S. ... Newark, NJ
Berkowitz, Jess Martin ... New York, NY
Berkowitz, Jonathan A.
West Palm Beach, FL
Berkowitz, June Freeman ... Gloucester, MA
Berkowitz, Kenneth A. ... Chatham, NJ
Berkowitz, Kenneth P. ... Nutley, NJ
Berkowitz, Larry W. ... Denver, CO
Berkowitz Law Firm, Inc. ... Tulsa, OK
Berkowitz, Lawrence M.
Kansas City, MO
Berkowitz, Lawrence S. ... New City, NY
Berkowitz, Lefkovits, Isom & Kushner, A Professional Corporation
Birmingham, AL
Berkowitz, Leonard ... Orchard Park, NY
Berkowitz, Leonard R. ... Houston, TX
Berkowitz, Leslie G. ... Denver, CO
Berkowitz, Lewis A. ... Tulsa, OK
Berkowitz, Lichtstein, Kuritsky, Giasullo & Gross, LLC ... Newark, NJ
West Orange, NJ
Berkowitz, Linda L. ... New York, NY
Berkowitz, Lisa A. ... New York, NY
Berkowitz, Lonalee A. ... Vestal, NY
Berkowitz, Malcolm W. ... Philadelphia, PA
Berkowitz, Malcolm W., & Assoc., P.C.
Philadelphia, PA
Berkowitz, Malowitz & Mullin
Greenwich, CT
Stamford, CT
Westport, CT
Berkowitz, Mark J. ... Fort Lauderdale, FL
Berkowitz, Mark J., P.A.
Fort Lauderdale, FL
Berkowitz, Marsha C. ... Los Angeles, CA
Berkowitz, Marsha S. ... Jamaica, NY
Berkowitz, Martin B. ... Torrance, CA
Berkowitz, Marvin C. ... Washington, DC
Berkowitz, Maurice ... Plantation, FL
Berkowitz, Melanie H. ... Chicago, IL
Berkowitz, Michael A. ... New York, NY
Berkowitz, Michael J. ... Philadelphia, PA
Berkowitz, Mitchell L. ... Singer Island, FL
Berkowitz, Mitchell L., P.A.
Singer Island, FL
Berkowitz, Morrell I. ... New York, NY
Berkowitz, Morrell I., P.C. ... New York, NY
Berkowitz, Morris ... New Haven, CT
Berkowitz, Nancy Jeanne ... Union, NJ
Berkowitz, Naomi ... Seattle, WA
Berkowitz, Norman R. ... New York, NY
Berkowitz & Pace ... Orchard Park, NY
Berkowitz, Patricia ... Concord, CA
Berkowitz, Paul ... Miami, FL
Berkowitz, Paul T. ... Chicago, IL
Berkowitz, Paul T. & Associates, Ltd.
Chicago, IL
Berkowitz, Philip J. ... Washington, DC
Berkowitz, Philip M. ... New York, NY
Berkowitz, Richard ... Westport, CT
Berkowitz, Richard E. ... Cleveland, OH
Berkowitz, Richard K. ... Miami, FL
Berkowitz, Robert ... Great Neck, NY
Berkowitz, Robert ... New York, NY
Berkowitz, Robert A. ... Pittsburgh, PA
Berkowitz, Robert J. ... Fairfield, CT
Berkowitz, Ron V. ... Dallas, TX
Berkowitz, Russell J. ... Stamford, CT
Berkowitz, Ruth M. ... San Francisco, CA
Berkowitz, Schagrin, Coonin & Cooper
Wilmington, DE
Berkowitz, Sean M. ... Chicago, IL
Berkowitz, Seymour ... New York, NY
Berkowitz, Sherri L. ... New York, NY
Berkowitz, Sheryl E. ... Miami, FL
Berkowitz, Solomon ... New York, NY
Berkowitz, Stephen N. ... Denver, CO
Berkowitz, Steven ... Beverly Hills, CA
Berkowitz, Steven ... Brooklyn, NY
Berkowitz, Steven ... New York, NY
Berkowitz, Steven E. ... Los Angeles, CA
Berkowitz, Steven H., (P.C.)
Southampton, PA
Berkowitz, Steven P. ... Brooklyn, NY
Berkowitz, Stuart R. ... St. Louis, MO
Berkowitz, Susan A.
Commodity Futures Trading Commission, Division of Enforcement, GV
Berkowitz, Susan B. ... Columbia, SC
Berkowitz, Susan Ellen Ferkin ... Bronx, NY
Berkowitz, Susan M. ... Atlanta, GA
Berkowitz, Ted A. ... Uniondale, NY
Berkowitz, Trager & Trager, LLC
Bridgeport, CT
Greenwich, CT
Stamford, CT
Westport, CT
Berkowitz, Warren ... East Meadow, NY
Berkowitz & Warren, Law Offices of
Lawrence, KS
Berkowitz, Wayne K. ... New York, NY
Berkowitz, Wendi J. ... San Francisco, CA
Berkowitz, Wendy H. ... Jacksonville, FL
Berkowitz, William C. ... Somerville, MA
Berkowitz, William N. ... Boston, MA
Berkowitz-Caballero, Esther
New York, NY
Berkowsky, Dennis S. ... Long Beach, NY
Berkowsky, Peter A. ... New York, NY
Berks, Martin K. ... Birmingham, AL
Berks, Melvyn H. ... Deerfield, IL
Berks, Robert J. ... Brockton, MA
Berks, Stuart ... Chicago, IL
Berkshire, James A. ... Peru, IN
Berkshire Law Firm ... Peru, IN
Berkshire, Richard N. ... Omaha, NE
Berkshire, Robert H. ... Omaha, NE
Berkshire, William C. ... Portland, OR
Berkshire, William F. ... Peru, IN
Berkson, Daniel B. ... Yonkers, NY
Berkson, Dennis A. ... Chicago, IL
Berkson, Gary M. ... Winter Park, FL
Berkson, Gorov & Levin, Ltd. ... Chicago, IL
Berkson, H. Neil ... Keene, NH
Berkson, Jacob B. ... Hagerstown, MD
Berkson, Jerome ... Chicago, IL
Berkson, Lester H. ... Zephyr Cove, NV
Berkson, Norman N. ... Chicago, IL
Berkson, Stuart M. ... Chicago, IL
Berkun, Alan M. ... Woodmere, NY
Berkun, Flora Marcus ... Pittsburgh, PA
Berkun, Jeffrey S. ... Albany, NY
Berkun, Susan J. ... Northbrook, IL
Berkwits, Roberta N. ... New York, NY
Berkwitt, Alison ... New York, NY
Berkwitt-Malefakis, Susan ... New York, NY
Berkwitz, Robert S. ... Minneapolis, MN
Berky, Robert ... Columbus, OH
Berl, Eugene L. ... Roseland, NJ
Berl, James F. ... Hilton Head Island, SC
Berl, James F., P.C., Law Offices of
Hilton Head Island, SC
Berl & Jones, P.A. ... Georgetown, DE
Berl, Joseph M. ... Washington, DC
Berl, Richard E. W., Jr. ... Georgetown, DE
Berlack, Evan R. ... Washington, DC
Berlack, Israels & Liberman LLP
Morristown, NJ
New York, NY
Berlage, Jan I. ... Hartford, CT
Berlan, Morton ... Chestnut Hill, MA
Berland, Abel E. ... Chicago, IL
Berland, Allan M. ... Kentfield, CA

Berland, Allan M. ... San Francisco, CA
Berland, Ava Holly
Federal Communications Commission, Office of the General Counsel, GV
Berland, Howard ... Evanston, IL
Berland, Judy L. ... New York, NY
Berland, Merrill J. ... Piscataway, NJ
Berland, Michael G. ... Chicago, IL
Berland, Richard B. ... Chicago, IL
Berland, Russell A. ... Kansas City, MO
Berland, Sanford N. ... New York, NY
Berland, William S. ... Berkeley, CA
Berlanga, Felicitas ... Chicago, IL
Berlanga, José A. ... Houston, TX
Berlanga, Mary Helen ... Corpus Christi, TX
Berlanstein, Martin R. ... Memphis, TN
Berlant, Gary A. ... Grants Pass, OR
Berlat, William L., Ltd. ... Tucson, AZ
Berle, Elihu M. ... Los Angeles, CA
Berle, Norman M. ... New York, NY
Berle, Peter A. A. ... Stockbridge, MA
Berlen, Carol A. ... Ocean Township, NJ
Berler-Khalouian, Julie ... Hauppauge, NY
Berlese, Margaret J. ... San Francisco, CA
Berlew, F. Kingston ... Boston, MA
Berlew, Randy E. ... Eatonton, GA
Berley, David R. ... Miami, FL
Berley, David R., P.A., Law Offices of
Miami, FL
Berley & DeVito ... Woodland Hills, CA
Berley, Diane E. ... Woodland Hills, CA
Berley, Richard M. ... Seattle, WA
Berliant, Jerry B. ... Chicago, IL
Berliant, Mark H. ... Cincinnati, OH
Berlie, Karen Margaret ... Los Angeles, CA
Berlik, Lee E. ... Tysons Corner, VA
Berlin, Abe M. ... Pompano Beach, FL
Berlin, Alan ... New York, NY
Berlin, Alan D. ... Washington, DC
White Plains, NY
Berlin, Amy G. ... New York, NY
Berlin, Anne D. ... Sudbury, MA
Berlin, Arthur E. ... Northbrook, IL
Berlin, Bertram J.
General Accounting Office, Office of the General Counsel, GV
Berlin, Boas & Isaacson ... Pittsburgh, PA
Berlin, Bob ... Macon, GA
Berlin & Braude ... Northbrook, IL
Berlin, Brenda Stacey ... Arlington, VA
Berlin, Brett J. ... Atlanta, GA
Berlin, Bruce A. ... Reading, PA
Berlin, Burgess L. ... Chatham, NJ
Berlin, Charles S. ... Woodbury, NY
Berlin, David M. ... Albuquerque, NM
Berlin, David S. ... New York, NY
Berlin, Donald L. ... Morristown, NJ
Berlin, Duane L. ... Norwalk, CT
New York, NY
Berlin, Edgar L. ... Austin, TX
Berlin, Edward ... Washington, DC
Berlin, Edward A. ... White Plains, NY
Berlin, Edward F. ... Greenfield, MA
Berlin, Emily ... New York, NY
Berlin, Eric P. ... Chicago, IL
Berlin, Evan N. ... Sarasota, FL
Berlin, Gerald A. ... Boston, MA
Berlin, Gerald L. ... Chicago, IL
Berlin, Harry ... Bayside, NY
Berlin and Hodges, P.C. ... Macon, GA
Berlin, Howard J. ... Miami, FL
Berlin, Jeffrey D. ... Mequon, WI
Berlin, Jeffrey S. ... Washington, DC
Berlin, Jennifer W. ... Cleveland, OH
Berlin, John D. ... Beulah, MI
Berlin, Kaplan, Dembling & Burke, A Professional Corporation
Morristown, NJ
Neptune, NJ
Berlin, Katharine M. ... Cambridge, MA
Berlin, Kenneth ... Washington, DC
Berlin, Kenneth A. ... New Brunswick, NJ
Berlin, Kurt ... Washington, DC
Berlin, Laurence M. ... Tucson, AZ
Berlin, Laurie Pamela ... Rockville Centre, NY
Berlin, Lawrence A. ... Reynoldsburg, OH
Berlin, Lee M. ... Naples, FL
St. Paul, MN
Berlin LLC ... Boston, MA
Berlin, Louise A. ... Lewiston, ME
Berlin, Maja A. ... Chicago, IL
Berlin, Marc D. ... Chicago, IL
Berlin, Marc S. ... Bloomfield Hills, MI
Berlin, Mark A. ... Boca Raton, FL
Berlin, Mark L.
Federal Communications Commission, Mass Media Bureau, GV
Berlin, Martin ... New York, NY
Berlin, Matthew A. ... Boston, MA
Berlin, Meredith Aland ... Chicago, IL
Berlin, Miriam ... Hartford, CT
Hartford, CT
Berlin, Mortimer A. ... Topeka, KS
Berlin, Nicole S. ... New York, NY
Berlin, Norman B. ... Philadelphia, PA
Berlin, Patricia ... Stratford, CT
Berlin, Peter ... Costa Mesa, CA
Berlin, Philip E. ... Burbank, CA
Berlin, Rachelle M. ... Dallas, TX
Berlin, Randy Lamm ... Chicago, IL
Berlin, Robert John ... Mount Clemens, MI
Berlin, Robert L. ... Boise, ID
Berlin, Robert L. ... Rutherford, NJ
Berlin, Ronald A. ... Pittsburgh, PA
Berlin, Roy ... Great Neck, NY
Berlin, Roy, P.C. ... Great Neck, NY
Berlin, Seth D. ... Washington, DC
Berlin, Sharon N. ... Mineola, NY
New York, NY
Berlin, Sherry Breuer ... Baltimore, MD
Berlin, Sidney L. ... Redwood City, CA
Berlin, Stanley G. ... Erie, PA
Berlin, Stanton H. ... Chicago, IL
Berlin, Stephen R. ... Winston-Salem, NC
Berlin, Stephen S. ... Tampa, FL
Berlin, Steven A. ... Newburyport, MA
Berlin, Steven B. ... San Francisco, CA
Berlin, Steven I. ... Chicago, IL
Berlin, Steven M. ... Princeton, NJ
New York, NY
Berlin, Susan J. ... Atlanta, GA
Berlin, Terry I., Mr. ... Southfield, MI
Berlin, William E. ... Department of Justice, Antitrust Division, GV
Berlin, William E. ... Birmingham, MI
Berlind, Mark H. ... New York, NY
Berline, Alexander J. ... San Francisco, CA
Berliner, Alan F. ... Columbus, OH
Berliner, Arnold D. ... Staten Island, NY
Berliner, Arthur I. ... New York, NY
Berliner, Brian M. ... Los Angeles, CA
Berliner, Candon & Jimison ... Berkeley, CA
Los Angeles, CA
Sacramento, CA
Washington, DC
Berliner Cohen ... San Jose, CA
Berliner, Corcoran & Rowe, L.L.P.
Washington, DC
Berliner, Cynthia K. ... Boston, MA
Berliner, Dana ... Washington, DC
Berliner, Dana Cox ... Mount Sterling, KY
Berliner, Diane Giles ... Los Angeles, CA
Berliner, Edward ... Austin, TX
Berliner, Eric L. ... Nevada City, CA
Berliner, Eric L. ... New York, NY
Berliner, Harold A. ... Nevada City, CA
Berliner, Henry A., Jr. ... Washington, DC
Berliner, Irv ... Cleveland, OH
Berliner, Jaimi ... New York, NY
Berliner, Jay ... Hempstead, NY
Berliner, Jerome M. ... New York, NY
Berliner, Jill H. ... Los Angeles, CA
Berliner, L. Jed ... Northampton, MA
Springfield, MA
Berliner, Laurie ... Vallejo, CA
Berliner Law Offices ... Nevada City, CA
Berliner, Lawrence W. ... Hartford, CT
Berliner, Liza R. ... New York, NY
Berliner, L. Jed ... Worcester, MA
Berliner, Lynn M. ... New York, NY
Berliner, M. Jay ... Richmond, VA
Berliner, Marie C. ... Austin, TX
Berliner, Martin M. ... Denver, CO
Berliner, Michael I. ... Livingston, NJ
Berliner, Michael R. ... New York, NY
Berliner, Norman S. ... Los Angeles, CA
Berliner, Robert ... Los Angeles, CA
Berliner, Robert M. ... New City, NY
Berliner, Robert W., Jr. ... Chicago, IL
Berliner, Roger A. ... Berkeley, CA
Los Angeles, CA
Sacramento, CA
Washington, DC
Berliner, Sanford A., (Inc.) ... San Jose, CA
Berliner, Shelly J. ... Foster City, CA
Berliner, Steven A. ... Los Angeles, CA
Berliner, Steven M. ... Los Angeles, CA
Berliner, Susan H. ... West Trenton, NJ
Berliner, Thomas M. ... San Francisco, CA
Berliner Zisser Walter & Gallegos, A Professional Corporation ... Denver, CO
Berling, Edward Everett ... Manakin-Sabot, VA
Berlinger, Richard W. ... Abington, PA
Berlinger & Small ... Abington, PA
Berlingeri Vincenty, Ina M. ... San Juan, PR
Berlingieri, Jennifer ... Garden City, NY
Berlingo & Carbone ... Port Chester, NY
Berlinsky, Bruce A. ... Charleston, SC
Berlinsky, Fred S. ... Cherry Hill, NJ
Berlinsky, Jay S. ... Chicago, IL
Berlinsky, Joshua A. ... Chicago, IL
Berlinsky, Joyce S. ... Deerfield, IL
Berlinsky, Philip A. ... North Charleston, SC
Berlinsky, Stephen J. ... Orlando, FL
Berlitz, Barbara Jean ... Pacific Grove, CA
Berlly, Bernard ... Great Neck, NY
Berlly, Susan G. ... Roslyn, NY
Berloff, Howard A. ... Northborough, MA
Berloff, Michael D. ... Boca Raton, FL
Berlon, Henry G. ... Fairfield, OH
Berlove, Harold J. ... Rochester, NY
Berlow, Rebecca ... New York, NY
Berlow, Robert A. ... Bloomfield Hills, MI
Berlow, Rosalind K. ... New York, NY
Berlowe, Andrea L. ... Department of Justice, Environment and Natural Resources Division, GV
Berlowe, Laura J. ... Coral Gables, FL
Berlowe, Peter Emerson ... Miami, FL
Berlowitz, Allan J. ... New York, NY
Berlowitz, David ... Rochester, NY
Berlowitz, Jeffrey S. ... Miami, FL
Berlowitz, William M. ... Lincoln, NE
Berlow-Lehner, Lisa ... Miami, FL
Berls, Bruce D. ... Los Angeles, CA
Berls, William H. ... New York, NY
Berlstein, Ann E. ... New York, NY
Berlstein, George ... New York, NY
Berluti, Robert R. ... Boston, MA
Berly, Joel Anderson, III ... Charleston, SC
Bermack, Eugene ... New York, NY
Bermack, Scott W. ... New York, NY
Bermak, Jacqueline N. ... Evanston, IL
Berman, A. Kyle ... Media, PA
Berman, Ada ... Beverly Hills, CA
Berman, Adam A. ... New York, NY
Berman, Adam E. ... Oak Brook, IL
Berman, Aisenberg & Platt
Washington, DC
Berman, Alan ... Pittsburgh, PA
Berman, Alan B. ... Las Vegas, NV
Berman, Alan J. ... Rockville Centre, NY
Berman, Alan M. ... New York, NY
Berman, Alan S. ... Los Angeles, CA
Berman, Alan S. ... Northbrook, IL
Berman, Alex ... Louisville, KY
Berman, Alexander S. ... New York, NY
Berman, Alison L. ... Boston, MA
Berman, Allison W. ... White Plains, NY
Berman, Andrew ... Longboat Key, FL
Berman, Andrew DiCarlo ... Boston, MA
Berman, Andrew E. ... San Diego, CA
Berman, Andrew H. ... Chicago, IL
Berman, Andrew J. ... San Francisco, CA
Berman, Andrew R. ... New York, NY
Berman, Andrew S.
North Miami Beach, FL
Berman, Anthony R. ... San Francisco, CA
Berman, Arnold L. ... West Palm Beach, FL
Berman, Arthur ... Harrisburg, PA
Berman, Arthur L. ... Chicago, IL
Berman, Arthur M. ... Chicago, IL
Berman, Asbel & Berman, L.L.P. ... Media, PA
Berman, Barbara A. ... Washington, DC
Berman, Barbara Miller ... Scarsdale, NY
Berman, Barbara P. ... Camden, NJ
Berman, Barbara Richmond ... Phoenix, AZ
Berman, Barrie D. ... Washington, DC
Berman, Barry D. ... Baltimore, MD
Berman, Barry D. ... West Orange, NJ
Berman, Barry J. ... Great Neck, NY
Berman, Bavero, Frucco, Gouz & Braunstein, P.C. ... New York, NY
White Plains, NY
Berman, Bayard F. ... Los Angeles, CA
Berman, Belinda I. ... Morris Plains, NJ
Berman, Ben H. ... East Liverpool, OH
Berman, Benjamin ... Santa Rosa, CA
Berman, Benjamin I.
Federal Trade Commission, Office of the Secretary, GV
Berman, Benjamin Z. ... Mahwah, NJ
Berman, Bennett I. ... Chicago, IL
Berman & Berkley, LLP
San Francisco, CA
Berman & Berman ... New York, NY
Berman, Berman & Berman, LLP
Los Angeles, CA
Berman, Bernard ... San Jose, CA
Berman, Bernard ... Boca Raton, FL
Berman, Bernard M. ... Media, PA
Berman, Bernard, P.A. ... Boca Raton, FL
Berman, Beth Hirsch ... Norfolk, VA
Berman, Betty Green ... Atlanta, GA
Berman, Blair I. ... Rockville, MD
Berman, Blanchard, Mausner & Resser, A Law Corporation ... Los Angeles, CA
Berman, Bourns & Currie, LLC
Hartford, CT
West Hartford, CT
Berman, Brad L. ... New York, NY
Berman, Bradley W. ... New York, NY
Berman, Brand & Goodman ... Ferndale, MI
Berman, Brent M. ... La Quinta, CA
Berman, Brian K. ... Las Vegas, NV
Berman, Brian K., Chtd. ... Las Vegas, NV
Berman, Bruce A. ... Los Angeles, CA
Berman, Bruce E. J. ... Los Angeles, CA
Berman, Bruce J. ... Miami, FL
Berman, Bruce M. ... Washington, DC
Berman, Bryan E. ... Houston, TX
Berman, Burt ... Universal City, CA
Berman, C. Martin ... Bridgton, ME
Lewiston, ME
Berman, Carol H.
Research Triangle Park, NC
Berman, Carol Sue ... Belvedere-Tiburon, CA
Berman, Cary Mark ... Chicago, IL
Berman, Charles ... Los Angeles, CA
Berman, Charles R. ... Summit, NJ
Berman, Clifford E. ... Northbrook, IL
Berman, Corey S. ... Chicago, IL
Berman, Craig ... Owings Mills, MD
Berman, Craig S. ... Santa Monica, CA
Berman, Cynthia ... Tarzana, CA
Berman, Cynthia A. ... Baltimore, MD
Berman, Dan J. ... Atlanta, GA
Berman, Daniel A. ... Los Angeles, CA
Berman, Daniel B. ... Syracuse, NY
Berman, Daniel J. ... Hagåtña, GU
Saipan, TT
Berman, Daniel L. ... Salt Lake City, UT
Berman, Daniel M. ... Washington, DC
Berman, Daniel Marc ... Orlando, FL
Berman, Daniel S. ... New York, NY
Berman, David ... Medford, MA
Berman, David A. ... East Meadow, NY
Berman, David C., A Professional Corporation ... Morristown, NJ
Berman, David Charles ... Morristown, NJ
Berman, David H. ... New York, NY
Berman, David Ira ... San Diego, CA
Berman, David J. ... San Francisco, CA
Berman, David J. ... Birmingham, MI
Berman, David M. ... Phoenix, AZ
Berman, David M. ... Miami, FL
Berman, David M. ... Dallas, TX
Berman, David M., P.A., Law Offices of
Miami, FL
Berman, David P. ... Solana Beach, CA
Berman, David S. ... Washington, DC
Berman, David S. ... Boston, MA
Berman, Deanna ... Denver, CO
Berman, Debbie L. ... Chicago, IL
Berman, Debra ... Long Island City, NY
Berman, DeLeve, Kuchan & Chapman, L.C.
Kansas City, MO
Berman, Delores M. ... St. Louis, MO
Berman, Dennis N. ... New York, NY
Berman, DeValerio & Pease, LLP
Boston, MA
Berman, DeValerio, Pease & Tabacco, LLP
San Francisco, CA
Berman, Diane L. ... Pittsburgh, PA
Berman, Douglas ... Brooklyn, NY
Berman, Douglas C. ... Trenton, NJ
Berman, Douglas M. ... Dallas, TX
Berman & Dowell ... Boston, MA
Berman, Edward A. ... Chicago, IL
Berman, Edward A. ... Morristown, NJ
Berman, Edward A., P.C. ... Chicago, IL
Berman, Edward J. ... Oak Park, IL
Berman, Edward M. ... New York, NY
Berman, Edward R. ... San Francisco, CA
Berman, Edwin M. ... Chicago, IL
Berman, Elihu H. ... Clearwater, FL
Berman, Elihu H., P.A. ... Clearwater, FL
Berman, Eliott M. ... New York, NY
Berman, Elise ... Edison, NJ
Berman, Elizabeth K. ... Deerfield, IL
Berman, Elliot H. ... Milwaukee, WI
Berman, Elliott ... Whitestone, NY
Berman & Emmerling ... East Liverpool, OH
Berman, Eugene B. ... Springfield, MA
Berman, Eugene D. ... Huntington, NY
Berman, Evan A. ... Los Angeles, CA
Berman, Frances R. ... Jamaica, NY
Berman, Frank R. ... Minneapolis, MN
Berman, Frank R., P.A. ... Minneapolis, MN
Berman, Fred J. ... Hollywood, FL
Berman, Fred M. ... Takoma Park, MD
Berman, Frederic S. ... New York, NY
Berman, Frederick J. ... New York, NY
Berman & Freedman ... Garden City, NY
Berman, G. Jean ... Minneapolis, MN
Berman, Garry C. ... New York, NY
Berman, Gary K. ... Durham, NC
Berman, Gary M. ... North Hollywood, CA
Berman, Gaufin, Tomsic, Savage & Campbell, A Professional Corporation
Salt Lake City, UT
Berman, George A. ... Boston, MA
Berman, Gerald S. ... Carlisle, MA
Berman, Glen E. ... Oakbrook Terrace, IL
Berman, Glenn & Haight
San Francisco, CA
Berman, Glenn J. ... New Brunswick, NJ
Berman, Gordon E. ... Las Cruces, NM
Berman, Gregg J. ... New York, NY
Berman, Gregory S. ... Louisville, KY
Berman, Harold B. ... Dallas, TX
Berman, Harold S. ... Boston, MA
Berman, Harris ... Ocean City, NY
Berman, Harris J. ... Louisville, KY
Berman, Harry S. ... Los Angeles, CA
Berman, Harvey ... Northbrook, IL
Berman, Harvey C. ... Syosset, NY
Berman, Harvey P. ... Blue Bell, PA
Berman, Harvey W. ... Ann Arbor, MI
Berman, Helen A. ... Los Angeles, CA
Berman, Henry S. ... White Plains, NY
Berman, Herbert E. ... Brooklyn, NY
Berman, Herbert L. ... Boston, MA
Berman, Herbert M., (Ltd.) ... Deerfield, IL
Berman, Howard ... Washington, DC
Berman, Howard A. ... Kingston, PA
Berman, Howard C. ... West Palm Beach, FL
Berman, Howard E. ... Yonkers, NY
Berman, Howard J. ... San Francisco, CA
Berman, Howard J. ... New York, NY
Berman, Howard Jay ... New York, NY
Berman, Howard R. ... San Diego, CA
Berman, Howard Z. ... Beverly Hills, CA
Berman, Ilana A. ... Voorhees, NJ
Berman, Ilene Weisbard ... Atlanta, GA
Berman, Ira E. ... St. Petersburg, FL
Berman, Ira L. ... New York, NY
Berman, Ira M. ... Cincinnati, OH
Berman, Ira P. ... Savannah, GA
Berman, Ira W. ... New York, NY
Berman, Jack ... Ferndale, MI
Berman, Jack K. ... San Francisco, CA
Berman, James ... Bridgeport, CT
Berman, James M. ... Oklahoma City, OK
Berman, Jane G. ... St. Louis, MO
Berman, Jane Sondgeroth ... Buffalo Grove, IL
Berman, Jay Harris ... Frazer, PA
Berman, Jay R. ... Brooklyn, NY
Berman, Jean C. ... New York, NY
Berman, Jed ... Winter Park, FL
Berman, Jeffrey ... Rockville, MD
Berman, Jeffrey A. ... Los Angeles, CA
Berman, Jeffrey A. ... Chicago, IL
Berman, Jeffrey B. ... Kansas City, MO
Berman, Jeffrey G. ... Washington, DC
Berman, Jeffrey N. ... Atlanta, GA
Berman, Jeffrey S. ... Greensboro, NC
Berman, Jeremy A. ... New York, NY
Berman, Jerold E. ... Brookline, MA
Berman, Jerome A. ... Los Angeles, CA
Berman, Jerome D. ... Louisville, KY
Berman, Jerome H. ... Rockville, MD
Berman, Jerrold ... Bronx, NY
Berman, Jesse ... New York, NY
Berman, Jill Nexon ... Miami, FL
Berman, Joanne H.
Environmental Protection Agency, Office of Enforcement and Compliance Assurance, GV
Berman, Joanne Schwartz ... New York, NY
Berman, Jodi D. ... Richmond, VA

Berman, Joel J., (P.C.) ....**Los Angeles, CA**
Berman, Joel S. ....Fort Lauderdale, FL
Berman, Joel S. ....New York, NY
Berman, John A. ....Denver, CO
Berman, John A. ....**West Hartford, CT**
Berman, John M. ....Tigard, OR
Berman, John R. ....Boston, MA
Berman, Jon D. ....South Windsor, CT
Berman, Jonathan ....**Washington, DC**
Berman, Joseph J. ....New York, NY
Berman, Joseph S. ....**Boston, MA**
Berman, Joshua ....**Atlanta, GA**
Berman, Joshua G. ....New York, NY
Berman, Joshua M. ....**New York, NY**
Berman, Judith A. ....**Phoenix, AZ**
Berman, Judy H. ....Flushing, NY
Berman, Judy L. ....Anchorage, AK
Berman, Julian L. ....**Chicago, IL**
Berman, Julius ....**New York, NY**
Berman, Karen M. ....Chicago, IL
Berman, Keevin ....Cleveland, OH
Berman, Keith ....New York, NY
Berman, Kenneth J.
Securities and Exchange Commission, Division of Investment Management, GV
Berman, Kenneth M. ....Gaithersburg, MD
Berman, Kenneth R. ....**Boston, MA**
Berman, Kenneth R. ....Las Vegas, NV
Berman, Laurence M. ....**Los Angeles, CA**
Berman, Laurence S. ....**Philadelphia, PA**
Berman, Lawrence E. ....Washington, DC
Berman, Leonard K. ....**Dearborn, MI**
Troy, MI
Berman, Leslie ....Morris Plains, NJ
Berman, Lester A. ....**Las Vegas, NV**
Berman, Linda C. ....**New York, NY**
Berman, Lisa ....**Newton, MA**
Berman, Loretta Lopez ....Albuquerque, NM
Berman, Lori B. ....Boca Raton, FL
Berman, Malcolm ....Houlton, ME
Berman, Marc R. ....**Hackensack, NJ**
Berman, Marc S. ....Clifton, NJ
Berman, Marcie E. ....**San Francisco, CA**
Berman, Marjorie E. ....**New York, NY**
Berman, Mark A. ....**Newark, NJ**
Berman, Mark A. ....**New York, NY**
Berman, Mark D. ....San Francisco, CA
Berman, Mark D. ....McLean, VA
Berman, Mark E. ....Pompano Beach, FL
Berman, Mark H. ....**McLean, VA**
Berman, Mark N. ....**Boston, MA**
Berman, Mark R., & Associates
Baltimore, MD
Berman, Mark S. ....Miami, FL
Berman, Marla A. ....New York, NY
Berman, Marla I. ....Miami, FL
Berman, Marlene J. ....Tustin, CA
Berman, Marshall F. ....**Washington, DC**
Berman, Martha A. H.
San Francisco, CA
Berman, Martin B. ....Beverly Hills, CA
Berman, Martin M. ....**Palm Desert, CA**
Berman, Martin R. ....Torrance, CA
Berman, Martin S. ....Boston, MA
Berman, Marvin D. ....**Chicago, IL**
Berman, Mathieu R. ....Newton, MA
Berman, Matthew B. ....**Los Angeles, CA**
Berman, Maxine S. ....Lawrenceville, NJ
Berman, Melanie N. Roe ....La Quinta, CA
Berman, Melinda M. ....**Sudbury, MA**
Berman, Michael ....**New York, NY**
Berman, Michael A.
Securities and Exchange Commission, Office of the General Counsel, GV
Berman, Michael A. ....Philadelphia, PA
Berman, Michael D. ....**Baltimore, MD**
Berman, Michael D. ....Needham, MA
Berman, Michael E. ....**New York, NY**
Berman, Michael H. ....**Chicago, IL**
Chicago, IL
Berman, Michael H. ....**Overland Park, KS**
Kansas City, MO
Berman, Michael J. ....**Hagåtña, GU**
Saipan, TT
Berman, Michael K. ....**New York, NY**
Berman, Michael P. ....**Phoenix, AZ**
Berman, Michael P. ....**Hartford, CT**
Berman, Michael S. ....Washington, DC
Berman, Milton ....Fort Lauderdale, FL
Berman, Mitchell D. ....Chicago, IL
Berman, Mitchell S. ....**Vineland, NJ**
Berman, Morris D. ....Madison, WI
Berman & Murray ....New York, NY
Berman, Myles D. (Mush) ....**Chicago, IL**
Berman, Myles L., Law Offices of
Los Angeles, CA
Newport Beach, CA
Thousand Oaks, CA
Berman, Myron B. ....North Miami Beach, FL
Berman, Myron J. ....Sarasota, FL
Berman, Myron J. ....New York, NY
Berman, Myron P. ....New York, NY
Berman, Nancy ....Baltimore, MD
Berman, Nancy E. ....**Denver, CO**
Berman, Nathaniel ....Boston, MA
Berman, Neil J. ....**Boca Raton, FL**
Miami, FL
Berman, Niles ....**Madison, WI**
Berman, Noel B. ....New York, NY
Berman, Nora Krasney ....Pepper Pike, OH
Berman, Norman ....Santa Ana, CA
Berman, Norman ....**Boston, MA**
Berman, Norman E. ....Denver, CO
Berman, O'Connor & Mann ....Hagåtña, GU
Kolonia, TT
Berman, Paley, Goldstein & Kanney, LLP
New York, NY
Berman, Pamela E., (P.C.) ....**Boston, MA**
Berman, Pamela J. ....Kailua, HI
Berman, Pamela L. ....Baltimore, MD
Berman, Paul B. ....Shaker Heights, OH
Berman, Paul E. ....Kansas City, MO
Berman, Paul Franklin ....**Miami, FL**
Berman, Paul J. ....**Washington, DC**
Berman, Paul M. ....**Philadelphia, PA**
Berman, Paul Schiff ....Hartford, CT
Berman, Peter E. ....**Mineola, NY**
New York, NY
White Plains, NY
Berman, Peter G. ....Providence, RI
Berman, Peter J. ....**Chicago, IL**
Berman, Peter J., Ltd. ....**Chicago, IL**
Berman, Philip M. ....Pompano Beach, FL
Berman, Phillip ....Milwaukee, WI
Berman & Rabin, P.A.
Overland Park, KS
Kansas City, MO
Berman, Rachael H. ....**Los Angeles, CA**
Berman, Ralph A. ....**New York, NY**
Berman, Ralph L. ....Minneapolis, MN
Berman, Randie S. ....**Roseland, NJ**
Berman, Raphael J. ....**New York, NY**
Berman, Richard A. ....Beverly Hills, CA
Berman, Richard A. ....**Rockford, IL**
Berman, Richard B. ....Lauderhill, FL
Berman, Richard B. ....Wailuku, HI
Berman, Richard B., P.A. ....Lauderhill, FL
Berman, Richard E. ....**Miami, FL**
Berman, Richard Jason ....**Washington, DC**
Berman, Richard M. ....**Minneapolis, MN**
Berman, Richard M. ....**Cherry Hill, NJ**
Berman, Richard M. ....Jamaica, NY
Berman, Richard P. ....**Fresno, CA**
Berman, Richard S. ....New York, NY
Berman, Robert A. ....West Chester, PA
Berman, Robert H. ....**New York, NY**
Berman, Robert J. ....**Fort Lauderdale, FL**
Berman, Robert J. ....Hackensack, NJ
Berman, Robert S. ....Department of Justice, Civil Rights Division, GV
Berman, Rod S. ....**Los Angeles, CA**
Berman & Roe ....La Quinta, CA
Berman, Ronald ....Tarzana, CA
Berman, Ronald C. ....**Madison, WI**
Berman, Ronald P. ....**New York, NY**
Berman, Ronald S. ....**Los Angeles, CA**
Berman, Ronnie Gouz ....**White Plains, NY**
Berman, Rosa ....Beverly Hills, CA
Berman, Russell S. ....**New York, NY**
Berman and Sable ....**Hartford, CT**
New Haven, CT
Berman, Samuel ....Laguna Hills, CA
Berman, Sanford L. ....Louisville, KY
Berman, Sanford Z. ....**New Carrollton, MD**
Rockville, MD
Berman, Sarah Bex ....Manlius, NY
Berman, Scott M. ....**New York, NY**
Berman, Seth C. ....**New York, NY**
Berman, Seymour W. ....Hingham, MA
Berman, Sharon Bauer ....**Atlanta, GA**
Berman, Sheila R. ....Clifton Park, NY
Berman, Sidney ....Union, NJ
Berman, Sidney M. ....**Detroit, MI**
Berman, Sidney S. ....New York, NY
Berman & Simmons, P.A. ....**Bridgton, ME**
Lewiston, ME
Portland, ME
South Paris, ME
Berman, Sobin & Gross ....Gaithersburg, MD
Berman, Stacy A. ....**Chicago, IL**
Berman, Stan ....**Seattle, WA**
Berman, Stanford W. ....Bethesda, MD
Berman, Stanley ....Nevada City, CA
Berman, Stanley ....**New York, NY**
Berman, Stanley M. ....**New York, NY**
Berman, Stephen ....Chandler, AZ
Berman, Stephen J. ....**Washington, DC**
Berman, Steve W. ....**Seattle, WA**
Berman, Steven ....New York, NY
Berman, Steven A. ....**New Haven, CT**
Berman, Steven A. ....**Chicago, IL**
Berman, Steven C. ....Portland, OR
Berman, Steven E. ....Santa Monica, CA
Berman, Steven E. ....Brooklyn, NY
Berman, Steven J. ....**Encino, CA**
Berman, Steven L. ....Torrance, CA
Berman, Steven L., A Prof. Corp., Law Offices of ....Torrance, CA
Berman, Steven M. ....**Tampa, FL**
Berman, Steven P. ....New Brunswick, NJ
Berman, Steven P. ....**Philadelphia, PA**
Berman, Steven Todd ....Herndon, VA
Berman, Stuart C. ....**New York, NY**
Berman, Stuart L. ....**Chicago, IL**
Berman, Sue E. ....Highland Park, IL
Berman, Susan L.
Securities and Exchange Commission, Office of Equal Employment Opportunity, GV
Berman, Susan Spalter
San Francisco, CA
Berman, Sussman & Forseter ....Bethesda, MD
Jericho, NY
Syosset, NY
Berman, Suzanne ....**New York, NY**
Berman, Teena ....New York, NY
Berman, Terry F. ....**Seattle, WA**
Berman, Thomas A. ....**Philadelphia, PA**
Berman, Tobias ....Huntington, NY
Berman, Todd ....San Francisco, CA
Berman, Tony ....**New York, NY**
Berman, U. Kelley ....**San Diego, CA**
Berman, Valerie Juster ....Greenwich, CT
Berman, Vicki L. ....**Orlando, FL**
Berman & Weiss ....**Palm Desert, CA**
Berman, William H. ....Washington, DC
Berman, William J. ....**Bedminster, NJ**
Morristown, NJ
Berman, William S. ....**San Francisco, CA**
Berman Wolfe Rennert Vogel & Mandler, P.A. ....Boca Raton, FL
Miami, FL
Berman, Zachary L. ....**Irvine, CA**
Berman, Zachary M. ....Jamaica, NY
Berman-Barrett, Sara J. .....Redondo Beach, CA
Bermann, George A. ....New York, NY
Bermant, George W. ....**Denver, CO**
Bermant, Tobias J. ....**New York, NY**
Bermanzohn, Frances R. ....New York, NY
Bermas, Peter I. ....East Islip, NY
Bermas, Roger E. ....Roslyn Heights, NY
Bermas, Stephen ....Norwalk, CT
Bermel, Jeanine R. ....**St. Louis, MO**
Bermel, Michele L. ....White Plains, NY
Bermeo, Eduardo E. ....Mission Hills, CA
Bermingham, Amy G. ....**New York, NY**
Bermingham, Ann B. ....Buffalo, NY
Bermingham, John E. ....**Oshkosh, WI**
Bermingham, John H. ....Princeton, NJ
Bermingham, John P. ....Oyster Bay, NY
Bermingham, John R. ....Denver, CO
Bermingham, Joseph D., Jr. ....Buffalo, NY
Bermudez, Angel M. ....Riverside, CA
Bermudez, Debbie ....**Guaynabo, PR**
Bermudez, Fernando ....**St. Louis, MO**
Bermudez, Joseph F. ....**Morristown, NJ**
Bermudez, Juan Carlos ....Miami, FL
Bermudez, Noe G. ....Buffalo Grove, IL
Bermudez Montenegro, Ruth
El Centro, CA
Bermúdez Torregrosa, Jorge
San Juan, PR
Bermudez-Velez, Rene M. ....San Juan, PR
Bern, David ....Phoenix, AZ
Bern, David S. ....Chicago, IL
Bern, Douglas M. ....**Fort Lee, NJ**
New York, NY
Bern, Marc Jay, Law Offices of
New York, NY
Bern, Martin D. ....**San Francisco, CA**
Bern, Medea M. Isphording ....San Mateo, CA
Bern, Nancy F. ....Boston, MA
Bernabe, Mary S. ....Des Moines, IA
Bernabei, Balestri & Fiocchi ....Ladd, IL
La Salle, IL
Spring Valley, IL
Bernabei, Ernest J., III ....**Cherry Hill, NJ**
Philadelphia, PA
Bernabei & Katz ....**Bethesda, MD**
Bernabei, Katz & Balaran, PLLC
Washington, DC
Bernabei, Lynne ....**Washington, DC**
Bernabei, Marc P. ....Princeton, IL
Bernabei, Vincent J. ....Brewster, OH
Bernabeo, Gregory S. ....**Philadelphia, PA**
Bernabo, Cathi L. ....Los Angeles, CA
Bernacchi, Doug A. ....**Michigan City, IN**
Bernacchi, Eugenia M. ....**Ventura, CA**
Bernacchi Legal Group
Michigan City, IN
Bernacchi, Michael B. ....**Los Angeles, CA**
Bernacchi, Richard L., (P.C.)
Los Angeles, CA
Bernacchi, Roger W. ....La Porte, IN
Bernacki, Barbara ....Bridgeport, CT
Bernacki, John E., Jr. ....Rochester, NY
Bernacki, Thomas M. ....Rochester, NY
Bernadicou, Michael A. ....**Sunnyvale, CA**
Bernadino, Joseph ....Fairfield, NJ
Bernadotte, Louis S. ....Southfield, MI
Bernak, Elliot D. ....**White Plains, NY**
Bernal, Abelardo P. ....El Paso, TX
Bernal, Albert L., II ....Livermore, CA
Bernal, Catherine L. ....San Jose, CA
Bernal, Celia R. ....**Sacramento, CA**
Bernal, David J. ....Houston, TX
Bernal, David V. ....Department of Justice, Civil Division, GV
Bernal, Eileen O'Connor ....**Andover, MA**
Bernal, Gilbert J., Jr. ....**Austin, TX**
Bernal, J. Arthur ....Pasadena, CA
Bernal, Jesus G. ....Los Angeles, CA
Bernal, Margaret Miller ....Whittier, CA
Bernal, Mark F. ....San Jose, CA
Bernal, Patrick C. ....**San Antonio, TX**
Bernal, Paul R. ....San Jose, CA
Bernal & Rigney, Inc. ....Berkeley, CA
Bernal, Sharon ....San Bernardino, CA
Bernal-Olson, Patricia ....Dayton, OH
Bernanke, Jessica R. ....**Washington, DC**
Bernanke, Seth M. ....Charlotte, NC
Bernard, Adrienne W. ....**New York, NY**
Bernard, Allyn A. ....Kula, HI
Bernard, Andrea J. ....**Grand Rapids, MI**
Bernard, Andrea P. ....**New York, NY**
Bernard & Angelle ....Lafayette, LA
Bernard, Anthony M. ....Youngstown, OH
Bernard, Aretta K. ....**Akron, OH**
Bernard, Balgley & Bonaccorsi .....Newark, CA
Bernard, Barton W. ....Lafayette, LA
Bernard, Brian Yusef ....Austin, TX
Bernard, Bruce D. ....Denver, CO
Bernard, Bruce W. ....**Erie, PA**
Bernard, Cassisa, Elliott & Davis, A Professional Law Corporation
Metairie, LA
New Orleans, LA
Oxford, MS
Bernard, Christopher D. ....**Bridgeport, CT**
Stamford, CT
Bernard, Christopher J. ....Reading, OH
Bernard, Christopher J.
The Woodlands, TX
Bernard, Claudia L. ....San Francisco, CA
Bernard, Corinne D. ....Harrison, NY
Bernard, Cynthia R. ....**Miami, FL**
Bernard, Dale A. ....**Cleveland, OH**
Bernard, Daniel F. ....**Longmont, CO**
Bernard, Daniel J. ....**Bingham Farms, MI**
Bernard, David K. ....Hazelwood, MO
Bernard, David L. ....Farmington Hills, MI
Bernard & Davidson ....Granite City, IL
Bernard, Debra Rae ....Chicago, IL
Bernard, Edward, (P.C.) ....Carson City, NV
Bernard, Elizabeth A. ....Youngstown, OH
Bernard, Elmer H. ....Alton, IL
Bernard, Eric P. ....**Manchester, NH**
Bernard, Eric P., P.C. ....**Manchester, NH**
Bernard, Eugene L. ....Washington, DC
Bernard, Gregory J. ....**Rapid City, SD**
Bernard, Haffey & Bohnert Co., L.P.A.
Beachwood, OH
Cleveland, OH
Highland Heights, OH
Mayfield, OH
Bernard, Henry A., Jr. ....Lafayette, LA
Bernard, Henry H., Jr. ....Baton Rouge, LA
Bernard, Howard ....Moorestown, NJ
Bernard, Hugh Y. ....Silver Spring, MD
Bernard, J. Michael ....**Detroit, MI**
Bernard, Jack M. ....Philadelphia, PA
Bernard, James H. ....**Kansas City, MO**
Bernard, James H., Jr. ....**Kansas City, MO**
Bernard, James L. ....**New York, NY**
Bernard, Janice McKimmie
Columbus, OH
Bernard, John Allen ....Lafayette, LA
Bernard, John M. ....**Philadelphia, PA**
Bernard, Joseph D. ....Springfield, MA
Bernard, Joseph J. ....Washington, DC
Bernard, Jules E., III
Federal Deposit Insurance Corporation, Regulation and Legislation Section, GV
Bernard, Julie J. ....**Boston, MA**
Bernard, Julie L. ....**Denver, CO**
Bernard, Kenneth G. ....Newport Beach, CA
Bernard, Kenneth R. ....Douglasville, GA
Bernard, Kent S. ....New York, NY
Bernard, Laura S. ....**San Francisco, CA**
Bernard Law Firm, The ....**Cleveland, OH**
Bernard, Lawrence B. ....**Washington, DC**
Bernard, Lawrence J., Jr. ....Washington, DC
Bernard, Lawrence Jay ....Jacksonville, FL
Bernard, Linda D. ....Detroit, MI
Bernard, Lloyd F. ....**Washington, DC**
Bernard, Louis A. ....Middleburg, VA
Bernard, Lynn M., (Miss) ....Youngstown, OH
Bernard, Lynne D. ....Bedford, NH
Bernard, Lyons & Gaddis ....**Denver, CO**
Longmont, CO
Bernard, Maria J. ....**Detroit, MI**
Bernard, Mariellsa A. ....Silver Spring, MD
Bernard, Mary A. ....**New York, NY**
Bernard, Mary S. ....**Chicago, IL**
Bernard, Maurice J., III ....Atlanta, GA
Bernard, Michael D. ....San Antonio, TX
Bernard, Michael Joey ....Metairie, LA
Bernard, Michael M. ....Newton, MA
Bernard, Michelle D. ....**Washington, DC**
Bernard, Pamela J. ....Gainesville, FL
Bernard, Paul L. ....**Manchester, NH**
Bernard, Paul R. ....**Detroit, MI**
Bernard, Peter ....Oakland, CA
Bernard, Phyllis E. ....Oklahoma City, OK
Bernard, Raymond E. ....Quincy, MA
Bernard, Rebecca L. ....Montesano, WA
Bernard, Richard A. ....Durham, NH
Bernard, Richard J. ....Orange, CA
Bernard, Richard J. ....**Miami, FL**
Bernard, Richard K. ....New York, NY
Bernard, Richard P. (IBA)...............................**New York, NY**
Bernard, Robert A. ....Jacksonville, FL
Bernard, Robert A. ....Brooklyn, NY
Bernard, Robert B. ....Newport Beach, CA
Bernard, Robert M. ....Columbus, OH
Bernard, Robert S. ....New York, NY
Bernard, Rodney, Jr. ....Baton Rouge, LA
Bernard, Roxie A. ....**Denver, CO**
Bernard, S. Butler, Jr.
West Memphis, AR
Bernard, Sharon Elaine
Farmington Hills, MI
Bernard, Stephen ....Los Angeles, CA
Bernard, Steven L. ....Denver, CO
Bernard, Steven M. ....Newark, CA
Bernard, Steven V. ....**Palo Alto, CA**
Bernard Stuczynski & Bonanti ....**Erie, PA**
Bernard, Terry V. ....Olympia, WA
Bernard, Thomas G. ....Colts Neck, NJ
Bernard, W. David ....**El Paso, TX**
Bernard, William D. ....**Chapel Hill, NC**
Bernard, William E. ....Fair Oaks, CA
Bernard, William E., A Professional Corporation ....Fair Oaks, CA
Bernard, William F. ....**Santa Ana, CA**
Bernard, William F. ....**Portland, OR**
Bernard, William L. ....**Eagan, MN**
Bernard, William N. ....Willmar, MN
Bernard, William R., Chrtd. ....Alexandria, VA
Bernard, William T. ....Kansas City, MO
Bernardi, Donald D. ....Bloomington, IL
Bernardi, Edward P. ....Portland, OR
Bernardi, Frederick A. ....Pekin, IL
Bernardi, Gina ....**Mineola, NY**
New York, NY
White Plains, NY
Bernardi, John A. ....Pekin, IL
Bernardi, John P. ....Los Angeles, CA
Bernardi, Joseph John ....**Detroit, MI**
Bernardi, Mark W. ....Harper Woods, MI
Bernardi, Richard L. ....Olympia Fields, IL
Bernardi, Robert D. ....Mount Holly, NJ

Bernstein, Barbara (Bobbi)
Department of Justice, Civil Rights Division, GV
Bernstein, Barbara W. ...Washington, DC
Bernstein, Barri E. ...Nashville, TN
Bernstein, Barry D. ...Basking Ridge, NJ
Bernstein, Barry M. ...New York, NY
Bernstein, Barry O. ...Long Beach, CA
Bernstein, Barry O. ...Los Angeles, CA
Bernstein, Barry O. ...Riverside, CA
San Bernardino, CA
Santa Ana, CA
Ventura, CA
Bernstein, Barry S. ...Encino, CA
Bernstein, Barry S. ...New York, NY
Bernstein, Beatrice ...New York, NY
Bernstein & Bell ...Chelmsford, MA
Bernstein, Benjamin ...Jamaica, NY
Bernstein & Berger ...Miami, FL
Bernstein, Bernard ...New York, NY
Bernstein, Bernard E. ...Knoxville, TN
Bernstein & Bernstein ...Detroit, MI
Bernstein & Bernstein ...New York, NY
Bernstein and Bernstein ...Rochester, NY
Bernstein & Bernstein ...White Plains, NY
Bernstein & Bernstein ...Columbia, SC
Bernstein Bernstein Krawec & Wymard P.C.
Harrisburg, PA
Bernstein Bernstein Krawec & Wymard, P.C. ...Pittsburgh, PA
Columbia, SC
Bernstein & Bernstein, P.A.
Charleston, SC
North Charleston, SC
Bernstein, Beth Elayne ...Columbia, SC
Bernstein, Bonnie G. ...Brooklyn, NY
Bernstein, Bradley ...New York, NY
Bernstein, Brenda Joy (B.J.) ...Atlanta, GA
Bernstein, Brenda Joy, P.C. ...Atlanta, GA
Bernstein, Brian K. ...New York, NY
Bernstein, Brooke Zykan ...New York, NY
Bernstein, Bruce ...New York, NY
Bernstein, Bruce C. ...Denver, CO
Bernstein, Bruce C., P.C. ...Denver, CO
Bernstein, Bruce D. ...New York, NY
Bernstein, Bruce G. ...Gulph Mills, PA
Bernstein, Bruce H. ...Reston, VA
Bernstein, Bruce R. ...Lafayette, CA
Bernstein, Burton M. ...Goleta, CA
Bernstein, Burwick & Tucker, LLC
Worcester, MA
Bernstein, Calvin A. ...Chicago, IL
Bernstein, Carl D. ...New York, NY
Bernstein, Carol W.
Department of Housing and Urban Development, Office of General Counsel, GV
Bernstein, Carolyn ...St. Louis, MO
Bernstein, Carolyn B. ...Flint, MI
Bernstein, Caryl S. ...Washington, DC
Bernstein, Cassandra B. ...Mill Valley, CA
Bernstein, Catherine P. ...Sacramento, CA
Bernstein & Chackman, P.A.
Hollywood, FL
Bernstein, Charles ...Garden City, NY
Bernstein, Charles G. ...Baltimore, MD
Bernstein, Charles S. ...Charleston, SC
North Charleston, SC
Bernstein, Christina A. ...San Diego, CA
Bernstein, Cindy Trellis ...Pittsburgh, PA
Bernstein, Claire B., (Mrs.) ...Philadelphia, PA
Bernstein, Cushner & Kimmell, P.C.
Boston, MA
Bernstein, Cyrus ...Washington, DC
Bernstein, Dale L. ...Bayonet Point, FL
Bernstein, Dana ...San Jose, CA
Bernstein, Daniel ...Bettendorf, IA
Bernstein, Daniel A. ...Princeton, NJ
Bernstein, Daniel J. ...Washington, DC
Bernstein, Daniel J. ...Boston, MA
Bernstein, Daniel L. ...New York, NY
Bernstein, Daniel P. ...Philadelphia, PA
Bernstein, Daniel S. ...Scotch Plains, NJ
Bernstein, Darren E. ...New York, NY
Bernstein, David ...Boynton Beach, FL
Bernstein, David ...Detroit, MI
Bernstein, David ...Norman, OK
Bernstein, David B. ...Boston, MA
Bernstein, David E. ...Arlington, VA
Bernstein, David H. ...New Orleans, LA
Bernstein, David H. ...New York, NY
Bernstein, David J. ...Akron, OH
Bernstein, David K. ...Wilmington, DE
Bernstein, David L. ...Washington, DC
Bernstein, David M. ...Atlantic City, NJ
Pleasantville, NJ
Bernstein, David M. ...Dallas, TX
Bernstein, David P. ...San Diego, CA
Bernstein, David P. ...Van Nuys, CA
Bernstein, David S.
Department of State, GV
Bernstein, David S. ...St. Petersburg, FL
Tampa, FL
Bernstein, David S. ...Roseland, NJ
Bernstein, David W. ...New York, NY
Bernstein, Deberah S. ...Barrington, IL
Bernstein, Debra Bodian ...New York, NY
Bernstein, Debra L. ...Barrington, IL
Bernstein, Deena R. ...Atlanta, GA
Bernstein, Dennis T. ...Tuckahoe, NY
Bernstein, Diane L. ...Bellerose, NY
Bernstein, Dina L. ...Dallas, TX
Bernstein, Donald C. ...St. Louis, MO
Bernstein, Donald M. ...New York, NY
Bernstein, Donald S. ...New York, NY
Bernstein, Dori K.
Equal Employment Opportunity Commission, Office of the General Counsel, GV
Bernstein, Douglas Carl
Farmington Hills, MI
Bernstein, Douglas N. ...New York, NY
Bernstein, Edward A. ...Merrick, NY
Bernstein, Edward A. ...New York, NY
Bernstein, Edward G. ...Carmel, CA
Bernstein, Edward G., P.C. ...Carmel, CA
Bernstein, Edward M. ...Las Vegas, NV
Bernstein, Edward M., & Assoc.
Las Vegas, NV
Bernstein, Edwin S.
Department of Agriculture, Office of Administrative Law Judges, GV
Bernstein, Elaine S. ...Dayton, OH
Bernstein, Eliot M. ...Milwaukee, WI
Bernstein, Elizabeth M. ...East Setauket, NY
Bernstein, Elvin R. ...Fort Worth, TX
Bernstein, Elyse B. ...Flushing, NY
Bernstein, Emanuel ...Glen Cove, NY
Bernstein, Eric D. ...Brooklyn, NY
Bernstein, Eric Martin ...Somerville, NJ
Bernstein, Eugene D. ...Chelmsford, MA
Bernstein, Eugene H. ...Chicago, IL
Bernstein, Eugene, Jr. ...Memphis, TN
Bernstein & Feldman, P.A.
Annapolis, MD
Bernstein, Florence ...Los Angeles, CA
Bernstein, Frank L. ...Menlo Park, CA
Washington, DC
Bernstein, Frederick L., (P.A.)
Hackensack, NJ
Bernstein, Fredric Ian ...Sherman Oaks, CA
Bernstein, Freya S. ...Boston, MA
Bernstein, G. Philip ...Boise, ID
Bernstein, Gaia ...New York, NY
Bernstein, Gail C. ...Washington, DC
Bernstein, Gary B. ...New York, NY
Bernstein, Gary S. ...Baltimore, MD
Bernstein, Gary S., P.A. ...Baltimore, MD
Bernstein, Geo. L. ...Philadelphia, PA
Bernstein, George Hutzler, Jr. ...Boston, MA
Bernstein, George K. ...Washington, DC
New York, NY
Bernstein, George L. ...Lynnfield, MA
Bernstein, Glen S. ...Washington, DC
Bernstein, Greg S. ...Beverly Hills, CA
Bernstein, Gregg D. ...Augusta, ME
Bernstein, Gregg L. ...Baltimore, MD
Bernstein, H. Bruce ...Chicago, IL
Bernstein, H. Carol ...Schaumburg, IL
Bernstein, Harlan ...Portland, OR
Bernstein, Harold F. ...Stamford, CT
Bernstein, Harold L. ...North Hills, NY
Bernstein, Harriet Magrish
San Francisco, CA
Bernstein, Harry S. ...Painesville, OH
Bernstein, Harvey N. ...Falls Church, VA
Bernstein, Henry M. ...Shreveport, LA
Bernstein, Henry, (P.C.) ...New Orleans, LA
Bernstein, Hiram H.
Department of Commerce, Patent and Trademark Office, GV
Bernstein, Hodsdon, Tannen & Korn, P.A.
Miami, FL
Bernstein & Hoffman, A Professional Corporation ...Scotch Plains, NJ
Bernstein, Honey ...Greenwood Lake, NY
Bernstein, Howard ...Buffalo Grove, IL
Bernstein, Howard ...Bethesda, MD
Bernstein, Howard ...Staten Island, NY
Bernstein, Howard I. ...New York, NY
Bernstein, Howard I. ...Madison, WI
Bernstein, Howard L. ...Chicago, IL
Bernstein, Howard L., (P.C.)
Washington, DC
Bernstein, Howard M. ...Tallahassee, FL
Bernstein, Howard M. ...Scarsdale, NY
Bernstein, Howard N. ...Indianapolis, IN
Bernstein, Howard O. ...Boulder, CO
Bernstein, Howard O. ...Denver, CO
Boulder, CO
Bernstein, Howard W. ...Painesville, OH
Bernstein, Hugh H., (P.A.) ...Miami, FL
Bernstein, Hugh M. ...Baltimore, MD
Bernstein, Ilisa B. G. ...Rockville, MD
Bernstein, Inga S. ...Boston, MA
Bernstein, Ira P. ...Oak Brook, IL
Bernstein, Irving A. ...Los Angeles, CA
Bernstein, Irwin L. ...Phoenix, AZ
Bernstein, Irwin S. ...Chicago, IL
Bernstein, Isadore M. ...Chicago, IL
Bernstein, Isadore S. ...Columbia, SC
Bernstein, J. Michael ...Celina, OH
Bernstein, Jack ...Hartsdale, NY
Bernstein, Jack A. ...Baltimore, MD
Bernstein, Jack N. ...Chicago, IL
Bernstein, Jack S. ...West Linn, OR
Bernstein, Jacob ...Oyster Bay, NY
Bernstein, James A ...Washington, DC
Bernstein, James E. ...Oregon City, OR
Bernstein, Jamie G. ...Treasury Department, Internal Revenue Service, GV
Bernstein, Jan L. ...Morristown, NJ
Bernstein, Jane A. ...Philadelphia, PA
Bernstein, Jane E. ...Westbury, NY
Bernstein, Jason A. ...Atlanta, GA
Bernstein, Jay H. ...Iselin, NJ
Bernstein, Jay L. ...New York, NY
Bernstein, Jay S. ...Silver Spring, MD
Bernstein, Jean ...Wayne, NJ
Bernstein, Jeanette K. ...Denver, CO
Bernstein, Jeff ...Flushing, NY
Bernstein, Jeffrey ...Boston, MA
Bernstein, Jeffrey ...Newark, NJ
Bernstein, Jeffrey A. ...Miami, FL
Bernstein, Jeffrey B. Arden
New York, NY
Bernstein, Jeffrey I. ...Philadelphia, PA
Bernstein, Jeffrey J. ...Department of Justice, Civil Division, GV
Bernstein, Jeffrey N. ...Great Neck, NY
Bernstein, Jeffrey R. ...Venice, CA
Bernstein, Jeffrey W. ...Laurel, MD
Bernstein, Jeffry A. ...San Francisco, CA
Bernstein, Jeremy B. ...Phoenix, AZ
Bernstein, Jeremy M. ...Aspen, CO
Bernstein, Jerry D. ...New York, NY
Bernstein, J. H. ...York, PA
Bernstein, Jill Kanoff ...Plainview, NY
Bernstein, Jill S. ...Bellingham, WA
Bernstein, Joan B. ...St. Louis, MO
Bernstein, Joan S. ...Sherman Oaks, CA
Bernstein, Joan Z.
Federal Trade Commission, Bureau of Consumer Protection, GV
Bernstein, Joel A. ...Wellesley, MA
Bernstein, Joel E. ...Hollywood, FL
Bernstein, Joel H. ...Washington, DC
Bernstein, Joel H. ...New York, NY
Bernstein, Joel J. ...Los Angeles, CA
Bernstein, Joel J. ...Napa, CA
Bernstein, Joel M. ...Los Angeles, CA
Bernstein, Johanna A. ...Danville, CA
Bernstein, John H. ...Denver, CO
Bernstein, John H ...Boston, MA
Bernstein, John T. ...Bloomington, IL
Bernstein, Jonathan A.
Federal Election Commission, Office of the General Counsel, GV
Bernstein, Jonathan A. ...New York, NY
Bernstein, Jonathan K. ...New York, NY
Bernstein, Jonathan K. ...Boston, MA
Bernstein, Jordan S. ...New York, NY
Bernstein, Joseph ...New Orleans, LA
Bernstein, Joseph C. ...Allentown, PA
Bernstein, Joseph E. ...New York, NY
Bernstein, Joseph J. ...Pittsburgh, PA
Bernstein, Joseph L. ...Fort Lauderdale, FL
Bernstein, Joseph L. ...Chicago, IL
Bernstein, Joseph L., P.A.
Fort Lauderdale, FL
Bernstein, Joseph M. ...Wilmington, DE
Bernstein, Joseph M. ...Milwaukee, WI
Bernstein, Joseph W. ...Chicago, IL
Bernstein, Joshua M. ...Philadelphia, PA
Bernstein, Joyce L.
Federal Communications Commission, Mass Media Bureau, GV
Bernstein, Jules ...Washington, DC
Bernstein, Karen ...Miami, FL
Bernstein, Karen L. ...Atlanta, GA
Bernstein, Keefe M. ...Dallas, TX
Bernstein, Kenneth A. ...Mineola, NY
Bernstein, Kenneth M. ...New York, NY
Bernstein, Kenneth M. ...Poughkeepsie, NY
Bernstein, Kenneth R. ...Aventura, FL
Bernstein, Kevin D. ...Memphis, TN
Bernstein, Kevin M. ...Syracuse, NY
Bernstein, Kimberly Grillo ...Norwalk, CT
Bernstein, Lara ...Great Neck, NY
Bernstein, Larry K. ...Rochester, NY
Bernstein, Lauren J. ...New York, NY
Bernstein, Lauren M. ...New York, NY
Bernstein, Laurie A. ...Roseland, NJ
Bernstein Law Corporation
Rancho Cucamonga, CA
Bernstein Law Firm, The, PLLC
Washington, DC
New York, NY
Bernstein Law Office ...Memphis, TN
Bernstein Law Office, The, P.A.
Miami, FL
Bernstein, Lawrence ...Washington, DC
Bernstein, Lawrence H. ...Bronx, NY
Bernstein, Leigh W. ...New York, NY
Bernstein, Leon ...Las Vegas, NV
Bernstein, Leonard ...Moriches, NY
Bernstein, Leonard A. ...Philadelphia, PA
Bernstein, Leone, (Ms.) ...Andover, MA
Bernstein, Liebhard & Lifshitz ...Fort Lee, NJ
Bernstein Liebhard & Lifshitz, LLP
New York, NY
Bernstein, Lionel ...New York, NY
Bernstein & Lipsett ...Washington, DC
Bernstein, Lisa Barse ...New York, NY
Bernstein Litowitz Berger & Grossmann LLP ...New York, NY
Bernstein, Lloyd ...San Francisco, CA
Bernstein, Lori ...Burbank, CA
Bernstein, Lori Merrill ...Durham, NC
Bernstein, Louis B. ...New York, NY
Bernstein, Louis D. ...Chicago, IL
Bernstein, Louise Roman ...New York, NY
Bernstein, Mara Block ...New York, NY
Bernstein, Mara L. ...San Rafael, CA
Bernstein, Marc A.
United States International Trade Commission, Office of the General Counsel, GV
Bernstein, Marc A. ...Albuquerque, NM
Bernstein, Marc A. ...New York, NY
Bernstein, Marc D. ...San Jose, CA
Bernstein, Marc E. ...New York, NY
Bernstein, Marc N. ...San Francisco, CA
Bernstein, Margrit S. ...Miami, FL
Bernstein, Maria Victoria
San Francisco, CA
Bernstein, Mark ...Farmington Hills, MI
Bernstein, Mark D., Attorney at Law, A Prof. Corp. ...Honolulu, HI
Bernstein, Mark F. ...Bronx, NY
Bernstein, Mark F. ...Philadelphia, PA
Bernstein, Mark I. ...Philadelphia, PA
Bernstein, Mark L. ...Fresno, CA
Bernstein, Mark R. ...Mineola, NY
Bernstein, Mark R. ...Charlotte, NC
Bernstein, Mark S. ...Chicago, IL
Bernstein, Mark W. ...Atlanta, GA
Bernstein & Marks ...Newark, NJ
Bernstein, Marlene J. ...Pittsburgh, PA
Bernstein, Marna E. ...Garden City, NY
Bernstein, Marshall A. ...Garden City, NY
Bernstein, Marshall A. ...Philadelphia, PA
Bernstein, Marshall E. ...New York, NY
Bernstein, Martin ...Milwaukee, WI
Bernstein, Martin B. ...North Salem, NY
Bernstein, Martina ...Wilmington, DE
Bernstein, Marvin ...New York, NY
Bernstein, Marvin N. ...Los Angeles, CA
Bernstein, Matthew C. ...Washington, DC
Bernstein, Matthew Ian ...Chicago, IL
Bernstein & McLean ...Bellingham, WA
Bernstein, Melanie Beth ...Las Vegas, NV
Bernstein, Melissa J. ...New York, NY
Bernstein, Melvin S. ...Baltimore, MD
Bernstein, Melvin S. ...Detroit, MI
Bernstein, Melvyn Louis ...Staten Island, NY
Bernstein, Merrick D. ...Atlanta, GA
Bernstein, Merril R. ...New York, NY
Bernstein, Merton C. ...St. Louis, MO
Bernstein, Michael A.
Fort Lauderdale, FL
Bernstein, Michael A., P.A.
Fort Lauderdale, FL
Bernstein, Michael D. ...Washington, DC
Bernstein, Michael E. ...Madison, WI
Bernstein, Michael H. ...Calhoun, GA
Bernstein, Michael H. ...New York, NY
Bernstein, Michael I., (P.C.)
New York, NY
Bernstein, Michael J. ...Peoria, IL
Bernstein, Michael L. ...Washington, DC
Bernstein, Michael R. ...Los Angeles, CA
Bernstein, Michael S. ...Richardson, TX
Bernstein, Michele B. ...New York, NY
Bernstein, Michelle M. ...Memphis, TN
Bernstein, Milton ...Harrisburg, PA
Bernstein, Mitchell D. ...New York, NY
Bernstein, Mitchell G. ...New York, NY
Bernstein, Mitchell H. ...Washington, DC
Bernstein, Murray ...Brooklyn, NY
Bernstein, N.W., & Associates, LLC
New York, NY
Bernstein, Naomi R.
Rancho Cucamonga, CA
Bernstein, Nathan ...Pompton Lakes, NJ
Bernstein, Neil N. ...St. Louis, MO
Bernstein, Neila R. ...Newport Beach, CA
Bernstein, Newton B. ...Southfield, MI
Bernstein, Norman ...East Meadow, NY
Bernstein, Norman W. ...New York, NY
Bernstein, Patricia E. ...Boston, MA
Bernstein, Paul ...Chicago, IL
Bernstein, Paul J. ...Seattle, WA
Bernstein, Paul S. ...Los Angeles, CA
Bernstein, Perry F. ...Boston, MA
Bernstein, Peter A. ...Boston, MA
Bernstein, Peter D. ...Washington, DC
Bernstein, Peter I. ...Garden City, NY
Bernstein, Philip B. ...Fresh Meadows, NY
Bernstein, Philip J. ...Chicago, IL
Bernstein, Philip M. ...Garden City, NY
Bernstein, R. Victor ...Basking Ridge, NJ
Bernstein, Radoff, Trachtenberg & Serafin, L.L.P. ...Houston, TX
Bernstein, Ralph ...New York, NY
Bernstein, Ralph M. ...Chicago, IL
Bernstein, Ralph M., & Associates
Chicago, IL
Bernstein, Raymond M. ...Stamford, CT
Bernstein, Rebecca Jane ...Philadelphia, PA
Bernstein, Rhonda H. ...Palm Harbor, FL
Bernstein, Richard A. ...New York, NY
Bernstein, Richard A. ...Rochester, NY
Bernstein, Richard D. ...Washington, DC
Bernstein, Richard F. ...New York, NY
Bernstein, Richard H. ...Alamo, CA
Bernstein, Richard H. ...New York, NY
Bernstein, Richard I. ...Hazleton, PA
Bernstein, Richard K., Associates, P.C.
New York, NY
Bernstein, Richard Kent ...New York, NY
Bernstein, Richard L. ...Brooklyn, NY
Bernstein, Richard M. ...Philadelphia, PA
Bernstein, Richard N. ...Miami, FL
Bernstein, Richard P. ...Sacramento, CA
Bernstein, Richard P. ...Dallas, TX
Bernstein, Richard P., Inc., P.C. ...Dallas, TX
Bernstein, Richard R. ...Bellevue, WA
Bernstein, Robert A. ...Boston, MA
Bernstein, Robert A. ...Morristown, NJ
Bernstein, Robert Alan ...Charleston, SC
North Charleston, SC
Bernstein, Robert B. ...New York, NY
Bernstein, Robert D. ...Houston, TX
Bernstein, Robert G. ...Fairfield, CA
Bernstein, Robert G. ...San Diego, CA
Bernstein, Robert H. ...Newark, NJ
Bernstein, Robert J. ...New York, NY
Bernstein, Robert L. ...Syosset, NY
Bernstein, Robert M. ...Los Angeles, CA
Bernstein, Robert M. ...Tuckahoe, NY
Bernstein, Robert S. ...Jacksonville, FL
Bernstein, Robert S. ...Pittsburgh, PA
Bernstein, Robert Steven ...New York, NY
Bernstein, Robert T. ...Chicago, IL
Bernstein, Robert T. ...Chicago, IL
Bernstein, Robin A. ...New York, NY
Bernstein, Robin J. ...Pittsburgh, PA
Bernstein, Roger J. ...New York, NY
Bernstein, Roger M. ...Miami, FL

Bernstein, Roger Scott ... New Orleans, LA
Raceland, LA
Bernstein, Roger Scott, A PLC
New Orleans, LA
Raceland, LA
Bernstein, Ronald J. ... Miami, FL
Bernstein, Roy J. ... New York, NY
Bernstein, Roy L. ... Chicago, IL
Bernstein, Ruth E., Law Offices of
New York, NY
Bernstein & Sakellaris ... Baltimore, MD
Bernstein, Samuel A. ... Brooklyn, NY
Bernstein, Samuel I. ... Farmington Hills, MI
Bernstein, Samuel J. ... Stamford, CT
Bernstein, Sandra ... Washington, DC
Bernstein, Sara L. ... Hartford, CT
Bernstein, Sarah M. ... Chicago, IL
Bernstein, Scot ... Sacramento, CA
Bernstein, Scott B. ... Scottsdale, AZ
Bernstein, Scott B. ... Plainsboro, NJ
Bernstein, Scott D. ... Beverly Hills, CA
Bernstein, Scott H. ... Great Neck, NY
Bernstein, Scott L. ... St. Louis, MO
Bernstein, Scott M. ... Miami, FL
Bernstein, Scott N. ... Princeton, NJ
Bernstein, Shari F. ... Media, PA
Philadelphia, PA
Bernstein, Shawn ... Baltimore, MD
Bernstein, Sheldon ... Kansas City, MO
Bernstein, Sheldon A. ... Milwaukee, WI
Bernstein, Shur, Sawyer & Nelson, A Professional Corporation ... Augusta, ME
Portland, ME
Bernstein, Simon ... Longboat Key, FL
Bernstein, Sol W. ... New York, NY
Bernstein, Stacy Renert
Fort Lauderdale, FL
Bernstein, Stair & McAdams LLP
Knoxville, TN
Bernstein, Stanley ... San Antonio, TX
Bernstein, Stanley D. ... New York, NY
Bernstein, Stanley J. ... Kentfield, CA
Bernstein, Stanley J. ... Waltham, MA
Bernstein, Stephen C. ... Englewood, FL
Bernstein, Stephen J. ... Warren, NJ
Bernstein, Stephen L. ... New York, NY
Bernstein, Stephen M. ... New Orleans, LA
Bernstein, Stephen M. ... New York, NY
Bernstein, Stephen N. ... Gainesville, FL
Bernstein, Stephen R. ... Compton, CA
Bernstein, Stephen R. ... Farmington Hills, MI
Bernstein, Stephen W. ... Boston, MA
Bernstein, Steven E. ... Jenkintown, PA
Bernstein, Steven J. ... Evanston, IL
Bernstein, Steven K.
Federal Trade Commission,
Bureau of Competition, GV
Bernstein, Steven M. ... Atlanta, GA
Bernstein, Steven M. ... Brooklyn, NY
Bernstein, Steven M. ... New York, NY
Bernstein, Stewart A. ... Philadelphia, PA
Bernstein, Stuart ... Chicago, IL
Bernstein, Stuart ... New York, NY
Bernstein, Stuart M. ... New York, NY
Bernstein, Sumner Thurman
Portland, ME
Bernstein, Susan
Federal Emergency Management Agency,
Office of the General Counsel, GV
Bernstein, Susan A. ... Kansas City, MO
Bernstein, Susan E. ... New York, NY
Bernstein, Susan F. ... Yonkers, NY
Bernstein, Susan M. ... Overland Park, KS
Bernstein, Suzanne C. ... Bloomfield Hills, MI
Bernstein, Talya ... Austin, TX
Bernstein, Terry S. ... Garden City, NY
Bernstein, Thomas A. ... New York, NY
Bernstein, Tina E. ... Trenton, NJ
Bernstein, Tobie ... Washington, DC
Bernstein, Tracey S. ... New York, NY
Bernstein, Vigdor D. ... New York, NY
Bernstein, Warren J. ... New York, NY
Bernstein, Weiss, Coplan, Weinstein & Lake
New York, NY
Bernstein, Willard ... Pennsville, NJ
Bernstein, William ... San Francisco, CA
Bernstein, William ... San Francisco, CA
Bernstein, William ... New York, NY
Bernstein, William E. ... Worcester, MA
Bernstein, William J. ... Atlanta, GA
Bernstein, William J. ... Melville, NY
Bernstein, William L. ... Chepachet, RI
Bernstein, William M.
National Labor Relations Board,
Office of the General Counsel, GV
Bernstein, William S. ... New York, NY
Bernstein-Baker, Judith A. ... Philadelphia, PA
Bernstein-Gaeta, Judith ... Washington, DC
Bernstein-Gold, Gail S. ... New York, NY
Bernstein Mathews, Lara
Washington, DC
Bernstone, Alvin M. ... New York, NY
Bernstone, Goldman & Tecklin
New York, NY
Bernstone, H. Louise ... Reno, NV
Bernt, C. John ... San Rafael, CA
Bernt, Lisa Jean ... Kenilworth, NJ
Bernthal, David G. ... Urbana, IL
Bernthal, Eric L. ... Washington, DC
Bernthol, Jason H. ... Los Angeles, CA
Bernton, William P. ... Washington, DC
Berntsen, Denis A. ... Chicago, IL
Berntsson, Robert H. ... Port Charlotte, FL
Bernuth, Terry ... Denver, CO
Bernys, Kevin M. ... Birmingham, MI
Bernz, David S. ... Newburgh, NY
Bero, Deborah J. ... Norwood, MA
Beroes, Elizabeth A. ... Pittsburgh, PA
Beroff, Carole Leavitt ... New York, NY
Berol, John A. ... La Jolla, CA
Berolzheimer, Karl ... Chicago, IL
Beron, Celeste ... Winston-Salem, NC
Beron, Gregory P. ... San Diego, CA
Beron, Helmut ... New York, NY
Beron, Joan D. ... Malden, MA
Beron, Thomas ... New Orleans, LA
Beronio, Janet S. ... Laveen, AZ
Beronio, Kirsten K.
Department of Transportation,
Federal Highway Administration, GV
Beronio, Walter J. ... Hoboken, NJ
Beroset, Barry W. ... Pensacola, FL
Beroset & Keene ... Pensacola, FL
Berotti, William G. ... Brooklyn, NY
Beroukas, Evdoxia ... Chicago, IL
Berowitz, Howard ... Clifton, NJ
Berowitz, Irwin ... New York, NY
Berowitz, Stephen S. ... Bloomfield, NJ
Berowitz, Susan L. ... Roseland, NJ
Beroza, Anne ... Livingston, NJ
Berozsky, Lisa S. ... Boston, MA
Berquist, Charles C. ... Minneapolis, MN
Berquist, Erin Murphy ... Baltimore, MD
Berquist, James D. ... Arlington, VA
Berquist, Jennifer ... Minneapolis, MN
Berquist, Stephen A. ... Boston, MA
Berquist, William J. ... Minneapolis, MN
Berra, Carolyn M. ... Overland Park, KS
Berra, Kenneth J. ... Kansas City, MO
Berra, Louis M. ... Chicago, IL
Berra, Paul J., III ... St. Louis, MO
Berra, Paul S. ... Los Angeles, CA
Berra, Richard C. ... San Mateo, CA
Berra • Spence ... San Mateo, CA
Berra, Thomas P., Jr. ... St. Louis, MO
Berrafato, Gabriel S. ... Morton Grove, IL
Berrafato & Porter ... Morton Grove, IL
Berran, Philip J. ... New York, NY
Berrane, Bradley E. ... Yorktown, VA
Berray, Robert W. ... Millbrook, NY
Berreckman & Berreckman, P.C. ... Cozad, NE
Berreckman, Claude E. ... Cozad, NE
Berreckman, Claude E., Jr. ... Cozad, NE
Berregaard, Suzie Anne ... Grimes, IA
Berrelez, Rolando
Federal Trade Commission,
Bureau of Consumer Protection, GV
Berreman, Thomas A. ... Minneapolis, MN
Berreman, Thomas H. ... St. Paul, MN
Berren, A. Larry ... Providence, RI
Berres, Gerald J. ... Beloit, WI
Berres, John R. ... Ashburn, VA
Berres, Karen Arndt ... South Barrington, IL
Berres, Roger E. ... Oak Brook, IL
Berres, Terrence R. ... Milwaukee, WI
Berresford, John W.
Federal Communications Commission,
Common Carrier Bureau, GV
Berresford, Theresa A. ... Bridgeton, NJ
Berreski, Barbara A. ... Trenton, NJ
Berres-Paul, Toni ... Portland, OR
Berret, Amy deGeneres ... Baton Rouge, LA
Berret, Theresa A. ... Kittanning, PA
Berret, Thomas A. ... Pittsburgh, PA
Berreteaga, Carlos ... San Juan, PR
Berreth, Steven P. ... Boca Raton, FL
Wichita, KS
Berrett, Barbara K. ... Salt Lake City, UT
Berrett, Bill A. ... Las Vegas, NV
Berrett, David M. ... Aurora, CO
Berrett, Edward J. ... Pocatello, ID
Berrett, Joel D. ... Roosevelt, UT
Berrett, John R. ... Menlo Park, CA
Berrett, Ralph E. ... Hanford, CA
Berretta, Frederick S. ... San Diego, CA
Berrey, Allen R. ... Merced, CA
Berrey, Robt G. ... San Diego, CA
Berrey, Robt. W., III ... Kansas City, MO
Berridge, George B. ... New York, NY
Berridge, Paula K. ... Fayetteville, AR
Berridge, Thomas E. ... Columbus, OH
Berridge, William P. ... Alexandria, VA
Berrien, Jacqueline A. ... New York, NY
Berrien, James D. ... Hillsboro, OR
Berrien, Matthew ... Modesto, CA
Berrien, Sylvia A. ... Fort Lauderdale, FL
Berrier, Billy G. ... San Diego, CA
Berrier, Erwin F., Jr. ... Fairfield, CT
Berrier, Mark L. ... Austin, TX
Berrier, Stephen W. ... Marysville, CA
Berrier, Willis Lee ... El Paso, TX
Berrigan, Helen G. ... New Orleans, LA
Berrigan, Joseph E., Jr. ... New Orleans, LA
Berrigan, Joseph J. ... Tunica, MS
Berrigan, Litchfield, Schonekas & Mann
New Orleans, LA
Berrigan, Patrick J. ... Slidell, LA
Berrigan, Patrick J. ... Kansas City, MO
Berrigan, Patrick J. ... Niagara Falls, NY
Berrigan, Patrick J., (P.L.C.)
New Orleans, LA
Slidell, LA
Berrigan, Robert B. ... Sacramento, CA
Berrigan, Thomas M. ... Pensacola, FL
Berriman, James J. ... Boston, MA
Berriman, Steven Patrick ... Livonia, MI
Berriman, W. Thomas ... Philadelphia, PA
Berrin, Robert G. ... Coral Gables, FL
Berringer, Howard G. ... Boise, ID
Berringer, John B. ... New York, NY
Berrington, Craig A. ... Washington, DC
Berrington, Howard M. ... Chicago, IL
Berrington, Lacy D. ... Washington, DC
Berrio, Itzel D. ... San Francisco, CA
Berrios, Ariel A. ... Los Angeles, CA
Berrios, Edgar A. ... Naranjito, PR
Berrios, Edgardo ... New York, NY
Berrios & Longo, P.S.C ... San Juan, PR
Berrios, Martha I. ... San Juan, PR
Berrios, Suzette Nanovic ... Princeton, NJ
Berrios-Amadeo, Luis ... San Juan, PR
Berríos Dávila, E. ... San Juan, PR
Berrios-Falcon, Ruben E. ... San Juan, PR
Berrios Perez, Edilberto ... San Juan, PR
Berrios Perez, Freddie ... San Juan, PR
Berris, Ellen D. ... Minneapolis, MN
Berris, Gordon I. ... Southfield, MI
Berris, Marc S. ... Minneapolis, MN
Berris, Norman ... Los Angeles, CA
Berris, Richard J. ... Cleveland, OH
Berritt, Gail J. ... Chicago, IL
New York, NY
Berritt, Harold E. ... Miami, FL
Berriz, Armando Juan ... Westlake Village, CA
Berrocal, Carlos J. ... Jupiter, FL
Berrocal & Wilkins, P.A. ... Jupiter, FL
Berrodin, Frank E. ... Grand Rapids, MI
Berrol, Bruce J. ... San Francisco, CA
Berrones, Alberto ... Indianapolis, IN
Berrones, Luis A. ... Chicago, IL
Berroya, Cesar Carbonell
San Francisco, CA
Berroya, Lawrence B. ... San Francisco, CA
Berruti, Gail ... Lindenhurst, NY
Berry, A. Franklin, Jr.
Bowling Green, KY
Berry, Ables, Tatum, Dick, Baxter, Parker & Hall, P.C. ... Athens, AL
Decatur, AL
Huntsville, AL
Scottsboro, AL
Berry, Adam Arthur ... Dallas, TX
Berry, Adrienne A. ... Louisville, KY
Berry, Alan M., (P.C.) ... Chicago, IL
Berry, Albert T. ... Department of Agriculture,
Office of the General Counsel, GV
Berry, Alison ... White Plains, NY
Berry, Allison L. ... Palo Alto, CA
Berry, Amy S. ... Burlington, NC
Berry, Anders Taylor ... Great Falls, MT
Berry, Andrew ... Orangeburg, SC
Berry, Andrew T. ... Newark, NJ
Berry, Anne C. ... Columbus, OH
Berry, Anthony D. "Butch" ... Jacksonville, FL
Berry, Appleman & Leiden, LLP
San Francisco, CA
Berry, Arthur C. ... Von Ormy, TX
Berry, Barbara A. ... Philadelphia, PA
Berry, Benj. I. ... Winnsboro, LA
Berry, Bernard J., Jr. ... Middletown, NJ
Berry, Bernard P., Jr. ... Minneapolis, MN
Berry and Berry ... Beverly Hills, CA
Berry & Berry, A Professional Corporation
Oakland, CA
Berry, Bobbi ... Tucson, AZ
Berry, Bonnie Eileen ... Beverly Hills, CA
Berry, Bradford M. ... Washington, DC
Berry, Bradley C. ... McMinnville, OR
Berry, Brett W. ... Wellington, KS
Berry, Bridget Ann ... West Palm Beach, FL
Berry, Bruce H. ... New York, NY
Berry, Bryan J. ... Rosemont, IL
Berry, Bryant ... Austin, TX
Berry, Bryon J. ... Warsaw, IN
Berry, Buford P. ... Dallas, TX
Berry, Burt ... Dallas, TX
Berry, Byrne & Randall ... Dallas, TX
Berry, Byron R. ... Denton, TX
Berry, C. Byron ... New Orleans, LA
Berry, C. Dewees ... Franklin, TN
Berry, C. Dewees, IV ... Nashville, TN
Berry, C. Nelson, III ... Seattle, WA
Berry, C. Nelson, III, P.S. ... Seattle, WA
Berry, Capper & Tulley
Crawfordsville, IN
Berry, Carl D. ... Lauderhill, FL
Berry, Carl D., P.A. ... Lauderhill, FL
Berry, Carol R. ... San Diego, CA
Berry, Carol Scott ... Phoenix, AZ
Berry, Carole C. ... Columbus, OH
Berry, Caroline E. ... New York, NY
Berry, Catherine R. ... Jacksonville, FL
Berry, Cavan J. ... Big Rapids, MI
Berry, Chad S. ... Baton Rouge, LA
Berry, Charles D. ... Mars, PA
Berry, Charles E. ... Denver, CO
Berry, Charles G. ... Albuquerque, NM
Berry, Charles G. ... New York, NY
Berry, Charles G., & Assocs., P.A.
Albuquerque, NM
Berry, Charles L. ... Houston, TX
Berry, Charles N., Jr. ... Oklahoma City, OK
Berry, Charles R. ... Scottsdale, AZ
Berry, Charles T. ... Fairmont, WV
Berry, Charlotte Howell ... Phoenix, AZ
Berry, Christel Ford ... Hartford, CT
Berry, Christine M. ... Chicago, IL
Berry, Christopher J. ... Phoenix, AZ
Berry, Christopher S. ... Madison, WI
Berry, Cinda ... Chicago, IL
Berry, Clair E. ... Athens, OH
Berry, Clark W. ... Fort Myers, FL
Berry, Claudia F. ... Salt Lake City, UT
Berry, Clay C. ... Juneau, AK
Berry, Cortland E. ... Reading, KS
Berry, Cynthia E. ... Washington, DC
Berry, D. Bowen ... Dallas, TX
Berry, D. Jeffrey ... Spring, TX
Berry, Dale E. ... Marco Island, FL
Berry, Dana A. ... Orleans, MA
Berry, Daniel F. ... Detroit, MI
Berry, Daniel G. ... Palos Hills, IL
Berry, Danielle E. ... Washington, DC
Berry, Daryl R. ... Chicago, IL
Berry, David B. ... Department of Justice,
Civil Rights Division, GV
Berry, David C. ... Washington, DC
Berry, David C. ... Boston, MA
Berry, David F. ... Los Angeles, CA
Berry, David F. ... Stanardsville, VA
Berry, David G. ... Palmer, AK
Berry, David G. ... Litchfield, MN
Berry, David H. ... Hilton Head Island, SC
Berry, David Luther ... San Diego, CA
Berry, David M. ... Indianapolis, IN
Berry, David P. ... San Francisco, CA
Berry, David P. L. ... Norfolk, VA
Berry, David T. ... Heber City, UT
Salt Lake City, UT
Berry, David W. ... Los Angeles, CA
Berry, David W. ... Birmingham, MI
Berry, David W. ... Raleigh, NC
Berry, Dawn Bradley ... Tijeras, NM
Berry, Day & McFee, P.A. ... Naples, FL
Berry, Dean C. ... New York, NY
Berry, Dean C. ... Newport News, VA
Berry, Dean L. ... Cleveland, OH
Berry, Dennis J. ... Encino, CA
Berry, Dolly Wisman ... Louisville, KY
Berry, Donald S. ... Boston, MA
Berry, Donna M ... Riverdale, MD
Berry, Doran J. ... Fayetteville, NC
Berry, Doris E. ... McKinney, TX
Berry, Douglas ... Nashville, TN
Berry, Douglas A. ... Monterey, CA
Berry, Douglas C. ... Seattle, WA
Berry, E. Janet ... New York, NY
Berry, Earl A., Jr. ... Dallas, TX
Berry, Earl T. ... Dallas, TX
Berry & Early ... Madison, VA
Stanardsville, VA
Berry, Edward D. ... Madison, VA
Berry, Edward F. ... Columbus, GA
Berry, Edward J. ... Birmingham, AL
Berry & Edwards ... Tampa, FL
Berry, Elizabeth A. ... Fort Worth, TX
Berry, Elva Bowden
Nuclear Regulatory Commission,
Office of the General Counsel, GV
Rockville, MD
Berry, Eric W. ... New York, NY
Berry, Eric W., P.C. ... New York, NY
Berry, Erica M. ... Florham Park, NJ
Berry, Ermlich & Lomax
Virginia Beach, VA
Berry, Eugene E., Jr. ... Library of Congress,
Copyright Office, GV
Berry, Eugene G. ... Pittsburgh, PA
Berry, Eugene S. ... Jackson, MS
Berry, F. Wilton ... Denver, CO
Berry & Floyd, P.S.C. ... New Castle, KY
Berry, Francine J. ... Basking Ridge, NJ
Berry, Francis, Salamey & Harris, PLC
Dearborn, MI
Berry, Frank D., Jr. ... San Jose, CA
Berry, Franklin H., Jr. ... Toms River, NJ
Berry, Frederick C., Jr. ... Phoenix, AZ
Berry, Frederick C., Jr., P.C. ... Phoenix, AZ
Berry, Frederick L. ... Greensboro, NC
Berry, Gene D. ... Jackson, MS
Berry, George Al ... San Francisco, CA
Berry, George C. ... Kansas City, MO
Berry, George E., Jr. ... Greensburg, PA
Berry, George J. ... Indianapolis, IN
Berry, George J., III ... Pittsburgh, PA
Berry, George T. ... Washington, DC
Berry, Gil I., Jr. ... Indianapolis, IN
Berry, Gina S. ... Ventura, CA
Berry, Gregory A. ... Beverly Hills, CA
Berry, Gregory J. ... White Plains, NY
Berry, Gregory K. ... Glasgow, KY
Berry & Greusel ... Marco Island, FL
Berry, H. Anderson, III ... Charlotte, NC
Berry, H. Dolph ... Fayetteville, NC
Berry, Harold W., Jr. ... Raleigh, NC
Berry, Harry W. ... Glasgow, KY
Berry & Henry, A Professional Law Corporation ... River Ridge, LA
Berry, Henry N., III ... South Portland, ME
Berry, Henry T. ... New York, NY
Berry, Howard C. ... Louisville, KY
Berry, Howard K. ... Oklahoma City, OK
Berry, Howard K., III ... Oklahoma City, OK
Berry, Howard K., Jr. ... Oklahoma City, OK
Berry, Hugh W. ... Rancho Cucamonga, CA
Berry, I. William, Inc. ... Katonah, NY
Berry, Ilona M. ... Chicago, IL
Berry, J. Ben ... Nashville, TN
Berry, J. Dale ... Chicago, IL
Berry, J. Daniel ... Washington, DC
Berry, J. Eric ... St. Louis, MO
Berry, J. Keith, Jr. ... Savannah, GA
Berry, J. Patrick ... Washington, DC
Berry, J. Stephen ... Atlanta, GA
Berry, Jack ... Dallas, TX
Berry, Jack K. ... Savannah, GA
Berry, James A. ... Springfield, OH
Berry, James C.P. ... New York, NY
Berry, James D. ... Shawnee, OK
Berry, James D., Jr. ... Shawnee, OK
Berry, James E. ... Houston, TX
Berry, James F. ... Chicago, IL
Berry, James F. ... Akron, OH
Berry, James G. ... Los Angeles, CA
Berry, James H., Jr. ... Los Angeles, CA
Berry, James I. Vance ... Nashville, TN
Berry, James I. Vance, Jr.
Jacksonville, FL
Berry, James P. ... Fresno, CA
Berry, James R. ... Albertville, AL
Berry, James W. ... Rayville, LA
Berry, James W. ... Bethany, OK

Berry, James W. ....**Oklahoma City, OK**
Berry, James W. "Bill", P.C. ....Bethany, OK
Berry, James W. "Bill" ....Bethany, OK
Berry, James W., Jr. ....Nashville, TN
Berry, James W., P.C. ....Enid, OK
Oklahoma City, OK
Berry, Jan A. ....Culver City, CA
Berry, Jan V. ....Des Moines, IA
Berry, Janet J. ....Reno, NV
Berry, Janet L. Rollins ....Columbia, MO
Berry, Janis M. ....Boston, MA
Berry, Jeannette Ellen ....Bozeman, MT
Berry, Jeffery R. ....Hartford, CT
Berry, Jeffrey D. ....Chicago, IL
Berry, Jeffrey G. ....Goshen, NY
Berry, Jerry ....Gonzalez, FL
Berry, Jerry ....Naples, FL
Berry, Jimmy D. ....Marietta, GA
Berry, Joe F., Jr. ....Columbia, SC
Berry, Joe M. ....Huntsville, AL
Berry, John A. ....North Chicago, IL
Berry, John A. ....River Ridge, LA
Berry, John C. ....Centreville, MI
Berry, John E. ....Hubbell, MI
Berry, John F. ....Portsmouth, OH
Portsmouth, OH
Berry, John F. ....Tyler, TX
Berry, John G. ....Madison, VA
Stanardsville, VA
Berry, John J., III ....New York, NY
Berry, John L. ....Tallahassee, FL
Berry, John M. ....Chicago, IL
Berry, John M. ....Louisville, KY
Berry, John M., Jr. ....New Castle, KY
Berry, John S. ....Tampa, FL
Berry, John Stevens ....Lincoln, NE
Berry, John T. ....Phoenix, AZ
Berry, John V. ....Phoenix, AZ
Berry, John V. ....Washington, DC
Berry, John W. ....New York, NY
Berry, John W. ....Kenedy, TX
Berry, John W., Jr. ....Sarasota, FL
Berry, Jonathan C. ....Harrisburg, PA
Berry, Joseph F. ....Three Lakes, WI
Berry, Joy Spencer ....Marshall, TX
Berry, Judith Lee ....Independence, MO
Berry, Judith M. ....Gorham, ME
Berry, Judy D. ....Camden, NJ
Berry, Kagan, Sahradnik & Kotzas, A Professional Corporation ....Toms River, NJ
Berry, Karen ....Portland, OR
Berry, Karen Renée ....New York, NY
Berry, Kathryn A. ....San Jose, CA
Berry, Kathy L. ....Houston, TX
Berry, Kelley & Hansen ....Lincoln, NE
Berry, Kenneth F. ....Coshocton, OH
Berry, Kessler, Crutchfield & Taylor
Moundsville, WV
Berry, Kevin D. ....Tulsa, OK
Berry, Kevin F. ....Philadelphia, PA
Berry, Kevin H. ....San Antonio, TX
Berry, Kevin M. ....Reno, NV
Berry, Kevin M. ....New York, NY
Berry, Kimberly ....Philadelphia, PA
Berry, Kimberly Briggs ....East Greenwich, RI
Berry, Kristina Gayle ....Nevada City, CA
Berry, L. Clyel ....Twin Falls, ID
Berry, Laura Kay W. ....Raleigh, NC
Berry, L. Clyel, (Chartered)
Twin Falls, ID
Berry, Lee Roy, Jr. ....Goshen, IN
Berry & Leftwich ....Washington, DC
Berry, Leigh Kennington ....Columbia, MS
Berry, Leo ....Helena, MT
Berry, L. G. ....Anchorage, AK
Berry, Linda Mallory ....Richmond, VA
Berry, Linda P. ....New York, NY
Berry, Lisa C. ....San Jose, CA
Berry, Loren C. ....New York, NY
Berry, Lynn E. ....Springfield, VA
Berry, M. Chad ....Bedford, TX
Berry, M. Daniel ....Lima, OH
Berry, M. Douglas ....Greensboro, NC
Berry, M. Paige ....Princeton, NJ
Berry, Marc H. ....Santa Clarita, CA
Berry, Marcia E. ....Norristown, PA
Berry, Margaret A. ....Brazil, IN
Berry, Mark ....El Paso, TX
Berry, Mark B. ....Sacramento, CA
Berry, Mark B. ....St. Louis, MO
Berry, Mark E. ....Stockton, CA
Berry, Mark G. ....Milwaukee, WI
Berry, Mark R. ....Vienna, VA
Berry, Mark S. ....Denver, CO
Berry, Mark V. ....Torrance, CA
Berry, Mark W. ....Bellevue, WA
Berry, Marla S. ....Nashua, NH
Berry, Mary Elizabeth ....Menlo Park, CA
Berry, Matthew B. ....Washington, DC
Berry, Matthew F. ....Clear Lake, IA
Berry, Max N., Law Offices of
Washington, DC
Berry & McKee ....Oklahoma City, OK
Berry, M. Daniel, L.P.A. ....Lima, OH
Berry, Melissa A. McGonigal ....Seattle, WA
Berry, Michael ....Dearborn, MI
Berry, Michael ....Austin, TX
Berry, Michael C., & Associates, P.A.
Washington, DC
Clearwater, FL
Berry, Michael C., Sr. ....Clearwater, FL
Berry, Michael Christian ....Houston, TX
Berry, Michael F. ....Vero Beach, FL
Berry, Michael G. ....Jefferson City, MO
Berry, Michael I. ....Los Angeles, CA
Berry, Michael L. ....Tallahassee, FL
Berry, Michael L., Jr.
Ponte Vedra Beach, FL

Berry, Michael R. ....Dallas, TX
Berry Moorman, Professional Corporation
Birmingham, MI
Detroit, MI
Berry, Nandita V. ....Houston, TX
Berry, Nazar ....San Diego, CA
Berry, Nickolas C. ....Miami, FL
Berry, Nolen W., P.C. ....Branson, MO
Berry and Oglesby ....Franklin, TN
Berry, Oran H., III ....San Angelo, TX
Berry, Pamela C. ....Department of Justice, Tax Division, GV
Berry, Patricia M. ....Los Angeles, CA
Berry, Patrick J. ....Cleveland, OH
Berry, Paul A. ....Dallas, TX
Houston, TX
Berry, Paul R. ....Syracuse, NY
Berry, Paul R. ....Pittsburgh, PA
Berry & Perkins, A Professional Corporation
Irvine, CA
Los Angeles, CA
Santa Ana, CA
Berry, Peter C. ....New York, NY
Berry, Peter J. ....Boston, MA
Berry, Phillip B. ....Placerville, CA
Berry, Phillip S. ....Oakland, CA
Berry, Quackenbush & Stuart, P.A.
Columbia, SC
Berry, R. Russell ....Atlanta, GA
Berry, R. Scott ....San Diego, CA
Berry, R. Stephen ....Washington, DC
Berry, Rachel E. ....Charlotte, NC
Berry, Ralph A., Jr. ....Medina, OH
Berry, Ray W. ....San Diego, CA
Berry, Rayburn ....Houston, TX
Berry, Raymond S. ....Salt Lake City, UT
Berry, Rena G. ....Roanoke, VA
Berry, Rex Darrell ....Seattle, WA
Berry, Richard B. ....Beebe, AR
Berry, Richard C. ....Troy, OH
Berry, Richard G. ....Los Angeles, CA
Berry, Richard J. ....Ottawa, IL
Streator, IL
Berry, Richard L., Jr. ....Toledo, OH
Berry, Richard L., Jr. ....Marshall, TX
Berry, Richard S. ....New York, NY
Berry, Richard W. ....Rockford, IL
Berry, Robert A. ....Houston, TX
Berry, Robert C. ....Newton, MA
Berry, Robert C. ....Wooster, OH
Berry, Robert F., Jr. ....Chicago, IL
Berry, Robert Gaynor ....Reno, NV
Berry, Robert H., Jr. ....Department of Defense, Defense Legal Services Agency, GV
Berry, Robert L. ....Rome, GA
Berry, Robert L. ....Omaha, NE
Berry, Robert L. ....Columbus, OH
Berry, Robert P. ....Kansas City, MO
Berry, Robert R. ....Melbourne, FL
Berry, Robert W. ....Denver, CO
Berry, Rodney T. ....Moundsville, WV
Berry, Roger L. ....New Smyrna Beach, FL
Berry, Ronald ....Catoosa, OK
Berry, Ronald C. ....Savannah, GA
Berry, Ronald C., P.C. ....Savannah, GA
Berry, Russell D. ....De Witt, AR
Berry, Rynn ....New York, NY
Berry, Sally F. ....Palo Alto, CA
Berry, Sammy, Jr. ....Lake Worth, FL
Berry, Sammy, Jr., P.A. ....Lake Worth, FL
Berry, Sandra Lee ....San Diego, CA
Berry, Sandra T. ....Little Rock, AR
Berry, Sarah E. ....Olathe, KS
Berry, Sarah E. ....Ocean Springs, MS
Berry, Sean R. ....Los Angeles, CA
Berry, Seth A. ....Boston, MA
Berry, Shari ....Houston, TX
Berry and Shelnutt, P.C. ....Phenix City, AL
Columbus, GA
Hamilton, GA
Talbotton, GA
Berry, Stephen L. ....Los Angeles, CA
Berry, Stephen L. ....Saint Marys, GA
Berry, Steven C. ....Holland, MI
Berry, Steven Gene ....Rockville, MD
Berry, Steven J. ....Dallas, TX
Berry, Sue A. ....Lumberton, NC
Berry, Theodore O. ....Oakland, CA
Berry, Theresa B. ....Virginia Beach, VA
Berry, Thomas A. ....Boothbay Harbor, ME
Berry, Thomas A., & Associates
Bloomington, IN
Berry, Thomas D. ....Dayton, OH
Berry, Thomas D., Jr. ....Gulfport, MS
Berry, Thomas E. ....St. Louis, MO
Berry, Thomas E. ....Houston, TX
Berry, Thomas J., Jr. ....Morristown, NJ
Berry, Thomas Leonard ....Princeton, WV
Berry, Thomas N. ....Cumberland, MD
Berry, Thomas O., Jr. ....St. George, SC
Berry, Thompson D., II ....San Francisco, CA
Berry & Thompson, L.L.P. ....Houston, TX
Berry, Timothy A. ....Orlando, FL
Berry, Timothy H. ....Leadville, CO
Berry, Timothy J. ....Plattsburgh, NY
Berry, Timothy J. ....Enon, OH
Berry, Tracy W. ....Dallas, TX
Berry, Travis R. ....Arkadelphia, AR
Berry, Turney P. ....Louisville, KY
Berry, Tyler, Jr. ....Franklin, TN
Berry & Van Meter Howard K. Berry, Jr.
Oklahoma City, OK
Berry, Victoria A. ....Huntington Beach, CA
Berry, Viktor H. ....Sacramento, CA
Berry, W. Douglas ....Tampa, FL
Berry, W. Scott ....Dallas, TX
Berry, Warner Bott ....San Francisco, CA
Berry, Wayne C. ....Philadelphia, PA

Berry, Wayne R. ....Department of Labor, Office of the Solicitor, GV
Berry, Weldon H. ....Houston, TX
Berry, William A. ....Oklahoma City, OK
Berry, William C. ....West Hartford, CT
Berry, William D. ....San Francisco, CA
Berry, William Everett, Jr. ....Odessa, TX
Berry, William G. ....Myrtle Beach, SC
Berry, William G., P.A. ....Myrtle Beach, SC
Berry, William L. ....Belleville, IL
Collinsville, IL
Berry, William R. ....Kingsport, TN
Berry, William Thomas ....Lovingston, VA
Berry, William W. ....Buffalo, NY
Berry, William W., IV ....Bedford, VA
Berry, William W., IV ....Bedford, VA
Berry, William W., Jr. ....Nashville, TN
Berry, Willis W., Jr. ....Philadelphia, PA
Berry, Wm. Todd ....Bakersfield, CA
Berry, W. W. ....Nashville, TN
Berry, Xanthe M. ....Oakland, CA
Berry-Goodfellow, Anne M. ....Westwood, MA
Berryhill, Bill B. ....Bellaire, TX
Berryhill, C. Douglas ....Jefferson City, TN
Berryhill, Cage & North, P.C.
Denver, CO
Telluride, CO
Berryhill, Jack W. ....Denver, CO
Berryhill, John A. ....Santa Barbara, CA
Berryhill, John C. ....Newark, OH
Berryhill, Jonathan L. ....Birmingham, AL
Berryhill, Stephen D. ....Haddon Heights, NJ
Berryhill & Williams, P.A.
Fort Lauderdale, FL
Berryman, Albert J. ....Fresno, CA
Berryman, B. Dan ....Fort Worth, TX
Berryman, Blake L. ....Dallas, TX
Berryman, Cathryn Anne ....Dallas, TX
Berryman, Charles F. ....Rochester, MN
Berryman, Emmett W. ....Dallas, TX
Berryman, Frank W. ....Madison, WI
Berryman, Franklin A. ....Nashville, TN
Berryman, G. Phil ....San Antonio, TX
Berryman, Hugh L. ....Dallas, TX
Berryman, James P. ....New London, CT
Berryman, Jerome W., II
Cleveland Heights, OH
Berryman, Jill E. ....San Rafael, CA
Berryman, Larry B. ....Worland, WY
Berryman, Leo, Jr. ....Tuscumbia, AL
Berryman, Melissa ....Morehead City, NC
Berryman, P. Brian ....San Antonio, TX
Berryman, Patrick D. ....Ann Arbor, MI
Berryman, R. Mitchell ....Winchester, KY
Berryman, R. Scott ....Atlanta, GA
Berryman, Richard B. ....Washington, DC
Berryman, Robert P. ....Hillsborough, CA
Berryman, William C., Jr. ....Athens, GA
Berryman, Wm. D. ....Centreville, VA
Berry-Smith, Bridgette A. ....Irvine, CA
Berryville, W. Wade ....Richmond, VA
Bers, Alan B. ....Chicago, IL
Bers, Mary M. ....Nashville, TN
Bers, Steven E. ....Baltimore, MD
Bersak, Robert A. ....Manchester, NH
Bersani, Frank A., Jr. ....Syracuse, NY
Bersani, James L. ....Columbus, OH
Bersani, John A. ....Syracuse, NY
Bersani, Kenneth ....Rochester, NY
Bersani, Leonard F. ....Syracuse, NY
Bersani, Mathilde C. ....Fayetteville, NY
Bersani, Michael D. ....Itasca, IL
Bersani, Michael G. ....Auburn, NY
Bersante, Monte ....Tacoma, WA
Bersch, Amy ....Beverly Hills, CA
Bersch, Blanche Cion ....Beverly Hills, CA
Bersch, Carl Richard, Jr.
Highland Heights, KY
Bersch, Deborah ....Williamsville, NY
Bersch, F. Joseph, III ....Seattle, WA
Bersch, Lynn A. ....San Francisco, CA
Bersch, Martha Tobin ....Houston, TX
Bersch & Rhodes, P.C. ....Roanoke, VA
Bersch, Robert S. ....Roanoke, VA
Bersch, Steven N. ....Beverly Hills, CA
Bersch, Timothy R. ....Houston, TX
Berschauer, Daniel J. ....Olympia, WA
Berschauer, David P. ....Laguna Hills, CA
Berschback, Don R. ....St. Clair Shores, MI
Bersche, Lynn J. ....Waterloo, IL
Berscheid, Karl J. ....San Luis Obispo, CA
Berscheidt, Thomas J. ....Great Bend, KS
Berschler, Arnold I. ....San Francisco, CA
Berschler, Jerold S. ....Norristown, PA
Bersell, Steven J. ....Chicago, IL
Bershad, Andrew D. ....Flourtown, PA
Bershad, David J. ....New York, NY
Bershad, Jack R ....Philadelphia, PA
Bershad, Lawrence ....Newark, NJ
Bershad, Russell B. ....Newark, NJ
Bershad, Stanley M. ....Southfield, MI
Bershin, Paul J. ....Van Nuys, CA
Bershin, Robert N. ....Orange, CA
Bershon, Nicole C. ....Los Angeles, CA
Bershtein, Bershtein & Bershtein, Professional Corporation ....Hamden, CT
Bershtein, Bruce E. ....Rockville, MD
Bershtein, Herman S. ....Hamden, CT
Bershtein, Jan ....Hamden, CT
Bershtein, Joy A. ....Hamden, CT
Bershtein, Lippman, Bachman & McKeon, P.C. ....New Haven, CT
Westport, CT
Bershtein, Raymond C. ....New Haven, CT
Bershtein, Richard A. ....Hamden, CT
Bersi, Ann ....Las Vegas, NV
Bersi, Mary Ann ....Las Vegas, NV
Bersin, Adam S. ....Syracuse, NY

Bersin, Alan D. ....San Diego, CA
Bersin, Andrew ....New York, NY
Bersin, Peter I. ....Beverly Hills, CA
Bersin, Richard A. ....Seattle, WA
Bersoff, Donald N. ....Haverford, PA
Berson, Bennett J. ....Madison, WI
Berson, Brian P. ....San Francisco, CA
Berson, Dale ....Brooklyn, NY
Berson, David J. ....Kansas City, MO
Berson, Eric C. ....Washington, DC
Berson, Joel I. ....New York, NY
Berson, Kimberly I. ....East Meadow, NY
Berson, Leonard R. ....New York, NY
Berson, Marc E. ....Roseland, NJ
Berson, Mark I. ....Greenfield, MA
Berson, Nancy S. ....Stamford, CT
Berson, Neil M. ....New York, NY
Berson, Norman S. ....Philadelphia, PA
Berson, Peter ....Philadelphia, PA
Berson, Robert M. ....New York, NY
Berson, Ronald ....New York, NY
Berson, Scott D. ....New York, NY
Berson, Sherry M. ....Bethesda, MD
Berson, Steven I. ....Palo Alto, CA
Berson, Susan A. ....Kansas City, MO
Berson, Susan W. ....New York, NY
Berss, Harvey G. ....Atlanta, GA
Berst, Robert A. ....Seattle, WA
Berstein, Richard W. ....Warwick, RI
Bersticker, Steven C. ....Cleveland, OH
Bert, Ellis Lawrence ....Dallas, TX
Bert, Jeffrey D. ....Davenport, IA
Berta, David J. ....Lorain, OH
Berta, Jeno M. ....Davenport, IA
Berta, Michael A. ....Washington, DC
Berta, Robert J. ....Trumbull, CT
Berta, T. Randall ....Fort Wayne, IN
Bertagno, Foster ....Wayne, NJ
Bertagnolli, Leslie A. ....Chicago, IL
Bertain, G. Joseph, Jr., Law Offices of
San Francisco, CA
Bertain, Lisa M. ....San Francisco, CA
Bertalan, Lisa N. ....Bend, OR
Bertan, David K. ....White Plains, NY
Bertan & LaRaus ....White Plains, NY
Bertani, Amy M. ....Joliet, IL
Bertani, Dante G. ....Greensburg, PA
Bertani, Louis R. ....Joliet, IL
Bertani, Mary Jo ....Austin, TX
Bertani, Matthew G. ....Morris, IL
Bertany, Thomas R. ....Roswell, GA
Bertas, Helen E. ....Philadelphia, PA
Bertaut, Carmelite M. ....New Orleans, LA
Bertch & Birch, East ....Heber City, UT
Salt Lake City, UT
Bertch, Daniel F. ....Heber City, UT
Salt Lake City, UT
Berté, Nancy A. ....Evanston, IL
Berteau, Alan J. ....Baton Rouge, LA
Berteau, John T. ....Sarasota, FL
Bertel, Numa V., Jr. ....New Orleans, LA
Bertele, Edward A. ....Secaucus, NJ
Bertell, John T. ....Buffalo, NY
Bertelle, Donald L. ....Chicago, IL
Bertelli, Catherine Hess ....Melrose, MA
Bertelli, Monty R. ....Des Moines, IA
Bertelsen, Bruce I. ....Washington, DC
Bertelsen, Karl H. ....Simi Valley, CA
Bertelsen, Mark A. ....Palo Alto, CA
Bertelsen, Michael W. ....St. Paul, MN
Bertelsen, Penny Rodeen ....San Rafael, CA
Bertelsen, Sharon M.
Federal Communications Commission, Mass Media Bureau, GV
Bertelsman, Kaufmann, Seidenfaden & Kolentse ....Fort Thomas, KY
Bertelsman, William O. ....Covington, KY
Bertelson, Richard William, III
Lexington, KY
Berten, David P. ....Chicago, IL
Bertenthal, David M. ....San Francisco, CA
Bertenthal, Philip J. ....Richmond, CA
Bertero, Edward Peter ....Garden City, NY
Bertero, James B. ....Santa Barbara, CA
Bertero, John B., III ....Concord, CA
Bertero, Karen E. ....Los Angeles, CA
Bertet, Jean-Claude ....Los Angeles, CA
Bertha, Nicholas J., III ....Florham Park, NJ
Berthel, Catherine M. ....Oneonta, NY
Berthel, Deborah A. ....Woodland Hills, CA
Berthel, K. Lee ....San Francisco, CA
Berthelot, Henry J. ....New Orleans, LA
Berthelot, Rita F. ....Kingwood, TX
Berthelot, Ronnie J. ....Baton Rouge, LA
Berthelsen, Alvin L. ....Lakewood, CO
Berthelsen, Gilbert J. ....Racine, WI
Berthelsen, Richard A. ....Washington, DC
Berthelsen, Richard G. ....McPherson, KS
Berthelsen, Wayne D. ....Fairfax, VA
Berthene, Sandra A. ....St. Louis Park, MN
Berthiaume, Blaise P. ......North Brookfield, MA
Spencer, MA
Berthiaume, David A.
Department of Education, Office of the General Counsel, GV
Berthiaume, Laura V. ....Rockville, MD
Berthiaume, M. Edward, Jr. ....Mahwah, NJ
Berthiaume, Mark A. ....Boston, MA
Berthiaume, Robert ....Boca Raton, FL
Berthiaume, Robert, P.A. ....Boca Raton, FL
Berthold, Fadette ....Boston, MA
Berthold, Margaret J. ....New Haven, CT
Berthold, Robert V., Jr. ....Charleston, WV
Berthold, Thomas R. ....San Jose, CA
Berthold, Tiano & O'Dell
Charleston, WV
Bertholf, Clifford L. ....Wichita, KS
Bertholf, Terry D. ....Hutchinson, KS

Besser, John E. .....Boston, MA
Besser, Kenneth R. .....Columbus, OH
Besser, Lawrence E. .....Miami, FL
Besser, Robert S. .....Los Angeles, CA
Besser, Stephen N. .....Los Angeles, CA
Besser, Steven V. .....Duluth, MN
Bessert, Gregory P. .....Vancouver, WA
Besses, Gerald S. .....San Francisco, CA
Bessette, Albert E., Jr. .....Holyoke, MA
Bessette, Frederick W. .....Milwaukee, WI
Bessette, James P. .....Malone, NY
Bessette, Maureen .....San Francisco, CA
Bessette, Paul M. .....San Francisco, CA
Bessette, Paul R. .....Austin, TX
Bessette, Roland L. .....Grosse Pointe Park, MI
Bessette, Steven M. .....Port St. Lucie, FL
Bessette, Thomas A. .....Springfield, MA
Bessette, Thomas E. .....Cambridge, MA
Bessette, Wendy W. .....Phoenix, AZ
Bessette-Smith, Suzanne .....Chicago, IL
Bessey, John D. .....Sacramento, CA
Bessey, John P. .....Columbus, OH
Bessey, Melissa A. .....Washington, DC
Bessey, Terrance L. .....Washington, DC
Bessho, David M. .....Atlanta, GA
Bessich, John A. .....Huntington Station, NY
New York, NY
Bessick, Elmer A. .....Elyria, OH
Bessinger, Janice F. .....Lake City, FL
Bessinger, John L. "Sam" .....Fresno, CA
Bessire, Todd DeWitt .....Salinas, CA
Besskó, Zsolt K. .....New York, NY
Bessler, John D. .....Minneapolis, MN
Bessler, Lisa M. .....Roseville, MN
Besso, David H. .....Bay Shore, NY
Besso, Michele .....Granger, WA
Bessolo, James P. .....Los Angeles, CA
Besson, Jann .....Los Altos, CA
Besson, Paul S. .....Washington, DC
Besson, Woodson Toliver, (P.C.)
Los Angeles, CA
Bessone, Luis Miguel .....Tampa, FL
Bessonette, George A. .....Homerville, GA
Best, Alice Rabinowitz .....Fort Lauderdale, FL
Best & Anderson, P.A. .....Crystal River, FL
Melbourne, FL
Orlando, FL
Best, Arthur M. .....Denver, CO
Best, Barry H. .....Providence, RI
Best, Benjamin H., II .....Pearland, TX
Best Best & Krieger LLP .....Ontario, CA
Rancho Mirage, CA
Riverside, CA
San Diego, CA
Best and Best, P.C. .....Birmingham, MI
Best, Bill, P.C., Attorney .....Brownsville, TX
Best, Charles D. .....Atlanta, GA
Best, Charles L. .....Portland, OR
Best, Charles W., III .....Norfolk, VA
Best, Charles W., III, P.C. .....Norfolk, VA
Best, Charles W., Jr. .....Norfolk, VA
Best, Charles W., Jr., P.C. .....Norfolk, VA
Best, Clem K., Jr. .....El Paso, TX
Best, Cynthia L. .....Phoenix, AZ
Best, Daniel E. .....Troy, MI
Best, David A. .....Bellevue, WA
Best, David L. .....Jacksonville, NC
Best, David R. .....Crystal River, FL
Melbourne, FL
Orlando, FL
Best, Deborah .....Seattle, WA
Best, Debra E. .....Los Angeles, CA
Best, Diane .....Pierre, SD
Best, Donald L., Jr. .....Pittsburgh, PA
Best, Douglas E. .....Denver, CO
Best, Edward S. .....Chicago, IL
Best, Eileen M. .....Toledo, OH
Best, Elizabeth Allaire .....Great Falls, MT
Best, Ellen S. .....Blue Hill, ME
Best & Flanagan LLP .....Minneapolis, MN
Best & Flanagan, LLP .....St. Paul, MN
Best, Franklin L., Jr. .....Horsham, PA
Best, Geoffry D. C. .....New York, NY
Best, George B., Jr. .....Kalispell, MT
Best, George C. .....Washington, DC
Best, Gerald R. .....McLean, VA
Best, Heyns & Klaeren, P.C. .....Jackson, MI
Best, Hollis G. .....Yosemite National Park, CA
Best, J. Donald .....Madison, WI
Best, J. Kinsley .....Brooksville, FL
Best, Jacque W. .....Sidney, MT
Best, James C. .....Miami, FL
Best, James F. .....Chicago, IL
Wheaton, IL
Best, James Jewell .....New Roads, LA
Best, James L. .....Lewisburg, PA
Best, James L., P.C. .....Lewisburg, PA
Best, Jamie M., III .....Columbia, SC
Best, Joan .....Hilo, HI
Best, Joanne L. .....Albion, NY
Best, John A. .....West Bend, WI
Best, John A., S.C. .....West Bend, WI
Best, Joseph M. .....Tulsa, OK
Best, Judah .....Washington, DC
Best, K. Candis .....Jamaica, NY
Best, Karen B. .....Denver, CO
Best, Kimberley Ann .....Washington, DC
Best, Kimberly M. .....Beaver Dam, WI
Best, Kimberly Y. .....Charlotte, NC
Best Koeppel .....Metairie, LA
New Orleans, LA
Houston, TX
Best, L. Dean .....Augusta, GA
Best, Landis Cox .....New York, NY
Best, Laurence E. .....New Orleans, LA
Houston, TX
Best Law Offices, P.C. .....Great Falls, MT
Best, Lawrence H. .....Birmingham, MI
Best, Lawrence P. .....Indio, CA
Best, Libbey W. Call .....Findlay, OH
Toledo, OH
Best & Lyons, P.A. .....Miami, FL
Best, Mangan & Langhenry .....Chicago, IL
Joliet, IL
Rockford, IL
Wheaton, IL
Best, Marilyn Dianne .....Oklahoma City, OK
Best, Mary M. .....Temecula, CA
Best, Michael A. .....Denver, CO
Best, Michael J. .....Great Falls, MT
Best, Miriam R. .....Brooklyn, NY
Best, Norma Hatfield .....Bowling Green, OH
Best, Pamela Weaver .....Raleigh, NC
Best, Patricia K. .....Chicago, IL
Best, Paula Whitney .....New York, NY
Best, Peter Farquhard .....Asheville, NC
Best, Peter J. .....Glenview, IL
Best, Philip M. .....Port Orchard, WA
Best, R. Bradley .....Oxford, MS
Best, R. Max .....Clovis, NM
Best, Richard E. .....San Francisco, CA
Best, Richard G. .....Denver, CO
Best, Richard R. .....Bronx, NY
Best, Rick .....Seattle, WA
Best, Robert B., Jr. .....Kansas City, MO
Best, Robert C. .....Manchester, WA
Best, Robert F. .....Jackson, MI
Best, Robert J. .....Chicago, IL
Best, Robert K. .....Sacramento, CA
Best, Robert P. .....Johnstown, NY
Best, Robert W. .....Owensboro, KY
Best, Roger E. .....Chicago, IL
Best, Ron .....Houston, TX
Best, Ronald S. .....Salt Lake City, UT
Best & Sharp, A Professional Corporation
Tulsa, OK
Best, Stacey L. .....Cheyenne, WY
Best, Stacey Ruda .....Woodland Hills, CA
Best, Stephen A. .....Washington, DC
Best, Stephen C. .....East Hartford, CT
Best, Stephen L. .....Fairfax, VA
Best, Steven J. .....Atlanta, GA
Best, Steven K. .....Metairie, LA
Best, Stuart A. .....Birmingham, MI
Best, Thomas E. .....Atlanta, GA
Best, Thomas G. .....San Francisco, CA
Best, Timothy G. .....Tulsa, OK
Best, Willard C. .....Geneva, NY
Best, William C., Jr. .....Brownsville, TX
Best, Zachary .....Oakland, CA
Bestard, Antonio J. .....Pomona, CA
Beste, Anne Bottini .....Washington, DC
Beste, Eric J. .....Department of Justice, Criminal Division, GV
Beste, James D. .....Cincinnati, OH
Beste, James G. .....Houston, TX
Beste, Robert K., Jr. .....Wilmington, DE
Bestebreurtje, Mary-Anne .....Tallahassee, FL
Besteiro, Donna R. .....Stamford, CT
Besterman, Kenneth A. .....New York, NY
Besterman, Marlene .....New York, NY
Bestine, Katherine J. .....Buffalo, NY
Bestol, Kay Lynn .....Cheyenne, WY
Bestor, Geoffrey .....Washington, DC
Bestor, John K. .....Kansas City, MO
Best-Parris, Karen .....Ellington, CT
Best Rendo, Jacqueline S. Best
Longwood, FL
Bestry, Sherwood L. .....Amherst, NY
Bestry, Sherwood L. .....Buffalo, NY
Bestrycki, Chester M., Jr.
Fort Lauderdale, FL
Bestul, Daniel P. .....Darlington, WI
Monroe, WI
Bestwick, Craig A. .....San Rafael, CA
Besu Law Firm, The .....Miami, FL
Besu, Roger .....Miami, FL
Besunder, Alfred .....Rockville Centre, NY
Besunder, Alison J. .....East Setauket, NY
Besunder, Harvey B., Law Offices of
Hauppauge, NY
Besunder, Harvey B., Law Offices of
Riverhead, NY
Besunder, Seymour .....Brooklyn, NY
Besvinick, Laura .....Miami, FL
Beswick, Albert L. .....Amherst, MA
Beswick, Brenda A. .....Los Angeles, CA
Beswick, George W. .....Havelock, NC
Morehead City, NC
Beswick, Jeffrey W. .....Grand Haven, MI
Beswick, Kevin Thomas .....Atlanta, GA
Beswick, Richard R. .....San Bernardino, CA
Beswick, Robert H. .....Beverly Hills, CA
Beswick, Thomas J. .....Irving, TX
Betancourt, Ana-Mita
Overseas Private Investment Corporation, GV
Betancourt, Brian A. .....New York, NY
Betancourt, Edward A. .....Department of State, Bureau of Consular Affairs, GV
Betancourt, Frank J. .....Waxahachie, TX
Betancourt, Glenn .....Schiller Park, IL
Betancourt, Julie Lynn Frederickson
Cypress, TX
Betancourt, Laura Lita .....Brownsville, TX
Betancourt, Neal L. .....Jacksonville, FL
Betancourt, Rafael J. .....Cranford, NJ
Betancourt, Sally .....White Plains, NY
Betancourt, Susana .....Miami, FL
Betancourt, Thomas R. .....Hackensack, NJ
Betancourt Pulliza, Rafael .....San Juan, PR
Betanzos, Christina L. .....Dallas, TX
Betanzos, Todd E. .....Dallas, TX
Betaque, Karen .....Santa Rosa, CA
Betar, Samuel J. .....Chicago, IL
Betbeze, J. Timothy, (P.C.)
New Orleans, LA
Betbeze, Jaime William .....Mobile, AL
Betcher, Edward J. .....New York, NY
Betcher, John L. .....Red Wing, MN
Betcher, Michael J. .....Lexington, MA
Betcher, Susan D. .....Seattle, WA
Betchkal, Gregory John .....Hudson, OH
Betebenner, Brad C. .....Salt Lake City, UT
Betenbough, Terry G. .....Lubbock, TX
Betensky, Elayne .....Los Angeles, CA
Betensky, Gary S. .....Miami, FL
West Palm Beach, FL
Betensky, Steven M. .....New York, NY
Beter, George D. .....Huntington, WV
Betesh, Joan Katz .....Philadelphia, PA
Betesh, Joanna P. .....Shrewsbury, NJ
Betesh, Marc E. .....Woodbridge, NJ
Betette, Robert V. .....Oakland, CA
Beth, Henry W. .....Worcester, MA
Beth, Kenneth N., (Ltd.) .....Champaign, IL
Beth, Steven N. .....Independence, MO
Beth, Steven N., P.C. .....Independence, MO
Bethancourt, J. Eric .....Arabi, LA
Bethancourt, Patricia A. .....New Orleans, LA
Bethancourt, Randall L., P.C. .....Houma, LA
Bethancourt, Van C., Jr. .....Mesa, AZ
Bethany, Brenda B. .....Jackson, MS
Bethard & Bethard, LLP .....Coushatta, LA
Bethard, Henry W., III .....Coushatta, LA
Bethard, James G. .....Coushatta, LA
Bethard, Robert E. .....Coushatta, LA
Bethards, Laureen A. .....Oakland, CA
Bethea, Black, Nishimura & Leithead
Hilo, HI
Bethea, Frances Blair .....Beaumont, TX
Bethea, J. Daryl .....Mesa, AZ
Bethea, John D. .....Phoenix, AZ
Bethea, Jordan & Griffin, P.A.
Bluffton, SC
Hilton Head Island, SC
Bethea, Maxwell & Waddell .....Memphis, TN
Bethea, Rhonda .....Los Angeles, CA
Bethea, Richard T. D. .....Memphis, TN
Bethea, Robert E. .....Hilo, HI
Bethea, Robert F. .....Jacksonville, FL
Bethea, Robert Partridge, Jr.
Columbia, SC
Bethea, Roderick .....Lake Forest, CA
Bethea, Susan .....Birmingham, AL
Bethea, William C. .....Little Rock, AR
Bethea, William D., III .....Gulfport, MS
Bethea, William L., Jr. .....Bluffton, SC
Hilton Head Island, SC
Bethea-Shields, Karen .....Durham, NC
Betheil, Richard M. .....New York, NY
Bethel, Alison .....Miami, FL
Bethel, Allan L., Jr. .....St. Louis, MO
Bethel, Allison K. .....Fort Lauderdale, FL
Bethel, Billie R., (Ms.) .....Gatlinburg, TN
Bethel, Cassandra M. .....Bronx, NY
Bethel, Charles F. .....San Diego, CA
Bethel, Dale K. .....Temecula, CA
Bethel, Douglas Wyatt .....Fairfax, VA
Bethel, Gary W. .....Fresno, CA
Santa Maria, CA
Bethel, George F., A Professional Corporation
Newport Beach, CA
Bethel, James E. .....Dalton, GA
Bethel, John E. .....Hampden, MA
Bethel & Nicastro, P.C. .....Washington, DC
Bethel, Pamela Elaine .....Plano, TX
Bethel, Pamela J. .....Washington, DC
Bethel, Terry A. .....Bloomington, IN
Bethel, Winston P. .....Decatur, GA
Bethell, Bruce H. .....Fort Smith, AR
Bethell and Cromwell, P.L.C.
Fort Smith, AR
Bethell, M. Clay .....Memphis, TN
Bethill, Charles D. .....New York, NY
Bethke, Erich L. .....Denver, CO
Bethke, William P. .....Lakewood, CO
Bethmann, Hollie E. .....Rensselaer, NY
Bethmann, Mark A. .....New York, NY
Bethoney, Cecilia Nedder .....Milton, MA
Bethscheider, Alan J. .....Houston, TX
Bethune, Brian D. .....Richardson, TX
Bethune, Downing M. .....Portland, OR
Bethune, Ed .....Washington, DC
Bethune, Gary L. .....Phoenix, AZ
Bethune, Gary L., & Associates, P.C.
Phoenix, AZ
Bethune, Marvin A. .....Charlotte, NC
Bethune, Scott S. .....Kansas City, MO
Bethune, William J. .....Vienna, VA
Bethurem, Nancye L. .....Honolulu, HI
Bethurem, Nancye L., P.C. .....Honolulu, HI
Betinsky, Marc E. .....Boston, MA
Betke, Christopher G. .....Boston, MA
Betke, James E. .....Chicago, IL
Betke, Todd W. .....Washington, DC
Betlach, Bradley J. .....Minneapolis, MN
Betlejeski, Diane D. .....New York, NY
Betleski, Adrian F. .....Lorain, OH
Betlesky, Richard .....New York, NY
Betley, Joseph F. .....Mount Laurel, NJ
Betley, Leonard J. .....Indianapolis, IN
Betley, William M. .....Orange, CA
Betlow, Pamela B. .....Short Hills, NJ
Betman, Ronald S. .....Chicago, IL
Bet-Mansour, E. Raman .....New York, NY
Betonti, Jayelene Danelle
Fairfax Station, VA
Betor, John G. .....Washington, DC
Betor-Rizzo, Janice M. .....Liberty Corner, NJ
Betournay, Karen T. .....Holyoke, MA
Betourney, Andrew E.
Department Of Veterans Affairs, Board of Veterans Appeals, GV
Betow, Gary L. .....Tulsa, OK
Betow, Joel .....Princess Anne, MD
Betras, David J. .....Youngstown, OH
Betras, Joseph D. .....Youngstown, OH
Betro, George L. .....Utica, NY
Betro, James W. .....Oneida, NY
Betsacon, Nicholas J. .....Columbus, OH
Betsill, Jerry .....Fort Worth, TX
Betsock, Barbara
Department of Transportation, Research and Special Programs Administration, GV
Betsworth, Nadine E. .....Riverside, CA
Bettac, Robert E. .....San Antonio, TX
Bettag, Jerome L. .....St. Charles, IL
Bettan, Jeffrey .....Westbury, NY
Bettasso, Katharine Lang .....Cleveland, OH
Bettasso, Kathryn A. .....Chicago, IL
Bettauer, Raija H. .....Treasury Department, Office of the Comptroller of the Currency, GV
Bettauer, Ronald J. .....Department of State, Office of the Legal Adviser, GV
Betteau, Bart M. .....New Albany, IN
Betten, Alan .....Baltimore, MD
Betten, Laura K. .....Melbourne, FL
Betten, Laura K., P.A. .....Melbourne, FL
Bettenberg, Robert T. .....Westminster, CO
Bettenburg, James R. .....St. Paul, MN
Bettenburg, Joan .....St. Paul, MN
Bettenburg Law Firm .....St. Paul, MN
Bettencourt, David .....Honolulu, HI
Bettencourt, Elizabeth C. .....Duxbury, MA
Bettencourt, Eugenia B. .....Boston, MA
Bettencourt, Jessica M. .....Boston, MA
Providence, RI
Bettencourt, M. Robert .....Visalia, CA
Bettencourt, Mark T. .....Boston, MA
Bettencourt, Scott E. .....Boston, MA
Bettendorf, Edward L. .....Chicago, IL
Bettendorf, Henry A. .....St. Louis, MO
Bettendorf, Margaret C. .....Columbus, OH
Bettendorf, Robert B. .....Ada, MI
Bettenga, Cory Larsen .....Minneapolis, MN
Bettenhausen, Barb L. .....Washington, DC
Bettenhausen, Donald I. .....Tinley Park, IL
Bettenhausen, Matthew R. .....Chicago, IL
Better, Herbert .....Baltimore, MD
Better, Lynda M. .....Oceanside, CA
Better, William J. .....Kinderhook, NY
Betteridge, Frances C. .....Tucson, AZ
Betterman & Dixon .....Omaha, NE
Betterman, James B. .....Overland Park, KS
Betterman, W. Patrick .....Omaha, NE
Betters, Nicole R.
Cranberry Township, PA
Betters, Robert C. .....Plymouth, MA
Bettersworth, James S. .....San Antonio, TX
Betterton, Dale Stuart .....Baltimore, MD
Betterton, Donald R .....Osceola, AR
Betterton, Greg .....Nokomis, FL
Betterton, Ken L. .....Salem, OR
Betterton, Kimberly C. .....Baltimore, MD
Bettes, Marjory Lou .....Dallas, TX
Bettex, Donald A. .....Palm Beach, FL
Bettex, John N. .....Atlanta, GA
Betti, Rosaire C. .....Pittsburgh, PA
Betti, Walter V. .....Commack, NY
Bettigole, Bridget M. .....Boston, MA
Bettigole, Bruce J. .....Franklin, MA
Wellesley, MA
Providence, RI
Bettigole, Bruce M.
Securities and Exchange Commission, Division of Enforcement, GV
Bettigole, Kara .....Boston, MA
Bettigole, Kyle A. .....Boston, MA
Bettilyon, Mark M. .....Salt Lake City, UT
Bettin, Bradly Roger .....Cocoa, FL
Bettin, Frederic .....Beverly Hills, CA
Bettinelli, William L. .....San Francisco, CA
Bettinger, Carl J. .....Albuquerque, NM
Bettinger, Michael J. .....San Francisco, CA
Bettinger, Nicholas S. .....Fort Worth, TX
Bettinger, Robert P. .....Las Vegas, NV
Bettinger, Wilmer C. .....Wilmington, DE
Bettini, Heidi L. .....New York, NY
Bettini, Joseph M. .....Phoenix, AZ
Bettino, Diane A. .....Princeton, NJ
Bettis, Barry Phillip .....Cumming, GA
Bettis, H. Wayne .....Houston, TX
Bettis, J. Warren .....Columbus, OH
Bettis, James M., Jr. .....Houston, TX
Bettis, Larry G. .....North Las Vegas, NV
Bettis, Lucy E. .....San Francisco, CA
Bettis, R. Mack .....Tulsa, OK
Bettis, Vance J. .....Columbia, SC
Bettis, Wade P. .....Canby, OR
Bettis, Wade P., Jr. .....La Grande, OR
Bettis, William Chad .....Greenwood, SC
Bettison, Dennis R. .....Galveston, TX
Bettius, Marc E. .....Arlington, VA
Bettle, Kara H. .....Sarasota, FL
Bettles, Thomas W. .....San Diego, CA
Bettman, Gary B. .....New York, NY
Bettman, Gerald S. .....Jacksonville, FL
Bettman, Gilbert .....Cincinnati, OH
Bettman, Jack W. .....Jacksonville, FL
Bettman, Marianna Brown .....Cincinnati, OH
Bettman, Ralph M. .....Tarrytown, NY
Bettman, William J. .....Chicago, IL
Bettmann, Frank A. .....Rapid City, SD
Bettridge, Ben .....Tacoma, WA
Bettridge, Scott E. .....New York, NY
Betts, A. Dean .....Georgetown, DE

Betts, A. Dean, Jr. ... Georgetown, DE
Betts, Alicia Rodriguez
West Palm Beach, FL
Betts, Anne E. Garry ... Minneapolis, MN
Betts, Barbara Lang ... Sacramento, CA
San Diego, CA
Betts & Beauregard, P.A. ... Georgetown, DE
Betts, Charlotte ... Garden City, NY
Betts, Christopher D. ... Findlay, OH
Betts, D. Michael ... Cleveland, OH
Betts, David M. ... Cleveland, OH
Betts, Derick W., Jr. ... New York, NY
Betts, Eugene N. ... Fort Lauderdale, FL
Betts, Frederick V. ... Seattle, WA
Betts, Gair G. ... Riverhead, NY
Betts, Gina E. ... Dallas, TX
Betts, Gina M. ... Teaneck, NJ
Betts, H. Rodger ... Kula, HI
Betts, Heather A. ... Detroit, MI
Betts & Holt ... Washington, DC
Betts, J. Edward ... Richmond, VA
Betts, J. Rod ... San Diego, CA
Betts, James B. ... Fresno, CA
Betts, James E. ... Cleveland, OH
Columbus, OH
Betts, James R. ... Tampa, FL
Betts, James T. ... Hartford, CT
Betts, Janet G. ... Phoenix, AZ
Betts, Jennifer S. ... San Diego, CA
Betts, John C. ... Mission, KS
Betts, Kenneth J. ... Chicago, IL
Betts, Kenneth L. ... Dallas, TX
Betts, Kenneth N. ... Davenport, IA
Betts, Kirk Howard ... Washington, DC
Betts Law Offices ... Pittsburgh, PA
Betts, Lowry M. ... Pittsboro, NC
Betts, Marilyn J. ... Manassas, VA
Betts, Michael A. ... Baton Rouge, LA
Betts, Michael D. ... Warminster, PA
Betts, Michael J. ... Pittsburgh, PA
Betts, Miller & Russo ... Findlay, OH
Betts, Patterson & Mines, P.S.
Seattle, WA
Betts, Raymond L., Jr. ... Denver, CO
Betts, Rebecca A. ... Charleston, WV
Betts, Robert I. ... Bellevue, WA
Betts, Roland W. ... New York, NY
Betts, Shawn M. ... Maplewood, MN
Betts, Stacey W. ... Ephrata, PA
Betts, Stephen C. ... Findlay, OH
Betts, Stephen C. ... Nashville, TN
Betts, Steven A. ... Phoenix, AZ
Betts, Virginia Trotter ... Nashville, TN
Betts, W. Furman, Jr. ... Palm Harbor, FL
Betts, Wendell ... Topeka, KS
Betts, William H., Jr. ... Brenham, TX
Betts, William J. ... Concord, CA
Betts & Wright, A Professional Corporation
Fresno, CA
Betts-Frankel, Marie ... Santa Monica, CA
Bettuo, Bart ... Martinsville, IN
Bettuzzi, Albert C. ... Chicago, IL
Bettuzzi & Van Der Horst, Ltd. ... Chicago, IL
Bettwy, Andrew J. ... New York, NY
Bettwy, Andrew L. ... Phoenix, AZ
Bettwy, Andrew W. ... Las Vegas, NV
Bettwy, Samuel W. ... San Diego, CA
Betty & Brantley, L.L.P. ... Fort Worth, TX
Betty, Dale A. ... Media, PA
Betty, Howard G. ... Winchester, TN
Betty, Jeffrey B. ... San Angelo, TX
Betty, Neuman & McMahon
Rock Island, IL
Davenport, IA
Betty, Randall E. ... Fort Worth, TX
Betz, Alan C. ... Lawrenceburg, TN
Betz, Alexander ... Southfield, MI
Betz, Brian Jennings ... Kalamazoo, MI
Betz, Carole Marino ... Wheaton, IL
Betz, Colonel F. ... Mount Vernon, WA
Betz, Colonel F. ... Seattle, WA
Betz, David F. ... Ludington, MI
Betz, Eleanor J. ... Philadelphia, PA
Betz, Gail M. ... Oxnard, CA
Betz, Gary L. ... Tampa, FL
Betz, Gerard G. ... New York, NY
Betz, Gilbert C. ... Miami, FL
Betz, Gilbert C., P.A. ... Miami, FL
Betz, Heidi Marie ... Troy, MI
Betz, Holly Hapak ... Indianapolis, IN
Betz, James E. ... Minneapolis, MN
Betz, Jan L. ... Portland, OR
Betz, Jean L. ... Bethesda, MD
Betz, John F. ... Brighton, MI
Betz, Kevin W. ... Indianapolis, IN
Betz, Kimberly A. ... Charlotte, NC
Betz, Larry R. ... Okemos, MI
Betz, Michael J. ... San Francisco, CA
Betz, Michael J. ... St. Louis, MO
Betz, Michael J. ... Dallas, TX
Betz, Michael W. ... Grand Rapids, MI
Betz, Richard F. ... Allentown, PA
Betz, Richard L. ... Naperville, IL
Betz, Robert J. ... Mineola, NY
New York, NY
White Plains, NY
Betz, Robert M. ... Dallas, TX
Betz, Ron Dale ... Bartlesville, OK
Betz, Steven G. ... Dearborn, MI
Betz, Thomas E. ... Urbana, IL
Betz, Thomas E. ... Cleveland, OH
Betz, Thomas F., Jr. ... Virginia Beach, VA
Betz, Thomas R. ... Philadelphia, PA
Betz, William E. ... Baldwin, NY
Betza, Edward J. ... Erie, PA
Betze, Deena L. ... Haddonfield, NJ
Betzel, Lissa S. ... Fort Worth, TX
Betzen, Mark E. ... Dallas, TX

Betzendorfer & Granoski ... Tacoma, WA
Betzendorfer, Jeanne E. ... Tacoma, WA
Betzendorfer, Joseph Q., Jr. ... Tacoma, WA
Betzer, S. I., Jr. ... Albuquerque, NM
Betzig, Susan E. ... Ann Arbor, MI
Betzina, Keith B. ... San Francisco, CA
Betzler, Bernadette ... Fort Washington, PA
Betzler, Kenneth R. ... Akron, OH
Betzold, Donald R. ... Brooklyn Center, MN
Beu, Patricia M. ... Brattleboro, VT
Beu, Richard C. ... Houston, TX
Beu, William R. ... Rockford, IL
Beuch, C. Scott ... Oklahoma City, OK
Beuche, James R. ... Ann Arbor, MI
Beuche, William A., Jr. ... Palo Alto, CA
Beuchel, Grant E. ... Rosamond, CA
Beuchert, Edward W. ... New York, NY
Beuchert, George H., Jr. ... Washington, DC
Beucke, Larry W. ... Kearney, NE
Beucler, Robert D., (P.C.) ... Phoenix, AZ
Beuerle, Robert J. ... Traverse City, MI
Beuerle, Stephen C. ... La Jolla, CA
Beuerlein, Michele E. ... Los Angeles, CA
Beugelmans, Jacques ... Los Angeles, CA
Beugen, Robert J. ... Minneapolis, MN
Beugen, Robert J., Ltd. Professional
Corporation ... Minneapolis, MN
Beugen, Valerie T. ... College Station, TX
Beuglet, Charles P. ... Newport Beach, CA
Beuhler & Beuhler ... San Antonio, TX
Beuhler, John W., Jr. ... Wenatchee, WA
Beuhler, Paul E. ... San Antonio, TX
Beuhler, Wm. W., Jr. ... San Antonio, TX
Beuk, Jelena ... Chicago, IL
Beukema, John F. ... Minneapolis, MN
Beulick, John S. ... St. Louis, MO
Beumler, Henry W. ... Portal, AZ
Beuning, James A. ... Mahnomen, MN
Beuoy, David L. ... Arab, AL
Beurman, Laura A. ... Cambridge, MA
Beurmann, Lloyd B., Jr. ... Brighton, MI
Beury, Robert N., Jr. ... Washington, DC
Beus, Edwin H. ... Sandy, UT
Beus, Gilbert & Devitt, P.L.L.C.
Phoenix, AZ
Beus, Karl S. ... Cleveland, OH
Beus, Leo R. ... Phoenix, AZ
Beusen, Jon ... St. Louis, MO
Beusse, James H. ... Orlando, FL
Beusse, Jeffrey H. ... Grand Rapids, MI
Beust, Lynne K. ... Reading, PA
Beustring, Glenn R. ... Tulsa, OK
Beustring, Russell V. ... Houston, TX
Beutel, Julie Restivo ... New City, NY
Beutel, Richard A. ... Round Rock, TX
Beutel, Susan Marie ... Detroit, MI
Beutelschies, John P. ... Denver, CO
Beutelschies, Mark E. ... Memphis, TN
Beuth, Philip ... Las Vegas, NV
Beutler, Christopher J. ... Lincoln, NE
Beutler, Ernest A., Jr.
Newport Beach, CA
Beutler, Gloria M. ... Napa, CA
Beutler, Mark J. ... Springfield, VA
Beutler, Robert A., Jr. ... Findlay, OH
Beutler, Stacy T. ... Chicago, IL
Beutler, Stanley ... Indianapolis, IN
Beutler, Todd M. ... Columbus, OH
Beutler, Toija J ... Portland, OR
Beutner, Brian K. ... Minneapolis, MN
Beuttenmuller, Donald J., Jr.
West Palm Beach, FL
Beuttenmuller, Kevin C.
West Palm Beach, FL
Beuttenmuller, Marilyn N.
West Palm Beach, FL
Beuttenmuller, Rudolf W. ... Dallas, TX
Beutter, Robert C. ... Mishawaka, IN
Beutz, Michael C. ... Littleton, CO
Bevacqua, Barry F. ... Philadelphia, PA
Bevacqua, Peter P. ... New York, NY
Bevacqua, Renee L. ... Hartford, CT
Bevacqua, Vincent E. ... Newark, NJ
Bevan, Clark R. ... San Ramon, CA
Bevan, G. Richard ... Twin Falls, ID
Bevan, George L., Jr. ... San Francisco, CA
Bevan, John M., III ... San Francisco, CA
Bevan, John P. ... San Francisco, CA
Bevan, John S. ... Philadelphia, PA
Bevan, Keith D. ... Northfield, OH
Bevan, Kenneth V. ... Orlando, FL
Bevan, Kent M. ... Kansas City, MO
Bevan, Murray E. ... Hackettstown, NJ
Morristown, NJ
Trenton, NJ
Bevan, P. Michelle ... Cincinnati, OH
Bevan, Philip R. ... Washington, DC
Bevan, Robert L. ... Kansas City, MO
Bevan, Robert S. ... White Plains, NY
Bevan, Thomas R. ... Philadelphia, PA
Bevan, William, III ... Pittsburgh, PA
Bevans, Elaine W. ... Tucson, AZ
Bevans, Jane ... New York, NY
Bevans & Katten ... New York, NY
Bevans, Lloyd I. ... Waverly, NE
Bevans & Peréz-Medrano, P.C.
Tucson, AZ
Bevans, Robert T. ... Waltham, MA
Bevans, Ronald T., Jr. ... Miami, FL
Bevans, Russell D. ... Eugene, OR
Bevans, William B. ... Lincoln, NE
Bevash, Suzanne E. ... Oakland, CA
Bevel, Gregory Haynes ... Dallas, TX
Bevel, Henry J., III ... Waterloo, IA
Bevelacqua, Charles A.
Department of Commerce, GV
Bevelheimer, Mary Jane ... Westland, MI
Bevelhymer, Darlene P. ... Bowling Green, OH

Bevelock, Gregory J. ... New York, NY
Bevens, Gordon E. ... Waverly, OH
Bevens, William W. ... Waverly, OH
Bever, Amelia M. ... Atlanta, GA
Bever, Darla A. ... Parkersburg, WV
Bever, David W. ... Seattle, WA
Bever, Dye, Mustard & Belin, L.C.
Wichita, KS
Bever, John H. ... Berea, OH
Bever, Lloyd W. ... Seattle, WA
Bever, Mark Stephen ... Cincinnati, OH
Bever, Patrick T. ... San Jose, CA
Bever, Robert L. ... Richmond, IN
Bever, Thomas D. ... Atlanta, GA
Beverage, Charles B., Jr. ... Richmond, VA
Beverage, Cynthia Lopez
San Antonio, TX
Beverage, Gerald G. ... Rockland, ME
Beverage, James W. ... Atlanta, GA
Beverage, Laura E. ... Denver, CO
Beverage, Peter J. ... San Antonio, TX
Beverage, Roger M. ... Oklahoma City, OK
Bevere, Daniel R. ... Nutley, NJ
Beverick, Timothy A. ... Wichita, KS
Beveridge, Albert J., III ... Washington, DC
Beveridge, Brent E. ... Fairmont, WV
Beveridge, Brett W. ... Atlanta, GA
Beveridge, Cathy J. ... Tampa, FL
Beveridge, Charles P., Jr. ... Chicago, IL
Beveridge, DeGrandi, Weilacher & Young, L.L.P. ... Washington, DC
Beveridge & Diamond ... Saddle Brook, NJ
Beveridge & Diamond LLP
Sacramento, CA
San Francisco, CA
Beveridge & Diamond, P.C.
Washington, DC
Baltimore, MD
New York, NY
Beveridge, Diane C. ... Westbury, NY
Beveridge, James E. ... Erie, PA
Beveridge, Mark S. ... Nashville, TN
Beveridge, Norwood P. ... Oklahoma City, OK
Beveridge, Norwood P., III ... New York, NY
Beveridge, Paul F. ... Omaha, NE
Beveridge, R. Paul ... Seattle, WA
Beveridge, Ron ... Solana Beach, CA
Beveridge, Susan A. ... Los Angeles, CA
Beveridge, Thomas R. ... Paoli, PA
Beveridge, William, Jr. ... Baltimore, MD
Beverlin, Wesley G. ... Los Angeles, CA
Beverly, Brian ... Oakland, CA
Beverly, Brian O. ... Raleigh, NC
Beverly, Carol J. ... West Bend, WI
Beverly, Don ... West Palm Beach, FL
Beverly, Frank E. ... Moneta, VA
Beverly, George Donald
West Palm Beach, FL
Beverly, Harolyn D. ... Detroit, MI
Beverly, J. W. ... Houston, TX
Beverly Law Corporation ... Torrance, CA
Beverly, Melvin E. ... South Lake Tahoe, CA
Beverly, Michael D. ... Richmond, VA
Beverly, O. Terry ... Conway, SC
Beverly & Pause ... Chicago, IL
Beverly, Philip C. ... Jacksonville, FL
Beverly, Philip C., Jr. ... Gainesville, FL
Beverly, Richard A. ... Washington, DC
Beverly, Robert G. ... Los Angeles, CA
Beverly, Stephen A. ... Alpharetta, GA
Beverly, Thomas M. ... Jacksonville, FL
Beverly, Virginia Q. ... Jacksonville, FL
Beverly, Walter E., Jr. ... Alexandria, VA
Beverly, William C., Jr. ... Torrance, CA
Beverly, William J. ... Torrance, CA
Bevers, Denzil ... Lubbock, TX
Bevers, Michael E. ... Birmingham, AL
Beversdorff, Lance ... Austin, TX
Beverstein, Jack ... Valdosta, GA
Beverung, M. Steven ... Lake Charles, LA
Bevevino, Jodi K. ... Warren, PA
Bevevino, Timothy R. ... Warren, PA
Bevevino, William A. ... Warren, PA
Bevez, Brian W. ... Lansing, MI
Bevier, Debra J. ... San Diego, CA
Bevier, Lillian R. ... Charlottesville, VA
Bevier, Michael J. ... Charlottesville, VA
Bevier, Robin C., Law Offices of
Rancho Cordova, CA
Bevier, Robin C., Law Offices of
Sacramento, CA
Bevil, John E. ... New Braunfels, TX
Bevilacqua, Anne Marie
United States Tax Court, GV
Bevilacqua, Anthony J. ... Philadelphia, PA
Bevilacqua, Daniel ... Santa Ana, CA
Bevilacqua, Gabriel L. I. ... Philadelphia, PA
Bevilacqua, Gary F. ... Westfield, MA
Bevilacqua, Gary J. ... Phoenix, AZ
Bevilacqua, John J. ... Providence, RI
Bevilacqua, John Paul ... New York, NY
Bevilacqua, Louis A. ... Stamford, CT
Bevilacqua, Louis J. ... New York, NY
Bevilacqua, Michael J. ... Boston, MA
Bevilacqua & Pesto ... Westfield, MA
Bevilacqua, Thomas M. ... Houston, TX
Bevill, Staci Shumpert ... Tupelo, MS
Bevill, Tom ... Jasper, AL
Bevill, Tom R. ... Breckenridge, TX
Beville, Gene ... Grand Junction, CO
Beville, Lisa M. ... San Antonio, TX
Beville, Norborne P., Jr. ... Manassas, VA
BeVille, Peggy Burke ... Clearwater, FL
Beving, Donald L. ... Des Moines, IA
Beving, Swanson & Forrest, P.C.
Des Moines, IA
Johnston, IA
Bevington, Anne M. ... Oakland, CA

Bevington, Elizabeth ... Tallahassee, FL
Bevington, Maria D. ... Amelia, OH
Bevington, Paula Lawton ... Atlanta, GA
Bevins, David E. ... Grand Rapids, MI
Bevins, Don C. ... Salem, OR
Bevins, Douglas G. ... Brooksville, FL
Bevins, Kevin B. ... San Bernardino, CA
Bevins, Mary E. ... Laguna Hills, CA
Bevins, Michael Lee ... Okemos, MI
Bevins, Ronald H. ... Orange, CA
Bevins, Ronald H., Jr. ... Orange, CA
Bevis, Antonia S. ... Wilmington, DE
Bevis, Cameron & Johnson, P.A.
Boise, ID
Bevis, Donald Prichard, Jr. ... Dallas, TX
Bevis, George R. ... New York, NY
Bevis, James A. ... Boise, ID
Bevis, John W. ... Fairfax, VA
Bevis, Milton H. ... Quincy, FL
Bevis, Thomas E. ... New Smyrna Beach, FL
Bevis Langevin, Judith ... Minneapolis, MN
Bevon, Loretta Gernon ... Santa Barbara, CA
Bevon, V. Brian ... Charleston, SC
Bevza, Denise ... New London, CT
Bewers, Michael D. ... New Orleans, LA
Bewick, Joseph F. ... Los Angeles, CA
Bewig, Matthew S. R. ... Washington, DC
Bewig, Theresa D. ... Lacombe, LA
Bewkes, E. Garrett, Jr. ... New York, NY
Bewley, Charles A. ... Denver, CO
Bewley, George N., Jr. ... Fort Wayne, IN
Bewley, J. Michael ... San Jose, CA
Bewley & Koday ... Fort Wayne, IN
Bewley, Lassleben & Miller
Los Angeles, CA
Santa Ana, CA
Whittier, CA
Bewley, Lillie B. ... Oklahoma City, OK
Bewley, Lonnie L. ... New Orleans, LA
Bewley, Peter D. ... Oakland, CA
Bewley, Suzette E. ... Indianapolis, IN
Bewley, Victor ... San Gabriel, CA
Bewley, Victor D. ... San Gabriel, CA
Bex, Richard E. ... Reno, NV
Bexley, Harry ... Atlanta, GA
Bexley, Kendall A. ... Avondale Estates, GA
Bexley & Osofsky ... Avondale Estates, GA
Bexten, Richd. C. ... San Antonio, TX
Bey, Jeffrey D. ... Los Angeles, CA
Bey, Kelly A. ... Los Angeles, CA
Bey, Sheryl ... Jackson, MS
Beyda, C. Richard ... Washington, DC
Beyda, Cathy S. ... San Jose, CA
Beyda, Daniel ... New York, NY
Beyda, David R. ... Binghamton, NY
Beydoun, Rindala ... Ann Arbor, MI
Beye, Bruce W. ... Stilwell, KS
Beyea, Alison ... Portland, ME
Beyel, John P. ... Morristown, NJ
Beyer, Aaron J. ... Philadelphia, PA
Beyer, Albert G. ... St. Louis, MO
Beyer, Anne Gretchen ... Palo Alto, CA
Beyer, Anthony G.
Environmental Protection Agency,
Office of the General Counsel, GV
Beyer, Bret C. ... Lafayette, LA
Beyer, Bridget ... Mineola, NY
Riverhead, NY
Beyer, Carolyn J. ... Cedar Rapids, IA
Beyer, Christine
Department of Transportation,
Federal Railroad Administration, GV
Beyer, Dana J. ... Seymour, CT
Beyer, Daniel G. ... Detroit, MI
Beyer, David A. ... Tampa, FL
Beyer, David J. ... Louisville, KY
Beyer, David W. ... Buffalo, NY
Beyer, Donald J. ... Madison, WI
Beyer, Dorianne ... New York, NY
Beyer, ElizaBeth Webb ... Reno, NV
Beyer, Elyse Renee ... New York, NY
Beyer, Eric W. ... Duluth, MN
Beyer, Eugene E., Jr. ... New York, NY
Beyer, G. Scott ... Yakima, WA
Beyer, Garrett J. ... Seattle, WA
Beyer, Gerald D., Jr. ... Chicago, IL
Beyer, Gerry W. ... San Antonio, TX
Beyer, Gregory R. ... Sacramento, CA
Beyer, Hans Christian ... Tampa, FL
Beyer, Harold G., Jr. ... Delmar, NY
Beyer, Henry A. ... Boston, MA
Beyer, James E. ... Dayton, OH
Beyer, James R. ... Chicago, IL
Beyer, Jennifer E. ... Lafayette, LA
New Orleans, LA
Beyer, John A. ... Pontiac, IL
Beyer, John H. ... Charlotte, NC
Beyer, John H. ... Memphis, TN
Beyer, John William ... Lancaster, PA
Beyer, Jonathan M. ... New York, NY
Beyer, Kenneth D. ... Olympia, WA
Beyer, Kent S. ... Los Angeles, CA
Beyer, Kimberly Lynn ... Santa Ana, CA
Beyer, Laura T. ... Charlotte, NC
Beyer, Lawrence F. ... Boca Raton, FL
Beyer, Linda M. ... New York, NY
Beyer, Marci E. ... Roswell, NM
Beyer, Martin A. ... Williston Park, NY
Beyer, Martin A. ... Dayton, OH
Beyer, Mary L. ... Seattle, WA
Beyer, Mary M. ... Madison, WI
Beyer, McMahon & La Rue ... Phoenix, AZ
Beyer, Melvin E. ... Brookfield, WI
Beyer, Michael J. ... Vienna, VA
Beyer, Michael K. ... Napa, CA
Beyer, Michael R. ... Seattle, WA
Beyer, Neil ... Austin, TX
Beyer, Patricia A. ... Fresno, CA

Beyer, Pongratz & Rosen, A Prof. Law Corp., The Law Offices of ...Sacramento, CA
Beyer, Richard A. ...**Chicago, IL**
Beyer, Richard W. ...Morganton, NC
Beyer, Robert D. ...Lancaster, PA
Beyer, Roberta ...Albuquerque, NM
Beyer, Russell, P.A. ...**Fort Lauderdale, FL**
Beyer, Russell T. ...**Fort Lauderdale, FL**
Beyer, Ruth A. ...**Portland, OR**
Beyer, Stanley C. ...**Houston, TX**
Beyer, Stanley J. ...New York, NY
Beyer, Stephan V. ...**Chicago, IL**
Beyer, Stephen L. ...Scottsdale, AZ
Beyer, Stephen W. ...**Huntington, NY**
Beyer, Steve D ...**Mountain View, CA**
Beyer, Steven R. ...Chicago, IL
Beyer, Susan V. ...Denver, CO
Beyer, Teresa A. ...West Des Moines, IA
Beyer, Theodore H. ...Baldwin, NY
Beyer, Timothy R. ...**Denver, CO**
Beyer, Vicki W. ...**Princeton, NJ**
Beyer, Wayne C. ...North Conway, NH
Beyer, Wayne C., & Associates, P.C. North Conway, NH
Beyer, Wayne R. ...Leming, TX
Beyer Weave Thomas & Nguyen, LLP Monterey, CA
Beyer Weaver Thomas & Nguyen, LLP Berkeley, CA **Mountain View, CA**
Beyer, William C. ...Warsaw, NY
Beyer, William D. ...**Cleveland, OH**
Beyer, William E. ...Denver, CO
Beyer, William G. ...Phoenix, AZ
Beyer, William G. Pension Benefit Guaranty Corporation, Office of the General Counsel, GV
Beyer, William H. ...Detroit, MI
Beyerhelm, Ruth W. ...Omaha, NE
Beyerl, Edwin J. ...Schenectady, NY
Beyerl, Frank C. ...Belen, NM
Beyerle, John J. ...Brooklyn, OH
Beyers, Costin & Case, A Professional Corporation ...**Santa Rosa, CA**
Beyers, James L. ...**Santa Rosa, CA**
Beyers, Kenneth P. ...**Houston, TX**
Beyers, Maureen ...**Phoenix, AZ**
Beyers, Melanie Ryan ...**Bay City, MI**
Beyers, Robert J. ...Champaign, IL
Beyers, William C. ...Loveland, CO
Beyer-Savoca, Christine A. ...**Princeton, NJ**
Beyersdorf, Larry S. ...San Diego, CA
Beyersdorff, Christopher Paul ...Southfield, MI
Beyer-Ulrich, Cynthia M. ...**Denver, CO**
Beyhum, Hayat ...Miami, FL
Beylen, Lawrence H. ...Van Nuys, CA
Beyler, Clifford A. ...**Indianapolis, IN**
Beyler, Keith H. ...Carbondale, IL
Beylerian, Elda ...**Newark, NJ**
Beylerian, Felicia ...**New York, NY**
Beylotte, Ronald J. ...Houston, TX
Beylus, Neal ...Boca Raton, FL
Beyma, Michael J. ...**Rochester, NY**
Beyman, Richard A. ...**New York, NY**
Beyman, Susan B. ...Norwalk, CT
Beymer, Robert O. ...Muncie, IN
Beynart, Robert W. ...**Atlanta, GA**
Beynon, Kathleen T. ...**Rockford, IL**
Beyoglides, Harry G., Jr. ...Dayton, OH
Bey-Proctor, Charlene D. Merit Systems Protection Board, Office of Appeals Counsel, GV
Beystehner, John J. ...**Louisville, KY**
Beyt, Bernard E. ...Lafayette, LA
Beyt & Beyt, A Prof. Law Corp. Lafayette, LA
Beyt, Janice Daigre ...Lafayette, LA
Beyt, Raymond A. ...Lafayette, LA
Beytagh, Ann Waters ...Dallas, TX
Beytagh, Francis X., Jr. ...Columbus, OH
Beytin, Kenneth A. ...**Tampa, FL**
Beytin, Susan A. ...Los Angeles, CA
Bez, Andrea T. ...**Houston, TX**
Bezack, Ira ...Melville, NY
Bezahler, Donald J. ...**New York, NY**
Bezaire, Maria ...Torrance, CA
Bezak, Elizabeth M. ...**Munster, IN**
Bezanson, Dennis G. ...Portsmouth, NH
Bezanson, Randall P. ...Iowa City, IA
Bezanson, Thomas E. ...**New York, NY**
Bezar, Nadeem A. ...**Philadelphia, PA**
Bezark, Brian R. ...Philadelphia, PA
Bezark, Fred ...Northbrook, IL
Bezark, Sean W. ...**Chicago, IL**
Bezas, G. Elaine Rochester, MI **Troy, MI**
Bezdecki, Edward F. ...Toms River, NJ
Bezdicek, Coreen K. ...**Des Moines, IA**
Bezdichek & Densberger ...Concord, MA
Bezdichek, Kathleen B. ...Concord, MA
Bezek, Peter J. ...**Santa Barbara, CA**
Bezemek, Robert J. ...Oakland, CA
Bezerra, Ryan S. ...**Sacramento, CA**
Bezet, Gary A. ...**Baton Rouge, LA**
Bezich, Anthony M. ...Haddonfield, NJ
Bezikos, Lynne A. ...**New York, NY**
Bezinque, Mark Chauvin ...**Rochester, NY**
Bezis, Cheryl D. ...Boston, MA
Bezjian, June E., (Miss) ...Medford, MA
Bezkorovainy, Anatoly ...Lincolnwood, IL
Bezman, Victor H., (P.C.) ...**Chicago, IL**
Bezman, Victoria ...Los Angeles, CA
Bezner, Karen E. ...Scotch Plains, NJ
Bezney, Michael A. ...Chicago, IL
Bezney, Paul A. ...**Dallas, TX**
Beznos, Harold ...Detroit, MI
Bezold, Clement L., Jr. ...Newport, KY
Bezold, George W. ...Milwaukee, WI
Bezold, Richard M. ...**Miami, FL**
Bezou, Jacques F., (A Prof. Law Corp.) **Covington, LA** **New Orleans, LA**
Bezou & Matthews ...**Covington, LA** **New Orleans, LA**
Bezouska, Robert F. ...Chicago, IL
Bezozi, Alan M. ...New York, NY
Bezozo, Kenneth K. ...**Dallas, TX**
Bezubka, John, Jr ...Providence, RI
Bezucha, Robert H. ...**Dallas, TX**
Bezuhly, Maureen ...**New York, NY**
Bezy, Vicki ...Worthington, OH
Bezz, Gregory J. ...**Hartford, CT**
Bezzeg, John E. ...Grants, NM
Bhachu, Amarjeet S. ...**Chicago, IL**
Bhagat, Nimmo ...**Memphis, TN**
Bhagwat, Ashutosh A. ...San Francisco, CA
Bhakar, Vid ...**Campbell, CA**
Bhakta, Kushal S. ...**Los Angeles, CA**
Bhalla, Amardeep S. ...**Cranford, NJ**
Bhalla, Ravinder S. ...Newark, NJ
Bhalla, Sabina ...**Los Angeles, CA**
Bhambhani, Frances M. ...**Washington, DC**
Bhambhani, Sanjay M. Department of Justice, Civil Division, GV
Bhamre, Hema Christine **Newport Beach, CA**
Bhandari, J. S. ...Pittsburgh, PA
Bhandari, Prabha Sipi ...**New York, NY**
Bhandari, Sanjay ...Menlo Park, CA
Bhanji, Azmeena ...Sacramento, CA
Bhansali, Asim M. ...**Houston, TX**
Bharam, Durga M. ...**Chicago, IL**
Bharara, Preetinder S. ...**New York, NY**
Bharara, Vinit ...**New York, NY**
Bharathi, S. Priya ...**Houston, TX**
Bhargava, Manoj ...**New York, NY**
Bhasin, Anoop K. ...Charleston, WV
Bhat, Shamala J. ...Silver Spring, MD
Bhatia, Karan ...**Washington, DC**
Bhatia, Shilpa ...**Seattle, WA**
Bhatia, Sudeep Kumar ...Barbourville, KY
Bhatia, Veenita ...**Philadelphia, PA**
Bhatia, Vineet ...**Houston, TX**
Bhatnagar, Mary E. ...San Mateo, CA
Bhatt, Minaksi ...**Seattle, WA**
Bhatt, Sanjay K. ...Columbus, OH
Bhatt, Sanjay L. ...Lihue, HI
Bhattacharya, Jay ...**Dallas, TX**
Bhattacharya, Rasmani ...**Houston, TX**
Bhattacharyya, Rupa ...Department of Justice, Civil Division, GV
Bhavsar & Comellas, P.A. ...Orlando, FL
Bhavsar, Kashmira I. ...Orlando, FL
Bhavsar, Samir A. ...**Dallas, TX**
Bhavsar, Saumya R. ...Treasury Department, Office of the Comptroller of the Currency, GV
Bhaya, Shakuntla L. ...**Wilmington, DE**
Bhayani, Minaz A. ...San Diego, CA
Bhirdo, Kelly W. ...Sunnyvale, CA
Bhisitkul, Thomas ...**Boston, MA**
Bhogal, Balbir ...**Santa Clara, CA**
Bhouraskar, Megha ...**New York, NY**
Bhowmik, Rachana ...Washington, DC
Bhumralkar, Shailendra C. Mountain View, CA
Bhushan, Raj ...Brooklyn, NY
Biaett, Kenneth ...Sun Lakes, AZ
Biafora, Joseph R. ...**Woodland Hills, CA**
Biafora, Weiner & Lampert **Los Angeles, CA** **Woodland Hills, CA**
Biafore, John D. ...**Providence, RI**
Biafore, Joseph F., Jr. ...San Jose, CA
Biafore, Joseph L., Jr. ...Stratford, CT
Biafore, Lani L. ...Visalia, CA
Biafore, Thomas J. ...**Atlanta, GA**
Biagas, Barbara E. ...San Francisco, CA
Biagetti, Peter A. ...**Boston, MA**
Biaggi Busquets & Mari Roca, Bufete Mayaguez, PR
Biaggi, Jaime V. ...Mayaguez, PR
Biaggi, Patricia A. ...**San Juan, PR**
Biaggi, Richard M. ...New York, NY
Biaggi, Scott K. ...**Tucson, AZ**
Biaggi García, Nelson ...San Juan, PR
Biagi, George N., III ...Atlantic City, NJ
Biagi, James B. ...**Goshen, NY**
Biagi, James F., Jr. ...**Seattle, WA**
Biagi, Joseph A. ...Shelbyville, KY
Biagi, Karen G. ...**Huntsville, AL**
Biagianti, Diane Wasil ...Orange, CA
Biagiarelli, Lisa Anne P. ...Stratford, CT
Biagini, Bruce J. ...**Macomb, IL**
Biagini, Marc J. ...Burr Ridge, IL
Biagini, Raymond B. ...**Washington, DC**
Biagini, Theodore J. ...**San Jose, CA**
Biagioli, John A. ...**Independence, MO**
Biagiotti, Marino, Montecallo & Farrington, P.C. ...Hackensack, NJ
Biagiotti, Robert M. ...Hackensack, NJ
Bial, Ernest L. ...**New York, NY**
Bialac, James T. ...**Phoenix, AZ**
Bialas, Irene E. ...Milwaukee, WI
Bialas, Kathleen M. Department of Housing and Urban Development, Office of General Counsel, GV
Bialas, Kimberly Thomas **Grand Rapids, MI**
Bialczak, Stanley T. ...Columbus, OH
Bialczak Musso, Patricia ...**Southfield, MI**
Bialecki, Bernard John, Jr. Kennett Square, PA
Bialecki, Gregory P. ...**Boston, MA**
Bialecki, Korleen Marie ...Holland, OH
Bialecki, Scott Robert ...Denver, CO
Bialek, Benjamin M. ...Rockville, MD
Bialek, Jay ...Nanuet, NY
Bialek, Mark Department of State, GV
Bialek, Mitchell R. ...Naperville, IL
Bialek, Scott E. ...San Antonio, TX
Bialek, Scott E. ...San Antonio, TX
Bialer, Bruce A. ...Cleveland, OH
Bialick, Barry E. ...San Jose, CA
Bialick, Mark E. ...**Oklahoma City, OK**
Bialick, Steven M., Law Office of **Minneapolis, MN**
Bialik, Ezra I. ...**New York, NY**
Bialik, Leslie J. ...Martinez, CA
Bialka, Walter S. ...Chicago, IL
Bialke, David M. ...**Minneapolis, MN**
Bialkin, Kenneth J. ...**New York, NY**
Bialkin, Lisa B. ...**New York, NY**
Bialko, Barbara A. ...Lansing, MI
Bialkowski, Charles V. ...Houston, TX
Bialkowski, Stephen W. ...Hackensack, NJ
Bialkowski, Zygmunt R., Jr. **Philadelphia, PA** **Scranton, PA**
Bialla, Rowley ...Northport, NY
Bialo, Katherine A. ...**Larchmont, NY**
Bialo, Kenneth M. ...**New York, NY**
Bialon, Franklin L. ...Monessen, PA
Bialo-Padin, Deirdre ...Brooklyn, NY
Bialosky, Adam Louis ...Treasury Department, Office of the Comptroller of the Currency, GV
Bialosky, David L. ...**Cleveland, OH**
Bialosky, Herbert S. ...Cleveland, OH
Bialostok, Lee ...New York, NY
Bialson, Annette G., (Inc.) ...**Palo Alto, CA**
Bialson, Bergen & Schwab ...**Palo Alto, CA** **San Jose, CA**
Bialson, James T. ...Campbell, CA
Bialy, Marjorie A. ...**Buffalo, NY**
Bialy, Rosalie J. ...Andover, MA
Bian, Eugene N. ...Springfield, IL
Bianca, Briana ...Shreveport, LA
Bianca, Daniel M. ...**New York, NY**
Biancamano, J. Keith ...**Los Angeles, CA**
Biancamano, John J. ...Columbus, OH
Biancardi, Linda D. ...Hackensack, NJ
Biancardi, Paul A. ...**Houston, TX**
Bianchi, A. Michael ...Omaha, NE
Bianchi, Albert ...**San Rafael, CA**
Bianchi, Albert V. ...Hauppauge, NY
Bianchi, Alden J. ...**Worcester, MA**
Bianchi, Alfred J. ...Seattle, WA
Bianchi, Angelo R. ...Nutley, NJ
Bianchi, Anthony G. ...Long Island City, NY
Bianchi & Bianchi ...Nutley, NJ
Bianchi, Bruno ...Bronx, NY
Bianchi, Carl F. ...Boise, ID
Bianchi, Carlos J. ...**New York, NY**
Bianchi, Christopher A. North Wildwood, NJ
Bianchi, David C., II ...Midland, TX
Bianchi, David J. ...**Peoria, IL**
Bianchi, David W. ...**Lancaster, CA**
Bianchi, David W. ...**Miami, FL**
Bianchi, Dominic L. ...**Washington, DC**
Bianchi, George L. ...Seattle, WA
Bianchi, George R. ...Oakland, CA
Bianchi, Gina L. ...Albany, NY
Bianchi, Henry E. ...Bakersfield, CA
Bianchi, Jaime A. ...**Miami, FL**
Bianchi, James L. ...Benicia, CA
Bianchi, James S. ...Los Angeles, CA
Bianchi, Janet S. ...Acton, MA
Bianchi, John F. ...Tarrytown, NY
Bianchi, Keegin, Talkington, Harrison & Schoppert LLP ...**San Rafael, CA**
Bianchi, Kerri E. ...Great Neck, NY
Bianchi & Lagarde, P.C. ...**Houston, TX**
Bianchi Law Firm, The ...Seattle, WA
Bianchi, LeRoy L. ...Schaumburg, IL
Bianchi, Louis A. ...**Woodstock, IL**
Bianchi, Marc D. ...Jenkintown, PA
Bianchi, Maria ...Albany, NY
Bianchi, Mark ...**Boston, MA** **Providence, RI**
Bianchi, Martha H. ...Dover, NJ
Bianchi & Paquin ...Hyannis, MA
Bianchi, Patricia E. ...Winfield, IL
Bianchi, Peter C., Jr. ...Miami, FL
Bianchi, Richard P. ...**Houston, TX**
Bianchi, Robert A. ...Hyannis, MA
Bianchi, Robert A. ...Nutley, NJ
Bianchi, Robert C. ...Cleveland, OH
Bianchi, Ronald B. ...White Plains, NY
Bianchi, Ronald F. ...Arlington, VA
Bianchi, Sal M. ...Oakbrook Terrace, IL
Bianchi, Timothy E. ...**Minneapolis, MN**
Bianchi-Jones, Erica ...Phoenix, AZ
Bianchin, Sheri L. ...Chicago, IL
Bianchini, Gino J. ...Coto De Caza, CA
Bianchini & McDonald **Hummelstown, PA** **York, PA**
Bianchini, Michael P. ...**York, PA**
Bianchini, Victor E. ...El Cajon, CA
Bianchino, Anthony J. ...Woodbury, NY
Bianchino, Bernard A. ...Denver, CO
Bianciella, Anthony J. ...**Florham Park, NJ**
Bianco, Alan Richard ...Mineola, NY
Bianco, Alfred J. ...**New York, NY**
Bianco, Angelo J. ...**New York, NY**
Bianco & Bianco ...Ridgewood, NY
Bianco, Chas. M. ...Brooklyn, NY
Bianco, Christopher J. ...Rochester, MN
Bianco, D. ...Bakersfield, CA
Bianco, David F. ...Forest City, PA
Bianco, Deborah A. ...Seattle, WA
Bianco, Deborah L. ...Denver, CO
Bianco, Dominic J. ...Steubenville, OH
Bianco, Dominic P. ...**Mineola, NY**
Bianco, Elizabeth Ashley ...**Riverside, CA** **San Bernardino, CA**
Bianco, Frank P. ...New Port Richey, FL
Bianco, Fred J., Jr. ...Peekskill, NY
Bianco, Gregory J. ...San Diego, CA
Bianco, Gregory O. ...**San Francisco, CA**
Bianco, James N. ...Santa Monica, CA
Bianco, James W. ...Golden Valley, MN
Bianco, Joanne M. ...Fairfield, NJ
Bianco, John G., III ...**Tampa, FL**
Bianco, John Philip ...Visalia, CA
Bianco, John V. ...**Boston, MA**
Bianco, Joseph F. ...New York, NY
Bianco, Joseph G. ...Short Hills, NJ
Bianco, Kathleen M. ...Riverwoods, IL
Bianco, Laura ...Brooklyn, NY
Bianco Law Firm ...Visalia, CA
Bianco, Lynne M. ...**Philadelphia, PA**
Bianco, Michele J. ...**Washington, DC**
Bianco & Murphy ...**San Francisco, CA**
Bianco, Paul D. ...**Washington, DC**
Bianco, Philip S. ...Visalia, CA
Bianco, Richard A. ...Tampa, FL
Bianco, Robert L. ...**San Francisco, CA**
Bianco, Robert M. ...Pittsburgh, PA
Bianco, Ronni S. ...Washington, DC
Bianco, S. Anthony ...**New York, NY**
Bianco, Sal A. ...White Plains, NY
Bianco, Theodore P. ...Lilburn, GA
Bianco, Theodore P., P.C. ...Lilburn, GA
Bianco, Thomas J. ...**Jericho, NY**
Bianco, Thomas M. ...Indiana, PA
Bianco, Vito L. ...**Parsippany, NJ**
Bianco, William A. ...**Denver, CO**
Bianco, William A. ...**Washington, DC**
Bianco, William F. ...Ridgewood, NY
Bianco, William J. ...Omaha, NE
Bianco, William T. ...Ridgewood, NY
Biancola, Frank A. ...**Short Hills, NJ**
Biancone, Louis ...New York, NY
Biancone & Wilinsky, LLP ...New York, NY
Bianconi, Lynne Schmidt ...Pittsburgh, PA
Bianculli, Joseph L. ...Arlington, VA
Bianculli, Pasquale E. ...Philadelphia, PA
Bianculli-Savage, Diane M. ...Cary, NC
Bianucci, Larry R. ...Reno, NV
Biard, David J. ...Plano, TX
Biard, John Andrew ...San Francisco, CA
Biard, Michael W. ...**Los Angeles, CA**
Biard, Robert F. ...**Austin, TX**
Biard, Webb ...Paris, TX
Biars, Mark M. ...Cleveland, OH
Bias, Dana G. ...Frankfort, KY
Bias, Sara F. ...Frankfort, KY
Biase, Lisa A. ...**Woodbridge, NJ**
Biasella, Joseph M., Jr. ...San Jose, CA
Biasetti, Jon ...**Chicago, IL**
Biasotti, David E. ...Hayward, CA
Biasotti, Robert E. ...**St. Petersburg, FL**
Biatch, Joel A. ...**Oakland, CA**
Biava, James E. ...**Malibu, CA**
Biba, Paul K. ...Bernardsville, NJ
Bibart, Richard L. ...**Columbus, OH**
Bibaud, Timothy M. ...Worcester, MA
Bibb, Ashley M. ...**Tulsa, OK**
Bibb, Benjamin C., Jr. ...Portland, OR
Bibb, Brenda M. ...Nashville, TN
Bibb, David H. ...Decatur, AL
Bibb, Edgar E., III ...**Beckley, WV**
Bibb, Eleanor B. ...Wichita Falls, TX
Bibb, John Randolph, Jr. ...**Nashville, TN**
Bibb, John T. ...**Houston, TX**
Bibb, Julian L. ...**Nashville, TN**
Bibb, Michael C. ...Sicklerville, NJ
Bibb, Peyton D., Jr. ...**Birmingham, AL**
Bibb, Robert C. ...**Everett, WA**
Bibb, William C. ...Anniston, AL
Bibbens, Lisa S. ...Tucson, AZ
Bibbens, Matthew G. ...**Greensboro, NC**
Bibbes, Gregory D. ...**San Francisco, CA**
Bibbins, Deborah M. ...**Hartford, CT**
Bibbins, Odessa Bradley ...Elizabeth City, NC
Bibbo, Jeffrey R. ...Columbus, OH
Bibbs, Peggy L. ...Terre Haute, IN
Bibby & Good ...**Charleston, WV**
Bibby, James A., Jr. ...**Charleston, WV**
Bibby, John F., Jr. ...**Chicago, IL**
Bibeau, Brian H. ...**Tallahassee, FL**
Bibeau, Fred A. ...Phoenix, AZ
Bibeau, Mark J. ...Tewksbury, MA
Bibeau, Paul H. ...Farmington Hills, MI
Biben, James H. ...Rochester, NY
Biben, Matthew Lee ...New York, NY
Biber, Aaron F. ...**Minneapolis, MN**
Biber, Michael J. ...Troy, MI
Biberaj & Associates ...Leesburg, VA
Biberaj, Buta ...Leesburg, VA
Biberfeld, Ellen J. ...San Francisco, CA
Biberfeld, Stefan Ernst ...**Seattle, WA**
Biberman, Serge ...**Chicago, IL**
Biberstein, Mark A. ...**Wichita, KS**
Biberstein & Nunalee Hampstead, NC **Burgaw, NC**
Biberstein, Richard von, Jr. ...**Burgaw, NC**
Biberstein, Robert L. ...Berne, IN
Bibey, Stephen A. ...Carthage, NC
Bibi, Mark L. ...Hackensack, NJ
Bibicoff, Hillary S. ...**Los Angeles, CA**
Bibik, Frederick P. ...Louisville, CO
Bibisi, Joseph W. ...Hartford, CT
Bibko, Edward A. ...**Chicago, IL**
Bibko, Peter N. ...Gramercy, LA

Bible, Hoy & Trachok, A Professional Corporation ... **Reno, NV**
Bible, Jerry B. ... Jasper, TX
Bible, John J. ... Redwood City, CA
Bible, Kathy J. ... Tallahassee, FL
Bible, Paul A. ... **Reno, NV**
Bible, Robert W., Jr. ... Tampa, FL
Bible, W. Thomas, Jr. ... **Chattanooga, TN**
Bibler, A. David ... Algona, IA
Bibler, Gregory A. ... **Boston, MA**
Bibler, R. Alan ... Topeka, KS
Bibler, R. Mark ... **Lancaster, OH**
Bibles, Camille D. ... Flagstaff, AZ
Biblin, Allan E., (A Professional Corporation) ... **Los Angeles, CA**
Biblin, Dina L.
Federal Deposit Insurance Corporation, Trial Litigation Section, GV
Biblo, Larry A. ... Plainview, NY
Biblow, Charlotte ... **Uniondale, NY**
Biblowit, Charles E. ... Jamaica, NY
Bibona, John M. ... **New York, NY**
Bibro, Mark ... **New York, NY**
Bibus, Thomas W. ... Apple Valley, MN
Bibus, Thomas Wm. ... Cincinnati, OH
Bica, Carole M. ... Salem, OH
Bice, Charles B. ... Winnfield, LA
Bice, David B. ... Lynchburg, VA
Bice, Debra L.
Department Of Health And Human Services, Social Security Administration, GV
Bice, Jean A. ... Ocala, FL
Bice, Keith A. ... **Indianapolis, IN**
Bice, Laurie J ... **Flemington, NJ**
Bice, Mark A. ... Windsor, NY
Bice, Michael R. ... **New York, NY**
Bice, Noley R., Jr. ... Waco, TX
Bice, Thomas J. ... **Fort Dodge, IA**
Bice, Timothy R. ... Santa Monica, CA
Bice, Todd L. ... **Las Vegas, NV**
Bice-Hightower, Diane ... Meridian, TX
Bichimer, Raymond A. ... **Columbus, OH**
Bichl, Francis G., Jr. ... La Salle, IL
Bichler, Charles M. ... **St. Paul, MN**
Bichler, Geoffrey ... Winter Park, FL
Bichler, Geoffrey, P.A. ... Winter Park, FL
Bichler, Howard J. ... Rice Lake, WI
Bichler, Randel I. ... Wells, MN
Bichler, Robert H. ... **Racine, WI**
Bichoupan, Abraham Abie ... New York, NY
Bichoupan, Carolyn Corn ... Carle Place, NY
Bick, Alan N. ... **Irvine, CA**
Bick, Catherine J. ... **Newark, NJ**
Bick, Donald A. ... Eugene, OR
Bick, James P., Jr. ... **St. Louis, MO**
Bick, Jeffrey R. ... **Indianapolis, IN**
Bick, John A. ... **New York, NY**
Bick, Jonathan D. ... **Roseland, NJ**
Bick, Kenneth R. ... Reno, NV
Bick, Kimberly L. ... **Irvine, CA**
Bick, Mario ... Davie, FL
Bick & Monte, P.C. ... Eugene, OR
Florence, OR
Bick, Robert S. ... **Birmingham, MI**
Bick, Stephen R. ... **Superior, WI**
Bick, Thomas K. ... **Washington, DC**
Bick, Vincent F., Jr. ... **Winston-Salem, NC**
Bickal, Ellen J. ... **New York, NY**
Bickal, Jean M. ... Trenton, NJ
Bickart, Allen B. ... Phoenix, AZ
Bickart, David O. ... **Washington, DC**
Bickel, Allison L. ... **Orlando, FL**
Bickel, Anne E. ... **Carlsbad, CA**
Bickel, Arthur S. ... Irvine, CA
Bickel & Associates ... **Piedmont, CA**
San Francisco, CA
Bickel, Branden E. ... **Piedmont, CA**
Bickel & Brewer ... **Chicago, IL**
New York, NY
Dallas, TX
Bickel, Bruce D. ... Fresno, CA
Bickel, Bruce P. ... Ames, IA
Bickel, David R. ... Department of Justice, Antitrust Division, GV
Bickel, Dwight A. ... Seattle, WA
Bickel, Dwight F. ... Meridian, ID
Bickel, James R. ... **Nevada, MO**
Bickel, John ... **Owensboro, KY**
Bickel, John H. ... **San Francisco, CA**
Bickel, John M. ... **Cedar Rapids, IA**
Bickel, John W., II ... **Chicago, IL**
New York, NY
Dallas, TX
Bickel, Lisa Morganstern ... **Phoenix, AZ**
Bickel, Louis P. ... **Dallas, TX**
Bickel, Lurline Sampson ... San Francisco, CA
Bickel, Mark P. ... **Traverse City, MI**
Bickel, Oliver Lincoln ... Plattsburgh, NY
Bickel, Riva Wenig ... Irvine, CA
Bickel, Robert D. ... St. Petersburg, FL
Bickel, Roger H. ... **Chicago, IL**
Springfield, IL
Bickel, Sandra K. ... **Indianapolis, IN**
Bickel, Stephen D. ... Houston, TX
Bickel, Steven B. ... Santa Ana, CA
Bickel, Todd A. ... **Chicago, IL**
Bickel, William W. ... Towson, MD
Bickelhaupt, Kathleen M. ... **Tampa, FL**
Bickelman, Richard D. ... **Boston, MA**
Bickenbach, Joan M. ... Los Angeles, CA
Bickenbach, Paul H. ... Manhattan Beach, CA
Bickerman Dispute Resolution Group, PLLC
Washington, DC
Bickerman, John G. ... Washington, DC
Bickerman, Peter B. ... **Augusta, ME**
Bickers, John M. ... Sackets Harbor, NY
Bickers, Kathleen Louise ... Portland, OR
Bickers, Thomas Alan ... **Knoxville, TN**
Bickerstaff, Alan D. ... Houston, TX
Bickerstaff, Heath, Smiley, Pollan, Kever & McDaniel, L.L.P. ... **Austin, TX**
Dallas, TX
Bickerstaff, Joan H. ... Melbourne, FL
Bickerstaff, Kelly R. ... Dallas, TX
Bickerstaff, Linda L. ... Cleveland, OH
Bickerstaff, Steve ... **Austin, TX**
Bickersteth, Kimberly A.
Bloomfield Hills, MI
Bickert, Russell G. ... **Mount Holly, NJ**
Bickerton, Brion A. ... Boston, MA
Bickerton & Gordon LLC ... Boston, MA
Bickerton, James J. ... **Honolulu, HI**
Bickerton, Marianne Hughes ... Boston, MA
Bickerton, Saunders, Dang & Bouslog
Honolulu, HI
Bickerton, Terry S. ... **San Antonio, TX**
Bickes, Kurt B. ... **Decatur, IL**
Bickes, Wayne L. ... **Decatur, IL**
Bickes, Wilson & Moss ... **Decatur, IL**
Bicket, Alexander P. ... **Pittsburgh, PA**
Bicket, Robin L. ... **Nashville, TN**
Bicket, Susan M. ... **Pittsburgh, PA**
Bickett, James L. ... Cleveland, OH
Bickett, Paula S. ... Phoenix, AZ
Bickett, Ronald P. ... Bakersfield, CA
Bickett, William W., II ... Akron, OH
Bickford, Ann ... **New York, NY**
Bickford, Barbara Jean ... Chapel Hill, NC
Bickford, Dorothy M. ... **Boston, MA**
Bickford, G. Thomas ... Greenwich, CT
Rye Brook, NY
Bickford, George B. ... East Granby, CT
Bickford, Harry L., Law Office
Ardmore, OK
Bickford, James D. ... Chambersburg, PA
Bickford, Magdalen Blessey ... Metairie, LA
Bickford, Marc A. ... Wautoma, WI
Bickford, Michael A. ... **Oklahoma City, OK**
Bickford, Nancy J. ... San Diego, CA
Bickford, Nathaniel J. ... **New York, NY**
Bickford, Peter H. ... **New York, NY**
Bickford, Robert C. ... Cold Spring, NY
Bickford, Robert D., Jr. ... **Parsippany, NJ**
New York, NY
Bickford, Rosemary A. ... Gretna, LA
Bickford, Scott R. ... **New Orleans, LA**
Bickford, Stephen M. ... **San Francisco, CA**
Bickford, Warren F., IV
Oklahoma City, OK
Bickham, Brent Marshall ... Pascagoula, MS
Bickham, Dana S. ... **Boulder, CO**
Bickham, David A. ... **Houston, TX**
Bickham, David A., P.C. ... **Houston, TX**
Bickham, Gary Draper ... **St. Louis, MO**
Bickham, J. David ... **Oakland, CA**
Bickham, J. David, Jr. ... **Austin, TX**
Bickham, Jeffrey E. ... Houston, TX
Bickham, Jonathan T. ... **Houston, TX**
Bickham, Luke F. ... **Tyler, TX**
Bickham, Timothy C. ... **Kansas City, MO**
Bickham, W. Bradley ... **Dallas, TX**
Bickham, W. Kent ... Midland, TX
Bickhaus, Michael A. ... **Quincy, IL**
Bicki, Richard C. ... Providence, RI
Bickle, Gregory L. ... Minneapolis, MN
Bickler, George L. ... Hartsdale, NY
Bickler, Marc H. ... Lauderhill, FL
Bickler, Sharon G. ... Great Neck, NY
Bickler, Timothy G. ... **Salem, OR**
Bickley, Don C. ... Cardiff-By-The-Sea, CA
Bickley & Hart ... Schaumburg, IL
Bickley, Jacobs & Barkus ... Charleston, WV
Bickley, Jennifer A. ... **Elkhart, IN**
Bickley, John H., III ... Schaumburg, IL
Bickley, John H., Jr. ... Libertyville, IL
Bickley, John J. ... Cincinnati, OH
Bickley, L. Rex ... Harrisburg, PA
Bickley, N. Alex ... Dallas, TX
Bickley, Neil A. ... Richardson, TX
Bickley, Nelson R. ... Charleston, WV
Bickley, Susan L. ... **Houston, TX**
Bickmore, Danford E. Lloyd ... Roanoke, TX
Bicknell, David G. ... Los Gatos, CA
Bicknell, Donald R., Jr.
North Palm Beach, FL
Bicknell, Donald W. ... **Eureka, CA**
Bicknell, Hughes and Winter, P.C. ... Clare, MI
Bicknell, James E. ... Denver, CO
Pueblo, CO
Bicknell, James S., III ... Clare, MI
Bicknell, John Harlow ... Huntington, WV
Bicknell, Kris D. ... Golden, CO
Bicknell, Mary D. ... **Shreveport, LA**
Bicknell & Smith ... Cambridge, MA
Bickner, Bruce P. ... De Kalb, IL
Bickner & Delves ... Jacksonville, FL
Orange Park, FL
Bickner, J. Bruce, P.A. ... Jacksonville, FL
Orange Park, FL
Bicknese, Jennifer A. ... Iowa Falls, IA
Bicknese, Karsten ... **Atlanta, GA**
Bicks, David P., (P.C.) ... **New York, NY**
Bicks, James H. ... **Stamford, CT**
Bicks, Jill D. ... New York, NY
Bicks, Mark S. ... **Washington, DC**
Bicks, Nathan A. ... **Memphis, TN**
Bicks, Peter A. ... **New York, NY**
Bicks, Robert A. ... **New York, NY**
Bicksler, Diana Guido ... San Francisco, CA
Bickwit, Leonard, Jr. ... **Washington, DC**
Bicocchi, LisaAnne Rega ... **New York, NY**
Bida, John F. ... Arlington, TX
Bidar, Mohammed J. ... **Cleveland, OH**
Bidari, Jayashree T. ... Cleveland, OH
Bidari, R. Thomas ... Wyandotte, MI
Bidari, R. Thomas, P.C. ... Wyandotte, MI
Bidart, Michael J., (P.C.) ... **Claremont, CA**
Biddinger, F. James ... Indianapolis, IN
Biddinger, Michael J. ... Ada, OH
Biddinger, Michelle P. ... Cass City, MI
Biddison, Alan M. ... Richmond, VA
Biddison, James A., Jr. ... Cockeysville, MD
Biddison, Mark E. ... **Boulder, CO**
Biddison, Thomas N., Jr. ... **Baltimore, MD**
Biddle, Anthony S. ... Texarkana, AR
Biddle, B. Diane ... Wartburg, TN
Biddle, Barbara Cozad
Department of Justice, Civil Division, GV
Biddle, Barry D. ... **Atlanta, GA**
Biddle, Carl M. ... Carmichaels, PA
Biddle, Charles R. ... Dallas, TX
Biddle, Claude L., Jr. ... Auburn, CA
Biddle & Colletti, P.C. ... **Ardmore, PA**
Philadelphia, PA
Biddle, Darol ... Pueblo, CO
Biddle, Delwyn G. ... Loon Lake, WA
Biddle, Elizabeth E. ... **Rockland, ME**
Biddle, Eric H., Jr. ... Arlington, VA
Biddle, Frank Oliver ... Laguna Beach, CA
Biddle, G. Brooks ... Bothell, WA
Biddle, Grafton M. ... Aurora, CO
Biddle & Hamilton ... Sacramento, CA
Biddle, J. Gary ... Santa Fe, NM
Biddle, James F. ... Dallas, TX
Biddle, James H. ... Indianapolis, IN
Biddle, Jeffrey A. ... San Francisco, CA
Biddle, Jonathan W., Law Offices of
Beverly Hills, CA
Biddle, Jonathan W., Law Offices of
Los Angeles, CA
Biddle, Laura Respess ... **Washington, DC**
Biddle, Mark H. ... **Ardmore, PA**
Biddle, Maurice F. ... Harrisonburg, VA
Biddle, Michael Gerald ... Emeryville, CA
Biddle, Oliver Caldwell ... Philadelphia, PA
Biddle, Ray E. ... Tustin, CA
Biddle, Rita J. ... Lansing, MI
Biddle, Robert W. ... Baltimore, MD
Biddle, Stephen F. ... Ketchum, ID
Biddle, Steven G. ... **Phoenix, AZ**
Biddle, Thomas W. ... Newark, NY
Biddle, Timothy M. ... **Washington, DC**
Biddle, Todd A. ... **Huntington, WV**
Biddle, Veronica M. ... Fort Lauderdale, FL
Biddle, W. Craig ... Sacramento, CA
Biddle, William P., III ... **Athens, TN**
Biddlecome, George W. ... Goshen, IN
Biddlecome, Mona W. ... Elkhart, IN
Biddlestone, William R., Jr. ... Athens, OH
Bideau, David J. ... Chanute, KS
Bideau, Edwin H., III ... Chanute, KS
Bideau Law Offices ... Chanute, KS
Bideau, Mark F. ... **West Palm Beach, FL**
Bideaux, Lisa A. ... Binghamton, NY
Bidegaray, Anna M. ... **Sidney, MT**
Bidegaray, Daniel B. ... **Sidney, MT**
Bidegaray Law Firm, LLP ... **Sidney, MT**
Bidelman, Marlene J. ... **Pittsburgh, PA**
Bidelspacher & Bidelspacher
Williamsport, PA
Bidelspacher, C. R. ... Williamsport, PA
Biden, Joseph R., Jr. ... Wilmington, DE
Biden, Sara Jones ... **Philadelphia, PA**
Biderman, David S. ... Washington, DC
Biderman, David T., A Prof. Corp.
Santa Monica, CA
Biderman, Joseph S. ... Los Angeles, CA
Biderman, Paul L. ... Albuquerque, NM
Biderman, Sidney ... Denver, CO
Biderman, Stanley D. ... Austin, TX
Biderman, Ted S. ... **Chattanooga, TN**
Bidgood, Charles S., III ... Meridian, MS
Bidgood, James K., Jr. ... **Atlanta, GA**
Bidinger, Jeri L. ... Anchorage, AK
Bidinger, Jerome R. ... **Fairfax, VA**
Bidjou, Brent V. ... Minneapolis, MN
Bidlingmaier, Robert L. ... Walnut Creek, CA
Bidna, Howard M. ... **Newport Beach, CA**
Bidna & Keys ... **Santa Ana, CA**
Newport Beach, CA
Bidner, Michael P. ... Garden City, NY
Bidol, James A. ... **Holland, MI**
Bidonde, Bridget Cawley ... **Buffalo, NY**
Bidstrup, Robert E. ... **St. Louis, MO**
Bidstrup, W. Richard ... **Washington, DC**
Bidwell & Beachler Co., L.P.A.
Columbus, OH
Bidwell, Charles W., Jr. ... Cicero, IL
Bidwell, Christopher A.
Belvedere-Tiburon, CA
Bidwell, David ... Columbus, OH
Bidwell, David M. ... San Francisco, CA
Bidwell, Gregory E. ... Anchorage, AK
Bidwell, Haakenson & Haakenson
Janesville, WI
Bidwell, J. Truman, Jr. ... **New York, NY**
Bidwell, Jane ... Irvine, CA
Bidwell, Mark E. ... Syracuse, NY
Bidwell, Paul Louis ... Asheville, NC
Bidwell, Robert H. ... Piscataway, NJ
Bidwell, Ronald R. ... **Tampa, FL**
Bidwell, Theo. P. ... Janesville, WI
Bidwill, James E. ... Chicago, IL
Bidwill, Martin J. ... Fort Lauderdale, FL
Bidwill, Michael J. ... Phoenix, AZ
Bidzinski, Zenon J. ... Rockford, IL
Bie, Eugene F., P.A. ... North Palm Beach, FL
Biebel, Ann M. ... New York, NY
Biebel, Anne H. ... Dunwoody, GA
Biebel, Christine M. ... **Chicago, IL**
Biebel & French, A Legal Professional Association ... **Dayton, OH**
Biebel, John H. ... Waltham, MA
Biebel, Martin Lee ... Chicago, IL
Biebel, Mary J. ... Venice, CA
Biebelberg, Keith N. ... Millburn, NJ
Biebelberg & Martin ... Millburn, NJ
Bieber, Alois R. ... **Columbus, KS**
Bieber, Brian H. ... **Coral Gables, FL**
Bieber, Bruce W. ... **Spring Valley, NY**
Bieber & Czechowski, P.C. ... Center Line, MI
Bieber, David L. ... Morris Plains, NJ
Bieber, Donald R. ... **Denver, CO**
Bieber, Donn K. ... Schuyler, NE
Bieber, Eric D. ... Albany, NY
Bieber, Gretta E. ... **Aurora, IL**
Bieber, James B. ... York, PA
Bieber, Jody M. ... Atlanta, GA
Bieber, Karen Ruth ... **Chicago, IL**
Bieber, Kelley Ann ... **New York, NY**
Bieber, Margaret J. ... **Cleveland, OH**
Bieber, Martin S. ... Lincolnwood, IL
Bieber, Melvin W. ... Madison, WI
Bieber, Paul J. ... Davenport, IA
Bieber, Raymond S. ... Hilo, HI
Bieber, Sander M. ... **Washington, DC**
Bieber, Scott ... **Chicago, IL**
Bieber, Seymour ... New York, NY
Bieber, Tammy P. ... **New York, NY**
Bieber, Theodore E. ... Nacogdoches, TX
Bieber, Walter ... Center Line, MI
Bieberich, Kent A. ... **Battle Creek, MI**
Biebesheimer, Charles H. ... Clear Lake, IA
Biebesheimer, Christina ... Washington, DC
Biechlin, Robert R., Jr. ... **San Antonio, TX**
Bieck, Erik E. ... Milwaukee, WI
Bieck, Robert B., Jr. ... **New Orleans, LA**
Bieda, Michael L. ... Seattle, WA
Biedak, Frank Edward ... **Fall River, MA**
Biedar, Sherry L. ... Chicago, IL
Biedenharn, F. Murray ... Monroe, LA
Biedenharn, John U., Jr. ... **Orlando, FL**
Biedenharn, Sarah W. ... Austin, TX
Bieder, Richard A. ... **Bridgeport, CT**
Biederman, Alan Philip ... **Rutland, VT**
Biederman, Blake T. ... Danbury, CT
Biederman, Charles J. ... **Nashville, TN**
Biederman, Daniel J. ... **Chicago, IL**
Biederman, Donald E. ... **Los Angeles, CA**
Biederman, Frana C., Ltd. ... Nordland, WA
Biederman & Hunter, LLP ... Atlanta, GA
Biederman, Janice K. ... Boston, MA
Biederman, Jerry H. ... **Chicago, IL**
Biederman, Laura K. ... **Washington, DC**
Biederman, Marc A. ... Tarzana, CA
Biederman & O'Keefe, Ltd. ... Chicago, IL
Biederman & Rakow PC ... **Rutland, VT**
Biederman, Robert L. ... Southfield, MI
Biederman, Robert W., (P.C.) ... **Dallas, TX**
Biederman, Robt. A. ... Lansing, IL
Biederman, Sharon R., & Associates
Santa Ana, CA
Biederman, W. James
General Services Administration, Office of the General Counsel, GV
Biedermann, William ... Chicago, IL
Biedermann, Alan H. ... Portland, OR
Biedermann, Hoenig, Massamillo & Ruff, A Professional Corporation ... **New York, NY**
Biedermann, John P. ... **New York, NY**
Biedermann, Kurt E. ... **New York, NY**
Biedler, L. Kite, Jr. ... **Monroe, NC**
Biedron, Jonathan J. ... **Bethesda, MD**
Biedrzycki, Richard C. ... **Philadelphia, PA**
Biedscheid, Bryan P. ... **Santa Fe, NM**
Biedul, Anthony C. ... Santa Barbara, CA
Biefeld, Diana L. ... Department of Commerce, Patent and Trademark Office, GV
Bieg, James P. ... **Santa Fe, NM**
Bieg, Kenn R. ... Livingston, NJ
Biega, John B. ... Bass River, MA
Bieganowski & Allen ... **Houston, TX**
Bieganowski, David A. ... **Traverse City, MI**
Bieganowski, Victor J. ... **Houston, TX**
Bieganski, Walter R. ... Cleveland, OH
Biege, Douglas L. ... **La Porte, IN**
Biege, Philip E. ... Enumclaw, WA
Biegel, Adam J. ... **Atlanta, GA**
Biegel, Alan A. ... Kettering, OH
Biegel, Alan A., Co., L.P.A. ... Kettering, OH
Biegel, Craig A. ... Daingerfield, TX
Biegel, Cristina Almada ... **Monterey, CA**
Biegel, Gregory A. ... **Rockford, IL**
Biegel, Joseph D. ... Washington, DC
Biegel, Lawrence E., Law Offices of
Monterey, CA
Biegel, Ronald L. ... Department of Commerce, Patent and Trademark Office, GV
Biegel, Stuart ... Los Angeles, CA
Biegeleisen, Alan J. ... New York, NY
Biegelman, Herbert ... New York, NY
Biegelman, Herbert, P.C. ... New York, NY
Biegelson, Alan R. ... Brooklyn, NY
Biegenwald, William ... **Honolulu, HI**
Biegenzahn, Stephen F. ... Woodland Hills, CA
Biegenzahn Weinberg ... Woodland Hills, CA
Bieger, Daniel R. ... **Abingdon, VA**
Bieger, Neil King ... **Bristol, VA**
Bieger, Peter A. ... Treasury Department, Office of the General Counsel, GV
Biegert, Matthew A. ... New Richmond, WI
Bieging, David A. ... **Washington, DC**
Bieging, I. Thomas ... **Denver, CO**
Bieglecki, Thomas R. ... Mount Clemens, MI
Biegler, Kent D. ... **Cambridge, OH**
Biegler, Opper & Ortiz ... Sacramento, CA
Biegler, Robert P. ... Sacramento, CA
Biegon, Bradford E. ... **Washington, DC**
Biehl, Adam J. ... **Columbus, OH**
Biehl, Cathleen S. ... **Milwaukee, WI**
Biehl, David J. ... **Great Neck, NY**
Biehl, Frederick C., III ... Roseland, NJ

Biehl, James .... **Princeton, NJ**
Biehl, John C. .... **Lexington, KY**
Biehl, John F. .... **Saipan, TT**
Biehl, Kathy Anne .... Jamaica, NY
Biehl, Michael L. .... **Honolulu, HI**
Biehl, Michael M. .... **Milwaukee, WI**
Biehl, Scott A.
Department of Transportation, Federal Transit Administration, GV
Biehl, Sheila .... **Stuart, FL**
Biehle, Debra W. .... **Houston, TX**
Biehler, Cindy Sue .... Santa Rosa, CA
Biehler, Gregory L. .... **Albuquerque, NM**
Biehler, Michael J. .... Buffalo, NY
Biehn, Denise E. .... Department of Justice, Criminal Division, GV
Biehn, Don .... **Lake Havasu City, AZ**
Biehn, Gary Paul .... **Philadelphia, PA**
Biehn, Kenneth G. .... Doylestown, PA
Biehn, Laurie Jankowski .... St. Paul, MN
Biehn, Mary A. .... Edgewood, KY
Biehn, Steven A. .... **Lake Havasu City, AZ**
Biehslich, Rebecca Prince .... **Mayfield, KY**
Biek, David L. .... Wayzata, MN
Biek, John A. .... **Chicago, IL**
Bieke, James R. .... **Washington, DC**
Bieke, Ronald J. .... Kalamazoo, MI
Bieker, Dennis L. .... **Hays, KS**
Bieker-Brady, Kristina .... **Boston, MA**
Biel, Albert A., Jr. .... El Paso, TX
Biel & Brehmer .... **Bakersfield, CA**
Biel & Clark, P.A. .... Hilton Head Island, SC
Biel, Eric R. .... United States Senate, Committee Legal Personnel, GV
Biel, Frederick J. .... **McAllen, TX**
Biel, Jack H. .... Hilton Head Island, SC
Biel, Joseph A. .... **Merrillville, IN**
Biel, Mark .... **Atlantic City, NJ**
Biel, Mary E. .... McMinnville, OR
Biel, Michael, (P.C.) .... Washington, DC
Biel, Phillip J. .... **Bakersfield, CA**
Biel, William R. .... Costa Mesa, CA
Biel, William S. .... **San Diego, CA**
Biela, Joseph A. .... Yorktown Heights, NY
Biela, Ronald W. .... Houston, TX
Biela, Ronald W., P.C. .... Houston, TX
Bielaczyc, Paul M. .... Santa Barbara, CA
Bielagus, John F. .... Bedford, NH
Bielak, Margaret .... **San Francisco, CA**
Bielamowicz, Maryann K. .... Trenton, NJ
Bielan, Judith Q. .... Bayonne, NJ
Bielanowski, Walter M. .... New Brunswick, NJ
Bielat, Jay S. .... **New York, NY**
Bielaus, Robert E. .... Plainsboro, NJ
Bielawa, Joseph R. .... **New York, NY**
Bielawski, Alan P. .... **Chicago, IL**
Bielawski, Diane Dillon .... **Chicago, IL**
Bielawski & Hegle .... Bay City, MI
Bielawski, Julia S. .... Albany, NY
Bielawski, Lawrence M. .... Bay City, MI
Bielawski, W. Mark .... Pleasanton, CA
Bielby, Jeanine Loehr .... Columbus, OH
Bielby, Lorence Jon .... **Tallahassee, FL**
Bielby, Mary Margaret S. .... Tallahassee, FL
Biele, Hugh I. .... Los Angeles, CA
Biele, Irving H. .... Salt Lake City, UT
Bielefeld, James R. .... Crown Point, IN
Bielefeld, Mary Elizabeth
Department of Justice, Tax Division, GV
Bielefeld, William J. .... New York, NY
Bielek, Melvin S. .... Glenshaw, PA
Bielek, Robt. E. .... Cleveland Heights, OH
Bielema, John R., Jr. .... **Atlanta, GA**
Bielen, Judith A. .... Mount Laurel, NJ
Bielen & Peterson .... Walnut Creek, CA
Bielen, Theodore J., Jr. .... Walnut Creek, CA
Bieler, I. Scott .... **New York, NY**
Bieler, Lawrence I. .... Miami, FL
Bieler, Philip H. .... New York, NY
Bieler, Seymour .... San Francisco, CA
Bieler, William R .... **Missoula, MT**
Bielfield, Bruce R. .... Miami, FL
Bielfield, Jay A., P.C. .... Detroit, MI
Bielfield, Jennifer A. .... **Detroit, MI**
Bielicke, Deborah E. .... Denver, CO
Bielinski, Joseph A. .... **Appleton, WI**
Bielinski, Peter .... **Houston, TX**
Bielli & D'Alessandro, P.C.
Philadelphia, PA
Bielli, Francis X. .... Philadelphia, PA
Bielli, Kara A. .... Philadelphia, PA
Bielory, Abraham M. .... **Brick, NJ**
Bielory & Hennes, P.C. .... **Brick, NJ**
Toms River, NJ
Whiting, NJ
Bielski, Donald J. .... Kenosha, WI
Bielski, Edward G. .... **Indianapolis, IN**
Bielski, John N., II .... **Wheaton, IL**
Bielski, Mozelle DeLong
Jefferson City, MO
Bielsky, Hyman K. .... Elgin, IL
Bieluch, William C. .... Hartford, CT
Bieluch, William C., Jr. .... Darien, CT
Biely & Biely .... **Santa Barbara, CA**
Santa Maria, CA
Biely, Charles S. .... Santa Maria, CA
Biely, Jennifer G. .... Seattle, WA
Biely, Suzanne K. .... **Santa Maria, CA**
Bieman, Richard W. .... Northfield, OH
Biemer, Bonnie K. .... Louisville, KY
Biemer, Thomas S. .... **Cherry Hill, NJ**
Philadelphia, PA
Biemiller, Richard E. .... **Virginia Beach, VA**
Bien, Elliot L. .... **Novato, CA**
Oakland, CA
Bien, Gregory J. .... **Topeka, KS**
Bien, Henry W., Sr. .... Woolford, MD
Bien, John R. .... Holyoke, MA

Bien, Lettie J. .... Miami, FL
Bien, Michael W. .... **San Francisco, CA**
Bien, Richard N. .... **Kansas City, MO**
Bien, Sherwood .... Fairfield, CT
Bien & Summers LLP .... **Novato, CA**
Oakland, CA
San Francisco, CA
San Mateo, CA
Bieneman, Bruce M. .... Grand Rapids, MI
Bieneman, Diane M. .... San Francisco, CA
Bienemann, Charles E., Jr.
Glen Burnie, MD
Bienen, Leigh B. .... Chicago, IL
Bienenfeld, Morris .... **Roseland, NJ**
Bienenfeld, Saul .... New York, NY
Bienenfeld & Wertman .... New York, NY
Bienenstock, Martin J. .... **New York, NY**
Bienenstock, Samuel .... Bingham Farms, MI
Biener, Alvin N. .... Providence, RI
Biener, Charles S. .... **New York, NY**
Biener, Ellen G. .... Cranston, RI
Biener, J. William .... Plantation, FL
Biener, Norman .... Little Ferry, NJ
Biener, Steven L. .... **Wilmington, DE**
Philadelphia, PA
Bienert, Thomas H., Jr.
Newport Beach, CA
Bienfang, George R. .... **Dallas, TX**
Bieniek, Michael E. .... **Chicago, IL**
Bieniek, Susan F. K. .... Minnetonka, MN
Bienstock, Andrea S. .... **Memphis, TN**
Bienstock & Clark .... **Los Angeles, CA**
Santa Monica, CA
Miami, FL
Chicago, IL
Kalamazoo, MI
Bienstock, Floyd P. .... **Phoenix, AZ**
Bienstock, Gregg L. .... **New York, NY**
Bienstock, Joshua .... Garden City, NY
Bienstock, Lori .... **New York, NY**
Bienstock, Michael .... Miami Beach, FL
Bienstock, Peter .... **New York, NY**
Bienstock, Peter .... Wallkill, NY
Bienstock, Robert H. .... New York, NY
Bienstock, Ronald S., & Associates
New York, NY
Bienstock, Steven J. .... Rockville, MD
Bienstock, Steven W. .... **Scottsdale, AZ**
Bienstock, Terry S., (P.A.) .... **Miami, FL**
Bienstock, Walter .... Woodmere, NY
Bienstock-Cohen, Jennifer .... **New York, NY**
Bienvenu, C. Thomas, Jr. .... **New Iberia, LA**
Bienvenu, Claudette .... **Kansas City, MO**
Bienvenu, David F. .... **New Orleans, LA**
Bienvenu, David M., Jr. .... **Baton Rouge, LA**
Bienvenu, Foster, Ryan & O'Bannon
New Orleans, LA
Bienvenu, J. Hunter .... Gretna, LA
Bienvenu, J. Hunter, A.P.L.C. .... Gretna, LA
Bienvenu, John C. .... **Santa Fe, NM**
Bienvenu, Leah L. .... Lafayette, LA
Bienvenu, Leonard P. .... Rockville, MD
Bienvenu, Leonard P., P.A. .... Rockville, MD
Bienvenu, Marvin A., Jr. .... Memphis, TN
Bienvenu, Michael P. .... **Baton Rouge, LA**
Bienvenu, P. Albert .... **New Orleans, LA**
Bienvenu, Staci A. .... Franklinton, LA
Bienvenu, Steven J. .... **Opelousas, LA**
Bienvenue, Dana A. .... Windham, ME
Bienvenue & Fenton, P.A. .... Windham, ME
Bien-Willner, Laura C. .... **Los Angeles, CA**
Bienz, Frederic Carl .... Smithtown, NY
Bier, Bernard H. .... New York, NY
Bier, Byron S. .... Quincy, IL
Bier, H. Barry .... Pittsburgh, PA
Bier, Jeffrey R. .... Haddon Heights, NJ
Bier, Jennifer C. .... **Arlington, VA**
Bier, Jessica .... New York, NY
Bier, Leonard T. .... New Brunswick, NJ
Bier, Lilian .... **Beaverton, OR**
Bier, Richard I. .... **Newark, NJ**
Bier, Robert J. .... Quincy, IL
Bier, Stephen H. .... **Roseland, NJ**
Bier & Wellborn .... Quincy, IL
Bierbach, Charles A. .... Huntingdon, PA
Bierbach, McDowell, McMinn & Zanic
Huntingdon, PA
Bierbaum, Amy B. .... Boston, MA
Bierbaum Law Offices .... **Boulder, CO**
Bierbaum, Mary-Margaret, Law Offices of
Aptos, CA
Bierbaum, Paul M., Jr. .... **Boulder, CO**
Bierbower, Mark B. .... **Washington, DC**
Bierbower, Robert J. .... David City, NE
Bierbower, William J. .... Washington, DC
Bierce, James M. .... Cuyahoga Falls, OH
Bierce & Kenerson, P.C. .... **New York, NY**
Bierce, Lyn C. .... San Francisco, CA
Bierce, William B. .... **New York, NY**
Bierek, William V., (P.C.) .... Hillsboro, OR
Bierenbaum, Susan .... **Los Angeles, CA**
Bierer, Allentoff & Margolis .... Baltimore, MD
Bierer, Frederick L. .... Baltimore, MD
Bierer, Joel D. .... Mill Valley, CA
Bierfeld, Charles M. .... Dallas, TX
Bierhans, Bruce A. .... Boston, MA
Stoughton, MA
Bierhans, Bruce A., A Professional Corporation .... **Stoughton, MA**
Bierhorst, Eugene K. .... New York, NY
Bieri & Ames .... **Detroit, MI**
Bieri, Diane E. .... **Washington, DC**
Bieri, James C. .... **Detroit, MI**
Bierig, Bobby L. .... Santa Barbara, CA
Bierig, Jack R. .... **Chicago, IL**
Bierig, N. Jaree .... **Dallas, TX**
Biering, Christopher P. .... Moncks Corner, SC

Biering, Christopher P., P.C.
Moncks Corner, SC
Biering, Raymond A. .... San Luis Obispo, CA
Biering, Ruth F. .... Los Osos, CA
Bieringer, Leonard M. .... Hartford, CT
Bierkamp, Mary M. .... Minneapolis, MN
Bierkan, Dean A. .... **Pittsburgh, PA**
Bierle, Don A. .... Yankton, SD
Bierlein Law Office, The, P.S. .... Issaquah, WA
Bierlein, Lawrence W. .... **Washington, DC**
Bierlein, Marna J. .... Issaquah, WA
Bierley, John C. .... **Tampa, FL**
Bierly, Denise M. .... **State College, PA**
Bierly, Mark F. .... McMinnville, OR
Bierly, Paul S. .... **Portland, OR**
Bierly, Richard A. .... **New Albany, IN**
Bierma, Lloyd W. .... Sioux Center, IA
Biermacher, Kenneth W. .... **Dallas, TX**
Bierman, Aimee E. .... **Boston, MA**
Bierman & Bierman, P.C. .... **Grinnell, IA**
Pella, IA
Bierman, Catherine Best .... McLean, VA
Bierman, Daniel J. B. .... Rehoboth Beach, DE
Bierman, David J. .... Seattle, WA
Bierman, Donald I. .... **Miami, FL**
Bierman, Donald L., Jr. .... **Fremont, CA**
Bierman, Donald L., Jr. .... **Fremont, CA**
Bierman, Ellen M. .... **Seattle, WA**
Bierman, Howard N. .... Bethesda, MD
Bierman, Ira M. .... **Great Neck, NY**
Bierman, Ivy Kagan .... **Los Angeles, CA**
Bierman, Jacquin D. .... Coral Gables, FL
Bierman, James N. .... **Washington, DC**
Bierman, Janice .... **Livingston, NJ**
Bierman, Jeffrey B. .... **Jacksonville, FL**
Bierman, John F. .... **Grinnell, IA**
Bierman, John F. (Rick), III .... **Grinnell, IA**
Pella, IA
Bierman, Jon A. .... **St. Louis, MO**
Bierman, Jordan B. .... **New York, NY**
White Plains, NY
Bierman, Joseph C. .... Albany, NY
Bierman, Karena J. .... **Chicago, IL**
Bierman, Kenneth T. .... **Hackensack, NJ**
Bierman, Lara K. .... Sacramento, CA
Bierman Law Offices .... St. Paul, MN
Bierman, Lawrence M. .... Mesa, AZ
Bierman, Leslie M. .... Hackensack, NJ
Bierman, Luke J. .... Albany, NY
Bierman, M. Elizabeth .... **Washington, DC**
Bierman, Michael H. .... **Los Angeles, CA**
Bierman, Michael T. .... Dallas, TX
Bierman, Mitchell A. .... **Miami, FL**
Bierman, Mitchell Alexander .... Miami, FL
Bierman, Mitchell S. .... Elizabeth, NJ
Bierman, Muserlian and Lucas
New York, NY
White Plains, NY
Bierman, Paul C. .... New York, NY
Bierman, Philip M. .... Manhattan, MT
Bierman, Richard E. .... **New York, NY**
Bierman, Rick S. .... New York, NY
Bierman, Sandra L. .... Phoenix, AZ
Bierman, Sheldon L.
Washington Grove, MD
Bierman, Shohat, Loewy & Klein, Professional Association .... **Miami, FL**
Bierman, Steven M. .... New York, NY
Bierman, Stuart Jon .... Oradell, NJ
Bierman, Susan .... **Washington, DC**
Bierman, Timothy R. .... Chicago, IL
Bierman, William A. .... St. Paul, MN
Bierman, William A., Jr. .... St. Paul, MN
Bierman, William D. .... **Hackensack, NJ**
Biermann, Carolyn J. .... Belen, NM
Biermann, Dirk T. .... **Denver, CO**
Biermann & Fretz, P.C. .... **Denver, CO**
Biermann, Sandra Lee .... Bettendorf, IA
Biermans, John T. .... Sacramento, CA
Biern, Herbert A.
Board of Governors Of The Federal Reserve System,
Division of Banking Supervision and Regulation, GV
Biernacki & Bauer, P.A. .... **DeLand, FL**
Biernacki, John V. .... **Troy, MI**
Biernacki, Raymond A., Jr. .... **DeLand, FL**
Biernacki, Stephenie M. .... **Tampa, FL**
Biernacki, Susan H. .... Albuquerque, NM
Biernat, James D. .... San Francisco, CA
Biernat, James M. .... Mount Clemens, MI
Biernat, Leonard F. .... St. Paul, MN
Biernat, Rebecca M. .... **San Francisco, CA**
Biernbaum, Alan S. .... Rochester, NY
Biernbaum, Inclima, Meyer & Ruby, LLP
Rochester, NY
Bierner, Michael H. .... Dallas, TX
Biersay, Lisagaye A. .... **Minneapolis, MN**
Bierschbach, Robert J. .... Redlands, CA
Biersdorf, Dan .... Minneapolis, MN
Biersdorf, Dan, P.A. .... Minneapolis, MN
Biersner, Robert J. .... Department of Labor, Office of the Solicitor, GV
Bierstedt, Peter R. .... **Los Angeles, CA**
Bierstedt, Robin .... **New York, NY**
Bierstein, Andrea .... **New York, NY**
Bierstein, Karin .... Washington, DC
Biersteker, Peter J. .... **Washington, DC**
Bierstock, Stephen P. .... **Sacramento, CA**
Bierut, Mary Beth .... Washington, DC
Biervliet, Julius C. .... New York, NY
Bierwirth, Joseph L., Jr. .... **Boston, MA**
Bierwirth, Leo .... Houston, TX
Biery, Biery, Myers & Armstrong, A Professional Corporation
San Antonio, TX
Biery, Charles E. .... **San Antonio, TX**

Biery, Evelyn H. (IBA) .... **Houston, TX**
San Antonio, TX
Biery, Fred .... San Antonio, TX
Biery, Galen E. .... Wichita, KS
Biery, James B. .... **Chicago, IL**
Biery, Samuel F. .... **San Antonio, TX**
Bies, Stanley .... **Rosemont, IL**
Biesanz, Steven T. .... Winona, MN
Bieschke, Walter B. .... Chicago, IL
Biese, Melita M. .... Mequon, WI
Milwaukee, WI
Racine, WI
Biesecker, Eric H. .... **Greensboro, NC**
Biesecker, Jean M. .... Bryn Mawr, PA
Biesecker, Joe E. .... **Lexington, NC**
Biesemeyer, David V. .... **San Francisco, CA**
Bieser, Charles D. .... Palm Beach Gardens, FL
Bieser, Greer & Landis .... **Dayton, OH**
Eaton, OH
Greenville, OH
Springfield, OH
Troy, OH
Xenia, OH
Bieser, Irvin G., Jr. .... **Dayton, OH**
Biesiada, John M. .... Chicago, IL
Biesinger, John W., III .... St. Petersburg, FL
Biesinger, L. Tasman .... Sandy, UT
Biesman, Sherwin F. .... Bellaire, TX
Biestek, John P., and Associates, Ltd.
Arlington Heights, IL
Biestek, John P., Jr. .... Arlington Heights, IL
Biestek, Kimberly C. .... Arlington Heights, IL
Biestek, Scott A. .... Arlington Heights, IL
Biester, David R. .... **New York, NY**
Biester, Edward G., III .... **Philadelphia, PA**
Biester, Mary K. .... Dallas, TX
Biester, Pamela Mayro .... **Media, PA**
Biesterfeld, Bryan D. .... **Denver, CO**
Minneapolis, MN
Biesterfeld, Craig S. .... **St. Louis, MO**
Biesterfeld, M. Dee .... **Denver, CO**
Biesterveld, Jeffrey L. .... Petersburg, IN
Biesty, James T. .... **Los Angeles, CA**
Biesty, McCool & Garretty, A Professional Corporation .... **Los Angeles, CA**
Bieter, Christopher M. .... Boise, ID
Bieter, David H. .... **Boise, ID**
Bieter, Thomas J. .... Duluth, MN
Biety, Dennis M. .... Oxnard, CA
Biever, Bennett H. H. .... **New Orleans, LA**
Bifano, Joseph N. .... West Mifflin, PA
Bifera, Frank V. .... Albany, NY
Bifferato, Bifferato & Gentilotti
Wilmington, DE
Bifferato, Ian Connor .... **Wilmington, DE**
Bifferato, Karen C. .... **Wilmington, DE**
Bifferato, Marie C. .... **Wilmington, DE**
Bifferato, Vincent A. .... Wilmington, DE
Bifferato, Vincent A., Jr. .... **Wilmington, DE**
Biffl, Elizabeth L. .... Fort Myers, FL
Bifone, Christopher P. .... **San Diego, CA**
Bifulco, Pasquale .... Staten Island, NY
Biga, Kay A. .... Superior, WI
Biga, Thomas A. .... Plymouth, MA
Bigalow, Tamara S. .... **New York, NY**
Bigane, Virginia M. .... Chicago, IL
Bigatel, Joel F. .... Narberth, PA
Bigay, Regina A. .... **San Francisco, CA**
Bigbee, Nancy P. .... Highlands Ranch, CO
Bigbee, Rebecca Joyce Knowles
Montgomery, AL
Bigby, Aaron D. .... **San Francisco, CA**
Bigby, Darren O. .... **Calabasas, CA**
Bigby, Terry D. .... Tahlequah, OK
Bigcraft, Susan L. .... **Portland, OR**
Bigel, Madeline K. .... New York, NY
Bigel, Mitchell S. .... **Raleigh, NC**
Bigeleisen, David Michael .... Daly City, CA
Bigeleisen, Marla B. .... **Lancaster, PA**
Philadelphia, PA
Bigeleison, Robin Lippitt .... Trenton, NJ
Bigelman, Jerrold M. .... Southfield, MI
Bigelow, Brian D. .... Berrien Springs, MI
Bigelow, Brian E. .... **Beckley, WV**
Bigelow, Bruce .... **Austin, TX**
Bigelow, Bruce C. .... **Honolulu, HI**
Bigelow, Charles L. .... Fort Myers, FL
Bigelow, Dana F. .... **Syracuse, NY**
Bigelow, David N. .... **Los Angeles, CA**
Bigelow, Donovan R. .... Seattle, WA
Bigelow, Erica Paquette .... Worcester, MA
Bigelow, Franklin T., Jr. .... Pasadena, CA
Bigelow, Gary W.
United States Postal Service, Law Department, GV
Bigelow, Glenn D., (A Prof. Corp.)
Oakland, CA
Bigelow, Gordon L. .... Conyngham, PA
Bigelow, James H. .... Altoona, PA
Bigelow, James W. .... Livonia, MI
Bigelow, John .... Gloucester, MA
Santa Fe, NM
Bigelow, John L. .... Conyngham, PA
Bigelow, Judith A. .... **Seattle, WA**
Bigelow, Jyce G. .... **New York, NY**
Bigelow, Katherine J. .... Oakland, CA
Bigelow, Kevin Lee .... **New York, NY**
Bigelow, Kirk L. .... New York, NY
Bigelow, Luke J. .... Jamaica, NY
Bigelow, M. Ross .... Los Angeles, CA
Bigelow, Michael B. .... Sacramento, CA
Bigelow, Michael P. .... **Indianapolis, IN**
Bigelow, Michelle L. .... Sacramento, CA
Bigelow, Molly A. .... Redding, CA
Bigelow, Moore & Tyre, LLP .... Pasadena, CA
Bigelow, Paige .... **Salt Lake City, UT**
Bigelow, Raymond C. .... New Orleans, LA
Bigelow, Robert P. .... Winchester, MA

Bigelow, Robert Wilson ....Bronx, NY
Bigelow, Ronald J. ....Houston, TX
Bigelow, Stephen D. ....Kalamazoo, MI
Bigelow, T. William ....Manchester, NH
Bigelow, Teresa V. ....Seattle, WA
Bigelow, V. Elise ....San Francisco, CA
Bigelow, Yvette E. ....Boston, MA
Bigelson, Alec P. ....New York, NY
Bigg, Dort S. ....Manchester, NH
Bigg, Dort S., III ....Washington, DC
Biggam, Charles M., III ....Chicago, IL
Biggam, Christensen & Minsloff
Santa Cruz, CA
Biggam, Fox & Skinner ....Montpelier, VT
Biggam, Lawrence P. ....Santa Cruz, CA
Biggam, Patrick L. ....Montpelier, VT
Biggane, Patrick J. ....Chicago, IL
Biggar, Barry P. ....New York, NY
Biggar, Ryan W. ....Las Vegas, NV
Biggar, Thomas W. ....Las Vegas, NV
Biggart, James G., II ....Tampa, FL
Biggart, Robert K. ....Purchase, NY
Biggart, Waddell A., II, (P.C.)
Washington, DC
Bigge, Robert J., Jr. ....Fort Lauderdale, FL
Bigger, Richard A., Jr. ....Charlotte, NC
Bigger, Stephen ....New York, NY
Bigger, Stephen R. ....Pocahontas, AR
Biggerman, Mark W. ....Lima, OH
Biggers, A. Susan ....Shelby, NC
Biggers, Beasley, Earle and Hightower, P.C.
Dallas, TX
Biggers, Deborah H. ....Tuskegee, AL
Biggers, Edward D. ....Dallas, TX
Biggers, Fred A. ....Concord, NC
Biggers, John ....Houston, TX
Biggers, John C. ....Dallas, TX
Biggers, John W. ....Tucson, AZ
Biggers, Kathryn Barton ....Dallas, TX
Biggers, Marc A. ....Greenwood, MS
Biggers, Michael G. ....New York, NY
Biggers, Neal B., Jr. ....Oxford, MS
Biggers, William T. ....Asheville, NC
Biggerstaff, Ralph A. ....Lakewood, CA
Biggerstaff, Robert E. ....Albany, NY
Biggert, Judith Borg ....Hinsdale, IL
Biggert, Rody P. ....Chicago, IL
Biggins, Arthur L. ....Alexandria, VA
Biggins & Associates ....Atlanta, GA
Biggins, Brian P. ....Rocky River, OH
Biggins, Daniel R. ....Tallahassee, FL
Biggins, Donna Shaw ....Tallahassee, FL
Biggins, Franklin N. ....Atlanta, GA
Biggins, James P. ....Urbana, IL
Biggins, John C. ....Washington, DC
Biggins, John J. ....Elmsford, NY
Biggins, Mary Janice ....Euclid, OH
Biggins, Nancy ....Ukiah, CA
Biggins, Sean W. ....Vero Beach, FL
Biggio, Charles E. ....New York, NY
Biggio, Jess ....New York, NY
Biggio, Timothy A. ....Dallas, TX
Biggs, A. George ....Carrollton, TX
Biggs, Alvin C. ....St. Matthews, SC
Biggs, Andrew S. ....Gilbert, AZ
Biggs, Andrew T. ....Bellevue, WA
Biggs and Battaglia ....Wilmington, DE
Biggs, Brent Austin ....Austin, TX
San Antonio, TX
Biggs, C. Thomas ....Durham, NC
Biggs, Carlton P. ....Laguna Niguel, CA
Biggs, Davis, Jr. ....St. Louis, MO
Biggs, Deborah L. ....Ann Arbor, MI
Biggs, Donald C. ....Indianapolis, IN
Biggs, Donald W. ....Albany, NY
Biggs, Eric ....Santa Fe, NM
Biggs, Eric, P.A. ....Santa Fe, NM
Biggs, F. Lewis ....Richmond, VA
Biggs, Faith Ford ....Dallas, TX
Biggs, G. Whitney ....Bridgeport, CT
Biggs, Gayla G. ....Lumberton, NC
Biggs, George N., III ....Malden Bridge, NY
Biggs, Gregory Marion ....Decatur, AL
Biggs, Hugh L. ....Portland, OR
Biggs, I. Murchison ....Lumberton, NC
Biggs, J. Patrick ....New Albany, IN
Biggs, James B. ....Topeka, KS
Biggs, James D. ....Chicago, IL
Biggs, James D. ....Amarillo, TX
Biggs, Jason R. ....Burlingame, CA
San Jose, CA
Biggs, Jo Ann ....Dallas, TX
Biggs, John, III ....Wilmington, DE
Biggs, John W., Jr. ....Chicago, IL
Biggs, Jonathan W ....Durham, NC
Biggs, Judith A. (Jude) ....Boulder, CO
Denver, CO
Biggs, Julie Hayward ....Los Angeles, CA
Riverside, CA
Biggs, Lee ....Searcy, AR
Biggs, M. Alexander ....Rocky Mount, NC
Biggs, Mary Coon ....Franklin, LA
Biggs, Mary Gregory ....Anaheim, CA
Biggs, Michael R. ....Wichita, KS
Biggs, Richard B. "Moe" ....Tucson, AZ
Biggs, Richard D. ....Atlanta, GA
Biggs, Richard L. ....Portland, OR
Biggs, Robert A., III ....Jackson, MS
Biggs, Robert M. ....Louisville, KY
Biggs & Stoehr, P.C. ....Omaha, NE
Biggs, Suzanne L. ....La Jolla, CA
Biggs, Thomas W. ....Fort Wayne, IN
Biggs, Tracy L. ....Arlington, VA
Biggs, Trowbridge, Supple, Cremaldi & Curet ....Franklin, LA
Morgan City, LA
New Iberia, LA
Biggs, William L., Jr., (P.C.) ....Omaha, NE
Bigham and Boyd ....Lewisburg, TN
Bigham, Brett L. ....Waxahachie, TX
Bigham, Donald ....Pinckneyville, IL
Bigham, Edward ....Philadelphia, PA
Bigham, Edward T., Jr. ....Waltham, MA
Bigham Englar Jones & Houston
Newark, NJ
Bronx, NY
New York, NY
Bigham, James E. ....Minneapolis, MN
Bigham, John R. ....Belton, TX
Bigham, Knox ....Lewisburg, TN
Bigham, Shannon Ireland ....Winter Park, FL
Bigham, Stephen M. ....New York, NY
Bigham, W. Harold ....Malibu, CA
Bigham, William J. ....Trenton, NJ
Bigheart, Michael C. ....Enid, OK
Bigi & Associates ....Charleroi, PA
Donora, PA
Bigi, Donna M. ....Irvine, CA
Bigi, Herman J. ....Charleroi, PA
Biging, Elizabeth K. ....Hicksville, NY
Biging, Peter J. ....New York, NY
Bigioni, Neil R. ....Philadelphia, PA
Bigknife, Tuari N. ....San Diego, CA
Biglen, G. Thomas ....Big Timber, MT
Biglen & Manos ....Big Timber, MT
Bigler, Berry, Johnston, Sztykiel & Hunt, P.C. ....Detroit, MI
Holland, MI
Troy, MI
Bigler, Bruce E. ....Troy, MI
Bigler, C. Stephen ....Wilmington, DE
Bigler, Debra N. ....Beaumont, TX
Houston, TX
Bigler, Glade S. ....Salt Lake City, UT
Bigler, James C. ....Studio City, CA
Bigler, Jo Anne ....Waterford, MI
Bigler, John C. ....Phillipsburg, NJ
Bigler, Michael F. ....Cincinnati, OH
Bigler, Robert C. ....Los Angeles, CA
Bigler, Thomas ....Denver, CO
Bigley, A. Donald ....Cherry Hill, NJ
Bigley, Anne L. ....Los Angeles, CA
Bigley, Donald J. ....Haddonfield, NJ
Bigley, Garland L. ....Richmond, VA
Bigley, Gerard M. ....Pittsburgh, PA
Bigley, John F. ....Stratford, CT
Bigley, Paul A. ....Los Angeles, CA
Bigley & Rosati ....Stratford, CT
Bigley, Thomas C., Jr. ....Columbus, IN
Biglin, Brian D. ....Columbus, OH
Biglow, John B. ....Minneapolis, MN
Biglow, Lucius H., Jr. ....Bellevue, WA
Biglow, Michael J. ....Fresno, CA
Biglow, Michael J. ....Minneapolis, MN
Biglow, Robt. R. ....Minneapolis, MN
Biglow, William A.
Department of Commerce,
Office of the General Counsel, GV
Bigman, Bennett A. ....Los Angeles, CA
Bigman, Jeffrey E. ....Daytona Beach, FL
Bigman, Laurie G. ....Syosset, NY
Bignall, Bliss O., Jr. ....Coeur d'Alene, ID
Bignall, John Earl ....Phoenix, AZ
Bignami, Francesca Elisabeth
Washington, DC
Bignault & Associates ....Savannah, GA
Bignault, W. Paschal ....Savannah, GA
Bigney, David Robert ....Orlando, FL
Bigoness, James Joseph ....Chicago, IL
Bigoness, Nicholas M. ....Oak Brook, IL
Bigonger, Jeffrey R. ....Yorba Linda, CA
Bigonger, Roland E. ....Yorba Linda, CA
Bigony, Bruce A. ....Los Angeles, CA
Bigos, Kathleen Boyle ....Seattle, WA
Bigosinski, Thomas C. ....Newark, NJ
Bigsby, Arthur J., Jr. ....Syracuse, NY
Bigsby, Laurie A. Lazich ....South Bend, IN
Bigsby, Lorna L. ....Everett, WA
Bigsby, Thomas D. ....Everett, WA
Bigsby & Willson ....Everett, WA
Bigus, Edward L. ....Overland Park, KS
Bigus, Kenneth E. ....Lenexa, KS
Bigus, Lawrence W. ....Overland Park, KS
Bigwood, Robert W. ....Fergus Falls, MN
Bigwood, Steven J.
Rancho Cucamonga, CA
Bihary, Joyce ....Atlanta, GA
Bihary, Paul J. ....Palm Beach, FL
Bihary, Sheila ....San Francisco, CA
Bihl, Victor A. ....Harrisburg, PA
Bihlmeyer, Lawrence ....Rapid City, SD
Bihn, George F., III ....Philadelphia, PA
Bihn, Jane F. ....Oregon, OH
Bihn, Martin A. ....Glendale, AZ
Bihr, Bernhard E. ....Los Angeles, CA
Bihr, Heather D. ....Oakland, CA
Bihr, Rebecca S. ....Overland Park, KS
Kansas City, MO
Bihun, Oksana R. ....Los Angeles, CA
Bijak, Bonnie B. ....Oak Forest, IL
Bijesse & Belford ....St. James, NY
Bijkersma, Paul C. ....Quincy, MA
Bijur, Jason ....New York, NY
Bik, Stephen P. ....Worcester, MA
Bikakis, Arneson & Karpuk
Sioux City, IA
Bikakis, Emmanuel S. ....Sioux City, IA
Bikales, Norman A. ....Boston, MA
Bikel, Dror ....New York, NY
Bikin, Bruce H. ....Philadelphia, PA
Bikkal, Cecilia G. ....White Plains, NY
Bikle, Robt. W. ....Dallas, TX
Biklen, David D. ....Hartford, CT
Biklen, Lisa L. ....Concord, NH
Bikman, Charla R. ....East Hampton, NY
Bikoff, David ....Indianapolis, IN
Bikoff, James L. ....Washington, DC
Bikoff, Russell A. ....Department of Justice,
Criminal Division, GV
Bikofsky, Aaron K. ....Framingham, MA
Bikofsky, David R. ....Newton, MA
Bikofsky and White ....Boston, MA
Framingham, MA
Biksa, Janis J. O. ....Palo Alto, CA
Bikus, Christopher M. ....Omaha, NE
Bila, Dennis W., II ....Bloomfield Hills, MI
Bila, William P. ....Chicago, IL
Bilac, Eva ....Brea, CA
Bilafer, John J. ....Arlington, MA
Bilaisis, Vilija A. ....Chicago, IL
Bilal, Joseph A. ....Kendall Park, NJ
Bilan, Michael J. ....Venice, CA
Bilanchone, Jill S. ....Fort Lauderdale, FL
Bilancini, Darrel A. ....Elyria, OH
Bilanzic, Peter J. ....Worth, IL
Bilas, Jay S. ....Charlotte, NC
Bilas, Jeffrey D. ....Orange, CA
Bilas, Jeffrey P. ....Chicago, IL
Bilas, Kurt W. ....Washington, DC
Bilas, Laura L. ....Chicago, IL
Bilas, Sharyl P. ....Irvine, CA
Bilava, Arthur J. ....Costa Mesa, CA
Bilawski, Rudy V. ....Stockton, CA
Bilawsky, Mark A. ....Princeton, NJ
Bilbao, Guillermo G. ....New York, NY
Bilbao, J. Raymond ....Richardson, TX
Bilbe, George L. ....New Orleans, LA
Bilbeaux, Nicole Kamian ....Palo Alto, CA
Bilbeaux, Ray ....Palo Alto, CA
Bilbeisi, Sharon L. ....Laguna Hills, CA
Bilbie, Richard L. ....Brownsville, TX
Bilbija, N. Amy ....New York, NY
Bilbo, Jimmy Wayne ....Cleveland, TN
Bilbray, James H. ....Las Vegas, NV
Bilbray, Robert P. ....Laughlin, NV
Bilbrew, Larry P. ....Glendale, CA
Bilbrew, Sharon L. ....Elkhart, IN
Bilbrey, Michael R. ....Wood River, IL
Bilbrey, Ross Logan ....Jacksonville, FL
Bilbrey, Thomas H. ....Lafayette, TN
Bilbro, Joe McCaleb ....New Orleans, LA
Bilby, Cindy ....Dayton, OH
Bilby, John W. ....Louisville, KY
Bilby, Richard M. ....Flagstaff, AZ
Bilcer, Brian W. ....Chicago, IL
Bilcheck, William B., Jr. ....Madison, CT
Bilchik, Gary B. ....Cleveland, OH
Bilchik, Shay
Department of Justice, GV
Bild, Brian Alan ....St. Louis, MO
Bild, John F. ....St. Louis, MO
Bilder, Anne Elizabeth ....Madison, WI
Bilder, Lawrence ....Jersey City, NJ
Bilder, Marshall D. ....Trenton, NJ
Bilder, Richard B. ....Madison, WI
Bilder, Seymour ....New York, NY
Bilder, Sheila Tralins ....Fairfield, NJ
Bilderback, Daniel S. ....Honolulu, HI
Bilderback, James William, II
Los Angeles, CA
Bilderback, Kip J. ....St. Louis, MO
Bilderback, Stering G. ....Quincy, IL
Bildersee, Robert A. ....Philadelphia, PA
Bildersee & Silbert LLP ....Philadelphia, PA
Bildhauer, Mathias G. ....Tucson, AZ
Bildner, Daniel I. ....New York, NY
Bildner, James L. ....Waltham, MA
Bildner, Philip ....Jericho, NY
Bildstein, Bernd ....Flushing, NY
Bildstein, Jeffrey W. ....Portland, OR
Bileci, Joseph E., Jr. ....Pacific Grove, CA
Bilek, Mary Lu ....Flushing, NY
Bilek, Thomas E. ....Houston, TX
Bilello, James G. ....Smithtown, NY
Bilello, Thomas C. ....Newport Beach, CA
Bilenker, Stephanie Anne
Philadelphia, PA
Bilenky, William S. ....Brooksville, FL
Biles, Barbara ....Los Angeles, CA
Biles, Bayless E. ....Bay Minette, AL
Biles, Blake A. ....Washington, DC
Biles, Dan ....Overland Park, KS
Biles, David W. ....Denton, TX
Biles, James F., Jr. ....Fayetteville, GA
Biles, James Richard ....Topeka, KS
Biles, James Richard, Chartered ....Topeka, KS
Biles, Michael J. ....Austin, TX
Bileti, Joseph J. ....Harper Woods, MI
Bilett, Joseph S. ....Denver, CO
Bilewich, Igor ....Uniondale, NY
Bilezerian, Keith D. ....Boston, MA
Bilfield, Murray D. ....Cleveland, OH
Bilfield & Sandel, Co., L.P.A.
Cleveland, OH
Bilford & Bilford, A Professional Law Corporation ....Van Nuys, CA
Bilford, David R. ....Van Nuys, CA
Bilford, Harriet K. ....Van Nuys, CA
Bilger, Bruce R. ....Houston, TX
Bilger, L. Victor, Jr. ....Los Angeles, CA
Bilgore, Donald L. ....Rochester, NY
Bilgore, Paul S. ....Los Angeles, CA
Bilgore, Reich, Levine, Kroll & Kantor
Rochester, NY
Bilheimer, John ....Nevada City, CA
Bilheimer, John A. ....Parsippany, NJ
Bilheimer, John M. ....Department of Justice,
Tax Division, GV
Bilheimer and Raquet ....Parsippany, NJ
Bilheimer, Stephen P. ....Little Rock, AR
Bilich, Charles A. ....Mineola, NY
Bilich, Edward K.M. ....Washington, DC
Bilicic, George W., Jr. ....New York, NY
Bilicki, Byron A. ....Jamestown, NY
Williamsville, NY
Bilicki, James T. ....Livonia, MI
Bilicki Law Firm, The, P.C. ....Jamestown, NY
Williamsville, NY
Bilicki & Simpson, P.C. ....Williamsville, NY
Bilik, Edward J. ....Greensburg, PA
Bilik, James D. ....New York, NY
Bilik, R. Eric ....Jacksonville, FL
Bilimoria, Neville M. ....Chicago, IL
Bilinkas, Edward J. ....Fairfield, NJ
Randolph, NJ
Bilinski, John N. ....Rutland, VT
Bilinski, Peter J. ....Syracuse, NY
Bilinsky, Matthew D. ....Springfield, IL
Bilisoly, F. Nash ....Norfolk, VA
Bilitski, Deborah A. ....Louisville, KY
Bilkis, David ....New York, NY
Bill, Arthur H. ....Washington, DC
Bill, Edmund G. ....Hempstead, NY
Bill, John H. ....Winter Park, FL
Bill, Karen Kraus ....Columbia, MO
Bill, Michael T. ....Pensacola, FL
Bill, Peter J. ....Detroit, MI
Billage, Judith ....Annapolis, MD
Billam, Dale J. ....Bartlesville, OK
Billam, Thomas D. ....Overland Park, KS
Billand, Michelle ....Washington, DC
Billard, Debra D. ....Jacksonville, FL
Billauer, Barbara P. ....Lido Beach, NY
Billawala, Omar N. ....San Jose, CA
Billbe, Ted D. ....Bellevue, WA
Billbe, Ted D., PLLC ....Bellevue, WA
Billbrough, G. Bartram, Jr. ....Miami, FL
Bille, Anthony J. ....North Andover, MA
Billeaud, Jean Ann ....Lafayette, LA
New Orleans, LA
Billeaud, Michael B. ....Lafayette, LA
Billeaud, Richard D. ....San Antonio, TX
Billek, Carl W. ....Newark, NJ
Billek, Maxwell L. ....Edison, NJ
Biller, Andrea R.
Securities and Exchange Commission,
Division of Corporation Finance, GV
Biller, Anthony J. ....Raleigh, NC
Biller, Dimitrios P. ....Los Angeles, CA
Biller, Jon D. ....North Haven, CT
Biller, Jonathan P. ....Washington, DC
Chicago, IL
Biller Law Firm, The ....North Haven, CT
Biller, Mark Drew ....Balsam Lake, WI
Biller, Stephen H. ....Memphis, TN
Biller, Stuart M. ....Oak Park, CA
Biller, Susan G. ....Woodbury, NY
Billescas, Roberto ....Alamo, TX
Billet, Barbara Gott ....Albany, NY
Billet & Billet ....New York, NY
Billet & Connor ....Turnersville, NJ
Philadelphia, PA
Billet, David S. ....New York, NY
Billet, Fern S. ....Philadelphia, PA
Billet, Jerome S., (A Professional Corporation) ....Los Angeles, CA
Billet, Kaplan, Sokol & Dawley
Los Angeles, CA
Billet, Kevin R. ....Atlanta, GA
Billet, Marvin ....New York, NY
Billet, Matthew S. ....Boston, MA
Fitchburg, MA
Billet, Melissa L. ....Glendale, CA
Billet, Rigopoulos & Levine
New Haven, CT
Boston, MA
Fitchburg, MA
Billet, Robert D. ....Turnersville, NJ
Philadelphia, PA
Billet, Van ....Newtown Square, PA
Billeter, J. David ....Park City, UT
Billett, Allan R. ....Tacoma, WA
Billett, Brian ....Washington, DC
Billett, Donald R. ....New York, NY
Billett, Donald Russell ....New York, NY
Billett, James D. ....Atlanta, GA
Billett, Jeffrey D. ....Department of Defense,
Defense Legal Services Agency, GV
Billey, Cynthia J. ....Los Angeles, CA
Billey, Eileen C. ....Greensburg, PA
Billey, James O. ....Ellendale, ND
Billheimer, Gordon ....Montgomery, WV
Billheimer, Gordon E., Jr. ....Carthage, MO
Billhimer, Mark A. ....Westbury, NY
Billhorn, John W. ....Chicago, IL
Billhymer, Julya ....Fort Worth, TX
Billian, Alan L. ....Baltimore, MD
Billick, Bernard M. ....Stroudsburg, PA
Billick, Brooke J. ....Milwaukee, WI
Billick, John T. ....Cleveland, OH
Billick, Timothy R. ....Mayfield Heights, OH
Billick, William ....Encino, CA
Billick & Wolf ....Stroudsburg, PA
Billiel, Michael D. ....Department of Justice,
Antitrust Division, GV
Billig, Andrew S. ....New York, NY
Billig, Darin S. ....New York, NY
Billig, Jack F. ....Baltimore, MD
Billig, Patrick G. ....Minneapolis, MN
Billig, Robert A. ....North Miami Beach, FL
Billig, Ronda L. ....Irvington, NY
Billik, Richard J. ....Brookfield, IL
Billik, Richard J., Jr. ....Chicago, IL
Billik, William M. ....Buffalo, NY
Billimack, SueAnn Sage ....Peoria, IL
Billing, Bernadette M. ....Cincinnati, OH
Billing, Beth ....Bartow, FL
Billing, Cochran, Heath, Lyles & Mauro, P.A. ....Fort Lauderdale, FL
Fort Myers, FL
Tampa, FL

Billing, Cochran, Heath, Lyles & Mauro, P.A.—Continued
West Palm Beach, FL
Billing, David B. ... Madison, WI
Billing, Mary Denise ... Salisbury, MD
Billinger, James L. ... Joint Committees And Commissions, GV
Billingham, Karen M. ... Dallas, TX
Billingham, Katherine L. ... Centerville, OH
Billingham & Marzelli ... Marshfield, MA
Billingham, William G. ... Marshfield, MA
Billings, Alan L. ... Marshfield, WI
Billings, Anne E. ... United States Senate, Senatorial Assistants, GV
Billings, Barbara R. ... Woodward, OK
Billings and Billings ... Wallingford, CT
Billings & Billings ... Woodward, OK
Billings, Bronwyn Erin ... San Diego, CA
Billings, Bruce A. ... Trinidad, CO
Billings, Bruce S. ... Limestone, ME
Billings, Bryan L. ... Woodward, OK
Billings, Bryce E. ... Valparaiso, IN
Billings, C. Thomas ... Greenfield, IN
Billings, Charles H. ... St. Louis, MO
Billings, Charles R. ... Dallas, TX
Billings, Charles R., P.C. ... Dallas, TX
Billings, Chester, Jr. ... New York, NY
Billings, Clyde A., Jr. ... Memphis, TN
Billings, Cunningham, Morgan & Boatwright, Professional Association
Kissimmee, FL
Orlando, FL
Sanford, FL
Billings, Cynthia Jo ... Southfield, MI
Billings, David A. ... San Diego, CA
Billings, David J. ... Los Angeles, CA
Billings, David M. ... New York, NY
Billings, Despena Fillios ... Boston, MA
Billings, Donald N. ... New York, NY
Billings, Donald R. ... Lewisville, NC
Billings, Douglas J. ... San Diego, CA
Billings, Eric R. ... Jacksonville, FL
Billings, Frank E. ... Houston, TX
Billings, Franklin S., Jr. ... Woodstock, VT
Billings, J. Hilary ... Bangor, ME
Billings, Jack A. ... Eugene, OR
Billings, James B. ... Oak Hill, WV
Billings, James G. ... Raleigh, NC
Billings, Jared M. ... Orlando, FL
Billings, Jeanne Lazarre
New Orleans, LA
Billings, Jeffery A. ... Chattanooga, TN
Billings, Jessie W.
Department of Commerce, Patent and Trademark Office, GV
Billings, John F. ... Ashland, KY
Billings, John P. ... Vermillion, SD
Billings, John V. P. ... Wallingford, CT
Billings, Jos. A. ... Johnston, IA
Billings, Joseph G. ... Landover, MD
Billings, Judith Mitchell ... Salt Lake City, UT
Billings, Julie H. ... Long Beach, CA
Billings, LaVon E. ... Red Oak, IA
Billings, Michael D. ... Oklahoma City, OK
Billings, Paige Evelyn ... Tallahassee, FL
Billings, Paul B., Jr. ... Memphis, TN
Billings, Peter W. ... Salt Lake City, UT
Billings, Rhoda B. ... Winston-Salem, NC
Billings, Richard A. ... Lakewood, CO
Billings, Richard W. ... Providence, RI
Billings, Roger R. ... Sacramento, CA
Billings & Solomon, P.C. ... Houston, TX
Billings, Thomas P. ... Boston, MA
Billings, Thomas T. ... Park City, UT
Salt Lake City, UT
Billings, William F., Law Offices of
Dallas, TX
Billings, William M. ... New York, NY
Billings, Wm. Compton ... Springfield, MO
Billingslea, Everett H. ... Olympia, WA
Billingslea, Sidney K. ... Anchorage, AK
Billingslea, Stephanie Colleen
Huntsville, AL
Billingslea, William, Jr. ... Chula Vista, CA
Billingsley, Ann B. Voorhees ... Cleveland, OH
Billingsley, C. Coleman, Jr. ... Raleigh, NC
Billingsley, Callan M. ... Boerne, TX
Billingsley, Curtis A. ... Tallahassee, FL
Billingsley, C. W. Tab, Jr. ... Atlanta, GA
Billingsley, Dana H. ... Montgomery, AL
Billingsley, Frances Newberry ... Chicago, IL
Billingsley, Gary M. ... Lockport, NY
Billingsley, H. Clay ... St. Louis, MO
Billingsley, Henry E., II ... Cleveland, OH
Billingsley, J. Michael ... Kingsport, TN
Billingsley, James H. ... Dallas, TX
Billingsley, James H. ... Plano, TX
Billingsley, Joanna V. ... Ozark, MO
Billingsley, John E. ... Baxter, IA
Newton, IA
Billingsley, John J. ... King George, VA
Billingsley, John R. ... Dallas, TX
Billingsley, Joseph A., Jr.
King George, VA
Billingsley, Kathleen ... Fort Worth, TX
Billingsley, Keith I. ... Little Rock, AR
Billingsley, Lance W. ... Annapolis, MD
Riverdale, MD
Billingsley, Larry R. ... Raytown, MO
Billingsley, Orzell, Jr. ... Birmingham, AL
Billingsley, Paul L. ... Hammond, LA
Luling, LA
Billingsley, Robbie L. ... Buffalo, NY
Billingsley, Rosario Bacon, (Ms.)
San Francisco, CA
Billingsley & Snead ... King George, VA
Billingsley, Stacey D. ... Nashville, TN

Billingsley, Stanley M. ... Carrollton, KY
Billings Vela, Linda M.
Colorado Springs, CO
Billington, Barry E. ... Atlanta, GA
Billington, Barry P., P.A.
Pompano Beach, FL
Billington and Billington ... Springfield, IL
Billington, David J. H. ... New York, NY
Billington, Glenn E. ... Cleveland, OH
Billington, John A. ... Springfield, IL
Billington, John W. ... Eugene, OR
Billington, John W., P.C. ... Eugene, OR
Billington, P. Daniel ... Union, MO
Billington, Patricia E. ... Honolulu, HI
Billington, Randall ... Riverside, CA
Billington, Randall J. ... Redlands, CA
Billington, Thomas R. ... Springfield, IL
Billinson, Craig J. ... Syracuse, NY
Billinson, George D. ... Baltimore, MD
Billinson, Jayne M. ... Philadelphia, PA
Billinson, Weinshenker and Balducci
Syracuse, NY
Billion, John H. ... Sioux Falls, SD
Billion, Michael M. ... Sioux Falls, SD
Billion, Richard E. ... Minneapolis, MN
Billips, Dale D. ... Pauma Valley, CA
Billips, Matthew C. ... Atlanta, GA
Billips, William M. ... Nashville, TN
Billiris, Tom H. ... Holiday, FL
Billman, Brookes D. ... New York, NY
Billman, Charles Ivey ... Arlington, VA
Billman, Donald L. ... Columbus, OH
Billman, Leslie G. ... Annapolis, MD
Billman, Martha Gray ... New York, NY
Billman, Robert E. ... Indianapolis, IN
Billman, Scott C. ... Buffalo, NY
Billmeier, Leonard Michael, Jr.
Tallahassee, FL
Billmeier, Robert C. ... Trenton, NJ
Billmeyer, Craig M. ... Cape Girardeau, MO
Billmyre, John G. ... Easton, MD
Billock, Wm. B. ... Allison Park, PA
Billon, Henri C. ... Rayne, LA
Billotte, Roger Griffin ... Denver, CO
Billotti, Annmarie ... Walnut Creek, CA
Billotti, Michael A. ... Princeton, NJ
Billow, Gerald J. ... Boston, MA
Billow, Patricia McQuillen ... Akron, OH
Billow, Paul H. ... Raleigh, NC
Bills, Alexander ... Stamford, CT
Bills, Charles W. ... Bethesda, MD
Bills, David J. ... Sacramento, CA
Bills, David S. ... Atlanta, GA
Bills, George William, Jr. ... Pittsburgh, PA
Bills, Kenneth T. ... Woodbridge, NJ
Bills, Liz ... Austin, TX
Bills, NinaLynne ... Salt Lake City, UT
Bills, Robert D., Jr. ... Costa Mesa, CA
Bills, Russell G. ... Marlow, OK
Billups, Paul A. ... Huntington, WV
Billups, Richard C. ... Rahway, NJ
Billups-Slone, Denise ... Walnut Creek, CA
Billy, Carrie L. ... United States Senate, Senatorial Assistants, GV
Billy, Catherine L. ... San Diego, CA
Billy, John M. ... La Jolla, CA
Billy, Michael, Jr. ... New York, NY
Billy, Stephen Mahone ... Brewton, AL
Billy, Steven T. ... Richmond, VA
Billyard, Roger E. ... Nunda, NY
Billyou, Jean D. ... Irvine, CA
Bilmes & Bilmes ... Pine Bush, NY
Bilmes, Frances E. ... Pine Bush, NY
Bilmes, Murray ... Pine Bush, NY
Bilms, Kevin P. ... Portsmouth, VA
Bilodeau, Christine ... Orlando, FL
Bilodeau, Doris A. ... South Deerfield, MA
Bilodeau, James R. ... Freeport, ME
Bilodeau, Jean Sheftic ... Baltimore, MD
Bilodeau, Kenneth D. ... Rochester, MI
Bilodeau, Nolin J. ... McLean, VA
Bilodeau, Thomas H., III ... Boston, MA
Bilodeau, Wallace A. ... Skowhegan, ME
Bilohavek, Bruce ... Washington, PA
Biloon & Associates ... Savannah, GA
Biloon, Audrey P. ... Savannah, GA
Biloon, Harold L. ... Wethersfield, CT
Bilott, Raymond L. ... Dayton, OH
Bilott, Robert A. ... Cincinnati, OH
Bilotta, Cassandra ... Suffern, NY
Bilotta, Gary L. ... Beaver, PA
Bilotta, Joseph ... Lake Worth, FL
Bilotti, Anthony J. ... Philadelphia, PA
Bilotti, Deborah L. ... Chicago, IL
Bilotti, Karen L. ... San Diego, CA
Bilotti, Sabino ... Springfield, MA
Bilotto, Gerard ... New York, NY
Bilow, Robert L. ... Boise, ID
Bilowz, Walter G. ... North Reading, MA
Bils, Charles F. ... Madison, WI
Bilse, Scott R. ... Hammond, IN
Bilsker, David L. ... Menlo Park, CA
Bilski, Christopher P. ... New York, NY
Bilski, Thomas James ... Osseo, WI
Bilsky, Bert L. ... Milwaukee, WI
Bilsky, Eric A. ... Washington, DC
Bilsky, Moses ... Chicago, IL
Bilsky, Steven F. ... Memphis, TN
Bilsky, Wayne W. ... Altamonte Springs, FL
Bilsky, Wayne W., P.A.
Altamonte Springs, FL
Orlando, FL
Bilson, Ira E. ... Santa Monica, CA
Bilson, Michael ... North Hollywood, CA
Bilstad, Blake T. ... San Diego, CA
Bilstad, Melissa L. ... San Francisco, CA
Bilstrom, Jon W. ... St. Louis, MO
Biltcliffe, David A. ... Fall River, MA

Biltekoff, Judith A. ... Buffalo, NY
Biltekoff, Robert A. ... Buffalo, NY
Biltekoff, Steven ... Buffalo, NY
Bilter, D. Keith ... San Francisco, CA
Bilton, Aaron Richard ... Chicago, IL
Bilton, Dean H. ... Chicago, IL
Bilton, Dwayne E. ... Houston, TX
Bilton, J. Philip ... Richardson, TX
Bilton, William David ... Columbia, SC
Bilus, Benjamin S. ... Stamford, CT
Bilus, Elizabeth Nickeson ... Purchase, NY
Bilut, Mark A. ... Chicago, IL
Bily, Kirkland J. ... Houston, TX
Bily, Raymond M., Jr. ... Philadelphia, PA
Bilyeu, Brigette ... Twin Falls, ID
Bilyeu, Byron L. ... Reno, NV
Bilyeu, Dana K. ... Carson City, NV
Bilyeu, Gregory Norman ... Bellingham, WA
Bilyeu, Marjorie ... Williamston, MI
Bilyeu, Marjorie, P.C. ... Williamston, MI
Bilyk, Thomas D. ... Chicago, IL
Bilynsky, Oleh V. ... Wilmington, DE
Bilzi, Carol J. ... Washington, DC
Bilzin, Brian L., (P.A.) ... Miami, FL
Bilzin, Marsha D. ... Miami, FL
Bilzin Sumberg Dunn Price & Axelrod LLP
Miami, FL
Bilzor, John C. ... Norfolk, VA
Bima-Reeves, Theresa ... Omaha, NE
Bimbela-Quiñones, Charles ... San Juan, PR
Bimber, Frederick R. ... Traverse City, MI
Bimber, Frederick R., P.C.
Traverse City, MI
Bimberg, Gary W. ... Southfield, MI
Bimberg, Rebecca D. ... Carleton, MI
Bimbler, Frederick P. ... New York, NY
Bimson, Bradford D. ... Virginia Beach, VA
Bimson, J. Dale ... Virginia Beach, VA
Bina, Daniel R. ... Pine City, MN
Bina, Hass, Saenger, Holm & Martin
Pine City, MN
Bina, Robert I. ... Batavia, IL
Binam, Robert M. ... Pasadena, CA
Binau, Dan J. ... Columbus, OH
Binczewski, Neal E. ... Albuquerque, NM
Bindas, Kathryn L. ... Washington, PA
Bindbeutel, Joseph P. ... Jefferson City, MO
Bindelglass, Howard ... New York, NY
Bindell, Francine L. ... Pittsburgh, PA
Bindeman, Sherry A. ... Washington, DC
Binder, Allan E. ... Mineola, NY
Binder, Allison ... Los Angeles, CA
Binder, Arlene ... Los Angeles, CA
Binder, Barry R. ... Encino, CA
Binder, Benjamin ... New York, NY
Binder, Bert ... Hackensack, NJ
Binder & Binder ... New York, NY
Binder, Bob ... Austin, TX
Binder, Brooks W. ... Atlanta, GA
Binder, Bruce S.
Environmental Protection Agency, Office of the General Counsel, GV
Binder, Carl A. ... Carle Place, NY
Binder, Charles E. ... Bay City, MI
Binder, Charles E. ... New York, NY
Binder, Darcy S. ... New York, NY
Binder, Darren T. ... Washington, DC
Binder, David A. ... Los Angeles, CA
Binder, David A. ... Reading, PA
Binder, David F. ... Philadelphia, PA
Binder, Denis ... Anaheim, CA
Binder Goldstein, Law Offices of
Paterson, NJ
Wayne, NJ
Binder, Harry J. ... New York, NY
Binder, Heinz ... San Jose, CA
Binder, Henry ... Houston, TX
Binder, Herman ... New York, NY
Binder, Ira D. ... Oxford, PA
Binder, Jane ... Minneapolis, MN
Binder, Janice B. ... Hazard, KY
Binder, Jennifer D. ... Stevens Point, WI
Binder, Jonathan Stuart
Environmental Protection Agency, Office of Enforcement and Compliance Assurance, GV
Binder, Joseph S. ... Bala Cynwyd, PA
Philadelphia, PA
Binder, Kalis & Proctor, P.C.
Norristown, PA
Pottstown, PA
Binder, Karen ... New York, NY
Binder, Karen Marie ... Detroit, MI
Binder, Kathleen ... St. Petersburg, FL
Binder, Kurt L. ... Worcester, MA
Binder, Laurie R. ... New York, NY
Binder Law Offices, P.A.
Minneapolis, MN
Binder, Lilli A. ... Harrisburg, PA
Binder, Lisa ... Los Angeles, CA
Binder & Malter ... San Jose, CA
Binder, Mark W. ... Minneapolis, MN
Binder, Martha L. ... Mission Viejo, CA
Binder, Martin W. ... Reading, PA
Binder, Mary Beattie ... Chicago, IL
Binder, Mary S. ... Chicago, IL
Binder, Maureen F. Wolfe
Los Angeles, CA
Binder & Milner ... Jackson, MS
Binder, Nancy R. ... Encino, CA
Binder, Paul K. ... Chicago, IL
Binder, Paul L. ... Cleveland, OH
Binder, Perry Z. ... Morrow, GA
Binder, Peter K. ... Gardner, MA
Binder, Richard L. ... Boston, MA
Binder, Richard L. ... Sheboygan, WI
Binder, Robert H. ... New York, NY
Binder, Robert L. ... Milwaukee, WI

Binder, Roy H. ... Wayne, NJ
Binder, Rudolph ... Chardon, OH
Binder, T. James ... Woodbridge, VA
Binder, Thomas J. ... Milwaukee, WI
Binder, Thomas M. ... Wyomissing, PA
Binder, Timothy R. ... San Diego, CA
Binder, Walter J., Jr. ... Cary, IL
Binder & Weiss, A Professional Corporation
Collingswood, NJ
Bala Cynwyd, PA
Philadelphia, PA
Binder, Wendy C. ... Chicago, IL
Binder, William M., Law Offices of
Milwaukee, WI
Binder-Arain, Laurel ... New York, NY
Binderman, William N. ... New York, NY
Philadelphia, PA
Philadelphia, PA
Binderow, Lawrence H. ... Del Mar, CA
Bindert, Thomas W. ... New York, NY
Bindes, Jack H. ... Southfield, MI
Bindewald, Kimberli D. ... North Platte, NE
Bindi, David E. ... Chicago, IL
Bindler, Deborah H. ... New York, NY
Bindler, M. Jill ... Fort Worth, TX
Bindler, Susan E. ... St. Louis, MO
Bindley, James F. ... Indianapolis, IN
Bindley, Richard S. ... Heath, OH
Bindner, Michael T. ... Indianapolis, IN
Bindner, Roger D. ... Orange City, IA
Paullina, IA
Bindner, Roseann Rene
Department of the Army, Office, Chief of Engineers/Headquarters, U.S. Army Corps of Engineers, GV
Bindock, D. Mark ... San Antonio, TX
Bindra, Saranjit S. ... New York, NY
Bindra, Tejinder S. ... Reston, VA
Bindrup, Scott L. ... Las Vegas, NV
Bindseil, James J. ... Charlotte, NC
Bindseil, Lori Dawn ... San Antonio, TX
Bine, Russell E. ... Birmingham, MI
Binegar, Daniel H. ... Dayton, OH
Binegar, G. David ... Davenport, IA
Binegar, G. Neil ... Covington, KY
Bineham, William D. ... San Antonio, TX
Binek, William W. ... Bismarck, ND
Binelli, Rudolph R., Jr. ... Hackensack, NJ
Bineman-Sowers, Martha Ann ... Ithaca, NY
Bines, Harvey E. ... Boston, MA
Binetsch, Joan M. ... East St. Louis, IL
Binetti, Luke F., (P.C.) ... Ridgefield, NJ
Binetti, Maureen S. ... Woodbridge, NJ
Binetti, Robert F. ... Ridgefield, NJ
Binetti, Robert F., P.A. ... Ridgefield, NJ
Binetti, William R. ... Racine, WI
Binford, F. Marshall ... Atlanta, GA
Binford, Gregory G. ... Cleveland, OH
Binford, Heidi M. ... Los Angeles, CA
Binford, Henry D. ... Dothan, AL
Binford, Howard M. ... Laguna Hills, CA
Binford, Joseph R. ... Houston, TX
Binford, W. Warren ... Sacramento, CA
Bing, Andrew D. ... Albany, NY
Bing, Anita K. ... Tampa, FL
Bing, Dan T. ... Memphis, TN
Bing, Jonathan L. ... New York, NY
Bing, Marie F. ... Saugerties, NY
Bing, Peter R. ... Los Angeles, CA
Bing, Richard G. ... Canton, OH
Bing, Richard M. ... Richmond, VA
Bing, Richard M., P.C. ... Richmond, VA
Bing, Robert K. ... Burlington, VT
Bing, Stephen R. ... Boston, MA
Bing, Stephen W. ... Houston, TX
Bing, Steven E. ... New York, NY
Bingaman, Anne K. ... McLean, VA
Bingaman, Charles C. ... Springfield, IL
Bingaman, Hess, Coblentz & Bell, A Professional Corporation ... Reading, PA
Bingaman, James H. ... Springdale, AR
Bingaman, Jeff ... Santa Fe, NM
Bingaman, John W. ... Austin, TX
Bingaman, Joseph P. ... Orinda, CA
Bingaman, Samuel Calvin, III
Chickasha, OK
Binge, Brent E. ... Washington, DC
Bingen, Lisa D. ... Richmond, VA
Bingen, Michael C. ... Kalamazoo, MI
Binger, Alan J. ... New City, NY
Binger, Charles H. ... St. Louis, MO
Binger, Cherie A. ... Key West, FL
Binger, James H. ... Wayzata, MN
Binger, Julia R. ... Northport, NY
Binger, Mark ... Newport Beach, CA
Binger, Ralph E. ... Superior, WI
Binger, Robert B. ... Spokane, WA
Binger, Ruth Ann ... St. Louis, MO
Binger, Steven R. ... Sioux Falls, SD
Binger, Thomas C. ... Milwaukee, WI
Bingham, A. Walker, III ... New York, NY
Bingham, Anthony B. ... Casa Grande, AZ
Bingham, Benjamin R. ... San Antonio, TX
Bingham, Bradley M. ... Houston, TX
Bingham, Carolyn J. ... Sanford, FL
Bingham, Charles W. ... Tacoma, WA
Bingham, Charlotte D. ... Lubbock, TX
Bingham, Clifton O., Jr. ... Baton Rouge, LA
Bingham Dana LLP ... Los Angeles, CA
Hartford, CT
Washington, DC
Boston, MA
New York, NY
Bingham, Darwin H. ... Salt Lake City, UT
Bingham, Donald E. ... Chicago, IL
Bingham, Donald M. ... Tulsa, OK
Bingham, Douglas A. ... La Jolla, CA
Bingham, Ellis Dean, III ... Birmingham, AL

Bird & Skibell, A Professional Corporation ... Dallas, TX
Bird, Stephen J. ... Rochester, NY
Bird, Stephen S. ... **Hilton Head Island, SC**
Bird, Steven R. ... Bryan, OH
Bird, Steven R. ... **Childress, TX**
Bird, Susan Willett ... Greenwich, CT
Bird, Susie Kim ... Treasury Department, Internal Revenue Service, GV
Bird, Svendsen, Brothers, Scheske & Pattison, P.C. ... **Coldwater, MI**; **Sturgis, MI**; **Three Rivers, MI**
Bird, T. Buckingham ... Monticello, FL
Bird, Terry C. ... Atlanta, GA
Bird, Terry W. ... **Los Angeles, CA**
Bird, Thomas C. ... **Albuquerque, NM**
Bird, Thomas L. ... **Minneapolis, MN**
Bird, Thomas L., & Associates, P.A. ... **Minneapolis, MN**
Bird, Timothy S. ... **Fairfax, VA**
Bird, Tina M. ... Chicago, IL
Bird, Warren J. ... Tallahassee, FL
Bird, Wendell R. ... **Atlanta, GA**
Bird, William E. ... Columbia, SC
Bird, William Q. ... **Atlanta, GA**
Bird, William Q., and Associates, P.C. ... **Atlanta, GA**
Bird, William R., Jr. ... **Orlando, FL**
Bird, William W. ... **St. Joseph, MO**
Birden, Paul B., Jr. ... Columbus, OH
Birder, Dudley D., Jr. ... **Gainesville, FL**
Birdlebough, Stephen C. ... Sacramento, CA
Birdoff, David C. ... **New York, NY**
Birdoff, Richard J. ... Union, NJ
Bird-Pico, Ana Marta ... **San Juan, PR**
Bird-Pocker, Beth ... Stamford, CT
Birdsall, Benjamin J. ... New Orleans, LA
Birdsall, Clark E. ... Dallas, TX
Birdsall, John A. ... **Milwaukee, WI**
Birdsall & Madigan ... Belmar, NJ
Birdsall, Phillip J. ... Mason, MI
Birdsall, Richard D. ... Sacramento, CA
Birdsall, Sandra J. ... Peoria, IL
Birdsall, William C. ... Farmington, NM
Birdsall, William C., P.C. ... Farmington, NM
Birdseye, Story ... San Jose, CA
Birdsong, Allen C ... Forsyth, MT
Birdsong, Andrew W., Jr. ... Atlanta, GA
Birdsong, Anne P. ... Lake Charles, LA; **New Orleans, LA**
Birdsong, Bret C. ... Department of Justice, Environment and Natural Resources Division, GV
Birdsong, Dan L. ... **Rolla, MO**
Birdsong, David W. ... Metairie, LA
Birdsong, George Y. ... Suffolk, VA
Birdsong, Jeffrey Layne ... Columbia, SC
Birdsong, Jimmy ... Oklahoma City, OK
Birdsong, Lindsey S. ... Tyler, TX
Birdsong, Samuel E., Jr. ... Jackson, MS
BirdSong Stapleton & Associates ... **Montgomery, AL**
BirdSong, Tracy G. ... **Montgomery, AL**
Birdt, Joan ... **Palos Verdes Estates, CA**
Birdt, Jonathan W. ... **Los Angeles, CA**
Birdwell & Associates ... **Oklahoma City, OK**
Birdwell, Carol A. ... Fort Worth, TX
Birdwell, Carol A., P.C. ... Fort Worth, TX
Birdwell, Daniel ... Chattanooga, TN
Birdwell, Dwight W. ... **Oklahoma City, OK**
Birdwell, J. Wade ... **Fort Worth, TX**
Birdwell, Janke & Durando, LLP ... **Portland, OR**
Birdwell, Jerry R. ... Dallas, TX
Birdwell, John W. ... Corydon, IA
Birdwell, Robt. L. ... Oklahoma City, OK
Birdwell, William A. ... **Tucson, AZ**; **Portland, OR**
Birdwell, William D. ... **Cookeville, TN**
Birdwell, Z. Scott ... Federal Deposit Insurance Corporation, Trial Litigation Section, GV
Birdwhistell, Nan Mead ... **New Haven, CT**
Birdwhistell, Wm. Barry ... Elizabethtown, KY
Birek, Stephen J., Jr. ... Department of Labor, GV
Biren, Andrea L. ... Oakland, CA
Biren, Brenda F. ... **San Francisco, CA**
Biren & Katzman ... **Los Angeles, CA**
Biren, Matthew B. F. ... **Los Angeles, CA**
Biren, Melissa H. ... **Parsippany, NJ**
Biren, Richard M. ... New York, NY
Biren, Sandra Bailey ... **Santa Monica, CA**
Biren, Steven R. ... Tarrytown, NY
Birenbach, Brian Alan ... **Buffalo, NY**
Birenbaum, Charles S. ... **Los Angeles, CA**; **San Francisco, CA**
Birenbaum, David B. ... Fairfax, CA
Birenbaum, David E. (IBA) ... **Washington, DC**
Birenbaum, Deborah B. ... Thousand Oaks, CA
Birenbaum, Herbert A. ... Long Beach, CA
Birenbaum, Jonathan ... **Stamford, CT**
Birenbaum, Martin S. ... Miami, FL
Birenbaum, Sam ... Malibu, CA
Birenbaum, Sara Gens ... **Cambridge, MA**
Birenbaum, Susan E. ... Pension Benefit Guaranty Corporation, Office of the General Counsel, GV
Birenbaum, Vicki A. ... **Houston, TX**
Birenboim, Bruce ... **New York, NY**
Birenz, Jerry S. ... **New York, NY**
Bires, David R. ... **Houston, TX**
Bires, Dennis E. ... New York, NY
Bires & Schaffer ... **Houston, TX**
Bires, Stephen L., Jr. ... Corpus Christi, TX
Biretta, Christine K. ... Denver, CO
Birg, Erika C. ... **Atlanta, GA**
Birgbauer, Bruce D. ... **Detroit, MI**
Birge, Andrew Byerly ... **Chicago, IL**
Birgé, Bradley D. ... Chicago, IL
Birge, Eric R. ... **Dallas, TX**
Birge, Gregory M. ... **Melbourne, FL**
Birge, James S. ... **Indianapolis, IN**
Birge, Jane E. ... Phoenix, AZ
Birge, Jonathan L. ... **Indianapolis, IN**
Birge, Jonathan Taggart ... **Indianapolis, IN**
Birge, Marian Helen ... Encinitas, CA
Birge & Mayers, P.C. ... **Denver, CO**; St. Louis, MO
Birge, Robert J. ... Cleveland, OH
Birge, Thomas D. ... **Denver, CO**
Birgel, Andreas, Jr. ... Encino, CA
Birgel, Anne ... Dover, NH
Birgel, Stephan ... Sherman Oaks, CA
Birgen, Deborah A. ... **Sioux Falls, SD**
Birgenheier, Hugh K. ... Tacoma, WA
Birgfeld, Frank J. ... Denver, CO
Birgisson, Gunnar ... **Washington, DC**
Biri, Lawrence E., Jr. ... New Orleans, LA
Biribauer, Richard F. ... New Brunswick, NJ
Biribin, Renato R. ... Plainfield, NJ
Biringer, Geoffrey M. ... Harrisburg, PA
Biringer, Hutchinson, Van Doren, Lillis & Bappert, P.C. ... **Coldwater, MI**; **Hillsdale, MI**; **Sturgis, MI**
Biringer, Richard F. ... **Coldwater, MI**
Birins, Sonja F. ... Mobile, AL
Birinyi, Richard G. ... **Bellevue, WA**
Birk, David J. ... Aurora, CO
Birk, David J., P.C. ... Aurora, CO
Birk, David R. ... Phoenix, AZ
Birk, Diane C ... Baltimore, MD; Woodbury, NJ
Birk, Edward L. ... **Jacksonville, FL**
Birk, John E. ... **Jasper, IN**
Birk, Joseph E. ... St. Louis, MO
Birk Kabrick, Attorneys at Law, A Professional Corporation ... **Jasper, IN**
Birk, Mary Price ... **Denver, CO**
Birk, Robert A. ... Portland, OR
Birk, Thomas H. ... **Jasper, IN**
Birka-White, David M., Law Offices of ... **Alamo, CA**
Birka-White, David M., Law Offices of ... **Oakland, CA**; **Sacramento, CA**; **San Francisco, CA**; **Walnut Creek, CA**
Birkbeck, A.J. Koerts ... Oak Park, IL
Birkby, John R. ... St. Louis, MO
Birkdale, Lisa M. ... **Boston, MA**
Birke, Charles L. ... **Los Angeles, CA**
Birke, Dennis P. ... **Madison, WI**
Birke, Richard ... Salem, OR
Birkedahl, Kara T. ... Denver, CO
Birkel, Bernard L. ... **Houston, TX**
Birkel, James L. ... David City, NE
Birkel, Julia L. ... **Malibu, CA**
Birkel, Walter G. ... **Washington, DC**
Birkel, William J. ... **Omaha, NE**
Birkeland, Anders ... Stoughton, WI
Birkeland, Bryan C. (IBA) ... **Dallas, TX**
Birkeland, Cathy A. ... **Chicago, IL**
Birkeland, John H. ... **Denver, CO**
Birkeland, Paul T. ... **Minneapolis, MN**
Birkelbach, John Steven ... **El Paso, TX**
Birkelund, James ... **San Francisco, CA**
Birken, Joel M. ... **Vienna, VA**
Birken, Mary Ann V. ... Houston, TX
Birkenbuel, Maria ... Great Falls, MT
Birkeness, William R. ... Liberty, MO
Birkenfeld, Douglas K. ... Boston, MA
Birkenholtz, Laura K. ... Des Moines, IA
Birkenholz, James D. ... Des Moines, IA
Birkenstein, David B. ... Chicago, IL
Birkenstock, Joseph M. ... Washington, DC
Birkenwald, Richard Paul ... North Miami Beach, FL
Birker, Craig C. ... **Los Angeles, CA**
Birkes, Keith A. ... Jefferson City, MO
Birkett, Joseph E. ... Wheaton, IL
Birkett, Peter W. ... Brooklyn, NY
Birkett, William C. ... Department of Justice, Immigration and Naturalization Service, GV
Birkhaeuser, Daniel E. ... **Walnut Creek, CA**
Birkhaeuser, David E. ... Springfield, MA
Birkhahn, Jonathan ... **New York, NY**
Birkhead, G. William ... **Kitty Hawk, NC**; **Norfolk, VA**
Birkhead, Geoffrey F. ... **Kitty Hawk, NC**; **Norfolk, VA**
Birkhead, Virginia F. ... Louisville, KY
Birkhimer, Dennis C. ... San Francisco, CA
Birkhimer, Dennis C., A Professional Corporation ... San Francisco, CA
Birkhimer, William R. ... Columbus, OH
Birkhoff, Neil V. ... **Roanoke, VA**
Birkhold & Charter, P.C. ... Kalamazoo, MI
Birkhold, Jeffrey O. ... **Grand Rapids, MI**
Birkhold, Thomas A. ... Kalamazoo, MI
Birkholz, Daniel A. ... St. James, MN
Birkholz, Frank W. ... **Seattle, WA**
Birkholz, Fred R. ... Jacksonville, FL
Birkholz, Gloria A. ... Albuquerque, NM
Birkie, Brooke K. ... **Santa Rosa, CA**
Birkin, Christopher L. ... **Las Vegas, NV**
Birkinsha, Jack E. ... Atchison, KS
Birkitt, Cynthia ... East Hanover, NJ
Birkland, Jack A. ... La Habra, CA
Birkland, Wendell R. ... **Portland, OR**
Birkman, Arlan H. ... Deerfield Beach, FL
Birkmeyer, Laura J. ... San Diego, CA
Birknes, John A., Jr. ... Dartmouth, MA
Birks, David C. ... **Chicago, IL**
Birks, Roger H. ... San Diego, CA
Birle, Hans Peter ... Boston, MA
Birle, Joann Berardo ... **New York, NY**
Birle, Noël C. ... **Philadelphia, PA**
Birley, Cindy S. ... **Denver, CO**
Birman, Caroline ... Forest Hills, NY
Birman, Joel D. ... Chicago, IL
Birman, Mindy Joan ... Bronx, NY
Birmelin, Robert C. ... Miami, FL
Birmiel, Howard A. ... Burke, VA
Birmingham, Alan ... **Hartford, CT**; **West Hartford, CT**; **Woodbury, CT**
Birmingham, Alison D. ... **Seattle, WA**
Birmingham, Ann E. ... Phoenix, AZ
Birmingham, Brad A. ... **Buffalo, NY**
Birmingham, Charles J. ... Tampa, FL
Birmingham, Cynthia K. ... **Hayward, CA**
Birmingham, Daniel ... **New York, NY**
Birmingham, Drue D., Jr. ... Olive Branch, MS
Birmingham, Edward ... Omaha, NE
Birmingham, Fletcher A. ... Independence, OH
Birmingham Group, The, LPA ... **Cleveland, OH**; **Rocky River, OH**
Birmingham, Hobart McK. ... Scotts Valley, CA
Birmingham, Jack ... Anchorage, AK
Birmingham, James B. ... **Orlando, FL**
Birmingham, James. F. ... White Plains, NY
Birmingham, Jennifer E. ... **Florham Park, NJ**
Birmingham, Joan A. ... Baltimore, MD
Birmingham, John D. ... Toledo, OH
Birmingham, John F., Jr. ... **Detroit, MI**
Birmingham, John T. ... Oberlin, OH
Birmingham, Lisa Nolen ... **Montpelier, VT**
Birmingham, Mark ... Kansas City, KS
Birmingham, Mary N. ... Tucson, AZ
Birmingham, Matthew T., III ... **Ludlow, VT**
Birmingham, Morley, Weatherford & Priore ... Tulsa, OK
Birmingham, Neal E. ... Atlanta, TX
Birmingham, Pat ... **Portland, OR**
Birmingham, Patrick J. ... Bloomfield, NE
Birmingham, Patrick Michael ... **Portland, OR**
Birmingham, Rebecca ... **Long Beach, CA**
Birmingham, Richard F. ... Staten Island, NY
Birmingham, Richard G. ... Clearwater, FL
Birmingham, Richard G. ... **Buffalo, NY**
Birmingham, Richard J. ... **Seattle, WA**
Birmingham, Suzanne Hornaday ... Concord, NC
Birmingham, Thomas F. ... Boston, MA
Birmingham, Thomas F. ... Tulsa, OK
Birmingham, Thomas P. ... St. Petersburg, FL
Birmingham, Thomas W. ... **Sacramento, CA**
Birmingham Thorson & Barnett, P.C. ... **Seattle, WA**
Birmingham, Tracy ... Chicago, IL
Birmingham, Virginia W. ... Oakmont, PA
Birmingham, William B. ... Los Angeles, CA
Birmingham, William T. ... Phoenix, AZ
Birn, Harold M. ... **New York, NY**
Birn, Jerome F., Jr. ... **Palo Alto, CA**
Birn, Linda S. ... Honolulu, HI
Birn, Sarah Walker ... **Albany, NY**
Birn, Stuart R. ... **Lansing, MI**
Birnant, Daniel A. ... New York, NY
Birnbach, Deborah S. ... **Boston, MA**
Birnbach, Howard R. ... Great Neck, NY
Birnbach, Ilyssa ... **New York, NY**
Birnbaum, Alan ... Department of Justice, Environment and Natural Resources Division, GV
Birnbaum, Arthur ... New York, NY
Birnbaum & Bloch ... New York, NY
Birnbaum, Bruce L. ... East Meadow, NY
Birnbaum, Courtney Lizabeth ... **New York, NY**
Birnbaum, Daniel ... Syracuse, NY
Birnbaum, Dave A. ... Whitestone, NY
Birnbaum, David ... Bronx, NY
Birnbaum, David M. ... New York, NY
Birnbaum, Deborah E. ... **New York, NY**
Birnbaum, Donald H. ... Mineola, NY
Birnbaum, Edward L. ... **New York, NY**
Birnbaum, Eric ... Philadelphia, PA
Birnbaum, Gary I. ... Mayfield Heights, OH
Birnbaum, Gary L. ... **Phoenix, AZ**
Birnbaum, George ... Los Angeles, CA
Birnbaum, George P. ... New York, NY
Birnbaum, Gerald L. ... O'Fallon, MO
Birnbaum, Ira M. ... Suffern, NY
Birnbaum, Irwin ... Syracuse, NY
Birnbaum, Jacalyn ... **Chicago, IL**
Birnbaum, James G. ... La Crosse, WI
Birnbaum, Janice L. ... New York, NY
Birnbaum, Jay L. ... **Washington, DC**
Birnbaum, Jill A. ... **St. Paul, MN**
Birnbaum, Julian R. ... **New York, NY**
Birnbaum, Julius ... New York, NY
Birnbaum, Katherine O. ... **Fort Lauderdale, FL**
Birnbaum, Kenneth J. ... New York, NY
Birnbaum, Lawrence H. ... Great Neck, NY
Birnbaum, Lenore S. ... Merrick, NY
Birnbaum, Leonard G. ... Redwood City, CA
Birnbaum, Leslie A. ... Boston, MA
Birnbaum, Lester H. ... Whippany, NJ
Birnbaum, Lester J. ... Shaftsbury, VT
Birnbaum, Lloyd C. ... **Philadelphia, PA**
Birnbaum, Mark ... **Santa Monica, CA**
Birnbaum, Mark D. ... Hempstead, NY
Birnbaum, Marsha ... New York, NY
Birnbaum, Michelle ... Washington, DC
Birnbaum, Mindy A. ... New York, NY
Birnbaum, Moe ... Puyallup, WA
Birnbaum, Morton ... Brooklyn, NY
Birnbaum, Owen ... Bethesda, MD
Birnbaum, Peter M. ... Atlanta, GA
Birnbaum, Renee ... Ann Arbor, MI
Birnbaum, Richard ... New York, NY
Birnbaum, Richard S. ... White Plains, NY
Birnbaum, Robby H. ... **Fort Lauderdale, FL**
Birnbaum, Robert ... Circle Pines, MN
Birnbaum, Robert ... Hicksville, NY
Birnbaum, Robert J. ... **Hartford, CT**
Birnbaum, Robert J. ... **San Antonio, TX**
Birnbaum, Robert L. ... **Boston, MA**
Birnbaum, Robert M. ... **New York, NY**
Birnbaum, Roy B. ... **Kalamazoo, MI**
Birnbaum, Scott A. ... **Boston, MA**
Birnbaum, Sheila L. ... **New York, NY**
Birnbaum, Sidney ... Aberdeen, NJ
Birnbaum & Skedelsky ... Whitestone, NY
Birnbaum, Stanley ... **Santa Rosa, CA**
Birnbaum, Steven M. ... San Francisco, CA
Birnberg & Associates, A Professional Corporation ... **San Francisco, CA**
Birnberg, Cory A. ... **San Francisco, CA**
Birnberg, Gerald M. ... Houston, TX
Birnberg, James R. ... **Los Angeles, CA**
Birnberg, Michael Ivan ... Little Falls, NJ
Birnberg, Paul ... Hopkins, MN
Birnboim, Jason L.S. ... New York, NY
Birnbrey, Henry ... Atlanta, GA
Birndorf, Beryl A. ... **Chicago, IL**
Birndorf & Birndorf ... **Chicago, IL**
Birndorf, Deborah F. ... **Chicago, IL**
Birndorf, Robert M. ... **Chicago, IL**
Birndorf, Theodore, and Associates ... Chicago, IL
Birne, Harvey L. ... Bayonne, NJ
Birne, Kenneth A. ... Cleveland, OH
Birne, Robert E. ... **Dallas, TX**
Birner & Birner ... La Place, LA
Birner, Brenda Braud ... La Place, LA
Birner, Donald K. ... Pekin, IL
Birner, Mitchell B. ... Washington, DC; **New York, NY**
Birner, Russell H. ... **Los Angeles, CA**
Birner, William B. ... La Place, LA
Birnesser, Gerald H. ... Miami Lakes, FL
Birney, Arthur A. ... Washington, DC
Birney, John C. ... Denver, CO
Birney, Philip R., (Inc.) ... **Sacramento, CA**
Birney, Thomas S. ... **Denver, CO**
Birney, William J. ... Department of Justice, Office of Professional Responsibility, GV
Birney, William J. ... **Garden City, NY**
Birney, William J., Jr. ... Norwalk, CA
Birney, William T. ... Department of the Army, Office of the Assistant Secretary of the Army (Installations, Logistics & Environment), GV
Birnhak, Adam Henry ... Oakland, CA
Birnhak, Carol M. ... San Francisco, CA
Birnholz, Alan C. ... Amherst, NY
Birnholz, Françoise ... New York, NY
Birnholz, Richard M. ... **Los Angeles, CA**
Birnholz, Standford P., (P.A.) ... Miami, FL
Birnie, Brian W. ... **Los Angeles, CA**
Birnie, Elizabeth B. ... Pasadena, CA
Birnie, George E. ... Portland, OR
Birnie, Tim ... Sebastopol, CA
Birnkrant & Birnkrant, P.C. ... **Farmington Hills, MI**
Birnkrant, Carol Nosanchuk ... Livonia, MI
Birnkrant, Henry J. ... **Washington, DC**
Birnkrant, Jon J. ... **Farmington Hills, MI**
Birnkrant, Sherwin M. ... **Farmington Hills, MI**
Birnkrant, Stephen S. ... Bloomfield Hills, MI
Birns, Richard D. ... Philadelphia, PA
Birns, Richard D., P.C. ... Philadelphia, PA
Birnsteel, C. Barret ... Louisville, KY
Biro, Emery J., III ... Houston, TX
Biro, Louis L. ... Chicago, IL
Biro, Michael G. ... **Pittsburgh, PA**
Biro, Nancy C. ... Chicago, IL
Biro, Susan Lori ... Environmental Protection Agency, Office of Administrative Law Judges, GV
Biron, Arnold L. ... Pittsburgh, PA
Biron, Celeste M. ... Portsmouth, NH
Biron, R. Bernard ... Blackstone, MA
Biron, Sara A. ... Saginaw, MI
Biron, Thomas E. ... **Philadelphia, PA**
Biros, Francis J. ... Department of Justice, Environment and Natural Resources Division, GV
Biros, Mark J. ... **Washington, DC**
Birotte, Andre ... **Los Angeles, CA**
Birov, Victoria A. ... **Chicago, IL**
Birr & Griffith, P.A. ... **Fort Lauderdale, FL**
Birr, James O., Jr. ... **Fort Lauderdale, FL**
Birr, Stephen G. ... **Fort Lauderdale, FL**; Tavares, FL
Birr, Stephen G., P.A. ... Tavares, FL
Birrane, Chartered ... **Towson, MD**
Birrane, Edward J., Jr. ... **Towson, MD**
Birrane, Kathleen A. ... **Baltimore, MD**
Birrell, Andrew Stuart ... Minneapolis, MN
Birrell & Birrell ... Warren, OH
Birrell, Bruce ... Warren, OH
Birrell, Dunlap & Ritts, Ltd. ... Minneapolis, MN
Birrell, George A. ... Wilmington, NC
Birrell, Jeffrey L. ... Flint, MI
Birrell, Richard W. ... Salt Lake City, UT
Birrell, Susan L. ... **Los Angeles, CA**

Bishop, Robert J. .... **New York, NY**
Bishop, Robert L. .... Winfield, KS
Bishop, Robert L. .... DeLancey, NY
Bishop, Robert W. .... **Washington, DC**
Bishop, Robert W. (Joe) .... **Louisville, KY**
Bishop, Ronald L. .... Waterville, ME
Bishop, Ronald T. .... Chicago, IL
Bishop, Rosemary .... San Diego, CA
Bishop, Ross H. .... Lansing, MI
Bishop, Rossi & Scarlati, Ltd.
Oak Brook, IL
Oakbrook Terrace, IL
Bishop, Russell .... Houston, TX
Bishop, S. Camille .... **Boston, MA**
Bishop, Sanford D., Jr. .... Columbus, GA
Bishop, Sharon D. .... Lawrenceburg, TN
Bishop, Sheila Doody .... Fairbanks, AK
Bishop, Sidney W. .... **Los Angeles, CA**
Bishop, Stefanie L. .... Easton, PA
Bishop, Stephen .... Garfield, WA
Bishop, Stephen L. .... **Stamford, CT**
Bishop, Stephen R. .... **Philadelphia, PA**
Bishop, Stephen R. .... **Dallas, TX**
Bishop, Steven M. .... San Diego, CA
Bishop, Stuart C. .... Tacoma, WA
Bishop, T. Brad .... Birmingham, AL
Bishop, T. Lee, Jr. .... Albany, GA
Bishop, Terrence E. .... **Minneapolis, MN**
Bishop, Thomas A. .... New London, CT
Bishop, Thomas E. .... Redwood City, CA
Bishop, Thomas E. .... **Jacksonville, FL**
Bishop, Thomas P. .... **Atlanta, GA**
Bishop, Thomas S. .... **Gainesville, GA**
Bishop, Thomas V. .... Fulton, MS
Bishop, Thomas Wayne .... Tallulah, LA
Bishop & Tiebauer, P.A. .... Waynesboro, MS
Bishop, Timothy A. .... **Trumbull, CT**
Bishop, Timothy S. .... **Chicago, IL**
Bishop, Toby Frances ...... Treasury Department, Departmental Offices, GV
Bishop, Tory M. .... **Omaha, NE**
Bishop, Tracy R. .... New Orleans, LA
Bishop & Warren .... Laguna Beach, CA
Bishop, Warren A. .... New Smyrna Beach, FL
Bishop, Wayne S. .... **Washington, DC**
Bishop, W. E., Jr. .... Ocala, FL
Bishop, Willard R. .... **Cedar City, UT**
Bishop, Willard R., P.C. .... **Cedar City, UT**
Bishop, William B. .... Shalimar, FL
Bishop, William D. .... Tempe, AZ
Bishop, William E. .... **Fayetteville, AR**
Bishop, William H., III .... Philadelphia, PA
Bishop, William L., Jr. .... **Seattle, WA**
Bishop, William Patrick .... **Houston, TX**
Bishop, William R. .... Leland, MI
Bishop, William T., III .... **Lexington, KY**
Bishop & Wilson .... **Louisville, KY**
Bishop, Wm. Thurmond .... Columbia, SC
Bishov, Jay .... Chicago, IL
Bishton • Gubernick .... **Los Angeles, CA**
Bishton, Norris J., Jr. .... **Los Angeles, CA**
Bisignani, Brian W. .... **Harrisburg, PA**
Bisignano, Christine A. .... Des Moines, IA
Bisignano, Christine A., P.C., Law Office of
Des Moines, IA
Bisignano & Harrison, L.L.P. .... Dallas, TX
Bisignano, Michael C. .... **Washington, DC**
Bisignano, Santo (Sandy), Jr. .... Dallas, TX
Bisio, Dennis P. .... Attleboro, MA
Bisio, Peter R. .... **Washington, DC**
Bisio, Richard .... **Detroit, MI**
Bisio, Susan M. .... **Detroit, MI**
Bisk & Fitch, L.L.P. .... **Houston, TX**
Bisk, Frank E. .... **New York, NY**
Bisk, Nathan M. .... Tampa, FL
Bisk, Nathan M., P.A. .... Tampa, FL
Bisk, Reuven M. .... **Houston, TX**
Biskamp, William T., Jr. .... Dallas, TX
Bisker, Steven R. .... Alexandria, VA
Biskind, Hunt & Taylor .... Phoenix, AZ
Biskind, Neil D., (P.C.) .... Phoenix, AZ
Biskup, Edward J. .... **Troy, MI**
Biskup, Kenneth George .... St. Louis, MO
Biskup, Robert T. .... Dearborn, MI
Biskup, Steven F. .... **Englewood, CO**
Biskupic, Vincent J. .... Naperville, IL
Bisman, Fredda J. .... Scottsdale, AZ
Bismarck, Astrid M. .... Miami, FL
Bismonte, Alfredo A. .... **San Jose, CA**
Bisnar & Associates .... Newport Beach, CA
Bisnar, John P. .... Newport Beach, CA
Bisnette, Dennis L. .... Laurel, MS
Bisno, Alice Cohen .... Costa Mesa, CA
Bisno, Barbara K. .... Miami, FL
Bisno, Edward J. .... Little Rock, AR
Bisno, Peter .... **Pasadena, CA**
Bisno, Robert H. .... Berkeley, CA
Bisno & Samberg .... **Los Angeles, CA**
Pasadena, CA
Bisnow, James S. .... Los Angeles, CA
Bisogno, Gloria L. .... **White Plains, NY**
Bisogno & Loeffler .... Basking Ridge, NJ
Bisogno, Vincent T. .... Basking Ridge, NJ
Bisol, Brian E. .... **San Diego, CA**
Bisom, Andrew S. .... Irvine, CA
Bisom-Rapp, Susan .... San Diego, CA
Bison, Henry J., Jr. .... Potomac, MD
Bison Jacobson Co., L.P.A. .... **Batavia, OH**
Cincinnati, OH
Dayton, OH
Hamilton, OH
Lebanon, OH
Portsmouth, OH
Bison, Michael H. .... **Boston, MA**
Bison Jacobson, Barbara .... **Cincinnati, OH**
Bisordi, Anthony C. .... **Shalimar, FL**
Bisordi, Sabrina A. .... **Destin, FL**
Bispels, William C. .... Reading, PA

Biss, Burton C. .... Anchorage, AK
Biss & Holmes .... Anchorage, AK
Bissada, Michele Marie .... **San Mateo, CA**
Bissaillon, Helen L. .... Duncanville, TX
Bissainthe, Pascale I. .... Washington, DC
Bissegger, Michael R. .... **Washington, DC**
Bissel, Eric R. .... Covington, LA
Bissell, Barry S. .... Columbus, OH
Bissell & Bissell .... Los Angeles, CA
Bissell & Bissell .... Gates Mills, OH
Bissell, Elisabeth Snarski .... Springfield, VA
Bissell, G. William .... Pittsburgh, PA
Bissell, Gina Marie .... Olympia, WA
Bissell, Henry M. (Chip), IV
Los Angeles, CA
Bissell, Henry M., III .... Los Angeles, CA
Bissell, Howard S. .... Gates Mills, OH
Bissell, Jack R. .... Sarasota, FL
Bissell, John G. .... **Houston, TX**
Bissell, John W. .... **East Lansing, MI**
Bissell, John W. .... Newark, NJ
Bissell, John W., P.C. .... **East Lansing, MI**
Lansing, MI
Bissell, Katherine E. .... Marietta, GA
Bissell, Keith .... Nashville, TN
Bissell, Luke .... Dallas, TX
Bissell, Marcia H. .... Anchorage, AK
Bissell, Marilyn R. .... Charlotte, NC
Bissell, Merlyn E. .... Attica, NY
Bissell, Michael S. .... Spokane, WA
Bissell, Richard A. .... Carlisle, MA
Bissell, Richard D. .... **Lexington, KY**
Bissell, Robert C. .... Maitland, FL
Bissell, Robert K. .... Gates Mills, OH
Bissell, Rolin P. .... **Philadelphia, PA**
Bissell, Scott D. .... **Seattle, WA**
Bissell, Thomas H. .... East Lansing, MI
Bissell, Thomas J. .... Denver, CO
Bissell, Thomas St. G. .... New York, NY
Bissell, Todd S. .... Sacramento, CA
Bissell, Whit .... **Palo Alto, CA**
Bissell, William G. .... Newport Beach, CA
Bissell, William G. .... Houston, TX
Bissell, William H. .... San Mateo, CA
Bissell-Ruggles, Laurie .... Rio Dell, CA
Bisset, Andrew W. .... Greenwich, CT
New York, NY
Bisset & Atkins .... Greenwich, CT
New York, NY
Bisset, Charles W. .... New York, NY
Bisset, Jennifer B .... Hood River, OR
Bisset, Jennifer E. .... Denver, CO
Bisset, Karen I. .... **Kansas City, MO**
Bisset, Sandra W. .... Southport, CT
Bisset, Thomas E. .... Washington, DC
Bisset, William T. .... **Los Angeles, CA**
Bissett, Brenda Adams .... **Los Angeles, CA**
Bissett, Colleen A. .... Oshkosh, WI
Bissett, Daniel J. .... Oshkosh, WI
Bissett, G. William .... **Miami, FL**
Bissett & Galli, Ltd., A Nevada Prof. Corp.
Reno, NV
Bissett, Gerald T. .... Houston, TX
Bissett, Robert T. .... Rahway, NJ
Bissett, Roger .... Reno, NV
Bissette, W. Louis, Jr. .... **Asheville, NC**
Bissex, Walter E. .... Austin, TX
Bissey, Brian P. .... Easton, PA
Bissig, Louis F. .... Hanford, CA
Bissinger, Charles C., Jr. .... **Cincinnati, OH**
Bissinger, David K. .... **Houston, TX**
Bissinger, Fredrick J. .... **Cookeville, TN**
Knoxville, TN
Bissinger, Julie F. .... Cincinnati, OH
Bissinger, Kristin F. .... **Roseland, NJ**
Bissinger, Mark C. .... **Cincinnati, OH**
Bissinger, Michael T. .... **Morristown, NJ**
Bissmeyer, Ramon D. .... **San Antonio, TX**
Bisso, Regel L. .... **Metairie, LA**
Bisson, Barry A. .... Huntington Beach, CA
Bisson, Donald E. .... Manchester, NH
Bisson, Gary B. .... Arlington, VA
Bisson, James H., III .... **Dalton, GA**
Bisson, Jeannette L.
United States Postal Service, Law Department, GV
Bisson, John F. .... Manchester, NH
Bisson, Leo A., Jr. .... **St. Johnsbury, VT**
Bisson, Randall W. .... Anaheim, CA
Bisson, Susan W. .... **Dalton, GA**
Bissonette, Aimée M. .... Minneapolis, MN
Bissonette, Lee R. .... **Minneapolis, MN**
Bissonette, Matthew J. .... **Washington, DC**
Bissonette, Nathan A. .... Maple Lake, MN
Bissonette, Norbert J. .... **Milwaukee, WI**
Bissonnet, Harold G. .... Kingwood, TX
Bissonnette, Andrew P. .... Juneau, WI
Bissonnette, Diane E. .... **Boston, MA**
Bissonnette, Guy R. .... Warwick, RI
Bissonnette, Karen L .... Los Angeles, CA
Bissonnette, L. Mark
South Lake Tahoe, CA
Bissonnette, Marsha O. .... Farmington, CT
Bissonnette, Maynard R. .... San Diego, CA
Bissonnette, Ronald L. .... **Lewiston, ME**
Bissonnette, Thomas E. .... Tampa, FL
Bissoon, Cathy .... **Pittsburgh, PA**
Bist, Michael P. .... **Tallahassee, FL**
Bistany, Alfred J. .... Richardson, TX
Bistany, Charles T. .... White Plains, NY
Bistany, Lawrence J. .... **Philadelphia, PA**
Bisted, Morris J., Jr. .... San Jose, CA
Bistline, Arthur M. .... Coeur d'Alene, ID
Bistline, Beverly B. .... Pocatello, ID
Bistline, Bruce S. .... Boise, ID
Bistline & Cohoon, A Law Corporation
Pasadena, CA
Torrance, CA

Bistline, F. Walter, Jr. .... **Houston, TX**
Bistline, Gregory D. .... **Pasadena, CA**
Bistline, Harold T., (P.A.) .... **Cocoa, FL**
Bistline, Jas. A. .... Alexandria, VA
Bistline, Maryann Joyce .... Altoona, PA
Bistline, Thomas M. .... St. Louis, MO
Bistram, Gregory M. .... **St. Paul, MN**
Bistran, Nancy A. .... Longmeadow, MA
Bistrow, Eric J. .... **Phoenix, AZ**
Bistrow, Mikel R. .... **San Diego, CA**
Bisulca, Andrew C. .... Springfield, VA
Bisulca, Anthony A. .... **Grand Rapids, MI**
Bisulca, Peter P. .... Northfield, NJ
Biswanger, Patricia Sons .... **Philadelphia, PA**
Biswas, Naomi Schupack
King Of Prussia, PA
Biswas, Naren .... Reynoldsburg, OH
Biswas, Sorojini J. .... **Raleigh, NC**
Biswurm, Robert J. .... Chicago, IL
Bisz, Daisy Richards .... Coral Gables, FL
Bitar, Douglas B. .... Hoquiam, WA
Bitar, Karen Y. .... **Stamford, CT**
Bitar, Nader .... San Diego, CA
Bitar, Paul A. .... Hoquiam, WA
Bitar, Raymond W. .... New Kensington, PA
Bitar, Thomas J. .... **Morristown, NJ**
Bitcon, Sharon J. .... Seattle, WA
Bite, Bite & Bite .... Birmingham, AL
Bite, Michael H., Jr. .... Birmingham, AL
Bite, Richard H. .... Birmingham, AL
Bitensky, Lorna .... Burbank, CA
Bitensky, Susan Helen .... East Lansing, MI
Bitetto, Eileen O'Boyle .... **East Meadow, NY**
Bitetto, James .... **New York, NY**
Bitetto, James Joseph .... **East Meadow, NY**
Bithell, Walter H. .... **Boise, ID**
Bither, Stephen D. .... Portland, ME
Bither, Thomas O. .... Houlton, ME
Bithorn, Edward G. .... **New York, NY**
Bitkower, Marshall L. .... Encino, CA
Bitler, Audrea J. Golding .... Encino, CA
Bitler, Margaret Holthusen
New York, NY
Bitman, Craig A. .... **New York, NY**
Bitman, David B. .... Hauppauge, NY
Bitman, Gerald .... Hauppauge, NY
Bitner, George E. .... **Oakton, VA**
Bitner, George E., Ltd. .... **Fairfax, VA**
Oakton, VA
Bitner, James E. .... **Oakton, VA**
Bitner, Jo Anne Sanderson
Falls Church, VA
Bitner, John H. .... **Chicago, IL**
Bitner, Julia Ann .... **Vienna, VA**
Bitner, Leslie Anne .... Dallas, TX
Bitner, Marc John .... Kenner, LA
Bitner, Maurice H. .... Parsippany, NJ
Bitner, R. Hunter, II .... **Orlando, FL**
Bitner, Richard E. .... Mesa, AZ
Bitner, William R. .... Alvin, TX
Bitney, J. Michael .... Spooner, WI
Bitney Law Firm, Ltd. .... **Barron, WI**
Eau Claire, WI
Hayward, WI
Rice Lake, WI
Siren, WI
Spooner, WI
Superior, WI
Bitney, Thomas J. .... **Spooner, WI**
Bitney, Woodrow W. .... **Spooner, WI**
Bitol, Solange .... Washington, DC
Bitonti, James V. .... McLean, VA
Bitsas, Pamela A. .... **Chicago, IL**
Bitseff, Tonie L. .... **Seattle, WA**
Bitses and Bitses .... Southold, NY
Bitses, James .... Southold, NY
Bitses, Katherine .... Southold, NY
Bitsimis, Gina Raio .... **Garden City, NY**
Bitsko, Gregory D. .... Freehold, NJ
Bitsky, Jason I. .... **New York, NY**
Bitsoli, Stephen L. .... Framingham, MA
Bittan, B. A., Jr. .... Fort Pierce, FL
Bittel, Beth A. .... **Fairfax, VA**
Bittel, Beth A., P.C., Law Offices of
Fairfax, VA
Bittel, Betty Ann .... Atlantic City, NJ
Bittel, Blake A. .... **Oklahoma City, OK**
Bittel, Jordan .... Miami, FL
Bittel, Patricia Thomas .... Cleveland, OH
Bittel, Timothy M. .... **Akron, OH**
Bittell, James E. .... **Midland, MI**
Bittenbender, Charles A.
Mayfield Heights, OH
Bittenbender, Heather S. .... **Harrisburg, PA**
Bittence, Mary M. .... **Cleveland, OH**
Bitter, Amy E. .... San Antonio, TX
Bitter, Gehart L. .... Burlingame, CA
Bitter, J. A., Jr. .... San Antonio, TX
Bitter, Joseph J. .... Dubuque, IA
Bitter Law Office .... Dubuque, IA
Bitter, Lisa Marie .... **Cincinnati, OH**
White Oak, OH
Bitter, Michelle R. Bernard
San Francisco, CA
Bitter, Steven B. .... **San Francisco, CA**
Bitterbaum, Adah R. .... Bethesda, MD
Bitterlich, Robert A. .... Sherman Oaks, CA
Bitterlin, Christopher George
San Diego, CA
Bitterman, Amy R. .... **Roseland, NJ**
Bitterman, Lawrence Y. .... New Brunswick, NJ
Bitterman, Leonard M. .... Clifton, NJ
Bitterman, Michael L. .... Trenton, NJ
Bitterman, Patrick J. .... **Chicago, IL**
Bitterman, Stephan A., Law Offices of
Upper Saddle River, NJ
Bitterman, Stephan A., Law Offices of
New York, NY

Bitters, Richard H. .... Pasadena, CA
Bittick, E. Kelly, Jr. .... **Tampa, FL**
Bittick, Peggy S., Law Offices .... Pearland, TX
Bittick, T. W. .... El Paso, TX
Bitticks, Robert R. .... Woodland Hills, CA
Bitting, Cynthia N. .... St. Louis, MO
Bitting, Daniel C. .... **Austin, TX**
Bitting, N. Staten, Jr. (P.C.) .... **Augusta, GA**
Bitting, Ronny M. .... **Clarinda, IA**
Bitting, Terry H. .... Tulsa, OK
Bitting, Timothy C. .... Reading, PA
Bitting, William M., (P.C.)
Los Angeles, CA
Bittinger, Ann M. .... **Kansas City, MO**
Bittker, Andrew M. .... Whitefish, MT
Bittker, Boris I. .... New Haven, CT
Bittker, Donald L. .... New York, NY
Bittker, Louise M. .... Birmingham, MI
Bittker, Morton L. .... **Rochester, NY**
Bittle, Edgar H. .... **Des Moines, IA**
Bittle, Lyndon F. .... **Dallas, TX**
Bittle, Ronald W. .... Alva, OK
Bittle, Timothy A. .... Sacramento, CA
Bittle, Todd P. .... **Harrisburg, IL**
Bittlingmaier, Fred T. .... Scarsdale, NY
Bittman, Howard .... **Boulder, CO**
Bittman, Michael J. .... **Orlando, FL**
Bittman, Mitchell D. .... **New York, NY**
Bittman, Robert J. .... **Washington, DC**
Bittman, William O. .... **Washington, DC**
Bittner, Amy M. .... **Syracuse, NY**
Bittner, Anthony M. .... Pittsburgh, PA
Bittner, Bernard .... Philadelphia, PA
Bittner, Bruce M. .... **Noblesville, IN**
Bittner, Carol Ann .... Glen Burnie, MD
Bittner, David T. .... Howell, MI
Bittner, Edward A., Jr. .... Pittsburgh, PA
Bittner, Eric M. .... **Clarksville, TN**
Bittner, Gary S. .... Acton, MA
Bittner, Gayle E. .... Oakland, CA
Bittner & Hahs, P.C. .... **Portland, OR**
Bittner, Hyrns, LaSata, Riemland & Daly, P.C. .... **St. Joseph, MI**
Bittner, J. Terrence .... **Portland, OR**
Bittner, Jacqueline .... Perth Amboy, NJ
Bittner, James U. .... Seattle, WA
Bittner, Jeffrey S. .... **Davenport, IA**
Bittner, Joel W. .... Des Moines, IA
Bittner, Kimberly Deciantis .... Providence, RI
Bittner, Mary Ellen .... Department of Justice, Drug Enforcement Administration, GV
Bittner, R. Richard, (P.C.) .... **Davenport, IA**
Bittner, Richard C. .... Glen Burnie, MD
Bittner, Robert E. .... **Pittsburgh, PA**
Bittner, Robert L. .... Milwaukee, WI
Bittner, Rodger V. .... **St. Joseph, MI**
Bittner, Scott P. .... **Somerset, PA**
Bittner, Thomas A. .... **Portland, OR**
Bittner, Thomas A. .... Farmers Branch, TX
Bittner, Vincent G. .... Mill Creek, WA
Bittner, Warren .... Miami, FL
Bittner, Wendy M. .... Boston, MA
Bittner, William H. .... **Anchorage, AK**
Bittourna, Bert K. .... Oak Brook, IL
Bitz, Dennis J. .... Springfield, MO
Bitzberger, Michelle L. .... Philadelphia, PA
Bitzegaio, Barry N. .... New Albany, IN
Bitzegaio, Harold J. .... Terre Haute, IN
Bitzer, Frank J. .... Cincinnati, OH
Bitzer, Jeffrey T. .... York, PA
Bitzer, John L. .... **Belleville, IL**
Collinsville, IL
Bitzer, Windy Cockrell .... **Mobile, AL**
Bitzko, Ann .... Upland, CA
Bitzonis, James .... North Haven, CT
Biunno, David B. .... Summit, NJ
Biunno, Francis A. .... Philadelphia, PA
Biunno, Mary Louise .... Mineola, NY
Biunno, Richard J. .... New Brunswick, NJ
Bius, Dana L. .... Fayetteville, NC
Bivans, Beth W. .... **Dallas, TX**
Bivans, Lorenzo A., Jr. .... **Philadelphia, PA**
Bivans, Roger W. .... **Dallas, TX**
Bivens, Allen R. .... **Buffalo, NY**
Bivens, Burney .... Orange Park, FL
Bivens, C. Phillip .... Dyersburg, TN
Bivens, Cull .... Tulsa, OK
Bivens, Don .... **Phoenix, AZ**
Bivens, Donald Whitlow .... **San Diego, CA**
Bivens, Frances E. .... **New York, NY**
Bivens, Harry R. .... Raleigh, NC
Bivens, Jerome A. .... Baltimore, MD
Bivens, John A. .... Tuscaloosa, AL
Bivens, Jones & Associates
Orange Park, FL
Bivens, Joseph Alton .... **Columbia, SC**
Bivens, Stephanie Ann .... Phoenix, AZ
Biviano, William R. .... Warren, OH
Bivin & McNamara .... **Kingwood, TX**
Bivin, Ruth Boren .... Houston, TX
Bivin, William W. .... **Kingwood, TX**
Bivins, Cynthia Glass .... **San Antonio, TX**
Bivins, Demetrius K. .... San Antonio, TX
Bivins, James D. .... Rockland, ME
Bivins, James M. .... Moultrie, GA
Bivins, Janet Y. .... **Wilmington, DE**
Bivins, J. C. .... Mount Vernon, GA
Bivins, John A. .... **Lafayette, LA**
Bivins, Julian M., Jr. .... Charlottesville, VA
Bivins, Ollie B., Jr. .... Flint, MI
Bivins, Renita K. .... New Orleans, LA
Bivins, Robert E. .... Albuquerque, NM
Bivins, Robert W. .... **Tampa, FL**
Bivins, Sonja F. .... **Atlanta, GA**
Bivins, Susan A. .... Newport News, VA
Bivins, William P., Jr. .... Augusta, GA
Bivona, Andrew P. .... Goshen, NY
Bivona, Beth Ann .... Newburgh, NY

Bivona & Cohen ... Philadelphia, PA
Bivona, Cohen, Kunzman, Coley, Yospin, Bernstein & DiFrancesco, A Professional Corporation ... Warren, NJ
Somerville, NJ
Bivona & Cohen, P.C. ... Los Angeles, CA
Brooklyn, NY
New York, NY
White Plains, NY
Bivona, Jake V. ... Bessemer, AL
Bivona, John C. ... Huntington, NY
Bivona, John V. ... New York, NY
Bix, Brian ... Hamden, CT
Bix, John H. ... Oakland, CA
Bix, Milton H. ... Minneapolis, MN
Bixby, Aaron R. ... Waterloo, IA
Bixby, Brian D. ... Boston, MA
Bixby, David M. ... Phoenix, AZ
Bixby, Frank L. ... Chicago, IL
Bixby, H. Richard ... Santa Ana, CA
Bixby, Joseph N. ... Geneva, NE
Bixby, Matilda B. ... Wilmington, DE
Bixby, Michael B. ... Boise, ID
Bixby, Phillip ... Rutland, VT
Bixby, Robert Hardwick ... Albany, NY
Bixby, Roger A. ... Chicago, IL
Bixby & Scott, P.C. A Professional Corporation Chicago, IL
Bixby, Thomas C. ... Quincy, MA
Bixby, William ... Valdez, AK
Bixenman, Scott L. ... Le Mars, IA
Bixenstine, Barton A. ... Cleveland, OH
Bixenstine, Kim F. ... Cleveland, OH
Bixler, Albert G. ... Philadelphia, PA
Bixler, Bruce M. ... Canton, OH
Bixler, C. Temple ... Oklahoma City, OK
Bixler, Diana Lee ... Chicago, IL
Bixler, Elizabeth J. ... Ithaca, NY
Bixler, Emanuel H., IV ... Birmingham, AL
Bixler, Esther Marie ... Cambridge, MA
Bixler, Gary A. ... Arroyo Grande, CA
Bixler, John Donovan ... Chicago, IL
Bixler, John Mourer ... Washington, DC
Bixler, Lee A. ... Dayton, OH
Bixler, Matthew W. ... Visalia, CA
Bixler, Neil J. ... Baltimore, MD
Bixler, R. Jeffrey ... Toledo, OH
Bixler, Robert ... Radnor, PA
Bixler, Sidney R. ... Washington, DC
Bixler, Timothy E. ... Atlanta, GA
Bixon, Michael I. ... Skillman, NJ
Bizal, Michael R. ... Overland Park, KS
Bizanos, Anastasia M. ... Boston, MA
Bizanos, Natasha M. ... Framingham, MA
Bizanovich, Mary Lee Moore Wheeling, WV
Bizar, Amy W. ... Mason, OH
Bizar, David M. ... Hartford, CT
Bizar, Irving ... New York, NY
Bizar, Leon ... Williston Park, NY
Bizar, Steven E. ... Philadelphia, PA
Bizer, Maxine E. ... Louisville, KY
Bizic, Eli W. ... Department of State, Bureau of Consular Affairs, GV
Bizik, Linley Clare ... Woodland Hills, CA
Bizios, Liana A. ... Chicago, IL
Bizot, John E. ... Chicago, IL
Bizousky, Beth ... Charlotte, NC
Bizzano, Joseph D., Jr. ... Minneapolis, MN
Bizzarri, Louis J. ... Camden, NJ
Bizzarro, Deborah L. ... Fort Lauderdale, FL
Bizzell, Kinchen C. ... New York, NY
Bizzell, Mark F. ... Owensboro, KY
Bizzell, Shannon L. ... Atlanta, GA
Bizzell, Susan D. ... Indianapolis, IN
Bizzell, William H. ... Cleveland, MS
Bizzell, Word G. ... Corsicana, TX
Bizzini, Karen L. ... Los Angeles, CA
Bizzoso, Irene M. ... Harrisburg, PA
Bjelajac, John M. ... Racine, WI
Bjelde, Richard L. ... Camden, NJ
Bjella, Arley ... Williston, ND
Bjella, Brian R. ... Bismarck, ND
Bjelland, Carol L. ... Thousand Oaks, CA
Bjelland, David N. ... San Bernardino, CA
Bjelland, Gary W. ... Great Falls, MT
Bjelland, Harley L. ... Mission Viejo, CA
Bjelland, Howard S. ... Montrose, CO
Bjerg, Robert J. ... Kansas City, MO
Bjerke, Alan A. ... Burlington, VT
Bjerke, Bruce T. ... Seattle, WA
Bjerke, Jack A. ... Columbus, OH
Bjerke, Michael L. ... Pine City, MN
Bjerke, Nathan H. ... Torrance, CA
Bjerke, Otto H. ... Olympia, WA
Bjerregaard, Kevin P. ... Irvine, CA
Bjertness, Donald E. ... Billings, MT
Bjertness, Mark A. ... Dearborn, MI
Bjerum, RaeAnn ... Irvine, CA
Bjes, Deborah E. ... Chicago, IL
Bjonerud, Deborah T. ... Oakland, CA
Bjorck, Catherine L. ... Dallas, TX
Bjorck, Dorothy H. ... Dallas, TX
Bjordammen, Stephen R. ... Wichita Falls, TX
Bjorgaard, David L. ... Tucson, AZ
Bjorge, Gerald H. ... Washington, DC
Bjorge, James R. ... New York, NY
Bjorgen, Thomas R. ... Olympia, WA
Bjorgum, A. Eric ... Los Angeles, CA
Bjork, Alan H. ... Des Moines, IA
Bjork, Amity A. ... Port Orchard, WA
Bjork, Charles H. ... Chicago, IL
Bjork, Dorothy L. ... Atlanta, GA
Bjork, John C. ... Minneapolis, MN
Bjork Lawrence ... Oakland, CA
Bjork, Lindley, Danielson & Baker, P.C. Denver, CO
Bjork, Mary Audi ... Albany, NY
Bjork, Peter A. ... Denver, CO
Bjork, Robert D., Jr. ... Oakland, CA
Bjork, Walter M. ... Scottsdale, AZ
Bjork, William E. ... Redwood City, CA
Bjorkholm, Jill K. ... Palo Alto, CA
Bjorklund, A. Leonard, Jr. San Rafael, CA
Bjorklund, Brenda A. ... Minneapolis, MN
Bjorklund, Christian C. ... Mill Valley, CA
Bjorklund, Donald C. ... Irvine, CA
Bjorklund, Graham, Martin & Taylor San Rafael, CA
Bjorklund, John W., Jr. ... Mays Landing, NJ
Bjorklund, Lucille G. ... Monarch Beach, CA
Bjorklund, Mary J. ... Edina, MN
Bjorklund, Mary J. Nierengarten Edina, MN
Bjorklund, Paul S. ... Sacramento, CA
Bjorklund, Sheila A. ... Minneapolis, MN
Bjorklund, Terrie M., Ms. ... Washington, DC
Bjorklund, Vernon E. ... Seattle, WA
Bjorklund, Victoria B. ... New York, NY
Bjorklund & Young ... Seattle, WA
Bjorkman, Dale A. ... St. Paul, MN
Bjorkman, Eric R. ... Boise, ID
Bjorkman, Eric R. ... Moscow, ID
Bjorkman, Henry C. ... Boston, MA
Bjorkman, Ian E. ... New Haven, CT
Bjorkman, James J. ... New York, NY
Bjorkman, John C. ... Seattle, WA
Bjorkman, John M. ... Minneapolis, MN
Bjorkman, Karen ... Minneapolis, MN
Bjorkman Law Office, P.C. ... Bridgewater, SD
Bjorkman, Louise Dovre ... St. Paul, MN
Bjorkman, Ron ... Emmett, ID
Bjorkman, Timothy W. ... Bridgewater, SD
Bjork-Tjornhom, Karin E. ... Auburn, CA
Bjorlic, John B. ... Gloucester, MA
Bjorlo, Philip A. ... McLean, VA
Bjorn, Teri A. ... Bakersfield, CA
Bjorndahl, Brian C. ... Tucson, AZ
Bjorndal, Lee A. ... Austin, MN
Bjornlund, Bruce ... Waterbury, VT
Bjornnes, Norman P., Jr. ... Minneapolis, MN
Bjornsen, James A. ... Newport, OR
Bjornson, David H. ... Missoula, MT
Bjornson, Erik ... Tacoma, WA
Bjornson, Hans I. E. ... Minneapolis, MN
Bjornson, Jodi Billing ... Bismarck, ND
Bjornstad, Christopher A. ... Spencer, IA
Bjornstad, Deborah H. ... Philadelphia, PA
Bjornstad, Edward Wallace ... Spirit Lake, IA
Bjornstad, Jennifer Schrader ... Knoxville, TN
Bjornstad, John M. ... Spencer, IA
Bjornstad Law Office ... Spirit Lake, IA
Bjornstrom, David G. ... Santa Rosa, CA
Bjorseth, Scott D. ... Alton, IL
Bjurberg, P. David ... Montgomery, AL
Bjurstrom, Callie A. ... San Diego, CA
Bjurstrom, F. Daniel ... Enumclaw, WA
Bjurstrom, Stanford M. ... St. Louis, MO
Bjurstrom, Stanley T. ... St. Louis, MO
Blaber, Leo B., Jr. ... Naperville, IL
Blaber, Thomas V. ... Amsterdam, NY
Blabey, David E. ... New York, NY
Blaboli, Sandee E. ... Columbus, OH
Blach, Donald Anthony ... San Jose, CA
Blache, Cecil J. ... Baton Rouge, LA
Blacher, Brian H. ... Milwaukee, WI
Blacher, Brian M. ... Washington, DC
Blacher, Jeffrey W. ... Miami, FL
Blacher Law Offices ... Milwaukee, WI
Blacher, Louis A. ... Lake Villa, IL
Blacher, Mark A. ... Elizabeth, NJ
Blacher, Philip ... North Palm Beach, FL
Blacher, Raquel ... West Palm Beach, FL
Blacher, Robert E. ... Chicago, IL
Blachinsky, Charles W. ... Kewanee, IL
Blachinsky, John M. ... Kewanee, IL
Blachinsky Law Offices ... Kewanee, IL
Blachly, David G. ... Indianapolis, IN
Blachly, Tabor, Bozik & Hartman Crown Point, IN
Fort Wayne, IN
La Porte, IN
Valparaiso, IN
Blachly, Thomas C. ... Hardwick, VT
Blachman, Irving ... Brooklyn, NY
Blachman, Marci J. ... Toledo, OH
Blachman, Michael J. ... Portsmouth, VA
Blachman, Rochel S. ... Los Angeles, CA
Blachor, Isaac ... Garden City, NY
Blacik, Benjamin J. ... Glendale, AZ
Black, A. Clifton ... Kissimmee, FL
Black, A. Clifton ... Orlando, FL
Black, A. Samuel ... Chicago, IL
Black & Adams ... Philadelphia, PA
Black, Adrienne ... Dunwoody, GA
Black, Alan M. ... Atlanta, GA
Black, Alan M. ... Allentown, PA
Black, Alexander C. ... Rochester, NY
Black, Allan A. ... Castroville, TX
Black, Allan R. ... Austin, TX
Black Allely Ryon & Maus, LLP Denver, CO
Black, Allen D. ... Philadelphia, PA
Black, Allen S. ... Williamson, WV
Black, Andrea ... Orlando, FL
Black, Andrew S. ... Brooklyn, NY
Black, Ann Young ... Miami, FL
Black, Anne Erskine ... Cincinnati, OH
Black, Anthony K. ... Tampa, FL
Black, Anthony M. ... Washington, DC
Black, Archibald W. ... Greenville, SC
Black, Archibald Wells, Jr. ... Greenville, SC
Black & Associates, P.C. ... Media, PA
Black, August B. ... Morris, IL
Black, Augustus Melton, Jr. ... Raleigh, NC
Black, Avis E. ... Lanham, MD
Black, Barbara ... White Plains, NY
Black, Barbara Aronstein ... New York, NY
Black, Barbara Canales Corpus Christi, TX
Black, Barbara E. ... Woodbridge, NJ
Black, Barbra I. ... Framingham, MA
Black, Benham M. ... Staunton, VA
Black, Bennie H. ... Atlanta, GA
Black, Bernard S. ... New York, NY
Black, Bert ... St. Paul, MN
Black, Bert ... Dallas, TX
Black, Beth A. ... Chicago, IL
Black and Black ... Santa Barbara, CA
Solvang, CA
Black & Black ... Commack, NY
Black & Black ... Port Arthur, TX
Black, Black and Black ... Port Huron, MI
Black, Black & Brown ... Washington, IL
Black & Black Lawyers ... Morris, IL
Black and Black, P.A. ... Coral Gables, FL
Black & Black, P.C. ... Logan, UT
Black, Blane A. ... Monongahela, PA
Black, Bonita K. ... Louisville, KY
Black, Bradley V. ... Irvine, CA
Black, Brandon K. ... Baton Rouge, LA
Black, Brian D. ... Alexandria, VA
Black, Brian S. ... Ephrata, PA
Black, Brian T. ... Chicago, IL
Black, Bronwyn M. ... Commack, NY
Black, Brown and Lanier ... El Cerrito, CA
Black, Bruce D. ... Albuquerque, NM
Black, Bruce E. ... Minneapolis, MN
Black, Bruce F. ... Denver, CO
Black, Bruce W. ... Pekin, IL
Black, Bryan Craig ... Harrisburg, PA
Black, Bryan M. ... Port Huron, MI
Black, C. Robert ... Chicago, IL
Black, Candace K. ... Brighton, CO
Black, Carl A. ... Ayer, MA
Black, Carl E. ... Cleveland, OH
Black, Carol A. ... Philadelphia, PA
Black, Caroline Kapusta ... Tampa, FL
Black, Catherine P. ... Moncks Corner, SC
Black, Chapman, Webber & Stevens Brookings, OR
Grants Pass, OR
Klamath Falls, OR
Medford, OR
Black, Charles E. ... San Diego, CA
Black, Charles G. ... Memphis, TN
Black, Charles L. ... Abilene, TX
Black, Charles L., Jr. ... New Haven, CT
Black, Charles M., Jr. ... Columbia, SC
Black, Charles W., Jr. ... Houston, TX
Black, Cheryl K. ... El Cerrito, CA
Black, Cheryl Lynn Department of Commerce, Patent and Trademark Office, GV
Black, Christina M. ... Sacramento, CA
Black, Christine H. ... New York, NY
Black, Christine M. ... Kansas City, KS
Black, Claire A. ... Tuscaloosa, AL
Black, Clare F. ... Tempe, AZ
Black, Claudia Pentony ... Marlton, NJ
Philadelphia, PA
Black, Clifford P., Jr. ... Savannah, MO
Black, Clinton R., IV ... Baltimore, MD
Black, Clyde O., II ... Roaring Spring, PA
Black Compean & Hall, A Limited Liability Partnership ... Los Angeles, CA
Black & Connolly, L.L.P. ... Austin, TX
Black, Creed C., Jr. ... Philadelphia, PA
Black, Cynthia R. ... Springfield, MO
Black, D. Carl, Jr. ... Jackson, MS
Black, D. Eric ... Rochester, NY
Black, D. Marcel ... Tuscumbia, AL
Black, D. Robert ... Atlanta, GA
Black, Dameron, Jr. ... Savannah, GA
Black, Daniel H. ... Beverly Hills, CA
Black, David ... Atlanta, GA
Black, David ... Norcross, GA
Black, David ... New York, NY
Black, David A. ... Louisville, KY
Black, David B. ... Del Rio, TX
Black, David B. ... Houston, TX
Black, David B. ... Richmond, TX
Black, David C. ... Johnson, KS
Black, David D. ... Port Huron, MI
Black, David D. ... Cincinnati, OH
Black, David H. ... Los Angeles, CA
Black, David H., Jr. ... Portland, OR
Black, David L. ... Denver, CO
Black, David L. ... Kansas City, MO
Black, David M. ... Washington, DC
Black, David M. ... Southfield, MI
Black, David R. ... Media, PA
Black, David S. ... Beaufort, SC
Black, David S. ... Falls Church, VA
Black, David T. ... Maryville, TN
Black, David W. ... Fort Lauderdale, FL
Black, David W. ... Dallas, TX
Black, Davis, Tierney & Steadman, LLC White River Junction, VT
Black and Davison ... Chambersburg, PA
Black, Deborah Miller ... Greenbrae, CA
Black, Debra Phillipes ... Beverly Hills, CA
Black, Dennis B. ... Chicago, IL
Black, Dennis G. ... Tyler, TX
Black, Dennis H. ... Brookings, OR
Grants Pass, OR
Klamath Falls, OR
Medford, OR
Black, Dennis M. ... Washington, DC
Black, Dennis R. ... Amherst, NY
Black, Dewitt T., III ... Purcellville, VA
Black, Don ... Dallas, TX
Black, Donald E. ... Detroit, MI
Black, Donald F. ... Jacksonville, FL
Black, Donald F. ... Morris, IL
Black, Donald G. ... Walnut Creek, CA
Black, Donald J. ... Santa Rosa, CA
Black, Donald S. ... Fresno, CA
Black, Donald W. ... Seattle, WA
Black, Donn L. ... Oakland, CA
Black, Donna R. ... Los Angeles, CA
Black, Donna Ward ... Mobile, AL
Black, Dorothy J. ... Washington, DC
Black, Douglas A. ... Memphis, TN
Black, Douglas Jon ... Redondo Beach, CA
Black, Dylan C. ... Birmingham, AL
Black, E. Garth ... San Francisco, CA
Black, Earl ... Port Arthur, TX
Black, Edward G. ... Boston, MA
Black, Edward J. ... Washington, DC
Black, Edward K. ... La Grange, KY
Black, Edward K., PSC ... La Grange, KY
Black, Edwin F. ... Commack, NY
Black, Elizabeth Lea ... Pittsburgh, PA
Black, Eric S. ... Berkeley Springs, WV
Black, Erik D. ... Santa Barbara, CA
Solvang, CA
Black, Eugene C., Jr. ... Albany, GA
Black, Eugene C., Sr. ... Albany, GA
Black, F. Evan ... Harrisburg, PA
Black, Felicia Duque ... Los Angeles, CA
Black, Fischer S. ... Tampa, FL
Black, Frank J. ... Morris, IL
Black, Franklin J. ... New Buffalo, MI
Black, Fred E. ... Eau Claire, WI
Black, Freda B. ... Durham, NC
Black, Frederick A. ... Hagåtña, GU
Black, Frederick E. ... Galveston, TX
Black, Frederick S. ... South Boston, VA
Black, G. Monroe, III ... Columbia, SC
Black, Gale Barron ... Department of Labor, Employment Standards Administration, GV
Black, Gary L. ... Williamsport, PA
Black, Gary M. ... Seal Beach, CA
Black, Gary R., Jr. ... El Paso, TX
Black, Geoffrey Scott ... Manchester, MD
Black, George C., Jr. ... The Colony, TX
Black, George C., Jr., P.C. ... The Colony, TX
Black, George R. ... Morris, IL
Black, Gerald J. ... Geneva, IL
Black & Gerngross, A Professional Corporation ... Marlton, NJ
Philadelphia, PA
Black, Giles T. ... Richmond, KY
Black, Gordon P. ... Adams, MA
Bennington, VT
Black, Gregory C. ... Butte, MT
Black, Gregory W. ... Chicago, IL
Black, Gregory W. ... Danville, IN
Black, H. Allen, III ... Washington, DC
Baltimore, MD
Black, H. Craig ... Greenville, TX
Black, Harold A. ... Lynchburg, VA
Black, Harris ... Stamford, CT
Black, Harry A. ... White River Junction, VT
Black, Harvey L., Jr. ... Bartlesville, OK
Black, Harvey N., Jr. ... Portland, OR
Black Helterline, LLP ... Portland, OR
Black, Henry H. ... Vicksburg, MS
Black, Herbert A., II ... Natick, MA
Black, Hilary P. ... Atlanta, GA
Black, Howard ... Jericho, NY
Black, Hugh E., III ... Chesapeake, VA
Black, Hugh L. ... Corona Del Mar, CA
Black, Hugh W. ... St. Joseph, MI
Black, Hugo L., III ... Miami, FL
Black, Hugo L., Jr. ... Miami, FL
Black, Hugo L., Jr., P.A. ... Miami, FL
Black, J. Barclay ... Augusta, GA
Black, J. David ... Palo Alto, CA
Black, J. David ... Winchester, VA
Black, J. Fern ... Denver, CO
Black, J. Michael ... Houston, TX
Texas City, TX
Black, J. Thomas, & Associates Houston, TX
Black, James ... Santa Barbara, CA
Solvang, CA
Black, James A., Jr. ... Tampa, FL
Black, James Bell, IV ... Raleigh, NC
Black, James G. ... Grand Rapids, MI
Black, James I., III ... New York, NY
Black, James J. ... Washington, DC
Black, James J., III ... Marlton, NJ
Philadelphia, PA
Black, James L., Jr. ... Boston, MA
Black, James M. ... Port Arthur, TX
Black, James M., II ... Islandia, NY
Black, James R. ... San Francisco, CA
Black, James R. ... Salt Lake City, UT
Black, James R., & Associates Salt Lake City, UT
Black, James R., Jr. ... Abilene, TX
Black, James S., Jr. ... Spokane, WA
Black, James W. ... Washington, DC
Black, Janet Ward ... Greensboro, NC
Black, Jared ... Seattle, WA
Black, Jason C. ... Orlando, FL
Black, Jeffrey A. ... Olean, NY
Black, Jeffrey H. ... Painesville, OH
Black, Jerry B. ... New York, NY
Black, Jerry K. ... Donelson, TN
Black, Joanna S. Lin ... Kirkland, WA
Black, Joe D. ... Vincennes, IN
Black, John A. ... Phoenix, AZ
Black, John A. ... Endicott, NY
Black, John A., Jr. ... Houston, TX
Black, John C. ... Fort Lauderdale, FL
Miami, FL
West Palm Beach, FL

Black, John C. ....Coeur d'Alene, ID
Spokane, WA
Black, John C. ....Anacortes, WA
Black, John C. ....Shawano, WI
Black, John E., Jr. ....Chicago, IL
Black, John F. ....Springfield, MO
Black, John G. ....Corning, AR
Black, John G. ....Treasury Department, Office of Regulations and Rulings, GV
Black, John H., Jr. ....Sacramento, CA
Black, John L. ....Salt Lake City, UT
Black, John M. ....San Antonio, TX
Black, John R., III ....Dallas, TX
Black, John S. ....Kansas City, MO
Black, John Scott ....Houston, TX
Black, John T. ....Birmingham, AL
Black, John T. ....Walterboro, SC
Black, John V. ....Pratt, KS
Black, John W. ....Coral Gables, FL
Black, John W. ....Monticello, FL
Black, John W. ....Tallahassee, FL
Black, John William ....Brownsville, TX
Black, Jonathan C. ....Boston, MA
Black, Jonathan R. ....Braintree, MA
Black, Jos. C. ....Jacksonville, FL
Black, Joseph A. ....Washington, DC
Black, Joseph M., Jr. ....Seymour, IN
Black, Joseph T. ....Worcester, MA
Black, Josiah M. ....Boston, MA
Black, Julia L. ....Flint, MI
Black, Jung & Sisco ....Tampa, FL
Black, K. Dean ....Denver, NC
Black, Karen A. ....Salina, KS
Black, Karen E. ....Escondido, CA
Black, Karen L. ....Chicago, IL
Black, Karen L. ....Philadelphia, PA
Black, Katherine D. ....Logan, UT
Black, Katherine M. ....Carbondale, IL
Black, Kathryn A. ....Anchorage, AK
Black, Kathryn J. ....Pasadena, CA
Black, Keith A. ....Chattanooga, TN
Black, Kelli L. ....Chattanooga, TN
Black, Kelly G. ....Mesa, AZ
Black, Kendell R. ....Little Rock, AR
Black, Kenneth A. ....Los Angeles, CA
Black, Kenneth B. ....Salt Lake City, UT
Black, Kenneth L. ....Washington, IL
Black, Kenneth W. ....Prospect Heights, IL
Black, Kenneth Wallace ....Washington, IL
Black, Kevin C. ....Woodstock, VA
Black, Kevin M. ....Cincinnati, OH
Black, Kimberley Dawn ....Lubbock, TX
Black, Kimberly J. ....Sacramento, CA
Black, Lambert, Coffin & Rudman
Portland, ME
Black, Larry G. ....Van Buren, AR
Black, Larry G. ....Austin, TX
Black, Laurel ....Chicago, IL
Black, L. C. ....Birmingham, AL
Black, Leonard D. ....Encino, CA
Black, Leonard D., A Professional Corporation ....Encino, CA
Black, Les ....Warwick, MA
Black, Leslie E., (Ms.) ....Johnson, VT
Black, Lewis S., Jr. ....Wilmington, DE
Black, Linda McIntyre ....Cleveland, OH
Black, Lisa M. ....San Diego, CA
Black, Lisa M. ....Westfield, NJ
Black, Lori Anne ....Dublin, OH
Black, Louis E. ....Jacksonville, FL
Black, Louis E. ....Melville, NY
New York, NY
Black, Loyd Hall, Jr. ....Atlanta, GA
Black, Lyle J. ....Eau Claire, WI
Black, Malcolm C. ....Wichita, KS
Black, Margaret F. ....Tallahassee, FL
Black, Margaret F. ....Newark, NJ
New York, NY
Black, Marjorie ....Bozeman, MT
Black, Mark A. ....Radford, VA
Roanoke, VA
Black, Martha L. ....Traverse City, MI
Black, Martha S. L. ....Maryville, TN
Black, Martin J. ....Philadelphia, PA
Black, Martin L. ....Tallahassee, FL
Black, Martin P. ....Arlington, VA
Black, Mary Ann ....Shawnee, OK
Black, Mary Beth ....Port Huron, MI
Black, Mary Margaret ....Dallas, TX
Black, Mary S. ....Dallas, TX
Black, Mary S., P.C. ....Dallas, TX
Black, Marylouise S. ....Westport, CT
Black, Matthew S. ....Raleigh, NC
Black, Matthew W., Jr. ....Rockville, MD
Black, Maureen Shaughnessy
New York, NY
Black, Maurice R. ....Carrollton, MS
Black, McCuskey, Hanhart, Deeds & Bauer, A Legal Professional Association
Dover, OH
New Philadelphia, OH
Black, McCuskey, Souers & Arbaugh, A Legal Professional Association
Canton, OH
Wooster, OH
Black & McLaren, A Professional Corporation ....Memphis, TN
Black, Melody R. ....Hendersonville, TN
Black, Melvin S. ....Miami, FL
Black, Melvin S., P.A. ....Miami, FL
Black, Michael C. ....Miami, FL
Black, Michael C. ....St. Paul, MN
Black, Michael C., Law Office, Ltd.
St. Paul, MN
Black, Michael G. ....Coeur d'Alene, ID
Spokane, WA
Black, Michael J. ....Bloomfield Hills, MI
Black, Michael John ....San Antonio, TX
Black, Michael V. ....Phoenix, AZ
Black, Michael W. ....Chicago, IL
Black, Milton ....Chicago, IL
Black, Milton, & Associates, Ltd.
Chicago, IL
Black and Morgan ....Birmingham, AL
Black, Nadia Rasheed ....Myrtle Beach, SC
Black, Nadia Rasheed, P.A.
Myrtle Beach, SC
Black, Nancy Fountain ....Raleigh, NC
Black, Nancy G. ....Baltimore, MD
Black, Nandia P. ....Oak Brook, IL
Black, Natalie A. ....Kohler, WI
Black, Nathalie V. ....Washington, DC
Black, Neal ....Seattle, WA
Black, Nicholas J. ....Albuquerque, NM
Black, Nicole L. ....Rochester, NY
Black, Noland & Read, P.L.C.
Staunton, VA
Black, Norman ....Sacramento, CA
Black, O. Earl, Jr. ....Tallahassee, FL
Black & Older ....Haddonfield, NJ
Bala Cynwyd, PA
Philadelphia, PA
Black, Pamela H. ....Los Angeles, CA
Black, Pamela K. ....Omaha, NE
Black, Patricia A. ....Fort Myers, FL
Black, Patricia Elizabeth ....San Francisco, CA
Black, Patricia M.
Federal Deposit Insurance Corporation, GV
Black, Patricia R. ....Ukiah, CA
Black, Paul E. ....Evansville, IN
Black, Paul F. ....St. Louis, MO
Black, Paul L. ....Woodbridge, NJ
Black, Paul M. ....Roanoke, VA
Black, Paul R. ....Indianapolis, IN
Black, Peter D. ....Jacksonville, FL
Black, Peter D., P.A. ....Jacksonville, FL
Black, Peter J. ....Boston, MA
Black, Peter L. ....Branford, CT
Black, Peter R. ....Grand Junction, CO
Black, Peter S. ....Portland, ME
Black, R. Andrew ....Houston, TX
Black, R. Drummond ....Midland, MI
Black, R. Russell ....Arlington, VA
Black, Ralph D. ....Sacramento, CA
Black, Ralph D. ....Hilo, HI
Black, Randall W. ....Los Angeles, CA
Black, Ray J. ....Waco, TX
Black, Ray J., Jr. ....Houston, TX
Black, Reginald ....Ocala, FL
Black, Renee Allee ....Eagle, CO
Black, Richard A. ....Phoenix, AZ
Black, Richard A., P.C. ....Phoenix, AZ
Black, Richard D. ....Walnut Creek, CA
Black, Richard D. ....Houston, TX
Black, Richard J. ....Morris, IL
Black, Richard M. ....Los Angeles, CA
Black, Richard W. ....Washington, DC
Minneapolis, MN
St. Paul, MN
Black, Robert ....Manhasset, NY
Black, Robert A. ....Beaumont, TX
Black, Robert B. ....Parkersburg, WV
Black, Robert C. ....Arlington, VA
Black, Robert C., Jr. ....Montgomery, AL
Black, Robert C., Sr. ....Montgomery, AL
Black, Robert D. ....Greenville, SC
Black, Robert E. ....Austin, TX
Black, Robert Gwyn ....Portland, OR
Black, Robert H. ....Los Angeles, CA
Black, Robert H. ....Bala Cynwyd, PA
Philadelphia, PA
Black, Robert J.
Department of Transportation, Federal Highway Administration, GV
Black, Robert J. ....Coral Gables, FL
Black, Robert J. ....Bogalusa, LA
Black, Robert L., Jr. ....Cincinnati, OH
Black, Robert M. ....Malden, MO
Black, Robert N. ....Crescent City, CA
Black, Robert N., Jr. ....Columbus, OH
Black, Robert R. ....Carlisle, PA
Black, Robert W. ....Wilmington, DE
Black, Robin J. ....Irvine, CA
Black, Ronald F. ....Anchorage, AK
Black, Ronald W. ....Orlando, FL
Black, Rosalind ....New York, NY
Black, Rosemary ....Detroit, MI
Black, Roy ....Miami, FL
Black, Roy T., III ....Dunwoody, GA
Black, Russell M. ....Charlotte, NC
Black's Law Office, P.A. ....Pratt, KS
Black, S. Norman ....Orange, CA
Black, Sam ....Washington, DC
Black, Samuel L. ....Boston, MA
Black, Sanford ....New Hyde Park, NY
Black, Sarah Donna ....Littleton, CO
Black, Scott B. ....East Meadow, NY
Black, Scott C. ....Department of the Army, Office of the Secretary, GV
Black, Scott L. ....New York, NY
Black, Scott T. ....Los Angeles, CA
Black, Sean A. ....Toccoa, GA
Black, Shane E. ....Birmingham, AL
Black, Shanise M. ....Los Angeles, CA
Black and Shaw, P.S.C. ....Louisville, KY
Middletown, KY
Black, Shawn P. ....Buffalo, NY
Black, Shelli J. ....Irvine, CA
Black, Shelly L. ....Riverside, CA
Black, Sherrie T. ....Baltimore, MD
Black, Sidney H., (Ltd.) ....Boynton Beach, FL
Black, Sims, Hubka, Burnett, Birch and Rawnsley, L.L.P. ....Daytona Beach, FL
Black, Srebnick & Kornspan, P.A.
Miami, FL
Black, Stanley A. ....Boulder, CO
Black, Stefanie A. ....Miami, FL
Black, Stephen F. ....Washington, DC
Black, Stephen Foster ....Birmingham, AL
Black, Stephen L. ....Cincinnati, OH
Black, Stephen R. ....Seattle, WA
Black, Stephen T. ....Logan, UT
Black, Stevan Lenoir ....Memphis, TN
Black, Steven G. ....Salt Lake City, UT
Black, Steven W. ....Denver, CO
Black, Steven W. ....Corvallis, OR
Black, Stith & Argyle, A Professional Corporation ....Park City, UT
Salt Lake City, UT
Black, Susan H. ....Jacksonville, FL
Black, Susan Neiswender ....Orlando, FL
Black, T. Keith ....Greensboro, NC
Black, Terrell L. ....Louisville, KY
Black, Terry R. ....Mount Vernon, IL
Black, Terry R. ....Lansing, MI
Black, Theodore N. ....Pittsburgh, PA
Black, Thomas C. ....Washington, DC
Black, Thomas E., Jr. ....Tulsa, OK
Black, Thomas E., Jr. ....Houston, TX
Black, Thomas L. ....Albany, OR
Black, Thomas M. ....Madison, TN
Black, Thomas V. ....Pratt, KS
Black, Thomas W. ....Tampa, FL
Black, Timothy A. ....Newport Beach, CA
Black, Timothy L. ....Indianapolis, IN
Black, Timothy T. ....Seattle, WA
Black, Tisha Reneé ....Las Vegas, NV
Black, Todd J. ....Champaign, IL
Black, Tom A. ....Plymouth, IN
Black, Travis G. ....Cameron Park, CA
Black, Val J. McLam ....Portland, OR
Black, Virgil C. ....Oklahoma City, OK
Black, W. Jerrold ....Savannah, GA
Black, Walter ....Great Neck, NY
Black, Walter E., Jr. ....Baltimore, MD
Black, Wayne V. ....Washington, DC
Black, William C. ....Woodland Hills, CA
Black, William C. ....Temple, TX
Black, William D., Law Offices of
Phoenix, AZ
Black, William E. ....Austin, TX
Black, William H., Jr. ....Philadelphia, PA
Black, William M., Jr. ....Raleigh, NC
Black, William R. ....Coto De Caza, CA
Black, William R.
Cumberland Foreside, ME
Black, W. L. Rivers, III ....Seattle, WA
Black, Wm. Stephen, II ....Tallahassee, FL
Black & Yund ....Seattle, WA
Blackaby Law Firm, P.C. ....Helena, MT
Blackaby, W. Dean ....Helena, MT
Blackall, Brewster ....Hartford, CT
Blackard, Caswell B., III ....Little Rock, AR
Blackard, Charles G., III ....Brentwood, TN
Blackard, Charles M.
Hot Springs National Park, AR
Blackard, Eugene C., Jr.
Walnut Creek, CA
Blackard, Fred K. ....Houston, TX
Blackard, J. T. ....Miami, FL
Blackard, Stovall & Murphy ....Brentwood, TN
Blackard, William R., Jr.
Fernandina Beach, FL
Blackard, William R., Jr. ....Jacksonville, FL
Blackard, William R., Jr.
St. Augustine, FL
Blackbird, Kathryn M. ....Austin, TX
Blackbourn, Lisle W. ....Elkhorn, WI
Blackburn, A. B., Jr. ....Jacksonville, FL
Blackburn, Ace J., Jr.
Fort Lauderdale, FL
Blackburn, Amy L. ....Atlanta, GA
Blackburn, Andrew H. ....Ogden, UT
Blackburn, Andrew J. ....San Diego, CA
Blackburn & Backus ....Tequesta, FL
East Lansing, MI
Blackburn, Barry C. ....Olive Branch, MS
Blackburn, Ben B., III ....Dalton, GA
Blackburn, Bill ....Corpus Christi, TX
Blackburn, Billy R. ....Albuquerque, NM
Blackburn & Blackburn ....Jacksonville, FL
Blackburn & Blackburn, P.C. ....Dalton, GA
Blackburn, Bob ....La Junta, CO
Blackburn, Brian L. ....Northampton, MA
Blackburn, Bruce E. ....Vanceburg, KY
Blackburn, Bruce W. ....Minneapolis, MN
Blackburn, Bryan E. ....Jacksonville, FL
Blackburn, Calon E., Jr. ....Mobile, AL
Blackburn, Calvin W., III ....Birmingham, AL
Blackburn, Carrie L. ....Baltimore, MD
Blackburn & Carter, P.C. ....Houston, TX
Blackburn, Catherine Elaine ....Tampa, FL
Blackburn, Charlene G. ....Worcester, MA
Blackburn, Charles D. ....Boston, MA
Blackburn, Charles F. ....Henderson, NC
Blackburn, Charles F. ....San Antonio, TX
Blackburn, Cherie W. ....Charleston, SC
Blackburn, Cheryl A. ....Nashville, TN
Blackburn & Company, L.C.
Jacksonville, FL
St. Augustine, FL
Blackburn, Crystal M. ....Oakland, CA
Blackburn, Daniel G. ....Bay Minette, AL
Blackburn, Daniel G., A Prof. Corp., Law Offices of ....Bay Minette, AL
Blackburn, David A. ....Plainview, TX
Blackburn, David Thomas ....Dalton, GA
Blackburn, Deborah D. ....Cedar City, UT
Blackburn, Dennis L. ....Jacksonville, FL
Blackburn, Donald W. ....Goshen, KY
Blackburn, Erich E. ....Pikeville, KY
Blackburn, Frank D. ....Baton Rouge, LA
Blackburn, G. Alan ....Atlanta, GA
Blackburn, George T. ....Henderson, NC
Blackburn, George T., II ....Henderson, NC
Raleigh, NC
Blackburn, Gerald L. ....Wynne, AR
Blackburn, Gregg S. ....Boston, MA
Blackburn, Gregory Joseph ....Tampa, FL
Blackburn, Gregory V. ....Mission Viejo, CA
Blackburn, Harry A. ....Chicago, IL
Blackburn, Harry R. ....Cherry Hill, NJ
Philadelphia, PA
Blackburn, Harry R. ....San Juan, PR
Blackburn, Harry R., & Associates
Cherry Hill, NJ
Philadelphia, PA
San Juan, PR
Blackburn, Hundley & Domene, LLP
Louisville, KY
Blackburn, J. Gilmer ....Decatur, AL
Blackburn, James B. ....Savannah, GA
Blackburn, James B. ....Houston, TX
Blackburn, James B., III ....Raleigh, NC
Blackburn, James B., Jr. ....Savannah, GA
Blackburn, James M. ....Tequesta, FL
Blackburn, James S. ....Los Angeles, CA
Blackburn, James S. ....Des Moines, IA
Blackburn, Janet Lynn Weaver
Lexington, VA
Blackburn, Janice K. ....Department of Labor, Office of Secretary, GV
Blackburn, J. E. ....Spearman, TX
Blackburn, Jean Ellen ....Menlo Park, CA
Blackburn, Joanne Thomas ....Seattle, WA
Blackburn, John F. ....Savannah, GA
Blackburn, John M. ....Arcadia, CA
Blackburn, John Marshall ....Valinda, CA
Blackburn, John P. ....Yankton, SD
Blackburn, John R. ....Seattle, WA
Blackburn, Joseph E. ....Richmond, VA
Blackburn, Joseph E., Jr. ....Richmond, VA
Blackburn, Joseph W. ....Birmingham, AL
Blackburn, Julie E. ....Chicago, IL
Blackburn, Julie Prlina ....New York, NY
Blackburn, June C. ....Jacksonville, FL
Blackburn, Kari Kardel ....Fallbrook, CA
Blackburn, Kerry ....Riverside, CA
Blackburn, Laurie J. ....Alexandria, VA
Blackburn, Lemuel H., Jr. ....Lawrenceville, NJ
Blackburn, Linda L. ....Hutchinson, KS
Blackburn, Lisa Galante ....Philadelphia, PA
Blackburn, Maloney and Schuppert, LLC
Decatur, AL
Blackburn, Mark B. ....Austin, TX
Blackburn, Marvin E., Jr. ....Junction, TX
Blackburn, Matthew K. ....New York, NY
Blackburn, Melissa A. ....San Diego, CA
Blackburn, Michael D.
Salt Lake City, UT
Blackburn, Michael P. ....Orange, CA
Walnut Creek, CA
Blackburn, Mitchell D.
Oklahoma City, OK
Blackburn and Muslin ....Arcadia, CA
Blackburn, Oris D., Jr. ....Valdosta, GA
Blackburn, Patrick J. ....Oakton, VA
Blackburn, R. Scott ....Dayton, OH
Blackburn, R. Thomas, Jr. ....Louisville, KY
Blackburn, Rex ....Boise, ID
Blackburn, Rhonda Jennings
Pikeville, KY
Blackburn, Richard W. ....Charlotte, NC
Blackburn, Robert E. ....Suffern, NY
Blackburn, Robert G. ....Atlanta, GA
Blackburn, Robert P. ....Emeryville, CA
Blackburn, Roger L. ....Miami, FL
Blackburn, Slobey, Freeman & Happell, P.C.
Nashville, TN
Blackburn, Stephen M. ....Fort Lauderdale, FL
Blackburn, Steven R. ....San Francisco, CA
Blackburn & Stoll, LC
Salt Lake City, UT
Blackburn, Stuart G. ....Windsor Locks, CT
Blackburn, Stuart G., Law Offices of
Windsor Locks, CT
Blackburn, Terence L. ....Newark, NJ
Blackburn, Thomas A. ....Allentown, PA
Doylestown, PA
Stroudsburg, PA
Blackburn, Thomas A. ....York, PA
Blackburn, Thomas E. ....Portland, ME
Blackburn, Thomas I. ....Columbus, OH
Blackburn, Thomas L. ....Washington, DC
Blackburn, Thomas L. ....Indianapolis, IN
Blackburn, Timothy W. ....Ogden, UT
Blackburn, W. Gary ....Nashville, TN
Blackburn, W. Stanley ....Atlanta, GA
Blackburn, Walther & Sloan ....Atlanta, GA
Blackburn, William G. ....Grand Island, NE
Blackburn, William H. ....Thomasville, GA
Blackburn, William M. ....Dallas, TX
Blackburn, William R. ....Deerfield, IL
Blackburn, Winfrey P., Jr. ....Louisville, KY
Blackburn, Wm. Keaton ....Junction, TX
Blackburn-Gardner, Elizabeth A.
Daytona Beach, FL
Blacke, Lawrence E. ....Fort Lauderdale, FL
Blacker, Harvey Darryl ....Columbia, MD
Blacker, Jonathan J. ....Boston, MA
Blacker, Jonathan L. ....Dallas, TX
Blacker, Lawrence L. ....Boston, MA
Blacker, Monica S. ....Dallas, TX
Blacker, Nathan ....Tamarac, FL
Blacker, Nordin F. ....San Francisco, CA
Blacker, Richard A. ....Los Angeles, CA
Blacker, Rick C. ....San Francisco, CA
Blacker, Sidney G. ....Sherman Oaks, CA
Blacker, Stanley ....New York, NY
Blacker, Stanley M.
Environmental Protection Agency, Program Office Attorneys, GV

Blackerby, Chris A. ... Austin, TX
Blackerby, R. Brittain ... New Bern, NC
Blacketer, Ashley N. ... Louisville, KY
Blacketer, Belinda ... Laguna Beach, CA
Blackett, Carolyn Wade ... Memphis, TN
Blackett, Hill, III ... San Francisco, CA
Blackett, Katherine N. ... Albuquerque, NM
Blackett, W. Ben ... Tacoma, WA
Blackey, T. David ... La Crosse, WI
Blackford, Barbara L. ... St. Louis, MO
Blackford, Gary D. ... Minneapolis, MN
Blackford, Jason C. ... Cleveland, OH
Blackford, John D. ... Tariffville, CT
Blackford, John R. ... Kansas City, MO
Blackford, Robert G. ... Gaithersburg, MD
Blackford, Robert N. ... Orlando, FL
Blackford, Sandra S. ... San Jose, CA
Blackford, Timothy ... San Diego, CA
Blackford, Wm. H. ... Dublin, OH
Blackhall, Jennifer Z. ... Clarence, NY
Blackham, Katherine S. ... Cleveland, OH
Blackham, Lowell E. ... St. Louis, MO
Blackham, Robert E. ... Akron, OH
Cleveland, OH
Blackham, Ross C. ... Manti, UT
Blackham, Sam R. ... El Paso, TX
Blackhurst, B. Kent ... Medford, OR
Blackhurst, Dennis P. ... Mesa, AZ
Blackhurst, Eric P. ... Midland, MI
Blackhurst, J. Hoyt ... Scottsdale, AZ
Blackhurst, John ... Medford, OR
Blackhurst, Scott D. ... Cleveland, OH
Blackhurst, Steven K. ... Portland, OR
Blackie, Jeffrey A. ... Newport Beach, CA
Blackie, William E., III ... Cleveland, OH
Blackiston, Henry C., III ... New York, NY
Blackiston, Luther ... Baltimore, MD
Blackledge, Frederick C. ... Minneapolis, MN
Blackledge, Joel L. ... Biloxi, MS
Blackler, Mia S. ... Walnut Creek, CA
Blackley, David E. ... Lockport, NY
Blackley, Mary L. Coon ... Shreveport, LA
Blacklidge, Gary L. ... Portland, OR
Blacklidge, Raymond M. ... West Chicago, IL
Blacklock, Bonnie ... New York, NY
Blacklock, Jan L. ... Lubbock, TX
Blacklock, William K. ... Missouri City, TX
Blacklocks, Stephen R. ... New York, NY
Blackman, A. Lee ... Encino, CA
Blackman, A. Lee, A Professional Law Corporation ... Encino, CA
Blackman, Albert L., Jr. ... Doylestown, PA
Blackman, Barbara R. ... Montpelier, VT
Blackman & Blackman, A Professional Corporation ... Sacramento, CA
Blackman, Brian Richard
Redwood City, CA
Blackman, Brian S. ... Pflugerville, TX
Blackman, Carol R. ... Philadelphia, PA
Blackman, Charles D. ... Boston, MA
Providence, RI
Blackman, Charles E., Jr. ... Chicago, IL
Blackman, Clifford A. ... Burlingame, CA
Redwood City, CA
Blackman, Clint C., III ... Dallas, TX
Blackman, Craig R. ... Philadelphia, PA
Blackman, Daniel J. ... West Palm Beach, FL
Blackman, David M. ... Sacramento, CA
Blackman, Gary I. ... Chicago, IL
Blackman, Gordon A. ... Columbus, OH
Blackman, Gordon N., Jr. ... Shreveport, LA
Blackman, Irving L. ... Chicago, IL
Blackman, James C. ... Warren, PA
Blackman, James W. ... Palo Alto, CA
Blackman, James W., A Professional Corporation ... Palo Alto, CA
Blackman, Jana Cohen ... Chicago, IL
Blackman, Jeffrey ... Tucson, AZ
Blackman, Jeffrey H. ... Glenview, IL
Blackman, Jennifer L. ... San Francisco, CA
Blackman, Jennifer Lynn
San Francisco, CA
Blackman, John C. ... Baton Rouge, LA
Blackman, John D. ... Woodland Hills, CA
Blackman, John N., Jr. ... New York, NY
Blackman, John S. ... San Mateo, CA
Blackman, Jonathan I. ... New York, NY
Blackman, Joshua D. ... New York, NY
Blackman, Joshua I. ... Lakewood, CO
Blackman, Keith ... Jonesboro, AR
Blackman, Kenneth R. ... New York, NY
Blackman, Laura S. ... Boca Raton, FL
Blackman Law Firm ... Jonesboro, AR
Blackman, Lawrence D. ... Denver, CO
Blackman, Lee L. ... Los Angeles, CA
Blackman, Lenard D. ... Westport, CT
Blackman, Lenard D., P.C. ... Westport, CT
Blackman & Levine, L.L.C. ... Denver, CO
Blackman, Linda Smith ... Bossier City, LA
Blackman, Marc D. ... Portland, OR
Blackman, Marc S. ... Chicago, IL
Blackman, Marianne ... Binghamton, NY
Blackman, Mark S. ... Encino, CA
Blackman, Martin E. ... Rye, NY
Blackman, Murray I. ... Philadelphia, PA
Blackman, Paul D. ... Kansas City, MO
Blackman & Perkins, L.L.C.
Bossier City, LA
Shreveport, LA
Blackman, Peter A. ... Sacramento, CA
Blackman, Peter W. ... Santa Monica, CA
Blackman, Philip L. ... Cherry Hill, NJ
Philadelphia, PA
Blackman, Philip M. ... Chicago, IL
Blackman, Robert B. ... Edison, NJ
Blackman, Robert B. ... New Brunswick, NJ
Blackman, Robert B. ... Paterson, NJ
Blackman, Robert I. ... Brooklyn, NY
Blackman, Robert M., Jr. ... San Antonio, TX
Blackman, Rodney J. ... Chicago, IL
Blackman, Sallie A. ... La Mesa, CA
Blackman, Scott H. ... Washington, DC
Blackman, Sidney W. ... Warren, PA
Blackman, Stephanie ... Santa Monica, CA
Blackman, Stephen E. ... Portland, OR
Blackman, Steven H. ... Beverly Hills, CA
Blackman, Susan Roussel ... Norfolk, VA
Blackmar, Charles B. ... Jefferson City, MO
Blackmar, David S. ... Boston, MA
Blackmar, George B. ... San Diego, CA
Blackmar, Principe & Schmelter, A Professional Corporation ... San Diego, CA
Blackmar, Thomas J. ... Burnsville, MN
Blackmer, Brian J. ... Okemos, MI
Blackmer, Jill K. ... Concord, NH
Blackmer, Mark R. ... Columbus, OH
Blackmer, Rebecca A. ... Washington, DC
Blackmer, S. Jonathan C.
Department of Justice, Environment and Natural Resources Division, GV
Blackmer, Steven G. ... Pittsburgh, PA
Blackmer, W. Scott ... Washington, DC
Blackmon, Carolee K. ... St. Petersburg, FL
Blackmon, Carolee K., P.A.
St. Petersburg, FL
Blackmon, Charles K. ... Greensboro, NC
Blackmon, Clyde M. ... Sacramento, CA
Blackmon, David H. ... Buffalo, NY
Blackmon, Edward B. ... Orangeburg, SC
Blackmon, Edward, Jr. ... Canton, MS
Blackmon, Jack R. ... Corpus Christi, TX
Blackmon, Joel D. ... Wardensville, WV
Blackmon, John A. ... Atlanta, GA
Blackmon, John G., Jr. ... Atlanta, GA
Blackmon, Leon C. ... West Simsbury, CT
Blackmon, Leslie A. ... Washington, DC
Blackmon, M. Paige ... Dallas, TX
Blackmon, Patricia A. ... Cleveland, OH
Blackmon, Patricia Speth ... Marion, SC
Blackmon, Phillip D., Jr.
Miami Lakes, FL
Blackmon, Robert C. ... Philadelphia, PA
Blackmon, Robert M. ... Corpus Christi, TX
Blackmon, Robert N. ... Arlington, VA
Blackmon, Sharon D. ... Detroit, MI
Blackmon, Shelby R. ... Little Rock, AR
Blackmon & Snellings, LLP
Sacramento, CA
Blackmon, Stacey L. ... Carrollton, GA
Blackmon, Tommy K. ... Brooksville, FL
Blackmond, Barbara A. ... Pittsburgh, PA
Blackmond, Don G. ... South Bend, IN
Blackmond, Don Gregory ... South Bend, IN
Blackmond, Frederick J. ... Lansing, MI
Blackmon-Milligan, Martha
Panama City, FL
Blackmon-Solis, Katherine E.
Little Rock, AR
Blackmon-Solis & Moak, L.L.P.
Little Rock, AR
Blackmore, Adele M.
Fort Lauderdale, FL
Blackmore & Blackmore
Fort Lauderdale, FL
West Palm Beach, FL
Blackmore & Grieshober ... Erie, PA
Blackmore, James C. ... Albany, NY
Blackmore, Josiah H. ... Columbus, OH
Blackmore, Margaret L. ... Columbus, OH
Blackmore, Robert F. ... Portland, OR
Blackmore, Robert W.
Fort Lauderdale, FL
Blackmore, Steven C. ... Pittsburgh, PA
Blackmun, Bomberger & Moran
Crown Point, IN
Hammond, IN
Highland, IN
Blackmun, Gilbert F. ... Highland, IN
Blackmun, Sally A. ... Orlando, FL
Blackmun, Scott A. ... Colorado Springs, CO
Blacknall, Willis H., III ... Waycross, GA
Blackner, David L. ... Salt Lake City, UT
Blacksberg, Robert L. ... Philadelphia, PA
Blacksburg, A. Brent ... Tappan, NY
Blackshaw, Betsy Wolf ... Barre, VT
Blackshaw, Julie Fox ... Los Angeles, CA
Blackshear, A. T., Jr. ... Houston, TX
Blackshear, Julian W., Jr. ... Nashville, TN
Blackshear, Patricia H. ... Austin, TX
Blackshear, W. Jere ... Dallas, TX
Blacksher, James U. ... Birmingham, AL
Blacksher, Wesley H. ... Mobile, AL
Blackshire, Elizabeth Ann ... Dallas, TX
Blackshire, Pamela Wray ... Charleston, WV
Blackstock, Benjamin W. ... Cedar Rapids, IA
Blackstock, Brent ... Tulsa, OK
Blackstock, Clayton R. ... Little Rock, AR
Blackstock, Craig ... Tulsa, OK
Blackstock, Daniel V. ... Oroville, CA
Blackstock, David S. ... Ventura, CA
Blackstock, James A. ... Angleton, TX
Blackstock, James F. ... Lebanon, TN
Blackstock, Jerry B. ... Atlanta, GA
Blackstock Law Offices, P.C.
Cedar Rapids, IA
Blackstock, LeRoy ... Tulsa, OK
Blackstock, Robert L. ... Walnut Creek, CA
Blackstock, Robert W. ... Hillsdale, MI
Blackstock, Ronald L. ... Weatherford, TX
Blackstock, Ronald L., P.C.
Weatherford, TX
Blackston, Joseph Walker ... New Orleans, LA
Blackston, Laura Leigh ... New Orleans, LA
Blackston, William M. ... New Orleans, LA
Blackstone, Adger Lee, III ... Columbia, SC
Blackstone, Craig Rodger
San Francisco, CA
Blackstone, David ... New York, NY
Blackstone, Edward R. ... Longview, TX
Blackstone, Franklin, III ... Washington, DC
Blackstone, Franklin, Jr.
Cranberry Township, PA
Pittsburgh, PA
Blackstone, George A. ... San Francisco, CA
Blackstone, J. Michael ... Crystal River, FL
Blackstone, James A. ... Cleveland, OH
Blackstone, Jay ... Youngstown, OH
Blackstone, Joan ... Pacifica, CA
Blackstone, Mary Louise ... Los Angeles, CA
Blackstone, M.F. ... Laramie, WY
Blackstone, Michael C. ... Washington, DC
Gaithersburg, MD
Arlington, VA
Blackstone, Raiford A., Jr. ... Chicago, IL
Blackstone, Robert A. ... Seattle, WA
Blackstone, Robert Craig ... Seattle, WA
Blackstone, Sandra Lee ... Parker, CO
Blackstone, Scott S. ... Tustin, CA
Blackstone, Stanley B., Law Office of
Lafayette, LA
Blackstone, William E. ... Nashville, TN
Blackstone, William Kenneth
Hazlehurst, GA
Blackstone, William M. ... Baltimore, MD
Blackwelder, Anna K. ... Charlotte, NC
Blackwelder, Brion L. ... Fort Lauderdale, FL
Blackwelder, Campbell & Leavitt
Indianapolis, IN
Blackwelder, Charles B. ... Indianapolis, IN
Blackwelder, Jeffrey A. ... Austin, TX
Blackwell, Albert, Jr. ... Upper Marlboro, MD
Blackwell, Allison Flom ... Minneapolis, MN
Blackwell, Amy Hackney ... Greenville, SC
Blackwell, Anthony J. ... Phoenix, AZ
Blackwell & Associates ... Garland, TX
Blackwell & Associates, P.C.
O'Fallon, MO
St. Louis, MO
Blackwell, Ayesha C. ... Morristown, NJ
Blackwell, Barbara J. Cullen ... Eugene, OR
Blackwell, Barbara W. ... Stamford, CT
Blackwell, Barry E. ... Dalhart, TX
Blackwell, Bert E. ... McCook, NE
Blackwell, Betty ... Austin, TX
Blackwell, Bradley K. ... Dallas, TX
Blackwell, Brian F. ... Baton Rouge, LA
Blackwell, Bruce B. ... Orlando, FL
Blackwell, Bryan S. ... Dothan, AL
Blackwell, Carroll M. ... Paris, MO
Blackwell, Cartledge W., Jr. ... Selma, AL
Blackwell, Chambliss, Henry, Caldwell & Cagle ... West Monroe, LA
Blackwell, Charles G. ... Laurel, MS
Blackwell, Charles L. ... Bethesda, MD
Blackwell, Charles W. ... Rock Hill, SC
Blackwell, Clifford E., III ... Madison, WI
Blackwell, Craig M. ... Department of Justice, Civil Division, GV
Blackwell, David A. ... Castle Dale, UT
Blackwell, David H. ... San Francisco, CA
Blackwell, David L. ... New Philadelphia, OH
Blackwell, Debbie L. ... Tulsa, OK
Blackwell, Debra W. ... Natchez, MS
Blackwell, Denise M. ... Plymouth, MN
Blackwell, Dennis M. ... Pittsburgh, PA
Blackwell & Diaco, P.A. ... Tampa, FL
Blackwell, Donald A. ... Miami, FL
Blackwell, Donald H. ... Lancaster, PA
Blackwell, Donald P. ... Richmond, VA
Blackwell, Douglas N., II
Chattanooga, TN
Blackwell, Earl R. ... Hillsboro, MO
Blackwell, Edith R. ... Rockville, MD
Blackwell, Elicia D. ... Fort Lauderdale, FL
Blackwell, Elizabeth ... Kansas City, MO
Blackwell, Floyd A. ... Garland, TX
Blackwell, Fred R. ... Gaithersburg, MD
Blackwell, Glenette ... Los Angeles, CA
Blackwell, Glenn L. ... Philadelphia, PA
Blackwell, Guy W., Jr. ... Greeneville, TN
Blackwell, Heather L. ... Beaumont, TX
Blackwell, Henry B., II ... Indianapolis, IN
Blackwell, Hugh A. ... Valdese, NC
Blackwell, Jacqueline M ... Indiana, PA
Blackwell, James L. ... Henderson, TX
Blackwell, Jean M. ... Chicago, IL
Blackwell, Jean S. ... Columbus, IN
Blackwell, Jeffrey G. ... Huntsville, AL
Blackwell, Jeffrey H. ... Wilmington, NC
Blackwell, Jerry W. ... Minneapolis, MN
Blackwell, Joan Ligocki ... Indianapolis, IN
Blackwell, Joel D. ... Washington, DC
Blackwell, John ... New Iberia, LA
Blackwell, John V., Jr. ... Fayetteville, NC
Blackwell, Jonathan Andrew ... Huntsville, AL
Blackwell, Joseph H. ... Cleveland, OH
Blackwell, Joseph W. ... Hubbard, OH
Blackwell, Judith Ashe ... Atlanta, GA
Blackwell, Karen J. ... Dayton, OH
Blackwell & Keith ... Selma, AL
Blackwell, Kendrick J. ... Tampa, FL
Blackwell, Landra D. ... Dallas, TX
Blackwell, Leo T. ... Indianapolis, IN
Blackwell, Leonard A., II ... Gulfport, MS
Blackwell, Luedeke, Hicks & Edwards, P.A.
Fayetteville, NC
Blackwell, Lynn C. ... Hartford, CT
Blackwell, Marianne ... Colorado Springs, CO
Blackwell, Mark C. ... Louisville, KY
Blackwell, Mary Kathleen M.
Allison Park, PA
Blackwell, Maxine ... Milledgeville, GA
Blackwell, Melinda D. ... Dallas, TX
Blackwell, Melineh B. ... Washington, DC
Blackwell, Menefee D. ... Kansas City, MO
Blackwell, Michelle A. ... Chicago, IL
Blackwell, Michelle A. ... Michigan City, IN
South Bend, IN
Blackwell, Michelle Davis ... Butler, PA
Blackwell, Monta Sharon ... Tulsa, OK
Blackwell, Murphy, Jr. ... West Monroe, LA
Blackwell, Nancy E. ... Lee's Summit, MO
Blackwell, Nancy N. ... Zionsville, IN
Blackwell, Nichelle L. ... Los Angeles, CA
Blackwell, Patricia A. ... Santa Ana, CA
Blackwell, R. Barrow ... Norfolk, VA
Blackwell, Richard A. ... Chicago, IL
Blackwell, Richard B. ... Hampton, VA
Blackwell, Richard M. ... Salina, KS
Blackwell, Robert A., Jr. ... Dallas, TX
Blackwell, Robert E. ... Baton Rouge, LA
Blackwell, Robert J. ... Washington, DC
Blackwell, Robert J. ... Minneapolis, MN
Blackwell, Robert J. ... O'Fallon, MO
Blackwell, Robert M. ... St. Louis, MO
Blackwell, Robert R. ... Yanceyville, NC
Blackwell, Ronald G. ... Marietta, GA
Blackwell, Ronald O. ... Garland, TX
Blackwell Sanders Peper Martin
Omaha, NE
Blackwell Sanders Peper Martin LLP
Edwardsville, IL
Overland Park, KS
Kansas City, MO
St. Louis, MO
Springfield, MO
Blackwell, Steven ... Mars Hill, NC
Blackwell, Steven A. ... University, MS
Blackwell, Susan Cullen ... Crystal Lake, IL
Blackwell, Suzette Wynn ... Silver Spring, MD
Blackwell, Thomas B. ... Indianapolis, IN
Blackwell, Thomas F. ... Grand Rapids, MI
Blackwell, Thomas F. ... Dallas, TX
Blackwell, Thomas F., P.C. ... Dallas, TX
Blackwell, Thomas F., Sr. ... Grand Rapids, MI
Blackwell, Thomas J. ... St. Louis, MO
Blackwell, Thomas Lewis, III ... Mobile, AL
Blackwell, Thos. D., Jr. ... Austin, TX
Blackwell, Victor ... Chicago, IL
Blackwell, Victoria T. ... Vancouver, WA
Blackwell & Walker, Attys. at Law, A Prof. Assn. ... Miami, FL
West Palm Beach, FL
Blackwell, Walter K. ... Daytona Beach, FL
Blackwell, Walter L., III ... Fontana, CA
Blackwell & White ... Biloxi, MS
Gulfport, MS
Jackson, MS
Blackwell, William L. ... Naples, FL
Blackwell, William W. ... Los Angeles, CA
Blackwell, Worth T. ... Tampa, FL
Blackwood, Alan G. ... Rock Island, IL
Blackwood, Amy A. ... Little Rock, AR
Blackwood Associates, P.C. ... Burlington, VT
Blackwood, Brett N. ... Birmingham, AL
Blackwood, Constance E. ... Hartford, CT
Blackwood, David M. ... Costa Mesa, CA
Blackwood, David P. ... Bethesda, MD
Blackwood, Dean ... Round Rock, TX
Blackwood, Donald J., Jr. ... Jackson, MS
Blackwood, Dora Anne ... Nashville, TN
Blackwood, Dorothy T. ... New Orleans, LA
Blackwood, Eileen M. ... Burlington, VT
Blackwood, George D., Jr.
Kansas City, MO
Blackwood, James E. ... Erie, PA
Blackwood, Jeffrey R. ... Jackson, MS
Blackwood, Jim ... Erlanger, KY
Blackwood, John F. ... Livingston, MT
Blackwood, John F. ... Nashville, TN
Blackwood, Jon K. ... Somerville, TN
Blackwood, Kristine ... Los Angeles, CA
Blackwood, L. James, II ... Greensboro, NC
Blackwood & Langworthy, L.C.
Kansas City, MO
Blackwood, Loyal R. ... Cocoa, FL
Blackwood, Raymond J. ... Houston, TX
Blackwood, Robert Lee ... Freeport, TX
Blackwood, Robin C.M. ... Irving, TX
Blackwood, Selwyn D. ... Atlanta, GA
Blackwood, Terry M. ... Richardson, TX
Blackwood, Thomas J., II ... Charlotte, NC
Blackwood, Timothy J. ... San Jose, CA
Blackwood, Toni Hays ... Kansas City, MO
Blackwood, Vincent
Equal Employment Opportunity Commission, Office of the General Counsel, GV
Blackwood, William B., Jr. ... Clearwater, FL
Blackwood, William M. ... Austin, TX
Blad, Karyn Schwartz ... Washington, DC
Blad, Leiv H., Jr. ... Washington, DC
Blade & Blade, P.A. ... Boca Raton, FL
Deerfield Beach, FL
Lighthouse Point, FL
Pompano Beach, FL
Blade, Bryan S. ... Cincinnati, OH
Blade, David A. ... Pompano Beach, FL
Blade, Judith S. ... Nashville, TN
Blade, Paul E. ... Deerfield Beach, FL
Blade, Thomas A. ... Moline, IL
Blade, William P. ... Deerfield Beach, FL
Bladen, Edwin M. ... Mercer Island, WA
Blader, Steven ... Lawrenceville, NJ
Bladergroen, Robert J. ... Fairfax, VA
Blades, Alexander B. ... New York, NY
Blades, Candace E. ... Richmond, VA
Blades, Carmichael, Rosser & Benz
Cedar Rapids, IA
Blades, Charles A. ... Cedar Rapids, IA
Blades, David R. ... Jay, OK

Blades, L. Showell, IV ..... Rock Hill, SC
Blades, Lawrence E. ..... Cedar Rapids, IA
Blades, Lester H., Jr. ..... Dover, DE
Blades, L. Showell, IV, P.A. ..... Rock Hill, SC
Blades, Reginald T., Jr.
Department of Justice, Civil Division, GV
Blades & Reisinger, P.A. ..... Dover, DE
Blades & Rosenfeld, P.A. ..... Baltimore, MD
Blades, Steven D. ..... Los Angeles, CA
Bladh, Wayne H. ..... Santa Fe, NM
Blado, Jonathan W. ..... Tacoma, WA
Blado Stratton, P.S. ..... Tacoma, WA
Bladow, Earl W. ..... Yakima, WA
Blady, I. Benjamin ..... Los Angeles, CA
Blaes, Stephen M. ..... Wichita, KS
Blaeser, Robert A. ..... Minneapolis, MN
Blaeser, Sandra S. ..... St. Paul, MN
Blaesing & Diaz, P.A. ..... New Port Richey, FL
Blaesing, Dionne Maria
New Port Richey, FL
Blaesing, Lois C. ..... Birmingham, MI
Blaesing, Lois C., P.C. ..... Birmingham, MI
Blaess, Mark J. ..... San Antonio, TX
Blaesser, Brian W. ..... Boston, MA
Blaetz, Peter T. ..... Burlington, NC
Blaeuer, Channing D. ..... Moberly, MO
Blageff, Lillian V. ..... Chesterland, OH
Blagg, Christopher J. ..... Washington, DC
Blagg, David A. ..... Omaha, NE
Blagg, Elizabeth C. ..... Warner Robins, GA
Blagg, James W. ..... San Antonio, TX
Blagg, John Lee ..... Brownwood, TX
Blagg Law Firm, P.A. ..... Clinton, AR
Blagg, Lester F. ..... Naples, FL
Blagg, Ralph J. ..... Clinton, AR
Blaha, Eric Peter ..... Mamaroneck, NY
Blaha & Hartford, A Professional Corporation
Castro Valley, CA
Pleasanton, CA
Blaha, Jerome A. ..... Castro Valley, CA
Pleasanton, CA
Blaha, Keith E. ..... Cleveland, OH
Blaha, L. Martin ..... San Mateo, CA
Blaha, Margaret (Peggy) M.
Columbus, OH
Blaha, Michael ..... Santa Monica, CA
Blaha, Stephen L. ..... Springfield, MA
Blaha, Thomas J. ..... Bowling Green, KY
Blaha, William J. ..... Southfield, MI
Blaher, Michael S. ..... Orlando, FL
Blaher, Neal J. ..... Orlando, FL
Blahnik, M. Pierre ..... San Luis Obispo, CA
Blahnik, Richard F. ..... Winona, MN
Blahnik, Robert E. ..... Spring Valley, MN
Blahovec, John E. ..... Greensburg, PA
Blahuta, Renee ..... Chicago, IL
Blaich, Elizabeth A. ..... Poplar Bluff, MO
Blaich, Grace C. ..... Poplar Bluff, MO
Blaich, Richard H. ..... Fort Wayne, IN
Blaies, Grant D. ..... Fort Worth, TX
Blaies, Gregory P. ..... Fort Worth, TX
Blaies & Hightower, L.L.P.
Fort Worth, TX
Blaik, Joan ..... Denver, CO
Blaiklock, A. Richard M. ..... Indianapolis, IN
Blain, Audrey ..... Uniondale, NY
Blain Bricklemyer & Smolker, P.A.
Tampa, FL
Blain, Clinton L. ..... San Diego, CA
Blain, James G., II ..... Houston, TX
Blain, L. M. Buddy ..... Tampa, FL
Blain, Lynne Jones ..... Richmond, VA
Blain, Michelle Farren ..... Baltimore, MD
Blain, Peter C. ..... Milwaukee, WI
Blain, Robert K., Law Offices
Chicago, IL
Blain, Russell M. ..... Tampa, FL
Blain, Sabrina ..... Poughkeepsie, NY
Blaine, Barbara S. ..... Washington, DC
Blaine, Belinda A.
Securities and Exchange Commission,
Division of Market Regulation, GV
Blaine, Carl P., (A Law Corporation)
Sacramento, CA
Blaine, Charles G. ..... Buffalo, NY
Blaine, Cheryl ..... Boston, MA
Blaine, Cheryl L. ..... Los Angeles, CA
Blaine, Craig J. ..... Westerville, OH
Blaine, David D. ..... Bakersfield, CA
Blaine & Dombrowski ..... Dearborn, MI
Blaine, Dorothea C. R., P.C. ..... Irvine, CA
Orange, CA
Santa Ana, CA
Blaine, Dorothea C. R. ..... Irvine, CA
Blaine, Dyann S. ..... San Francisco, CA
Blaine, George J. ..... Treasury Department,
Internal Revenue Service, GV
Blaine, George W. ..... Lutherville, MD
Blaine, Jack H. ..... Washington, DC
Blaine, Jack L. ..... San Rafael, CA
Blaine, Jonathan E. ..... Hartford, CT
Blaine, Kent R. ..... Louisville, KY
Blaine, Kevin F. ..... Alton, IL
Blaine, Michelle A. ..... Houston, TX
Blaine, Paul A. ..... Camden, NJ
Blaine, Quentin ..... Plymouth, NH
Blaine, Stephen E. ..... Santa Ana, CA
Blaine, Steven W. ..... Charlottesville, VA
Blaine, Timothy M. ..... Sacramento, CA
Blaine, Victor R. ..... Houston, TX
Blaine, William E., Jr. ..... Columbus, OH
Blaine, William L. ..... Berkeley, CA
Blair, A. Dwight ..... Pell City, AL
Blair, Adrianne May ..... Columbus, OH
Blair, Albert ..... Miami, FL
Blair, Alison Cornell ..... Chicago, IL
Blair, Allen S. ..... Memphis, TN
Blair, Allen W. ..... Kansas City, MO

Blair, Andrew J. ..... Clifton, NJ
Blair, Andrew L. ..... Charleston, WV
Blair, Andrew L., Jr. ..... Denver, CO
Blair, Angela J. ..... Dallas, TX
Blair, Anita K. ..... Arlington, VA
Blair, Anna ..... Sheffield, AL
Blair, Basil L. ..... Detroit, MI
Blair, Becky ..... Cleveland, OH
Blair, Benj. F. ..... Topeka, KS
Blair, Bernard Joseph, II ..... New Orleans, LA
Blair, Bernice M. ..... Washington, DC
Blair, Billy C. ..... Fort Worth, TX
Blair, Bobby Joe ..... Memphis, TN
Blair & Bondurant, P.A. ..... Jackson, MS
Blair, Bonnie S. ..... Washington, DC
Blair, Bowen, Jr. ..... Portland, OR
Blair, Brian C. ..... Orlando, FL
Blair, C. William ..... Fort Worth, TX
Blair, Carl F., Jr. ..... Littleton, CO
Blair, Channing K. ..... Chicago, IL
Blair, Charles H. ..... Troy, MI
Blair, Charles T. ..... Washington, DC
Blair, Charles V. ..... Bakersfield, CA
Blair, Chester L. E. ..... Chicago, IL
Blair, Christopher G. ..... Kansas City, MO
Blair, Clarence E. ..... Compton, CA
Blair, Clifford J. ..... Oklahoma City, OK
Blair Conaway Bograd & Martin, P.A.
Charlotte, NC
Blair, Courtney A. ..... Columbia, MD
Blair, Cynthia A. ..... East Hartford, CT
Blair, D. Kevin ..... Aurora, IL
Chicago, IL
Blair, D. Marianne ..... Tulsa, OK
Blair, D. Thomas ..... Danville, VA
Blair, Dallas L., III ..... Kingsport, TN
Blair, Dan G. ..... House of Representatives,
Committee on Post Office & Civil Service,
GV
Blair, Danya W. ..... Houston, TX
Blair, David A. ..... San Francisco, CA
Blair, David B. ..... Washington, DC
Blair, David H. ..... New York, NY
Blair, David J. ..... Sioux City, IA
Blair, David J., P.C., Law Office of
Sioux City, IA
Blair, David M. ..... Tualatin, OR
Blair, Dennis T. ..... South Hampton, NH
Blair, Donald K. ..... Monticello, IN
Blair, Donald W. ..... Cincinnati, OH
Blair, Duncan B. ..... Birmingham, AL
Blair, Duncan Wardman ..... Alexandria, VA
Blair, Edward E. ..... Huntsville, AL
Blair, Edward H., Jr. ..... Lenoir, NC
Blair, Edward T. ..... Hamden, CT
Blair, Frank J. ..... Baltimore, MD
Blair, George A., III ..... New Orleans, LA
Blair, George R., Jr. ..... Buffalo, NY
Blair, George R., Sr. ..... Buffalo, NY
Blair, Gerald E., Jr. ..... Huntington, WV
Blair, Gerald F. ..... Boston, MA
Blair, Gerald F. ..... Newton, MA
Blair, Gilson H. ..... Akron, OH
Blair, Graham Kerin ..... Houston, TX
Blair, Gregory S. ..... Round Rock, TX
Blair, H. David ..... Batesville, AR
Blair, Hardcastle & O'Connor, P.A.
Baltimore, MD
Blair, Harry A. ..... Fort Myers, FL
Blair, Harry A., P.A. ..... Fort Myers, FL
Blair, Harry C. J. ..... Bangor, PA
Blair, Harry F. ..... New York, NY
Blair, Homer O. ..... San Angelo, TX
Blair, Isabel ..... Gaithersburg, MD
Blair, J. Donald ..... Louisville, KY
Blair, Jack C. ..... Minneapolis, MN
Blair, Jacke L. ..... Spokane, WA
Blair, James A., III ..... Greenville, SC
Blair, James B. ..... Springdale, AR
Blair, James E., Jr. ..... Mesa, AZ
Blair, James F. ..... Lima, OH
Blair, James G. ..... Seattle, WA
Blair, James L. ..... Phoenix, AZ
Blair, James N. ..... New York, NY
Blair, James R. ..... Parachute, CO
Blair, James V. ..... Department of Labor,
Office of the Solicitor, GV
Blair, James W. ..... Delaware, OH
Blair, Janyce K.I. ..... El Segundo, CA
Blair, Jeffrey N. ..... New York, NY
Blair, Jeffry Mason ..... Dallas, TX
Blair, Jennifer ..... Dubuque, IA
Blair, Jennifer E. ..... Vienna, WV
Blair, Jerri Ann ..... Tavares, FL
Blair, Jerri Ann, P.A. ..... Tavares, FL
Blair, Jerrold E. ..... Universal City, CA
Blair, Jerry M. ..... Live Oak, FL
Blair, Jim ..... The Woodlands, TX
Blair, John Alan, III ..... San Antonio, TX
Blair, John Alan, III, P.C. ..... San Antonio, TX
Blair, John B. ..... Key West, FL
Blair, John G. ..... Chillicothe, OH
Blair, John Houston ..... Dallas, TX
Blair, John M. ..... Rogers, AR
Blair, John N. ..... Tonawanda, NY
Blair, John R. ..... Clarendon Hills, IL
Blair, John R. ..... Wichita, KS
Blair, Jolene Carman ..... Fort Collins, CO
Blair, Joyce ..... San Francisco, CA
Blair, Julie H. ..... Jefferson, MD
Blair, Karen E. ..... Califon, NJ
Blair, Katherine J. ..... Beverly Hills, CA
Blair, Kathleen D. ..... Germantown, TN
Blair, Keith J. ..... Long Beach, CA
Blair, Keith W. ..... Lawrenceburg, TN
Nashville, TN
Smithville, TN
Blair, Kevin S. ..... Roanoke, VA

Blair, Koren ..... New York, NY
Blair, Kristin R. ..... Virginia Beach, VA
Blair, Lance P. ..... Seattle, WA
Blair, Laurel R. S. ..... Greenville, SC
Blair, Laurence I. ..... Hollywood, FL
Blair, L. D. ..... Little Rock, AR
Blair, Les M., III ..... Dubuque, IA
Blair, Leslie H. ..... Rocky River, OH
Blair, Linda B.
Federal Communications Commission,
Mass Media Bureau, GV
Blair, Lori L. ..... Towson, MD
Blair, Lynne P. ..... Oakland, CA
Blair, M. Wayne ..... Seattle, WA
Blair, Margaret L.
Spring Lake Heights, NJ
Blair, Mark ..... Murrieta, CA
Blair, Matthew C. ..... Midland, TX
Blair, Matthew J. ..... Niles, OH
Blair, Michael F. ..... Abingdon, VA
Blair, Michael T. ..... Chicago, IL
Blair, Michael W. ..... New York, NY
Blair, Mitchell G. ..... Cleveland, OH
Blair, Nancy E. ..... Stamford, CT
Blair, Nelda Luce ..... The Woodlands, TX
Blair, Nicola S. ..... San Diego, CA
Blair, Noel ..... New York, NY
Blair, Nora F. ..... Harrisburg, PA
Blair and Parsons ..... Ashville, AL
Birmingham, AL
Oneonta, AL
Pell City, AL
Talladega, AL
Blair, Paul R. ..... Fountain Valley, CA
Blair, Paul W. ..... Morehead, KY
Blair, Penelope C. ..... Honolulu, HI
Blair, Peter H., Jr. (P.C.) ..... Denver, CO
Blair, Philip E. ..... San Jose, CA
Blair, Philip Michael ..... Bryan, TX
Blair & Potts ..... Greenwich, CT
Norwalk, CT
Stamford, CT
Blair & Quesinberry ..... Morehead, KY
Blair, Randolph N., Jr. ..... Baltimore, MD
Blair, Rebecca C. ..... Nashville, TN
Blair, Rebecca R. ..... Argyle, TX
Blair, Richard B. ..... Youngstown, OH
Blair, Richard G. ..... Walnut Creek, CA
Blair & Roach ..... Tonawanda, NY
Blair, Robert A., (P.C.) ..... Washington, DC
Blair, Robert E. ..... Welch, WV
Blair, Robert J. ..... San Diego, CA
Blair, Robert R. ..... Selma, AL
Blair, Robert S., Jr. ..... Charlotte, NC
Blair, Robin C. ..... Raton, NM
Blair, Rod ..... Irvine, CA
Blair, Ronald E. ..... Clarendon Hills, IL
Blair, Ronda J. ..... Fort Worth, TX
Blair, Ross W. ..... Irving, TX
Blair, Russell ..... Honolulu, HI
Blair, Russell J. ..... Hartford, CT
Blair, Sam B., Jr. ..... Memphis, TN
Blair, Samuel R. ..... Koloa, HI
Blair, Sandra ..... San Francisco, CA
Blair, Schaefer, Hutchison & Wolfe, LLP
Vancouver, WA
Blair, Scott E. ..... Kansas City, MO
Blair, Shannon B. ..... Minneapolis, MN
Blair, Sloan B. ..... Fort Worth, TX
Blair, Stephen S. ..... Austin, TX
Blair, Steven ..... Lancaster, PA
Blair, Steven A. ..... New York, NY
Blair, Steven E. ..... Enterprise, AL
Blair, Stroud & Davidson ..... Batesville, AR
Newport, AR
Blair, Teresa A. ..... Trenton, NJ
Blair, Terry B. ..... Baltimore, MD
Blair, Theodore T. ..... Pittsburgh, PA
Blair, Thomas Michael ..... Washington, DC
Blair, Thomas R. ..... Tonawanda, NY
Blair, Thomas W. ..... Philadelphia, PA
West Chester, PA
Blair, Thomas W. ..... Lancaster, SC
Blair, Timothy Allen ..... Little Rock, AR
Blair, Timothy L. ..... Portland, OR
Blair, Trace R. ..... San Antonio, TX
Blair, Vernon ..... Louisville, KY
Blair, Vernon W., II ..... Corydon, IN
Blair, W. Bradley, II ..... Charlotte, NC
Blair, W. Robert ..... Crete, IL
Blair, Warren A., III ..... Braintree, MA
Blair, Watson B. ..... Seattle, WA
Blair, Wayne H. ..... Klamath Falls, OR
Blair, William A. ..... Winter Haven, FL
Blair, William F. ..... Jackson, MS
Blair, William G. ..... Salem, OR
Blair, William H. ..... Stamford, CT
Blair, William Henry ..... Fort Worth, TX
Blair, William J. ..... Hagåtña, GU
Blair, William M., III ..... Longview, TX
Blair, William McC., Jr. ..... Washington, DC
Blair, William P. ..... Canton, OH
Blair, William Paul ..... Pasadena, CA
Blair, William S. ..... Birmingham, AL
Blair, Wm. L. ..... Little Rock, AR
Blair, Wolf, Kaiser & Sunderman Co., L.P.A.
Delaware, OH
Blair-Davis, JoAnn ..... Virginia Beach, VA
Blaire, Bonnie ..... Miami, FL
Blaire & Cole, P.A. ..... Miami, FL
Blair-Kijewski, Cheryl C.
Department of Labor,
Office of the Solicitor, GV
Blais, Beverly A. ..... Corona Del Mar, CA
Blais Cunningham and Crowe Chester
Pawtucket, RI
Blais, Earle C. ..... Burbank, CA
Blais, Edward L. ..... Pawtucket, RI

Blais, Henry J., III ..... Pawtucket, RI
Blais, Jan David ..... Gloucester, MA
Blais, Lawrence F. ..... Fort Worth, TX
Blais, Linda L. ..... Spring Lake, MI
Blais, Michael K. ..... Dallas, TX
Blais, Norman R. ..... Burlington, VT
Blais, Patricia ..... Philadelphia, PA
Blais, Robert H. ..... Seattle, WA
Blais, Simone M.L. ..... Santa Monica, CA
Blais, William E. ..... Rock Island, IL
Blaisch, Harold ..... Encino, CA
Blaisdell & Blaisdell ..... Ellsworth, ME
Blaisdell, Bruce F. ..... Boston, MA
Blaisdell, Charles Andrew ..... Salem, MA
Blaisdell, Charles O. ..... White Plains, NY
Blaisdell, Christopher M. ..... Palm Desert, CA
Blaisdell & Church ..... Salt Lake City, UT
Blaisdell, David F. ..... Moreno Valley, CA
Blaisdell, David R. ..... Salt Lake City, UT
Blaisdell, Kenneth W. ..... Ellsworth, ME
Blaisdell, Lori A. ..... Madison, ME
Blaisdell, Nancy S. ..... Minneapolis, MN
Blaisdell, Robert K. ..... Boston, MA
Blaisdell, William B., IV ..... Ellsworth, ME
Blaise, Michael R. ..... Ventura, CA
Blaise, Michael W. ..... Houston, TX
Blaise, Oliver N., III ..... Binghamton, NY
Blaiss, Sam ..... Cordova, TN
Blaivas, David G. ..... New York, NY
Blaivas, Jay ..... New York, NY
Blaize, Charles G., Jr. ..... Baton Rouge, LA
Lafayette, LA
Blaize, Marci L. ..... Baton Rouge, LA
Blaize, Michael P. ..... Valparaiso, IN
Blaize, Tony V. ..... Boston, MA
Blajwas, Harold ..... Belvedere-Tiburon, CA
Blake, A. John ..... Roseland, NJ
Blake, Albert P., Jr. ..... Redwood City, CA
Blake, Alexia Kita ..... Scranton, PA
Blake, Allen M. ..... Clearwater, FL
Blake, Allen M., P.A. ..... Clearwater, FL
Blake, Amy Lyn ..... Boston, MA
Blake, Anita Straubhaar ..... Strongsville, OH
Blake, Anne ..... Lowell, MA
Blake, Anne M.
Department Of Health And Human Services,
GV
Blake, Archie E. ..... Yerington, NV
Blake, Arthur J. ..... Asbury Park, NJ
Blake & Ball ..... Galesburg, IL
Blake, Barry A. ..... Encino, CA
Blake, Benjamin F. ..... Detroit, MI
Blake, Benjamin S., III ..... Boston, MA
Blake, Benjamin S., III, P.C. ..... Boston, MA
Blake, Benton L. ..... Phoenix, AZ
Blake, Beverly D. ..... New York, NY
Blake & Blake ..... Overland Park, KS
Blake, Brad L. ..... St. Louis, MO
Blake, Bradford C. ..... St. Louis, MO
Blake, Carlton A. ..... Westfield, NJ
Blake, Catherine C. ..... Baltimore, MD
Blake, Charles T. ..... Raleigh, NC
Blake, Charlotte Gail ..... Boone, NC
Blake, Chey Phleshette ..... New York, NY
Blake, Christophe David ..... Brea, CA
Blake, Christopher J. ..... San Diego, CA
Blake, Christopher J. ..... Raleigh, NC
Blake, Christopher J. ..... Fairfax Station, VA
Blake, Christopher Lee ..... Jamaica Plain, MA
Blake, Coleen A. ..... Chicago, IL
Blake, Curtis D. ..... Seattle, WA
Blake, D. Owen, Jr. ..... Birmingham, AL
Blake, D. Steven ..... Sacramento, CA
Blake, Daniel J. ..... Boston, MA
Blake, Daniel T. ..... Attleboro, MA
Blake, Daniel W. ..... Pine City, MN
Blake, David A. ..... Washington, DC
Blake, David B. ..... Irving, TX
Blake, David D. ..... Pleasantville, NJ
Blake, David G. ..... Media, PA
Blake, David R. ..... Oceanside, CA
Blake, Dennis P. ..... Camden, NJ
Westmont, NJ
Blake, Dennis W. ..... Oakland, CA
Blake, Dexter B., Jr. ..... Far Hills, NJ
Blake, Dionne Wilson ..... Miami, FL
Blake, Donald M. ..... Jericho, NY
Blake, Duane C. ..... Cambridge, MA
Blake, Eaddy H. ..... Durham, NC
Blake, Edw. J. ..... Philadelphia, PA
Blake, Edward J., Jr. ..... Belleville, IL
Blake, Edward J., Jr., P.C. ..... Belleville, IL
Blake, Erica ..... Boston, MA
Blake, Ernest L., Jr. (P.C.)
Washington, DC
Blake, F. Peter ..... Detroit, MI
Blake, Frances M. ..... Bronxville, NY
Blake, Francis E. ..... Frederick, MD
Blake, Francis S. ..... Schenectady, NY
Blake, Geff ..... Scranton, PA
Blake, George P. ..... Chicago, IL
Blake, Guy S. ..... Los Angeles, CA
Blake, Harlan M. ..... New York, NY
Blake, Harold N. ..... Palo Alto, CA
Blake, Harold W. ..... Danville, IN
Blake, Hartwell H. K. ..... Kaumakakai, HI
Blake & Hazard ..... Belfast, ME
Blake, Helen Holt ..... Tulsa, OK
Blake, Helenemarie ..... Miami, FL
Blake, Henry H. ..... Suwanee, GA
Blake, James F. ..... Oakland, CA
Blake, James Michael ..... Hopkinton, MA
Blake, James P. ..... Murray Hill, NJ
Blake, James R. ..... Canton, OH
Blake, James T. ..... Detroit, MI
Blake, Jayson Edward ..... Detroit, MI
Blake, Jeanne ..... Beverly Hills, MI
Blake, Jeff D. ..... Chicago, IL

Blake, Jeffrey A. .... Gahanna, OH
Blake, Jerome D. .... New York, NY
Blake, Jerome J. .... Baltimore, MD
Blake, Joanna L. .... Las Vegas, NV
Blake, John A. .... Pauls Valley, OK
Blake, John C. .... Jonesboro, LA
Blake, John E., Jr. .... Overland Park, KS
Blake, John F. .... Kettering, OH
Blake, John H. .... San Jose, CA
Blake, John J. .... Galesburg, IL
Blake, John J. .... Kansas City, KS
Blake, John R. .... Worcester, MA
Blake, John R., Jr. .... Boston, MA
Blake, Jonathan D. .... Washington, DC
Blake, Jos. A., Jr. .... Chicago, IL
Blake, Joseph J., Jr. .... Greenville, SC
Blake, Joseph P., Jr. .... Manhasset, NY
Blake, K. Steven .... Barrington, IL
Blake, Karin, (P.C.) .... Franklin, MA
Blake, Kent A. .... Gilbert, AZ
Blake, Kevin M. .... Bridgeport, CT
Philadelphia, PA
Blake, Kimberly Ann .... Oakland, CA
Blake, Kirchner, Symonds, MacFarlane, Larson & Smith, P.C. .... Detroit, MI
Blake, Kristin N. .... Clifton, VA
Blake, Kurt A. .... York, PA
Blake, Laura Lee .... Irvine, CA
Blake, Lawrence E. .... Prince George, VA
Blake, Lawrence J. .... Los Angeles, CA
Blake, Lee P. .... Phoenix, AZ
Blake, Linda Donoghue .... Warwick, NY
Blake, Lise R. Connell
North Chelmsford, MA
Blake, Lorraine .... St. Paul, MN
Blake, Lynn M. .... Schenectady, NY
Blake, Lystra G. .... Department of Justice, Criminal Division, GV
Blake, M. David .... Boston, MA
Blake, Marcy .... Mamaroneck, NY
Blake, Margaret R. .... Washington, DC
Blake, Mark D. .... San Francisco, CA
Blake, Marlene Dixon .... Wilson, NC
Blake, Marlowe J. .... Hallandale Beach, FL
Blake, Marlowe J., P.A.
Hallandale Beach, FL
Miami, FL
Blake, Martin .... San Francisco, CA
Blake, Martin C. .... Cleveland, OH
Blake, Mary Beth .... Overland Park, KS
Blake, Matthew P. .... Cary, NC
Blake, Maurice N. .... Woodland Hills, CA
Blake, Maxine .... New York, NY
Blake, M. David, A Professional Association
Boston, MA
Blake, Melvyn A. .... Marlton, NJ
Blake, Meredith L. .... Santa Monica, CA
Blake, Michael A. .... Santa Monica, CA
Blake, Michael J. .... Los Angeles, CA
Blake, Michael J. .... Kansas City, MO
Blake, Michael J. .... Kingsport, TN
Blake, Michael W. .... Batavia, IL
Blake, Michael W. .... Beckley, WV
Blake, Michelle Lalley .... Albuquerque, NM
Blake, Milton .... Houston, TX
Blake, Mona .... Washington, DC
Blake, Natalie .... Los Angeles, CA
Blake, Patricia G. .... Detroit, MI
Blake, Paul M., Jr. .... Fayetteville, WV
Blake, Paul N., III .... Wilson, NC
Blake, Penelope M. .... San Jose, CA
Blake & Phillips .... St. Paul, MN
Blake, R. Mason .... Melbourne, FL
Blake, Ralph J., III .... Phoenix, AZ
Blake, Randall B. .... Sioux Falls, SD
Blake, Randall L. .... Woodland, CA
Blake, Randy B. .... Montgomery, AL
Blake, Ray E., II .... Wilmington, NC
Blake, Richard C. .... New York, NY
Blake, Richard F. .... New York, NY
Blake, Richard L. .... Murphysboro, IL
Blake, Richard M., Sr. .... Vista, CA
Blake, Robert A., Jr. .... Charlotte, NC
Blake, Robin M. .... Danvers, MA
Blake, Rodney R. .... Sidney, OH
Blake, Rodney R., Jr. .... Sidney, OH
Blake, Roger F. .... Belfast, ME
Blake, Roger J. .... Phoenix, AZ
Blake, Ronald A. .... Boca Raton, FL
Blake, Ronald K. .... Tempe, AZ
Blake, Roy G. .... Fayetteville, GA
Blake, Sallie A. .... Tucson, AZ
Blake, Samantha E. .... Los Angeles, CA
Blake, Scott A. .... Toledo, OH
Blake, Sean R. .... Doylestown, PA
Blake, Sharon L. .... Miami, FL
Blake & Shields .... Phoenix, AZ
Blake, Stanford .... Miami, FL
Blake, Stephen R. .... Chewelah, WA
Blake, Susanna Rowsell .... Boston, MA
Blake, T. Michael .... Oklahoma City, OK
Blake, Thomas A. .... San Francisco, CA
Blake, Thomas A. .... Sioux Falls, SD
Blake, Thomas R. .... Miami, FL
Blake, Thomas W. .... Grand Junction, CO
Blake, Thomas W. .... Houston, TX
Blake, Timothy Carl .... Miami, FL
Blake, Timothy Carl, P.A. .... Miami, FL
Blake, Timothy J. .... Phoenix, AZ
Blake, Trina M. .... Seattle, WA
Blake & Uhlig, P.A. .... Kansas City, KS
Blake, Walter R. .... Coral Springs, FL
Blake, Walter R., P.A. .... Coral Springs, FL
Blake, Ward M. .... Stone Mountain, GA
Blake, Weldon M. .... Washington, DC
Blake, Wendy L. .... Department of Justice, Environment and Natural Resources Division, GV
Blake, Wesley C. .... San Diego, CA
Blake, William A. .... Arlington, VA
Blake, William C., Jr. .... Tampa, FL
Blake, William F., Jr., Co., L.P.A.
Steubenville, OH
Blake, William G. .... Lincoln, NE
Blake, William J. .... Audubon, NJ
Blake, William J. .... Cleveland, OH
Blake, William L. .... Springfield, IL
Blake, William L. .... Cleveland, OH
Blake, Wynne M. .... Lewiston, ID
Blake and Zemis .... Montgomery, AL
Blakeboro, Alan A. .... Santa Barbara, CA
Blakeburn, Dave L. .... Muskogee, OK
Blakeburn, J. Robert .... Oklahoma City, OK
Blake-Greenaway, Veronica .... Iselin, NJ
Blake Hook, Carla .... Leesburg, VA
Blake-Larson, Sylvia L. .... Fort Worth, TX
Blakeley, Amy E. .... Newark, NJ
Blakeley, Bradley D. .... Los Angeles, CA
Blakeley, Brian L. .... San Antonio, TX
Blakeley, Brian L., & Associates, P.C.
San Antonio, TX
Blakeley & Brinkman .... Los Angeles, CA
Blakeley, Charles H. .... New York, NY
Blakeley, Craig J. .... McLean, VA
Blakeley, Dick A. .... Tulsa, OK
Blakeley, John W. .... South Bend, IN
Blakeley & Ramey .... Dallas, TX
Blakeley, Scott E. .... Los Angeles, CA
Blakeley, Tom .... Dallas, TX
Blakelock, Frederick E. .... Philadelphia, PA
Blakelock & Stringer .... Provo, UT
Blakely, Bruce W. .... Mill Valley, CA
Blakely, Caroline E. .... Washington, DC
Blakely, Dean & Wagner .... Madison, OH
Blakely, Elizabeth B. .... Los Angeles, CA
Blakely, George .... Beloit, WI
Blakely, James C., Jr. .... Greenville, SC
Blakely, James C., Jr., P.A. .... Greenville, SC
Blakely, John M. .... Chula Vista, CA
Blakely, John R. .... Los Angeles, CA
Blakely, John T. .... Clearwater, FL
Naples, FL
Tampa, FL
Blakely, Jonathan P. .... Cleveland, OH
Blakely, Joseph A. .... Oakland, CA
Blakely, Joshua A. .... Milwaukee, WI
Blakely, Laura MacKallor .... Santa Clara, CA
Blakely, Marvin .... Rutherford, NJ
Blakely, Nelson M. .... Perkasie, PA
Blakely, Newell H. .... Houston, TX
Blakely, Nicole S. .... La Jolla, CA
Blakely, P. Arnsen .... Costa Mesa, CA
Blakely, Richard A. .... Erie, PA
Blakely, Richard S. .... Oakland, CA
Blakely, Robert G. .... Beloit, WI
Blakely, Roger W., Jr. .... Costa Mesa, CA
La Jolla, CA
Blakely, Sokoloff, Taylor & Zafman
Costa Mesa, CA
La Jolla, CA
Los Angeles, CA
Sunnyvale, CA
Denver, CO
Lake Oswego, OR
Austin, TX
Kirkland, WA
Blakely, Sokoloff, Taylor & Zafman LLP
Palo Alto, CA
San Francisco, CA
Portland, OR
Blakely, Steven L. .... Covington, IN
Blakely, Susan Smith .... Great Falls, VA
Blakely, Timothy L. .... Red Wing, MN
Blakely, Todd P. .... Denver, CO
Blakely, William D. .... Washington, DC
Blakeman, Bradley A. .... Valley Stream, NY
Blakeman, Bruce A. .... Valley Stream, NY
Blakeman, C. Thomas .... Pontiac, IL
Blakeman, Cletus W. .... Omaha, NE
Blakeman, Harold C. .... Longmeadow, MA
Blakeman, Janet L. .... New York, NY
Blakeman, Mark E. .... Hartford, CT
Blakeman, Richard R. .... Boca Raton, FL
Blakeman, Robert M. .... Valley Stream, NY
Blakeman, Royal E., (P.C.)
Valley Stream, NY
Blakeman, S. Lynn .... Dallas, TX
Blakeman, William S. .... Bartow, FL
Blakeman, William S. .... Lakeland, FL
Blakemore, Allison B. .... Akron, OH
Blakemore, Catherine J. .... Glendale, CA
Blakemore, Christopher W. .... Boulder, CO
Blakemore, David L. .... Wichita, KS
Blakemore, Jerry D. .... Chicago, IL
Blakemore, Margaret A. .... Plano, TX
Blakemore, Meeker & Bowler, L.P.A.
Akron, OH
Blakemore, Robert W. .... Akron, OH
Blakemore, T. Mark .... Brownsville, TX
Blakemore, Thomas F. .... Chicago, IL
Blakemore, Trina L. .... Columbus, OH
Blakemore, William K. .... Sacramento, CA
Blakeney, Blackburn and Oliver, L.L.P.
Dallas, TX
Blakeney, Charles W. .... Geneva, AL
Blakeney, E. Troy .... Houston, TX
Blakeney, James R. .... Palm Desert, CA
Blakeney, M. Robert .... Dallas, TX
Blakeney, Michael L. .... Beaumont, TX
Blakeney, Ralph H. .... Costa Mesa, CA
Blakeney, Robert W. .... Needham, MA
Blakeney, Shellie N.
Federal Communications Commission, Wireless Telecommunications Bureau, GV
Blaker, Evan A. .... Cherry Hill, NJ
Blaker, Jeffrey A. .... Miami Beach, FL
Blaker, Jill .... Chatham, NJ
Blaker, Richard Hathaway .... New York, NY
Blakeslee, Aimee .... Chatham, NJ
Blakeslee, Anita F. .... West Palm Beach, FL
Blakeslee, Brian E. .... South Dennis, MA
Blakeslee & Chambers, P.C.
Traverse City, MI
Blakeslee, Cynthia Boyer .... Leola, PA
Blakeslee, Donald P. .... Bronxville, NY
Blakeslee, Edward E. .... New York, NY
Blakeslee, H. James .... Simsbury, CT
Blakeslee, Jack A. .... Caldwell, OH
Canton, OH
Blakeslee, Jack A., Co., L.P.A.
Caldwell, OH
Canton, OH
Blakeslee, John R. .... Traverse City, MI
Blakeslee, Julia .... Bingham Farms, MI
Blakeslee, Katherine T. .... Wilton, CT
Blakeslee, Marian C. .... San Rafael, CA
Blakeslee, Melise R. .... Washington, DC
Blakeslee, Merritt R. .... Washington, DC
Blakeslee, Neil C., & Associates
Rockford, MI
Blakeslee, Wesley D. .... Westminster, MD
Blakeslee, William D. .... Gulfport, MS
Hattiesburg, MS
Blakesley, Donald W. .... Springfield, MA
Worcester, MA
Blakesley, Leonard E., Jr. .... El Segundo, CA
Blakesley, Rodney E. .... Feeding Hills, MA
Blakesley, Scott E. .... Kansas City, MO
Blake-Thomas, David E.
Department of Justice, Antitrust Division, GV
Blakeway, Judith R. .... San Antonio, TX
Blakeway, Victor D.
Federal Energy Regulatory Commission, Office of the General Counsel, GV
Blakewell, Richard D. .... Walnut Creek, CA
Blakey, A. Craig, II .... Phoenix, AZ
Blakey, Albert G., III .... York, PA
Blakey, Daniel R. .... Los Angeles, CA
Blakey, Elizabeth E. .... Notre Dame, IN
Blakey, G. Robert .... Notre Dame, IN
Blakey, John C. .... Lubbock, TX
Blakey, Michael H. .... Riverhead, NY
Blakey, Milton K. .... Colorado Springs, CO
Blakey, Robert, Jr. .... Prescott, AZ
Blakey, Robert, Jr., P.C. .... Phoenix, AZ
Prescott, AZ
Blakey, Robert M. .... Long Beach, CA
Blakey, Robert M., A Professional Law Corporation .... Long Beach, CA
Blakey, Thomas H. .... Miami, FL
Blakey, Walker J. .... Chapel Hill, NC
Blakey, William A. .... Washington, DC
Blakey, Yost, Bupp & Schaumann, LLP
York, PA
Blakinger, Byler & Thomas, P.C.
Lancaster, PA
Blakinger, Charles B. .... Philadelphia, PA
Blakinger, Dan A. .... Lancaster, PA
Blakinger, Richard J. .... Lancaster, PA
Blakley, Allison C. .... Chicago, IL
Blakley, Benjamin S., III .... Du Bois, PA
Blakley, Donna N. .... Oklahoma City, OK
Blakley, J.E. Mayla .... Honolulu, HI
Blakley, Jones & Mohney .... Du Bois, PA
Blakley, K. Girard .... Maumee, OH
Blakley, Kenneth H. .... Oklahoma City, OK
Blakley, Kevin J. .... Phoenix, AZ
Blakley, Mark E. .... Huntsville, TN
Blakley, Terri K. .... Oklahoma City, OK
Blakney, Diana V. .... Seattle, WA
Blakney, William E. .... Seattle, WA
Blakslee, Dana C. .... Boston, MA
Blalack, Cynthia A. .... New Ulm, MN
Blalack, Joe R. .... Gladewater, TX
Blalack, Michael .... Dallas, TX
Blalock, A. Milling .... Clinton, SC
Blalock, Amy R. .... Tyler, TX
Blalock & Associates .... Las Vegas, NV
Blalock, Candace L. .... Pauls Valley, OK
Blalock, David G. .... Newport News, VA
Blalock, Edward L. .... Las Vegas, NV
Blalock, Howard R. .... Springfield, IL
Blalock, J. Breck .... Washington, DC
Blalock, J. Harry .... Birmingham, AL
Blalock, Jack B., Jr. .... Houston, TX
Blalock, James A., III .... Washington, DC
Blalock, Joyce .... Santa Fe, NM
Blalock, Landers, Walters and Vogler, P.A.
Bradenton, FL
Longboat Key, FL
Sarasota, FL
Blalock, Larry W. .... New Martinsville, WV
Wheeling, WV
Blalock, Lois L. .... San Francisco, CA
Blalock, Lorraine H. .... Redding, CA
Blalock, Michael D. .... Birmingham, AL
Blalock, Myron G., Jr. .... Houston, TX
Blalock, Pamela C. .... Birmingham, AL
Blalock, Robert G. .... Bradenton, FL
Blalock, S. Gordon .... Ponte Vedra Beach, FL
Blalock, Sandra G. .... Atlanta, GA
Blalock, Steven F. .... Albemarle, NC
Blalock, Steven W. .... Los Angeles, CA
Blalock, Steven W., A Law Corporation
Los Angeles, CA
Blalock, Thomas J. .... Oklahoma City, OK
Blalock, Tim D. .... Natchez, MS
Blalock, William H., Jr. .... Gainesville, GA
Blalock, William S. .... Orlando, FL
Blamer, Robert L. .... Livonia, MI
Blamires, Bradley R. .... Los Angeles, CA
Blan, Kennith William, Jr. .... Danville, IL
Blan, Ollie L., Jr. .... Birmingham, AL
Blanar, Robt. G. .... Houston, TX
Blanarik, Edward S., Jr.
State College, PA
Blanc, David M. .... Pendleton, OR
Blanc, Diane E. .... New York, NY
Blanc, Erik I. .... Pekin, IL
Blanc, Peter D. .... West Palm Beach, FL
Blanc, Robert .... Melville, NY
Blanc, Robert S. .... Plandome, NY
Blanc, Robert S. .... Houston, TX
Blanc, Roger D. .... New York, NY
Blanc, Ronald L., (P.C.) .... Los Angeles, CA
Blanc, Steven D. .... Beverly Hills, CA
Blanc, Susan M. .... New York, NY
Blanc Williams Johnston & Kronstadt, LLP
Los Angeles, CA
BlancaFlor, Dawn C. .... Boise, ID
Blancaflor, Eliseo M. .... Rego Park, NY
Blancarte, James E. .... Los Angeles, CA
Blancarte, James E., A Professional Corporation, Law Offices of
Los Angeles, CA
Blancato, Lydia Cox .... Wilmington, DE
Blancato, Maria .... Summit, NJ
Blancato, Richard T. .... Tarrytown, NY
Blancato, William A. .... Winston-Salem, NC
Blance, Robert B. .... Brewster, MA
Blancett, Cary S. .... Memphis, TN
Blancett, George E. .... Memphis, TN
Blancett, John W. .... New York, NY
Blancett-Maddock, David D. .... Pittsburgh, PA
Blancett-Maddock, Diane .... Pittsburgh, PA
Blanch, James T. .... Salt Lake City, UT
Blanch, Joey L. .... Los Angeles, CA
Blanch, Julianne .... Salt Lake City, UT
Blanch, Philip F. .... Fairfield, NJ
Blanch, Robert J., Jr. .... Palo Alto, CA
Blanch, Sandra I. .... Boston, MA
Blanchar, Jon W. .... Edina, MN
Blanchard, Alice L. .... Langley, WA
Blanchard, Anna Neal .... Raleigh, NC
Blanchard, Arthur .... Dallas, TX
Blanchard, Barbara A. .... Somers, NY
Blanchard, Brian W. .... Madison, WI
Blanchard, Bruce M. .... Fairfax, VA
Blanchard, Catherine A. .... Manchester, NH
Blanchard, Cathey and Bowen
Hendersonville, NC
Blanchard, Charles A.
Executive Office Of The President, Office of National Drug Control Policy, GV
Blanchard, Charles F. .... Raleigh, NC
Blanchard, Charles J. .... Dallas, TX
Blanchard, Charles P. .... New Orleans, LA
Blanchard, Christopher .... Willimantic, CT
Blanchard, Christopher M. .... Athens, GA
Blanchard, Clayton H., Jr. .... Eustis, FL
Blanchard, Daniel F., III .... Charleston, SC
Blanchard, Dock A. .... Ocala, FL
Blanchard, Donald E. .... Denver, CO
Blanchard, Donald H. .... Coraopolis, PA
Blanchard, E. John .... Lansing, MI
Blanchard, E. Troy .... Milwaukee, WI
Blanchard, Elmer F. .... Madeira Beach, FL
Blanchard, Eric A. .... Franklin Park, IL
Blanchard, Eugene V. .... Rockland, MA
Blanchard, Gerald L. .... Atlanta, GA
Blanchard, Gregory B. .... Hampton, VA
Blanchard, Gregory B., P.C. .... Hampton, VA
Blanchard, Hal R. .... Denver, CO
Parker, CO
Blanchard, Hartman E., Jr.
Washington, DC
Blanchard, James B. .... Chicago, IL
Blanchard, James E. .... Augusta, GA
Blanchard, James E., P.C. .... Augusta, GA
Blanchard, James G. (Jim), Jr.
Augusta, GA
Blanchard, James H. .... Columbus, GA
Blanchard, James J. .... Washington, DC
Blanchard, Janelle M. .... McLean, VA
Blanchard, Jenkins & Miller, P.A.
Raleigh, NC
Blanchard, John A. .... Flint, MI
Blanchard, John Ben .... Amarillo, TX
Blanchard, John J. ....
Department of the Navy, GV
Blanchard, John J. .... Montvale, NJ
Blanchard, John R., Law Offices of
Burbank, CA
Blanchard, John T. .... Mission Viejo, CA
Blanchard, John T. .... Seattle, WA
Blanchard, Judith E. .... Webster, TX
Blanchard, Karl W. .... Joplin, MO
Blanchard, Karl W., Jr. .... Joplin, MO
Blanchard, Kathleen .... Wayne, PA
Blanchard, Kim D. .... Los Angeles, CA
Blanchard, Kimberly S. .... New York, NY
Blanchard, Krasner & French, A Professional Corporation .... La Jolla, CA
Blanchard, Kyla M. .... Baton Rouge, LA
Blanchard, L. Kristen .... Philadelphia, PA
Blanchard, Laricke D. .... Washington, DC
Blanchard, Larry Donell .... Atlanta, GA
Blanchard, Lawrence E., Jr. .... Richmond, VA
Blanchard, Leslie S. .... Abingdon, VA
Blanchard, Lester L. .... Gardena, CA
Blanchard, Lonnie C., III
Los Angeles, CA
Blanchard, M. Robert .... Pensacola, FL
Blanchard, Mary Margaret .... Visalia, CA
Blanchard, Melvin F. .... Towson, MD
Blanchard, Merriam, Adel & Kirkland, P.A.
Ocala, FL
Blanchard, Michael A. .... Norwich, CT
Blanchard, Michael D. .... Boston, MA
Blanchard, Michael D. .... Fort Worth, TX
Blanchard, Norwood P., III .... Raleigh, NC

Blanchard, Patrick C. .... Wichita, KS
Blanchard, Patrick M. .... Chicago, IL
Blanchard, Petra H. .... Halifax, VA
Blanchard, Philip J. .... Costa Mesa, CA
Blanchard, R. Edward .... New Orleans, LA
Blanchard, Raymond P. .... Portsmouth, NH
Blanchard, Robert W. .... La Jolla, CA
Blanchard, Robertson, Mitchell & Carter, P.C. .... Cassville, MO
Joplin, MO
Mount Vernon, MO
Blanchard, Roderick D. .... Minneapolis, MN
Blanchard, Ronald G. .... Hendersonville, NC
Blanchard, Scott L. .... Taholah, WA
Blanchard, Suzanne E. .... Camden, NJ
Blanchard, Tara Weinstock
Washington, DC
Blanchard, Terry J. .... Lafayette, LA
Blanchard, Timothy P. .... Los Angeles, CA
Blanchard, Van .... Coshocton, OH
Blanchard, Vye .... Portland, OR
Blanchard, Walker, O'Quin & Roberts, A Professional Law Corporation
Bossier City, LA
Shreveport, LA
Blanchard, Wendy T. .... Houston, TX
Blanchard, William .... Encino, CA
Blanchard, William B. .... Geneva, IL
Blanchard, William C. .... Kirkland, WA
Blanchard, William E. .... Treasury Department, Internal Revenue Service, GV
Blanchard, William R. .... Montgomery, AL
Blanchard-Saiger, Gail M.
Sacramento, CA
Blanche, Bradley D. .... Irvine, CA
Blanche, Fred A., III .... Baton Rouge, LA
Blanche, Fred A., Jr. .... Baton Rouge, LA
Blanche, Gregory W. .... Traverse City, MI
Blanchet, Benjamin B. .... Lafayette, LA
Blanchet, David A. .... Lafayette, LA
Blanchet, Donna Jean .... Boulder, CO
Blanchet, Harold J., Jr. .... Saginaw, MI
Blanchet, Joel A. .... Chicago, IL
Blanchet, Kimberly Williams
Indianapolis, IN
Blanchet, Sharon .... San Diego, CA
Blanchett, Neal J. .... Minneapolis, MN
Blanchette, Antoinette Wavene
New York, NY
Blanchette, David J. .... Phoenix, AZ
Blanchette, James G., Jr. .... Dallas, TX
Blanchette, James G., Jr., A Professional Corporation .... Dallas, TX
Blanchette, Janis LaRoche .... Berkeley, CA
Blanchette, Patti .... Portsmouth, NH
Blanchette, Raymond A. .... Monson, MA
Blanchette, Robert W. .... Washington, DC
Blanchette, Thomas A. .... Pawtucket, RI
Blanchfield, Andrew .... Baton Rouge, LA
Blanchfield, Francis J., Jr. .... Charlotte, NC
Blanchfield, Garrett D., Jr. .... St. Paul, MN
Blanchfield, James .... Stamford, CT
Blanchfield, Linda A. .... Philadelphia, PA
Blanchfield, Mark William .... Albany, NY
Blanchfield, Robert J., Jr. .... Severna Park, MD
Blanchfield, Thomas M. .... Palos Hills, IL
Blanchini, Patricia .... New York, NY
Blanck, Eugene L. .... Redlands, CA
Blanck & Grybowski .... Miami, FL
Blanck, Herbert F. .... Santa Rosa, CA
Blanck, Jeffrey S. .... Zephyr Cove, NV
Blanck, John I., Jr. .... Washington, DC
Blanck, Katherine L. .... San Diego, CA
Blanck, Peter David .... Iowa City, IA
Blanck, Richard J. .... Boonville, MO
Blanck, Richard L. .... Salt Lake City, UT
Blanck, Robert F. .... Philadelphia, PA
Blanck, Robert W. .... South Miami, FL
Blanck, Roselyn Komisar
Farmington Hills, MI
Blanck, Russell A. .... Circle Pines, MN
Blancke, Clare .... Boston, MA
Blanckenburg, William L. .... Napa, CA
Blanco, Alan Carlos .... Pittsburgh, PA
Blanco, Alicia Yoko .... Los Angeles, CA
Blanco & Associates, P.C. .... Detroit, MI
Troy, MI
Blanco, Caroline M. .... Department of Justice, Environment and Natural Resources Division, GV
Blanco & Company .... Fresno, CA
Blanco, David B. .... Winston-Salem, NC
Blanco, Franklin A. .... Coral Gables, FL
Fort Lauderdale, FL
Blanco, Ileana M. .... Houston, TX
Blanco, James Anthony .... Lake Charles, LA
Blanco, Jeanette H. .... Charlotte, NC
Blanco, Jesse, Jr. .... Clinton, MS
Blanco, Jim L. .... Chicago, IL
Blanco, Jorge E. .... Coral Gables, FL
Blanco, Juan, Jr. .... Arlington, TX
Blanco, Katherine V. .... Tampa, FL
Blanco, Leslie .... Chicago, IL
Blanco, Leyza Florin .... Miami, FL
Blanco, Louis .... Hollywood, FL
Blanco, Louis .... Woodside, NY
Blanco, Lourdes J. .... New York, NY
Blanco, Luis R. P. .... El Segundo, CA
Blanco, Marco A. .... New York, NY
Blanco, Maria C. .... Atlanta, GA
Blanco, Orlando L. .... Troy, MI
Blanco, Pablo N. .... South Orange, NJ
Blanco, Patricia .... Chattanooga, TN
Blanco, Pedro A. .... Miami, FL
Blanco, Salvador M. .... Fresno, CA
Blanco, Steven J. .... El Paso, TX
Blanco Tackabery Combs & Matamoros, P.A. .... Winston-Salem, NC

Blanco Fuertes, Miguel Agustín
San Juan, PR
Blanco-Reyes, Marilyn .... Memphis, TN
Bland, Amelia L. .... Marion, VA
Bland, Amy L. .... Jackson, MS
Bland, Ardie A. .... Kansas City, MO
Bland & Associates, P.C. .... Marion, VA
Bland & Bland .... Charleston, WV
Bland, Catherine L. .... Carlsbad, CA
Bland, Charles N., Jr. .... Los Angeles, CA
Bland, Cynthia Sax .... Pittsboro, NC
Bland, Daniel D. .... Calabasas, CA
Bland, David E. .... Minneapolis, MN
Bland, David H. .... Chapel Hill, NC
Bland, David S. .... New Orleans, LA
Bland, Deborah Irene .... Fayetteville, NC
Bland, Donna A. .... Montgomery, AL
Bland, Douglas S. .... Houston, TX
Bland, Eric M. .... New York, NY
Bland, Eric S. .... Columbia, SC
Bland, Harris & McClellan .... Cullman, AL
Bland, Howard & Birdwhistell
Elizabethtown, KY
Bland, Hugh G., Jr. .... Nashville, TN
Bland, J. Goodwin .... New York, NY
Bland, J. Richard .... Minneapolis, MN
Bland, James T. .... Cordova, TN
Bland, James T., Jr. & Associates
Memphis, TN
Bland, Jane Nenninger .... Houston, TX
Bland, John L. .... Houston, TX
Bland, John W., Jr. .... Decatur, GA
Bland, John W., Jr. .... Elizabethtown, KY
Bland, Juliet Puissegur .... New Orleans, LA
Bland, Karen L. .... Washington, DC
Bland, Lisa C. .... Raleigh, NC
Bland, Michael D. .... Matthews, NC
Bland, Michael J. .... Springfield, IL
Bland, Paul C. .... Petersburg, VA
Bland, Phillip B. .... Walnut Creek, CA
Bland, Richard B. .... Hyattsville, MD
Upper Marlboro, MD
Bland, Richard G. .... Tyler, TX
Bland, Richard L. .... Louisville, CO
Bland, Richard L., Jr. .... Atlanta, GA
Bland, Richard N. .... Montpelier, VT
Bland, Richard Trabue .... Gulfport, MS
Bland, Richard W., II .... Boston, MA
Bland, Richard W. E. .... Richmond, VA
Bland, Robert Ivan .... Arlington, TX
Bland, Ronald J. .... Seattle, WA
Bland, Shannon M. .... Charleston, WV
Bland, Sheryl Clarkson .... Gaffney, SC
Bland, Stephanie N. .... Princeton, NJ
Bland, Stewart E. .... Louisville, KY
Bland, T. Steven .... Elizabethtown, KY
Bland, Terry D. .... Carrollton, TX
Bland, Timothy S. .... Memphis, TN
Bland, Victor L. .... Kalamazoo, MI
Bland, William R. .... Williamsburg, VA
Bland, William W. .... Goldsboro, NC
Bland, Wilton E., III .... New Orleans, LA
Blanda, Alisun Smith .... Lake Forest, IL
Blanda, John J. .... Columbus, OH
Blanda, Philip J., Jr. .... Holmdel, NJ
Blanda, Robert A. .... Sayreville, NJ
Blanda, Robert A., Jr. .... Hazlet, NJ
Blander, Andrea .... Seattle, WA
Blander, Stuart A. .... New York, NY
Blandford, Alfred L. .... Twin Falls, ID
Blandford, Colleen M. .... Cincinnati, OH
Blandford, Daniel M. .... Grand Rapids, MI
Blandford, David B. .... Louisville, KY
Blandford, James F.
Federal Labor Relations Authority, Office of the Solicitor, GV
Blandford, Jaron P. .... Lexington, KY
Blandford, Jefferson B. .... Atlanta, GA
Blandford, John R. .... Johns Island, SC
Blandford, Joseph E. .... Louisville, KY
Blandford and Werbin, P.C. .... Chamblee, GA
Blandford, William J. .... Racine, WI
Blandin, Stephan David .... Chicago, IL
Blanding, Durand .... St. Croix Falls, WI
Blandino, Alan G. .... Gibsonia, PA
Blandino, Frank A. .... Cranford, NJ
Blando, Edward M. .... Cedar Rapids, IA
Blando, Frank P. .... Stratford, CT
Blando, Mark J. .... Washington, DC
Blandon, Elizabeth R. .... Miami, FL
Blane, Christine .... Valparaiso, IN
Blane & Frank .... Newark, NJ
Blane, James L. .... Charlotte, NC
Blane, James L., PLLC .... Charlotte, NC
Blane, Kenneth R. .... Newark, NJ
Blane, Lyle L. .... Glendale, CA
Blane & O'Hara .... Petersburg, IL
Blane, Richard G., II .... Des Moines, IA
Blane, Roger S. .... New York, NY
Blane, Samuel S. .... Petersburg, IL
Blaney, Brian H. .... Phoenix, AZ
Blaney, Casey & Walton .... Demotte, IN
Morocco, IN
Rensselaer, IN
Blaney, Daniel C. .... Morocco, IN
Blaney, Doyle O. .... Los Angeles, CA
Blaney, Gerald N., Jr. .... Lawrenceville, GA
Blaney, J. Kevin .... Oklahoma City, OK
Blaney, James B. .... Jackson Heights, NY
Blaney, James E. .... St. Paul, MN
Blaney, James M. .... Manasquan, NJ
Toms River, NJ
Blaney, Jerri M. .... Palm Beach Gardens, FL
Blaney, Jerri M., P.A.
Palm Beach Gardens, FL
Blaney, Kevin B. .... Utica, NY
Blaney, Lloyd J. .... Madison, WI
Blaney, Michael .... Bloomfield, NJ

Blaney, Michael C. .... Enfield, CT
Blaney, Michael C. .... Houston, TX
Blaney, Michael J. .... Kansas City, MO
Blaney, Natalie Talbott .... New York, NY
Blaney, Susan B. .... Kansas City, KS
Blanford, Albert T. .... Ventura, CA
Blanford, Frederick L. .... Lincoln, IL
Blanford, Kristen B. .... Dallas, TX
Blanford, S. Dianne .... Lexington, KY
Blanford, Theodore J. .... Indianapolis, IN
Blanford, Thomas D. .... Washington, DC
Blangiardo, Frank J. .... Coram, NY
Blank, A. Russell .... Atlanta, GA
Blank, A. Russell, & Associates, P.C.
Atlanta, GA
Blank, Adam S. .... New York, NY
Blank, Alan R. .... Portland, OR
Blank, Allan A. .... New York, NY
Blank, Arnold .... Rockville, MD
Blank, Arthur J., Jr. .... New York, NY
Blank, Bess .... Los Angeles, CA
Blank, Beverly L. .... Washington, DC
Blank & Blank .... Bridgeport, CT
Blank, Charles E. .... Bloomfield Hills, MI
Blank, Christopher E. .... Concord, NH
Blank, Christopher L.
Newport Beach, CA
Blank, Christopher P. .... Brooklyn, NY
Blank, Cynthia F. .... Cincinnati, OH
Blank, Daniel P. .... San Francisco, CA
Blank, Daniel W. .... Superior, WI
Blank, David Jeffrey .... New York, NY
Blank, David M. .... Covington, KY
Blank, Diane Serafin .... New York, NY
Blank, Douglas S. .... San Diego, CA
Blank, Eleanor, (A P.C.) .... Encino, CA
Blank, Ellen I. .... Freehold, NJ
Blank, Eric I. .... Boulder, CO
Blank, Eric P. .... Seattle, WA
Blank, Errol .... West Nyack, NY
Blank, Ethan J. .... New York, NY
Blank, F. Philip .... Tallahassee, FL
Blank, Gerald .... San Diego, CA
Blank, Goolnick & Dittenhoefer
New York, NY
Blank, Harold J. .... Portland, OR
Blank, Harvey P.
Department Of The Interior, Office of the Solicitor, GV
Blank, Helene E. .... Brooklyn, NY
Blank, Ira L. .... St. Louis, MO
Blank, Irving M. .... Richmond, VA
Blank, James S. .... New York, NY
Blank, Jennifer Jo .... New York, NY
Blank, Jennifer S. .... Washington, DC
Blank, Jeremy David .... San Jose, CA
Blank, Joel H. .... Huntington Beach, CA
Blank, John B. .... Bridgeport, CT
Blank, Jonathan .... Washington, DC
Blank, Jonathan .... New York, NY
Blank, Jonathan T. .... Richmond, VA
Blank, Joseph B. .... New York, NY
Blank, Judith A. .... Hartford, CT
Blank, Julie E. .... San Francisco, CA
Blank, Karen L. .... Woodland, CA
Blank, Karen N. .... Department of Labor, Office of the Solicitor, GV
Blank, Kathleen Alice .... Washington, DC
Silver Spring, MD
Blank, Laura J. .... New York, NY
Blank, Leslie Nanette .... New York, NY
Blank, Lester E. .... Bridgeport, CT
Blank, Linda M. .... Los Angeles, CA
Blank, Lisa S. .... Boston, MA
Blank, Mark
Pension Benefit Guaranty Corporation, Office of the General Counsel, GV
Blank, Mark, Jr. .... Paoli, PA
Blank, Martin E. .... Ann Arbor, MI
Blank, Martin H., Jr., Law Office of
Los Angeles, CA
Blank, Martin J. .... Chevy Chase, MD
Blank, Matthew A. .... Spring Valley, NY
Blank, Maura Scott .... Seattle, WA
Blank, Michael A. .... Palm Beach, FL
Blank, Michael A., P.A. .... Palm Beach, FL
Blank, Michael Carl .... San Luis Obispo, CA
Blank, Mitchell .... New York, NY
Blank, Nelson D. .... Tampa, FL
Blank, Norma Hudson .... Canton, OH
Blank, Owen D. .... Portland, OR
Blank, Paul .... Bronx, NY
Blank, Peter L. .... Washington, DC
Blank, Philip B. .... White Plains, NY
Blank, Raymond E. .... Bridgeport, CT
Blank, Rhonda .... Washington, DC
Blank, Richard M. .... New York, NY
Blank, Richard N. .... Fort Lauderdale, FL
Blank, Richard S. .... Boston, MA
Blank, Rigsby & Meenan, P.A.
Tallahassee, FL
Blank, Robert C. .... Freehold, NJ
Blank, Robert G. .... Soulsbyville, CA
Blank, Robert H. .... Miami, FL
Blank, Robert L. .... Tampa, FL
Blank, Robert P. .... New York, NY
Blank Rome Comisky & McCauley LLP
Wilmington, DE
Washington, DC
Boca Raton, FL
Baltimore, MD
Cherry Hill, NJ
Trenton, NJ
Allentown, PA
Media, PA
Philadelphia, PA
Blank, Samuel S. .... Media, PA
Blank, Shari M. .... Kansas City, MO

Blank, Stacy D. .... Tampa, FL
Blank, Stephen P. .... New York, NY
Blank, Stephen P., P.C. .... New York, NY
Blank, Susan Foster .... Eighty Four, PA
Blank, Suzanne M. .... Superior, WI
Blank, Thomas C. .... Toledo, OH
Blank, Thomas J. .... Cincinnati, OH
Blank, Thomas W. .... Rochester, NY
Blank, Timothy C. .... Boston, MA
Blank, Vicki L. .... Nashville, TN
Blank, Wayne A. .... Atlanta, GA
Blanke, Beverly A. .... Manhattan Beach, CA
Blanke, David P. .... Dallas, TX
Blanke, Jordan M. .... Atlanta, GA
Blanke, Melvin H. .... Plymouth, WI
Blanke, Richard B. .... St. Louis, MO
Blanke, Robert H. .... Olivette, MO
Blanke, Stacey M. .... New Orleans, LA
Blank-Ecker, Tammi L. .... Yonkers, NY
Blankemeyer, Anna Mae .... Ottawa, OH
Blanken, Donald .... Philadelphia, PA
Blankenau, Don .... Omaha, NE
Blankenbaker, Robert .... Chicago, IL
Blankenbeckler, F. A., Jr. .... Waxahachie, TX
Blankenheimer, Alan H. .... Phoenix, AZ
Blankenheimer, Susan Leslie
Treasury Department, Office of the Comptroller of the Currency, GV
Blankenhorn, Frederick L. .... Neptune, NJ
Blankenhorn, J. Christian .... Valencia, CA
Blankenhorn & Ragan .... Neptune, NJ
Blankenship, Alan M. .... Branson West, MO
Blankenship, Albert L., Jr. .... Tucson, AZ
Blankenship, Alice K. .... Columbus, OH
Blankenship & Associates .... Riverside, CA
Blankenship, Beth J. .... Nashville, TN
Blankenship and Blankenship
Murfreesboro, TN
Nashville, TN
Blankenship, Brent A. .... Rochester, MI
Blankenship, Brent A., P.C. .... Rochester, MI
Blankenship, C. Mark .... Murray, KY
Blankenship, Carmen .... Irving, TX
Blankenship, Carmichael, Staubus, Wiland & Randall, P.C. .... Dallas, TX
Blankenship, Carolyn H. .... New York, NY
Blankenship, Clyde Alan .... Huntsville, AL
Blankenship & Company
Birmingham, AL
Blankenship & Conlon .... Huntsville, AL
Blankenship, Cooper .... Dallas, TX
Blankenship, David B. .... Huntsville, AL
Blankenship, David B., Attorney-at-Law, P.C.
Huntsville, AL
Blankenship, David W. .... Kingsport, TN
Blankenship, Dick .... Austin, TX
Blankenship, Donald E. .... Birmingham, AL
Blankenship, Douglas L. .... Fairbanks, AK
Blankenship, G. Thomas .... Indianapolis, IN
Blankenship, Gerald, Jr. .... Riverside, CA
Blankenship, G. T. .... Oklahoma City, OK
Blankenship, Harley N. .... Louisville, KY
Blankenship, J. Lawrence
Oklahoma City, OK
Blankenship, James C., III
Fayetteville, WV
Blankenship, Jap W. .... Oklahoma City, OK
Blankenship, Jennifer Clower
Nashville, TN
Blankenship, Jeri .... Huntsville, AL
Blankenship, John T. .... Murfreesboro, TN
Blankenship, Joseph W. .... Atlanta, GA
Blankenship, Julie K. .... Dallas, TX
Blankenship, Kimberly A. .... St. Louis, MO
Blankenship, Kurt S. .... Metairie, LA
New Orleans, LA
Blankenship, Kyra K. .... Lubbock, TX
Blankenship Law Firm .... Batesville, AR
Blankenship Law Firm, The .... Seattle, WA
Blankenship, Leroy .... Batesville, AR
Blankenship, Leroy W. .... Salinas, CA
Blankenship, Malcolm B., Jr.
Salisbury, NC
Blankenship, Mark I. .... Riverside, CA
Blankenship, Mark O. .... Lubbock, TX
Blankenship, Marlena M. .... Los Angeles, CA
Blankenship, Marshall L. .... Chicago, IL
Blankenship, Mercer J., Jr. .... Charlotte, NC
Blankenship, Michael Keith .... Wytheville, VA
Blankenship, Michele M. .... Osage Beach, MO
Blankenship, Michelle R. .... Detroit, MI
Blankenship, N. Jeffrey .... Florence, KY
Blankenship, Pamela Anita .... Grambling, LA
Blankenship, Patricia A.
Murfreesboro, TN
Blankenship, Patrick .... Knox, IN
Blankenship, Randall G. .... Winter Haven, FL
Blankenship, Randall G., P.A.
Winter Haven, FL
Blankenship, Randy J. .... Cincinnati, OH
Blankenship, Richard F. .... De Ridder, LA
Blankenship, Rodney B. .... Winter Haven, FL
Blankenship, Scott C.G. .... Seattle, WA
Blankenship, Sherry L. .... Del City, OK
Oklahoma City, OK
Blankenship, Stacey Ann .... Paducah, KY
Blankenship, Suzanne .... Pensacola, FL
Blankenship, Thomas L. .... Benton, KY
Blankenship, Trace .... Nashville, TN
Blankenship, William F., III .... Houston, TX
Blankenstein, Paul .... Washington, DC
Blanker, Alan H. .... Greenfield, MA
Blanket, Robert S. .... Fort Lauderdale, FL
Blankfein, Lloyd C. .... New York, NY
Blankfein, Richard S. .... Oyster Bay, NY
Blankingship, A. Hugo, III
Alexandria, VA

Blankingship, A. Hugo, Jr. ... **Fairfax, VA**
Blankingship & Keith, A Professional Corporation ... **Alexandria, VA**
Fairfax, VA
Leesburg, VA
Blankingship & Koomey, P.C.
Alexandria, VA
Blankinship, Ramona L. ... Lakeland, FL
Blankman, Douglas A. ... Fort Lauderdale, FL
Blankmeyer, Kurt V. ... **Wilton, CT**
Blankner, Francis W. ... Orlando, FL
Blankopf, Marion ... **Rochester, NY**
Blanks, Betty E. ... Visalia, CA
Blanks, Clifton D. ... San Marcos, TX
Blanks, Edel F., III ... Harahan, LA
Blanks, Edel F., Jr. ... **Monroe, LA**
Blanks, Greenfield & Rhodes ... **Temple, TX**
Blanks, Joseph C. ... Beaumont, TX
Blanks, Mickey J. ... **Temple, TX**
Blanks, T. Michael ... **Chesterfield, VA**
Glen Allen, VA
Blanks, William F. ... Montezuma, GA
Blankshain, Michael R. ... Chicago, IL
Blanks-Smart, Miriam
Bloomfield Hills, MI
Blankstein, Jeffrey ... **Los Angeles, CA**
New York, NY
Blankstein, Michael J. ... **Chicago, IL**
Blankstein, Mitchell ... Washington, DC
Blankstein, Richard K., P.C. ... **Boston, MA**
Blanock, F. Paul ... Mathews, VA
Blanos, Geo. N. ... Atlanta, GA
Blanpied, Lloyd E., Jr. ... Orange, CA
Blanscet, Gary W. ... Dallas, TX
Blanscet, Glen A. ... Dallas, TX
Blanscet, Joan ... Dallas, TX
Blansett, Eual D., Jr. ... Stockton, CA
Blansit, Lin L. ... **Austin, TX**
Blansitt, H. Don ... Schulenburg, TX
Blansky, David Adam ... Hempstead, NY
Blanson, Vincent P., A Professional Law Corporation ... New Orleans, LA
Blant, Erwin M. ... Port Chester, NY
Blant, Ian L. ... **New York, NY**
Blanton, Alex ... **Washington, DC**
Blanton, A. M. ... Jasper, AL
Blanton, Amelia Norman ... Memphis, TN
Blanton, Ben W. ... **Indianapolis, IN**
Blanton, Bill D. ... Dallas, TX
Blanton & Blanton ... Bakersfield, CA
Blanton, Bruce C. ... **East Lansing, MI**
Southfield, MI
Blanton, C. Hugh, Jr. ... Jacksonville, FL
Blanton, C. Terry ... Decatur, GA
Blanton, Charles A., II ... Richmond, VA
Blanton, Charles A., III ... Glen Allen, VA
Blanton, Christopher ... **Sherman, TX**
Blanton, Christopher M. ... **St. Louis, MO**
Blanton, Clay B. ... Quinton, VA
Blanton, Darrell D. ... Memphis, TN
Blanton, David E. ... **Sikeston, MO**
Blanton, Donna E. ... **Tallahassee, FL**
Blanton, Edward L., Jr. ... **Baltimore, MD**
Blanton, Edward L., Jr., P.A., Law Office of
Baltimore, MD
Blanton, Edward P., Jr. ... Aiken, SC
Blanton, Edwin F. ... **Tallahassee, FL**
Blanton, Fred, Jr. ... Fultondale, AL
Blanton, G. Derek ... Surfside Beach, SC
Blanton, Gary L. ... Wichita, KS
Blanton, Hoover C. ... **Columbia, SC**
Blanton, J. Charles ... **Boise, ID**
Blanton, Jack S. ... Houston, TX
Blanton, Jacqueline L. ... **Sarasota, FL**
Blanton, James A. ... Denton, TX
Blanton, James C. ... West Palm Beach, FL
Blanton, James T. ... **Fort Worth, TX**
Blanton, John C. ... San Antonio, TX
Blanton, Jonathan D. ... **Jackson, OH**
Blanton, Joseph C., Jr. ... **Sikeston, MO**
Blanton, Kevin S. ... **Harrisburg, PA**
Blanton, Larry R. ... Jeffersonville, IN
Blanton, Leenetta ... Tampa, FL
Blanton, Lewis M. ... Cape Girardeau, MO
Blanton, M. Eldridge, III ... **Richmond, VA**
Blanton, M. Stanford ... **Birmingham, AL**
Blanton, Mary R., & Associate
Salisbury, NC
Blanton, Mary Rutherford ... **Salisbury, NC**
Blanton, Michael S. ... **Los Angeles, CA**
Blanton, Nancy S. ... Bakersfield, CA
Blanton, Patricia L. ... Los Angeles, CA
Blanton, Philip C. ... Bakersfield, CA
Blanton, Rice, Sidwell & Nickell, L.L.C.
Cape Girardeau, MO
Sikeston, MO
Blanton, Richard S. ... Farmville, VA
Blanton, Robin A. ... **Vero Beach, FL**
Blanton, Stephanie Leigh ... **Columbia, SC**
Blanton, Steve A. ... Frankfort, KY
Blanton, Teresa O. ... Fort Worth, TX
Blanton, Theodore A. (Ted) ... Salisbury, NC
Blanton, Thomas P. ... Juneau, AK
Blanton, Thomas R., III ... **Morganton, NC**
Blanton, Thomas R., III, P.A.
Morganton, NC
Blanton, Timothy D. ... Palo Alto, CA
Blanton, Tobey D. ... **Houston, TX**
Blanton, Tom ... Austin, TX
Blanton, Vicki D. ... Dallas, TX
Blanton, W. C. ... **Minneapolis, MN**
Blanton, Wendy M. ... Fort Myers, FL
Blanton, William N., Jr. ... Houston, TX
Blas, Alfred F. ... Morris Plains, NJ
Blas, Kimberly J. ... **Boise, ID**
Blasbalg, Arnold Leo ... Providence, RI
Blasband, David ... **New York, NY**
Blasband, Denise P. ... **San Diego, CA**
Blasberg, Arthur, Jr. ... Boston, MA
Blasberg, Teresa A., & Associates
Los Angeles, CA
Blasberg, William H. ... **Philadelphia, PA**
Blaschak, Thomas R. ... Dayton, OH
Blaschka, Francis L. ... Cleveland, OH
Blaschke, Harold G. ... Houston, TX
Blaschke, Michael J. ... Oklahoma City, OK
Blasco, Anthony S. ... Easton, PA
Blasco, Richard E. ... **Pasadena, CA**
Blasco, Robert ... **Juneau, AK**
Blascovich, Ralph S. ... San Francisco, CA
Blasdel, Diane C. ... **Palm Springs, CA**
Blasdel, W. Mark ... Oklahoma City, OK
Blasdell, Daniel A. ... East Palestine, OH
Blasdell, Thomas L. ... **Los Angeles, CA**
Blase, Aaron T. ... Wichita, KS
Blase & Blase, P.A. ... Wichita, KS
Blase, David R. ... Point Richmond, CA
Blase, DeWitt F. ... Ventura, CA
Blase, Guy ... Palo Alto, CA
Blase, Henry H. ... Wichita, KS
Blase, James G. ... St. Louis, MO
Blase, John C. ... St. Louis, MO
Blase, Kurt E. ... **Washington, DC**
Blase, Marcia K.
Commodity Futures Trading Commission, Office of the General Counsel, GV
Blase, Nicholas B. ... Niles, IL
Blase, Tamatha Ann ... Denver, CO
Blaser, Anne C. ... Seattle, WA
Blaser, Arthur W. ... Orange, CA
Blaser, Charles F. ... **Lawrence, KS**
Blaser, Michael R. ... Des Moines, IA
Blaser, Ronna Iris Wineberg ... Nashville, TN
Blaser, Sorensen & Hansen, Chartered
Blackfoot, ID
Blaser, Stephen J. ... Blackfoot, ID
Blaser, Terry A. ... Waterville, KS
Blaser, William B. ... Tucson, AZ
Blasey, Ralph G., III ... **Washington, DC**
Blasey, Thomas M. ... **McLean, VA**
Blasgen, Sharon W. ... San Jose, CA
Blash, Justin Samuel ... **New York, NY**
Blash, Michelle N. Lewis ... **New York, NY**
Blashek, Robert D., III ... **Los Angeles, CA**
Blasi, Andrew B. ... Boca Raton, FL
Blasi, Andrew B., P.A., Law Offices of
Boca Raton, FL
Blasi, Anna M. ... Fort Worth, TX
Blasi, Anthony C. ... West Orange, NJ
Blasi, Arthur M. ... Boston, MA
Blasi, Carol A. ... Trenton, NJ
Blasi, David ... Downers Grove, IL
Blasi, Frank T. ... **Scranton, PA**
Blasi, Gary L. ... Los Angeles, CA
Blasi, Gerald J. ... Endicott, NY
Blasi, Gregory J. ... **New York, NY**
Blasi, John J. ... **Chicago, IL**
Blasi, John R. ... **Westfield, NJ**
Blasi, Joseph F., Jr. ... New Orleans, LA
Blasi, Linda Manney ... Binghamton, NY
Blasi & O'Day ... Endicott, NY
Blasi, Robert R. ... Spring Lake Heights, NJ
Blasi, Ronald W. ... New York, NY
Blasi, Suzanne M. ... Westford, MA
Blasi, Thomas J. ... New Orleans, LA
Blasi, Vincent A. ... New York, NY
Blasi & Walsh ... **Scranton, PA**
Blasiak, George S. ... **Syracuse, NY**
Blasiak, James L. ... **Washington, DC**
Blasier, Peter C. ... **Pittsburgh, PA**
Blasik, Michael J. ... Boston, MA
Blasik-Miller, Susan ... **Dayton, OH**
Blasi-Lamendola, Agnes B.
New Orleans, LA
Blasingame, Burch, Garrard, Bryant & Ashley, P.C. ... **Athens, GA**
Atlanta, GA
Elberton, GA
Gainesville, GA
Greensboro, GA
Lawrenceville, GA
Blasingame, Chad ... Houston, TX
Blasingame, David A. ... Riesel, TX
Blasingame, Ernest N., Jr. ... Florence, AL
Blasingame, Gary B. ... **Athens, GA**
Blasingame, Jack W.
Department Of Veterans Affairs, Board of Veterans Appeals, GV
Blasingame, Karen ... Chicago, IL
Blasingame, Oscar ... **St. Petersburg, FL**
Blasingim-Stenzel, Arla H. ... Glendale, AZ
Blasini, Jorge F. ... **San Juan, PR**
Blasini, Peter B. ... New Haven, CT
Blasius, Gordon A. ... New York, NY
Blasius, Myra V. ... **Jamestown, NY**
Blask, James F. ... Milwaukee, WI
Blask, Jerome K. ... **Washington, DC**
Blaska, Thomas C., & Associates
Atlanta, GA
Blaske and Blaske ... Ann Arbor, MI
Battle Creek, MI
Blaske, E. Robert ... Ann Arbor, MI
Battle Creek, MI
Blaske, Steven A. ... **Norcross, GA**
Blaske, Thomas H. ... Ann Arbor, MI
Battle Creek, MI
Blaskey, Mark S. ... **West Conshohocken, PA**
Blaskey, Richard J. ... Long Beach, CA
Blaskey, Samuel B. ... Lafayette Hill, PA
Blasko, Eugene K. ... Marlton, NJ
Blasko, J.P., Professional Corporation
Doylestown, PA
Blasko, John P. ... **Doylestown, PA**
Blasko, John W. ... **Harrisburg, PA**
State College, PA
Blasko, Joseph C. ... **Columbus, OH**
Blaskopf, Lawrence ... Department of Justice, Tax Division, GV
Blaskovich, David M. ... **Merrillville, IN**
Blasky, Aaron E. ... Cincinnati, OH
Blasland, Warren V. ... Liverpool, NY
Blass, Betty R. ... Marietta, GA
Blass, Douglas J. ... Fort Lauderdale, FL
Blass & Driggs ... **New York, NY**
Blass & Frankel, P.A. ... Miami, FL
Blass, Harold ... White Plains, NY
Blass, Jonathan A. ... New York, NY
Blass, Michael S. ... **New York, NY**
Blass, Norman ... New York, NY
Blass, Rebecca B. ... Little Rock, AR
Blass, Robert A. ... **Montvale, NJ**
Blass, Ronald C., Jr. ... **Poughkeepsie, NY**
Blass, Scott S. ... Wheeling, WV
Blass, Stephen A. ... Miami, FL
Blass, W. Joel ... **Biloxi, MS**
Gulfport, MS
Blass, William Joe ... Santee, CA
Blassberg, Franci J. ... **New York, NY**
Blassingame, Janet W. ... Washington, DC
Blassingame, J. D. ... Groveton, TX
Blassingame, Kenneth E. ... Dallas, TX
Blassingame-Brown, Charlesetta ... Detroit, MI
Blastic, Nancy A. ... **Orlando, FL**
Blasy, Jill ... Midland, MI
Blaszak, James S. ... **Washington, DC**
Blaszak, Michael W. ... Oak Brook, IL
Blaszak, Nancy Janus ... Orchard Park, NY
Blaszcyk, Theodore W. ... Patchogue, NY
Blatch, Maralyn Lyn ... Washington, DC
Blatcher, Frank S. ... **Media, PA**
Blatcher, Pamela W. ... **Media, PA**
Blatchford, Howard P., Jr. ... **Boston, MA**
Blatchford, Joseph H. ... Washington, DC
Blatchford, Kevin F. ... **Chicago, IL**
Blatchley, Jill T. ... San Diego, CA
Blatchley, Robert L. ... Baltimore, MD
Blatchley, William E. ... **San Diego, CA**
Blatchly, Bruce D. ... **New Paltz, NY**
Blatchly & Simonson, P.C. ... **New Paltz, NY**
Blate, Gary T. ... Oakhurst, CA
Blatman, Bettye Ann ... Concord, MA
Blatner, Lita O. ... Visalia, CA
Blatner, Margaret ... Los Angeles, CA
Blatner, Sherry D. ... Phoenix, AZ
Blatnik, Frances P. ... Birmingham, MI
Blatnik, Lawrence E.
Federal Mine Safety and Health Review Commission, Office of the Commissioners, GV
Blatnikoff, Alan G. ... **Southfield, MI**
Blatt & Associates, P.C., Law Offices of
Washington, DC
Baltimore, MD
Blatt, Dana L. ... Encino, CA
Blatt, David ... Gloversville, NY
Blatt, David S. ... **Washington, DC**
Blatt, David S. ... Gloversville, NY
Blatt, Elaine S. ... **Chicago, IL**
Blatt, Eric Kennedy ... **San Francisco, CA**
Blatt, Franklin R., Law Offices of
Harrisonburg, VA
Blatt, Gayle Meryl ... **San Diego, CA**
Blatt, George J. ... Cleveland, OH
Blatt, Gregory R. ... **New York, NY**
Blatt, Hammesfahr & Eaton ... **Chicago, IL**
New York, NY
Blatt, Harold G. ... **St. Louis, MO**
Blatt, Hasenmiller, Leibsker, Moore & Pelletteiri ... **Cherry Valley, IL**
Chicago, IL
Normal, IL
Blatt, Ira S. ... Arcata, CA
Blatt, Jason ... **Philadelphia, PA**
Blatt, Jason Dennis ... **Alexandria, VA**
Blatt, Jeffrey J. ... Los Angeles, CA
Blatt, Lisa Kaye ... Chantilly, VA
Blatt, Lisa Schiavo ... Department of Justice, Office of the Solicitor General, GV
Blatt, Mara Asya ... **El Paso, TX**
Blatt, Melinda Kay ... Brentwood, TN
Blatt, Michele S. ... New York, NY
Blatt, Mindy L. ... Brooklyn, NY
Blatt, Norman E., Jr. ... Allentown, PA
Blatt, P. Andrew ... **Cincinnati, OH**
Blatt, Peter A. ... **West Palm Beach, FL**
Blatt, Regina K. ... Sacramento, CA
Blatt, Richard L. ... **Chicago, IL**
Blatt, Richard L. ... Red Bank, NJ
New York, NY
Blatt, Robert ... Cincinnati, OH
Blatt, Robert A. ... Larchmont, NY
Blatt, Robert, Jr. ... Redwood City, CA
Blatt, Robert S. ... **Fort Smith, AR**
Blatt, Robert S. ... **Chicago, IL**
Blatt, Shannon L. ... Fort Smith, AR
Blatt, Shawn M. ... **Dayton, OH**
Blatt, Sol, Jr. ... Charleston, SC
Blatt, Steven H. ... **Garden City, NY**
Blatt, Steven M. ... Harrisonburg, VA
Blatt, Stuart R. ... **Baltimore, MD**
Blatt, Susanne R. ... Worcester, MA
Blatt, Timothy J. ... Mercer, PA
Blatt, William S. ... Fort Lauderdale, FL
Blattberg, Alan ... **New York, NY**
Blatte, Bernard Baruch ... San Francisco, CA
Blatte, Lawrence A. ... **New York, NY**
Blatte, Pamela B. ... **Boston, MA**
Blatteis, Charles S. ... **Memphis, TN**
Blatteis, David S. ... New York, NY
Blattel, Jesse ... Beverly Hills, CA
Blatter, Andrew Z. ... **New York, NY**
Blatter, Cherilynn M. ... **Los Angeles, CA**
Blatter, William J. ... Chicago, IL
Blattmachr, Jonathan G. ... **New York, NY**
Portland, OR
Blattner, Christopher C. S. ... **Portland, OR**
Blattner, David J., Jr. ... **Boston, MA**
Blattner, David K. ... **Fort Lauderdale, FL**
Blattner, Elisabeth R. ... **Salt Lake City, UT**
Blattner, Elizabeth Hurley ... **Dayton, OH**
Blattner, J. Wray ... **Dayton, OH**
Blattner, Jeffrey H. ... United States Senate, Senatorial Assistants, GV
Blattner, John C. ... **Ann Arbor, MI**
Blattner, Robert A. ... **Cleveland, OH**
Blaty, Anthony J. ... South Miami, FL
Blaty, Donald M. ... Dearborn, MI
Blatz, Frank H., Jr. ... Westfield, NJ
Blatz, Paul B. ... Ojai, CA
Blatz, Robert E., Jr. ... Reno, NV
Blatz, Robert F. ... Gary, IN
Blau, Allan I. ... Mill Valley, CA
Blau, Arthur M. ... New York, NY
Blau, Barbara J. ... Weston, CT
Blau, Bernard J. ... **Cold Spring, KY**
Blau & Blau ... Springfield, NJ
Blau & Bonavich ... **Chicago, IL**
Blau, Cecile Anne ... Jeffersonville, IN
Blau, Charles E. ... Springfield, NJ
Blau, Charles W. ... **Dallas, TX**
Blau, Craig ... **New York, NY**
Blau, David M. ... **Bloomfield Hills, MI**
Blau, David M. ... Milwaukee, WI
Blau, David S. ... Los Angeles, CA
Blau, Denise L. ... **New York, NY**
Blau, Eddie E. ... Culver City, CA
Blau, Edward, Law Offices of
Los Angeles, CA
Blau, Ellen A. ... St. Louis, MO
Blau, Gary A. ... Boston, MA
Blau, George G. ... Atlanta, GA
Blau, George L. ... Fort Collins, CO
Blau, H. Andre ... Oakland, CA
Blau, Harvey R. ... **Jericho, NY**
Blau, Herbert H. ... Larchmont, NY
Blau, Howard L. ... New York, NY
Blau, J. Gordon, (P.A.) ... Orlando, FL
Blau, J. Nathan ... Atlanta, GA
Blau, J. Nathan, P.C. ... Atlanta, GA
Blau, Jeffrey A., (P.A.) ... Tampa, FL
Blau, Joel ... Delmar, NY
Blau, Jonathan A. ... **San Jose, CA**
Santa Monica, CA
Blau, Keith J. ... Universal City, CA
Blau, Kramer, Wactlar & Lieberman, P.C.
Jericho, NY
Mineola, NY
Blau, Laurence A. ... San Francisco, CA
Blau, Leslie A. ... **Winter Park, FL**
Blau, Leslie A. ... **Chicago, IL**
Blau, Louis C. ... Los Angeles, CA
Blau, Marc ... **Los Angeles, CA**
Blau, Maura E. ... **Westfield, NJ**
Blau, Michael Jay ... Warren, MI
Blau, Michael L. ... **Boston, MA**
Blau, Orit ... Beverly Hills, CA
Blau, Randall M. ... **Southfield, MI**
Blau, Richard D. ... **Phoenix, AZ**
Blau, Richard M. ... **Tampa, FL**
Blau, Richard Newton ... Manchester, MA
Blau, Robert D. ... Springfield, NJ
Blau, Robert E. L. ... **Cold Spring, KY**
Blau, Russell M. ... **Washington, DC**
Blau, Sharon ... **New York, NY**
Blau, Steven B. ... New York, NY
Blau, Steven N. ... **Torrance, CA**
Blauch, Kevin C. ... **New York, NY**
Blauer, Heather ... **Bethesda, MD**
Blauer, Joanne ... New York, NY
Blauer, Lorin R. ... Bountiful, UT
Blauer-Jones, Brad ... Havertown, PA
Blauert, Paul F. ... Seattle, WA
Blaufarb, Gerard A. ... Los Altos, CA
Blaufarb, Jonathan K. ... **Beverly Hills, CA**
Blaufeld, Samuel S. ... Pittsburgh, PA
Blaufeld & Schiller ... Pittsburgh, PA
Blaufus, Daniel Allen ... **Portland, OR**
Blaufuss, John A. ... Toledo, OH
Blaufuss, Marjorie A. ... Topeka, KS
Blaugrund, Clifford E. ... Albuquerque, NM
Blaugrund, Daniel J. ... Herkimer, NY
Blaugrund, David S. ... **Dublin, OH**
Blaugrund, Herbert & Martin, Incorporated
Columbus, OH
Delaware, OH
Dublin, OH
New Albany, OH
Blaugrund, Stuart E. ... **Dallas, TX**
Blauhut, Linda E. ... Washington, DC
Blaum, Janet H. ... **Wilkes-Barre, PA**
Blaum, William M. ... **Scranton, PA**
Scranton, PA
Blauman and McCabe ... Bronx, NY
White Plains, NY
Blauman, Simon L. ... Bronx, NY
White Plains, NY
Blauner, Earl M. ... San Francisco, CA
Blauner, Michelle H. ... **Boston, MA**
Blauner, Stephen J. ... **New York, NY**
Blauschild, Doreen J. ... Los Angeles, CA
Blaushield, Julius ... Rosedale, NY
Blaustein, Alan P. ... New York, NY
Blaustein, Alan S. ... Los Angeles, CA
Blaustein, Andrea M. ... Los Angeles, CA
Blaustein, Caryn F. ... **New City, NY**
Blaustein & D'Ambra, P.C. ... East Hills, NY
Blaustein, David P. ... Albany, NY
Blaustein, Donna R. ... **Miami Beach, FL**
Blaustein, Gary Alan ... Bedminster, NJ
Union, NJ
Blaustein, Gerald ... Dix Hills, NY

Blaustein, Herbert ..... Union, NJ
Blaustein, Howard Alan ..... New York, NY
Blaustein, Joette Milians ..... Jamaica, NY
Blaustein, Jon G. ..... Atlanta, GA
Blaustein, Joseph B. ..... Long Beach, CA
Blaustein, Lisa S. ..... East Hills, NY
Blaustein, Martin S. ..... Ogden, UT
Blaustein, Randy B. ..... Woodmere, NY
Blaustein, Richard P. ..... Newton, MA
Blaustein, Robert S. ..... New York, NY
Blaustein, Rochelle S. ..... McLean, VA
Blaustein, Roni B. ..... New York, NY
Blaustein, Shella Wolff ..... Atlanta, GA
Blaustein, Stacey E. ..... White Plains, NY
Blaut, Milton S. ..... Boca Raton, FL
Hollywood, FL
Blauvelt, Arthur A., III ..... Aberdeen, WA
Blauvelt, George M. ..... Menomonie, WI
Blauvelt, James N. ..... Bloomfield, NJ
Blauvelt, Janet I. ..... Kansas City, MO
Blauvelt & Kouretchian, LLP
New York, NY
Blauvelt, Peter M. ..... Rochester, NY
Blauvelt, Thomas C. ..... New York, NY
Blauw, Daniel L. ..... Grand Rapids, MI
Blauwet, Roger C. ..... Omaha, NE
Blavatt, Blavatt & Blavatt, LLC
Owings Mills, MD
Blavatt, Jason A. ..... Owings Mills, MD
Blavatt, Jeffrey M. ..... Owings Mills, MD
Blavatt, Ronald ..... Owings Mills, MD
Blavin, Sheree A. ..... Santa Monica, CA
Blawie, Elias J. ..... Menlo Park, CA
Blawie, James L. ..... Fremont, CA
Blawie, John F. ..... Bridgeport, CT
Blaxberg & Grayson, P.A. ..... Miami, FL
Blaxberg, I. Barry ..... Miami, FL
Blaxill, David Charles ..... New York, NY
Blaxter, H. Vaughan, III ..... Pittsburgh, PA
Blaxter, J.T. Wells ..... San Francisco, CA
Blay, Barry C. ..... Fresno, CA
Blay & Liss ..... Brooklyn, NY
Blay, Michele T. ..... Chicago, IL
Blay, Robert D. ..... Palm Desert, CA
Blaya, Robbin K. ..... Washington, DC
Blaydes, Lonnie E., Jr. ..... Dallas, TX
Blaylock, Barbara F. ..... Dallas, TX
Blaylock, Bruce A. ..... Bethesda, MD
Blaylock, Bruce A., and Associates, Chartered, Law Offices of
Washington, DC
Bethesda, MD
Blaylock, Charles R. ..... Monroe, LA
Blaylock & Cleous, Chtd.
Overland Park, KS
Wichita, KS
Blaylock, Connie ..... Dalton, GA
Blaylock, Cynthia Ward ..... Laguna Beach, CA
Blaylock, Gary H. ..... Pomona, CA
Blaylock, Gwendolyn C. ..... Chicago, IL
Blaylock, Jeffrey H. ..... Columbia, MO
Blaylock, John David ..... Memphis, TN
Blaylock, Michael I. ..... Los Angeles, CA
Blaylock, Paul D. ..... Portland, OR
Blaylock, Richard L. ..... New York, NY
Blaylock, Robert J. ..... Los Angeles, CA
Blaylock, Roger S. ..... Salt Lake City, UT
Blaylock, Stephen J. ..... Wichita, KS
Blaylock, Terry P. ..... Plano, TX
Blaylock, Thomas M. ..... Roanoke, VA
Blaylock, Thomas M. ..... Salem, VA
Blaylock, William B. ..... Dallas, TX
Blaymore, Michael D.
Roslyn Heights, NY
Blayney, Mark William ..... Louisville, KY
Blayney, Michael J. ..... Dallas, TX
Blayton, Oscar H. ..... Hampton, VA
Blaz, Norman Yale ..... Encino, CA
Blazak, Robert S. ..... Canandaigua, NY
Blaze, R. Scott ..... Department of Justice, Civil Division, GV
Blazek, Frank ..... Huntsville, TX
Blazek, George T. ..... Omaha, NE
Blazek, James E. ..... New Orleans, LA
Blazek, James Nicholas ..... Dublin, OH
Blazek, James T. ..... Omaha, NE
Blazek, Keith G. ..... Indianapolis, IN
Blazek, Mark J. ..... Valparaiso, NE
Blazek, Miles J., Jr. ..... New Orleans, LA
Blazek, Paula H. ..... Beaumont, TX
Blazek, Robert G. ..... Brookfield, WI
Blazek-White, Doris ..... Washington, DC
Blazel, John M. ..... Ripon, WI
Blazer, Brenda L., P.C. ..... Bismarck, ND
Blazer, Gregory H. ..... Decatur, GA
Blazer, John A. ..... Fairfax, VA
Blazer, Jonathan ..... Philadelphia, PA
Blazer, Kristi ..... Helena, MT
Blazer, Lawrence C. ..... Oakland, CA
Blazer, Marci A. ..... New York, NY
Blazevic, Donna J. ..... Minneapolis, MN
Blazey, Douglas R. ..... Reading, PA
Blazey, Scott A. ..... Jasper, IN
Blazi, Anthony J. ..... Elkhart, IN
Blazi, Geoffrey L. ..... Lafayette, IN
Blazi, John A., Law Offices of
Waterbury, CT
Blazick, Leonard R. ..... Philadelphia, PA
Blazier, Christensen & Bigelow, A Professional Corporation ..... Austin, TX
Blazier, John C. ..... Austin, TX
Blazier, T. Glynn ..... Lake Charles, LA
Blazina, James A., (Chtd.) ..... Chicago, IL
Blazina, Michael Martin ..... Sacramento, CA
Blazkovec, Jacob M. ..... Algoma, WI
Blazkovec, Jacob P. ..... Algoma, WI
Blazs, Kevin A. ..... Jacksonville, FL
Blazsek, Otto F. ..... Clifton, NJ

Blazure, G. Frederick ..... Trenton, NJ
Blazusiak, Thomas J. ..... Allentown, PA
Blazy, Kelly ..... Anchorage, AK
Seattle, WA
Blazzard, Grodd & Hasenauer, P.C.
Westport, CT
Lauderdale-By-The-Sea, FL
Blazzard, Norse N. ..... Westport, CT
Lauderdale-By-The-Sea, FL
Blea, Dale J. ..... Oakhurst, CA
Blea, David P. ..... New York, NY
Blea, Jacob, III ..... Livermore, CA
Blea, Lori S. ..... Bronxville, NY
Bleach, Robert T. ..... Fort Walton Beach, FL
Panama City, FL
Pensacola, FL
Bleakley, Cypher, Parent, Warren & Quinn
Grand Rapids, MI
Bleakley, Frederick W. ..... Grand Rapids, MI
Bleakley, Frederick W. ..... Muskegon, MI
Bleakley, Peter K. ..... Washington, DC
Bleakley Platt Remsen Millham & Curran
New York, NY
Bleakley Platt & Schmidt, LLP
Greenwich, CT
Bleakley Platt & Schmidt LLP
White Plains, NY
Bleakley, Richard R. ..... Hackensack, NJ
Bleakley, Robert W. ..... Tampa, FL
Bleakley, Sarah M. ..... Tallahassee, FL
Bleakley, William M. ..... Springfield, IL
Bleakley, William P. ..... Oklahoma City, OK
Bleakney, Cheryl A. ..... Seattle, WA
Bleakney, Robert G., Jr. ..... Boston, MA
Bleaman, Marc D. ..... Tucson, AZ
Blears, Norman J. ..... Palo Alto, CA
Blease, Coleman A. ..... Sacramento, CA
Blease, J. Russell ..... Pawtucket, RI
Blease, Jeffrey R. ..... St. Cloud, MN
Blease Law Firm, Ltd. ..... St. Cloud, MN
Blease, Rochelle F. ..... St. Cloud, MN
Bleattler, Karen L. ..... Charleston, WV
Bleau, Andrew G. ..... New York, NY
Bleau, Denise J. ..... West Palm Beach, FL
Bleau, Fox & Associates, A Professional Law Corporation ..... Los Angeles, CA
Bleau, Richard E. ..... Carmichael, CA
Bleau, Thomas J. ..... Bay City, MI
Bleau, Thomas P. ..... Los Angeles, CA
Blech, Kenneth A. ..... Strongsville, OH
Blech, Samuel H. ..... Arlington, VA
Blecha, Kirk S. ..... Omaha, NE
Blecharczyk, Mary L. ..... East Providence, RI
Blecher & Collins, A Professional Corporation ..... Los Angeles, CA
Blecher, Ivy K. ..... Bronx, NY
Blecher, Jonathan B. ..... Miami, FL
Blecher, Joseph J. ..... New York, NY
Blecher, M. David ..... Lincolnshire, IL
Blecher, Maxwell M. ..... Los Angeles, CA
Blecher, Melvin ..... Washington, DC
Blecher, Mendel & Fedele ..... New York, NY
Blecher, Robert B., P.C. ..... Scottsdale, AZ
Blecher, Stuart H. ..... San Rafael, CA
Blecher, Tedd ..... New York, NY
Blechl, James J. ..... Indianapolis, IN
Blechman, Beth ..... Tallahassee, FL
Blechman, Jay A. ..... Pittsburgh, PA
Blechman, Jon S. ..... Binghamton, NY
Blechman, Mark S. ..... Orlando, FL
Blechman, Mark S., P.A. ..... Orlando, FL
Blechman, Michael D. ..... New York, NY
Blechman, Michael S. ..... Pittsburgh, PA
Blechman, Noah G. ..... San Francisco, CA
Blechman, Rachel ..... Miami, FL
Blechman, William J. ..... Miami, FL
Blechner, Paul A. ..... Los Angeles, CA
Blechschmidt, Bart M. ..... San Diego, CA
Las Vegas, NV
Bleck, Daniel S. ..... Boston, MA
Bleck, Michael J. ..... Minneapolis, MN
Blecke, James C. ..... Miami, FL
Blecker, Herbert ..... New York, NY
Blecker, Ira D. ..... Hopewell Junction, NY
Blecker, Jodi H. ..... Chevy Chase, MD
Blecker, Marcia Z. ..... Roslyn, NY
Blecker, Robert I. ..... New York, NY
Blecker, Sol ..... Broomall, PA
Bleckley, Jeanette A. ..... Sacramento, CA
Bleckman and Blair ..... El Segundo, CA
Bleckman, John H. ..... St. Louis, MO
Bleckman, Martin J. ..... El Segundo, CA
Bleckner, David J. ..... New York, NY
Bleckwenn, A. Theodore ..... Madison, WI
Bledsaw, Lynette M. ..... Detroit, MI
Bledsoe, Barry ..... Montgomery, AL
Bledsoe, Baxter, Jr. ..... London, KY
Bledsoe & Bledsoe, P.L.L.C.
Charlotte, NC
Bledsoe, Bradley W. ..... Anderson, SC
Bledsoe and Bryson, P.S.C. ..... London, KY
Bledsoe, Cathcart, Diestel, Livingston & Pedersen, LLP ..... San Francisco, CA
Bledsoe, Catherine A. ..... Baltimore, MD
Bledsoe, Chad ..... Lawton, OK
Bledsoe, Charles A., Jr. ..... Blythewood, SC
Bledsoe, Clint G. ..... El Paso, TX
Bledsoe, Craig G. ..... Caldwell, ID
Bledsoe, D. Gregory ..... Tulsa, OK
Bledsoe, David A. ..... Portland, OR
Bledsoe, David I. ..... Alexandria, VA
Bledsoe, Dennis ..... Houston, TX
Bledsoe, Gary L. ..... Austin, TX
Bledsoe, Henry, Jr. ..... Chicago, IL
Bledsoe, James A., Jr. ..... Jacksonville, FL
Bledsoe, Janet L. ..... Rogers, AR
Bledsoe, John A. ..... Laguna Niguel, CA
Bledsoe, John H. ..... Memphis, TN

Bledsoe, John P. ..... Portland, OR
Bledsoe, John W., III, P.A. ..... Hartsville, SC
Bledsoe, Louis A., III ..... Charlotte, NC
Bledsoe, Louis A., Jr. ..... Charlotte, NC
Bledsoe, Mark S. ..... Anchorage, AK
Bledsoe, Michael L. ..... Jackson, GA
Bledsoe, Michael N. ..... Chicago, IL
Bledsoe, Michael N., & Associates, Ltd.
Chicago, IL
Bledsoe, Monalie E.
Merit Systems Protection Board, Office of Appeals Counsel, GV
Bledsoe, Murff F. ..... Belton, TX
Bledsoe, Philip W. ..... Kansas City, MO
Bledsoe, Robert C. ..... Midland, TX
Bledsoe, Robert T. ..... San Jose, CA
Bledsoe, Schmidt, Lippes, Moonly & Roberson, P.A. ..... Jacksonville, FL
Bledsoe, Stephen M. ..... Kansas City, MO
Bledsoe, Stephen V. ..... Jacksonville, FL
Bledsoe, Steven E. ..... Los Angeles, CA
Bledsoe, Steven R. ..... Kansas City, MO
Bledsoe, Susan G. ..... Chicago, IL
Bledsoe, Terry L., P.A., Law Offices of, The
Altamonte Springs, FL
Orlando, FL
Bledsoe, Terry Lytle
Altamonte Springs, FL
Bledsoe, Thos. D., Jr. ..... San Angelo, TX
Bledsoe, William F. ..... Highland Park, MI
Bledstein, I. Mark ..... Encino, CA
Bledstein & Lauber ..... Encino, CA
Blee, Janette M. ..... Washington, DC
Blee, Michael G. ..... St. Cloud, MN
Blee, Michael J. ..... Atlantic City, NJ
Blee, Michael T. ..... Fort Wayne, IN
Blee & Reep, P.A. ..... St. Cloud, MN
Blee, Thomas J. ..... Fort Wayne, IN
Bleecker, Anne Frances ..... Charleston, SC
Bleecker, Anne Frances, LLC, Law Offices
Charleston, SC
Bleecker & Bleecker ..... Rockville, MD
Bleecker, Brodey & Andrews
Indianapolis, IN
Bleecker & Clarke, LLC ..... Charleston, SC
Bleecker, James S., Jr. ..... Sacramento, CA
Bleecker, John M., Jr. ..... Charleston, SC
Bleecker, Kathryn A. ..... Department of Justice, Civil Division, GV
Bleecker, Lloyd M. ..... Massapequa, NY
Bleecker, Lorin H. ..... Cabin John, MD
Bleecker, Rebecca Ryder ..... Rockville, MD
Bleecker, Renaud T. ..... New York, NY
Bleecker, Stanley A. ..... Providence, RI
Bleecker, Steven S. ..... Rockville, MD
Bleeke & Associates ..... Fort Wayne, IN
Bleeke, James F. ..... Indianapolis, IN
Bleeke, Richard Ray ..... Fort Wayne, IN
Bleeker, Douglas R. ..... Mitchell, SD
Bleeker, Harry M. ..... Great Bend, KS
Bleeker, Ronald A. ..... Fairfax, VA
Bleemendaal, Susan V. ..... Tampa, FL
Bleemer, Russell E. ..... Newark, NJ
Blees, Jonathan ..... Sacramento, CA
Blefeld, Bruce A. ..... Houston, TX
Blegen, Bryce C. ..... Broadview, IL
Blegen, Daniel Eric ..... Kansas City, MO
Blegen, Douglas A. ..... Mequon, WI
Blegen, Douglas A., S.C. ..... Mequon, WI
Blegen, Jon A. ..... Rio Vista, CA
Blegen-McCoy, Leanne E. ..... Elgin, IL
Blehart, Bruce D. ..... Chicago, IL
Blehm, Mark A. ..... Russell, KS
Blehr, Barbara Warner ..... Saugus, CA
Bleiberg, Charles M. ..... New York, NY
Bleiberg, Isadore C. ..... Brooklyn, NY
Bleiberg, Richard Beverly ..... New York, NY
Bleiberg, Robert P. ..... Atlanta, GA
Bleiberg, Victoria L. ..... Palo Alto, CA
Bleich, Clifford G. ..... Tucson, AZ
Bleich, David L. ..... New York, NY
Bleich, Donald L. ..... St. Joseph, MI
Bleich, E. Joseph ..... Ruston, LA
Bleich, Eva Helena ..... Westmont, NJ
Philadelphia, PA
Bleich, Jeffrey L. ..... San Francisco, CA
Bleich, Joe ..... Monroe, LA
Bleich, Martin ..... Albany, NY
Bleich, Ronald ..... New Brunswick, NJ
Bleich, Sanford J. ..... Brooklyn, NY
Bleicher, Ann Goldstein ..... Wayne, NJ
Bleicher, Marianne Eliopoulos
San Mateo, CA
Bleicher, Paul Andrew ..... Albuquerque, NM
Bleicher, Richard D. ..... Berkeley Heights, NJ
Bleicher, Robert A. S. ..... San Francisco, CA
Bleicher, Samuel A. ..... Washington, DC
McLean, VA
Bleichert Lee, Maura ..... New York, NY
Bleichfeld, Howard S. ..... Washington, DC
Bleichman, Joshua N. ..... Inwood, NY
Bleichmar, Javier ..... New York, NY
Bleichner, Brad D. ..... Los Angeles, CA
Bleidorn, Melissa J. ..... Milwaukee, WI
Bleidt, John J. ..... Louisville, KY
Bleier, Arthur ..... Jamaica, NY
Bleier, Bradford A. ..... Folsom, CA
Bleier, Brenton A. ..... Folsom, CA
Bleier & Cox ..... Encino, CA
Los Angeles, CA
Bleier, Cyndi ..... Old Bridge, NJ
Bleier, David Scott ..... Brooklyn, NY
Bleier, Elizabeth A. ..... Encino, CA
Bleier Law Firm, The ..... Folsom, CA
Bleier, Lisa J. ..... Arlington, VA
Bleier, Michael E. ..... Pittsburgh, PA
Bleifer, Candace Connart
Los Angeles, CA

Bleifer, Craig B. ..... Morristown, NJ
New York, NY
Bleifer, Cynthia A. ..... Beverly Hills, CA
Bleifer, Paul E. ..... Fort Lee, NJ
Bleifer, Scott D. ..... Los Angeles, CA
Bleifuss, Edward L. ..... West Linn, OR
Bleifuss, Leslie Gregory ..... Lisle, IL
Bleikamp, Joan B. ..... Saratoga Springs, NY
Bleil, Charles M. ..... Fort Worth, TX
Bleil, Walter G. ..... Pittsburgh, PA
Bleiler, Charles A. ..... San Diego, CA
Bleiler, Charles A., A Professional Corp.
San Diego, CA
Bleiler, Susan Ann ..... Pensacola, FL
Bleimaier, John Kuhn ..... Princeton, NJ
Bleimaier, John Kuhn ..... Trenton, NJ
Bleiman, Wendy A. ..... Irvine, CA
Bleisch, Barbara D., Law Offices of
Clayton, MO
Bleisch, Barbara D., Law Offices of
St. Louis, MO
Bleisch, N. David ..... Cleveland, OH
Bleisch, William R. ..... Detroit, MI
Bleise, Bernhard Jürgen ..... Denver, CO
Bleiwas, Pamela B. ..... Ithaca, NY
Bleiwas, Victor ..... New York, NY
Bleiweis, Jerome L. ..... Albuquerque, NM
Bleiweiss, Irene
Federal Communications Commission, Mass Media Bureau, GV
Bleiweiss, Shell J. ..... Chicago, IL
Blejec, Ivan F., Jr. ..... New York, NY
Blejwas, David I. ..... New York, NY
Blek, Charles L., Jr. ..... Laguna Hills, CA
Blek, Scott W. ..... Burbank, CA
Blen, Berta A. ..... Los Angeles, CA
Blencowe, Paul S. ..... Los Angeles, CA
Blend, Julie Edwards ..... Dallas, TX
Blend Law Firm, The, A Professional Corporation ..... Dallas, TX
Blend, Maryann Faith ..... Decatur, GA
Blend, Robert M. ..... Dallas, TX
Blend, Stanley L. ..... San Antonio, TX
Blendell, Elizabeth A. ..... Los Angeles, CA
Blendell, James ..... Latham, NY
Blenden, Dick A. ..... Carlsbad, NM
Blenden Law Firm ..... Carlsbad, NM
Blenden Law Firm ..... Bedford, TX
Dallas, TX
Blenden, Lawrence P. ..... Union, NJ
Blenden, Mark P. ..... Bedford, TX
Dallas, TX
Blenden, Paul L. ..... Ocean Township, NJ
Blenden, Phil ..... Carlsbad, NM
Blender, Penny A. ..... Bensalem, PA
Blender, Richard P. ..... Paterson, NJ
Blenis, Bonnie A. ..... Rochester, NY
Blenke, John W., Jr. ..... Prospect Heights, IL
Blenkhorn, Amy E. ..... Bay Village, OH
Blenkhorn, Tamara ..... Tallahassee, FL
Blenko, Andrew W. ..... North Huntingdon, PA
Blenko, Walter J., Jr. ..... Pittsburgh, PA
Blenman and Netzloff ..... Birmingham, MI
Blenner, Stuart J. ..... Chicago, IL
Blenner, Walter W. ..... Palm Harbor, FL
Blenstroub, Rachael Ann ..... Eastman, GA
Blesch, Elizabeth J. ..... Atlanta, GA
Blesch, Robert W. ..... Phoenix, AZ
Blesener, Susan C. ..... Madison, WI
Bleser, Donald ..... Cincinnati, OH
Bleser, Rita E. ..... St. Louis, MO
Bleshman, Joseph M. ..... New York, NY
Blesi, Samuel D. ..... Department of Justice, Environment and Natural Resources Division, GV
Bleskoski, Karen A. ..... Syracuse, NY
Blesoff, Marc S. ..... Chicago, IL
Blessen, Richard P. ..... Chicago, IL
Blessey, Caroline M. ..... New Orleans, LA
Blessey, Gerald ..... Biloxi, MS
Gulfport, MS
Blessey, Gerald, & Associates ..... Biloxi, MS
Gulfport, MS
Blessey, Raymond L. ..... Los Angeles, CA
Blessey, Robert L. ..... New York, NY
Blessey, Walter J., IV ..... Ocean Springs, MS
Blessing, Alison K. ..... Liberty, MO
Blessing, Anne H. ..... Oakton, VA
Blessing, Cecile Fernandez ..... Orlando, FL
Blessing, David B. ..... Orlando, FL
Blessing, David G. ..... Monte Sereno, CA
Blessing, Donald C. ..... Farmville, VA
Blessing, Joan ..... Belle Mead, NJ
Blessing, Keven G. ..... Bernardsville, NJ
Blessing, Maribeth ..... Abington, PA
Blessing, Maribeth, LLC, Law Offices of
Abington, PA
Blessing, Peter H. ..... New York, NY
Blessing, Thomas J. ..... Ann Arbor, MI
Blessing, Thomas William
Indianapolis, IN
Blessing, Todd M. ..... Phoenix, AZ
Blessinger, Jeffrey M. ..... Baraboo, WI
Blessinger, Peter J. ..... New York, NY
Blessington, G. Michael, (P.C.)
Oklahoma City, OK
Blessington, John C. ..... Boston, MA
Blessington, Patrick J. ..... Norristown, PA
Blessington, Thomas J. ..... Moorestown, NJ
Philadelphia, PA
Blessis, Lisa Billy ..... Simsbury, CT
Blessum, A. Zane ..... Winterset, IA
Bletcher, Robert L. ..... Santa Barbara, CA
Blethen, Bailey W. ..... Mankato, MN
Blethen Gage & Krause ..... Mankato, MN
Blethen, Marilyn E. ..... Duncanville, TX
Bletsas, Charles ..... Chicago, IL
Bletter, Gloria A. ..... New York, NY

Bletzer & Bletzer, P.C. ....Brighton, MA
Bletzer, Conrad J. ....Brighton, MA
Bletzer, Conrad J., Jr. ....Brighton, MA
Bletzer, Curt F ....Brighton, MA
Bletzer, Kimberly A. ....Brighton, MA
Bleuel, Bartley S. ....Ventura, CA
Bleuel & Muirhead ....Ventura, CA
Bleuer, Keith T. ....Rochester, MN
Bleuler, Christina C. ....San Jose, CA
Blevans, Brandon R. ....Santa Rosa, CA
Blevans, Robert E. ....Napa, CA
Blevens, Ivan A. ....Seward, NE
Blevens, Robert I. ....Seward, NE
Blevins, Allen W. ....Knoxville, TN
Blevins, Beth A. ....Pine Bluff, AR
Blevins & Blevins, P.C. ....Dalton, GA
Blevins, Bryan O., Jr. ....Beaumont, TX
Blevins, Chesley N. ....Austin, TX
Blevins, Clifton D. ....San Diego, CA
Blevins & Costanza, P.A.
Southern Pines, NC
Blevins, David C. ....Independence, MO
Blevins, David J. ....Dalton, GA
Blevins, Dennis E. ....Nashville, TN
Blevins, Don W. ....Washington, DC
Blevins, F. Bryant ....Miami, FL
Blevins, Gary L. ....Oklahoma City, OK
Blevins, Hugh T., Jr. ....Dallas, TX
Blevins, J. Donald ....Washington, DC
Blevins, James B. ....Oklahoma City, OK
Blevins, Jeffrey A. ....Chicago, IL
Blevins, Jerome B. ....St. Petersburg, FL
Blevins, Jerry M. ....Montgomery, AL
Blevins, John ....Edmonton, KY
Blevins, John M. ....Anderson, IN
Blevins, John O. ....Yuba City, CA
Blevins Law Firm ....North Little Rock, AR
Blevins, Melissa J. ....Farmington, MO
Blevins, Michael D. ....Walnut Creek, CA
Blevins, Michael F. ....Salina, KS
Blevins, Michael W. ....Sayre, OK
Blevins, Nancy Nesbitt ....Pryor, OK
Blevins, Paul E. ....Elyria, OH
Blevins, Paul E. ....Pryor, OK
Blevins & Pietz, P.C. ....Independence, MO
Blevins, Sandra L. ....Indianapolis, IN
Blevins, Sheri H. ....Dalton, GA
Blevins & Sordahl, Inc. A Professional Corporation ....Pryor, OK
Blevins, Staci ....Los Angeles, CA
Blevins, Steven W. ....Southern Pines, NC
Blevins, Valerie J. ....Kansas City, MO
Blevins, William B. ....North Little Rock, AR
Blevins, William J. ....Knoxville, TN
Blevins, William Ward ....Flower Mound, TX
Blevit, Stephen D. ....Los Angeles, CA
Blew, John C. ....Chicago, IL
Blew, William B., III ....Oklahoma City, OK
Blewer, Edwin L., III ....Shreveport, LA
Blewer, Edwin L., Jr. ....Shreveport, LA
Blewer, Julie E. ....Shreveport, LA
Blewett, Alex ....Great Falls, MT
Blewett, Alexander (Zander), III
Great Falls, MT
Blewett & Allen-Garibaldi, Inc.
Stockton, CA
Blewett, Nancy Taylor ....Butler, PA
Blewett, Paul F. ....Ventura, CA
Blewett, Richard N. ....Buffalo, NY
Blewett, Robert N. ....Stockton, CA
Blewett, Ron T. ....Lewiston, ID
Blewitt, Dennis L. ....Boulder, CO
Blewitt, J. Justin, Jr. ....Los Angeles, CA
Blewitt, Thomas M. ....Scranton, PA
Blews, Scott G. ....Atlanta, GA
Blews, William F. ....St. Petersburg, FL
Blews, William F., P.A. ....St. Petersburg, FL
Bley, Barry H. ....Brier Hill, NY
Bley and Bley ....San Francisco, CA
Bley, Gail Potysman ....Chicago, IL
Bley, John L. ....Olympia, WA
Bley, Kenneth B. ....Los Angeles, CA
Bley, Lorin E. ....Austin, TX
Bley, Paul N. ....Department of Defense, Defense Legal Services Agency, GV
Bley & Pfeiffer, P.C. ....Columbia, MO
Bley, Stephen Bruce ....San Francisco, CA
Bley, Walter H., Jr. ....Columbia, MO
Bleyer and Bleyer ....Marion, IL
Murphysboro, IL
Bleyer, Brad K. ....Benton, IL
Bleyer, Brad K. ....Marion, IL
Bleyer, Brad K. ....Murphysboro, IL
Bleyer, James B. ....Marion, IL
Bleyer, Joseph A. ....Marion, IL
Bleyer, Kenneth A. ....Herrin, IL
Bleyer, Knute Rockne ....Marion, IL
Bleyhl, Philip L. ....Oak Harbor, WA
Bleyman, Anne ....Pittsboro, NC
Bleynat, Edward L., Jr. ....Asheville, NC
Bleznick, Jordan L. ....New York, NY
Bliablias, Dino D. ....Livingston, NJ
Blibaum, Samuel ....Towson, MD
Blicht, Steven M. ....Cliffside Park, NJ
Blick, C. Samuel ....Rancho Santa Fe, CA
Solana Beach, CA
Blick, C. Samuel ....San Diego, CA
Blick, Clayton L. ....Litchfield, CT
Blick, Edward A. ....Silver Spring, MD
Blick, Joseph A., Jr. ....Greenville, NC
Blick, Judith A. ....San Diego, CA
Blick, Stephen L. ....San Jose, CA
Blickensderfer, Charles Thomas ....Denver, CO
Blickensderfer, Matthew C. ....Chicago, IL
Blickensderfer, Michael C. ....Massapequa, NY
Blickensderfer, Patricia A. ....Eliot, ME
Blickenstaff, Dale A. ....Fresno, CA
Blickenstaff, David C. ....Chicago, IL
Blickenstaff, Jennifer A. ....Chicago, IL
Blickenstaff, Kathleen M.
Grandview Heights, OH
Blickenstaff, Kenneth L. ....Indianapolis, IN
Blickenstaff, Leslie S. ....Boston, MA
Blickenstaff, Scott D. ....San Francisco, CA
Blicker, David M. ....Sacramento, CA
Blicker and Manchee, P.L.L.C. ....Dallas, TX
Blicker, Zola B. ....Dallas, TX
Blickhan, Lawrence W. ....Quincy, IL
Blickman, Daniel R. ....New York, NY
Blickman, Michael A. ....Indianapolis, IN
Blickman, Neil J.
Federal Trade Commission, Bureau of Consumer Protection, GV
Blicksilver, Harvey ....Lantana, FL
Bliden, David S. ....Annapolis, MD
Blied, Timothy J. ....Irvine, CA
Blieden, Lawrence H. ....Phoenix, AZ
Blier, Carl J. ....Knoxville, TN
Blier, Teresa Sleppy ....Alexandria, VA
Blier, William M. ....Washington, DC
Bliesner, Lawrence D. ....Portland, OR
Bliessner, Diane M. ....Denver, CO
Bliessner, Edward J.
Greenwood Village, CO
Bligh, Jennifer Ilene ....San Antonio, TX
Bligh, Jennifer M. ....Phoenix, AZ
Bligh, Robert A. ....Lincoln, NE
Bligh, William J. ....Chicago, IL
Blight, Wendy R. ....Dallas, TX
Bliley, Paul S., Jr. ....Richmond, VA
Blim, John M. ....Chicago, IL
Blincoe, Elizabeth M.
Highland Heights, KY
Blincow, John K., Jr. ....Charleston, SC
Blindauer, Donald J. ....Middleton, WI
Blinder, Aaron I. ....Brooklyn, NY
Blinder, Albert A. ....New York, NY
Blinder, D. Lilah ....San Francisco, CA
Blinder, Henry D. ....Durham, NC
Blinder, Karen L. ....Newark, NJ
Blinder, Robert ....New York, NY
Blinder, Robert D. ....Encino, CA
Blinder, Steven P. ....Newton, MA
Blinderman, Barbara S. ....Los Angeles, CA
Blinderman, Harold M. ....Hartford, CT
Blinderman, Jonathan L.
Los Angeles, CA
Blinderman, Richard I. ....Miami, FL
Blinderman, Robert L. ....Amarillo, TX
Blindman, Stanley ....Scarsdale, NY
Bline, Ralph A. ....Sarasota, FL
Blink, Robert J. ....Des Moines, IA
Blinka, Caren E. ....Houston, TX
Blinken, Antony J.
Executive Office Of The President, National Security Council, GV
Blinken, Sally S. ....New York, NY
Blinkoff, Jeffrey L. ....Mineola, NY
Blinkoff, Michael M. ....Buffalo, NY
Blinkoff, Sharon A. ....Montclair, NJ
New York, NY
Blinks, Scott E. ....Chehalis, WA
Blinn, C. Duane ....Hartford, CT
Blinn, Daniel S. ....Rocky Hill, CT
Blinn, David L. ....San Francisco, CA
Blinn, Donald P. ....San Antonio, TX
Blinn, George A. ....Chelsea, AL
Blinn, James R., Jr. ....Yakima, WA
Blinn, Judith I. ....Lansing, MI
Blinn, Linda Segal ....Springfield, MA
Blinn, Marguerite E. ....Chicago, IL
Blinn, Mark A. ....Dallas, TX
Blinn, Peter C. ....Ocala, FL
Blinn, Robert O. ....Wichita, KS
Blinn, S. David ....Irvine, CA
Los Angeles, CA
Blinston, Steven C. ....Winter Park, FL
Blinstrub, Ralph W. ....Kansas City, MO
Blinstrub, Robert L. ....Birmingham, MI
Blischak, John W. ....Phoenix, AZ
Blischak, Matthew P. ....Alexandria, VA
Blischak, Michael ....Steubenville, OH
Blish & Cavanagh ....Providence, RI
Blish, John H. ....Providence, RI
Blish, Nelson A. ....Rochester, NY
Blisko, Larry ....Elmont, NY
Bliss, Albert A. ....New York, NY
Bliss, Amy ....Dubuque, IA
Bliss, Bradford F. K. ....Honolulu, HI
Bliss, Charles R. ....Atlanta, GA
Bliss, Daniel H. ....Troy, MI
Bliss, Deborah Pike
North Little Rock, AR
Bliss, Dennis L. ....Trenton, NJ
Bliss, Donald T., Jr. ....Washington, DC
Bliss, Erik S. ....San Diego, CA
Bliss, F. Allen ....Boston, MA
Bliss, Harold J., Jr. ....Phoenix, AZ
Bliss, Harold J., Jr. ....Scottsdale, AZ
Bliss, Herbert J. ....Valhalla, NY
Bliss, Homer A. C., P.A. ....Jacksonville, FL
Bliss, Homer A.C. ....Jacksonville, FL
Bliss & Hoty-Bliss ....Cleveland, OH
Bliss, Ina N. ....Los Angeles, CA
Bliss, James I. ....Bloomington, IL
Bliss, James R. ....Stamford, CT
Bliss, James W. ....Lansing, MI
Bliss, Janet H. ....Lake Placid, NY
Bliss, Jason J. ....Mesa, AZ
Bliss, John E. ....Wausau, WI
Bliss, John Gerard ....White Plains, NY
Bliss, John M. ....Wausau, WI
Bliss, Judith A. ....Cleveland, OH
Bliss, Lisa Radtke ....Atlanta, GA
Bliss, Loa Elaine ....Newton, MA
Bliss, Mary Ellen ....Rockville, MD
Bliss McGlynn, P.C. ....Detroit, MI
Troy, MI
Bliss, Michael D. ....Boston, MA
Bliss, Michael E. ....Washington, DC
Bliss, Patrick J. ....White Plains, NY
Bliss, Raymond C. ....Wethersfield, CT
Bliss, Richard E. ....Philadelphia, PA
Pittsburgh, PA
Bliss, Richard H. ....New York, NY
Bliss, Richard J. ....Milwaukee, WI
Bliss, Richard W. ....Washington, DC
Bliss, Robert C. ....North Attleboro, MA
Bliss, Robert Harms ....Dallas, TX
Dallas, TX
Bliss, Ronald G. ....Houston, TX
Bliss, Ronald L. ....Anchorage, AK
Bliss, Shirlee L. ....Burbank, CA
Bliss, T. Stevens ....Danbury, CT
Bliss, Thomas P. ....Cleveland, OH
Bliss, Vanessa L. ....Buffalo, NY
Bliss, Victoria ....Yucca Valley, CA
Bliss, Walter R., Jr. ....Princeton, NJ
Bliss & Wilkens, LLC ....Anchorage, AK
Blissard, Judith M. ....Houston, TX
Blissard, Louis B. ....Kaunakakai, HI
Blissert, Jane A. ....Los Angeles, CA
Blissett, Frances ....North Miami Beach, FL
Blissman, Bruce W. ....East McKeesport, PA
Blissman, Geo. C., Jr. ....East McKeesport, PA
Blissman, Scott ....Media, PA
Blitch, Anne Lindgren ....Atlanta, GA
Blitch, Brooks E., III ....Homerville, GA
Blitch, Elizabeth P. ....New Orleans, LA
Blitch, James Daniel, IV ....Rome, GA
Blitch, Joseph E. ....Orlando, FL
Blitch, Stephen G. ....Oakland, CA
Blitch, Susan K. ....Oakland, CA
Blitenthal, Ronald J. ....Chicago, IL
Blitman, Bruce Alan ....Pembroke Pines, FL
Blitman, Charles E. ....Syracuse, NY
Blitman and King LLP ....Albany, NY
Rochester, NY
Syracuse, NY
Blitman, Lisa H ....New York, NY
Blits, Marie Corlett ....San Francisco, CA
Blitshtein, Iriana ....Huntingdon Valley, PA
Blitshtein & Weiss, A Prof. Corp., Law Offices of ....Huntingdon Valley, PA
Blitstein, Lee A. ....Woodland Hills, CA
Blitstein, Lori P. ....Chicago, IL
Blitstein, Sherwood E. ....Chicago, IL
Blitstien, Lori S. ....Los Angeles, CA
Blittner, David M. ....New York, NY
Blitz, Alvin H. ....Harrisburg, PA
Blitz, Arthur ....New York, NY
Blitz, Arthur H. ....Bethesda, MD
Blitz, Bert A. ....New York, NY
Blitz & Blitz, P.A. ....Owings Mills, MD
Blitz, Brian A. ....Owings Mills, MD
Blitz, C. Akin ....Portland, OR
Blitz, Eric J. ....Lutherville, MD
Blitz, Gary P. ....Washington, DC
Blitz, Herman ....Bronx, NY
Blitz & Humphreys ....North Bergen, NJ
Blitz, James S. ....Washington, DC
Blitz, Jeffrey S. ....Mays Landing, NJ
Blitz, Jeffrey W. ....Montgomery, AL
Blitz, Marcy G. ....Boca Raton, FL
Blitz, Nelson ....Fairfax, VA
Blitz, Robert ....North Bergen, NJ
Blitz, Robert D. ....St. Louis, MO
Blitz, Robert H. ....Laguna Hills, CA
Blitz, Sandra J. ....New York, NY
Blitz, Scott E. ....Owings Mills, MD
Blitz, Stephen M. ....Denver, CO
Blitz, William J. ....Eugene, OR
Blitzer, Carol A. N. ....Baton Rouge, LA
Blitzer, Christine B. ....New Orleans, LA
Blitzer, Craig M. ....Eden, NC
Blitzer, Daniel S. ....Mount Laurel, NJ
Blitzer, Julie C. ....Princeton, NJ
Blitzer, Sidney M., Jr. ....Baton Rouge, LA
Blitzman, Jay David ....Boston, MA
Blivaiss, David H. ....New York, NY
Bliven, Mark A. ....Dallas, OR
Bliwas, Stuart M. ....Harrisburg, PA
Bliwise, Lester M. ....New York, NY
Bliwise, Matthew S. ....New York, NY
Blix, Fay ....Laguna Hills, CA
Blixseth, Stephen R. ....Eugene, OR
Blixt, Charles A. ....Winston-Salem, NC
Blixt, Gerald ....Colorado Springs, CO
Blizard & Blizard ....Middletown, NY
Blizard, F. Daniel, III ....Middletown, NY
Blizard, Frank D., Jr. ....Middletown, NY
Blizard, Janet L. ....Department of Justice, Civil Rights Division, GV
Blizman, Paul J. ....Farmington Hills, MI
Bliznik, Mary Ann ....Batavia, NY
Blizzard, Edward F. ....Houston, TX
Blizzard, George D., II ....Madison, WV
Blizzard, Henry W. ....Athens, AL
Blizzard, Henry Wallace, III ....Decatur, AL
Blizzard, Joseph ....Houston, TX
Blizzard, Kathleen L. ....Tallahassee, FL
Blizzard & McCarthy, L.L.P.
Houston, TX
Blizzard, Patricia A. ....St. Petersburg, FL
Blizzard, Susan J. ....Atlanta, GA
Blizzard, Thadd A. ....Sacramento, CA
Bloch, Alan N. ....Pittsburgh, PA
Bloch, Anne C. ....Philadelphia, PA
Bloch, Barry H. ....Raleigh, NC
Bloch, Beate ....Washington, DC
Bloch, Beverly J. ....Anaheim, CA
Bloch, Bruce E. ....Miami, FL
Bloch, Bruce M. ....New York, NY
Bloch, Carolyn J. ....Pittsburgh, PA
Bloch, Charles Bennett ....New York, NY
Bloch, David A. ....Belleville, IL
Bloch, David J. ....Washington, DC
Bloch, David P. ....Department of Justice, Tax Division, GV
Bloch, David S. ....Palo Alto, CA
Bloch, Denise H. ....St. Louis, MO
Bloch, Donald M. ....Boston, MA
Bloch, Edward S. ....Scotch Plains, NJ
Bloch, Elizabeth G. (Heidi) ....Austin, TX
Bloch, Emily A. ....Portland, ME
Bloch, Evan A. ....Pittsburgh, PA
Bloch, Frank S. ....Nashville, TN
Bloch, Gerald D. ....Aliso Viejo, CA
Bloch, Gerald J. ....Milwaukee, WI
Bloch, Helen Iris ....Salem, OR
Bloch, Howard A. ....Rochester, NY
Bloch, Israel ....Swampscott, MA
Bloch, James J.
Pension Benefit Guaranty Corporation, Other Lawyers in Staff or Executive Positions, GV
Bloch, Janine D. ....San Francisco, CA
Bloch, Jason E. ....Miami, FL
Bloch, Jeffrey M. ....Jersey City, NJ
Bloch, Jeffrey P.
Federal Deposit Insurance Corporation, Resolutions Section, GV
Bloch, Jonathan, (P.C.) ....Los Angeles, CA
Bloch, Kate E. ....San Francisco, CA
Bloch, Kathleen Borrero ....Palo Alto, CA
Bloch, Kenneth A. ....Seattle, WA
Bloch, Laura J. ....San Francisco, CA
Bloch, Leo D. ....Seattle, WA
Bloch, Leon E., Jr. ....Kansas City, MO
Bloch, Linda E. ....Bloomfield Hills, MI
Bloch, Marc J. ....Cleveland, OH
Bloch, Marla R. ....New York, NY
Bloch, Matthew D. ....New York, NY
Bloch, Meric Craig ....Basking Ridge, NJ
Bloch, Michael F. ....Maitland, FL
Bloch & Minerley, P.L. ....Boca Raton, FL
Bloch, Mitchell J. ....Beverly Hills, CA
Bloch, Mitchell R. ....New York, NY
Bloch, Norman A. ....New York, NY
New York, NY
Bloch, Norman L. ....Chicago, IL
Bloch, Pamela S. ....Omaha, NE
Bloch, Patricia Kathleen ....Corona, CA
Bloch, Peter B.
Nuclear Regulatory Commission, Atomic Safety and Licensing Board Panel, GV
Bloch, Peter M.
Department of Transportation, Office of the General Counsel, GV
Bloch, Peter M. ....New York, NY
Bloch, Randal S. ....Cincinnati, OH
Bloch, Richard ....Towson, MD
Bloch, Richard I. ....Washington, DC
Bloch, Robert E. ....Washington, DC
Bloch, Robert E. ....Chicago, IL
Bloch, Ronald A. ....Washington, DC
Bloch, Sandra A. ....Philadelphia, PA
Bloch, Scott J. ....Lawrence, KS
Bloch, Stanley E. ....New York, NY
Bloch, Stefanie Z. ....Camden, NJ
Philadelphia, PA
Bloch, Steven ....Omaha, NE
Bloch, Steven L. ....New York, NY
Bloch, Stuart E. ....Boca Raton, FL
Bloch, Susan E. ....San Francisco, CA
Bloch, Susan Low ....Washington, DC
Bloch, Thomas P. ....Boston, MA
Bloch, William W. ....Beverly Hills, CA
Blocher, Arch C., Jr. ....Carrollton, TX
Blocher, Del A. ....Bayport, MN
Hastings, MN
Blocher, James A. ....Harrisburg, PA
Blocher, Joseph P. ....Silver Spring, MD
Blocher, Lawrence R. ....Santa Monica, CA
Blocher, Mark D. ....Cincinnati, OH
Blocher, Nelson David ....Chicago, IL
Block, Adam K. ....River Edge, NJ
Block, A. J., Jr. ....Atlanta, GA
Block, Alan B. ....Buffalo, NY
Block, Alan D. ....Torrance, CA
Block, Alan F. ....Chicago, IL
Block, Alan M. ....Boston, MA
Block, Alan P. ....Los Angeles, CA
Block, Alan Robert ....Los Angeles, CA
Block, Alan Robert, A Prof. Corp., Law Offices of ....Los Angeles, CA
Block, Alan S. ....Washington, DC
Fairfax, VA
Block, Albert W., Jr. ....Monroe, LA
Block, Alvin L. ....Napa, CA
Block, Alvin W., & Associates ....Chicago, IL
Block, Alvin W., & Associates
Waukegan, IL
Wheaton, IL
Block, Andrew A. ....Chicago, IL
Block, Andrew David ....Birmingham, AL
Block, Andrew T. ....Norwalk, CT
Block, Ann ....Mineola, NY
Block, Ann E. ....Sacramento, CA
Block, Annemarie Harris ....Miami, FL
Block, Arnold S. ....Philadelphia, PA
Block, Arthur R. ....New York, NY
Block, Arthur R. ....Philadelphia, PA
Block, Arthur S. ....Palm Springs, CA
Block and Associates, Ltd., A Professional Corporation ....Monroe, LA
Block & Balestri, P.C. ....Addison, TX
Dallas, TX
Block, Barry H. ....Forest Hills, NY
Block, Barry M. ....Dayton, OH
Block, Bernard N. ....Chicago, IL

Block, Beth S. .... **Shrewsbury, NJ**
New York, NY
Block & Bouterie .... **Thibodaux, LA**
Block, Bradford E. .... **Deerfield, IL**
Block, Bradley S. .... Oak Brook, IL
Block, Brandon A. .... **Miami, FL**
Block, Bret L. .... **Atlanta, GA**
Block, Brian T. .... Culver City, CA
Block, Bruce A. .... **Cleveland, OH**
Block, Bruce D. .... **Baltimore, MD**
Block, Bruce H. .... Chicago, IL
Block, Bruce T. .... **Milwaukee, WI**
Block, Byron B. .... **Tallahassee, FL**
Block Caron & Lyon .... **Deerfield, IL**
Block, Carrie .... **Irvine, CA**
Block, Cathy Wintersteen .... Joliet, IL
Block, Charles J. .... Voorhees, NJ
Block, Charles J. .... **New York, NY**
Block, Cheryl D. .... Washington, DC
Block, Christine Cooper .... **Washington, DC**
Block, Christopher B. .... Livingston, NJ
Block, Clem H. .... Louisville, KY
Block, CLifford P. .... Little Rock, AR
Block & Colucci, P.C. .... **Jupiter, FL**
Buffalo, NY
Clifton Park, NY
Rochester, NY
Block, Craig E. .... Ankeny, IA
Block, Cristobel .... Norfolk, VA
Block, Crouch, Keeter & Huffman, L.L.P.
Wilmington, NC
Block, Daniel .... Waterloo, IA
Block, Daniel J. .... **Pearl River, NY**
Block, David B. .... **Huntsville, AL**
Block, David E. .... **Miami, FL**
Block, David J. .... **San Francisco, CA**
Block, Deborah S. .... Oklahoma City, OK
Block, Debra S. .... Boca Raton, FL
Block, Debra S. .... Annapolis, MD
Block, Dennis E. .... Berlin, NJ
Block, Dennis H. .... Glenview, IL
Block, Dennis J. .... **New York, NY**
Block, Devon W. .... **Los Angeles, CA**
Block, Dirk V., (P.C.) .... **Omaha, NE**
Block, Donald B. .... Phoenix, AZ
Block, Donald V. .... Panorama City, CA
Block, Donna .... Rosemead, CA
Block, Edward J. .... **Kenosha, WI**
Block, Edward M. .... Las Vegas, NV
Block, Edward T. .... Spokane, WA
Block, Elaine .... Houston, TX
Block, Elaine L. .... Washington, DC
Block, Eli .... Venice, FL
Block, Elizabeth .... New York, NY
Block, Elizabeth Cooper .... Baltimore, MD
Block, Ellen G. .... **Washington, DC**
Block, Ellen Sue .... **Miami, FL**
Block, Elliott J. .... Corona Del Mar, CA
Block, Emil H. .... Springfield, NJ
Block, Fern H .... **New York, NY**
Block, Franklin L. .... **Wilmington, NC**
Block, Frederic .... Brooklyn, NY
Block, Frederick E.
Department of Housing and Urban Development,
Office of General Counsel, GV
Block, Frederick H. .... New York, NY
Block, Frederick L. .... Brooklyn, NY
Block, Gary E. .... Washington, DC
Block, Gary R. .... West Chester, PA
Block, Geoffrey A. .... Sparta, NJ
Block, Gerald .... Garden Grove, CA
Block, Gerald J. .... Lafayette, LA
Block, Greg M. .... Moraga, CA
Block, Gregory A. .... **Grand Rapids, MI**
Block, Gus .... **Houston, TX**
Block, Hal G. .... **Costa Mesa, CA**
Block, Harold D., Law Office of
Milwaukee, WI
Block, Harold M. .... **Thibodaux, LA**
Block, Harold Paul .... Las Vegas, NV
Block, Harry .... New York, NY
Block, Howard .... Liberty, NY
Block, Howard S. .... Tustin, CA
Block, Ilene Goldman
Department of Justice,
Antitrust Division, GV
Block, Ilene Goldstein .... Sacramento, CA
Block, Ira H. .... Moonachie, NJ
Block, Irwin J. .... **Miami, FL**
Block, J. Randolph .... Chicago, IL
Block, Jack .... Miami, FL
Block, Jack L. .... **Chicago, IL**
Block, Janet .... Florham Park, NJ
Block, Janice L. .... Chicago, IL
Block, Jason .... **New York, NY**
Block, Jay Irwin .... Westminster, MD
Block, Jay Sherman .... Columbia, MD
Block, Jeffrey A. .... New York, NY
Block, Jeffrey B. .... **Philadelphia, PA**
Block, Jeffrey C. .... **Boston, MA**
Block, Jennifer Y. .... New York, NY
Block, Jerald P. .... **Thibodaux, LA**
Block, Jerold M. .... Massapequa, NY
Block, Jerome H. .... Appleton, WI
Block, Jessica .... **Boston, MA**
Block, Jill D. .... **New York, NY**
Block, Jocelyn .... Camden, NJ
Block, Joel Jay .... Morton Grove, IL
Block, Jonathan A. .... **Portland, ME**
Block, Jonathan David .... **Detroit, MI**
Block, Jonathan L. .... Camarillo, CA
Block, Jonathan M. .... **Palo Alto, CA**
Block, Joseph D. .... Los Angeles, CA
Block, Joseph G. .... **Washington, DC**
Block, Julian .... Larchmont, NY
Block, Julie A. .... Brooklyn, NY
Block, Julie Thalen .... New Haven, CT

Block, Justin M. .... Mineola, NY
Block, Karen J. .... Ventura, CA
Block, Karl E. .... **Los Angeles, CA**
Block, Keith .... **Denver, CO**
Portland, OR
Block, Kenneth J. .... Santa Ana, CA
Block, Kenneth L. .... Los Angeles, CA
Block, Kenneth L. .... Chicago, IL
Block, Kenneth M. .... **New York, NY**
Block, Kevin P. .... Napa, CA
Block, Krockey, Cernugel and Cowgill, P.C.
Chicago, IL
Joliet, IL
Block, Lance J., Jr. .... **West Palm Beach, FL**
Block & Landsman .... **Chicago, IL**
Block, Lauren .... New York, NY
Block, Lawrence P. .... **Washington, DC**
Block, Lawrence, (P.C.) .... **Chicago, IL**
Block Lepore Sanders, LLP .... Atlanta, GA
Block, Leslie F. .... Phoenix, AZ
Block, Lonny R. .... **New York, NY**
Block, Lynn .... **Fargo, ND**
Block, Manfred S. .... **Norfolk, VA**
Block, Marc C. .... Tustin, CA
Block, Marc Sandy .... Thornwood, NY
Block, Marcene B. .... Little Rock, AR
Block, Marian S. .... Bethesda, MD
Block, Mark A. .... San Diego, CA
Block, Mark A. .... **Atlanta, GA**
Block, Mark B. .... Portland, OR
Block, Mark E. .... **Norwich, CT**
Block, Mark L. .... **Los Angeles, CA**
Block Markus Williams, L.L.C.
Denver, CO
Portland, OR
Cheyenne, WY
Block, Martha A. .... Fort Lauderdale, FL
Block, Martha Magee .... Royersford, PA
Block, Martin .... Mineola, NY
Block, Marvin I. .... Merchantville, NJ
Philadelphia, PA
Block, Mary Anne Kinney
Hoffman Estates, IL
Block, Matthew A. .... **Atlanta, GA**
Block, Matthew F. .... **Thibodaux, LA**
Block, Maureen Shaughnessy
San Francisco, CA
Block, Max .... Westhampton Beach, NY
Block, Max, Jr. .... New York, NY
Block, Michael .... Merrick, NY
Block, Michael D. .... **Joliet, IL**
Block, Michael J. .... **Haddonfield, NJ**
Philadelphia, PA
Block, Michael L. .... **Philadelphia, PA**
Block, Michael N. .... Hackensack, NJ
Mineola, NY
New York, NY
Block, Mitchell J. .... Los Angeles, CA
Block, Mitchell S. .... **Atlanta, GA**
Block, Nancy J. .... **New York, NY**
Block, Neal J. .... **Chicago, IL**
Block, Neil M. .... Northport, NY
Block, Nelson R. .... **Houston, TX**
Block and New .... West Chester, PA
Block, Noah .... New York, NY
Block, Norman L. .... Walled Lake, MI
Ypsilanti, MI
Block, Norman M. .... Hawthorne, NY
Block, Norman M., P.C. .... Hawthorne, NY
Block, Osofsky & Berkowitz .... Torrance, CA
Block, Patricia K. .... Columbus, OH
Block, Patrick L. .... **Portland, OR**
Block, Paul S. .... New York, NY
Block, Paula .... Basking Ridge, NJ
Block, Philip M. .... Hartford, CT
Block, Phyllis Shuster
North Palm Beach, FL
Block, Ralph L. .... Los Angeles, CA
Block, Randall D. .... **Dallas, TX**
Block, Randall G. .... **San Francisco, CA**
Block, Rebecca W. .... **Birmingham, AL**
Block, Richard A. .... **Tucson, AZ**
Block, Richard A. .... **Encino, CA**
Block, Richard A. .... Los Altos Hills, CA
Block, Richard A. .... **Westlake Village, CA**
Block, Richard A. .... **Woodland Hills, CA**
Block, Richard H. .... **New York, NY**
Block, Richard J. .... Tarrytown, NY
Block, Richard L. .... Anchorage, AK
Block, Richard L. .... Hartsdale, NY
Scarsdale, NY
Block, Richard M. .... New York, NY
Block, Richard R. .... Philadelphia, PA
Block, Robert C. .... Platteville, WI
Block, Robert C., Law Offices
Platteville, WI
Block, Robert G. .... Cincinnati, OH
Block, Robert H. .... Chicago, IL
Block, Robert N. .... Los Angeles, CA
Block, Ronald M. .... Barrington, NJ
Block, Ronald S. .... Stafford, TX
Block, S. Lester .... Princeton, NJ
Block, Samuel A. .... Vero Beach, FL
Block, Samuel A., P.A. .... Vero Beach, FL
Block, Samuel B. .... Washington, DC
Block, Samuel P. .... Long Beach, CA
Block, Seymour & Samson, S.C.
Appleton, WI
Block, Sharon D. .... Philadelphia, PA
Block, Sharon I.
National Labor Relations Board,
Office of the General Counsel, GV
Block, Simon .... **New York, NY**
Block, Sondra Harans .... **Rockville, MD**
Block, Stanley B. .... **Chicago, IL**
Block, Stanley H. .... Baltimore, MD
Block, Stephen A. .... New York, NY
Block, Stephen H. .... New York, NY

Block, Stephen Hale .... **Atlanta, GA**
Block, Stephen Jay .... Chicago, IL
Block, Stephen M. .... Washington, DC
Block, Stephen M. .... **Houston, TX**
Block, Steven A., The Law Office of
Sacramento, CA
Block, Steven C. .... Kansas City, MO
Block, Steven H. .... Towson, MD
Block, Steven H. .... Dallas, TX
Block, Steven J. .... Kansas City, MO
Block, Steven P. .... **Mineola, NY**
Block, Steven R. .... **Addison, TX**
Block, Steven W. .... **Seattle, WA**
Block, Stewart A.
Federal Communications Commission,
Office of the General Counsel, GV
Block, Stuart I. .... **San Francisco, CA**
Block, Susan .... Clayton, MO
Block, Susan C. .... Washington, DC
Block, Suzanne A. .... **Kansas City, MO**
Block, Teri L. .... **Gold River, CA**
Block, Timothy M. .... **Chicago, IL**
Block, Walter S. .... La Crosse, WI
Block, Wayne B. .... **Miami, FL**
Block, Wendy H. .... Boulder, CO
Block, William C. .... Dallas, TX
Block, William H. .... **Seattle, WA**
Block, William K. .... **New York, NY**
Block, Winston J. .... **Joliet, IL**
Blocker, Adrienne S. .... High Point, NC
Blocker, Brad W. .... **Redwood City, CA**
Blocker, Chad C. .... **New York, NY**
Blocker, Denise Savoie .... Portola Valley, CA
San Francisco, CA
Blocker, Edward M. .... **Tarrytown, NY**
Blocker, Mark B. .... **Chicago, IL**
Blocker, Mikel R. .... Springdale, AR
Blocker, Robert L. .... Decatur, GA
Blocker, Walter L., III .... Birmingham, AL
Blocker, Wendy J. .... Woodbourne, NY
Blockhus, Victoria McBride .... San Jose, CA
Blockinger, Jeffrey C. .... **Washington, DC**
Block-Lieb, Susan .... Newark, NJ
Blockman, Arnold F. .... Urbana, IL
Blockovich, Brian .... Chicago, IL
Blockson, Taua Jenielle .... Baltimore, MD
Blockwick, Craig N. .... Boulder, CO
Blodgett & Blodgett, P.C. .... **Boston, MA**
Worcester, MA
Blodgett, Bryan E. .... Medford, OR
Blodgett, D. Bradley .... **Springfield, IL**
Blodgett, Donald E. .... Rock Falls, IL
Blodgett, Gerry A. .... **Worcester, MA**
Blodgett, Henry D. .... Dallas, TX
Blodgett, J. Kevin .... **Houston, TX**
Blodgett, James A. .... Newport Beach, CA
Blodgett, James N. .... Boston, MA
Blodgett, Jotham T. .... St. Paul, MN
Blodgett, Kimberly .... **Louisville, KY**
Blodgett, Lester W. .... Redwood City, CA
Blodgett, Lisa H. .... **Oklahoma City, OK**
Blodgett, Makechnie & Vetne
Peterborough, NH
Blodgett, Mary .... **Los Angeles, CA**
Blodgett, Maurice M. .... Peterborough, NH
Blodgett, Peter S. .... Watertown, NY
Blodgett, Stephen S. .... Burlington, VT
Blodgett, Thomas W. .... Irvine, CA
Blodgett, Timothy P. .... **Rochester, NY**
Blodgett, Verne E. .... Bloomfield, CT
Blodgett, Watts & Volk, P.C. .... Burlington, VT
Blodgett, William A. .... Duluth, MN
Blodgett, William A., Jr. .... **Louisville, KY**
Blodgett, William L. .... Treasury Department,
Internal Revenue Service, GV
Blodgett-Ford, Sayoko .... Redmond, WA
Blodig, Gregory John
Fort Lauderdale, FL
Blodinger, Robt. H. .... Charlottesville, VA
Blodnick, Edward K. .... Jericho, NY
Blodnick, Gordon, Blodnick & Zelin
Jericho, NY
Blodnick, Peter L. .... Jericho, NY
Bloedel, Ellen H. .... Salt Lake City, UT
Bloedel, Kurt R. .... New York, NY
Bloedorn, Cathleen A. .... **Chicago, IL**
Bloedorn, Philip E. .... Milwaukee, WI
Bloedorn, Robert E. .... West Columbia, SC
Bloem, Gordon M. .... Mount Pleasant, MI
Bloem, James H. .... Allegan, MI
Bloemendaal, Dirk C., Jr. .... **Ada, MI**
Bloemer, Donna M. .... **Cincinnati, OH**
Bloemers, Ralph O. .... **Portland, OR**
Bloemker, Clyde H. .... Louisville, KY
Bloemker, R. William .... Kansas City, MO
Bloemker, Russell K. .... Lincoln, NE
Bloemsma, Michiel A. .... **New York, NY**
Bloesch, Calvin Paul .... Belleville, IL
Bloesch, Jeffrey M. .... Calumet City, IL
Bloese, Kevin William .... Wheaton, IL
Bloeser, Philip .... Woodland Hills, CA
Bloethe, Orville W. .... Victor, IA
Bloethe - Van Zee Law Office .... Victor, IA
Bloetscher, Carl, III .... Detroit, MI
Blofelo, Leah Tuffanelli .... Novato, CA
Blofield, Tiffany A. .... **Minneapolis, MN**
St. Paul, MN
Bloh, Dennis M. .... Bala Cynwyd, PA
Bloh, Timothy J. .... **Philadelphia, PA**
Blohm, D. Randall .... Minneapolis, MN
Blohm, Dori S. .... **Tulsa, OK**
Blohm, Helen Marinak .... San Francisco, CA
Blohm, Kenneth E. .... **San Francisco, CA**
Blohm, Linda E. .... Department of Commerce,
Patent and Trademark Office, GV
Blohowiak, Bruce J. .... Spokane, WA
Bloink, Robin L. .... **Summit, NJ**
Blois, Marsden S. .... San Jose, CA

Bloise, John R. .... Painted Post, NY
Bloise, Michael .... **Washington, DC**
Bloksberg, Frank D. .... Nevada City, CA
Blom, Brenda Bratton .... Baltimore, MD
Blom, Daniel C. .... **Seattle, WA**
Blom, David E. .... New Berlin, WI
Blom, Deborah A. .... Wilmington, DE
Blomberg, Alfred A. .... Mount Clemens, MI
Blomberg, Anderson, Moore & Bahorski, P.C. .... **Mount Clemens, MI**
Blomberg, Elizabeth A. .... **Palo Alto, CA**
Blomberg, Jeffrey A. .... **Stamford, CT**
Blomberg, Jill Heitler .... New York, NY
Blomberg, Philip D. .... Chicago, IL
Blomberg, Steven T. .... **Gaithersburg, MD**
Blomberg, Thomas G., Jr.
San Francisco, CA
Blome, Donald A. ....
Department of State, GV
Blome, William H. .... North Palm Beach, FL
Blome, William O.
Federal Energy Regulatory Commission,
Office of the General Counsel, GV
Blomeley, James L., Jr. .... **Murphy, NC**
Blomer, Philip J. .... Cincinnati, OH
Blomerth & Payne .... Lockhart, TX
Blomerth, Todd .... Lockhart, TX
Blomgren, Douglas C. .... **Portland, OR**
Blomgren, Gilbert E. .... **Columbus, OH**
Blomgren, James Q. .... Oskaloosa, IA
Blomkalns, Andy .... New Orleans, LA
Blomme, Edward J. .... **Minneapolis, MN**
Blommel, Denise M. .... Mesa, AZ
Blomo, James Thomas .... Phoenix, AZ
Blomquist, Claire Prin .... **Bel Air, MD**
Havre de Grace, MD
Blomquist, Daniel T. .... Minneapolis, MN
Blomquist, Edwin R., Jr. .... Wellesley, MA
Blomquist, Eric R. .... San Francisco, CA
Blomquist, Erika B. .... **Dallas, TX**
Blomquist, Ernest R., III
Arlington Heights, IL
Blomquist, Harry L., III .... San Antonio, TX
Blomquist, Hiram E. .... Prairie Village, KS
Blomquist, Jack Edward .... Frederick, MD
Blomquist, James A. .... **Minneapolis, MN**
Blomquist, Jefferson L. .... Bel Air, MD
Blomquist, John D. .... **Newark, NJ**
New York, NY
Blomquist, Kristin J. .... Topeka, KS
Blomquist, Michelle R.
Salt Lake City, UT
Blomquist, Peter C. .... **Austin, TX**
Blomquist, Robert F. .... Valparaiso, IN
Blomquist, Sonja E. .... **San Francisco, CA**
Blomquist, Wallace V. .... Minneapolis, MN
Blomquist, William K. .... **Chicago, IL**
Blomstrom, James L. .... **Youngstown, OH**
Blomstrom, John J. .... **Casper, WY**
Blond & Allison, P.C., Law Offices of
Overland Park, KS
Kansas City, MO
Blond, Barton S. .... **Kansas City, MO**
Blond, Hyman J. .... Silver Spring, MD
Blond, Irwin E. .... **Kansas City, MO**
Blond, Peter Eric .... **New York, NY**
Blondeau, Alexander L., Jr.
Baton Rouge, LA
Blondeau, Caire & Gregorie, A Professional Law Corporation .... Baton Rouge, LA
Blondell, John A. .... Glen Burnie, MD
Blondell, William J., Jr. .... Baltimore, MD
Blonder, David .... Los Angeles, CA
Blonder, Martha Lynne .... New York, NY
Blonder, Martin K. .... **Chicago, IL**
Blonder, Meir Y. .... New York, NY
Blonder, Nicholas .... Mill Valley, CA
Blonder, Steven P. .... **Chicago, IL**
Blondes, Cliff M. .... Rockville, MD
Blondes, Leonard S. .... Bethesda, MD
Blondes, Stacy J. .... Rockville, MD
Blondet, Melissa Negron
Fort Lauderdale, FL
Blondin, Audrey B. .... Torrington, CT
Blondin, Carl A. .... **Oakdale, MN**
Blondin, Carl A. .... **St. Paul, MN**
Blondin, Carmen Joseph .... Lottsburg, VA
Blondin, Karen N. .... Honolulu, HI
Blondin, Kevin G. .... **Longview, WA**
Blondin, Philip E. .... Department of Justice,
Tax Division, GV
Blondis, Robert H. .... Milwaukee, WI
Blondman, Mark .... **Washington, DC**
Philadelphia, PA
Blongewicz, Jon A. .... Overland Park, KS
Blongewicz, Mark K. .... **Tulsa, OK**
Blonien, John S. .... Goldendale, WA
Blonien, Rodney J. .... Sacramento, CA
Blonigen, Michael A. .... Casper, WY
Blonquist, Thomas R. .... Salt Lake City, UT
Blonsky, Daniel F. .... **Miami, FL**
Blonsky, Joseph .... Miami, FL
Blonsky, Joseph, P.A. .... Miami, FL
Blonstein, Marc D. .... **Scottsdale, AZ**
Blood, Boose & Brizuela .... St. Charles, IL
Blood, C. Kenneth .... St. Charles, IL
Blood, Charles W. .... St. Louis, MO
Blood, Curtis L. .... Collinsville, IL
Blood, Deborah J. .... **Essex, CT**
Blood and Duncanson .... Jamestown, NY
Blood, John J. .... **New York, NY**
Blood, Laura .... **Washington, DC**
Blood, Margaret H. .... New York, NY
Blood, Perkins & Warnick, P.C.
Casper, WY
Blood, Peter Stuart .... Pueblo, CO
Blood, Robert K. .... Muskogee, OK
Blood, Russell M. .... **Casper, WY**

Blood, Timothy G. ....San Diego, CA
Blood, William R. ....Jamestown, NY
Bloodgood, Charles F., Jr. ....Sacramento, CA
Bloodgood, Leon E. ....Torrance, CA
Bloodgood, Nancy ....**Charleston, SC**
Bloodgood, Patricia A. ....**Minneapolis, MN**
Bloodhart, Ann K. ....**Minneapolis, MN**
Bloodsaw, Tracey A. ....New York, NY
Bloodstein, Daniel ....Albany, NY
Bloodworth & Associates
Oklahoma City, OK
Bloodworth, A. W. Franklin ....**Atlanta, GA**
Bloodworth, Darryl M. ....**Orlando, FL**
Bloodworth, Garland ....Oklahoma City, OK
Bloodworth, John H. ....Poplar Bluff, MO
Bloodworth Law Offices
Poplar Bluff, MO
Bloodworth, Louis R., Jr. ....Silver Spring, MD
Bloodworth & McSwain ....**Atlanta, GA**
Bloodworth, Ralph R., Jr.
Poplar Bluff, MO
Bloodworth, Susan S. ....**Jacksonville, FL**
Bloodworth, Ted A. ....Tucson, AZ
Bloodworth, Thomas L. ....**Dallas, TX**
Bloodworth, William D., II ....Huntsville, TX
Bloodworth, Wm. H. ....**Poplar Bluff, MO**
Bloom, Alan ....Los Angeles, CA
Bloom, Alan J. ....Towson, MD
Bloom, Alan S. ....Washington, DC
Bloom, Alice ....Mamaroneck, NY
Bloom, Allan ....Los Angeles, CA
Bloom, Allan E. ....**Fort Wayne, IN**
Bloom, Allan S. ....**New York, NY**
Bloom, Allen ....**Princeton, NJ**
Bloom, Allen J. ....East St. Louis, IL
St. Louis, MO
Bloom, Allen R. ....San Diego, CA
Bloom, Allyn M. ....Greenvale, NY
Bloom, Alton Dale ....**Fort Wayne, IN**
Bloom, Andrea ....**Denver, CO**
Bloom, Anne R. ....Miami, FL
Bloom, Anne W. ....Washington, DC
Bloom, Arnold ....**Boston, MA**
Bloom, Arnold S. ....Oakland, NJ
Bloom, Arthur L. ....**Philadelphia, PA**
Pittsburgh, PA
Bloom, Barbara Butler ....**Minneapolis, MN**
Bloom, Barri ....**Portland, ME**
Bloom, Barry L. ....New York, NY
Bloom, Barry M. ....Dallas, TX
Bloom, Barry M., P.C. ....Dallas, TX
Bloom, Barry S. ....**New York, NY**
Bloom, Barton W. ....Middletown, NY
Bloom, Benjamin M. ....**Medford, OR**
Bloom, Bloom, More and Miller
Fort Wayne, IN
Bloom & Bloom, P.C. ....**New Windsor, NY**
Bloom Borenstein, P.C. ....Springfield, NJ
Bloom, Brian R. ....**Houston, TX**
Bloom, Bruce E. ....Deerfield, IL
Bloom, Bryan E. ....Morristown, NJ
Bloom & Buell ....**Boston, MA**
Bloom, Charles E. ....Miami, FL
Bloom, Charles E. ....Toledo, OH
Bloom, Charles J. ....**Philadelphia, PA**
Wayne, PA
Bloom, Charles S. ....Fort Collins, CO
Bloom, Christopher A. ....**Chicago, IL**
Bloom, Clifford H. ....**Grand Rapids, MI**
Bloom, Cliffton E. ....Tucson, AZ
Bloom, Craig ....**New York, NY**
Bloom, Cyrus J. ....**Roseland, NJ**
Bloom, Daniel J. ....**New Windsor, NY**
Bloom, Daniel J. ....New York, NY
Bloom, Dara L. ....Spring, TX
Bloom, David ....New York, NY
Bloom, David B. ....**Los Angeles, CA**
Bloom, David B., A Prof. Corp., Law Offices of ....**Bakersfield, CA**
Los Angeles, CA
Orange, CA
San Bernardino, CA
Ventura, CA
Bloom, David E. ....New York, NY
Bloom, David I. ....**Washington, DC**
Bloom, David S. ....**Pittsburgh, PA**
Bloom, David Seth ....Mountain View, CA
Bloom, Deborah A. ....**Springfield, MA**
Bloom, Deborah M. ....Milpitas, CA
Bloom, Dena L. ....**Los Angeles, CA**
Bloom, Dennis D. ....Red Oak, IA
Bloom, Diane S.
Treasury Department, GV
Bloom, Donald E. ....San Francisco, CA
Bloom, Donald L. ....Huntington Beach, CA
Bloom, Duff ....Eugene, OR
Bloom, E. Martin ....**Birmingham, AL**
Bloom, Earl C., Jr. ....**Birmingham, AL**
Bloom, Edward A. ....**Washington, DC**
Bloom, Edward C. ....Greenwich, CT
Bloom, Edward D. ....**Rochester, NY**
Bloom, Edward I. ....**San Francisco, CA**
Bloom, Edward M. ....**Boston, MA**
Bloom, Elias ....Indianapolis, IN
Bloom, Elise M. ....**New York, NY**
Bloom, Ellen S. ....Cherry Hill, NJ
Bloom, Elmer E. ....Muscatine, IA
Bloom, Ely ....Greenville, NC
Bloom, Emanuel ....New York, NY
Bloom, Eric W. ....**Washington, DC**
Bloom, Evan T. ....Department of State, Office of the Legal Adviser, GV
Bloom, F. Walter, III ....**Oil City, PA**
Bloom, Francis W. ....Wilbraham, MA
Bloom, G. Duff ....Albany, OR
Eugene, OR
Bloom, Gary L. ....Oklahoma City, OK
Bloom, Gary M. ....Livonia, MI
Bloom, Gary N. ....Spokane, WA
Bloom Gates & Whiteleather
Columbia City, IN
South Whitley, IN
Bloom, George E. ....**Hammond, IN**
Bloom, George M. ....**Livingston, NJ**
Bloom, Gerald E., III ....Fairless Hills, PA
Bloom, Gerson D. ....Galveston, TX
Bloom, Gordon F. ....Newton, MA
Bloom, Greg E. ....**Great Neck, NY**
Bloom, Gregg S. ....Miami, FL
Bloom, Gwen D. ....**Orlando, FL**
Bloom, Gwen S. ....Brooklyn, NY
Bloom, Heidi C. ....**Raleigh, NC**
Bloom, Herbert A. ....San Mateo, CA
Bloom, Hergott, Cook, Diemer & Klein, LLP
Beverly Hills, CA
Los Angeles, CA
Bloom, Herman ....Philadelphia, PA
Bloom, Herman J. ....West Bloomfield, MI
Bloom, Herschel M. ....**Atlanta, GA**
Bloom, Howard B. ....Union, NJ
Bloom, Howard M. ....**Boston, MA**
Bloom, Ilene Lin ....**Chicago, IL**
Bloom, Ira J. ....Charleston, SC
Bloom, Ira Mark ....Albany, NY
Bloom, Ira W. ....**Westport, CT**
Bloom, Irwin ....**New York, NY**
Bloom, Irwin N. ....Los Angeles, CA
Bloom, Jack L. ....Greenville, SC
Bloom, Jacob ....Chicago, IL
Bloom, Jacob A. ....**Beverly Hills, CA**
Bloom, Jane M. ....**Goshen, NY**
Bloom, Janette M. ....Carson City, NV
Bloom, Jay B. ....Springfield, NJ
Bloom, Jay Robert ....New York, NY
Bloom, Jay S. ....Encino, CA
Bloom, Jeffrey B. ....**New York, NY**
Bloom, Jeffrey C. ....San Diego, CA
Bloom, Jeffrey Charles ....Bronx, NY
Bloom, Jeffrey M. ....**Palo Alto, CA**
Bloom, Jeffrey P. ....**Washington, DC**
Bloom, Jeffrey P. ....Columbia, SC
Bloom, Jennifer E. ....**Houston, TX**
Bloom, Jerold L. ....Sherman Oaks, CA
Bloom, Jerome M. ....Baltimore, MD
Bloom, Jerome P. ....Englewood, OH
Bloom, Jerry R. ....**Los Angeles, CA**
Bloom, Joan Vaughan ....Marietta, GA
Bloom, JoAnne Gazarek ....Chicago, IL
Bloom, Joel R. ....**Boston, MA**
Bloom, John ....Columbia City, IN
Bloom, John A. ....Santa Rosa, CA
Bloom, Jonathan ....**Boca Raton, FL**
White Plains, NY
Bloom, Jonathan ....**New York, NY**
Bloom, Jonathan A. ....**New York, NY**
Bloom, Jonathan F. ....**Philadelphia, PA**
Bloom, Jonathan, P.A., Law Offices of
Boca Raton, FL
White Plains, NY
Bloom, Jordan L. ....**San Francisco, CA**
Bloom, Jos. ....Salinas, CA
Bloom, Joshua A. ....**San Francisco, CA**
Bloom, Joyce ....Los Alamitos, CA
Bloom, Judith Ilene ....**Los Angeles, CA**
Bloom, Karen J. ....Boston, MA
Bloom, Karen S. ....San Francisco, CA
Bloom, Kavanaugh & Lonnerstater
Livonia, MI
Bloom, Kenith D. ....Newark, NJ
Bloom, Kenneth A. ....**New York, NY**
Bloom, Kenneth M. ....**Miami, FL**
Bloom, Kenneth M. ....Chicago, IL
Northbrook, IL
Bloom, Kevin D. ....Miami, FL
Bloom, Laura E. ....**Southfield, MI**
Bloom, Lauren M. ....Washington, DC
Bloom, Lauren S. ....**Chicago, IL**
Bloom, Laurence J. ....**Boston, MA**
Bloom, Laurie Styka ....**Buffalo, NY**
Bloom, Lawrence H. ....New York, NY
Bloom, Lee H. ....Larchmont, NY
Bloom, Leonard ....**Towson, MD**
Bloom, Leonard, & Associates, LLC
Baltimore, MD
Towson, MD
Bloom, Leonard H., (P.A.) ....**Miami, FL**
Bloom, Linda S. ....**Albuquerque, NM**
Bloom, Linda S., P.A. ....**Albuquerque, NM**
Bloom, Linda Wilson ....Sacramento, CA
Bloom, Lisa ....Los Angeles, CA
Bloom, Lois S. ....New York, NY
Bloom, Louis H. ....Charleston, WV
Bloom, Margaret L. ....**Washington, DC**
Washington, DC
Bloom, Marissa F. ....**Los Angeles, CA**
Bloom, Marjorie Rosenthal
Pension Benefit Guaranty Corporation, Office of the General Counsel, GV
Bloom, Mark A. ....**New York, NY**
Bloom, Mark D. ....**Miami, FL**
Bloom, Mark G. ....Madison, WI
Bloom, Mark N. ....**Larchmont, NY**
Bloom, Mark W. ....**Worcester, MA**
Bloom, Martin A. ....**Denver, CO**
Bloom, Marvin I. ....Aurora, IL
Bloom, Marvin J. ....Great Neck, NY
Bloom, Marvin S. ....Hartford, CT
Bloom, Michael ....Westlake Village, CA
Bloom, Michael A. ....**Philadelphia, PA**
Bloom, Michael A. ....Dallas, TX
Bloom, Michael B. ....**Minneapolis, MN**
Bloom, Michael David ....Orangeburg, NY
Bloom, Michael H. ....**Miami, FL**
Bloom, Michael H. ....**Portland, OR**
Bloom, Michael J. ....**Tucson, AZ**
Bloom, Michael J. ....New York, NY
Bloom, Michael J. ....Pittsburgh, PA
Bloom, Michael J., P.C. ....**Tucson, AZ**
Bloom, Michael S. ....North Miami, FL
Bloom, Michael S. ....**Boston, MA**
Bloom, Michael S. ....Voorhees, NJ
Philadelphia, PA
Bloom, Michael S., P.A. ....North Miami, FL
Bloom, Michael W. ....Marshalltown, IA
Bloom, Millard D. ....Towson, MD
Bloom & Minsker ....**Miami, FL**
Bloom & Mintz ....New York, NY
Bloom, Mitchell S. ....**Boston, MA**
Bloom, Morris ....Federal Trade Commission, Bureau of Competition, GV
Bloom, Morton J. ....Playa Del Rey, CA
Bloom, Morton W. ....New York, NY
Bloom Murr & Associates, P.C.
Denver, CO
Bloom, Murray A.
Department of Transportation, Maritime Administration, GV
Bloom, Myron A. ....**Philadelphia, PA**
Bloom, Norman D., Jr. ....**Alamogordo, NM**
Bloom, Oscar J. ....Mount Sinai, NY
Bloom, Paul ....Longmeadow, MA
Bloom, Paul J. ....**Melville, NY**
Bloom, Paul L. ....**Santa Fe, NM**
Bloom, Paul M. ....Los Angeles, CA
Bloom, Peter E. ....**New Windsor, NY**
Bloom, Peter J.
Agency for International Development, Other Offices of A.I.D., GV
Bloom, Peter M. ....**Washington, DC**
Bloom, Philip ....Miami, FL
Bloom, Philip M. ....Chicago, IL
Uniondale, NY
Bloom, Randall Lane
Fort Lauderdale, FL
Bloom, Rebecca J. ....**Walla Walla, WA**
Bloom, Richard D. ....Los Angeles, CA
Bloom, Richard I. ....Southfield, MI
Bloom, Richard J. ....Detroit, MI
Bloom, Richard S. ....Cleveland, OH
Bloom, Robert ....Washington, DC
Bloom, Robert A. ....**Hoffman Estates, IL**
Bloom, Robert A. ....New York, NY
Bloom, Robert H. ....New York, NY
Bloom, Robert J. ....New York, NY
Bloom, Robert L. ....Baltimore, MD
Bloom, Robert M. ....Chesterland, OH
Bloom, Robert T. ....Mineola, NY
Bloom, Roger F. ....**New York, NY**
Bloom, Ronald I. ....Northfield, NJ
Bloom, Ronald L., (P.A.) ....Jacksonville, FL
Bloom & Rosenfield ....Westborough, MA
Bloom, Rubenstein, Karinja & Dillon, P.C.
Livingston, NJ
Newark, NJ
Bloom, Rudibaugh & Gunn ....**Hemet, CA**
Temecula, CA
Bloom & Ruttenberg ....Los Angeles, CA
Bloom, Sam ....Miami, FL
Bloom, Samuel R. ....**Minneapolis, MN**
Bloom, Sandra P. ....Summit, NJ
Bloom, Sara Lynne ....Washington, DC
Bloom, Sara Nelson ....Washington, DC
Bloom, Scott M. ....**San Francisco, CA**
Bloom, Seth E. ....Department of Justice, Antitrust Division, GV
Bloom, Sidney H. ....Boynton Beach, FL
Bloom, Sigmund L. ....Albuquerque, NM
Bloom, Simon H. ....**Atlanta, GA**
Bloom, Simon H., Jr. ....Miami, FL
Bloom, Stanley S. ....Hazlet, NJ
Bloom, Stephen D. ....**Emporia, VA**
Bloom, Stephen E. ....Cleveland, OH
Bloom, Stephen L. ....**Carlisle, PA**
Bloom, Stephen M. ....**Pendleton, OR**
Bloom, Steven ....Boston, MA
Bloom, Steven A. ....**Phoenix, AZ**
Bloom, Steven D. ....**New York, NY**
Bloom, Steven E. ....Monterey Park, CA
Bloom, Steven N. ....**Los Angeles, CA**
Bloom, Susan Frank ....**New York, NY**
Bloom, Susan K. ....**New York, NY**
Bloom, Susan L. ....Oakland, CA
Bloom, Suzanne Jaffe ....New York, NY
Bloom, Tammara Sue ....San Jose, CA
Bloom, Theodore G. ....Annapolis, MD
Bloom, Theodore S. ....Columbus, OH
Bloom, Thomas F. ....**Nashville, TN**
Bloom, Thomas S. ....Newark, NJ
Bloom, Timothy J. ....Columbia City, IN
South Whitley, IN
Bloom, Timothy J. ....**Grand Haven, MI**
Bloom, Todd A. ....New Orleans, LA
Bloom, Warren S. ....Orlando, FL
Bloom, Wendy L. ....**Chicago, IL**
Bloom, William M. ....Columbia City, IN
Bloom, William R. ....**Miami, FL**
Bloom, William R. ....Westborough, MA
Bloom, William R. ....Clackamas, OR
Bloom & Witkin ....**Boston, MA**
BloomBecker, Jay J. ....Santa Cruz, CA
Bloomberg, Andrea L. ....**Chicago, IL**
Bloomberg, Burton ....New York, NY
Bloomberg, Cheryl R. ....**New York, NY**
Bloomberg, Coe A., (A Professional Corporation) ....**Los Angeles, CA**
Bloomberg, David C. ....Northampton, MA
Bloomberg, Edward S. ....**Buffalo, NY**
Bloomberg, Jeffrey M. ....**New York, NY**
Bloomberg, Jeffry L. ....Deadwood, SD
Bloomberg, Jonathon H.
Minneapolis, MN
Bloomberg, Judith A. ....**San Francisco, CA**
Bloomberg, Judith A. ....**Sausalito, CA**
Bloomberg, Lisa I. ....New York, NY
Bloomberg, Mark H. ....**New York, NY**
Bloomberg, Mitchell R. ....**Miami, FL**
Bloomberg, Morris J. ....Albany, NY
Bloomberg, Nancy E. ....**Philadelphia, PA**
Bloomberg & O'Hara ....**Burlington, VT**
Bloomberg, Robert L. ....Miami, FL
Bloomberg, Ronald W. ....**Lansing, MI**
Bloomberg, Samuel S. ....**Burlington, VT**
Bloomberg, Sheri E. ....**New York, NY**
Bloomberg, Steinberg & Bader
New York, NY
Bloomberg, Steven A. ....Chicago, IL
Bloomberg, Steven P. ....**Bolingbrook, IL**
Bloomberg, Vivian Rigdon
Los Angeles, CA
Bloomberg, Warner S., III ....San Jose, CA
Bloome, Jerrad D. ....Houston, TX
Bloomenthal & Associates P.C.
Boston, MA
Bloomenthal, Harold S. ....**Denver, CO**
Bloomenthal, Leslie E. ....**Boston, MA**
Bloomenthal, Melvin Lee ....**Stamford, CT**
Bloomenthal, Nowell Z. ....Waltham, MA
Bloomer, Andrew B. ....**Chicago, IL**
Bloomer, Bloomer & Bloomer ....Osborne, KS
Bloomer & Bloomer, P.C. ....Rutland, VT
Bloomer, David A. ....Houston, TX
Bloomer, H. Franklin, Jr. ....**New York, NY**
Bloomer, John E. ....**Dallas, TX**
Bloomer, John H., Jr. ....Rutland, VT
Bloomer, Julianne ....**Beverly Hills, CA**
Bloomer, Keith G ....Shelby, NC
Bloomer, Lloyd C. ....Osborne, KS
Bloomer, Paul W. ....**Carlinville, IL**
Bloomer, Richard S. ....Rutland, VT
Bloomer, Richard S., P.C. ....Rutland, VT
Bloomer, Robert A. ....Osborne, KS
Bloomer, Robert A. ....Rutland, VT
Bloomer, Shelley D. G. ....Osborne, KS
Bloomer, Suzanne M. ....Bronxville, NY
Bloomer, Thomas M. ....**Elmsford, NY**
New York, NY
Bloomer, William F. ....Boston, MA
Bloomer, William J. ....Rutland, VT
Bloomfield, Alan P. ....Brooklyn, NY
Bloomfield, Allan R. ....Forest Hills, NY
Bloomfield, Anne H. ....Bartlesville, OK
Bloomfield, B. Edwin ....**Springfield, MO**
Bloomfield, David C. ....New York, NY
Bloomfield, David J. ....Los Angeles, CA
Bloomfield, David S. ....Columbus, OH
Bloomfield, David S., Jr. ....**Columbus, OH**
Bloomfield, Donald R. ....New York, NY
Bloomfield, Elaine
Equal Employment Opportunity Commission, Office of Federal Operations, GV
Bloomfield Group, P.C.
Bloomfield Hills, MI
Bloomfield, Jay ....**New York, NY**
Bloomfield, Karl ....Beverly Hills, CA
Bloomfield, Keith M. ....**New York, NY**
Bloomfield, Kevin L. ....St. Louis, MO
Bloomfield, Lee J. ....**Memphis, TN**
Bloomfield, Leon M. ....San Francisco, CA
Bloomfield, Louis J. ....Mayfield Village, OH
Bloomfield, Mark A. ....Washington, DC
Bloomfield, Marshall E. ....Bronx, NY
Bloomfield, Maxwell H., III
Washington, DC
Bloomfield, Micah W. ....**New York, NY**
Bloomfield, Neil Jon, Law Office of
Napa, CA
San Francisco, CA
Bloomfield, Neil Jon, Law Office of
San Rafael, CA
Bloomfield, Richard Andrew ....San Jose, CA
Bloomfield, Roger E. ....**Dayton, OH**
Bloomfield, Sally W. ....**Columbus, OH**
Bloomfield, Stephanie L. ....**Tacoma, WA**
Bloomfield, Susan Berry ....**Bethesda, MD**
Bloomfield, Tammy Cain ....Los Angeles, CA
Bloomfield, Theresa Hand ....Shreveport, LA
Bloomfield, Thomas A. ....San Francisco, CA
Bloomfield, Timothy J. ....**Washington, DC**
Bloomgarden, Craig S. ....**Los Angeles, CA**
Bloomgarden, David ....Los Angeles, CA
Bloomgarden, Ellen M. ....Glenside, PA
Bloomgarden, Nancy L. ....New York, NY
Bloomgarden, Paul M. ....Fort Lauderdale, FL
Bloomgarden, Paul M., P.A.
Fort Lauderdale, FL
Bloomgarden-White, Inc. ....Glenside, PA
Bloomgren, Brynn K.
Department Of Veterans Affairs, Board of Veterans Appeals, GV
Bloomingdale, A. Lee, Jr. ....Omaha, NE
Bloomingdale, Bruce C. ....**Chicago, IL**
Bloomquist, Amy Peterson ....**Austin, TX**
Bloomquist, Christine E. ....**Washington, DC**
Bloomquist, Dennis H. ....**Fairfax, VA**
Bloomquist, Elizabeth W. ....Fairmont, MN
Bloomquist & Halper, P.A.
Minneapolis, MN
Bloomquist, John Eric ....**Helena, MT**
Bloomquist, John S. ....Eagan, MN
Bloomquist, Katherine C.
Minneapolis, MN
Bloomquist, Mark A. ....**Minneapolis, MN**
Bloomquist, Michael ....**Washington, DC**
Bloomquist, P. Richard
West Palm Beach, FL
Bloomquist, Terrence H. ....Grayling, MI
Bloomquist, Timothy R. ....Mora, MN
Bloom-Rudibaugh, Kathlyn J. ....**Hemet, CA**
Temecula, CA

Bloomstein, Alexander W.
Great Barrington, MA
Hillsdale, NY
Bloomstein, Joshua M. ....New York, NY
Bloomstein, Lawrence D. ....New York, NY
Bloomstein, Morris J. ....New York, NY
Bloomston, Brett M. ....Birmingham, AL
Bloomstone, Amy ....Newton, MA
Bloomstrom, Gregory J. ....Two Harbors, MN
Bloor, Daniel G. ....Richmond, VA
Bloor, Stephen Michael
Department of Defense,
Defense Legal Services Agency, GV
Bloor, Terry J. ....Kennewick, WA
Bloor, William E. ....Waitsburg, WA
Bloore, Suzanne W. ....Boston, MA
Bloostein, Marc J. ....Boston, MA
Blooston, Arthur ....Washington, DC
Blooston, Mordkofsky, Jackson & Dickens
Washington, DC
Blos, Richard B. ....San Jose, CA
Blose, James P. ....Bridgeport, CT
Blosh, Marie ....Castro Valley, CA
Bloshinsky, Gregory S. ....Aventura, FL
Boca Raton, FL
Fort Lauderdale, FL
West Palm Beach, FL
Bloskey, Jeffrey S. ....Overland Park, KS
Bloss, David J. ....Grand Rapids, MI
Bloss, George F., III ....Gulfport, MS
Bloss, James R. ....Treasury Department,
Office of Thrift Supervision, GV
Bloss, John F. ....Greensboro, NC
Bloss, Julie Lanier ....Dallas, TX
Bloss, Marian C. ....Austin, TX
Bloss, William M. ....New Haven, CT
Bloss-Baum, Linda
House of Representatives,
Committee Legal Personnel, GV
Blosser, David J., & Associates ....Angola, IN
Blosser, G. Harley ....St. Louis, MO
Blosser, James J. ....Fort Lauderdale, FL
Blosser, Keith D. ....Columbus, OH
Blosser, Larry A. ....Washington, DC
Blosser, Leslie L. ....Minneapolis, MN
Blossfeld, Darcy C. ....Dallas, TX
Blossman & Hand ....Covington, LA
Blossman, Jack A. ....Covington, LA
Blossman, Roy E. ....New Orleans, LA
Blossner, Robert ....New York, NY
Blossom, David R. ....Jamestown, NY
Blossom, William C. ....Wallace, NC
Blostein, Arnold T. ....Fort Lauderdale, FL
Blostein, Arnold T., P.A.
Fort Lauderdale, FL
Blostein, Harold L. ....Cochiti Lake, NM
Blostein, Jeffrey L. ....West Palm Beach, FL
Blotch, Alan T. ....Seattle, WA
Blotner, David A. ....Department of Justice,
Antitrust Division, GV
Blotner, J. Joseph ....Gretna, LA
Blotner, Norman D. ....New Rochelle, NY
Blotney, Frank J., Jr. ....West Palm Beach, FL
Blotnik, Michael M. ....Buffalo, NY
Blott, Jacquelyn W. ....Bryan, TX
Blotter, Scott T. ....Salt Lake City, UT
Blouch, John W. ....Washington, DC
Blough, Eric J. ....Charlotte, NC
Blough, Janis L. ....Lansing, MI
Blough, Jim C. ....Natchez, MS
Blough, Lynn E. ....Hillsboro, OR
Blough, Marcine A. ....Atherton, CA
Blough, Philip K., II ....Tulsa, OK
Blough, Richard J. ....Novi, MI
Blough, Robert E. ....Indianapolis, IN
Blougouras, Daniel W. ....Louisville, KY
Blouin, C. Denis ....Los Angeles, CA
Blouin, Daniel M. ....Chicago, IL
Blouke, Milton B. ....Seattle, WA
Blount, Barry D. ....Houston, TX
Blount, Charles W., III ....Dallas, TX
Blount, Clarence D. ....Waycross, GA
Blount, Cliff ....Austin, TX
Blount, Crisp, Mills & Economos, LLP
Greenville, NC
Blount, David E. ....Bradenton, FL
Blount, David L. ....Portland, OR
Blount & Duke ....Greenville, NC
Blount, Edward C., Jr. ....Mobile, AL
Blount, Elissa J. ....New York, NY
Blount, Gregory W. ....Atlanta, GA
Blount, Gwendolyn A. .... Washington, DC
Blount, James D., Jr. ....Raleigh, NC
Blount, James E., IV ....Memphis, TN
Blount, James E. (Jeb), III ....Memphis, TN
Blount, Jane Woodruff ....Atlanta, GA
Blount, Jay T. ....Pittsburgh, PA
Blount, John F. ....Atlanta, GA
Blount, John T. ....Miami, FL
Blount, Joseph L. ....Jackson, MS
Blount, Judson H., III ....Greenville, NC
Blount, Kristen A. ....Flint, MI
Blount, Larry C. ....Sulphur Springs, TX
Blount Law Firm ....Memphis, TN
Blount Law Firm, The, P.L.L.C.
Greenville, NC
Blount, Mae S. ....Roosevelt, NY
Blount, Marvin K., III ....Greenville, NC
Blount, Marvin K., Jr. ....Greenville, NC
Blount, Michael E. ....Chicago, IL
Blount, Nancy ....Detroit, MI
Blount, Nancy M. ....Miami, FL
Blount, Percy J. ....Augusta, GA
Blount, R. E. Peppy ....Longview, TX
Blount, Robert A. ....Newport News, VA
Blount, Robert A., & Associates, P.C.
Newport News, VA
Blount, Sherri N. ....Washington, DC
Blount, Stephen W., III ....San Antonio, TX
Blount, Steven V. ....Naples, FL
Blount, Susan L. ....Newark, NJ
Blount, Thomas ....Bellevue, NE
Blount, Uriel, Jr. ....DeLand, FL
Blount, William F., Jr. ....Mineral, VA
Blount Craig, Margaret ....Richmond, VA
Blount-Powell, Barbara ....Gainesville, FL
Bloustein, Elise A. ....Brooklyn, NY
Bloustein, Marc C. ....Albany, NY
Bloustein, Oscar A. ....White Plains, NY
Bloustein-Schutz, Judith ....Bronx, NY
Blow, B. Clifton ....McLemoresville, TN
Blow, Carroll E., Jr. ....Mobile, AL
Blow, David S. ....Hackensack, NJ
Blow, George ....Washington, DC
Blow, George W., III ....Panama City, FL
Blow, Marcellus I. ....St. Louis, MO
Blow, Steven ....Albany, NY
Blower, Bradley H.
Federal Trade Commission,
Bureau of Consumer Protection, GV
Blower, Earl ....Idaho Falls, ID
Blower, Richard C. ....Sparks, NV
Blowers, Erik B. ....Charlotte, NC
Blowers, Grant ....New Haven, MO
Blowers, Lynn Marie ....Yorktown, VA
Bloxham, Steven J. ....Window Rock, AZ
Bloxham, Thomas L. ....Oakland, CA
Bloxom, John E. ....Pocomoke City, MD
Bloxom, John M., IV ....Newark, DE
Bloxom, R. Norris ....Accomac, VA
Bloxom, Richard R. ....Snow Hill, MD
Bloyd, Melissa M. ....Washington, DC
Bloyer, Raymond K. ....Washington, DC
Bloyer, William P. ....Minneapolis, MN
Bloys, Allen K. ....Whitehouse Station, NJ
Bloys, John V. ....Bethlehem, PA
Blozan, Leslie A. ....Encino, CA
Blubaugh, Marc S. ....Columbus, OH
Blubaugh, Ronald E. ....Sacramento, CA
Blucher, Hope Knight ....Rutland, VT
Blucher, Jonathan P. ....Dayton, OH
Blucher, Paul A. ....Sarasota, FL
Blucher, Paul A., P.A., Law Office of
Sarasota, FL
Bluck, James H. ....New York, NY
Bludman, Peter D. ....Philadelphia, PA
Bludworth & Associates, P.C.
Houston, TX
Bludworth, Bill R. ....Houston, TX
Bludworth, Darnell ....New Orleans, LA
Bludworth, David H.
West Palm Beach, FL
Blue, Ahndrea L. ....Seattle, WA
Blue, Allan Marshall ....Lewis Center, OH
Blue, Arthur C., III ....Gastonia, NC
Blue, Arthur M. ....Carthage, NC
Blue, Barbara P. ....North Hollywood, CA
Blue, Beth D. ....San Diego, CA
Blue, Claire
Federal Communications Commission,
Common Carrier Bureau, GV
Blue, D. Laird ....Denver, CO
Blue, Dane N. ....Memphis, TN
Blue, Daniel T., Jr. ....Raleigh, NC
Blue, David J. ....New York, NY
Blue, Deborah J. ....Sarasota, FL
Blue, Donald M. ....Plymouth, MI
Blue, Douglas J. ....Columbus, OH
Blue & Edwards, P.A. ....Baltimore, MD
Towson, MD
Blue, Eleanore C. ....Kansas City, MO
Blue, Elizabeth E. Appel ......Washington, DC
Blue, Emerson E. ....Chicago, IL
Blue, F. Lloyd, Jr. ....Destin, FL
Blue, Frank W. ....Dallas, TX
Blue, Gary D. ....Huron, SD
Blue, Geoffrey Neff ....Philadelphia, PA
Blue, George ....Huron, SD
Blue, George R., Jr. ....Metairie, LA
Blue, Gregory A. ....New York, NY
Blue & Haeder ....Huron, SD
Blue, Henry W., Jr. ....San Diego, CA
Blue, Ivy P., Jr. ....Hanover, VA
Blue, J. William, Jr. ....Chapel Hill, NC
Blue, James M. ....Tampa, FL
Blue, Janet Roberts ....Indianapolis, IN
Blue, Jason A. ....Columbus, OH
Blue, John A. ....Los Angeles, CA
Blue, John R. ....Lakeland, FL
Blue, Jon C. ....New Haven, CT
Blue, Keith F. ....Knoxville, TN
Blue, Lacy W. ....Charlotte, NC
Blue, Lisa A. ....Dallas, TX
Blue, Lori E. ....Lansdale, PA
Blue, M. Muffy ....Decatur, GA
Blue, Martha ....Flagstaff, AZ
Blue, Michael E. ....Salt Lake City, UT
Blue, Michael E. ....Seattle, WA
Blue, Michael M. ....Oklahoma City, OK
Blue, Norman E. ....Lake Geneva, WI
Blue, Rachel ....Tulsa, OK
Blue, Randy E. ....Springfield, IL
Blue, Rob, Jr. ....Destin, FL
Panama City, FL
Blue, Robert E. ....Fresno, CA
Blue, Robert G. ....Towson, MD
Blue, Robert M. ....Washington, DC
Blue, Steven J. ....Edon, OH
Blue, Thomas C. ....Roanoke, VA
Blue, Thomas D., Jr. ....Raleigh, NC
Blue, Thomas Wilcox ....Richmond, VA
Blue, Timothy D. ....Seattle, WA
Blue, Tyson ....Lyons, NY
Blue, Warren G. ....Columbus, OH
Blue, William A., Jr. ....Nashville, TN
Blue, William D. ....Lincoln, NE
Blue, William F. ....Towson, MD
Blue, William W. (Bill) ....Perry, FL
Tallahassee, FL
Blue Williams, L.L.P. ....Metairie, LA
New Orleans, LA
Bluebond, Sheri A. ....Los Angeles, CA
BlueDog, Kurt V. ....Minneapolis, MN
BlueDog, Olson & Small, P.L.L.P.
Minneapolis, MN
Bluedorn, Donald C., II ....Pittsburgh, PA
Bluedorn and Ohlin Co., L.P.A. ......Warren, OH
Bluedorn, Samuel F. ....Warren, OH
Bluefeld, Judith L. ....Gaithersburg, MD
Blueher, Thomas F. ....Albuquerque, NM
Bluemel, Mark-Robert ....San Diego, CA
Bluemke, Eric G. ....Santa Ana, CA
Bluemle, Roland E. ....New York, NY
Bluer, Philip ....San Jose, CA
Blue Sky, Chester D. T. ....Denver, CO
Bluespruce, Leisah C. ....East Brunswick, NJ
Bluestein, Bryan ....Columbia, SC
Bluestein, Craig B. ....Jenkintown, PA
Bluestein, David ....Conroe, TX
Bluestein, Ed, Jr. ....Houston, TX
Bluestein, Elizabeth S. ....Los Angeles, CA
Bluestein, Gary ....Buffalo, NY
Bluestein, Harold ....Miami, FL
Bluestein, Irwin ....Mineola, NY
Bluestein, Jeffrey S. ....Highland Heights, KY
Bluestein, Joseph S. ....Birmingham, AL
Bluestein, Lisa M. ....New York, NY
Bluestein, Lisa N. ....New York, NY
Bluestein, Louis A. ....Denver, CO
Bluestein, Louis H. ....Chicago, IL
Bluestein, Margaret Miles ....Columbia, SC
Bluestein, Mark R. ....Pennsauken, NJ
Bluestein, Martin J. ....Pound Ridge, NY
Bluestein, Natalie Parker ....Charleston, SC
Bluestein, Philip M. ....Cincinnati, OH
Bluestein, Richard M. ....Boston, MA
Bluestein, Ronald ....Philadelphia, PA
Bluestein, S. Scott ....Charleston, SC
Bluestein & Sander ....New York, NY
Pound Ridge, NY
Bluestein and Wayne, P.A. ....Miami, FL
Bluestone, Andrew Lavoott
New York, NY
Bluestone, Arthur B. ....Chicago, IL
Bluestone, Charles L. ....Columbus, OH
Bluestone, Marshall E. ....Santa Rosa, CA
Bluestone, Max D. ....Cedarhurst, NY
Bluestone, Norman ....New York, NY
Bluestone, Saul ....Detroit, MI
Southfield, MI
Bluestone, Stephen L. ....Bethesda, MD
Bluestone, Stuart M. ....Santa Fe, NM
Blueweiss, Jeffrey A. ....Bridgeport, CT
Blueweiss, Nancy I. ....Boston, MA
Bluff, Guy W., P.C. ....Cottonwood, AZ
Phoenix, AZ
Bluff, Guy Wm. ....Cottonwood, AZ
Phoenix, AZ
Bluher, John H. ....New York, NY
Bluhm, D. Rodney ....Milwaukee, WI
Bluhm, Diane E. ....New Albany, IN
Louisville, KY
Bluhm, George P. ....Schenectady, NY
Bluhm, Gerald M. ....Lexington, MA
Bluhm, Graham A. ....Toledo, OH
Bluhm, Lori Grigg ....Troy, MI
Bluhm, Mark A. ....Kansas City, MO
Bluhm, Mary Ann ....Fresno, CA
Bluhm, Peter M. ....Montpelier, VT
Bluhm, Robert J. ....Salt Lake City, UT
Bluhm, Shirley L. ....Olympia, WA
Bluish, Pamela M. ....Toms River, NJ
Bluitt, Hollistyne C. ....Orange, NJ
Blum, Alan ....New York, NY
Blum, Alan A. ....Waukegan, IL
Blum, Alfred S. ....Denver, CO
Blum, Alison R. ....Los Angeles, CA
Blum, Amy D. ....Jacksonville, TX
Blum, André ....Madison, WI
Blum, Andrew C. ....Houston, TX
Blum, Andrew T. ....Grand Rapids, MI
Blum, Annette Hana ....New York, NY
Blum, Bambi G. ....Miami, FL
Blum, Bambi G., P.A. ....Miami, FL
Blum, Beverly Wald ....Jericho, NY
Blum and Blum, P.A. ....Baltimore, MD
Blum, Branden S. .....Department of Commerce,
National Oceanic and Atmospheric
Administration, GV
Blum, Brian M. ....Washington, DC
Blum, Bruce S. ....Palm Beach Gardens, FL
Blum, Charles F. ....New York, NY
Blum, Charles J. ....Columbus, OH
Blum, Christopher V. ....New York, NY
Blum, Cynthia A. ....Newark, NJ
Blum, Daniel B. ....Boulder, CO
Blum, Dave E. ....Wilton, CA
Blum, David ....Baltimore, MD
Blum, David C. ....Chicago, IL
Blum, David C. ....Salt Lake City, UT
Blum, David D. ....Atlanta, GA
Blum, David E. ....Washington, DC
Blum, David E. ....Laurel, MD
Blum, David M. ....Baltimore, MD
Blum, David Marc ....New York, NY
Blum, David S. ....Northbrook, IL
Blum, David S. ....Philadelphia, PA
Blum, Debra J. ....Decatur, GA
Blum, Debra Spotts ....Lakeport, CA
Blum, Dennis E. ....San Francisco, CA
Blum, Dylana Leigh ....Washington, DC
Blum, E. Joan ....Newton, MA
Blum, Edward ....Katonah, NY
Blum, Edward F., Jr. ....Anaheim, CA
Blum, Edward L. ....Oakland, CA
Blum, Eric S. ....Irvine, CA
Blum, Eva Tansky ....Pittsburgh, PA
Blum, Frances J. ....Minneapolis, MN
Blum, Frank A. ....Finleyville, PA
Blum, Frank B., Jr. ....San Bruno, CA
Blum, Fred M. ....San Francisco, CA
Blum, Frederic G. ....Rochester, NY
Blum, Gary B. ....Denver, CO
Blum, Gary L. ....Boca Raton, FL
Blum, George L. ....Rochester, NY
Blum, Gersen & Wood ....New York, NY
Blum, Gersen, Wood & Blakeman
Boca Raton, FL
Blum, Gretchen R. ....Cincinnati, OH
Blum, Harry N. ....Los Angeles, CA
Blum, Helaine M. ....Orlando, FL
Blum, Henry J. ....Houston, TX
Blum, Herbert H. ....New York, NY
Blum, Howard ....Boca Raton, FL
Blum, Howard ....New York, NY
Blum, Howard A. ....Philadelphia, PA
Blum, Howard J. ....Golden Valley, MN
Blum, Howard S. ....Tarzana, CA
Blum, Hyman ....Brooklyn, NY
Blum, Ian R. ....New York, NY
Blum, Irving R. ....Southfield, MI
Blum, Irwin E. ....North Miami Beach, FL
Blum, Israel ....New York, NY
Blum, Ivon B. ....Los Angeles, CA
Blum, Jack A. ....Washington, DC
Blum, James A. ....Pharr, TX
Blum, James P., Jr. ....Atlanta, GA
Blum, James R. ....Boston, MA
Blum, Jeffrey Austin ....Boston, MA
Blum, Jeffrey H. ....New York, NY
Blum, Jeffrey P. ....Redwood City, CA
Blum, Jeffrey S. ....Harrisburg, PA
Pittsburgh, PA
Blum, Jenifer S. ....Overland Park, KS
Blum, Jennifer A. ....Camden, NJ
Blum, Jennifer L. ....Washington, DC
Blum, Jerome ....Baltimore, MD
Blum, John D. ....Chicago, IL
Blum, John R. H. ....Lakeville, CT
Blum, Jonathan ....Forty Fort, PA
Blum, Jonathan D. ....New York, NY
Blum, Joseph H. ....Cherry Hill, NJ
Philadelphia, PA
Blum, Julie A. ....Washington, DC
Blum, Keith Jeffrey ....Miami, FL
Blum, Kevin ....Cleveland, OH
Blum, Kristina Hammer ....Norcross, GA
Blum, L. Amy ....Los Angeles, CA
Blum, Larry E. ....Baltimore, MD
Blum, Laurel D. ....Columbus, OH
Blum, Lee B. ....Hampton, IA
Blum, Leo ....Green Valley, AZ
Blum, Leonard ....New York, NY
Blum, Leonard C. ....Southport, CT
Blum, Linda J. ....New York, NY
Blum, Lorin B., Law Offices of
Oakland, CA
Walnut Creek, CA
Blum, Lorin B., Law Offices of
Walnut Creek, CA
Blum, Madelon ....Anchorage, AK
Blum, Malcolm ....Hackensack, NJ
Blum, Marc P. ....Baltimore, MD
Blum, Mark A. ....Fresno, CA
Kerman, CA
Blum, Mark A. ....Monterey, CA
Blum, Mark G. ....Waukesha, WI
Blum, Mark R. ....Rochester, NY
Blum, Marla R. ....Greensburg, PA
Blum, Martha P. ....Santa Barbara, CA
Blum, Marvin E., & Associates, P.C.
Fort Worth, TX
Blum, Marvin Elliott ....Fort Worth, TX
Blum, Mathew C.
Executive Office Of The President,
Office of Management and Budget, GV
Blum, Matthew D. ....Philadelphia, PA
Blum, Maurice Henry ....New York, NY
Blum, Melanie R. ....Orange, CA
Blum, Melvin A. ....Chicago, IL
Blum, Melvin C. ....Delray Beach, FL
Blum, Michael Charles ....Baltimore, MD
Blum, Michael G. ....Belvedere-Tiburon, CA
Blum, Michael Joel ....Fort Lee, NJ
Blum, Michael R. ....Detroit, MI
Blum, Michelle M. ....Irvine, CA
Blum, Milton ....Chicago, IL
Blum, Milton R. ....Miami Beach, FL
Blum & Minicus ....Katonah, NY
Blum, Mitchell E. ....Elkins Park, PA
Blum, Monica ....New York, NY
Blum, Paul J. ....Phoenix, AZ
Blum, Peter R. ....Hartford, CT
Blum, Propper & Hardacre, Incorporated
Los Angeles, CA
Blum, Rachel M. ....Chicago, IL
Blum, Richard A. ....New York, NY
Blum, Richard B. ....San Clemente, CA
Blum, Richard Clarke ....Burlington, VT
Blum, Robert A. ....San Francisco, CA
Blum, Robert A. ....New York, NY
Blum, Robert C. ....Freehold, NJ
Blum, Robert L. ....Mount Pleasant, PA
Blum, Robert M. ....San Francisco, CA
Blum, Robert M. ....New York, NY
Blum, Ronald G. ....New York, NY
Blum and Roseman ....Orange, CA
Blum, Royal I. ....Washington, DC
Blum, Samuel S. ....Miami, FL
Blum, Sean ....Houston, TX
Blum, Selwyn ....Chicago, IL
Blum, Seth Mitchell ....Gainesville, FL

Blum, Seymour H. ... Northbrook, IL
Blum, Shelley ... Charlotte, NC
Blum, Sidney ... Baltimore, MD
Blum, Stephanie I. ... Los Angeles, CA
Blum, Steven ... Washington, DC
Blum, Steven A. ... Los Angeles, CA
Blum, Steven A. ... Wellesley, MA
Blum, Steven B. ... Ambler, PA
Blum, Steven G. ... Washington, DC; Swarthmore, PA
Blum, Steven T. ... Chicago, IL
Blum, Stuart M. ... Baltimore, MD
Blum, Susan B. ... Hauppauge, NY
Blum, Susan M. ... Boston, MA
Blum, Theodore I. ... Atlanta, GA
Blum, Thomas R. ... New Orleans, LA
Blum, Tibby ... New York, NY
Blum, Vickie Voukidis ... Chicago, IL
Blum, W. Barry ... Miami, FL
Blum, Warren I. ... Los Angeles, CA
Blum & Weisbaum, P.A. ... Baltimore, MD
Blum, William G. ... Dubuque, IA
Blum, William, Jr. ... Washington, DC
Blum, William L. ... Denver, CO; New York, NY; Charlotte Amalie, St. Thomas, VI
Blum, William S. ... Des Moines, IA
Blum, Yumkas, Mailman, Gutman & Denick, P.A. ... Baltimore, MD
Blumberg, Aaron D. ... Philadelphia, PA
Blumberg, Alan G. ... New York, NY
Blumberg, Allan B. ... Baltimore, MD
Blumberg, Anthony E. ... Chicago, IL
Blumberg & Associates ... Arlington, TX
Blumberg & Blumberg, P.C. ... Charlevoix, MI; Gaylord, MI; Petoskey, MI
Blumberg, Bruce A. ... Somerville, NJ
Blumberg, Bruce L. ... San Francisco, CA
Blumberg, Canter, Cohen & Nemiroff ... Van Nuys, CA
Blumberg & Carrig ... Little Falls, NY
Blumberg, Cherkoss, Fitz Gibbons & Blumberg ... Amityville, NY
Blumberg, Craig A. ... New York, NY
Blumberg, Daniel E. ... Arlington, TX
Blumberg, David ... Goffstown, NH
Blumberg, David ... New York, NY
Blumberg, David A. ... Monsey, NY
Blumberg, David J. ... Van Nuys, CA
Blumberg, Donna Kaye ... Raleigh, NC
Blumberg, Edgar ... Albany, NY
Blumberg, Edith ... New York, NY
Blumberg, Edward R. ... Miami, FL
Blumberg, Elliot J. ... Gaylord, MI
Blumberg, Eric M. ... Rockville, MD
Blumberg, Ernest ... Brockton, MA
Blumberg, Eugene J. ... Amityville, NY
Blumberg, G. John ... Neenah, WI
Blumberg, Gerald ... New York, NY; Yorktown Heights, NY
Blumberg, Gerald ... Cincinnati, OH
Blumberg, Gerald & Lawrence, LLP ... New York, NY; Yorktown Heights, NY
Blumberg, Grace Ganz ... Los Angeles, CA
Blumberg, H. Lee ... Amityville, NY
Blumberg, Henry ... New York, NY
Blumberg, Herbert H. ... East Amherst, NY
Blumberg, Jane Stacy ... Burlingame, CA
Blumberg, Jay J. ... Woodbury, NJ
Blumberg, Jeffrey S. ... Baltimore, MD
Blumberg, Jill H. ... Roseland, NJ
Blumberg, Joel B. ... West Palm Beach, FL
Blumberg, John P. ... Long Beach, CA
Blumberg, Jonathan A. ... Raleigh, NC
Blumberg & Kaufman, P.C. ... Philadelphia, PA
Blumberg, Larry M. ... Des Moines, IA
Blumberg Law Corporation ... Long Beach, CA; Mammoth Lakes, CA; **Newport Beach, CA**
Blumberg, Lawrence ... Van Nuys, CA
Blumberg, Lawrence S. ... New York, NY; Yorktown Heights, NY
Blumberg, Leonard R. ... Manville, NJ
Blumberg, Malcolm M. ... Philadelphia, PA
Blumberg, Mark ... Department of Justice, Civil Rights Division, GV
Blumberg, Matthew D. ... Milford, PA
Blumberg, Maxine Ames ... San Francisco, CA
Blumberg, Morris B. ... Terre Haute, IN
Blumberg, Myron ... Long Beach, CA; Mammoth Lakes, CA
Blumberg, Patricia H. ... Atlanta, GA
Blumberg, Peter D. ... Washington, DC
Blumberg, Peter G. ... Federal Election Commission, Office of the General Counsel, GV
Blumberg, Richard A. ... Melville, NY; Mineola, NY
Blumberg, Richard E. ... Berkeley, CA
Blumberg, Richard J. ... New York, NY
Blumberg, Richard M. ... Houston, TX
Blumberg, Richard P. ... Seattle, WA
Blumberg, Robert C. ... Department of State, Bureau of Oceans, International Environmental & Scientific Affairs, GV
Blumberg, Robert H. ... New York, NY
Blumberg, Robert S. ... Los Angeles, CA
Blumberg, Ronald H. ... Solana Beach, CA
Blumberg & Rosenberg, P.A. ... Manville, NJ; Somerville, NJ
Blumberg, Sara B. ... Boynton Beach, FL
Blumberg, Sara, P.A. ... Boynton Beach, FL
Blumberg, Stanley B. ... New York, NY
Blumberg, Stephen M. ... Fresno, CA
Blumberg, Theresa Z. ... Denver, CO
Blumberg, Tracey A. ... New York, NY
Blumberg-Cohen, Gail ... Van Nuys, CA
Blume, Abraham ... Monsey, NY
Blume, Anne L. ... Chicago, IL
Blume, Arlene A. ... New Orleans, LA
Blume & Blume, Attorneys at Law, P.C. ... Tuscaloosa, AL
Blume, Bruce M. ... Seattle, WA
Blume, Charles E. ... Pasadena, CA
Blume, Connelly, Jordan, Stucky & Ulmer ... Fort Wayne, IN
Blume, Daniel ... West Hartford, CT
Blume, Daniel H. ... San Francisco, CA
Blume, Edward L. ... Philadelphia, PA
Blume, Elbaum & Collins, P.C. ... Glastonbury, CT; Hartford, CT; Washington Depot, CT; West Hartford, CT
Blume, Fred ... Philadelphia, PA
Blume, Gary L. ... Tuscaloosa, AL
Blume, Gary R. ... Phoenix, AZ
Blume, George B. ... Mars Hill, NC
Blume, Gerald W. ... New York, NY
Blume, Gloria S. ... Santa Monica, CA
Blume, Goldfaden, Berkowitz, Donnelly, Fried & Forte, A Professional Corporation ... Chatham, NJ; Elizabeth, NJ; Hackensack, NJ; Jersey City, NJ; Morristown, NJ; Newark, NJ; North Bergen, NJ; Paterson, NJ; Princeton, NJ; Somerville, NJ
Blume, Gregory V. ... Overland Park, KS
Blume, Helene Campbell ... Everett, WA
Blume, Herbert L. ... Belleair, FL
Blume, Howard Reed ... Plymouth, MA
Blume, Jack P. ... Washington, DC
Blume, James D. ... Dallas, TX
Blume, John H. ... Columbia, SC
Blume, John M. ... Chatham, NJ
Blume, Karolyn Vreeland ... Allentown, PA
Blume Law Firm, P.C. ... Phoenix, AZ
Blume, Lawrence D. ... New York, NY
Blume, Lawrence K. ... Honolulu, HI
Blume, Lisa A. ... Great Barrington, MA
Blume, Michael ... San Francisco, CA
Blume, Michael S. ... Philadelphia, PA
Blume, Myrna ... Roseland, NJ
Blume, Nancy B. ... Stamford, CT
Blume, Nettie Cohen ... Tuscaloosa, AL
Blume, Paul C., Sr. ... Chicago, IL
Blume, Peter K. ... Pittsburgh, PA
Blume, Ralph R. ... Fort Wayne, IN
Blume, Richard L. ... Stamford, CT
Blume, Richard N. ... Boston, MA
Blume, Robert S. ... Port Jefferson, NY
Blume & Stoddard ... Dallas, TX
Blume, T. Kevin ... Wheelersburg, OH
Blume, Thomas M. ... Lakewood, CO
Blume, W. Paul ... Little Rock, AR
Blumel, Diane B. ... Spokane, WA
Blumel, Jeffrey J. ... Omaha, NE
Blumel, Joseph A., III ... Spokane, WA
Blumen, Andrew S. ... Las Vegas, NV
Blumen, Elizabeth Wolman ... New Bedford, MA
Blumen, Lee I. ... Santa Ana, CA
Blumen, Norman H. ... Oceanside, CA
Blumen, Rick D. ... Atlanta, GA
Blumen, Scott M. ... San Diego, CA
Blumenberg, Amy B. ... Brisbane, CA
Blumenberg, Sidney ... New York, NY
Blumencranz, Eric S. ... Lake Success, NY
Blumenfeld, Andrew B. ... Baltimore, MD
Blumenfeld, Barbara Pinkerton ... Albuquerque, NM
Blumenfeld, Barry E. ... Chicago, IL
Blumenfeld, Charles R. ... Seattle, WA
Blumenfeld & Cohen ... San Francisco, CA; Washington, DC
Blumenfeld, Daniel M. ... Kings Beach, CA; Incline Village, NV
Blumenfeld, David A. ... Los Angeles, CA
Blumenfeld, David I. ... San Francisco, CA
Blumenfeld, David, (Ltd.) ... Chicago, IL
Blumenfeld, Edgar A., (Ltd.) ... Chicago, IL
Blumenfeld, Eli ... Beverly Hills, CA
Blumenfeld, Eli, Law Corporation ... Beverly Hills, CA
Blumenfeld, Elizabeth deGrazia ... Dulles, VA
Blumenfeld, Eric ... Morristown, NJ
Blumenfeld, Franklin H. ... Bronx, NY
Blumenfeld, Gerald M. ... New City, NY
Blumenfeld, Glenn D. ... Philadelphia, PA
Blumenfeld, Jack A. ... Dothan, AL
Blumenfeld, Jack B. ... Wilmington, DE
Blumenfeld, Jack R. ... Miami, FL
Blumenfeld, Jack R., P.A. ... Miami, FL
Blumenfeld, Jeffrey ... Washington, DC
Blumenfeld, Jeffrey ... Philadelphia, PA
Blumenfeld, Jeremy P. ... Cincinnati, OH
Blumenfeld, Joel L. ... Long Island City, NY
Blumenfeld, John A. ... St. Louis, MO
Blumenfeld, John A., Jr. ... Minneapolis, MN
Blumenfeld & Kaplan ... New City, NY
Blumenfeld, Kaplan & Sandweiss, P.C. ... St. Louis, MO
Blumenfeld, Laura Ross ... Department of Justice, Federal Bureau of Investigation, GV
Blumenfeld, Louis B. ... Hartford, CT
Blumenfeld, Martin Lee ... Pittsburgh, PA
Blumenfeld, Michael ... Los Angeles, CA
Blumenfeld, Michael B. ... Washington, DC
Blumenfeld, Michael E. ... Baltimore, MD
Blumenfeld, Michael J. ... Oakland, CA
Blumenfeld, Michael J., A Professional Corporation ... Oakland, CA
Blumenfeld, Michael T. ... New York, NY
Blumenfeld, Norman L., Law Offices of ... Washington, DC
Blumenfeld, Richard ... Riverside, CA
Blumenfeld, Richard L. ... Albuquerque, NM
Blumenfeld, Robert L. ... El Paso, TX
Blumenfeld, Seth D. ... Rye Brook, NY
Blumenfeld, Sherry ... Nyack, NY
Blumenfeld, Stan ... Los Angeles, CA
Blumenfeld, Sue D. ... Washington, DC
Blumenfeld, Susan Bahme ... Philadelphia, PA
Blumenfield, Charles S. ... Milwaukee, WI
Blumenkopf, Alan ... Albany, NY
Blumenkopf, Jack ... Detroit, MI
Blumenkopf, Jay S. ... Boca Raton, FL
Blumenkopf, Norman ... New York, NY
Blumeno, Judith H. ... Farmington Hills, MI
Blumenreich, Gene A. ... Boston, MA
Blumenreich, Linda B. ... Federal Trade Commission, Bureau of Competition, GV
Blumenreich, Marc W. ... Los Angeles, CA
Blumenreich, Mordecai H. ... Oceanside, NY
Blumenshine, Scott A. ... Chicago, IL
Blumenson, Eric D. ... Boston, MA
Blumenson, Randi H. ... Suffolk, VA
Blumenson, Robert ... Jamaica, NY
Blumenstein, Adam ... New York, NY
Blumenstein, Carl L. ... San Francisco, CA
Blumenstein, Charles F., II ... Cherry Hill, NJ
Blumenstein, Karen S. ... Chicago, IL
Blumenstein, Paul A. ... Palo Alto, CA
Blumenstein, Randall S. ... Birmingham, MI
Blumenstiel, Huhn, Wood, Adams & Hemmer Co., L.P.A. ... Columbus, OH
Blumenstiel, James B. ... Columbus, OH
Blumenstiel, Laura C. ... Akron, OH
Blumenstock, Hyman ... Darien, CT
Blumenstock, John U. H. ... New York, NY
Blumenthal, Allen ... Los Angeles, CA
Blumenthal, Amy M. ... Chicago, IL
Blumenthal, Amy M. ... Dallas, TX
Blumenthal, Andrew F. ... New York, NY
Blumenthal, Anita G. ... Washington, DC
Blumenthal, Arthur J. ... Mequon, WI
Blumenthal, Barbara Z. ... Denver, CO
Blumenthal, Carol S. ... Washington, DC
Blumenthal, Dan M. ... Garden City, NY
Blumenthal, David A. ... Los Angeles, CA; Washington, DC
Blumenthal, David M. ... Wellesley, MA
Blumenthal, David M. ... New York, NY
Blumenthal, Delavan & Williams, P.A. ... Annapolis, MD
Blumenthal, Diane L. ... San Diego, CA
Blumenthal, Don M. ... Cleveland, OH
Blumenthal, Ellen ... Los Angeles, CA
Blumenthal, Elliot J. ... New York, NY
Blumenthal, Emily S. ... Atlanta, GA
Blumenthal, Gabriel H. ... Titusville, FL
Blumenthal, Gail ... Lawrence, NY
Blumenthal, Gary M. ... Dayton, OH
Blumenthal, Grant ... Chicago, IL
Blumenthal & Gruber, P.C. ... Dallas, TX
Blumenthal, Harry C. ... Annapolis, MD
Blumenthal, Henry ... New York, NY
Blumenthal, Herman B., III ... Seminole, FL
Blumenthal, Howard M. ... Department of Justice, Antitrust Division, GV
Blumenthal, Jeanne B., & Associates ... Merrillville, IN
Blumenthal, Jeffrey C. ... Chicago, IL
Blumenthal, Jeffrey M. ... Blue Bell, PA
Blumenthal, Jeffrey S. ... Chicago, IL
Blumenthal, Jerome H. ... Oklahoma City, OK
Blumenthal, John D. ... Doylestown, PA
Blumenthal, Jon E. ... Omaha, NE
Blumenthal, Kenneth S. ... Columbus, OH
Blumenthal, Linda C. ... Thousand Oaks, CA
Blumenthal & Lomazow, A Professional Law Corporation ... Riverside, CA
Blumenthal & Lynne, A Professional Corporation ... New York, NY
Blumenthal, Marc J. ... Buffalo Grove, IL
Blumenthal, Marc Nelson ... Park Ridge, IL
Blumenthal, Martin A. ... Northfield, IL
Blumenthal, Martin E. ... Riverside, CA
Blumenthal, Max E. ... Baltimore, MD
Blumenthal, Mel D. ... Santa Monica, CA
Blumenthal, Michael L. ... Chicago, IL
Blumenthal, Michael L. ... Kansas City, MO
Blumenthal, Michael R. ... Cleveland, OH
Blumenthal, Michael S., Law Offices of ... New Carrollton, MD
Blumenthal, Michael V. ... New York, NY
Blumenthal, Mitchell ... Sunnyvale, CA
Blumenthal, Ned ... Atlanta, GA
Blumenthal, Norman B. ... San Diego, CA
Blumenthal, Norman R. ... Los Angeles, CA
Blumenthal, Ostroff & Markham ... San Diego, CA
Blumenthal, Pamela Morris ... Washington, DC
Blumenthal, Paul S. ... Washington, DC
Blumenthal, Richard ... Stamford, CT
Blumenthal, Richard A. ... Malvern, PA
Blumenthal, Richard L. ... Beverly Hills, CA; **New York, NY**
Blumenthal, Richard L. ... Boston, MA
Blumenthal, Robert B. ... Riverside, CA
Blumenthal, Robert B., P.C. ... Riverside, CA
Blumenthal, Robert Henry ... San Francisco, CA
Blumenthal, Robert L. ... Dallas, TX
Blumenthal, Robert P. ... Memphis, TN
Blumenthal, Ronnie ... Equal Employment Opportunity Commission, Office of Federal Operations, GV
Blumenthal, Steven E. ... West Palm Beach, FL
Blumenthal, Steven E. ... Atlanta, GA
Blumenthal, Steven H. ... Chicago, IL
Blumenthal, Steven J. ... Mount Laurel, NJ; Philadelphia, PA
Blumenthal, Susan G. ... Washington, DC
Blumenthal, Susan K. ... Teaneck, NJ
Blumenthal, Thomas ... Denver, CO
Blumenthal, Thomas M. ... St. Louis, MO
Blumenthal, Virginia M. ... Riverside, CA
Blumenthal, Warren S. ... Milwaukee, WI
Blumenthal, William ... Washington, DC
Blumenthal-Stechman, Jane Ellen ... Garden City, NY
Blumer, Barbara J. ... St. Paul, MN
Blumer, Frederick T. ... Atlanta, GA
Blumer International, P.C. ... Atlanta, GA
Blumer, Kenneth R. ... Los Angeles, CA
Blumer, L. Celeste H. ... Clayton, MO
Blumer, Mark E. ... Lansing, MI
Blumer Nally & Siro ... Kansas City, KS; Kansas City, MO
Blumer, Stacey M. ... Department Of Health And Human Services, Office of the General Counsel, GV
Blumer, William R. ... Wyomissing, PA
Blumers, John M. ... Florham Park, NJ
Blumert, Stephen J. ... New York, NY
Blumfield, Darrin Ari ... Los Angeles, CA
Blumfield, Ronald A. ... Philadelphia, PA
Blumhardt, Kristi ... Denver, CO
Blumhardt, W. Eric ... Walnut Creek, CA
Bluming, Sidney D. ... New York, NY
Bluming, Sidney D., P.C. ... New York, NY
Blumkin, Anna Y. ... Boston, MA
Blumkin, Joy A. ... Ithaca, NY
Blumkin, Linda R. ... New York, NY
Blumling & Gusky, LLP ... Pittsburgh, PA
Blumling, Robert J. ... Pittsburgh, PA
Blumling, Sheldon J. ... Atlanta, GA
Blumm, Michael ... Portland, OR
Blumner, James ... Equal Employment Opportunity Commission, Office of Federal Operations, GV
Blumner, Linda Butler ... Baltimore, MD
Blumofe, Robt. F. ... Los Angeles, CA
Blumreich, Craig C. ... Topeka, KS
Blumrosen, Alfred William ... Newark, NJ
Blumrosen, Amy Jo ... Houston, TX
Blumrosen, Eric A. ... Houston, TX
Blumsack, Alan P. ... Somerville, MA
Blumsack & Canzano ... Woburn, MA
Blumsack, Charles E. ... Woburn, MA
Blum-Shore, Deborah K. ... Attleboro, MA
Blumson, Sarr J. ... Ann Arbor, MI
Blumstein, Allan ... New York, NY
Blumstein, Andree Sophia ... Nashville, TN
Blumstein, Block and Pease ... Merchantville, NJ; **Philadelphia, PA**
Blumstein & Dunn, A Professional Corporation ... Anchorage, AK
Blumstein, Edward ... Merchantville, NJ; **Philadelphia, PA**
Blumstein, Glenn J. ... Redmond, WA
Blumstein, James F. ... Nashville, TN
Blumstein, Jeffrey P. ... Lawrenceville, NJ
Blumstein, Joel G. ... Boston, MA
Blumstein, Mark I. ... Fort Lauderdale, FL
Blumstein, Mark I., P.A. ... Fort Lauderdale, FL
Blumstein, Nancy E. ... Minneapolis, MN
Blumstein, Philip ... Anchorage, AK
Blumstein, Stuart I. ... San Bruno, CA
Blunck, Christopher R. ... Environmental Protection Agency, Program Office Attorneys, GV
Blunck, Elaine N. ... Tempe, AZ
Blunck, Tedde R. ... Herndon, VA
Blunda, Christina F. ... Brick, NJ
Blunda, Mark J. ... Liberty Corner, NJ
Blunda, Stephen K. ... New York, NY
Blundall, George W. ... United States Court Of Appeals For The Federal Circuit, GV
Blundell, Isabelle A.S. ... Boston, MA
Blundell, Richard K. ... Greeley, CO
Blunden, Anthony A. ... Orinda, CA
Blundetto, Sandra G. ... New York, NY
Blundo, Frank G. ... Encino, CA
Blundon, Jill M. ... Pittsburgh, PA
Blunk, Christian R. ... Omaha, NE
Blunk, Forrest S. ... Denver, CO
Blunk, Richard A. ... Dallas, TX
Blunt, A. Paul ... Scottsdale, AZ
Blunt, Amy R. ... Liberty, MO
Blunt & Associates, Ltd. ... Edwardsville, IL
Blunt & Associates, P.C. ... Phoenix, AZ; Scottsdale, AZ
Blunt, David H. ... Salem, OR
Blunt, David L. ... Edwardsville, IL
Blunt, Jennifer M. ... Lusby, MD
Blunt, John L. ... Fairview, NJ
Blunt, Kathleen S. ... Thousand Oaks, CA
Blunt, Laurence C. ... Sacramento, CA

Blunt, Lawrence G. ... San Jose, CA
Blunt, Peter H. ... Sausalito, CA
Blunt, Richard S. ... Tampa, FL
Blunt, Shelton D. ... Baton Rouge, LA
Blunt, Steven A., Law Offices of
Pasadena, CA
Blunt, William W., Jr. ... Blue Bell, PA
Bluntson, Craig D. ... Jackson, MS
Bluntzer, Charles K. ... Victoria, TX
Blush, Susan A. ... Newport Beach, CA
Bluso, Linda L. ... Cleveland, OH
Blust, John M. ... Greensboro, NC
Blust, Larry D. ... Chicago, IL
Blust, Matthew L. ... West Palm Beach, FL
Blust, Thomas L. ... Batavia, OH
Blustein, Andrew E. ... Great Neck, NY
Blustein, Benjamin J. ... Department of Justice, Civil Rights Division, GV
Blustein, Burt J. ... Middletown, NY
Blustein, Michael S. ... Middletown, NY
Blustein, Philip Rubin ... Beverly Hills, CA
Blustein, Samuel J. ... Houston, TX
Blustin, L. Sanford ... Lincolnwood, IL
Blustin, Sholly A. ... Minneapolis, MN
Blut, Elliot S., Law Offices of
Los Angeles, CA
Blut, Jerome L. ... Las Vegas, NV
Blut, Jerome L., Chartered
Las Vegas, NV
Blut, Monica A. ... Los Angeles, CA
Blute, Joseph G. ... Boston, MA
Bluth, Arlene P. ... New York, NY
Bluth, Joseph P. ... Mankato, MN
Bluth, Lawrence ... Great Neck, NY
Bluth, Lawrence N. ... Detroit, MI
Bluth, Michael B. ... Buffalo, NY
Bluth, Robert E. ... Medford, OR
Bluth, Thomas J. ... Peoria, IL
Bluth, Thomas M. ... Fort Lauderdale, FL
Bluth, William H. ... Columbus, OH
Bluthardt, Edw. E. ... Franklin Park, IL
Blutman, Alan T. ... New York, NY
Blutman, Paul E. ... New York, NY
Blutrich, Falcone & Miller ... Somerset, NJ
Blutstein, Allan ... New York, NY
Blutstein, Elizabeth S. ... Milwaukee, WI
Blutstein, George J. ... Miami, FL
Blutter, Arthur I. ... Hicksville, NY
Blutter, Joanne Diamond ... Hicksville, NY
Bluver, Howard C. ... New York, NY
Bluver, Mark H. ... Springfield, MA
Bly, Herman O. ... Fort Myers, FL
Bly, James W. ... Columbia Heights, MN
Bly, L. Michael ... Dayton, OH
Bly, Loren L. ... Jamestown, NY
Bly, Paul M. ... Denver, CO
Bly, Rece, P.C. ... Portland, OR
Bly, Robert M. ... Knoxville, TN
Bly, Scott Alan ... Hershey, PA
Bly, Sheffield & Bargar ... Jamestown, NY
Bly, Virginia Rae Ott ... St. Paul, MN
Bly, William F. ... Los Angeles, CA
Blydenburgh, Candace A. ... Richmond, VA
Blydenburgh, Donald R. ... Central Islip, NY
Blye, Cecil A., Jr. ... Louisville, KY
Blye, Cecilia D.
Securities and Exchange Commission, Division of Corporation Finance, GV
Blye, Jeffrey D. ... Los Angeles, CA
Blye, Steven P. ... Norwalk, CA
Blyer, Alvin P. ... New York, NY
Blyer, Steven R. ... Valley Stream, NY
Blyler, Howard J. ... Cowen, WV
Blyler, Richard W. ... St. Petersburg, FL
Blyler, William E. ... Pisgah Forest, NC
Blyn, Arthur E. ... New York, NY
Blyn, Gary M. ... Roseland, NJ
Blyn, Kathy ... New York, NY
Blynn, Guy M. ... Winston-Salem, NC
Blynn, Ian J. ... Harrisburg, PA
Blynn, Michael R. ... Miami, FL
Blynn, Terry Peyser ... Harrisburg, PA
Blystone & Blystone ... Meadville, PA
Blystone, Bradley P. ... Orlando, FL
Blystone, Curtis E. ... Meadville, PA
Blystone, Kelly T. ... Orlando, FL
Blystone, Peter E. ... Meadville, PA
Blyth, Bradley C. ... Beaverton, OR
Blyth, Jesse J.M. ... San Diego, CA
Blyth, John E. ... Rochester, NY
Blyth, John W. ... Des Moines, IA
Blyth, Peter R. ... Beaverton, OR
Blyth, Porcelli & Blyth ... Beaverton, OR
Blyth, Stanley D. ... Napa, CA
Blythe, Angela M ... Oakland, MD
Blythe, Carol Beth
Department of Labor, GV
Blythe, Daniel G. ... Cheyenne, WY
Blythe, David J. ... Northfield, VT
Blythe, E. Bruce, III ... Louisville, KY
Blythe, Edward E. ... Chicago, IL
Blythe, James D., II ... Indianapolis, IN
Blythe, Kenneth A. ... Allentown, PA
Blythe, M. Keith ... Fort Smith, AR
Blythe & Ost ... Indianapolis, IN
Blythe, Richard M. ... Decatur, AL
Blythe, Robert B. ... Charlotte, NC
Blythe, Robert E. ... Los Angeles, CA
Palm Desert, CA
Blythe, Robert G. ... Tallahassee, FL
Blythe, Robert W. ... New Haven, CT
Blythe & Steiner, P.C. ... Cheyenne, WY
Blythe, Stephanie C. ... Lynchburg, VA
Blythe, Stephen E. ... Oklahoma City, OK
Blythe, Stephen E. ... Temple, TX
Blythe & Taylor ... Northfield, VT
Blythe, Wendy E. ... New York, NY

Blyveis, Barry ... Department of Justice, Criminal Division, GV
Blyweiss, Daniel A. ... Philadelphia, PA
B.-Mauritz, Jamie ... Andover, MA
Bninski, Roman A. ... New York, NY
Boackle & Associates ... Jackson, MS
Boackle, K. F. ... Jackson, MS
Boada, J. Alberto ... Los Angeles, CA
Boadi, Richard Yaw Keynes ... New York, NY
Boado, Andrea M. ... Chicago, IL
Boadwee, Harry ... Mountain View, CA
Boagni, Charles F., III ... Opelousas, LA
Boagni, Kenneth, Jr. ... Opelousas, LA
Boags, Charles D. ... Los Angeles, CA
Boak, Alison T. ... Atlanta, GA
Boak, Ethelyn A.B. (Lynn) ... Cheyenne, WY
Boak, Jeffrey L. ... Greenwich, CT
Boak, Robert I. ... Whitehouse, NJ
Boak, Ronald W. ... Philadelphia, PA
Boak, Scott W. ... Atlanta, GA
Boak, Stephen A. ... El Segundo, CA
Boak, Stephen H. ... Plymouth, MI
Boakes, Robert E. ... Woodbury, NJ
Boal, David W. ... Kansas City, KS
Boal, Dennis M. ... Evanston, WY
Boal, Ellis ... Detroit, MI
Boal, Jennifer F. ... Los Angeles, CA
Boal & Jeserich ... Kansas City, KS
Boal, Robert T., III ... Kent, WA
Boal & Spangler ... Evanston, WY
Boals, Heather M. ... Washington, DC
Boan, James ... Bolingbrook, IL
Boan, Jason Preston ... Spartanburg, SC
Boan, Joseph E. ... Pittsburgh, PA
Boan, Robert E. ... Miami, FL
Boanerges, James ... Houston, TX
Boano, Michael L. ... Youngstown, OH
Board, April Lee ... Merrillville, IN
Board, Charles L. ... Wilmington, DE
Board, Dwight V. ... Boise, ID
Board, John ... Guymon, OK
Board, John B. ... Amarillo, TX
Board, Joseph B., Jr. ... Scotia, NY
Board, Joseph W. ... Pickens, SC
Board, Wilmarth & Barela, L.L.P.
Amarillo, TX
Boardingham, Brian F. ... Nutley, NJ
Boardman, Carol Ann ... Stockton, CA
Boardman, Carr & Weed, P.C.
Birmingham, AL
Boardman, Charles T. ... Portland, OR
Boardman, Clifford A. ... Philadelphia, PA
Boardman, Dorothy Lowe ... Jacksonville, FL
Boardman, Ellen O. ... Washington, DC
Boardman, Gordon C. ... East Lansing, MI
Boardman, Harold F., Jr. ... Collegeville, PA
Boardman, J. Kevin ... Dallas, TX
Boardman, James E. ... St. Joseph, MI
Boardman, James M. ... Anchorage, AK
Boardman, James P. ... Saginaw, MI
Boardman, Joan T. ... Manassas, VA
Boardman, Joseph, P.C. ... Philadelphia, PA
Boardman, Kristi L. ... St. Louis, MO
Boardman, Mark S. ... Birmingham, AL
Boardman, Michael N. ... Ridgewood, NJ
Boardman, Radmore & Glassman, P.C.
Cherry Hill, NJ
Newtown, PA
Philadelphia, PA
Plymouth Meeting, PA
Boardman, Richard C. ... Boise, ID
Boardman, Richard J. ... St. Louis, MO
Boardman, Robert A. ... Chicago, IL
Boardman, Roger W., (P.S.)
Goldendale, WA
Boardman & Spiller, P.A. ... Immokalee, FL
Boardman, Suhr, Curry & Field LLP
Madison, WI
Boardman, Thomas A. ... St. Paul, MN
Boardman, Thomas K. ... Immokalee, FL
Boardman, William J. ... Washington, DC
Boardman, William M. ... Seattle, WA
Boardman, William T. ... Sandwich, MA
Boardman, Wm. F. ... Calais, ME
Boarman, Charles H. ... Newark, DE
Boarman, Charles V. ... Lexington, KY
Boarman, Donald J. ... Johnson City, TN
Boarman, Donald J., P.C. ... Johnson City, TN
Boarman, Roberta ... Chicago, IL
Boarnet, Barbara S. ... Irvine, CA
Boas, Arlene L. ... West Hempstead, NY
Boas, Christopher B. ... San Jose, CA
Boas, Craig ... Baltimore, MD
Boas, Hans F. ... The Woodlands, TX
Boas, Maxwell S. ... Fullerton, CA
Boas, Paul D. ... Pittsburgh, PA
Boas, Robert A. ... Atlanta, GA
Boas Schneider & Walsh ... St. Louis, MO
Boasberg, Albert L. ... San Francisco, CA
Boasberg, James E. ... Washington, DC
Boase, Ian A. ... Rancho Cordova, CA
Boat, John S. ... Oakland, CA
Boaten, H., P.A., Law Office of ... Topeka, KS
Boaten, Henry Osei ... Topeka, KS
Boateng, Agyenim ... Frankfort, KY
Boates, Scott K. ... Houston, TX
Boates, Scott K., P.C. ... Houston, TX
Boath, George W., Jr. ... Stratford, CT
Boatman, Boscarino, Grasso & Twachtman
Glastonbury, CT
Hartford, CT
Boatman, Edgar R. ... Okmulgee, OK
Boatman, James A., Jr. ... Winter Park, FL
Boatman, Mark A. ... St. Louis, MO
Boatman, Patrick W. ... Glastonbury, CT
Boatman, Robert W. ... Phoenix, AZ
Boatman, Suzan E. ... San Luis Obispo, CA
Boatman, W. Scott ... Indianapolis, IN

Boatner, Amy J. ... Dallas, TX
Boatner, B. Herbert, Jr. ... Tampa, FL
Boatner, John A., Jr. ... Bunkie, LA
Boatright, Brian D. ... Golden, CO
Boatright, Daniel B. ... Overland Park, KS
Boatright, David M. ... Austin, TX
Boatright, Douglas Craig ... Columbus, OH
Boatright, Gerald E. ... Wheat Ridge, CO
Boatright, J. Laddie ... Brunswick, GA
Boatright, J. Robert ... Kingsport, TN
Boatright, Jimmy J. ... Waycross, GA
Boatright, Lori N. ... Los Angeles, CA
Boatright, Peter L. ... Oklahoma City, OK
Boatright & Ripp, PLLC ... Wheat Ridge, CO
Boatright, Virgil A. ... Wheat Ridge, CO
Boatti, Robert P. ... New York, NY
Boatti, Stephen J. ... New York, NY
Boatwright, Adams & Bechelli
Concord, CA
Boatwright, Camille G. ... Coronado, CA
Boatwright, Daniel E. ... Concord, CA
Boatwright, David C. ... San Diego, CA
Boatwright, John B., III ... Richmond, VA
Boatwright, Joseph E., Jr. ... Orlando, FL
Boatwright, Marc W. ... Washington, DC
Boatwright, Richard H. ... Manassas, VA
Boatwright, Robert Scott ... Greenville, SC
Boatwright, Stephen E. ... Carlsbad, NM
Boatwright, Stephen R. ... Phoenix, AZ
Boatwright, William A. ... Des Moines, IA
Boaz & Associates, P.C.
Oklahoma City, OK
Boaz, Daniel Y. ... Paducah, KY
Boaz, Dennis L. ... Hagåtña, GU
Boaz, Joe Edd ... El Paso, TX
Boaz, Richard Earl ... Charleston, WV
Boaz, Samuel S. ... Paducah, KY
Boaz, Stephen S. ... Oklahoma City, OK
Boba, Matthew C. ... Chicago, IL
Boback, James M. ... Crystal Lake, IL
Boback, Karen J.
Christiansted, St. Croix, VI
Charlotte Amalie, St. Thomas, VI
Bobadilla, D. Fernando ... Miami, FL
Bobadilla, Doris T. ... New Orleans, LA
Bobak, Donald J. ... Akron, OH
Bobak, M. Lois ... Orange, CA
Bobak, Mark T. ... St. Louis, MO
Bobak, Thomas R. ... South Holland, IL
Bobango & Chance, A Professional Corporation ... Memphis, TN
Bobango, Gerald J. ... Fairmont, WV
Bobango, John A. ... Memphis, TN
Bobay, John R. ... San Anselmo, CA
Bobay, Kaechele & Wilensky, P.C.
Lansing, MI
Bobay, Thomas P. ... Lansing, MI
Bobb, Aviva K. ... Los Angeles, CA
Bobb, Donald K. ... Reading, PA
Bobb, Gordon M. ... Los Angeles, CA
Bobb, Howard L. ... Philadelphia, PA
Bobb, Merrick J. ... Los Angeles, CA
Bobb, Patricia C. ... Chicago, IL
Bobb, Patricia C., & Associates, P.C.
Chicago, IL
Bobb, Robert J. ... Gary, IN
Bobb, Sylvette C. ... Houston, TX
Bobbe, Cherie L. ... Aptos, CA
Bobber, Bernard J. ... Milwaukee, WI
Bobber, Peter C. ... Chicago, IL
Bobber, Thomas K. ... Green Bay, WI
Bobbink, Michael ... Bellingham, WA
Bobbish, Laury E. ... Department of Justice, Antitrust Division, GV
Bobbitt & Associates, P.C. ... Atlanta, GA
Bobbitt, Barton C. ... Portland, OR
Bobbitt, Blakeney A. ... San Francisco, CA
Bobbitt, Bradford A., (P.A.) ... Ocala, FL
Bobbitt, Calhoun ... Laredo, TX
San Antonio, TX
Bobbitt, David T. ... Miami, FL
Bobbitt, Elizabeth Knight ... Macon, GA
Bobbitt, Everett L. ... San Diego, CA
Bobbitt, Halter & Watson
San Antonio, TX
Bobbitt, Howard I. ... Portland, OR
Bobbitt, Jay C. ... Dallas, TX
Bobbitt, Julian D., Jr. ... Raleigh, NC
Bobbitt, Lawrence A., III ... Cheyenne, WY
Bobbitt, Lawrence C. ... Columbus, OH
Bobbitt, Leroy ... Santa Monica, CA
Bobbitt, Loren M. ... Springfield, IL
Bobbitt, Mary R. ... Ransom Canyon, TX
Bobbitt, Phillip L. ... Atlanta, GA
Bobbitt, Robert Lee, Jr. ... San Antonio, TX
Bobbitt & Roberts ... Santa Monica, CA
Bobbitt, Robin S. ... Houston, TX
Bobbitt, Ronald A. ... Chicago, IL
Bobbitt, Thomas C., III ... Dublin, GA
Bobbitt, Wesley Reid ... Albuquerque, NM
Bobbitt, Wesley Reid, A Professional Corporation ... Albuquerque, NM
Bobbitt, William E., Jr. ... Staunton, VA
Bobby, Charles H. ... El Macero, CA
Bobby, Theodore N. ... Pittsburgh, PA
Bobchin, Peter C. ... New York, NY
Bobeck, Glenn J. ... Buffalo, NY
Bobeck, Joshua Michael
General Services Administration, GV
Bobek, Barry A., Professional Association
Jacksonville, FL
Bobel, Anthony M. ... Niles, IL
Bobelian, Michael ... New York, NY
Bobell, Gordon F. ... Department of the Army, U.S. Army Legal Services Agency, GV
Boben, Barbara M. ... Lancaster, PA
Bobenhausen, Gale M. ... Safety Harbor, FL
Bobenhausen & Torrie ... Safety Harbor, FL

Bobenhouse, James E. ... Cedar Rapids, IA
Bober, Alan M. ... Irvine, CA
Bober, Carlton A. ... Fort Lauderdale, FL
Bober, Gerald Marvin
Occupational Safety and Health Review Commission, Administrative Law Judges, GV
Bober, Herbert J. ... Chatham, MA
Bober, Joanne L. ... Muskegon, MI
Bober, Leanne Myers ... Washington, DC
Bober, Peter J. ... Fort Lauderdale, FL
Bober, Ruth K. ... Floral Park, NY
Bober, Wayne J. ... Philadelphia, PA
Boberg, Charles P. ... Sandgate, VT
Boberg, John R. ... Mineola, NY
Boberg, Kenneth J. ... Red Bank, NJ
Boberg, Wayne D. ... Chicago, IL
Boberick, Donald H. ... Anchorage, AK
Boberschmidt, Philip F. ... Indianapolis, IN
Bobertz, Bradley C. ... Uniondale, NY
Bobetsky, Theodore J. ... Greenfield, MA
Bobetsky, William B. ... Benicia, CA
Concord, CA
Bobetsky, William B. ... Benicia, CA
Bobholz, Clifford D. ... Eau Claire, WI
Bobick, Bridget ... Atlanta, GA
Bobier, Katherine F. ... Reno, NV
Bobik, Ralph M. ... Tarzana, CA
Bobiles, Lazaro L. ... Sacramento, CA
Bobinets, Deborah L. ... Akron, OH
Bobinette, Charles W. ... St. Louis, MO
Bobinis, Charles E. ... Pittsburgh, PA
Bobinski, Mary Anne ... Houston, TX
Bobinski, Peter S. ... Department of Justice, Federal Bureau of Investigation, GV
Bobinsky, Syl F. ... Berea, OH
Bobis, Carmen, (Mrs.) ... Irvington, NY
Bobis, Daniel H. ... Westfield, NJ
Bobit, Janet J. ... Boston, MA
Bobitt, Thomas D., II ... Tuscaloosa, AL
Bobko, Noel A. ... Stuart, FL
Boblick, Shelby S. ... Chicago, IL
Bobman, Steven M. ... Lakewood, WA
Bobnak, George Stephen ... Philadelphia, PA
Bobner, William B. ... St. Louis, MO
Bobo, A. Russell ... North Palm Beach, FL
Bobo, Anne Roberts ... Little Rock, AR
Bobo, Christopher ... San Pedro, CA
Bobo, Fincher G. (Jack) ... Clarksdale, MS
Bobo, George M. ... Atlanta, GA
Bobo, Hunt & Bobo ... Murfreesboro, TN
Shelbyville, TN
Bobo, J. Allen ... Sarasota, FL
Bobo, J. Timothy ... Knoxville, TN
Bobo, J. A. (Jim) ... Odessa, TX
Bobo, James A. ... Brandon, MS
Florence, MS
Bobo, James E. ... Houston, TX
Bobo, John T. ... Shelbyville, TN
Bobo, Leslie Joyner ... Jackson, MS
Bobo, Malcolm P. ... Little Rock, AR
Bobo, Matthew ... Fort Worth, TX
Bobo, O.W., III ... Topeka, KS
Bobo, Patricia W.
Department Of Health And Human Services, Office for Civil Rights, GV
Bobo, Spicer, Ciotoli, Fulford, Bocchino & DeBevoise, P.A. ... Clearwater, FL
North Palm Beach, FL
Orlando, FL
Bobo, Stephen T. ... Chicago, IL
Bobo, William, Jr. ... Charleston, SC
Bobolia, George ... Santa Barbara, CA
Bobolia, Stephen J. ... Katonah, NY
Bobonis, Bobonis & Rodriguez Poventud
San Juan, PR
Bobonis, Clemente ... Carolina, PR
Bobonis, Guillermo J. ... San Juan, PR
Bobonis Gonzalez, Carlos A.
San Juan, PR
Bobonis-Zequeira, María del Pilar
San Juan, PR
Bobosky, W. Brand ... Naperville, IL
Bobotek, H. Mark ... Columbia, MD
Bobotek, James P. ... Washington, DC
Bobotek, Susan Teresa Treadwell
Department of State, Bureau of Consular Affairs, GV
Bobowick, Morton ... Toledo, OH
Bobowski, Richard P. ... Dallas, TX
Bobrick, Edward A. ... Chicago, IL
Bobrick, Sandra B. ... Tacoma, WA
Bobrin, George M. ... Philadelphia, PA
Bobrin, Linda G. ... Southfield, MI
Bobrink, Jeannie M. ... Kansas City, MO
Bobrinskoy, George V., Jr. ... Chicago, IL
Bobroff, Harold ... Woodmere, NY
Bobroff, Hesse, Lindmark & Martone, P.C.
St. Louis, MO
Bobroff, Michael J. ... St. Louis, MO
Bobroff, Seth B. ... San Diego, CA
Bobrosky, David B. ... Encino, CA
Bobrow, Adam F. ... Washington, DC
Bobrow, Alvan L. ... New York, NY
Bobrow, Arlene S. ... Denver, CO
Bobrow Greenapple Skolnik & Shakarchy
New York, NY
Bobrow, Henry B. ... White Plains, NY
Bobrow, Holly Nacht ... New York, NY
Bobrow, Howard J. ... Cleveland, OH
Bobrow, Irving S. ... New York, NY
Bobrow, Jared ... Menlo Park, CA
Bobrow, Kenneth L. ... Clinton, NY
Bobrow, Morris D. ... San Francisco, CA
Bobrow, Myla Denise ... Chicago, IL
Bobrow, Oscar Jacob ... Richmond, CA
Bobrow, Patricia Shaffer ... Utica, NY
Bobrow, Robert Dmitri ... Louisville, KY

Bobrow, Robert I. .... Morristown, NJ
Bobrow & Rosen .... New York, NY
Bobrow & Sosis .... New Rochelle, NY
Bobrow, Stuart Joseph .... Chicago, IL
Bobrow, Susan .... Sacramento, CA
Bobrow, Walter A. .... New Rochelle, NY
Bobrowiecki, John S., Jr. .... Gardiner, ME
Borowski, John J. .... Southfield, MI
Bobrowski, Mark .... Boston, MA
Bobrowsky, Kim R. .... Pittsburgh, PA
Bobruff, Neal M. .... Groton, CT
Bobruff, Paul A. .... Wethersfield, CT
Bobrycki, Kenneth J. .... Syracuse, NY
Bobryk, Michal L. .... Hartford, CT
Bobryk, Shirlee M. .... Okemos, MI
Bobula, Marilyn A. .... Cleveland, OH
Bobulsky, William P. .... Jefferson, OH
Bobus, Randall J. .... Santa Rosa, CA
Bobys, Hugh M. .... Los Angeles, CA
Bobys, Marc P. .... Los Angeles, CA
Bobzien, Andrew James .... Vancouver, WA
Bobzien, David P. .... Fairfax, VA
Bobzien, James A. .... St. Paul, MN
Boc, William E. .... Dover, NH
Bocage, Ronald J. .... Boston, MA
Bocamazo, Steven J. .... New York, NY
Bocamazo, Susan A. .... Boston, MA
Bocan, David E. .... Los Angeles, CA
Bocanegra Ocasio, Joanna .... San Juan, PR
Bocarsly, Lance S. .... Los Angeles, CA
Boccabella, John A. .... Reading, PA
Boccaccio, Christopher J. .... Hartford, CT
Boccalatte, John L. .... Middletown, CT
Boccardi, Maria .... Cleveland, OH
Boccardi, Susan M. .... New York, NY
Boccardo, James F. .... Los Gatos, CA
Boccardo Law Firm, The .... San Jose, CA
Boccarosse, Ralph N., Jr. .... Fairfax, VA
Boccassini, Joseph T. .... Newark, NJ
Boccella, Kathryn J. .... Fort Worth, TX
Boccher, Edward J. .... Westfield, NJ
Boccher, Geralyn A. .... Morristown, NJ
Bocchi, Linda Rosa .... Washington, DC
Bocchieri, Breton A. .... Los Angeles, CA
Bocchini, Suzanne S. .... Hartford, CT
West Hartford, CT
Bocchino, Amato J., Jr. .... Boston, MA
Bocchino, Anthony J. .... Pittsburgh, PA
Bocchino, John W. .... Clearwater, FL
North Palm Beach, FL
Orlando, FL
Bocchino, Linda Shafer .... Philadelphia, PA
Bocchino, Ralph P. .... Philadelphia, PA
Bocchino, Robert L., Jr. .... Boston, MA
Bocci, Frank E. .... Eugene, OR
Bocci, Frank E., P.C. .... Eugene, OR
Bocci & Hoffmann .... Portland, OR
Bocci, Mark R. .... Lake Oswego, OR
Bocci, Paul R., Jr. .... Portland, OR
Boccia, Barbara .... Daly City, CA
Boccia, Barbara, Law Office of, Inc.
Daly City, CA
Boccia, Julius S. .... Beacon, NY
Boccia, Michael R. .... Brooklyn, NY
Boccieri, Thomas E. .... Norwood, NJ
Boccio, David S. .... New York, NY
Boccio, Lynn A. .... Garden City, NY
Boccio, Richard A. .... Buffalo, NY
Boccio, Rosemary .... San Francisco, CA
Boccio, Virginia Ann .... Massapequa, NY
Boccio, William R. .... Mineola, NY
Boccippio, Frank W., Jr. .... Metuchen, NJ
Bocco, Veronica A. .... Cherry Hill, NJ
Boccumini, Carole Mae .... Yonkers, NY
Boccuti, Ascanio S. .... Towson, MD
Boccuto, Martin J. .... Honolulu, HI
Boccuzzi, Carmine D., Jr. .... New York, NY
Bocek, John R. .... Auburn, WA
Boch, Brian R. .... Chicago, IL
Boch, David C. .... Boston, MA
Bochanis, John T. .... Bridgeport, CT
Bochat & Keenan, P.C. .... Garden City, NY
Bochat, Kenneth F. .... San Francisco, CA
Bochat, Lawrence J. .... Garden City, NY
Bochenek, Casimir W. .... Cleveland, OH
Bochenek, Michael P .... New York, NY
Bochenek, Stephen J. .... Springfield, IL
Bocher, Sheri L. .... Atlanta, GA
Bocher, Sheri L., P.C. .... Atlanta, GA
Bochert, Linda H. .... Madison, WI
Boches, Barry H. .... Waukegan, IL
Boches, Barry H. & Associates, P.C.
Waukegan, IL
Bochet, William C. .... Fair Lawn, NJ
Bochetto, George .... Philadelphia, PA
Bochetto & Lentz, A Professional Corporation .... Cherry Hill, NJ
Philadelphia, PA
Bochicchio, Paul J. .... Boston, MA
Bochicchio, Vito S. .... Pittsburgh, PA
Bochino, Harold A. .... Danbury, CT
Bochinski, Julianne Blair, Law Office of
Canton, CT
Bochinski, Pamela D. .... Westport, CT
Bochis, George John .... Lakeland, FL
Bochis, Joanne Salvatore .... Little Falls, NJ
Bochis, Vincent J. .... Little Falls, NJ
Bochner, Lisa J. .... New York, NY
Bochner, Paul M. .... Ardsley, NY
Bochner, Ron K. .... Oakland, CA
Bochner, Steven E. .... Palo Alto, CA
Bochner, Suzanne .... Jamaica, NY
Bochnewich, Marie A. .... Palm Desert, CA
Bochnewich, Peter M. .... Palm Springs, CA
Bochniak, Lori J. .... Madison, WI
Bochte & Kuzniar .... St. Charles, IL
Bochte, William F. .... St. Charles, IL
Bocian, David A. .... Washington, DC
Bocianowski, Michael W. .... Redmond, WA
Bocik, Edward J. .... Sylvania, OH
Bock, A. David .... Fayetteville, NC
Bock, Aaron C. .... Hawthorne, NY
Bock, Amy K. .... Dallas, TX
Bock, Bennie, II .... New Braunfels, TX
Bock, Brian D. .... Riverside, CA
Bock, Dale E. .... Bloomington, IL
Bock, Daniel A. .... Phoenix, AZ
Bock, Diana K. .... Tampa, FL
Bock, Elizabeth A. .... Springfield, MO
Bock, Eric J. .... Parsippany, NJ
Bock, Eric P. .... Washington, DC
Bock and Finkelman, P.C. .... Ardmore, PA
Bock, Frederic W. .... Warrensburg, MO
Bock, G. Roger .... Boulder, CO
Bock, George M. .... Kansas City, MO
Bock, H. Riley .... New Madrid, MO
Bock, Harris T. .... Philadelphia, PA
Bock, Harry H. .... New Madrid, MO
Bock, Harvey N. .... Riverwoods, IL
Bock, Henry E., Jr. .... Boston, MA
Bock, James E. .... San Antonio, TX
Bock, Jane Sujen .... New York, NY
Bock, Jeffrey B. .... Clearwater, FL
Bock, Jeffrey W. .... Portland, OR
Bock, Joel H. .... Chicago, IL
Bock, Joel N. .... New York, NY
Bock, John A., Jr. .... Belleville, IL
Bock, John Gordon .... Houston, TX
Bock, Joseph R. .... Newark, NJ
Bock, Joseph R. .... Pittsburgh, PA
Bock, Kathleen M. .... Fairfield, CA
Napa, CA
Bock, Kim E. .... New Boston, NH
Bock, Leonard A. .... Palm Springs, CA
Bock, Les .... Boise, ID
Bock, Leslie S. .... Boston, MA
Bock, Louis .... Woodbury, NY
Bock, Lynn N. .... New Madrid, MO
Bock, Mary Milan .... Denver, CO
Bock, Maureen Ann .... Wichita, KS
Bock, Michael G. .... Pittsburgh, PA
Bock, Morton M. .... New York, NY
Bock, Nicole Theophilus .... Kansas City, MO
Bock, Norman P. .... New York, NY
Bock, P. Maureen .... Boise, ID
Bock, Patricia Y. .... Sacramento, CA
Bock, Paul S. .... Washington, DC
Bock, Phillip A. .... Chicago, IL
Bock, Phyllis A. .... Bozeman, MT
Bock, R. Stewart .... Seattle, WA
Bock, Richard C. .... Tucson, AZ
Bock, Richard P. .... Springfield, MA
Bock, Robert Jonathan .... Phoenix, AZ
Bock, Simon .... New York, NY
Bock, Stephen J. .... Farmington Hills, MI
Bock, Thomas E. .... Bay City, MI
Bock, Tracy Heslin .... Plainfield, IN
Bock, Wallace .... New York, NY
White Plains, NY
Bock, William F. .... Elkhorn, WI
Bock, William, III .... Indianapolis, IN
Bockanic, William N. .... Hudson, OH
Bockelie, Nanci Snow .... Salt Lake City, UT
Bockelman, C. William, Jr. .... Lake Forest, IL
Bockelman, J. Richard .... Chicago, IL
Bockelman, Robert J. .... San Francisco, CA
Bocken, R. Charles .... Honolulu, HI
Bocker, Karen Ann .... Mineola, NY
Bockes, Kurt R. .... Oakland, CA
Bocketti, Brian J. .... Buffalo, NY
Bockhop, Bryan William .... Atlanta, GA
Bockhorst, Thomas A. .... Boston, MA
Bockian, Jonathan M. .... Boston, MA
Bockley, Kathryn M. .... Atlanta, GA
Bockman & Bockman .... Tuscaloosa, AL
Bockman, Craig R. .... Los Angeles, CA
Bockman, Cynthia Helene Moore
Columbus, MS
Bockman, Cynthia M. .... Tuscaloosa, AL
Bockman, Harlan R. .... Brighton, CO
Bockman, Henry W. .... Sherman Oaks, CA
Bockman, John E. .... Tuscaloosa, AL
Bockman, Lori L. .... St. Louis, MO
Bockman, Robert T. .... Columbia, SC
Bockman, Stuart Fink .... Torrance, CA
Bockmon, Fred .... Phoenix, AZ
Bockmon, Julia Barrows .... Anchorage, AK
Bockmon, Matthew C. .... Sacramento, CA
Bockner, Gordon Judd .... Stamford, CT
Bocko, Robert J. .... Seattle, WA
Bockoff, Henry .... Southfield, MI
Bockol, Richard Max .... Narberth, PA
Bockrath, Joseph T. .... Baton Rouge, LA
Bocks, Nathan .... Holland, MI
Bocksch, Rochelle .... Fort Lauderdale, FL
Bockstein, Herbert .... New York, NY
Bockstein, Mark P. .... Fort Lauderdale, FL
Bockstein, Mark P. .... Plantation, FL
Bockstein, Martin H. .... New York, NY
Bockus, Jane .... San Antonio, TX
Bock-Vavroch, Martha, (Mrs.) .... Belleville, IL
Boco, Robert L. .... Sunnyvale, CA
Bocock, Candice H. .... Austin, TX
Bocock, Joseph H. .... Oklahoma City, OK
Bocock, Kerry L. .... Oklahoma City, OK
Bocook, Bret K. .... Durham, NC
Bocott, James C. .... North Platte, NE
Bocskor, Catherine E. .... Rockville, MD
Boczar, Barbara A. .... Davis, CA
Boczar, James J., (P.A.) .... Indianapolis, IN
Boczenowski, Anthony Paul .... Lexington, MA
Boda, Daniel K. .... Columbus, OH
Boda, Steven J. .... Edison, NJ
Boda, Veronica C. .... Philadelphia, PA
Boda, Wm. Paul .... Wichita, KS
Bodach, L. Barrett .... Chicago, IL
Bodach, Robert C. .... Joliet, IL
Bodager, Barbara Aileen .... San Francisco, CA
Bodager, Bill W. .... Media, PA
Bodager, Bradley E. .... Elkview, WV
Bodager, Brian R. .... Green Bay, WI
Bodah, Scott F. .... Camillus, NY
Bodamer, A. Bradley .... Kansas City, MO
Bodansky, Joel N. .... Seattle, WA
Bodansky, Robert L. .... Washington, DC
Bodanza & Bodanza .... Leominster, MA
Bodanza, David P. .... Leominster, MA
Bodanza, Mark C. .... Leominster, MA
Bodary, James W. .... Southfield, MI
Bodas, Margie R. .... Minneapolis, MN
Bodden & Muraoka, Attorneys at Law, A Law Corporation .... Wailuku, HI
Bodden, Thomas A. .... Wailuku, HI
Boddicker, Clinton R. .... Keokuk, IA
Boddicker, Joan M. .... Minneapolis, MN
Boddicker, Joe L. .... Charter Oak, IA
Denison, IA
Boddie, Arvin .... Chicago, IL
Boddie, Deborah D. .... Washington, DC
Boddie, Elise C. .... New York, NY
Boddie, James H., Jr. .... Bastrop, LA
Boddie, John H. .... Greensboro, NC
Boddie, Needham J., II .... Raleigh, NC
Boddie, Richard F. .... Springfield, VA
Boddie, Rodney B. .... Falls Church, VA
Boddington & Brown, Chartered
Kansas City, KS
Kansas City, MO
Boddington, Edward M., Jr.
Kansas City, KS
Boddy, Carla Denine .... Cleveland, OH
Boddy, Charles D., Jr. .... Manchester, NH
Boddy, Elizabeth J. .... Oak Brook, IL
Boddy, James E., Jr. .... San Francisco, CA
Bode, Allen Lee .... Kew Gardens, NY
Bode & Beckman, L.L.P. .... Washington, DC
Bode, C. Brett .... Peoria, IL
Bode, Call & Stroupe, L.L.P. .... Raleigh, NC
Bode, Carroll, McCoy, Hoefle & Mihal, S.C.
Milwaukee, WI
Waukesha, WI
Bode, Charles M. .... Columbia, MD
Bode, Clive D. .... Fort Worth, TX
Bode, Dale L. .... Belleville, IL
Edwardsville, IL
Bode, Dawn E. .... Chicago, IL
Bode, Denise Anne .... United States Senate, Senatorial Assistants, GV
Bode, Eileen Ann .... Mineola, NY
Bode, Frederick W., III .... Pittsburgh, PA
Bode, George A. .... Tallahassee, FL
New Orleans, LA
Bode, H. Christian .... Phoenix, AZ
Bode, Hugh J. .... Cleveland, OH
Bode, Jay L. .... Marietta, GA
Bode, Jeannette R. .... Chicago, IL
Bode, John R. .... Chattanooga, TN
Bode, John T. .... Raleigh, NC
Bode, John Theiler .... Waukesha, WI
Bode, John W. .... Washington, DC
Bode, Joy R. .... Austin, TX
Bode, Keith A. .... Lynden, WA
Bode, Keith F., (LTD.) .... Chicago, IL
Bode, Kirk W. .... Pekin, IL
Bode, Matthew S. .... Department of Justice, Criminal Division, GV
Bode, Michael J. .... Mineola, NY
Bode, Nancy .... St. Paul, MN
Bode, Philip L. .... Phoenix, AZ
Bode, Richard L. .... Rapid City, SD
Bode, Robert C. .... Richmond, VA
Bode, Robert V. .... Raleigh, NC
Bode, William H. .... Washington, DC
Bodeau, A. Scott .... Carson City, NV
Bodeau, Andrew .... Los Angeles, CA
Bodeau, Sandra Yaeger .... Minneapolis, MN
Bodeen, Diana Hilary .... Paterson, NJ
Bodek, Arthur W. .... New York, NY
Bodek, David N. .... New York, NY
Bodek, Efraim J. .... Far Rockaway, NY
Bodell, Bové , Grace & Van Horn, A Professional Corporation .... Cherry Hill, NJ
Bodell, Bové, Grace & Van Horn, A Professional Corporation
Philadelphia, PA
Bodell, Bové , Grace & Van Horn, A Professional Corporation .... Pittsburgh, PA
Bodell, Gerald E. .... Bridgeport, CT
New York, NY
Bodell, Gerald E. .... Greenwich, CT
Hartford, CT
New Haven, CT
Norwalk, CT
Bodell, Joseph T., Jr. .... Philadelphia, PA
Bodem, Loren E. .... Stuart, FL
Bodem, Loren E., Chartered .... Stuart, FL
Bodemer, Jo Ann .... Uniondale, NY
Boden, Barbara M. .... Boston, MA
Boden, L. Donald .... Santa Barbara, CA
Boden, Martha L. .... Albany, NY
Boden, Stephanie L. .... Farmingdale, NY
Boden, Suzan E. .... Sioux City, IA
Boden, Suzanne M. .... Vero Beach, FL
Bodendorf, Andrew F. .... Washington, DC
Bodenger, George W. .... Philadelphia, PA
Bodenhamer, Don P. .... Fort Worth, TX
Bodenhamer, Katrina S. .... Tulsa, OK
Bodenhamer, Kenneth D. .... Tulsa, OK
Bodenhamer & Levinson, P.A. .... Tulsa, OK
Bodenhamer, M. J. .... Philadelphia, MS
Bodenheimer, David Z. .... Washington, DC
Bodenheimer, Howard S. .... Encino, CA
Bodenheimer, James P. .... Shreveport, LA
Bodenheimer, John T. .... Aiken, SC
Bodenheimer, Jones & Szwak, L.L.P.
Shreveport, LA
Bodenheimer, Stephen M., Jr.
Charlotte, NC
Bodenhofer, Paul J. .... Niantic, CT
Bodenrader, Edw. W. .... Lawrence, MA
Bodenstab, Richard G. .... Chicago, IL
Bodenstedt, Kristin J. .... Washington, DC
Bodenstein, Diane .... New York, NY
Bodenstein, Gail M. .... New York, NY
Bodenstein, Janette S. .... Los Angeles, CA
Bodenstein, Jordan H. .... Las Vegas, NV
Bodensteiner, Dominic T. .... Washington, DC
Bodensteiner, Ivan E. .... Valparaiso, IN
Bodensteiner, Lisa M. .... San Jose, CA
Bodensteiner, William L. .... Austin, MN
Boder, Robert M. .... New York, NY
Bodet, Marcus .... Miami, FL
Bodet, Nancy O. .... St. Louis, MO
Bodet, Richard L. .... Kenner, LA
Bodeux, Reginald P. .... St. Charles, MO
Bodewes, Christine M. .... Chicago, IL
Bodewes, Herman G. .... Springfield, IL
Bodholt, Seanna M. .... Spokane, WA
Bodi, Attila I. .... New York, NY
Bodi, Lynn J. .... Madison, WI
Bodi, Steven Richard .... Medfield, MA
Bodian & Bodian, LLP .... White Plains, NY
Bodian, David H. .... White Plains, NY
Bodian & Eames, L.L.P. .... New York, NY
Bodian, Helen .... New York, NY
Bodian, Martin H. .... Melville, NY
Bodian, Robert I. .... New York, NY
Bodick, John K. .... Anchorage, AK
Bodie, Carroll A. .... Hunt Valley, MD
Bodie, Gary J. .... Prineville, OR
Bodie, James C. .... Richmond, VA
Bodie, Jeffrey C. .... Portland, OR
Bodie, John F., Jr. .... Toledo, OH
Bodie, Nagle, Dolina, Smith & Hobbs, P.A.
Bel Air, MD
Reisterstown, MD
Towson, MD
Bodie, T. Lee .... Tampa, FL
Bodie, Thomas G. .... Bel Air, MD
Reisterstown, MD
Towson, MD
Bodien, Bernard L. .... Grand Rapids, MN
Bodiford, Christopher L. .... Arlington, VA
Bodiford, James G. .... Marietta, GA
Bodiford, James W., Jr. .... Mobile, AL
Bodiford, Joseph C. .... Tampa, FL
Bodiford, Larry A. .... Panama City, FL
Bodiford, Raymond O. .... Orlando, FL
Bodiford, Robin L. .... Fort Lauderdale, FL
Bodik, Colleen D. .... West Palm Beach, FL
Bodik, Michael G. .... West Palm Beach, FL
Bodiker, David H. .... Columbus, OH
Bodily, Timothy A. .... Las Vegas, NV
Bodin, Gregory E. .... Baton Rouge, LA
Bodin, James F. .... Duluth, MN
Bodin, James Gerard .... Montgomery, AL
Bodin, Kristi .... Springfield, MA
Bodin, Mark N. .... New Orleans, LA
Bodin, Paul David .... Coral Gables, FL
Bodin, Philippe .... Portland, OR
Bodin, Vincent J. .... Jackson, MS
Bodine, Brian G. .... Seattle, WA
Bodine, David .... Bridgeport, CT
Bodine, J. Joseph, Jr. .... Columbus, OH
Bodine, Jennifer B. .... Denton, MD
Bodine, John D. .... Sullivan, IN
Bodine, John W. .... Gwynedd, PA
Bodine, Laurence .... Chicago, IL
Bodine, Margot R. .... Rye Brook, NY
Bodine, Mark V. .... Overland Park, KS
Bodine, Susan Hunt .... New York, NY
Bodinet, Nancy R. .... Phoenix, AZ
Bodinson, Ron .... Overland Park, KS
Bodker, Brian D. .... Atlanta, GA
Bodker, Drew M. .... Spokane, WA
Bodker, Ramsey & Andrews, A Professional Corporation .... Atlanta, GA
Bodker, Stuart E. .... Kansas City, MO
Bodkin, Henry G., Jr. .... Los Angeles, CA
Bodkin, Laurence G., Jr. .... New York, NY
Bodkin, Lynn M. .... New York, NY
Bodkin, Michael N. .... Coos Bay, OR
Bodkin, R. Thomas .... Evansville, IN
Bodlander, Linda M. .... Los Angeles, CA
Bodlander, Linda M., Law Offices of
Los Angeles, CA
Bodle, David J. .... Indianapolis, IN
Bodle, John F. .... Lafayette, IN
Bodley, Alice L.
Federal Labor Relations Authority, Authority Member Staff, GV
Bodley, David W. .... Pocomoke City, MD
Bodley, James C. .... Cincinnati, OH
Bodley, John M. .... Sacramento, CA
Bodley, Michelle L. .... Vienna, VA
Bodman, James F., Jr. .... Mobile, AL
Bodman, Longley & Dahling LLP
Ann Arbor, MI
Cheboygan, MI
Detroit, MI
Troy, MI
Bodman, Matthew Day .... Columbia, SC
Bodmer, Bradley William Brian .... Albany, NY
Bodmer, Isabelle H. .... New York, NY
Bodmer, Kathleen Lawler .... Andover, MA
Bodnam, Elizabeth A. .... St. Louis, MO
Bodnar, Alexandra A. .... Los Angeles, CA
Bodnar, Andrew G. .... New York, NY
Bodnar, Brenda T. .... Cleveland, OH
Bodnar, James R. .... Medford, NJ
Bodnar, John C. .... St. Louis, MO

Bodnar, Joseph J. .... Bethany Beach, DE
Wilmington, DE
Bodnar, Julie M. .... **Cincinnati, OH**
Bodnar, Laura W. .... **St. Louis, MO**
Bodnar, Martin J. .... Akron, OH
Bodnar, Melisa L. .... **Macon, GA**
Bodnar, Peter O. .... **White Plains, NY**
Bodnar, Priscilla M. .... Philadelphia, PA
Bodnar, Raymond L., (P.C.) .... Guttenberg, NJ
Bodnar, Thomas L. .... South Bend, IN
Bodne, Michael D. .... North Miami Beach, FL
Bodner, Bruce, (P.C.) .... New York, NY
Bodner, Bruce W. .... San Antonio, TX
Bodner, Charles D. .... **Elmwood Park, NJ**
Bodner, Diane .... **Washington, DC**
Bodner, Fredric L. .... **Albany, NY**
Bodner, Gerald A. .... Bronx, NY
Bodner, Gerald T. .... **Syosset, NY**
Bodner, Hal .... Los Angeles, CA
Bodner, Jacob .... **New York, NY**
Bodner, Joan B. .... Brookline, MA
Bodner, John, Jr. .... **Washington, DC**
Bodner, Karen E. .... Los Angeles, CA
Bodner, Leigh R. .... Atlanta, GA
Bodner, Leonard S. .... Boston, MA
Bodner, Linda O. .... New York, NY
Bodner, Marcella M. .... **Morristown, NJ**
Bodner, Mark H. .... Fairfax, VA
Bodner, Mark L. .... New York, NY
Bodner, Mark S. .... **Framingham, MA**
Bodner, Michael J. .... **Pittsburgh, PA**
Bodner, Paul M. .... New York, NY
Bodner, Randall W. .... **Boston, MA**
Bodner, Susan P. .... New York, NY
Bodney, David J. .... **Phoenix, AZ**
Bodney, Howard E. .... **Overland Park, KS**
Bodney, John A. .... **Chico, CA**
Paradise, CA
Bodnieks, Lars O. .... **Miami, FL**
Bodo, C. Eric .... Chicago, IL
Bodo, Maureen M. .... San Rafael, CA
Bodoff, Amy P. .... New York, NY
Bodoff, Fred A. .... Brooklyn, NY
Bodoff, Jeffrey .... **New York, NY**
Bodoff, Joseph S. U. .... **Boston, MA**
Providence, RI
Bodoff, Lippman .... Glen Rock, NJ
Bodoff, Stuart M. .... **Uniondale, NY**
Bodoh, Devon M. .... Detroit, MI
Bodoh, Keith D. .... **Marietta, GA**
Bodoh, William T. .... Youngstown, OH
Bodoin, Robert R. .... **Arlington, TX**
Bodolay, Stephen M. .... Treasury Department, Federal Law Enforcement Training Center, GV
Bodolay, Teresa S. .... **Clearwater, FL**
Bod ón, Zulma A. .... Woodside, NY
Bodor, Brian R. .... **Washington, DC**
Bodor, C. Andrew .... Warren, OH
Bodor, C. Andrew, Co., L.P.A. .... Warren, OH
Bodor, Frank R. .... Warren, OH
Bodorff, Richard J. .... **Washington, DC**
Bodovitz, James P. .... New York, NY
Bodow, Joel M. C. .... Los Angeles, CA
Bodow, Wayne R. .... **Syracuse, NY**
Bodrato, Michael F. .... Tenafly, NJ
Bodron, Mark A. .... **Houston, TX**
Bodson, Bruce R. .... Seabrook, TX
Bodson, Michael E.
Department of Commerce, Patent and Trademark Office, GV
Bodtker, Willard .... Albany, OR
Bodurtha, James K. .... **Springfield, MA**
Bodwell, John W. .... Connersville, IN
Bodwell, Lori M. .... Fairbanks, AK
Bodwin, Randolph L. .... East Lansing, MI
Bodwitch, William P. .... Syracuse, NY
Body, David W. .... Des Moines, IA
Body, James B. .... Fort Worth, TX
Bodycombe, Paul A. .... Hilliard, OH
Bodyfelt, E. Richard .... Portland, OR
Bodyfelt, Mount, Stroup & Chamberlain
Portland, OR
Vancouver, WA
Bodzin, Gary A. .... North Miami Beach, FL
Bodzin, Martin I. .... Boca Raton, FL
Bodzin, Robert B. .... **Philadelphia, PA**
Bodzin, Robert M. .... **Oakland, CA**
Bodzin, Sidney M. .... Miami, FL
Bodzin, Stephen A. .... Washington, DC
Bodziner, Steven .... Brooklyn, NY
Boe, Elliott O. .... Fergus Falls, MN
Boe, Kathleen M. .... **Burlington, VT**
Boe, Marianne Guerrini .... Chicago, IL
Boe, P. Nathaniel .... **Chicago, IL**
Boe, Randall J. .... **Dulles, VA**
Boe, Rodger C. .... **Hartford, CT**
Boe, Ryan N. .... **Aberdeen, SD**
Boe, Susan M. .... West Des Moines, IA
Boe, Tim .... **Little Rock, AR**
Boe, William .... Seattle, WA
Boebel, Norman L. .... Mukwonago, WI
Boechler, Jeanette .... Fargo, ND
Boeck, Daniel P. .... Buffalo, NY
Cheektowaga, NY
Lancaster, NY
Boeck, David .... Bismarck, ND
Boeck, Tamara L. .... **Gold River, CA**
Boeck, William A. .... **Los Angeles, CA**
Boecke, Donald W. .... **Boston, MA**
Boeckel, Craig A. .... Bismarck, ND
Boeckeler, John C. .... Nashua, NH
Boecker, Jeffrey A. .... Washington, DC
Boecker, Sylvia J. .... Virginia Beach, VA
Boecker, Sylvia J., P.C. .... Virginia Beach, VA
Boecker, Theodore R. .... **Clive, IA**
Boecker, Theodore R., Jr. .... Omaha, NE
Boeckman, Bradley L. .... Redding, CA
Boeckman, Daniel V. .... St. Peters, MO
Boeckman, Duncan E. .... Dallas, TX
Boeckman, James W. .... **Austin, TX**
Boeckman, Joseph P. .... **Columbus, OH**
Boeckman, Philip J. .... **New York, NY**
Boeckman, Richard A. .... **Great Bend, KS**
Boeckman, Sara Jane .... Kingfisher, OK
Boeckmann, Fred .... Columbia, MO
Boeckmann, O. Joseph, Jr. .... Wynne, AR
Boeckmann, Terry B. .... Bowling Green, KY
Boedecker, Aviva Shiff .... Berkeley, CA
Boedecker, James G. .... **San Francisco, CA**
Boedecker, K. Judson .... Sarasota, FL
Boedecker, Katrina I. .... Olympia, WA
Boedeker, Edgar G. .... **St. Louis, MO**
Boedeker, E. W. .... Levelland, TX
Boedeker, Joseph F. .... Roseville, MI
Boedeker, Thomas R. .... Soldotna, AK
Boedekker, Joe .... Roseville, MI
Boeder, Bruce A. .... Minneapolis, MN
Boeder, Thomas L. .... **Seattle, WA**
Boedigheimer, Robert D. .... Minneapolis, MN
Boeding, Jo Diane R. .... Kansas City, KS
Boeding, Paul R. .... Gladstone, MO
Boeding, Thomas L. .... Kansas City, KS
Boegel, Ellen K. .... New York, NY
Boeger, Elmore L. .... Riverside, IL
Boeger, Heerwagen, Lusthoff & Brendemuhl, P.C. .... Riverside, IL
Boeger, John L. .... St. Louis, MO
Boeggeman, George, Hodges & Corde, P.C.
Stamford, CT
Albany, NY
New York, NY
White Plains, NY
Boeglin, Brian J. .... Chicago, IL
Boeglin, Daniel L. .... **Indianapolis, IN**
Boeglin, G. James .... **Fort Wayne, IN**
Boeglin, Timothy J. .... Chicago, IL
Boeglin & Troyer .... **Fort Wayne, IN**
Boegner, Carolyn Crandall .... Flint, MI
Boeh, Alan M. .... Troy, KS
Boeh, Cynthia Ann Adamson
St. Paul, MN
Boeh, John D. .... St. Joseph, MO
Boehk, Robert P. .... Bryan, OH
Boehl Stopher & Graves .... **New Albany, IN**
Lexington, KY
Louisville, KY
Paducah, KY
Prestonsburg, KY
Boehle, Joelle Schulze .... **Austin, TX**
Boehle, Wayne J. .... **Santa Monica, CA**
Boehlefeld, Heidi A. .... Cleveland, OH
Boehler, Anne Marie
Department of Commerce, Patent and Trademark Office, GV
Boehler, Christopher T. .... **Houston, TX**
Boehler, James R. .... Rochester, NY
Boehlert, C. Richard .... Falls Church, VA
Boehlert, Garry R. .... **Washington, DC**
Boehlert, Jeffrey A. .... **Des Moines, IA**
Boehley, Lisa E.
Federal Communications Commission, Common Carrier Bureau, GV
Boehling, D.E. .... **Washington, DC**
Boehling, George A. .... **Mineola, NY**
Boehling, Lawrence S. .... Burgaw, NC
Boehlje, Boyd W. .... Pella, IA
Boehlje, Todd M. .... **St. Louis, MO**
Boehm, Ann M.
Federal Labor Relations Authority, Office of the Solicitor, GV
Boehm, Arthur R., Jr. .... San Ramon, CA
Boehm & Associates, P.C. .... Chicago, IL
Boehm & Boehm .... Barrington, IL
Boehm, Brian B. .... Manhasset, NY
Boehm, Brown, Seacrest, Fischer & LeFever, P.A. .... **Daytona Beach, FL**
Ocala, FL
Orlando, FL
Tallahassee, FL
Tampa, FL
Boehm, Bruce J. .... **Stockton, CA**
Boehm, Carl R. .... **Charlotte, NC**
Boehm, Carolyn Grace .... **Rolla, MO**
Boehm, Casper P., Jr. .... Sayreville, NJ
Boehm, Christopher Charles .... Norwalk, CT
Boehm, Claudette .... Manhattan Beach, CA
Boehm, David F. .... **Cincinnati, OH**
Boehm, David O. .... **Rochester, NY**
Boehm, Donald R. .... Houston, TX
Boehm, Edward N. .... **Chattanooga, TN**
Boehm, Frederick A. .... **Pittsburgh, PA**
Boehm, Gabrielle T. .... East Troy, WI
Boehm, Garrett L. .... Barrington, IL
Boehm, H. G. .... Northridge, CA
Boehm, J. Richard .... **Daytona Beach, FL**
Boehm, Jack E., Jr. .... **Chicago, IL**
Boehm, Jeffrey D. .... **Chattanooga, TN**
Boehm, Joel T. .... **San Diego, CA**
Boehm, John C., Jr. .... **Austin, TX**
Boehm, John M. .... **Lincoln, NE**
Boehm, Kenneth L. .... Upper Marlboro, MD
Boehm, Kenneth L., P.C.
Upper Marlboro, MD
Boehm, Kurtz & Lowry .... **Cincinnati, OH**
Boehm, Lisa S. .... **Portland, ME**
Boehm, Mary Alice C. .... **Edinburg, TX**
Boehm, Michelle M. .... **Kansas City, MO**
Boehm, Paul J. .... Cincinnati, OH
Boehm, Rachel E. .... **San Francisco, CA**
Boehm, Richard G. .... Hamburg, NY
Boehm, Robert C. .... **Miami, FL**
Boehm, Robert C. .... **Buffalo, NY**
Boehm, Robert G. .... Chico, CA
Boehm, Robert I. .... Chicago, IL
Boehm, Robert J. .... **Chattanooga, TN**
Boehm, Robert L. .... New York, NY
Boehm, Sandra R. .... St. Paul, MN
Boehm, Sandra R., Ltd., & Associates
St. Paul, MN
Boehm, Scott E. .... **Phoenix, AZ**
Tucson, AZ
Boehm, Steven B. .... **Washington, DC**
Boehm, Thomas .... Fresno, CA
Boehm, Thomas M. .... San Jose, CA
Boehm, William C. .... Morton, WA
Boehm, Wm. J. .... Crownsville, MD
Boehmcke, Daniel E. .... Philadelphia, PA
Boehmcke, Elizabeth Q. .... **New York, NY**
Boehme, Donna C. .... **Murray Hill, NJ**
Boehme, Mark Thomas .... Concord, CA
Boehmer, Clifford B. .... Mission Viejo, CA
Boehmer, Colette .... Medford, OR
Boehmer, Raymond .... La Jolla, CA
Boehmer, Richard A. .... **Los Angeles, CA**
Boehmer, Robert G. .... Athens, GA
Boehmer, Steven E. .... **El Cajon, CA**
Boehnen, Daniel A. .... **Chicago, IL**
Boehnen, David L. .... **Eden Prairie, MN**
Boehner, Donald H. .... Greenvale, NY
Boehner, Leonard B. .... **New York, NY**
Boehner, Russell J. .... **Pittsburgh, PA**
Boehnert, John M. .... **Providence, RI**
Boehning, H. Christopher .... **New York, NY**
Boehning, Richard A. .... **Lafayette, IN**
Boehning, Stuart P. .... **Lafayette, IN**
Boehnke, Yvette .... San Pedro, CA
Boehnlein, Mary A. .... Waukesha, WI
Boehrer, Charles B. .... **Chicago, IL**
Boehringer, C. Shawn .... Miami, FL
Boehringer, Kelly M. .... Owings Mills, MD
Boehringer, Lynne Therese
North Chicago, IL
Boeing, William L. .... **Dallas, TX**
Boeke, Lee E. .... **Atlanta, GA**
Boeke, Noel .... **Tampa, FL**
Boeke, Robert M. .... Midland, MI
Boekeloo, Charles F. .... Grand Rapids, MI
Boekeloo, Charles F., P.C.
Grand Rapids, MI
Boek-Werness, Sandra .... Alexandria, VA
Arlington, VA
Boelcke, Mary Lou .... Eugene, OR
Boeldt, James M. .... Adell, WI
Boelhouwer, Annette M. .... **Boston, MA**
Boelio, Robert W. .... Palm Springs, CA
Royal Oak, MI
Boelio, Sharon .... **Pontiac, MI**
Boelk, Christine Vierra .... Pleasant Hill, CA
Boellert, Karl E. .... Lake Charles, LA
Boelte, Kathleen M. .... Englewood, CO
Boelter, Allen B. .... Marina Del Rey, CA
Boelter, Arthur H. .... **Seattle, WA**
Boelter & Associates .... **Seattle, WA**
Boelter, Jay A. .... **Atlanta, GA**
Boelter, John D. .... Minneapolis, MN
Boelter and Perry .... Marina Del Rey, CA
Boelter, Philip F. .... **Minneapolis, MN**
Boelter, Richard W. .... Wautoma, WI
Boelzner, David E. .... **Richmond, VA**
Boemanns, R. John .... Blairsville, GA
Boemanns, Virginia A. .... Blairsville, GA
Boemer, Robert B. .... **Houston, TX**
Boemig, Madison K. .... Wells River, VT
Boemig & Taylor .... Wells River, VT
Boenig, Leonard D. .... Menlo Park, CA
Boeniger, Stacie A. .... **Boston, MA**
Boening, Amy E. .... Dallas, TX
Boennighausen, Mark V. .... San Francisco, CA
Boennighausen, Susan Roeder .... San Jose, CA
Boenning, Franklin W. .... **Roseland, NJ**
Boenning, Henry O. .... **Haddonfield, NJ**
Boensch, A. Cranwell .... Walterboro, SC
Boepple, Elizabeth A. .... **Bennington, VT**
Manchester Center, VT
Boer, Cindy C. .... **Denver, CO**
Boer, Ellen S. .... Greenwich, CT
Boer, Gina Dashman .... **Berkeley, CA**
Boer, Katarina K. .... **Washington, DC**
Böer, Ralf-Reinhard .... **Milwaukee, WI**
Boer, Roger W. .... **Grand Rapids, MI**
Boer, Tom J.
Environmental Protection Agency, Office of the General Counsel, GV
Boerger, George H. .... Columbus, OH
Boergers, David P.
Federal Energy Regulatory Commission, Office of the General Counsel, GV
Boericke, J. Bradley .... **Philadelphia, PA**
Boericke, William H. .... **New York, NY**
Boerigter, Daniel W. .... **Minneapolis, MN**
Boerigter, James C. .... **Kalamazoo, MI**
Boeringer, William R. .... **Miami, FL**
Boerio, Michael S. .... **San Mateo, CA**
Boerman, Mary Jo .... Grand Rapids, MI
Boerner, David .... Tacoma, WA
Boerner & Dennis .... **Lubbock, TX**
Boerner, Gene G., III .... **Tulsa, OK**
Boerner & Goldsmith, P.C. .... **Ida Grove, IA**
Boerner, Joe V., Jr. .... **Lubbock, TX**
Boerner, John E. .... Towson, MD
Boerner, Laurel L. .... **Ida Grove, IA**
Odebolt, IA
Boerner Law Firm .... Odebolt, IA
Boerner, Margaret .... Philadelphia, PA
Boerner, Robert S. .... Sheboygan, WI
Boerner, Roger L. .... **Milwaukee, WI**
Boerner, William D. .... **Brookhaven, MS**
Boers, Alan E. .... Manlius, NY
Boersch, Martha .... Berkeley, CA
Boerschig, John P. .... Katy, TX
Boerschinger, Thomas H. .... **Chicago, IL**
Boersig, Thomas C., Jr.
Maryland Heights, MO
Boersma, David J. .... Wheaton, IL
Boersma, Diana Lurie .... Tarrytown, NY
Boersma, Wilhelmina .... Detroit, MI
Boerstler, Heidi .... Denver, CO
Boerstler, Herbert W. .... Houston, TX
Boertzel, Gail S. .... **Morristown, NJ**
Boes, C. Todd .... **Boston, MA**
Boes, Carol S. .... **Palo Alto, CA**
Boes, Charles W. .... Dallas, TX
Boes, Helge P. .... **Washington, DC**
Boes, Janet M. .... Saginaw, MI
Boes, Judith R. "Lynn" .... **Des Moines, IA**
Boes, Lawrence E. .... **New York, NY**
Boes, Lawrence W. .... **New York, NY**
Boesch, Charles H. .... Dayton, OH
Boesch, Lawrence M. .... San Jose, CA
Boesch, Lydia O. .... San Francisco, CA
Boesch, Philip W., Jr., (Professional Corporation) .... **Los Angeles, CA**
Boesch, Terry R. .... Valparaiso, IN
Boesch, William L. .... **Boston, MA**
Boesch, William S. .... **Manchester, NH**
Portsmouth, NH
Boesche, McDermott & Eskridge
Bartlesville, OK
Muskogee, OK
Tulsa, OK
Boeschenstein, Edward A. .... **St. Louis, MO**
Boeschenstein, Eric .... Muskegon, MI
Boeschenstein, William S. .... San Diego, CA
Boese, Douglas A. .... **Rochester, MN**
Boese, J. Lynn .... Indianapolis, IN
Boese, John A. .... Freehold, NJ
Boese, John T. .... **Washington, DC**
Boese, Kerrie A. .... Denver, CO
Boese, Max .... Bainbridge Island, WA
Boese, Michael James .... **Duluth, MN**
Boese, Randall .... **Los Angeles, CA**
Boese, Robert L. .... **Baton Rouge, LA**
Boesel, Milton C., Jr. .... **Toledo, OH**
Boesen, Jon C. .... Denver, CO
Boesen, Martha E. .... Des Moines, IA
Boeshart, Paul D. .... Lincoln, NE
Boesiger, Robert F. .... **Detroit, MI**
Boesky, Julie A. .... **Portland, ME**
Boesky, Keith D. .... San Diego, CA
Boesky, Roger .... San Diego, CA
Boesman, William C. .... Library of Congress, Congressional Research Service, GV
Boespflug, John F., Jr. .... **Seattle, WA**
Boessenecker, Edward J. .... San Francisco, CA
Boessenecker, Janet M. .... San Francisco, CA
Boessenecker, John E. .... San Francisco, CA
Boester, Kevin L. .... Pinckneyville, IL
Boester, Robert A. .... Hampton, VA
Boetcher, Martin J. .... **Youngstown, OH**
Boetsch, Mary E. .... Reno, NV
Boettcher, Charles C. .... **Dallas, TX**
Boettcher, Cynthia J. .... Tulsa, OK
Boettcher, David F. .... Fresno, CA
Boettcher & Drummond .... Tulsa, OK
Boettcher, Fred L. .... Ponca City, OK
Boettcher, LaLonde, Kleweno, Rutledge, Jahn & Holtmann, P.S. .... Vancouver, WA
Boettcher Law Offices, Inc. .... Ponca City, OK
Boettcher, Matthew J. .... **Detroit, MI**
Boettcher, Roger W. .... Madison, WI
Boettcher, Ryan & Martin
Oklahoma City, OK
Ponca City, OK
Tulsa, OK
Boettcher, Thomas D. .... Tulsa, OK
Boettcher, Wayne M. .... Muskogee, OK
Boettcher, Werner .... Puyallup, WA
Boettcher, William C. .... Vancouver, WA
Boettcher, William H. .... Mesa, AZ
Phoenix, AZ
Boetter, Bruce William .... **San Diego, CA**
Boettge, Douglas R. .... **Minneapolis, MN**
Boettger, Thomas E. .... Pittsburgh, PA
Boetticher, Albert V. .... Chestertown, MD
Boetticher, Kristin L. .... **Minneapolis, MN**
Boettinger, Stephen W. .... **Milwaukee, WI**
Boettler, Louis A. .... **Canton, OH**
Boetto & Boetto .... Joliet, IL
Boetto, Dominic F. .... Joliet, IL
Boetto, Paul V. .... Joliet, IL
Boever, Virginia .... Alexandria, MN
Boevers, James A. .... **Salt Lake City, UT**
Boex, Steven R. .... Green Bay, WI
Boex-Jordan, Kathleen M.
Madisonville, KY
Boeye, John Billings .... Red Oak, IA
Boeye, John F. .... Red Oak, IA
Boeye, Robert P. .... **Moline, IL**
Boezeman, Richard A. .... Las Vegas, NV
Boezi, Henry V., III .... Providence, RI
Boffa, Jeffrey R. .... **New York, NY**
Boffa, Robert C. .... Beverly Hills, CA
Boffa, William, Jr. .... Roselle Park, NJ
Boffey, Christopher .... **Chicago, IL**
Bofill, Jose Carlos .... Miami, FL
Bofill & Vilar, P.A. .... Miami, FL
Bofinger, Charlene .... McLean, VA
Bofinger, Theodore F. .... Carmichael, CA
Bofshever, Harold S. .... **Fort Lauderdale, FL**
Boga, Terence R. .... **Los Angeles, CA**
Bogaard, Jonathan H. .... **Chicago, IL**
Bogaard, Laurie Hall .... Fair Haven, NJ
Bogaard, Peter A. .... **Newark, NJ**
Bogaard, William J. .... Pasadena, CA
Bogaards, Debra F. .... **San Francisco, CA**
Bogaards, Pieter .... **San Rafael, CA**
Bogacz, Stephen J. .... Brooklyn, NY
Bogaczyk, David M. .... Detroit, MI
Bogaczyk, David M. .... Blossburg, PA
Bogad & Lyte .... South Plainfield, NJ
Bogad, Suzanne T. .... South Plainfield, NJ

Bogaert, William T. ... **Boston, MA**
Bogaerts, Andree ... **New York, NY**
Bogage, Jedd E. ... San Diego, CA
Bogan, Brett C. ... **Overland Park, KS**
Bogan, Bruce R. ... **Orlando, FL**
Bogan, Charles E. ... Abilene, KS
Bogan, David B. ... Arlington Heights, IL
Bogan, David W. ... **Stamford, CT**
Bogan, Donald T. ... Greensboro, NC
Bogan, J. Steedley ... **Columbia, SC**
Bogan, James F., III ... **Atlanta, GA**
Bogan, John J. ... **Blue Bell, PA**
Bogan, Joseph ... Rancho Mirage, CA
Bogan, Linzie F. ... Savannah, GA
Bogan, Lisa M. ... Washington, DC
Bogan, Mary Ann Pelly
Point Pleasant Beach, NJ
Bogan, Mary Elizabeth ... **Philadelphia, PA**
Bogan, Nancy Nicholson ... **Albany, NY**
Bogan, Robert ... Albany, NY
Bogan, Robert E. ... Columbia, SC
Bogan, Robin C. ... **Hackensack, NJ**
Bogan, Thomas P. ... Clinton, NY
Bogan, Willie C. ... San Francisco, CA
Bogar, James D. ... Shiremanstown, PA
Bogar, Thomas J. ... **Wilmington, DE**
Bogarad, Sharon N. ... **Weirton, WV**
Bogard, Aimee B. ... **Birmingham, AL**
Bogard, Brian K. ... Jefferson City, MO
Bogard, David B. ... Little Rock, AR
Bogard, Donald P. ... Plainfield, IN
Bogard, Hal Nance ... **Louisville, KY**
Bogard, Howard E. ... **Birmingham, AL**
Bogard, Lawrence J. ... **Washington, DC**
Bogard, Mark D. ... **Phoenix, AZ**
Bogard, Robert S. ... **St. Louis, MO**
Bogardus, David P. ... Chesterfield, VA
Bogardus, Frank E. ... Albany, NY
Bogardus, John H. ... Lakeview, OR
Bogardus, Kristina ... **Albuquerque, NM**
Bogardus & Nichols, P.C. ... Lakeview, OR
Bogardus, Peter B., Jr. ... Gunnison, CO
Bogardus, Phyllis L. ... Kansas City, MO
Bogart, Amy L. ... **Washington, DC**
Bogart & Bogart, P.C. ... **Atlanta, GA**
Bogart, Christian B. ... **Metairie, LA**
Bogart, Christine Clark ... **Atlanta, GA**
Bogart, Christopher P. ... **New York, NY**
Bogart, Daniel B. ... Des Moines, IA
Bogart, Edward J. ... **Jersey City, NJ**
Bogart, Elizabeth R. ... **Stockton, CA**
Bogart, Ernest F., Jr. (P.C.) ... Bastrop, TX
Elgin, TX
Bogart, George ... General Accounting Office, Office of the General Counsel, GV
Bogart, James W. ... Salinas, CA
Bogart, Jeffrey B. ... **Atlanta, GA**
Bogart, Jeffrey H. ... **San Diego, CA**
Bogart, John G. ... Tucson, AZ
Bogart, John H. ... **Salt Lake City, UT**
Bogart, Joshua ... **New York, NY**
Bogart, Kelly Cambre ... **Metairie, LA**
Bogart, Larry I. ... **Atlanta, GA**
Bogart, Leonard B. ... Sun City, AZ
Bogart, Mark I. ... **Chicago, IL**
Bogart, Marni ... **Buffalo, NY**
Bogart, Matthew R. ... **Minneapolis, MN**
Bogart, Nelson ... New York, NY
Bogart, Phyllis ... Santa Monica, CA
Bogart, Ryan and Campisano
Jersey City, NJ
Bogart, Steffi K. ... **New York, NY**
Bogart, Steven P. ... **Milwaukee, WI**
Bogart, Susan ... **Chicago, IL**
Bogart, Vincent L. ... **Wichita, KS**
Bogart, William H. ... Syracuse, NY
Bogart, William H., P.C. ... Syracuse, NY
Bogartz, Amy Haas ... Atlanta, GA
Bogas, Kathleen L. ... Detroit, MI
Bogas, Paul
Equal Employment Opportunity Commission, Office of Legal Counsel, GV
Bogash, Morris ... New Rochelle, NY
Bogason, Robert S. ... Mill Valley, CA
Bogatin, Corman & Gold
San Francisco, CA
Bogatin, Irvin, (P.C.) ... **Memphis, TN**
Bogatin Law Firm, The, PLC
Memphis, TN
Bogatin, Marc ... **New York, NY**
Bogatin, M. J. ... **San Francisco, CA**
Bogatto, Barron P. ... **Houston, TX**
Bogatto, Richard P. ... **Houston, TX**
Bogaty, A. Paul ... New York, NY
Bogaty, McEwen & Sparks, P.C.
Grove City, PA
Bogaty, Raymond H. ... Grove City, PA
Bogaty, William J. ... Fairfax, VA
Bogatz, Harold ... Hightstown, NJ
Bogatz, I. Scott ... **Las Vegas, NV**
Bogatz, James A. ... Lincoln, NE
Bogatz, Neil B. ... Hightstown, NJ
Bogatz and Shore, A Professional Corporation
Hightstown, NJ
Bogatz, Susan A. ... **New York, NY**
Bogda, Russell W. ... Los Angeles, CA
Bogda-Cleveland, Hedi E. ... Chicago, IL
Bogdan, Edward A., III ... Albany, NY
Bogdan, Edward A., Jr. ... Albany, NY
Bogdan, Eric A.V. ... Houston, TX
Bogdan and Faist, P.C. ... Albany, NY
Bogdan, Francis G. ... Milford, CT
Bogdan, Frederick W. ... **New York, NY**
Bogdan, Henry W. ... Baltimore, MD
Bogdan, Joseph J. ... **Chicago, IL**
Bogdan, Kenneth A. ... Bel Air, MD
Bogdan, Robert Anthony
Pompano Beach, FL
Bogdan, Robert P. ... **Buffalo, NY**
Bogdan, Robert P. ... **Sackets Harbor, NY**
Bogdan, Robert P ... **Watertown, NY**
Bogdan, Suzanne K. ... **Fort Lauderdale, FL**
Bogdan, William A. ... **San Francisco, CA**
Bogdanchik, Mark David V. ... Pasadena, CA
Bogdanoff, Charles Jay ... Philadelphia, PA
Bogdanoff & Charles, LLC ... Greenwich, CT
Bogdanoff, John N. ... Daytona Beach, FL
Bogdanoff, Karen J. ... Greenwich, CT
Bogdanoff, Lee R. ... **Los Angeles, CA**
Bogdanoff, Michael S. ... Philadelphia, PA
Bogdanoff, Philip ... Akron, OH
Bogdanoff, Robert J. ... Delray Beach, FL
Bogdanoff, Suzanne ... **White Plains, NY**
Bogdanos, Claudia T. ... **New York, NY**
Bogdanos, Matthew F. ... Bayside, NY
Bogdanos, Tula ... **San Francisco, CA**
Bogdanovich, Guy ... **Olympia, WA**
Bogdanow, Alan J. ... **Dallas, TX**
Bogdanow, Michael B. ... **Boston, MA**
Bogdanowicz, Kathryn A. ... **Chicago, IL**
Bogdanski, Donna, (P.C.) ... Macedon, NY
Bogdanski, John A. ... Portland, OR
Bogdanski, John J. ... **Hartford, CT**
Bogdanski, Joseph W. ... New Haven, CT
Bogden, Edward K. ... Troy, MI
Bogden, James M. ... **Seattle, WA**
Bogden, Kenneth E. ... Sandusky, OH
Bogdon, Bernard D. ... Raleigh, NC
Bogdon, Donald L. ... Glendale, CA
Bogdon, Paul ... Pittsburgh, PA
Bogdon, Steven N. ... **Vancouver, WA**
Bogdonoff, Glenn ... Treasury Department, Internal Revenue Service, GV
Bogdonoff, Michael A. ... **Philadelphia, PA**
Boge, William A. ... Manassas, VA
Bogeaus, Geoffrey Forsythe
Los Angeles, CA
Bogen, Andrew E. ... **Los Angeles, CA**
Bogen, Andrew S. ... **New York, NY**
Bogen, Charles ... **New York, NY**
Bogen, Curt P. ... Niles, OH
Bogen, David S. ... Baltimore, MD
Bogen, Edward J., Jr. ... **Leland, MS**
Oxford, MS
Bogen, Evelyn K. ... Amherst, MA
Bogen, Gloria Elizabeth ... St. Paul, MN
Bogen, Gordon ... **Dallas, TX**
Bogen, Judy ... **Los Angeles, CA**
Bogen, Kimberlee S. ... **San Francisco, CA**
New York, NY
Bogen, Mark D. ... Boca Raton, FL
Bogen, Mark D., P.A. ... Boca Raton, FL
Bogen, Mark R. ... Lebanon, OH
Bogen, Robert L. ... **Fort Lauderdale, FL**
Bogen, Roy A. ... Minneapolis, MN
Bogen, William ... Cresskill, NJ
Bogenreif, Darcy J. ... Chicago, IL
Bogenrief, Paul A. ... **Torrance, CA**
Bogenschutz & Dutko, P.A.
Fort Lauderdale, FL
Bogenschutz, J. David
Fort Lauderdale, FL
Bogenschutz, Michael ... Humble, TX
Bogenschutz, Stephen A. ... Cedarville, OH
Boger, Brent D. ... Bellevue, WA
Boger, Brian L., Law Offices of
Columbia, SC
Boger, Gene S. ... **Orlando, FL**
Boger, John Charles ... Chapel Hill, NC
Boger, John R., Jr. ... **Concord, NC**
Boger, John W. ... Albany, NY
Boger, Keith A. ... Delaware, OH
Boger, Kenneth S. ... **Boston, MA**
Boger, William H., III ... Washington, DC
Bogert, Albert Z. ... New Cumberland, PA
Bogert, Jeffrey C. ... Los Angeles, CA
Bogert, Jeffrey F. D. ... **Miami, FL**
Bogert, Laurence M. ... Sacramento, CA
Bogetto, Philip D. ... Fort Collins, CO
Boggan, Ricky L. ... Jackson, MS
Boggess, D. Brian ... Las Vegas, NV
Boggess, G. Carl ... Bedford, VA
Boggess, Jeffrey A. ... Crawfordsville, IN
Boggess, Jeffrey A., P.C. ... Crawfordsville, IN
Boggess, Lovett T. ... Anderson, TX
Boggess, Rhonda B. ... **Jacksonville, FL**
Boggess, Thomas Phillip ... River Forest, IL
Boggess, Timothy D. ... Princeton, WV
Boggess, William V. ... Fairbanks, AK
Boggia, Eugene S. ... Philadelphia, PA
Boggia, Peter F. ... Hackensack, NJ
Boggia, Philip N. ... **Ridgefield Park, NJ**
Boggia, Priscilla M. ... **Ridgefield Park, NJ**
Boggie, Jean C. ... **Clinton, NJ**
Boggins, John F. ... Canton, OH
Boggins, Joseph C. ... **Austin, TX**
Boggio, Bernard C. ... Cincinnati, OH
Boggio, Dorothy A. ... New Wilmington, PA
Boggio, Gail Marie ... **White Plains, NY**
Boggio, Linda Maria ... New York, NY
Boggio, Louis J. ... Denver, CO
Boggio, Randy F. ... Bloomington, MN
Boggs, A. Michael ... Bossier City, LA
Boggs, Anthony R. ... **Atlanta, GA**
Boggs, Archie ... New Orleans, LA
Boggs, B. Jefferson, Jr. ... **Alexandria, VA**
Boggs, Backer & Bates, LLC
Belleville, IL
Kansas City, MO
St. Louis, MO
Boggs, Beth C. ... **St. Louis, MO**
Boggs, Bhavana S. ... **Washington, DC**
Boggs, Byron W. ... Missoula, MT
Boggs, Cameron G. (Bozzie) ... Greenville, SC
Boggs, Carol Ann ... Washington, DC
Boggs, Celene M.E. ... **Fresno, CA**
Boggs, Charles A., (A Law Corporation)
New Orleans, LA
Boggs, Craig T. ... **Chicago, IL**
Boggs, Danny J. ... Louisville, KY
Boggs, David C. ... **Charlotte, NC**
Boggs, David M. ... **Tampa, FL**
Boggs, Dean ... Jacksonville, FL
Boggs, Don A. ... Tallahassee, FL
Boggs, Don P. ... Havana, IL
Boggs, Donald A. ... Jacksonville, FL
Boggs, Douglas C. ... **Washington, DC**
Boggs, Duane A. ... **Cincinnati, OH**
Boggs, E. Jackson ... **Tampa, FL**
Boggs, Edward Cunningham
Columbia, SC
Boggs, Edward V. ... Detroit, MI
Boggs, Elaine M.
Securities and Exchange Commission, Division of Investment Management, GV
Boggs & Fishel ... **Panama City, FL**
Boggs, George T. ... **Washington, DC**
Boggs, H. Glenn, II ... Tallahassee, FL
Boggs, Howard W. ... Sylvania, OH
Boggs, J. Caleb, III ... **Wilmington, DE**
Washington, DC
Philadelphia, PA
Boggs, Jacqueline A. ... Los Angeles, CA
Boggs, James D. ... **Kansas City, MO**
Boggs, James D. ... **Platte City, MO**
Boggs, James N. ... Los Angeles, CA
Boggs, James T. ... Greensburg, PA
Boggs, John A. ... Tallahassee, FL
Boggs, John H. ... **Toledo, OH**
Boggs, John N. ... **Panama City, FL**
Boggs, John Phillip ... **Redwood City, CA**
Boggs, John S., Jr. ... Pawhuska, OK
Boggs, Jonathan D. ... Jacksonville, FL
Boggs, Kelly A. ... **Columbus, OH**
Boggs, Kenneth M. ... Barbourville, KY
Boggs, Kenneth R. ... Columbus, OH
Boggs, Kimberly R. ... **Dayton, WA**
Boggs & Knuppel, P.C. ... Havana, IL
Boggs, L. Kennedy ... Columbia, SC
Boggs, Larry A. ... **Fairfield, CT**
Boggs, Loehn & Rodrigue
New Orleans, LA
Boggs, Louise Cobb ... Richmond, VA
Boggs, Michael P. ... Waycross, GA
Boggs, N. Cornell, III ... **St. Louis, MO**
Boggs, Patrick H. ... **Columbus, OH**
Boggs, Paul R., III ... **Newport, KY**
Boggs, Paula E. ... **Round Rock, TX**
Boggs, Ralph S. ... Toledo, OH
Boggs, Robert M. ... **Yakima, WA**
Boggs, Ronald L. ... St. Charles, MO
Boggs, Roy E., Jr. ... Chicago, IL
Boggs, Steven E. ... Honolulu, HI
Boggs, Steven Parker ... **Harlan, KY**
Boggs, Steven W. ... College Station, TX
Boggs, T. Hale ... **Palo Alto, CA**
Boggs, Thad E. ... Dalton, GA
Boggs, Theodore A. ... **Columbus, OH**
Boggs, Thomas A. M. ... **Spartanburg, SC**
Boggs, Thomas H., Jr. ... **Demopolis, AL**
Boggs, Thomas Hale, Jr. ... **Washington, DC**
Boggs, Travis G. ... Albany, NY
Boggs, Virginia R. ... Washington, DC
Boggs, William H., Sr. ... Jasper, GA
Boggs, William P. ... Clanton, AL
Boggs, William S. ... **San Diego, CA**
Bogguss, J. Scott ... **Cedar Rapids, IA**
Boggy, S. Nicholas ... **Fremont, NE**
Bogh, Richard J. ... Alhambra, CA
Bogh, Stacy R. ... Sacramento, CA
Boghetich, Tony ... Oklahoma City, OK
Boghigian, Gregory R. ... **Nashua, NH**
Boghosian, Robert A. ... **New York, NY**
Boghosian, Vorton B. ... Latham, NY
Boghossian, Berg A. ... New York, NY
Boghossian, Leon C., III ... **Boston, MA**
Providence, RI
Bogiages, Stephen A. ... Cambridge, MA
Bogie, Robert Reid ... Brookfield, CT
Bogie, Terence J. ... Delran, NJ
Bogigian, Janet G. ... Los Angeles, CA
Bogigian, Robert G. ... Greenfield, IN
Bogin, Asher ... **Dayton, OH**
Bogin, Bonnie I. ... **Beverly Hills, CA**
Bogin, Bruce M. ... **Orlando, FL**
Bogin, Linda ... **New York, NY**
Bogin, Matthew B. ... **Washington, DC**
Bogin, Michael S. ... **New York, NY**
White Plains, NY
Bogin, Munns & Munns ... **Deltona, FL**
Kissimmee, FL
Ocala, FL
Orlando, FL
Bogin, Patterson & Bohman LLP
Dayton, OH
Bogins-McDowell, Sharon ... Biddeford, ME
Bogisch, Karen A. ... **Austin, TX**
Bogle, Bill F. ... **Fort Worth, TX**
Bogle, Carol A. ... Poughkeepsie, NY
Bogle, Charles R. ... **New York, NY**
Bogle & DeAscentis, P.C. ... **Fall River, MA**
Mattapoisett, MA
Bogle, Edgar F. ... **Gastonia, NC**
Bogle, Elizabeth Bentley
Merit Systems Protection Board, Washington, D.C. Regional Office, GV
Bogle, Gavin T. ... **New York, NY**
Bogle, Horace R., Jr. ... Lyndhurst, NJ
Bogle & Howle ... **Charlotte, NC**
Gastonia, NC
Bogle, James G., Jr. ... Columbia, SC
Bogle, Jerry D. ... **Wichita, KS**
Bogle, Joe M., Jr. ... Wichita, KS
Bogle, Julie M. ... **Madison, WI**
Bogle, Peter C. ... **Fall River, MA**
Mattapoisett, MA
Bogle, Richard B. ... Orlando, FL
Bogle, Richard Thomas ... New York, NY
Bogle, Ronald E. ... Hickory, NC
Bogle & Schulman, P.A.
Altamonte Springs, FL
Orlando, FL
Sanford, FL
Bogle, Sean F. ... **Altamonte Springs, FL**
Bogle, William F., Jr. ... **Poughkeepsie, NY**
Bogli, Jason E. ... **New York, NY**
Boglioli, Bernard F. ... West Long Branch, NJ
Boglioli & Stein ... West Long Branch, NJ
Boglivi, Lauren K. ... **New York, NY**
Bogna, Annette ... Pasadena, CA
Bognanno, Kellee A. ... Indianapolis, IN
Bogner, Eugene P. ... Cincinnati, OH
Bogner, Ira G. ... **New York, NY**
Bogner, James B. ... **Orlando, FL**
Bogner, Jon ... **Dickinson, ND**
Bogner, William E. ... Chicago, IL
Bognet, Frank ... Hazleton, PA
Bogni, Jason R. ... **San Diego, CA**
Bogniard, John ... **Canton, OH**
Salem, OH
Bogollagama, Chandra Mahinda
McLean, VA
Bogomolny, Richard J. ... Gates Mills, OH
Bogomolny, Robert L. ... **Skokie, IL**
Bogorad, Cynthia Schneider
Washington, DC
Bogorad, Saml. ... Washington, DC
Bogorad, Stephen A. ... **Washington, DC**
Bogos & Bogos ... Detroit, MI
Bogos, Frederick M. ... Philadelphia, PA
Bogos, Lawrence ... Detroit, MI
Bogos, Nicholas G. ... Treasury Department, Internal Revenue Service, GV
Bogos, Paul G. ... Detroit, MI
Bogos, Paul M. ... **Sterling Heights, MI**
Bogoshian, Matthew K. ... Salinas, CA
Bogosian, Donald P. ... Berkeley Heights, NJ
Bogosian, Gary P. ... Carmel, NY
Bogosian, Margaret C. ... Upton, NY
Bogosian, Matthew R. ... **Los Angeles, CA**
Bogosian, Paul J., Jr. ... **Providence, RI**
Bogosian & Power, Chartered
Vero Beach, FL
Bogosian, Richard P. ... **Vero Beach, FL**
Bogoslavsky, Abraham ... **Little Rock, AR**
Bogoslow & Jones, P.A. ... **Walterboro, SC**
Bogossian, Gail ... Hartford, CT
Bogost, Jeffrey N. ... Dallas, TX
Bogot, William ... **Chicago, IL**
Bograd, Edward ... **Charlotte, NC**
Bograd, Harriet M. ... New York, NY
Bograd, Sandra L. ... **Roseland, NJ**
Bogran, John P. ... San Antonio, TX
Bogren, Elizabeth T. ... New York, NY
Bogren, John J. ... Albuquerque, NM
Bogren, Michael S. ... **Kalamazoo, MI**
Bogris, George D. ... **Towson, MD**
Boguchwal, Freda Weiner ... Pound Ridge, NY
Boguchwal, Stephen F. ... Holmdel, NJ
Bogucki, Edw. A. ... Chicago, IL
Bogucki Knoebel & Vice P.S.C.
Augusta, KY
Florence, KY
Maysville, KY
Bogucki, Raymond A. ... Los Angeles, CA
Bogucki, Raymond S. ... Augusta, KY
Florence, KY
Maysville, KY
Bogucki, Robert H. ... Garden City, NY
Bogue, A. Stevenson ... **Omaha, NE**
Bogue, Andrew W. ... Rapid City, SD
Bogue and Bogue ... Dupree, SD
Faith, SD
Bogue, Bonnie G. ... Albany, CA
Bogue, Elizabeth ... Williamston, MI
Bogue, Eric H. ... Dupree, SD
Faith, SD
Bogue, Jeffrey A. ... **Denver, CO**
Bogue Koury & Marylander LLC
Denver, CO
Bogue, Maureen K. ... **Palo Alto, CA**
Bogue, Richard ... **Providence, RI**
Bogue, Richard A.
Federal Deposit Insurance Corporation, Compliance and Enforcement Section, GV
Bogue, Richard E. ... Canton, SD
Bogue, Roger W. ... San Antonio, TX
Bogue, Russell S., III ... **Atlanta, GA**
Bogue, Susanna I. ... San Francisco, CA
Bogue, Weeks, Collier & Reed
Vermillion, SD
Bogues, Wm. N. ... Royal Oak, MI
Bogus, Thomas C. ... Cheyenne, WY
Boguski, Gary W. ... Mount Laurel, NJ
Boguslaski, Mary G. ... **Morristown, NJ**
Boguslavsky, Maya M. ... **Philadelphia, PA**
Boguslawski, George W., Jr.
Pittsburgh, PA
Bogust, Henry J. ... Los Angeles, CA
Bogusz, Richard P. ... Chicago, IL
Bogut, John C., Jr. ... **Pittsburgh, PA**
Bogut, John F. ... Jericho, NY
Bogut, Linda L. ... Minneapolis, MN
Bogut & O'Brien ... Jericho, NY
Bogutz, Allan D. ... **Tucson, AZ**
Bogutz & Gordon, P.C. ... **Tucson, AZ**
Bogutz, Jerome E. ... **Philadelphia, PA**
Bogutz, Marc L. ... **Philadelphia, PA**
Bogutz, Tami L. ... **Philadelphia, PA**
Bogy, John W. ... San Francisco, CA

Bogy, Peter E. ......Department of the Air Force, Office of the Judge Advocate General, GV
Bogy, Vernon C., III ....Los Angeles, CA
Bohac, Martin M. ....Omaha, NE
Bohac, Paul ....Black River Falls, WI
Bohach, George P. ....Weirton, WV
Bohach, Russell D. ....Milwaukee, WI
Bohachek, Earl L., III ....San Francisco, CA
Bohacz, Steven J. ....Barrington, IL
Boham, William D. ....Oak Park, MI
Bohan, Anthony ....Newport Beach, CA
Bohan, Barry F.
Department Of Veterans Affairs, Board of Veterans Appeals, GV
Bohan, David C. ....Chicago, IL
Bohan, David L. ....Boston, MA
Bohan, Gerald F. ....Westerville, OH
Bohan, Jack L. ....San Jose, CA
Bohan, James A. ....Torrance, CA
Bohan, James F. ....Harrisburg, PA
Bohan, Joseph P., Jr. ....Larchmont, NY
Bohan, L. Stewart ....Rocky Hill, CT
Bohan, Mary R. ....Department of Justice, Civil Division, GV
Bohan, Richard W. ....Houston, TX
Bohan, Richard W., (P.C.) ....Sarasota, FL
Bohan, Robert Z. ....Annapolis, MD
Bohan, Thomas E. ....Round Rock, TX
Bohan, Thomas L. ....Macon, GA
Bohan, Thomas L. ....Portland, ME
Bohan, Trask, Bohan and Winter
Larchmont, NY
New York, NY
White Plains, NY
Bohana, Jack ....Sunrise, FL
Bohana, Lawrence J. ....Glendale, CA
Bohanan, David R. ....Boston, MA
Bohanan, Ralph, Jr. ....Birmingham, AL
Bohanan, Stephanie Dawn ....Newport, AR
Bohannon, Bohannon & Hancock, P.C.
Norfolk, VA
Bohannon, C. Tad ....Little Rock, AR
Bohannon, Dale ....Cookeville, TN
Bohannon, David L. ....Richmond, KY
Bohannon, Edward A. ......Treasury Department, Office of Regulations and Rulings, GV
Bohannon, Frederick G. ....Tallahassee, FL
Bohannon, Joe M. ....Tulsa, OK
Bohannon, John E. ....Topeka, KS
Bohannon, Karen A. ....Burbank, CA
Bohannon, Lawrence J. ......Fort Lauderdale, FL
Bohannon, Marcia L. ....Reston, VA
Bohannon, Mark ......Department of Commerce, Office of the General Counsel, GV
Bohannon, Marshall T., Jr. ....Norfolk, VA
Bohannon, Michael D. ....Poulsbo, WA
Bohannon, Paul M. ....Houston, TX
Bohannon, Ralph ....Clarksburg, WV
Bohannon, Robert L. ....Norfolk, VA
Bohannon, Rogers & Fox
Fort Lauderdale, FL
Bohannon, Scott M. ....Washington, DC
Bohannon, Suzanne M. ....Philadelphia, PA
Bohannon-Gaunty, Karen ....Burbank, CA
Bohanon, David A. ....Oklahoma City, OK
Bohanon, John C. ....Minneapolis, MN
Bohanon, Philip L. ....Oklahoma City, OK
Bohanon, Philip L., P.C.
Oklahoma City, OK
Bohanon, Richard L. ....Oklahoma City, OK
Bohanic, Robert V. ....Chicago, IL
Bohart, Gerald L. ....San Diego, CA
Bohatch, Colette K. ....Washington, DC
Bohatch, John S. ....Coral Gables, FL
Key West, FL
Bohatch, Therese I. ....San Francisco, CA
Bohaty, Karen M. ....St. Paul, MN
Bohcali, Barbara A. ....Arlington, VA
Bohdan, John C., II ....Fort Wayne, IN
Bohdan, William J. ....Bethpage, NY
Bohde, David S. ....Harper Woods, MI
Bohde, Edw. L. ....St. Clair Shores, MI
Bohe, Mark E. ....Seattle, WA
Bohe, Mark E., & Associates, Law Offices of
Seattle, WA
Bohen, Mary Catherine M.
Los Angeles, CA
Bohensky, Jay ....New York, NY
Bohigas, Adelmis ....Miami, FL
Bohikian, Dickron ....Southfield, MI
Bohl, Charles A. ....Albany, NY
Bohl, Charles H. ....Milwaukee, WI
Bohl, Della Rocca & Dorfman, P.C.
Albany, NY
Bohl, James C. ....Baraboo, WI
Bohl, Joan C. ....Los Angeles, CA
Bohl, Laurel L. ....Albany, NY
Bohl, Phillip C. ....Malibu, CA
Bohl, Phillip W. ....Minneapolis, MN
Bohl, R. Martin ....San Diego, CA
Bohl, Richard K. ....Delmar, NY
Bohl, Robert D. ....Torrance, CA
Bohl, Steven C. ....Toledo, OH
Bohl, Thomas M. ....Ventura, CA
Bohland, Angelyn M. ....New York, NY
Bohland, Michael L. ....Brookville, IN
Bohlander, Richard W. ....El Centro, CA
Bohleber, Steven L. ....Evansville, IN
Bohlen, Charles E., Jr. ....Glendale, CA
Bohlen, Christopher W. ....Kankakee, IL
Bohlen, Edward G. ....Boston, MA
Bohlen, John E., Jr. ....Baltimore, MD
Bohlen, Jonathan A. ....Chicago, IL
Bohlen, Lawrence G. ....Cambridge, MD
Bohlen, Monica R. ....Cincinnati, OH
Bohlen, Reiner D. ....Forest Park, IL
Bohlen, William F. ....Philadelphia, PA
Bohlender, Hugh D. ....Northbrook, IL
Bohlender, Lori Kim ....Salida, CO
Bohlender, Loura K. ....Denver, CO
Bohler, Jack K. ....East Point, GA
Bohler, Leesa A. ....Savannah, GA
Bohler, William J. ....Palo Alto, CA
Bohlig, John D. ....St. Paul, MN
Bohlig, Robert M. ....Cambridge, MA
Bohling, Frederick A. ....Eagan, MN
Bohling, Gayle E.
Department of Housing and Urban Development, Office of General Counsel, GV
Bohling, Joseph E. ....Denver, CO
Bohling, Martha J. ....Denver, CO
Bohling, Richard C. ....Laramie, WY
Bohling, Tara J. ....Milwaukee, WI
Bohling, William B. ....Salt Lake City, UT
Bohlke, C. Douglas ....Olympia, WA
Bohlke, Gary L. ....Washington, DC
Bohlke, Wendy ....Bellingham, WA
Bohlken, Alfred B. ....Omaha, NE
Bohlken, Donald Walter ....Des Moines, IA
Bohlman, Bruce E. ....Grand Forks, ND
Bohlman, Erick ....Chicago, IL
Bohlman, Herbert M. ....Tempe, AZ
Bohlmann, Andrew J. ....Tampa, FL
Bohm, Alex A. ....New York, NY
Bohm, Carlota M. ....Pittsburgh, PA
Bohm, David Allen ....Chicago, IL
Bohm, David R. ....St. Louis, MO
Bohm, Elyse K. ....Brooklyn, NY
Bohm, Gerald ....Nutley, NJ
Bohm, Jack N. ....Overland Park, KS
Bohm, James G. ....Irvine, CA
Bohm, Jeff ....Austin, TX
Bohm, Joel L. ....Brooklyn, NY
Bohm, Lori Beckman ....Beachwood, OH
Bohm, Mark D. ....Miami, FL
Bohm, Martin ....Evanston, IL
Bohm, Richard D. ....New York, NY
Bohm, Robert D. ....Phoenix, AZ
Bohm, Roberto A. ....Santa Ana, CA
Bohm, Stephanie A. ....Atlanta, GA
Bohm, Theresa A. ....Lake Success, NY
Bohman, Brent A. ....Salt Lake City, UT
Bohman, Jerome B. ....Dayton, OH
Bohman, John F. ....Gardner, MA
Bohman, John L. ....Washington, DC
Bohman, Martin S. ....Baton Rouge, LA
Bohmann, Angela M. ....Minneapolis, MN
Bohmart, Joel K. ....New York, NY
Bohmart & Sacks, P.C. ....New York, NY
Bohme, Robert J. ....Washington, DC
Bohmer, John T. ....Naperville, IL
Bohmer, Robert W. ....Toledo, OH
Bohms, Ruth Bauer ....Fairbanks, AK
Bohn & Bohn, LLP ....San Jose, CA
Bohn, Charles R. ....Cupertino, CA
Bohn, Corinn Jo ....Phoenix, AZ
Bohn, David C. ....Eden Prairie, MN
Bohn, Donna F. ....Wichita, KS
Bohn, Douglas J. ....New York, NY
Bohn, Elizabeth M. ....Miami, FL
Bohn, Jay Bently ....Berkeley Heights, NJ
Bohn, Joallyn ....Walnut Creek, CA
Bohn, John A., Jr. ....Hagåtña, GU
Bohn, Jon P. ....Houston, TX
Bohn, Joseph P. ....Chicago, IL
Bohn, Mark ....Phoenix, AZ
Bohn, Michael ....Las Vegas, NV
Bohn, Michael G. ....Denver, CO
Bohn, Paul Francis ....Northville, MI
Bohn, Richard N. ....Miami, FL
Bohn, Robert H. ....San Jose, CA
Bohn, Robert H., Jr. ....San Jose, CA
Bohn, Robert H., Jr. ....Boston, MA
Bohn, Russell S. ....West Palm Beach, FL
Bohn, Timothy John ....Lake Orion, MI
Bohn, Wilford J. ....Arlington, TX
Bohn, Yale H. ....Princeton, NJ
Bohnaker, James P. ....Hampton, VA
Bohne, Christopher M. ....Tampa, FL
Bohne, Edward D. ....Alton, IL
Bohne, Karl W., Jr. ....Melbourne, FL
Bohne, Russell L. ....Palo Alto, CA
Bohne, Susan M. ....Tampa, FL
Bohne, Teresa ....Irving, TX
Bohnen, Michael J. ....Boston, MA
Bohnen, Rosenthal & Dusenbury
Monterey, CA
Bohnen, Thomas P. ....Monterey, CA
Bohnenfield, Murray ....Brooklyn, NY
Bohnenkemper, Sharon L. ....Indianapolis, IN
Bohnenstengel, Robin K. ....Baltimore, MD
Bohnenstiehl, Ray L. ....Southfield, MI
Bohner, Anthony J. ....Boise, ID
Bohner, Chasan & Walton ....Boise, ID
Bohner, Dale K. ....Tampa, FL
Bohner, Edward J. ....Anchorage, AK
Bohner, Hal J. ....Palo Alto, CA
Bohner, Kathleen ....Southfield, MI
Bohner, Leslie Gillin ....Philadelphia, PA
Bohner, Robert C. ....Los Angeles, CA
Bohner, Robert J. ....Garden City, NY
Bohner, Robert J., Jr. ....Philadelphia, PA
Bohnert, Edward G. ....Cleveland, OH
Bohnert, Kenneth A. ....Louisville, KY
Bohnert, Lester L. ....Rock Island, IL
Bohnert, Robert J. ....Louisville, KY
Bohnett, William H. ....New York, NY
Bohnhoff, Henry M. ....Albuquerque, NM
Bohnhoff, Karl A.H. ....Lansing, MI
Bohnhorst, Mark A. ....Minneapolis, MN
Bohning, Larry L. ....Denver, CO
Bohnsack, Paul E., II ....Minnetonka, MN
Boho, Dan L. ....Chicago, IL
Bohon, Kate E. ....Platte City, MO
Bohon, Scott E. ....Memphis, TN
Bohonnon, David M. ....New Haven, CT
Bohonnon, K. Wynne ....New Haven, CT
Bohonnon Law Firm, The, LLC
New Haven, CT
Westport, CT
Bohonnon, R. William ....New Haven, CT
Bohorad, James C. ....Pottsville, PA
Bohorad, Robert N. ....Mahanoy City, PA
Pottsville, PA
Bohorquez, Claudia C., Law Offices of
Burbank, CA
Bohorquez, Claudia C., Law Offices of
Los Angeles, CA
Bohorquez, Elizabeth
.......................................Houston, TX
Bohr, David M. ....Wenatchee, WA
Bohr, Paul J. ....Washington, DC
Bohr, Sarah H. ....Jacksonville, FL
Bohreer, E. Michelle Evans ....Houston, TX
Bohren, J. Keith ....Phoenix, AZ
Bohrer, Abram I. ....New York, NY
Bohrer, Barry A. ....New York, NY
Bohrer, Brad Rodriguez ....La Jolla, CA
Bohrer, Bruce B. ....Ottawa, OH
Bohrer, David ....Northbrook, IL
Bohrer, David C. ....Chicago, IL
Bohrer, David N. ....St. Louis, MO
Bohrer, Edward J. ....Minneapolis, MN
Bohrer, James F. ....Bloomington, IN
Bohrer, Jeremy I. ....New York, NY
Bohrer, Joseph A. ....Springfield, MO
Bohrer, Mason L. ....Winnetka, IL
Bohrer, Morton H. ....Verona, NJ
Bohrer, Nancy King ....Wilmette, IL
Bohrer, Philip ....Baton Rouge, LA
New Orleans, LA
Bohrer, Robert A. ....San Diego, CA
Bohrer, Robert A. ....Seattle, WA
Bohrer, Roger H. ....Elwood, NY
Bohrer, Sanford L. ....Miami, FL
Bohrer, Thomas H. ....Manhattan Beach, CA
Bohrer, William C. ....Pocatello, ID
Bohrnsen, Andrew C. ....Spokane, WA
Bohrnsen, Andrew C., P.S., The Law Offices of ....Spokane, WA
Bohrod, Elaine M. ....Newark, NJ
Bohrod, Malcolm M. ....Newark, NJ
Bohrod, Robert ....Elizabeth, NJ
Bohrofen, Eldon L. ....Sheboygan, WI
Bohse, Frederick H. ....Dover, OH
Bohy, Ronald L. ....Lake Oswego, OR
Bohyer, John E. ....Missoula, MT
Boiarsky, Kenneth R. ....Houston, TX
Boiarsky, Kenneth R., P.C. ....Houston, TX
Boice, James E. ....Houston, TX
San Antonio, TX
Boice, William H. ....Atlanta, GA
Boicourt, Michael L. ....Jefferson City, MO
Boiczyk, Michael P. ....New Britain, CT
Boie, Wesley L. ....Anna, IL
Boies, Caryl Louise ....Hollywood, FL
Armonk, NY
Boies, Christopher A. ....Armonk, NY
Boies, David ....Armonk, NY
Boies, David B. ....Wayzata, MN
Boies, John H. ....Sycamore, IL
Boies, Judith ....New York, NY
Boies, Lewis W., Jr. ....Santa Monica, CA
Boies, Mary McInnis ....Bedford, NY
Boies, Schiller & Flexner LLP
Hollywood, FL
Orlando, FL
Armonk, NY
New York, NY
White Plains, NY
Boies & Schiller LLP ....Washington, DC
Hanover, NH
Boies, Wilber H. ....Chicago, IL
Boigon, Howard L. ....Denver, CO
Boigon, Irving I. ....Southfield, MI
Boikan, Sergius M. ....San Francisco, CA
Boiko, Bruce M. ....Miami, FL
Boiko, Stephan A. ....Albany, NY
Boileau, Alain E. ....Fort Lauderdale, FL
Boileau, E. Burdette ....Claremont, CA
Boileau, John P. ....Lock Haven, PA
Boileau, Lynne J. ....Crofton, MD
Greenbelt, MD
Boileau, Raymond G.
Department of Agriculture, Farm Service Agency, GV
Boileau, Steven A. ....Scarborough, ME
Boiler, Jeffrey H. ....Eugene, OR
Boiler & Kelly ....Eugene, OR
Boillot, David A. ....New York, NY
Boinski, Patricia M. ....Washington, DC
Boire, Fredrique B. ....Tampa, FL
Boire, Harold A. ....Tampa, FL
Boire, Martin C. ....Ormond Beach, FL
Boire, Richard G. ....Davis, CA
Boire, Richard L. ....Rochester, NH
Bois, Maurice P. ....Manchester, NH
Bois, Thomas J., II, (P.C.) ....Irvine, CA
Boisaubin, Alfred L. ....St. Louis, MO
Boisclair, James B. ....Denver, CO
Boisclair, Yvette M. ....Providence, RI
Boise, Barry H. ....Philadelphia, PA
Boise, Craig M. ....Cleveland, OH
Boise, Whitney P. ....Portland, OR
Boisi, Jas. O. ....New York, NY
Boisits, Gerald S. ....Muskego, WI
Boisseau, Charles H. ....Providence, RI
Boisseau, Eldon L. ....Great Bend, KS
Overland Park, KS
Wichita, KS
Kansas City, MO
Springfield, MO
Boisseau, George C., Law Offices of
Santa Rosa, CA
Boisseau, Jane ....New York, NY
Boisseau Leonard & Dean LLP
Providence, RI
Boisseau, Marvin E., Jr.
University City, MO
Boisseau, Richard R. ....Atlanta, GA
Boisselle, Armand P. ....Cleveland, OH
Boissevain, Benjamin M. ....New York, NY
Boissoneault, Kevin J. ....Toledo, OH
Boissonneault, Diane ....Boston, MA
Boisture, J. Bruce ....Farmington, CT
Boisture, Robert A. ....Washington, DC
Boisvert, David L. ....Lowell, MA
Boisvert, Erin R. ....Concord, MA
Boisvert, Laurence S. ....Concord, MA
Boisvert, M. Elissa ....Boston, MA
Boisvert, Robert C., Jr. ....Minneapolis, MN
Boisvert, Russell B. ....Bridgton, ME
Boisvert-Guay, Monique ....Portland, ME
Boiter, M. Eric ....Barnwell, SC
Boitmann, Robert J. ....New Orleans, LA
Boitnott, Jarrod S. ....Lincoln, NE
Boitnott, John T. ....Rocky Mount, VA
Boitos, Matthew J. ....Watersmeet, MI
Boitz, Elwyn F. ....Wayne, NJ
Boivin, Daniel J. ....Minneapolis, MN
Boivin, Harry D. ....Klamath Falls, OR
Boivin, Jones, Uerlings, DiIaconi & Oden, P.C. ....Klamath Falls, OR
Bojack, Audrey D. ....Mountain View, CA
Bojanowski, Richard F. ....Salt Lake City, UT
Bojanowski, Thaddeus J. ....Summit, IL
Bojanowski, Timothy J. ....Ashtabula, OH
Bojarski, Jill M. ....Tustin, CA
Bojarski, Valerie Hope ....Princeton, NJ
Bojazi, Dolores M. ....Philadelphia, PA
Bojczuk, Scott J. ....Parsippany, NJ
Boje, Bruce A. ....Noblesville, IN
Boje, Debra L. ....Tampa, FL
Bojko, Andrew Mark ....Columbus, OH
Bojorquez, Alan J. ....Austin, TX
Bojum, Frederick A. ....North Plainfield, NJ
Bok, Alexander T. ....Boston, MA
Bok, Derek C. ....Cambridge, MA
Bok, Geoffrey R. ....Boston, MA
Bok, Joan T., (Mrs.) ....Boston, MA
Bok, John F. ....Boston, MA
Bok, Marion Monaghan ....Boston, MA
Bokan, William A. ....Sacramento, CA
Bokar, Gregory M. ....Argonne, IL
Bokar, Michael S. ....Trenton, NJ
Bokat, Karen G.
Federal Trade Commission, Bureau of Competition, GV
Bokat, Stephen A. ....Washington, DC
Bokelman & Benjamin, A Professional Law Corporation ....San Francisco, CA
Bokelman, Robert U. ....San Francisco, CA
Boken, Constance ....Augusta, GA
Bokeno, David ....Baltimore, MD
Boker, David E. ....Niles, OH
Bokermann, Joan Patrice ....Ottawa, KS
Bokert, Mark ....New York, NY
Bokhari, Zulfiqar ....Chicago, IL
Bokides, Nicholas T. ....Weiser, ID
Boklage, Adam David ....Shawnee, KS
Bokma, Richard A. ....Trenton, NJ
Bokman, David I. ....Atlanta, GA
Bokor, Bruce H. ....Clearwater, FL
Tampa, FL
Bokor, Claude H. ....Cedarhurst, NY
Bokor, Jonathan D. ....New York, NY
Bokor, Richard A. ....Tampa, FL
Bokos, C. Charles ....Westland, MI
Bokota, Gregory M. ....Crown Point, IN
Bokota, Paul A. ....Irvine, CA
Bokota, Paul A. ....Indianapolis, IN
Bokovoy, Don E. ....Ramona, CA
Boksa, Mary Lou Anne ....Oak Brook, IL
Bokser, Andrew Arnold ....Brooklyn, NY
Bola, Stephen L. ....Indianapolis, IN
Bolach, Anthony M. ....Detroit, MI
Bolam, Brian M. ....Cincinnati, OH
Bolan, Debbie S. ....North Andover, MA
Bolan Jahnsen ....Shrewsbury, NJ
Bolan, James S. ....Boston, MA
Needham, MA
Bolan, John J. ....Millburn, NJ
Bolan, Michael Buckley ....Chicago, IL
Bolan, Michael J. ....Irvine, CA
Bolan, Terrence J. ....Shrewsbury, NJ
Bolan, Thomas A. ....Los Angeles, CA
Bolan, Thomas A. ....New York, NY
Bolan, Thomas A., P.C. ....New York, NY
Bolan, William F., Jr. ....Trenton, NJ
Bolanca, Marijana ....Woodbury, NY
Boland, Amy Schweer ....Bellbrook, OH
Boland, Ann M. ....Buffalo, NY
Boland, Barbara A. ....New Brunswick, NJ
Boland, Bernard E. ....St. Cloud, MN
Boland, Beth I. Z. ....Boston, MA
Boland, Boyd N. ....Denver, CO
Boland, Brian F. ....Reading, PA
Boland, Brian P. ....New York, NY
Boland & Brooks ....Smithtown, NY
Boland, Christopher T. ....Washington, DC
Boland, Claire E. ....New York, NY
Boland, Constance M. ....New York, NY
Boland, Dale Lorraine, (Ms.) ....Denver, CO
Boland, Daniel D. ....Little Rock, AR
Boland, Daniel P. ....Niagara Falls, NY
Boland, David J. ....West Orange, NJ
Boland, Donald J. ....Mineola, NY
Boland, Edmund P. ....Chicago, IL
Boland, Elizabeth A. ....Tampa, FL
Boland, Francis H. ....Lowell, MA

Boland, Frank K. ......Treasury Department, Internal Revenue Service, GV
Boland, Gary L. ......Baton Rouge, LA
Boland, George A. ......San Bernardino, CA
Boland, J. William ......Richmond, VA
Boland, James H. ......Rego Park, NY
Boland, James J. ......Chicago, IL
Boland, Jill C. ......Cleveland, OH
Boland, John D. ......Putnam, CT
Boland, John F. ......Mineola, NY
Boland, John F. ......Vienna, VA
Boland, John L. ......Rockville, MD
Boland, John M. ......Providence, RI
Boland, John P. ......Cleveland, OH
Boland Law Firm, L.L.C.
Baton Rouge, LA
Boland, Lois E. ......Department of Commerce, Patent and Trademark Office, GV
Boland, Lyn ......Smithtown, NY
Boland, Marc W. ......Bethesda, MD
Boland, Mark ......Washington, DC
Boland, Mary B. ......New York, NY
Boland, Mary Egan ......Springfield, MA
Boland, Mary L. ......Darien, IL
Boland, Maureen Kelly ......Belleville, IL
Boland, Michael A. ......Brandon, MS
Boland, Michael Cleary ......Reading, PA
Boland, Michael J. ......San Francisco, CA
Boland, Michael J. ......Washington, DC
Boland, Michael J. ......Chicago, IL
Boland, Nicholas J. ......Smithtown, NY
Boland, Pamela A. ......Detroit, MI
Boland, Patricia J. ......Phoenix, AZ
Boland, Patrick E. ......New York, NY
Boland, Patrick J., III ......Philadelphia, PA
Boland, Patrick Michael ......Warren, MI
Boland, Paul ......Los Angeles, CA
Boland, Paul A. ......San Diego, CA
Boland, Robert A. ......Redwood City, CA
Boland, Robert W., Jr. ......Kansas City, MO
Boland, Rochelle E. ......Lexington, KY
Boland, St. Onge & Brouillard
Putnam, CT
Willimantic, CT
Boland, Sean F. X. ......Washington, DC
Boland, Sharon M. ......New York, NY
Boland, Shelley A. ......Secaucus, NJ
Boland, Susan J.
Judicial Panel On Multidistrict Litigation, GV
Boland, Tara ......Washington, DC
Philadelphia, PA
Boland, Thomas E. ......Great Falls, MT
Boland, Thomas R. ......Washington, DC
Boland & Tighe ......New York, NY
Boland, Veronica Maloney ......Mineola, NY
Boland, William H. ......Portland, OR
Boland, William T., Jr. ......New York, NY
Bolander, Bruce D. ......St. Paul, MN
Bolander, David L. ......St. Joseph, MO
Bolander, Diana Gayle ......Wolfeboro Falls, NH
Boland-Hurt, Deedy ......Tupelo, MS
Boland Steier, Mary ......Omaha, NE
Bolane, John L. ......Rochester, NY
Bolaños, Anita ......Chicago, IL
Bolanos, Bernard ......Houston, TX
Bolaños, José A., Jr. ......Miami, FL
Bolanos, Raymond P. ......San Francisco, CA
Bolanos, Richard C. ......Mountain View, CA
Bolaños, Truxton & Youngs, P.A.
Coral Gables, FL
Fort Myers, FL
Miami, FL
Bolanovich, John W. ......Windermere, FL
Bolanovich, Mirko ......Kansas City, MO
Bolanowski & Brennan ......Sterling Heights, MI
Bolanowski, Eugene R. ......Sterling Heights, MI
Bolanowski, Raymond T. ......Elizabeth, NJ
Bolas, Donald M. ......Palm Desert, CA
Bolas, Michael A. ......Clarence, NY
Bolash, Brian W. ......Erie, PA
Bolash, Nancy Kahn ......Yorktown, VA
Bolasina, Michael C. ......Seattle, WA
Bolasny, Sheldon I.
Department Of Veterans Affairs, VA Regional Counsel Office, Washington, D.C., GV
Bolatti & Griffith ......New York, NY
Bolatti, Silvia L. ......New York, NY
Bolbach, Cynthia J. ......Washington, DC
Bolbrock, Mary Patricia ......Stamford, CT
Bolcato, Angelo J. ......Sparta, NJ
Bolce, Louis H., II ......Cincinnati, OH
Bolch, Laurie ......Boca Raton, FL
Bolch, Laurie, P.A. ......Boca Raton, FL
Bolch, Thomas J. ......Raleigh, NC
Bolchoz, J. Robert, Jr. ......Columbia, SC
Bold, Frederick, Jr. ......Walnut Creek, CA
Bold, Lawrence R. ......Kansas City, MO
Bold, Polisner, Maddow, Nelson & Judson
Walnut Creek, CA
Bolde, Mark Allen ......Indianapolis, IN
Bolden, A. Scott ......Washington, DC
Bolden, Carl B., Jr. ......Detroit, MI
Bolden, Clarence D. ......Indianapolis, IN
Bolden, Cynthia K. ......Chula Vista, CA
Bolden, Dwight M. ......Los Angeles, CA
Bolden, Elizabeth ......Bronx, NY
Bolden, Frank A. ......New Brunswick, NJ
Bolden, James A. ......Philadelphia, PA
Bolden & Martin ......Los Angeles, CA
Bolden, Raymond A. ......Joliet, IL
Bolden, Ruth de V. ......San Francisco, CA
Bolden, Stephanie R. ......Oakland, CA
Bolden, Stephen R. ......Tulsa, OK
Bolden, Stephen R. ......Philadelphia, PA
Bolden, Timothy F. ......Phoenix, AZ
Bolden, Timothy H. ......Chattanooga, TN
Bolden, Victor C. ......Altadena, CA
Bolding, Edward P. ......Tucson, AZ
Bolding, E. W., Jr. ......Las Vegas, NV
Bolding, Grady M. ......San Francisco, CA
Bolding, James M. ......Plano, TX
Boldingh, Mary Jo ......Chicago, IL
Boldizsar, Juan L. ......Chicago, IL
Boldizsar, Juan L., P.C. ......Chicago, IL
Boldizsar, Laszlo ......Melrose Park, IL
Boldman, Christopher T.
West Palm Beach, FL
Boldra & Klueger ......Encino, CA
Los Angeles, CA
Boldra, Patricia E. ......Los Angeles, CA
Boldrey, R. Lance ......Lansing, MI
Boldrick, Clifton, Holland & Essman, A Professional Corporation ......Midland, TX
Odessa, TX
Boldrick, Henry G. ......Lebanon, KY
Boldrick, James P. ......Midland, TX
Boldrick, Margaret Corning
San Antonio, TX
Boldrick, Margaret Corning, P.C.
San Antonio, TX
Boldrick, Neill, Jr., P.C. ......San Antonio, TX
Boldt, Bruce F., Jr. ......Louisville, KY
Boldt, Burleigh E. ......Sioux Falls, SD
Boldt, C. Robert ......Los Angeles, CA
Boldt, Chris ......Dripping Springs, TX
Boldt, Christopher Eric ......Wauchula, FL
Boldt, Clarence J., Jr. ......Bloomfield Hills, MI
Boldt, Daniel James ......Toledo, OH
Boldt, David R. ......North Royalton, OH
Boldt, Elizabeth Ashley ......Kansas City, MO
Boldt, James H. ......Grants Pass, OR
Boldt, Kimberly L. ......Miami, FL
Boldt, Margaret M. ......Rochester, NY
Boldt, Melvin W. ......Palatine, IL
Boldt, Michael H. ......Indianapolis, IN
Boldt, Michael O'B. ......Secaucus, NJ
Boldt, Richard C. ......Baltimore, MD
Boldt, Richd. W. ......Toledo, OH
Boldt, Ronald M. ......Los Angeles, CA
Boldt, Wendy L. ......St. Louis, MO
Bolduan, Linda M. ......Portland, OR
Bolduan, Stephen C. ......St. Paul, MN
Bolduc, Andrew R. ......Little Falls, NJ
Bolduc, David ......Austin, TX
Bolduc, Gregory B. ......Chicago, IL
Bolduc, Lori Ann ......Newton, MA
Bolduc, Lynne ......Irvine, CA
Bolduc, Michael J. ......Dover, NH
Boldys, Walter ......Boston, MA
Bole, Brad, Law Office of ......Tampa, FL
Bole, David B. ......Paramus, NJ
Bole, David L. ......Louisville, KY
Bole, Frank H. ......Wilmerding, PA
Bole, Linda Marie ......Cheyenne, WY
Bolecek, Jessica French ......Richmond, VA
Bolechowski, Michael W. ......Emeryville, CA
San Francisco, CA
Bolek, Cathleen M. ......Cleveland, OH
Bolek, Joseph E., Jr. ......Cleveland, OH
Boleky, Thomas F. ......Chicago, IL
Bolema, Theodore R.
Department of Justice, Antitrust Division, GV
Bolen, Alan L. ......Worthington, OH
Bolen, Anne E. ......San Francisco, CA
Bolen, Charles E. ......Medford, OR
Bolen, Daniel Patrick ......Kansas City, MO
Bolen, David ......Houston, TX
Bolen, David E. ......New York, NY
Bolen & Erwin, Ltd., A Prof. Law Corp.
Alexandria, LA
Bolen, Fransen & Boostrom LLP
Clovis, CA
Fresno, CA
Bolen, Hal H., II ......Fresno, CA
Bolen, James A., Jr. ......Alexandria, LA
Bolen, James B., Jr. ......Moraga, CA
Bolen, John P. ......Houston, TX
Bolen, M. Christopher ......Raleigh, NC
Bolen, Mary S. ......Senatobia, MS
Bolen, Michael J. ......Edina, MN
Bolen, R. Michael ......Jackson, MS
Bolen, Richard J. ......Charleston, WV
Huntington, WV
Bolen, Richard Lee ......West Columbia, SC
Bolen, Steven C. ......Martinez, CA
Bolen, T. G. ......Decatur, IL
Bolen, T.G., Jr. ......Jackson, MS
Bolen, Virginia R. ......Morris, IL
Bolen, William C. ......Chattanooga, TN
Bolen-Almquist, Jennifer ......Cayce, SC
Bolenbaugh, Gary E. ......Fort Wayne, IN
Bolender, Jeffrey S. ......Los Angeles, CA
Bolender, Julie A. ......Akron, OH
Bolender, Mark J. ......Redmond, WA
Bolender, Shawn ......Des Moines, IA
Bolender, Sue Ellen ......West Des Moines, IA
Boler, James R. ......Arlington, VA
Boler, James T. ......Omaha, NE
Boler, Jean M. ......Minneapolis, MN
Boler, Nancy H. ......Houston, TX
Bolerjack, Stephen D. ......Dearborn, MI
Boles, Alan E., Jr. ......Boulder, CO
Boles, B. B., III ......Pensacola, FL
Boles, Bennie C. ......Center, TX
Boles, Boles & Ryan, A Professional Corporation ......New Orleans, LA
Baton Rouge, LA
Monroe, LA
Boles, Calvin F., IV ......Richmond, VA
Boles, Carla L. ......North Hills, CA
Boles, Darin J. ......San Diego, CA
Boles, Donald M. ......Doylestown, PA
Boles, Edgar H. ......Cleveland, OH
Boles, Everett F. ......Holbrook, MA
Boles, Garrett C. ......Groton, MA
Boles, George M. ......Birmingham, AL
Boles, Grady W. ......Liberal, KS
Boles, Gregory J. ......Harrisburg, PA
Philadelphia, PA
Boles, H. Hampton ......Birmingham, AL
Boles, Harry A. ......Kernersville, NC
Boles, Herbert F. ......Midland, TX
Boles, James André ......Reno, NV
Boles, James K. ......Bradenton, FL
Boles, Janet S. ......Baton Rouge, LA
Boles, Joan Cain ......Wimauma, FL
Boles, John S. ......Houston, TX
Boles, Jos. E. ......Joliet, IL
Boles, Joseph D. ......River Falls, WI
Boles, Joseph L., Jr. ......St. Augustine, FL
Boles, J. V. ......Danville, IN
Boles, Kent J., Jr. ......Baltimore, MD
Boles, Martin R. ......Los Angeles, CA
Boles, Matthew ......Des Moines, IA
Boles, Mitchel Hampton ......Montgomery, AL
Boles, Richard J. ......Durham, NC
Boles, Robert L. ......San Diego, CA
Boles, Susan Clancy ......St. Charles, IL
Boles, W. Joel ......Pensacola, FL
Boles, William A. ......St. Louis, MO
Boles, William R. ......Monroe, LA
Boles, William R., Jr. ......Monroe, LA
Bolesky, Tracy H. ......Naples, FL
Bolesky, Tracy H., P.A. ......Naples, FL
Bolet, Albert J., III ......Atlanta, GA
Boleware, Michael W. ......New Orleans, LA
Boley, Benjamin W. ......Washington, DC
Boley, James D. ......San Diego, CA
Boley, John N. ......Chicago, IL
Boley, Leisa R. ......Columbus, OH
Boley, Leslie J. ......Redwood City, CA
Boley & McKellar, A Professional Corporation ......Cheyenne, WY
Boley, Patrick ......St. Paul, MN
Boley, Richard P. ......Cheyenne, WY
Boley, Thomas R. ......Barberton, OH
Boley, Todd ......San Jose, CA
Boley, William F. ......Midland, MI
Boleyn, David F. ......Arlington, VA
Boleyn, Susan V. ......Atlanta, GA
Bolf, Thomas R. ......Fort Lauderdale, FL
Bolfango, Lauren M. S.
San Francisco, CA
Bolfing, Gerald L. ......Waco, TX
Bolgar, Peter L. ......Southfield, MI
Bolgard, Robert D. ......Hartford, CT
Bolgard, Roger D. ......Monterey, CA
Redwood City, CA
Bolgatz, Abraham E. ......Troy, NY
Bolgatz, Michael Glenn ......San Francisco, CA
Bolgen & Bolgen ......Woburn, MA
Bolgen, Claudia Leis ......Woburn, MA
Bolgen, Stig W. ......Woburn, MA
Bolger, Bernadette L. ......San Francisco, CA
Bolger, Bruce S. ......Los Angeles, CA
Bolger, David T. ......Harrisburg, PA
King Of Prussia, PA
Bolger & Gosser ......Woodstock, IL
Bolger, Janet Marie ......Worcester, MA
Bolger, Jeanne P. ......New York, NY
Bolger, Joel H. ......Valdez, AK
Bolger, John D. ......Woodstock, IL
Bolger, Kathleen M. ......Washington, DC
Bolger, Kevin P. ......Chicago, IL
Bolger, Marifrances Dant
Philadelphia, PA
Bolger, Michael William ......Chicago, IL
Bolger, Nancy A. ......Syosset, NY
Bolger, Richard J. ......Toms River, NJ
Bolger, Richard Owen ......Fairfax, VA
Bolger, Rita M. ......New York, NY
Bolger, Robert J., Jr. ......Washington, DC
Baltimore, MD
Bolger, Shawn M. ......Franklin Park, IL
Bolger, Vincent J. ......Lisle, IL
Bolger, William A. ......Gloucester, VA
Bolger, William J. ......Putnam Valley, NY
Bolgert, James J. ......Sheboygan, WI
Bolgert, John ......Sheboygan, WI
Bolgiano, David G. ......Baltimore, MD
Bolgrien, Rentz, Mineau, Koepke & Kimes, S.C. ......Beloit, WI
Bolgrien, William A. ......Beloit, WI
Bolhouse, Richard L. ......Grandville, MI
Boli, Louis A. "Michael", IV ......Alameda, CA
Bolick, E. Douglas ......Newburyport, MA
Bolick, H. Arthur, II ......Greensboro, NC
Bolick, Jennifer L. ......Greensboro, NC
Raleigh, NC
Bolick, Robert L. ......Las Vegas, NV
Bolick, Robert L., Ltd. ......Las Vegas, NV
Bolick, Thomas N. ......Washington, DC
Boliek, David L., Jr. ......Dunn, NC
Boliek, Virginia S. ......Birmingham, AL
Bolig, Ronald R. ......Sellersville, PA
Telford, PA
Bolin, Barbara L. ......Phoenix, AZ
Bolin, Britta J. ......Chicago, IL
Bolin, Bruce M. ......Minden, LA
Bolin, Cornelius J., Jr. ......Shreveport, LA
Bolin, David G. ......Murfreesboro, TN
Smyrna, TN
Bolin, Dexter L., Jr. ......Terre Haute, IN
Bolin, Duane E. ......Denver, CO
Bolin, Imogene Wright ......Smyrna, TN
Bolin, J. Harold ......High Point, NC
Bolin, James E., Jr. ......Shreveport, LA
Bolin, James E., Sr. ......Shreveport, LA
Bolin, James H. ......Jackson, MS
Bolin, James H., Jr. ......Basking Ridge, NJ
Bolin, Jane Nelson ......State College, PA
Bolin, Joseph W. ......Murray, KY
Bolin, L. Robert ......Cincinnati, OH
Bolin, Linda S. ......Dallas, TX
Bolin, Michael F. ......Birmingham, AL
Bolin, Ngozi E. ......New York, NY
Bolin, Norma Maret ......St. Louis, MO
Bolin, Randy Doran ......Des Moines, IA
Bolin, Richard F. ......Birmingham, AL
Bolin, Richard G. ......Jeffersonville, IN
Bolin, Roger C. ......Hennepin, IL
Bolin, Sandra A. ......Berea, KY
Bolin, Stephen J. ......Washington, DC
Bolin, Travis Nicholas ......Cypress, TX
Bolin & Ward ......Murfreesboro, TN
Smyrna, TN
Bolin, William B. ......Garden City, KS
Bolind, Lawrence E., Jr. ......Imperial, PA
Bolinder, Clint R. ......Boise, ID
Bolinder, Erik J. ......Boise, ID
Boline, Floyd E. ......Minneapolis, MN
Boling, Andrea White ......Beltsville, MD
Boling, Andrew J. ......Chicago, IL
Boling, Christopher G. ......Memphis, TN
Boling, Deborah K. ......Chicago, IL
Boling, Edward A. ......Department of Justice, Environment and Natural Resources Division, GV
Boling, Jefferson D. ......Birmingham, AL
Boling, John L. ......Jacksonville, FL
Boling, John W. ......Meridian, MS
Boling, Larry B. ......Jonesboro, AR
Boling, Leon ......Cumming, GA
Boling, Leroy ......Pensacola, FL
Boling, Mark C. ......Danville, CA
Boling & McCart, A Professional Association
Jacksonville, FL
Boling, Michael R. ......Dallas, TX
Boling, R. Lucas ......Jefferson City, MO
Boling, Rice, Bettis & Martin, L.L.P.
Cumming, GA
Boling, Richard ......Hopkinsville, KY
Boling, Robert C. ......Downers Grove, IL
Boling, Tammy ......El Reno, OK
Boling, William C. ......Los Angeles, CA
Boling, William H., Jr. ......Rome, GA
Bolinger & Associates, A P.C.
Pleasant Hill, CA
Bolinger, Blake W. ......Freehold, NJ
Bolinger, Brad L. ......Washington, DC
Bolinger, Bradley Drew ......Middletown, OH
Bolinger, Bradley R. ......Chambersburg, PA
Bolinger, Christopher N. ......Chicago, IL
Bolinger, Darlene M.
Department of Agriculture, Office of the General Counsel, GV
Bolinger, Donald J. ......Kokomo, IN
Bolinger, Donald J., II ......Kokomo, IN
Bolinger, Georgianne Fackelman ......Marion, IN
Bolinger, H. A., Jr. ......Bigfork, MT
Bolinger, Jackson B. ......Lafayette, LA
Bolinger, Kenneth W. ......Pleasant Hill, CA
Bolinger Law Firm, The, A Professional Corporation ......Lafayette, LA
Bolinger, Michael O. ......Kokomo, IN
Bolinger, Norman J. ......Jacksonville, FL
Bolinger, R. Stephen ......Anaheim, CA
Bolinger, Randall M. ......Tampa, FL
Bolinger, Thomas L. ......San Diego, CA
Bolinger, William H. ......Versailles, MO
Bolinske, Robert V. ......Bismarck, ND
Bolinsky, Dorothy E. ......Princeton, NJ
Bolint, Mary Elisabeth ......Tampa, FL
Bolio, Wayne M. ......Menlo Park, CA
Bolis, Marie E. ......San Diego, CA
Boliver, Gail E. ......Marshalltown, IA
Omaha, NE
Boliver Law Firm ......Marshalltown, IA
Omaha, NE
Bolk, David R. ......Terre Haute, IN
Bolkcom, Jerome V. ......Washington, DC
Bolkcom, Mary E. ......Minneapolis, MN
Bolkema, Gerald K. ......Chicago, IL
Bolker, Sandra A. ......Ventura, CA
Bolkin, Bruce I. ......Los Angeles, CA
Bolkin, Eve B. ......New York, NY
Boll, Cynthia A. ......Columbus, IN
Franklin, IN
Boll, Frederick L. ......South Amboy, NJ
Boll, George A. ......Dallas, TX
Boll, James C. ......Madison, WI
Boll, James C., Jr. ......Madison, WI
Boll, John P. ......Shrewsbury, NJ
Boll, Karen Ann ......Grosse Pointe, MI
Boll, Lyle L. ......Englewood, CO
Boll, Paul J. ......Clayton, MO
Boll, Thomas L. ......Bartow, FL
Bolla, Alexander J., Jr. ......Birmingham, AL
Bolla, Lawrence C. ......Erie, PA
Bolla, William J. ......Doylestown, PA
Bolland, Katharine S. ......Boston, MA
Bolland, Marvin O. ......Woodburn, OR
Bollar, Carlos M. ......Cherry Hill, NJ
Bollar, Marla Grace ......Lake Forest, CA
Bollar, Rick L. ......Rupert, ID
Bollar, Robert W. ......Orange, CA
Bollard, Donald C., III ......Leawood, KS
Bollard, William C. ......Irvine, CA
Bollato, Jerome T. ......St. Louis, MO
Bolle, William E. ......Troy, MI
Bollella, Donald ......Irvine, CA
Bollenbacher, James A. ......Pittsburgh, PA
Bollenbeck, Richard E. ......Appleton, WI
Bollendorf, Jodi Dabson ......Beloit, WI
Bollengier, Alfred E. ......Warwick, RI
Bollengier, Robert E. ......Warwick, RI
Boller, Charles A. ......Pittston, PA
Boller, David B. ......Glendale, CA
Boller, Diane F. ......Charlottesville, VA

Boller, Harvey R. ... Chicago, IL
Boller, M. William ... Buffalo, NY
Boller, Matthew Hubly
West Palm Beach, FL
Boller, Michael F. ... Sidney, OH
Boller, Rosemary B. ... New York, NY
Boller, Thomas R. ... Mobile, AL
Boller, Timothy C. ... Waterloo, IA
Boller, Timothy L. ... Wichita, KS
Seattle, WA
Boller, W. Steven ... Milford, OH
Bollero, Barbara L. ... Seattle, WA
Bollero, Jennifer Leisner ... St. Charles, IL
Bollert, Joe A. ... Los Angeles, CA
Bollerup, M. Therese Kennedy ... Lincoln, NE
Bolles, Becky J. ... Mount Pleasant, MI
Bolles, David M. ... Albany, NY
Bolles, Donald S. ... King City, CA
Bolles, John A. ... New Orleans, LA
Bolles, R. Brad ... Ardmore, OK
Bollettieri, Jill Hutchinson
Minneapolis, MN
Bollettieri, Joseph H. ... St. Paul, MN
Bollhauer, Raymond G. ... Cincinnati, OH
Bollheimer, Valerie K. ... Bedminster, NJ
Bollhofer, Joseph A. ... St. James, NY
Bollhoffer, Allan J. ... Redwood City, CA
Bollier, Eugenie S. ... Gretna, LA
Bolliger, John C. ... Rancho Cordova, CA
Kennewick, WA
Bolliger, Ralph W. ... Portland, OR
Bollin, Kip T. ... Cleveland, OH
Bollin, Kurt S. ... Glendale, CA
Bolling, Anne D. ... Washington, DC
Bolling & Bolling, Attorneys, P.C.
Dalton, GA
Bolling, Carl R. ... Abingdon, VA
Bolling, Harold D. ... Whitesburg, KY
Bolling & Hearl, A Professional Corporation
Abingdon, VA
Bolling, James A., Jr. ... Jacksonville, FL
Bolling, Julie Coldren ... Indianapolis, IN
Bolling, K. Stephen ... Huntsville, AL
Bolling, Nora T. ... New Orleans, LA
Bolling, Robert Stephen ... Huntsville, AL
Bolling, Rodger A. ... Sheldon, IL
Bolling & Tackett ... Whitesburg, KY
Bolling, Theodore D., Jr. ... Sacramento, CA
Bolling, Thomas Newton ... Washington, DC
Bolling, Walter & Gawthrop, A Professional Corporation ... Sacramento, CA
Bolling, Walter H., Jr. ... Dalton, GA
Bolling, William D. ... Mobile, AL
Bollinger, Barry G. ... Chicago, IL
Bollinger, Ben ... Panama City, FL
Bollinger, Bernard D., Jr.
Los Angeles, CA
Bollinger, Beth M. ... Spokane, WA
Bollinger, Bobby L., Jr. ... Charlotte, NC
Bollinger, Brett M. ... Covington, LA
Bollinger, C. Michael ... Alexandria, LA
Bollinger, Catherine Parker ... Tulsa, OK
Bollinger, Chris L. ... Chicago, IL
Bollinger, Debra M. ... Pierre, SD
Bollinger, Donald E. ... Glendora, CA
Bollinger, Dorothy M. ... Lansdale, PA
Bollinger, Douglas L. ... Carlsbad, CA
Bollinger, Frank L. ... Oklahoma City, OK
Bollinger, Gary D. ... St. Louis, MO
Bollinger, Gerald A. ... Oklahoma City, OK
Bollinger, Gerald E. ... Lead, SD
Bollinger, Howard M. ... Stamford, CT
Bollinger, James M. ... New York, NY
Bollinger, John J. ... Vienna, VA
Bollinger, Jolee Hancock
Birmingham, AL
Bollinger, Lee ... Chicago, IL
Bollinger, Mark R.
Federal Communications Commission, Wireless Telecommunications Bureau, GV
Bollinger, Maura Cantrill ... New Haven, CT
Bollinger, Robert C. ... Decatur, IL
Bollinger, Robert F. ... Miami, FL
Bollinger, Ronald G. ... Salt Lake City, UT
Bollinger, Ruberry & Garvey ... Chicago, IL
Bollinger, Sheryl L. ... Englewood, CO
Bollington, John R. ... Brea, CA
Bollington, Lounsbury and Chase ... Brea, CA
Bollini, Julia Alessandra ... Washington, DC
Bollish, Lynn Allison ... Fort Worth, TX
Bollman, J. Michael ... San Diego, CA
Bollman & Lesser, Law Offices of
Lake Forest, IL
Waukegan, IL
Bollman, Michael F. ... New Orleans, LA
Bollman, Patricia A. ... New Orleans, LA
Bollman, Robert M. ... Lake Forest, IL
Bollman, William H. ... Washington, DC
Bollmann, Bradford P. ... Louisville, KY
Bollo, Paul L. ... Danbury, CT
Bollom, James C. ... Houston, TX
Bollong, Christine B. ... Key West, FL
Bollow, Fred D. ... Shelbyville, MO
Bollow, Richard C. ... Chicago, IL
Bolls, R. David, III ... Modesto, CA
Bollt, Jerry M. ... West Palm Beach, FL
Bollwerk, G. Paul, III
Nuclear Regulatory Commission, Atomic Safety and Licensing Board Panel, GV
Bollwerk, Helen M. ... Department of Justice, Office of the Pardon Attorney, GV
Bollwerk, Jill S. ... St. Louis, MO
Bolly, Virgil E. ... Sellersburg, IN
Bolm, David A. ... Santa Fe, NM
Bolm, Robert J. ... Buffalo, NY
Bolmarcich, Gene ... Peoria, IL
Bolmer, John E., II ... Denver, CO

Bolmeyer, Frank G., Jr. ... Cleveland, OH
Bolner, Lesli S. ... Metairie, LA
Bolnick, Garry M. ... New City, NY
Bolnick, Ira ... Albuquerque, NM
Bolock, Frank J., Jr. ... Scranton, PA
Bolocofsky, David N. ... Englewood, CO
Bolocofsky, David N., P.C. ... Englewood, CO
Bolog, Debra Helfand ... Potomac, MD
Bolog, Erik D. ... Washington, DC
Bologna, Christine A. ... Sacramento, CA
Bologna, Harris & Nunheimer, P.C.
Boston, MA
Bologna, Jeannete Lewis ... Miami, FL
Bologna, Jennifer A. Magyar
Stamford, CT
Bologna, John R. ... Boston, MA
Bologna, John V. ... Greenwich, CT
Bologna, Michael T. ... Fairfield, CT
Bologna, William F. ... New Orleans, LA
Bolognese, Anthony J. ... Philadelphia, PA
Bolognese, Robert E ... Philadelphia, PA
Bolognesi, Joseph W. ... Annandale, VA
Bolognini, Louis T. ... West Lafayette, IN
Bolognone, Angela M. ... Columbus, OH
Bologovsky, Ingrid M. ... Boston, MA
Bolon, Gordon K. ... Columbus, OH
Bolon, Laurence J. ... Chicago, IL
Bolon, Thomas M. ... Columbus, OH
Bolon, Thomas M., Jr. ... Columbus, OH
Bolong, Heidi Gahler ... Yakima, WA
Bolotin, Jay A. ... Cincinnati, OH
Bolotin, Jeffrey W. ... Bethesda, MD
Bolotin, Joan M. ... Miami, FL
Bolotin, Samuel G. ... Toledo, OH
Bolotin, Sandra Campo ... Toledo, OH
Bolotin, Steven J. ... Boston, MA
Bolotin, Steven L. ... Bartow, FL
Bolotin, William J. ... Chicago, IL
Bolotow, Norman Jay ... Providence, RI
Bolour, Ally ... Beverly Hills, CA
Boloyan, Myron B. ... Lake Wylie, SC
Bolser, Clark Mead ... Englewood, CO
Bolser, Sean J. ... New York, NY
Bolsinger, Hiram C., Jr. ... Cincinnati, OH
Bolsinger, Markus P. ... New York, NY
Bolson, David A. ... South Orange, NJ
Bolson, James D. ... Running Springs, CA
Bolson, Jeffrey T. ... Los Angeles, CA
Bolson, John H. ... San Bernardino, CA
Bolson Kuntz & Serembe
San Bernardino, CA
Bolstad, Andrea P. ... Liberty, MO
Bolstad, David C. ... Los Angeles, CA
Bolstad & Porembski ... Liberty, MO
Bolstein, Arthur ... Department of Labor, Office of the Solicitor, GV
Bolstein, M. Joel ... Philadelphia, PA
Bolstein, Philip ... Elizabeth, NJ
Bolster and Bruder ... Jamesburg, NJ
Bolster, George F. ... Jamesburg, NJ
Bolster, Jeffrey S. ... Charlotte, NC
Bolster, John R. ... Tyler, TX
Bolster, William M. ... St. Louis, MO
Bolt, Andrew W., II ... Anniston, AL
Birmingham, AL
Bolt, Cassandra Shoemaker ... Waverly, OH
Bolt, Curtis E. ... Garden City, KS
Bolt, David M. ... Anoka, MN
Bolt, Deborah L. ... Hartford, KY
Bolt, Donald B., III ... Tulsa, OK
Bolt, Eduardo Guerini ... Costa Mesa, CA
Bolt, J.D., P.C. ... Independence, VA
Bolt, J. Dennis ... Columbia, SC
Bolt, James A. ... New Berlin, WI
Bolt, Jan Eric ... Santa Rosa, CA
Bolt, J.D. ... Independence, VA
Bolt, John F. ... New Smyrna Beach, FL
Bolt, John R. ... Tucson, AZ
Bolt, Julie K. ... Portland, OR
Bolt Law Offices ... Anniston, AL
Birmingham, AL
Bolt, Paula Cobia ... Anniston, AL
Birmingham, AL
Bolt, R. Preston, Jr. ... Mobile, AL
Bolt, Robert K. ... Oakland, CA
Walnut Creek, CA
Bolt, Robert S. ... Tampa, FL
Bolt, Thomas P.
Federal Deposit Insurance Corporation, Liquidation Branch, GV
Bolt, Thurlow & Hall, P.A.
New Smyrna Beach, FL
Bolt, Tom
Charlotte Amalie, St. Thomas, VI
Bolt, Tom, & Associates, P.C.
Cruz Bay, St. John, VI
Charlotte Amalie, St. Thomas, VI
Boltacz, Susan R. ... Atlanta, GA
Boltax, Jack J. ... San Diego, CA
Boltax, Phyllis E. ... Barre, VT
Bolte, Bethann K. ... Alamo, CA
Bolte, Carrick E. ... Temecula, CA
Bolte, Frank R. ... Pittsburgh, PA
Bolte, Lee W. ... Ocean City, MD
Bolter, Howard L. ... Minneapolis, MN
Bolter, Marci L. ... Glendale, CA
Bolthouse, Laret D. ... Clarksville, MI
Boltin, William G., III ... Orlando, FL
Bolton, Anne H. ... Whitehouse Station, NJ
Bolton, Arthur K. ... Griffin, GA
Bolton, Arthur P., III ... Flourtown, PA
Bolton, Averill H. ... North Plains, OR
Bolton, Barbara Elizabeth ... Boston, MA
Bolton, Barry W. ... Bogalusa, LA
Bolton, Beverly A. ... Jackson, MS
Bolton, Brian B. ... Maitland, FL
Bolton, Bruce ... Syracuse, NY
Bolton, Bryan D. ... Baltimore, MD

Bolton, Craig J. ... Phoenix, AZ
Bolton, Cynthia E. ... Troy, MI
Bolton, Dan C., Law Offices of
San Francisco, CA
Bolton, Dana James ... New York, NY
Bolton, Darold D. ... Marysville, KS
Bolton, David A. ... Orlando, FL
Bolton, David, (P.A.) ... Miami, FL
Bolton, Debra Raggio ... Washington, DC
Bolton, Donald E. ... Miami, FL
Bolton, Dunn & Yates, A Professional Corporation ... Malibu, CA
Bolton, Edward J. ... Suffern, NY
Bolton, Frank C. ... Denver, CO
Bolton, Frank R., Jr. ... Alexandria, LA
Bolton, George W., Jr. ... Rayville, LA
Bolton, Gregory J.
Department of Housing and Urban Development, Office of General Counsel, GV
Bolton, James G. ... Delaware, OH
Bolton, James M. ... Burlington, MA
Methuen, MA
Bolton, James R. ... Omaha, NE
Bolton, Jason Wayne ... Springfield, MO
Bolton, John F. ... Garden City, NY
Bolton, John J. ... Providence, RI
Bolton, John M., III ... Montgomery, AL
Bolton, John R. ... Washington, DC
Bolton, Joseph D. ... Miami, FL
Bolton, Julian T. ... Memphis, TN
Bolton, Karen D. ... Fairview Heights, IL
Bolton & Kearney, P.A. ... Aberdeen, MD
Bel Air, MD
Bolton, Keith A. ... Seattle, WA
Bolton, Larry A. ... Hutchinson, KS
Bolton Law Offices, P.A. ... Nashua, NH
Bolton Law Offices, P.A. ... Greensboro, NC
Bolton, Lawrence B. ... Sacramento, CA
Bolton, Lawrence E. ... Raleigh, NC
Bolton, Mary Lou ... Phoenix, AZ
Bolton, Michael ... Florham Park, NJ
Bolton, Michael J. ... Sacramento, CA
Bolton, Michael J. ... Deerfield, IL
Bolton, Michael K. ... Houston, TX
Bolton, Michael P. ... Troy, MI
Bolton & Park ... Griffin, GA
Bolton, Paul F. ... Worcester, MA
Bolton, Peter C. ... Detroit, MI
Bolton, Phillip B. ... Bernardsville, NJ
Bolton, Phillip E. ... Greensboro, NC
Bolton, Richard L. ... Chicago, IL
Bolton, Richard L. ... Madison, WI
Bolton, Richard M. ... Detroit, MI
Bolton, Robert A. ... San Clemente, CA
Bolton, Robert M. ... Dallas, TX
Bolton, Robert R. ... Hauppauge, NY
Bolton, Robert S. ... Detroit, MI
Bolton, Russell K., Jr. ... Palm Desert, CA
Bolton, Stacey Beth ... Red Wing, MN
Bolton, Stephen F. ... Pensacola, FL
Bolton, Stephen G., (P.A.)
Overland Park, KS
Bolton, Stephen T. ... Youngstown, OH
Bolton, Steven A. ... Nashua, NH
Bolton, Steven G. ... Frankfort, KY
Bolton, Steven H. ... Park Rapids, MN
Bolton, Susan Ritchie ... Phoenix, AZ
Bolton, W. Donald, Jr. ... Foley, AL
Bolton, W. Donald, Jr., P.C.
Bay Minette, AL
Foley, AL
Bolton, Warren R. ... North Chatham, MA
Bolton, Wayne ... Selmer, TN
Bolton, Wilbur W., III ... Aberdeen, MD
Bel Air, MD
Bolton, William R. ... Temecula, CA
Bolton, Wyman John ... Warren, MI
Bolton-Munach, Lorin, P.A. ... Hollywood, FL
Bolton-Smith, Carlile, Jr. ... Washington, DC
Bolts, Irene R. Epstein ... Wynnewood, PA
Boltuch, Burton F. ... San Francisco, CA
Boltwood, Russell Lewis ... Alameda, CA
Boltz & Boltz ... Green Bay, WI
Boltz, Carole L. ... Lincolnshire, IL
Boltz, Earl F., Jr. ... Phoenix, AZ
Boltz, G. Brian ... Lancaster, OH
Boltz, Gerald E. ... Santa Monica, CA
Boltz, Howard O., Jr. ... Santa Monica, CA
Boltz, John R. ... Green Bay, WI
Boltz, Jon D. ... San Juan, PR
Boltz, Michael C. ... Santa Fe, NM
Boltz, Paul A. ... Green Bay, WI
Boltz, Paul William, Jr. ... Philadelphia, PA
Boltz, Russ E. ... Washington, DC
Detroit, MI
Boltzman, Amy W. ... St. Louis, MO
Bolus, John N. ... Birmingham, AL
Bolus, Michael Tommy ... Charleston, SC
Bolus, Paul P. ... Birmingham, AL
Bolus, Philip W.
General Services Administration, Office of the General Counsel, GV
Bolves, Brian A. ... Tampa, FL
Bolves, Eric L. ... Orlando, FL
Bolvig, Axel, III ... Birmingham, AL
Bolvig, C. Peter ... Birmingham, AL
Bolvin, Janet Lee ... Anchorage, AK
Bolvin, Kenneth W. ... Richardson, TX
Boly, Jeffrey E. ... Portland, OR
Bolyard, Dana R. ... Kansas City, MO
Bolyard, David L. ... Department of Justice, Executive Office for Immigration Review, GV
Bolyard & Gutsell, P.L.L.C.
Morgantown, WV
Bolyard, Jeffrey S. ... Morgantown, WV
Bolz, Charles S. ... Boca Raton, FL

Bolz, Farrell ... Houston, TX
Bolz, Farrell, P.C. ... Houston, TX
Bolz, Frank A. ... Rego Park, NY
Bolz, Henry H., III ... Miami, FL
Bolz, Herbert F. ... Sacramento, CA
Bolz, James M. ... West Dundee, IL
Bolz, Julia M. ... Seattle, WA
Bolz, Nan Blumenfeld
West Palm Beach, FL
Bolze, Cheryl A. ... Rockville, MD
Bolze, Duane W. ... Phoenix, AZ
Bolze, Ray S. ... Washington, DC
Bölzle, Gregory A. ... Louisville, KY
Bom, Kathleen A. ... Chicago, IL
Bom, R. Steve ... La Porte, IN
Boma, James R. ... Denver, CO
Boman, Carol R. ... San Francisco, CA
Boman, Christopher J. ... Los Angeles, CA
Boman, David L. ... Kansas City, MO
Boman, J. Marcus ... San Francisco, CA
Boman, John H., Jr. ... Atlanta, GA
Boman, Marc A. ... Seattle, WA
Boman, Michael L. ... Kansas City, MO
Bomar, Anne E. ... Washington, DC
Bomar, Deric J. ... Detroit, MI
Bomar, Ellie G. ... Dallas, TX
Bomar, H. Leland ... Spartanburg, SC
Bomar, James L., Jr. ... Shelbyville, TN
Bomar, Joy Tanner ... Memphis, TN
Bomar, Kimberly A. ... Palo Alto, CA
Bomar, Kurt J. ... Sarasota, FL
Bomar, Kurt J., P.A. ... Sarasota, FL
Bomar, L. Wayne ... Shelbyville, TN
Bomar, Robert S. ... Atlanta, GA
Bomar, Thomas H. ... San Francisco, CA
Bomar, Valarie Tatem ... Detroit, MI
Bomar, William A. ... Oak Ridge, TN
Bomar, William L. ... Memphis, TN
Bomarito, Douglas M. ... Portland, OR
Bomarito, Douglas M., P.C. ... Portland, OR
Bomba, Christopher A. ... Cedar Mountain, NC
Bomba, Thomas F. ... Staten Island, NY
Bombaci, Barbara A. ... Milwaukee, WI
Bombaci, Santina M. ... Warren, NJ
Bombalier, Silvia ... South Gate, CA
Bombara, John C. ... Hartford, CT
Bombara, Robert G. ... Garden City, NY
Bombard, Steven Robert ... New York, NY
Bombardier, Colleen B.
Federal Deposit Insurance Corporation, Appellate Litigation Section, GV
Bombaugh, Robert L.
Department of Justice, Civil Division, GV
Bombeck, Scott C. ... Warren, OH
Bomberg, Alison T. ... Boston, MA
Bomberg, Margaret ... Chico, CA
Bomberger, Gregory ... Armonk, NY
Bomberger, Jon A. ... Fort Wayne, IN
Bomberger, Margaret M. ... Indianapolis, IN
Bomberger, Peter C. ... Highland, IN
Bomberger, R. Michael ... San Diego, CA
Bomberger, Russell B. ... Monterey, CA
Bombich, Lorene J. ... Stone Mountain, GA
Bombik, Richard John ... Cleveland, OH
Bombino, Isabel P. ... Miami, FL
Bomchill, Fern C. ... Chicago, IL
Bomengen, Kristen F. ... Juneau, AK
Bomes, Stephen D. (IBA) ... Los Angeles, CA
Bomgardner, Clyde R. ... Mifflintown, PA
Bomgardner, David J. ... Woodbridge, VA
Bomgardner, John H., II
San Francisco, CA
Bomgardner, Sharon J. ... Treasury Department, Internal Revenue Service, GV
Bomgardner & Winder ... Mifflintown, PA
Bomher, John T. ... Springfield, IL
Bomhoff, Margaret A.
Oklahoma City, OK
Bomhoff, Timothy J. ... Oklahoma City, OK
Bomier, Jerome T. ... Neenah, WI
Bomier, Samuel J. ... Neenah, WI
Bomkamp, Gary W. ... St. Louis, MO
Bommarito, Michael J. ... Lansing, MI
Bommarito, Michael J. ... Southfield, MI
Bommer, Timothy J. ... Jackson, WY
Bompart, Timothy L. ... Forest Hills, NY
Bompey, Mitchell S. ... New York, NY
Bomrind, Zev M. ... New York, NY
Bomse, Audrey J. ... Piscataway, NJ
Bomse, Stephen V. ... San Francisco, CA
Bomser, Alan H. ... New York, NY
Bomson, Scott J. ... Department of Justice, Bureau of Prisons, GV
Bomstein, Anna E. ... New York, NY
Bomstein, Brian E. ... Miami, FL
Bomstein, Michael S. ... Philadelphia, PA
Bomze, Jay I. ... Philadelphia, PA
Bomze, Paul E. ... Philadelphia, PA
Bon & Kaszynski ... St. Paul, MN
Bon, Michael D. ... Miami, FL
Bon, Nicolett M. ... St. Paul, MN
Bon, William A., Jr. ... Southfield, MI
Bon, William S. ... Casper, WY
Bona, Kathy L. ... Yakima, WA
Bona, Thomas M. ... Newburgh, NY
Uniondale, NY
White Plains, NY
Bona, Thomas M., P.C. ... Bronx, NY
Newburgh, NY
New York, NY
Uniondale, NY
White Plains, NY
Bonacarti, Alexandra M. ... Brooklyn, NY
Bonacci, Anthony A. ... Phoenix, AZ
Bonacci, Edward, Jr. ... New York, NY
Bonacci, JoAnne M. ... Livingston, NJ
Bonacci, John A. ... Pittsburgh, PA
Bonacci, Louis M. ... Cleveland, OH

Bonacci, Maria Salcedo ... Chicago, IL
Bonacci, Muchow & Redman, Law Offices of ... Pittsburgh, PA
Bonaccio, Cecilia ... Cleveland, OH
Bonaccorsi, David Paul ... Newark, CA
Bonaccorsi, Joseph P. ... Chicago, IL
Bonaccorsi, Mary Clare ... Chicago, IL
Bonaccorso, Samuel ... Boston, MA
Bonaccorso, William S. ... Boston, MA
Bonaccorsy, John J. ... Daytona Beach, FL
Bonacic, Andrew M. ... Glens Falls, NY
Bonacic, Blustein & Krahulik, LLP
Middletown, NY
Warwick, NY
Bonacic, J. Scott ... Middletown, NY
Bonacic, John J. ... Middletown, NY
Bonacker, Donald E. ... Springfield, MO
Bonacore, Joseph ... Uniondale, NY
Bonacorsa, Michael V. ... New York, NY
Bonacorsi, Ellen E. ... St. Louis, MO
Bonacorsi, Louis F. ... St. Louis, MO
Bonacorsi, Mary M. ... St. Louis, MO
Bonacquist, Harold F. ... New York, NY
Bonacquist, Mark R. ... Albany, NY
Bonacquisti, Mark ... Miami, FL
Bonacum, John J., III ... New York, NY
Bonadies, Anthony S. ... Hamden, CT
Bonadies, Doreen J. ... North Haven, CT
Bonadies, Paul N. ... Chicago, IL
Bonadio, Anthony F. ... Rochester, NY
Bonadio, Anthony M. ... Port Huron, MI
Bonadonna, Eileen M. Cornell
Kissimmee, FL
Bonady, Mark S. ... New Berlin, WI
Bonafede, Michael C. I. ... Loveland, CO
Bonafede, Samuel J. ... Marion, NY
Bonaffini, Josephine M. ... Andover, MA
Bonafide, Philip P. ... Laconia, NH
Bonafield, James J. ... Clifton, NJ
Bonagofsky, John S. ... Berkeley, CA
Bonagofsky, Kristy Wheeler
San Francisco, CA
Bonaguide, Christine A. ... Buffalo, NY
Bonaguidi, Lawrence P. J., & Associates, P.C.
New York, NY
Bonaguidi, Lawrence P. J. ... New York, NY
Bonagura, Salvatore R. ... Floral Park, NY
Bonaguro, Lester A. ... Chicago, IL
Bonaguro, Mark N. ... Westlake, OH
Bonahoom & Bonahoom ... Fort Wayne, IN
Bonahoom, Joseph G. ... Fort Wayne, IN
Bonahoom, Otto M. ... Fort Wayne, IN
Bonaiuto, Frank F. ... Cleveland, OH
Bonaldes, Melissa E. ... Kew Gardens, NY
Bonaldi, Alfred R. ... Belleville, IL
Bonaldi and Clinton, Ltd. ... Belleville, IL
Bonamarte, Michael F., III
Highland Park, IL
Bonamassa, Michael A. ... Marlton, NJ
Bonami, E. Andre ... Chicago, IL
Bonamo, Richard R. ... Woodbridge, NJ
Bonan and Bonan ... McLeansboro, IL
Bonan, Donna L. ... Benton, IL
Bonan, Elizabeth P. ... Stuart, FL
Bonan, F. William ... McLeansboro, IL
Bonan, Seon P. ... New York, NY
Bonan, W. Martin ... Stuart, FL
Bonander, Lachlan M. ... Larchwood, IA
Bonander, Lachlan M., P.C. ... Larchwood, IA
Bonander, Rodney B. ... Larchwood, IA
Bonanni, Louis S. ... New York, NY
Bonanni, Marc ... Tustin, CA
Bonanni, Maureen Sullivan ... Albany, NY
Bonanni, Megan ... Detroit, MI
Bonanno, Anthony Michael ... Norwood, MA
Bonanno, Edward R. ... Trenton, NJ
Bonanno, Felicia M. ... Shrewsbury, NJ
Bonanno, Gale Carney
Environmental Protection Agency, Program Office Attorneys, GV
Bonanno, Jack F. ... San Francisco, CA
Bonanno, James Bautz ... Tenafly, NJ
Bonanno, Jennifer A. ... Washington, DC
Bonanno, Joseph G. ... Malden, MA
Bonanno, Lisa ... Washington, DC
Bonanno, Mark A. ... Portland, OR
Bonanno, Nona Jean ... Washington, DC
Rockville, MD
Bonanno, Peter V. ... Washington, DC
Bonanno, Robert H. ... Tampa, FL
Bonanno, Santo J. ... Ridgewood, NJ
Bonanno, Stephen M. ... Carrollton, GA
Bonanno, Steven R. ... Chicago, IL
Bonanno, Thomas S. ... Brooklyn, NY
Bonanno, William S. ... Madison, NJ
Bonano, William E. ... San Francisco, CA
Bonansinga, Tim J. ... Hood River, OR
Bonanti, John M. ... Erie, PA
Bonanto, Paul J. ... Wilmington, DE
Bonapart, Alan D. ... San Francisco, CA
Bonapart, Barri Kaplan ... Mill Valley, CA
Bonaparte, Elliott, Ostrander & Preston, P.C. ... Portland, OR
Seattle, WA
Bonaparte & Miyamoto, A Professional Law Corporation ... Los Angeles, CA
Newport Beach, CA
Bonaparte, Nell Hoffman ... Portland, OR
Bonaparte, Robert E. L. ... Portland, OR
Bonaparte, Ronald H. ... Los Angeles, CA
Newport Beach, CA
Bonapfel, Paul W. ... Atlanta, GA
Bonaquist, James A., Jr. ... Naples, FL
Bonar, Barbara Dahlenburg
Covington, KY
Bonar, Delbert E. ... Findlay, OH
Bonar, Jason J. ... Chelsea, AL
Bonar, Jennifer M. ... Washington, DC
Bonar, John A. ... Covington, KY
Bonar, Robert Bruce ... Louisville, KY
Bonard, Glenn R. ... Washington, DC
Bonarigo, Benjamin J. ... Batavia, NY
Bonaros, Thomas Patrick ... Utica, NY
Bonarrigo, Anthony ... New York, NY
Bonarti, Michael A. ... Roseland, NJ
Bonasera, Richard F. ... Carver, MA
Bonasera, Thomas J. ... Columbus, OH
Bonassar, Joseph M. ... Danbury, CT
Bonasso, Michael ... Charleston, WV
Bonasso, Steven J. ... Detroit, MI
Bonath, Keane A. ... Robbinsdale, MN
Bonato, Donald J. ... Lansing, MI
Bonato, Sandra ... Alamo, CA
Bonau, Jose' Antonio ... New Orleans, LA
Bonaventura, Ellen Mary ... New York, NY
Bonaventura, Mark G. ... Columbus, OH
Bonaventura, Mary Beth ... Gary, IN
Bonaventure, Frank C., Jr.
Baltimore, MD
Bonavia, Andrew J. ... Ithaca, NY
Bonavich, Peter R. ... Chicago, IL
Bonavita Law Firm, The ... Austin, TX
Bonavita, Neil M. ... Austin, TX
Bonavita, Paul N. ... North Brunswick, NJ
Bonavita, Samuel F. ... Warren, PA
Bonavita, Thomas J. ... Warren, PA
Bonavitacola, Alex. ... Philadelphia, PA
Bonavitacola, Portia A. ... Philadelphia, PA
Bonazzi, John J. ... Wellesley, MA
Bonazzola, Mark L. ... Long Beach, CA
Boncek, Edward ... Land O'Lakes, FL
Boncheck, Daniel H. ... Lancaster, PA
Boncher, Frederick J. ... Caledonia, MI
Grand Rapids, MI
Bonchi, Keith A. ... Atlantic City, NJ
Bonchonsky, Michael P. ... Somerville, NJ
Bonchonsky, Peter R. ... Garden City, NY
Bonciolini, Dennis J. ... Gresham, OR
Boncore, Philip R. ... Boston, MA
Bonczek, Robert R. ... Wilmington, DE
Bonczek, Stanley R. ... Edison, NJ
Bonczyk, Bruce S. ... Springfield, IL
Bond, A. Gordon, Jr. ... Coral Springs, FL
Bond, Adam M. ... New York, NY
Bond, Adrienne Randle ... Houston, TX
Bond, Allen C. ... Lake Success, NY
Bond, Andrea M. ... Minneapolis, MN
Bond, Andy L. ... St. Louis Park, MN
Bond, Ann T. ... Metairie, LA
Bond, Anthony R. ... Elyria, OH
Bond, Arnett & Phelan, P.A. ... Ocala, FL
Bond, Baron ... New York, NY
Bond, Betty Blue Keeler ... Montgomery, AL
Bond, Betty Jean ... Kansas City, MO
Bond, Beverly S. ... New York, NY
Bond & Bond ... El Dorado, KS
Bond, Botes & McCormick, P.C. ... Biloxi, MS
Bond, Brian C. ... Phoenix, AZ
Bond & Bridenhager ... Liberty, IN
Bond, Brook Bernard ... San Francisco, CA
Bond, C. Guy ... Jacksonville Beach, FL
Bond, C. James ... Pittsburgh, PA
Bond, Calhoun ... Baltimore, MD
Bond, Cary R. ... San Diego, CA
Bond, Cathy L. ... Indianapolis, IN
Bond, Cecily ... Sacramento, CA
Bond, Charles ... Berkeley, CA
Bond, Charles H. ... Farmingdale, NJ
Bond, Chas. S. ... San Antonio, TX
Bond, Christopher ... Portland, ME
Bond, Christopher S. ... Kansas City, MO
Bond, Clifford J. ... New York, NY
Bond, Conte & Norman, P.L.L.C.
Washington, DC
Bond, Cynthia D. ... Ithaca, NY
Bond, Daniel Earl ... Chardon, OH
Bond, David D. ... Livingston, NJ
Bond, David E. ... Burlington, VT
Bond, David M. ... Washington, DC
Bond, David M. ... Houston, TX
Bond, David R. ... Rockford, IL
Bond, Deke W. ... Houston, TX
Bond, Dianna K. ... Dayton, OH
Bond & Domb, A Professional Association
Pembroke Pines, FL
Bond, Donald H. ... Yakima, WA
Bond, Donald W. ... Winona, MS
Bond, Douglas C. ... Canton, OH
New Philadelphia, OH
Bond, Douglas W. ... Orlando, FL
Bond, E. Clifton, Jr. ... Monticello, AR
Bond, Edward C. ... Floral Park, NY
Bond, F. Hooper ... Easton, MD
Bond, Ferris R. ... Washington, DC
Bond, Floyd William, III ... Park Forest, IL
Bond, Frank Kevin ... Salt Lake City, UT
Bond, Frank M. ... Santa Fe, NM
Bond, Fred W. ... Shelbyville, KY
Bond, Gamma and Associates, P.C.
Berkeley, CA
Bond, Gary K. ... Chattanooga, TN
Bond, Gary L., Jr. ... Dallas, TX
Bond, Gary M. ... Chicago, IL
Bond, Gene Perry
Department Of The Interior, GV
Bond, George T. ... Houston, TX
Bond, Gilbert A. ... Los Angeles, CA
Bond, Gregory W. ... Oklahoma City, OK
Bond, Ida Elizabeth ... Knoxville, TN
Bond, J. Trenton ... Beaumont, TX
Bond, James A. ... Stuart, FL
Bond, James A., P.A. ... Stuart, FL
Bond, James B. ... Bryan, TX
Bond, James E., II ... Welch, WV
Bond, James O. ... Lebanon, TN
Bond, Jan ... St. Louis, MO
Bond, Jane ... Akron, OH
Bond, Jane E. ... Orlando, FL
Bond, Jason A. ... Piscataway, NJ
Bond, Jason R. ... Madison, WI
Bond, Jay D., Jr. ... Daytona Beach, FL
Bond, Jay R. ... Oklahoma City, OK
Bond, Jeannette M. ... Newark, NJ
Bond, Jill K. ... Buffalo, NY
Bond, Johanna E. ... Washington, DC
Bond, John A. ... Pembroke Pines, FL
Bond, John D., III ... Charlotte, NC
Bond, John E. ... Whittier, CA
Bond, John L. A. ... Pembroke Pines, FL
Bond, John M. ... Oklahoma City, OK
Bond, John M., Jr. ... New York, NY
Bond, Jon Patterson ... Tulsa, OK
Bond, Joseph R. ... Santa Clara, CA
Bond, Julia L. ... San Leandro, CA
Bond, Katharyn ... San Francisco, CA
Bond, Katherine Cook ... Austin, TX
Bond, Katherine F. ... Augusta, GA
Bond, Keith N. ... Buffalo, NY
Bond, Kenneth W. ... New York, NY
Bond, Kevin W. ... Winter Park, FL
Bond, Langhorne M. ... Washington, DC
Bond, Laura J. ... Overland Park, KS
Kansas City, MO
Bond, Laurence B. ... Salt Lake City, UT
Bond, Lisa ... Los Angeles, CA
Bond, Lyn, Jr. ... Charlotte, NC
Bond, M. Thomas, Jr. ... Ocala, FL
Bond, Madison E. ... Englewood, CO
Bond, Malcolm Joseph ... Baltimore, MD
Bond, Malcolm Joseph, P.A.
Baltimore, MD
Bond, Marc D. ... Anchorage, AK
Bond, Marcia ... Stockbridge, GA
Bond, Margaret E. ... Ewing, NJ
Bond, Margaret E. ... Dallas, TX
Bond, Mark W. ... Biloxi, MS
Bond, Martin W. ... Philadelphia, PA
Bond and McDonald, P.C. ... Geneva, NY
Bond, Megan M. ... Clifton Park, NY
Bond, Melissa V. ... Doylestown, PA
Bond, Meridith C. ... Knoxville, TN
Bond, Michael J. ... Burbank, CA
Bond, Michael J. ... Seattle, WA
Bond, Michael W. ... Fort Myers, FL
Bond, Michelle J. ... Hartford, CT
Bond, Monte M. ... Dallas, TX
Bond & Morris ... Englewood, CO
Denver, CO
Bond, Nathan L. ... Tallahassee, FL
Bond, Nathan L., P.A. ... Tallahassee, FL
Bond & O'Brien ... Jacksonville, AR
Bond, Patrick K. ... Wheaton, IL
Bond, Patterson ... Tulsa, OK
Bond, Peggy A. ... Eugene, OR
Bond, Peggy A., P.C. ... Eugene, OR
Bond, Philippa ... New York, NY
Bond, R. Douglass ... Chicago, IL
Bond, R. Keith ... Elizabethtown, KY
Bond, R. Wayne ... Atlanta, GA
Bond, Randall S. ... Bryan, TX
Bond, Rebecca ... San Francisco, CA
Bond, Richard C., Jr. ... Wayne, IL
Bond, Richard E. ... Wakarusa, IN
Bond, Robert J., Jr. ... Lafayette Hill, PA
Bond, Robert L. ... Pasadena, CA
Bond, Robert M. ... Indianapolis, IN
Bond, Robert M. ... El Dorado, KS
Bond, Ronald M. ... Phoenix, AZ
Bond, Russ W. ... Englewood, CO
Bond, Sarah A. ... Helena, MT
Bond, Schoeneck & King, LLP
Overland Park, KS
Albany, NY
Buffalo, NY
Oswego, NY
Saratoga Springs, NY
Syracuse, NY
Bonita Springs, FL
Naples, FL
Bond, Stanley V. ... Fayetteville, AR
Bond, Stephanie K ... Tucson, AZ
Bond, Stephen A. ... San Diego, CA
Bond, Stephen P. ... Elyria, OH
Bond, Stuart H. ... Roswell, GA
Bond, Susan G. ... Department of the Army, Office, Chief of Engineers/Headquarters, U.S. Army Corps of Engineers, GV
Bond, T. David ... New Orleans, LA
Bond, T. Norton ... Pensacola, FL
Bond & Taylor, L.L.P. ... Houston, TX
Bond, Terrence A. ... St. Louis, MO
Bond, Thaddeus M., Jr. ... Waukegan, IL
Bond, Thaddeus M., Sr. ... Waukegan, IL
Bond, Thaddeus M., Jr. & Associates, P.C.
Waukegan, IL
Bond, Thomas D. ... Milwaukie, OR
Bond, Thomas J., (P.C.) ... Austin, TX
Bond, Thomas M. ... Boston, MA
Bond, Thomas R. ... Philadelphia, PA
Bond, Tully M., Jr. ... Macon, GA
Bond, W. Ellis ... Lake Charles, LA
Bond, W. Michael ... Washington, DC
Bond, Will ... Jacksonville, AR
Bond, William A. ... Dallas, TX
Bond, William E., Jr. ... Pensacola, FL
Bond, William H. ... Buffalo, NY
Bond, William J. ... St. Paul, MN
Bond, William W., Jr. ... Ellenwood, GA
Bonda, Dana L. ... Los Angeles, CA
Bondada, Vijay V. ... Philadelphia, PA
Bondar, Barbara S. ... Denver, CO
Bondar, Nancy L. ... Saginaw, MI
Bondareff, Richard F. ... Dumfries, VA
Bondarenko, Gregory P.
Grand Rapids, MI
Bond-Collins, Rhonda D. ... Washington, DC
Bondelie, P. Anne ... San Francisco, CA
Bondelie, Rolf Marcus ... Los Gatos, CA
Bondell, Jay A. ... New York, NY
Bondell, Stuart M. ... New York, NY
Bonder, Daniel L. ... Cleveland, OH
Bonder, Dawn Morgenthal ... Uniondale, NY
Bonder, Kimberly B. ... Melbourne, FL
Bonder, Louis D. ... Austin, TX
Bonder, Sandra L. ... New York, NY
Bonder, Scott L. ... Atlanta, GA
Bonder, Teresa Thebaut ... Atlanta, GA
Bonder, Todd W. ... Beverly Hills, CA
Bonderman, David ... Fort Worth, TX
Bonderman, Judith A. ... Washington, DC
Bondhus, JoAnn E. ... Wayne, NE
Bondi, Harry G. ... Casper, WY
Bondi, Harry G., P.C., Law Offices
Casper, WY
Bondi & Iovino ... Mineola, NY
Bondi, Joseph C. ... Mineola, NY
Bondi, Kathleen Buchanan
Oakbrook Terrace, IL
Bondi, Michael A. ... Chicago, IL
Bondi, Steven A. ... Hartford, CT
Bondies, Walton P., Jr.
Farmers Branch, TX
Bondi-Stoddard, Annamarie
Great Neck, NY
Bondoc, N. Rommel ... San Francisco, CA
Bondonno, Franklin E. ... San Jose, CA
Bondor, Paul A. ... New York, NY
Bondorowsky, Barry R. ... Brooklyn, NY
Bondroff, Ronald D. ... Baltimore, MD
Bonds, A. Camp ... Muskogee, OK
Bonds, A. Camp, Jr. ... Muskogee, OK
Bonds, Alexander ... Joliet, IL
Bonds, Alva F., Jr. ... Memphis, TN
Bonds, Barbara E. ... Cheyenne, WY
Bonds, Barbara P. ... Little Rock, AR
Bonds, Bruce L. ... Urbana, IL
Bonds, Emily Sides ... Birmingham, AL
Bonds, George R. ... Nashville, TN
Bonds, Harriet Ashby ... Walterboro, SC
Bonds, Jeff M. ... Muskogee, OK
Bonds, John W., Jr. ... Atlanta, GA
Bonds, John Y., III ... Fort Worth, TX
Bonds, Kurt R. ... Las Vegas, NV
Bonds, Marlene Kriewald ... Burton, TX
Bonds, Matthews, Bonds & Hayes
Muskogee, OK
Bonds, Paula ... Atlanta, GA
Bonds, Robert J. ... Walterboro, SC
Bonds, Russell S. ... Atlanta, GA
Bonds, Suzanne M. ... Chicago, IL
Bonds, W. Collins ... Milan, TN
Bonds, W. Ronald ... Chicago, IL
Bonds, William T. ... Avon Lake, OH
Bondura, Julie M. ... Greenville, SC
Bondura, Stephen E. ... Greenville, SC
Bondurant, Alyce Alane ... Iowa Park, TX
Bondurant, Amy C. ... Atlanta, GA
Bondurant, B. Elliott ... West Point, VA
Bondurant & Benson, P.C. ... Richmond, VA
BonDurant, Bruce J. ... South Bend, IN
Bondurant, Charles J. ... San Antonio, TX
Bondurant, Elizabeth J. ... Atlanta, GA
Bondurant, Emmet J., II ... Atlanta, GA
Bondurant, Frank E. ... Marianna, FL
Bondurant and Fuqua, P.A.
Marianna, FL
Bondurant, James E. ... Hodgenville, KY
Bondurant, James E., Jr. ... Knoxville, TN
Bondurant, John T. ... Louisville, KY
Bondurant, John W. ... Medford, OR
Bondurant, Mary Williams ... Atlanta, GA
Bondurant, Mixson & Elmore, LLP
Atlanta, GA
BonDurant, Robert E. ... Palm Beach, FL
Bondurant, Si M. ... Jackson, MS
Bondurant, Stacy C. G. ... Milledgeville, GA
Bondurant, Susan ... Long Island City, NY
Bondurant, Thomas J. ... Lebanon, VA
Bondurant, Thomas J., Jr. ... Roanoke, VA
Bondurant, Thomas O., Jr. ... Richmond, VA
Bondurant, Walton G., Jr. ... Portsmouth, VA
Bondurant, Ward S. ... Atlanta, GA
Bondurant, Wiley M. ... San Antonio, TX
Bondurant, Wm. L. ... Davidson, NC
Bondy, Esther S. ... Short Hills, NJ
Bondy, Eugene L., Jr. ... New York, NY
Bondy, Jonathan S. ... Roseland, NJ
Bondy, Robert M. ... Milford, MI
Bondy & Schloss LLP ... New York, NY
Bondy, Thomas L. ... New York, NY
Bone, Bill, P.A., The Law Office of
West Palm Beach, FL
Bone, Charles W. ... Nashville, TN
Bone, Dani Victor ... Gadsden, AL
Bone, David D. ... Sarasota, FL
Bone, David H. ... Belleville, IL
Bone, Gary J. ... Gadsden, AL
Bone, J. David ... Jacksonville, IL
Bone, J. Roger ... Bradenton, FL
Bone, James H. ... Atlanta, GA
Bone, Jan M. E. ... East Orleans, MA
Bone, Jesse V., Jr. ... Gastonia, NC
Bone, Katherine K. ... Atlanta, GA
Bone, Lea ... Birmingham, AL
Bone, Maurice E. ... Belleville, IL
Bone, Richard A. ... Southfield, MI
Bone, Robert E. ... Houston, TX
Bone, Robert E., Jr. ... Cape Coral, FL
Bone, Robert Murray ... Santa Rosa, CA
Bone, Steven R. ... Carmel, IN

Bone, William Dudley "Bill"
West Palm Beach, FL
Boneau & Lewis .... Port Arthur, TX
Boneau, Melvin J. .... Port Arthur, TX
Bonebakker, Erno R. .... Portland, ME
Bonebakker, Victoria B. .... Portland, ME
Boneberg, Robert C. .... New York, NY
Bonebrake, Alan C. .... Hillsboro, OR
Bonebrake, Carol B. .... Topeka, KS
Bonebrake, D. Scott .... Philadelphia, PA
Bonebrake, James G. .... Chicago, IL
Bonebrake, Stephen J. .... Chicago, IL
Bonecutter, Brenda L. .... Newport, KY
Bonee, John L. .... Hartford, CT
Bonee, John L., III .... Hartford, CT
Bonee Law Offices, LLP .... Hartford, CT
Bonekemper, Edward H., III
Department of Transportation, Research and Special Programs Administration, GV
Bonell, Brian Paul .... Englewood, CO
Bonella, Michael J. .... Philadelphia, PA
Bonelli, Benjamin P. .... Belvedere-Tiburon, CA
Bonelli, Dave R. .... San Francisco, CA
Bonelli, David J. .... San Francisco, CA
Bonelli, Margaret .... South Windsor, CT
Bonelli, William Jeffrey .... Malibu, CA
Bonello, Carol L. .... Norristown, PA
Bonello, Francis V. .... Eatontown, NJ
Woodbridge, NJ
Bonello, John A. .... Washington, DC
Bonello, John L. .... West End, NJ
Bonem, David W. .... Portales, NM
Bonem, Franklin S. .... New York, NY
Bonem, Robert E. .... Wilmette, IL
Bonem, Stuart J. .... Chicago, IL
Bonenberger, Gregory H. .... Branford, CT
Bonenberger, Landers P.
Martinsburg, WV
Wheeling, WV
Bonenfant, Mark A. .... Los Angeles, CA
Boneno, David J. .... Baton Rouge, LA
Boneparth, Harvey M. .... New York, NY
Boner, D. Stephen .... San Diego, CA
Boner, Eleanor K. .... White Plains, NY
Boner, Mary Eftink .... Jackson, MO
Boner, Richard D. .... Charlotte, NC
Boner & Stern, A Professional Corporation
San Diego, CA
Bonertz, Margaret A. .... Pasadena, CA
Bones, Amy S. .... Omaha, NE
Bonesch, Christie F. .... Allentown, PA
Bonesio, Elizabeth Eaton .... Dallas, TX
Bonesio, W. Michael .... Dallas, TX
Boness, Christine M. .... Boston, MA
Boness, Frederick H. .... Anchorage, AK
Bonessa, Dennis R. .... Pittsburgh, PA
Bonessa, Rita J. .... Denver, CO
Bonesso, William F. .... Melville, NY
Mineola, NY
Bonesteel, Damon B. .... Los Angeles, CA
Bonesteel, Michael J., (A Professional Corporation) .... Santa Monica, CA
Bonesteel, Scott M. .... San Diego, CA
Bonesteel, Virginia A. (IBA) **.... Lexington, MA**
Bonet, Charles O. .... Socorro, NM
Boneta, John A. .... Arlington, VA
Boneta, Roberto .... San Juan, PR
Bonetati, Marilyn L. .... Orange, CA
Bonett, Linda M. .... Fresno, CA
Bonetti, A. Edward, Jr. .... Akron, OH
Bonetti, Dennis J. .... Harrisburg, PA
Bonetti, Veronica A. .... Elk Grove, CA
Bonevac, Judy Barringer
Fort Lauderdale, FL
Bonevac, Judy Barringer, P.A.
Fort Lauderdale, FL
Bonewitz, Richard D. .... Mishawaka, IN
Boney, Durham T. .... Columbia, SC
Boney, F. H. .... Summerville, GA
Boney, H. Robert, Jr. .... Somers Point, NJ
Boney, Harold A. .... Beaufort, SC
Boney, Howard S., Jr. .... Tarboro, NC
Boney, Jacqueline M. .... Findlay, OH
Toledo, OH
Boney, Kecia .... Washington, DC
Boney, N. Bruce, Jr. .... Charlotte, NC
Boney, Sandra Reid .... Columbia, SC
Boney, Steven P. .... Austin, TX
Boney, Timothy G. .... Trenton, NJ
Boney, Warren X. .... Tyler, TX
Boney, William J., Jr. .... Wilmington, NC
Bonezzi Switzer Murphy & Polito, Co. L.P.A. .... Cleveland, OH
Bonezzi, William D. .... Cleveland, OH
Bonfa, Don P. .... Huntington Beach, CA
Bonfanti, Anthony J. .... New Orleans, LA
Bonfanti, Anthony J., Sr. .... Metairie, LA
Bonfanti, James I. .... Somerville, MA
Bonfanti, Leonard A. .... Peabody, MA
Bonfatti, Timothy J. .... North Falmouth, MA
Bonfeld, Roberta Gail .... Brooklyn, NY
Bonfield, Arthur E. .... Iowa City, IA
Bonfield, Howard S. .... New York, NY
Bonfield, Lauren B. .... New York, NY
Bonfield, Susan D. .... Trenton, NJ
Bonfiglio, Barbara Wixon
Washington, DC
Bonfiglio, David C. .... Elkhart, IN
Bonfiglio, David T. .... Phoenix, AZ
Bonfiglio, Gregory A. .... Palo Alto, CA
Bonfiglio, Joel D. .... Washington, DC
Bonfiglio, Kristi S. .... Phoenix, AZ
Bonfiglio, Michael A. .... Toledo, OH
Bonfiglio, Paul R. .... Toledo, OH
Bonfiglio, Peter J., III .... Laurel Springs, NJ
Bonfiglio, Richard S. .... Brooklyn, NY
Bonfiglio, Rosa .... New York, NY

Bonfiglio, Suzette D. .... Mount Laurel, NJ
Philadelphia, PA
Bonfilio, Gregory J. .... San Francisco, CA
Bonfilio, Victor P. .... San Francisco, CA
Bonfini, Emilio M. .... Bellaire, OH
Bonfoey, Michael .... Waynesville, NC
Bonga, David C. .... Usk, WA
Bongaardt, J. Clark .... Media, PA
Bongar, Charles A., Jr. .... Waldorf, MD
Bongard, Charles Mark .... Lexington, KY
Bongard, Charles R. .... San Diego, CA
Bongard, Helen L. .... Lexington, KY
Bongard, William O. .... Minneapolis, MN
Bongartz, Seth B. .... Manchester Center, VT
Bonges, Robert C. .... Chicago, IL
Bongi, Thomas M. .... San Francisco, CA
Bongiorni, Vincent A. .... Springfield, MA
Bongiorno, Andrew W. .... Basking Ridge, NJ
Bongiorno, Anthony A. .... Boston, MA
Bongiorno, Anthony M. .... New York, NY
Bongiorno, Joseph .... Yonkers, NY
Bongiorno, Joseph R. .... New York, NY
Bongiorno, Joseph S. .... Wheaton, IL
Bongiorno, Michael .... Woodland Hills, CA
Bongiorno, Michael G. .... Boston, MA
Bongiorno, Salvatore J. .... Chicago, IL
Bongiovanni, Anthony M. .... Linwood, NJ
Bongiovanni, Anthony M., A Prof. Corp.
Linwood, NJ
Bongiovanni, Arthur E. .... Naples, FL
Syracuse, NY
Bongiovanni & Berger .... Philadelphia, PA
Bongiovanni, Collins & Warden, A Professional Corporation .... Denville, NJ
Bongiovanni, David A. .... Princeton, NJ
Bongiovanni, Ernest .... Howell, NJ
Bongiovanni, Joseph N., III
Philadelphia, PA
Bongiovanni, Joseph N., Jr.
Philadelphia, PA
Bongiovanni, Kim Rice .... Jacksonville, FL
Bongiovanni, Mark .... Cedar Knolls, NJ
Bongiovanni, Patricia A. .... Northbrook, IL
Bongiovi, Donald J. .... Rego Park, NY
Bongiovi, Henry J. .... Santa Barbara, CA
Bongiovi, Joseph J., III .... Las Vegas, NV
Bongiovi, Lisa A. .... Springfield, MA
Bonhag, Cornelia L. .... New York, NY
Bonhage, Thomas F., Jr. .... Jacksonville, FL
Bonham, Craig Anthony .... Plano, TX
Bonham, David B. .... Washington, DC
Bonham, David B., (P.C.) .... Nederland, TX
Bonham, David L. .... Miami, FL
Bonham, Geoffrey R. .... Columbia, SC
Bonham, J. Ted .... Oklahoma City, OK
Bonham, James D. .... Houston, TX
Bonham, Jenny A. .... Huntington, WV
Bonham, John D. .... Montgomery, AL
Bonham, John T., II .... Charleston, WV
Bonham, Kenneth C. .... South Lake Tahoe, CA
Bonham, Larry M. .... Charleston, WV
Bonham, Mark E. .... Palo Alto, CA
Bonham, Mitchell W. .... Mason, OH
Bonham, Robert G. .... Denver, CO
Bonham, Robert W., III
Federal Election Commission, Office of the General Counsel, GV
Bonham, Terrence J. .... Ventura, CA
Bonham, Thomas L. .... Albuquerque, NM
Bonham, William D. .... Houston, TX
Bonham, William E. .... Sacramento, CA
Bonham, William T. .... Gahanna, OH
Bonhaus, Laurence A. .... Cincinnati, OH
Bonheim, Karl E. .... Riverhead, NY
Bonheyo, Patricia L. .... San Francisco, CA
Bonhomme, Evelyne V.
Treasury Department, Office of Thrift Supervision, GV
Boni, Bruce J. .... McKees Rocks, PA
Boni, Michael J. .... Philadelphia, PA
Boni, Paul .... Marlton, NJ
Philadelphia, PA
Bonial, Hilary B. .... Dallas, TX
Bonica, John R. .... Houston, TX
Bonica, John R., P.C. .... Houston, TX
Bonicoro, Karin E. .... Austin, TX
Bonidy, Austin O. .... Miami, FL
Bonidy, Jos. K. .... New Kensington, PA
Bonie, Anjele D. .... New York, NY
Boniello, Anton, Conti & Boniello
Niagara Falls, NY
Boniello, David G. .... Niagara Falls, NY
Boniello, Dorothea M. .... Billings, MT
Boniello, Ralph A. .... Niagara Falls, NY
Boniello, Ralph A., III .... Niagara Falls, NY
Boniello, Thomas R. .... Westfield, NJ
Boniface, John Frederick
Oklahoma City, OK
Bonifacic, Frank M. .... Chicago, IL
Bonifant, James A. .... Gaithersburg, MD
Bonifas, James J. .... Wauwatosa, WI
Bonifay, Cecelia .... Orlando, FL
Bonifaz, Cristobal, Law Offices of
Amherst, MA
Bonifaz, Cristobal, Law Offices of
Boston, MA
Bonifaz, John C. .... Boston, MA
Bonifazio, Jack .... Los Angeles, CA
Bonifer, A. Joseph, Sr. .... Alexandria, VA
Bonifield, Amy E. .... Durham, NC
Bonifield, Jerald J. .... Belleville, IL
Bonifield & Rosenstengel, P.C.
Belleville, IL
Bonilla, Armando O. .... Department of Justice, Civil Division, GV
Bonilla & Berlanga, Inc. .... Corpus Christi, TX
Bonilla, Christie Moon .... Pasadena, CA
Bonilla, David Andrew .... El Paso, TX

Bonilla, Gregory L. .... Great Falls, MT
Bonilla, Jon .... Corpus Christi, TX
Bonilla, Leigh H. .... Lincoln, MA
Bonilla, Marilyn .... Boca Raton, FL
Bonilla, Mark A. .... Garden City, NY
Bonilla, Noel Christopher, II .... Mineola, NY
Bonilla, Rafael S. .... San Juan, PR
Bonilla, Raymond, Jr. .... Austin, TX
Bonilla, Ruben, Jr. .... Corpus Christi, TX
Bonilla, Rudy J. .... Santa Rosa, CA
Bonilla, Tony .... Corpus Christi, TX
Bonilla, William D. .... Corpus Christi, TX
Bonilla, William David, Jr.
Corpus Christi, TX
Bonilla Ortiz, Fernando J. .... San Juan, PR
Bonime, Jonathan D. .... Pittsburgh, PA
Bonime-Blanc, Andrea .... Ridgewood, NJ
Bonin, Adam C. .... Philadelphia, PA
Bonin, Albert M. .... Denver, CO
Bonin, Charles V. .... Morristown, NJ
Bonin, Franklin A. .... Encino, CA
Bonin, John R. .... Wenatchee, WA
Bonin, L. Hill, Jr. (A P.L.C.) .... Lafayette, LA
Bonin, Leslie A. .... New Orleans, LA
Bonin, Paul A., (A Professional Law Corporation) .... New Orleans, LA
Bonin, Robert M., (P.C.) .... Boston, MA
Bonin, Ronald L. .... Cranston, RI
Bonin, William O. .... New Iberia, LA
Bonin & Zalcman .... Boston, MA
Bonina, Andrea E. .... Brooklyn, NY
Bonina & Bonina, P.C. .... Brooklyn, NY
New York, NY
Bonina, Diane I. .... Schaumburg, IL
Bonina, Elizabeth .... Brooklyn, NY
Bonina, John Anthony .... Brooklyn, NY
Bonina, John, III .... Brooklyn, NY
Bonine, John E. .... Eugene, OR
Boning, Charles Richard .... Tallahassee, FL
Bonini, Aleta M. .... Toledo, OH
Bonini, Frank J., Jr. .... Philadelphia, PA
Bonini, Griffin M. J. .... San Jose, CA
Bonini, Jean F. .... Culver City, CA
Bonini, John E. .... Hartford, CT
Bonino, John M. .... Los Angeles, CA
Bonino, Mark G. .... Redwood City, CA
Bonis, Ann C. .... Boston, MA
Bonis, Daniel J. .... Des Plaines, IL
Bonis, Francine D. .... Lincoln Park, NJ
Bonis, Peter H. .... San Francisco, CA
Boniske, Nina L. .... Miami, FL
Bonistalli, John J. .... Boston, MA
Bonistalli, Joseph J. .... Pittsburgh, PA
Bonistalli, Joseph W., II .... Norfolk, VA
Bonito, Robert A. .... Irvine, CA
Bonitz, Susan M. .... San Luis Obispo, CA
Boniuk, Vivien .... New York, NY
Boni-Vendola, Corrine A. .... New Haven, CT
Bonjean, Robert V., Jr. .... Jacksonville, IL
Bonjiovi, Henry J. .... Santa Barbara, CA
Bonjorni, Duncan A. .... Auburn, WA
Bonjour, Bruce A. .... Chicago, IL
Bonjour, Jules F., Jr. .... Hayward, CA
Bonjour & Thorman .... Hayward, CA
Bonk, Colleen M .... Columbus, OH
Bonk, David T. .... Princeton, NJ
Bonk, Joseph C. .... Edison, NJ
Bonk, Joseph J. .... Wayne, NJ
Bonke, Mark Harold .... Denver, CO
Bonko, Robert J. .... Cleveland, OH
Bonkoski, Stina A. .... Denver, CO
Bonkosky, Richard .... San Francisco, CA
Bonkowski, Michael F. .... Wilmington, DE
Bonn, Bernard J., III .... Boston, MA
Bonn, Denise .... Washington, DC
Bonn, Elizabeth Currin .... Costa Mesa, CA
Bonn, Evelyn M. .... Boston, MA
Bonn, Jeffrey D. .... Phoenix, AZ
Bonn, Jeffrey D., P.C. .... Phoenix, AZ
Bonn, John R. .... Los Angeles, CA
San Diego, CA
Bonn, Karen I. .... Whitman, MA
Bonn, Luscher, Padden & Wilkins, Chartered .... Phoenix, AZ
Bonn, Michael .... Chicago, IL
Bonn, Paul V. .... Phoenix, AZ
Bonn, William A. .... Newark, NJ
Bonnabeau, Raymond R.
Golden Valley, MN
Bonnaffons, Louis P. .... New Orleans, LA
Bonnaffons, Robert L. .... New Orleans, LA
Bonnaig & Thomas .... New York, NY
Bonnar, R. Paul .... Pleasant Hill, CA
Bonnard, Colette .... New York, NY
Bonne, Bridges, Mueller, O'Keefe & Nichols, Professional Corporation
Los Angeles, CA
Riverside, CA
San Francisco, CA
San Luis Obispo, CA
Santa Ana, CA
Santa Barbara, CA
Ventura, CA
Bonne, Bruce J. .... Los Angeles, CA
Bonneau & Geismar, L.L.C.
Lewiston, ME
Bonneau, Hunt .... Dallas, TX
Bonneau, John V. .... Lewiston, ME
Bonneau Law Firm, The .... Carrollton, TX
Dallas, TX
Bonneau, Sonya G. .... Syracuse, NY
Bonnefil, Pierre G. .... New York, NY
Bonnefin, Janet M. .... Irvine, CA
Bonnefoy-Lev, Linda R. .... Santa Fe, NM
Bonnell, Fraser A. .... Berkeley, CA
Bonnell, Gerald W. .... Lexington, MA
Bonnell, Larry .... Purcell, OK
Bonnell, Paul F. .... Seattle, WA

Bonnell, Paula .... Boston, MA
Bonnell, Paula, A Professional Corporation
Boston, MA
Bonnell, Sara L. .... Glendale, AZ
Bonnell, Sylvia E. .... San Francisco, CA
Bonnell, William M. .... Richmond, CA
Bonnen, David C. .... Angleton, TX
Bonnen, Susan Desmarais .... Erie, PA
Bonner, Alice A. W. .... Houston, TX
Bonner, Alice D. .... Atlanta, GA
Bonner, Angelene .... Hayward, CA
Bonner, Arthur H. .... New York, NY
Bonner and Bonner .... Media, PA
Bonner & Bonner .... Harlingen, TX
Bonner, Bradley D. .... Powell, WY
Bonner, Bradley D., P.C. .... Powell, WY
Bonner, Byrd L. .... San Antonio, TX
Bonner, Carl .... Siloam Springs, AR
Bonner, Christopher J. .... Syracuse, NY
Bonner, Curtis .... Harlingen, TX
Bonner, Cynthia A. .... Irvine, CA
Bonner, Dale E. .... Los Angeles, CA
Bonner, Daniel F. .... Muskegon, MI
Bonner, Daniel J. .... Short Hills, NJ
Bonner, Dennis G. .... Denver, CO
Bonner, Dennis G., P.C. .... Denver, CO
Bonner, Douglas G. .... Washington, DC
Bonner, Douglas W., Jr. .... Little Rock, AR
Bonner, Ellen C. .... Gulfport, MS
Bonner, Ellen C., & Associates, P.A.
Gulfport, MS
Bonner, Eugene A. .... Media, PA
Bonner, E. V. (Chip), Jr.
Corpus Christi, TX
Bonner, G. Larry .... Martinez, GA
Bonner, Gail .... Boston, MA
Providence, RI
Bonner, Grace Linnell .... St. Louis, MO
Bonner Hogan, A Professional Corporation
Clearwater, FL
Bonner, Hugh .... Media, PA
Bonner, Hugh P. .... Boston, MA
Bonner, James P. .... New York, NY
Bonner, James P. .... Wilmington, NC
Bonner, Janet M. .... El Paso, TX
Bonner, Joel E., III .... Los Angeles, CA
Bonner, John F., III .... Minneapolis, MN
Bonner, John R. .... Williamsport, PA
Bonner, John R., Sr. .... Clearwater, FL
Bonner, Judith A.
General Services Administration, Office of Regional Counsel, GV
Bonner, Karin L. .... New York, NY
Bonner, Keith M. .... Washington, DC
Baltimore, MD
Rockville, MD
Bonner, Kevin J. .... Phoenix, AZ
Bonner, Kim Carlton .... Sarasota, FL
Bonner, Kimberly M. .... Washington, DC
Bonner Law Firm, A Professional Association
Little Rock, AR
Bonner, Leonard J. .... Washington, DC
Bonner, Leslie R. .... Richardson, TX
Bonner, Lewis Mark .... Enid, OK
Bonner, Lisa L. .... Boston, MA
Bonner, Lola L. .... Rockport, TX
Bonner, Margy .... Billings, MT
Bonner, Mark .... Enid, OK
Bonner, Mark H. .... Department of Justice, Criminal Division, GV
Bonner, Mary C. .... Fort Lauderdale, FL
Bonner, Michael B. .... Nacogdoches, TX
Bonner, Michael H. .... San Francisco, CA
Bonner, Michael J. .... Las Vegas, NV
Bonner, Michael P. .... Westfield, NJ
Bonner, Michael P. .... Philadelphia, PA
Bonner, Michael Patrick
Coral Gables, FL
Bonner, Michael R. .... Vicksburg, MS
Bonner, Michael S. .... Boston, MA
Bonner, Nancy M. .... Bensalem, PA
Bonner, Norman M. .... Austin, TX
Bonner, Patrick D., Jr. .... New York, NY
Bonner, Patrick J. .... New York, NY
Bonner, Paul B. .... Washington, DC
Bonner, Peter T. .... Department of Agriculture, Office of the General Counsel, GV
Bonner, R. Lawrence .... Miami, FL
Bonner, Raymond A. .... Washington, DC
Bonner, Richard A. .... El Paso, TX
Bonner, Richard W. .... Newport Beach, CA
Bonner, Richard W., A Professional Corporation .... Newport Beach, CA
Bonner, Robert A.
United States Court Of Appeals District Of Columbia Circuit, GV
Bonner, Robert A. .... Wellesley Hills, MA
Bonner, Robert C. .... Los Angeles, CA
Washington, DC
Bonner, Robert E. .... Orlando, FL
Bonner, Robert J. .... Milwaukee, WI
Bonner, S. Smith .... Jackson, MS
Bonner, Sigrid K.J. .... New Orleans, LA
Bonner, Stayton M. .... Henderson, TX
Bonner, Stayton M., Jr. .... Henderson, TX
Bonner, Stephen W. .... Norman, OK
Bonner, Stephen W., P.C. .... Norman, OK
Bonner, Thomas C. .... Atlantic City, NJ
Bonner, Thomas J. .... New York, NY
Bonner, Timothy R. .... Grove City, PA
Bonner, Tricia K. .... New York, NY
Bonner, Victor M. .... Houston, TX
Bonner, Wallace D., Jr. .... Albany, GA
Bonner, Walter J. .... Washington, DC
Bonner, William Adair .... Media, PA
Bonner, William J. .... Camarillo, CA
Bonner, William J. .... Lexington, KY
Bonner, William J., Jr. .... Camden, AL

Boone, F. Stephen ...... Los Alamos, NM
Boone, Francine Thornton ...... Philadelphia, PA
Boone, Francis B. ...... San Francisco, CA
Boone, Gayle A. ...... Dallas, TX
Boone, George Street ...... Elkton, KY
Boone, Gregory K. ...... Culver City, CA
Boone, Grover L. ...... Jackson, MS
Boone, Haley S. ...... Graham, NC
Boone, Harold T. ...... Towson, MD
Boone, Heidi B. ...... Seattle, WA
Boone, J. Alexander ...... Roanoke, VA
Boone, J. Fred ...... Portales, NM
Boone, J. Fred, P.C. ...... Portales, NM
Boone, J. Sidney, Jr. ...... Charleston, SC
Boone, J. William ...... Atlanta, GA
Boone, Jack B. ...... Austin, TX
Boone, Jack E., Jr. ...... Augusta, GA
Boone, James A. ...... Jackson, MS
Boone, James A. ...... Houston, TX
Boone, James B. ...... Fort Lauderdale, FL
Boone, James B. ...... Sunrise, FL
Boone, James C., Jr. ...... Palestine, TX
Boone, James P. ...... Biddeford, ME
Boone, James S. ...... Santa Cruz, CA
Boone, J. E. ...... New Albany, MS
Boone, Jefferson W. ...... Allston, MA
Boone, Jeffery A. ...... Venice, FL
Boone, Jeffrey S. ...... St. Louis, MO
Boone, Jennette L. ...... Houston, TX
Boone, Jerry ...... Atlantic City, NJ
Boone, Jess Street ...... Birmingham, AL
Boone, Jill E. ...... Okemos, MI
Boone, Joel A. ...... Quincy, MA
Boone, John H. ...... San Francisco, CA
Boone, John T., III ...... Atlanta, GA
Boone, Joseph A. ...... Irwinton, GA
Boone, Karlberg and Haddon P.C.
Deer Lodge, MT
Hamilton, MT
Missoula, MT
Polson, MT
Boone, Karsten S. ...... San Diego, CA
Boone, Kimberly Keefer ...... Birmingham, AL
Boone, L. Daniel ...... Houston, TX
Boone, LaBarron Nelson
Montgomery, AL
Boone, Latham, III ...... Anderson, TX
Boone, Laurel Lee Pope ...... Enka, NC
Boone Law Firm, P.A. ...... Cleveland, MS
Boone, Levi, III ...... Cleveland, MS
Boone, Linda F. ...... Newport, AR
Boone, Lucinda C. ...... Salinas, CA
Boone, Lynn Hudson ...... Hoffman Estates, IL
Boone, Mary Ann ...... Lancaster, OH
Boone, Mary Beth ...... Nashville, TN
Boone, Merrill Debs
Pension Benefit Guaranty Corporation, Office of the General Counsel, GV
Boone, Michael M. ...... Dallas, TX
Boone, Michael N. ...... Houston, TX
Boone, Michael R. ...... San Francisco, CA
Boone, Michael Scott ...... Atlanta, GA
Boone, Mordecai D. ...... San Francisco, CA
Boone, Nicola J. ...... Stuart, FL
Boone, Oval B. ...... Tallahassee, FL
Boone, Patrick H. ...... Birmingham, AL
Boone, Patrick H., Jr. ...... Littlefield, TX
Boone, Paul Stanley ...... Jacksonville, FL
Boone, Pedro L. ...... Bethlehem, PA
Boone, Philip S., Jr. ...... San Francisco, CA
San Jose, CA
Boone, Quentin H. ...... Sharon Springs, KS
Boone & Quigley ...... Florence, AL
Boone, Richard W., Law Offices of
Fairfax, VA
Boone, Rita H. ...... St. Louis, MO
Boone, Robert E., III ...... Santa Monica, CA
Boone, Robert E., Jr. ...... Washington, DC
Boone, Sam W., Jr. ...... Gainesville, FL
Boone, Sandra Arcelia
Department of Labor, GV
Boone, Sandra Neisser ...... Austin, TX
Boone, Scott & Boone ...... Irwinton, GA
Boone, Shacara N. ...... Roseland, NJ
New York, NY
Boone, Smith, Davis, Hurst & Dickman, A Professional Corporation ...... Tulsa, OK
Boone, Stanley A. ...... Fresno, CA
Boone, Stephen K. ...... Venice, FL
Boone, Stephen T. ...... Asheville, NC
Boone, Susan E. ...... Newport, AR
Boone, Sydney K., Jr. ...... Houston, TX
Boone, Taylor S. ...... San Antonio, TX
Boone, Terry S. ...... Fort Worth, TX
Boone, Theodore S. ...... Washington, DC
Boone, Thomas H. ...... Missoula, MT
Boone, Thomas K. ...... Dallas, TX
Boone, Thomas W. ...... Leavenworth, KS
Boone, Tim ...... Little Rock, AR
Boone, Timothy J. ...... Columbus, OH
Boone, Vicki L. ...... Omaha, NE
Boone, Victor J. ...... Raleigh, NC
Boone, W. Bradford ...... Lexington, KY
Boone, W. Dan ...... New York, NY
Boone, W. Daniel ...... Oakland, CA
Boone, W. Kennedy, III ...... Hagerstown, MD
Boone, Walter H. ...... Jackson, MS
Boone, Wheeler B. ...... Lexington, KY
Boone, William B. ...... Santa Rosa, CA
Boone, William C., Jr. ...... Louisville, KY
Boone, William P. ...... Austin, TX
Boone, William R., A Prof. Law Corp.
Many, LA
Boone, William W. ...... Oklahoma City, OK
Boonin, Robert A. ...... Ann Arbor, MI
Detroit, MI
Boonshoft, Stephen ...... New York, NY
Boonstra, Earl R. ...... Detroit, MI
Boonstra, Mark T. ...... Detroit, MI
Boonstra, Michael E. ...... Logansport, IN
Boonstra, Richard D. ...... Chicago, IL
Boonswang, Chad G. ...... Philadelphia, PA
Boop, Arlene F. ...... New York, NY
Boop, Gregory K. ...... Cleveland, OH
Boop, Thomas E. ...... Sunbury, PA
Boor, William, Jr. ...... Houston, TX
Boorady, Carol L. ...... Wichita, KS
Booras, James K. ...... Waukegan, IL
Booras, Ted S. ...... West Palm Beach, FL
Booras, Theodore Steve
West Palm Beach, FL
Boord, L. Roger ...... Chicago, IL
Boorer, Amy ...... Encino, CA
Boorman, Erie V., Jr. ...... Provo, UT
Boorman, Michael R. ...... Atlanta, GA
Boorman, Peter J. ...... Newington, CT
Boornazian, James G. ...... Oakland, CA
Boornazian, Jensen & Garthe, A Professional Corporation ...... Oakland, CA
Walnut Creek, CA
Boorsch, James T. ...... Brooklyn, NY
Boorstein, Barry ...... Houston, TX
Boorstein, Frank ...... Stone Mountain, GA
Boorstein, Harry ...... Hollywood, FL
Boorstein, Ronald L. ...... Chicago, IL
Boorstyn, Neil ...... San Francisco, CA
Boortz, Donald L. ...... Newport Beach, CA
Boortz, Neal A., Jr. ...... Dunwoody, GA
Boortz, Steven L. ...... South Pasadena, CA
Boos, Arthur C. ...... Dallas, TX
Boos, Brian G. ...... Kansas City, MO
Boos, Carole J. ...... Milbank, SD
Boos, Charles G. ...... Traverse City, MI
Boos, Francis H., Jr. ...... Rochester, NY
Boos, George B. ...... Milbank, SD
Boos & Grajczyk, L.L.P. ...... Milbank, SD
Boos, Jack, P.C. ...... Peoria, IL
Boos, James C. ...... Duluth, MN
Boos, Jean E. ...... Eagan, MN
Boos, J. H. "Skip" ...... Plantation, FL
Boos, John F. ...... Peoria, IL
Boos, John L. ...... San Francisco, CA
Boos & Laurans, L.L.C. ...... Kansas City, MO
Boos, Mark L. ...... Indianapolis, IN
Boos, Matthew T. ...... Minneapolis, MN
Boos, Robert W. ...... Tampa, FL
Boose Casey Ciklin Lubitz Martens McBane & O'Connell ...... Palm Beach, FL
West Palm Beach, FL
Boose, Clyde R. ...... Akron, OH
Boose, Jerry D. ...... St. Charles, IL
Boose, Justin R. ...... Portland, OR
Boose & McSwain ...... Fayetteville, NC
Boose, Michael C. ...... Fayetteville, NC
Boose, R. Andrew ...... New York, NY
Boose, Robert I., II ...... Somerset, PA
Boose, William R., III (P.A.)
West Palm Beach, FL
Boose and Young, P.C. ...... Somerset, PA
Booser, Michael C. ...... Woodland Hills, CA
Booska, Steven A. ...... Sacramento, CA
San Francisco, CA
Boostrom, Donna ...... Fresno, CA
Boot, Jeannette K. ...... New York, NY
Boote, Richard H. ...... Department of Justice, Environment and Natural Resources Division, GV
Boote, Robert McLaurin ...... Philadelphia, PA
Booten, Ralph L., II ...... Huntington, WV
Bootes, RaMona G. ...... Albuquerque, NM
Bootes, Wendi S. ...... Columbus, OH
Bootey, E. Robert ...... Jamestown, NY
Booth, Alexander H. ...... Atlanta, GA
Booth, Alexander, Jr. ...... Union City, NJ
Booth, Alfred Q. ...... Prattville, AL
Booth, Anna-Marie ...... San Francisco, CA
Booth, Anne Cawthon ...... Tallahassee, FL
Booth, Arnold & Perez, P.A.
Fernandina Beach, FL
Jacksonville, FL
Booth Banning LLP ...... Los Angeles, CA
San Diego, CA
San Francisco, CA
Booth, Bate, Grieco and Briody
Montclair, NJ
Newark, NJ
Booth, Bernard H. ...... Jackson, MS
Booth, Betsy L. ...... Dallas, TX
Booth, Bradley G. ...... Sacramento, CA
Booth, Brian G., (P.C.) ...... Portland, OR
Booth, Britt S. ...... Montgomery, AL
Booth, Bryan H. ...... Salt Lake City, UT
Booth, Brynja McDivitt ...... Easton, MD
Booth, C. Harley ...... Williamsburg, VA
Booth, Carol ...... Amherst, MA
Booth, Charles A. ...... New York, NY
Booth, Charles E. ...... Ormond Beach, FL
Booth, Chesley P. W. ...... Corning, NY
Booth, Chris H. ...... Beaumont, TX
Booth, Christine W. ...... Washington, DC
Booth, Christopher ...... Bronx, NY
Booth, Christopher C. ...... Albany, NY
Booth, Christopher R., Jr. ...... Philadelphia, PA
Booth & Cook, Ltd. ...... North Aurora, IL
Booth & Cook, P.A. ...... Port Richey, FL
Booth, Curtis H. ...... Annapolis, MD
Easton, MD
Booth, Cynthia Edgar ...... Tallahassee, FL
Booth, Cynthia K. ...... Indianapolis, IN
Booth, D. Randolph, Jr. ...... Corpus Christi, TX
Booth, Daniel T. ...... Bridgeport, WV
Booth, David ...... Golden, CO
Booth, David C. ...... Paducah, KY
Booth, Dawn R. ...... Washington, DC
Booth, Dean ...... Atlanta, GA
Booth & Dillon, A Prof. Corp. ...... Austin, TX
Booth, Douglas A. ...... Austin, TX
Booth, Douglas G. ...... Santa Fe, NM
Booth, Douglas M. ...... Santa Ana, CA
Booth, Edgar C. ...... Tallahassee, FL
Booth, Edgar H. ...... New York, NY
Booth, Edmund A., Jr. ...... Augusta, GA
Booth, Edward ...... Decatur, IL
Booth, Edward M. ...... Jacksonville, FL
Booth, Edward M., Jr. ...... Jacksonville, FL
Booth, Eileen ...... Sacramento, CA
Booth, Eugene A. ...... Baton Rouge, LA
Booth, Fenton C. ...... Chicago, IL
Booth & Finch ...... Sacramento, CA
Booth, Forrest ...... San Francisco, CA
Booth, Frank R. ...... Austin, TX
Booth, Freret, Imlay & Tepper, P.C.
Washington, DC
Booth, Geo. E., Jr. ...... Shaker Heights, OH
Booth, Gregory A. ...... St. Paul, MN
Booth, Guy P. ...... Cedar Rapids, IA
Booth, Harold W. ...... Gladwyne, PA
Booth Harrington Johns & Toman, L.L.P.
Greensboro, NC
High Point, NC
Booth, Henry H. ...... Treasury Department, Office of the General Counsel, GV
Booth, Herbert J. ...... Flint, MI
Booth, Hillary Arrow ...... Los Angeles, CA
Booth, Horace G. ...... Weatherford, TX
Booth & Horton, P.A. ...... Tallahassee, FL
Booth, J. Phillip ...... Atlanta, GA
Booth, James C. ...... Costa Mesa, CA
Booth, James C. ...... Minneapolis, MN
Booth, James C. ...... Kingsport, TN
Booth, James C., Inc., A Professional Corporation ...... Costa Mesa, CA
Booth, James D. ...... Salem, OR
Booth, James W. ...... Sierra Madre, CA
Booth, Jane E. ...... New York, NY
Booth, Janet Carroll ...... Richmond, KY
Booth, Jason L. ...... Chicago, IL
Booth, Jason Michael ...... Los Angeles, CA
Booth, Joe T., III ...... Montgomery, AL
Booth, John C. ...... Farmington, NM
Booth, John C., P.C. ...... Farmington, NM
Booth, John F. ...... Dallas, TX
Booth, John L., II ...... Detroit, MI
Booth, John P. ...... Tallahassee, FL
Booth, John T. ...... Litchfield, CT
Booth, John W. ...... Leesburg, FL
Booth, John William (Bill) ...... Dallas, TX
Booth, Joseph H. ...... Jefferson, GA
Booth, Joseph P., III ...... Greensboro, NC
Booth, Joseph T., IV ...... Montgomery, AL
Booth, Joseph W. ...... Overland Park, KS
Booth, Joyce A. ...... Kew Gardens, NY
Booth, Karyn A. ...... Washington, DC
Booth, Kerrin S. ...... St. Louis Park, MN
Booth, Kevin E. ...... Hartford, CT
Booth, Kimberly A. ...... Omaha, NE
Booth & Koskoff ...... Torrance, CA
Booth, Laura M. ...... Irvine, CA
Booth, Laura Tubbs ...... Minneapolis, MN
Booth Law Firm, L.L.P. ...... Sumter, SC
Booth Law Offices, P.A. ...... Montgomery, AL
Booth, Lawrence R. ...... Torrance, CA
Booth, Little & Antoline ...... Decatur, IL
Booth, Lockard, Politz, LeSage & D'Anna, L.L.C. ...... Shreveport, LA
Booth, Mark F. ...... Fort Lauderdale, FL
Booth, Mary Foushee ...... St. Petersburg, FL
Booth, Matthew J. ...... Austin, TX
Booth & McCarthy ...... Bridgeport, WV
Booth, Michael A. ...... Dayton, OH
Booth, Michael H. ...... Peachtree City, GA
Booth, Michael J. ...... Austin, TX
Booth, Mitchel & Strange
Costa Mesa, CA
Los Angeles, CA
San Diego, CA
Booth, Mitchell B. ...... New York, NY
Booth, Monti Rice ...... Lubbock, TX
Booth, Monty J. ...... Everett, WA
Booth, Patricia Hubert ...... McAllen, TX
Booth Patterson, P.C. ...... Auburn Hills, MI
Pontiac, MI
Rochester, MI
Waterford, MI
Booth, Paul M. ...... Washington, DC
Booth, Peter W. ...... Colorado Springs, CO
Booth, Rainey C. ...... Pensacola, FL
Booth, Richard B. ...... Aberdeen, MS
Booth, Richard C. ...... Tallahassee, FL
Booth, Richard E. ...... Midland, TX
Booth, Richard H. ...... Denver, CO
Booth, Richard H. ...... Lexington, KY
Booth, Richard L. ...... Sumter, SC
Booth, Richard N. ...... Conway, SC
Booth, Richard P., Jr. ...... Irvine, CA
Booth, Richard P., Jr., P.C. ...... Irvine, CA
Booth, Richard R. ...... Miami, FL
Booth, Richard S. ...... Ithaca, NY
Booth, Robert A., Jr. ...... Shreveport, LA
Booth, Robert K., Jr. ...... Mountain View, CA
Booth, Robert P. ...... North Aurora, IL
Booth, Robert T. ...... Plattsburgh, NY
Booth, Roger E. ...... Torrance, CA
Booth, Russell H., Jr. ...... Cambridge, OH
Booth, Samuel M. ...... Winston-Salem, NC
Booth, Sandra E. ...... Columbus, OH
Booth, Stephen C. ...... Port Richey, FL
Booth, Stephen H. ...... Pleasanton, CA
Booth, Stephen M. ...... Phoenix, AZ
Booth, Stephen P. ...... San Francisco, CA
Booth, Susan J. ...... Los Angeles, CA
Booth, Terry J. ...... Milwaukee, WI
Booth, Thomas C., III, Law Office of
San Diego, CA
Booth, Thomas R. ...... Pleasanton, CA
Booth, Thomas T., Jr. ...... Cherry Hill, NJ
Philadelphia, PA
Booth, Unes J. ...... Osceola, IA
Booth, Victoria M. ...... Lancaster, OH
Booth, Vincent J. ...... Metairie, LA
Booth, W. Richard ...... Pittsburgh, PA
Booth, Wadleigh, Langdell, Starr & Peters
Manchester, NH
Booth, Walter S. ...... Bethesda, MD
Booth, Wayne C., Jr. ...... Seattle, WA
Booth, Wayne C., Sr. ...... Seattle, WA
Booth, William A. ...... Los Osos, CA
Booth, William D. ...... Bloomfield Hills, MI
Booth, William D. ...... New York, NY
Booth, William E. ...... Boston, MA
Booth, William E., III ...... Columbia, SC
Booth, William H. ...... San Francisco, CA
Booth, William H. ...... Walnut Creek, CA
Booth, William H. ...... East Elmhurst, NY
Booth, William Keith ...... Birmingham, AL
Booth, William W. ...... West Palm Beach, FL
Booth, William W. ...... Albany, NY
Booth-Barton, Elisabeth ...... Danbury, CT
Boothby, Albert C., Jr. ...... Brunswick, ME
Boothby, Carol A. ...... Olympia, WA
Boothby, Colleen L. ...... Washington, DC
Boothby, J. Lee ...... San Diego, CA
Boothby, Lee ...... Washington, DC
Berrien Springs, MI
Boothby, Nelleene A. ...... Anchorage, AK
Boothby & Yingst ...... Washington, DC
Berrien Springs, MI
Boothe, Ben B. ...... Arlington, TX
Boothe, Brownell K. ...... Scottsdale, AZ
Boothe, Dennis E. ...... Tallahassee, FL
Boothe, Dennis E., P.A. ...... Tallahassee, FL
Boothe, Dennis H. ...... Lancaster, CA
Boothe, Dian H. ...... Norcross, GA
Boothe, Ferris F. ...... Portland, OR
Boothe, Garland C., Jr. ...... Westfield, NJ
Boothe, Jeffrey F. ...... Washington, DC
Boothe, Johnny R. ...... Winnsboro, LA
Boothe, Lawrence I. ...... Dillonvale, OH
Boothe, Leo ...... Harrisonburg, LA
Boothe, Marilyn A. ...... Fernandina Beach, FL
Boothe, Myles S. ...... Marietta, GA
Boothe, Patrick L. ...... Jonesville, LA
Boothe, Roger K. ...... St. Louis, MO
Boothe, Thomas A. ...... Cordova, TN
Boothe, Thomas S. ...... Portland, OR
Boothe-Perry, Nicola A. ...... Orlando, FL
Booth-Gulley, Pamela K. ...... West Covina, CA
Boothman, Claud O. ...... Dallas, TX
Boothman, Hebert & Eller, P.C.
Detroit, MI
Boothman, Richard C. ...... Detroit, MI
Boots, Clydene ...... Murrieta, CA
Boots, Daniel L. ...... Indianapolis, IN
Boots, Paul M. ...... Portland, ME
Boots, Robin E. ...... Concord, NH
Boots, Valerie Kent ...... Indianapolis, IN
Bootsma, Eric R. ...... Stamford, CT
Bootsma, Ernest G. ...... Portland, OR
Booty, Kelvin H., Jr. ...... Oakland, CA
Bootz, Andrew J. ...... Mount Prospect, IL
Bootzin, Joel H. ...... Chicago, IL
Booxbaum, Donald M. ...... Jensen Beach, FL
Booye, Sherri L. ...... Washington, DC
Booz, Mark L. ...... Falls Church, VA
Boozang, Kathleen M. ...... St. Louis, MO
Booze, Robert J. ...... Annapolis, MD
Boozell, Jeffrey N. ...... Los Angeles, CA
Boozer, Elizabeth L. ...... Columbia, SC
Boozer, F. Vernon ...... Towson, MD
Boozer, Gordon B. ...... Grand Rapids, MI
Boozer, Jadie M., Jr. ...... Jacksonville, AL
Boozer, Linda Baggett ...... Pascagoula, MS
Boozer, Marilynn L. ...... Saginaw, MI
Boozer, Martin H. ...... Austin, TX
Boozer, Robert C. ...... Atlanta, GA
Boozer, Timothy A. ...... Little Rock, AR
Boozer, Travis Pelham ...... Arlington, VA
Bopeley, Thomas R. ...... Zanesville, OH
Bopp, Alexander H. ...... San Juan, PR
Bopp, Bryan Christopher ...... Poughkeepsie, NY
Bopp, Coleson & Bostrom
Terre Haute, IN
Bopp, Edward S. ...... Arabi, LA
Bopp, Eric A. ...... Arabi, LA
Bopp, Fred W., III ...... Portland, ME
Bopp, Gerald L. ...... Seattle, WA
Bopp, Gregory M. ...... Houston, TX
Bopp, James, Jr. ...... Washington, DC
Terre Haute, IN
Bopp, Kevin Coffman ...... Springfield, MA
Bopp, Lyle R. ...... Forman, ND
Bopp, R. Jon ...... Ballwin, MO
Bopp, Thomas R. ...... Tampa, FL
Boppart, Paul D. ...... Kansas City, MO
Boquet, Jules D. ...... Houma, LA
Boquist, Walter A., II ...... Wyomissing, PA
Bor, Aaron J. ...... New Bedford, MA
Bor, Andrew ...... Seattle, WA
Bor, Fredric L., P.C. ...... Cherry Hill, NJ
Bor, Robert M. ...... Washington, DC
Bor, Stephen ...... Haddonfield, NJ
Philadelphia, PA
Bor, Victoria L. ...... Washington, DC
Bora, Peter G. ...... Chicago, IL
Boraas, Karlyn Vegoe ...... Minneapolis, MN
Boraas, Russell L. ...... Richmond, VA
Borababy, George M. ...... Washington, DC
Borack, Alan N. ...... Patchogue, NY
Borack, David E. ...... Miami, FL
Borack, Jerilyn L. ...... Sacramento, CA
Boradiansky, Tina S. ...... Santa Fe, NM
Borah, Brett A. ...... Sunnyvale, CA

Borges, Evan C. ....Irvine, CA
Borges, Fredrick M. ....Tustin, CA
Borges, George W. ....San Francisco, CA
Borges, Guy D. ....Fairfield, CA
Borges, Joaquina L. ....New Haven, CT
Borges, Joseph J. ....Brooklyn, NY
Borges, Joseph K., Jr. ....Pomona, CA
Borges, Judith A. ....Fall River, MA
Borges, Kent H. ....Colorado Springs, CO
Borges Law Center, PSC ....San Juan, PR
Borges Law Corporation ....Visalia, CA
Borges, Mark A. ....Santa Clara, CA
Borges, Paul C. ....Providence, RI
Borges, Richard C. ....New Bedford, MA
Borges, Richard C., Jr. ....New Bedford, MA
Borges, Saundra A. Kee ....Hartford, CT
Borges, Wanda ....New Hyde Park, NY
Borgeson, Amy L. ....Minneapolis, MN
Borgeson, Bruce W. ....New York, NY
Borgeson & Burns, P.C. ....Fairbanks, AK
Borgeson, Cory R. ....Fairbanks, AK
Borgeson, Earl C. ....Sherborn, MA
Borgeson, Jay M. ....Santa Barbara, CA
Borgeson, Pamela ....New York, NY
Borgeson, Richard D. ....Armonk, NY
Borgeson, Steven E. ....Boston, MA
Borgeson, William B. ....Beaverton, OR
Borges Ruiz, Luis R. ....Minneapolis, MN
Borgestad, James T. ....Minneapolis, MN
Borgfeld, Walter L., Jr. ....Lufkin, TX
Borggaard, Andrew P. ....Boston, MA
Borggaard, Jennifer M. ....Boston, MA
Borghesani, Paul D. ....Elkhart, IN
South Bend, IN
Borghesani, William H., Jr.
Washington, DC
Borghese Law Firm ....Philadelphia, PA
Borghese, Louis A. ....Gulf Shores, AL
Borghese, Mark R. ....Las Vegas, NV
Borghese, Robert J. ....Philadelphia, PA
Borghesi, Brian P. ....Wolcott, CT
Borghesi, Brian P., and Associates
Wolcott, CT
Borghesi, Vera ....Brick, NJ
Borghetti, Ann F., P.A. ....St. Petersburg, FL
Borghetti, Anne F. ....St. Petersburg, FL
Borghetti, Peter J. ....Danvers, MA
Borghi, Albert C. ....Hanover, MD
Borghoff, John J. ....Omaha, NE
Borgia, Eric M. ....Erie, PA
Borgiotti, Sergio I. ....Washington, DC
Borgman, Charles L. ....Denver, CO
Borgman, Charles L. ....Bardonia, NY
Borgman, Mark W. ....Newton, IA
Borgman, Richard B. ....Prineville, OR
Borgman, Steven R. ....Houston, TX
Borgmann, Daniel J. ....Fort Wayne, IN
Borgmann, James P. ....Muncie, IN
Borgmann, Ronald F. ....St. Louis, MO
Borgmann, W. F. ....Savannah, GA
Borgna, Theodore J. ....Springfield, VA
Borgo, John R. ....Fort Lauderdale, FL
Miami, FL
Borgogni, Lorenzo ....New York, NY
Borgognoni, Gregory P. ....Miami, FL
Borgos, Susan H. ....Denver, CO
Borgoyn, Robert G., Jr. ....Pittsburgh, PA
Borgquist, Carl Eric ....Bozeman, MT
Borgsdorf, Charles W. ....Ann Arbor, MI
Borgstahl, Gene T. ....Toledo, OH
Borgstrom, Karen Creighton ....Lebanon, NH
Borgula, Matthew G. ....Detroit, MI
Borgwardt, John P. ....Portland, OR
Borhart, Robert J. ....Minneapolis, MN
Bori, Evelyn M. ....Orlando, FL
Boriack, Winfred G. ....Houston, TX
Borich, Joseph R., III ....Leawood, KS
Borich, Joseph R., III ....Kansas City, MO
Borich, Peter T. ....Urbana, IL
Borie, John D. ....Murrieta, CA
Borie, Peter ....New York, NY
Borik, Michael J., Jr. ....New York, NY
Borin, Aldo ....Penngrove, CA
Borin, D. Samuel ....Kansas City, MO
Borin, Francis J. ....Teaneck, NJ
Borin, Garry I. ....Novi, MI
Borin, Glenn ....New York, NY
Borin, Howard M. ....Bloomfield Hills, MI
Borin, James L. ....Troy, MI
Borin, Marsha Zutz ....Rockland, DE
Borin, Meri Craver ....Troy, MI
Boring & Coy, Professional Corporation
Fountaintown, IN
Boring, Dennis Edgar ....Greensboro, NC
Boring, Dix ....San Francisco, CA
Boring, Gary L. ....Fountaintown, IN
Boring, George W. ....Bedford, TX
Boring, George W., III ....Maitland, FL
Boring, James L. ....Vienna, VA
Boring, James "Mike" ....Guymon, OK
Boring, Kirby L. ....Pittsburgh, PA
Boring & Leach ....Guymon, OK
Boring & Pilger, P.C. ....Alexandria, VA
Fairfax, VA
McLean, VA
Vienna, VA
Boring, Rachel C. ....Atlanta, GA
Boring, Richard L. ....Columbus, OH
Borino, Ronald A. ....Boston, MA
Borins, Halpern, Stromberg & Paskowitz
Buffalo, NY
Niagara Falls, NY
Borins, Jennifer G. ....Brookline, MA
Borins, Setel, Snitzer & Brownstein
Buffalo, NY
Borinsky, A. David ....Baltimore, MD
Borinsky, Daniel H. ....Woodbridge, VA

Borinsky, Elizabeth Marzo
Baltimore, MD
Borinsky, Susan C. ....Fairfax Station, VA
Boris, Andrew S. ....Chicago, IL
Boris, Anthony J. ....Philadelphia, PA
Boris & Associates ....Oceanside, CA
San Diego, CA
Boris, Donna M. ....Oceanside, CA
Boris, Fran R. ....Chicago, IL
Boris, Howard L. ....Rego Park, NY
Boris, John A., Law Offices of
Philadelphia, PA
Boris, Larry ....Denver, CO
Boris, Lawrence, P.C. ....Denver, CO
Boris, Richard S. ....New York, NY
Boris, Saml. C. ....Lakewood, CO
Boris, Steven B. ....Framingham, MA
Boris, Timothy P. ....Santa Barbara, CA
Boris, Walter R. ....Jackson, MI
Borish, Michael N. ....Philadelphia, PA
Borish, Warren J. ....Haddonfield, NJ
Philadelphia, PA
Borisky, S. Douglas ....New York, NY
Borislow, Kerri Lin ....Philadelphia, PA
Boris-Marchetti, Lynda A. ....San Jose, CA
Indianapolis, IN
Borisoff, Richard S. ....New York, NY
Borison, Alison S. ....New Orleans, LA
Borison, Jerome ....Denver, CO
Borison, Margaret L. ....Denver, CO
Borison, Scott C.I. ....Frederick, MD
Borison, Susan R. ....Cleveland, OH
Boriss, Madeleine ....Santa Cruz, CA
Boris-Schacter, William ....Boston, MA
Borja, Carlos F. ....Fair Oaks, CA
Borja, Jesus ....Saipan, TT
Borja, Mary E. ....Washington, DC
Borja, Mary Ellen Murphy ....Clearwater, FL
Borja, Mary Ellen, P.A. ....Clearwater, FL
Borja, Paul D. ....Washington, DC
Borja, William A. ....Clearwater, FL
Borjeson, Eric S. ....Philadelphia, PA
Bork, Christopher J. ....Phoenix, AZ
Bork, Derek D. ....Cleveland, OH
Bork, James T. ....Bloomfield Hills, MI
Bork, Jeffrey S. ....Silverthorne, CO
Bork, John K. ....Topeka, KS
Bork, Lisa Kathryn ....Irving, TX
Bork, N. Larry ....Topeka, KS
Bork, Paul ....Boston, MA
Providence, RI
Bork, Paul M. ....Midland, MI
Bork, Richard W. ....New York, NY
Bork, Terry A. ....Los Angeles, CA
Borkan, Howard ....New York, NY
Borkan, Steven Blair ....Chicago, IL
Borkan & Toback, P.C. ....New York, NY
Borke, Susan ....Washington, DC
Borkenhagen, Joyce E. ....Las Vegas, NV
Borkenhagen, Lynn ....San Diego, CA
Borker, Wallace J. ....Red Bank, NJ
New York, NY
Borkholder, John ....San Francisco, CA
Borkholder, Kathi W. ....Orlando, FL
Borkin, Albert M. ....Detroit, MI
Borkland, Michael J. ....Austin, TX
Borko, Mariane Kern ....Scarsdale, NY
Borko, Susan Lynn ....Forest Hills, NY
Borkon, Bard D. ....Minneapolis, MN
Borkon, Edward H. ....Minneapolis, MN
Borkon, Ramstead, Mariani & Letourneau, Ltd. ....Minneapolis, MN
Borkovic, David A. ....Pittsburgh, PA
Borkow, Allan J. ....New York, NY
Borkowski, Angela F. ....Belvidere, NJ
Borkowski, Catherine ....Indianapolis, IN
Borkowski, Edward J. ....Pittsburgh, PA
Borkowski, George M., (A Professional Corporation) ....Los Angeles, CA
Borkowski, Glenn E. ....Little Rock, AR
Borkowski, James W. ....White Plains, NY
Borkowski, John Joseph
Federal Communications Commission,
Wireless Telecommunications Bureau, GV
Borkowski, John W. ....New Orleans, LA
Borkowski, Joseph S. ....Middletown, CT
Borkowski, Randall J. ....Seattle, WA
Borkowski, Thomas J. ....Ramsey, NJ
Borkowski, Thomas J., Jr.
Bloomfield Hills, MI
Borkowski, Thomas P. ....Pennington, NJ
Borkowski, Winston K. ....Ormond Beach, FL
Borkowski, Winston K., P.A.
Ormond Beach, FL
Borkowsky, Mitchell T. ....Westbury, NY
Borkowsky, Taras G. ....New York, NY
Borkson, Elliot P. ....Fort Lauderdale, FL
Borkum, David N. ....Jonesboro, AR
Borla, North & Associates, P.C.
Downers Grove, IL
Borla, Robert V. ....Downers Grove, IL
Borlack, Alan R. ....Chicago, IL
Borlam, Anne J. ....Brooklyn, NY
Borland, Andy ....Hibbing, MN
Borland & Borland ....Wilkes-Barre, PA
Borland & Borland ....Midland, TX
Borland, Cheryl L. ....Cincinnati, OH
Borland, David Lawrence ....Little Rock, AR
Borland, Elizabeth G. ....Atlanta, GA
Borland and Haver ....Defiance, OH
Borland, Jack A. ....Kirkland, WA
Borland, James A. ....Albuquerque, NM
Borland, James Andrew ....Springfield, IL
Borland, James S. ....Defiance, OH
Borland, Kimberly D. ....Wilkes-Barre, PA
Borland, Lorelei J. ....New York, NY
Borland, Mac, Jr. ....Dothan, AL
Borland, Marie Attaway ....Tampa, FL

Borland, R. Mike ....Midland, TX
Borland, Richard S. ....Chicago, IL
Borland, Ruth Slamon ....Wilkes-Barre, PA
Borland, Tamara Morrison ....Cedar Rapids, IA
Borland, Tressa J. ....Department of Justice,
Criminal Division, GV
Borland, Vi Lea ....Midland, TX
Borland, William K. ....Chicago, IL
Borland de Marneffe, Katrin ....Boston, MA
Borley, Robert L. ....Springfield, OH
Borlin, Craig H. ....Omaha, NE
Borling, David C. ....Grafton, OH
Borlund, Amy ....Los Angeles, CA
Borman, Amy J. ....Ann Arbor, MI
Findlay, OH
Toledo, OH
Borman, Amy Singer
West Palm Beach, FL
Borman, Bernard N. ....Boston, MA
Borman, Bonnie M. ....Bentleyville, OH
Borman, Channa Erin ....College Station, TX
Borman, Deborah L. ....Chicago, IL
Borman, Edward H., Jr. ....Orange Beach, AL
Borman, Franklin C. ....Farmington Hills, MI
Borman, Hyman D. ....Lake Worth, FL
Borman, John ....Winona, MN
Borman, Joseph R. ....St. Paul, MN
Borman, Judith L. ....Newark, NJ
Borman, Keith T. ....Washington, DC
Borman, Marvin ....Minneapolis, MN
Borman, Matthew S.
Department of Commerce,
Office of the General Counsel, GV
Borman, Paul D. ....Detroit, MI
Borman, Susan D. ....Detroit, MI
Borman, Thomas H. ....Minneapolis, MN
Borman, Wendelin K. ....Old Greenwich, CT
Bormann, Buckmeier, Bauer & Todd
McLaughlin, SD
Bormann, Buckmeier, Bauer & Todd
Mobridge, SD
Bormann, Clark J. ....Bismarck, ND
Bormann, Donald J. ....Emmetsburg, IA
Bormann, I. F. ....Mobridge, SD
Bormann Law Office ....Bismarck, ND
Bormann, Marsha Weg ....Davenport, IA
Bormaster, Melody B. ....Los Angeles, CA
Bormes, James X. ....Chicago, IL
Bormet, Richard A. ....Houston, TX
Bormuth Freeman & Stinson, LC
Cody, WY
Bormuth, M. Cole ....Cody, WY
Bormuth, William K. ....Cody, WY
Born, Brooksley ....Washington, DC
Born, D. Timothy ....Evansville, IN
Born, David P. ....Fairmont, WV
Born, Dawn S. ....Houston, TX
Born, Eileen McCarthy ....Newton, NJ
Born, Ellen Corey ....San Diego, CA
Born, J. Wm. ....Atlanta, GA
Born, Jack D. ....Lansing, MI
Born, Jeanne Marie ....Columbia, SC
Born, Joseph H. ....Boston, MA
Born, Martha ....Boston, MA
Born, Mary Ann ....Hingham, MA
Born, Michael E. ....Columbus, OH
Born, Michael W. ....Vernon Hills, IL
Born, Nancy K. ....Kansas City, MO
Born, Richard W. ....Danville, KY
Born, Robert C. ....Northbrook, IL
Born, Robert E. ....Norcross, GA
Born, Ross J. ....Bethlehem, PA
Born, S. R. ....Indianapolis, IN
Born, Suzanne ....Minneapolis, MN
Born, Timothy ....Clovis, CA
Borncamp, Thomas ....Los Angeles, CA
Borne, Allen H., Jr. ....New Orleans, LA
Borne, Allen J. ....Franklin, LA
Borne, Clayton J., III ....Metairie, LA
Borne, James ....Austin, TX
Borne, Keith M. ....Lafayette, LA
Borne, Philip J. ....New Orleans, LA
Borne, Troy Allen ....Cincinnati, OH
Borne, Wilkes & Brady, L.L.P.
Lafayette, LA
Bornefeld, Bruce K. ....Port Arthur, TX
Borneman, Walter R. ....Evergreen, CO
Bornemann, Kristian J. ....New York, NY
Bornemeier, Walter C., II ....Bountiful, UT
Borneo, Catherine A. ....New York, NY
Borner, Thomas A. ....Putnam, CT
Borner, William J. ....Mount Vernon, NY
Bornes, Marjorie E. ....New York, NY
Bornes, Patricia ....Redmond, WA
Bornfeld, Michael J. ....Mammoth Lakes, CA
Borngesser, C. Vance ....Detroit, MI
Bornheimer, Allen M., (P.C.) ....Boston, MA
Bornhoft, B. B., Jr. ....Las Vegas, NV
Bornhoft & Berkenstadt ....San Diego, CA
Bornhoft, LaDonna D. ....Little Rock, AR
Bornhoft, Raymond ....Fayetteville, AR
Bornhoft, Robert S. ....Phoenix, AZ
Bornhoft, Robert W. ....San Diego, CA
Bornholdt, Bruce A. ....Salem, OR
Bornholdt, Gary W. ....Treasury Department,
Internal Revenue Service, GV
Bornholdt, Kenneth C.
San Luis Obispo, CA
Bornholdt, Thomas H. ....Olathe, KS
Bornhorst, Amanda Spies
New Philadelphia, OH
Bornhorst, Kathleen F. ....Hartford, CT
Bornhorst, Nicole K. ....Cleveland, OH
Bornhorst, Thomas H. ....Baltimore, MD
Bornhouser, Michael E. ....Waco, TX
Borniger, Thomas D. ....Wichita, KS
Bornman, Tracy L. ....Kansas City, MO
Bornmann, Priscilla G. ....Alexandria, VA

Bornn, David A. ....Cruz Bay, St. John, VI
Charlotte Amalie, St. Thomas, VI
Bornn, Edith L., Law Offices of
Charlotte Amalie, St. Thomas, VI
Bornn Handy Law Firm, The
Cruz Bay, St. John, VI
Charlotte Amalie, St. Thomas, VI
Bornn, Nancy ....Santa Monica, CA
Bornn, Nancy, A Law Corporation
Santa Monica, CA
Bornong, Joseph H. ....Minneapolis, MN
Borns, Clarence ....Palo Alto, CA
Merrillville, IN
Borns, Lawrence W. ....Daytona Beach, FL
Borns, Mark F. ....Madison, WI
Bornscheuer, Diane L. ....Scottsdale, AZ
Bornstein, Alan ....Seattle, WA
Bornstein, Alan A. ....Edgewater, NJ
Bornstein, Alan B. ....St. Louis, MO
Bornstein, Alfred ....North Hollywood, CA
Bornstein, Arnold N. ....Hawthorne, NJ
Bornstein, Aron L. ....Chicago, IL
Bornstein, Benjamin A. ....Danbury, CT
Bornstein, Benjamin J. ....Treasury Department,
Office of Regulations and Rulings, GV
Bornstein & Bornstein, P.C. ....Chicago, IL
Bornstein, Brian D. ....New York, NY
Bornstein, Bruce H. ....Chicago, IL
Bornstein, Carl M., Law Offices of
New York, NY
Bornstein, Coleman L. ....Boston, MA
Bornstein, Daniel M. ....San Rafael, CA
Bornstein, Daniel Marc ....San Francisco, CA
Bornstein, David ....Rockaway Park, NY
Bornstein, David J. ....Los Angeles, CA
Bornstein, Deborah H. ....Chicago, IL
Bornstein, Elizabeth A. ....Chicago, IL
Bornstein, George F. ....Hawthorne, NJ
Bornstein, H. Edwin ....Louisville, KY
Bornstein, Henry A. ....Farmington Hills, MI
Bornstein, Henry I. ....San Francisco, CA
Bornstein & Hovermale ....Portland, ME
Bornstein, Ira J. ....Chicago, IL
Bornstein, Isidoor ....San Rafael, CA
Bornstein, Jack I. ....Garden City, NY
Bornstein, Jeffrey L. ....San Francisco, CA
Bornstein, Joseph L. ....Portland, ME
Bornstein, Joseph P. ....Rockville, MD
Bornstein, Joshua Andrew
Monterey Park, CA
Bornstein Law Offices ....San Rafael, CA
Bornstein, Lewis R. ....Cherry Hill, NJ
Bornstein, Margery T. ....Denver, CO
Bornstein, Marvin T. ....Hollywood, FL
Bornstein, Maureen ....Chicago, IL
Bornstein, Michael D. ....Columbus, OH
Bornstein, Mindi ....New York, NY
Bornstein, Mitchell M. ....Chicago, IL
Bornstein, Morris Victor ....St. Petersburg, FL
Bornstein & Oppenheimer ....Louisville, KY
Bornstein, Peter H. ....Berlin, NH
Bornstein, Peter R., Law Offices of
Denver, CO
Bornstein & Petree, P.A. ....Orlando, FL
Bornstein, Philip J. ....Astoria, NY
Bornstein, Richard A. ....New York, NY
Bornstein, Robert A. ....Morristown, NJ
Bornstein, Robert J. ....Louisville, KY
Bornstein, Ronald ....Milwaukee, WI
Bornstein, Ronald E. ....San Francisco, CA
Bornstein, Ronald L. ....Jupiter, FL
Bornstein, Samuel D. ....Paramus, NJ
Bornstein, Samuel D., A Professional Corporation ....Hackensack, NJ
Paramus, NJ
Paterson, NJ
Bornstein, Scott J. ....New York, NY
Bornstein, Shari D. ....Southington, CT
Bornstein & Smith ....Fort Lauderdale, FL
Hollywood, FL
Bornstein, Stephen A. ....New York, NY
Bornstein, Steven L. ....Cooper City, FL
Bornstein, Theodore H. ....Washington, DC
Bornstein, Tim L. ....Amherst, MA
Bornstein, Wendy S. ....Bridgewater, NJ
Bornstein, William S. ....Louisville, KY
Bornstein/Marin, LLC, Attorneys at Law
Rockville, MD
Borntrager, Ezra Eli ....Fortuna, CA
Boro, Lauren I. ....Palo Alto, CA
Borochoff, Douglas M. ....Tulsa, OK
Borock, Jacqueline ....Philadelphia, PA
Borod, Donald L. ....Hartford, CT
Borod & Kramer, P.C. ....Memphis, TN
Borod, Richard M. ....Providence, RI
Borod, Ronald S. ....Boston, MA
Borodach, Andrew S. ....New York, NY
Borodach, Patricia M. ....New York, NY
Borodach, Samuel ....New York, NY
Borodkin, Lisa J. ....Los Angeles, CA
Borodkin, Marvin ....Tucson, AZ
Borof, Irwin J. ....Walnut Creek, CA
Boroff, Alan E. ....Blue Bell, PA
Boroff, Jensen & Klein ....Santa Cruz, CA
Boroff, Ralph W. ....Santa Cruz, CA
Borofsky, Gary M. ....Los Angeles, CA
Borofsky, Jennifer L. ....Newark, NJ
New York, NY
Borofsky, Lewis A. ....Goshen, NY
Borofsky, Lewis & Amodeo-Vickery, P.A.
Manchester, NH
Borofsky, Mark H. ....Franklin Lakes, NJ
Borofsky, Marvin ....Danbury, CT
Borofsky, Michael P.
Department of Commerce,
Office of the General Counsel, GV
Borofsky, Stephen E. ....Manchester, NH
Boron, Krystna M. ....Washington, DC

Boron, Krystyna
Export-Import Bank of The United States, Office of the General Counsel, GV
Boron, Martin C. ... Cleveland, OH
Boron, Robert A. ... Chicago, IL
Boron, Robert A., Ltd. ... Chicago, IL
Boron, Sandra ... Schaumburg, IL
Boronkay, Carl ... Los Angeles, CA
Boros, Andrew Anthony ... Chicago, IL
Boros, Donna Platt ... Phoenix, AZ
Boros & Garofalo, P.C. ... Washington, DC
Boros, Howard S. ... Washington, DC
Boros, Jerome S. ... New York, NY
Boros, Joan E. ... Washington, DC
Boros, Sally P. ... Des Plaines, IL
Boros, Stuart A. ... Los Angeles, CA
Boros, William B. ... Wheaton, IL
Borosh, Lawrence P. ... Cleveland, OH
Boroski, Marilee C. ... Columbus, OH
Borosko, Martin L. ... Roseland, NJ
Boroughs, Lewis E. ... Greensboro, NC
Boroughs, Thomas ... Orlando, FL
Boroumand, Mehrnaz ... San Francisco, CA
Borovas, George ... Washington, DC
Borovich, Susan M. ... Port Huron, MI
Borovina, Anton J. ... Garden City, NY
Borovoy, Roger S. ... Menlo Park, CA
Borovsky & Ehrlich, A Professional Corporation ... Chicago, IL
Borovsky, Herbert L. ... Chicago, IL
Borow, Hilary C. ... Houston, TX
Borow, Jennifer L. ... Los Angeles, CA
Borow, Lloyd J. ... Mulberry, FL
Borow, Malke ... Newark, NJ
Borow, Philip Allan ... New Brunswick, NJ
Borow, Richard H., (P.C.)
Los Angeles, CA
Borowick, Howard R. ... White Plains, NY
Borowick, Jeffrey Mark ... Roslyn, NY
Borowiec & Borowiec ... Sierra Vista, AZ
Borowiec, Francis B. ... Chamblee, GA
Borowiec, Joel P. ... Sierra Vista, AZ
Borowiec, Matthew W. ... Bisbee, AZ
Borowiec, Thaddeus E. ... New York, NY
Borowiec, William M. ... Sierra Vista, AZ
Borowiecki, Lawrence R. ... Chicago, IL
Borowitz, Albert I. ... Cleveland, OH
Borowitz, Barry Edward ... Encino, CA
Borowitz & Goldsmith, PLC
Louisville, KY
Borowitz, Morris B. ... Louisville, KY
Borowitz, Paul J. ... Zanesville, OH
Borowitz, Peter L. ... New York, NY
Borowski, Daniel J. ... Milwaukee, WI
Borowski, Dannie R. ... Palmdale, CA
Borowski, Irwin M. ... Washington, DC
Borowski, John M. ... West Orange, NJ
Borowski, John P. ... Glen Ridge, NJ
Borowski, Marcia ... Atlanta, GA
Borowski, Paul A. ... Akron, OH
Borowski, T. A., Jr. ... Pensacola, FL
Borowsky, Frank E., Jr. ... Sea Girt, NJ
Borowsky, Jay ... Philadelphia, PA
Borowsky, Milton M. ... Wyncote, PA
Borowsky, Paulina A.
West Long Branch, NJ
Borowsky, Philip ... Los Angeles, CA
San Francisco, CA
Borowsky, Philip, A Prof. Corp., Law Offices of ... Los Angeles, CA
San Francisco, CA
Borowsky, Scott C. ... Upper Darby, PA
Borowsky, Victor ... Dearborn Heights, MI
Borowy, Frank R. ... Newington, CT
Borquez, Robert P. ... Denver, CO
Borra, James C. ... Bethesda, MD
Borra, Janice L. ... Albuquerque, NM
Borrack, E.J. ... New York, NY
Borradaile, Earl E. ... Davison, MI
Borras, Anthony B. ... Lauderhill, FL
Borras, Christopher W. ... Concord, NC
Borrasca, Adelia S. ... Washington, DC
Borrasso, Ava ... Miami, FL
Borré, Alexander P. ... Brockton, MA
Borre, Glen V. ... Grand Rapids, MI
Borre, Peterson, Fowler & Reens, P.C.
Grand Rapids, MI
Borrebach, William B., Jr. ... Media, PA
Borreca, Christopher P. ... Houston, TX
Borregard, Leo E. ... Asheville, NC
Borreggine, Angela ... New York, NY
Borrego & Clark, LLP ... Houston, TX
Borrego, Fernando A. ... Wyandotte, MI
Borrego, John ... San Diego, CA
Borrego, John C. ... Fort Lauderdale, FL
Borrego, Jose A. ... Sacramento, CA
Borrego, Theodore R. ... Houston, TX
Borreliz, Ellen R. ... Southborough, MA
Borreliz, Mark A. ... Boston, MA
Borrell, Jeffrey F. P. ... Staten Island, NY
Borrell, Mark S. ... Ventura, CA
Borrelle, Robert J. ... Moorestown, NJ
Borrelli, Carmela L. ... Greenport, NY
Borrelli, Cynthia J. ... Florham Park, NJ
New York, NY
Borrelli, Damon J. ... Needham, MA
Borrelli, Edward P. ... New York, NY
Borrelli, Jody M. ... Los Angeles, CA
Borrelli, Lisa A. ... Pittsburgh, PA
Borrelli, Mark ... Chicago, IL
Borrelli, Michael ... Brookline, MA
Borrelli, Michael J., Jr. ... White Plains, NY
Borrelli, Salvatore L., (P.C.)
West Paterson, NJ
Borrelli, Steve ... Encino, CA
Borrello, Bruce J. ... Metairie, LA
Borrello, Donna M. ... New Orleans, LA
Borrello, Joel L. ... New Orleans, LA
Borrello, Leopold P. ... Saginaw, MI
Borrello, Ralph T. ... Washington, DC
Borrello, Robert J. ... Miami, FL
Borrello, Roger F. ... Plantation, FL
Borrello, Stephen L. ... Saginaw, MI
Borrero, Michael W. ... Fresno, CA
Borresen, Rand A. ... Irvine, CA
Borresen, Thomas H. ... Jerome, ID
Borrett, Lloyd M. ... El Paso, TX
Borrevik, Jason D. ... Palo Alto, CA
Borri, Gregg J. ... Bloomfield, NJ
New York, NY
Borrillo, Matthew A. ... Portland, OR
Borrillo, Theodore A. ... Littleton, CO
Borrino, David F. ... Santa Monica, CA
Borris, Jeffrey ... Beverly Hills, CA
Borris, Robert C., Jr. ... Castro Valley, CA
Borris, Thomas J. ... Santa Ana, CA
Borrok, Howard E. ... Jamaica, NY
Borrok, Linderman, Weissman & Steingart
New York, NY
Borrok, Peter A. ... White Plains, NY
Borromeo, Glenn J. ... Palo Alto, CA
Borromeo, Karina Q. ... Kansas City, KS
Borromeo, Theodore C. ... Sunnyvale, CA
Borron & Delahaye, A Professional Law Corporation ... Plaquemine, LA
Borron, John A., Jr. ... Kansas City, MO
Borron, Jorgé ... Coral Gables, FL
Borron, Paul G., III ... Plaquemine, LA
Borrone, Edward J. ... Newark, NJ
Borror, Caywood J. ... San Bernardino, CA
Borror, David S. ... Dublin, OH
Borroto, Heriberto (Herb) R. ... Miami, FL
Borrow, Ellen Carol ... Princeton Junction, NJ
Borrow, J. Stewart ... New York, NY
Borrowdale, Robert J. ... Battle Creek, MI
Borrowman, Aaron T.
Woodland Hills, CA
Borrus, Bruce J. ... Seattle, WA
Borrus, Goldin & Foley, A Professional Corporation ... New Brunswick, NJ
Borrus, Goldin, Foley, Vignuolo, Hyman, Stahl & Clarkin, A Professional Corporation ... Elizabeth, NJ
Freehold, NJ
North Brunswick, NJ
Princeton, NJ
Somerville, NJ
Trenton, NJ
Borrus, Jack ... North Brunswick, NJ
Borrus, Michael Glen ... Berkeley, CA
Borruso, Christopher Thomas
Farmingdale, NY
Borruso, Michael T. ... Cambridge, MA
Borruso, Santo ... New York, NY
Bors, E. Daniel, Jr. ... Laguna Hills, CA
Bors, James E. ... Brookfield, WI
Borsack, Scott P. ... Lawrenceville, NJ
Borsand, Steven F. ... Rolling Meadows, IL
Borsari, George R., Jr. ... Washington, DC
Borsari, J. Thomas ... Lake Isabella, CA
Borsari & Paxson ... Washington, DC
Borsberry, Joseph M. ... Peoria, IL
Borschel, Susan J. ... McLean, VA
Borschke, August J. ... Winston-Salem, NC
Borseth, Eric ... Des Moines, IA
Borseth & Genest ... Des Moines, IA
Borsetti, Charles V. ... Garden City, NY
Borsheim, Curtis A. ... Appleton, WI
Borsheim, Eric R. ... Austin, TX
Borsich, Douglas G.
North Charleston, SC
Borsini, Shari M. ... Detroit, MI
Borska, Elliot F. ... Encino, CA
Borska, Lawrence E. ... Philadelphia, PA
Borsky, Linda B. ... Memphis, TN
Borsky, Robert ... Torrance, CA
Borsman, LanEe ... Emerald Isle, NC
Borsody, Robert P. ... New York, NY
Borsody, Robert P., P.C. ... New York, NY
Borson, D. Benjamin ... San Francisco, CA
Borsos, John J. ... Salt Lake City, UT
Borsos, Robert B. ... Kalamazoo, MI
Borsos, Robert L. ... Mattawan, MI
Borst, Alan W., Jr. ... New York, NY
Borst, Deborah A. ... Chicago, IL
Borst, G. Edward, Jr. ... Warrenton, VA
Borst, Jack L. ... Lansing, MI
Borst, Mark V. ... Waltham, MA
Borst, Mary Lou ... Brandon, MS
Borst, Richard T. ... Portland, OR
Borst, Samuel D. ... Hamilton, OH
Borst, Stephen L. ... Worcester, MA
Borst, Thomas G. ... San Ramon, CA
Borst, Vincent T. ... Chicago, IL
Borst, William V. ... Hebron, CT
Borstad, Hans B. ... Staples, MN
Borstein, Carole A. ... New York, NY
Borstein, Leon Baer ... Ghent, NY
New York, NY
Borstein, Scott R. ... Chicago, IL
Borstein & Sheinbaum ... Ghent, NY
New York, NY
Borsuk, Esther Atara
Department of Commerce, Patent and Trademark Office, GV
Borsuk, Jeffery L. ... Walnut Creek, CA
Borsuk, Lynne Y. ... Decatur, GA
Borsykowsky, David ... Burlington, VT
Bort, Daniel C. ... Boston, MA
Bort, Ina R. ... New York, NY
Bort, Peter E. ... Norristown, PA
Bort, Samuel ... San Francisco, CA
Borta, Daniel F. ... Waukesha, WI
Borteck, Robert D. ... Morristown, NJ
Bortel, Aaron R. ... San Francisco, CA
Borten, Cathy G. ... Bethesda, MD
Borten, Mark S. ... New York, NY
Borth, Charles K. ... Spencer, IA
Borth, Donald M. ... Warrensburg, NY
Borth, James R. ... Olathe, KS
Borth, Ray L. ... Overland Park, KS
Borth, Scott J. ... Seattle, WA
Borthwick & Associates ... Cheyenne, WY
Borthwick, Dean W. ... Cheyenne, WY
Borthwick, Douglas M. ... Santa Ana, CA
Borthwick, James ... Kansas City, MO
Borthwick, Robert J. ... Los Angeles, CA
Borthwick, Wm. Harold, (P.C.)
Los Angeles, CA
Bortin, Ava M. ... Milwaukee, WI
Bortin, David N. ... Walnut Creek, CA
Bortka, Lynn Alan ... Houston, TX
Bortman, David ... Los Angeles, CA
Bortner, David F. ... West Chester, PA
Bortner, Jeffrey C. ... York, PA
Bortner, Michael E. ... Harrisburg, PA
Bortner, Oscar S. ... Doylestown, PA
Bortner, Patricia Lee ... Mount Holly, NJ
Bortner, Peter E. ... Bethlehem, PA
Bortner, R. Brooke ... Greenbelt, MD
Bortner, Robert Mark ... St. Petersburg, FL
Bortner, Scott R. ... Foster City, CA
Bortnick, Blaine H. ... New York, NY
Bortnick, Caryn ... Oakland, CA
Bortnick, Janet Edelstein ... Camden, NJ
Bortnick, Jeffrey S. ... New York, NY
Bortnick, Jonathan A. ... Kansas City, MO
Bortnick, Komoroski, McKeon & Sakoulas, P.C. ... Kansas City, MO
Bortnick, Richard Jon ... Philadelphia, PA
Bortnick, Robin G. ... Potomac, MD
Bortnick, Steven D. ... New York, NY
Bortolan, Eleanor N. ... Hartford, CT
Bortolazzo, Richard A. ... Benicia, CA
Bortolot & LaBrecque ... Stratford, CT
Bortolot, Richard V., Jr ... Stratford, CT
Borton, Joseph W. ... Meridian, ID
Borton, Mark E. ... Longwood, FL
Borton, Petrini & Conron, LLP
Bakersfield, CA
Fresno, CA
Los Angeles, CA
Modesto, CA
Redding, CA
Sacramento, CA
San Bernardino, CA
San Diego, CA
San Francisco, CA
San Jose, CA
San Luis Obispo, CA
Santa Ana, CA
Ventura, CA
Borton, Richard C. ... Haddonfield, NJ
Borton, Robert E. ... San Francisco, CA
Borton, Thomas B. ... Bloomington, IL
Bortstein, Lawrence ... New York, NY
Bortuer, Scott R. ... Foster City, CA
Bortz, Arnold L. ... Cincinnati, OH
Bortz, David G. ... Olympia, WA
Bortz, David L. ... Reisterstown, MD
Bortz, Edward D. ... Englewood Cliffs, NJ
Bortz, Jason K. ... Washington, DC
Bortz, Laurie R. ... Baltimore, MD
Bortz, Lee ... Cincinnati, OH
Bortz, Michael W. ... Vancouver, WA
Bortz, Milton H. ... Cincinnati, OH
Bortz, Patricia L. ... Birmingham, AL
Bortzfield, Ruth N. ... Boxford, MA
Boruchin, Diana ... Miami, FL
Borucke, David C. ... Tampa, FL
Borucki, Andrea T. ... Indianapolis, IN
Borucki, Joseph W. ... Cherry Hill, NJ
King Of Prussia, PA
Borud, Randall D. ... Lithonia, GA
Borukhov, Aron B. ... New York, NY
Borum, Howard L. ... Greensboro, NC
Borum, J. Owen ... Denver, CO
Borum, Joy B. ... Scottsdale, AZ
Borum, Marian L. ... Fair Lawn, NJ
Borum, Winston L. ... Dallas, TX
Borun, Michael F. ... Chicago, IL
Borunda, Ernest ... Chula Vista, CA
Borus, Joseph S. ... Denver, CO
Borushok, Edith Auster ... Hollywood, FL
Boruszak, Bruce L. ... Chicago, IL
Borut, Ezra B. ... New York, NY
Boruta, Mark A. ... Chicago, IL
Borvice, W. A. ... San Francisco, CA
Borwick, Anthony S.
General Services Administration, Board of Contract Appeals, GV
Borwick, Rodney J. ... Denver, CO
Boryla, Michael J. ... Englewood, CO
Borys, Lawrence, (Professional Corporation)
Los Angeles, CA
Borza, Americo ... Sarasota, FL
Borzeka, Peter J., & Associates
Chicago, IL
Borzelli, Theresa ... West Orange, NJ
Borzi, Phyllis C. ... Washington, DC
Borzillo, Michelle M.
Federal Deposit Insurance Corporation, Corporate Affairs Section, GV
Borzillo, Rita Kathryn ... Exton, PA
Borzone, Robert J., Jr. ... New York, NY
Borzym, Alice Donna ... Chicago, IL
Bos, Andrew D. ... Rochester Hills, MI
Bos, Anne Elizabeth ... Topeka, KS
Bos & Associates, P.A. ... Orlando, FL
Bos, C. Peter ... Bangor, ME
Bos, Carey N. ... Orlando, FL
Bos, Carole D. ... Grand Rapids, MI
Bos, Gerard Alford ... Charlotte, NC
Bos & Glazier, P.L.C. ... Grand Rapids, MI
Bos, John E. ... Lansing, MI
Bosa, Gordon J. ... Alamosa, CO
Bosacco, John E. ... New York, NY
Bosack, Sean O'D. ... Milwaukee, WI
Bosacki, Ann Marie ... Tampa, FL
Bosacki, Steven M. ... Morristown, NJ
Bosakowski, James A. ... Annapolis, MD
Bosanac, Paul ... Milwaukee, WI
Bosard, McCutcheon & Rau, L.T.D.
Minot, ND
Bosau, Christine R. ... Crestview, FL
Bosben, Donald D. ... Reston, VA
Bosbyshell, Edward C., Jr. ... Los Angeles, CA
Bosca, D'orsi ... Springfield, OH
Boscarino, Gina M. ... Washington, DC
Boscarino, Thomas C. ... Glastonbury, CT
Bosch, Allan R. ... Boise, ID
Bosch, Anita Lechner ... New Orleans, LA
Bosch, Anthony R. ... Pittsburgh, PA
Bosch, Brenda H. ... Rockville, MD
Bosch, Brian A. ... Chicago, IL
Bosch, Burton O. ... Havre, MT
Bosch, Clement A. ... Palo Alto, CA
Bosch, Dennis B. ... Independence, MO
Bosch, Donald A. ... Knoxville, TN
Bosch, Edward J. ... Minot, ND
Bosch, G. Randolph ... San Diego, CA
Bosch, Gerald W. ... Minneapolis, MN
Bosch, Gerard R. ... Jackson, WY
Bosch, Guillermo L. ... Collegeville, PA
Bosch, John F. ... Clay Center, KS
Bosch, Kuhr, Dugdale, Martin & Kaze, PLLP ... Havre, MT
Bosch Law Firm, The, P.C. ... Knoxville, TN
Bosch, Lisa Zima ... Fort Lauderdale, FL
Bosch, Mari Carmen ... San Juan, PR
Bosch, Michael W. ... Hammond, IN
Bosch, Michele C. ... Washington, DC
Bosch, Peter D. ... Grand Rapids, MI
Bosch, Richard J. ... Kalamazoo, MI
Bosch, Ronald R.
Department Of Veterans Affairs, Board of Veterans Appeals, GV
Bosch, Warren B. ... Denver, CO
Bosch, William J., III ... Pompano Beach, FL
Bosch, William M. ... Washington, DC
Bosche, Kelly B. ... Newport Beach, CA
Bosché, Thomas S. ... Newport Beach, CA
Boschee, Catherine ... Minneapolis, MN
Boschee, Larry L. ... Bismarck, ND
Boschert, Curtis D. ... Clarksdale, MS
Boschert, Lawrence W. ... St. Charles, MO
Boschert, Neville H. ... Jackson, MS
Boschert, Rosemary C. ... Billings, MT
Boschert, Theresa F. ... Billings, MT
Boschetto, David R. ... Boston, MA
Boschini, Peter C. ... Greensburg, PA
Boschken, Laura ... New York, NY
Boschwitz, Kenneth S. ... San Diego, CA
Boschwitz, Rudy E. ... Fridley, MN
Boscia, James D. ... Merrillville, IN
Boscia, Sandra L. ... Charlotte, NC
Boscio, Juan L. ... Ponce, PR
Boscio, Roberto ... Ponce, PR
Bosco, Anthony J. ... Chicago, IL
Bosco, Anthony J. ... New York, NY
Bosco, Blau, Ward & Nopar
Los Angeles, CA
Santa Monica, CA
New York, NY
Bosco, Carol A. ... Plainview, NY
Bosco, Celia S. ... Livingston, NJ
Bosco, Dana M. ... Hartford, CT
Bosco, David D. ... Wantagh, NY
Bosco, Diane Elizabeth ... Hackensack, NJ
Bosco, Don M. ... New York, NY
Bosco, Douglas H. ... Santa Rosa, CA
Bosco, Francis L. ... Patchogue, NY
Bosco, Gary E. ... Bay City, MI
Bosco, Jenifer ... Lowell, MA
Bosco, John I. ... New Rochelle, NY
Bosco, John P. ... West Chicago, IL
Bosco, Joseph A. ... Washington, DC
Bosco, Joseph A. ... Chicago, IL
Bosco, Joseph P. ... Harrisburg, PA
Bosco, Louis C., Jr. ... Orchard Lake, MI
Bosco, Mark S. ... Phoenix, AZ
Bosco, Mary Elizabeth ... Washington, DC
Bosco, Michael A., Jr. ... Phoenix, AZ
Bosco, Paul Jhoseph ... Washington, DC
Bosco, Philip R. ... Washington, DC
Bosco, Ronald T. ... Chicago, IL
Boscoe, Donald D. ... Stockton, CA
Boscoe, Donald D., Professional Corporation
Stockton, CA
Boscoe, Mark H. ... Denver, CO
Boscolo, Benjamin T. ... Greenbelt, MD
Boscovich, Richard D. ... Miami, FL
Bose, Arup K. ... Arlington, VA
Bose, Henry E. ... Aptos, CA
Bose, Kimberly A.
Federal Energy Regulatory Commission, Office of the General Counsel, GV
Bose Law Firm, PLLC ... Arlington, VA
Bose, Lewis C. ... Indianapolis, IN
Bose McKinney & Evans LLP
Indianapolis, IN
Bose, Romi N. ... Chicago, IL
Bose, Sanjoy K. ... Washington, DC
Bose, Sudeep ... Arlington, VA
Bose, William A. ... Menlo Park, CA
Bosecker, Kelley A. ... Tampa, FL
Bosee, John K., 4th ... New York, NY
Bosek, Edward S. ... New York, NY
Bosek, Elizabeth M. ... Daytona Beach, FL
Bosek Law Firm ... Washington, DC
Bosek, Ruth A. ... Washington, DC
Bosek, Saul ... Chatham, NJ

Boselli, Kathryn .... San Francisco, CA
Boselli, Rita M. .... Haddonfield, NJ
Bosen, Harry F., Jr. .... Salem, VA
Bosen, Harry F., Jr., P.C. .... Roanoke, VA
Salem, VA
Bosen, John K. .... Portsmouth, NH
Bosen, Theodore L. .... Plymouth, MA
Boser, George F. .... Melbourne Beach, FL
Boser, Peter J. .... Freehold, NJ
Boserup, Viggo .... Los Angeles, CA
Bosetti, Guy C. .... Richmond, VA
Bosh, Michael A. .... Minot, ND
Boshak, Heather R. .... Roseland, NJ
New York, NY
Boshar, Mark F. .... Cambridge, MA
Boshardy, John V. .... Springfield, IL
Boshart, Nicole L. .... Utica, NY
Boshaw, Deborah H. .... Detroit, MI
Boshea, Kevin V. .... New Orleans, LA
Boshears, B.J. .... Kingsport, TN
Boshears, Edward E. .... Brunswick, GA
Bosher, George M. .... Richmond, VA
Boshes, Jeffrey P. .... Phoenix, AZ
Boshes, Ralph W. .... Los Angeles, CA
Boshinski, Thomas A. .... Smyrna, GA
Boshkoff, Douglass G. .... Bloomington, IN
Boshkoff, Ellen E. .... Indianapolis, IN
Boshkov, Stefan R. .... New York, NY
Boshnaick, Michael H. .... San Francisco, CA
Boshnick, William S. .... Reston, VA
Bosiak, Ann A. .... Concord, NH
Bosick, Joseph J. .... Pittsburgh, PA
Bosien, Brian K. .... Beaumont, TX
Corpus Christi, TX
Houston, TX
Bosik, James E. .... Denver, CO
Bosilevac, Fred N., Jr. .... Overland Park, KS
Bosilovic, Robert J. .... Eighty Four, PA
Bosin, Andrew S. .... Hackensack, NJ
Bosin, Stephen R. .... River Edge, NJ
New York, NY
Bosinoff, Philip .... Winchester, MA
Bosio, Christopher J. .... Rochester, MI
Bosio, Jos. F. .... Solana Beach, CA
Bosis, Daniel D., Jr. .... Daly City, CA
Boskey, Bennett .... Washington, DC
Boskey, James B. .... Newark, NJ
Boskey, Jill Ann .... New York, NY
Boskey, Richard S. .... Boston, MA
Bosko, Daniel P. .... Stow, OH
Bosko, David M. .... Costa Mesa, CA
Bosko, Gianna M. .... Palo Alto, CA
Bosko, Marybeth .... Columbus, OH
Bosko, Michael G. .... Newport Beach, CA
Boskoff, Catherine G. .... San Francisco, CA
Boskovich, Anthony, Law Offices of
San Jose, CA
Boskovich, Anthony M. .... San Jose, CA
Boskovich, John J. .... Sacramento, CA
Boskovich, Martin A. .... Los Angeles, CA
Boskovich, Violet M. .... Long Beach, CA
Bosl, Phillip L. .... Los Angeles, CA
Bosland, Carl C. .... Salt Lake City, UT
Bosland, Christopher .... Washington, DC
Boslaugh, Leslie .... Lincoln, NE
Bosler, Christy .... Oklahoma City, OK
Bosler, Mark S. .... Bloomfield Hills, MI
Bosler, Timothy H. .... Kansas City, MO
Bosley, Dale E.
Supreme Court Of The United States, GV
Bosley, David Joseph .... Columbus, OH
Bosley, Eric D. .... Port Orchard, WA
Bosley, Freeman R., Jr. .... St. Louis, MO
Bosley & Hutzelman, P.C.
Washington, DC
Alexandria, VA
Fairfax, VA
Bosley, Janine H. .... Alexandria, VA
Bosley, Jeffrey S. .... San Francisco, CA
Bosley, Paul B. .... North Aurora, IL
Bosley, Robert C. .... McCook, NE
Bosley & Schatz .... Marion, IN
Bosley, Wade R. .... Marion, IN
Boslin, Jay Cannon .... Scottsdale, AZ
Bosma, Brian C. .... Indianapolis, IN
Bosman, Calvin L. .... Grand Haven, MI
Bosman, Erin .... San Diego, CA
Bosman, Lisa J. .... Austin, TX
Bosman, Michelle P.
Pension Benefit Guaranty Corporation, Office of the General Counsel, GV
Bosmans, Bertrand G. .... Buffalo, NY
Bosniak, Linda S. .... Camden, NJ
Bosnic, Michael Louis .... Walled Lake, MI
Bosomworth, Bradley D. .... Los Gatos, CA
Bosque, Ada E. .... Baltimore, MD
Bosque, William F., Jr. .... San Francisco, CA
Bosques, Olga L. .... Columbus, OH
Bosquez-Flores, Linda .... Fresno, CA
Boss, Alyssa V. .... Boston, MA
Providence, RI
Boss, Amelia H. .... Philadelphia, PA
Boss, Anderson & James, Chartered
Laurel, MD
Boss, Charles M. .... Maumee, OH
Boss, Donald Edwin .... Covina, CA
Boss, Donald J. .... Los Angeles, CA
Boss, Evelyn Patrick .... San Diego, CA
Boss, Fred L., Jr. .... Tulsa, OK
Boss, Frederick M. .... Salem, OR
Boss, George .... Hempstead, NY
Boss, Gregory A. .... Los Angeles, CA
Boss, Hugh M. .... Santa Barbara, CA
Boss, Jerre .... Atlanta, GA
Boss, Lorraine Stacknowitz .... New York, NY
Boss, Maria Kathleen .... Culver City, CA
Boss, Mark H. .... Toledo, OH
Boss, Marlene L. .... Menlo Park, CA

Boss, Patti Lynn .... Hartford, CT
Boss, Ralph H., Jr. .... Rochester, NY
Boss, Shaun K. .... San Diego, CA
Boss, Shaun K., A Professional Corporation
San Diego, CA
Boss & Vitou .... Maumee, OH
Boss, Willard I., Jr. .... Houston, TX
Boss, William R. .... Tulsa, OK
Bossange, Anne .... Palo Alto, CA
Bossard, Scott T. .... New Port Richey, FL
Bossard, Sterling R. .... Bountiful, UT
Bossart, David R. .... Fargo, ND
Bossart, James A., Jr. .... Tallahassee, FL
Bossart, Janet E. .... Ridgewood, NJ
Bossart, Jeffrey H. .... Chester, NJ
Bosse, Ann Norman .... Baltimore, MD
Bosse, David R. .... Phoenix, AZ
Bosse, Diane F. .... Buffalo, NY
Bosse, E. Peter .... Millis, MA
Bosse, Fred C. .... San Antonio, TX
Bosse, Frederick M. .... Houston, TX
Bosse, Frederick M., P.C. .... Houston, TX
Bosse, Gregory L. .... Orange, CA
Bosse, Jeff, & Associates .... Evansville, IN
Bosse, Jeffrey A. .... Evansville, IN
Bosse, Leigh D. .... Hillsborough, NH
Bosse, Linda .... United States Senate,
Senatorial Assistants, GV
Bosse, Linda R. .... Boston, MA
Bosse, Mark Lawrence .... Foster City, CA
Bosse, Michael R. .... Portland, ME
Bosse, Peter L. .... Boston, MA
Bosse, Richard C., Jr. .... New York, NY
Bosse, Richard E. .... Henning, MN
Bosse, Richard E., Chtd. .... Henning, MN
Bossé, Steven L. .... Tucson, AZ
Bosse, Thomas W. .... Cincinnati, OH
Bosselait, Rosemary A. .... Ashland, MA
Bosseler, Gregory J. .... Fort Myers, FL
Bosselman, Fred P. .... Evanston, IL
Bossen, Roy M. .... Chicago, IL
Bossen, William A. .... Los Angeles, CA
Bossenbroek, David L. .... Muskegon, MI
Bossenbrook, Arlyn J. .... East Lansing, MI
Bossenmaier, Paul V. .... Sacramento, CA
Bosser, Steven J. .... Fort Worth, TX
Bosserman, David .... Angleton, TX
Bosserman, Gordon E. .... Los Angeles, CA
Bossert, John Keith .... Liberty, IN
Bossert, Patricia L. .... Denver, CO
Bossert, Terry R. .... Bala Cynwyd, PA
Harrisburg, PA
Bossert, Walter A., Jr. .... New York, NY
Bosses, Stevan J. .... New York, NY
Bosset, Eric C. .... Washington, DC
Bosshard & Assoc. .... La Crosse, WI
Bosshard, Jeffrey J. .... Soquel, CA
Bosshard, John, III .... Valdez, AK
Bosshard, Sabina .... La Crosse, WI
Bosshardt & Edwards, P.A.
Fort Lauderdale, FL
Bosshardt, John P. .... Rickreall, OR
Bosshardt, Kurt E. .... Fort Lauderdale, FL
Bosshardt, Stacey M. .... Washington, DC
Bosshart, Daniel J. .... Oakland, CA
Bossi, Mark V. .... St. Louis, MO
Bossi, Vittoria Monica .... Stockton, CA
Bossie, Kelly & Hodes, P.A.
Manchester, NH
Bossie, Melanie L. .... Tampa, FL
Bossie, Robert F. .... Manchester, NH
Bossier, Albert L., Jr. .... Kenner, LA
Bossier, Brian C. .... Metairie, LA
New Orleans, LA
Bossier-Phillips, Donna .... Kenner, LA
Bossin, Joanna B. .... Atlanta, GA
Bossin, Kenneth A. .... Cleveland, OH
Bossin, Phyllis G. .... Cincinnati, OH
Bossin, Phyllis G., Co., L.P.A.
Batavia, OH
Cincinnati, OH
Hamilton, OH
Lebanon, OH
Bossio, Cheryl D. .... San Francisco, CA
Bosslet, Robert W., Jr. .... Granite City, IL
Bosslet, Timothy M. .... St. Louis, MO
Bossley, Burton B., Jr. .... Houston, TX
Bossmeyer, Raymond F. .... Louisville, KY
Bosso, Bosso & Pardo .... Riviera Beach, FL
Bosso, Robert E. .... Santa Cruz, CA
Bosso, William J., Jr. .... Riviera Beach, FL
Bosso, Williams, Sachs, Book, Atack & Gallagher, A Professional Corporation
Santa Cruz, CA
Bossolina, Joseph M. .... Hackensack, NJ
Bossolt, Robert J. .... Upper Saddle River, NJ
Bosson, Paul R.
Hot Springs National Park, AR
Bosson, Richard C. .... Santa Fe, NM
Bossong, Brooks F. .... Asheboro, NC
Greensboro, NC
Bossong, Kenneth J. .... Trenton, NJ
Bosso-Pardo, Sandra
West Palm Beach, FL
Bossov, Adam E. .... Chicago, IL
Bossow, Garth E. .... Dallas, TX
Bosswick, Mark G. .... New York, NY
Bosswick, Pamela .... New York, NY
Bost, Alison R. .... Winston-Salem, NC
Bost, Burton T. .... Orangevale, CA
Bost, Deborah J. .... Greensboro, NC
Bost, Donald Webb, Jr. .... Baltimore, MD
Bost, Glenn E., II .... Pittsburgh, PA
Bost, James A. .... Tulsa, OK
Bost, Janice Wilson .... Edmond, OK
Bost, John C. .... Carlsbad, CA
Bost, Merrilee J. .... Oklahoma City, OK

Bost, Richard B. .... Cherry Hill, NJ
Philadelphia, PA
Bost, Robert K. .... Oklahoma City, OK
Bost, S. Fraley .... Winston-Salem, NC
Bost, Stephen A. .... Los Angeles, CA
Bost, Thomas G. .... Los Angeles, CA
Bost, Tiffany M. .... Charleston, WV
Bost, Wayne W. .... Austin, TX
Bost, William Clarence "Bill" .... Pinehurst, NC
Bost, William L., Jr. .... Atlanta, GA
Bost, William M., Jr. .... Jackson, MS
Bost, William M., Jr. .... Vicksburg, MS
Bost, William S., III .... Raleigh, NC
Bostany, John P. .... Newark, NJ
New York, NY
Bostany Law Firm, The .... Newark, NJ
New York, NY
Bostelman, John T. .... New York, NY
Boster, B. Scott .... Cincinnati, OH
Boster, Michael D. .... Denver, CO
Boster, Stanford R. .... Cincinnati, OH
Bostetter, Judith M. .... Elm Grove, WI
Bostetter, Martin V. B., Jr. .... Alexandria, VA
Bostian, William J. .... Salisbury, MD
Bostic, Amy L. .... Columbus, OH
Bostic, Betzi M. .... Harrisonburg, VA
Bostic, Cindy K. Pulley .... Oxford, NC
Bostic, J. Nicholas .... Hart, MI
Bostic, James N. .... Austin, TX
Bostic, Michael J. .... Dallas, TX
Bostic, R. Darren .... Harrisonburg, VA
Bostic, Terrance A. .... Tampa, FL
Bostick, Blake M. .... Oklahoma City, OK
Bostick, Bradley L. .... Oakland, CA
Bostick, Brian Roberts .... Birmingham, AL
Bostick, Bush-Joseph & Horwich
Chicago, IL
Bostick, C. Dent .... Nashville, TN
Bostick, Carolyn F. .... Menlo Park, CA
Bostick, Catherine M. .... Lapeer, MI
Bostick, Christine N. .... Richmond, VA
Bostick, G. Fred .... Thomasville, GA
Bostick, George H. .... Washington, DC
Bostick, Mark S. .... Oakland, CA
Bostick, Maurice E. .... New Orleans, LA
Bostick, Robert A. .... Dayton, OH
Bostick, Robert L. .... Piedmont, CA
Bostick, Shelley Ballard .... Chicago, IL
Bostick, Tara T. .... Birmingham, AL
Bostick, W.G., Jr. .... St. Petersburg, FL
Bostjancich, John .... Chicago, IL
Bostleman, William L. .... Holland, OH
Bostock, Catherine E. .... Hackensack, NJ
Bostock, Dean G. .... Boston, MA
Bostock, Susan L. .... Phoenix, AZ
Bostock, Thomas R. .... Kalispell, MT
Boston, Alicia .... Dallas, TX
Boston, Allen S. .... St. Louis, MO
Boston, Ben .... Lawrenceburg, TN
Boston, Bever, Klinge, Cross & Chidester
Richmond, IN
Boston, Charles D. .... Houston, TX
Boston, Christina M. .... Philadelphia, PA
Boston, David K. .... New York, NY
Boston, David W. .... San Francisco, CA
Boston, Derrick O. .... Santa Monica, CA
Boston, Ellis A. .... Washington, DC
Boston, George B. .... Bowling Green, KY
Boston, Gerald W. .... Lansing, MI
Boston, Holt & Sockwell, PLLC
Lawrenceburg, TN
Boston, Hugh Chester, III
Birmingham, AL
Boston, James R., & Associates, P.C.
Houston, TX
Boston, James R., Jr. .... Houston, TX
Boston, Jennifer Caillier .... Philadelphia, PA
Boston, Julia L. .... Milwaukie, OR
Boston, Kirby L. .... Houston, TX
Boston, Krista D. .... Jefferson City, MO
Boston, Lucille J. .... Marina Del Rey, CA
Boston, Lucille J., Inc., A Prof. Law Corp.
Marina Del Rey, CA
Boston, P. Talmage, Jr. .... Dallas, TX
Boston, Richard E. .... Richmond, IN
Boston, Robert B. .... Mount Shasta, CA
Weed, CA
Boston, Robert E. .... Nashville, TN
Boston, Ronald E. .... Columbia, SC
Boston, Roy L. .... Chicago, IL
Boston, Russell M., (P.C.) .... Macon, GA
Boston, Shannon C. .... Cincinnati, OH
Boston, Sheila S. .... New York, NY
Boston, Ted J. .... Spring, TX
Boston, Thomas R. .... Atlanta, GA
Boston, Wiley S. .... Orlando, FL
Boston, William C., Jr.
Oklahoma City, OK
Boston, William C., P.L.L.C.
Oklahoma City, OK
Boston, William Clayton, III
Oklahoma City, OK
Boston, William E. .... Lawrenceburg, TN
Bostos, Stephanie R. .... Columbus, OH
Bostrom, Barry A. .... Terre Haute, IN
Bostrom, Brent D. .... St. Paul, MN
Bostrom, Lisa Klaiman .... New York, NY
Bostrom, Lori E. .... New York, NY
Bostrom, Patricia Lynn .... Redmond, WA
Bostrom, Robert Everett .... New York, NY
Bostrom Sands & Sander, P.C.
Denver, CO
Bostrom, William A. .... Denver, CO
Bostron, Catherine A. .... New York, NY
Bostwick & Associates .... San Francisco, CA
Denver, CO
Honolulu, HI
Tulsa, OK

Bostwick, Chas. W. .... Jacksonville, FL
Bostwick, Cynthia .... Port Huron, MI
Bostwick, Darrel J. .... Salt Lake City, UT
Bostwick, Donald W. .... Wichita, KS
Bostwick, Dwight P. .... Washington, DC
Bostwick, Frederick deB., III .... Waco, TX
Bostwick, Gary L. .... Santa Monica, CA
Bostwick & Hoffman LLP
Santa Monica, CA
Bostwick, James S. .... San Francisco, CA
Denver, CO
Honolulu, HI
Tulsa, OK
Bostwick, Janet C. .... Tucson, AZ
Bostwick, Janet E. .... Boston, MA
Bostwick, Jarrett T. .... Bellevue, WA
Bostwick, John .... Guntersville, AL
Bostwick, Michael E. .... Salt Lake City, UT
Bostwick, Michael G. .... Portland, OR
Bostwick, Phillip D., (P.C.) .... Washington, DC
Bostwick, Reese V. .... Tucson, AZ
Bostwick, Richard R. .... Casper, WY
Bostwick, Richard T. .... Sandy Spring, MD
Bostwick, Sarah Moore .... Salem, OR
Bostwick, Thomas C. .... Salem, OR
Bostwick, Thomas H. .... Towson, MD
Bostwick, Wendy A. .... Philadelphia, PA
Boswell, Allen B. .... Athens, TX
Boswell, Anthony O. .... Hurst, TX
Boswell, Archie L. .... Norfolk, VA
Boswell, Aubrey .... Laguna Park, TX
Boswell, Bryce M. .... St. Louis, MO
Boswell, C. A. .... Bartow, FL
Boswell, C. A., Jr. .... Babson Park, FL
Boswell, Christopher H. .... Harlingen, TX
Boswell, D. Kirk .... New Orleans, LA
Boswell, Daniel C. .... Huntsville, AL
Boswell, Daphne W. .... Winter Haven, FL
Boswell, David A. .... Rehoboth Beach, DE
Boswell, Don R. .... Palm Beach, FL
Boswell, Donna A. .... Washington, DC
Boswell & Dunlap, LLP .... Bartow, FL
Boswell, Elizabeth W. .... Atlanta, GA
Boswell, G. Thomas .... Fort Worth, TX
Boswell, George Harvey .... Jackson, TN
Boswell, George T. .... Mineola, TX
Boswell, Gerald P. .... Trenton, NJ
Boswell, Hallmark & Brothers, A Professional Corporation .... Houston, TX
Boswell, Harry D. .... Tallahassee, FL
Boswell, J. David .... Paducah, KY
Boswell, J. Derek .... Palo Alto, CA
Boswell, James W., II .... Terre Haute, IN
Boswell, James W., III .... Atlanta, GA
Boswell, Jeffrey G. .... Fresno, CA
Boswell, Jeffrey R. .... Harrisburg, PA
Boswell, John G. .... Cary, NC
Boswell, John H. .... Houston, TX
Boswell, John I. .... Hanover, NH
Boswell, John M. .... Crewe, VA
Boswell, Joseph J. .... Mobile, AL
Boswell, Julie A. .... Nashville, TN
Boswell, Kelley O. .... Albany, GA
Boswell & Kober, P.C. .... Dallas, TX
Fort Worth, TX
Haslet, TX
Boswell Law Firm .... Bryant, AR
Little Rock, AR
Memphis, TN
Boswell, Lawrence O. .... Tucson, AZ
Boswell, Lola .... Collins, MO
Boswell, Lorin A., Jr. .... Fort Worth, TX
Boswell, Mark R. .... San Luis Obispo, CA
Boswell, Mark W. .... De Kalb, IL
Boswell, Mary Jane .... Washington, DC
Boswell, Michael Allen .... Sumner, WA
Boswell, Michael Lawrence
Altamonte Springs, FL
Boswell, Oscar W., II .... Lafayette, LA
Boswell, Paul H. .... Dover, DE
Rehoboth Beach, DE
Wilmington, DE
Boswell, Peyton, III .... Mineola, NY
Boswell, Richard A. .... San Francisco, CA
Boswell, Richard A. .... Lincoln, NE
Boswell, Richard V. .... Westminster, MD
Boswell, Robert C. .... Floyd, VA
Boswell, Robin Reid .... Pascagoula, MS
Boswell, Ross A. .... Memphis, TN
Boswell, Sherrie Lynn .... Auburn, WA
Boswell, Sherry L. .... Greenville, SC
Boswell & Sims .... Paducah, KY
Boswell, Stella Anne .... Durham, NC
Boswell, Stephen E. .... Jonesboro, GA
Boswell, Stephen E., P.C. .... Jonesboro, GA
Boswell, Susan G. .... Tucson, AZ
Boswell, Ted .... Bryant, AR
Memphis, TN
Boswell, Thomas H. .... Rockford, IL
Boswell, Tintner, Piccola & Wickersham
Harrisburg, PA
Boswell, Wade M. .... New York, NY
Boswell, Wade M. .... Knoxville, TN
Boswell, William D. .... Harrisburg, PA
Boswell, William E., Jr. .... Norman, OK
Boswell, William P. .... Pittsburgh, PA
Boswell & Williamson .... Crewe, VA
Bosworth, Allen .... Fort Lauderdale, FL
Bosworth, Arthur H., II .... Denver, CO
Bosworth, Carolyn Mitchell .... Tustin, CA
Bosworth, Claude F. .... New Orleans, LA
Bosworth, David Alan .... San Antonio, TX
Bosworth, David B. .... Charlotte, NC
Bosworth, Duane A., II .... Portland, OR
Bosworth, Frank M., Jr. .... Largo, FL
Bosworth, Gray & Fuller .... Bronxville, NY
White Plains, NY
Bosworth, Greer C. .... Los Angeles, CA

Boudreaux, Tina M. ... **New Orleans, LA**
Boudreaux, Todd, P.C. ... **Augusta, GA**
Boudreaux, William R. ... **Indianapolis, IN**
Boudro, Beate ... **Albuquerque, NM**
Boudrot, Susan M. ... San Francisco, CA
Boudwin, Carol A. ... Dayton, NJ
Boudwin, Judith A. ... Wilmington, DE
Boudwin and Yurchenco ... Dayton, NJ
Boue, Adelqui J. ... Lincolnwood, IL
Bou, Edward C., P.C. ... Washington, DC
Bouer, Jodie F. ... **Newark, NJ**
Bouer, Robert ... Chicago, IL
Bouey, Donald J. ... **San Francisco, CA**
Bouey, Pamela S. ... San Bruno, CA
Bouffard, Andre D. ... **Burlington, VT**
Bouffard, Chris S. ... **San Diego, CA**
Bouffard, Dean K. ... Kittery, ME
Bouffard, Henry P. ... **Norfolk, VA**
Bouffard, Janet S. ... **Denver, CO**
Bouffard, Robert S. ... Boardman, OH
Bougen, Harriet S. ... Albany, NY
Bougere, Walter C., Jr. ... New Orleans, LA
Bough, Brad ... **Terre Haute, IN**
Bough, Stephen R. ... Kansas City, MO
Bougher, Frederick C. ... Medina, OH
Bougher, J. Scott ... Silverdale, WA
Boughey, Garvie & Bushner
San Francisco, CA
Honolulu, HI
Boughey, James D. ... **San Francisco, CA**
Honolulu, HI
Boughey Law Firm ... Minot, ND
Boughman, Barry ... **Denver, CO**
Boughman, Harold Lee, Jr.
Fayetteville, NC
Boughner, Jackson L. ... Naples, FL
Boughner, James R. ... Pittsburgh, PA
Boughner, Stephen T. ... **Washington, DC**
Boughton, Barry D. ... **Lansing, MI**
Boughton, Bert D. ... Silverdale, WA
Boughton, F. Sherman, Jr.
Lake Providence, LA
Boughton, Keith ... Grand Junction, CO
Boughton, Nancy L. ... **Washington, DC**
Bougie, Laurent A. ... Denver, CO
Bougie, Laurent A., P.C. ... Denver, CO
Bougie, Roger M. ... Stratford, CT
Bouhaben, Sarah J. ... Pacific Grove, CA
Bouhall, Robert C. ... Cleveland, OH
Bouhan, Richard M. ... Kansas City, MO
Bouhan, Williams & Levy LLP
Brunswick, GA
Savannah, GA
Bouhassis, Leila M. ... Dallas, TX
Bouillion, Frances M. ... Lafayette, LA
Boujoukos, G. Jeffrey ... **Philadelphia, PA**
Boukalik & Linden ... **Cleveland, OH**
Boukalik, William T. ... **Cleveland, OH**
Bouker, Edward E. ... Hays, KS
Bouker, Jon S., Jr. ... House of Representatives, Congressional Assistants, GV
Boukidis, Constance E. ... **Los Angeles, CA**
Boukidis, Constantine M. ... Pasadena, CA
Boukis, Christ ... **Cleveland, OH**
Boukis, Kenneth ... **Cleveland, OH**
Bouknight, Doni M. ... **Columbia, SC**
Bouknight, J. A., Jr. ... **Washington, DC**
Bouknight, Robert K. ... **Lexington, SC**
Boukus, Charles P., Jr. ... **Arlington, VA**
Boul, Harry D. ... Columbia, MO
Boul, John L. ... Oklahoma City, OK
Boulac, Mary Ann ... **South Bend, IN**
Boulahanis, Gregory J. ... Dearborn, MI
Boulahanis, Gregory J., P.C. ... Dearborn, MI
Bouland & Brush, L.L.C. ... **Baltimore, MD**
Columbia, MD
Bouland, H. Dean ... **Baltimore, MD**
Bouland, John T. ... **Ocala, FL**
Bouland & Smith, L.L.P. ... **Ocala, FL**
Boulanger, Carol Seabrook
New York, NY
Boulanger, Jean Alfred ... Coventry, RI
Boulanger, Joseph E. ... **Andover, MA**
Boulanger, Michael R. ... Rockford, IL
Boulanger, Raymond M., Jr. ... Buffalo, NY
Boulanger, Raymond P., (P.C.)
Boston, MA
Boulay, Donna-Marie ... St. Paul, MN
Boulay, Sandra J. MacCormack
Lowell, MA
Boulbol, Charles E. ... **New York, NY**
Bould, Roger M. ... **Pittsburgh, PA**
Boulden, Jeffrey C. ... **Chicago, IL**
Boulden, John D. ... Orlando, FL
Boulden, Judith A. ... Salt Lake City, UT
Boulden, Michael R. ... **Dallas, TX**
Boulden, Patrick T. ... Tulsa, OK
Boulden, Richard S. ... Durham, NC
Boulden, Thomas A. ... **Norristown, PA**
Boulden, William L.
Merit Systems Protection Board, Washington, D.C. Regional Office, GV
Boulder, Linda L. ... Durango, CO
Bouldin & Bouldin ... **Murfreesboro, TN**
Bouldin, G. Sumner R., Jr.
Murfreesboro, TN
Bouldin, Granville S. R.
Murfreesboro, TN
Bouldin, James L. S. ... **San Francisco, CA**
Bouldin, Michael William ... Covington, KY
Bouldin, Steven H. ... **High Point, NC**
Bouldin, W. Mercer ... Tucson, AZ
Bouldin, William M. ... **Russellville, AL**
Boulding, Mark E. ... Washington, DC
Bouldon, Allyson ... **Chicago, IL**
Boule, Eugene T. ... New York, NY
Bouler, Nicholas ... Birmingham, AL
Boulet, Jeanette M. ... Tucson, AZ

Boulet, Virginia ... **New Orleans, LA**
Boulet, William P., Jr. ... Denver, CO
Boulette, Jason S. ... **Austin, TX**
Bouley, Gerard J. ... Danvers, MA
Bouley, Robert L. ... **Cambridge, MA**
Bouley, Sara E. ... **Salt Lake City, UT**
Boulger, James T. ... **Chillicothe, OH**
Boulger, John V. ... **Fargo, ND**
Boulger, Sean T. ... **Boston, MA**
Boulger, William C. ... **Chillicothe, OH**
Boulhosa, Michael L. ... **New York, NY**
Boulia, Trudy L. ... **Albany, NY**
Boulier, Perry D. ... **Spartanburg, SC**
Bouligny, James A. ... El Campo, TX
Boulineau, Robert M., Jr. ... Milledgeville, GA
Boullion, Lois Ann ... Houston, TX
Boulos, James G. ... **Saco, ME**
Boulos, Nader R. ... **Chicago, IL**
Boulos, Nichols & Webb ... **Saco, ME**
Bouloukos, George J. ... **Birmingham, AL**
Bouloukos & Oglesby ... **Birmingham, AL**
Boulris, Amy Brigham
Fort Lauderdale, FL
Miami, FL
Boulris, Mark J. ... **Miami, FL**
Boulris, Mark J., P.A. ... **Miami, FL**
Boult, Cummings, Conners & Berry, PLC
Nashville, TN
Boult, John W. ... **Tampa, FL**
Boult, Reber ... Albuquerque, NM
Boult, Reber M. ... **Nashville, TN**
Boulter, Beau ... Amarillo, TX
Boulter, Stuart L. ... Arvada, CO
Boulton, Amy Fernand
East Hartford, CT
Boulton, Barbara D. ... **Knoxville, TN**
Boulton, Florence Berger ... Spencer, MA
Boulton, Gerald R. ... Canby, MN
Boulton, J. Stephen ... Cranston, RI
Boulton, Leila B. ... Jerome, AZ
Boulton, Scot W. ... St. Louis, MO
Boulton, Stephen F. ... **Chicago, IL**
Boulton, Wayne T. ... **Hartford, CT**
Boulware, Clay H. ... Austin, TX
Boulware, Dan M. ... **Cleburne, TX**
Boulware, Leilani ... **Nashville, TN**
Boulware, Margaret A. ... **Houston, TX**
Boulware, Melissa Parks ... **Houston, TX**
Boulware, R. Dan ... **St. Joseph, MO**
Boulware, Richard W. ... Everett, MA
Boulware, Rolin T. ... Shelbina, MO
Boulware, Thomas M. ... **Barnwell, SC**
Bouma, H. B. ... **Washington, DC**
Bouma, Hermann B. ... **Washington, DC**
Bouma, John J. ... **Phoenix, AZ**
Bouma, John Jeffrey ... Phoenix, AZ
Bouma, Ralph R., Jr. ... Wheaton, IL
Bouma, Richard L. ... **Grand Rapids, MI**
Bouma, Robert E. ... **Chicago, IL**
Bouman, John K. ... **Rochester, NY**
Bouman, John M. ... Chicago, IL
Bouman, Peter H. ... **Binghamton, NY**
Owego, NY
Bouman, Stacy P. ... Edina, MN
Boumann, Robert L. ... Golden, CO
Boumil, S. James ... Lowell, MA
Boumstein, Mark N. ... Skokie, IL
Bound, A. Edward, Jr. ... Clearwater, FL
Boundas, John T. ... **Houston, TX**
Boundas, Theodore A. ... **Chicago, IL**
Bounds & Bounds ... Ellicott City, MD
Bounds, Bruce M., Law Offices of
Coral Gables, FL
Bounds, Bruce M., Law Offices of
Miami, FL
Bounds, Curtis P. ... **Wilmington, DE**
Bounds & Dorsey ... **Roanoke, VA**
Bounds, George L. ... Rochester, NY
Bounds, J. Clancey ... **Orlando, FL**
Bounds, James K. ... Warrenton, VA
Bounds, John K. ... Hugo, OK
Bounds, Joseph P. ... Roanoke, VA
Bounds, Richard ... **Mobile, AL**
Bounds, Robert I. ... Yakima, WA
Bounds, Roland R. ... Ellicott City, MD
Bounds, Ronald J. ... Austin, TX
Bounds, Ronnie Earl, Jr. ... Shreveport, LA
Bounds, Scott ... **Huntsville, TX**
Bounds, Stephen C. ... Ellicott City, MD
Bounds-Olsen, Pamela Michelle
Ocala, FL
Boundy, David E. ... **New York, NY**
Boundy, Frederick Ross ... **Seattle, WA**
Boneff, Bobby B. ... Portland, OR
Bouneff & Chally ... Portland, OR
Bounty, Thomas M. ... **Hartford, CT**
Bouquet, Brian D. ... **St. Louis, MO**
Bouquet, Christopher C. ... **Washington, DC**
Bouquet, Edouard Jean-Pierre
Bethesda, MD
Bouquet, Eugene A. ... Lake Charles, LA
Bouquet, John K. ... **Minneapolis, MN**
Bour, Elmer F. ... Monmouth, IL
Bour, John W. ... **Scranton, PA**
Bouras, James ... New York, NY
Bourassa, Beth A. ... **Albany, NY**
Bourassa, David E. ... Salem, OR
Bourassa, Donald J. ... Augusta, ME
Bourassa, Donald R. ... Genoa, NV
Bourassa, M. Gary ... Tustin, CA
Bourassa & Petersen, P.A. ... Augusta, ME
Bourassa-Diaz, Sharon ... Fort Lauderdale, FL
Bourbeau, Mark S. ... Boston, MA
Bourbeau, Michael C. ... Boston, MA
Bourbeau, Sheryl M. ... **Boston, MA**
Bourbeau, Tocchio & Floyd ... Boston, MA
Bourbin, Bryan M. ... Los Angeles, CA
Bourbois, Joseph A. ... **San Antonio, TX**

Bourbon, M. Theresa ... **Wheaton, MD**
Bourbon, Richard W. ... Philadelphia, PA
Bourbon, Robert S. ... **Wheaton, MD**
Bourbon, Robert S., and M. Theresa
Bourbon, Law Offices of ... **Wheaton, MD**
Bourbon, Sandra M. ... Atlanta, GA
Bourcy, Bernetta A. ... Penn Yan, NY
Bourdeau, Carrie S. ... **Las Vegas, NV**
Bourdeau, Gayle A. ... Boston, MA
Bourdeau, J. Fred ... Great Falls, MT
Bourdeau, James O. ... **Rochester, NY**
Bourdeau, Karl S. ... **Washington, DC**
Bourdeau, Paul L. ... **Hartford, CT**
Bourdeaux and Jones ... **Meridian, MS**
Bourdelais, Scott A. ... Santa Ana, CA
Bourdet, Jodie M. ... **San Francisco, CA**
Bourdette, Miriam R. ... Visalia, CA
Bourdette & Partners ... Visalia, CA
Bourdette, Philip C. ... Visalia, CA
Bourdon, Charles F. ... San Francisco, CA
Bourdon, Curtis L. ... **Woodstock, VT**
Bourdon, Glenda Sue ... Prescott, AZ
Bourdon & Mayhew, P.C. ... **Woodstock, VT**
Bourdon, Paul A. ... Woodstock, VT
Bourdon, R. Edward, Jr.
Virginia Beach, VA
Bourdow & Bowen, P.C. ... Midlothian, VA
Bourdow, Carolyn A. H. ... Midlothian, VA
Bourdreau, Alfred H. O., Jr. ... Elizabeth, WV
Bouregy, Thomas K., Jr. ... Hackensack, NJ
Bouregy, William L. ... Deep River, CT
Bouregy, Zane ... Hackensack, NJ
Bourelly, Alex J.
Securities and Exchange Commission, Division of Enforcement, GV
Bouressa & Patteson, S.C. ... Green Bay, WI
Bouressa, Terence J. ... Green Bay, WI
Bouret, Marc P. ... **Walnut Creek, CA**
Bourette Schuur, Pamela ... **Long Beach, CA**
Bourey, Alan D. ... Decatur, IL
Bourg, Baron B. ... Houma, LA
Bourg, David J. ... Round Rock, TX
Bourg, Kari Levine ... Washington, DC
Bourgault, Dennis P. ... Washington, DC
Bourgault, Lynne S. ... **Los Angeles, CA**
San Francisco, CA
Bourg Brown, Christi ... **Houston, TX**
Bourgeacq, Christian A. ... St. Louis, MO
Bourgeau, David C., Jr. ... Naples, FL
Bourgeois, Alexandre P. ... **Austin, TX**
Bourgeois, Amelie Yvette ... Austin, TX
Bourgeois, André G. ... **Baton Rouge, LA**
Bourgeois, Brent J. ... **Baton Rouge, LA**
Bourgeois, David A. ... **New York, NY**
Bourgeois, David J. ... **Metairie, LA**
Bourgeois, Denise L. ... Santa Fe Springs, CA
Bourgeois, Dresser & White ... Worcester, MA
Bourgeois, George S., Jr. ... Opelousas, LA
Bourgeois, Gerard J. ... Morgan City, LA
Bourgeois, Glenn Michael ... **New York, NY**
Bourgeois, Gregory T. ... **Austin, TX**
Bourgeois, J. Rion ... **Tigard, OR**
Bourgeois, John Augustine
Baltimore, MD
Bourgeois, John T. ... Thibodaux, LA
Bourgeois, L. Robert ... **Tampa, FL**
Bourgeois, Lucien L. ... **Jackson, MS**
Bourgeois, Richard D. ... Springfield, MA
Bourgeois, Richard Pierre ... **New York, NY**
Bourgeois, Roy A. ... Worcester, MA
Bourgeois, Susan V. A. ... New York, NY
Bourgeois, Travis Louis ... **New Orleans, LA**
Bourgeois, Wilfred A. ... Omaha, NE
Bourgeois, William E. ... **Monroe, LA**
Bourgeois, Yolande M. ... Chicago, IL
Bourgerie, Alexia Kent ... **Rockville, MD**
Bourgerie, Richard P. ... **New York, NY**
Bourget, Anthony J. ... **Eau Claire, WI**
Bourget & Bourget, P.A. ... Augusta, ME
Bourget, Cynthia M. ... **Falmouth, MA**
Bourget & Kenney ... **Falmouth, MA**
Bourget, Marc J. ... Stockton, CA
Bourget, Nancy J. ... **Detroit, MI**
Bourget, Norman C. ... Augusta, ME
Bourget, Paul L. ... Augusta, ME
Bourget, Ronald W. ... Augusta, ME
Bourget, Stephen J. ... Augusta, ME
Bourgoignie, P. Tristan ... **Miami, FL**
Bourgoin, David L. ... Honolulu, HI
Bourgoin, David L., Law Offices of
Honolulu, HI
Bourgoin, Jennifer A. ... **Detroit, MI**
Bourgoin, Robert D. ... East Harwich, MA
Bourgois, Nancy K. ... Seattle, WA
Bourgon, George M. ... Novi, MI
Bourgon, George M., Jr. ... Detroit, MI
Bourgon, Joseph H. ... Birmingham, MI
Bourgon, Joseph H. ... **Southfield, MI**
Bourgon, Richard W. ... Bingham Farms, MI
Bourguignon, Barbara Y. ... Gainesville, FL
Bourguignon, Henry ... Toledo, OH
Bourguignon, Robert L. ... **New York, NY**
Bourhis, Ray ... San Francisco, CA
Bouril, James ... Lombard, IL
Bouril, James, & Associates ... Lombard, IL
Bourjaily, Monte F., IV ... Washington, DC
Bourk, Gilbert P., III ... Olathe, KS
Bourke, Brian J. ... Palm Springs, CA
Bourke, Flanagan & Asato, P.C.
East Hampton, NY
Southampton, NY
Bourke, John J. ... Chicago, IL
Bourke, Mary W. ... **Wilmington, DE**
Bourke, Michael A. ... Prescott, AZ
Bourke, Miriam Krell ... **Greenfield, MA**
Bourke, Patricia M. ... Walnut Creek, CA
Bourke, Robert M. ... North Haven, CT
Bourke, Terence T. ... Sheboygan, WI

Bourke, Thomas J. ... **Southampton, NY**
Bourke, Thomas K. ... **Los Angeles, CA**
Bourke, William B. ... Abilene, TX
Bourke, William C. ... Palo Alto, CA
Bourke, William J. ... **Denver, CO**
Bourland, Albert D. ... Vienna, VA
Bourland, Cindy Olson ... **Austin, TX**
Bourland, Dana Brooks ... **Irving, TX**
Bourland, David L. ... **Memphis, TN**
Bourland, Donald E. ... **Memphis, TN**
Bourland, Heflin, Alvarez & Minor, P.L.C.
Memphis, TN
Bourland, J. David ... Baton Rouge, LA
Bourland, John A. ... Tulsa, OK
Bourland, John Kent ... Ann Arbor, MI
Bourland, Kirkman, Seidler & Evans, L.L.P.
Fort Worth, TX
Bourland, Michael E. ... **Fort Worth, TX**
Bourland, Michael V. ... **Fort Worth, TX**
Bourland, R. Brent ... Natchez, MS
Bourland, Richard L. ... **Fort Worth, TX**
Bourland, Smith, Wall & Wenzel, A Professional Corporation
Fort Worth, TX
Bourland, Stephanie ... **Fort Worth, TX**
Bourn, Mark A. ... St. Cloud, MN
Bourn, Stefan G. ... **Jackson, MS**
Bournazian, J. David ... **Los Angeles, CA**
Bournazian, Jack V. ... **San Diego, CA**
Bournazian & Luna ... **San Diego, CA**
Bournazos, Steven ... **New York, NY**
Bourne, Alfia M. ... North Olmsted, OH
Bourne, Amanda Dalton ... **Los Angeles, CA**
Bourne, Andrea S. ... **Dallas, TX**
Bourne, Aynsley B. ... **Milwaukee, WI**
Bourne, Brian D. ... Clarendon Hills, IL
Bourne, Carla R.D. ... Visalia, CA
Bourne, David L. ... **Milwaukee, WI**
Bourne, Dinah H. ... **Roseland, NJ**
Bourne, Donald ... Russellville, AR
Bourne, Gordon M. ... Coudersport, PA
Bourne, James E. ... **New Albany, IN**
Bourne, Joel K. ... Tarboro, NC
Bourne, Jon C. ... Denver, CO
Bourne, Jonathan F. ... **Montclair, NJ**
Bourne, Judith L.
Charlotte Amalie, St. Thomas, VI
Bourne, Laurence N.
Federal Communications Commission, Office of the General Counsel, GV
Bourne, Nancy B. ... **San Francisco, CA**
Bourne, Noll & Kenyon, A Professional Corporation ... **Elizabeth, NJ**
Summit, NJ
Bourne, Patrick J. ... Omaha, NE
Bourne, Philip J. ... Columbus, OH
Bourne, Richard ... College Park, MD
Bourne, Richard ... Boston, MA
Bourne, Richard P. ... Belgium, WI
Bourne, Richard W. ... Baltimore, MD
Bourne, Robert B. ... **Summit, NJ**
Bourne, Robert D. ... Fairfax, VA
Bourne, Robert E. ... Cumming, GA
Bourne, Robert E. ... Midland, MI
Bourne, Robert E., Jr. ... **Lake Worth, FL**
Bourne, Robert F. ... San Diego, CA
Bourne, Robert J. ... Meriden, CT
Bourne, Steven Reid ... **Boston, MA**
Bourne, Sumner A. ... Peoria, IL
Bourne, Susan A. Fair ... Louisville, KY
Bourne-Vanneck, Richard P.
Charlotte Amalie, St. Thomas, VI
Bourns, Courtney B. ... **West Hartford, CT**
Bourque, Arthur J. ... Phoenix, AZ
Bourque & Associates, P.A. ... **Concord, NH**
Manchester, NH
Portsmouth, NH
Bourque, Charles C., Jr. ... **Houma, LA**
Bourque & Clegg ... Sanford, ME
Bourque, Daniel J. ... **Manchester, NH**
Bourque, Denise M. ... New Haven, CT
Bourque, Elmer T. ... Manchester, NH
Bourque, Gerald E. ... The Woodlands, TX
Bourque, Jude David ... New Orleans, LA
Bourque, Kevin J. ... **Worcester, MA**
Bourque, Michael Th. ... **New York, NY**
Bourque, Michelle A. ... **New Orleans, LA**
Bourque, Reule P. ... Kaplan, LA
Bourque, Robert A. ... **New York, NY**
Bourque, Ronald D. ... Sanford, ME
Bourque, Shari-Ellen ... **Baltimore, MD**
New York, NY
Bourque, Starr H. ... Wheaton, IL
Bourque, Stephanie L. ... **Washington, DC**
Bourque, Stephen A. ... San Jose, CA
Bourque, Thomas B. ... **Ann Arbor, MI**
Bourque, William Michael ... New Haven, CT
Bourquin, Dennis M. ... Redwood City, CA
Bourquin, Linda J. ... New Orleans, LA
Bourret, Amy J. ... **Dallas, TX**
Bours, Reginald W., III ... **Rockville, MD**
Bours, Reginald W., III, P.C.
Rockville, MD
Boursereau, Dominique Guy ... New York, NY
Bourstein, Bonnie ... New York, NY
Bourstein, Ira ... New York, NY
Bour-Stokes, Joann M. ... Columbus, OH
Boursy, John J., Jr.
Department of State, GV
Bourtin, Nicolas ... **New York, NY**
Bousanti, Anthony J. ... Staten Island, NY
Bouscaren, Anthony G. ... New York, NY
Bouscaren, Winslow F. ... **Baltimore, MD**
Towson, MD
Bouschor, David S. ... Duluth, MN
Bouschor, David S. ... Denton, TX
Bouschor, Royal G., II (P.C.) ... Tucson, AZ
Bouse, Bartlett Andrew ... Woodward, OK

Bouse, Cornell Van Nos ... Huntington, NY
Bouse, F. Courts ... Setauket, NY
Bouse, Robert H., Jr. ... Baltimore, MD
Bousfield, Nan S. ... Slidell, LA
Boush, Joseph M. ... Springfield, VA
Boushka, Cheryl C. ... Overland Park, KS
Bouska, James W. ... Overland Park, KS
Bousley, Denise I. ... Los Angeles, CA
Bouslog, Christopher S. ... Honolulu, HI
Bouslog, Harriet ... Honolulu, HI
Bouslog, Jeffrey J. ... Minneapolis, MN
Bouslog, Thomas D. ... Buffalo Grove, IL
Bousquet, Francis J. ... Boston, MA
Bousquet & Jackson, P.C. ... Houston, TX
Bousquet, Laurence G. ... Syracuse, NY
Bousquet, Pamela G. S. ... San Rafael, CA
Bousquet, Philip S. ... Syracuse, NY
Bousquet, Thomas G. ... Houston, TX
Bousquette, Elizabeth A. (Bridge)
New York, NY
Bousquette, William C., Jr. ... Belleville, IL
Boustani, Eric Bakri ... Monterey, CA
Boustany, Alfred Frem, II ... Lafayette, LA
Boustany, Jon Eric ... Baltimore, MD
Boustead, Cheryl Leo ... White Plains, NY
Boustead, John ... Ho-Ho-Kus, NJ
Boustead, Michael ... York, PA
Boustead, Thomas ... White Plains, NY
Boustead, William H. ... New Orleans, LA
Bouta, Robert F. ... Garden City, NY
Boutall, John C. ... Metairie, LA
Boutchee, Kathy D. ... Houston, TX
Boutcher, Robert F. ... East Setauket, NY
Boutchyard, Theresa I. ... Bel Air, MD
Bouteiller, William Lewis ... Albany, NY
Boutel, Adrian ... New York, NY
Boutell, David G. ... Kalamazoo, MI
Boutell, Michael D. ... Detroit, MI
Boutell, William T., Jr. ... Phoenix, AZ
Bouterie, Richard J., Jr. ... Thibodaux, LA
Bouthilet, Kirby O. ... Green Bay, WI
Bouthillette, Max L. ... Sugar Land, TX
Bouthillette, Staci Reeves ... Houston, TX
Bouthillier, Reginald L., Jr.
Tallahassee, FL
Boutilier, Elaine M.
Board of Governors Of The Federal Reserve System,
Office of the General Counsel, GV
Boutilier, Emory L. ... San Diego, CA
Boutillier, James J. ... Montclair, NJ
Boutillier, James M. ... Yakima, WA
Boutillier, Robert A. ... Princeton, NJ
Boutin, Ann Simmons ... Pasadena, CA
Boutin, Arturo M. ... New York, NY
Boutin & Associates, P.L.L.C.
Londonderry, NH
Manchester, NH
Salem, NH
Boutin, Charles R. ... Aberdeen, MD
Boutin, Daniel W. ... Portland, ME
Boutin, Dentino, Gibson Di Giusto, Hodell & West, A Professional Corporation
Sacramento, CA
Boutin, Edmund J. ... Londonderry, NH
Boutin, Marc M. ... Melrose, MA
Boutin, Michelle L. ... Anchorage, AK
Boutin, Peter R. ... San Francisco, CA
Boutin, Roderick A. ... Oregon City, OR
Boutin, Stephen F. ... Sacramento, CA
Bouton, Alexandre B. ... Washington, DC
Bouton, Daniel R. ... Stanardsville, VA
Bouton, Melanie A. ... Richmond, VA
Bouton, Paul E. ... Boston, MA
Bouton, Peter M. ... Cedar Knolls, NJ
Bouton, Scott ... Austin, TX
Bouton, William W., III ... Hartford, CT
Boutris, Basil J. ... Walnut Creek, CA
Boutris, Demetrios A. ... Sacramento, CA
Boutrous, James Joseph, II ... Detroit, MI
Boutrous, Theodore J., Jr.
Los Angeles, CA
Washington, DC
Boutsis, Eve A. ... Miami, FL
Boutte, David Gray ... Fairfax, VA
Boutton, Mary L. ... Rocky River, OH
Boutwell, C. Everette, Ltd. ... Laurel, MS
Boutwell, Charles D. ... Northbrook, IL
Boutwell & Connick ... Deerfield Beach, FL
Boutwell, Fay & Fabricant, LLP ... Irvine, CA
Boutwell, Gary N., II ... Hammond, LA
Boutwell, John D. ... Charlotte, NC
Boutwell Law Offices, PLLC
Lexington, MS
Boutwell, Marc ... Lexington, MS
Boutwell, Raymond O., Jr. ... Brookhaven, MS
Boutwell, Robert E., (P.A.)
Deerfield Beach, FL
Boutwell, Rufus C., Jr. ... Durham, NC
Boutwell, Sherrie M. ... Irvine, CA
Boutz, S. James ... Atlanta, GA
Boutzoukas, Michael E. ... Tampa, FL
Bouveron, Ernest A. ... Sequim, WA
Bouvette, Linda S. ... Taylorsville, KY
Bouvette, Ralph E. ... Shepherdsville, KY
Taylorsville, KY
Bouvier, Christopher B.
San Francisco, CA
Bouvier, Gerald ... Buffalo, NY
Bouvier, J. Peter ... San Francisco, CA
Bouvier, Joseph F. ... Westmont, NJ
Philadelphia, PA
Bouvier, Joseph T. ... Lexington, KY
Bouvier, Lynn A. ... North Smithfield, RI
Bouvier, O'Connor ... Buffalo, NY
Bouwens, James W. ... Holland, MI
Bouwens, Joel G. ... Holland, MI
Bouwer, Greg A. ... Merrillville, IN
Bouwers, Delia A. ... Pittsburgh, PA
Bouwkamp, Alan A. ... Indianapolis, IN
Bouwkamp, Stephen C. ... Livonia, MI
Bouxsein, Dennis G. ... Chicago, IL
Bouza, Cynthia Eder ... Los Angeles, CA
Bouzaglou, Lydia Ruth ... Orange, CA
Bouzane, John Edward ... San Bernardino, CA
Bouzari, Eloise Henderson ... Denver, CO
Bouzeos, Darcy L. ... Chicago, IL
Bova, Anthony M. ... Oakland, CA
Bova, Barry W. ... Bellevue, OH
Bova, Judith A. ... Santa Fe, NM
Bova, Karen ... Albuquerque, NM
Bova, V. Arthur, Jr. ... Albuquerque, NM
Bova-Hiatt, Lisa Ann ... New York, NY
Bovaird, Brendan P. ... King Of Prussia, PA
Bovan, Patricia M. ... Santa Clara, CA
Bovard, Gilbert K. ... Mason City, IA
Bovard, Kenneth C. ... Los Angeles, CA
Bovard, Mark E. ... Mattoon, IL
Bovard, Thomas A.
Department Of The Interior,
Office of the Solicitor, GV
Bovarnick, Bennett ... Pompano Beach, FL
Bovarnick, Bennett, P.A.
Pompano Beach, FL
Bovarnick, Karen Z. ... San Francisco, CA
Bovarnick, Paul S. ... Portland, OR
Bovarnick, Richard A. ... Denver, CO
Bovarnick, Robert M. ... Philadelphia, PA
Bovarnick, Steven H. ... San Francisco, CA
Bovasso, Louis J. ... Los Angeles, CA
Bovay, John C. ... Gainesville, FL
Bove, Alexander A., Jr. ... Boston, MA
Bove, Alexander A., Jr., P.C. ... Boston, MA
Bove, Beverly L. ... Wilmington, DE
Bové, Edward J. ... Rockville, MD
Bove, Emil J., Jr. ... Seneca Falls, NY
Bove, Frank J. ... Alexandria, VA
Bove & Fry ... Mansfield, OH
Bove, James J. ... Remsenburg, NY
Bove, Jeffrey B. ... Wilmington, DE
Bove, John G. ... New York, NY
Bove, John J. ... Norwalk, CT
Bove, John Jay ... Schenectady, NY
Bove, Josem & Josem ... Norwalk, CT
Bové, Kevin A. ... Escondido, CA
Bove, Leigh J. ... Haddonfield, NJ
Bové, Louis A. ... Cherry Hill, NJ
Philadelphia, PA
Bove, Matthew J. ... San Francisco, CA
Bove, Nicholas J., Jr. ... Stamford, CT
Bove, Patricia A. ... Chicago, IL
Bove, Ralph R. ... Mansfield, OH
Bove, Thomas F. ... Indianapolis, IN
Boveda, Olimpia T. ... Boston, MA
Bovee, Bonnie L. ... Southfield, MI
Bovee, Kenneth T. ... Leland, MI
Bovee, Lucinda R. ... Albuquerque, NM
Bovée, Megan E. ... Toledo, OH
Bovee, Michael R. ... Spencer, IA
Bovee, Philip S. ... Los Angeles, CA
Bovée, Scott A. ... Concord, CA
Bovee, Susan B.
Commodity Futures Trading Commission,
Division of Enforcement, GV
Bovee, Warren R. ... St. Paul, MN
Boveia, Gary J. ... Waverly, IA
Boveia Law Firm ... Waverly, IA
Boveland, Wilson C. ... New Orleans, LA
Bovell & Settle ... Chattanooga, TN
Bovell, Steve A. ... Chattanooga, TN
Boven, Douglas G. ... Oakland, CA
Boven, Thomas M. ... Grand Haven, MI
Bovender, William C. ... Johnson City, TN
Kingsport, TN
Bovenkamp, Christopher T. ... Dallas, TX
Bovenzi & Donovan ... Springfield, MA
Bovenzi, Giorgio ... New York, NY
Bovenzi, Moriarty & Mullaney
Leominster, MA
Bovenzi, Thomas M. ... Leominster, MA
Springfield, MA
Boveri, Mark D. ... South Bend, IN
Boverie, Glenda B. ... Lubbock, TX
Bovett, Robert E. ... Newport, OR
Bovey, Cary L. ... Round Rock, TX
Bovey, Richard O. ... Lafayette, IN
Bovia, Lester G., Jr. ... Chicago, IL
Bovich, John P. ... San Francisco, CA
Bovich, Valerie L. ... Chicago, IL
Bovie, George F., III ... Stuart, FL
Bovik, Erick A. ... Austin, TX
Bovill, John, III ... Saginaw, MI
Bovill, William S. ... Saginaw, MI
Bovilsky, Jay E. ... New Haven, CT
Bovino, Charles A. ... Garden City, NY
Bovino, Matthew A. ... Stamford, CT
Bovino, Scott C. ... Philadelphia, PA
Bovis, John M., (P.C.) ... Atlanta, GA
Bovis, Kyle & Burch, LLC ... Atlanta, GA
Bovitz, J. Scott ... Los Angeles, CA
Bovitz & Spitzer ... Los Angeles, CA
Bovone, Charles P. ... New York, NY
Bovos, Marc L. ... Poteau, OK
Bovshow, Aaron G. ... Canoga Park, CA
Bovshow, Robert ... Van Nuys, CA
Bovshow, Robert, A Prof. Corp.
Van Nuys, CA
Bovy, David L. ... Seattle, WA
Bovy, Wampold & Munro ... Seattle, WA
Bow, James ... San Francisco, CA
Bow, James T., II ... Portland, OR
Bow, Susan E. ... Calabasas, CA
Bowbeer, Hildy ... St. Paul, MN
Bowcock, Matthew H. ... Rhinebeck, NY
Bowcock & Morgan, L.L.P. ... Austin, TX
Bowcock, Patricia L. ... Austin, TX
Bowdach, Elliott J. ... Agoura Hills, CA
Bowden, A. Bruce ... Pittsburgh, PA
Bowden, Aaron K. ... Jacksonville, FL
Bowden, Albert J., III ... Tallahassee, FL
Bowden, Andrew J. ... Baltimore, MD
Bowden, Benjamin M. ... Andalusia, AL
Bowden, Benjamin U. ... Gulfport, MS
Bowden, Brett H. ... Ossining, NY
Bowden, C. Paul ... Tifton, GA
Bowden, C. Wade ... West Palm Beach, FL
Bowden, David H. ... Winston-Salem, NC
Bowden, David O. ... Little Rock, AR
Bowden, David O. ... Fairfax, VA
Bowden, Edwin W. ... Winston-Salem, NC
Bowden, Ellen M. ... Department of Justice,
Civil Rights Division, GV
Bowden, Elliott ... New York, NY
Bowden, George E., III
Treasury Department,
Internal Revenue Service, GV
Bowden, George N. ... Everett, WA
Bowden, Gerald D. ... Scotts Valley, CA
Bowden, Gloria K. ... Atlanta, GA
Bowden, Henry L., Jr. ... Atlanta, GA
Bowden, J. Thomas ... Ramona, CA
Bowden, J. Thomas ... Maitland, FL
Bowden, Janet Carol ... Rancho Santa Fe, CA
Bowden, Janine Coy ... Cynthiana, KY
Bowden, Jeanne Johnson ... Atlanta, GA
Bowden, John B. ... Spartanburg, SC
Bowden, John J. ... Minneapolis, MN
Bowden, John W. ... Chicago, IL
Bowden, Jon M. ... Houston, TX
Bowden, Kathleen M. ... Fort Myers, FL
Bowden, Kendel & Jones, PLLC
Little Rock, AR
Bowden, Kimberly L. ... Bala Cynwyd, PA
Bowden, Kurt M. ... Traverse City, MI
Bowden Law Firm, The, P.C. ... Atlanta, GA
Bowden, Leslie J. ... Kenwood, CA
Bowden, Matthew W. ... Birmingham, AL
Bowden, Michael M. ... Providence, RI
Bowden, Mona M. ... Iowa Falls, IA
Bowden, Otto R. T. ... Jacksonville, FL
Bowden, Peter C. ... Houston, TX
Bowden, Phyllis B. ... Goleta, CA
Bowden, Ralph T., Jr. ... Decatur, GA
Bowden, Richard B. ... Palo Alto, CA
Bowden, Robert L. ... Clayton, AL
Bowden, Stephanie M.L. ... Russellville, AR
Bowden, Stephanie M.L., P.A.
Russellville, AR
Bowden, Stephen S. ... Lewisburg, TN
Bowden, Steven W. ... Pensacola, FL
Bowden, Susan J. ... Stillwater, MN
Bowden, Teresa G. ... Winston-Salem, NC
Bowden, Thomas A. ... Baltimore, MD
Bowden, Tim L. ... Goodlettsville, TN
Bowden, Tracy H. ... Irving, TX
Bowden, Vivian G. ... Wilmington, DE
Bowden, Wendell L. ... Macon, GA
Bowden, William P. ... Wilmington, DE
Bowden, William P., Jr. ... New York, NY
Bowden, William R., Jr. ... Odessa, TX
Bowden-Hollis, Ann ... Gulfport, MS
Bowdery, Allan G. ... New York, NY
Bowdich, John W. ... Dallas, TX
Bowdish, James L. S. ... Stuart, FL
Bowditch & Dewey, LLP ... Boston, MA
Framingham, MA
Springfield, MA
Worcester, MA
Bowditch, James A. ... Missoula, MT
Bowditch, Lynn Spann ... Richmond, ME
Bowditch, Mark I. ... Washington, DC
Bowditch, René Roark ... Williamsburg, VA
Bowdoin, Douglas C. ... Orlando, FL
Bowdoin, E. Seavey ... Boston, MA
Bowdoin, W. Roderick, (P.A.)
Lake City, FL
Bowdre, J. Birch ... Birmingham, AL
Bowdre, Karon O. ... Birmingham, AL
Bowdren, Kelly A.M. ... Waltham, MA
Bowdry, Irene Patterson, Law Offices of
Moreno Valley, CA
Bowdry, Irene R. ... Moreno Valley, CA
Palm Desert, CA
Bowe, Ann T. ... Milwaukee, WI
Bowe, Caruso & Epstein, A Professional Corporation ... Neptune, NJ
Bowe, Curtis L., III ... Charlotte, NC
Bowe, Debra A. ... North Highlands, CA
Bowe, James F., Jr. ... Washington, DC
Bowe, James R. ... Tamaqua, PA
Bowe, Jeffrey P. ... Tamaqua, PA
Bowe, John J. ... Norwell, MA
Bowe, John J., Attorney at Law, P.C.
Norwell, MA
Bowe, Karolyn N. ... Elkton, MD
Bowe, Larry S. ... Hood River, OR
Bowe, Lisella & Bowe ... Tamaqua, PA
Bowe, Mary T. ... Boston, MA
Bowe, Michael J. ... New York, NY
Bowe, Michelle K. ... New York, NY
Bowe, Philip Paul ... San Francisco, CA
Bowe, Richard A. ... Guttenberg, NJ
Bowe, Richard W. ... Washington, DC
Bowe, Sara Jane ... Des Moines, IA
Bowe, Tracy Flynn ... St. Joseph, MN
Bowe, William J. ... Chicago, IL
Bowe, William J. ... Neptune, NJ
Bowe, William L. ... Philadelphia, PA
Bowein, Lloyd L. ... Naples, FL
Bowein, Lloyd L., P.A. ... Naples, FL
Bowen, Alanson G., Jr. ... Wilmington, DE
Bowen, Albert C., Jr. ... Birmingham, AL
Bowen, Albert R. ... Parkton, MD
Bowen, Alden Earl ... Pittsburgh, PA
Bowen, Anita ... New York, NY
Bowen, Ann L. ... New York, NY
Bowen, Anne-Marie L. ... Atlanta, GA
Bowen & Associates ... Houston, TX
Bowen, Berry D. ... Houston, TX
Bowen & Berry, PLLC ... Lumberton, NC
Bowen & Bowen ... Columbus, OH
Bowen, Bowen & Bowen, P.C.
Tazewell, VA
Bowen, Bradley Wm. ... Salt Lake City, UT
Bowen, Brian K. ... Plymouth, MA
Bowen, Bruce ... Reno, NV
Bowen, C. Ben ... Greenville, SC
Bowen & Campione, P.A. ... Vero Beach, FL
Bowen, Carl P. ... Miami, FL
Bowen, Carol Ewald ... Charlotte, NC
Bowen, Carolyn R. ... Bronx, NY
Bowen, Cary B. ... Richmond, VA
Bowen, Chad S. ... Tampa, FL
Bowen, Charles B., Jr. ... Greenville, SC
Bowen, Charles H. ... Half Moon Bay, CA
Bowen, Charles P. ... Bozeman, MT
Bowen, Charles S. ... Binghamton, NY
Bowen, Christopher K. ... New York, NY
Bowen, Christopher R. ... Richmond, CA
Bowen & Cohen ... Newton, MA
Bowen, Colin T. ... Oakland, CA
Bowen, Dan C. ... Reno, NV
Bowen, Dana C. ... Wagoner, OK
Bowen, Daniel A. ... Temple, TX
Bowen, Daniel C. ... Fullerton, CA
Bowen, Darrell L. ... Plattsburgh, NY
Bowen, David C. ... Norfolk, VA
Bowen, David F. ... Pittsford, NY
Bowen, David N. ... Washington, DC
Bowen, David R. ... Salt Lake City, UT
Bowen, David T. ... Muskegon, MI
Bowen, Debra L. ... Redondo Beach, CA
Bowen, Deirdre M. ... Washington, DC
Bowen, Donald H. ... Camano, WA
Bowen, Donald R. ... Hazel Park, MI
Bowen, Donna J. ... Austin, TX
Bowen, Duane C. ... Carlsbad, CA
Bowen, Dudley H., Jr. ... Augusta, GA
Bowen, Dwight R. ... Idaho Falls, ID
Bowen, E. Howland ... Little Compton, RI
Providence, RI
Bowen, Eddie H. ... Raleigh, MS
Bowen, Edward J. ... Hackensack, NJ
Bowen, Elizabeth Karen
Department of the Army,
Office, Chief of Engineers/Headquarters,
U.S. Army Corps of Engineers, GV
Bowen, Eric A. ... Montgomery, AL
Bowen, Forrest A. ... Bridgeport, WV
Bowen, Frances C. ... Binghamton, NY
Bowen, Frank M. ... St. Helena, CA
Bowen, Frederick ... Department of Labor,
Office of the Solicitor, GV
Bowen, G. Thomas ... Salem, NJ
Bowen, Gary L. ... Houston, TX
Bowen, Gary N. ... Baltimore, MD
Bowen, Gene P. ... Troy, MI
Bowen, Gerald L. ... Elkins Park, PA
Bowen, Geraldine S. ... Newark, NJ
Bowen, Glenn W. ... Eagan, MN
Bowen, Henry C. ... Charleston, WV
Bowen, Howard Wesley ... Jackson, MS
Bowen, J. Donald ... Houston, TX
Bowen, J. Thomas ... Las Vegas, NV
Bowen, J. Thomas ... Midvale, UT
Salt Lake City, UT
Bowen, Jack E. ... Lake Worth, FL
Bowen, James A. ... Juneau, AK
Bowen, James B. ... Phoenix, AZ
Bowen, James C. ... Doylestown, PA
Bowen, James Carl ... Tulsa, OK
Bowen, James Curran Davis ... Atlanta, GA
Bowen, James L. ... Weatherford, TX
Bowen, James M. ... Santa Fe, NM
Bowen, James M. ... New York, NY
Bowen, James M. ... Rutherfordton, NC
Bowen, James T., III ... Lincolnton, NC
Bowen, James W. ... Dallas, TX
Bowen, Jay S. ... Nashville, TN
Bowen, Jeffrey H. ... Rochester, NY
Bowen, Jennifer D. ... Buffalo, NY
Bowen, Jerome R. ... Las Vegas, NV
Bowen, Joan M. ... Wichita, KS
Bowen, Jo-Ann Leigh ... Boise, ID
Bowen, Joanna F. ... Darien, CT
Bowen, Joe M. ... Tazewell, VA
Bowen, John A. ... Fitchburg, MA
Bowen, John E. ... Vacaville, CA
Bowen, John E. ... Boston, MA
Bowen, John F. ... Minneapolis, MN
Bowen, John R. C.
Hilton Head Island, SC
Bowen, John W. ... Largo, FL
Bowen, John W., III ... Valparaiso, FL
Bowen, John W. E. ... Columbus, OH
Bowen, John W.E., IV ... Columbus, OH
Bowen, Joseph D. ... Mount Vernon, WA
Bowen, Joy Hand, (P.C.) ... Lithia Springs, GA
Bowen, Julia A. ... Herndon, VA
Bowen, Karen L. ... San Francisco, CA
Bowen, Kate ... Blue Bell, PA
Bowen, Kenneth B. ... Northampton, MA
Bowen, Kenneth D. ... Kansas City, MO
Bowen, Kenneth R. ... New Orleans, LA
Bowen, Kevin F. ... Providence, RI
Bowen, Kim ... Hartford, CT
Bowen, Krista R. ... Charlotte, NC
Bowen, L. Irene ... Department of Justice,
Civil Rights Division, GV
Bowen, Lawrence H. ... Fairfax, VA
Bowen, Lecora ... College Park, GA
Bowen, Lennon E., III ... Eustis, FL

Bowen, Leslie ... **Costa Mesa, CA**
Bowen, Leslie Charles, (Mr.) ... Muskegon, MI
Bowen Lhota & Firtell, P.A.
Fort Lauderdale, FL
Pompano Beach, FL
Bowen, Lisa J. ... **Alexandria, MN**
Bowen, Lisa R. ... Twinsburg, OH
Bowen, Lori A. ... Wilkes-Barre, PA
Bowen, Louis R., Jr. ... Winter Park, FL
Bowen, Lowell R. ... **Baltimore, MD**
Bowen, M. John, Jr. ... **Columbia, SC**
Bowen, Magdalena "Mitzi" Cain
Bozeman, MT
Bowen, Margretta Jeffers ... New York, NY
Bowen, Mark David ... **Pompano Beach, FL**
Bowen, Mark Holdsworth ... Pikesville, MD
Bowen, Martin W. ... **Little Rock, AR**
Bowen, Maurice R., Jr. ... **Chattanooga, TN**
Bowen, McKenzie and Bowen
Greenville, SC
Bowen, Michael A. ... **Milwaukee, WI**
Bowen, Michael G. ... Doylestown, PA
Bowen, Michael G. ... Midlothian, VA
Bowen, Michael G., & Associates
Doylestown, PA
Bowen, Michael L. ... Titusville, FL
Bowen, Michael P. ... New York, NY
Bowen, Michael S. ... **Bloomington, IL**
Bowen, Nancy T. ... **Houston, TX**
Bowen, Neal D. ... Kissimmee, FL
Bowen, Pat Kerry ... Simi Valley, CA
Bowen, Patrick H. ... Bridgeport, CT
Bowen, Paul H. ... **Tampa, FL**
Bowen, Paul H., P.A. ... **Tampa, FL**
Bowen, Paul T. ... **Alexandria, VA**
Bowen, Perry G., Jr. ... Prince Frederick, MD
Bowen, Philip M. ... Omaha, NE
Bowen, Phillip C. ... **El Paso, TX**
Bowen, Phillip J. ... **Ann Arbor, MI**
Bowen, R. William ... San Diego, CA
Bowen, Radabaugh, Milton & Brown, P.C.
Detroit, MI
Troy, MI
Bowen, Randall K. ... **Alexandria, VA**
Bowen, Ray B., Jr. ... Tarzana, CA
Bowen, Rees T., III ... **Dallas, TX**
Bowen, Richard ... **Boston, MA**
Bowen, Richard A. ... St. Paul, MN
Bowen, Richard D. ... **Booneville, MS**
Bowen, Richard John ... Andover, MA
Bowen, Richard K. ... **Springfield, VT**
Bowen Riley Warnock & Jacobson, PLC
Nashville, TN
Bowen, Robert B. ... Lunenburg, MA
Bowen, Robert E. ... Minneapolis, MN
Bowen, Robert J. ... **Lynchburg, VA**
Bowen, Robert M. ... Chanhassen, MN
Bowen, Robert O. ... Plymouth, IN
Bowen, Robin R. ... **Hendersonville, NC**
Bowen & Rutty, P.C. ... Bronx, NY
Bowen, Sara A. ... Milwaukee, WI
Bowen, Scott W. ... **Los Angeles, CA**
Bowen, Sean A. H. ... **Kingsport, TN**
Bowen, Sharon Y. ... **New York, NY**
Bowen, Sherfield P. ... Bronx, NY
Bowen & Siegel ... **Northampton, MA**
Bowen, Stephanie ... **San Luis Obispo, CA**
Bowen, Stephen D., III ... Columbia, SC
Bowen, Stephen P. ... **San Francisco, CA**
Bowen, Stephen S. ... **Chicago, IL**
Bowen, Stephen W. ... **Tucumcari, NM**
Bowen, Steven Holmes ... Lowell, MA
Bowen, Stuart W., Jr. ... Austin, TX
Bowen, Tammy L., P.C. ... Savannah, GA
Bowen, Tammy Lee ... Savannah, GA
Bowen, T. C., III ... **Tazewell, VA**
Bowen, T. C., Jr. ... **Tazewell, VA**
Bowen, Ted B. ... Yuma, AZ
Bowen, Terry D. ... Prattville, AL
Bowen, Terry R. ... **Chicago, IL**
Bowen, Thomas A. ... Harrisburg, PA
Bowen, Thomas R. ... **Troy, MI**
Bowen, Travis L. ... Idaho Falls, ID
Salt Lake City, UT
Bowen, Travis L., P.C. ... Idaho Falls, ID
Salt Lake City, UT
Bowen, Valerie H. ... Norfolk, VA
Bowen, Veronica L. ... **Rapid City, SD**
Bowen, Vincent ... **Washington, DC**
Bowen, Vinton D. ... Newton, MA
Bowen, W. Andrew ... **Savannah, GA**
Bowen, Wes ... Memphis, TN
Bowen, Wiley F. ... Dunn, NC
Bowen, Willard G. ... Richmond, IN
Bowen, William A. ... Aberdeen, SD
Bowen, William C. ... Olney, IL
Bowen, William D. ... Milan, TN
Bowen, William H. ... Little Rock, AR
Bowen, William L. ... Middletown, OH
Bowen, William M.
Hilton Head Island, SC
Bowen, William M., Jr. ... **Birmingham, AL**
Bowen, William M., P.A. ... **Beaufort, SC**
Hilton Head Island, SC
Bowen, William T. ... Des Moines, IA
Bowen, Woodberry L. ... **Lumberton, NC**
Bowens, Florence A. ... Durham, NC
Bowens, John M. ... **Bedminster, NJ**
Bowens, Marilyn ... Durham, NC
Bowens, Robert Laurence ... Framingham, MA
Bowens, Sandra Walton ... Memphis, TN
Bowens, Stephon John ... Smithfield, NC
Bowen-Slaven, Lisa M. ... **Fort Wayne, IN**
LaGrange, IN
Bower, Allan M. ... **Santa Monica, CA**
Bower, Amelia A. ... Cleveland, OH
Bower, Anita M. ... **Los Angeles, CA**
Bower, Ann ... Austin, TX
Bower, Barbara K. ... Junction City, OR
Bower, Barbara K., P.C. ... Junction City, OR
Bower, Barbara L. ... **Pittsburgh, PA**
Bower, Beth Romans ... **Kansas City, MO**
Bower, Blair A. ... Millersburg, OH
Bower & Bower ... Oklahoma City, OK
Bower, Brian L. ... **Charleston, IL**
Bower, Bruce Duncan ... Pleasanton, CA
Bower, Bruce L. ... **Chicago, IL**
Bower, Bryant H. ... Fitzgerald, GA
Bower, Bryant H., Jr. ... **Waycross, GA**
Bower, David ... River Rouge, MI
Bower, David A. ... Bangor, ME
Bower, David E. ... Santa Monica, CA
Bower, David H. ... Oklahoma City, OK
Bower, David I. ... **Washington, DC**
Bower, Dennis H. ... **Berwyn, PA**
Bower, Diane Y. ... **Jackson, MI**
Bower, Earl W. ... St. Clair Shores, MI
Bower, Eileen King ... **Chicago, IL**
Bower & Falk ... Kentland, IN
Bower, Frederick J. ... Frederick, MD
Bower, George C., Jr. ... **Wadesboro, NC**
Bower, Glen L. ... Chicago, IL
Bower, Glenn L. ... **Dayton, OH**
Bower Greer & Panzarella, PC ... **Erie, PA**
Greensburg, PA
Harrisburg, PA
Pittsburgh, PA
Sharon, PA
Washington, PA
Bower, Greg H. ... Boise, ID
Bower, Henry E. ... **Houston, TX**
Bower, Hubert O. ... Yuba City, CA
Bower, J. Leeds ... **Charleston, IL**
Bower, J. Patrick ... **Clarksburg, WV**
Bower, James H. ... Bloomfield Hills, MI
Bower, Jean R. ... Washington, DC
Bower, Jeffrey M. ... State College, PA
Bower, John E., Jr. ... **Los Angeles, CA**
Bower, John J. ... **New York, NY**
Bower, Joseph D. ... Pueblo, CO
Bower, Joseph Sidney ... **Kinston, NC**
Bower, Karen A. ... **Washington, DC**
Bower, Kathy S. ... **Bethel, CT**
Southbury, CT
Waterbury, CT
Bower, Keith C., Law Offices of
Santa Clara, CA
Bower, Kenneth J. ... **Galveston, TX**
Bower, Lennox C. ... Dallas, TX
Bower, Mark D. ... **Columbia, SC**
Bower, Mark R. ... **New York, NY**
Bower, Marshall T. ... Bradenton, FL
Bower, Mary E. ... Pittsburgh, PA
Bower, N. Russell ... Panama City, FL
Bower, Pamela A. ... **Redwood City, CA**
Bower & Parker ... Bozeman, MT
Bower, Patricia W. ... **Casselberry, FL**
Bower, Paul G. ... **Los Angeles, CA**
Bower, Peter R. ... **New York, NY**
Bower, Philip A. ... Morgantown, WV
Bower, R. Bruce ... **Atlanta, GA**
Bower, Ralph ... Kentland, IN
Bower, Raymond C. ... Carmel, IN
Bower, Richard E. ... Connellsville, PA
Bower, Richard W. ... Sacramento, CA
Bower, Robert A. ... **Chicago, IL**
Bower, Robert S. ... **Costa Mesa, CA**
Bower, Robert W., Jr. ... **Portland, ME**
Bower, Sandra S. ... Jacksonville, FL
Bower Sanger & Futterman, P.C.
New York, NY
Bower, Stephen C. ... **Merrillville, IN**
Bower, Susan ... **Palo Alto, CA**
Bower, Terry L. ... Akron, OH
Bower, Theodore D. ... Chicago, IL
Bower, Thomas K. ... Dallas, TX
Bower, Thomas L., III ... Gainesville, GA
Bower, Thomas M. ... **Lake Success, NY**
New York, NY
Bower, Thomas N. ... Waterloo, IA
Bower, Walter M., P.C. ... Oklahoma City, OK
Bower, Ward ... Newtown Square, PA
Bower, William A. ... **San Diego, CA**
Bower, William B. ... **Chicago, IL**
Bower, William J., III ... Baltimore, MD
Bowerbank, W. W. ... Salt Lake City, UT
Bowerfind, Robin B. ... **Baltimore, MD**
Bowerman, Bowden & Moothart, P.C.
Traverse City, MI
Bowerman, Cathy Rogers ... **Southfield, MI**
Bowerman, Donald B. ... Oregon City, OR
Bowerman, Faust N. ... Dallas, TX
Bowerman, Gary L. ... **Traverse City, MI**
Bowerman, Larry K. ... Plymouth, MI
Bowerman, Michael E. ... Virginia Beach, VA
Bowerman, Neil Edwin ... Minneapolis, MN
Bowerman, Richard H. ... West Haven, CT
Bowerman, Richard W. ... **New Haven, CT**
Bowerman, Ronald A. ... Des Moines, IA
Bowerman, Seth E. ... **Providence, RI**
Bowerman & Willis ... Virginia Beach, VA
Bowers, Albert D. ... **Washington, DC**
Bowers, Alicia Almeida ... **Charlotte, NC**
Bowers, Angela P. ... Anniston, AL
Bowers, Anthony J. ... Lima, OH
Bowers, Barbara J. ... **Lexington, KY**
Bowers, Barrie Biddison ... Richmond, VA
Bowers, Beverly B. ... Harrisonburg, VA
Bowers, Bill E. ... **Fort Worth, TX**
Bowers, Bob W. ... **Lexington, NC**
Bowers, Booth H. ... Oceanside, CA
Bowers & Bowers ... Clanton, AL
Bowers & Bowers ... New Orleans, LA
Bowers, Bowers & Mastin
New Philadelphia, OH
Bowers, Brenda K. ... Columbus, OH
Bowers, Brewer, Garrett & Wiley
Huntington, IN
Warren, IN
Bowers, Brock C. ... **Oklahoma City, OK**
Bowers, Burt A. ... Shreveport, LA
Bowers, Burt A., A Prof. Law Corp.
Shreveport, LA
Bowers, Burton W. ... Ottawa, KS
Bowers, Carl W. ... Marietta, GA
Bowers, Caryl M. ... **Bloomington, IN**
Bowers, Catherine M. ... **Warrenton, VA**
Bowers, Charles Allston ... **Cleveland, OH**
Bowers, Charles F., Jr. ... Ambridge, PA
Bowers, Charles Fredric, III ... Ambridge, PA
Bowers, Charles R. ... **Portland, OR**
Bowers, Christopher D. ... Dallas, TX
Bowers, Dan R. ... Harrison, AR
Bowers, Dana L. ... Medford, MA
Bowers, Daniel H. ... **Kansas City, MO**
Bowers, David ... Galveston, TX
Bowers, David A. ... Arnold, MD
Bowers, David A. ... **Jackson, MS**
Bowers, David A. ... **Roanoke, VA**
Bowers, David Alan ... **Schaumburg, IL**
Bowers, David C. ... **Macon, GA**
Bowers, David F. ... **West Palm Beach, FL**
Bowers, David E. ... Lima, OH
Bowers, David L. ... Towson, MD
Bowers, Deborah J. ... **Greensboro, NC**
Bowers, Debra A. ... **Morgantown, WV**
Bowers, Debra Lee ... Philadelphia, PA
Bowers, Donald J. ... **Bridgeport, CT**
Bowers, Donald S. ... Fort Smith, AR
Bowers, Edgar R. ... Oak Ridge, TN
Bowers, Edmond F. ... **Medina, OH**
Bowers, Edward B., Jr. ... **Myrtle Beach, SC**
Bowers, F. Daniel ... Buffalo, NY
Bowers, F. Wesley ... **Evansville, IN**
Bowers, Forrest, P.C. ... **Lubbock, TX**
Bowers, Fred ... **Lubbock, TX**
Bowers, Gary A. ... Shreveport, LA
Bowers, Gary R. ... Raleigh, NC
Bowers, Gerald Roger ... Philadelphia, PA
Bowers, Glenn ... **Columbia, SC**
Bowers, Gordon G., Jr. ... Waconia, MN
Bowers, Gregory H. ... Elizabethton, TN
Bowers, Gwendolyn Ruth ... Dayton, OH
Bowers, H. Alan ... Des Moines, IA
Bowers, H. Michael ... **Charleston, SC**
Bowers, H. Paxton ... Bloomington, IL
Bowers, H. Thad ... New Philadelphia, OH
Bowers, Harold F., Jr. ... Wadsworth, OH
Bowers, Harrison, Kent & Miller, LLP
Evansville, IN
Bowers, Herbert B., III ... New Orleans, LA
Bowers, J. David ... **Kansas City, MO**
Bowers, Jack E. ... Villa Park, IL
Bowers, Jack W. ... Knoxville, TN
Bowers, James C., Jr. ... **Kansas City, MO**
Bowers, James H. ... **Babylon, NY**
New City, NY
Bowers, James L., Jr. ... Chicago, IL
Bowers, James R. ... **Des Moines, IA**
Bowers, James W. ... **Huntington, IN**
Warren, IN
Bowers, James W. ... Purchase, NY
Bowers, James W. ... Lubbock, TX
Bowers, Jeanette M. ... **Kirkland, WA**
Bowers, Jeffrey S. ... **Franklin, WV**
Bowers, Jeryl A. ... **Los Angeles, CA**
Bowers, Jill ... Sacramento, CA
Bowers, John ... San Francisco, CA
Bowers, John E. ... Circleville, OH
Bowers, John H. ... Madison, WI
Bowers, John J. ... **Winston-Salem, NC**
Bowers, John L., III ... Elizabethton, TN
Bowers, John L., Jr. ... Elizabethton, TN
Bowers, John M. ... **Los Angeles, CA**
Bowers, John M. ... Minneapolis, MN
Bowers, John S. ...
Department Of Health And Human Services, GV
Bowers, John S. ... Columbus, OH
Bowers, John W ... **Fort Wayne, IN**
Bowers, John W. ... **Charlotte, NC**
Bowers, Joshua F. ... Washington, DC
Bowers, Joshua F., P.C., Law Offices of
Washington, DC
Bowers, Joyce M. ... Parsippany, NJ
Bowers, Karl S. ... **Columbia, SC**
Bowers, Keith D. ... Herkimer, NY
Bowers, Kelly C. ... Los Angeles, CA
Bowers, Kellye J. ... **Cincinnati, OH**
Bowers, Kenneth R., Jr. ... Phoenix, AZ
Bowers, Kent ... Harrisonburg, VA
Bowers, Kimberly S. ... **San Antonio, TX**
Bowers, Kirsten Hughes ... Hillsboro, OR
Bowers, Lacie L. ... Las Vegas, NV
Bowers Law Office ... **Lubbock, TX**
Bowers, Lawrence D., Jr. ... Harrisonburg, VA
Bowers, Lawrence R. ... Wellesley, MA
Bowers, Lee M., II ... **Huntington, IN**
Warren, IN
Bowers, Lee S. ... Estill, SC
Bowers, Lesly A. ... Columbia, SC
Bowers, Lynn A. ... **Washington, DC**
Bowers, Margaret M. ... Dearborn, MI
Bowers, Mark E. ... Beverly Hills, CA
Bowers, Mark E., Law Office of
Beverly Hills, CA
Bowers, Martin J. E. ... Lynbrook, NY
Bowers, Melody A. ... Fort Myers, FL
Bowers, Michael J. ... **Atlanta, GA**
Bowers, Michelle D. ... **Chicago, IL**
Bowers, Mikel J., (P.C.) ... **Dallas, TX**
Bowers, Murphy, Lieberman & Lambo
Somerville, NJ
Bowers, Neal E. ... Lodi, OH
Bowers Orr & Dougall, L.L.P.
Columbia, SC
Bowers, Patricia A. ... Austin, TX
Bowers, Patricia Nalley ... New Orleans, LA
Bowers, Peter C. ... Philadelphia, PA
Bowers, Peter C., & Associates, P.C.
Philadelphia, PA
Bowers, Philip R. ... **Atlanta, GA**
Bowers, Phillipa L. ... New Orleans, LA
Bowers, Quinton R. ... Birmingham, AL
Bowers, Ralph E. ... Lake Forest, IL
Bowers, Richard Allen ... Lakewood, CO
Bowers, Richard E. ... Alpine, TX
Bowers, Richard K., Jr. ... **Tampa, FL**
Bowers, Richard L. ... Morgan Hill, CA
Bowers, Richard M. ... DeLancey, NY
Bowers, Richard N. ... **New York, NY**
Bowers, Richard S., Jr. ... **Elkhart, IN**
Bowers, Richard W. ... Sunrise, FL
Bowers, Robert C. ... **Winston-Salem, NC**
Bowers, Robert D. ... Nashville, IL
Bowers, Robert E., Jr. ... **New London, NH**
Bowers, Robert G. ... El Cajon, CA
Bowers, Robert G. ... New Bern, NC
Bowers, Robert J. ... **Cleveland, OH**
Bowers, Robert L. ... Clanton, AL
Bowers, Robert L., Jr. ... Clanton, AL
Bowers, Robert S. ... Fairfield, CA
Bowers, Robert Vic, Jr. ... **Owensboro, KY**
Bowers, Robt. F. ... Marco Island, FL
Bowers, Roger Gallup ... **Richmond, VA**
Bowers, Ronald E. ... Los Angeles, CA
Bowers, Ronald J. ... Salisbury, NC
Bowers, Russell E. ... **Flint, MI**
Bowers, Sally A. ... St. Louis, MO
Bowers, Sarah Clark ... Sylacauga, AL
Bowers, Scott R. ... Evansville, IN
Bowers, Sheldon ... Montpelier, VT
Bowers, Sherry Barnette ... Truckee, CA
Bowers, Stacey L. ... **Denver, CO**
Bowers, Stacey V. ... Chicago, IL
Bowers, Stephen A. ... **Woodland Hills, CA**
Bowers, Stephen Michael ... **Atlanta, GA**
Bowers, Stephen R. ... Elkhart, IN
Bowers, Steven M. ... Austin, TX
Bowers & Stevenson, P.C.
Fort Worth, TX
Bowers, Susan ...
Department of Education, GV
Bowers, Susan L. ... Shreveport, LA
Bowers, Terree Allan ... Los Angeles, CA
Bowers, Theodore R. ... Panama City, FL
Bowers, Thomas ... Bloomington, IN
Bowers, Thomas J., III ... El Dorado Hills, CA
Honolulu, HI
Bowers, Todd ... **Dallas, TX**
Bowers, Todd A. ... Seattle, WA
Bowers, Verner L., Jr. ... Palacios, TX
Bowers, Vicki J. ... **Jacksonville, FL**
Bowers, W. Kent ... Harrisonburg, VA
Bowers, W. Reynolds ... **Rochester, NY**
Bowers, William C. ... **New York, NY**
Bowers, William L., Jr. ... **Houston, TX**
Bowers, William P. ... **Dallas, TX**
Bowers, Wm. E. ... Minneapolis, MN
Bowers, Wm. O., III ... San Antonio, TX
Bowers, Wm. S. ... Ottawa, KS
Bowersock, Barbara E. ... Van Nuys, CA
Bowersock, Richard K. ... **Wichita Falls, TX**
Bowersock, W. Scott ... Santa Monica, CA
Bowersox, Barbara G.
Oklahoma City, OK
Bowersox, Brian M. ... Westminster, MD
Bowersox, David K. ... **Westminster, MD**
Bowersox, Jeffrey A. ... Lake Oswego, OR
Bowersox, Kim C. ... Monterey, CA
Bowersox & Ostrander ... Westminster, MD
Bowersox, Thomas H. ... **Conroe, TX**
Bowersox, W. Timothy ... **Conroe, TX**
Bowes, Alan T. ... New York, NY
Bowes & Associates, P.C. ... Pittsburgh, PA
Bowes, Bonnie L. ... **Dallas, TX**
Bowes, Brian P. ... **Monroe, LA**
Bowes, Charles A., Jr. ... **Allentown, PA**
Bowes, Charles F. ... **Houston, TX**
Bowes, Cheri Lane ... New York, NY
Bowes, Donald C. ... Troy, NY
Bowes, Fred S. ... Gretna, LA
Bowes, Gregory P. ... Indianapolis, IN
Bowes, Hallinan & Derosier ... Salem, MA
Bowes, James ... Parlin, NJ
Bowes, Jerry J. ... Sylmar, CA
Bowes, John C. ... Lakewood, CO
Bowes, John J. ... Oxford, MA
Bowes, Karen J. ... Chicago, IL
Bowes, Leslie P. ... Berwyn, PA
Bowes, Mary Jane ... Pittsburgh, PA
Bowes, Patricia Crehan ... Alpharetta, GA
Bowes, Perkins & Hutchison, P.C.
Indianapolis, IN
Bowes, Robert C. ... Cleveland, OH
Bowes, Robert D., Sr. ... Boston, MA
Bowes, Roy M. ... Gretna, LA
Bowes, Thomas F. ... Plympton, MA
Bowes, Thomas P. ... **Houston, TX**
Bowes, William P., Jr. ... **Houston, TX**
Bowhan, Brett R. ... Idaho Falls, ID
Bowhay, James H. ... **Chicago, IL**
Bowick, Stephanie M. ... Oakland, CA
Bowie, A. Gwynn, Jr. ... **Annapolis, MD**
Baltimore, MD
Bowie, Alexander ... Newport Beach, CA
Bowie, April D. ... Miami, FL
Bowie Arneson Wiles & Giannone
Newport Beach, CA
Bowie & Bruegmann ... Walnut Creek, CA
Bowie, C. Keating ... **Baltimore, MD**
Bowie, Candace H. ... Boulder, CO

Bowman, Phyllis Huang ....Albuquerque, NM
Bowman, Quinton V. ....Washington, DC
Bowman, R. H. Tibaut, P.C.
San Antonio, TX
Bowman, Rebecca Anne ....McMurray, PA
Bowman, Rebecca D. ....Auburn, CA
Bowman, Rebecca G. ....Baltimore, MD
Bowman, Reddick A., Jr. ....Orangeburg, SC
Bowman, Reid C. ....Morristown, NJ
Bowman, R. H. Tibaut ....San Antonio, TX
Bowman, Richard A. ....Minneapolis, MN
Bowman, Richard P. ....New York, NY
Bowman, Robert A. ....Frankfort, KY
Bowman, Robert L. ....Knoxville, TN
Bowman, Roberta K.
Department of Defense,
Defense Legal Services Agency, GV
Bowman & Robinson, Ltd. ....Reno, NV
Bowman, Robyn Katzman
Harrisburg, PA
Bowman, Rodger N. ....Clarksville, TN
Bowman, Ronald ....International Falls, MN
Bowman, Roy G. ....Washington, DC
Bowman, Royce V., Jr. ....Mount Clemens, MI
Bowman, Russell J. ....Dallas, TX
Bowman, S. Andrew ....Indianapolis, IN
Bowman, Scott ....Memphis, TN
Bowman, Scott G. ....Minneapolis, MN
Bowman, Scott M. ....Salem, OH
Bowman, Sharon C. ....Dallas, TX
Bowman, Sheila N. ....Saipan, TT
Bowman & Smith, P.C. ....Phoenix, AZ
Yuma, AZ
Bowman, Stacy H. ....Bakersfield, CA
Bowman, Stanley D. ....Redondo Beach, CA
Bowman, Stephen L. ....Dallas, TX
Bowman, Stephen M. ....Ithaca, NY
Bowman, Steven C. ....Boise, ID
Bowman, Susan D. ....Morristown, NJ
Bowman, Susan L. ....Seneca, KS
Bowman, Tamra L. ....Santa Monica, CA
Bowman, Terri L. ....Cleveland, OH
Bowman, Theodore A. ....Toledo, OH
Bowman, Thomas A. ....Conyers, GA
Bowman, Thomas G. ....Corpus Christi, TX
Bowman, Thomas M. ....Battle Creek, MI
Bowman, Timothy M. ....Painesville, OH
Bowman, Tom J. ....Richmond, MO
Bowman & Tracey, LLP ....Bakersfield, CA
Bowman, Victor L. ....Detroit, MI
Bowman, Walter D. ....Buffalo, NY
Bowman, Walter W. ....Beltsville, MD
Bowman, William ....San Francisco, CA
Bowman, William ....New York, NY
Bowman, William Hammond, III
Columbia, SC
Bowman, William J. ....Washington, DC
Bowman, William J., Jr. ....Charlotte, NC
Bowman, William S. ....Louisville, KY
Bowmar, Larkin, Lilly & Barton, P.C.
Ayer, MA
Littleton, MA
Bowmar, Robert Henry ....Albany, NY
Bowmer, Carl F. ....Richmond, VA
Bowmer, Jim D. ....Temple, TX
Bown, David M. ....Salt Lake City, UT
Bown, Jill A. ....Ambler, PA
Bown, Paul ....Springfield, IL
Bown, Robert T. ....North Haven, CT
Bownas, James H. ....Columbus, OH
Bownas, Pearson N. ....Cleveland, OH
Bowne, Blaine ....Denver, CO
Bowne, J. Thomas ....Santa Ana, CA
Bowne, Laura L. ....Houston, TX
Bowne, Lynn D. ....Owosso, MI
Bowne, Robert R. ....Burbank, CA
Bowne, Robert R., II ....Burbank, CA
Bowne, William H., III
Department of Justice,
Criminal Division, GV
Bownes, Hugh H. ....Boston, MA
Bownes, Michael A. ....Montgomery, AL
Bownes, Carmela M. ....Pacific Grove, CA
Bowring, Douglas B. ....Edgartown, MA
Bowron, Bushnell & Henderson
Birmingham, AL
Bowron, Edward G. Isaacs ....Mobile, AL
Bowron, Frank L. ....Casper, WY
Bowron, Harold A., III ....Birmingham, AL
Bowron, Harold A., Jr. ....Birmingham, AL
Bowron, Leah Harper ....Birmingham, AL
Bowron, Les ....Casper, WY
Bowron, Robert H., Jr. ....Birmingham, AL
Bowron, Scott G. ....Dorr, MI
Bowron, Thomas W., II ....Birmingham, AL
Bowron, William C. ....Traverse City, MI
Bowron-White, Susan C. ....Indianapolis, IN
Bows, Harry I. ....Concord, CA
Bowse, Michael A. ....San Diego, CA
Bowser, Alan Steele ....Silver Spring, MD
Bowser, Angela P. ....Richmond, VA
Bowser, Charles H. ....Lexington Park, MD
Bowser, Charles J., Jr. ....Boston, MA
Bowser, Charles W. ....Philadelphia, PA
Bowser, Danielle Gotwols ....Miami, FL
Bowser, Elmer Earl, Jr.
New Martinsville, WV
Bowser, Kyle D. ....Van Nuys, CA
Bowser, Leslie A. Gorman ....Manlius, NY
Bowser, Patrick Arthur ....Lubbock, TX
Bowser, Philip G., Jr. ....San Francisco, CA
Bowser, Renee Luvonia ....Washington, DC
Bowser, Richard ....Sacramento, CA
Bowser, Richard Thomas ....Buies Creek, NC
Bowser, Sharyn Shaw ....Tallmadge, OH
Bowser, William D. ....Sonoma, CA
Bowser, William E. ....Kalamazoo, MI
Bowser, William W. ....Wilmington, DE
Bowsher, John M. ....Columbus, OH
Bowsher, Matthew R. ....Washington, DC
Bowsher, Robert T. ....Baton Rouge, LA
Bowshier, Stephen J. ....Grove City, OH
Bowsman, Thomas E. ....Tallahassee, FL
Bowyer, Brent ....Berkley, MI
Bowyer, Charles T. ....Towson, MD
Bowyer, Elizabeth A. ....Brookline, MA
Bowyer, Raymond C. ....Walton, IN
Bowyer, Timothy E. ....Braselton, GA
Bowytz, Eliot Glantz ....Leesburg, VA
Bowytz Law Group ....Washington, DC
Bethesda, MD
Bowytz, Robert B. ....Washington, DC
Bethesda, MD
Bowytz, Steven H. ....Pittsburgh, PA
Bowz, Danny N. ....Metairie, LA
Box, Anne Louise ....Dallas, TX
Box, Bennett A. ....Edmonds, WA
Box and Box ....Ottumwa, IA
Box, Bradford David ....Jackson, TN
Box, Charles E. ....Rockford, IL
Box, Craig L. ....Enid, OK
Box, David A. ....Claremore, OK
Box, Dennis R. ....Oklahoma City, OK
Box, Dwain D. ....Oklahoma City, OK
Box, Gary ....Edmonds, WA
Box, Gaylen L. ....Pocatello, ID
Box, Glenn E. ....Dallas, TX
Box, Gregory C. ....Cleveland, OH
Box, Herbert F. ....Ottumwa, IA
Box, J. Calvin ....Metairie, LA
Box, James M. ....Ottumwa, IA
Box, Jerre E. ....Sacramento, CA
Box, Jerry D. ....Austin, TX
Box, John D. ....San Antonio, TX
Box, John R. ....Chicago, IL
Box, Kenneth L. ....Houston, TX
Box, Murray L. ....Evanston, IL
Box, Robert E., Jr. ....Jackson, MS
Box, Robert M. ....Ottumwa, IA
Box, Ruth Ann ....Dallas, TX
Box, Susan S. ....Akron, OH
Box, Thomas D. ....Dallas, TX
Boxberger, Bruce O. ....Fort Wayne, IN
Boxberger, Gina R. ....Columbia, MO
Boxell, Charles K. ....Toledo, OH
Boxer, A. Matthew ....Roseland, NJ
Boxer, Aaron ....Boca Raton, FL
Boxer, Andrew C. ....Springfield, VT
Boxer, Barbara K. ....Milwaukee, WI
Boxer, Barry J. ....New York, NY
Boxer, Daniel E. ....South Portland, ME
Boxer, Elkind & Gerson ....Oakland, CA
Boxer, Harold S. ....White Plains, NY
Boxer, Harriette N. ....New York, NY
Boxer, Jason T. ....New York, NY
Boxer, Jeffrey ....New York, NY
Boxer, Joel E. ....Los Angeles, CA
Boxer, Jonathan A. ....Redondo Beach, CA
Boxer, Karen S. ....New York, NY
Boxer, Lawrence A. ....Oakland, CA
Boxer, Leonard ....New York, NY
Boxer, Lester ....Los Angeles, CA
Boxer, Mark H. ....Palo Alto, CA
Boxer, Matthew ....Kenilworth, NJ
Boxer, Michael A. ....Port Washington, NY
Boxer, Nelson A. ....New York, NY
Boxer, Saml. ....Royal Palm Beach, FL
Boxer, Sandor T. ....Los Angeles, CA
Boxer, Sidney ....Brooklyn, NY
Boxer, Sidney ....Peekskill, NY
Boxer, Stewart N. ....Oakland, CA
Boxer, Terri S. ....Milwaukee, WI
Boxer, Vicki F. ....Milwaukee, WI
Boxer, Walter H. ....New York, NY
Boxerman, Marc Jay ....Chicago, IL
Boxerman, Michael J. ....Chicago, IL
Boxerman, Samuel B. ....Washington, DC
Boxerman, Sanford J. ....St. Louis, MO
Boxeur, Dennis S. ....Oklahoma City, OK
Boxill, Brent B. ....Baton Rouge, LA
Boxley, Bolton & Garber, L.L.P.
Raleigh, NC
Boxley, J. Michael ....Albany, NY
Boxley, John Maclachlan ....Raleigh, NC
Boxley, Norman F., Law Offices of
Pasadena, CA
Boxwell, Nancy L. ....Beverly Hills, CA
Boxx, Amy L. ....Monett, MO
Boxx, Karen E. ....Seattle, WA
Boxx, Timothy John ....Tiptonville, TN
Boy, Fred P., III ....New York, NY
Boy, Shannon L. ....Little Rock, AR
Boyack, Alan D. ....St. George, UT
Boyack, Andrea J. ....Washington, DC
Boyack, Dean C. ....Los Angeles, CA
Boyack, Douglas C. ....Sonora, CA
Boyack, Edward D. ....Las Vegas, NV
Boyack, Edward D. ....Las Vegas, NV
Boyack, Heidi ....Portsmouth, NH
Boyack, M. Wayne ....Seattle, WA
Boyack, Robert M. ....Joliet, IL
Boyadjian, Kohar M. ....Union, NJ
Boyadjian, Livia ....New York, NY
Boyadjis, Andreas A. ....Florham Park, NJ
Boyadjis, Anthony A. ....Florham Park, NJ
Boyadjis, Eleni ....Cherry Hill, NJ
Boyajan, Leon M., II ....Inverness, FL
Boyajan, Leon M., II, P.A. ....Inverness, FL
Boyajian, Aaron D. ....Longmeadow, MA
New York, NY
Boyajian, Berj ....Los Angeles, CA
Boyajian, Donald W. ....Albany, NY
Boyajian, Harrington & Richardson
Providence, RI
Boyajian, John ....Providence, RI
Boyajian, Judith A. ....San Francisco, CA
Boyajian, Karnig ....Boston, MA
Boyajian, Lynn Ciolino
Florham Park, NJ
Boyajian, Michael G. ....Brooklyn, NY
Boyajian, Michael J.
San Luis Obispo, CA
Boyajian, Thomas M. ....Fresno, CA
Boyajian, Victor H. ....Newark, NJ
Boyaki, Walter L. ....El Paso, TX
Boyan, James W. ....Paramus, NJ
Boyan, Joseph M. ....Morristown, NJ
Boyan, Robert S. ....High Point, NC
Boyan, Susan ....Vernon, CT
Boyan, William L. ....Trenton, NJ
Boyanton, Janet ....DeSoto, TX
Boyapati, Anuradha Y ....Chicago, IL
Boyar, Andrew ....Eldred, NY
Boyar, David A. ....New York, NY
Boyar, Edward ....Brooklyn, NY
Boyar, Gabriel ....New York, NY
Boyar, Higgins & Hayden, P.A.
Morristown, NJ
Boyar, J. William ....Houston, TX
Boyar & Miller, A Professional Corporation
Houston, TX
Boyar, Robert M. ....Morristown, NJ
Boyarin, Jonathan ....New York, NY
Boyaris, Karen L. ....Chicago, IL
Boyarsky, Jay S. ....San Jose, CA
Boyarsky, Jeffery L. ....Menlo Park, CA
Boyarsky, Mitchell ....New York, NY
Boyarsky, Saul ....St. Louis, MO
Boyazis, James ....Akron, OH
Boyce, Albert G. ....Baltimore, MD
Boyce, Andrew S. ....Detroit, MI
Boyce, Arthur W. ....Frederick, MD
Boyce, Arthur W., P.A. ....Frederick, MD
Boyce & Atkinson ....Duluth, GA
Lawrenceville, GA
Lilburn, GA
Monroe, GA
Boyce, Beaumont S. ....Amarillo, TX
Boyce, Beth A. ....Pittsburgh, PA
Boyce & Boyce ....Stillwater, OK
Boyce & Boyce, A Professional Association
Newport, AR
Boyce, Bret T. ....Washington, DC
Boyce, Brian P. ....Little Rock, AR
Boyce, Charles A. ....Dallas, TX
Boyce, Coreen L. ....Scarsdale, NY
Boyce, Cynthia L. ....Brooklyn, NY
Boyce, Daniel J. ....Gibbsboro, NJ
Philadelphia, PA
Boyce, David B. ....Eagan, MN
Boyce, David B. ....Salt Lake City, UT
Boyce, David P. ....Austin, TX
Boyce, David S. ....Los Angeles, CA
Boyce, Dawn E. ....Fairfax, VA
Boyce, Donna L. ....Frankfort, KY
Boyce, Donna L. ....Memphis, TN
Boyce, Edward W., III ....Newport, AR
Boyce, Ekonomou & Atkinson ....Atlanta, GA
Lilburn, GA
Boyce, G. Eugene ....Raleigh, NC
Boyce, G. Judson ....East Providence, RI
Boyce, George R. ....Fall River, MA
Boyce, Gerard R. ....New York, NY
Boyce, Gilbert W. ....Washington, DC
Boyce, Henry H. ....Newport, AR
Boyce Horne & Jones, L.C. ....St. Louis, MO
Boyce & Isley, PLLC ....Raleigh, NC
Boyce, James A. ....Murray Hill, NJ
Boyce, Jeffrey C. ....Las Vegas, NV
Boyce, John Clark ....Baton Rouge, LA
Boyce, John, Jr. ....Carlsbad, CA
Boyce, John K., III ....San Antonio, TX
Boyce, John P. ....Philadelphia, PA
Boyce, John R. ....St. Louis, MO
Boyce, Justin F. ....Palo Alto, CA
Boyce, Katharine R. ....Washington, DC
Boyce, Kevin D. ....Cleveland, OH
Boyce, Kiersten L. ....Washington, DC
Boyce, Kimberly A. ....Seattle, WA
Boyce Law Firm ....Newport, AR
Boyce Law Firm ....Carlsbad, CA
Boyce, LeRoy C. ....Kailua-Kona, HI
Boyce, Leslie Ann ....Venice, CA
Boyce, Margaret M. ....Philadelphia, PA
Boyce, Maria Wyckoff ....Houston, TX
Boyce, Michael D. ....Chicago, IL
Boyce, Michael T. ....Mineola, NY
Boyce, Murphy, McDowell & Greenfield,
L.L.P. ....Sioux Falls, SD
Boyce, P. Joseph ....Turnersville, NJ
Boyce, Peter F. ....Lilburn, GA
Boyce, Phillip R. ....Roseland, NJ
Boyce, R. Daniel ....Raleigh, NC
Boyce, Richard G. ....Alpena, MI
Boyce, Richard J. ....San Francisco, CA
Boyce, Richard L. ....Tecumseh, MI
Boyce, Richard M. ....Alliance, OH
Boyce, Robert E. ....San Diego, CA
Boyce, Ronald N. ....Salt Lake City, UT
Boyce, Roy W.
Federal Communications Commission,
Mass Media Bureau, GV
Boyce, Sam H. ....Newport, AR
Boyce & Schaefer ....San Diego, CA
Boyce, Sharon E. ....Knoxville, TN
Boyce, Sheldon W. ....Rochester, NY
Boyce, Sherry L. ....Stillwater, OK
Boyce, Steven E. ....Billerica, MA
Boyce, Steven L. ....Burlington, KS
Boyce, Susan B. ....Rockville, MD
Boyce, Thomas W., Jr. ....New London, CT
Boyce, Timothy J. ....Hartford, CT
Boyce, Valerie F. ....Little Rock, AR
Boyce, W. LaRue, Jr. ....Atlanta, GA
Boyce, Wayne ....Newport, AR
Boyce, Wendell H. ....Bartlesville, OK
Boyce, White, Werth & Mack ....Alpena, MI
Boyce, William C., Jr. ....Manassas, VA
Boyce, William H. ....Stillwater, OK
Boyce, William J. ....Houston, TX
Boyce, William J., Law Office of
St. Petersburg, FL
Boyce, William R. ....Los Angeles, CA
Boyce-Iassogna, Patricia ....New Haven, CT
Boychuck, Stanley V. ....Chicago, IL
Boychuk, George E. ....New York, NY
Boychuk, Jos. M. ....New York, NY
Boyd, Aaron Ray ....Claremont, CA
Boyd Agnew Dryer & Storaasli, Ltd.
Duluth, MN
Boyd, Alan B. ....Columbus, OH
Boyd, Alan C. ....Toledo, OH
Boyd, Alan M. ....Washington, DC
Boyd, Alan S. ....Washington, DC
Boyd, Alan T. ....Wilmington, DE
Boyd, Albert H. ....Memphis, TN
Boyd, Alec Hunter ....San Francisco, CA
Boyd, Alvin ....Mesquite, TX
Boyd, Anne Nauful ....Atlanta, GA
Boyd, Arch B., III ....Memphis, TN
Boyd, Arch B., III & Associates
Memphis, TN
Boyd, Arthur E., Jr. ....San Francisco, CA
Boyd & Associates ....Dallas, TX
Boyd, B. Randolph ....Richmond, VA
Boyd, Barbara J. ....Seattle, WA
Boyd & Bazil, LLP ....Aspen, CO
Boyd, Ben Harlan ....Alexandria, VA
Boyd, Benjamin S. ....Washington, DC
Boyd, Benson & Hendrickson
Baltimore, MD
Towson, MD
Boyd, Bethany R. ....Charleston, WV
Boyd, Bill C. ....Houston, TX
Boyd & Boyd ....Dallas, TX
Frisco, TX
Plano, TX
Boyd & Boyd Co., L.P.A. ....Columbus, OH
Boyd & Boyd, P.C. ....Centerville, MA
Boyd & Boyd, P.C. ....Chesapeake, VA
Norfolk, VA
Virginia Beach, VA
Boyd, Brandon J. ....Amsterdam, NY
Boyd, Brent A. ....Houston, TX
Boyd, Brent M. ....Columbia, SC
Boyd, Brian Carter ....Anchorage, AK
Boyd, Brook D. ....New York, NY
Boyd, Bruce M. ....San Francisco, CA
Boyd, Bruce W. ....Ashland, OH
Boyd, Bruce W. ....Sioux Falls, SD
Boyd, C. Anthony ....Santa Barbara, CA
Boyd, C. Everett, Jr. ....Tallahassee, FL
Boyd, Cami L. Dawson ....Dallas, TX
Boyd, Carl B., Jr. ....Henderson, KY
Boyd, Carol ....Los Angeles, CA
Boyd, Carolyn A. ....Denver, CO
Boyd, Catherine Leigh ....Columbia, SC
Boyd, Cecilia Redding ....Panama City, FL
Boyd & Chang, L.L.P. ....Irvine, CA
San Francisco, CA
Boyd, Charles M. ....Scottsdale, AZ
Boyd, Charles P., Jr. ....Little Rock, AR
Boyd, Charles W. ....Conroe, TX
Boyd, Charles Y. ....Gadsden, AL
Boyd, Chester Hugh ....Baton Rouge, LA
Boyd, Christine O. ....Philadelphia, PA
Boyd, Christopher P. ....Jacksonville, FL
Boyd, Christopher S. ....Saginaw, MI
Boyd, Claudia L. ....Moorestown, NJ
Philadelphia, PA
Boyd, Clinton D. ....Middletown, OH
Boyd, Craig S. ....Boyertown, PA
Boyd, Craig T. ....Chicago, IL
Boyd & Crane ....Chicago, IL
Boyd, Damon L. ....Phoenix, AZ
Boyd, Dan R. ....Santa Ana, CA
Boyd, Dan S. ....Dallas, TX
Boyd, Dana G.
Department of Housing and Urban
Development,
Office of General Counsel, GV
Boyd, Daniel P. ....Hillsdale, MI
Boyd, David B. ....Putnam, CT
Boyd, David C. ....Dallas, TX
Boyd, David E. ....Sacramento, CA
Boyd, David Henry ....Cincinnati, OH
Boyd, David Hugh ....Woodbridge, VA
Boyd, David J. ....Chicago, IL
Boyd, David J. ....Cincinnati, OH
Boyd, David L. ....Santa Ana, CA
Boyd, David R. ....Montgomery, AL
Boyd, David R. ....Washington, DC
Boyd, Debra L. ....Los Angeles, CA
Boyd, Delores R. ....Montgomery, AL
Boyd, Denis J. ....Two Harbors, MN
Boyd, Dennis ....Houston, TX
Boyd, Dennis R. ....New York, NY
Boyd, Derrick S. ....Bridgeport, TX
Decatur, TX
Boyd, Dianne C. ....Fayetteville, AR
Boyd, Don A. ....Wilmington, DE
Boyd, Donald A. ....Yakima, WA
Boyd, Donald Bruce, Jr. ....Chicago, IL
Boyd, Donald J. ....Vancouver, WA
Boyd, Douglas F. ....Springfield, MA
Boyd, Douglas L. ....Tulsa, OK
Boyd, Douglas R., Sr. ....El Monte, CA
Boyd, D. W. ....Newkirk, OK
Boyd, Earl E. ....Los Angeles, CA
Boyd, Edward John, V ....Southold, NY
Boyd, Eric ....Columbus, OH
Boyd, Eric E. ....Chicago, IL

Boyd & Ericksen ....Encino, CA
Boyd, Erin H. ....Metairie, LA
New Orleans, LA
Boyd, Ernest W. ....Beaumont, TX
Boyd, Eva-Marie ....Laguna Beach, CA
Boyd, F. Gillar, Jr. ....Palm Springs, CA
Boyd, F. Keats, III ....Centerville, MA
Boyd, F. Keats, Jr. ....Centerville, MA
Boyd, Federico A. ....Atlanta, GA
Boyd, Felicia J. ....Minneapolis, MN
Boyd & Fernambucq, P.C.
Birmingham, AL
Boyd, Foster S. ....Tallahassee, FL
Boyd, Fred, Jr. ....Fremont, CA
Pleasanton, CA
San Jose, CA
Boyd, Frederick C.C., III ....Atlanta, GA
Boyd, Frederick L., Jr. ....San Jose, CA
Boyd, Gail H. ....Tempe, AZ
Boyd, Geo. R., Jr. ....East Point, GA
Boyd, Geoffrey J. C. ....Baltimore, MD
Boyd, George ....Mesa, AZ
Boyd, George G., Jr. ....Columbus, GA
Boyd, George M. ....Cleveland, OH
Boyd, Gerald R., Jr. ....Tampa, FL
Boyd, Graham G. ....Washington, DC
Boyd, H. Michael ....Charlotte, NC
Boyd, Hal J. ....Memphis, TN
Boyd, Harry ....Tyler, TX
Boyd, Hollie ....Indianapolis, IN
Boyd, Holly Anderson ....Tyler, TX
Boyd, Howard T., III ....Houston, TX
Boyd, Ian K. ....San Francisco, CA
Boyd, J. Curtis ....Fort Pierce, FL
Boyd, J. Curtis, P.A. ....Fort Pierce, FL
Boyd, J. Kip ....Midland, TX
Boyd, J. Pamela ....Santa Ana, CA
Boyd, J. Ronald ....Birmingham, AL
Boyd, Jack L. ....Indianapolis, IN
Boyd, Jack N., Jr. ....Texarkana, TX
Boyd, Jacqueline Ann ....Santa Monica, CA
Boyd, James A. ....Wytheville, VA
Boyd, James A., Jr. ....Panama City, FL
Boyd, James B. ....Aspen, CO
Boyd, James E. ....Frankfort, KY
Boyd, James E. ....Houston, TX
Boyd, James G. ....Charleston, SC
Boyd, James J. ....St. Paul, MN
Boyd, James M. ....Norfolk, VA
Boyd, James M. ....Camas, WA
Boyd, James M., Jr. ....Sacramento, CA
Boyd, James O. ....Temple, TX
Boyd, James R. ....Long Beach, CA
Boyd, James W. ....Traverse City, MI
Boyd, James W. ....Wynnewood, PA
Boyd, James W. ....Rock Hill, SC
Boyd, James W., Sr. ....Columbus, OH
Boyd, Jamie C. ....Canyon Lake, TX
Boyd, Jamie Taylor ....Tulsa, OK
Boyd, Janet C. ....Washington, DC
Boyd, Janet E. ....Stafford, VA
Boyd, Jean Hudson ....Fort Worth, TX
Boyd, Jeffery H. ....Norwalk, CT
Boyd, Jeffrey D. ....Columbus, OH
Boyd, Jeffrey D. ....Worthington, OH
Boyd, Jeffrey G. ....Tulsa, OK
Boyd, Jeffrey P. ....Chattanooga, TN
Jackson, TN
Boyd, Jeffrey S. ....Austin, TX
Boyd & Jenerette, P.A. ....Jacksonville, FL
Boyd, Jennifer Anne ....Nashville, TN
Boyd, Jennifer N. ....Darien, CT
Greenwich, CT
Boyd, Jerry K. ....Spokane, WA
Boyd, Jim H. ....Fayetteville, AR
Boyd, Joanne E. ....Birmingham, AL
Boyd, Joel E. ....Melbourne, FL
Boyd, John A. ....Riverside, CA
Boyd, John A. ....Stone Harbor, NJ
Boyd, John B. ....Independence, MO
Boyd, John C. ....Youngstown, OH
Boyd, John D. ....Lansing, MI
Boyd, John E. ....New York, NY
Boyd, John J. ....Kankakee, IL
Boyd, John J. ....Baltimore, MD
Boyd, John L. ....Tulsa, OK
Boyd, John L., Jr. ....Sun City Center, FL
Boyd, John M., Jr. ....Washington, DC
Boyd, John R. ....Santa Fe, NM
Boyd, John Richard ....Independence, MO
Boyd, John Roberts ....Irvine, CA
Boyd, John T. ....Amarillo, TX
Boyd, John T., II ....Monroeville, PA
Boyd, John T., Jr. ....Amarillo, TX
Boyd, John W. ....Westport, CT
Boyd, John W. ....Indianapolis, IN
Boyd, John W. ....Albuquerque, NM
Boyd, John W. ....Cleveland, OH
Boyd, Jon R. ....Dallas, TX
Boyd, Joseph A., Jr. ....Tallahassee, FL
Boyd, Joseph M., Jr. ....Nashville, TN
Boyd, Joseph R. ....Tallahassee, FL
Boyd, Joseph R. ....New Orleans, LA
Boyd, Karen Barry ....Dallas, TX
Boyd, Karen I. ....Menlo Park, CA
Boyd, Karla L.
Securities and Exchange Commission, Division of Corporation Finance, GV
Boyd & Karver ....Boyertown, PA
Boyd, Katherine R. ....Modesto, CA
Boyd, Kathleen Doyle ....Buffalo, NY
Boyd, Keith Y. ....Medford, OR
Boyd, Kelly Alvis ....Houston, TX
Boyd, Kelly R. ....Palo Alto, CA
Boyd, Kenneth E. ....Toledo, OH
Boyd, Kenneth T. ....Mineola, NY
Boyd, Kenneth W. ....Cleburne, TX
Boyd, Kenter & Stewart, P.C.
Independence, MO
Boyd, Kevin W. ....Austin, TX
Boyd, Kier T. ....Clinton, MD
Boyd, Kurt ....Encino, CA
Boyd, La Merle M., and Associates
Santa Fe, NM
Boyd, Larry C. ....Irvine, CA
Boyd, Larry P. ....Houston, TX
Boyd, Larry R. ....McKinney, TX
Boyd, Lauren D. ....San Diego, CA
Boyd, Laurence E. ....Angleton, TX
Boyd, Lauri G. ....Ferriday, LA
Boyd Law Associates, A Professional Corporation ....Lancaster, PA
Boyd Law Office, P.C.
South Sioux City, NE
Boyd, Lawrence G. ....Dallas, TX
Boyd, Leo J. M. ....Richmond, VA
Boyd, Lewis F. ....Paris, TX
Boyd, Lindsey & Branch, P.A., Law Firm of
Tallahassee, FL
Boyd, Lois Willson ....Pine Mountain, GA
Boyd, Lon V. ....Kingsport, TN
Boyd, Luke H., Jr. ....Winchester, VA
Boyd, Lundy L. ....Memphis, TN
Boyd, Luther R. ....Gulfport, MS
Boyd, Marcia J. ....Rochester, NY
Boyd, Marion S., Jr. ....Memphis, TN
Boyd, Mark ....Moran, KS
Boyd, Mark R. ....Fort Lauderdale, FL
Boyd, Martha P. ....Greensboro, NC
Boyd & Martin, P.C. ....Westport, CT
Boyd, Mary Ann Kinnebrew ....Houston, TX
Boyd, Mary Margaret ....Pittsburgh, PA
Boyd, Mary Olert ....Nashville, TN
Boyd, Matthew A. ....Nashville, TN
Boyd and McKay ....San Francisco, CA
Boyd, Michael A. ....New York, NY
Boyd, Michael A. ....Houston, TX
Boyd, Michael G. ....Englewood, NJ
Boyd, Michael J. ....Libertyville, IL
Boyd, Michael M. ....Lewisburg, TN
Boyd, Michael P. ....Portland, ME
Boyd, Michael W. ....Magnolia, AR
Boyd, Michael W. ....Oakland Park, FL
Boyd, Michael W. ....Greenville, MS
Boyd, Michael W. ....New York, NY
Boyd, Michele L. ....Salt Lake City, UT
Boyd, Nancy Shimanek ....Des Moines, IA
Boyd, Nathaniel W., IV ....York, PA
Boyd, Patrick R., P.C. ....Irvine, CA
Boyd, Paul M. ....Boise, ID
Boyd, Paul M. ....Tyler, TX
Boyd, Paul M., P.C. ....Tyler, TX
Boyd, Peter J. ....Boise, ID
Boyd, Philip C. ....Simsbury, CT
Boyd, Phillip Larry ....Rogersville, TN
Boyd, Phillip Larry, P.C. ....Rogersville, TN
Boyd, R. Craig ....Tyler, TX
Boyd, R. Eugene ....Bellevue, WA
Boyd, Ralph C. ....Glen Burnie, MD
Boyd, Ralph F., Jr. ....Boston, MA
Boyd, Randall S. ....Denton, TX
Boyd, Rebecca J. ....Washington, DC
Boyd, Reel A. ....Sioux Falls, SD
Boyd, Reese R., III ....Boston, MA
Boyd, Rex Neil ....Birmingham, AL
Boyd, Richard C. ....Durham, NC
Boyd, Richard, Jr. ....Harrisonburg, LA
Boyd, Rita M. ....Dallas, TX
Boyd, Robert A. ....Binghamton, NY
Boyd, Robert A. ....Cleveland, OH
Boyd, Robert C. ....Jackson, MS
Boyd, Robert D. ....Atlanta, GA
Boyd, Robert E., III ....Columbus, OH
Boyd, Robert E., Jr. ....Columbus, OH
Boyd, Robert F. ....Littleton, CO
Boyd, Robert Friend ....Norfolk, VA
Boyd, Robert J. ....Tallahassee, FL
Boyd, Robert P. ....Ardmore, PA
Boyd, Robert S. ....Santa Rosa, CA
Boyd, Robert T. ....San Francisco, CA
Boyd, Robert T. ....Torrington, CT
Boyd, Robert W. ....Orlando, FL
Boyd, Robert W. ....Kankakee, IL
Boyd, Robert W. ....Duluth, MN
Boyd, Robert W., Jr. ....McMinnville, TN
Boyd, Robt. J. ....Anaconda, MT
Boyd, Roger N. ....Washington, DC
Boyd, Roy J., Jr. ....Brunswick, GA
Boyd, Russell A., Jr. ....Folkston, GA
Boyd, S. Jeff, Jr. ....Columbia, SC
Boyd, Sally W. ....Columbus, OH
Boyd, Samuel L. ....Dallas, TX
Boyd, Sandra N. "Sissy" Gorden
Houston, TX
Boyd, Scott M. ....Rockford, IL
Boyd, Shannon R. ....Irvine, CA
Boyd, Shawn ....Poplar Bluff, MO
Boyd, Sheena Jones ....Durham, NC
Boyd, Shirley R. ....Minneapolis, MN
Boyd, Stacey L. ....Baltimore, MD
Boyd, Steven D. ....Wilmington, DE
Boyd, Steven J. ....Kansas City, MO
Boyd, Steven S. ....Houston, TX
Boyd, Stuart D. ....Lakeland, FL
Boyd, Teresa A. ....Memphis, TN
Boyd, Thomas A., Jr., (P.A.)
Jacksonville, FL
Boyd, Thomas C. ....Racine, WI
Boyd, Thomas H. ....Minneapolis, MN
St. Paul, MN
Boyd, Thomas M. ....Washington, DC
Boyd, Timothy W. ....Atlanta, GA
Boyd, Todd D. ....Clear Lake, SD
Estelline, SD
Boyd, Tony Lee ....Fort Wright, KY
Boyd • Veigel, P.C. ....McKinney, TX
Boyd, Victoria L. ....Palo Alto, CA
Boyd, W. Howard, Jr. ....Greenville, SC
Boyd, W. Thomas, Jr. ....Wilson, NC
Boyd, W. Todd ....Miami, FL
Boyd, Walter M. ....Greenfield, MA
Boyd, Walter Y., Jr. ....Washington, DC
Boyd, Watkins & Patrick ....Frankfort, KY
Boyd, Wayne E. ....South Sioux City, NE
Boyd, Will C., Jr. ....Cherryfield, ME
Boyd, Willard L. ....Iowa City, IA
Boyd, Willard L., III ....Des Moines, IA
Boyd, William A. ....Cleveland, OH
Boyd, William C. ....Columbia, SC
Boyd, William C. ....Houston, TX
Boyd, William E. ....Tucson, AZ
Boyd, William E. ....San Francisco, CA
Boyd, William E., Jr. ....Springfield, MA
Boyd, William F. ....Coeur d'Alene, ID
Boyd, William G. ....Rossville, GA
Boyd, William J., P.C. ....Oak Brook, IL
Boyd, William L. ....Trenton, NJ
Boyd, William M. ....McKinney, TX
Boyd, William O. ....Casselberry, FL
Mount Dora, FL
Boyd, William O., P.A. ....Casselberry, FL
Mount Dora, FL
Boyd, William S. ....San Francisco, CA
Boyd, William S. ....Las Vegas, NV
Reno, NV
Boyd, William S., III ....Gulfport, MS
Boyd, William S., III, & Associates, P.A.
Biloxi, MS
Gulfport, MS
Hattiesburg, MS
Jackson, MS
Boyd, William Stephen ....Dallas, TX
Boyd, William Stewart ....Chicago, IL
Boyd, William W. ....Lancaster, PA
Boyd & Young ....Greencastle, IN
Boyda, John M. ....Southfield, MI
Boyda, Robert G. ....Oak Brook, IL
Boyda, Stephen W. ....Marysville, KS
Boydell, Earl M. J., Jr. ....New Orleans, LA
Boyden, Bruce E. ....New York, NY
Boyden, Bruce R. ....Spokane, WA
Boyden, Cary C. ....Sacramento, CA
Boyden, Christopher W.
North Palm Beach, FL
Boyden, Jacquelyn K. ....Durham, NC
Boyden, Joel M. ....Grand Rapids, MI
Boyden, John C. ....Reno, NV
Boyden, John S., Jr. ....Salt Lake City, UT
Boyden, Julie Ann ....Brockton, MA
Boyden, Kenneth J. D. ....Media, PA
Boyden, Stephen G. ....Salt Lake City, UT
Boyden, Timmons, Dilley & Haney PLC
Grand Rapids, MI
Boyden, W. Lincoln ....Boston, MA
Boyden, Wendi L. ....Hartford, CT
Boyd-Obarski, Rebecca ....Naperville, IL
Boydoh, Robert E., Jr. ....Greensboro, NC
Boydston, Brian ....Los Angeles, CA
Boydston, Karla J. ....Fort Worth, TX
Boydston, M. Brent ....Durant, OK
Boydston, M. Brent, P.C. ....Durant, OK
Boydston, Michelle D. ....Santa Monica, CA
Boydston, Richard ....Cincinnati, OH
Boydstun, C. Bryant, Jr.
St. Petersburg, FL
Boydstun, Dabroski, Lyle & Wood, P.A.
Clearwater, FL
St. Petersburg, FL
Tampa, FL
Boydstun, Robert L. ....New York, NY
Boydstun, R. W., Jr. ....Louisville, MS
Boye, Deborah T. ....Chicago, IL
Boye, Helen ....Sausalito, CA
Boye, Lee A. ....Chicago, IL
Boye, Tiffany A. ....Elgin, IL
Boyer, Alan I. ....Skokie, IL
Boyer, Albert C. ....Chula Vista, CA
Boyer, Allen W. ....Charlotte, NC
Boyer, Amy Smith ....Atlanta, GA
Forsyth, GA
Boyer, Andrew Ben ....Joliet, IL
Boyer, Anna B. ....Boston, MA
Boyer, April L. ....Pittsburgh, PA
Boyer, Ardwin Eugene ....Chicago, IL
Boyer & Bade, A Professional Corporation
Phoenix, AZ
Boyer, Barbara L. ....Cheyenne, WY
Boyer, Barbara S. ....Macon, GA
Boyer, Bari ....Worcester, MA
Boyer, Barry B. ....Buffalo, NY
Boyer, Beverly J. ....Brookfield, WI
Boyer, Bradley P. ....Los Angeles, CA
Boyer, Brent ....Marion, KS
Boyer, Brett ....Pleasant Grove, UT
Boyer, Bruce A. ....Chicago, IL
Boyer, Bruce S. ....St. Petersburg, FL
Boyer, Burton ....Boston, MA
Boyer, Carmellia C. ....Houston, TX
Boyer, Cathy S. ....Butler, PA
Boyer, Charles R. ....Atlanta, GA
Boyer, Christine ....Iowa City, IA
Boyer, Churilla & Dawson, P.C.
Detroit, MI
Mount Clemens, MI
Sterling Heights, MI
Boyer, Clell C., Jr. ....Kalamazoo, MI
Boyer, Cynthia J. ....Sterling Heights, MI
Boyer, D. Randall ....San Francisco, CA
Boyer, Daniel J. ....Hoffman Estates, IL
Boyer, Danny D. ....Salina, KS
Boyer, Darryl L. ....Brookfield, WI
Boyer, David C., Jr. ....Portland, ME
Boyer, David D. ....Costa Mesa, CA
Boyer, David G. ....Chicago, IL
Boyer, David W. ....Philadelphia, PA
Boyer, Dennis L. ....Madison, WI
Boyer, Diann Basler ....Carbondale, IL
Boyer, Donaldson & Stewart, LLP
Wichita, KS
Boyer, Douglas Charles ....Dedham, MA
Boyer, Edward F. ....Seattle, WA
Boyer, Edward Franklin ....Seattle, WA
Boyer, Edwin M. ....Sarasota, FL
Boyer, Elizabeth M. ....Novelty, OH
Boyer, Elroy G. ....Chestertown, MD
Boyer, Eric R. ....Torrington, WY
Boyer, Eric W. ....Miami, FL
Boyer, Ethan T. ....San Diego, CA
Boyer, Ewing & Harris, Incorporated
Houston, TX
Boyer & Ferrell, P.A. ....Sarasota, FL
Boyer, George P. ....Department of Commerce, Patent and Trademark Office, GV
Boyer, Gilda L. ....Cedar Rapids, IA
Boyer, Gregory F. ....Tampa, FL
Boyer, Gregory L. ....Providence, RI
Boyer, H. Stacey ....Baltimore, MD
Boyer, Helen Anne ....Seattle, WA
Boyer & Holzinger ....Bethlehem, PA
Boyer, J. Alton ....Washington, DC
Boyer, James G. ....Lake Charles, LA
Boyer, James R. ....Sarasota, FL
Boyer, James R., P.A. ....Sarasota, FL
Boyer, Joel Steven ....Costa Mesa, CA
Boyer, John ....New York, NY
Boyer, John K. ....Omaha, NE
Boyer, John R., Jr. ....Houston, TX
Boyer, John S. ....Moorestown, NJ
Boyer, John Scott ....Moorestown, NJ
Boyer, John W. ....Las Vegas, NV
Boyer, John W., Ltd. ....Las Vegas, NV
Boyer, Joseph A. ....Southfield, MI
Boyer, Kenneth H. ....Charlotte, NC
Boyer, Kenneth M. ....Troy, MI
Boyer, Kerri L. ....Washington, DC
Boyer, Kristin Fisher ....Marion, KS
Boyer, Kristin Morgan ....Chicago, IL
Boyer, Lee W. ....Lake Charles, LA
Boyer, Lloyd L. ....Englewood, CO
Boyer, Madeleine ....Washington, DC
Boyer, Marc F. ....Menands, NY
Boyer, Mark K. ....Hagerstown, MD
Boyer, Mary Devitt ....Columbus, OH
Boyer, Matthew F. ....Wilmington, DE
Boyer, Maurice L. ....Knoxville, TN
Boyer, Max K. ....Phoenix, AZ
Boyer, Michael K. ....Moberly, MO
Boyer, Morris S. ....Jonesboro, GA
Boyer, Nancy Eshcoff ....Fort Wayne, IN
Boyer, Neil A. ....Department of State, Bureau of International Organization Affairs, GV
Boyer, Neil J. ....Chicago, IL
Boyer, Neil J. ....Wheaton, IL
Boyer, Norman A. ....Santa Rosa, CA
Boyer, Paul W.
Export-Import Bank of The United States, Office of the General Counsel, GV
Boyer, Peter G. ....Toledo, OH
Boyer, Peter J. ....Moorestown, NJ
Philadelphia, PA
Boyer, Phoebe Bennet ....New Haven, CT
Boyer, R. Bruce ....New Braunfels, TX
Boyer, R. David ....Fort Wayne, IN
Boyer, R. David, II ....Fort Wayne, IN
Boyer, Reynolds & DeMarco, Ltd.
Providence, RI
Boyer, Richard F. ....Bethlehem, PA
Boyer, Richard L. ....San Diego, CA
Boyer, Robert C. ....Bloomfield Hills, MI
Boyer, Robert E. ....Fort Smith, AR
Boyer, Robert L. ....Franklin, PA
Boyer, Robert P. ....Scottdale, PA
Boyer, Robert W. ....Grants Pass, OR
Boyer, Ron ....Martinez, CA
Boyer, Ronald E. ....Watseka, IL
Boyer, Ronald L. ....Rogers, AR
Boyer, Ronald L. ....McAlester, OK
Boyer, Royald E., P.C. ....Watseka, IL
Boyer, Ryan W. ....Idaho Falls, ID
Boyer, Ryan W., P.A. ....Idaho Falls, ID
Boyer and Schiltz, P.A. ....Clearwater, FL
St. Petersburg, FL
Tampa, FL
Boyer, Schrantz, Rhoads & Teague, PLC
Bentonville, AR
Rogers, AR
Boyer, Shelli L. ....Chicago, IL
Boyer, Spencer H. ....Washington, DC
Boyer, Susan E. ....Marietta, OH
Boyer, Susan E. ....Philadelphia, PA
Boyer, Tamara P. Eifler ....Maryville, TN
Boyer, Tanzler & Boyer ....Jacksonville, FL
Boyer, Ted ....Salt Lake City, UT
Boyer, Thomas G. ....Milwaukee, WI
Boyer, Thomas L. ....Troy, MI
Boyer, Thomas P. ....Fort Wayne, IN
Boyer, Timothy H. ....Evanston, IL
Boyer, Tyrie A. ....Jacksonville, FL
Boyer, Tyrie W. ....Jacksonville, FL
Boyer, W. Chris ....Lubbock, TX
Boyer, W. Patric ....Pittsburgh, PA
Washington, PA
Boyer, Wayne J. ....Clearwater, FL
Boyer, Wesley J. ....Macon, GA
Boyer, William G. ....Sterling Heights, MI
Boyer, William G., Jr.
Sterling Heights, MI
Boyer-Ryan, Beth ....Brookfield, WI
Boyers, Carla Dionne ....Chicago, IL
Boyers, James M. ....Indianapolis, IN

Boyers, Marissa ... Philadelphia, PA
Boyers, Martin R. ... Las Vegas, NV
Boyers, Rand G. ... New York, NY
Boyers, Robert B. ... Miami, FL
Boyers, Seymour ... New York, NY
Boyers, Steven R. ... Santa Monica, CA
Boyers, William C. ... Hendersonville, TN
Boyer-Vine, Diane F. ... Sacramento, CA
Boyer-Zager, Laura L. ... Salt Lake City, UT
Boyes, Arvid C. ... Boerne, TX
Boyes & Associates, P.A. ... Gainesville, FL
Boyes & Farina, Professional Association
Palm Beach, FL
Stuart, FL
West Palm Beach, FL
Boyes, Patrice Flinchbaugh ... Gainesville, FL
Boyes, William E. ... West Palm Beach, FL
Boyes, William L. ... Camarillo, CA
Boyett, Christopher W. ... Miami, FL
Boyett, Comer ... Searcy, AR
Boyett, David A., III ... Mobile, AL
Boyett, James E. ... Atlanta, GA
Boyett, Morgan & Killough, P.A.
Searcy, AR
Boyett, Victoria Rose ... Stockton, CA
Boyett, William T. ... Dalton, GA
Boyette & Boyette ... Carthage, NC
Boyette, David L. ... Sarasota, FL
Boyette, Judith W. ... Oakland, CA
Boyette, K. Wade, Jr. ... Clermont, FL
Boyette, Mosley G., Jr. ... Carthage, NC
Boyette, Richard T. ... Raleigh, NC
Boyette, Van R. ... Memphis, TN
Boyette, Wayne S. ... Tarboro, NC
Boyhan, David M. ... New York, NY
Boyhan, Robert O. ... Mineola, NY
Boyk, Carol S. ... Los Angeles, CA
Boyk, Charles E. ... Toledo, OH
Boyk, Fredric M. ... Toledo, OH
Boyke, Stephen T. ... Portland, OR
Boyken, Quentin R. ... Des Moines, IA
Boykin, Barry C. ... Chicago, IL
Boykin, Brenda J. ... Washington, DC
Boykin & Casano, P.C. ... Washington, DC
Boykin, Charles J. ... Columbia, SC
Boykin, Cue D. ... Austin, TX
Boykin, Curtis A. ... Washington, DC
Boykin, Deloris M. ... Birmingham, AL
Boykin, Donald W. ... Jackson, MS
Boykin, Hamilton H. ... Washington, DC
Boykin, Jeffery P. ... Los Angeles, CA
Boykin, Jerry William ... Alexandria, VA
Boykin, John D., (P.A.)
West Palm Beach, FL
Boykin, John W. ... Atlanta, GA
Boykin, Lisa M. ... Alexandria, VA
Boykin, Mark H. ... Woodland Hills, CA
Boykin, Marshall, III ... Corpus Christi, TX
Boykin, Noble L., Jr. ... Savannah, GA
Boykin, Rigdon H. ... New York, NY
Boykin, Roberta M. ... New York, NY
Boykin, Suzanne M. ... Norcross, GA
Boykin, Terrill W. ... New Orleans, LA
Boykin, Todd W., (P.C.) ... Amarillo, TX
Boykin, Yvette S. ... Cincinnati, OH
Boykins, Genora Kendrick ... Houston, TX
Boykins, James R. ... Washington, DC
Boykins, Michael L. ... Chicago, IL
Boyko, Andrew ... Parma, OH
Boyko & Boyko ... Parma, OH
Boyko, Christopher A. ... Cleveland, OH
Boyko, David R. ... Palo Alto, CA
Boyko, Edgar Paul, & Associates
Anchorage, AK
Boyko, Gregory A. ... Collinsville, CT
Boyko, Ihor N. ... Indianapolis, IN
Boyko, John, Jr. ... Grand Rapids, MI
Boyko, John M. ... Torrance, CA
Boyko, Philip W. ... Houston, TX
Boyko, Stephen A. ... New York, NY
Boyko, Timothy A. ... Parma, OH
Boyko, William ... Cleveland, OH
Boykoff, Emanuel ... Boca Raton, FL
Boyl, Charleen Cirese ... La Jolla, CA
Boyl, John Patrick ... San Diego, CA
Boylan, A. Jackson ... Chester, VA
Boylan, Alfred G. ... Rochester, NY
Boylan, Andrew J. ... Port Jefferson, NY
Boylan, Arthur J. ... Willmar, MN
Boylan, Brian P. ... New York, NY
Boylan, Brown, Code, Vigdor & Wilson, LLP
Rochester, NY
Boylan, Christopher W. ... Terryville, CT
Boylan, Darlene A. ... Milwaukee, WI
Boylan, E. Richard ... Bridgewater, NJ
New Brunswick, NJ
Boylan, George W. ... Raleigh, NC
Boylan, Geraldine M. ... New York, NY
Boylan, James G. ... McLean, VA
Boylan, James J. ... New York, NY
Boylan, James O., III ... Del Mar, CA
Boylan, Jean M. ... Los Angeles, CA
Boylan, John C. ... Minneapolis, MN
Boylan, John J. ... Jersey City, NJ
Boylan, John J., III ... Springfield, VT
Boylan, John J., Jr. ... Burlington, VT
Boylan, Kim Marie Kozaczek
Washington, DC
Boylan, Laurence W. ... Le Roy, NY
Boylan, Mark S. ... Le Roy, NY
Boylan, Matthew J. ... Newark, NJ
Boylan, Matthew P. ... Roseland, NJ
Boylan, Michael G., (P.C.) ... Geneva, IL
Boylan, Michael J. ... Pleasanton, CA
Boylan, Michael J. ... Cincinnati, OH
Boylan, Michael L. ... Louisville, KY
Boylan, Morton & Whiting, LLP
Batavia, NY
Le Roy, NY
Boylan, Nicholas A. ... Las Vegas, NV
Boylan, Patrick J. ... Bellevue, NE
Boylan, Paul G. ... Boston, MA
Boylan, Paul Nicholas ... Sacramento, CA
Boylan, Paul S. ... Le Roy, NY
Boylan, Richard L. ... Cleveland, OH
Boylan & Richards, P.C. ... Springfield, VT
Boylan, Robert J. ... Department of Justice,
Federal Bureau of Investigation, GV
Boylan, Robert T. ... Chicago, IL
Boylan, Scott P. ... Department of Justice,
Criminal Division, GV
Boylan & Serpico ... Doylestown, PA
Boylan, Thomas C. ... Southfield, MI
Boylan, Thomas P. ... Chicago, IL
Boylan, Valerie J. ... Setauket, NY
Boylan, Virginia Walker ... Washington, DC
Boylan, Wayne M. ... Westfield, MA
Boylan, William E. ... Wheaton, IL
Boylan, Winnifred P. ... Bay City, MI
Boyland, Herbert ... Longview, TX
Boyland, Joseph E. ... Boston, MA
Boyland, Mark C. ... New York, NY
Boyland, William E. ... Palm Desert, CA
Boyland, William E. ... Palm Springs, CA
Boylan-Hill, Pamela ... Macon, GA
Boyle & Anderson, P.C. ... Auburn, NY
Boyle, Ann M. ... St. Augustine, FL
Camden, NJ
Norristown, PA
Boyle, Ann M. ... Philadelphia, PA
Boyle, Antoinette ... Billings, MT
Boyle, Arion R. ... Metairie, LA
Boyle, Ashby D., II ... Salt Lake City, UT
Boyle & Associates, P.C. ... Omaha, NE
Boyle, B. Irvin ... Charlotte, NC
Boyle, Bain & Downer ... Charlottesville, VA
Boyle, Barbara D. ... Pacific Palisades, CA
Boyle, Bernard G. ... Orange, CA
Boyle, Bernard J. ... Indianapolis, IN
Boyle & Boyle ... Denver, CO
Boyle, Boyle & Smith, S.C.
Milwaukee, WI
Boyle, Bradford W. ... Attleboro, MA
Boyle, Brian A. ... Chicago, IL
Boyle, Brian D. ... Washington, DC
Boyle, Brian D. ... Philadelphia, PA
Boyle, Brian H. ... Chicago, IL
Boyle, Brian J. ... Glendale, CA
Boyle, Bridget E. ... Milwaukee, WI
Boyle, Bruce Alan ... Greensburg, PA
Boyle, Carter & Gaines ... Wilmington, NC
Boyle, Catherine A. ... Harrisburg, PA
Boyle, Cecil F., Jr. ... Southfield, MI
Boyle, Celine M ... Boston, MA
Boyle, Charles A. ... Chicago, IL
Boyle, Charles A., & Associates, Ltd.
Chicago, IL
Boyle, Charles E. ... Cambridge, MA
Boyle, Charles E. ... Pittsburgh, PA
Boyle, Charles T. ... Port Charlotte, FL
Boyle & Chernick, P.C. ... Springfield, MA
Boyle, Christine G. ... Philadelphia, PA
Boyle, Christopher ... Newport, RI
Boyle, Christopher W. ... Philadelphia, PA
Boyle, Colleen E. ... Metairie, LA
Boyle, Conrad J. ... Fort Lauderdale, FL
Boyle, Cordes & Brown ... De Kalb, IL
Oregon, IL
Boyle, Cynthia Good ... Baltimore, MD
Boyle, Cynthia W. ... Bethesda, MD
Boyle, Daniel B. ... Irvine, CA
Boyle, Daniel M. ... Chicago, IL
Chicago Heights, IL
Boyle, Daniel W. ... Iowa City, IA
Boyle, David ... Los Angeles, CA
Boyle, David C. ... Albany, NY
Boyle, David F. ... San Francisco, CA
Boyle, Denis J. ... Bronx, NY
Boyle, Dennis E. ... Harrisburg, PA
Boyle, Dennis R. ... Burlington, WI
Boyle, Donald P., Jr. ... Atlanta, GA
Boyle, E. Thomas ... Uniondale, NY
Boyle, Edward G., III ... Abington, MA
Boyle, Edward J. ... New York, NY
Boyle, Edward J., Jr. ... New Orleans, LA
Boyle, Edward J., Sr. ... New Orleans, LA
Boyle, Edward L. ... Mesa, AZ
Boyle, Edward M. ... Overland Park, KS
Boyle, Edward P. ... New York, NY
Boyle, Elaine I. ... Farmington, CT
Boyle, Elizabeth Hunt ... Champaign, IL
Boyle, Ellen M. ... Yonkers, NY
Boyle, Ellen Mikorski ... Summit, NJ
Boyle, Emily R. ... Los Angeles, CA
Boyle, Eugene A. ... Chicago, IL
Boyle, Eugene F. ... Mansfield, MA
Boyle, Eugene H., Jr. ... Detroit, MI
Boyle, F. Ladson ... Columbia, SC
Boyle, Francis A. ... Champaign, IL
Boyle, Francis J. ... Providence, RI
Boyle, Francis M., Jr. ... Marinette, WI
Boyle, Gary ... Littleton, NH
Boyle, Gary W. ... Tulsa, OK
Boyle, George A., (A Prof. Corp.)
Bakersfield, CA
Boyle, George B. ... Raleigh, NC
Boyle, George D. ... Bloomington, IL
Boyle, George W., II ... Arvada, CO
Boyle, Gerald P. ... Milwaukee, WI
Boyle, Gerald J. ... Plymouth, NH
Boyle, Germain P. ... Denver, CO
Boyle, Goldsmith & Bolin ... Hennepin, IL
Boyle, Gregory M. ... Chicago, IL
Boyle, Gregory W. ... Tinton Falls, NJ
Boyle, Howard R. ... Houston, TX
Boyle, Iwona K. ... Chicago, IL
Boyle, Jacque ... Los Angeles, CA
Boyle, James B., Jr. ... Pasadena, CA
Boyle, James Brian ... White Plains, NY
Boyle, James D. ... Bellevue, WA
Boyle, James F. ... Los Angeles, CA
Boyle, James F. ... Grand Prairie, TX
Boyle, James F. ... Milwaukee, WI
Boyle, James Fenton ... Boston, MA
Boyle, James J. ... Washington, DC
Boyle, James J. ... Miami, FL
Boyle, James J., III ... Malden, MA
Boyle, James M. ... Washington, DC
Boyle, James P. ... Chicago, IL
Boyle, James P. ... Cleveland, OH
Boyle, James P., Jr. ... Prescott, AZ
Boyle, James R. ... East Rochester, NY
Boyle, James W. ... Honolulu, HI
Boyle, James William ... Freehold, NJ
Boyle, Jane A. ... Hartford, CT
Boyle, Jane Jackson ... Dallas, TX
Boyle, Janet ... Houston, TX
Boyle, Janet E. ... Markham, IL
Boyle, Janet E. ... Cambridge, MA
Boyle, Jean M. ... Boston, MA
Boyle, Jeanine ... New York, NY
Boyle, Jeffrey L. ... Rolling Hills Estates, CA
Boyle, Jerome E. ... Chicago, IL
Boyle, Jim, Law Offices of ... Austin, TX
Boyle, Johanna L. ... La Plata, MD
Boyle, John D. ... Los Angeles, CA
Boyle, John Delano ... Boston, MA
Boyle, John E. ... Denver, CO
Boyle, John E. ... Edgartown, MA
Boyle, John F. ... Plymouth, NH
Boyle, John F. ... Purchase, NY
Boyle, John F., Jr. ... Braintree, MA
Boyle, John F., Jr. ... Irving, TX
Boyle, John G. ... St. Louis, MO
Boyle, John J. ... Miami, FL
Boyle, John J. ... Cincinnati, OH
Boyle, John M. ... Elizabeth, NJ
Boyle, John O. ... San Diego, CA
Boyle, John P. ... Minneapolis, MN
Boyle, John P. ... Eatontown, NJ
Boyle, John P. ... New York, NY
Boyle, John W. ... Pittsburgh, PA
Boyle, Jos. P. ... Greenfield, MA
Boyle, Joseph A. ... Parsippany, NJ
New York, NY
Boyle, Joseph M. ... Phoenix, AZ
Boyle, Joseph M. ... Washington, DC
Boyle, Joseph M. ... International Falls, MN
Boyle, Joseph T. ... Fremont, MI
Boyle, Judith A. ... Phoenix, AZ
Boyle, Karen J. ... Seattle, WA
Boyle, Karen Krom ... San Diego, CA
Boyle, Karen Paden ... Wilmington, NC
Boyle, Kathleen Corkin ... Okemos, MI
Boyle, Kathleen Dempsey ... Chicago, IL
Boyle, Kenneth R. ... Springfield, IL
Boyle, Kevin Charles ... Washington, DC
Boyle, Kevin M. ... Burke, VA
Boyle, Kevin R. ... Washington, DC
Boyle, Kevin R. ... Malvern, PA
Boyle, Kevin V. ... Chicago, IL
Boyle, Kim Maria ... New Orleans, LA
Boyle, Kristine M. ... Toledo, OH
Boyle, Larry M. ... Boise, ID
Boyle Law Firm, The, A Professional
Corporation ... York, PA
Boyle Law Office ... Burlington, WI
Boyle Law Office, P.C. ... Plymouth, NH
Boyle, Lawrence F. ... Boston, MA
Boyle, Leo J. ... Wilmington, DE
Boyle, Leo V. ... Boston, MA
Boyle, Lester J., 3d ... Springfield, MO
Boyle & Leyhane, Ltd. ... Chicago, IL
Boyle, Lisa Kaas ... Los Angeles, CA
Boyle, Lisa M. ... Hartford, CT
Boyle, Louis L. ... Harrisburg, PA
Boyle & Lowry, L.L.P. ... Dallas, TX
Fort Worth, TX
Irving, TX
Boyle, Lynnette Z. ... Omaha, NE
Boyle, Marie Mariscalco ... Newport, KY
Boyle, Mark A. ... Fort Myers, FL
Boyle, Mark C. ... Milwaukee, WI
Boyle, Mark H. ... Chicago, IL
Boyle, Mark S. ... Chicago, IL
Boyle, Mark S. ... Cincinnati, OH
Boyle, Martin L. ... La Mesa, CA
Boyle, Mary Ellen T. ... Boston, MA
Boyle, Mary Jane ... Cleveland, OH
Boyle, Matthew ... Irving, TX
Boyle, Matthew A. ... South Hackensack, NJ
Boyle, Matthew T., (P.S.C.) ... Seattle, WA
Boyle, Matthew Wade ... Timonium, MD
Boyle & McClain ... Springfield, IL
Boyle, Michael ... Omaha, NE
Boyle, Michael C. ... Eagle Pass, TX
Uvalde, TX
Boyle, Michael F. ... San Diego, CA
Boyle, Michael H. ... New Ulm, MN
Boyle, Michael J. ... New Haven, CT
Boyle, Michael J. ... Pittsburgh, PA
Boyle, Mindy L. ... Oradell, NJ
Boyle & Morrissey, P.C. ... Boston, MA
Boyle, Olson & Robinson
Los Angeles, CA
Pasadena, CA
Boyle, Patricia J. ... Detroit, MI
Boyle, Patrick E. ... Chicago, IL
Boyle, Patrick J. ... St. Louis, MO
Boyle, Patrick J. ... Goshen, NY
Boyle, Patrick J. ... New York, NY
Boyle, Patrick O. ... East Alton, IL
Florissant, MO
Boyle, Paul M. ... Tacoma, WA
Boyle, Pecharich, Cline & Whittington,
P.L.L.C. ... Prescott, AZ
Boyle, Peter K. ... San Francisco, CA
Boyle, Peter M. ... Washington, DC
Boyle, Philip G. ... Boston, MA
Boyle, Raymond E. ... Chicago, IL
Boyle, Regina M. ... Modesto, CA
Boyle, Regina M., A Law Corporation
Modesto, CA
Boyle, Richard E. ... Belleville, IL
St. Louis, MO
Boyle, Richard E., Jr. ... Charleston, WV
Boyle, Richard F., Jr. ... Greensburg, PA
Boyle, Richard R. ... Salt Lake City, UT
Boyle, Robert D. ... Chicago, IL
Boyle, Robert E. A. ... Peoria, AZ
Boyle, Robert G. ... Pittsburgh, PA
Boyle, Robert G., Jr. ... Richmond, VA
Boyle, Robert K. ... New York, NY
Boyle, Roger ... New York, NY
Boyle, Sandra D. ... Nicholson, PA
Boyle, Sarah Parke ... Southfield, MI
Boyle, Seamus ... Mountainside, NJ
Boyle, Stacey Lynne ... Secaucus, NJ
Boyle, Stephen H. ... Bakersfield, CA
Boyle, Stephen J., III ... Virginia Beach, VA
Boyle, Susan ... Washington, DC
Boyle, Susan J. ... San Diego, CA
Boyle, Suzanne ... Los Angeles, CA
Boyle, Terence, (Mr.) ... Jersey City, NJ
Boyle, Terence P. ... Denver, CO
Boyle, Teresa ... New York, NY
Boyle, Terrance K. ... Detroit, MI
Boyle, Terrence J. ... Washington, DC
Boyle, Terrence M. ... Albany, NY
Boyle, Terrence T. ... Troy, MI
Boyle, Terrence W. ... Elizabeth City, NC
Boyle, Thomas ... Denver, CO
Boyle, Thomas A. ... Syracuse, NY
Boyle, Thomas A., III ... Bedford, MA
Boyle, Thomas C ... Melbourne, FL
Boyle, Thomas C. ... St. Louis, MO
Boyle, Thomas D. ... Dallas, TX
Boyle, Thomas E. ... Columbus, OH
Boyle, Thomas E. ... Pittsburgh, PA
Boyle, Thomas J. ... San Francisco, CA
Boyle, Thomas J. ... San Jose, CA
Boyle, Thomas J. ... Chicago, IL
Boyle, Timothy D. ... Burlington, WI
Boyle, Timothy E. ... Washington, DC
Boyle, Tyburski, & Rosenblatt ... Denver, CO
Boyle, Vervian Elaine ... Baton Rouge, LA
Boyle, Wallace H. ... North Hills, NY
Boyle, Walter Durley ... Hennepin, IL
Boyle, William C. Adrian ... York, PA
Boyle, William E. ... Atwater, CA
Boyle, William J. ... Springfield, MA
Boyle, William M. ... Brooklyn, NY
Boyle-Ebersole, Danielle ... Camden, NJ
Boyle Lewis, Amy ... Hauppauge, NY
Boyles, Charles M. ... Glenview, IL
Boyles, Charles O. ... Richmond, VA
Boyles, Jack C. ... Clinton, MS
Boyles, Jean Winborne ... Raleigh, NC
Boyles, John D. ... Grand Rapids, MI
Boyles, John H. ... Washington, DC
Boyles, John W. ... Skokie, IL
Boyles, John W., P.C. ... Skokie, IL
Boyles, Karl W., Jr. ... Pensacola, FL
Boyles, Kevan ... Palm Beach, FL
Boyles, Kevan, P.A., Law Office of
Palm Beach, FL
Boyles, Kristen L. ... Seattle, WA
Boyles, Laurel O. ... Winston-Salem, NC
Boyles, Peter J. ... Traverse City, MI
Boyles, Raymond E. ... Little Rock, AR
Boyles, Rodney W. ... Tyler, TX
Boyles, Stephen L. ... Palatka, FL
Boyles, Susan Holdsclaw
Winston-Salem, NC
Boyles, William A. ... Orlando, FL
Boyles, William H. ... Dallas, TX
Boyll, Jeffrey A. ... Terre Haute, IN
Boylston, Deborah T. ... Seattle, WA
Boylston, Louise M. ... Columbia, SC
Boylston, Patrick G. ... Portland, OR
Boylston, Richard W. ... Tavares, FL
Boylston, Robert J. ... Bradenton, FL
Boylston, Samuel L. ... Columbia, SC
Boymel, Paul E.
Equal Employment Opportunity
Commission,
Office of Legal Counsel, GV
Boyn, Gary D. ... Elkhart, IN
Boyne, James J. ... Oakbrook Terrace, IL
Boyne, Kathryn L. ... Minneapolis, MN
Boyne, Kevin ... Belleville, IL
Boyne, Shawn M. ... Farmington, NM
Boyne, Steven J. ... Miami, FL
Boynovska, Tzvetelina Tzvetanova
Chicago, IL
Boyns, Sara B. ... Monterey, CA
Boynton, Alan R., Jr. ... Harrisburg, PA
Boynton, Bruce, III ... Grants, NM
Boynton, Carroll A., (Mr.) ... Far Hills, NJ
Boynton, Christopher S. ... Portsmouth, VA
Boynton, Daniel R. ... Troy, MI
Boynton, David A. ... Rockville, MD
Boynton & Earle ... Milwaukee, WI
Boynton, Edwin R. ... Philadelphia, PA
Boynton, Elizabeth L. ... Portland, ME
Boynton, Esmont & Zawalich
South Bend, IN
Boynton, Esther G. ... Beverly Hills, CA
Boynton, Frederick C. ... South Bend, IN

Boynton, Frederick G. ... Atlanta, GA
Boynton, Gary J. ... Orlando, FL
Boynton, George H. ... Tuxedo Park, NY
Boynton, Henry J. ... Lansing, MI
Boynton, Jack E. ... Traverse City, MI
Boynton, Jacqueline E ... Milwaukee, WI
Boynton, James S. ... New York, NY
Boynton, Jay C. ... Andover, NH
Boynton, Joe ... Worcester, MA
Boynton, John R. ... Dover, OH
Boynton, Jonathan A. ... San Diego, CA
Boynton, Julie A. ... Chicago, IL
Boynton, Lisa A. ... Chicago, IL
Boynton, Lynn Caudle ... Gaithersburg, MD
Boynton, Mark D. ... Winston-Salem, NC
Boynton, Michael S. ... Milford, CT
Boynton, Michelle M. ... Minneapolis, MN
Boynton, Paul W. ... San Anselmo, CA
Boynton, Ralph W. ... Casper, WY
Boynton, Richard J. ... Cincinnati, OH
Boynton, Robert F. ... Boston, MA
Boynton, Robert H. ... Milford, CT
Boynton, Robert H., P.C. ... Milford, CT
Boynton, Robert L. ... Troy, MI
Boynton, Roger E. ... Abbeville, LA
Boynton, Sally J. ... White Plains, NY
Boynton, Theodore K. ... San Jose, CA
Boynton, Victoria L. ... Westport, CT
Boynton, Waldron, Doleac, Woodman & Scott, Professional Association
Portsmouth, NH
Boysaw, Bryan K. ... Palm Beach Gardens, FL
Boysaw, Marsha A. ... Los Angeles, CA
Boysen, Connie J. ... Overland Park, KS
Kansas City, MO
Boysen, Connie J., P.A., P.C.
Overland Park, KS
Kansas City, MO
Boysen, David C. ... Rochester, NY
Boysen, Douglas R. ... Milwaukee, WI
Boyson, Frank A. ... Elyria, OH
Boyson, Mark A. ... Bellingham, WA
Boyson, Phyllis D. ... Sacramento, CA
Boyt, Jefferson E. ... Austin, TX
Boyte, G. Griffin ... Humboldt, TN
Boyte, Gregory S. ... Los Angeles, CA
Boyte, Katherine (Kitty) D. ... Nashville, TN
Boyte, Mary Katherine ... Yuma, AZ
Boyte, Samuel F. ... Atlanta, GA
Boyuk, Walter C. ... Columbus, OH
Boyum, Arne F. ... Rolla, ND
Boyum, William ... Asheville, NC
Boywid, E.T., P.A. ... Pensacola, FL
Boywid, Edward T. ... Pensacola, FL
Bozajian, James R. ... Los Angeles, CA
Bozanian, Elton J. ... Hackensack, NJ
Bozanich, Dinko J. ... Los Angeles, CA
Bozanich, Peter Andre ... Los Angeles, CA
Bozarth, Bennett E. ... Marlton, NJ
Bozarth, James H. ... Roswell, NM
Bozarth, Keith S. ... Jefferson City, MO
Bozarth, Lisa Dianne ... Oklahoma City, OK
Bozarth, Margaret A. ... Harrisburg, PA
Bozarth, Melinda Hoyle ... Austin, TX
Bozarth, R. Drake ... Des Moines, WA
Bozarth, Rick ... Taloga, OK
Bozarth, Robert S. ... Richmond, VA
Bozarth, Ronald L. ... Seattle, WA
Bozarth, Ross B. ... Sacramento, CA
Bozarth, Shawn A. ... Harrisburg, PA
Bozarth, Stephen J. ... Orlando, FL
Bozarth, Troy A. ... Edwardsville, IL
Bozarth & Vickers, A Professional Corporation ... Roswell, NM
Bozarth, William C. ... Vienna, VA
Boze, John L. ... Sacramento, CA
Bozeat, Jennifer M. ... San Francisco, CA
Bozeat, Sally H. ... Camillus, NY
Bozek, Adam S. ... Stamford, CT
Bozek, Joan L. ... New London, CT
Bozek, Laura L. ... Chicago, IL
Bozek, Matthew J. ... New York, NY
Bozeka, George Angelo ... Akron, OH
Bozelko, Ronald F. ... Orange, CT
Bozelko, Ronald F., P.C. ... Orange, CT
Bozell, Douglas Allen
Maryland Heights, MO
Bozeman, A. Ted ... Hayneville, AL
Bozeman, Alzetta L. ... Chicago, IL
Bozeman, Bruce L. ... Mount Vernon, NY
Bozeman, C. Howard ... Knoxville, TN
Bozeman, Frank C., III
Fort Walton Beach, FL
Panama City, FL
Pensacola, FL
Bozeman, Frank C., Jr.
Fort Walton Beach, FL
Panama City, FL
Pensacola, FL
Bozeman, Jenkins & Matthews, P.A.
Fort Walton Beach, FL
Milton, FL
Panama City, FL
Pensacola, FL
Bozeman, John R. ... Aiken, SC
Bozeman, Marc H. ... Los Angeles, CA
Bozeman, Marcus Neil ... Memphis, TN
Bozeman, Neighbour, Patton & Noe
Moline, IL
Rock Island, IL
Davenport, IA
Bozeman, Robert J. ... Monroe, LA
Bozeman, Thomas H. ... Greenville, SC
Bozeman & Trott, LLP ... Mount Vernon, NY
Bozeman, Virgil ... Moline, IL
Bozeman, W. Steve ... Pascagoula, MS
Bozeman, William T. ... Nashville, TN
Bozemore, Joseph A. ... Sylvania, GA
Bozen, Nicholas L. ... Lansing, MI
Bozenhard, Robert W., Jr.
West Springfield, MA
Bozenhard, Socha & Ely
West Springfield, MA
Bozentka, Lynn M. ... Bethesda, MD
Bozer, Alan J. ... Buffalo, NY
Bozetarnik, Cecelia C. ... Brattleboro, VT
Bozgoz, Enver ... Klamath Falls, OR
Bozian, Robin A. ... Marietta, OH
Bozic, Martha ... Chicago, IL
Bozicevic, Field & Francis, LLP
Palo Alto, CA
Bozicevic, Karl ... Palo Alto, CA
Bozich, Bruce M. ... Palos Heights, IL
Bozich, Darinco ... Indio, CA
Bozich-Di Luigi, Maryann ... Mars, PA
Bozick, Gary W. ... Chicago, IL
Bozik, Gillian T. ... Allentown, PA
Bozik, James S. ... Valparaiso, IN
Bozik, Margaret Joanne ... Alburg, VT
Bozimowski, Walter A.
Clinton Township, MI
Bozkaya, Terri D. ... Anchorage, AK
Bozman-Moss, Barbara L. ... Santa Rosa, CA
Bozman-Moss & Watson ... Santa Rosa, CA
Boznos, William P. ... Long Grove, IL
Bozof, Richard P. ... Washington, DC
Bozoian, Harry D. ... Jefferson City, MO
Bozonie, Barbara A. ... St. Paul, MN
Bozorgi, Guita ... Chicago, IL
Bozorgi, Tracie Militano ... Chicago, IL
Bozorth, Squire N. ... New York, NY
Bozorth, Susan L. ... Monroe, OH
Bozovich, Vesna ... St. Louis, MO
Bozung, Linda J. ... Los Angeles, CA
Bozych, Paul ... Chicago, IL
Bozza, Guido V. ... Gates Mills, OH
Bozza, Joseph D. ... Spring Lake, NJ
Bozza, Kenneth R ... New York, NY
Bozza, Mario ... Boston, MA
Bozza, Mary Kaye ... Cleveland, OH
Bozza, Michael J. ... Trenton, NJ
Bozzacco, Glenn S. ... Philadelphia, PA
Bozzelli, Karen A. ... Akron, OH
Bozzetti, Domnick ... Jacksonville, FL
Bozzi, Nicholas C. ... Philadelphia, PA
Bozzo, Bruce J. ... San Francisco, CA
Bozzo, Frank J. ... Fayetteville, AR
Bozzo, George L. ... Boulder Creek, CA
Bozzo, Paul P. ... Rego Park, NY
Bozzo, Stephen E. ... Arlington, VA
Bozzone, Cynthia R. ... Huntington Beach, CA
Bozzuffi, William J. ... Tuxedo Park, NY
Bozzuto, David J. ... Waterbury, CT
Bozzuto, Elizabeth A. ... Waterbury, CT
Bozzuto, Jacqueline ... Orlando, FL
Braa, Michael W., Sr. ... Fresno, CA
Braaf, Estelle M. ... Los Angeles, CA
Braafladt, Arnie Rolf ... San Jose, CA
Braaksma, Calvin L. ... Bozeman, MT
Braasch, Debra L. ... Irvine, CA
Braasch, George H. ... Downers Grove, IL
Braaten, Gena A. ... Minneapolis, MN
Braaten, James S. ... Toms River, NJ
Braaten, Karen K., Ltd. ... Grand Forks, ND
Braaten, Karen Kosanda ... Grand Forks, ND
Braatz, David E. ... Crown Point, IN
Braatz, John R. ... New York, NY
Braatz, William B. ... Carmel, NY
Braband, Sandi Monroe ... Houston, TX
Brabant, Gerard F. ... Roscommon, MI
Brabant, Gerard F., P.C. ... Roscommon, MI
Brabant, Lisa ... New York, NY
Brabant, Thomas C. ... Lexington, KY
Brabbit, Lisa Montpetit ... Minneapolis, MN
Brabbit, Robert T. ... Minneapolis, MN
Brabec, Mark E. ... Schaumburg, IL
Brabec, Thomas A. ... Stevens Point, WI
Brabec, Thomas E. ... Chicago, IL
Brabec, Todd W. ... Lexington, KY
Brabec, William C. ... Jackson, MS
Brabeck, Jean M. ... Chicago, IL
Brabender, Daniel J., Jr. ... Erie, PA
Brabender, Danna C. F. ... Eugene, OR
Brabender, David J. ... Eugene, OR
Brabender, Robert C. ... Erie, PA
Brabham, B. J. ... Richmond, VA
Brabham, David S. ... Longview, TX
Brabham, Thomas M. ... Mc Comb, MS
Brabson, Ben D. ... Sevierville, TN
Brabson, Catherine L. ... Salt Lake City, UT
Brabston, Eugene W. ... Birmingham, AL
Brabston, James K. ... Huntsville, AL
Brabston, Jamie Manasco ... Huntsville, AL
Brabston, Suzanne ... Little Rock, AR
Brabyn, Thomas Paul ... Memphis, TN
Bracaglia, John F. ... Somerville, NJ
Bracaglia, John F., Jr. ... Somerville, NJ
Bracaglia, Thomas P. ... Collingswood, NJ
Philadelphia, PA
Bracaglia, Wendy Johnston
Philadelphia, PA
Bracaglia, William L. ... Secaucus, NJ
Bracamonte, Eugene R. ... Tucson, AZ
Bracanovich, Judith Ann ... Portland, OR
Bracci, Leo J. ... Avon, NY
Braccialarghe, Randolph
Fort Lauderdale, FL
Bracciale, Vito A. ... Newton, MA
Braccio, Joseph L. ... Buffalo, NY
Bracco, Michael A. ... San Mateo, CA
Bracco, Robert A., & Associates
Columbus, OH
Bracco, Steven ... Jericho, NY
Brace, Anna C. ... Irvine, CA
Brace & Crowdis, A Prof. Law Corp.
Sacramento, CA
Brace, Danny D., Jr. ... Sacramento, CA
Brace, David A. ... Moline, KS
Brace, Douglas A. ... Nashville, TN
Brace, Frederic F., Jr. ... Chicago, IL
Brace, Frederic F., Jr., Law Firm of
Chicago, IL
Brace, Glenn E. ... Boston, MA
Brace, Michael W. ... Vancouver, WA
Brace, Robert L. ... Santa Barbara, CA
Brace, William A. ... Santa Barbara, CA
Braceful, Brenda E. ... Detroit, MI
Bracegirdle, Thad J. ... Wilmington, DE
Braceras, Andrew M. ... Falmouth, MA
Braceras, Jennifer Cabranes ... Boston, MA
Braceras, Roberto M. ... Boston, MA
Bracewell, Bradley F. ... Houston, TX
Bracewell, Fentress ... Houston, TX
Bracewell & Patterson, L.L.P.
Washington, DC
Austin, TX
Corpus Christi, TX
Dallas, TX
Fort Worth, TX
Houston, TX
San Antonio, TX
Bracewell, R. M. ... St. Paul, MN
Bracewell, Searcy ... Houston, TX
Bracey, Bill E., Jr. ... Blytheville, AR
Bracey, Destafhino S. ... Washington, DC
Bracey, Earl ... Macomb, IL
Bracey, Faye Machen ... San Antonio, TX
Bracey, Kali N. ... Washington, DC
Bracey, Lucius H., Jr. ... Charlottesville, VA
Bracey, Thomas D., Law Office of
San Antonio, TX
Brach, Eichler, Rosenberg, Silver, Bernstein, Hammer & Gladstone, A Professional Corporation ... Roseland, NJ
Brach, Gilbert E., Jr. ... Racine, WI
Brach, Norma Darshan ... Boston, MA
Brach, Richard S. ... New York, NY
Brach, William L. ... Roseland, NJ
Bracher, John A. ... York, PA
Bracher, Pamela Blass ... Chattanooga, TN
Brachfeld, Emanuel ... New York, NY
Brachfeld, Erica ... Los Angeles, CA
Brachfeld, Joseph ... Stamford, CT
Brachfeld, Martin ... Westlake Village, CA
Brachfeld, Sheppard & Colman
Westlake Village, CA
Brachfeld, Susan ... Westlake Village, CA
Brachman, Lisa ... Raleigh, NC
Brachman, Mitchell S. ... Beverly Hills, CA
Bracht, Daniel P. ... West Point, NE
Bracht, David L. ... Omaha, NE
Bracht, Gerald L. ... Houston, TX
Brachtenbach, Robert F. ... Olympia, WA
Brachtl, Martis Ann ... New York, NY
Brachtl, Susan Porter ... New York, NY
Brachvogel, Paul A. ... Tacoma, WA
Brack, Brian P. ... Clovis, NM
Brack, Charles S. ... Anahuac, TX
Brack, Gregory H. ... Marietta, GA
Brack, Joe B. ... Baytown, TX
Brack, Kurt S. ... Merriam, KS
Brack, Lindsay R. ... San Diego, CA
Brack & Mason ... San Diego, CA
Brack, Sarah Lovejoy ... Charleston, WV
Brack, William T. ... Washington, DC
Brackbill, Andrew M. ... Seattle, WA
Brackbill, Charles L., Jr.
Boynton Beach, FL
Brackbill & Livengood ... Seattle, WA
Bracke, Anthony Joseph ... Covington, KY
Bracke, Dona ... Glendale, CA
Bracke, Michelle M. ... Chicago, IL
Brackeen, Bill L. ... Houston, TX
Brackeen, Herbert P. ... Wichita, KS
Brackel, Walter F. ... Dearborn, MI
Brackelmanns, Lisa Anne ... Los Angeles, CA
Brackemyre, Jayne F. ... Atlanta, GA
Bracken, Andrew J. ... Des Moines, IA
Bracken, Anne Margaret ... New York, NY
Bracken and Baram ... Boston, MA
Bracken, Beverly Willis ... Waco, TX
Bracken, Carol Ware ... Fort Worth, TX
Bracken, Clyde ... Dallas, TX
Bracken, David S. ... Alexandria, VA
Bracken, Douglas C. ... Dallas, TX
Bracken, Edward P., Jr. ... Mineola, NY
Bracken, Frank A. ... Indianapolis, IN
Bracken, Gary L. ... Ponca City, OK
Bracken, Geoffrey H. ... Houston, TX
Bracken, Hugh J. ... Media, PA
Bracken, Hugh J. ... Philadelphia, PA
Bracken, J. Owen, Jr. ... Baltimore, MD
Bracken, James P. ... Buffalo, NY
Bracken, Jeffrey W. ... Lansing, MI
Bracken, John H. ... Providence, RI
Bracken, John J., III ... Hartford, CT
Bracken, John P. ... Islandia, NY
Bracken, Kelly L. ... Philadelphia, PA
Bracken, L. Robert ... Dallas, TX
Bracken, Larry C. ... Fort Worth, TX
Bracken, Lawrence J. ... Brooklyn, NY
Bracken, Lawrence J., II ... Atlanta, GA
Bracken, Linda J. ... Mission Viejo, CA
Bracken, Linda K. ... Bellevue, WA
Bracken & Margolin, LLP
Central Islip, NY
Hauppauge, NY
Islandia, NY
Riverhead, NY
Bracken, Mary J. ... Edina, MN
Bracken, Michael ... New York, NY
Bracken, Morris & Powell, L.L.P.
Ponca City, OK
Bracken, Nanette Beattie ... Ridgefield, CT
Bracken, Paul M. ... El Paso, TX
Bracken, Robert ... Frankfort, IN
Bracken, Roger W. ... Bailey's Crossroads, VA
Bracken, Thomas B. ... Boston, MA
Bracken, Thomas E. ... Newton, NJ
Bracken, Thomas H. ... La Crosse, WI
Bracken, Thomas J. ... New York, NY
Bracken, Truly F. ... Atlanta, GA
Bracken, W. Christopher ... Atlanta, GA
Bracken, W. Earl, Jr. ... Waco, TX
Bracken, William Lee ... Okeechobee, FL
Bracken-Emerson, Jill ... Indianapolis, IN
Brackenridge, Dean R. ... Indianapolis, IN
Bracker, Beverly K. ... San Diego, CA
Bracker, I. Henry ... Savannah, GA
Bracker, Lorraine K. ... Flushing, NY
Brackett, A. William ... Fort Worth, TX
Brackett, Alan Guy ... New Orleans, LA
Brackett, Alexander P.
Bloomfield Hills, MI
Brackett, B. Michael ... Columbia, SC
Brackett, Barbara L. ... Fairfax, VA
Brackett & Brackett, P.C. ... Great Falls, VA
Brackett, Charles M. ... Houston, TX
Brackett, Claud F., Jr. ... Norcross, GA
Brackett, Colquitt P., Jr. ... Athens, GA
Brackett, David G.H. ... Atlanta, GA
Brackett, Deke W. ... Knoxville, TN
Brackett, Douglas A. ... Charlotte, NC
Brackett, Douglas Anthony ... Columbia, SC
Brackett & Ellis, A Professional Corporation
Fort Worth, TX
Brackett, Gary S. ... Worcester, MA
Brackett, J. Steven ... Hickory, NC
Brackett, J. Steven, Law Office ... Hickory, NC
Brackett, Laura J. ... Seattle, WA
Brackett Lucas ... Worcester, MA
Brackett, Martin L., Jr. ... Charlotte, NC
Brackett, Scott Douglas ... Cleveland, OH
Brackett, Shaker ... Flint, MI
Brackett, Terry O. ... Great Falls, VA
Brackett, Tim Leonard, Jr. ... McLean, VA
Brackett, William D. ... Treasury Department,
Internal Revenue Service, GV
Brackett, William F. ... Norcross, GA
Brackett, William W. ... Great Falls, VA
Brackey, Channing E. ... Fort Lauderdale, FL
Brackey, Dean L. ... Pepin, WI
Brackin, Cathy Lee ... Audubon, NJ
Brackin, Charles R. ... Lake Providence, LA
Brackin, Julian B., Jr. ... Foley, AL
Brackin, Steven K. ... Dothan, AL
Brackins, Charles G. ... Los Angeles, CA
Brackins-Willett, Linda ... Los Angeles, CA
Brackle, Ronald R. ... Fairbury, NE
Bracklein, Steven E. ... Oklahoma City, OK
Brackley, Albert J. ... Brooklyn, NY
Brackley, John C. ... Sheridan, WY
Brackley, Marguerite ... Rockland, MA
Brackley, Patrick J. ... New York, NY
Brackley, Ryan W. ... New York, NY
Brackley, Suzanne M. ... Great Neck, NY
Brackman & Associates, P.C. ... St. Louis, MO
Brackman, Jody H. ... New York, NY
Brackman, John C. ... Union, MO
Brackman, Paul ... St. Louis, MO
Brackman, Robert S. ... Houston, TX
Brackman, Robert S., P.C. ... Houston, TX
Brackman, Roberta R. ... New York, NY
Brackman, Thomas G. ... St. Louis, MO
Brackmann, Dawn D. ... Grand Rapids, MI
Brackmann, Douglas J. ... Hudsonville, MI
Bracknell, Rebecca Chesno
Treasury Department,
Internal Revenue Service, GV
Brackney, Charles P. ... Denver, CO
Brackney, Megan L. ... Jefferson City, MO
Brackney, Ruth J. ... Kansas City, MO
Brackney, William A. ... Winston-Salem, NC
Brackshaw, Susan L. ... Washington, DC
Brackx, Charles ... Harper Woods, MI
Brackx, Charles, P.C. ... Harper Woods, MI
Bracnaro, James W. ... Shelton, CT
Bracuti, Guy A. ... Treasury Department,
Internal Revenue Service, GV
Bracy, Carol Ratsamy ... Bakersfield, CA
Bracy, Delars J. ... Chicago, IL
Bracy, H. Burton ... Simpsonville, SC
Bracy, John C. ... Kingsport, TN
Bracy & Kuhl, A Legal Professional Association ... Toledo, OH
Bracy, Lance B. ... Nashville, TN
Bracy, Lorenzo E. ... Chicago, IL
Bracy, Matthew T. ... Houston, TX
Bracy, Stephen L. ... Atlanta, GA
Bracy & Vanderpool ... Houston, TX
Bracy, Warren D. ... Durham, NC
Bracy, William H. ... Toledo, OH
Brada, Robert ... Santa Monica, CA
Bradach, John F. ... Portland, OR
Bradach Law Offices ... Portland, OR
Vancouver, WA
Bradak & Clark ... Palm Springs, CA
Bradak, Glen R. ... Palm Springs, CA
Bradberry, Darlene P. ... Norfolk, VA
Bradberry, Homer W. ... Dresden, TN
Bradberry, James E. ... Newport News, VA
Bradberry, James H. ... Dresden, TN
Bradberry, Ted H. ... Columbia, SC
Bradbrooke, Timothy Dane
Valley Stream, NY
Bradburn, Wayne E., Jr. ... York, PA
Bradbury, Erin O'Neil ... Boston, MA
Bradbury, Gary Todd ... Lexington, KY
Bradbury, James D. ... Jonesboro, AR
Bradbury, J. C. ... Boston, MA
Bradbury, Lauren A. ... Pittsburgh, PA
Bradbury, Mark L. ... San Clemente, CA

Bradbury, Mary Jo ....Atlanta, GA
Bradbury, Michael A. ....Charlotte, NC
Bradbury, Michael D. ....Ventura, CA
Bradbury, Petra J. ....Cleveland, OH
Bradbury, Philip J. ....Madison, WI
Bradbury, Richard R. ....Los Angeles, CA
Bradbury, Shannon E. ....Milwaukee, WI
Bradbury, Stephen A. ....Boise, ID
Bradbury, Stephen Douglas ....Susanville, CA
Bradbury, Steven Gill ....Washington, DC
Bradbury, Timothy ....Seattle, WA
Bradbury, Victor J. ....Metairie, LA
Bradbury, William H., III ....Blue Bell, PA
Bradbury, William H., III ......Norristown, PA
Bradbury, William S. ....Falls Church, VA
Braddick, Henderson B. ....Harrison, NY
Braddock, Anne M. ....Bath, NY
Braddock, Christopher ....Denver, CO
Braddock, David B. ....Altus, OK
Braddock, Donald L. ....Jacksonville, FL
Braddock, Gerald E. ....Vicksburg, MS
Braddock, Gerald Talmadge ....Madison, MS
Braddock, Isaac H. ....Beverly Hills, CA
Braddock, James D. ....Austin, TX
Braddock, James L. ....Monroe, LA
Braddock, John R. ....Houston, TX
Braddock Law Firm, PLLC ....Madison, MS
Braddock, Maurine A. ....Iowa City, IA
Lone Tree, IA
Braddock, Patricia Finn ....Austin, TX
Braddock, Paul A. ....St. Augustine, FL
Braddock, Theda ....Annapolis, MD
Braddock, William A. ....Minneapolis, MN
Braddom, Sylvia Leong ....Dallas, TX
Braddy, G. Galen ....Greenville, NC
Braddy, Gill ....Fitzgerald, GA
Braddy, Thomas M. ....Omaha, NE
Brademan, Victoria J. ....Purchase, NY
Braden, Berwyn B. ....Lake Geneva, WI
Braden, Brenda L. ....Tualatin, OR
Braden, Brett E. ....Houston, TX
Braden, Colleen A. ....Orlando, FL
Braden, Dale S. ....Russellville, AR
Braden, Dana D., (P.A.)
West Palm Beach, FL
Braden, David E. T. ....Milwaukee, WI
Braden, David R., IV ....Denver, CO
Braden, David R., Jr. ....Golden, CO
Braden, Deborah S. ....Birmingham, AL
Braden, Donald E. ....Fountain Hills, AZ
Braden, E. Mark ....Washington, DC
Braden, Elaine Wallace ....Albany, NY
Braden, Everette A. ....Chicago, IL
Braden, Frindt, Stinar & Stageman, LLC
Colorado Springs, CO
Braden, George D. ....Scarborough, ME
Braden, Glenn A. ....Neoga, IL
Braden, Gonzalez & Associates
New Orleans, LA
Braden, Gregory C. ....Atlanta, GA
Braden, Henry E., IV, (A Law Corporation)
New Orleans, LA
Braden, J. Donald ....Stevensville, MD
Braden, J. Scott ....Faribault, MN
Braden, John A. ....Muskegon, MI
Braden, Julie E. ....San Diego, CA
Braden, Kathleen S. ....Los Angeles, CA
Ventura, CA
Braden Law Firm, A Professional Corporation
Billings, MT
Braden, Magdalen ....Philadelphia, PA
Braden, Michael T. ....Dallas, TX
Braden, Morris J. ....Billings, MT
Braden & Olson ....Lake Geneva, WI
Braden, Paul A. ....El Paso, TX
Braden, Paul E. ....Tulsa, OK
Braden, Ralph A., Jr. ......Colorado Springs, CO
Braden, Richard A. ....Buffalo, NY
Braden, Roger A. ....Wenatchee, WA
Braden, Roger N. ....Covington, KY
Cincinnati, OH
Braden, Scott W. ....Tallahassee, FL
Braden, Stanton C. ....Iselin, NJ
Braden, Susan G. ....Washington, DC
Braden & Varner, P.C. ....Dallas, TX
Braden, Victor J. ....Lawrence, KS
Braden, William C., Jr. ....Houston, TX
Bradenham, Robert E., II ....Norfolk, VA
Brader, Ruth J. ....Philadelphia, PA
Braderman, Jay R. ....Harrisburg, PA
Bradfield, Christine A. ....Atlanta, GA
Bradfield, Donald L., (P.C.)
Gaithersburg, MD
Bradfield, Eugene R. ....South Amboy, NJ
Bradfield, Jennifer ....Denver, CO
Bradfield, Mark M. .....West Palm Beach, FL
Bradfield, Mark M., P.A.
West Palm Beach, FL
Bradfield, Michael ....Washington, DC
Bradfield, Robert J., III ....Laconia, NH
Bradfield, Albert N. ....Walla Walla, WA
Bradford, Anne Marie ....Department of Justice, Executive Office for Immigration Review, GV
Bradford, B. Allen, Jr. ....Hooksett, NH
Bradford, Barbara J.
Lake Buena Vista, FL
Bradford & Barthel, LLP ....Fresno, CA
Rancho Cucamonga, CA
Sacramento, CA
Salinas, CA
Tarzana, CA
Bradford & Bradford, P.A. ....Chester, SC
York, SC
Bradford, Brady & Johnson ....Provo, UT
Bradford, Bruce O. ....Chicago, IL
Bradford, C. Steven ....Lincoln, NE
Bradford, Camille Q. ....Denver, CO
Bradford, Carl O. ....Portland, ME
Bradford, Carter A. ....Orlando, FL
Bradford, Charles E., Jr. ....Aberdeen, MD
Bradford, Charles L., Jr. ....Weatherford, TX
Bradford, Charles S. ....Greenwich, CT
Bradford, Charles S. ....York, SC
Bradford, Chris M. ....Los Angeles, CA
Bradford, Christina L. ....Louisville, KY
Bradford, Christopher J. ....Boston, MA
Bradford, Christopher T.
Los Angeles, CA
Bradford, Clarence L. ....Woodland, CA
Bradford, Coenen & Welsh ....Omaha, NE
Bradford, Curtis M. ....Hutchinson, MN
Bradford, Cynthia C. ....San Francisco, CA
Bradford, Dale A. ....Cleveland, OH
Bradford, Dana E. Walton
Federal Communications Commission, Common Carrier Bureau, GV
Bradford, Dana G., II ....Jacksonville, FL
Bradford, Daniel P. ....Boston, MA
Bradford, Darryl M. ....Chicago, IL
Bradford, David J. ....Chicago, IL
Bradford, David John ....Chicago, IL
Bradford, David R. ....Orem, UT
Bradford, David T. ....Nashville, TN
Bradford, David W. ....Buffalo, NY
Bradford, D.C. "Woody" ....Omaha, NE
Bradford & Decker ....Tulsa, OK
Bradford & Donahue, P.C. ......Birmingham, AL
Bradford, Donald E. ....Baton Rouge, LA
Bradford, Donald R. ....Tulsa, OK
Bradford, Douglas J. ....Batavia, OH
Bradford, Elizabeth J. ....Oklahoma City, OK
Bradford, Eric Kempton ....Boston, MA
Bradford, Frank ....Marietta, GA
Bradford, Fredrick J. ....Galveston, TX
Bradford, Gail Smith ....Nashville, TN
Bradford, George E. ....Pittsburgh, PA
Bradford, George E., Jr. ....Houston, TX
Bradford, George J. ....Westport, CT
Bradford, Glenn E. ....East Alton, IL
Bradford, Glenn E. ....Kansas City, MO
Bradford, Glenn E., & Associates, P.C.
Kansas City, MO
Bradford, Hal R. ....Winter Park, FL
Bradford, Harold F. ....Markleeville, CA
Bradford, Harold K., Jr. ....St. Paul, MN
Bradford, Ian A. ....Buffalo, NY
Bradford, Ira F., Jr. ....Coraopolis, PA
Bradford, J. Michael ....Beaumont, TX
Bradford, J. William ....Greenwood, SC
Bradford, James A. ....Birmingham, AL
Bradford, James J. ....Montgomery, AL
Bradford, James K. ....Springfield, MA
Bradford, James L., III ....Covington, LA
Bradford, James R. ....Redford, MI
Bradford, James W., Jr. ....York, SC
Bradford, James W., Jr. ....Angleton, TX
Bradford, Janet E. ....Fort Lauderdale, FL
Bradford, Jas. N. ....St. Paul, MN
Bradford, Jas. P. ....Birmingham, AL
Bradford, Jeffrey L. ....Phoenix, AZ
Bradford, Jerome ....Los Angeles, CA
Bradford, Jerry G. ....Dallas, TX
Bradford, J.H. Brad, III ....Atlanta, GA
Bradford, Jill L. ....Boston, MA
Bradford, John D. ....Kennebunk, ME
Bradford, John P. ....Fort Worth, TX
Bradford, John Stanton
Lake Charles, LA
Bradford, Julie A. ....Fort Worth, TX
Bradford, Keith L. ....Henderson, NV
Bradford, Kent M. ....Van Wert, OH
Bradford, Kimberly A. ....Indianapolis, IN
Bradford, Koenig, Sheppard & Kerr, L.L.P.
Houston, TX
Bradford, Koger McIntosh
Spartanburg, SC
Bradford, Laura R. ....New York, NY
Bradford, Lisa J. ....Boston, MA
Bradford, Lowell J. ....Washington, DC
Bradford, M. Ray, Jr. ....Bangor, ME
Bradford, Mark D. ....Los Angeles, CA
Rolling Hills Estates, CA
Bradford, Martina L. ....Washington, DC
Bradford, Mary Ferguson ....Beaumont, TX
Bradford, Mary R.
Department Of The Interior, National Park Service, GV
Bradford, Matthew C. ....Sacramento, CA
Bradford, Melinda K. ....Athens, OH
Bradford, Meredith ....Walnut Creek, CA
Bradford, Michael E., Law Offices of
Phoenix, AZ
Bradford, Michael E., Law Offices of
Yuma, AZ
Bradford, Michael J. ....Tampa, FL
Bradford, Michele G. ....Gadsden, AL
Bradford, Michele M. ....Philadelphia, PA
Bradford, Nancyjean ....Abingdon, VA
Bradford, Oliver F., Jr. ....Covington, LA
Bradford, Pamela G. ....New York, NY
Bradford, Patricia C. ....Milwaukee, WI
Bradford, Patrick A. ....New York, NY
Bradford, Paul D. ....Fort Worth, TX
Bradford, Peggie J. ....Los Angeles, CA
Bradford, Peter B. ....Oklahoma City, OK
Bradford, Peter C. ....Newport Beach, CA
Bradford, Philip L. ....New York, NY
Bradford & Prochnow ....Hutchinson, MN
Bradford, R. James, III ....New York, NY
Bradford, R. Larry ....Birmingham, AL
Bradford, R. Verne ....Winchester, MA
Bradford, Randall B. ....Pineville, LA
Bradford, Richard D. ....Provo, UT
Bradford, Richard L. ....Tampa, FL
Bradford, Robert A. ....Oklahoma City, OK
Bradford, Robert (Robin) H. ....Dallas, TX
Bradford, Robert T. ....Washington, DC
Bradford, Robert W., Jr.
Montgomery, AL
Bradford, Roberts J., Jr. ......Daytona Beach, FL
Bradford, Roger V. ....Valparaiso, IN
Bradford, Rufus ....Los Angeles, CA
Bradford, Rutledge M. ....Maitland, FL
Bradford, Scott F. ....Los Angeles, CA
Bradford, Stacey A. ....Washington, DC
Bradford, Standish, Jr. ......South Hamilton, MA
Bradford, Stephen L. ....Los Angeles, CA
Bradford, Steven M. ....Dallas, TX
Bradford, Susan C. ....Salt Lake City, UT
Bradford, Thomas R. ....Los Angeles, CA
Bradford, Thomas W.
Rancho Cucamonga, CA
Bradford, Timothy B. ....Los Angeles, CA
Bradford, Tracy L. ....Chicago, IL
Bradford & Trew ....Weatherford, TX
Bradford, Tudruj and Tomasky
Westport, CT
Bradford, William A., Jr.
Washington, DC
Bradford, William H., Jr.
Washington, DC
Bradford, William J. ....Sun City, AZ
Bradham, Bennett & Korth, P.A.
St. Petersburg, FL
Bradham, John M. ....Washington, DC
Bradham, Joseph W., Jr. ....St. Petersburg, FL
Bradham, Sharmaine ....Philadelphia, PA
Bradican, Michael F.
Department Of Veterans Affairs, Board of Veterans Appeals, GV
Bradican, William F. ....Scranton, PA
Bradicich, R. Barton, Jr ....Victoria, TX
Bradie, Anna B. ....Houston, TX
Bradie, Bradie & Bradie ....Houston, TX
Bradie, Michell S. ....Houston, TX
Bradie, Peter R. ....Houston, TX
Bradigan, Brian J. ....Columbus, OH
Bradin, David S.
Research Triangle Park, NC
Brading, Edward T. ....Johnson City, TN
Brading, Edwin B. ....Columbia, SC
Brading, James E., II ....Johnson City, TN
Brading, Stanley G., Jr. ....Atlanta, GA
Bradish, J. Robert ....Oxnard, CA
Bradish, Margo N. ....San Francisco, CA
Bradisse, Anthony J. ....Altadena, CA
Bradlau, George F. ....New York, NY
Bradley, A. Jane
Executive Office Of The President, Office of the U.S. Trade Representative, GV
Bradley, Adam T. ....Hawthorne, NY
Bradley, Al L., Jr. ....Houston, TX
Bradley, Andrea Fish ....Washington, DC
Bradley, Andrea J. ....Fort Lauderdale, FL
Bradley, Andrew G. ....New Canaan, CT
Bradley, Ann B. ....Long Branch, NJ
Bradley, Ann K. ....San Diego, CA
Bradley, Annette L. ....Las Vegas, NV
Bradley, Ansel L. ....Ellenwood, GA
Bradley Arant Rose & White LLP
Birmingham, AL
Huntsville, AL
Washington, DC
Bradley, Aubrey J., Jr. ....Wichita, KS
Bradley, Audrey Lewchik ....Boston, MA
Bradley, Barry A. ....Los Angeles, CA
Bradley, Bernard E., Jr. ....Cambridge, MA
Bradley, Bertram ....Berkeley, CA
Bradley, Beth D. ....Dallas, TX
Bradley, Beth Weems ....Memphis, TN
Bradley, Betty C. ....Houston, TX
Bradley, Bill ....Gadsden, AL
Bradley, Bill ....Reno, NV
Bradley, Billy S. ....Treasury Department, Office of the General Counsel, GV
Bradley & Blanton ....Paris, KY
Bradley & Bradley ....Chicago, IL
Bradley & Bradley ....Georgetown, KY
Bradley and Bradley ....Cleburne, TX
Bradley & Bradley, A Prof. Corp., Law Offices of ....Dallas, TX
Southlake, TX
Bradley, Bradley & Halford, L.C.
Lexington, MO
Odessa, MO
Bradley, Brendan ....Nashville, TN
Bradley, Brent D. ....Los Angeles, CA
Bradley, Brent F. ....Pensacola, FL
Bradley, Brian J. ....Chicago, IL
Bradley, Brian Scott ....Fort Worth, TX
Bradley, Bruce A. ....Hagåtña, GU
Bradley, Bryan A. ....Valparaiso, IN
Bradley & Burke, Ltd. ....Chicago, IL
Bradley, Burke W., Jr. ....Fremont, CA
Bradley, Burnett & Kinyon, Professional Association ....Keene, NH
Bradley, Byron K. ....Chicago, IL
Bradley, C. Allen, Jr. ....De Ridder, LA
Bradley, C. Craig, Jr. ....Louisville, KY
Bradley, C. Harvey, Jr. ....Indianapolis, IN
Bradley, C. William, Jr. ......New Orleans, LA
Bradley, Campbell, Carney & Madsen, Professional Corporation ....Golden, CO
Bradley, Carole W. ....Pasadena, CA
Bradley, Carrell F. ....Portland, OR
Bradley, Catherine M. ....San Diego, CA
Bradley, Cecilia ....Tallahassee, FL
Bradley, Charles A. ....Billings, MT
Bradley, Charles A., III ....White Plains, NY
Bradley, Charles H., III ....Concord, NH
Bradley, Charles H. D., II ....New Haven, CT
Bradley, Charles W. ....Edgard, LA
Bradley, Charles W. ....New York, NY
Bradley, Charlotte A. ....Washington, DC
Bradley, Cheryl J. ....White Plains, NY
Bradley, Chester A., III ....Monroe, LA
Bradley, Christine M.
Federal Deposit Insurance Corporation, Liquidation Branch, GV
Bradley, Christopher K. ....Decatur, IL
Bradley, Christopher T. ....New York, NY
Bradley, Clay P. ....San Francisco, CA
Bradley & Coleman ....Blytheville, AR
Jonesboro, AR
Bradley, Craig C. ....Chicago, IL
Bradley, Craig M. ....Bloomington, IN
Bradley, Curley, Asiano & McCarthy, A Prof. Corp. ....Sacramento, CA
Newport Beach, CA
San Francisco, CA
San Rafael, CA
Denver, CO
Bradley, Dan P. ....Anahuac, TX
Bradley, Dan R. ....Waverly, TN
Bradley, Daniel L. ....Belleville, IL
Bradley, Daniel Michael, Jr. ....Woburn, MA
Bradley, Daniel O. ....Atlanta, GA
Bradley, David B. ....Amarillo, TX
Bradley, David E. ....Department of Justice, Foreign Claims Settlement Commission of the United States, GV
Bradley, David H. ....Hanover, NH
Norwich, VT
Bradley, David H. ....Dallas, TX
Bradley, David Paul ....Cleveland, OH
Bradley, David V.L. ....Buffalo, NY
Bradley & Dees ....Clarksdale, MS
Bradley & Deike ....Edina, MN
Bradley, Dennis A. ....Lexington, KY
Bradley, Diane
Equal Employment Opportunity Commission, Office of Federal Operations, GV
Bradley, Don R. ....Austin, TX
Bradley, Donald E. ....Irvine, CA
Bradley, Donald E. ....Palo Alto, CA
Bradley, Donald F. ....Manchester, CT
Bradley, Donald J. ....St. Petersburg, FL
Bradley, Dorothy M. ....Bozeman, MT
Bradley, Drendel & Jeanney ....Reno, NV
Bradley, Duncan L. ....Arvada, CO
Bradley, E. Michael ....New York, NY
Bradley, E. Rex ....Bowling Green, MO
Bradley, E. Rex ....Louisiana, MO
Bradley, E. Ronald ....St. Petersburg, FL
Bradley, E. Scott ....Georgetown, DE
Wilmington, DE
Bradley, Earl M. ....Knoxville, TN
Bradley, Edmund J. ....Santa Ana, CA
Bradley, Edward ....Philadelphia, PA
Bradley, Edward F. ....Naugatuck, CT
Bradley, Edward F., Jr. ....Portland, ME
Bradley, Edward J. ....Chicago, IL
Bradley, Edward J. ....Philadelphia, PA
Bradley, Edward J., Jr. ....Chicago, IL
Bradley, Edwin J. ....Davis, CA
Bradley, Edwin J. ....Tampa, FL
Bradley, Edwin L., II ....San Francisco, CA
Bradley, Eileen ....Washington, DC
Bradley, Elisabeth Stewart ....New York, NY
Bradley, Elizabeth A. ....Edwardsville, IL
Bradley, Elizabeth Franco
Beverly Hills, CA
Bradley, Elizabeth Franco
Los Angeles, CA
Bradley, Elizabeth L. ....Beverly Hills, CA
Bradley, Eric L. ....Pittsburgh, PA
Bradley, Eric R. ....Dallas, TX
Bradley, E. T., Jr. ....Roswell, GA
Bradley, Eugene J. ....Bala Cynwyd, PA
Bradley, F. James ....Cedar Rapids, IA
Bradley & Farris ....Columbus, OH
Bradley, Francis M. ....Melbourne, FL
Bradley, Francis R., III ....Houston, TX
Bradley, Frank E. ....San Antonio, TX
Bradley, Franklyn D., II ....Philadelphia, PA
Bradley, Fred F. ....Frankfort, KY
Bradley, Frederick W. ....San Francisco, CA
Bradley, Frederick W. ....New Orleans, LA
Bradley & Freed, P.S.C. ....Paducah, KY
Bradley, Gail E., Jr. ....Greencastle, IN
Bradley, Galen A. ....Merrillville, IN
Bradley, Garrett J. ....Boston, MA
Bradley, Gary A. ....Englewood, CO
Bradley, Gary J. ....Benicia, CA
Bradley, Gary R. ....Lexington, MO
Odessa, MO
Bradley, Geoffrey J. ....Wilmington, OH
Bradley, Georganne W. ....Las Vegas, NV
Bradley, George C. ....Carlisle, PA
Bradley, George E. ....Laguna Hills, CA
Bradley, George H. ....Treasury Department, Internal Revenue Service, GV
Bradley & Geren ....Groesbeck, TX
Bradley & Giardini ....Lorain, OH
Bradley, Gina A. ....Dayton, OH
Bradley, Gorman, Jr. ....Paducah, KY
Bradley, Gregory L. ....Indianola, PA
Bradley, G.S. Stephen ....Lafayette, LA
Bradley, Guthery, Turner & Curry
Charlotte, NC
Bradley, Harry J. ....Media, PA
Bradley & Hatcher ....Columbus, GA
Bradley, Helene Gorman ....Chicago, IL
Bradley, Herman D., (P.C.) ....Nashville, TN
Bradley, Hilbert L. ....Gary, IN
Bradley, Homer S., Jr. ....Keene, NH
Bradley, J. Albert ....North Andover, MA
Bradley, J. Chris ....North Little Rock, AR
Bradley, J. Craig, Jr. ....Georgetown, KY
Paris, KY

Brady, Bruce M. ....New York, NY
Brady, C. Michael ....Morristown, NJ
Brady, Carole E. ....Lansing, MI
Brady, Carolyn Barnett
Morehead City, NC
Brady, Carolyn C. ....New Haven, CT
Brady, Catherine M. ....Cleveland, OH
Brady, Cathleen Russell ....Washington, DC
Brady, Celeste Stahl ....Newport Beach, CA
Brady, Charles A., III ....Lenoir, NC
Brady, Charles E. ....River Falls, WI
Brady, Charles J. ....Flushing, NY
Brady, Charles R. ....Laguna Beach, CA
Brady, Cheryl Hellmann ....Houston, TX
Brady, Christine Marie ....Chesterfield, VA
Brady, Christopher ....Bloomfield, NJ
New York, NY
Brady, Christopher G. ....Dallas, TX
Brady, Christopher J. ....Charlotte, NC
Brady, Christy L. ....Miami, FL
Brady, Clifford C. ....Mobile, AL
Brady, Connolly & Masuda, P.C.
Chicago, IL
Brady, Coyle and Schmidt ....Toledo, OH
Brady, Cynthia Antonak ....Winnetka, IL
Brady, Daniel J. ....Westmont, IL
Brady, Daniel O. ....Freeport, NY
Brady, David A. ....Orange, CA
Brady, David B. ....Morristown, NJ
Brady, David M. ....Redding, CA
Brady, David N. ....Cookeville, TN
Brady, David S. ....Camp Hill, PA
Brady, David S. ....Sugar Land, TX
Brady, Denise A. ....Austin, TX
Brady, Dennis A. ....Marcus, IA
Remsen, IA
Brady, Dennis C. ....Annapolis, MD
Brady, Dennis C., P.C. ....Annapolis, MD
Brady, Dennis J. ....Merrick, NY
Brady, Diane Webster ....Plattsburgh, NY
Brady, Donald A., Jr. ....Bella Vista, AR
Springdale, AR
Brady, Donald E. ....Wilmot, NH
Brady, Donald S. ....Fillmore, CA
Brady, Donley L. ....Los Angeles, CA
Brady, Donna L. ....Irvine, CA
Brady, Donna M. ....Mineola, NY
Brady, Donna M. ....Westbury, NY
Brady, Douglas A.
Christiansted, St. Croix, VI
Brady, Douglas J. ....Philadelphia, PA
Brady, Douglas W. ....Dallas, TX
Brady, Douglas W., & Associates, A Prof.
Corp., The Law Offices of ....Dallas, TX
Brady, Edmund M., Jr. ....Detroit, MI
Brady, Edw. L. ....Hollister, CA
Brady, Edward J. ....Haddon Heights, NJ
Brady, Edward J. ....Columbus, OH
Brady, Edward L. ....Hazleton, PA
Brady, Edward P., III ....Bridgeport, CT
Brady, Edward T., Jr. ....Louisville, KY
Brady, Edward Thomas ....Fayetteville, NC
Brady, Edward W. ....Baltimore, MD
Brady, Eileen M. ....Holyoke, MA
Brady, Elaine Caprio ....Boston, MA
Brady, Elizabeth M. ....San Diego, CA
Brady, Enoch C. ....New York, NY
Brady, Erin M. ....Pittsburgh, PA
Brady, Francis A., III ....Kew Gardens, NY
Brady, Francis J. ....Hartford, CT
Brady, Francis M. ....Chicago, IL
Brady, Frank J. ....Yankton, SD
Brady, Frank J., Jr. ....West Paterson, NJ
Brady, Frank P. ....Overland Park, KS
Brady, Frank R. ....Boca Raton, FL
Brady, Gary P. ....Boston, MA
Brady, George M., III ....Washington, DC
Brady, George T. ....Charlotte, NC
Brady, Gerald W., Jr. ....Metamora, IL
Peoria, IL
Brady, Gerard P. ....Cranford, NJ
White Plains, NY
Brady, Ginger K. ....Tulsa, OK
Brady, Gregory C. ....Department of Justice,
Office of Justice Programs, GV
Brady, H. Howell, Jr. ....Georgetown, KY
Brady, Harold E., Jr. ....Glendale, AZ
Brady, Hathaway, Brady & Bretz,
Professional Corporation ....Detroit, MI
Brady, Holly A. ....Fort Wayne, IN
Brady, J. John, Jr. ....Austin, TX
Brady, J. Scott ....Wilkes-Barre, PA
Brady, Jack E. ....Dallas, TX
Brady, Jack J. ....Toledo, OH
Brady, Jack Morgan ....Sugar Land, TX
Brady, James ....Orange, CA
Brady, James ....Lafayette, LA
Brady, James Austin ....Austin, TX
Brady, James C. ....Long Beach, CA
Brady, James C. ....Fort Lauderdale, FL
Brady, James C., P.A. ....Fort Lauderdale, FL
Brady, James D. ....Philadelphia, PA
Brady, James F. ....Newark, NJ
Brady, James H. R. ....Alexandria, VA
Brady, James J. ....Baton Rouge, LA
Brady, James J. ....Barnstable, MA
Framingham, MA
Brady, James J. ....Buffalo, NY
Brady, James J. ....New York, NY
Brady, James J. ....Huntsville, TX
Brady, James M. ....Joliet, IL
Brady, James M. ....Kansas City, MO
Brady, James P. ....Toms River, NJ
Brady, James S. ....Grand Rapids, MI
Brady, James W., Jr. ....Washington, DC
Brady, Jane R. ....San Francisco, CA
Brady, Jas. F. ....St. Louis, MO
Brady, Jason M. ....Palo Alto, CA

Brady, Jeanne C. ....Boca Raton, FL
Brady, Jennifer Gimler ....Wilmington, DE
Brady & Jensen ....Elgin, IL
Brady, Jerry M. ....Idaho Falls, ID
Brady, Jill R. ....Henderson, KY
Brady, Joan E. ....Chicago, IL
Brady, Joan M. ....Glen Ellyn, IL
Brady, Joan P. ....Covington, KY
Brady, JoAnn M. ....Santa Barbara, CA
Brady, Joanne Canitia ....South Euclid, OH
Brady, John A. ....San Diego, CA
Brady, John A. ....Lexington, KY
Brady, John B., Jr. ....New York, NY
Brady, John C. ....Peoria, IL
Brady, John D. ....Jacksonville, FL
Brady, John D. ....Baton Rouge, LA
Brady, John D. ....Jackson, MS
Brady, John D., Jr. ....Mobile, AL
Brady, John E. ....Columbus, OH
Brady, John F. ....Palo Alto, CA
Brady, John F. ....Rehoboth Beach, DE
Brady, John F. ....Detroit, MI
Brady, John G. ....Tampa, FL
Brady, John J. ....Tucson, AZ
Brady, John J. ....Silver Spring, MD
Brady, John P. ....Wilmington, DE
Brady, John P. ....Chicago, IL
Brady, John P. ....Concord, MA
Brady, John P. ....Milwaukee, WI
Brady, John Steven ....Warren, NJ
Brady, John T. ....Peoria, IL
Brady, John W. ....Mauston, WI
Brady, Jon E. ....Casper, WY
Brady, Joseph E. ....Howard Beach, NY
Brady, Joseph H. ....Central Islip, NY
Brady, Joseph J., Jr. ....Poway, CA
Brady, Joseph T. ....Boston, MA
Brady, Joseph V. ....Lexington, MS
Brady, Karen A. ....Kansas City, MO
Brady, Karen L. ....Arvada, CO
Brady, Karen, P.C. ....Arvada, CO
Brady, Katherine A. ....San Francisco, CA
Brady, Kathleen Callan ....Milwaukee, WI
Brady, Kay M. ....Pittsburgh, PA
Brady, Keith A. ....New York, NY
Brady, Keith R. ....Wilmington, DE
Brady, Kelly H. ....Charlotte, NC
Brady, Kenneth P. ....Richmond, VA
Brady, Kevin F. ....Wilmington, DE
Brady, Kevin G. ....Anchorage, AK
Seattle, WA
Brady, Klein & Weissman, LLP
Los Angeles, CA
New York, NY
Brady, Larry O. ....Waco, TX
Brady, Laura ....Department of Justice,
Executive Office for Immigration Review,
GV
Brady, Laura A. ....Florham Park, NJ
Brady, Laura J. ....Wilsonville, OR
Brady, Lawrence M. ....Rosemont, IL
Brady, Lawrence P., Jr. ....Kearny, NJ
Brady, Leonard V. ....Milwaukee, WI
Brady Lerma, Chartered ....Boise, ID
Brady, Linn A. ....New York, NY
Brady, Lisa O. ....Cut Off, LA
Brady, Lois I. ....Oakland, CA
Brady, Lynne Ellen ....Cedar Rapids, IA
Brady, M. James ....Provo, UT
Brady, M. Jane ....Wilmington, DE
Brady, Marcia P. ....Fountain Valley, CA
Brady, Margaret M. ....New York, NY
Brady, Mark F. ....Kansas City, MO
Brady, Marsha ....Hillsboro, MO
Brady, Martin J. ....Sparta, NJ
Brady, Mary Ann ....Spokane, WA
Brady, Mary E. ....Madison, IN
Brady, Mary Jo ....New York, NY
Brady, Mathew M. ....Bakersfield, CA
Brady, Matthew J. ....Simsbury, CT
Brady, Matthew O. ....Chicago, IL
Brady, Matthew T. ....Cleveland, OH
Brady, Matthew V. ....Sacramento, CA
Brady, Melanie R. ....Washington, DC
Brady, Michael ....Grosse Pointe Park, MI
Brady, Michael A. ....Buffalo, NY
Brady, Michael A. ....Kingston, PA
Brady, Michael A. ....Memphis, TN
Brady, Michael G. ....San Diego, CA
Brady, Michael G. ....Largo, FL
Brady, Michael G. ....Boise, ID
Brady, Michael G. ....Detroit, MI
Brady, Michael G., P.A. ....Largo, FL
Brady, Michael H., (P.C.)
Oklahoma City, OK
Brady, Michael J. ....Redwood City, CA
Brady, Michael J. ....Southfield, MI
Brady, Michael J. ....Hackensack, NJ
Brady, Michael L. ....Detroit, MI
Lansing, MI
Brady, Michael L. ....Bellefontaine, OH
Brady, Michael S. ....Lake Success, NY
Brady, Michael T. ....Washington, DC
Brady, Michael V. ....Sacramento, CA
Brady, Nancy M. ....Albany, OR
Brady, Norman C. ....Houston, TX
Brady & Orseck, L.L.P. ....Waldwick, NJ
Brady & O'Shea, P.C. ....Cedar Rapids, IA
Brady, Owen J. ....Pasadena, CA
Brady, P. John ....Kansas City, MO
Brady & Paduano ....Toms River, NJ
Brady, Patricia A. ....Honolulu, HI
Brady, Patricia A. ....Madison, WI
Brady, Patricia M. ....Charlottesville, VA
Brady, Patricia S. ....Los Angeles, CA
Brady, Patrick D. ....Lansing, MI
Brady, Patrick E. ....Chicago, IL
Brady, Patrick G. ....Newark, NJ

Brady, Patrick M. ....Wausau, WI
Brady, Patrick O. ....Waco, TX
Brady, Patrick S. ....Seattle, WA
Brady, Patti Austin ....Pickens, SC
Brady, Paul E. ....Wheaton, IL
Brady, Paul R., III ....Philadelphia, PA
Brady, Peggy Surabian
Farmington Hills, MI
Brady, Peter F. ....Boston, MA
Brady, Peter F. ....Holyoke, MA
Brady, Peter F. ....Amherst, NY
Brady, Peter F., Jr. ....Boston, MA
Brady, Peter Ryan ....New York, NY
Brady, Philip L. ....Columbus, OH
Brady, Phillip D. ....Washington, DC
Brady, R. Daniel ....Raleigh, NC
Brady, Randy D. ....Norman, OK
Brady, Raymond F. ....Gainesville, FL
Brady & Reade ....Yankton, SD
Brady, Richard A. ....Washington, DC
Brady, Richard A. ....Whippany, NJ
Brady, Richard D. ....Costa Mesa, CA
Brady, Richard D. ....Tampa, FL
Brady, Richard J. ....Waldwick, NJ
Brady, Richard P. ....Greeley, CO
Brady, Richard T. ....San Antonio, TX
Brady, Richard W. ....New York, NY
Brady, Robert A. ....Port Washington, NY
Brady, Robert A. ....Cary, NC
Brady, Robert D. ....Hastings-On-Hudson, NY
Brady, Robert J. ....La Jolla, CA
Brady, Robert J. ....Redwood City, CA
Brady, Robert J. ....Denver, CO
Brady, Robert J. ....Jersey City, NJ
Brady, Robert J., Jr. ....Bowie, MD
Brady, Robert L. ....Madison, CT
Brady, Robert L. ....St. Louis, MO
Brady, Robert L. ....St. Louis, MO
Brady, Robert M. ....Cincinnati, OH
Brady, Robert M. ....Cincinnati, OH
Brady, Robert M. ....East Providence, RI
Brady, Robert P. ....Washington, DC
Brady, Robert P. ....Bismarck, ND
Brady, Robert S. ....Wilmington, DE
Brady, Robert S. ....Department of Defense,
Defense Legal Services Agency, GV
Brady, Roger M. ....Wilmette, IL
Brady, Rupert J. ....Falls Church, VA
Brady & Schaefer, LLP ....Amherst, NY
Brady, Schaulat & Falsetti, Professional
Association ....Oklahoma City, OK
Brady, Schilawski & Ingram, P.L.L.C.
Cary, NC
Raleigh, NC
Brady, Scott E. ....Baton Rouge, LA
Brady, Sean Michael ....Wilmington, DE
Brady, Spencer R. ....Santa Rosa, CA
Brady, Stacey A. ....Greensboro, NC
Brady, Stephani Brett ....Fayetteville, AR
Brady, Stephen R. ....San Francisco, CA
Brady, Steven G. ....Orlando, FL
Brady, Steven J. ....Overland Park, KS
Brady, Steven M. ....Miami, FL
Brady, Steven W. ....Dallas, TX
Brady, Terence M.
Department of Agriculture,
Office of the General Counsel, GV
Brady, Terence S. ....Mount Holly, NJ
Brady, Teresa P. ....Bensalem, PA
Brady, Terrence J. ....Waukegan, IL
Brady, Terrence R. ....Chicago, IL
Brady, Terry F. ....Toms River, NJ
Brady, Terry J. ....Kansas City, MO
Brady, Theresa L. ....Jackson, MS
Brady, Thomas A. ....San Francisco, CA
Brady, Thomas C. ....Ellicottville, NY
Salamanca, NY
Brady, Thomas E. ....Spearfish, SD
Brady, Thomas E., P.C. ....Spearfish, SD
Brady, Thomas F. ....Walpole, MA
Brady, Thomas J. ....Jersey City, NJ
Brady, Thomas J. ....Pikeville, TN
Brady, Thomas M. ....Pensacola, FL
Brady, Thomas P. ....Detroit, MI
Brady, Thomas Peter ....Worcester, MA
Brady, Thomas T. ....Tiverton, RI
Brady, Thos. J. ....Chicago, IL
Brady, Thos. P. ....Chicago, IL
Brady, Timothy ....Columbia, MO
Fulton, MO
Holts Summit, MO
Brady, Timothy Patrick ....Hartford, CT
Brady, Vickie J. ....Omaha, NE
Brady, Vivian Lee ....New York, NY
Brady, Vorwerck & Ryder ....Orange, CA
Walnut Creek, CA
Brady, W. Blair ....Fayetteville, AR
Brady, Wallace ....Fort Worth, TX
Brady, Wallace A. ....Mauston, WI
Brady, Wallace & Associates, P.C.
Fort Worth, TX
Brady, William A. ....Havertown, PA
Brady, William H. ....Honolulu, HI
Brady, William J. ....Denver, CO
Brady, William J. ....Center Line, MI
Brady, William J., III ....New York, NY
Brady, William J., Jr. ....Philadelphia, PA
Brady, William P. ....Wilmington, DE
Brady, William P. ....De Kalb, IL
Sycamore, IL
Brady, William P. ....New York, NY
Brady, William T., Jr. ....Miami, FL
Brady and Witters, P.A. ......Fort Lauderdale, FL
Braedyn, James M. ....Orlando, FL
Braegelmann, Jeffry C. ....New Ulm, MN
Braegger, Troy R. ....Denver, CO
Braem, Lee A. ....Teterboro, NJ

Braeman, Kathryn M.
Department of Defense,
Defense Legal Services Agency, GV
Braemer, Richard J. ....Philadelphia, PA
Braendel, Addison D. ....Chicago, IL
Braender, Lori J. ....Morristown, NJ
Braendle, James T. ....Cambridge, IL
Braeseke, John O. ....Morton Grove, IL
Braeuer, Wayne M.
Department Of Veterans Affairs,
Board of Veterans Appeals, GV
Braeuninger, William F. ....Monroe, MI
Braff, Adam ....Washington, DC
Braff, Andrew C., P.S. ....Colville, WA
Braff, David H. ....New York, NY
Braff, Donna Levinston ....Somerville, NJ
Braff, Harold ....New York, NY
Braff, Harold I. ....Livingston, NJ
New York, NY
Braff, Harris & Sukoneck ....Elizabeth, NJ
Livingston, NJ
Morristown, NJ
Newark, NJ
New York, NY
Braff, Jeffrey L. ....Philadelphia, PA
Braff, Jonathan L. ....Philadelphia, PA
Braff, Michael D. ....New York, NY
Braff, Sharman ....Pleasanton, CA
Braffett, Fielding G. ....Grand Junction, CO
Braff-Guajardo, Ellen L. ....Gilroy, CA
Braffman, Elaine Albom ....Orange, CT
Braffman, Gerald H. ....Orange, CT
Braffman, Susannah J. ....Los Angeles, CA
Brafford, Anne ....Washington, DC
Brafford, William C. ....Trevose, PA
Brafman, Benjamin ....New York, NY
Brafman, Bruce J. ....Irving, TX
Brafman, David S. ....New York, NY
Brafman, Frank ....Hilton Head Island, SC
Brafman, Howard J. ....Miami Lakes, FL
Brafman, Leslie R. ....Delray Beach, FL
Brafman, Neil J. ....Towson, MD
Brafman & Ross, P.C. ....New York, NY
Brafman, Stuart M. ....Chicago, IL
Brafman, Wendy S. ....St. Louis, MO
Braford, L. Brad ....Roanoke, VA
Braford, L. Brad, P.C. ....Roanoke, VA
Braga, Jamie Lee Brands ....San Jose, CA
Braga, Kathleen M. ....Lake Ridge, VA
Braga, Linda J., A P.L.C. ....Garland, TX
Braga, Linda Jean ....Garland, TX
Braga, M. Thereza ....Los Angeles, CA
Braga, Russell M. ....Orlando, FL
Braga, Stephen L. ....Washington, DC
Bragalone, Jeffrey R. ....Dallas, TX
Bragalone, Jon A. ....Fort Wayne, IN
Bragalone, Mickie S. ....Dallas, TX
Bragalone, Robert A. ....Dallas, TX
Bragan, Judith M. ....Fairfax, VA
Bragan, Judith M., P.C. ....Fairfax, VA
Bragança, Celiza P. ....Chicago, IL
Bragar, Raymond A. ....New York, NY
Bragar Wexler Eagel & Morgenstern, LLP
New York, NY
Bragaw, Rexford T., III
Department of Defense,
Defense Commissary Agency, GV
Bragdon, Alexander B. ....Detroit, MI
Bragdon Berkson Davis & Klein, P.C.
Keene, NH
Bragdon, Edwin W. ....Boston, MA
Bragdon, F. Jefferson ....Pittsburgh, PA
Bragdon, Peter J. ....Portland, OR
Bragdon, Stephen B. ....Keene, NH
Bragdon, Trina M. ....Philadelphia, PA
Brage, John R. ....St. Joseph, MO
Brager, Bernard ....Baltimore, MD
Brager, Dennis N. ....Los Angeles, CA
Brager, Dennis N., A Prof. Corp., Law
Offices of ....Los Angeles, CA
Brager, Elliott A. ....Randallstown, MD
Brager, Jeannine ....Los Angeles, CA
Brager, Marcia J. ....McLean, VA
Brager, Michelle L. ....San Francisco, CA
Brager, Robert ....Washington, DC
Baltimore, MD
Bragg, Alfred O., III ....Tallahassee, FL
Bragg, Alice Carlton ....Charlotte, NC
Bragg, Alice M. ....Houston, TX
Bragg & Baker, P.C. ....Denver, CO
Bragg, Brian E. ....Short Hills, NJ
Bragg, Caprice H. ....Cleveland, OH
Bragg, David F. ....Austin, TX
Bragg, Douglas E. ....Denver, CO
Bragg & Dziesinski ....San Francisco, CA
Bragg, Ellis M., Jr. ....Charlotte, NC
Bragg, Gary L. ....Plymouth Meeting, PA
Bragg, Gilbert T. ....Austin, TX
Bragg, Holly J. ....Miamisburg, OH
Bragg, James B. ....New York, NY
Bragg, Jeffrey M. ....Richardson, TX
Bragg, Jennifer L. ....Rockville, MD
Bragg, Jennifer L. ....Philadelphia, PA
Bragg, J. J. ....Beaumont, TX
Bragg, John C. ....Grandview, MO
Bragg, Kristi ....Summit, NJ
Bragg, Lawrence D., III ....Boston, MA
Bragg, Lee K. ....Augusta, ME
Bragg, Michael E. ....Bloomington, IL
Bragg, Michael J. ....Portland, OR
Bragg, Michael W. ....Toledo, OH
Bragg, Morgan S. ....West Palm Beach, FL
Bragg, O. Randolph ....Chicago, IL
Bragg, Patricia Dunmire ....Tulsa, OK
Bragg, Ralph ....Toledo, OH
Bragg, Robert A. ....Los Angeles, CA
Newport Beach, CA
San Francisco, CA

Bragg, Robert Lawrence .... Sacramento, CA
Bragg, Sherry S. .... Newport Beach, CA
Bragg, Short, Serota & Kuluva
Los Angeles, CA
Newport Beach, CA
Bragg, Smithers & Curry .... Austin, TX
Bragg, Suzanne E. .... Mount Laurel, NJ
Bragg, Tara L. .... Hutchinson, KS
Bragg, William K., Jr. .... Charleston, WV
Bragg, William R. .... Eureka, CA
Braggins, Todd R. .... Rochester, NY
Braghirol, David .... Columbia, SC
Bragin, Mitchell J. .... Washington, DC
Bragin, Ronald A. .... Los Angeles, CA
Braginsky, Julius .... Los Angeles, CA
Bragman, Jeffrey L. .... East Hampton, NY
Bragman, Karen Barris .... Atlanta, GA
Bragman, Lawrence Wayne
San Rafael, CA
Bragman, Melvin .... Laguna Hills, CA
Bragorgos, Nicholas E. .... Memphis, TN
Brague, Norman E. .... Wadsworth, OH
Braguner, Amy J. .... La Plata, MD
Braham, Denis C. .... Houston, TX
Braham, Lisa A. .... Los Angeles, CA
Braham, W. Walter, Jr. .... Pittsburgh, PA
Brahan, Jeffrey P. .... Pittsburgh, PA
Brahaney, Edwin L. .... Midland, TX
Brahin, H. Jeffrey .... Doylestown, PA
Brahin, Lynn Hirschfeld .... Chicago, IL
Brahinsky, David S. .... Sherman Oaks, CA
Brahm & Jenkins .... Norfolk, VA
Brahm, John W. .... Milwaukee, WI
Brahm, Michael H. .... Tarzana, CA
Brahm, R. Nash .... Norfolk, VA
Brahm, Richard C. .... Columbus, OH
Brahm, Rochelle D. .... Miami, FL
Brahm, Russell N., III .... Norfolk, VA
Brahm, Samuel B. .... St. Petersburg, FL
Brahman, Pouneh Nina .... Los Angeles, CA
Brahmbhatt, Sunil A. .... Santa Ana, CA
Brahms, David Michael .... Carlsbad, CA
Brahms & Duxbury .... Carlsbad, CA
Brahms, Ronald Jay .... San Diego, CA
Brahms, Sharon A. .... San Francisco, CA
Brahms, William A. .... Brecksville, OH
Brahmst, Oliver C. .... New York, NY
Brahn, Kathleen M. K.
Woodland Hills, CA
Brahney, Thomas M., III .... New Orleans, LA
Brahos, O. John .... Chicago, IL
Braico, Nicholas R. .... Irvine, CA
Braid, Frederick D. .... Mineola, NY
New York, NY
Braida, Charlene A. .... Philadelphia, PA
Braidwood, G. Christopher .... Chicago, IL
Braidwood, Milton R. .... Caseville, MI
Braier, Paul A. .... Reston, VA
Braig, Kevin P. .... Cincinnati, OH
Braiker-Gordon, Bonnie
Woodland Hills, CA
Brail, Herbert A. .... Dearborn, MI
Braile, Deborah L. .... Fort Lauderdale, FL
Brailey, Susan Heine .... White Plains, NY
Brailsford, Amanda K. .... Boise, ID
Brailsford, Daniel T. .... Columbia, SC
Brailsford, James M., III .... Columbia, SC
Braiman, Arthur W. .... Poughkeepsie, NY
Braiman, Arthur W., P.C. .... Poughkeepsie, NY
Braiman, Edward M. .... Rochester, NY
Braiman, Jeffrey S. .... Arlington Heights, IL
Brain, Christopher I. .... Seattle, WA
Brain, Deborah D.
Department of Housing and Urban Development,
Office of General Counsel, GV
Brain, Mark H. .... Phoenix, AZ
Brain, Michael A. .... Anchorage, AK
Brain, Paul E. .... Seattle, WA
Brain, Robert Donald .... Los Angeles, CA
Brain, Romney R. .... Seattle, WA
Brainard, Barbara A. .... Portland, OR
Brainard, C. Scott .... St. Petersburg, FL
Brainard, Calvin A. .... Seneca Falls, NY
Brainard, Charles R. .... New York, NY
Brainard, Christopher M.
Los Angeles, CA
Brainard, Eron J. .... Shreveport, LA
Brainard, Kathleen R. .... El Cajon, CA
Brainard, Kenneth .... Van Nuys, CA
Brainard, Larrie R. .... El Cajon, CA
Brainard, Lauren R. .... Los Angeles, CA
Brainard Law Offices, The .... Charleston, IL
Lawrenceville, IL
Marshall, IL
Mattoon, IL
Paris, IL
Robinson, IL
Shelbyville, IL
Sullivan, IL
Tuscola, IL
Brainard, Mark Thomas .... Dover, DE
Brainard, Norton H., III .... Philadelphia, PA
Brainard, Patrick J. .... Cleveland, OH
Brainard, Robert L. .... Long Beach, CA
Brainard, Thomas D. .... North Chicago, IL
Brainard, Todd L. .... Warren, OH
Brainerd, Alexander L. .... Palo Alto, CA
Brainerd, Betsy Boyce .... Denver, CO
Brainerd, Byron .... Wichita, KS
Brainerd, Frank J., Jr. .... Denver, CO
Brainerd, James R., Jr. .... Watertown, MA
Brainerd, John H. .... Irvine, CA
Brainerd, Richard W. .... Vega, TX
Brainerd, Scott A. .... Chicago, IL
Brainerd, Scott A., Ltd. .... Chicago, IL
Brainerd, Stanley J. .... Tallahassee, FL
Brainerd, Stephanie M. .... Portland, OR
Brainerd, Stephen M. .... Denver, CO
Brainerd, Wm F. .... Roswell, NM
Brainich, Marc .... San Francisco, CA
Brainin, David N. .... New York, NY
Brainin, Marvin H. .... Elizabeth, NJ
Brainin, Stacy L. .... Dallas, TX
Brainis, Steven M. .... Shreveport, LA
Brais, Keith S. .... Miami, FL
Brais, Louise McAlpin .... Miami, FL
Braislin, John P. .... Seattle, WA
Braisted & Braisted .... Staten Island, NY
Braisted, Charles H. B. .... New York, NY
Braisted, Christina K. .... Atlanta, GA
Braisted, David W. .... Staten Island, NY
Braisted, James P. .... Staten Island, NY
Braisted, James P., Jr. .... Staten Island, NY
Braisted, John M., III .... Staten Island, NY
Braisted, John M., Jr. .... Staten Island, NY
Braisted, Lawrence E. .... Vero Beach, FL
Braisted, Sharon Hochberg .... Cupertino, CA
Braiterman, Andrew H. .... New York, NY
Braiterman, David J. .... Concord, NH
Braiterman, Stuart N. .... Baltimore, MD
Braithwaite, Bridget A. .... Arlington, TX
Braithwaite, David G. .... Boston, MA
Braithwaite, David R. .... Madison, WI
Braithwaite, Fabian .... Nashua, NH
Braithwaite, J. William .... Chicago, IL
Hoffman Estates, IL
Braithwaite, John N. .... Salt Lake City, UT
Braithwaite, Kelley M. .... Columbia, SC
Braithwaite, Linda I. .... Tarpon Springs, FL
Braithwaite, Linda I., P.A.
Tarpon Springs, FL
Braithwaite, Robert T. .... Cedar City, UT
Braithwaite, Robin A. .... Aiken, SC
Braithwaite Smith, P.A. .... Aiken, SC
Barnwell, SC
Edgefield, SC
Saluda, SC
Braithwaite, Susan W. .... Highland Park, IL
Braithwaite, William T. .... Annapolis, MD
Braitman, Arthur R. .... Lafayette Hill, PA
Norristown, PA
Braitman, Barry H. .... Chicago, IL
Braitman, Mary Beth .... Indianapolis, IN
Braitman, Susan Irene .... Riverhead, NY
Braiwick, Robert M., Jr. .... New Orleans, LA
Brajcich, Douglas J. .... Spokane, WA
Brajcich, Gary D. .... Spokane, WA
Braje, Craig V. .... Michigan City, IN
Braje, Karen A. .... San Francisco, CA
Braje & Nelson, LLP .... Michigan City, IN
Brajevich, Joseph A. .... Beverly Hills, CA
San Pedro, CA
Brajevich, Nikki
Department of State, GV
Brajevich, Sally Patrone .... Los Angeles, CA
Brajkovich, Steven .... Covina, CA
Brake, Andrew T. .... Englewood, CO
Brake, Andrew T., P.C. .... Denver, CO
Englewood, CO
Brake, Brian K. .... Glen Allen, VA
Brake, Charles A., Jr. .... Atlanta, GA
Brake, Daniel J. .... Columbus, OH
Brake, David R. .... Lansing, MI
Brake, David S. .... Chanute, KS
Brake, Eileen M. .... Coral Gables, FL
Brake, Larry G. .... Columbus, OH
Brake, P. Joseph .... San Antonio, TX
Brake, Pamela Downing .... Watertown, MA
Brake, R. Edward .... Arlington, VA
Brake, Richard J. .... Lansing, MI
Brake, Robert M. .... Coral Gables, FL
Brake, Ryan G. .... Birmingham, AL
Florence, AL
Brake, Stephen J. .... Boston, MA
Brake, Timothy L. .... Kansas City, MO
Brake, Timothy L., P.C. .... Kansas City, MO
Brakebill, Carol A. .... New York, NY
Brakebill, David A. .... Houston, TX
Brakebill, Kenneth W. .... San Francisco, CA
Brakefield, James Cain .... Jasper, AL
Brakefield, Richard E. M. .... Palm Springs, CA
Brakefield, W. Marcus .... Tuscaloosa, AL
Brakeman, Jill B. .... Bantam, CT
Brakemeyer, Doane .... Lancaster, CA
Brakensiek, Carlyle R. .... Sacramento, CA
Brakensiek, Warren N. .... Los Angeles, CA
Braker, Debra A. .... Kansas City, MO
Braker, Gregory S. .... Washington, DC
Braker, Herbert .... Philadelphia, PA
Braker, Herbert, P.A. .... Philadelphia, PA
Braker, Jeffrey L. .... Los Angeles, CA
Braker, Robert N. .... Philadelphia, PA
Brakewood, Robert E. .... Sherman Oaks, CA
Brakke, Jon R. .... Fargo, ND
Brakoniecki, David A. .... Pittsburgh, PA
Brakora, Henry R. .... Stanwood, MI
Brakora, James M. .... Detroit, MI
Brakora, John R. .... Manistee, MI
Brakowiecki, Lester E. .... Citrus Heights, CA
Bral, J. John .... Los Angeles, CA
Braland, Samuel H. .... Earlham, IA
Braley, Barbara A. .... Parkston, SD
Braley, Bruce L. .... Waterloo, IA
Braley, Christopher M. .... Parkston, SD
Braley, Gayle Morrell .... Concord, NH
Braley, Kevin C. .... Minneapolis, MN
Braley Law Office .... Parkston, SD
Braley, Leslie A. .... Placentia, CA
Braley, Mark D. .... Richmond, VA
Braley, Michael V. .... Parkston, SD
Braley, Nan B. .... Dallas, TX
Braley, Philip R. .... Hooksett, NH
Braley, Ronald E. .... Seattle, WA
Braley, Timothy Shawn .... Enid, OK
Bralliar, Thomas B., Jr. .... Cleveland, OH
Bralove, David H. .... Washington, DC
Bralove Group, The .... Washington, DC
Bralow, David S. .... Orlando, FL
Bralow, Maxwell P. .... Plymouth Meeting, PA
Braly, Angela Fick .... St. Louis, MO
Braly & Braly and Coyne, A Partnership of Prof. Corps. .... Ada, OK
Braly, Cynthia J. .... Tulsa, OK
Braly, George W. .... Ada, OK
Braly, Hunt .... Valencia, CA
Braly, Mack Muratet .... Broken Arrow, OK
Bram, Adam N. .... West Conshohocken, PA
Bram, Adam Scott .... Los Angeles, CA
Bram, Andrew E. .... Cambridge, MA
Bram, Eric M. .... Peoria, IL
Bram, Kimberly G. .... Richmond, VA
Bram, Leslie D. .... Gainesville, FL
Braman, Darrell N., Jr. .... Baltimore, MD
Braman, James E. .... Albany, NY
Braman, John C. .... Bellevue, WA
Braman, Leonard .... Washington, DC
Braman, Michael B. .... Minneapolis, MN
Braman, Richard G. .... Minneapolis, MN
Braman, Susan J. .... Rochester, NY
Braman, William M. .... Indianapolis, IN
Bramante, Mark S. .... New York, NY
Brambach, A. Gretchen .... Walnut Creek, CA
Brambil, Joseph R. .... New York, NY
Brambilla, Robert C.
Treasury Department, GV
Brambl, Ronald M., Jr. .... Tucson, AZ
Bramble, Barbara J. .... Washington, DC
Bramble, Barry B. .... Mount Holly, NJ
Bramble, Forrest F., Jr. .... Baltimore, MD
Bramble, Mark A. .... Charleston, WV
Bramblett and Bramblett, P.C. .... El Paso, TX
Bramblett, Coll, (Mr.) .... El Paso, TX
Bramblett, C. R. Kit .... El Paso, TX
Bramblett, Debra Rhodes .... Augusta, GA
Bramblett, Edward L. .... Houston, TX
Bramblett, Eric C. .... Austin, TX
Bramblett, Eugene D. .... Camden, AR
Bramblett, Eugene, P.A. .... Camden, AR
Bramblett, George W., Jr. .... Dallas, TX
Bramblett, Karen R. .... Philadelphia, PA
Bramblett, Mary Anne .... El Paso, TX
Bramblett, McDonald & Stiles, P.C.
Augusta, GA
Bramblett, Walker H. .... Cumming, GA
Brame, Catherine G. .... Alexandria, LA
Brame, Frank A., III .... Denver, CO
Brame, Frank M. .... Lake Charles, LA
Brame, J. Robert, III
National Labor Relations Board,
Board Members, GV
Brame, Joseph A. .... Lake Charles, LA
Brame, Kenyatta Lumumba
Grand Rapids, MI
Brame & McCain .... Lake Charles, LA
Brame, Nancy O. .... Salt Lake City, UT
Brame, Patricia M. .... Las Vegas, NV
Brame, Robert G. .... San Antonio, TX
Brame, Scott M. .... Alexandria, LA
Brame, Stephen C. .... Lawrenceville, NJ
Brame, Thomas Q., Jr. .... Bay Springs, MS
Brame, Wendy J. .... Tulsa, OK
Bramell, James S. .... Nashville, TN
Bramer, James D. .... Fort Collins, CO
Bramer, Lisan H. .... Sunnyvale, CA
Bramer, Richard M. .... Sullivan, IN
Brames, Arnold H. .... Terre Haute, IN
Brames & Oldham .... Terre Haute, IN
Bramesco, Julienne W. .... Oakland, CA
Bramfeld, John F. .... Champaign, IL
Bramfeld & Wong .... Champaign, IL
Bramhall, Christopher E. .... Salt Lake City, UT
Bramhall, Eugene H. .... Provo, UT
Bramhall, R. Douglas .... Sacramento, CA
Bramhall, Samuel E. .... Los Angeles, CA
Bramhall, Thomas M. .... Fayetteville, AR
Bramhall, Thomas M., Ltd. .... Fayetteville, AR
Bramham, Charles .... New York, NY
Bramham, R. Michael .... Redding, CA
Bramlage, Gregory J. .... Los Angeles, CA
Bramlage, Julia Louise .... Detroit, MI
Bramlet, Eric .... Mount Carmel, IL
Bramlet, Robert E. .... Rochester, NY
Bramlett, Alec .... Dallas, TX
Bramlett, Brenda S. .... Shelbyville, TN
Bramlett & Bush .... Medford, OK
Bramlett, Jeffrey O. .... Atlanta, GA
Bramlett, Ken R., Jr. .... Charlotte, NC
Bramlett Law Offices .... Nashville, TN
Bramlett, Paul Kent .... Nashville, TN
Bramlett, Rick M. .... Medford, OK
Bramlett, Sharon Crawley .... Columbia, SC
Bramlette, David C., III .... Biloxi, MS
Bramlette, Robert C., Jr. .... Flossmoor, IL
Bramlette, Robert W. .... Houston, TX
Bramley, Bruce C. .... Albany, NY
Bramley, Craig Andrew .... Lewiston, ME
Bramley, Jeffrey L. .... Medina, OH
Bramley, Russell .... Warwick, RI
Bramley, William A., III .... San Diego, CA
Brammell Law Office, P.S.C.
New Castle, KY
Brammell, Rebecca A. .... Irwin, PA
Brammell, Sally A. .... New York, NY
Brammell, Stephen H. .... Las Vegas, NV
Brammell, William Hartman
New Castle, KY
Brammer, Diana Merewether .... Arlington, MA
Brammer, Florence I. .... Minneapolis, MN
Brammer, J. Wm., Jr. .... Tucson, AZ
Brammer, James E. .... Washington, DC
Brammer, James E. .... Valparaiso, IN
Brammer, Jay M. .... Sterling, CO
Brammer Law Office, P.C. .... Sterling, CO
Brammer, M. Susan .... Maysville, KY
Brammer, Matthew V. .... Cincinnati, OH
Brammer, Peggy J. .... San Francisco, CA
Brammer, Ravi .... Fort Lauderdale, FL
Brammer, Ray Ann .... Sterling, CO
Brammer, Scott W. .... McHenry, IL
Brammer, Steven Caines .... Memphis, TN
Bramnick, Andrew .... Washington, DC
Bramnick, Gale A. .... Miami, FL
Bramnick, James S. .... Miami, FL
Orlando, FL
Bramnick, Jon M. .... Plainfield, NJ
Bramnick, Jon M. .... Scotch Plains, NJ
Bramnick, Mario .... Hollywood, FL
Bramnick, Michael R. .... Horsham, PA
Bramnik, Robert P. .... Chicago, IL
Brams, Alan B. .... Waltham, MA
Brams, Craig L. .... Maitland, FL
Brams, Daniel J. .... West Palm Beach, FL
Brams, Jeffrey Brent .... West Palm Beach, FL
Brams, Marianne E. .... Portland, OR
Brams, Robert S. .... Washington, DC
Brams, Warren B. .... West Palm Beach, FL
Brams, Young & Levinson .... Norwell, MA
Waltham, MA
Bramscher, Robert G. .... Kenosha, WI
Bramson, David H. .... Los Angeles, CA
Bramson, Edwin M. .... Kansas City, MO
Bramson, Howard F. .... Washington, DC
Bramson, Howell .... White Plains, NY
Bramson, James R. .... Dulles, VA
Bramson, Janet K. .... Inglewood, CA
Bramson, Laura .... New York, NY
Bramson, Melvin R. .... Chicago, IL
Bramson, Nanci S. .... Department of Justice,
Tax Division, GV
Bramson, Philip A. .... New York, NY
Bramson & Pressman .... Conshohocken, PA
Bramson, Robert M. .... Walnut Creek, CA
Bramson, Robert S. .... Conshohocken, PA
Bramson, Victoria C. .... Trenton, NJ
Bramwell, George Y. .... New York, NY
Bramwell, Henry .... Brooklyn, NY
Bramwell, M. Russell .... Palatine, IL
Bramwell, Neil D. .... New York, NY
Bramwell, William M., Jr. .... New York, NY
Bramwit, Melinda Fellner .... Baltimore, MD
Morristown, NJ
Bran, Paul Bennett .... Washington, DC
Branagan, James J. .... Shaker Heights, OH
Branam, James T. .... Antlers, OK
Branam, Richard E. .... Coalgate, OK
Branaman, Amy .... Dallas, TX
Branan, Anne Novick, (P.A.)
Fort Lauderdale, FL
Branan, Debra Pace .... Hernando, MS
Southaven, MS
Branan, Homer B., III .... Memphis, TN
Branan, Jon Gary .... Macon, GA
Branand, David C. .... Annapolis, MD
Brana-Todd, Annemarie .... Hackensack, NJ
Branaugh, Preston J. .... Denver, CO
Branca, John G. .... Los Angeles, CA
Branca, Joseph D. .... Aston, PA
Branca, Michael A. .... Alexandria, VA
Branca, Robert G., Jr. .... Providence, RI
Branca, Ross M. .... Brooklyn, NY
Branca, Thomas C. .... Norristown, PA
Branca, William J. .... Boston, MA
Brancaccio, Marian Lyia .... Dallas, TX
Brancard, William R. .... Santa Fe, NM
Brancart, Edmond Dean .... Dodge City, KS
Brancatelli, Frank R. .... Willoughby, OH
Brancati, George A. .... Wilmington, DE
Brancato, Brancato & Brancato
Garden City, NY
Brancato, Brian P. .... New Orleans, LA
Brancato, Cynthia C.
Department of the Navy, GV
Brancato, Frank A. .... Kansas City, MO
Brancato, Frank A. .... Lancaster, OH
Brancato, Gilda .... Department of State,
Office of the Legal Adviser, GV
Brancato, Jennifer .... New York, NY
Brancato, John J. .... New York, NY
Brancato, John R. .... Navarre, FL
Brancato, Joseph A. .... Garden City, NY
Brancato, Joseph A., Jr. .... Garden City, NY
Brancato, Louis J. .... Garden City, NY
Brancato, Mark F. .... King Of Prussia, PA
Brancato, Mark J. .... Cedar Knolls, NJ
Brancato, Salvatore A. .... Jersey City, NJ
Brancato, Steven M. .... Stamford, CT
Branch, Aldo P. O. .... Campbell, CA
Branch & Associates .... Glendale, CA
Branch, Bartram C., Jr. .... Manchester, NH
Branch, Brian Kern .... Albuquerque, NM
Branch, Clifford Lanier .... Montgomery, AL
Branch, Cynthia Cleland .... Metairie, LA
Branch, Dale E. .... Bogalusa, LA
Branch, Daniel H. .... Dallas, TX
Branch, David F., Jr. .... Lumberton, NC
Branch, Deborah Fairley .... Houston, TX
Branch, Deborah K. .... New York, NY
Branch, Dewart & Wise .... Rochester, NY
Branch, Douglas A. .... Oklahoma City, OK
Branch, Dustin P. .... San Diego, CA
Branch, E. Thomas, Jr. .... Atlanta, GA
Branch, E. B. .... San Antonio, TX
Branch, Elizabeth L. .... Atlanta, GA
Branch, Eugene T. .... Atlanta, GA
Branch, Felicia L. .... Jacksonville, FL
Branch, George S. .... Atlanta, GA
Branch & Greenhalge, Prof. Assn.
Concord, NH
Branch, Harllee, Jr. .... Atlanta, GA
Branch, J. Powers .... Longview, TX
Branch, James A., III .... Atlanta, GA

Branch, James A., Jr. ....Albuquerque, NM
Branch, James Vaughan ....Gainesville, GA
Branch, Jeffrey T. ....Paragould, AR
Branch, Jennifer L. ....Cincinnati, OH
Branch, Joan E. ....Omaha, NE
Branch, John C. ....Oklahoma City, OK
Branch, John C., P.C. ....Oklahoma City, OK
Branch, John W. ....Redlands, CA
Branch, John W. ....Rochester, NY
Branch, John W. ....Seattle, WA
Branch, Johnie E., Jr. ....Baton Rouge, LA
Branch, Joseph C. ....Milwaukee, WI
Branch, Judith ....San Francisco, CA
Branch, K. Christopher ....Glendale, CA
Branch, Kathryn H. ....New York, NY
Branch, Kenneth J. ....Castro Valley, CA
Branch, Kerry E. ....Los Angeles, CA
Branch, Kimberly Dee ....New York, NY
Branch, Lanier, P.C. ....Montgomery, AL
Branch, LaShanda D. ....Washington, DC
Branch Law Firm ....Durango, CO
Albuquerque, NM
Santa Fe, NM
Houston, TX
Branch, Malcolm Howell
Broken Arrow, OK
Branch, Margaret Moses
Albuquerque, NM
Branch, Marilyn M. ....Salt Lake City, UT
Branch, Michael L. ....San Diego, CA
Branch, Michelle N. ....Palo Alto, CA
Branch, Paul R. ....San Francisco, CA
Branch, Rebecca C. ....Albuquerque, NM
Branch, Richard L. ....Las Vegas, NM
Branch, Robert D. ....Concord, NH
Branch, Robert William ....Fresno, CA
Branch, Sarah M. ....Nashville, TN
Branch, Sujatha J. ....Los Angeles, CA
Branch, Susan Konecny ....Los Gatos, CA
Branch, Tanya M. ....New York, NY
Branch, Thomas B., III ....Atlanta, GA
Branch, Thompson, Philhours & Warmath, A Professional Association
Paragould, AR
Branch, Tom D. ....Draper, UT
Branch, Turner W., (P.A.) ....Durango, CO
Albuquerque, NM
Houston, TX
Branch, Victor F. ....Houston, TX
Branch, Victor F., Law Offices of
Houston, TX
Branch & Weingartner ....Albuquerque, NM
Branch, William F. ....Warren, MI
Branch, William F. ....Richmond, VA
Branch, William H. ....Tallahassee, FL
Brancheau, Stacey Nichols ....Fenton, MI
Branchfield, Edward ....Newport, OR
Branchflower, Stephen E. ....Anchorage, AK
Branciforte, Carl ....New Brunswick, NJ
Branciforte, Jason M. ....Washington, DC
Brancio, Marya Louise ....Denver, CO
Branconier, Michael A. ....Pasadena, CA
Brand, Abraham ....Los Angeles, CA
Brand, Adam J. ....Boston, MA
Brand, Andrew ....New London, CT
Brand, Ariela Z. ....New York, NY
Brand, Arthur S. ....Ferndale, MI
Brand, Ascher T. ....Jamaica, NY
Brand, Audrey W. ....Jackson, MS
Brand, Barbara G.
Department of the Air Force, Office of the Judge Advocate General, GV
Brand, Barbara M. ....Indio, CA
Brand, Bart S. ....St. Louis, MO
Brand, Bethany S. ....Minneapolis, MN
Brand, Brand, Minter & Burke
New York, NY
Ossining, NY
Brand, Cayea & Brand, LLC
Garden City, NY
New York, NY
Brand, Charles J. ....Newton, NJ
Brand, Chrystal Sommers ....Juneau, AK
Brand, Cindy A. ....San Diego, CA
Brand, Corinne L. ....Springfield, IL
Brand, Craig A. ....Miami, FL
Brand, Daryl J. ....Nashville, TN
Brand, David Britton ....Knoxville, TN
Brand, David E. ....Wilmington, DE
Brand, David H. ....Denver, CO
Brand, David L. ....Church Hill, TN
Brand, David W. ....Garden City, NY
New York, NY
Brand, Deborah ....West Chester, PA
Brand, Del Herman ....New York, NY
Brand, Donald E. ....Bel Air, MD
Brand, Dulcie D. ....Los Angeles, CA
Brand, Eric H. ....Greenville, OH
Brand, Eric S. ....Los Angeles, CA
Brand, Esta L. ....San Francisco, CA
Brand, Etzion ....Baltimore, MD
Brand, Evelyn G. ....Sacramento, CA
Brand Farrar & Buxbaum LLP
Los Angeles, CA
Brand Farrar Buxbaum LLP
New York, NY
Brand & Frulla, A Professional Corporation
Washington, DC
Brand, Garret A. ....Rockford, MI
Brand, George E., Jr. ....Detroit, MI
Brand, Gervais R. ....Phoenix, AZ
Brand, Harold J., Jr. ....Buffalo, NY
Brand, Irving ....Tamarac, FL
Brand, Irving ....New York, NY
Brand, Jack Irwin ....Cincinnati, OH
Brand, Jack W. ....Jackson, MS
Newton, MS
Brand, Jane Treen ....Boston, MA

Brand, Jeanine R. ....Breckenridge, MN
Brand, Jennifer S.
Small Business Administration, Office of the General Counsel, GV
Brand, Jeremy L. ....Southfield, MI
Brand, John W., Jr. ....Lawrence, KS
Brand, Jonathan M. ....Concord, CA
Brand, Joseph L. ....Washington, DC
Brand, Judith P. ....Pittsburgh, PA
Brand, Julia W. ....Los Angeles, CA
Brand, Karen F. ....Bartlesville, OK
Brand, Karen L. ....Hartford, CT
Brand, Kaye D. ....McMinnville, OR
Brand, Kenneth N. ....Fairfax, VA
Brand, Malcolm L. ....Salem, OR
Brand, Marc E. ....Jackson, MS
Brand, Mark ....Passaic, NJ
Brand, Mark A. ....Chicago, IL
Brand, Mark E. ....Buffalo, NY
Brand, Marsha Raimi ....West Bloomfield, MI
Brand, Martha C. ....Minneapolis, MN
Brand, Michael A. ....Los Angeles, CA
Brand, Michael E. ....Washington, DC
Brand, Michael E. ....Miami, FL
Brand, Milton L. ....Houston, TX
Brand, Mitchell M. ....New York, NY
Brand, Norman ....San Francisco, CA
Brand & Novak, Ltd. ....Chicago, IL
Brand, Richard L. ....Calabasas, CA
Brand, Richard L. ....Washington, DC
Brand, Robert C., Jr. ....Columbus, GA
Brand, Robert J. ....Milwaukee, WI
Brand, Ronald A. ....Pittsburgh, PA
Brand, Russell ....Chicago, IL
Brand, Sam M. ....Jackson, MS
Brand, Stanley M. ....Washington, DC
Brand, Stefanie A. ....Newark, NJ
Brand, Stephen S. ....Sacramento, CA
Brand, Steve A. ....Minneapolis, MN
Brand, Susan E. ....New York, NY
Brand, Susan F. ....Woburn, MA
Brand, Thomas B. ....Portland, OR
Brand, Thomas J. ....Carmel, CA
Brand, Torris M. ....Las Vegas, NV
Brand, Wallace Edward ....Washington, DC
Brand, Walter J. ....Jackson, MS
Brand, W. W., Jr. ....Houston, MS
Branda, Christopher, Jr. ....Philadelphia, PA
Branda, Jacqueline I. ....Houston, TX
Branda, James E. ....Lisle, IL
Branda, Joyce R. ....Department of Justice, Civil Division, GV
Branda, Rose Ann ....Brooklyn, NY
Brandabur, Campbell, Finlay, Johnson, Weckstein & Beard ....Xenia, OH
Brandabur, James F. ....Xenia, OH
Brandabur Law Office ....Hamilton, OH
Brandabur, Michael J. ....Hamilton, OH
Brandalise, Matthew D. ....San Jose, CA
Brandao, Anderson W. ....Houston, TX
Brandao, Edward J. ....Metairie, LA
Brandau, Ann I. ....La Crosse, WI
Brandau, Douglas Ryan ....Richmond, VA
Brandau, Herman ....Bloomington, IL
Brandau, Lori A. ....Des Moines, IA
Brandau, Rebecca J. ....St. Louis, MO
Brand-Ballard, Jeffrey ....Chicago, IL
Brande, Lewis M. ....Alta Loma, CA
Brandeberry, Mike E. ....Kirkland, WA
Brandecker, Smull & Graham
Columbia, MO
Brandecker, William, Jr. ....Columbia, MO
Brandeis, Clifford A. ....New York, NY
Brandeis, Jack E. ....Haddonfield, NJ
Brandeis, Jennifer R. ....Dallas, TX
Brandeis-Roman, Tracy, Law Office of
Philadelphia, PA
Brandel, Jeffrey R. ....Denver, CO
Brandel, Lawrence S. ....Medina, OH
Brandel, Nancy ....Los Angeles, CA
Brandel, Roland E. ....San Francisco, CA
Brandell, David A. ....Eden Prairie, MN
Branden, James M. ....New York, NY
Brandenberg, Henry D. ....Bayville, NJ
Brandenberg, Pamela H. ....Fort Worth, TX
Brandenberg, Barry W. ....Vancouver, WA
Brandenburg & Brandenburg, P.C.
Albuquerque, NM
Brandenburg, Brent L. ....New York, NY
Brandenburg, Cynthia L. ....Springboro, OH
Brandenburg, Dan S. ....Washington, DC
Brandenburg, Dennis L. ....Brush, CO
Brandenburg, Edgar H. ....Brush, CO
Brandenburg, Gary M.
West Palm Beach, FL
Brandenburg, George P. ....Cincinnati, OH
Brandenburg, James C. ....St. Louis, MO
Brandenburg, James L.
Albuquerque, NM
Brandenburg, James M. ....Taos, NM
Brandenburg, Jay W. ....La Palma, CA
Brandenburg, John P.
Securities and Exchange Commission, Division of Investment Management, GV
Brandenburg, John R. ....Chicago, IL
Brandenburg, John R., & Associates, Ltd.
Chicago, IL
Brandenburg & Johnson ....Taos, NM
Brandenburg, Kari E. ....Albuquerque, NM
Brandenburg & Lownsdale
St. Louis, MO
Brandenburg, Mark Coats ....Charleston, SC
Brandenburg, Mark, Esq. ....Las Vegas, NV
Brandenburg, Paul Mangan ....Lansing, MI
Brandenburg, R. E. ....Belle Fourche, SD
Rapid City, SD
Brandenburg, Robert C. ....Southfield, MI
Brandenburg, Ronald W. ....St. Cloud, MN

Brandenburg & Schultz ....Brush, CO
Brandenburg, Steven M. ....Palo Alto, CA
Brandenburg, Valerie ....Willoughby, OH
Brandenburger, Linda ....Sacramento, CA
Brandenburger, Mark ....Hamilton, OH
Brandenburger, Stephen A. ....Sacramento, CA
Brandenburg-Rees, Jacqueline
Carlinville, IL
Brandenburg-Rees & Rees ....Carlinville, IL
Brandenhoff, Gerald H. ....Bloomington, MN
Brandenstein, Edward G. ....Pittsburgh, PA
Brandenstein, Henry F., Jr. ....Vienna, VA
Brandenstein, Richard ....Woodbury, NY
Brander, Reynolds A., Jr. ....Grand Rapids, MI
Brander, Shelly F. ....Kalispell, MT
Brander, Susan ....Boston, MA
Branderbit, Jay D. ....Philadelphia, PA
Brandes, Barbara J. ....New York, NY
Brandes, David ....New York, NY
Brandes, Elisa A. ....San Diego, CA
Brandes, Gregory J. ....Boulder, CO
Brandes, Howard P. ....Department of Labor, Office of Secretary, GV
Brandes, Joanne ....Sturtevant, WI
Brandes, Joel R. ....Garden City, NY
Brandes, Joel R., P.C., The Law Firm of
Garden City, NY
Brandes, Karl J. ....Tampa, FL
Brandes & Lane, P.C. ....Phoenix, AZ
Brandes, Lawrence I. ....New York, NY
Brandes, Lewis A. ....Bethesda, MD
Brandes, Mark ....Denver, CO
Brandes, Matthew J. ....Cedar Rapids, IA
Brandes, Paul D. ....Philadelphia, PA
Brandes, Philip O. ....New York, NY
Brandes, Ramona Coral ....Port Orchard, WA
Brandes, Randall S. ....Harrisburg, PA
Brandes, Richard N. ....Phoenix, AZ
Brandes, Robert M. ....Phoenix, AZ
Brandes, Robert W., Jr. ....Fort Collins, CO
Brandes, Roy ....Hillsdale, MI
Brandes, Wendy L. ....New York, NY
Brandes, William F., Jr. ....Naples, FL
Brandes-Gibbs, Robin ....Santa Ana, CA
Brandewie, David J. ....Merrillville, IN
Brandfass, Paula Koenig ....Charleston, WV
Brandfass, Robert L. ....Charleston, WV
Brandfield, Julie ....New York, NY
Brandfon, Martin ....Redwood City, CA
Brandfonbrener, Eric D. ....Chicago, IL
Brandhorst, Daniel R. ....Los Angeles, CA
Brandhuber, Walter F. ....Houston, TX
Brandi, Dianne Dolores ....New York, NY
Brandi, Michael J. ....Hartford, CT
New Haven, CT
Brandi, Thomas J., Law Offices of
San Francisco, CA
Brandiet, Leon J. ....Phoenix, AZ
Brandimarte, A. Paul, Jr. ....New York, NY
Brandimore, Stanley A. ....St. Petersburg, FL
Brandin, Alf R. ....San Francisco, CA
Brandin, Patricia A. ....Chicago, IL
Branding, Frederick H. ....Chicago, IL
Brandis, Barbara ....San Jose, CA
Brandis, Bernardine ....Burbank, CA
Brandis, Michael F. ....San Francisco, CA
Brandl, Anne M ....South Weymouth, MA
Brandl, James D. ....Buffalo, NY
Brandl, Jean M. ....San Diego, CA
Brandler, Bruce ....Harrisburg, PA
Brandler, Jonathan M., (P.C.)
Los Angeles, CA
Brandley, David F. ....Caldwell, NJ
Brandley, David F., Jr. ....New York, NY
Brandley and Kleppe ....Caldwell, NJ
Brandlin, Brian Robert ....Torrance, CA
Brandlin, Bruce R. ....Carson, CA
Brandlin, J. J. ....Los Angeles, CA
Brandlin, John J., Jr. ....Irvine, CA
Brandlin, William T.
Rolling Hills Estates, CA
Brandman, Etta ....New York, NY
Brandman, Lawrence S. ....New York, NY
Brandman, Michael F. ....Cranford, NJ
White Plains, NY
Brandman, Scott L. ....New York, NY
Brandmeyer, Brian K., Law Offices of
Long Beach, CA
Brandmeyer, Brian K., Law Offices of
Los Angeles, CA
Brandmeyer, Kent T. ....Los Angeles, CA
Brandmeyer, Stanley M. ....St. Louis, MO
Brandner, Geoffrey S. ....Stamford, CT
Brandner & Ponzini ....Stamford, CT
Brandner, Renee A. ....New Rochelle, NY
Brandner, Robert L. ....Medford, WI
Brandoff, Mark A. ....Garden City, NY
Brandoff, Mark A., P.C. ....Garden City, NY
Brandofino, Elaine Marie ....New York, NY
Brandolino, Joseph A. ....Los Angeles, CA
Brandolph, Arthur N. ....Philadelphia, PA
Brandolph, David B. ....Washington, DC
Brandom, C. Dudley ....Sun City, AZ
Brandom, David A. ....Beaumont, TX
Brandon, Agnes E.C. ....Minneapolis, MN
Brandon, Amy Y. ....Medina, OH
Brandon, Anne D. ....San Francisco, CA
Brandon, Barbara H. ....Pittsburgh, PA
Brandon & Brandon ....Lewisburg, TN
Brandon, Cynthia J.
Hot Springs National Park, AR
Brandon, D. Rhett ....New York, NY
Brandon, David E. ....Nashville, TN
Brandon, David L. ....Los Angeles, CA
Brandon, Deanna L. ....Cleveland, OH
Brandon, Deborah A. ....Memphis, TN
Brandon, Donald R. ....Herrin, IL
Brandon, Douglas C. ....Lexington, KY

Brandon, George Ian ....Phoenix, AZ
Brandon, Glenn E., Jr. ....Birmingham, AL
Brandon & Hilton ....Los Angeles, CA
Brandon, Hutton S. ....Waleska, GA
Brandon, J. Elliott ....Sebring, OH
Brandon, Jack ....Los Angeles, CA
Brandon, Jack L. ....Oklahoma City, OK
Brandon, Jack P. ....Lakeland, FL
Lake Wales, FL
Winter Haven, FL
Brandon, James E. ....Tulsa, OK
Brandon, James E. ....Amarillo, TX
Brandon, James R. ....Canton, OH
Brandon, Jay ....San Antonio, TX
Brandon, Jean ....Westbury, NY
Brandon, Joel S. ....Greenville, SC
Brandon, John B. ....Reynoldsville, PA
Brandon, John E. ....Franklin, TN
Brandon, Jon ....Chicago, IL
Brandon, Keith F. ....Atlanta, GA
Brandon, Kelly K. ....Omaha, NE
Brandon, Kevin P. ....Washington, DC
Brandon, Larry R. ....Amarillo, TX
Brandon, Linda M. ....New York, NY
Brandon, Lisa E. ....Long Beach, CA
Brandon, Lonnie J. ....Los Angeles, CA
Brandon, M. Stephen, (P.C.)
Memphis, TN
Brandon, Mark L., (Inc.) ....San Diego, CA
Brandon, Marvin ....South Brunswick, NJ
Brandon, Merwin McGehee, Jr. ....Bastrop, LA
Brandon, Miles L. ....Huntsville, AL
Brandon, Richard A. ....Chicago, IL
Brandon, Robert A. ....New York, NY
Brandon, Robert W., III ....Union City, TN
Brandon, Roger E. ....Lewisburg, TN
Brandon, Roger R. ....San Jose, CA
Brandon, S. Mark ....Brea, CA
Brandon, Schmidt, Goffinet & Solverson
Carbondale, IL
Brandon, Scott A. ....Brea, CA
Brandon, Susan K. ....New York, NY
Brandon, Susan Stidham ....Muskogee, OK
Brandon, Suzanne ....Minnetonka, MN
Brandon, Thomas B., III ....Williamston, NC
Brandon, Thomas S., Jr. ....Fort Worth, TX
Brandon, W. Scott ....Myrtle Beach, SC
Brandon, Walter J. ....Hampstead, NC
Brandon, William H. ....Avondale Estates, GA
Brandon, Wm. Kent ....Carbondale, IL
Brandon & Yarc, LLP ....Long Beach, CA
Los Angeles, CA
Newport Beach, CA
Brandon-Arnold, Cynthia M.
United States Court Of Veterans Appeals, GV
Brandon-Brown, Elizabeth, Law Office of
Torrance, CA
Brandow, John G., Jr. ....Miami, FL
Brandow, John M. ....New York, NY
Brandow, Laura White ....Boston, MA
Brandow, Michael K. ....Peoria, IL
Brandow, Peter A. ....Warminster, PA
Brandow, Peter B. ....New York, NY
Brandow, Wayne R. ....Marina Del Rey, CA
Brandriet, Leon J. ....Phoenix, AZ
Brandriet, Leon J., P.C., Law Offices of
Phoenix, AZ
Brandrup, Douglas W. ....New York, NY
Brands, Annette L. ....Chicago, IL
Brands, Bethany Verhoef ....Estherville, IA
Brands, Henk ....Washington, DC
Brands, James V. ....Poughkeepsie, NY
Brandsdorfer, Mark Michael
Gaithersburg, MD
Brandser, Kristin J. ....Iowa City, IA
Brandsness, Andrew C.
Klamath Falls, OR
Brandsness, Brandsness & Rudd, P.C.
Klamath Falls, OR
Brandsness, William P.
Klamath Falls, OR
Brandstatter, Doris ....Hackensack, NJ
Brandstetter, Allison ....Tampa, FL
Brandstetter, Brian J. ....Dallas, TX
Fort Worth, TX
Brandstetter, Dean C. ....Idaho Falls, ID
Brandstetter, Gary W. ....Snohomish, WA
Brandstetter & Green ....San Francisco, CA
Brandstetter, Jeffrey ....San Francisco, CA
Brandstrader, Karen Ann ....San Francisco, CA
Brandstrader, Thomas C.
Mount Prospect, IL
Brandt, Adam K. ....Columbus, OH
Brandt, Alan C. (Peter), Jr.
Fort Lauderdale, FL
Brandt, Albert ....San Diego, CA
Brandt, Albert R., Jr. ....Lockport, NY
Brandt, Alf W. ....Sacramento, CA
Brandt, Alfred P. ....Jackson, MI
Brandt, Amy R. ....Cherry Hill, NJ
Philadelphia, PA
Brandt, Ann ....Portland, ME
Brandt, Arthur F. ....Chicago, IL
Brandt, Avalon S. ....Baltimore, MD
Brandt, Barry ....Upland, CA
Brandt and Beeson, P.C.
Johnson City, TN
Brandt, Bernard B. ....Greenwich, CT
Brandt, Brendan W. ....Riverside, CA
Brandt, Brian K. ....Upland, CA
Brandt, Brian Stuart ....New York, NY
Brandt, Carl L. ....San Jose, CA
Brandt, Charles ....Wilmington, DE
Brandt, Charles ....Lafayette, LA
Brandt, Charles A. ....Oklahoma City, OK
Brandt, Charles H. ....Westfield, NJ
Brandt, Charles J., Jr. ....Austin, TX

Brandt, Charles T. ... **Aspen, CO**
Brandt, Charles T., & Associates, P.C.
Aspen, CO
Brandt, Christine C. ... **Birmingham, AL**
Brandt, Christopher D. ... **Kansas City, MO**
Brandt, Christopher M.
Colorado Springs, CO
Brandt, Cindi R. ... **New York, NY**
Brandt, Colleen L. ... **Brick, NJ**
Brandt, Craig A. ... Oakland, CA
Brandt, Craig A. ... **Minneapolis, MN**
St. Paul, MN
Brandt and Dalton, P.A. ... Wilmington, DE
Brandt, David L. ... Windham, ME
Brandt, David P. ... Franklin, PA
Brandt, Derek Y. ... **Chicago, IL**
Brandt, Donald A. ... Traverse City, MI
Brandt, Edward N., III, Law Offices of
Dallas, TX
Brandt, Elen Pass ... San Rafael, CA
Brandt, Elisabeth C. ... Sacramento, CA
Brandt, Ellen F. ... **West Palm Beach, FL**
Brandt, Ellen F. ... Defiance, OH
Brandt, Elysa Teric ... **New York, NY**
Brandt, Eric S. ... Boston, MA
Brandt, Eugene H. ... **West Palm Beach, FL**
Brandt Fisher Alward & Roy, P.C.
Elk Rapids, MI
Traverse City, MI
Brandt, Fisher and Harvey ... Defiance, OH
Brandt, Fred W. ... Pasadena, CA
Brandt, Frederic H. ... **Johnson City, TN**
Brandt, Frederic T., III ... **Rockford, IL**
Brandt, Gail F. ... **Minneapolis, MN**
Brandt, Garret S. ... **Aspen, CO**
Brandt, Gary ... Greenwich, CT
Brandt, George, III ... **Spartanburg, SC**
Brandt, George J., Jr. ... **Mount Vernon, NY**
Brandt, George W. ... **Honolulu, HI**
Brandt & Gerber ... Palmyra, PA
Brandt, Gina Francesca ... Los Angeles, CA
Brandt, Gina M. ... **Hutchinson, MN**
Minneapolis, MN
Brandt, Greggory C. ... **Oakland, CA**
Brandt, Guy N. ... **St. Louis, MO**
Brandt, Haughey, Penberthy, Lewis & Hyland, P.A. ... **Moorestown, NJ**
Mount Holly, NJ
Philadelphia, PA
Brandt, Hazel Marlee ... **San Francisco, CA**
Brandt, Horan, Hallstrom & Sedlacek
Syracuse, NE
Brandt, Hubert J. ... **New York, NY**
Brandt & Hull ... Grove City, OH
Brandt, James ... Greenwich, CT
Brandt, James E. ... **Newark, NJ**
Brandt, James E. ... **New York, NY**
Brandt, James J. ... **Mason City, IA**
Brandt, James W. ... St. Peter, MN
Brandt, Jane Politz ... **Dallas, TX**
Brandt, Janice F. ... **Dallas, TX**
Brandt, Jay A. ... **Dallas, TX**
Brandt, Jeffrey L. ... **Stamford, CT**
Brandt, Jeffrey P. ... **Glendale, CA**
Brandt, Jennifer A. ... **Philadelphia, PA**
Brandt, Jennifer D. ... **Fort Worth, TX**
Brandt, Jennifer L. ... Cranford, NJ
Brandt, Jennings, Roberts, Davis & Snee, PLLC ... **Falls Church, VA**
Brandt, Joel A. ... **Madison, NJ**
Brandt, John E. ... **St. Paul, MN**
Brandt, John H. ... **Fort Wayne, IN**
Brandt, John J. ... **Falls Church, VA**
Brandt, John T. ... Hopkins, MN
Brandt, John W. ... Oswego, NY
Brandt, Jonathan F. ... Peru, IL
Brandt, Katherine D. ... **Cleveland, OH**
Brandt, Kathleen L. ... **Stamford, CT**
Brandt, Kathryn Weg ... **New York, NY**
Brandt, Kevin M. ... **Los Angeles, CA**
Brandt, Larry C. ... **Walhalla, SC**
Brandt, Larry C., P.A. ... **Anderson, SC**
Walhalla, SC
Brandt, Laura McCabe ... Uniondale, NY
Brandt, Laura R. ... **New York, NY**
Brandt, Laurel H. ... Springfield, MA
Brandt, Linda A. ... Columbia, MD
Brandt, Loren A. ... San Diego, CA
Brandt, Mark P. ... Santa Monica, CA
Brandt, Mark W. ... Dunedin, FL
Brandt, Maryanna E. ... Harrisburg, PA
Brandt, Michael D. ... **Bellevue, WA**
Brandt, Michael J. ... **Birmingham, AL**
Brandt, Michael K. ... Champaign, IL
Brandt, Michael Richard ... **Bridgeport, CT**
Brandt, Michael T. ... Grove City, OH
Brandt, Milnes, Rea & Wise ... Pittsburgh, PA
Brandt, Mitchell D. ... Westbury, NY
Brandt, Nancy E. ... **Orlando, FL**
Brandt, Nancy L. ... **San Jose, CA**
Brandt, Natasha E. ... Brook Park, OH
Brandt, Norman C. ... Burbank, CA
Brandt, Patricia A. ... East Lansing, MI
Brandt, Peter F. ... New Orleans, LA
Brandt, Peter W. ... **Bloomington, IL**
Brandt, Philip D. ... **Washington, DC**
Brandt, Philip H. ... Tacoma, WA
Brandt, Phillip ... West Liberty, OH
Brandt, Ralph E., Jr. ... New Orleans, LA
Brandt, Ralph F. ... Yuma, AZ
Brandt, Raymond J. ... Metairie, LA
Brandt, Raymond J., P.L.C., Law Offices of
Metairie, LA
Brandt, Richard E. ... **Sacramento, CA**
Brandt, Richard K., & Associates
Pittsburgh, PA
Brandt, Richard K., & Associates
Sewickley, PA
Brandt, Robert C. ... **Los Angeles, CA**
Brandt, Robert C. ... Slidell, LA
Brandt, Robert C., A Prof. Corp., Law Offices of ... **Los Angeles, CA**
Brandt, Robert J. ... Lake Forest, IL
Brandt, Robert S. ... **Nashville, TN**
Brandt, Robert W. ... **Salt Lake City, UT**
Brandt, Robt. M. ... Geneva, NY
Brandt, Ronald E. ... Lake Villa, IL
Brandt, Ronald L. ... **Boston, MA**
Brandt, Ronald L. ... **Wellesley, MA**
Brandt, S. David ... **Moorestown, NJ**
Brandt, Scott H. ... Philadelphia, PA
Brandt, Shelley L. ... **Olympia, WA**
Brandt, Stacie L. ... **Costa Mesa, CA**
Brandt, Steinberg & Lewis LLP
New York, NY
Brandt, Stephen D. ... Holland, OH
Brandt, Stephen M. ... Rochester, NY
Brandt, Sterrett J. ... Oakland, CA
Brandt, Susan H. ... **Bloomington, IL**
Brandt, Susan J. ... **Houston, TX**
Brandt, Susan Mascette ... **Rochester, NY**
Brandt, T. Marshall ... Ellicott City, MD
Brandt, Thomas H. ... **Lockport, NY**
Brandt, Thomas J. ... **Houston, TX**
Brandt, Thomas K. ... Minneapolis, MN
Brandt, Thomas P. ... **Dallas, TX**
Brandt, Uclair W. ... Punta Gorda, FL
Brandt, W. Perry ... **Kansas City, MO**
Brandt, William A., Jr. ... **New York, NY**
Brandt, William D. ... Salem, OR
Brandt, William R. ... **Bloomington, IL**
Brandt, William S. ... Eden Prairie, MN
Brandt, William S. ... **Rochester, NY**
Brandt, William W. ... Palmyra, PA
Brandt, Wm. B. ... Syracuse, NE
Brandt-Erichsen, Scott A. ... Anchorage, AK
Brandt-Erichsen, Svend A. ... **Seattle, WA**
Brandt-Hawley, Susan L. ... Glen Ellen, CA
Brandveen, Antonio I. ... Mineola, NY
Brandwein, Abraham J.J. ... Boston, MA
Brandwein, David I. ... Bloomfield, CT
Brandwein, Debra J. ... Boulder, CO
Brandwein, Michael K. ... Lincolnshire, IL
Brandwein, Richard E. ... **Chicago, IL**
Brandwein, Roger ... New York, NY
Brandwein, William A. ... **Monterey, CA**
Columbus, OH
Brandwein, William A., A Professional Law Corporation ... **Monterey, CA**
Columbus, OH
Brandwene, Jason David ... **Palo Alto, CA**
Brandwine, Jeffrey A. ... Buffalo, NY
Brandy, Dominic L. ... **Fort Lauderdale, FL**
Brandys Carson & Pritchard, P.C.
El Paso, TX
Brandys, Karin Armen ... **El Paso, TX**
Brandys, Roy R. ... **El Paso, TX**
Braner, Matthew Curt ... San Diego, CA
Branfeld & Associates, P.S. ... Tacoma, WA
Branfeld, Gary H. ... Tacoma, WA
Branfman, Eric J. ... **Washington, DC**
Branford, Thomas O. ... Newport, OR
Brang, Robert F. ... Redford, MI
Brangaccio, Peter J. ... Tulsa, OK
Branhagen, Darrel R. ... DeSoto, TX
Branham, Andrew C. ... **Memphis, TN**
Branham, C. Michael ... **Charleston, SC**
Branham, Chasity Brooks ... Bartow, FL
Branham & Day, P.C. ... **Nashville, TN**
Branham, Elizabeth C.
San Francisco, CA
Branham, Hudson ... Richmond, VA
Branham, Hudson, P.C. ... Richmond, VA
Branham, James L. ... Honolulu, HI
Branham, Jeb T. ... **Atlanta, GA**
Branham, Jeffry J. ... **Orlando, FL**
Branham, John F. ... **Huntington, IN**
Warren, IN
Branham, John P. ... **Nashville, TN**
Branham, Kenneth W. ... Tampa, FL
Branham, Marcy F. ... Phoenix, AZ
San Antonio, TX
Branham, Melanie J., Law Offices of
Olathe, KS
Branham, Norris G. ... Fort Worth, TX
Branham, Retha M. ... Greenville, VA
Branick & Branick ... **Port Arthur, TX**
Branick, Jeff R. ... **Port Arthur, TX**
Branick, Jesse E. ... **Port Arthur, TX**
Braniff, Wendall Corrigan ... Austin, TX
Braniff, William ... **San Diego, CA**
Branigan, Alan E. J. ... **Arlington, VA**
Richmond, VA
Branigan, John J. ... Voorhees, NJ
Philadelphia, PA
Branigan & Ortiz, L.L.C., P.C.
Voorhees, NJ
Philadelphia, PA
Branigan, Terence P. ... Chicago, IL
Branigan, Thomas P. ... **Detroit, MI**
Branigan, Timothy P. ... **Washington, DC**
Branigan, William A., Jr. ... Arlington, VA
Branigin, Roger D. ... Columbus, OH
Branigin, Roger D., Jr. ... **Lafayette, IN**
Branigin, Wm. A. ... Seattle, WA
Branin, Joan ... Sacramento, CA
Branin, Linda S. ... San Francisco, CA
Branin, Theodore W. ... York, PA
Branine, Brian ... Sacramento, CA
Branine, Chalfant & Hill ... **Hutchinson, KS**
Branine, Suzanne L. ... West Sacramento, CA
Branion, John M., III ... Newport Beach, CA
Branisa, Michael ... **Houston, TX**
Branit, James R. ... **Chicago, IL**
Branitsky, Herbert S. ... Rockville Centre, NY
Branitsky, Randy ... **Washington, DC**
Brank, Laura M. ... **New York, NY**
Branker, Raymond A. ... Santa Ana, CA
Brankey, Edward W. ... Charleston, IL
Brankey, George E. ... Boston, MA
Brankey, Smith & Glasson, P.C.
Charleston, IL
Brankin, Patrick T. ... **Chicago, IL**
Brankin, Paul John ... Sisseton, SD
Brankman, Anthony C. ... Albany, NY
Branley, Patricia E. ... Brooklyn, NY
Branman, Kathryn H. K. ... Irvine, CA
Branman, Meyer ... Beverly Hills, CA
Branman, Robert J. ... Department of Justice, Tax Division, GV
Brann, Albert M. ... Lubbock, TX
Brann, Amy ... Cincinnati, OH
Brann, David J. ... **Troy, PA**
Brann, Gerald W. ... Canton, PA
Troy, PA
Brann & Isaacson, LLP ... **Lewiston, ME**
Portland, ME
Brann & Light, P.C. ... **Lewisburg, PA**
Brann, Matthew W. ... **Troy, PA**
Brann, Paul W. ... **Lewisburg, PA**
Brann, Peter J. ... **Lewiston, ME**
Brann, Richard R. ... **Houston, TX**
Brann, Scott R. ... Sarasota, FL
Brann, Williams, Caldwell & Sheetz
Canton, PA
Troy, PA
Brannagan, Shawn M. ... Clearwater, FL
Brannan, Arthur D. ... **Atlanta, GA**
Brannan, Derick J. ... Sacramento, CA
Brannan, Donald J. ... **New Orleans, LA**
Brannan, Douglas D. ... Santa Ana, CA
Brannan, G. Bryan ... Encino, CA
Brannan & Guy, P.C. ... **Montgomery, AL**
Brannan, J. Bernard, Jr.
Montgomery, AL
Brannan, James W. ... Rockland, ME
Brannan, Jane LeCroy ... Montgomery, AL
Brannan, John C., Jr. ... **Dallas, TX**
Brannan, Lynette T. ... **Sacramento, CA**
Brannan, Patricia A. ... **Washington, DC**
Brannan, Samuel T. ... **Atlanta, GA**
Brannan, Stephen G. ... **Sarasota, FL**
Brannan, Stephen L. ... Odessa, TX
Brannan, Suzanne S. ... **McLean, VA**
Brannan, T. Daniel ... **Atlanta, GA**
Brannan, Thomas J. ... **Beardstown, IL**
Virginia, IL
Brannan, Trevor ... Los Angeles, CA
Brannan, W. Scott ... Greensboro, NC
Brannan, William B. ... **New York, NY**
Brannelly, Catherine Caroline
Waterbury, CT
Brannelly, Colleen ... **Fort Lauderdale, FL**
Brannen, Barney L.
White River Junction, VT
Brannen, Barney L., Jr. ... Athens, GA
Brannen, Chas. J. ... Covington, KY
Brannen, D. Albert ... **Atlanta, GA**
Brannen, Daniel E., Jr. ... Washington, DC
Brannen, David G. ... San Antonio, TX
Brannen, Dian Hixon ... Temecula, CA
Brannen, Frank P. ... **Savannah, GA**
Brannen, Franklin P., Jr. ... **Atlanta, GA**
Brannen, George W., (P.C.) ... St. Charles, IL
Brannen, Jeffrey A. ... **Dallas, TX**
Brannen, Jeffrey R. ... **Santa Fe, NM**
Brannen, Jennifer R. ... **Dallas, TX**
Brannen, Joe G. ... Humble, TX
Brannen, Joe S. ... Inverness, FL
Brannen, John H. ... **Canton, OH**
Brannen, Joseph Chad ... Marietta, GA
Brannen, Laura J. ... Germantown, WI
Brannen, Perry, Jr. ... Savannah, GA
Brannen, Robert B., Jr. ... **Savannah, GA**
Brannen, Robert W. ... **Menlo Park, CA**
Brannen, Russell C., Jr. ... **Milwaukee, WI**
Brannen, Sam L. ... **Statesboro, GA**
Brannen, Sam L., Jr. ... **Atlanta, GA**
Brannen, Sam L., P.C. ... **Statesboro, GA**
Brannen, Searcy & Smith ... **Savannah, GA**
Brannen, Stephan A. ... Denison, IA
Brannen, Stillwell & Perrin, P.A.
Inverness, FL
Branner, Don M. ... Salinas, CA
Branner & Kuster ... Sherman Oaks, CA
Branner, Mark S. ... Sherman Oaks, CA
Branney, Hillyard and Barnhart, L.L.P.
Denver, CO
Englewood, CO
Branney, Joseph J. ... **Englewood, CO**
Brannian, Lawrence J. ... **Dallas, TX**
Brannick, Alvin P. ... North Huntingdon, PA
Brannick, George J. ... Jackson, MI
Brannick, Patricia M. ... New York, NY
Brannigan, Cathy L. ... Grove City, PA
Brannigan, Eugene J. ... Williston Park, NY
Brannigan, James W., Jr. ... San Diego, CA
Brannigan, John M. ... Flossmoor, IL
Brannigan, Joseph P. ... San Diego, CA
Brannigan, Mary Ellen ... **Canfield, OH**
Brannigan, Robert L. ... Mamaroneck, NY
Brannigan, Susan ... **Chicago, IL**
Brannigan, Thomas E. ... **Chicago, IL**
Brannigan, Vincent M. ... Washington, DC
Branning, Earl C.
Department Of Health And Human Services, GV
Branning & Harrison ... **Sarasota, FL**
Branning, Peter S., (P.A.) ... **Sarasota, FL**
Brannock, B. E. ... **Staunton, VA**
Brannock, G. Steven ... West Palm Beach, FL
Brannock, Keith W. ... Columbus, OH
Brannock, Keith W. Co., L.P.A.
Columbus, OH
Brannock, Steven L. ... **Tampa, FL**
Brannock, V. Gail ... **Atlanta, GA**
Brannom, Thos. M., Jr. ... Houston, TX
Brannon, Anita C. ... **Tampa, FL**
Brannon, Anthony M. ... Durham, NC
Brannon, Barry N. ... Florence, AL
Brannon, Ben W. ... Atlanta, GA
Brannon, Berkley M ... Salinas, CA
Brannon, Brown, Haley, Robinson & Bullock, P.A. ... **Lake City, FL**
Brannon, C. John ... **Indianapolis, IN**
Brannon, Camille Wright ... **Atlanta, GA**
Brannon, Carol Rice ... Roseville, CA
Brannon, Charles W., Jr. ... **Savannah, GA**
Brannon, Clifton W., Sr. ... Longview, TX
Brannon, Curtis W. ... **Shalimar, FL**
Brannon, Dave Lee ... Miami, FL
Brannon, Derwin T. ... **Charleston, SC**
Brannon, Doris E. ... Savannah, GA
Brannon, Dwight A. ... Gilmer, TX
Brannon, Dwight D. ... **Dayton, OH**
Brannon, Ellis B. ... Sharon Center, OH
Brannon, G. Sims ... Irwindale, CA
Brannon, Gail L. ... Bradenton, FL
Brannon, George T., Sr. ... Germantown, TN
Brannon, Grayling E. ... Jacksonville, FL
Brannon, J. Richardson ... Gainesville, GA
Brannon, James Graham ... Houston, TX
Brannon, James H. ... Houston, TX
Brannon, James P. ... Paris, KY
Brannon, James S. ... Peoria, IL
Brannon, Jane ... **Lexington, KY**
Brannon, Jeanna A. ... **Atlanta, GA**
Brannon, J. L., (P.C) ... **Dallas, TX**
Brannon, John S. ... **Houston, TX**
Brannon, Joseph A. ... Bowling Green, MO
Brannon, L. Travis, Jr. ... Atlanta, GA
Brannon Law Office, The ... Gainesville, GA
Brannon & Lowe ... **Dayton, OH**
Brannon, Marie Kirk ... Frankfort, KY
Brannon, P. David ... **Tallahassee, FL**
Brannon, Robert M., Jr. ... Memphis, TN
Brannon, Thomas L. ... **Memphis, TN**
Brannon, William A. ... Las Vegas, NV
Brannon, William B., Jr. ... Lake City, FL
Brannon, William D.
Fort Walton Beach, FL
Brannon, William D., P.A.
Fort Walton Beach, FL
Brannon, William Earl ... Lindale, GA
Brannon, Wm. Bert ... **Columbia, SC**
Brannum, C. Mark ... **Dallas, TX**
Branom, Debra E. ... **Plano, TX**
Branom, R. Henry, Jr., (P.C.)
St. Louis, MO
Branom, Robert H. ... Clayton, MO
Branom, Steven A. ... **Seattle, WA**
Branon, R. Frost, Jr. ... Savannah, GA
Branon, R. Frost, Jr. ... Charlotte, NC
Branower, Andrew J. ... New York, NY
Brans, Kenneth R. ... **Martinez, CA**
Brans, Neil ... Arlington, TX
Branscom, Tara A. ... **Roanoke, VA**
Branscomb, Anne W. ... Cambridge, MA
Branscomb, Harvie, Jr.
Corpus Christi, TX
Branscome, John B. ... **Washington, DC**
Branscum, David A. ... **Oklahoma City, OK**
Branscum, Herby, Jr. ... Perryville, AR
Branscum, Valley M. ... Sapulpa, OK
Bransdorfer & Bransdorfer, P.C.
Grand Rapids, MI
Bransdorfer, David C. ... **Grand Rapids, MI**
Bransdorfer, Elizabeth K.
Grand Rapids, MI
Bransdorfer, Mark S. ... **Grand Rapids, MI**
Bransdorfer, Stephen C.
Grand Rapids, MI
Branse, Debra ... **San Diego, CA**
Branse, Herman I. ... Lauderhill, FL
Branse, Mark K. ... **Glastonbury, CT**
Bransfield, John P. ... Chicago, IL
Bransfield, Kirk W. ... Lynn, MA
Bransfield, Stephanie C. ... Chicago, IL
Bransfield, Thomas D. ... Chicago, IL
Bransford & Kalperis, P.C. ... Boston, MA
Bransford, Mark H. ... Tulsa, OK
Bransford, Mary ... Boston, MA
Bransford, R. Alexander, Jr. ... **Atlanta, GA**
Bransford, Stephen D. ... St. Louis, MO
Bransford, William L. ... **Washington, DC**
Bransgrove, Stanley J. ... Tiburon, CA
Bransilver, Edward ... **Washington, DC**
Bransky, Aaron ... **Duluth, MN**
Bransky, Harlan L. ... Yucca Valley, CA
Bransky, James A. ... Traverse City, MI
Bransky, Philip L. ... Crete, IL
Bransley, Robert A. ... Chicago, IL
Branson & Bearman ... Memphis, TN
Branson Brinkop Griffith & Strong LLP
Redwood City, CA
San Francisco, CA
San Jose, CA
San Mateo, CA
Branson, Charles Edward ... Lawrence, KS
Branson, Charles R. ... Seattle, WA
Branson, Christopher B. ... **Portland, ME**
Branson, David J. ... **Washington, DC**
Washington, DC
Branson, Debbie D. ... **Dallas, TX**
Branson, Douglas M. ... Tacoma, WA
Branson, Frank L. ... **Dallas, TX**
Branson, Frank L., P.C., Law Offices of
Dallas, TX
Branson, Hershel ... Jackson, KY
Branson, J. A. ... Redwood City, CA
Branson, James O., III ... Midland, MI
Branson, John R. ... Memphis, TN

Branson, Jones & Stedelin ... Centralia, IL
Branson, Kristin M. ... New York, NY
Branson, Lindley S. ... Minneapolis, MN
Branson, Richard H. ... Galveston, TX
Branson, Richard P. ... Boston, MA
Branson, Robert Bailey ... Orlando, FL
Branson, Robert E. ... Washington, DC
Branson, Robert E. ... Sterling, IL
Branson, Steven A. ... Norwood, MA
Branson, Susan L. ... Tallahassee, FL
Branson, Thomas A. ... Redwood City, CA
Branson, Timothy E. ... Minneapolis, MN
Branson, Timothy K. ... Redwood City, CA
Branson, Uzzell S., III, Law Offices of Pasadena, CA
Branstad, Christine E. ... Des Moines, IA
Branstad, Terry E. ... Des Moines, IA
Bransten, Eileen ... New York, NY
Bransten, Peter M. ... Los Angeles, CA
Branstetter, C. Burton ... Houston, TX
Branstetter, C. Dewey, Jr. ... Nashville, TN
Branstetter, Cecil D. ... Nashville, TN
Branstetter, Kilgore, Stranch & Jennings Nashville, TN
Branstetter, Marlin E. ... Anaheim, CA
Branstetter, Michael K. ... Wallace, ID
Branstetter, Ross W., III ... Washington, DC
Branstine, Daniel L. ... Costa Mesa, CA
Branstiter, George W. ... Lexington, SC
Branstool, W. David ... Newark, OH
Brant & Associates ... Pittsburgh, PA
Brant and Baldwin ... Lake Park, FL
Brant, Charles E. ... Columbus, OH
Brant, Clayton H. ... Lincoln, NE
Brant, David R. ... Topeka, KS
Brant, Donald B., Jr. ... New York, NY
Brant, George H. ... Chicago, IL
Brant, Jay E. ... Detroit, MI
Brant, Jerome E. ... Liberty, MO
Brant, Joanne C. ... Ada, OH
Brant, Joel S. ... Cincinnati, OH
Brant, John G. ... Wheat Ridge, CO
Brant, John G., Professional Corporation Golden, CO
Wheat Ridge, CO
Brant, John J., Jr. ... Queens Village, NY
Brant, John M. ... Albuquerque, NM
Brant, John W. ... Reynoldsburg, OH
Brant, Jonathan ... Cambridge, MA
Brant, Joseph A. ... Cincinnati, OH
Brant, Kimberly L. ... San Francisco, CA
Brant, Kirby ... Watertown, WI
Brant, Larry J. ... Portland, OR
Brant, Lisa R. ... Los Angeles, CA
Brant, Marilyn Dawkins ... Louisville, IL
Brant, Marjorie H. ... Columbus, OH
Brant, Michael L. ... Klamath Falls, OR
Brant, Michael W. ... Pittsburgh, PA
Brant, Michelle ... San Francisco, CA
Brant, Moore, Macdonald & Wells, P.A. Jacksonville, FL
Brant and Pettitt ... Los Angeles, CA
Brant, Robert E. ... Cincinnati, OH
Brant, Robert L., Jr. ... Collegeville, PA
Brant, Thomas A. ... Cambridge, MA
Brant, Todd E. ... Fort Lauderdale, FL
Brant, Travis W. ... Toledo, OH
Brant, William Allen ... San Antonio, TX
Brant, William E. ... Lake Park, FL
Brant, William P. ... Jacksonville, FL
Branthoover, Carolyn M. ... Pittsburgh, PA
Branthover, Ned W. ... New York, NY
Branting, Leland R. ... Parker, CO
Brantingham, Paul J. ... Nipomo, CA
Brantingham, Shirley A. ... St. Paul, MN
Brantl, James S. ... Worcester, MA
Brantl, Winafred R. ... Washington, DC
Brantley, Allison S. ... Atlanta, GA
Brantley, Bethany Lynne New Orleans, LA
Brantley, C. Robert, Jr. Federal Communications Commission, Wireless Telecommunications Bureau, GV
Brantley, Charles B. ... Boise, ID
Brantley, Charles Steven ... Macon, GA
Brantley, Darrell N. ... Alamogordo, NM
Brantley, Dora A. ... Detroit, MI
Brantley, Ellen Bass ... Little Rock, AR
Brantley, Emily J. ... Atlanta, GA
Brantley, Eugene L. ... Columbia, SC
Brantley, F. Cooper ... Greensboro, NC
Brantley, G. Grant ... Atlanta, GA
Brantley, Gerald L. ... Austin, TX
Brantley & Holt, L.L.P. ... Bryan, TX
Brantley, Hugh F. ... Rochester, NY
Brantley, J. Christopher ... Goldsboro, NC
Kinston, NC
Brantley, J. Michael ... Fort Worth, TX
Brantley, James ... Atlanta, GA
Brantley, James C. ... Dawson Springs, KY
Brantley, Jeffrey A. ... Detroit, MI
Brantley, John ... Playa Del Rey, CA
Brantley, John R. ... Houston, TX
Brantley, Joseph P., IV ... Baton Rouge, LA
Brantley, Keen K. ... Scott City, KS
Brantley, Larry Wayne ... Huntsville, AL
Nashville, TN
Brantley, Laurie A. ... Tuscaloosa, AL
Brantley, Luther T., III ... Jackson, MS
Brantley, Overtis Hicks ... Atlanta, GA
Brantley, Patricia N. ... Las Vegas, NM
Brantley, Paul A. ... Montgomery, AL
Brantley, Phillip M. ... Houston, TX
Brantley, R. Jack, P.A. ... Ridgeland, MS
Brantley, Rickey J. ... Fort Worth, TX
Brantley, Robert J., Jr. ... Ridgeland, MS
Brantley, Roy D. ... Bryan, TX
Brantley, Samuel K., Jr. ... Merced, CA
Brantley, Sandra J. ... Cleveland, OH
Brantley, Scott, Jr. ... Bay Village, OH
Brantley, Suzanne B. ... Tallahassee, FL
Brantley, Teresa M. ... Ontario, CA
Brantley, Terry O. ... Marietta, GA
Brantley, Thomas H. ... Boston, MA
Brantley & Wilkerson, P.C. Montgomery, AL
Brantley, William L. ... Bay Minette, AL
Brantlinger-Angus, Elizabeth G. Hartford, CT
Brantman, Dina L. ... Chicago, IL
Brantman, Robert J. ... Chicago, IL
Brantmeier, Bennett J. ... Reedsburg, WI
Brantner, Andrea J. ... Stamford, CT
Brantner, Jeffrey W. ... Columbus, OH
Brantner, Jerry O. ... Fargo, ND
Brantner, Robert J., Law Offices of Ventura, CA
Branton & Bitner ... Alvin, TX
Branton, Brian Edward ... Washington, DC
Branton, Calvin F., Jr. ... St. Paul, MN
Branton, Gary G. ... Beverly Hills, CA
Las Vegas, NV
Branton & Hall, P.C. ... San Antonio, TX
Branton, Harold D. ... Myrtle Beach, SC
Branton, James ... Atlanta, GA
Branton, James L. ... San Antonio, TX
Branton, Lawrence S. ... San Diego, CA
Branton, Leo, Jr. ... Los Angeles, CA
Branton, Mary K. ... Alvin, TX
Branton, Stanley E. ... St. Francisville, LA
Branton, Thomas M. ... Alvin, TX
Branton, Victoria L. ... Houston, TX
Branton & Wilson, A Professional Corporation ... San Diego, CA
Brants, Harry M. ... Fort Worth, TX
Brants, Lucy ... Fort Worth, TX
Brantseg, Wallace R. ... Sisseton, SD
Brantz, George M. ... Philadelphia, PA
Brantz, James A. ... Boulder, CO
Branum, Kyle L. ... Seattle, WA
Branum, Lowell E. ... Midland, TX
Branyan, Lawrence O., Jr. ... Natchez, MS
Branyan, Margaret E. ... Springfield, MO
Branyan, Tyson E. ... Cushing, OK
Branyon, Michael Keith ... Fort Worth, TX
Branyon, Steven M. ... Orlando, FL
Branz, Andrew ... Boston, MA
Branz, Louis R. ... St. Louis, MO
Branzburg, Morton R. ... Cherry Hill, NJ
Philadelphia, PA
Braquet, Sidney J. ... Houston, TX
Brar, Vikram ... Glendale, CA
Braren, Richard ... Sarasota, FL
Bras, Robert W. ... Minneapolis, MN
Round Rock, TX
Brasacchio, Anthony R. ... Pottstown, PA
Brascetta, Gary J. ... Philadelphia, PA
Brasch, Henry C. ... New York, NY
Brasch, Jane Akin ... Harlingen, TX
Brasch, Justin C. ... New York, NY
Brasch, Michele Murray ... New York, NY
Brasch, Norvell E. ... Denver, CO
Brasch, Richard A. ... Arlington, VA
Brasch, Robert E. ... North Bend, OR
Brasch & Taylor, L.L.P. ... Harlingen, TX
Brasco, Christopher J. ... McLean, VA
Brase, David E. ... Denver, CO
Brasee, Mark L. ... Omaha, NE
Brasel, Gary G. ... Tulsa, OK
Brasel, Nancy E. ... Minneapolis, MN
Braselton, Forrest G. ... Nacogdoches, TX
Braselton, James T. ... Phoenix, AZ
Brasfield, Craig E. ... Jackson, MS
Brasfield, Evans B. ... Richmond, VA
Brasfield, Fuller, Freeman, Lovell & O'Hern, P.A. ... St. Petersburg, FL
Brasfield, J. Hunt ... Alexandria, VA
Brasfield, J. Scott ... St. Petersburg, FL
Brasfield, Julia H. ... Alexandria, VA
Brasfield, Kathy Perry ... Montgomery, AL
Brasfield, Lois N. ... Montgomery, AL
Brash, David F., III ... Monroeville, PA
Brash, Edmond J. ... Coolidge, AZ
Brash, William W., III ... Cedarburg, WI
Brashares, James C. ... Hilliard, OH
Brashares, William C. ... Washington, DC
Brashear, Ann R. ... Washington, DC
Brashear, Bruce ... Gainesville, FL
Brashear, Christian A. ... Culpeper, VA
Brashear, Crystal Stull Mount Sterling, KY
Brashear & Ginn ... Omaha, NE
Brashear, J. Preston, III ... Dallas, TX
Brashear, J. Preston, III ... Garland, TX
Brashear, James F. ... Fort Worth, TX
Brashear, James T. ... Fresno, CA
Brashear, Kermit A. ... Omaha, NE
Brashear, Kermit A., III ... Omaha, NE
Brashear, Kris Victor ... Omaha, NE
Brashear, Kurth A. ... Omaha, NE
Brashear, Leonard H. ... Hyden, KY
Brashear, Tangora and Spence, LLP Canton, MI
Livonia, MI
Brashear, William R. ... Livonia, MI
Brasher, Celynda L. ... St. Louis, MO
Brasher, D. Clinton ... Beaumont, TX
Brasher, John D., Jr. ... Denver, CO
Brasher, Joseph T. ... Atlanta, GA
Brasher, Lance T. ... Washington, DC
Brasher Law Firm, L.C. ... St. Louis, MO
Brasher, Mary Copeland ... Wichita Falls, TX
Brasher, Patricia Daly ... St. Louis, MO
Brasher, Rex L., Jr. ... Memphis, TN
Brasher, William A. ... St. Louis, MO
Brashers-Krug, Gail ... Towson, MD
Brashers-Krug, Patricia ... Towson, MD
Brashich, Deyan R. ... New York, NY
Brashier, Clifton A., Jr. ... Atlanta, GA
Brashier, Jeffery J. ... Houston, TX
Brashier, Philip ... Houston, TX
Brashler, Thomas R. ... Chicago, IL
Brasier, Ernie ... St. Louis, MO
Brasier, Karen E. ... Las Vegas, NV
Brasier, Lindley A. ... Dallas, TX
Brasier, Marilyn J. ... Greenbelt, MD
Brasier, Susan M. ... Dayton, OH
Brasil, Elisa C. ... San Francisco, CA
Brasington, David Scott ... Houston, TX
Brask, Gretchen M. ... Lake Oswego, OR
Braskey, James F. ... Frostburg, MD
Grantsville, MD
Braskey Law Offices, P.A. ... Frostburg, MD
Grantsville, MD
Braskich, Keith J. ... Peoria, IL
Brasley, John A. ... Bath, NY
Braslow, Albert C. ... Philadelphia, PA
Braslow, Dean G. ... New York, NY
Braslow, Denis A. ... Pensacola, FL
Braslow, Derek T. ... Pennsauken, NJ
Braslow, Ingrid S. ... White Plains, NY
Braslow, John ... North Babylon, NY
Braslow, Paul ... Mill Valley, CA
Braslow, Richard M. ... Toms River, NJ
Braslow, Stephen L. ... Islip, NY
Brasman, Michael M. ... Boston, MA
Brasman, Michael M., P.C., Law Offices of Boston, MA
Brasno, Andrew T., Jr. (A Prof. Corp.) South River, NJ
Brass, Edward K. ... Salt Lake City, UT
Brass, Eric A. ... Boston, MA
Brass, M. Francis ... Suisun City, CA
Brass, Mary M. ... Chicago, IL
Brass, Michele Carroll ... San Francisco, CA
Brass, Rick ... Houston, TX
Brass, Robert J. ... Trenton, NJ
Brassard, Peter G. ... Boston, MA
Brassard, Raymond J. ... Boston, MA
Brassard, Raymond M. ... Beaumont, TX
Brassart, Raymond A. ... Muncie, IN
Brass-Corey, Sharon ... Warrington, PA
Brasseale, Kent A., II ... Evansville, IN
Brasseaux, Calvin P. ... Covington, LA
Brasseaux, Lorna ... Baton Rouge, LA
Brassel & Baldwin, P.A. ... Annapolis, MD
Baltimore, MD
Towson, MD
Brassel, Jon W. ... Annapolis, MD
Brassel, Mary V. ... Staten Island, NY
Brasseler, Hans J. ... Palo Alto, CA
Brassell, Bowen H. ... Phenix City, AL
Brassell, Comer C., Jr. ... Marshall, TX
Brasselle, Susan Curry ... Charleston, WV
Brassett, Leo L. ... Baton Rouge, LA
Brasseur, Gary V. ... Saginaw, MI
Brasseur, Gary W. ... Lansing, MI
Brassey, Andrew C. ... Boise, ID
Brassey, Carol Lynn ... Boise, ID
Brassey, John Michael ... Boise, ID
Brassey, Wetherell, Crawford & McCurdy, L.L.P. ... Boise, ID
Caldwell, ID
Twin Falls, ID
Brassfield, Cowan & Howard ... Rockford, IL
Streator, IL
Brassfield, David James ... Rockford, IL
Brassfield, Eugene E. ... Rockford, IL
Streator, IL
Brassil, Elise Ann ... Boston, MA
Brassil & Rohlfing, P.C. ... St. Louis, MO
Brassil, Timothy B ... St. Louis, MO
Brassington, Andrew S. ... Pasco, WA
Brassington, Stanley J. Schuylkill Haven, PA
Braswell, Bradley S. ... Union Springs, AL
Braswell, Bruce W. ... Poughkeepsie, NY
Braswell, David W. ... St. Louis, MO
Braswell, Dennis William ... Atlanta, GA
Braswell, E. Maurice ... Fayetteville, NC
Braswell, Edwin M., Jr. ... Kinston, NC
Braswell, Fred O., III ... Montgomery, AL
Braswell, Glenn E. ... Woodbridge, VA
Braswell, Jason M. ... Decatur, GA
Braswell, Jefferson Monroe Gainesville, FL
Braswell, John M. ... Alexandria, VA
Braswell, Julian H. ... Miami, FL
Braswell, Linda S. ... Miami, FL
Braswell, Louis E. ... Mobile, AL
Braswell, M. Roy ... Huntsville, AL
Braswell, Marina Utgoff ... Washington, DC
Braswell, Mark K. Securities and Exchange Commission, Division of Enforcement, GV
Braswell, Mark W. Administrative Office Of The United States Courts, GV
Braswell, Nicholas T., III Montgomery, AL
Braswell, Paul K. ... Dallas, TX
Braswell, R. Gene ... Goldsboro, NC
Braswell, Telo General Services Administration, Office of the General Counsel, GV
Braswell, Walter M. ... Westfield, NJ
Braswell, William C., Jr. ... Birmingham, AL
Braszo, John J. ... Pittsburgh, PA
Brat, James L. ... Los Angeles, CA
Bratcher, Alford A. ... Marlow, OK
Bratcher, Bennett F. ... Nashville, TN
Bratcher & Bratcher ... Edmond, OK
Oklahoma City, OK
Bratcher, Gerald T. ... Oakland, CA
Bratcher & Gockel, L.C. ... Kansas City, MO
Bratcher, John A. W. ... Murfreesboro, TN
Bratcher, Kelly L. ... Oklahoma City, OK
Bratcher, Kent ... Waco, TX
Bratcher, Lynne J. ... Kansas City, MO
Bratcher, Michael C. ... Louisville, KY
Bratcher, Monty L. ... Oklahoma City, OK
Bratcher, Pamela Carolyn Bowling Green, KY
Bratcher, Steven T. ... Treasury Department, Office of Regulations and Rulings, GV
Bratcher, Susan Dianne ... Gladstone, MO
Bratcher, Thomas O. ... McMinnville, TN
Bratcher, Timothy W. ... Louisville, KY
Bratcher, W C ... Lubbock, TX
Braten, Maxine A. ... Stuart, FL
Braten, Steven Robert Fort Lauderdale, FL
Bratfisch, Paul R. ... Colorado Springs, CO
Brath, Marilyn S. ... Malibu, CA
Brathwaite, Janette M ... Houston, TX
Brathwaite, Michelle C. ... Los Angeles, CA
Brathwaite, Van M. ... Washington, DC
Bratka, Dan W. ... Bellefontaine, OH
Bratke, Steven R. ... Parkersburg, WV
Bratkowsky, Joan Gloria ... Westbury, NY
Bratland, Scott R. ... Watertown, SD
Bratman, Cheryl Joy ... Los Angeles, CA
Bratman, J. Robert ... Princeton, NJ
Bratman, Marc P. ... Los Angeles, CA
Bratsafolis, Jeanne M. ... Union, NJ
Bratsafolis, Michelle S. ... New York, NY
Bratsafolis, Nicholas A. ... New York, NY
Bratschie, Steven E. ... Grand Rapids, MI
Bratschun, Thomas D. ... Englewood, CO
Bratt, Barrie R. ... Southfield, MI
Bratt, Carol ... Redmond, WA
Bratt, Carolyn S. ... Lexington, KY
Bratt, Charles B. ... Pascagoula, MS
Bratt, David A. ... Lexington, KY
Bratt, Douglas J. ... Vancouver, WA
Bratt, Herbert S. ... Milwaukee, WI
Bratt, Holly ... San Francisco, CA
Bratt, Ira M. ... Yorktown Heights, NY
Bratt, Ira M., P.C. ... Yorktown Heights, NY
Bratt, Jay I. ... Department of Justice, Civil Division, GV
Bratt, Mark Lowell ... Pierre, SD
Bratt, Max A. ... Valley Stream, NY
Bratt, Pamela K. ... Grand Rapids, MI
Bratt, William F. ... Hilton Head Island, SC
Brattain, Bruce D. ... Indianapolis, IN
Brattain, George A. ... Terre Haute, IN
Brattain & Minnix ... Indianapolis, IN
Brattain & Nattkemper ... Terre Haute, IN
Brattain, Richard H. ... Las Vegas, NV
Brattain, William F., II ... Anchorage, AK
Brattan, Joseph Y., III ... Baltimore, MD
Hunt Valley, MD
Brattebo, Susan N. ... West Palm Beach, FL
Bratter, Jack E., A Law Corporation Encino, CA
Bratter, Joshua ... Miami, FL
Bratter, Susanne ... Oakland, CA
Bratti, Dominick ... Los Angeles, CA
Roseland, NJ
New York, NY
Brattin, Helen ... Houston, TX
Brattin, John ... Okemos, MI
Bratton, Alison Offutt ... Little Rock, AR
Bratton, Andral N. ... New York, NY
Bratton, Barham ... Austin, TX
Bratton & Bethel ... Gatlinburg, TN
Bratton, Bonnie ... Austin, TX
Bratton, Bruce F. ... Harrisburg, PA
Bratton, Cardelle ... Chicago, IL
Bratton, Dale L. ... San Francisco, CA
Bratton, Darrell D. ... San Diego, CA
Bratton, David D. ... Rochester Hills, MI
Bratton, Elaine M. ... Houston, TX
Bratton, Eleanor Katherine Albuquerque, NM
Bratton, Frances D. ... Las Cruces, NM
Bratton, G. Ray ... Memphis, TN
Bratton, George R., Jr. ... Nashville, TN
Bratton, Howard C. ... Las Cruces, NM
Bratton, James H., Jr. ... Atlanta, GA
Bratton, Jeff ... Covington, LA
Bratton, L. Richard ... Gunnison, CO
Bratton & McClow, LLC ... Gunnison, CO
Bratton, P. Scott ... Lowell, MA
Bratton, Paula W. ... Tulsa, OK
Bratton, Robert L. ... Austin, TX
Bratton, Robert M., Jr. Highland Heights, KY
Bratton, Sam G., II ... Tulsa, OK
Bratton, Sam I., Jr. ... Little Rock, AR
Bratton, Sheryl L. ... Santa Rosa, CA
Bratton, William A., III ... Dallas, TX
Bratton, William W., Jr. ... Newark, NJ
Bratun, Juliana J. ... Boulder, CO
Bratvold, Diane B. ... Minneapolis, MN
Bratvold, Larry K. ... Springfield, MO
Bratz, David C. ... Seattle, WA
Bratzel, Andrew D. ... Downers Grove, IL
Brau, Germán J. ... Mayaguez, PR
Brau, Paul D. ... Norwalk, CA
Braubach, Robert P. ... San Antonio, TX
Brauch, Jeffrey A. ... Virginia Beach, VA
Brauch, William L. ... Des Moines, IA
Braucher, Jean ... Tucson, AZ
Braucher, Richard H. ... Richardson, TX
Braucher, Warren D. ... Englewood, CO
Braucher, William M. ... Boston, MA
Brauchle, Jeffrey R. ... Orono, MN
Brauchle, Kristen ... Houston, TX
Brauchle, Paul ... Dallas, TX
Brauchler, George H. ... Golden, CO

Brauchler, Reta Anne ... Littleton, CO
Brauchli & Brauchli, P.C. ... Tucson, AZ
Brauchli, Christopher R. ... Boulder, CO
Brauchli, Robert C. ... Tucson, AZ
Brauchli - Snyder, LLC ... Boulder, CO
Brauchli, William A. ... Tucson, AZ
Braud, Andrée M. ... New Orleans, LA
Braud, Bert S. ... Kansas City, MO
Braud, Brenda ... Independence, LA
Braud, Charles H., Jr. ... Baton Rouge, LA
Braud, Jeffery P. ... Gonzales, LA
Braud, John O. ... Dayton, OH
Braud, Rene S. ... Bellaire, TX
Braud, Rudolph M., Jr. ... Springfield, IL
Braud, Stephen C. ... Belle Chasse, LA
Braud, Stephen H. ... Houma, LA
Braud, Walter D. ... Rock Island, IL
Braud/Westensee, Ltd. ... Rock Island, IL
Braude, Evan A. ... Los Angeles, CA
Braude, Herman M. ... Washington, DC
Braude, Jacob ... Brooklyn, NY
Braude & Margulies, P.C.
Washington, DC
Braude, Mervyn T. ... Phoenix, AZ
Braude, Michael E. ... Northbrook, IL
Braudes, Michael R. ... Baltimore, MD
Braudrick, Arthur C., Jr. ... Los Angeles, CA
Brauer, Andrea I. ... Los Angeles, CA
Brauer, Anne Kristen ... San Mateo, CA
Brauer, Buescher, Valentine, Goldhammer & Kelman, P.C. ... Denver, CO
Brauer, David A. ... Chicago Heights, IL
Brauer, David A. ... Detroit, MI
Brauer, David P. ... Medfield, MA
Brauer, David W. ... Howell, MI
Brauer, Donald E. ... Cambria, CA
Brauer, Eric B. ... Holland, PA
Brauer, Hugh D. ... Munster, IN
Brauer, Ingo ... San Jose, CA
Brauer, James W. ... Indianapolis, IN
Brauer, Jeffrey A. ... Cleveland, OH
Brauer, Kurt M. ... Detroit, MI
Brauer, Larry L. ... Seward, NE
Brauer, Laurel B. ... Beverly Hills, CA
Brauer, Laurel B., A Prof. Corp., Law Offices of ... Beverly Hills, CA
Brauer Law Office ... Kearney, NE
Brauer, Lawrence M. ... Washington, DC
Brauer, M. Jacqueline ... St. Louis, MO
Brauer, Marc J. ... Woodland Hills, CA
Brauer, Marlena J. ... New York, NY
Brauer, Martin R. ... Roslyn, NY
Brauer, Mary A. ... Denver, CO
Brauer, Mary Mansfield ... Belleville, IL
Brauer, Matthew A. ... Detroit, MI
Brauer, Rhonda L. ... New York, NY
Brauer, Robert E. ... Bonne Terre, MO
Brauer, Robert F. ... New York, NY
Brauer, Robert H. ... Thousand Oaks, CA
Brauer, Siegfried H., III ... Kearney, NE
Brauer & Solar ... Holland, PA
Brauer, Walter C., III ... Denver, CO
Brauer, Walter F., Jr. ... New Orleans, LA
Brauer, William J. ... Oakland, CA
Brauer-Palacios, Inge ... Fontana, CA
Braufman, Bertram ... Wantagh, NY
Braufman, James R. ... Encino, CA
Braufman, Sid ... New York, NY
Braugh, Christine Emerson ... Houston, TX
Braugh, Gary M. ... Nederland, TX
Braugh, Roger S., Jr. ... Corpus Christi, TX
Braugh, Scott S. ... Plano, TX
Braughton, Rodney L. ... San Jose, CA
Braukmann, Curtis J. ... Kansas City, MO
Brault, Adelard L. ... Fairfax, VA
Brault, Albert D. ... Rockville, MD
Brault, Albert E. ... Washington, DC
Rockville, MD
Brault, Darcie R. ... Detroit, MI
Brault, David L. ... Orange, CA
Brault, Graham, Scott & Brault, LLC
Rockville, MD
Fairfax, VA
Washington, DC
Brault, James J. ... New Haven, CT
Brault, James M. ... Rockville, MD
Brault, Joan F. ... Rockville, MD
Brault, Lisa Joy ... Los Angeles, CA
Brault, Mark A. ... Racine, WI
Brault, Melissa G. ... Baltimore, MD
Brault, Palmer, Grove, Zimmerman, White & Steinhilber ... Washington, DC
Alexandria, VA
Fairfax, VA
Manassas, VA
Brault, Patrick J. ... Glendale, CA
Braum, Scott L. ... Dayton, OH
Braumiller, Adrienne Brevard ... Dallas, TX
Braumiller & Rodriguez ... Dallas, TX
Braumuller, Robert ... New York, NY
Braun, Alfred E. ... Carmel, NY
Braun, Andrew A. ... New Orleans, LA
Braun, Barrett B. ... Walnut Creek, CA
Braun • Becker • Kruzel, A Professional Corporation ... Scottsdale, AZ
Braun, Bennett J. ... Joliet, IL
Braun, Bernard ... Commack, NY
Braun, Bernard, P.C. ... Commack, NY
Braun, Berton G. ... Chicago, IL
Braun, Bradley S. ... Scottsdale, AZ
Braun, Brent A. ... Los Angeles, CA
Braun, Brian A. ... Monticello, IL
Braun, Bruce R. ... Chicago, IL
Braun, Charles G. ... Oklahoma City, OK
Braun, Charles H. ... Chicago, IL
Braun, Christopher J. ... Indianapolis, IN
Braun, Christopher M. ... Wichita, KS
Braun, Cory L. ... Denver, CO
Braun, Craig D. ... Bakersfield, CA
Braun, Cynthia A. ... Albuquerque, NM
Braun, Dana F. ... Savannah, GA
Braun, Daniel A. ... Washington, DC
Braun, Daniel C. ... Roseland, NJ
Braun, Daniel R. ... Covington, KY
Braun, David A. ... Los Angeles, CA
Braun, David A. ... Norcross, GA
Braun, David B. ... Detroit, MI
Braun, David C. ... Tampa, FL
Braun, David L. ... Pierre, SD
Braun, David P. ... Tucson, AZ
Braun, Dianne Blocker ... Canton, OH
Braun, Donald ... Yorktown Heights, NY
Braun, Donald N. ... Los Angeles, CA
Braun, Edgar J. ... San Francisco, CA
Braun & Edwards ... Flossmoor, IL
Braun, Eric A. ... Louisville, KY
Braun, Eric Jon ... East Aurora, NY
Braun, Eric M. ... Washington, DC
Braun, Eric M. ... Greensboro, NC
Braun, Ernest ... San Pedro, CA
Braun, Ernest A. ... Pacific Palisades, CA
Braun, Frederick C. ... Boca Raton, FL
Braun, Gary A. ... Nashua, NH
Braun, Gary L. ... Warren, OH
Braun, George F. ... San Diego, CA
Braun, George W. ... Philadelphia, PA
Braun, Glenn R. ... Hays, KS
Braun & Goldberg ... New York, NY
Braun, Harland W. ... Los Angeles, CA
Braun, Harland W., Professional Corporation ... Los Angeles, CA
Braun, Herbert A. ... Woodland Hills, CA
Braun, Herman L. ... South Orange, NJ
Braun, Howard J. ... Washington, DC
Braun, Hugh R. ... Milwaukee, WI
Braun, Hugo E., Jr. ... Saginaw, MI
Braun, Jacob G. ... Brooklyn, NY
Braun, Jean E. B. ... Milwaukee, WI
Braun, Jeffrey I. ... Orange, CA
Braun, Jeffrey L. ... New York, NY
Braun, Jeffrey N. ... Detroit, MI
Braun, Jeffrey W. ... Des Plaines, IL
Braun, Jennifer ... Los Angeles, CA
Braun, Jerome ... San Francisco, CA
Braun, Jerome I. ... San Francisco, CA
Braun, John C., Jr. ... Morristown, NJ
Braun, John D. ... Colorado Springs, CO
Braun, John J. ... Garden City, NY
Braun, John R. ... Eureka, CA
Braun, John W. ... Louisville, KY
Braun, Jonathan A. ... Detroit, MI
Braun, Joseph J. ... Cincinnati, OH
Braun, Joseph Patrick ... Charles City, IA
Cresco, IA
New Hampton, IA
Braun, Joy Goldberg ... New Orleans, LA
Braun, Judith K. ... Nutley, NJ
Braun, Karen M. ... New York, NY
Braun, Karl M. ... Atlanta, GA
Braun, Keith B. ... West Palm Beach, FL
Braun, Keith S. ... Great Neck, NY
Braun, Kelly M. ... Tampa, FL
Braun Kendrick Finkbeiner PLC
Ann Arbor, MI
Bay City, MI
Midland, MI
Mount Pleasant, MI
Saginaw, MI
Braun, Kenneth A. ... Los Angeles, CA
Braun, Kevin P. ... Hartford, CT
Braun, Kristine Leigh ... Los Angeles, CA
Braun, Laurie Ellen ... New York, NY
Braun Law Office ... Mount Calvary, WI
Braun, Lawrence H. ... Columbus, OH
Braun, Lawrence M. ... Los Angeles, CA
Braun, Leon M., Jr. ... Hinesville, GA
Braun, Lillian M. ... Cleveland, OH
Braun, Linda Osberg ... Miami, FL
Braun, Lisa J. ... Detroit, MI
Braun, Lisa M. ... St. Louis, MO
Braun, Lloyd J., (A Professional Corporation)
Beverly Hills, CA
Braun, Lonnie R. ... Rapid City, SD
Braun, Louis J. ... Mount Kisco, NY
Braun, Lucy W. ... Ann Arbor, MI
Braun, Lynch, Smith & Strobel, Ltd.
Chicago, IL
Braun, Lynda M. ... New York, NY
Braun, Marc W. ... St. Louis, MO
Braun, Marcia ... Morris Plains, NJ
Braun, Marily A. ... Fair Grove, MO
Braun, Mark A. ... Chicago, IL
Braun, Mark S. ... Des Moines, IA
Braun, Mark Stafford ... Topeka, KS
Braun, Marlys Kinnel, II ... Orange, CA
Braun, Marvin R. ... St. Paul, MN
Braun, Maryls K. ... Irvine, CA
Braun, Melucci & Bright, LLP
San Diego, CA
Braun, Michael A. ... Chicago, IL
Braun, Michael D. ... Los Angeles, CA
Braun, Michael F. ... Chicago, IL
Braun, Michael O. ... New York, NY
Braun, Michael P. ... New York, NY
Braun, Michael P. ... Hamilton, OH
Braun, Michael R. ... Atlanta, GA
Braun, Michael S. ... Redondo Beach, CA
Braun, N. Barrett ... St. Louis, MO
Braun, Nancy E. ... Charlotte, NC
Braun, Neil S. ... Short Hills, NJ
Braun, Patrick E. ... Rockford, IL
Braun, Paul D. ... Milwaukee, WI
Braun, Paul S. ... Flossmoor, IL
Braun, Peter ... Boston, MA
Braun, Peter D. ... Buffalo, NY
Braun, Philip James ... Leesburg, FL
Braun, Richard A. ... Glenview, IL
Braun, Richard F. ... New York, NY
Braun, Richard H. ... Portland, OR
Braun, Richard J. ... Nashville, TN
Braun, Richard J., & Associates
Nashville, TN
Braun, Richard L. ... Williamsburg, VA
Braun, Richard L., II ... Detroit, MI
Braun, Robert A. ... Commack, NY
Braun, Robert C. ... Costa Mesa, CA
Braun, Robert E. ... New York, NY
Braun, Robert E., (P.C.) ... Los Angeles, CA
Braun, Robert T. ... Irvine, CA
Braun, Robert W. ... Waterloo, IA
Braun, Robt. E. ... Columbus, OH
Braun, Ronald W. ... Brodhead, WI
Braun, Scott D. ... Chicago, IL
Wheaton, IL
Braun, Seymour ... New York, NY
Braun, Sheldon L. ... Northbrook, IL
Braun, Sheri Dee ... Fort Lauderdale, FL
Braun, Stephen J. ... Waldorf, MD
Braun, Stephen T. ... Nashville, TN
Braun, Steven E. ... Paterson, NJ
Braun, Steven John ... Kansas City, MO
Braun, Steven K. ... Tenafly, NJ
Braun, Theodore A. ... Washington, DC
Braun, Thomas K. ... Rosemead, CA
Braun, Thomas W. ... Boston, MA
Braun, Timothy A. ... St. Charles, MO
Braun, Timothy M. ... Mount Calvary, WI
Braun, Tracey E.
Export-Import Bank of The United States, Office of the General Counsel, GV
Braun, Traci M. ... Chicago, IL
Braun, W. David ... Chicago, IL
Braun, William D. ... Department of Justice, Criminal Division, GV
Braun, William J., (P.E.) ... San Diego, CA
Braun, William N. ... Naperville, IL
Braun, William P., Jr. ... Madison, NJ
Braun, William R. ... La Jolla, CA
Braun, Wm. H. ... Huntington, NY
Braunberger, Wayne H. ... Sandy, UT
Brauneisen, Gregg A. ... Danbury, CT
Brauner Baron Rosenzweig & Klein, L.L.P.
New York, NY
Brauner, David A. ... New York, NY
Brauner, Kelli B. ... Boise, ID
Brauner, Lillian A. Loveland ... Manhattan, KS
Brauner, Saul H. ... Chicago, IL
Brauner, Wm. J. ... Caldwell, ID
Brauner, Wm. J., P.A. ... Caldwell, ID
Braunfeld, Andrew L. ... Norristown, PA
Braunfotel, Keith I. ... New City, NY
Braunlich, Jeffrey Scott ... Lansing, MI
Braunlich, Mark S., Law Offices of
Monroe, MI
Braunlich, Paul E. ... Monroe, MI
Braunlich, Russow & Braunlich, A Professional Corporation ... Adrian, MI
Ann Arbor, MI
Monroe, MI
Braunlich, William H. ... Monroe, MI
Braun-Pritzker, Michele J. ... Chicago, IL
Braunreuther, Joseph G. ... Jamaica, NY
Braunschneider, Karl ... Grand Rapids, MI
Braunschweig, Martin ... New York, NY
Braunschweig & Osborne ... New York, NY
Braunschweig, Robert ... New York, NY
Braunschweig, Robt. S. ... New York, NY
Braunschweig, Sonya R.
Minneapolis, MN
Braunschweig, T. J. ... Algona, IA
Braunsdorf, Mary ... Norwalk, CT
Braunsdorf, Paul R. ... Rochester, NY
Braunstein, Alan L. ... Boston, MA
Braunstein, Barry G. ... Boston, MA
Braunstein & Chase, L.L.P. ... Hempstead, NY
Braunstein, Donnie ... Providence, RI
Braunstein, Frank ... New York, NY
Braunstein, Harry P. ... New York, NY
Braunstein, Jacob ... Brooklyn, NY
Braunstein, Jerrold B. ... Sacramento, CA
Braunstein, Jill T. ... Uniondale, NY
Braunstein, Joseph ... Boston, MA
Braunstein, Kenneth ... Washington, DC
Braunstein, Lawrence Jay
White Plains, NY
Braunstein, Lee S. ... Hempstead, NY
Braunstein, Lisa ... Quincy, MA
Braunstein, Maurice M. ... Pittsburgh, PA
Braunstein, Michael D. ... Houston, TX
Braunstein, Mordecai B. ... New York, NY
Braunstein, Neil H. ... Florham Park, NJ
Braunstein, Perry M. ... New York, NY
Braunstein, Richard ... Palm Coast, FL
Braunstein, Richard A. ... New York, NY
Braunstein, Richard L. ... Washington, DC
Braunstein, Robin B. ... Syracuse, NY
Braunstein, Ronald N. ... Boston, MA
Braunstein, Samuel L. ... Fairfield, CT
Braunstein, Sharon I. ... Bronx, NY
Braunstein & Todisco, LLC
Bridgeport, CT
Fairfield, CT
Trumbull, CT
Braunstein-Burgett, Karen L.
Washington, DC
Brauntuch, Michelle Bloom ... Tenafly, NJ
Braus, David N. ... New York, NY
Braus, Jessica L. ... Westport, CT
Braus, Susan B. ... Hingham, MA
Brause, Cheryl Vigder ... New York, NY
Brause, Fred S., Jr. ... Metuchen, NJ
Brausen, Timothy Paul ... Minneapolis, MN
Brauser, Jason M. ... Portland, OR
Brauser, Linda ... Beaverton, OR
Braut, Bradley Seth ... New York, NY
Brauth, Marvin J. ... Woodbridge, NJ
Brautigam & Brautigam ... Fredonia, NY
Brautigam, Daryl P. ... Fredonia, NY
Brautigam, David C. ... Houghton, NY
Brautigam, Jane S. ... Loveland, CO
Brautigam, John B. ... Meadville, PA
Brautigam, Michael G. ... Cincinnati, OH
Brautigam, Peter B. ... Anchorage, AK
Brautigam, Sharon E. ... Fredonia, NY
Brautigam, Steven N. ... New York, NY
Brauweiler, Daniel Charles ... Dallas, TX
Brauwerman & Associates, P.A.
Fort Lauderdale, FL
Miami, FL
Brauwerman, Jeffrey N.
Fort Lauderdale, FL
Miami, FL
Brauwerman, Suzan C. ... Miami, FL
Brav, Nelson P. ... San Diego, CA
Brav, Peter G. ... Valley Stream, NY
Brav & Schwartz, A Professional Corporation ... San Diego, CA
Brav, Steven A. ... Cambridge, MA
Bravacos, John G., III ... West Chester, PA
Bravacos, Linda K. ... King Of Prussia, PA
Bravard, Walter E., Jr. ... Indianapolis, IN
Bravard, Wyman N. ... Mountain View, CA
Brave, Georgine, Law Office of
San Diego, CA
Brave, Michael A. ... St. Paul, MN
Braveman, David ... Philadelphia, PA
Braveman, Peter E. ... Los Angeles, CA
Braveman, Wayne S. ... Los Angeles, CA
Braver, Andrew F ... Newport Beach, CA
Braver, Cleo P. ... Baltimore, MD
Braver, Samuel W. ... Tampa, FL
Pittsburgh, PA
Braverman, Alan Jay
Fort Lauderdale, FL
Braverman, Alan N. ... New York, NY
Braverman, Alvin M. ... Owings Mills, MD
Braverman, Arthur ... Boca Raton, FL
Braverman & Associates, P.C.
New York, NY
Braverman, Bennett ... Fort Lauderdale, FL
Braverman, Bruce E. ... Chicago, IL
Braverman, Burt A. ... Washington, DC
Braverman, Daniel S. ... New York, NY
Braverman, David L. ... Cherry Hill, NJ
Philadelphia, PA
Braverman & Dedrick ... Fort Lauderdale, FL
Braverman, Edward T. ... New York, NY
Braverman, Elliott K. ... Philadelphia, PA
Braverman, Fred R. ... Medford, NJ
Braverman, Gordon L. ... Hackensack, NJ
Braverman, Helen Mandel
Cherry Hill, NJ
Philadelphia, PA
Braverman, Herbert L. ... Cleveland, OH
Braverman, Howard H. ... Springfield, IL
Braverman, Irving M. ... New York, NY
Braverman, Jill I. ... New York, NY
Braverman, Joel J. ... Bridgeport, NY
Braverman, Jonathan ... Braintree, MA
Braverman, Jonathan J. ... Mineola, NY
Braverman, Jonathan J. ... New York, NY
Braverman, Jonathan W. ... Oceanside, CA
Braverman, Joseph K. ... Washington, DC
Braverman, Julie ... New York, NY
Braverman, Larry J. ... Sunnyvale, CA
Braverman, Les C., P.C. ... Lincoln Park, MI
Southfield, MI
Braverman, Leslie Cary, Mr.
Lincoln Park, MI
Southfield, MI
Braverman & Lester ... Hackensack, NJ
Braverman, Lori J. ... New York, NY
Braverman, Mark ... Portland, OR
Braverman, Michael E. ... Baltimore, MD
Braverman, Morton S.
North Miami Beach, FL
Braverman, Morton S, P.A.
North Miami Beach, FL
Braverman, Nathan ... Baltimore, MD
Braverman, Paul ... Framingham, MA
Braverman, Paul J. ... New York, NY
Braverman, Peter ... New York, NY
Braverman, Philip ... Englewood Cliffs, NJ
Braverman, Richard ... Boston, MA
Braverman, Richard ... New Hyde Park, NY
Braverman, Robert J. ... New York, NY
Braverman, Robert N. ... Cherry Hill, NJ
Braverman and Rossi, P.A., Law Offices of
Fort Lauderdale, FL
Braverman, Samuel Michael ... Bronx, NY
Braverman, Samuel W. ... Lincoln Park, MI
Braverman, Shari Helene
New Hyde Park, NY
Braverman, Sheldon L. ... Cleveland, OH
Braverman, Stanley Alan ... Philadelphia, PA
Braverman, Stanton ... Arlington, VA
Braverman, Stephen C. ... Philadelphia, PA
Braverman, Steven D. ... Fort Lauderdale, FL
Braverman, Tobie ... Cincinnati, OH
Braverman, Todd J. ... New York, NY
Braverman, Wayne R. ... Chicago, IL
Braverman, William A. ... New York, NY
Braverman, William C. ... Homewood, IL
Bravin, Mark N. ... Washington, DC
Bravo, Alan E. ... Littleton, CO
Bravo, Anthony J., Jr. ... Boston, MA
Bravo, Carmine M. ... Sanford, FL
Bravo, Carmine M., P.A., Attorney Mediation Group ... Sanford, FL
Bravo, David D. ... New Orleans, LA
Bravo, Dominique ... New York, NY
Bravo, Eric Steven ... Columbus, OH

Bravo, Joseph K. ....San Francisco, CA
Bravo, Karen E. ....Boston, MA
Bravo, Kenneth A. ....Cleveland, OH
Bravo, Leonardo L. ....Washington, DC
Bravo & Margulies ....San Francisco, CA
Bravos, James William ....San Diego, CA
Bravo-Ugarte, Sherry ....San Antonio, TX
Brawer, Lynnette ....San Rafael, CA
Brawer, Marc H. ....Fort Lauderdale, FL
Brawer, Steven E. ....Roseland, NJ
Brawerman, Richard S. ....Los Angeles, CA
Brawka, Judith M. ....St. Charles, IL
Brawley & Brawley ....Durham, NC
Brawley, Catherine McCabe
Charlotte, NC
Raleigh, NC
Columbia, SC
Brawley, Charles A., III ....Philadelphia, PA
Brawley, Cheryl R. ....Honolulu, HI
Brawley, Dan Phillip ....Lakeland, FL
Brawley, Dan Phillip, P.A. ....Lakeland, FL
Brawley, Daniel Lee ....New Bern, NC
Wilmington, NC
Brawley, Edward T. ....Durham, NC
Brawley, James L. ....Hartford, CT
Brawley, Joanne ....Arlington, MA
Brawley, P.B., P.A. ....Mooresville, NC
Brawley, P.B., Jr. ....Mooresville, NC
Brawley, Sumter C., Jr. ....Durham, NC
Brawley, Suzanne M. ....Houston, TX
Brawner, Barbara M. ....San Francisco, CA
Brawner, Carolyn ....Fort Wayne, IN
Brawner, Gerald T. ....Philadelphia, PA
Brawner, Jeffrey B. ....Dallas, TX
Brawner, Larry C., (P.C.)
Oklahoma City, OK
Brawner Law Firm, A Professional Corporation ....Oklahoma City, OK
Brawner, Philip L. ....Miami, FL
Brawner, Robert E. ....Memphis, TN
Braxter, Milton J. ....Cleveland, OH
Braxton, Cathy Ann ....Chicago, IL
Braxton, George P., II ....Washington, DC
Braxton, Gladys E. ....Goshen, NY
Braxton, H. Harrison, Jr. .....Fredericksburg, VA
Braxton, Jeffrey M. ....Fort Lauderdale, FL
Braxton, Lisa M. ....Atlanta, GA
Braxton, Lonnie ....New London, CT
Braxton, Meredith C. ....Greenwich, CT
Braxton, Michael ....Miami, FL
Braxton, Michael E. ....Pittsburgh, PA
Braxton, Patricia D. ....Cincinnati, OH
Braxton, Sharon W. ....Lewisville, TX
Braxton, Wayne G. ....Chipley, FL
Bray, A. F., Jr. ....Martinez, CA
Bray, Aisha Tinker ....Cheyenne, WY
Bray, Alice M. ....New York, NY
Bray, Allan D. ....Las Vegas, NV
Bray, Amy H. ....Atlanta, GA
Bray, Ana Marie Castle ....Hartford, CT
Coral Gables, FL
Bray, Andrew W. ....Hartford, CT
Bray, Ann D. ....St. Paul, MN
Bray, Austin C., Jr. ....Austin, TX
Bray, Bernard P. ....San Jose, CA
Bray and Bray ....Martinez, CA
Bray, Brett G. ....Dripping Springs, TX
Bray, Carroll F., Jr. ....Atlanta, GA
Bray & Chappell, Incorporated
San Antonio, TX
Bray, Chiocca, Rappaport & Rothstadt, L.L.C.
Parsippany, NJ
Bray, Christopher D. ....Boise, ID
Bray, Clarence V. ....San Antonio, TX
Bray, Daniel L. ....Iowa City, IA
Bray, David G. ....Phoenix, AZ
Bray, Debra L. ....Los Angeles, CA
Bray, Debra S. ....Alexandria, VA
Bray, Donald H. ....Albany, NY
Bray, Doris R. ....Greensboro, NC
Bray, Douglas M. ....Woodland Hills, CA
Bray, Garth W. ....New York, NY
Bray, Geiger, Rudquist & Nuss
Stockton, CA
Bray, Geri R. ....Auburn, CA
Bray, Gregory A. ....Los Angeles, CA
Bray, H. Allen ....Maryville, TN
Bray, H. Michael ....Canton, GA
Bray, Harry C. ....Highland, MD
Bray, Holly Jean ....Hartford, CT
Bray, J. Robert ....Norfolk, VA
Bray, James C. ....Jacksonville, FL
Bray, James R., Jr. ....Corpus Christi, TX
Bray, Jana W. ....Los Angeles, CA
Bray, Janet L. ....Austin, TX
Bray, Jeff ....Dallas, TX
Bray, Jerry G., Jr. ....Virginia Beach, VA
Bray, Jim G., Jr. ....Plano, TX
Bray, John A. ....Commack, NY
Bray, John D. ....San Antonio, TX
Bray, John H. ....Duluth, MN
Bray, John M. ....Washington, DC
Bray, John R. ....Buffalo, NY
Bray, John T. ....Carlsbad, CA
Bray & Johnson ....Canton, GA
Bray, Joni M. ....Louisville, KY
Bray, Karen E. S. ....Department of Labor, Office of the Solicitor, GV
Bray, Karen M. ....Santa Monica, CA
Bray, Kathleen S. ....Duluth, MN
Bray, Keith J. ....Sacramento, CA
Bray & Klockau, P.L.C.
Cedar Rapids, IA
Iowa City, IA
Bray, L. Steve ....Houston, TX
Bray, Larry E. ....New York, NY
Bray, Larry R ....Memphis, TN
Bray, Laurack D. ....Washington, DC

Bray, Lindsay L. ....Detroit, MI
Bray, Lisa ....Charleston, WV
Bray, M. Craig ....Everett, WA
Bray, Mary C. ....Houston, TX
Bray & McDermitt ....Plano, TX
Bray, Michael ....Winter Park, FL
Brooklyn, NY
Bray, Michael L. ....Clarksburg, WV
Bray, Nick R. ....Waco, TX
Bray, Oliver W. ....Martinez, CA
Bray, Pamela W. ....Lexington, KY
Bray, Patricia C. ....Treasury Department, Internal Revenue Service, GV
Bray, Patrick ....Denver, CO
Bray, Paul M. ....Albany, NY
Bray, Peter R. ....Parsippany, NJ
Bray, Philip J. ....Hagerstown, MD
Bray, Reona F. ....Fort Lauderdale, FL
Bray, Richard D. ....Martinsville, IN
Bray, Richard S. ....Chesapeake, VA
Bray, Robert J. ....Greenfield, MA
Bray, Robert J., Jr. ....Philadelphia, PA
Bray, Robert L. ....West Des Moines, IA
Bray, Roy H. ....Houston, TX
Bray, Roy H., & Associates, Inc.
Houston, TX
Bray & Singletary, P.A. ....Jacksonville, FL
Bray, Stephanie A. ....Manchester, NH
Bray, Steven L. ....Miami, FL
Bray, Susan Elizabeth ....Greensboro, NC
Bray, Thomas L. ....St. Paul, MN
Bray, Thomas W. ....Floral Park, NY
Bray, W. Lowell, Jr. ....New Port Richey, FL
Bray, Ward C. ....Magnolia, TX
Bray, Waymond D.
Department of Commerce, Patent and Trademark Office, GV
Bray, William B. ....Colonial Heights, VA
Bray, Wm. Terry ....Austin, TX
Braybrooke, Scott E. ....Los Angeles, CA
Braybrooks, Colin S. ....Atlanta, GA
Brayer, Janet M. ....San Francisco, CA
Brayer, Jo Saxton ....Albuquerque, NM
Brayer, William H., Jr. ....New York, NY
Brayley, Nancy E. ....Rochester, NY
Brayman, Glenda K. ....Rochester, NY
Brayman, Paul M. ....Chicago, IL
Braymer, John A. ....Baton Rouge, LA
Braymer, Mary Anne ....Denver, CO
Braynard, Nathan C. ....Petaluma, CA
Braynon, Harold L. ....Miami, FL
Brayshaw, David D. ....Woodside, CA
Brayshaw, Jon W. ....New York, NY
Brayshaw, William E. ....Denver, CO
Brayton, Alan R. ....Novato, CA
Brayton, Gary L. ....Santa Cruz, CA
Brayton, Lincoln D. ....Swansea, MA
Brayton, Michael D. ....San Jose, CA
Brayton, Nathanael R. ....Boston, MA
Brayton, Purcell, Curtis & Geagan
El Segundo, CA
Novato, CA
Portland, OR
Brayton, Thomas C. ....Claremont, CA
Brayton, Thomas J. ....Long Beach, CA
Brayton, Thomas L. ....Waterbury, CT
Braz, Antonio B. ....Farmington, CT
Braz, Darline Kristina ....New York, NY
Braz, Rose ....Santa Cruz, CA
Braz, Sharon M. ....Oakland, CA
Walnut Creek, CA
Braza, James E. ....Milwaukee, WI
Braza, Mary Kathryn ....Milwaukee, WI
Braze, Gail Stimmell ....Petaluma, CA
Sacramento, CA
San Francisco, CA
Braze, James J. ....Petaluma, CA
Sacramento, CA
San Francisco, CA
Braze Law Offices ....Petaluma, CA
Sacramento, CA
San Francisco, CA
Brazeal, C. Ellis, III ....Birmingham, AL
Brazeal, Margaret Napier ....Franklin, TN
Brazeal, Mark D. ....Palo Alto, CA
Brazeale, Diana P. ....Kansas City, MO
Brazeau, James E. ....Toledo, OH
Brazeau, Nicholas J.
Wisconsin Rapids, WI
Brazeau, Nicholas John, Jr.
Wisconsin Rapids, WI
Brazeau, Potter, Wefel & Nettesheim
Wisconsin Rapids, WI
Brazeau, Robert James ....Salem, OR
Brazee & Associates ....Lafayette, LA
Brazee, James L. ....Lafayette, LA
Brazel, Melinda J. ....Clearwater, FL
Brazel, Robert E. ....Tampa, FL
Brazell, Cindy A. ....Atlanta, GA
Brazell, Ida H. ....Corpus Christi, TX
Brazell, James E. ....White Plains, NY
Brazell, James Z. ....Austin, TX
Brazelton, James C. ....Modesto, CA
Brazelton, Robert S. ....Downey, CA
Brazen, Lionel I. ....Chicago, IL
Braziel, Derek ....Dallas, TX
Braziel, L. M. ....Emory, TX
Braziel, Scherry Ann Perkins
Mount Pleasant, TX
Brazier, Donald H. ....Seattle, WA
Brazier & Erdmann ....Grass Valley, CA
Brazier, Geoffrey L. ....Helena, MT
Brazier, Jimmy B. ....Lumpkin, GA
Brazier, John R. ....Grass Valley, CA
Brazier, Robert G. ....Atlanta, GA
Brazier, Thomas S. ....San Jose, CA
Brazil, Adlong & Osment, PLC
Conway, AR

Brazil, Amy ....Conway, AR
Brazil, Anthony G. ....Los Angeles, CA
Brazil, Dan M. ....Lufkin, TX
Brazil, Eugene F. ....Fort Washington, PA
Brazil, F. Kevin ....Costa Mesa, CA
Brazil, Harold E. ....Washington, DC
Brazil, J. Patrick ....Topeka, KS
Brazil, Joseph H. ....New York, NY
Brazil, K. Scott ....Houston, TX
Brazil, Leonard ....Los Angeles, CA
Brazil, Michael P. ....Bridgeton, MO
Brazil, Susan B. ....Providence, RI
Brazil, Timothy E. ....Chanute, KS
Brazil, Wayne D. ....Oakland, CA
Brazil, William C. ....Conway, AR
Brazil, W. O., III ....Asheville, NC
Brazil-Breashears, Karen ....Chicago, IL
Brazilian, John H. ....Boston, MA
Brazill, John L. ....Seal Beach, CA
Brazill, Timothy P. ....Indianapolis, IN
Braziller, Scott L. ....Flushing, NY
Brazinski, John A. ....Jackson, WY
Brazis, William E., Jr.
Department of Defense, Defense Legal Services Agency, GV
Brazitis, George E. ....Champaign, IL
Brazle, Kenneth D. ....New Braunfels, TX
Brazle & Pfeuffer, L.L.P.
New Braunfels, TX
Brazlin, Hyman ....Phoenix, AZ
Braznell, Barbara A. ....St. Joseph, MO
Brazner, Kevin Howard ....Milwaukee, WI
Brazzel, Crystal R. ....Austin, TX
Brazzel-Massaro, Barbara ....Bridgeport, CT
Brazzil, Angela J. ....Huntington Beach, CA
Brazzil, Cynthia E. ....Troy, MI
Brcak, Frank ....Cleveland, OH
Brdar, Robert Allan ....Euclid, OH
Breaden, Randall E. ....Greenville, OH
Breading, Lee Ann ....Denton, TX
Breads, Michael D. ....Silver Spring, MD
Bready, Donald F. ....Wilbraham, MA
Bready, G. Galt ....Falls Church, VA
Bready, George G., Jr. ....Irving, TX
Break, Robert K. ....Costa Mesa, CA
Breakell & Couch, P.C. ....Albany, NY
Saratoga Springs, NY
Breakell, Walter G. ....Albany, NY
Saratoga Springs, NY
Breaker, Laura Lee ....Denver, CO
Breakman, Denise M. ....Beverly Hills, CA
San Gabriel, CA
Breakman, Paul M. ....Washington, DC
Breakstone, Donald S. ....Chicago, IL
Breakstone, Douglas M. ....Danbury, CT
Breakstone, Jay L. T. ....Bellmore, NY
Breakstone, Jeffrey L. ....Marina Del Rey, CA
Breakstone, Marc L. ....Boston, MA
Breakstone, Mark D. ....Clearwater, FL
Breakstone, Rhonda Wiener ....Bellmore, NY
Breakstone, Robert J. ....San Francisco, CA
Breakstone, Stuart B. ....Memphis, TN
Breakstone, White-Lief & Gluck, P.C.
Boston, MA
Breall, Joseph M. ....San Francisco, CA
Breall, Max R. ....Santa Rosa, CA
Breall, Susan M. ....San Francisco, CA
Bream, James M. ....Chicago, IL
Bream, John H. ....Harrisburg, PA
Bream, Shannon Depuy ....Tampa, FL
Brean, Lawrence ....Pittsburgh, PA
Brean, Richard J. ....Pittsburgh, PA
Brear, Joseph A., Jr. ....Boston, MA
Breard, Kent ....Monroe, LA
Breard, L. Christopher ....Gulfport, MS
Breard, L. Kent, Jr. ....Monroe, LA
Breard Law Firm, Ltd. ....Gulfport, MS
Brearley, David B. ....Hacienda Heights, CA
Brearley, Jennifer S. ....Charlotte, NC
Brearley, Purvis ....Trenton, NJ
Brearton, Christopher D.
Los Angeles, CA
Brearton, James E. ....Troy, NY
Brearton, James J. ....Latham, NY
Breathitt, Douglas H. ....Lakeland, FL
Breathitt, Edward T. ....Lexington, KY
Breathouwer & Gilman ....Portland, OR
Breathouwer, James G. ....Portland, OR
Breathwit, John J. ....Oklahoma City, OK
Breaud, Alan K. ....Lafayette, LA
Breaud & Lemoine, A Professional Law Corporation ....Baton Rouge, LA
Lafayette, LA
New Iberia, LA
New Orleans, LA
Breault & Associates, P.C. ....Pittsburgh, PA
Breault, Douglas L. ....Valley, AL
Breault, Pamela M.
Treasury Department, GV
Breault, Stephanie R. ....Piedmont, CA
Breault, Theodore E. ....Pittsburgh, PA
Breaune, Joseph G. ....Miami, OK
Breaux, Anne H. ....New Orleans, LA
Breaux, Claire E. ....Metairie, LA
Breaux & Hornstein ....St. Gabriel, LA
Breaux, Huey Henry ....Lafayette, LA
Breaux, Jean C., Jr. ....Lafayette, LA
Breaux, Jean C., Jr. & Associates, A Prof. Law Corp. ....Lafayette, LA
Breaux, Joseph N. ....Gretna, LA
Breaux, Kerry McHugh ....Dallas, TX
Breaux, Kreig A. ....New Iberia, LA
Breaux, Mack E. ....New Orleans, LA
Breaux, Marie ....New Orleans, LA
Breaux, Marjorie Briley ....Lafayette, LA
Breaux, Melvin C. ....Doylestown, PA
Breaux, Melvin D. ....Lake Forest, CA
Breaux, Michael D. ....Baton Rouge, LA

Breaux, Michael J. ....Lafayette, LA
Breaux, Paul J. ....Lafayette, LA
Breaux, Paul P., Jr. ....St. Gabriel, LA
Breaux, Paul W. ....Baton Rouge, LA
Breaux, Ralph G. ....New Orleans, LA
Breaux, Richard A. ....Houma, LA
Breaux, Robert S. ....Houston, TX
Breaux, Ronald W. ....Dallas, TX
Breaux, Steven T. ....Atlanta, GA
Breaux, Terry G. ....Franklin, LA
Breay, Christopher J. ....Detroit, MI
Breay, James H. ....Grand Rapids, MI
Breazeale, Elizabeth Chumney
San Antonio, TX
Breazeale, Francis I. ....Nashville, TN
Breazeale, Sachse & Wilson, L.L.P.
Baton Rouge, LA
Covington, LA
New Orleans, LA
Brebberman, James A. ....Toledo, OH
Brebbia, John Henry ....Las Vegas, NV
Brebner, Bartlet A. ....Phoenix, AZ
Brebner, Dennis A. ....Waukegan, IL
Brebner, Graeme D. ....Anchorage, AK
Brebner & Kellers, P.C. ....Phoenix, AZ
Brebneer, Cole D. ....Portland, OR
Brecheen, Leigh C. ....Beverly Hills, CA
Brecher, Allison ....Phoenix, AZ
Brecher, Armin G. ....Atlanta, GA
Brecher, Arthur D. ....Needham, MA
Brecher, Barbara E. ....Sacramento, CA
Brecher, Dan, Law Offices of
New York, NY
Brecher, David ....New York, NY
Brecher, David J. ....Palo Alto, CA
Washington, DC
Brecher, David S. ....Jacksonville, FL
Brecher, Elliot E. ....New York, NY
Brecher, Ephraim M. ....Morristown, NJ
Brecher, Ethan A. ....New York, NY
Brecher Fishman Pasternack Popish Feit Heller Rubin & Reiff ....Brooklyn, NY
Garden City, NY
Hauppauge, NY
New York, NY
White Plains, NY
Brecher, George ....New York, NY
Brecher, Harvey ....New York, NY
Brecher, Howard A. ....New York, NY
Brecher, James O. ....Roswell, GA
Brecher, Jeffrey W. ....Phoenix, AZ
Brecher, Joseph J. ....Oakland, CA
Brecher, Marc G. ....Philadelphia, PA
Brecher, Mitchell F. ....Washington, DC
Brecher, Stephanie L. Siegel
Santa Clara, CA
Brecher, Stuart G. ....Mountainside, NJ
Brecher, Susan W. ....Larchmont, NY
Brecher, Todd S. ....San Francisco, CA
Brecher, Valerie ....Washington, DC
Brecher, Wyner, Simons & Bolan LLP
Boston, MA
Needham, MA
Brechin, John H. ....Oakbrook Terrace, IL
Brechner, Howard E. ....Parsippany, NJ
Brechner, Judith ....Tallahassee, FL
Brecht, Jeff C. Duncan ....Portland, OR
Brecht, Julius J. ....Anchorage, AK
Brechtel, Timothy P. ....New Orleans, LA
Brechtelsbauer, Catherine McLaughlin
Lansing, MI
Breci, Samuel J. ....Columbia, SC
Breck, David F. ....Pontiac, MI
Breck, David R. ....Philadelphia, PA
Breck, Deborah S. ....Bridgeport, CT
Southport, CT
Stamford, CT
Breck, John H., III ....Boston, MA
Breck, Kathleen Tarpey ....Springfield, MA
Breck, Kevin H. ....Birmingham, MI
Breck, Linda C. ....Corpus Christi, TX
Breck, William H. ....Winter Springs, FL
Breck, William H., P.C. ....Winter Springs, FL
Brecka, Judith A. ....Schuyler, NE
Breckberg, Robert L. ....Anchorage, AK
Brecke, Allen D. ....Kennewick, WA
Breckenfeld, William G. ....Washington, DC
Breckenfelder, Ted E. ....Davenport, IA
Breckenridge, Alan S. ....St. Louis, MO
Breckenridge, Bryan C. ....Nevada, MO
Breckenridge, Donald O. ....Grove City, OH
Breckenridge, Francine Wilkins
Austin, TX
Breckenridge, Franklin E., Jr.
Indianapolis, IN
Breckenridge, Franklin E., Sr. ....Elkhart, IN
Breckenridge, Hugh, Law Offices of
Irvine, CA
Breckenridge, James R. ....New York, NY
Breckenridge, J. B. ....Evansville, IN
Breckenridge, Jeniphr A.E. ....Seattle, WA
Breckenridge, John E.
Newport Beach, CA
Breckenridge, John H. ....Coupeville, WA
Breckenridge, John L. ....Warren, OH
Breckenridge, Jonathan E. ....New York, NY
Breckenridge, Kenneth
Hot Springs National Park, AR
Breckenridge, Kenneth, P.A.
Hot Springs National Park, AR
Breckenridge Law Office ....New York, NY
Breckenridge, Lee P. ....Boston, MA
Breckenridge, Patricia ....Kansas City, MO
Breckenridge, Paul G., Jr. ....Glendale, CA
Breckenridge, Ray E. ....St. Louis, MO
Breckenridge, Robert E., II ....Ottumwa, IA
Breckenridge, Russell L. ....New Orleans, LA
Brecker, Charles D. ....Miami, FL

Brecker, Jeffrey R. .... **New York, NY**
Brecker, Mark Lewis .... New York, NY
Brecker, Martin F. .... New York, NY
Breckinridge, Alexander N., IV
New Orleans, LA
Breckinridge, Davis & Sproles, PLLC
Summersville, WV
Breckinridge, Jeanne Provosty
Austin, TX
Breckinridge, John S., Jr. .... **New York, NY**
Breckinridge, S. D., Jr. .... Lexington, KY
Breckir, Joseph .... Salinas, CA
Breckler, Mark J. .... San Francisco, CA
Breckner, Andrea S. .... **Minneapolis, MN**
Breclaw, John D. .... Griffith, IN
Brecount, S. Todd .... **Springfield, OH**
Breczinski, Michael J. .... Burton, MI
Breda, Mary C. .... Fort Lauderdale, FL
Bredahl, Jeff A. .... Fargo, ND
Bredar, James K. .... Baltimore, MD
Bredberg, Karl A. .... Aledo, IL
Breddan, Matthew Adam
Sherman Oaks, CA
Breddan, Wendi .... Thousand Oaks, CA
Bredder, Roy S. .... Vienna, VA
Brede, J. Daniel .... **Boca Raton, FL**
Brede, J. Daniel, P.A. .... **Boca Raton, FL**
Bredeck, Jeffrey W. .... **Baltimore, MD**
Bredehoft, Charles M. .... McLean, VA
Bredehoft, Elaine Charlson .... **Reston, VA**
Bredehoft, J. Patrick .... **Dallas, TX**
Bredehoft, John M. .... **McLean, VA**
Bredehoft, Joseph M. .... Trenton, NJ
Bredell and Bredell .... **Ypsilanti, MI**
Bredell, John H. .... **Ypsilanti, MI**
Bredell, Lynn Marie .... **Ypsilanti, MI**
Bredemann, Richard W. .... Scottsdale, AZ
Bredemeier, Daryl K. .... Independence, MO
Bredemeier, Melvin W. .... Fort Wayne, IN
Bredemeyer, Arthur C. .... Springfield, IL
Bredenbeck, Arthur H. .... Half Moon Bay, CA
Bredenbeck, Cheryl A. .... Minneapolis, MN
Bredenberg, Michael David
Department of Justice,
Bureau of Prisons, GV
Atlanta, GA
Bredensteiner, Gregg R. .... Indianapolis, IN
Bredesen, Karsten E. .... Springfield, MO
Bredesen, Robert Joseph .... **Anchorage, AK**
Bredhoff, Audrey Carter
Securities and Exchange Commission,
Office of the General Counsel, GV
Bredhoff, Elliot .... **Washington, DC**
Bredhoff & Kaiser, P.L.L.C.
Washington, DC
Bredhoff, Robert L. .... **Washington, DC**
Bredice, Steven A. .... **Burlington, VT**
Bredimus, Frank B., Jr. .... Leesburg, VA
Bredimus, Frank, P.C. .... Leesburg, VA
Bredin, Ann Marie .... **Chicago, IL**
Bredlau, Richard R. .... Ventura, CA
Bredle, James A., Jr. .... Martinsville, IN
Bredlie, Kirsten R. .... St. Paul, MN
Bredt, Alan M. .... Wilmington, DE
Philadelphia, PA
Bredthauer, Trudy Saunders .... Omaha, NE
Bredthauer, William G. .... **Fort Worth, TX**
Bree, Dermot .... Basking Ridge, NJ
Bree, Joseph S. .... New York, NY
Bree, Martin J. .... Philadelphia, PA
Breece, Carol Jolene "Jodie" .... Miami, FL
Breece, Charles E.
Environmental Protection Agency,
Office of Enforcement and Compliance
Assurance, GV
Breece, Conrad D. .... **San Francisco, CA**
Breece, Marline R. .... **Indianapolis, IN**
Breece, R. William, Jr. .... St. Louis, MO
Breecher-Breen, Sheila R. .... Phoenix, AZ
Breecker, Robert E. .... Oakland, CA
Breeckner, Randall J. .... **New Milford, CT**
Breed Abbott & Morgan .... **New York, NY**
Breed, Alexandra T. .... **Manchester, NH**
Breed, Dale Pennell .... Lebanon, NH
Breed, E. Mark, III .... **Sebring, FL**
Breed, E. Mark, III, P.A. .... **Sebring, FL**
Breed, George G. .... San Francisco, CA
Breed, James Harrington .... **Fairfax, VA**
Breed, Jerome A. .... **Washington, DC**
Breed, John C. .... Katy, TX
Breed, Joseph R. .... Boston, MA
Breed, Nathaniel P., Jr. (P.C.)
Washington, DC
Breed, Pamela M. .... Department of Commerce,
Office of the General Counsel, GV
Breed, Paul L. .... Portland, OR
Breed, Paul L., P.C. .... Portland, OR
Breed, Rebecca S. .... Greenwich, CT
Breed, Richard P., III .... **Boston, MA**
Breed, Susan K. .... Granbury, TX
Breed, Thomas J. .... **Cincinnati, OH**
Breede, Michael E. .... **New York, NY**
Breeden, Barbara H. .... **Irvington, VA**
Breeden & Breeden, L.L.P., Law Offices
New Orleans, LA
Breeden, Edward L., III .... **Norfolk, VA**
Breeden, James C. .... **Irvington, VA**
Breeden, James S. .... Dallas, TX
Breeden, James T. .... **San Francisco, CA**
Breeden, John L., Jr. .... Conway, SC
Breeden, Leon .... **San Marcos, TX**
Breeden, Linda L. .... Piedmont, CA
Breeden, MacMillan & Green, P.L.C.
Chesapeake, VA
Norfolk, VA
Portsmouth, VA
Virginia Beach, VA
Breeden, Margaret C. .... New Orleans, LA

Breeden, Mel J., Jr. .... Jackson, MS
Breeden, Michael .... **Roseville, CA**
Pendleton, OR
Breeden, Patrick D. .... **New Orleans, LA**
Breeden, Thomas R. .... **Manassas, VA**
Breeden, Thomas R., P.C. .... **Manassas, VA**
Breeding, Barbara A. .... Houston, TX
Breeding, Barbara, & Associates, A Prof. Law
Corp. .... Houston, TX
Breeding, Bradford L. .... **Corbin, KY**
Breeding, Carl W. .... **Frankfort, KY**
Breeding, Clark W. .... Dallas, TX
Breeding, J. Mark .... **Houston, TX**
Breeding, Mark S. .... **Little Rock, AR**
Breeding, Paul R. .... Dallas, TX
Breedlove, Brian H. .... **Clifton Park, NY**
Breedlove, Gary T. .... Metairie, LA
Breedlove, Gregory B. .... **Mobile, AL**
Breedlove, Irvin P., Jr. .... **Durham, NC**
Breedlove, James T. .... **Devon, PA**
Breedlove, Jill M. .... **Schenectady, NY**
Breedlove, John P. .... **Eden Prairie, MN**
Breedlove, Kathy A. .... San Diego, CA
Breedlove, Melanie .... San Antonio, TX
Breedlove, Roger J. .... Alexandria, LA
Breedlove, Roy C. .... **Tulsa, OK**
Breedlove, Scott W. .... **Dallas, TX**
Breedlove, Wm. R. .... Portsmouth, VA
Breedveld, Jay .... **Austin, TX**
Breedy-Richardson, Wilberta
Los Angeles, CA
Breeland, A. Wayne .... Dallas, TX
Breeland, Durwood J. .... **Brookhaven, MS**
Breeland, Lyn T. .... Dallas, TX
Breeland, Patrick K. .... **Austin, TX**
Breeling & Assocs., P.C. .... Omaha, NE
Breeling, Roy G., Jr. .... Omaha, NE
Breems, Timothy S. .... **Chicago, IL**
Breen, Aviva .... St. Paul, MN
Breen, Barbara A. .... Lake Grove, NY
Breen, Barry N.
Environmental Protection Agency,
Office of Enforcement and Compliance
Assurance, GV
Breen & Bartlett, P.C. .... Darien, CT
Breen, Bradford S. .... **New York, NY**
Breen, Clarke Laurence .... New York, NY
Breen, Daniel J. .... **Murray Hill, NJ**
Breen, David .... Warrendale, PA
Breen, David A. .... Philadelphia, PA
Breen, David H. .... Myrtle Beach, SC
Breen, David H., P.A. .... Myrtle Beach, SC
Breen, David J. .... New York, NY
Breen, David V. .... Mishawaka, IN
Breen, Debra Fiala .... **Omaha, NE**
Breen, Dennis A. .... **New York, NY**
Breen, Dorothy M. .... **Naples, FL**
Breen, Eileen F. .... White Plains, NY
Breen, F. R. .... Reno, NV
Breen, Fredrick E. .... Fort Dodge, IA
Breen, Gail R. .... Tonawanda, NY
Breen, George B. .... **Washington, DC**
Breen, J. Daniel .... Jackson, TN
Breen, J. Timothy .... Lake George, NY
Breen, James J., Jr. .... **Cincinnati, OH**
Breen, James Lane .... Farmingdale, NY
Breen, James M. .... **Miami, FL**
Breen, James M. .... **Chicago, IL**
Breen, James P., Jr. .... Richmond, VA
Breen, Jean Marie
Pension Benefit Guaranty Corporation,
Office of the General Counsel, GV
Breen, John E. .... **Los Angeles, CA**
Breen, John E. .... Plymouth, MI
Breen, John E. .... Columbus, OH
Breen, John F. .... Flint, MI
Saginaw, MI
Breen, John J. .... Sea Cliff, NY
Breen, John J. .... **West Chester, PA**
Breen, John M. .... Chicago, IL
Breen, John Paul .... Indianapolis, IN
Breen, Joseph B. .... Darien, CT
Breen, Joseph P. .... **San Francisco, CA**
Breen, Joseph R. .... **Chicago, IL**
Breen, Joseph W. .... Woburn, MA
Breen, Kelly S. .... Omaha, NE
Breen, Kevin J. .... **Akron, OH**
Breen, Kevin W. .... **Burbank, CA**
Breen, Lauren E. .... Buffalo, NY
Breen, Leo M. .... Evanston, IL
Breen, Lisa A. .... **Morristown, NJ**
Breen, Lisa C. .... **Chicago, IL**
Breen, Lori L. .... Pittsburgh, PA
Breen, Margaret M. .... Seattle, WA
Breen, Mary Elizabeth .... Brooklyn, NY
Breen, Mary P. .... New York, NY
Breen, Maura .... **New York, NY**
Breen, Maurice C. .... Fort Dodge, IA
Breen, Maurice M. .... Plymouth, MI
Breen, Michael A. .... **Bowling Green, KY**
Breen, Michael A., P.S.C.
Bowling Green, KY
Breen, Michael Kevin .... **Woodcliff Lake, NJ**
Breen, Michael L. .... Middleburgh, NY
Breen, Michael T. .... Atlanta, GA
Breen, Neil T. .... **Chicago, IL**
Breen, Norman Paul .... San Diego, CA
Breen, Patrick E. .... **Los Angeles, CA**
Breen, Patrick L. .... **Elkhart, IN**
Breen, Paul W. .... **San Jose, CA**
Breen & Person, Ltd., Professional
Corporation .... **Brainerd, MN**
Breen, Peter I. .... Reno, NV
Breen, Philip L. .... Department of Justice,
Civil Rights Division, GV
Breen, Philip T. .... Sutton, MA
Breen, Ramona A. .... Ogdensburg, NY
Breen, Richard F., Jr. .... Salem, OR

Breen, Richard H. .... **Brainerd, MN**
Breen, Richard M. .... **La Grange, KY**
Breen, Richard M. .... **Louisville, KY**
Breen, Richard T. .... **Los Angeles, CA**
Breen, Robert D. .... **Houston, TX**
Breen, Samson .... Baton Rouge, LA
Breen, Scott E. .... **San Antonio, TX**
Breen, Sean E. .... **Austin, TX**
Breen, Susan K. .... **Encino, CA**
Breen, Terry H. .... Vista, CA
Breen, Thomas F. .... **New York, NY**
Breen, Thomas M. .... **Chicago, IL**
Oak Park, IL
Breen, Thomas P. .... Hollister, CA
Breen, Timothy P. .... Cincinnati, OH
Breen, W. David .... Woodlyn, PA
Breen, Walter E. .... **New York, NY**
Providence, RI
Breen, William J., III .... **Omaha, NE**
Breen, William P., Jr. .... Boston, MA
Breene, Paul E. .... **Newark, NJ**
Breene, Roger J. .... **Roseland, NJ**
Breene, William E. .... Franklin, PA
Breen-Greco, Ann .... Chicago, IL
Breer, Charles A. .... **Denver, CO**
Brees, Benjimin M. .... Glendale, CA
Brees, Eugene W., II .... **Austin, TX**
Brees, Mina A. .... **Austin, TX**
Dallas, TX
Breese, Betsy A. .... Shaker Heights, OH
Breese, Claude R. .... Savannah, GA
Breese, Donald .... **Los Angeles, CA**
Breese, Donald E. .... Toledo, OH
Breese, Kenneth B. .... **Holland, MI**
Breese, William P. S. .... Boulder, CO
Breese-Jaeck, JoAnne .... **Racine, WI**
Breeser, Jeffrey W. .... **Norfolk, VA**
Breeskin, Michael W. .... Denver, CO
Breeskin, Nathan
National Labor Relations Board,
Office of the General Counsel, GV
Breeswine, Garry Lee .... Albuquerque, NM
Breetz, Bethany A. .... **Louisville, KY**
Breetz, Matthew W. .... **Louisville, KY**
Breetz, Robert G. .... Louisville, KY
Breetz, William R. .... **Farmington, CT**
Breeze, Colin M. .... **New York, NY**
Breeze, Dean .... Las Vegas, NV
Breeze, Fred .... Tallahassee, FL
Breeze, John H. .... Slingerlands, NY
Breeze, John W. .... **El Centro, CA**
Breeze, Kurt D. .... Hillsboro, MO
Breeze, Lynda M. .... Simi Valley, CA
Breeze, Michael A.M. .... Phoenix, AZ
Breeze and Rhodes-Devey, P.C.
Slingerlands, NY
Breeze, Ward .... **New York, NY**
Breg and Breg .... Waterbury, CT
Breg, Noël Ruggiero .... Waterbury, CT
Breg, William F. .... Waterbury, CT
Brega, Charles F. .... **Denver, CO**
Brega, Matthew A. .... San Diego, CA
Brega & Winters P.C. .... **Denver, CO**
Greeley, CO
Bregande, Julie A. .... **St. Louis, MO**
Bregande, Mathieu D. .... St. Louis, MO
Bregante, Richard D. .... San Diego, CA
Bregel, Calvert Ross .... Towson, MD
Bregel, Kerr, Davis & Dantes .... Towson, MD
Bregenzer, David N., Jr. .... Hopewell, NJ
Bregenzer, Michael P. .... **Chicago, IL**
Bregenzer, Neil S. .... Bend, OR
Breger, Edward E. .... New York, NY
Breger, Eli .... North Miami Beach, FL
Breger, Gorin & Leuzzi .... New York, NY
Breger, Kimberly D. .... Rego Park, NY
Breger, Richard P. .... Aventura, FL
Bregg, Herbert .... Boca Raton, FL
Breggia, Stephen E. .... Providence, RI
Breggin, Janie .... Denver, CO
Breggin Law Firm, The, P.C. .... Denver, CO
Breggin, Linda K. .... **Washington, DC**
Bregianes, Geo. .... Springfield, MA
Bregianes, James J. .... **Springfield, MA**
Breglio, John F. .... **New York, NY**
Bregman, Arthur Randolph .... Washington, DC
Bregman, Berbert & Schwartz, L.L.C.
Washington, DC
Bethesda, MD
Hyattsville, MD
Bregman & Burt, A Professional Association
Scottsdale, AZ
Bregman, David N. .... **San Diego, CA**
Bregman, Douglas M. .... **Bethesda, MD**
Bregman, Eleanor T. .... San Diego, CA
Bregman, Eric .... **New York, NY**
White Plains, NY
Bregman, Gary H. .... Glendale, CA
Bregman, Herbert M. .... Burbank, CA
Bregman, Howard .... **Boca Raton, FL**
West Palm Beach, FL
Bregman, Jacqueline D.
Albuquerque, NM
Bregman, Joseph P. .... Encino, CA
Bregman, Judy E. .... Grand Haven, MI
Bregman, Keith A. .... North Hollywood, CA
Bregman, Keith A. .... **Wayne, NJ**
Bregman Law Firm, The, P.C.
Albuquerque, NM
Bregman, Lynn .... **Washington, DC**
Bregman, Mark A. .... **Scottsdale, AZ**
Bregman, Martin J. .... Topeka, KS
Bregman, Martin S. .... Telluride, CO
Bregman, Norie Rand .... **New York, NY**
Bregman, Paula G. .... **Wilkes-Barre, PA**
Wilkes-Barre, PA
Bregman, Paula G., A Professional
Corporation .... **Wilkes-Barre, PA**

Bregman, Peter R. .... Long Beach, CA
Bregman, Robert J. .... New York, NY
Bregman, Sam .... **Albuquerque, NM**
Bregman, Sandra K. .... **Scottsdale, AZ**
Bregman, Stanley I., Law Office of
Washington, DC
Bregman, Theodore G. .... Encino, CA
Bregman, Theodore G., A Law Corp.
Encino, CA
Bregman & Welch .... Grand Haven, MI
Bregoff, Denise A. .... **Fort Lauderdale, FL**
Bregovic, Boyana .... **New York, NY**
Bregstein, Henry .... **Newark, NJ**
New York, NY
Bregstein, Nancy J. .... **Philadelphia, PA**
Bregy, Lawrence .... Camden, ME
Breh, Donald J. .... **Glenview, IL**
Brehany, E. Jane .... **Pensacola, FL**
Breheney, Mary Fern .... Poughkeepsie, NY
Breheny, Brian V. .... **New York, NY**
Breheny, Peter F. .... **New York, NY**
Brehl, Edmund Kenneth .... Sacramento, CA
Brehl, James W. .... **Minneapolis, MN**
Brehl, Theresa M. .... **San Diego, CA**
Brehm, Alison J. .... **Louisville, KY**
Brehm, David J. .... **Delaware, OH**
Brehm, Diane Elizabeth .... **Philadelphia, PA**
Brehm, Douglas Gerard .... **Knoxville, TN**
Brehm, Gregory A. .... **New York, NY**
Brehm, J. Fred .... Knoxville, TN
Brehm, James Francis .... Greenville, SC
Brehm, James G. .... **Heathrow, FL**
Brehm, John E., Jr. .... Cincinnati, OH
Brehm, Karen S. .... **Wilmington, DE**
Brehm, L. Andrew .... **Chicago, IL**
Brehm, Peter C. .... **Green Bay, WI**
Brehm, Philip J. .... Janesville, WI
Brehm, Philip R. .... **Green Bay, WI**
Brehman, Delbert J. .... **Chicago, IL**
Brehmer, Charles R. .... **Bakersfield, CA**
Brehmer, Earle E. .... Norton, KS
Brehmer, George W. .... Monterey, CA
Brehmer, Karl S. .... Columbia, SC
Brehmer, Marcia L. .... Columbus, OH
Brehn, Russell P. .... Conway, SC
Brei, Jeffrey T. .... **San Diego, CA**
Breibart & Lichtenstein, P.C.
Birmingham, AL
Breibart & McCauley .... Lexington, SC
Breibart, Richard .... Birmingham, AL
Breibart, Richard J. .... Lexington, SC
Breidbart, Randy M. .... Jericho, NY
Breidbord, Paul L. .... Stamford, CT
Breidenbach, Breidenbach & Troncelliti
Norristown, PA
Pottstown, PA
Breidenbach, Buckley, Huchting, Halm &
Hamblet, A Law Corporation
Diamond Bar, CA
Los Angeles, CA
Breidenbach, Douglas B. .... Pottstown, PA
Breidenbach, Francis .... **Los Angeles, CA**
Breidenbach, Heidi S. .... **Dayton, OH**
Breidenbach, John E., & Associates
Dayton, OH
Breidenbach, Johnson, Douple, Beyoglides,
Leve & Hansen .... Dayton, OH
Breidenbach, Paul .... Shaker Heights, OH
Breidenbach, Robert A. .... **St. Louis, MO**
Breidenbach, Scott F. .... Pottstown, PA
Breidenbaugh, J. Christopher .... Dayton, OH
Breidenstein, Ralph .... St. Charles, MO
Breidenthal, Robert E. .... Wichita, KS
Breiding, Leonard J., II .... **Akron, OH**
Breier Deutschmeister & Urban, P.C.
New York, NY
Breier, Eileen G. .... Coral Gables, FL
Breier, Gary A. .... Oregon, OH
Toledo, OH
Breier, Gregory J. .... Toledo, OH
Breier, Marcus I. .... New York, NY
Breier, Miriam M. .... New York, NY
Breier, Robert G. .... **Miami, FL**
Breier and Seif, P.A. .... **Coral Gables, FL**
Miami, FL
West Palm Beach, FL
Breier, Vivian .... **Mineola, NY**
Breig, Joseph P. .... Millville, NJ
Breighner, Martin B. .... Harbor Springs, MI
Breighner, Martin, III .... Harbor Springs, MI
Breihan, John R. .... **Austin, TX**
Breiland, Lance M. .... **New York, NY**
Breiling, John J. .... Portland, OR
Breimann, Robert J. .... **Grundy, VA**
Breimayer, Joseph F. .... Minneapolis, MN
Breimer, Stephen F. .... **Beverly Hills, CA**
Breindel & Ferstendig, P.C.
New York, NY
Breindel, Howard .... **New York, NY**
Breindel, Robert A. .... Anaheim, CA
Breiner, Alexander .... **Fairfield, CT**
Breiner, Alfred W. .... **Alexandria, VA**
Breiner & Breiner .... **Alexandria, VA**
Breiner, Christina M. .... **Melville, NY**
Breiner, Deborah L. .... San Rafael, CA
Breiner, Mary J. .... **Alexandria, VA**
Breiner, Myles Steven .... Honolulu, HI
Breiner, Theodore A. .... **Alexandria, VA**
Breiner, William J. .... Kenilworth, NJ
Breines, Andrew S. .... **Boston, MA**
Breinholt, Jeffrey A. .... Department of Justice,
Criminal Division, GV
Breinholt, Margaret M.
Department of Agriculture,
Office of the General Counsel, GV
Breinig, Alfred O., Jr. .... Jenkintown, PA
Breinin, Bartley J. .... **New York, NY**
Breininger, Ryan S. .... **Bryan, OH**

Breininger, Thomas M. ... **Naperville, IL**
Breisach, Eric E. ... **Kalamazoo, MI**
Breisblatt, Robert B. ... **Chicago, IL**
Breisky, Laura R. ... Corte Madera, CA
Breit, Billy ... Chesapeake, VA
Breit, Billy, & Associates, PC
Chesapeake, VA
Breit, Bosch, Levin & Coppola, P.C.
Denver, CO
Breit, Carol An ... Richmond, VA
Breit, Donald H. ... Sioux Falls, SD
Breit, Drescher & Breit, P.C.
Chesapeake, VA
Newport News, VA
Norfolk, VA
Portsmouth, VA
Virginia Beach, VA
Breit, Gene R. ... New York, NY
Breit, Jeffrey A. ... **Norfolk, VA**
Breit, Michelle G. ... Palo Alto, CA
Breit, Mitchell M. ... **New York, NY**
Breit, Richard H. ... **Fort Lauderdale, FL**
Breit, Steven L. ... Manheim, PA
Breitbach, John T. ... **Cedar Rapids, IA**
Breitbart, David ... New York, NY
Breitbart, Douglas L. ... New York, NY
Breitbart, Gregg J. ... **Miami, FL**
Breitbart, Jeffrey W. ... Los Angeles, CA
Breitbart, Kenneth J. ... Baltimore, MD
Breitbart, Kenneth J., & Associates, P.A.
Baltimore, MD
Breitbart, Robert S. ... Woodbury, NY
Breitbeil, Kenneth R. ... **Houston, TX**
Breitburg, David ... **Los Angeles, CA**
Breitenbach, Douglas L. ... Washington, DC
Breitenbach, Edwin E.
Huntington Beach, CA
Breitenbach, Gene L. ... Grand Junction, CO
Breitenbach, Jerold W. ... Kenosha, WI
Breitenbach, Robert B. ... Evergreen, CO
Breitenbach, Roy W. ... **Great Neck, NY**
Breitenbach, Thomas A. ... **Cincinnati, OH**
Breitenbach, William H. ... Cleveland, OH
Breitenberg, John F.
House of Representatives, Committee on Post Office & Civil Service, GV
Breitenbucher, James E. ... **Seattle, WA**
Breitenecker, Rudiger L. ... **New York, NY**
Breiteneicher, Henry S.
National Labor Relations Board, Office of Solicitor, GV
Breitenfield, Victor H. ... Tomah, WI
Breitenstein & Browne, A Professional Corporation ... Closter, NJ
Breitenstein, Gerald ... Closter, NJ
Breitenstein, Jonathan Earl ... Louisville, KY
Breitenstein, Laurie K. ... **Barrington, IL**
Breitenstein, Peter F. ... **Denver, CO**
Breitenwischer, Scott R. ... **Houston, TX**
Breiter, Jeanne C. ... Hempstead, NY
Breiter, Lorna M. ... St. Paul, MN
Breiter, Randee Godofsky ... Coral Gables, FL
Breitfeller, Ralph E. ... **Columbus, OH**
Breithart, Richard O.
Palm Beach Gardens, FL
Breithaupt, Eric J. ... **Birmingham, AL**
Breithaupt, H. Diane ... Alameda, CA
Breithaupt, Harry J., Jr. ... Washington, DC
Breithaupt, Henry C. ... **Portland, OR**
Breithaupt, James F. ... Satellite Beach, FL
Breithaupt, Jeffrey L. ... Santa Rosa, CA
Breithaupt, R. Alan ... Monroe, LA
Breithaupt, Richard W. ... Denver, CO
Breithoff, Carole A. ... New Orleans, LA
Breitholle, Howard F. ... Cincinnati, OH
Breitkopf, David J. ... Newark, NJ
Breitkopf, Herman L.
New Brunswick, NJ
Breitkopf, Laurel D. ... North Chicago, IL
Breitkopf, Scott Alan ... Miami, FL
Breitkreutz, Anne M. ... **Omaha, NE**
Breitkreutz, Brenda M. ... **Cincinnati, OH**
Breitkreutz, Carolyn R. ... Auburn, CA
Breitlauch, Linda ... Saylorsburg, PA
Breitling, Duane R. ... **Fargo, ND**
West Fargo, ND
Breitling, Peter M. ... **Philadelphia, PA**
Breitman, Alan M. ... Livingston, NJ
Breitman, Craig R. ... **Los Angeles, CA**
Breitman, Frank ... Philadelphia, PA
Breitman, Julia M. ... Los Angeles, CA
Breitman, Lori C. ... Short Hills, NJ
Breitman, Lorraine R. ... Hackensack, NJ
Breitman, Mark L. ... South Amboy, NJ
Breitman, Matthew K. ... **New York, NY**
Breitman, Milton M. ... **Livingston, NJ**
Breitman, Peter N. ... St. Louis, MO
Breitman, Reid Hunter ... **Los Angeles, CA**
Breitman, Steven E. ... Jamaica, NY
Breitmoser, Katharine A. ... **Jacksonville, FL**
Breitner, Carol S. ... Falls Church, VA
Breitner, Dennis A., Law Offices of
Mineola, NY
Breitner, Lauren Elizabeth ... Garden City, NY
Breitner, Paul D. ... **Miami, FL**
Breitner, Renee A. ... Merrick, NY
Breitner, Steven S. ... **Harrington Park, NJ**
Breitowitz, Irving A. ... Baltimore, MD
Breitsameter, George W. ... Boise, ID
Breitstadt, Charles P. ... Columbus, OH
Breitstein, Joel M. ... Baltimore, MD
Breitstein, Norman ... Wickatunk, NJ
Breitstein, Paul T. ... **Woodcliff Lake, NJ**
Breitstone, Peter C. ... Cedarhurst, NY
Breitstone, Stephen M. ... **Mineola, NY**
Breitwieser, Richard J. ... **Martinez, CA**
Breitwieser, Richard J. ... **Oakland, CA**

Breitwisch, Corilynn ... Los Angeles, CA
Breivogel, Kenneth R. ... Falmouth, MA
Brejcha, Barrie L. ... **Chicago, IL**
Brejcha, Robert Allen ... Tulsa, OK
Brejcha, Roger J. ... La Grange, IL
Brejcha, Ronald J. ... Milwaukee, WI
Brejcha, Thomas ... Chicago, IL
Brejcha, William D. ... **Chicago, IL**
Brejt, Sara Naiman ... Cleveland, OH
Brekhus, Elizabeth Ann ... **Greenbrae, CA**
Brekhus, Matthew D. ... Greenbrae, CA
Brekhus, Peter B. ... **Greenbrae, CA**
Brekhus, Peter B., and Associates, Law Offices of ... **Greenbrae, CA**
Brekka & Brekka ... Hubbardston, MA
Brekka, Clare Frain ... Hubbardston, MA
Brekka, Kenneth L. ... Hubbardston, MA
Brekke & Angerer ... Citrus Heights, CA
Brekke, Edgar A. ... Malibu, CA
Brekke, George O. ... Citrus Heights, CA
Brekke, Janet F. ... Sioux Falls, SD
Brekke, Jeffrey D. ... **Sioux Falls, SD**
Brekke, Richard A. ... **Billings, MT**
Brekken, Deppe, Wynia & Cook, P.C.
Jewell, IA
Story City, IA
Brekken, Judean C. ... Story City, IA
Brekus, Andrew J. ... Turnersville, NJ
Breland & Breland ... Houston, TX
Breland, Curtis ... Leakesville, MS
Breland, David J. ... Decatur, AL
Breland, Harvey Breece ... Greenville, SC
Breland, James T. ... Jackson, MS
Breland, John M. ... **Jackson, MS**
Breland, Nancy L. ... Houston, TX
Breland, Norman L. ... **Gulfport, MS**
Breland, Norman L., P.A. ... **Biloxi, MS**
Gulfport, MS
Breland, Patton H., Jr. ... Houston, TX
Breland, Paula Jan ... Austin, TX
Breland, Suzette F. ... Jackson, MS
Breland and Whitten ... Sumner, MS
Brelje, Christopher J. ... **Phoenix, AZ**
Brell, Werner ... New York, NY
Brelo, Clayton E. ... Cleveland, OH
Brelsford, Gregg B. ... Anchorage, AK
Brelsford, Harry G. ... Seattle, WA
Brelsford, Harry W. ... Santa Barbara, CA
Brelsford, James F. ... **Menlo Park, CA**
Brelsford, William L., Jr.
Walnut Creek, CA
Brelsford, William M. ... San Antonio, TX
Brelvi, Farah S. ... New York, NY
Brem, Katherine Butler ... **Houston, TX**
Brem, Michael Lamar ... **Houston, TX**
Brem, Samantha A. ... **St. Petersburg, FL**
Breman, Joseph E. ... Boca Raton, FL
Breman, Matthew C. ... **Indianapolis, IN**
Breman, Vicki A. ... Department of Agriculture, Office of the General Counsel, GV
Bremer, Brent M. ... Atlanta, GA
Bremer, C. Dawson ... **San Antonio, TX**
Bremer, Catherine Ward ... Oak Park, IL
Bremer, Celeste F. ... Des Moines, IA
Bremer, Charles A. ... St. Louis, MO
Bremer, Christine A. ... Wausau, WI
Wisconsin Rapids, WI
Bremer & Cook ... Greencastle, IN
Bremer, Daniel D. ... Burton, MI
Bremer, David H. ... **San Francisco, CA**
Bremer, Duncan S. ... Colorado Springs, CO
Bremer, Frederick S. ... Indianapolis, IN
Bremer, Howard W. ... **Denver, CO**
Bremer, Howard W. ... Madison, WI
Bremer, James ... **McLean, VA**
Bremer, Jane E. ... **Minneapolis, MN**
Bremer, John L. ... Wheeling, WV
Bremer, John M. ... **Milwaukee, WI**
Bremer, Keith G. ... **Orange, CA**
San Diego, CA
Bremer, Lance R. ... **Houston, TX**
Bremer, Laura C. ... **San Francisco, CA**
Bremer, LeAnne ... **Vancouver, WA**
Bremer, Lisa ... Department of Commerce, Economic Development Administration, GV
Bremer, Marcia G. ... Olivia, MN
Bremer, Mark J. ... **St. Louis, MO**
Bremer, Michael Francis ... St. Petersburg, FL
Bremer & Nelson LLP ... Grand Rapids, MI
Bremer, Ralph M. ... Seattle, WA
Bremer, Richard C. ... **Dearborn, MI**
Bremer, Richard C., Jr. ... Dedham, MA
Bremer, Richard D. ... Calabasas, CA
Bremer, Robert J. ... Greencastle, IN
Bremer, Scott A. ... **Chicago, IL**
Bremer, Thomas R. ... Norwalk, CT
Bremer & Whyte, LLP ... **Los Angeles, CA**
Orange, CA
San Diego, CA
Bremer, William B. ... Park Ridge, IL
Bremer, William D. ... San Francisco, CA
Bremer, William M. ... Grand Rapids, MI
Bremer, William R. ... Tiburon, CA
Bremer-Kugle, Julianne F. ... **Houston, TX**
Bremermann, H. John, III ... Timonium, MD
Bremner, Anne Melani ... **Seattle, WA**
Bremner, Janus & Cook ... **Chesterfield, VA**
Richmond, VA
Bremner, John E. ... Philadelphia, PA
Bremner, Joseph P. ... Milwaukee, WI
Bremond, Harry B. ... **Palo Alto, CA**
Brems, John N. ... **Salt Lake City, UT**
Bremser, Annmarie Clausen ... Westford, MA
Bremser, Steve ... Victorville, CA
Bremseth, Fredric A. ... Wayzata, MN
Bremson, Francis L. ... Sacramento, CA
Bremus, Scott M. ... **Cumming, GA**
Bremyer, Jay K. ... **McPherson, KS**

Bremyer, John K. ... **McPherson, KS**
Bremyer & Wise, P.A. ... **McPherson, KS**
Bremyer-Archer, Jill ... **McPherson, KS**
Bren, Gerald H. ... St. Louis Park, MN
Bren, Roberta S. ... **Arlington, VA**
Bren, Vicki L. ... Rockville, MD
Brena, Bell & Clarkson, P.C.
Anchorage, AK
Brena, Robin O. ... **Anchorage, AK**
Brenan, C. Erin ... **San Francisco, CA**
Brenan, C. Kane ... New York, NY
Brenan, Denis V. ... **Philadelphia, PA**
Brenan, Henton S. ... Carmel, CA
Brenan, Kevin D. ... Warren, NJ
Brenan, Michael S. ... San Antonio, TX
Brencher, George, III ... Branford, CT
Brencher, George, IV ... **New Haven, CT**
Brenckle, Carol A. ... Kenai, AK
Brend, Jeffrey W. ... Chicago, IL
Brendamour, Douglas P. ... Cincinnati, OH
Brendamour, Reeta H. ... **Cincinnati, OH**
Brende, Arlie J. ... **Sioux Falls, SD**
Brende, Kelly Dean ... **Lincoln, NE**
Brende & Schroeder Law Office, L.L.P.
Sioux Falls, SD
Brendel, Cory C. ... **Glendale, CA**
Brendel, John G. ... Houston, TX
Brendel, John K. ... Brookfield, WI
Brendel, John M. ... Newark, NJ
Brendel, John Patrick ... **St. Paul, MN**
Brendel, John S. ... **Pittsburgh, PA**
Brendel, Joseph R. ... **Pittsburgh, PA**
Brendel, Neal R. ... **Pittsburgh, PA**
Brendel and Zinn, Ltd. ... **St. Paul, MN**
Brendemuehl, Curtis A. ... Oconomowoc, WI
Brendemuehl, Lynn Coffin ... Natick, MA
Brendemuhl, James L. ... Riverside, IL
Brendemuhl, Ruth Anne ... Riverside, IL
Brendemuhl, William J., Jr. ... Denver, CO
Brenden, Ann E. ... Des Moines, IA
Brenden, Peggy A. ... Minneapolis, MN
Brender, Art ... **Fort Worth, TX**
Brendle, Wayne M. ... Charlotte, NC
Brendza, Robert P. ... Exton, PA
Brendze, Elizabeth ... Philadelphia, PA
Brendzel, Henry T. ... Middletown, NJ
Brendzel, Michael L. ... **New York, NY**
Brendzel, Rachel ... **Philadelphia, PA**
Brendzel, Ronald Irwin ... Aliso Viejo, CA
Breneisen, Albert J. ... **New York, NY**
Breneman, Diane M. ... **Kansas City, MO**
Breneman, Gary M. ... Reston, VA
Breneman & Georges ... **Washington, DC**
Alexandria, VA
Breneman, William D. ... **Alexandria, VA**
Brenemen, Jack B. ... Brandon, MS
Brenengen, Matthew M.
Minneapolis, MN
Brener, Herbert ... Philadelphia, PA
Brener, Judith M. ... New York, NY
Brener, Michael Scott ... St. Paul, MN
Brener, Richard J. ... **Miami, FL**
Brener, Robert J. ... **New York, NY**
Brenes, Neil F. ... **New York, NY**
Brengle, James K. ... **Philadelphia, PA**
Brengle, John E. ... **New Albany, IN**
Brengle, William A. ... **Grand Rapids, MI**
Brenham, Robert P. ... Baton Rouge, LA
Brenhouse, Arnold A. ... Irvington, NY
Brenia, Bruce W. ... Waterbury, CT
Brenizer, Jon W. ... Syracuse, NY
Brenker, Scott Mitchell ... Commack, NY
Brenker, William A. ... Denver, CO
Brenlla, George F. ... **New York, NY**
Brenlove, Nicholas P. ... Bridgeville, PA
Brenman, Abraham ... Fair Lawn, NJ
Brenman, Albert ... **Denver, CO**
Brenman, Andrew H. ... Fair Lawn, NJ
Brenman Bromberg & Tenenbaum, P.C.
Denver, CO
Brenman, David W. ... Denver, CO
Brenman, Eric B. ... Newton, MA
Brenman, Irving I. ... Merrillville, IN
Brenman, Jeffrey M. ... **Denver, CO**
Brenman, Lawrence H. ... **Chicago, IL**
Brenman, Lisa R. ... **Chapel Hill, NC**
Brenman, Paul Jonathan
Philadelphia, PA
Brenman & Piper ... Fair Lawn, NJ
Brenman, Stephen M. ... Merrillville, IN
Brenna & Brenna ... **Rochester, NY**
Brenna, Daniel R. ... Trenton, NJ
Brenna, Nathan P. ... **Minneapolis, MN**
Brenna, Robert L., Jr. ... **Rochester, NY**
Brennaman, Patrick A. ... Minneapolis, MN
Brennan, Alfred L., Jr. ... Baltimore, MD
Brennan, Alfred L., Sr. ... Towson, MD
Brennan, Alice C. ... **New York, NY**
Brennan, Andrew J. ... Salt Lake City, UT
Brennan, Ann Amer ... **Akron, OH**
Brennan, Anne Talbot ... **Towson, MD**
Brennan, Annemarie ... **Washington, DC**
Brennan, Anthony L. ... Baltimore, MD
Brennan, Arthur D. ... Concord, NH
Brennan, Arthur D. ... Bronx, NY
Brennan & Associates ... **Houston, TX**
Brennan, Babette L. ... **Quincy, IL**
Brennan & Barnard ... **Quincy, IL**
Brennan, Bernard A. ... Sanger, CA
Brennan & Bernardin, A Professional Corporation ... **Collingswood, NJ**
Brennan, Bonnie C. ... New York, NY
Brennan & Brennan ... Milwaukee, WI
Brennan and Brennan, Attorneys of Law, P.A.
Baltimore, MD
Brennan & Brennan, P.C. ... South Bend, IN
Brennan, Bridget A. ... **Philadelphia, PA**
Brennan, Bridget G. ... New York, NY

Brennan, Bruce A. ... De Kalb, IL
Brennan, Bruce J. ... Washington, DC
Brennan & Burns ... Brighton, MI
Brennan, Carey M. ... **Pittsburgh, PA**
Brennan, Carol A. ... Woodland Hills, CA
Brennan, Caron, Lenehan & Iacopino
Concord, NH
Manchester, NH
Brennan, Carrie J. ... **Phoenix, AZ**
Brennan, Cates & Constance, P.C.
Belleville, IL
Brennan, Catherine E. ... Salinas, CA
Brennan, Catherine Margaret ... Baltimore, MD
Brennan, Charles F. ... Garden City, NY
Brennan, Charles J. ... Nokomis, FL
Brennan, Charles W. ... Wayland, MA
Brennan, Chas. E. ... Brookhaven, MS
Brennan, Christopher John ... Bethesda, MD
Brennan, Clayton Lane ... Ukiah, CA
Brennan & Collins ... **Milwaukee, WI**
Brennan, Cristina M. ... **New York, NY**
Brennan, Cynthia J. ... **Orlando, FL**
Brennan, Cynthia L.
Plymouth Meeting, PA
Brennan, Dan ... Laguna Hills, CA
Brennan, Daniel C. ... Albany, NY
Brennan, Daniel E., Jr. ... Trumbull, CT
Brennan, Daniel Edward ... Trumbull, CT
Brennan, Daniel H., Jr. ... Bedford Park, IL
Brennan, Daniel J. ... **King Of Prussia, PA**
Brennan, Daniel J. ... **Round Rock, TX**
Brennan, Daniel S. ... **Chicago, IL**
Brennan, Daniel T. ... Raleigh, NC
Brennan, Danolda J. ... Chicago, IL
Brennan, David C. ... Orlando, FL
Brennan, David. C. ... **Albany, NY**
Brennan, David F. ... Commerce, CA
Brennan, David K. ... **Philadelphia, PA**
Brennan, David L. ... **Akron, OH**
Brennan, David R. ... **Minneapolis, MN**
Brennan, David T. ... **Denver, CO**
Brennan, David W. ... **La Jolla, CA**
Brennan, Dawn R. ... **San Diego, CA**
Brennan, Denise Peters ... Des Moines, IA
Brennan, Dennis J.
Agency for International Development, Other Offices of A.I.D., GV
Brennan, Dennis J. ... Worcester, MA
Brennan, Dennis J. ... **Cherry Hill, NJ**
Philadelphia, PA
Brennan, Dennis M. ... South Bend, IN
Brennan, Dichter & Brennan ... Stamford, CT
Brennan, Donald J. ... **Amherst, MA**
Brennan, Donald J. ... **Pittsfield, MA**
Brennan, Donna S. ... **Baltimore, MD**
Brennan, Douglas F. ... Harrisburg, PA
Brennan, E. Gaynor, Jr. ... Stamford, CT
Brennan, E. Thomas ... St. Paul, MN
Brennan, E. Thomas, Jr. ... Sea Girt, NJ
Brennan, Edmund J. ... Taunton, MA
Brennan, Edmund J., Jr. ... **Taunton, MA**
Brennan, Edward F., Jr. ... Belleville, IL
Brennan, Edward F., Jr. ... Wellesley, MA
Brennan, Edward J. ... St. James, NY
Brennan, Edward J., Jr. ... **Boston, MA**
Brennan, Edward M. ... **Tampa, FL**
Brennan, Edward M. ... Pottsville, PA
Brennan, Edward P. ... Albany, NY
Brennan, Edward T. ... **Savannah, GA**
Brennan, Edward V. ... **La Jolla, CA**
San Diego, CA
Brennan, Eileen A. ... New York, NY
Brennan, Elise Dunitz ... **Tulsa, OK**
Brennan, Elizabeth A. ... **Missoula, MT**
Brennan, Elizabeth L. ... **Stamford, CT**
Brennan, Enda T. ... Santa Cruz, CA
Brennan, Erin Flood ... Sauk City, WI
Brennan, Eugene G. ... **New York, NY**
Brennan, Eugene J. ... Calico Rock, AR
Brennan, Eugenia M. ... Coxsackie, NY
Brennan, Evelyn B. ... Houston, TX
Brennan, Fabriani and Novenstern
Mount Kisco, NY
Brennan & Fitzgerald ... Mount Clemens, MI
Brennan & Francis
New Martinsville, WV
Brennan, Francis J. ... **Albany, NY**
Brennan, Francis J., III, Law Office of
Cranbury, NJ
Brennan, Francis W. ... Modesto, CA
Brennan, Francis X. ... Media, PA
Brennan, Frank P. ... **Cherry Hill, NJ**
Brennan, Frederick H. ... Napa, CA
Brennan, Frederick, Vouros & Black
Youngstown, OH
Brennan, G. Arthur ... Alfred, ME
Brennan, George B. ... Littleton, CO
Brennan, George J. ... Glendale, CA
Brennan, George K. ... Baltimore, MD
Brennan, Gerald D. ... Kissimmee, FL
Brennan, Gerard M. ... **Somerville, NJ**
Brennan, Gordon W. ... Lansing, MI
Brennan, H. Randal ... **Vero Beach, FL**
Brennan, Harris & Rominger
Brunswick, GA
Hinesville, GA
Savannah, GA
Statesboro, GA
Waycross, GA
Brennan, Hayskar, Jefferson, Walker & Schwerer, Professional Association
Fort Pierce, FL
Brennan, Henry J., III ... **Detroit, MI**
Brennan, J. Brian ... West Palm Beach, FL
Brennan, J. Lorraine ... Miami, FL
Brennan, J. Martin, Jr. ... Sterling Heights, MI
Brennan, J. Michael ... **Irvine, CA**
Brennan, J. Michael ... Fort Pierce, FL

Brennan, J. Michael ... Towson, MD
Brennan, J. Michael, P.A. ... Fort Pierce, FL
Brennan, Jacquie ... Houston, TX
Brennan, James A. ... Reading, MA
Brennan, James A. ... Las Vegas, NV
Brennan, James C. ... Baltimore, MD
Brennan, James C. ... Aston, PA
Media, PA
Brennan, James C. ... Falls Church, VA
Brennan, James E. ... Janesville, WI
Brennan, James F. ... New London, CT
Brennan, James F. ... Ramsey, NJ
Brennan, James F., III ... Plainfield, CT
Brennan, James G. ... Albany, NY
Brennan, James J. ... Chicago, IL
Brennan, James J. ... Worcester, MA
Brennan, James Joseph ... Rego Park, NY
Brennan, James M. ... San Francisco, CA
Brennan, James M. ... Dayton, OH
Brennan, James N., IV ... Charlotte, NC
Brennan, James P. ... Waterbury, CT
Brennan, James P. ... Mount Clemens, MI
Brennan, James P. ... New York, NY
Brennan, James P. ... Milwaukee, WI
Brennan, James P., Sr. ... Los Angeles, CA
Brennan, James T. ... Anchorage, AK
Brennan, James Thomas ... West Haven, CT
Brennan, Jane M. ... Buffalo Grove, IL
Brennan, Janis H. ... Washington, DC
Brennan, Janna Ellen ... Orlando, FL
Brennan, Jason C. ... New York, NY
Brennan, Jean T. ... Englewood, CO
Brennan, Jeanne S. ... Brockton, MA
Brennan, Jeffrey C. ... New Orleans, LA
Brennan, Jeffrey W. ... Washington, DC
Brennan, Jennifer A. ... Boston, MA
Brennan, Jerry G. ... Middlesboro, KY
Brennan, Jerry L. ... Quincy, IL
Brennan, Joan S. ... Palo Alto, CA
Brennan, Johanna French ... Rochester, NY
Brennan, John B. ... Mount Holly, NJ
Brennan, John C. ... Southfield, MI
Brennan, John C. ... New York, NY
Brennan, John D., III ... East Hartford, CT
Brennan, John F. ... Chicago, IL
Brennan, John F. ... Chicago, IL
Brennan, John F. ... Agawam, MA
Brennan, John F. ... Royal Oak, MI
Brennan, John H. ... Minneapolis, MN
Brennan, John J. ... Daly City, CA
Brennan, John J. ... Washington, DC
Brennan, John J. ... Herkimer, NY
Brennan, John J. ... Philadelphia, PA
Brennan, John J. ... Milwaukee, WI
Brennan, John J., III ... Washington, DC
Baltimore, MD
Rockville, MD
Vienna, VA
Brennan, John J., III ... New Orleans, LA
Brennan, John L. ... Wichita, KS
Brennan, John M. ... Orlando, FL
Brennan, John M. ... Camp Springs, MD
Brennan, John Michael ... Savannah, GA
Brennan, John O. ... Floral Park, NY
Brennan, John P. ... Chicago, IL
Brennan, John R. ... Brighton, MI
Brennan, John R. ... Syracuse, NY
Brennan, John S. ... Lansing, MI
Brennan, John T. ... Fort Pierce, FL
Brennan, John T. ... New York, NY
Brennan, John T. ... White Plains, NY
Brennan, John T. ... Sugar Land, TX
Sugar Land, TX
Brennan, John T., Jr. ... Washington, DC
Brennan, John W. ... Arlington, VA
Brennan, Jonathan J. ... New York, NY
Cincinnati, OH
Brennan, Joseph F. ... Hartford, CT
Brennan, Joseph F. ... Worcester, MA
Brennan, Joseph K. ... Milwaukee, WI
Brennan, Joseph M. ... Albany, NY
Brennan, Joseph P. ... Savannah, GA
Brennan, Joseph P., Jr. ... West Orange, NJ
Brennan, Joseph R. ... Wall Township, NJ
Brennan, Joseph R. ... Glens Falls, NY
Brennan, Joseph T. ... Overland Park, KS
Oklahoma City, OK
Brennan, Joseph V.
Grosse Pointe Farms, MI
Brennan, Julie B. ... Andover, MA
Brennan, Juliet N. ... Muskogee, OK
Brennan, Kathleen M. ... East Hartford, CT
Brennan, Kathleen Michaela
Minneapolis, MN
Brennan, Kenneth J. ... St. Louis, MO
Brennan, Kerry Ann ... New York, NY
Brennan, Kevin C. ... Washington, DC
Brennan, Kevin J. ... New York, NY
Brennan, Kevin T. ... Burlington, VT
Brennan, Kevin V ... Cornwall, NY
Brennan, Kevin W. ... Peoria, IL
Brennan, Kimberly A. ... Cleveland, OH
Brennan, Laura C. ... Raleigh, NC
Brennan, Lawrence B. ... New York, NY
Brennan, Lawrence J. ... Kansas City, KS
Brennan, Lawrence J. ... Westbury, NY
Brennan, Lawrence P., Jr.
Los Angeles, CA
Brennan, Leoniede M. ... Minneapolis, MN
Brennan, Lisa M.S. ... Rockville, MD
Brennan, Lorraine M. ... New York, NY
Brennan, Lucille B. ... Worcester, MA
Brennan, Luke A. ... Grand Junction, CO
Brennan, Luke A., LLC
Grand Junction, CO
Brennan, Lynne M. ... San Diego, CA
Brennan, Margaret A. ... Chicago, IL
Brennan, Margaret J. ... Libertyville, IL

Brennan, Mark C. ... Minneapolis, MN
Brennan, Mark E. ... Littleton, CO
Brennan, Mark E. ... Seattle, WA
Brennan, Mark E., P.C. ... Denver, CO
Littleton, CO
Brennan, Mark M. ... Chicago, IL
Brennan, Mark P. ... Salisbury, MD
Brennan, Mark S. ... Richmond, VA
Brennan, Mark W. ... Kansas City, MO
Brennan, Martin M., Jr. ... Charlotte, NC
Brennan, Mary Anna ... Newark, DE
Brennan, Mary Anne ... Cincinnati, OH
Brennan, Mary E. ... New Orleans, LA
Brennan, Mary Lynn ... San Francisco, CA
Brennan, Mary M. ... Boston, MA
Brennan, Mary Siobhan ... Trenton, NJ
Brennan, Mary Siobhan, P.A. ... Trenton, NJ
Brennan, Mary Susan ... Short Hills, NJ
Brennan, Mary V. ... DeLand, FL
Brennan, Maryanne Connors ... Boonton, NJ
Brennan, Mary-Lou ... Milton, MA
Brennan, Matranga, Hopping & Carmody, P.C.
Utica, MI
Brennan, Matthew A., III ... Oakton, VA
Brennan, Matthew J. ... New York, NY
Brennan, Maureen A. ... Cleveland, OH
Brennan, Maureen R. ... Columbus, OH
Brennan, Maureen V. ... Los Angeles, CA
Brennan, McNamara & Baldwin, P.C.
Fairfield, CT
Trumbull, CT
Brennan, Michael B. ... South Bend, IN
Brennan, Michael C. ... New York, NY
Brennan, Michael D. ... Southborough, MA
Brennan, Michael D. ... Cleveland, OH
Brennan, Michael D. ... Elkhorn, WI
Brennan, Michael G. ... Chicago, IL
Brennan, Michael G. ... Collingswood, NJ
Brennan, Michael G. ... Philadelphia, PA
Brennan, Michael J. ... Chicago, IL
Brennan, Michael J. ... Holyoke, MA
Brennan, Michael J. ... Staten Island, NY
Brennan, Michael J. ... Fairless Hills, PA
Brennan, Michael J. ... Jackson, WY
Brennan, Michael P. ... Troy, MI
Brennan, Michael R. ... Delray Beach, FL
Brennan, Michael W. ... Albuquerque, NM
Santa Fe, NM
Brennan, Michael W. ... Neillsville, WI
Brennan, Michele ... Monmouth Beach, NJ
Brennan, Molly ... Maynard, MA
Brennan, Molly K. ... San Francisco, CA
Brennan, Noel A. ... Washington, DC
Brennan, Noelle C. ... Chicago, IL
Brennan, Norman E. ... Indianapolis, IN
Brennan, Patricia A., (Mrs.) ... Farmington, MI
Brennan, Patricia B. ... New York, NY
Brennan, Patricia F. ... New York, NY
Brennan, Patricia T. ... West Chester, PA
Brennan, Patrick ... South Bend, IN
Brennan, Patrick Cavanaugh ... Milwaukee, WI
Brennan, Patrick J. ... Birmingham, MI
Brennan, Patrick J. ... New York, NY
Brennan, Patrick McKinley ... Tempe, AZ
Brennan, Patrick Spahr ... Cranbury, NJ
Brennan, Patrick W. ... Milwaukee, WI
Brennan, Paul ... New York, NY
Brennan, Paul A. ... San Juan Capistrano, CA
Brennan, Paul C. ... Boston, MA
Brennan, Paul C. ... Woburn, MA
Brennan, Paul F. ... Pittsfield, MA
Brennan, Paul L.
Department of Transportation,
Federal Highway Administration, GV
Brennan, Paul M. ... Richmond, VA
Brennan, Peter ... Hoffman Estates, IL
Brennan, Peter H. ... Princeton, NJ
Brennan, Peter J. ... Philadelphia, PA
Brennan, Peter Justin ... Chicago, IL
Brennan, Peter L. ... East Hartford, CT
Brennan, Peter T. ... Oakland, CA
Brennan, Philip I. ... Falls Church, VA
Brennan, Pierce V. ... Bronx, NY
Brennan, Ramirez, Wilmouth & Sesini, L.L.P.
Milwaukee, WI
Brennan, Raymond M. ... Putnam Valley, NY
Brennan, Recupero, Cascione, Scungio &
McAllister ... Taunton, MA
Providence, RI
Brennan, Rehfuss and Liguori, P.C.
Albany, NY
Brennan, Richard E. ... Florham Park, NJ
Brennan, Richard F. ... Birmingham, MI
Brennan, Richard J. ... Salinas, CA
Brennan, Richard J. ... Chicago, IL
Brennan, Richard R. ... Scottsdale, AZ
Brennan, Richard S. ... Chicago, IL
Racine, WI
Brennan, Robert E. ... Rochester, NY
Brennan, Robert F., A Professional
Corporation ... Glendale, CA
Los Angeles, CA
Brennan, Robert Francis ... Glendale, CA
Brennan, Robert J. ... Morristown, NJ
New York, NY
Brennan, Robert J., Jr. ... Fairfield, CT
Trumbull, CT
Brennan, Robert L., Jr. ... Brockton, MA
Brennan, Robert M. ... Providence, RI
Brennan, Robert W. ... Des Moines, IA
Brennan, Robins & Daley, P.C.
Pittsburgh, PA
Washington, PA
Brennan, Sandra David ... Vista, CA
Brennan, Scott M. ... Des Moines, IA
Brennan, Sean J. ... Lincoln, NE
Brennan, Sean J., P.C. ... Lincoln, NE
Brennan, Sean P. ... Dallas, TX

Brennan, Shane J. ... Washington, DC
Brennan, Sheila M. ... Austin, TX
Brennan, Sidney L., Jr. ... Minnetonka, MN
Brennan, Steil, Basting & MacDougall, S.C.
Delavan, WI
Janesville, WI
Madison, WI
Monroe, WI
Brennan, Stephan Y. ... Baltimore, MD
Brennan, Stephen P. ... Wallingford, CT
Brennan, Stephen W. ... New York, NY
Brennan, Sterling A. ... Irvine, CA
Brennan, Steven W. ... Torrance, CA
Brennan, Susan E. ... Belleville, IL
Brennan, Susan Fox ... Hackensack, NJ
Brennan, Susan L. ... Wyoming, MI
Brennan, Sylvia M. ... Alexandria, VA
Brennan, Terence F. ... Orlando, FL
Brennan, Terence P. ... Tulsa, OK
Brennan, Terrence L. ... New Orleans, LA
Brennan, Terrence L. ... Shaker Heights, OH
Brennan, Terrence Patrick ... Gainesville, VA
Brennan, Tess ... Trenton, NJ
Brennan, Theresa A. ... St. Louis, MO
Brennan, Theresa M. ... Brighton, MI
Brennan, Theresa Milore ... Allentown, PA
Brennan, Thomas A. ... Cincinnati, OH
Brennan, Thomas A., Jr. ... New York, NY
Brennan, Thomas C. ... United States Senate,
Committee Legal Personnel, GV
Brennan, Thomas C., III ... Houston, TX
Brennan, Thomas E. ... Atlanta, GA
Brennan, Thomas E. ... Lansing, MI
Brennan, Thomas E., Jr. ... Mason, MI
Brennan, Thomas F. ... Minneapolis, MN
Brennan, Thomas I. ... New City, NY
Brennan, Thomas J. ... Palm City, FL
Brennan, Thomas J., Jr. ... Montauk, NY
Brennan, Thomas M. ... Bedford, MA
Brennan, Thomas M. ... Utica, MI
Brennan, Thomas P. ... Edina, MN
Brennan, Thomas P. ... Wilkes-Barre, PA
Brennan, Thomas P., (P.C.)
Los Angeles, CA
Brennan, Thomas R. ... Reno, NV
Brennan, Timothy J. ... Mount Kisco, NY
Brennan, Timothy L. ... Indianapolis, IN
Brennan, Timothy P. ... New York, NY
Brennan, Timothy R. ... Atlanta, GA
Brennan, Timothy S. ... L'Anse, MI
Brennan, V. Jude ... Vero Beach, FL
Brennan, Vaughn C. ... Gretna, LA
Brennan, W. John ... Albuquerque, NM
Brennan & Waite, P.L.C. ... Arlington, VA
Fairfax, VA
Oakton, VA
Vienna, VA
Brennan & Wasden LLP ... Brunswick, GA
Hinesville, GA
Savannah, GA
Statesboro, GA
Brennan, Weldon "Web" Earl ... Tampa, FL
Brennan, William C., Jr.
Upper Marlboro, MD
Brennan, William E. ... Royal Oak, MD
Brennan, William E. ... Manchester, NH
Brennan, William G. ... Sacramento, CA
Brennan, William H. ... Syracuse, NY
Brennan, William J. ... Denver, CO
Brennan, William J. ... Marlborough, MA
Brennan, William J. ... Buffalo, NY
Brennan, William J. ... Toledo, OH
Brennan, William J. ... King Of Prussia, PA
Norristown, PA
Brennan, William J., III ... Princeton, NJ
Brennan, William J., IV ... Philadelphia, PA
Brennan, William J., Jr. ... Decatur, GA
Brennan, William J., Jr. ... Omaha, NE
Brennan, William J., Law Offices of
Philadelphia, PA
Brennan, William J., P.C. ... Denver, CO
Brennan, William Jay, Jr. ... New York, NY
Brennan, William L. ... Shrewsbury, NJ
New York, NY
Brennan, William R. ... New York, NY
Brennan, William S. ... Portland, OR
Brennan, William T. ... Laurelton, NY
Brennand, James L. ... El Paso, TX
Brennan-Rotolo, Cynthia Ann
Lebanon, NJ
Brennecke, Allen E. ... Marshalltown, IA
Brennecke, Stephen T. ... Grinnell, IA
Brenneis, John E. ... Atlanta, GA
Brenneise, Craig S. ... Dallas, TX
Brenneise & Wise ... Dallas, TX
Brenneke, Andrea ... Seattle, WA
Brenneman, Deborah S. ... Cincinnati, OH
Brenneman, Delbert J. ... Portland, OR
Brenneman, Diane M. ... Washington, DC
Brenneman, Fleet B. ... Orrville, OH
Brenneman, Frederica S. ... Westport, CT
Brenneman, Gerald W. ... Kansas City, MO
Brenneman, Hugh W., Jr. ... Grand Rapids, MI
Brenneman, Keith O. ... Mechanicsburg, PA
Brenneman, Matthew C. ... Baltimore, MD
Brenneman, Michael J. ... Iowa City, IA
Kalona, IA
Brenneman, Reagan L.
Salt Lake City, UT
Brenneman, Richard C. ... Santa Maria, CA
Brenneman, Richard C., A Professional
Corporation ... Santa Maria, CA
Brenneman, Russell L. ... Hartford, CT
Brenneman, Sandra L. ... Charleston, WV
Brenneman, Stephen R. ... Sacramento, CA
Brenneman, Steven L. ... Chicago, IL
Brenneman & Waltman ... Orrville, OH
Brennen, Amy S. Lundy ... Norristown, PA

Brennen, David A. ... Richmond, VA
Brennen, Kevin E. ... Amarillo, TX
Brennen, Ray R. ... Allentown, PA
Brennen, Richard P. ... Pasadena, CA
Brennen, Robert S. ... Baltimore, MD
Brennenstuhl, H. Brent
Bowling Green, KY
Brenner, Aaron M. ... Saratoga Springs, NY
Brenner, Alan ... Department of Justice,
Environment and Natural Resources
Division, GV
Brenner, Alana C. ... Orlando, FL
Brenner, Andrew S. ... Palo Alto, CA
Brenner, Andrew S. ... Miami, FL
Brenner, Anita S. ... Pasadena, CA
Brenner, Barbara A. ... Sacramento, CA
Brenner, Barbara Carolina ... Latham, NY
Brenner, Barbara S. ... Washington, DC
Albany, NY
Brenner & Brenner ... Philadelphia, PA
Brenner, Brenner & Wall ... Waukesha, WI
Brenner, Brown, Golian & McCaffrey Co.,
L.P.A. ... Columbus, OH
Brenner, Daniel G. ... Alexandria, LA
Brenner, Daniel L. ... Washington, DC
Brenner, Daniel L. ... Kansas City, MO
Brenner, Daniel W. ... Murphysboro, IL
Brenner, David E. ... Philadelphia, PA
Brenner, David J. ... New York, NY
Brenner, David L. ... Austin, TX
Brenner, David M. ... Chicago, IL
Brenner, David M. ... Seattle, WA
Brenner, David N. ... Houston, TX
Brenner, Dean R. ... Washington, DC
Brenner, Deborah A. ... Brooklyn, NY
Brenner & Dienstag ... Miami, FL
Brenner, Dohnal, Evans & Yoffy, P.C.
Chesterfield, VA
Goochland, VA
Hanover, VA
Midlothian, VA
Petersburg, VA
Richmond, VA
Brenner, Donald ... Tappan, NY
Brenner, Donald B. ... Princeton, NJ
Brenner, Donald R. ... Washington, DC
Brenner, Edgar H. ... Arlington, VA
Brenner, Edward R., Law Offices of
Sacramento, CA
Brenner, Elizabeth E. ... Pawtucket, RI
Brenner, Elliot M. ... Philadelphia, PA
Brenner, Eric J. ... Armonk, NY
Brenner, Frank ... New York, NY
Brenner, Frederick W., Jr. ... Detroit, MI
Brenner, Gail V. ... Northbrook, IL
Brenner, Gary Allan ... San Diego, CA
Brenner, Gary R. ... San Mateo, CA
Brenner, Gerald M. ... Woonsocket, RI
Brenner, Irving M. ... Charlotte, NC
Brenner, James D. ... Eggertsville, NY
Brenner, James E. ... Detroit, MI
Brenner, Janet M. ... Washington, DC
Brenner, Jean S. ... New York, NY
Brenner, Jeffrey S. ... Kansas City, MO
Brenner, Jeffrey S. ... Cherry Hill, NJ
Brenner, Jeffrey S. ... Providence, RI
Brenner, Jerry H. ... Wilmington, DE
Brenner, Jesse H. ... Montclair, NJ
Brenner, Joan ... Department of Labor,
Office of the Solicitor, GV
Brenner, Joan B. ... Dayton, OH
Brenner, Jodi B. ... Fort Lee, NJ
Brenner, Joel A. ... East Northport, NY
Brenner, Joel F. ... Washington, DC
Brenner, John F. ... Newark, NJ
Brenner, Jonathan A. ... New York, NY
Brenner, Jonathan M. ... Los Angeles, CA
Brenner, Jonathan S. ... New York, NY
Brenner, Joseph, Jr. ... Nashville, TN
Brenner, Joseph K. ... Washington, DC
Brenner, Joseph M. ... New York, NY
Brenner, Joyce ... New York, NY
Brenner, Karen M. ... Austin, TX
Brenner, Karl A. ... Pleasanton, CA
Brenner, Laura A. ... Milwaukee, WI
Brenner, Lawrence
Federal Energy Regulatory Commission,
Office of the Administrative Law Judges, GV
Brenner, Lawrence H. ... Miami, FL
Brenner, Lawrence J. ... Allentown, PA
Brenner, Lawrence M. ... Santa Cruz, CA
Brenner, Lawrence Richard ... New York, NY
Brenner, Lee S. ... Los Angeles, CA
Brenner, Leona ... Short Hills, NJ
Brenner, Leonard ... New York, NY
Brenner, Leonard J. ... Chicago, IL
Brenner, Lina M. ... San Francisco, CA
Brenner, Lisa R. ... Denver, CO
Brenner, Lockwood & Peterson
Kansas City, MO
Brenner, Lori Ella ... Pittsburgh, PA
Brenner, Lou W., Jr. ... Treasury Department,
U.S. Customs Service, GV
Brenner, Louis ... Portsmouth, VA
Brenner, Louis W., Sr. ... Eagan, MN
Brenner, Madeleine A. F. ... Seattle, WA
Brenner, Mania C. ... Columbus, OH
Brenner, Marc J. ... Morristown, NJ
Brenner, Marc S. ... Chicago, IL
Brenner, Margaret Twomey ... Houston, TX
Brenner, Margo R. ... Philadelphia, PA
Brenner, Mark B. ... New York, NY
Brenner, Mark E. ... Canoga Park, CA
Brenner, Mark Howard
Hastings-On-Hudson, NY
Brenner, Martin J. ... Livingston, NJ
Brenner, Marvin J. ... Salinas, CA
Brenner, Matthew G. ... Orlando, FL

Brenner, Mavrias & Alm ... Chicago, IL
Brenner, Michael ... West Palm Beach, FL
Brenner, Michael J. ... San Francisco, CA
Brenner, Michael L. ... Pittsburgh, PA
Brenner, Micheal Terry ... Livonia, MI
Brenner, Michelle Silverman ... New York, NY
Brenner & Moltzen, Ltd. ... Chicago, IL
Joliet, IL
Kankakee, IL
Morris, IL
Waukegan, IL
Wheaton, IL
Brenner, Monika Rice ... Treasury Department, Office of Regulations and Rulings, GV
Brenner, Mory K. ... Pittsfield, MA
Brenner, Nancy ... Princeton, NJ
New York, NY
Brenner, Nathan G., Jr. ... Chicago, IL
Brenner, Newton D., (P.C.)
New Haven, CT
Brenner, Oren Z. ... Miami Beach, FL
Brenner, Paul R. ... New York, NY
Brenner, Paul S. ... New York, NY
Brenner, Ralph W. ... Philadelphia, PA
Brenner, Regina Esteras
La Canada Flintridge, CA
Brenner, Richard L. ... Great Neck, NY
Brenner, Richard M. ... Miami, FL
Brenner, Robert ... New York, NY
Brenner, Robert A. ... Woodland Hills, CA
Brenner, Robert M. ... Gering, NE
Brenner, Ronald ... Miami, FL
Brenner, Ronald G. ... Huntington Woods, MI
Brenner, Roseann Lynn ... Philadelphia, PA
Brenner, Roy D. ... Catonsville, MD
Brenner, Saltzman & Wallman LLP
Hartford, CT
New Haven, CT
Brenner, Saml. B. ... Philadelphia, PA
Brenner, Saul B. ... New York, NY
Brenner, Saul D. ... Beverly Hills, CA
Brenner, Scott D. ... Mamaroneck, NY
Brenner, Scott F. ... Pompano Beach, FL
Brenner, Sheldon A. ... Chicago, IL
Brenner, Stephen A. ... New York, NY
Brenner, Stephen G. ... New York, NY
Brenner, Steven A. ... Chicago Heights, IL
Brenner, Steven G. ... Los Angeles, CA
Brenner, Stewart W. ... New York, NY
Brenner, Susan W. ... Dayton, OH
Brenner, T. Webster, Jr. ... Baltimore, MD
Brenner, Talmadge G. ... Quincy, IL
Brenner, Teresa M. ... Charlotte, NC
Brenner, Terrill M. ... New Brunswick, NJ
Brenner, Theodore I. ... Richmond, VA
Brenner, Thomas E. ... Harrisburg, PA
Brenner, Thomas F. ... New York, NY
Brenner, Thomas S. ... Waukesha, WI
Brenner, Todd Austin ... Columbus, OH
Brenner, Victoria P. ... Pinehurst, NC
Brenner, Wendy ... Palo Alto, CA
Brenner, William J. ... Stryker, OH
Brenner, William R. ... Hollidaysburg, PA
Brenner-Deangelo, Nancy
Greenwood Lake, NY
Brenners, Steven R., Law Offices of
Coral Springs, FL
Brenners, Steven R., Law Offices of
Fort Lauderdale, FL
Brennglass, Samuel Lawrence
New York, NY
Brennick, Joan M. ... Wilmington, MA
Brennick, William F. ... Dedham, MA
Brennig, Charles C., II ... Houston, TX
Brennig, Tammy W. ... Houston, TX
Brenniman, Kathleen F. ... Evanston, IL
Brenningmeyer, David Allen ...
Department Of Veterans Affairs, GV
Brennock, Michael W. ... Chicago, IL
Brennwald, James Quinn ... Chicago, IL
Brennwald, Stephen Frederic ... Laurel, MD
Brennwasser, Rhea L. ... Fort Lauderdale, FL
Brenny, Gregory P. ... Minneapolis, MN
Brenon, John G. ... Williamsville, NY
Brenot, C. Alexei ... Glendale, CA
Brensilber, David M. ... New York, NY
Brensinger, Joseph B. ... Pompton Lakes, NJ
Brenske & Christensen ... Las Vegas, NV
Brenske, William R. ... Las Vegas, NV
Brenskelle, David P. ... McDonough, GA
Brenson, Ian ... La Grange, IL
Brent, A. Strode, Jr. ... Fairfax, VA
Brent, Albert ... White Plains, NY
Brent, Anthony R. ... Bakersfield, CA
Brent, Bert L. ... Ashville, AL
Brent, Craig H. ... Franklin, TN
Brent, Darren J. ... Miami, FL
Brent, David J. ... Chicago, IL
Brent, David L. ... Santa Ana, CA
Brent, Debra Presti ... Naples, FL
Brent, Douglas F. ... Louisville, KY
Brent, Duncan K. ... Washington, DC
Brent, James Burkhart ... Knoxville, TN
Brent, Jason G. ... Tehachapi, CA
Brent, John F. ... Detroit, MI
Brent, John William ... Atlanta, GA
Brent, Joseph P. ... Chicago, IL
Brent, Mark D. ... Aurora, IL
Brent, Mary H. ... Metairie, LA
Brent, Michael D. ... Nashville, TN
Brent, Nancy J. ... Chicago, IL
Brent, Paul M. ... Santa Monica, CA
Woodland Hills, CA
Brent, Philip D. ... Encino, CA
Brent, Philip D., Professional Corporation
Encino, CA
Brent, Robert L. ... Encino, CA
Brent & Roberts ... Rochester, NY
Brent, Stephen M. ... Rochester, NY
Brent, Theodore W., Jr. ... Doylestown, OH
Brent, Woodland & Sweetnam, P.C.
Atlanta, GA
Brentani, William B. ... New York, NY
Brente, Cory M. ... Los Angeles, CA
Brentin, John O. ... Houston, TX
Brentlinger, Richard P. ... Denver, CO
Brentnall, Gerald J., Jr. ... Loomis, CA
Brenton, Constance R. ... Boulder, CO
Brenton, Craig C. ... Salem, OR
Brenton, Dean T. ... Cincinnati, OH
Brenton, Lawrence M. ... Kalamazoo, MI
Brenton, Michael S. ... East Lansing, MI
Brenton, Roberta C. ... Aurora, IL
Brenton, Ruth A. ... Houston, TX
Brenton, Thomas G. ... Danville, IN
Brents, Alan Harrison ... Orlando, FL
Brents, Melinda Heath ... Houston, TX
Brents, Walker A., Jr. ... Fort Worth, TX
Brentwood Law Offices ... Brentwood, TN
Brentzel, Cathy M. ... Ligonier, PA
Brenza, Lindley J. ... Denver, CO
Chicago, IL
Breon, Cary R. ... Philadelphia, PA
Breon, Keith V. ... San Francisco, CA
Breon & Leffler ... Warrensburg, MO
Breon, Leonard K. ... Warrensburg, MO
Brereton, Brad C. ... Santa Cruz, CA
Brereton, Hugh E. ... Modesto, CA
Brereton, Julian B. P. ... Philadelphia, PA
Brereton, William R. ... Naples, FL
Bres, Thomas A. ... Houston, TX
Bresch, Jeffrey J. ... Pittsburgh, PA
Bresch, Saul R. ... Danbury, CT
Brescher, George A. ... Fort Lauderdale, FL
Brescher, John B., Jr. ... Newark, NJ
Breschi, Anthony J. ... Towson, MD
Breschi, David R. ... Towson, MD
Harrisburg, PA
Brescia, August J. ... Oxnard, CA
Brescia, Duane J. ... Indianapolis, IN
Dallas, TX
Brescia, James A. ... Boston, MA
Brescia, Ralph P. ... Los Angeles, CA
Brescia, Raymond Henry ... New York, NY
Brescia, Robert T. ... Jersey City, NJ
Brescia, Vincent A. ... New York, NY
Brescoll & Associates, P.C.
Birmingham, MI
Mount Clemens, MI
Brescoll, Daniel S. ... New York, NY
Brescoll, Dennis P. ... Birmingham, MI
Brescoll, James A. ... Mount Clemens, MI
Bresee, Edward C., Jr. ... Atlanta, GA
Bresee, Gary A. ... San Francisco, CA
Bresee, James R. ... Lebanon, NH
Bresee, Mark R. ... Irvine, CA
Bresee, Patricia ... Redwood City, CA
Bresee, William F. ... Yorba Linda, CA
Breseman, Ross E. ... Columbus, OH
Bresenham, David ... Los Angeles, CA
Bresenham, Maurice L., Jr. ... Houston, TX
Bresenoff, Marc R. ... Norfolk, VA
Breshears, Joseph W. ... Dallas, TX
Breshears, Randall A.
Oklahoma City, OK
Bresin, Robert A. ... Hackensack, NJ
Breski, Gregory W. ... Erie, PA
Breskin, David E. ... Seattle, WA
Breskin, Howard B. ... Seattle, WA
Breskin, Lawrence J. ... Detroit, MI
Breskin, Marvin ... Bloomfield Hills, MI
Breskin, William Adam ... Washington, DC
Breskin & Witenberg ... Seattle, WA
Breskman, Samuel ... Narberth, PA
Bresko, Andrew G. ... Youngstown, OH
Bresky, Hunt F. ... Mineola, NY
Bresky, Lisa M. ... Middletown, NY
Breslau, Brad W. ... Denver, CO
Breslau, David E. ... Philadelphia, PA
Breslau, Nancy B. ... San Rafael, CA
Breslau, William E. ... Vernon, CT
Breslauer, Alison P. ... Chicago, IL
Breslauer, Gerald M. ... Miami, FL
Breslauer, James E. ... Lawrence, MA
Breslauer, Michael D. ... San Diego, CA
Breslauer, Nathan ... Levittown, NY
Breslauer, Peter ... Philadelphia, PA
Breslaw, April Anne
Federal Deposit Insurance Corporation, GV
Bresler, Andrea J. ... Chicago, IL
Bresler, Barry M. ... Albany, NY
Bresler, Catherine M. ... Lake Forest, IL
Bresler, David L. ... St. Petersburg, FL
Bresler, Emily ... Santa Monica, CA
Bresler, George ... New York, NY
Bresler Goodman & Unterman, LLP
Westport, CT
New York, NY
Bresler & Harvick, Ltd. ... Chicago, IL
Bresler, Jean C. ... New York, NY
Bresler, Judith A. ... New York, NY
Bresler, Judith S. ... Rockville, MD
Bresler, Marc S. ... Encino, CA
Bresler, Martin B. ... Chicago, IL
Bresler, Peter H. ... San Francisco, CA
Bresler, Sidney M. ... Washington, DC
Breslerman, Lee H. ... Wall, NJ
Breslin, Allan C. ... Covington, LA
Breslin, Allan C., A Professional Corporation
Covington, LA
Breslin, Auty and Preziosi
Hackensack, NJ
Breslin and Breslin, P.A. ... Hackensack, NJ
Breslin, Dana McBride ... Brookhaven, PA
Breslin, Edward F. ... Englewood Cliffs, NJ
Breslin, Eileen M. ... Garden City, NY
Breslin, Elvira Madden ... Chalfont, PA
Breslin, Emily K. ... Atlanta, GA
Breslin, Eric R. ... Newark, NJ
Breslin, Frank J., Jr. ... Glendale, CA
Breslin, H. Paul ... Walnut Creek, CA
Breslin, J. Kent ... Cleveland, OH
Breslin, James A., Jr. ... Lyndhurst, NJ
Breslin, James J., III ... Trenton, NJ
Breslin, James, Jr. ... St. Petersburg, FL
Breslin, Jennifer S. ... Philadelphia, PA
Breslin, Joanne M. ... Annapolis, MD
Breslin, John G. ... Brooklyn, NY
Breslin, John J. ... Yonkers, NY
Breslin, John J., III ... Hackensack, NJ
Breslin, John M. ... Hackensack, NJ
Breslin, John X. ... Ottawa, IL
Breslin, Kathleen M ... Plymouth Meeting, PA
Breslin, Kenneth A. ... Garden City, NY
Breslin, Kevin P. ... Chicago, IL
Breslin, Leo J. ... Cincinnati, OH
Breslin, M. Christine ... Dedham, MA
Breslin, Mary E. ... Hackensack, NJ
Breslin & McNerney ... Hackensack, NJ
Breslin, Michael F., Law Offices of
King Of Prussia, PA
Breslin, Michael F., Law Offices of
Philadelphia, PA
Breslin, Michael G. ... Albany, NY
Breslin, Michael J., Jr. ... Hackensack, NJ
Breslin, Neil D. ... Albany, NY
Breslin, Patricia ... Cranston, RI
Breslin, Richard W. ... Norwich, NY
Breslin, Robert H., Jr. ... Warwick, RI
Breslin, Robert J., Jr. ... Brookhaven, PA
Breslin, Roger W., Jr. ... Montvale, NJ
Breslin, Sweeney & Earle ... Warwick, RI
Breslin, T. Peter, Jr. (Professional Law Corporation) ... Metairie, LA
Breslin, Thomas A. ... Albany, NY
Breslin, Thomas P., II ... Los Angeles, CA
Breslin, Thomas R. ... Glendale, CA
Breslin, Walter I. ... Media, PA
Breslin Stachura, M. Elizabeth
Middletown, RI
Breslo, James A. ... Los Angeles, CA
Breslo, John C. ... Los Angeles, CA
Breslow, Allan J. ... Vernon, NJ
Breslow, Allen B. ... Farmingdale, NY
Breslow, Andrew B. ... Irving, TX
Breslow, Barry L. ... Reno, NV
Breslow, Howard S. ... Jericho, NY
New York, NY
Breslow, Jeffrey Reid ... Washington, DC
Breslow, Jeffrey S. ... Miami, FL
Breslow, Jerome W. ... Bethesda, MD
Breslow, Jordan J. ... Seattle, WA
Breslow, Karen ... Culver City, CA
Breslow, Leonard J. ... Jericho, NY
New York, NY
Breslow, Nancy ... New York, NY
Breslow, Richard H. ... Miami, FL
Breslow, Richard M. ... New York, NY
Breslow, Ronald A. ... Wayne, NJ
Breslow, Roy W. ... Verona, NJ
Breslow, Stephanie R. ... New York, NY
Breslow, Steven Harley ... New York, NY
Breslow, Stuart ... New York, NY
Breslow, Stuart G. ... Hunt Valley, MD
Breslow & Walker, LLP ... Jericho, NY
New York, NY
Bresnahan, Arthur S. ... Chicago, IL
Bresnahan, Arthur W. ... Chicago, IL
Bresnahan, Daniel J. ... Minneapolis, MN
Bresnahan, Frances M. ... Atlanta, GA
Bresnahan & Garvey ... Chicago, IL
Bresnahan, James R. ... St. Paul, MN
Bresnahan, Jeremiah J., Jr. ... Boston, MA
Bresnahan, Jill A. ... Eagan, MN
Bresnahan, John V. ... New York, NY
Bresnahan, Lisa M. ... Medfield, MA
Bresnahan, Mark P. ... McLean, VA
Bresnahan, Maureen A. ... Boston, MA
Bresnahan, Pamela A. ... Washington, DC
Bresnahan, Richard C. ... St. Louis, MO
Bresnahan, Robert J. ... Meridian, MS
Bresnahan, Roger G. ... San Antonio, TX
Bresnahan, Roger G., P.C.
San Antonio, TX
Bresnahan, Terrance M. ... Berkeley, CA
Bresnahan, Victoria C. ... Chicago, IL
Bresnahan, William P. ... Pittsburgh, PA
Bresnan, Dennis M. ... New York, NY
Bresnan, Joseph E. ... Ambler, PA
Bresnan, Maureen Ann ... Stamford, CT
Bresnan, Peter H.
Securities and Exchange Commission, Office of the General Counsel, GV
Bresnan, Robert V. ... White Plains, NY
Bresnan Gibson, Paula M.
Washington, DC
Bresnehan, Elizabeth G. ... Springfield, MA
Bresney, Todd A. ... Chicago, IL
Bresnick, Laurene Blanche
San Francisco, CA
Bresnick, Mara J. ... Sacramento, CA
Bresnick, Michael J. ... New York, NY
Bresnick, Michele L. ... Baltimore, MD
Bresnick, Sandra A. ... New York, NY
Bresnick, Sidney R. ... New York, NY
Bresnick, William ... Ashland, MA
Bresnick, William O. ... Washington, DC
Bresnicky, James John ... Washington, DC
Rockville, MD
Bress, Allen ... Boston, MA
Bress & Boynton, LLP ... White Plains, NY
Bress, Dean S. ... White Plains, NY
Bress, Frank A. ... White Plains, NY
Bress, Joseph M. ... Washington, DC
Bress, Kathy L. ... Elkins Park, PA
Bress, Kevin F. ... Havre de Grace, MD
Bress, Michael E., (P.A.)
Minneapolis, MN
Bress, Pamela M. ... Satellite Beach, FL
Bress, Richard P. ... Washington, DC
Bressack, Alfred ... Nanuet, NY
Bressan, Paul L. ... Los Angeles, CA
Bressaw, H. William ... Fords, NJ
Bressel, Jerold A. ... Overland Park, KS
Bresser, Jeffrey W. ... Norfolk, VA
Bresset, Stephen G. ... Honesdale, PA
Bressi, Jess R. ... Irvine, CA
Bressi, Nicholas S., Law Office of
Austin, TX
Bressie, Kent D. ... Washington, DC
Bressler, Alfred W. ... New York, NY
Bressler, Amery & Ross, A Professional Corporation ... Florham Park, NJ
Morristown, NJ
New York, NY
Bressler, Arnold N. ... New York, NY
Bressler, Barbara B. ... Chicago, IL
Bressler, Barry E. ... Philadelphia, PA
Bressler, Bernard ... Florham Park, NJ
New York, NY
Bressler, Brett M. ... Winter Park, FL
Bressler, Carla J. ... Solana Beach, CA
Bressler, Curcio & Stout, P.C. ... Bristol, VA
Bressler, David J. ... Lisle, IL
Bressler, David N. ... Blue Bell, PA
Bressler, David S. ... Edison, NJ
Bressler, Eric J. ... Mattituck, NY
Bressler, Felice M. ... Chicago, IL
Bressler, G. Walter ... Bristol, VA
Bressler, Gary D. ... Philadelphia, PA
Bressler, Gregory N. ... New York, NY
Bressler, Harold J. ... Oakbrook Terrace, IL
Bressler, H. J. ... Hamilton, OH
Bressler, Howard J. ... Los Angeles, CA
Bressler, Howard L. ... New York, NY
Bressler, Jane C. ... New York, NY
Bressler, Joshua R. ... New York, NY
Bressler, Kenneth L. ... New York, NY
Bressler, Kenneth L. ... Dallas, TX
Bressler Law Firm ... Edison, NJ
Bressler, Marc J. ... Edison, NJ
Bressler, Mark S. ... Boston, MA
Bressler, Martin ... New York, NY
Bressler, Marvin ... Garden City, NY
Bressler, Melvin ... Rochester, NY
Bressler, Michael A. ... Southfield, MI
Bressler, Michael R. ... New York, NY
Bressler, Robert G. ... Roseland, NJ
Bressler, Robert N. ... Staten Island, NY
Bressler, Sandra E. ... Oakland, CA
Bressler, Shanks & Gedling ... Hamilton, OH
Bressler, Stacy Hope ... Miami, FL
Bressler, Stephen A. ... San Antonio, TX
Bressler, Stephen M. ... Phoenix, AZ
Bressler, Stuart L. ... Schaumburg, IL
Bressler, Todd N. ... Los Angeles, CA
Bresslour, Gerald ... Seattle, WA
Bressman, Charles M., Jr. ... Omaha, NE
Bressman, David Allan ... Columbus, OH
Bressman, David L. ... New York, NY
Bressman, Jerold A. ... West Orange, NJ
Bressman, Marc I. ... Cherry Hill, NJ
Short Hills, NJ
Philadelphia, PA
Bressman, Michael B. ... Nashville, TN
Bressman, Robert I. ... New York, NY
Bressman, Stuart ... New York, NY
Bressner, S. Earl ... Evansville, IN
Bresson, Michael K. ... Portsmouth, NH
Bresson, Michael P. ... Houston, TX
Brest, Iris, (Mrs.) ... Palo Alto, CA
Brest, Paul ... Palo Alto, CA
Brestal, Willard F. ... Naperville, IL
Bresticker, Bert ... San Diego, CA
Bresticker & Chow ... San Diego, CA
Brestoff, Nelson E. ... Los Angeles, CA
Breston, Michael P. ... Houston, TX
Breston, Michael P., P.C. ... Houston, TX
Bret, Thomas V. ... Oakland, CA
Bret, William N. ... Dallas, TX
Bret, William N., III ... Dallas, TX
Bretan, Harold ... Basking Ridge, NJ
Bretan, Neil F. ... West Palm Beach, FL
Breth, Thomas E. ... Butler, PA
Bret Harte, Lawrence K. ... Sebring, FL
Brethauer, Troy M. ... Oak Brook, IL
Bretoi, Jeffrey S. ... Whittier, CA
Bretoi & Raleigh ... Whittier, CA
Breton, Debra J. ... Cambridge, MA
Breton, Gary G. ... Springfield, MA
Breton, Michael P. ... East Hartford, CT
Breton, Peter L. ... West Palm Beach, FL
Breton, Robert O. ... Schenectady, NY
Bretscher, Carl P. ... Washington, DC
Bretscher, Carol Ann ... Valley Stream, NY
Bretscher, Mark Howard
Commodity Futures Trading Commission, Division of Enforcement, GV
Bretschneider, Barry E. ... Washington, DC
Bretschneider, William L. ... San Jose, CA
Bretsen, Stephen N. ... Harrisburg, PA
Bretsnyder, Lance Christian
Webster Groves, MO
Bretsnyder, Robert C. ... Allison Park, PA
Bretsnyder, Robert C., P.C. ... Allison Park, PA
Brett, Anthony H. ... Winston-Salem, NC
Brett, Barry J. ... New York, NY
Brett, Bradford A. ... Mexico, MO
Brett, Brenden E. ... Doylestown, PA
Brett, Charles R. ... Tupelo, MS
Brett & Daugert, P.L.L.C.
Bellingham, WA

Brett, Dean R. ... Bellingham, WA
Brett, Derek B. ... Washington, DC
Brett, Erdel, Van Matre, Tanzey & Lovekamp, P.C. ... Mexico, MO
Brett, Gregory L. ... Los Angeles, CA
Brett, H. James "Bo" ... Dunnellon, FL
Ocala, FL
Orlando, FL
Brett, Harry P. ... New York, NY
Brett, James A. ... Boston, MA
Brett, Jay Andrew ... Fort Myers, FL
Brett, Jay E. ... Niagara Falls, NY
Brett, Joel D. ... St. Charles, MO
Brett, John P. ... Norwalk, CT
Brett, Julie P. ... Chicago, IL
Brett & Kaestner, P.A. ... Oklahoma City, OK
Brett, Kenneth W. ... Watertown, NY
Brett, Kim A. ... St. Petersburg, FL
Brett, Kirk L. ... New York, NY
Brett, Laura U. ... New York, NY
Brett, Mary Ryder ... Washington, DC
Brett, Matthew S. ... New York, NY
Brett & Reynolds, P.A. ... Dunnellon, FL
Ocala, FL
Brett, Stephen M. ... Englewood, CO
Brett, Thomas F., II ... Chicago, IL
Brett, Thomas J. ... New York, NY
Brett, Thomas R. ... Tulsa, OK
Brett, Tybe A. ... Pittsburgh, PA
Brett, William T. ... Oklahoma City, OK
Brettauer, Karin H. ... Los Angeles, CA
Bretthauer, Cynthia M. ... Paducah, KY
Bretting, Denise A. ... Loveland, CO
Brett-Major, Lin ... Boca Raton, FL
Brett-Major, Lin, P.A. ... Boca Raton, FL
Brettner, Christopher S. ... St. Petersburg, FL
Bretton, James C. ... New York, NY
Bretton-Granatoor, Marianne ... New York, NY
Brettschneider & Brettschneider
Huntington, NY
Brettschneider, Eric B. ... New York, NY
Brettschneider, Joel H. ... Brooklyn, NY
Brettschneider, Joseph M.
Huntington, NY
Brettschneider, Rita R. F. ... Huntington, NY
Bretz & Coven, LLP ... New York, NY
Bretz, Daniel J. ... Detroit, MI
Bretz, Eileen Collins ... New York, NY
Bretz, Jennifer ... Montvale, NJ
Bretz, Kerry ... New York, NY
Bretz, Linda L. ... Albuquerque, NM
Bretz, Matthew L. ... Hutchinson, KS
Bretz, Rebecca A.A. ... St. Paul, MN
Bretz, Robert H. ... Los Angeles, CA
Bretz, Robert H., A Professional Corporation
Los Angeles, CA
Bretz, Ronald J. ... Lansing, MI
Bretzmann & Aldridge, L.L.P.
High Point, NC
Bretzmann, Raymond A. ... High Point, NC
Breuch, David A. ... Detroit, MI
Breuch, Thomas F. ... Maquoketa, IA
Breuder, Drew E. ... Los Angeles, CA
Breuel, Brian H. ... Princeton, NJ
Breuer, Frank G. ... Lake Oswego, OR
Breuer, Jennifer R. ... Chicago, IL
Breuer, Julie Exum ... Jacksonville, FL
Ponte Vedra Beach, FL
Breuer, Krista C. ... Sacramento, CA
Breuer, Lanny A. ... Washington, DC
Breuer, Louis A. ... Toledo, OH
Breuer, Matthew G. ... Jacksonville, FL
Breuer, Nancy Robinson ... Washington, DC
Breuer, Teri L. ... Encino, CA
Breuer, Wiebke ... Dallas, TX
Houston, TX
Breuer, William J. ... Ridgewood, NY
Breuleux, F. Michael ... San Jose, CA
Breuner, Andrew J. ... Truckee, CA
Breuner, Katrina L. ... Los Angeles, CA
Breuner, Susan Beth ... Truckee, CA
Breunig, Chad O. ... Charlotte, NC
Breunig, Craig T. ... Wahoo, NE
Breunig, Daniel A. ... Madison, WI
Breunig, Erin Lang ... Charlotte, NC
Breunig, Kurt A. ... Elyria, OH
Breunig, Mark R. ... Rancho Cordova, CA
Breunig, Preston T. ... Indianapolis, IN
Breunig, Richard A. ... Albany, NY
Breunig, Robert J. ... South St. Paul, MN
Breuning, Jonathan R. ... Omaha, NE
Breuninger & Fellman ... Fanwood, NJ
Breuninger, Patricia ... Fanwood, NJ
Breur & Breur ... Wayne, NJ
Breur, G. Thomas ... Wayne, NJ
Breur, George A. ... Wayne, NJ
Brevard, Jacqueline E.
Whitehouse Station, NJ
Brever, Peggy E. ... Milwaukee, WI
Brever, Thomas E. ... Minneapolis, MN
Brevetti, Laura A., Law Offices
New York, NY
Brevetti, Louis A. ... New York, NY
Brevik & Associates ... Minneapolis, MN
Brevik, Christopher E. ... Minneapolis, MN
Breviu, John A. ... West Fargo, ND
Brevorka, Peter J. ... Greensboro, NC
Brew, Alexandra J. ... Los Angeles, CA
Brew, Dorothy V. ... Los Angeles, CA
Brew, Eugene J., Jr. ... Erie, PA
Brew, Gerard G. ... Newark, NJ
Brew, James W. ... Washington, DC
Brew, John B. ... Washington, DC
Brew, Julian ... Los Angeles, CA
Brew, Lindsay E. ... Tucson, AZ
Brew, Michael R. ... New York, NY
Brew, Richard Douglas ... Modesto, CA
Brew, Richard Douglas, A Professional Law Corporation ... Modesto, CA
Brew, Sarah L. ... Minneapolis, MN
Brew, Sean ... San Diego, CA
Brewbaker, Robert S., Jr. ... Norfolk, VA
Brewbaker, William S., Jr. ... Montgomery, AL
Brewe, Franklin D. ... Aurora, IL
Brewe, Helen K. ... Chicago, IL
Brewe, Kenneth E. ... Everett, WA
Brewe Layman, A Professional Services Corporation ... Everett, WA
Brewer, A. Horace ... Ridgeland, MS
Brewer, Albert P. ... Birmingham, AL
Brewer, Alice A. ... West Haven, CT
Brewer, Alison E. ... Brookfield, WI
Brewer, Amy L. ... Breckenridge, CO
Brewer, Andrea B. ... Murray Hill, NJ
Brewer, Andrew M. ... Haddonfield, NJ
Brewer, Anna Elliott ... Alexandria, LA
Brewer, Anthony D. ... Lexington, KY
Brewer, Arthur M. ... Baltimore, MD
Brewer & Associates ... Douglasville, GA
Brewer & Auer ... White Plains, NY
Brewer, Benjamin M. ... Show Low, AZ
Brewer, Bennie F. ... Knoxville, TN
Brewer, Brad E. ... Dallas, TX
Brewer, Brendan Patrick ... San Rafael, CA
Brewer & Brewer ... Newport Beach, CA
Brewer & Brewer ... Wilkesboro, NC
Brewer, Brewer, Anthony & Middlebrook
Dallas, TX
Fort Worth, TX
Irving, TX
Brewer, Burleigh J. ... Newport Beach, CA
Brewer, C. Madison ... Department of Justice, Executive Office for United States Attorneys, GV
Brewer, C. William ... Fresno, CA
Brewer & Cahill ... Oconomowoc, WI
Brewer, Carol M. ... Miami, FL
West Palm Beach, FL
Brewer, Celia A. ... Solana Beach, CA
Brewer, Charles A. ... Jackson, MS
Brewer, Charles M. ... Phoenix, AZ
Brewer, Charles M., Ltd. ... Phoenix, AZ
Brewer, Charles R. ... Asheville, NC
Brewer, Chester A. ... Bartlesville, OK
Brewer, Christopher ... Pittsburgh, PA
Brewer, Christopher P. ... Raleigh, NC
Brewer, Christopher W. ... Tampa, FL
Brewer, Cindy G. ... Mount Pleasant, MI
Brewer, Coy E., Jr. ... Fayetteville, NC
Brewer, Craig W. ... Covington, LA
Metairie, LA
Brewer, Curtis ... Oconomowoc, WI
Brewer, Curtis C., IV ... Raleigh, NC
Brewer, D. Brett ... Jacksonville, TX
Brewer, Dana ... Concordia, KS
Brewer, Daniel A. ... Norwood, MA
Brewer, Daniel H. ... South Bend, IN
Brewer, Danielle K. ... West Palm Beach, FL
Brewer, David A. ... La Jolla, CA
Brewer, David J. ... Fairfax, VA
Brewer, David L. ... Huntington, IN
Warren, IN
Brewer, David Madison ... New York, NY
Brewer, David R., Jr. ... New York, NY
Brewer, Deanna H. ... Houston, TX
Brewer, Deaton & Bowman, PLLC
Greenwood, MS
Brewer, Deborah T. ... Sarasota, FL
Brewer, Deedra M. ... Douglasville, GA
Brewer, Delbert H. ... Greencastle, IN
Brewer, Dennis C. ... Perryville, MO
Brewer, Dennis G., Jr. (P.C.) ... Irving, TX
Brewer, Dennis G., Sr. ... Irving, TX
Brewer, Donald R. ... Jacksonville, FL
Brewer, Donald R., (Chtd.) ... Dundee, IL
Brewer, Dori E. Lee ... Seattle, WA
Brewer, Douglas R. ... Salt Lake City, UT
Brewer, Edward S., Jr. ... Boston, MA
Brewer, Edward Y. ... Clemmons, NC
Brewer, Edwin E. ... Angleton, TX
Brewer, F. Holcomb, III ... Philadelphia, PA
Brewer, Felice Berkman ... New York, NY
Brewer, Gary A. ... Nashville, TN
Brewer, Gary B. ... Caruthersville, MO
Brewer, Gary E. ... Morristown, TN
Brewer, George W. ... Fairfield, CA
Brewer, George W. ... San Mateo, CA
Brewer, Gilbert W. ... Augusta, ME
Brewer, Glenda O. ... Dallas, TX
Brewer, Graydon R. ... Pittsburgh, PA
Brewer, Gregory J. ... Wilkesboro, NC
Brewer, Gregory T. ... Dallas, TX
McKinney, TX
Brewer, Herbie ... Birmingham, AL
Brewer, Hollis B., III ... Washington, DC
Brewer, J. Clark ... Raleigh, NC
Brewer, J. Mark ... Houston, TX
Brewer, James A. ... Ames, IA
Brewer, James F. ... Arbutus, MD
Brewer, James F., II ... Westminster, MD
Brewer, James K. ... Corvallis, OR
Brewer, James L. ... Seattle, WA
Brewer, James N. ... Los Angeles, CA
Brewer, James S. ... West Hartford, CT
Brewer, James W. ... El Paso, TX
Brewer, Janet L. ... Palo Alto, CA
Brewer, Jeffery R. ... Wichita, KS
Brewer, Jerry L. ... Orlando, FL
Brewer, Joe O. ... Wilkesboro, NC
Brewer, Joel H. ... Roxboro, NC
Brewer, Joel N. ... Federal Trade Commission, Bureau of Consumer Protection, GV
Brewer, John B., Jr. ... Fort Myers, FL
Brewer, John Brian ... Phoenix, AZ
Brewer, John E. ... Lake Worth, FL
Brewer, John H. ... Birmingham, AL
Brewer, John N. ... Las Vegas, NV
Brewer, John N. ... Oklahoma City, OK
Brewer, John W. ... San Diego, CA
Brewer, John W. ... New York, NY
Brewer, Joseph J. ... San Diego, CA
Brewer, Joy H. ... Cary, NC
Brewer, Julian S., Jr. ... Baltimore, MD
Brewer, Katherine ... Pittsburgh, PA
Brewer, Kathleen A. ... Westlake Village, CA
Brewer, Kevin R. ... Cincinnati, OH
Brewer, Krause & Brooks ... Nashville, TN
Brewer, Kristin G. ... Salt Lake City, UT
Brewer, Kurt Forrest ... Orlando, FL
Brewer, Lance A. ... Newport Beach, CA
Brewer, Larry W. ... Austin, TX
Brewer, Lee M. ... Westerville, OH
Brewer, Lynn Kelly ... Atlanta, GA
Brewer, Margaret Tirza ... Long Beach, CA
Brewer, Mark ... Lansing, MI
Brewer, Mark P. ... Tallahassee, FL
Brewer, Mary Barrett ... Nashville, TN
Brewer, Michael A. ... Los Angeles, CA
Brewer, Michael C. ... Eden Prairie, MN
Brewer, Michael E. ... Walnut Creek, CA
Brewer, Michael L. ... New Smyrna Beach, FL
Brewer, Michael W. ... Phoenix, AZ
Brewer, Michael W. ... Oklahoma City, OK
Brewer, Michelle D. ... San Francisco, CA
Brewer, N. Craig, III ... Greenwood, MS
Brewer, Nancy ... San Jose, CA
Brewer, Oby T., III ... Atlanta, GA
Brewer, Oscar S. ... Kansas City, MO
Brewer, Patti Davis ... Wiscasset, ME
Brewer, Paul G. ... Minneapolis, MN
Brewer, Paul M. ... Dallas, TX
Brewer, Peter J. ... Great Barrington, MA
Brewer, Peter L. ... Knoxville, TN
Brewer, Peter N., Law Offices of
Palo Alto, CA
Brewer, Phil ... Roswell, NM
Brewer & Pritchard, A Professional Corporation ... Houston, TX
Brewer, R. Kent ... Walnut Creek, CA
Brewer, Rachelle Lyn ... Santa Monica, CA
Brewer, Ralph ... Baton Rouge, LA
Brewer, Rebecca Hendricks
McKinney, TX
Brewer, Renee Giacomini ... San Rafael, CA
Brewer, Robert G. ... Glendale, CA
Brewer, Robert G., Jr. ... Bethesda, MD
Brewer, Robert M. ... Lexington, KY
Brewer, Robert R. ... Quitman, TX
Brewer, Robert S., Jr. ... San Diego, CA
Brewer, Robin A. ... Mill Valley, CA
Oakland, CA
Brewer, Robin E. ... Medford, MA
Brewer, Ronald J. ... Clio, MI
Brewer, Ronald J., P.C. ... Clio, MI
Brewer, Roy E. ... Sacramento, CA
Brewer, Roy G. ... Seattle, WA
Brewer, Russell L. ... Allentown, PA
Brewer, Rustin A. ... Hermiston, OR
Brewer, Scott T. ... Rockingham, NC
Brewer, Sherman T., Jr. ... New York, NY
Brewer, Silas H., Jr. ... Little Rock, AR
Brewer, Stephen C. ... Hurst, TX
Brewer, Stephen J. ... Covington, KY
Cincinnati, OH
Hamilton, OH
Brewer, Stephen M. ... Titusville, FL
Brewer, Stephen M., P.A. ... Titusville, FL
Brewer, Stephen W. ... Norfolk, VA
Brewer, Steven J. ... Oakland, CA
Brewer, Steven L. ... Cleveland, OH
Brewer, Susan H. ... Richmond, VA
Brewer, Susan M. ... Southaven, MS
Brewer, Susan Slenker ... Morgantown, WV
Brewer and Terry, P.C. ... Morristown, TN
Brewer, Thomas J. ... Seattle, WA
Brewer, Thomas K. ... Pekin, IL
Brewer, Timothy Fraser ... Eugene, OR
Brewer, Todd B. ... Houston, TX
Brewer, Tommy ... Chicago, IL
Brewer, Travis G. ... Austin, TX
Brewer, W. Chester, Jr.
West Palm Beach, FL
Brewer, W. Chester, Jr., P.A.
West Palm Beach, FL
Brewer, W. Dennis ... Belvedere-Tiburon, CA
Brewer, Walter L. ... Bartow, FL
Brewer, Wendy D. ... Tallahassee, FL
Brewer, Wilburn, Jr. ... Columbia, SC
Brewer, William A. ... Mobile, AL
Brewer, William A., III ... Chicago, IL
New York, NY
Dallas, TX
Brewer, William, & Associates
San Diego, CA
Brewer, William C., & Associates
Morgantown, WV
Brewer, William C., III ... Livingston, AL
Brewer, William C., III ... Nashville, TN
Brewer, William Clarence, Jr.
Greenville, NC
Brewer, William D. ... New York, NY
Brewer, William D. ... Eugene, OR
Brewer, William E. ... Atlanta, GA
Brewer, William E. ... Marmora, NJ
Brewer, William E., Jr., Law Offices of
Raleigh, NC
Brewer, William G. ... West Des Moines, IA
Brewer, William H. ... Tupelo, MS
Brewer, William J. ... Northfield, IL
Brewer, William J. & Assoc., Ltd.
Northfield, IL
Brewer, William K. ... San Diego, CA
Brewer, William L. ... Stamford, CT
Brewer, William M., III ... New Orleans, LA
Brewer, William R., Jr. ... Maryville, TN
Brewer, Worten, Robinett
Bartlesville, OK
Pawhuska, OK
Brewers, Gregory T. ... Beresford, SD
Brewerton, John Lee, III ... Orlando, FL
Brewerton, John Lee, III, P.A.
Orlando, FL
Brewi, Stephen T. ... New York, NY
Brewick, Lorelei H. ... Des Moines, IA
Brewin, Katherine S. ... Chicago, IL
Brewin, William F., Jr. ... Marlborough, MA
Brewington, Dana L.
Environmental Protection Agency, Program Office Attorneys, GV
Brewington, Elizabeth S. ... Greensboro, NC
Brewington, Kathleen Ann ... Santa Cruz, CA
Brewington, Pamela D.
Department of Justice, Civil Rights Division, GV
Brewis, Jesse A. ... Indianapolis, IN
Brewsaugh, Gary D. ... Lake Forest, CA
Brewster, André W. ... San Francisco, CA
Brewster, Andre W. ... Baltimore, MD
Brewster, Arthur J. ... Metairie, LA
Brewster, Beverly Brown ... San Rafael, CA
Brewster, Bradley S. ... Trenton, NJ
Brewster & Brewster ... Kansas City, MO
Brewster, Charles D. ... Kearney, NE
Brewster, Chas. F. ... Bangor, ME
Brewster, Chris ... Lee's Summit, MO
Brewster, Christopher R. ... Washington, DC
Brewster, Clark O. ... Tulsa, OK
Brewster, Clark S. ... Bryant, AR
Brewster, Cynthia E. ... Denver, CO
Brewster, David A. ... Orange, CA
Brewster, David F. ... Columbus, KS
Brewster, David M. ... Detroit, MI
Brewster, David T. ... Boston, MA
Brewster, Donald P. ... Minneapolis, MN
Brewster, Elizabeth A. ... New York, NY
Brewster, Erin R. ... Charleston, WV
Brewster, Evans V. ... White Plains, NY
Brewster, F. Anthony ... Madison, WI
Brewster, George L. ... Los Angeles, CA
Brewster, George W., Jr. ... San Diego, CA
Brewster, Geri Ann ... Torrance, CA
Brewster, Gerry L. ... Towson, MD
Brewster, Harold D., Jr. ... Bluefield, WV
Brewster, Harris ... Fort Worth, TX
Brewster, Henry H., Jr. ... Mobile, AL
Brewster, J. Leland, II ... Cincinnati, OH
Brewster, James M. ... Overland Park, KS
Brewster, James P. ... Ransom Canyon, TX
Brewster, James R. ... Tallahassee, FL
Brewster, Jessica Y. ... Washington, DC
Brewster, Jody J. ... Washington, DC
Brewster, Jody Moser ... Garden Grove, CA
Brewster, Joe G. ... Stuart, NE
Brewster, John E., Jr. ... Houston, TX
Brewster, John S. ... Marion, IL
Brewster, Lawrence ... San Francisco, CA
Brewster, Lee ... Los Angeles, CA
Brewster, Mark P. ... San Antonio, TX
Brewster, Michael J. ... Marietta, GA
Brewster, Michael J., P.C. ... Atlanta, GA
Marietta, GA
Brewster, Miriam E. ... San Diego, CA
Brewster, Morhous & Cameron, PLLC
Bluefield, WV
Brewster, Paul M. ... Marquette, MI
Sault Ste. Marie, MI
Brewster, Richard T., Jr. ... Kansas City, MO
Brewster, Richard W. ... New York, NY
Brewster, Richard W., P.C. ... New York, NY
Brewster, Robert T. C.
Hallandale Beach, FL
Brewster, R. T. ... Kansas City, MO
Brewster, Rudi M. ... San Diego, CA
Brewster, Seth W. ... Portland, ME
Brewster, Seward B. ... Augusta, ME
Brewster, Shallcross and DeAngelis
Tulsa, OK
Brewster, Susan Aileen ... Bend, OR
Brewster, Sydney Eddy ... Salem, OR
Brewster, Sylvia F. ... Portland, ME
Brewster, Walter R., Jr. ... New York, NY
Brewster, Wayne R. ... Clayton, MO
Brewster, William D. ... Decatur, IL
Brewster, William H. ... Atlanta, GA
Brewster, William M. ... Portland, OR
Brewton, Benjamin H. ... Augusta, GA
Brewton, Eric A. ... Atlanta, GA
Brewton, Peter M. ... Houston, TX
Brewton, Robert D. ... Navasota, TX
Brewton, Wilbur E. ... Tallahassee, FL
Brewton, William F. ... Dade City, FL
Brey, Diane Richards ... Columbus, OH
Brey, Donald C. ... Columbus, OH
Brey, Ingrid K. ... Grosse Pointe Park, MI
Brey, Lewis ... Stamford, CT
Breyer, Arnold David ... Mount Shasta, CA
Breyer, George E. ... Chicago, IL
Breyer, George E., Ltd. ... Chicago, IL
Breyer, John F., Jr. ... Washington, DC
Breyer, Karl J. ... Minneapolis, MN
Breyer, Robert Clark ... Mineola, NY
Breyer, Stephen G.
Supreme Court Of The United States, GV
Breyer, Suzanne M. ... Oshkosh, WI
Breyer, Wayne S. ... New York, NY
Breyfogle, Douglas B. ... Kansas City, MO
Breyfogle, Edwin H. ... Massillon, OH
Breyfogle, John W., Jr. ... Olathe, KS
Breyfogle, Jon W. ... Washington, DC
Breyfogle, Ross E. ... Denver, CO
Breyfogle & Sell ... Massillon, OH

Breymeier, Joseph A. .... Cherry Hill, NJ
Philadelphia, PA
Breza, John Michael .... **Detroit, MI**
Breza, Scott M. .... Baltimore, MD
Brezel, Samuel .... **New York, NY**
Brezic, Richard F. .... Bratenahl, OH
Brezina, Barbara Y. .... Abington, MA
Brezina & Buckingham, P.C. .... Oak Brook, IL
Brezina, David C. .... **Chicago, IL**
Brezina, George R., Jr. .... Tampa, FL
Brezina, John C. .... Oak Brook, IL
Brezina, Joseph E. .... Philadelphia, PA
Brezine, Adam P. .... **New York, NY**
Brezine, Donald F. .... Fairborn, OH
Brezinski, Steven A. .... **Madison, WI**
Brezinsky, Helene .... **Newark, NJ**
New York, NY
Brezinsky, Jerome C. .... Orlando, FL
Brezinsky, Leann M. .... **Orlando, FL**
Breznai, Theodore A. .... Cleveland, OH
Breznay, Deborah B. .... **Boston, MA**
Breznay, George B. .... Department of Energy, Office of Hearings and Appeals, GV
Brezner, David J. .... **San Francisco, CA**
Breznick, Martin F. .... New York, NY
Breznik, Leo .... Shenandoah, PA
Brezosky, Brian E. .... Louisville, KY
Brhel, Martin C., Jr. .... Indio, CA
Bria, Robert S. .... **Wilmington, DE**
Briach, George G. .... Youngstown, OH
Briamonte, Barbara E. .... **New York, NY**
Brian, A. Morgan, Jr. .... **New Orleans, LA**
Brian, A. Morgan, Jr., A Professional Law Corporation .... **New Orleans, LA**
Brian, Aaron M. .... **Portland, OR**
Brian, Bard K. .... **Benton, KY**
Brian, Brad D. .... **Los Angeles, CA**
Brian & Brian .... Akron, OH
North Canton, OH
Brian, Conley E., Jr. .... New York, NY
Brian Dailey Law Firm, P.C. .... **Cadillac, MI**
Detroit, MI
Farmington Hills, MI
Grand Rapids, MI
Mount Clemens, MI
Brian, Edward Alan .... Sunrise, FL
Brian, Jeannette M. .... **Philadelphia, PA**
Brian, John G., III .... **St. Paul, MN**
Brian, Michael .... Medford, OR
Brian, Pat B. .... Salt Lake City, UT
Brian, Richard F. .... North Canton, OH
Brian, Robert M. .... West Palm Beach, FL
Brian, Steven J. .... Akron, OH
North Canton, OH
Brian, Tom J. .... Crosbyton, TX
Brian, W. H., Jr. .... **Amarillo, TX**
Brian, William J., Jr.
Research Triangle Park, NC
Brian, W. J. .... Montgomery, AL
Briandi, Jody E. .... **Buffalo, NY**
Briansky, Daniel .... Boston, MA
Briansky, Richard E. .... **Boston, MA**
Briant, Judith E. .... Trenton, NJ
Briars, Eugene J. .... Chicago, IL
Bribiesca, Joseph .... Wichita, KS
Bribiesco, John T. .... Davenport, IA
Bribriesco, William J., & Associates
Bettendorf, IA
Bricca, Wm. C. .... Ross, CA
Briccetti & Calhoun .... **White Plains, NY**
Briccetti, Vincent L. .... **White Plains, NY**
Brice, Aimée D. .... Seattle, WA
Brice, Amy L. .... El Paso, TX
Brice, Barbara D.
Equal Employment Opportunity Commission, Office of the General Counsel, GV
Brice, Bill E. .... **Dallas, TX**
Brice and Brice, P.A. .... York, SC
Brice, Calvin N. .... Phoenix, AZ
Brice, Charles B., A Professional Law Corporation .... Winnfield, LA
Brice, Christina Chadwick .... York, SC
Brice, Donald Lee, Jr. .... Bossier City, LA
Shreveport, LA
Brice, Edward T. .... Chardon, OH
Brice, Elizabeth Ryan .... Nacogdoches, TX
Brice, Franklin B., Jr.
Environmental Protection Agency, Office of Congressional and Legislative Affairs, GV
Brice, Gary .... Los Angeles, CA
Brice, Harry L. .... Chicago, IL
Brice, James C., III .... Greenville, SC
Brice, James D. .... **Greenville, SC**
Brice, James P. .... Roanoke, VA
Brice, John C. .... Garrettsville, OH
Brice, John P., II .... **Lexington, KY**
Brice, John R. .... **Clarksville, TN**
Brice Legal Group, The, P.C. .... **Dallas, TX**
Brice, Leonard Rider, III .... Breckenridge, CO
Brice, Lynn S. .... **Richmond, VA**
Brice, Mark J. .... **Washington, DC**
Brice, Michael P. .... Oskaloosa, IA
Brice, Michael P., P.C. .... Oskaloosa, IA
Brice, Nina Rose .... Santa Ana, CA
Brice, Richard T., IV .... Annapolis, MD
Brice, Roger T. .... **Chicago, IL**
Brice, Susan .... **Chicago, IL**
Brice, Thomas R. .... **Jacksonville, FL**
Brice, Vinson .... Los Angeles, CA
Brice, W. Robins .... **Houston, TX**
Brice, William M., III .... York, SC
Brice, William M., Jr. .... York, SC
Brice-Heames, Teresa .... Mesa, AZ
Bricely, Deborah M. .... **Troy, MI**
Briceno, Frank S. .... Santa Rosa, CA
Briceno, Freed & Bader, P.C.
Santa Rosa, CA
Briceno-Hawkins, Rose A.
Department of Justice, Criminal Division, GV
Brichacek, John I. .... New Carlisle, OH
Brick, Adam B. .... Washington, DC
Brick, Alan W. .... Annandale, VA
Brick, Angela C. .... Des Moines, IA
Brick, Ann .... San Francisco, CA
Brick, Ann Marie .... Des Moines, IA
Brick, Barrett L.
Federal Communications Commission, Mass Media Bureau, GV
Brick, Brick & Elmer, P.C.
North Tonawanda, NY
Brick, Christine .... Minneapolis, MN
Brick, Daniel E. .... North Tonawanda, NY
Brick, David .... Santa Cruz, CA
Brick, Diana L. .... **Paramus, NJ**
Brick, Gentry, Bowers, Swartz, Stoltze, Schuling & Levis, P.C. .... **Des Moines, IA**
Brick, Howard A. .... **Boston, MA**
Brick, James .... Cambridge, MA
Brick, James E. .... **Des Moines, IA**
Brick, James T. .... Sioux Falls, SD
Brick, Jon S. .... **San Diego, CA**
Brick, Joseph S. .... **Des Moines, IA**
Brick, Lawrence S. .... West Hartford, CT
Brick, Lyndean Lenhoff .... Joliet, IL
Brick, Patrick W. .... **Des Moines, IA**
Brick, Peter O. .... Port Richey, FL
Brick, Peter O. & Associates
Port Richey, FL
Brick, Philip D. .... Cleveland, OH
Brick, Ralph B. .... Louisville, KY
Brick, Samuel T., Jr. .... Department of Defense, Defense Legal Services Agency, GV
Brick, Steven A. .... **San Francisco, CA**
Brick, Steven P. .... **Des Moines, IA**
Brick, Timothy T. .... **Cleveland, OH**
Brick, William D. .... **Woodbridge, NJ**
Brick, William R., Jr. .... Warren, NJ
Brickates & Brickates .... Biddeford, ME
Brickates, Robt. E. .... Biddeford, ME
Brickell, Beatrice A. .... **Washington, DC**
Brickell, Bradley D. .... **Oklahoma City, OK**
Brickell, Elisa Schaefer .... **New York, NY**
Brickell, Jamie M. .... **New York, NY**
Brickell, Julia L. .... **New York, NY**
Brickell, Scott .... Beverly Hills, CA
Bricken, Charles .... Department of Justice, Tax Division, GV
Bricken, Daniel M. .... Charlotte, NC
Bricken, Kathleen C. .... **Portland, OR**
Bricken, Richard P. .... **Frederick, MD**
Germantown, MD
Bricken, Richard P., P.A. .... **Frederick, MD**
Germantown, MD
Bricken, Thomas L. .... **Fredericksburg, VA**
Bricken, Thomas L., A Professional Corporation .... **Fredericksburg, VA**
Bricker, A. Austin .... Jackson, MS
Bricker, Amy .... Philadelphia, PA
Bricker, Andrea H. .... **Los Angeles, CA**
Bricker, Cary A. .... New York, NY
Bricker, Charles E. .... Dayton, OH
Bricker, Christine A. .... **Columbus, OH**
Bricker, Dale E. .... Youngstown, OH
Bricker, David .... **Santa Monica, CA**
Bricker, David L. .... **Harrisburg, PA**
Bricker, Diane W. .... **Addison, TX**
Bricker, Diane W. .... **Dallas, TX**
Bricker, Douglas M. .... **Columbus, OH**
Bricker & Eckler LLP .... **Columbus, OH**
Bricker, Elizabeth A. .... Tacoma, WA
Bricker, Elizabeth Anne .... Northridge, CA
Bricker, Gary R. .... El Segundo, CA
Bricker, Harry L., Jr. .... **Harrisburg, PA**
Bricker, Jennie L. .... **Portland, OR**
Bricker, Joann M. .... **Jacksonville, FL**
Bricker, Jonathan P. .... Troy, MI
Bricker, Jules R. .... **Rockville, MD**
Bricker, Jules R., P.A. .... **Rockville, MD**
Bricker, Leigh C. .... Wilkesboro, NC
Bricker, Lew R.C. .... **Chicago, IL**
Bricker, Mary L. .... Des Moines, IA
Bricker, Monte .... **Portland, OR**
Bricker, Myrna D. .... Miami, FL
Bricker, Paul L. .... Detroit, MI
Bricker, Robert G. .... Souderton, PA
Bricker, Ross B. .... **Chicago, IL**
Bricker, Stephen W. .... Richmond, VA
Bricker, Timothy R. .... **Columbus, OH**
Bricker, Todd A. .... **Nashville, TN**
Bricker, William L., Jr. .... **New York, NY**
Bricker, William T. S. .... Baltimore, MD
Bricker Zakovics Querin Thompson & Ritchey PC .... **Portland, OR**
Bricker, Zakovics, Querin, Thompson & Ritchey, P.C. .... Missoula, MT
Brickett, Bonnie .... Ann Arbor, MI
Brickey, James N. .... **St. Louis, MO**
Brickey, William E. .... Salem, OR
Brickfield, Burchette & Ritts, P.C.
Washington, DC
Austin, TX
Brickfield, Cyril F. .... Washington, DC
Brickfield, Elizabeth .... **Las Vegas, NV**
Brickfield, Francis X. .... Brooklyn, NY
Brickfield, Paul B. .... **River Edge, NJ**
Brickfield, Paul B., A Professional Corporation .... **Hackensack, NJ**
River Edge, NJ
Brickfield, Peter J. P. .... **Washington, DC**
Brickhill, Michael J. .... Appomattox, VA
Brickhouse, Beatrice Jackson
Farmington, NM
Brickhouse, Gennice D.
Pension Benefit Guaranty Corporation, Office of the General Counsel, GV
Bricking, Dennis E. .... Louisville, KY
Brickle, Gregory S. .... **Charleston, SC**
Columbia, SC
Bricklemyer, Eugene C., Jr. .... Beaufort, SC
Bricklemyer, Keith W. .... **Tampa, FL**
Bricklemyer Smolker & Bolves,, P.A.
Orlando, FL
Bricklemyer Smolker & Bolves, P.A.
Tampa, FL
Brickler, John W. .... **St. Louis, MO**
Brickley, Barry F. .... Mansfield, OH
Brickley, David G. .... Woodbridge, VA
Brickley, James H. .... Lansing, MI
Brickley, James M. .... St. Petersburg, FL
Brickley, John T. .... New York, NY
Brickley, Kathleen K. .... **South Bend, IN**
Brickley, L. Crawford, Jr. .... **New York, NY**
Brickley, Richard L. .... **Boston, MA**
Brickley, Richard L., Jr. .... **Boston, MA**
Brickley, Samuel D., II .... **Wilmington, DE**
Brickley, Sears & Sorett .... **Boston, MA**
Brickley, William J. .... **Grand Blanc, MI**
Bricklin, Anne M. .... Seattle, WA
Bricklin, Bernice K. .... Norristown, PA
Bricklin, David A. .... Seattle, WA
Bricklin & Gendler, LLP .... Seattle, WA
Bricklin, Louis E. .... **Philadelphia, PA**
Bricklin, Susan Dein .... Philadelphia, PA
Brickman, Alan M. .... Syracuse, NY
Brickman, Bernard S. .... New York, NY
Brickman, Boaz M. .... **Los Angeles, CA**
Brickman & Brickman .... Charleston, SC
Brickman, David .... Albany, NY
Brickman, Heather .... Arlington Heights, IL
Brickman, Howard .... Salinas, CA
Brickman, Jack P. .... Charleston, SC
Brickman, James T. .... **New York, NY**
Brickman, Jeffrey H. .... Decatur, GA
Brickman, Jeffrey M. .... **Chicago, IL**
Brickman, Joel J. .... Manchester, NH
Brickman, John M. .... **Great Neck, NY**
Brickman, Kenneth A. .... Springfield, IL
Brickman, Leon .... Brooklyn, NY
Brickman, Lester .... New York, NY
Brickman, Lowell .... **Wayne, NJ**
Brickman, Martin .... Albany, NY
Brickman, Michael J. .... Charleston, SC
Brickman, Neal, Law Offices of
New York, NY
Brickman, Philip C. .... **Houston, TX**
Brickman, Richard Ian .... Manchester, NH
Brickman, Robert D. .... Norfolk, VA
Brickman, Robert I. .... Scottsdale, AZ
Brickman, Robert J. .... Boca Raton, FL
Brickman, Sharon M. .... Brooklyn, NY
Brickman, Stephen K. .... Albany, NY
Brickman, Steven A. .... **Birmingham, AL**
Brickman, Walter A. .... Malden, MA
Bricknell, Sarah M. .... Philadelphia, PA
Brickner, Barry L. .... Bingham Farms, MI
Brickner, David H. .... Santa Ana, CA
Brickner, Deborah C. .... **Costa Mesa, CA**
Brickner, J. Scott .... **Houston, TX**
Brickner, Jed W. .... **New York, NY**
Brickner, Laurianne .... Woodstock, MD
Brickner, Lisa M. .... **Cincinnati, OH**
Brickner, Lynne M. O. .... **Simi Valley, CA**
Brickner, Paul .... Cleveland, OH
Brickner, Stuart H. .... West Bloomfield, MI
Brickson, Herbert O. .... River Ridge, LA
Brickson, Richard A. .... St. Louis, MO
Brickwedde, Richard J. .... **Syracuse, NY**
Brickwood, Gary C. .... Redding, CA
Brickwood & Underwood .... Redding, CA
Bricmont, Daniel .... **Pittsburgh, PA**
Bricmont, Robert J., Jr. .... **Denver, CO**
Bricmont, Robert J., Jr., A Professional Corporation .... **Denver, CO**
Brictson, David N. .... Golden, CO
Brida, S. Renee .... San Antonio, TX
Brida, Thomas R. .... **San Francisco, CA**
Bride, James D. .... **Cedar Knolls, NJ**
Bride, James Rafferty .... Washington, DC
Bride, John W. .... Portland, ME
Bride, Robert F. .... **Ventura, CA**
Brideau, Charles J. .... Albuquerque, NM
Bridegroom, Bruce D. .... Tucson, AZ
Bridegroom & Hayes .... Tucson, AZ
Bridell, John R. .... Minneapolis, MN
Briden, James A. .... Pawtucket, RI
Briden, Mark W. .... Redding, CA
Bridenbaugh, Thomas D.
Washington, DC
Bridenhagen, Paul W. .... Department of Justice, Executive Office for United States Trustees, GV
Bridenhager, Franklin .... Liberty, IN
Bridenstine, David M. .... Canton, OH
Bridenstine, K. M. .... Polson, MT
Bridenstine, Louis H., Jr. .... Warren, MI
Bridenstine, Paul J. .... Kalamazoo, MI
Bridenstine, William A., Jr. .... Richmond, VA
Bridewell & Bridewell .... Lake Village, AR
Bridewell, David A. .... Chicago, IL
Bridewell, Dennis W. .... Cleburne, TX
Bridewell, Laurie A. .... Lake Village, AR
Bridewell, Robert G. .... Lake Village, AR
Bridewell, Sherry H. .... Richmond, VA
Bridge, Adam E. .... Burlington, VT
Bridge, Alan L. .... Storm Lake, IA
Bridge, Andrew A. .... Washington, DC
Bridge, Auburn J. .... Walterboro, SC
Bridge, Barbara .... Green Cove Springs, FL
Bridge, Bobbe Jean .... Seattle, WA
Bridge and Bridge .... Buffalo, NY
Bridge, Burneatta L. .... Madison, WI
Bridge, Catherine L. .... **Indianapolis, IN**
Bridge, Catherine S. .... **Los Angeles, CA**
Bridge, Charles P. .... Buffalo, NY
Bridge, Diane L.
National Labor Relations Board, Office of the General Counsel, GV
Bridge, Elisabeth Townsend .... **Racine, WI**
Bridge, Elizabeth G. .... Buffalo, NY
Bridge, Ellen Fishler .... **Ellicott City, MD**
Bridge, G. Michael .... Indianapolis, IN
Bridge, Gregg E. .... **Milwaukee, WI**
Bridge, James M. .... St. Louis, MO
Bridge, James Martin .... Bedford, TX
Bridge, John B. (IBA) .... **Indianapolis, IN**
Bridge, John W. .... Troy, MI
Bridge, Jonathan J. .... Seattle, WA
Bridge, Mark M. .... Woodbury, NJ
Wayne, PA
Bridge, Mark M., PC .... Woodbury, NJ
Wayne, PA
Bridge, Neely Roe .... Cleburne, TX
Bridge, Richard L. .... **St. Louis, MO**
Bridge, Robert L.
Department of the Air Force, Office of the General Counsel, GV
Bridge, Samuel G., Jr. .... **Louisville, KY**
Bridge, Tracy B. .... Minneapolis, MN
Bridge, Wade .... **Cincinnati, OH**
Bridge, William J. .... Dallas, TX
Bridge, William J. .... Richmond, VA
Bridge, Winston J. .... North Port, FL
Bridgefarmer, Larry J., (P.C.) .... **Dallas, TX**
Bridgeford, Jerylyn R. .... **Omaha, NE**
Bridgeford, Mark Kent .... Glendale, CA
Bridgeford, Rebecca J. .... **Wilmington, DE**
Bridgeforth, Henry C., Jr. .... Memphis, TN
Bridgeland, James R., Jr. .... **Cincinnati, OH**
Bridgeman, Andrea L. .... **McLean, VA**
Bridgeman, Ann Curtright .... Montrose, AL
Bridgeman, Ann Curtright, P.C.
Montrose, AL
Bridgeman, Arthur R. .... San Francisco, CA
Bridgeman, Benet E., Jr. .... Mineola, NY
Bridgeman, James D. .... **Washington, DC**
Bridgeman, Lester M. .... **Mobile, AL**
Washington, DC
Bridgeman, Randy A. .... **Chicago, IL**
Bridgen, William J. .... Los Angeles, CA
Bridger, John W. .... **Houston, TX**
Bridger, R. Jeffrey .... **New Orleans, LA**
Bridger-Riley & Associates, P.C. .... Tulsa, OK
Bridger-Riley, N. Kay .... Tulsa, OK
Bridgers, Ben Oshel .... **Sylva, NC**
Bridgers, Betty Alice .... Studio City, CA
Bridgers, Daniel F., (P.C.) .... **Decatur, GA**
Bridgers, Darrell M. .... **New York, NY**
Bridgers, David A. .... Louisville, KY
Bridgers, David C., Jr. .... Jackson, NC
Bridgers & Gill .... **Pensacola, FL**
Bridgers, Horton, Rountree & Boyette
Tarboro, NC
Bridgers, J. Dixon, III .... **Pensacola, FL**
Bridgers, Katharine B. .... Tarboro, NC
Bridgers, Lanny B. .... **Atlanta, GA**
Bridgers, Stringfellow, Bland & Peters, Law Offices of .... **Atlanta, GA**
Decatur, GA
Bridgers, William David .... **Nashville, TN**
Bridges, Alison A. .... Atlanta, GA
Bridges, Allen K. .... Pasadena, CA
Bridges, Alvin L., Jr. .... Atlanta, GA
Bridges, Andrew P. .... **Palo Alto, CA**
Bridges, Annita M. .... Oklahoma City, OK
Bridges, Bebe .... Ardmore, OK
Bridges, Benjamin H., III .... **Salisbury, NC**
Bridges, Brandon G. .... **Nashville, TN**
Bridges and Bridges .... **Houghton, MI**
Iron Mountain, MI
Marquette, MI
Negaunee, MI
Bridges, Caroline .... **Negaunee, MI**
Bridges, Chandler R. .... **Roswell, GA**
Bridges, Charles .... Washington, DC
Bridges, Charles E. .... **St. Charles, MO**
Bridges, Dan'L W. .... **Tacoma, WA**
Bridges, David L. .... Dallas, TX
Bridges, David M. .... **Houston, TX**
Bridges, Donald, Jr. .... Treasury Department, Departmental Offices, GV
Bridges, Douglas R. .... Bloomington, IN
Bridges, E. Nickolas .... **Marquette, MI**
Negaunee, MI
Bridges, Earl A., Jr. .... New Orleans, LA
Bridges, Edson L., III .... Omaha, NE
Bridges, Florence N. .... Washington, DC
Bridges, Frank L. .... **Boston, MA**
Providence, RI
Bridges, G. Wayne .... **Covington, KY**
Independence, KY
Bridges, G. Wayne, P.S.C. .... **Covington, KY**
Independence, KY
Bridges, Gailen Wayne, Jr.
Covington, KY
Bridges, Gary L. .... Odessa, TX
Bridges, Gene .... Honolulu, HI
Bridges & Gilbert .... **Rutherfordton, NC**
Shelby, NC
Bridges, Gregory R. .... Neosho, MO
Bridges, Hallie Gail .... Belzoni, MS
Bridges, Harold A. .... **Los Angeles, CA**
Bridges, J. Michael .... **Springfield, MO**
Bridges, Jack T. .... **Sanford, FL**
Bridges, James E., II .... **Auburn, AL**
Tuskegee, AL
Bridges, James E., III .... **Opelika, AL**
Bridges, James L. .... North Charleston, SC
Bridges, James R. .... **San Francisco, CA**

Bridges, Jeffrey D. .... Macon, GA
Bridges, Jennifer du Quant
New York, NY
Bridges, Joe Doyle .... Rockwall, TX
Bridges, John .... Newberg, OR
Bridges, John E. .... Waterville, WA
Bridges, John S. .... Monterey, CA
Bridges, Judy C. .... Charleston, SC
Bridges, Kamela .... Austin, TX
Bridges, Kandice K. .... Dallas, TX
Bridges, Karen E. .... Detroit, MI
Bridges, Kathleen H. .... Denver, CO
Bridges, Kenneth D. .... Louisville, MS
Bridges, Kenneth D. .... Shelby, NC
Bridges, Kenneth H. .... Chicago, IL
Bridges, Kevin M. .... Albemarle, NC
Bridges, Lance W. .... San Diego, CA
Bridges Law Firm .... Salisbury, NC
Bridges, Lewis Z. .... Jefferson City, MO
Lake Ozark, MO
Bridges, Louis Emerson, III .... Atlanta, GA
Bridges, Michael B. .... Greenville, SC
Bridges, Michael D. .... Columbus, OH
Bridges, Michael J. .... Detroit, MI
Bridges, Miller & Green, P.C. .... Macon, GA
Bridges, Misti M. .... Washington, DC
Bridges, N. Darrell .... Chattanooga, TN
Bridges, Oliff D. .... Jefferson City, TN
Bridges, Orr, Derrick & Ervin
Darlington, SC
Dillon, SC
Florence, SC
Kingstree, SC
Marion, SC
Sumter, SC
Bridges, R. Scott .... Spokane, WA
Bridges, Richard E. .... Augusta, ME
Bridges, Richard T. .... Thomaston, GA
Bridges, Richd. W. .... Santa Cruz, CA
Bridges, Ried .... Santa Barbara, CA
Ventura, CA
Bridges, Rikard L. .... Athens, GA
Bridges, Robert G. .... Des Moines, IA
Bridges, Robert L. .... Lakeport, CA
Bridges, Robert L. .... Marysville, OH
Bridges, Robert M. .... Rockville Centre, NY
Bridges, Russell B. .... Austin, TX
Bridges, S. Powell .... Wilmette, IL
Bridges, Saunders M. .... Florence, SC
Bridges, Saunders M., Jr. .... Florence, SC
Bridges & Seibel, P.C. .... St. Charles, MO
Bridges, Steven J. .... Evanston, IL
Bridges, Terry C. .... Atlanta, GA
Bridges, Terry, Law Offices of
Riverside, CA
Bridges, Thomas A. .... Springfield, MA
Bridges, Thomas L. (Tom) .... Sinton, TX
Bridges, Thomas S. .... Owosso, MI
Bridges, Tracy T. .... Omaha, NE
Bridges, Tyrone M. .... Atlanta, GA
Bridges, Walter G. .... Bessemer, AL
Bridges, Young, Matthews & Drake PLC
Pine Bluff, AR
Bridges-Fortson, Peggy Y. .... Waterford, MI
Bridges Hazen, Marilee B. .... Sacramento, CA
Bridgesmith, Larry W. .... Nashville, TN
Bridgett, Arthur T. .... San Francisco, CA
Bridgetts, Kevin R .... Golden, CO
Bridgewater, Bradley S. .... Denver, CO
Bridgewater, Carroll C., Jr. .... Kelso, WA
Bridgewater, Christiana J. .... New York, NY
Bridgewater, Erle .... Athens, OH
Bridgewater, Shawn M. .... Metairie, LA
Bridgford, Clifford R. .... Frederick, MD
Bridgford, Knottnerus & Gleason
Newport Beach, CA
Bridgford, Richard K.
Newport Beach, CA
Bridgforth, Allen C., II .... Yazoo City, MS
Bridgforth, Barry W., Jr. .... Southaven, MS
Bridgforth & Beal, P.C. .... Las Cruces, NM
Bridgforth & Buntin .... Southaven, MS
Bridgforth, David R. .... Pine Bluff, AR
Bridgforth, Dudley B., Jr. .... Southaven, MS
Bridgforth, E. Barry .... Yazoo City, MS
Bridgforth, Joe K. .... Atlanta, GA
Bridgforth, John D. .... Forrest City, AR
Bridgforth, John D., P.A. .... Forrest City, AR
Bridgforth, Love, Norquist & Rohman
Yazoo City, MS
Bridgforth, Stephen .... Las Cruces, NM
Bridgforth, William C. .... Pine Bluff, AR
Bridgforth, William M. .... Pine Bluff, AR
Bridgham, Paige E. .... Springfield, MA
Bridgham, Ruth Tompkins .... Nassau, NY
Bridgham, Tracy E.
Federal Communications Commission,
Common Carrier Bureau, GV
Bridgman & Bridgman
San Francisco, CA
Bridgman, Casey N.
Wessington Springs, SD
Bridgman, David A. .... Cary, NC
Bridgman, G. Ross .... Columbus, OH
Bridgman, Gary L. .... Southbridge, MA
Bridgman, Geoffrey J. .... Seattle, WA
Bridgman, George R. .... Santa Rosa Beach, FL
Bridgman, Gerri S. .... Yarmouth, ME
Bridgman, James C. .... San Francisco, CA
Bridgman, Kurt D. .... San Francisco, CA
Bridgman, Linda B. .... Washington, DC
Bridgman, Richard D. .... San Francisco, CA
Bridgman, Robyne R. Lau .... Richmond, VA
Bridgman, Stan W. .... Los Angeles, CA
Bridgman, Susan R. .... Dayton, OH
Bridgman, Terence J. .... Wauwatosa, WI
Bridgman, Thomas F. .... Chicago, IL
Bridgman, Vickie A. .... Santa Ana, CA
Bridgman, Victor H., III .... Wilmington, DE
Bridgwater, Kerri .... Houston, TX
Bridgwater, Roger .... Houston, TX
Bridgwater, Roger, P.C. .... Houston, TX
Bridi & Bridi .... Beckley, WV
Bridi, Constance M. .... Boston, MA
Bridi, Ghassan G. .... San Diego, CA
Bridi, John L. .... Beckley, WV
Bridston, J. Kevin .... Denver, CO
Bridwell, Amy K. .... Atlanta, GA
Bridwell, Clifford .... Wichita Falls, TX
Bridwell, Kent M. .... Los Angeles, CA
Bridwell, Mark R. .... Atlanta, GA
Bridwell, Michael T. .... Beaumont, TX
Bridwell, R. Randall .... Charleston, SC
Bridwell, Robert Kennedy
Parsippany, NJ
Bridwell, Robert V. .... Indianapolis, IN
Brieant, Charles L. .... White Plains, NY
Brieant, Charles L., III .... New York, NY
Brieant, Victoria E. .... San Francisco, CA
Briechle, Michael .... Wilkes-Barre, PA
Bried, Abby .... Houston, TX
Bried, William P. .... Allentown, PA
Briede, Robert M. .... Walloon Lake, MI
Briede & Spoerl .... Walloon Lake, MI
Briedis, Robert A. .... New York, NY
Brief, Anna Lynn .... Los Angeles, CA
Brief, Howard .... Seal Beach, CA
Brief Kesselman & Knapp .... New York, NY
Brief, Matthew J. .... New York, NY
Briefman, Karen A. .... Pembroke Pines, FL
Briegel Baylard, P.C. .... Chesterfield, MO
Union, MO
Briegel, Daniel J. .... Union, MO
Briegel, Davis, Arand & Fischer, LLC
Union, MO
Briegel, Michael W. .... Newton, NJ
Briegleb, B. John .... Sacramento, CA
Brielmann, Joseph J. .... Media, PA
Brien, Charles W. .... Benton, KY
Brien, David R. .... Santa Monica, CA
Brien, Edward R. .... Santee, CA
Brien, James B., Jr. .... Mayfield, KY
Brien, Jon Derek .... Hoboken, NJ
Brien, Rex F. .... Philadelphia, PA
Brien, Ronald F. .... Spring City, PA
Brien, Russell A. .... Kansas City, MO
Briendel, William D. .... New York, NY
Brienes, Harold .... Bridgeport, CT
Brienza, Catherine .... Ridgewood, NJ
Brienza, Gary A. .... Orefield, PA
Brienza, Susan D. .... Denver, CO
Brier, Arnold Evan .... Dallas, TX
Brier, Beth J. .... Summit, NJ
Brier, Bonnie S. .... Philadelphia, PA
Brier, Bruce D. .... Summit, NJ
Brier, Carol M. .... Scottsdale, AZ
Brier, Daniel T. .... Scranton, PA
Brier, David .... New York, NY
Brier, David E. .... Cherry Hill, NJ
Philadelphia, PA
Brier, Frank Joseph .... Scranton, PA
Brier, Freya Rachel .... Boulder, CO
Brier & Irish, P.L.C. .... Phoenix, AZ
Brier, Jennifer Molish .... Lansdale, PA
Brier, John J. .... Scranton, PA
Brier, Kenneth P. .... Boston, MA
Brier, M. Claire S. .... Washington, DC
Brier, Matthew J. .... Pawtucket, RI
Brier, Patrick J. .... Scranton, PA
Wilkes-Barre, PA
Brier, Robert N. .... Phoenix, AZ
Brier, Stephen S. .... Portland, OR
Brier, Tina E. .... San Francisco, CA
Brier, Wilma A. .... Washington, DC
Briere, William J. .... Minneapolis, MN
Brierley, Douglas S. .... Morristown, NJ
Brierly Law Office, L.L.P. .... Grinnell, IA
Newton, IA
Sully, IA
Brierly, Tracey J. .... Las Vegas, NV
Brierly, William H. .... Denver, CO
Brierre, Eugene D. .... New Orleans, LA
Brierton, B. James .... San Diego, CA
Brierton, Jones & Jones, LLP
San Diego, CA
Brierton, Robert S. .... Johnstown, PA
Bries, Maria A. .... Chicago, IL
Briese, H. Gregory .... Bogalusa, LA
Briese, Joanne M. .... Billings, MT
Briese, June Maria .... Mineola, NY
Briese, Shawn L. .... Daytona Beach, FL
Briesemeister, Wilfred E. .... Whittier, CA
Brieske, Brian Andrew .... Denver, CO
Brieske, James T. .... Atlanta, GA
Brieske, Terri L. .... Chicago, IL
Brietkrenz, Ronald .... Akron, OH
Briffa, Gerald E., Law Offices of
Red Hook, NY
Briffault, Richard A. .... New York, NY
Brifman, Mark A. .... Encino, CA
Brifman, Martin B. .... Plymouth, CA
Brigagliano, Christine .... Palo Alto, CA
San Francisco, CA
Brigagliano, James A.
Securities and Exchange Commission,
Office of the General Counsel, GV
Brigance, Gerald L. .... Kansas City, MO
Brigance, Steven A. .... Arlington, TX
Brigance, William G., Sr. .... Sacramento, CA
Brigandi, John E. .... New York, NY
Brigandi, Stephen M. .... San Diego, CA
Briganti, Kelly A. .... Westfield, NJ
Briganti, Lorraine .... New York, NY
Briganti, Vincent .... White Plains, NY
Briganti, William R. .... Library of Congress,
Copyright Office, GV
Brigantic, Patricia E. .... New York, NY
Brigati, Joseph J. .... Washington, DC
Brigden, John F. .... Mountain View, CA
Brigden & Petajan, S.C. .... Milwaukee, WI
Briger & Associates .... New York, NY
Briger, Paul H. .... New York, NY
Briger, Peter L. .... New York, NY
Brigg, John Michael .... Independence, MO
Briggerman, Steven L. .... Washington, DC
Briggett, Marlissa S.
Commission on Civil Rights,
Office of the General Counsel, GV
Briggle, Charles G., Jr. .... Springfield, IL
Briggle, Robert D. .... Colorado Springs, CO
Briggs, Alan L. .... Washington, DC
Briggs, Alice C. .... Peterborough, NH
Briggs, Allen R. .... Cathedral City, CA
Briggs, Andrew Holbrook .... Harrisburg, PA
Briggs, Barbara B. .... Sarasota, FL
Briggs, Barbara J. .... New York, NY
Briggs, Barbara L. .... Philadelphia, PA
Briggs, Barry J. .... Seattle, WA
Briggs, Basil M. .... Detroit, MI
Briggs, Bettina A. .... Taunton, MA
Briggs & Briggs .... Tacoma, WA
Briggs, Bruce B. .... Mars Hill, NC
Briggs, C. Donald, III .... Rockport, ME
Briggs, Cara M. .... Rochester, NY
Briggs, Carole Williams .... Glastonbury, CT
Briggs, Charles A. .... Memphis, TN
Briggs, Charles H. .... Sacramento, CA
Briggs, Christopher J. .... San Diego, CA
Briggs, Church E. .... Exton, PA
Briggs, Coralee .... El Paso, TX
Briggs, Craig A. .... Pittsburgh, PA
Briggs, Curtis G. .... Houston, TX
Briggs, Dale J. .... Tulsa, OK
Briggs, Dale L. .... Dallas, TX
Briggs, David .... Kirksville, MO
Briggs, David B. .... Huntsville, AL
Briggs, David C. .... Dallas, TX
Briggs, David J. .... Cleveland, OH
Briggs, David W. .... Washington, DC
Briggs, David William .... Seattle, WA
Briggs, Don F. .... Tavares, FL
Briggs, Donald L. .... Santa Barbara, CA
Briggs, Donald R. .... Berkeley, CA
Briggs, Douglas E. .... Grand Junction, CO
Briggs, E. Ray .... Raleigh, NC
Briggs, Eddie J. .... De Kalb, MS
Briggs, Ellen M. .... Philadelphia, PA
Briggs, Emerson V., III .... Washington, DC
Briggs, Florence A. .... Flora, IN
Briggs, Garrett L. .... Daytona Beach, FL
Briggs, Gina M. .... New York, NY
Briggs, Glenn L. .... Costa Mesa, CA
Briggs, Heather .... Burlington, VT
Briggs, Jack L. .... Sioux Falls, SD
Briggs, James A. .... Carmel, IN
Briggs, James R. .... Tulsa, OK
Briggs, Janet Molahan .... Portland, OR
Briggs, Jeffery A. .... Reno, NV
Briggs, Jeffrey C. .... Los Angeles, CA
Briggs, Jeffrey T. .... Santa Monica, CA
Briggs, Jerome C. .... Minneapolis, MN
Briggs, Joan Stefanec .... Daytona Beach, FL
Briggs, John B. .... Atlanta, GA
Briggs, John C. .... Daytona Beach, FL
Maitland, FL
Briggs, John D. .... St. Louis, MO
Briggs, John D. .... Salem, NY
Briggs, John D. .... York, PA
Briggs, John D., II .... Baltimore, MD
McLean, VA
Briggs, John DeQ., III .... Washington, DC
Briggs, John H. .... Taos, NM
Briggs, John L. .... Atlantic Beach, FL
Briggs, John M., III .... Muskegon, MI
Briggs, John R. .... Sacramento, CA
Briggs, John T. .... New Bern, NC
Briggs, Jonathan R. .... Sugar Land, TX
Briggs, Keith E. .... Spokane, WA
Briggs, Kevin B. .... Fresno, CA
Briggs, Kevin R. .... Las Vegas, NV
Briggs, Knoepfel & Ronca
Charlotte Amalie, St. Thomas, VI
Briggs, Larry B. .... Houston, TX
Briggs, Larry N. .... Greenville, SC
Briggs, Laura Lee .... Walnut Creek, CA
Briggs, Laurie A. .... Columbus, OH
Briggs, Lincoln W. .... New York, NY
Briggs, M. Courtney .... Oklahoma City, OK
Briggs, Marissa K. .... Buffalo, NY
Briggs, Marjorie Crowder .... Columbus, OH
Briggs, Mark G. .... El Paso, TX
Briggs, Mark K. .... Phoenix, AZ
Briggs, Michael G. .... Houston, TX
Briggs, Michael W. .... Charlotte, NC
Briggs and Morgan, Professional Association
Minneapolis, MN
St. Paul, MN
Briggs, Nancy K. .... Merrillville, IN
Briggs, Norma .... Madison, WI
Briggs, Norman W. .... Cherry Hill, NJ
Marmora, NJ
Philadelphia, PA
Briggs, Orin G. .... Irmo, SC
Briggs, Pamela E. B. .... Austin, TX
Briggs, Patrick J. .... San Diego, CA
Briggs, Patrick Timothy .... Redwood City, CA
Briggs, Patterson & Associates .... Tulsa, OK
Briggs, Paul .... Schenectady, NY
Briggs, Paul M. .... Phoenix, AZ
Tucson, AZ
Briggs & Pry .... Akron, OH
Briggs, R. David .... Akron, OH
Briggs, Randy R. .... Ocala, FL
Briggs, Rawle R. .... New York, NY
Briggs, Rebecca Lynn .... Frankfort, KY
Briggs, Richard O. .... Los Angeles, CA
Briggs, Robert B. .... Juneau, AK
Briggs, Robert F. .... Atlanta, GA
Briggs, Robert G. .... Stillwater, MN
Briggs, Robert H. .... Costa Mesa, CA
Briggs, Robert L. .... Tulsa, OK
Briggs, Robert L., P.C. .... Tulsa, OK
Briggs, Robert R. .... Tacoma, WA
Briggs, Robert W. .... Anaheim, CA
Briggs, Robert W. .... Akron, OH
Briggs, Robt. .... Lake Oswego, OR
Briggs, Rodney A.
Palos Verdes Peninsula, CA
Briggs, Rodney D. .... Chevy Chase, MD
Briggs, Ronald J. .... Elizabethtown, NY
Briggs, Sandra S. .... Hartford, CT
Briggs, Scott A. .... Oklahoma City, OK
Briggs, Shawn B. .... Tacoma, WA
Briggs, Stephanie K. .... Charlotte, NC
Briggs, Stephen J. .... St. Joseph, MO
Briggs, Steve C. .... Denver, CO
Briggs, Steven E. .... Newport Beach, CA
Briggs, Stuart C. .... Davenport, IA
Briggs, Stuart R. .... Seattle, WA
Briggs, Susan Hunt .... Charlotte, NC
Briggs, Susan S. .... San Francisco, CA
Briggs, Taylor R., (P.C.) .... New York, NY
Briggs, Templeton, Jr. .... Newport Beach, CA
Briggs, Terrence J. .... Portland, ME
Briggs, Thomas A. .... Cleveland, OH
Briggs, Thomas W. .... Fort Worth, TX
Briggs, Timothy H. .... Irvine, CA
Briggs, Timothy Ray .... Albuquerque, NM
Briggs, Todd E. .... Detroit, MI
Briggs, Tom P. .... Dallas, TX
Briggs, Virginia L. .... Denver, CO
Briggs, Virginia P. .... Palo Alto, CA
Briggs, W. Winston .... Atlanta, GA
Briggs, Walter D. .... Middletown, CT
Briggs, Ward D. .... South St. Paul, MN
Briggs, Wendy Gerlach .... Phoenix, AZ
Briggs, William B. .... New York, NY
Briggs, William H. .... Detroit Lakes, MN
Briggs, William H., Jr. .... Washington, DC
Briggs, William J. .... Flora, IN
Briggs, William J., II .... Beverly Hills, CA
Briggs, William L. .... Fort Wayne, IN
Briggs, William M. .... Pismo Beach, CA
Briggs, William P. .... Kittery, ME
Briggs, Wilson & Tomasi .... Salem, NY
Briggs, York Mcmillan .... Lubbock, TX
Briggs-Bunting, Jane L. .... Rochester, MI
Briggs-Redissi, Lois .... Dearborn, MI
Briggum, Sue M. .... Washington, DC
Brigham, Andrew Prince .... Jacksonville, FL
Tampa, FL
Brigham, Bradley L. .... Seattle, WA
Brigham & Brigham, A Legal Professional
Association .... Cincinnati, OH
Brigham & Brigham, P.A. .... Miami, FL
Brigham, Brooke A. .... Oakland, CA
Brigham, Carla Folz .... Boston, MA
Brigham, Carol A. .... Danielson, CT
Brigham, Charles A, III .... Cincinnati, OH
Brigham, Charles A., Jr. .... Cincinnati, OH
Brigham, Christopher L. .... Hartford, CT
New Haven, CT
Brigham, Constance G., Law Offices of
Torrance, CA
Brigham, Dana P. .... Miami, FL
Brigham, David P. .... Mount Laurel, NJ
Brigham, Donald P. .... Laguna Hills, CA
Brigham, Edward, (P.A.) .... Baltimore, MD
Brigham, Elizabeth J. .... Bryson City, NC
Brigham, G. Andrew .... Dover, TN
Brigham, Geoffrey R. ....
Department of Justice, GV
Brigham, H. Day, Jr. .... Boston, MA
Brigham, Jack K. .... Tempe, AZ
Brigham, Johan Van't Hul .... Boston, MA
Brigham & Kane .... Waukegan, IL
Brigham, Karen Berg .... Miami, FL
Brigham, Karen L. .... Waukegan, IL
Brigham, Katharine S. .... West Chester, PA
Brigham, Leroy Weathers .... Augusta, GA
Brigham, Martin K. .... Philadelphia, PA
Brigham, Matthew J. .... San Jose, CA
Brigham Moore Gaylord Schuster Merlin &
Tobin LLP .... Fort Lauderdale, FL
Jacksonville, FL
Miami, FL
Orlando, FL
Sarasota, FL
Tampa, FL
Winter Park, FL
Brigham, Neala C. .... Shawnee, KS
Brigham, Paul L., Jr. .... Framingham, MA
Brigham, Robert H. .... Madison, WI
Brigham, Robert J. .... Palo Alto, CA
Brigham, S. T. Jack, III .... Palo Alto, CA
Brigham, Stephen S. .... Milwaukee, WI
Brigham, Thomas B., Jr. .... Rochester, NY
Brigham, Thomas S. .... Ukiah, CA
Brigham, Toby Prince, (P.A.)
Fort Lauderdale, FL
Jacksonville, FL
Miami, FL
Sarasota, FL
Tampa, FL
Winter Park, FL
Brigham and Trevor, P.C.
Philadelphia, PA
Brigham, William H. .... Mobile, AL
Brigham, William H. .... Burleson, TX
Brigham-Allen, Tara K. .... Malibu, CA
Brighenti, Simon J., Jr. .... Springfield, MA
Brighoff, William F. .... Chesterfield, MO

Bright, Arlette K. ....Annapolis, MD
Bright, B. Andrew ....Hagerstown, MD
Bright, B. Andrew, Chtd.
Hagerstown, MD
Bright, Barry D. ....Flora, IL
Bright, Barton R., III ....Atlanta, GA
Bright, Bobby Neal ....Montgomery, AL
Bright and Brown ....Glendale, CA
Los Angeles, CA
Bright, Bruce F. ....Annapolis, MD
Bright, Charles T. ....Orange, CA
Bright & Chimera, P.A. ....Delray Beach, FL
Bright, Christi L. ....Kansas City, MO
Bright, Christopher P. ....Revere, MA
Bright, Craig B. ....Manakin-Sabot, VA
Bright, Cynthia T. ....Palo Alto, CA
Bright, Daniel E. ....State College, PA
Bright, David A. ....Boston, MA
Bright, David S. ....Escondido, CA
Orange, CA
Bright, David T. ....Corpus Christi, TX
Bright, Dennis A. ....Victorville, CA
Bright, Earl A., II ....Menlo Park, CA
Bright, Fletcher W. ....Chattanooga, TN
Bright, Francis E. ....Newton, NJ
Bright, Frank ....Shreveport, LA
Bright, Fred, Jr. ....Knoxville, TN
Bright, Fredric D. ....Milledgeville, GA
Bright, Gail Ellen ....Topeka, KS
Bright, Gary M. ....Carpinteria, CA
Bright, Gerald V. ....Dallas, TX
Bright, Gibson & Nipert, P.C. ....Denver, CO
Bright, Gregory P. ....Santa Monica, CA
Bright, H. C., III ....Chattanooga, TN
Bright, Helen ....Austin, TX
Bright, Hugh B., Jr. ....Knoxville, TN
Bright, Izetta F. ....Detroit, MI
Bright, J. Converse ....Valdosta, GA
Bright, J. Reeve ....Delray Beach, FL
Bright, James M. ....Houston, TX
Bright, James R. ....Cleveland, OH
Bright, James S. ....Glendale, CA
Bright, Jane M. ....Hartford, CT
Bright, Joel M. ....Baltimore, MD
Bright, John B. ....El Paso, TX
Bright, John D. ....Goshen, NY
Bright, John H. ....Seattle, WA
Bright, Jonathan K. ....New York, NY
Bright, Joseph ....Wilmette, IL
Bright, Joseph C. ....Philadelphia, PA
Bright, Joshua L. ....San Francisco, CA
Bright, Laura B. ....Escondido, CA
Bright, Lloyd D. ....Evansville, IN
Bright & Long, P.C. ....Montgomery, AL
Bright & Lorig, A Professional Corporation
Los Angeles, CA
Bright, Lucy P. ....Abingdon, VA
Bright, Lynn Clardy ....Montgomery, AL
Bright, Maldrick E. ....Milton, FL
Bright, Maldrick E. ....Pensacola, FL
Bright, Marilyn S. ....Atlanta, GA
Bright, Mark E. ....Oklahoma City, OK
Bright, Mary S. ....Cleveland, OH
Bright, Maureen J. ....Glendale, CA
Bright, Melvin J. ....Department of Labor, Employment & Training Administration, GV
Bright, Michael T. ....Riverside, CA
Bright, Myron H. ....Fargo, ND
Bright, Patrick F. ....Los Angeles, CA
Bright, Peter L. ....El Paso, TX
Bright & Powell ....Carpinteria, CA
Bright, Raymond E. ....San Francisco, CA
Bright, Richard G. ....Philadelphia, PA
Bright, Robert ....Clarksburg, WV
Bright, Robert C., Law Offices of
Oklahoma City, OK
Bright, Robert E. ....San Diego, CA
Bright, Robert R. ....Delray Beach, FL
Bright, Robt. E. ....East Tawas, MI
Bright, Royal E. ....Philadelphia, PA
Bright, Ruth E. ....Department of State, Foreign Service Officers (Overseas), GV
Bright, Scott E. ....Center Line, MI
Bright, Stanley R. ....Jersey City, NJ
Bright, Stephen B. ....Atlanta, GA
Bright, Stephen F. ....Langhorne, PA
Bright, Steven ....Chicago, IL
Bright, Steven A. ....Farmington Hills, MI
Bright, Steven F. ....Dallas, TX
Bright, Ted R. ....Denver, CO
Bright, Teresa A. ....San Francisco, CA
Bright, Thomas A. ....Greenville, SC
Bright, Thomas L. ....Shippensburg, PA
Bright, Tracey W. ....Odessa, TX
Bright, W. Edward ....New York, NY
Bright, William C. ....Pulaski, TN
Bright, William D. ....Portland, IN
Bright, William D. ....Paola, KS
Bright, William H., Jr. ....Hartford, CT
Brightbill, David J. ....Lebanon, PA
Brightbill, Donna Long ....Lebanon, PA
Brightbill, James E. ....Akron, OH
Brightbill, Peter L. ....New York, NY
Brightbill, Timothy C. ....Washington, DC
Bright-Coleman, Kim L.
Federal Election Commission, Office of the General Counsel, GV
Brightman, David R. ....Los Angeles, CA
Brightman, J. Timothy ....McKinney, TX
Brightman, Kathleen Carlisle
Wilmington, DE
Brightman, Richard J. ....Paramus, NJ
Brightman, Richard S. ....Tallahassee, FL
Brightman, Robert G. ....Orlando, FL
Brightman, Tracy B. ....Dallas, TX
Brightmire, Jon E. ....Tulsa, OK
Brightmire, Kristen L. ....Tulsa, OK
Brightmire, Paul W. ....Tulsa, OK

Brighton, Abbie L. ....Flint, MI
Troy, MI
Brighton, Anthony R. ....Cleveland, OH
Brighton, Jo Ann J. ....Manchester, NH
Brighton, Joel T. ....Manchester, NH
Brighton, Kenneth A. ....Peterborough, NH
Brighton, Kenneth C. ....Peterborough, NH
Brighton, Nancy A. ....Redwood City, CA
Brighton, Robert C., Jr.
Fort Lauderdale, FL
Brighton & Runyon, P.A. ......Peterborough, NH
Brighton, William D. ....Department of Justice, Environment and Natural Resources Division, GV
Brighton, Wm. Curtis ....Terre Haute, IN
Brightwell, Bruce A. ....Louisville, KY
Brightwell, Jeffery A. ....Calabasas, CA
Brightwell, Julie Mann ....Columbus, OH
Brightwell, Kim Edward ....Austin, TX
Brightwell, Thomas P. ....Englewood, CO
Brightwell, Thomas P., P.C. ....Englewood, CO
Brigida, Peter ....Chicago, IL
Briglia & Hundley, P.C. ....Fairfax, VA
Briglia, Joseph P. ....Philadelphia, PA
Briglia, Shannon J. ....Washington, DC
Vienna, VA
Briglia, Steven D. ....Fairfax, VA
Briglia & Taglianetti ....Philadelphia, PA
Brigliadoro, Richard ....Parsippany, NJ
Brigman, Fred C., III ....Alpine, TX
Brigman, Fred C., Jr. ....San Angelo, TX
Brigman, James Rhett ....Seattle, WA
Brigman, Lillian D. ....Houston, TX
Brigman, Myron W. ....Springfield, IL
Brignac, Ericka Schexnayder
New Orleans, LA
Brignac, Julian P. ....New Orleans, LA
Brignac, Len R. ....Baton Rouge, LA
New Orleans, LA
Brignac, Trent S. ....Lafayette, LA
New Orleans, LA
Brigner, Julie E ....Columbus, OH
Brigner, Nancy A. ....Columbus, OH
Brigner, V. Michael ....Dayton, OH
Brignola, Dominick J. ....Albany, NY
Brignola, Erin K. ....Bear, DE
Brignole & Bush ....Granby, CT
Hartford, CT
Brignole, Timothy ....Granby, CT
Hartford, CT
Brignon, Walter L. ....Midland, TX
Brignone, Andrew S. ....Las Vegas, NV
Reno, NV
Brigsted, Annette ....Middletown, CT
Brigtsen, N. Craig, Jr. ....New Orleans, LA
Briguglio, Anthony J. ....Yonkers, NY
Briguglio, Salvatore
Rancho Cucamonga, CA
Brihammar, B. Niklas ....Key West, FL
Brilbeck, Thomas J. ....Rochester, NY
Briles, Christina L. ....Ventura, CA
Briles, Margaret S. ....Davenport, IA
Briles, Rita M. ....Salisbury, MD
Briles, Scott C. ....Atlanta, GA
Briles, Tracy D. ....Santa Ana, CA
Briley, C. David ....Nashville, TN
Briley, Jacqueline Roullier ....Toledo, OH
Briley, John A., Jr. ....Washington, DC
Briley, Joseph H. ....Gray, GA
Briley, Len G., Jr ....San Antonio, TX
Briley, Michael M. ....Toledo, OH
Briley, Robert ....Nashville, TN
Briley, Robert L. ....Chanute, KS
Briley, Steve ....Wichita Falls, TX
Briley, Wm. F. ....Raleigh, NC
Brilhante, Gregory A. ....Fall River, MA
Briliant, Seth H. ....Atlantic City, NJ
Brill, Aaron P. ....Chicago, IL
Brill, Alan B. ....Suffern, NY
Brill, Alan B., P.C. ....Suffern, NY
Brill, Alan J. ....New York, NY
Brill, Allen H. ....New York, NY
Brill, Anthony S. ....Los Angeles, CA
Brill, Arthur W. ....Kalamazoo, MI
Brill, Arthur W. ....New York, NY
Brill, B. Kastle ....Buffalo, NY
Brill, Barbara A. ....San Francisco, CA
Brill, Carole L. ....San Francisco, CA
Brill, Charles A. ....Dallas, TX
Brill, Christopher J. ....Newtown, PA
Brill, Cynthia M. ....New York, NY
Brill, Daliah ....Atlanta, GA
Brill, David ....New York, NY
Brill, David ....Houston, TX
Brill, David A. ....Louisville, KY
Brill, David W. ....Coral Gables, FL
Brill, Douglas M. ....Elyria, OH
Brill, Edward A. ....New York, NY
Brill, Eli R. ....Philadelphia, PA
Brill, Elyse Arnow ....Pound Ridge, NY
Brill, Eric A. ....San Francisco, CA
Brill, Gerow D. ....Windsor, CT
Brill, Gerrilyn G. ....Atlanta, GA
Brill, Haydn J. ....New York, NY
Brill, Howard R. ....Hempstead, NY
Brill, Howard W. ....Fayetteville, AR
Brill, Jack C. ....Tamarac, FL
Brill, James E. ....Houston, TX
Brill, James E., P.C. ....Houston, TX
Brill, Jane M. ....Coronado, CA
Brill, Jeffrey ....Palo Alto, CA
Brill, Jeffrey A. ....New York, NY
Brill, Jennifer L. ....San Francisco, CA
Brill, Jesse M. ....San Francisco, CA
Brill, Josiah E., Jr. ....Minneapolis, MN
Brill, Julie S. ....Montpelier, VT
Brill, Kevin M. ....Chicago, IL
Brill, Kevin M. ....Providence, RI

Brill, Laura W. ....Los Angeles, CA
Brill, Lawrence J. ....Columbia, MD
Brill, Leroy A. ....Wilmington, DE
Brill, Lori ....Atlanta, GA
Brill, Lori A. ....Germantown, MD
Brill, Martin J. ....Los Angeles, CA
Brill, Matthew A. ....Washington, DC
Brill, Maurice ....Brooklyn, NY
Brill & Meisel ....New York, NY
Brill, Michael J., (P.C.) ....Los Angeles, CA
Brill, Moore & Wagoner, P.C.
West Plains, MO
Brill, Nancy L. ....New York, NY
Brill, Nathan Lee
Department of Justice, GV
Brill, Nelson ....Brookline, MA
Brill, Newton C. ....West Plains, MO
Brill, Norma Hand ....North Fort Myers, FL
Brill, Norma Hand, P.A.
North Fort Myers, FL
Brill, Peter E. ....Palm Desert, CA
Brill, Rachel ....San Juan, PR
Brill, Ralph L. ....Chicago, IL
Brill, Richard H. ....Glenview, IL
Brill, Robert J. ....Chicago, IL
Brill, Robert M. ....Sun Prairie, WI
Brill, Robert M., Law Offices of
New York, NY
Brill, Robert S. ....Minneapolis, MN
Brill, Robin A. ....New York, NY
Brill, Steven C. ....New York, NY
Brill, Steven J. ....New York, NY
Brill, Theodore F. ....Plantation, FL
Brill, Theodore F., P.A. ....Plantation, FL
Brill, Thomas A. ....Newport Beach, CA
Brill, Thomas F. ....Southfield, MI
Brill, Thomas H. ....Leawood, KS
Brill, Thomas J. ....Leawood, KS
Brill, Thomas R. ....Los Angeles, CA
Brill, Vanessa M. ....Morristown, NJ
Brill, Walter A. ....Atlanta, GA
Brill, Wayland M. ....Menlo Park, CA
Brill, Wendy Oglander ....New York, NY
Brill, William L. ....Columbus, OH
Brille, Michael A. ....Washington, DC
Brilleman, Louis A. ....New York, NY
Briller, David D. ....Cleveland, OH
Briller, Julius ....New York, NY
Brilley & Brewster ....Decatur, IL
Brilley, Donald E. ....Decatur, IL
Brillhart, Burton Dean ....San Antonio, TX
Brillhart, Ember A. ....Washington, DC
Brillhart, Michael J. ....York, PA
Brillhart, Roy W., Jr. ....Overland Park, KS
Brilliant, Allan S. ....Chicago, IL
Brilliant, Corinne L. ....Rockaway Park, NY
Brilliant, Dina ....Philadelphia, PA
Brilliant, Jon A. ....Deerfield Beach, FL
Brilliant, Marsha C. ......Westlake Village, CA
Brilliant, Meyer M., (P.A.) ....Miami, FL
Brilliant, Neil L. ....Chicago, IL
Brilliant, Robert J. ....Annapolis, MD
Brilliant, Robert J., P.A. ....Annapolis, MD
Brilliant, Robert M. ....El Cerrito, CA
Brilliant, Shalom ....Department of Justice, Civil Division, GV
Brilliant, Todd Steven ....Boston, MA
Brilling, Jaclyn A. ....Albany, NY
Brillinger, Joseph G., Jr. ....Norwich, NY
Brilz, Stephen E. ....Englewood, CO
Brim, Arnett & Robinett, P.C. ....Austin, TX
Brim, Daniel S. ....Fernandina Beach, FL
Brim, James C., Jr. ....Camilla, GA
Brim, James C., Jr. ....Newton, GA
Pelham, GA
Brim, James Ernest, III ....Gainesville, GA
Brim, Jefferson K., III ....Austin, TX
Brim, Phyllis T. Turner ....Chicago, IL
Brim, Randall L. ....Houston, TX
Brim, Thomas P. ....Charlotte, NC
Brim, William J. ....Las Vegas, NV
Brimacombe, Robert M. ....Ann Arbor, MI
Brimberg, Barnett J. ....Houston, TX
Brimberry, Jerry W. ....Albany, GA
Brimberry, Jerry W. (Jay) ....Albany, GA
Brimberry, Kaplan & Brimberry, P.C.
Albany, GA
Brimberry, Mark D. ....Albany, GA
Brimberry, Paul L. ....Sacramento, CA
Brimberry, Robert W. ....Sugar Land, TX
Brimble, Philip J. ....Encino, CA
Brimer, Jeffrey A. ....St. Louis, MO
Brimer, John W. ....Wichita, KS
Brimer, Lynn M. ....Southfield, MI
Brimhall, T. Wayne ....Franklin, TX
Brimley, J. Bruce ....Findlay, OH
Brimley & Kostyo, L.P.A. ....Findlay, OH
Brimley, Michael W. ....Las Vegas, NV
Brimlow, Joan P. ....Rochester, NY
Brimmage, Amy ....Dallas, TX
Brimmage, Maurice (Marty) L., Jr.
Dallas, TX
Brimmeier, Bonnie ....Pittsburgh, PA
Brimmer, Andrew Franklin
San Francisco, CA
Brimmer, Carol Teresa ....Cheektowaga, NY
Brimmer, Clarence A. ....Cheyenne, WY
Brimmer, Geraldine A. ....Denver, CO
Brimmer, Janette K. ....St. Paul, MN
Brimmer, Karen A. ....Miami, FL
Brimmer, Leslie R. ....Hartford, CT
Brimmer, Mark A. ....San Diego, CA
Brimmer, Philip A. ....Denver, CO
Brimner, Teresa Foster ....Fairbanks, AK
Brimo, Anthony N., Jr. ....Satellite Beach, FL
Brimsek, John R., (P.C.) ....Washington, DC
Brin, Barbara J. ....Longview, TX
Brin, Barry ....San Antonio, TX

Brin, Benjamin A. ....Los Angeles, CA
Brin & Brin, P.C. ....Brownsville, TX
Corpus Christi, TX
Edinburg, TX
San Antonio, TX
Brin, George G. ....San Antonio, TX
Brin, Kaylene Mae ....Hays, KS
Brin, Marla B.
Environmental Protection Agency, Office of Enforcement and Compliance Assurance, GV
Brin, Philip ....Longview, TX
Brin, R. Nathan ....Dallas, TX
Brin, Ronald B. ....Corpus Christi, TX
Brin, Royal H., Jr., (P.C.) ....Dallas, TX
Brin, Theodore W. ....Denver, CO
Brina, Robert R., Jr. ....Costa Mesa, CA
Brinberg, Simeon ....Great Neck, NY
Brinberg, Todd M. ....New York, NY
Brincefield, Barbara O. ....Washington, DC
Brincefield, Hartnett, Tompkins & Clark, P.C. ....Washington, DC
Alexandria, VA
Arlington, VA
Fairfax, VA
Brincefield, James C. "Beau", Jr.
Alexandria, VA
Brinck, Sandra J. ....Santa Fe, NM
Brinckerhoff, Clarke W.
Federal Trade Commission, Bureau of Consumer Protection, GV
Brinckerhoff, Matthew D. ....New York, NY
Brinckerhoff, Nelson F.
North Kingstown, RI
Brinckerhoff, Philip G. ....Chicago, IL
Brinckerhoff, Richard L. ....Stamford, CT
Brinckloe, William B., Jr.
Costa Mesa, CA
Brinckman, Douglas E. ....Christiansburg, VA
Brinckman, Jeff P. ....Prairie du Chien, WI
Brinckman, John M. ....La Crosse, WI
Brinckman Law Office, S.C.
Prairie du Chien, WI
Brincks, Lon J. ....Kansas City, MO
Brincks, Michael T.
General Services Administration, Office of Regional Counsel, GV
Brind, David H. ....Geneva, NY
Brind, Ira ....Philadelphia, PA
Brindell, James R. ....West Palm Beach, FL
Brindisi, Louis T. ....Utica, NY
Brindisi, Louis T., & Anthony A. Murad, Law Offices of ....Utica, NY
Brindisi, Nicholas S. ....Clifton, NJ
Brindisi, Nicholas S., P.C. ....Clifton, NJ
Brindisi, Richard M. ....Tampa, FL
Brindisi, Thomas J. ....Los Angeles, CA
Brindle, Alec W. ....Seattle, WA
Brindle, Alec W., Jr. ....Seattle, WA
Brindle, Garrett W. ....Philadelphia, PA
Brindle, Judith A. ....Nassau, NY
Brindle, Sheryl Lee ....Norfolk, VA
Brindle, Theodore M. ....Portland, OR
Brindle, Thomas J. ....Oakland, CA
Brindley, Brent M. ....St. George, UT
Brindley, James A. ....Milwaukee, WI
Brindley, Joseph H. ....Westlake Village, CA
Brindley, Katharine Witter ....Seattle, WA
Brindley, R. Lane ....Austin, TX
Brindley, Ralph J. ....Seattle, WA
Brindza, Robert A., II ....Cleveland, OH
Brindze, Paul L. ....Los Angeles, CA
Brine, Aubrey C. ....Beverly, MA
Brine, Bridget A. ....Duluth, MN
Brine, Gerald J. ....Brainerd, MN
Crosslake, MN
Brine, Philip A., Jr. ....Marblehead, MA
Brine, Russell A. ....Olympia, WA
Brinen, Jeffrey S. ....Denver, CO
Briner, Drew ....Tahoe City, CA
Briner, Fred E. ....Benton, AR
Briner, Fred E., P.A. ....Benton, AR
Briner, Karl D. ....Waterloo, IA
Brines, Teresa ....Lakewood, CO
Briney, Bruce R. ....Janesville, WI
Briney & Foret ....Lafayette, LA
Briney, Laurence D. ....Spokane, WA
Briney, Michael D. ....Portland, OR
Briney, Patrick J. ....Lafayette, LA
Briney, Roger A. ....Atlanta, GA
Briney and Welborn ....Bloomfield, MO
Bring, Dale V. ....Columbus, OH
Bring, Jason E. ....Jonesboro, GA
Bring, Karl E. ....Fort Collins, CO
Bring, Mark B. ....Grand Forks, ND
Bring, Martin R. ....New York, NY
Bring, Murray H. ....New York, NY
Bring, Robert D. ....New York, NY
Bringard, Jerry D. ....Dearborn, MI
Bringard, Kara L. ....Irvine, CA
Bringardner, Bruce W. ....Dallas, TX
Bringardner, Daniel E. ....Columbus, OH
Bringardner, Richard D. ....Columbus, OH
Bringas, Martha C. ....Los Angeles, CA
Bringer, Paul A. ....Bloomfield Hills, MI
Bringer, Rachel L. ....Palmyra, MO
Bringewatt, Kevin M. ....Charlotte, NC
Bringgold, Blake D. ....Tampa, FL
Bringgold, Donald R. ....Newport Beach, CA
Bringle, Douglas Scott ....Winter Park, FL
Bringle, Kathryn L. ....Winston-Salem, NC
Bringman, Joseph E. ....Seattle, WA
Bringman, William P., Co., L.P.A.
Fredericktown, OH
Bringman, William Paul ....Fredericktown, OH
Bringuel, Kevin M. ....Los Angeles, CA
Bringus, Diane M. ....Lawrence, KS
Brinich, Ken ....Bend, OR

Brister, James L., P.L.L.C., Law Offices of ... Universal City, TX
Brister, John W. ... Boston, MA
Brister, Kenneth A. ... Lake Providence, LA
Brister, Laurie R. ... Lake Providence, LA
Brister, LaVerne M. ... Owego, NY
Brister, Richard C. ... Houston, TX
Brister, Scott A. ... Houston, TX
Brister & Zandrow, L.L.P. ... Boston, MA
Bristley, Calvin W., Jr. ... Fremont, OH
Bristol, Alan M. ... Corsicana, TX
Bristol, Craig J. ... San Jose, CA
Bristol, D. Ian ... Miami, FL
Bristol, Daniel D. ... Metairie, LA
Bristol, David C. ... Litchfield, CT
Bristol, David G. ... Portland, OR
Bristol, David J. ... Treasury Department, Office of Thrift Supervision, GV
Bristol, Dawn L. ... New York, NY
Bristol, Douglas ... Chicago, IL
Bristol, Fred R. ... San Antonio, TX
Bristol, Gary Lee ... New York, NY
Bristol, George ... Harrisburg, PA
Bristol, Hope Tieman ... Fort Lauderdale, FL
Bristol, James B. ... Nashville, TN
Bristol, James D. ... Waukon, IA
Bristol, Jonathan S. ... Morristown, NJ
Bristol, Kappy K., Law Offices of ... Los Angeles, CA
Bristol, Kathleen M. ... South Burlington, VT
Bristol, Lauren B. ... Mineola, NY
Bristol, Lynn A. ... Washington, DC
Bristol, Murray L. ... Tulsa, OK
Bristol, Norman ... Kalamazoo, MI
Bristol, Patrick S. ... Hartford, CT
Bristol, Robert Matthew ... Roswell, NM
Bristol, Steven P. ... Brunswick, GA
Bristol, Valarie S. ... Austin, TX
Bristol, William H. ... Rochester, NY
Bristoll, B. Gene ... Victorville, CA
Bristor, Katherine M. ... New York, NY
Bristow, Albert C. ... Haddonfield, NJ
Bristow, B. Daryl ... Houston, TX
Bristow, Bill W. ... Jonesboro, AR
Bristow & Coyne ... Providence, RI
Bristow, David T. ... Los Angeles, CA
Bristow, Edgar Thomas ... Lyons, CO
Bristow, Herbert S. ... Waco, TX
Bristow, Kevin J. ... Providence, RI
Bristow, Laurel K. ... Providence, RI
Bristow, Mary F. ... Manchester, TN
Bristow, Stephen E. ... Graham, TX
Bristow, Susan Lee ... Portland, OR
Bristow, Walter J., Jr. ... Columbia, SC
Bristow, Walter S., III ... Portland, OR
Bristow, Walter S., III, P.C. ... Portland, OR
Bristow, William C. ... Tupelo, MS
Bristow, William M. ... Marietta, GA
Britain Flynn, P.S. ... Bellingham, WA
Britain, Howard W. ... Tyler, TX
Britain, James E. ... Bellingham, WA
Britain, Timothy E. ... Concord, NH
Britan, Scott S. ... Miami, FL
Britcher, E. Drew ... Morristown, NJ
Britchkow, Lisa M. ... Berwyn, PA
Brite and Butler ... Hardinsburg, KY
Brite, J. Taylor ... Pleasanton, TX
Brite, Paul Clifford ... Newburgh, NY
Brite, Thomas C. ... Hardinsburg, KY
Britell, Peter S. ... New York, NY
Britnell, Vonda L. ... Columbiana, AL
Britner, Paul ... Office of Personnel Management, Compensation Division, GV
Brito, Alejandro ... Miami, FL
Brito, Carlos D. ... New Bedford, MA
Brito, Eduardo A. ... Los Angeles, CA
Brito, Leonardo F. ... Miami, FL
Brito, Michael J. ... Plano, TX
Brito, Patricia Ann ... Houston, TX
Brito, Tonya L. ... Tempe, AZ
Brito, Wanda M. ... Fall River, MA
Briton, Roger H. ... Woodbury, NY
Britos, Cesar R. ... Portland, ME
Britschge, Robert S. ... Hamilton, NJ
Britschgi, Richard F. ... Newport Beach, CA
Britson, Dennis N. ... Des Moines, IA
Britson, Richard E. ... Pensacola Beach, FL
Britt, Amy E. ... Anaheim, CA
Britt, Amy M. ... Davenport, IA
Britt, Anne M. ... Newark, NJ
Britt, Anthony ... Tampa, FL
Britt, B A, Jr. ... Texarkana, TX
Britt & Britt, PLLC ... Lumberton, NC
Pinehurst, NC
Britt, Burl R., III ... Astoria, NY
Britt, Campbell, Nagel & Sproat ... Columbus, OH
Britt, Carl L., Jr. ... Fayetteville, NC
Britt, Charles W. ... Alvin, TX
Britt, Christopher Dorian ... Savannah, GA
Britt, Clifford ... Winston-Salem, NC
Britt, Cynthia E. ... Chattanooga, TN
Britt, David B. ... Waco, TX
Britt, David M. ... Raleigh, NC
Britt, Dennis J. ... Davenport, IA
Britt, Dennis J. ... Everett, WA
Britt, Dewey D. ... Odessa, TX
Britt, Diane J. ... Lansing, MI
Britt, Donald E., Jr. ... Wilmington, NC
Britt, Donald S. ... Sacramento, CA
Britt, Dudley H., Jr. ... Columbia, SC
Britt, Earl T. ... Philadelphia, PA
Britt, Elaine C. ... Trenton, NJ
Britt, Evander M., III ... Lumberton, NC
Britt, George Everett ... Austin, TX
Britt • Getty Law Offices ... Cumberland, MD

Britt & Gnapp, P.C. ... Richmond, VA
Britt, Hankins, Schaible & Moughan ... Philadelphia, PA
Plymouth Meeting, PA
Britt, J. Stephen ... McLean, VA
Britt, James C., Jr. ... Columbus, OH
Britt, James J., Jr. ... Princeton, NJ
Britt, James W. ... Denver, CO
Britt, James W. ... Eugene, OR
Britt, James W., P.C. ... Eugene, OR
Britt, Jennifer A. ... San Diego, CA
Britt, Jill Starling ... Graham, NC
Britt, Joe Freeman ... Wilmington, NC
Britt, John G. ... Durham, NC
Britt, John K. ... Boston, MA
Britt, John M. ... Tarboro, NC
Britt, John R. ... Hartford, CT
Britt, John Y. ... Securities and Exchange Commission, Division of Corporation Finance, GV
Britt, Jonathan D. ... Morris Plains, NJ
Britt, Joyce E. ... San Francisco, CA
Britt, Kent A. ... Cincinnati, OH
Britt, L. Johnson, III ... Lumberton, NC
Britt Law Firm ... Wilmington, NC
Britt, Lon A. ... Waterloo, IA
Britt, Louis P., III ... Memphis, TN
Britt, Lynn M. ... Fort Lauderdale, FL
Britt, Margurete R. ... Chapel Hill, NC
Britt, Marjorie Payne ... Houston, TX
Britt, Marjorie Payne, P.C. ... Houston, TX
Britt, Michael A. ... Kenner, LA
Britt, Michael C. ... Myrtle Beach, SC
Britt, Patrick S. ... Syracuse, NY
Britt, Paul A., Jr. ... Englewood, CO
Britt, Philip J. ... Syracuse, NY
Britt, Phillip M. ... Kennett, MO
Britt & Riehl, P.C. ... Freehold, NJ
Britt, Robert E. ... St. Louis, MO
Britt, Robert J. T. ... Hartford, CT
Britt, Ronald J. ... Sacramento, CA
Britt, Roy F. ... Freehold, NJ
Britt, Sharon R. ... Nashville, NC
Britt, Stephen J. ... Norristown, PA
Britt, Susan Fagen ... Carle Place, NY
Britt, Terrance L. ... Cumberland, MD
Britt, Tobin Lee ... Elgin, IA
Britt, Veda L. ... Chicago, IL
Britt, W. Derrick ... Palo Alto, CA
Britt, W. Earl ... Raleigh, NC
Britt, Wade H., III ... Columbia, SC
Britt, Walt M., (P.C.) ... Buford, GA
Britt, Walter T. ... Clinton, NC
Britt, Warren H. ... Richmond, VA
Britt, William C. ... Minneapolis, MN
Britt, William Dean ... Houston, TX
Britt, William J. ... Southport, CT
Britt, William Ross ... Smithfield, NC
Britt, William S. ... Lumberton, NC
Pinehurst, NC
Britt, William S. ... Salt Lake City, UT
Brittain, Brian K. ... Cleveland, OH
Brittain, Carol A. ... San Francisco, CA
Brittain, Charles M., III ... Fayetteville, NC
Brittain, Clay D., III ... Myrtle Beach, SC
Brittain, David D., Jr. ... Houston, TX
Brittain, David R. ... Tampa, FL
Brittain, Emma Ruth ... Conway, SC
Brittain, Eric M. ... El Paso, TX
Brittain, Gary W. ... Corbin, KY
Brittain, George Robert, II ... Tazewell, VA
Brittain, Greg ... Lavaca, AR
Brittain, Greg, P.A. ... Lavaca, AR
Brittain, Gregory W. ... San Bernardino, CA
Brittain, J. Mark ... Stockbridge, GA
Brittain, Jack O., Sr. ... Natchitoches, LA
Brittain, James D., P.C. ... Taylor, MI
Brittain, James Dale ... Taylor, MI
Brittain, John A. ... Natchitoches, LA
Brittain, John C. ... Hartford, CT
Brittain, John J. ... Elgin, IL
Brittain, John S. ... Philadelphia, PA
Brittain, Kenneth F. ... Anchorage, AK
Brittain, Kerry R. ... Fort Worth, TX
Brittain & Ketcham, P.C. ... Elgin, IL
Brittain, Lurline G. ... Tucson, AZ
Brittain, Max G., Jr. ... Chicago, IL
Brittain, Michael E. ... Cleveland, OH
Brittain, Paige ... Amarillo, TX
Brittain & Pentlarge ... Anchorage, AK
Brittain, Richard L. ... Atlanta, GA
Brittain, Robert R., Jr. ... Wilkes-Barre, PA
Brittain, Ronald J. ... Eaton Rapids, MI
Brittain Sledz Morris & Slovak, A Professional Corporation ... Chicago, IL
Brittain, Steve ... Austin, TX
Brittain, Steven T. ... Honolulu, HI
Brittain & Sylvester ... Natchitoches, LA
Brittain, T. Daniel ... Dallas, TX
Brittain, Thomas C. ... Conway, SC
Myrtle Beach, SC
Brittain, Thomas M., Jr. ... Hendersonville, NC
Brittain, Vicki K. ... San Marcos, TX
Brittain, William H., II ... Montgomery, AL
Brittan, Jillisa ... Chicago, IL
Brittan, William C. ... Denver, CO
Britten, Gary W. ... Spring Arbor, MI
Britten, Gordon W. ... Jackson, MI
Britten, John W. ... Schenectady, NY
Britten, Lacy D. ... Bedford, TX
Britten Law Firm, The ... Bedford, TX
Brittenham, Dann R. ... Gaithersburg, MD
Brittenham, David A. ... New York, NY
Brittenham, Donald A., Jr. ... Arlington, VA
Brittenham, Harry M. ... Los Angeles, CA
Brittenham, Raymond L. ... New York, NY
Brittenum, Dedrick, Jr. ... Memphis, TN
Brittian, R. Bradford ... Knoxville, TN

Brittigan, Robert L. ... Department of Defense, Defense Legal Services Agency, GV
Brittin, Alexander J. ... Washington, DC
Brittin, Jocelyn West ... McLean, VA
Brittin, Michael D. ... Washington, DC
Brittin, Peter B. ... Montpelier, VT
Brittin, W. Don, Jr. ... Des Moines, IA
Brittingham, Debra S. ... Department of Commerce, Patent and Trademark Office, GV
Brittingham, Francis M. ... Danville, IL
Brittingham, Galen Lee, P.C. ... Tulsa, OK
Brittingham, J. David ... Cincinnati, OH
Brittingham, John M. ... Nashville, TN
Brittingham, Lyvonne ... San Antonio, TX
Brittingham, Mark A. ... St. Louis, MO
Brittingham, Michael T. ... Raleigh, NC
Columbia, SC
Brittingham & Sadler ... Danville, IL
Brittingham, Smith R., III ... Oberlin, OH
Brittingham, Smith R., IV ... United States International Trade Commission, Office of Unfair Import Investigations, GV
Brittingham, S. R., Jr. ... Virginia Beach, VA
Brittle, Aubrey B. ... Richmond, VA
Brittle, Timothy N. ... Portland, OR
Brittman, Shelley L. ... San Francisco, CA
Brittner, Eldon W. ... Walnut Creek, CA
Britto, Gregory N. ... Fairfax, VA
Britton, A. Paul ... Rochester, NY
Britton, Andrew J. ... Venice, FL
Britton, Andrew J., P.A. ... Venice, FL
Britton, Anita M. ... Lexington, KY
Britton, Ann H. ... Wilmington, DE
Britton & Bossenbroek, P.C. ... Muskegon, MI
Britton, Brent C.J. ... San Francisco, CA
Britton, Brigid Conybeare ... Seattle, WA
Britton, Burnett ... San Francisco, CA
Britton, Christopher Q. ... San Diego, CA
Britton, Clifton J. ... Warrensburg, MO
Britton, Daniel ... Brewton, AL
Britton, Daniel E. ... Brookline, MA
Britton, David W., Jr. ... Baltimore, MD
Britton, Diane ... New York, NY
Britton, Douglas A. ... Norfolk, VA
Britton, Douglas F ... Portland, ME
Britton and Douglas, P.C. ... Brookline, MA
Britton, Edward C. ... Washington, DC
Britton, Elaine ... Lynchburg, VA
Britton, Eric D. ... Toledo, OH
Britton, G. Dale ... Los Angeles, CA
San Diego, CA
Britton, Gary C. ... Santa Cruz, CA
Britton, Gary T. ... Muskegon, MI
Britton, Glen H. ... Columbus, OH
Britton, Gray and Hill, P.C. ... Oklahoma City, OK
Britton, Harold F. ... Chicago, IL
Britton, Homer C. ... Chicago, IL
Britton, Homer C., Ltd. ... Chicago, IL
Britton, I. Ripon, Jr. ... Birmingham, AL
Britton, Jack B. ... St. Maries, ID
Britton, James E. ... Oklahoma City, OK
Britton, Jeanne M. ... Trenton, NJ
Britton, John E. ... Cleveland, OH
Britton, John E. ... Erie, PA
Britton, John H. ... Fayetteville, NC
Britton, John J. ... Knoxville, TN
Britton, John M. ... Phenix City, AL
Britton, John P. ... Sumter, SC
Britton, Joseph A. ... Euclid, OH
Britton, Joseph S. ... Bristol, PA
Langhorne, PA
Britton, Joyce S. ... Chicago, IL
Britton, Kathryn Howe ... Aptos, CA
Britton, Kathy M. ... Baltimore, MD
Britton, Keith L. ... New York, NY
Britton, Larry J. ... Milwaukee, WI
Britton Law Firm, The, LLC ... Sumter, SC
Britton, Layne Leslie ... Los Angeles, CA
Britton, Louis F. ... Terre Haute, IN
Britton, Mark D. ... St. Paul, MN
Britton, Mark S. ... Seattle, WA
Britton, Mary E. ... Washington, DC
Britton, Matthew J. ... Fairfax, VA
Britton, Michael ... Philadelphia, PA
Britton, Michael S. ... Dallas, TX
Britton, Patricia Ann ... Magna, UT
Britton, Patricia R. ... Atlanta, GA
Britton, Raymond L. ... Houston, TX
Britton, Rebecca J. ... Fayetteville, NC
Britton, Robert M. ... Philadelphia, PA
Britton, Ronald P. ... Milwaukee, WI
Britton, Ronald P., S.C., Law Office of ... Milwaukee, WI
Britton, Samuel P. ... Torrance, CA
Britton, Scott R. ... Chicago, IL
Britton, Sean M. ... Southfield, MI
Britton, Shawn M. ... Alameda, CA
Britton Silberman & Cervantez LLP ... San Francisco, CA
Britton, Susan G. ... New York, NY
Britton, Thomas C. ... Carbondale, IL
Britton, Valeda J. ... Boston, MA
Britton, William L. ... Olympia, WA
Britton, William R., Jr. ... Cape Elizabeth, ME
Britton-Mehlisch, Scott A. ... Independence, MO
Britts, George M. ... Charlotte, NC
Britts, Kimberly A. ... Sherman Oaks, CA
Britvan, Aaron ... Woodbury, NY
Britvan, Jerrold ... Southfield, MI
Britvan, Lawrence P. ... New York, NY
Britwar, Marilyn D. ... Atlanta, GA
Britz, Harland M. ... Toledo, OH
Britz, Juliene A. ... Westmont, IL
Britz, Robert J. ... Elburn, IL

Britz, Stephen J. ... Annapolis, MD
Britz & Zemmelman ... Toledo, OH
Britzman, Steven J. ... Brookings, SD
Britzmann, Brad ... Seattle, WA
Brivanlou, Margaret Bolce ... New York, NY
Brix, Cheri L. ... Minneapolis, MN
Brixius, Frank J. ... Minneapolis, MN
Brixius, Frank J. ("Chip"), Jr. ... Wayzata, MN
Brizan, Glena T. ... Baltimore, MD
Brizee, Clarence W. ... Tucson, AZ
Brizee, Jennifer Kauth ... Twin Falls, ID
Brizek, Ida Rose ... Hackensack, NJ
Brizel, Michael A. ... Pleasantville, NY
Brizel, Steven I. ... New York, NY
Brizendine, Austin W., Jr. ... Columbia, MD
Brizendine, James D. ... Oklahoma City, OK
Brizendine, Paul A. ... Louisville, KY
Brizendine, Richard A. ... Long Beach, CA
Brizendine, Richard C. ... Long Beach, CA
Brizendine, Robert E. ... Atlanta, GA
Brizendine, Victor W., III ... Shelbyville, KY
Brizgys, Vincent L. ... Chicago, IL
Brizius, Charles O. ... Reeseville, WI
Brizuela, M. Caroline ... St. Charles, IL
Brizzee, Bart W. ... Riverside, CA
San Bernardino, CA
Brizzi, Francis J., Jr. ... Department Of Veterans Affairs, Office of the General Counsel, GV
Brizzolara, Anthony M. ... Cleveland, OH
Brizzolara, Charles A. ... Chicago, IL
Brizzolara, Christopher ... Los Angeles, CA
Brizzolara, L. E. (Ted), III ... Dallas, TX
Brizzolara, Margaret M. ... Washington, DC
Huntington, WV
Brizzolara, Paul T. ... Amelia, OH
Brkich, Milan ... Sarasota, FL
Brkich, Samuel T. ... Chicago, IL
Brkich, Susan A. ... San Francisco, CA
Brnilovich, David ... Phoenix, AZ
Brnovich, Mark ... Phoenix, AZ
Bro, Brian E. ... Houston, TX
Bro, Ruth Hill ... Chicago, IL
Bro, Theodore J. ... Los Angeles, CA
Broach, Judith P. ... New York, NY
Broach, Kent M. ... Indianapolis, IN
Broach, Robert E. ... Jacksonville, FL
Broach, Roger H. ... Houston, TX
Broach & Stulberg, LLP ... New York, NY
Broache, Pamela Thomas ... Baltimore, MD
Broad, Alan H., P.C., Law Offices ... Grosse Pointe Woods, MI
Broad, Alan Hugh ... Grosse Pointe Woods, MI
Broad, Andrea R. ... Philadelphia, PA
Broad, Barry ... Sacramento, CA
Broad, Brian W. ... Boca Raton, FL
Broad, Brian W., P.A. ... Boca Raton, FL
Broad and Cassel ... Boca Raton, FL
Fort Lauderdale, FL
Miami, FL
Orlando, FL
Tallahassee, FL
Tampa, FL
West Palm Beach, FL
Broad, Donald K. ... Indianapolis, IN
Broad, Henry S. ... Princeton, NJ
Broad, John W. ... San Francisco, CA
Broad, Matthew R. ... Boise, ID
Broad, Michael ... San Leandro, CA
Broad, Norman ... Miami, FL
Broad, Robert L., Jr. ... Research Triangle Park, NC
Broad, Sally J. ... Buffalo, NY
Broad, Shepard ... Miami, FL
Broad, Stacy L. ... Philadelphia, PA
Broad, Thos. K. ... Dallas, TX
Broad, William L. ... Syracuse, NY
Broadaway, Brad ... Paragould, AR
Broadaway, Mary Lile ... Paragould, AR
Broadaway, Randy D. ... Silver Creek, GA
Broadbear, Michael W. ... Atlanta, GA
Broadbelt, Evan W. ... Allenwood, NJ
Broadbelt, Patricia ... Brooklyn, NY
Broadbelt, Robert B. ... Beverly Hills, CA
Broadbent, Amy S. ... Louisville, KY
Broadbent, Berne S. ... Salt Lake City, UT
Broadbent, Cynthia A. ... Santa Rosa, CA
Broadbent, David K. ... Salt Lake City, UT
Broadbent, Howard W. ... Cleveland, OH
Broadbent, Peter E., Jr. ... Richmond, VA
Broadbent, Phillip E. ... Chandler, AZ
Broadbent, Rebecca A. ... Boise, ID
Broadbent, William W. ... Maplewood, NJ
Broaddus, Andrew L. ... Westbrook, ME
Broaddus, Arthur B. ... Ukiah, CA
Broaddus, Colleen M. ... Seattle, WA
Broaddus & Ferrucci ... Westbrook, ME
Broaddus, Francis C., Jr. ... El Paso, TX
Broaddus, Francis C., Jr., P.C. ... El Paso, TX
Broaddus, J. Morgan, III ... El Paso, TX
Broaddus, John McN. ... Washington, DC
Broaddus, Margaret Cuthbert ... Petersburg, VA
Broaddus, Mark ... Chicago, IL
Broaddus, Marla ... Austin, TX
Broaddus, Mary Lane (Chapman) ... El Prado, NM
Broaddus, Michael D. ... Seattle, WA
Broaddus, T. Warner R. ... Carlsbad, CA
Broaddus, William G. ... Richmond, VA
Broaddus, W. R., III ... Martinsville, VA
Broadfield, Donald E., Jr. ... Washington, DC
Broadfoot, Alexander L. ... Phoenix, AZ
Broadfoot, Cynthia L. ... Burlington, VT
Broadfoot, Frederick M. ... Red Bank, NJ

Broda, Samuel ....Department of Commerce, Patent and Trademark Office, GV
Brodack, Michael A. ....New York, NY
Brodarick, Michael V. ....Louisville, KY
Brodbeck, Alan L. ....O'Neill, NE
Brodbeck, Charles R. ....Pittsburgh, PA
Brodbeck, Donald E. ....Riviera Beach, FL
Brodbeck, Richard L. ....Springfield, MO
Brodbeck, Sally Drews ....Lorain, OH
Brodbeck, Susan C. ....Chatham, NJ
Brodbeck, William P. ....Sacramento, CA
Brodbeck, William P. ....Woodland Hills, CA
Brodbine, Anju Chandra ....Cleveland, OH
Brodbine, John J. ....Boston, MA
Brodbine, Michael S. ....Southfield, MI
Brodd, Joel W. ....Baldwin, WI
Brodd, Mary J. ....Bellevue, WA
Brode, David M. ....Ravenna, OH
Brode, George, Jr. ....Chicago, IL
Brode, George, Jr., Ltd. ....Chicago, IL
Brode, Kevin W. ....Pittsburgh, PA
Brode, Marvin J. ....Memphis, TN
Brode, Rick P. ....Southfield, MI
Brodegaard, Robert F. ....New York, NY
Brodehl, Kevin R. ....San Leandro, CA
Brodek, Ann Hinke ....Racine, WI
Brodek, Gregory A. ....Augusta, ME
Bangor, ME
Brodek, Jeffrey R. ....Racine, WI
Brodek, Richard C. ....Racine, WI
Brodell, A. Peter ....Richmond, VA
Broden, Broden & Walker ......Devils Lake, ND
Broden, Douglas L. ....Devils Lake, ND
Broden, F. Clinton ....Dallas, TX
Broden, John E. ....South Bend, IN
Broden, Leo ....Devils Lake, ND
Broden, Thomas, Jr. ....Notre Dame, IN
Broden, Willard Cannell ....Bradenton, FL
Broder, Aaron J. ....New York, NY
Broder, Andrew J. ....Bingham Farms, MI
Broder, Bernard J., III ....Caribou, ME
Broder, Betsy ....Federal Trade Commission, Bureau of Consumer Protection, GV
Broder & Butts, LLP ....Colchester, CT
Broder, Douglas F. ....New York, NY
Broder, Elena N. ....Washington, DC
Broder, Eric J. ....New York, NY
Broder, Gary L. ....Waterbury, CT
Broder, Gerald D. ....New York, NY
Broder, H. Neil ....Livingston, NJ
Broder, Howard K. ....Rochester, NY
Broder, James N. ....Portland, ME
Broder, James P. ....Las Vegas, NV
Broder, Jamie ....Los Angeles, CA
Broder, Jonathan M. ....Philadelphia, PA
Broder, Joseph A. ....Colchester, CT
Broder, Kimberly Janelle ....Atlanta, GA
Broder, Lisa Schatz ....Farmington Hills, MI
Broder, Marcy B. ....Seattle, WA
Broder, Marian C. ....Longmeadow, MA
Broder, Myron ....Morganville, NJ
Broder, Richard P. ....Garden City, NY
Broder, Richard P., P.C. ....Garden City, NY
Broder, Robert M. ....Philadelphia, PA
Broder, Shari B. ....Freeport, ME
Broder, Sherry P. ....Honolulu, HI
Broder, Sherry P., A Law Corporation, Law Office of ....Honolulu, HI
Broder, Stewart A. ....Westborough, MA
Broder, William I. ....East Norwich, NY
Broderick, Bancroft & Goldberg
Boston, MA
Cambridge, MA
Broderick, Brenda N. ....Chicago, IL
Broderick, Brett Michael
Los Angeles, CA
Broderick, Brian C. ....Boston, MA
Broderick, Brian D. ....Southfield, MI
Broderick and Broderick ....Lincoln, ME
Broderick, Camilla L. ....Los Angeles, CA
Broderick, Carole A. ....Philadelphia, PA
Broderick, Carole D. (Parisot)
St. Petersburg, FL
Broderick, Caroline R. ....Boston, MA
Broderick, Catherine A.
Securities and Exchange Commission, Office of the General Counsel, GV
Broderick, Christopher Peter
Los Angeles, CA
Broderick, Daniel P. ....Cambridge, MA
Broderick, David F. ....Bowling Green, KY
Broderick, David F. ....Newark, NJ
Broderick, David J. ....Great Neck, NY
New York, NY
Broderick, Dennis J. ....Cincinnati, OH
Broderick, Desireé M. ....New York, NY
Broderick, Donald J. ....Livonia, MI
Broderick, Edward A. ....Boston, MA
Broderick, Edward F., Jr. ....Morristown, NJ
Broderick, Edward M., III ....Chicago, IL
Broderick, Edwin T. ....New York, NY
Broderick, Francis L. ....Stratham, NH
Broderick, Jack F. ....Davenport, IA
Broderick, James A. ....Madison, WI
Broderick, James A., Jr. ....Los Angeles, CA
Broderick, James H., Jr. ....Los Angeles, CA
Broderick, James M. ....Boston, MA
Broderick, James V. ....Manchester, NH
Broderick, Jill Lanman ....East Burke, VT
Broderick, J.J. ....Charlotte, NC
Broderick, John C. ....Crownsville, MD
Broderick, John Carroll ....Hunt Valley, MD
Broderick, John J. ....Syosset, NY
Broderick, John M. ....Chicago, IL
Broderick, John R.
Rancho Palos Verdes, CA
Broderick, John T., Jr. ....Concord, NH

Broderick, Katherine Shelton
Washington, DC
Broderick, Kevin P. ....Lowell, MA
Broderick, Kieran P. ....Albany, NY
Broderick, Kilian ....Dallas, TX
Broderick, Mark ....Tampa, FL
Broderick, Mark P. ....Waukegan, IL
Broderick, Martha A. ....Lincoln, ME
Broderick, Matthew J. ....Philadelphia, PA
Broderick, Michael F. ....Honolulu, HI
Broderick, Michael, III ....Waterbury, CT
Broderick, Michael L. ....Buffalo, NY
Broderick, Michael P. ....Silver Spring, MD
Broderick, Michael W. ....Peabody, MA
Broderick, Newmark & Grather, A Professional Corporation ....Morristown, NJ
Broderick, Patrick A. ....San Francisco, CA
Broderick, Patrick F. ....Bayside, NY
Broderick, Patrick G. ....New York, NY
Broderick, Patrick J., II ....Norristown, PA
Broderick, Patrick M. ....Santa Rosa, CA
Broderick, Paul E. ....Bluemont, VA
Broderick, Paul W. ....Chicago, IL
Broderick, Peter F. ....New York, NY
Broderick, Peter L. ....Lewiston, NY
Broderick, Peter P. ....Williamsville, NY
Broderick, Peter R. ....San Antonio, TX
Broderick, Phillip R. ....Banning, CA
Broderick, Raymond J. ....Philadelphia, PA
Broderick, Richard H. ....Lincoln, ME
Broderick, Richard H., Jr. ....Lincoln, ME
Broderick, Robert E. ....Ludlow, VT
Broderick, Robert L. ....Belleville, IL
Broderick, Roger J. ....Santa Monica, CA
Broderick, Sherril Elder ....Muskogee, OK
Broderick, Stacy R. ....Green Bay, WI
Broderick, Susan M. ....New York, NY
Broderick, Tamara M. ....Providence, RI
Broderick, Thomas ....Braintree, MA
Broderick, Thomas C. ....Chicago, IL
Broderick, Thomas F. ....Peoria, IL
Broderick, Thomas F. ....Seattle, WA
Broderick, Thomas J., Jr. ....Anderson, IN
Broderick & Thornton
Bowling Green, KY
Broderick, Timothy B. ....Palo Alto, CA
Broderick, Vernon ....New York, NY
Broderick, William A. ....Clarendon Hills, IL
Broderick, William D. ....New York, NY
Broderick, William D. ....Niagara Falls, NY
Broderick, William D., Jr.
Niagara Falls, NY
Broderick, William M. ....New York, NY
Brodermann, M. Cristina ....Miami, FL
Broders, John J. ....New Orleans, LA
Broders, Laura Comiskey ....New Orleans, LA
Brodersen, Charles E. ....Lanham, MD
Brodersen, Daniel N. ....Orlando, FL
Brodersen, Daniel N., P.A. ....Orlando, FL
Brodersen, Randall E. ....Westminster, CO
Brodersen, Thomas C. ....Visalia, CA
Broderson, G. Sidnor ....Franklin, KY
Brodeur, Donald E. ....Sacramento, CA
Brodeur, Lawrence Albert ....Worcester, MA
Brodeur, Margaret R. ....Hartford, CT
Brodeur, Mark C. ....Dallas, TX
Brodeur, Paul E. ....Coventry, RI
Brodeur & Reina, P.C. ....Dallas, TX
Brodeur, Richard J., P.A. ....Sanibel, FL
Brodeur, Richard John ....Sanibel, FL
Brodeur-McGan, Lisa ....Springfield, MA
Brodey, Jami L. ....Chicago, IL
Brodey, Jay Michael ....Indianapolis, IN
Brodey, Jeffrey Ronald ....Beverly Hills, CA
Brodey, Jessica M. ....Washington, DC
Brodey & Price ....Beverly Hills, CA
Brodey, Ronald B., (P.C.) ....Indianapolis, IN
Brodhead, Ben C. ....Atlanta, GA
Brodhead, Cynthia ....Berlin, CT
Brodhead, David C. ....New York, NY
Brodhead, Peter J. ....Cleveland, OH
Brodhead, Richard J. ....Lebanon, TN
Brodhead, William M. ....Bloomfield Hills, MI
Brodich, Nicholas ....Concord, NH
Brodie, Alan R. ....Chicago, IL
Brodie, Brad A. ....Aiken, SC
Brodie, Cathryn L. ....Jackson, WY
Brodie, David H. ....Boca Raton, FL
Brodie, David L. ....San Diego, CA
Brodie, Donald W. ....Eugene, OR
Brodie, Edward F. ....Ventura, CA
Brodie, Ellen E. ....Rancho Cucamonga, CA
Brodie, Eric L. ....Boston, MA
Brodie, Frederick A. ....New York, NY
Brodie, Jean A. ....Kalamazoo, MI
Brodie, Jordan ....Brooklyn, NY
Brodie, Julie R. ....Alexandria, VA
Brodie, Katherine D. ....Washington, DC
Brodie, Keith J. ....Grand Rapids, MI
Brodie, Lawrence P. ....Stuart, FL
Brodie, Maia ....St. Louis, MO
Brodie, Margo K. ....New York, NY
Brodie, Martha J. ....Sunrise, FL
Brodie & Massey Lawyers, P.A.
Aiken, SC
Brodie, Michael ....Philadelphia, PA
Brodie, Michael A. ....Los Angeles, CA
Brodie, Michael J. ....Oakland, CA
Brodie, Nancy F. ....New York, NY
Brodie & Pawluc ....Stuart, FL
Brodie, Ralph G., Ltd. ....Little Rock, AR
Brodie, Robert B. ....Jackson, WY
Brodie, Ronald ....Miami Beach, FL
Brodie, Sidney Z. ....Fort Lauderdale, FL
Brodie, Sidney Z. ....Miami, FL
Miami, FL
Brodie, Stephen D. ....New York, NY
Brodie, Steven J. ....Miami, FL

Brodie, Steven S. ....Sherman Oaks, CA
Brodie, T. Furman ....Florence, SC
Brodie Techner & Rubinsky
Philadelphia, PA
Brodie, Thomas P. ....Englewood Cliffs, NJ
Brodie, Warren H. ....Wellesley, MA
Brodie, Warren H., P.C. ....Wellesley, MA
Brodigan, George D. ....West Hartford, CT
Brodigan, Joseph J. ....Boston, MA
Brodigan, Joseph J., Jr. ....Boston, MA
Brodigan, Michael ....Boston, MA
Brodin, Drake T. ....Fairfax, VA
Brodin, Jeffrey C. ....Phoenix, AZ
Brodin, Mark S. ....Newton, MA
Brodin, Robert A. ....St. Paul, MN
Brodin, Rodney G. ....Duluth, MN
Brodinsky, Robin L. ....Owings Mills, MD
Brodish, Joan E. ....Winston-Salem, NC
Brodka, Mark A. ....Los Angeles, CA
Brodkey, Andrew A. ....Tucson, AZ
Brodkey, Bruce H., (P.C.) ....Omaha, NE
Brodkey, Cuddigan, Peebles & Kaplan
Omaha, NE
Brodkey, Hugh A. ....Chicago, IL
Brodkey, Jill Hack ....Milwaukee, WI
Brodkey, Lawrence R. ....Omaha, NE
Brodkin, Alan L., & Associates ......El Toro, CA
Brodkin, Dennis ....Roseland, NJ
Brodkin, Jeffrey A. ....Philadelphia, PA
Brodkin, Karen ....Los Angeles, CA
Brodkin, Martin F. ....Chicago, IL
Brodkin, Richard ....Los Angeles, CA
Brodl, Raymond F. ....Des Plaines, IL
Brodley, Joseph F. ....Boston, MA
Brodlieb, Judith Hanson ....Carlsbad, CA
Brodman, Alan L. ....East Brunswick, NJ
Brodman, Barry ....New York, NY
Brodman, Christopher A. ....Pittsburgh, PA
Brodman, Roger E. ....Phoenix, AZ
Brodman, Steven J. ....Middletown, NJ
Brodnax, Matilda A. ....Washington, DC
Brodnax, Samuel A., Jr. ....New York, NY
Brodnax, William Bland ....North Hills, CA
Brodner, Joseph M. ....St. Charles, IL
Brodney, Fern J. ....Rockville, MD
Brodnick, Andrew D. ....White Plains, NY
Brodnick, Deborah A. ....Juno Beach, FL
Brodnicki, Gretchen A. ....Boston, MA
Brodnik, Martyn T. ....Columbus, OH
Brodnik, Thomas A. ....Indianapolis, IN
Brodovsky, Alan A. ....Sacramento, CA
Brodovsky, William B. ....Sacramento, CA
Brodow, Nora J. ....Paramus, NJ
Brodoway, Barbara A. ....Wilmington, DE
Brodowski, Brian M. ....Pennsauken, NJ
Brodowski, Michael E. ....Huntsville, AL
Brodowski, Michael H. ....Boston, MA
Brodowski, Michael L. ....Irving, TX
Brodrick, Dorothy L. ....Union Gap, WA
Brodrick, R. Brian ....New York, NY
Brodrick, Richard G. ....Stamford, CT
Brodrick, Robert H. ....Garden City, NY
Brodrick, William S. ....Kittery, ME
Brodsky, Aaron S. ....Boulder, CO
Denver, CO
Brodsky, Adam ....New York, NY
Brodsky, Adam J. ....Rockland, MA
Brodsky, Altman & McMahon, L.L.P.
New York, NY
Brodsky, Athena C. ....Boston, MA
Brodsky, Barry Z. ....Santa Monica, CA
Brodsky, Baskin & Miller, Inc.
San Francisco, CA
Brodsky, Charles E. ....Camp Hill, PA
Brodsky, Charles I. ....Marlboro, NJ
Brodsky, Cheryl L. ....Oakland, CA
Brodsky, Craig Stephen ....Washington, DC
Brodsky, Dale L. ....Orinda, CA
Brodsky, David A. ....Chester, NY
Brodsky, David E. ....New York, NY
Brodsky, David M. ....New York, NY
Brodsky, David N. ....Boston, MA
Brodsky, Deborah M. ....Farmington, MI
Brodsky, Dennis A. ....Troy, MI
Brodsky, Dmitry D. ....Los Angeles, CA
Brodsky, Donald W. ....Houston, TX
Brodsky, Edward ....New York, NY
Brodsky, Ethan M. ....Fort Lee, NJ
Brodsky, Eugene A. ....San Francisco, CA
Brodsky, Felice A. ....Lockport, NY
Brodsky, Grace L. ....New York, NY
Brodsky, Greenblatt & Renehan, Chartered
Gaithersburg, MD
Rockville, MD
Brodsky, Harry E. ....Huntingdon Valley, PA
Brodsky, Herbert E. ....Richmond, VA
Brodsky, Irvin J. ....Towson, MD
Brodsky, Irving ....Byram, CT
Brodsky, Irving ....Providence, RI
Brodsky, Irwin A. ....New York, NY
Brodsky, Jackson ....Gaithersburg, MD
Brodsky, James A. ....Washington, DC
Brodsky, Jamie ....Los Angeles, CA
Brodsky, Jason Lawrence ....Cherry Hill, NJ
Allentown, PA
Bala Cynwyd, PA
Philadelphia, PA
Brodsky, Jeffrey H. ....Chicago, IL
Brodsky, Jeffrey L. ....Huntington Woods, MI
Brodsky, Jerry ....Huntingdon, PA
Brodsky, Jerry Peter
Fort Lauderdale, FL
Brodsky, Joan P. ....Philadelphia, PA
Brodsky, Jodi S. ....Roseland, NJ
Brodsky, Joel A. ....Chicago, IL
Brodsky, Joel A. ....Chicago, IL
Brodsky, Judith T. ....Brooklyn, NY
Brodsky, Julie M. ....Sherman Oaks, CA

Brodsky, Lawrence A. ....Atlantic City, NJ
Brodsky, Lawrence B. ....Chicago, IL
Brodsky, Leonard ....Brooklyn, NY
Brodsky, Lisa J. ....Chicago, IL
Brodsky, Marc Seewald ....New York, NY
Brodsky, Margaret Stone ....Miami, FL
Brodsky, Mark ....St. Louis, MO
Brodsky, Mark W. ....West Hartford, CT
Brodsky, Marshall D., Law Office of
Denver, CO
Brodsky, Michael P. ....Everett, WA
Brodsky, Neal P. ....Norfolk, VA
Brodsky, Neil ....Lakewood, NJ
Brodsky, Neil L. ....Boston, MA
Providence, RI
Brodsky, Nina I. ....New York, NY
Brodsky & Peck ....Mamaroneck, NY
Brodsky, Philip R. ....Cleveland, OH
Brodsky, Reed Michael ....Washington, DC
Brodsky, Rhonda L. ....Atlanta, GA
Brodsky, Richard E. ....Miami, FL
Brodsky, Richard E., P.A. ....Miami, FL
Brodsky, Rick ....Ocean Township, NJ
Brodsky, Robert A. ....Mamaroneck, NY
Brodsky, Ronald D. ....Long Beach, CA
Brodsky, Samuel ....New York, NY
Brodsky & Smith, LLC ....Cherry Hill, NJ
Allentown, PA
Bala Cynwyd, PA
Philadelphia, PA
Brodsky, Stacy R. ....West Bloomfield, MI
Brodsky, Stephen ....New York, NY
Brodsky, Stephen R. ....San Diego, CA
Brodsky, Steven ....Department of Justice, Antitrust Division, GV
Brodsky, Valerie J. ....Norfolk, VA
Brodsky, William M. ....New York, NY
Brodt, Charles E. ....Edmond, OK
Brodt, David I. ....Palm Beach, FL
Brodt, Eric ....Indianapolis, IN
Brodt, William F., Jr. ....Bethlehem, PA
Brodtmann, James W. ....Chalmette, LA
Brody, Aaron L. ....New York, NY
Brody, Alan J. ....Woodbridge, NJ
Brody, Alan J. ....New York, NY
Brody, Allen S. ....Palm Springs, CA
Brody, Allison A. ....Jacksonville, FL
Brody, Alton A., Jr. ....Modesto, CA
Brody, Alvan ....Boston, MA
Brody, Alvin J. ....Taunton, MA
Brody, Anita B. ....Philadelphia, PA
Brody, Arthur ....Los Angeles, CA
Brody, Barry L. ....Phoenix, AZ
Brody, Barry L., P.C. ....Phoenix, AZ
Brody, Barry T. ....Lincolnwood, IL
Brody, Bernard B. ....Wilmette, IL
Brody, Betty ....New Orleans, LA
Brody & Brody, P.A. ....Miami, FL
Brody, Burton H. ....East Hanover, NJ
Brody, Carol R. ....Lincolnshire, IL
Brody, Christopher W. ....Washington, DC
Brody, Cynthia I. ....Detroit, MI
Brody, David A. ....Washington, DC
Brody, David A. ....Buffalo, NY
Brody, David E. ....Denver, CO
Brody, David H. ....Washington, DC
Brody, David J. ....Lexington, MA
Brody, David R. ....New York, NY
Brody, David V. ....Trenton, NJ
Brody, David W. ....La Jolla, CA
Brody, Denis ....Jericho, NY
Brody, Elizabeth S. ....Roselle, NJ
Brody, Ellen Seiler ....New York, NY
Brody, Evelyn ....Chicago, IL
Brody Fabiani & Cohen ....New York, NY
Brody, Fred M. ....Chicago, IL
Brody, Frederic S. ....Stamford, CT
Brody, Gerald J. ....Bethesda, MD
Brody, Gore & Fineberg, Ltd. ....Chicago, IL
Brody, Hardoon, Perkins & Kesten
Boston, MA
Brody, Harold M. ....Los Angeles, CA
Brody, Harry P. ....Sarasota, FL
Brody, Harry, P.A. ....Sarasota, FL
Brody, Howard P. ....Los Angeles, CA
Brody, J. Kenneth ....Portland, OR
Brody, Jacobs & FitzGerald ....Boston, MA
Brody, James P. ....Milwaukee, WI
Brody, Jamie A. ....Phoenix, AZ
Brody, Jan Alan ....Roseland, NJ
Brody, Jane L. ....Livingston, NJ
Brody, Janet ....San Francisco, CA
Brody, Jay Howard ....Farmington Hills, MI
Brody, Jay Howard, P.C.
Farmington Hills, MI
Brody, Jeffrey A. ....Chicago, IL
Brody, Jeffrey M. ....Kingston, NY
Brody, Jeffrey S. ....Boston, MA
Brody, Jerry A. ....Rosemead, CA
Brody, Joan P. ....New York, NY
Brody, Jodie Schaffer ....New York, NY
Brody, John P. ....Columbus, OH
Brody, John P., Jr. ....Port Orchard, WA
Brody, Jonathan E. ....Miami, FL
Brody, Joseph D. ....Detroit, MI
Brody, Jules ....New York, NY
Brody, Karen L. ....Denver, CO
Brody, Kenneth E. ....Harrisburg, PA
Brody, Kenneth N. ....Sacramento, CA
Brody, Kevin J. ....Pasadena, CA
Brody, Lauren Reiter ....New York, NY
Brody, Lawrence ....St. Louis, MO
Brody, Leonard ....Venice, FL
Brody, Leslie Ann ....New York, NY
Brody, Leslie Paul ....New York, NY
Brody, Lisa E. ....Philadelphia, PA
Brody, Mark A. ....New York, NY
Brody, Mark Steven ....New York, NY

Brody, Mary Beth ... **Minneapolis, MN**
Brody, Mary P. ... **Boston, MA**
Brody, Michael C. ... Alexandria, VA
Brody, Michael J. ... **Los Angeles, CA**
Brody, Michael L. ... **Chicago, IL**
Brody, Michael P. ... **San Francisco, CA**
Brody, Michael T. ... **Chicago, IL**
Brody, Michael W. ... Merrick, NY
Brody, Miriam Kahan ... Roseland, NJ
Brody, Morton A. ... Bangor, ME
Brody, Myron L. ... **San Francisco, CA**
San Jose, CA
Brody, Nancy S. ... Framingham, MA
Brody, Neal S. ... Richboro, PA
Brody, Neil ... **New York, NY**
Brody, Norman M. ... Minneapolis, MN
Brody, Patricia S. ... **San Francisco, CA**
Brody, Paul I. ... Willimantic, CT
Brody, Peter M. ... **Washington, DC**
Brody, Philip S. ... New York, NY
Brody, Raymond ... **New York, NY**
Brody, Reed K. ... New York, NY
Brody, Richard A. ... **San Francisco, CA**
Brody, Richard E. ... **Boston, MA**
Brody, Richard H. ... **Atlanta, GA**
Brody, Richd. S. ... Boston, MA
Brody, Robert ... West Palm Beach, FL
Brody, Robert E. ... Philadelphia, PA
Brody, Robert S. ... Glendale, CA
Brody, Robert S., (Ltd.) ... Chicago, IL
Brody, Robyn Maddox ... **Twin Falls, ID**
Brody, Ronald S. ... **New York, NY**
Brody, Sara B. ... **San Francisco, CA**
Brody, Scott A. ... Jericho, NY
Brody, Seth O. L. ... **Southport, CT**
Brody, Stanley M. ... Tamarac, FL
Brody, Stanton ... Glencoe, IL
Brody, Stephen D. ... Washington, DC
Brody, Steven G. ... **New York, NY**
Brody, Steven I. ... Skokie, IL
Brody, Steven M. ... Boston, MA
Brody, Stuart H. ... **New York, NY**
Brody, Stuart L. ... **Los Angeles, CA**
Brody, Stuart M. ... Chicago, IL
Brody, Susan L. ... Chicago, IL
Brody, Todd D. ... **New York, NY**
Brody, Todd E. ... **San Francisco, CA**
Brody, Warren ... Springfield, NJ
Brody, Wayne ... **Melville, NY**
Brody, Wilkinson and Ober, P.C.
Bridgeport, CT
Fairfield, CT
Norwalk, CT
Southport, CT
Stamford, CT
Westport, CT
Brody, William G. ... Providence, RI
Brody, William J. ... **Minneapolis, MN**
Brody, William S. ... **Los Angeles, CA**
Brody, Wm. ... Miami Beach, FL
Brodyaga, Elisabeth (Lisa) S. ... Harlingen, TX
Brodzansky, Karl ... Carle Place, NY
Brodzinski, Carrie A. ... **Simsbury, CT**
Brodzinski, Kenneth ... Boston, MA
Broe, Karen-Ann ... Fairfax, VA
Broeckaert, Steven A.
Federal Communications Commission,
Cable Services Bureau, GV
Broeckel, Janet A. ... **Washington, DC**
Broecker, Edwin J. ... **Indianapolis, IN**
Broecker, Howard W. ... Carol Stream, IL
Geneva, IL
Broeder, Gary G. ... Billings, MT
Broege, Neumann & Fischer
Manasquan, NJ
Broege, Peter J. ... Manasquan, NJ
Broege, Robert D. ... **Little Silver, NJ**
Broehl, Margo E. ... Wooster, OH
Broeker, Douglas C. ... **Miami, FL**
Broeking, James M. ... **Chicago, IL**
Broeking, Lawrence E. ... Marion, IL
Broekstra, Scott D. ... **Grand Rapids, MI**
Broeman, Dwight W. ... Cincinnati, OH
Broeman, Peter I. ... **Morristown, NJ**
New York, NY
Broemel, W. Davidson ... **Nashville, TN**
Broemer, W. Fulton ... Houston, TX
Broemer, W. Fulton & Associates, L.C.
Houston, TX
Broemmel, Michael ... Topeka, KS
Broening, James R. ... **Phoenix, AZ**
Broening, Oberg, Woods, Wilson & Cass, P.C. ... **Phoenix, AZ**
Broenniman, Margaret ... Miami, FL
Broeren, P. Robert, Jr. ... **Washington, DC**
Broering-Jacobs, Carolyn ... **Cleveland, OH**
Broerman, Kevin J. ... **Orange, CA**
Broerman, Michael W. ... Oskaloosa, IA
Broers, Lynette Alaine ... Peoria, IL
Broersma, Amy-Hannah ... Los Angeles, CA
Broersma, Dirk P. ... **Los Angeles, CA**
Broesche, Travis C. ... Houston, TX
Broesder, Jason C. ... **Medford, OR**
Broetsky, John G. ... Yonkers, NY
Brof, Julie K. ... **Washington, DC**
Broffman, Scott L. ... Los Angeles, CA
Broffman, Sidney ... Los Angeles, CA
Brofman, Michael D. ... **East Meadow, NY**
Brofman, Robert B. ... New York, NY
Brofman, Susan Bauer ... Carmel, NY
Brofsky, Marc Alan ... Westwood, MA
Brog, Avron I. ... **New York, NY**
Brog, Steven J. ... **Atlantic City, NJ**
Brogan, Allan J. ... Maumee, OH
Brogan, Amy G. ... Shrewsbury, NJ
Brogan, Ann Burke ... **Portsmouth, VA**
Brogan, Barbara J. ... Lexington, NE
Brogan, Beauchamp E. ... Knoxville, TN
Brogan, Brian L. ... Kansas City, MO
Brogan & Brogan, P.C. ... Shrewsbury, NJ
Brogan, Byron J. ... Gainesville, FL
Brogan, Christopher J. ... **Farmington, CT**
Brogan, Dennis D. ... **Downingtown, PA**
Reading, PA
West Chester, PA
Brogan, Doris Del Tosto ... Villanova, PA
Brogan, Edward E. ... Phoenix, AZ
Brogan, Eileen M. ... Lawrence, MA
Brogan, F. William, Jr. ... Weirton, WV
Brogan, Francis B., Jr.
Fort Lauderdale, FL
Brogan, Geo. E. ... Evergreen Park, IL
Brogan, James A. ... Dayton, OH
Brogan, James F. ... Madison, NE
Brogan, James M. ... **Philadelphia, PA**
Brogan, James P. ... **Irvine, CA**
Brogan, Jodi A. ... Lancaster, PA
Brogan, John A. ... **Roseland, NJ**
Brogan, John J. ... Shrewsbury, NJ
Brogan, John J. ... Tenafly, NJ
Brogan, John R. ... York, NE
Brogan, Jonathan W. ... **Portland, ME**
Brogan, Julie A. ... **Boston, MA**
Brogan, Kathleen B. ... **Nashua, NH**
Brogan, Kathryn A. ... **Fort Wayne, IN**
Brogan, Kelly Ann ... **Philadelphia, PA**
Brogan, Kevin H., (P.C.) ... **Los Angeles, CA**
Brogan, Kim R. ... Bonita, CA
Brogan, Laura L. ... Fort Lauderdale, FL
Brogan, Laura L., P.A. ... Fort Lauderdale, FL
Brogan, Leo J. ... Silver Spring, MD
Brogan, Lisa Sopata ... **Chicago, IL**
Brogan, Marilyn Matthes ... **New York, NY**
Brogan, Michael P. ... Oklahoma City, OK
Brogan, Michael T. ... Norfolk, NE
Brogan, Patrick M. ... **Norfolk, VA**
Brogan, Peter R. ... Cranford, NJ
Brogan, Sean H. ... **Philadelphia, PA**
Brogan & Stafford, P.C. ... Norfolk, NE
Tilden, NE
Brogan, Stephen J. ... **Washington, DC**
Brogan, Thomas E. ... Norfolk, NE
Tilden, NE
Brogan, Thomas F. ... Passaic, NJ
Brogan, Thomas P. ... **Harrisburg, PA**
Brogan, Timothy E. ... Norfolk, NE
Brogan, William J. ... **Washington, DC**
Brogden, Annette T. ... **Indianapolis, IN**
Brogden, Blackwell M., Jr. ... Raleigh, NC
Brogden, Edward (E.H.), Jr.
Montgomery, AL
Brogden, Joseph B. ... Brewton, AL
Brogden, Reid A. ... Nashville, TN
Brogden, Robert H. ... **Ozark, AL**
Brogden & Stevens ... **Daleville, AL**
Ozark, AL
Brogden, William H. ... Oklahoma City, OK
Brogdon, James E., Jr. ... Marion, SC
Brogdon, Leigh Green ... Macon, GA
Brogdon, M. Gino, Sr. ... Atlanta, GA
Brogdon, Quentin ... Dallas, TX
Brogdon, Ralph E. ... San Jose, CA
Brogdon, Randy E. ... **Phoenix, AZ**
Brogdon, Siobhan S.
Department Of Veterans Affairs,
Board of Veterans Appeals, GV
Brogdon, William A. ... Memphis, TN
Brogdon, W.M. "Rowe" ... **Statesboro, GA**
Brogelman, Wayne H. ... Milwaukee, WI
Brogger, Gregory B. ... Palo Alto, CA
Broghammer, John D. ... **Sacramento, CA**
Broghammer, Stephen P. ... Omaha, NE
Broglio, Dennis N. ... **Charleston, WV**
Brogna, Carmine A. ... **Tucson, AZ**
Brogna, Denise Abundis ... **Ventura, CA**
Brogna, Victor ... Boston, MA
Brogna, Vincent R. ... Andover, MA
Brognano, Dominick J.
Department of Defense,
Defense Legal Services Agency, GV
Brohard, Jonathan T. ... **Phoenix, AZ**
Brohel, Jeffrey C. ... **White Plains, NY**
Brohman, Mark A. ... Lincoln, NE
Brohman, Michael B. ... **Chicago, IL**
Lincolnwood, IL
Broich, Michael J. ... **Minneapolis, MN**
Broida, Charles J. ... **Columbia, MD**
Broida and Farrow ... **Naperville, IL**
Broida, Joel D. ... St. Petersburg Beach, FL
Broida, Peter B. ... Arlington, VA
Broida, Ronald J. ... **Naperville, IL**
Broido, Julie Brock
National Labor Relations Board,
Office of the General Counsel, GV
Broido, Michael W. ... New York, NY
Broidy, Alan F. ... Los Angeles, CA
Broidy, Steven D. ... Los Angeles, CA
Broihier, Jeffrey T. ... **Seattle, WA**
Broihier, John C. ... Naperville, IL
Broihier & Wotipka ... **Seattle, WA**
Broikos, Gregory G. ... **Rochester, NY**
Broiles, R. David ... Fort Worth, TX
Broiles, Steven A. ... Los Angeles, CA
Broiles & Timms, LLP ... Los Angeles, CA
Broili, Robert H., Law Offices of
Reno, NV
Broillet, Bruce A. ... **Santa Monica, CA**
Broitman, Joshua S. ... **New York, NY**
Brok, Sergio Fabian ... Sunrise, FL
Brokamp, Lawrence J. ... Fairfax, OH
Brokans, Edmunds J. ... **Ambler, PA**
Brokans, Edmunds J. ... **Philadelphia, PA**
Brokate, Brian W. ... **New York, NY**
Brokaw, Adelyn D. ... Annandale, NJ
Brokaw, Clifford V., III ... Southampton, NY
Brokaw, Glenn J. ... Independence, OH
Brokaw, James L. ... Treasury Department,
Internal Revenue Service, GV
Brokaw, Jed E. ... **Davenport, IA**
Brokaw, Kenneth A. ... **Oklahoma City, OK**
Brokaw, Mary Ann ... Kirkland, WA
Broker, Ann René ... Fairbanks, AK
Broker, Anne E. ... Department of Energy,
Office of the General Counsel, GV
Broker & Charton ... **Santa Ana, CA**
Broker, Jeffrey W. ... **Santa Ana, CA**
Broker, Kenneth S. ... Encino, CA
Broker, Leah M. ... Asheville, NC
Broker, Linda ... Greensburg, PA
Broker, Michael J. ... San Antonio, TX
Broker, Phyllis J. ... Boston, MA
Broker, William K. ... Savannah, GA
Brokke, Mervin ... **Groton, CT**
Brokl, Matthew K. ... Eagan, MN
Brolick, Peter W. ... **Tulsa, OK**
Brolin, William A. ... Anaconda, MT
Broline, Patricia F. ... San Marcos, TX
Broll, Michael J. ... Austin, TX
Broll, William F. ... **San Francisco, CA**
Brollesy, Hany S. ... **New York, NY**
Brolley, Vincent D. ... Peru, IL
Brollier, C. Daniel ... Clarksville, TN
Brollier, David S. ... Richmond, VA
Brollier, Gary E. ... Bellevue, NE
Brollier & Wolf ... **Hugoton, KS**
Ulysses, KS
Brolly, Kelly Himes ... **Philadelphia, PA**
Brom, John M. ... Chicago, IL
Brom, Joseph P. ... Cincinnati, OH
Bromagen, William L. ... Fort Lauderdale, FL
Bromagen, William L., P.A.
Fort Lauderdale, FL
Bromall, George C., II ... Pittsburgh, PA
Bromall & Simon ... Pittsburgh, PA
Broman, Amy J. ... Ann Arbor, MI
Broman, Dorothea Allen ... Detroit, MI
Broman, Paul A. ... New York, NY
Broman, Stacy A. ... **Minneapolis, MN**
Bromander, Bruce C. ... Bloomington, MN
Bromann, Scott ... Wheaton, IL
Bromberek, James J. ... **Naperville, IL**
Bromberg, Alan R. ... **Dallas, TX**
Bromberg, Arthur D. ... Livingston, NJ
Bromberg, Barbara Schwartz
Cincinnati, OH
Bromberg, Brian L. ... New York, NY
Bromberg, Bruce L. ... Atlanta, GA
Bromberg, Cathy L. ... **Stamford, CT**
Bromberg, Daniel H. ... **Washington, DC**
Bromberg, Dennis M. ... Fresno, CA
Bromberg, Henri Louie, Jr. ... Dallas, TX
Bromberg, James S. ... Albuquerque, NM
Bromberg, Jeffrey A. ... New York, NY
Bromberg, John E. ... **Dallas, TX**
Bromberg, Jonathan R. ... **Rockville, MD**
Bromberg, Karen H. ... New York, NY
Bromberg, Kenneth K. ... San Francisco, CA
Bromberg, Laurence J. ... **New York, NY**
Bromberg, Lee Carl ... **Boston, MA**
Bromberg, Leo E. ... Beverly Hills, CA
Bromberg, Lisa Murtha ... **Morristown, NJ**
New York, NY
Bromberg, Louis J. ... Hartford, CT
Bromberg, Michael A. ... **Blue Bell, PA**
Bromberg, Michael D. ... Washington, DC
Bromberg, Michael S. ... Los Angeles, CA
Bromberg & Miller ... Pittsburgh, PA
Bromberg, Myron J. ... **Morristown, NJ**
New York, NY
Bromberg, Neil S. ... **Washington, DC**
Bromberg, Richard S. ... Washington, DC
Bromberg, Robert S. ... Cincinnati, OH
Bromberg, Rosenthal & Siegel
Washington, DC
Bromberg, Rosenthal, Siegel & Goodman
Rockville, MD
Bromberg, Roy G. ... New York, NY
Bromberg, S. George ... Lexington, MA
Bromberg, Stephen A. ... **Birmingham, MI**
Bromberg, Steven D. ... Newport Beach, CA
Bromberg & Sunstein LLP ... **Boston, MA**
Bromberg, Thomas R. ... **Denver, CO**
Bromberg, Todd Andrew ... **New York, NY**
Bromberg & Yaeger ... Newport Beach, CA
Bromberger, Allen R. ... New York, NY
Bromby, Craig A. ... **Raleigh, NC**
Brome, Robert H. ... New York, NY
Brome, Thomas R. ... **New York, NY**
Bromell, Jan Benature ... Georgetown, SC
Bromell, Thomas C. ... Mount Pleasant, MI
Bromer, Nick ... **Washington, DC**
Bromfeld, Andrea C. ... **New York, NY**
Bromfield, David H. ... **San Francisco, CA**
Bromfield, Harold A. ... San Diego, CA
Bromfield, Katherine M. ... Liberty, MO
Bromfield, Lise A. ... **New York, NY**
Bromfield, Wayne A. ... Lewisburg, PA
Bromfield, William H. ... Seattle, WA
Bromiel, Jerome J. ... **Tucson, AZ**
Bromiley, J. Kirk ... **Wenatchee, WA**
Bromiley, Jennifer Erin ... **Los Angeles, CA**
Brominski, Bernard F. C. ... Wilkes-Barre, PA
Bromley, Alexander H. ... **Los Angeles, CA**
Bromley, C. Corwin ... **Englewood, CO**
Bromley, David A. ... Walnut Creek, CA
Bromley, Dennis K. ... **Piedmont, CA**
Bromley, Edward P., III ... **Princeton, NJ**
Bromley, Ellen E. ... Stamford, CT
Bromley, Emily Sarah ... Boston, MA
Bromley, George W. ... Tucson, AZ
Bromley, Ira J. ... Cedarhurst, NY
Bromley, J. Robert ... **Stamford, CT**
Bromley, James F. ... **Washington, DC**
Bromley, James L. ... **New York, NY**
Bromley, Jennifer Arbittier
New York, NY
Philadelphia, PA
Bromley, Kyra K. ... **New York, NY**
Bromley, Mark ... Lancaster, WI
Bromley, Marvin L. ... Huntington Woods, MI
Bromley, Michael R.
Colorado Springs, CO
Bromley, Michael R., P.C.
Colorado Springs, CO
Bromley, N. Paul ... Huntington, WV
Bromley, Nancy Johnson
Prospect Heights, IL
Bromley, Rebecca Snyder
Colorado Springs, CO
Bromley, Richard ... **Chicago, IL**
Bromley, Richard A. ... San Francisco, CA
Bromley, Richard E. ... **Los Angeles, CA**
Bromley, Tarquin Jay ... Scotch Plains, NJ
Bromley, Verna P. ... Seattle, WA
Bromley, Wendy J.N. ... **Baraboo, WI**
Bromley, William R. ... Houston, TX
Bromley, William W. ... Eugene, OR
Bromm, Curtis A. ... **Wahoo, NE**
Bromm, F. Whittemore ... Roanoke, VA
Bromm, Susan E.
Environmental Protection Agency,
Office of Enforcement and Compliance
Assurance, GV
Bromme, Jeffrey S.
Consumer Product Safety Commission,
Office of the General Counsel, GV
Broms, Willard L. ... Leonardtown, MD
Bromsen, Ellen K. ... Englewood Cliffs, NJ
Bromson, Burton N. ... Highland Beach, FL
Bromson, Christopher W.
Windsor Locks, CT
Bromson, Debra L. ... Wilmington, DE
Bromson, Lois V. ... East Hartford, CT
Bromson and Reiner ... **Windsor Locks, CT**
Bromund, Dave C. ... **Indianapolis, IN**
Bromwell, W. Wade ... Charlottesville, VA
Bromwich, Michael R. ... **New York, NY**
Bronaugh, John H. ... Lexington, KY
Bronaugh, John W. ... Washington, DC
Bronchick, Frank ... Central Islip, NY
Bronchick, Kenneth C. ... Fort Lauderdale, FL
Bronchick, Kenneth C., P.A.
Fort Lauderdale, FL
Bronchick, William ... Denver, CO
Bronczyk, Arthur F. ... Camden, NJ
Brondfield, Ellen S. ... Washington, DC
Brondyk, Daniel J. ... **Grand Rapids, MI**
Brondyke, Donald V. ... Modesto, CA
Brondyke, Ronald Dale ... **Asheville, NC**
Brondyke, Valerie Jayne ... New York, NY
Broneill, William M. ... Manchester, CT
Brones, Lisa ... Des Moines, IA
Bronesky, Joseph J. ... **Denver, CO**
Bronfeld, Allen S. ... New York, NY
Bronfin, Edward D. ... **Denver, CO**
Bronfin, Fred ... **New Orleans, LA**
Bronfin, Michael E. ... Kew Gardens, NY
Bronfman, Andrew I. ... West Hartford, CT
Bronfman, Jillisa ... **San Francisco, CA**
Bronfman, Matt M. ... Atlanta, GA
Brong, Joyce Collier ... **Cherry Hill, NJ**
Philadelphia, PA
Brongo, William J. ... Rochester, NY
Bronikowski, Lisa A. ... New York, NY
Bronis, Barbara W. ... **Stuart, FL**
Bronis, Barbara W., P.A. ... **Stuart, FL**
Bronis, Stephen J. ... **Miami, FL**
Bronitsky, Martha G. ... Hayward, CA
Bronk, Daniel A. ... **Syracuse, NY**
Bronk, Eric C. ... Newport Beach, CA
Bronkesh, Noah ... **Atlantic City, NJ**
Newark, NJ
New York, NY
Bronn, Clyde L. ... Long Beach, CA
Bronnenberg, Bobbi D. Renner
Cheyenne, WY
Bronnenkant, Anna Collis ... Scottsdale, AZ
Bronnenkant, Rex P. ... **Phoenix, AZ**
Bronner, David A., (P.C.) ... **Chicago, IL**
Bronner, Deborah R. ... Los Angeles, CA
Bronner, Howard C. ... Columbus, OH
Bronner, James R. ... Northbrook, IL
Bronner, Mary Lynn M. ... Montgomery, AL
Bronner, William ... Chicago, IL
Bronner, William R. ... Hightstown, NJ
Bronosky, W. Joseph ... **Huntington, WV**
Bronowski, Clare ... **Los Angeles, CA**
Bronsdon, James F., Jr. ... Stamford, CT
Bronska, Laurence R. ... **Chicago, IL**
Bronski, Donna M. ... Phoenix, AZ
Bronsky, A. J. ... **Belleville, IL**
St. Louis, MO
Bronsnick, Andrew R. ... **Livingston, NJ**
Bronsnick, Sarit Keinan
Florham Park, NJ
Bronsnick, Warren J. ... Short Hills, NJ
Bronson, Albert M. ... Austin, TX
Bronson, Andrew G. ... Laconia, NH
Bronson, Barbara J. ... **Franklin, OH**
Springboro, OH
Bronson, Bill ... **Dallas, TX**
Bronson, Bill, P.C. ... **Carrollton, TX**
Dallas, TX
Denton, TX
Bronson, Clarissa H. ... Cambridge, MA
Bronson, Cynthia ... Oak Brook, IL
Bronson, Daniel R. ... **Chicago, IL**
Bronson, Edward D., Jr. ... Lakeport, CA
Bronson, Eric E. ... **Los Angeles, CA**
Bronson, Franklin C. ... Lincoln, MA
Bronson, Glenn B. ... Philadelphia, PA
Bronson, Glenn R. ... **Salt Lake City, UT**

Bronson, Gordon M. .... Honolulu, HI
Bronson, H. Bruce, Jr. .... Purchase, NY
Bronson, Harry Bernard .... Rochester, NY
Bronson, Jeanelle G. .... Orlando, FL
Bronson, Jeffrey I. .... East Orange, NJ
Bronson, Jill E. .... Philadelphia, PA
Bronson, John L. .... Newark, NJ
Bronson, John W. .... Gibsonburg, OH
Bronson & Kahn .... Chicago, IL
Bronson, Kenneth .... Chelsea, MI
Bronson, Kent A. .... New York, NY
Bronson, Kristin M. .... Denver, CO
Bronson, Mark I. .... St. Louis, MO
Bronson, Martha .... Stockton, CA
Bronson, Meridith J. .... Hackensack, NJ
Bronson & Migliaccio .... New York, NY
Purchase, NY
White Plains, NY
Bronson, Neal B. .... Lebanon, OH
Bronson, Peter C., (P.C.) .... Los Angeles, CA
Bronson, Phillip I. .... Encino, CA
Bronson, Rice & Simon .... Bethany, CT
Bronson, Richard A. .... Lakeland, FL
Bronson, Shannon I. .... Portland, OR
Bronson, Theotis .... Orlando, FL
Bronson, Todd M. .... Monroe, MI
Bronson, Vicki S. .... Fayetteville, AR
Bronson, William O. .... Great Falls, MT
Bronspiegel & Zeman .... New Bedford, MA
Bronstein, Alvin J. .... Washington, DC
Bronstein, Benjamin .... Towson, MD
Bronstein, Bernard .... Las Vegas, NV
Bronstein, Carlson, Gleim & Smith, P.A.
St. Petersburg, FL
Bronstein, Caryn .... Forest Hills, NY
Bronstein, Craig Penner .... Santa Ana, CA
Bronstein, Daniel A. .... East Lansing, MI
Bronstein, David A. .... Hollywood, FL
Bronstein, David R. .... Philadelphia, PA
Bronstein, Donald S. .... Boston, MA
Bronstein, Eric J. .... Blue Bell, PA
Bronstein, Eric S. .... Detroit, MI
Bronstein, Gary R. .... Washington, DC
Bronstein, Glen M. .... New York, NY
Bronstein, Harold .... Bainbridge Island, WA
Bronstein, Jay S. .... Sharon, MA
Bronstein, Joel D. .... St. Petersburg, FL
Bronstein, John D. .... Los Angeles, CA
Bronstein, Lisa Ann .... Santa Ana, CA
Bronstein, Marc A., Law Offices of
Los Angeles, CA
Bronstein, Marc A., Law Offices of
Santa Monica, CA
Bronstein, Mark .... Boston, MA
Bronstein, Mark P. .... Portland, OR
Bronstein, Paul A. .... Los Angeles, CA
Bronstein, Peter C. .... Marina Del Rey, CA
Bronstein, Peter E. .... Miami, FL
Bronstein, Peter E. .... New York, NY
Bronstein, Peter H. .... Salem, NH
Bronstein, Philip L. .... Chicago, IL
Bronstein, Richard J. .... New York, NY
Bronstein, Richard M. .... Central Islip, NY
Bronstein, Robert .... Denver, CO
Bronstein, Ronald S. .... Kansas City, MO
Bronstein, Ronald W. .... Succasunna, NJ
Bronstein, Sewall P., (P.C.)
Marlborough, MA
Bronstein, Stanley F. .... Houston, TX
Bronstein, Stuart A. .... San Francisco, CA
Bronstein, Van Veen & Bronstein, P.C.
New York, NY
Bronster, Jeffrey A. .... Livingston, NJ
Bronster, Margery S. .... Honolulu, HI
Bronsther, Brian H. .... Clifton Park, NY
Bronsther, Judith A. .... New York, NY
Bronston, Benjamin William .... Metairie, LA
Bronston, Byron E., Jr. .... Wausau, WI
Bronston, David E. .... New York, NY
Bronston, Edythe L., Law Offices of
Los Angeles, CA
Bronston, Jack E. .... Albany, NY
New York, NY
Bronston, Kenneth A. .... Salt Lake City, UT
Bronston, Lloyd Burke .... Overland Park, KS
Bronston, Robert L. .... Washington, DC
Bronstrup, Charles Lewis, II .... Mogadore, OH
Bronte, Patricia A. .... Chicago, IL
Bronzaft, Bertram .... New York, NY
Bronzi, Luca R. .... Miami, FL
Bronzo, John F. .... New York, NY
Broock, Richard A. .... Dayton, OH
Broock, Scott S. .... New York, NY
Broocks, Baker & Lange, L.L.P.
Houston, TX
Broocks, Ben C. .... Houston, TX
Broocks, John H. .... Kerrville, TX
Broocks, Linda .... Houston, TX
Broodo, Kenneth Chaim .... Dallas, TX
Brook, Bradley E. .... Los Angeles, CA
Brook, Byron .... Glenview, IL
Brook, Claudia L. .... Westbury, NY
Brook, David .... Media, PA
Brook, David E. .... Lexington, MA
Brook, Debra J. .... Savannah, GA
Brook, Doris J. .... Portland, OR
Brook, Fiona A. .... Los Angeles, CA
Brook, Harold N. .... Burbank, CA
Brook, Henry W. .... Santa Clara, CA
Brook, Jack Pierce .... New Orleans, LA
Brook, James F., and Associates
Mesa, AZ
Phoenix, AZ
Scottsdale, AZ
Sun City, AZ
Brook, Jeannette MacLeod
Indianapolis, IN
Brook, Jennifer J. .... Laconia, NH
Brook, Jonathan .... Houston, TX
Brook, Jonathan A. .... Houston, TX
Brook, Jonathan, & Company, A Professional Corporation .... Houston, TX
Brook, Julie Hammel .... San Francisco, CA
Brook, Laurel W. .... Concord, NH
Brook, Lisa S. .... Norfolk, VA
Brook, Martin C. .... Detroit, MI
Brook, Michael John Middleton
San Francisco, CA
Brook, Mitchell P. .... San Diego, CA
Brook, Nyda S. .... New Orleans, LA
Brook, Pizza & Van Loon, L.L.P.
Baton Rouge, LA
New Orleans, LA
Slidell, LA
Brook, Randall H. .... Seattle, WA
Brook, Richard A. .... Mineola, NY
Brook, Richard E. .... Great Neck, NY
Brook, Richard S. .... Mineola, NY
Brook, Robert D. .... Department of Justice, Environment and Natural Resources Division, GV
Brook, Rodney L. .... Muskogee, OK
Brook, Roger S. .... Fairfax, VA
Brook, Sanford M. .... Indianapolis, IN
Brook, Scott J. .... Fort Lauderdale, FL
Brook, Stephen D. .... Boston, MA
Brook, Steven R. .... San Antonio, TX
Brook, V. John, Jr. .... St. Petersburg, FL
Brook, V. John, P.A. .... St. Petersburg, FL
Brooke, Alban E. .... Jacksonville, FL
Brooke, Allan F., II .... Jacksonville, FL
Brooke & Brooke .... China Grove, NC
Brooke, Bruce D. .... Memphis, TN
Brooke, Carole Carlton .... China Grove, NC
Brooke, Charles P. .... Missoula, MT
Brooke, Charles W. .... Davenport, IA
Brooke & Cloyd .... Muncie, IN
Brooke, Curtis .... Redmond, WA
Brooke, Darrell G. .... Los Angeles, CA
Pasadena, CA
Brooke, Edward W. .... Washington, DC
Brooke, Eve Lynn .... Newport Beach, CA
Brooke, Francis C., Jr. .... Chevy Chase, MD
Brooke, James R. .... Reno, NV
Brooke, Jeffrey F. .... Virginia Beach, VA
Brooke, Jeffrey R. .... Phoenix, AZ
Brooke, Jerry .... Fort Benton, MT
Brooke, John A. .... Baltimore, MD
Brooke, John C., IV .... San Antonio, TX
Brooke, John H. .... Muncie, IN
Brooke, John R. .... Portland, OR
Brooke, Laura M. .... Ocean Township, NJ
Brooke, Lawrence T. .... Fairfax, VA
Brooke, Lewis, Jr. .... Traverse City, MI
Brooke, Mary Ellen .... Baltimore, MD
Brooke, Morris R. .... Flourtown, PA
Brooke, Nelson A. .... Philadelphia, PA
Brooke & O'Brien, P.L.C. .... Davenport, IA
Brooke, P. Cynthia .... Middlebury, CT
Brooke, Paul A. .... Honolulu, HI
Brooke, Peter M. .... Miami, FL
Brooke, Philip S., III .... Spokane, WA
Brooke, Phillip L. .... Memphis, TN
Brooke, Robert L. .... Nederland, TX
Brooke, Robert L. .... Richmond, VA
Brooke, Samuel P. .... Poughkeepsie, NY
Brooke & Shaw, LLP .... Minden, NV
Reno, NV
Brooke, Shirley J. .... Costa Mesa, CA
Brooke, Susan Rogers .... Indianapolis, IN
Brooke, T. Scott .... Minden, NV
Brooke, Thomas M. .... China Grove, NC
Brooke, Thomas M.L. .... Beaverton, OR
Brooke, Thomas R. .... Department of Defense, Defense Legal Services Agency, GV
Brooke, Thomas W. .... Washington, DC
Brooke, William M. .... Bozeman, MT
Brooke-Davidson, C. Carrick .... Austin, TX
Brooke-Devlin, Morgan .... Falls Church, VA
Brookens, Benoit O., II ....
Department of Labor, GV
Brookens & Collett .... Marion, KS
Brookens, J. Robert .... Marion, KS
Brookens, John W. .... Westmoreland, KS
Brookens, Kalynne .... Shelbyville, IN
Brookens, Marilyn E. .... Treasury Department, Internal Revenue Service, GV
Brooker, Clay C. .... West Palm Beach, FL
Brooker, Elizabeth Stewart .... Fort Pierce, FL
Brooker, Grant R. .... Kennesaw, GA
Brooker, Gregory G. .... Bloomington, MN
Brooker, James K. .... Canton, OH
Brooker, Jeanne J. .... Columbia, SC
Brooker, Jeff Z., III .... Columbia, SC
Brooker, Joseph M. .... Denver, CO
Brooker, Norton W., Jr. .... Mobile, AL
Brooker, Renee
Department of Justice, GV
Brooker, Rod T., Law Offices of
Tampa, FL
Brooker, Rosalind Poll .... Fall River, MA
Brooker, Thurmond .... Florence, SC
Brookes, A. Anders .... Rockville, MD
Brookes, Anne E. .... Dallas, TX
Brookes, Craig A. .... Atlanta, GA
Brookes, Lawrence V. .... Berkeley, CA
Brookes, Mark Charles .... Columbus, OH
Brookes, Robert J. .... Philadelphia, PA
Brookes, Steven J. .... Lakeport, CA
Brookes, Timothy R. .... East Liverpool, OH
Brookes, Valentine .... Orinda, CA
Brookey, Brian Kent .... Los Angeles, CA
Brookhart, Charles E.
Department of Justice, Tax Division, GV
Brookhart, Dan M. .... Lancaster, PA
Brookhart, Walter R. .... Houston, TX
Brookhiser, Robert J., Jr.
Washington, DC
Brookhouse, Andrew R. .... Kenosha, WI
Brookhouse, Eugene J. .... Kenosha, WI
Brookhouse, Richardson & Parise
Kenosha, WI
Brookhouser, Patrick E., Jr. .... Omaha, NE
Brookhyser, Donald E. .... Las Vegas, NV
Brookie, Terrence L. .... Indianapolis, IN
Brooking, Cheryl Rawls .... Anchorage, AK
Brooking, Frederick R. .... Clarksburg, WV
Brooking, John R. S. .... Covington, KY
Brooking, John S. "Brook"
Covington, KY
Brookings, Deborah D. .... Seattle, WA
Brookins and Cook .... Atlanta, GA
Brookins, Ernest D. .... Atlanta, GA
Brookins, Francine A. .... Oakland, CA
Brookins, Phillip J. .... Jackson, MS
Brooklier, Anthony P. .... Los Angeles, CA
Brooklyn, Daniel P., Jr. .... New York, NY
Brookman, Adam L. .... Milwaukee, WI
Brookman, Andrew J. .... Philadelphia, PA
Brookman, Anthony R. .... Walnut Creek, CA
Brookman & Brookman, P.C.
New York, NY
Brookman, Daniel F. .... Santa Monica, CA
Brookman, Kenneth H. .... Clifton, NJ
Brookman, Marc D. .... Philadelphia, PA
Brookman, Matthew P. .... St. Louis, MO
Brookman, Melvin .... Philadelphia, PA
Brookman, Michael D. .... New York, NY
Brookman, Raymond C. .... Martinez, CA
Brookman, Robert K. .... Chicago, IL
Brookman, Rosenberg, Brown & Sandler
Voorhees, NJ
Philadelphia, PA
Brookman, Steven L. .... Beverly Hills, CA
Brookman, Stewart S. .... Beverly Hills, CA
Brookman & Talbot, Inc. .... Walnut Creek, CA
Brookman, William M. .... San Antonio, TX
Brookman & Wroten .... Sacramento, CA
Stockton, CA
Brookmeyer, Stephen J. .... Garden City, NY
Melville, NY
New York, NY
Brookmyer, Gary .... Palm Beach Gardens, FL
Brookner, Jason S. .... Dallas, TX
Brookner, Jeffrey J. .... Morristown, NJ
Brookner, Marvin A. .... Fairfield, CA
Brookner, Steve E. .... Miami, FL
Brookner, Steve E., P.A. .... Miami, FL
Brookoff, Bruce M. .... New York, NY
Brookover, Fleischmann & Carr, P.C.
East Lansing, MI
Lansing, MI
Brookover, George M. .... East Lansing, MI
Brookover, Thomas W. .... Bloomfield Hills, MI
Brooks, Aaron W. .... Rockford, IL
Brooks, Adams and Tarulis .... Chicago, IL
Geneva, IL
Naperville, IL
Brooks, Aileen K. .... Chicago, IL
Brooks, Albert .... Philadelphia, PA
Brooks, Alison A. .... Costa Mesa, CA
Brooks, Allan Arthur, III
Oklahoma City, OK
Brooks, Allyn A., (Mr.) .... Evanston, IL
Brooks, Alphonso D. .... New York, NY
Brooks, Alvin G. .... Evanston, IL
Brooks, Alvin G., Jr. .... Chicago, IL
Brooks, Amy M. .... Detroit, MI
Brooks, Andrew D. .... San Diego, CA
Brooks, Ann .... Oklahoma City, OK
Brooks, Anna Marie F. Bourgeois
Edina, MN
Brooks, Annalisa .... Laurel, MD
Brooks, Arthur L. .... Lexington, KY
Brooks, Arthur V.N. .... Cleveland, OH
Brooks, B. Jeffrey .... Washington, DC
Brooks, Barnett Quinton .... Baltimore, MD
Brooks, Barnett Quinton, & Associates LLC
Baltimore, MD
Brooks, Barry A. .... New York, NY
Brooks, Barry J. .... Nacogdoches, TX
Brooks, Beach A., Jr. .... Winter Haven, FL
Brooks, Ben A., III .... Dallas, TX
Brooks, Benjamin H., III .... Mobile, AL
Brooks, Benjamin J. .... Atlanta, GA
Brooks, Bennie R. .... Landover, MD
Brooks, Beth Sprecher .... Elmhurst, IL
Brooks, B.G. .... Washington, DC
Brooks, Billy C. .... Newport News, VA
Brooks, Bradley & Kenney .... Media, PA
Brooks, Brenda G. .... Knoxville, TN
Brooks, Brian Keith .... Pembroke, NC
Brooks, Brian P. .... Washington, DC
Brooks, Brion J. .... Grand Rapids, MI
Brooks & Brooks .... Montrose, CO
Brooks & Brooks .... Edina, MN
Brooks, C.E., & Associates, P.C.
Denver, CO
Brooks, C. Robert .... Beverly Hills, CA
Brooks, C. Robert .... Los Angeles, CA
Brooks, Campbell & Grubbs, L.L.P.
Wichita Falls, TX
Brooks, Caroline Hyman .... Narberth, PA
Brooks, Cary W. .... Detroit, MI
Brooks, Catherine M. .... Omaha, NE
Brooks, Charlene Canvasser .... Okemos, MI
Brooks, Charles A. .... Wrightsville Beach, NC
Brooks, Charles B., II .... Monroe, NC
Brooks, Charles C. .... Savannah, GA
Brooks, Charles D., Jr. .... Merrillville, IN
Brooks, Charles E. .... Towson, MD
Brooks, Charles W., Jr. .... Louisville, KY
Brooks, Chester R. .... Sun City Center, FL
Brooks, Christopher F. .... Butler, PA
Cranberry Township, PA
Brooks, Christopher W. .... Cary, NC
Brooks, Christy Ann .... Milwaukee, WI
Brooks, Clare J. .... Baltimore, MD
Brooks, Clarence H. .... Suffolk, VA
Brooks, Clifford A. .... Greenbelt, MD
Brooks, Cody H. .... Scranton, PA
Brooks, Collins E. .... Grand Rapids, MI
Brooks, Conrad D. .... Atlanta, GA
Brooks, Constance E. .... Denver, CO
Brooks, Cornell W.
Federal Communications Commission, Office of the General Counsel, GV
Brooks, Craig M. .... Pittsburgh, PA
Brooks, Craig T. .... Santa Rosa, CA
Brooks, Cynthia .... Newark, NJ
Brooks, Cynthia W. .... Houston, TX
Brooks, Dana Carli .... Los Angeles, CA
Brooks, Daniel J. .... New York, NY
Brooks, Daniel M. .... Roseland, NJ
Brooks, Daniel R. .... Boston, MA
Brooks, Daniel T. .... Washington, DC
Springfield, VA
Brooks, Daniel T. .... Wichita, KS
Brooks, Danny S. .... Suitland, MD
Brooks, Darin L. .... Houston, TX
Brooks, Darren L. .... San Diego, CA
Brooks, David .... United States Senate, Committee Legal Personnel, GV
Brooks, David .... Sayre, OK
Brooks, David A. .... Sherman Oaks, CA
Brooks, David A. .... Valparaiso, IN
Brooks, David A. .... Springfield, NJ
Brooks, David B. .... Austin, TX
Brooks, David E. .... Ellwood City, PA
Brooks, David K. .... Durango, CO
Brooks, David L. .... North Berwick, ME
Brooks, David M. .... Indianapolis, IN
Brooks, David M. .... New York, NY
Brooks, David M. .... New York, NY
Brooks, David P. .... Mesa, AZ
Brooks, David P., PLC, Law Offices of
Mesa, AZ
Brooks, David R. .... Camden, NJ
Brooks, David Victor .... Cary, NC
Brooks, David W. .... Kansas City, MO
Brooks, Dean A. .... Miami, FL
Brooks, Deborah Lorraine .... Knoxville, TN
Brooks, Deborah Lynn .... Oklahoma City, OK
Brooks, Dennis D. .... Jonesborough, TN
Brooks, Dexter .... Lumberton, NC
Brooks, Dexter R. .... Department of Labor, Office of Secretary, GV
Brooks, Diana A. .... Bel Air, MD
Brooks, Dianne L. .... Springfield, MA
Brooks & Distler .... New York, NY
Brooks, Donald B. .... Atlanta, GA
Brooks, Donald J. .... Chicago, IL
Brooks, Donald J., Jr. .... Philadelphia, PA
Brooks, Donald L. .... North Palm Beach, FL
Brooks, Donald L., P.A.
North Palm Beach, FL
Brooks, Donald R. .... Poland, OH
Brooks, Donald S. .... Roseland, NJ
Brooks, Donna .... Jacksonville, FL
Brooks, Donna Eich .... Birmingham, AL
Brooks, Donna J. .... Winsted, CT
Brooks, Donna J. B. .... Dallas, TX
Brooks, Donna L. .... Hartford, CT
Brooks, Donna Miller
Fort Lauderdale, FL
Brooks, Dorothy L. .... Charlottesville, VA
Brooks, Douglas J. .... Dallas, TX
Brooks, Douglas L. .... Atlanta, GA
Brooks, Douglas M. .... Louisville, KY
Brooks, Douglas M. .... Boston, MA
Brooks, Douglas S. .... Boston, MA
Brooks, Eavelyn T. .... New Orleans, LA
Brooks, Edward A., Jr. .... Hauppauge, NY
Brooks, Edward George .... Oakland, CA
Brooks, Edward J., III .... Minneapolis, MN
Brooks, Edward M. .... Washington, DC
Brooks, Edward R. .... Honolulu, HI
Brooks, Edwin E. .... Chicago, IL
Brooks, Edwin F. .... Richmond, VA
Brooks, Elaine .... Decatur, GA
Brooks, Eleanor I. .... Montgomery, AL
Brooks, Elizabeth A. .... New York, NY
Brooks, Elizabeth C. .... Wyndmoor, PA
Brooks, Elizabeth G. .... Seattle, WA
Brooks, Elizabeth M. .... Little Rock, AR
Brooks, Ellen M. .... Cleveland, OH
Brooks, Elliot R. .... West Palm Beach, FL
Brooks, Eric M. .... Beverly Hills, CA
Brooks, Erin O. .... Birmingham, AL
Brooks, Ernie L. .... Southfield, MI
Brooks, Eugene C., III .... Durham, NC
Brooks, Eugene C., IV .... Savannah, GA
Brooks, Evelyn E. .... Fayetteville, AR
Brooks, Faye Dottheim .... New York, NY
Brooks & Fitzpatrick .... Lexington, KY
Brooks, Fred A. .... Springfield, MO
Brooks, Fredric M. .... Washington, DC
New York, NY
Brooks, G. Edwin .... Houston, TX
Brooks, Gary A. .... New York, NY
Brooks, Gary L.
National Archives And Records Administration, General Counsel Staff, GV
Brooks, Gary L. .... Dayton, OH
Oklahoma City, OK
Brooks, Gary S. .... Miami, FL
Brooks, Gary T. .... Norwich, VT
Brooks, Gary T., PLC .... Norwich, VT
Brooks, Gene E. .... Evansville, IN
Brooks, George L .... Oxon Hill, MD

Broome, John Spooner .... Lumpkin, GA
Broome, Jonathan J., Jr. .... Vienna, VA
Broome, Julian F., Jr. .... Venice, FL
Broome Law Firm, The, P.A.
Titusville, FL
Broome, Lissa Lamkin .... Chapel Hill, NC
Broome, Richard Crofton .... Titusville, FL
Broome, Shannon S. .... Fairfield, CT
Broome, Stanley Dale .... New Orleans, LA
Broome, Stephen F. .... Maitland, FL
Broome, Stephen F., P.A. .... Maitland, FL
Broome, Thomas J. .... Oakland, CA
Broome, Virginia Gay .... West Palm Beach, FL
Broome, William H. .... Anniston, AL
Broome, William R. H., P.A.
West Palm Beach, FL
Broome, William R. H.
West Palm Beach, FL
Broomfield, David D. .... Wichita, KS
Broomfield, Larri J. .... Milwaukee, WI
Broomfield, Michael A. .... New York, NY
Broomfield, Robert C. .... Phoenix, AZ
Broos, Gregory R. .... St. Paul, MN
Brooslin, Andrew S. .... Boston, MA
Brooslin, Richard A. .... Springfield, MA
Brooten, Kenneth E., Jr. .... Marianna, FL
Brooten, Kenneth E., Jr., Chartered
Marianna, FL
Brophey, Alicia .... Canton, MA
Brophy, Carl M., (P.C.) .... Medford, OR
Brophy, Carol René .... San Francisco, CA
Brophy, Christine Moriarty
Elmwood Park, NJ
Brophy, D. Richard, (P.C.) .... Oakland, CA
Brophy, Daniel E. .... Fort Wayne, IN
Brophy, Fiona A. .... Menlo Park, CA
Brophy, Frank C., Jr. .... Phoenix, AZ
Brophy, Gilbert T. .... Jupiter, FL
Brophy, J. Stephen
Department of Transportation, U. S. Coast Guard, GV
Brophy, James E., III .... Phoenix, AZ
Brophy, Joan Edmonds .... Chicago, IL
Brophy, John .... Boston, MA
Brophy, Joseph F. .... Austin, TX
Brophy, Joseph J. .... White Plains, NY
Brophy, Joseph M. .... Westport, CT
Brophy, Karen Hayes .... Garland, TX
Brophy, Katie M. .... Louisville, KY
Brophy & Laub .... White Plains, NY
Brophy, Mary Ray .... Birmingham, MI
Brophy, Michael D. .... New York, NY
Philadelphia, PA
Brophy, Michael J. .... Phoenix, AZ
Brophy, Michael J. .... Warwick, RI
Brophy, Michael S. .... Los Angeles, CA
Brophy, Michael V. .... Houston, TX
Brophy, Mills, Schmor, Gerking & Brophy, LLP .... Medford, OR
Brophy, Moira L. .... Mount Olive, NJ
Brophy, Patrick J. .... Plano, TX
Brophy, Patrick W. .... New York, NY
Brophy, Philip N. .... Falls Church, VA
Brophy & Pleasant, L.L.P. .... Houston, TX
Brophy, Pollyann L. .... Los Angeles, CA
Brophy, R. Gregory .... Atlanta, GA
Brophy, Richard E., Jr. .... Waco, TX
Brophy & Roebuck .... Fort Wayne, IN
Brophy, Stephen W. .... Washington, DC
Brophy, Thomas A. .... Norristown, PA
Brophy, Thomas F. .... Windsor, CT
Brophy, Thomas J. .... Chicago, IL
Brophy, Timothy E. .... Medford, OR
Brophy, Virginia A. .... Cohasset, MA
Brophy, Walter R., Jr. .... Redding, CA
Brophy Bair, Teresa C. .... Buffalo, NY
Brorby & Crozier, P.C. .... Austin, TX
Brorby, Donna .... San Francisco, CA
Brorby, Robert P. .... Richmond, CA
Brorby, Thomas J. .... Austin, TX
Brorby, Wade .... Cheyenne, WY
Bros, Carol L. .... St. Paul, MN
Brosch, Kevin J. .... Department of Agriculture, Foreign Agricultural Service, GV
Broschak, Thomas J. .... Columbus, OH
Broschay, Paul W. .... Detroit, MI
Brosche, Wm. F., Jr. .... Seattle, WA
Broscious, Glynn & Fischer, A Professional Corporation .... Belvidere, NJ
Washington, NJ
Broscious, James W. .... Washington, NJ
Broscious, William A. .... Richmond, VA
Broscius, Patricia C. .... Easton, PA
Brosco, Anthony J. .... Providence, RI
Brosco & Brosco, P.C. .... Providence, RI
Brosco, Dino A. .... Providence, RI
Brosco, Gian F. .... Providence, RI
Brosco, Matthew J. .... Providence, RI
Broscritto, Anthony, Jr. .... Central Islip, NY
Brose, Ann E. .... Minneapolis, MN
Brose, Christian .... Dallas, TX
Brose, E. Jerome .... Easton, PA
Brose, Gregory W. .... Ventura, CA
Brose, James F. .... Media, PA
Brose, Jonathan P. .... New York, NY
Brose, Michael J. .... New Richmond, WI
Brose, R. Christian .... Fort Worth, TX
Brose, Steven H. .... Washington, DC
Broseman, George W. .... Rosemont, PA
Brosey, Richard L. .... Chehalis, WA
Brosgol, David S. .... New York, NY
Brosh, John J., III .... Bel Air, MD
Brosha, William H. .... Princeton, NJ
Broshears, Lee .... Morro Bay, CA
Broshot, James A. .... Steelville, MO
Brosi, Kathleen B. .... Baltimore, MD
Brosio, Frederick M., Jr. .... Pasadena, CA
Brosio, Robert L. .... Los Angeles, CA
Brosius, Donald F. .... Columbus, OH
Brosius, E. Eugene .... Northumberland, PA
Brosius, Edward J. .... Chicago, IL
Brosius, Robert M., Jr. .... Tarzana, CA
Brosk, Joel .... Northbrook, IL
Broski, Gerald F. .... Maple Heights, OH
Brosky, David J. .... Pittsburgh, PA
Brosky, John C. .... Washington, DC
Brosky, John G. .... Pittsburgh, PA
Brosky, Michael E. .... Lorain, OH
Brosky, Robert E. .... Amherst, OH
Broslovsky, Allen .... Visalia, CA
Brosman, Wayne Bennett .... Santa Ana, CA
Brosnahan, Brian P. .... San Francisco, CA
Brosnahan, Carol S., (Mrs.) .... Berkeley, CA
Brosnahan, Helen R. .... South St. Paul, MN
Brosnahan, James J. .... San Francisco, CA
Brosnahan, Jennifer R. .... Washington, DC
Brosnahan, John J. .... San Francisco, CA
Brosnahan, John J. .... Falls Church, VA
Brosnahan, Joseph & Suggs, P.A.
Minneapolis, MN
Brosnahan, Mary M. .... Chicago, IL
Brosnahan, Paul F. .... Winona, MN
Brosnahan, Roger P. .... Minneapolis, MN
Brosnan, David J. .... Campbell Hall, NY
Brosnan, Denis A., Jr. .... Columbia, SC
Brosnan, Doris E. .... Milwaukee, WI
Brosnan & Hegler .... Garden City, NY
Brosnan, John D. .... Fairfax, VA
Brosnan, John F. .... Chicago, IL
Brosnan, John F. .... Boston, MA
Brosnan, John G. .... General Accounting Office, Office of the General Counsel, GV
Brosnan, Joseph G. .... New City, NY
Brosnan, Kathleen A. .... Chicago, IL
Brosnan, Margaret A. .... Cleveland, OH
Brosnan, Mark J. .... Garden City, NY
Brosnan, Martin J. .... Warren, MI
Brosnan, Mary Hensey .... Garden City, NY
Brosnan, Pegeen .... Fremont, CA
Brosnan, S. Elizabeth .... Columbia, SC
Brosnan, Sharon L. .... Appleton, WI
Brosnan, Thomas F. .... Washington, DC
Brosnan, Tiffany .... Irvine, CA
Brosnan, Tracy J. .... New City, NY
Brosnick, Richard B. .... New York, NY
Bross, David S. .... Philadelphia, PA
Bross, Donald C. .... Denver, CO
Bross, Elliot M. .... Newark, NJ
Bross, Gary W. .... Norcross, GA
Bross, John A. .... Chicago, IL
Bross, Joseph J. .... Columbia, MD
Bross, Michael D. .... Newark, NJ
Bross, Phyllis E. .... Trenton, NJ
Bross & Saginar .... Norcross, GA
Bross, Sheldon .... Newark, NJ
Bross, Stephen W. .... Burke, VA
Bross, Stephenie .... New York, NY
Bross, Steward R., Jr. .... New York, NY
Bross Underwood & Zipkin .... Newark, NJ
Bross, Walter Indulis .... Philadelphia, PA
Brossard, Kay L. .... Seattle, WA
Brossart, John W. .... Indianapolis, IN
Brosse, Michael A. .... New York, NY
Brosse, Peter D. .... Cleveland, OH
Brosseau, Jon H. .... Drayton, ND
Brosseau, Marc R. .... Denver, CO
Brosseit, A. Kimberly .... Wilmington, DE
Brossman, Douglas S. .... Lancaster, PA
Brossman, Eric L. .... Harrisburg, PA
Brossman, Larry A. .... Chicago, IL
Brossman, Mark E. .... New York, NY
Brost, C. Robert .... St. Paul, MN
Brost, Dallas E. .... Presho, SD
Brost, Frank D. .... Pierre, SD
Brost, Kenneth E. .... Madison, WI
Brost, Linda Newbauer .... St. Paul, MN
Brost, Margaret H. .... Olympia, WA
Brost, Will R. .... St. Cloud, MN
Brosteau, Clarence A. .... Willard, OH
Brosterhous, Patricia .... Chicago, IL
Brosterhous, Patricia, Ltd. .... Chicago, IL
Brosterhous, Raymond L., II
Sacramento, CA
Brosterman, Melvin A. .... New York, NY
Brostoff, Alan S. .... Milwaukee, WI
Brostoff, Ben C. .... Buffalo Grove, IL
Brostoff, Sandra N., Law Office of
Schaumburg, IL
Brostoff, Steve .... New York, NY
Brostrom, David W. .... Bridgeport, NE
Brostrom, Ellen R. .... Minneapolis, MN
Brostrom, Kevin A. .... Grand Island, NE
Brostron, Judith C. .... St. Louis, MO
Brostron, Kenneth C. .... St. Louis, MO
Brot, Ronald F. .... Los Angeles, CA
Brot, Ronald F. .... Woodland Hills, CA
Broth, Mark T. .... Manchester, NH
Brotherhood, Randal J. .... Milwaukee, WI
Brothers, Alan W. .... Chicago, IL
Brothers & Ash .... Bend, OR
Brothers, Bruce J. .... Bend, OR
Brothers, Carter R. .... Nashville, TN
Brothers, Catherine E. .... Morehead City, NC
Brothers, Charles A. .... Austin, TX
Brothers, D. Douglas .... Austin, TX
Brothers, David E. .... Houston, TX
Brothers, Henry J., II .... Washington, DC
Brothers, James E. .... Boston, MA
Brothers, James R. .... Fargo, ND
Brothers, Jeffery Patrick .... Gretna, LA
Brothers, Kenneth W. .... Washington, DC
Brothers, Kieran J. .... Roseville, CA
Brothers, Lynda L. .... Seattle, WA
Brothers, Martin L. .... New York, NY
Brothers, Matthew .... Nashville, TN
Brothers, Norman M., Jr. .... Atlanta, GA
Brothers, Richard T. .... Seattle, WA
Brothers, Robert A. .... Indianapolis, IN
Brothers, Robert P. .... Sturgis, MI
Brothers, Roger J. .... Walnut Creek, CA
Brothers, Ronald J. .... Plainfield, IN
Brothers, Rudolph, Jr. .... Huntsville, TX
Brothers & Thomas, L.L.P. .... Austin, TX
Brothers, Thomas W. .... Nashville, TN
Brothers & Thompson, P.C. .... Chicago, IL
Brotherson, James R. .... Elkhart, IN
Brotherson, Larry B. .... Denver, CO
Brotherton, Allen C. .... Charlotte, NC
Brotherton, Beth E. .... Taylorville, IL
Brotherton, Carolyn Ogden
New London, CT
Brotherton & Colbert PLLC .... Dallas, TX
Denton, TX
Lewisville, TX
Brotherton, Joseph F. .... Greensboro, NC
Brotherton, Joseph L. .... Seattle, WA
Brotherton, Robert P. .... Wichita Falls, TX
Brotherton, Ronald P. .... Wilton, CT
Brotherton, William J. .... Lewisville, TX
Brotherton, William L., Jr. .... Phoenix, AZ
Brotherton, William T., III
Charleston, WV
Brothman, Phillip .... Angola, NY
Brotkin, Linda M. .... Dallas, TX
Brotman, Alison B. .... Bedminster, NJ
Brotman, David B. .... Sherman Oaks, CA
Brotman, Dennis S. .... Trenton, NJ
Brotman & Graziano, A Professional Corporation .... Trenton, NJ
Brotman Group, The .... La Jolla, CA
Brotman, Harris F. .... La Jolla, CA
Brotman, Jeffrey F. .... Philadelphia, PA
Brotman, Jeffrey H. .... Kirkland, WA
Brotman, Marc C. .... Boca Raton, FL
Brotman, Michele V. .... Philadelphia, PA
Brotman & Nusbaum .... Boca Raton, FL
Fort Lauderdale, FL
Miami, FL
Brotman, Robert .... Elizabeth, NJ
Brotman, Saul H. .... Delray Beach, FL
Brotman, Stanley S. .... Camden, NJ
Brotman, Susan .... New York, NY
Brotman, Susan J. .... Boca Raton, FL
Brotman, Susan J., P.A. .... Boca Raton, FL
Brotmann, Andrew K. .... White Plains, NY
Brotmann & Freedman .... Stamford, CT
White Plains, NY
Brotmann, S. Lawrence .... White Plains, NY
Brotmann, Stephen J. M. .... White Plains, NY
Broton, Edward R. .... Syracuse, NY
Brott, Andrea Adam .... Berkeley, CA
Brott, Cara L. .... Detroit, MI
Brott, Donald J. .... Wauconda, IL
Brott, Eugene E. .... San Francisco, CA
Brott, Gary N. .... Canfield, OH
Brott, Irving D., Jr. .... Buffalo, NY
Brott, Irving H. .... Los Angeles, CA
Brott, James W. .... Orange, CA
Brott, Lizabeth Fox .... Okemos, MI
Brott, Robert W. .... Acme, MI
Brott, Steven R. .... Falls City, NE
Brott, Wilson D. .... Acme, MI
Brotter, Ralph .... Great Neck, NY
Brotz, Beth Y. .... Los Angeles, CA
Brotz, Kevin R. .... Bedminster, NJ
Brotzen, Peter P. .... Los Angeles, CA
Brotzman, Buchholz & McDowell
Boulder, CO
Brotzman, Daniel L. .... Denver, CO
Brotzman, Donald G. .... Washington, DC
Brotzman, Ronald J. .... Boulder, CO
Brou, Dale J. .... Boutte, LA
Brou, John F. .... New Orleans, LA
Broucek, Christine Elizabeth
Overland Park, KS
Broucek, Eric F. .... Overland Park, KS
Kansas City, MO
Broucek, F. J., Jr. .... Mount Prospect, IL
Broucek, Karen A. .... Chicago, IL
Brouch, Robert F. .... Aurora, IL
Broude & Hochberg .... Boston, MA
Broude, John S. .... Fort Worth, TX
Broude, Joseph .... Boston, MA
Broude, Mark Allen .... New York, NY
Broude, Paul D. .... Boston, MA
Broude, Smith & Jennings, P.C.
Fort Worth, TX
Broudny, Roy .... Garden City, NY
Great Neck, NY
Broudy & Associates, P.C. .... New York, NY
Broudy, Joshua P. .... Philadelphia, PA
Broudy, Leonard C. .... Los Angeles, CA
Broudy, Louis L. .... New York, NY
Broudy, Mitchell D. .... Virginia Beach, VA
Broudy, Richard F. .... Virginia Beach, VA
Broudy, William K. .... New York, NY
Brough, Gregory .... St. Louis, MO
Brough, Michael B., & Associates
Chapel Hill, NC
Brough, Wendy .... Santa Ana, CA
Brough, William R. .... Metairie, LA
Broughal, Christine M. .... Creedmoor, NC
Durham, NC
Greensboro, NC
Raleigh, NC
Broughal & DeVito, L.L.P. .... Bethlehem, PA
Broughal, James L. .... Bethlehem, PA
Brougham, David C. .... Los Angeles, CA
Brougham, David R. .... Denver, CO
Brougham, Crystal Theresa .... Jacksonville, FL
Broughel, Andrew J. .... Milford, CT
Broughel, David B. .... Boston, MA
Brougher, Brent W. .... San Francisco, CA
Brougher, James L. .... Danville, IL
Broughman, William A. .... Tucker, GA
Broughton, Agee S., III .... Mobile, AL
Broughton, Albert K., Jr. .... Salisbury, MD
Broughton, Albert K., Jr., P.A.
Salisbury, MD
Broughton, Allen L. .... Atlanta, GA
Broughton, Angela .... Minneapolis, MN
Broughton, Barry .... Austin, TX
Broughton, Ben .... Muskegon, MI
Broughton & Broughton, L.L.P.
Southern Pines, NC
Broughton, Darren C. .... New York, NY
Broughton, Elliott P. .... Montgomery, AL
Broughton, H. Chalk, Jr.
Southern Pines, NC
Broughton, Howard C.
Southern Pines, NC
Broughton, J. Kevin .... Jackson, MS
Broughton, Jacqulynn M. .... Cherry Hill, NJ
Broughton, Janet C. S.
Southern Pines, NC
Broughton, Kenneth E., Jr. .... Houston, TX
Broughton & Kyser, P.C. .... Austin, TX
Broughton, Marcia Allen
Clarksburg, WV
Broughton, Matthew W. .... Roanoke, VA
Broughton, N. Reid .... Roanoke, VA
Broughton, Phillip C. .... New York, NY
Broughton, Richard E. .... Montgomery, AL
Broughton, Robert B. .... Raleigh, NC
Broughton, Sharon A. .... La Mesa, CA
Broughton, Terence D. .... Dublin, CA
Broughton, Terry V. .... Fort Myers, FL
Broughton, Terry V., P.A. .... Fort Myers, FL
Broughton, Turner Anderson
Richmond, VA
Broughton, Wilkins, Webb & Sugg, P.A.
Raleigh, NC
Broughton, Willa C. .... Plymouth, MI
Brouhard, Julia R. .... Cleveland, OH
Brouillard, Adam M. .... Hartford, CT
Brouillard & Brouillard .... Laconia, NH
Brouillard, Claude M. .... Hartford, CT
Brouillard, Mark R. .... Putnam, CT
Brouillard, Philip A. .... Laconia, NH
Brouillard, Richard P. .... Laconia, NH
Brouillard, Robert P. .... Syracuse, NY
Brouillard, William L. .... Boston, MA
Brouillet, Nancy A. .... Norwich, CT
Brouillette, Brain F. .... Iron Mountain, MI
Brouillette, Francis D. .... Iron Mountain, MI
Brouillette, Gary J. .... Kansas City, MO
Brouillette, Grace C. .... Banning, CA
Brouillette, Harold J. .... Marksville, LA
Brouillette, James Everet
New Orleans, LA
Brouillette, John D. .... Breaux Bridge, LA
Brouillette, Timothy P. .... North Platte, NE
Brouillette, William R. .... Iron Mountain, MI
Broujos, Frank Nicholas, Jr.
Wilmington, DE
Broujos & Gilroy, P.C. .... Carlisle, PA
Broujos, John H. .... Carlisle, PA
Broukhim, Bejan D. .... Los Angeles, CA
Broullire, Peter J., III .... Albuquerque, NM
Brouman, Alvin .... Pepper Pike, OH
Broumas & Broumas .... Baltimore, MD
Westminster, MD
Broumas, J. Michael .... Baltimore, MD
Westminster, MD
Broumas, Jill Schlessinger .... Baltimore, MD
Westminster, MD
Broun, Amanda Rachel .... Washington, DC
Broun, Charles W., III .... Atlanta, GA
Brouner, Frederic J. .... Madison, WI
Brouner, James S. .... Dallas, TX
Brounoff, J. Michael .... Dallas, TX
Brountas, Nicholas P. .... Bangor, ME
Brountas, Nicholas P., Jr. .... New York, NY
Brountas, Paul P. .... Boston, MA
Brountas, Paul P., Jr. .... Boston, MA
Brourman, Michael .... Los Angeles, CA
Brourman, Phyllis R. .... Beverly Hills, CA
Brous, Joel P. .... Kansas City, MO
Brous, Thomas R. .... Kansas City, MO
Brousaides, Eric C. .... Columbia, MD
Brousard, Jack D. .... Chicago, IL
Brouse McDowell, A Legal Professional Association .... Akron, OH
Cleveland, OH
Brouse, Michael S. .... Fosston, MN
Brouse, Robert C. .... Delray Beach, FL
Broussard, Aaron F. .... Kenner, LA
Broussard, Andre C., Jr.
New Orleans, LA
Broussard, AndréC. .... Baton Rouge, LA
Broussard, Barry D. .... New Orleans, LA
Broussard, Bart A. .... Covington, LA
Broussard, Bob .... Lafayette, LA
Broussard, Bob, A Professional Law Corporation .... Lafayette, LA
Broussard, Bolton, Halcomb & Vizzier
Alexandria, LA
Broussard & Broussard, Ltd. .... Abbeville, LA
Broussard, C. Gweneyette .... Houston, TX
Broussard, Camille .... New York, NY
Broussard, Candace J. .... Houston, TX
Broussard, Charles C. .... Sulphur, LA
Broussard, Christopher D. .... Beaumont, TX
Broussard, Collis Anthony, Jr.
Houston, TX
Broussard & Condry .... Orlando, FL
Broussard, Daniel E., Jr. .... Alexandria, LA
Broussard, David & Daigle, A Professional Law Corporation .... Lafayette, LA
Broussard, Debra K. .... Houston, TX
Broussard, Edward B. .... Abbeville, LA

Broussard, Edward M.
Department of Justice, Federal Bureau of Investigation, GV
Broussard, Eugene D., Sr. ... New Iberia, LA
Broussard, Evest A., III ... Baton Rouge, LA
Broussard, Francis C. ... Monroe, LA
Broussard, Francis J. ... New Orleans, LA
Broussard, Hal J. ... Lafayette, LA
Broussard, Jennifer A. ... Houston, TX
Broussard, John E. ... Chicago, IL
Broussard, Joseph E. ... Beaumont, TX
Broussard, Judy K. ... Cleveland, OH
Broussard, Lester H. ... Gastonia, NC
Broussard, Lloyd ... Austin, TX
Broussard, Marcus A. ... Abbeville, LA
Broussard, Marcus A., Jr. ... Abbeville, LA
Broussard, Margaret E. ... San Ramon, CA
Broussard, Marianna ... Lafayette, LA
Broussard, Martin L., Jr. ... New Orleans, LA
Broussard, Mary Jane ... Dallas, TX
Broussard, Melissa D. ... Lafayette, LA
Broussard, Michael ... Orlando, FL
Broussard, Michael A. ... Metairie, LA
Broussard, Natalie B. ... New Iberia, LA
Broussard, Peter O. ... Charlotte, NC
Broussard, Richard C., (A Professional Law Corporation) ... Lafayette, LA
Broussard, Robert ... Huntsville, AL
Broussard, Robert L. ... St. Martinville, LA
Broussard, Robert P. ... Spring, TX
Broussard, Robert R. ... Bethpage, NY
Broussard, Stephen J. ... Metairie, LA
Broussard, Steven A. ... Tulsa, OK
Broussard, Terrel J. ... New Orleans, LA
Broussard, Thomas A. ... Austin, TX
Broussard, Thomas R., Ltd.
Los Angeles, CA
Broussard, Thomas Rollins
Los Angeles, CA
Broussard, Tim ... Ontario, CA
Broussard, Todd J. ... Houston, TX
McAllen, TX
Broussard, Troy A. ... Lafayette, LA
Broussard, Whitney C. ... New York, NY
Broussard, William Arren ... Austin, TX
Broussard, Wilmore J., Jr. ... Schriever, LA
Broussard-Baloney, Geri ... Garyville, LA
Brousseau & Associates, A Professional Corporation ... Dallas, TX
Brousseau, Jankovich & Ormiston
Seattle, WA
Brousseau, John C. ... Washington, DC
Brousseau, Justine H. ... Boston, MA
Brousseau, MaryAnn Sarris ... Dallas, TX
Brousseau, Paul Bradford ... Springfield, MA
Brousseau, Robert L. ... Seattle, WA
Brousseau, Robert T. ... Dallas, TX
Brousseau, Shawn F. ... Albany, NY
Brousseau, Ted ... Naples, FL
Brousseau, Thomas W. ... Dudley, MA
Brouwer, Deborah L. ... Detroit, MI
Brouwer, Francisca J.M. ... Danville, CA
Brouwer, Gerard ... Leland, IL
Brouwer, Mark E. ... Grand Rapids, MI
Brouwer, Wendy B. ... New York, NY
Brovarone, Dennis ... Broomfield, CO
Brovender, Lisa J. ... New York, NY
Brover, Richard D. ... Long Beach, CA
Broverman, Jonathan A. ... Pittsfield, MA
Broverman & Podeschi, Professional Corporation ... Taylorville, IL
Broverman, Quinn M. ... Taylorville, IL
Broverman, Robert ... Taylorville, IL
Broverman, Robert Lee ... Shelbyville, IL
Brovey, Jennifer P. ... Washington, DC
Brovins, Joan M. ... Northport, MI
Brovins & Oehmke, P.C. ... Northport, MI
Brovitz, Richard S. ... Rochester, NY
Brovner, Lesley Allison ... Kew Gardens, NY
Brovold, Bruce J. ... Arcadia, WI
Brovold, Jay V. ... Medora, ND
Brow, Geoffrey G. B. ... New York, NY
Brow, Gregory S. ... Atlanta, GA
Brow, Michael S. ... Burlington, VT
Browarsky, Phillip ... Toledo, OH
Browd, Rudolph ... Miami, FL
Browd, Rudolph, P.A. ... Miami, FL
Browde, Michael B. ... Albuquerque, NM
Browde, Sanford ... Jersey City, NJ
Browder, Bannister R., Jr.
Winston-Salem, NC
Browder, Brian R. ... Nashville, TN
Browder, David, Jr. ... Clearwater, FL
Browder, Francis E. ... Greenville, PA
Browder, Herbert E. "Chip"
Tuscaloosa, AL
Browder & Higginbotham, L.L.P.
Austin, TX
Browder, J. Tyrone ... King, NC
Browder, J. Tyrone, P.A. ... King, NC
Browder & Kenney, P.C. ... Phoenix, AZ
Browder, Leslie E. ... Winston-Salem, NC
Browder, Mary Elizabeth M.
Bethany Beach, DE
Wilmington, DE
Browder, Olin L., Jr. ... Ann Arbor, MI
Browder, Paul K. ... Austin, TX
Browder, Robert D. ... Fort Worth, TX
Browder, Robert W. ... Phoenix, AZ
Browder, T. Martin, Jr. ... Kingsport, TN
Browder, Thomas M., III ... Macon, GA
Browder, W. Christopher ... Orlando, FL
Browder, William B. ... Wilmette, IL
Browder, William Barr, Jr. ... Midland, TX
Browder, William H., Jr. ... Portland, ME
Browdie, Alison S. ... Portland, OR
Browdy, Alvin ... Sarasota, FL
Browdy, Brian L. ... Chicago, IL
Browdy, Joseph E. ... New York, NY
Browdy, Michelle H. ... Chicago, IL
Browdy and Neimark ... Washington, DC
Browdy, Roger L. ... Washington, DC
Browdy, Scott A. ... Chicago, IL
Browe, Kathleen P. ... Richmond, VA
Browell, Douglas K. ... Columbus, OH
Brower, Alan G. ... New York, NY
Brower, Alfred W. ... Pearl River, NY
Brower, Anne T. ... New York, NY
Brower, Charles F. ... Torrington, CT
Brower, Charles H. ... Honolulu, HI
Brower, Charles H., and Associates, A Law Corporation ... Honolulu, HI
Brower, Charles H., II ... Minneapolis, MN
Brower, Charles N. ... Washington, DC
Brower, Christian S. ... Troy, MI
Brower, David A. P. ... New York, NY
Brower, David J. ... Chapel Hill, NC
Brower, David L. ... Nome, AK
Brower, David S. ... Santa Ana, CA
Brower, D.E., Jr. ... Oklahoma City, OK
Brower, Dereck R. ... Minneapolis, MN
Brower, Elizabeth Adolff ... Stamford, CT
Brower, Floyd A. ... Roundup, MT
Brower, Gary J. ... Trenton, NJ
Brower, Gregory A. ... Reno, NV
Brower, Gregory E. ... Baldwin, NY
Brower, Harold E. ... St. Petersburg, FL
Brower, Hillary L. ... East Brunswick, NJ
Brower, Hugh T. ... Las Cruces, NM
Brower, James M. ... San Diego, CA
Brower, John E. ... Minneapolis, MN
Brower, John F. ... Brighton, MI
Brower, John M. ... Fullerton, NE
Brower, Joshua C. Allen ... Seattle, WA
Brower, Karren ... Wheaton, IL
Brower, Kimberly S. ... Detroit, MI
Brower, Linda R. ... Somerville, NJ
Brower, Lynn ... Paris, ID
Brower, Murry S. ... Latham, NY
Brower, Nancy C. ... Charlotte, NC
Brower, Pat ... El Paso, TX
Brower, Pieter A. ... Kansas City, MO
Brower, Pieter A., P.C. ... Kansas City, MO
Brower, Prentice W. ... Hilton Head Island, SC
Brower, Richard L. ... San Diego, CA
Brower, Robert C. ... Blackfoot, ID
Brower, Robert D., Jr. ... Grand Rapids, MI
Brower, Robert G. ... Detroit, MI
Brower, Robert L. ... Lewiston, ID
Brower, Robert W. ... El Sobrante, CA
Brower, Ronald G. ... Santa Ana, CA
Brower, Ronald P. ... Washington, DC
Brower, Sam R., (P.C.) ... Omaha, NE
Brower, Sandra J. ... San Diego, CA
Brower, Scot S., Law Offices of
Honolulu, HI
Brower, Scott W. ... Kalamazoo, MI
Brower & Slavin, P.C. ... El Paso, TX
Brower, Stephen E. ... Trenton, NJ
Brower, Steve ... Treasury Department, Internal Revenue Service, GV
Brower, Steven ... Costa Mesa, CA
Brower, Steven D. ... Melville, NY
Brower, Thomas D. ... Scottsbluff, NE
Brower, Todd C. ... Roseland, NJ
Browers, William L. ... Elgin, IL
Browitt, David H. A. ... Roslyn, WA
Brown, A. Craig ... Springfield, MA
Brown, A. Kay Stanfield ... Troy, MI
Brown, A. Russell ... Gallatin, TN
Brown, A. Russell ... Lafayette, TN
Brown, A. Russell ... Lebanon, TN
Brown, A. Steven ... Los Angeles, CA
Brown, A. Todd ... Charlotte, NC
Brown, A. Vincent, Jr. ... Bessemer, AL
Brown, Aaron C., Jr. ... Paris, TN
Brown, Aaron, Jr. ... Portland, OR
Brown, Abbott S. ... South Orange, NJ
Brown, Abraham R. ... Burlingame, CA
Brown, Adam M. ... New York, NY
Brown, Adam R. ... Teaneck, NJ
Brown, Adele Burt ... Lexington, KY
Brown & Adkins ... Houston, TX
Brown, Adolph A. ... Skokie, IL
Brown, Adrian W. ... Atlanta, GA
Brown, Adrienne S. ... Torrance, CA
Brown, Agnes Marie ... Department of Justice, Civil Division, GV
Brown, Alan ... San Antonio, TX
Brown, Alan C. ... Tustin, CA
Brown, Alan C. ... Washington, DC
Brown, Alan C. ... Chicago, IL
Brown, Alan E. ... Tyler, TX
Brown, Alan I. ... New York, NY
Brown, Alan I. ... Dayton, OH
Brown, Alan J. ... Midland, TX
Brown, Alan M. ... New York, NY
Brown, Alan S. ... Indianapolis, IN
Brown, Alan S. ... Concord, NH
Brown, Alanna R. ... Golden, CO
Brown, Albert ... Boca Raton, FL
Brown, Albert D. (Trey), III
San Antonio, TX
Brown, Albert T., Jr. ... Cincinnati, OH
Brown, Alec H. ... New York, NY
Brown, Alexander E. ... Boulder Junction, WI
Eagle River, WI
Brown, Alexander Lee ... Roanoke, VA
Brown, Alexia E. ... Rancho Santa Fe, CA
Brown, Alfred A. ... Philadelphia, PA
Brown, Algie D. ... Shreveport, LA
Brown, Alice A. ... Houston, TX
Brown, Alicia M. ... Boston, MA
Brown, Alicia M. ... Charlotte, NC
Brown, Alison J. ... Washington, DC
Brown, Alison M. ... Raleigh, NC
Brown, Alison P. ... New York, NY
Brown, Allan E.
Executive Office Of The President, Office of Management and Budget, GV
Brown, Allan M. ... Schenectady, NY
Brown, Allan William ... Pittsburgh, PA
Brown, Allen ... Sharonville, OH
Brown, Allen B. ... Dell Rapids, SD
Brown, Allen C. ... El Cajon, CA
Brown, Allen J. ... Wellesley, MA
Brown, Allen K. ... Whittier, CA
Brown, Allen R. ... Louisville, KY
Brown, Allen S. ... Venice, FL
Brown, Allen Tupper ... Gill, MA
Brown, Allen V. ... Woodbridge, NJ
Brown, Allen W. ... Greensboro, NC
Brown, Allison I. ... Chicago, IL
Brown, Allyn E. ... Newberg, OR
Brown, Allyn L., Jr. ... Norwich, CT
Brown, Alton R., Jr. ... Mobile, AL
Brown, Altshuler and Spiro, A Ptnrshp. incl. A Prof. Corp. ... Beverly Hills, CA
Brown, Alvin H. ... New York, NY
Brown, Alvin S. ... Treasury Department, Internal Revenue Service, GV
Brown, Alyson C. ... Irving, TX
Brown, Amelia Logan ... Washington, DC
Brown and Amodio, A Legal Professional Association ... Medina, OH
Brown, Amy C. ... New York, NY
Brown, Amy J.
General Services Administration, Office of the General Counsel, GV
Brown, Amy L. ... Washington, DC
Brown, Amy L. ... Prairie Village, KS
Brown, Amy Lesserson ... Lake Success, NY
Brown, Andrea ... New York, NY
Brown, Andrea Marie ... Washington, DC
Brown, Andrew ... Washington, DC
Brown, Andrew B. ... Sacramento, CA
Brown, Andrew B. ... York, PA
Brown, Andrew Coy ... Houston, TX
Brown, Andrew J., Law Offices of
San Diego, CA
Brown, Andrew M. ... Anchorage, AK
Brown, Andrew M. ... Washington, DC
Brown, Andrew M., Jr. ... Newport, RI
Brown, Andrew Melton ... Tampa, FL
Brown, Andrew P. ... Beverly, MA
Brown, Andrew, Signorelli & Zallar, P.A.
Duluth, MN
Brown, Angela D. ... Houston, TX
Brown, Angela H. ... Greenville, NC
Brown, Angela J. ... Crown Point, IN
Brown, Angela K. ... Long Beach, CA
Brown, Angela M. ... Lansing, MI
Brown, Angela M. ... New York, NY
Brown, Angela Ranel ... Baltimore, MD
Brown, Ann Stoloff ... Anchorage, AK
Brown, Anna J. ... Portland, OR
Brown, Anna L. ... Naples, FL
Brown, Anna L. ... New York, NY
Brown, Anna Lee ... Carson City, NV
Brown, Anne ... Raleigh, NC
Brown, Anne E. ... St. Paul, MN
Brown, Anne E. ... Eau Claire, WI
Brown, Anne Elise ... New Orleans, LA
Brown, Anne Graff ... Des Moines, IA
Brown, Anne Greenwood ... Lake Elmo, MN
Brown, Anne H. ... Santa Rosa, CA
Brown, Anne Krilla ... Old Bridge, NJ
Brown, Anthony P. ... San Francisco, CA
Brown, Anthony P. ... Galveston, TX
Brown, Anthony W. ... Rocky Mount, NC
Brown, Arenofsky & Squire ... Mesa, AZ
Brown, Arlene P. ... Rockville Centre, NY
Brown, Arlyss E. ... Lincoln, NE
Brown, Arnold A. ... Miami, FL
Brown, Arnold E., II ... San Francisco, CA
Brown, Arnold H. ... Westwood, KS
Brown, Arnold I. ... Brooklyn, NY
Brown, Arnold S. ... Boston, MA
Brown, Arthur A. ... Thousand Oaks, CA
Brown, Arthur C. ... New Castle, IN
Brown, Arthur E. ... New York, NY
Brown, Arthur F. ... Bradenton, FL
Brown, Arthur H., Jr. ... New York, NY
Brown, Arthur J. ... Washington, DC
Brown, Arthur L. ... Encinitas, CA
Brown, Arthur M. ... Atlantic City, NJ
Brown, Arthur R., Jr. ... Cocoa, FL
Orlando, FL
Brown, Arthur S. ... Carlsbad, CA
Brown, Arthur V. ... Natick, MA
Brown, Arthur Wm., Jr. ... Los Angeles, CA
Brown, Aryeh Y. ... Seattle, WA
Brown, Ashley C. ... Columbus, OH
Brown, Ashley Haus ... Tulsa, OK
Brown, Ashley Haus, P.C. ... Tulsa, OK
Brown & Associates ... San Diego, CA
Brown & Associates ... Belleville, IL
Brown & Associates, LLP ... Pasadena, CA
Brown & Associates, P.A.
Riviera Beach, FL
Brown, Aubrey C. ... Louisville, KY
Brown, Aubrey Lee, Jr. ... Memphis, TN
Brown, Audrey A. ... Delta Junction, AK
Brown, Augustus F. ... Bel Air, MD
Brown, Avery L.
Department of Labor, GV
Brown, Avery R. ... Los Angeles, CA
Brown, Avry L. ... Hartford, CT
Brown, B. Andrew ... Minneapolis, MN
Brown, B. Blaine, III ... Montgomery, AL
Brown, B. Ervin, II ... Washington, DC
Winston-Salem, NC
Brown, B. Lane ... Hammond, LA
Brown, B. Lane ... Warren, OH
Brown, B. Mackay ... Miami, FL
Brown, B. Mahlon ... Las Vegas, NV
Brown, B. Mahlon, III ... Las Vegas, NV
Brown, Bachman S., Jr. ... Kannapolis, NC
Brown & Bain, A Professional Association
Phoenix, AZ
Tucson, AZ
Brown, Baird A. ... Los Angeles, CA
Brown, Baird A., A Professional Corporation
Los Angeles, CA
Brown, Baird B. ... Grand Junction, CO
Brown, Baird B., P.C.
Grand Junction, CO
Brown, Banks ... New York, NY
Brown, Barbara ... Los Angeles, CA
Brown, Barbara ... Garden City, NY
Brown, Barbara A. ... Sharon, MA
Brown, Barbara A. ... Albuquerque, NM
Brown, Barbara Ann ... Mobile, AL
Brown, Barbara Anne ... Atlanta, GA
Brown, Barbara Berish ... Washington, DC
Brown, Barbara Block ... New York, NY
Brown, Barbara Bulla ... Potomac, MD
Brown, Barbara E. ... Washington, DC
Brown, Barbara F. ... San Diego, CA
Brown, Barbara J. ... Lansing, MI
Brown, Barbara M. ... Cincinnati, OH
Brown, Barbara M. ... Cleveland, OH
Brown, Barbara S. ... Baltimore, MD
Brown, Bari G. ... Potomac, MD
Brown, Barrett Keith ... Sherman, TX
Brown, Barry ... Boston, MA
Brown, Barry ... Rochester, NY
Brown, Barry Allan ... Houston, TX
Brown, Barry Cummins ... East Lansing, MI
Brown, Barry D. ... Los Angeles, CA
Redwood City, CA
Brown, Barry H. ... Santa Monica, CA
Brown, Barry S. ... Seal Beach, CA
Brown, Barry S. ... Baltimore, MD
Brown, Barry S. ... Dallas, TX
Brown, Barry Spencer ... Bloomington, IN
Brown, Bart A., Jr. ... Fort Thomas, KY
Brown, Barton ... Overland Park, KS
Brown, Bartram S. ... Chicago, IL
Brown and Beaufait, P.S. ... Seattle, WA
Brown, Becky J. ... Shelby, NC
Brown, Bemiller, Murray & McIntyre
Bucyrus, OH
Mansfield, OH
Mt. Gilead, OH
Brown, Ben H., Jr. ... Alexandria, VA
Brown, Benjamin Charles
Oklahoma City, OK
Brown, Benjamin D. ... San Francisco, CA
Brown, Benjamin L. ... Silver Spring, MD
Brown, Benjamin P.
West Palm Beach, FL
Brown, Benjamin W. ... Des Moines, IA
Brown, Bennett A. ... Fairfax, VA
Brown, Bennett D. ... Long Island City, NY
Brown, Berardini & Dunning, P.C.
Denver, CO
Brown & Bergman ... Atlantic City, NJ
Brown, Bernard E. ... Kansas City, MO
Brown, Bernard L. ... Fairfax, VA
Brown, Bernie J., Jr. ... Memphis, TN
Brown, Bert M., IV ... Las Vegas, NV
Brown, Bertram ... New York, NY
Brown, Beth A. ... Northbrook, IL
Brown, Bettina Schiebler ... Atlanta, GA
Brown, Betty L. ... Flower Mound, TX
Brown, Betty R. ... Waunakee, WI
Brown, Beverley S. ... Norwalk, OH
Brown, Bill Wardlaw ... Fort Worth, TX
Brown & Bins ... Rochester, MN
Brown, Blair A. ... Decatur, IN
Brown, Blair G. ... Washington, DC
Brown & Boland ... San Francisco, CA
Brown, Boniard I. ... West Covina, CA
Brown, Boniard I., Inc. ... West Covina, CA
Brown, Bonita Kneeland ... Tampa, FL
Brown, Bonnie M. ... Louisville, KY
Brown, Bowden V. ... Bloomfield Hills, MI
Brown, Bowdy J. ... Montgomery, AL
Brown, Bowman, (P.A.) ... Miami, FL
Brown, Boyd Janney ... Fairfax, VA
Leesburg, VA
Brown, Bradford C. ... Davidson, NC
Brown, Bradford D. ... Santa Barbara, CA
Brown, Bradford S. ... Los Angeles, CA
Brown, Bradford T. ... Tucson, AZ
Brown & Bradley ... Vallejo, CA
Brown, Bradley J. ... Wichita, KS
Brown, Bradley L. ... Portland, OR
Brown, Bradshaw, Anderson & Moffat, LLP
Salt Lake City, UT
Brown, Brandon A. ... New Orleans, LA
Brown, Brandy Oliver ... Berea, KY
Brown, Branford D. ... Cincinnati, OH
Brown Brasher & Smith ... Memphis, TN
Brown & Brehmer ... Columbia, SC
Brown, Brenda K. ... Dallas, TX
Brown, Brent L. ... McKinney, TX
Brown, Brett S. ... De Kalb, IL
Brown, Brian ... Melville, NY
Brown, Brian ... New York, NY
Brown, Brian A. ... Little Rock, AR
Brown, Brian David ... Wellesley, MA
Brown, Brian E. ... Austin, TX
Brown, Brian Edward ... New Rochelle, NY
Brown, Brian I. ... Burton, MI
Brown, Brian M. ... Baltimore, MD
Brown, Brian M. ... Reno, NV
Brown, Brian Michael ... Detroit, MI
Brown, Brian N. ... Kansas City, MO
Brown, Brian R. ... Durham, NC
Brown, Brian S. ... Baltimore, MD

Brown, Brian T. ... Blue Ash, OH
Brown, Brickford Y. ... Richmond, VA
Brown, Brit T. ... Houston, TX
Brown, Britt A. ... Decatur, IL
Brown, Brook Bennett ... Austin, TX
Brown, Brooks R. ... Boston, MA
Brown & Brown ... Palo Alto, CA
Brown & Brown ... San Diego, CA
Brown & Brown ... Ventura, CA
Brown & Brown ... Jonesboro, GA
Brown & Brown ... New Castle, IN
Brown & Brown ... Rochester, IN
Brown and Brown ... Cheboygan, MI
Newberry, MI
St. Ignace, MI
Sault Ste. Marie, MI
Brown & Brown ... Kearney, MO
Brown & Brown ... St. Louis, MO
Brown & Brown ... Las Vegas, NV
Brown and Brown ... Ballston Spa, NY
Brown & Brown ... Smithtown, NY
Brown and Brown ... Medina, OH
Brown & Brown ... McAlester, OK
Brown & Brown ... Seattle, WA
Brown & Brown, Attorneys at Law, P.C.
Merrillville, IN
Brown, Brown & Brown ... Albemarle, NC
Troy, NC
Brown, Brown & Brown, A Professional Association ... Baltimore, MD
Bel Air, MD
Elkton, MD
Towson, MD
Brown, Brown, Chandler & Townend
Garland, TX
Brown & Brown Law Offices, P.C.
Eagar, AZ
Holbrook, AZ
Pinetop, AZ
St. Johns, AZ
Brown & Brown, P.C. ... Highland Park, IL
Brown & Brown, P.C. ... Bedford, MA
Brown & Brown, P.C. ... Omaha, NE
Brown & Brown, P.C. ... Jersey City, NJ
Newark, NJ
Brown, Brown, Solt & Ferretti
Allentown, PA
Bethlehem, PA
Easton, PA
Brown, Brown & White, Chartered
Baltimore, MD
Brown, Bruce ... Washington, DC
Brown, Bruce A. ... Aurora, IL
Brown, Bruce A. ... Las Vegas, NV
Brown, Bruce A. ... New York, NY
Brown, Bruce B. ... Kearney, MO
Brown, Bruce B. ... Clyde, NC
Brown, Bruce D. ... Washington, DC
Brown, Bruce D. ... Baltimore, MD
Brown, Bruce G. ... Amherst, MA
Brown, Bruce I. ... Los Angeles, CA
Brown, Bruce J. ... Asheville, NC
Brown, Bruce L. ... Anchorage, AK
Brown, Bruce L. ... Seattle, WA
Brown, Bruce M. ... Fresno, CA
Brown, Bruce M. ... Miles City, MT
Brown, Bruce P. ... Atlanta, GA
Brown, Bruce S. ... Great Neck, NY
Brown, Bruce V. ... Detroit, MI
Brown, Bryan F. ... Santa Ana, CA
Brown, Bryan K. ... Los Angeles, CA
Brown, Bryan K. ... Houston, TX
Brown & Bunch ... Chapel Hill, NC
Durham, NC
Raleigh, NC
Brown, Burgoon & Hartnagel
New City, NY
Brown & Burke ... Portland, ME
Brown, Burl C. ... Gainesville, TX
Brown, Burton ... Rossville, GA
Brown, Burton A. ... Chicago, IL
Brown, Byrd R. ... Pittsburgh, PA
Brown, Byron E. (Rusty) ... Tulsa, OK
Brown, C. Baird ... Philadelphia, PA
Brown, C. Brandon ... Baton Rouge, LA
Brown, C. Chester, Jr. ... Spartanburg, SC
Brown, C. Christopher ... Baltimore, MD
Brown, C. Christopher ... Athens, TN
Brown, C. Clifton ... Sapulpa, OK
Brown, C. Collins ... Allentown, PA
Brown, C. David, II, (P.A.) ... Orlando, FL
Brown, C. Douglas ... Panama City, FL
Brown, C. Edward, IV ... St. Louis, MO
Brown, C. Harold ... Fort Worth, TX
Brown, C. Kyle ... Phoenix, AZ
Brown, C. Mitchell ... Columbia, SC
Brown, C. Palmer, Jr. ... Wilmington, NC
Brown, C. Randolph ... Monroe, LA
Brown, C. Reed, P.C. ... Sandy, UT
Brown, C. Scott ... Salt Lake City, UT
Brown, C. Thomas ... Baltimore, MD
Elkton, MD
Brown, C. Thomas ... Fairfax, VA
Brown, C. Vincent ... Greenville, SC
Brown, Cahill, Gawne & Miller, P.C.
St. Albans, VT
Brown, Caleb, Jr. ... Cincinnati, OH
Brown, Calissa W. ... Wilmington, DE
Brown, Calvin B. ... Vero Beach, FL
Brown, Canda L. ... West Palm Beach, FL
Brown, Cara L. ... Las Vegas, NV
Brown & Carby ... Natchez, MS
Brown, Carl C., Jr. ... Augusta, GA
Brown, Carl H., Jr. ... Pittsburgh, PA
Brown, Carl L. ... Fresno, CA
Brown, Carl O., Jr. ... New Orleans, LA
Brown, Carl R. ... San Diego, CA
Brown, Carla L. ... West Palm Beach, FL

Brown, Carla L., A Prof. Assoc., Law Offices of ... West Palm Beach, FL
Brown, Carlos F. ... Sacramento, CA
Brown & Carlson, P.A. ... Minneapolis, MN
Brown, Carlton L. ... Richmond, VA
Brown, Carlton S. ... Lumpkin, GA
Brown, Carol A. ... Sacramento, CA
Brown, Carol A. ... New Haven, CT
Brown, Carol C. ... Boston, MA
Brown, Carol C., and Associates, P.C.
Boston, MA
Brown, Carol N. ... Birmingham, AL
Brown, Carole Dominguin ... Wilton, CT
Brown, Carole J. ... Lawton, OK
Brown, Caroline M. ... Washington, DC
Brown, Caroline N. ... Chapel Hill, NC
Brown, Carolyn A. ... Dallas, TX
Brown, Carolyn A. ... Kennewick, WA
Brown, Carolyn J. ... Chicago, IL
Brown, Carolyn J., P.C. ... Chicago, IL
Brown, Carolyn M. ... Lexington, KY
Brown, Carrie L. ... Oakland, CA
Brown, Carroll E. ... Amarillo, TX
Brown, Carson V. ... Lock Haven, PA
Brown & Casey ... Brookfield, MO
Brown, Catherine ... Orlando, FL
Brown, Catherine ... Trenton, NJ
Brown, Catherine Agnello
Orchard Park, NY
Brown, Catherine E. ... West Orange, NJ
Brown, Catherine M. ... Louisville, KY
Brown, Catherine M. ... Morristown, NJ
Brown, Catherine M., L.L.C.
Morristown, NJ
Brown, Catherine R. ... Mankato, MN
Brown, Catherine T. ... Washington, DC
Brown, Catherine W. ... Department of State, Office of the Legal Adviser, GV
Brown, Cathrynn Novich ... Carlsbad, NM
Brown, Cathy K. ... Morristown, NJ
Brown, Cecil N. ... Tucson, AZ
Brown, Cedric A. ... Jamaica, NY
Brown, Cedric R. ... Portland, OR
Brown, Celia A. ... Humble, TX
Brown, Celia Reznick ... Greenwich, CT
Brown & Chapman ... St. Louis, MO
Brown, Charles A. ... Lewiston, ID
Brown, Charles A. ... Pasadena, TX
Brown, Charles A., Jr. ... Westfield, NJ
Brown, Charles A., P.A. ... Little Rock, AR
Brown, Charles Asa ... Portsmouth, OH
Brown, Charles B. ... Northbrook, IL
Brown, Charles Bruce ... Starkville, MS
Brown, Charles C. ... Salt Lake City, UT
Brown, Charles C., Jr. ... Bellefonte, PA
Brown, Charles C. W. ... Santa Monica, CA
Brown, Charles D. ... San Diego, CA
Brown, Charles D. ... New York, NY
Brown, Charles D. ... New York, NY
Brown, Charles D. ... Greensboro, NC
Brown, Charles D. ... Seattle, WA
Brown, Charles E. ... Salisbury, NC
Brown, Charles E. ... Alliance, OH
Hartville, OH
Brown, Charles E. ... Columbus, OH
Brown, Charles E. ... Austin, TX
Brown, Charles E. ... Dallas, TX
Brown, Charles E. ... San Antonio, TX
Brown, Charles E., II ... Gainesville, MO
Brown, Charles Earl ... Toledo, OH
Brown, Charles Edward ... Troy, MI
Brown, Charles F. ... Washington, DC
Brown, Charles G. ... De Kalb, IL
Brown, Charles G. ... Pittsburgh, PA
Brown, Charles G., III ... Charleston, WV
Brown, Charles Gordon ... Chapel Hill, NC
Brown, Charles H. ... Statesboro, GA
Brown, Charles H. ... Detroit, MI
Brown, Charles H. ... Kingwood, WV
Brown, Charles H., II ... Los Angeles, CA
Brown, Charles H., III ... Atlanta, GA
Brown, Charles H., III ... Cincinnati, OH
Brown, Charles J. ... Windham, NY
Brown, Charles J., III ... Salisbury, MD
Brown, Charles J., Jr. ... Houma, LA
Brown, Charles L. ... West Palm Beach, FL
Brown, Charles M. ... St. Ignace, MI
Brown, Charles M. ... Mansfield, OH
Brown, Charles N. ... Utica, NY
Brown, Charles P. ... Glenarm, MD
Brown, Charles P. ... Albemarle, NC
Brown, Charles P. ... Memphis, TN
Brown, Charles, (P.C.) ... Galveston, TX
Brown, Charles R. ... Kansas City, MO
Brown, Charles R. ... Brevard, NC
Brown, Charles R. ... Salt Lake City, UT
Brown, Charles R. P. ... Fort Pierce, FL
Brown, Charles S. ... Southlake, TX
Brown, Charles S. C.
National Science Foundation, Office of the General Counsel, GV
Brown, Charles Stuart ... Cheyenne, WY
Brown, Charles W. ... Atlanta, GA
Brown, Charles W. R. ... Houston, TX
Brown, Charlie R. ... Clearwater, FL
Brown, Chas. S., Jr. ... New Castle, IN
Brown, Cherie J. ... Placerville, CA
Brown, Cheryl A. ... Atlanta, GA
Brown, Chester H., Jr. ... San Antonio, TX
Brown, Chewanney A. ... College Park, MD
Brown & Childress, L.L.C. ... East Orange, NJ
Brown, Chris Marie ... Fresno, CA
Brown, Christa L. ... Austin, TX
Brown, Christi L. ... Lima, OH
Brown, Christian D. ... Boise, ID
Brown, Christian T. ... New Orleans, LA
Brown, Christina L. ... Evanston, IL
Brown, Christine A. ... Elmira, NY

Brown, Christine Donahue ... Trumbull, CT
Brown, Christine P. ... Portland, OR
Brown, Christopher ... Walnut Creek, CA
Brown, Christopher ... Glen Burnie, MD
Brown, Christopher A. ... Fresno, CA
Brown, Christopher A. ... Indianapolis, IN
Brown, Christopher A. ... Atlantic City, NJ
Brown, Christopher C. ... Pontiac, MI
Brown, Christopher D. ... Miami, FL
Brown, Christopher E. ... Boston, MA
Brown, Christopher J. ... Springfield, MA
Brown, Christopher L. ... Boston, MA
Brown, Christopher M. ... Prestonsburg, KY
Brown, Christopher M. ... Eden Prairie, MN
Brown, Christopher M. ... Houston, TX
Brown & Christopher ... Starke, FL
Brown, Christopher R. ... Hazlet, NJ
Red Bank, NJ
Brown, Christopher S. ... Seattle, WA
Brown, Christopher T. ... Medina, OH
Brown, Christopher T. ... Austin, TX
Brown, Christopher W. ... Alexandria, VA
Brown, Christy C. ... Phoenix, AZ
Brown, Chuck D. ... Joplin, MO
Brown, Chuck Ragan ... Houston, TX
Brown, Clarence B., III ... Dallas, TX
Brown, Clarence O'Neill ... New York, NY
Brown, Clarence S. ... Sacramento, CA
Brown Clark, A Professional Association
Sarasota, FL
Brown, Clarke C. ... Salem, OR
Brown, Clarkson F. ... San Antonio, TX
Brown, Claude Duffey ... Fort Worth, TX
Brown, Claudia D. ... San Antonio, TX
Brown and Clemens ... Kewanee, IL
Brown, Clement ... Fall River, MA
Brown, Clifford ... Forestville, MD
Brown, Clifford F. ... Norwalk, OH
Brown, Clifford H.
Agency for International Development, Legal Advisers-Overseas, GV
Brown, Clifford L. ... Boise, ID
Brown, Clifford S. ... Springfield, MO
Brown, Clifford W. ... Lubbock, TX
Brown, Clifton G. ... Sumter, SC
Brown, Clint M., Jr. ... Houston, TX
Brown, Colin W. ... Deerfield Beach, FL
Brown, Colleen A. ... Canandaigua, NY
Rochester, NY
Brown & Connery, LLP ... Camden, NJ
Westmont, NJ
Brown, Connis O., III
Fort Lauderdale, FL
Brown, Constance M. ... New Orleans, LA
Brown, Corey C. ... Houston, TX
Brown, Corey I. ... Sacramento, CA
Brown, Corinne Alison ... Simsbury, CT
Brown, Cornelius P. ... Chicago, IL
Brown, Courtney Burge ... Birmingham, AL
Jacksonville, FL
Atlanta, GA
Brown & Cox ... Temple, TX
Brown, Craig ... Dallas, TX
Brown, Craig A. ... Alexandria, VA
Brown, Craig E. ... Oklahoma City, OK
Brown, Craig J.
Federal Communications Commission, Common Carrier Bureau, GV
Brown, Craig L. ... New York, NY
Brown, Craig M. ... San Jose, CA
Brown, Craig M. ... Boston, MA
Brown, Craig M. ... Cleveland, OH
Brown, Craig M., Inc. ... San Jose, CA
Brown, Craig R. ... New York, NY
Brown, Craig T. ... Irvine, CA
Brown, Craig W. ... Sausalito, CA
Brown, Craig W. ... Binghamton, NY
Brown, Creighton & Peckham
Atwood, KS
Brown & Crouppen, P.C. ... St. Louis, MO
Brown, Cummins & Brown Co., L.P.A.
Cincinnati, OH
Brown, Curtis D. ... Minneapolis, MN
Brown, Curtis L. ... Orlando, FL
Brown, Curtis L. ... Elm Mott, TX
Brown, Curtiss E. ... Lompoc, CA
Brown, Cynthia A. ... Woodridge, IL
Brown, Cynthia A. ... Boston, MA
Brown, Cynthia Anne ... Lubbock, TX
Brown, Cynthia Briscoe ... Atlanta, GA
Brown, Cynthia Buck ... Greenville, SC
Brown, Cynthia J. ... Irvine, CA
Brown, Cynthia L. ... McLean, VA
Brown, D. Craig ... Florence, SC
Brown, D. Gerald ... Palo Alto, CA
Brown, D. Keith ... Newtown, PA
Brown, D. Randall ... Fort Wayne, IN
Brown, D. Scott ... Kansas City, KS
Brown, D. Scott ... Mansfield, LA
Brown, D. Tyner ... Westchester, IL
Brown, D. Wayne ... Breckenridge, CO
Brown, Dale F. ... Painesville, OH
Brown, Dale L. ... San Diego, CA
Brown, Dale M. ... Washington, PA
Brown, Dale Martin ... Winston-Salem, NC
Brown, Dama ... Dearborn, MI
Brown, Damon R. ... Lexington, KY
Brown, Dan R. ... Lawton, OK
Brown, Dana ... Louisville, KY
Brown, Dana B., Mr. ... Baton Rouge, LA
Brown, Dana M. ... Dallas, TX
Brown, Dana M. ... Richmond, VA
Brown, Daniel ... Lisle, IL
Brown, Daniel A. ... Washington, DC
Brown, Daniel A. ... Columbus, OH
Brown, Daniel A. ... Dayton, OH
Brown, Daniel A. ... Beaverton, OR
Brown, Daniel A. ... Seattle, WA

Brown, Daniel B. ... Nashville, TN
Brown, Daniel C. ... Tallahassee, FL
Brown, Daniel C. ... Detroit, MI
Brown, Daniel D. ... Danville, IL
Brown, Daniel F. ... Buffalo, NY
Brown, Daniel G. ... San Mateo, CA
Brown, Daniel G. ... Louisville, KY
Brown, Daniel G. ... New York, NY
Brown, Daniel H. ... Emeryville, CA
Brown, Daniel H. ... New York, NY
Brown, Daniel H. ... North Baltimore, OH
Brown, Daniel J. ... St. Louis, MO
Brown, Daniel J. ... Spokane, WA
Brown, Daniel James ... Columbia, SC
Brown, Daniel K. ... Fort Collins, CO
Brown, Daniel L. ... Phoenix, AZ
Brown, Daniel L. ... New York, NY
Brown, Daniel L. ... San Antonio, TX
Brown, Daniel L., P.C. ... San Antonio, TX
Brown, Daniel P., Jr. ... Hartford, CT
Brown, Daniel R. ... Los Angeles, CA
Brown, Daniel R. ... Kansas City, MO
Brown, Daniel R. ... Portland, OR
Brown, Daniel S. ... Danville, CA
Brown, Daniel S. ... New York, NY
Brown, Daniel S. ... Roanoke, VA
Brown, Daniel T. ... Chicago, IL
Brown, Darla Sue ... Bloomington, IN
Brown, Darrel G. ... Muskegon, MI
Brown, Darrell E. ... Tulsa, OK
Brown, Darrell F. ... Little Rock, AR
Brown, Darren ... Beaumont, TX
Brown, Darryl ... Dallas, TX
Brown, Darryl K. ... Atlanta, GA
Brown, Darven L. ... Tulsa, OK
Brown, Darven L., P.C. ... Tulsa, OK
Brown, Daryl J. ... Sarasota, FL
Brown, David ... Meriden, CT
Brown, David ... Murphysboro, IL
Brown, David A. ... Pinetop, AZ
St. Johns, AZ
Brown, David A. ... El Cerrito, CA
Brown, David A. ... Walnut Creek, CA
Brown, David A. ... Boston, MA
Brown, David A. ... Charlotte, NC
Brown, David A. ... Aiken, SC
Brown, David A. ... Florence, SC
Brown, David A., A Professional Corporation
Walnut Creek, CA
Brown, David Allen, (A Professional Corporation) ... Irvine, CA
Brown, David Anthony ... Washington, IL
Brown, David B. ... Wilmington, DE
Brown, David B. ... Jonesboro, GA
Brown, David B. ... Dallas, TX
Brown, David C. ... Los Angeles, CA
Brown, David C. ... Pasadena, CA
Brown, David C. ... Louisville, KY
Brown, David C. ... Glen Burnie, MD
Brown, David D. ... Chicago, IL
Brown, David D. ... Abingdon, VA
Brown, David D., III ... New York, NY
Brown, David E. ... Sacramento, CA
Brown, David E. ... Kenilworth, IL
Brown, David E. ... Iowa City, IA
Brown, David E. ... Rochester, NY
Brown, David E., Jr. ... Washington, DC
Brown, David F. ... Irvine, CA
Brown, David F. ... Modesto, CA
Brown, David F. ... San Antonio, TX
Brown, David G. ... San Diego, CA
Brown, David Glenn ... Martinez, CA
Brown, David Gregory ... Jefferson City, MO
Brown, David H. ... Houston, TX
Brown, David I. ... Sacramento, CA
Brown, David I. ... San Rafael, CA
Brown, David Irving ... New York, NY
Brown, David J. ... San Francisco, CA
Brown, David J. ... Rochelle, IL
Rockford, IL
Brown, David J. ... Lawrence, KS
Brown, David J., (P.C.) ... Boston, MA
Brown, David James ... Lewisville, TX
Brown, David K. ... Scranton, PA
Brown, David Keith ... Houston, TX
Brown, David L. ... Des Moines, IA
Brown, David L. ... New York, NY
Brown, David L. ... Greensboro, NC
Brown, David L. ... Philadelphia, PA
Brown, David L. ... Granbury, TX
Brown, David M. ... Seal Beach, CA
Brown, David M. ... Atlanta, GA
Brown, David M. ... St. Peters, MO
Brown, David Marshall
Fort Lauderdale, FL
Brown, David Marshall, P.A.
Fort Lauderdale, FL
Brown, David N. ... Washington, DC
Brown, David N. ... Medina, OH
Brown, David O. ... Harrisburg, PA
Brown, David P. ... Mill Valley, CA
Brown, David P. ... Henderson, TX
Brown, David P. ... Kingwood, WV
Brown, David P., III ... Haverford, PA
Brown, David R. ... Deerfield, IL
Brown, David R. ... Niles, IL
Brown, David R. ... Pittsburgh, PA
Brown, David Rodney ... Jacksonville, FL
Brown, David S. ... Carlsbad, CA
Brown, David S. ... Los Angeles, CA
Brown, David S. ... Torrance, CA
Brown, David S. ... Manchester, NH
Brown, David S. ... New York, NY
Brown, David Simon ... Buffalo, NY
Brown, David S. J. ... Washington, DC
Brown, David T. ... Chicago, IL
Brown, David W. ... Monterey, CA
Brown, David W. ... Washington, DC

Brown, David W. ... St. Louis, MO
Brown, David W. ... Huntingdon Valley, PA
Brown, David W., P.C. ... Portland, OR
Brown, David W. T. ... Los Angeles, CA
Brown, Dawn B. ... Manchester, NH
Brown, Dean ... Oklahoma City, OK
Brown, Dean A. ... Fort Wayne, IN
Brown, Dean R. ... New York, NY
Brown, Dean S. ... Encino, CA
Brown, Deane B. ... Chicago, IL
Brown, Deanna M. ... San Bernardino, CA
Brown, Debora Nilsen ... Wyckoff, NJ
Brown, Deborah C. ... San Francisco, CA
Brown, Deborah Casey ... Greenville, SC
Brown, Deborah D. ... Atlanta, GA
Brown, Deborah Janco ... Lakewood, OH
Brown, Deborah L. ... Lubbock, TX
Brown, Debra K. ... Exeland, WI
Brown, Debra L. ... Portland, ME
Brown, Debra M. ... Jackson, MS
Brown, Dee Kincaid ... Larchmont, NY
Brown, Deirdra J. ... Chattanooga, TN
Brown, Delmar L. ... Richmond, VA
Brown, Deloris A. ... Los Angeles, CA
Brown, Delphine W. Knight
New York, NY
Brown, Dena Gavant ... Smithtown, NY
Brown, Dengler, Good & Rider, L.C.
Wichita, KS
Brown, Denise ... Arlington, VA
Brown, Denise C. ... Stuart, FL
Brown, Denise Gorges ... Burbank, CA
Brown, Denise Langlois ... New Orleans, LA
Brown, Denise R. ... Washington, DC
Brown, Dennis A. ... Wyomissing, PA
Brown, Dennis C. ... Washington, DC
Brown, Dennis C. ... East Syracuse, NY
Brown, Dennis C., (A Professional Corporation) ... Los Angeles, CA
Brown, Dennis D. ... San Jose, CA
Brown, Dennis D. ... Tulsa, OK
Brown, Dennis K. ... Greenwood, IN
Brown, Dennis L. ... Houston, TX
Brown, Dennis L., P.C. ... Houston, TX
Brown, Dennis M. ... San Jose, CA
Brown, Dennis M. ... Ronkonkoma, NY
Brown, Dennis O. ... Pittsburgh, PA
Brown, Dennis R. ... Laguna Hills, CA
Brown, Dennis Woodfin ... Denver, CO
Brown, Denny L. ... Rancho Santa Fe, CA
Brown, Derek R.
Department Of Veterans Affairs, Board of Veterans Appeals, GV
Brown, Desmond P. ... Modesto, CA
Brown, Destiny A. ... Towson, MD
Brown, Diana K. ... Los Angeles, CA
Brown, Diana S. ... Columbus, OH
Brown, Diane ... Austin, TX
Brown, Diane C. ... Chicago, IL
Brown, Diane C. ... Kansas City, MO
Brown, Diane G. ... San Diego, CA
Brown, Diane M. ... Campbell, CA
Brown, Dick Terrell ... Austin, TX
Brown, Dickson G. ... New York, NY
Brown & Dierdorf ... Watertown, NY
Brown, Diffenderffer & Kearney, LLP
Towson, MD
Brown, Diffenderffer, Wagonheim & Kearney, LLP ... Baltimore, MD
Brown, Diven & Hentschke
Solana Beach, CA
Brown, Don C. ... San Bernardino, CA
Brown, Don C. ... Wilmington, DE
Brown, Don D. ... Woodward, OK
Brown, Don E. ... Pratt, KS
Brown, Don E. ... Houston, TX
Brown, Don P. ... Chagrin Falls, OH
Brown, Don P. ... Cleveland, OH
Brown, Don P., Jr. ... Boulder, CO
Brown, Don R. ... Pocahontas, AR
Brown, Donald ... Detroit, MI
Brown, Donald ... Plymouth Meeting, PA
Brown, Donald A. ... Washington, DC
Brown, Donald A. ... Dolton, IL
Brown, Donald A. ... Columbus, OH
Brown, Donald B. ... San Jose, CA
Brown, Donald B. ... Torrance, CA
Brown, Donald C. ... Lake Charles, LA
Brown, Donald C. ... Woodbury, NJ
Brown, Donald C., Jr. ... Washington, DC
Brown, Donald D. ... Cambridge, OH
Brown, Donald D., Jr. ... Fishkill, NY
Poughkeepsie, NY
Brown, Donald E. ... Jacksonville, FL
Brown, Donald E. ... Dearborn, MI
Brown, Donald F. ... Bangor, ME
Brown, Donald J. ... Des Moines, IA
Brown, Donald J. ... Minneapolis, MN
St. Paul, MN
Brown, Donald J., Jr. ... Chicago, IL
Brown, Donald K., Jr. ... Louisville, KY
Brown, Donald Killian ... Louisville, KY
Brown, Donald N. ... Chicago, IL
Brown, Donald, (P.C.) ... Boston, MA
Brown, Donald R. ... Los Angeles, CA
Brown, Donald R. ... Alexandria, LA
Brown, Donald R. ... Monroe, LA
Brown, Donald R. ... Trenton, NJ
Brown, Donald W. ... San Francisco, CA
Brown, Donald W. ... St. Charles, MO
Brown, Donise Edwards
North Palm Beach, FL
Brown, Donna ... Austin, TX
Brown, Donna J. ... New York, NY
Brown, Donna Jean ... Concord, NH
Brown, Donna M. ... Springfield, MA
Brown, Donna P. ... College Park, MD
Brown, Donnaldson K. ... Brooklyn, NY

Brown, Dora M. ... Dallas, TX
Brown, Doris M. ... Kansas City, KS
Brown, Doris V. ... Kissimmee, FL
Brown, Dorothy A. ... New York, NY
Brown, Dorothy J. Lindsey
Oklahoma City, OK
Brown, Douglas A. ... Houston, TX
Brown, Douglas B. ... Orlando, FL
Brown, Douglas B. ... Cleveland, OH
Brown, Douglas & Brown ... St. Joseph, MO
Brown, Douglas C. ... San Diego, CA
Brown, Douglas D. ... Hammond, LA
Brown, Douglas E. ... Eagar, AZ
Pinetop, AZ
Brown, Douglas E. ... Detroit, MI
Brown, Douglas G. ... Denver, CO
Brown, Douglas G. ... Greenville, SC
Brown, Douglas G., P.C. ... Springfield, IL
Brown, Douglas H. ... Olympia, WA
Brown, Douglas J. ... Minneapolis, MN
Brown, Douglas J. ... Nashville, TN
Brown, Douglas L. ... Mobile, AL
Brown, Douglas M. ... Chicago, IL
Brown, Douglas R. ... Southport, CT
Brown, Douglas R. ... Wauconda, IL
Brown, Douglas R. ... Evansville, IN
Brown, Douglas R. ... Indianapolis, IN
Brown, Douglas R. ... Somerville, NJ
Brown, Douglas S. ... Newport Beach, CA
Brown, Douglas S. ... Ventura, CA
Brown, Douglas S. ... Naugatuck, CT
Brown, Douglas W. ... Sacramento, CA
Brown, Douglas W. ... Denver, CO
Brown, Douglas W. ... Shelbyville, IN
Brown, Douglas W., Jr. ... Atlanta, GA
Brown, Drew M. ... Phoenix, AZ
Brown, Drew & Massey, LLP
Casper, WY
Brown, D. Scott ... Shreveport, LA
Brown, Duane B. ... Detroit, MI
Brown, Duane E. ... Albuquerque, NM
Brown, Duane K. ... Wichita, KS
Brown, Duncan Hall ... Southfield, MI
Brown, Dwayne L. ... Montgomery, AL
Brown, Dyke ... Orinda, CA
Brown, E. Blair ... Alexandria, VA
Brown, E. Cooper ... Department of Labor, Office of Secretary, GV
Brown, E. Edward ... Garden City, KS
Brown, E. Lawson, Jr. ... Burlington, NC
Brown, E. Parker ... Richmond, VA
Brown, E. Parker, II ... Syracuse, NY
Brown, E. Scott, Jr. ... Baldwinsville, NY
Brown, E. Terry ... Montgomery, AL
Brown, Earl A., Jr. ... Houston, TX
Brown, Earl D., Jr. ... New York, NY
Brown, Earl, Jr. ... Indianapolis, IN
Brown, Earl T., Law Office of
Greenville, NC
Brown, Earl V. ... Boxford, MA
Brown, Earl V., Jr. ... Washington, DC
Brown, Earl W. ... Orono, ME
Brown, Earl W., III ... Springfield, MO
Brown, Earle O., III ... Fort Worth, TX
Brown, Earnest Edward, Jr. ... Pine Bluff, AR
Brown, Earnest H. ... Houston, TX
Brown, E. B., (Ms.) ... Atlanta, GA
Brown, Eddie W. ... Florence, KY
Brown, Edgar A. ... Fort Pierce, FL
Brown, Edgar N. ... Department of Justice, Criminal Division, GV
Brown, Edith Juanita ... Wheaton, IL
Brown, Edmund Gerald, Jr. ... Oakland, CA
Brown, Edmund S., Jr. ... Buffalo, NY
Brown, Edsel M., Jr. ... Washington, DC
Brown, Edw. T., Jr. ... Lilburn, GA
Brown, Edward A. ... Brighton, CO
Brown, Edward A. ... Alexandria, VA
Brown, Edward Allen ... Brunswick, ME
Brown, Edward D. ... Denver, CO
Brown, Edward D., Jr. ... Manlius, NY
Brown, Edward E. ... Indianapolis, IN
Brown, Edward E. ... Richmond, IN
Brown, Edward G. ... Pittsburgh, PA
Brown, Edward H. ... Atlanta, GA
Brown, Edward H. ... New Rochelle, NY
Brown, Edward J. ... Rockville, MD
Brown, Edward J. ... Malverne, NY
Brown, Edward J. ... Chillicothe, OH
Brown, Edward L., Jr. ... Wichita, KS
Brown, Edward M. ... Syracuse, NY
Brown, Edward M. ... Huntingdon, PA
Brown, Edward R. ... Oxnard, CA
Brown, Edward R. ... Cleveland, OH
Brown, Edward R. ... Columbiana, OH
Brown, Edward T. ... Mineola, NY
Brown, Edward T. ... Smithtown, NY
Brown, Edward W. ... Milwaukee, WI
Brown & Edwards, Chartered ... Boise, ID
Brown, Edwin B. ... Irvine, CA
Brown, Edwin C., Jr. ... Alexandria, VA
Brown, Edwin C., Sr. ... Alexandria, VA
Brown, Edwin P., Jr. ... Department of State, Director General—Foreign Service, GV
Brown, Edwin S. ... Chicago, IL
Brown, Edwin T., Jr. ... Merrillville, IN
Brown, Eileen A. ... Los Angeles, CA
Brown, Eileen McCarthy ... New Orleans, LA
Brown, Eileen P. ... Washington, DC
Brown, Eilene ... Washington, DC
Brown, Elaine ... San Jose, CA
Brown, Elaine Aten ... Columbus, OH
Brown, Elaine J. ... Portland, OR
Brown, Eleanor W. ... Providence, RI
Brown, Eli H., IV ... Prospect, KY
Brown, Elissa J. ... Oakland, CA
Brown, Elizabeth ... Oklahoma City, OK
Brown, Elizabeth A. ... San Francisco, CA

Brown, Elizabeth A. ... Wilmington, DE
Brown, Elizabeth Allison
Administrative Office Of The United States Courts, GV
Brown, Elizabeth A.S. ... Chicago, IL
Brown, Elizabeth C. ... New Orleans, LA
Brown, Elizabeth Coppage
Los Angeles, CA
Brown, Elizabeth E. ... Denver, CO
Brown, Elizabeth H. G. ... Ann Arbor, MI
Brown, Elizabeth J. ... Los Angeles, CA
Brown, Elizabeth Kemp
Oklahoma City, OK
Brown, Elizabeth M.
Executive Office Of The President, Office of the Vice President, GV
Brown, Elizabeth M. ... Fort Wayne, IN
Brown, Elizabeth M. ... Monroe, NC
Brown, Elizabeth Rockwell ... Seattle, WA
Brown, Elizabeth S. ... Kansas City, MO
Brown, Ella L. ... Portland, ME
Brown, Ella Marie ... Cleveland, OH
Brown, Ellen Ann ... Bremerton, WA
Tacoma, WA
Brown, Ellen C. ... Groton, CT
Brown, Ellen Sterns ... Philadelphia, PA
Brown, Elliot H. ... New York, NY
Brown, Elliot N. ... Los Angeles, CA
Brown, Elliott J. ... Bordentown, NJ
Brown, Ellis F. ... Wrentham, MA
Brown, Ellis Ray ... Atlanta, GA
Jonesboro, GA
Brown, Ellyn L. ... Towson, MD
Brown, Ellyn L., Chartered ... Towson, MD
Brown, Elvin J. ... Norman, OK
Brown, Elwood L. ... Port Huron, MI
Brown, Emily Burks ... Danville, KY
Brown, Emma Crowder ... Doylestown, PA
Brown, Emmett E., III ... Stamford, CT
Brown, Enola T. ... Tampa, FL
Brown Environmental Law Group, P.C., The
Chicago, IL
Brown, Eric ... Pasadena, CA
Brown, Eric ... Austin, TX
Brown, Eric B. ... Lincoln, NE
Brown, Eric G., A Prof. Corp., Law Office of
Austin, TX
Brown, Eric J. ... Anchorage, AK
Brown, Eric L. ... Columbus, OH
Brown, Eric L., Co., L.P.A. ... Columbus, OH
Brown, Eric M. ... Chicago, IL
Brown, Eric R. ... Stockton, CA
Brown, Eric S. ... New York, NY
Brown, Eric S. ... Columbus, OH
Brown, Eric V., Jr. ... Kalamazoo, MI
Brown, Eric V., Sr. ... Kalamazoo, MI
Brown, Erica D. ... Washington, DC
Brown, Erica I. ... Des Moines, IA
Brown, Erik S. ... Commission on Civil Rights, Office of the General Counsel, GV
Brown, Ernest C. ... Sacramento, CA
San Diego, CA
San Francisco, CA
Brown, Ernest & Company, A Professional Corporation ... Phoenix, AZ
Brown, Ernest, & Company, A Professional Corporation ... Los Angeles, CA
Brown, Ernest & Company, A Professional Corporation ... Sacramento, CA
San Diego, CA
Brown, Ernest, & Company, A Professional Corporation ... San Francisco, CA
Brown, Ernest L. ... Brooksville, MS
Brown, E. T., Jr. ... Birmingham, AL
Brown, Ethan J. ... Boston, MA
Brown, Eugene, Jr. ... Oakland, CA
Brown, Evelina Coker ... Batesville, IN
Brown, Everette T., Jr. ... Tulsa, OK
Brown, F. Keith ... Elgin, IL
Brown, F. Keith ... Frankfort, KY
Shepherdsville, KY
Brown, F. Mackenzie ... Newport Beach, CA
Solana Beach, CA
Brown, F. Montgomery ... Clive, IA
Brown, F. Morgan ... Pinetop, AZ
Brown, F. Patrick ... Overland Park, KS
Brown & Farris ... Nashville, TN
Brown Feehan & Cline, P.C. ... Rapid City, SD
Brown, Fletcher ... Arcadia, FL
Brown Fletcher & Associates
Los Angeles, CA
Brown, Fletcher H. ... Austin, TX
Brown, Florenceruth J. ... Santa Fe, NM
Brown, Floyd ... Houston, TX
Brown, Floyd R. ... Carlsbad, CA
Brown, Floyd W., Jr. ... Corpus Christi, TX
Brown, Forrest Walworth ... Santa Monica, CA
Brown & Fortunato, P.C. ... Amarillo, TX
Brown & Fox, P.C. ... New York, NY
Brown, Frances R. ... Orlando, FL
Brown, Frances Smylie ... Denver, CO
Brown, Franchot A. ... Columbia, SC
Brown, Francis A. ... Calais, ME
Brown, Francis B. ... Providence, RI
Brown, Francis C., Jr. ... New York, NY
Brown, Francis H., III ... New Orleans, LA
Brown, Francis Shunk, 3rd ... Wyndmoor, PA
Brown, Frank A. ... San Diego, CA
Brown, Frank B., IV ... Austin, TX
Brown, Frank C. ... Charlotte, NC
Brown, Frank E. ... Tampa, FL
Brown, Frank E., Jr. ... McLean, VA
Brown, Frank I. ... Birmingham, AL
Brown, Frank I. ... Spring Valley, NY
Brown, Frank J. ... Hartford, CT
Brown, Frank J. ... Seattle, WA
Brown, Frank O., Jr. ... Atlanta, GA
Brown, Frank Overton, Jr. ... Richmond, VA

Brown, Frank R. ... Granada Hills, CA
Brown, Frank R. ... Tarboro, NC
Brown, Franklin C. ... Harrisburg, PA
Brown, Franklyn N. ... Tigard, OR
Brown, Fred A. ... San Francisco, CA
Brown, Fred B. ... Baltimore, MD
Brown, Fred G. ... Fairbanks, AK
Brown, Fred L. ... Department of Energy, Office of Hearings and Appeals, GV
Brown, Frederic E. ... Fairbanks, AK
Brown, Frederic N. ... Rochester, MN
Brown, Frederick A. ... Omaha, NE
Brown, Frederick C., Jr.
Minneapolis, MN
Brown, Frederick H. ... Charleston, SC
Brown, Frederick L. ... Boston, MA
Brown, Frederick W. ... Burbank, CA
Brown & Freeston ... Washington, DC
Brown, G. Chris ... Harrisonburg, VA
Brown, G. Daniel ... Alexander City, AL
Brown, G. Frank ... Dallas, TX
Brown, G. Hank ... Greeley, CO
Brown, G. Michael ... Irvine, CA
Brown, G. Michael ... Atlantic City, NJ
Brown, G. Page, Jr. ... Exeter, NH
Brown, G. Richard ... Sacramento, CA
Brown, G. Steven ... Orlando, FL
Brown, G. Steven ... Helena, MT
Brown, G. William, Jr. ... New York, NY
Brown, Gail L. ... Kansas City, MO
Brown, Galen S. ... New Orleans, LA
Brown, Garrett E., Jr. ... Trenton, NJ
Brown, Garry ... Alamo, TN
Brown, Garry D. ... Dallas, TX
Brown, Garry D. ... Waxahachie, TX
Brown, Garth W. ... Findlay, OH
Brown, Garthe ... Portland, OR
Brown, Gary ... Los Angeles, CA
Brown, Gary A. ... Springfield, IL
Brown, Gary C. ... Tempe, AZ
Brown, Gary E. ... Rialto, CA
Brown, Gary E. ... Live Oak, FL
Brown, Gary E. ... Columbus, OH
Brown, Gary L. ... Aventura, FL
Brown, Gary L. ... Greenville, OH
Brown, Gary L. ... Seattle, WA
Brown, Gary Louis ... Miami, FL
Brown, Gary M. ... Nashville, TN
Brown, Gary M. ... Anson, TX
Brown, Gary N. ... Houston, TX
Brown, Gary R. ... Estes Park, CO
Brown, Gary R. ... Wewoka, OK
Brown, Gary Randall ... Woodstock, VT
Brown, Gary S. ... Fairfield, CT
Brown, Gary S. ... New Orleans, LA
Brown, Gary W. ... Newnan, GA
Brown, Gary W. ... Fairfax, VA
Brown Gavalas & Fromm LLP
Clifton, NJ
New York, NY
Brown, Gavin A. ... Waynesville, NC
Brown, Gayle J. ... Anchorage, AK
Brown, Gene ... Meridian, MS
Brown, Gene D. ... Tallahassee, FL
Brown, Gene I. ... Bozeman, MT
Brown, Gene L. ... Grants Pass, OR
Brown, Geo. A. ... Boston, MA
Brown, Geo. A. ... Manchester, NH
Brown, Geo. C. ... St. Paul, MN
Brown, Geo. E. ... Miami, FL
Brown, Geoffrey C. ... Los Angeles, CA
Brown, Geoffrey F. ... Skowhegan, ME
Brown, Geoffrey R. S. ... New York, NY
Brown, George A. ... Mobile, AL
Brown, George A. ... Fresno, CA
Brown, George C.
Securities and Exchange Commission, Office of the General Counsel, GV
Brown, George E. ... LaGrange, IN
Brown, George E., Jr. ... Baltimore, MD
Brown, George E., Jr. ... American Fork, UT
Brown, George F. ... Hicksville, NY
Brown, George H. ... Palo Alto, CA
Brown, George H. ... St. Petersburg, FL
Brown, George H., III ... Brooksville, FL
Brown, George H., Jr. ... Memphis, TN
Brown, George K., Jr. ... Bradenton, FL
Brown, George L., Jr. ... Berryville, AR
Brown, George M. ... Boca Raton, FL
Brown, George R. ... Tucson, AZ
Brown, George R., V ... New York, NY
Brown, George T., Jr. ... Jonesboro, GA
Brown, George W. ... Washington, DC
Brown, George W. ... Worcester, MA
Brown, George William, III ... Madison, GA
Brown, Gerald ... San Diego, CA
Brown, Gerald F. (Geff) ... Chicago, IL
Brown, Gerald (Geff) ... Chicago, IL
Brown, Gerald J. ... Duluth, MN
Brown, Gerald J. ... Houston, TX
Brown, Gerald L. ... Pensacola, FL
Brown, Gerald M. ... Temple, TX
Brown, Gerald Q. ... Department of Defense, Defense Legal Services Agency, GV
Brown, Geraldine ... Merced, CA
Brown, Geraldine Reed ... Montclair, NJ
Brown, Geraldine Soat ... Chicago, IL
Brown, Gerard S. ... Rancho Cucamonga, CA
Brown and German ... Albuquerque, NM
Brown, Gerry M. ... El Paso, TX
Brown, Gian A. ... Atlanta, GA
Brown, Gilbert T. ... San Jose, CA
Brown, Gilbert T., Jr. ... Monroe, LA
Brown, Gildenhorn & Jacobs
Washington, DC
Brown, Gillian David ... Buffalo, NY
Brown, Gillian P. ... Garden City, NY
Brown, Gina M. ... Los Angeles, CA

Brown, G. L. (Gary), III ....Enid, OK
Brown, Gladys M. ....Harrisburg, PA
Brown, Glen J. ....San Mateo, CA
Brown, Glenn A. ....Atlanta, GA
Brown, Glenn A., Jr. ....Tarzana, CA
Brown, Glenn C. ....Bend, OR
Portland, OR
Brown, Glenn E. ....Tampa, FL
Brown, Glenn J. ....Quakertown, PA
Brown, Glenn L. ....Des Plaines, IL
Brown, Glenn R. ....Troy, MI
Brown, Glenn W. ....Waynesville, NC
Brown & Godbold ....Rock Hill, SC
Brown, Goldstein & Levy, LLP
Baltimore, MD
Brown, Gordon F. ....Oklahoma City, OK
Brown, Gordon H. ....Winston-Salem, NC
Brown, Gordon W. ....Beverly, MA
Brown, Grayson H. ....Baton Rouge, LA
Brown, Grayson H., Law Firm of
Baton Rouge, LA
Brown & Green, P.A. ....Orlando, FL
Brown, Gregg C. ....Fort Worth, TX
Brown, Gregg R. ....Austin, TX
Beaumont, TX
Brown, Gregory A. ....Westchester, IL
Brown, Gregory B. ....Benton, AR
Brown, Gregory B. ....Portland, ME
Brown, Gregory B., P.A. ....Portland, ME
Brown, Gregory C. ....Glendale, CA
Brown, Gregory D. ....Oakland, CA
Brown, Gregory G. ....Irvine, CA
Brown, Gregory J. ....Glendale, NY
Brown, Gregory J. ....Eau Claire, WI
Brown, Gregory K. ....Chicago, IL
Brown, Gregory L. ....Chicago, IL
Brown, Gregory L. ....Buffalo, NY
Brown, Gregory M. ....Washington, DC
Brown, Gregory P. ....Tampa, FL
Brown, Gregory P. ....Dearborn, MI
Brown, Gregory R. ....Des Moines, IA
Brown, Gregory S. ....Denver, CO
Brown, Gregory V. ....Houston, TX
Brown, Gregory W. ....Merrillville, IN
Merrillville, IN
Brown, Gregory W. ....Raleigh, NC
Brown, Grover C. ....Wilmington, DE
Brown & Guilbert ....New York, NY
Brown, H. Barksdale ....Oakland, CA
Brown, H. Blanton ....Oklahoma City, OK
Brown, H. Blanton, & Associates, P.C.
Oklahoma City, OK
Brown, H. Eugene ....Jonesboro, GA
Brown, H. Fletcher ....Houston, TX
Brown, H. Gordon ....Tucson, AZ
Brown, H. Grady, III ....Beaufort, SC
Brown, H. Harding ....Chatham, NJ
Brown, H. Lanier, II ....Birmingham, AL
Brown, H. Lowell ....Los Angeles, CA
Brown, H. Stephen ....Memphis, TN
Brown, H. Stewart ....Albany, GA
Brown, H. Thomas ....Cincinnati, OH
Brown, Hal M. ....Chicago, IL
Brown, Hall, Shore & McKinley, LLP
Stockton, CA
Brown, Harley ....Racine, WI
Brown, Harley M., P.L.C. ....Baton Rouge, LA
Brown, Harley Mark ....Baton Rouge, LA
Brown, Harmon A. ....Chicago, IL
Brown, Harold A. ....Beverly Hills, CA
Brown, Harold, & Associates, Law Offices of
Boston, MA
Brown, Harold Hansen, (A Professional Corporation) ....Santa Monica, CA
Brown, Harold J. ....Bloomfield, NJ
Brown, Harold N. ....Fairbanks, AK
Brown, Harold P. (Bo), Jr. ....Lubbock, TX
Brown, Harold R., III ....Alexandria, VA
Brown, Harriette Campbell ....Winchester, VA
Brown, Harris ....Jacksonville, FL
Brown, Harry ....Boca Raton, FL
Brown, Harry D. ....Department of the Army, U.S. Army Court of Criminal Appeals, GV
Brown, Harry E. ....Riverside, CA
Brown, Harry E., Jr. ....Oklahoma City, OK
Brown, Harry J. ....Pottsville, PA
Brown, Harry L. ....Warsaw, NY
Brown, Harry M. ....Cleveland, OH
Brown, Harry R. ....Riverhead, NY
Brown, Hart, Reed, Golowich & Kaplan, LLP ....Amherst, MA
Brown, Hartford O. ....San Jose, CA
Brown, Harvey ....San Pedro, CA
Brown, Harvey A. ....Pepper Pike, OH
Brown, Harvey G., Jr. ....Houston, TX
Brown, Harvey R. ....White Plains, NY
Brown, Harvey S. ....Phoenix, AZ
Brown, Harvey S. ....New York, NY
Brown Hastings & Clutter ....Indianapolis, IN
Brown, Hawkins, Basola & Mattingley
Decatur, IL
Maroa, IL
Sandoval, IL
Brown, Hay & Stephens ....Springfield, IL
Brown, Hayden D. ....Charlotte, NC
Brown, Hayes D., II ....Birmingham, AL
Brown, Hazen D. ....Cortez, CO
Brown, Heather A. Palmer ....McLean, VA
Brown, Heather Anne ....Kansas City, MO
Brown, Heather E. ....Tulsa, OK
Brown, Heather L. ....Roseland, NJ
Brown, Heather L. ....Houston, TX
Brown, Heather M. ....Darien, CT
Brown, Heather M., LLC, Law Office of
Darien, CT
Brown, Heidi A. ....St. Louis, MO
Brown, Heidi E. ....San Diego, CA
Brown, Heidi K. ....Columbia, SC

Brown, Heidi L. ....Oklahoma City, OK
Brown, Helen P. ....New York, NY
Brown, Helene F. ....New York, NY
Brown, Henry A., III ....Menlo Park, CA
Brown, Henry E. ....Clarksburg, WV
Brown, Henry G. ....Omaha, NE
Brown, Henry L. (Roy) ....Huntsville, AL
Brown, Henry M. ....Longwood, FL
Brown, Henry Otis ....Petersburg, VA
Brown, Henry W. ....Columbia, SC
Brown, Herbert H. ....Radnor, PA
Brown, Herbert L. ....Orinda, CA
Brown, Herbert Olan ....Brooklyn, NY
Brown, Herbert R. ....Columbus, OH
Brown, Herbert S. ....Trenton, MO
Brown, Herbert T., Jr. ....Grasonville, MD
Brown, Herbert W., III ....San Juan, PR
Brown, Herman Cubbage, Jr. ....Dover, DE
Brown, Herman, Dean, Wiseman, Liser & Hart, L.L.P. ....Fort Worth, TX
Brown, Hermione K. ....Beverly Hills, CA
Brown & Hewitt, P.A. ....Sebring, FL
Brown & Hill, PLLC ....Corbin, KY
London, KY
Brown & Holland ....Haverford, PA
Brown, Holly Anne ....New York, NY
Brown, Holly B. ....Bozeman, MT
Brown, Holly B., P.C. ....Bozeman, MT
Brown, Horace M. ....Maryville, TN
Brown, Hosmer A. ....Minneapolis, MN
Brown, Houston L. ....Birmingham, AL
Brown, Howard B. ....Los Angeles, CA
Brown, Howard Carter, Jr. ....Kensington, MD
Brown, Howard M. ....Boston, MA
Brown, Howard M. ....Media, PA
Brown, Hubert L., Law Offices, Professional Corporation ....Norwich, NY
Brown, Hubert R. ....Tallahassee, FL
Brown, Hudgens, P.C. ....Bay Minette, AL
Chatom, AL
Mobile, AL
Brown, Hugh B. ....Chester, MT
Brown, Hugh D. ....Cleveland, OH
Brown, Hugh L. ....Starkville, MS
Brown, Hughes, Bird & Rote
Grants Pass, OR
Brown, Hulon B. ....Jacksonville, TX
Rusk, TX
Brown, Hunt Sevier ....Nashville, TN
Brown, Huntington C. ....Denver, CO
Brown and Huss, P.C. ....Miles City, MT
Brown & Hutchinson ....Rochester, NY
Brown, I. Sylvan ....Phoenix, AZ
Brown, Ian ....Tallahassee, FL
Brown, Ian A. ....Lewiston, ME
Brown & Iawen ....Great Bend, KS
Brown, Ifigenia T., (Mrs.) ....Ballston Spa, NY
Brown, Ilene S. ....Bethpage, NY
Brown, Ira A., Jr. ....Calistoga, CA
Brown, Ira L. ....Great Neck, NY
Brown, Ira P. ....Nyack, NY
Brown, Iris June ....Hartford, CT
Brown, Irma J. ....Compton, CA
Brown, Isaac, III ....Dallas, TX
Brown, Isabel Lee ....San Francisco, CA
Brown, Isabelle M. ....Lakeport, CA
Brown, J. Anthony ....Knoxville, TN
Brown, J. Bowen ....Tampa, FL
Brown, J. Chris ....Mauldin, SC
Brown, J. Clint ....Tampa, FL
Brown, J. Craig ....Valley View, TX
Brown, J. Curtiss ....Houston, TX
Brown, J. David ....Dallas, TX
Brown, J. Devon, (Ms.) ....Carmichael, CA
Brown, J. Douglas ....Columbus, OH
Brown, J. Glenn ....Athens, GA
Eatonton, GA
Brown, J. Jack ....New York, NY
Brown, J. Jeffrey ....Indianapolis, IN
Brown, J. Kenneth ....Los Angeles, CA
Brown, J. Kent ....West Palm Beach, FL
Brown, J. Kirk ....Huntsville, TX
Brown, J. Lawrence, Jr. ....Wilkes-Barre, PA
Brown, J. Lawson, Jr. ....Albany, NY
Brown, J. Lee, (P.A.) ....Little Rock, AR
Brown, J. Melissa ....San Jose, CA
Brown, J. Michael ....Eureka, CA
Brown, J. Michael ....Pleasanton, CA
Brown, J. Michael ....Washington, DC
Brown, J. Michael ....Louisville, KY
Brown, J. Michael ....Bolivar, MO
Brown, J. Michael ....Richmond, VA
Brown, J. Mike ....Dalton, GA
Brown, J. Mitchell ....Washington, DC
Brown, J. Norman ....Forest, MS
Brown, J. Patrick ....Bellevue, WA
Brown, J. Patten, III ....Lafayette, LA
Brown, J. Rick ....Portsmouth, OH
Brown, J. Robert ....Costa Mesa, CA
Brown, J. Robert ....Atlanta, GA
Brown, J. Robert ....Timonium, MD
Brown, J. Robert ....El Paso, TX
Brown, J. Robert, Jr. ....Santa Ana, CA
Brown, J. Robert, Jr. ....Denver, CO
Brown, J. Russell, Jr. ....Los Angeles, CA
Brown, J. Russell, Jr., A Law Corporation
Los Angeles, CA
Brown, J. Scott ....Shawnee, KS
Brown, J. Scott ....Norman, OK
Oklahoma City, OK
Brown, J. Scott ....Salt Lake City, UT
Brown, J. Stephen ....Lebanon, TN
Brown, J. Thomas, Jr. ....Goldsboro, NC
Brown, J. Winston ....Houston, MS
Brown, Jack C. ....Indianapolis, IN
Brown, Jack D. ....Yuba City, CA
Brown, Jack E. ....Phoenix, AZ
Brown, Jack L. ....Los Angeles, CA

Brown, Jack L. ....Tulsa, OK
Brown, Jack R. ....Shreveport, LA
Brown, Jack R. ....Chattanooga, TN
Brown, Jacki C. ....Santa Ana, CA
Brown, Jackson M. ....Starkville, MS
Brown, Jackson M., Ltd. ....Starkville, MS
Brown, Jacob ....Kansas City, MO
Brown, Jacobson, Tillinghast, Lahan & King, P.C. ....New London, CT
Norwich, CT
Putnam, CT
Brown, Jacqueline Cherveny, P.C.
Elmont, NY
Brown, Jacqueline Cherveny ....Elmont, NY
Brown, Jacqueline Cherveny ....Elmont, NY
Brown, Jacqueline FitzGerald
Department of Justice, Federal Bureau of Investigation, GV
Brown, Jacqueline Ley ....Tampa, FL
Brown, Jaime ....Denver, CO
Brown, James ....Louisville, KY
Brown, James A. ....New Orleans, LA
Brown, James A. ....Silver Spring, MD
Brown, James A. ....Elk City, OK
Brown, James A. ....Wenatchee, WA
Brown, James Albert ....United States Senate, Committee Legal Personnel, GV
Brown, James Alvin ....Milledgeville, GA
Brown, James B. ....Stockton, CA
Brown, James B. ....Punta Gorda, FL
Lansing, MI
Brown, James B. ....Pittsburgh, PA
Brown, James B., Jr. ....East Brunswick, NJ
Brown, James C. ....Sacramento, CA
San Luis Obispo, CA
Brown, James D. ....Delta, CO
Brown, James D., Jr. ....Coral Gables, FL
Brown, James E. ....Bakersfield, CA
Brown, James E. ....Los Angeles, CA
Brown, James E. ....Denver, CO
Brown, James E. ....Washington, DC
Brown, James E. ....Chicago, IL
Brown, James E. ....Joplin, MO
Brown, James E. ....Kansas City, MO
Brown, James E. ....Depew, NY
Brown, James E. ....Macedonia, OH
Brown, James E. ....Blue Bell, PA
Brown, James E. ....Honesdale, PA
Brown, James E. ....Philadelphia, PA
Brown, James E., & Associates, P.C.
Denver, CO
Brown, James E. "Buster"
Lake Jackson, TX
Brown, James E. "Jeb", II ....Austin, TX
Brown, James E., Jr. ....Houston, TX
Brown, James E., (P.C.) ....Arlington, TX
Austin, TX
Dallas, TX
Houston, TX
Brown, James F. ....Menlo Park, CA
Brown, James F. ....Moorestown, NJ
Brown, James F. ....Charlotte, NC
Brown, James F., III ....Charleston, WV
Brown, James F., IV ....Charleston, WV
Brown, James F., Jr. ....Atlanta, GA
Brown, James G. ....Orlando, FL
Brown, James Glenn ....Indianapolis, IN
Brown, James H. ....Louisville, KY
Brown, James H., Jr. ....New Orleans, LA
Brown, James H., Jr. ....Philadelphia, PA
Brown, James Howe, Jr. ....Fairfax, VA
Brown, James J. ....Washington, DC
Brown, James J.
Federal Communications Commission, Mass Media Bureau, GV
Brown, James J. ....St. Petersburg, FL
Brown, James J. ....Chicago, IL
Brown, James J. ....Indianapolis, IN
Brown, James J. ....St. Ignace, MI
Brown, James J. ....Las Vegas, NV
Brown, James J., Jr. ....San Diego, CA
Brown, James J., Professional Corporation, Ltd.
Las Vegas, NV
Brown, James K. ....Boston, MA
Brown, James Knight ....Charleston, WV
Brown, James L.
Department of Transportation, Surface Transportation Board, GV
Brown, James Leonard ....Las Vegas, NV
Brown, James M. ....Temple Hills, MD
Brown, James M. ....Salem, OR
Brown, James M. ....Aberdeen, WA
Brown, James Martin ....Brooksville, FL
Brown, James Michael ....Beckley, WV
Brown, James Mitchell ....Cleveland, OH
Brown, James N., III ....Medina, OH
Brown, James O. ....Grand Haven, MI
Holland, MI
Brown, James P. ....Zanesville, OH
Brown, James P., Jr. ....McDonough, GA
Brown & James, P.C. ....Belleville, IL
Kansas City, MO
St. Louis, MO
Springfield, MO
Brown, James R. ....West Palm Beach, FL
Brown, James R. ....Mason City, IA
Brown, James R. ....Grand Rapids, MI
Brown, James R. ....Kearney, MO
Brown, James R. ....Farmers Branch, TX
Brown, James R. ....Houston, TX
Brown, James R. ....Salt Lake City, UT
Brown, James R. ....Ephrata, WA
Brown, James R., III ....Baltimore, MD
Brown, James R., Jr. ....Boston, MA
Brown, James S. ....San Francisco, CA
Brown, James S. ....New York, NY
Brown, James T. ....Houston, TX
Brown, James W. ....Santa Barbara, CA

Brown, James W. ....Newark, DE
Brown, James W. ....Savannah, GA
Brown, James W. ....Osceola, IA
Brown, James W. ....New York, NY
Brown, James W. ....Columbus, OH
Brown, James W. ....Harrisburg, PA
Brown, James W. R. ....Omaha, NE
Brown, Jamie E. ....Washington, DC
Brown, Jan H. ....New York, NY
Brown, Jan H., P.C. ....New York, NY
Brown, Jane ....Dallas, TX
Brown, Jane A. Johanningsmeier
Oklahoma City, OK
Brown, Jane E. ....Spokane, WA
Brown, Jane L. ....Dallas, TX
Brown, Jane Pansing ....Liberty, MO
Brown, Janet A. ....Washington, DC
Vienna, VA
Brown, Janet C. ....New York, NY
Brown, Janet E. ....Oakland, CA
Brown, Janet E. ....Goochland, VA
Brown, Janet K. ....Riverview, MI
Brown, Janet Klein ....Baltimore, MD
Brown, Janet L. ....Orlando, FL
Brown, Janet L. ....Lafayette, LA
Brown, Janice ....San Francisco, CA
Brown, Janice J. ....Las Vegas, NV
Brown, Janice Patrice ....San Diego, CA
Brown, Janice Y. ....Knoxville, TN
Brown, Janine ....Atlanta, GA
Brown, Jared ....New York, NY
Brown, Jarvis W. ....Faulkton, SD
Brown, Jas. F., Jr. ....Department of Labor, Office of Secretary, GV
Brown, Jason ....Boston, MA
Brown, Jason K. ....New York, NY
Brown, Jason O. ....New Smyrna Beach, FL
Brown, Jason R. ....Springfield, MO
Brown, Jay D. ....Glendale, CA
Brown, Jay H. ....Las Vegas, NV
Brown, Jay J. ....Oceanside, CA
Brown, Jay M. ....Chicago, IL
Brown, Jay M. ....Teterboro, NJ
Brown, Jay Patrick ....Austin, TX
Brown, Jay S. ....Washington, DC
Brown, Jay S. ....Seattle, WA
Brown, Jay W. ....San Francisco, CA
Brown, Jay W. ....Houston, TX
Brown, Jay Ward ....Washington, DC
Brown, Jean Anne ....Louisville, KY
Brown, Jean R. ....Sacramento, CA
Brown, Jeff K. ....Prairie Village, KS
Brown, Jeff M. ....Boca Raton, FL
Brown, Jefferies and Boulware ....Aiken, SC
Barnwell, SC
Brown, Jefferson B. ....Portsmouth, VA
Brown, Jefferson W. ....Charlotte, NC
Brown, Jeffery B. ....Amherst, MA
Brown, Jeffery L. ....Madison, WI
Brown, Jeffrey ....Tallahassee, FL
Brown, Jeffrey ....Minneapolis, MN
Brown, Jeffrey A. ....Columbus, GA
Brown, Jeffrey A. ....Chicago, IL
Brown, Jeffrey A. ....Binghamton, NY
Brown, Jeffrey A. ....Columbus, OH
Brown, Jeffrey B. ....Salt Lake City, UT
Brown, Jeffrey C. ....Albuquerque, NM
Brown, Jeffrey C. ....El Paso, TX
Brown, Jeffrey G. ....New Port Richey, FL
Palm Harbor, FL
Tampa, FL
Brown, Jeffrey Grant ....Chicago, IL
Brown, Jeffrey Grant, P.C. ....Chicago, IL
Brown, Jeffrey H. ....Chicago, IL
Brown, Jeffrey Howard
Bloomfield Township, MI
Brown, Jeffrey J. ....Bloomfield Hills, MI
Brown, Jeffrey K. ....Irvine, CA
Brown, Jeffrey K. ....Austin, TX
Brown, Jeffrey L. ....Columbus, OH
Brown, Jeffrey M. ....La Jolla, CA
Brown, Jeffrey M. ....Chicago, IL
Brown, Jeffrey M. ....Columbus, OH
Brown, Jeffrey M. ....Houston, TX
Brown, Jeffrey N. ....Los Angeles, CA
Brown, Jeffrey O. ....Palo Alto, CA
Brown, Jeffrey O. ....Steubenville, OH
Brown, Jeffrey P. ....Atlanta, GA
Brown, Jeffrey R. ....San Francisco, CA
Brown, Jeffrey R. ....Manhasset Hills, NY
Brown, Jeffrey S. ....Decatur, AL
Brown, Jeffrey S. ....Bethel, AK
Brown, Jeffrey S. ....Greenfield, MA
Brown, Jeffrey S. ....Hackensack, NJ
Brown, Jeffrey S. ....Lynbrook, NY
Brown, Jeffrey T., Sr. ....Lanham, MD
Brown, Jeffrey V. ....Houston, TX
Brown, Jeffrey W. ....Atlanta, GA
Brown, Jenifer M. ....Washington, DC
Brown, Jennifer Backes ....Boston, MA
Brown, Jennifer Gerarda ....Hamden, CT
Brown, Jennifer L. ....San Francisco, CA
Brown, Jennifer L. ....Shreveport, LA
Brown, Jennifer L. ....Kansas City, MO
Brown, Jennifer L. ....Circleville, OH
Brown, Jennifer S. ....Orlando, FL
Brown, Jennifer Walters ....Blue Bell, PA
Brown, Jerald K. ....Garland, TX
Brown, Jeremy M. ....Newark, NJ
Brown, Jerilyn J. ....Princeton, NJ
Brown, Jerome A. ....Victoria, TX
Brown, Jerome J. ....New York, NY
Brown, Jeromy E. ....Chickasha, OK
Oklahoma City, OK
Brown, Jerrold S. ....Buffalo, NY
Brown, Jerry A. ....New Orleans, LA
Brown, Jerry A., Jr. ....Los Angeles, CA
Brown, Jerry D. ....Chicago, IL

Brown, Jerry K. ... Encino, CA
Brown, Jerry K. ... McMinnville, OR
Brown, Jerry K., P.C. ... McMinnville, OR
Brown, Jerry M. ... Belmont, MA
Brown, Jesselyn Alicia
Department of Justice, Civil Division, GV
Brown, Jessica T. ... Lubbock, TX
Brown, Jill ... Interlachen, FL
Brown, Jill ... Indianapolis, IN
Brown, Jill Cannon ... Bethesda, MD
Brown, Jill I. ... Los Angeles, CA
Brown, Jill N. ... Minneapolis, MN
Brown, Jim B. ... Highland, IN
Brown, Jim B. ... Canyon, TX
Brown, Jimmie H. ... Albany, GA
Brown, Jo Ann ... Des Moines, IA
Brown, Jo Ann ... St. Louis, MO
Brown, Jo Beth ... St. Louis, MO
Brown, Joachim J. ... La Grange, IL
Brown, Joan L. ... New York, NY
Brown, Joan M. ... New York, NY
Brown, Joan S. ... Baltimore, MD
Brown, Joan S. ... Columbia, SC
Brown, Joan T. ... San Francisco, CA
Brown, Joanne E. ... Madison, WI
Brown, Joanne M. ... Oakland, CA
Brown, Joe B. ... Nashville, TN
Brown, Joe B. ... Dallas, TX
Brown, Joe D. ... San Antonio, TX
Brown, Joe Frazier ... San Antonio, TX
Brown, Joe Frazier, Jr. ... San Antonio, TX
Brown, Joel A. ... Coral Gables, FL
Brown, Joel E. ... Birmingham, AL
Brown, Joel F. ... Chicago, IL
Brown, Joel R. ... Wilmington, DE
St. Petersburg, FL
Brown, Johill (Joel) H. ... Miami, FL
Brown, John ... Oxnard, CA
Brown, John B. ... Fort Worth, TX
Brown, John C. ... Bozeman, MT
Brown, John C., III ... San Francisco, CA
Brown, John Christopher ... Baltimore, MD
Brown, John Clark, Jr. ... Inglewood, CA
Brown, John Clark, Jr. ... Los Angeles, CA
Brown, John D. ... Emmetsburg, IA
Brown, John D. ... Lincoln, NE
Brown, John D. ... Cleveland, OH
Brown, John E. ... Glendale, CA
Brown, John E. ... Sarasota, FL
Brown, John E. ... Lake Charles, LA
Brown, John E. ... Lincoln, NE
Brown, John E., (P.C.) ... Riverside, CA
Brown, John Edgar, III ... Cleveland, TN
Brown, John F. ... Baltimore, MD
Brown, John F. ... Houston, TX
Brown, John F., Jr. ... Philadelphia, PA
Brown, John F., Jr. ... Elkins, WV
Brown, John H. ... Denver, CO
Brown, John H. ... Ada, MI
Brown, John H. ... East Greenwich, RI
Brown, John L. ... West Des Moines, IA
Brown, John L. ... Pierre, SD
Brown, John Lee ... Middlesboro, KY
Brown, John Lewis ... New York, NY
Brown, John M. ... Lansing, MI
Brown, John M. ... Amarillo, TX
Brown, John Michael ... Augusta, GA
Brown, John Michael, P.C. ... Augusta, GA
Brown, John M. L. ... Nashville, TN
Brown, John N. ... Okemos, MI
Brown, John O. ... Baker, LA
Brown, John P. ... Naples, FL
Brown, John P. ... St. Louis, MO
Brown, John P. ... Nashville, TN
Brown, John Patrick, Jr. ... Washington, DC
Brown, John Quincy, III ... Sacramento, CA
Brown, John Quincy, Jr. ... Sacramento, CA
Brown, John R. ... Troy, MI
Brown, John R. ... Philadelphia, PA
Brown, John S. ... Boston, MA
Brown, John T. ... Fort Walton Beach, FL
Brown, John T. ... Commerce, GA
Brown, John T. ... Mansfield, OH
Brown, John T., P.A. ... Fort Walton Beach, FL
Brown, John Thompson ... Chicago, IL
Brown, John Thos. ... Hagåtña, GU
Brown, John W. ... Pittsburgh, PA
Brown, John W. ... Chesapeake, VA
Brown, John W., Jr. ... Towson, MD
Brown, John W., P.C. ... Chesapeake, VA
Brown, John Wilson ... San Diego, CA
Brown, Johnine J. ... Chicago, IL
Brown, Johnnie E. ... Charleston, WV
Brown, Johnny ... Miami, FL
Brown, Johnny M. ... Houston, TX
Brown, Johnny R. ... Sherman, TX
Brown, Jon Ed ... Idabel, OK
Brown, Jon L. ... San Francisco, CA
Brown, Jon L. ... Charleston, WV
Brown, Jon M. ... Bluffton, IN
Brown, Jon Michael, Jr. ... Chicago, IL
Brown, Jonathan A. ... Vernon, AL
Brown, Jonathan D. ... San Francisco, CA
Brown, Jonathan D. ... Omaha, NE
Brown, Jonathan D. ... Riverhead, NY
Brown, Jonathan M. ... Indianapolis, IN
Brown, Jonathan P. ... Sioux Falls, SD
Brown, Jonna S. ... Miami, FL
Palm Beach, FL
Brown, Jordan ... New Orleans, LA
Brown, José Tomas ... Flint, MI
Brown, Josef B. ... Hyattsville, MD
Brown, Joseph A. ... Garden City, NY
Brown, Joseph B. ... East Hanover, NJ
Brown, Joseph C. ... Chicago, IL
Brown, Joseph C. ... Houston, TX
Brown, Joseph C., Jr. ... Seattle, WA
Brown, Joseph D. ... McKinney, TX
Brown, Joseph E. ... Fort Worth, TX
Brown, Joseph E., III ... Wilson, NC
Brown, Joseph G. ... Belmont, NC
Brown, Joseph J. ... Eugene, OR
Brown, Joseph M. ... Parkersburg, WV
Brown, Joseph M., Jr. ... Mobile, AL
Brown, Joseph N. ... Detroit, MI
Brown, Joseph R. ... Sherman Oaks, CA
Brown, Joseph R., Jr. ... Edwardsville, IL
Brown, Joseph W. ... Las Vegas, NV
Brown, Joshua M. ... Dallas, TX
Brown, Joyce A. ... Gastonia, NC
Brown, Joyce M. ... Honolulu, HI
Brown, Joyce R. ... Detroit, MI
Brown, Joyce S. ... Newark, NJ
Brown, Judith A. ... Hartford, CT
Brown, Judith Ann ... Sterling, VA
Brown, Judith Austin ... San Rafael, CA
Brown, Judith E. ... Palo Alto, CA
Brown, Judith Helen ... Norwood, NY
Brown, Judith K. ... Indianapolis, IN
Brown, Judith Olans ... Boston, MA
Brown, Judith T. ... Oakland, CA
Brown, Judy ... Austin, TX
Brown, Judy Harris ... Duluth, MN
Brown, Judy S. ... Kenner, LA
Brown, Jules F. ... Lancaster, WI
Brown, Julia Stallings ... Atlanta, GA
Brown, Julian Sylvester ... McLean, VA
Brown, Juliana M. ... Louisville, CO
Brown, Julie A. ... San Diego, CA
Brown, Julie K. ... Milwaukee, WI
Brown, Julie Malone ... Baton Rouge, LA
Brown, Julie Turner ... Springfield, MO
Brown, June Blanchard
United States International Trade Commission, Office of the General Counsel, GV
Brown, June Hobby ... Knoxville, TN
Brown, Junious D., III ... Tallahassee, FL
Brown & Justh ... Coeur d'Alene, ID
Brown, Justin Lewis ... Los Angeles, CA
Brown, J. W. ... Houston, TX
Brown, K. Bellamy ... Phoenix, AZ
Brown, K. Kathy ... Oxford, MS
Tupelo, MS
Brown, K. Scott ... Treasury Department, Internal Revenue Service, GV
Catonsville, MD
Brown, Karen B. ... Minneapolis, MN
Brown, Karen Cochrane ... Albany, NY
Brown, Karen Elizabeth ... Atlanta, GA
Brown, Karen K. ... Houston, TX
Brown, Karen Kendrick ... Washington, DC
Brown, Karen M. ... Torrance, CA
Brown, Karen Napua ... Hilo, HI
Brown, Karen R. ... Commack, NY
Brown, Karen S. D. ... Newport News, VA
Brown Karosen & Ballan, LLP
Bloomfield, NJ
Brown & Karp ... Alexandria, VA
Brown, Katharine B. ... New York, NY
Brown, Katharine Mason
Administrative Office Of The United States Courts, GV
Brown, Katherine ... Jacksonville, FL
Brown, Katherine ... Portland, OR
Brown, Katherine A. ... Nashville, TN
Brown, Katherine Walsh ... Dallas, TX
Brown, Kathleen ... Sacramento, CA
Brown, Kathleen ... Bloomington, IL
Brown, Kathleen A. ... San Francisco, CA
Brown, Kathleen A. ... Fort Lauderdale, FL
Brown, Kathleen Curran ... Woodbridge, NJ
Brown, Kathleen Dowling ... St. Louis, MO
Brown, Kathryn
Equal Employment Opportunity Commission, Office of Federal Operations, GV
Brown, Kathryn C.
Department of Commerce, National Telecommunications & Information Administration, GV
Brown, Kathryn J. ... San Francisco, CA
Brown, Kathryn J. ... Sycamore, IL
Brown, Kathryn M.
Fort Walton Beach, FL
Brown, Kathryn Paull ... Bethesda, MD
Brown, Kathy A. ... Department of Defense, Office of the General Counsel, GV
Brown, Kay Millicent ... Washington, DC
Brown, Keith ... Nevada, MO
Brown, Keith Adrian ... Birmingham, AL
Brown, Keith D. ... Spokane, WA
Brown, Keith E. ... Anchorage, AK
Brown, Keith L. ... Edwards, CO
Brown, Keith O'Brien ... Department of Justice, Executive Office for Immigration Review, GV
Brown, Keith Patrick ... Melville, NY
Brown, Keith S. ... Boston, MA
Brown, Kelleher, Zwickel & Wilhelm, L.L.P.
Catskill, NY
Windham, NY
Brown, Kelley Marie ... San Diego, CA
Brown, Kelley R. ... Rochester, NY
Brown, Kelli E. ... Bowling Green, KY
Brown, Kelly ... Phoenix, AZ
Brown, Kelly A. ... Department of Commerce, Office of the General Counsel, GV
Brown, Kelly C. ... Topeka, KS
Brown, Kelly D. ... Houston, TX
Brown, Kelly Kennedy ... Portland, OR
Brown & Kelly, L.L.P. ... Buffalo, NY
Niagara Falls, NY
Brown, Kelly M. ... San Francisco, CA
Brown, Kelly M. ... St. Louis, MO
Brown, Kelly Michele ... Woodbridge, NJ
Brown, Kelly N. ... Pullman, WA
Brown & Kelly, P.A. ... Baltimore, MD
Brown, Ken D. ... Metairie, LA
Brown, Kennedy F. ... Gainesville, FL
Brown, Kenneth Allen ... Melville, NY
Brown, Kenneth B. ... New York, NY
Brown, Kenneth C. ... Manchester, NH
Nashua, NH
Brown, Kenneth C. ... White Plains, NY
Brown, Kenneth D. ... Ottawa, IL
Brown, Kenneth D. ... Newark, NJ
Brown, Kenneth D. ... Bronx, NY
Brown, Kenneth D. ... Williamsport, PA
Brown, Kenneth Douglas ... Greenwich, CT
Brown, Kenneth E. ... Woodbridge, VA
Brown, Kenneth G. ... Bernalillo, NM
Brown, Kenneth H. ... San Francisco, CA
Brown, Kenneth I. ... Columbia, MD
Brown, Kenneth J. ... Seattle, WA
Brown, Kenneth L. ... Uniondale, NY
Brown, Kenneth M. ... Nashua, NH
Brown, Kenneth M. ... Murray Hill, NJ
Brown, Kenneth M. ... Parsippany, NJ
Brown, Kenneth M. ... Oak Ridge, TN
Brown, Kenneth R. ... Ventura, CA
Brown, Kenneth R. ... Fairburn, GA
Brown, Kenneth R. ... Boston, MA
Brown, Kenneth R. ... Salt Lake City, UT
Brown, Kenneth S. ... New York, NY
Brown, Kenneth T. ... Laramie, WY
Brown, Kenneth W. ... Louisville, KY
Brown, Kenneth W. ... Houston, TX
Brown, Kenneth William
San Antonio, TX
Brown, Kent H. ... Slingerlands, NY
Brown, Kent L. ... Jefferson City, MO
Brown, Kent Masterson ... Washington, DC
Danville, KY
Brown, Kent Masterson, Law Offices of
Lexington, KY
Brown, Kerdock & Associates, P.C.
Exton, PA
Quakertown, PA
Brown, Kermit C., P.C. ... Laramie, WY
Rawlins, WY
Brown, Kerr & King ... Quitman, TX
Brown, Kerry H. ... Tampa, FL
Brown, Kerry K. ... Dallas, TX
Brown, Kevin ... New York, NY
Brown, Kevin B. ... Dallas, TX
Brown, Kevin C. ... Alexandria, VA
Brown, Kevin E. ... Twinsburg, OH
Brown, Kevin E. ... Middlebury, VT
Brown, Kevin Harold ... Baltimore, MD
Brown, Kevin J., Law Offices of
Syracuse, NY
Carlisle, PA
Brown, Kevin L. ... Los Angeles, CA
Brown, Kevin L. ... Denver, CO
Brown, Kevin M. ... Department of Justice, Tax Division, GV
Brown, Kevin M. ... Springfield, MA
Brown, Kevin M. ... Albuquerque, NM
Brown, Kevin P. ... Chicago, IL
Brown, Kevin R. ... Hemet, CA
Brown, Kevin R ... Beaverton, OR
Brown, Kevin S. ... Livingston, MT
Brown, Kevin T. ... Macon, GA
Brown, Kevin T. ... Columbia, SC
Brown, Kevin W. ... Boston, MA
Brown, Kevin W. ... Columbus, OH
Brown, Kieran George ... Philadelphia, PA
Brown, Kim A. ... Nashville, TN
Brown, Kim C. ... Fort Myers, FL
Brown, Kim D. ... Austin, TX
Brown, Kim M. ... St. Louis, MO
Brown, Kimbel L. ... New Braunfels, TX
Brown, Kimberly ... Irvine, CA
Brown, Kimberly ... Memphis, TN
Brown, Kimberly A. ... Pittsburgh, PA
Brown, Kimberly J. ... Chicago, IL
Brown, Kimberly J. ... Columbus, OH
Brown, Kimberly K. ... Oklahoma City, OK
Brown, Kimberly N. ... Washington, DC
Brown, Kimberly W. ... Houston, TX
Brown, Kinsey & Funkhouser, P.L.C.
Mason City, IA
Brown, Kirk P. ... Pueblo, CO
Brown, Kirtley W. ... Marion, AL
Brown, Krista E. ... St. Louis, MO
Brown, Kristen E ... Chicago, IL
Brown, Kristen J. ... Columbus, OH
Brown, Kristen W. ... Harrisburg, PA
Brown, Kristi L. ... Fort Wayne, IN
Brown, Kristin Nordeck ... Longmont, CO
Brown, Kristopher D. ... New York, NY
Brown, Kristy C. ... Orlando, FL
Brown, Kurtis L.V. ... Flint, MI
Brown, Kyle D., (P.C.) ... Los Angeles, CA
Brown, Kyle T. ... St. Johnsbury, VT
Brown, L. Douglas ... Los Angeles, CA
Brown, L. Edward ... Elma, WA
Brown, L. Ross ... Eugene, OR
Brown, L. Sheldon ... Lincolnshire, IL
Brown, L. Stanley ... Charlotte, NC
Brown, L. Vance ... Oklahoma City, OK
Brown, L.A. "Smokey", Jr.
Greenwood, SC
Brown & Lacallade, P.C. ... Austin, TX
Brown, Lakresa Mecole ... Houston, TX
Brown, LaMar B. ... San Diego, CA
Brown, Lane R. ... Los Angeles, CA
Brown and LaPointe, P.A. ... Exeter, NH
Brown, Larrie Ann ... Topeka, KS
Brown, Larry A. ... Eugene, OR
Brown, Larry D. ... Prestonsburg, KY
Brown, Larry F. ... Fort Worth, TX
Brown, Larry R. ... Canton, OH
Brown, Larry T. ... Winston-Salem, NC
Brown, Larry W. ... Bethesda, MD
Brown & Laskin ... Wellesley, MA
Brown, Latane' Ware ... Norfolk, VA
Brown, Laura Elizabeth ... Waco, TX
Brown, Laura Hobson ... New Orleans, LA
Brown, Laura M. ... Milwaukee, WI
Brown, Laura Sanders ... Jackson, MS
Brown, Laurence A. ... Grand Rapids, MI
Brown, Laurence, & Associates, P.C., Law Firm of ... Arlington, VA
Brown, Laurence H. ... Philadelphia, PA
Brown, Laurence K. ... Los Angeles, CA
Brown, Laurence K. ... Chappaqua, NY
Brown, Laurence R. ... Arlington, VA
Brown, Laurence W. ... Washington, DC
Brown, Laurie Melissa ... Dallas, TX
Brown Law Firm ... Oklahoma City, OK
Brown Law Firm, P.C. ... Billings, MT
Bozeman, MT
Brown Law Firm, P.C. ... Tyler, TX
Brown Law Firm, The ... Los Angeles, CA
Brown Law Firm, The ... Kansas City, MO
Brown Law Firm, The ... Albemarle, NC
Brown Law Office ... Rochester, IN
Brown Law Office, Gary L., P.L.L.C.
Enid, OK
Brown, Lawrence A. ... Norristown, PA
Brown, Lawrence B. ... Point Richmond, CA
Brown, Lawrence B. ... Malvern, PA
Brown, Lawrence C. ... Minneapolis, MN
Brown, Lawrence C. ... Buffalo, NY
Brown, Lawrence G. ... Sacramento, CA
Brown, Lawrence H. ... Chicago, IL
Brown, Lawrence I. ... Westport, CT
Brown, Lawrence M. ... Rochester, IN
Brown, Lawrence N. ... Salem, OR
Brown, Lawrence P. ... Bridgeport, NY
Brown, Lawrence R. ... Portland, OR
Brown, Lawrence R., Jr. ... Radnor, PA
Brown, Lawson M. ... Van Nuys, CA
Brown, Layne G., Jr. ... Palisade, CO
Brown, Layne G., Jr., P.C. ... Palisade, CO
Brown, Leanne P. ... Tampa, FL
Brown, Lee ... Upland, CA
Brown, Lee Catherine ... Cambridge, MA
Brown, Lee H. ... Tucson, AZ
Brown, Lee R. ... Birmingham, AL
Brown, Leigh Lani T.
Department of Justice, Antitrust Division, GV
Brown, Leila R. ... Los Angeles, CA
Brown, Lelus B. ... Newton, KS
Brown, Leon F. ... Fair Oaks, CA
Brown, Leon F. ... Fort Thomas, KY
Brown, Leonard G. ... Flagstaff, AZ
Brown, Leonard G., III ... Greenville, NC
Brown, Leonard L., Jr. ... Chesapeake, VA
Brown, Leonard Scott ... Dallas, TX
Brown, LeRoy E., III ... Richmond, VA
Brown, Lesile Dean ... London, KY
Brown, Leslie ... Coudersport, PA
Brown, Leslie D. ... Provo, UT
Brown, Leslie E. ... Los Angeles, CA
Brown, Leslie McLellan ... Amherst, MA
Brown, Lester J. ... Sacramento, CA
Brown, Lester O. ... Los Angeles, CA
Brown, Letitia M. ... Atlanta, GA
Brown & Levicoff, P.C. ... Pittsburgh, PA
Beckley, WV
Brown, Lewis F. ... Vallejo, CA
Brown Lewis Janhunen & Spencer, A Professional Service Corporation
Aberdeen, WA
Montesano, WA
South Bend, WA
Brown, Lewis N. ... Miami, FL
Brown, Liane L. ... Honolulu, HI
Brown, Libby A. ... Houston, TX
Brown, Lillian E. ... Sterling, VA
Brown, Lillian M. ... Washington, DC
Brown, Linda J. ... San Francisco, CA
Brown, Linda M. ... Brooklyn, NY
Brown, Linda Marie ... New York, NY
Brown, Linda Prine ... Oklahoma City, OK
Brown, Linda S. ... Westport, CT
Brown, Linder & DePrez ... Shelbyville, IN
Brown, Linnea ... Denver, CO
Brown, Lippert, Heile & Evans
Cincinnati, OH
Brown, Lisa ... Stockton, CA
Brown, Lisa A. ... Atlanta, GA
Brown, Lisa A. ... Chicago, IL
Brown, Lisa A. ... Houston, TX
Brown, Lisa Bagley ... Houston, TX
Brown, Lisa C. ... Portland, OR
Brown, Lisa D. ... Albuquerque, NM
Brown, Lisa F. ... Birmingham, AL
Brown, Lisa J. ... Los Angeles, CA
Brown, Lisa M. ... Oakland, CA
Brown & Livingston, P.C. ... Statesboro, GA
Brown, Lloyd E., Jr. ... Ocala, FL
Brown, Lloyd L., Jr. ... Ringgold, GA
Brown, Lloyd W., II ... New York, NY
Brown, Lonnie T., Jr. ... Atlanta, GA
Brown, Lora L. ... Seattle, WA
Brown, Loren H. ... New York, NY
Brown, Loren N. ... Saratoga Springs, NY
Brown, Loren W. ... Placentia, CA
Brown, Lorenzo ... Dallas, TX
Brown, Lorenzo, & Associates, P.C.
Dallas, TX
Brown, Lori Ann ... San Francisco, CA
Brown, Lori Anne ... Miami, FL
Brown, Lori J. ... Washington, DC
Brown, Lori Lei ... Houston, TX
Brown, Lori Lipman ... Las Vegas, NV
Brown, Lori Root ... Scarsdale, NY

Brown, Lorna Alksne ....San Diego, CA
Brown, Lorna Patton ....Oakland, CA
Brown, Lorne J. ....Pasadena, CA
Brown, Louis C., III ....Mission, TX
Brown, Louis J. ....Philadelphia, PA
Brown, Louise Allen ....Waterbury, CT
Brown, Louise F. ....Sharon, CT
Brown, Louise M. ....Augusta, KY
Brown, Louise M., P.S.C. ....Augusta, KY
Brown, Lowell C. ....Los Angeles, CA
Brown, Lucy Chernow ....Delray Beach, FL
Brown, Lucy T. ....Burlington, VT
Brown, Luke H. ....
Department of Housing and Urban Development, GV
Brown, Luke N., Jr. ....Ridgeland, SC
Brown, Luke S. ....Fort Lauderdale, FL
Brown, Luke S., P.A. ....Fort Lauderdale, FL
Brown, Lundgren & Goldthorpe
Alliance, OH
Canton, OH
Hartville, OH
Brown, Lyle B. ....Columbus, OH
Brown, Lynn M. ....New York, NY
Brown, Lynn W. ....Elizabethton, TN
Brown, Lynne Thaxter ....Fresno, CA
Brown, M. Cory ....San Diego, CA
Brown, M. Haynes ....Erwin, TN
Brown, M. Kingsley ....San Francisco, CA
Brown, M. Lawrence ....Phoenix, AZ
Brown, M. Scott ....McLean, VA
Brown, M. Shannon ....Martinsburg, WV
Brown, Mabel W. ....Geneseo, IL
Brown, Mackintosh, (P.C.) ....Denver, CO
Brown, Maeve Elise ....Berkeley, CA
Brown, Malcolm D. ....Troy, MI
Brown, Malcolm H. ....Bismarck, ND
Brown, Malcolm H., P.C. ....Bismarck, ND
Mandan, ND
Brown, Malcolm P. ....Chicago, IL
Brown, Malcolm T. ....New York, NY
Brown, Manley F. ....Atlanta, GA
Macon, GA
Brown, Mara A. ....Ogden, UT
Salt Lake City, UT
Brown, Marc A. ....Fairfax, VA
Brown, Marc A. ....Federal Way, WA
Brown, Marc E. ....Los Angeles, CA
Brown, Marc E. ....Boston, MA
Brown, Marc L. ....Los Angeles, CA
Brown, Marc L. ....Park Ridge, IL
Brown, Marc R. ....Elizabeth, NJ
Brown, Marcus A. ....St. Louis, MO
Brown, Marcus V. ....New Orleans, LA
Brown, Margaret A. ....Fort Collins, CO
Brown, Margaret A. ....Boston, MA
Brown, Margaret Ann ......Tysons Corner, VA
Brown, Margaret D. ....San Francisco, CA
Brown, Margaret Miller ....Santa Fe, NM
Brown, Margaret Scanlan ....Libertyville, IL
Brown, Margaret W. ....Houston, TX
Brown, Margaret Y. ....Auburn, AL
Brown, Margery H. ....Missoula, MT
Brown, Margo M. ....Oklahoma City, OK
Brown and Margolius ....Cleveland, OH
Brown, Marguerite L. ....Agoura Hills, CA
Brown, Marianne E. ....Cherry Hill, NJ
Philadelphia, PA
Brown, Marianne Mandell ....Cincinnati, OH
Brown, Marietta E. ....Omaha, NE
Brown, Marilyn Moody ....Provo, UT
Brown, Marion L. ....Burlingame, CA
Brown, Marjorie A. ....Blue Bell, PA
Brown, Marjorie E. R. ....El Centro, CA
Brown, Marjorie Randall
New Orleans, LA
Brown, Mark ....Washington Crossing, PA
Brown, Mark A. ....Santa Monica, CA
Brown, Mark A. ....Department of Justice, Environment and Natural Resources Division, GV
Brown, Mark A. ....Tampa, FL
Brown, Mark A. ....Knoxville, TN
Brown, Mark A. ....Seattle, WA
Brown, Mark Adams ....San Angelo, TX
Brown, Mark C. ....Pasadena, CA
Brown, Mark C. ....Lincoln, NE
Brown, Mark D. ....Oklahoma City, OK
Brown, Mark E. ....Kansas City, MO
Brown, Mark E. ....Kansas City, MO
Brown, Mark J. ....Las Vegas, NV
East Aurora, NY
Brown, Mark J., Ltd., Law Offices of
Las Vegas, NV
East Aurora, NY
Brown, Mark K. ....Los Angeles, CA
Brown, Mark L. ....St. Louis, MO
Brown, Mark R. ....Palm Beach, FL
Brown, Mark R. ....St. Petersburg, FL
Brown, Mark R. ....Baltimore, MD
Brown, Mark S. ....Washington, DC
Brown, Mark S. ....Minneapolis, MN
Brown, Mark S. ....Madison, WI
Brown, Mark T. ....Marietta, GA
Brown, Mark W. ....Latham, NY
Mechanicville, NY
Brown, Mark Y. ....Logansport, IN
Brown, Marlene G. ....Trenton, NJ
Brown, Marna L. ....East Brunswick, NJ
Brown, Marni K. ....Atlanta, GA
Brown, Marshall B. ....Houston, TX
Brown, Marshall B., P.C. ....Houston, TX
Brown, Marshall D., Jr. ....Houston, TX
Brown, Marshall J. ....Chicago, IL
Brown, Marshall K. ....Chicago, IL
Brown, Marston C. ....Marietta, GA
Brown, Marston C., P.C. ....Marietta, GA
Brown, Martha G. ....Albuquerque, NM
Brown, Martha K. ....Fort Worth, TX
Brown, Martha L. ....London, KY
Brown, Martha L. ....Lubbock, TX
Brown, Martha P. ....Greensboro, NC
Brown, Martha S. ....Chicago, IL
Brown, Martin B. ....Baltimore, MD
Brown, Martin D. ....Littleton, CO
Brown, Martin, Haller & McClain
San Diego, CA
Brown, Martin Robert ....Caledonia, MI
Brown, Martin Shallenberger, Jr.
Nashville, TN
Brown, Martin W., The Law Firm of
Memphis, TN
Brown, Marty Young ....Pittsburgh, PA
Brown, Marvin H., III ....Wichita Falls, TX
Brown, Marvin J. ....Merced, CA
Brown, Marvin L. ....Steamboat Springs, CO
Brown, Marvin M. ....New York, NY
Brown, Mary Ann ....Burlington, IA
Brown, Mary C. ....Dallas, TX
Brown, Mary Jennifer ....Little Rock, AR
Brown, Mary J. T. ....Wayland, MA
Brown, Mary Kay ....Philadelphia, PA
Brown, Mary L. ....Washington, DC
Brown, Mary Lee Walker ....Hernando, MS
Brown, Mary M. ....Indianapolis, IN
Brown, Mary R. ....Mashpee, MA
Brown, Mary Vinciguerra ....Latham, NY
Brown, Maryjane Elizabeth ....Bloomfield, NJ
Brown, Marylou ....Baltimore, MD
Brown, Mary-Patrice ....Washington, DC
Brown, Massey, Evans, McLeod & Haynsworth, Attorneys at Law, P.A.
Greenville, SC
Brown, Matthew ....Boston, MA
Brown, Matthew D. ....San Francisco, CA
Brown, Matthew G. ....Dallas, TX
Brown, Matthew K. ....New Orleans, LA
Brown, Matthew M. ....Springfield, OH
Brown, Matthew S. ....Chicago, IL
Brown, Matthew T. ....New Orleans, LA
Brown, Matthew T. ....New York, NY
Brown, Matthew W. ....Houston, TX
Brown, Maura Jane ....Fairfax, VA
Brown, Max D. ....Chicago, IL
Brown, Max J. ....United States Senate, Senatorial Assistants, GV
Brown, Maynard M. ....Wilmington, NC
Brown McCarroll Oaks Hartline & Carll
The Woodlands, TX
Brown McCarroll & Oaks Hartline, L.L.P.
Austin, TX
Dallas, TX
Houston, TX
Longview, TX
Brown McCarroll Sheets & Crossfield, L.L.P.
Round Rock, TX
Brown, McDonald, Conolly & Davis
Galesburg, IL
Brown, McDonnell & Romaker, A Professional Law Corporation ....La Jolla, CA
Brown, Medford J., III ....Philadelphia, PA
Brown, Megan ....Oak Harbor, WA
Brown, Melanie L. ....Petersburg, VA
Brown, Melinda J. ....Cambridge, MA
Brown, Melissa C. ....Sacramento, CA
Brown, Melissa C. ....Chicago, IL
Brown, Melissa Dianne Hutcheson
Decatur, AL
Brown, Melissa Fuller ....Mount Pleasant, SC
Brown, Melissa K. ....San Francisco, CA
Brown, Melitha Lynn (Mitzi) ....Dallas, TX
Brown, Melvin A. ....Billings, MT
Brown, Melvin F. ....St. Louis, MO
Brown, Meredith L. ....San Diego, CA
Brown, Meredith M. ....New York, NY
Brown, Merilyn D. ....Chicago, IL
Brown, Meyer W. ....Kansas City, MO
Brown, Michael A. ....San Bernardino, CA
Brown, Michael A. ....Washington, DC
Brown, Michael A. ....Baltimore, MD
Brown, Michael A. ....Cincinnati, OH
Brown, Michael A. ....Moncks Corner, SC
Brown, Michael B. ....Dothan, AL
Brown, Michael B. ....St. Petersburg, FL
Brown, Michael B. ....Sarasota, FL
Brown, Michael Barrett ....Truckee, CA
Brown, Michael C. ....Cleveland, OH
Brown, Michael D. ....Los Angeles, CA
Brown, Michael D. ....Lyons, CO
Brown, Michael D. ....Riviera Beach, FL
Brown, Michael D. ....Baton Rouge, LA
Brown, Michael D. ....New York, NY
Brown, Michael D. ....Lubbock, TX
Brown, Michael Duane ....Salem, OR
Brown, Michael E. ....Scottsdale, AZ
Brown, Michael E. ....San Francisco, CA
Brown, Michael E. ....Vallejo, CA
Brown, Michael E. ....Indianapolis, IN
Brown, Michael E. ....Baltimore, MD
Brown, Michael F. ....Floral Park, NY
Brown, Michael F. ....Ithaca, NY
Brown, Michael F. ....Harrisburg, PA
Brown, Michael F. ....Philadelphia, PA
Brown, Michael Francis ....Los Gatos, CA
Brown, Michael G. ....New York, NY
Brown, Michael G. ....Dallas, TX
Brown, Michael H. ....Covington, KY
Cincinnati, OH
Brown, Michael H.M. ....Hartford, CT
Brown, Michael I. ....Chicago, IL
Brown, Michael I., Ltd. ....Chicago, IL
Brown, Michael J. ....Pinetop, AZ
Brown, Michael J. ....Tucson, AZ
Brown, Michael J. ....Tucson, AZ
Brown, Michael J. ....San Diego, CA
Brown, Michael J. ....San Diego, CA
Brown, Michael J. ....Washington, DC
Brown, Michael J. ....Lansing, MI
Brown, Michael J. ....New York, NY
Brown, Michael J. ....Portland, OR
Brown, Michael J. ....Philadelphia, PA
Brown, Michael Jay ....Seattle, WA
Brown, Michael K. ....Los Angeles, CA
Brown, Michael K. ....Walnut Creek, CA
Brown, Michael K. ....Concord, NH
Brown, Michael K., Law Office of
Westport, CT
Brown, Michael L. ....Tucson, AZ
Brown, Michael L. ....Atlanta, GA
Brown, Michael L. ....Emmetsburg, IA
Brown, Michael L. ....Oklahoma City, OK
Brown, Michael L. ....Houston, TX
Brown, Michael L., Jr. ....Rock Hill, SC
Brown, Michael L., (P.C.) ....Houston, TX
Brown, Michael M., (A Professional Law Corporation) ....Manteca, CA
Brown, Michael N. ....Tampa, FL
Brown, Michael N. ....Oklahoma City, OK
Brown, Michael O. ....Chicago, IL
Brown, Michael O. ....Dearborn, MI
Brown, Michael P. ....San Francisco, CA
Brown, Michael R. ....Irvine, CA
Brown, Michael R. ....Pasadena, CA
Brown, Michael R. ....Fairfield, IA
Brown, Michael R. ....Boston, MA
Brown, Michael S. ....New York, NY
Brown, Michael S., (P.C.) ....Alameda, CA
Brown, Michael Stewart ....Athens, GA
Brown, Michael T. ....Washington, DC
Brown, Michael T. ....Upper Marlboro, MD
Brown, Michael T. ....Washington, VA
Brown, Michael V. ....Harrisburg, PA
Brown, Michael W. ....Diamond Bar, CA
Brown, Michael W. ....Kansas City, MO
Brown, Michael W. ....Union, MO
Brown, Michael William ....Seattle, WA
Brown, Michele A. ....Buffalo, NY
Brown, Michele Schwartz ....Atlanta, GA
Brown, Michelle B. ....Kansas City, MO
Brown, Michelle L. ....Baltimore, MD
Brown, Mike ....Lubbock, TX
Brown & Miller ....Cleveland, TN
Brown, Milton, Jr. ....Tuscaloosa, AL
Brown, Milton, Jr., P.C. ....Tuscaloosa, AL
Brown, Milton K., Jr. ....Richmond, VA
Brown, Mirka ....Los Angeles, CA
Brown, Mitchell W. ....Pocatello, ID
Brown, Molly M.A. ....Albany, NY
Brown, Monica M. ....Dallas, TX
Brown, Monte L. ....Auburn, IN
Brown, Monte R. ....McAlester, OK
Brown, Morris ....Woodbridge, NJ
Brown, Morris C. ....West Palm Beach, FL
Brown, Morton B. ....Boston, MA
Brown, Morton P. ....Miami, FL
Brown & Moss, P.A. ....Fayetteville, NC
Brown, Myra J. ....Chicago, IL
Brown, Myron D. ....El Paso, TX
Brown, Myron S. ....Santa Ana, CA
Brown, Myron Timothy ....Baltimore, MD
Brown, N. Cristian ....Wesley Chapel, FL
Brown, N. Jack ....Kansas City, KS
Brown, N. Jeffrey ....New York, NY
Brown & Nachman, L.L.C.
Kansas City, MO
Brown, Nagel, Waters & Hiser, LLC
Laramie, WY
Rawlins, WY
Brown, Naida L. ....Los Angeles, CA
Brown, Nancy ....Los Angeles, CA
Brown, Nancy ....San Pedro, CA
Brown, Nancy E. ....Salem, OR
Brown, Nancy G. ....Columbus, OH
Brown, Nancy J. ....San Pedro, CA
Brown, Nancy Jean Hoffman
Houston, TX
Brown, Nancy Newman ....Philadelphia, PA
Brown, Nancy S. ....New Castle, IN
Brown, Nancy Viano ....Boston, MA
Brown, Nancy W. ....Clarksburg, WV
Brown, Narcisse A., (Mr.) ....Chicago, IL
Brown, Nat ....Stockton, CA
Brown, Nata K. ....Washington, DC
Brown, Natalie ....Denver, CO
Brown, Natalie D. ....Frankfort, KY
Lexington, KY
Brown, Nathan M. ....Alexandria, VA
Brown, Nathan T. ....Dickson, TN
Brown, Nathaniel G. ....Hartford, CT
Brown, Nathaniel K. ....Bedford, MA
Brown, Neal A. ....New York, NY
Brown, Neal M. ....Lutherville, MD
Brown & Neier ....Fayetteville, NC
Brown, Neil A. ....Cleveland, OH
Brown, Neil H. ....Santa Ana, CA
Brown, Neill S. ....Nashville, TN
Brown, Nela ....Houston, TX
Brown, Nelson Anthony ....Chicago, IL
Brown Newson & Córdova ....San Juan, PR
Brown, Nicholas D. ....Manchester, NH
Brown, Nicholas N. ....Bowling Green, KY
Brown, Nicholas R. ....New York, NY
Brown, Nicole Y. ....Westfield, NJ
New York, NY
Brown, Nicolette L. ....Chicago, IL
Brown Nietert & Kaufman, Chartered
Washington, DC
Brown, Nina Kole ....Miami, FL
Brown, Nina Williams ....Harrisburg, IL
Brown, Norbert H., Jr. ....Poughkeepsie, NY
Brown, Norman R. ....Buffalo, NY
Brown, O. Hampton, III ....West Chester, PA
Brown, Obringer, Beardsley & DeCandio, Professional Association ...Jacksonville, FL
Brown, Odine Michay ....New York, NY
Brown, Ogden R. ....Buffalo, NY
Brown, Olson & Wilson, Professional Corporation ....Concord, NH
Lebanon, NH
Manchester, NH
Brown, Omer F., II ....Washington, DC
Brown, Onalee ....Denver, CO
Brown, Orran Lee ....Richmond, VA
Brown, Orrin J. ....Greenville, ME
Brown, Ossie, Law Offices of
Baton Rouge, LA
Brown, Owen S. ....Oklahoma City, OK
Brown, P. Brent ....Roanoke, VA
Brown, P. Robert, Jr. ....Detroit, MI
Brown, Paindiris & Scott, LLP
Glastonbury, CT
Hartford, CT
Brown, Pamela A. ....Englewood, CO
Brown, Pamela Charles ....Seattle, WA
Brown, Pamela D. ....Charleston, SC
Brown, Pamela J. ....Washington, DC
Brown, Pamela M. ....Austin, TX
Brown, Pamela Platt ....Northbrook, IL
Brown, Pamila J. ....Baltimore, MD
Brown, Pat ....Seattle, WA
Brown, Patrice M. ....Kansas City, KS
Brown, Patricia A. ....Treasury Department, Departmental Offices, GV
Brown, Patricia Ann ....Tucson, AZ
Brown, Patricia G. ....Portland, OR
Brown, Patricia H. ....Boulder, CO
Brown, Patricia I. ....Boston, MA
Brown, Patricia L. ....Cary, NC
Brown, Patricia L. ....North Kingstown, RI
Brown, Patricia L. ....Round Rock, TX
Brown, Patricia M. ....Chicago, IL
Brown, Patricia Mary Clare ....Baltimore, MD
Brown, Patricia Robinson ....Carlisle, PA
Brown, Patricia Russell ....Washington, DC
Brown, Patrick ....Oklahoma City, OK
Brown, Patrick D. ....Twin Falls, ID
Brown, Patrick E. ....Albany, NY
New York, NY
Brown, Patrick F. ....Charlotte, NC
Brown, Patrick J. ....Treasury Department, Departmental Offices, GV
Brown, Patrick J. ....Buffalo, NY
Brown, Patrick N. ....West Palm Beach, FL
Brown, Patrick S. ....Los Angeles, CA
Brown, Patrick T. ....Fairbanks, AK
Brown, Patsy H. (Pat) ....Bethany, OK
Brown, Paul ....Mobile, AL
Brown, Paul ....Sherman, TX
Brown, Paul A. ....Syracuse, NY
Brown, Paul D. ....St. Paul, MN
Brown, Paul D. ....Washington, VA
Brown, Paul D., P.C. ....Mobile, AL
Brown, Paul E. ....Des Moines, IA
Brown, Paul E. ....Lockport, IL
Brown, Paul E. ....Massillon, OH
Brown, Paul F. ....Hartford, CT
Brown, Paul F. ....Chicago, IL
Brown, Paul F. ....Ballston Spa, NY
Brown, Paul H. ....Washington, DC
Brown, Paul L. ....Chicago, IL
Brown, Paul M. ....St. Louis, MO
Brown, Paul M. ....Omaha, NE
Brown, Paul M. ....New York, NY
Brown, Paul Michael ....Department of Justice, Civil Division, GV
Brown, Paul R. ....Bangor, ME
Brown, Paul R ....Seattle, WA
Brown, Paul S. ....St. Louis, MO
Brown, Paul S. ....New York, NY
Brown, Paul Truett ....Lewisburg, TN
Brown, Paul V., Jr. ....Portsmouth, NH
Brown, Paul W. ....Hutchinson, KS
Brown, Paul W. ....New York, NY
Brown, Paul W. ....Columbus, OH
Brown, Paul W. ....Memphis, TN
Brown, Paul W. ....Dallas, TX
Brown, Paul W., P.C. ....Dallas, TX
Brown, Paul Westfall ....Watertown, NY
Brown, Paula A. ....Pleasanton, CA
Brown, Paula Baiman ....Philadelphia, PA
Brown, Paula J. ....New York, NY
Brown, Paulette ....East Orange, NJ
Brown, Payne D. ....Fort Wayne, IN
Brown & Peel ....Fresno, CA
Brown, Peggy L. ....Olympia, WA
Brown, Penny ....Chicago, IL
Brown, Penny Jill ....Wailuku, HI
Brown and Percival Co., L.P.A.
Canton, OH
Massillon, OH
Brown, Pernila (Penny) S. ....Jackson, MS
Brown, Perry E. ....Jackson, MS
Brown, Peter ....New York, NY
Brown, Peter B. ....Phoenix, AZ
Tucson, AZ
Brown, Peter C. ....Orange, CA
Las Vegas, NV
Brown, Peter C. ....Lexington, KY
Brown, Peter C., Jr. ....Armonk, NY
Brown, Peter C., Law Offices Of
Las Vegas, NV
Brown, Peter David ....Mount Pleasant, SC
Brown, Peter E. ....Lexington, KY
Brown, Peter J. ....Los Angeles, CA
Brown, Peter J. ....West Hartford, CT
Brown, Peter L. ....Washington, DC
Brown, Peter M. ....San Francisco, CA
Brown, Peter M. ....Albany, NY
Saratoga Springs, NY
Brown, Peter M., P.C. ....San Francisco, CA
Brown, Peter Megargee ....New York, NY
Brown, Peter N. ....Santa Barbara, CA

Brown, Peter O. ... **Rochester, NY**
Brown, Peter R. ... **Boston, MA**
Brown, Peter T. ... Independence, OH
Brown, Peter W. ... **Kansas City, MO**
Brown, Peter W. ... **Concord, NH**
Brown & Peyton ... **Charleston, WV**
Brown, Phil W., Jr. ... Houston, TX
Brown, Philip A. ... Gooding, ID
Brown, Philip A. ... St. Joseph, MI
Brown, Philip A. ... **Columbus, OH**
Brown, Philip A., P.C. ... St. Joseph, MI
Brown, Philip F. ... **Columbus, OH**
Brown, Philip M. ... **Atlanta, GA**
Macon, GA
Brown, Philip M. ... Houston, TX
Brown, Philip R., Law Offices of
Honolulu, HI
Brown, Philip S. ... Brooklyn, NY
Brown, Philip W. ... Arlington Heights, IL
Brown, Philip Y. ... **Boston, MA**
Brown, Phillip C. ... **Moberly, MO**
Brown, Phillip C., P.C. ... **Moberly, MO**
Brown, Phillip E. ... **San Francisco, CA**
Brown, Phillip E. ... Roanoke, VA
Brown, Phillip L. ... **Dallas, TX**
Brown, Phillip S. ... Detroit, MI
Brown, Phillip S. ... **Kansas City, MO**
Brown, Phillip S. ... **Dallas, TX**
Brown, Phillip W. ... Shelbyville, IN
Brown, Phoebe W. ... **Washington, DC**
Brown, Phyllis C. ... Long Beach, CA
Brown, Phyllis E. ... Los Angeles, CA
Brown, Phyllis E. ... **Cincinnati, OH**
Brown, Phyllis I. ... Kansas City, MO
Brown, Phyllis W. ... Baltimore, MD
Brown, Pinnisi & Michaels, P.C.
Ithaca, NY
Syracuse, NY
Brown, Porter K. ... Hutchinson, KS
Brown, Portia K. ... Rapid City, SD
Brown, Prentiss M., III ... St. Ignace, MI
Brown, Prentiss M., Jr. ... **St. Ignace, MI**
Brown, Preston ... **Washington, DC**
Brown, Priscilla ... **San Francisco, CA**
Brown Professional Group
Salt Lake City, UT
Brown, Prothro & Williamson, A Professional Corporation
Wichita Falls, TX
Brown, Queen, Patten & Jenkins, P.A.
Waynesville, NC
Brown, Quentin L. ... Overland Park, KS
Brown, Quentin Q., Jr. ... Birmingham, AL
Brown, R. Andrew ... Miami, FL
Brown, R. Christine ... **Torrance, CA**
Brown, R. Donald, (Law Offices of)
Los Angeles, CA
Brown, R. Edward ... Van Nuys, CA
Brown, R. Edwin ... **Rockville, MD**
Brown, R. Grady ... Houston, TX
Brown, R. Joshua ... Lexington, OH
Brown, R. Kent ... **Charlotte, NC**
Brown, R. Kevin, Jr. ... Pittsburgh, PA
Brown, R. Lewis, Jr. ... Butte, MT
Brown, R. Michael ... **Champaign, IL**
Brown, R. Romer ... **Coeur d'Alene, ID**
Brown, R. Scott ... Tampa, FL
Brown, R. Scott ... **Raleigh, NC**
Brown, R. Steven ... Springfield, MO
Brown, Rachel A. ... **Las Cruces, NM**
Brown, Rachel Townsend
Lee's Summit, MO
Brown, Ralph ... Maryville, TN
Brown, Ralph ... San Antonio, TX
Brown, Ralph, & Associates ... Maryville, TN
Brown, Ralph E. ... **Chicago, IL**
Brown, Ralph Evan ... San Diego, CA
Brown, Ralph H. ... Westerville, OH
Brown, Ralph K., Jr. ... Omaha, NE
Brown, Ralph R. ... **Dallas Center, IA**
Brown, Ralph S. ... New Haven, CT
Brown, Ralph S., Jr. ... New York, NY
Brown, Ralph T., Jr. ... Chattanooga, TN
Brown, Ralph W. ... **Portland, ME**
Brown, Ramon E. ... Camano, WA
Brown, Randal B. ... Suquamish, WA
Brown, Randal Lynn ... Grand Junction, CO
Brown, Randall C. ... **Dallas, TX**
Brown, Randall E. ... Farmers Branch, TX
Brown, Randall W. ... **Kansas City, MO**
Brown, Randolph A. ... **Louisville, KY**
Brown, Randolph T. ... **Long Prairie, MN**
Brown, Randolph T., P.A.
Long Prairie, MN
Brown, Randy L. ... Grand Junction, CO
Brown & Ray ... **Cambridge, IL**
Brown and Ray ... **Geneseo, IL**
Brown, Ray C. ... Sedona, AZ
Brown, Ray G. ... Columbus, OH
Brown, Ray R. ... **Anchorage, AK**
Brown, Raymond A. ... Jersey City, NJ
Newark, NJ
Brown, Raymond A., III ... Bloomfield, NJ
Brown, Raymond A., Jr. ... Newark, NJ
Brown, Raymond A., Jr., (P.C.) ... Newark, NJ
Brown, Raymond E. ... **Irvine, CA**
Brown, Raymond F. ... Georgetown, KY
Brown, Raymond L. ... **Biloxi, MS**
Pascagoula, MS
Brown, Raymond L., Jr. ... **Alexandria, LA**
Brown, Raymond M. ... Newark, NJ
Brown, Raymond R. ... Basking Ridge, NJ
Brown, Raymond R. ... Houston, TX
Brown, Raymond W. ... **Prescott, AZ**
Brown Raysman Millstein Felder & Steiner LLP ... **Los Angeles, CA**
Hartford, CT
Morristown, NJ
New York, NY
Uniondale, NY
Brown, Reagan Chelsea ... **Atlanta, GA**
Brown, Reagan M. ... **Houston, TX**
Brown, Reba ... **Nashville, TN**
Brown, Rebecca Craycraft
Huntington, WV
Brown, Rebecca K., P.A. ... Benton, AR
Brown, Rebecca L. ... Nashville, TN
Brown, Rebecca L. (Berkeley)
St. Louis, MO
Brown, Regina J. ... New York, NY
Brown, Reginald C., Jr. ... **Florence, SC**
Brown, Reginald J. ... Tallahassee, FL
Brown, Reid G. ... Waynesville, NC
Brown, Rendell F. ... West Palm Beach, FL
Brown, Rex D., Jr. ... Greenwich, CT
Brown, Rex L. ... Decatur, IL
Maroa, IL
Brown, Rexford T. ... Jackson, MS
Brown, Rhonda R. ... **Washington, DC**
Brown, Rhonda S. ... New York, NY
Brown, Rhonda Simpson ... Minnetonka, MN
Brown, Rhonda T. ... Rochester, NY
Brown, Richard ... Parsippany, NJ
Brown, Richard ... Exton, PA
Quakertown, PA
Brown, Richard A. ... **Tucson, AZ**
Brown, Richard A. ... **Los Angeles, CA**
New York, NY
Brown, Richard A. ... San Diego, CA
Brown, Richard A. ... Sunnyvale, CA
Brown, Richard A. ... Chester, IL
Brown, Richard A. ... Rochester, IN
Brown, Richard A. ... Kew Gardens, NY
Brown, Richard A., Jr.
Newport Beach, CA
Brown, Richard A., Jr. ... **Brunswick, GA**
Brown, Richard B. ... **Anchorage, AK**
Brown, Richard B. ... San Francisco, CA
Brown, Richard B. ... **Mineola, NY**
Brown, Richard C. ... Dayton, OH
Brown, Richard D. ... **Bakersfield, CA**
Brown, Richard D. ... **West Des Moines, IA**
Brown, Richard D. ... Malden, MA
Brown, Richard D. ... Morristown, NJ
Brown, Richard D. ... **Columbus, OH**
Brown, Richard E. ... Atlanta, GA
Brown, Richard E. ... Oneonta, NY
Brown, Richard E. ... Bellaire, TX
Brown, Richard E, Jr ... Plainfield, NJ
Brown, Richard E., Jr. (P.C.) ... Watchung, NJ
Brown, Richard E. (Rick)
Daytona Beach, FL
Brown, Richard F. ... **Amarillo, TX**
Brown, Richard G. ... **Salt Lake City, UT**
Brown, Richard H. ... Schenectady, NY
Brown, Richard H. ... **Cleveland, OH**
Brown, Richard H., III ... **Morristown, NJ**
Brown, Richard H., Jr. ... **New York, NY**
Brown, Richard I. ... **Denver, CO**
Brown, Richard J. ... Matawan, NJ
Brown, Richard J. ... **Princeton, NJ**
New York, NY
Brown, Richard J. ... **New York, NY**
Brown, Richard K. ... **New York, NY**
Brown, Richard L. ... Tempe, AZ
Brown, Richard L. ... **Irvine, CA**
Brown, Richard L. ... **Washington, DC**
Brown, Richard L. ... **Vero Beach, FL**
Brown, Richard L. ... Beech Grove, IN
Brown, Richard L. ... **Fort Worth, TX**
Brown, Richard L., II ... Camden, NJ
Brown, Richard L., Jr. ... Indianapolis, IN
Brown, Richard L., P.A. ... **Vero Beach, FL**
Brown, Richard Lane, III ... **Albemarle, NC**
Brown, Richard M. ... **Chicago, IL**
Brown, Richard M. ... Minneapolis, MN
Brown, Richard N. ... Brookfield, MO
Brown, Richard O. ... **Birmingham, AL**
Brown, Richard P. ... Englewood, CO
Brown, Richard P., Jr. ... **Philadelphia, PA**
Brown, Richard R. ... **Hartford, CT**
Brown, Richard R. ... Department of Justice, Civil Division, GV
Brown, Richard R. ... Upper Sandusky, OH
Brown, Richard S. ... San Diego, CA
Brown, Richard S. ... Rockville, MD
Brown, Richard S. ... **New York, NY**
Philadelphia, PA
Brown, Richard S. ... Waukesha, WI
Brown, Richard S., Jr. ... New York, NY
Brown, Richard Scott ... **San Francisco, CA**
Brown, Richard T. ... East Longmeadow, MA
Brown, Richard T. ... Fairborn, OH
Brown, Richard T. ... Westlake, OH
Brown, Richard T., III ... **Cincinnati, OH**
Brown, Richard T., Jr. ... Philadelphia, PA
Brown, Richard W. ... Atlanta, GA
Brown, Richard W. ... Great Bend, KS
Brown, Richard W. ... Bogalusa, LA
Brown, Richard Warren ... Midland, MI
Brown, Richd. A. ... Glen Burnie, MD
Brown, Rick ... Dalton, GA
Brown, Ricklin ... **Charleston, WV**
Brown, Rickman P. ... **Atlanta, GA**
Brown, Ridgely W. ... Darien, CT
Brown, R. J. ... Little Rock, AR
Brown, Robert ... **San Francisco, CA**
Brown, Robert A. ... Delta, CO
Brown, Robert A. ... Key Largo, FL
Brown, Robert A. ... Northbrook, IL
Brown, Robert A. ... Stillwater, OK
Brown, Robert A. ... La Vergne, TN
Brown, Robert A., Jr. ... **St. Joseph, MO**
Brown, Robert B. ... Stevensville, MT
Brown, Robert B. ... **Richmond, VA**
Brown, Robert B., Jr. ... **Pittsburgh, PA**
Brown, Robert Baldwin, III ... **Miami, FL**
Brown, Robert Bruce ... **Birmingham, MI**
Detroit, MI
Brown, Robert C. ... Florence, AZ
Brown, Robert C. ... **Phoenix, AZ**
Brown, Robert C. ... **Denver, CO**
Brown, Robert C. ... Danbury, CT
Brown, Robert C. ... **Wichita, KS**
Brown, Robert C. ... **Mayfield, KY**
Brown, Robert C. ... Ellicott City, MD
Brown, Robert C. ... Farmington Hills, MI
Brown, Robert C. ... Duluth, MN
Brown, Robert C. ... **Butte, MT**
Brown, Robert C. ... Columbia, SC
Brown, Robert C. ... **Dallas, TX**
Brown, Robert C., Jr. ... **Easton, PA**
Brown, Robert Charles ... Old Bridge, NJ
Brown, Robert Clarke ... New York, NY
Brown, Robert D. ... **Oxnard, CA**
Brown, Robert D. ... **Miami, FL**
Brown, Robert D. ... **Merrillville, IN**
Brown, Robert D. ... Mount Laurel, NJ
Brown, Robert D. ... **Houston, TX**
Brown, Robert D., Jr. ... **Totowa, NJ**
Brown, Robert E. ... San Francisco, CA
Brown, Robert E. ... **Charleston, IL**
Brown, Robert E. ... **Rochester, NY**
Brown, Robert E. ... King George, VA
Brown, Robert E. ... **Norfolk, VA**
Brown, Robert Erven ... Scottsdale, AZ
Brown, Robert Erven, P.A. ... Scottsdale, AZ
Brown, Robert F. ... **Cincinnati, OH**
Brown, Robert F. ... **Dallas, TX**
Brown, Robert G. ... Yarmouth Port, MA
Brown, Robert G. ... Tulsa, OK
Brown, Robert Grattan, Jr. ... **Memphis, TN**
Brown, Robert H. ... **Chicago, IL**
Brown, Robert H. ... **South Bend, IN**
Brown, Robert H. ... Somerset, KY
Brown, Robert H. ... **Akron, OH**
Brown, Robert Hutton, III ... **Atlanta, GA**
Brown, Robert I. ... Detroit, MI
Brown, Robert J. ... Pasadena, CA
Brown, Robert J. ... **San Diego, CA**
Brown, Robert J. ... **San Diego, CA**
Brown, Robert J. ... Department of Justice, Immigration and Naturalization Service, GV
Brown, Robert J. ... North Vernon, IN
Brown, Robert J. ... **Lexington, KY**
Brown, Robert J. ... **Clifton, NJ**
New York, NY
Brown, Robert J. ... **New York, NY**
Brown, Robert J. ... Denver, NC
Brown, Robert J. ... **Dayton, OH**
Brown, Robert J. ... Wooster, OH
Brown, Robert J. ... York, PA
Brown, Robert J., Jr. ... **West Trenton, NJ**
Brown, Robert Joseph ... **San Francisco, CA**
Brown, Robert, Jr. ... Durham, NC
Brown, Robert K. ... **Chatham, NJ**
Brown, Robert K. ... **New York, NY**
Brown, Robert L. ... Little Rock, AR
Brown, Robert L. ... **Denver, CO**
Brown, Robert L. ... **Louisville, KY**
Brown, Robert L. ... Arnold, MO
Brown, Robert L. ... St. Louis, MO
Brown, Robert L. ... Bucyrus, OH
Brown, Robert L. ... **Cleveland, OH**
Brown, Robert L. ... Chattanooga, TN
Brown, Robert L., III ... **Corbin, KY**
Brown, Robert L., (P.C.) ... Orange, NJ
Brown, Robert Larry ... **Memphis, TN**
Brown, Robert M. ... Denver, CO
Brown, Robert M. ... Ormond By The Sea, FL
Brown, Robert M. ... **Albany, NY**
Brown, Robert M. ... Winston-Salem, NC
Brown, Robert M. ... Dayton, OH
Brown, Robert M., II ... Davie, FL
Brown, Robert M., Jr. ... Roanoke, VA
Brown, Robert N. ... Wellesley, MA
Brown, Robert O. ... Omaha, NE
Brown, Robert P. ... **Lewiston, ID**
Brown, Robert P. ... Wells, ME
Brown, Robert P. ... East Lansing, MI
Brown, Robert Preston ... **Atlanta, GA**
Brown, Robert R. ... **Seymour, IN**
Brown, Robert Raymond ... **Chicago, IL**
Brown, Robert S. ... San Gabriel, CA
Brown, Robert S. ... Highland Park, IL
Brown, Robert S. ... **New York, NY**
Brown, Robert S. ... **Cincinnati, OH**
Brown, Robert Sims ... Columbia, SC
Brown, Robert T. ... Jacksonville, FL
Brown, Robert Tim ... **New York, NY**
Brown, Robert V., P.S. ... Seattle, WA
Brown, Robert V., P.S. ... Seattle, WA
Brown, Robert W. ... **Coral Gables, FL**
Brown, Robert W. ... Kansas City, MO
Brown, Robert W. ... **Akron, OH**
Brown, Robert W. ... **Allentown, PA**
Brown, Robert W. ... Pittsburgh, PA
Brown, Robert W. ... **Sumter, SC**
Brown, Robert W. ... **Sheridan, WY**
Brown, Robert W., Jr. ... Libertyville, IL
Brown, Robert W., Jr. ... Washington, IL
Brown, Robert Warren ... Belgrade, MT
Brown, Roberta ... Encino, CA
Brown, Roberta S. ... Highland Park, IL
Brown, Roberta T. ... Boston, MA
Brown, Robin Shively ... **Little Rock, AR**
Brown, Robt. J. ... Carrollton, GA
Brown, Robt. Pershing ... New York, NY
Brown, Rockwood ... **Billings, MT**
Brown, Roddey Middleton, III
Hampstead, NC
Brown, Roderick E. ... Ventura, CA
Brown, Rodney Alan ... **New York, NY**
Brown, Rodney D. ... Danbury, CT
Brown, Rodney F. ... San Diego, CA
Brown, Rodney L., Jr. ... **Seattle, WA**
Brown, Rodney M. ... Detroit, MI
Southfield, MI
Brown, Rodney M. ... Greenville, SC
Brown, Roger A. ... Birmingham, AL
Brown, Roger A. ... Sonora, CA
Brown, Roger A. ... Harleysville, PA
Brown, Roger D. ... **San Diego, CA**
Brown, Roger D., Law Offices of
Fort Worth, TX
Brown, Roger G. ... Jefferson City, MO
Brown, Roger K. ... Des Moines, IA
Brown, Roger L. ... **Fort Lauderdale, FL**
Brown, Roger L. ... Boise, ID
Brown, Roger L. ... Calumet City, IL
Brown, Roger M. ... **San Francisco, CA**
Brown, Roger M. ... Treasury Department, Internal Revenue Service, GV
Brown, Roger W. ... Jasper, IN
Brown, Roger W. ... Baltimore, MD
Brown, Roland G. ... Jacksonville, TX
Brown & Romeo ... Jonesboro, GA
Brown, Ron D. ... **Salt Lake City, UT**
Brown, Ronald ... **Indianapolis, IN**
Brown, Ronald A. ... **Waldorf, MD**
Brown, Ronald A. ... St. Louis, MO
Brown, Ronald A., Jr. ... **Wilmington, DE**
Brown, Ronald B. ... Fort Lauderdale, FL
Brown, Ronald Boyd ... **Cleveland, OH**
Brown, Ronald C. ... Honolulu, HI
Brown, Ronald D. ... **New York, NY**
Brown, Ronald D. ... Cincinnati, OH
Brown, Ronald E. ... **Morristown, NJ**
Brown, Ronald G. ... Seattle, WA
Brown, Ronald J. ... **Minneapolis, MN**
Brown, Ronald J. ... **Pittsburgh, PA**
Brown, Ronald J. ... Leesburg, VA
Brown, Ronald K., Jr., (A Professional Corporation) ... **Newport Beach, CA**
Brown, Ronald L. ... Los Angeles, CA
Brown, Ronald L. ... Fort Collins, CO
Brown, Ronald L. ... Lincoln, NE
Brown, Ronald L. ... Oklahoma City, OK
Brown, Ronald L., P.C. ... Oklahoma City, OK
Brown, Ronald L., P.C. ... **Dallas, TX**
Brown, Ronald M. ... Chicago, IL
Brown, Ronald Nelson ... Houston, TX
Brown, Ronald R. ... Kingwood, WV
Brown, Ronald W. ... **Sacramento, CA**
Brown, Ronald W ... **St. Augustine, FL**
Brown, Ronda L. ... **McLean, VA**
Brown, Ronda R. ... Rockville, IN
Brown, Ronna D. ... New York, NY
Brown, Roosevelt ... Lakewood, CA
Brown, Roseta, Long, McConville, Kilcullen & Carlson ... **Eugene, OR**
Brown, Roslyn G. ... Norfolk, VA
Brown, Ross E. ... Stow, MA
Brown, Ross G. ... Honolulu, HI
Brown, Rowine Hayes ... Chicago, IL
Brown, Rowland C. W. ... Columbus, OH
Brown, Roy C., Jr. ... Montgomery, AL
Brown, Roy E. ... Alvin, TX
Brown, Roy J. ... Birmingham, AL
Brown, Roy L. ... Satanta, KS
Brown, Roy W. ... Kearney, MO
Brown, Royce H. ... Marshall, TX
Brown, Ruby Y., (Mrs.) ... Pocatello, ID
Brown, Rudnick, Freed & Gesmer
Hartford, CT
Boston, MA
Providence, RI
Brown, Rudy M. ... Brooklyn, NY
Brown, Rufus E. ... **Portland, ME**
Brown, Russell C. ... **Phoenix, AZ**
Brown, Russell C. ... **Henderson, TX**
Brown, Russell N. ... **Buffalo, NY**
Brown, Ryan Douglas ... **Nashville, TN**
Brown, Ryan K. ... Kennewick, WA
Brown, S. Brad ... **Dallas, TX**
Brown, S. Phillip ... Macon, GA
Brown, Sacha M. ... **Orlando, FL**
Brown, Sally ... San Francisco, CA
Brown, Sam'l E. ... Lubbock, TX
Brown, Sampson A. ... La Jolla, CA
Brown, Samuel ... Dillon, CO
Brown, Samuel Henry ... **Los Angeles, CA**
Brown, Samuel J. ... **Annapolis, MD**
Brown, Samuel R., II ... Virginia Beach, VA
Brown, Samuel S., (Ltd.) ... Chicago, IL
Brown, Samuel W. ... **Knoxville, TN**
Brown, Samuel Z. ... **Cherry Hill, NJ**
Philadelphia, PA
Brown, Sandra A. ... **Pittsburgh, PA**
Brown, Sandra L. ... **Washington, DC**
Brown, Sandra L. ... Atlanta, GA
Brown, Sandra L. ... **Seattle, WA**
Brown, Sanford D. ... **Freehold, NJ**
Brown, Sanford M. ... **Dallas, TX**
Brown, Sara Beth ... Reno, NV
Brown, Sarah A. ... **Irvine, CA**
Brown, Sarah A. ... Overland Park, KS
Brown, Sarah E. ... Sierra Vista, AZ
Brown, Sarah Z. ... **Dallas, TX**
Brown, Schottelkotte & Tweedell
Delta, CO
Brown and Schwaninger ... Washington, DC
Brown Schwartz Patterson & Ankers, P.C.
Detroit, MI
Troy, MI
Brown & Scoccimaro, P.C. ... Albany, GA
Brown, Scott A. ... **San Francisco, CA**
Brown, Scott A. ... **Washington, DC**
Brown, Scott A. ... **Cambridge, MA**
Brown, Scott D. ... **Mason City, IA**
Brown, Scott D. ... **New York, NY**
Brown, Scott D. ... Midvale, UT
Brown, Scott Edmondson ... Des Moines, IA

Brown, Scott F. ... New York, NY
Brown, Scott G. ... Mobile, AL
Brown, Scott G. ... Pittsburgh, PA
Brown, Scott J. ... Chicago, IL
Brown, Scott M. ... Santa Barbara, CA
Brown, Scott M. ... Thousand Oaks, CA
Brown, Scott M. ... Omaha, NE
Brown, Scott M. ... Derby, NY
Brown, Scott N., Jr. ... Chattanooga, TN
Brown, Scott P. ... Wrentham, MA
Brown, Scott R. ... Palo Alto, CA
Brown, Scott R. ... Cincinnati, OH
Brown and Seelye, PLLC ... Bremerton, WA
Tacoma, WA
Brown, Seth E. ... Washington, DC
Brown, Seymour R. ... Cleveland, OH
Brown, Shad Louis ... Pueblo, CO
Brown & Shamp ... Atlanta, GA
Brown, Shanetta Y. ... Department of Justice, Civil Rights Division, GV
Brown, Sharie A. ... Fairfax, VA
Brown, Sharon ... Fort Lauderdale, FL
Miami, FL
Brown, Sharon E. ... Anchorage, AK
Brown, Sharon Jacobs ... Plantation, FL
Brown, Sharon K. ... Los Angeles, CA
Brown, Sharon Lorraine ... New York, NY
Brown, Sharon M. ... Richland, WA
Brown, Sharon S. ... San Antonio, TX
Brown, Shaunna F. ... Secaucus, NJ
Brown, Shawn M. ... New City, NY
Brown, Shawna L. ... Dallas, TX
Brown, Sheila D. ... Memphis, TN
Brown, Sheila E. ... Los Alamos, NM
Brown, Sheldon R. ... Annandale, MN
Brown, Shelly R. ... Seattle, WA
Brown, Sheridan H. ... Palo Alto, CA
Brown, Sherri P. ... Lexington, KY
Brown, Sherrie ... White Plains, NY
Brown, Sherrie Willman ... Decatur, AL
Brown, Sheryl J. ... Washington, DC
Brown, Shiels & Chasanov ... Dover, DE
Georgetown, DE
Rehoboth Beach, DE
Brown, Shirley Hastings ... Asheville, NC
Brown, Shirley K. ... Helena, MT
Brown, Shirley Z. ... Montgomery, AL
Brown, Sidford Lewis ... Los Angeles, CA
Brown, Sidney D. ... Edmond, OK
Oklahoma City, OK
Brown, Sidney R. ... Atlanta, GA
Brown, Simon R. ... Nashua, NH
Brown, Sims, Wise & White, A Professional Corporation ... Houston, TX
Brown, Sommers T. ... Washington, DC
Brown & Spence, LLP
Overland Park, KS
Brown, Spencer J. ... Kansas City, MO
Brown, Spencer L. ... New York, NY
Brown, Spencer W. ... Kerrville, TX
Brown, Stacie L. ... Las Vegas, NV
Brown, Stacy Smith ... New Orleans, LA
Brown, Stacy V. ... St. Louis, MO
Brown, Stan ... Abilene, TX
Brown, Stan Derwin ... Lanham, MD
Brown, Stanley D. ... Los Angeles, CA
Brown, Stanley E. ... Harrisburg, PA
Brown, Stanley H. ... Reno, NV
Brown, Stanley H., Jr. ... Reno, NV
Brown, Stanley H., Jr., Chartered
Reno, NV
Brown, Stanley J. ... Rockville, MD
McLean, VA
Brown, Stansel A., III ... Pell City, AL
Brown, Stefanie M. ... Mill Valley, CA
Brown, Stephanie ... West Palm Beach, FL
Brown, Stephanie E. ... Pittsburgh, PA
Brown, Stephen A. ... Westbury, NY
Brown, Stephen A. ... Alexandria, VA
Brown, Stephen B. ... Stamford, CT
Brown, Stephen B. ... Treasury Department, Office of the Comptroller of the Currency, GV
Brown, Stephen B. ... Raleigh, NC
Brown, Stephen C. ... Windsor, CT
Brown, Stephen C. ... Boise, ID
Brown, Stephen C. ... Oak Brook, IL
Brown, Stephen C. ... Rochester, NH
Brown, Stephen D. ... Washington, DC
Brown, Stephen D. ... Columbus, OH
Brown, Stephen D. ... Medford, OR
Brown, Stephen D. ... Philadelphia, PA
Brown, Stephen D. ... Madison, WI
Brown, Stephen E. ... Birmingham, AL
Brown, Stephen E. ... Memphis, TN
Brown, Stephen E. ... Montesano, WA
Brown, Stephen F. ... San Luis Obispo, CA
Brown, Stephen H. ... Washington, DC
Brown, Stephen H. ... Augusta, GA
Brown, Stephen H. ... Greenville, SC
Brown, Stephen J. ... Chicago, IL
Brown, Stephen J. ... Boston, MA
Brown, Stephen J. ... Worcester, MA
Brown, Stephen J. ... Medina, OH
Brown, Stephen L. ... Charleston, SC
Brown, Stephen M. ... Memphis, TN
Brown, Stephen M. ... Yakima, WA
Brown, Stephen P. ... Detroit, MI
Brown, Stephen P. ... Uniondale, NY
Brown, Stephen R. ... San Diego, CA
Brown, Stephen R. ... Walnut Creek, CA
Brown, Stephen R., Jr. ... Havre, MT
Brown, Stephen Ross ... Missoula, MT
Brown, Stephen S. ... Washington, DC
Silver Spring, MD
Brown, Stephen S. ... Kansas City, MO
Brown, Stephen T. ... Miami, FL
Brown, Stephen W. ... Pratt, KS
Brown, Stephen W. ... Valley Forge, PA
Brown, Stephenie L. ... New York, NY
Brown, Steven A. ... Kalamazoo, MI
Brown, Steven Ames ... San Francisco, CA
Brown, Steven C. ... Sebring, FL
Brown, Steven C. ... New York, NY
Brown, Steven Clyde Reed
Birmingham, AL
Brown, Steven D. ... Richmond, VA
Brown, Steven D. ... Seattle, WA
Brown, Steven E. ... Westlake Village, CA
Brown, Steven G. ... Overland Park, KS
Brown, Steven G. ... Salem, NH
Brown, Steven G. ... Media, PA
Brown, Steven J. ... Phoenix, AZ
Brown, Steven J. ... Claremont, CA
Brown, Steven J. ... Cedarhurst, NY
Brown, Steven J. ... Gig Harbor, WA
Brown, Steven Jay ... Phoenix, AZ
Brown, Steven K. ... Idaho Falls, ID
Brown, Steven K. ... St. Louis, MO
Brown, Steven L. ... New York, NY
Brown, Steven L. ... Rochester, NY
Brown, Steven L. ... Norfolk, VA
Brown, Steven L., Jr. ... Danville, CA
Brown, Steven M. ... Indianapolis, IN
Brown, Steven M. ... Columbus, OH
Brown, Steven Michael ... Kalamazoo, MI
Brown, Steven R. ... Gonzales, TX
Brown, Steven R. ... Gonzales, TX
San Marcos, TX
Brown, Steven S. ... Chicago, IL
Brown, Steven S. ... Buffalo, NY
Clifton Park, NY
Brown, Steven W. ... Newport Beach, CA
Brown, Steven W. ... Ventura, CA
Brown, Steven W. ... Chicago, IL
Brown, Steven W. ... Salina, KS
Brown, Steven W., Chartered ... Salina, KS
Brown, Stewart H. ... Vail, CO
Brown, Stewart M. ... San Diego, CA
Brown, Stratton S. ... Detroit, MI
Brown & Streza, LLP ... Irvine, CA
Newport Beach, CA
Brown, Stuart ... Dallas, TX
Brown, Stuart E., Jr. ... Berryville, VA
Brown, Stuart L. ... Treasury Department, Internal Revenue Service, GV
Brown, Stuart M. ... Portland, OR
Brown, Stuart M. ... Philadelphia, PA
Brown, Stuart P. ... Augusta, KY
Florence, KY
Maysville, KY
Brown, Stuart W. ... Dallas, TX
Brown & Sturm ... Rockville, MD
Brown & Sullivan, LLP ... Alameda, CA
Brown, Susan A. ... New York, NY
Brown, Susan Claire ... Chevy Chase, MD
Brown, Susan Cultice ... Zanesville, OH
Brown, Susan D. ... Treasury Department, Departmental Offices, GV
Brown, Susan D. ... Columbus, OH
Brown, Susan E. ... Denver, CO
Brown, Susan E. ... Columbus, OH
Brown, Susan I. ... Albuquerque, NM
Brown, Susan L. ... Rochester, IN
Brown, Susan Leigh ... Troy, MI
Brown, Susan McMenamin ... Atlanta, GA
Brown, Susan Tucker ... Washington, DC
Brown, Susan Vogt ... Newton, MA
Brown, Susanna Albaugh ... Des Moines, IA
Brown, Susanna M. ... Oak Brook, IL
Brown, Susannah Leslie ... Hanover, MA
Brown, Susanne Meyer ... Oakland, CA
Brown, Suzanne ... St. Louis, MO
Brown, Suzanne M. ... Minneapolis, MN
Brown, Suzanne R. ... Burlington, VT
Brown, Sylvia F. ... Savannah, GA
Brown & Szaller Co., L.P.A.
Cleveland, OH
Brown, T. Alan ... Buffalo, NY
Brown, T. Andrew ... Rochester, NY
Brown, T. Carroll ... Bel Air, MD
Brown, T. Lee, Jr. ... Richmond, VA
Brown, T. Logan ... Miami, OK
Brown, T. Michael ... Birmingham, AL
Brown, Tamara Y. ... Washington, DC
Brown, Tami Lewis ... Atlanta, GA
Brown, Tammy A. ... Oakland, CA
Brown, Tammy L. ... Southfield, MI
Brown, Tammy L. ... Mount Vernon, NY
Brown, Tanisha L. ... Raleigh, NC
Brown & Tarantino ... Buffalo, NY
Rochester, NY
White Plains, NY
Brown, Tarlow & Berry, P.C. ... Newberg, OR
Brown, Ted R. ... Orlando, FL
Brown, Terence M. ... Sacramento, CA
Brown, Terence M. ... Starke, FL
Brown, Teresa L. ... Charleston, WV
Brown, Terrell, Hogan, Ellis, McClamma & Yegelwel, P.A. ... Fernandina Beach, FL
Jacksonville, FL
Jacksonville Beach, FL
Orange Park, FL
St. Augustine, FL
Brown, Terrell N. ... Denver, CO
Brown, Terrence C. ... Bellevue, WA
Brown, Terrence D. ... Des Moines, IA
Brown, Terrence L. B. ... Arlington, VA
Brown, Terry D. ... Charlotte, NC
Brown, Terry G. ... Oakland, CA
Brown, Terry L. ... Aliso Viejo, CA
Brown, Terry L. ... Charleston, MO
Brown, Terry N. ... Belleville, IL
Brown, Terryl L. ... New York, NY
Brown, Theodore A. ... Trenton, NJ
Brown, Theodore C. ... Springfield, MA
Brown, Theodore C., Jr. ... Raleigh, NC
Brown, Theodore G., III ... Palo Alto, CA
Brown, Theodore, Jr. ... Atlanta, GA
Brown, Theresa A. ... Denver, CO
Brown, Theresa D. ... Camden, NJ
Brown, Theresa V. ... New York, NY
Brown, Thomas ... Abilene, TX
Brown, Thomas A. ... Palos Heights, IL
Brown, Thomas A. ... Hartford City, IN
Brown, Thomas A. ... Covington, KY
Frankfort, KY
Lexington, KY
Louisville, KY
Cincinnati, OH
Nashville, TN
Brown, Thomas A. ... Aberdeen, WA
Brown, Thomas A., II ... New York, NY
Brown, Thomas B. ... Auburn, CA
Brown, Thomas B. ... Edina, MO
Brown, Thomas C. ... Kansas City, MO
Brown, Thomas C. ... Cleveland, OH
Brown, Thomas C. ... Geneva, OH
Brown, Thomas C. ... El Paso, TX
Brown, Thomas C., Jr. ... McLean, VA
Brown, Thomas D. ... St. Louis, MO
Brown, Thomas Daniel ... Charlotte, NC
Brown, Thomas E. ... Pine Bluff, AR
Brown, Thomas E. ... Washington, DC
Brown, Thomas E. ... Wichita, KS
Brown, Thomas E. ... Omaha, NE
Brown, Thomas E. ... Trenton, NJ
Brown, Thomas E. ... Milwaukee, WI
Brown, Thomas E., III ... Albuquerque, NM
Brown, Thomas E., Jr.
Department Of Health And Human Services, Office of the General Counsel, GV
Brown, Thomas F. ... New Haven, CT
Brown, Thomas G. ... Palo Alto, CA
Brown, Thomas G. ... Denver, CO
Brown, Thomas G. ... West Palm Beach, FL
Brown, Thomas G. A. ... New York, NY
Brown, Thomas H. ... Birmingham, AL
Brown, Thomas H. ... Kilgore, TX
Brown, Thomas Howard ... Boston, MA
Brown, Thomas J. ... Tyler, TX
Brown, Thomas J., III ... Jefferson City, MO
Brown, Thomas Jacob ... Santa Ana, CA
Brown, Thomas John ... Pontiac, IL
Brown, Thomas K. ... Irvine, CA
Brown, Thomas K. ... Houston, TX
Brown, Thomas L., Jr. ... Tequesta, FL
Brown, Thomas Leo ... Lansing, MI
Brown, Thomas M. ... Los Angeles, CA
Brown, Thomas M. ... Bangor, ME
Brown, Thomas M. ... Minneapolis, MN
Brown, Thomas M. ... Trenton, NJ
Brown, Thomas P. ... San Francisco, CA
Brown, Thomas P. ... Chicago, IL
Brown, Thomas P. ... Cuba, NY
Brown, Thomas P., III ... Washington, DC
Brown, Thomas P., III ... Bethesda, MD
Brown, Thomas P., III ... Chevy Chase, MD
Brown, Thomas P., IV ... Los Angeles, CA
Brown, Thomas R. ... Jacksonville, FL
Brown, Thomas R. ... Naples, FL
Brown, Thomas R. ... Burlington, IA
Brown, Thomas R. ... Omaha, NE
Brown, Thomas S. ... Philadelphia, PA
Brown, Thomas S. ... Providence, RI
Brown, Thomas W. ... Lake City, FL
Brown, Thomas W. ... Albany, NY
Brown, Thomas W. ... Bartlesville, OK
Brown, Thomas W. ... Portland, OR
Brown Thompson Pruitt & Peterson, P.C. A Professional Corporation ... Dallas, TX
Fort Worth, TX
Brown, Timothy ... Washington, DC
Brown, Timothy B. ... Baltimore, MD
Brown, Timothy C. ... Columbus, OH
Brown, Timothy D. ... Phoenix, AZ
Brown, Timothy D.
House of Representatives, Office of Legislative Counsel, GV
Brown, Timothy Dale ... College Park, MD
Brown, Timothy E. ... Tonopah, NV
Brown, Timothy F. ... Washington, DC
Brown, Timothy J. ... Perrysburg, OH
Brown, Timothy J. ... Philadelphia, PA
Brown, Timothy L. ... Austin, TX
Brown, Timothy N. ... San Francisco, CA
Brown, Timothy P. ... Chambersburg, PA
Hanover, PA
Lancaster, PA
Brown, Timothy R. ... Atlanta, GA
Brown, Timothy R. ... Cincinnati, OH
Brown, Timothy R. ... Dallas, TX
Brown, Timothy R., (P.C.) ... Houston, TX
Brown, Timothy S. ... Harbor Springs, MI
Brown, Timothy W. ... Atlanta, GA
Brown, T.K. ... Conyers, GA
Brown, Toby D. ... Mobile, AL
Brown, Todd Allen ... Montgomery, AL
Brown, Todd D. ... Silver Spring, MD
Brown, Todd G. ... Eugene, OR
Brown, Todd & Heyburn PLLC
New Albany, IN
Covington, KY
Lexington, KY
Louisville, KY
Nashville, TN
Brown, Todd Lowell ... Boston, MA
Brown, Tom ... Livingston, TX
Brown, Tom C. ... Oregon, WI
Brown, Tom Fairfield ... Tampa, FL
Brown, Tom N. ... Santa Cruz, CA
Brown, Tom Watson ... Atlanta, GA
Brown, ToNola D. ... Greensboro, NC
Brown, Tonya Moten ... Austin, TX
Brown, Tracey L.
Federal Trade Commission, Bureau of Consumer Protection, GV
Brown, Tracey Skinner ... Miami, FL
Brown, Tracie L. ... San Francisco, CA
Brown, Tracy C. ... New York, NY
Brown, Tracy L. ... Rochester, NY
Brown, Tracy M. ... Larkspur, CA
Brown, Travis T. ... Washington, DC
Brown, Trevor A. ... Honolulu, HI
Brown, Tricia ... Phoenix, AZ
Phoenix, AZ
Brown, Troy A., Jr. ... Tampa, FL
Brown, Troy C. ... El Paso, TX
Brown, Troy R. ... Cleveland, OH
Brown, Troy S. ... Philadelphia, PA
Brown, T. W. ... Chapel Hill, NC
Brown, Tyler A. ... San Francisco, CA
Brown, Tyler P. ... Richmond, VA
Brown, Tyler S. ... Washington, DC
Brown, Tyra T. ... Rochester Hills, MI
Brown, Tyrone ... Washington, DC
Brown & Ubarri ... San Juan, PR
Brown, Udell C., Sr. ... Pensacola Beach, FL
Brown, Usher Larry ... Orlando, FL
Brown, V. Emile, Law Office of
Los Angeles, CA
Brown, Valentine A ... Philadelphia, PA
Brown, Valerie A. ... Los Angeles, CA
Brown, Valerie G. ... Denver, CO
Brown, Valerie Susan ... Kansas City, MO
Brown, Vance F.
Research Triangle Park, NC
Brown, Vance R. ... Boston, MA
Brown, Vanessa Thornton ... Pittsburgh, PA
Brown, Venel D.
Research Triangle Park, NC
Brown, Vera G. ... Spring Valley, NY
Brown, Verne E. ... St. Paul, MN
Brown, Vernon A. ... Tulsa, OK
Brown, Veryl E. ... Seguin, TX
Brown, Vickie Yates ... Louisville, KY
Brown, Victor ... Chicago, IL
Brown, Victor Emmanuel ... Oakland, CA
Brown, Victor K. ... Dumont, NJ
Brown, Victor Manuel ... Bronx, NY
Brown, Victoria J. ... Burlington, VT
Brown, Vincent ... Princeton, NJ
Brown, Vincent D. ... Lincoln, NE
Brown, Vincent Tyrone ... Miami, FL
Brown, Virgil E., Jr. ... Cleveland, OH
Brown, Virgil L. ... Zebulon, GA
Brown, Virgil L. ... Albuquerque, NM
Brown, Virginia L. ... Treasury Department, Office of Regulations and Rulings, GV
Brown, Virginia M. ... New York, NY
Brown, Virginia S. ... Cleveland, OH
Brown, Vivian F. ... Portsmouth, VA
Brown, W. Baxter ... Coeur d'Alene, ID
Brown, W. Campbell ... West Frankfort, IL
Brown, W. Charles ... Mansfield, LA
Brown, W. Clark ... Los Angeles, CA
Brown, W. Clint, Jr. ... Decatur, AL
Brown, W. Clint, Jr., & Associates, P.C.
Decatur, AL
Brown, W. Colby ... Rocky Mount, VA
Brown, W. Denis, IV ... Monroe, LA
Brown, W. Douglas ... Allentown, PA
Brown, W. Frank, III ... Chattanooga, TN
Brown, W. Gerald ... Stockton, CA
Brown, W. Hayes, III ... Baltimore, MD
Brown, W. James ... Chicago, IL
Brown, W. Jay ... Saginaw, MI
Brown, W. Jeffrey ... Atlanta, GA
Brown, W. Kendall ... Des Moines, IA
Brown, W. Kirk, (P.A.) ... Tallahassee, FL
Brown, W. Lewis ... Louisville, KY
Brown, W. Neil ... Freeport, IL
Brown, W. Rodes ... Frankfort, KY
Lexington, KY
Brown, W. Scott ... New Orleans, LA
Brown, W. Scott ... Houston, TX
Brown, W. Ted ... Storm Lake, IA
Brown, W. Tracy ... Charleston, SC
Brown, W. Tynan ... Drayton Plains, MI
Brown & Waldron ... Arcadia, FL
Brown, Wallace W. ... Chandler, AZ
Brown, Waller & Gibbs, P.C.
Anchorage, AK
Brown, Walston S. ... New York, NY
Brown, Walter ... Natchez, MS
Brown, Walter A., Jr. ... Oakland, CA
Brown, Walter B., Jr. ... Winnsboro, SC
Brown, Walter F., Jr. ... San Francisco, CA
Brown, Walter J. ... Natchez, MS
Brown, Walter M. ... Kansas City, MO
Brown, Walter R. ... Des Moines, IA
Brown, Walter W. ... Washington, DC
Brown, Wanda L. ... Orlando, FL
Brown, Ward ... Seattle, WA
Brown, Ward & Haynes, P.A.
Waynesville, NC
Brown, Ward K. ... Kansas City, MO
Brown, Ward, Salzman & Weiss, P.A.
Kissimmee, FL
Orlando, FL
Brown and Warnock ... Cincinnati, OH
Brown, Warren ... Fort Lauderdale, FL
Brown, Warren L. ... Covina, CA
Brown, Warren R. ... Phoenix, AZ
Brown, Wash H. ... Kansas City, KS
Brown, Watt & Buchanan, P.A.
Biloxi, MS
Gulfport, MS
Hattiesburg, MS
Jackson, MS
Pascagoula, MS
Brown, Wayne B. ... San Diego, CA

Brown, Wayne D. .... Dallas, TX
Brown & Weikert .... Jasper, IN
Brown & Welsh, P.C. .... Meriden, CT
Brown, Wendell O. .... Kingstree, SC
Brown, Wendy G. .... Kew Gardens, NY
Brown, Wendy L. .... Torrance, CA
Brown, Wendy Lea .... Berkeley, CA
Brown, Wendy R. .... Brooklyn, NY
Brown, Wesley .... McAlester, OK
Brown, Wesley E. .... Wichita, KS
Brown, Wesley L. .... Gaffney, SC
Brown Westbrook, A Professional Corporation Birmingham, AL
Brown & Wichmer, P.C. .... St. Louis, MO
Brown & Wicker .... Monroe, LA
Brown, Wilda M. .... Decatur, GA
Brown, Willbrand, Simon & Powell, P.C. Columbia, MO
Brown, William A. .... Rochester, MN
Brown, William A. .... Hernando, MS
Brown, William A. .... Dallas, TX
Brown, William A. .... Houston, TX
Brown, William B. .... Atlanta, GA
Brown, William B. .... Minneapolis, MN
Brown, William C. .... Los Angeles, CA
Brown, William C. .... Vernon, CT
Brown, William C. .... Department of Justice, Criminal Division, GV
Brown, William C. .... Des Moines, IA
Brown, William C. .... Owosso, MI
Brown, William C. .... Omaha, NE
Brown, William C. .... Portland, OR
Brown, William C., III .... New York, NY
Brown, William D. .... Solana Beach, CA
Brown, William D. .... Monroe, LA
Brown, William D. .... Cleveland, OH
Brown, William D. .... Johnson City, TN
Brown, William D. .... Austin, TX
Brown, William E. .... San Francisco, CA
Brown, William E. .... Fayetteville, NC
Brown, William E., II .... Lexington, KY
Brown, William F. .... Moorestown, NJ
Brown, William F. .... Mount Laurel, NJ
Brown, William F. .... Dallas, TX
Brown, William F., Jr. .... San Jose, CA
Brown, William F., Jr. .... Waco, TX
Brown, William G. .... Chicago, IL
Brown, William G. .... Brazil, IN
Brown, William H. .... Fort Collins, CO
Brown, William H. .... Baton Rouge, LA
Brown, William H., III .... Philadelphia, PA
Brown, William H., Jr. .... Memphis, TN
Brown, William Horner .... Pawling, NY
Brown, William Houston .... Memphis, TN
Brown, William J. .... Washington, DC
Brown, William J. .... Miami, FL
Brown, William J. .... Buffalo, NY
New York, NY
Brown, William J. .... Columbus, OH
Brown, William J. .... Dayton, OH
Brown, William J. .... Cleveland, TN
Brown, William J., Jr. .... Los Angeles, CA
Brown, William J. T. .... New York, NY
Brown, William K. .... Colorado Springs, CO
Brown, William K. .... Peoria, IL
Brown, William Kent Fort Lauderdale, FL
Brown, William L. .... San Luis Obispo, CA
Brown, William L. .... Newton, KS
Brown, William L. .... Binghamton, NY
Brown, William L. .... Charlotte, NC
Brown, William L. .... Chattanooga, TN
Brown, William L. .... Arlington, TX
Brown, William L. .... Alexandria, VA
Brown, William L., Jr. .... Crown Point, IN
Brown, William L., Jr. .... Tacoma, WA
Brown, William Lee .... Knoxville, TN
Brown, William M. .... Sacramento, CA
Brown, William M. .... Fort Worth, TX
Brown, William M., Jr. .... Versailles, KY
Brown, William R. .... Phoenix, AZ
Brown, William R. .... Indianapolis, IN
Brown, William R. .... Traverse City, MI
Brown, William R. .... Hempstead, NY
Brown, William R. .... Erie, PA
Brown, William R. .... Mansfield, TX
Brown, William R., P.C. .... Phoenix, AZ
Brown, William R., P.C. .... Mansfield, TX
Brown, William R., Sr. .... Morristown, NJ
Brown, William Reid, Jr. .... Palo Alto, CA
Brown, William S. .... Delray Beach, FL
Brown, William S. .... Greenville, SC
Brown, William Thomas .... Nashville, TN
Brown, William V., Jr. .... Texarkana, TX
Brown, William W. .... St. Louis, MO
Brown, William W. .... Columbus, OH
Brown, William W. .... Seattle, WA
Brown, Willie R. .... Santa Fe, NM
Brown, Willis D. .... Fayetteville, NC
Brown, Willis E. .... Chicago, IL
Brown, Wilma Jean .... Las Vegas, NM
Brown, Wilson M., III .... Philadelphia, PA
Brown, Winfield & Canzoneri, Incorporated Los Angeles, CA
Brown, Winfield J., Jr. .... Somers, NY
Brown, Winick, Graves, Gross, Baskerville and Schoenebaum, P.L.C. Des Moines, IA
Pella, IA
Brown, Winn D., Jr. .... Southaven, MS
Brown, Winston P. .... Milwaukee, WI
Brown, Winthrop N., (P.C.) Washington, DC
Brown, W. K. (Bo) .... McKinney, TX
Brown, Wm. F. .... Columbus, OH
Brown & Wolff, P.C. .... Omaha, NE
Brown, Wood, III .... New Orleans, LA
Brown & Wood LLP .... Los Angeles, CA
San Francisco, CA
Washington, DC
New York, NY
Brown, W. W. .... Calhoun City, MS
Brown & Wyrick .... Leavenworth, KS
Brown, W. Z. Jefferson .... Chico, CA
Brown, Yvette Mcgee .... Columbus, OH
Brown, Yvette Rodriguez .... Orlando, FL
Brown, Yvonne .... Deerfield Beach, FL
Brown, Zan Colson, Ms. .... San Antonio, TX
Brown, Zane A., Jr. .... Seattle, WA
Brown, Zhonette .... Washington, DC
Brown, Zina Pickens .... St. Louis, MO
Brown, Zina Pickens, P.C. .... St. Louis, MO
Brownback, Peter Evans .... Fayetteville, NC
Brown-Barrett, LaRhonda .... New York, NY
Brown-Burton, Lorna E. Fort Lauderdale, FL
Brown-Casalino, Patricia A. Los Angeles, CA
Browndorf, Eric A. .... Atlantic City, NJ
Browndorf, Matthew C. .... Harrisburg, PA
Browndorf, Stephen A. .... Northfield, NJ
Browne, Alfred L. .... Boston, MA
Browne, Allan .... Beverly Hills, CA
Browne, Alyce T. .... Waukegan, IL
Browne, Anne Porter .... Albuquerque, NM
Browne, Audrey A. .... New York, NY
Browne, Audrey N. .... New Orleans, LA
Browne, Beneth Anderson .... Sacramento, CA
Browne, Bernice Darcy .... Allentown, PA
Browne, Berniece A. Department of Commerce, Office of the General Counsel, GV
Browne, Bettina B. .... Atlantic Beach, NY
Browne, Bitner .... Springfield, OH
Browne, Brian L. .... West Palm Beach, FL
Browne & Browne .... Bridgeport, CT
Beaumont, TX
Browne, Bruce C. .... Rochester, MI
Browne, C. Willing .... Denver, CO
Browne, Carmen M. .... Denver, CO
Browne, Carol L. .... Chicago, IL
Browne, Carolyn H. .... Albany, NY
Browne, Cecil .... New York, NY
Browne, Charles L., III .... Cheverly, MD
Browne, Charles T. .... Asheboro, NC
Browne, Christopher M. .... Worcester, MA
Browne, Christopher P. .... Hoboken, NJ
New York, NY
Browne, Claudia E. .... Grants Pass, OR
Browne, Craig R. .... Boston, MA
Browne, David Joseph .... Upper Sandusky, OH
Browne, David L. .... New Orleans, LA
Browne, David M. .... Los Angeles, CA
Browne, David P. .... Bonita Springs, FL
Browne, Dennis Andrew .... Washington, DC
Browne, Diana G. .... New York, NY
Browne, Donald A. .... Bridgeport, CT
Browne, Douglas F. .... Hannibal, MO
Browne, E. Robert .... Duxbury, MA
Browne, Edmond R., Jr. .... Rocky Hill, CT
Browne, Elizabeth W. .... Eugene, OR
Browne, Ellen L. .... Closter, NJ
Browne, Ernest J. .... Beaumont, TX
Browne, Ernest J., Jr. .... Beaumont, TX
Browne, Ernest J. "Trey" .... Beaumont, TX
Browne, F. Sedgwick .... New York, NY
Browne, Flebotte, Wilson & Horn, P.L.L.C.
Creedmoor, NC
Durham, NC
Greensboro, NC
Raleigh, NC
Browne, Frances K. .... New York, NY
Browne, Francis J. .... Hartford, CT
Browne, Fred .... Los Angeles, CA
Browne & Galluccio .... Paterson, NJ
Browne, Graham .... Albuquerque, NM
Browne, H. Howard, III .... Cary, NC
Browne, Hal M. .... Dallas, TX
Browne, Harvey R. .... Paterson, NJ
Browne, Henry H. .... Round Lake, IL
Browne, Herbert H., Jr. .... Charlotte, NC
Browne, J. Austin .... New York, NY
Browne, J. Danforth .... Tampa, FL
Browne, J. Douglas .... Sacramento, CA
Browne, J. Patrick .... Cleveland, OH
Browne, Jack E. .... Little Rock, AR
Browne, James B. .... Oklahoma City, OK
Browne, James M. .... Irving, TX
Browne, James R. .... Indianapolis, IN
Browne, James R. .... Irving, TX
Browne, Jennifer M. .... Little Rock, AR
Browne, Jo-Ann P. .... Mineola, NY
Browne, John Henry .... Seattle, WA
Browne, John J .... New York, NY
Browne, John J. .... Houston, TX
Browne, John P. .... Melville, NY
Browne, John R. .... Oklahoma City, OK
Browne, John R., III .... San Francisco, CA
Browne, John R., Jr. .... Marion, IN
Browne, John T. .... Los Angeles, CA
Browne, Juliet T. .... Portland, ME
Browne, Kathleen R. .... Boston, MA
Browne, Kathryn Neville .... Bronx, NY
Browne, Kenneth N. .... Kew Gardens, NY
Browne, Kingsbury, Jr. .... Boston, MA
Browne, Kristi L. .... Chicago, IL
Browne, LaFleur C. .... Minneapolis, MN
Browne, Larry W. .... Wilbraham, MA
Browne, Lawrence C. .... New York, NY
Browne, Leslie Braginsky .... Wayne, NJ
Browne, Leslie M. .... San Francisco, CA
Browne, M. Neil .... Bowling Green, OH
Browne, M. Warren .... Waccabuc, NY
Browne, Margaret A. .... Richmond, VA
Browne, Maria T. .... Washington, DC
Browne, Marijane Benner .... Boston, MA
Browne, Mary E. .... Indianapolis, IN
Browne, Matthew J. .... Dallas, TX
Browne, Matthew James, III .... Tulsa, OK
Browne, Matthew T. .... New York, NY
Browne, Maureen F. .... Washington, DC
Browne, Michael L. .... Philadelphia, PA
Browne, Nancy D. .... New York, NY
Browne, Nancy L. .... Cape Girardeau, MO
Browne, Noëlle Stevens .... Raleigh, NC
Browne, P. Scott .... Grass Valley, CA
Browne, Patrick J. .... New Orleans, LA
Browne, Patrick J., Jr. .... Washington, DC
Browne, Patrick Paul .... Shoreline, WA
Browne, Patrick W., Jr. .... New Orleans, LA
Browne, Pierce B. .... Concord, MA
Browne, Rachelle V. .... Washington, DC
Browne, René E. .... Washington, DC
Browne & Ressler .... Seattle, WA
Browne, Richard A. .... Valparaiso, IN
Browne, Richard C. .... Washington, DC
Browne, Richard F. .... Atlanta, GA
Browne, Richard H. .... Pontiac, MI
Browne, Robert E. .... Chicago, IL
Browne, Robert E., III .... Spartanburg, SC
Browne, Robert L. .... Manassas, VA
Browne, Robt. L. .... Bangor, ME
Browne, Rochelle .... Los Angeles, CA
Browne, Ryan J. .... Dallas, TX
Browne, Scott Andrew .... Tampa, FL
Browne, Shannon T. .... Stamford, CT
Browne, Sharlene W. .... Bronx, NY
Browne, Shawnee S. .... Lakewood, CA
Browne, Spencer I. .... Denver, CO
Browne Spitzer Herriman Stephenson Holderead & Musser .... Marion, IN
Browne, Stanhope S. .... Philadelphia, PA
Browne, Steven A. .... Washington, DC
Browne, Steven C. .... Boston, MA
Browne, Steven D. .... San Antonio, TX
Browne, Susanne M. .... Los Angeles, CA
Browne, T. Christopher .... Fort Worth, TX
Browne, T. Marcus, III .... Creedmoor, NC
Durham, NC
Greensboro, NC
Raleigh, NC
Browne, Tamra D. .... San Francisco, CA
Browne, Theodore W., II .... East Alton, IL
Browne, Thomas L. .... Chicago, IL
Browne, Vincent B. .... Chicago, IL
Browne, Vincent P. .... Newark, NJ
Browne, William H., III .... Lincoln, NE
Browne, William T. .... Bridgeport, CT
Browne & Woods LLP .... Beverly Hills, CA
Los Angeles, CA
Browne-Barbour, Vanessa S. .... Pittsburgh, PA
Brownell, Anne L. .... Folsom, CA
Brownell, Carlton K. .... Geneva, NY
Brownell, Carlton K., III .... Buffalo, NY
Brownell, Christopher W. .... Hastings, MN
Brownell, Daniel D. .... New York, NY
Brownell, Donald C. .... Detroit, MI
Brownell, Edmund B. .... Flint, MI
Brownell, Eileen L. .... Washington, DC
Brownell, F. William .... Washington, DC
Brownell, Gary F. .... Black River Falls, WI
Brownell, George R. .... Washington, DC
New York, NY
Brownell, Gordon Stewart .... St. Helena, CA
Brownell, John R. .... Grand Island, NE
Brownell, Keith .... Duluth, MN
Brownell, Michael E. .... Sacramento, CA
Brownell and Moeser .... Springfield, VT
Brownell, Robert D. .... Palo Alto, CA
Brownell, Robert L. .... Silver Spring, MD
Brownell, Scott MacKenzie .... Bradenton, FL
Brownell, Thomas M. .... Falls Church, VA
Brownell, Todd D. .... Folsom, CA
Brownell, Washburn & Truswell Northampton, MA
Brownell, William M., Jr. .... Gainesville, GA
Brownelle, Raymond L. .... Fairfax, VA
Browne-Matherly, Valerie .... Boston, MA
Browne-Pindilli, Kathleen .... Newark, NJ
Browner, Betty J. .... Hayward, CA
Browner, Carol M. .... Washington, DC
Browner, Julius H. .... Fort Lauderdale, FL
Browner, Lawrence J. Westhampton Beach, NY
Browner, Pulido & Sheehan .... Hayward, CA
Browner, William A. .... Providence, RI
Brownfeld, Gail M. .... Houston, TX
Brownfield, C. William, & Associates Columbus, OH
Brownfield, Charles E., Jr. .... Stamford, TX
Brownfield, Erin K. .... Chattanooga, TN
Brownfield, Faye-Marie Morgan New York, NY
Brownfield, Gail Wade .... Alamogordo, NM
Brownfield, Gary L. .... Chicago, IL
Brownfield, George E. North Hollywood, CA
Brownfield, Gina J. Roso .... Lancaster, PA
Brownfield, Gregory C. .... Topeka, KS
Brownfield, Lyman .... Columbus, OH
Brownfield, M. Lea .... Mesilla, NM
Brownfield, Mathew D. .... Chattanooga, TN
Brownfield, Matthew .... Cincinnati, OH
Brownfield, Michael L. .... Fort Payne, AL
Brownfield, Sandra M. .... Irvine, CA
Brownfield, Thomas L. .... Havana, IL
Brownfield, Todd A. .... Pittsburgh, PA
Brown Fletcher, Lolita .... Los Angeles, CA
Brown-Hebert, Marjorie R. .... Chicago, IL
Brown Hilburn, Elizabeth Ellen Alexandria, LA
Brownhill, Burnett & Associates, P.C. Houston, TX
Brownhill, David B. .... McMinnville, OR
Portland, OR
Brownhill, J. Steve .... Houston, TX
Brownhill, Schmidt & Associates Houston, TX
Brownhill, Thomas E. .... Eugene, OR
Browning, Allen H. .... Idaho Falls, ID
Browning, Ashley E. .... Raleigh, NC
Browning, Bart D. .... Twin Falls, ID
Browning & Bradshaw-Hull .... Houston, TX
Browning Bushman, A Professional Corporation .... Houston, TX
Browning, Carol Dan .... Louisville, KY
Browning, Charlene Guller .... Key West, FL
Browning, Charles A. .... San Francisco, CA
Browning, Charles F. .... Houston, TX
Browning, Charles R. .... Livonia, LA
Browning, Charles W. .... Detroit, MI
Browning, Chauncey H., Jr. .... Charleston, WV
Browning, Cheryl M. .... Washington, DC
Browning, Christopher C. .... Tucson, AZ
Browning, Christopher G., Jr. Raleigh, NC
Browning, Clifford W. .... Indianapolis, IN
Browning & Colas Attorneys, P.C. Forest Grove, OR
Browning & Cooke .... Columbus, OH
Browning, Corbett J. .... Merced, CA
Browning, Courtenay C. .... Austin, TX
Browning, D. Lea .... Washington, DC
Browning, David S. .... New York, NY
Browning, Duke Nguyen .... Houston, TX
Browning, E. Bailey, III .... Madison, FL
Browning, Eden, Sireci, Guller & Klitenick, P.A. .... Key West, FL
Browning, Edmund L., Jr. .... Washington, DC
Browning, Francis A. .... Detroit, MI
Browning, George D. .... Westminster, CO
Browning, George, III .... Sarasota, FL
Browning, George, III, P.A. .... Sarasota, FL
Browning, Harrell Z. .... Corpus Christi, TX
Browning, Heather R. .... Atlanta, GA
Browning, Hess K. .... Arlington, TX
Browning & Hill, L.L.P. .... Greenville, NC
Browning, Hillary Brooke .... Nashville, TN
Browning, J. Taylor .... Los Angeles, CA
Browning, J. Willmont, Jr. .... Alexandria, VA
Browning, Jackson B., Jr. .... New York, NY
Browning, James L., Jr. .... San Carlos, CA
Browning, James O. .... Albuquerque, NM
Browning, James P., Jr. .... Dallas, TX
Browning, James R. .... Fair Oaks, CA
Browning, James R. .... San Francisco, CA
Browning, Jason Trevor .... Fort Smith, AR
Browning, Jay D. .... San Antonio, TX
Browning, Jeffery H. .... Austin, TX
Browning, Jennifer L. .... Chicago, IL
Browning, Jennifer S. .... Columbus, OH
Browning, Jill Michele .... Reston, VA
Browning, Jimmy Lee .... Breckenridge, TX
Browning, John Dent .... Harrisonburg, VA
Browning, John G. .... Dallas, TX
Browning, John R. .... Los Angeles, CA
Browning, John W. .... Towson, MD
Browning, Jon M. .... Columbus, OH
Browning, Joseph W. .... New Orleans, LA
Browning, Judith W. .... Helena, MT
Browning, Julie A. .... Hoffman Estates, IL
Browning, Kaleczyc, Berry & Hoven, P.C. Billings, MT
Helena, MT
Browning, Kenneth L. .... Beverly Hills, CA
Browning, Kent J. .... Houston, TX
Browning, Kimberly A. Commodity Futures Trading Commission, Division of Economic Analysis, GV
Browning, Lamie & Sharp, P.C. Lebanon, VA
Browning, Larry G. .... Lebanon, VA
Browning, Linda K. .... Birmingham, AL
Browning & Lipton .... Dallas, TX
Browning, Marc D. .... Cleveland, OH
Browning, Margaret L. .... Plymouth, MI
Browning, Marilyn .... La Porte, TX
Browning, Mark William .... Charleston, WV
Browning, Martin R. .... Milwaukee, WI
Browning, Michael F. .... Boulder, CO
Browning, Michael L. .... Key West, FL
Browning, Monica R. .... Carlsbad, CA
Browning, Nicholas, III .... Los Angeles, CA
Browning, Pamela Broer .... Columbus, OH
Browning, Patrick L. .... Cypress, CA
Browning, Paul M. .... Lancaster, PA
Browning & Peifer, P.A. Albuquerque, NM
Browning, Philip M., Jr. Department Of Health And Human Services, Social Security Administration, GV
Browning, R. Stephen .... Helena, MT
Browning, Renita Diane .... White Plains, NY
Browning, Renona C. .... Morgantown, KY
Browning, Rex C. .... Seattle, WA
Browning, Richard E. .... Mobile, AL
Browning, Richard E., P.C. .... Mobile, AL
Browning, Rick .... Odessa, TX
Browning, Robert A. .... Kansas City, MO
Browning, Robert A. .... Forest Grove, OR
Browning, Robert, Jr. .... Pineville, WV
Browning, Robert, Jr., L.C. .... Pineville, WV
Browning, Robert L. .... Indianapolis, IN
Browning, Robert L. .... Portland, OR
Browning, Robert M. .... Houston, TX
Browning, Robert P. .... Scranton, PA
Browning, Robert R. .... Greenville, NC
Browning, Robert W. .... Atlanta, GA
Browning, Robert W., Jr. .... Sarasota, FL
Browning, Robin Wayne .... Middlesex, NJ
Browning, Roger A. .... Beverly Hills, CA

Browning, Ronald D .... Portland, OR
Browning, Sally Specht
Maryland Heights, MO
Browning, Sarah L. .... Concord, NH
Browning, Scott Alton .... Mobile, AL
Browning, Scott M. .... Denver, CO
Browning, Shelley .... Beverly Hills, CA
Browning, Sheri C. .... Portland, OR
Browning, Sondra Pike .... El Dorado, CA
Browning, Stephen D. .... Columbus, OH
Browning, Susan J. .... Washington, DC
Browning & Tanksley, LLP .... Atlanta, GA
Marietta, GA
Browning, Thomas J. .... Marietta, GA
Browning, Walter G. .... Birmingham, AL
Browning, Warren .... Bethesda, MD
Browning, Warren W. .... Lake Bluff, IL
Browning, Wholey & Lenvin
San Francisco, CA
Browning, William D. .... Tucson, AZ
Browning, William Elkins .... Houston, TX
Browning, William E. S. .... New York, NY
Browning, William J. .... Columbus, OH
Browning, William K. .... San Diego, CA
Browning, William R. .... Culpeper, VA
Browning, William Scott .... Greenville, NC
Browning, William V. .... Wichita Falls, TX
Browning, William W. .... Durham, NC
Brown-Inz, Steven .... Bayside, NY
Brooklyn, NY
New York, NY
Brown-James, Lori A. .... Anniston, AL
Brown-Jeffries, Frederica E.
Kew Gardens, NY
Brownjohn, William A. .... Rumford, RI
Brown-Jones, Pamela .... West Orange, NJ
Brownlee, David A. .... Pittsburgh, PA
Brownlee, David W. .... Pittsburgh, PA
Brownlee, E. Gardner .... Florence, MT
Brownlee, Eileen A. .... Fennimore, WI
Brownlee, Fambrough LaMonte, III
Baltimore, MD
Brownlee, Gary S. .... Indianapolis, IN
Brownlee, Hunter J. .... Tampa, FL
Brownlee, Jackson O. .... Orlando, FL
Brownlee, Jamie M. .... Atlanta, GA
Brownlee, J. E. .... Denton, TX
Brownlee, John H., III .... Kingsland, TX
Brownlee, John Leslie .... Washington, DC
Brownlee, John R. .... Bakersfield, CA
Brownlee, Joseph L. .... Phoenix, AZ
Brownlee, Joseph L., P.C., Law Offices of
Phoenix, AZ
Brownlee, Karen M. .... Pittsburgh, PA
Brownlee, Mark S. .... Fort Dodge, IA
Brownlee, Michelle .... San Francisco, CA
Brownlee, Patricia Lynne .... St. Louis, MO
Brownlee, Richard S., III
Jefferson City, MO
Brownlee, Robert H. .... St. Louis, MO
Brownlee, Ronald A. .... Houston, TX
Brownlee, Steven H. .... Chevy Chase, MD
Brownlee, Thomas R., Jr. .... Columbus, OH
Brownlee, Timothy R. .... Kansas City, MO
Brownless, Suzanne S. .... Tallahassee, FL
Brownley, Robert M. .... Grand Rapids, MI
Brownley, William L. P. .... Ashburn, VA
Brownlie, James D. .... Denver, CO
Brownlie, Robert W. .... San Diego, CA
Brownlow, Brad .... Decatur, GA
Brownlow, Joree G. .... Dyersburg, TN
Brownlow, Richard A. .... Atlanta, GA
Brownlow & Schaefer .... Decatur, GA
Brownlow, Terri .... Sacramento, CA
Brownman, Charles H. .... Houston, TX
Brownman, Joseph S.
Federal Trade Commission,
Bureau of Competition, GV
Brown-McAfee, Karen .... Washington, DC
Brown-Noel, Denise J. .... New York, NY
Brown-oglesby, Bonnie J. .... Marietta, GA
Brownridge, Lawrence B. .... New York, NY
Brownridge-Tucker, Byrdie .... Chicago, IL
Brownrigg, John C. .... Omaha, NE
Brownrout, Harvey M. .... Stamford, CT
Browns, Cheryl L. .... Fresno, CA
Brownsberger, William N. .... Boston, MA
Brown-Schwart, Mary Anne .... Columbus, OH
Brownsell, Brian R. .... St. Petersburg, FL
Brownshadel, Elton L. .... Houston, TX
Brownshadel, Elton L., P.C. .... Houston, TX
Brown-Singh, Lillian M. .... Bogalusa, LA
Brown-Smith, Heather M. .... Orange, CA
Brownson, Beth A. .... Syracuse, NY
Brownson, Lore W. .... Atlanta, GA
Brownson, Richmond Jay .... Tulsa, OK
Brownson, Robert D. .... Minneapolis, MN
Brownson, Robert S. .... Barrington, IL
Brownson, Ronald L. .... Upland, CA
Brown-Spencer, G. Thomas .... Centreville, AL
Brownstein, Adam R. .... Arlington, VA
Brownstein, Adrianne J. .... Los Angeles, CA
Brownstein, Alan E. .... Davis, CA
Brownstein, Amy R. .... Los Angeles, CA
Brownstein, Andrew R. .... New York, NY
Brownstein, Andrew S. .... Richmond, VA
Brownstein, Bernard .... New York, NY
Brownstein, Bettina E. .... Little Rock, AR
Brownstein, Charles S. .... Flushing, NY
Brownstein, Daniel J. .... Great Neck, NY
Brownstein, David C. .... San Francisco, CA
Brownstein, David I. .... San Francisco, CA
Brownstein, David K. .... Beverly Hills, CA
Brownstein, Elfreda G. .... New York, NY
Brownstein, Gary .... Collingswood, NJ
Philadelphia, PA
Brownstein, Howard B. .... Union City, NJ
Brownstein, Howard B. .... Philadelphia, PA
Brownstein, Howard K. .... Bronx, NY
Brownstein Hyatt & Farber, P.C.
Denver, CO
Glenwood Springs, CO
Washington, DC
Brownstein, Iris Davis .... Philadelphia, PA
Brownstein, Irwin .... New York, NY
Brownstein, Irwin, Law Firm of
New York, NY
Brownstein, Ivan L. .... Chicago, IL
Brownstein, James S. .... New Haven, CT
Brownstein, Jerome D. .... New York, NY
Brownstein, Joel .... Buffalo, NY
Brownstein, Judy B. .... White Plains, NY
Brownstein, Kenneth R. .... Bellevue, WA
Brownstein, Lawrence E. .... Delray Beach, FL
Brownstein, Linda Susan .... Holliston, MA
Brownstein, Mark .... Orange, CA
Brownstein, Mark J. .... Philadelphia, PA
Brownstein, Michael A. .... New York, NY
Brownstein, Michael Z. .... New York, NY
Brownstein, Norman .... Denver, CO
Brownstein, Paul .... Southampton, PA
Brownstein, Paul H. .... Morristown, NJ
Brownstein, Philip N. .... Washington, DC
Brownstein, Rask, Arenz, Sweeney, Kerr &
Grim, LLP .... Portland, OR
Brownstein, Rhonda .... Montgomery, AL
Brownstein, Richard A. .... Tarzana, CA
Brownstein, Richard J. .... Portland, OR
Brownstein, Richard S. .... Studio City, CA
Brownstein, Steven R. .... Coral Gables, FL
Brownstein & Vitale, P.C. .... Collingswood, NJ
Brownstein & Vitale, P.C. .... Philadelphia, PA
Brownstein and Washko .... Southampton, PA
Brownstein & Weingarten, P.C.
Great Neck, NY
Brownstein, William H. .... Los Angeles, CA
Brown-Steiner, Terrence C. .... Rochester, NY
Brown-Stohler, Michelle .... Bluffton, IN
Brownston, John .... Sacramento, CA
Brownstone, Susan E. .... Boulder, CO
Brownwood, Randall L. .... San Diego, CA
Brownyard, Debora D. .... Walthill, NE
Brownyard, Richard J. .... Mount Pleasant, SC
Browser, Adam L. .... Mineola, NY
Brox, Stephen M. .... Dracut, MA
Broxterman, Burton F. .... Albuquerque, NM
Broxterman, Christina Maria
Atlanta, GA
Broxton, G. Allen .... Gainesville, GA
Broyde, Channah S. .... Atlanta, GA
Broyde, Jeffrey .... San Bernardino, CA
Broydes, Mark .... New York, NY
Broyhill, Linda S. .... Washington, DC
Broyles, A. H. .... Shreveport, LA
Broyles, Bruce Martin .... Warren, OH
Broyles, Bryan T. .... Department of the Army,
U.S. Army Legal Services Agency, GV
Broyles, D. Scott .... Charlotte, NC
Broyles, Deborah J. .... San Francisco, CA
Broyles, Dona K. .... Tulsa, OK
Broyles, Edward Arnold .... Fairfax, VA
Broyles, Elizabeth K. .... Frankfort, KY
Broyles, Eric C. .... Washington, DC
Broyles, Frank L. .... Dallas, TX
Broyles, Gaston M., Jr.
Corpus Christi, TX
Broyles, Harvey .... Shreveport, LA
Broyles, J. Larry .... Augusta, GA
Broyles, J. Larry, P.C. .... Augusta, GA
Broyles, James D. .... Atlanta, GA
Broyles, James Hunter, Jr. .... Farmington, AR
Broyles, John A. .... Indianapolis, IN
Broyles, Joseph A. .... Newport Beach, CA
Broyles, JulieAnn M. .... St. Louis, MO
Broyles, Keith E. .... Atlanta, GA
Broyles, Kevin E. .... Atlanta, GA
Broyles, Mark K. .... Rochester, NY
Broyles, Michael A.
Hot Springs National Park, AR
Broyles, Michelle Coe
Hot Springs National Park, AR
Broyles, Paul J. .... Spring, TX
Broyles, Phillip L. .... Cleveland, OH
Broyles & Pratt, A Professional Corporation
Austin, TX
Corpus Christi, TX
Broyles, Robert E.
Department Of Veterans Affairs,
Office of the General Counsel, GV
Broyles, Samuel G., Jr. .... Irvine, CA
Las Vegas, NV
Broyles, Scott C. .... Clarkston, WA
Broyles, Stephen E. .... Baton Rouge, LA
Broyles, Susan I. .... Denver, CO
Broyles, Ted R. .... Leesville, LA
Broyles, Ted R., II .... Leesville, LA
Broyles, Thomas C. .... Virginia Beach, VA
Broyles, Tommy L. .... Austin, TX
Broyles, Vernadette R. .... Atlanta, GA
Broz, Alycia N. .... Columbus, OH
Broz, Dean .... Raleigh, NC
Broz, Debra L. .... Bowling Green, KY
Broz, Frank P. .... Sun City, AZ
Broz, Glenn A. .... North Royalton, OH
Broz, Glenn A. .... Strongsville, OH
Broz, John F. .... Cedar Rapids, IA
Broz, Jonathan E. .... Kansas City, MO
Broz, Mitchell A. .... Seattle, WA
Broz, Richard A. .... Hooks, TX
Broz, Richard F. .... Seattle, WA
Broz, Vickie S. .... Mobridge, SD
Brozan, Ralph M. .... New York, NY
Brozdowski, Paul L. .... Bridgeport, CT
Cortlandt Manor, NY
Broze, Lee .... Houston, TX
Brozek, Jerome S. .... Chicago, IL
Brozena, Sarah Harrison .... Arlington, VA
Brozinsky, Edward .... Huntington, NY
Brozinsky & Singer .... Huntington, NY
Brozio, Gerhart W. .... San Diego, CA
Brozman, Andrew P. .... New York, NY
Brozman, Tina L. .... New York, NY
Brozosky, Martin M. .... Northbrook, IL
Brozost, Jay A. .... Bethesda, MD
Brozovich, William C. .... Dixon, IL
Brozyna, Jeffry H. .... Allentown, PA
Bru, Julie Ofelia .... Miami, FL
Brualdi, Richard B. .... New York, NY
Brubacher, Marshall L.
San Bernardino, CA
Brubaker, Alan K., (A Professional
Corporation) .... San Diego, CA
Brubaker, Brad C. .... Wayne, PA
Brubaker, Bruce H. .... Akron, OH
Brubaker, C. Richard .... Mentor, OH
Brubaker, Charlene .... Hays, KS
Brubaker, Christopher M.
Philadelphia, PA
Brubaker, Daniel C. .... Grand Rapids, MI
Lowell, MI
Brubaker, Emily .... Los Angeles, CA
Brubaker, Flynn & Darland, P.C.
Davenport, IA
Eldridge, IA
Brubaker, Fredk. O. .... Reading, PA
Brubaker, George T. .... Lancaster, PA
Brubaker, Gregory C. .... Indianapolis, IN
Brubaker, Jennifer S. .... Tallahassee, FL
Brubaker, Malvin W. .... Lancaster, PA
Brubaker, Marcus J. .... Toledo, OH
Brubaker, Margaret R. .... Boulder, CO
Brubaker, Mark E. .... Irvine, CA
Brubaker, Mark E. .... Los Angeles, CA
Brubaker, Raina E. .... Washington, DC
Brubaker, Richard Alan
North Hollywood, CA
Brubaker, Robert L. .... Columbus, OH
Brubaker, Ronald C. .... Red Creek, WV
Brubaker, Sara K. Wetherholt
Traverse City, MI
Brubaker, Stephanie P. .... Belvidere, NJ
Brubaker, Theodore L. .... Lancaster, PA
Brubaker, Thomas C. .... Kent, WA
Brubaker, Warren E. .... Chicago, IL
Brubeck, David H., Law Office of
Jeffersonville, IN
Brucato, Charles J., Jr. .... Milford, MA
Bruccoleri, Stephen .... Voorhees, NJ
Philadelphia, PA
Brucculeri, Frank C. .... Long Beach, CA
Brucculeri, Louis .... Houston, TX
Bruce, Alan P. .... Pennsauken, NJ
Bruce, Andrea M. .... Washington, DC
Bruce, Anthony M. .... Buffalo, NY
Bruce, B. Allan .... Burlington, VT
Bruce, Barrett N. .... Austin, TX
Bruce, Benjamin A. .... Rochester, NY
Bruce, Bill J. .... Oklahoma City, OK
Bruce, Blair A. .... Houston, TX
Bruce, Bruce & Holt, L.L.C. .... Wichita, KS
Bruce, Carol Elder .... Washington, DC
Bruce, Carole Watkins .... Greensboro, NC
Bruce, Charles A. (Tony), Jr.
Princess Anne, MD
Bruce, Charles B., Jr. .... Denver, CO
Bruce, Charles M. .... Washington, DC
Bruce, Dale W. .... Wichita, KS
Bruce, Dan A. .... Houston, TX
Bruce, Dana G. .... Rockwall, TX
Bruce, Daniel G. .... Juneau, AK
Bruce, David R. .... Palo Alto, CA
Corvallis, OR
Bruce, David R. .... Winston-Salem, NC
Bruce, Davis C. .... Watertown, MA
Bruce, Deborah J. .... Oklahoma City, OK
Bruce, Debra L. .... Houston, TX
Bruce, Derek Eliot .... Orlando, FL
Bruce, Devon C. .... Chicago, IL
Bruce, Donald G. .... Vermillion, SD
Bruce, Duane N. .... Chicago, IL
Bruce, E. Edward .... Washington, DC
Bruce, Elizabeth G. .... Kansas City, MO
Bruce, Ellen A. .... Boston, MA
Bruce, Eric B. .... Washington, DC
Bruce, Eric D. .... Bradenton, FL
Bruce, Eric D. .... Wichita, KS
Bruce, Eric D., P.A. .... Bradenton, FL
Bruce, Erika L. .... Dallas, TX
Bruce, Gary J. .... St. Joseph, MI
Bruce, Gary O. .... Columbus, GA
Bruce, George C. .... Wichita, KS
Bruce, Gerald Roger
Department of the Air Force,
Office of the Judge Advocate General, GV
Bruce, Greg .... Santa Barbara, CA
Bruce, Harrison, Jr. .... Richmond, VA
Bruce, Homer L., Jr. .... Houston, TX
Bruce, J. Donald .... Jacksonville, FL
Bruce, Jackson M. .... Blacksburg, VA
Pulaski, VA
Bruce, Jackson M., Jr. .... Naples, FL
Milwaukee, WI
Bruce, James .... Fairfield, CT
Bruce, James .... Santa Fe, NM
Bruce, James E., Jr. .... Boise, ID
Bruce, James E., Jr. .... Hopkinsville, KY
Bruce, James L. .... Ketchikan, AK
Bruce, James M. .... Denver, CO
Bruce, James S. .... Phoenix, AZ
Bruce, James S. .... Atlanta, GA
Bruce, James T., III .... Washington, DC
Bruce, James W. .... Harrisburg, PA
Bruce, James W., III .... Oklahoma City, OK
Bruce, Jason W. .... Chicago, IL
Bruce, Jeffrey A. .... St. Paul, MN
Bruce, Jeffrey W. .... Belton, MO
Kansas City, MO
Bruce, Jillian R. .... Portland, OR
Bruce, Jim R., II .... Kennett, MO
Bruce, John D. .... Cambridge, MA
Bruce, John F. .... Washington, DC
Bruce, John M. .... Manitowoc, WI
Bruce, John T. .... Woodland Park, CO
Bruce, John Thomas .... Richmond, VA
Bruce, Joseph Franklin .... Annapolis, MD
Bruce, Joseph J. .... Rockford, IL
Bruce, Joseph J., P.C. .... Rockford, IL
Bruce, Kenneth D. .... Summerville, GA
Bruce, Kenneth R. .... Pittsburgh, PA
Bruce, Kimberly Hunter .... Pittsburgh, PA
Bruce, Larry B., (A P.L.C.)
Huntington Beach, CA
Bruce, Laura B. ....
Office Of Special Counsel, GV
Bruce, Laurie B., (Mr.) .... New York, NY
Bruce Law Firm, The .... Belton, MO
Kansas City, MO
Bruce, Lawrence H., Jr. .... St. Albans, VT
Bruce, Leslie A. .... Nashville, TN
Bruce, Lisa E. .... Reno, NV
Bruce, Lisa LeDoux .... Houston, TX
Bruce, Lisbeth P. .... Bradenton, FL
Bruce & Logan .... Denver, CO
Bruce, Louise A. .... St. Paul, MN
Bruce, Louise Anne .... St. Paul, MN
Bruce, M. Celeste .... Greenbelt, MD
Bruce, Marc M. .... Statesboro, GA
Bruce, Mark C. .... Santa Ana, CA
Bruce, Mark F. .... Reno, NV
Bruce, Mary Frances
Department of Commerce,
Patent and Trademark Office, GV
Bruce & McCoy .... Oakland, CA
Bruce, Megan M. .... Culver City, CA
Bruce, Michael J. .... Oroville, CA
Bruce, Michael M. .... Eugene, OR
Bruce & Mooney, P.C. .... Georgetown, DE
Bruce, Neil C. .... Colorado Springs, CO
Bruce, Pamela .... Albany, NY
Bruce, Patricia E. .... Washington, DC
Bruce, Patricia G. .... New Bern, NC
Bruce, Paul N. .... Independence, CA
Bruce, Peter W. .... Milwaukee, WI
Bruce, Phillip N. .... Sacramento, CA
Bruce, R. Michael .... Danbury, NC
Bruce, Randall E. .... Nashville, TN
Bruce, Rebecca S. .... Muncie, IN
Bruce, Richard A. .... Boston, MA
Bruce, Richard A. .... Oklahoma City, OK
Bruce, Robert A. .... Rock Hill, SC
Bruce, Robert D. .... Mineola, TX
Bruce, Robert J. .... Denver, CO
Bruce, Robert L. .... Irvine, CA
Bruce, Robert P. .... Destrehan, LA
Bruce, Robert R. .... Downers Grove, IL
Bruce, Ronald D. .... Boise, ID
Bruce, Ronald G. .... Greer, SC
Bruce, Ronald K. .... Greenville, KY
Madisonville, KY
Bruce, Scott G. .... Bala Cynwyd, PA
Bruce, Sherry R. .... Syracuse, NY
Bruce, S. T. .... Memphis, TN
Bruce, Stephen L. .... Oklahoma City, OK
Bruce, Stephen R. .... Washington, DC
Bruce, Steven .... San Francisco, CA
Bruce, Susan E. .... Harrisburg, PA
Bruce, Suzanne L. .... Paoli, PA
Bruce, Tammy Lesta .... Tulsa, OK
Bruce, Terry L. .... Olney, IL
Bruce, Theodore A. .... Jefferson City, MO
Bruce, Thomas G. .... Vancouver, WA
Bruce, Weathers, Corley & Lyle
Clarksville, TN
Nashville, TN
Bruce, William A. .... Bakersfield, CA
Bruce, William Billington .... Nashville, TN
Bruce, William C. .... Wethersfield, CT
Bruce, William L. .... Bourne, MA
Bruce, William R. .... Memphis, TN
Bruce, William R. .... Nashville, TN
Bruce-Chinery, Jacqueline A.
Los Angeles, CA
Bruce-Erickson, Caroline J. .... Lansing, MI
Bruce-Watson, Abigale .... Greenbelt, MD
Bruch, Carl E. .... Washington, DC
Bruch, Carol S. .... Davis, CA
Bruch, Elizabeth M. .... Minneapolis, MN
Bruch, G. Daniel, Jr. .... Philadelphia, PA
Bruch, Gregory S.
Securities and Exchange Commission,
Division of Enforcement, GV
Bruch, Joshua D. .... New York, NY
Bruch, Julie A. .... Northbrook, IL
Bruch, Karen Perme .... Butler, PA
Bruch, Michael J. .... Milwaukee, WI
Bruch, Sarah Fry .... Stevens Point, WI
Bruchal, Richard S. .... Ansonia, CT
Brucher, Peter V. .... Arroyo Grande, CA
Bruchez, Ernest V. .... Bryan, TX
Bruchez, Goss, Thornton, Meronoff &
Hawthorne, P.C. .... Bryan, TX
College Station, TX
Bruchler, Bruce B. .... Lakeport, CA
Bruchs, Amy O. .... Madison, WI
Brucia, Gregory F. .... New York, NY
Bruck, Christina M. .... Omaha, NE
Bruck, David I. .... Columbia, SC
Bruck, David L. .... Woodbridge, NJ
Bruck, Deborah Krusche .... Milwaukee, WI
Bruck, Edw. G. .... Hamilton, OH
Bruck, Michael C. .... Chicago, IL
Bruck, Michael R. .... Oakland, CA

Bruck, Richard H. ....Newport Beach, CA
Bruck, Roberta D. ....New Orleans, LA
Bruck, Sarah M. ....Irvine, CA
Bruckart, David L. ....Huntington, NY
Brucken, Robert M. ....Cleveland, OH
Brucker, Alex M. ....Los Angeles, CA
Brucker, Andrew G. ....Norwalk, CT
Southport, CT
Brucker, Andrew P. ....New York, NY
Brucker, Carol R. ....Denver, CO
Brucker, Daniel T. ....Arcata, CA
Brucker, Edward ....Coconut Creek, FL
Brucker, H. Michael ....Emeryville, CA
Brucker, Heinrich A. ....Aitkin, MN
Brucker, Joseph C. ....Springfield, OH
Brucker, Mary Wicks ....Seattle, WA
Brucker Morra & Hiltunen, A Professional Corporation ....Los Angeles, CA
Brucker, Nancy J. ....Eugene, OR
Brucker, Scott Evan ....Philadelphia, PA
Brucker, Stephen F. ....Kingston, NY
Brucker, Thomas H. S. ....Seattle, WA
Brucker, Thomas L. ....Fairbury, IL
Brucker, Wilber M., III ....Detroit, MI
Brucker, Wilber M., Jr. ....Detroit, MI
Brucker, William G. ....Bethel Park, PA
Brucker, William J. ....Laguna Hills, CA
Brucker-Kennedy, Gwen E.
Newport Beach, CA
Bruckert, Eileen R. ....Richfield, MN
Bruckert, George L., Jr. ....Chicago, IL
Bruckert, Jennifer Kay
San Francisco, CA
Bruckert, Terry I. ....Belleville, IL
Bruckhaus Westrick Heller Löber
New York, NY
New York, NY
Brucklacher, James F. ....Findlay, OH
Bruckman, David B. ....White Plains, NY
Bruckman, George T. ....New York, NY
Bruckman, Randall S. ....Rahway, NJ
Bruckman, Thomas R. ....Clearwater, FL
Bruckmann, Barbara O. ....Washington, DC
Bruckmann, Joseph G. ....Stamford, CT
Bruckmann, Mark F. ....New York, NY
Bruckner, Arnold D. ....Columbia, MD
Greenbelt, MD
Bruckner & Bruckner, P.A. ....Columbia, MD
Greenbelt, MD
Bruckner, Dale W. ....Wheaton, IL
Bruckner, Don ....Albuquerque, NM
Bruckner, Frederic N. ....Garden City, NY
Bruckner, James D. ....Carle Place, NY
Bruckner, John H. ....Cincinnati, OH
Bruckner, John J. ....Palo Alto, CA
Bruckner, Joyce Ann ....Columbia, MD
Greenbelt, MD
Bruckner, Lawrence L. ....Dixon, IL
Bruckner, M.J. "Jim" ....Lincoln, NE
Bruckner, Paul F. ....Geneva, IL
Bruckner, Rosemary A. ....Santa Barbara, CA
Bruckner, Sandra Petras ....Aurora, IL
Bruckner, Stephen M. ....Omaha, NE
Bruckner & Sykes, L.L.P. ....Houston, TX
Bruckner, W. Joseph ....Minneapolis, MN
Bruckner, William H. ....Houston, TX
Bruckner, William L. ....San Diego, CA
Bruckner, Wm. Joseph ....Atlanta, GA
Bruckner, Ziva P. ....Augusta, GA
Bruckno, Kimberle ....Cherry Hill, NJ
Bruder, Arthur Perry ....Department of Energy, Office of the General Counsel, GV
Bruder, Beverly Shwetz ....Cleveland, OH
Bruder, Dale R. ....Visalia, CA
Bruder, Elizabeth Martens ....Bellwood, IL
Bruder, Gary A. ....Ann Arbor, MI
Bruder, Gentile & Marcoux, L.L.P.
Washington, DC
Bruder, George F. ....Washington, DC
Bruder, Glenn P. ....Edina, MN
Bruder, Glenn P., P.A. ....Edina, MN
Bruder, Jerome J. ....Jamesburg, NJ
Bruder, John E. ....New Brunswick, NJ
Bruder, Kathleen Duffy ....Harrisburg, PA
Bruder, Mark S. ....New York, NY
Bruder, Melvyn Carson ....Dallas, TX
Bruder, Paul J., Jr. ....Harrisburg, PA
Bruder, Richard C. ....Southfield, MI
Bruder, Susan M. ....Marion, OH
Bruder, Walter F., Jr. ....Los Angeles, CA
Bruderle, Gerard ....Philadelphia, PA
Bruderle, Stephen J. ....Philadelphia, PA
Brudie, Barbara A. ....Garden City, NY
Brudie, Donald T. ....Garden City, NY
Brudie, Jeff M. ....Lewiston, ID
Brudner, Alan J. ....New York, NY
Brudner, R.M. & Associates, P.C.
Houston, TX
Brudner, Russ M. ....Houston, TX
Brudney, James J. ....United States Senate, Committee Legal Personnel, GV
Brudney, Victor ....Cambridge, MA
Brudno, Mitchell K. ....Elkins Park, PA
Brudno, Susan J. ....Mount Laurel, NJ
Brudnoy, Katherine, (Miss)
Minneapolis, MN
Brudny, James J., Jr. ....Columbus, OH
Brudny, Michael J. ....Clearwater, FL
Tampa, FL
Brudny, Peter J. ....Tampa, FL
Brudny, Peter J., P.A. ....Tampa, FL
Brudny & Rabin, P.A. ....Clearwater, FL
Tampa, FL
Brudvig, Thomas M. ....Roseville, MN
Brudvik, Jackie D. ....Seattle, WA
Brudvik, William J. ....Mayville, ND
Brudy, Lawrence D. ....Pittsburgh, PA
Brudz, John J. ....Plainville, CT
Brudzinski, Daniel L. ....Fremont, OH
Brudzinski, Walter J. ....Virginia Beach, VA
Brue, Frederick A. ....Flushing, NY
Brue, Nordahl L. ....Burlington, VT
Bruech, Valerie M. ....Hillsboro, OR
Brueck, Carl W., Jr. ....Pittsburgh, PA
Brueck, George F. ....Grand Rapids, MI
Brueck, Nancy L. ....Monroeville, PA
Brueckel, Becky ....Chicago, IL
Bruecker, Richd. G. ....New York, NY
Brueckheimer, David R. ....Valrico, FL
Brueckheimer, Deborah K. ....Bartow, FL
Brueckner, Karen N. ....San Bernardino, CA
Brueckner, Kurt M. ....Scottsdale, AZ
Brueckner, Leslie A. ....Washington, DC
Brueckner, Matthew E. ....Sacramento, CA
Brueckner, William E., III ....Rochester, NY
Brue-Clopton, Denice E. ....Riverside, CA
Bruegel, David R. ....Bloomfield Hills, MI
Bruegge, Robert T. ....Edwardsville, IL
Brueggeman, Jeffry A. ....Denver, CO
Brueggeman, Larry B. ....Milwaukee, WI
Brueggemann, James R. ....Los Angeles, CA
Brueggemann, Lewis ....Billings, MT
Brueggemann, Mark A. ....Collinsville, IL
Bruegger, Joseph F. ....Dallas, TX
Bruegmann, William J. ....Walnut Creek, CA
Brueher, Gary ....Othello, WA
Bruehl, Mary Sheely ....Oklahoma City, OK
Bruehl, Timothy J. ....Bokeelia, FL
Bruel, John C. ....Great Neck, NY
Bruemmer, Margaret Barr ....Milwaukee, WI
Bruemmer, Russell J. ....Washington, DC
Bruen, Alexander J. ....Narragansett, RI
Bruen, Edw. F. L. ....New York, NY
Bruen & Gordon, A Professional Corporation ....Walnut Creek, CA
Bruen, James A. ....San Francisco, CA
Bruen, James A. ....San Francisco, CA
Bruen, James G., Jr. ....Department of Justice, Civil Division, GV
Bruen, John P. ....Short Hills, NJ
Bruen, Thomas M. ....Walnut Creek, CA
Bruenderman, J. Warren ....Louisville, KY
Bruenell, Deborah D. ....Culver City, CA
Brueneman, A. J., Jr. ....Cincinnati, OH
Bruening, Allen F. ....Albuquerque, NM
Bruening, Francine M. ....Painesville, OH
Bruening, Glen T. ....Albany, NY
Bruening, Richard P. ....Kansas City, MO
Bruenn, Christine A. ....Augusta, ME
Bruenner, Eric W. ....New Brunswick, NJ
New York, NY
Bruenner, Frederick H. ....New York, NY
Bruenning, Daniel G. ....Big Bear City, CA
Bruens, Craig A. ....New York, NY
Bruer, Donald H. ....Edina, MN
Bruer, Galen L. ....Minneapolis, MN
Bruer, Kristine L. ....Minneapolis, MN
Bruer, Robert L. ....Springfield, MO
Bruer, Robert S. ....Kansas City, MO
Bruer, Rudolph H. ....Southold, NY
Bruer, Wooddell & Bates, P.C.
Springfield, MO
Bruers, Stuart E. ....Torrance, CA
Bruesehoff, Kristen T. ....San Diego, CA
Brueseke, Harold E. ....South Bend, IN
Bruesewitz, Terry B. ....Crested Butte, CO
Brueske, Curtis B. ....La Crosse, WI
Bruess, Charles E. ....Indianapolis, IN
Bruess, Steven C. ....Minneapolis, MN
Bruestle, Eric G. ....Cincinnati, OH
Bruestle, Glenn H. ....Princeton, NJ
Bruetsch, Patrick J. ....Birmingham, MI
Bruett, Keith A. ....Milwaukee, WI
Bruewer, Henry J. ....Fairfield, OH
Bruff, John B. ....Mount Clemens, MI
Bruffee, Anthea H. ....Brooklyn, NY
Bruffett, John W. ....Ava, MO
Bruffey, John C., Jr. ....Atlanta, GA
Bruffey, Michael E. ....Gulfport, MS
Brufsky, Allen D. ....Matlacha, FL
Naples, FL
Brufsky, Allen D., P.A. ....Matlacha, FL
Naples, FL
Brug, Peggy ....New Brunswick, NJ
Bruge-Holland, Kara M. ....Philadelphia, PA
Bruge-Holland, Kara M. ....Philadelphia, PA
Brugess, George T. ....Chicago, IL
Brugg, Betsy Davis ....Rochester, NY
Brugge, Parker E. ....Washington, DC
Brugge, Robert D. ....Glendale, CA
Bruggeman, Alan R. ....Chicago, IL
New Lenox, IL
Bruggeman, Amie L. ....Akron, OH
Bruggeman, Burton L. ....Orlando, FL
Bruggeman, Clair J. ....Tacoma, WA
Bruggeman, Dan R. ....Adrian, MI
Bruggeman, Dan R., P.C. ....Adrian, MI
Bruggeman, George, Jr.
San Bernardino, CA
Bruggeman, Gretchen ....Beverly Hills, CA
Bruggeman, Linda S. ....Washington, DC
Bruggeman, Marcia Ann ....New York, NY
Bruggeman, Patrick ....Fort Wayne, IN
Bruggeman, Smith & Peckham, LLP
Indio, CA
Rancho Cucamonga, CA
Riverside, CA
San Bernardino, CA
Victorville, CA
Brugger, Carol R. ....Bonita Springs, FL
Brugger, Eugene C. ....Dallas, TX
Brugger, George A. ....Greenbelt, MD
La Plata, MD
Brugger, Gregg W. ....Santa Monica, CA
Brugger, Joern-Eric W. ....San Mateo, CA
Brugger, John N., III ....Lexington, KY
Brugger, John N., Jr. ....Naples, FL
Brugger, Mark William ....Vienna, VA
Brugger, Richard P. ....Lake Geneva, WI
Brugger, Susan Shay ....Pierre, SD
Bruggink, Craig A. ....Grand Rapids, MI
Bruggink, Eric G.
United States Court of Federal Claims, GV
Bruggink & Fagan, P.C. ....Grand Rapids, MI
Bruggman, Peggy E. ....Palo Alto, CA
Brugh, George E. ....York, NE
Brugh, Jim ....Logansport, IN
Brugh, Lynn K., IV ....Richmond, VA
Brugh, Mark P. ....Hagerstown, MD
Brugh, Timothy C. ....San Jose, CA
Brugler & Levin ....Lewistown, PA
Brugman, John W. ....Portland, OR
Brugman, William E.
Rancho Palos Verdes, CA
Bruguera, S. Paul ....Torrance, CA
Brugueras, Jaime ....San Juan, PR
Bruh, Saul D. ....New York, NY
Bruha, John C. ....Grand Rapids, MI
Bruhn, Barry R. ....Peoria, IL
Bruhn, David E. ....Minneapolis, MN
Bruhn, Gary D. ....Detroit, MI
Bruhn, J. Michael, Jr. ....Kingston, NY
Bruhn, James D. ....Clinton, IA
Bruhn, Julie A. ....San Jose, CA
Bruhn, Stanley K. ....Mount Vernon, WA
Bruhns, Gary R. ....San Francisco, CA
Bruhschwein, Glen R. ....Dickinson, ND
Bruice, Alec W. ....Santa Barbara, CA
Bruin, James L. ....Roswell, NM
Bruin, Linda L. ....Lansing, MI
Bruin, William J., Jr. ....St. Louis, MO
Bruiniers, Terence L. ....San Francisco, CA
Bruinooge & Associates ....Hackensack, NJ
Rutherford, NJ
Bruinooge, Thomas H. ....Rutherford, NJ
Bruins, David R. ....Haledon, NJ
Bruins, Faith K. ....Boston, MA
Bruinsma, Dirk ....Laguna Hills, CA
Bruinsma & Hewitt, Trial Lawyers
Laguna Hills, CA
Bruinsma, James C. ....Grand Rapids, MI
Bruinsma, James R. ....Chicago, IL
Bruinsma, Tim C. ....Los Angeles, CA
Brukner, John S., (P.C.) ....Houston, TX
Brukoff, William M. ....Southfield, MI
Bruks, Patrick J. ....Chicago, IL
Bruksch, Terri L. ....Indianapolis, IN
Bruland, Joan V. ....San Francisco, CA
Brule, David E. ....Walnut Creek, CA
Brule, Paul A. ....Cumberland, RI
Brule & Rooney, LLP ....Walnut Creek, CA
Brule, Thomas R. ....Cleveland, OH
Brull & Piccionelli ....Los Angeles, CA
Brull, Richard P. ....Los Angeles, CA
Brum, Adam ....Tampa, FL
Brum, Bryan M. ....Atlanta, GA
Brum, Irvin ....Mineola, NY
Brum, Kenneth A. ....Warren, RI
Brum, Nancy Edwards ....Marietta, OH
Brumagin, Grace Morse ....Tustin, CA
Bruman, Elizabeth Meador ....Houston, TX
Brumbach, Aaron A. ....Reading, PA
Brumbach, Allison Ann ....Sacramento, CA
Brumbach, Charles P. ....Twin Falls, ID
Brumbach, Gabrielle Harner ....Pasadena, CA
Brumbach, Mancuso & Fegley, P.C.
Reading, PA
Brumbach, Marissa J. ....Philadelphia, PA
Brumback, Charles T., Jr. ....Orlando, FL
Brumback, Eileen P. ....New York, NY
Brumback, Gordon J. ....Greenbelt, MD
Brumback, Mary Helen Skinner
Norman, OK
Brumback, Melissa Dewey ....Raleigh, NC
Brumback, Oscar B. ....Monroeville, PA
Brumbaugh, Alice A. ....Baltimore, MD
Brumbaugh, Anne Jenkins ....Greenville, OH
Brumbaugh, Christopher T.
St. Louis, MO
Brumbaugh, Clay A. ....Elizabethtown, NC
Fayetteville, NC
Jacksonville, NC
New Bern, NC
Shallotte, NC
Wilmington, NC
Brumbaugh, D. Forrest ....Dallas, TX
Brumbaugh, George E., Jr.
Mount Clemens, MI
Brumbaugh, Granville M., Jr.
New York, NY
Brumbaugh, James P. ....Wailuku, HI
Brumbaugh & Jenkins ....Wailuku, HI
Brumbaugh, John M. ....Miami, FL
Brumbaugh, John M. ....Baltimore, MD
Brumbaugh, John Patterson ....Atlanta, GA
Brumbaugh, Kay Lynn ....Dallas, TX
Brumbaugh, Kirk Edward ....Omaha, NE
Brumbaugh, Mark S. ....Longview, WA
Brumbaugh, Michael L. ....Greenville, OH
Brumbaugh, Mu & King, P.A.
Elizabethtown, NC
Fayetteville, NC
Jacksonville, NC
New Bern, NC
Shallotte, NC
Wilmington, NC
Brumbaugh, Philip J. ....Greenville, OH
Brumbaugh & Quandahl, P.C.
Omaha, NE
Brumbaugh, R. Bruce ....Hollidaysburg, PA
Brumbaugh, Richard H. ....Spencer, WV
Brumbaugh, Robert B. ....Dayton, OH
Brumbaugh, Roland J. ....Denver, CO
Brumbaugh, Thomas D. ....Lafayette, LA
Brumbaugh, Wm. M. ....Tulsa, OK
Brumbeloe, Nancy L.S. ....Topeka, KS
Brumbelow, Jeremy Scott ....Little Rock, AR
Brumbelow, John R. ....Tyler, TX
Brumbelow, Leah S. ....Douglasville, GA
Brumbelow, Paula L. ....Nacogdoches, TX
Brumberg, Bruce S. ....Brookline, MA
Brumberg, Dennis P. ....Radford, VA
Roanoke, VA
Brumberg, Harriet R. ....Philadelphia, PA
Brumberg, Mackey & Wall, P.L.C.
Radford, VA
Roanoke, VA
Brumberger, Jill F. ....Houston, TX
Brumby, Andrew M. ....Orlando, FL
Brumby, John T. ....Atlanta, GA
Brumby, Otis A. ....Marietta, GA
Brumby, Sewell R. ....Atlanta, GA
Brumby, William E., II ....Marietta, GA
Brumby, William E., II, P.C. ....Marietta, GA
Brumel, Warren ....Keyport, NJ
Brumer, Ari ....Los Angeles, CA
Brumer, Herbert S. ....Los Angeles, CA
Brumer & Kaufman, P.A.
Boca Raton, FL
Fort Lauderdale, FL
Miami, FL
Brumer, Marc L. ....Boca Raton, FL
Fort Lauderdale, FL
Miami, FL
Brumer, Michael ....Boca Raton, FL
Fort Lauderdale, FL
Miami, FL
Brumfield and Austin ....Mc Comb, MS
Brumfield, Brad J. ....Lake Charles, LA
Brumfield, Bruce J., Jr. ....Yazoo City, MS
Brumfield, Chris N. ....San Luis Obispo, CA
Brumfield, David C. ....Pittsburgh, PA
Brumfield, Douglas H. ....Jackson, MS
Brumfield, G. David ....Charleston, WV
Welch, WV
Brumfield, James B. ....Navarre, FL
Brumfield, Jerry W. ....Kansas City, MO
Brumfield, Jimmie A., II ....Baton Rouge, LA
Brumfield, Lorna Hislop ....Bakersfield, CA
Brumfield, Margaret Ann ....Richmond, TX
Brumfield, Noah A. ....Palo Alto, CA
Brumfield, R. Carlton ....Muncie, IN
Brumfield, Robert H., III ....Bakersfield, CA
Brumfield, Robert W. ....Mc Comb, MS
Brumfield, Ronald J. ....Franklinton, LA
Brumfield & Watson ....Bluefield, WV
Charleston, WV
Welch, WV
Brumit, David Benjamin ....Buena Vista, VA
Brumitt, Lee B. ....Kansas City, MO
Bruml, Charles R. ....Cleveland, OH
Brumleve, Ronald J. ....Midlothian, VA
Brumleve, Ronald J., P.C. ....Midlothian, VA
Brumleve, Wilson L. ....Cincinnati, OH
Brumley, A. Neal ....Charlotte, NC
Brumley, Alison M. ....Lafayette, LA
Brumley, Bill V., Jr., P.C. ....Bartlesville, OK
Tulsa, OK
Brumley & Bishop ....Bartlesville, OK
Tulsa, OK
Brumley, Bruce Alan ....Topeka, KS
Brumley, Christopher A. ....Charleston, WV
Brumley, Janet Phillips ....Dallas, TX
Brumley, Paul ....Dallas, TX
Brumley, Philip ....Jersey City, NJ
Patterson, NY
Brumley, S. Ray ....Treasury Department, Internal Revenue Service, GV
Brumley, Steven D. ....Duncanville, TX
Brumlik, Charles Joseph ....Princeton, NJ
Brumlow, Terry ....Calhoun, GA
Brumm, James E. ....New York, NY
Brumm, Margaret M. ....Naperville, IL
Brumm, Marguerite Melo ....Visalia, CA
Brumme, Carl A., III ....Lexington, SC
Brummer, Arlene ....Miami, FL
Brummer, Bennett H. ....Miami, FL
Brummer, George L. ....Oakland, CA
Brummer, Richard H. ....Effingham, IL
Brummer, Terry E. ....Kansas City, MO
Brummett, Dwight D. ....Loveland, CO
Brummett, Craig ....Lubbock, TX
Brummett, Duane L. ....Fort Walton Beach, FL
Brummett, Gregory P. ....Washington, DC
Brummett, Hac, III ....Ventura, CA
Brummett, Michael L. ....Dallas, TX
Brummett, Raymond L. ....Wichita, KS
Brummett, Suzanne G. ....Irvine, CA
Brummett, William R. ....Albuquerque, NM
Brummett, Winston P. ....Lubbock, TX
Brummitt, Daniel T. ....Oklahoma City, OK
Brummitt, Randall C. ....Walnut Creek, CA
Brummond, David J. ....Naperville, IL
Brummond, Robert J. ....St. Louis, MO
Brummund, Matthew P. ....Muskegon, MI
Brumsey, William, III ....Currituck, NC
Brumskine, Margaret Deconte
New York, NY
Brumund & Jacobs ....Joliet, IL
Brumund, James R. ....Joliet, IL
Brumund, Paul F. ....Joliet, IL
Brumund, Robert P. ....Joliet, IL
Brun, James H. ....Cincinnati, OH
Brun, Jean-Marc ....Washington, DC
Brun, Monica Fat ....San Francisco, CA
Brun, Roy L. ....Shreveport, LA
Brunault, Harold F. ....Holyoke, MA
Brunault-McGuinness, Andrea L.
Holyoke, MA
Brunavs, G. Alfred ....Atlanta, GA
Brunda, Bruce B. ....Laguna Hills, CA
Brundage, Albert ....Burbank, CA

Brundage, Barbara E. .... Paducah, KY
Brundage, Carla J. .... Newark, NJ
Brundage, Cory .... Indianapolis, IN
Brundage, Dianne S. .... Winter Park, FL
Brundage, Donald L., P.C. .... Westminster, CO
Brundage, John M. .... Marshall, MI
Brundage, Lew D. .... Yakima, WA
Brundage, Maureen S. .... New York, NY
Brundage, Michael P. .... Tampa, FL
Brundage, Paul D.
National Aeronautics And Space Administration, GV
Brundage, Robert A. .... San Francisco, CA
Brundage, Robert J. .... Jefferson City, MO
Brundage, Samuel G. .... Rochester, NY
Brundage, Stephen A. .... Wheaton, IL
Brundage, Warner F., Jr. .... Richmond, VA
Brundage & Zellmann .... San Diego, CA
Brundidge, Arthurice T. .... Memphis, TN
Brundidge, Carl I. .... Arlington, VA
Brundige, Dennis J. .... Kansas City, MO
Brundige, Harold T. .... Martin, TN
Brundige, Maurice L. .... Pasadena, CA
Brundige, Robert W., Jr. .... New York, NY
Brundige, Winston T. .... Baltimore, MD
Brundin, Barbara L. .... Denver, CO
Brundin, Brian J. .... Anchorage, AK
Brundin, Inc. .... Anchorage, AK
Brundirks, James E. .... Kalamazoo, MI
Brundrett, George L., Jr. .... Houston, TX
Brundrett and Moutinho .... Ludlow, MA
Brundrett, Roberta Loring .... Ludlow, MA
Brundy, James M. .... San Francisco, CA
Brune, David A. .... Baltimore, MD
Brune, David H. .... Irving, TX
Brune, Edward I. .... Indianapolis, IN
Brune, Kenneth L. .... Tulsa, OK
Brune, Michael J. .... Coolidge, AZ
Brune & Neff, A Professional Corporation
Tulsa, OK
Brune & Richard LLP .... New York, NY
Brune, Susan .... New York, NY
Brune, Tracy A. .... Syracuse, NY
Brune, Walter F., Jr. .... Ponca City, OK
Brune, William J. .... Evansville, IN
Brunea, Chris T. .... Buffalo, NY
Bruneau, Brooks R. .... Princeton, NJ
Bruneau, Charles E., Jr. .... New Orleans, LA
Bruneau, Christopher T. .... Washington, DC
Bruneau, David H. .... Port Angeles, WA
Bruneel, Anne E. .... South Bend, IN
Brunel, André J. .... Dallas, TX
Brunel, Dean C. .... Somerville, MA
Brunell, Alan R. .... Chicago, IL
Brunell, Albert L. .... Demarest, NJ
Brunell, David Charles
Dearborn Heights, MI
Brunell, Janet F. .... Jericho, NY
Brunell, Norman E. .... Los Angeles, CA
Brunell, Richard M. .... Boston, MA
Brunell, Roger A. .... New Orleans, LA
Brunelle, George .... New York, NY
Brunelle & Huch, Ltd. .... Minneapolis, MN
Brunelle, Jan P. .... San Francisco, CA
Brunelle, John O. .... Minneapolis, MN
Brunelle, Roger J. .... Worcester, MA
Brunelle, Suzanne .... Boston, MA
Brunelli, Robert R. .... Denver, CO
Bruneman, Steven W. .... Dallas, TX
Brunenkant & Haskell, LLP
Washington, DC
Brunenkant, Jon L. .... Washington, DC
Bruner, Barry T. .... Carroll, IA
Bruner, Becky M. .... Washington, DC
Bruner, Ben E. .... Montgomery, AL
Bruner, Bradley .... San Francisco, CA
Bruner, Brooks, Koch & Sorg
Indianapolis, IN
Bruner & Bruner .... Carroll, IA
Bruner & Bruner .... San Antonio, TX
Bruner, Bryan D. .... Fort Worth, TX
Bruner, Cecelia J. .... Dallas, TX
Bruner, Cheryl E. .... Cincinnati, OH
Bruner, Christopher M. .... Bethesda, MD
Bruner, David E. .... Marco Island, FL
Bruner, David S. .... Carroll, IA
Bruner, Faith Winsborough .... Dallas, TX
Bruner, Frederick M. .... Alexandria, VA
Bruner, Gina M. .... Fort Worth, TX
Bruner, Harry C., Jr. .... Charleston, WV
Bruner, Harvey B. .... Cleveland, OH
Bruner, Henry B. .... Chagrin Falls, OH
Bruner, J. William .... Boonville, IN
Bruner, James A. .... Rockville, IN
Bruner, James D. .... Phoenix, AZ
Bruner, James H. K. .... Albany, NY
Pattersonville, NY
Bruner, James L. .... Columbia, SC
Bruner, James L. .... San Antonio, TX
Bruner, James R. .... Greenville, NC
Bruner, James W. .... Springfield, IL
Bruner, Jamieson & Pappas, L.L.P.
Fort Worth, TX
Bruner, Janet .... Washington, DC
Bruner, Jeffrey A. .... Shelton, CT
Bruner, Jerry L. .... Laurinburg, NC
Bruner, John J. .... Atlanta, GA
Bruner, Joseph E. .... High Point, NC
Bruner, Judith C. .... San Diego, CA
Bruner, Kenneth R. .... Emporia, KS
Bruner, Larry A. .... San Antonio, TX
Bruner, Leslie M. .... Laurinburg, NC
Bruner, N. Lucinda .... Brighton, CO
Bruner & Nash, Professional Corporation
Moraga, CA
Bruner, Omar S., Jr. .... Indianapolis, IN
Bruner, P. Daniel .... Washington, DC
Bruner, Patricia Taylor .... Knoxville, TN
Bruner, Paula R.
Equal Employment Opportunity Commission, Office of the General Counsel, GV
Bruner, Philip L. .... Minneapolis, MN
Bruner, Powell, Robbins, Wall & Mullins, LLC .... Columbia, SC
Bruner, Robert B. .... Dallas, TX
Bruner, Robert C. .... Indianapolis, IN
Bruner, Robert S. .... Carroll, IA
Bruner, Scott V. .... Chicago, IL
Bruner, Sharon A. .... Lansing, MI
Bruner, Stephen C. .... Chicago, IL
Bruner, T. Lee .... Butte, MT
Bruner, Thomas M. .... Midland, TX
Bruner, Tom H. .... Tulsa, OK
Bruner, Vincent M., & Associates
Fort Walton Beach, FL
Panama City, FL
Bruner, William .... San Diego, CA
Bruner, William G., III .... Towson, MD
Brunero, John S. .... Coventry, RI
Brunero, John S., Jr. .... Coventry, RI
Brunero, Stephen J. .... West Warwick, RI
Bruness, Wayne C. .... Indianapolis, IN
Brunet, Craig W. .... Los Angeles, CA
Brunet, Edward J. .... Portland, OR
Brunet, Francois .... Richmond Hill, NY
Brunet, William J. .... New York, NY
Brunett, Jozef L. .... Sacramento, CA
Brunette, John S. .... Reston, VA
Brunette, Julie .... Middleton, WI
Brunette, Paul H. .... Wichita Falls, TX
Brunette, Richard W., Jr.
Los Angeles, CA
Brunette, Ricky L. .... Portland, ME
Brunette, Robert A.
La Canada Flintridge, CA
Brunette, Stephen A.
Colorado Springs, CO
Brunette, Steven E. .... Carson, CA
Brunette, Vicky Marie Jeannette
Buffalo, NY
Brunette Anthony, Vicky-Marie .... Buffalo, NY
Brunetti, Alfred J. .... New Haven, CT
Brunetti, Angela M. .... Southfield, MI
Brunetti, Christopher G.
San Francisco, CA
Brunetti, Frank L. .... Hackensack, NJ
Brunetti, Kenneth A. .... San Francisco, CA
Brunetti, Melvin .... Reno, NV
Brunetti, Robert C. .... Danbury, CT
Brunetto, Joseph A. .... Columbus, OH
Brunetto, Nadia Walker .... Newark, NJ
Bruney, David C. .... Gainesville, FL
Bruney, Ronald A. .... Austin, TX
Brunfect, Mitchell J. .... Virginia, MN
Brungard, Randy P. .... Lock Haven, PA
Brungard, Richard G. .... Koror, TT
Brungardt, John K. .... Kansas City, MO
Brunger, Melinda Held .... Houston, TX
Brungess, Julia Ann .... Fresno, CA
Brungo, Michael L. .... Pittsburgh, PA
Bruni, A. Victor .... Torrance, CA
Bruni, Christopher B. .... San Francisco, CA
Bruni, Domenic .... Oshkosh, WI
Bruni, Gennaro .... New York, NY
Bruni, John W. .... Pittsburgh, PA
Bruni, S. Elizabeth Lamar .... Dallas, TX
Brunick, Alvarez & Battersby, Prof. Corp.
Redlands, CA
Riverside, CA
San Bernardino, CA
Brunick, Kevin M. .... Virginia Beach, VA
Brunick, Timothy S. .... Norfolk, VA
Brunick, William J. .... Redlands, CA
San Bernardino, CA
Brunig, Robert A. .... Fort Worth, TX
Bruning, Anthony S. .... St. Louis, MO
Bruning, Deonne L. .... Lincoln, NE
Bruning, Eric J. .... Stuart, FL
Bruning, Gregory W. .... Overland Park, KS
Bruning, Jon C. .... Elkhorn, NE
Bruning, Kevin W. .... Crystal Lake, IL
Bruning, Olga M. .... Arnold, MD
Bruning, Richard C. .... Orlando, FL
Bruning, Robert M. .... Pasadena, CA
Bruning, Robert M., Law Offices of
Pasadena, CA
Bruning, Susan B. .... Dallas, TX
Bruning, William J. .... Leawood, KS
Bruning, William L. .... Leawood, KS
Brunini, Edmund L., Jr. .... Jackson, MS
Brunini, Grantham, Grower & Hewes, PLLC .... Jackson, MS
Brunjes, David H. .... Treasury Department, Federal Law Enforcement Training Center, GV
Brunjes, Gary M. .... Amityville, NY
Brunjes, John A. .... Cheshire, CT
Brunk, Edward W. .... Kansas City, KS
Brunk, J. Dale .... Phoenix, AZ
Brunk, Richard K. .... Chesterfield, MO
Brunk, Stephen K. .... La Jolla, CA
Brunk, Wilfred N. .... Plymouth, MI
Brunkenhoefer Law Firm, P.C.
Corpus Christi, TX
Brunkenhoefer, Robert Blake
Corpus Christi, TX
Brunkenhoefer, Robert Edward
Corpus Christi, TX
Brunn, Alan R. .... Owings Mills, MD
Brunn, Charles K. .... Modesto, CA
Brunn, Elizabeth K. .... Baltimore, MD
Brunn & Flynn, A Professional Corporation
Merced, CA
Modesto, CA
Brunn, George .... Berkeley, CA
Brunn, Gerald E. .... Modesto, CA
Brunn, Herbert .... Bronxville, NY
Brunn, Larry K. .... Portland, OR
Brunn Law Firm, The, LPA .... Cleveland, OH
Brunn, McKnight .... Oakland, CA
Brunn, Richard C. .... Canton, OH
Brunn, Thomas L., Jr. .... Cleveland, OH
Brunn, Thomas L., Sr. .... Cleveland, OH
Brunner, Anne Marie L. .... Northbrook, IL
Brunner & Brunner Co., L.P.A.
Alliance, OH
Columbus, OH
Brunner, Conver & Conver .... Lansdale, PA
Brunner, Daniel H. .... Spokane, WA
Brunner, Donald A. .... Norwalk, CT
Brunner, Douglas J. .... Springfield, MA
Brunner, Edward R. .... Barron, WI
Brunner, Frances Re'Nee .... Topeka, KS
Brunner, Gail A. .... Philadelphia, PA
Brunner, George H., Jr. .... King Of Prussia, PA
Brunner, H. Frank .... Cullman, AL
Brunner, James E. .... Jackson, MI
Brunner, Jennifer L. .... Columbus, OH
Brunner, John D. .... Wapakoneta, OH
Brunner, John M. .... Woodcliff Lake, NJ
Brunner, Joseph M. .... Bellwood, IL
Brunner, Julie M. .... St. Paul, MN
Brunner, Kathleen T. .... Torrance, CA
Brunner, Kathryn L. .... Orange, CA
Brunner, Kim M. .... Bloomington, IL
Brunner, Major O. .... Asheville, NC
Brunner, Mark J. .... West Bend, WI
Brunner, Maurice T. .... Rochester, NY
Brunner, Rick L. .... Alliance, OH
Columbus, OH
Brunner, Robert H. .... Indianapolis, IN
Brunner, Roger .... Fairbanks, AK
Brunner, S. Dresden .... Naples, FL
Brunner, Seth P. .... Sacramento, CA
Brunner, Stephen C. .... Columbus, OH
Brunner, Stephen P. .... San Francisco, CA
Brunner, Steven M. .... Chicago, IL
Brunner, Sultra E. .... Pasadena, CA
Brunner, Susan Davis .... Chicago, IL
Brunner, Thomas J. .... Wausau, WI
Brunner, Thomas J., Jr. .... South Bend, IN
Brunner, Thomas N. .... Manistee, MI
Brunner, Thomas W. .... Washington, DC
Brunner, William L. .... Portland, OR
Brunnock & Cicchetti, LLC .... Waterbury, CT
Brunnock, Thomas P. .... Waterbury, CT
Brunnock, Timothy J. .... Morristown, NJ
Bruno, Aileen F. .... Thousand Oaks, CA
Bruno, Alfred P. .... New Haven, CT
Wallingford, CT
Bruno, Alice A. .... Branford, CT
Bruno, Anne L. .... Boston, MA
Bruno, Anthony D. .... Morris Plains, NJ
Bruno, Anthony T. .... Lakewood, NJ
Bruno, Barbara J. .... Detroit, MI
Bruno, Bernard J. .... River Forest, IL
Bruno, Brooks & Goldberg, P.C.
Bullhead City, AZ
Kingman, AZ
Lake Havasu City, AZ
Parker, AZ
Bruno & Bruno .... New Orleans, LA
Bruno, Bruno & Colin, P.C. .... Denver, CO
Bruno, Charles .... Easton, PA
Bruno, Chastity Carter .... Paoli, PA
Bruno, Christopher
Securities and Exchange Commission, Division of Enforcement, GV
Bruno, Christopher J. .... New Orleans, LA
Bruno, Christopher J. .... New York, NY
Bruno, Cirino M. .... New York, NY
Bruno, Clarke .... New York, NY
Bruno, Craig J. .... Melville, NY
Bruno, David J. .... Denver, CO
Bruno, Dominic M. .... Toledo, OH
Bruno, Dorothy P. .... York, PA
Bruno, Edward C. .... Newburgh, NY
Bruno, Edward S. .... Scarsdale, NY
Bruno, Eli T. .... New York, NY
Bruno, Erasmo S. .... White Plains, NY
Bruno, Eugene G. .... San Diego, CA
Bruno, Ferdinand A. .... Bristol, RI
Bruno, Francisco G. .... San Juan, PR
Bruno, Frank A. .... New Orleans, LA
Bruno, Frank L. .... Winthrop, MA
Bruno, Frank P. .... New York, NY
Bruno, Frank S. .... New Orleans, LA
Bruno, Frederic, & Associates
Minneapolis, MN
Bruno, Gary F. .... Oneida, NY
Bruno, Gary R. .... Shawano, WI
Bruno, George .... Manchester, NH
Bruno, Gerbino & Macchia, LLP
Melville, NY
Bruno, Gino J. .... Newport Beach, CA
Bruno, Goldberg & Ventura .... Floral Park, NY
Bruno, Gregory D. .... Melrose Park, IL
Bruno, Harold R., III .... Denver, CO
Bruno, Harry R., Jr. .... Hayward, CA
Bruno, James C. .... Detroit, MI
Bruno, James J. .... Erie, PA
Bruno, James P. .... Secaucus, NJ
Bruno, James S. .... Glenside, PA
Bruno, John .... Columbus, OH
Bruno, John E. .... Boston, MA
Bruno, John J. .... New York, NY
Bruno, Jonathan B. .... Boston, MA
Bruno, Joseph C. .... Philadelphia, PA
Bruno, Joseph F. .... New York, NY
Bruno, Joseph M. .... New Orleans, LA
Bruno, Judy A. .... Pittsburgh, PA
Bruno, Keith M. .... Plattsburgh, NY
Bruno, Kevin J. .... Newark, NJ
Bruno, Kevin R. .... Woodsville, NH
Bruno, Kim G.
Federal Energy Regulatory Commission, Office of the General Counsel, GV
Bruno, Klint .... Chicago, IL
Bruno, Lee E. .... Kingman, AZ
Bruno, Lori Ann .... New York, NY
Bruno, Louis B. .... Denver, CO
Bruno, Louis G. .... Escondido, CA
Bruno, Louis G. .... Los Angeles, CA
San Diego, CA
Bruno, Lucas F., Jr. .... New Orleans, LA
Bruno, Lynn Sfara .... Youngstown, OH
Bruno, Marian R.
Federal Trade Commission, Bureau of Competition, GV
Bruno, Marilyn Joan .... Department of State, Bureau of Economic and Business Affairs, GV
Bruno, Mary E. .... Phoenix, AZ
Bruno, Michael A. .... Middletown, NJ
Bruno, Michael A. .... New York, NY
Bruno, Michael A. .... Toledo, OH
Bruno, Michael D. .... San Francisco, CA
Bruno, Michael E.
Charlotte Amalie, St. Thomas, VI
Bruno, Michael George .... San Diego, CA
Bruno, Nicholas J., Jr. .... Albany, NY
Bruno, Patrick L. .... Floral Park, NY
Bruno, Paul A. .... San Jose, CA
Bruno, Philippe M. .... Washington, DC
Bruno, Richard .... Waterbury, CT
Bruno, Richard J. .... Miami, FL
Bruno, Richard S. .... Martinez, CA
Bruno, Richard T. .... Denver, CO
Bruno, Robert J. .... Phoenix, AZ
Bruno, Robert J. .... New Orleans, LA
Bruno, Robert J. .... Burnsville, MN
Bruno, Rocco J., Jr. .... Niagara Falls, NY
Bruno, Rosemary J. .... Newark, NJ
Bruno, Saml. A. .... Butler, PA
Bruno, Stephen P. .... New Orleans, LA
Bruno, Susan J. .... Philadelphia, PA
Bruno, Suzanne Gouveia .... Arlington, MA
Bruno, Teresa P. .... Raleigh, NC
Bruno, Theresa A. .... Kingman, AZ
Bruno, Thomas A. .... Urbana, IL
Bruno, Thomas C. .... Mineola, NY
Bruno, Thomas, II .... Philadelphia, PA
Bruno, Toni Rae .... Los Angeles, CA
Bruno, Vincent J. .... Northfield, NJ
Bruno, Vincent J. .... Red Bank, NJ
Brunoforte, Louis J. .... Largo, FL
Brunoforte, Louis J., P.A. .... Clearwater, FL
Largo, FL
New Port Richey, FL
St. Petersburg, FL
Tampa, FL
Brunon, Bradley W. .... Los Angeles, CA
Brunow, Sandra L. .... Houston, TX
Bruns, Christopher Lee .... Cedar Rapids, IA
Bruns, Craig R. .... San Ramon, CA
Bruns, David A. .... St. Louis, MO
Bruns, David E. .... Topeka, KS
Kansas City, MO
Bruns, David Wm. .... Coldwater, OH
Bruns, Donald B. .... Madison, WI
Bruns, Elizabeth Patricia .... Alexandria, VA
Bruns, Emerson E. .... New York, NY
Bruns, Irving V. .... St. Paul, MN
Bruns, Jeanne Marie .... Cincinnati, OH
Bruns, Joe H. .... Seguin, TX
Bruns, Julie A. .... Dayton, OH
Bruns, Kevin P. .... LaGrange, IN
Bruns, Kevin T. .... United States Senate, Senatorial Assistants, GV
Bruns, Norman J. .... Seattle, WA
Bruns, Phillip T. .... Houston, TX
Bruns, Robert C. .... Peace Dale, RI
Bruns, Robert T. .... Cincinnati, OH
Bruns, Robert W. .... Phoenix, AZ
Bruns, Scott A. .... Yakima, WA
Bruns, Stephen R. .... Eaton, OH
Bruns, Steven H. .... St. Paul, MN
Bruns, Thomas B. .... Cincinnati, OH
Bruns, William G. .... Muncie, IN
Bruns, William G. .... St. Louis, MO
Brunsell, Clayton W. .... Oakland, CA
Brunsell, Paul F. .... Madison, WI
Brunsell, Robert .... Emeryville, CA
Brunsell, Wm. C. .... Evansville, WI
Brunsman, John J. .... Springfield, IL
Brunsman, Robert Burt .... Boston, MA
Brunsman, Theresa M. .... Cincinnati, OH
Brunson, C. Matthew .... Elba, AL
Brunson, Denise M. .... Minneapolis, MN
Brunson, Eva H. .... Allendale, SC
Brunson, Hugh E. .... Crowley, LA
Brunson, James A. .... Bay City, MI
Brunson, James D. .... Spring, TX
Brunson, Jeffery L. .... Crowley, LA
Brunson, John Morgan .... Clearwater, FL
Brunson, John S. .... Houston, TX
Brunson, Kent B. .... Montgomery, AL
Brunson, Melvin W. .... Mobile, AL
Brunson, N. Deane .... Charlotte, NC
Brunson, Nolen L. .... Travelers Rest, SC
Brunson, Paul W., Jr. .... Clayton, AL
Brunson, Robert H. .... Columbia, SC
Brunson, Samuel T. .... Florence, SC
Brunson, Steve P. .... Gadsden, AL
Brunson, Ted Brett .... Natchitoches, LA
Brunson, William L., Jr. .... Elba, AL
Brunson-Wheeler, Natalie Y.
Bloomington, IL
Brunstad, G. Eric, Jr. .... Hartford, CT
Brunstad, Sheryl Kim .... Glastonbury, CT
Brunstad, William D. .... Atlanta, GA

Brunstein, Anna G. .... **New York, NY**
Brunstein, Irene Y. .... Brooklyn, NY
Brunsten, William S., (P.C.)
Los Angeles, CA
Brunstetter, Peter S. .... **Winston-Salem, NC**
Brunsting, Suzanne L. .... **Rochester, NY**
Brunstrom, Keith W. .... Jefferson City, MO
Brunsvold, Ben E. .... Moorhead, MN
Brunsvold, Brian G. .... **Washington, DC**
Brunswick, Alan M. .... **Los Angeles, CA**
Brunswick, Max F. .... New Haven, CT
Brunswick, Rhonda M. .... San Diego, CA
Brunt, Constance P. .... Harrisburg, PA
Brunt, George B. .... Plano, TX
Brunt, T. Neal .... **Cartersville, GA**
Brunt, Thomas F. .... **Passaic, NJ**
Brunt, Thomas F. .... **Paterson, NJ**
Bruntel, Kenneth M. .... **Washington, DC**
Brunton, Bruce D. .... Bainbridge Island, WA
Brunton, Diane L. .... Carlinville, IL
Brunton & Jagger .... Glendale, CA
Brunton, James E. .... Glendale, CA
Brunton, Michael F. .... Topeka, KS
Brunton, Michael J. .... Belleville, IL
Brunton, Paul D. .... Tulsa, OK
Brunton, Robert G. .... **Atlanta, GA**
Brunton, Scott A. .... **Peoria, IL**
Brunton, Shari M. .... **Belleville, IL**
Brunton, Susan Beth .... Seattle, WA
Bruntrager & Billings, P.C. .... St. Louis, MO
Bruntrager, Daniel J. .... St. Louis, MO
Bruntrager, Karen C. .... **Chicago, IL**
Bruntrager, Mary Butts .... St. Louis, MO
Bruntrager, Neil J. .... St. Louis, MO
Bruntrager, Raymond A. .... St. Louis, MO
Brunts, Eve M. .... **Boston, MA**
Bruntz, John E. .... Des Moines, IA
Bruntz, Julie Kron .... West Des Moines, IA
Brunvand, Bjorn E. .... **Clearwater, FL**
Brunvand, Bjorn E., P.A. .... **Clearwater, FL**
Brunwasser, Allen N. .... Pittsburgh, PA
Brunwasser, Arthur .... San Francisco, CA
Brunwasser, Ina C. .... New York, NY
Brunwasser, Marta .... Newburgh, NY
Brunwin, Christopher M. .... Los Angeles, CA
Bruny, Roger H. .... **Charlotte, NC**
Bruozas, Anthony J. .... **Chicago, IL**
Brupbacher, Allyson N. .... Houston, TX
Brupbacher, Emil D., Jr. .... Baton Rouge, LA
Brusavich, Bruce M. .... **Torrance, CA**
Brusca, Richard L. .... **Washington, DC**
Brusca, Sandra E. .... Rockville, MD
Bruscato, Anthony J. .... Monroe, LA
Bruscato, Joseph Peter .... Rockford, IL
Brusch, Cameil Rainford
Charlotte Amalie, St. Thomas, VI
Bruschi, Dale Alan .... **Fort Lauderdale, FL**
Bruscino, David A. .... **Cleveland, OH**
Brusco, F. Robert .... **New Brunswick, NJ**
New York, NY
Brusco, Mario .... New York, NY
Brusco, Nicholas .... New York, NY
Brusco, Paul A. .... New York, NY
Bruse, J. Charles .... **Washington, DC**
Bruser, B. Aven .... **New Orleans, LA**
Bruser, Henry B., III .... **Alexandria, LA**
Brusewitz, Mary Rose .... **New York, NY**
Brusewitz, Wayne R. .... Independence, MO
Brusgul, Justin C. .... Voorheesville, NY
Brush, Barbara J. .... Fort Lauderdale, FL
Brush, Barbara J., P.A. .... Fort Lauderdale, FL
Brush, Bart Anderson .... **Portland, OR**
Brush, Bradford M. .... **Philadelphia, PA**
Brush, C. Bernard .... Pataskala, OH
Brush, David D. .... **Minneapolis, MN**
Brush, Edward J. .... **Baltimore, MD**
Brush, George B. .... West Tisbury, MA
Brush, Hunter B. .... Tyler, TX
Brush, Jason D. .... Waltham, MA
Brush, Joseph M., II .... Little York, NJ
Brush, Kimberly Swoyer .... Lakeland, FL
Brush, Kirk .... **Fort Collins, CO**
Brush, Leon H. .... San Ysidro, CA
Brush, Leslie Sands .... Wayne, PA
Brush, Mason H. .... Los Angeles, CA
Brush, Michael A. .... Venice, CA
Brush, Murray P., III .... Oakland, CA
Brush, Peter N.
Department of State, GV
Brush, Robert M. .... **Lakeland, FL**
Brush, Roger A. .... Huntingdon Valley, PA
Brush and Sacks .... Venice, CA
Brush, Thomas B. .... Cincinnati, OH
Brush, Thomas H. .... Charleston, SC
Brush, Thomas H. .... **Madison, WI**
Brush, Thomas H., P.A. .... Charleston, SC
Brush, Victoria S. .... **San Diego, CA**
Brushwood, David B. .... Gainesville, FL
Brushwood, E. Thomas .... **Panama City, FL**
Tallahassee, FL
Brushwood and Gruver, P.A.
Fort Walton Beach, FL
Panama City, FL
Tallahassee, FL
Thomasville, GA
Brusic, Joseph A. .... Port Orchard, WA
Brusiloff, Paul D. .... **New York, NY**
Brusilow, David E. .... **Dallas, TX**
Brusini, Stephen M. .... **Providence, RI**
Brusk & Brusk .... **Columbus, OH**
Reynoldsburg, OH
Brusk, Norman .... **Reynoldsburg, OH**
Brusk, Susan Pam .... **Reynoldsburg, OH**
Bruskin, Robert M. .... **Washington, DC**
Bruskin, Samuel B., (P.C.) .... **Boston, MA**
Brusky, Andrew P. .... **Milwaukee, WI**
Brusky, George J. .... **Miami, FL**
Brusky, Peter N. .... **Milwaukee, WI**
Brusky & Sjostrom SC .... **Milwaukee, WI**
Brusnahan, Kreig J. .... Avon Lake, OH
Brusniak Clement Harrison & McCool, P.C.
Austin, TX
Dallas, TX
El Paso, TX
Houston, TX
San Antonio, TX
Brusniak, John, Jr. .... **Dallas, TX**
Bruso, Daniel E. .... **Springfield, MA**
Bruso, Peter L. .... Pleasantville, NJ
Bruso, William F., Jr. .... Albany, NY
Brusoski, Donna J.
Equal Employment Opportunity Commission,
Office of the General Counsel, GV
Bruss, Elroy A. .... Germantown, WI
Bruss, Howard G. .... **Toledo, OH**
Bruss, Robert J. .... Burlingame, CA
Brussack, Robert D. .... Athens, GA
Brusseau, Phillip J. .... **Los Angeles, CA**
Brussel, Gabrielle S. .... New York, NY
Brussel, Leo B. .... Beverly Hills, CA
Brusslan, Dan .... **Chicago, IL**
Brusslan, James D. .... Chicago, IL
Brusso, Charles N. .... Chicago, IL
Brusso, Charles T., Jr. .... **Providence, RI**
Brusstar, John W. .... Detroit, MI
Brusstar, Thomas A. .... **Chicago, IL**
Brust, Barry A. .... **Los Angeles, CA**
Brust, Clayton P. .... **Reno, NV**
Brust, Douglas .... **San Diego, CA**
Brust, Jennifer A. .... **Arlington, VA**
Brust, Jennifer M. .... Department of Commerce,
Patent and Trademark Office, GV
Brust, Kim E. .... **Fargo, ND**
Brust, Michael E. .... **Marshfield, MA**
Brust, Steven E. .... **Jacksonville, FL**
Brustad, George H. .... Lake Oswego, OR
Brustad, Orin D. .... **Detroit, MI**
Brustein, Abraham E. .... **Park Ridge, IL**
Brustein, Carole N. .... Montgomery, AL
Brustein, David S. .... Honolulu, HI
Brustein & Manasevit .... **Washington, DC**
Brustein, Michael L. .... **Washington, DC**
Brustein, Mitchell R. .... **Philadelphia, PA**
Brustein-Kampel, Lynn J. .... New City, NY
Brustin, Arnold B. .... Los Angeles, CA
Brustin, Gary C. .... **San Jose, CA**
Brustin, Gary C. .... **Santa Rosa, CA**
Brustin, Marvin A. .... Chicago, IL
Brustin, Marvin A., Ltd. .... Chicago, IL
Brustin, Nick .... **New York, NY**
Brustkern, Daniel J. .... **Austin, TX**
Brustman, Frederick Henry .... Newton, MA
Brustman, James .... Anaheim, CA
Brustman, Stacie .... **Toms River, NJ**
Brustofski, Paul A. .... **Durham, NC**
Brustowicz, Celeste .... **New Orleans, LA**
Brusven, Arland D. .... Minneapolis, MN
Bruther, Grace .... **Atlantic City, NJ**
Brutinel & Jones .... Prescott, AZ
Brutinel, Robert M. .... Prescott, AZ
Brutkiewicz, Donald E. .... Mobile, AL
Brutkiewicz, Donald E., Jr. .... Mobile, AL
Brutkiewicz, John Clement .... Mobile, AL
Brutlag, Hartmann & Okoneski, P.A.
Minneapolis, MN
Brutlag, Michael L. .... **Minneapolis, MN**
Brutlag, Paul .... **Elbow Lake, MN**
Brutman, Laura C. .... **Washington, DC**
Brutocao, Desiree .... **Los Angeles, CA**
Brutocao, Scott A. .... **Los Angeles, CA**
Brutocao, Terrence J. .... West Covina, CA
Brutocao, William J. .... **Pasadena, CA**
Brutoco, Roberto G., (P.C.) .... Irvine, CA
Bruton, Burt .... **Miami, FL**
Bruton, Charles R. .... **Philadelphia, PA**
Bruton, Daniel C. .... **Winston-Salem, NC**
Bruton, David P. .... **Philadelphia, PA**
Bruton, Elizabeth A. .... **Pittsburgh, PA**
Bruton, Francis X., III .... **Dover, NH**
Bruton, Frayda L. .... **Sacramento, CA**
Bruton, James A., III .... **Washington, DC**
Bruton, Jefferson H. .... Hendersonville, NC
Bruton, Jennifer J. .... Washington, DC
Bruton, John C., Jr. .... **Columbia, SC**
Bruton, Karen K. .... Atlanta, GA
Bruton, Linda M. .... **Detroit, MI**
Bruton, Michael G. .... **Chicago, IL**
Bruton, O. Grant .... **Louisville, KY**
Bruton, Roger N. .... Flint, MI
Brutsch, Sheri Gonda .... Philadelphia, PA
Brutscher, Brutscher & Foley
Kennett Square, PA
Brutscher, George A. .... **Kennett Square, PA**
Brutten, Alan .... Brooklyn, NY
Brutten, Caren S. .... New York, NY
Bruttomesso, Raymond I. .... Atlanta, GA
Bruttomesso, Raymond I., Jr.
Lexington, MA
Brutts, Deanne M. .... York, PA
Brutus, Phillip J. .... Miami, FL
Brutz, James M. .... **Warren, OH**
Brutz, Michael James .... Melbourne, FL
Brutzkus, Mark D. .... Encino, CA
Bruu, Christen Culligan
Department Of Veterans Affairs,
Board of Veterans Appeals, GV
Bruun, Lance K. .... **Corpus Christi, TX**
Bruun, Lance K. .... **Kingsville, TX**
Portland, TX
Rockport, TX
Bruyere, Michael P. .... **Atlanta, GA**
Bruyere, William R. .... Houston, TX
Bruyn, Wayne D. .... Southampton, NY
Bruyneel, Laura G. .... San Francisco, CA
Bruyneel, Thomas E. .... **Riverside, CA**
Bruynes, Jan-Paul "JP" .... **New York, NY**
Bruyninckx, F. J., III .... Monroe, LA
Bruza, Dean R. .... Plymouth, MI
Bruzas, Diane M. .... Chicago, IL
Bruzga, Charles E. .... New York, NY
Bruzga, Jill M. .... New York, NY
Bruzga, Paul W. .... Manchester, NH
Bruzonsky, Steven J. .... Mesa, AZ
Bruzzano, Melissa A. .... **Oakland, CA**
Bruzzese, Frank J. .... Steubenville, OH
Bruzzese, James J. .... Houston, TX
Bruzzese, Joseph J., Jr. .... Steubenville, OH
Bruzzese, Joseph J., Sr. .... Steubenville, OH
Bruzzese, M. Lynne .... Saipan, TT
Bruzzese, Michael J. .... **Pittsburgh, PA**
Bruzzese, Thomas M. .... Warwick, RI
Bruzzi, Robert S. .... Providence, RI
Bruzzichesi, Gina M. .... **Princeton, NJ**
Bruzzone, Kathryn A. .... Lafayette, CA
Bruzzone, Lauren C. .... Thornwood, NY
Bruzzone, Leland J. .... San Leandro, CA
Bruzzone, Richard A. .... **Oakland, CA**
Bry, Douglas Louis .... Denver, CO
Brya, Lara M. .... **Irvine, CA**
Brya, Larry F. .... Lansing, MI
Bryan, A. Lorenzo .... **New York, NY**
Bryan, Albert V., Jr. .... Alexandria, VA
Bryan, Amee B. .... Tampa, FL
Bryan, Anna M. .... **Philadelphia, PA**
Bryan, Arthur E., Jr. .... **Chicago, IL**
Bryan & Atkins .... Bozeman, MT
Bryan, Bahnmuller, Goldman and McElveen, L.L.P. .... **Sumter, SC**
Bryan, Barbara Block .... **Long Grove, IL**
Bryan, Barry R. .... **New York, NY**
Bryan, Barry R. .... Lufkin, TX
Bryan, Bates W. .... Chattanooga, TN
Bryan, Bates W., Jr. .... Chattanooga, TN
Bryan, Benjamin L., Jr. .... Fort Pierce, FL
Bryan, Bernard H. .... Albany, NY
Bryan, Boyd A. .... **Lafayette, LA**
Bryan, Bradric T. .... Cleveland, OH
Bryan, Brice E. .... Westlake Village, CA
Bryan, Bruce R. .... Syracuse, NY
Bryan and Bryan .... Muncie, IN
Bryan & Bryan .... Cranesville, PA
North East, PA
Bryan, C. Clark .... Elmhurst, IL
Bryan, C. Gregory .... **Augusta, GA**
Bryan, Carl D. .... Sulphur Springs, TX
Bryan, Carl F., II .... Nevada City, CA
Bryan, Carson Nicholas .... Dallas, WV
Bryan Cave LLP .... **Phoenix, AZ**
Irvine, CA
Los Angeles, CA
Santa Monica, CA
Washington, DC
Overland Park, KS
Jefferson City, MO
Kansas City, MO
St. Louis, MO
New York, NY
Bryan, Charles E. .... **Washington, DC**
Bryan, Cheryle Thompson .... **Ashburn, GA**
Bryan, Christian E. .... Omaha, NE
Bryan, Christina A. .... **Houston, TX**
Bryan, Clarice A.
Charlotte Amalie, St. Thomas, VI
Bryan & Coleman .... Winchester, VA
Bryan, Connie M. .... **Oklahoma City, OK**
Bryan, Daniel E. .... Geneva, NE
Bryan, Darrell L. .... **Lexington, NE**
Bryan, David A. .... **Toledo, OH**
Bryan, David C. .... **Easton, MD**
Bryan, David C. .... **New York, NY**
Bryan, David C., Jr. .... West Columbia, SC
Bryan, David M. .... Wichita, KS
Bryan, David McLane .... Overland Park, KS
Bryan, David Newman .... **Kinston, NC**
Bryan, David W. .... Stillwater, OK
Bryan, Douglas L. .... Marksville, LA
Bryan, Douglas L. .... **New York, NY**
Bryan, E. Blay .... Richmond, VA
Bryan, Edward G. .... Painesville, OH
Bryan, F. Murray .... Harrisburg, PA
Bryan, F. C. .... Mount Sterling, KY
Bryan & Flynn-O'Brien .... Albuquerque, NM
Bryan & Fogle .... Mount Sterling, KY
Bryan, Frank J. .... **Lake City, SC**
Surfside Beach, SC
Bryan, Frank Wingfield, Jr. .... Austin, TX
Bryan, Garry W. .... **Clinton, IL**
Bryan, Geoffrey L. .... **Los Angeles, CA**
Bryan, George G. .... **Urbana, IL**
Bryan, George R. "Pat", III
Albuquerque, NM
Bryan, George W. .... Atlanta, GA
Bryan, González Vargas y González Baz, P.C.
Chicago, IL
Bryan, González Vargas y González Baz., Inc. .... **New York, NY**
Bryan, González Vargas y González Baz, Inc.
New York, NY
Bryan, Greyson Lee .... **Los Angeles, CA**
Bryan, Grover L. .... Liberal, KS
Bryan & Haar .... **Surfside Beach, SC**
Bryan, Henry W. .... Greenville, DE
Bryan, Hinshaw & Barnet, A Professional Corporation .... **San Francisco, CA**
Walnut Creek, CA
Bryan, Howard F., III .... Montgomery, AL
Bryan, Howard F., IV .... Lafayette, AL
Bryan, J. Anthony .... Van Nuys, CA
Bryan, J. Chase .... **Jackson, MS**
Bryan, J. Shepard, Jr. .... **Jacksonville, FL**
Bryan, J. Stockton, (P.A.) .... Stuart, FL
Bryan, James E. .... Annandale, VA
Bryan, James E., Jr. .... Laurens, SC
Bryan, James N., Jr. .... **Nashville, TN**
Bryan, James N., Jr., P.C. .... **Nashville, TN**
Bryan, James S. .... **Los Angeles, CA**
Bryan, James S. .... Cranesville, PA
North East, PA
Bryan, James T., III .... Chapel Hill, NC
Bryan, James W. .... **Greensboro, NC**
Bryan, Jas. C. .... Columbia, SC
Bryan, Jay B. .... **Atlanta, GA**
Bryan, Jeffrey L. .... **San Antonio, TX**
Bryan, Jennie Boldish .... Grand Rapids, MI
Bryan, Jennifer .... Burnsville, MN
Bryan, Jennifer H.
Department of Commerce,
Office of the Inspector General, GV
Bryan, Jerry E. .... Oklahoma City, OK
Bryan, Jerry M. .... **Youngstown, OH**
Bryan, Jill T. .... Turnersville, NJ
Bryan, Jim B. .... Lubbock, TX
Bryan, Joan Marie .... De Soto, MO
Bryan, Joe Dale .... Lubbock, TX
Bryan, Joel R., Jr. .... Westlake Village, CA
Bryan, John A. .... Salem, OR
Bryan, John C. .... Washington C. H., OH
Bryan, John Douglas .... Walterboro, SC
Bryan, John G. .... San Diego, CA
Bryan, John J. (Jim) .... Topeka, KS
Bryan, John K. .... **Pittsburgh, PA**
Bryan, John L., Jr.
Palm Beach Gardens, FL
Bryan, John M. .... Alexandria, VA
Bryan, John N., Jr. .... Birmingham, AL
Bryan, John T. .... Denver, CO
Bryan, John T., Jr. .... Anniston, AL
Bryan, Johnathan W. .... **Sumter, SC**
Bryan, Jonathan M. .... **Columbus, OH**
Bryan, Joseph R. .... Youngstown, OH
Bryan, Joseph W. .... **Atlanta, GA**
Bryan, Judkins M. .... **Montgomery, AL**
Bryan, Julie A. .... **Salt Lake City, UT**
Bryan & Jupiter, A Prof. Law Corp.
New Orleans, LA
Bryan, Karen LaMoreaux .... Tuscaloosa, AL
Bryan, Karen Smith .... **Los Angeles, CA**
Bryan, Kathleen A. .... Scottsdale, AZ
Bryan, Kelly E. .... San Francisco, CA
Bryan, Kelly N. .... Muncie, IN
Bryan, Kelly R. .... **Philadelphia, PA**
Bryan, Kennon W. .... **Fairfax, VA**
Bryan, Kerry H. .... Treasury Department,
Internal Revenue Service, GV
Bryan, Kimberly W. .... **Raleigh, NC**
Bryan, Laura A. .... Woodside, CA
Bryan Law Office .... Angola, IN
Bryan, Lem C. .... Fort Smith, AR
Bryan, Leslie J. .... **Atlanta, GA**
Bryan, Levitin & Bab, LLP
New York, NY
Bryan, Linda Logan .... **St. Augustine, FL**
Bryan, Lon D. .... Muncie, IN
Bryan, Lonnie .... Minneapolis, MN
Bryan, Lykins & Hejtmanek, P.A.
Topeka, KS
Bryan, MacDonald .... **Salinas, CA**
Bryan, Marcy L. .... **Jackson, MS**
Bryan, Marguerite Patrick .... **Atlanta, GA**
Bryan, Mario E.
Charlotte Amalie, St. Thomas, VI
Bryan, Mark A. .... Bozeman, MT
Bryan, Mark C. .... **Jacksonville, FL**
Bryan, Mary Lowndes .... Columbia, SC
Bryan, Maureen O. .... **St. Louis, MO**
Bryan, Melissa K. .... **Tacoma, WA**
Bryan, Michael B. .... Arab, AL
Bryan, Michael D. .... St. Louis, MO
Bryan, Michael L. .... Winchester, VA
Bryan, Michelle V. .... Arlington, VA
Bryan, Mikel D. .... Santa Rosa, CA
Bryan, Mitchell .... **Chicago, IL**
Bryan, Monica D. .... Louisville, KY
Bryan, Nancy Benfield .... Richmond, VA
Bryan, Nat .... **Birmingham, AL**
Bryan, Nelson, Randolph and Weathers, P.A.
Columbia, MS
Hattiesburg, MS
Jackson, MS
Bryan, Nelson, Schroeder, Castigliola & Banahan .... **Biloxi, MS**
Gulfport, MS
Jackson, MS
Lucedale, MS
Pascagoula, MS
Bryan, Norwood E., Jr. .... Fayetteville, NC
Bryan, Patricia L. .... Chapel Hill, NC
Bryan, Patricia M. .... United States Senate,
Office of Senate Legal Counsel, GV
Bryan, Patrick M. .... Juno Beach, FL
Bryan, Paul F. .... Orlando, FL
Bryan, Paul S. .... Lake City, FL
Bryan, Penelope Eileen .... Denver, CO
Bryan, Penelope T. .... **St. Petersburg, FL**
Bryan, Phyllis J. .... **Ventura, CA**
Bryan, R. David .... Tifton, GA
Bryan, R. Timothy .... **Washington, DC**
Bryan, Randy C .... **Winter Park, FL**
Bryan, Raymond Charles .... Anniston, AL
Bryan, Rebecca Shows .... Montgomery, AL
Bryan, Reed A. .... **Fort Lauderdale, FL**
Bryan, Richard C. .... **Westmont, NJ**
Bryan, Richard H. .... Carson City, NV
Bryan, Richard J. .... Lansing, MI
Bryan, Richard M. .... **San Francisco, CA**
Bryan, Richard W. .... **Washington, DC**
Baltimore, MD
Rockville, MD
Vienna, VA
Bryan, Rick .... **New York, NY**
Bryan, Robert A. .... San Francisco, CA

Bryan, Robert A., Jr. ....Raleigh, NC
Bryan, Robert C. ....Dunn, NC
Bryan, Robert J. ....Tacoma, WA
Bryan, Robert J., (P.A.) ....Miami, FL
Bryan, Robert M. ....Charlotte, NC
Bryan, Robert N. ....Honesdale, PA
Bryan, Robert O. ....Jasper, AL
Bryan, Robert P., III ....Charlotte, NC
Bryan, Robert R. ....San Francisco, CA
Bryan, Robert S. ....Seattle, WA
Bryan & Robinson, Inc. ....Oklahoma City, OK
Bryan, Roland T. ....Oxford, MD
Bryan, Rosemarie Luise ....Chattanooga, TN
Bryan, Russ C. ....McLean, VA
Bryan, Ruth A. ....Chicago, IL
Bryan, Sandra G.
Equal Employment Opportunity Commission, Office of Federal Operations, GV
Bryan, Sean A. ....Fort Worth, TX
Bryan, Sharon A. ....Torrance, CA
Bryan, Stanley G. ....Chesapeake, VA
Bryan, Steven J. ....Newfoundland, NJ
Bryan, T. James ....New York, NY
Bryan, Thomas A. ....Hicksville, NY
Bryan, Thomas H. ....Evansville, IN
Bryan, Thomas J., Jr. ....San Diego, CA
Bryan, Thomas L. ....Mahwah, NJ
Bryan, Tim G. ....Casselton, ND
Bryan, Tom E. ....Plano, TX
Bryan, Tommy E. ....Montgomery, AL
Bryan, Travis B., III ....Bryan, TX
Bryan, Trevor G. ....New Orleans, LA
Bryan, Vincent E., III ....Kent, WA
Bryan, Vincent E. III, III., P.S. ....Kent, WA
Bryan, Virginia A. ....Billings, MT
Bryan, W. Brad ....Houston, TX
Bryan, W. Burton ....Canfield, OH
Bryan, W. Gilbert ....Hobbs, NM
Bryan, W. Wheeler ....Atlanta, GA
Bryan, Wayne P. ....Grand Rapids, MI
Bryan, Wendell Hobdy, II ....Amory, MS
Bryan, William A. ....Surfside Beach, SC
Bryan, William B. ....Angola, IN
Bryan, William Bradley ....Houston, TX
Bryan, William J. ....Homewood, IL
Bryan, William L., Jr. ....Foothill Ranch, CA
Bryan-Caron, M. Courtney ....Boston, MA
Bryans & Bryans ....Denver, CO
Bryans, David M. ....Englewood, CO
Westminster, CO
Bryans, Henry S. ....Philadelphia, PA
Bryans, Joseph W. ....El Cajon, CA
Bryans, Richard W. ....Denver, CO
Bryans, Richard W., Jr. ....Denver, CO
Bryant, A. Dale ....Jackson, KY
Bryant, Aaron Christopher
United States Senate, Office of Senate Legal Counsel, GV
Bryant, Alan O. ....Louisville, KY
Bryant, Alfred S. ....Beaufort, NC
Emerald Isle, NC
Bryant, Alton E., Jr. ....Richmond, VA
Bryant, Amy Davidson ....McLean, VA
Bryant, Andrea Pair ....Austin, TX
Bryant, Andrew J. ....Baraboo, WI
Bryant, Angela Perella ....Tampa, FL
Bryant, Anita
Charlotte Amalie, St. Thomas, VI
Bryant, Ann Lake ....Washington, DC
Bryant, Arthur H. ....Washington, DC
Bryant & Associates, P.C. ....Millheim, PA
Bryant, B. Seth ....New York, NY
Bryant, Barbara S. ....Oakland, CA
Bryant, Barnes & Simpson, P.C.
Christiansted, St. Croix, VI
Cruz Bay, St. John, VI
Charlotte Amalie, St. Thomas, VI
Bryant, Barry A. ....Texarkana, AR
Bryant, Beth M. ....Wilmington, NC
Bryant, Beverly ....Hopkins, MN
Bryant, Bill L., Jr. ....Tallahassee, FL
Bryant, Bradley ....Naples, FL
Bryant, Brandon S. ....New York, NY
Bryant, Brenda G. ....Metropolis, IL
Bryant, Brenda J. ....New Bern, NC
Bryant, Brenton Doyle ....Fayetteville, AR
Bryant, Brian D. ....Chicago, IL
Bryant, Britain H.
Christiansted, St. Croix, VI
Bryant, Bruce C. ....Oak Ridge, TN
Bryant, Bruce K. ....Brooklyn, NY
Bryant, B. T. ....Houston, TX
Bryant, Bunyan
Agency for International Development, Office of the General Counsel, GV
Bryant, Calvin B. ....High Point, NC
Bryant, Carina E. ....Lake Forest, IL
Bryant, Carl A. ....Albany, GA
Bryant, Carl P. ....St. Marys, WV
Bryant, Carleton E., IV ....Knoxville, TN
Bryant, Cecilia ....Jacksonville, FL
Bryant, Cecilia, P.A. ....Jacksonville, FL
Bryant, Charles A. ....Smyrna, GA
Bryant, Charles Daniel ....Brundidge, AL
Bryant, Charles F., II ....Federal Way, WA
Bryant, Cheryl A. ....Helena, MT
Bryant, Chrysti Lynn ....Fort Worth, TX
Bryant, Clarence ....Chicago, IL
Bryant, Clark, Dukes, Blakeslee, Ramsay & Hammond, P.L.L.C. ....Gulfport, MS
Hattiesburg, MS
Bryant, Clohan, Eller, Maines & Baruh, LLP
Palo Alto, CA
San Jose, CA
Bryant, Corbet F., Jr. ....Dallas, TX
Bryant, Craig ....Tulsa, OK
Bryant, Craig I. ....Goldsboro, NC
Bryant, Craig I., P.A. ....Goldsboro, NC
Bryant, Cynthia ....Sacramento, CA
Bryant, D. Mitchell ....Cleveland, TN
Bryant, Dan T. ....McMinnville, TN
Bryant, Daniel A. ....Ruidoso, NM
Bryant, Daniel A., P.A. ....Ruidoso, NM
Bryant, Daniel C. ....Boston, MA
Bryant, Daniel James
House of Representatives, Committee Legal Personnel, GV
Bryant, Daniel M., Jr. ....Mankato, MN
Bryant, Darrel W. ....Council Grove, KS
Bryant, David ....Dallas, TX
Bryant, David E. ....Naples, FL
Bryant, David J. ....Chicago, IL
Bryant, David L. ....Tulsa, OK
Bryant, Davis & Cowden, P.C.
Atlanta, GA
Bryant, Dawn S. ....Raleigh, NC
Bryant, Deborah A. ....Brooklyn, NY
Bryant, Deborah L. ....Phoenix, AZ
Bryant, Deborah Smith ....Houston, TX
Bryant, Dennis L. ....Washington, DC
Bryant, D. Mitchell ....Athens, TN
Bryant, Donald C., Jr. ....Redwood City, CA
Bryant, Donald L., Jr. ....St. Louis, MO
Bryant, Donald R. ....Dover, NH
Bryant, Doris ....Northbrook, IL
Bryant, Douglas K. ....Laramie, WY
Bryant, Dwane H. ....Mauldin, SC
Bryant, Edward C., Jr. ....Springfield, MA
Bryant, Edward H., Jr. ....Petersburg, VA
Bryant, Edward R., Jr. ....Naples, FL
Bryant, Edward R., Jr., P.A. ....Naples, FL
Bryant, Eileen E. ....Troy, NY
Bryant, Elizabeth A. ....Denver, CO
Bryant, Elizabeth Beach
Minneapolis, MN
Bryant, Ellen M. ....Greenbelt, MD
Bryant, Emerson & Fitch ....Redmond, OR
Bryant, Eric A. ....Phoenix, AZ
Bryant, Eric J. ....Augusta, ME
Bryant, Eric L. ....Baltimore, MD
Bryant, Everett Clay ....Athens, GA
Bryant, Fanning and Shuler
Lexington, SC
Orangeburg, SC
Bryant, Farris ....Tallahassee, FL
Bryant, Frank L. ....Charlotte, NC
Bryant, Frederick L. ....Baltimore, MD
Bryant, Frederick M. ....Tallahassee, FL
Bryant, Frederick W. ....Kansas City, MO
Bryant, G. David ....Oklahoma City, OK
Bryant, G. Watson, Jr. ....Atlanta, GA
Bryant, Garry B. ....Tucson, AZ
Bryant, Gary ....Sarasota, FL
Bryant, Gary A. ....Oklahoma City, OK
Bryant, Gary A. ....Norfolk, VA
Bryant, Genevieve Frazier ....Atlanta, GA
Bryant, Geo. W., Jr. ....Richmond, VA
Bryant, George H. ....Hartwell, GA
Bryant, George M. ....New York, NY
Bryant, Gregory E. ....Little Rock, AR
Bryant, H. Paul ....Concord, CA
Bryant, Hall B., III ....Huntsville, AL
Bryant, Harry S. ....Orangeburg, SC
Bryant, Harvey L., III ....Norfolk, VA
Bryant, Herman V. ....Cincinnati, OH
Bryant, Herschel ....Kansas City, MO
Bryant and Higby, Chartered
Panama City, FL
Bryant, Hubert Hale ....Tulsa, OK
Bryant, J. Carroll ....Aiken, SC
Bryant, J. Carroll, P.A. ....Aiken, SC
Bryant, J. Phillip ....St. Louis, MO
Bryant, J. Winston ....Little Rock, AR
Malvern, AR
Bryant, Jack H. ....Abilene, TX
Bryant, Jackson C. ....Newport Beach, CA
Bryant, Jacqueline Shim ....Chicago, IL
Bryant, James D. ....Tulsa, OK
Bryant, James David ....Bowling Green, KY
Bryant, James L. ....Boston, MA
Bryant, James M., II ....Little Rock, AR
Bryant, James Milton ....Schoharie, NY
Bryant, James N. ....Millheim, PA
State College, PA
Bryant, James R., Jr. ....Western Springs, IL
Bryant, James Sears ....Washington, DC
Oklahoma City, OK
Bryant, J. D. ....Wilmington, OH
Bryant, Jeanne B. ....Nashville, TN
Bryant, Jeffrey M. ....San Francisco, CA
Bryant, Jennifer Adelle ....Houston, TX
Bryant, Jennifer Ann ....Seattle, WA
Bryant, Jerald D. ....Okeechobee, FL
Bryant, Jerry M. ....Middletown, OH
Bryant, Joel R. ....San Diego, CA
Bryant, John Addison ....Arkadelphia, AR
Bryant, John C., Jr. ....Kaneohe, HI
Bryant, John D. ....Hendersonville, NC
Bryant, John M., Jr. ....Nashville, TN
Bryant, John N. ....Jacksonville, FL
Bryant, John S. ....Orangeburg, SC
Bryant, John S. ....Nashville, TN
Bryant, John W. ....Chatham, MA
Bryant, John W. ....Troy, MI
Bryant, John W. ....Lansdale, PA
Bryant, John W. ....Dallas, TX
Bryant, John Walter ....Raleigh, NC
Bryant, Joseph R. ....Tampa, FL
Bryant, Josephine ....Macon, GA
Bryant, Judith E. ....Austin, TX
Bryant, Julian A., Jr. ....Virginia Beach, VA
Bryant, Karen ....Houston, TX
Bryant, Karyn Crigler ....Nashville, TN
Bryant, Katherine L. ....Denver, CO
Bryant & Kautz, P.S.C. ....Paducah, KY
Bryant, Kenneth A. ....Santa Ana, CA
Bryant, Kenneth C., (A Professional Corporation) ....San Jose, CA
Bryant, Kenneth M. ....Nashville, TN
Bryant, Kenneth W. ....Houston, TX
Bryant, Kevin C. ....Rochester, NY
Bryant, L. Edward, Jr. ....Chicago, IL
Bryant, Larry J. ....Des Moines, IA
Bryant, Larry S. ....Atlanta, GA
Bryant Law Firm ....Tulsa, OK
Bryant Law Offices ....Wilmington, OH
Bryant, Lawrence H. ....Virginia Beach, VA
Bryant, Lisa Koch ....Louisville, KY
Bryant, Lon Grayston ....Atlanta, GA
Bryant, Lon N. ....Wilsonville, OR
Bryant, Lovlien & Jarvis, P.C. ....Bend, OR
Bryant, Loy E. ....Spartanburg, SC
Bryant, M. Christopher ....Tallahassee, FL
Bryant, Malcolm F., Jr. ....Vidalia, GA
Bryant, Marc R. ....Stamford, CT
Bryant, Margaret R. ....White Plains, NY
Bryant, Marianne ....Cherry Hill, NJ
Bryant, Marilynne Regan ....Walpole, MA
Bryant, Mark ....Kansas City, MO
Bryant, Mark L. ....Englewood, CO
Bryant, Mark P. ....Paducah, KY
Bryant, Mary C. ....Chicago, IL
Bryant, Mary L. ....Austin, TX
Bryant, Matthew H. ....Winston-Salem, NC
Bryant, Matthew N. ....Altadena, CA
Bryant, Meredith L. ....Newark, NJ
Bryant, Michael A. ....Fort Lauderdale, FL
Bryant, Michael A. ....Eden Valley, MN
Bryant, Michael D. ....Bloomfield Hills, MI
Bryant, Michael E. ....Orange, CA
Bryant, Michael E. ....Vienna, VA
Bryant, Michael Kevin ....Dallas, TX
Bryant, Michael P. ....Newport Beach, CA
Bryant, Michel J. ....Sacramento, CA
Bryant, Michele S. ....Evansville, IN
Bryant, Miller and Olive, P.A.
Tallahassee, FL
Tampa, FL
Atlanta, GA
Bryant, N. Randolph ....Winchester, VA
Bryant, Nancy L. ....Stockton, CA
Bryant, Neil R. ....Bend, OR
Bryant, Nichole ....Tulsa, OK
Bryant, Nicole K. ....Cuyahoga Falls, OH
Bryant, Noel F. ....Pine Bluff, AR
Bryant, Noel F., P.A. ....Pine Bluff, AR
Bryant, O'Dell & Basso, L.L.P.
Syracuse, NY
Bryant, Olen C., Jr. ....Brookhaven, MS
Bryant, Olen C., Jr. ....Hazlehurst, MS
Bryant, Orene ....Flint, MI
Bryant, Ottie Andre ....Chicago, IL
Bryant, Patricia S. ....Elberton, GA
Bryant, Patrick S. ....Charlotte, NC
Bryant, Patrick S. ....Houston, TX
Bryant, Patterson, Covington & Idol, P.A.
Durham, NC
Bryant, Paul M., Jr.
Rancho Cucamonga, CA
Bryant, Paula Perkins ....St. Louis, MO
Bryant, Peggy Lynn ....Columbus, OH
Bryant, Philip E. ....Houston, TX
Bryant, Philip E., P.C. ....Houston, TX
Bryant, Philip P. ....Gladwin, MI
Bryant, Phillip D. ....Oxford, MS
Bryant, Quillian L., Jr. ....Louisville, GA
Bryant, R. Michael, Jr. ....Houston, TX
Bryant, Randall D. ....Farmington Hills, MI
Bryant, Randolph W. ....Houston, TX
Bryant, Randy A. ....Miami, FL
Bryant, Rebecca ....Boston, MA
Bryant, Rebecca A. ....Owings Mills, MD
Bryant, Rebecca A., P.A. ....Owings Mills, MD
Bryant, Richard N. ....South Portland, ME
Bryant, Richard T. ....Kansas City, MO
Bryant, Richard T., & Associates, P.C.
Overland Park, KS
Kansas City, MO
Bryant, Robert A. ....Southfield, MI
Bryant, Robert A. ....Carrollton, MO
Bryant, Robert L. ....Williamsburg, VA
Bryant, Robert M. ....Department of Justice, Federal Bureau of Investigation, GV
Bryant, Robert P. ....Costa Mesa, CA
Bryant, Robert P. ....Atlanta, GA
Bryant, Robert W., Jr. ....Selma, NC
Bryant, Robinzina ....Detroit, MI
Bryant, Robt. E. ....Chicago, IL
Bryant, Ronald L. ....Redmond, OR
Bryant, Rosa Jean ....Addison, TX
Bryant, Roscoe C., III ....Department of Labor, Office of the Solicitor, GV
Bryant, Roslyn Bell ....Houston, TX
Bryant, Rowlett W. ....Panama City, FL
Bryant, Russell T., Law Offices of
Lawrenceville, GA
Bryant, S. Benjamin ....Charleston, WV
Bryant, Sandy Leviticus ....Indianapolis, IN
Bryant & Sanzone ....Middletown, OH
Bryant, Shannon M. ....Reno, NV
Bryant, Shawn D. ....Washington, DC
Bryant & Stanley ....Beaufort, NC
Emerald Isle, NC
Bryant, Stearns J., Jr. ....New Haven, CT
Bryant, Stephen A. ....Fremont, MI
Bryant, Stephen A. ....Richmond, VA
Bryant, Steve A. ....Houston, TX
Bryant, Steven D. ....Redmond, OR
Bryant, Steven J. ....Waynesville, NC
Bryant, Susan ....Longmont, CO
Bryant, Susan E. ....Farmington, CT
Bryant, Susan E., P.C. ....Farmington, CT
Bryant, Susan J. ....Hempstead, NY
Bryant, Teresa DeLoatch ....Greenville, NC
New Bern, NC
Bryant, Theodore G. ....Seattle, WA
Bryant, Theresa J. ....Portland, ME
Bryant, Thomas B., III ....Orangeburg, SC
Bryant, Thomas F. ....Lima, OH
Bryant, Thomas L.
Corporation for National and Community Service, Office of the General Counsel, GV
Bryant, Thomas V., Jr. ....Bend, OR
Bryant, Timothy J. ....Portland, ME
Bryant, Timothy R. M. ....Chicago, IL
Bryant, Valerie Thomas ....Valdosta, GA
Bryant & Van Nest, LLC ....Denver, CO
Bryant, Victor S., Jr. ....Durham, NC
Bryant, W. Joel ....Houston, TX
Bryant, W. Keith ....Dallas, TX
Bryant, Wanda ....Raleigh, NC
Bryant, Wayne R. ....Cherry Hill, NJ
Bryant, Weyman C. ....Fayetteville, GA
Bryant & White ....St. Marys, WV
Bryant, William B.
United States District Court For The District Of Columbia, GV
Bryant, William C. ....Austin, TX
Bryant, William H. ....Palo Alto, CA
Bryant, William J. ....Birmingham, AL
Bryant, William L. ....Birmingham, AL
Bryant, William R., Jr. ....Kiawah Island, SC
Bryant, Winifred L. ....Lexington, KY
Bryant, Yvette M. ....Baltimore, MD
Bryant, Yvonne N. ....Chicago, IL
Bryant-Fields, Regina L.
San Francisco, CA
Bryant-Kambe, Madeleine ....Newhall, CA
Bryant-Ojeda, Wendy E. ....Ooltewah, TN
Bryan-Toledo, Lina A. ....New York, NY
Bryant-Walker, Tara ....Jackson, MS
Bryar, Marcel A. ....Arlington, VA
Bryce, Crandall & Coleman, P.C.
Knoxville, TN
Bryce, David D. ....Georgetown, TX
Bryce, Douglas D. ....Georgetown, TX
Bryce, Geoffrey A. ....Chicago, IL
Bryce, James D. ....Tuscaloosa, AL
Bryce, James D. ....Decatur, GA
Bryce, James Y. ....Austin, TX
Bryce, Mark R. ....Far Rockaway, NY
Bryce, Mark S. ....Safford, AZ
Bryce, Martin C., Jr. ....Philadelphia, PA
Bryce, Philip J. ....Knoxville, TN
Bryce, Philip R. ....Brooklyn, NY
Bryce, Rita ....Department of Justice, Antitrust Division, GV
Bryce, Robert W. ....Oregon, OH
Toledo, OH
Bryce, Shauna C. ....Newark, NJ
Bryce, Susan M. ....Lancaster, MA
Bryce, Teresa A. ....Charlotte, NC
Bryce & Udall ....Safford, AZ
Bryce, William D. ....Georgetown, TX
Bryceland, Linda A ....Chicago, IL
Brychel, Michael J. ....Chicago, IL
Bryck, Cathryn ....Atherton, CA
Bryde, Gary A. ....Hockessin, DE
Bryde, Gary A., P.A. ....Hockessin, DE
Wilmington, DE
Bryde, Stevem P. ....New York, NY
Bryden, John R. ....Andover, MA
Bryden, Leslie W. ....Sunbury, PA
Brydger, Gordon C. ....Fort Lauderdale, FL
Brydger, Gordon C., P.A.
Fort Lauderdale, FL
Brydges, Earl W., Jr. ....Lewiston, NY
Brydges, James E., Jr. ....Norfolk, VA
Brydges, Janet Blake ....Virginia Beach, VA
Brydges, Jerauld E. ....New York, NY
Brydges, Louis W., Jr. ....Waukegan, IL
Brydges, Louis W., Sr. ....Waukegan, IL
Brydges, Mahan, O'Brien & Frucci, P.C.
Norfolk, VA
Virginia Beach, VA
Brydges, Richard G. ....Virginia Beach, VA
Brydges, Thomas E. ....Buffalo, NY
Brydon, David V. G. ....Jefferson City, MO
Brydon, Deb ....North Liberty, IA
Brydon, John C. ....Erie, PA
Brydon, John H. ....Butler, PA
Brydon, John R. ....San Francisco, CA
Brydon, S. Joseph ....Slippery Rock, PA
Brydon, Swearengen & England, Professional Corporation
Jefferson City, MO
Bryen, Eric R. ....Farmington Hills, MI
Bryen, Eric R., P.C. ....Farmington Hills, MI
Bryenton, Gary L. ....Cleveland, OH
Bryer, Andrea S. ....Chicago, IL
Bryer, Barry A. ....New York, NY
Bryer and David ....New York, NY
Bryer & Freedman ....Chicago, IL
Bryer, Hyman ....Chicago, IL
Bryer, Lanning Gerald ....New York, NY
Bryer, Paul R. ....Arlington Heights, IL
Bryer, Stanley ....New York, NY
Bryer, Terry A. ....North Ridgeville, OH
Bryers, William J. ....Spring House, PA
Brygider, Brandon R. ....Old Westbury, NY
Bryk, Dale S. ....New York, NY
Bryk, John R. ....Bridgeport, CT
Bryk, Kenneth H. P. ....Albany, NY
Bryk, William M. ....Staten Island, NY
Bryks, Helene ....New York, NY
Bryks, Jacqueline E. ....New York, NY
Bryla, Carroll J. ....Fredericksburg, TX
Bryla & Schoessow, A Professional Corporation
Fredericksburg, TX

Brylawski, E. Fulton, (P.C.) Alexandria, VA
Brylawski, Henry H. .... Washington, DC
Brylski, Mark D. ....Jersey City, NJ
Bryman, David N. ....Atlanta, GA
Bryman, Harold ....Woodland Hills, CA
Bryn, Brenda Greenberg ....Miami, FL
Bryn, Mark J. ....Miami, FL
Brynan, Jeffrey ....Beverly Hills, CA
Bryne, James R. ....New Haven, CT
Brynelson, Herrick, Bucaida, Dorschel & Armstrong ....Madison, WI
Brynelson, Julia D. ....Sacramento, CA
Bryner, Alexander O. ....Anchorage, AK
Bryner, Bryce K. ....Price, UT
Bryner, Carrie K. Croft ....Cedar Rapids, IA
Bryner, G. Michael ....New York, NY
Bryner, M. Candice ....Newport Beach, CA
Bryner, William M. ....Winston-Salem, NC
Brynes, Erica L. ....Ithaca, NY
Brynestad, Lorens Q. .....Brooklyn Park, MN
Red Wing, MN
Bryngil, Judith Anne ....New York, NY
Bryniczka, Jacob P. ....Westport, CT
Brynie, Tammy ....Newton, MA
Bry-Nildsen, Martin, Jr. ....Washington, NJ
Brynn, Frederick J. ....Washington, DC
Brynn, Frederick J., P.C. ....Washington, DC
Brynteson, Mark D. ....Chesapeake, VA
Brynteson, Timothy P. ....Denver, CO
Brysh, Paul J. ....Pittsburgh, PA
Bryski, Kathleen K. ....Walnut Creek, CA
Bryson, Alton Dan ....Birmingham, AL
Bryson, Arthur J. ....Lexington, KY
Bryson, Brent H. ....Phoenix, AZ
Bryson, Bruce ....San Rafael, CA
Bryson & Bryson ....Eugene, OR
Bryson, Carl V. ....Lansing, MI
Bryson, Carroll N. ....Centralia, MO
Bryson, Cary B. ....Lafayette, LA
Bryson, Cheryl Blackwell ....Chicago, IL
Bryson, Christiana G. ....Chino, CA
Bryson, Daniel K. ....Raleigh, NC
Bryson, David A. ....Dallas, TX
Bryson, David B. ....Oakland, CA
Bryson, David C. ....Boston, MA
Bryson, Dean F. ....Salem, OR
Bryson, E. Brent ....Las Vegas, NV
Bryson, E. Brent, Ltd. ....Las Vegas, NV
Bryson, E. C., Jr. ....Raleigh, NC
Bryson, Elizabeth A. ....New York, NY
Bryson, Eugene W., III ....Shreveport, LA
Bryson, Eugene W., Jr. ....Shreveport, LA
Bryson, Fred L. ....Pickens, SC
Bryson, Gary A. ....Cincinnati, OH
Bryson, George P., P.C. ....Longmont, CO
Bryson, George Philip ....Longmont, CO
Bryson, Jeffrey L. ....San Jose, CA
Bryson, John A. ....Department of Justice, Environment and Natural Resources Division, GV
Bryson, John C., Jr. ....Chicopee, MA
Bryson, John D. ....High Point, NC
Bryson, John E. ....Rosemead, CA
Bryson, John M., II ....Washington, DC
Bryson, Judy Dyke .....Department of the Army, Office, Chief of Engineers/Headquarters, U.S. Army Corps of Engineers, GV
Bryson, Kevin R. ....Cherry Hill, NJ
Bryson, Kyle A. ....Tucson, AZ
Bryson, Larry A. ....Columbia, MO
Bryson, Larry G. ....London, KY
Bryson, Molly R. ....Washington, DC
Bryson, Nancy S. ....Washington, DC
Bryson, Neil F. ....Middleboro, MA
Bryson, Phillip E. ....Charleston, SC
Bryson, Rance ....Dallas, TX
Bryson, Randall ....Eugene, OR
Bryson, Richard ....Sugar Hill, GA
Bryson, Richard ....Eugene, OR
Bryson, Richard W. ....San Diego, CA
Bryson, Rick N. ....Phoenix, AZ
Bryson, Robert T. ....Orange, CA
Bryson, Rodney S. ....Covington, KY
Bryson, Rodney W. ....Davie, FL
Bryson, Royson L. ....Westmont, NJ
Bryson, Steven L. ....Los Angeles, CA
Bryson, Susan J. ....New Haven, CT
Bryson, Terry W. ....Stillwater, OK
Bryson, Thomas M. ....Jackson, MS
Bryson, Timothy C. ....San Diego, CA
Bryson, W. Hamilton ....Richmond, VA
Bryson, William C. United States Court Of Appeals For The Federal Circuit, GV
Bryson, William H. ....Woodbury, TN
Bryson, William P. ....Anchorage, AK
Bryton, Cindy M. ....Washington, DC
Bryza, Mark L. ....Dallas, TX
Brzeczek, Richard J. ....Chicago, IL
Brzezenski, Lynne A. ....Prospect Heights, IL
Brzezenski, Thomas J. ....McHenry, IL
Brzezinski, Edwin B. ....St. Louis, MO
Brzezinski, Elaine Victoria ....Dallas, TX
Brzezinski, Mark F. ....Washington, DC
Brzezinski, Patricia Hawpetoss ....Oneida, WI
Brzezinski, Robert B. ....Livonia, MI
Brzezinski, Robert E. ....San Antonio, TX
Brzezinski, Robert Edward Eden Prairie, MN
Brzezinski, Stephen R. ....Detroit, MI
Brzezynski, Lora A. ....Washington, DC
Brzon, Jonathan C. ....Leavenworth, KS
Brzostowski, John S. ....Baltimore, MD
Brzovic, Daniel P. ....Fullerton, CA
Brzustowicz, John C. ....McMurray, PA
Brzuszek, Joseph L. ....Monroeville, PA
Brzuziewski, Glenn E. ....Bath, OH

Brzytwa, E. John ....Cleveland, OH
Brzytwa, James J. ....Riverside, CA
Bschorr, Paul J. ....New York, NY
Bsharah, Perry A. ....Minneapolis, MN
B'Smith, John D. ....Boston, MA
Bu, John Jongbae ....New York, NY
Bua, Carmine J. ....San Diego, CA
Bua, Nicholas J. ....Chicago, IL
Bua, Ronald J. ....Pittsburgh, PA
Buafo, Althea Lorriane ....Macon, GA
Buan, Brenda A. ....Boston, MA
Buatt, Louis E. ....Baton Rouge, LA
Buatti, Maryanne ....Garden City, NY
Bub, David P. ....St. Louis, MO
Bub, Laura Gerdes ....St. Louis, MO
Bub, Leo J. ....St. Louis, MO
Bub, Michael E. ....St. Louis, MO
Bub, Ronald L. ....Fairfax, VA
Buba, Barbara J. ....Philadelphia, PA
Buba, Vicki L. ....Louisville, KY
Bubak, Mark W. ....Omaha, NE
Buba-Kruer, Lise ....Louisville, KY
Bubalo, Gregory J. ....Louisville, KY
Buban, Theodore A. ....Las Vegas, NV
Bubany, Charles P. ....Lubbock, TX
Bubar, Katherine W. ....Bangor, ME
Bubb, Brian D. ....Los Angeles, CA
Bubb, Christopher G. ....Trenton, NJ
Bubb, Frank W., III ....Irving, TX
Bubb, Gary A. ....Jacksonville, FL
Bubb, Gary A. P.A. ....Jacksonville, FL
Bubb, Gary C. ....Boston, MA
Bubb, Michael S. ....Morristown, NJ
Bubb, Michael S. ....New York, NY
Bubba, Joseph A. ....Allentown, PA
Bubeck, Thomas F. ....New York, NY
Bubel, Henry P. ....New York, NY
Bubel, Neil F. ....Rochester, NY
Buben, John R., Jr. ....Charlotte, NC
Bubenik, Mark L. ....Tacoma, WA
Bubenik, Sharron M. ....Tulsa, OK
Bubenzer, William I., (P.S.C.) Covington, KY
Bubier, Jill L. ....Hyde Park, VT
Bublewicz, John J. ....Mercerville, NJ
Bubley & Bubley, P.A. ....Tampa, FL
Bubley, Daniel B. ....Tampa, FL
Bubley, Martin A. ....Tampa, FL
Bublick, Bruce W. ....Northbrook, IL
Bublick, Jordan E. ....Cutler Ridge, FL
Hialeah, FL
Miami, FL
Bublick, Jordan E., P.A. ....Cutler Ridge, FL
Hialeah, FL
Miami, FL
Bublis, James Fredric ....Norman, OK
Bublitz, Kevin L. ....Brookfield, WI
Bubman, Michael E. ....Los Angeles, CA
Bubna, Walter P. ....Parma, OH
Bubolz, Danford J. ....Verona, WI
Bubp, Danny Ray ....West Union, OH
Bubrick, Sam ....Los Angeles, CA
Bubrig, Darryl W., Sr. ....Buras, LA
Bubrig & Waid ....Buras, LA
Bubrow, Jonathan ....Hackensack, NJ
Bubsey, William E. ....Tallahassee, FL
Bubul, Stephen J. ....Minneapolis, MN
Buc & Beardsley ....Washington, DC
Buc, Nancy L. ....Washington, DC
Bucaida, Frank J. ....Madison, WI
Bucalo, John C. ....Cleveland, OH
Bucalo, Patricia ....Naples, FL
Bucalos, Dean W. ....Lexington, KY
Bucar, Jacqueline DeAndrus New Haven, CT
Bucar, Thomas N. ....New Bedford, MA
Bucari, Robert T. ....Madison, NJ
Bucaria, Stephen A. ....Mineola, NY
Bucaria, Thomas A. ....Mineola, NY
Bucaro, Andrew G. ....New Orleans, LA
Bucaro, Thomas ....Chicago, IL
Bucca, Anthony C. ....Tannersville, NY
Bucca, Benjamin S., Jr. ....New Brunswick, NJ
Bucca & Campisano ....New Brunswick, NJ
Buccafurni, Marian Blanche Santa Clara, CA
Buccarelli, Richard A. ....Princeton, NJ
Buccat, Betty O. ....Oakland, CA
Buccella, William V. ....Boston, MA
Buccellato, Eugene C. ....Baldwin, NY
Buccellato, James V. ....Red Bank, NJ
Bucceri, Benjamin F., Jr. ....Sacramento, CA
Bucceri, Louis ....Clifton, NJ
Bucceri and Pincus ....Clifton, NJ
Buccero, Samuel J. ....Kansas City, MO
Bucchi, Mark P. ....Troy, MI
Bucchianeri, Virgil A. ....Carson City, NV
Bucchino, Gary P. ....Omaha, NE
Bucci, Amy ....Jericho, NY
Bucci, Angela B. ....Providence, RI
Bucci, Anthony J., Jr. ....Providence, RI
Bucci, Bailey & Javins, L.C. Charleston, WV
Bucci, Carol A. ....Greensburg, PA
Bucci, Christin M. ....Arlington, VA
Bucci, Dean C. ....Marietta, GA
Bucci, Earl M. ....Schenectady, NY
Bucci, Elaine T. ....North Providence, RI
Bucci, Frank P. ....Punta Gorda, FL
Bucci, Gregg ....White Plains, NY
Bucci, Guy R. ....Charleston, WV
Bucci, James ....Jenkintown, PA
Bucci, James M. ....Reading, PA
Bucci, Joseph H. ....Pittsburgh, PA
Bucci, Linda M. ....Newton, MA
Bucci & Lockwood ....Baldwinsville, NY

Bucci, Lori Rae Securities and Exchange Commission, Division of Market Regulation, GV
Bucci, Michael A. ....Hartford, CT
Bucci, Michael A. ....Providence, RI
Bucci, Michael A., II ....Schenectady, NY
Bucci, Michael R., Jr. ....Pittsburgh, PA
Bucci, Peter ....New York, NY
Bucci, Rames J. ....Philadelphia, PA
Bucci, Rosemary E. ....Baldwinsville, NY
Bucci, Ruth E. ....North Providence, RI
Bucci, Thomas W. ....Bridgeport, CT
Bucci, Thomas W., Jr. ....Bridgeport, CT
Bucci, V. Paul, II ....Charleston, WV
Bucciarelli, S. Thomas ....Ardmore, PA
Bucciere, Robert L. ....Cincinnati, OH
Buccieri, M. Elaine ....Nashville, TN
Buccieri, Shirley Hanna ....San Francisco, CA
Buccigross, James H. ....Peabody, MA
Buccina, Bonnie Angela ....Syracuse, NY
Buccino, Ernest J., Jr. ....Philadelphia, PA
Buccino, Sharon M. ....Chicago, IL
Buccino, Terri N.A. ....Phoenix, AZ
Buccitelli, Marcia D. ....Hingham, MA
Bucco, Anthony Mark ....Boonton, NJ
Bucco, Paul A. ....Spring House, PA
Buccola, Robert A. ....Sacramento, CA
Buccola, Teri Ann ....Los Angeles, CA
Bucek, Maureen ....Austin, TX
Bucella, Donna ....Department of Justice, Executive Office for United States Attorneys, GV
Bucelo, Armando J., Jr. ....Coral Gables, FL
Bucey, David R. ....Atlanta, GA
Bucey & Junker, A Professional Corporation Pittsburgh, PA
Bucey, Wiley A., Jr. ....Pittsburgh, PA
Buch, David ....Buffalo, NY
Buch, Harry L. ....Wheeling, WV
Buch, Jerome F. ....Chicago, IL
Buch, Leslie N. ....New York, NY
Buch, Robert E. ....Los Angeles, CA
Buch, Sandra Bolz ....Austin, TX
Bucha, Jason P. ....San Rafael, CA
Bucha, Sandra L. ....Chicago, IL
Buchaca, John D. ....San Diego, CA
Buchal, James L. ....Portland, OR
Buchalter, Alan R. ....Eugene, OR
Buchalter, Daniel D ....San Leandro, CA
Buchalter, Howard M. ....Denver, CO
Buchalter, Irving H. ....Birmingham, AL
Buchalter, Irwin R. ....Los Angeles, CA
Buchalter, Neil J. ....Titusville, FL
Buchalter, Nemer, Fields & Younger, A Professional Corporation ....Irvine, CA
Los Angeles, CA
San Francisco, CA
Buchalter, Stephen ....Poughkeepsie, NY
Buchalter, Stuart D. ....Los Angeles, CA
Buchalter, Terri Lynn ....Miami, FL
Buchan, Charles J. ....Little Rock, AR
Buchan, Debra S. ....Wyndmoor, PA
Buchan, Frederick, Jr. Department of Justice, Civil Division, GV
Buchan, John J. ....Ebensburg, PA
Johnstown, PA
Buchan, Jonathan E., Jr. ....Charlotte, NC
Buchan, Laurie ....Malibu, CA
Buchan, Mary E. ....Marion, SC
Buchan, Robert B. ....Dallas, TX
Buchanan, A. Deane ....Cleveland, OH
Buchanan, Alexander Blackman Nashville, TN
Buchanan, Alexander S. ....Nashua, NH
Buchanan, Alida R. ....Santa Clara, CA
Buchanan, Allan D. ....Willmar, MN
Buchanan, Annette M. Office of Personnel Management, Merit Systems Division, GV
Buchanan, Barbara ....Sandpoint, ID
Buchanan, Barbara ....Seattle, WA
Buchanan, Barbara Eckert ....Detroit, MI
Buchanan & Barry, S.C. ....Milwaukee, WI
Buchanan, Bob ....Pawnee, OK
Buchanan & Bolte ....Fenwick Island, DE
Ocean City, MD
Buchanan, Bradford L. Colorado Springs, CO
Buchanan, Brenda K. ....Austin, TX
Buchanan, Brenda M. ....Portland, ME
Buchanan, Brian F. ....Los Angeles, CA
Buchanan, Brittan Lance ....Austin, TX
Buchanan, Brooks R. ....Jackson, MS
Buchanan, Bruce ....Duluth, MN
Buchanan, Bruce E. ....Little Rock, AR
Buchanan, Bryan K. ....Fort Worth, TX
Buchanan & Buchanan ....Lebanon, IN
Rockville, IN
Buchanan, Buchanan, Bibler, Buchanan & Handsaker ....Algona, IA
Lakota, IA
Swea City, IA
Buchanan, Butler, III ....Philadelphia, PA
Buchanan, Byron M. ....Houston, TX
Buchanan, C. Duffy ....Sherman Oaks, CA
Buchanan, C. Steven ....Duluth, GA
Buchanan, Candace L. ....Walnut Creek, CA
Buchanan, Charles E. ....Joplin, MO
Buchanan, Charlotte S. ....Albany, NY
Buchanan, Christine ....Alpharetta, GA
Buchanan, Christine H. ....Norfolk, VA
Buchanan, Christopher T. ....Charlotte, NC
Buchanan, Dale L. ....Chattanooga, TN
Buchanan, Dale L., & Assocsiates, P.C. Chattanooga, TN
Buchanan, Dan E. ....Riverside, CA
Buchanan, Daniel E. ....Jamestown, ND
Buchanan, David H. ....Atlanta, GA

Buchanan, David R. ....Kansas City, MO
Buchanan, David R. ....New York, NY
Buchanan, Debra C. ....Tacoma, WA
Buchanan, Donald R. ....Tustin, CA
Buchanan, Douglas ....Bishop, CA
Buchanan, Douglas M. San Luis Obispo, CA
Buchanan, Douglas W. ....Irving, TX
Buchanan, Edward Allen ....Torrington, WY
Buchanan, Elizabeth ....Birmingham, MI
Buchanan, Elizabeth A. ....Tucson, AZ
Buchanan, Elizabeth F. Department of the Army, Office of the General Counsel, GV
Buchanan, Eric Spencer ....Little Rock, AR
Buchanan, Eustace W. ....Beverly, MA
Buchanan, G. Kevin ....Dallas, TX
Buchanan, G. Sidney ....Houston, TX
Buchanan, Gregg A. ....Algona, IA
Buchanan, Henry S. ....Roseland, NJ
Buchanan Ingersoll, Professional Corporation ....Washington, DC
Aventura, FL
Miami, FL
Tampa, FL
Lexington, KY
Princeton, NJ
Buffalo, NY
New York, NY
Bryn Mawr, PA
Harrisburg, PA
Philadelphia, PA
Pittsburgh, PA
Buchanan, J. Scott ....Sacramento, CA
Buchanan, J. Vincent ....Rising Sun, OH
Buchanan, James F. ....Corpus Christi, TX
Buchanan, James J. ....San Diego, CA
Buchanan, James L., II ....Las Vegas, NV
Buchanan, James L., II, Prof. Corp. Las Vegas, NV
Buchanan, James P. ....Lebanon, IN
Buchanan, James R. ....Houston, TX
Buchanan, James Randall Washington, DC
Buchanan, James T. ....North Easton, MA
Buchanan, James W. ....Denver, CO
Buchanan, James W. ....Lenoir, NC
Buchanan, James W., III ....Denver, CO
Buchanan, Jeffrey D. ....Tempe, AZ
Buchanan, Jerry A. ....Columbus, GA
Buchanan, Joe M. ....Indianola, MS
Buchanan, John A. ....La Plata, MD
Buchanan, John B. ....Lebanon, IN
Rockville, IN
Buchanan, John C. ....Grand Rapids, MI
Buchanan, John D. ....Rosemead, CA
Buchanan, John D., Jr. ....Tallahassee, FL
Buchanan, John F. ....Houston, TX
Buchanan, John G., III ....Washington, DC
Buchanan, John M. ....Garden City, KS
Buchanan, Joseph H. ....Story City, IA
Buchanan, Joseph P. ....Dayton, OH
Buchanan, Joseph R. ....Miami, FL
Buchanan, Julia C. Federal Communications Commission, Wireless Telecommunications Bureau, GV
Buchanan, Julie K. ....Austin, TX
Buchanan, Julie M. ....Milwaukee, WI
Buchanan, Jurdem & Zulauf, P.C. Denver, CO
Buchanan Kent, P.C. ....Tyler, TX
Buchanan, Kevin D. ....Bartlesville, OK
Buchanan, Kevin Patrick ....St. Louis, MO
Buchanan, Kimberly A. ....Las Vegas, NV
Buchanan, Kyle L. ....Oklahoma City, OK
Buchanan & Land, L.L.P. ....Columbus, GA
Buchanan, Larry E. ....Stuart, FL
Buchanan, Laura L. ....San Francisco, CA
Buchanan, Lauren G. ....West Chester, PA
Buchanan Law Offices ....Jamestown, ND
Buchanan, Lawrence C. ....Santa Rosa, CA
Buchanan, Lee E. ....New Albany, IN
Buchanan, Leslie Stobbs ....Springfield, OH
Buchanan, Lisa Manget .....New Orleans, LA
Buchanan, M. Patricia ....Detroit, MI
Buchanan, Maria Quinto ....Toledo, OH
Buchanan, Mark A. ....St. Cloud, MN
Buchanan, Mark A. ....Kansas City, MO
Buchanan, Marla K. ....Jacksonville, FL
Buchanan, Marvin ....Oak Harbor, WA
Buchanan, Melanie M. ....Ocean City, MD
Buchanan, Michael A. ....Morgantown, WV
Buchanan, Michael J. ....Madison, WI
Buchanan, Michael R. ....Dallas, TX
Buchanan, Michael Ray ....Gainesville, FL
Buchanan, Michele A. ....Los Angeles, CA
Buchanan, Michele S. Wugalter Phoenix, AZ
Buchanan, Mickey J. ....Ashdown, AR
Buchanan, Minor F. ....Jackson, MS
Buchanan, Nancy L. ....Denver, CO
Buchanan, Neal G. ....Klamath Falls, OR
Buchanan Neville Stouffer, A Professional Corporation ....Boulder, CO
Lakewood, CO
Denver, CO
Buchanan, Norman H. ....Portland, ME
Buchanan, Patricia K. Fenske Seattle, WA
Buchanan, Patrick C., Jr. ....Roanoke, VA
Buchanan, Patrick R. ....Biloxi, MS
Pascagoula, MS
Buchanan, Paul ....Wichita, KS
Buchanan, Paul C. ....Portland, OR
Buchanan, Paul H., Jr. ....Indianapolis, IN
Buchanan, Paul M. ....Nashville, TN
Buchanan, Paul M. ....Fort Worth, TX
Buchanan, R. Scott ....Jefferson City, MO

Buchanan, Raymond L., Jr. ... Indianapolis, IN
Buchanan, Richard A. ... Chicago, IL
Buchanan, Richard W. ... Laguna Hills, CA
Buchanan, Richard W. ... New York, NY
Buchanan, Richard W. ... Seattle, WA
Buchanan, Robert A. ... Grand Rapids, MI
Buchanan, Robert B. ... Tucson, AZ
Buchanan, Robert B. ... Orlando, FL
Buchanan, Robert G., Jr. ... Dallas, TX
Buchanan, Robert J. ... Grand Rapids, MI
Buchanan, Robert Kelly, Jr.
Palo Alto, CA
Buchanan, Robert L., Jr. ... Aiken, SC
Buchanan, Robert L., Jr. ... Edgefield, SC
Buchanan, Robert M. ... Boston, MA
Buchanan, Robert M., Jr. (P.C.)
Boston, MA
Buchanan, Robert Norman, III
Nashville, TN
Buchanan, Ronald B. ... Hendersonville, TN
Buchanan, Ross B. H. ... Denver, CO
Buchanan, Russell G. ... Algona, IA
Lakota, IA
Buchanan, Scott G. ... Algona, IA
Buchanan, Shellee E. ... Newtown Square, PA
Buchanan, Sherry ... Puyallup, WA
Buchanan, Silver & Beckering, P.L.C.
Allegan, MI
Grand Haven, MI
Grand Rapids, MI
Holland, MI
Kalamazoo, MI
Muskegon, MI
St. Joseph, MI
Traverse City, MI
Buchanan, Stuart P. ... Winter Park, FL
Buchanan, Susan ... Burlington, VT
Buchanan, Susan Fox ... Denver, CO
Buchanan, Susan S. ... Burlington, VT
Buchanan, Terry Anne ... Oxnard, CA
Buchanan, Thomas D. ... Latham, NY
Buchanan, Thomas G. ... Pittsburgh, PA
Buchanan, Thomas G., III ... Dallas, TX
Buchanan, Thomas H. ... Tyler, TX
Buchanan, Thomas Jay ... Blountsville, AL
Buchanan, Thomas M. ... Washington, DC
Buchanan, Thomas M. ... Marengo, IA
North English, IA
Williamsburg, IA
Buchanan, Thomas R.
Overland Park, KS
Kansas City, MO
Buchanan, Thomas T. ... Laurel, MS
Buchanan, Timothy J. ... Fresno, CA
Buchanan, Timothy R. ... Arvada, CO
Buchanan, Timothy R., P.C. ... Arvada, CO
Buchanan, Todd R. ... Algona, IA
Buchanan, Vicki Marolt
Newport Beach, CA
Buchanan, Victor W. ... Asheville, NC
Buchanan, Victoria ... Jackson, MS
Buchanan, Virginia M. ... Pensacola, FL
Buchanan, Walter A. ... New York, NY
Buchanan, Walter W. ... Indianapolis, IN
Buchanan, Whitney ... Albuquerque, NM
Buchanan, William A. ... Redmond, WA
Buchanan, William C. ... Lambertville, NJ
Buchanan, William E. ... Arlington, VA
Buchanan, William F. ... Bend, OR
Buchanan, William H., Jr. ... Wilton, CT
Buchanan, William J., P.A. ... Columbia, SC
Buchanan, William Jennings ... Columbia, SC
Buchanan, William R., Sr. ... Lutherville, MD
Buchanan-Sidorski, Maria T. ... Buffalo, NY
Buchanio, Charles P. ... Lebanon, PA
Buchansky-Francesco, Amy
Staten Island, NY
Buchardt, Todd W. ... Skokie, IL
Buchband, Richard D. ... New York, NY
Buchbauer & McGuire, P.C.
Winchester, VA
Buchbauer, Peter W. ... Winchester, VA
Buchberg, Carl G. ... Los Angeles, CA
Buchberg, Paul D. ... Los Angeles, CA
Buchberger, Paul M. ... Wausau, WI
Buchbinder, Darrell ... New York, NY
Buchbinder & Elegant, P.A. ... Miami, FL
Buchbinder, Elizabeth N. ... Washington, DC
Buchbinder, Gedalia ... Brooklyn, NY
Buchbinder, Harris J. ... Miami, FL
Buchbinder, Lori R. ... New York, NY
Buchbinder, Mark ... Miami, FL
Buchbinder, Richard E. ... Newark, NJ
Buchbinder, Robert C. ... Columbus, OH
Buchbinder, Stephen J. ... Newton, MA
Buchdahl, Micah U. ... Voorhees, NJ
Buche, Craig M. ... Goshen, IN
Buchel, Rudolph J. ... Dallas, TX
Buchele, James P. ... Topeka, KS
Buchele, Thomas C. ... Chicago, IL
Buchen, David A. ... Claremont, CA
Buchen, Jean Roger ... Frederick, MD
Buchen, John G. ... Sheboygan, WI
Buchen, Judith M. ... Glendale, CA
Buchen, Katarzyna A. ... New York, NY
Buchen, Marvin ... New York, NY
Buchen, Philip W. ... Washington, DC
Buchen, Wise & Dorr ... Hanover, PA
Buchenau, Thomas M. ... El Cajon, CA
Buchenau, Thomas M. ... San Diego, CA
Buchenberger, Thomas E. ... Wantagh, NY
Buchenhorner, Michael J. ... Miami, FL
Buchenroth, Stephen R. ... Columbus, OH
Bucher, Andrew M. ... Miami, FL
Bucher, Bradley Roger ... Springfield, IL
Bucher, David E. ... Department of Commerce, Patent and Trademark Office, GV

Bucher, Donald C. ... Minneapolis, MN
Seattle, WA
Bucher, Donald E. ... Kansas City, MO
Bucher, Donna L. ... Mitchell, SD
Bucher, Eden R. ... Reading, PA
Bucher, Elaine M. ... Aventura, FL
Boca Raton, FL
Fort Lauderdale, FL
West Palm Beach, FL
Bucher, Elliott D. ... West Union, OH
Bucher Firm, P.C. ... Charleston, SC
Bucher, James I. ... Marine, IL
Bucher, James R. ... Upper Marlboro, MD
Bucher, Jeffrey M. ... San Francisco, CA
Bucher, Jennifer D. ... Seattle, WA
Bucher, John V., Jr. ... Albany, NY
Bucher, Kathryn ... Washington, DC
Bucher, Larry Dean ... Pittsburgh, PA
Bucher, Linda ... Kew Gardens, NY
Bucher, Paul E. ... Waukesha, WI
Bucher, Paul W. ... Rochester, MN
Bucher, Ronald E. ... Omaha, NE
Bucher, Stephen ... Charleston, SC
Bucher, Steven J. ... Plankinton, SD
Bucher, William D. ... Park City, KY
Bucher, Wilson ... Lancaster, PA
Buchert, Cheryl Prestenback ... Metairie, LA
Buchert, Christopher B. ... Cincinnati, OH
Buchert, Kenneth D. ... Monterey, CA
Buchert, Terrence S. ... St. Petersburg, FL
Buchert, Thomas R. ... Middletown, OH
Buchet, Michael M. X. ... Washington, DC
Buchfirer, Alan H. ... Lexington, MA
Buchhammer, Curtis B. ... Cheyenne, WY
Buchhammer & Kehl, P.C.
Cheyenne, WY
Buchheister, Carl W. ... Prince Frederick, MD
Sunderland, MD
Buchheit, Eugene N. ... Louisville, KY
Buchheit, Lee C. ... New York, NY
Buchheit, Scott Edward ... Haddonfield, NJ
Buchheit, Teresa C. ... Louisville, KY
Buchholdt, Titania ... Berkeley, CA
Buchholtz, David P. ... Albuquerque, NM
Buchholtz, Bernard ... New York, NY
Buchholz, Briana C. ... Nutley, NJ
Buchholz, Carl D., III ... Philadelphia, PA
Buchholz, Carl M. ... Philadelphia, PA
Buchholz, Charles ... Chicago, IL
Buchholz, David O. ... Department of Justice, Civil Division, GV
Buchholz, Diane K. ... Matteson, IL
Buchholz, Edward J. ... St. Louis, MO
Buchholz, James P. ... Fort Wayne, IN
Buchholz, James Thomas ... Chicago, IL
Buchholz, John R. ... Miami, FL
Buchholz, Keith A. ... Bremerton, WA
Buchholz, Kristin M. ... Chicago, IL
Portland, OR
Buchholz, Mark A. ... Lincoln, NE
Buchholz, Roger A. ... Boulder, CO
Buchholz, Scott D. ... San Diego, CA
Buchholz & Sias ... Waupun, WI
Buchholz, Steven D. ... Palo Alto, CA
Buchholz, Steven R. ... Anaheim, CA
Buchholz, William E. ... Waupun, WI
Buchholz, William G., II ... St. Louis, MO
Buchholz-McIntosh, Carolyn L.
Denver, CO
Buchi, Mark K. ... Salt Lake City, UT
Buchicchio, Michael F. ... Scarsdale, NY
Buchignani, Alvin G. ... San Francisco, CA
Buchignani, Antony E. ... Los Angeles, CA
Buchignani, J. Richard ... Memphis, TN
Buchinger, Melody ... Chilton, WI
Buchinsky, M. Frances ... New York, NY
Buchinsky, Mark T. ... Philadelphia, PA
Buchko, John P. ... Department of Justice, Civil Rights Division, GV
Buchko, Laura Ellen ... Charleston, WV
Buchko, William E. ... Monaca, PA
Buchleitner, John R. ... Ellicott City, MD
Buchler and Buchler ... Metairie, LA
Buchler, Conrad A. ... Metairie, LA
Buchler, D Ari ... Newton, MA
Buchler, Harold A. ... Metairie, LA
Buchler, Harold A., Jr. ... Metairie, LA
Buchler, Howard A. ... Schaumburg, IL
Buchler, Peter R. ... Houston, TX
Buchli, Jeffry R., Law Offices of
Honolulu, HI
Buchli, Richard I., II ... Kansas City, MO
Buchmaier, Wolfgang ... Columbia, SC
Buchman, Abraham M. ... New York, NY
Buchman, Adele S. ... Houston, TX
Buchman, Arnold E. ... Phoenix, AZ
Buchman, Barry I. ... Washington, DC
Buchman & Buchman Attorneys at Law, P.A.
Tampa, FL
Buchman, Danny F. ... Southfield, MI
Buchman, David M. ... Columbus, OH
Buchman, Donald G. ... Sacramento, CA
Buchman, Gary D. ... Newton, MA
Buchman, Harold ... Reisterstown, MD
Buchman, J. Miles ... Tampa, FL
Buchman, Janice Carole ... Tampa, FL
Buchman, Jason A. ... Houston, TX
Buchman, Jennifer L. ... New York, NY
Buchman, Joel ... New York, NY
Buchman, John A. ... Washington, DC
Buchman, John F. ... Canton, OH
Buchman, John T. ... Anoka, MN
Buchman, Joseph P. ... Los Angeles, CA
Buchman, Joshua T. ... Chicago, IL
Buchman, Kenneth W. ... Plant City, FL
Buchman, Kenneth W., P.A. ... Plant City, FL
Buchman, Lawrence J. ... Mineola, NY
Buchman, Michael M. ... New York, NY

Buchman, Mitchell J. ... Houston, TX
Buchman & O'Brien, LLP
San Francisco, CA
Washington, DC
Edison, NJ
New York, NY
Buchman, Paul Lewis ... Delray Beach, FL
Buchman, Robert A., (P.C.)
Walnut Creek, CA
Buchman, Stephen L. ... New York, NY
Buchman, Steven E. ... Simsbury, CT
Buchmann, Alan P. ... Cleveland, OH
Buchmann, George A. ... Miami, FL
Buchmann, Matthew A., (P.A.)
Overland Park, KS
Buchmeier & Brost,, P.L.C. ... St. Paul, MN
Buchmeier, Joseph M. ... St. Paul, MN
Buchmeier, Ronald W. ... Indianapolis, IN
Buchmeier, Thomas R. ... Edmonds, WA
Buchmeier, Thomas R., P.S. ... Edmonds, WA
Buchmeyer, Jerry L. ... Dallas, TX
Buchmiller, Ginger M. ... Chicago, IL
Buchmiller, James E. ... Greenville, IL
Buchmiller, James E., Ltd. ... Greenville, IL
Buchmiller, Lawrence T. ... Albuquerque, NM
Buchmiller, Timothy L. ... Los Angeles, CA
Buchner, Donald R. ... Follett, TX
Buchner, Mark E. ... Tulsa, OK
Buchner, Marvin ... Jericho, NY
Buchner, Robert J. ... Fort Lauderdale, FL
Buchner, Susan A. ... Paramus, NJ
Bucholtz, Alan H. ... Denver, CO
Bucholtz & Bull, P.C. ... Denver, CO
Bucholtz, Harold R. ... Washington, DC
Bucholtz, Jeffrey S. ... Washington, DC
Bucholtz, Roy J. ... Reston, VA
Bucholtz, Roy J., P.C. ... Reston, VA
Bucholtz, Sara R. ... New York, NY
Bucholz, Seymour H. ... New York, NY
Buchovecky, John J. ... Washington, DC
Buchsbaum, Aaron L. ... Savannah, GA
Buchsbaum, Alan H. ... New York, NY
Buchsbaum, Andrew ... Boston, MA
Buchsbaum, Andrew V. ... New York, NY
Buchsbaum, Craig M. ... San Francisco, CA
Buchsbaum, David A. ... Miami, FL
Buchsbaum and Lowe ... Savannah, GA
Buchsbaum, Michael C. ... Washington, DC
Buchsbaum, Norman R. ... Baltimore, MD
Buchsbaum, Peter A. ... Woodbridge, NJ
Buchsbaum, Richard A. ... White Plains, NY
Buchsbaum, Robert L. ... Hollywood, FL
Buchsbaum, Stanley ... Brooklyn, NY
Buchschacher, Paul W. ... Arlington, TX
Buchser, Linda E. ... San Francisco, CA
Buchstab, Klaus J. ... Charlotte, NC
Buchta, Alfred H., Jr. ... Alamo, CA
Buchta, Barbara F. ... Roseland, NJ
Buchter, John S. ... Camptonville, CA
Buchter, Jonathan F. ... Cleveland, OH
Buchter, Richard L. ... Kew Gardens, NY
Buchwach, Michael D. ... Pittsburgh, PA
Buchwald, Ave ... Long Beach, CA
Buchwald, Deborah-Beth ... West Hartford, CT
Buchwald, Don, LLP, Law Offices of
New York, NY
Buchwald, Gerald J. ... Redwood City, CA
Buchwald, Herbert ... Denver, CO
Buchwald, Jules ... New York, NY
Buchwald, Naomi Reice ... New York, NY
Buchwald, Todd F. ... Department of State, Office of the Legal Adviser, GV
Buchwalter, Douglas M. ... Clearwater, FL
Buchwalter, Steve Alan ... Encino, CA
Buchy, John J., Jr. ... Harrisburg, PA
Buchyn & Buchyn ... Schenectady, NY
Buchyn, Joseph J. ... Schenectady, NY
Buchyn, Steven A. ... Schenectady, NY
Buck, Alan ... Louisville, IL
Buck, Alice M. ... San Diego, CA
Buck, Allison V. ... Boston, MA
Buck, Anderson & Assocs., P.C.
Alexandria, VA
Stafford, VA
Woodbridge, VA
Buck, Andrew L. ... New York, NY
Buck, Arthur N. ... San Diego, CA
Buck, Berry, Landau & Breunig, P.A.
Indianapolis, IN
Buck, Bradford H. ... Hartford, CT
Buck, Brannon J. ... Birmingham, AL
Buck, Bruce ... Eureka, CA
Buck & Buck ... McMinnville, TN
Smithville, TN
Buck, Byron, II ... Peoria, IL
Buck, C. Brantly ... Little Rock, AR
Buck, Carl V., III ... New Brunswick, NJ
Buck, Carolyn J. ... Treasury Department, Office of Thrift Supervision, GV
Buck, Cecilia J. ... New Milford, CT
Buck, Christopher D. ... Annapolis, MD
Buck, Craig E. ... Alexandria, VA
Stafford, VA
Woodbridge, VA
Buck, D. Reuben ... San Diego, CA
Buck, Dale A. ... Martinsburg, WV
Buck, Danaher, Ryan and McGlenn
Elmira, NY
Buck, David Clyde ... Houston, TX
Buck, David D. ... Seattle, WA
Buck, David J. ... San Antonio, TX
Buck, David P. ... Riva, MD
Buck, Donald E. ... St. Augustine, FL
Buck, Dorothy Defore ... Chattanooga, TN
Buck, Douglas I. ... Flint, MI
Buck, Douglas I., II, P.C. ... Flint, MI
Buck, Douglas Irvine, II ... Flint, MI
Buck, Douglas S. ... Chicago, IL

Buck, E. Rhett ... Houston, TX
Buck, Ed L. ... Alamogordo, NM
Buck, Elizabeth J. ... New Rochelle, NY
Buck, Emory W. ... Lansdale, PA
Buck, F. Dane, Jr. ... Concord, NH
Buck, Francis L. ... Charlottesville, VA
Buck, Frank ... Smithville, TN
Buck, Frank M., Jr. ... New Orleans, LA
Buck, Frank S. ... Birmingham, AL
Buck, Frank S., P.C. ... Birmingham, AL
Buck, Frank W. ... Cleveland, OH
Buck, Fred B. ... Philadelphia, PA
Buck, Frederick J. ... Redmond, WA
Buck, G. Joseph ... Torrance, CA
Buck, George L., Jr. ... Port Angeles, WA
Buck, George R., Jr. ... Cortez, CO
Buck, George Thad, II ... West Point, MS
Buck, Gertrude J. ... Bayside, NY
Buck, Gladys Rogers ... Philadelphia, PA
Buck & Gordon LLP ... Seattle, WA
Buck, Gurdon H. ... Hartford, CT
Buck, Gwendolen S. ... Monterey, CA
Buck, Harvey S. ... West Point, MS
Buck, James A. ... Indianapolis, IN
Buck, James B. ... Denver, CO
Buck, James E. ... New York, NY
Buck, James J. ... Seattle, WA
Buck, James Lee, II
Securities and Exchange Commission, Division of Enforcement, GV
Buck, James M. ... Santa Monica, CA
Buck, James R. ... Sycamore, IL
Buck, Jane R. ... New York, NY
Buck, Joanna H. ... Dallas, TX
Buck, John A., II ... Chicago, IL
Buck, John D. ... Radford, VA
Buck, John E. ... Britt, IA
Buck, John H. ... Elkton, MD
Buck, John H. ... Houston, TX
Buck, John K. ... Lawrence, MA
Buck, Joseph C. ... Elmira, NY
Buck, Juliet F. ... New York, NY
Buck, Kara Brown ... Washington, DC
Buck, Karen A. ... Washington, DC
Buck, Karen C. ... Philadelphia, PA
Buck, Karen Schaefer ... Denver, CO
Buck, Kathleen A. ... Washington, DC
Buck, Keenan & Owens, L.L.P.
Houston, TX
Buck, Keith A. ... Des Moines, IA
Buck, Keri A. ... Lodi, CA
Buck, Kevin E. ... Boston, MA
Buck, Ky Ann ... St. John, KS
Buck, Laurie C. ... Boston, MA
Buck Law Firm, P.C. ... Alamogordo, NM
Buck Law Office ... Britt, IA
Buck, Lena Ann ... Smithville, TN
Buck, Lisa Marie ... Minneapolis, MN
Buck, Lori A. ... Minneapolis, MN
Buck, Lynne Haddad ... Cleveland, OH
Buck, Mark A. ... Topeka, KS
Buck, Marshall D. ... Youngstown, OH
Buck, Mary Louise Dague ... Muncie, IN
Buck, Max H. ... Marshalltown, IA
Buck, Maynard A., III ... Cleveland, OH
Buck, Michael A. ... Midlothian, IL
Buck, Michael L. ... Allegan, MI
Buck, Michael L.F. ... Sacramento, CA
Buck, Michael P. ... New York, NY
Buck, Migdal & Myers, Chartered
Annapolis, MD
Buck, Milton A. ... Newark, NJ
Buck, Minna R. ... Syracuse, NY
Buck, Mitchel ... Sun City West, AZ
Buck, Morison ... Tampa, FL
Buck, Nelson D. ... Red Bluff, CA
Buck, Perry E. ... Vancouver, WA
Buck, Peter A. ... Sacramento, CA
Buck, Peter C. ... Charlotte, NC
Buck, Peter L. ... Seattle, WA
Buck, R. Bruce ... Hope, AR
Buck, Ralph D., Jr. ... Dallas, TX
Buck, Richard E. ... Costa Mesa, CA
Buck, Richard E. ... Odessa, TX
Buck, Richard S., IV
Federal Emergency Management Agency, GV
Buck, Richard W. ... Jacksonville, FL
Buck, Robert ... Long Beach, CA
Buck, Robert B. ... Carmel, CA
Buck, Robert C. ... Atlanta, GA
Buck, Robert E. ... Greenville, MS
Buck, Robert E. ... Pomeroy, OH
Buck, Robert E., P.A. ... Greenville, MS
Buck, Robert F. ... Seattle, WA
Buck, Robert R. ... Oklahoma City, OK
Buck, Robert W., Jr. ... Houston, TX
Buck, Rodney L. ... Tulsa, OK
Buck, Royce W. ... Mayfield, KY
Buck, Sarah H. ... Buffalo, NY
Buck, Sharon Klein ... Malvern, PA
Buck & Sheeran ... Cortez, CO
Buck, Signe M. ... Venice, CA
Buck, Stephen M. ... Peoria, IL
Buck, Steven D. ... Philadelphia, PA
Reading, PA
Buck, Steven E. ... Zanesville, OH
Buck, T. Kernahan ... Cambridge, MA
Buck, Teresa J. ... Fort Worth, TX
Buck & Tereskerz, Ltd. ... Charlottesville, VA
Buck, Teri Anderson ... Stafford, VA
Woodbridge, VA
Buck, Theron A. ... Seattle, WA
Buck, Thomas B., III ... Columbus, GA
Buck, Thomas E. ... Wheeling, WV
Buck, Thomas G. ... Metairie, LA
New Orleans, LA
Buck, Thomas K. ... Los Angeles, CA

Bucklin, Kerry S. .... **Seattle, WA**
Bucklin, Klemin & McBride, P.C.
Bismarck, ND
Bucklin, Leonard H. .... **Bismarck, ND**
Bucklin, Leonard W. .... York Harbor, ME
Bucklin, Mark R. .... **Seattle, WA**
Bucklin, Patricia K. .... Albany, NY
Bucklin, Robert V. .... Las Vegas, NV
Bucklin, Stephen L. .... Los Angeles, CA
Bucklo, Elaine E. .... Chicago, IL
Bucklo, Michael P. .... **Deerfield, IL**
Buckly, Ronald W. .... **Santa Monica, CA**
Buckman, David I. .... Philadelphia, PA
Buckman, Deborah F. .... Highland Park, IL
Buckman, Donald K. .... **Fort Worth, TX**
Buckman & Farris, PSC .... Shepherdsville, KY
Buckman, Herbert .... **Cleveland, OH**
Buckman, James E. .... **Parsippany, NJ**
Buckman, Jeffrey W. .... **Holland, MI**
Buckman, Jennifer T. .... **Riverside, CA**
Buckman, John B., IV .... **Morristown, NJ**
Buckman & Lotstein, P.C.
Chevy Chase, MD
Buckman, Mary L. .... **Norristown, PA**
Buckman, Melvin J. .... **Radnor, PA**
Buckman, Michael L. .... Brookline, MA
Buckman, Richard C. .... Raleigh, NC
Buckman, Sally A. .... **Washington, DC**
Buckman, Steven M. .... **Washington, DC**
Buckman, Steven V. .... **Tulsa, OK**
Buckman, Steven V., P.C.
Oklahoma City, OK
Tulsa, OK
Buckman, Thomas W. .... **Glenview, IL**
Buckman, William H. .... Moorestown, NJ
Buckman, Yardley D., II .... Sarasota, FL
Buckmann, Carol I. .... **New York, NY**
Buckmaster and Macy, LLP
Belle Fourche, SD
Buckmaster, Robert E.
Altamonte Springs, FL
Buckmaster, Wesley W. .... **Belle Fourche, SD**
Buckmeier, A. N. .... McLaughlin, SD
Mobridge, SD
Buckmeier, Brian E. .... **Sioux City, IA**
Buckmeier & Daane .... **Sioux City, IA**
Buckmeier, Maxine M. .... **Sioux City, IA**
Buckmelter, Vincent .... Denver, CO
Buckmir, Elizabeth M. .... **New Haven, CT**
Buckna, Susan A. .... Appleton, WI
Bucknam, Andrew G. .... **Hartford, CT**
Bucknam, Deborah T. .... St. Johnsbury, VT
Bucknam, Heather Wilson .... **Hartford, CT**
Bucknam, James R. .... **New York, NY**
Bucknam, Ralph E. .... Garden City, NY
Bucknam, Robert W., Jr. .... **Haddonfield, NJ**
Bucknam, William E. .... Deerfield Beach, FL
Bucknell, Allen D. .... **Phoenix, AZ**
Bucknell, James M. .... Bessemer, MI
Bucknell, Robin .... Phoenix, AZ
Bucknell Stehlik .... **Seattle, WA**
Bucknell, Thomas N. .... **Seattle, WA**
Buckner, Adair M. .... **Amarillo, TX**
Buckner, Alan C. .... **Houston, TX**
Buckner, Alan G. .... Marina Del Rey, CA
Buckner, Alan G., A Professional Corporation
Marina Del Rey, CA
Buckner, Alani & Young .... **Costa Mesa, CA**
Buckner, Andrew C. .... **Winston-Salem, NC**
Buckner, Andrew P. .... Greenbelt, MD
Buckner & Buckner, P.C.
Overland Park, KS
Buckner, Carole J. .... Irvine, CA
Buckner, Charles A., Jr. .... Nashville, TN
Buckner, Dale A. .... West Palm Beach, FL
Buckner, David M. .... Washington, DC
Buckner, David R. .... Chicago, IL
Buckner, David W. .... **Dallas, TX**
Buckner, Deborah G. .... Overland Park, KS
Buckner, Donald A. .... Houston, TX
Buckner, Edward F. .... Stockton, CA
Buckner, Edwin E., Jr. .... Marshall, TX
Buckner, Fillmore .... Seattle, WA
Buckner, Gayley M. .... **Woodland Hills, CA**
Buckner, Henry K., Jr. .... Nashville, TN
Buckner, James N. .... New York, NY
Buckner, James R. .... **Chattanooga, TN**
Buckner, James W. .... Murfreesboro, TN
Buckner, Jerry .... Weatherford, TX
Buckner, J. N., Jr. .... Prattville, AL
Buckner, Joseph M. .... Hillsborough, NC
Buckner, Kathryn A. .... **Southfield, MI**
Buckner, Kenneth E., P.A. .... Pine Bluff, AR
Buckner & Kourofsky .... Rochester, NY
Buckner, L. Rachel .... **Washington, DC**
Buckner, Laurel Marie Vidmar
Seattle, WA
Buckner, L. J., Jr. .... **Kansas City, MO**
Buckner, Mary A. .... Columbus, GA
Buckner, Mary A., P.C. .... Columbus, GA
Buckner, Melissa Spirt .... Miami, FL
Buckner, Michael L. .... **Jacksonville, FL**
Buckner, Michael S. .... **Washington, DC**
Buckner, Michael W. .... **Waterloo, IA**
Buckner, Mike S., (P.A.)
West Palm Beach, FL
Buckner, Perry M., Law Offices of
Walterboro, SC
Buckner, Raymond T., Jr. .... Rochester, NY
Buckner, Richard G. .... **Rockingham, NC**
Buckner, Richard W. .... **Los Angeles, CA**
Buckner, Robert P., Jr. .... Giddings, TX
Buckner, Robin S. .... Miami, FL
Buckner, Rosanne .... Tacoma, WA
Buckner & Shifrin, P.A. .... Miami, FL
Buckner, Shyla R. .... **Amarillo, TX**
Buckner, Simon B. .... Overland Park, KS
Buckner, Steven R. .... **Bethesda, MD**

Buckner, Thomas R. .... **Memphis, TN**
Buckner, William D. .... **Costa Mesa, CA**
Buckner-Davis, Pamela N. .... Santa Ana, CA
Bucknum, Susan L. .... **Philadelphia, PA**
Bucknum, Thomas J. .... Cambridge, MA
Bucko, Benjamin J. .... Groton, NY
Bucko, Lisa J. .... **Atlanta, GA**
Bucko, Michael J. .... Chicago, IL
Buckovich, Mark E. .... Irvine, CA
Buckridge, Charles R. .... Stuart, FL
Buckrop, Bruce A. .... **Rock Island, IL**
Buckser, Lisa K. .... **New York, NY**
Buckson, Marlee .... **Portland, OR**
Buckstad, Erik K. .... Rochester Hills, MI
Buckstein, Brian D. .... **New York, NY**
Buckstein, Evelyn .... **New York, NY**
Buckstein, Mark A. .... Fort Lauderdale, FL
Buckun, Anthony H. .... Grayslake, IL
Buckun, Anthony T. .... Grayslake, IL
Buckun & Buckun, P.C. .... Grayslake, IL
Buckvar, Eric J. .... New York, NY
Buckvar, Morton .... New York, NY
Buckvar, Norman S. .... St. Louis, MO
Buckwalter, Charles Quimby, Jr.
Alcoa Center, PA
Buckwalter, Gary L. .... Dallas, TX
Buckwalter, John H. .... Shelton, WA
Buckwalter, Kenneth D. .... Auburn, CA
Buckwalter, Michael A. .... Beavercreek, OH
Buckwalter, Michelle B. .... Morrison, IL
Buckwalter, Paul T., II .... Midlothian, VA
Buckwalter, Ronald L. .... Philadelphia, PA
Buckwalter, Thomas M. .... Alturas, CA
Buckwalter, Wayne C. .... Exton, PA
Wayne, PA
West Grove, PA
Buckworth, Mark D. .... Wilmington, DE
Bucsi, Frank J. .... Belvidere, NJ
Bucur, Karyn Hilde .... **Laguna Hills, CA**
Bucur, Nicholas A. .... Cleveland, OH
Bucuvalas, Michael G. C. .... Quincy, MA
Bucy, G. Rhea .... **Nashville, TN**
Bucy, Pamela D. .... Helena, MT
Bucy, Winifred L. .... Beckley, WV
Buczak, Douglas C. .... Birmingham, MI
Buczek, Jennifer .... **New York, NY**
Buczek, Wilma J. .... Tucson, AZ
Buczko, Thaddeus .... Salem, MA
Buczkowski, Arthur W. .... Lathrup Village, MI
Buczkowski, David J. .... Boston, MA
Buczkowski, Eugene V. .... Buffalo, NY
Buczynski, Frank A., Jr. .... Toms River, NJ
Buczynski, Joseph J. .... **Washington, DC**
Buda, David M. .... Columbus, OH
Buda, David N. .... Montvale, NJ
Buda, Denise .... **New York, NY**
Buda, Frank M. .... Woodland Hills, CA
Buda, Ian Stewart .... Beverly Hills, CA
Buda, James B. .... **Peoria, IL**
Buda, Mark Christopher .... Lynbrook, NY
Buda, Philip H. .... Redwood City, CA
Buda, Terrence J. .... Harrisburg, PA
Buda, Thaddeus J., Jr. .... **Lansing, MI**
Budach, Deborah L. .... **Palo Alto, CA**
Budagher & Associates .... Albuquerque, NM
Budagher, John A. .... Albuquerque, NM
Budaj, Steven T. .... **Detroit, MI**
Budaj, Steven T., P.C., Law Offices of
Detroit, MI
Budakian, Mary Alice .... Woodcliff Lake, NJ
Budanitsky, Sander .... Ridgewood, NJ
Budarapu, Amar N. .... **Houston, TX**
Budare, Justin E. .... **Los Angeles, CA**
Buday, David M. .... **Kalamazoo, MI**
Buday, Gwen E. .... **Grand Rapids, MI**
Buday, Lisa J. .... Washington, PA
Buday, Lynne M. .... Traverse City, MI
Buday, Paul V. .... Spotsylvania, VA
Buday, Raymond C., Jr. .... Atlanta, GA
Buday, Robert T. .... Indianapolis, IN
Budd and Bennett .... **Naples, FL**
Budd & Bertas .... Philadelphia, PA
Budd, C. Burcham .... Dallas, TX
Budd, Carlotta M. .... Madison, NJ
Budd, David G., (P.A.) .... **Naples, FL**
Budd and Gardner .... Madison, NJ
Budd, Geck Yong .... West Bloomfield, MI
Budd, James T. .... **Atlanta, GA**
Budd, John H. .... **Worcester, MA**
Budd, John H., Jr. .... Phoenix, AZ
Budd, John J. .... Short Hills, NJ
Budd, Jordan C. .... San Diego, CA
Budd Larner Gross Rosenbaum Greenberg & Sade, A Professional Corporation
Cherry Hill, NJ
Short Hills, NJ
New York, NY
Philadelphia, PA
Budd, Macdonald .... **New York, NY**
Budd, Martin L. .... **Stamford, CT**
Budd, Nancy J. .... **Lihue, HI**
Budd, Paige E. .... **Los Angeles, CA**
Budd, Patricia A. .... Bethpage, NY
Budd, Patrick N. .... Trenton, NJ
Budd, Regina M.
General Services Administration, Office of the General Counsel, GV
Budd, Rick .... Aurora, CO
Budd, Rick, P.C. .... Aurora, CO
Budd, Robert A. .... Woodland Hills, CA
Budd, Russell Wills .... **Dallas, TX**
Budd, Steven W. .... Somers, NY
Budd, Terry .... **Pittsburgh, PA**
Budd, Thomas J., II .... Ashland, OH
Budd, Thomas W. .... **New York, NY**
Budd, Timothy Allan .... San Diego, CA
Budd, Toni Turner .... **Tulsa, OK**
Budd, William K. .... Clearwater, FL

Budde, Alan F. .... Los Angeles, CA
Budde, Anna M. .... **Troy, MI**
Budde, Denae Hildebrand .... Visalia, CA
Budde, Frank J. .... Tyler, TX
Budde, Frederick L. .... Minneapolis, MN
Budde, Joanna K. .... **Erie, PA**
Budde, Oliver M. .... **New York, NY**
Buddell, Brian H. .... **San Francisco, CA**
Budden, Harry E., Jr. .... Paris, KY
Buddenbaum, James A. L.
Indianapolis, IN
Buddenbohm, Leonard L. .... **Atchison, KS**
Overland Park, KS
Buddenhagen, Scott J. .... Shelton, CT
Budd-Falen, Karen .... Cheyenne, WY
Budd-Falen Law Offices, P.C.
Cheyenne, WY
Buddie, James A. .... Pittsburgh, PA
Buddie, Raymond M. .... **San Francisco, CA**
River Edge, NJ
New York, NY
Buddin, Richard L. .... **Denver, CO**
Buddingh, Gerrit Jan .... West Sacramento, CA
Buddingh, Jan K., Jr. .... **San Diego, CA**
Buddington, Leonard, Jr .... White Plains, NY
Buddington, Perry C. .... Northford, CT
Buddock, Peter J. .... Bethlehem, PA
Budds, Denis W. .... Flat Rock, MI
Bude, George J. .... **St. Louis, MO**
Budeiri, Priscilla R. .... Richmond, VA
Budell, Andrew Mark .... Lincoln, NE
Budelman, Robert B., Jr. .... **New York, NY**
Budelmann, Scott Allen .... Canton, NY
Budenholzer, Robert T. .... St. Louis, MO
Budensiek, Mark D. .... **Costa Mesa, CA**
Buder, Donald D. .... **San Francisco, CA**
Buder, Eugene H. .... St. Louis, MO
Buderwitz, Joseph M. .... **White Plains, NY**
Budesa, Robert D. .... Toms River, NJ
Budesheim, Thomas L. .... Kansas City, MO
Budetti, Joseph Bart .... Overland Park, KS
Budewitz, Leslie Ann .... Polson, MT
Budewitz, Thomas A. .... **Helena, MT**
Budge, Alan T. .... Walnut Creek, CA
Budge, Donald M. .... Newton, MA
Budge, Hamilton W. .... San Francisco, CA
Budge, Hamilton W., Jr. .... Eugene, OR
Budge, James R.
Securities and Exchange Commission, Division of Corporation Finance, GV
Budge, Randall C. .... **Pocatello, ID**
Budicak, Joseph M. .... New Brighton, PA
Budike, Marianthe L. .... Wallingford, PA
Budilovsky, John A., Jr. .... Batavia, IL
Budin, Arnold I. .... Union, NJ
Budin, Beverly R. .... **Philadelphia, PA**
Budin, Greenman & Greenman .... Union, NJ
Budin, Harlan Scott .... New York, NY
Budin, Jay .... New York, NY
Budin, Jerome N. .... Modesto, CA
Budin, John Joseph .... Chicago, IL
Budin & Lipkin .... Chicago, IL
Budin, Michael Allan .... **Wilmington, DE**
Budin, Nathaniel .... **Philadelphia, PA**
Budin, Pamela Ivy .... **New York, NY**
Budin, Paul D. .... New York, NY
Budin, Reisman & Schwartz, P.C.
New York, NY
Budinetz, James A. .... **Hartford, CT**
Budinsky, Robert .... Youngstown, OH
Budish, Adam E. .... New York, NY
Budish, Andrew M. .... **Prospect Heights, IL**
Budish, Armond D. .... Cleveland, OH
Budish, James G. .... Wauwatosa, WI
Budish, Lawrence H. .... **New York, NY**
Budish, Robert P. .... Boca Raton, FL
Budish and Solomon, Ltd. .... Cleveland, OH
Budjac Corvette, Barbara A. .... Alexandria, VA
Budka, David M. .... **Southfield, MI**
Budka, Michael J. .... **Litchfield, MN**
Budke, Kurt A. .... **Oklahoma City, OK**
Budlong, C. Michael .... Hartford, CT
Budlong, John, Law Offices of
Seattle, WA
Budman, Alan D. .... Abington, PA
Budman, Brian .... Englewood, CO
Budman, Donald J. .... **Charleston, SC**
Budman, Robert L. .... Los Angeles, CA
Budman, Theodore M. .... Garden City, NY
Budmen, Donald E. .... **Syracuse, NY**
Budner, Bruce A., & Associates
Dallas, TX
Budner, Craig W. .... **Dallas, TX**
Budner, Dawn Ryan .... **Dallas, TX**
Budney, Alan F. .... Newington, CT
Budney, Jerold I. .... **Fort Lauderdale, FL**
Budney, Richard R., Jr. .... **Philadelphia, PA**
Budnick, Leo T., Jr. .... Bridgeport, CT
Budnick, Martin .... Melbourne Beach, FL
Budnick, Myron H. .... Miami, FL
Budnick, Sandra J. .... Kalamazoo, MI
Budnick, Victor R. .... Fairfield, CT
Budnik, John Raymond .... San Bernardino, CA
Budnitz, Mark E. .... Atlanta, GA
Budny, Clement L., Jr. .... **Racine, WI**
Budny, Joseph F. .... **Waterbury, CT**
Budny, Judith M. .... West Allis, WI
Budny, Terrence E. .... **Chicago, IL**
Budnyk, Rita H. .... North Palm Beach, FL
Budo, Tami C. .... **Las Vegas, NV**
Budoff, Irving N. .... Utica, NY
Budoff, Marc .... Phoenix, AZ
Budoff, Robert A. .... Phoenix, AZ
Budoff, Robert S. .... **Washington, DC**
Budoff & Ross, P.C. .... Phoenix, AZ
Budoff, Scott Alan .... Goldens Bridge, NY
Budoff, Sheila Kraft .... Washington, DC
Budofsky, Daniel N. .... **New York, NY**

Budow, Leonard N. .... Great Neck, NY
Budow, Michael J. .... **Bethesda, MD**
Budow and Noble, P.C. .... **Washington, DC**
Bethesda, MD
Ellicott City, MD
Rockville, MD
Budow, Stephen I. .... **New York, NY**
Budow, Terri H. .... **Irving, TX**
Budra, Michael K. .... Kilauea, HI
Budreau, James H. .... Boston, MA
Budros, Barbara D. .... Traverse City, MI
Budrys, Ramona .... San Jose, CA
Budsberg, Brian L. .... **Olympia, WA**
Budwick, Michael S. .... **Miami, FL**
Budwick, Philip H.
Department of Transportation, Maritime Administration, GV
Budwig, Mark G. .... **San Diego, CA**
Budwig, Mark W. .... New York, NY
Budyak, Carole A. .... Chicago, IL
Budz, Chester H., Jr. .... Fort Myers, FL
Budzak, James E. .... Pittsburgh, PA
Budzik, James A. .... **Cleveland, OH**
Budzik, Matthew J. .... **Hartford, CT**
Budzik, Valerie J. .... New York, NY
Budzinski, Elizabeth M. .... **Chicago, IL**
Budzinski, Henry A. .... Chicago, IL
Budzinski, Michael A. .... Anchorage, AK
Budzyn, Ludomir A. .... **New York, NY**
Budzyn, Michael J. .... **Pasadena, CA**
Budzynski, Thomas J. .... Mount Clemens, MI
Bue, Carl O., Jr. .... Houston, TX
Bue, Kara L. .... **Washington, DC**
Buebendorf, Jeffrey F. .... **Norwich, CT**
Bueche, Failer, O'Callaghan & Zintsmaster
Flushing, MI
Bueche, Gregory J. .... **Chicago, IL**
Bueche, Gregory J. .... **Wheaton, IL**
Bueche, Howard J. .... Flushing, MI
Bueche, Kenneth G. .... Denver, CO
Bueche, Robin Ward .... Baton Rouge, LA
Buechel, Charles A., Jr. .... **Pittsburgh, PA**
Buechel & Conley .... **Covington, KY**
Buechel, D. Robert, Jr.
San Francisco, CA
Buechel, Edward J. .... **Covington, KY**
Buechel, William B. .... Concordia, KS
Buechele, Robert H. .... **Providence, RI**
Buecheler, Richard J. .... Syracuse, NY
Buecher, Glen G. .... Boca Raton, FL
Buechl, James L. .... **Boston, MA**
Buechler, Bruce .... **Roseland, NJ**
Buechler, Christopher L.
Department of the Navy, GV
Buechler, David M. .... Parker, SD
Buechler, Elizabeth M. .... United States Senate, Committee Legal Personnel, GV
Buechler, Gary M. .... **Parsippany, NJ**
New York, NY
Buechler, Gerald B., Jr. .... Dallas, TX
Buechler, Julie Marie .... Helena, MT
Buechler, Lisa .... Lincoln, NE
Buechler, Ruth Anne .... **Denver, CO**
Buechler, William M. .... Austin, TX
Buechley, Susan E. .... New York, NY
Buechner, C. Suzanne .... Haverford, PA
Buechner, Elizabeth J. .... Baltimore, MD
Buechner, Haffer, O'Connell, Meyers & Healey Co., L.P.A. .... **Covington, KY**
Cincinnati, OH
Buechner, Jack W. .... **Washington, DC**
Buechner, Paul E., III .... Menlo Park, CA
Buechner, Robert W. .... **Cincinnati, OH**
Buechner, William H., Jr. .... **Atlanta, GA**
Buechsenschuetz, Gretchen K.
Boston, MA
Buecker, Bernard John .... San Antonio, TX
Buecker, Thomas J. .... **Piqua, OH**
Buecker, Thomas J., Co., L.P.A.
Piqua, OH
Buege, Robert M. .... **Waukegan, IL**
Buegler, Larry D. .... St. Paul, MN
Buegler, Paul W. .... Brea, CA
Buehl, Robert T. .... Bargersville, IN
Buehl, Stephen T. .... **St. Helena, CA**
Buehler Atkins Associates .... Indianapolis, IN
Buehler, Barry R. .... Zephyr Cove, NV
Buehler, Bettina V. .... **Brattleboro, VT**
Buehler, Brice E., P.C. .... Phoenix, AZ
Buehler & Buehler .... **Lake Oswego, OR**
Portland, OR
Buehler, Charles L. .... Great Bend, KS
Buehler, Craig R. .... Lewistown, MT
Buehler, David A. .... **Columbus, GA**
Buehler, Donald R. .... Seattle, WA
Buehler, E. Marvin .... Arlington Heights, IL
Buehler, Earl G. .... Madison, WI
Buehler, George W. .... **Los Angeles, CA**
Buehler, J. Scott .... Ogden, UT
Buehler, J. Scott, Law Offices of .... Ogden, UT
Buehler, James C. (J.C.) .... Indianapolis, IN
Buehler, John E., Jr. .... Boston, MA
Buehler, John W. .... **Lake Oswego, OR**
Buehler, Joseph S. .... Chesterfield, MO
Buehler, Karen J. .... **Lake Oswego, OR**
Buehler, Kevin S. .... New York, NY
Buehler, Lauren C.
Environmental Protection Agency, Program Office Attorneys, GV
Buehler, Mark B. .... Costa Mesa, CA
Buehler, Rance V. .... West Dundee, IL
Buehler, Robert B. .... New York, NY
Buehler, Sara L. .... Chicago, IL
Buehler, Scott D. .... St. Charles, MO
Buehler, Stephen E. .... Chicago, IL
Buehler, Terrence, Law Offices of
Chicago, IL
Buehler, Thomas L. .... Cincinnati, OH

Buehler, Trevor K. ... New Philadelphia, OH
Buehne, Gregory J. ... Spokane, WA
Buehner, Candace Cavanaugh
Grosse Pointe Woods, MI
Buehner, Heidrun Marina ... St. Louis, MO
Buehner, John E. ... Atlanta, GA
Buehner, Lloyd R. ... Joplin, MO
Buehner, Lloyd R., III ... Joplin, MO
Buehner, Robert W., Jr. ... Bloomsburg, PA
Buehner, Robt. C. ... Monona, WI
Buehner, Ronald D. ... Houston, TX
Buehrer, Timothy S. ... Kolonia, TT
Buehrle, Edward V. ... Akron, OH
Bueide, Daniel A. ... Fargo, ND
Bueing, Ronald L. ... Seattle, WA
Buek, Richard W., Jr. ... Washington, DC
Bueker, John ... Boston, MA
Buel, Robert ... Manhattan, KS
Buel, Sarah M. ... Boston, MA
Buell, Ardin P. ... Chicago, IL
Buell, Barbara Hayes ... Boston, MA
Buell & Berner ... Larkspur, CA
Palo Alto, CA
San Francisco, CA
Buell, Bruce T. ... Colorado Springs, CO
Buell, Carol L. ... New York, NY
Buell, Curtiss N. ... Port Chester, NY
Buell, Deborah M. ... New York, NY
Buell, E. Rick, II, (P.C.) ... Larkspur, CA
Palo Alto, CA
Buell, Erika J. S. ... Boston, MA
Buell, Guy T. ... Austin, TX
Buell, James G. ... St. Louis, MO
Buell, Joseph P. ... Chicago, IL
Buell Law Firm ... Colorado Springs, CO
Buell, Lucille Polk ... Bronxville, NY
Buell, Maile E. ... Milwaukee, WI
Buell, Mark P. ... Tampa, FL
Buell, Michael D. ... Marietta, OH
Buell, Robert D. ... San Diego, CA
Buell, Robert M. ... Richmond, VA
Buell, Rodd R. ... Miami, FL
Buell, Rodd R., P.A. ... Coral Gables, FL
Miami, FL
Buell, Samuel W. ... Brooklyn, NY
Buell, Scott A. ... Brooklyn, NY
Buell & Sipe Co., L.P.A. ... Marietta, OH
Buell, Thor E. ... Mountain View, CA
Buell, Willis A. ... Sioux City, IA
Buellesbach, Richard P. ... Milwaukee, WI
Buelow, Clifford B. ... Milwaukee, WI
Buelow, Gary A. ... Painted Post, NY
Buelow, Henry D. ... St. Cloud, MN
Buelow, Roger M. ... Bakersfield, CA
Buelt, David L. ... Omaha, NE
Bueltel, Joseph A ... Owatonna, MN
Buemi, Sally J. ... North Haven, CT
Buenaventura, M. Rosalie Locsin
New York, NY
Buenaventura, Ricardo F. ... Tacoma, WA
Buenaventura, Servideo T. ... Quincy, MA
Buendia, Raymond ... San Diego, CA
Buendo, Frank P., Jr. ... Springfield, MA
Buenger, Caroline Broun ... Cincinnati, OH
Buenger, Julian V. ... Dallas, TX
Buenger, Julian V., P.C. ... Dallas, TX
Buenger, Michael L. ... Pierre, SD
Buenger, O. Charles, III ... Waco, TX
Buenker, Josef F. ... Houston, TX
Bueno, Antonio G. ... Los Angeles, CA
Bueno & Dresselhaus ... Los Angeles, CA
Bueno, Edgar D.
Department Of Health And Human Services, GV
Bueno, Irene B. ... United States Senate, Senatorial Assistants, GV
Bueno-Flores, Mary H. ... Inglewood, CA
Buente, Benjamin E., Jr. ... Evansville, IN
Buente, David T., Jr. ... Washington, DC
Buenzle, Desirée ... New York, NY
Buenzle, Robert J. ... Reston, VA
Buenzli, Howard M. ... Madison, WI
Buenzli, William L. ... Madison, WI
Buerger, Christian A. ... Washington, DC
Buerger, Moseley, Carson & Byrd, PLC
Franklin, TN
Buerger, Paul T., Jr. ... Buffalo, NY
Buerger, Richard A. ... Franklin, TN
Buerk, Caroline Hassett ... Buffalo, NY
Fredonia, NY
Buerkert, John E., Jr. ... Charlotte, NC
Buerkett, Lorilea ... Springfield, IL
Buerkle, Beeson, Ludwig, Jackson & Boner, L.C. ... Jackson, MO
Buerkle, Joe T. ... Jackson, MO
Buerle, Karen M. ... New Brunswick, NJ
Buerman, Gunther K. ... Rochester, NY
Buermann, Eric ... Miami, FL
Buermann, George H.
Upper Montclair, NJ
Buerstatte, Jon V. ... Eugene, OR
Buerstetta, Grant E. ... New York, NY
Buerstetta, Kristen Skog ... Newark, NJ
Bueschel, Richard Frederick ... Ellensburg, WA
Bueschel, Thomas A. ... Rockford, IL
Buescher, Charles M., Jr. ... Albuquerque, NM
Buescher, Daniel M. ... Washington, MO
Buescher, Joseph H., Jr. ... Tucson, AZ
Buescher, Mary Elizabeth O'Keefe
Grand Junction, CO
Buescher, Sarah A.
Securities and Exchange Commission, Division of Investment Management, GV
Buescher, Stephen L. ... Cleveland, OH
Buescher, Terry (Mary Therese)
St. Louis, MO
Buescher, Thomas B. ... Denver, CO
Buesing, Carl K. ... Sheboygan, WI
Buesing, Karen Meyer ... Tampa, FL
Buesing, Robert H. ... Tampa, FL
Buess, Terese M. ... Houston, TX
Buess, Thomas E. ... Chicago, IL
Buesser, Anthony C. ... Birmingham, MI
Buesser, Buesser, Black, Lynch, Fryhoff & Graham, P.C. ... Bloomfield Hills, MI
Detroit, MI
Buesser, Frederick G., III
Birmingham, MI
Buesser, Jennifer G. ... New York, NY
Buesser, William R. ... Bloomfield Hills, MI
Buestrin, Lisa M. ... Mequon, WI
Buetens & Buetens ... Hobe Sound, FL
Buetens, Eric D. ... Hobe Sound, FL
Buetens, Melvin W. ... Hobe Sound, FL
Bueter, Randall S. ... Little Rock, AR
Buethe, Bradley K. ... Tampa, FL
Buethe, Cynthia G. ... Lincoln, NE
Buethe, Neal T. ... St. Paul, MN
Buether, Eric W. ... Dallas, TX
Buetow, David R. ... Chicago, IL
Buetow, Herbert R. ... Schaumburg, IL
Buetow, Jennifer A. ... Hauppauge, NY
Buettner, Brian C. ... Rochester, NY
Buettner, Diane M. ... Bloomfield Hills, MI
Buettner, Kenneth L. ... Oklahoma City, OK
Buettner, Mary E. ... Waterloo, IL
Buettner, Mary E., P.C. ... Waterloo, IL
Buettner, Michael M. ... Fresno, CA
Buettner, Peter F. ... New York, NY
Buettner, Robert A. ... Birmingham, AL
Buettner, Robert D. ... Denver, CO
Buettner, Susan P. ... Lincoln, NE
Bufalini, David A. ... Tacoma, WA
Bufalini, David A., P.S., Inc. ... Tacoma, WA
Bufalino, Angelo J. ... Chicago, IL
Bufalino, Brian A. ... West Pittston, PA
Bufalino, Charles J. ... West Pittston, PA
Bufalino, Marie A. (Nanette) ... Naperville, IL
Bufalino, William E. ... Southfield, MI
Bufano, Anthony P. ... Jersey City, NJ
Bufano, Michelle M. ... Florham Park, NJ
Bufe, Eric T. ... Cleveland, OH
Bufe, John F. ... Tyler, TX
Buff, Ernest D. ... Morristown, NJ
Buff, Gary M. ... Department of Labor, Office of the Solicitor, GV
Buff, Merle Rubin ... New York, NY
Buff, Ralph M. ... Sacramento, CA
Buff, Robert C. ... Rockville Centre, NY
Buff, Shelly C. ... St. Charles, MO
Buffa, Bette M. ... Creve Coeur, MO
Buffa, Dudley W. ... Corvallis, OR
Buffa, Michael A. ... Commack, NY
Buffa, Thomas A. ... Chicago, IL
Buffalo, Henry M. ... Minneapolis, MN
Buffalo Road Professionals, P.C. ... Erie, PA
Buffalo, Vaughn J. ... New York, NY
Buffalo, William L. ... Las Vegas, NV
Buffaloe, Jane J. ... Nashville, TN
Buffalow, Gregory C. ... Mobile, AL
Buffam, David J. ... Shelton, CT
Buffardi, Linda E. ... Providence, RI
Buffardi, Louis J. ... Forest Park, IL
Buffardi, Louis P. ... Chicago, IL
Buffen, David L. ... Chicago, IL
Buffenstein, Allan S. ... Richmond, VA
Buffenstein, Daryl R. ... Atlanta, GA
Buffenstein, E. Bernard ... Cave Creek, AZ
Buffer, Pete F. ... Kalona, IA
Buffett, Jane B. ... Madison, WI
Buffett, Roger ... Madison, WI
Buffin, Robert J. ... San Francisco, CA
Buffington & Aaron, A Law Corporation
San Francisco, CA
Buffington, Alice A. ... Southfield, MI
Buffington, B. Scott ... Magee, MS
Buffington, Blake ... Austin, TX
Buffington, Bobbi K. ... Los Angeles, CA
Buffington, C. Phillip, Jr. ... Jackson, MS
Buffington, Carolyn Brown ... Cincinnati, OH
Buffington, Connie H. ... Marietta, GA
Buffington, Conrad ... Trussville, AL
Buffington, Damita G. ... Chicago, IL
Buffington, David N. ... San Francisco, CA
Buffington, Forrest G. ... Gallup, NM
Buffington, George N. ... San Francisco, CA
Buffington, G. N. ... Santa Fe, NM
Buffington, John E. ... Eureka, CA
Buffington, John Larry ... Collins, MS
Buffington, John R., III ... Woodlawn, MD
Buffington, John V. ... Philadelphia, PA
Buffington, Kimberly L. ... Los Angeles, CA
Buffington, Lamont E. ... Detroit, MI
Buffington, Lori A. ... Chowchilla, CA
Buffington, M. Dean ... Boise, ID
Buffington, Milton P. ... Washington, DC
Buffington, N. David
Saint Simons Island, GA
Buffington, Rahn R. ... Lykens, PA
Buffington, Robert W. ... Columbia, SC
Buffington, Sharon L. ... Hudson, WI
Buffington, Susan H. ... Richmond, VA
Buffington, Teresa Burkett ... Cheyenne, WY
Buffington, Wendy ... Tampa, FL
Buffmyer, Raymond G. ... Charlotte, MI
Buffo, Patricia M. ... Chicago, IL
Buffomante, Angelo A. ... Elma, NY
Buffomante, Frank J. ... Williamsville, NY
Buffon, Charles E. ... Washington, DC
Buffon, Kathleen V.
Farm Credit Administration, Legal Counsel Division, GV
Buffone, Samuel J. ... Washington, DC
Buffone, Steven P. ... New York, NY
Bufford, Dan F. ... Little Rock, AR
Bufford, Patrick H. ... East Hartford, CT
Bufford, Robyn Graham ... Birmingham, AL
Bufford, Samuel ... Los Angeles, CA
Buffum, Carol L. ... Atlanta, GA
Buffum, Paul ... Nashua, NH
Buffum, Theresa A., II ... Rockland, MA
Bufill, Lourdes M.
Environmental Protection Agency, Office of Enforcement and Compliance Assurance, GV
Bufkin, Cary E. ... Jackson, MS
Bufkin, Elizabeth T. ... Clarksdale, MS
Bufkin, James A. ... Lufkin, TX
Bufkin, Louis D. ... Lake Charles, LA
Bufkin, Michael E. ... Dundee, IL
Bufkin, Michael J. ... Louisville, KY
Bufkin & Peterson ... Dundee, IL
Bufkin, Richard L. ... Dallas, TX
Bufkin, Thomas Gerry ... Jackson, MS
Bufogle & Associates ... Tulsa, OK
Bufogle, Joseph F. ... Tulsa, OK
Buford, A. Walter ... Memphis, TN
Buford, Albert D., III ... Buchanan, VA
Buford, Andrea M. ... Chicago, IL
Buford & Associates, P.C. ... Fairfax, VA
Buford & Buford ... Macon, GA
Roberta, GA
Buford, C. Douglas, Jr. ... Little Rock, AR
Buford, Calvin D. ... Cincinnati, OH
Buford, Charles A. ... Clearwater, FL
Buford, Charlotte L.
Securities and Exchange Commission, Office of Municipal Securities, GV
Cleveland, OH
Buford, Daniel S. ... Tulsa, OK
Buford, Darryll A. ... New York, NY
Buford, Dorman ... Greenwood, MS
Buford, Floyd M., Jr. ... Macon, GA
Roberta, GA
Buford & Gonzalez, L.L.P. ... Austin, TX
Houston, TX
Buford, Henderson L. "Sam", III
Austin, TX
Buford & Jordan ... Austin, TX
Buford, Mary L. ... Omaha, NE
Buford, Michelle Keadle
New Orleans, LA
Buford, Mischa D. ... Overland Park, KS
Buford, Patrick O'B. ... Fairfax, VA
Buford, Peters & Ware, LLC ... Chicago, IL
Buford, Rivers, Jr. ... Tallahassee, FL
Buford, Robert P. ... Richmond, VA
Buford, Tasha O. ... Tallahassee, FL
Buford, Thomas C. ... Cleveland, OH
Buford, Thomas G. ... San Luis Obispo, CA
Buford, Winston V. ... Kimberling City, MO
Buford III, Robert L. ... Austin, TX
Houston, TX
Bufton, J. Kelly ... Chicago, IL
Bugaisky, Lawrence B. ... Washington, DC
Bugaj and Henry ... Honesdale, PA
Bugaj, Ronald M. ... Honesdale, PA
Bugalla, Brendi Kaplan ... Nashville, TN
Bugas, Theodore T. ... Astoria, OR
Bugatto, B. John ... San Francisco, CA
Bugay, Arthur L. ... Philadelphia, PA
Bugay, Hope Switkay ... Jenkintown, PA
Bugay, John J. ... Santa Barbara, CA
Bugay, Paul E. ... Owensboro, KY
Bugay, Scott R. ... North Miami Beach, FL
Bugbee & Conkle ... Toledo, OH
Bugbee, Jesse D. ... St. Albans, VT
Bugdanowitz, Bradley A.
San Francisco, CA
Bugden, Collins & Morton, L.C.
Salt Lake City, UT
Bugden, Walter F., Jr. ... Salt Lake City, UT
Bugeja, Harry P. ... Farmington Hills, MI
Bugen, Paul ... Glenside, PA
Bugg, A. Davis, Jr. ... Irvington, VA
Bugg, Alan L. ... Colorado Springs, CO
Bugg, Christopher ... Madison, WI
Bugg, Clifford N. ... Chillicothe, OH
Bugg, Glenda Gail ... Atlanta, GA
Bugg, J. Bruce, Jr. ... San Antonio, TX
Bugg, J. Bruce, Jr., A Professional Corporation
San Antonio, TX
Bugg, John A. ... Tulsa, OK
Bugg, John E. ... Durham, NC
Bugg, Mary Margaret ... Durham, NC
Bugg, Robert E. ... Clearwater, FL
Bugg, Steven W. ... Oklahoma City, OK
Bugg, Thomas H. ... Clinton, KY
Bugg, Todd E. ... Bloomington, IL
Bugg, Wolf & Wilkerson, P.A.
Durham, NC
Bugge, Lawrence J. ... Madison, WI
Buggs, Corey D. ... Lexington, NC
Buggs, Harrel T. ... Jacksonville, FL
Buggs, Mary Elizabeth ... Milwaukee, WI
Buggs, Stephen R. ... Platteville, WI
Buggy, Kenneth J. ... Harrisburg, PA
Buggy, Sean P. ... Philadelphia, PA
Bugh, Carolyn Elaine ... Miami, FL
Bugh, Claudia J ... South Bend, IN
Buginas, Scott J. ... Livermore, CA
Buglass, Georgia A. ... Chicago, IL
Bugley, Richard L. ... Westborough, MA
Buglio, Anthony S. ... Warwick, RI
Buglione, Albert C. ... Wayne, NJ
Buglione, Victor A. ... Ozone Park, NY
Bugliosi, Vincent T., Jr. ... Beverly Hills, CA
Bugna, LaVerne June, (Mrs.)
Newport Beach, CA
Bugner, J. O. ... Cave Creek, AZ
Bugni, Michael W. ... Seattle, WA
Bugoni, Paul F. ... New York, NY
Bugos, Joseph T. ... Lisle, IL
Bugos, Robert A. ... Anderson, SC
Bugosh, Pamela ... Brunswick, ME
Buh, Peter A. ... Rockford, IL
Buhai, Barbara J. ... Chicago, IL
Buhan, Elaine ... Tuckerton, NJ
Buharin, Amelia A. ... Minneapolis, MN
Buhay, William C. ... Marietta, GA
Buhite, Russell S. ... Tampa, FL
Buhl, B. Kingsley ... Bloomfield Hills, MI
Buhl, Diane M. ... Lexington, MA
Buhl, Herbert E., III ... Columbia, SC
Buhl, Lynn Yerges ... Auburn Hills, MI
Buhl, Paul D. ... East Haddam, CT
Middletown, CT
Buhl, William C. ... Paw Paw, MI
Buhle, Warren T. ... New York, NY
Buhler, Allen C. ... Racine, WI
Buhler, Bruce G. ... Marietta, GA
Buhler, Emile J., III ... New Orleans, LA
Buhler, Forrest A. ... Manhattan, KS
Buhler, Frank S., III ... Victoria, TX
Buhler, Gregory W. ... Peekskill, NY
Buhler, Joan E. ... Englewood, CO
Buhler, John Lockwood ... Racine, WI
Buhler, Kim H. ... Provo, UT
Buhler Law Firm, The ... Memphis, TN
Buhler, Lynn ... Memphis, TN
Buhler, Mark J. ... Orlando, FL
Buhler, Michelle ... Seattle, WA
Buhler, Phillip A. ... Jacksonville, FL
Buhler, Roman P. ... House of Representatives, Committee on House Administration, GV
Buhler, Stephen J. ... West Valley City, UT
Buhler, Violetta Kapsalis ... Chicago, IL
Buhlinger, P. Scott ... Bartlesville, OK
Buhlman, Robert A. ... Boston, MA
Buhman, Camille R. ... St. George, UT
Buholtz, Eileen E. ... Rochester, NY
Buholz, Laddie Allen ... Orlando, FL
Buholz, Steven Wm. ... Dallas, TX
Buhr, Gerald T. ... Lutz, FL
Buhr, Stephen M. ... Richmond, VA
Buhrer, R. Scott ... New Orleans, LA
Buhrfiend, Richard M. ... Elmhurst, IL
Buhring, Debra M. ... Chicago, IL
Buhrman, Jeffrey P. ... Portland, ME
Buhrman & Maddux ... Chattanooga, TN
Buhrman, Richard B. ... Alexandria, VA
Buhrman, Richard W. ... Chattanooga, TN
Buhrmann, David L. ... Abilene, TX
Buhrmann, James H. ... Crete, NE
Buhrow, Bonnie J. ... Milwaukee, WI
Buhrow, Kenneth H. ... Edgerton, WI
Milton, WI
Buhrow, Kimberly Y. Smith
Cleveland, OH
Buhrow, Kimberly Y. S. ... Akron, OH
Buhyoff, Marilyn B. ... Blacksburg, VA
Bui, Hung H. ... Arlington, VA
Bui, Mai-Phuong N. ... Los Angeles, CA
Bui, Marguerite L. ... Los Angeles, CA
Bui, Thuy T. ... Los Angeles, CA
Buice, B. Carl ... Milledgeville, GA
Buice, Kevin B. ... Atlanta, GA
Buice, R. Avon ... Macon, GA
Buice, R. Edward ... Wakefield, MA
Buice, William T., III ... New York, NY
Buick, Kevin E. ... De Kalb, IL
Waterman, IL
Buie, Alan M. ... Washington, DC
Buie, Craig Pennington ... Charlotte, NC
Buie, David Richard ... Kansas City, MO
Buie, Donald R. ... Winston-Salem, NC
Buie, Jane B. ... New Orleans, LA
Buie & Thompkins ... Winston-Salem, NC
Buie, William T. ... Livonia, MI
Bui-Eve, Hanna ... Palo Alto, CA
Buigas, Gabriel ... Miami, FL
Buigas, Hector ... Miami, FL
Buik, Richard D. ... Washington, DC
Buikema, Dirk H. ... Austin, TX
Buikema, Eric A. ... Birmingham, MI
Buikema, Hiskes, Dillner, O'Donnell & Marovich, Ltd. ... Orland Park, IL
South Holland, IL
Buikema, Paul R. ... Orland Park, IL
Buikema, Robert H. ... Milwaukee, WI
Buikema, Ronald ... South Holland, IL
Buikus, Donald H. ... Margate, FL
Builder, J. Lindsay, Jr. ... Winter Park, FL
Builta, James A. ... Austin, TX
Builta, Jonathan R. ... Anderson, IN
Buis, J. Stephen ... Richmond, VA
Buis, Pequita Jay ... Indianapolis, IN
Buisson, Andre J. ... Jennings, LA
Buisson, Andre J., P.L.C. ... Jennings, LA
Buist, Arthur L. ... Baltimore, MD
Buist & Byars, L.L.C. ... Charleston, SC
Kiawah Island, SC
Buist, Moore, Smythe & McGee, P.A.
Charleston, SC
Buist, Thomas G. ... Charleston, SC
Buitendorp, Rita Dawn ... Grand Rapids, MI
Buiteweg, Johannes A. ... Rochester Hills, MI
Buiteweg, Lori A. ... Ann Arbor, MI
Buiteweg, Thomas ... Detroit, MI
Buitron, Oscar ... Austin, TX
Bujalski, Zbigniew B. ... Atlanta, GA
Bujan, Jesus F. ... Miami, FL
Bujan, John M. ... Eden Prairie, MN
Bujarski, Richard J. ... Omaha, NE
Bujdud, Christian William ... Stamford, CT
Bujkovsky, Gustav G. ... San Diego, CA
Bujnoch, Dennis P. ... San Antonio, TX
Bujnowski, Mary Lynn ... Tampa, FL
Bujold, Frank J. ... Troy, MI
Bujold, Lawrence R. ... San Diego, CA
Bujold, Mark J. ... Brunswick, GA
Bujold, Michael J. ... Manchester, NH

Bujold, Robt. J. .... Iron Mountain, MI
Bujold, Thos. J. .... Duluth, MN
Bujold, Tyrone P. .... Minneapolis, MN
Buk, Robert J. .... Utica, MI
Bukac, James E. .... Oil City, PA
Bukar, Nancy A. .... Washington, DC
Bukata, Dianne H. .... Pasadena, CA
Bukata, Laura .... Chicago, IL
Bukata, Marta C. .... Chicago, IL
Bukaty, Edward F., III, (P.L.C.)
Metairie, LA
Bukaty, Edward F., III, Prof. Law Corp.
Metairie, LA
New Orleans, LA
Bukaty, John J. .... Kansas City, KS
Bukaty, John J., Jr. .... Kansas City, KS
Bukaty, Jos. A. .... Kansas City, KS
Bukaty, Mark A. .... Dallas, TX
Bukaty, Steve, A.J. .... Overland Park, KS
Bukaty, Steve A. J. .... Overland Park, KS
Bukawyn, Walter Michael .... Short Hills, NJ
Buker, Charles E., III .... Atlanta, GA
Buker, Charles E., Jr. .... Burnsville, NC
Buker, Daniel J. .... Tallahassee, FL
Buker, Jones, Morton & Haley, P.C.
Atlanta, GA
Buker, Katharine .... Beloit, WI
Buker, Margaret R. .... Alpharetta, GA
Buker, Michael .... Indianapolis, IN
Buker, Robert H., Jr. .... Clewiston, FL
Bukey & Bentley .... Seattle, WA
Bukey, David B. .... Seattle, WA
Bukhman, Dina .... Chicago, IL
Bukhman, Emil .... New York, NY
Buki, Dennis G. .... Philadelphia, PA
Buki, Gary A. .... New York, NY
Bukiet, Michael S. .... Clifton, NJ
Bukis, Joseph P. .... Philadelphia, PA
Buklad and Buklad .... South Orange, NJ
Buklad, Henry A., Jr. .... South Orange, NJ
Buklad, M. Theodora .... South Orange, NJ
Bukolt, Mary Anne F. .... Plattsburgh, NY
Bukorovic, Natasha .... Merrillville, IN
Bukosky, Michael A. .... Red Bank, NJ
Bukovac, Daniel .... Kansas City, MO
Bukovan, Deborah L. .... Columbus, OH
Bukowczyk, Robert J. .... Somerville, NJ
Bukowski, Chester J., Jr. .... Hartford, CT
Bukowski, Elaine Marie .... Prospect, KY
Bukowski, Gerard T. .... Kansas City, MO
Bukowski, Jacqueline Hansen
New York, NY
Bukowski, Jeffrey D. .... Reading, PA
Bukowski, John A., Jr. .... Bloomfield, NJ
Bukowski, Kenneth A. .... Oakland, CA
Bukowski, Kenneth J. .... Green Bay, WI
Buksbaum, Gregg S. .... Washington, DC
Bukuras, George P .... Boston, MA
Buky, Stanley V. .... West Palm Beach, FL
Bula, Michael S. .... Milwaukee, WI
Bula, Robert M. .... Kingman, AZ
Bulan, Cynthia L. .... Tampa, FL
Bulan, Harold P. .... Buffalo, NY
Bulan, Lynn A. .... Washington, DC
Bulan, Toby-Lee G. .... Buffalo, NY
Buland, Vali .... Cambridge, MA
Bulasko, Elizabeth E. .... Northbrook, IL
Bulasky, Louis .... San Francisco, CA
Bulavsky, Jerome E. .... Santa Monica, CA
Bulbow, David .... Dallas, TX
Bulbulia, Naim Dutch .... New York, NY
Bulchis, Edward W. .... Seattle, WA
Bulecza, Linda Griffiths .... Tallahassee, FL
Bulen, L. Keith .... Greenwood, IN
Bules, June E. .... Plymouth, IN
Bules, Raymond T. .... Canton, OH
Buley, Jeffrey T. .... Albany, NY
Buley, Joseph E. .... Portland, OR
Buley, Richard R. .... Missoula, MT
Bulfin, John J. .... West Palm Beach, FL
Bulfin, Robert M. .... Fort Lauderdale, FL
Bulfin, Robert M., P.A. .... Fort Lauderdale, FL
Bulfinch, Susan R. .... Simi Valley, CA
Bulford, Robert E. .... Akron, OH
Bulgarelli, Harold M. .... Novi, MI
Bulgatz, Joseph S. .... New York, NY
Bulgawicz, Susan L. .... Houston, TX
Bulger, Berube, McDermott & McOsker
Boston, MA
Bulger, Brian W. .... Chicago, IL
Bulger, Craig .... Department of Labor,
Office of Secretary, GV
Bulger, Harold W., Jr. .... Detroit, MI
Bulger, J. Brian .... Great Falls, MT
Bulger, Jay M. .... San Diego, CA
Bulger & Jensen .... Bridgeport, NE
Bulger, John .... Rochester, NY
Bulger, John R. .... Ludington, MI
Bulger, Michele L. .... Washington, DC
Bulger, Paul S. .... Portland, ME
Bulger, Richard F. .... Chicago, IL
Bulger, Robert J. .... Bridgeport, NE
Bulger, Robert W. .... New York, NY
Bulger, William M., Jr. .... Boston, MA
Bulger, William M., (P.C.) .... Boston, MA
Bulgin, Andrew D. .... Baltimore, MD
Bulian, Joseph .... New York, NY
Bulich, Antone S., Jr. .... Bakersfield, CA
Bulinski, Gregory P. .... Minneapolis, MN
Bulitt, David L. .... Greenbelt, MD
Bulka, Shmuel R. .... New York, NY
Bulkeley, Craig S. .... Miami, FL
Asheville, NC
Bulkeley, Craig S., P.A., Law Offices of
Miami, FL
Asheville, NC
Bulkeley, Harry C. .... Galesburg, IL
Bulkeley, J. Russell .... New York, NY
Bulkeley, Lewis E. .... Chicago, IL
Bulkeley, Charles S. .... Needham, MA
Bulkley, David R. .... Philadelphia, PA
Bulkley, James .... Aspen, CO
Bulkley, Josephine A. .... Washington, DC
Bulkley, Kimmberly M. .... Atlanta, GA
Bulkley, Richardson and Gelinas, LLP
Northampton, MA
Springfield, MA
Bulkley, Robert D., Jr. .... Salem, OR
Bulkley, Roy L. .... Topeka, KS
Bulko, Joseph N. .... Syracuse, NY
Bulko, Kenneth J. .... Schenectady, NY
Bull, Amanda E. .... Towson, MD
Bull, Amy Jo .... San Francisco, CA
Bull, Andrea .... Philadelphia, PA
Bull and Associates, P.A. .... Orlando, FL
Bull, Bartle .... New York, NY
Bull, Benjamin .... Phoenix, AZ
Bull, Beverly L. .... Stone Mountain, GA
Bull & Bull .... Berwick, PA
Bull, Charles L., Jr. .... Welsh, LA
Bull, Cohn and Associates
Santa Barbara, CA
Bull, Constance D. .... Houston, TX
Bull, Constance J. .... Lake Oswego, OR
Bull, David S. .... Raleigh, NC
Bull, Edward M., III .... San Francisco, CA
Bull, Edwin C. .... Phoenix, AZ
Bull, Eric .... Minneapolis, MN
Bull, Eugene H.
Federal Election Commission,
Office of the General Counsel, GV
Bull, Harrison E. .... Santa Barbara, CA
Bull, Harry C. .... Chicago, IL
Bull, Holly Weston .... Chicago, IL
Bull, Howard L. .... Palo Alto, CA
Bull, Ingall W., Jr. .... Pasadena, CA
Bull, James C. .... Denver, CO
Bull, James M. .... Sacramento, CA
Bull, Jan Arthur .... Bullhead City, AZ
Bull, Joy A. .... San Diego, CA
Bull, Kelly L. .... San Diego, CA
Bull, Kenneth W. .... Gaylord, MN
Bull, Lawrence L. .... Worcester, MA
Bull, Leland L., Jr. .... Seattle, WA
Bull, Marcia K. .... Montgomery, AL
Bull, Michael D. .... Lancaster, PA
Bull, Morreale & Judelson, P.C.
Middletown, NY
Bull, Nicholas .... Portland, ME
Bull, Peter D. .... New York, NY
Bull, Robert A. .... Berwick, PA
Bull, Robert E. .... Chicago, IL
Bull, Robert E. .... Berwick, PA
Bull, Robert J. .... Milwaukee, WI
Bull, Samuel T. .... Reno, NV
Bull, Stephen .... Lynchburg, VA
Bull, Stephen M. .... Orlando, FL
Bull, Stephen N. H. .... New York, NY
Bull, Stratton .... Jackson, MS
Bulla, Bonnie A. .... Las Vegas, NV
Bullano, Joseph V. .... New Castle, PA
Bullard, A. F. .... San Pedro, CA
Bullard, Anderson & Anderson, PLLC
Auburn Hills, MI
Clarkston, MI
Flint, MI
Pontiac, MI
Bullard, Andrew C. .... Kennett, MO
Bullard & Bullard .... Austin, TX
Bullard, Bullard & Spencer, L.L.C.
Dothan, AL
Bullard, Charles E. .... Fort Mitchell, KY
Bullard, Cheryl H. .... Columbia, SC
Bullard, Christopher K. .... Houston, TX
Bullard, Daniel, IV .... Macon, GA
Bullard, Dennine .... New York, NY
Bullard, Donald A. .... Oklahoma City, OK
Bullard, Edward T. .... Kansas City, MO
Bullard, Elizabeth M. .... Sugar Land, TX
Bullard, Garry R. .... Portland, OR
Bullard, Gregory E. .... Hanford, CA
Bullard, Gregory H. .... Chicago, IL
Bullard, H. Todd .... Rochester, NY
Bullard, H. Todd, Esq., P.C.
Rochester, NY
Bullard & Hayes .... Fort Mitchell, KY
Bullard & Hoehner, P.C.
Oklahoma City, OK
Bullard, Holly H. .... Los Angeles, CA
Bullard, J. Rhett .... Lake City, FL
Bullard, J. Warren .... Ocala, FL
Bullard, J. Warren, P.A., Law Office of
Ocala, FL
Bullard, Jacqueline L. .... Springfield, IL
Bullard, James C. .... Kennett, MO
Bullard, James E. .... Orange, CA
Bullard, James G. .... Minneapolis, MN
Bullard, James L. .... Marietta, GA
Bullard, Jane E. .... Austin, TX
Bullard, Jeffrey .... Troy, MI
Columbus, OH
Bullard, Jennie K. .... Greensburg, PA
Bullard, Jerry Douglas .... Fort Worth, TX
Bullard, John .... Parsons, KS
Bullard, John S. .... San Antonio, TX
Bullard, Kevin Jarrett .... Whiteville, NC
Bullard, Korshoj, Smith & Jernstedt, A Professional Corporation .... Portland, OR
Bullard, Larsen & Plock, P.C.
Fort Collins, CO
Bullard, Lisa Wallace .... Greensboro, NC
Bullard, Louisa J. .... Chevy Chase, MD
Bullard, Lyman G., Jr. (P.C.) .... Boston, MA
Bullard, Madison E., Jr. .... Raleigh, NC
Bullard, Marcia J .... Cleveland, OH
Bullard, Mercer E.
Securities and Exchange Commission,
Division of Investment Management, GV
Bullard, Norman D. .... Wilmington, NC
Bullard, Patrick S. .... Houston, TX
Bullard, Peter C. .... New Bedford, MA
Bullard, Peter W. .... Fort Collins, CO
Bullard, Randolph A. .... Miami, FL
Bullard, Robert K. .... Lake City, FL
Bullard, Robert L. .... Minneapolis, MN
Bullard, Rockwood W., III .... Clarkston, MI
Bullard, Ruby Warren .... Fayetteville, NC
Bullard, Susan F. .... Minneapolis, MN
Bullard, Thomas R. .... Limon, CO
Bullard, Trant .... Dothan, AL
Bullard, Valerie Alexander .... Mineola, NY
Bullard, W. Terry .... Dothan, AL
Bullard, Wayne A. .... Wilmington, NC
Bullard, William J. .... Oklahoma City, OK
Bullard, Willis C., Jr. .... Milford, MI
Bullard-Ferguson, Stephanie Rowenia
Bowie, MD
Bullaro & Carton, Chartered .... Chicago, IL
Wheaton, IL
Munster, IN
Bullaro, John J., Jr. .... Chicago, IL
Bullat, G. Nicholas .... Chicago, IL
Bulleit, Donald V. .... St. Petersburg, FL
Bulleit, Edward B. .... Gettysburg, PA
Bulleit, Kristy A. Niehaus
Washington, DC
Bulleit, Thomas E., Jr. .... Lexington, KY
Bulleit, Thomas N., Jr. .... Washington, DC
Bullen, D. Benjamin .... Memphis, TN
Bullen, Dana R. .... Alexandria, VA
Bullen, Frederick H. .... La Jolla, CA
Bullen, James L. .... Baton Rouge, LA
Lafayette, LA
Bullen, Jeffrey A. .... Colorado Springs, CO
Bullen, Joseph W., III .... Media, PA
Bullen, K. Anne .... Houston, TX
Bullen, Lawrence L. .... Jackson, MI
Bullen, Linda M. .... Chicago, IL
Bullen, Thomas K. .... Clarkston, MI
Buller, Carolyn J. .... Cleveland, OH
Buller, Carter R. .... Philadelphia, PA
Buller, Galen M. .... Santa Fe, NM
Buller, Pierce E. .... Cherry Hill, NJ
Philadelphia, PA
Buller, Terry D. .... Oakland, CA
Buller, Terry D., Professional Corporation
Oakland, CA
Buller, Thomas L. .... Mount Clemens, MI
Bullerdick, Kathie .... St. Louis, MO
Bullerdick, Kim H. .... Scottsdale, AZ
Bullerdieck, Michael J. .... Perryville, MO
Bulliard, Philip .... Metairie, LA
Bulliner, P. Alan .... New York, NY
Bullington, David B. .... Vinton, VA
Bullington, John T. .... Hillsboro, IL
Bullington, Michael G. .... Indianapolis, IN
Bullington, Paul E. .... New Orleans, LA
Bullington, R. Steven .... Pike Road, AL
Bullington, Sandra R. .... Monterey, VA
Bullington, Stephen A. .... Phoenix, AZ
Bullington, Tom W., Sr. .... Austin, TX
Bullington, Walter G., Jr. .... Brandon, FL
Bullington, White, McPhail, Jarmanand Evans, P.C. .... Hillsboro, IL
Bullion, Andrew B. .... Philadelphia, PA
Bullion, Bruce T. .... Little Rock, AR
Bullion, J. W. .... Dallas, TX
Bullion, Thomas M. .... Taylor, TX
Bullion, Thomas M., III .... Austin, TX
Bullion-Gascoyne, Deborah J.
Houston, TX
Bullis, Gary G., Ltd. .... Reno, NV
Bullis, James R. .... Moorhead, MN
Fargo, ND
Bullis, Jo Louise .... Mancelona, MI
Bullis, John .... Wahpeton, ND
Bullis, Paul A. .... Phoenix, AZ
Bullis, Robert G. .... Binghamton, NY
Bullis, Steven F. .... Port Kent, NY
Bullis, William H. .... Bakersfield, CA
Bullis, William M. .... Los Angeles, CA
Bullitt, Pascale Georgia .... New York, NY
Bullitt, Richard S. .... Morristown, NJ
Bullitt, Stimson .... Seattle, WA
Bullitt, William C. .... Philadelphia, PA
Bullivant Houser Bailey, A Professional Corporation .... Gold River, CA
Irvine, CA
Sacramento, CA
San Francisco, CA
Portland, OR
Seattle, WA
Vancouver, WA
Bullivant, Robert A. .... Virginia Beach, VA
Bullman, Barbara E. .... Gaithersburg, MD
Bullman & Bullman .... Charleston, WV
Bullman, Daniel T. .... Springfield, MA
Bullman, Edward L. .... Charleston, WV
Bullman, John P. .... Fort Wayne, IN
Bullman, Mark B. .... Atlanta, GA
Bullman, Sandra Sisson .... Charleston, WV
Bulloch, Donald M., Jr. .... Murfreesboro, TN
Bulloch, John T. .... Cleveland, OH
Bulloch, Steven N. .... Cleveland, OH
Bullock, Alexander McMillan
Stamford, CT
Washington, DC
Bullock, Alice Gresham .... Washington, DC
Bullock, Amy C. .... Raeford, NC
Bullock, Betty C. .... San Francisco, CA
Bullock, Brentley M. .... Portland, OR
Bullock, Bruce S. .... Jacksonville, FL
Bullock and Bullock .... Tulsa, OK
Bullock, Bunny .... Russellville, AR
Bullock, Charles E.
Environmental Protection Agency,
Office of Administrative Law Judges, GV
Bullock, Childs, Pendley, Reed, Herzfeld & Rubin .... Jacksonville, FL
St. Augustine, FL
Bullock, Christopher R. .... Richmond, VA
Bullock, Clinton J. .... Salt Lake City, UT
Bullock, Cynthia Anne .... Virginia Beach, VA
Bullock, Danne L. .... New York, NY
Bullock, Darlene D.
Department of Commerce,
Patent and Trademark Office, GV
Bullock, David M. .... Nashville, TN
Bullock, Deborah K. .... Dallas, TX
Bullock, Donald L. .... Shreveport, LA
Bullock, Edwin C. .... New York, NY
Bullock, Elza V., Jr. .... Houston, TX
Bullock, Fly and Hornsby .... Murfreesboro, TN
Bullock, Forman .... New Bedford, MA
Bullock, Frank W., Jr. .... Greensboro, NC
Bullock, Freeman M. .... Houston, TX
Bullock, Gary M. .... Portland, OR
Bullock, Howard N. .... Columbus, OH
Bullock, J. Jay .... Salt Lake City, UT
Bullock, J. Jerome .... Washington, DC
Bullock, J. Robert .... Provo, UT
Bullock, Jack T., II .... Winnemucca, NV
Bullock, Jacquelyn R. .... Brooklyn, NY
Bullock, James .... Houston, TX
Bullock, James F. .... Dallas, TX
Bullock, James N. .... Jackson, MS
Bullock, James R. .... La Junta, CO
Bullock, James S. .... St. Paul, MN
Laramie, WY
Bullock, Jay .... Lake Buena Vista, FL
Bullock, Jim E. .... Austin, TX
Bullock, Joan R. .... Toledo, OH
Bullock, John T. .... San Francisco, CA
Bullock, Kenneth E. .... Laurel, MS
Bullock Law Firm .... Salt Lake City, UT
Bullock Law Office .... La Junta, CO
Bullock Law Offices, Ltd.
Winnemucca, NV
Bullock, Loren J. .... Bessemer, AL
Bullock, Louis W. .... Tulsa, OK
Bullock, Maurice R. .... Midland, TX
Bullock, Miriam E. Joos .... Wayne, MI
Bullock, Monica Hyman .... Calumet City, IL
Bullock, Patricia W. .... Tulsa, OK
Bullock and Regier, P.C. .... Portland, OR
Vancouver, WA
Bullock, Reginald, Jr. .... New York, NY
Bullock, Richard P. .... Baton Rouge, LA
Bullock, Robert (Bob) .... Austin, TX
Bullock, Robert S. .... Washington, DC
Bullock, Robert V. .... Frankfort, KY
Bullock, Robin L. .... Springfield, MO
Bullock, Roddy M. .... Cincinnati, OH
Bullock, Roger H. .... Salt Lake City, UT
Bullock, Samuel H. .... Pitman, NJ
Bullock, Scott G. .... Washington, DC
Bullock, Scott & Neisig, A Professional Corporation .... Midland, TX
Odessa, TX
Bullock, Stafford G. .... Raleigh, NC
Bullock, Stephen C. .... Lake City, FL
Bullock, Stephen C. .... Syracuse, NY
Bullock, Stephen G. .... New Orleans, LA
Bullock, Steve .... Miami, FL
Bullock, Steven C. .... Inkster, MI
Bullock, Terry L. .... Topeka, KS
Bullock, Thomas D. .... Lexington, KY
Bullock, Thomas F. .... Milmay, NJ
Bullock, Valerie A. .... Bastrop, TX
Bullock & Van Kleef .... Dardanelle, AR
Russellville, AR
Bullock, Victor A. .... Los Angeles, CA
Bullock, W. Brent .... American Fork, UT
Bullock, Willard T., IV .... Atlanta, GA
Bullock, William B. .... Murfreesboro, TN
Bullock, William E., Jr. .... Fairfield, AL
Bullock, William G. .... Texarkana, TX
Bullock, William R. .... Dardanelle, AR
Bullock, Wm. O. .... Memphis, TN
Bulloff, Aaron H. .... Cleveland, OH
Bulloff, Frances W. .... Cleveland, OH
Bulloff, Steven M. .... Indianapolis, IN
Bullon, Kathryn M. .... Fond du Lac, WI
Bullowa, Arthur M. .... New York, NY
Bulls, Mary L. .... Atlanta, GA
Bulluck, Dona Smith .... Albany, NY
Bulluck, Jacqueline R.
Federal Mine Safety and Health Review Commission,
Office of the Administrative Law Judges, GV
Bullwinkel, Aaron J. .... Boston, MA
Bullwinkel, George E. .... Chicago, IL
Bullwinkel, Jeffrey G.
Department of Justice,
Criminal Division, GV
Bullwinkel, Kristen A. .... Boston, MA
Bullwinkel Partners, Ltd. .... Chicago, IL
Bulmahn, T. Paul .... Denver, CO
Bulman, Cornelius, Jr. .... Columbus, OH
Bulman, Dunie, Burke & Feld, Chartered
Washington, DC
Bethesda, MD
Bulman, James C. .... Portsmouth, RI
Bulman, John E. .... Cambridge, MA
Providence, RI
Bulman, John G. .... Scituate, MA
Bulman, Joseph D. .... Bethesda, MD
Bulman, Joseph Robert .... South Amboy, NJ
Bulman, Lawrence Z. .... Bethesda, MD
Bulman, Leonard Z. .... Annapolis, MD
Bulman, Michael S. .... Amherst, MA

Buonassissi, Henning, Campbell & Moffet, A Professional Corporation **Washington, DC**
Fairfax, VA
Buonassissi, Joseph V., II ....**Fairfax, VA**
Buonauro, Robert J. ....**Orlando, FL**
Buonauro, Robert J., P.A. ....**Orlando, FL**
Buoncristiani, David ....**San Francisco, CA**
Buondelmonte, Charles ....Woodbury, NY
Buongiorno, Ernest A. ....**Tarzana, CA**
Buoniconti, Nicholas A., III ....**Orlando, FL**
Buoniconti, Stephen John ....Springfield, MA
Buono, Anthony F. ....Framingham, MA
Buono, Anthony G. ....Kinderhook, NY
Buono, Arthur C. ....Vienna, VA
Buono, Barbara J. ....Morristown, NJ
Buono Block P.C. ....**Portland, OR**
Buono, David A., II ....**Dallas, TX**
Buono, David J. ....**Portland, OR**
Buono, Dean J. ....**Marlton, NJ**
Buono, Francis M. ....**Washington, DC**
Buono, Frank A. ....Brooklyn, NY
Buono, John F., Jr. ....Alameda, CA
Buono, Kathryn M. ....**Milwaukee, WI**
Buonocore, Ann E. ....San Antonio, TX
Buonocore, Colleen E. ....Amherst, NY
Buonocore, Ernest S. ....**White Plains, NY**
Buonocore, John H., Jr. ....**Morristown, NJ**
Buonocore, Kristine J. ....Yonkers, NY
Buonocore, Peter A. ....**New York, NY**
Buonocore, Thomas A. ....**Parsippany, NJ**
Buonocore & Trevisan, P.C.
Morristown, NJ
Parsippany, NJ
Buonodono, Patricia K. ....Marietta, GA
Buonomo, Donald G. ....Mount Kisco, NY
Buonomo, Lawrence S. ....**Detroit, MI**
Buonopane, Edward B. ....Chatham, NJ
Buonopane, Michael M. ......**Glastonbury, CT**
Buonpastore, Alan N. ....New York, NY
Buoscio, Angelo A. ....Merrillville, IN
Buoscio, F. Ronald ....Chicago, IL
Buoscio, Harry R. ....Bridgeview, IL
Buoscio, Pera, Kramer & Nowak
Merrillville, IN
Buoymaster, John W. ....San Francisco, CA
Bupp, C. Randall ....**Oakland, CA**
Bupp, David Wm. ....**York, PA**
Buppert, Carolyn Knight ....Annapolis, MD
Buppert, Stuart G., II ....Baltimore, MD
Buquicchio, Frank L. ....**Westbury, NY**
Burach, Ellen A. ....Brooklyn, NY
Burack, Emanuel ....Columbia, SC
Burack, James ....Washington, DC
Burack, Jeffrey P. ....New York, NY
Burack, Marshall R. ....**Miami, FL**
Burack, Michael L. ....**Washington, DC**
Burack, Mitchell E. ....**Philadelphia, PA**
Burack, Thomas S. ....**Concord, NH**
Manchester, NH
Buraglio, Rockne J. ....Highlands Ranch, CO
Burak Anderson & Melloni, PLC
Burlington, VT
Burak & Berg ....San Francisco, CA
Burak, Blackie, Law Office of
Walnut Creek, CA
Burak, Brian A. ....Evanston, IL
Burak, Charis M. ....**Harrisburg, PA**
Burak, H. Paul (IBA) ....**New York, NY**
Burak, Janet J. ....**Liberty Corner, NJ**
Burak, Janet L. ....**Prospect Heights, IL**
Burak, Mark H. ....**Boston, MA**
Burak, Michael L. ....**Burlington, VT**
Burakoff, Linda Kim ....Los Angeles, CA
Burakoff, Michael P. ....Wayne, NJ
Burakoff, William L. ....**Irvine, CA**
Burakreis, Dorothy R. ....Department of Justice, Environment and Natural Resources Division, GV
Buraks, Kevin H. ....**Philadelphia, PA**
Buran, David C. ....**Burlington, VT**
Buran, John P. ....Manitowoc, WI
Buran Law Offices ....Manitowoc, WI
Buran, Reginald P. ....Manitowoc, WI
Burandt, Robert B. ....Cape Coral, FL
Buranich, William P. ....**San Francisco, CA**
Buranosky, Thomas ....**Chicago, IL**
Buras, A. Wayne ....**Covington, LA**
Buras, Gilbert R., Jr. ....New Orleans, LA
Buras, Robert V. J. ....New Orleans, LA
Buratti, Barbara K. ....**Oklahoma City, OK**
Buratti, Roberta N. ....Kenosha, WI
Buratto, Raymond J. ....Rochester Hills, MI
Burau, James K. ....**Reno, NV**
Burba, Christopher M. ....Cleveland, OH
Burbach, Barbara L. ....**Milwaukee, WI**
Burbach, Charles P. ....Southfield, MI
Burbach, Edward D. ....**Houston, TX**
Burbach, George V. ....Brooklyn, NY
Burbach, Jeffrey D. ....**The Woodlands, TX**
Burbach, John P. ....**Huntsville, AL**
Burbach, Max J. ....**Omaha, NE**
Burbach, Paul J. ....Milwaukee, WI
Burbach, Robert ....Omaha, NE
Burbach & Stansbury, S.C.
Milwaukee, WI
Burbach, Stephen D. ....**Los Angeles, CA**
Burbach, William F. ....San Francisco, CA
Burbacher, Charles R., II ....Linville, NC
Burback, Bradley Allen ....Arvada, CO
Burbage, Jesse S., III ....**Atlanta, GA**
Burbage, Lindsay L. ....Trenton, NJ
Burbage, Paul ....Costa Mesa, CA
Burbage and Ramsey ....Trenton, NJ
Burbage & Weddell, L.L.C. ....**Atlanta, GA**
Burban, Elizabeth M. ....New York, NY
Burban, Peter ....Chicago, IL
Burbank, C. Todd ....**Orlando, FL**
Burbank & Collins ....**Louisville, KY**
Burbank, David O. ....Pittsfield, MA
Burbank Dodson & McDonald
El Dorado, AR
Burbank, Donald B. ....Shingle Springs, CA
Burbank, Gary R. ....El Dorado, AR
Burbank, Harold Haley, II ....Kennebunk, ME
Burbank, Jeffrey R. ....Logan, UT
Burbank, Kelton M. ....Pittsfield, MA
Burbank, Linda E. ....Portland, OR
Burbank, Paul Whittaker ....Rochester, NY
Burbank, Priscilla A. ....Richmond, VA
Burbank, Robert J. ....St. Louis, MO
Burbank, Rosalind A. ....**Chicago, IL**
Burbank, Stephen B. ....Philadelphia, PA
Burbank, Virginia R. Collins
Louisville, KY
Burbank, William F. ....**Louisville, KY**
Burbank, Winston S. ....Fairbanks, AK
Burbidge, Brinton R. ....Salt Lake City, UT
Burbidge, Carnahan, Ostler & White, L.L.C.
Salt Lake City, UT
Burbidge, David ....**Cedar Rapids, IA**
Iowa City, IA
Waterloo, IA
Burbidge, James E. ....Ventura, CA
Burbidge and Mitchell
Salt Lake City, UT
Burbidge, Richard D. ....**Salt Lake City, UT**
Burbidge, Sarah ....San Francisco, CA
Burbine, R. A. ....Holbrook, MA
Burbott, James E., II ....San Dimas, CA
Burbott, Pamela J. ....Royal Oak, MI
Burbridge, Glen A. ....**Denver, CO**
Burbrink, Roy D. ....Plymouth, IN
Burby, William E., Jr. ....Los Angeles, CA
Burcat, Bruce H. ....King Of Prussia, PA
Burcat, Joel R. ....**Harrisburg, PA**
Burcat, Peter S., Law Offices of
Burlingame, CA
Morgan Hill, CA
Medford, NJ
Aston, PA
Burcat, Peter S., Law Offices of
San Francisco, CA
San Jose, CA
Cherry Hill, NJ
Philadelphia, PA
Burce, Gregory C. ....**Milwaukee, WI**
Burch, Alan R. ....Treasury Department, Office of the Comptroller of the Currency, GV
Burch, Andrew J. ....Benton Harbor, MI
Burch, Ashley S. ....**Monroe, LA**
Burch & Associates, P.C. ....Dallas, TX
Burch, Carleton R. ....**Los Angeles, CA**
Burch, Charles B. ....Moraga, CA
Burch, Charles H. ....Hardin, IL
Burch, Clarence L. ....Chicago, IL
Burch, Clyde M. ....Shelbyville, MO
Burch & Cracchiolo, P.A. ....**Mesa, AZ**
Phoenix, AZ
Scottsdale, AZ
Tempe, AZ
Burch, Cynthia B. ....Charlotte, NC
Burch, Cynthia L. ....**Los Angeles, CA**
Burch, Dana A. ....Tulsa, OK
Burch, David R. ....Los Angeles, CA
Burch, Dean ....Washington, DC
Burch, Denice Sayers ....**Atlanta, GA**
Burch, Derek K. ....**Oklahoma City, OK**
Burch, Donald V. ....**Jackson, MS**
Burch, Dorothy Bass ....**Raleigh, NC**
Burch, Dorothy N. ....Los Angeles, CA
Burch, E. Davison ....**Athens, GA**
Burch, Edward Davison, Jr. ....**Atlanta, GA**
Burch, Eric J. ....**Manchester, TN**
Burch, Francis B., Jr. ....**Baltimore, MD**
Burch, Frank Haze ....**Phoenix, AZ**
Burch & George, A Professional Corporation
Oklahoma City, OK
Burch, Gregory F. ....**Houston, TX**
Burch, Heidi L. ....**San Francisco, CA**
Burch, J. Thomas, Jr. ....Alexandria, VA
Burch, James L. ....Moraga, CA
Burch, James W. ....Salt Lake City, UT
Burch, John V., (P.C.) ....**Atlanta, GA**
Burch, Jonathan W. ....**Oklahoma City, OK**
Burch, Jonathan W., P.C.
Oklahoma City, OK
Burch, Joseph T. ....Lexington, KY
Burch, Kenneth W. ....Houston, TX
Burch, Kevin P. ....Detroit, MI
Burch, Kristan B. ....**Norfolk, VA**
Burch, Kyle A. ....Media, PA
Burch, Larry N. ....Greenbelt, MD
Burch, Laurie J. ....Raleigh, NC
Burch, LeAnne P. ....**Monticello, AR**
Burch, Marjorie A. ....Modesto, CA
Burch, Marsha A. ....**Sacramento, CA**
Burch, Micah ....**New York, NY**
Burch, Paul M. ....Pageland, SC
Burch, Porter & Johnson ....**Memphis, TN**
Burch, Preston R. ....**Columbia, SC**
Burch, R. A. "Rick" ....Gulfport, MS
Burch, Randy T. ....**Reading, PA**
Burch, Richard C. ....**Towson, MD**
Burch, Richard J. (Rex) ....**Houston, TX**
Burch, Richard K. ....Santa Barbara, CA
Burch, Robert B., Jr. ....Los Angeles, CA
Burch, Robert D. ....**Los Angeles, CA**
Burch, Robert E. ....Charlotte, TN
Burch, Robert J. ....Coquille, OR
Burch, Robert L. ....New Philadelphia, OH
Burch, Sarena D. ....**Columbia, SC**
Burch, Stanley E. ....Dallas, TX
Burch, Stephanie L. ....**Chicago, IL**
Burch, Stephen R. ....**Windsor, NC**
Burch, Susan E. ....Denver, CO
Burch, Susan R. ....High Point, NC
Burch, Thomas C. ....**San Francisco, CA**
Burch, Thomas G., Jr. ....**Atlanta, GA**
Burch, Thomas J., III ....Albany, NY
Burch, Thomas W., III ....**Houston, TX**
Burch, Timothy E. ....Charlotte, NC
Burch, Timothy J. ....**Washington, DC**
Baltimore, MD
Burch, Tracy A. ....Shreveport, LA
Burch, V. Reagan ....**Houston, TX**
Burch, W. Jeffrey ....**Irvine, CA**
Burch, William A. ....**Morrison, IL**
Burch, William R. ....Chicago, IL
Burch, William T., Jr. ....Syracuse, NY
Burch, Wm. E. ....Chicago, IL
Burcham, Charles Lee ....**Reno, NV**
Burcham, Dan H. ....Long Beach, CA
Burcham, Jack ....Austin, TX
Burcham, Jeffrey G. ....Martinsburg, WV
Burcham, Scott A. ....**Lincoln, NE**
Burcham, Thomas H. ....Berkeley, CA
Burcham, Tom R., III ....**Farmington, MO**
Burchanowski, Peter ....Williamsport, PA
Burchard, Daniel L. ....**Burlington, VT**
Burchard, Dennis D. ....National City, CA
Burchard, John G., Jr. ....Okanogan, WA
Burchard, Robert K. ....Gonzales, TX
Burchell, John J. ....Omaha, NE
Burchell, Patricia W. ....**Hattiesburg, MS**
Burcher, E. Andrew ....**Alexandria, VA**
Burcher, Thomas A. ....Hampton, VA
Burcheri, Russell C. ....Mineola, NY
Burchett, Alan E. ....**Chico, CA**
Burchett, Albert A. ....Prestonsburg, KY
Burchett, Brian L. ....**San Diego, CA**
Burchett, Charla McNally ....**Sarasota, FL**
Burchett, Charles Richard ....Glasgow, KY
Burchett, Curtis Allen ....Pueblo, CO
Burchett, Dale ....Glasgow, KY
Burchett, Dewey E., Jr. ....Benton, LA
Burchett, Marjorie J. ....**San Diego, CA**
Burchett, Paul P. ....Prestonsburg, KY
Burchett, Philip Ely ....Lebanon, VA
Burchett, Robert L. ....**Rockville, MD**
Burchett, Sam P. ....**Lexington, KY**
Burchett, Stephen D. ....San Diego, CA
Burchett, Stephen S. ....**Ashland, KY**
Burchett, Warren F. ....Citrus Heights, CA
Burchetta, Collins & Hanley, LLP
Carmel, NY
New York, NY
White Plains, NY
Burchetta, James D. ....**Carmel, NY**
White Plains, NY
Burchetta, Joseph L. ....**Carmel, NY**
Burchette, Anastasia ....Los Angeles, CA
Burchette, Robert L. ....**Charlotte, NC**
Burchette, William H. ....**Washington, DC**
Burchfiel, Kenneth J. ....**Washington, DC**
Burchfiel, Robert B. ....**San Jose, CA**
Burchfiel, Robert E. ....Wichita, KS
Burchfield, Bobby R. ....**Washington, DC**
Burchfield & Burchfield ....Columbus, OH
Burchfield, Cynthia L. ....Tacoma, WA
Burchfield, Donna C. ....**Atlanta, GA**
Burchfield, John W. ....Sugar Land, TX
Burchfield, Kenneth E. ....**Brighton, MI**
Burchfield, Laura ....Columbus, OH
Burchfield, Martin D. ....**Van Wert, OH**
Burchfield, Marvin ....Greenville, MS
Burchfield, Park & Heddon, P.C.
Brighton, MI
Howell, MI
Burchfield, Patricia A., (Mrs.)
Bloomington, IN
Burchfield, Randy ....Columbus, OH
Burchfield, Thomas E. ....Barrington, IL
Burchik, Mary H. ....Lebanon, PA
Burchill, Andrew S. ....**New York, NY**
Burchill, John J. ....Boston, MA
Burchill, William R., Jr. ....Administrative Office Of The United States Courts, GV
Burchinow, Elsa Djab ....Denver, CO
Burchinow, Naran U. ....St. Louis, MO
Burchmore, David W. ....**Cleveland, OH**
Burchstead, Harry B., Jr. ....Sumter, SC
Burchuk, Hillary B. ....Department of Justice, Antitrust Division, GV
Burciaga, Eloy ....Chicago, IL
Burcik, Richard W. ....West Chester, PA
Burcin, Steve W. ....Richmond, VA
Burck, Cyril B., Jr. ....Metairie, LA
Burck, H. Mark ....**Houston, TX**
Burck, Lapidus & Lanza, P.C.
Houston, TX
Burck, William A., III ....Westborough, MA
Burcke, Joseph R. ....**St. Louis, MO**
Burckle, Alton G. ....Tustin, CA
Burcz, Roberta Anne ....Bay Head, NJ
Burczak, Alan J. ....Plattsburgh, NY
Burczyk, Raymond ....Racine, WI
Burd & Associates, P.C. ....Houston, TX
Burd, Bartz & Gutenkauf
Minneapolis, MN
Burd, Daniel H. ....**Washington, DC**
Burd, Gene ....Houston, TX
Burd, Gene M. ....Philadelphia, PA
Burd, James M. ....Louisville, KY
Burd, James P. ....Andover, NY
Burd, John S. ....Carmel, CA
Burd, L. Paul ....**Minneapolis, MN**
Burd, Lee R. ....**Sioux Falls, SD**
Burd Magathan Lozano & Zacherl, L.L.P.
Miami, FL
Burd & Naylor ....**Los Angeles, CA**
Santa Ana, CA
Burd, Ronald P. ....Hermosa Beach, CA
Burd, Stuart ....Elkins Park, PA
Burd, Warren M. ....Hempstead, NY
Burd, William G. ....**Miami, FL**
Burd, William M. ....**Santa Ana, CA**
Burda, Christi L. ....Grand Rapids, MI
Burda, Joan M. ....Elyria, OH
Burda, John A. ....**Chicago, IL**
Burda, Robert T. ....Dublin, OH
Burdack, Karen A. ....**Fort Worth, TX**
Burde, Howard A. ....Harrisburg, PA
Burde, Laura I. ....New York, NY
Burdeaux, Charles M. ....Houston, TX
Burdeaux, Paul F. ....Dallas, TX
Burdega, M. Dave ....Deer Park, WA
Burdelik, Thomas L. ....Chicago, IL
Burdelik, Thomas L. & Associates
Chicago, IL
Burdell, Charles S., Jr. ....Seattle, WA
Burdell, Jody M. ....Pittsburgh, PA
Burden, Alice E. ....**Irvine, CA**
Burden, Beverly M. ....Lexington, KY
Burden, Brad W. ....Lincoln, NE
Burden, Brian A., P.A. ....**Tampa, FL**
Burden, Brian Anthony ....**Tampa, FL**
Burden, Carter ....New York, NY
Burden, Christian C. ....**Tampa, FL**
Burden, Christopher W. ....**New York, NY**
Burden, Crystal J. ....Brooklyn, NY
Burden, David G. ....**Winnetka, IL**
Burden, Dianne S. ....Boston, MA
Burden, Donna L. ....**Buffalo, NY**
Burden, Elizabeth S. (Betsy)
Palm Beach, FL
Burden, Gregory L. ....Hermosa Beach, CA
Burden, James E. ....**Oakland, CA**
San Francisco, CA
Burden, James E. ....New York, NY
Burden, James E., Inc. A Professional Law Corporation ....**San Francisco, CA**
Burden, Jared L. ....Washington, DC
Burden, Jeffry C. ....Richmond, VA
Burden, Joseph ....**New York, NY**
Burden, Linda J. ....Santa Ana, CA
Burden, Mark M. ....**Chicago, IL**
Burden, Ronald G. ....**New York, NY**
Burden, Thomas H. ....Ypsilanti, MI
Burden, W. Cotton ....Niwot, CO
Burden, Winfred E., Jr. ....Bellevue, WA
Burdett, Christopher C. ....**Stamford, CT**
Burdett, Christopher C., P.C., Law Offices of
Stamford, CT
Burdett, Gilbert U. ....**Billings, MT**
Burdett, James C. ....**Chicago, IL**
Burdett, James E. ....Portland, OR
Burdett, James R. ....**Washington, DC**
Burdett, Joseph W. ....**Los Angeles, CA**
Burdett Law Firm, P.C. ....**Billings, MT**
Burdett, Morgan & Thomas, L.L.P.
Amarillo, TX
Burdett, Russell L. ....Demopolis, AL
Burdett, Thomas Lee, (P.C.) ....Amarillo, TX
Burdette, Alan ....Birmingham, AL
Burdette, Bradford K. ....**Dallas, TX**
Burdette, Brooks R. ....**New York, NY**
Burdette, Cathy J. ....Department of Justice, Civil Division, GV
Burdette, Dee-Ann ....Kenova, WV
Burdette, Douglas Lee ....**Seattle, WA**
Burdette, Elliott E. ....Dallas, TX
Burdette, H. Carter ....**Fort Worth, TX**
Burdette, J. Dexter ....Kansas City, KS
Burdette, Jeffrey Thomas
Mount Vernon, KY
Burdette, John N. ....**Frederick, MD**
Burdette, Kathleen A. ....Boston, MA
Burdette, Kristine A. ....Fairmont, WV
Burdette, Mary Clariday ....**Dallas, TX**
Burdette, Michael J. ....**West Des Moines, IA**
Burdette, R. Milo ....Austin, TX
Burdette, Rebecca P. ....Houston, TX
Burdette, Robert B. ....Library of Congress, Congressional Research Service, GV
Burdette, Timothy J. ....**Pittsburgh, PA**
Burdette, Virginia Andrews ....Mukilteo, WA
Burdette, William J. ....**Houston, TX**
Burdge, Clifford S., Jr. ....**Hartford, CT**
West Hartford, CT
Burdge, Michael J. ....**Dayton, OH**
Burdge, Richard J., Jr. ....**Los Angeles, CA**
Burdge, Richard W. ....Indianapolis, IN
Burdge, Ronald L. ....Dayton, OH
Burdi, James F. ....Garden City, NY
Burdick, Ben L. ....Oklahoma City, OK
Burdick, Brian L. ....**Indianapolis, IN**
Burdick, Bruce E. ....**St. Louis, MO**
Burdick, Burton E. ....Fort Lauderdale, FL
Burdick, Burton E., P.A.
Fort Lauderdale, FL
Burdick, Carl R. ....**St. Joseph, MI**
Burdick, Christopher D.
San Francisco, CA
Burdick, Christopher W. ....**New York, NY**
Burdick, Clifton D. ....San Diego, CA
Burdick & DiLeo, P.C. ....**Worcester, MA**
Burdick, Eugene A. ....Sarasota, FL
Williston, ND
Burdick, Fretel & Piombino ....Madison, CT
Burdick, Geoffrey C. ....West Palm Beach, FL
Burdick, Glen M. ....**Oklahoma City, OK**
Burdick, Gregory S. ....West Palm Beach, FL
Burdick, Harold A. ....Boulder, CO
Burdick, James W. ....**Bloomfield Hills, MI**
Burdick, John A., Jr. ....**Worcester, MA**
Burdick, John O. ....Green Bay, WI
Burdick, John W. ....Yucca Valley, CA
Burdick, Kenneth A. ....Austin, TX
Burdick, Kevin J. ....Auburn, CA

Burgess, T. David ..... Williamsburg, OH
Burgess, T. David, Co., L.P.A.
Williamsburg, OH
Burgess, Thomas C. ..... Akron, OH
Burgess, Thomas J.
Federal Energy Regulatory Commission, Office of the General Counsel, GV
Burgess, Tim L. ..... Houston, TX
Burgess, Tim L., P.C. ..... Houston, TX
Burgess, Timothy C. ..... Anniston, AL
Burgess, Timothy C. ..... Montgomery, AL
Burgess, Timothy M. ..... Anchorage, AK
Burgess, Todd ..... Phoenix, AZ
Burgess, Virginia Vance ..... Portland, OR
Burgess, W. Gregg ..... Department of Energy, Office of the General Counsel, GV
Burgess, Wells D. ..... Department of Justice, Environment and Natural Resources Division, GV
Burgess, William E. ..... Virginia Beach, VA
Burgess, William P. ..... Huntsville, AL
Burgess, William T. ..... Detroit, MI
Burgess, William T. ..... Hendersonville, TN
Burgess-Farrell, Susan L. ..... New York, NY
Burgess Lawson, Yvonne ..... Wilsonville, OR
Burgess-Solomon, Jennifer ..... Miami, FL
Burget, Mark E. ..... Oklahoma City, OK
Burgett, Dalton J. ..... Jamestown, NY
Burgett, David W. ..... Washington, DC
Burgett, Donald H., Jr. ..... Willmar, MN
Burgett, George L. ..... Chicago, IL
Burgett, Henry A. ..... Ponte Vedra Beach, FL
Burgett, John M. ..... Washington, DC
Burgett, John Michael ..... Lafayette, IN
Burgett, Jonas Q. ..... Denver, CO
Burgett, Keith E. ..... Council Bluffs, IA
Burgett, Paul R. ..... Coquille, OR
Burgett & Robbins ..... Dunkirk, NY
Jamestown, NY
Mayville, NY
Westfield, NY
Warren, PA
Burgett, Stacy L. ..... Cocoa, FL
Burgett, Susanna C. ..... Boston, MA
Burgett, Timothy S. ..... Monrovia, CA
Burgfechtel, R. Jeffrey ..... Menomonie, WI
Burggraf, Norman L. ..... Granger, IN
Burgh, Balian & Bergstein
Sherman Oaks, CA
Burgh, Dianna M. ..... Los Angeles, CA
Burgh, Edward M. ..... Sherman Oaks, CA
Burghardt, Ingo F. ..... McLean, VA
Burghardt, James T., (P.C.) ..... Denver, CO
Burghardt, John L. ..... Chico, CA
Burghardt, Kathleen L. ..... Cherry Hill, NJ
Burghardt, Rita C. ..... New York, NY
Burghart, Gary R. (IBA) ..... Englewood, CO
Burghart, Mark A. ..... Topeka, KS
Burghart, William T. ..... Phoenix, AZ
Burgher, Gopal M. ..... New York, NY
Burgi, Kenneth S. ..... Newport Beach, CA
Burgin, Anthony D. ..... Kansas City, MO
Burgin, Charles E. ..... Marion, NC
Burgin, Cynthia R. ..... Cincinnati, OH
Burgin, Gina M. ..... Richmond, VA
Burgin, Harold L. ..... Baltimore, MD
Burgin, John C., Jr. ..... Knoxville, TN
Burgin, John S. ..... Raleigh, NC
Burgin, Jon B. ..... Dallas, TX
Burgin, Lester J. ..... Cincinnati, OH
Burgin, Max N. ..... North Little Rock, AR
Burgin, Meryl Davis ..... Owings Mills, MD
Burgin, Michael Alexander ..... Dearborn, MI
Burgin, Sara Marquis ..... Austin, TX
Burgin, Stephen M. ..... Los Angeles, CA
Burgin, William G., III ..... Greensboro, NC
Burgio, James P. ..... Buffalo, NY
Burgio, John E. ..... Caldwell, NJ
Burgio, Kita & Curvin ..... Buffalo, NY
Burgio, Salvatore ..... Roanoke, VA
Burgio, Stephen E. ..... Kew Gardens, NY
Burglass & Associates, L.L.C.
Metairie, LA
New Orleans, LA
Burglass, Bruce D., Jr. ..... Metairie, LA
Burglin, Paul R. ..... Mill Valley, CA
Burgmeier, L. Dale ..... Washington, DC
Annapolis, MD
Owings Mills, MD
Burgmeier, Timothy W. ..... Baton Rouge, LA
Burgner, Bobby L. ..... Atlanta, GA
Burgo, Rosemary R. ..... Mount Laurel, NJ
Burgon, Barre G. ..... Brigham City, UT
Burgon, Steven L. ..... Seattle, WA
Burgoon, Brian D. ..... Atlanta, GA
Burgoon, Denis M. ..... Jacksonville, FL
Burgoon, James W., Jr. ..... Greenwood, MS
Burgoon, Joseph J. ..... Atlanta, GA
Burgoon, Kelly A. ..... New City, NY
Burgoon & Oakes, P.C. ..... Greenwood, MS
Burgoon, Richard P., Jr. ..... Pittsburgh, PA
Burgoon, Samuel M. ..... Fallbrook, CA
Burgoon, Stephen S. ..... Baltimore, MD
Frederick, MD
Burgos, Arlene ..... New York, NY
Burgos & Burgos ..... Washington, DC
Gaithersburg, MD
Silver Spring, MD
Fairfax, VA
Burgos, Caroline Heindel
Los Angeles, CA
Burgos, Edwin A. ..... Woodland Hills, CA
Burgos, Jorge A. ..... Santa Ana, CA
Burgos, Juan ..... Bridgeton, NJ
Burgos, Kara M. ..... La Crosse, WI
Burgos, Kedra L. ..... Buffalo, NY
Burgos, Linda F. ..... Silver Spring, MD
Burgos, Nelson I. ..... Gaithersburg, MD
Silver Spring, MD
Fairfax, VA
Burgos, Olivia A. ..... Los Angeles, CA
Burgos, Raymond P. ..... San Juan, PR
Burgos, Rosemarie ..... Long Beach, CA
Burgos, Vivian ..... Denver, CO
Burgos-Gandia, Juan L. ..... Richardson, TX
Burgos-Pérez, Heriberto J. ..... San Juan, PR
Burgott, George A. ..... Eugene, OR
Burgott, Susan L. ..... Eugene, OR
Burgower, Wendy S. ..... Houston, TX
Burgoyne, Allen G. ..... Pelham, NY
Burgoyne, Grant T. ..... Boise, ID
Burgoyne, James M. ..... Worcester, MA
Burgoyne, John D.
National Labor Relations Board, Office of the General Counsel, GV
Burgoyne, Michael H. ..... Towson, MD
Burgoyne, Michael H., P.A., Law Office of
Towson, MD
Burgoyne, Paul J. ..... Philadelphia, PA
Burgoyne, Robert Anthony
Washington, DC
Burgoyne, Shirley J. ..... Ann Arbor, MI
Burgoyne, Shirley J., P.C. ..... Ann Arbor, MI
Burgoz, Mark A. ..... Phoenix, AZ
Burgrabe, Nick F. ..... Lincoln, IL
Burgraff, Carolyn Cox ..... Charleston, WV
Burgraff, Craig R. ..... Harrisburg, PA
Burgraff, Michelle M. ..... Janesville, WI
Burgreen, Mark S. ..... Augusta, GA
Aiken, SC
Burgs, Robert D. ..... Plantation, FL
Burguieres, Ernest A., III
New Orleans, LA
Burguieres, John B., Jr. ..... Torrance, CA
Burguieres, Robert E., P.A.
St. Petersburg, FL
Burgujian, Richard V. ..... Washington, DC
Burgum, Bradley J. ..... Casselton, ND
Burgum & Irby Law Firm, P.C.
Casselton, ND
Burgund, Reynolds ..... New York, NY
Burgunder, Herbert, III ..... Baltimore, MD
Burgunder, Herbert, Jr. ..... Baltimore, MD
Burgunder, Karl A. ..... Oviedo, FL
Burgunder, Karl A., P.A. ..... Oviedo, FL
Burgunder, Lee B. ..... San Luis Obispo, CA
Burgunder, Thomas J. ..... Pittsburgh, PA
Burgweger, Francis J., Jr. ..... New York, NY
Burgwyn, Henry H. ..... Raleigh, NC
Burgwyn, W. H. S., Jr. ..... Woodland, NC
Burgy, Dennis M. ..... Boulder Junction, WI
Eagle River, WI
Burgy, Kathryn ..... Oklahoma City, OK
Burhans, Debra L. ..... Batavia, NY
Burhans, Glenn T., Jr. ..... New York, NY
Burhans, John T. ..... St. Joseph, MI
Burhans, Kenneth L. ..... Louisville, KY
Burhans, Mark Eugene ..... Lockport, NY
Burhenn, David W. ..... Los Angeles, CA
Burhorn, Charles ..... Leakesville, MS
Burhyte, Janet G. ..... Buffalo, NY
Buri, Charles E. ..... Scottsdale, AZ
Buri, Mark D. ..... Buffalo, NY
Buri, Philip J. ..... Bellingham, WA
Buri, Wayne C. ..... North Miami Beach, FL
Buri, Wayne C., P.A.
North Miami Beach, FL
Burian, Lawrence J. ..... New York, NY
Burian, Philip A. ..... Cedar Rapids, IA
Burian, Saul Eliot ..... New York, NY
Burianek, Clarence A. ..... Pueblo, CO
Burianek, Francis P. ..... Allentown, PA
Burianek, Lisa Marie ..... Albany, NY
Burianek, Todd D. ..... Grafton, ND
Buric, John A. ..... Phoenix, AZ
Buric, John Robert ..... Charlotte, NC
Burick, Elizabeth A. ..... Canton, OH
Burick, Elliot D. ..... Redding, CA
Burick, Lawrence T. ..... Dayton, OH
Burick, Monica J. ..... Irvine, CA
Buries, Glen A. ..... San Diego, CA
Burijon, Robert W., Jr. ..... Orlando, FL
Burik, Michael A. ..... Los Angeles, CA
Buring, Donald C. ..... Covington, KY
Buringrud, Jay E. ..... Bismarck, ND
Buringrud, Ward E. ..... Seattle, WA
Burish, Mark D. ..... Madison, WI
Burk, Bernard A. ..... San Francisco, CA
Burk, Bernard E., (A Law Corp.)
New Orleans, LA
Burk, Beverly ..... Richardson, TX
Burk & Burk ..... Denver, CO
Burk, Daniel R. ..... Falls Church, VA
Burk, Eric L. ..... Charlotte, NC
Burk, Eugene S. ..... Denver, CO
Burk, Faith G. ..... Dallas, TX
Burk, Howard J. ..... Philadelphia, PA
Burk, James E. ..... Washington, DC
Burk, James W. ..... Akron, OH
Burk, Jana Rork ..... Austin, TX
Burk, Jason M. ..... Las Vegas, NV
Burk, Jerry C. ..... Denver, CO
Burk, Jo Ann ..... Parsippany, NJ
Burk, John Rogers ..... Roseville, CA
Burk, John Rogers, A Law Corporation
Roseville, CA
Burk & Koda, PLLC ..... Washington, DC
Burk, Laurel Anne ..... New York, NY
Burk Law Firm, The, A Professional Corporation ..... Austin, TX
Burk Law Office, P.C. ..... Choteau, MT
Burk, Michael G. ..... Austin, TX
Burk, Michael R. ..... San Jose, CA
Burk, Michael R., A Professional Corporation
San Jose, CA
Burk, Nancy L. ..... Toledo, IA
Burk, Patrick T. ..... Des Moines, IA
Burk, Peter W. ..... Waterloo, IA
Burk, Richard B. ..... West Palm Beach, FL
Burk, Robert A. ..... Tulsa, OK
Burk, Robert L. "Stoney" ..... Choteau, MT
Burk, Robert M. ..... Los Angeles, CA
Burk, Robert S. ..... Chevy Chase, MD
Burk, Robert S. ..... Minneapolis, MN
Burk, Russell C. ..... Denver, CO
Burk & Seaton, P.A. ..... Minneapolis, MN
Burk, Steven E. ..... Globe, AZ
Burk, Susan M. ..... St. Augustine, FL
Burk, Walter E. ..... Los Angeles, CA
Burk, Warren W. C. ..... Viera, FL
Burk, William A. ..... Salt Lake City, UT
Burk, William L. ..... Burlington, CO
Burka, Alfred ..... Washington, DC
Burka, Diane P. ..... Hanover, MD
Burka, Robert A. ..... Washington, DC
Burkam, Jeffrey A. ..... Delaware, OH
Burkam, Yost & Fuller ..... Delaware, OH
Burkamp, Wayne L. ..... North Hollywood, CA
Burkan, Nathan, Jr. ..... New York, NY
Burkard, Arthur C.E. ..... New York, NY
Burkard, Herbert G. ..... Menlo Park, CA
Burkard, Joseph R. ..... Paulding, OH
Burkard, Peter H. ..... Southbury, CT
Burkard, Richard P.
General Accounting Office, Office of the General Counsel, GV
Burkard, Timothy A. ..... Manitowoc, WI
Burkardt, Meg L. ..... Oakmont, PA
Burkardt, Robert F. ..... Oakmont, PA
Burkart, Barbara W. ..... Amherst, MA
Burkart, Eugene J. ..... Waltham, MA
Burkart, Francis W., III ..... Salem, VA
Burkart, Frederick ..... New Orleans, LA
Burkart, Glenn A. ..... Springfield, MO
Burkart & Hunt, P.C. ..... Springfield, MO
Burkart, Karen ..... Edwardsville, IL
Burkart, Michael M. ..... Mineola, NY
Burkart, Raymond C., Jr. ..... New Orleans, LA
Burkart, Robert L. ..... Evansville, IN
Burkart, Thomas W. ..... Hamel, IL
Maryville, IL
Burkart, Timothy C. ..... Seattle, WA
Burkart, William ..... Eastpointe, MI
Burkdall, Lisa M. ..... Los Angeles, CA
Burkdoll, Elizabeth A. ..... St. Louis, MO
Burke, Adam F. ..... Los Angeles, CA
Burke, Adrienne J. ..... East Hanover, NJ
Burke, Aimee L. ..... Prospect Heights, IL
Burke, Alfair S. ..... Buffalo, NY
Burke, Alan D. ..... Rochester, IN
Burke, Albright, Harter & Rzepka, LLP
Rochester, NY
Burke, Alexander J. ..... Princeton, NJ
Burke, Alice Estill ..... Chicago, IL
Burke, Amy Sudaley ..... Teaneck, NJ
Burke, Ann M. ..... Fort Lauderdale, FL
Burke, Ann Marie ..... Washington, DC
Burke, Ann Marie ..... Edison, NJ
Burke, Ann Marie ..... Lancaster, PA
Burke, Ann Marie V. ..... New York, NY
Burke, Anne M. ..... Chicago, IL
Burke, Anne Pilati ..... Houston, TX
Burke, Arnold L. ..... Chicago, IL
Burke, Arthur J. ..... New York, NY
Burke, Arthur W., Jr. ..... Grand Lake, CO
Burke & Associates ..... Braintree, MA
Burke, Barbara A. ..... Los Angeles, CA
Burke, Barbara A. ..... Minneapolis, MN
Burke, Barbara P. ..... Orlando, FL
Burke, Bari R. ..... Missoula, MT
Burke, Barry E. ..... Chicago, IL
Burke, Basil C., Jr. ..... Madison, VA
Burke, Bernard J., Jr. ..... Burr Ridge, IL
Burke, Betsy E. ..... Department of Justice, Criminal Division, GV
Burke, Betty Speer ..... Austin, TX
Fort Worth, TX
Houston, TX
Burke & Beuoy ..... Arab, AL
Burke, Beverly J. ..... Washington, DC
Burke & Blue, P.A. ..... Destin, FL
Panama City, FL
Burke, Bob ..... Oklahoma City, OK
Burke, Brendan ..... Philadelphia, PA
Burke, Brian ..... Fort Wayne, IN
Burke, Brian B. ..... Madison, WI
Burke, Brian E.
Department of Agriculture, GV
Burke, Brian E. ..... Boston, MA
Burke, Brian E. ..... Boston, MA
Burke, Brian F. ..... Washington, DC
Burke, Brian G. ..... San Francisco, CA
Burke, Brian H. ..... Santa Barbara, CA
Burke, Brian K. ..... Indianapolis, IN
Burke, Brian T. ..... Bentonville, AR
Burke, Bridget A. ..... Peoria, IL
Burke, Bridgit ..... Albany, NY
Burke, Bruce A. ..... Tucson, AZ
Burke, Bruce A., P.C. ..... Tucson, AZ
Burke, Bruce T. H. ..... Oakland, CA
Burke & Burke ..... Buffalo, NY
Burke & Burke ..... New York, NY
Burke & Burke ..... Forty Fort, PA
Wilkes-Barre, PA
Burke & Burke ..... Fairfax, VA
Burke, Burke & Burke ..... New York, NY
Burke & Burke, Ltd. ..... Chicago, IL
Downers Grove, IL
Burke Burns & Pinelli, Ltd. ..... Chicago, IL
Burke, C. Nicholas ..... Lebanon, NH
Burke, Carl P. ..... Boise, ID
Burke, Carol A. ..... Chicago, IL
Burke, Carol M. ..... Houston, TX
Burke, Carolyn Moll ..... Los Angeles, CA
Burke, Carroll A. ..... Bowling Green, KY
Burke & Casserly, P.C. ..... Albany, NY
Burke & Cestia ..... New Iberia, LA
Burke, Charlene E. ..... Canfield, OH
Burke, Charles A. ..... Winston-Salem, NC
Burke, Charles R. ..... Pittsburgh, PA
Burke, Charles R. ..... Virginia Beach, VA
Burke, Charles T. ..... Livonia, MI
Burke, Charles W. ..... St. Petersburg, FL
Burke, Cherie M.D. ..... Albany, NY
Burke, Cheryl C. ..... Washington, DC
Burke, Christine F. ..... Hallowell, ME
Burke, Christine Houlihan ..... Hopkinton, MA
Burke, Christopher C. ..... Boise, ID
Burke, Christopher J. ..... Providence, RI
Burke, Christopher J. ..... Salt Lake City, UT
Burke, Christopher L. "Kipper"
San Antonio, TX
Burke, Christopher R. ..... Portland, OR
Burke, Claudia Mary ..... Salem, OR
Burke, Coleman P. ..... New York, NY
Burke, Colin T. ..... New York, NY
Burke, Colman J. ..... New York, NY
Burke, Constance Marie ..... Marco Island, FL
Naples, FL
Burke Costanza & Cuppy LLP
East Chicago, IN
Hammond, IN
Merrillville, IN
Valparaiso, IN
Burke, Craig C. ..... Indianapolis, IN
Burke, Cristin A. ..... Myrtle Beach, SC
Burke, Cullen M. ..... Ocean City, MD
Burke, Cullen M., P.A. ..... Ocean City, MD
Burke, Curtis S. ..... Chicago, IL
Burke, Curtis S., P.C. ..... Chicago, IL
Burke, D. Barlow ..... Washington, DC
Burke, D. Michael ..... Martinsburg, WV
Burke, Dan ..... Alexandria, VA
Burke, Daniel B., Jr. ..... New Albany, IN
Burke, Daniel C. ..... Mineola, NY
New York, NY
Burke, Daniel E. ..... Florence, KY
Cincinnati, OH
Burke, Daniel F., Jr. ..... Cincinnati, OH
Burke, Daniel K. ..... Dallas, TX
Burke, Daniel P. ..... Hauppauge, NY
Burke, Daniel R. ..... Boston, MA
Burke, Daniel R. ..... Rochester, NY
Burke, Daniel V. ..... Carlsbad, CA
Burke, Daniel V. ..... Vista, CA
Burke, Daniel W. ..... Menlo Park, CA
Burke, David E. ..... Cleveland, OH
Burke, David J. ..... Stamford, CT
Burke, David M. ..... Englewood, CO
Burke, David P. ..... San Diego, CA
Burke, David P. ..... Danbury, CT
Burke, David P. ..... Tampa, FL
Burke, David R. ..... Baltimore, MD
Burke, Deborah S. ..... Marion, IN
Burke, Deirdre K. ..... Greenfield, MA
Burke, Delia A. ..... Washington, DC
Burke, Denis P. ..... Omaha, NE
Burke, Denise ..... Andover, MA
Burke, Denise A. ..... Hempstead, NY
Burke, Denise D. ..... Memphis, TN
Burke, Denise M. ..... Alpena, MI
Burke, Denise Mary ..... Wichita Falls, TX
Burke, Dennis A. ..... San Diego, CA
Burke, Dennis C. ..... Liberty Corner, NJ
Burke, Dennis Clay ..... Louisville, KY
Burke, Dennis E. ..... Fairfax, VA
Burke, Dennis E. ..... Madison, WI
Burke, Dennis J. ..... Chicago, IL
Burke, Dennis K. ..... United States Senate, Committee Legal Personnel, GV
Burke, Dennis M. ..... Riverside, CA
Burke, Dennis P. ..... Los Angeles, CA
Burke, Derek David ..... Newark, NJ
Burke, Dominick F. ..... Fairfield, CT
Burke, Donald ..... New York, NY
Burke, Donald F. ..... Baltimore, MD
Burke, Donald F. ..... New York, NY
Burke, Donovan W. ..... New York, NY
Burke, Dorothy Bonner ..... New York, NY
Burke, Dracos D. ..... New Iberia, LA
Burke, E. James ..... Cheyenne, WY
Burke, E. James, III ..... Lewiston, ME
Burke, E. Jeffrey ..... San Luis Obispo, CA
Burke, E. Patrick, Jr. ..... Rutland, VT
Burke, Earle Wm. ..... Costa Mesa, CA
Burke, Edmund ..... Honolulu, HI
Burke, Edmund A. ..... Putney, VT
Burke, Edmund B. ..... Atlanta, GA
Burke, Edmund J. ..... Chicago, IL
Burke, Edmund P. ..... Chicago, IL
Downers Grove, IL
Burke, Edmund W. ..... Washington, DC
Burke, Edmund W. ..... Buffalo, NY
Burke, Edward ..... Braintree, MA
Burke, Edward A. ..... Cincinnati, OH
Burke, Edward D. ..... Southampton, NY
Burke, Edward D., Jr. ..... Shawano, WI
Burke, Edward J. ..... Chicago, IL
Burke, Edward J. ..... Keene, NH
Burke, Edward J. ..... New York, NY
Burke, Edward L. ..... Merrillville, IN
Burke, Edward L. ..... Framingham, MA
Burke, Edward M. ..... Chicago, IL
Burke, Edward M. ..... Hopewell Junction, NY
Burke, Edward P. ..... Clayton, MO
Burke, Erin E. ..... Charlotte, NC
Burke, Erin K. ..... Des Moines, IA
Burke, Erin K. ..... Paramus, NJ
Burke, Erin L. ..... Los Angeles, CA
Burke, Eugene E. ..... Buffalo, NY
Burke, Eugene Vincent ..... Williamsville, NY

Burke, Theodore E. ... Walpole, MA
Burke, Theresa Counts ... St. Louis, MO
Burke, Theresa F. ... New York, NY
Burke, Thomas ... La Mesa, CA
Burke, Thomas A., III ... St. Charles, MO
Burke, Thomas B. ... Fayetteville, AR
Burke, Thomas B. ... Milwaukee, WI
Burke, Thomas C. ... St. Louis, MO
Burke, Thomas C. ... Bellmawr, NJ
Burke, Thomas C. ... New York, NY
Burke, Thomas C. ... Rochester, NY
Burke, Thomas E. ... Tucson, AZ
Burke, Thomas E., (P.C.) ... New York, NY
Burke, Thomas F. ... Oakland, CA
Burke, Thomas F. ... Washington, DC
Burke, Thomas F. ... Chicago, IL
Burke, Thomas F. ... Belmont, MA
Burke, Thomas F. ... Dartmouth, MA
New Bedford, MA
Burke, Thomas F. ... Albany, NY
Burke, Thomas F. ... North Bend, OR
Burke, Thomas F. ... Trevose, PA
Burke, Thomas F. ... Sioux Falls, SD
Burke, Thomas F., Jr. ... Wilkes-Barre, PA
Burke, Thomas G. ... Seattle, WA
Burke, Thomas H. ... Des Moines, IA
Burke, Thomas J. ... Batavia, IL
Burke, Thomas J. ... Lawrence, MA
Burke, Thomas J. ... White Bear Lake, MN
Burke, Thomas J. ... White Plains, NY
Burke, Thomas J., Jr. ... Denver, CO
Burke, Thomas J., Jr. ... Chicago, IL
Burke, Thomas J., Jr. ... Ardmore, PA
Burke, Thomas M. ... Orlando, FL
Burke, Thomas M. ... Maple Grove, MN
Burke, Thomas M. ... St. Louis, MO
Burke, Thomas M. ... Buffalo, NY
Burke, Thomas M., P.C., Law Offices
St. Louis, MO
Burke, Thomas P. ... Los Angeles, CA
Burke, Thomas P. ... Chicago, IL
Waukegan, IL
Burke, Thomas P. ... Anderson, IN
Burke, Thomas P. ... New York, NY
Burke, Thomas P. ... New York, NY
Burke, Thomas P. ... New York, NY
Burke, Thomas P., II ... Phoenix, AZ
Burke & Thomas, PLLP ... St. Paul, MN
Burke, Thomas R. ... San Francisco, CA
Burke, Thomas R. ... Omaha, NE
Burke, Timothy C. ... Langhorne, PA
Burke, Timothy Charles ... Westminster, MD
Burke, Timothy E. ... Montclair, NJ
Burke, Timothy F., Jr. ... Pittsburgh, PA
Burke, Timothy J. ... Phoenix, AZ
Burke, Timothy J. ... Braintree, MA
Burke, Timothy L. ... Buffalo, NY
Burke, Timothy M. ... St. Paul, MN
Burke, Timothy M. ... Cincinnati, OH
Burke, Timothy P. ... Boston, MA
Burke, Timothy P. ... Olympia, WA
Burke, Toby W. ... Fort Worth, TX
Burke, Vincent C., III ... Chevy Chase, MD
Burke, Virginia L. ... Virginia Beach, VA
Burke, Virginia M. ... Providence, RI
Burke, W. Dale ... Monett, MO
Burke, W. Lewis ... Columbia, SC
Burke, W. Patrick ... San Antonio, TX
Burke, Walker D. ... Warner Robins, GA
Burke, Walter T. ... Sherborn, MA
Burke, Walter T. ... Albany, NY
Burke, Ward R. ... Lufkin, TX
Burke, Warren, MacKay & Serritella, P.C.
Chicago, IL
Burke, Weaver & Prell ... Boca Raton, FL
Chicago, IL
Burke, Whitney A. ... Orlando, FL
Burke, William A., III ... Billings, MT
Burke, William I. ... Lincoln Park, MI
Burke, William J. ... El Segundo, CA
Burke, William J. ... Chicago, IL
Burke, William J. ... Princeton, NJ
Burke, William J. ... New York, NY
Burke, William J., III ... West Chester, PA
Burke, William J., Jr. ... Pawtucket, RI
Burke, William L. ... Hamilton, NY
Burke, William L. ... New York, NY
Burke, William L. ... Shenandoah, PA
Burke, William M. ... Mesa, AZ
Burke, William M. ... Denver, CO
Burke, William M. ... Naples, FL
Burke, William M. ... New York, NY
Burke, William R., Jr. ... Houston, TX
Burke, William S. ... Providence, RI
Burke, William T. ... Poughkeepsie, NY
Burke, William T. ... Krum, TX
Burke, William T. ... Seattle, WA
Burke, William T., Jr. ... Dallas, TX
Burke, William T. J. ... San Jose, CA
Burke, Williams & Sorensen, LLP
Camarillo, CA
Costa Mesa, CA
Irvine, CA
Los Angeles, CA
Riverside, CA
Burke & Wilson ... Kimball, NE
Burke, W. L., Jr. ... Abilene, TX
Burke, Wm. J. ... Syracuse, NY
Burke, Woodard & O'Donnell, P.C.
Cheyenne, WY
Burke, W. T., Sr. ... Portsmouth, NH
Burke, Yvonne Brathwaite ... Los Angeles, CA
Burke-Cain, Melissa A. ... Olympia, WA
Burke Carroll, Grace ... Fairfax, VA
Burkeen, Daniel ... Groesbeck, TX
Burkel, James T. ... Ann Arbor, MI
Burkemper, J. Ira ... Irvine, CA
Burkemper Law Firm, L.L.P. ... Troy, MO
Burkemper, T. Bennett, Jr. ... Troy, MO
Burkemper, Thomas B. ... Troy, MO
Burkenheim, Marie Sabath
North Hollywood, CA
Burkenroad, David C. ... Santa Monica, CA
Burkenstock, Susan J. ... New Orleans, LA
Burker, Richard S. ... New York, NY
Burkert & Hart ... Fort Myers, FL
Naples, FL
Burkert, Peter C. ... Fort Myers, FL
Burkert-Brist, Monica ... Madison, WI
Burkes, Jennifer P. ... Jackson, MS
Burkes, Rebecca Lynne ... Bentonville, AR
Burket, Dale A. ... Orlando, FL
Burket, George E., III ... Kingman, KS
Burket, John L. ... Troy, MI
Burket, Patricia Krise ... Harrisburg, PA
Burkett, Aubrey V. ... Fort Worth, TX
Burkett, Barbara A. ... Gainesville, FL
Burkett, Bradford C. ... White Plains, NY
Burkett, Bradley K. ... Portland, IN
Burkett & Burdette ... Seattle, WA
Burkett, Charles W. ... Atherton, CA
Burkett and Chevallier ... Many, LA
Burkett, Craig M. ... Reno, NV
Burkett, Cynthia M. ... Brownwood, TX
Burkett, D. Morgan ... New York, NY
Burkett, David C. ... Seattle, WA
Burkett, David I. ... Monroe, LA
Burkett, Denise R. ... Neenah, WI
Burkett, Don M. ... Many, LA
Burkett, Elizabeth Schorpp
Columbus, OH
Burkett, F. Michael, Jr. ... Boise, ID
Burkett, Gwendolyn Yeager ... Garland, TX
Burkett, J. Kristin ... Newark, OH
Burkett, James R. ... Glens Falls, NY
Burkett, Joseph W., Jr. ... Kerrville, TX
Burkett, Laurie J. ... Monroe, LA
Burkett, Lawrence V., Jr. ... Springfield, MA
Burkett, Lex J. ... Wilmington, DE
Burkett, Loreen M. ... Lebanon, PA
Burkett, Martin G. ... Miami, FL
Burkett, Michael E. ... Santa Ana, CA
Burkett, Michael J. ... Charleston, SC
Burkett, Michael L. ... Fremont, OH
Burkett, Michael R. ... Fort Worth, TX
Burkett, Patrick J. ... Southfield, MI
Burkett, Paul A. ... Washington, DC
Burkett, Perry C. ... Bronx, NY
Burkett, Perry E. ... Corpus Christi, TX
Burkett, Rebecca M. ... Chicago, IL
Burkett, Robert E., Jr. ... Carmel, IN
Burkett, Robert L. ... Ventura, CA
Burkett, Robert W. ... Sumter, SC
Burkett and Ross ... Dimmitt, TX
Burkett, Scott T. ... Houston, TX
Burkett, Stephen L. ... Corpus Christi, TX
Burkett, Steven P. ... Cherry Hill, NJ
Bensalem, PA
Burkett, Teresa Meinders ... Tulsa, OK
Burkett, Tracey E. ... Hazard, KY
Burkett, Traci ... Atlanta, GA
Burkett, William A. ... Watertown, MA
Burkett, William B. ... Washington, DC
Burkett, William R. ... Oklahoma City, OK
Burkett-Norey, Stacey A.
East Bridgewater, MA
Burkett-O'Hern, Linda
Oklahoma City, OK
Burkey, Ann L. ... Long Grove, IL
Burkey, Bruce A. ... Altamont, IL
Effingham, IL
Burkey & Burkey, P.C. ... Roswell, GA
Burkey, Catherine C. ... Grand Junction, CO
Burkey, Donna R. ... Rockford, IL
Burkey, Franklin ... Joliet, IL
Burkey, Frederick D. ... Roswell, GA
Burkey, J. Brent ... Marietta, GA
Burkey, Jennifer Austin ... Roswell, GA
Burkey, Lee M. ... Chicago, IL
Burkey, Lee M., Jr. ... La Grange, IL
Burkey, Louis J. ... Tacoma, WA
Burkey, Max ... Des Moines, IA
Burkey, Michael J. ... Moundsville, WV
Burkey, Michael R. ... Cumberland, MD
Burkey, Robert F. ... Warren, OH
Burkey, Tessa ... Atlanta, GA
Burkey, Todd C. ... Austin, TX
Burkhalter, Alton G. ... Irvine, CA
Burkhalter, Bob ... New Smyrna Beach, FL
Burkhalter, Carl S. ... Birmingham, AL
Burkhalter, Clermon O. ... Gordo, AL
Burkhalter, David A., II ... Knoxville, TN
Burkhalter, Hunter W. ... Austin, TX
Burkhalter, Karahan, Palmer & Armstrong, L.L.P. ... Houston, TX
Burkhalter, Kay L. ... Houston, TX
Burkhalter, Lawrence E. ... Miami, FL
Burkhalter, Paul B. ... Dallas, TX
Houston, TX
Burkhalter, Rene R. ... Marinette, WI
Burkhalter, William H., Jr.
North Augusta, SC
Burkhalter, William H., Jr., P.A.
North Augusta, SC
Burkhard, Jack H. ... Greeneville, TN
Burkhard, James R. ... Columbia, SC
Burkhard, Phyllis B. ... Columbia, SC
Burkhard, Robert V. ... Omaha, NE
Burkhardt, A.J. ... St. Louis, MO
Burkhardt & Associates ... Boston, MA
Burkhardt, Catherine M. ... Chicago, IL
Burkhardt, Craig S. ... Springfield, IL
Burkhardt, Daniel W.
Executive Office Of The President, GV
Burkhardt, Diane L. ... Denver, CO
Burkhardt, Donald A. ... Denver, CO
Burkhardt, Donald H. ... Denver, CO
Burkhardt, Donald M. ... Denver, CO
Burkhardt, Edwin R., Jr. ... Towson, MD
Burkhardt, Ellen ... Boston, MA
Burkhardt, Eric W. ... Santa Barbara, CA
Burkhardt, Gwenda M. ... Deerfield, IL
Burkhardt, James G. ... Toledo, OH
Burkhardt, James I. ... Alexandria, VA
Burkhardt, James M. ... Cannon Falls, MN
Burkhardt, James M. ... Frackville, PA
Burkhardt, Jennifer A. ... Seattle, WA
Burkhardt, Jill L. ... San Diego, CA
Burkhardt, John A. ... Tulsa, OK
Burkhardt, John F. ... White Plains, NY
Burkhardt, Julianne C. ... Bozeman, MT
Burkhardt, Kyle R. ... Chicago, IL
Burkhardt & Larson
Rancho Santa Fe, CA
Burkhardt Law Firm, The, LLP
Denver, CO
Burkhardt, Michael S. ... Philadelphia, PA
Burkhardt, Minnie ... Denison, TX
Burkhardt, Philip ... Rancho Santa Fe, CA
Burkhardt, William J. ... Rosemead, CA
Burkhart, Alfred W. ... Norwalk, CT
Burkhart, Barry G. ... Oklahoma City, OK
Burkhart, Charles A. ... Birmingham, AL
Burkhart, David E. ... Memphis, TN
Burkhart, Diane M. ... Baton Rouge, LA
Burkhart, Errol A. ... Uniondale, NY
Burkhart, Francis H. ... Zanesville, OH
Burkhart, Frederick S.
Grand Rapids, MI
Burkhart, George F. ... Woodsfield, OH
Burkhart, Glenn D. ... Demotte, IN
Burkhart, Gordon R. ... Riverside, CA
Burkhart, John J. ... Toledo, OH
Burkhart, Madeleine Marie ... Nashville, TN
Burkhart, Mary-Ann R. ... Miami, FL
Burkhart, Matthew J. ... Columbus, OH
Burkhart, Paul J. ... Redlands, CA
Burkhart, Steven A. ... Milford, CT
Burkhart, Susan K. ... Raleigh, NC
Burkhart, Terry F. ... Escanaba, MI
Marquette, MI
Burkhart, Thomas D. ... Saginaw, MI
Burkhart, Tiderington & Loeffler
Saginaw, MI
Burkhart, William H. ... Seattle, WA
Burkhart, William R. ... Canton, OH
Burkhead, David D. ... Phoenix, AZ
Burkhead, Harlan D. ... Kansas City, MO
Burkhead, Leah Brown ... Mission, KS
Burkhead, Melvin Dean ... Lawrence, KS
Burkholder, Bruce H. ... Columbus, OH
Burkholder, Christen W. ... Bristol, VA
Burkholder, Christen W., P.C. ... Bristol, VA
Burkholder, Evan A. ... Chicago, IL
Richmond, VA
Burkholder, John A. ... Los Angeles, CA
Burkholder, John C. ... Cleveland, OH
Burkholder, Joy M. ... Milwaukee, WI
Burkholder, Kurt B. ... Portland, OR
Burkholder, Paul C. ... Los Angeles, CA
Burkholder, Robert M., Jr. ... Exton, PA
Burkholder, Samuel P. ... Washington, DC
Burkholder, Thomas B. ... Williamsport, PA
Burkholder, Vaughn ... Wichita, KS
Burkholz, Alan E. ... Morganville, NJ
Burkholz, Robert C. ... Kalamazoo, MI
Burkholz, Spencer A. ... San Diego, CA
Burkholz, Zoe S. ... Benton Harbor, MI
Burkhouse, Nolan C. ... Norwich, VT
Burkin, Alice B. ... Boston, MA
Burkin, Mary Ann ... Glendale, CA
Burkin, Michael J. ... Waltham, MA
Burkins, V. Jean ... Columbia, SC
Burkinshaw, Matthew J. ... Walpole, MA
Burkinshaw, Robert W. ... Newton, MA
Burkitt, Susan Kelly ... Irvine, CA
Burkitt, William D. ... Bellingham, WA
Burkitt, William R. ... Pasadena, CA
Burkland, Adriane W. ... Chicago, IL
Burkland, Derik M. ... Salem, OR
Burkland, Elizabeth A ... New York, NY
Burkland, Mark E. ... Chicago, IL
Burkland, Miriam Leskovar ... Chicago, IL
Burkle, Kurt E. ... Guilford, CT
Burkley, Bruce D. ... McLean, VA
Burkley, Diane E. ... New York, NY
Burkley, John H. ... Purchase, NY
Burkley, Kenneth B. ... Greensburg, PA
Burkley, Walter R., Jr. (A Professional Corporation) ... Torrance, CA
Burklund, Hollis W. ... Austin, TX
Burkman, Alicia Guevara ... Dallas, TX
Burkman, John M. ... Washington, DC
Burko, Elliott J. ... New York, NY
Burko, Harvey ... Brooklyn, NY
Burko, Paula ... Buffalo, NY
Burkoff, John M. ... Pittsburgh, PA
Burkoff, Nancy M. ... Pittsburgh, PA
Burkoff, Susan ... Bronx, NY
Burkow, Steven H. ... Los Angeles, CA
Burks, Adra E. ... Lawrence, KS
Burks, Ann T. ... Richmond, VA
Burks, Ashby Q. ... Brentwood, TN
Burks, Charles C., Jr. ... Knoxville, TN
Burks, Delos H. ... Picayune, MS
Burks, Donald M. ... Richmond, VA
Burks, Garnett R., Jr. ... Las Cruces, NM
Burks, Harold S. ... Harrodsburg, KY
Burks, Janet Getty ... Little Rock, AR
Burks, John M. ... Birmingham, AL
Burks, Kristine L. ... Sacramento, CA
Burks, L. Lee, Jr. ... Chicago, IL
Burks, Larry W., (P.A.) ... Little Rock, AR
Burks, Margaret A. ... Cincinnati, OH
Burks, Robert ... Lynden, WA
Burks, Sheila A. ... Norcross, GA
Burks, Sylvia K. ... Palo Alto, CA
Burks, Tracy L. ... Dallas, TX
Burks, Winston W., III ... Roanoke, VA
Burkwit, Charles F. ... Rochester, NY
Burkwit, Robert L. ... Clifton Springs, NY
Ontario, NY
Rochester, NY
Webster, NY
Burky & Burky ... Canfield, OH
Burky, Christopher M. ... Chicago, IL
Burky, Elton A. ... Hartland, ME
Pittsfield, ME
Burky, Elton B. ... Canfield, OH
Burky & McCarthy, Law Office of
Hartland, ME
Pittsfield, ME
Burkybile, Karen L. ... Paris, IL
Burlage, Gerald J. ... Virginia Beach, VA
Burlake, John M. ... Crescent City, CA
Burland, Barry P. ... New York, NY
Burland, Dan ... San Jose, CA
Burland, Jacob ... San Francisco, CA
Burland, James S. ... Baton Rouge, LA
Burland, Jan E. ... San Jose, CA
Burlant, Brian L. ... New York, NY
Burlant, Gail A. ... New York, NY
Burlant, Paul ... Mineola, NY
Burlazzi, Susan Y. ... Dallas, TX
Burleigh, Charles L., Jr. ... Detroit, MI
Burleigh, David W. ... Covington, KY
Burleigh, Jack F. ... Lafayette, LA
Burleigh, Jennifer J. ... New York, NY
Burleigh, John F. ... New York, NY
Burleigh, Lawrence K., Jr. ... Lafayette, LA
Burleigh, Lawrence K., Ltd., A Prof. Law Corp. ... Lafayette, LA
Burleigh, Lawrence K., Sr. ... Lafayette, LA
Burleigh, Lewis A. ... Boston, MA
Burleigh, Paul H. ... Los Angeles, CA
Burleigh, Peter Shane ... Port Huron, MI
Burleigh, Reginald E. ... Caribou, ME
Burleigh, Richard B. ... Boise, ID
Burleigh, Robert C., Jr. ... Memphis, TN
Burleigh, Roger S. ... Dallas, TX
Burleigh, Timothy A. ... Jacksonville, FL
Burleigh, Tracy A. ... Wilmington, DE
Burlein, Steven Erik ... Honesdale, PA
Burleson, Bob ... Temple, TX
Burleson, Bruce ... Temple, TX
Burleson, David G. ... Duncan, SC
Burleson, David S. ... St. Paul, MN
Watertown, WI
Burleson, David T. ... El Paso, TX
Burleson, Denice Michelle Culver
Wetumpka, AL
Burleson, Hopson Ned, II ... Prague, OK
Burleson, Ira L. ... Birmingham, AL
Burleson, Jane ... Fairfield, CA
Burleson, Joan B. ... Denver, CO
Burleson, John ... Waco, TX
Burleson, John D. ... Jackson, TN
Burleson, L. Frank, Jr. ... Murfreesboro, NC
Burleson, Lea M. ... Austin, TX
Burleson, Leigh ... Kansas City, MO
Burleson, Lynn P. ... Raleigh, NC
Burleson, Lynn T. ... Washington, DC
Burleson, Pate & Gibson ... Dallas, TX
Burleson, Richard L. ... Houston, TX
Burleson, William G. ... Lansing, MI
Burlett, Cherie T. ... New Orleans, LA
Burlew & Caliman ... Cincinnati, OH
Burlew, Candace L. ... Columbia, SC
Burlew, Daniel M., II ... Owensboro, KY
Burlew, John H. ... Cincinnati, OH
Burley & Bailey, A Professional Corporation
Sherman, TX
Burley Barton & Misko, P.C. ... Trenton, MI
Burley, Brent D. ... Baton Rouge, LA
Burley, C. Melvin, Jr. ... Trenton, MI
Burley, Don O. ... Washington, DC
Burley, Edward G. ... Washington, DC
Burley, Jeffrey J. ... Sherman, TX
Burley, John C. ... Leonia, NJ
Burley, John D. ... Columbus, OH
Burley, John L. ... Chicago, IL
Burley, Lynn M. ... Minneapolis, MN
Burley, Michael J. ... Tequesta, FL
Burley, Robert A., (P.C.) ... Davison, MI
Burley, Robert N. ... Buena Vista, CO
Burley, Thomas A. ... Douglas, WY
Burlie, Todd R. ... Cherokee, OK
Burling, James C. ... Boston, MA
Burling, James S. ... Sacramento, CA
Burling, Peter Hoe ... Claremont, NH
Burling, Philip ... Boston, MA
Burlingame, Alexander G. ... Cleveland, OH
Burlingame, Alvah W., III
Shelter Island Heights, NY
Burlingame, Beverly Ray ... Dallas, TX
Burlingame, Claude I. ... Thompson Falls, MT
Burlingame, Daniel W.
Bloomfield Hills, MI
Burlingame, Daniel W., P.C.
Bloomfield Hills, MI
Burlingame, David G. ... Denver, CO
Burlingame, Glenn D. ... Boston, MA
Burlingame, James M. ... New Orleans, LA
Burlingame, James M., IV
New Orleans, LA
Burlingame, Jason ... Chicago, IL
Burlingame, John A. ... Washington, DC
Burlingame, John H. ... Cincinnati, OH
Cleveland, OH
Burlingame, Margaret Best
Indianapolis, IN

Burlingame, Paul William, Jr. ... Beaver Falls, PA
Burlingame, Robert B. ... Mountain View, CA
Burlingame, Roger G. ... Concord, NH
Burlingame, Stephen J. ... Danielson, CT
Burlingame, Stephen L. ... Lansing, MI
Burlingame, Thomas E. ... West Des Moines, IA
Burlingame, Todd L. ... Walnut Creek, CA
Burlingham, Carol ... Bartow, FL
Burlingham, Charles, Jr. ... Cambridge, MA
Burlingham, Nicholas W. ... New London, CT
Burlingham, Rebecca A. ... Chicago, IL
Burlingham, Ruth D. ... DeLand, FL
Burlingham, Steven R. ... Sacramento, CA
Burlingham Underwood LLP ... New York, NY
Burlington, Bill ... Butner, NC
Burlington, David Robert ... Greenville, SC
Burlington, Linda B. ... Department of Commerce, National Oceanic and Atmospheric Administration, GV
Burlington, Philip M. ... West Palm Beach, FL
Burlington, Robert K. ... Miami, FL
Burlington, Robert M. ... Fairfax, VA
Burlinson, Alice G. ... Christiansburg, VA
Burlison, Bill D. ... Crofton, MD
Burlison, David P., Jr. ... Memphis, TN
Burlison, James David ... Bowling Green, MO
Burlison & Luostari ... La Canada Flintridge, CA
Burlison, Rex M. ... O'Fallon, MO
Burlison, Rex. M., Law Offices of ... O'Fallon, MO
Burlison, Robert A. ... Salinas, CA
Burlison, Robert C., Jr. ... La Canada Flintridge, CA
Burlock, Stephen J. ... Bangor, ME
Burman, Brenda Wren ... Phoenix, AZ
Burman, Critton & Luttier ... North Palm Beach, FL
Burman, Cynthia N. ... Chicago, IL
Burman, Darryl Michael ... Houston, TX
Burman, David B. ... Los Angeles, CA
Burman, David J. ... Seattle, WA
Burman, Dennis Lee ... Marysville, WA
Burman, Harold S. ... Department of State, Office of the Legal Adviser, GV
Burman, Ira M. ... Chicago, IL
Burman, J. Michael, (P.A.) ... North Palm Beach, FL
Burman, Jeffrey S. ... Newark, NJ
New York, NY
Burman, John M. ... Laramie, WY
Burman, Lisa M. ... Chicago, IL
Burman, Louis ... Buffalo, NY
Burman & Manning ... Chicago, IL
Burman, Marshall L. ... Chicago, IL
Burman, Martin ... Malvern, PA
Burman, Michael L. ... Hopkinsville, KY
Burman, Peter ... Santa Fe, NM
Burman, Robert N. ... Columbus, OH
Burman, Roberta ... New York, NY
Burman & Robinson ... Columbus, OH
Burman, Russell S. ... Brooklyn, NY
Burman, Sheldon V., Law Offices, P.C. ... New York, NY
Burman, Sheldon V., (P.C.) ... New York, NY
Burmaster, Jeffrey M. ... New Orleans, LA
Burmaster, Joan Winters ... Metairie, LA
Burmaster, Melvin J. ... New Orleans, LA
Burmaster, Paul William ... Overland Park, KS
Burmeister, Angela L. ... Omaha, NE
Burmeister, Charles J. ... Lincoln, NE
Burmeister, Dale R. ... Troy, MI
Burmeister, Edward D. ... San Francisco, CA
Burmeister, Eric W. ... Des Moines, IA
Burmeister, Jeffrey A. ... Atlanta, GA
Burmeister, Jon B. ... Beaumont, TX
Burmeister, Klaus H. ... San Francisco, CA
Burmeister, Michael T. ... Ridgecrest, CA
Burmeister, Richard R. ... Glastonbury, CT
Burmeister, Steve D. ... Independence, MO
Burmeister, Theodore Hyde ... Washington, DC
Burmeister, William L. ... New York, NY
Burmila, Edward A., Jr. ... Joliet, IL
Burmila & Thomas ... Joliet, IL
Burmon, David L. ... Weston, MA
Burmood, Brent C. ... Omaha, NE
Burn, David N. ... Nashville, TN
Burn, Denise S. ... Chicago, IL
Burn, Glen P. ... Peachtree City, GA
Burn, James R., Jr. ... Pittsburgh, PA
Burn, Keith S. ... Albuquerque, NM
Burn & Littlefield ... Albuquerque, NM
Burn, Steven A. ... New York, NY
Burn, William C. ... Marietta, GA
Burnaford, Nina L.S. ... Philadelphia, PA
Burnaine, Wayne L. ... Lawrenceville, GA
Burnam, H. Warren, Jr. ... Arlington, VA
Burnam, John A. ... Hattiesburg, MS
Burnam, Thompson, Weldon, Simons and Dunlap, P.S.C. ... Richmond, KY
Burnaman, Phillip R. ... Falls Creek, PA
Burnaman, Ross S. ... Tallahassee, FL
Burnard, George W. ... Troy, MI
Burnat, Lawrence S. ... Atlanta, GA
Burnat, Michael A. ... Virginia Beach, VA
Burnaugh, Rebecca L. ... Atlanta, GA
Burnazian, Lara M. ... New York, NY
Burnbaum, Edward H. ... New York, NY
Burnbaum, Marian C. ... New York, NY
Burne, Christopher F. ... Dunmore, PA
Burnell, William L. ... El Cajon, CA
Burnell, Wilson D. ... Aurora, IL
Burner, Burnie ... Austin, TX
Burner, Charles R. ... Warsaw, IN
Burner, Eric ... New York, NY
Burner, Faye A. ... Asheville, NC
Burner, Nancy ... Port Jefferson, NY
Burner, Susan L., (P.C.) ... Los Angeles, CA
Burnes, Albert P. ... Omaha, NE
Burnes & Burnes ... Alexandria, LA
Burnes, Cynthia F. ... Nashville, TN
Burnes, Dennis M. ... St. Louis, MO
Burnes, Dmitrc Ian ... Alexandria, LA
Burnes, Edward M. ... Chicago, IL
Burnes, James P. ... Columbus, OH
Burnes, James T. ... Irvine, CA
Burnes, Joan E. ... Upper Darby, PA
Burnes, John H., Jr. ... Washington, DC
Burnes, Maryanne E. ... Boston, MA
Burnes, Richard V. ... Alexandria, LA
Burnes, Sam ... Evanston, IL
Burness, Robert E., III ... Walnut Creek, CA
Burness, Robert E., Jr. ... Chico, CA
Burness, Stephen W. ... Kalamazoo, MI
Burnet, Terry ... St. Louis, MO
Burnett, Abner, Law Office of ... Odessa, TX
Burnett, Andrew G. ... Carson City, NV
Burnett, Anne E. ... Athens, GA
Burnett, Anne K. ... Omaha, NE
Burnett, Arthur L., Sr. ... Washington, DC
Burnett, Barbara A. ... Syracuse, NY
Burnett, Barbara L. ... Houston, TX
Burnett, Bart B. ... Denver, CO
Burnett, Betty C. ... Rosemead, CA
Burnett, Bobby ... Munday, TX
Burnett, Boyd P. ... Portland, OR
Burnett, Bradley P. ... Denver, CO
Burnett, Bradley P., P.C. ... Denver, CO
Burnett, Brandy J. ... Richmond, VA
Burnett, Brent A. ... Salt Lake City, UT
Burnett, Brian W. ... Salt Lake City, UT
Burnett & Burnett ... Sinton, TX
Burnett, Burnett & Allen ... San Jose, CA
Burnett, Byron K. ... New York, NY
Burnett, Caroline Y. ... Washington, DC
Burnett, Charles B. ... Treasury Department, Internal Revenue Service, GV
Burnett, Charles D. ... Osceola, AR
Burnett, Charles V. ... Issaquah, WA
Burnett, Charlotte ... Calabasas, CA
Burnett, Craig A. ... Santa Rosa, CA
Burnett, Craig V. ... Irvine, CA
Burnett, Cynthia H. ... Houston, TX
Burnett, David B. ... Redwood City, CA
Burnett, David T. ... Issaquah, WA
Burnett, Dennis J. ... Washington, DC
Burnett, Donald L. ... Larned, KS
Burnett, Donald L., Jr. ... Louisville, KY
Burnett, Donna S., (P.C.) ... Houston, TX
Burnett, Douglas R. ... New York, NY
Burnett, E. C., III ... Spartanburg, SC
Burnett, Elizabeth B. ... Boston, MA
Burnett, Elizabeth J. ... San Diego, CA
Burnett, Eric C. ... Boston, MA
Burnett, F. Gerald ... Birmingham, AL
Burnett, Francisca A. ... San Jose, CA
Burnett, Fred A. ... Port Sanilac, MI
Burnett, Frederick W., Jr. ... Dallas, TX
Burnett, G. Michael ... Jacksonville, FL
Burnett, Gary Boyd ... Las Vegas, NV
Salt Lake City, UT
Burnett, Gary, P.C. ... Las Vegas, NV
Salt Lake City, UT
Burnett, Gilbert H. ... Wilmington, NC
Burnett Godette & Burnett, LLC ... Washington, DC
Burnett, Grove T. ... Taos, NM
Burnett, Henry ... Miami, FL
Burnett, Henry G. ... New York, NY
Burnett, Howard D. ... Pocatello, ID
Burnett, Jack W. ... Billings, MT
Burnett, James A. ... Shreveport, LA
Burnett, James E. ... Allegan, MI
Burnett, James E. ... Jefferson, TX
Burnett, James E., Jr. ... Clinton, AR
Burnett, James F. ... Wilmington, DE
Burnett, James J. ... Houston, TX
Burnett, James O. ... Fayetteville, AR
Burnett, James P. ... Chilton, WI
New Holstein, WI
Burnett, James R. ... Boston, MA
Burnett, Jane ... New Canaan, CT
Burnett, Jason B. ... Jacksonville, FL
Burnett, Jay W. ... Houston, TX
Burnett, Jeffrey I. ... Parsippany, NJ
Burnett, Jody K. ... Salt Lake City, UT
Burnett, Joe B. ... Dallas, TX
Burnett, John J. ... New York, NY
Burnett, John L. ... Little Rock, AR
Burnett, John P. ... Independence, MO
Burnett, John S. ... St. Petersburg, FL
Burnett, John T. ... Columbia, SC
Burnett, John W. ... Boston, MA
Burnett, Jonathan H. ... Knoxville, TN
Burnett, Joshua E. ... Tampa, FL
Burnett, K. King ... Salisbury, MD
Burnett, Kastran & Klein ... Allegan, MI
Burnett, Katie G. ... Miami, FL
Burnett, Kevin W. ... Edmond, OK
Burnett, Lane T., P.A. ... Jacksonville, FL
Burnett, Lauren A. ... Avon, CO
Burnett, Lauren A., P.C., The Law Office of ... Avon, CO
Burnett, Lawrence J. ... Milwaukee, WI
Burnett, Lawrence W. ... New York, NY
Burnett, LeAnne ... Oklahoma City, OK
Burnett, L.G. "Buddy", Jr. ... Nashville, TN
Burnett, Lisa C.S. ... Philadelphia, PA
Burnett, Lisa Sudderth ... Atlanta, GA
Burnett, Loretta A. ... Colorado Springs, CO
Burnett, Louis J. ... Birmingham, MI
Burnett, Louis J., P.C. ... Birmingham, MI
Burnett, Malcolm W., Jr. ... Northbrook, IL
Burnett, Malvern C. ... New Orleans, LA
Bay St. Louis, MS
Burnett, Margaret J. ... Environmental Protection Agency, Program Office Attorneys, GV
Burnett, Margaret M. ... Jacksonville, FL
Burnett, Marjorie A. ... Washington, DC
Burnett, Marjorie Ann ... Rowayton, CT
Burnett, Mark H. ... Boston, MA
Burnett, Martin L. ... North Miami, FL
Burnett, Marva Ann ... New York, NY
Burnett, Marvin A. ... Los Angeles, CA
Burnett, Mary Elise ... Kankakee, IL
Burnett, Mary Frances ... Fort Myers, FL
Burnett, Mary Parham ... Jacksonville, FL
Burnett, Michael J. ... Rockville Centre, NY
Burnett, Michael Lance ... Houston, TX
Burnett, Michael L.R. ... Austin, TX
Burnett, Michael O. ... Washington, DC
Burnett, Michael T. ... Chicago, IL
Burnett, Nancy ... Troy, NY
Burnett, Nancy P. ... Securities and Exchange Commission, Office of Equal Employment Opportunity, GV
Burnett, Nelson ... Montgomery, AL
Burnett, Paula ... Albuquerque, NM
Burnett, Peter C. ... Leesburg, VA
Winchester, VA
Burnett, Philip D. ... Crossville, TN
Burnett, Philip L. ... Fort Myers, FL
Burnett, Philip L., P.A. ... Fort Myers, FL
Burnett, R. Alan ... Portland, OR
Burnett, R. George ... Green Bay, WI
Burnett, Ralph M. ... Oakland, MD
Burnett, Rand S. ... Keene, NH
Burnett, Random R. ... Daytona Beach, FL
Maitland, FL
Burnett, Robert A. ... Atlanta, GA
Burnett, Robert A., Jr. ... Des Moines, IA
Burnett, Robert A., P.C. ... Atlanta, GA
Burnett, Robert J. ... Fort Lauderdale, FL
Burnett, Robert J. ... Pittsburgh, PA
Burnett, Robert J. ... Tacoma, WA
Burnett, Robert L., Jr. ... Beaumont, TX
Burnett, Robert M. ... Fort Worth, TX
Burnett, Robert W. ... San Francisco, CA
Burnett, Robert W. ... Naperville, IL
Burnett, Roger Guy ... Liberty, MO
Burnett, Ronald S. ... Texarkana, TX
Burnett, Russell A. ... Atlanta, GA
Burnett, S. Margene ... Kansas City, MO
Burnett, Sheldon J. ... Fort Lauderdale, FL
Burnett, Sheldon J. ... Miami, FL
Burnett, Sherry D. ... Hot Springs National Park, AR
Burnett, Stephen W. ... Dallas, TX
Burnett, Susan E. ... Austin, TX
Burnett, Susan Jan ... Dallas, TX
Burnett, Theresa Lynn ... Trenton, NJ
Burnett, Thomas H. ... Lexington, KY
Burnett, Travis E. ... Bellaire, TX
Burnett, Vincent A. ... Wichita, KS
Burnett, W. Jefferson ... Dallas, TX
Burnett, Walker, & Baker, L.L.C. ... Shreveport, LA
Burnett, Warren ... Odessa, TX
Burnett, Wayne A. ... Brandon, MS
Burnett, William J. ... Philadelphia, PA
Burnett, William L. ... Houston, TX
Burnett & Williams, P.C. ... Leesburg, VA
Winchester, VA
Burnett, Wm. G. ... Sinton, TX
Burnett, Yancey N. ... Mobile, AL
Burnette, Angela T. ... Atlanta, GA
Burnette, Carolyn G. ... Sacramento, CA
Burnette, Charles B., III ... Rock Hill, SC
Burnette, Cynthia P. ... Tampa, FL
Burnette, Dobson & Hardeman ... Chattanooga, TN
Burnette, Erica Littlejohn ... Waco, TX
Burnette, Frank L., II ... Des Moines, IA
Burnette, G. Sam ... Macon, GA
Burnette, Graham ... Sunnyvale, CA
Burnette, Guy E., Jr. ... Tallahassee, FL
Burnette, Harry F. ... Chattanooga, TN
Burnette, J. Thomas ... Oxford, NC
Burnette & Kelley ... Des Moines, IA
Burnette & Leclair ... Columbia, SC
Lexington, SC
Burnette, M. Malissa ... Columbia, SC
Burnette, Marbi L. ... Moreno Valley, CA
Burnette, Mark G. ... Decatur, GA
Burnette, R. Edwin, Jr. ... Lynchburg, VA
Burnette, R. Kim ... Knoxville, TN
Burnette, Roberta J. ... Moorpark, CA
Burnette, Sarah Katherine Kelly ... Oxford, NC
Burnette, Susan Lynn ... Amarillo, TX
Dallas, TX
Burnette, Suzanne M. ... Department of Labor, Office of the Solicitor, GV
Burnette, Viola A. ... Mission, SD
Burnette, W. Brian ... Frankfort, KY
Burnette, W. Mark ... Lewisburg, WV
Burnette, Weldon M. ... Lewisburg, WV
Burnetti, Dean ... Lakeland, FL
Burnetti, Douglas K. ... Lakeland, FL
Burnetti, P.A., Law Office of ... Lakeland, FL
Burney, Billy C. ... Decatur, AL
Burney, Burney & Jones ... Wilmington, NC
Burney, David G. ... Washington, DC
Burney, Deitra Pleshette ... Atlanta, GA
Burney, Frank B. ... San Antonio, TX
Burney & Herthneck Co., L.P.A. ... Rocky River, OH
Burney, James Brent ... Decatur, AL
Burney, Janet E. ... Cleveland, OH
Burney, John J., Jr. ... Wilmington, NC
Burney, Jon R. ... Rocky River, OH
Burney, Laura H. ... San Antonio, TX
Burney, Louis A. ... Wilmington, NC
Burney, Nathaniel ... New York, NY
Burney, Nona M. ... Cleveland, OH
Burney, Philip G. ... Denver, CO
Burney, Raymond ... New York, NY
Burney, Rhett D. ... Laurens, SC
Burney, Robert S. ... Westfield, NJ
Burney, Thomas R. ... Chicago, IL
Burney, W. Travis ... Lincoln, NE
Burnham, A. Danzey ... New York, NY
Burnham, Albert C. ... Belvedere-Tiburon, CA
Burnham, Alicia C. ... Irvine, CA
Burnham, Anne More ... San Antonio, TX
Burnham, Annemarie ... West Hartford, CT
Burnham & Brown, A Professional Corporation ... Oakland, CA
Sacramento, CA
San Francisco, CA
San Jose, CA
Burnham, Carl, Jr. ... Ontario, OR
Burnham, Carson G. ... Boston, MA
Burnham, Clark J. ... Oakland, CA
Burnham, D. Jeffrey ... Seattle, WA
Burnham, Daniel C. ... Costa Mesa, CA
Burnham, Daniel J. ... Chicago, IL
Burnham, Donald S. ... Boston, MA
Burnham, Ernest C., Jr. ... Clinton, CT
Burnham, Francis N. ... Cleveland, OH
Burnham, Hathorne A. ... Golden, CO
Burnham & Hines ... Boston, MA
Burnham, H. R. ... Anniston, AL
Burnham, James A. ... Chicago, IL
Burnham, Janice L., Law Offices of ... Newport Beach, CA
Burnham, Jay B. ... Farmington, NM
Burnham, Jeffrey L. ... Kansas City, MO
Burnham, Jim ... Dallas, TX
Burnham, John T. ... Los Osos, CA
Burnham, Judson D. ... Barre, VT
Burnham, Kelly ... Las Cruces, NM
Burnham & Klinefelter, P.C. ... Anniston, AL
Gadsden, AL
Burnham, Lauren Z. ... Atlanta, GA
Burnham, Margaret A. ... Boston, MA
Burnham, Margaret Shea ... Greensboro, NC
Burnham, Mary K. ... Collins, MS
Burnham, Noel C. ... Wilmington, DE
Burnham, P. Anthony ... Newport Beach, CA
Burnham, Patrick S. ... Anniston, AL
Burnham, Paul H. ... Darien, CT
Burnham, Perry H. ... San Antonio, TX
Burnham, Priscilla S. ... Marquette, MI
Burnham, Ralph E. ... Cincinnati, OH
Burnham, Richard B. ... Phoenix, AZ
Burnham, Richard E. ... Framingham, MA
Burnham, Richard M. ... Madison, WI
Burnham, Scott J. ... Missoula, MT
Burnham, Sharon ... Honolulu, HI
Burnham, Shawn E. ... Seattle, WA
Burnham, Steven A. ... Louisville, KY
Burnham, Steven E. ... Port Huron, MI
Burnham, Teresa Bodwell ... Missoula, MT
Burnham, Thomas N. ... Ann Arbor, MI
Burnham, Timothy B. ... Shreveport, LA
Burnham, William ... Detroit, MI
Burnham, W. R. ... Eufaula, OK
Burnham Pieroni, Rebecca ... Phoenix, AZ
Burnheimer + Company, P.C. ... Traverse City, MI
Burnheimer, Mark A. ... Traverse City, MI
Burnhill, Clifford ... Oakland, CA
Burnick, Barrie Sue ... Bethesda, MD
Burnick, Daniel J. ... Birmingham, AL
Burnick, Dean C. ... San Francisco, CA
Burnick, Gregory S. ... Detroit, MI
Burnight, Gregory J. ... Long Beach, CA
Burnight, Susan R. ... Minneapolis, MN
Burnim, Ira A. ... Washington, DC
Burningham, Branden T. ... Salt Lake City, UT
Burningham & Burningham ... Salt Lake City, UT
Burningham, Guy R. ... Provo, UT
Burningham, Kay ... Lafayette, CO
Burningham, Kent S. ... Salt Lake City, UT
Burningham, L. David ... Salt Lake City, UT
Burningham, Leonard W. ... Salt Lake City, UT
Burningham, Marilynn K. ... Salt Lake City, UT
Burningham, Ross L. ... San Diego, CA
Burnison, Boyd E. ... Oakland, CA
Burnison, Chantal S. ... Los Angeles, CA
Burniston, Thomas Knowles ... Croton-On-Hudson, NY
Burnite, John T., Jr. ... Walnut Creek, CA
Burnley, James H., IV ... Washington, DC
Burnley, Kenneth W. ... Federal Communications Commission, Wireless Telecommunications Bureau, GV
Burnley, Tracy L. ... Cherry Hill, NJ
Burnovski, Ron H. ... Los Angeles, CA
Burns, Aimee R. ... Beaumont, TX
Burns, Alan R. ... Orange, CA
Burns, Albert H. ... Boston, MA
Burns, Alice Ann ... Miami, FL
Burns, Alice R. ... Cedar City, UT

Burns, Alisa B. ....Denver, CO
Burns, Allison E. ....Newport Beach, CA
Burns, Amy C. ....Boston, MA
Burns, Amy Elizabeth ....Topeka, KS
Burns Anderson Jury & Brenner, L.L.P.
Austin, TX
Burns, Andrew Joseph ....Baltimore, MD
Burns, Andrew M. ....Rochester, NY
Burns, Andrew T. ....Portland, OR
Burns, Ann Barry ....Minneapolis, MN
Burns, Ann Forest, Law Offices of
Seattle, WA
Burns, Ann K. ....Houston, TX
Burns, Annette T. ....Phoenix, AZ
Burns & Arneke, L.L.P.
Winston-Salem, NC
Burns, Arnold I. ....New York, NY
Burns & Associates ....Cleveland, OH
Burns, B. Darren ....Annapolis, MD
Burns, B. John ....Des Moines, IA
Burns, Barbara ....East Brunswick, NJ
Burns, Barbara M. ....Ann Arbor, MI
Burns, Barton C. ....Chattanooga, TN
Burns, Belinda A. ....Dayton, OH
Burns, Ben A. ....Nashville, TN
Burns, Bethany Moir ....Washington, DC
Burns, Beverly Hall ....Detroit, MI
Burns, Bobby D. ....Treasury Department, Internal Revenue Service, GV
Burns, Brad T. ....Dallas, TX
Burns, Brandi ....Clifton Park, NY
Burns, Brent A. ....New York, NY
Burns, Brian ....New York, NY
Burns, Brian D. ....Florham Park, NJ
Burns, Brian D. ....Oneonta, NY
Burns, Brian E. ....New York, NY
Burns, Brian J. ....Boston, MA
Burns, Brian P. ....San Francisco, CA
Burns, Brian R. ....Washington, DC
Burns, Brian T. ....Providence, RI
Burns and Brown ....De Kalb, IL
Burns, Bruce A. ....New York, NY
Burns, Bruce W. ....San Jose, CA
Burns, Bryant, Hinchey, Cox & Rockefeller, P.A. ....Dover, NH
Burns & Burns ....Redding, CA
Burns, Burns, Burns & Morgan
Anniston, AL
Gadsden, AL
Burns and Burns, P.C. ....Phoenix, AZ
Burns, Burns, Walsh & Walsh, P.A.
Lyndon, KS
Osage City, KS
Burns, C. Christine ....Phoenix, AZ
Burns, C. Craig ....Little Rock, AR
Burns, C. David ....New Orleans, LA
Burns, Cara R. ....Los Angeles, CA
Burns, Carol S. ....Los Angeles, CA
Burns & Carpinello ....Delmar, NY
Burns, Catherine ....Redding, CA
Burns, Catherine Ann ....Annandale, VA
Burns, Catherine L. ....Boston, MA
Burns, Charles ....Jupiter, FL
Burns, Charles B., Jr. ....Cleveland, TN
Burns, Charles P. ....San Francisco, CA
Burns, Charles P. ....Chicago, IL
Burns, Charles Robert Douglas, Jr.
Gadsden, AL
Burns, Christopher G. ....Jacksonville, FL
Burns, Christopher J. ....Buffalo, NY
Burns, Clara B. ....El Paso, TX
Burns, Claude M., Jr. ....Tuscaloosa, AL
Burns, Clement E., Jr. ....St. Louis, MO
Burns, Clyde M. ....Lyndon, KS
Osage City, KS
Burns, Coleen A. ....Madison, WI
Burns, Columbus B., III ....Savannah, GA
Burns, Craig B. ....Mandan, ND
Burns, Craig P. ....Toledo, OH
Burns, Cunningham & Mackey, P.C.
Mobile, AL
Burns, Daniel J. ....Chicago, IL
Burns, Daniel J., Jr. ....Kimberly, WI
Burns, Daniel L. ....Grand Rapids, MI
Burns, Daniel M. (Matt) ....Austin, TX
Burns, Daniel R. ....Schenectady, NY
Burns, Daniel T. ....Chicago, IL
Burns, Danny D. ....Fort Worth, TX
Burns, Darla J. ....Columbus, OH
Burns, Darlene E. ....Bronx, NY
Burns, David ....Dedham, MA
Burns, David A. ....Clarksdale, MS
Burns, David Alan ....Houston, TX
Burns, David C. ....Newton, KS
Burns, David D. ....Washington, DC
Burns, David E. ....New York, NY
Burns, David H. ....Tallahassee, FL
Burns, David J. ....Salt Lake City, UT
Burns, David J.T. ....Concord, NH
Burns, David Penn ....Washington, DC
Burns, David S. ....New York, NY
Burns, David W. ....Medford, NJ
Burns, David W. ....Coshocton, OH
Burns, David W. ....Houston, TX
Burns, Dawn D. ....Collingdale, PA
Burns, Day & Presnell, P.A. ....Raleigh, NC
Burns, Dean D. ....Petoskey, MI
Burns, Deanna A. ....Kansas City, MO
Burns, Deborah J. ....Santa Monica, CA
Burns, Debra Linn ....Indianapolis, IN
Burns, Denis C. ....St. Louis, MO
Burns, Dennis D., Law Offices of
La Jolla, CA
Burns, Dennis R. ....Oklahoma City, OK
Burns, D. F. ....Cambridge, MA

Burns, Doane, Swecker & Mathis, L.L.P.
Redwood City, CA
San Francisco, CA
Washington, DC
Research Triangle Park, NC
Alexandria, VA
Burns, Don C. ....Columbia, LA
Burns, Donald A. ....Manchester, NH
Burns, Donald A., P.C. ....Portland, OR
Burns, Donald E. ....Los Angeles, CA
Burns, Doreen Emily ....Treasury Department, Departmental Offices, GV
Burns, Douglas C. ....Brunswick, OH
Burns, Douglas E. ....Springfield, NJ
Burns, Douglas E. ....Oklahoma City, OK
Burns, Douglas F. ....Pittsburgh, PA
Burns, Douglas J. ....Highlands, NC
Burns, Douglas T. ....Garden City, NY
Burns, Douglass W. ....Denver, CO
Burns, Duane A. ....Grand Island, NE
Burns, Dwight T., III ....Boston, MA
Burns, E. Grantland ....Greenville, SC
Burns, Eban D. ....Hartford, CT
Burns, Edmund C. ....New York, NY
Burns, Edmund J. ....New York, NY
Burns, Edward E. ....Lenexa, KS
Burns, Edward J. ....Rochester, NY
Burns, Edward M. ....Long Grove, IL
Burns, Edward M. ....Cambridge, MA
Burns, Edward M., II ....Waynesboro, VA
Burns, Edward M., II, P.C., The Law Offices of
Waynesboro, VA
Burns, Edward T. ....Madison, CT
Burns, Edward William ....Pasadena, CA
Burns, Eileen T. ....Mount Laurel, NJ
Philadelphia, PA
Burns, Eleanor R. ....Dexter, NY
Burns, Elizabeth ....Syracuse, NY
Burns, Elizabeth A. ....San Francisco, CA
Burns, Elizabeth A. ....Portland, ME
Burns, Elizabeth A. ....Lyndhurst, NJ
Burns, Elkanah J. ....Toluca Lake, CA
Burns, Ellen B. ....New Haven, CT
Burns, Emily G. ....Phoenix, AZ
Sun City, AZ
Burns, Eric Grimsley ....Boston, MA
Burns, Eric H. ....Lafayette, IN
Burns, Eugene M. ....Yorktown Heights, NY
Burns, Eugene P. ....Boston, MA
Burns, F. Kent ....Raleigh, NC
Burns, F. Shaun ....La Jolla, CA
Burns, Faith B. ....Cincinnati, OH
Burns & Farrey ....Boston, MA
Springfield, MA
Worcester, MA
Burns, Figa & Will, P.C. ....Denver, CO
Burns, Francis C. ....Watertown, SD
Burns, Francis P., III ....Philadelphia, PA
Burns, Frank J. ....Los Angeles, CA
Burns, Frederick J. ....Springfield, MA
Burns, Fredric B. ....Miami, FL
Burns, G. Lee ....Prairie Village, KS
Burns, G. Lee, Jr. ....San Francisco, CA
Burns, G. Webster ....Torrance, CA
Burns, Gary A. ....Tacoma, WA
Burns, Gary F. ....Gadsden, AL
Burns, Geoffrey J. ....Lyndon Station, WI
Burns, George C. ....San Antonio, TX
Burns, George D. ....Falls Church, VA
Burns, George E., Jr. ....Baltimore, MD
Burns, George F. ....Portland, ME
Burns, George J. ....New York, NY
Burns, George S. ....Costa Mesa, CA
Burns, Gerald A. ....Fort Wayne, IN
Burns, Gerald E. ....New York, NY
Burns, Gerald E., III ....Philadelphia, PA
Burns, Gerald F. ....Grand Rapids, MI
Burns, Gerald M. ....Madisonville, KY
Burns, Glen C. ....Ardmore, OK
Burns & Goldstone, P.C. ....Los Angeles, CA
Burns, Gordon B. ....Sacramento, CA
Burns, Gregory N. ....Fort Myers, FL
Burns, Guy C. ....Tracy, CA
Burns, Guy L., Jr. ....Mountain Brook, AL
Burns, Guy M. ....Clearwater, FL
Tampa, FL
Burns & Hammerly ....Issaquah, WA
Burns, Harmon E. ....San Mateo, CA
Burns, Harold H., Jr. ....Baltimore, MD
Burns, Harry A., III ....Clarks Summit, PA
Burns, Harry E., II ....St. Cloud, MN
Burns, Harry H. ....Seminole, FL
Burns, Harry J. ....San Antonio, TX
Burns, Haunani F. ....Honolulu, HI
Burns, Heather M.
Federal Maritime Commission, Bureau of Enforcement, GV
Burns, Heather M. ....Manchester, NH
Burns & Henry ....Pomeroy, WA
Burns, Howard ....Athens, AL
Burns, Howard C. ....Pittsburgh, PA
Burns, Howard W., Jr. ....New York, NY
Burns, Hugh A. ....Denver, CO
Burns, Hugh L. ....New York, NY
Burns, Hugh R. ....Los Angeles, CA
Burns, Ian F. ....Reno, NV
Burns, Ian F., & Associates, P.C.
Reno, NV
Burns, J. Benjamin ....Columbus, GA
Burns, J. Benjamin, P.C. ....Columbus, GA
Burns, J. Daran, The Law Offices of
Marietta, GA
Burns, J. Franklin ....Atlanta, GA
Burns, J. Scott ....Phoenix, AZ
Burns, J. Scott ....Boston, MA
Burns, Jack L. ....Muscatine, IA
Burns, Jack R. ....Issaquah, WA
Burns, James ....Decorah, IA

Burns, James ....New York, NY
Burns, James A. ....Phoenix, AZ
Burns, James A. ....Birmingham, MI
Burns, James A. ....Detroit, MI
Burns, James A., Jr. ....Chicago, IL
Burns, James B. ....Chicago, IL
Burns, James B. ....Philadelphia, PA
Burns, James C., Jr. ....Shelbyville, TN
Burns, James D. ....Seattle, WA
Burns, James E. ....Cleveland, OH
Cleveland, OH
Burns, James E., Jr. ....San Francisco, CA
Burns, James H. ....Bath, NY
Burns, James J. ....Albany, NY
Burns, James J. ....New York, NY
Burns, James J. ....Barre, VT
Burns, James J. ....Richmond, VA
Burns, James J., Jr. ....Rye, NY
Burns, James L. ....New York, NY
Burns, James L. ....Cleveland, OH
Burns, James M. ....Washington, DC
Burns, James M. ....Livingston, NJ
Burns, James M. ....Portland, OR
Burns, James P., 3rd ....Rochester, NY
Burns, James S. ....Honolulu, HI
Burns, James S. ....Philadelphia, PA
Burns, James T. ....Kankakee, IL
Burns, James T. ....Indianapolis, IN
Burns, James W. ....Angola, IN
Burns, James W. ....Cherry Hill, NJ
Burns, James W. ....Garden City, NY
Burns, Jane Clarke ....St. Louis, MO
Burns, Janice L. ....Detroit, MI
Burns, Jean W. ....Provo, UT
Burns, Jeanette Byrum ....Lilburn, GA
Burns, Jeff ....Huron, SD
Burns, Jeffrey A. ....Kansas City, MO
Burns, Jeffrey P. ....Philadelphia, PA
Burns, Jeffrey R. ....Greeley, CO
Burns, Jeffrey S. ....Chicago, IL
Burns, Jerome E., P.C. ....Saginaw, MI
Burns, Jerry A. ....Gainesville, FL
Burns, Jerry A. ....Bowling Green, KY
Burns, Joel D. ....Milledgeville, GA
Burns, Joel D., P.C. ....Milledgeville, GA
Burns, John ....Seattle, WA
Burns, John A. ....Columbus, OH
Burns, John A. ....Seattle, WA
Burns, John A., Jr. ....Melville, NY
Mineola, NY
Burns, John Brister ....Jackson, TN
Burns, John D. ....Raleigh, NC
Burns, John D. ....Portland, OR
Burns, John Douglas ....Greenbelt, MD
Burns, John E. ....Peekskill, NY
Burns, John F. ....Detroit, MI
Burns, John F. ....St. Joseph, MO
Burns, John F. ....Athens, OH
Burns, John G. ....Trenton, MI
Burns, John J. ....Fairbanks, AK
Burns, John J.
Agency for International Development, Other Offices of A.I.D., GV
Burns, John J. ....Cleveland, OH
Burns, John Kendrick ....Wilmington, NC
Burns, John L. ....Tequesta, FL
West Palm Beach, FL
Burns, John M. ....Omaha, NE
Burns, John M. ....Portland, OR
Burns, John M., III ....New York, NY
Burns, John P. ....Costa Mesa, CA
Burns, John P. ....Santa Ana, CA
Burns, John R. ....Department of Defense, Defense Legal Services Agency, GV
Burns, John R., III ....Fort Wayne, IN
Burns, John T., Jr. ....Burnsville, MN
Burns, John V. ....Perth Amboy, NJ
Burns, John V. ....Milwaukee, WI
Burns, John W. ....Palo Alto, CA
Burns, John W. ....Birmingham, MI
Burns, John W. ....New York, NY
Burns, Jonathan B. ....Charlottesville, VA
Burns, Joseph A. ....San Bernardino, CA
Burns, Joseph B. ....Hartford, CT
Burns, Joseph H. ....North Brunswick, NJ
Burns, Joseph L. ....Ferrysburg, MI
Burns, Joseph M. ....Chicago, IL
Burns, Josephine Amato
Pension Benefit Guaranty Corporation, Office of the General Counsel, GV
Burns, J. T. ....Wedowee, AL
Burns, Julia V. ....Pittsburgh, PA
Burns, Julie Rissman ....Owings Mills, MD
Burns, Karen ....New York, NY
Burns, Karen K. ....Boston, MA
Burns, Karen Romero ....San Francisco, CA
Burns, Karen Saraco ....Bristol, PA
Langhorne, PA
Burns & Kasmen, A Professional Corporation ....Jenkintown, PA
Burns, Katherine Mills ....McIntosh, FL
Burns, Katherine Stoll ....Sherman Oaks, CA
Burns, Kathleen Sholette ....Voorhees, NJ
Burns, Keith ....Portland, OR
Burns, Keith D. ....Durham, NC
Burns, Keith J. ....Woodbridge, NJ
Burns, Kendra Joss ....Laramie, WY
Burns, Kennedy, Schilling & O'Shea
New York, NY
Burns, Kenneth A. ....Las Vegas, NV
Burns, Kenneth B. ....Cleveland, OH
Burns, Kenneth D. ....Fayetteville, NC
Burns, Kenneth H. ....Houston, TX
Burns, Kenneth J., Jr. ....Northbrook, IL
Burns, Kenneth M. ....Okolona, MS
Burns, Kenneth N. ....San Francisco, CA
Burns, Kevin L. ....Phoenix, AZ
Burns, Kevin L. ....Trumbull, CT

Burns, Kevin M. ....Dayton, OH
Burns, Kevin R. ....Little Rock, AR
Burns, Kirk Lee ....Miami, FL
Burns, Kristin L. ....Atlanta, GA
Burns, Kristina A. ....Albany, NY
Burns, L. Newton ....Rockwall, TX
Burns, Larry A. ....San Diego, CA
Burns Law Firm ....Omaha, NE
Burns Law Firm ....Sioux Falls, SD
Burns Law Firm, The, LLC
Greenbelt, MD
Burns, Lawrence A. ....Cape Coral, FL
Burns, Lawrence F. ....Jersey City, NJ
Burns, Lawrence P. ....Grand Rapids, MI
Burns, Lawrence R. ....Greensburg, PA
Burns, Lee N. ....Janesville, WI
Burns, Leighton R. ....Utica, NY
Burns, Leo T. ....Logansport, IN
Burns, Leon C., Jr. ....Cookeville, TN
Burns & Levinson LLP ....Boston, MA
Hingham, MA
Burns, Ligerie P. ....Ridgewood, NJ
Burns, Lisa A.
Federal Communications Commission, Office of the General Counsel, GV
Burns, Lisa Anne ....La Jolla, CA
Burns, Lisa Weinstein ....Boston, MA
Burns, Lois Amphtor ....Harrisburg, PA
Burns, Loraine J. ....Roseland, NJ
Burns, Loretta M. ....New York, NY
Burns, Lori R. ....Chicago, IL
Burns, Luke K., Jr. ....Westminster, MD
Burns, M. Brett ....Dallas, TX
Burns, M. Edward, Jr. ....Englewood, CO
Burns, M. Elizabeth (Lisa) ....Phoenix, AZ
Burns, M. Susan ....Chisago City, MN
Burns, Malcolm R. ....Lawrence, KS
Burns, Margaret A. ....Alexandria, VA
Burns, Marian M. ....Lyndon, KS
Osage City, KS
Burns, Mark E. ....Salt Lake City, UT
Burns, Mark G. ....St. Louis, MO
Burns, Mark W. ....Chicago, IL
Burns & Marks ....Bowling Green, KY
Burns & Marshall LLP ....St. Louis, MO
Burns, Marshall S., Jr. ....Lansing, MI
Burns, Martha Masteller ....Phoenix, AZ
Burns, Martin ....Tacoma, WA
Burns, Martin J. ....Chicago, IL
Burns, Marvin G., (Professional Corporation) ....Los Angeles, CA
Burns, Mary Elizabeth ....New York, NY
Burns, Mary Ellen ....Stamford, CT
Burns, Mary L. ....Albany, NY
Burns, Mary P. ....Minot, ND
Burns, Mary Patricia ....Chicago, IL
Burns, Mary Spalding ....Chicago, IL
Burns, Matthew ....Jersey City, NJ
Burns, Matthew W. ....Destin, FL
Burns, Maureen E. ....Sacramento, CA
Burns, Maureen E. ....New Haven, CT
Burns, McDonald, Bradford, Patrick & Tinsley, L.L.P. ....Abbeville, SC
Greenwood, SC
Laurens, SC
Burns, Meade ....Atlanta, GA
Burns, Megan E. ....Virginia Beach, VA
Burns, Meghan Catherine ....Arlington, VA
Burns, Melina J. ....Oakland, CA
Burns, Melissa L. ....Los Angeles, CA
Burns, Michael ....Columbus, OH
Burns, Michael ....Hayward, WI
Burns, Michael A. ....Pasadena, CA
Burns, Michael D. ....West Haven, CT
Burns, Michael E. ....Bethlehem, PA
Burns, Michael F. ....Riverside, CA
Burns, Michael J. ....Sacramento, CA
Burns, Michael J. ....Chicago, IL
Burns, Michael J. ....Easton, MD
Burns, Michael J. ....Columbus, OH
Burns, Michael J. ....Philadelphia, PA
Burns, Michael M. ....Fort Lauderdale, FL
Burns, Michael O. ....St. Cloud, MN
Burns, Michael P. ....St. Helena, CA
San Francisco, CA
Burns, Michael P. ....Hastings, NE
Burns, Michael S. ....Lombard, IL
Burns, Michael W. ....Pittsburgh, PA
Burns, Michael W. ....Greenville, SC
Burns, Michael Wm. ....Chicago, IL
Burns, Mitchell ....Rockville, MD
Burns, Mitchell S. ....Gold River, CA
Burns, Moultrie B., Jr. ....Camden, SC
Burns, Nancy J. ....Cincinnati, OH
Burns, Nancy Weinberg ....Brooklyn, NY
Burns, Natalie L. ....Portland, ME
Burns, Neil ....Boston, MA
Burns, Norman L. ....Gonzales, TX
Burns, O'Gorman, Black & Weyand, L.L.C.
San Antonio, TX
Burns, Patrick A. ....New York, NY
Burns, Patrick G. ....Chicago, IL
Burns, Patrick J. ....Indianapolis, IN
Burns, Patrick J., Jr. ....New York, NY
Burns, Patrick M. ....Kankakee, IL
Burns, Paul A. ....Martinsburg, WV
Burns, Paul B. ....Boston, MA
Burns, Paul D. ....Cedar Rapids, IA
Burns, Paul E. ....Phoenix, AZ
Burns, Paul E. ....Brighton, MI
Burns, Paul G. ....New York, NY
Burns, Paul J. ....Largo, FL
Burns, Paul J. ....Spokane, WA
Burns, Paul J., P.S. ....Spokane, WA
Burns, Peggy Ann ....Northglenn, CO
Burns, Peter F. ....Mobile, AL
Burns, Peter M. ....Hartford, CT
Burns, Peter S. ....Pearce, AZ

Burris, Victoria Ehret ... Decatur, IL
Burris, William E. ... St. Louis, MO
Burris, William J. ... Franklinton, LA
Burriss & Monahan, A Professional Corporation ... Mountain View, CA
Burriss, Richard S. ... Mountain View, CA
Burriss, Susan Howie ... Mountain View, CA
Burritt, Nancy L. ... Albany, NY
Burr-Jones, A. Elizabeth ... Burley, ID
Burro, C. Peter ... Somers Point, NJ
Burroff, Teresa J. ... Austin, TX
Burron, Keith ... Cheyenne, WY
Burroughs, Allison Dale ... Philadelphia, PA
Burroughs, Amy E. ... Nashville, TN
Burroughs, Benton, Jr. ... Falls Church, VA
Burroughs, Blair B. ... Seattle, WA
Burroughs, Carol E. ... Washington, DC
Burroughs, Charles E. ... Milwaukee, WI
Burroughs & Damast ... New York, NY
Burroughs, Davis C., Jr. ... Pittsburgh, PA
Burroughs, Edward R. ... Stockton, CA
Burroughs, F. Randolph
Alamogordo, NM
Burroughs, Froneberger & Humber
Point Reyes Station, CA
Burroughs, G. Gordon ... Edwardsville, IL
Burroughs, Gail ... New Rochelle, NY
Burroughs, Geoffrey ... Sacramento, CA
Burroughs & Guin, LLP ... Tuscaloosa, AL
Burroughs, H. Franklin ... Conway, SC
Myrtle Beach, SC
Burroughs, Harold R. ... St. Louis, MO
Burroughs, Hepler, Broom, MacDonald & Hebrank ... Belleville, IL
East St. Louis, IL
Edwardsville, IL
St. Louis, MO
Burroughs, J. David ... Dawsonville, GA
Burroughs, J. David ... Dawsonville, GA
Burroughs, J. David ... Gainesville, GA
Burroughs, James B. ... Indianapolis, IN
Burroughs, James C. ... Vienna, VA
Burroughs, James C., II ... Minneapolis, MN
Burroughs, James D. ... Philadelphia, PA
Burroughs, James T. ... San Francisco, CA
Burroughs, John D. ... Point Reyes Station, CA
Burroughs, John Robert ... Oakland, CA
Burroughs, Joseph O., Jr. ... Conway, SC
Burroughs, Katherine A. ... Hartford, CT
Burroughs, Kathryn Hillebrands
Fort Wayne, IN
Burroughs, Keith H. ... Knoxville, TN
Burroughs Law Firm, A Professional Association ... Conway, SC
Myrtle Beach, SC
Burroughs, Lisa ... Sacramento, CA
Burroughs, Mark A. ... Denton, TX
Burroughs, Michael S. ... Tuscaloosa, AL
Burroughs, Nancy Haas ... Chagrin Falls, OH
Burroughs, Patricia Small ... Conroe, TX
Burroughs, Patrick R. ... Lansing, MI
Burroughs, Paul F. ... Erie, PA
Burroughs, Philip D. ... Indianapolis, IN
Burroughs, R. Alexander
Winston-Salem, NC
Burroughs, Ralph C. ... Tuscaloosa, AL
Burroughs, Raymond H. ... Collinsville, IL
Burroughs & Rhodes ... Alamogordo, NM
Burroughs, Richard R. ... Cleveland, TX
Burroughs, Rick C. ... Mobile, AL
Burroughs, Robert C. ... Ault, CO
Burroughs, Robert C., P.C. ... Ault, CO
Burroughs, Robert M. ... Charlotte, NC
Burroughs, Susan B. ... Dallas, TX
Burroughs, Wendy ... Waterbury, VT
Burroughs, William S., Jr. ... Arlington, VA
Burrous, Beth A. ... Washington, DC
Burrow, Alan G. ... Boise, ID
Burrow, Christina Hosp ... Washington, DC
Burrow, D. Brett ... Nashville, TN
Burrow, Darrell Lee ... College Park, GA
Burrow, David H. ... Houston, TX
Burrow, Hance W., III ... Dallas, TX
Burrow, Harlan & Childers
Blytheville, AR
Osceola, AR
Burrow, John L ... Springdale, AR
Burrow, Lance ... San Jose, CA
Burrow, Leon ... Blytheville, AR
Burrow, Linda M. ... Los Angeles, CA
Burrow, Michael R. ... Greenfield, IN
Burrow & Parrott, L.L.P. ... Houston, TX
Burrow, Patrick A. ... Little Rock, AR
Burrow, Robert H. ... Baltimore, MD
Burrow, Robert Harold ... Silver Spring, MD
Burrow, Stephen ... New York, NY
Burrow, Stephen W. ... Pascagoula, MS
Burrow, Timothy W. ... Nashville, TN
Burrow, William F., Jr. ... Austin, TX
Burrowes, David T. ... Chicago, IL
Burrowes, Andrew E. ... Palo Alto, CA
Burrows, Ann Lee ... Little Falls, NY
Burrows, Cecil J. ... Pittsfield, IL
Burrows, Dale A. ... Denton, TX
Lewisville, TX
Burrows, Damon, II ... Washington, DC
Burrows, Dana D. ... Provo, UT
Burrows, Daniel W. ... Amarillo, TX
Burrows, Dennis R., (P.C.) ... Lubbock, TX
Burrows, Ellen K. ... Philadelphia, PA
Burrows, Ernest J. ... Portland, OR
Burrows, Gordon A. ... New York, NY
Burrows, Gordon W. ... White Plains, NY
Burrows & Hall ... Wallace, NC
Burrows, James A. ... Watertown, NY
Burrows, Jay E. ... Shelby, MI
Burrows, Jennifer L. ... New Orleans, LA
Burrows and Jester, P.A.
Merritt Island, FL
Burrows, Karrick A. ... Pueblo, CO
Burrows, Kenneth David ... New York, NY
Burrows, Kenneth G. ... Tacoma, WA
Burrows Law Offices ... Pittsburgh, PA
Burrows, Lawton A., Jr. ... Driggs, ID
Burrows, Lee E. ... Irvine, CA
Burrows, Matthew H. ... Oakland, CA
Burrows, Matthew J. ... Beverly Hills, CA
Burrows, Meade G. ... Northampton, MA
Burrows, Melinda ... Washington, DC
Burrows, Michael ... New York, NY
Burrows, Michelle R. ... Salem, OR
Burrows, Nancy E. ... Woburn, MA
Burrows, Peter ... Irvine, CA
Burrows, Quentin C. ... Naperville, IL
Burrows, Randall A. ... San Francisco, CA
Burrows, Richard H. ... Providence, RI
Burrows, Richard L. ... Wallace, NC
Burrows, Robert D. ... Laguna Niguel, CA
Burrows, Robert E. ... La Grange, IL
Burrows, Robert M. ... Grants Pass, OR
Burrows, Ronni K. ... Pittsburgh, PA
Burrows, Sharon Elizabeth ... Seattle, WA
Burrows, Stephen H. ... Mount Pleasant, MI
Burrows, Steven W. ... Chicago, IL
Burrows, Suzanne I. ... Washington, DC
Silver Spring, MD
Burrows, Thomas J. ... Jamaica, NY
Burrows, Thomas N. ... Department of Justice, Criminal Division, GV
Burrows, Tom G. ... Merritt Island, FL
Burrows, Weiss & Bloomberg
Northampton, MA
Burrows, William P. ... Syracuse, NY
Burruano, Joseph D. ... Mineola, NY
Burruano, Samuel Joseph, Jr.
Buffalo, NY
Burruezo, Carlos J. ... Orlando, FL
Burrus, E. Dale ... Houston, TX
Burrus, Eugene A. ... Dallas, TX
Burrus, James H., Jr. ... Maitland, FL
Burrus, John E. ... Denver, CO
Burrus, John H. ... Lexington, KY
Burrus, Judith E. ... Nashville, TN
Burrus, Otis C. ... Zionsville, IN
Burrus, Robert L., Jr. ... Richmond, VA
Burrus, Roger L. ... Zionsville, IN
Burrus, S. T. ... New Braunfels, TX
Burruss, Darrell E. ... Bakersfield, CA
Burruss, Mary Jane ... Fairfax, VA
Burruss, Melvin ... New York, NY
Burruss, Ray B. ... Lawrenceville, GA
Burry, Brenton G. ... Columbia, SC
Burry, Daniel C. ... Decatur, IN
Burry, Douglas E. ... Haddonfield, NJ
Burry, H. H. ... Fort Myers, FL
Burry, Kenneth L. ... Los Angeles, CA
Burry, Mark S. ... Decatur, IN
Bursa, Brian M., (P.A.)
St. Petersburg, FL
Bursack, Linda Merens ... Beaumont, TX
Bursavich, Jude C. ... Baton Rouge, LA
Bursch, John J. ... Grand Rapids, MI
Burse, David T. ... San Jose, CA
Burse, LaTina Luvette ... Baltimore, MD
Burse, Raymond M. ... Louisville, KY
Bursell, Jeffrey D. ... St. George, UT
Burseth, Steve ... Anchorage, AK
Burshtyn, James H. ... Austin, TX
Burshtyn, Laurence I. ... Houston, TX
Bursi, F. Michael ... Memphis, TN
Bursiek, Paul G. ... Denver, CO
Bursik, David H.E., Law Offices of
Wayne, NJ
Bursik, Julie L. ... Minneapolis, MN
Bursk, Bonnie Marie ... Granada Hills, CA
Burski, James L.
Department Of The Interior, Office of Hearings & Appeals, GV
Bursky, Robert M. ... New York, NY
Bursky-Stillman, Alicia ... New York, NY
Bursley, Kathleen A. ... Chestnut Hill, MA
Burson, Alan H. ... Oceanside, CA
Burson and Beck ... Carey, OH
Burson, Charles W.
Executive Office Of The President, Office of the Vice President, GV
Burson, I. Jackson, Jr. ... Eunice, LA
Burson, I. Jackson, Jr., A Professional Law Corporation ... Eunice, LA
Burson, John H. ... Toledo, OH
Burson, John Stephen ... Fairfax, VA
Burson, Kaye G. ... Memphis, TN
Burson, Leo R. ... Memphis, TN
Burson, Margo E. ... Topeka, KS
Burson, Norma L. ... Dallas, TX
Burson, Patrick A. ... Miami, FL
Burson, Paul A. ... Carey, OH
Burson, Paul L. ... Memphis, TN
Burson, Richard O. ... Laurel, MS
Burson, Robert A. ... Stuart, FL
Burson, Robert A., P.A. ... Stuart, FL
Burson, Robert J. ... Chicago, IL
Burson, S. Bradley ... Silver Spring, MD
Burson, Timothy J. ... Atlanta, GA
Burson, Valerie Lynne ... Houston, TX
Burstein, Alan S. ... Syracuse, NY
Burstein, Albert ... Hackensack, NJ
Burstein, Ari ... Washington, DC
Burstein, Arthur ... Putnam Valley, NY
Burstein, Barbara S. ... Tucson, AZ
Burstein, Beatrice S. ... Mineola, NY
Burstein, Bernardo ... Miami, FL
Burstein, Carole Hyman ... Metairie, LA
Burstein, Cheryl H. ... Wayne, NJ
Burstein, David ... New York, NY
Burstein, David H. ... Springfield, MA
Burstein, Deborah S. ... New York, NY
Burstein, Diane B. ... Washington, DC
Burstein, Eleanor C. ... Forest Hills, NY
Burstein, Emanuel S. ... Washington, DC
Burstein, Fred ... Minneapolis, MN
Burstein, Harry H. ... New York, NY
Burstein, Harvey ... Boston, MA
Burstein, Herbert ... Beverly Hills, CA
Burstein, Hertogs & McFarland, P.A.
Hastings, MN
Minneapolis, MN
Burstein, Jack B. ... Vallejo, CA
Burstein, James A. ... Chicago, IL
Burstein, Jeffrey C. ... Newark, NJ
Burstein, Joel V. ... Santa Fe, NM
Burstein, Joseph ... Washington, DC
Burstein, Joshua ... New York, NY
Burstein, Judd ... New York, NY
Burstein, Karen S. ... New York, NY
Burstein, Laurie E. ... Los Angeles, CA
Burstein, Lawrence E. ... Boston, MA
Burstein, Lucien ... New York, NY
Burstein, Marc S. ... Clayton, MO
Burstein, Mark ... Los Angeles, CA
Burstein, Mark A. ... Bloomfield Hills, MI
Farmington Hills, MI
Burstein, Maurice I. ... Bethesda, MD
Burstein & McPherson, LLP
New York, NY
Burstein, Melvin L. ... Minneapolis, MN
Burstein, Merwyn J. ... Springfield, MA
Burstein, Michael D. ... Chicago, IL
Burstein, Michael I. ... Los Angeles, CA
Burstein, Neil A. ... New York, NY
Burstein, Noah M. ... Elmwood Park, NJ
Burstein, Richard D., (A Professional Corporation) ... Los Angeles, CA
Burstein, Richard I. ... Randolph, VT
Burstein, Richard J. ... Detroit, MI
Burstein, Richard L. ... Albany, NY
Burstein, Robert A. ... New York, NY
Burstein, Robert J. ... Bethesda, MD
Burstein, Robert S. ... Stratford, CT
Burstein, Ronald B. ... West Dundee, IL
Burstein, Steven M. ... Minneapolis, MN
Burstein, William M. ... Albany, NY
Burstin, Brian J. ... New York, NY
Burstiner, Gil Y. ... Atlanta, GA
Burstyn, David H. ... Miami, FL
Burstyn, Harold L. ... Rome, NY
Burstyn, Lee J. ... Potomac, MD
Bursztynsky, Susan Lynn ... Ottawa, IL
Burt, Alexander D., III ... Chestertown, MD
Burt, Alice G. ... Wayne, PA
Burt, Antony S. ... Chicago, IL
Burt, B. Steven ... Terry, MS
Burt, Barbara Kelley ... Bolivar, NY
Burt, Blee, Dixon & Sutton, LLP
Fort Wayne, IN
Burt, Brian J. ... Pittsburgh, PA
Burt, Brian R. ... Phoenix, AZ
Burt & Burt, P.A. ... Albany, GA
Burt, C. Fredrick ... Salem, OR
Burt, C. Oliver, III ... West Palm Beach, FL
Burt, Carolyn L. ... Newburyport, MA
Burt, Charles R. ... Chesterfield, MO
Burt, Chris ... Los Angeles, CA
Burt, Christine A. ... Walpole, MA
Burt, Cleon L. ... St. Louis, MO
Burt, Dan ... Washington, DC
Burt, David A. ... Daytona Beach, FL
Burt, David H. ... Wilmington, DE
Burt, David R. ... Charlestown, MA
Burt, Donald F. ... Lincoln, NE
Omaha, NE
Burt, E. Daniel, Jr. ... Shreveport, LA
Burt, Edward C., Jr. ... Hamden, CT
Burt, Edward J. ... Oak Forest, IL
Burt, Elsen K. ... Dunedin, FL
Burt, Eric M. ... New York, NY
Burt, Erin C. ... Columbia, SC
Burt, Forrest W. ... Chardon, OH
Burt, Frank D. ... Boston, MA
Burt, Franklin G. ... Washington, DC
Miami, FL
Burt, Gary M. ... Manchester, NH
Burt, George R. ... Jonesboro, GA
Burt, Henry J., Jr. ... Wheaton, IL
Burt, Henry M. ... Louisville, KY
Burt, Hilliard P. ... Albany, GA
Burt, J. Chandini ... New York, NY
Burt, J. Keith ... Washington, DC
Burt, J. Philip ... Fort Wayne, IN
Burt, James A. ... Springfield, MO
Burt, James E., IV ... Miami, FL
Burt, James L., III ... Fort Worth, TX
Burt, Jasper N. ... Marion, OH
Burt, Jeffrey A. ... Washington, DC
Burt, Jeffrey C. ... Los Angeles, CA
Burt, Jennifer A. ... Washington, DC
Burt, John W. ... Boston, MA
Burt, Jon G. ... Kaufman, TX
Burt, Joseph P. ... Erie, PA
Burt, Karen A. ... Fresno, CA
Burt, Laura B. ... Charlotte, NC
Burt, Laurie ... Boston, MA
Burt, Loann Quinn ... Pickerington, OH
Burt, Maner & Miller ... Washington, DC
Burt, Margaret A. ... Pittsford, NY
Burt, Marianna Inga ... Baltimore, MD
Burt, Mark E. ... Chicago, IL
Burt, Marshall J. ... Chicago, IL
Burt, Mary J. ... Washington, DC
Burt, Michael D. ... North Palm Beach, FL
Burt, Michael E. ... New Haven, CT
Burt, Michael L. ... Charlotte, NC
Burt, Michael N. ... San Francisco, CA
Burt, Nancy ... Beverly Hills, CA
Burt, Pamela S. ... Harrisville, MI
Burt, Paul J. ... Baltimore, MD
Burt & Pucillo, LLP
West Palm Beach, FL
Burt, R. Neal ... Lubbock, TX
San Antonio, TX
Burt, Richard A. ... Daytona Beach, FL
Burt, Richard Alexander ... San Diego, CA
Burt, Richard F. ... Cleveland, OK
Tulsa, OK
Burt, Richard G. ... San Jose, CA
Burt, Richard M. ... Norwalk, CT
Windsor, CT
Burt, Robert A. ... New Haven, CT
Burt, Robert G. ... Portland, OR
Burt, Robert G., P.C. ... Portland, OR
Burt, Ryan J. ... Minneapolis, MN
Burt, Sandra ... Scottsdale, AZ
Burt, Sarah R. ... Broomfield, CO
Burt, Scott W. ... Dallas, TX
Burt, Stephen A. ... Lincoln, NE
Burt, Sue M. ... St. Cloud, MN
Burt & Swan ... Albany, GA
Burt, Swanson, Lathen, Alexander, McCann & Smith, P.C. ... Salem, OR
Burt, Tammy A. ... Evanston, WY
Burt, Theodore M. ... Trenton, FL
Burt, Theodore M., P.A. ... Trenton, FL
Burt, Thomas H. ... New York, NY
Burt, Thomas W. ... Redmond, WA
Burt, Val J., II ... Linden, VA
Burt, Wallace L. ... Ormond Beach, FL
Burt, Walter H., III ... Albany, GA
Burt, Warren B. ... Hockessin, DE
Burt, William E., Jr. ... Stanton, KY
Burt, William P. ... New York, NY
Burt, Winston S. ... Conway, MA
Burt, Woodruff A. ... Freeport, IL
Burt, Yumeka C. ... Jackson, MS
Burtch, Jack W., Jr. ... Richmond, VA
Burtch, James M., III ... Columbus, OH
Burtch, Jeoffrey L. ... Newark, DE
Wilmington, DE
Burtch, John H. ... Columbus, OH
Burtch, Kirk A. ... Phoenix, AZ
Burtchaell, John W. ... Venice, FL
Burtchaell, Margaret M. ... Elkhart, IN
Burt-Edwards, Barbara ... Miami, FL
Burten, Barry L., P.C. ... Los Angeles, CA
Burtenshaw, Rick D. ... Salt Lake City, UT
Burthe, Jack H. ... San Bernardino, CA
Burthey, Grover C., Jr. ... Durham, NC
Burti, Christopher L. ... Farmville, NC
Burtin, Brent J. ... St. Louis, MO
Burtis, Jill E. ... El Segundo, CA
Burtis, John A. ... Minneapolis, MN
Burtis, John M. ... Charlotte, NC
Burtis, Paul F. ... Toledo, OH
Burtis, William C., Jr. ... Binghamton, NY
Burtka, Karen J. ... Troy, MI
Burtker, David C. ... Chicago, IL
Burtker, John C. ... Chicago, IL
Burtker, Robert S. ... Chicago, IL
Burtless-Creps, Rebecca L. ... Dearborn, MI
Burtner, Ann ... Fresno, CA
Burtner, David D. ... Pensacola, FL
Burtner, Mark ... Paris, TX
Burtner, Rebecca L. ... McKinney, TX
Burtness, Janet L.
Hot Springs National Park, AR
Burtnett, Steven C. ... San Bernardino, CA
Burtoff, Bruce D. ... Washington, DC
Burton, A. Paul ... Hampton, VA
Burton, Alan G. ... Wilmington, DE
Burton, Alan R. ... Fort Lauderdale, FL
Burton, Alfred G. ... Chicago, IL
Burton & Anderson, LLP ... Atlanta, GA
Burton, Anne M. ... Chicago, IL
Burton & Associates ... Pittsburgh, PA
Burton & Associates, P.C. ... Melville, NY
Burton, B. Scott ... Atlanta, GA
Burton, Barbara North ... Miami, FL
Burton, Barbara Yolette ... Springfield, MA
Burton, Bartlett & Glogovac
Las Vegas, NV
Reno, NV
Burton, Bernard L. ... Melville, NY
Burton, Beverly A. ... Richmond, VA
Burton, Beverly Chewning ... Austin, TX
Burton, Billy B. ... Fairfield, CA
Burton, Blair F. ... El Cerrito, CA
Burton, Bradford Arthur ... Chicago, IL
Burton, Brandon J. ... Oklahoma City, OK
Burton, Brent O. ... Clarksburg, WV
Burton, Brian Ray ... Sherman, TX
Burton, Brian T. ... Portland, OR
Burton, Bruce Kent ... Malvern, AR
Burton, Bruce W. ... Houston, TX
Burton & Burton, P.A. ... Wauchula, FL
Burton, Busch & Garcin ... Loveland, CO
Burton, C. Robert, IV ... Tulsa, OK
Burton, C. Thomas, Jr. ... Reno, NV
Burton, Calvin A. ... Eagle River, WI
Burton, Carol W. ... Denver, CO
Burton, Carolyn Beasley
San Francisco, CA
Burton, Catherine M.
Oklahoma City, OK
Burton, Charles ... New York, NY
Burton, Charles A. ... Rushville, IL
Burton, Charles B. ... Phoenix, AZ
Burton, Charles E. ... Fort Lauderdale, FL
Burton, Charles H. ... Bethesda, MD
Burton, Charles M. ... Colorado Springs, CO
Burton, Charles P. ... Paramus, NJ
New York, NY
Burton, Charles R. ... Austin, TX

Burton, Charles William ... Dallas, TX
Burton, Christopher W. ... Bedford, IN
Burton, Clay C. ... Tucson, AZ
Burton, Cleve ... Rome, GA
Burton & Cork ... Indianapolis, IN
Burton, D. Clark ... San Francisco, CA
Burton, Daniel E. ... Hartford, CT
Burton, Daniel N. ... Tampa, FL
Burton, Danny R. ... Dallas, TX
Burton, David ... Princeton, WV
Burton, David A. B., (P.C.)
Los Angeles, CA
Burton, David C. ... Richmond, VA
Burton, David E. ... Los Angeles, CA
Burton, David E. ... Whittier, CA
Burton, David E., A Professional Corporation
Los Angeles, CA
Burton, David J. ... Richmond, IN
Burton, David J. ... New York, NY
Burton, David K. ... Philadelphia, PA
Burton, David R. ... Baltimore, MD
Burton, David W. ... De Ridder, LA
Burton & Davis, LLP ... Milwaukee, WI
Burton, Dean ... Bronx, NY
Burton, Dean O. ... Elkhart, IN
Burton, Debra F. ... Washington, DC
Burton, Dennis E. ... Indianapolis, IN
Burton, Deron Cornell ... Washington, DC
Burton, Donald E. ... Dayton, OH
Burton, Douglas L. ... Boston, MA
Burton, Dudley ... Fort Myers, FL
Burton, Dwayne L. ... Phoenix, AZ
Burton, Edward G. ... Lewiston, ID
Burton, Edward L., III ... Salt Lake City, UT
Burton, Elaine Minow ... Tucson, AZ
Burton, Elinor Dejez ... Van Nuys, CA
Burton, Emma K. ... Washington, DC
Burton, Everett ... Portsmouth, OH
Burton, Frank R. ... Monterey Park, CA
Burton, Freddie G., Jr. ... Detroit, MI
Burton, Fred'k W. ... Yreka, CA
Burton, G. Bill ... Dublin, OH
Burton, Gabe W. ... Fredericksburg, VA
Burton, Gerry L. ... Indianapolis, IN
Burton, Glenn M. ... Tampa, FL
Burton, Grant T. ... Los Angeles, CA
Burton & Greenberg ... Bronx, NY
Burton, Gregory C. C. ... Washington, DC
Burton, H. Coleman ... Huntsville, AL
Burton, H. Dickson ... Salt Lake City, UT
Burton, Harry W. ... Washington, DC
Burton & Hickman ... Bedford, IN
Burton, Ira T. ... Weiser, ID
Burton, J. Bayne ... Anderson, IN
Burton, J. Mark ... Lexington, KY
Burton, J. Riley ... Twin Falls, ID
Burton, James A. ... New Orleans, LA
Burton, James A. ... Seattle, WA
Burton, James D. ... Chicago, IL
Burton, James L. ... Oklahoma City, OK
Burton, James M. ... Pittsburgh, PA
Burton, James Ralph ... Chicago, IL
Burton, James W. ... Costa Mesa, CA
Burton, Jane ... Palo Alto, CA
Burton, Jane A. ... Aptos, CA
Burton, Jeffrey H. ... Norfolk, VA
Burton, Jeffry Richards ... Ogden, UT
Burton, Jennifer A.
Federal Communications Commission, Wireless Telecommunications Bureau, GV
Burton, Jerry M. ... Indianapolis, IN
Burton, Jill E. ... Durham, NC
Burton, Jim R. ... Jonesboro, AR
Burton, Joan H. ... Oldsmar, FL
Burton, Jocelyn ... San Francisco, CA
Burton, Jody Berke
General Services Administration, Office of the General Counsel, GV
Burton, Joel S. ... Washington, DC
Burton, John ... Phoenix, AZ
Burton, John A., Jr. ... Minneapolis, MN
Burton, John C. ... Los Angeles, CA
Burton, John C. ... Pasadena, CA
Burton, John D. ... New York, NY
Burton, John F., Jr. ... New Brunswick, NJ
Burton, John H., Jr. ... Birmingham, AL
Burton, John L. ... San Francisco, CA
Burton, John P. ... Santa Fe, NM
Burton, John R. ... Palm City, FL
Burton, John Robt. ... Sacramento, CA
Burton, John S. ... Santa Cruz, CA
Burton, John W. ... Wauchula, FL
Burton, John W. H. ... Wauchula, FL
Burton, Jon K. ... Mansfield, OH
Burton, Jon William ... Atlanta, GA
Burton, Joseph B. ... Los Angeles, CA
Burton, Joseph J., Jr. ... Atlanta, GA
Burton, Joseph M. ... San Francisco, CA
Burton, J. R. ... Hauppauge, NY
Burton, Julienne M. ... Houston, TX
Burton, Kelly M. ... Dillon, CO
Burton, Kenneth C. ... Seattle, WA
Burton, Kenneth R., Jr. ... Chicago, IL
Burton, Kent ... Hermosa Beach, CA
Burton, Kevin T. ... Anchorage, AK
Burton & Kilgore ... Princeton, WV
Burton, Kimiko C. ... San Francisco, CA
Burton & Kroll ... Weiser, ID
Burton, LaDonna L. ... Clinton, NJ
Burton & Lamey ... Indianapolis, IN
Burton, Larry L. ... Treasury Department, Office of Regulations and Rulings, GV
Burton, Laura Deddish ... Greensboro, NC
Burton & Leather & Associates
Phoenix, AZ
Burton, Leslie A. ... San Francisco, CA
Burton, Lester S. ... Birmingham, MI
Burton, Linda J. ... Gary, IN

Burton, Lisa Stephanian ... Boston, MA
Burton, Louis W. ... Houston, TX
Burton, Lura L. ... Los Angeles, CA
Burton, Lynda M. ... Redwood City, CA
Burton, M. David ... Columbus, OH
Burton, M. David ... Dallas, TX
Burton, M. Faith ... Department of Justice, Office of Legislative Affairs, GV
Burton, Malcolm B. ... Warren, NJ
Burton, Marcia Y. ... Raleigh, NC
Burton, Margaret Ann ... Redwood City, CA
Burton, Marion B. ... Little Rock, AR
Burton, Mark C. ... Fort Lauderdale, FL
Burton, Mark E., Jr. ... San Francisco, CA
Burton, Mark P. ... Gretna, LA
Burton, Mark S. ... Encino, CA
Burton, Mark S. ... San Francisco, CA
Burton, Martha Young ... Port Charlotte, FL
Burton, Martin N. ... Los Angeles, CA
Burton, Marvin O. ... Glenbrook, NV
Burton, Matthew R. ... Minneapolis, MN
Burton, Michael D. ... St. Louis, MO
Burton, Michael I. ... San Anselmo, CA
Burton, Michael K. ... Murray, UT
Burton, Michael L. ... Washington, DC
Burton, Michael Ray ... Milwaukee, WI
Burton, Michelle LeRoux ... San Diego, CA
Burton, Mike ... San Antonio, TX
Burton, Mona L. ... Salt Lake City, UT
Burton, Morris E. ... Frankfort, KY
Burton & Murphy ... Tampa, FL
Burton, Nancy E. ... Washington, DC
Burton, Nancy Winston ... Fresno, CA
Burton, Otis R., Jr. ... Talladega, AL
Burton, Ottway, (P.A.) ... Asheboro, NC
Burton, P. Scott ... Los Angeles, CA
Burton, Parker & Schramm
Mount Clemens, MI
Burton, Patricia A. ... Fort Lauderdale, FL
Burton, Paul H. ... Beaverton, OR
Burton, Preston ... Washington, DC
Alexandria, VA
Burton, R. Dal ... Atlanta, GA
Burton, R. Don ... Loveland, CO
Burton, R. Edw. ... San Francisco, CA
Burton, R. Nicholas ... Decatur, IL
Burton, Ralph M. ... Southfield, MI
Burton, Ramon L. ... Minneapolis, MN
Burton, Randall J. ... Sacramento, CA
Burton, Randy ... Houston, TX
Burton, Raymond P., Jr. ... Auburn, CA
Burton, Rebecca L. ... Las Vegas, NV
Burton, Richard ... Nevada City, CA
Burton, Richard A. ... Dallas, TX
Burton, Richard Arthur ... Bethesda, MD
Burton, Richard C., Jr. ... Aiken, SC
Burton, Richard H. ... Fountain Valley, CA
Burton, Richard H. ... Richmond, VA
Burton, Richard J. ... Beverly Hills, CA
Burton, Richard J. ... Sacramento, CA
Burton, Richard J. ... Aventura, FL
Burton, Richard J., & Associates, P.A.
Aventura, FL
Burton, Richard L. ... Ottawa, IL
Burton, Robbyn E. ... Colorado Springs, CO
Burton, Robert A. ... Department of Defense, Defense Legal Services Agency, GV
Burton, Robert A. ... Salt Lake City, UT
Burton, Robert C. ... Sugar Land, TX
Burton, Robert D. ... Austin, TX
Burton, Robert E. ... San Francisco, CA
Burton, Robert G. ... San Francisco, CA
Burton, Robert G. ... Richmond, IN
Burton, Robert S. ... Cleveland, OH
Burton, Robert T. ... Dallas, TX
Burton, Robert W. ... Havertown, PA
Burton, Roger D. ... Birmingham, AL
Burton, Ronald A. ... San Francisco, CA
Burton, Ronald E. ... New York, NY
Burton, Ross Alan ... Winnsboro, SC
Burton, Rulon T. ... Salt Lake City, UT
Burton, Scott A. ... Danville, VA
Burton, Scott A., P.C. ... Danville, VA
Burton, Sean O. ... Burbank, CA
Burton and Simkin ... Richmond, IN
Burton, Staci A. ... Chicago, IL
Burton, Stephanie Holmes ... Greenville, SC
Burton, Stephen J. ... Minneapolis, MN
Burton, Stephen L. ... Sherman Oaks, CA
Burton, Steven ... Central Islip, NY
Burton, Steven G. ... Tampa, FL
Burton, Steven M. ... Waco, TX
Burton & Sue, L.L.P. ... Greensboro, NC
Burton, Susan P. ... Austin, TX
Burton, Susanne L. ... San Antonio, TX
Burton, Ternon ... Richmond, VA
Burton, Terry C. ... Buffalo, NY
Burton, Thomas H. ... Buffalo, NY
Burton, Thomas H. ... Houston, TX
Burton, Thomas J. ... Winnsboro, TX
Burton, Thomas M. ... Irvine, CA
Martinez, CA
Burton, Thomas M. ... Pleasanton, CA
Burton, Thomas M. ... Walnut Creek, CA
Burton, Thomas R., III ... Boston, MA
Burton, Thomas W. ... Newport Beach, CA
Burton, Thomas W. ... Dallas, TX
Burton, Tracey E. ... St. Paul, MN
Burton, Tracey G. ... Bath, ME
Burton, Volkmann & Schmal, LLP
Monterey, CA
Salinas, CA
San Jose, CA
Santa Cruz, CA
Burton, W. Amon, Jr. ... Austin, TX
Burton, Walter K. ... Greensboro, NC
Burton, Walter M., Jr. ... Olympia, WA
Burton, Wayne L. ... Albany, NY

Burton, Wilford M. ... Salt Lake City, UT
Burton, William C. ... New York, NY
Burton, William E., III ... Greensboro, NC
Burton, William F. ... Washington, DC
Burton, William L. ... Marietta, OH
Burton, William R. ... Chapel Hill, NC
Burton, William W. ... Murfreesboro, TN
Burton & Williams, P.C. ... Rome, GA
Burton-Clark, Leslie ... Brick, NJ
Burton-Goldman, Charlyn ... Boston, MA
Burton Jensen, Joan ... Miami, FL
Burts, Robert M. ... Rutledge, TN
Burts, Turner, Rhodes & Thompson
Spartanburg, SC
Burtschi, Kathleen Furst
Department of Housing and Urban Development, Office of General Counsel, GV
Burtschi, Mark R. ... Reston, VA
Burtt, David R., Jr. ... Portland, ME
Burtt, David Richard ... Palo Alto, CA
Burtt, Michael S. ... Pensacola, FL
Burttram, Bruce A. ... Birmingham, AL
Burttram & Henderson ... Birmingham, AL
Burtz, Samuel P. ... Canton, GA
Burtzel, Cheryl M. ... Round Rock, TX
Burtzlaff, Robert A. ... Palo Alto, CA
Burtzos, Stephanie M. Funteas ... Chicago, IL
Buruunsuzyan, Maro ... Glendale, CA
Burusco, Christophe H. ... Los Angeles, CA
Burvant, Andre B. ... Baton Rouge, LA
Burvant, Robert J. ... New Orleans, LA
Burville, Michael D. ... Minneapolis, MN
Burwell, Bruce M. ... Alamogordo, NM
Burwell, Burwell & Nebout, L.L.P.
Houston, TX
Texas City, TX
Burwell, Clayton L. ... Washington, DC
Burwell, Curt Eugene ... St. Louis, MO
Burwell, Donald Steven ... Tampa, FL
Burwell, Emily Pryor ... Huntsville, AL
Burwell, F. Merrimon ... Rutherfordton, NC
Burwell, G. Todd ... Jackson, MS
Burwell, George A. ... Warrenton, NC
Burwell, Gladys B. ... Texas City, TX
Burwell, Henry M. ... Greenville, SC
Burwell, J Lance ... Snowmass Village, CO
Burwell, Jack G. ... Farmington Hills, MI
Burwell, Jackson P. ... Huntsville, AL
Burwell, Jackson P., P.C. ... Huntsville, AL
Burwell, James H., Jr. ... Rutherfordton, NC
Burwell, Jane E. Hugo ... Fairfield, CT
Burwell, Joseph R. ... Dallas, TX
Burwell, Karen E. ... Ironton, OH
Burwell, Kaye Woodard ... Atlanta, GA
Burwell, Linda G. ... Detroit, MI
Burwell, Lloyd W. ... Ironton, OH
Burwell, Michael D. P. ... Bloomfield Hills, MI
Burwell and Nahikian, A Professional Corporation ... Bloomfield Hills, MI
Burwell, Patrick P. ... Phoenix, AZ
Burwell, Peters & Houston ... Washington, DC
Burwell, Robert E. ... San Diego, CA
Burwell, Russell G. ... Houston, TX
Texas City, TX
Burwell, Russell G., III ... Texas City, TX
Burwell, Steven R. ... New York, NY
Burwell, Walter Brodie, Jr. ... Raleigh, NC
Burwell, William H. ... Franklin, PA
Burwell, William R. ... Gainesville, FL
Burwen, Norman ... Fort Lauderdale, FL
Burwick, Douglas L. ... Leominster, MA
Burwick, Jerald D. ... Boston, MA
Burwick, Michael C. ... Buffalo, NY
Burwick, Stephen D. ... Worcester, MA
Bury, Andrew G., Jr. ... Fairfax, VA
Urbanna, VA
Woodbridge, VA
Bury & Associates ... Mountainside, NJ
Bury, Bradford M. ... Mountainside, NJ
Bury, Christopher Allan ... Pasadena, CA
Bury, David C. ... Tucson, AZ
Bury, John F. ... Spokane, WA
Bury, Mark W.
Department of Transportation, Federal Aviation Administration, GV
Bury, Moeller, Humphrey & O'Meara, P.C.
Tucson, AZ
Bury, Richard J. ... Mitchellville, MD
Bury, Stephen J. ... New York, NY
Bury, Stephen J., P.C. ... New York, NY
Burza, Vernon R. ... Chicago, IL
Burzawa, Jeffrey W. ... Greensburg, PA
Burzawa, Susan Kay ... Evanston, IL
Burzawa and Wiltman ... Greensburg, PA
Burzio, John M. ... Washington, DC
Burzio & McLaughlin ... Washington, DC
Burzych, Diane L. ... Wilmette, IL
Burzych, Mark J. ... Lansing, MI
Burzynski, Daniel A ... Naples, FL
Burzynski, Irwin P. ... Millburn, NJ
Burzynski, Jill Jacob ... Naples, FL
Burzynski, Martin A. ... Sarasota, FL
Burzynski and Pfeuffer ... Naples, FL
Bus, Helen M. ... West Chicago, IL
Bus, Steven F. ... Reno, NV
Busacca, Jeanne L. ... Denver, CO
Busacca, Jeanne, P.C., Law Offices of
Denver, CO
Busacca, Joseph F. ... Philadelphia, PA
Busack, Frederick L. ... Tallahassee, FL
Busacker, Dale H. ... St. Paul, MN
Busailah, Muna ... Pasadena, CA
Busald, E. André ... Florence, KY
Busald Funk Zevely, P.S.C. ... Florence, KY
Cincinnati, OH
Busam, David R. ... Columbus, OH
Busam, Thomas C. ... Gallipolis, OH

Busani, Adriana M. ... New York, NY
Busansky, Alexander Hendler
Department of Justice, Civil Rights Division, GV
Busath, Douglas C. ... Sacramento, CA
Busath, Lynn Earl ... New York, NY
Busatto, Max T. ... Pittsburgh, PA
Busbee, Annarita McGovern ... Atlanta, GA
Busbee, Dan ... Dallas, TX
Busbee, George D. ... Atlanta, GA
Busbee, Hunter & Griffith ... Aiken, SC
Edgefield, SC
Busbee, Jacqueline Fogle ... Wagener, SC
Busbee, O. Dantzler, II ... Aiken, SC
Busby, A. Jerry ... Phoenix, AZ
Busby, A. Jerry, P.C. ... Phoenix, AZ
Busby, Austin, Cooper & Farr
Anderson, IN
Busby, Bell & Biggs, P.C. ... Tucson, AZ
Busby, Bonnie L. ... Salisbury, NC
Busby, Celeste Ann ... Universal City, CA
Busby, Charles T. ... Edenton, NC
Busby, Charles T., P.A. ... Edenton, NC
Busby, Curtis J. ... Las Vegas, NV
Busby, David ... Washington, DC
Busby, Deborah T. ... Houston, TX
Busby, Floy M. ... Tallahassee, FL
Busby, "Ginger" M. ... Birmingham, AL
Busby, Howard L. ... Dallas, TX
Busby, J. Brett
Supreme Court Of The United States, GV
Busby, Jack K. ... Pinehurst, NC
Busby, James G. ... Tucson, AZ
Busby, James G., Jr. ... Phoenix, AZ
Busby, Jerry S. ... Las Vegas, NV
Busby, John G. ... Santa Barbara, CA
Busby, John W., II ... Lafayette, CA
Busby, John W., II, P.C. ... Lafayette, CA
Busby, J.S. Scott ... Atlanta, GA
Busby, Kathryn L. ... Phoenix, AZ
Busby, Leonard A. ... Philadelphia, PA
Busby, Mary Alice ... Wyomissing, PA
Busby, Paul M. ... Meridian, MS
Busby, Richard G. ... Memphis, TN
Busby, Robert F. ... Salisbury, NC
Busby, Robert W., Jr. ... Washington, DC
Busby, Russell C. ... Comfort, TX
Busby, Scott W. ... Department of Justice, Immigration and Naturalization Service, GV
Busby, Spencer S. ... San Diego, CA
Busby, Thomas L. ... Corpus Christi, TX
Busby, Thomas William ... Gulfport, MS
Busby, W. Dawn
Department of Commerce, GV
Busby, William W., III ... Bartlesville, OK
Busby, Wilson H. ... Jenks, OK
Busca, Morris J. ... New London, CT
Buscaglia, Anne M. ... New York, NY
Buscaglia, Frank M. ... Wayne, NJ
Buscaglia, Fred A. ... Buffalo, NY
Buscaglia, T.H., and Associates
Miami, FL
Buscaglia, Thomas H. ... Miami, FL
Buscaglia, William K., Jr. ... Buffalo, NY
Buscail-Smith, Carol ... Marietta, GA
Buscarello, Maria E. ... New York, NY
Buscemi, Gary ... New York, NY
Buscemi, Lawrence ... Centereach, NY
Buscemi, Leonard P. ... Arlington, VA
Buscemi, Nancy S. ... Brooklyn, NY
Buscemi, Paul ... New York, NY
Buscemi, Peter ... Washington, DC
Buscemi, Peter P. ... Brookfield, CT
Busceti, Rocco ... New York, NY
Busch, Alan L. ... Dallas, TX
Busch, Alan L., P.C., Law Offices of
Dallas, TX
Busch, Alfred B. ... Chicago, IL
Busch, Allison Jill ... New York, NY
Busch, Andrew E. ... Wichita, KS
Busch, Arthur A. ... Flint, MI
Busch, Bertram E. ... North Brunswick, NJ
Busch, Betty L. ... Dayton, OH
Busch, Bruce R. ... Olympia, WA
Busch and Busch, LLP
East Brunswick, NJ
New Brunswick, NJ
North Brunswick, NJ
South Brunswick, NJ
Busch, Carl J. ... El Segundo, CA
Busch, Charlene A. ... Laguna Hills, CA
Busch, Christine Pellegrini
Philadelphia, PA
Busch, David J. ... Tallahassee, FL
Busch, David L. ... Richmond, MO
Busch, David R. ... Minneapolis, MN
Busch, Diane Matassino ... Marietta, GA
Busch, Don G. ... Springfield, MO
Busch, Douglas Dale ... La Jolla, CA
Busch, Edward F. ... Louisville, KY
Busch, Edward P. ... Miami, FL
Busch, Edward R. ... Hilton Head Island, SC
Busch, Elizabeth Susan ... Santa Ana, CA
Busch, Ellen C. ... Bloomfield Hills, MI
Busch, Eric E. ... Spring City, PA
Busch, Eric S. ... Portland, OR
Busch Firm, The ... Irvine, CA
Las Vegas, NV
Busch, Gary M. ... Southfield, MI
Busch, Glenn A. ... New York, NY
Busch, Gretchen Miller ... Denver, CO
Busch, Harold R. ... Dallas, TX
Busch, Henry ... North Brunswick, NJ
Busch, Henry M. ... Fallbrook, CA
Busch, Howard B. ... East Meadow, NY
Busch, James C. ... Marietta, GA
Busch, James C. ... St. Louis, MO
Busch, James R. ... Arlington Heights, IL

Busch, Janine R. .... Sacramento, CA
Busch, Jeffrey S. .... New York, NY
Busch, Jerome A. .... Newport Beach, CA
Busch, Jethro S. .... San Francisco, CA
Busch, John A. .... Milwaukee, WI
Busch, John E. .... Elkins, WV
Busch, John R. .... White Plains, NY
Busch, Johnson & Mank .... Wichita, KS
Busch, Joseph P., III .... Irvine, CA
Busch, Julie D. .... Louisville, KY
Busch, Kelly Vaughan .... Lafayette, IN
Busch, Kevin M. .... Minneapolis, MN
Busch, Kevin T. .... Geneva, IL
Busch, Leonard R. .... North Brunswick, NJ
Busch, Lisa Nathanson .... New York, NY
Busch, Malcolm R. .... North Brunswick, NJ
Busch, Mark L. .... Portland, OR
Busch, Mark N. .... North Brunswick, NJ
Busch, Mark R. .... Charlotte, NC
Busch, Mary Ellen .... Chicago, IL
Busch, Maura .... Long Island City, NY
Busch, Michael E. .... San Diego, CA
Busch, Nancy K. .... Allentown, PA
Busch, Nancy K., P.C. .... Allentown, PA
Busch, Peter J. .... San Francisco, CA
Busch, Philip B. .... Department of Justice, Immigration and Naturalization Service, GV
Busch Professional Corporation
Golden, CO
Lakewood, CO
Busch, Raymond W. .... Mount Prospect, IL
Busch, Raymond Warren .... Fairfax, VA
Busch, Richard F. .... Morristown, NJ
Busch, Richard F., II .... Denver, CO
Busch, Richard J. .... Seattle, WA
Busch, Richard L. .... Brooklyn, NY
Busch, Richard S. .... Calabasas, CA
Busch, Richard S. .... Nashville, TN
Busch, Robert G. .... Golden, CO
Busch, Robert G. .... Golden, CO
Busch, Robert L. .... Orange Park, FL
Busch, Robert L., and Associates, P.A.
Orange Park, FL
Busch, Ronald J. .... North Brunswick, NJ
Busch, Stephen D. .... Richmond, VA
Busch, Susannah M. Dudley
Calabasas, CA
Busch & Talbott, L.C. .... Buckhannon, WV
Elkins, WV
Marlinton, WV
Parsons, WV
Philippi, WV
Busch, Theodore P. .... Fort Stockton, TX
Busch, Thomas A. .... Sacramento, CA
Busch, Thomas H. .... Lafayette, IN
Busch, Thomas H. .... Springfield, OH
Busch, Thomas P. .... Portland, OR
Busch, Thomas S. .... Merriam, KS
Busch, Timothy R. .... Irvine, CA
Busch, Valerie Y. .... Charlotte, NC
Busch, Wendolyn S. .... Tampa, FL
Busch, William M., Jr. .... Loveland, CO
Busch, William P., Jr. .... Atlantic City, NJ
Busch, William R. .... St. Paul, MN
Busch, William R., Jr. .... Minneapolis, MN
Busch, William S. .... New York, NY
Busch, William W. .... Kansas City, MO
Buschardt-Pisarczyk, Karen .... Chicago, IL
Buschbacher, Michael .... Milford, OH
Buschbom, Ronald L. .... Fort Myers, FL
Busch-Ell, Alana .... Waupun, WI
Buschenfield, D. A. .... Signal Hill, CA
Buscher, Daniel R. .... Marshall, MI
Buscher, Glendon J., Jr. .... Squantum, MA
Buscher, Hurschel .... Erie, KS
Buscher, Mark R. .... Washington, DC
Buscher, Sally A. .... Lincoln, NE
Busching, Alice L. .... San Francisco, CA
Busching, Laurence E. .... New York, NY
Busching, Marcia J. .... Scottsdale, AZ
Busching, William W. .... Jackson, MS
Buschle, Martin W. .... Grand Rapids, MI
Buschman, Ahern, Persons & Bankston
Jacksonville Beach, FL
Buschman, Albert E., Jr.
Jacksonville Beach, FL
Buschman, Francis X., Jr. .... Souderton, PA
Buschman, Howard C., III .... New York, NY
Buschman, Howard C., Jr. .... Hackettstown, NJ
Buschman, Thomas W. .... Arlington, VA
Buschmann, Carr & Shanks, Professional Corporation .... Fishers, IN
Indianapolis, IN
Buschmann, Gail M. .... Dedham, MA
Buschmann, James R. .... Detroit, MI
Buschmann, Jeffrey S. .... St. Louis, MO
Buschmann, Karl H.
National Labor Relations Board, Division of Administrative Law Judges, GV
Buschmann, Nicholas T. .... Indianapolis, IN
Buschmann, Odette N. .... Staten Island, NY
Buschmann, Paul .... Boca Raton, FL
Buschmann, Raymond P. (IBA) .... Chicago, IL
Buschmann, Robert M. .... New York, NY
Buschmann, Stephen R. .... Fishers, IN
Indianapolis, IN
Buschmann, Waldemar G.
Waterville, ME
Buschner, Arlys L. .... Orlando, FL
Buschner, Arlys L., P.A. .... Orlando, FL
Buschner, Traci L. .... Washington, DC
Buscho, Tami J. .... Sacramento, CA
Busch-Rubalcava, Rachel .... Chicago, IL
Busciglio, Peter D. .... Santa Ana, CA
Busconi, Frederick A. .... Southborough, MA
Busconi, Ronald G. .... Boston, MA
Busdicker, Gordon G. .... Minneapolis, MN
Busé, Glenn A. .... Milwaukee, WI

Buse, Isabel Elizabeth .... Central Islip, NY
Buse, Jennifer Dietz .... Cincinnati, OH
Buse, Michele .... Los Angeles, CA
Buse, Susan Bradley .... Belleville, IL
St. Louis, MO
Buseck, Donald C. .... Erie, PA
Buseck, Gary D. .... Boston, MA
Buseck, Michael C. .... Richmond, VA
Buseck, Thomas J. .... Erie, PA
Busek, Charles T. .... Norwalk, CT
Busek, Charles T., P.C. .... Norwalk, CT
Busek, Jeannette R. .... Los Angeles, CA
Busell, Sandra Noreen .... New York, NY
Busemeyer, Gale K. .... Avon, CT
Busemeyer, William A. .... Cincinnati, OH
Busenburg, J. Robt. .... Danville, OH
Busenlener, James T. .... Metairie, LA
Buser, James D. .... Omaha, NE
Buser, John P., (P.C.) .... Dallas, TX
Buser, Joseph R. .... Crawfordsville, IN
Buser, Michael B. .... Kansas City, MO
Buser, Paul J. .... Scottsdale, AZ
Buser, Robin D., (Mr.) .... Mount Laurel, NJ
Buser, Stephen C. .... Columbia, IL
Buser, Stephen C., Ltd., Law Office of
Columbia, IL
Buser, Sue A. .... Baton Rouge, LA
Buser, Thomas E. .... Fort Lauderdale, FL
Buser, Wade A. .... Atlanta, GA
Busette, Julie Matsumoto .... Palo Alto, CA
Busey, G. Brian .... Washington, DC
Busey, J. Craig .... Elk Grove Village, IL
Busey, Rodney H. .... Wichita, KS
Busey, Roxane C. .... Chicago, IL
Busey, Stephen D. .... Jacksonville, FL
Busey & Tolle, Chartered .... Wichita, KS
Busey, Ward A. .... Houston, TX
Busfield, Julia L. .... Little Rock, AR
Bush, Ackley, Milich & Hallinan
Oakdale, CA
Bush, Allen J. .... Blytheville, AR
Bush, Allen S. .... Escanaba, MI
Iron Mountain, MI
Bush, Alvin B. .... Northfield, IL
Bush, Anna Markley .... Barrington, IL
Bush, Anthony E. .... Trenton, NJ
Bush, Anthony Gerard .... Kansas City, MO
Bush, Antoinette Cook .... Washington, DC
Bush, Barbara A. .... Department of Justice, Justice Management Division, GV
Bush, Bernetta D. .... Chicago, IL
Bush, Betty L. .... East Point, GA
Bush, Bing I., Jr. .... San Diego, CA
Lexington, KY
Bush, Bing I., Sr. .... Georgetown, KY
Bush, Bradley M. .... Woodland Hills, CA
Bush, Brent A. .... Wheeling, WV
Bush, Brian X. .... Department of the Army, Office of the Judge Advocate General, GV
Bush, Bryan E., Jr. .... Baton Rouge, LA
Bush, Bryan R. .... Orange, CA
Bush & Bush .... Constantine, MI
Sturgis, MI
Bush & Bush .... Elkins, WV
Bush, Bush & Larsen .... Fountain Valley, CA
Bush, Bush & Shanelec .... Lyons, KS
Sterling, KS
Bush, C. Glen .... Jackson, MS
Bush, Cameron C. .... Henderson, NC
Bush, Catherine McCartney .... Lancaster, PA
Bush, Charles .... San Francisco, CA
Bush, Charles .... Philadelphia, PA
Bush, Charles R. .... Seattle, WA
Bush, Cheri L. .... Boise, ID
Bush, Cheryl A. .... Bloomfield Hills, MI
Bush, Christina J. .... Elkins, WV
Bush, Christopher R. .... Boston, MA
Bush, Clinton G. .... Weston, WV
Bush Craddock & Reneker, L.L.P.
Dallas, TX
Marshall, TX
Bush, Craig R. .... Cleveland, OH
Bush, Crowley, Leverett & Leggett, LLP
Macon, GA
Bush, Crystal Pruess .... Chicago, IL
Bush, D. Michael .... Los Angeles, CA
Bush, David A. .... Grand Island, NE
Bush, David J. .... Tyler, TX
Bush, David T. .... Media, PA
Bush, David W. .... Granby, CT
Hartford, CT
Bush, David W. .... Elizabethton, TN
Bush, Derek M. .... Washington, DC
Bush, Diane Wegner .... Glendale, CA
Bush, Diedre Jane Josephine, Law Offices of
Modesto, CA
Bush, Don D. .... Dallas, TX
Marshall, TX
Bush, Don P. .... Roswell, GA
Bush, Donald C. .... Pittsburgh, PA
Bush, Donald D. .... Philadelphia, PA
Bush & Donlon, P.A.
Palm Beach Gardens, FL
Bush, Douglas R. .... Washington, DC
Bush, Duane A. .... Bonita Springs, FL
Bush, E. Philip .... Dallas, TX
Bush, E. Thomas, S.C. .... Milwaukee, WI
Bush, Edward B. .... Toms River, NJ
Bush, Edwin F., II .... Appleton, WI
Bush, Eleanor L. .... Harrisburg, PA
Bush, F. Brad .... Charlotte, NC
Bush, F. Clay .... Atlanta, GA
Bush, Florence G. .... Salem, OH
Bush, Floyd E. (Gene) .... Livingston, TX
Bush, F. M., III .... Tupelo, MS
Bush, Frank P., Jr. .... Elkins, WV
Bush, Fred M., Jr. .... Tupelo, MS
Bush, Gary L. .... Houston, TX

Bush, Gary M. .... Oklahoma City, OK
Bush, Gayle E. .... Seattle, WA
Bush, George C. .... Saginaw, MI
Bush, George D. .... Augusta, GA
Bush, George M. .... Doylestown, PA
Bush, George W., Jr.
Palm Beach Gardens, FL
Bush, Gerald V. .... Garden Grove, CA
Bush, Graeme W. .... Washington, DC
Bush, Granville M. .... Lyons, KS
Sterling, KS
Bush, Granville M., IV .... Lyons, KS
Sterling, KS
Bush, Gregory A. .... Parsippany, NJ
Bush, Guy K. .... Washington, DC
Bush, H. Michael .... New Orleans, LA
Bush, Harold J. .... Flemington, NJ
Bush, Harrison .... Richmond, VA
Bush, Hartley H. .... Oakdale, CA
Bush, Harvey J. .... Medford, OK
Bush, Hauder & Adkerson .... Dallas, TX
Bush, Heather Butler
West Palm Beach, FL
Bush, Heather M. .... Davison, MI
Bush & Heise .... Barrington, IL
Bush, Hobert H. .... Columbus, OH
Bush, Howard .... Constantine, MI
Bush, Howard J. .... Sturgis, MI
Bush, Howard S. .... Augusta, GA
Bush, Howard S., P.C. .... Augusta, GA
Bush, Ilsa K. .... Washington, DC
Bush, Irving T. .... New York, NY
Bush, J. Steven .... Dallas, TX
Bush, J. Steven .... Fort Worth, TX
Bush, Jack G. .... Oklahoma City, OK
Bush, James A. .... Phoenix, AZ
Bush, James Daniel .... Department of State, Office of the Legal Adviser, GV
Bush, James H. .... Tacoma, WA
Bush, James L. .... Hiawatha, KS
Bush, James M. .... Phoenix, AZ
Bush, James, P.C., Law Offices of
Phoenix, AZ
Bush, James R. .... Houston, TX
Bush, James T. .... Dallas, TX
Bush, Janice Mulligan .... Tallahassee, FL
Bush, Jason L. .... Overland Park, KS
Bush, Jeffrey W. .... Juneau, AK
Bush, Jennifer Ann Mims .... Prattville, AL
Bush, Jesse W. .... Macon, GA
Bush, Jill Stevens .... Grosse Pointe Woods, MI
Bush, Jimmie Carl .... Nashville, TN
Bush, Joanna Rudnicki .... Van Nuys, CA
Bush, Joel D., II .... Atlanta, GA
Bush, John A. .... Boise, ID
Bush, John B. .... Wetumpka, AL
Bush, John C. .... Dallas, TX
Bush, John D. .... Amsterdam, NY
Bush, John E., Jr. .... Littleton, CO
Bush, John K. .... Louisville, KY
Bush, John M. .... Louisville, KY
Bush, John P. .... Sturgis, MI
Bush, John R. .... Tampa, FL
Bush, Joseph E. .... Jackson, MS
Bush, Joseph J., III .... Youngstown, OH
Bush, Joseph S. .... Muskegon, MI
Bush, Judith K. .... Fairbanks, AK
Bush, Julian L. .... St. Louis, MO
Bush, Julian S. .... Isle of Palms, SC
Bush, K. Dale .... Fountain Valley, CA
Bush, Karen K. .... Washington, DC
Bush, Karen L. .... Washington, DC
Bush, Kathleen Carol .... San Diego, CA
Bush, Kenneth J. .... Miami, FL
Bush, Kenneth M. .... Birmingham, AL
Bush, Kenny R. .... Kosciusko, MS
Bush, Keri Lynn .... Los Angeles, CA
Bush, Kevin D. .... San Diego, CA
Bush, Kevin R. .... Columbus, OH
Bush, Kurstin B. .... San Diego, CA
Bush, L. Leslie .... Portland, OR
Bush, LaDonne .... Denver, CO
Bush, Larry S. .... University, MS
Bush, Laura C. .... Newark, NJ
Bush Law Group, The, P.A. .... Orlando, FL
Tallahassee, FL
Bush Law Office .... Louisville, KY
Bush, Lawrence A. .... Los Angeles, CA
Bush, Lawrence P. .... Fort Walton Beach, FL
Bush, Leland .... Tyler, MN
Bush, Leo J. .... Sunriver, OR
Bush & Leonard .... Oklahoma City, OK
Bush, Lewis & Roebuck, P.C.
Beaumont, TX
Bush, Lucinda A. .... Munster, IN
Bush, Lynn J. .... Washington, DC
Bush, Mari C. .... Boulder, CO
Bush, Mari C., LLC .... Boulder, CO
Bush, Mark A. .... Lansing, MI
Bush, Martha W. .... Harrisburg, PA
Bush, Martin James .... Great Neck, NY
Bush, Mary J. .... Auburn, CA
Bush, Matthew M. .... Savannah, GA
Bush, Michael J. .... Landover, MD
Bush, Michael J. .... Lebanon, VA
Bush, Michael K. .... Davenport, IA
Bush, Michael L. .... Morton, IL
Bush, Michael P. .... Fountain Valley, CA
Bush, Michael R. .... Chico, CA
Bush, Michael S. .... Dallas, TX
Bush, Milton W. .... Port Huron, MI
Bush, Milton W., Jr. .... Durham, CT
Bush & Morrison, P.C. .... Arlington, TX
Bush, Myron .... Eastchester, NY
Bush, Nancy J. .... Dallas, TX
Bush, Neal .... Detroit, MI
Bush & O'Brien, P.C. .... Houston, TX
Bush, Pearson C. J. .... East St. Louis, IL

Bush, Peter J. .... Avon, NY
Bush, Philip H. .... Lakeland, FL
Bush, Philip L. .... San Francisco, CA
Bush, Phillip L. .... Fountain Valley, CA
Bush, R. Benjamin .... Columbus, IN
Bush, Raymond G. .... Phillipsburg, NJ
Bethlehem, PA
Bush, Raymond G., Law Offices
Phillipsburg, NJ
Allentown, PA
Easton, PA
Stroudsburg, PA
Bush, Rebecca A. .... New Orleans, LA
Bush, Richard A. .... New Haven, CT
Bush, Richard A. .... Parkersburg, WV
Bush, Richard Burton .... Tallahassee, FL
Bush, Richard D. Tim .... Cheyenne, WY
Bush, Richard L. .... Hartford, CT
Bush, Richard N. .... Louisville, KY
Bush, Richard S. .... Alexandria, LA
Bush, Richard T. .... Youngstown, OH
Bush, Robert A. .... Burbank, CA
Bush, Robert A. .... Elizabeth, IL
Bush, Robert A. Baruch .... Hempstead, NY
Bush, Robert B. .... Indianapolis, IN
Bush, Robert B. .... Dallas, TX
Bush, Robert D. .... Staten Island, NY
Bush, Robert E. .... Youngstown, OH
Bush, Robert G., III .... Sherman, TX
Bush, Robert J. .... Elmsford, NY
Bush, Robert J. .... Media, PA
Bush, Robert K. .... Chicago, IL
Bush, Robert L. Russell .... Arlington, TX
Bush, Robert W. .... Conway, AR
Bush, Robert W. .... Fort Worth, TX
Bush, Robin C. .... Philadelphia, PA
Bush, Robin Z. .... Baltimore, MD
Bush, Roger D. .... Marshall, TX
Bush, Ronald E. .... Tampa, FL
Bush, Ronald E. .... Pocatello, ID
Bush, Ronald P. .... Eugene, OR
Bush Ross Gardner Warren & Rudy, P.A.
Tampa, FL
Bush, Roy A. .... Davenport, IA
Bush, Russell K. .... Auburn, AL
Bush, Russell K. .... Opelika, AL
Bush, Samuel D. .... Stamford, CT
Bush, Scott C. .... Springfield, MA
Bush, Scott K. .... Honolulu, HI
Bush, Scott W. .... Albany, NY
Bush, Shelby J. .... Dallas, TX
Bush, Shelley A., (PC) .... Houston, TX
Bush & Smith .... Jackson, GA
Bush, Snow E., Jr. .... Longview, TX
Bush, Snow E., Jr., P.C. .... Longview, TX
Bush, Stacy E. .... New York, NY
Bush, Stephen W. .... East Peoria, IL
Bush, Steven M. .... Englewood, CO
Bush, Steven M. .... Valparaiso, IN
Bush Strout & Kornfeld .... Seattle, WA
Bush, Susan A. .... San Francisco, CA
Bush, Terri Lynn .... Shreveport, LA
Bush, Thomas A. .... Wichita, KS
Bush, Thomas E., S.C. .... Milwaukee, WI
Bush, Thomas F., Jr. .... Chicago, IL
Bush, Thurman & Wilson, P.A.
Charlotte, NC
Bush, Timothy .... Hudson, NH
Bush, Timothy A. .... Birmingham, AL
Bush, Tom, Law Office of .... Charlotte, NC
Bush, Toxie L., Jr. .... Abbeville, LA
Bush & Trippel .... Parkersburg, WV
Bush, Virginia A. .... Atlanta, GA
Bush, W. Don .... Beaumont, TX
Bush, W. Joe .... Santa Barbara, CA
Bush, W. Randall .... Riverdale, NJ
Bush, Walter H., Jr. .... Atlanta, GA
Macon, GA
Bush, Walter L., Jr. .... Maple Grove, MN
Bush, Walter W. .... Oshkosh, WI
Bush, Warren L. .... Wall Lake, IA
Bush, Wendell E. .... Little Rock, AR
Bush, William .... New York, NY
Bush, William B., Jr. .... Atlanta, GA
Bush, William C. .... Gaithersburg, MD
Bush, William David, III .... Orange City, FL
Bush, William G., III .... Dover, DE
Bush, William G., IV .... Dover, DE
Bush, William J. .... San Francisco, CA
Bush, William J. .... Davenport, IA
Bush, William L. .... Wellsville, OH
Bush, William M. .... Fullerton, CA
Bush, William O. W. .... Cookeville, TN
Bush, William S. .... Houston, TX
Bush, Willis W. .... Andalusia, AL
Bush, Wilson H. .... Jackson, GA
Bush, Zoe A. .... Washington, DC
Bushala, Jim J. .... San Antonio, TX
Busharis, Barbara J. .... Philadelphia, PA
Bushaw, Amy C. .... Portland, OR
Bushay, Vance O. .... Minneapolis, MN
Bushee, James M. .... Washington, DC
Bushee, Linda Woodward .... Washington, DC
Bushek, David W. .... Kansas City, MO
Bushek, Kimberly Breda
Kansas City, MO
Bushel, Glenn E. .... Baltimore, MD
Bushell, Andrew .... Chicago, IL
Bushell, Elizabeth D. .... Tucson, AZ
Bushell, James R. .... Portland, ME
Bushell, Kleczka, Minasi & O'Connor
Northport, NY
Bushell, Michael A. .... Denver, CO
Bushell, Stephanie M. .... Morristown, NJ
Bushell, Theodore G. .... Northport, NY
Bushell, Victor C. .... New York, NY
Bushelli, Scott C. .... Cranford, NJ
Bushelman, Lisa O. .... Edgewood, KY

Bushemi, John P., & Associates
Crown Point, IN
Bushemi, John P., & Associates
Merrillville, IN
Busher, Joseph M., Jr. ....**Hartford, CT**
Bushey, Jennifer L. ....**Fort Lauderdale, FL**
Bushey, Maribeth A. ....San Francisco, CA
Bushey, Martha L. ....**Youngstown, OH**
Bushfield, John P. ....Miller, SD
Bushie, Lee H. ....Rolla, MO
Bushin, Howard I. ....New York, NY
Bushinski, Stephen J., P.C. ....Ringtown, PA
Bushinsky, Steven J. ....**Haddonfield, NJ**
Philadelphia, PA
Bush-Joseph, Victoria L. ....Chicago, IL
Bushkin, Henry I. ....Los Angeles, CA
Bushkin & Hiaasen, P.A.
Fort Lauderdale, FL
Bushkin, Regina S. ....Fort Lauderdale, FL
Bushkin, Robert J. ....Sells, AZ
Bushkofsky, Linda Post ....Wescosville, PA
Bushling, Bryant E. ....Los Angeles, CA
Bushlow, Alan L. ....Ridgewood, NY
Bushlow, Bruce E. ....Ridgewood, NY
Bushlow, Irving B. ....Brooklyn, NY
Bushmaker, Larry W. ....Countryside, IL
Bushmaker, Sandra Jean ....Sausalito, CA
Bushman, C. James ....**Houston, TX**
Bushman, David M. ....Nanuet, NY
Bushman, Heather L. ....**Santa Ana, CA**
Bushman, Howard M. ....**Arlington, VA**
Bushman, Howard M., Ltd.
Arlington, VA
Bushman, Ira W. ....**Philadelphia, PA**
Bushman, Kay ....Fort Belvoir, VA
Bushman, Martin B. ....Salt Lake City, UT
Bushman, Melvin C. ....Phoenix, AZ
Bushman, Meyer A. ....**Philadelphia, PA**
Bushman, Patricia F. ....Houston, TX
Bushman, Patricia F., P.C. ....Houston, TX
Bushman, Richard Lewis ....Spring Run, PA
Bushman, Ronald M. ....Mill Valley, CA
Bushman, Teresa Gear ....**Houston, TX**
Bushman, Willard M. ....Berkeley, CA
Bushmann, Eugene G. ......**Jefferson City, MO**
Bushmiller, Ann E. ....**Washington, DC**
Bushnaq, Darek S. ....**Baltimore, MD**
Bushnaq, Faith S. ....**Charlotte, NC**
Bushnell, Andrea L. ....Salem, OR
Bushnell, Blake W. ....**Honolulu, HI**
Bushnell, Caplan & Fielding
San Francisco, CA
Bushnell, Dan S. ....Salt Lake City, UT
Bushnell, Deborah A. ....Dunedin, FL
Bushnell, Gene R. ....**Rapid City, SD**
Bushnell, George E., III ....New York, NY
Bushnell, George E., Jr. ....**Detroit, MI**
Bushnell, James J., Jr. ....Birmingham, AL
Bushnell, James T. ....**Palo Alto, CA**
Bushnell, Laura I. ....**Menlo Park, CA**
Bushnell, Prudence ....Silver Spring, MD
Bushnell, R.E., & Law Firm
Washington, DC
Bushnell, Richard ....**Chicago, IL**
Bushnell, Robert E. ....**Washington, DC**
Bushnell, Robert L. ....Martinsville, VA
Bushnell, Roderick P. ....**San Francisco, CA**
Bushnell, Victoria Coombs
Salt Lake City, UT
Bushnell, William C. ....Athens, GA
Bushner, Nicholas J. ....**Philadelphia, PA**
Bushner, Ronald S. ....**San Francisco, CA**
Bushofsky, Jeffrey J. ....**Chicago, IL**
Bushong, Larry T. ....**St. Louis, MO**
Bushong, Miller A., III ....Charleston, WV
Bushong, R.M. Joe ....**Phoenix, AZ**
Bushong, Stephen K. ....Portland, OR
Bushong, Steven J. ....**Boulder, CO**
Bushor, Edward L. ....San Diego, CA
Bushor, Robert B. ....Tempe, AZ
Bushor, Susan P. ....**San Diego, CA**
Bushore, Michelle L. ....**Chicago, IL**
Bushorr, Gregory J. ....Rochester, NY
Bushueff, B. Paul, Jr. ....Southborough, MA
Bushway, Gregory L. ....Milledgeville, GA
Bushway, Todd C. ....Buffalo, NY
Bushy, Willard F. ....Westbrook, CT
Bushyeager, Amy L. ....**Washington, DC**
Busi, V. Kumar ....Redlands, CA
Busichio, Edward P. ....Scotch Plains, NJ
Busick, Denzel R. ....**Grand Island, NE**
Busick, Mark B ....Fresno, CA
Busick, Steven L. ....Vancouver, WA
Busico, Louis R. ....Lawrenceville, NJ
Newtown, PA
Philadelphia, PA
Busillo, Anthony C., II ....Harrisburg, PA
Busillo, John J. ....**New York, NY**
Business Law Group, The, A Professional Corporation ....**Los Angeles, CA**
Business Litigation Counsel, LLP
San Francisco, CA
Business & Technology Law, P.C.
Albuquerque, NM
Businga, Floyd ....Denver, CO
Businger, Peter A. ....**New York, NY**
Busis, Richard J. ....**Philadelphia, PA**
Busis, William L. ....Washington, DC
Busk, Chadwick C. ....**Grand Rapids, MI**
Busker, Gary L. ....Marshall, MO
Busker, Stephen E. ....Plantation, FL
Buskey, Lynn A. ....South Weymouth, MA
Buskirk, Bruce A. ....Silverdale, WA
Buskirk, George A., Jr. ....**Indianapolis, IN**
Buskirk, Jeffrey Eugene ....Grove City, OH
Buskirk Province, Inc., P.S. ....Silverdale, WA
Buskirk-Peeler, Mandy ....Westfield, NJ
Busko, Gregory J. ....**Roseland, NJ**
Buskop, Wendy K. B. ....**Houston, TX**
Buskus, Michael S. ....Albany, NY
Buslee, Christopher H. ....Ladysmith, WI
Buslee, Henry ....Fond du Lac, WI
Buslepp, Richard C. ....**Detroit, MI**
Busler, David E. ....Mansfield, OH
Busler, Robert H. ....Prairie Village, KS
Busler, Timothy W. ....New York, NY
Busman & Busman, P.C.
Fairfax Station, VA
Busman, Kenneth ....White Plains, NY
Busman, Marc A. ....**Fairfax Station, VA**
Busman, Rosalyn R. ....**Fairfax Station, VA**
Busnardo, Geralyn T. ....Compton, CA
Busner, Philip H. ....Port Washington, NY
Busny, Elise ....**Boston, MA**
Busó, Eduardo L. ....**Miami, FL**
Buso, John N. ....**West Palm Beach, FL**
Buso, John N., P.A. ....**West Palm Beach, FL**
Buso, Raymond ....Salem, MA
Busó-García, Carmen H. ....**San Juan, PR**
Busot, Aldo G. ....Coral Gables, FL
Busot, Aldo J. ....Coral Gables, FL
Busot & Busot, P.A. ....Coral Gables, FL
Busot, Maria Victoria ....Coral Gables, FL
Busquets, Carlos R. ....Miami, FL
Busroe, Frederick M., Jr. ....London, KY
Buss, Adam J. ....**Jacksonville, FL**
Buss, Brian K. ....**Austin, TX**
Buss, Charles A. ....Grand Junction, CO
Buss, Charles A. ....Cleveland, OH
Buss, Charlyn J. ....Department of Justice, Executive Office for Immigration Review, GV
Buss, David B. ....**New York, NY**
Buss, Dennis A. ....Chagrin Falls, OH
Buss, Donald A. ....Portland, OR
Buss, E. Robert ....**Tulsa, OK**
Buss, Eric J. ....**Minneapolis, MN**
Buss, Gregory A. ....Mount Clemens, MI
Buss, Gregory A., P.C. ....Mount Clemens, MI
Buss, Jeffrey D. ....**New York, NY**
Buss, John W., Jr. ....Pittsburgh, PA
Buss, Jonathan H. ....Salt Lake City, UT
Buss, Lindsey F. ....**Washington, DC**
Buss & Long ....Whitehall, PA
Buss, Mary Lynn ....Lansing, MI
Buss, Patricia M. ....Eagan, MN
Buss, Richard C. ....Whitehall, PA
Buss, Sara Davis ....**Pittsburgh, PA**
Buss, Todd C. ....Watertown, WI
Buss, William D., II
Cleveland Heights, OH
Buss, William G., Jr. ....Iowa City, IA
Bussan, Matthew J. ....Rochester, MN
Bussard, Alan R. L. ....**Towson, MD**
Bussard, Donald A. ....**Wilmington, DE**
Bussard, James W. ....Grand Haven, MI
Bussard & Sielski ....Grand Haven, MI
Bussard, Vicki L. ....**Denver, CO**
Bussart, Ford T. ....**Rock Springs, WY**
Bussart, James C. ....Atlanta, GA
Bussart & Medley ....Lewisburg, TN
Bussart, Walter W. ....Lewisburg, TN
Bussart, West, Rossetti, Piaia & Tyler, P.C.
Rock Springs, WY
Busscher, A. Brad ....Chicago, IL
Busse & Busse, P.C. ....**Chicago, IL**
Busse, C. William ....**Chicago, IL**
Busse, C. William, Jr. ....**Chicago, IL**
Busse & Hunt ....**Portland, OR**
Busse, James F. ....Omaha, NE
Busse, Kent V. ....Chicago, IL
Busse, Melanie D. ....Olathe, KS
Busse, Michele McMahon
Cedar Rapids, IA
Busse, Norma V. ....San Antonio, TX
Busse, Paul W. ....**St. Paul, MN**
Busse, Richard A. ....Newhall, CA
Busse, Richard C., Jr. ....**Portland, OR**
Busse, Robert J. ....**Charleston, WV**
Busse, Robert L. ....Toledo, OH
Bussell, Jerry W. ....Sugar Land, TX
Bussell, Joel G. ....Southfield, MI
Bussell, Leah R. ....San Diego, CA
Bussell, Leland C. ....**Springfield, MO**
Bussell, Lillian M. ....Southfield, MI
Bussell, O'Neal & Hall ....Springfield, MO
Bussell, Ronald L. ....Carmel, IN
Bussell, Sally Carney ....**Pensacola, FL**
Bussell, Sally Carney, P.A. ....**Pensacola, FL**
Bussell, Sheryl A. ....Chanute, KS
Bussell, Wayne (IBA) ....Lexington, KY
Busselle, James R. ....**Palo Alto, CA**
Busselman, Robert L. ....Kenedy, TX
Busser, Jo L. ....Philadelphia, PA
Busser, Norine ....**Costa Mesa, CA**
Busser, Scott M. ....**Denver, CO**
Bussert, Christopher P. ....**Atlanta, GA**
Bussert, Deborah Schmitt ....**Chicago, IL**
Bussert, Margaret M. ....Atlanta, GA
Bussert, Ronald E. ....Oklahoma City, OK
Bussey, Carl W. ....Kansas City, MO
Bussey, David T. ....Monmouth, ME
Bussey, Dean L. ....Minneapolis, MN
Bussey, Douglas M. ....Chico, CA
Bussey & Giudice ....Atlanta, GA
Bussey, John W., III ....**Orlando, FL**
Bussey, John W., III and Associates, P.A.
Orlando, FL
Bussey, L. Davis, (P.S.C.) ....Lexington, KY
Bussey & Lauve, LLC ....**Alexandria, LA**
Bussey, Lynn M. ....Bath, ME
Bussey, Mark E. ....Atlanta, GA
Bussey, Nichelle ....**New York, NY**
Bussey, Reginald ....Houston, TX
Bussey, Reginald, PLLC ....Houston, TX
Bussey, Richard A. ....**Washington, DC**
Bussey, Robert L. ....Alexandria, LA
Bussey, Ronald H. ....**Anchorage, AK**
Bussey, Stuart ....Walnut Creek, CA
Bussey, Susan ....Norman, OK
Bussey, Teri A. ....**Tallahassee, FL**
Bussey, William D. ....Bayfield, WI
Bussian, James R. ....**Birmingham, AL**
Bussian, John A., III ....**Durham, NC**
Bussian, John A., P.A., The Law Firm of
Durham, NC
Bussian, Robert A. ....**Houston, TX**
Bussiere, Alice ....San Francisco, CA
Bussiere & Bussiere, P.A. ....Manchester, NH
Bussiere, Donald K. ....San Francisco, CA
Bussiere, Emile R. ....Manchester, NH
Bussiere, Emile R., Jr. ....Manchester, NH
Bussing, Kathryn B. ....**Kansas City, MO**
Bussler, Richard ....Milwaukee, WI
Bussman, David L. ....Lake Oswego, OR
Bussman, Donald H. ....Chicago, IL
Bussman, James R. ....Cuyahoga Falls, OH
Bussman, Stephen P. ....Fort Payne, AL
Bussmann, Frank A. ....St. Louis, MO
Busson, Berenice ....**New York, NY**
Busson & Sikorski, L.L.C. ....**New York, NY**
Bussone, Fran M. ....**Campbell, CA**
Bussone, Joseph D. ....**Los Angeles, CA**
Bust, Edward J. ....St. Louis, MO
Bustamante, Alberto S., III ....**Orlando, FL**
Bustamante, Andrés Z. ....Los Angeles, CA
Bustamante, Antonius Kieran ....**Reston, VA**
Bustamante, David ....**Irvine, CA**
Bustamante, Ernest S. ....Phoenix, AZ
Bustamante, Fernando M. ....**Chicago, IL**
Bustamante, Karen S. ....Houston, TX
Bustamante, Luis C. ....**Knoxville, TN**
Bustamante, Manuel ....Worcester, MA
Bustamante, Michael D. ....Albuquerque, NM
Bustamante, Nestor, III
Fort Lauderdale, FL
Bustamante, Patricia E. ....Santa Fe, NM
Bustamante, Peter V. ....**Chicago, IL**
Bustamante, Rebecca ....**San Antonio, TX**
Bustamante, Robert M. ....San Jose, CA
Bustamante, Vincent ....Houston, TX
Bustamante, William M. ....Miami, FL
Bustamante, Rodrigo ....Minneapolis, MN
Bustard, R. David ....**Sarasota, FL**
Buster, Debra Minker ....**Atlanta, GA**
Buster, Donald L. ....Carrollton, TX
Buster, J. Kevin ....**Atlanta, GA**
Buster, James L. ....Santa Ana, CA
Busterna, Stephen J. ....Harrisburg, PA
Busterud, John A. ....San Francisco, CA
Busterud, John W. ....**San Francisco, CA**
Bustillo, Eric I. ....Miami, FL
Bustin, Jerry L. ....Forest, MS
Bustin, Thomas A. ....New Port Richey, FL
Busto, Felice ....Washington, DC
Busto & Jennings, Professional Association
Miami, FL
Busto, Mark R. ....**Bellevue, WA**
Busto, Mercedes ....**Miami, FL**
Bustos, Arthur L. ....Las Vegas, NM
Bustos, Fernando Manuel ....**Lubbock, TX**
Bustos, Karen Bell ....San Bernardino, CA
Bustraan, Kathleen M. ....**Baltimore, MD**
Busuttil, Edward Joseph ....Stockton, CA
Busuttil, James J. ....Jamaica, NY
Buswell, Anna ....Boston, MA
Buswell, Jack D. ....Sparta, WI
Butaitis, Stephen A. ....**Charleston, SC**
Butala, Richard M. ....**St. Paul, MN**
Butalla, David Paul ....North Huntingdon, PA
Butani, Kash M. ....Tylertown, MS
Butanis, Barry Anthony ....Towson, MD
Butanis, Victor K. ....Bel Air, MD
Butash, Glenn Eric ....**Morristown, NJ**
Butash, Michael G. ....New Port Richey, FL
Butaud, Andrea F. ....Bellevue, WA
Butaud, Jo Ann ....Lenexa, KS
Butauski, Joseph A. ....**Columbus, OH**
Butbul, David ....Skokie, IL
Butch, Mariann E. ....**Cleveland, OH**
Butch, Mary Sue ....**New York, NY**
Butch, Peter J., III ....**Philadelphia, PA**
Butch, Quinn, Rosemurgy, Jardis, Bush, Burkhart & Parks, P.C. ....**Escanaba, MI**
Gladstone, MI
Houghton, MI
Iron Mountain, MI
Marquette, MI
Sault Ste. Marie, MI
Butch, Thomas L. ....**Escanaba, MI**
Gladstone, MI
Butchart, Elizabeth Ann ....Jackson, MS
Butcher, Allan K. ....Fort Worth, TX
Butcher, Allan K., Jr. ....Stephenville, TX
Butcher, Ball & Lowry ....Kokomo, IN
Butcher, Billy J. ....Fort Worth, TX
Butcher, Bruce A. ....**Seattle, WA**
Butcher & Butcher ....**Glenville, WV**
Butcher, Catherine Curran
Washington, DC
Butcher, Clarence C., Jr.
Department of Transportation, Federal Aviation Administration, GV
Butcher, Connie J. ....Carol Stream, IL
Butcher & Croley ....Williamsburg, KY
Butcher, Curtis J., Law Offices ....Carmel, IN
Butcher, Daniel E. ....San Diego, CA
Butcher, Daniel L. ....**Dallas, TX**
Butcher, David A. ....**Indianapolis, IN**
Butcher, Dennis D. ....Santa Barbara, CA
Butcher, Herbert P. ....Oil City, PA
Butcher, James R. ....Kokomo, IN
Butcher, Jane Royce ....Williamsburg, KY
Butcher, Janet T. ....**Columbia, SC**
Butcher, Joe D. ....Blue Springs, MO
Butcher, John F. ....**Los Angeles, CA**
Butcher, John R. ....Richmond, VA
Butcher, John S. ....**Denver, CO**
Butcher, Johnny H. ....Wellsboro, PA
Butcher, Julie A. ....**Lexington, KY**
Butcher, Karen A. ....**Washington, DC**
Butcher, Keith D. ....**Charlotte, NC**
Butcher, Kimiko K. ....Boston, MA
Butcher, Larry E. ....Kearney, MO
Butcher, Lynn M. ....**South Bend, IN**
Butcher, Marcy Kay Katherine ....Eugene, OR
Butcher, Nancy Nawas ....**Shreveport, LA**
Butcher, Peter C. ....**Pittsburgh, PA**
Butcher, Peter F. ....**Washington, DC**
Butcher, R. Terry ....**Glenville, WV**
Butcher, Robert J. ....Homewood, IL
Butcher, Roger B. ....Orlando, FL
Butcher, Samuel V. ....**Cleveland, OH**
Butcher, Sharon A. ....**Houston, TX**
Butcher, Steve, Sr. ....Rochester, NY
Butcher, Terry J. ....Baton Rouge, LA
Butcher, Thomas A. ....Allendale, MI
Butcher, Timothy B. ....**Glenville, WV**
Butcher, William C. ....Melrose Park, IL
Butcher, William P. ....Homewood, IL
Butcher & Williams, P.S. ....**Seattle, WA**
Butchko, Andrew M. ....Trenton, NJ
Butchko, John T. ....Glendale, CA
Butchko, Robert C.
Commodity Futures Trading Commission, Division of Enforcement, GV
Butchma, James T. ....Richmond, VA
Butchman, Alan A. ....Washington, DC
Butcka, Walter ....Sanford, FL
Bute, Daniel J. ....Ottawa, IL
Bute, David W. ....**Denver, CO**
Butel, Francis Joseph ....Jefferson City, MO
Buten, Gerald L. ....Chicago, IL
Butenas, John P. ....Gaithersburg, MD
Butenhof, Ann N. ....Manchester, NH
Butenkoff, George G. ....Warehouse Point, CT
Butensky, Debra S. ....Arlington, VA
Butensky, Howard ....Tuckerton, NJ
Butensky & Pepe, P.A. ....Tuckerton, NJ
Buter, Buzard & Dunaetz, LLP
Los Angeles, CA
Buter, Irwin ....Los Angeles, CA
Butera & Andrews ....**Washington, DC**
Butera, August R. ....Chicago, IL
Butera, Beausang, Cohen & Brennan, Professional Corporation
King Of Prussia, PA
Norristown, PA
Butera, Celeste M. ....**Uniondale, NY**
Butera, Charles V. ....Niagara Falls, NY
Butera, Constance D. ....Canton, OH
Butera, Cynthia Oteri ....Covington, LA
Butera, H. Kenneth ....**King Of Prussia, PA**
Butera, James J. ....**Washington, DC**
Butera, John C. ....King Of Prussia, PA
Butera & Jones, L.L.P. ....King Of Prussia, PA
Butera, Karen D. ....**Canton, OH**
Butera, Michael I. ....**Pittston, PA**
Butera, Michael I. ....**Wilkes-Barre, PA**
Butera, Paul J. ....**Chicago, IL**
Butera, Richard M. ....Rockford, IL
Butera, Robert J. ....Philadelphia, PA
Butera, Thomas L. ....Pittsburgh, PA
Butera, William C. ....New City, NY
Buteyn, Debra K. ....Aliso Viejo, CA
Buth, George S. ....Grand Rapids, MI
Buthod & Buthod ....Evansville, IN
Buthod, Charles Tynan ....**Houston, TX**
Buthod, James M. ....Evansville, IN
Buthod, John J. ....**Evansville, IN**
Buthod, Therese ....**Tulsa, OK**
Buthusiem, Edward J. ....**Philadelphia, PA**
Butigan Law Firm ....**Seattle, WA**
Butigan, William C. ....**Seattle, WA**
Butin, Barry ....**Fort Lauderdale, FL**
Butin, Charles S. ....Great Neck, NY
Buting, Walter E.
South San Francisco, CA
Butkin, Robert A. ....Oklahoma City, OK
Butkovic, Denis ....**New York, NY**
Butkovich, John E. ....Cincinnati, OH
Butkovich, Joseph A. ....Cincinnati, OH
Butkovich, Schimpf, Schimpf & Ginocchio, A Legal Professional Association
Cincinnati, OH
Butkovitz, Alan L. ....**Elkins Park, PA**
Butkowski, Corinne R. ....**Cedar Rapids, IA**
Butkus, Carl J. ....**Albuquerque, NM**
Butkus, J. Steven ....**Wheaton, IL**
Butkus & Reimer, P.C. ....**Albuquerque, NM**
Butleman, Bernard J. ....Brooklyn, NY
Butler, A. Bates, III ....**Tucson, AZ**
Butler, A. Hays ....Wilmington, DE
Butler, A. Jerry ....Logan, UT
Butler, Alan L. ....Dallas, TX
Butler, Albert R. ....**Milwaukee, WI**
Butler, Algernon L., Jr. ....Wilmington, NC
Butler, Algernon Lee, III ....Wilmington, NC
Butler, Alicia D. ....**Dallas, TX**
Butler, Alison L. ....West Palm Beach, FL
Butler, Alison M. ....**Chicago, IL**
Butler, Allen ....**Dallas, TX**
Butler, Allen D. ....Tempe, AZ
Butler, Andrew H. ....**Boston, MA**
Butler, Anita B. ....Kansas City, MO
Butler, Anita L. ....New Britain, CT
Butler, Anita M. ....Clearwater, FL
Butler, Ann L. ....Santa Cruz, CA
Butler, Annette G. ....Cleveland, OH
Butler, Anthony M. ....Baton Rouge, LA
Butler, Arthur A. ....**Seattle, WA**
Butler, Arthur R. ....**Plymouth, MI**

Butler, Arthur V. ... Wheaton, MD
Butler, & Associates ... Tallahassee, FL
Butler & Associates ... Anchorage, AK
Butler, & Associates, P.A. ... Topeka, KS
Butler, Avo Stevens ... Sherman, TX
Butler, B. Davis, Jr. ... Atlanta, GA
Butler, B. Janelle ... Toledo, OH
Butler, Barry A. ... Hartford, CT
Butler, Barry Ben, Sr. ... Tampa, FL
Butler, Barry Ben, Sr., P.A. ... Tampa, FL
Butler, Benjamin J. ... Harrisburg, PA
Butler, Benjamin M. ... Winchester, VA
Butler, Benjamin T. ... Washington, DC
Butler, Betsy S. ... Nags Head, NC
Butler, Blaine S. ... Bountiful, UT
Butler, Blake & Robinson, P.A.
Baltimore, MD
Butler, Bonnie J. ... Baltimore, MD
Butler, Bradly M. ... Peoria, IL
Butler, Brent K. ... Jefferson City, MO
Butler, Brett ... Louisville, KY
Butler, Brian E. ... Madison, WI
Butler, Brian J. ... Syracuse, NY
Butler, Brian T. ... Baton Rouge, LA
Butler, Brian T. ... Farmville, VA
Butler, Bruce A. ... Knoxville, TN
Butler, Bruce B. ... Lima, OH
Butler, Bruce M. ... Rancho Cucamonga, CA
Butler, Bruce T. ... Hardinsburg, KY
Butler, Bryan W. ... Palo Alto, CA
Butler Burgott Leslie & Stine
Coos Bay, OR
Eugene, OR
Butler Burnette Pappas ... Miami, FL
Tallahassee, FL
Tampa, FL
Butler & Butler ... San Diego, CA
Butler & Butler ... Lawton, OK
Butler, Butler & Hudson ... Greensburg, KY
Butler & Butler, P.A. ... Baltimore, MD
Butler & Butler, P.A. ... Wheaton, MD
Butler & Butler, P.A. ... Albuquerque, NM
Butler, Butler & Rosenberger, A Professional Corporation ... Salem, NJ
Butler, C. David ... Atlanta, GA
Butler, C. Victor, Jr. ... Orlando, FL
Butler, Carl A. ... New Orleans, LA
Butler, Carolyn Lazar ... Madison, WI
Butler, Cass C. ... Salt Lake City, UT
Butler, Cathleen T. ... Newark, NJ
Butler, Cecil C. ... Chicago, IL
Butler, Cecile A. ... Springfield, MA
Butler, Charles A., Jr. ... South Boston, VA
Butler, Charles Bradley ... Woodland, CA
Butler, Charles C. ... Dublin, GA
Vidalia, GA
Butler, Charles C. ... Bryan, OH
Butler, Charles E. ... Pueblo, CO
Butler, Charles E. ... Wilmington, DE
Butler, Charles E., III ... Fort Lauderdale, FL
Butler, Charles E., P.C. ... Pueblo, CO
Butler, Charles J. ... Washington, DC
Butler, Charles R. ... Corpus Christi, TX
Butler, Charles R., Jr. ... Mobile, AL
Butler, Charles S. ... Cleveland, OH
Butler, Cheryl A. ... Department of Commerce, Patent and Trademark Office, GV
Butler, Christine A. ... Sarasota, FL
Butler, Christine L. ... Cambridge, MA
Butler, Christopher ... Chicago, IL
Butler, Christopher A. ... Onalaska, WI
Butler, Christopher E. ... Tampa, FL
Butler, Christopher J. ... New York, NY
Butler, Christopher Price
Chattanooga, TN
Butler, Christy L. ... Tulsa, OK
Butler, Cincione, DiCuccio, Dritz & Barnhart
Columbus, OH
Butler, Clarke & Feighan Co., L.P.A.
Cleveland, OH
Butler, Clint W. ... Huntsville, AL
Butler, Clinton V., Jr. ... Jackson, TN
Butler, Colleen Connors ... Chicago, IL
Butler, Colleen Elizabeth
San Francisco, CA
Butler, Craig V. ... San Diego, CA
Butler, Cynthia Calibani ... Lawton, OK
Butler, Cynthia Jeanne ... Murfreesboro, NC
Butler, Cynthia S. ... Pompton Plains, NJ
Butler, Dale E. ... Dallas, TX
Butler, Dana Elizabeth ... Pasadena, CA
Butler, Dana H. ... Houma, LA
Butler, Daniel J. ... Topsfield, MA
Butler, Daniel T. ... Hempstead, NY
Butler, Danny P. ... Greensburg, KY
Butler, Daphne E. ... San Francisco, CA
Butler, David ... San Bruno, CA
Butler, David ... Denver, CO
Butler, David ... Lawton, OK
Butler, David A., Jr. ... San Bruno, CA
Butler, David C. ... Marietta, GA
Butler, David C. ... Enid, OK
Butler, David C., P.C. ... Marietta, GA
Butler, David D. ... Des Moines, IA
Butler, David E. ... Vestal, NY
Butler, David F. ... Magnolia, AR
Butler, David G. ... Kalamazoo, MI
Butler, David J. ... Washington, DC
Butler, David J. ... Richfield, MN
Butler, David J. ... Columbus, OH
Butler, David L. ... San Antonio, TX
Butler, David M. ... Quincy, MA
Butler, David N. ... Trenton, NJ
West Orange, NJ
Butler, David R. ... Waterville, ME
Butler, David T., Jr. ... Baton Rouge, LA
Butler, Dean V. ... Seattle, WA
Butler, Deanna M. ... Palo Alto, CA

Butler, Deborah A. ... Treasury Department, Internal Revenue Service, GV
Butler, Deborah Sirotkin ... Arlington, MA
Butler, Debra K. ... Pasadena, CA
Butler, Denis J. ... Jamaica, NY
Butler, Dennis ... Lawton, OK
Butler, Dennis E. ... Lafayette, IN
Butler, Dennis E. ... Sugar Land, TX
Butler, Dennis F. ... Cleveland, OH
Butler, Dewey R. ... Dunn, NC
Butler, Diane M. ... Seattle, WA
Butler, Diane T. ... Minneapolis, MN
Butler, Dianne Drew ... Stockton, CA
Butler, Don R. ... Austin, TX
Butler, Donald F., Jr. ... Kansas City, MO
Butler, Donald K. ... Richmond, VA
Butler, Donald P. ... Houston, TX
Butler, Doug K. ... Dallas, TX
Butler, Douglas ... Torrance, CA
Butler, Douglas, A Professional Corporation
Torrance, CA
Butler, Douglas D. ... Novato, CA
Butler, Duane E. ... Overland Park, KS
Butler, Duge ... Indianapolis, IN
Butler, Durham & Willougby
Kalamazoo, MI
Butler, E. Bruce ... Pleasanton, CA
Butler, E. William ... Columbus, OH
Butler, Earl D. ... Vestal, NY
Butler, Earl D., P.C. ... Vestal, NY
Butler, Earle Lee, (P.A.)
Fort Lauderdale, FL
Butler, Edmund P. ... Blue Bell, PA
Butler, Edward J. ... Colorado Springs, CO
Butler, Edward J., Jr. ... Newark, NJ
Butler, Edward M. ... Eugene, OR
Butler, Edward T. ... San Diego, CA
Butler, Edward T. ... Naples, FL
Butler, E. J. ... Forrest City, AR
Butler, Elana R. ... New York, NY
Butler, Elizabeth ... Boston, MA
Butler, Elizabeth Ann ... New York, NY
Butler, Elizabeth E. ... New York, NY
Butler, Elizabeth R. ... Portland, ME
Butler, Ellyn S. ... Baltimore, MD
Butler, Elvira O. ... Chapel Hill, NC
Butler, Emily Holsinger ... New York, NY
Butler, Ernest W. ... Youngstown, OH
Butler, Eugene R. ... Columbus, OH
Butler, Eugene W. ... Columbus, OH
Butler, Evelyn G. ... Livonia, MI
Butler, Everett S. ... Phoenix, AZ
Butler, F. David ... Columbia, SC
Butler, F. Elmore ... Richmond, VA
Butler, F. Lee ... Houston, TX
Butler, F. Prince ... Arlington, VA
Virginia Beach, VA
Butler, F. E. ... McAllen, TX
Butler, Felicita Therese ... Los Angeles, CA
Butler, Fitzgerald & Potter, A Professional Corporation ... New York, NY
Butler, Floyd L. ... Jackson, MS
Butler, Francis P. ... Palos Park, IL
Butler, Frank ... Meadowbrook, PA
Butler, Frank B. ... Minneapolis, MN
Butler, Frank D. ... Pinellas Park, FL
Butler, Frank D., P.A. ... Clearwater, FL
Pinellas Park, FL
St. Petersburg, FL
Tampa, FL
Butler, Frank L. ... Chicago, IL
Butler, Frank L., III ... Macon, GA
Butler, Franklin C. ... Stanwood, WA
Butler, Fred D. ... San Francisco, CA
Butler, Frederick K. ... Providence, RI
Butler, G. Brian ... Atlanta, GA
Butler, Galter & O'Brien Law Firm
Lincoln, NE
Butler, Garey F. ... Fort Myers, FL
Butler, Gary A. ... Pittsburgh, PA
Butler, Gary Frank ... Livingston, TX
Butler, Gary L. ... Daytona Beach, FL
Butler, Gary W. ... Department of Agriculture, Office of the General Counsel, GV
Butler, G. C. ... Bonham, TX
Butler, George A. ... Greensburg, PA
Butler, George E. ... Chattanooga, TN
Butler, George E., II ... Atlanta, GA
Dahlonega, GA
Butler, George E., II ... Cumming, GA
Dawsonville, GA
Gainesville, GA
Butler, George E., Jr. ... Fayetteville, AR
Butler, George H.
United States Postal Service, Law Department, GV
Butler, George M. ... Hagåtña, GU
Butler, George P., III ... Detroit, MI
Butler, George W., III ... Houston, TX
Butler, George W., Jr. ... Tallahassee, FL
Butler, Gerald J. ... Scranton, PA
Butler, Gerard A. ... Boston, MA
Butler, Gilbert E., Jr. ... Roanoke, VA
Butler, Gordon T. ... Miami, FL
Butler, Greene S. ... New Orleans, LA
Butler, Gregory B. ... Cambridge, MA
Butler, Gregory C. ... Clinton, NC
Butler, Griffen & Mannix
West Chester, PA
Butler, H. William ... Detroit, MI
Butler & Hailey, P.C. ... Houston, TX
Butler & Harris ... Houston, TX
Butler, Harris D., III ... Richmond, VA
Butler, Harrison R. ... Upper Darby, PA
Butler, Harry F. ... Elyria, OH
Butler, Herbert H. ... Salem, NJ
Butler, Herbert H., Jr. ... Salem, NJ
Butler, Hicky & Long ... Forrest City, AR

Butler & Hosch, P.A. ... Orlando, FL
Butler, Howard B., Jr. ... Houston, TX
Butler, Howard G. ... Jacksonville, FL
Butler, Ilbert I. ... Berkeley, CA
Butler, Ira, Jr. ... Fort Worth, TX
Butler, J. Bradway ... Washington, DC
Butler, J. David ... Barnwell, SC
Butler, J. Dudley ... Laramie, WY
Butler, J. Keith ... Oklahoma City, OK
Butler, J. Lance ... Oxford, MS
Butler, J. Patrick ... Tucson, AZ
Butler, J. Preston ... Dallas, TX
Butler, J. Stewart, III ... Fayetteville, NC
Butler, J. Thomas ... Shreveport, LA
Butler, J. Todd ... Atlanta, GA
Butler, Jack A., Law Offices of
Nashville, TN
Butler, Jack C. ... Columbus, OH
Butler, James B. ... Columbia, MD
Butler, James C. ... New Orleans, LA
Butler, James D ... Bessemer, AL
Butler, James D. ... Denver, CO
Butler, James D. ... Bethesda, MD
Butler, James D. ... Jersey City, NJ
New York, NY
Butler, James D., P.A. ... Hackensack, NJ
Jersey City, NJ
New York, NY
Butler, James E. ... Bridgeport, CT
Butler, James E. ... Detroit, MI
Butler, James E. ... St. Louis, MO
Butler, James E. ... Las Vegas, NV
Butler, James E. ... Cincinnati, OH
Butler, James E. ... Dickinson, TX
Butler, James E., Jr. ... Atlanta, GA
Columbus, GA
Butler, James F. ... Uniondale, NY
Butler, James F. ... Jackson, TN
Butler, James F., III ... Atlanta, GA
Butler, James G. ... Los Angeles, CA
Butler, James G. ... San Francisco, CA
Butler, James G., A Professional Corporation
Los Angeles, CA
Butler, James G., Jr. ... Overland Park, KS
Butler, James J. ... Alexandria, VA
Butler, James J., III ... Stuart, FL
Butler, James L. ... Washington C. H., OH
Butler, James N., Jr. ... Asbury Park, NJ
Butler, James Neve, III ... Kenai, AK
Butler, James R. ... Columbus, OH
Butler, James R., Jr. (P.C.)
Los Angeles, CA
Butler, James T. ... Tampa, FL
Butler, James T., & Associates, P.A.
Tampa, FL
Butler, James W., III ... Atlanta, GA
Butler, James W. (Woody) ... Austin, TX
Butler, Jana C. ... Harrisburg, PA
Butler, Jason M. ... New York, NY
Butler, Jay W. ... Bountiful, UT
Butler, Jean Smith ... Glendora, CA
Butler, Jeff E. ... New York, NY
Butler, Jeffrey J. ... Lansing, MI
Butler, Jeffrey M. (IBA) ... New York, NY
Butler, Jeffrey M. ... Walterboro, SC
Butler, Jeffry ... Los Angeles, CA
Butler, Jenna Fruechtenicht
New Bern, NC
Wilmington, NC
Butler, Jennifer ... Stamford, CT
Butler, Jennifer Anne ... New Haven, CT
Butler, Jennifer Kang ... West Orange, NJ
Butler, Jennifer Lynch ... Nashville, TN
Butler, Jerald L. ... Dallas, TX
Butler, Jeremy E. ... Phoenix, AZ
Butler, Jerome M. ... Chicago, IL
Butler, Jesse H. ... Kansas City, MO
Butler, Jesse L. ... Clinton, NC
Butler, Jim ... Salt Lake City, UT
Butler, Jimmie ... Tampa, FL
Butler, JoAnn C. ... Boise, ID
Butler, Joanne L. ... Morristown, NJ
Butler, Joel M. ... Los Angeles, CA
Butler, John A., III ... San Jose, CA
Butler, John B., III ... Columbia, SC
Butler, John B., III, P.A. ... Columbia, SC
Butler, John B., Jr. ... Columbia, SC
Butler, John Carleton ... Robbins, CA
Butler, John E. ... Ithaca, NY
Butler, John E. ... Syracuse, NY
Butler, John F. ... Mobile, AL
Butler, John F. ... Hackensack, NJ
Butler, John G. ... Morristown, NJ
Phillipsburg, NJ
Butler, John G. ... Union, NJ
Butler, John G., III ... Washington, DC
Butler, John H. ... New York, NY
Butler, John H., II ... New Orleans, LA
Butler, John J. ... Uxbridge, MA
Butler, John J. ... New York, NY
Butler, John J. ... Raleigh, NC
Butler, John K. ... Twin Falls, ID
Butler, John K. ... Princeton, NJ
Butler, John K. ... Tacoma, WA
Butler, John L. ... Brooklyn, NY
Butler, John M ... New York, NY
Butler, John M. ... St. Marys, WV
Butler, John Mack ... Tulsa, OK
Butler, John R. ... Aptos, CA
Butler, John R., Jr. ... Atlanta, GA
Butler, John S. ... Greenwood, IN
Butler, John S. ... Austin, TX
Butler, John T. ... Miami, FL
Butler, John W. ... Washington, DC
Butler, John W. ... Knoxville, TN
Butler, John Wm., Jr. ... Chicago, IL
Butler, Jolyan A. ... Hartford, CT
Butler, Jolynn Barry ... Columbus, OH

Butler, Jonathan K. ... Salt Lake City, UT
Butler, Joseph ... La Grange, IL
Butler, Joseph F. ... Los Angeles, CA
Butler, Joseph G. ... Boston, MA
Butler, Joseph J., Jr. ... Marco Island, FL
Butler, Joseph M. ... Rapid City, SD
Butler, Julia R. ... Harleysville, PA
Butler, Julian D. ... Huntsville, AL
Butler, Karen ... San Diego, CA
Butler, Karen A. ... Albany, NY
Butler, Katharine A. ... Richland, WA
Butler, Katharine I. ... Columbia, SC
Butler, Katharine S. ... Atlanta, GA
Butler, Katherine ... Houston, TX
Butler, Katherine E. ... Rockville, MD
Butler, Katherine L. ... Houston, TX
Butler, Kathleen ... Lansing, MI
Butler, Kathlynn Lea ... Atlanta, GA
Butler, Kathy H. ... St. Louis, MO
Butler, Kay Rivest ... Birmingham, MI
Butler, Keith E. ... Newport Beach, CA
Butler, Keith R. ... Milwaukee, WI
Butler, Kenneth ... Okmulgee, OK
Butler, Kenneth B. ... El Paso, TX
Butler, Kenneth D. ... Duluth, MN
Butler, Kenneth V. ... Overland Park, KS
Butler, Kerry J. ... Louisville, KY
Butler, Kevin J. ... South Bend, IN
Butler, Kimberly M. ... Littleton, NH
Butler, Kristine L. ... Newark, NJ
Butler, L. Chris ... Houston, TX
Butler, L. Daniel ... Augusta, GA
Butler & LaBelle ... Scranton, PA
Butler, Landrum and Pierce, P.C.
Lakewood, CO
Butler, Lara ... Memphis, TN
Butler, Larry A. ... Jackson, TN
Butler, Larry D. ... Healdsburg, CA
Butler, Larry E. ... Kearney, NE
Butler, Larry G. ... Kansas City, MO
Butler, Larry J. ... Shreveport, LA
Butler, Larry Kent ... Atlanta, GA
Jasper, GA
Butler, Laura Peterson ... Roanoke, VA
Butler, Lauranne S. ... Boston, MA
Butler, Laurie J., (P.C.) ... Los Angeles, CA
Butler, Lawr. J. ... Decatur, GA
Butler, Lawrence E. ... San Francisco, CA
Butler, Leland E. ... Penn Valley, CA
Butler, Leo J. ... San Francisco, CA
Butler, Lewis H. ... San Francisco, CA
Butler, Linda M. ... Havana, IL
Butler, Linda M. ... Huntingdon, TN
Butler & Linger ... Tulsa, OK
Butler, Lisa ... Chicago, IL
Butler, Lisa F. ... San Diego, CA
Butler, Lisa M. ... Princeton, NJ
Butler, Lisa Reeves ... Bella Vista, AR
Bentonville, AR
Butler & Looney, P.C. ... Vale, OR
Butler, Louis B., Jr. ... Milwaukee, WI
Butler, Louis M. ... Metairie, LA
Butler, Ludlow S., Jr. ... San Diego, CA
Butler, Lynda L. ... Williamsburg, VA
Butler, Lynda R. ... Bellevue, WA
Butler, M. Caldwell ... Roanoke, VA
Butler, M. Tyus, Jr. ... Savannah, GA
Butler, M. Warren ... Mobile, AL
Butler & MacDougald ... Atlanta, GA
Jasper, GA
Butler, Macon, Williams & Pantele, P.C.
Richmond, VA
Butler, Malcolm L. ... Savannah, GA
Butler, Mara Schechter ... Virginia Beach, VA
Butler, Margaret K. ... Santa Rosa, CA
Butler, Marguerite Louise ... Houston, TX
Butler, Marie ... Red Lake, MN
Albuquerque, NM
Butler, Marie D. ... Metairie, LA
Butler, Marilyn E. ... Los Angeles, CA
Butler, Marilyn L. ... Manchester, NH
Butler, Mark Allen
United States Court Of Appeals District Of Columbia Circuit, GV
Butler, Mark C. ... Buffalo, NY
Butler, Mark E. ... New York, NY
Butler, Mark F. ... Hollywood, FL
Butler, Mark J. ... Irvine, CA
St. Louis, MO
Butler, Mark S. ... Morris Plains, NJ
Butler, Mark T. ... Detroit, MI
Butler, Martin C. ... Covington, KY
Butler, Mary Cathryn ... Washington, DC
Butler, Mary K. ... Miami, FL
Butler, Mary Taylor ... Dallas, TX
Butler & McNamara, P.C. ... Media, PA
Norristown, PA
Philadelphia, PA
Butler, Means, Evins & Browne, P.A.
Gaffney, SC
Spartanburg, SC
Butler, Melinda A. ... Houston, TX
Butler, Michael ... San Francisco, CA
Butler, Michael E. ... Arlington, VA
Butler, Michael J. ... Tucson, AZ
Butler, Michael J. ... Philadelphia, PA
Butler, Michael J. ... Dallas, TX
Butler, Michael P.
Department Of Veterans Affairs, Office of the General Counsel, GV
Butler, Michael P. ... Dallas, TX
Butler, Michael R. ... Lake Oswego, OR
Butler, Michael S. ... Harrisburg, PA
Lancaster, PA
Butler, Michael V. ... Mission Viejo, CA
Butler, Michael W. ... Garden City, NY
Butler, Michelle L. ... Washington, DC
Butler, Milton C. ... Los Angeles, CA

Butler, Mireille O. .... **Seattle, WA**
Butler, Molly E. .... Lakewood, CO
Butler and Monks .... Cambridge, MA
Butler, Moon & Hosch, P.A. .... **Orlando, FL**
Butler, Morgan Robert .... Waukesha, WI
Butler, Morris .... Greensburg, KY
Butler, Moss M. .... Jonestown, MS
Butler, Nancy Michelle .... Hartsville, SC
Butler, Nancy O'Hare .... New York, NY
Butler, Nathanial Paxton .... Statesville, NC
Butler, Nathaniel E. .... Washington, DC
Butler, Neil H. .... **Tallahassee, FL**
Butler Norris & Gold .... Hartford, CT
Butler, Oliver J., Jr. .... Houston, TX
Butler, Ollie B., Jr. .... Tampa, FL
Butler, Patricia Ann .... Boulder, CO
Butler, Patricia G. .... **Washington, DC**
Butler, Patricia Greene .... **Atlanta, GA**
Butler, Patrick C. .... Fallbrook, CA
Butler, Patrick D. .... **Louisville, CO**
Butler, Patrick H. .... Indianapolis, IN
Butler, Patrick J., Jr. .... **New Orleans, LA**
Butler, Patrick M. .... **Boston, MA**
Hyannis, MA
Butler, Patrick R. .... Wichita, KS
Butler, Patrick S. .... St. Louis, MO
Butler, Paul .... Jersey City, NJ
Butler, Paul A. .... Houston, TX
Butler, Paul B. .... Boise, ID
Butler, Paul B., Jr. .... **Tampa, FL**
Butler, Paul Edward .... New York, NY
Butler, Paul M., Jr. .... **New York, NY**
Butler, Paul T. .... Treasury Department,
Internal Revenue Service, GV
Butler, Paul V. .... Washington, DC
Butler, Penn Ayers .... Palo Alto, CA
Butler, Peter J. .... **New Orleans, LA**
Butler, Peter J. .... **Seattle, WA**
Butler, Peter J., Jr. .... **New Orleans, LA**
Butler, Philip H. .... **Montgomery, AL**
Butler, Phyllis .... Warren, MI
Butler, Pierce L. .... Washington, NJ
Butler, R. David, II .... Vale, OR
Butler, R. Frank .... Fresno, CA
Butler, R. Kevin .... Oklahoma City, OK
Butler, Ralph D. .... Monmouth, IL
Butler, Randall E. .... **Houston, TX**
Butler, Randall E., P.C. .... **Houston, TX**
Butler, Raymond S. .... Baltimore, MD
Butler, Rebecca F. .... Elkhart, IN
Butler, Regina M. .... **Toms River, NJ**
Butler, Rene Bassett .... Wood River, IL
Butler, Rex Lamont .... **Anchorage, AK**
Butler, Richard A. .... Lawrenceburg, IN
Butler, Richard B. .... Union, NJ
Butler, Richard C. .... Little Rock, AR
Butler, Richard C., Jr. .... Little Rock, AR
Butler, Richard D. .... Arlington, MA
Butler, Richard J. .... **Lincoln, NE**
Butler, Richard L. .... **Falls Church, VA**
Butler, Richard L. .... Seattle, WA
Butler, Richard M. .... **San Antonio, TX**
Butler, Richard W. .... **Eugene, OR**
Butler, Richard W., Jr. .... **Grand Rapids, MI**
Butler, Rick .... Hillsborough, NC
Butler, Rick S. .... **Houston, TX**
Butler, Robert A. .... Danbury, CT
Butler, Robert A. .... Columbus, OH
Butler, Robert A. .... Shawnee, OK
Butler, Robert B., A Professional Law Corporation .... **Houma, LA**
Butler, Robert B., III .... **Houma, LA**
Butler, Robert D. .... Vale, OR
Butler, Robert E., II .... Bardstown, KY
Butler, Robert F. .... Reno, NV
Butler, Robert H. .... Fayetteville, NC
Butler, Robert H., III .... Detroit, MI
Butler, Robert J. .... **Washington, DC**
Butler, Robert J. .... Flossmoor, IL
Butler, Robert M. .... Tulsa, OK
Butler, Robert O., Jr. .... **St. Francisville, LA**
Butler, Robert S. .... San Diego, CA
Butler, Robert T. .... **Cincinnati, OH**
Butler, Robert T. .... **Fredericksburg, VA**
Butler, Robert W. .... Granite City, IL
Butler, Robert Y. .... Arcadia, LA
Butler, Robyn .... Overland Park, KS
Kansas City, MO
Butler Rodgers Law Offices
Milwaukee, WI
Butler, Roger C. .... Corpus Christi, TX
Butler, Roger N., Jr. .... **Tulsa, OK**
Butler, Ron M. .... Marlin, TX
Butler, Ronald .... **Chicago, IL**
Butler, Ronald D. .... Harrisburg, PA
Butler, Ronald E. .... Lexington, KY
Butler, Ronald P. .... High Point, NC
Butler, Rubin, Saltarelli & Boyd
Chicago, IL
Butler, Russell P. .... Camp Springs, MD
Butler, Ryan L. .... Vero Beach, FL
Butler, Samuel C. .... **New York, NY**
Butler, Scot, III .... Phoenix, AZ
Butler, Scott A. .... **Roanoke, VA**
Butler, Scott C. .... **Cherry Hill, NJ**
Blue Bell, PA
Butler, Scott D. .... **Indianapolis, IN**
Butler, Scott J. .... Rushville, IL
Butler, Seletha Rochell .... **Atlanta, GA**
Butler, Sharon K. .... Spartanburg, SC
Butler, Sheryl A. .... Department of the Army,
U.S. Army Legal Services Agency, GV
Butler and Simeri, P.C. .... South Bend, IN
Butler, Snow, O'Mara, Stevens & Cannada, PLLC .... **Gulfport, MS**
Jackson, MS
Memphis, TN
Butler, Sophia Cason .... **Baxley, GA**
Butler, Stacy G. .... Baton Rouge, LA
Butler & Stein, P.C. .... **Phoenix, AZ**
Tucson, AZ
Butler, Stephanie A. .... **San Francisco, CA**
Butler, Stephen B. .... Old Greenwich, CT
Butler, Stephen D. .... San Francisco, CA
Butler, Stephen G. .... **Winchester, VA**
Butler, Stephen J. .... **Cincinnati, OH**
Butler, Stephen K. .... **Santa Rosa, CA**
Butler, Stephen R. .... Los Angeles, CA
Butler, Stephen R. .... **Memphis, TN**
Rosenberg, TX
Butler, Stephen R. .... Broadway, VA
Butler, Stephen W. .... Rogers, AR
Butler, Steven E. .... Department of Justice,
Civil Rights Division, GV
Butler, Steven E. .... Morgantown, IN
Butler, Stewart C. .... Albuquerque, NM
Butler, Susan A. .... Corona Del Mar, CA
Butler, Susan Hickman .... Morton, IL
Butler, Susan M. .... **Washington, DC**
Butler, T. Sean .... **Los Angeles, CA**
Butler, Talmadge .... Fort Payne, AL
Butler, Teresa L. .... **Atlanta, GA**
Butler, Terrence L. .... Beverly Hills, CA
Butler, Terrence Lamont .... Brooklyn, NY
Butler, Terrence R. .... Elyria, OH
Butler, Theresa M. .... Wheaton, MD
Butler, Thomas A. .... **San Diego, CA**
Butler, Thomas A. .... **New York, NY**
Butler, Thomas D. .... Cavalier, ND
Butler, Thomas E. .... Buffalo, NY
Butler, Thomas E. .... **New York, NY**
Butler, Thomas E., Jr. .... **Philadelphia, PA**
Butler, Thomas G. .... New York, NY
Butler, Thomas J. .... New York, NY
Butler, Thomas J., Jr. .... Union, NJ
Butler, Thomas L. .... Austin, TX
Butler, Thomas R. .... Albert Lea, MN
Butler, Thomas S. K. .... Nahant, MA
Butler, Timothy F. .... Bridgeport, CT
New York, NY
Butler, Timothy H. .... **Seattle, WA**
Butler, Timothy L. .... Santa Fe, NM
Butler, Timothy P. .... New York, NY
Butler, Timothy R. .... **Dayton, OH**
Butler, Tobin A. .... **Cherry Hill, NJ**
Butler, Todd B. .... **Topeka, KS**
Butler, Tommy H. .... Helena, MT
Butler, Tyrone T. .... Albany, NY
Butler, Van L. .... **Salt Lake City, UT**
Butler, Victoria A. .... Tampa, FL
Butler, Victoria A. .... New York, NY
Butler, Vines and Babb, P.L.L.C.
Knoxville, TN
Butler, Virginia Pipes .... Department of Justice,
Environment and Natural Resources
Division, GV
Butler, Voigt & Stewart, P.C.
Kearney, NE
Butler, Wallace W. .... **Waterloo, IA**
Butler, Warren .... **Knoxville, TN**
Butler, W. C. .... Eupora, MS
Butler, Wendy .... **Atlanta, GA**
Butler, Wesley R. .... **Lexington, KY**
Butler, Whittier, LaLiberty & Mitchell, P.A.
Waterville, ME
Butler, William A. .... **Washington, DC**
Butler, William A. .... Kirkland, WA
Butler, William B. .... Westfield, NJ
Butler, William C. .... Mount Clemens, MI
Butler, William F. .... Sun City Center, FL
Butler, William F., III .... Hyannis, MA
Butler, William, 4th .... West Chester, PA
Butler, William G. .... Detroit, MI
Butler, William J. .... **Chicago, IL**
Butler, William J. .... New York, NY
Butler, William J., Jr. .... **Washington, DC**
Butler, William Joseph "Joey"
Lafayette, TN
Butler, William M. .... Tuscaloosa, AL
Butler, William M. .... Campbell, CA
Butler, William M., Jr. .... Louisville, KY
Butler, William N. .... Towson, MD
Butler, William O., III .... Montgomery, AL
Butler, William P. .... Philadelphia, PA
Butler, William T. .... Houston, TX
Butler, Wm. J. .... Savannah, GA
Butler, Wooten, Overby, Fryhofer, Daughtery & Sullivan .... **Atlanta, GA**
Columbus, GA
Butler, Wycliffe V. .... Albuquerque, NM
Butler, Zane B. .... Dallas, TX
Butler-Graves, Dawn .... St. Louis, MO
ButleRitchie, David T. .... Shrewsbury, NJ
Butler-Truesdale, Tonya M. .... Washington, DC
Butman, Charles B., (P.A.)
Fort Lauderdale, FL
Butman, David C. .... **Chicago, IL**
Butner, Blain B. .... **Washington, DC**
Butner & Butner, Inc. .... Wewoka, OK
Butner, Carol Steib .... **Houston, TX**
Butner, Christopher A. .... **Dallas, TX**
Butner, George W. .... Wewoka, OK
Butner, Lawrence .... New York, NY
Butner, Richard E. .... Wewoka, OK
Butner, Robin L. .... New York, NY
Butner, William E. .... Hickory, NC
Butnick, Roland .... Livermore, CA
Butow, David C. .... **New York, NY**
Butowsky, Michael R. .... **New York, NY**
Butrum, Roy W. .... **Washington, DC**
Butrus, Carol Willis .... Paoli, PA
Butrus, Gregory P. .... **Birmingham, AL**
Butrus, John J., Jr. .... **Dallas, TX**
Butrus, Khoshbin & Wilson, L.L.P.
Dallas, TX
Butrym, Edward J. .... **Pennington, NJ**
Butsavage & Associates, P.C.
Washington, DC
Butsavage, Carey R. .... **Washington, DC**
Butsch, David T. .... **St. Louis, MO**
Butsch, William M. .... **Atlanta, GA**
Butsch, William M., P.C. .... **Atlanta, GA**
Butscher, Alisa C. .... Cleveland, OH
Butschky, Wilfred W. .... Mount Airy, MD
Butson, Gilbert D. .... **Honolulu, HI**
Butswinkas, Dane H. .... **Washington, DC**
Butt, Edward T., Jr. .... **Chicago, IL**
Butt, George F. .... South Bend, IN
Butt, James Carroll .... Lone Star, SC
Butt, Jeffrey Drew .... **Tampa, FL**
Butt, JoAnne B. .... Alexandria, VA
Butt, Layne J. .... **Las Vegas, NV**
Butt, Louis M., Jr. .... New Brockton, AL
Butt, Nathan W., Jr. .... Jamaica, NY
Butt, Paul L. .... **Albuquerque, NM**
Butt, Richard H. .... San Jose, CA
Butt, Thomas F. .... Fayetteville, AR
Butt, Thornton & Baehr, P.C.
Albuquerque, NM
Butt, William Jackson, II .... **Fayetteville, AR**
Butta, Matthew C. .... Canoga Park, CA
Buttafuoco, Daniel P. .... Woodbury, NY
Buttafuoco, Joseph .... Kearny, NJ
Buttafuoco, Karpf & Arce .... Kearny, NJ
Buttafuoco, Nicholas R. .... Kearny, NJ
Buttar, Abid A. .... Philadelphia, PA
Buttar, Rashda M. .... **Chicago, IL**
Buttarazzi, H. Ronald .... Rochester, NY
Buttarazzi, Ronald J. .... Fairport, NY
Buttaro, Patricia A. .... Fayetteville, GA
Buttaro, Patricia A. .... Fayetteville, GA
Buttars, Rodney T. .... Boise, ID
Butte, Dagmar .... Tualatin, OR
Buttell, Chadwick I. .... **Chicago, IL**
Buttell, Deborah H. .... **Chicago, IL**
Buttell, George J., III .... Chicago Heights, IL
Buttenwieser, Lawrence B. .... **New York, NY**
Butter, Gary M. .... **New York, NY**
Butter, John A. .... Vernon, CT
Butter, Stephen H. .... Miami, FL
Butterall & Greene, LLC .... Hanover, MA
Butterall, Joanne .... Hanover, MA
Butterbrodt, Robert D. .... **St. Paul, MN**
Butterer, Karl Werner, Jr.
Grand Rapids, MI
Butterfass, Stephen E. .... Fishkill, NY
Butterfield, Benjamin P. .... **Orlando, FL**
Butterfield, C. Robert .... **Dallas, TX**
Butterfield, David .... **Shreveport, LA**
Butterfield, David A. .... Valparaiso, IN
Butterfield, Edwin L. .... Lake Success, NY
Butterfield, Evan M. .... Deerfield, IL
Butterfield, Frank R. .... **Wayne, NJ**
Butterfield, Grant C. .... **Denver, CO**
Butterfield, Joachim, Schaedler & Kelleher
Bethlehem, PA
Butterfield, John S., Jr. .... Sacramento, CA
Butterfield, Jonathan E. .... **Williamsport, PA**
Butterfield, Kathleen .... Boise, ID
Butterfield, Kenneth C. .... Huntington, NY
Butterfield, Kevin W. .... **Durham, NC**
Butterfield Law Offices .... Valparaiso, IN
Butterfield, Lisanne M. .... Portland, OR
Butterfield, Lloyd H. .... Roanoke, VA
Butterfield, Louis B. .... **Portland, ME**
Butterfield, Mark D. .... Black River Falls, WI
Butterfield, Mark, P.C. .... Rutland, VT
Butterfield, Mark R. .... Rutland, VT
Butterfield, Mark W. .... Newark, CA
Butterfield, Peter T. .... **Boston, MA**
Butterfield, Randall J. .... **Atlanta, GA**
Butterfield, Rhonda F. .... Anchorage, AK
Butterfield, Robert K., Jr. .... **San Diego, CA**
Butterfield, Robert L., Jr. .... **Orlando, FL**
Butterfield Schechter LLP .... **San Diego, CA**
Butterfield, Steven B. .... **Tulsa, OK**
Butterfield, Thomas K. .... **Lapeer, MI**
Butterfield, Toby M.J. .... **New York, NY**
Butterfield, Wayne A., (Inc.) .... Arcadia, CA
Butterfield, William .... Dallas, TX
Butterfield, William H. .... **Washington, DC**
Butterfield, William P. .... **Washington, DC**
Butterfoss, Edwin J. .... St. Paul, MN
Butterklee, Neil H. .... **New York, NY**
Butterly, Sean C. .... Watertown, CT
Butterman, Alexander H.
Department of Commerce,
Patent and Trademark Office, GV
Butterman, Irene .... Denver, CO
Butterman, Jay R. .... **New York, NY**
Butterman Kahn & Gardner, LLP
New York, NY
Butterman, Mark B. .... **Chicago, IL**
Butterman, Michael D. .... **Miami, FL**
New York, NY
Buttermore & Boggs, P.S.C. .... **Harlan, KY**
Buttermore, Christopher L.
Coral Springs, FL
Buttermore, Grant M. .... **Westfield, NJ**
Buttermore, H. King, III .... **Atlanta, GA**
Buttermore, Mullen, Jeremiah and Phillips
Westfield, NJ
Buttermore, Rodney E., Jr. .... **Harlan, KY**
Butters, Brazilian & Small, LLP
Boston, MA
Butters, Frederick F. .... **Bloomfield Hills, MI**
Butters, John C. .... Atlanta, GA
Butters, Kenneth L. .... **Des Moines, IA**
Butters, Robert D. .... **Chicago, IL**
Butters, Thomas J., (P.C.) .... **Boston, MA**
Butterwick, Bright & O'Laughlin, Inc., A Professional Law Corporation
Riverside, CA
Butterwick, J. D. .... **Riverside, CA**
Butterwick, Kirk D. .... Laguna Beach, CA
Butterworth, Alan R. .... St. Louis, MO
Butterworth, Alfred Zachariah
St. Francisville, LA
Bay St. Louis, MS
Butterworth, Ann V. .... Nashville, TN
Butterworth, Bradley .... Hopewell, VA
Butterworth & Campbell PC .... Hoboken, NJ
Philadelphia, PA
Butterworth, David G. .... **Philadelphia, PA**
Butterworth, Edward L.
Santa Fe Springs, CA
Butterworth, Eric M. .... Kennewick, WA
Butterworth, George W., III .... **Boston, MA**
Butterworth, George W., Sr. .... El Paso, TX
Butterworth, George W., Sr., P.C.
El Paso, TX
Butterworth, Guerin L. .... Long Beach, CA
Butterworth, H. Curtis .... Hopewell, VA
Butterworth, Joel D. .... Prague, OK
Butterworth, Kenneth J. .... **Lowell, MA**
Butterworth, Michael M.
New Orleans, LA
Butterworth, Richard R.
General Services Administration,
Office of the General Counsel, GV
Butterworth, Robert A. .... Tallahassee, FL
Butterworth, Robert Martin .... Oakton, VA
Butterworth, S. Kendall .... **Atlanta, GA**
Butterworth, Sandra E. .... **Duluth, MN**
Butterworth, Stephanie M.
San Francisco, CA
Butterworth, Thomas C. .... Rowayton, CT
Buttery, James C. .... **San Luis Obispo, CA**
Buttery, James Frank, Jr. .... Fairfax, VA
Buttery, Miles E., II .... San Antonio, TX
Buttery, Miles E., II, P.C. .... San Antonio, TX
Buttigieg, Brian J. .... Old Greenwich, CT
Buttiglieri, Joseph P. .... **Troy, MI**
Buttimer, Anne E. .... Barre, VT
Buttimer, Edward M. .... Savannah, GA
Buttimer, Richard J. .... Milledgeville, GA
Buttita, John J. .... **Chicago, IL**
Buttitta, Claudio .... **New York, NY**
Buttitta, Joseph J. .... Streamwood, IL
Buttitta, Sandra Lynn .... Los Angeles, CA
Buttler, Donna L. .... Windsor, CT
Buttler, John H. .... Portland, OR
Buttles, Lewis .... San Antonio, TX
Buttles, Rebecca J. .... Atlanta, GA
Buttner, Frederic A. .... Jacksonville, FL
Buttner, Indrek H. .... **Hartford, CT**
Buttner, Robert M. .... **Scranton, PA**
Buttnick, Morris A. .... Seattle, WA
Butto, Natalie .... Bradenton, FL
Buttolph, Katherine .... Princeton, NJ
Button, Alan L. .... Buies Creek, NC
Button, Christine A. .... **New York, NY**
Button, Christine P. .... Cortlandt Manor, NY
Button, David R. .... **Cleveland, OH**
Button, Don P. .... **Kokomo, IN**
Button, Edward N. .... Hagerstown, MD
Button, Hillis & Oaks .... **Kokomo, IN**
Button, James A. .... Milwaukee, WI
Button, Kenneth R. .... **Los Angeles, CA**
Button, Kristin K. .... Washington, DC
Button, Robert A., Jr. .... Louisville, KY
Button, Roger D. .... **Round Rock, TX**
Buttone, Cheryl D. .... New York, NY
Buttorff, Cynthia S. .... **Louisville, KY**
Butto-Solan, Lisa .... Marietta, GA
Buttram & Davis, L.L.C. .... Gadsden, AL
Buttram, H. Dean .... Birmingham, AL
Buttram, Kimberly Anne .... **Dallas, TX**
Buttram, Reuel B. .... Atlanta, GA
Buttram, Stephen V. .... **Houston, TX**
Buttram, Walden M. .... Gadsden, AL
Buttress, Amanda M. .... Champaign, IL
Buttress, Christine A. .... **Florence, KY**
Cincinnati, OH
Buttrey, Carol W. .... Nashville, TN
Buttrey, Claude T. .... Lebanon, NH
Buttrey, Donald W. .... **Indianapolis, IN**
Buttrey, James D. A. .... Howell, MI
Buttrey, Marisa M. .... New York, NY
Buttrey, William D. .... United States Senate,
Committee Legal Personnel, GV
Buttrick, John A. .... **Phoenix, AZ**
Buttrick, John W. .... **New York, NY**
Buttrick, Marshall A. .... Nashua, NH
Buttrick, Matthew W. .... **Miami, FL**
Buttridge, Joseph W. .... Albany, NY
Buttrill, Gerald H., (P.C.) .... Houston, TX
Buttrill & Kuhn .... Houston, TX
Buttross, Jayne L. .... Jackson, MS
Buttry, James A., (P.A.) .... **Little Rock, AR**
Butts, Allison F., (Mr.) .... Chevy Chase, MD
Butts, Benjamin J. .... **Oklahoma City, OK**
Butts, Bernard H., Jr., (P.A.) .... Hialeah, FL
Butts, Bertie N., III .... Midland, MI
Butts & Butts .... **Boydton, VA**
South Hill, VA
Butts, C. Glasgow .... **South Hill, VA**
Butts, C. William, Jr. .... Galesburg, IL
Butts, Charles A. .... **Poughkeepsie, NY**
Butts, Charles D. .... San Antonio, TX
Butts, Charles G., Jr. .... **South Hill, VA**
Butts, Clyde I. .... Walnut Creek, CA
Butts, David O. .... Tupelo, MS
Butts, David W. .... **Kansas City, MO**
Butts, Derek .... Martinez, CA
Butts, Diana Fay .... Galena, OH
Butts, Duncan R. .... **Denver, CO**
Butts, Edna Ramón .... **Austin, TX**
Butts, Edward A. .... Chicago, IL
Butts, Elliot W. .... Jacksonville, FL
Butts, Gary A. .... Whittier, CA
Butts, George B. .... **Austin, TX**

Butts, Greg E. ... Dallas, TX
Butts, Halleck A. ... Columbia, SC
Butts, J. Crawford ... Oklahoma City, OK
Butts, James A., III ... South Hill, VA
Butts, James A., IV ... South Hill, VA
Butts, James S. ... Warsaw, IN
Butts, Jeffery Hornor ... Norfolk, VA
Butts, John W. ... Colchester, CT
Butts, Karlton C. ... Los Angeles, CA
Butts, Lampkin H. ... Laurel, MS
Butts & Lenora ... Chandler, OK
Butts, Lorraine D. ... Hartford, CT
Butts, Mark C. ... Canton, MA
Butts, Melanie C. ... Los Angeles, CA
Butts, Michael J. ... New Braunfels, TX
Butts, Michael T. ... Akron, OH
Butts, Michele R. ... Boise, ID
Butts, Nancy L. ... Williamsport, PA
Butts, Robert J., (P.C.) ... Cheboygan, MI
Butts, Robert R. ... New York, NY
Butts, Robert R. ... Poughkeepsie, NY
Stanfordville, NY
Butts, Roland E. ... Poughkeepsie, NY
Butts, Samuel Arthur, III ... Nashville, TN
Butts, Stacie L. ... Newport Beach, CA
Butts, Stephen Gilbert ... New Bedford, MA
Butts, Tamorah Christine ... Houston, TX
Butts, Terry L. ... Elba, AL
Butts, Thomas J. ... San Jose, CA
Buttweiler, Thomas, Ltd. ... St. Cloud, MN
Butz, Robert A. ... Devils Lake, ND
Buturla, Richard J. ... Milford, CT
Butuyan, Joel Ruiz ... Williamsburg, VA
Butvinik, Jeffrey I. ... Fairfax, VA
Butwin, Bradley J. ... New York, NY
Buty, Madeline L. ... Oakland, CA
Butya, Ernest ... Pittsburgh, PA
Butz, Andrew ... Washington, DC
Fairfax, VA
Butz, Carla J. ... Minneapolis, MN
Butz, David E. ... Canton, OH
Salem, OH
Butz, Donald F. ... Bakersfield, CA
Butz, Douglas M. ... Irvine, CA
San Diego, CA
Butz Dunn DeSantis & Bingham, A Professional Corporation ... Irvine, CA
San Diego, CA
Butz, Edward H. ... Allentown, PA
Butz, James A. ... Fort Wayne, IN
Butz, John R. ... Springfield, OH
Butz, Joseph T. ... Chicago, IL
Butz, Kelly P. ... Winter Haven, FL
Butz & Kraft, P.C. ... Rugby, ND
Butz, M. Kathleen ... Nevada City, CA
Butz, Mark J. ... Rugby, ND
Butz, Richard C. ... Toms River, NJ
Butz, Thomas M. ... Pittsburgh, PA
Butz, Thomas P. ... Toms River, NJ
Tuckerton, NJ
Butz, Vernon G. ... Kankakee, IL
Butz, Walter H. ... Bellevue, OH
Butzbaugh, Alfred M. ... St. Joseph, MI
Butzbaugh & Dewane, P.L.C.
St. Joseph, MI
Butzbaugh & Ehrenberg ... St. Joseph, MI
Butzbaugh, Elden W., Jr. ... St. Joseph, MI
Butzbaugh, T.D. ... Detroit, MI
Butzel, Albert K. ... New York, NY
Butzel, Laura E. ... New York, NY
Butzel Long, A Professional Corporation
Boca Raton, FL
Naples, FL
Palm Beach Gardens, FL
Ann Arbor, MI
Birmingham, MI
Detroit, MI
Grosse Pointe Farms, MI
Okemos, MI
Butzen, David Richard ... Chicago, IL
Butzen, Philip J. ... Poway, CA
Butzer, Carl C. ... Dallas, TX
Butzi, Fred F. ... Wilmington, DE
Butzier, Stuart R. ... Albuquerque, NM
Butzner, John D., Jr. ... Richmond, VA
Butzon, Christophe A. ... Jackson, MN
Buuck, David L. ... Knoxville, TN
Buus, William Lee ... Santa Ana, CA
Buvens, John L. ... Wimberley, TX
Buvens, John L., Jr. ... Houston, TX
Buvinger, Margaret S. ... Enid, OK
Buwalda, Annigje J. ... Annandale, VA
Bux, Robert J. ... Medina, OH
Bux, William John ... Dallas, TX
Houston, TX
Buxbaum, Amy M. ... Harrisburg, PA
Buxbaum & Chakmak, A Law Corporation
Claremont, CA
Newport Beach, CA
Buxbaum, David A. ... Claremont, CA
Newport Beach, CA
Buxbaum, David M. ... Oak Ridge, TN
Buxbaum, Debra A. ... Boston, MA
Buxbaum & Dix, PLLC ... Butte, MT
Helena, MT
Buxbaum, Douglas A. ... Butte, MT
Helena, MT
Buxbaum, Edward M. ... Baltimore, MD
Buxbaum, Ellen R. ... New York, NY
Buxbaum, Gloria Lynn ... Morristown, NJ
Buxbaum, Hannah L. ... Bloomington, IN
Buxbaum, James M. ... San Luis Obispo, CA
Buxbaum, Michael A. ... New York, NY
Buxbaum, Moira J. ... San Francisco, CA
Buxbaum, Richard M. ... Berkeley, CA
Buxbaum, Scott A. ... Elmsford, NY
Buxbaum, Steven A. ... Houston, TX
Buxbaum, William ... Newbury Park, CA
Buxeda, Nikos ... New York, NY
Buxman, Darrin L. ... Pueblo, CO
Buxner, Evan D. ... St. Louis, MO
Buxo, Zoraida ... San Juan, PR
Buxton, Anne P. ... United States Senate, Senatorial Assistants, GV
Buxton, Anthony W. ... Augusta, ME
Buxton, C. Michael ... Washington, DC
Buxton, Donald L. ... Sacramento, CA
Buxton, Eileen J. ... Sacramento, CA
Buxton, Fred M. ... Tulsa, OK
Buxton, George H., III ... Oak Ridge, TN
Buxton, George N. ... New York, NY
Buxton, James H. ... Edmond, OK
Buxton, Janet A. ... Denver, CO
Buxton, Joseph T., III ... Urbanna, VA
Yorktown, VA
Buxton, Joseph T., III, P.C. ... Urbanna, VA
Yorktown, VA
Buxton, Kristen R. ... Salem, MA
Buxton Law Office ... Oak Ridge, TN
Buxton, Mary Perrin ... Fort Lauderdale, FL
Buxton, Ralph W. ... Portsmouth, VA
Buxton, Renee Ann ... McHenry, IL
Buxton, Rex L. ... Eden Prairie, MN
Buxton, Robin L. ... Walnut Creek, CA
Buxton, Susan E. ... Boise, ID
Buxton, Timothy G. ... Denver, CO
Buxton, W. Robert ... San Francisco, CA
Buxton, William B. ... Duncan, OK
Buyama, Tyrus S. ... Honolulu, HI
Buyan, Robert Dean ... Irvine, CA
Buyck, Hugh Willcox ... Charleston, SC
Buyck, John A. ... Rochester, NY
Buyck, Mark W., III ... Florence, SC
Buyck, Mark W., Jr. ... Florence, SC
Buydens & Anderson, P.C. ... Detroit, MI
Buydens, Robert G. ... Detroit, MI
Buyer, Deborah Ann ... New York, NY
Buyer, Dennis ... Glenview, IL
Buyers, Russell A. ... Farmington, MI
Buyle, Kristy L. ... Overland Park, KS
Buyle, Mark P. ... Overland Park, KS
Buynak, Brian B. ... Washington, NJ
Buynak, D. Michael ... Monterey Park, CA
Buynak, Michael F. ... Kenilworth, NJ
Buynak, S. Timothy, Jr.
Santa Barbara, CA
Buyrn & Crook ... Chesapeake, VA
Buyrn, Richard L. ... Chesapeake, VA
Buyrn, William E. ... Chesapeake, VA
Buys, Cunera M. ... Chicago, IL
Buys, Kenneth R. ... Philadelphia, PA
Buyske, Marc G. ... Shelby, MT
Buysse, Cheryl A. ... Los Angeles, CA
Buysse, David F. ... Chicago, IL
Buytendyk, Michael G. ... Wooster, OH
Buyum, Curt D. ... New York, NY
Buza, Lori Ann ... Woodbridge, NJ
Buzaid, Laurence E. ... Thousand Oaks, CA
Buzaid, Lisa L. ... New Milford, CT
Buzaid, Norman A. ... Danbury, CT
Buzak, Edward J. ... Montville, NJ
Buzan, Richard P. ... McLean, VA
Buzard, A. Vincent ... Rochester, NY
Buzard, Brian L. ... Mount Morris, IL
Buzard, David A. ... Virginia Beach, VA
Buzard, Donald S. ... Milwaukee, WI
Buzard, George D., III ... Chicago, IL
Buzard, Glenn S. ... Los Angeles, CA
Buzard, Robert R. ... New York, NY
Buzard, William D., Jr. ... Spokane, WA
Buzas, John S. ... Long Beach, CA
Buzash, George E. ... Dublin, OH
Buzawa, Carl G. ... Wilmington, MA
Buzbee & Hawk, PLLC ... Little Rock, AR
Buzbee, James H., (P.A.) ... Plant City, FL
Buzbee, John P. ... Anadarko, OK
Hinton, OK
Buzbee, J.R. ... Little Rock, AR
Buzbee, Lester R., III ... Conroe, TX
Buzbee & Upchurch ... Anadarko, OK
Hinton, OK
Buzby, Anne K. ... Jacksonville, FL
St. Augustine, FL
Buzby, Brian L. ... Columbus, OH
Buzecky, Jennifer Drury ... Milwaukee, WI
Buzek, Vincent J. ... Broomfield, CO
Buzgon, Bernerd A. ... Lebanon, PA
Buzgon, Davis, Ltd. ... Lebanon, PA
Buzhardt, Joseph R., III
United States Senate, Committee Legal Personnel, GV
Buzin, Heath T. ... New York, NY
Buzin, Randi M. ... New York, NY
Buzin, Stephen H. ... Oklahoma City, OK
Buzo, William R. ... Lexington, KY
Buzogany, J. Barry ... Malvern, PA
Buzulencia, Michael D. ... Warren, OH
Buzunis, Constantine D. ... San Diego, CA
Buzydlowski, Frank P. ... Philadelphia, PA
Buzza, E. John ... Stevens Point, WI
Buzzanca, Kristen Marie ... Lakeland, FL
Lake Wales, FL
Winter Haven, FL
Buzzard & Allen ... Olympia, WA
Buzzard, Erik D. ... Irvine, CA
Buzzard, Gene C. ... Tulsa, OK
Buzzard, J. David ... East Liverpool, OH
Buzzard, Jerome L. ... Olympia, WA
Buzzard Law Firm, A Professional Corporation
Pampa, TX
Buzzard, Lynn Robert ... Buies Creek, NC
Buzzard, Mark N. ... Pampa, TX
Buzzard, Robert A. ... Lillington, NC
Buzzard, Steven R. ... Centralia, WA
Buzzard, Vanessa A. ... Pampa, TX
Buzzell, Arthur L. ... Davenport, IA
Buzzell, Charles M. ... San Francisco, CA
Buzzell, David W. ... Philadelphia, PA
Buzzell, Graham & Welsh ... Macon, GA
Milledgeville, GA
Buzzell, Joseph F. ... Melville, NY
Mineola, NY
Buzzell, R. William ... Macon, GA
Buzzell, Stephen L. ... Saranac Lake, NY
Buzzelli, Laurence F. ... Cleveland, OH
Buzzelli, Russell A. ... Akron, OH
Buzzello, Eileen R. ... Omaha, NE
Buzzendore, Robert L. ... York, PA
Buzzett, William Archer ... Tallahassee, FL
Buzzetta, Daniel J. ... New York, NY
Buzzetti, Albert L. ... Englewood Cliffs, NJ
Buzzetti, Lisa M. ... Tampa, FL
Buzzi, Paul F. ... Akron, OH
Buzzi, William P. ... Pittsburgh, PA
Buzzini, Bertram G. ... Sacramento, CA
Buzzinotti, Elaine M. ... Pittsburgh, PA
Buzzy, George E. ... Halifax, VA
Byabagye, Juliet K. ... Mountain View, CA
Byalin, Joan Tenzer ... Albany, NY
Byam, Clark R., (P.C.) ... Pasadena, CA
Byam, Clayton ... Omaha, NE
Byam & Hoarty ... Omaha, NE
Byam, John T. ... Washington, DC
Byam, Joseph C. ... Omaha, NE
Byard, Paul S. ... New York, NY
Byard, Robert Reed ... Columbus, OH
Byarlay, Thomas W. ... Little Rock, AR
Byars, Alex ... Columbus, GA
Byars, Ann Bishop ... Atlanta, GA
Byars, Custis M. ... Charleston, SC
Byars, G. Rice, Jr. ... Memphis, TN
Byars, George S. ... Jasper, AL
Byars, Joe D., Jr. ... Fort Smith, AR
Byars, Roy William ... Tulsa, OK
Byars, Samuel D. ... Austin, TX
Byars, Walter R. ... Montgomery, AL
Byars, Whitney J. ... Jackson, MS
Byars, William R., Jr. ... Camden, SC
Byars, Wilton V., III ... Oxford, MS
Byassee, Jean L. ... Nashville, TN
Byassee, William Sam ... Raleigh, NC
Byassee, Wm. David ... Denver, CO
Bybee, Charles D. ... Denver, CO
Bybee, D. Kirk ... Pocatello, ID
Bybee, David A.
Department of Justice, GV
Bybee, Don L. ... Salt Lake City, UT
Bybee, Duane A. ... Pocatello, ID
Bybee, Edward J. ... Honolulu, HI
Bybee, Elizabeth Bashaw ... Anderson, IN
Bybee, Gerald G. ... Amarillo, TX
Bybee, Jack D. ... Walnut Creek, CA
Bybee, Jay S. ... Baton Rouge, LA
Bybee, John M. ... Farmington, UT
Bybee, Michael E. ... Birmingham, AL
Bybee, Richard D. ... Charleston, SC
Bybee, Robert B. ... Walnut Creek, CA
Bybee, Sally J. ... Dallas, TX
Bybee, Shannon L., Jr. ... Las Vegas, NV
Bybel, Nicholas, Jr. ... Harrisburg, PA
Byberg, Gregory B. ... Beverly Hills, CA
Bycel, Benjamin ... Los Angeles, CA
Byck, Edwin R. ... Savannah, GA
Byck, Harrison Ross ... Cherry Hill, NJ
Bala Cynwyd, PA
Byck, Larry S. ... Marlton, NJ
Bycraft, John T. ... Chicago, IL
Byczek, Christopher S ... Lake Success, NY
Bydalek, David T. ... Lincoln, NE
Bydalek, Michael K. ... Omaha, NE
Byde, Jennifer N. ... Salt Lake City, UT
Byde, Sheldon E. ... Salt Lake City, UT
Bye, B. Iver ... Phelan, CA
Bye, Chuck ... River Falls, WI
Bye, David ... Fort Collins, CO
Bye, Don L. ... Duluth, MN
Bye, Don L., P.A. ... Duluth, MN
Bye, Dori N. ... New Haven, CT
Bye, Gareth D. ... Hartford, CT
Bye, Goff & Rohde, Ltd. ... River Falls, WI
Bye, Howard D. ... San Antonio, TX
Bye, James E. ... Denver, CO
Bye, Jonathan M. ... Minneapolis, MN
Bye, Kermit Edward ... Fargo, ND
Bye, Richard L. ... Duluth, MN
Bye, Robert A. ... Shawnee, KS
Bye, Roland E. ... Irvine, CA
Bye, Vaccaro & Winsten LLP ... Irvine, CA
Byelas, Leslie ... Westport, CT
Byelick, Robert P. ... St. Petersburg, FL
Tampa, FL
Byer, Albert A. ... Summit, NJ
New York, NY
Byer, Andrew A. ... Fort Lauderdale, FL
Byer & Byer ... Anderson, IN
Byer, C. William, Jr. ... Anderson, IN
Byer, David J. ... Boston, MA
Byer, Evan Jay ... Miami, FL
Byer, Jeffrey M. ... San Diego, CA
Byer, Joan L. ... Louisville, KY
Byer, Matthew R. ... St. Louis, MO
Byer, Peter ... New York, NY
Byer, Robert L. ... Pittsburgh, PA
Byer, Timothy G. ... Los Angeles, CA
Byer, Valerie K. ... Glendale, CA
Byer, Willard E., Jr. ... West Orange, NJ
Byer, William, Sr. ... Anderson, IN
Byergo, Anthony B. ... Chicago, IL
Byerley, David C. ... Kansas City, MO
Byerley, Mary Ruth ... Wichita, KS
Byerley, Thomas K. ... Niles, MI
Byerly, Bruce L. ... Portland, OR
Byerly, David S. ... Greenbelt, MD
Byerly, James A. ... Houston, TX
Byerly, John A. ... Aspinwall, PA
Byerly Law Offices ... High Point, NC
Byerly, Lisa M. ... Menlo Park, CA
Byerly, Radford ... Houston, TX
Byerly, Steven E. ... High Point, NC
Byerly, T. Edw. ... Timonium, MD
Byerly, W. B. Jack, Jr. ... High Point, NC
Byerly-Padden, Jean-Marie ... Baltimore, MD
Byers, Adrienne M. ... Los Angeles, CA
Byers, Andrew Robert ... Lake Orion, MI
Byers, Boyd A. ... Wichita, KS
Byers, Bruce K. ... Ridgewood, NJ
Middlebury, VT
Byers & Byers, P.A. ... Ridgewood, NJ
Byers, Carl N. ... Salem, OR
Byers, Charlotte ... New York, NY
Byers, Christopher D. ... Ridgewood, NJ
Byers, Christopher L. ... San Francisco, CA
Byers, David A. ... Dearborn, MI
Byers, David C. ... Encino, CA
Byers, David E. ... Tulsa, OK
Byers, David J. ... Burlingame, CA
Byers, David J. ... Sparta, MI
Byers, David L. ... Beech Grove, IN
Byers, David W. ... Sacramento, CA
Byers, David W. ... Plano, TX
Byers, Duane M. ... Arlington, VA
Byers, Frank H., II ... Decatur, IL
Byers, Frank H., II, Ltd. ... Decatur, IL
Byers, Frank S. ... Joliet, IL
Byers, Fred C., Jr. ... New York, NY
Byers, Fritz ... Toledo, OH
Byers, Garrick A. ... Fresno, CA
Byers, Gary L. ... Maumee, OH
Byers, H. Steven ... Humble, TX
Byers, Henry E. ... Rochester, NY
Byers, J. Darren, A Prof. Assoc., Law Offices of ... Winston-Salem, NC
Byers, James Darren ... Winston-Salem, NC
Byers, James T. ... Roseland, NJ
Byers, Jane ... St. Louis, MO
Byers, Jay C. ... Round Rock, TX
Byers, Jay R. ... Indianapolis, IN
Byers, Jeri DeMontford ... Anchorage, AK
Byers, Joan H. ... Raleigh, NC
Byers, John K. ... Knoxville, TN
Byers, John M. ... Milwaukee, WI
Byers, John R. ... Jacksonville, FL
Byers, Jonathan R. ... Bismarck, ND
Byers, Kevin P. ... Columbus, OH
Byers, Kevin P., Co., LPA ... Columbus, OH
Byers & Lyden, A Professional Corporation
Agoura Hills, CA
Byers, Matthew T. ... Carlsbad, NM
Byers, Michael A. ... Columbus, OH
Byers, Michael W. ... Agoura Hills, CA
Byers, Nisha Poth ... Dallas, TX
Byers, Paul R. ... Aurora, IN
Byers, Rhonda ... Atlanta, GA
Byers, Robbie A. ... Tupelo, MS
Byers, Robert D. ... San Antonio, TX
Byers, Robin A. ... Boulder, CO
Byers, Robt. J. ... Jackson, MI
Byers, Ronald G. ... Independence, MO
Byers, Shauna L. ... Portland, OR
Byers, Shirley C. ... Greenville, MS
Byers, Stephen M. ... Washington, DC
Byers, Thomas L. ... Tulsa, OK
Byers, Torrie M. ... Pasadena, CA
Byers, Vic L., III ... Bakersfield, CA
Byers, Wayne C. ... Houston, TX
Byers, William F. ... Northridge, CA
Byers, William R. ... Adel, IA
Byers-Emmerling, Melissa
East Liverpool, OH
Byerts, Robert C. ... Tallahassee, FL
Byford, Kenneth W. ... Fort Worth, TX
Byford, Kenneth W., P.C., Law Firm of
Fort Worth, TX
Byham, Edgar K. ... New York, NY
Byington, Alberto, Jr. ... Palacios, TX
San Antonio, TX
Byington, Dennis R. ... Burley, ID
Byington, Holloway, Whipple & Jones, Chartered ... Burley, ID
Byington, Janice M. ... Corpus Christi, TX
Byington, John H., III ... Mineola, NY
Byington, John H., Jr. ... New York, NY
Byington, Lisa M. ... McLean, VA
Byington, Robert L. ... Hastings, MI
Byington, William W., Jr. ... Rome, GA
Byk, Joseph J., Jr. ... Peterborough, NH
Bykerk, Donald N. ... Prague, OK
Bykofsky, Irving R. ... Boca Raton, FL
Bykowski, Anthony ... Bloomington, IL
Byl, John V. ... Grand Rapids, MI
Bylenga, Dan E., Jr. ... Grand Rapids, MI
Bylenga, Thomas L. ... Kentwood, MI
Byler, Alex M. ... Pendleton, OR
Byler, Anthony L. ... Philadelphia, PA
Byler, Celia S. ... Westborough, MA
Byler, Charles A. ... Department of Justice, Drug Enforcement Administration, GV
Byler, Gary C., The Law Office of
Virginia Beach, VA
Byler Goldman Goodley Winkle & Hetrick
Lancaster, PA
Byler, J. Daryl ... Meridian, MS
Byler, Janet Sharpe ... Huntington, NY
Byler, Philip A. ... New York, NY
Byler, W. Bryan ... Lancaster, PA
Byles, Daniel W ... Nutley, NJ
Byles, Deborah A. ... Fort Lauderdale, FL
Bylinsky, Gregory E. ... New York, NY
Bylsma, Jon M. ... Grand Rapids, MI
Bylsma, Michael S. ... Treasury Department, Office of the Comptroller of the Currency, GV

Byrne, Sean M. ... Chicago, IL
Byrne, Sean P. ... Detroit, MI
Byrne, Sean P. ... Richmond, VA
Byrne, Shane M. ... San Francisco, CA
Byrne, Sheri A. ... San Francisco, CA
Byrne, Steven ... Farmington, CT
Byrne, Stewart C. ... Houston, TX
Byrne & Storm, P.C. ... Hartford, CT
Byrne, Suzanne R. ... New York, NY
Byrne, Tara A. ... New York, NY
Byrne, Terrence B. ... Baltimore, MD
Byrne, Terrence J. ... Fresno, CA
Byrne, Terrence J. ... Wausau, WI
Byrne, Theodore P. ... Las Vegas, NV
Byrne, Thomas ... Morristown, NJ
Byrne, Thomas E. ... Castle Rock, CO
Byrne, Thomas E. ... Arlington, VA
Byrne, Thomas F. ... Santa Rosa, CA
Byrne, Thomas J. ... Denver, CO
Byrne, Thomas J. ... Bridgeport, CT
Byrne, Thomas J. ... Lansing, MI
Byrne, Thomas J. ... Goshen, NY
Byrne, Thomas J. ... New York, NY
Byrne, Thomas J. ... Columbus, OH
Byrne, Thomas J., Jr. ... St. Louis, MO
Byrne, Thomas M. ... Beverly Hills, CA
Byrne, Thomas M. ... Atlanta, GA
Byrne, Thomas M. ... St. Louis, MO
Byrne, Thomas P. ... San Francisco, CA
Byrne, Thomas P. ... Farmington, CT
Byrne, Timothy J. ... Princeton, NJ
Byrne, Victoria ... Chicago, IL
Byrne, Walter R., Jr. ... Lexington, KY
Byrne, William ... New Orleans, LA
Byrne, William B. ... Catskill, NY
Byrne, William E. ... Cameron Park, CA
Byrne, William M., Jr. ... Los Angeles, CA
Byrne, William P. ... New York, NY
Byrne, William T. ... West Orange, NJ
Byrne, William T. ... New York, NY
Byrne, Wm. D. ... Monona, WI
Byrnes, Andrew C. ... Palo Alto, CA
Byrnes, B. Rebecca ... Oakland, CA
Byrnes, Bernard C. ... New York, NY
Byrnes, Brian D ... Amery, WI
Byrnes, Bruce J. ... New York, NY
Byrnes, Bryant H. ... Oakland, CA
Byrnes, Cynthia C. ... Salem, OR
Byrnes, Daniel M. ... Amery, WI
Byrnes, Daniel P. ... Braintree, MA
Byrnes, David A. ... Los Angeles, CA
Byrnes, David F. ... San Francisco, CA
Byrnes, Deborah Sweet ... Towson, MD
Byrnes, Debra A. ... Patchogue, NY
Byrnes, Dennis P. ... Cleveland, OH
Byrnes, Diane Marie Soccorso ... Melrose, MA
Byrnes, Don R. ... Houston, TX
Byrnes, Donald J. ... Altoona, PA
Byrnes, Edward J. ... Wilmington, MA
Byrnes, Elbert N. ... New Orleans, LA
Byrnes, Gentry B. ... St. Petersburg, FL
Byrnes, George T. ... Fargo, ND
Byrnes, J. Norris ... Towson, MD
Byrnes, James ... San Diego, CA
Byrnes, James J. ... Union, NJ
Byrnes, James L.
Department Of The Interior, Office of Hearings & Appeals, GV
Byrnes, James M. ... Chicago, IL
Byrnes, James M. ... Rochester, NY
Byrnes, Jo Anne ... Flemington, NJ
Byrnes, John ... New York, NY
Byrnes, John Carroll ... Baltimore, MD
Byrnes, John E. ... Vienna, VA
Byrnes, John R. ... Sayville, NY
Byrnes, John R. ... Milwaukee, WI
Byrnes, John S., Jr. ... Alhambra, CA
Byrnes, John T., Jr. ... Washington, DC
Byrnes, Joseph L. ... Santa Ana, CA
Byrnes & Keller, LLP ... Seattle, WA
Byrnes, Kevin P. ... Charlotte, NC
Byrnes, Lawrence I. ... Beachwood, OH
Byrnes, Lawrence P. ... Blue Bell, PA
Byrnes, Leo A. ... Brewster, MA
Byrnes, Logan B. ... Los Angeles, CA
Byrnes, Martha C. ... Salt Lake City, UT
Byrnes, Michael J. ... Ann Arbor, MI
Byrnes, Michael T. ... Milwaukee, WI
Byrnes, Nathan A. ... Springfield, MA
Byrnes, Noelle Anne ... Boston, MA
Byrnes, Norman T. ... Boston, MA
Byrnes, Pamela G. ... Ypsilanti, MI
Byrnes, Patricia G. ... Lyndhurst, NJ
Byrnes, Peter D. ... Seattle, WA
Byrnes & Reish, P.C. ... Ypsilanti, MI
Byrnes, Richard J. ... Woodbridge, NJ
Byrnes, Robert E. ... Los Angeles, CA
Byrnes, Robert F. ... Scottsdale, AZ
Byrnes, Robert J. ... Brooklyn, NY
Byrnes, Ronald G. ... Houston, TX
Byrnes, Sean F. ... Red Bank, NJ
Byrnes, Sondra J. ... Chicago, IL
Byrnes, Stacey M. ... Beverly Hills, CA
Byrnes & Sullivan ... New York, NY
Byrnes, Thomas J. ... Department of Justice, Civil Division, GV
Byrnes, Thomas N., Jr. ... Quincy, MA
Byrnes, Thomas Scott ... Beverly Hills, CA
Byrnes, Timothy J. ... Turtle Lake, WI
Byrnes, Timothy R. ... Anchorage, AK
Byrnes, Virginia ... Crownpoint, NM
Byrnes, William ... Manasquan, NJ
Byrnes, William F. ... Los Angeles, CA
Byrnes, William G. ... Washington, DC
Byrnes, William J. ... Timonium, MD
Byrnes, William J. ... McLean, VA
Byrnes-Ales, Sylvia K. ... Joplin, MO
Byrns, Amy Ejercito ... Honolulu, HI
Byrns, Chester J. ... St. Joseph, MI
Byrns, Lisa Ann ... New York, NY
Byrns, William C. ... Honolulu, HI
Byrns, Zack H. ... Merritt Island, FL
Byrom, Chris Scott ... Oklahoma City, OK
Byrom, Christina M ... Waterbury, VT
Byrom, Donald H. ... Jamestown, KY
Byrom, James E. ... Austin, TX
Byrom, Jennifer ... Milton, FL
Byrom, Joe A. ... Dallas, TX
Byrom, Robert G. ... Columbus, OH
Byron, Barry M. ... Willoughby, OH
Byron, Barry M., Co., L.P.A.
Willoughby, OH
Byron, C. Elton, Jr. ... Beckley, WV
Byron, Chris ... New Bedford, MA
Byron, Christopher W. ... St. Louis, MO
Byron, Daniel P. ... Indianapolis, IN
Byron, David J. ... Fremont, CA
Byron, David J. ... Minneapolis, MN
Byron, Deborah A. ... Fresno, CA
Byron, Earl T. ... Chicago, IL
Byron, H. Joseph ... Philadelphia, PA
Byron, H. Thomas, III
Department of Justice, Civil Division, GV
Byron, Harvey E. ... Los Angeles, CA
Byron, Herbert Mark ... Los Angeles, CA
Byron, James R. ... Elkhart, IN
Mishawaka, IN
Byron, Jana ... New York, NY
Byron, John E. ... Aurora, CO
Byron, John P. ... Minneapolis, MN
Byron, Keith P. ... Poughkeepsie, NY
Byron, Leo J. ... Fergus Falls, MN
Byron, Linda ... Columbus, OH
Byron, Michael J. ... Janesville, WI
Byron, Michael R. ... Philadelphia, PA
Byron, Nicholas G. ... Edwardsville, IL
Byron, Paul G. ... Orlando, FL
Byron, Ricardo A. ... Philadelphia, PA
Byron, Richard J. ... Wausau, WI
Byron, Richard M. ... Dallas, TX
Byron, Robert E., Jr. ... East Hartford, CT
Byron, Robert G. ... Chicago, IL
Byron, Robert W. ... Binghamton, NY
Byron & Roberts ... Owingsville, KY
Byron, Roger A. ... Owingsville, KY
Byron, Stephen L. ... Willoughby, OH
Byron, Stuart D. ... New York, NY
Byron, Susan A. ... Tampa, FL
Byron, Theresa A. ... Radnor, PA
Byron, Thomas W. ... San Diego, CA
Las Vegas, NV
Byrtus, Paul H. ... Department Of The Interior, Office of Hearings & Appeals, GV
Byrum, Charles L. ... Chicago, IL
Byrum, David E. ... Charlotte, NC
Byrum, Douglas S. ... Indianapolis, IN
Byrum, Henry C., Jr. ... Charlotte, NC
Byrum & Holland, LLP ... Bakersfield, CA
Byrum, James A., Jr. ... Wheeling, WV
Byrum, Jill Quattlebaum ... New Bern, NC
Byrum, John K., Jr. ... Richmond, VA
Byrum, Kenneth M. ... Bakersfield, CA
Byrum Law Offices, P.C. ... Alexandria, VA
Byrum, Lesa L. ... Washington, DC
Byrum, Mark W., Jr. ... Alexandria, VA
Byrum, Marni E. ... Arlington, VA
Byrum, Porter B. ... Charlotte, NC
Byrum, Richard W. ... Kansas City, MO
Byrum, Robert G. ... Chesapeake, VA
Byrum, Thomas G. ... Wheeling, WV
Byrum, William K. ... Indianapolis, IN
Byse, Clark ... Cambridge, MA
Byset, J. Fred ... Manassas, VA
Bysfield & Bysfield ... Prairie Village, KS
Bysfield, Frank E., III ... Prairie Village, KS
Bysfield, Todd Andrew ... Prairie Village, KS
Bysiewicz, Karen ... Princeton, NJ
Bysshe, Frederick H., Jr., Law Offices of
Ventura, CA
Bystrom, Carl E. ... Brunswick, GA
Bystrom, Carl E., Co., L.P.A.
Brunswick, GA
Bystrom, Frederick C. ... Simi Valley, CA
Bystrom, Keith ... Norman, OK
Bystrowski, Robert S. ... Hartford, CT
Bystrynski, William B. ... Raleigh, NC
Bytof, Linda R. ... San Francisco, CA
Byun, Chai B. ... Los Angeles, CA
Byun, Il Young ... San Diego, CA
Byung-Cho Chang, Kenneth
La Canada Flintridge, CA
Byvoets, Simone ... Chicago, IL
Bywater, Douglas E. ... Washington, DC
Vienna, VA
Bywater, Gordon E. ... Las Vegas, NV
Bywater, Joseph G. ... Lakeland, FL
Bywater, Stephen A. ... Burley, ID
Bywaters, Phyllis K. ... Houston, TX
Bzdok, Christopher M. ... Traverse City, MI
Bzdyk, Karen L. ... Miami, FL
Bzura, Adrienne J. ... North Plainfield, NJ

Caamano, Daniel ... St. Petersburg, FL
Cabada, José A. ... Austin, TX
Cabal, Alvaro A.
Panama Canal Commission, Office of the General Counsel, GV
Caballero, Alberto ... Harrington Park, NJ
Caballero, Alexander ... Tampa, FL
Caballero, Anna M. ... Salinas, CA
Caballero, Dilia M. ... Washington, DC
Caballero, George ... New York, NY
Caballero, George G. ... Baton Rouge, LA
Caballero, Horace R. ... San Diego, CA
Caballero, John H. ... Santa Fe Springs, CA
Caballero, Marcia B. ... Miami, FL
Caballero, Mario ... San Antonio, TX
Caballero, Matcham & McCarthy, A Professional Partnership ... Salinas, CA
Caballero, Michael J. ... Treasury Department, Departmental Offices, GV
Caballero, Michele S. ... Lake Charles, LA
Caballero, Pilar ... Tampa, FL
Caballero, Richard ... Panorama City, CA
Caballero, Rick A. ... Baton Rouge, LA
Caballero, Thomas Edward
Department of Justice, Civil Division, GV
Cabán, Mildred ... San Juan, PR
Cabana, Douglas R. ... Boonton, NJ
Cabanas, Dante Alconcel
San Bernardino, CA
Cabanas, Karen K. ... Key West, FL
Cabanas, Oscar J. ... Miami, FL
Cabañas, Roberto L. ... San Juan, PR
Cabanday, Orlando F. ... Beverly Hills, CA
Cabanel, Lawrence A. ... Philadelphia, PA
Cabanillas Galiano, E. A. ... Mayaguez, PR
Cabaniss & Adkins, A Professional Association ... Atlanta, GA
Cabaniss, Boyce C. ... Austin, TX
Cabaniss, Charles D. ... Dallas, TX
Cabaniss, David B. ... Albany, NY
Cabaniss, Ellis ... Clinton, OK
Cabaniss, George M., Jr. ... Atlanta, GA
Cabaniss, John C., Law Office of
Milwaukee, WI
Cabaniss, John T. ... Houston, TX
Cabaniss, Johnston, Gardner, Dumas & O'Neal ... Birmingham, AL
Gulf Shores, AL
Mobile, AL
Cabaniss, Joseph W. ... Charleston, SC
Cabaniss, Judith M. ... Albuquerque, NM
Cabaniss, Kevin C. ... Dallas, TX
Cabaniss, McDonald, Smith & Wiggins, P.A.
Orlando, FL
Atlanta, GA
Cabaniss, Ronald E. ... Orlando, FL
Cabaniss, Thomas E. ... Charlotte, NC
Cabanski, Robert W. ... Toledo, OH
Cabanski-Evers, Mary ... Palo Alto, CA
Cabarrocas, Jaime ... Forest Hills, NY
Cabassa, Angela Carter ... Lutz, FL
Cabassa, Luis ... Tampa, FL
Cabassa-Sauri, Leopoldo J. ... San Juan, PR
Cabasso, Sheryl L. ... New York, NY
Cabatic, Linda A. ... Sacramento, CA
Cabbage, Elwin F. ... Hutchinson, KS
Cabbell, Diane Benedict ... Ann Arbor, MI
Cabbibo, Ronald ... Park Ridge, NJ
Cabble, Robert H. ... Hauppauge, NY
Cabe, James Y. ... Franklin, NC
Cabe, James Y., P.A. ... Franklin, NC
Cabe Law Offices ... Sacramento, CA
Cabe, Meredith Elizabeth
Executive Office Of The President, GV
Cabe, Paige C. ... Wilmington, NC
Cabe, Phillip A. ... Sacramento, CA
Cabe, Robert D. ... Little Rock, AR
Cabe, Williams & Slusser, P.A.
Wilmington, NC
Cabeca, Anthony John Vieira ... Boston, MA
Cabell, Andrea Elaine ... Gulfport, MS
Cabell, Benjamin, IV ... Newark, DE
Cabell, Charles L. ... Richmond, VA
Cabell, Diane Thilly ... Boston, MA
Cabell, Donald L. ... Boston, MA
Cabell, Nathaniel W. ... Charleston, SC
Cabell, R. Baird ... Franklin, VA
Cabell, Robert, & Associates
Powhatan, VA
Richmond, VA
Cabell, Royal E., Jr. ... Manakin-Sabot, VA
Cabell, Temple W. ... Norfolk, VA
Richmond, VA
Cabell, Walter B. ... Los Angeles, CA
Cabell, William ... Kilmarnock, VA
Cabello, Rufino ... Carrizo Springs, TX
Cabelly, Alan S. ... Elmhurst, NY
Cabert, Dianne E. ... Mount Vernon, WA
Cabes, Robert J., (P.C.) ... Lafayette, LA
Cabey, Edwin H. ... Chicago, IL
Cabeza, Manuel E., (P.A.) ... Coral Gables, FL
Cabeza, Orlando ... Miami, FL
Cabezas, Fabio R. ... Irvine, CA
Cabezas-Gil, Rosa M., P.C.
San Antonio, TX
Cabezas-Gil, Rosa Maria ... San Antonio, TX
Cabi, Lisa Cerino ... San Francisco, CA
Cabianca, Brian A. ... Phoenix, AZ
Cabianca, Daniel R. ... Houston, TX
Cabibi and Cabibi, A Professional Law Corporation ... Metairie, LA
Cabibi, Charles E., Jr. ... Metairie, LA
Cabibi, S. Philip ... Pueblo, CO
Cabillot, Jean Marie ... Santa Monica, CA
Cabiness, R. Flay ... Brunswick, GA
Cabitt, Jill I. ... Boston, MA
Cabiya Morales, Jose L. ... San Juan, PR
Cablao, Elena N. ... Austin, TX
Cable, Chad ... Sulphur Springs, TX
Cable, Curtis W. ... Sacramento, CA
Cable, Dale Aaron ... Pittsburgh, PA
Cable & Dobnicker ... Lima, OH
Cable, Donald A. ... Seattle, WA
Cable, Howard W., Jr. ... Akron, OH
Cable Huston Benedict Haagensen & Lloyd LLP ... Corvallis, OR
Portland, OR
Cable, J. Franklin, P.C. ... Portland, OR
Cable, J. Laurence ... Portland, OR
Cable, Jane ... New London, CT
Cable, Langenbach, Kinerk & Bauer, LLP
Seattle, WA
Cable, Michael A. ... San Francisco, CA
Cable, Michael W. ... Ivanhoe, MN
Lake Benton, MN
Marshall, MN
Cable, Monte B. ... Joplin, MO
Cable, Neil A. ... Seattle, WA
Cable, Patrice E. ... Bremerton, WA
Cable, Randall L. ... Indianapolis, IN
Cable, Ronald G. ... Des Moines, IA
Cable, Stuart M. ... Boston, MA
Cable, Susan Kathryn ... Rochester, NY
Cable, W. Thomas ... Dallas, GA
Cabler, Roy William, III ... Brownsville, TX
Cabler, Thomas B. "Dale"
Spartanburg, SC
Cabodi, K. J. ... Laguna Niguel, CA
Caborn, David A. ... Columbus, OH
Caborn, Michael Craig ... Maitland, FL
Cabos, Julie A. ... Los Angeles, CA
Cabot, Anthony N. ... Las Vegas, NV
Cabot, Cesar C. ... Hagåtña, GU
Cabot, Charles C., Jr. ... Boston, MA
Cabot, Christopher ... Boston, MA
Cabot, Edward S. ... Brooklyn, NY
Cabot, Elizabeth A. ... Detroit, MI
Cabot, George S. ... Walnut Creek, CA
Cabot, Howard Ross ... Phoenix, AZ
Cabot, Katherine H. ... Cortez, CO
Cabot Law Offices ... Millbrae, CA
Cabot, Linwood ... Fort Lauderdale, FL
Cabot, Mitchell S. ... Chicago, IL
Cabot, Rochelle ... Millbrae, CA
Cabot, Sarah S. ... Boston, MA
Cabot, Stephen J. ... Philadelphia, PA
Cabotaje, Michael A. ... Los Angeles, CA
Cabou, Christian G. ... Waukesha, WI
Cabou, Julie L. ... Milwaukee, WI
Cabra, Edwin L. ... Leesville, LA
Cabraal, Shirin H. ... Milwaukee, WI
Cabraja, Kathleen J. ... Pittsburgh, PA
Cabraja & Silverberg, P.C.
Pittsburgh, PA
Cabral, Alan B. ... Los Angeles, CA
Cabral, Alfonso Sonny ... Denver, CO
Cabral, Alfred A. ... Richmond, CA
Cabral, Allen M. ... Akron, OH
Cabral, Andrea J. ... Boston, MA
Cabral, Bernardo J. ... New Bedford, MA
Cabral & Cabral ... Metairie, LA
Cabral, Carlos C. ... Los Angeles, CA
Cabral, Charlene Denise Oliveira
Framingham, MA
Cabral, Douglas M. ... New Bedford, MA
Cabral, Elizabeth A. ... Juneau, AK
Cabral, Harry Craig ... Metairie, LA
Cabral, Harry R., Jr. ... Metairie, LA
Cabral, Kristin A. ... Department of Justice, Civil Division, GV
Cabral, Michael Joseph ... Los Angeles, CA
Cabral, Miles America ... Denver, CO
Cabral, Natalie ... New Bedford, MA
Cabral, Neal J. ... Washington, DC
Cabral, Susan C. ... Salisbury, MD
Cabral, Suzanne T. ... Tracy, CA
Cabral, Ted M. ... Modesto, CA
Cabral, Theresa L. ... San Ramon, CA
Cabral, Thomas J. ... Cleveland, OH
Cabral-Daniels, René
Department Of Health And Human Services, Office of the General Counsel, GV
Cabrales, Carlos A. ... New York, NY
Cabrales, David G. ... Dallas, TX
Cabral-Mackenzie, Lisa M.
Buzzards Bay, MA
Cabranes, Jose A. ... New Haven, CT
Cabraser, Elizabeth J. ... San Francisco, CA
Cabrera, Anna M. ... New York, NY
Cabrera, Anthony S. ... Atlanta, GA
Cabrera, Charles R. ... San Francisco, CA
Cabrera, Esmeralda ... New York, NY
Cabrera, Guillermo ... San Diego, CA
Cabrera, Henry Garcia, Jr. ... Tucson, AZ
Cabrera, Ivan F. ... Fort Lauderdale, FL
Cabrera, Ivonne M. ... New York, NY
Cabrera, Jacqueline ... New York, NY
Cabrera, Joel ... Chicago, IL
Cabrera, Joseph, Jr. ... Springfield, MA
Cabrera, Juan E., Jr. ... Houston, TX
Cabrera, Karen Ocasio ... San Juan, PR
Cabrera, Orlando J. ... Miami, FL
Cabrera, Pamela J. ... Bolton, CT
Cabrera, Peter R. ... Indio, CA
Cabrera, Raul D. ... Miami, FL
Cabrera, Ricardo C. ... Miami, FL
Cabrera, Rodney ... Alexandria, LA
Cabrera, Rose I. ... Santa Monica, CA
Cabrera-Arana, Arianna M.
Fort Lauderdale, FL
Cabrera-Rodriguez, Orlando
San Juan, PR
Cabreré, Eleanor P. ... Chicago, IL
Cabret, Maria M.
Christiansted, St. Croix, VI
Cabrey, Brian J., Law Offices of
Jacksonville, FL
Cabrinha, Neal A. ... San Jose, CA
Cabush, Thomas A. ... Milwaukee, WI
Cacace, Karen ... San Francisco, CA
Cacace, Michael J. ... Stamford, CT
Cacace, Perry A. ... New York, NY
Cacace, Tusch & Santagata ... Stamford, CT
Cacace-Coyne, Bridget ... New York, NY
Cacace-Diggini, Susan Marie
White Plains, NY
Cacavas, Elena ... Brooklyn, NY
Caccamise, William C., Jr. ... New York, NY

Cagle, Mary Terpstra .... Miami, FL
Cagle, Michael R. .... Lake Charles, LA
Cagle, Molly .... Austin, TX
Cagle, Peter B. .... Miami, FL
Cagle, R. Hunter .... Knoxville, TN
Cagle, Ralph M. .... Madison, WI
Cagle, Richard A. .... Alton, IL
Cagle, Stephen H. .... Houston, TX
Cagle, Timothy R. .... Methuen, MA
Cagle, William B. .... Asheville, NC
Cagley, James J. .... Rockville, MD
Caglianone, Jeffrey A. .... Brooksville, FL
Tampa, FL
Caglianone & Miller, P.A. .... Brooksville, FL
Tampa, FL
Cagliostro, Anthony .... Schenectady, NY
Cagliotti, Michael .... Washington, DC
Cagna, Robert A. .... Washington, DC
Cagnassola, Gregory J. .... Indianapolis, IN
Cagnetta, Steven J. .... Boston, MA
Cagney, Gail .... Pittsburgh, PA
Cagney, Joan .... Bronx, NY
Cagney, Joseph B. .... Evanston, IL
Cagney, Lawrence K. .... New York, NY
Cagney, Mary Ellen .... Chicago, IL
Cagney, Richard B., Jr. .... Houston, TX
Cagney, William C. .... Iselin, NJ
New York, NY
Cagney, William P., III .... Delray Beach, FL
Chicago, IL
Cagney, William P., III, P.A.
Delray Beach, FL
Chicago, IL
Cagnoli, Joseph, Jr. .... Norristown, PA
Cagnoli, Sheryl A.
United States Postal Service,
Law Department, GV
Cahal, Mac F. .... Prairie Village, KS
Cahalan, Christina .... Nashville, TN
Cahalan, Geo. M. .... Oakland, CA
Cahalan, James L. .... Schaumburg, IL
Cahalan, James T. .... Sacramento, CA
Cahalan, Jordan Lee .... Sacramento, CA
Cahalan, Lynn Theresa .... Northport, NY
Cahalan, Richard D. .... Los Angeles, CA
Cahalan, Robert P .... Syracuse, NY
Cahalan, Scott D. .... Atlanta, GA
Cahalan, Suzanne M. .... Wheaton, IL
Cahalan, Thomas C. .... Newark, NJ
Cahalane, Denise K. .... Boston, MA
Cahalane, Patrick H. .... Manasquan, NJ
Cahalane, Vincent P. .... Brockton, MA
Cahalane, Vincent P., P.C. .... Brockton, MA
Middleboro, MA
Plymouth, MA
Quincy, MA
Taunton, MA
Cahalin, Philip H. .... Boston, MA
Cahalin, Philip H. .... Middleton, MA
Cahaly, Joy Anne .... Boston, MA
Cahaly, Richard F., Sr. .... Lexington, MA
Cahaly, Ronald F. .... Allston, MA
Cahan, Bruce B. .... New York, NY
Cahan, Earl L. .... Philadelphia, PA
Cahan, Eric .... Tucson, AZ
Cahan, James N. .... Chicago, IL
Cahan, Jerry R. .... San Luis Obispo, CA
Cahan, Judith E. .... Englewood, CO
Cahan, Michael A. .... Washington, DC
Cahan, Regina .... Seattle, WA
Cahan, Richard J. Alan .... Miami, FL
Cahen, Daniel .... Chicago, IL
Cahen, Donald M. .... San Francisco, CA
Cahen, Jessica L. .... San Francisco, CA
Cahen, Stephen A. .... Miami, FL
Caher, James P. .... Eugene, OR
Cahill, Agnes M. .... Rockfall, CT
Cahill, Allan D. D. .... Norfolk, VA
Cahill, Allison Findley .... Chicago, IL
Cahill, Anne B. .... White Plains, NY
Cahill, Arla D. .... Morristown, NJ
Cahill, August H., Jr. .... Boise, ID
Cahill, Barton J. .... Moorhead, MN
Cahill & Beehm .... Binghamton, NY
Endicott, NY
Cahill & Branciforte .... New Brunswick, NJ
Cahill, Brendan J. .... Bloomfield Hills, MI
Cahill, Brian F. .... Issaquah, WA
Cahill, Brian G. .... Racine, WI
Cahill, Carol Lynn .... Salem, MA
Cahill, Cathy F. .... Chicago, IL
Cahill, Christian & Kunkle, Ltd.
Chicago, IL
Cahill, Christine E. .... San Francisco, CA
Cahill, Christopher E. .... Kingston, NY
Cahill, Christopher M. .... Chicago, IL
Cahill, Christopher S. .... Galveston, TX
Cahill, Daniel E. .... Burlington, IA
Cahill, Daniel G. .... Raleigh, NC
Cahill, Daniel J. .... Atlantic City, NJ
Cahill, Daniel J. .... Albany, NY
Cahill, Daniel J., Jr. .... Athens, GA
Cahill, Daniel M. .... Mill Valley, CA
Cahill, David A. .... Naugatuck, CT
Cahill, David J. .... Wheaton, IL
Cahill, David P. .... Ann Arbor, MI
Cahill, David R. .... New York, NY
Cahill, Dennis P. .... Alta, UT
Cahill, Dieterich & Schilling .... Burlington, IA
Cahill, Donal A., Jr. .... Bridgeport, CT
Cahill, Donna L. .... Treasury Department,
United States Secret Service, GV
Cahill, Edward F. .... Boston, MA
Cahill, Elena L. .... Shelton, CT
Cahill, Elwood F., Jr. .... New Orleans, LA
Cahill, F. Everett .... San Francisco, CA
Cahill, Frank J., Law Offices of .... Pelham, NY
Cahill, Gary P. .... Shelton, CT
Cahill, George F. .... Boston, MA
Cahill, George J., Jr. .... New Haven, CT
Cahill, Gerald E. .... Louisville, KY
Cahill, Goetsch & DiPersia, P.C.
New Haven, CT
Cahill Gordon & Reindel
Washington, DC
New York, NY
Cahill, H. Frank .... Anchorage, AK
Cahill, Harry L., III .... New Orleans, LA
Cahill, J. Kevin .... Redmond, WA
Cahill, James E., III .... Dallas, TX
Cahill, James E., Jr. .... Senatobia, MS
Cahill, James F. .... Garden City, NY
Cahill, James J. .... Albany, NY
Cahill, James M. .... New Brunswick, NJ
Cahill, James N. .... Endicott, NY
Cahill, James S. .... Los Angeles, CA
Cahill, Jeffrey D. .... Minneapolis, MN
Cahill, Jennifer L. .... Palo Alto, CA
Cahill, Jill A. .... Oakland, CA
Cahill, John A. .... Brooklyn, NY
Cahill, John A. .... New York, NY
Cahill, John D. .... Los Angeles, CA
Cahill, John D. .... Alta, UT
Cahill, John F. .... Washington, DC
Baltimore, MD
Cahill, John J., III .... Slingerlands, NY
Cahill, John J., Jr. .... Philadelphia, PA
Cahill, John M. .... Menlo Park, CA
Cahill, John P., Jr. .... Houston, TX
Cahill, John R. .... New York, NY
Cahill, John S. .... New York, NY
Cahill, Joseph F., Jr. .... St. Albans, VT
Cahill, Joseph M. .... Washington, DC
Cahill, Joseph R. .... Nevada, IA
Cahill, Julie A. Cahalane .... Brockton, MA
Cahill, Kathleen .... Baltimore, MD
Cahill, Kathleen G. .... San Francisco, CA
Cahill, Kathleen, LLC, The Law Offices of
Baltimore, MD
Towson, MD
Cahill, Kathleen P. .... Wayne, PA
Cahill, Kelly A. .... Crystal Lake, IL
Cahill, Kenneth Jude .... Painesville, OH
Cahill, Kevin A. .... San Diego, CA
Cahill, Kevin A. .... Kingston, NY
Cahill, Kim E. Hutchinson .... Phoenix, AZ
Cahill, Laura Anne .... Hartford, CT
Cahill Law Offices .... Nevada, IA
Cahill, Lawrence R., (P.C.) .... Boston, MA
Cahill, Linda B. .... New York, NY
Cahill, Lisa A. .... New York, NY
Cahill, Lisabeth Peck .... Weaverville, CA
Cahill, Loretta (Laurie) A.
Grand Junction, CO
Cahill, M. Cornelia .... Albany, NY
Cahill, Madeline Clark .... San Diego, CA
Cahill, Margaret M. .... Chicago, IL
Cahill, Mark D., (P.C.) .... Boston, MA
Cahill & Marquart, P.A. .... Moorhead, MN
Fargo, ND
Cahill, Martin G. .... Omaha, NE
Cahill, Mary Denise .... Chicago, IL
Cahill, Mary E.
Department of Justice, GV
Cahill, Mary Patricia .... Chicago, IL
Cahill, Maura R. .... New York, NY
Cahill, Michael B. .... Bellevue, WA
Cahill, Michael E. .... Los Angeles, CA
Cahill, Michael J. .... Hauppauge, NY
Cahill, Michael J. .... Hauppauge, NY
Cahill, Michael J., P.C. .... Hauppauge, NY
Cahill, Michael P. .... Toms River, NJ
Cahill, Michael S., Jr.
West Bridgewater, MA
Cahill, Michael W. .... New Haven, CT
Cahill, Nancy L. .... Seattle, WA
Cahill & O'Neill .... Honolulu, HI
Kailua-Kona, HI
Wailuku, HI
Cahill, Patrick J. .... Leavenworth, KS
Cahill, Patrick T. .... Hamtramck, MI
Cahill, Peter .... Globe, AZ
Cahill, Peter J. .... New York, NY
Cahill, Peter T. .... Wailuku, HI
Cahill, Philip H. R. .... Boston, MA
Cahill, Richard F. .... Irvine, CA
Cahill, Richard M. .... Irving, TX
Cahill, Robert A. .... Washington, DC
Cahill, Robert E., Jr. .... Towson, MD
Cahill, Robert E., Sr. .... Towson, MD
Cahill, Robert G. .... Birmingham, AL
Cahill, Robert T. .... McLean, VA
Cahill, Robert V. .... Los Angeles, CA
Cahill, Robin L. .... San Diego, CA
Cahill, Ronald E. .... Boston, MA
Cahill, Sean T. .... San Diego, CA
Cahill, Sheila J. .... Lincoln, NE
Cahill, Steven J. .... Moorhead, MN
Cahill, Steven John .... Palo Alto, CA
Cahill, Susan Lynne .... Greensburg, PA
Cahill, Susannah .... New York, NY
Cahill, Sutton & Thomas, P.L.C.
Phoenix, AZ
Tucson, AZ
Cahill, Terance P. .... Chicago, IL
Cahill, Terence P. .... Oconomowoc, WI
Cahill, Thomas B. .... Schaumburg, IL
Cahill, Thomas J. .... Palo Alto, CA
Cahill, Thomas J. .... Greenwich, CT
Cahill, Thomas J. .... Nevada, IA
Cahill, Thomas J. .... New York, NY
Cahill, Thomas J., P.C. .... Greenwich, CT
Cahill, Timothy F. .... Sacramento, CA
Cahill, Timothy Francis .... Westford, MA
Cahill, Tracy L. Thornburg, (A Professional Corporation) .... Los Angeles, CA
Cahill, Victoria B. .... San Francisco, CA
Cahill, Virginia A. .... Sacramento, CA
Cahill, Wilinski & Rhodes .... Camden, NJ
Haddonfield, NJ
Cahill, William A., Jr. .... Woodbury, NY
Cahill, William A., Sr. .... Woodbury, NY
Cahill, William C. .... Phoenix, AZ
Cahill, William E. .... New York, NY
Cahill, William F., Jr. .... Boston, MA
Cahill, William J. .... Burlington, IA
Cahill, William S. .... Burlington, IA
Cahill, William T. .... Greenwich, CT
Cahill, William T. .... Chicago, IL
Cahill, William T., Jr. .... Haddonfield, NJ
Cahill, William W., Jr. .... Baltimore, MD
Cahill, Wm. A. .... Brooklyn, NY
Cahill Zimmer & DeCarlo, LLP
Garden City, NY
Cahillane, Christopher W. .... Pittsburgh, PA
Cahillane, James M. .... New York, NY
Cahillane, Maurice M. .... Springfield, MA
Cahillane, Thomas E. .... Griffith, IN
Cahilly, D. Bruce .... Coudersport, PA
Cahir, MaryLou .... Torrance, CA
Cahlan, J. Forest .... Tonopah, NV
Cahlan, John F. .... Las Vegas, NV
Cahn, Aaron R. .... New York, NY
Cahn, Arthur S.
Department Of Health And Human Services,
Social Security Administration, GV
Cahn, Avram J. .... New York, NY
Cahn, Bruce H. .... Portland, OR
Cahn, Charles, II .... Baltimore, MD
Cahn, Charles M., Jr. .... Baltimore, MD
Cahn, Cory Rabin .... New Orleans, LA
Cahn, David L. .... Washington, DC
Cahn, Edward N. .... Allentown, PA
Philadelphia, PA
Cahn, Frank Bernard .... Baltimore, MD
Cahn, Frank Bernard, P.A. .... Baltimore, MD
Cahn, Harris A. .... West Orange, NJ
Cahn, Herman .... New York, NY
Cahn, James M. .... Worcester, MA
Cahn, James S. .... Cleveland, OH
Cahn, Jeffrey Barton .... Newark, NJ
New York, NY
Cahn, Jeffrey H. .... Westminster, CO
Cahn, Jerry .... Rego Park, NY
Cahn, June B. .... New Orleans, LA
Cahn, Lauren S. .... New York, NY
Cahn, Linda J. .... New York, NY
Cahn, Mark D. .... Washington, DC
Cahn, Matthew J. .... Paramus, NJ
Cahn, Maurice U. .... Washington, DC
Rockville, MD
Cahn, Michael D. .... Providence, RI
Cahn, Penelope B. .... Mineola, NY
Cahn, Reuben C. .... Fort Lauderdale, FL
Cahn, Richard C. .... Melville, NY
Cahn, Robert .... Albertson, NY
Cahn, Robert A.
Judicial Panel On Multidistrict Litigation,
GV
Cahn, Robert F., Jr. .... Atlanta, GA
Cahn & Samuels, LLP .... Washington, DC
Rockville, MD
Cahn, Sheryl A. Haarmann
Milwaukee, WI
Cahn, Stanley M. .... Chicago, IL
Cahn, Stephen J. .... Cleveland, OH
Cahn, Stephen M. .... Worcester, MA
Cahn, Steven D. .... Edison, NJ
Cahn, Timothy R. .... Emeryville, CA
Cahn, William .... Mineola, NY
Cahn Wishod & Knauer, LLP
Melville, NY
Cahners, John D. .... Los Gatos, CA
Cahnmann, Leonard .... Chicago, IL
Cahn-Roth, Tracey E. .... Wayne, NJ
Cahoon, Bradley R. .... Salt Lake City, UT
Cahoon, Colin P. .... Dallas, TX
Cahoon, David .... Jonesboro, AR
Cahoon, David L. .... Silver Spring, MD
Cahoon, Donald B., Jr. .... Scranton, PA
Cahoon, Howard C., Jr. .... Harwich, MA
Cahoon, James P. .... Van Wert, OH
Cahoon, John E., Jr. .... Houston, TX
Cahoon, Ladd .... San Francisco, CA
Cahoon, Marilyn .... Greensboro, NC
Cahoon, Peter T. .... Akron, OH
Cahoon, Richard C., (P.C.)
Salt Lake City, UT
Cahoon, Richd. C. .... Salt Lake City, UT
Cahoon, Robert S. .... Greensboro, NC
Cahoon, Susan A. .... Atlanta, GA
Cahoon & Swisher .... Greensboro, NC
Cahoone, David K., (P.A.) .... Sarasota, FL
Cahouet, Ann P. .... Pittsburgh, PA
Cahow, Bradley E. .... Elgin, IL
Cahoy, Daniel R. .... New York, NY
Cahr, Darren S. .... Chicago, IL
Cahr, Jill M. .... Chicago, IL
Cahraman, Thomas H. .... Riverside, CA
Cai, Rongwei .... Seattle, WA
Cai, Tien T. .... Minneapolis, MN
Caiaccio, Kevin T. .... Atlanta, GA
Caiafa, Douglas .... Los Angeles, CA
Caiafa, Douglas, A Professional Law Corporation .... Los Angeles, CA
Caiati, Emanuel Joseph .... Houston, TX
Caiazza, Donald Michael .... Boston, MA
Caiazza, Francis X. .... New Castle, PA
Caiazza, Pasquale P. .... Orange, CA
Caiazzo, Anthony J. .... Philadelphia, PA
Caiazzo, Christopher C.
White Plains, NY
Caiazzo, Mary E. .... Nashville, TN
Caiazzo, Nicholas R. .... New York, NY
Caid, Brian V. .... Denver, CO
Caietti, Robert A. .... Hanford, CA
Caietti, Robert M. .... San Diego, CA
Caietti, William .... Cameron Park, CA
Caietti (Emme), Carolyn M.
San Diego, CA
Cail & Associates, P.C. .... Washington, DC
Cail & Cail .... Savannah, GA
Cail, Kenneth H. .... Savannah, GA
Cail, Kenneth H., Jr. .... Savannah, GA
Cail, Nicole Jones .... Indianapolis, IN
Cail, Paula Fuhrman .... Oklahoma City, OK
Cail, Sylvester, Jr. .... Washington, DC
Caillaud, Paul A. .... Miami, FL
Cailleteau, Caryn L. .... Friendswood, TX
Caillouet, Clyde C. .... Thibodaux, LA
Caillouet, Clyde C., Jr. .... Pensacola, FL
Caillouet, L. Charles .... Thibodaux, LA
Caillouet, Martin J. .... Thibodaux, LA
Caillouet, Stephen E. .... Thibodaux, LA
Caillouette, Richard A. .... Diamond Bar, CA
Cailteux, Konrad L. .... New York, NY
Caimi, August W. .... El Segundo, CA
Caimi, Paul A. .... Beachwood, OH
Cain, Ackerman & McCormick, P.C.
Pittsburgh, PA
Cain, Aimee .... New York, NY
Cain, Alan F. .... Helena, MT
Cain, Andrea L. .... Orlando, FL
Cain, B. Frank .... Fort Worth, TX
Cain, Barry S. .... Chicago, IL
Cain, Bernest H., Jr. .... Oklahoma City, OK
Cain, Billy R. .... Buford, GA
Cain, Brennan P. .... Anchorage, AK
Cain, Brent A. .... Carlinville, IL
Cain, Brian P. .... Atlanta, GA
Cain, C. Jean .... Sacramento, CA
Cain, C. Joseph .... Austin, TX
Cain, C. Larry .... Sherman, TX
Cain, C. Marshall
Environmental Protection Agency,
Office of Enforcement and Compliance
Assurance, GV
Cain & Cain .... Houston, TX
Katy, TX
Cain, Cain and Ritchey .... Canton, MS
Cain, Camille D. .... Houston, TX
Katy, TX
Cain, Candace .... Pittsburgh, PA
Cain, Chap B., III .... Liberty, TX
Cain, Charles E. .... Washington, DC
Cain, Charles J. .... Houston, TX
Cain, Charles L. .... High Point, NC
Cain, Christopher C. .... Madison, WI
Cain, Christopher Lee .... Tuscaloosa, AL
Cain, Craig W. .... Colorado Springs, CO
Cain, Cynthia Smith .... Denver, CO
Cain, Daniel J. .... Rockford, IL
Cain, David .... San Francisco, CA
Cain, David C. .... Dallas, TX
Cain, David H. .... Dallas, TX
Cain, David M. .... Hartford, CT
Cain, David P. .... Lewisburg, TN
Cain, David R.
Federal Energy Regulatory Commission,
Office of the General Counsel, GV
Cain, David W. .... Wailuku, HI
Cain, Deanne M. .... Colorado Springs, CO
Cain, Delmar L. .... Austin, TX
Cain, Dennis .... Houston, TX
Cain, Dennis L. .... Boise, ID
Cain, Derek E. .... Washington, DC
Cain, Don E. .... Pampa, TX
Cain, Donald L. .... Kansas City, MO
Cain, Donna Craft .... Villa Park, IL
Cain, Douglas M. .... Denver, CO
Cain, Eileen M. .... Norristown, PA
Cain, Elizabeth A. .... Cleveland, OH
Cain, Ellen M. .... Tuscaloosa, AL
Cain, Ellen P. .... Springfield, MA
Cain, Emory P. .... Jacksonville, FL
Cain, Erwin A. .... Dallas, TX
Cain, Erwin A., P.C. .... Dallas, TX
Cain, Esta L. .... Wilmington, DE
Cain & Ewald, P.A. .... Orlando, FL
Cain, Francis A. .... Knoxville, TN
Cain, Frank E., Jr. .... Bennettsville, SC
Cain, Gene Austin .... Walnut Creek, CA
Cain, George E., Jr. .... New Orleans, LA
Cain, George H. .... Hartford, CT
Cain, Gordon R. .... New Orleans, LA
Cain & Gruning .... Brooklyn, NY
Cain, Harvey D. .... Sacramento, CA
Cain, Henry M. .... Gainesville, FL
Cain, Hibbard, Myers & Cook, P.C.
Great Barrington, MA
Pittsfield, MA
Cain, Howard G., Jr. .... Huntsville, AR
Cain, Hugh J. .... Des Moines, IA
Cain, Ian .... Houston, TX
Cain, J. Thomas, Jr. .... Texas City, TX
Cain, J. William, Jr. .... Little Rock, AR
Cain, Jack S. .... Stroudsburg, PA
Cain, James D., Jr. .... Lake Charles, LA
Cain, James F. .... Elkins, WV
Cain, James H. .... Auburn, NE
Cain, James M. .... Washington, DC
Cain, James P. .... Raleigh, NC
Cain, James T. .... Manchester, NH
Cain, Janet E. .... Milwaukee, WI
Cain, Jason Morgan .... Chicago, IL
Cain, Jeffery A. .... Belleville, IL
Cain, Jennifer Z. .... Parkersburg, WV
Cain, Jerry Bruce .... Laredo, TX
Cain, Jerry D. .... Blacksburg, VA
Cain, Jerry W., Jr. .... Atlanta, GA
Cain, Jimmy E. .... Greenwell Springs, LA
Cain, John C. .... Houston, TX

Cain, John D. ... Flora Vista, NM
Cain, John E. ... Milwaukee, WI
Cain, John M. ... Orlando, FL
Cain, John P. ... Burlington, VT
Cain, Jonathan T. ... Tysons Corner, VA
Cain, Jos. B., Jr. ... Montgomery, AL
Cain, Joseph B. ... Boonton, NJ
Cain, Joseph D. ... Pittsburgh, PA
Cain, Joseph L. ... Gallipolis, OH
Cain, Joseph T. ... Dallas, TX
Cain, Josephine M. ... Brooklyn, NY
Cain, Joyce D. ... Huntington, NY
Cain, Julia A. ... Rittman, OH
Cain, Julie Kareeé ... Liberty, TX
Cain, Juliet ... New York, NY
Cain, Karen ... Placentia, CA
Cain, Karen K. ... Cleveland, OH
Cain, Kenneth R., Jr. ... Birmingham, AL
Cain, Kerry Ayers
Department Of Health And Human Services, Office of the General Counsel, GV
Cain, Kevin C. ... Boston, MA
Providence, RI
Cain, L. John ... Burlington, VT
Cain, Larry D. ... Houston, TX
Katy, TX
Cain, Larry, Law Office of ... Sherman, TX
Cain, Leroy, Jr. ... Nashville, TN
Cain, Lillian Pike ... Newton, MA
Cain, M. David, Jr. ... Gurnee, IL
Cain, Marion W. ... San Antonio, TX
Cain, Mark S. ... Santa Ana, CA
Cain, Mark T. ... Charlotte, NC
Cain, Marty G. ... Oklahoma City, OK
Cain, Mary S. ... San Francisco, CA
Cain, Maureen A. ... Denver, CO
Cain, May L. ... Miami, FL
Cain, Michael A. ... Washington, DC
Cain, Michael Edward ... Fort Worth, TX
Cain, Michael J. ... Madison, WI
Cain, Michael K. ... Chesapeake, VA
Cain, Michelle M. ... St. Louis, MO
Cain, Mildred Boellner ... Richmond, VA
Cain, Moira E. ... Pittsburgh, PA
Cain, Morrison G. ... Arlington, VA
Cain, Noel R. ... Belton, TX
Cain, Pamela M. ... Santa Monica, CA
Cain, Patricia Ann ... Iowa City, IA
Cain, Patricia S. ... Chicago, IL
Cain, Patrick J. ... Los Angeles, CA
Cain, Paul J. ... Newark, OH
Cain, Preston L. ... Kansas City, MO
Cain, Randall W. ... Lee's Summit, MO
Cain, Randy C. ... Austin, TX
Cain, Richard J. ... Harwich Port, MA
Cain, Richard R. ... Collinsville, IL
Cain, Richard R., Jr. ... St. Louis, MO
Cain, Rick A. ... Mobridge, SD
Cain, Robert G. ... Burlington, VT
Cain, Robert T., Jr. ... Lufkin, TX
Cain, Roger M. ... Lebanon, NJ
Cain, Rose M. ... Natick, MA
Cain, Scott Carl ... Edwardsville, IL
Cain, Sheila T. ... New York, NY
Cain, Simon L. ... Washington, DC
Cain & Snihur ... Hollywood, FL
Miami, FL
Cain, Steven M. ... Grafton, WI
Cain, Steven T. ... Upper Marlboro, MD
Cain, Sue Lynn Boyd ... Nashville, TN
Cain, Tamara Beam ... Norman, OK
Cain, Tamara K. ... Washington, DC
Cain, Thomas Wm. ... San Jose, CA
Cain, Tim J. ... LaGrange, IN
Cain, Timothy D. ... Oklahoma City, OK
Cain, Timothy F. ... Escanaba, MI
Cain, Timothy M., (P.A.) ... Seneca, SC
Cain, Tom ... Lawrenceville, GA
Cain, Tom M., Jr. ... Dallas, TX
Cain, Vanessa Zecher ... San Jose, CA
Cain, W. Clayton ... Victoria, TX
Cain, William B. ... Nashville, TN
Cain, William G. ... Greenville, SC
Cain, William, Jr. ... Little Rock, AR
Cain, William S. ... Canton, MS
Cain, William S., Jr. ... Columbus, GA
Cain, William T. ... Somerset, KY
Cain & Wyrough, P.C. ... Upper Marlboro, MD
Cain, Yvette Y. ... Nashville, TN
Caine, Alva C. ... Birmingham, AL
Caine, Andrew W. ... Los Angeles, CA
Caine, Angela G. ... Birmingham, AL
Caine, Arthur S. ... Minneapolis, MN
Caine, Burton ... Philadelphia, PA
Caine & Caine ... Naugatuck, CT
Caine, Carol R. ... Philadelphia, PA
Caine, Cecil ... Moulton, AL
Caine, Christopher John ... Fresno, CA
Caine, Clifford J. ... St. Paul, MN
Caine, Daniel M. ... Seattle, WA
Caine, Edward A. ... Washington, DC
Arlington, VA
Caine, Gidon M. ... Palo Alto, CA
Caine, Howard R. ... Silver Spring, MD
Caine, Jack E. ... Evansville, IN
Caine, John Dixon ... Washington, DC
Caine, John T. ... Ogden, UT
Caine, M. Leonard, III ... Naugatuck, CT
Caine, Margaret Moore
Securities and Exchange Commission, Office of Compliance Inspections and Examinations, GV
Caine, Martin L. ... New York, NY
Caine, Maureen S. ... Naugatuck, CT
Caine, Melvin E. ... Media, PA
Caine, Patrick R. ... Department of Justice, Executive Office for Immigration Review, GV
Caine, Patrick T. ... Providence, RI
Caine, Richard B. ... San Francisco, CA
Caine, Robert S. ... Mineola, NY
Caine, Shawn E. ... San Diego, CA
Caine, Stephen M. ... Santa Monica, CA
Caine & Taleisnik ... Fresno, CA
Caine, Thomas Durkee ... Tavares, FL
Lexington, KY
Caine, Wesley K. ... Washington, DC
Caines, Dennis E. ... San Francisco, CA
Cainkar, Louis F., (Ltd.) ... Chicago, IL
Cainkar, Vincent ... Burbank, IL
Cain-Lofton, Frances ... Charleston, SC
Cain-Wallace, Rosemary A.
Atlantic City, NJ
Caiola, Frank L. ... Norristown, PA
Caiola, Michelle A. ... Chicago, IL
Caiola, Paul S. ... Baltimore, MD
Caione, Kristen M. ... New York, NY
Caira, Mark ... Woodbury, NJ
Caira, Paula J. ... Washington, DC
Caira, Richard J., Jr. ... Raleigh, NC
Caire, D. Agna ... Slidell, LA
Caire, G. Walton ... Harvey, LA
Caire, Gregorie & Whitehead, L.C.
Baton Rouge, LA
Caire, Philip G. ... Baton Rouge, LA
Caire, Stephen J. ... Gretna, LA
Cairncross & Hempelmann, A Professional Service Corporation ... Seattle, WA
Cairney, Roberta ... San Francisco, CA
Cairnie, Hilary Stephen ... Washington, DC
Cairns, Ann B. ... Philadelphia, PA
Cairns & Associates, P.C. ... Denver, CO
Cairns, Carolyn ... Seattle, WA
Cairns, David A. ... Vero Beach, FL
Cairns, David A., P.A. ... Vero Beach, FL
Cairns, David M. ... Redwood City, CA
Cairns, Donald J. ... Milwaukee, WI
Cairns, Eileen ... Chicago, IL
Cairns, Gregory B. ... Denver, CO
Cairns, J. Donald ... Cleveland, OH
Cairns, J. Thomas, Jr. ... Los Angeles, CA
Cairns, James A. ... Wilmington, DE
Cairns, James R. ... Los Angeles, CA
Cairns, Jay R. ... Yuma, AZ
Cairns, Jeffrey P. ... Minneapolis, MN
Cairns, J. H. ... Portland, OR
Cairns, John A. ... Minneapolis, MN
Cairns, John B. ... New York, NY
Cairns, John D. ... Pasadena, CA
Cairns, Kevin S. ... Parsippany, NJ
Cairns & Lans ... Los Angeles, CA
Pasadena, CA
Cairns & Levin ... Chicago, IL
Cairns, Norman ... Albuquerque, NM
Cairns, Pamela A. ... Seattle, WA
Cairns, R. Matthew ... Concord, NH
Cairns, Richard H., (P.C.) ... Denver, CO
Cairns, Richard J. ... New York, NY
Cairns, Richard W. ... Department of the Army, U.S. Army Court of Criminal Appeals, GV
Cairns, Robert F. ... Houston, TX
Cairns, S. Matthew ... Philadelphia, PA
Cairns, Scott S. ... Jacksonville, FL
Cairo, Joseph M. ... Waterford, NY
Cairo, Louis C. ... Chicago, IL
Cairo, Marc J. ... Chicago, IL
Cairo, Richard A. ... Harrisburg, PA
Cairone, Matthew C. ... Pittsburgh, PA
Caisley, William T. ... Bloomington, IL
Caison, Heather Paige ... Mount Pleasant, SC
Caisse, Joseph G. ... Leominster, MA
Caisse, Kenneth E. ... Norwich, CT
Caissie, Jennie Lynn ... Southbridge, MA
Caitlin, Catherine R. ... Minneapolis, MN
Caito, Gregory A. ... Albany, NY
Caito, Harry J. ... Westlake, OH
Caits, William B. ... New York, NY
Caivano, Anthony P. ... Denville, NJ
Cajacob, John T., Jr. ... Faribault, MN
Cajacob, Kathleen D. ... Lakewood, OH
Cajacob, Kristin M. ... Minneapolis, MN
Cajoleas, Pete J. ... Jackson, MS
Cajthaml, Faron L. ... Orlando, FL
Cake, Lee W. ... Oakland, CA
Cake & Rhoades, P.C. ... Alexandria, VA
Cakmis, Rosemary T. ... Orlando, FL
Cal, Peter A. ... Denver, CO
Cala, Pamela J. ... Reading, PA
Cala, Philip A. ... Jamestown, NY
Calaba, Frank V. ... Los Angeles, CA
Calabrase, Mark ... Berea, OH
Calabrese, Alex M. ... New York, NY
Calabrese, Anthony ... Washington, DC
Calabrese, Anthony O., III ... Cleveland, OH
Calabrese, Anthony O., Jr. ... Cleveland, OH
Calabrese, Antonio J. ... McLean, VA
Calabrese, Arnold J. ... Florham Park, NJ
Calabrese, Arnold J., A Prof. Corp., Law Offices of ... Florham Park, NJ
Calabrese Associates, P.C. ... Dallas, TX
Plano, TX
Calabrese, Carla M. ... Farmington Hills, MI
Calabrese, Carla M. ... Dallas, TX
Calabrese, Christina A. ... Feeding Hills, MA
Calabrese, Christopher J. ... Rochester, NY
Calabrese, Constance A. ... Pottsville, PA
Calabrese, David ... New York, NY
Calabrese, Dominic J. ... Astoria, NY
Calabrese, Frank ... Chicago, IL
Calabrese, Gary A. ... Austin, TX
Calabrese, Gina M. ... Santa Monica, CA
Calabrese, Jeffrey J. ... Rochester, NY
Calabrese, Jennifer M. ... Philadelphia, PA
Calabrese, John F. ... College Park, MD
Calabrese, Joseph A. ... Los Angeles, CA
Calabrese, Joseph C. ... Mineola, NY
Calabrese, Joseph L. ... Brooklyn, NY
Calabrese, Joseph S. ... Buffalo, NY
Calabrese, Kyle W. ... Buffalo, NY
Calabrese, Margaret M. ... Valley Forge, PA
Calabrese, Marianne ... Florham Park, NJ
Calabrese, Mary Conway ... Geneseo, NY
Calabrese, Mary Sullivan
Garden City, NY
Calabrese, Michael ... New York, NY
Calabrese, Michael A. ... Washington, DC
Calabrese, Michael J. ... Wheaton, IL
Calabrese, Michael J. ... Milwaukee, WI
Calabrese, Michael R. ... Washington, DC
Calabrese, Nicholas J. ... Pittsburgh, PA
Calabrese, Richard A. ... Rochester, NY
Calabrese, Salvatore J. ... White Plains, NY
Calabrese & Torn ... New York, NY
Calabresi, Guido ... New Haven, CT
Calabretta, Joseph W., (Co., L.P.A.)
Canton, OH
Calabria, Ann Marie ... Raleigh, NC
Calabria, Donald J. ... Encino, CA
Calabria, Jose L. ... San Juan, PR
Calabria, Joseph T. ... Roseland, NJ
Calabria, Michael J. ... Steubenville, OH
Calabria, Nicholas P. ... Rockville Centre, NY
Calabria, Rebecca L. ... Kaufman, TX
Calabro, Alfred A. ... Glendale, CA
Calabro, Anthony J. ... Glendale, CA
Calabro, Calabro & Calabro ... Glendale, CA
Calabro, Daniel F. ... Glendale, CA
Calabro, Edward H. ... Glendale, CA
Calabro, Gregory G. ... New York, NY
Calabro & Jennette ... Atlanta, GA
Calabro, Michael J. ... Boston, MA
Calabro, Michael M. ... Atlanta, GA
Calabro, Michael V. ... Montclair, NJ
Calabro, Miriam ... New York, NY
Calabro, Pershing N. ... Philadelphia, PA
Calabro, Rachel F. ... Chicago, IL
Calaby, Cecelia A. ... Washington, DC
Calafell, Alberto L. ... New York, NY
Calafell, Ray ... Tampa, FL
Calafell, Ray, Jr., P.A. ... Tampa, FL
Calaff, Robert A.
Federal Communications Commission, Wireless Telecommunications Bureau, GV
Calafiore, Frances Z. ... Hartford, CT
Calaf-Legrand, Federico ... Philadelphia, PA
San Juan, PR
Calagione, Angelo A. ... Milford, MA
Calagione, Robert B. ... Milford, MA
Calagiovanni, Alicia S. ... Syracuse, NY
Calahan, Mark C. ... Los Angeles, CA
Calahan, P. Charles ... New Iberia, LA
Calaiaro, Corbett & Bower, P.C.
Pittsburgh, PA
Calaiaro, Donald R. ... Pittsburgh, PA
Calais, Barbara ... Sacramento, CA
Calaluca, Laura Hamilton
Washington, DC
Calamare, Andrew J. ... Boston, MA
Calamari, Andrew M. ... Bronx, NY
Calamari, Andrew M. ... New York, NY
Calamari & Calamari ... Bronx, NY
Calamari, John D. ... New York, NY
Calamari, Joseph A. ... Kinnelon, NJ
Calamari, Joseph A. ... Jamaica, NY
Calamari, Joseph L. ... Bronx, NY
Calamari, Peter E. ... New York, NY
Calamari, Rita ... Laconia, NH
Calamari, Robert ... Lancaster, NH
Calamari, Robert C. ... Myrtle Beach, SC
Calamari & Saltarelli ... New York, NY
Calamari, Stephen A. ... New York, NY
Calamari-Righi, Maryellen
Washington, DC
Calamaro, Raymond S. ... Washington, DC
Calame, John C. ... Selma, AL
Calame, Larry M. ... Austin, TX
Calame, Parmele Price ... Charlotte, NC
Calame, Richard A. ... Boston, MA
Calametti, Kimberly J. ... Mobile, AL
Calamia, Joseph A. ... El Paso, TX
Calamita, F. Paul, III ... Richmond, VA
Calamita, Grace M. ... Springfield, MA
Calamita, Nicolas Jansen ... New York, NY
Calamunci, Anthony J. ... Toledo, OH
Calamunci, Groth & Joelson Co., L.P.A.
Temperance, MI
Toledo, OH
Calamusa, Rocco, Jr. ... Birmingham, AL
Calamusa, Steven G.
West Palm Beach, FL
Calande, Pauline E. ... San Francisco, CA
Calandra & Castaldi ... Bronx, NY
Calandra, Claire L. ... Morristown, NJ
Calandra, Joanne M. ... Chester, NJ
Calandra, John J. ... New York, NY
Calandra, John P. ... Cleveland, OH
Calandra, Marisa ... White Plains, NY
Calandra, Michael A. ... Bronx, NY
Calandra, Thomas D. ... Brockport, NY
Calandrillo, Steve P. ... Seattle, WA
Calandrino, Philip K. ... Orlando, FL
Calandrino, Philip K., P.A. ... Orlando, FL
Calandrino, Stephen A. ... New York, NY
Calandro, Michele Stewart
Baton Rouge, LA
Calano & Calano ... New York, NY
Calano, Janet Madonia ... New York, NY
Calano, Michael A. ... New York, NY
Calantoni, Holly V. ... Easton, PA
Calapai, Dominique M. ... Washington, DC
Calarco, Michael D. ... Newark, NY
Calarco, Santo ... Jersey City, NJ
Calardo, Stephen P. ... Cincinnati, OH
Calarese, Norma Carr ... Springfield, MA
Calarie, Cindy L. ... Kittanning, PA
Calarie, Peter ... Kittanning, PA
Calati, Anthony J. ... Detroit, MI
Calati, Hope L. ... Detroit, MI
Calatrello, Frederick J. ... Cleveland, OH
Calautti, Susan M. ... Ashley, IL
Calaway, Martin Curtis ... Los Angeles, CA
Calaway, Richard B. ... Little Rock, AR
Calaway, Scott M. ... Springfield, OH
Calaway, Stephen G. ... Winston-Salem, NC
Calaway, Todd E. ... Springfield, OH
Calaway, Tonit M. ... Milwaukee, WI
Calaway-McLean, Kathleen A.
Beverly Hills, CA
Calbo-Jackson, Rosanne ... Oakland, CA
Calbom, Harry R., Jr. ... Longview, WA
Calbom & Schwab, P.S.C. ... Brewster, WA
Chelan, WA
Ellensburg, WA
Kennewick, WA
Moses Lake, WA
Wenatchee, WA
Calcagni, Anthony M. ... Portland, ME
Calcagni, Jeffrey M. ... Huntingdon Valley, PA
Calcagni, John R. ... Hauppauge, NY
Calcagni, Luann Louise ... Somerville, MA
Calcagni, Thomas Richard
Morristown, NJ
Calcagnie, Kevin F. ... Newport Beach, CA
San Diego, CA
Calcagnini, George J. ... Mount Kisco, NY
Calcagnini, Regina A. ... Falls Church, VA
Calcagno, Andrew John ... Nutley, NJ
Calcagno, Carla C. ... Washington, DC
Calcagno, Dennis John ... Quincy, MA
Calcagno, Elizabeth M. ... Harrisburg, PA
Calcagno & Garruto ... Nutley, NJ
Calcagno, Joseph ... Lombard, IL
Calcagno, Steven R. ... Staten Island, NY
Calcagno, Valerie ... Oxford, MS
Calcara, Mark D. ... Great Bend, KS
Calcara, Richard L. ... Kansas City, KS
Calcaterra, Craig ... Columbus, OH
Calcaterra, Mark P. ... Auburn Hills, MI
Calcaterra, Regina Marie ... Newark, NJ
Calciano, Elizabeth M. ... Los Angeles, CA
Calciano, Elizabeth Spedding
Pasadena, CA
Calcines, Joaquin, Jr. ... Passaic, NJ
Paterson, NJ
Calcote, Keith D. ... Fort Worth, TX
Calcutt Cunningham Davison Rogers Boynton & Petterson, P.L.L.C.
Traverse City, MI
Calcutt, Kathleen M. ... St. Petersburg, FL
Calcutt, Patrick B. ... St. Petersburg, FL
Calcutt, William B. ... Traverse City, MI
Caldarazzo, Richard J. ... Oak Brook, IL
Caldarelli, Albert A. ... Boston, MA
Caldarelli, Paul A. ... Washington, DC
Caldarelli, William J. ... San Diego, CA
Caldarola, Charles ... New York, NY
Caldarola, Michael A. ... San Jose, CA
Caldarone, Thomas J., Jr.
North Providence, RI
Caldart, Charles C. ... Boston, MA
Caldbeck, Gareth H. ... Shelburne, VT
Caldbeck & Schweitzer ... Burlington, VT
Shelburne, VT
Caldbeck, Thomas K. ... San Antonio, TX
Caldbeck, Weldon S. ... Cheyenne, WY
Caldcleugh, Elizabeth R. ... Dallas, TX
Caldecott, E. J. ... Pasadena, CA
Caldecott, Richard R. ... Minneapolis, MN
Caldecott, Wheeler & Searles, P.L.C.
Minneapolis, MN
Caldeira, Charlene A. ... Boston, MA
Calder, C. Lynn ... Raleigh, NC
Calder & Calder ... Wilmington, NC
Calder, Cynthia A. ... Wilmington, DE
Calder, Daniel N. ... Valley Forge, PA
Calder, David L. ... Batesville, MS
Calder, Eugene B. ... Ypsilanti, MI
Calder, Eugene B., III ... Falls Church, VA
Calder, Gary L. ... Aurora, CO
Calder, Gordon S., Jr. ... Newark, NJ
Calder, Gregory C. ... Idaho Falls, ID
Calder, Howard M. ... Montpelier, VT
Calder, J. Keith ... Wilmington, NC
Calder, James J. ... New York, NY
Calder, J.D. ... New York, NY
Calder, Joseph A. ... Garner, NC
Calder, Kathleen Duggan
Redwood City, CA
Calder, Linda D. ... Riverhead, NY
Calder, Mary M. ... New London, WI
Calder, Meta ... Tallahassee, FL
Calder, Robert ... Wilmington, NC
Calder, Robert, Jr. ... Wilmington, NC
Calder, Stephen M. ... Camden, NJ
Philadelphia, PA
Calder, Stephen P. ... Aurora, CO
Calder, Stephen P., P.C. ... Aurora, CO
Calder, Thomas M. ... Warren, MI
Calder, Thomas S. ... Cincinnati, OH
Calder, Tracy E. ... Weehawken, NJ
Calder, Wallace J. ... Salt Lake City, UT
Calder, Watkins, McWilliam & Beaver, P.L.L.C.
Garner, NC
Calder, William B., Jr. ... Harrisburg, PA
Caldera, Donald L. ... Lake Placid, NY
Caldera, Eva Orlebeke ... Los Angeles, CA
Caldera, Hella V. ... San Antonio, TX
Calderaro, Ralph T. ... Kingston, MA
Calderas, Erica L. ... Cleveland, OH
Calderazzi, Kathrine L. ... Washington, DC
Calderbank, Timothy J. ... Portland, OR
Calderhead, David C. ... Milford, OH

Calderola, Barbara ... Seattle, WA
Calderon, Alvaro R., Jr. ... San Juan, PR
Calderon, Andrew Michael ... Reston, VA
Calderon, Bruce Robert ... New York, NY
Calderón, Byron ... El Paso, TX
Calderon, Carlos M. ... Mount Vernon, NY
Calderon, Charles M. ... Los Angeles, CA
Calderon, Dennis ... San Diego, CA
Calderon, Eddie R., Jr. ... Houston, TX
Calderón, Ernest ... Phoenix, AZ
Calderon, Gerard A. ... San Antonio, TX
Calderon, Joseph ... Bronx, NY
Calderon, Joseph ... New York, NY
Calderon, Joseph D. ... Indianapolis, IN
Calderon, Joseph E. ... Oak Park, IL
Calderon, Joseph E., Ltd. ... Oak Park, IL
Calderon, Joseph H. ... Turlock, CA
Calderon, Karen Gianas ... Phoenix, AZ
Calderon, Lewis Scott ... Uniondale, NY
Calderon, Michele Johnson ... Indianapolis, IN
Calderon, Nicholas T. ... San Diego, CA
Calderon, Peter J. ... Washington, DC
Calderon, Raul M. ... San Antonio, TX
Calderon, Reina A. ... Bowling Green, OH
Calderon, Ricardo E., Law Offices of
Del Rio, TX
Calderon, Ricardo E., Law Offices of
Eagle Pass, TX
Calderon, Ricardo R. ... Springfield, MA
Calderon, Rosa E. Permuy ... San Juan, PR
Calderon, Virginia Y. ... El Centro, CA
Calderon, Yuri A. ... Houston, TX
Calderon-Bartolomei, Jose M. ... San Juan, PR
Calderone, Adrian Thomas
Uniondale, NY
Calderone, Andrew J. ... Akron, OH
Calderone, Anthony M. ... Battle Creek, MI
Calderone, Cary J. ... San Francisco, CA
Calderone, Chris E. ... Lafayette, CA
Calderone, Donald A. ... Cleveland, OH
Calderone, Fred P., P.C.
Farmington Hills, MI
Calderone, Frederick P.
Farmington Hills, MI
Calderone, Kenneth A. ... Akron, OH
Calderone Law Offices, P.C.
Battle Creek, MI
Coldwater, MI
Kalamazoo, MI
Calderone, Lynda L. ... Philadelphia, PA
Calderone, Philip D. ... Old Brookville, NY
Calderone, Philip F. ... Albany, NY
Calderone, Vincent ... Woodland Hills, CA
Calders, William A. ... San Diego, CA
Calderwood, Bruce ... Murphys, CA
Calderwood, Gail C. ... Pittsburgh, PA
Calderwood, James A. ... Washington, DC
Calderwood, Rebbecca F. ... Ventura, CA
Calderwood, Richard C. ... Santa Clara, CA
Calderwood, Terry W. ... Camden, ME
Calderwood, W. Scott ... Warren, PA
Calderwood, William A. ... New York, NY
Caldes, Theodore G. ... Nassau, NY
Caldes, William Gerald ... New York, NY
Philadelphia, PA
Caldevilla, David M. ... Tampa, FL
Caldin, Debra G. ... Los Angeles, CA
Caldis & Caldis ... St. Paul, MN
Caldis, Gordon ... Grand Forks, ND
Caldis, Harry S. ... St. Paul, MN
Caldis, Steven H. ... St. Paul, MN
Caldis & Tingum, Ltd. ... Grand Forks, ND
Caldis, Todd G. ... St. Paul, MN
Caldito, Laura M. "Ray" ... Los Angeles, CA
Caldon, David T. ... Calabasas, CA
Caldwell, Adam S. ... Washington, DC
Caldwell, Alan L. ... Austin, TX
Caldwell, Ann M. ... Ardmore, PA
Caldwell, Anna E. ... Winston-Salem, NC
Caldwell, Anna E., P.A. ... Winston-Salem, NC
Caldwell, Anna M. ... Grand Rapids, MI
Caldwell, Anthony J. ... Los Angeles, CA
Caldwell Associates ... Washington, DC
Caldwell, Barbara Lee ... Phoenix, AZ
Caldwell, Barry H. ... United States Senate,
Senatorial Assistants, GV
Caldwell, Berner & Caldwell
Woodstock, IL
Caldwell, Brent L. ... Lexington, KY
Caldwell, Brent R. ... Houston, TX
Caldwell, Brent T. ... Seattle, WA
Caldwell, Brian ... Topeka, KS
Caldwell, Bryan M. ... Belmont, NY
Caldwell & Caldwell ... Thomaston, GA
Baltimore, MD
Caldwell & Caldwell ... Incline Village, NV
Caldwell & Caldwell ... Dallas, TX
Caldwell, Caldwell & Caldwell, P.L.C.
Newton, IA
Caldwell & Caldwell, P.A. ... Salisbury, MD
Caldwell, Cannon-Ryan & Riffee
Charleston, WV
Caldwell, Carolyn Bielefeld
Indianapolis, IN
Caldwell, Carrie L. ... Little Canada, MN
Caldwell, Catharine A. ... Miami, FL
Caldwell, Charles E. ... Birmingham, AL
Caldwell, Charles F. ... Raleigh, NC
Caldwell, Charles F. ... Houston, TX
Caldwell, Charles M.
Department of Justice, GV
Caldwell, Charles M. ... Omaha, NE
Caldwell, Charles Y., III ... Richmond, VA
Caldwell, Chester A., III ... Abilene, TX
Caldwell, Chris D. ... Oklahoma City, OK
Caldwell, Christopher G.
Los Angeles, CA
Caldwell, Claud R. ... Augusta, GA

Caldwell, Clifford C. ... El Centro, CA
Caldwell & Clinton, PLLC ... Houston, TX
Caldwell, Connie
Federal Energy Regulatory Commission,
Office of the General Counsel, GV
Caldwell, Connie S. ... Atlanta, GA
Caldwell, Craig A. ... Sacramento, CA
Caldwell, Craig D. ... Rusk, TX
Caldwell, Craig D., P.C. ... Rusk, TX
Caldwell, Craig H. ... Bristol, TN
Caldwell, Craig H., Jr. ... Bristol, TN
Caldwell, Cynthia O'Bryant
San Angelo, TX
Caldwell, D. Faye ... Houston, TX
Caldwell, Dan O., III ... Thermopolis, WY
Caldwell, Daniel D. ... Hawthorne, NJ
Caldwell, Daniel H. ... Abingdon, VA
Caldwell, David ... Dallas, TX
Caldwell, David A. ... San Jose, CA
Caldwell, David A. ... Cincinnati, OH
Caldwell, David B. ... San Francisco, CA
Caldwell, David C. ... Upper Montclair, NJ
Caldwell, Deborah A. ... Cleveland, OH
Caldwell, Derek R. ... Wilmington, NC
Caldwell, Diana M. ... Macedonia, OH
Caldwell, Diana Weaks ... Tallahassee, FL
Caldwell, Don S., Jr. ... Mexia, TX
Caldwell, Donald B. ... Hartford, CT
Caldwell, Donald Harrison, Jr.
Charlotte, NC
Caldwell, Donald Harrison, Jr., P.A.
Charlotte, NC
Caldwell, Donald S. ... Roanoke, VA
Caldwell, Doris A. ... Oakland, CA
Caldwell, Douglas C. ... West Monroe, LA
Caldwell, Edea M. ... Stockbridge, GA
Caldwell, Edmond W., Jr. ... Raleigh, NC
Caldwell, Edwin T., (P.C.)
San Francisco, CA
Caldwell, Ehrsam, Kennedy & Lavery
Bridgeport, CT
Caldwell, Elizabeth J. M. ... Charlotte, NC
Caldwell, Ethan Awbrey ... Seattle, WA
Caldwell, Everett D. ... Scottsmoor, FL
Caldwell, Excetral K. ... Washington, DC
Caldwell, F. John, Jr. ... Atlantic City, NJ
Caldwell, G. Ernest ... Galveston, TX
Caldwell, G. Wade ... San Antonio, TX
Caldwell, Gary L. ... Santa Maria, CA
Caldwell, Gene W. ... Whitehouse, TX
Caldwell, Gerard Vernon, Jr. ... Baltimore, MD
Caldwell, Gilbert R., III ... Newton, IA
Caldwell, Gisela ... San Diego, CA
Caldwell, Glenn J. ... New York, NY
Caldwell, Gregory D. ... Lake Oswego, OR
Caldwell, Gregory L. ... Noblesville, IN
Caldwell, H. Allan ... Wichita, KS
Caldwell, H. Dwane, Jr. ... Houston, TX
Caldwell, H. Lee ... Abilene, TX
Caldwell, H. Michelle ... Dallas, TX
Caldwell, Harmon W., Jr. ... Atlanta, GA
Caldwell, Harold G. ... Troy, PA
Caldwell, Harold L. ... Cincinnati, OH
Caldwell, Harry M. ... Malibu, CA
Caldwell, Henry H. ... South Barrington, IL
Caldwell, Herman Mallory ... Houston, TX
Caldwell, Herman S., Jr. ... Adelphi, MD
Caldwell, Hugh M., Jr. ... Tucson, AZ
Caldwell, J. Christopher ... Detroit, MI
Caldwell, J. Daffan ... Houston, TX
Caldwell, J. Edward ... Bridgeport, CT
Caldwell, J. Richard, Jr. ... Tampa, FL
Caldwell, J. Thomas, Law Offices of
Ripley, TN
Caldwell, J. Todd ... Anniston, AL
Caldwell, Jack C. ... Lafayette, LA
Caldwell, Jacqueline Bollas ... Canton, OH
Salem, OH
Caldwell, James D. ... Shreveport, LA
Caldwell, James D. ... Corpus Christi, TX
Caldwell, James David ... Tallulah, LA
Caldwell, James E. ... Chicago, IL
Caldwell, James G. ... Kansas City, MO
Caldwell, James N. ... Columbia, SC
Caldwell, James Patrick ... Tupelo, MS
Caldwell, Jerry W. ... Jesup, GA
Caldwell, Jesse B., III ... Gastonia, NC
Caldwell, J.I.M., Jr. ... Oklahoma City, OK
Fort Worth, TX
Caldwell, Joe ... Taos, NM
Caldwell, Joe R., Jr. ... Washington, DC
Caldwell, John ... Pasadena, CA
Caldwell, John B. ... West Union, OH
Caldwell, John C. ... Oregon City, OR
Caldwell, John H. ... Washington, DC
Caldwell, John H. ... Houston, TX
Caldwell, John L. ... Beaverton, OR
Caldwell, John R. ... Fayetteville, TN
Caldwell, John W. ... Philadelphia, PA
Caldwell, John W., Jr. ... El Paso, TX
Caldwell, John W., Jr. ... San Angelo, TX
Caldwell, Johnnie L. ... Thomaston, GA
Caldwell, Johnnie L., Jr. ... Thomaston, GA
Caldwell, JoLynn Campbell
Kansas City, MO
Caldwell, Joseph D. ... New Hartford, NY
Caldwell, Joseph W. ... Charleston, WV
Caldwell, Karen K. ... Lexington, KY
Caldwell, Karen S. ... Incline Village, NV
Caldwell, Karen Skeens ... Houston, TX
Caldwell, Kathleen K. ... Sioux Falls, SD
Caldwell, Kathleen Laird ... Memphis, TN
Caldwell & Kearns, A Professional
Corporation ... Harrisburg, PA
Caldwell & Kennedy, A Professional
Corporation ... Barstow, CA
Big Bear City, CA
Riverside, CA
San Bernardino, CA
Victorville, CA
Caldwell, Kenneth N. ... Incline Village, NV
Caldwell, Kirk W., (A Law Corporation)
Honolulu, HI
Caldwell, Lance A. ... Portland, OR
Caldwell, Larry ... Sacramento, CA
Caldwell, Laura A. ... Chicago, IL
Caldwell Law Firm, P.A. ... Fort Myers, FL
Naples, FL
Caldwell Law Firm, P.C. ... Houston, TX
Caldwell, Leslie Ann ... Birmingham, AL
Caldwell, Leslie, Newcombe & Pettit, A Professional Corporation
Los Angeles, CA
Caldwell, Leslie R. ... New York, NY
Caldwell, Lisa J. ... Winston-Salem, NC
Caldwell, Lisa M. ... Portland, OR
Caldwell, Lisa Woodbury ... Charleston, SC
Caldwell, Lori Jean ... Orlando, FL
Caldwell, M. Dan ... Oklahoma City, OK
Caldwell, M. Dwayne ... Philadelphia, PA
Caldwell, Manley P., Jr. ... Palm Beach, FL
Caldwell, Maria-Lisa ... Nashville, TN
Caldwell, Mark M., III ... Radford, VA
Caldwell, Mark R. ... Phoenix, AZ
Caldwell, Mark S. ... Denver, CO
Caldwell, Mary Ellen ... Cambridge, OH
Caldwell & McCarty, P.C.
Oklahoma City, OK
Caldwell Megna ... Trenton, NJ
Caldwell, Melvin J. ... Salisbury, MD
Caldwell, Melvin J., Jr. ... Salisbury, MD
Caldwell, Michael A. ... Atlanta, GA
Caldwell, Michael L. ... Detroit, MI
Farmington Hills, MI
Caldwell, Michael R. ... Muleshoe, TX
Caldwell, Michael T. ... Woodstock, IL
Caldwell, Michael Train ... San Francisco, CA
Caldwell & Moll, L.C.
Overland Park, KS
Kansas City, MO
Caldwell, Nancy E. ... Atlanta, GA
Caldwell, Neil ... Angleton, TX
Caldwell, Nellie Jane ... Columbus, OH
Caldwell, O. Richard ... Silver Spring, MD
Caldwell & Pacetti ... Palm Beach, FL
West Palm Beach, FL
Caldwell & Patterson ... Houston, TX
Caldwell, Paul M. ... Clermont, FL
Caldwell, Paul R. ... Fort Myers, FL
Naples, FL
Caldwell, Paulette M. ... New York, NY
Caldwell, Peggy J. ... Atlanta, GA
Caldwell, Peter D. ... New York, NY
Caldwell, Peter M. ... Oakland, CA
Caldwell, R. Michael ... Baton Rouge, LA
Caldwell, Randal B. ... Newton, IA
Caldwell, Rex S., III ... Annapolis, MD
Caldwell, Richard H. ... Houston, TX
Caldwell, Richard J. ... Miami, FL
Caldwell, Rick L. ... Virginia Beach, VA
Caldwell, Robert J. ... Lewiston, ID
Caldwell, Robert L. ... San Antonio, TX
Caldwell, Robert S. ... Overland Park, KS
Caldwell, Robt. E. ... Tulsa, OK
Caldwell, Robt. H., Jr. ... Denton, TX
Caldwell, Robt. L. ... Dallas, TX
Caldwell, Rodney K. ... Houston, TX
Caldwell, Ronald Mark ... Canton, OH
Caldwell, Roy W. ... Clermont, FL
Caldwell, Sally J. ... Philadelphia, PA
Caldwell, Sara ... Daytona Beach, FL
Orlando, FL
Caldwell, Sara ... Lake Mary, FL
Palm Coast, FL
Sanford, FL
Caldwell, Sean M. ... Cincinnati, OH
Caldwell, S. F. ... Lumberton, NC
Caldwell, Sharon Lee Stine
Rancho Cucamonga, CA
Caldwell & Singleton LLC ... St. Louis, MO
Caldwell, Stacey E. ... Lisle, IL
Caldwell, Stokely G., Jr. ... Charlotte, NC
Caldwell, Susan L. ... Los Angeles, CA
Caldwell, T. Eugene ... Jackson, MS
Caldwell, Terry E. ... Victorville, CA
Caldwell, Terry Joe ... Tulsa, OK
Caldwell, Theodore J., Jr.
Philadelphia, PA
Caldwell, Thomas A. ... Chattanooga, TN
Caldwell, Thomas B. ... San Mateo, CA
Caldwell, Thomas D., Jr. ... Harrisburg, PA
Caldwell, Thomas E. ... Port Orange, FL
Caldwell, Thomas J. ... Miami, FL
Caldwell, Thomas J. ... Monroe, NC
Caldwell, Thomas K. ... Indianapolis, IN
Caldwell, Tom P. ... Hattiesburg, MS
Caldwell, Victor F. ... New York, NY
Caldwell, Victoria B. ... Boston, MA
Caldwell, W. Eugene ... Brunswick, GA
Caldwell, W. Eugene, P.C. ... Brunswick, GA
Saint Simons Island, GA
Caldwell, W. VanD. ... Upper Marlboro, MD
Caldwell, W. Wilson ... Cleveland, OH
Caldwell, Wallace F. ... Stockton, CA
Caldwell & Watson, LLP ... Atlanta, GA
Caldwell, Wesley S., III ... Trenton, NJ
Caldwell, William A. ... Boston, MA
Caldwell, William A. ... Tulsa, OK
Caldwell, William C., Jr.
St. Francisville, LA
Caldwell, William E. ... Fairbanks, AK
Caldwell, William I., Jr. ... Woodstock, IL
Caldwell, William J. ... Clinton, NJ
Plainfield, NJ
Caldwell, William R. ... Houston, TX
Caldwell, William W. ... Vero Beach, FL

Caldwell, William W. ... Harrisburg, PA
Caldwell, Wm. M. ... Denver, CO
Caldwell, Worsham N., Jr. ... St. Louis, MO
Caldwell, Wylie H., Jr. ... Florence, SC
Caldwell, Yolanda S. ... Houston, TX
Caldwell-Bono, Deborah S. ... Roanoke, VA
Caldwell-Stone, Deborah ... Chicago, IL
Cale, E. Barclay, Jr. ... Miami, FL
Cale, Edgar B. "Chip" ... Philadelphia, PA
Cale, Melinda ... Bristow, OK
Caleb, Edwin I. ... Klamath Falls, OR
Caleb, Vanessa ... Nevada, MO
Calebrese, Victoria A.
West Palm Beach, FL
Caleca, Johanna E. ... East Hampton, NY
Caleca & Towner ... East Hampton, NY
Calechman, Jack H. ... Boston, MA
Caleel, Richard A. ... Los Angeles, CA
Caleen, R. L., Jr. ... Tallahassee, FL
Calegan, Denise S. ... Boca Raton, FL
Calegari, Kevin R. ... San Francisco, CA
Calella, Joseph G. ... Morristown, NJ
Calello, Marc A. ... Wayne, NJ
Calello Martinez, P.C. ... Nutley, NJ
Calello, Sheila E. ... Newark, NJ
Calem, Andrea R. ... Washington, DC
Calem, Flora L. ... San Diego, CA
Calenda, Daniel A. ... Providence, RI
Calenda & Iacoi, Ltd. ... Providence, RI
Calender, John G. ... Washington, DC
Calender, Thomas E.D. ... Atlanta, GA
Calendo, Puckett, Sheedy & DiCorrado
Fresno, CA
Glendale, CA
Los Angeles, CA
Ventura, CA
Calendo, Stephen P. ... Glendale, CA
Caleo, Paul D. ... Oakland, CA
Caler, Margaret S. ... Escondido, CA
Calero, Anthony J. ... San Francisco, CA
Calero, Frank ... Seattle, WA
Calero Blanco, Jorge ... San Juan, PR
Calero-Cerezo, Sylvia I. ... Aguadilla, PR
Cales, Gloria L. ... Phoenix, AZ
Cales, Gloria L., P.C. ... Phoenix, AZ
Cales, James A., III ... Norfolk, VA
Cales, James A., Jr. ... Portsmouth, VA
Calesaric, Robert E. ... Newark, OH
Calescibetta, C.C. ... Long Beach, CA
Caleshu, James T. ... San Francisco, CA
Caletti, Helen S. ... San Francisco, CA
Calevas, Harry A. ... Bethesda, MD
Calewarts, Kenneth G. ... Green Bay, WI
Caley & Associates ... Orange, CA
Caley, Eldon F. ... Roseburg, OR
Caley, Eldon F., Lawyer, P.C.
Roseburg, OR
Caley, James W. ... Hartford, CT
Caley, Rebecca A. ... Orange, CA
Caley, Steven D. ... Atlanta, GA
Caley, Steven P. ... New York, NY
Caley, Sylvia B. ... Atlanta, GA
Caley, Thomas G. ... Metamora, MI
Calfa, Jeffrey P. ... Chicago, IL
Calfas, Ann K. ... Beverly Hills, CA
Calfas, John A. ... Los Angeles, CA
Calfas, John A., A Professional Corporation
Los Angeles, CA
Calfas, Neil ... San Antonio, TX
Calfas, Scott J. ... Los Angeles, CA
Calfee, David W. ... Meadow Vista, CA
Calfee, David W., III ... Woodland, CA
Calfee, Dennis A. ... Gainesville, FL
Calfee, Halter & Griswold LLP
Cleveland, OH
Columbus, OH
Calfee, John B. ... Cleveland, OH
Calfee, Kent N. ... Woodland, CA
Calfee, Robert D. ... Williamson, WV
Calfee, William L. ... Cleveland, OH
Calfee & Young, A Professional Corporation
Woodland, CA
Calfin, Mike M. ... Lubbock, TX
Calfo, Alexander G. ... Los Angeles, CA
Calfo, Angelo J. ... Seattle, WA
Calgaro, Robert A. ... Rockford, IL
Calger, Arthur R. ... White Plains, NY
Calhelha, Moacyr R. ... Newburgh, NY
Calhelha, Nancy D.
Cornwall-On-Hudson, NY
Calhoon, Clyde R. ... Brookings, SD
Calhoon, Jerry L. ... Palestine, TX
Calhoon, Ken F. ... Little Rock, AR
North Little Rock, AR
Calhoon & Kratochvil ... Brookings, SD
Calhoon, Melissa ... San Francisco, CA
Calhoon, Michael L. ... Houston, TX
Calhoon, Ralph E. ... Waco, TX
Calhoon, Ronald L. ... Harrisburg, PA
Calhoun, Alexander D.
San Francisco, CA
Calhoun, Austin J. ... Memphis, TN
Calhoun, Bridget ... New York, NY
Calhoun, Bridget E. ... Washington, DC
Baltimore, MD
Calhoun, Candace K. ... Cumberland, MD
Calhoun, Carol A. ... New York, NY
Calhoun, Carol V. ... Washington, DC
Calhoun, Catherine F. ... Baton Rouge, LA
Calhoun, Cerbone & Sapp, L.L.C.
Savannah, GA
Calhoun, Charles L. ... Macon, GA
Calhoun, Clifford J. ... Boulder, CO
Calhoun, Clinton W., III
White Plains, NY
Calhoun, Cynthia M. ... Anniston, AL
Calhoun, Cynthia Miller
Department of the Army,

Office, Chief of Engineers/Headquarters, U.S. Army Corps of Engineers, GV
Calhoun, D. Allen ... St. Louis, MO
Calhoun, D. Keith ... Atlanta, GA
Calhoun, Daima A. ... Riverside, CA
Calhoun, David A. ... Louisville, KY
Calhoun, David M. ... Atlanta, GA
Calhoun, Donald E., Jr. ... Columbus, OH
Calhoun, Douglas M. Spring Lake Heights, NJ
Calhoun, Edgar P. ... Blountville, TN
Calhoun, Elizabeth C. ... Augusta, GA
Calhoun, Emilie Manning San Francisco, CA
Calhoun, Emily ... Boulder, CO
Calhoun, Eric G. ... Dallas, TX
Calhoun, Faulk, Watkins & Faircloth, L.L.C. Luverne, AL
Troy, AL
Calhoun, Frank K. ... Jacksonville, FL
Calhoun, Frank K., P.A. ... Jacksonville, FL
Calhoun, Frank L. Department of Transportation, Federal Highway Administration, GV
Calhoun, Frank W. ... Austin, TX
Calhoun, Galloway, Jr. ... Tyler, TX
Calhoun, George R., V ... Baltimore, MD
Calhoun, Gordon J. ... Los Angeles, CA
Calhoun, Howard L. ... Akron, OH
Calhoun, J. Rockne ... Louisiana, MO
Calhoun, James P. ... Tampa, FL
Calhoun, Jas. R. C. ... Dillon, SC
Calhoun, Joe ... Portland, OR
Calhoun, John C., Jr. ... Birmingham, AL
Calhoun, John C., Jr. ... Little Rock, AR
North Little Rock, AR
Calhoun, John L. ... Baltimore, MD
Calhoun, John P. ... El Paso, TX
Calhoun, John P., P.C. ... El Paso, TX
Calhoun, John R. ... Long Beach, CA
Calhoun, John R. ... Savannah, GA
Calhoun, Jon Robert ... Los Angeles, CA
Calhoun, Jose M. ... Hartford, CT
Calhoun, Joseph D., III ... Little Rock, AR
Calhoun, Kademenos & Heichel Co., L.P.A. Ashland, OH
Bucyrus, OH
Mansfield, OH
Mt. Gilead, OH
Mt. Vernon, OH
Norwalk, OH
Sandusky, OH
Wooster, OH
Calhoun, Kendall R. ... Crownsville, MD
Calhoun, Kenneth A. ... Savannah, GA
Calhoun, Kevin C. ... Rochester Hills, MI
Calhoun, Laura E. ... Dallas, TX
Calhoun, Marcus B. ... Thomasville, GA
Calhoun, Marcus B., Jr. ... Columbus, GA
Calhoun, Mark Alan ... Dallas, TX
Calhoun, Martin C. ... Washington, DC
Calhoun, Michael D. ... Durham, NC
Calhoun, Mildred L. ... Chicago, IL
Calhoun, Monica Dodd ... New York, NY
Calhoun & Murray ... Vidalia, LA
Calhoun, Murray A. ... New Orleans, LA
Calhoun, Murray A., & Associates, L.L.C. New Orleans, LA
Calhoun, Nancy J. ... Chatsworth, GA
Calhoun, Nathan M. ... Vidalia, LA
Calhoun, O. G., Jr. ... Greenville, SC
Calhoun, O. M. ... Amarillo, TX
Calhoun, Pamela Ann ... Houston, TX
Calhoun, R. Gilbert ... Bellaire, TX
Calhoun, R. Steven ... Alexandria, LA
Calhoun, Richard F. ... Troy, AL
Calhoun, Richard W. ... Marietta, GA
Calhoun, Robert K., Jr. ... San Francisco, CA
Calhoun, Robert L. ... Alexandria, VA
Calhoun, Ronald J., P.C. Sterling Heights, MI
Calhoun, Ronald James Sterling Heights, MI
Calhoun, Ronald L., Law Office of Hanford, CA
Calhoun, Ronald R. ... Gallipolis, OH
Calhoun, Ronald R. ... El Paso, TX
Calhoun, Rory R. ... Garden City, NY
Calhoun, Rosemary L. ... Daytona Beach, FL
Calhoun, S. Bart ... Eureka, MO
St. Louis, MO
Washington, MO
Calhoun, Sally J. ... Peabody, MA
Calhoun, Samuel W. ... Tacoma, WA
Calhoun, Scott D. ... Atlanta, GA
Calhoun, Sonya J. ... Perry, GA
Calhoun & Stacy ... Dallas, TX
Calhoun, Stephen L. ... Nez Perce, ID
Calhoun, Tania L. General Accounting Office, Office of the General Counsel, GV
Calhoun, Thomas H. ... Warner Robins, GA
Calhoun, Todd B. ... Lewiston, ID
Calhoun, Tom P., III ... Greenwood, MS
Calhoun, W. Crisler ... Cupertino, CA
Calhoun, W. McCall, Jr. ... Americus, GA
Calhoun, Waddell, Ufholz & Hunt Akron, OH
Calhoun, Walter S. ... Chicago, IL
Calhoun, Walter W. ... Alpharetta, GA
Calhoun, Weldon O. ... Cameron, TX
Calhoun, William A. ... Mansfield, OH
Calhoun, William A., II ... Irvine, CA
Calhoun, William C. ... Augusta, GA
Calhoun, William F. ... Staten Island, NY
Calhoun, William G. ... Nashville, TN
Calhoun, William H. ... San Diego, CA
Calhoun, William Leland, Jr. ... Roseville, MN
Calhoun, William R., Jr. ... Columbia, SC
Calhoun, William W. ... Atlanta, GA
Calhoun, Wilson ... Corpus Christi, TX
Calhoun, Wm. Daniel ... Fairhope, AL
Calhoun-O'Neal, Bonnie L. ... Greensboro, NC
Cali, Andrea J. Department of Housing and Urban Development, Office of Administrative Law Judges, GV
Cali, Brian J. ... Dunmore, PA
Cali, Diane Marie Deutch ... Hawthorne, NJ
Cali, Leonard J. ... Basking Ridge, NJ
Cali, Mark L. ... Paso Robles, CA
San Luis Obispo, CA
Cali, Mary Catherine ... Baton Rouge, LA
Cali, Michael T. ... New Orleans, LA
Cali, Stephen L. ... Oakland, CA
Cali, Vincent Marc ... New York, NY
Calia, Kurt G. ... Washington, DC
Calia, Lauren R. ... Baltimore, MD
Calianos, Jonathan C. ... Providence, RI
Calibey, Kathryn ... Hartford, CT
Caliboso, Carlito P. ... Honolulu, HI
Calica, Jerome H. ... Miami, FL
Calica, Leah Clifton ... San Diego, CA
Temecula, CA
Calica, Robert M. ... Garden City, NY
Calicchio, Thomas A. ... New York, NY
Calico, Paul B. ... Cincinnati, OH
Caliendo, Anthony R. ... Arlington, MA
Caliendo, Carla S. ... New York, NY
Caliendo, Charles P. ... Melville, NY
Caliendo, Charles T. ... New York, NY
Caliendo, Craig A. ... Milwaukee, WI
Caliendo, Craig M. ... Philadelphia, PA
Caliendo, G. D. ... Pearl River, NY
Caliendo, Madeline Equal Employment Opportunity Commission, Office of Federal Operations, GV
Caliendo, Maura M. ... Scarsdale, NY
Caliendo, Nicholas C. ... Freehold, NJ
Caliendo, Sam C., Law Offices of Boca Raton, FL
Califano, Joseph A., Jr. ... New York, NY
Califano, Mark G. ... Washington, DC
Califano, Peter C. ... San Francisco, CA
Califano, Petra-Kate ... Miami, FL
Califano, Richard T. ... New York, NY
Califano, Thomas R. ... New York, NY
Califf & Harper, P.C. ... Moline, IL
Rock Island, IL
Davenport, IA
Califf, Joan L. ... Department of Justice, Civil Division, GV
Califf, John C. ... Short Hills, NJ
Califf, Junius P. ... Moline, IL
Califf, Paul M. ... Kinnelon, NJ
Calig & Handelman, Co., L.P.A. Columbus, OH
Lancaster, OH
Newark, OH
Calig, Samuel L. ... Columbus, OH
Caligari, Gregory B. ... San Francisco, CA
Caligiuri, Debra N. ... Encinitas, CA
Caligiuri, Hilary L. ... St. Paul, MN
Caligiuri, Maria Antonia Newport Beach, CA
Caligiuri, Sam S.F. ... Hartford, CT
Caliguire, Todd R. ... Englewood Cliffs, NJ
Caliguiri, Michael ... New York, NY
Calihan, Brown, Burgardt, Wurst & Daniel Garden City, KS
Calihan, Patrick J. ... Chicago, IL
Calihan, Ray H., Jr. ... Garden City, KS
Calihan, Robert Barnes ... Rochester, NY
Calikusu, Ioakim Michael ... Bedford, TX
Calille, Albert ... Temecula, CA
Calimafde, George J. ... Mount Prospect, IL
Calimafde, John M., (P.C.) ... New York, NY
Calimafde, Paula A. ... Bethesda, MD
Caliman, A. Noel ... Cincinnati, OH
Caliman, Judith E. ... Detroit, MI
Caliman, Meredith L. ... Los Angeles, CA
Calimlim, Rowene L. ... Winston-Salem, NC
Calin, Sandra ... Anaheim, CA
Calinda, Claire M. ... Toms River, NJ
Calinoff & Katz ... New York, NY
Calinoff, Robert A. ... New York, NY
Calio, Joseph E. Securities and Exchange Commission, Division of Corporation Finance, GV
Calior, John E. ... Hermitage, PA
Caliri, David J. ... Southern Pines, NC
Caliri, Joseph L. ... Wilmette, IL
Caliri, Robert R. ... Chicago, IL
Calise, Christina L. ... Stamford, CT
Calise, Michael R. ... Providence, RI
Calise, Nicholas J. ... Richfield, OH
Calise, William J., Jr. ... Costa Mesa, CA
Calisher, Daniel K. ... San Francisco, CA
Calisoff, Adam Scott ... Chicago, IL
Calisoff, Charles I. ... Chicago, IL
Calister, Richard W. ... San Diego, CA
Calistri, Brian L. ... Philadelphia, PA
Calistri, Ronalyn S. ... Fort Washington, PA
Calistri, Susan A. ... Vero Beach, FL
Calistro, Eugene R., Jr. ... New Haven, CT
Calistro, Roger B. ... New Haven, CT
Calistro, Valerie B. ... New York, NY
Calitre, Philip C. ... Boulder, CO
Caliva, Michael J. ... Chicago, IL
Calivas, Chris W. ... Dover, NH
Calix, Charles T. ... Pasadena, CA
Calix, Sharon J. ... West Palm Beach, FL
Calk, Charles L. ... De Bary, FL
Calk, James I. ... Longview, TX
Calk, Jeffrey A. ... Nashville, TN
Calkin, Judith A. ... Harrisburg, PA
Calkins, Benjamin ... Cleveland, OH
Calkins & Calkins ... Eugene, OR
Calkins & Campbell ... Harrisburg, PA
Calkins, Charles B. ... Shrewsbury, PA
York, PA
Calkins, Charles W. ... Winston-Salem, NC
Calkins, Christopher C. ... Carlsbad, CA
Calkins, Colleen Daphne, (P.C.) Los Angeles, CA
Calkins, Donald A. ... Bradenton, FL
Calkins, Donn L. ... Denver, CO
Calkins, Douglas H. ... Redding, CA
Calkins, George D., II ... Los Angeles, CA
Calkins, Hugh ... Portland, ME
Calkins, J. Scott ... Harrisburg, PA
Calkins, James C. ... Austin, TX
Calkins, James H., Jr. ... Indianapolis, IN
Calkins, John J. ... Washington, DC
Calkins, John W. ... San Francisco, CA
Calkins, Judson W. ... St. Louis, MO
Calkins, Judy Ann ... Eugene, OR
Calkins, Kenneth E. ... Glendale, CA
Calkins, Kevin R. ... Baraboo, WI
Calkins, Lynn Estes ... Washington, DC
Calkins, Mark H. ... Tacoma, WA
Calkins, Mary Beth Voelker New Orleans, LA
Calkins, Mary Craig ... Los Angeles, CA
Calkins, Mary Lynne ... New York, NY
Calkins & Pouravelis ... Portland, ME
Calkins, R. Ronald ... Indianapolis, IN
Calkins, Raymond K. ... Lincoln, NE
Calkins, Richard M. ... Des Moines, IA
Calkins, Robert S. ... Peoria, IL
Calkins, Sarah M. ... Boston, MA
Calkins, Scott A. ... Omaha, NE
Calkins, Scott D. ... Los Angeles, CA
Calkins, Scott R. ... Pittsburgh, PA
Calkins, Sheila Marie ... Cambridge, MA
Calkins, Stephen ... Washington, DC
Calkins, Stephen R. ... Charlotte, NC
Calkins, Steven P. ... New York, NY
Calkins, Susan W. ... Dover-Foxcroft, ME
Calkins, Thomas D. ... Gainesville, GA
Calkins, Thomas W. ... Waterbury, CT
Calkins, Troy M. ... Chicago, IL
Calkins, William D. ... Appleton, WI
Calkins, Win ... Eugene, OR
Calkins-Thompson, Katheryne Midlothian, VA
Calko, Steven ... Los Angeles, CA
Call, Alan C. ... Santa Monica, CA
Call, Barrett & Burbank, A Professional Corporation ... Fairbanks, AK
Call, Blake H. ... Anchorage, AK
Call, Bradley F. ... Washington, DC
Call, Brian D. ... Monterey, CA
Call, C. Bradley ... Venice, CA
Call, Charles G. ... Boston, MA
Call, Christian B. ... Venice, CA
Call, Christopher Douglas ... Salem, OR
Call, Clayton & Jensen, A Professional Corporation ... Newport Beach, CA
Call, Craig M. ... Roy, UT
Call, Cynthia E. ... Athens, GA
Call, Cynthia E., P.C. ... Athens, GA
Call, David G. ... Stamford, CT
Call, David H. ... Fairbanks, AK
Call, David M. ... Phoenix, AZ
Call, David M. ... Hartford, CT
Call, David W. ... San Bernardino, CA
Call, Dawn M. ... Salt Lake City, UT
Call, Deidre J. ... Las Vegas, NV
Call, Elizabeth A. Schallop ... Phoenix, AZ
Call, Ellen Cox ... Louisville, KY
Call, Gary L. ... Charleston, WV
Call, Gregory D. ... Los Angeles, CA
San Francisco, CA
Call, Gregory L. ... North Sioux City, SD
Call, J. Randall ... Park City, UT
Salt Lake City, UT
Call, Jan Fink ... Philadelphia, PA
Call, Jason L. ... St. Louis, MO
Call, John A. ... Edmond, OK
Call, John L., Jr. ... Mount Holly, NJ
Call, John R. ... Los Angeles, CA
Call, John R. ... Denver, CO
Call, John S., Jr. ... West Palm Beach, FL
Call, John W. ... Salt Lake City, UT
Call, Keith A. ... Salt Lake City, UT
Call, Kelly M. ... Alexandria, VA
Call, Kevin L. ... Lionville, PA
Call, Merlin W. ... Los Angeles, CA
Call, Omer J. ... Brigham City, UT
Call, R. Dayton ... Fairfield, CA
Call, Revis T. ... Burbank, CA
Call, Scott A. ... Salt Lake City, UT
Call, Steven W. ... Salt Lake City, UT
Call, Susan H. ... Richmond, VA
Call, W. Davidson ... Raleigh, NC
Call, W. Douglas ... Batavia, NY
Call, Wayne W. ... Newport Beach, CA
Calladine, Guy D. ... San Francisco, CA
Callaghan, Anthony P. ... Newark, NJ
Callaghan, Brian J. ... Atlantic City, NJ
Callaghan & Callaghan, PLLC Summersville, WV
Callaghan, D. Craig ... Philadelphia, PA
Callaghan, Dan O. ... Summersville, WV
Callaghan, Daniel J. ... Manchester, NH
Callaghan, Edward M. ... Oakland, CA
Callaghan, Gerald P. ... Chicago, IL
Callaghan, Hana S. ... Los Altos, CA
Callaghan, Hannah M. ... Portland, OR
Callaghan, John Daniel ... Salem, OR
Callaghan, John L. ... Washington, DC
Callaghan, John P. ... New Bedford, MA
Callaghan, Julia R. ... Summersville, WV
Callaghan, Katherine ... Northampton, MA
Callaghan, Kathleen R. ... Baton Rouge, LA
Callaghan, Kevin ... Missoula, MT
Callaghan, Kevin M. ... White Plains, NY
Callaghan, Lawrence A. San Francisco, CA
Callaghan, Martin J. ... Alexandria, VA
Callaghan, Mary P. ... Katonah, NY
Callaghan, Matthew F., Jr. North Kingstown, RI
Callaghan, Michael O. ... Charleston, WV
Callaghan, Paul S. ... Providence, RI
Callaghan, Peter G. ... Concord, NH
Callaghan, Richard S., Jr. Charlottesville, VA
Callaghan, Richard S., Jr., Ltd. Charlottesville, VA
Callaghan, Robert M. ... Charlottesville, VA
Callaghan, Stephen O. ... Summersville, WV
Callaghan, Susan J. ... Butte, MT
Callaghan, Terry S. ... Grand Rapids, MI
Callaghan, Thomas A. ... Albany, NY
Callaghan, Thomas O. ... Cleveland, OH
Callaghan & Thompson ... Atlantic City, NJ
Callaghan, Thos. M. ... Cleveland, OH
Callaghan, William S. ... Dallas, TX
Callagy, John M. ... Stamford, CT
New York, NY
Callagy, Paul G. ... Poughkeepsie, NY
Callagy, Robert M. ... New York, NY
Callaham, James F., Jr. ... Atlanta, GA
Callaham, William C. ... Sacramento, CA
Callahan, A. Renée ... Washington, DC
Callahan, Albert J. ... Hartford, CT
Callahan, Anne N. ... Wray, CO
Callahan & Arnold ... Columbus, WI
Callahan, Beth A. ... Roseland, NJ
Callahan, Bette P. ... Walnut Creek, CA
Callahan & Blaine, A Professional Law Corporation ... Irvine, CA
Los Angeles, CA
Santa Ana, CA
Callahan, Brian Gerard ... Boston, MA
Callahan, Brian M. ... Schenectady, NY
Callahan, Brian P. ... Smithtown, NY
Callahan, Brian T. ... Boston, MA
Callahan, C. Patrick ... San Diego, CA
Callahan & Callahan ... Wray, CO
Callahan & Callahan ... Lake St. Louis, MO
Callahan & Callahan ... Longview, TX
Callahan & Callahan, P.C. ... Crofton, MD
Callahan, Calley D. ... Austin, TX
Callahan, Candace Hamann Santa Fe, NM
Callahan, Caren ... Santa Rosa, CA
Callahan, Carol A. ... North Brunswick, NJ
Callahan, Carroll B. ... Columbus, WI
Callahan, Catherine A. ... Minnetonka, MN
Callahan, CeeAnn ... Portland, OR
Callahan, Celine T. ... Washington, DC
Callahan, Charles M. ... Phoenix, AZ
Callahan, Charles T. ... Boston, MA
Callahan, Chas. G. ... Dedham, MA
Callahan, Chris ... Rutherfordton, NC
Callahan, Christie M. ... Cherry Hill, NJ
Philadelphia, PA
Callahan, Christine D. ... Concord, CA
Callahan, Christopher J. ... Chicago, IL
Callahan, Christopher L. ... Phoenix, AZ
Callahan, Connie M. ... Sacramento, CA
Callahan, Cornelius P., Jr. ... Chicago, IL
Callahan, Courtney A. Fort Lauderdale, FL
Callahan, Craig A. ... Newport Beach, CA
Callahan, Curtiss, Carey and Gates Greenfield, MA
Callahan, Cynthia ... Rockville, MD
Callahan, Cynthia Light ... Petaluma, CA
Callahan, Daniel F. ... Baltimore, MD
Callahan, Daniel F. ... New York, NY
Callahan, Daniel J. ... Santa Ana, CA
Callahan, Daniel L. ... Fairbanks, AK
Callahan, Daniel P. ... Dallas, TX
Callahan, David K. ... Chicago, IL
Callahan, David P. ... New York, NY
Callahan, David Patrick ... Oxnard, CA
Callahan, Dawnvolynn D. ... Omaha, NE
Callahan & Deacon ... Sacramento, CA
Callahan, Deirdre Julia ... Fort Washington, PA
Callahan, Dennis J. ... Chicago, IL
Callahan, Dennis L. ... St. Louis, MO
Callahan, Dennis R. ... Fort Washington, PA
Callahan, Dennis W. ... Atwater, CA
Callahan, Douglas J. ... Fenton, MI
Callahan, Dwight P. ... Florence, AZ
Callahan, Edward D. ... Westlake Village, CA
Callahan, Edward J., Jr. Minneapolis, MN
Callahan, Edward M., Jr. ... Roseland, NJ
Callahan, Edward T. ... Scarsdale, NY
Callahan, Elizabeth O. ... Southfield, MI
Callahan, Ellen Ann ... Gaithersburg, MD
Callahan, Elletta Sangrey ... Syracuse, NY
Callahan, Eugene G. ... Oak Brook, IL
Callahan, Eugene J. ... Loveladies, NJ
Callahan, Eugene J. ... New York, NY
Callahan, F. Murray ... Rockville, MD
Callahan, F. Sullivan ... Norfolk, VA
Callahan, F. Terry ... San Antonio, TX
Callahan, F. Terry, P.C., Law Office of San Antonio, TX
Callahan, G. Kevin Spring Lake Heights, NJ
Callahan, Gary B., (Inc.) ... Sacramento, CA
Callahan, Gary W. ... Greeley, CO
Callahan, George M. Hot Springs National Park, AR

Callahan, Gerald W. .... Oil City, PA
Callahan, Glenn P. .... Cherry Hill, NJ
Philadelphia, PA
Callahan, H. Patrick .... Indianapolis, IN
Callahan & Hamann, P.C. .... Santa Fe, NM
Callahan, J. Christopher .... Springfield, VT
Callahan, J. Kevin .... St. Paul, MN
Callahan, J. Kim .... Longview, TX
Callahan, J. Patrick, P.C. .... Trenton, IL
Callahan, J. William .... Detroit, MI
Callahan, Jack W. .... Wichita Falls, TX
Callahan, James A. .... Detroit, MI
Callahan, James Byrne .... Newport, RI
Callahan, James J. .... Cedar Rapids, IA
Callahan, James J. .... Jersey City, NJ
Callahan, James J. .... New York, NY
Callahan, James J., III .... Baldwin, NY
Callahan, James M. .... Portland, OR
Callahan, James P. .... Trenton, IL
Callahan, James V. .... Chicago, IL
Callahan, Jane A. .... Rochester, MN
Callahan, Jane Dunlap .... Orlando, FL
Callahan, Janet D. .... Syracuse, NY
Callahan, Jeffrey R. .... Miami Springs, FL
Callahan, Jennifer H.
Oklahoma City, OK
Callahan, Jennifer M. .... Boston, MA
Callahan, Jennifer Timmeney
Scranton, PA
Callahan, Joanne M.
Environmental Protection Agency,
Office of Enforcement and Compliance
Assurance, GV
Callahan, John G. .... Scarsdale, NY
Callahan, John H. .... Syracuse, NY
Callahan, John J. .... Washington, DC
Callahan, John J. .... Glen Burnie, MD
Callahan, John J. .... Elizabeth, NJ
Callahan, John J. .... Buffalo, NY
Callahan, John J. .... Toledo, OH
Callahan, John J., Jr. .... Huntsville, AL
Callahan, John K. .... Monroe, WI
Callahan, John M. .... Chicago, IL
Callahan, John M. .... Northampton, MA
Callahan, John M. .... Southfield, MI
Callahan, John P. .... Geneva, IL
Callahan, John P., Jr. .... Oak Brook, IL
Callahan, John R. .... Boston, MA
Callahan, John T. .... Washington, DC
Callahan, John T., III .... Norfolk, VA
Callahan, John W. .... West Hartford, CT
Callahan, Joseph F. .... St. Louis, MO
Callahan, Joseph M. .... Syracuse, NY
Callahan, Joseph P. .... New York, NY
Callahan, Joseph P. .... Richmond, VA
Callahan, Joseph T. .... Wray, CO
Callahan, Joyce Balich .... Dedham, MA
Callahan, Karen L. .... Tulsa, OK
Callahan, Karin E. .... Altadena, CA
Callahan, Katherine C. .... Hartford, CT
Callahan, Kathleen A. .... Marblehead, MA
Callahan, Kathleen Joy .... Syracuse, NY
Callahan, Kathleen M. .... Omaha, NE
Callahan, Kelley C. .... Oklahoma City, OK
Callahan, Kelly Patrick .... Albert Lea, MN
Callahan, Kenneth E. .... Albuquerque, NM
Callahan, Kerry R. .... Hartford, CT
Callahan, Kevin G. .... Jersey City, NJ
Callahan, Kevin K. .... Pasadena, CA
Callahan, Kevin L. .... Minneapolis, MN
Callahan, Kevin O'Leary .... Denver, CO
Callahan, Kimmer W. .... Coeur d'Alene, ID
Callahan, Kirsten Nelson .... Boston, MA
Callahan, Laura Marie .... Chicago, IL
Winnetka, IL
Callahan Law Firm
Hot Springs National Park, AR
Callahan Law Firm .... Tallahassee, FL
Callahan Law Offices, A Professional
Corporation .... Newport, RI
Callahan, Lawrence .... Williamstown, MA
Callahan, Leslie D. .... Liberty Corner, NJ
Callahan, Little & Sullivan .... San Diego, CA
Callahan, Lori M. .... Topeka, KS
Callahan, M. James .... Phoenix, AZ
Callahan, Marc K. .... Irvine, CA
Callahan, Margaret C. .... Des Moines, IA
Callahan, Margaret W. .... Toledo, OH
Callahan, Marian Hyler
Department of Justice,
Bureau of Prisons, GV
Callahan, Mark B. .... Harrisonburg, VA
Callahan, Mary Ann .... Chicago, IL
Callahan, Mary Ellen .... Washington, DC
Callahan, Matilda Radalj .... Los Angeles, CA
Callahan, Maureen A. .... Baldwin, NY
Callahan, Maureen Theresa .... Atlanta, GA
Callahan, McCune & Willis, LLP
Los Angeles, CA
San Diego, CA
Tustin, CA
Callahan, Michael E. .... Overland Park, KS
Callahan, Michael F. .... Chevy Chase, MD
Callahan, Michael F. .... Boston, MA
Callahan, Michael J. .... Foster City, CA
Callahan, Michael J. .... Detroit, MI
Callahan, Michael J. .... Union, NJ
Callahan, Michael K. .... Cambridge, MA
Callahan, Michael R. .... Chicago, IL
Callahan, Michael R. .... Concord, NH
Callahan, Michael S. .... Kentwood, MI
Callahan, Michael S. .... San Antonio, TX
Callahan, Michael T. .... Tallahassee, FL
Callahan, Michael T. .... Overland Park, KS
Callahan, Michael T. .... Akron, OH
Callahan, Michael W. .... Pueblo, CO
Callahan, Nancy Kay .... New York, NY
Callahan, Neal J. .... Columbus, GA

Callahan, Nicholas P., III .... Fairhope, AL
Callahan, Nicholas P., Jr. .... Fairfield, AL
Callahan, Patrice M. .... Los Angeles, CA
Callahan, Patricia E. .... New York, NY
Callahan, Patricia M. .... New York, NY
Callahan, Patrick .... Kailua-Kona, HI
Callahan, Patrick J. .... Crofton, MD
Callahan, Patrick K. .... Portland, OR
Callahan, Patrick M. .... Newark, NJ
Callahan, Paul F. .... Brooklyn, NY
Callahan, Paul M. .... Duanesburg, NY
Schenectady, NY
Callahan, Paul W. .... Norristown, PA
Callahan, Peter F. X. .... Media, PA
Callahan, Peter M. .... Tustin, CA
Callahan & Prohaska, Chtd.
Coeur d'Alene, ID
Sandpoint, ID
Callahan, Randall C. .... St. Petersburg, FL
Callahan, Raymond F. .... Denver, CO
Callahan, Rebecca .... Newport Beach, CA
Callahan, Rebecca, A Professional Law
Corporation .... Newport Beach, CA
Callahan, Richard G. .... Jefferson City, MO
Callahan, Richard J. .... Williamsport, PA
Callahan, Richard M., Jr. .... Pasadena, CA
Callahan, Richard P.
West Palm Beach, FL
Callahan, Richard W. .... Hamden, CT
Callahan, Robert A. .... Kalamazoo, MI
Callahan, Robert E. .... Irvine, CA
Callahan, Robert F. .... Bridgewater, NJ
Callahan, Robert J. .... Hartford, CT
Callahan, Robert J. .... Chicago, IL
Callahan, Robert J. .... New York, NY
Callahan, Robert J., Jr. .... Lake St. Louis, MO
Callahan, Robert L., III .... Atlanta, GA
Callahan, Robert L., Jr. .... Atlanta, GA
Callahan, Robert M. .... Farmingdale, NY
Callahan, Robert P. .... New York, NY
Callahan, Sally K. .... Sacramento, CA
Callahan, Scott P. .... Houston, TX
Callahan, Sean E. .... Washington, DC
Callahan & Shears, P.C. .... Portland, OR
Callahan, Stephen J. .... Boston, MA
Callahan, Stephen P. .... Houma, LA
Callahan, Steven B. .... New York, NY
Callahan, Teresa A. .... Princeton, NJ
Callahan, Thomas A., Jr. .... Newark, NJ
Callahan, Thomas E. .... Woburn, MA
Callahan, Thomas J. .... Wray, CO
Callahan, Thomas J. .... Holbrook, MA
Callahan, Thomas J. .... Tenafly, NJ
Callahan, Thomas J. .... Cleveland, OH
Callahan, Thomas R. .... Crofton, MD
Callahan, Timothy .... Walnut Creek, CA
Callahan, Timothy J. .... Los Angeles, CA
Callahan, Timothy J. .... Kenilworth, NJ
Callahan, Timothy J. .... Vienna, VA
Callahan, Timothy Neal .... Seattle, WA
Callahan, Timothy P. .... Chicago, IL
Callahan, Timothy W. .... Winter Park, FL
Callahan, Timothy W., II
Philadelphia, PA
Callahan, Tracy Glenn .... East Hanover, NJ
Callahan, W. Scott .... Orlando, FL
Callahan, Wendy E. .... Wellesley Hills, MA
Callahan, William B. .... Norristown, PA
Callahan, William E., Jr. .... Roanoke, VA
Callahan, William E., Jr. .... Milwaukee, WI
Callahan, William F., III .... New York, NY
Callahan, William L. .... Beltsville, MD
Ellicott City, MD
Callahan, William P. .... New York, NY
Callahan & Wolkoff, P.C. .... New York, NY
Callahan-Brown, Linda J. .... Findlay, OH
Callahan-Freeberg, Bobbie Y. .... Tulsa, OK
Callais, Lee A. .... Lockport, LA
Callam, Alexandra K. .... Boston, MA
Providence, RI
Callam, Dorothy Eileen
West Palm Beach, FL
Callam, Paul A. .... Ann Arbor, MI
Callan, Ann Penland .... San Francisco, CA
Callan, Bernard T. .... Bay Shore, NY
Callan & Byrnes .... New York, NY
Callan, Cesar .... New York, NY
Callan, Edward W. .... San Diego, CA
Callan, Erin M. .... New York, NY
Callan, James M., Jr. .... Clearwater, FL
Spring Hill, FL
Callan, James M., Jr., P.A. .... Clearwater, FL
Spring Hill, FL
Callan, James Michael .... El Paso, TX
Callan, James R. .... White Plains, NY
Callan, Jennifer F. .... El Paso, TX
Callan, Joan S. .... Chicago, IL
Callan, John C., Jr. .... San Francisco, CA
Callan, John F. .... Milwaukee, WI
Callan, John Marsden .... Lowell, MA
Callan, John P., Sr. .... Cocoa Beach, FL
Callan, John Thomas .... Irvine, CA
Callan, Kathleen M. .... Cumberland, MD
Callan, Laura E. .... Madison, WI
Callan, Mary Beth .... Green Bay, WI
Callan, Michael J. .... Fort Smith, AR
Callan, Michael K. .... Springfield, MA
Callan, Michael T. .... Bellevue, WA
Callan, Michelle L. .... Rochester, NY
Callan, Norman D. .... Hollidaysburg, PA
Callan, Paul F. .... Shrewsbury, NJ
New York, NY
Callan, Paul R. .... Middleboro, MA
Callan, Philip J., Jr. .... Springfield, MA
Callan, Regenstreich, Koster & Brady
Shrewsbury, NJ
Garden City, NY
New York, NY

Callan, Robert E. .... Rolling Meadows, IL
Callan, Robin .... Bellevue, WA
Callan, Scott .... Rome, GA
Callan, Sean P. .... Cincinnati, OH
Callan, Sullivan & Burke, P.C. .... Lowell, MA
Callan, Susan E. .... Middleboro, MA
Callan, Terrence A. .... San Francisco, CA
Callan, Thomas J. .... Round Rock, TX
Callan, Thomas P. .... Orlando, FL
Callan, Thomas P., P.A. .... Orlando, FL
West Palm Beach, FL
Callan, Thos. L. .... Milwaukee, WI
Callan & Willis, Professional Corporation
Breckenridge, CO
Callanan, Casey E. .... Buffalo, NY
Callanan, Charles F. .... Los Angeles, CA
Callanan, Christopher A. .... Boston, MA
Callanan, Evan H., Jr. .... Plymouth, MI
Callanan, Gailyc Sonia .... Boston, MA
Callanan, Geo. T. .... Los Angeles, CA
Callanan, Jane E. .... New York, NY
Callanan, John P., Sr. .... Watkins Glen, NY
Callanan, John W. .... Pine Bush, NY
Callanan, Karen Smith .... Rochester, NY
Callanan, Kevin B., Law Office of
Boston, MA
Callanan, Kevin B., Law Office of
Norwell, MA
Callanan, Margaret C. .... Buffalo, NY
Callanan, Margaret M. .... Boston, MA
Callanan, Richard F. .... New York, NY
Calland, Dean A. .... Pittsburgh, PA
Calland, Warren W. .... Phoenix, AZ
Callander, Amanda Lee .... Mount Pleasant, SC
Callander, Diane .... Denton, TX
Callander, Douglas L. .... Kalamazoo, MI
Callanen, Foley & Hobika .... Marcy, NY
Utica, NY
Callard, Elizabeth C. .... Ignacio, CO
Callard, George D. .... Chicago, IL
Callard, Tracy Taylor .... Wichita, KS
Callari, Andrew C. .... Irvine, CA
Callari, Joseph A. .... Wall, NJ
Callas, Christopher L. .... Charleston, WV
Callas, Darcy G. .... Rock Island, IL
Callas, Felopulos & Ditelberg, LLP
Boston, MA
Callas, Franklin G. .... Palm Beach, FL
Callas, George N. .... Hartford, CT
Callas, Gretchen M. .... Charleston, WV
Callas, Gust .... Canton, OH
Callas, James C. .... Ontario, CA
Callas, John S. .... Rock Island, IL
Callas, Nicholas G. .... Columbia, SC
Callas, Perry G. .... Crystal Lake, IL
Callaway, Ann M. .... Warrenton, VA
Callaway, Ann M., P.C. .... Warrenton, VA
Callaway and Associates .... Houston, TX
Callaway, Barbara J. .... Prescott, AZ
Callaway and Bradley .... Huntsville, AL
Callaway, Bryan H. .... Greenwood, MS
Callaway, Carol G. .... Houston, TX
Callaway, Carolyn .... Albuquerque, NM
Callaway, Carolyn, P.C.
Albuquerque, NM
Callaway, Carrie M. .... San Francisco, CA
Callaway, Catherine Balon .... Houston, TX
Callaway, Charles C. .... Walters, OK
Callaway, Charles C., Jr.
Oklahoma City, OK
Callaway, Claudia Treadwell
Washington, DC
Callaway, C. W. (Dugan), Jr.
Birmingham, AL
Callaway, Douglas D. .... Richmond, VA
Callaway, E. Stephen .... Georgetown, DE
Callaway, Edward Moye .... Nashville, TN
Callaway, Ellen C. .... Department of Defense,
Defense Legal Services Agency, GV
Callaway, Eugene V. .... Houston, TX
Callaway, F.M., P.C. .... Colorado Springs, CO
Callaway, Frank Thomas .... Knoxville, TN
Callaway, Fredrick M.
Colorado Springs, CO
Callaway, Gregory W. .... Nashville, TN
Callaway, Harold D., III .... Gulf Shores, AL
Callaway, Henry A., III .... Mobile, AL
Callaway, Howe & Detro .... Omak, WA
Callaway, J. Brice .... Huntsville, AL
Callaway, James A., Jr. .... Davis, CA
Callaway, Joe I. .... Dallas, TX
Callaway, Jon S. .... Madison, WI
Callaway, Joseph Newton
Rocky Mount, NC
Callaway, Lawrence C., III .... Ocala, FL
Callaway, M. Catherine .... Huntsville, AL
Callaway, Mark R. .... Cleveland, TN
Callaway, Mary M. .... Pensacola, FL
Callaway, Mary M., P.A. .... Pensacola, FL
Callaway, Michael E. .... Cleveland, TN
Callaway, Neal S. .... Fort Worth, TX
Callaway, Neville & Brinson .... Claxton, GA
Metter, GA
Statesboro, GA
Callaway, Patrick T. .... Overland Park, KS
Callaway, Patrick T., P.C.
Overland Park, KS
Callaway, Paul R. .... Pittsford, NY
Callaway, Peg R. .... Omak, WA
Callaway, R. Boone .... San Francisco, CA
Callaway, Richard F., Jr. .... Houston, TX
Callaway, Richard J. .... Madison, WI
Callaway, Robert L. .... Dallas, TX
Callaway, Saml. R. .... Dunwoody, GA
Callaway, Sharon E. .... San Antonio, TX
Callaway, Stephen V. .... Shreveport, LA
Callaway, Steve M. .... Birmingham, AL
Callaway, Timothy F., III .... Savannah, GA

Callaway, William E., Jr. .... Claxton, GA
Metter, GA
Statesboro, GA
Callaway, William H. .... Tucson, AZ
Callaway, William H. .... Los Altos, CA
Callaway, William H., Jr.
Washington, DC
Callaway, William O., Jr. .... Fort Worth, TX
Callaway & Wolf .... San Francisco, CA
Callcott, Cynthia M. .... Dallas, TX
Callcott, John R. .... Nashville, TN
Callcott, W. Hardy
Securities and Exchange Commission,
Office of the General Counsel, GV
Calle, Jim E. .... Tucson, AZ
Callea, Carol Ann .... Waterbury, VT
Callea, Louis J. .... Greene, NY
Callear, Charles L. .... Rochester, NY
Callear, James Y.
Federal Mine Safety and Health Review
Commission,
Office of the General Counsel, GV
Callegary & Callegary .... Baltimore, MD
Callegary, Claude L. .... Baltimore, MD
Callegary, Ellen .... Baltimore, MD
Callegary, Peter M. .... Baltimore, MD
Callegary, Raymond E. .... Baltimore, MD
Callegary & Steedman, P.A. .... Baltimore, MD
Callegher, Nancy L. .... Washington, DC
Calleja, Kristen M. .... Richmond, VA
Callejas, Esteban R. .... Bowling Green, OH
Callejo, Adelfa B., (Mrs.) .... Dallas, TX
Callejo & Callejo .... Dallas, TX
Callejo, Ricardo A. .... San Francisco, CA
Callejo, William F. .... Dallas, TX
Callen, Bernard A. .... Jersey City, NJ
Callen, Craig R. .... Jackson, MS
Callen, Danielle .... New Orleans, LA
Callen, Dennis M. .... Jersey City, NJ
Callen, Eldon A. .... Morgantown, WV
Callen, George M., III .... Birmingham, AL
Callen, Jed Z. .... Henniker, NH
Callen, Mark B. .... Spokane, WA
Callen, Michael E. .... Kansas City, KS
Callen, Michael K. .... Morgantown, WV
Callen, Paul C. .... House of Representatives,
Office of Legislative Counsel, GV
Callen, R. Scott .... Tallahassee, FL
Callen, Ralph I. .... Anaheim, CA
Callen, Richard B. .... Rochester, NY
Callender, Alvin, Jr. .... Houston, TX
Callender, Arlene B. .... Dothan, AL
Callender, C. Duane .... Toledo, OH
Callender, Dale E. .... New York, NY
Callender, J. Holligan .... New Rochelle, NY
Callender, James S., Jr. .... Mentor, OH
Callender, John F. .... Jacksonville, FL
Callender, Lynnette E. James
Jacksonville, FL
Callender, Mark R. .... Greensburg, LA
Callender, M.C.
Charlotte Amalie, St. Thomas, VI
Callender, Sidney D. .... San Antonio, TX
Callender, William C. .... Columbia, MS
Callender, William L. .... Los Angeles, CA
Callens, Christian P. .... Houston, TX
Caller, Aldo P. .... Overland Park, KS
Calleri, Angelo T. .... Rochester, NY
Calleri, Angelo T., P.C. .... Rochester, NY
Calleros, Charles R. .... Tempe, AZ
Callery, Bart J., Jr. .... Lowell, MA
Callery, Catherine M. .... Rochester, NY
Callery, Raymond J. .... Peoria, IL
Callery, T. Grant .... Washington, DC
Callery, Thomas W. .... Lewiston, ID
Calles, John E. .... Miami, FL
Callesen, Margaret S. .... Cleveland, OH
Callesen, Phillip M. .... Cleveland, OH
Callet, David P., (P.C.) .... Washington, DC
Calleton, Theodore E. .... Pasadena, CA
Calleton & Trytten, LLP .... Pasadena, CA
Calley, C. Leon .... Houston, TX
Calley, Cyril D. .... Alexandria, VA
Calley, Daniel P. .... New York, NY
Calli, Robert Ross .... Utica, NY
Calli, William S. .... Utica, NY
Calli, William S., Jr. .... Utica, NY
Callicotte, Harry D., P.S.C.
Elizabethtown, KY
Fort Knox, KY
Radcliff, KY
Callicotte, Harry Don .... Radcliff, KY
Callicutt, K. Hayes .... Jackson, MS
Callier, Charles E., Jr. .... St. Louis, MO
Callier & Garza .... Houston, TX
Callier, Jefferson C. .... Columbus, GA
Callier, Joseph Alan .... Houston, TX
Callier, Linda H. .... Columbus, GA
Callies, David L. .... Honolulu, HI
Callies, Lisa E. .... Hauppauge, NY
Callies, Paula A. .... Eden Prairie, MN
Callies, Robert W. .... Seattle, WA
Calligan, Michael D. .... Seattle, WA
Calligar, Dee M. .... New York, NY
Calligaro, Julie A. .... Taylor, MI
Calligaro, Lee .... Washington, DC
Callihan, Michael B. .... Bryan, TX
Callihan, Brent L. .... Alabaster, AL
Callihan, Cherry Owens .... Lexington, KY
Callihan, David L. .... Harrisburg, PA
Callihan, Lorey L. .... Greenville, SC
Callinan, John F.
Cape May Court House, NJ
Callinan, John W. .... Springfield, NJ
Callinan, Maureen .... Pittsford, NY
Callinan, Thomas V., Jr. .... Woburn, MA
Callion, Luther .... Los Angeles, CA
Calliotte, Clyde D., (Mrs.) .... Little Rock, AR

Callipari, Marc D. ....Denver, CO
Callis, Ann E. ....Granite City, IL
Callis, Cheryl ....St. Louis, MO
Callis, Clifford L., Jr. ....Rainbow City, AL
Callis, James P. ....Fraser, MI
Callis, John Harlan, III Prestonsburg, KY
Callis, Lance ....Granite City, IL
Callis, P. ....Oakland, CA
Callis, Papa, Jackstadt & Halloran, P.C. Granite City, IL
Callis, Robert L. ....Mount Juliet, TN
Callis & Stover ....Gadsden, AL
Rainbow City, AL
Callison, Donald M. ....Arlington, VA
Callison, Dorn, Thomason & Knott, P.A. Greenwood, SC
Callison, George Preston (G.P.), Jr. Greenwood, SC
Callison, Glenn B. ....Dallas, TX
Callison, G. P. ....Greenwood, SC
Callison, J. William ....Denver, CO
Callison, Jack R. ....Cayce, SC
Callison, John C. ....Nashville, TN
Callison, John M. ....Saginaw, MI
Callison, Laura A. ....Jacksonville, FL
Callison, Linda A. F. ....Palo Alto, CA
Callison, Orion Gray, III ....Miami, FL
Callison, Preston H. ....West Columbia, SC
Callison, Richard H. ....Houston, TX
Callison, Russell J. ....San Francisco, CA
Callison, Susan, (P.C.) ....Memphis, TN
Callison, Thomas E. ....Denver, CO
Callison Tighe & Robinson, LLP Columbia, SC
Callison, William A. ....Chicago, IL
Callison, William A. ....Brewster, OH
Callister & Callister ....Glendale, CA
Callister, Daniel Q. ....Washington, DC
Callister, Douglas L. ....Glendale, CA
Callister & Hendricks, A Professional Law Corporation ....Merced, CA
Callister, Janet L. ....Newport Beach, CA
Callister, Jerry E. ....Merced, CA
Callister, John C. ....Pasadena, CA
Callister, Louis H. ....Salt Lake City, UT
Callister, Marion J. ....Boise, ID
Callister, Mark L. ....Salt Lake City, UT
Callister, Matthew Q. ....Las Vegas, NV
Callister Nebeker & McCullough, A Professional Corporation Salt Lake City, UT
Callister, Paul D. ....Glendale, CA
Callister & Reynolds ....Las Vegas, NV
Callister, Richard C. ....Pasadena, CA
Callister, Robert ....Las Vegas, NV
Callister, Stephen R. ....Glendale, CA
Callister, Susan P. ....San Ramon, CA
Callister, Tad R. ....Glendale, CA
Callister, Thomas K. ....Newport Beach, CA
Callner, Bruce W. ....Atlanta, GA
Callo, Armin R. ....San Diego, CA
Callo, Dominick F. ....New York, NY
Callobre, Anthony R. ....Los Angeles, CA
Callon, Kathleen ....San Francisco, CA
Callon, Linda A. ....San Jose, CA
Callon, Mark ....Kirkland, WA
Callori, Frederick P. ....Boston, MA
Callow, Amy Gasser ....Cincinnati, OH
Callow, James M. ....New Orleans, LA
Callow, Joseph M., Jr. ....Cincinnati, OH
Callow, Keith M. ....Olympia, WA
Callow, Mary E. ....Wheaton, IL
Callow, Thomas E. ....Bloomfield Hills, MI
Callow, Wm. G. ....Madison, WI
Callow, Wm. Grant ....Anchorage, AK
Callow, Wm. Grant, A Professional Corporation ....Anchorage, AK
Calloway & Calloway, P.C. ....Atlanta, GA
Calloway, Claude R. ....Waukegan, IL
Calloway, Curtis A. ....Baton Rouge, LA
Calloway, Curtis C. ....St. Louis, MO
Calloway, Dean A. ....Atlanta, GA
Calloway, Deborah A. ....Hartford, CT
Calloway, Diane S. ....Atlanta, GA
Calloway, George C. ....Atlanta, GA
Calloway & Hofmann, P.C. Hilton Head Island, SC
Calloway, James A. ....Oklahoma City, OK
Calloway, James R. ....United States Senate, Committee Legal Personnel, GV
Calloway, Jerelene ....Riverside, CA
Calloway, Jocelyn L. ....Mount Holly, NJ
Calloway, K. Brian ....Houston, TX
Calloway, Karen M. ....Fayetteville, GA
Calloway, Kenneth E. ....Wildwood, NJ
Calloway, Kenneth E., A Professional Corporation ....Wildwood, NJ
Calloway, Laura A. ....Montgomery, AL
Calloway, Mark T. ....Charlotte, NC
Calloway, Nan Shelby ....Nashville, TN
Calloway, Norris & Burdette ....Dallas, TX
Calloway, R.W. ....Dallas, TX
Calloway, S. Marcus ....Atlanta, GA
Calloway, S. Marcus, P.C. ....Atlanta, GA
Calloway, Shirley R. ....Chicago, IL
Calloway, Sidney C. ....Fort Lauderdale, FL
Calloway, Sue Dill ....Columbus, OH
Calloway, Valerie L. ....Richfield, OH
Calloway, Vern D., Jr. ....Tallahassee, FL
Calloway, W. E. ....Columbia, SC
Callsen, Julie A. ....Cleveland, OH
Callum, Alice W. ....Ypsilanti, MI
Callum, Thomas E. ....Wheaton, IL
Calluori, Joseph ....New York, NY
Callwood, June B. ....New York, NY
Calma, John Cardona ....Kapaa, HI
Calmann, Arnold B. ....Newark, NJ
Calmar, Harry E. ....New London, CT
Calmes, Jeffrey C. ....Baton Rouge, LA
Calmes, Joseph C. ....Bellevue, WA
Calnan, Alan ....Los Angeles, CA
Calnan, Cornelius J. ....Houston, TX
Calnan, Cornelius J. and Associates, Law Offices of, P.C. ....Houston, TX
Calnan, Mary Ann ....Lynnfield, MA
Calnan, Mary E. ....Cambridge, MA
Calnan, Sean C. ....Springfield, MA
Calnan, William E. ....West Palm Beach, FL
Calnan, William H., IV ....Parsippany, NJ
Calne, Max ....New York, NY
Calnero, Carl J. ....Sacramento, CA
Calo, Dena B. ....Philadelphia, PA
Calo, Dennis ....Hackensack, NJ
Calo, Frank F., III ....Cherry Hill, NJ
Calo, Robert R. ....Philadelphia, PA
Calobrisi, Carla ....Washington, DC
Caloca-Johnson, Dawn ....Tallahassee, FL
Caloca-Johnson, Dawn, P.A. ....Tallahassee, FL
Calocci, Kelly K. ....Denver, CO
Caloccia, Mary Elizabeth ....Homewood, IL
Calof, Alvin ....Riverside, CA
Calof, Lawrence ....Palo Alto, CA
Calof, Manly D. ....Van Nuys, CA
Calof, Michael P. ....Woodland Hills, CA
Calof, Michael P., Inc. ....Woodland Hills, CA
Caloger, Philip D. ....Chicago, IL
Calogero, David J. ....Lafayette, LA
Calogero, Gina A. ....Hackensack, NJ
Calogero, Gina Rush ....Lafayette, LA
Calogero, Michael G. ....Metairie, LA
Calogero, Michael G., LLC ....Metairie, LA
Calogero, Pascal F., Jr. ....New Orleans, LA
Calogero, Stefano ....Parsippany, NJ
New York, NY
Calogero, Stephen A. ....Dayton, OH
Calogero, Thomas M. ....New Orleans, LA
Calogero, Valerie P. ....Department of Justice, Federal Bureau of Investigation, GV
Caloia, Houpt & Light, P.C. Glenwood Springs, CO
Caloia, Sherry A. ....Glenwood Springs, CO
Caloir, Helene O. ....Bronx, NY
Calomeni, Dale A. ....Roswell, GA
Calomiris & Calomiris, P.A. ....Bethesda, MD
Calomiris, Carol L. ....Bethesda, MD
Calomiris, James G. ....Bethesda, MD
Calone, Richard S. ....Stockton, CA
Calone, Richard S., Inc. ....Stockton, CA
Calonge, Gloria ....Falls Church, VA
Calongne, R. J., Jr. ....Baton Rouge, LA
Calonita, Timothy ....Garden City, NY
Calore, Lynda J. L. ....New York, NY
Calore, Patricia A. ....Lansing, MI
Calore, William J. ....Wayne, NJ
Calos, Stefan Mitchell ....Hopewell, VA
Calotta, John G. ....New York, NY
Calotta Levine Samuel, LLP ....New York, NY
Caloway, Mary F. ....Wilmington, DE
Caloyer, Mark T. ....Pittsburgh, PA
Calrow, Paul E. ....Walnut Creek, CA
Calsada, Glenn Ward ....Los Angeles, CA
Caltagirone, James V. ....Tampa, FL
Caltagirone, James V., & Associates, P.A. Tampa, FL
Caltagirone, Librande P. ....Drexel Hill, PA
Caltagirone, Paul ....Poughkeepsie, NY
Calto, Joseph T. ....New York, NY
Calton & Calton ....Eufaula, AL
Calton, Calvin A. ....Billings, MT
Calton, Deborah A. ....Kansas City, MO
Calton, Frances M. ....Billings, MT
Calton Hamman & Wolff, A Professional Corporation ....Billings, MT
Calton, James B. ....Joplin, MO
Webb City, MO
Calton, Jimmy S., Jr. ....Eufaula, AL
Calton, Jimmy S., Sr. ....Eufaula, AL
Calton, John L. ....Englewood, CO
Calton, Judy B. ....Detroit, MI
Calton, Roger W. ....Laguna Niguel, CA
Calton, Walter B. ....Eufaula, AL
Caltrider, Arthur P., Jr. ....Baltimore, MD
Caltrider, Joseph L. ....Charles Town, WV
Martinsburg, WV
Caltrider, Steven P. ....Indianapolis, IN
Calucchia, Danielle M. ....Chicago, IL
Caluwaert, John M. ....Elmhurst, IL
Caluwaert, Kristen R. ....Elmhurst, IL
Caluwaert & Panegasser ....Elmhurst, IL
Calvacca, Anthony S. ....Mineola, NY
Calvacca, Lynn ....Flushing, NY
Calvacca, Stephen J. ....Orlando, FL
Calvagna, John J. ....Los Angeles, CA
Calvanese, Peter J. ....Garden City, NY
Calvani, Terry ....Washington, DC
Calvanico, Thomas P. ....Jersey City, NJ
Calvarese, Joseph A. (Jay), Jr. ....Denver, CO
Calvarese, Stephen C. ....Tulsa, OK
Calvaruso, Andrea L. ....New York, NY
Calvaruso, Edmund A. ....Rochester, NY
Calvaruso, Joseph A. ....New York, NY
Calve, Andrea U. ....Allen, TX
Calve, James P. ....Department of Commerce, Patent and Trademark Office, GV
Calve, Rosalie ....New York, NY
Calvelli, Gina M. ....Los Angeles, CA
Calvelli, John F. ....House of Representatives, Congressional Assistants, GV
Calvelli, Maria Dimeo ....New York, NY
Calvelli, Rick T. ....Milwaukee, WI
Calvelli, Rocke A. ....Milwaukee, WI
Calvello, Donald C. ....San Jose, CA
Calver, Merlin G. ....Ogden, UT
Calver, Tracey A. ....Los Angeles, CA
Calverley, David J. ....Phoenix, AZ
Calverley, Helen M. ....Santa Clara, CA
Calvert & Associates, P.C. ....Fairfax, VA
Manassas, VA
Calvert & Bryant ....Englewood, CO
Calvert, C. Douglas ....Dallas, TX
Calvert, C. Tok ....Burbank, CA
Calvert, Camille ....San Francisco, CA
Calvert, Carey Cobb ....Tulsa, OK
Calvert, Carl A. ....Albuquerque, NM
Calvert, Carrie M. ....Tucson, AZ
Calvert, Clay ....Sacramento, CA
Calvert, Curtis R. ....Chicago, IL
Calvert, Cynthia S. ....Fresno, CA
Calvert, Cynthia Thomas Washington, DC
Calvert, David P. ....Wichita, KS
Calvert, David R. ....Greenwood Village, CO
Calvert, David W. ....Berkeley, CA
Calvert, Donna L. ....Chicago, IL
Calvert, Elizabeth W. ....Atlanta, GA
Calvert, Frank D. ....Beaumont, TX
Calvert, Frank M. ....Oconto, WI
Calvert, George W. ....Doraville, GA
Calvert, Gerry L. ....Lexington, KY
Calvert, Gina K. ....Louisville, KY
Calvert, Gordon L. ....Bethesda, MD
Calvert, Gregory A. ....Tulsa, OK
Calvert, Horace K. ....Oklahoma City, OK
Calvert, Ian A. ....Department of Commerce, Patent and Trademark Office, GV
Calvert, James S., Jr. ....Houston, TX
Calvert, Jay H., Jr. ....Philadelphia, PA
Calvert, Jeffrey Robert ....San Diego, CA
Calvert, Jesse R., Jr. ....Grants Pass, OR
Calvert, Jill N. ....Salisbury, NC
Calvert, Jimmy R. ....Birmingham, AL
Calvert, Joan D. ....Denver, CO
Calvert, John H. ....Kansas City, MO
Calvert, John P. ....Alexandria, VA
Calvert, John S. ....New York, NY
Calvert, Joseph J. ....Cleveland, OH
Calvert Law Offices, P.C. ....Pearland, TX
Calvert, Lawrence L., Jr. Federal Election Commission, Office of the General Counsel, GV
Calvert, Loretta ....New York, NY
Calvert, Louise M. ....Chicago, IL
Calvert, Mark D. ....Rolla, MO
Calvert, Mark S. ....Knoxville, TN
Calvert, Matthew J. ....Atlanta, GA
Calvert, Melanie A. ....Pasadena, CA
Calvert Menicucci, P.C. Albuquerque, NM
Calvert, Rae Venable ....Pearland, TX
Calvert, Randall K. ....Oklahoma City, OK
Calvert, Randall K., P.C. Oklahoma City, OK
Calvert, Randall M. ....Englewood, CO
Calvert, Robert A. ....Englewood, CO
Calvert, Robert J. ....Berkeley, CA
Calvert, Robert J. ....Covington, KY
Calvert, Roy M. L. ....Lawton, OK
Calvert, Samuel V. ....St. Cloud, MN
Calvert, Samuel V., P.A. ....St. Cloud, MN
Calvert, Sarah K. ....Fairfax, VA
Calvert, Sean R. ....Albuquerque, NM
Calvert, Stacey S. ....Dallas, TX
Calvert, Stanley A. ....San Diego, CA
Calvert, T. Marc ....Houston, TX
Calvert, Thomas B. ....Metairie, LA
Calvert, Thomas B., P.L.C. ....Metairie, LA
Calvert, Virginia F. ....North Syracuse, NY
Calvert, W. Logan ....Madisonville, KY
Calvert, Walter R. ....Baltimore, MD
Calvert, William B. ....Elkton, MD
Calvert, William L. ....Defiance, OH
Calvert, William M. ....Colorado Springs, CO
Calvert-Banks, Eunice M. San Francisco, CA
Calvesbert, Paul E. ....San Juan, PR
Calvet, Pamela C. ....Santa Monica, CA
Calvete, Michael L. ....North Chili, NY
Calvetti, Frederick F. ....Washington, DC
Calvey, Brian J. ....New York, NY
Calvey, Faye L. ....Minocqua, WI
Calvey, Kevin J. ....Oklahoma City, OK
Calvey Law Offices, S.C. ....Minocqua, WI
Calvey, Lee F. ....Minocqua, WI
Calvey, Michael J. ....New York, NY
Calvi, Carlo J. ....Yonkers, NY
Calvi, Julius M. ....North Adams, MA
Calviera, Peter V. ....Newark, NY
Calvillo, Stevan R. ....Long Beach, CA
Calvin, Aubrey B. ....Houston, TX
Calvin, C. Joseph ....Rector, AR
Calvin, Charles D. ....Denver, CO
Calvin, Dain K., (P.C.) ....Phoenix, AZ
Calvin, Edward E. ....Cape Girardeau, MO
Calvin, Edward E., A Professional Corporation Cape Girardeau, MO
Calvin, Gary W. ....Fort Washington, PA
Calvin, Joe ....Decatur, AL
Calvin, Joseph H., III ....Birmingham, AL
Calvin, Joyce ....New York, NY
Calvin, Karen Duboc ....Kansas City, MO
Calvin, Loran A. ....South Pasadena, CA
Calvin, Mark E. ....Jacksonville, FL
Calvin, Michael B. ....St. Louis, MO
Calvin, Neil P. ....Redmond, WA
Calvin, Richardson & Verner, A Professional Corporation ....Houston, TX
Calvin, Shirley K. ....Garden City, KS
Calvin, William C. ....Clinton, IL
Calvino, John N. ....Providence, RI
Calvit, Brian D. ....Baton Rouge, LA
Calvit, H. Bradford ....Alexandria, LA
Calvit, Michael T. ....Vero Beach, FL
Calvo, Arthur Talley ....Gaston, SC
Calvo, James W. ....Chicago, IL
Calvo, James W., P.C. Law Offices of Chicago, IL
Calvo, Janet M. ....New York, NY
Calvo, John A. ....Princeton, NJ
Calvo, Joseph A. ....Hagåtña, GU
Calvo, Larry A. ....Granite City, IL
Calvo, Lisa M. ....Philadelphia, PA
Calvo & Mateyka ....Granite City, IL
Calvo, Theodore E. ....San Diego, CA
Calvocoressi & Gale ....Hartford, CT
Calvocoressi, John L. ....Hartford, CT
Calvocoressi, Thomas J. ....Hartford, CT
Calvy, Joe Ann Matthews ....Kingstree, SC
Calwell, Stuart, PLLC, The Law Offices of Charleston, WV
Calwell, W. Stuart, Jr. ....Charleston, WV
Calzacorta, Carmen M. ....Portland, OR
Calzaretta, Marylou ....St. Louis, MO
Calzaretta, Victor ....Portland, OR
Calzone, David B. ....Bingham Farms, MI
Cama, Franklin A. ....Melville, NY
Smithtown, NY
Camacho, Aileen ....Philadelphia, PA
Camacho, Alejandro E. ....Los Angeles, CA
Camacho, Alejandro E. ....New York, NY
Camacho, Andy M. ....Encino, CA
Camacho, Anthony R. ....Hagåtña, GU
Camacho, Cesar R. ....Key Biscayne, FL
Camacho, Domenique ....New York, NY
Camacho, Edwin ....New York, NY
Camacho, Elizabeth A. ....Los Angeles, CA
Camacho, Jennifer A. ....Boston, MA
Camacho, Joseph D. ....Albuquerque, NM
Camacho, Luis F. ....Cayey, PR
Camacho, Michelle P. ....Haddon Heights, NJ
Camacho, Mike, Jr. ....Los Angeles, CA
Camacho, Renee Lyn ....Albuquerque, NM
Camacho, Robert P. ....Fremont, CA
Camacho, Roger L. ....Newark, NJ
Camacho, Timothy M. ....Modesto, CA
Camacho, Vincent Sablan ....Berkeley, CA
Camacho Izquierdo, Gilben ....Yauco, PR
Camacho Nowlin, Marlene I. ....Irvine, CA
Camahort, Steve L. ....Palo Alto, CA
Camak, Stephen N. ....Raleigh, NC
Camalier, Charles A., III ....Washington, DC
Bethesda, MD
Camann, John R. ....Sandy Creek, NY
Camann, Richard L. ....Lynn, MA
Camara, Joan E. ....Portsmouth, RI
Camara, Mario ....Los Angeles, CA
Camara, Valerie J. ....Rahway, NJ
Camara, William G. ....Fall River, MA
Camara, William G., P.C. ....Fall River, MA
Camarata, Cristina ....Addison, TX
Camarata, Kerry P. ....Thibodaux, LA
Camarda, Diego R. ....Scarsdale, NY
Camardella & Brown, LLC Great Neck, NY
Camardella, James V. ....Great Neck, NY
Camardella, L. F. ....Manhasset, NY
Camardella, Matthew J. ....Woodbury, NY
Camardi, Thomas C., Jr. ....Anaheim, CA
Camardo, Carolyn L. ....Portsmouth, VA
Camardo, Ralph D. ....Albany, NY
Camarella, Judith K. ....Springfield, VA
Camarena, Anna M. ....Vista, CA
Camarena, Enrique E. ....San Diego, CA
Camarena, Lucila L. Flores ....Austin, TX
Camarena, Timothy ....Camarillo, CA
Camarillo, Gerardo A. ....Houston, TX
Camarillo, Laura ....Houston, TX
Camarinos, Tasso E. ....Pittsburgh, PA
Camarot, Henry J., (P.C.) Sun City West, AZ
Camarota, Michael V. ....Kalamazoo, MI
Camarota, Michele L. ....Lynnfield, MA
Camarra, Christopher L. Washington, DC
Camarra, Joseph A. ....Chicago, IL
Camassa, John A. ....Manasquan, NJ
Camassar, Garon ....New London, CT
Camassar, Scott D. ....New London, CT
Camasto, Nicholas A., (Ltd.) Mount Prospect, IL
River Forest, IL
Camastra, Ralph A. ....Glendale, CA
Camaur, Elisabeth ....Santa Monica, CA
Camaur, Richard ....Fairfax, VA
Camazine, Alisse C. ....St. Louis, MO
Camba, Romeo G. ....Boston, MA
Cambareri, Dom ....Syracuse, NY
Cambareri, Joseph V. ....Garden City, NY
Cambareri, Mark Philip ....Liberty, NY
Cambareri, Stefano ....Syracuse, NY
Cambas, Donald S. ....Tampa, FL
Camber, Michael A. ....Santa Ana, CA
Camber, Rachel A. ....Miami, FL
Camber, Stephen J. ....San Francisco, CA
Camberg, Roy A. ....Houston, TX
Cambest, John F. ....Pittsburgh, PA
Cambiano, George J. ....Morrilton, AR
Cambiano, Joe ....Morrilton, AR
Cambiano, Joseph A. ....Kansas City, MO
Cambiano, Mark S. ....Morrilton, AR
Cambiano, Mark S., P.A. ....Morrilton, AR
Cambio, David A. ....New York, NY
Camblos, James L., III ....Charlottesville, VA
Cambon, Leon F. ....New Orleans, LA
Cambosos, Richard T. General Accounting Office, Office of the General Counsel, GV
Cambouris, Arthur T. ....New York, NY
Cambourogiou, Kimon ....New York, NY
Cambra, Laurie A. ....San Pedro, CA
Cambray, Joan M. ....Oakland, CA
Cambre, David M. ....New Orleans, LA

Cambre, Susanne M. ....Covington, LA
Metairie, LA
Cambria, Anthony R. ....Newark, NJ
Cambria, David G. ....Chicago, IL
Cambria, John F. ....New York, NY
Cambria, Paul J., Jr. ....Beverly Hills, CA
Buffalo, NY
Cambria, William A. ....Newark, NJ
Cambridge, Beatrice W. ....Mineola, NY
Cambridge, Feilmeyer, Landsness, Chase & Jones, P.L.C. ....Atlantic, IA
Griswold, IA
Cambridge, James R. ....Detroit, MI
Cambridge, Jill H. ....Worcester, MA
Cambridge, Robert M. ....Arlington, VA
Cambridge, Teresa P. ....Indianapolis, IN
Cambridge, Teresa P., P.C. ....Indianapolis, IN
Cambridge, William G. ....Omaha, NE
Cambron, Beverly R. ....Houston, TX
Cambron, Catherine A. ....Berkeley, CA
Cambron, Cynthia L. ....Vero Beach, FL
Cambron, James S. ....Louisville, KY
Cambron, Kelly ....Vero Beach, FL
Cambron, Mark R. ....Louisville, KY
Cambronne, Karl L. ....Minneapolis, MN
Cambs, Denise P. ....Syracuse, NY
Cambs, Peter J. ....Syracuse, NY
Camche, Joel T. ....New York, NY
Camden, Bonnie G. ....Cincinnati, OH
Camden, Gregory E. ....Norfolk, VA
Camden, Kevin Patrick ....Canton, IL
Camden, Stephen R. ....Vallejo, CA
Camden, William D. ....Grand Rapids, MI
Camechis, Karen M. ....Tallahassee, FL
Camel, David J. ....Los Angeles, CA
Camel, Kevin L. ....Lake Charles, LA
Camel, Lisa M. ....San Antonio, TX
Cameli, Mark A. ....Milwaukee, WI
Cameli, Mary N. ....Chicago, IL
Cameli, Thomas F. ....Chicago, IL
Camello, Marlowe O. ....Sun City, CA
Camelo, Dianne M. ....New York, NY
Camen, Toby P. ....Gladwyne, PA
Camenisch, J. Mel, Jr. ....Lexington, KY
Camenisch, Robert L. ....Sun City, AZ
Camenisch, Shela C. ....Orinda, CA
Camenker, Ellen Sarafan ....Apopka, FL
Camens, Barbara L. ....Washington, DC
Camenson, David M. ....Fresno, CA
Camera, Michael J. ....Lorain, OH
Camera, Nicholas J. ....New York, NY
Camera, Paul ....San Rafael, CA
Camera, Robert J. ....Newburgh, NY
Cameranesi, Remo Z. ....Elm Grove, WI
Camerer, G. Glenn ....Gering, NE
Camerieri, Christopher J. ....Norcross, GA
Camerik, Howard M. ....Boca Raton, FL
Camerik, Nellie P. ....Miami, FL
Camerini, David C. ....New York, NY
Camerini, Ezequiel A. ....New York, NY
Camerino, James ....Princeton, NJ
Camerino, Michael V. ....Somerville, NJ
Camerino, Steven V. ....Concord, NH
Camerlengo, George F. ....Burlingame, CA
Camerlengo, Joseph V., Jr.
Jacksonville, FL
Camerlingo, Pepi ....Chicago, IL
Camerlo, Diane Berry ....St. Louis, MO
Cameron, A. Craig ....Orlando, FL
Cameron, Aimee L. ....Springfield, MA
Cameron, Alan B. ....Denver, CO
Cameron, Alan D., II ....Boise, ID
Cameron, Alex B. ....Stone Lake, WI
Cameron, Andrew D. ....San Francisco, CA
Cameron, Andrew L. ....Orlando, FL
Cameron, Andrew L., P.A. ....Orlando, FL
Cameron, Andy, Law Offices of ......Denver, CO
Cameron, Angela E. ....Trenton, NJ
Cameron, Anna Victoria ....Los Angeles, CA
Cameron, Anthony B. ....Quincy, IL
Cameron, Arthur E. ....Washington, DC
Cameron & Associates ....Saginaw, MI
Cameron, Bonnie L. ....Atlanta, GA
Cameron, Bradley J. ....Wilkesboro, NC
Cameron, Brenda M. ....Olathe, KS
Cameron, Brent H. ....Salt Lake City, UT
Cameron, Brian E. ....New York, NY
Cameron, Brodnax, Jr. ....Bel Air, MD
Cameron, Bruce L. ....Columbus, OH
Cameron, Bruce N. ....Springfield, VA
Cameron, Caitlin J. ....Chicago, IL
Cameron and Cameron ....Montgomery, AL
Cameron & Cameron ....Cleveland, OH
Cameron, Catherine Anne .....Albuquerque, NM
Cameron and Chaffin ....Cookeville, TN
Cameron, Charles E., Jr. ....San Jose, CA
Cameron, Cheralyn S ....Reston, VA
Cameron, Cheryl A. ....Cambridge, MA
Cameron, Christie Speir ....Raleigh, NC
Cameron, Christopher David Ruiz
Los Angeles, CA
Cameron, Clark H. ....Calabasas, CA
Cameron, Connie M ....Saginaw, MI
Cameron, Craig C. ....Tucson, AZ
Cameron, Cynthia T. ....Houston, TX
Cameron, D. Steve ....Beverly Hills, CA
Cameron, Dallas A., Jr. ....Raleigh, NC
Cameron, Dane A. ....Chico, CA
Cameron, Daniel M. ....Sacramento, CA
Cameron, David C. ....Tulsa, OK
Cameron, David K. ....Cleveland, OH
Cameron, David L. ....Salem, OR
Cameron & Davis, P.A.
West Palm Beach, FL
Cameron, Dean C. ....Chicago, IL
Cameron, Deborah Shelles ....Portland, ME
Cameron, Denise R. ....Cleveland, OH
Cameron, Dennis A. ....Clarksville, AR
Hot Springs National Park, AR
Cameron, Dennis A., P.A. ....Clarksville, AR
Hot Springs National Park, AR
Cameron, Dennis C. ....Tulsa, OK
Cameron, Dennis S. ....Linthicum, MD
Cameron, Diana ....Houston, TX
Cameron, Donald B. ....Slidell, LA
Cameron, Donald B., Jr. ....Washington, DC
Cameron, Donald D. ....Tulsa, OK
Cameron, Donald H. ....Toledo, OH
Cameron, Donna L. ....Burlington, MA
Cameron, Donna M., P.C. ....Portland, OR
Cameron, Donna W. ....Houston, TX
Cameron, Douglas E. ....Pittsburgh, PA
Cameron, Douglas G. ....Bethlehem, PA
Cameron, Douglas W.
Yorktown Heights, NY
Cameron & Dreyfuss ....Santa Ana, CA
Cameron, Duncan Gordon
Saddle River, NJ
Cameron, Duncan H. ....Washington, DC
New York, NY
Cameron, Duncan J. ....Denver, CO
Cameron, E. Colby ....Providence, RI
Cameron, Edward J. ....Philadelphia, PA
Cameron, Edward R. ....Brookfield, WI
Cameron, Edward W. ....Fairfax, VA
Cameron, Elizaeth ....Alma, MI
Cameron, Elvis C. ....Jonesboro, IL
Cameron, F. Morton ....San Diego, CA
Cameron, F. Robert ....Birmingham, MI
Cameron, Florence F. ....Los Angeles, CA
Cameron, Francis X.
Nuclear Regulatory Commission,
Office of the General Counsel, GV
Cameron, Gary L. ....Fairfield, IA
Cameron, George B. ....New York, NY
Cameron, George, III ....Ann Arbor, MI
Cameron, George W., Jr.
Montgomery, AL
Cameron, Glenn S. ....West Palm Beach, FL
Cameron, H. Mal ....Pleasanton, CA
Cameron, Hal B., Jr., Law Offices of
Tyler, TX
Cameron, Heather ....Washington, DC
Cameron & Hoffman ....Fullerton, CA
Cameron & Hornbostel LLP
Washington, DC
New York, NY
Cameron, Hugh R. ....Baltimore, MD
Cameron, Hugh R., P.A. ....Baltimore, MD
Cameron, J. Harvey ....Jasper, TN
Cameron, J. Harvey, P.C. ....Jasper, TN
Cameron, J. Scott ....Montpelier, VT
Cameron, J. Vincent ....Portland, OR
Cameron, Jack G. ....Fort Worth, TX
Cameron, James A. ....Tulsa, OK
Cameron, James D. ....Harrisburg, PA
Cameron, James Duke ....Phoenix, AZ
Cameron, James K. ....San Francisco, CA
Cameron, James K., & Associates, A Prof. Corp. ....San Francisco, CA
Cameron, James M., Jr. ....Ann Arbor, MI
Cameron, James R. ....New York, NY
Cameron, James S. ....Fayetteville, GA
Cameron, James T. ....Austin, TX
Cameron, James W. ....Montgomery, AL
Cameron, James W., III ....Nashville, TN
Cameron, Jas. L., Jr. ....Birmingham, MI
Cameron, Jeffrey M. ....Houston, TX
Cameron, Jennifer E. ....Madison, WI
Cameron, Jennifer S. ....Jonesboro, AR
Cameron, Jerry J. ....Bluefield, WV
Cameron, Jill A. ....Chicago, IL
Cameron, John A., Jr. ....Portland, OR
Cameron, John B. ....Goshen, NY
Cameron, John Brooks, & Associates
Medina, OH
Cameron, John C. ....Malvern, PA
Cameron, John D. ....New Berlin, NY
Cameron, John F. ....Montgomery, AL
Cameron, John G., Jr. ....Grand Rapids, MI
Cameron, John O. ....Montgomery, AL
Cameron, Jose M. ....Perth Amboy, NJ
Cameron, Joseph A. ....North Andover, MA
Cameron, Josephine L. ....Okemos, MI
Cameron, Keith C. ....Waco, TX
Cameron, Kelley E. ....Boston, MA
Cameron, Kelly ....Washington, DC
Cameron, Kelly A. ....Washington, DC
Cameron, Ken ....Santa Monica, CA
Cameron, Kerry M. ....Sisseton, SD
Cameron, Laureen Adele ....Sarasota, FL
Cameron, Lee L., Jr. ....Dallas, TX
Cameron, Lenore H. ....Harrisburg, PA
Cameron, Lisa M. ....Boston, MA
Cameron, Lori A. ....Irving, TX
Cameron, Lynn C. ....Minneapolis, MN
Cameron, Margaret M. ....San Marino, CA
Cameron, Mark A. ....Monterey, CA
Cameron, Mark A. ....Walnut Creek, CA
Cameron, Marriott, Walsh, Hodges & Coleman, P.A. ....Daytona Beach, FL
Ocala, FL
Orlando, FL
Cameron, Mary Margaret ....Livonia, MI
Cameron, MaryBeth ....Melville, NY
Cameron McKenna LLP
San Francisco, CA
Washington, DC
Cameron, Michael G. ....Houston, TX
Cameron, Michael Kevin
Department of Justice,
Immigration and Naturalization Service, GV
Cameron, Michele Ann ....Portsmouth, RI
Cameron & Mittleman LLP
Providence, RI
Cameron, Nancy L. ....St. Paul, MN
Cameron, Nelson W. ....Shreveport, LA
Cameron, Nina Rao ....New York, NY
Cameron, O. Winston ....Meridian, MS
Cameron, Pamela ....Sequim, WA
Cameron, Parry Glenn ....Los Angeles, CA
Cameron, Patrick K. ....Baltimore, MD
Cameron, Pearlson & Gale
Long Beach, CA
Los Angeles, CA
Cameron & Penegor ....Brookfield, WI
Cameron, Philip D. ....Dublin, OH
Cameron, Phillip F. ....Cincinnati, OH
Cameron, Richard Kip ....Hopkinsville, KY
Cameron, Richard R. ....Washington, DC
Cameron, Robert ....Helena, MT
Cameron, Robert G. ....Harrisburg, PA
Cameron, Robert H. ....Washington, DC
Cameron, Robert S. ....Sacramento, CA
Cameron, Robert W. ....Pittsburgh, PA
Cameron, Roderick A. ....Seattle, WA
Cameron, Roderick A. ....Chippewa Falls, WI
Cameron, Roger P. ....Philadelphia, PA
Cameron, Ronald Brooks ....Fullerton, CA
Cameron, Ronald G. ....Auburn, CA
Cameron Rowe ....Birmingham, MI
Cameron, Roy L., Jr. ....Philadelphia, PA
Cameron, Sarah T. ....Inverness, CA
Cameron, Scott W. ....Provo, UT
Cameron, Sondra R. ....Cleveland, OH
Cameron, Stephanie Yost
Los Angeles, CA
Cameron, Stephen R. ....Sacramento, CA
Cameron, Steven R. ....Santa Ana, CA
Cameron, Streetar ....Des Moines, IA
Cameron, Suzon Landeck
Federal Communications Commission,
Compliance and Information Bureau, GV
Cameron, Thomas ....Ozona, TX
Cameron, Thomas C. ....Milton, MA
Cameron, Thomas C. ....Kalamazoo, MI
Cameron, Timothy C. ....Long Beach, CA
Cameron, Timothy W. ....Boston, MA
Cameron, Toryah S. ....Washington, DC
Cameron, W. Fred ....Houston, TX
Cameron, William A. ....Cookeville, TN
Cameron, William D. ....Seattle, WA
Cameron, William J., Jr.
Castleton-on-Hudson, NY
Cameron, William L. ....Kennewick, WA
Cameron, William M., III ....Richlands, NC
Cameron, William M., Jr. ....Jacksonville, NC
Cameron, William Mack ....Jackson, MS
Cameron, William P. ....Houston, TX
Cameron, William W. ....Minnetonka, MN
Cameron, Yolanda L. ....Atlanta, GA
Cameron-Joseph, Mila K. ....Austin, TX
Cameron-Kelley, Susan ......Newport Beach, CA
Cameron-Stuart, James B. ....Houston, TX
Camerota, Frank P. ....New Castle, DE
Camerota, Michele C. ....Cheshire, CT
Camerson, Donald J., II
Florham Park, NJ
Cames, Paul L. ....Warner Robins, GA
Camet, Gregory W. ....Washington, DC
Camet, Lily A. ....Washington, DC
Camfield, Gray M., P.A. ....Palm Bay, FL
Camfield, Roland E., Jr. ....Sonora, CA
Camhi & Camhi ....Sherman Oaks, CA
Camhi, Donald N. ....Philadelphia, PA
Camhi, Howard I. ....Sherman Oaks, CA
Camhi, Jason A. ....New York, NY
Camhi, Rina E. ....Houston, TX
Camhi, Ronald R. ....Sherman Oaks, CA
Camhi, Stanley A. ....Garden City, NY
Camhi, Steven K. ....Sherman Oaks, CA
Camhy Karlinsky & Stein LLP
New York, NY
Camhy, Sheldon D. ....New York, NY
Camic, David E. ....Aurora, IL
Camic, Johnson, Wilson & Bloom
Aurora, IL
Camic, Nina L. ....Madison, WI
Camick, Daniel G. ....Toledo, OH
Camiel, Peter A. ....Seattle, WA
Camilleri, Kenneth J. ....Trenton, MI
Camilleri, Lynn M. ....Livonia, MI
Camilleri, Mary Ann ....Cheshire, CT
Camilleri, Paul J. ....New York, NY
Camilleri, Philip S. ....San Jose, CA
Camilletti, David A. ....Martinsburg, WV
Camilletti, George P. ....Akron, OH
Camilletti, Ollar & Santa Barbara
Martinsburg, WV
Camilletti, Paul C. ....Wheeling, WV
Camilletti, Paul T. ....Wheeling, WV
Camilletti, Sacco & Pizzuti ....Wheeling, WV
Camilli, Michelle L. ....Moorhead, MN
Camilli, Thomas A. ....Green Bay, WI
Camillo, Jack J. ....Westfield, NJ
Camillo, John A. W. ....Inglis, FL
Camillo, John R. ....Plano, TX
Camillo, Lynne ....Treasury Department,
Internal Revenue Service, GV
Camillo, Susan M. ....Boston, MA
Camillo, William M. ....Boothwyn, PA
Camilo-siracusa, Fior ....Chicago, IL
Camin, Cheryl S. ....Dallas, TX
Camiña, Ophelia F. ....Dallas, TX
Caminer, Brian F. ....Chicago, IL
Caminero, Rafael ....Lancaster, PA
Caminez, Jon D. ....Tallahassee, FL
Caming, H. W. Wm. ....Summit, NJ
Caminiti & Caminiti ....Chicago, IL
Caminiti, Donald A. ....Hackensack, NJ
Caminiti, Kathleen McLeod ....Somerset, NJ
Caminiti, Michael Joseph ....Chicago, IL
Caminiti, Paul A. ....Southold, NY
Caminiti, Peter David ....Chicago, IL
Caminker, Evan H. ....Los Angeles, CA
Camino, Carmine ....Cleveland, OH
Camino, George J. ....Schenectady, NY
Camino, Paula E. ....Cleveland, OH
Caminsky, Jeffrey ....Detroit, MI
Camisa, Stephen E. ....Frankfort, KY
Camisa, Vance G. ....Whitehouse Station, NJ
Camishion, Nancy C. ....West Palm Beach, FL
Camitta, Hugh Douglas ....Detroit, MI
Cammack, Ann Burgess
Treasury Department,
Internal Revenue Service, GV
Cammack, Cecil C. ....Tyler, TX
Cammack, Cecil C., Jr. ....Nemo, TX
Cammack, Christopher M. ....Houston, TX
Cammack, Christopher M., P.C.
Houston, TX
Cammack, James W. ....Dallas, TX
Cammack, John L. ....Stockton, CA
Cammack, Kent E. ....Phoenix, AZ
Cammack, Kerry N. ....Austin, TX
Cammack, Mark Elwin ....Los Angeles, CA
Cammack, Rex ....Houston, TX
Cammack, Sharon D. ....Houston, TX
Cammack, Stephen T. ....Sacramento, CA
Cammack & Strong ....Austin, TX
Cammack, Virgil E., Jr. ....Pasadena, TX
Cammaker, Joshua R. ....New York, NY
Cammaker, Sheldon I. ....Norwalk, CT
Cammarano & Cammarano ....Wayne, NJ
Cammarano, Dennis A. ....Long Beach, CA
Los Angeles, CA
New York, NY
Cammarano, Michael J. ....Reading, PA
Cammarano, Peter J. ....Wayne, NJ
Cammarano, Robert J. ....Wayne, NJ
Cammarano & Tract ....Reading, PA
Cammarano, Vincent J. ....Chelsea, MA
Cammarata, Anthony ....Tallahassee, FL
Cammarata, Barbara Looney
San Diego, CA
Cammarata, Carl D. ....San Francisco, CA
Cammarata, John M. ....Trenton, NJ
Cammarata, Joseph ....Washington, DC
Cammarata, Kimberly Stanton
Baltimore, MD
Cammarata, Michael R. ....Falls Church, VA
Cammarata, Naomi F ....Brockton, MA
Cammarata, Ross J. ....Rochester, NY
Cammarata, Susan Tycer ....Pittsburgh, PA
Cammarata, Thomas J. ....Jersey City, NJ
Cammarato, Kenneth J. ....Pittsfield, MA
Cammarn, Scott A. ....Charlotte, NC
Cammarosano, Joseph R. ....New York, NY
Cammarota, Michael J. ....Charlotte, NC
Cammarota, Nicholas J. ....Carmichael, CA
Cammer, Margaret ....New York, NY
Cammer, Robert ....New York, NY
Cammerano, Linda J. ....Rutherford, NJ
Cammerzell, Frederick E., III ....Princeton, NJ
Cammisa, Agostino ....Philadelphia, PA
Cammon, Dale L. ....St. Louis, MO
Cammon, Roger E. ....St. Louis, MO
Cammon, Tonya Kennedy
Chattanooga, TN
Camner, Alfred R. ....Miami, FL
Camner, Anne Shari ....Miami, FL
Camner, Lipsitz and Poller, Professional Association ....Coral Gables, FL
Miami, FL
Fort Lauderdale, FL
West Palm Beach, FL
Camodeca, Frank R. ....Des Plaines, IL
Camomot, Dino R. ....Louisville, KY
Camoriano & Associates ....Louisville, KY
Camoriano, Theresa Fritz ....Louisville, KY
Camors, Robert E., Jr. ....San Jose, CA
Camougis, Sarah N.A. ....Boston, MA
Camozzi, John J. ....Walnut Creek, CA
Camp, Alida D. ....Los Angeles, CA
Camp, Alissa J. ....Springfield, IL
Camp, Allen F. ....Oxnard, CA
Camp, Ashby L. ....Memphis, TN
Camp, Bryan T. ....Treasury Department,
Internal Revenue Service, GV
Camp & Camp ....Sparta, TN
Camp & Camp, P.A.
Fort Lauderdale, FL
Camp, Carol René ....Fort Worth, TX
Camp, Charles E. ....Smyrna, GA
Camp, Charles H. ....Washington, DC
Camp, Charles R. ....Little Rock, AR
Camp, Christopher J. ....Berwyn, PA
Camp, Collins C., Jr. ....Houston, TX
Camp, Courtney Chanin ....Atlanta, GA
Camp, Daniel ....Santa Monica, CA
Camp, Daniel P. ....Carrollton, GA
Camp, David C. ....Denver, CO
Camp, David Danielson ....St. Louis, MO
Camp, David L. ....Midland, MI
Camp, David W. ....Jackson, TN
Memphis, TN
Camp, Dennis D. ....Ocala, FL
Camp, Dennis D., P.A. ....Ocala, FL
Camp, Donald J. ....Austin, TX
Camp, Elizabeth W. ....Rome, GA
Camp, Elwood H. ("Woody"), III
Nashville, TN
Camp, Emory C. ....Cameron, TX
Rockdale, TX
Camp, Gary L. ....Rock Island, IL
Camp, Gayle Y. ....Kennesaw, GA
Camp, George ....Oklahoma City, OK
Camp, Gregory S. ....Rocky Mount, NC
Camp, Gus R. ....Piggott, AR
Camp, H. Nelson ....Huntsville, AL
Camp, H. Ward, III ....Albuquerque, NM
Camp, Harry W. ....McMinnville, TN

Campbell, Donald ... Dallas, TX
Campbell, Donald D. ... Berkeley Heights, NJ
Campbell, Donald F. ... East Lansing, MI
Campbell, Donald F. ... Toms River, NJ
Campbell, Donald F. ... Dallas, TX
Campbell, Donald G. ... Minneapolis, MN
Campbell, Donald J. ... Pinedale, CA
Campbell, Donald J. ... Las Vegas, NV
Campbell, Donald K., III (P.A.)
Little Rock, AR
Campbell, Donald R. ... Binghamton, NY
Campbell, Donald R., Jr. ... Fort Worth, TX
Campbell, Donald S. ... White Plains, NY
Campbell, Donald T. ... Minot, ND
Campbell, Donna G. ... Covington, KY
Campbell, Donna J. ... Philadelphia, PA
Campbell, Donna J., & Associates, P.C.
Philadelphia, PA
Campbell, Donovan, Jr. ... Dallas, TX
Campbell, Dorothy L. ... Kansas City, MO
Campbell, Douglas A. ... Pittsburgh, PA
Campbell, Douglas G. ... Tazewell, VA
Campbell, Douglas M. ... Santa Ana, CA
Campbell, Douglas M. ... Chattanooga, TN
Campbell, Douglas N. ... Atlanta, GA
Campbell, Douglas P. ... Ulysses, KS
Campbell, Douglas W. ... Milford, OH
Campbell, Dow L. ... Findlay, OH
Campbell, Drew A.(Sandy) ... Dallas, TX
Campbell, Drew H. ... Columbus, OH
Campbell, Duncan A., III ... Boulder, CO
Campbell, Durrant & Beatty, P.C.
Pittsburgh, PA
Campbell, Dutro E., II ... St. Louis, MO
Campbell, Dwight Conrad ... Memphis, TN
Campbell, Dwight, Jr. ... Buffalo, NY
Campbell, E. Wayne ... San Antonio, TX
Campbell, Edgar P. ... Fishkill, NY
Stone Ridge, NY
Valhalla, NY
Campbell, Edgar P. ... New York, NY
White Plains, NY
Campbell, Edgar T.
Manchester Center, VT
Campbell, Edmund J., Jr. ... Norristown, PA
Campbell, Edward A. ... Boonville, IN
Campbell, Edward F., Jr. ... New York, NY
Campbell, Edward K., Jr. ... Denver, CO
Campbell, Edward L. ... Kirksville, MO
Campbell, Edward L., Jr. ... Fairfax, VA
Campbell, Edward S., III ... Tampa, FL
Campbell, Eileen Kerry ... New York, NY
Campbell, Elizabeth A. ... Portland, ME
Campbell, Elizabeth A. ... Buffalo, NY
Campbell, Elizabeth Herlong
Columbia, SC
Campbell, Elizabeth Todd ... Birmingham, AL
Campbell, Emily ... New York, NY
Campbell, Eric P. ... San Diego, CA
Campbell, Eugene R. ... York, PA
Campbell, Eugene R. ... Houston, TX
Campbell, Eva L. ... Irvine, CA
Campbell, F. Lee ... Seattle, WA
Campbell, Ferrin C., Sr., (P.A.)
Crestview, FL
Campbell & Flores LLP ... San Diego, CA
Seattle, WA
Campbell, Foley, Lee, Murphy & Cernigliaro, A Professional Corporation
Asbury Park, NJ
Campbell, Forrest E. ... Greensboro, NC
Campbell, Forrest W., Jr.
Greensboro, NC
Campbell, Frances D. ... Denver, CO
Campbell, Francis J. ... Neptune, NJ
Campbell, Frank A. ... Pacific Palisades, CA
Campbell, Frank A. ... Greensboro, NC
Campbell, Frank A. S. ... Department of Justice, Federal Bureau of Investigation, GV
Campbell, Frank J. ... Vicksburg, MS
Campbell, Frank P. ... Los Angeles, CA
Campbell, Fred G. ... Davenport, WA
Campbell, Fred M. ... Columbus, OH
Campbell, Frederick B. ... Garnett, KS
Campbell, Frederick B. ... New York, NY
Campbell, Frederick H.
Colorado Springs, CO
Campbell, Frederick K. ... Little Rock, AR
Campbell, Frederick R. ... Metairie, LA
Campbell, Fuchsia ... St. Paul, MN
Campbell, G. Anthony ... Thomasville, GA
Campbell, G. Blake ... San Francisco, CA
Campbell, G. Jefferson, Jr. ... Medford, OR
Campbell, G. Jefferson, Jr., P.C.
Medford, OR
Campbell, Gail ... New York, NY
Campbell, Gail Inman ... Harrison, AR
Campbell, Gary J. ... Medford, MA
Campbell, Gary J. ... Sherman, TX
Campbell, Gary R. ... Saginaw, MI
Campbell, Gary T. ... West Orange, NJ
Campbell, Gary T., P.C. ... West Orange, NJ
Campbell, Gene C. ... Harrison, AR
Campbell, George B. ... Portland, OR
Campbell, George E. ... Little Rock, AR
Campbell, George G. ... Reno, NV
Campbell & George, LLP ... Houston, TX
Campbell, George P. ... Grand Ledge, MI
Lansing, MI
Campbell, George T., III ... Manchester, NH
Campbell, George W., Jr. ... Arlington, VA
Campbell, George W., Jr., & Assoc., A P.C., Law Offices of ... Arlington, VA
Campbell, Gilbert R., Jr. ... Nashville, TN
Campbell, Glenn C. ... Washington, DC
Campbell, Glenn J. ... Oxnard, CA
Campbell, Glenn M. ... Philadelphia, PA
Campbell, Gordon ... Carmel, CA
Campbell, Gordon ... Salt Lake City, UT
Campbell, Graham G. ... San Francisco, CA
Campbell, Greg A. ... St. Louis, MO
Campbell, Gregory J. ... Charleston, WV
Campbell, H. Alexander ... Louisville, KY
Campbell, H. Gregory, Jr. ... Blacksburg, VA
Campbell, H. Wayne ... Denver, CO
Campbell, Hank B. ... Lakeland, FL
Campbell, Hardesty & Douglas
Frankfort, IN
Campbell, Harold E. ... Phoenix, AZ
Campbell Harrison & Wright L.L.P.
Houston, TX
Campbell, Harry E. ... Huntington, NY
Campbell, Harvey B., Jr. ... Montgomery, AL
Campbell, Harvey R. ... San Diego, CA
Campbell, Heather A. ... Houston, TX
Campbell, Helen I. ... Lansing, MI
Campbell, Henry G., Jr. ... Eugene, OR
Campbell, Herman C. ... Utica, MI
Campbell, Holt & McCue
Kansas City, MO
Campbell and Hooper ... Newport, TN
Campbell & Hopkins ... Anniston, AL
Campbell, Horace E. ... Cornelia, GA
Campbell, Hornbeck, Chilcoat & Veatch, LLC ... Columbus, OH
Campbell, Howard Gregory
Little Rock, AR
Campbell, H. R. ... Scottsboro, AL
Campbell, Hudson & Brannon, L.L.C.
Atlanta, GA
Campbell, Hugh ... Ashland, VA
Campbell, Hugh B., III ... Mount Airy, NC
Campbell, Hugh B., Jr. ... Charlotte, NC
Campbell, Hugh D. ... San Diego, CA
Campbell, Hugh S. ... West Hartford, CT
Campbell, Hugh S. ... Ashland, VA
Campbell, I. Matthew, Jr. ... Rockville, MD
Campbell, Ilene Baxt ... Fairfax, VA
Campbell, Inlow H. ... Lancaster, CA
Campbell, Ivor E. ... New Albany, OH
Campbell, J. Alan ... Durham, NC
Campbell, J. Brian ... Needles, CA
Campbell, J. Colin ... Independence, VA
Campbell, J. Kenneth ... Delray Beach, FL
Campbell, J. Michael ... Columbiana, AL
Campbell, J. Michael ... Atlanta, GA
Campbell, J. Timothy ... Xenia, OH
Campbell, Jack ... Vista, CA
Campbell, Jack D. ... Reno, NV
Campbell, Jack D., P.C., & Associates
Reno, NV
Campbell, Jack L. ... Kansas City, MO
Campbell, Jack Robert ... Toledo, OH
Campbell, Jack V. ... Youngstown, OH
Campbell, Jack W., IV ... Washington, DC
Campbell, Jacqueline A.
West Sacramento, CA
Campbell, Jacqueline A. ... Metairie, LA
Campbell, Jamee S. ... Tulsa, OK
Campbell, James ... Portland, OR
Campbell, James A. ... Council Bluffs, IA
Campbell, James C.
Hot Springs National Park, AR
Campbell, James C. ... Shalimar, FL
Campbell, James D. ... Tucson, AZ
Campbell, James D. ... Falls Church, VA
Campbell, James D., Jr. ... Harrisburg, PA
Campbell, James Farragher
San Francisco, CA
Campbell, James G. ... Louisville, KY
Campbell, James H. ... Shreveport, LA
Campbell, James K. ... Dallas, TX
Campbell, James M. ... Anniston, AL
Campbell, James M. ... Hartford, CT
Portland, ME
Boston, MA
Concord, NH
Providence, RI
Campbell, James M. ... Orlando, FL
Campbell, James M. ... Akron, OH
Campbell, James P. ... Leesburg, VA
Campbell, James P., & Associates, P.C.
Leesburg, VA
Campbell, James R. ... Burlington, KS
Campbell, James R. ... Middle Island, NY
Campbell, James R., Jr. ... New York, NY
Campbell, James R. C.
New Port Richey, FL
Campbell, James S. ... Washington, DC
Campbell, James S. ... Pensacola, FL
Campbell, James S. ... Honolulu, HI
Campbell, James T. ... Amarillo, TX
Campbell, James W. ... Denver, CO
Campbell, James W. ... Hingham, MA
Campbell, James W. ... Richardson, TX
Campbell, James W., Jr. ... Lima, NY
Campbell, Jamie Thompson ... Carmel, IN
Campbell, Jan N. ... Indianapolis, IN
Campbell, Jane F. ... Jackson, MI
Campbell, Janet B. ... Cincinnati, OH
Campbell, Janet S. ... Atlanta, GA
Campbell, Janice G. ... Cambridge, MA
Campbell, Janice Parker ... Metairie, LA
Campbell, Jason A. ... Britton, SD
Campbell, Jason E. ... Jacksonville, FL
Campbell, Jason T. ... Raleigh, NC
Campbell, Jay R. ... Cleveland, OH
Campbell, Jean H. ... Pullman, WA
Campbell, JeanMarie ... New York, NY
Campbell, Jeffrey A. ... Washington, DC
Campbell, Jeffrey A. ... Boston, MA
Campbell, Jeffrey C. ... Dublin, CA
Campbell, Jeffrey J. ... Phoenix, AZ
Tucson, AZ
Campbell, Jeffrey M. ... Saginaw, MI
Campbell, Jennifer ... Charlotte, NC
Campbell, Jennifer Katze ... Atlanta, GA
Campbell, Jennifer L. ... Los Angeles, CA
Campbell, Jerald M., Jr. ... Trenton, TN
Campbell, Jerry A. ... Taylorsville, NC
Campbell, Jerry M. ... Portland, TX
Campbell, Jerry P. ... Waco, TX
Campbell, Jess D. ... Knoxville, TN
Campbell, Jill A. ... Cincinnati, OH
Campbell, Joan Marie ... New York, NY
Campbell, Joanne Driscoll ... Lynn, MA
Campbell, Joe B. ... Lexington, KY
Campbell, Joe W. ... Huntsville, AL
Campbell, Joel R. ... Columbus, OH
Campbell, John ... Miami, FL
Campbell, John ... Albuquerque, NM
Campbell, John ... Midland, TX
Campbell, John A. ... Kalamazoo, MI
Campbell, John A., III
Fort Lauderdale, FL
Campbell, John A.L. ... Tulsa, OK
Campbell, John B. ... San Diego, CA
Campbell, John C. ... Montgomery, AL
Campbell, John C. ... Minden, LA
Campbell, John C. ... Stoneham, MA
Campbell, John D. ... New York, NY
Campbell, John Daniel (Dan) ... Phoenix, AZ
Campbell, John E. ... Middletown, MD
Campbell, John E., Jr. ... Duncan, OK
Campbell, John F. ... Austin, TX
Campbell, John F. ... Quechee, VT
Campbell, John G. ... Chicago, IL
Campbell, John H. ... Atlanta, GA
Campbell, John H. ... Ware, MA
Campbell, John H. ... Galveston, TX
Campbell, John Harl ... Kansas City, MO
Campbell, John J. ... Denver, CO
Campbell, John J. ... Cambridge, MA
Campbell, John, Jr. ... Honolulu, HI
Campbell, John L. ... Cincinnati, OH
Campbell, John L. ... Rogersville, TN
Campbell, John M. ... Goldenrod, FL
Campbell, John M. ... Haddonfield, NJ
Philadelphia, PA
Campbell, John M., Jr. ... Greenville, SC
Campbell, John N. ... Philadelphia, PA
Campbell, John P. ... York, ME
New York, NY
Campbell, John P., III ... Metairie, LA
Campbell, John P., III, P.L.C. ... Metairie, LA
Campbell, John R. ... Tampa, FL
Campbell, John R. ... Boston, MA
Campbell, John R. ... Kansas City, MO
Campbell, John R. ... Charlotte, NC
Campbell, John R., Jr. ... Kansas City, MO
Campbell, John Robert ... Huntsville, AL
Campbell, John Russell ... Birmingham, AL
Campbell, John S. ... Newark, DE
Campbell, John S. ... Portland, ME
Campbell, John S. ... Carrollton, OH
Campbell, John S., III ... Baton Rouge, LA
Campbell, John S., Jr. ... Baton Rouge, LA
Campbell, John T. ... Birmingham, AL
Campbell, John T. ... Memphis, TN
Campbell, John W. ... Washington, DC
Campbell, John W. ... Jacksonville, FL
Lakeland, FL
Tampa, FL
Campbell, John W. ... Atlanta, GA
Campbell, John W. ... Indianapolis, IN
Campbell, John W. ... Marion, IN
Campbell, John W. ... Topeka, KS
Campbell, John W. ... Memphis, TN
Campbell, John W. ... Memphis, TN
Campbell, John W. ... Spokane, WA
Campbell, John W., III
San Francisco, CA
Campbell, John Wishart ... Lumberton, NC
Campbell, Jon P. ... Jersey City, NJ
Campbell, Jonathan D. ... Dallas, TX
Campbell, Joseph B. ... Augusta, ME
Campbell, Joseph E. ... Philadelphia, PA
Campbell, Joseph H. Jr. ... Baton Rouge, LA
Campbell, Joseph Patrick ... New York, NY
Campbell, Joseph W. ... Oakland, CA
Campbell, Joyce Ann ... Lakeport, CA
Campbell, Joyce Ann ... Middletown, OH
Campbell, Julia Bell ... Washington, DC
Campbell, Julian C., Jr. ... Chicago, IL
Campbell, Julie A. ... Washington, DC
Campbell, Julie A. ... Cortland, NY
Tully, NY
Campbell, Julie M. ... Chicago, IL
Campbell, June K. ... Seattle, WA
Campbell, Justin Marvin, III
Houston, TX
Campbell, K. Ray ... Houston, TX
Campbell, Karen D. ... Oakland, CA
Campbell, Karen L. ... New York, NY
Campbell, Karen M. ... Louisville, KY
Campbell, Karen Martin ... Memphis, TN
Campbell and Karlik, P.A.
Palm Beach Gardens, FL
West Palm Beach, FL
Campbell, Karmen Kimsey ... Sweetwater, TN
Campbell, Katherine A., (P.C.)
Palos Verdes Estates, CA
Campbell, Katherine E. ... Reedsburg, WI
Campbell, Kathleen E. ... Valhalla, NY
Campbell, Kathleen M. ... San Francisco, CA
Campbell, Kathleen S. ... Binghamton, NY
Campbell, Kathrin D. ... Cleveland, OH
Campbell, Kathryn Stocks
Fort Smith, AR
Campbell, Keenan, Harry, Cooney & Karlstrom
Clarkston, MI
Campbell, Keino ... Atlanta, GA
Campbell, Keith H. ... Spokane, WA
Campbell, Keith R. ... Department of Justice, Executive Office for Immigration Review, GV
Campbell, Kelley E. ... Washington, DC
Campbell, Kelly A. ... Knoxville, TN
Morristown, TN
Campbell, Kelly B. ... Denver, CO
Campbell, Kelly L. ... Atlantic City, NJ
Campbell, Kenneth ... St. Albans, NY
Campbell, Kenneth A., Jr. ... Walterboro, SC
Campbell, Kenneth G. ... Rapid City, SD
Campbell, Kenneth L. ... Nashville, TN
Campbell, Kenneth R. ... San Diego, CA
Campbell, Kenneth R. ... Southport, NC
Campbell, Kenneth W. ... Monroe, LA
Campbell, Kent N. ... Fort Collins, CO
Campbell, Kenton P. ... Austin, TX
Campbell, Kerri Kim ... Kalamazoo, MI
Campbell, Kevin ... Chicago, IL
Campbell, Kevin ... Charleston, SC
Campbell, Kevin B ... Lake Success, NY
Campbell, Kevin B. ... Nashville, TN
Campbell, Kevin D. ... Los Angeles, CA
Campbell, Kevin R. ... Cleveland, OH
Campbell, Kimberley E.
Surfside Beach, SC
Campbell, Kimberley S. ... Fort Worth, TX
Campbell Knutson, Professional Association
Eagan, MN
Campbell, Kristen E. ... Canton, OH
Campbell, Kristin A. ... Westborough, MA
Campbell, Kurt U. ... Los Angeles, CA
San Diego, CA
Campbell Kyle Proffitt ... Carmel, IN
Campbell Kyle & Proffitt ... Fishers, IN
Indianapolis, IN
Campbell Kyle Proffitt ... Noblesville, IN
Campbell, L. Cooper ... Burbank, CA
Campbell, L. Don, Jr. ... Memphis, TN
Campbell, L. Webb, II ... Nashville, TN
Campbell, LaBudde & Weston, L.L.C.
Montgomery, AL
Campbell, Lael E ... Dallas, TX
Campbell, Laird ... Denver, CO
Campbell, Lana Wiltshire ... Los Angeles, CA
Campbell, Latiolais & Ruebel
Denver, CO
Campbell, Laura J. ... Detroit, MI
Campbell, Laura R. ... Cleveland, OH
Campbell, Laurie G. ... Bossier City, LA
Campbell Law Firm, P.A. ... Charleston, SC
Campbell Law Firm, The ... Sycamore, IL
Campbell Law Office ... Ely, MN
Campbell Law Offices ... Oakland, CA
Campbell Law Offices ... Mount Pleasant, MI
Campbell, Lawrence G. ... Detroit, MI
Campbell, Lawrence M. ... Durham, NC
Campbell, Lawrence W. ... San Diego, CA
Campbell, Leah ... New York, NY
Campbell, Lee A. ... Lincolnshire, IL
Campbell, Lee A., P.C. ... Lincolnshire, IL
Campbell, Leon E. ... La Jolla, CA
Campbell, Leon L. ... Spartanburg, SC
Campbell, Leonard M. ... Denver, CO
Campbell, Leonard W. D. ... Montrose, CO
Campbell, Leslie D., Jr. ... Ashland, VA
Campbell, Levin H. ... Boston, MA
Campbell & Levine, LLC
Greensburg, PA
Pittsburgh, PA
Campbell, Lewis O. ... Albuquerque, NM
Campbell, Linda L. ... Naples, FL
Campbell, Linda M. ... Syracuse, NY
Campbell, Lionel T. ... Lancaster, CA
Campbell, Lisa J. ... North Palm Beach, FL
Campbell, Lisa J. ... Hamilton, MA
Campbell, Lisa M. ... Washington, DC
Campbell, Lon Overton ... Nashville, TN
Campbell, Lora U. ... West Trenton, NJ
Campbell, Loren W. ... Ann Arbor, MI
Campbell, Loudon L. ... Harrisburg, PA
Campbell, Louis K. ... Fincastle, VA
Campbell, Lucien B. ... San Antonio, TX
Campbell, M. Douglas, Jr. ... Knoxville, TN
Campbell, M. Steven ... Cornelia, GA
Campbell, M. Trant ... Springfield, MA
Campbell, Malcolm J., Jr. ... New York, NY
Campbell, Margaret Claiborne
Atlanta, GA
Campbell, Margaret Hutchins
Atlanta, GA
Campbell, Margaret M. ... New York, NY
Campbell, Margaret R. ... Rock Island, IL
Campbell, Margaret S. ... Painesville, OH
Campbell, Maria B. ... Birmingham, AL
Campbell, Maria W. ... Jefferson City, MO
Campbell, Maria Wagstaff
Jefferson City, MO
Campbell, Marion L. ... Titusville, FL
Campbell, Marisa S. ... Raleigh, NC
Campbell, Mark A. ... Sacramento, CA
Campbell, Mark A. ... Sioux City, IA
Campbell, Mark A. ... Fishkill, NY
Stone Ridge, NY
Valhalla, NY
Campbell, Mark C. ... Beckley, WV
Campbell, Mark D. ... Los Angeles, CA
Campbell, Mark H. ... Manchester, NH
Campbell, Mark R. ... Long Beach, CA
Campbell, Mark R. ... Durant, OK
Campbell, Marshall S. ... Houston, TX
Campbell, Martha M. ... Newton, MA
Campbell, Martha R. ... Beaumont, TX
Campbell, Martin J. ... Tavares, FL
Campbell, Martin & Manley, L.L.P.
Atlanta, GA
Campbell, Marvin H., II
Montgomery, AL

Campbell, Marvin L. ....Greeneville, TN
Campbell, Marvin N. ....Stamford, CT
Campbell, Mary Ann ....Reading, PA
Campbell, Mary Demopoulos ....Nashville, TN
Campbell, Mary Jo ....Deerfield, IL
Campbell, Mary Koch ....Portland, OR
Campbell, Mary M. ....Lincoln, NE
Campbell, Mary R. ....Sacramento, CA
Campbell, Mary Sue ....San Jose, CA
Campbell, Maryann ....Clark, NJ
Campbell, Matthew A. ....Scarsdale, NY
Campbell, Matthew C. ....Warren, NJ
Campbell, Matthew E. ....Portsmouth, NH
Campbell, Matthew W. ....Joliet, IL
Campbell, Max L. ....Lakewood, CO
Campbell & McArdle, P.A. ....Portland, ME
Campbell, McCranie, Sistrunk, Anzelmo & Hardy, P.C. ....Metairie, LA
New Orleans, LA
Campbell, Melissa A. ....Chicago, IL
Campbell, Melissa L. ....Chattanooga, TN
Campbell, Merideth L., Jr ....Chula Vista, CA
Campbell, Merrick I. ....Norfolk, VA
Campbell, Michael A. ....Fresno, CA
Campbell, Michael A. ....Chicago, IL
Campbell, Michael A. ....St. Louis, MO
Campbell, Michael A. ....Beaverton, OR
Campbell, Michael B. ....Santa Fe, NM
Campbell, Michael D. ....Washington, DC
Campbell, Michael G. ....Grand Rapids, MI
Campbell, Michael G. ....Philadelphia, PA
Campbell, Michael Gert ....Rockville, MD
Campbell, Michael I. ....Decatur, IL
Campbell, Michael J. ....Philadelphia, PA
Campbell, Michael R. ....Morehead, KY
Campbell, Michael Ray ....McDonough, GA
Campbell, Michael Roame ....Portland, OR
Campbell, Michael Ross ....Chattanooga, TN
Campbell, Michael T. ....Albuquerque, NM
Campbell, Michael W. ....Lafayette, LA
New Iberia, LA
Campbell, Michelle ....Philadelphia, PA
Campbell, Michelle C. ....Los Angeles, CA
Campbell, Mildred Carolyn "Carol"
Austin, TX
Campbell, Moberg, Canessa, Faber & Hooley,, P.C. ....Seaside, OR
Campbell, Molly A. ....Spokane, WA
Campbell, Molly Jo ....Honolulu, HI
Campbell, Monterey ....Lakeland, FL
Campbell & Morgan, P.C. ....Austin, TX
Campbell, Morgan W. ....Falls Church, VA
Campbell, Moxley & Campbell, LC
Salt Lake City, UT
Campbell, Murray C. ....Niles, MI
Campbell, Nancy Duff ....Washington, DC
Campbell, Nancy E. ....Bronx, NY
Campbell, Nancy E. ....Philadelphia, PA
Campbell, Nancy Kay ....Phoenix, AZ
Campbell, Nancy W. ....Hillsboro, OR
Campbell, Naomi S., (Mrs.) ....Honolulu, HI
Campbell, Naomi Sylvia ....Honolulu, HI
Campbell, Natasha I. ....Philadelphia, PA
Campbell, Nedra D. ....Detroit, MI
Farmington Hills, MI
Campbell, Neva T. ....Portland, OR
Campbell, Newman & Associates, P.A.
Panama City, FL
Campbell, Nicole Lefcourt ....Baltimore, MD
Campbell, Noelle D. ....Dayton, OH
Campbell, Norman A. ....Kingston, RI
Campbell, O'Brien & Mistele, P.C.
Detroit, MI
Troy, MI
Campbell, Orbie M. ....Atlanta, GA
Campbell, Orland, Jr. ....Manchester, VT
Campbell, P. Brian ....Roswell, GA
Campbell, P. David ....Los Angeles, CA
Campbell, Paige P. ....Hammond, LA
Campbell, Pamela A. M., P.A.
St. Petersburg, FL
Campbell, Pamela A. M.
St. Petersburg, FL
Campbell, Pamela J. ....New York, NY
Campbell, Pamela W. ....Paris, TX
Campbell, Patricia A. ....Austin, TX
Campbell, Patricia B. ....Detroit, MI
Campbell, Patricia C. ....Denver, CO
Campbell, Patricia E. ....Philadelphia, PA
Campbell, Patricia Gardner ....Nashville, TN
Campbell, Patricia J. ....Los Angeles, CA
Campbell, Patrick A. ....Lincoln, NE
Campbell, Patrick C. ....Oakland, CA
Campbell, Patrick C. ....Bryn Mawr, PA
Campbell, Patrick C., Jr. ....Philadelphia, PA
Campbell, Patrick D. ....La Mesa, CA
Campbell, Patrick J. ....Cupertino, CA
Campbell, Patrick M. ....New City, NY
Campbell, Patrick S. ....Washington, DC
Campbell, Patsy ....Doylestown, PA
Campbell, Paul B. ....Lakewood, OH
Campbell, Paul C. ....Auburn, NY
Campbell, Paul E. ....Willoughby, OH
Campbell, Paul G. ....Lancaster, PA
Campbell, Paul, III ....Chattanooga, TN
Campbell, Paul J. ....Chicago, IL
Campbell, Paul, Jr. ....Chattanooga, TN
Campbell, Paula A. ....Boston, MA
Campbell, Paula A. ....Norristown, PA
Campbell, Paula Ann ....Batavia, NY
Campbell, Paulette ....Miami, FL
Campbell, Peter C. ....Wilmington, DE
Campbell, Peter Dow, II ....Orleans, MA
Campbell, Phil ....Little Rock, AR
North Little Rock, AR
Campbell, Phil W. ....Van Wert, OH
Campbell, Philip R. ....Tulsa, OK
Campbell, Phillip J. ....Sacramento, CA
Campbell, Phillip S. ....Oakland, CA
Campbell, Phyllis A. ....Des Moines, IA
Campbell, Pollyann S. ....Atlanta, GA
Campbell, R. Colin ....Buffalo, NY
Campbell, R. Edgar ....Albany, GA
Campbell, R. Edward ....West Palm Beach, FL
Campbell, R. Holland ....Washington, DC
Campbell, R. Randall
Department Of Veterans Affairs, Office of the General Counsel, GV
Campbell, R. Scott
Hot Springs National Park, AR
Campbell, Rachel A. ....Dallas, TX
Campbell, Rachel Danish
Washington, DC
Campbell, Ralph J. ....Mariposa, CA
Campbell, Randall B., The Law Offices of
Roanoke, VA
Campbell, Randy A. ....Hindman, KY
Campbell, Ray A., III ....Boston, MA
Campbell, Ray Worthy ....Chicago, IL
Campbell, Raymond W. ....Beloit, WI
Campbell, Rebecca Holland
Washington, DC
Campbell, Rebecca Stack ....Washington, DC
Campbell, Regina M. ....Trumbull, CT
Campbell, Renee L. ....Los Angeles, CA
Campbell, Reynolds H. ....Mount Pleasant, MI
Campbell, Rhett G. ....Houston, TX
Campbell, Richard A. ....Norcross, GA
Campbell, Richard A. ....Chicago, IL
Campbell, Richard A. ....Clarkston, MI
Campbell, Richard B. ....Aurora, CO
Campbell, Richard B. ....Tampa, FL
Campbell, Richard D. ....Elberton, GA
Campbell, Richard Duncan ....Spokane, WA
Campbell, Richard E. ....San Diego, CA
Campbell, Richard F. ....Slidell, LA
Campbell, Richard F. ....Buffalo, NY
Campbell, Richard G., Jr. ....Reno, NV
Campbell, Richard G., Sr. ....Reno, NV
Campbell, Richard H., Jr. ....Danville, KY
Campbell, Richard J., Jr. ....Chicago, IL
Campbell, Richard L. ....Denver, CO
Campbell, Richard L. ....Clarence, NY
Campbell, Richard L. ....New York, NY
Campbell, Richard L. ....Bellefonte, PA
State College, PA
Campbell, Richard M. ....Oakland, CA
Campbell, Richard M. ....Monroe, LA
Campbell, Richard N. ....Nevada City, CA
Campbell, Richard O. ....Denver, CO
Campbell, Richard P. ....Chicago, IL
Campbell, Richard P. ....Portland, ME
Boston, MA
Concord, NH
Providence, RI
Campbell, Richard T. ....Phoenix, AZ
Campbell, Richard W. ....Portsmouth, OH
Campbell, Richard W. ....Ogden, UT
Campbell & Riggs, A Professional Corporation ....Aiken, SC
Houston, TX
Campbell, Robert ....Redding, CA
Campbell, Robert A. ....Wytheville, VA
Campbell, Robert A. ....Charleston, WV
Campbell, Robert B. ....Winston-Salem, NC
Campbell, Robert B. ....Brunswick, OH
Campbell, Robert C. ....Sacramento, CA
Campbell, Robert C. ....Department of State, Foreign Service Officers (Overseas), GV
Campbell, Robert C., III ....Mobile, AL
Campbell, Robert Cleaver, III
Los Angeles, CA
Campbell, Robert D. ....Chicago, IL
Campbell, Robert D. ....Atchison, KS
Campbell, Robert D. ....Colonia, NJ
Campbell, Robert D. ....Dallas, TX
Campbell, Robert D. ....Puyallup, WA
Campbell, Robert D. ....Parkersburg, WV
Campbell, Robert E. ....Los Angeles, CA
Campbell, Robert E. ....Taylorsville, NC
Campbell, Robert E. ....Gettysburg, PA
Campbell, Robert F. ....Oakland, CA
Campbell, Robert F. ....Carmel, IN
Campbell, Robert F. ....South Padre Island, TX
Campbell, Robert G. ....Los Angeles, CA
Campbell, Robert H. ....Clare, MI
Campbell, Robert H. ....Seattle, WA
Campbell, Robert J. ....Denver, CO
Campbell, Robert J. ....Kansas City, MO
Campbell, Robert J. ....Springfield, MO
Campbell, Robert J. ....Helena, MT
Campbell, Robert J. ....Beaver, PA
Campbell, Robert J., Jr.
Oklahoma City, OK
Campbell, Robert James
Birmingham, AL
Campbell, Robert L. ....Clayton, MO
Campbell, Robert L. ....Pittsburgh, PA
Campbell, Robert M. ....Chino Valley, AZ
Campbell, Robert M. ....Ann Arbor, MI
Campbell, Robert M. ....Jackson, MS
Waco, TX
Campbell, Robert O. ....The Woodlands, TX
Campbell, Robert P. ....Akron, OH
Campbell, Robert R. ....Knoxville, TN
Campbell, Robert R., Jr. ....Nashville, TN
Campbell, Robert S. ....Baltimore, MD
Campbell, Robert S., Jr.
Salt Lake City, UT
Campbell, Robert T. ....Fairfax, VA
Campbell, Robert V. ....San Anselmo, CA
Campbell, Robert V. ....Duluth, MN
Campbell, Robert W. ....Rocky River, OH
Campbell, Robin C. ....Los Angeles, CA
Campbell, Robin Corwin
Fort Lauderdale, FL
Campbell & Robinson ....Decatur, IL
Campbell, Robt. N., Jr. ....San Antonio, TX
Campbell, Roger C. ....New York, NY
Campbell, Roger L.
Cruz Bay, St. John, VI
Charlotte Amalie, St. Thomas, VI
Campbell & Rogers ....Batavia, NY
Campbell, Roland P. ....Boulder, CO
Campbell, Ronald ....Wichita, KS
Campbell, Ronald A. ....Louisville, KY
Campbell, Ronald D. ....Pierre, SD
Campbell, Ronald E. ....Evergreen Park, IL
Campbell, Ronald J. ....Princeton, NJ
Campbell, Ronald P. ....Atlanta, GA
Campbell, Rory J. ....San Francisco, CA
Campbell, Ross E. ....Palo Alto, CA
Campbell, Ross W. ....Ann Arbor, MI
Campbell & Rowell, L.L.P., Law Offices of
Birmingham, AL
Campbell, Roxanna S. ....Newark, NJ
Campbell, Roy D., III ....Nashville, TN
Campbell, Roy D., Jr. ....Greenville, MS
Campbell, Roy T., Jr. ....Newport, TN
Campbell, Ruairidh William
Salt Lake City, UT
Campbell, Rutherford B, Jr. ....Lexington, KY
Campbell, Ryan T. ....Reno, NV
Campbell, Sallyanne ....San Francisco, CA
Campbell, Sam ....Hopewell, VA
Campbell, Sam G., III ....Palo Alto, CA
Campbell, Samuel D. ....Pulaski, VA
Campbell, Samuel G., III ....Austin, TX
Campbell, Sandra J. ....Talladega, AL
Campbell, Sarah Grace ....Syracuse, NY
Campbell, Sarah Jane ....Natchitoches, LA
Campbell, Sarah P. ....Ashland, VA
Campbell, Scot R. ....Reno, NV
Campbell, Scott ....Oskaloosa, IA
Campbell, Scott ....Montesano, WA
Campbell, Scott A. ....Columbus, OH
Campbell, Scott B. ....Santa Barbara, CA
Campbell, Scott F. ....Seattle, WA
Campbell, Scott G. ....New York, NY
Campbell, Scott H. ....Los Angeles, CA
Campbell, Scott J. ....Milwaukee, WI
Campbell, Scott L. ....Boise, ID
Campbell, Scott L. ....Platte City, MO
Campbell, Scott M. ....Denver, CO
Campbell, Scott R. ....San Francisco, CA
Campbell, Scott W. ....San Francisco, CA
Campbell, Sean E. ....New York, NY
Campbell, Sharon ....Dallas, TX
Campbell, Sherry Herrera
Warner Robins, GA
Campbell & Sink, A Prof. Corp., The Law Offices of ....Cloverdale, CA
Santa Rosa, CA
Campbell & Smith ....Seattle, WA
Campbell & Snyder LLP ....Albuquerque, NM
Campbell, Spiller, Jr. ....Nashville, TN
Campbell, Stacey A. ....Kansas City, MO
Campbell, Staci D. ....Fresno, CA
Campbell, Stanley L. ....Fort Wayne, IN
Campbell, Stanley T. ....St. Petersburg, FL
Campbell, Stanley W., Jr.
Hallandale Beach, FL
Pompano Beach, FL
Campbell, Stephen A., Law Offices of
Claremont, CA
Campbell, Stephen D. ....Grants Pass, OR
Campbell, Stephen G. ....Phoenix, AZ
Campbell, Stephen J. ....Kansas City, MO
Campbell, Stephen P. ....Boston, MA
Campbell, Stephen Robert
Department of Justice, Civil Division, GV
Campbell, Steven L. ....Indianapolis, IN
Campbell, Steven T. ....Seaside, OR
Campbell, Steven V. ....Greenville, NC
Campbell & Stone ....Carson City, NV
Reno, NV
Campbell, Stuart C. ....Seattle, WA
Campbell, Stuart D. ....Tulsa, OK
Campbell, Susan Clark ....Cornelia, GA
Campbell, Susan Curtis ....King, NC
Campbell, Susan D. ....Towson, MD
Campbell, Susan E. Duffey
Colorado Springs, CO
Campbell, Susan M. ....Carson City, NV
Campbell, Susan Millington
New York, NY
Campbell, Susan V. ....Coeur d'Alene, ID
Campbell, T. Chuck ....Houston, TX
Campbell, T. Joseph ....Cartersville, GA
Campbell, T. Kyle, III ....Albuquerque, NM
Campbell, Tammy ....Denver, CO
Campbell, Tammy Lynn ....Pikeville, KY
Campbell, Tena ....Salt Lake City, UT
Campbell, Terence H. ....Chicago, IL
Campbell, Teresa L. ....Southlake, TX
Campbell, Terrence J. ....Kansas City, KS
Campbell, Terry L. ....Modesto, CA
Campbell, Terry L. ....Milwaukee, WI
Campbell, T. H., III ....Gainesville, FL
Campbell, Thomas ....Chicago, IL
Campbell, Thomas A. ....Santa Rosa, CA
Campbell, Thomas A. ....Cortland, OH
Campbell, Thomas A. ....Houston, TX
Campbell, Thomas A. ....Auburn, WA
Campbell, Thomas A., Jr. ....Newark, NJ
Campbell, Thomas D. ....Washington, DC
Campbell, Thomas E. ....Atlanta, GA
Campbell, Thomas E. ....Fairfax, VA
Campbell, Thomas E. ....Douglas, WY
Campbell, Thomas E., P.C. ....Douglas, WY
Campbell, Thomas F. ....Birmingham, AL
Campbell, Thomas F. ....Northville, MI
Campbell, Thomas G. ....St. Paul, MN
Campbell, Thomas H. ....Phoenix, AZ
Campbell, Thomas H. ....Fairfax, VA
Campbell, Thomas J. ....Redwood City, CA
Campbell, Thomas J. ....Indianapolis, IN
Campbell, Thomas J. ....Eagan, MN
Campbell, Thomas J. ....St. Louis, MO
Campbell, Thomas J. ....Pittsburgh, PA
Campbell, Thomas K. ....Newark, OH
Campbell, Thomas K., II ....Roswell, NM
Campbell, Thomas L. ....Washington, DC
Campbell, Thomas L. ....Fort Pierce, FL
Campbell, Thomas L. ....Chicago, IL
Campbell, Thomas L., Jr. ....Naples, FL
Campbell, Thomas M. ....Harrisonville, MO
Campbell, Thomas M. ....New York, NY
Campbell, Thomas N. ....Los Angeles, CA
Campbell, Thomas R. ....Lansing, MI
Campbell, Thomas R. ....Gettysburg, PA
Campbell, Thomas R., Jr. ....Roswell, GA
Campbell, Thomas T.C. ....Rawlins, WY
Campbell, Tim J., Jr. ....Newton, IA
Campbell, Tim L. ....Golden, CO
Campbell, Timothy C. ....Panama City, FL
Campbell, Timothy C. ....Akron, OH
Campbell, Timothy F. ....Lakeland, FL
Campbell, Timothy F. ....Godfrey, IL
Campbell, Timothy J. ....Hoboken, NJ
Philadelphia, PA
Campbell, T. K. ....Las Cruces, NM
Campbell, Todd A. ....Kansas City, MO
Campbell, Todd J. ....Nashville, TN
Campbell, Todd M. ....Atlanta, GA
Campbell, Tom ....Malvern, PA
Campbell, Tracey A, ...Paoli, PA
Campbell, Tracey E. ....Bloomfield, NJ
Campbell, Truman F. ....Fresno, CA
Campbell & Turkaly ....Charleston, WV
Campbell, Venessa V. ....Birmingham, AL
Campbell, Vicki J. ....Huntington Beach, CA
Campbell, Victoria Brace ....Port Jervis, NY
Campbell, Victoria L. ....Bel Air, MD
Campbell, Vincent B. ....Rochester, NY
Campbell, Vivian D. Vines
Birmingham, AL
Campbell, Vivian L. ....Washington, DC
Campbell, W. Arthur ....Ho-Ho-Kus, NJ
Campbell, W. Charles ....Dallas, TX
Campbell, W. Clark, Jr. ....Montgomery, AL
Campbell, W. Douglas ....United States Senate, Committee Legal Personnel, GV
Campbell, W. Loy ....Scottsboro, AL
Campbell, W. Matthew ....New Orleans, LA
Campbell, W. Scott ....Wheeling, WV
Campbell, Wallace L. ....Tallahassee, FL
Campbell, Waller & McCallum, L.L.C.
Birmingham, AL
Campbell, Wallis L. ....Arvada, CO
Campbell, Walter G., Jr.
Fort Lauderdale, FL
Campbell, Walter S. ....College Station, TX
Campbell, Warburton, Fitzsimmons, Smith, Mendell & Pastore, A Professional Corporation ....San Jose, CA
Campbell, Ward A. ....Sacramento, CA
Campbell, Warren B. ....Irvine, CA
Campbell, Warren D. ....Dallas, TX
Campbell, Wendi S. ....Dallas, TX
Campbell, West H. ....Yakima, WA
Campbell, West H., P.L.L.C. ....Yakima, WA
Campbell and White ....Gettysburg, PA
Campbell, Willard R. ....Santa Cruz, CA
Campbell, William ....New York, NY
Campbell, William ....St. Clairsville, OH
Campbell, William A. ....Philadelphia, PA
Campbell, William B. ....Los Angeles, CA
Campbell, William C. ....Atlanta, GA
Campbell, William C. ....Woburn, MA
Campbell, William C. ....Portland, OR
Campbell, William D. ....Newport Beach, CA
Campbell, William D. ....Normal, IL
Campbell, William D. ....Steubenville, OH
Campbell, William F. ....San Francisco, CA
Campbell, William F., III ....Morristown, NJ
Campbell, William F., Jr. ....Denver, CO
Campbell, William G. ....Ely, MN
Campbell, William H. ....Peoria, IL
Campbell, William H.
Oklahoma City, OK
Campbell, William J. ....Denver, CO
Campbell, William J. ....Mount Pleasant, MI
Okemos, MI
Campbell, William J. ....Jamestown, TN
Campbell, William J. ....Houston, TX
Campbell, William J., Jr. ....Chicago, IL
Campbell, William Kent ....Covington, GA
Campbell, William L. ....Arlington, TX
Campbell, William R.
North Palm Beach, FL
Campbell, William Scott ....Charleston, WV
Campbell, William W. ....Quarryville, PA
Campbell & Williams ....Las Vegas, NV
Campbell & Williams, L.L.C. ....Dallas, TX
Campbell, Winfield M ....Houston, TX
Campbell, Wm. A. ....Chapel Hill, NC
Campbell, Wm. D.
North Richland Hills, TX
Campbell, Wolfenzon, Souhrada & Volk
San Diego, CA
Campbell, Woodley C. ....Montgomery, AL
Campbell, Woodrow W., Jr.
New York, NY
Campbell, Woods, Bagley, Emerson, McNeer & Herndon, P.L.L.C. ....Ashland, KY
Charleston, WV
Huntington, WV
Campbell, W. T., Jr. ....Sylacauga, AL
Campbell-Brunson, Kirsten V.
Department of the Army, U.S. Army Legal Services Agency, GV

Campbell-Mohn, Frederick S. ..... Montpelier, VT
Campbell-O'Conor, Jill R. ..... Chicago, IL
Campe, Christine A. ..... Chicago, IL
Campe, Rene Robertson ..... Chicago, IL
Campe, Thomas D., Jr. ..... Waukegan, IL
Campeau, Joseph O. ..... Moorpark, CA
Campeau, Kenneth J. ..... San Jose, CA
Campeau & Thomas, A Law Corporation ..... San Jose, CA
Campedel, Robert V. ..... Bloomfield Hills, MI
Pittsburgh, PA
Campellone, Paul A. ..... Providence, RI
Campen, George B. ..... Union City, NJ
Campen, Henry C., Jr. ..... Raleigh, NC
Campen, Howard W. ..... San Jose, CA
Campen, Sidney S., Jr. ..... Easton, MD
Campen, Steven D. ..... Rockville, MD
Campen & Walsworth, P.A. ..... Easton, MD
Salisbury, MD
Camper, Anne B. ..... Washington, DC
Camper, Beverly M. ..... Hemet, CA
Camper, Clarke Dryden ..... Washington, DC
Camper, Deborah Fontaine ..... Hurlock, MD
Camper, Harry G., Jr. ..... Charleston, WV
Camper, Stephen P. ..... Dallas, TX
Camper, William L. ..... Tallahassee, FL
Campero, Adolfo, Jr. ..... Houston, TX
Campese, Matthew C. ..... New York, NY
Campf, Brian S. ..... New York, NY
Campfield, Ann Brakke ..... Richmond, VA
Campfield, John M. ..... Greensburg, PA
Campfield, Kristen M. ..... Harrisburg, PA
Campfield, Regis W. ..... Dallas, TX
Camphouse, John G. ..... Bishop, CA
Campi, Kathleen McCormick ..... Upper Montclair, NJ
Campiche, Hepburn, McCarty & Bianco, P.L.L.C. ..... Seattle, WA
Campiche, Jeffery M. ..... Seattle, WA
Campiere, Margaret S. ..... New Orleans, LA
Campillo, Ralph A. ..... Los Angeles, CA
Campilongo, Lisa F. ..... San Francisco, CA
Campilongo, Michael
Small Business Administration, Office of the General Counsel, GV
Campion, Bernard L. ..... San Antonio, TX
Campion, Brian T. ..... Hackensack, NJ
Campion, Charles E. ..... San Antonio, TX
Campion, Curran, Rausch, Gummerson & Dunlop, P.C. ..... Crystal Lake, IL
Woodstock, IL
Campion, Douglas J. ..... San Diego, CA
Campion, George G. ..... Newark, NJ
Campion, James A. ..... Crystal Lake, IL
Campion, James E., Jr. ..... Philadelphia, PA
Campion, Jeff ..... Miami, FL
Campion, John E.
Research Triangle Park, NC
Campion, John E., III ..... Orange, CA
Campion, Kenneth G. ..... Whittier, CA
Campion, Kenneth G., A Professional Corporation ..... Whittier, CA
Campion, Kevin John ..... Washington, DC
Campion, Phyllis ..... Hauppauge, NY
Campion, Reneé ..... Towson, MD
Campion, Robert C. ..... Framingham, MA
Campion, Rodolff, Van Riper & Procopio LLP ..... Orange, CA
Campion, Thomas B. ..... Ketchum, ID
Campion, Thomas F. ..... Florham Park, NJ
Campione, Christine E. ..... Broadalbin, NY
Campione, Christopher C. ..... Vero Beach, FL
Campione, John J. ..... Vero Beach, FL
Campione, Leslie Shamrock ..... Eustis, FL
Campione, Matthew J. ..... Fairfax, VA
Campione, Trent Edward
Los Angeles, CA
Campisano, Anthony M.
New Brunswick, NJ
Campisano, Anthony W. ..... Sarasota, FL
Valrico, FL
Campisano, Frank P. ..... Louisville, KY
Campisano, Frank R. ..... Montclair, NJ
Campisano, Gina M. ..... Pittsburgh, PA
Campisano, Guy A., Jr.
San Francisco, CA
Campisano, Joseph M. ..... Montclair, NJ
Campisano, Mark Stephen ..... New York, NY
Campisano, Richard N. ..... Jersey City, NJ
Campise, James F. ..... New York, NY
Campisi, Dominic J. ..... San Francisco, CA
Campisi, Gregory G. ..... Roseland, NJ
Campisi, Jeffrey ..... Roseland, NJ
Campisi, Jon J. ..... Santa Clara, CA
Campisi, Joseph ..... New York, NY
Campisi, Mary Lynn ..... Birmingham, AL
Campisi, P. Joseph, Jr. ..... New York, NY
Campisi, Samuel Chris ..... Birmingham, AL
Campiti, Anthony J. ..... Dallas, TX
Campiti, Vincent M. ..... South Bend, IN
Campitiello, Lawrence G. ..... Carlsbad, CA
Campito, Laurie A. ..... Albany, NY
Campito, Paul J. ..... Schenectady, NY
Camp-Lee, Susan ..... Round Rock, TX
Camplese, Albert S. ..... Ashtabula, OH
Camplese, Nicole M. ..... Harrisburg, PA
Campney, A. Michelle
Oklahoma City, OK
Campo Anderson, LLP ..... Boston, MA
Campo, Anthony M. ..... Indianapolis, IN
Campo, Anthony M. ..... Boston, MA
Campo, Benjamin Paul ..... New York, NY
Campo, Charles M., Jr. ..... Boston, MA
Campo, Elizabeth F. ..... Gainesville, FL
Campo, Fred A. ..... Staten Island, NY
Campo, Henry A. (drew)
Oklahoma City, OK
Campo, John, III ..... Phoenix, AZ
Campo, John P. ..... New York, NY
Campo, John R. ..... Redwood City, CA
Campo, Joseph C. ..... Los Angeles, CA
Campo, Karen R. ..... Garden City, NY
Campo, Laurent M. ..... Washington, DC
Campo, Maria C. ..... Fort Wayne, IN
Campo, Mary Ann ..... New York, NY
Campo, Paul V. ..... Clifton, NJ
Campo, Paul V. L. ..... Vista, CA
Campo, Richard M. ..... New York, NY
Campo, Robert A. ..... Cheektowaga, NY
Campo, Robin L. ..... Fairfield, CA
Campo, Stephen J. ..... Chicago, IL
Campo, Stephen V. ..... New York, NY
Campo, Thomas G. ..... Woodbury, NJ
Campo, Tina L. ..... Pittsburgh, PA
Campoamor-Sanchez, Fernando
Department of Justice, Civil Division, GV
Campobasso, Carina J.
Department of Justice, Tax Division, GV
CampoBasso Law Office, The
Leominster, MA
CampoBasso & McGuirk ..... Athol, MA
Leominster, MA
CampoBasso, Peter A. ..... Leominster, MA
CampoBasso, Stephen M. ..... Leominster, MA
CampoBasso, Vincent J. ..... Leominster, MA
Campodonico, J. Dominic
San Francisco, CA
Campoli, Andrew T. ..... North Adams, MA
Pittsfield, MA
Campoli & Campoli
Great Barrington, MA
North Adams, MA
Pittsfield, MA
Campoli, J. Peri ..... North Adams, MA
Pittsfield, MA
Campoli, Thomas L. ..... North Adams, MA
Pittsfield, MA
Campolieto, John M. ..... Rochester, NY
Campolieto, Joseph M. ..... Taylor, PA
Campolo, Donald C. ..... Paterson, NJ
Campolo, Joseph N. ..... Melville, NY
Campolongo & Bosworth, L.L.P. ..... Tustin, CA
Campolongo, Jeffrey ..... Philadelphia, PA
Campolongo, John ..... Melville, NY
Campolongo, Joy ..... Tustin, CA
Campolongo, Robert P. ..... New York, NY
Campolucci, Roger L. ..... Seattle, WA
Camponovo, Christopher N.
Los Angeles, CA
Campora, Steven M. ..... Jackson, CA
Sacramento, CA
Camporeale, Carlo J. ..... River Edge, NJ
Campos, Alfred ..... Washington, DC
Campos, Alfredo J., Jr. ..... Irving, TX
Campos, Alice G. ..... Reno, NV
Campos, Atanacio ..... New Braunfels, TX
Campos, David F. ..... San Francisco, CA
Campos, David N. ..... Grand Rapids, MI
Campos, Dennis M. ..... Sacramento, CA
Campos, Elizabeth ..... Oakland, CA
Campos, Ellen ..... Santa Cruz, CA
Campos, George ..... Flushing, NY
Campos, Guillermo ..... Los Angeles, CA
Campos, Jesse B. ..... San Antonio, TX
Campos, John L. ..... San Antonio, TX
Campos, Joseph Michael ..... Seattle, WA
Campos, Lorie A. ..... Los Angeles, CA
Campos, Luis R. ..... Dallas, TX
Campos, Maricela (Mari) ..... Edinburg, TX
Campos, Marta ..... Department of Justice, Civil Rights Division, GV
Campos, Michael A. ..... Fresno, CA
Sacramento, CA
San Francisco, CA
Campos, Miguel P. ..... Albuquerque, NM
Campos, Paul ..... San Ramon, CA
Campos, Raymond Q. ..... Los Angeles, CA
Campos, Rolando ..... East Grand Forks, MN
Campos, Ruben D. ..... San Antonio, TX
Campos, Santiago E. ..... Santa Fe, NM
Campos, Sara T. ..... San Francisco, CA
Campos, Stacy A. ..... San Francisco, CA
Campos, Victor M. ..... Santa Cruz, CA
Campos, Victor Miguel ..... Brentwood, NY
Camposano, Eugene ..... Marlton, NJ
Philadelphia, PA
Camposeo, Elaine N. ..... Manchester, CT
Campos-Marquetti, Roberto ..... New York, NY
Campoy, Bret E. ..... Santa Rosa, CA
Campoy, Cynthia D ..... Phoenix, AZ
Campoy, Joe, Jr ..... Sacramento, CA
Campriello, Austin V. ..... New York, NY
Campsen & Campsen ..... Charleston, SC
Campsen, George E. "Chip", III
Charleston, SC
Campsen, George E., Jr. ..... Charleston, SC
Campsen, Paul K. ..... Norfolk, VA
Campson, Paul J. ..... White Plains, NY
Campwala, Tasneem ..... Los Angeles, CA
Camras, Barbara J. ..... Los Angeles, CA
Camras, Michael J. ..... Los Angeles, CA
Camras, Michael J., Inc. ..... Los Angeles, CA
Camrud, Maddock, Olson & Larson, Ltd.
Grand Forks, ND
Camrud, Susan ..... Farmington, NM
Camrud, Theodore M. ..... Grand Forks, ND
Camson, Barry S. ..... Cambridge, MA
Camuel, Cynthia H. ..... Plano, TX
Camunez, Betty A. ..... Albuquerque, NM
Camuñez, Michael C. ..... Los Angeles, CA
Camuñez, Rosanne ..... Las Cruces, NM
Camus, Constance A. ..... Greenbelt, MD
Camus, Edward P. ..... Riverdale, MD
Camus, Glenn Emil ..... Atlanta, GA
Camvel, Patricia C. ..... Harrisburg, PA
Can, Errol Anthony ..... Kent, OH
Canaan, Mary ..... Sacramento, CA
Canaan II, Gerald C. ..... Richmond, VA
Canada, A. Joseph, Jr. ..... Virginia Beach, VA
Canada, Bradley Seth ..... England, AR
Canada, Christopher ..... Clark, NJ
Canada, Cynthia M. ..... New Orleans, LA
Canada, Denise D. ..... Oklahoma City, OK
Canada, G. Vann, Jr. ..... Rockville, MD
Canada, Jerry ..... Boston, MA
Canada, Kent ..... Amarillo, TX
Canada, Kursten L. ..... Vail, CO
Canada, Larry G. ..... New Orleans, LA
Houston, TX
Canada, Mark P. ..... Indianapolis, IN
Canada, Meredith ..... Houston, TX
Cañada, Rachel Maria ..... Cleveland, OH
Canada, Robert ..... Evansville, IN
Canaday, Arthur C. ..... Blowing Rock, NC
Canaday & Canaday, P.A. ..... Benson, NC
Canaday, C. C., Jr. ..... Benson, NC
Canaday, Claude C., III ..... Benson, NC
Canaday, Harry E. ..... Benson, NC
Canaday, Marjorie Sibley ..... Raleigh, NC
Canaday, Mary Alice S. ..... Westport, CT
Canaday, Nicholas, III ..... Baton Rouge, LA
Canaday, Richard A., P.C. ..... Portland, OR
Canaday, Russell D. ..... Independence, KS
Canaday, Theresa A. ..... Chicago, IL
Canaday, Thomas B. ..... Detroit, MI
Canade, Austen Donald ..... Brooklyn, NY
Canade, Terrence P. ..... Chicago, IL
Canady, A. Britten ..... Charlotte, NC
Canady & Canady ..... St. Pauls, NC
Canady, Charles T. ..... Lakeland, FL
Canady, Clinton, III ..... Lansing, MI
Canady, Donald R. ..... Fayetteville, NC
Canady, Donald W. ..... Vista, CA
Canady, Jack F. ..... Winston-Salem, NC
Canady, Karen S. ..... Los Angeles, CA
Canady, Kelly Lynn ..... San Francisco, CA
Canady Law Offices ..... Lansing, MI
Canady, Mark H. ..... Lansing, MI
Canady, Paul T. ..... St. Pauls, NC
Canady, Paul T., II ..... St. Pauls, NC
Canady, Richard W. ..... San Francisco, CA
Canady, Thornton, Burge, Brown & Laws, L.L.P. ..... Winston-Salem, NC
Canafax, James D. ..... New Orleans, LA
Canafax, Thomas, Jr. ..... Chicago, IL
Canala, John Steven ..... Mentor, OH
Canala, Robert L. ..... Cleveland, OH
Canale, Anthony P. ..... Dallas, TX
Canale, Daniel D. ..... Memphis, TN
Canale, David A. ..... Atlanta, GA
Canale, David M. ..... Columbus, OH
Canale, Francis X. ..... Chevy Chase, MD
Canale, Gregory V. ..... Glens Falls, NY
Canale, John F. ..... Buffalo, NY
Canale, John Ford, III ..... Memphis, TN
Canale, Michelle R. ..... Irvine, CA
Canale, Phil M., Jr. ..... Memphis, TN
Canale, Stuart J. ..... Memphis, TN
Canale, William V. ..... Glens Falls, NY
Canales, Adolph P. ..... Dallas, TX
Canales, H. Paul ..... San Antonio, TX
Canales, Hector A. ..... Houston, TX
Canales, Homero C. ..... Alice, TX
Canales, Ignacio E. ..... Brownsville, TX
Canales, J. A. "Tony" ..... Corpus Christi, TX
Canales, L. G. (Jerry) ..... Edinburg, TX
Canales, Olivero E. ..... Laredo, TX
Canales, Patricia N. ..... Corpus Christi, TX
Canales & Simonson, P.C.
Corpus Christi, TX
Canales, Terry A. ..... Alice, TX
Canales, Viola I. ..... San Francisco, CA
Canalia, Peter B. ..... Lansing, IL
Canalia & Valerius, P.C. ..... Lansing, IL
Canan, Bruce A. ..... Kirkwood, MO
Canan, Michael J. ..... Orlando, FL
Canan, Patrick T. ..... St. Augustine, FL
Canan, Russell F. ..... Washington, DC
Canant, Fred C. ..... Modesto, CA
Canant & Woodall ..... Modesto, CA
Canar, Deanne R. ..... Sacramento, CA
Canar, John R. ..... Rochester, MI
Canar, Michael G. ..... Rocklin, CA
Canaras, Barry T. ..... Baltimore, MD
Canaras, George T. ..... Lutherville, MD
Canarick, Bernard D. ..... Tamarac, FL
Canarick, Bernard D., P.A., Law Offices ..... Tamarac, FL
Canarick, Jeffrey ..... New York, NY
Canarick, Robert J. ..... Cranford, NJ
Canarie, J. David, Jr. ..... Portland, ME
Canaris, Jas. E. ..... Cleveland, OH
Canarte, MaryKay ..... Gaithersburg, MD
Canary, Barbara ..... Boston, MA
Canary, Bonni Cherrick ..... Salem, OR
Canary, David L. ..... Portland, OR
Canary, Janet M. Cook
Equal Employment Opportunity Commission, Office of the General Counsel, GV
Canary, Nancy H. ..... Palm Beach, FL
Cleveland, OH
Canary, Thomas L., Jr. ..... Louisville, KY
Cañas, David L. ..... Los Angeles, CA
Cañas, David P. ..... Nashville, TN
Cañas, Eduardo ..... Fort Worth, TX
Cañas, Norma E. ..... New York, NY
Cañas, Roberto, Jr. ..... Dallas, TX
Canata, Anthony J. ..... Boston, MA
Canatella, Richard A. ..... San Francisco, CA
Canavan & Boehm ..... Manhasset, NY
Canavan, Cathleen M. ..... Boston, MA
Canavan, Charles F. ..... Sun City, AZ
Canavan, Gerard F. ..... White Plains, NY
Canavan, James Jeffrey ..... Chicago, IL
Canavan, John A., Jr. ..... Winthrop, MA
Canavan, John G., Jr. ..... Shawnee, OK
Canavan, Kelly M. ..... Sag Harbor, NY
Canavan, Kevin ..... Philadelphia, PA
Canavan, Matthew J. ..... Rochester, NY
Canavan, Michael J. ..... Princeton, NJ
Canavan, Patrick D. ..... New York, NY
Canavan, R. Lawrence ..... Wheaton, IL
Canavan, Robert T. ..... Iselin, NJ
Canavan, Thomas J., Jr. ..... Manhasset, NY
Canavello, Susan Smith ..... New Orleans, LA
Canavesi, Karl J. ..... Rockford, IL
Canavor, Frederick C., Jr. ..... Seattle, WA
Canbaz, Janet ..... Reseda, CA
Canby, Caleb H., III ..... Barrington, IL
Canby, John A. ..... Phoenix, AZ
Canby, Margaret (Meg) L. ..... New York, NY
Canby, Rhonda ..... Sacramento, CA
Canby, William C., Jr. ..... Phoenix, AZ
Canby, William Nathan ..... Beverly Hills, CA
Cancel, Carlos Misael ..... Rockville, MD
Cancell, Nadine ..... New York, NY
Cancellare, Michael Whitney
Glen Head, NY
Cancelli, Dante A. ..... Scranton, PA
Cancelliere, Michael A., Jr.
Philadelphia, PA
Cancelmi, Harry J., Jr. ..... Waynesburg, PA
Cancelosi, Susan Evans ..... Dallas, TX
Canciamilla, Joseph E. ..... Pittsburg, CA
Canciello, Niru ..... Pittsburgh, PA
Canciello, Richard S. ..... Pittsburgh, PA
Cancienne, L. Milton, Jr. ..... Houma, LA
Cancienne, L. Milton, Jr., A Professional Law Corporation ..... Houma, LA
Cancienne, Phyllis Guin
New Orleans, LA
Cancila, Joseph A., Jr. ..... Chicago, IL
Cancilla, Braden ..... Los Angeles, CA
Cancilla, Michael J. ..... Whitesboro, NY
Cancio & Cancio Reichard ..... Aguadilla, PR
Cancio, Elvira ..... San Juan, PR
Cancio, Hiram R. ..... San Juan, PR
Cancio, Humberto, Jr. ..... Miami, FL
Cancio, Mariana L. ..... Miami, FL
Cancio, Marili ..... Miami, FL
Cancio, Nadal, Rivera, Díaz & Berrios
San Juan, PR
Cancio, Pablo R. ..... Aguadilla, PR
Cancio-Bello, Carla ..... North Miami, FL
Cancio-Bello, Emilio D. ..... San Juan, PR
Cancio-Bigas, Jose R. ..... San Juan, PR
Cancio-Bigas, Miguel P. ..... San Juan, PR
Cancio-Gonzalez, Jose R. ..... Aguadilla, PR
Cancio Gonzalez, Sylvia E. ..... San Juan, PR
Cancio-Ortiz, Juan Ramón ..... San Juan, PR
Cancio Reichard, Pablo G. ..... Aguadilla, PR
Cancio-Sifre, Ramon ..... San Juan, PR
Candalino, Courtney ..... Minneapolis, MN
Candan, Ipek N. ..... New York, NY
Candaux, David L. ..... Encino, CA
Candaux, Mary J. ..... Department of Justice, Civil Division, GV
Candaux, Pauline A. ..... Philadelphia, PA
Candea-Ramsey, Jayne
Colorado Springs, CO
Candee, Hamilton ..... San Francisco, CA
Candee, Marshall G. ..... San Jose, CA
Candee, Richard S. ..... Mount Kisco, NY
Candee, Robert M. ..... Dallas, TX
Candee, William J., III ..... Uniondale, NY
Candee, William J., IV ..... Dallas, TX
Candela, Ana Maria ..... Miami, FL
Candela, Anthony W. ..... Detroit, MI
Candela, Gregory P. ..... New York, NY
Candela, John C. ..... Mount Clemens, MI
Candela, Joseph ..... Forest Hills, NY
Candela, Michael P. ..... Oroville, CA
Candela, Steven ..... New York, NY
Candelaria, Anita ..... Bakersfield, CA
Candelaria, Christopher E. ..... Holbrook, AZ
Candelaria, James M. ..... Denver, CO
Candelaria, Jerome Fitch ..... Oakland, CA
Candelaria, Maria T. ..... Staten Island, NY
Candelaria, Neil ..... Albuquerque, NM
Candelaria, Roger M. ..... Durango, CO
Candelaria, William A. ..... New York, NY
Candelario, Mary Ann ..... New York, NY
Candelas-Perez, Veronica ..... San Juan, PR
Candell, Donald D. ..... Gonzales, LA
Candelmo, Amanda M. ..... Boston, MA
Candelmo, James A. ..... Department of Justice, Criminal Division, GV
Candelmo, Stephen P. ..... Washington, DC
Candelora, Joseph N. ..... Madison, MS
Candelora, Richard ..... Tampa, FL
Candelora, Vincent J. ..... New Haven, CT
Candelore, Craig A. ..... San Diego, CA
Candeloro, Carlos M. ..... Los Angeles, CA
Canders, Stephen A. ..... Kennebunk, ME
Candeto, Michael A. ..... Jacksonville, FL
Candeub, Adam ..... Washington, DC
Candeub, Douglas N. ..... Philadelphia, PA
Candido, Anthony M. ..... New York, NY
Candido, Domna L. ..... New York, NY
Candido, John C. ..... Burbank, CA
Candido, Larry S. ..... New York, NY
Candido, Michael A., Jr. ..... Armonk, NY
Candido, Robert J. ..... Cedar Grove, NJ
Candiello, Martha E. ..... Philadelphia, PA
Candiello, Susan K. ..... Lemoyne, PA
Candiello, Vedo R. ..... Toledo, OH
Candiello, Vincent ..... Harrisburg, PA
Candioto, Sara J. ..... Los Angeles, CA
Candiotti, Howard ..... Levittown, NY

Candiotti, Michael H. ... Encino, CA
Candiotty, Max ... Los Angeles, CA
Candito, Joseph ... Cincinnati, OH
Candito, Marianne Norato ... Oakdale, NY
Candito, Steven A. ... Calverton, NY
Candland, D. Stuart ... Danville, CA
Candland, Richard W. ... Los Angeles, CA
Candler, Clark E. ... Decatur, GA
Candler, Elizabeth ... Findlay, OH
Candler, George Scott, III ... Decatur, GA
Candler, James N., Jr. ... Detroit, MI
Candler, John B. ... Baltimore, MD
Candler, John S., II ... Atlanta, GA
Candler, Lynne M. ... Dallas, TX
Candler, Richard Boyer ... Vero Beach, FL
Candler, Rick L. ... Ruston, LA
Candler, Sheila ... New York, NY
Candler, Terri A. ... Decatur, GA
Candlin, Bruce P. ... Bloomington, MN
Candlish, Elizabeth L. ... San Francisco, CA
Candlish, Richard W. ... Costa Mesa, CA
Candoli, Julie Ann ... Austin, TX
Candon, Charles A. ... Baltimore, MD
Candon, John C. ... Norwich, VT
Candon, Kevin P. ... Rutland, VT
Candon, Kevin P., P.C. ... Rutland, VT
Candon, Mary Eva ... Washington, DC
Candor, Alan F. ... Narberth, PA
Candor, Monique Ballard ... San Diego, CA
Candor, Richard D. ... San Diego, CA
Candor, Youngman, Gibson and Gault
Williamsport, PA
Candreva, Jeremiah H. ... New York, NY
Candreva, Karen F. ... New York, NY
Candrick, Thomas R., Jr. ... New Haven, CT
Candris, Laura A. ... Pittsburgh, PA
Candy, Peter L. ... Santa Barbara, CA
Cane, Alexander R. ... New York, NY
Cane, Allan M. ... Fairfield, CT
Cane, Barbara H. ... Nyack, NY
Cane, David E. ... Santa Ana, CA
Cane & Firstenberg ... New York, NY
Cane, Joseph C., Jr. ... Los Angeles, CA
Cane, Leora ... Anaheim, CA
Cane, Marilyn Blumberg
Fort Lauderdale, FL
Cane, Michael A. ... Las Vegas, NV
Cane, Myles A. ... New York, NY
Cane, Paul F. ... Seattle, WA
Cane, Paul W., Jr. ... San Francisco, CA
Cane, Ronald S. ... San Jose, CA
Cane, Stuart
Environmental Protection Agency,
Environmental Appeals Board, GV
Cane, Thomas ... San Antonio, TX
Cane, Thomas ... Wausau, WI
Cane & Walker LLP ... Santa Ana, CA
Canedo, Saundra K. ... Annapolis, MD
Canegaly, Amelia A. ... Idaho Falls, ID
Caneiro, Raul ... Short Hills, NJ
Canel, Davis & King ... Chicago, IL
Canel, James H. ... Chicago, IL
Canel, James H., Ltd., & Associates
Chicago, IL
Canel, Jay A. ... Chicago, IL
Canel, Jennifer S. ... Chicago, IL
Canel, Richard L., Jr. ... Philadelphia, PA
Canel, Robert L. ... Chicago, IL
Canel, Scott I. ... Chicago, IL
Canelias, Peter S. ... New York, NY
Canellis, Barbara Ann ... Westfield, NJ
Canellis, George W. ... Westfield, NJ
Canellos, Angela E. ... Milwaukee, WI
Canellos, Areti P. ... Squantum, MA
Canellos, Peter C. ... New York, NY
Canelo, Adolph B., III ... Merced, CA
Canelo, Hansen, Wilson, Wallace & Padron,
Professional Corporation ... Merced, CA
Canelos, Nicholas S. ... Stamford, CT
Canepa & Cummins, P.C. ... Chicago, IL
Canepa, James V. ... Columbus, OH
Canepa, Joseph F. ... Santa Fe, NM
Canepa, Kristine M. ... Worcester, MA
Canepa, Marianne L. ... Fresno, CA
Canepa, Mark B. ... Fresno, CA
Canepa, Scott K. ... Las Vegas, NV
Canepa, Thomas V. ... Chicago, IL
Canepa & Vidal, P.A. ... Santa Fe, NM
Caner, George C., Jr. ... Boston, MA
Caner, Kelly Smith ... Chicago, IL
Canerday, Jon J.
National Credit Union Administration,
Office of General Counsel, GV
Caneris, Adonis A. ... Canton, OH
Canero-Davies, Antonia ... Miami, FL
Canero-Davis, Antonia, P.A. ... Miami, FL
Canessa, William R. ... Seaside, OR
Canestrano, Michael R. ... Syracuse, NY
Canestrari, Ronald ... Cohoes, NY
Canestraro, C. Russell ... Columbus, OH
Canestraro, Donald C. ... Maple Heights, OH
Canestraro, Eugene F. ... Toledo, OH
Canet, Carlos A. ... Miami, FL
Canetti, Craig W. ... Washington, DC
Canetti, Isaac S. ... Nanuet, NY
Caneva, Ronald L. ... Lockport, IL
Canevari, Thomas M. ... Stamford, CT
New York, NY
Canevazzi, Russell P. ... Plymouth, MA
Canevi, Mehmet I. ... New York, NY
Caney, David A. ... Deale, MD
Caney, Lee D. ... New York, NY
Canez, Raul A. ... Fort Worth, TX
Canfield, Andrew T. ... Washington, DC
Canfield, Ann Therese ... Los Angeles, CA
Canfield, Arnold W. ... Sarasota, FL
Canfield, Austin F., Jr. ... Solomons, MD
Canfield, Christopher M. ... New York, NY
Canfield, Damon H. ... Arlington, WA
Canfield, David C. ... Arlington, VA
Canfield, David Joseph ... Douglaston, NY
Canfield, Dianna G. ... Charleston, WV
Canfield, Douglas B. ... Wilmington, DE
Canfield, Edgar H. ... Bainbridge Island, WA
Canfield, Edward F. ... Washington, DC
Philadelphia, PA
Canfield, Elizabeth F. ... Rockford, IL
Canfield, Elmer E. ... Olympia, WA
Canfield, Gregory W. ... San Antonio, TX
Canfield, Gregory W., P.C., Law Offices of
San Antonio, TX
Canfield, Helen K. ... Tulsa, OK
Canfield, James B. ... Troy, NY
Canfield, James J. ... Syracuse, NY
Canfield, James R. ... San Jose, CA
Canfield, James W. ... Douglaston, NY
Fort Washington, PA
Canfield, Jeffrey F. ... Chicago, IL
Canfield, Jerry L. ... Fort Smith, AR
Canfield, Jill M. ... Washington, DC
Canfield, John M. ... Dunbar, WV
Canfield, Kenneth S. ... Atlanta, GA
Canfield, Laura E.
Department Of Health And Human Services,
Office of the General Counsel, GV
Canfield, Laura M. ... Lansing, MI
Canfield, Lisa K. ... Raleigh, NC
Canfield, Madden, Rossi, Ruggiero &
Crowley, LLP ... Douglaston, NY
New York, NY
Canfield, Maryann ... New York, NY
Canfield, Michael L. ... Roseburg, OR
Canfield, Peter C. ... Atlanta, GA
Canfield, Robert A. ... Richmond, VA
Canfield, Robert C. ... Kansas City, MO
Canfield, Robert E. ... Rockford, IL
Canfield, Robert E. ... South Bend, IN
Canfield, S. Paige ... St. Louis, MO
Canfield, Shapiro, Baer & Heller
Chesterfield, VA
Hanover, VA
Richmond, VA
Canfield, Thomas C. ... New York, NY
Canfield, William B., III ... Washington, DC
Canganelli, Michael ... Chicago, IL
Cangelosi, A. Edward ... New Orleans, LA
Cangelosi, Celia R. ... Baton Rouge, LA
Cangelosi, Linda ... Austin, TX
Cangelosi, Randal R. ... New Orleans, LA
Cangelosi, Robert L. ... Baton Rouge, LA
Cangelosi & Robin, L.L.C.
New Orleans, LA
Cangelosi, Roy F., Jr. ... Baton Rouge, LA
Cangelosi, Victor L. ... Washington, DC
Cangemi, Andrew G. ... Garden City, NY
Cangemi, Maria C. ... Metairie, LA
Cangemi, Salvador J. ... Metairie, LA
Canges, E. Michael ... Denver, CO
Canges, Iwashko & Bethke, A Professional
Corporation ... Denver, CO
Cangialosi, Thomas J., Jr.
Hackensack, NJ
Cangiano, Christian V. ... New York, NY
Cangiano, Nina ... New York, NY
Cangilos, John J. ... Burbank, CA
Cangilos-Ruiz, Margaret ... Albany, NY
Cangin, Stephanie ... Roanoke, VA
Cangro, Charles V. ... Gainesville, FL
Cangro, Larry ... St. Petersburg, FL
Canham, John J. ... East Greenwich, RI
Canham, John J., Jr. ... North Kingstown, RI
Canham, Thomas R. ... Chicago, IL
Caniff, Charles E., Jr. ... Philadelphia, PA
Caniglia, Joseph P. ... Omaha, NE
Caniglia, Lawrence S., (P.A.)
Moorestown, NJ
Caniglia, Phil R. ... Council Bluffs, IA
Caniglia, Saml. P. ... Omaha, NE
Caniglia, William T. ... Albuquerque, NM
Caniglia, William T., P.C. ... Albuquerque, NM
Canino, Cheryl Ann ... Hartford, CT
Canino, Edna E. ... Miami, FL
Canino, Edna E., P.A. ... Miami, FL
Canino, Felix F. ... West Palm Beach, FL
Canino, John R. ... Amenia, NY
Canino, Joseph L. ... Kingston, NY
Canino, Robert A. ... Dallas, TX
Canino, Valerie A. ... Rockville, MD
Canipelli, Kevin V. ... Jacksonville, FL
Canis, Jonathan E. ... Washington, DC
Canivan, James T. ... Glastonbury, CT
Canizio, Candida L. ... New York, NY
Canizio, Mark ... New York, NY
Canjar, Gary J. ... Lansing, MI
Canjar, Geo. A. ... Denver, CO
Canli, Suzan, Law Offices of
San Francisco, CA
Canmann, David L. ... Chicago, IL
Cann, Alexander L. ... Savannah, GA
Cann, Brian ... Worcester, MA
Cann, Carmine J. ... Clarksburg, WV
Cann, David P.
Hot Springs National Park, AR
Cann, Douglas W. ... Bemidji, MN
Cann, Emily ... Baltimore, MD
Cann, Frederic E. ... Portland, OR
Cann, Haskell, D'Albani, Schueppert, Hazelton
& Rodgers, P.A. ... Bemidji, MN
Cann, James F. ... Omaha, NE
Cann, James V. ... Clarksburg, WV
Cann, John D. ... St. Paul, MN
Cann, Lawrence B., III ... Richmond, VA
Cann, Martin J. ... Plainfield, IL
Cann, Ralph H., Jr. ... Detroit, MI
Cann, Samuel A. ... Savannah, GA
Cann, William F. ... Concord, NH
Canna, John F. ... Orland Park, IL
Canna, Thomas J. ... Orland Park, IL
Cannada, Don B. ... Jackson, MS
Cannada, R. Barry ... Jackson, MS
Cannada, Robert C. ... Jackson, MS
Cannaday, Barry F. ... Dallas, TX
Cannaday, Jennifer B. ... Salt Lake City, UT
Cannaday, Michael W. ... Collinsville, VA
Cannady, Cynthia C. ... Menlo Park, CA
Cannady, Gregg R. ... Dallas, TX
Cannady, Michael P. ... Augusta, KS
Cannady, Michael R. ... Portland, OR
Cannady, Thomas B. ... Belleville, IL
Cannady, Walter J. ... Emeryville, CA
Cannain, Lester C. ... Albuquerque, NM
Cannan, Mark J. ... San Antonio, TX
Cannarella, Paul V. ... Hartsville, SC
Cannariato, Sam J. ... Rockford, IL
Cannarozzi, E. Gregory M. ... Oradell, NJ
Cannata, F. Richard, Jr. ... Phoenix, AZ
Cannata, Gregory J. ... New York, NY
Cannata, Jack C., Jr. ... Houston, TX
Cannata, Kenneth S. ... Houston, TX
Cannata, Linda J. ... Middletown, CT
Cannata, Michael E. ... Staten Island, NY
Cannata, Steven J. ... Los Angeles, CA
Cannata, Steven J. ... Tampa, FL
Cannata, Therese Y. ... Walnut Creek, CA
Cannataro, Frank E. K.
Rockville Centre, NY
Cannatella, Anthony S. ... New York, NY
Cannatella, Joseph A., Jr. ... Bossier City, LA
Cannatelli, Frank P. ... Branford, CT
Cannatti, Michael R. ... Austin, TX
Cannava, Ernest J. ... East Islip, NY
Cannavino, John W. ... Stamford, CT
Cannavino, Thomas F. ... Endicott, NY
Cannavo, Jack J. ... Central Islip, NY
Cannavo, John J. ... New York, NY
Cannavo, John Nicholas ... Brockton, MA
Plymouth, MA
Cannavo, Judith M. ... Long Beach, CA
Cannavo, Thomas J. ... Buffalo, NY
Cannavo, Vito A. ... Mineola, NY
New York, NY
Cannedy, Marty K. ... Wichita Falls, TX
Cannell, Brian G. ... Logan, UT
Cannell, John R. ... New York, NY
Cannell, Julian E. ... Peoria, IL
Cannell, Marian L. ... Newark, NJ
Cannell, Susan T. ... Ann Arbor, MI
Cannella, Andrew S. ... Stamford, CT
Cannella, David E. ... Orlando, FL
Cannella, Debra ... Newark, NJ
Cannella, Dewey V. ... Edison, NJ
Cannella, Emilia Francesca ... Chicago, IL
Cannella, James L. ... Gretna, LA
Cannella, Joseph L. ... New York, NY
Cannella, Lisa ... Norwalk, CT
Cannella, Marie R. ... Rocklin, CA
Cannella, Michael ... New York, NY
Cannella, Nicholas M. ... New York, NY
Cannella, Norman S. ... Tampa, FL
Cannella, Renée Mayerson ... Stamford, CT
Cannella, Robert A. ... Tampa, FL
Cannella, Robert T. ... Omaha, NE
Cannella, Stephen J. ... Richmond, VA
Cannello, Steven J. ... Newberry, MI
Sault Ste. Marie, MI
Cannelora, Louis ... Martinez, CA
Canner, Alan J. ... Boulder, CO
Canner, Demmon F.
Department of the Army,
Office of the Judge Advocate General, GV
Canner, Gary F. ... Miami, FL
Canner, Glen A. ... Stamford, CT
Canner, Julie C. ... Southfield, MI
Canner, Robert A. ... Bloomfield Hills, MI
Canner, Steven G. ... New York, NY
Cannerelli, Carol A. ... Cherry Hill, NJ
Philadelphia, PA
Canney, Edward J. ... Boston, MA
Canney, John R., III ... Rutland, VT
Canney, John R., III, P.C. ... Rutland, VT
Canney, Vincent P.
Department of Commerce,
Patent and Trademark Office, GV
Cannick, Devereaux L. ... Flushing, NY
Canniff, Brian P. ... Media, PA
Canniff, John J. ... Boston, MA
Canning, Barbara Condit ... Chicago, IL
Canning, Brent R. ... Boston, MA
Providence, RI
Canning, Charles A. ... Elgin, IL
Canning, Christopher S. ... Chicago, IL
Canning, David R. ... Miami, FL
Canning, Dennis J. ... New York, NY
Canning, Ernest A., (A P.C.)
Westlake Village, CA
Canning, Frederic D. ... Oregon City, OR
Canning, Gordon T., Jr. ... Cleveland, OH
Canning, John B. ... Stamford, CT
Canning, John W.C. ... Sea Cliff, NY
Canning, Kathleen H. ... Upper Marlboro, MD
Canning, Kevin J. ... Boston, MA
Canning, Kimberly M. ... Simsbury, CT
Canning, Marcia Joan ... San Francisco, CA
Canning, Michael J. ... Middletown, NJ
Canning, Michael J. ... New York, NY
Canning & Murray, P.A. ... Miami, FL
Canning, Patrick T. ... Chicago, IL
Canning, Robert C. ... Quincy, MA
Canning, Timothy A. ... San Francisco, CA
Cannington, Weyman E., Jr. ... Lumpkin, GA
Cannistraci, Andrea F. ... New York, NY
Cannistraci, Carmela ... Roseland, NJ
Cannistraci, Dina ... New York, NY
Cannistraci, John A. ... New York, NY
Cannistraci, Sharonrose ... Los Gatos, CA
Cannito, Danielle ... Andover, MA
Cannito, John A. ... Pine Brook, NJ
Cannizzaro & Ballard ... Chicago, IL
Cannizzaro, Cindy ... Chicago, IL
Cannizzaro, Dale C. P. ... New Orleans, LA
Cannizzaro, Domenic J. ... San Francisco, CA
Cannizzaro, Frank ... Los Angeles, CA
Cannizzaro, Fraser & Bridges
Marysville, OH
Cannizzaro, John F. ... Marysville, OH
Cannizzaro, John R. ... Staten Island, NY
Cannizzaro, Joseph R. ... Cohoes, NY
Cannizzaro, Leon A., Jr. ... New Orleans, LA
Cannizzaro, Sam F. ... Chicago, IL
Cannizzo, Craig J. ... San Francisco, CA
Cannoles & Clasing, Chartered
Baltimore, MD
Cannoles, Raymond J. ... Baltimore, MD
Cannon, A. Clark ... Geneva, NY
Cannon, Alan W. ... Palo Alto, CA
Cannon, Allan T. ... New York, NY
Scarsdale, NY
Cannon, Allan T., P.C. ... New York, NY
Scarsdale, NY
Cannon, Allen, III ... Washington, DC
Cannon, Allen L. ... Fort Lauderdale, FL
Cannon, Alton L. ... Leitchfield, KY
Cannon, Anthon S., Jr. ... Los Angeles, CA
Cannon, Beth A. ... Cherry Hill, NJ
Philadelphia, PA
Cannon, Brenda J. ... De Bary, FL
Cannon, Brian C. ... Palo Alto, CA
Cannon, Bruce L. ... Lenoir, NC
Cannon & Bruns ... Muncie, IN
Cannon, Bryan Thomas ... Arlington, TX
Cannon, Bryan W. ... Sandy, UT
Cannon and Cannon ... Clemson, SC
Cannon & Cannon ... Milwaukee, WI
Cannon, Cannon & Cooper, P.C.
Nashville, TN
Cannon, Catesby Berry, III ... Salinas, CA
Cannon, Catherine M. ... San Diego, CA
Cannon, Cathlynn H. ... Dallas, TX
Cannon, Charles B. ... Dallas, TX
Cannon, Charles E. ... Painesville, OH
Cannon, Charles J. ... Department of Justice,
Tax Division, GV
Cannon, Cheryl Hughes ... Houston, TX
Cannon, Christopher C. ... Santa Ana, CA
Cannon, Christopher J. ... San Francisco, CA
Cannon, Christopher L. ... Princeton, NJ
Cannon, Christopher M.
Fort Lauderdale, FL
Cannon, Clayton C. ... Houston, TX
Cannon, Corinne B. ... Clemson, SC
Cannon, Craig J. ... Ocala, FL
Cannon, D. Kay ... Department of Defense,
Defense Legal Services Agency, GV
Cannon, Daniel E. ... Chicago, IL
Cannon, Daniel W. ... Washington, DC
Cannon, David A. ... New York, NY
Cannon, David A. ... East Greenwich, RI
Cannon, David C. ... Detroit, MI
Cannon, David C., Jr. ... Pittsburgh, PA
Cannon, David D. ... Minneapolis, MN
Cannon, David J. ... Milwaukee, WI
Cannon, David L. ... Canton, GA
Cannon, David Rees ... Charlotte, NC
Cannon, Dean H. ... Washington, DC
Cannon, Dennis A., (A L.C.) ... Lancaster, CA
Cannon, Devereaux D., Jr. ... Nashville, TN
Cannon, Douglas ... Greensboro, NC
Cannon, Douglas B. ... Salt Lake City, UT
Cannon, Douglas C. ... Chicago, IL
Cannon & Dunphy, S.C. ... Brookfield, WI
Madison, WI
Milwaukee, WI
Cannon, E. Bedford ... Statesville, NC
Cannon, Edward V., Jr. ... Medfield, MA
Cannon, Ellis G. ... Pittsburgh, PA
Cannon, Ernest ... Houston, TX
Cannon, Ernest H. ... Houston, TX
Cannon, Evelyn O. ... Baltimore, MD
Cannon, Gary C. ... San Diego, CA
Cannon, Gayle E. ... Dallas, TX
Cannon, Geoffrey J. ... Albany, NY
Cannon, George B. ... Springfield, MA
Cannon, George D., Jr. ... Washington, DC
Cannon, George T. ... Merritt Island, FL
Cannon, George W., Jr.
Frederiksted, St. Croix, VI
Cannon, Glen E. ... Winston-Salem, NC
Cannon, Glenn M. ... Pittsburgh, PA
Cannon, Gomer L. ... Lake Stevens, WA
Cannon, Gordon T. ... Lubbock, TX
Cannon, Grayson Smith ... Nashville, TN
Cannon, Gregory L. ... Plymouth, MI
Cannon, H. Leroy ... San Francisco, CA
Cannon, Henrietta R. ... Sandston, VA
Cannon, Hiram A. ... Tucson, AZ
Cannon, Hiram A., P.C. ... Tucson, AZ
Cannon, Howard W. ... Las Vegas, NV
Reno, NV
Cannon, Hugh ... Raleigh, NC
Charleston, SC
Cannon, Hugh ... Mount Pleasant, SC
Cannon, Hugh W. ... Hartsville, SC
Cannon, J. Norman ... Arlington, TX
Cannon, J. Phillip ... Albany, GA
Cannon, James E. ... Salt Lake City, UT
Cannon, James F. ... Dayton, OH
Cannon, James F. ... Dayton, OH
Cannon, James H. ... Fairbanks, AK
Cannon, James J., Jr.
Manchester Center, VT
Cannon, James P. ... Kansas City, MO
Cannon, James R. ... Cedar Bluff, AL

Cannon, James R. ..... Mount Morris, NY
Cannon, James R. ..... Raleigh, NC
Cannon, James R., Jr. ..... Washington, DC
Cannon, James T. ..... Union City, TN
Cannon, James W., Jr. ..... Austin, TX
Cannon, Jamie R ..... Hagerstown, MD
Cannon, Jari Carlton ..... Washington, DC
Cannon, Jeffrey Steven ..... Beverly Hills, CA
Cannon, Jerry M. ..... San Diego, CA
Cannon, Joan M. ..... Omaha, NE
Cannon, Joe ..... Groesbeck, TX
Cannon, Joe F. ..... Houston, TX
Cannon, Joel A., Jr. ..... Knoxville, TN
Cannon, John F. ..... Newport Beach, CA
Cannon, John F. ..... New York, NY
Cannon, John G. ..... Houston, TX
Cannon, John J. ..... Villanova, PA
Cannon, John J., III ..... New York, NY
Cannon, John K. ..... Bloomfield Hills, MI
Cannon, John M. ..... Nashville, TN
Cannon, John R., Jr. ..... Memphis, TN
Cannon, John V., III ..... Sarasota, FL
Cannon, John W. ..... Tulsa, OK
Cannon, Jonathan H. ..... Orange, CA
Cannon, Jonathan Z. ..... Washington, DC
Cannon, Joseph ..... Colorado Springs, CO
Cannon, Julia Taylor ..... Leesburg, VA
Cannon, Karen E. ..... Dallas, TX
Cannon, Karl R. ..... Sandy, UT
Cannon, Kathleen Weaver
Washington, DC
Cannon, Kelly ..... Seattle, WA
Cannon, Kevin, Law Office of, P.A., The
Orlando, FL
Cannon, Kevin S. ..... Orlando, FL
Cannon, Kim D. ..... Cheyenne, WY
Sheridan, WY
Cannon, Kimberly A. ..... Jacksonville, FL
Cannon, Kimble C. ..... Washington, DC
Cannon, Kristine W. ..... Bemidji, MN
Cannon, L. Kinder, III ..... Jacksonville, FL
Cannon Law Offices ..... Des Moines, IA
Cannon Law Offices ..... Salt Lake City, UT
Cannon, Leon H. ..... New Port Richey, FL
Cannon, Lisa Marie ..... Los Angeles, CA
Cannon, Maeve E. ..... Trenton, NJ
Cannon, Marci L. ..... Kansas City, MO
Cannon, Margaret Anne ..... Cleveland, OH
Cannon, Maria E. ..... New York, NY
Cannon, Martin A., Jr. ..... Omaha, NE
Cannon, Mary E. ..... San Diego, CA
Cannon, Matthew J. ..... Chicago, IL
Cannon, Melvin R. ..... Bay Shore, NY
Cannon, Meyer Von Bremen & Goss, LLP
Albany, GA
Cannon, Michael ..... Fairfax, VA
Cannon, Michael J. ..... Palos Heights, IL
Cannon, Michael J. ..... New York, NY
Cannon, Michael P. ..... Chicago, IL
Cannon, Michael R. ..... St. Louis, MO
Cannon, Neal D., Jr. ..... Houston, TX
Cannon, Ned A. ..... Lewiston, ID
Cannon, Neil E., III ..... Dallas, TX
Cannon, Olin B. ..... Louisville, GA
Cannon, Patrick C. ..... Salt Lake City, UT
Cannon, Patrick G. ..... Richmond, CA
Cannon, Patrick J. ..... Oneonta, NY
Cannon, Patrick M. ..... Hatboro, PA
Cannon, Patrick W. ..... Melville, NY
Cannon, Paul L. ..... Abilene, TX
Cannon, Peter J. ..... Madison, WI
Cannon, Peter S. ..... Des Moines, IA
Cannon, Peter W. ..... Mahnomen, MN
Cannon, R. Carl ..... Atlanta, GA
Cannon, R. Dean, Jr. ..... Orlando, FL
Cannon, Rachel M. ..... Chicago, IL
Cannon, Ralph J. ..... Glen Burnie, MD
Cannon, Raymond E. ..... Palo Alto, CA
Cannon, Raymond J., Jr. ..... Andover, MA
Cannon, Raymond Lee ..... Tallulah, LA
Cannon, Richard Kirk ..... San Francisco, CA
Cannon, Richard Kirk & Associates, The Law Offies of ..... San Francisco, CA
Cannon, Richard L., III ..... Greenville, NC
Cannon, Richard N. ..... Salt Lake City, UT
Cannon, Robert A. ..... Lincoln, NE
Cannon, Robert C. ..... Salem, OR
Cannon, Robert E. ..... Elba, AL
Cannon, Robert H. ..... Chicago, IL
Cannon, Robert L. ..... Santa Monica, CA
Cannon, Robert M.
Federal Communications Commission,
Wireless Telecommunications Bureau, GV
Cannon, Robert T. ..... Hyannis, MA
Cannon, Robert W. ..... Redlands, CA
San Bernardino, CA
Cannon, Robert W. ..... Baltimore, MD
Cannon, Robt. P. ..... Salisbury, MD
Cannon, Ross W. ..... Helena, MT
Cannon, Roy ..... San Diego, CA
Cannon, Russell A. ..... Vista, CA
Salt Lake City, UT
Cannon, Sally Cobb ..... Atlanta, GA
Cannon, Scott A. ..... New Orleans, LA
Cannon, Scott D. ..... Mount Morris, NY
Cannon, Scott D. ..... Tulsa, OK
Cannon & Sheehy ..... Helena, MT
Missoula, MT
Cannon, Shelton
Federal Energy Regulatory Commission,
Office of Electric Power Regulation, GV
Cannon & Simmons ..... Groesbeck, TX
Cannon, Stacey M. ..... Waltham, MA
Cannon, Stan Decker ..... Rock Springs, WY
Cannon, Stern, Aveni and Loiacono Co., L.P.A. ..... Mentor, OH
Painesville, OH
Cannon, Stewart L., Jr. ..... Johnson City, TN

Cannon, Susan C. ..... Mattituck, NY
Cannon, Teresa Chmielewski ..... Houston, TX
Cannon, Terrence L. ..... Lompoc, CA
Cannon, Terri L. ..... Baton Rouge, LA
Cannon, Therese A. ..... Inglewood, CA
Cannon, Thomas A. ..... Muncie, IN
Cannon, Thomas A., Jr. ..... Muncie, IN
Cannon, Thomas G. ..... Milwaukee, WI
Cannon, Thomas P. ..... Philadelphia, PA
Cannon, Thomas R. ..... Charlotte, NC
Cannon, Timothy P. ..... Painesville, OH
Cannon, Tina Roberts ..... Sacramento, CA
Cannon, Todd R. ..... Salt Lake City, UT
Cannon, Tracy A. ..... Baltimore, MD
Cannon, Tristan C. ..... Beverly Hills, CA
Cannon & Vaughan ..... Elba, AL
Cannon, Victor R. ..... Santa Ana, CA
Cannon, Vincent T. ..... Providence, RI
Cannon, Virginia M. ..... Philadelphia, PA
Cannon, W. Stephen ..... Richmond, VA
Cannon, Wade K. ..... Chattanooga, TN
Cannon, Walter R. ..... Las Vegas, NV
Cannon, William E., Jr. ..... Albany, GA
Cannon, William H. ..... Clinton, MI
Cannon, William H. ..... Charlotte, NC
Cannon, William H., P.A. ..... Charlotte, NC
Cannon, William M. ..... Brookfield, WI
Cannon, William P. ..... Houston, TX
Cannon, William S. ..... San Diego, CA
Cannon, William T. ..... Philadelphia, PA
Cannon, William T., P.C.
Philadelphia, PA
Cannone, Frank T. ..... New York, NY
Cannon-Geary, Irene S. ..... New York, NY
Cannon II, Kenneth L.
Salt Lake City, UT
Cannonito, Christopher E. ..... Tinley Park, IL
Cannon-Ryan, Susan ..... Charleston, WV
Cannova, Frank S. ..... St. Petersburg, FL
Cannuscio, Michael Vincent ..... Boston, MA
Cannuscio, Robert E. ..... Philadelphia, PA
Canny, Joan Marie ..... New Orleans, LA
Canny, John G. ..... Evergreen, CO
Canny, Michael J. ..... Garden City, NY
Canny, Thomas M. ..... Kalamazoo, MI
Cano, Alice ..... Mary Esther, FL
Cano, Christopher M. ..... Chicago, IL
Cano, Edward P. ..... San Antonio, TX
Cano, José ..... McAllen, TX
Cano, Kristin M. ..... Newport Beach, CA
Cano, Kristin M. ..... San Diego, CA
Santa Barbara, CA
Cano, Liliana ..... South Miami, FL
Cano, Mario S. ..... Miami, FL
Cano, Matthew B. ..... Corpus Christi, TX
Cano, Rudy ..... Houston, TX
Cano, Thomas N. ..... Woodland Hills, CA
Cano, Yvette ..... Irvine, CA
Canoff, Karen Huston ..... San Diego, CA
Canoles, Leroy T., Jr. ..... Norfolk, VA
Canon, George A. ..... Lubbock, TX
Canon, Jack A. ..... Tulsa, OK
Canon, Michael J. ..... Midland, TX
Canon, Short & Gaston ..... Midland, TX
Canon, William L. ..... Oklahoma City, OK
Canoni, John C. ..... New York, NY
Canoni, John D. ..... New York, NY
Canonico, Robert A. ..... Waco, TX
Canotas, Vasiliki M. ..... Manchester, NH
Canouse, Joseph P. ..... Maitland, FL
Canova, Christopher P. ..... Tallahassee, FL
Canova, L. Phillip, Jr. ..... Plaquemine, LA
Canova, Thomas A. ..... New York, NY
Canova-Parker, Ann ..... Santa Barbara, CA
Canovas, Anita C. ..... Washington, DC
Canovas, M. Colleen Foley ..... Scranton, PA
Cánovas, María Luisa ..... New York, NY
Canowitz, Howard Jay ..... Columbus, OH
Canowitz, Robin L. ..... Columbus, OH
Canseco, Francisco R. ..... Laredo, TX
Canseco, Jorge E. ..... San Antonio, TX
Canseco, Jose S. ..... New Orleans, LA
Cansino, Carl ..... Cordele, GA
Cansler, Linda Cheryl ..... Beaumont, TX
Cansler, Lockhart, Campbell, Evans, Bryant & Garlitz, P.A. ..... Charlotte, NC
Cansler, Robert E. ..... Concord, NC
Cantacuzene, Rodion, Jr. ..... Midland, TX
Cantafio and Hardy-Moore ..... Craig, CO
Steamboat Springs, CO
Cantafio, Ralph A. ..... Craig, CO
Steamboat Springs, CO
Cantagallo, Phillip J. ..... Ashtabula, OH
Cantalin, James R. ..... St. Louis, MO
Cantalin, Jeanne L. ..... St. Louis, MO
Cantalupo, Anthony A., Jr. ..... Rockville, MD
Cantalupo, Charles, Jr. ..... West Orange, NJ
Cantalupo, Dominic ..... Santa Monica, CA
Cantanno, James E. ..... Jericho, NY
Cantara, Michael P. ..... Alfred, ME
Cantara, Paul D. ..... Buffalo, NY
Cantarella, Eva T. ..... Bloomfield Hills, MI
Cantarelli, Pat ..... Chicago, IL
Cantella, Kathleen M. ..... Los Angeles, CA
Cantelme, David J. ..... Phoenix, AZ
Cantens, Gaston I. ..... Coral Gables, FL
Canter, Bram D. E. ..... Tallahassee, FL
Canter, Bruce M. ..... Newport Beach, CA
Canter, Carrie C. ..... Fort Worth, TX
Canter, David H. ..... Los Angeles, CA
Orange, CA
Canter, David S. ..... Beverly Hills, CA
Canter, David S. ..... Chicago, IL
Canter, Douglas M. ..... Washington, DC
Canter, Edith F. ..... Chicago, IL
Canter, Eric Geoffrey ..... Fort Lauderdale, FL
Canter, Howard P. ..... Van Nuys, CA
Canter, Jacqueline H. ..... Philadelphia, PA

Canter, Jane Ann ..... Baltimore, MD
Canter, Jonathan D. ..... Cambridge, MA
Canter, Jonathan H. ..... New York, NY
Canter, Julius D. ..... Jersey City, NJ
Canter, MacKenzie, III ..... Washington, DC
Kansas City, MO
Canter, Mark A. ..... Rockville, MD
Canter, Michael J. ..... Columbus, OH
Canter, Mitchell J. ..... Suffern, NY
Canter, Nelson E. ..... White Plains, NY
Canter, Pamela R. ..... San Mateo, CA
Canter, Richard J. ..... Milwaukee, WI
Canter, Richard L. ..... New Boston, OH
Canter, Robert B. ..... Rockville, MD
Canter, Robert S. ..... Beverly Hills, CA
Canter, Ronald M. ..... Los Angeles, CA
Canter, Ronald S. ..... Bethesda, MD
Canter, Ronda Silberberg ..... Boston, MA
Canter, Susan E. ..... New York, NY
Canter & Valvano LLP ..... New City, NY
Suffern, NY
Canter, Zel ..... Santa Maria, CA
Canterberry, Lisa Baker ..... Dallas, TX
Canterberry, Lisa Baker ..... McKinney, TX
Plano, TX
Canterbury, Christopher C.
Anchorage, AK
Canterbury, Joseph F., Jr. ..... Dallas, TX
Canterbury, Keith A. ..... Tuscaloosa, AL
Canterbury and Raub ..... Mill Valley, CA
San Francisco, CA
Canterbury, Ross E. ..... Peoria, IL
Canterbury, Stuber, Elder, Gooch & Surratt, P.C. ..... Dallas, TX
Canterbury, Thomas ..... Beckley, WV
Canterbury, Wayne S. ..... San Francisco, CA
Canterino, Kimberly Marie ..... Middletown, NY
Canterman, Robert S. ..... Washington, DC
Cantero, Raoul G., III ..... Miami, FL
Cantero-Frau, Pedro A. ..... San Juan, PR
Cantey & Hanger ..... Dallas, TX
Fort Worth, TX
Cantey & Hanger Roan & Autrey L.L.P.
Austin, TX
Cantey & Hanger Travis & Gooch
Washington, DC
Cantey, Nicole Paul ..... Columbia, SC
Cantey, William Childs, III ..... Columbia, SC
Cantieri, Thomas B. ..... Virginia Beach, VA
Cantilo & Bennett, L.L.P. ..... Austin, TX
Cantilo, Patrick H., (P.C.) ..... Austin, TX
Cantin, Eileen J. ..... Newington, CT
Cantin, Lucian C. ..... Cumming, GA
Cantin, Raynald B. ..... Hartford, CT
Cantino, Ronald J. ..... Hilton Head Island, SC
Cantion, James D. ..... Niagara Falls, NY
Cantius, Carole J. ..... Roslyn Heights, NY
Cantleberry, Jill C. ..... Cincinnati, OH
Cantley, Beckett G. ..... Atlanta, GA
Cantlin, John L. ..... Ottawa, IL
Cantlin, Richard A. ..... Portland, OR
Cantoli, Dennis J. ..... Point Pleasant Beach, NJ
Canton, Doreen ..... Cincinnati, OH
Canton, Gregory S. ..... United States Senate,
Committee Legal Personnel, GV
Canton, Leonardo A. ..... Coral Gables, FL
Canton, Mirta (Mikki) ..... Miami, FL
Canton, Wm. ..... New Rochelle, NY
Cantone, Dale E. ..... Baltimore, MD
Cantone, Daniel G. ..... Camillus, NY
Cantone, Robert A. ..... New York, NY
Cantone, Thomas S. ..... Baltimore, MD
Cantoni, Linda ..... Kew Gardens, NY
Cantoni, Maurizia M. ..... San Diego, CA
Cantoni, Michelle Finger ..... Conroe, TX
Cantonwine, Steven R. ..... Arnold, MO
Cantor, Abraham ..... Willoughby, OH
Cantor, Abraham, & Associates
Willoughby, OH
Cantor, Adam B. ..... Newark, NJ
Cantor, Adryenn ..... Ventura, CA
Cantor, Alan I. ..... Washington, DC
Cantor, Alan I. ..... Manchester, NH
Cantor, Alan L. ..... Boston, MA
Cantor, Alena ..... Phoenix, AZ
Cantor, Amy R. ..... New York, NY
Cantor, Andrew B. ..... Blue Bell, PA
Cantor, Andrew M. ..... Baltimore, MD
Cantor, Arkema & Edmonds, A Professional Corporation ..... Richmond, VA
Cantor, Arthur I. ..... Washington, DC
Cantor, Bernard H. ..... Johnson City, TN
Cantor, Bernard H., and Associates, P.C.
Johnson City, TN
Cantor, Bernard J. ..... Troy, MI
Cantor, Brian S. ..... Fairfield, CT
Cantor & Cantor ..... Richmond, VA
Cantor, Clifford A., Law Offices of
Redmond, WA
Cantor Colburn LLP ..... Hartford, CT
Windsor, CT
Springfield, MA
Cantor, Daniel A. ..... Washington, DC
Cantor, Daniel L. ..... New York, NY
Cantor, Darren R. ..... Denver, CO
Cantor, Darren R. ..... Vail, CO
Cantor, David M. ..... Louisville, KY
Cantor, David Michael ..... Mesa, AZ
Cantor, David Michael, P.C., Law Offices of
Mesa, AZ
Phoenix, AZ
Cantor, Debra Denison ..... Camp Hill, PA
Cantor, Donald J. ..... Hartford, CT
Cantor, Donna M. ..... Wilmington, DE
Cantor, Eddie ..... Richmond, VA
Cantor, Epstein, Bailey & Degenshein, LLP
New York, NY

Cantor, Eugene H. ..... Treasury Department,
Office of the Comptroller of the Currency,
GV
Cantor, Floman, Gross, Kelly, Amendola & Sacramone, P.C. ..... Orange, CT
Cantor, Gary E. ..... Philadelphia, PA
Cantor, Herbert I. ..... Washington, DC
Cantor, Irvin V. ..... Richmond, VA
Cantor, Irwin I. ..... Memphis, TN
Cantor, James E. ..... Anchorage, AK
Cantor, Jane Bruskin ..... East Brunswick, NJ
Cantor, Jay A. ..... Santa Rosa, CA
Cantor, Jay M. ..... Washington, DC
Cantor, Jay S. ..... Poughkeepsie, NY
Cantor, Jerald C., (P.A.) ..... Hollywood, FL
Cantor, Jesse ..... Seattle, WA
Cantor, Jonathan E. ..... New York, NY
Cantor, Jonathan R. ..... Baltimore, MD
Cantor, Kim A. .....
Treasury Department, GV
Cantor, Linda E. ..... Indianapolis, IN
Cantor, Linda F. ..... Los Angeles, CA
Cantor, Lorne S. ..... Miami, FL
Cantor, M. Daniel ..... Lawrenceville, NJ
Cantor, Madelyn Shohen ..... Wynnewood, PA
Cantor, Marc J. ..... Boston, MA
Cantor, Mark A. ..... Southfield, MI
Cantor, Mark H. ..... Buffalo, NY
Cantor, Mark I. ..... Owings Mills, MD
Cantor, Mark I., P.A. ..... Owings Mills, MD
Cantor, Matthew L. ..... New York, NY
Cantor, Melvyn L. ..... New York, NY
Cantor, Michael ..... Windsor, CT
Cantor, Michael D. ..... Newton, MA
Cantor, Michael J. ..... Southfield, MI
Cantor, Michael L. ..... Phoenix, AZ
Cantor, Mitchell ..... New York, NY
Cantor, Norman L. ..... Newark, NJ
Cantor, Patricia A. ..... Boston, MA
Cantor, Paul A. ..... Seattle, WA
Cantor, Paul S. ..... Fall River, MA
Seekonk, MA
Providence, RI
Cantor, Phyllis M. ..... San Francisco, CA
Cantor, Richard Alan ..... Washington, DC
Cantor, Richard I. ..... Poughkeepsie, NY
Cantor, Richard L. ..... Kennett Square, PA
Malvern, PA
Cantor, Robert I. ..... New York, NY
Cantor, Robt. ..... Richmond, VA
Cantor, Ronald L. ..... Oakhurst, NJ
Cantor, Samuel C. ..... Greenwich, CT
Cantor, Samuel J. ..... Boca Raton, FL
Cantor, Scott Michael ..... Las Vegas, NV
Cantor, Shari J. ..... West Hartford, CT
Cantor, Shauna Altwegg ..... Arlington, VA
Cantor, Shawn ..... Wyckoff, NJ
Cantor, Stefanie D. ..... Boston, MA
Cantor, Steven L. ..... Miami, FL
Naples, FL
Cantor, Steven L., P.A. ..... Miami, FL
Naples, FL
Cantor, Stirley Newell ..... Phoenix, AZ
Cantore, Anthony S. ..... Albany, NY
Cantore & Cantore ..... Oak Park, IL
Cantore, Harold A. ..... Oak Park, IL
Cantore, J. Michael, Jr. ..... Stamford, CT
Cantore, Jami L. ..... Los Angeles, CA
Cantore, Preston H. ..... Oak Park, IL
Cantore, Robert A. ..... Los Angeles, CA
Cantorna, Bernard F. ..... Baraboo, WI
Cantos, Earl J. ..... San Diego, CA
Cantos, Earl J., Jr. ..... San Diego, CA
Cantrall, J. Robert
Department of the Air Force,
Office of the Judge Advocate General, GV
Cantrel, Francis J., Jr. ..... United States Senate,
Committee Legal Personnel, GV
Cantrell, Anthony Benjamin
San Antonio, TX
Cantrell, Ben H. ..... Nashville, TN
Cantrell, C. Bryan ..... College Station, TX
Cantrell, C. E. ..... San Antonio, TX
Cantrell, Charles C. ..... Mountain View, MO
Cantrell, Charles L. ..... Oklahoma City, OK
Cantrell, Constance H. ..... Norcross, GA
Cantrell, Crispin G. ..... Milwaukee, WI
Cantrell, Dail R. ..... Clinton, TN
Cantrell, Daphene L. ..... Charlotte, NC
Cantrell, David D., Jr. ..... Easley, SC
Cantrell, Deborah J. ..... Albuquerque, NM
Cantrell, Dennis F. ..... Indianapolis, IN
Cantrell, Don W. ..... Groesbeck, TX
Cantrell, Frank S. ..... Memphis, TN
Cantrell, Garry Philip ..... Irving, TX
Cantrell, Glenda Ruth ..... Wichita, KS
Cantrell, Green, Pekich, Cruz & McCort, A Professional Corporation
Long Beach, CA
Cantrell, Harry E., Jr. ..... New Orleans, LA
Cantrell, James B., Sr. ..... Orlando, FL
Cantrell, Jay A. ..... Wichita Falls, TX
Cantrell, Jeffrey P. ..... Charlotte, NC
Cantrell, Jennifer ..... Chicago, IL
Cantrell, Lana ..... New York, NY
Cantrell, Larry D. ..... Athens, TN
Cantrell, Luther E., Jr. ..... Nashville, TN
Cantrell, Malinda D. ..... St. Petersburg, FL
Cantrell, Mark Lea (Beau) ..... El Reno, OK
Cantrell, Mary Beth ..... Orlando, FL
Cantrell, Michael E. ..... Garland, TX
Cantrell, Michael H. ..... Fairfax, VA
Cantrell, Michael T. ..... Baltimore, MD
Cantrell, P. Michelle ..... Alexandria, VA
Cantrell, Paul R. ..... Indianapolis, IN
Cantrell, Pfenne P. ..... Indianapolis, IN
Cantrell, Pratt & Varsalona ..... Clinton, TN
Cantrell, Robert M. ..... Oklahoma City, OK

Cantrell, Rose Park ... Nashville, TN
Cantrell, Sharon Simmons ... Houston, TX
Cantrell, Thomas L. ... Dallas, TX
Cantrell, Timothy A. ... Amarillo, TX
Cantrell, Valerie Maguire ... Sparta, TN
Cantrell, W. Patrick ... Houston, TX
Cantrell, Wendell G. ... Spartanburg, SC
Cantrell, William H. ... Santa Ana, CA
Cantrell, William H., Jr. ... Weatherford, TX
Cantrelle, J. Norris ... Raceland, LA
Cantrelle, Nelson J., Jr. ... Gretna, LA
Cantrelle, Nelson J., Jr., A Professional Law Corp. ... Gretna, LA
Cantrick, Joel W. ... Denver, CO
Cantrill, David W. ... Boise, ID
Cantrill, J. Campbell, III ... Georgetown, KY
Cantrill, Skinner, Sullivan & King ... Boise, ID
Cantrill, Thomas H. ... Dallas, TX
Cantu, Alejandro ... New York, NY
Cantú, Amadeo F., Jr. ... Los Angeles, CA
Cantu, Antonio G. ... San Antonio, TX
Cantu, Arturo R. ... McAllen, TX
Cantu, Charles E. ... San Antonio, TX
Cantu, David ... Fort Worth, TX
Cantu, David A. ... Edinburg, TX
Cantu, David O. ... Seattle, WA
Cantu, Felix M., Jr. ... Houston, TX
Cantu, Jose, Jr. ... Houston, TX
Cantu, Kristin L. ... Chicago, IL
Cantu, Martin T., Jr. ... Austin, TX
Cantu, Mary Chapman ... Houston, TX
Cantu, Mary Jo ... Houston, TX
Cantu, Norma J. ... Amarillo, TX
Cantu, Oscar R. ... Miami, FL
Cantu, Patricia Ann ... Los Angeles, CA
Cantu, Ramon M. ... Houston, TX
Cantu, Reynaldo S., Jr. ... Brownsville, TX
Cantu, Richard A. ... McAllen, TX
Cantu, Ruben ... San Antonio, TX
Cantú, Sylvia ... Dallas, TX
Cantú, Sylvia ... Denton, TX
Cantú-Hertzler, Daniel W. ... Philadelphia, PA
Cantwell, C. Bradford ... Springfield, MO
Cantwell & Cantwell ... Walnut Creek, CA
Cantwell & Cantwell ... Chicago, IL
Cantwell & Cantwell ... Malone, NY
Cantwell, Clay ... Branson, MO
Cantwell, Donald W. ... Arlington, TX
Cantwell, E. Carey, (P.C.) ... Buffalo, NY
Cantwell, Frances I. ... Charleston, SC
Cantwell, Frank P., Jr. ... Morristown, TN
Cantwell, Jack ... Walnut Creek, CA
Cantwell, James B. ... Albany, NY
Cantwell, Jerry P. ... Albuquerque, NM
Cantwell, John E. ... Walnut Creek, CA
Cantwell, L. Yager ... Chicago, IL
Cantwell, Laurie J. ... Reston, VA
Cantwell, Lawrence W. ... Concord, CA
Cantwell, Lori A. ... Plattsburgh, NY
Cantwell, Marianne ... Department of Justice, Bureau of Prisons, GV
Cantwell, Michael J., Jr. ... Newtown Square, PA
Cantwell, Paul M., Jr. ... Malone, NY
Cantwell, Peter A. ... Chicago, IL
Cantwell, Richard E. ... Plattsburgh, NY
Cantwell, Robert D. ... St. Louis, MO
Cantwell, Smith & Trokey, LLP ... Branson, MO
Cantwell, Thomas P. ... Barnstable, MA
Cantwell, William ... Saranac Lake, NY
Cantwell, William H., II ... Melbourne, FL
Cantwell, William J. ... New York, NY
Cantwell, William M. ... East Islip, NY
Cantwell, William P. ... Denver, CO
Canty, Brendan T. ... Milford, CT
Canty, David J. ... Myrtle Beach, SC
Canty,David, P.A. ... Myrtle Beach, SC
Canty, Dawn M. ... Chicago, IL
Canty, Elaine ... Upland, CA
Canty, F. Douglas ... Charlotte, NC
Canty, Frank George ... Philadelphia, PA
Canty, James E. ... North Reading, MA
Canty, James M. ... San Francisco, CA
Canty, Jon Marshal ... Pittsburgh, PA
Canty, Joseph D., Jr. ... Rancho Cucamonga, CA
Canty, Kenneth P. ... Oxford, MA
Canty, Patrick J. ... Colorado Springs, CO
Canty, Robert D., Jr. ... Dorchester, MA
Canty, Ross M. ... Wenona, IL
Canty, Trecia M. ... New York, NY
Canty, W. P. Timothy ... Lakewood, CO
Canty-Letsome, Rosezella ... Environmental Protection Agency, Program Office Attorneys, GV
Canuel, Edward T. ... Boston, MA
Canulli, Michael D. ... Oak Brook, IL
Canup, James W. C. ... Richmond, VA
Canuso, Anthony V. ... Ventnor City, NJ
Canuso & Canuso, P.C. ... Ventnor City, NJ
Canuso, Joseph A. ... Ventnor City, NJ
Canuso, Joseph A. ... Philadelphia, PA
Canuso, Joseph P. ... Cherry Hill, NJ / Philadelphia, PA
Canuso, Vito A., III ... Newport Beach, CA
Canuso, Vito F., Jr. ... Philadelphia, PA
Canuteson, Donald G. ... Dallas, TX
Canvel, Henry P. ... San Francisco, CA
Canzano, Diane M. ... Department of Commerce, GV
Canzano, Donna L. ... Tallahassee, FL
Canzano, Peter L. ... Washington, DC
Canzano, Richard M. ... Woburn, MA
Canzano, Roger S. ... Auburn Hills, MI
Canzius, Preston M. ... Morristown, NJ
Canzoneri, Anthony ... Los Angeles, CA
Canzoneri, Jack J. ... Southborough, MA
Canzoneri, Joseph ... Franklin Square, NY
Canzoneri, Patricia M. ... New York, NY
Canzoneri, Vincent J. ... Boston, MA
Cao, Lan ... New York, NY
Cao, Yanping ... New York, NY
Caola, Victor J. ... Toms River, NJ
Caolo & Chapman ... Dallas, TX
Caolo, Jack P. ... Dallas, TX
Caolo, Michael, Jr. ... Dallas, TX
Caouette, Cory Christian ... Treasury Department, Office of the Comptroller of the Currency, GV
Cap, Allen A. ... Las Vegas, NV
Cap, Marcy E. ... Chicago, IL
Cap, Robert J. ... Chicago, IL
Capabianco, Jennifer J. ... San Francisco, CA
Capacci, John G. ... Lyons, NY / **Sodus, NY**
Capaccoli, Walter P. ... San Jose, CA
Capace, Charles R. ... Boston, MA
Capace, Steven F. ... New York, NY
Capadano, Harry L., III ... Omaha, NE
Capalbo, Barry N. ... Warwick, RI
Capalbo & Capalbo ... Westerly, RI
Capalbo, Joseph A. ... Columbia, SC
Capalbo, Joseph J., II ... Stamford, CT
Capalbo, Kevin M. ... Durham, NC
Capalbo, M. Lee ... Seekonk, MA / Providence, RI
Capalbo, Richard M. ... Fort Lauderdale, FL
Capalbo, Thomas E. ... Los Angeles, CA
Capalbo, Thomas J., Jr. ... Westerly, RI
Capalbo, William S. ... Woodside, NY
Capaldi, Mark ... Southfield, MI
Capaldi, Michael D. ... Newport Beach, CA
Capallo, Thomas E. ... Baltimore, MD
Capanegro, Michael J. ... Great Neck, NY
Capanna & Capanna ... Fairport, NY
Capanna, Nicholas D. ... Fairport, NY
Capanna, Paloma A. ... Fairport, NY
Capano & Dejoie ... Lynn, MA
Capano, Mario C. ... Lynn, MA
Capano, Thomas J. ... Wilmington, DE
Caparas, Armando T. ... Mountain View, CA
Caparell, Barbara S. ... Plymouth, MA
Caparell & DiGregorio, The Family Law Group ... Plymouth, MA
Caparello, Dominic M. ... Tallahassee, FL
Caparosa, Kyle M. ... Palm Beach, FL
Capassakis, Evelyn M. ... New York, NY
Capasse, Edward J. ... Westport, CT
Capasso, Andrew M. ... Brooklyn, NY
Capasso, Burns & Massaroni ... Schenectady, NY
Capasso, David A ... New Orleans, LA
Capasso, Jane B. ... Wilmington, DE
Capasso, John M. ... Linwood, NJ
Capasso, John M., P.C. ... Linwood, NJ
Capasso, Mary T. ... Oakbrook Terrace, IL
Capasso, Michael M. ... Coram, NY
Capasso, Robert C. ... Norwood, MA
Capasso, Thomas A. ... Coram, NY
Capasso, Vincent, Jr. ... Schenectady, NY
Capata, Julian Eli ... Los Angeles, CA
Capatides, Michael G. ... New York, NY
CaPaul, Erik ... Waunakee, WI
Capawana, Anthony L. ... East Hanover, NJ
Capazzi, Louis A., Jr. ... Oradell, NJ
Capdeville, Andrew L. ... Charlotte Amalie, St. Thomas, VI
Capdeville, Andrew L., P.C. ... Christiansted, St. Croix, VI / Cruz Bay, St. John, VI / Charlotte Amalie, St. Thomas, VI
Capdeville, Charles R. ... Metairie, LA
Capdeville, Douglas L., Law Offices of ... Christiansted, St. Croix, VI
Capdeville, Douglas L., Law Offices of ... Charlotte Amalie, St. Thomas, VI
Cape, Billie J., (Ms.) ... Bullard, TX
Cape, Grant ... Harrisburg, IL
Cape, Joel Edwin ... New Orleans, LA
Cape, John A. ... Grass Valley, CA
Cape, Julie A. ... Katy, TX
Cape, Randall E. ... Sacramento, CA
Capece, Colleen Lagan ... New York, NY
Capece, Frank G. ... Secaucus, NJ / Trenton, NJ
Capece, Nancy ... Elizabeth, NJ
Capecelatro, Mark J. ... Canaan, CT
Capecelatro & Nelligan ... Canaan, CT
Capecelatro, Salvador J., III ... Utica, NY
Capeci, Susan M. ... Bronxville, NY
Capehart, Blaine E. ... Mount Laurel, NJ
Capehart, Brent A. ... Tulsa, OK
Capehart, Craig Earl ... Indianapolis, IN
Capehart, Lynne C. ... Gainesville, FL
Capehart, Marvin (Chip), II ... Huntington, WV
Capehart & Scatchard, P.A. ... Mount Laurel, NJ / Trenton, NJ
Capehart, Thomas A. ... Allentown, PA
Capeheart, Ted C. ... Ashdown, AR
Capek, John C. ... Philadelphia, PA
Capel, Christopher Blair ... Raleigh, NC
Capel, Susan Pauline ... Atlanta, GA
Capel, Wallace, Jr. ... Flint, MI
Capeles, Nina S. ... Beverly, MA
Capeless, David F. ... Pittsfield, MA
Capeless, Robert T. ... Boston, MA
Capeless, Rosanne Gervasi ... Tallahassee, FL
Capeling, Curtis ... Nashville, TN
Capell, David C. ... San Francisco, CA
Capell, Fredrick G. ... Newberg, OR
Capell, Howard J. ... Lake Success, NY / New York, NY
Capell & Howard, P.C. ... Dothan, AL / Greenville, AL / Hayneville, AL / Luverne, AL / Montgomery, AL / Opelika, AL / Prattville, AL / Selma, AL / Troy, AL / Tuskegee, AL / Union Springs, AL / Wetumpka, AL
Capell, Jack L. ... Montgomery, AL
Capell, John L., III ... Montgomery, AL
Capell, Philip J. ... Lake Success, NY / New York, NY
Capell & Vishnick ... Lake Success, NY
Capell, Vishnick & Odierno ... Melville, NY
Capell, Walter R. ... Rochester, NY
Capella, Richard A. ... Los Angeles, CA / Pleasanton, CA
Capella, Robert A. ... Pickerington, OH
Capelle, A. Anna ... San Francisco, CA
Capelle, Ben ... Dallas, TX
Capelle & Burdette ... Dallas, TX
Capelle, Louis C. ... Dayton, OH
Capelle, Stephen H. ... Austin, TX
Capelle, Thomas A. ... San Francisco, CA
Capelli, Christopher J. ... Stamford, CT
Capelli, John J., Jr. ... Alameda, CA
Capellini, Albert A. ... Yorktown Heights, NY
Capello, Danette M. ... Portland, OR
Capello, Deno C., Jr. ... Lexington, KY
Capello, Gene A. ... New York, NY
Capello, Joseph F. ... Denver, CO
Capello, Kim Thomas ... Novi, MI
Capello, Lloyd A., Jr. ... Donaldsonville, LA
Capello, Susan A. ... Franklin Lakes, NJ
Capellupo, Mirella F. ... Chicago, IL
Capelo, Jaime L., Jr. ... Corpus Christi, TX
Capeloto, Allen J., Law Office of ... San Mateo, CA
Capeloto, J. Sheldon ... Pasadena, CA
Capeloto, Jeffrey H. ... Everett, WA
Capeloto, Joanne V. ... Atlanta, GA
Capelotti-Clougher, Marie-Catherine ... Sandwich, MA
Capelouto, Richard ... Palo Alto, CA
Capener, Cole R. ... Palo Alto, CA
Capener, Jeffery Howard ... Portland, OR
Caperna, Aldo J. ... Merrick, NY
Capers, Bobby ... Lebanon, TN
Capers, Dunbar, Sanders & Bruckner ... Appling, GA / Atlanta, GA / Augusta, GA / Aiken, SC
Capers, Jean M. ... Cleveland, OH
Capers, John D. ... Augusta, GA
Capers, John D., Jr. ... Atlanta, GA
Capers, Robert A. ... Dallas, TX
Capers, Robert L. ... New York, NY
Caperton, Anderson Drew ... Charlotte, NC
Caperton, Charles L. ... Dallas, TX
Caperton, Charles L., A Professional Corporation ... Dallas, TX
Caperton, Eva P. ... Roseville, MN
Caperton, G. Coble ... Memphis, TN
Caperton, Kent A. ... Austin, TX
Caperton, Mark ... Austin, TX / Caldwell, TX
Caperton, Michael O. ... London, KY
Caperton, Susan Mosser ... Martinsburg, WV
Caperton, Virginia L. ... Middlesboro, KY
Caperton-Walling, Kelly ... Dallas, TX
Capes, Daniel K. ... Naples, FL
Capes, David V. ... St. Louis, MO
Capes, Hubbard C. ... Cleveland, OH
Capes, Jerry O. ... Covington, GA
Capes, Nelson R. ... Minneapolis, MN
Capestro, Andrew J. ... Monterey, CA
Capetanakis, Charles ... New York, NY
Capetanakis, John G. ... Long Island City, NY
Capetola, Anthony A. ... Williston Park, NY
Capetola & Doddato ... Williston Park, NY
Capetola, Dolores ... Williston Park, NY
Capetola, Joseph J. ... Williston Park, NY
Capetta, John T. ... Stamford, CT
Capetz, Martin R. ... Salem, OR
Capezio, Joseph G. ... Point Pleasant, NJ
Capezza, Michelle ... New York, NY
Capezzera, Frank M. ... Boston, MA
Capezzera, Vincent M. ... Jacksonville, FL
Capezzuto, Joseph A. ... Boston, MA
Capezzuto, Louis J. ... New York, NY
Capicotto, Rina M. ... Mineola, NY
Capilli, John D. ... Westbury, NY
Capillo, James J. ... Lexington, KY
Capin, John A. ... Boston, MA
Capineri, Jos. A. ... Pawtucket, RI
Capineri, Stephen J. ... Providence, RI
Capio, Ralph J. ... St. Louis, MO
Capiro and Associates ... Los Angeles, CA
Capiro, Rafael M. ... Los Angeles, CA
Capistran, Adriana ... San Francisco, CA
Capistran, Armand ... Manchester, NH
Capistrano, Robert P. ... San Francisco, CA
Capistrant, Joseph M. ... Minneapolis, MN
Capistrant, Theresa A. ... Minneapolis, MN
Capitani, Joseph S. ... Chicago, IL
Capitano, A. Todd ... Charlotte, NC
Capitano, Francesca M. ... Merrick, NY
Capitano, John H. ... Charlotte, NC
Capitano, Michelle Fava ... Tampa, FL
Capitel, Irving S. ... Park Ridge, IL
Capitelli, Ralph ... New Orleans, LA
Capitelli & Wicker ... Metairie, LA / New Orleans, LA
Capitina, Michael F. ... Mountain View, CA
Capitina, Nevo F. ... Mountain View, CA
Capitol District Law Offices ... Raleigh, NC
Capizola, Fineman & Lapham, A Professional Corporation ... Vineland, NJ
Capizola, Michael D. ... Vineland, NJ
Capizzi, Anthony ... Dayton, OH
Capizzi, Mary E. Devlin ... Washington, DC
Capizzi, Michael R. ... Santa Ana, CA
Capizzi, Robert L. ... Chicago, IL
Capizzi, Samuel J. ... Depew, NY
Capko, Robert J. ... Lake Mary, FL
Capko, William G. ... West Palm Beach, FL
Caplan, Alan ... Seattle, WA
Caplan, Alan M. ... San Francisco, CA
Caplan, Alan M. ... Northbrook, IL
Caplan, Andrea L. ... Chicago, IL
Caplan, Andrew F. ... Boston, MA
Caplan, Andrew M. ... Department Of Health And Human Services, Office of the General Counsel, GV
Caplan, Andrew M. ... Houston, TX
Caplan, Arnold H. ... Pittsburgh, PA
Caplan, Barry P. ... Portland, OR
Caplan, Bennett A. ... Washington, DC
Caplan, Brian D. ... Kalamazoo, MI
Caplan, Brian D. ... New York, NY
Caplan, Brian D., P.C. ... Kalamazoo, MI
Caplan, Buckner, Rohrbaugh & Kostecka, Chtd. ... Washington, DC / Bethesda, MD / Rockville, MD / Arlington, VA
Caplan & Caplan, P.C. ... Albany, NY
Caplan & Chester ... Pittsburgh, PA
Caplan, Corina R. ... Washington, DC
Caplan, Darryl S. ... Mount Laurel, NJ
Caplan, Daryl Sue ... Bethesda, MD
Caplan, David ... Phoenix, AZ
Caplan, David ... Beverly Hills, CA
Caplan, David E. ... Grand Rapids, MI
Caplan, David I. ... Murray Hill, NJ
Caplan, David L. ... Beverly Hills, CA
Caplan, David L. ... New York, NY
Caplan, David S. ... Palo Alto, CA
Caplan, Deborah Barthel ... Sacramento, CA
Caplan, Denise B. ... Chicago, IL
Caplan, Donald M. ... Bethesda, MD
Caplan, Donna ... Sun City, CA
Caplan and Earnest LLC ... Boulder, CO
Caplan, Evan B. ... Philadelphia, PA
Caplan, Fern Brown ... Exton, PA / Norristown, PA / Philadelphia, PA
Caplan, Frank S. ... Walnut, CA
Caplan, Franklin H. ... Miami, FL
Caplan, Fred M. ... Chicago, IL
Caplan, Gail R. ... Albany, NY
Caplan, Gale Rasin ... Baltimore, MD
Caplan, Gary S. ... Chicago, IL
Caplan, George T. ... Los Angeles, CA
Caplan, Gerald A. ... Boulder, CO
Caplan, Gerald M. ... Sacramento, CA
Caplan, Goodman L. ... Houston, TX
Caplan, Gordon R. ... New York, NY
Caplan, Herbert Lee ... Chicago, IL
Caplan, Hilary D. ... Baltimore, MD
Caplan, Howard A. ... Jacksonville, FL
Caplan, Howard A., P.A. ... Jacksonville, FL
Caplan, Howard J. ... Boston, MA
Caplan, Irvin N. ... Baltimore, MD
Caplan, James F. ... Boca Raton, FL
Caplan, James M. ... Norfolk, VA
Caplan, Jeffrey E. ... Reston, VA
Caplan, Jerome E. ... Hartford, CT
Caplan, John D. ... New York, NY
Caplan, Jonathan S. ... New York, NY
Caplan, Julian ... Palo Alto, CA
Caplan, Julian W. ... New York, NY
Caplan, Karen J. ... Mount Laurel, NJ
Caplan, Kathleen McHenry ... Chicago, IL
Caplan, Larry, Law Offices of ... Baltimore, MD
Caplan, Larry, Law Offices of ... Towson, MD
Caplan, Lawrence A. ... Miami, FL
Caplan, Leah M. ... Cleveland, OH
Caplan, Lee A. ... Cumberland, MD
Caplan, Lee H. ... Baltimore, MD
Caplan, Lee H., P.C. ... Baltimore, MD
Caplan, Lee, P.A. ... Cumberland, MD
Caplan, Lorraine S. ... Pittsburgh, PA
Caplan, Louis ... West Palm Beach, FL
Caplan & Luber, LLP ... Cherry Hill, NJ / Paoli, PA / Philadelphia, PA
Caplan, Maia R. ... Washington, DC
Caplan, Marjorie M. ... Lansdale, PA
Caplan, Martin J. ... Schenectady, NY
Caplan, Melvin ... Ellwood City, PA
Caplan, Michael J. ... Grants, NM
Caplan, Michael S. ... Baltimore, MD
Caplan, Michael S. ... Pittsburgh, PA
Caplan, Milton I. ... New Haven, CT
Caplan, Mindy ... Austin, TX
Caplan, Mitchell H. ... Chicago, IL
Caplan, Morton L. ... Long Beach, CA
Caplan, Muriel Alix ... New York, NY
Caplan, Murray N. ... Albany, NY
Caplan, Nancy J. ... Cambridge, MA
Caplan, Parrel A. ... Minneapolis, MN
Caplan, Peter A. ... Detroit, MI
Caplan, Renee S. ... Virginia Beach, VA

Caplan, Richard H., (A Law Corp.) Los Angeles, CA
Caplan, Richard L. ....Paoli, PA
Caplan, Richard V. ....Jersey City, NJ **New York, NY**
Caplan, Robert ....San Diego, CA
Caplan, Robert A. ....New Orleans, LA
Caplan, Robert L. ....Clarendon Hills, IL
Caplan, Robert L., P.C. ....Clarendon Hills, IL
Caplan, Robert M. ....Philadelphia, PA
Caplan, Robert Wayne ....Atlanta, GA
Caplan, Russell L. ....Arlington, VA
Caplan, Sara L. ....Los Angeles, CA
Caplan, Sheri J. ....New York, NY
Caplan, Sherri G. ....New York, NY
Caplan, Stacey L. ....Chicago, IL
Caplan, Stephen R. ....Orlando, FL
Caplan, Steven M. ....Towson, MD
Caplan, Stuart A. ....New York, NY
Caplan, Stuart H. ....Hamden, CT
Caplan, William J. ....Costa Mesa, CA
Caplan, William L. ....Akron, OH
Caplan, William V. ....Burlingame, CA
Caple, Steven W. ....Dallas, TX
Caplea, Don E., (L.P.A.) ....Canton, OH
Caplea, Nicholas G. ....Canton, OH
Caplener, Harold D. ....Morgan Hill, CA
Caples, D. Elwood ....Vancouver, WA
Caples, Michael D. ....Jackson, MS
Caples, Michael E. ....San Francisco, CA
Caples, Patrick W. ....Fresno, CA
Caples, Richard J. ....New York, NY
Caples, William F. ....Bedford, MA
Caples, William F., Law Offices Of Bedford, MA
Caplette, Michael V. ....Southbridge, MA
Caplette, Nancy J. ....Phoenix, AZ
Capley, Gerald W. ....Melbourne, FL
Caplice, Byron D. ....Greenfield, MA
Caplice, Kristin S. ....Richmond, VA
Caplice, William F. ....Chicago, IL
Caplicki, Dennis P. ....Florida, NY
Caplicki, Edmund V., III ....Seattle, WA
Caplicki, Edmund V., Jr. LaGrangeville, NY **Poughkeepsie, NY**
Caplicki, Patricia M. ....New York, NY
Caplin & Drysdale, Chartered Washington, DC New York, NY
Caplin, Michael A. ....Falls Church, VA
Caplin, Mortimer M. ....Washington, DC
Caplin, Stephen B. ....Englewood, CO Indianapolis, IN
Caplin, Susan ....Mount Kisco, NY
Capling, Peter B. ....Bad Axe, MI
Caplinger, Daniel J. ....Seattle, WA
Caplinger, Derek L. ....Pendleton, OR
Caplinger, Don S. ....Harrisburg, AR
Caplinger, James M. ....Topeka, KS
Caplinger, James M., Chartered Topeka, KS
Caplinger, James M., Jr. ....Topeka, KS
Caplinger, Leta J. ....Van Buren, AR
Caplinger, Mark E. ....Topeka, KS
Caplinger, Nancy M. ....Topeka, KS
Caplinger, Roy T. ....New York, NY
Caplis, Daniel J. ....Denver, CO
Caplis, Kevin J. ....Chicago, IL
Caplis, Stephen B. ....Baltimore, MD
Caplis, Thomas M. ....Southfield, MI
Caploe, Fred ....Richmond, CA
Caplow, Sheldon R. ....Encino, CA
Caplow, Sheldon R., Inc., A Prof. Corp. Encino, CA
Caplow, Stacy ....Brooklyn, NY
Caplow, Steven P. ....Seattle, WA
Caplow & Zimmerman ....Skokie, IL
Capo, John J. ....Atlanta, GA
Capo, Joy H. ....Locust Valley, NY
Capo', Maria D. ....Houston, TX
Capo, Marilyn ....Coral Gables, FL
Capobianco, Anthony ....Los Angeles, CA
Capobianco, Charles ....Rochester, NY
Capobianco, Daniel B. ....Metairie, LA Boston, MA
Capobianco, David A. ....Framingham, MA
Capobianco, Donald A. Port Washington, NY
Capobianco, Donald A., P.C. Port Washington, NY
Capobianco, Edward J. ....Providence, RI
Capobianco & Gentili, P.C. ....Natick, MA
Capobianco, James L. ....Philadelphia, PA
Capobianco, Joseph ....Garden City, NY
Capobianco, Linda E. ....Stuart, FL
Capobianco, Neil A. ....New York, NY
Capobianco, Robert R. ....Natick, MA
Capobianco, Robert W. ....Atlanta, GA
Capobres, Judy S. ....Chicago, IL
Capoccia, Andrew F. ....Albany, NY
Capoccia, Christopher D. ....Livonia, MI
Capoccia, Rachel M. ....Los Angeles, CA
Capodanno, Joseph F., Jr. ....Wilmington, DE
Capodilupo, Daniel ....Boston, MA
Capodilupo, Daniel L. ....Boston, MA
Capoferri, Anita ....Department of Energy, Office of the General Counsel, GV
Capogrosso, Eleanor ....New York, NY
Capogrosso, Eric ....Beverly Hills, CA
Capolupo, Pasquale A. ....Clairton, PA
Capó-Matos, Jorge L. ....San Juan, PR
Capon, Craig J. ....Eugene, OR
Capon, Virginia F. ....New York, NY
Capone, Andrew N. ....Watertown, NY
Capone, Bert J. ....Boston, MA Providence, RI
Capone, Dorothea M. ....Morristown, NJ New York, NY
Capone, Fred ....Everett, MA
Capone, James J., Jr. ....Hackettstown, NJ
Capone, Jerome M. ....Wilmington, DE
Capone, John W. ....Worcester, MA
Capone, Joseph A. ....Department of Justice, Antitrust Division, GV
Capone, Lori A. ....McKees Rocks, PA
Capone, Lucien, III ....Greensboro, NC
Capone, Michael S. ....Winthrop, MA
Capone, Ralph N. ....West Orange, NJ
Capone, Richard M. ....Watertown, NY
Capone, Stephen F. ....Pittsburgh, PA
Capone, Victoria A. ....Yonkers, NY
Capone, Vincent S. ....Philadelphia, PA
Caponera, Philip S. ....Albany, NY
Caponera, Victor A., Jr. ....Albany, NY
Caponi, Steven L. ....Wilmington, DE
Caponigro, John P. ....Bloomfield Hills, MI
Caporael, Francis T. ....Redlands, CA
Caporal, John P. ....Oklahoma City, OK
Caporale, D. Nick ....Omaha, NE
Caporale, Lawrence James ....Annapolis, MD
Caporale, Michael R., Jr. North Branford, CT
Caporale, Robert L. ....Boston, MA
Caporale, Seb ....Omaha, NE
Caporaletti, Wanda G. ....Silver Spring, MD
Caporizzo, A. William ....Boston, MA
Caporizzo, Cynthia A. ....Department of Justice, GV
Caporossi, Robert W. ....Cleveland, OH
Caporrino, James A. ....Fort Lee, NJ
Caporusso, Catherine A. ....Chicago, IL
Caposela, Ernest Michael ....Clifton, NJ
Capossela, Joseph P. ....Vernon, CT
Capossere, Julie Karowe ....Rochester, NY
Capo-Suria, Miglisa L. ....San Juan, PR
Capote, Beatriz "Betty" M., P.A. ....Miami, FL
Capote, Beatriz M. ....Miami, FL
Capote, Nibaldo J. ....Miami, FL
Capotorto, Paul J ....Toms River, NJ
Capotosto, Donald H. ....West Bend, IA
Capouano, Albert D. ....Orlando, FL
Capouano, Leon M. ....Montgomery, AL
Capouano, Smith, Warren & Klinner, P.C. Montgomery, AL
Capousis, Nicholas D. ....Annapolis, MD Manassas, VA
Capousis, Nicholas D., P.C. Annapolis, MD Manassas, VA
Capowski, John J. ....Harrisburg, PA
Capowski, Timothy Robert Great Neck, NY
Capoziello, James L. ....New York, NY
Capozza, Frank C. ....Indianapolis, IN
Capozza, Richard R. ....Syracuse, NY
Capozzi, Anthony G. ....Brooklyn, NY
Capozzi, Anthony P. ....Fresno, CA
Capozzi & Associates, P.C. Harrisburg, PA
Capozzi, Barbara A. ....Philadelphia, PA
Capozzi, David A. ....Fort Washington, PA
Capozzi, Louis J., Jr. ....Harrisburg, PA
Capozzi, Robert J. ....Boston, MA
Capozzi, Robin K. ....Pittsburgh, PA
Capozziello, Edward ....Milford, CT
Capozzola, Damian D. ....Los Angeles, CA
Capozzoli, Diane J. ....Milton, MA
Capozzoli, Matthew J. ....Louisville, KY
Capozzolo, Anthony ....New York, NY
Capp, Alvin ....Fort Lauderdale, FL
Capp, Alvin, P.A. ....Fort Lauderdale, FL
Capp, Barry M. ....Sayreville, NJ
Capp, David ....Dyer, IN
Capp, Dean J. ....Sugar Land, TX
Capp, Jonathan Charles ....Long Beach, CA
Capp, Lynn M. ....Grosse Pointe, MI
Capp, Michael W. ....Tucson, AZ
Capp, William A. ....Atlanta, GA
Cappa, James A. ....Bayside, NY
Cappa, John R. ....St. Petersburg, FL
Cappa, John R., II ....St. Petersburg, FL
Cappa, John R., P.A. ....St. Petersburg, FL
Cappa, Joseph T. ....Springfield, NJ
Cappabianca, Rosemarie ....New York, NY
Cappadona, Louis A. ....Oxnard, CA
Cappadonna, Carol ....Phoenix, AZ
Cappai, Ronald E. ....Los Angeles, CA
Cappalli, Lisa J. ....Hartford, CT
Cappalli, Richard A. ....Woonsocket, RI
Cappalli, Richard B. ....Philadelphia, PA
Capparella, Donald ....Nashville, TN
Capparella, Richard D. Securities and Exchange Commission, Executive Staff, GV
Capparis, Michael C. ....Piscataway, NJ
Cappas, Craig A. ....Chicago, IL
Cappas, Samuel L. ....Highland, IN
Cappas, Thomas S. ....East Chicago, IN
Cappel, Andrew J. ....New Haven, CT
Cappel, Carolyn M. ....Cleveland, OH
Cappel, Charles W. ....Santa Barbara, CA
Cappel, Frederick L. ....Lake Charles, LA
Cappel, Harry W. ....Cincinnati, OH
Cappel Law Offices ....Costa Mesa, CA
Cappel, Richard B. ....Lake Charles, LA
Cappel, Timothy R. ....Costa Mesa, CA
Cappell, Cynthia A. ....Hackensack, NJ
Cappell, Robert E. ....Bowie, MD
Cappella, Elena A. ....Philadelphia, PA
Cappella, Kerri Lee ....Pittsburgh, PA
Cappellani, Jerome E. ....Kew Gardens, NY
Cappellano, Edward Louis Castleton-on-Hudson, NY
Cappellanti, Ellen S. ....Charleston, WV
Cappelli, Allen P. ....New York, NY
Cappelli, Emil J. ....Buffalo, NY
Cappelli, Joseph J. ....Blue Bell, PA
Cappelli, Louis, Jr. ....Collingswood, NJ Philadelphia, PA
Cappelli, Louis, Jr., A Professional Corporation Collingswood, NJ
Cappelli, Michael J. ....Laguna Niguel, CA Riverside, CA
Cappelli, Michael R. ....Bronx, NY
Cappelli, Richard M. ....Glen Mills, PA Media, PA
Cappellini, Bruno ....New York, NY
Cappellini, Douglas G. ....Allentown, PA
Cappellini, Gifford S. ....Wilkes-Barre, PA
Cappellini, Jeffrey S. ....Scottsdale, AZ
Cappello, A. Barry ....Santa Barbara, CA
Cappello, Cynthia J. ....Chicago, IL
Cappello, Dennis S. ....Elmhurst, NY
Cappello, Francis P. ....Potsdam, NY
Cappello, George M. ....Cranston, RI
Cappello, George M., Ltd. ....Cranston, RI
Cappello, Henry J. ....Alexandria, VA
Cappello, John C. ....Walden, NY
Cappello & Linden ....Potsdam, NY
Cappello & McCann LLP Santa Barbara, CA Ventura, CA
Cappelluti, Kris Ann E. ....Trenton, NJ
Cappelluti, Lisa M. ....Oakland, CA
Cappelmann, Claude M. ....Beaufort, SC
Capper, Cary W. ....Miami, FL
Capper, Donald R. ....Proctorville, OH
Capper, Holland C., (Ltd.) ....Chicago, IL
Capper, Jean Marie ....Chicago, IL
Capper, John S., IV ....Crawfordsville, IN
Capper, Thomas A. ....Wynnewood, PA
Capper, Virginia B. ....Dearborn, MI
Cappetta, Anthony G. ....Chicago, IL
Cappetta, Frederick C. ....Oakbrook Terrace, IL
Cappetta & Shadle, Ltd. Oakbrook Terrace, IL
Cappiello, Daniel M. ....Concord, NH
Cappiello, George J., Jr. San Francisco, CA **New York, NY**
Cappiello Hofmann & Katz, P.C. San Francisco, CA **Newark, NJ New York, NY**
Cappillino, Donald ....Pawling, NY Poughkeepsie, NY
Cappillino, Donald, Law Offices of Pawling, NY Poughkeepsie, NY
Cappillo, David V. ....Atlanta, GA
Cappio, James ....New York, NY
Capplis, Sean E. ....Worcester, MA
Cappocchi, Raymond A. ....Beverly Hills, CA
Cappola, Jeffrey W. ....Teaneck, NJ
Cappolella, Lisa J. ....Pottstown, PA
Cappolino, Dodd & Krebs ....Cameron, TX
Cappolino, Timothy R. ....Cameron, TX
Cappozzo, Frank M. ....Waukesha, WI
Cappozzo, Fred J. ....Chatham, NY
Capps, Ancelet, Stoverink & Clark Carthage, IL
Capps, Bryan L. ....Orlando, FL
Capps, Cantwell & Capps Morristown, TN
Capps, Catherine Brown ....Burkesville, KY
Capps, Christopher P. ....Morristown, TN
Capps & Cobb ....Melbourne, FL
Capps, Damon R. ....Houston, TX
Capps, Damon R., P.C. ....Houston, TX
Capps, David L. ....Houston, TX
Capps, Deborah G. ....Jasper, AL
Capps, Douglas L. ....Portland, OR
Capps, Gregory S. ....Moorestown, NJ Philadelphia, PA
Capps, J. Christopher ....Dothan, AL
Capps, J. deR. ....St. Petersburg, FL
Capps, James L., II Altamonte Springs, FL
Capps, Jeffrey D. ....Pendleton, OR
Capps, Jeremy D. ....Holland, MI
Capps, John E. ....Roswell, NM
Capps, Julie Ann ....Fort Worth, TX
Capps, Kelly J. ....Washington, DC
Capps, Kendall Earl ....Burbank, CA
Capps, Marshall D. ....Crowell, TX
Capps, Noel C. ....Kansas City, MO
Capps, Pamela M. ....New York, NY
Capps, Paul R. ....Morristown, TN
Capps, Peter T. ....Berwyn, IL
Capps, R. Fred ....Burkesville, KY
Capps, Steven D. ....Charlotte, MI
Capps, Stewart B. ....Melbourne, FL
Capps, Stewart B., P.A. ....Melbourne, FL
Capps, Thomas C. ....Liberty, MO
Capps, Thomas H. ....St. Louis, MO
Capps, W. Ross ....Gulfport, MS
Capps, William F., (P.C.) ....Los Angeles, CA
Cappucci, Debora A. ....Los Angeles, CA **San Diego, CA**
Cappucci, Robert N. ....New York, NY
Cappucci, Vincent R. ....New York, NY
Cappuccilli, Timothy J. ....Syracuse, NY
Cappuccio, Joseph G. ....New York, NY
Cappuccio, Marie Ann ....Hammonton, NJ
Cappuccio, Mark S. ....Lansdale, PA
Cappuccio, Paul T. ....Washington, DC
Cappuccio, Ronald J. ....Cherry Hill, NJ
Cappuccio, William S. ....Hammonton, NJ
Cappuyns, Elisabeth ....New York, NY
Cappuzzo, Robert A ....Secaucus, NJ
Cappy, George B. ....Tampa, FL
Cappy, George B., P.A. ....Tampa, FL
Cappy, Rod J. ....Los Angeles, CA
Capra, Daniel J. ....New York, NY
Capra, George J. ....Kansas City, MO
Capra, James J., Jr. ....New York, NY
Capra, Shari M. ....Phoenix, AZ
Capra, Susan A. ....Chicago, IL
Caprara, Alfonso ....Philadelphia, PA
Caprara, Joseph A. ....Philadelphia, PA
Capraro, Jacob S. ....Metairie, LA
Capraro, Joseph A., Jr. ....Boston, MA
Caprera & Caprera ....Southbridge, MA
Caprera, David A. ....Denver, CO
Caprera, Dorothy Allison ....Southbridge, MA
Caprera, Robert G. ....Southbridge, MA
Caprera, S. Anthony ....Southbridge, MA
Capretz & Associates ....Newport Beach, CA
Capretz, Colette M. ....Washington, DC
Capretz, Donald A. ....Lafayette, LA
Capretz, Donald A., A Professional Law Corporation ....Lafayette, LA
Capretz, James T. ....Newport Beach, CA
Capria, Mary Ann ....Falls Church, VA
Capriano, Lichtman & Flach ....New York, NY
Capriano, Michael P. ....New York, NY
Capriglione, Dennis J. ....Clayton, MO
Caprigliore, Scott J. ....Ewing, NJ
Caprile, James Andrew ....Sacramento, CA
Capriles, Robert ....Omaha, NE
Caprini, Elizabeth J. ....Chicago, IL
Caprio, Christine Wallace ....Pittsburgh, PA
Caprio, Frank ....Providence, RI
Caprio, Frank M. ....Huntsville, AL
Caprio, Frank T. ....Providence, RI
Caprio, Joseph R., P.C. ....West Point, VA
Caprio, Kathleen Huettner Huntington Woods, MI
Caprio, Michael R., Jr. ....Norfolk, VA
Caprio, Nicholas E. ....West Orange, NJ
Caprioglio, Paul E., (A Prof. Corp.) Fresno, CA
Capriola, Charles E., Jr. ....Bennington, VT
Capriola, Martin S. ....Willows, CA
Capriola, Richard J. ....Atlanta, GA
Caprioli, Madeline ....Philadelphia, PA
Capriolo, Ralph A. ....Akron, OH
Capriotti, Arnold E., Jr. ....Cherry Hill, NJ Wynnewood, PA
Capriotti & Associates ....Portland, OR
Capriotti & Associates International Law Minnetonka, MN
Capriotti, David M. ....Syracuse, NY
Capriotti, F.J. (Franco), III ....Minnetonka, MN Portland, OR
Capriotti, Roger P. ....Los Angeles, CA
Capriotti, Trieste L. ....Schwenksville, PA
Capristo, Claire C. ....Pittsburgh, PA
Capristo, Joseph C. ....California, MD
Capristo, Robert C. ....Pittsburgh, PA
Capritto, A. J. ....New Orleans, LA
Capritto & Gillette ....New Orleans, LA
Capritto, Maria ....Ventura, CA
Capritto, Phillip T. ....Ventura, CA
Capro, Henry J. ....West Bloomfield, MI
Capron, Alexander M. ....Washington, DC
Capron & Avgerinos, P.C. ....Chicago, IL
Capron, Cheryl Y. ....Chapel Hill, NC
Capron, Daniel F. ....Chicago, IL
Capron, David ....Merced, CA
Capron, Jack B. ....Skaneateles, NY
Capron, John M. ....Atlanta, GA
Capron, John R. ....San Francisco, CA
Capron, Mark G. ....Lakeland, FL
Capron, Maryanne H. ....Chicago, IL
Capron, Robert E. ....San Francisco, CA
Capron, Stephen J. ....Tulsa, OK
Caproni, Valerie E. ....Brooklyn, NY
Capruso, James M. ....Hoboken, NJ
Caps, Thomas L. ....Los Angeles, CA
Capsalis, Carole H. ....Alexandria, VA Arlington, VA
Capsalis, John N. ....New York, NY
Capsalis, Manuel A. ....Alexandria, VA Arlington, VA
Capshaw, Donald W. ....Texarkana, TX
Capshaw, Goss & Bowers, L.L.P. Dallas, TX
Capshaw, Joyce M. ....St. Louis, MO
Capshaw, Laura Cormier ....Boston, MA
Capshaw, Richard A., (P.C.) ....Dallas, TX
Capshaw, S. Calvin, III ....Longview, TX
Capshaw, Tom D. ....Evansville, IN
Capshaw, William K. ....Elmsford, NY
Capshew, Thomas F. ....Tallahassee, FL
Capt, Patricia E. ....Chicago, IL
Captain, Felicia ....Lawrence, MA
Capua, Andrea N. ....Boone, NC
Capua, Craig A. ....Dallas, TX
Capua & Kaeiser ....Miami, FL
Capua, Paul A. ....Miami, FL
Capua, Peter M. ....Miami, FL
Capua, Robert M. ....Chicago, IL
Capua, S. Peter ....Miami, FL
Capuano, Christopher ....Reston, VA
Capuano, Daryl C. ....Hartford, CT
Capuano, Deborah A.S. ....Westborough, MA
Capuano, Donald J. ....Washington, DC
Capuano, Earl F. ....Westport, CT
Capuano, Eugene R. ....Everett, MA
Capuano, Mark D. ....Waterbury, CT
Capuano, Michael E. ....Somerville, MA
Capuano, Philip V. ....San Diego, CA
Capuano, Robert M. ....Cherry Hill, NJ
Capuano, Susan T. ....Reston, VA
Capuder & Arnoff, P.C. ....New York, NY
Capuder, Douglas M. ....New York, NY
Capuder, Drew M. ....Houston, TX
Capurro, Adolph J. ....San Francisco, CA
Capurro, Christina M. ....Saratoga, CA

Cardenas, Susan M. ..... **Key West, FL**
Cardenas, Valerie R. ..... **San Diego, CA**
Cardenas, Whitis & Stephen, L.L.P.
McAllen, TX
Cardenas Conn, Gloria ..... Los Angeles, CA
Cardente, Douglas T. ..... Portland, ME
Carder, Brad A. ..... Eau Claire, WI
Carder, Charles L., III ..... **Atlanta, GA**
Carder, Deborah O'Connell ..... Largo, FL
Carder, Elizabeth B. ..... **Washington, DC**
Carder, J. Keith ..... Birmingham, AL
Carder, Mark S. ..... **Kansas City, MO**
Carder, Michael D. ..... Indianapolis, IN
Carder, Shelley A. ..... San Diego, CA
Carder, William H. ..... San Francisco, CA
Cardey, Keith R. ..... Elmhurst, IL
Cardey-Yates, Lynn R. ..... Magna, UT
Cardi, Dawn M., & Associates
New York, NY
Cardi, Martha J. ..... **Denver, CO**
Cardi, Patricia M. ..... **New York, NY**
Cardi, Philip B. ..... **Denver, CO**
Cardi, Stephen A. ..... Warwick, RI
Cardiello, Frank X. ..... Trenton, NJ
Cardieri, Joseph V. ..... Brooklyn, NY
Cardiff, David J. ..... San Francisco, CA
Cardiff, Mary ..... Fort Bragg, CA
Cardile, John J. ..... **Garfield, NJ**
Cardile, Julius J. ..... Brooklyn, NY
Cardilli, Lisa ..... Coventry, RI
Cardillo, Anthony T.
Office Of Special Counsel,
Dallas Field Office, GV
Cardillo, Christopher A. ..... **Buffalo, NY**
Cardillo & Corbett ..... **New York, NY**
Cardillo, Harry A. ..... **Brooklyn, NY**
Cardillo, James D. ..... New York, NY
Cardillo, John P. ..... **Naples, FL**
Cardillo, Keith & Bonaquist, A Professional Association ..... **Naples, FL**
Cardillo, Matthew J. ..... **Tampa, FL**
Cardillo, Paul T. ..... Tampa, FL
Cardillo, Peter M. ..... **Tampa, FL**
Cardillo, Raymond F., Jr. ..... **Arlington, VA**
Cardimen, Jeffrey S. ..... Farmington Hills, MI
Cardin, Benjamin L. ..... Baltimore, MD
Cardin, Frank G. ..... San Clemente, CA
Cardin & Gitomer ..... Baltimore, MD
Cardin, Howard L. ..... Baltimore, MD
Cardin, Jan H. K. ..... Stevenson, MD
Cardin, Leslie J. ..... **Duluth, GA**
Cardin, Leslie J. ..... **Lawrenceville, GA**
Cardin, Mary Beth ..... Hartford, CT
Cardin & Parmley, P.A. ..... Farmington, NM
Cardin, Patricia ..... Vernon, CT
Cardin, Robert ..... Farmington, NM
Cardin, Sanford R. ..... **Washington, DC**
Cardin, Tom W. ..... Cassville, MO
Cardin, Tommie S. ..... **Jackson, MS**
Cardinal, Gary A. ..... **Reno, NV**
Cardinal, James ..... New York, NY
Cardinal, John G. ..... Ashtabula, OH
Cardinal, Joseph John ..... Evergreen Park, IL
Cardinal, Kenneth J. ..... Sebring, OH
Cardinal, Laura A. ..... **Sierra Vista, AZ**
Cardinal Law Office ..... Sebring, OH
Cardinal, Marc J. ..... **San Jose, CA**
Cardinal, Paul A. ..... Glens Falls, NY
Cardinale, Anthony M. ..... Boston, MA
Cardinale & Cardinale ..... Jamesport, NY
Cardinale, Christine Marie ..... Pittsburgh, PA
Cardinale, Christopher T.
Washington, DC
Cardinale, Frank C., Jr. ..... Orange, CA
Cardinale, Nancy L. ..... Jefferson City, MO
Cardinale, Philip J. ..... Jamesport, NY
Cardinale, Richard ..... Brooklyn, NY
Cardinale, Robert T. ..... Boston, MA
Cardinale, Susan M. P. ..... Jamesport, NY
Cardinali, Debra R. ..... **Westport, CT**
Cardine, G. Joseph ..... Casper, WY
Cardinez, Benjamin F. ..... Farmington, CT
Cardino & Cardino ..... Amityville, NY
Cardino, Frank J. ..... Amityville, NY
Cardino, Joseph, Jr. ..... Amityville, NY
Cardis, Francis J. ..... Franklin, IN
Cardis, Joel ..... Blue Bell, PA
Cardis, Kraut & Harris, P.C. ..... Blue Bell, PA
Cardman, Denise A. ..... Washington, DC
Cardman, Philip N. ..... Folsom, CA
Cardon, Andrea L. ..... **Boise, ID**
Cardon, David A. ..... **Virginia Beach, VA**
Cardon, John A. ..... Bethesda, MD
Cardon, Jonathan G. ..... New York, NY
Cardon, Kelly G. ..... Ogden, UT
Cardon, Lawrence M. ..... **Norfolk, VA**
Cardon, Marriner ..... Phoenix, AZ
Cardon, Marriner, P.C. ..... Phoenix, AZ
Cardon, P. Craig ..... **San Francisco, CA**
Cardon, Robert L. ..... Annandale, VA
Cardona, Anthony V. ..... Albany, NY
Cardona, Anthony V., Jr. ..... **Albany, NY**
Cardona, Carlos M. ..... Isla Verde, PR
Cardona, Cesar G. ..... Brooklyn, NY
Cardona, Diane M. ..... Cedar Rapids, IA
Cardona, Elena ..... Los Angeles, CA
Cardona, George S. ..... Los Angeles, CA
Cardona, Joseph V. ..... Philadelphia, PA
Cardona, Laura Estela ..... Syracuse, NY
Cardona, Marian Palma ..... Kansas City, MO
Cardona, Marisol ..... **New York, NY**
Cardona, Mildred ..... **Peoria, IL**
Cardona, Troy A. ..... Herculaneum, MO
Cardona, Victor A. ..... **Albany, NY**
Cardona, Virginia S. ..... Hockessin, DE
Cardona Alvarez, Alfredo ..... San German, PR
Cardone, Barbara A. ..... **Bangor, ME**
Cardone, Clifford E. ..... **New Orleans, LA**
Cardone, Clifford E., A Professional Law Corporation ..... **New Orleans, LA**
Cardone, Joseph V. ..... Medina, NY
Cardone, Kathleen ..... El Paso, TX
Cardone, Kenneth A. ..... Las Vegas, NV
Cardone, Lucia A. ..... **New York, NY**
Cardone, Maurice A. ..... Nanticoke, PA
Cardone, Nunzio J. ..... Lynbrook, NY
Cardone, Rosanna Miseo
Berkeley Heights, NJ
Cardone, Sandra L. ..... Cambridge, MA
Cardone, Vincent D. ..... Medina, NY
Cardoni and Associates ..... **Kingston, PA**
Scranton, PA
Wilkes-Barre, PA
Cardoni, Douglas J. ..... New York, NY
Cardoni, Harry V. ..... **Kingston, PA**
Cardoni, Horace R. ..... Mountainside, NJ
Cardoni, Susan D. ..... **Portland, OR**
Cardonick, Andrew R. ..... **Chicago, IL**
Cardonne, Gisela ..... Miami, FL
Cardono, James ..... Pawtucket, RI
Cardonsky, Robert J. ..... Elizabeth, NJ
Cardosi, John P. ..... **San Jose, CA**
Cardosi, Julie A. ..... Springfield, IL
Cardoso, Flavio A. ..... **New York, NY**
Cardoso, Linda T. ..... Newport Beach, CA
Cardoso, Patricia ..... New York, NY
Cardot, John M. ..... **Fresno, CA**
Cardot, Richard W. ..... Elkins, WV
Cardoza, Adele K. ..... **Costa Mesa, CA**
Cardoza, Anthony R. ..... Chico, CA
Cardoza, Brian A. ..... **Rosemead, CA**
Cardoza, Edward R. ..... **Indianapolis, IN**
Cardoza, John L. ..... **San Francisco, CA**
Cardoza, Marvin E. ..... San Francisco, CA
Cardoza, Max S. ..... Eureka, CA
Cardoza, Paula F. ..... Indianapolis, IN
Cardoza, Rafael Y. ..... Hayward, CA
Cardoza, Steven W. ..... **Costa Mesa, CA**
Cardoza, Thomas M. ..... Garden City, NY
Cardoza, Victor M. ..... Las Vegas, NV
Cardoza, William A.
Merit Systems Protection Board,
Office of the General Counsel, GV
Cardozo, A. A., Jr. ..... Modesto, CA
Cardozo, Benjamin M. ..... New York, NY
Cardozo, Benjamin S. ..... **Los Angeles, CA**
Cardozo, Caesar Pina ..... Boston, MA
Cardozo & Cardozo ..... Modesto, CA
Cardozo & Cardozo, P.C. ..... New York, NY
Cardozo, Danforth, III ..... Montpelier, VT
Cardozo, Daniel L.
South San Francisco, CA
Cardozo, Enid ..... Albuquerque, NM
Cardozo, Joseph L. ..... Sarasota, FL
Cardozo, Michael A. ..... **New York, NY**
Cardozo, Michael H., IV ..... Washington, DC
Cardozo, Michael H., V ..... Washington, DC
Cardozo, Richard A. ..... Modesto, CA
Cardozo, Richard S. ..... Cumberland, RI
Card-Smith, Virginia L. ..... Denver, CO
Carducci, David A. ..... Solana Beach, CA
Carducci, Leonard A., Jr. ..... Hackettstown, NJ
Carduff, Wendell L. ..... West Springfield, MA
Cardulla, Richard J. ..... San Diego, CA
Cardullo, Cindy Merten ..... Sacramento, CA
Cardwell, Allison A. ..... Chattanooga, TN
Cardwell & Associates, P.C. ..... Denver, CO
Cardwell, C. Patteson, IV ..... **Parsippany, NJ**
Cardwell, Cardwell & Smoragiewicz
Hartford, CT
Cardwell, Christopher W. ..... **Nashville, TN**
Cardwell, David E. ..... **Orlando, FL**
Cardwell, Elaine K. ..... Phoenix, AZ
Cardwell, Garland D. ..... **Sherman, TX**
Cardwell, Gary L. ..... Martinsville, VA
Cardwell & Hart ..... **Austin, TX**
Cardwell, J. Thomas ..... **Orlando, FL**
Cardwell, J. William ..... Dallas, TX
Cardwell, Jerry E. ..... Denver, CO
Cardwell, John A. ..... **Austin, TX**
Cardwell, John G., Jr. ..... Columbus, OH
Cardwell & Knight ..... **Madison, NC**
Cardwell, Kristina M. ..... Virginia Beach, VA
Cardwell, M. Donald ..... Hartford, CT
Cardwell, Mary Jane ..... Waycross, GA
Cardwell, Nicholas P. ..... Hartford, CT
Cardwell, Richard A. ..... **Columbus, OH**
Cardwell, Richard B. ..... New York, NY
Cardwell, Richard W. ..... Indianapolis, IN
Cardwell, Robert A. ..... **Irvine, CA**
Cardwell, Robert L. ..... San Jose, CA
Cardwell, Robert W., Jr. ..... Spring House, PA
Cardwell, Ronald E. ..... **Greenville, SC**
Cardwell, Ronald O. ..... **Burlington, NC**
Cardwell, Samantha ..... Columbia, MO
Cardwell, Suzan K. ..... **Houston, TX**
Cardwell, Timothy L. ..... Norwalk, OH
Cardwell, Vernon E. ..... **Madison, NC**
Cardwell, Victor O. ..... **Roanoke, VA**
Cardwell, Walter W., III ..... Austin, TX
Cardwell, William A. ..... **Honolulu, HI**
Cardwell, William W., Jr. ..... Gadsden, AL
Care, Chester P. ..... Lexington, KY
Care, Terry John ..... **Las Vegas, NV**
Careaga, Richard ..... Vernon Hills, IL
Careaga, Victor A., P.A. ..... **Coral Gables, FL**
Careaga, Victor Armando
Coral Gables, FL
Carel, B. Kay ..... **Oklahoma City, OK**
Carel, Robert Douglas ..... Oklahoma City, OK
Carell, Edith C. ..... Nashville, TN
Carella, Byrne, Bain, Gilfillan, Cecchi, Stewart & Olstein, A Professional Corporation ..... **Roseland, NJ**
Carella, Charles C. ..... **Roseland, NJ**
Carella, Charles M. ..... **Roseland, NJ**
Carella, John ..... San Mateo, CA
Carella, Keri A. ..... Florham Park, NJ
Carellas, Theodore T. ..... Rincon, GA
Carelli, Paul V., III ..... Las Vegas, NV
Carelli, Paul V., IV ..... **San Diego, CA**
Carelli, Sandra E. ..... **San Diego, CA**
Las Vegas, NV
Carello, William J. ..... Plano, TX
Carello, William M. ..... **Darien, CT**
Caren, Mark S. ..... **New York, NY**
Carena, Lori H. ..... Brooklyn, NY
Carenbauer, George E. ..... **Charleston, WV**
Carens, Thomas J. ..... **Boston, MA**
Carenza, Christopher J. ..... St. Louis, MO
Careri, Frank, Jr. ..... Hackensack, NJ
Carero, William M. ..... Los Angeles, CA
Cares, Robert P. ..... Detroit, MI
Caresani, Ann M. ..... **Cleveland, OH**
Caress, Jeffrey L. ..... New York, NY
Caress, John H. ..... Indianapolis, IN
Caress, Timothy C. ..... **Indianapolis, IN**
Carestia, Dominic P. ..... Butte, MT
Caretti, Beth A. ..... **Dearborn, MI**
Caretti, Louis S. ..... **Vallejo, CA**
Caretti, Richard L. ..... Bloomfield Hills, MI
Carew, Allan J. ..... **Dubuque, IA**
Carew, Colleen F. ..... New York, NY
Carew Law Office ..... **Seattle, WA**
Carew, Robert J. ..... Toledo, OH
Carew, Shane C. ..... **Seattle, WA**
Carew, Thomas E. ..... **Kansas City, MO**
Carew, Tina M. ..... **New York, NY**
Carew, William J. ..... Montauk, NY
Carew, William J., P.C. ..... Montauk, NY
Carew, William L. ..... Colorado Springs, CO
Carey, Alice Ann ..... Bridgeport, CT
Carey, Ann D. ..... **Denver, CO**
Carey, Ann M. ..... Seattle, WA
Carey, Anne E. ..... Hollywood, CA
Carey, Anthony ..... **Chicago, IL**
Carey, Anthony M. ..... **Washington, DC**
Baltimore, MD
Carey & Associates ..... Rumford, ME
Carey, Austin, Jr. ..... **Hartford, CT**
Carey, Austin, Jr., P.C. ..... **Hartford, CT**
Carey, Barbara Jane ..... **New York, NY**
Carey, Bill ..... Roanoke, VA
Carey, Bradford D. ..... **Metairie, LA**
Carey, Brian C. ..... New Britain, CT
Carey, Brian P. ..... New York, NY
Carey, Brigid E. ..... **Scranton, PA**
Carey, Bruce C. ..... Eagle, CO
Carey, Bruce D. ..... Grosse Pointe Farms, MI
Carey, Bruce D., P.C.
Grosse Pointe Farms, MI
Carey & Carey ..... Blue Island, IL
Carey, Carey & Carey ..... Easthampton, MA
Carey, Caroline Marnock ..... **Portland, OR**
Carey, Catherine ..... **Honolulu, HI**
Carey, Catherine A. ..... New York, NY
Carey, Chad L. ..... **Wilmington, OH**
Carey, Charles B. ..... Laguna Hills, CA
Carey, Charles B. ..... Montclair, NJ
Carey, Charles B., Law Offices of, A Prof. Corp. ..... Laguna Hills, CA
Carey, Charles E. ..... **Boston, MA**
Carey, Charles G. ..... Escondido, CA
Carey, Chris D. ..... Medina, OH
Carey, Christen Civiletto ..... **Atlanta, GA**
Carey, Christopher
Department of the Air Force,
Office of the Judge Advocate General, GV
Carey, Christopher C. ..... Alexandria, VA
Carey, Christopher E. ..... **New Orleans, LA**
Carey, Christopher J. ..... New Bedford, MA
Carey, Christopher J. ..... **Newark, NJ**
Carey, Crystal L. ..... **Dover, DE**
Carey, Cynthia Truesdell ..... Auburn Hills, MI
Carey, Daniel D. ..... Springfield, OH
Carey, Daniel J. ..... West Orange, NJ
Carey & Danis, L.L.C. ..... **St. Louis, MO**
Carey, Darrell R. ..... Canyon, TX
Carey, David E. ..... **Bel Air, MD**
Carey, David L. ..... New York, NY
Carey, David W. ..... Julian, CA
Carey, Deborah L. ..... Dover, DE
Carey, Dennis F., III ..... Montclair, NJ
Carey, Diana K. ..... **Seattle, WA**
Carey, Diane P. ..... **Irvine, CA**
Carey & Dobson, LLC ..... **Atlanta, GA**
Carey, Donald F. ..... **Idaho Falls, ID**
Carey, Doreen R. ..... Fort Lauderdale, FL
Carey, Doreen Renzulli, P.A.
Fort Lauderdale, FL
Carey, Douglas E. ..... Suffolk, VA
Carey, Douglas F. ..... New Orleans, LA
Carey, Douglas G. ..... Maitland, FL
Carey, Dru Bronwyn ..... Bronx, NY
Carey, Earl L., Jr. ..... Baltimore, MD
Carey, Edmond J. ..... Seattle, WA
Carey, Edward J. ..... Abingdon, MD
Carey, Edward J. ..... Albany, NY
Carey, Edward L.
Department Of Health And Human Services,
Social Security Administration, GV
Carey, Edward P. ..... Pittsburgh, PA
Carey, Edwin J., JR ..... Duncan, OK
Carey, Elizabeth L. ..... Long Grove, IL
Carey, Ellen M. Chiocca ..... Easton, MA
Carey, Emerson, Jr. ..... **Atlanta, GA**
Carey & Emmings, Ltd. ..... **Fairfax, MN**
Carey, Erma J. ..... Houston, TX
Carey, Filter, White & Boland
Chicago, IL
Carey, Florence A. ..... **Boston, MA**
Carey, Francis J. ..... Rosemont, IL
Carey, Francis J. ..... **Pittsburgh, PA**
Carey, Francis J. ..... Pittsburgh, PA
Carey, Frank T., Jr. ..... Blue Island, IL
Carey, George D. ..... Boise, ID
Carey, Gerard M. ..... Newark, NJ
Carey, Glenn B. ..... Newark, NJ
Carey, Gordon T., Jr. ..... **Portland, OR**
Carey, Gordon T., Jr., P.C. ..... **Portland, OR**
Vancouver, WA
Carey, H. Bissell, III ..... **Boston, MA**
Carey, Hala L. ..... **Dallas, TX**
Carey, Harland E. ..... Phoenix, AZ
Carey, Harry L.
Department of Housing and Urban Development,
Office of General Counsel, GV
Carey, Harry M., Jr. ..... **Cambridge, MA**
Carey & Hilbert ..... **Clearwater, FL**
Gainesville, FL
St. Petersburg, FL
Carey, Howard J., Jr. ..... Hutchinson, KS
Carey, Hugh L. ..... **Fort Lauderdale, FL**
New York, NY
Carey, J. Kevin ..... **Tampa, FL**
Carey, J. Kevin ..... **Fort Worth, TX**
Carey, J. Matthew ..... Louisville, KY
Carey, J. Robert ..... Silver Spring, MD
Carey, Jack ..... **Belleville, IL**
Carey, Jack M. ..... **Gainesville, GA**
Carey, Jack S. ..... **St. Petersburg, FL**
Carey, James A. ..... Manasquan, NJ
Carey, James A., Jr. ..... **Hackensack, NJ**
Carey, James D. ..... Durham, NC
Carey, James F.
Federal Maritime Commission,
Other Offices of the Commission, GV
Carey, James F. ..... Easthampton, MA
Carey, James F. ..... **Dallas, TX**
Carey, James L. ..... **Chicago, IL**
Carey, James P. ..... Chicago, IL
Carey, James P. ..... **Minneapolis, MN**
Carey, James P. ..... **Helena, MT**
Carey, James R. ..... **Chicago, IL**
Carey, James R. ..... East Alton, IL
Carey, James S., Jr. ..... Pittsburgh, PA
Carey, James T. ..... Louisville, KY
Carey, James T. ..... **Weirton, WV**
Carey, Jana Howard, (P.C.)
Baltimore, MD
Carey, Jane E. ..... **Emeryville, CA**
San Francisco, CA
Carey, Jarrard & Walker ..... **Cleveland, GA**
Dahlonega, GA
Gainesville, GA
Carey, Jay ..... Arlington, WA
Carey, Jeffrey C. ..... Portland, OR
Carey, Jeffrey J. ..... Overland Park, KS
Carey, Jeffrey L. ..... Seattle, WA
Carey, Jeffrey M. ..... **Chicago, IL**
Carey, Jennifer L. ..... **Duluth, MN**
Carey, Jenny B. ..... **Boise, ID**
Carey, Jessica C. ..... **Anchorage, AK**
Carey, Joel E. ..... Sacramento, CA
Carey, Johanna C. ..... **Lansing, MI**
Carey, John ..... **New York, NY**
Carey, John ..... White Plains, NY
Carey, John A. ..... Albuquerque, NM
Carey, John C. ..... **Miami, FL**
Carey, John C. ..... New York, NY
Carey, John C. ..... Austin, TX
Carey, John D. ..... **Macon, GA**
Carey, John D., Jr. ..... **Dallas, TX**
Carey, John E., Jr. ..... **San Francisco, CA**
Carey, John H. ..... Colorado Springs, CO
Carey, John J. ..... **St. Louis, MO**
Carey, John J. ..... Thoreau, NM
Carey, John L. ..... **South Bend, IN**
Carey, John M. ..... **Boston, MA**
Carey, John M. ..... **Toledo, OH**
Carey, John P., III
Federal Emergency Management Agency,
Office of the General Counsel, GV
Carey, John R. ..... New York, NY
Carey, John T. ..... Chicago, IL
Carey, John T. P. ..... New London, CT
Carey, John W. ..... **Fairfax, MN**
Minneapolis, MN
Carey, Joseph ..... **Stamford, CT**
Carey, Joseph E. ..... Bowie, MD
Carey, Joseph Patrick ..... Fishkill, NY
Carey, Joseph Patrick, P.C. ..... Fishkill, NY
Carey, Joseph W. ..... **Miami, FL**
Carey, Karen Estelle ..... **Winston-Salem, NC**
Carey, Kate ..... **Washington, DC**
Carey, Katherine A. ..... **Newport Beach, CA**
Omaha, NE
Carey, Katherine Ott ..... **Los Angeles, CA**
Carey, Kathleen A. ..... **Washington, DC**
Carey, Kelly Mack ..... **Roseland, NJ**
Carey, Kevin A. ..... San Diego, CA
Carey, Kevin F. ..... **New York, NY**
Carey, Kevin J. ..... **Philadelphia, PA**
Carey, Kevin M. ..... Seattle, WA
Carey, Kimball H. ..... **Columbus, OH**
Carey, Kimberly Lynn ..... Richmond, VA
Carey, Leslie ..... **Chicago, IL**
Carey, Lewis P., Jr. ..... Miami, FL
Carey, Lisa A. ..... Patchogue, NY
Carey, Lisa Agresti ..... Newark, NJ
Carey, Lisa J. ..... Chardon, OH
Carey, Louise E. ..... Buffalo, NY
Carey, Lynn G. ..... **St. Louis, MO**
Carey, Marcus S. ..... Erlanger, KY
Carey, Margaret A. ..... Chicago, IL
Carey, Margaret L. ..... Montrose, CO
Carey, Maria A. ..... Rockville, MD
Carey, Mark P. ..... **Westport, CT**
Carey, Marla S. ..... Spokane, WA
Carey, Mary P. ..... Richmond, CA

Carey, Meismer & McKeon, PLLP
Anaconda, MT
Missoula, MT
Carey, Michael D. ... Blue Island, IL
Carey, Michael J. ... Easthampton, MA
Carey, Michael L. ... Walden, NY
Carey, Michael M. ... Warren, MI
Carey, Michael P. ... Denver, CO
Carey, Michael P. ... Norwich, CT
Carey, Michael Q. ... New York, NY
Carey, Michael R. ... Tampa, FL
Carey, Michael W. ... Charleston, WV
Carey, Michele Stark
Colorado Springs, CO
Denver, CO
Carey, Michelle ... Elmhurst, IL
Carey, Michelle L. ... New York, NY
Carey, Michelle M.
Federal Communications Commission, Common Carrier Bureau, GV
Carey & Mooney, P.C. ... Stoneham, MA
Carey, Moses, Jr. ... Chapel Hill, NC
Carey, Nada M. ... Tallahassee, FL
Carey, Nancy L. ... Chicago, IL
Carey & Nelson ... Silver Spring, MD
Carey, Niemi, Skaggs, McKinley & Stout
Louisville, KY
Carey, Nina Collins ... Traverse City, MI
Carey, Norman C. ... Springfield, OH
Carey, O'Malley, Whitaker & Manson, P.A.
Tampa, FL
Carey, Patrick ... Glendale, CA
Carey, Patrick A. ... Orlando, FL
Carey, Patrick A., P.A. ... Orlando, FL
Carey, Patrick B. ... Northville, MI
Carey, Patrick C. ... Scranton, PA
Carey, Patrick M. ... Erie, PA
Carey, Patrick T. ... Flossmoor, IL
Carey, Paul D. ... Seattle, WA
Carey, Paul E. ... Des Moines, IA
Carey, Paul G. ... Napa, CA
Carey, Paul G. ... Syracuse, NY
Carey, Paul J. ... Harrisburg, PA
Carey, Paul W. ... Worcester, MA
Carey, Paula M. ... Stoneham, MA
Carey, Paulette R. ... Edison, NJ
New York, NY
Carey, Penny L. ... Indianapolis, IN
Carey, Peter B. ... Chicago, IL
Carey, Philip E. ... Sacramento, CA
Carey, Philip J. ... Markham, IL
Carey, Phillip L. ... Hilo, HI
Carey, R. Peter ... Chicago, IL
Carey, Rachel C. ... Spokane, WA
Carey, Ralph P. ... Scranton, PA
Carey, Ralph P., & Associates ... Scranton, PA
Carey, Raymond ... Woodbury, NY
Carey, Raymond J. ... Detroit, MI
Carey, Raymond R. ... Madison, WI
Carey, Richard J. ... Easthampton, MA
Carey, Richard P. ... Springfield, OH
Carey, Richard W. ... Des Moines, IA
Carey, Risdon & Kirk ... Kalamazoo, MI
Carey, Robert B. ... Colorado Springs, CO
Carey, Robert E., Law Office of
Stanton, DE
Carey, Robert G. ... Wilmington, DE
Carey, Robert H. ... New York, NY
Carey, Robert J. ... Kalkaska, MI
Carey, Robert J. ... Berwyn, PA
Carey, Robert J., P.C. ... Kalkaska, MI
Carey, Robert L. ... Portland, OR
Carey, Robert P. ... Cincinnati, OH
Carey, Robert R. ... Greenfield, MA
Carey, Robert S. ... Boston, MA
Carey, Robert S., Jr. ... East Hartford, CT
Carey, Robert W. ... Binghamton, NY
Carey, Robert W. ... Houston, TX
Carey, Robt. E. ... Palo Alto, CA
Carey, Rodger M. ... Mission Viejo, CA
Carey, Roger E. ... Helena, MT
Carey, Ronald C. ... Wilmington, OH
Carey & Ruszczyk ... Buffalo, NY
Carey, Sarah C. ... Washington, DC
Carey, Scott D. ... Nashville, TN
Carey, Scott & Douglas, PLLC
Charleston, WV
Carey, Scott L. ... Chicago, IL
Carey, Scott T. ... Santa Clara, CA
Carey, Shawn W. ... Buffalo, NY
Carey, Steven S. ... Anaconda, MT
Missoula, MT
Carey, Stevens A. ... Los Angeles, CA
Carey, Susan C. ... Syracuse, NY
Carey, Susan M. ... Universal City, CA
Carey, Susan West ... Nashville, TN
Carey, Suzanne Valdez ... Kansas City, KS
Carey, Taylor S. ... Sacramento, CA
Carey, Terry M. ... Dothan, AL
Carey, Thomas C. ... Boston, MA
Carey, Thomas C. ... Inkster, MI
Carey, Thomas D. ... Kalamazoo, MI
Carey, Thomas E. ... Joliet, IL
Carey, Thomas F. ... Napa, CA
Carey, Thomas F. ... Chicago, IL
Carey, Thomas G., Jr. ... Warren, OH
Carey, Thomas H. ... Minneapolis, MN
Carey, Thomas P. ... San Francisco, CA
Carey, Thomas R. ... Chicago, IL
Carey, Thomas S. ... Rumford, ME
Carey, Thomas W. ... Clearwater, FL
Carey, Timothy J. ... Chicago, IL
Carey, Timothy M. ... Cleveland, OH
Carey, Tracey Shaffer ... Department of Justice, Executive Office for United States Attorneys, GV
Carey, W. David P., III ... Honolulu, HI
Carey, Wayne J. ... Wilmington, DE
Carey, Wilford K. ... Hood River, OR
Carey, Willard K. ... La Grande, OR
Carey, William A. ... Boston, MA
Carey, William B. ... Berkeley Springs, WV
Carey, William Barker ... Anchorage, AK
Carey, William C. ... Morristown, NJ
Carey, William C. ... Parsippany, NJ
Carey, William H. ... St. Petersburg, FL
Carey, William H. ... New Bedford, MA
Carey, William J. ... Honolulu, HI
Carey, William L. ... Grayling, MI
Carey, William L. ... Fairfax, VA
Carey, William L., Law Offices of
Grayling, MI
Carey-Wilson, Jacqueline
San Bernardino, CA
Carfagno, Jim, Jr. ... Russellville, AR
Carfagno, Jim, Jr., P.A., Law Offices of
Russellville, AR
Carfley, John R. ... Philipsburg, PA
Carfley, Stephanie ... Lancaster, PA
Carfrae, Dorothy L. ... Downey, CA
Cargas, Martin dePorres ... St. Louis, MO
Cargerman, Alan W. ... Oregon, IL
Cargie, Thomas ... Chicago, IL
Cargil, Meloney J. ... Dallas, TX
Cargile, Ann Peldo ... Nashville, TN
Cargill, Amanda J. ... Spokane, WA
Cargill, Christiane E. ... Los Angeles, CA
Cargill, Emilia K. ... Las Vegas, NV
Cargill, Gary B. ... Charlottesville, VA
Cargill, Harvey, Jr. ... Abilene, TX
Cargill, James P. ... Vinton, VA
Cargill, James P., P.C. ... Vinton, VA
Cargill, Kenneth R. ... North Conway, NH
Cargill, Lance W. ... Oklahoma City, OK
Cargill, Lynn E. ... Mount Clemens, MI
Cargill, Mark W. ... Palestine, TX
Cargill, Michael L. ... Troy, OH
Cargill, R. Mason ... Atlanta, GA
Cargill, Randy V. ... Roanoke, VA
Cargill, Rolin L., III ... Minneapolis, MN
Cargill, Stephen C. ... Oklahoma City, OK
Cargnelutti, Daniel H., Law Offices of
San Diego, CA
Cargo, David F. ... Albuquerque, NM
Cargo, Patrick Michael ... Houston, TX
Cargo, Wm. Andrew ... Denver, CO
Carhart, Edward A. ... Miami, FL
Carhart, Edward A., P.A.
Coral Gables, FL
Miami, FL
Carhart, Judd J. ... Boston, MA
Carhart, Lynette J. ... Morristown, NJ
Carhart, Thaddeus E. ... San Francisco, CA
Cari, Alexander R. ... Newport, RI
Cari, Joseph A., Jr. ... Washington, DC
Chicago, IL
Cari, Samuel R. ... Hudson, WI
Carian, Armand T. ... Albuquerque, NM
Carian, Jacob ... Albuquerque, NM
Cariappa, Padma Tatta ... Cincinnati, OH
Cariati, John J. ... Encino, CA
Carickhoff, David W., Jr ... Wilmington, DE
Carico, Charles Calvert ... Sunland, CA
Carico, Christopher D.
Manhattan Beach, CA
Carico, David B. ... Huntington Park, CA
Carico, Joseph Ray ... Norton, VA
Caridad, Jacquelyn Anne
Philadelphia, PA
Caridad, Miguel ... Miami, FL
Caridad, Roger R. ... Danielson, CT
Cariddi, John J. ... Hackensack, NJ
Carideo, James V. ... Tampa, FL
Carideo, Saml. S. ... Dennis Port, MA
Caridi, Anthony D. ... Houston, TX
Caridi, Carmella ... New York, NY
Caridi, Charles J. ... Springfield, VA
Caridi, Joan ... New York, NY
Caridi, Michael J. ... Washington, DC
Caridi, Nino D. ... Hackensack, NJ
Cariello, Bari B. ... New York, NY
Cariello, William J. ... Garden City, NY
Cariello, William J., III ... New York, NY
Carifa, Cyri K. ... Chicago, IL
Carifa, Kenneth J. ... New Britain, CT
Cariglia, Joseph J. ... Worcester, MA
Cariglio & Associates Co., L.P.A.
North Olmsted, OH
Cariglio, Gennaro, Jr. ... Miami Beach, FL
Cariglio, Terrence L. ... North Olmsted, OH
Carignan, Joseph A. ... San Francisco, CA
Carignan, Katherine Fagan
North Andover, MA
Carignan, Philip J. ... Avon, CT
Carignan, Raymond ... Severna Park, MD
Carignan, Robert A. ... Rochester, NH
Carilli, Albert F. A. ... Hackensack, NJ
Carilli, Joseph F. ... West Haven, CT
Carillo, Christopher ... Dallas, TX
Carimi, Darryl J. ... Metairie, LA
Carimi Law Firm, A Law Corporation
Metairie, LA
Carine, Francis V. ... Albany, NY
Carington, Andrew C. ... Richmond, VA
Carinhas, Jack G., Jr. ... Brownsville, TX
Carinhas & Saldaña, L.L.P. ... Brownsville, TX
Carini, Daniel J. ... Elk Grove Village, IL
Carini, Joseph B., III ... Chicago, IL
Carini, Maria ... Chicago, IL
Carino, Anthony J., Jr. ... Pittsburgh, PA
Carino, Francis J. ... South Windsor, CT
Carino, Lynn ... Philadelphia, PA
Carino, Philip J. ... Cleveland, OH
Cario, Jeffrey P. ... Spring Hill, FL
Cario, Peter ... San Antonio, TX
Carion, Elsa ... New York, NY
Cariotto, John D. ... Lincoln, NE
Caris, Gary Owen ... Los Angeles, CA
Caris, Theodore A. ... Fremont, MI
Carisch, Christian B. ... Indianapolis, IN
Carissimi, Mark M. ... Cleveland, OH
Carissimi, Vincent V. ... Philadelphia, PA
Carita, Joseph A. ... Marlton, NJ
Carita, Michael J. ... Fairfax, VA
Carithers, Hugh A., Jr. ... Jacksonville, FL
Carithers, Kelly P. ... Fayetteville, AR
Carithers, Robert P. ... Evansville, IN
Carius, Jeffrey R. ... St. Louis, MO
Carkhuff, Denise A. ... Cleveland, OH
Carkhuff, Timothy J. ... Topeka, KS
Carkner, Ronald E. ... White Plains, NY
Carl, B. Jeffrey ... Seattle, WA
Carl, Barbara Balling ... Greensburg, PA
Uniontown, PA
Carl, Bernard J. ... New York, NY
Carl, Beverly M. ... Santa Fe, NM
Carl, Colin "C.J." ... Austin, TX
Carl, Daniel R. ... Emeryville, CA
Carl, Dorothy E. ... Philadelphia, PA
Carl, Elizabeth A. ... Reno, NV
Carl, Emory T. ... Bellaire, TX
Carl, Fred, III ... Elkhart, IN
Carl, Gary Robert ... Eugene, OR
Carl, Greta Fell ... Chicago, IL
Carl, H. Charles, III ... Romney, WV
Carl, Head & Triplett ... Louisville, KY
Simpsonville, KY
Carl, Herbert R. ... Cleveland, OH
Carl and Hiza ... Chicago, IL
Carl, Jack D. ... Birmingham, AL
Carl, James F. ... Harrisburg, PA
Carl, James M. ... Sacramento, CA
Carl, Jean P., (Miss) ... Grand Blanc, MI
Carl, John J. ... Newark, NJ
Carl, Kenneth J. ... Los Angeles, CA
Carl, Lee & Coselli, P.C. ... Houston, TX
Carl, Linda Rae ... Los Angeles, CA
Carl, M. Denise Melton ... Richmond, VA
Carl, Matthew J. ... Pittsburgh, PA
Carl, Norma B. ... Richmond, VA
Carl, Norman H. ... Rolling Meadows, IL
Carl, R. Richard, II ... Knoxville, TN
Carl, Robert J., Jr. ... Sioux Falls, SD
Carl, Ronald A. ... La Jolla, CA
Carl, Samuel B. ... Louisville, KY
Simpsonville, KY
Carl, Scott E. ... Escondido, CA
Carl, Stephen J. ... Rochester, NY
Carl, Thomas S. ... West Columbia, TX
Carl, Wilminor M., (Mrs.) ... Sugar Land, TX
Carlacio, Judith Scott ... La Mesa, CA
Carlamere, David F. ... Cherry Hill, NJ
Carlamere, Rowan & Schemanski
Cherry Hill, NJ
Carlan, Andrew E. ... Farmingdale, NY
Carlan, Janine A. ... Washington, DC
Carland, Edward J. ... Amherst, NY
Carland, J. Paul, II ... Fort Lauderdale, FL
Carland, John P., II ... Fort Lauderdale, FL
Carland, Timothy M. ... Beaver, PA
Carlberg, Gene B. ... Bakersfield, CA
Carlberg, Gwendolyn Jo M.
Alexandria, VA
Carlberg, Gwendolyn Jo M. ... Fairfax, VA
Carlberg, James E. ... Indianapolis, IN
Carlburg, Carolyn Hopkins ... Pasadena, CA
Carlburg, Katherine Beecher
New York, NY
Carle, Curtis ... Salem, MO
Carle, Edward S. ... Louisville, KY
Carle, Gina Bilangi ... Teaneck, NJ
Carle, Henry M. ... Des Moines, IA
Carle, John R. ... Claremore, OK
Carle, Keith ... Jonesboro, AR
Carle, Mackie, Power & Ross, LLP
Napa, CA
Santa Rosa, CA
Carle & Mosier ... Claremore, OK
Carle, Stephen D. ... Zephyrhills, FL
Carle, Susan D. ... Washington, DC
Carle, Willard A., III ... Santa Rosa, CA
Carle, William D., III ... Cleveland, OH
Carlebach, P. David ... New York, NY
Carlee, Robert D. ... Anniston, AL
Carleen & Bohanon ... Minneapolis, MN
Carleen, Donald P. ... New York, NY
Carleen, John C. ... Boston, MA
Carleen, John C. ... Minneapolis, MN
Carleen, John C., P.C., Law Office of
Boston, MA
Carlen, Leon C. ... Bethpage, NY
Carlen, Nancy J. ... Carmel, CA
Carleno, Harry E. ... Littleton, CO
Carleno & Parsley, P.C. ... Littleton, CO
Carleo, Anne Marie ... Cambridge, MA
Carleo, James A. ... Pueblo, CO
Carleo, Robert A., Jr. ... Boston, MA
Carles, Alice J. ... South Orange, NJ
Carles, Jenny Ann ... New York, NY
Carles, Robert S. ... Charlotte, NC
Carles, Thomas S., (P.A.) ... Parsippany, NJ
Carlesimo, Anthony G. ... Birmingham, MI
Carlesimo, Mark T. ... Miami, FL
Carlet, David C. ... Chicago, IL
Carlet, Frank A. ... Clifton, NJ
Carlet, Garrison & Klein ... Clifton, NJ
Carleton, Brenda Ford
Department of Justice, GV
Carleton, C. Elaine ... Denver, CO
Carleton, Charles E. ... San Francisco, CA
Carleton, David P. ... Los Angeles, CA
Carleton, Dennis M. ... Pittsburgh, PA
Carleton, Doris Bruton ... Santa Fe, NM
Carleton, Douglas C. ... Los Angeles, CA
Carleton, Eva J. ... Gig Harbor, WA
Carleton, Frederick J. ... Bandon, OR
Carleton, Joseph G., Jr. ... Wells, ME
Carleton, Michael D. ... Lake Charles, LA
Carleton, Michael S. ... San Diego, CA
Carleton, Neil L. ... Sterling, CO
Carleton, Stephen C. ... Baton Rouge, LA
Carletta, Charles F. ... Troy, NY
Carletta, Dennis C. ... Garden City, NY
Carletta, Salvatore J. ... Brooklyn, NY
Carletti, Christopher M. ... Seattle, WA
Carletti, James S. ... San Diego, CA
Carley, Ann Terrell ... Tallahassee, FL
Carley, Anne M. ... New York, NY
Carley, Arthur F. ... Aspen Hill, MD
Carley, Christopher ... Aurora, CO
Carley, David W. ... Baton Rouge, LA
Carley, Deborah L. ... Pontiac, MI
Carley, Dennis E. ... Providence, RI
Carley, Donald M. ... San Francisco, CA
Carley, Francine Roth ... Martinez, CA
Carley, Garry G. ... Troy, MI
Carley, George H. ... Atlanta, GA
Carley, James L.
Commodity Futures Trading Commission, GV
Carley, John H. ... Parsippany, NJ
Carley, John L. ... New York, NY
Carley, Linde Hodson ... Charlotte, NC
Carley, Margaret Murphy ... Portland, OR
Carley, Patricia R. ... Roseland, NJ
Carley, Richard T. ... Trenton, NJ
Carley, Stephen F. ... Atlanta, GA
Carley, Stephen R. ... Charlotte, NC
Carley, Warren E. ... Boston, MA
Carley, William P.
Federal Deposit Insurance Corporation, Division of Bank Supervision, GV
Carlick, Samuel ... Paducah, KY
Carlidge, Mark T. ... Haddonfield, NJ
Philadelphia, PA
Carlier, Lawrence W. ... Batavia, OH
Carlile, Bruce A. ... Killeen, TX
Carlile & Carlile ... Killeen, TX
Carlile, Craig ... Provo, UT
Carlile, Jason S. ... Albany, OR
Carlile, Larry L. ... Denver, CO
Carlile, Maria L. ... San Francisco, CA
Carlile Patchen & Murphy LLP
Columbus, OH
Carlile, Richard F. ... Dayton, OH
Carlile, Robert T. ... Palm City, FL
Carlile, Stephen B. ... Marshall, TX
Carlile, Stephen D. ... Salem, OR
Carlile, Tom A. ... Killeen, TX
Carlin, Allan H. ... New York, NY
Carlin, Amy D. ... New York, NY
Carlin, Andrew C. ... Yonkers, NY
Carlin, Angela G. ... Cleveland, OH
Carlin, Barbara A. ... Lewiston, ME
Portland, ME
Carlin, Barbara M. ... Pittsburgh, PA
Carlin, Bradshaw, Thomas & Yeatman L.L.P. ... Washington, DC
Bethesda, MD
Carlin, Brian E. ... Carmel, NY
Carlin, Brian J. ... Burlington, NJ
Huntingdon Valley, PA
Carlin, C. Brian ... Bethesda, MD
Carlin & Ceccia ... Long Beach, CA
Carlin, Christine F. ... Libertyville, IL
Carlin, Cindy ... Marina Del Rey, CA
Carlin, Clair M. ... Youngstown, OH
Carlin, David H. ... New York, NY
Carlin, David P. ... Columbus, OH
Carlin, Dennis J. ... Chicago, IL
Carlin, Donald P. ... Binghamton, NY
Carlin, E. Austin ... Bethesda, MD
Carlin, Elliot ... New York, NY
Carlin, Francine Galante ... New York, NY
Carlin, Gary R. ... Long Beach, CA
Carlin, Gary R., A Professional Corporation
Long Beach, CA
Carlin, Haral E. ... Fayetteville, NC
Carlin, Hellstrom & Bittner ... Moline, IL
Rock Island, IL
Davenport, IA
Carlin, Hugh A. ... Lakewood, OH
Carlin, Hugh C. ... Buffalo, NY
Carlin, Ira S. ... Escondido, CA
Carlin, Ira S., A Professional Corporation
Escondido, CA
Carlin, J. Christopher ... Notre Dame, IN
Carlin, J. David ... Washington, DC
Carlin, Jack G. ... Santa Barbara, CA
Carlin, James H. ... Santa Monica, CA
Carlin, James M. ... Sioux City, IA
Carlin, James T. ... Davenport, IA
Carlin, Jane D. ... New York, NY
Carlin, Jay Strike ... Harrisburg, PA
Carlin, Jeffrey J. ... Kansas City, KS
Carlin, John B., Jr. ... Bloomfield Hills, MI
Carlin, John C., Jr. ... Pittsburgh, PA
Carlin, John D. ... New York, NY
Carlin, John H. ... Cleveland, OH
Carlin, John J. ... Davenport, IA
Carlin, John J. ... Binghamton, NY
Carlin, John J. ... Forty Fort, PA
Carlin, John J., III ... Baltimore, MD
Carlin, John J., Jr. ... Florham Park, NJ
Carlin, John S. ... Fort Myers, FL
Carlin, Joseph J. ... Huntingdon Valley, PA
Carlin, Joseph S. ... Washington, DC
Carlin, Kevin J. ... Hackensack, NJ
Carlin & Kienitz, P.A. ... Lewiston, ME
Portland, ME
Carlin, Kimberly ... Independence, MO
Carlin, Kimberly, P.C. ... Independence, MO

Carlin, Larry M. ... New York, NY
Carlin, Lee S. ... Jacksonville, FL
Carlin, Lyndell M., Jr. ... Basking Ridge, NJ
Carlin, M. Roger ... Pineville, MO
Carlin, Maddock, Fay & Cerbone, P.C.
Florham Park, NJ
Morristown, NJ
Newark, NJ
Carlin, Mark S. ... Washington, DC
Carlin, Marnie S. ... Los Angeles, CA
Carlin, Michael B. ... Albany, NY
Carlin, Michael L. ... New York, NY
Carlin, Mitchell I. ... New York, NY
Carlin, Montgomery R. ... New York, NY
Carlin, Nancy G. ... Long Beach, CA
Carlin, Nicholas A. ... San Francisco, CA
Carlin, Nicholas W. ... Louisville, KY
Carlin, Norman F. ... San Francisco, CA
Carlin, Paul V. ... Baltimore, MD
Carlin, Paul V., III ... Spokane, WA
Carlin, Philip R. ... West Orange, NJ
Carlin, Robert Michael ... Los Angeles, CA
Carlin, Robin H. ... New York, NY
Carlin, Roy H. ... New York, NY
Carlin, Sarah R. ... Chicago, IL
Carlin, Sean M. ... Morristown, NJ
Carlin, Stanley ... Teaneck, NJ
Carlin, Stephen C. ... Dallas, TX
Carlin, Steven B. ... New York, NY
Carlin, Susan Marcotte ... Providence, RI
Carlin, Thomas F. ... Spring Lake, NJ
Carlin, Timothy J. ... Minneapolis, MN
Carlin, Tracy S. ... Jacksonville, FL
Carlin & Vasvari, LLC ... Youngstown, OH
Carlin, Victor E. ... Albuquerque, NM
Carlin, Wayne M. ... New York, NY
Carlin, William J. ... Bristol, PA
Langhorne, PA
Carline, Joseph J. ... New York, NY
Carline, William T., III ... Warwick, RI
Carlineo, Daniel S. ... Washington, DC
Carliner, David ... Washington, DC
Carliner, David Daniel ... Towson, MD
Carliner, Remes and Mirbagheri-Smith, P.C.
Washington, DC
Carling, Francis ... New York, NY
Carling, Richard J. ... Salt Lake City, UT
Carling-Smith, Malcolm R. ... Sacramento, CA
Carlini, Anthony C., Jr.
Poughkeepsie, NY
Carlini, Lawrence J. ... Cleveland, OH
Carlino, Anthony M. ... Hackensack, NJ
Carlino, Christine A. ... Encinitas, CA
Carlino, James C. ... Indianapolis, IN
Carlino, Jodi-Ann ... Wilmington, DE
Carlino, Joseph F. ... Melville, NY
Mineola, NY
Carlino, Mark A. ... Phoenix, AZ
Carlino, V. Lynn ... Eastpointe, MI
Carlins, David J. ... Chicago, IL
Carlins, Joel M. ... Chicago, IL
Carlins and Moss ... Chicago, IL
Carlin-Sasaki, Julie B. ... New York, NY
Carlinsky, Michael B. ... New York, NY
Carlinsky, Mitchell J. ... Garden City, NY
Carlis, Brian A. ... Princeton, NJ
Carlis, George W. ... Milwaukee, WI
Carlis, Michael D. ... Baltimore, MD
Carlise, Andrea S. ... Oakland, CA
Carlisi, Joseph ... Atlanta, GA
Carlisi, Roy, Jr. ... Buffalo, NY
Carlisle, Alan ... Rancho Cucamonga, CA
Carlisle, Calvin E. ... Atlanta, GA
Carlisle & Carlisle, P.C. ... Birmingham, AL
Carlisle, Catherine M. ... Redondo Beach, CA
Carlisle, Dale L. ... Tacoma, WA
Carlisle, Daniel T. ... Wadena, MN
Carlisle, David R. ... Miami, FL
Carlisle, Debra L. ... Treasury Department, Internal Revenue Service, GV
Carlisle, Edward Lane ... Jackson, MS
Carlisle, Elaine L. ... Atlanta, GA
Carlisle, Frances B. ... New York, NY
Carlisle, Gerald K. ... Cleveland, OH
Carlisle, Jack E., Jr. ... Shreveport, LA
Carlisle, James R., II ... Pittsburgh, PA
Carlisle, James T. ... West Palm Beach, FL
Carlisle, Jay C., II ... White Plains, NY
Carlisle, Jeffrey J. ... Washington, DC
Carlisle, Jennifer ... Little Rock, AR
Carlisle, Joe Y. ... Macon, GA
Carlisle, John C. ... Grosse Pointe Farms, MI
Carlisle, John Wright ... Atlanta, GA
Carlisle, Jonathan D. ... Greenwich, CT
Carlisle, Judith L. ... Vallejo, CA
Carlisle, Keith McLain ... New York, NY
Carlisle, Kevin L. ... Seattle, WA
Carlisle Law Office ... Fort Lauderdale, FL
Carlisle, Linda E. ... Washington, DC
Carlisle, Lynn ... Dallas, TX
Carlisle, Marshall N. ... Fayetteville, AR
Carlisle, Matthew C. ... Dayton, OH
Carlisle, McNellie & Rini Co., L.P.A.
Cleveland, OH
Columbus, OH
Carlisle, Peter S. ... Portland, ME
Carlisle, R. Jeff ... Los Angeles, CA
Carlisle, Ralph E. ... Decatur, GA
Carlisle, Randall A. ... Chicago, IL
Carlisle, Richard G., (P.C.)
Kansas City, MO
Carlisle, Richard L. ... Treasury Department, Internal Revenue Service, GV
Carlisle, Robert M., Jr. ... Winston-Salem, NC
Carlisle, Rose-Marie T. ... Columbia, SC
Carlisle, Russell E., (P.A.)
Fort Lauderdale, FL
Campton, NH
Carlisle, Russell E., P.A., Law Offices of
Campton, NH
Carlisle, Sam Q., II ... Rocky Mount, NC
Carlisle, Sarah J. ... Birmingham, AL
Carlisle, Sheila A. ... Indianapolis, IN
Carlisle, Stephen M., (P.A.)
Fort Lauderdale, FL
Carlisle, Terry ... Birmingham, AL
Carlisle, Thomas J. ... Springfield, IL
Carlisle, Thos. F. ... Dallas, TX
Carlisle, Valerie Lynn ... Grenada, MS
Jackson, MS
Oxford, MS
Carlisle, Von Allan ... Biloxi, MS
Carlisle, W. Scott, III ... Portland, ME
Carlisle, W. Todd ... Birmingham, AL
Carlisle, William O. ... Running Springs, CA
Carlisle, Wm. L. ... New York, NY
Carlitz, Debbie A. ... South Plainfield, NJ
South Plainfield, NJ
Feasterville, PA
Carlitz & Eisenberg, P.C.
South Plainfield, NJ
Feasterville, PA
Carlitz, William M. ... Philadelphia, PA
Carlitz, William M., P.C. ... Philadelphia, PA
Carll, Connie Preslar ... The Woodlands, TX
Carll, James H. ... Haddonfield, NJ
Carll, Lloyd H. ... The Woodlands, TX
Carll, Robert W. ... Richmond, VA
Carlman, Leonard R. ... Jackson, WY
Carlo, Alan M. ... Baltimore, MD
Hunt Valley, MD
Carlo, Armando, III ... Chicago, IL
Carlo, Christopher J. ... San Jose, CA
Carlo, Dorothy ... Northampton, MA
Carlo & Dubos ... New York, NY
Carlo, Gerardo A. ... New York, NY
San Juan, PR
Carlo, James N. ... Buffalo, NY
Carlo, Jorge S. ... San Juan, PR
Carlo, Juan C. ... Washington, DC
Carlo, Katherine D. ... Alexandria, VA
Carlo, L. Heather ... Los Angeles, CA
Carlo, Meredith A. ... Washington, DC
Carlock, Chad ... Davis, CA
Carlock, Charles ... Indianapolis, IN
Carlock, David, P.C. ... Dallas, TX
Carlock, G. David ... Dallas, TX
Carlock, J. Gregory ... Melville, NY
New York, NY
Carlock, Kevin B. ... Marietta, GA
Carlock, Lisa T. ... Sacramento, CA
Carlock, Mahlon W., II ... Indianapolis, IN
Carlock, Steve ... Indianapolis, IN
Carlock, Thomas E. ... Englewood, CO
Carlock, Thomas R. ... Ardmore, OK
Carlock, Thomas S., (P.C.) ... Atlanta, GA
Carlo Linares, Osvaldo ... San Juan, PR
Carlon, Cynthia A. ... Bloomington, IL
Carlon, James E. ... Pierre, SD
Carlon, John A. ... Bloomington, IL
Carlon, John T., Jr. ... Fort Lauderdale, FL
Carlonas, Jane M. ... Scranton, PA
Carlone, John J. ... Brielle, NJ
Carloni, August G. ... Los Angeles, CA
Carloni, Carla J. ... Washington, DC
Carloni, Linda L. ... San Francisco, CA
Carlos, Bertha J. ... San Diego, CA
Carlos, Guillermo A. ... Lexington, KY
Carlos, Jennifer M. ... Louisville, KY
Carlos, John C. ... Pittsburgh, PA
Carlos, Kelly A. ... Atlanta, GA
Carlos, Kimberly C. ... Kansas City, MO
Carlos Law Firm, The, A Professional Corporation ... Orange, CA
Carlos, Marc X. ... San Diego, CA
Carlos, Mary Jo ... Orange, CA
Carlos, Natalie J. ... Miami, FL
Carlos, Pamela A. ... Philadelphia, PA
Carlos, Thomas P. ... Miami, FL
Carlos, Thomas P., P.A. ... Miami, FL
Carlos, Tierney Michael
Department of the Navy, Office of the Judge Advocate General, GV
Carlotti, Carl M. ... Erie, PA
Carlotti, Stephen J. ... Boston, MA
Providence, RI
Carlotto, Thomas E. ... Boston, MA
Providence, RI
Carlough, Leslie A. ... Portland, OR
Carlovsky, Michael A. ... Bakersfield, CA
Carlow, Donald N. ... Hartford, CT
Carlow, Jack ... Los Angeles, CA
Carlow, Kathleen M. ... Albuquerque, NM
Carlow, Nina C. ... Bronx, NY
Carlowicz, Andrew J., Jr.
New Brunswick, NJ
Carlozzi, Jane M. ... Farmington, CT
Carlozzi, Joanne ... New York, NY
Carlozzi, Joyce E. ... Columbus, OH
Carlozzi, Linda R. ... New York, NY
Carlozzi, Mark J. ... Costa Mesa, CA
Carlquist, Mark S. ... Los Gatos, CA
Carls, David H. ... Wellesley, MA
Carls, David R. ... Atlanta, GA
Carls, Harry W., III ... Orlando, FL
Carls, Krista Pyle ... Aurora, IL
Carls, Laurie Paro ... Canton, NY
Carlsen, Christopher ... New York, NY
Carlsen, Christopher, Law Offices of
Santa Fe, NM
Carlsen, David R. ... Minneapolis, MN
Carlsen, Elliot J. ... Seattle, WA
Carlsen, Ernest G. ... Sioux Falls, SD
Carlsen, Errol ... Portland, OR
Carlsen, James ... Linthicum, MD
Carlsen, Nicki Marie Varyu
Los Angeles, CA
Carlsen, Robert B. ... North Port, FL
Greenfield, MA
Carlsen, Robert C. ... Glendale, NY
Carlsen, Robert C. ... Sleepy Hollow, NY
Carlsen, Susan B. ... Sacramento, CA
Carlsmith Ball ... Los Angeles, CA
Washington, DC
Hagåtña, GU
Hilo, HI
Honolulu, HI
Kailua-Kona, HI
Kapolei, HI
Wailuku, HI
Saipan, TT
Carlsmith, Donn W. ... Honolulu, HI
Carlsmith, Robert W. ... Kamuela, HI
Carlson, A. David ... Houston, TX
Carlson, Alan ... San Francisco, CA
Carlson, Alan B. ... San Jose, CA
Carlson, Alan D. ... Fort Collins, CO
Carlson, Alan G. ... Minneapolis, MN
Carlson, Alan L. ... Austin, TX
Carlson, Alan R. ... Bartlesville, OK
Carlson, Alan S. ... Philadelphia, PA
Carlson, Alex E. ... Miami Springs, FL
Carlson, Alfred J. ... Philadelphia, PA
Carlson, Amy L. ... Washington, DC
Carlson, Anita P. ... Boston, MA
Carlson, Ann Farrissey ... White Plains, NY
Carlson, Anne D. ... Milaca, MN
Carlson, Ann-Marie ... Rockford, IL
Carlson, Arthur B. ... Harvard, IL
Carlson, Arthur W., (A P.C.)
Santa Barbara, CA
Carlson, Beth A. ... West Palm Beach, FL
Carlson, Beth E. ... Minneapolis, MN
Carlson, Brent A. ... Grand Junction, CO
Carlson, Brett A. ... Phoenix, AZ
Carlson, Brian Alan ... Dallas, TX
Carlson, Brian D. ... New York, NY
Carlson, Brian T. ... Bloomington, MN
Carlson, Brian T., P.A. ... Bloomington, MN
Carlson, Bruce H. ... Fargo, ND
Carlson, Bruce L. ... Springfield, IL
Carlson, C. Craig ... Newport Beach, CA
Carlson, C. Kent ... Seattle, WA
Carlson, C. Ray ... Valencia, CA
Carlson, C. Ray, A Law Corporation
Valencia, CA
Carlson, C. Theodore ... Albany, NY
Carlson, C. William, Jr.
Huntington Beach, CA
Carlson, C. William, Jr., Inc., A Professional Corp. ... Huntington Beach, CA
Carlson, Calladine & Peterson LLP
Los Angeles, CA
San Francisco, CA
Carlson, Candace J. ... Cheyenne, OK
Carlson, Carl J. ... Seattle, WA
Carlson & Carlson, P.C.
Breckenridge, CO
Frisco, CO
Carlson, Carol ... Chicago, IL
Carlson, Carol D. ... Grand Rapids, MI
Carlson, Carol E. ... Dayton, OH
Carlson, Carolyn ... Fort Lauderdale, FL
Carlson, Caryl L. ... Wilmington, DE
Carlson, Casey K. ... Clearwater, FL
Carlson, Charles A. ... Tampa, FL
Carlson, Charles A., III ... Harlingen, TX
Carlson, Charles D. ... Eugene, OR
Carlson, Charles D. ... Vancouver, WA
Carlson, Charles E., Jr. ... Greensboro, NC
Carlson, Charles M. ... Annapolis, MD
Carlson, Cheryl Fandel ... Tacoma, WA
Carlson, Chris ... Plano, TX
Carlson, Chris A. ... Los Angeles, CA
Carlson, Christina M. ... Los Angeles, CA
Carlson, Christopher A. ... Bismarck, ND
Carlson, Christopher J. ... Philadelphia, PA
Carlson, Christopher S. ... Detroit, MI
Carlson, Christopher T. ... Franklin, MA
Wellesley, MA
Carlson, Christopher T. ... Columbus, OH
Carlson, Clair A. ... Santa Cruz, CA
Carlson, Clair A., Jr. ... Boston, MA
Carlson, Claire F. ... Fort Dodge, IA
Carlson, Claire W. ... Esopus, NY
Carlson, Clare ... Saratoga, CA
Carlson, Clarence G. ... Birmingham, MI
Carlson, Clint D. ... Fort Worth, TX
Carlson, Crafton N. ... Fort Lauderdale, FL
Carlson, Craig A. ... Anchorage, AK
Carlson, Craig R. ... Columbus, OH
Carlson, Craig W. ... Georgetown, TX
Killeen, TX
Round Rock, TX
Temple, TX
Waco, TX
Carlson, Curtis ... Miami, FL
Carlson, Curtis G. ... Richmond, VA
Carlson, Curtis W. ... Cos Cob, CT
Carlson, Cynthia D. ... Eugene, OR
Carlson, D. Bret ... New York, NY
Carlson, Dale A. ... Mazomanie, WI
Prairie Du Sac, WI
Carlson, Dale Alan ... Harvard, IL
Carlson, Dale L. ... New Haven, CT
Carlson, Dana James ... Fairfax, VA
Carlson, Darin W. ... Portland, OR
Carlson, Darren R. ... Omaha, NE
Carlson, David A. ... Fairbanks, AK
Carlson, David A. ... Farmington, MN
Carlson, David B. ... Chicago, IL
Carlson, David B. ... Evanston, IL
Carlson, David G. ... New York, NY
Carlson, David George ... Springfield, MA
Carlson, David J. ... Short Hills, NJ
Carlson, David J. ... New Berlin, WI
Carlson, David John ... Spokane, WA
Carlson, David L. ... Salem, OR
Carlson, David L. ... Richmond, VA
Carlson, David M. ... Salt Lake City, UT
Carlson, David P. ... Berlin, NH
Carlson, David R. ... Chicago, IL
Carlson, David R. ... Vale, OR
Carlson, David R. ... Spokane, WA
Carlson, David R. ... Portage, WI
Carlson, David V. ... Seattle, WA
Carlson, Deborah DiVerdi ... Boston, MA
Carlson, Deborah W. ... Chicago, IL
Carlson, Dee Kevin ... Salem, OR
Carlson, Dennis E. ... Chicago, IL
Carlson, Dennis G. ... St. Paul, MN
Carlson, Dennis R. ... Grand Rapids, MI
Carlson, Don D. ... Minneapolis, MN
Carlson, Donald H. ... Milwaukee, WI
Carlson, Donald L. ... Glen Ellyn, IL
Carlson, Donald R. ... Washington, DC
Carlson, Donald W. ... San Francisco, CA
Carlson, Douglas C. ... Cleveland, OH
Carlson, Douglas Fred ... Berkeley, CA
Carlson, Douglas R. ... Chicago, IL
Carlson, Douglas R. ... West Des Moines, IA
Carlson, Duane D. ... Scottsdale, AZ
Carlson, Eben B. ... Seattle, WA
Carlson, Edward D. ... Clearwater, FL
Carlson, Edward R. ... Phoenix, AZ
Carlson, Edwin A. ... Los Angeles, CA
Carlson, Eileen E. ... Riverton, NJ
Carlson, Eileen Shannon ... Washington, DC
Carlson, Eldon R. ... Kent, WA
Carlson, Ellen C. ... Norfolk, VA
Carlson, Eric ... San Francisco, CA
Carlson, Eric B. ... Los Angeles, CA
Carlson, Eric D. ... Milwaukee, WI
Carlson, Eric H. ... Lake Oswego, OR
Carlson, Eric J. ... Chicago, IL
Carlson, Eric Jon ... Edwardsville, IL
Carlson, Eric Matthew ... Los Angeles, CA
Carlson, Eric S. (Rick) ... Seattle, WA
Carlson, Erik B. ... Denver, CO
Carlson, Erin C. ... North Adams, MA
Carlson & Fabish, P.S. ... Seattle, WA
Carlson, Frank K. ... Union, MO
Carlson, Frank S. ... Elyria, OH
Carlson, Gary E. ... St. Paul, MN
Carlson, Gary E. ... Santa Fe, NM
Carlson, Gary G. ... St. Paul, MN
Carlson, Gary L. ... Medford, WI
Carlson, Gary M. ... Beaverton, OR
Carlson, Gary W. ... Andover, MA
Carlson, Gayle B., P.A. ... Tampa, FL
Carlson, Gayle Buttram ... Tampa, FL
Carlson, George C., Jr. ... Batesville, MS
Carlson, George L. ... Minneapolis, MN
Carlson, Glenn A. ... Jefferson City, MO
Carlson, Glenn A. ... East Greenwich, RI
Carlson, Glenn H. ... Washington, DC
Carlson, Gordon G. ... Roseburg, OR
Carlson, Grady K. ... McLean, VA
Carlson, Gregory ... Faribault, MN
Carlson, Hammond & Paddock, L.L.C.
Denver, CO
Carlson, Hans K. ... Jackson, MN
Carlson, Harry L. ... Boston, MA
Carlson, Harry V., Jr. ... Milwaukee, WI
Carlson, Herbert E., Jr. ... Hartford, CT
Carlson, J. Kem ... Dallas, TX
Carlson, Jack A. ... Cable, WI
Washburn, WI
Carlson, Jack W. ... Minneapolis, MN
Carlson, James B. ... Birmingham, AL
Carlson, James B. ... New York, NY
Carlson, James Edgar ... Blossburg, PA
Wellsboro, PA
Carlson, James F. ... Chicago, IL
Carlson, James L. ... Elkhorn, WI
Carlson, James R. ... Chicago, IL
Carlson, James R. ... Rochester, MN
Carlson, James R. ... Cleveland, OH
Carlson, James R., Jr. ... Grand Forks, ND
Carlson, Jane ... Greeley, CO
Carlson, Jane Fisher ... Franklin, MA
Carlson, Janet R. ... Chicago, IL
Carlson, Janet R. ... Boston, MA
Carlson, Janis Felder ... Fort Lauderdale, FL
Carlson, Janis Felder, P.A.
Fort Lauderdale, FL
Carlson, Jared M.
Federal Communications Commission, Common Carrier Bureau, GV
Carlson, Jay D. ... Fargo, ND
Carlson, Jay L. ... Washington, DC
Carlson, Jeffery E. ... Tulsa, OK
Carlson, Jeffery J. ... Los Angeles, CA
Carlson, Jeffrey B. ... Eden Prairie, MN
Carlson, Jeffrey G. ... Minneapolis, MN
Carlson, Jeffrey R. ... Rockford, IL
Carlson, Jennie P. ... Cincinnati, OH
Carlson, Jennifer Anne Slater
Milwaukee, WI
Carlson, Jerome Gaylord ... Camarillo, CA
Carlson, Jo Ann M. ... Traverse City, MI
Carlson, Joel ... Kew Gardens, NY
Carlson, John ... New York, NY
Carlson, John A. ... Southfield, MI
Carlson, John A., Jr. ... Louisville, CO
Carlson, John B. ... Nashville, TN
Carlson, John C. ... Reading, PA
Carlson, John C. ... Friday Harbor, WA
Carlson, John C. ... Madison, WI
Carlson, John Charles, Jr. ... Madison, WI
Carlson, John D. ... Bakersfield, CA

Carmel, Thomas D. ....Houston, TX
Carmel, Timothy J. ....San Luis Obispo, CA
Carmeli, Margaret B. ....Middletown, NJ
Carmeli, Michele ....Trabuco Canyon, CA
Carmell, David Laurence ....Deerfield, IL
Carmell, Sherman M. ....Chicago, IL
Carmell, William A. ....New York, NY
Carmella, Angela C. ....Newark, NJ
Carmella, Bradley R. ....Hamilton, OH
Carmella, James D. ....Indiana, PA
Carmellino, Joseph S. ....San Diego, CA
Carmely, Klara ....Pasadena, CA
Carmen, Bruce L. ....Chicago, IL
Carmen, Christopher S. ....Redlands, CA
Carmen, D. Anderson
Winston-Salem, NC
Carmen, Dennis V. ....Houston, TX
Carmen, Diane M. ....Edgewater, CO
Carmen, Joseph A. ....Haddonfield, NJ
Carmen, Kathleen P. ....Media, PA
Carmen, Lynn ....Los Angeles, CA
Carmen, Melinda L. ....Washington, DC
Carmen & Muss, P.L.L.C. ....Washington, DC
Carmen, Peter D. ....Syracuse, NY
Carmen, Robert M. ....Great Neck, NY
New York, NY
Carmical, J. Stanley ....Lumberton, NC
Carmical, Lee A. ....Brunswick, GA
Carmichael, Andrew J., Jr.
Virginia Beach, VA
Carmichael, B. Jay, Jr. ....Dallas, TX
Carmichael, Beverly K. ....Dallas, TX
Carmichael, Brian Q. ....Houston, TX
Carmichael, Carson, III ....Raleigh, NC
Carmichael, C. E., Jr. ....Tuscumbia, AL
Carmichael, Daniel P. ....Indianapolis, IN
Carmichael, David E. ....Eugene, OR
Carmichael, David H. ....Scottsdale, AZ
Carmichael, David P. ....Covina, CA
Carmichael, David R.
Newport Beach, CA
Carmichael, Fred M. ....New Bern, NC
Carmichael, Gardner, Turner and Brown
Springfield, MO
Carmichael, H. Alan ....Lubbock, TX
Carmichael, H. Wayne ....Bloomington, IL
Pekin, IL
Carmichael, Hope Derby ....Raleigh, NC
Carmichael, J. Dwight ....Hillsboro, TX
Carmichael, Jacquelynn D.
Salt Lake City, UT
Carmichael, James E. ....St. Charles, MO
Carmichael, James T. ....Washington, DC
Carmichael, Jay S. ....Tomah, WI
Carmichael, Jeffery L. ....Wichita, KS
Carmichael, Jeffrey L. ....Indianapolis, IN
Carmichael, Jill A. ....Taunton, MA
Carmichael, John B., III ....Irvine, CA
Carmichael, John B., Jr. ....Las Vegas, NV
Carmichael, John H. ....Los Angeles, CA
Carmichael, John H. ....Charlotte, NC
Carmichael, John L. ....Wichita, KS
Carmichael, Joseph P. ....Salem, MA
Carmichael, Kepten D. ....Indianapolis, IN
Carmichael, Kevin ....Naples, FL
Carmichael Law Offices, S.C. ....Tomah, WI
Carmichael, Lawrence R. ....Somerset, KY
Carmichael, LeRoy ....Trenton, NJ
Carmichael, Linda M. ....Wilmington, DE
Carmichael, Lloyd Joseph
Springfield, MO
Carmichael, Lynne A. ....San Francisco, CA
Carmichael, Malcolm N.
Montgomery, AL
Carmichael, Martin ....Westport, CT
Carmichael, Martin, III, (P.C.)
Boston, MA
Carmichael, Michelle Davis
Indianapolis, IN
Carmichael, Patricia Ann
Newport Beach, CA
Carmichael, Paul D. ....Cupertino, CA
Carmichael, Peter G. ....Baton Rouge, LA
Carmichael & Powell, Professional
Corporation ....Phoenix, AZ
Carmichael, R. Cartwright, Jr. .....Charlotte, NC
Carmichael, Ralph W. ....New York, NY
Carmichael, Rebecca S. ....Austin, TX
Carmichael, Robert A. ....Bellingham, WA
Carmichael, Ronald W. ....Phoenix, AZ
Carmichael, Shaleim M. ....Washington, DC
Carmichael, Tamara ....Miami, FL
Carmichael, Terri Lyn ....New Orleans, LA
Carmichael, Thomas L. ....Jasper, AL
Carmichael, V. F. ....Knoxville, TN
Carmichael, Vicki L. ....Jeffersonville, IN
Carmichael, W. Russell ....Media, PA
Carmichael, William C., II ....Atlanta, GA
Carmichael, William G. ....Clinton, LA
Carmichael, William H. ....Cedar Rapids, IA
Carmichael, William K. ....Atlanta, GA
Carmicino, Benedict G. ....Roseland, NJ
Carmicino, Bonny J. Schwenke
Florham Park, NJ
Carmick, Stephen T. ....Chehalis, WA
Carmien, Donald C. ....Vestal, NY
Carmignani, Marco Hygino ....Chatham, NJ
Carmignani, Robert D. ....Philadelphia, PA
Carmikle, Jan ....Davis, CA
Carmin, M. Donald ....Toledo, OH
Carmin, Michael L. ....Bloomington, IN
Carmine, Alison A. ....Fort Lauderdale, FL
Carmine, Colton C. ....Oakland, CA
Carmine, Ferrell D.
Department of Commerce,
Patent and Trademark Office, GV
Carmine, Kenneth F. ....Newark, DE
Wilmington, DE

Carminucci, James A.
Saratoga Springs, NY
Carmody, Arthur R., Jr. ....Shreveport, LA
Carmody, Brendan P. ....Charlotte, NC
Carmody, Brian James ....Mineola, NY
Carmody, Carolyn P. ....Washington, DC
Carmody, Charles E. ....Utica, MI
Carmody, David C. ....West Haven, CT
Carmody, Don T. ....Woodstock, NY
Carmody, Donald P.
Department Of Health And Human Services,
Public Health Service, GV
Carmody, Donald R. ....St. Louis, MO
Carmody, Edward L. ....Davenport, IA
Carmody, Ellen S. ....Grand Rapids, MI
Carmody, Francis Michael
Shreveport, LA
Carmody, Frederick A. ....Marco Island, FL
Carmody, Gerard T. ....St. Louis, MO
Carmody, James A. ....Houston, TX
Carmody, James C. ....Yakima, WA
Carmody, James P. ....Clayton, MO
Carmody, James P. ....Richlands, VA
Carmody, James R. ....Elmira, NY
Carmody, Jane H. ....New York, NY
Carmody, Jerry L. ....La Mesa, CA
Carmody, John J., Jr. ....Bethesda, MD
Carmody, John J., Jr. ....Albuquerque, NM
Carmody, John T., Jr. ....Miami, FL
Stuart, FL
Carmody, Kathleen Marie ....Buffalo, NY
Carmody Law Offices ....Albuquerque, NM
Carmody, Lisa A. ....San Jose, CA
Carmody MacDonald, P.C. ....St. Louis, MO
Carmody, Michael ....New York, NY
Carmody, Michael J. ....McLean, VA
Carmody, Michelle C. ....Denver, CO
Carmody, Nikki Nagori ....Dallas, TX
Carmody, Patrick ....West Chester, PA
Carmody, Patrick J. ....New York, NY
Carmody, Patrick L. ....Omaha, NE
Carmody, Patrick M. ....Elgin, IL
Carmody, Patrick M., Jr.
Dearborn Heights, MI
Carmody, Richard P. ....Birmingham, AL
Carmody, Roger T. ....San Francisco, CA
Carmody, Sean J. ....Pittsburgh, PA
Carmody, Sheila ....Phoenix, AZ
Carmody, Stephanie Morris
Washington, DC
Carmody, Stephen J. ....Jackson, MS
Carmody, Stephen R. ....Carlinville, IL
Carmody, Susan L. ....New York, NY
Carmody, Thomas E. ....Phoenix, AZ
Carmody, Thomas H. ....Stoughton, MA
Carmody, Thomas P. ....Carlinville, IL
Carmody, Timothy J. ....Olathe, KS
Carmody, Timothy R. ....Waterbury, CT
Carmody & Torrance LLP
New Haven, CT
Southbury, CT
Waterbury, CT
Carmody, Victor W., Jr. ....Jackson, MS
Carmody, Victor W., Jr., P.A.
Jackson, MS
Carmody, Vincent J. ....Newtonville, NY
Troy, NY
Carmody & Welch ....La Mesa, CA
Carmody, William Christopher
Dallas, TX
Carmody, William F. ....Glen Ellyn, IL
Carmody, William J. ....Washington, DC
Carmody, William W. ....Munising, MI
Carmody & Yokubaitis, L.L.P.
Houston, TX
Carmody-Roberts, Linda ....Katonah, NY
Carmodys L.L.P. ....Dallas, TX
Carmon, Angela Ingram .....Winston-Salem, NC
Carmon & Carmon ....New York, NY
Carmon, Haggai ....New York, NY
Carmon, Rakeffet ....New York, NY
Carmona, Anthony G. ....Daytona Beach, FL
Carmona, Frank T. ....Galveston, TX
Carmona, Gale P. ....Valparaiso, IN
Carmona, Lisa A. ....West Palm Beach, FL
Carmona, Paul D. ....Austin, TX
Carmona de Polanco, Migdalia
San Juan, PR
Carmosino, Albert A. ....Denver, CO
Carmosino, John ....Lyndhurst, OH
Carmouche, Charles H. ....Houston, TX
Carmouche, Donald T. ....Gonzales, LA
Carmouche, H. Purvis, Jr. ....Amite, LA
Carmouche, Hamilton L. ....Merrillville, IN
Carmouche, John H. ....Gonzales, LA
Carmouche Law Firm, The, A Professional
Corporation ....Lake Charles, LA
Carmouche, Paul J. ....Shreveport, LA
Carmouche, Virginia M. ....Lake Charles, LA
Carn, Daniel L. ....York, PA
Carn, William C., III ....Dothan, AL
Carnabuci, Joseph S. ....Brockton, MA
Carnaby, Clark W. ....Tarpon Springs, FL
Carnaby, Henry N. ....Omaha, NE
Carnagey, Roger A. ....Oakland, CA
Carnaghan, Robert D. ....Baltimore, MD
Carnago, Gerald J. ....Troy, MI
Carnago, James V. ....Troy, MI
Carnago, James V., P.C., Law Offices of
Detroit, MI
Troy, MI
Carnahan, A. Vernon ....New York, NY
Carnahan, Burt K. ....New Orleans, LA
Carnahan, Carole Deeny ....Fort Collins, CO
Carnahan, Colin J. ....Nashville, TN
Carnahan, Debra Ann ....St. Louis, MO
Carnahan, Debrha J. ....Boise, ID
Carnahan, Donald Dean ....Dedham, MA

Carnahan, Douglas G. ....Torrance, CA
Carnahan, Edward J. ....Mission Hills, CA
Carnahan, Elizabeth A. ....Nashville, TN
Carnahan, Evans, Cantwell & Brown, P.C.
Springfield, MO
Carnahan, Frank C. ....Springfield, MO
Carnahan & Garvin, L.L.C.
St. Louis, MO
Carnahan, George ....New York, NY
Carnahan, Hickle & Calvert, L.L.C.
Rolla, MO
Carnahan, J. Aron ....Chicago, IL
Carnahan, J. Russell ....St. Louis, MO
Carnahan, James G. ....London, KY
Carnahan, JoAnn E. ....Salt Lake City, UT
Carnahan, John A. ....Columbus, OH
Carnahan, John H. ....Brattleboro, VT
Carnahan, John M., III ....Springfield, MO
Carnahan, Laurie S. ....New Berlin, WI
Carnahan, Mary E. ....Columbia, MO
Carnahan, Melvin E. ....Jefferson City, MO
Carnahan, Michael S. ....Dallas, TX
Carnahan, Michael W. ....Phoenix, AZ
Carnahan, Mike ....Houston, TX
Carnahan, Nancy Forbis ....Dallas, TX
Carnahan & Perry, PLC ....Phoenix, AZ
Carnahan, Richard A. ....De Soto, KS
Carnahan, Robert N. ....Corpus Christi, TX
Carnahan, Roger A. ....Rolla, MO
Carnahan, Russell E. ....Columbus, OH
Carnahan, Susan Bush ....Palo Alto, CA
Carnahan, Thomas S. ....St. Louis, MO
Carnahan, Timothy D. ....Cleveland, OH
Carnahan, William A. ....Washington, DC
Carnahan, William H. ....Colorado Springs, CO
Carnahan, William H., P.C.
Colorado Springs, CO
Carnal, Gary A. ....St. Petersburg, FL
Carnal & Mansfield, P.A.
St. Petersburg, FL
Carnal, Sallie Christian ....Austin, TX
Carnall, Andrew J. ....Bluffton, IN
Carnall, George H., II ....Olive Branch, MS
Carnall, Ned R. ....Bluffton, IN
Carnall, Ned R., Andrew J., P.C.
Bluffton, IN
Carnam, Allyn Myles ....Ridgefield, CT
Carnaroli, Denise A. ....Sacramento, CA
Carnaroli, Rudolph E. (Rick) ....Pocatello, ID
Carnathan, Gary L. ....Tupelo, MS
Carnathan & Malski ....Amory, MS
Pontotoc, MS
Tupelo, MS
Carnathan, Sean T. ....Boston, MA
Carnazzo, Mary M. ....Omaha, NE
Carnazzo, William P. ....Sacramento, CA
Carne, John E. ....Oakland, CA
Carneal, Drew St. John ....Richmond, VA
Carneal, George U. ....Washington, DC
Carneal, George U., III ....Washington, DC
Carneal, John T. ....Paducah, KY
Carneal, Samuel G. ....Lexington, KY
Carnecchia, Baldo M., Jr.
Philadelphia, PA
Carnegie, Annette P. ....San Francisco, CA
Carnegie, Jack G. ....Houston, TX
Carnegie, R. Adam ....Tampa, FL
Carneiro, Jeannette D. ....Boston, MA
Carnell, Darrel ....Ormond Beach, FL
Carnell, Eric Scott ....Kirkland, WA
Carnell, Joseph L. ....Oklahoma City, OK
Carnell, Kent I. ....Madison, WI
Carnell, Richard M., Jr. ....Ocala, FL
Carnell, Richard S. ....United States Senate,
Committee Legal Personnel, GV
Carnell, Susanne ....Washington, DC
Carnell, Teresa Burt ....Baltimore, MD
Carnell, William S. ....Washington, DC
Carnelli, Christopher M. ....Trenton, NJ
Carnemolla, Diana M.A. ....New York, NY
Carner, Bert M., Jr. ....Modesto, CA
Carner, Gretchen S. ....Los Angeles, CA
Carner, Michael ....Commack, NY
Carner, Ronald S. ....Commack, NY
Carnero, Manuel, Jr. ....Houston, TX
Carnes, Burt ....Georgetown, TX
Carnes & Carnes, Attorneys, P.C.
Albertville, AL
Carnes, Carolyn J. ....Newark, OH
Carnes, Charles N. ....Fayetteville, AR
Carnes, Charlie L. ....Atlanta, GA
Carnes, David B. ....Gadsden, AL
Carnes, Donald F., (P.C.) ....Austin, TX
Carnes, Douglas N. ....Austin, TX
Carnes, Ed ....Montgomery, AL
Carnes, Everette C. ....Marion, NC
Carnes & Franklin, P.A. ....Marion, NC
Carnes, James R. ....Toledo, OH
Carnes, James S. ....Cleveland, OH
Carnes, Jerry W. ....Nashville, TN
Carnes, Jimmy F. ....Albertville, AL
Carnes, John E. ....Augusta, ME
Carnes, John S., Jr. ....West Chester, PA
Carnes, Kelly H. ....Washington, DC
Carnes, Lamar ....Dallas, TX
Carnes, Lawrence L. ....Tallahassee, FL
Carnes, Lynore M.
Merit Systems Protection Board,
Office of Board Members, GV
Carnes, Melinda P. ....Boston, MA
Carnes, Paul F., (Inc.) ....Dallas, TX
Carnes, Robert J. ....Pittsfield, MA
Carnes, Steven Lee ....San Antonio, TX
Carnes, Terry ....Dallas, TX
Carnes, Thomas ....Ravenna, OH
Carnes, Thomas M. ....San Francisco, CA
Carnes, Thomas P. ....Houston, TX
Carnes, Thomas S. ....Virginia Beach, VA

Carnes, Tiffany ....Austin, TX
Carnes, T. J. ....Albertville, AL
Carnes, Todi S. ....Shalimar, FL
Carnes, Vanessa L. ....Boston, MA
Carnes, Wamsley, Waid & Hyman, P.C.
Gadsden, AL
Carnes, William E. ....Pawtucket, RI
Carnes, William J. ....Tampa, FL
Carnes, William N. ....Kansas City, MO
Carnes, William W. ....Dallas, TX
Carnese, Charles W. ....Portland, OR
Carnese, Charles W., P.C. ....Portland, OR
Carnese, Gregory P. ....Old Lyme, CT
Carnese and Heck ....Old Lyme, CT
Carnessale, Thomas Williams
San Diego, CA
Carnevale, Barbara Grose ......New York, NY
Carnevale, Dario V. ....Miami, FL
Carnevale, Flavia ....North Miami, FL
Carnevale, James M. ....Wakefield, MA
Carnevale, James Michael
North Andover, MA
Carnevale, Lawrence F. ....New York, NY
Carnevale, Matthew Robert, Jr.
Manchester, NH
Carnevale, Michael F., II ....Princeton, NJ
Carnevale, Robert J. ....Lowell, MA
Carnevale, Robert J., P.C. ....Lowell, MA
Carnevale, Steven J. ....Los Angeles, CA
Carnevale, Vito ....Maplewood, NJ
Carnevali, Ronald P., Jr. ....Johnstown, PA
Carney, Alfonso L., Jr. ....Washington, DC
Carney, Ann S. ....Geyserville, CA
Carney, Anne ....Fort Wayne, IN
Carney, Anne M. ....Portland, ME
Carney, Appleby & Brewick, P.L.C.
Des Moines, IA
Carney Badley Smith & Spellman, P.S.
Olympia, WA
Seattle, WA
Carney & Bassil, A Professional Corporation
Boston, MA
Carney, Bradford G. Y. ....Towson, MD
Carney, Brent T. ....Short Hills, NJ
Carney, Brian ....Midland, TX
Carney, Brian S. ....Athens, GA
Carney, Bruce E. ....Crystal River, FL
Carney, Buckley & Hays ....Portland, OR
Carney & Carney ....Washington, DC
Carney & Carney ....Cleveland, OH
Carney and Carney ....Norristown, PA
Carney, Christine V ....Geneva, IL
Carney, Christopher J. ....New York, NY
Carney, Christopher J. ....Cleveland, OH
Carney, Clair R. ....Traverse City, MI
Carney, Clifford M. ....Downers Grove, IL
Carney, Clifton J., Jr. ....Boulder, CO
Carney, Cormac J. ....Newport Beach, CA
Carney, Daniel F. ....Reston, VA
Carney, Daniel W. ....North Scituate, MA
Carney, Daniel W. ....Weatherford, TX
Carney, David A. ....Columbia, MD
Carney, David J. ....Waltham, MA
Carney, David J. ....Cleveland, OH
Carney, Deborah Turner ....Golden, CO
Carney & Delany, LLP ....Riverside, CA
Carney, Demetrius E. ....Chicago, IL
Carney, Dianne B. ....Indio, CA
Carney, Donald F., Jr. ....Troy, MI
Carney, Donald J. ....Washington, DC
Carney, Douglas J. ....Minneapolis, MN
Carney, Edmund M. ....Pittsburgh, PA
Carney, Edw. H. ....Erie, PA
Carney, Edward J., Jr. ....Wayne, PA
Carney, Edwin ....Glendale, CA
Carney, Elizabeth ....Denver, CO
Carney, Erin M. ....New York, NY
Carney, Eva Marie ....Washington, DC
New York, NY
Carney, Francis J. ....Salt Lake City, UT
Carney, Frank N. Stockdale
Memphis, TN
Carney, Fred D., Jr. ....Washington, DC
Carney, G. Daniel ....Pittsburgh, PA
Carney, Gary R., Jr. ....New York, NY
Carney, George V. ....Portland, OR
Carney, Gerald B. ....Waverly, IA
Carney, Gerard B. ....Boston, MA
Carney & Good ....Erie, PA
Carney, Gregory R. ....New York, NY
Carney, Hayden A. ....Pasadena, CA
Carney, Howard A., Jr. ....Atlanta, TX
Carney, J. Allen ....Little Rock, AR
Carney, Jack E., Jr. ....Pembroke, GA
Carney, James A. ....Lake Forest, IL
Carney, James A. ....Cleveland, OH
Carney, James A. ....Janesville, WI
Carney, James F. ....Norristown, PA
Carney, James J. ....West Palm Beach, FL
Carney, James L. ....Woodbridge, VA
Carney, James M. ....Scottsbluff, NE
Carney, James T., II ....Pittsburgh, PA
Carney, James W. ....Des Moines, IA
Carney, Jane W. ....Riverside, CA
Carney, Janet M. ....Vero Beach, FL
Carney, Janis A. ....Los Gatos, CA
Carney, Jeffrey T. ....Hackensack, NJ
Carney, Jodi G. ....Mountain Home, AR
Carney, John ....Washington, DC
Carney, John F. ....Washington, DC
Carney, John F. ....Garden City, NY
Carney, John G. ....Harrison, NY
Carney, John J. ....Boston, MA
Carney, John J. ....Buffalo, NY
Carney, John James ....Cleveland, OH
Carney, John R. ....Livonia, MI
Carney, John R. ....Ludington, MI
Carney, John R., P.C. ....Livonia, MI

Carpenter, Jerry W.
Securities and Exchange Commission, Division of Market Regulation, GV
Carpenter, Jessica ... Mesa, AZ
Carpenter, JoAnn ... Washington, DC
Carpenter, Joel R. ... Boston, MA
Carpenter, John A. ... Sunbury, PA
Carpenter, John C. ... Los Angeles, CA
Mountain View, CA
Carpenter, John D. ... Pasadena, CA
Carpenter, John E. ... Wheat Ridge, CO
Carpenter, John J. ... Brookline, MA
Carpenter, John Joseph ... Charlotte, NC
Carpenter, John L. ... Portland, ME
Carpenter, John R. ... Cedar Rapids, IA
Carpenter, John R. ... Seattle, WA
Carpenter, John T. ... Omaha, NE
Carpenter, John W. ... San Francisco, CA
Carpenter, John W. ... San Francisco, CA
Carpenter, Jordan R. ... Philadelphia, PA
Carpenter, Joseph E., Jr. ... Sunrise, FL
Carpenter, Joseph F. ... Carson City, NV
Carpenter, Joseph T., Law Offices of
Montgomery, AL
Carpenter, Julia A. ... Indianapolis, IN
Carpenter, Julia K. ... Lake Forest, IL
Carpenter, Julia M. ... Washington, DC
Carpenter, Karen B. ... North Syracuse, NY
Carpenter, Kathleen F.
Walnut Creek, CA
Carpenter, Kathryn A. ... Sugar Land, TX
Carpenter, Keith D. ... St. Paul, MN
Milwaukee, WI
Carpenter, Keith E.
Securities and Exchange Commission, Office of International Affairs, GV
Carpenter, Kelly ... New York, NY
Carpenter, Kenneth ... Arlington, TX
Carpenter, Kenneth D. ... Davenport, WA
Odessa, WA
Ritzville, WA
Spokane, WA
Carpenter, Kenneth M. ... Topeka, KS
Carpenter, Kenneth W. ... Decatur, GA
Carpenter, Kerry D. ... Denham Springs, LA
Carpenter, Kerry J. ... Bismarck, ND
Carpenter, Kevin S. ... St. Cloud, MN
Carpenter, Kimberly R. D. ... Southfield, MI
Carpenter, Kirk D. ... Auburn, IN
Carpenter & Klatskin, P.C. ... Denver, CO
Carpenter, Kristen D. A. ... Atlanta, GA
Carpenter, L. Deborah ... Framingham, MA
Carpenter, Laura A. ... Phoenix, AZ
Carpenter, Laura A. ... Odessa, TX
Carpenter, Laura Heitner ... Houston, TX
Carpenter, Laura M. ... Dallas, TX
Carpenter Law Firm ... Minneapolis, MN
Carpenter Law Office ... Great Bend, KS
Carpenter Law Office, P.A. ... Bemidji, MN
Carpenter Law Offices ... Bismarck, ND
Carpenter, Leah J. ... Cass Lake, MN
Carpenter & Lessley, LLP
Los Angeles, CA
Mountain View, CA
Carpenter, Linda G. ... Atlanta, GA
Carpenter, Linda Jean ... Brooklyn, NY
Carpenter, Linda M. ... Redding, CA
Carpenter Lourie & Associates
Washington, DC
Carpenter, M. Ellen ... Boston, MA
Carpenter, M. John ... Great Bend, KS
Carpenter, M. Michael ... Beverly Hills, CA
Carpenter, Margaret M. ... Lexington, MA
Carpenter, Mark E. ... Charlotte, NC
Carpenter, Mark J. ... Minneapolis, MN
Carpenter, Martha L. ... San Diego, CA
Carpenter, Martin Dee ... Washington, DC
Carpenter, Martin L. ... Los Angeles, CA
Carpenter, Mary Todd ... Alexandria, VA
Carpenter, Mason and McGowan
Oklahoma City, OK
Tulsa, OK
Carpenter & Mayfield ... San Jose, CA
Carpenter, Melanie Lynn ... Sioux Falls, SD
Carpenter, Michael David ... Midland, MI
Carpenter, Michael H. ... Columbus, OH
Carpenter, Mikel W. ... Orlando, FL
Carpenter, Mikel W., P.A. ... Orlando, FL
Carpenter, Molly ... Chicago, IL
Carpenter, Nanaruth H. ... Grand Rapids, MI
Carpenter & Nixon, LLP ... Santa Fe, NM
Carpenter, Noel P. ... Herkimer, NY
Carpenter, Norman R. ... Minneapolis, MN
Carpenter & O'Connor ... Knoxville, TN
Carpenter & Ortega, P.C. ... Houston, TX
Carpenter, Otha T. ... Houston, TX
Carpenter, P. Brooks ... Brimfield, MA
Carpenter, Paffenbarger & Meyerhoefer
Norwalk, OH
Carpenter, Paige M. ... Tuscaloosa, AL
Carpenter, Parks G. ... St. Louis, MO
Carpenter & Parrish, P.A. ... Gainesville, FL
Carpenter, Patricia A. ... Stamford, CT
Carpenter, Patrick E. ... Gillette, WY
Carpenter, Paul D. ... Spring Valley, NY
Carpenter, Paul E. ... Pepper Pike, OH
Carpenter, Paul Philip ... Tierra Verde, FL
Carpenter, Paul S. ... Shrewsbury, MA
Carpenter, Peter F. ... Far Hills, NJ
Carpenter, Phillips B. ... Townshend, VT
Carpenter & Poston ... Tulsa, OK
Carpenter & Precup ... Alexandria, VA
Carpenter Professional Association
Topeka, KS
Carpenter, R. Scott ... Knoxville, TN
Carpenter, R. Todd ... Houston, TX
Carpenter, Randle B., Jr. ... New York, NY
Carpenter, Raymond A., Jr. ... Rockville, VA

Carpenter, Raymond P. ... Atlanta, GA
Carpenter, Richard A. ... San Diego, CA
Carpenter, Richard J., Jr. ... Spokane, WA
Carpenter, Richard L., Jr. ... Tulsa, OK
Carpenter, Richard N. ... Santa Fe, NM
Carpenter, Richard W. ... Park Ridge, IL
Carpenter, Richd. M. ... Racine, WI
Carpenter, Robert A. ... Cincinnati, OH
Carpenter, Robert B. ... Boston, MA
Carpenter, Robert C. ... Larkspur, CA
Carpenter, Robert D. ... Los Angeles, CA
Carpenter, Robert E. ... Des Moines, IA
Carpenter, Robert H. ... Denver, CO
Carpenter, Robert H., Jr. ... Baton Rouge, LA
Carpenter, Robert H., Jr. ... Minneapolis, MN
Carpenter, Robert K. ... Alexandria, VA
Carpenter, Robert M. ... Jackson, MS
Carpenter, Robert R. ... Rock Hill, SC
Carpenter, Robert T. ... Chicago, IL
Carpenter, Robert W. ... Boston, MA
Carpenter, Rolland T. ... Tallahassee, FL
Carpenter, Ronald A. ... Gainesville, FL
Carpenter, Ronald G. ... Ann Arbor, MI
Carpenter, Ronald K. ... Bemidji, MN
Carpenter, Ronald K. ... Camdenton, MO
Osage Beach, MO
Carpenter, Ronald R. ... Olympia, WA
Carpenter, Rosemary G. ... Cincinnati, OH
Carpenter & Rothans ... Los Angeles, CA
Carpenter & Rowen, P.C. ... Omaha, NE
Carpenter, Roy E., Jr. ... Starkville, MS
Carpenter & Russell ... Townshend, VT
Carpenter, Russell Bruce ... Vida, OR
Carpenter, Russell H., Jr.
Washington, DC
Carpenter, Samuel ... San Diego, CA
Carpenter, Samuel D. ... Battle Creek, MI
Carpenter, Sandra D. ... Arlington, TX
Carpenter, Scott B. ... Scottsdale, AZ
Carpenter, Scott R. ... Irvine, CA
Carpenter, Scott R. ... Salt Lake City, UT
Carpenter, Sheila J. ... Washington, DC
Carpenter, Sonja L. ... Huntington, WV
Carpenter, Stacy ... Denver, CO
Carpenter, Stacy R. ... Grand Junction, CO
Carpenter, Stanley H. ... Waterbury, VT
Carpenter, Stephen L. ... Knoxville, TN
Carpenter, Stephen W. ... Janesville, WI
Carpenter, Steven J. ... Grand Rapids, MI
Carpenter, Steven J., P.C. ... Grand Rapids, MI
Carpenter, Steven M. ... Portland, OR
Carpenter, Susan Caroline ... New York, NY
Carpenter, Susan K. ... Indianapolis, IN
Carpenter, Terri L. ... Broomfield, CO
Carpenter, Thomas B. ... Philadelphia, PA
Carpenter, Thomas L., Jr. ... Gautier, MS
Carpenter, Thomas M., (P.C.) ... Hemet, CA
Sun City, CA
Carpenter, Thomas Milton ... Little Rock, AR
Carpenter, Thomas T. ... Los Angeles, CA
Carpenter, Thomas W. ... Des Moines, IA
Carpenter, Thomas W. ... Newport News, VA
Carpenter, Timothy W. ... Bellingham, WA
Carpenter, Toby R. ... Knoxville, TN
Carpenter, Vernon J. ... Pittsburgh, PA
Carpenter & Visser ... Grand Rapids, MI
Carpenter, W. Geoffrey ... Sparks, MD
Carpenter, W. Kyle ... Knoxville, TN
Carpenter, W. Scott ... Houston, TX
Carpenter, Walker & Hardesty
Bellingham, WA
Carpenter, Walter C. ... Hendersonville, NC
Carpenter, Walter N. ... Orlando, FL
Carpenter, Walter T., Jr. ... Lenoir, NC
Carpenter & Wegner ... Cincinnati, OH
Carpenter, William ... St. Paul, MN
Carpenter, William A., Jr. ... Newark, NJ
Carpenter, William C., Jr. ... Wilmington, DE
Carpenter, William Charles, Jr. ... Eugene, OR
Carpenter, William F., III ... Nashville, TN
Carpenter, William G. ... Columbus, OH
Carpenter, William H. ... Albuquerque, NM
Carpenter, William H. ... Pepper Pike, OH
Carpenter, William L. ... Broomfield, CO
Carpenter, William L. ... Las Vegas, NV
Carpenter, William O. ... Arlington, VA
Carpenter, William R. ... Topeka, KS
Carpenter, William R. ... Norristown, PA
Carpenter, Williard C., Jr.
San Francisco, CA
Carpenter, Willis V. ... Denver, CO
Carpenter, W. S., Jr. ... Dallas, TX
Texarkana, TX
Carpenter Emery, Kimberly A.
Charlottesville, VA
Carpenter-Holmes, Amy K.
Washington, DC
Carpentier, Deborah Ann
Washington, DC
Carpentier, Diane M. ... St. Clair Shores, MI
Carpentier, Elizabeth A. ... Columbia, SC
Carpentier, H. Frank ... Asbury Park, NJ
Carpentier, Joan-Elisse ... New York, NY
Carpentier, Jos. G. ... Moline, IL
Carpentier, Nancy B. ... Dallas, TX
Carpentier, Peter F. ... Andover, MA
Carpentier, Robert A., (P.C.) ... Mineola, NY
Carpentier, Victor L. ... Jamaica, NY
Carpentiere, Mary Emmanuella
Stony Brook, NY
Carpentieri, Christopher ... New York, NY
Carper, Anderson L. ... Phoenix, AZ
Carper, Donald L. ... Sacramento, CA
Carper, Gayle Tronvig ... Macomb, IL
Carper, Joseph Ray ... Danville, VA
Carper, Michael D. ... Kearney, NE
Carper, Michael H. ... Lubbock, TX
Carper, Michael R. ... Denver, CO

Carper, Nancy ... Chicago, IL
Carper, Nichole ... Sioux Falls, SD
Carper, Raymond E. ... Denver, CO
Carper, Roy ... Borger, TX
Carper & Rubesh ... Chicago, IL
Carper, Stephen K. ... Frederick, MD
Carper, W. Kent ... Charleston, WV
Carperos, Melissa A. ... Atlanta, GA
Carpey, Stuart A. ... Philadelphia, PA
Carpi, Janice E. ... Richmond, VA
Carpiac, Lou ... Ventura, CA
Carpien, Alan H.
Environmental Protection Agency, Office of the General Counsel, GV
Carpignano, Julius ... Newfoundland, NJ
Carpinelli, Ralph R. ... Cleveland, OH
Carpinello, Beth Davies ... Albany, NY
Carpinello, George F. ... Albany, NY
New York, NY
Carpinello, Melissa A. ... Delmar, NY
Carpineti, Walter I ... San Francisco, CA
Carpiniello, Nina V. ... Philadelphia, PA
Carpini-Pace, Laura ... Manhattan Beach, CA
Carpino, Cathleen M. ... Boston, MA
Carpio, J. Graham ... Bedford Park, IL
Carpio, Philip F. ... McLean, VA
Carpman, Stephen M. ... Detroit, MI
Carpol, Steven J. ... Redwood City, CA
Carponelli & Krug ... Chicago, IL
Carponelli, Stephen P. ... Chicago, IL
Carponter, Candace C. ... New York, NY
Carr, Adam E. ... Twinsburg, OH
Carr, Alan J. ... New York, NY
Carr, Albert V., Jr. ... Lexington, VA
Carr, Alford, Clausen & McDonald, L.L.C.
Mobile, AL
Carr, Alisa N. ... Pittsburgh, PA
Carr, Allen Lane, (Inc., P.S.) ... Edmonds, WA
Carr, Allison, Pugh, Howard, Oliver & Sisson, P.C. ... Birmingham, AL
Florence, AL
Mobile, AL
Carr, Andrew R., Jr. ... Memphis, TN
Carr, Anita C. ... New York, NY
Carr, Ann, Law Offices of ... Lancaster, PA
Carr, Ann, Law Offices of
Philadelphia, PA
Carr, Ann Smith ... St. Louis, MO
Carr, Anthony P. ... Cleveland, OH
Carr, Anthony R. ...
Department of Defense, GV
Carr, Arthur G., III ... St. Louis, MO
Carr, Aute L. ... Sun City, AZ
Carr, Barry A. ... Palo Alto, CA
Carr, Benjamin H., Jr. ... Harrisonburg, VA
Carr, Bernard B. ... Montgomery, AL
Carr, Bessie M. ... San Diego, CA
Carr, Betsy Ryan ... Washington, DC
Carr & Boyette, PLLC ... Memphis, TN
Carr, Brian E. ... New York, NY
Carr, Brian K. ... St. Marys, WV
Carr, Brian L. ... San Jose, CA
Carr, Brian L. ... Richmond, VA
Carr, Brian T., Law Offices of ... Metairie, LA
Carr, Bruce A. ... Lake Station, IN
Carr, Bruce G. ... Glens Falls, NY
Carr, C. Randall ... Dallas, TX
Carr, C. Robert ... Templeton, CA
Carr, Calvin ... Boston, MA
Carr, Caroline M. ... Orange, CA
Carr, Carolyn L. ... Pittston, PA
Carr & Carr ... Manchester, IA
Tulsa, OK
Carr, Catherine A. ... Roseland, NJ
Carr, Catherine C. ... Philadelphia, PA
Carr, Cathleen Vaune ... Cleveland, OH
Carr, Charles F. ... Mobile, AL
Carr, Charles L., II ... Houston, TX
Carr, Charles M., III ... Houston, TX
Carr, Charles T., III ... New Orleans, LA
Carr, Cherylyn D. ... New York, NY
Carr, Chris A. ... San Luis Obispo, CA
Carr, Christina S. ... Camden, AR
Carr, Christine L. ... Portland, OR
Carr, Christine Schleibaum
Los Angeles, CA
Carr, Christopher A. ... Pasadena, CA
Carr, Christopher J. ... San Francisco, CA
Carr, Christopher K. ... Washington, DC
Carr, Christopher L. ... Lillington, NC
Carr, Christopher P. ... Boston, MA
Carr, Christopher T. ... Flushing, NY
Carr, Christopher W. ... Dallas, TX
Carr, Claire C. ... Richmond, VA
Carr, Claude E. ... Chicago, IL
Carr, Clay R. ... Birmingham, AL
Carr, Colleen Klonaris ... Birmingham, AL
Carr, Connie S. ... Cleveland, OH
Carr, Conrad J. ... Bloomington, MN
Carr, D. Kay ... Ruskin, FL
Carr, Dabney J., IV ... Richmond, VA
Carr, Daniel ... New York, NY
Carr, Daniel Hartman ... San Jose, CA
Carr, Daniel L. ... San Mateo, CA
Carr, Daniel W. ... Denver, CO
Carr, Danny M. ... Detroit, MI
Carr, Darol H. M. ... Port Charlotte, FL
Carr, Darwin K. ... Dallas, TX
Carr, David ... San Francisco, CA
Carr, David A. ... Arlington, VA
Carr, David Brian ... Hartford, CT
Carr, David C ... Burlingame, CA
Carr, David C. ... Burlingame, CA
Carr, David J. ... Indianapolis, IN
Carr, David Wilkinson, Jr.
Charlottesville, VA
Carr, Davis ... Mobile, AL
Carr, Davis H. ... Nashville, TN

Carr, Dawna R. ... San Antonio, TX
Carr, Debra A. ... Department of Justice, Civil Rights Division, GV
Carr, Debra L. ... Hattiesburg, MS
Carr, Denine K. ... Rochester, NY
Carr, Dennis M., Law Offices of
San Francisco, CA
Carr, Diane S. ... East Lansing, MI
Carr, Diane Wagner ... Tallahassee, FL
Carr, Dolores Ann ... San Jose, CA
Carr, Donald A. ... Washington, DC
Carr, Donald A. ... Chicago, IL
Carr, Douglas S. ... Portland, ME
Carr, Duane A. ... Greenville, MI
Carr, Dudley R. ... Tupelo, MS
Carr, E. Michael ... Manchester, IA
Carr, Eddie L. ... Tulsa, OK
Carr, Edmund A. ... Arcadia, MI
Carr, Edward A. ... Houston, TX
Carr, Edward J. ... Fayetteville, NY
Carr, Edwin J. ... Boston, MA
Carr, Eric M. ... New York, NY
Carr, Eugene M., III ... Hendersonville, NC
Carr, Feneli & Carbone, Co., L.P.A.
Mayfield Heights, OH
Carr & Ferrell LLP ... Palo Alto, CA
Carr, Flora & Carroll, P.C. ... El Paso, TX
Carr, Francis T. ... New York, NY
Carr, Frank ... Department of the Army, Office, Chief of Engineers/Headquarters, U.S. Army Corps of Engineers, GV
Carr, Frank B. ... Nine Mile Falls, WA
Carr, Fred S., Jr. ... Kankakee, IL
Carr, Frederick J. ... San Francisco, CA
Carr, G. Michael ... Doylestown, PA
Carr, Gary T. ... St. Louis, MO
Carr, Gayl Branum ... Fairfax, VA
Carr, Gayle C. ... Derby, CT
Litchfield, CT
Carr, Geoffrey T. ... Redwood City, CA
Carr, George E., (P.A.) ... Orlando, FL
Carr, George F., Jr. ... Highland Heights, KY
Carr, George M. ... San Francisco, CA
Carr, George R. ... White Marsh, MD
Carr & Goodman ... Tupelo, MS
Carr Goodson Warner, A Professional Corporation ... Washington, DC
Baltimore, MD
Rockville, MD
Vienna, VA
Carr, Gregory A. ... Montgomery, AL
Carr, Gregory W. ... Dallas, TX
Carr, H. Judson ... Essex, CT
Carr, H. Palmer, Jr. ... Crawfordville, FL
Carr, Harold D. ... Olympia, WA
Carr, Harry J. ... Silver Spring, MD
Carr, Henry V., III
Charlotte Amalie, St. Thomas, VI
Carr, Hunt & Joy L.L.P. ... Amarillo, TX
Lubbock, TX
Carr, Ian ... Chicago, IL
Carr, J. Craig ... Youngstown, OH
Carr, J. Danielle ... Chicago, IL
Carr, J. David ... Pittsburgh, PA
Carr, J. Philip ... Milledgeville, GA
Carr, J. Richard ... Attalla, AL
Carr, J. Richard ... Chevy Chase, MD
Carr, J. Robert ... Washington, DC
Carr, J. Russell ... Chicago, IL
Carr, J. Scott ... Atlanta, GA
Carr, Jack D. ... Birmingham, AL
Carr, James A. ... Columbus, OH
Carr, James Byron ... Davis, CA
Carr, James C. ... Atlanta, GA
Carr, James C., Jr. ... Atlanta, GA
Carr, James D. ... Houlton, ME
Carr, James E., P.C. ... Leesburg, VA
Carr, James F. ... Denver, CO
Carr, James G. ... Toledo, OH
Carr, James L. ... Durham, NC
Carr, James M. ... Department of Defense, Defense Legal Services Agency, GV
Carr, James M.
Federal Communications Commission, Office of the General Counsel, GV
Carr, James M. ... Indianapolis, IN
Carr, James P. ... Los Angeles, CA
Carr, James P., A Professional Corporation
Los Angeles, CA
Carr, James Q., II ... Memphis, TN
Carr, James R. ... Roseville, CA
Carr, James R. ... Waukegan, IL
Carr, James R. ... Louisville, KY
Carr, James S. ... Parsippany, NJ
New York, NY
Carr, James T. ... Birmingham, AL
Carr, James T. ... Miles City, MT
Carr, James W. ... Hallettsville, TX
Carr, Jane Childs ... Atlanta, GA
Carr, Jeffrey A. ... Cherry Hill, NJ
Carr, Jeffrey B. ... Mobile, AL
Carr, Jeffrey R. ... Nashville, TN
Carr, Jeffrey W. ... Houston, TX
Carr, Jennifer M. ... Baltimore, MD
Carr, Jerome D. ... Baltimore, MD
Carr, Jody Allison ... San Francisco, CA
Carr, Joel L. ... Mineola, NY
Carr, John ... Manchester, IA
Carr, John B. ... Pensacola, FL
Carr, John C. ... Bethesda, MD
Carr, John David ... Van Nuys, CA
Carr, John F. ... Washington, DC
Carr, John H., Jr. ... Salem, MA
Carr, John J. ... New York, NY
Carr, John L. ... Napa, CA
Carr, John L. ... Newport Beach, CA
Carr, John L. ... Indianapolis, IN
Carr, John L. ... Quakertown, PA

Carrillo, Luis A. ... Montebello, CA
Carrillo, Martha A. ... Santa Cruz, CA
Carrillo, Michael A. ... Chicago, IL
Carrillo, Pablo E. ... New Orleans, LA
Carrillo, Raúl A., Jr. ... Las Cruces, NM
Carrillo, Ricardo Oscar ... Benavides, TX
Carrillo, Wilma ... Lakeland, FL
Carrillo-Cotto, Mayra ... San Juan, PR
Carrillo Rey, Yuisa ... New York, NY
Carringer, Christine A. ... Fairfield, CA
Oakland, CA
Carrington, Ann-Marie D. ... Washington, DC
Carrington & Carrington, P.A.
Clearwater, FL
Carrington, Charles C. ... Orlando, FL
Carrington, Claudia R. ... San Jose, CA
Carrington, Coleman, Sloman & Blumenthal, L.L.P. ... Dallas, TX
Carrington, Cristyn E. ... Yuma, AZ
Carrington, Dean D. ... Cedar Rapids, IA
Carrington, Deborah R. ... Raleigh, NC
Carrington, Donine Marie ... Rockville, MD
Carrington, Frederick ... Clearwater, FL
Carrington, Grover A.
Mount Sterling, KY
Carrington, James E. ... Tulsa, OK
Carrington, Janis L. ... Olympia, WA
Carrington, Jerrold B. ... Evanston, IL
Carrington, John F. ... Houston, TX
Carrington, John L. ... Harlingen, TX
Carrington, Joseph H. ... Richmond, VA
Carrington, Kenneth M. ... Greensboro, NC
Carrington, Mark ... Waterbury, CT
Carrington, M. C. ... Beaumont, TX
Carrington, Mcken Vincent ... Houston, TX
Carrington & Nye ... Santa Barbara, CA
Carrington, Patricia I. ... Buffalo, NY
Carrington, Paul D. ... Durham, NC
Carrington, Richard A. ... Santa Barbara, CA
Carrington, T. Michael ... Denver, CO
Carrington, Terron M. ... Clearwater, FL
Carrion, Al J. ... Arbuckle, CA
Carrion, Albert A., Jr. ... Austin, TX
Carrion, Audrey J. S. ... Baltimore, MD
Carrion, Jose M. ... Orlando, FL
Carrion, Ramon ... Clearwater, FL
Carrion-Christiansen, M. Georgina
San Juan, PR
Carrithers, Charmaine I. ... Houston, TX
Carrithers, David W. ... Louisville, KY
Carrithers, Dennis R. ... Louisville, KY
Carrithers, Judith A. ... Honolulu, HI
Carrithers, Richard C. ... Bellevue, WA
Carriuolo, Anthony J.
Fort Lauderdale, FL
Carriuolo, Richard A. ... Portland, ME
Carrle, Gunther O. ... Cherry Hill, NJ
Harrisburg, PA
King Of Prussia, PA
Carrns, Douglas R. ... Boston, MA
Carro, J. Dean ... Akron, OH
Carro, John ... New York, NY
Carro, John P. ... New York, NY
Carro, John S. ... New York, NY
Carro, Michael J. ... New York, NY
Carro, Richard S. ... Treasury Department, Office of the General Counsel, GV
Carro, Sergio G. ... Denville, NJ
Carro, Velez, Carro & Mitchell
New York, NY
Carroccio, A. Thomas ... Washington, DC
Carroccio, Benjamin ... Mineola, NY
Carroccio, Charles S., Jr. ... Rockville, MD
Carrol, Jed L. ... Buffalo, NY
Carrol, Robert Kelton ... San Francisco, CA
Seattle, WA
Carrol, Thomas J. ... Crystal Lake, IL
Carroll, Alfred B., Jr. ... Philadelphia, PA
Carroll, Alice O. ... Lexington, MA
Carroll, Amy E. ... Washington, DC
Carroll, Andrew J. ... San Francisco, CA
Carroll, Andrew S. ... Sedalia, MO
Carroll, Andrew S. ... Warrensburg, MO
Carroll, Anita L. ... White Plains, NY
Carroll, Ann M. ... Dallas, TX
Carroll, Anne Berrill ... New York, NY
Carroll, Anne L. ... Rydal, PA
Carroll, Anthony J. ... New York, NY
Carroll, April Dawn ... Clinton, TN
Carroll & Associates ... Dalton, GA
Rome, GA
Carroll Associates ... Wellesley, MA
Carroll & Associates, P.A. ... Miami, FL
Carroll & Associates, P.C. ... Denver, CO
Carroll, Barbara A. ... Santa Barbara, CA
Carroll, Benjamin L., III ... Honolulu, HI
Carroll, Benjamin Sam ... Birmingham, AL
Carroll, Beverly A. ... Rock Hill, SC
Carroll, Bradley S. ... Tucson, AZ
Carroll, Brenda Mary ... Wheaton, IL
Carroll, Brett D. ... Fort Lauderdale, FL
Carroll, Brian G. ... Waukesha, WI
Carroll, Brian K. ... Evansville, IN
Carroll, Brian P. ... Boston, MA
Carroll, Brian S. ... Marysville, KS
Carroll, Bruce K. ... Ukiah, CA
Carroll, Bryant S., III ... Metairie, LA
Carroll, Bryant S., Jr. ... Jacksonville, FL
Carroll, Burdick & McDonough LLP
Los Angeles, CA
Sacramento, CA
San Francisco, CA
Walnut Creek, CA
Carroll, C. Daniel ... Carlsbad, CA
Carroll, C. Joseph ... Department of Justice, United States Marshals Service, GV
Carroll, Candace M. ... San Diego, CA
Carroll, Carrie L. ... Harrisburg, PA
Carroll, Carrie V. ... Raleigh, NC
Carroll, Carroll, Davidson & Young, P.C.
Syracuse, NY
Carroll and Carroll, P.A.
Minneapolis, MN
Carroll & Carroll, P.C. ... Birmingham, AL
Carroll, Catherine ... Mountain View, CA
Carroll, Catherine ... Washington, DC
Carroll, Catherine N. ... Portland, OR
Carroll & Cedrone ... Philadelphia, PA
Carroll, Charles F. ... New York, NY
Carroll, Charles M. ... St. Clair Shores, MI
Carroll, Charles O. ... Seattle, WA
Carroll, Charles P. ... Coral Gables, FL
Carroll, Charles T. ... Ocean City, NJ
Carroll, Charles T., Jr. ... United States Senate, Committee Legal Personnel, GV
Carroll, Charles V. ... Spokane, WA
Carroll, Christina L. ... Jackson, MS
Carroll, Christine M. ... Chicago, IL
Carroll, Christopher F. ... Wailuku, HI
Carroll, Christopher Robert
Gladstone, NJ
New York, NY
Carroll, Christy ... Jackson, MS
Carroll, Clement J., Jr. ... Chicago, IL
Carroll, Colleen ... Boston, MA
Carroll, Colleen Anne
Department of Agriculture, Office of the General Counsel, GV
Carroll, Connie Griffin ... Little Rock, AR
Carroll, Courtney R. ... Washington, DC
Carroll, Courtney R. ... San Juan, PR
Carroll, Curtis L. ... Eagle Butte, SD
Carroll, Cynthia L. ... Newark, DE
Carroll, Cynthia Y. ... New Bern, NC
Carroll, D. David, II ... Columbus, OH
Carroll, Dan L. ... Sacramento, CA
Carroll, Dana ... New York, NY
Carroll, Daniel B. ... Florham Park, NJ
Carroll, Daniel C. ... Walkersville, MD
Carroll, Daniel G. ... Chicago, IL
Carroll, Daniel J. ... Topeka, KS
Carroll, Daniel L. ... New York, NY
Carroll, Daniel M. ... Boston, MA
Carroll, Daniel P. ... Pittsburgh, PA
Carroll, Daniel R. ... Indianapolis, IN
Carroll, Danielle Lynnette Deloache
McKinney, TX
Carroll, Darren J. ... Indianapolis, IN
Carroll, David B. ... Irvine, CA
Carroll, David B. ... Walpole, MA
Carroll, David C. ... Ada, MI
Carroll, David H. ... Austin, TX
Carroll, David J. ... Phoenix, AZ
Carroll, David R. ... Palm Beach Gardens, FL
Carroll, David S. ... Denver, CO
Carroll, David S. ... New York, NY
Carroll, David W. ... Lawrenceville, NJ
Carroll, David W. ... Providence, RI
Carroll, David Wm. T. ... Gahanna, OH
Carroll, Dennis D. ... Anderson, IN
Carroll, Dennis F. ... Chevy Chase, MD
Carroll, Dennis M. ... Willingboro, NJ
Carroll, Diane C. ... Melville, NY
Carroll, Dionè Cherie ... Miami, FL
Carroll, Donald C. ... San Francisco, CA
Carroll, Donald K. ... Oak Grove, LA
Carroll, Donald L., Jr. ... Lakewood, CO
Carroll, Donald R. ... Pittsburgh, PA
Carroll & Donaldson ... Crown Point, IN
Carroll, Dorothy A. ... Fresno, CA
Carroll, Douglas J. ... Milwaukee, WI
Carroll, E. Randolph ... Greensboro, NC
Carroll, Earl H. ... Phoenix, AZ
Carroll, Edgar S. ... Sedalia, MO
Carroll, Edmund H., Jr. ... Davenport, IA
Carroll, Edward, III ... Spokane, WA
Carroll, Edward J. ... Kingston, NY
Carroll, Edward J. ... Burlington, VT
Carroll, Edward J., III ... Springfield, MA
Carroll, Edward M. ... Hayward, CA
Carroll, Edward P. ... Stamford, CT
Carroll, Eileen Monahan ... New York, NY
Carroll, Eileen P. ... La Jolla, CA
Carroll, Elaine Dajani ... Linwood, NJ
Carroll, Elena T.
Merit Systems Protection Board, Office of Appeals Counsel, GV
Carroll, Elizabeth A. ... Los Angeles, CA
Carroll, Elizabeth B. ... Danville, VA
Carroll, Elizabeth Hughes ... Washington, DC
Carroll, Elizabeth Jahncke ... New York, NY
Carroll, Elizann ... Dallas, TX
Carroll, Ernest L. ... Artesia, NM
Carroll, F. Andrew, III ... Alexandria, VA
Carroll, F. Michael ... Phoenix, AZ
Carroll, Faye K. ... Fairfax, VA
Carroll & Ferguson ... Walkersville, MD
Carroll, Frances M. ... Elk Grove Village, IL
Carroll, Francis J. ... Troy, NY
Carroll, Francis J., Jr.
Daytona Beach, FL
Carroll, Francis W. ... Stamford, CT
Carroll, Francis X. ... Buffalo, NY
Carroll, Frank J. ... Des Moines, IA
Carroll, Frank K. ... Shreveport, LA
Carroll, Frank T. ... Philadelphia, PA
Carroll, Frankie Jeanne ... Murray, KY
Carroll, Franklin L. ... Santa Ana, CA
Carroll, Franklin L. ... Cumberland, MD
Carroll, Frederic ... Dallas, TX
Carroll, Frederick A. ... El Monte, CA
Carroll, Gale E. ... Weston, WV
Carroll, Gary Michael ... Birmingham, AL
Carroll, Gay L. ... Sacramento, CA
Carroll, George ... Pittsburgh, PA
Carroll, George D. ... Richmond, CA
Carroll, George F., Jr. ... Norwalk, CT
Carroll, George M. ... Eau Claire, WI
Carroll, Gerald J., Jr. ... Syracuse, NY
Carroll, Gerald K. ... San Francisco, CA
Carroll, Gerald T. ... Minneapolis, MN
Carroll, Gilbert & Bachor, A Prof. Law Corp.
Brea, CA
Carroll, Grace Burke ... Fairfax, VA
Carroll, Gregory Alan ... West Union, OH
Carroll & Gross, L.L.P. ... Austin, TX
Carroll, Gwen V. ... Chicago, IL
Carroll, Gwen Veronica, Ltd., The Law Offices of ... Chicago, IL
Carroll, Hal O. ... Detroit, MI
Carroll, Harold J. ... Boston, MA
Carroll, Harry G. ... Bogota, NJ
Carroll, Harry P. ... Springfield, MA
Carroll, Hartigan, Farmer, Cerney & McGillen, Ltd. ... Chicago, IL
Carroll, Helen S. ... Akron, OH
Carroll, Holly A. ... West Haven, CT
Carroll, Holly Wilson ... Coral Springs, FL
Carroll, Howard R. ... Mount Clemens, MI
Carroll, Hunter C. ... Birmingham, AL
Carroll, Irene S. ... Los Angeles, CA
Carroll, J. Jay ... Yakima, WA
Carroll, J. Speed ... New York, NY
Carroll, J. Thomas, Jr. ... Harrisville, MI
Carroll, Jack P. ... Beaumont, TX
Carroll, Jacqueline M. ... West Chester, PA
Carroll, Jacqueline Musto ... Kingston, PA
Carroll, James A., Jr. ... Newport Beach, CA
Carroll, James Brendan, III ... Dallas, TX
Carroll, James E. ... Chicago, IL
Carroll, James E. ... Boston, MA
New York, NY
Providence, RI
Carroll, James E. ... Poulsbo, WA
Carroll, James F. ... Fort Lauderdale, FL
Carroll, James F. ... Suffern, NY
Carroll, James F. ... Middlebury, VT
Carroll, James Frederick ... Wayne, NJ
Carroll, James H. ... Boulder, CO
Denver, CO
Carroll, James Houlihan
Fort Lauderdale, FL
Carroll, James J. ... Branford, CT
Carroll, James J. ... Hartford, CT
Carroll, James J. ... Chicago, IL
Carroll, James J. ... Cincinnati, OH
Carroll, James J. ... Cleveland, OH
Carroll, James J., III ... Los Angeles, CA
Carroll, James K. ... New Orleans, LA
Carroll, James L. ... Jackson, MS
Oxford, MS
Tupelo, MS
Carroll, James L. ... Austin, TX
Carroll, James L. ... El Paso, TX
Carroll, James M. ... Laconia, NH
Carroll, James M. ... Columbus, OH
Carroll, James P. ... Sacramento, CA
Carroll, James P. ... Washington, DC
Charlotte, NC
Carroll, James P. ... Rutland, VT
Carroll, James R. ... Brea, CA
Carroll, James R. ... Chicago, IL
Carroll, James R. ... Boston, MA
Carroll, James S., III
Charlotte Amalie, St. Thomas, VI
Carroll, James T., III ... Detroit, MI
Carroll, James T., Jr. ... Raymond, ME
Carroll, James V., III ... Houston, TX
Carroll, James W. ... Phoenix, AZ
Carroll, James W. ... Ithaca, NY
Carroll, James W., Jr. ... Pittsburgh, PA
Carroll, Jameson B. ... Atlanta, GA
Carroll, Jan M. ... Indianapolis, IN
Carroll, Jane Skelley ... Chicago, IL
Carroll, Janet ... Fair Oaks, CA
Carroll, Janice C. ... Cambridge, MA
Carroll, Jeanne A. ... Denver, CO
Carroll, Jeffrey P. ... Minneapolis, MN
Carroll, Jennifer S. ... West Palm Beach, FL
Carroll, Jennifer S., P.A., Law Offices of West Palm Beach, FL
Carroll, Jenny Elizabeth ... Tyler, TX
Carroll, Jeremy E. ... Danville, VA
Carroll, Joan L. ... Boston, MA
Carroll, Joe ... Belton, TX
Carroll, Joe C. ... Birmingham, AL
Carroll, John A. ... Hauppauge, NY
Carroll, John B. ... Plandome Manor, NY
Carroll, John Benjamin, (P.C.)
Syracuse, NY
Carroll, John Byrne ... Chelmsford, MA
Carroll, John C. ... Roselle, IL
Carroll, John F. ... Winston-Salem, NC
Carroll, John F. ... San Antonio, TX
Carroll, John F., IV ... Virginia Beach, VA
Carroll, John F., Jr. ... Shepherdsville, KY
Carroll, John Francis ... San Pedro, CA
Carroll, John G. ... Louisville, KY
Carroll, John G. ... Tappan, NY
Carroll, John J. ... Breezy Point, NY
Carroll, John J., Jr. ... Boston, MA
Carroll, John K. ... New York, NY
Carroll, John L. ... Montgomery, AL
Carroll, John L. ... Evansville, IN
Carroll, John M. ... Chicago, IL
Carroll, John M. ... Davenport, IA
Carroll, John M. ... New York, NY
Carroll, John P. ... Indio, CA
Carroll, John P., Jr. ... New York, NY
Carroll, John R. ... San Jose, CA
Carroll, John R. ... Minneapolis, MN
Carroll, John S. ... Tucson, AZ
Carroll, John S. ... Chicago, IL
Carroll, John T., III ... Philadelphia, PA
Carroll, John W.
Palm Beach Gardens, FL
Carroll, John W. ... New York, NY
Carroll, John W. ... Harrisburg, PA
Carroll, Jon ... Dallas, TX
Carroll, Joseph F. ... Fort Worth, TX
Carroll, Joseph G., III ... Spokane, WA
Carroll, Joseph G., P.S. ... Spokane, WA
Carroll, Joseph J. ... New York, NY
Carroll, Joseph P. ... Annapolis, MD
Carroll, Joseph P. ... Woonsocket, RI
Carroll, Joseph R. ... Eggertsville, NY
Carroll, Joseph T., Jr. ... Fort Collins, CO
Carroll, Joseph W., III ... West Chester, PA
Carroll, Julian M. ... Frankfort, KY
Carroll, Julie M. ... Rochester, MI
Carroll, Karen A. ... Cincinnati, OH
Carroll, Karen E. ... Ventura, CA
Carroll, Karen J.
Environmental Protection Agency, Office of the General Counsel, GV
Carroll, Karen Margaret ... Boston, MA
Carroll, Karen R. ... Brattleboro, VT
Carroll, Kathleen F. ... Basking Ridge, NJ
Carroll, Kathryn G. ... Chapel Hill, NC
Carroll, Kelley R. ... Truckee, CA
Reno, NV
Carroll, Kelly & Murphy ... Providence, RI
Carroll, Kelly & Trotter ... Long Beach, CA
Carroll, Ken ... Dallas, TX
Carroll, Kenneth E. ... Rego Park, NY
Carroll, Kenneth G.
Research Triangle Park, NC
Carroll, Kenneth P. ... Rochelle Park, NJ
Carroll, Kevin ... Rocky Hill, CT
Carroll, Kevin J. ... Tallahassee, FL
Carroll, Kevin J. ... Plattsburgh, NY
Carroll, Kevin James ... Manchester, NH
Carroll, Kevin M. ... Washington, DC
Baltimore, MD
Carroll, Kevin M. ... Lowell, MA
Carroll, Kevin M. ... Watertown, MA
Carroll, Kevin P. ... Rosemount, MN
Carroll, Kevin P. ... New York, NY
Carroll, Kimberly Gray ... Fairport, NY
Carroll, Kirk Bradley ... Durango, CO
Carroll, Kline & Wall ... Chicago, IL
Carroll, Krispen S. ... Rochester, MI
Carroll & Lane ... Norwalk, CT
Carroll, Larry ... Denver, CO
Carroll, Laura Emily ... Kew Gardens, NY
Carroll, Laura J. ... Los Angeles, CA
Carroll, Laura L. ... Boston, MA
Carroll, Laurence B., III ... Portland, ME
Carroll, Laurie A. ... Philadelphia, PA
Carroll, Laurie A. ... Dallas, TX
Carroll Law Office, Ltd. ... Rosemount, MN
Carroll Law Office, S.C. ... Cedarburg, WI
Carroll, Lawrence W. ... Markham, IL
Carroll, Lawrence W., Jr.
Altamonte Springs, FL
Carroll, Lawrence W., Jr., P.A.
Altamonte Springs, FL
Carroll, Lee ... Syracuse, NY
Carroll, Lee ... Houston, TX
Carroll, Leo P. ... Milford, CT
Carroll, Leslie A. ... Newark, NJ
Carroll, Lewis ... McLean, VA
Carroll, Linda L. ... Miami, FL
Carroll, Linda Law ... Pittsburgh, PA
Carroll, M. Lyle ... Jackson, MS
Carroll & Manges ... Fort Collins, CO
Carroll, Marcel E. ... Montgomery, AL
Carroll, Marci R. ... Fairmont, WV
Carroll, Marcus ... Tyler, TX
Carroll, Marcy L. Kozacek ... Denver, CO
Carroll, Margaret Ann ... Washington, DC
Carroll, Margaret C. ... Santa Monica, CA
Carroll, Marianne ... Austin, TX
Carroll, Marilyn M. ... Milwaukee, WI
Carroll, Mark ... Chicago, IL
Carroll, Mark Bennett
Fort Lauderdale, FL
Carroll, Mark C. ... Jackson, MS
Carroll, Mark J. ... Washington, DC
Carroll, Mark J. ... Dallas, TX
Carroll, Mark M. ... Miami, FL
Carroll, Mark M., & Associates, P.C.
Miami, FL
Carroll, Mark T. ... Philadelphia, PA
Carroll, Martha W. ... Boston, MA
Carroll, Martin B., (P.C.) ... Chicago, IL
Carroll, Mary C. ... Oakmont, PA
Carroll, Mary Lynn ... Northampton, MA
Carroll, Mary M. ... New York, NY
Carroll, Mary S. ... Tallahassee, FL
Carroll, Mary Vozzola ... Chicago, IL
Carroll, Matthew F. ... Houston, TX
Carroll, Maura ... Concord, NH
Carroll, Maureen ... Norwood, MA
Carroll, Maureen A. ... Flushing, NY
Carroll, Maureen English ... Minneapolis, MN
Carroll, Maurine A. ... Franklin, TN
Carroll, McNulty & Kull L.L.C.
Far Hills, NJ
Gladstone, NJ
Morristown, NJ
Peapack, NJ
Somerville, NJ
New York, NY
Carroll, Megan J. ... Palo Alto, CA
Carroll, Melanie J. ... Rockingham, NC
Carroll, Michael Andrew ... Hackensack, NJ
Carroll, Michael B. ... Denver, CO
Carroll, Michael Brooks
San Francisco, CA
Carroll, Michael C. ... New York, NY
Carroll, Michael D. ... Detroit, MI

Carson, Phillip L. ....Chicago, IL
Carson, Randee K. ....Clearwater, FL
Carson, Richard C. ....Los Alamitos, CA
Carson, Richard M. ....Tulsa, OK
Carson, Robert A. ....Chicago, IL
Carson, Robert J. ....Baltimore, MD
Carson, Robert J., P.A. ....Baltimore, MD
Carson, Robert M. ....Birmingham, MI
Carson, Robert O. ....Bedford, OH
Carson, Robert W. ....Fort Gratiot, MI
Carson, Rosa H. ....Tallahassee, FL
Carson, Roy R. ....Prescott, AZ
Carson, Russell D. ....Tulsa, OK
Wagoner, OK
Carson, Ruth P. ....Denver, CO
Carson, Sandra Pirie ....New York, NY
Carson, Sheree Strom ....Bellevue, WA
Carson, Steven L. ....Lisle, IL
Carson, Susan M. ....Alameda, CA
Carson, Tami L. ....Tulsa, OK
Carson, Timothy J. ....Philadelphia, PA
Carson, Van ....Cleveland, OH
Carson, Vincent D. ....El Paso, TX
Carson, Virginia S. ....Silver Spring, MD
Carson, W. Scott ....Denver, CO
Carson, Wallace P., Jr. ....Salem, OR
Carson, Wallis M. ....Tampa, FL
Carson, Walter E. ....Silver Spring, MD
Carson, Wendy B. ....Los Angeles, CA
Carson, William A., II ....Memphis, TN
Carson, William E. ....Covington, VA
Carson, William F. ....Birmingham, MI
Carson, William H. ....Eureka, CA
Carson, William W., Jr. ....Warrenton, VA
Carsonie, Frank W. ....Columbus, OH
Carsons, Theo ....Lawrence, NY
Carson-Selman, Mark L. ....New York, NY
Carss, D. Bradley ....Escondido, CA
Carssow, Tim ....Atlanta, GA
Carssow, William Benton ....Austin, TX
Carstarphen, Edward M. ....Houston, TX
Carstarphen, Lisa R. ....Miami, FL
Carstarphen, M.L. ....Washington, DC
Miami, FL
Carstarphen, Oktavia Dertinger
Galveston, TX
Carstedt, William D. ....Chicago, IL
Carsten, Douglas H. ....Los Angeles, CA
Carstens, Anne P., (Mrs.) ....Beatrice, NE
Carstens, David W. ....Dallas, TX
Carstens, Donald ....Newport Beach, CA
Carstens, Fred W. ....Beatrice, NE
Carstens, John H. ....Washington, DC
Fairfax, VA
Carstens, Kurt ....Newport, OR
Carstens, Philip J., Jr. ....Spokane, WA
Carstens, Rand Dunn ....Los Angeles, CA
Carstens, Theresa L. ....San Diego, CA
Carstens, Yee & Cahoon, L.L.P.
Dallas, TX
Carstensen, J. William ....Salt Lake City, UT
Carstensen, Jack E. ....Cocoa, FL
Orlando, FL
Carstensen, Paula M. ....Chicago, IL
Carstensen, Peter C. ....Madison, WI
Carstensen, Richard J. ....Billings, MT
Carstenson, Larry G. ....Kearney, NE
Carswell, Bruce ....Stamford, CT
Carswell, Kenneth R. ....Jesup, GA
Carswell, Matthew E. ....St. Louis, MO
Carswell, Robert ....New York, NY
Carta, John J., Jr. ....Essex, CT
Carta, Mark R. ....Darien, CT
Carta, Salvadore ....Omaha, NE
Carta, Steven ....Fort Myers, FL
Cartafalsa, John B., Sr. ....New York, NY
Cartafalsa, Joseph B. ....Iselin, NJ
New York, NY
Cartafalsa, Lisa A. ....New York, NY
Cartagena, Angel M., Jr.
Federal Communications Commission, Common Carrier Bureau, GV
Cartagena, Juan ....New York, NY
Cartagena-Santiago, Edgar ....San Juan, PR
Cartall, Bryan P. ....San Antonio, TX
Cartall Law Firm, The ....San Antonio, TX
Cartano, David J. ....Los Angeles, CA
Cartano, John D. ....Bellevue, WA
Cartaya, Carmen Y. ....Miami, FL
Carte, Gene ....Fayetteville, WV
Cartee, David S. ....Atlanta, GA
Cartee, Eric Scott ....Madison, TN
Cartee, Gary L. ....Charleston, SC
Cartee, Jonathan W. ....Birmingham, AL
Cartee, Joseph B. ....Birmingham, AL
Cartee, Martha J. Carpenter ....Lenoir, NC
Cartee, Michael J. ....Tuscaloosa, AL
Cartee, S. Joel ....Atlanta, GA
Carteen, Lisa I. ....Raleigh, NC
Cartelli, Carolynn Auber ....Cambridge, MA
Cartelli, James A. ....White Plains, NY
Cartelli, Lawrence P. ....New York, NY
Cartelli, Michael A. ....Pasadena, CA
Cartelli, Salvatore J. ....Middletown, CT
Cartelli, Thomas ....Middletown, CT
Cartelli, Thomas ....Bronx, NY
Carten, Francis N. ....New York, NY
Cartenuto, David J. ....Somers, NY
Carter, A. Wayne ....Las Vegas, NV
Carter, Adam Augustine ....Washington, DC
Carter, Adrianna L.
Research Triangle Park, NC
Carter, Allan P. ....Vallejo, CA
Carter, Allen G., Sr. ....Canton, OH
Carter, Allen G., Sr. Co., L.P.A.
Canton, OH
Carter, Allison Molony ....Charleston, SC
Carter, Amanda C. ....Montgomery, AL

Carter, Amie Peele ....Indianapolis, IN
Carter, Amy M. ....Dallas, TX
Carter, Anderson, II ....Las Cruces, NM
Carter, Anderson, II, P.C. ....Las Cruces, NM
Carter, Andrea G. ....New Brunswick, NJ
Carter, Andrew B. ....Memphis, TN
Carter, Andrew W. ....The Dalles, OR
Carter, Anne Marie ....Atlanta, GA
Carter, Anne Michele ....Manchester, NH
Carter & Ansley ....Atlanta, GA
Carter, Anthony O. ....Flushing, NY
Carter, Anthony Todd ....Montgomery, AL
Carter, Antoinette D ....New York, NY
Carter, Archie & Hassell ....Washington, NC
Carter, Arthur F. ....Guilford, CT
Carter, Arthur M. ....Indianapolis, IN
Carter, Arthur T. ....Dallas, TX
Carter, Austin E. ....Atlanta, GA
Carter, Barry E. ....Washington, DC
Carter & Bauer ....St. Louis, MO
Carter, Behnke, Oglesby and Bacik
Eureka, CA
Fort Bragg, CA
Lakeport, CA
Santa Rosa, CA
Ukiah, CA
Carter, Ben D. ....Lansing, MI
Carter, Benjamin E. ....Riverhead, NY
Carter, Bernard A. ....Crown Point, IN
Carter, Betsy I. ....Plano, TX
Carter, Billy L. ....Montgomery, AL
Carter, Brenda J. ....Fort Lauderdale, FL
Carter, Bret R. ....Los Angeles, CA
Carter, Brett James ....Clovis, NM
Carter, Brett R.
United States Tax Court, GV
Carter, Brian ....Corona Del Mar, CA
Carter, Brian C. ....Ukiah, CA
Carter, Brian M. ....San Francisco, CA
Carter, Brock & Hinman, P.A.
Idaho Falls, ID
Carter, Brown & Osborne, P.C.
Roanoke, VA
Carter, Bruce ....Burbank, CA
Carter, Bruce ....Monroe, OH
Carter, Bruce R. ....Reisterstown, MD
Carter, Burney J. ....Sebastian, FL
Carter, Burney J., P.A. ....Sebastian, FL
Carter, Byron R. ....Orlando, FL
Carter, C. Kent ....Bloomington, IN
Carter, C. Michael ....Westport, CT
Oceanport, NJ
New York, NY
Carter, C. Philip ....Knoxville, TN
Carter, C. Scott ....Metairie, LA
Carter, C. Scott ....Kansas City, MO
Carter, C. Stuart ....Indianapolis, IN
Carter, Callan G. ....San Francisco, CA
Carter, Candy L. ....Hanover, MD
Carter, Carl Q. ....Memphis, TN
Carter & Carlson, LLP ....Pasadena, CA
Carter, Carlton C. ....Canton, GA
Carter, Carol Elizabeth
Colorado Springs, CO
Carter, Carrie M. Coppinger ....Seattle, WA
Carter & Carter ....San Francisco, CA
Carter & Carter ....Sioux City, IA
Carter & Carter ....Boston, MA
Carter & Carter ....Wilmington, NC
Carter & Carter ....Enid, OK
Carter and Carter ....Johnson City, TN
Carter & Carter ....Fort Worth, TX
Carter & Cates ....New Orleans, LA
Carter, Catherine C. ....Atlanta, GA
Carter, Catherine J. ....Los Angeles, CA
Carter, C.D., III ....Albuquerque, NM
Carter, Chad C. ....Arlington, TX
Carter, Charles B., Jr. ....Gainesville, FL
Carter, Charles C., Jr. ....Stockton, CA
Carter, Charles E. ....Owenton, KY
Carter, Charles E. ....Danville, VA
Carter, Charles E., Jr. ....La Grange, KY
Owenton, KY
Carter, Charles G. ....Milwaukee, WI
Carter, Charles H. ....Corona, CA
Perris, CA
Carter, Charles L., Jr. ....Crockett, TX
Carter, Charles P. ....Clinton, TN
Carter, Charles P. ....Kirkland, WA
Carter, Chelo Zepeda ....Houston, TX
Carter, Cheryl Roche ....Houston, TX
Carter, Chris A. ....Berea, KY
Carter, Christina M. ....Orinda, CA
Carter, Christopher H. M. ....Concord, NH
Carter, Christopher O'Hara ....Flippin, AR
Carter, Christopher O'Hara, P.A., Law Offices of ....Flippin, AR
Carter & Civitello ....New Haven, CT
Woodbridge, CT
Carter, Clara A. ....Chicago, IL
Carter, Clarence W. ....Danbury, NC
Carter, Claude D. ....Roanoke, VA
Carter, Clay ....Midland, MI
Carter, Clayton C. ....Centreville, MD
Carter, Clement D. ....Clarksburg, WV
Carter, Clifford C. ....Midland, MI
Carter, Clifford L. ....Sacramento, CA
Carter, Clifton B. ....Fort Worth, TX
Carter, Clinton C. ....Montgomery, AL
Carter & Coleman ....Washington, DC
Alexandria, VA
Arlington, VA
Fairfax, VA
Carter, Colyn E. ....Eagle River, WI
Carter, Conboy, Case, Blackmore, Napierski and Maloney, P.C. ....Albany, NY
Carter, Courtney D. ....Chicago, IL

Carter, Craig, Bass, Blair & Kushner, P.C.
Danville, VA
Carter, Craig D. ....Oklahoma City, OK
Carter, Cristina ....San Antonio, TX
Carter, Cynthia Elaine Kinser ....Nashville, TN
Carter, D. Jeffrey ....Racine, WI
Carter, D. Reeves ....New York, NY
Carter, Dan T. ....Atlanta, GA
Carter, Daniel P. ....Cleveland, OH
Carter, Daniel P. ....Warwick, RI
Carter, Daniel R. ....Little Rock, AR
Carter, Daniel R. ....Chicago, IL
Carter, Daniel R. ....Warrensburg, MO
Carter, Daniel R. ....Houston, TX
Carter, Darnell E. ....Springfield, OH
Carter, Darrel B. ....Bellevue, WA
Carter, Darrell ....Bemidji, MN
Carter, Darryl K. ....Houston, TX
Carter, David A. ....Boca Raton, FL
Carter, David A. ....Annapolis, MD
Riverdale, MD
Carter, David A. ....Spokane, WA
Carter, David A., P.A. ....Boca Raton, FL
Carter, David B., Jr. ....Lansing, MI
Carter, David C. ....Boulder, CO
Carter, David C. ....Jacksonville, FL
Carter, David C. ....Charlottesville, VA
Carter, David E. ....Batavia, OH
Carter, David G. ....Charlotte, NC
Carter, David Kelly ....Tompkinsville, KY
Carter, David M. ....Vero Beach, FL
Carter, David M. ....Atlanta, GA
Carter, David M. ....Uniondale, NY
Carter, David M. ....Asheville, NC
Carter, David O. ....Los Angeles, CA
Carter, David O. ....Sioux Falls, SD
Carter, David P. ....Largo, FL
Carter, David P. ....San Antonio, TX
Carter, David R. ....New Port Richey, FL
Carter, David R., P.A. ....New Port Richey, FL
Carter, David S. ....Anchorage, AK
Carter, David W. ....London, OH
Carter, David W. ....Lawton, OK
Carter, David Wayne ....Columbia, TN
Carter & Davidson ....Columbus, MS
Carter & Deaton ....Yuma, AZ
Carter, Deborah L. ....Evergreen, CO
Carter, Deborah M. ....Atlanta, GA
Carter, Denise Mullens ....East Orange, NJ
Carter, Derb, Jr. ....Charlottesville, VA
Carter, Diane Tripp ....Austin, TX
Carter, Dianna K. ....Indio, CA
Carter, Dianne T. ....Newport News, VA
Carter, Don G. ....Portland, OR
Carter, Donald D., Jr. ....Department of Labor, Office of the Solicitor, GV
Carter, Donald L. ....Portland, ME
Carter and Donnelly, P.C.
Port Jefferson Station, NY
Carter, Doris Adkins ....Wheaton, IL
Carter, Dorval R., Jr.
Department of Transportation, Federal Transit Administration, GV
Carter, Douglas ....Tompkinsville, KY
Carter, Douglas A. ....Burbank, CA
Carter, Douglas Alan ....Oklahoma City, OK
Carter, Douglas J. ....Johnson City, TN
Carter & Drylie, P.A. ....Gainesville, FL
Carter, Dudley H. ....Columbus, MS
Carter, E. Beale, Jr. ....Boykins, VA
Carter, E. Leon ....Dallas, TX
Carter, Earl F. ....Rialto, CA
Carter, Edward B., Jr. ....Wilmington, DE
Carter, Edward C., III ....Chicago, IL
Carter, Edward Carlton ....Columbus, GA
Carter, Edward E. ....Doraville, GA
Carter, Edward E., P.C. ....Doraville, GA
Carter, Edward Keith ....Shreveport, LA
Carter, Edwin F. (Ted) ....Novato, CA
Carter, Elizabeth Ashley ....Covington, LA
Carter, Elizabeth Blair ....Charlottesville, VA
Carter, Elizabeth Brannen
Montgomery, AL
Carter, Elizabeth Taylor ....Farmville, VA
Carter, Eric C. ....Kansas City, MO
Carter, Eric H. ....Portland, OR
Carter, Erik ....Shelbyville, IN
Carter, Erin L. ....Department of Justice, Antitrust Division, GV
Carter, Ernest R., Jr. ....Ahoskie, NC
Carter, Eugenia G. ....Madison, WI
Carter, Evans J. ....Framingham, MA
Carter, E.W. "Skip" ....Pocatello, ID
Carter, Ewing, III ....High Point, NC
Carter, Farah K. ....Atlanta, GA
Carter, Francis D., Law Offices of
Washington, DC
Carter, Francis L. ....Miami, FL
Carter, Frank M. ....Fairfax, VA
Carter, Frank N., Jr. ....St. Louis, MO
Carter, Frederick W. H. ....Denver, CO
Carter, G. Todd ....Brunswick, GA
Carter, Gaines P. ....Duluth, GA
Carter, Gary J. ....Dayton, OH
Carter, Gebauer & Waldman
Southfield, MI
Carter, Gene ....Portland, ME
Carter, Geo S. ....Boston, MA
Carter, Geoffrey N. ....Oakland, CA
Carter, George C. ....Lancaster, NH
Carter, George M. ....Benton, KY
Carter, George R. ....Louisville, KY
Carter, George R. ....Las Vegas, NV
Carter, George R., Ltd. ....Las Vegas, NV
Carter, Georgia B. ....Clarksburg, WV
Carter, Gerald W. S. ....Richmond, VA
Carter, Geraldine C. ....Los Angeles, CA

Carter, Geraldine C., Law Offices of
Los Angeles, CA
Carter, Geronda Vertasha ....Union City, GA
Carter & Getty, P.C. ....Locust Grove, VA
Orange, VA
Carter, Gideon T., III ....Baton Rouge, LA
Carter, Gilbert H. ....Nevada, MO
Carter, Gina ....Greenwood Village, CO
Carter, Glenn Dale ....Shawnee, OK
Carter, Glenn J. ....Phoenix, AZ
Carter, Glenn Thomas ....Silver Spring, MD
Carter, Gordon T. ....Montgomery, AL
Carter, Grace A. ....San Francisco, CA
Carter, Greg B. ....Joplin, MO
Carter, Gregory C.
Department of Transportation, Federal Aviation Administration, GV
Carter, Gregory Erwin ....Newark, OH
Carter, Gregory S. ....Terre Haute, IN
Carter & Grimsley ....Peoria, IL
Carter, H. Bruce ....Burbank, CA
Carter, H. Byron, III ....Jackson, MS
Carter, H. Sanders, Jr. ....Atlanta, GA
Carter, H. A. Bud ....Oklahoma City, OK
Carter, H.A., III ....Oklahoma City, OK
Carter, Halle ....Broomfield, CO
Carter, Harold B., Jr. (IBA)
New Orleans, LA
Carter, Harold M., Jr. ....Rochester, NY
Carter, Harold R. ....Belfast, ME
Carter, Harold R. ....Majuro, TT
Carter, Harriet H. ....San Diego, CA
Carter, Harrod & Cunningham
Athens, TN
Cleveland, TN
Dayton, TN
Carter, Harry L. ....San Diego, CA
Carter, Henry Lee ....Orange, VA
Carter, Henry S. ....Richmond, VA
Carter, Henry Wolfgang ....Washington, DC
Carter & Hinman, P.A. ....Boise, ID
Carter, Hunter T. ....Washington, DC
Carter, J. Denise ....Kansas City, MO
Carter, J. Don ....Fort Worth, TX
Carter, J. Kenneth, Jr. ....Columbia, SC
Carter, J. Montgomery ....Fresno, CA
Carter, J. Robert, Jr. ....Memphis, TN
Carter, J. Ross ....Redding, CA
Carter, J. Steven ....Tallahassee, FL
Carter, Jack Ellison ....Texarkana, TX
Carter, James A. ....San Francisco, CA
Carter, James A. ....San Angelo, TX
Carter, James A., & Associates, A Prof. Corp.
San Angelo, TX
Carter, James C. ....Beaverton, OR
Carter, James D., Jr., Law Office of
Bradenton, FL
Carter, James E. ....Phoenix, AZ
Carter, James E. ....Santa Ana, CA
Carter, James E. ....Madison, GA
Carter, James E. ....Cherry Hill, NJ
Carter, James H. ....Cedar Rapids, IA
Carter, James H. ....Coralville, IA
Carter, James H. ....Charlotte, NC
Carter, James H., Jr. ....New York, NY
Carter, James J. ....Castle Rock, CO
Carter, James L., Jr. ....Salisbury, NC
Carter, James Lee ....San Francisco, CA
Carter, James M. ....Albuquerque, NM
Carter, James M. ....Columbus, OH
Carter, James Oliver ....Wilmington, NC
Carter, James P. ....Irvine, CA
Carter, James P. ....Milwaukee, WI
Carter, James R. ....Peoria, IL
Carter, James R. ....Hopkinsville, KY
Carter, James R. ....New Orleans, LA
Carter, James S. ....Albany, NY
Carter, James W. ....Port Jefferson Station, NY
Carter, James W., IV ....San Antonio, TX
Carter, James W., Jr. ....Schaumburg, IL
Carter, Janet L. ....Myrtle Beach, SC
Carter, Jason D. ....Beverly Hills, CA
Carter, Jason E. ....Department of Justice, Criminal Division, GV
Carter, J. B. ....Kirkwood, MO
Carter, Jean Gordon ....Raleigh, NC
Carter, Jean Turner ....Little Rock, AR
Carter, Jean W. ....San Francisco, CA
Carter, Jeanne M. ....Oklahoma City, OK
Carter, Jeff J. ....Salem, OR
Carter, Jeff J., P.C. ....Salem, OR
Carter, Jeffery J. ....Tucson, AZ
Carter, Jeffrey A. ....Dallas, TX
Carter, Jeffrey C. ....Los Angeles, CA
New York, NY
Carter, Jennifer A. ....New York, NY
Carter, Jennifer C. ....Orlando, FL
Carter, Jennifer Williams ....Easton, MD
Carter, Jeremy M. ....Mashpee, MA
Carter, Jerome Christopher ....Mobile, AL
Carter, Jerry C. ....Reno, NV
Carter, Jessica Schaetzl ....New York, NY
Carter, Jill Herron ....Deerfield, IL
Carter, Jim H. ....Fort Lauderdale, FL
Carter, Jimmy Ira ....Dallas, TX
Carter, Jo Ann ....Houston, TX
Carter, Joan S. ....Department of Justice, Environment and Natural Resources Division, GV
Carter, Joanne L. ....San Jose, CA
Carter, Joel S. ....Moline, IL
Carter, John ....New York, NY
Carter, John Allen ....Macomb, IL
Carter, John B., Jr. ....Lumberton, NC
Carter, John C. ....Harlan, KY
Carter, John D. ....San Francisco, CA
Carter, John E. ....Boca Raton, FL
Carter, John E. ....Nashville, TN

Carter, John E. ... Fairfax, VA
Carter, John E., P.C. ... Fairfax, VA
Carter, John F., III ... Wilmington, NC
Carter, John Henry, Jr. ... New York, NY
Carter, John J. ... Milwaukee, WI
Carter, John Jeffery, Law Office ... Chico, CA
Carter, John K. ... Louisville, KY
Carter, John Kinnley ... New York, NY
Carter, John L. ... Houston, TX
Carter, John M. ... Roseau, MN
Carter, John M. ... Alexandria Bay, NY
Clayton, NY
Carter, John M. ... New York, NY
Carter, John M. ... Portsmouth, VA
Carter, John M. ... Richmond, VA
Carter, John M. ... Richmond, VA
Carter, John M., P.A. ... Roseau, MN
Carter, John Penn, III ... El Centro, CA
Carter, John R. ... Georgetown, TX
Carter, John R. ... San Antonio, TX
Carter, John T. ... Auburn Hills, MI
Carter, John T., Jr. ... Jacksonville, NC
Carter, John W. ... St. Louis, MO
Carter, John W. ... Danville, VA
Carter, Johnny W. ... Houston, TX
Carter, Jon M. ... Melbourne, FL
Carter, Jonathan P. ... Boise, ID
Carter, Jos. S. ... Boston, MA
Carter, Joseph C., III ... Richmond, VA
Carter, Joseph C., Jr. ... Richmond, VA
Carter, Joseph H. ... Omaha, NE
Carter, Joseph I. ... Tifton, GA
Carter, Joseph T. ... Marshalltown, IA
Carter, Joyce E. ... Springfield, IL
Carter, Julia Vance ... New York, NY
Carter, Julianne H. ... Phoenix, AZ
Carter, Julie A. ... Sacramento, CA
Carter, Julie Behm ... New Haven, CT
Carter, Karen B. ... Culver City, CA
Carter, Karen R. ... New Orleans, LA
Carter, Karin W. ... Harrisburg, PA
Carter, Katharine Mull ... Warsaw, IN
Carter, Katharine S. ... Hudson, OH
Carter, Katherine Keeton ... Boston, MA
Carter, Katherine L. ... Los Angeles, CA
Carter, Kathleen A. ... Newport Beach, CA
Carter, Kathleen D. ... Albuquerque, NM
Carter, Kathleen Mary Kushi ... Santa Ana, CA
Carter, Kathryn ... Jamestown, KS
Carter, Kayla D. ... Dallas, TX
Carter, Keith C. ... Austin, TX
Carter, Keith M. ... Ventura, CA
Carter, Keith M. ... Tampa, FL
Carter, Kelly A. ... Detroit, MI
Carter, Kenford O. ... Flippin, AR
Carter, Kenneth B. ... Santa Ana, CA
Carter, Kenneth M., (A Professional Law Corporation) ... New Orleans, LA
Carter, Kenneth P. ... New Orleans, LA
Carter, Kevin A. ... Pittsburgh, PA
Carter, Kevin B. ... Los Angeles, CA
Carter, Kevin M. ... Buffalo, NY
Carter, Kevin W. ... Department of the Army, U.S. Army Court of Criminal Appeals, GV
Carter, Kim M. ... Lancaster, PA
Carter, Kirk A. ... Worcester, MA
Carter & Kirk, P.C. ... Oklahoma City, OK
Carter & Kramer, P.C. ... Alexandria, VA
Carter, Kris O. ... Washington, DC
Carter & Kropelnicki, P.A. ... Asheville, NC
Carter, Lana ... Orange, CA
Carter, Laurel A. ... Palmer, AK
Carter, Laurie Aleta ... New York, NY
Carter Law Firm, P.C. ... Albuquerque, NM
Carter Law Office ... Gillette, WY
Carter, Lawrence A. ... Quincy, MA
Carter, Lawrence B. ... Fort Worth, TX
Carter, Ledyard & Milburn ... Washington, DC
New York, NY
Carter, Lee C. ... Washington, DC
Carter, Lee R. ... Santa Barbara, CA
Carter, Leigh H. ... Cleveland, OH
Carter, Leland E. ... Memphis, TN
Carter, Leland W. ... Dallas, TX
Carter, Leonard H. ... New York, NY
Carter, Leroy K. ... Dallas, TX
Carter, Lesa Landry ... Washington, DC
Carter, Lester G., Jr. ... Fayetteville, NC
Carter, Lewis C. ... Topeka, KS
Carter, Lewis N. ... Tulsa, OK
Carter, Linda C. ... Annapolis, MD
Riverdale, MD
Carter, Linda E. ... Sacramento, CA
Carter, Linda Kelleher ... San Diego, CA
Carter, Lisa D. ... Benton, KY
Carter, Lisette F. ... Spokane, WA
Carter, Lloyd V. ... Waukesha, WI
Carter, Lori A. ... Savannah, GA
Carter, Louis J. ... Philadelphia, PA
Carter, Lynda ... Jackson, MS
Carter, Lynn E. ... Austin, TX
Carter, Lynn J. ... Lake Forest, IL
Carter, Lynn P. ... Houston, TX
Carter, Mabee & Paris ... Chattanooga, TN
Carter, Mac Bradley ... Seminole, OK
Carter, Macauley, Jr. ... Marshalltown, IA
Carter, Malaika D. ... Washington, DC
Carter Mancini & Sermet ... Los Angeles, CA
Carter, Margaret H. ... Boston, MA
Carter, Marie D. ... Richmond, VA
Carter, Marie W. ... Placerville, CA
Carter, Marjorie K. ... St. Louis, MO
Carter, Mark A. ... Chicago, IL
Carter, Mark A. ... Charleston, WV
Carter, Mark F. ... Wilmington, NC
Carter, Mark H. ... Madison, WI
Carter, Mark S. ... Phenix City, AL
Carter, Mark S. ... Little Rock, AR
Carter, Marsha Dunning ... Eastville, VA
Carter, Mary Renae ... Charlottesville, VA
Carter, Mary Wiesman ... Houston, TX
Carter, Matthew C. ... Fort Smith, AR
Carter, Matthew J. ... Burlington, VT
Carter, Matthew M., II ... Tallahassee, FL
Carter, Maxine L. ... North Hollywood, CA
Carter, Maxwell D. ... Birmingham, AL
Carter, Melanie S. ... Chicago, IL
Carter, Melissa W. ... Alpharetta, GA
Carter, Melody ... Cincinnati, OH
Carter, Michael A. ... Fort Worth, TX
Carter, Michael C. ... Fort Smith, AR
Carter, Michael D. ... Oklahoma City, OK
Carter, Michael G. ... Milwaukee, WI
Carter, Michael H. ... Phoenix, AZ
Carter, Michael J. ... Orlando, FL
Carter, Michael L. ... Indianapolis, IN
Carter, Michael L. ... Mayaguez, PR
Carter, Michael W. ... Danville, CA
Carter, Michele D. ... Los Angeles, CA
Carter, Michelle Qvale ... San Francisco, CA
Carter, Mike ... Crawfordville, FL
Carter, Mike ... Nashville, TN
Carter, Mikele S. ... Blairsville, GA
Carter, Miller Kent ... Pikeville, KY
Carter, Milton J., Jr. ... Seattle, WA
Carter, Mitchel M. ... Peralta, NM
Carter, Nancy Carol ... San Diego, CA
Carter, Nancy L. ... Huntsville, AL
Carter, Nancy Lee ... Neenah, WI
Carter, Nancy Rink ... Ottawa, IL
Carter, Nathan P. ... Orlando, FL
Carter, Nicala R. ... Chicago, IL
Carter, Nicholas B. ... Boston, MA
Carter, Nicholas B. ... St. Louis, MO
Carter, Nicholas H. ... Gillette, WY
Carter, Nick ... Huntington, WV
Carter, Nolan ... Orlando, FL
Carter, Nolan, Jr. ... Lexington, KY
Carter, Nolan, P.A. ... Orlando, FL
Carter, Norman M., Jr. ... Plainfield, NJ
New York, NY
Carter, Odell C. ... Star City, AR
Carter, Orbin F. ... Charlottesville, VA
Carter, Osborne ... Newark, NJ
Carter, Otis C., Jr. ... Walterboro, SC
Carter, Ottowa E., Jr. ... Jackson, MS
Carter, Pamela W. ... New Orleans, LA
Carter, Patrice P. ... Raleigh, NC
Carter, Patricia I. ... Minneapolis, MN
Carter, Patricia Winn ... Winter Park, FL
Carter, Patrick J., Law Offices of ... San Francisco, CA
Carter, Paul B. ... San Antonio, TX
Carter, Paul J. ... Los Angeles, CA
Carter, Paul N. ... Mohawk, NY
Carter, Peggy L. ... Guymon, OK
Carter, Peter H. ... Norwich, VT
Carter, Peter W. ... Minneapolis, MN
Carter, Philip L., (P.S.) ... Kirkland, WA
Carter, Philip R. ... New York, NY
Carter, Philip T. ... Bloomfield Hills, MI
Carter, Philip V. ... Chicago, IL
Carter, Phillip C. ... Jackson, MS
Carter, Phillip N. ... Sidney, MT
Carter, Phyllis H. ... Charleston, WV
Carter, Phyllis H., L.C. ... Charleston, WV
Carter, Priscilla D. ... New York, NY
Carter, R. Bruce ... Oklahoma City, OK
Carter, R. Douglas ... Dayton, OH
Carter, R. Michael ... Tulsa, OK
Carter, R. Thomas ... Louisville, KY
Carter, R. Trevor ... Indianapolis, IN
Carter, Raines Felton ... Atlanta, GA
Carter, Ralph D. ... Hazard, KY
Carter, Ralph F. ... Grand Forks, ND
Carter, Ramseier, & Holcombe ... Alexandria Bay, NY
Clayton, NY
Carter, Randall A. ... Denver, CO
Carter, Randolph W. ... Norcross, GA
Carter, Randy J. ... Dallas, TX
Carter, Ray C. ... Madison, MS
Carter, Raymond D. ... Gulfport, MS
Carter, Renée ... Oakland, CA
Carter, Rex L. ... Greenville, SC
Greer, SC
Carter, Richard B. ... Tustin, CA
Carter, Richard C. ... Cooper City, FL
Carter, Richard D. ... Los Angeles, CA
Carter, Richard D. ... Washington, DC
Alexandria, VA
Carter, Richard E. ... New York, NY
Carter, Richard E. ... Philadelphia, PA
Carter, Richard E. ... Charlottesville, VA
Carter, Richard J., Jr. ... Atlanta, GA
Carter, Richard J., Jr. ... New York, NY
Carter, Richard M. ... Marietta, GA
Carter, Richard M. ... Memphis, TN
Carter, Richard S. ... Denver, CO
Carter, Richard W. ... Bradenton Beach, FL
Carter, Richard W. ... San Antonio, TX
Carter & Richbourg, L.L.P. ... Tifton, GA
Carter, Rick K. ... Yuma, AZ
Carter, Robert A. ... Newark, NJ
Carter, Robert A. ... Fort Worth, TX
Carter, Robert A., P.C. ... Fort Worth, TX
Carter, Robert B. ... Johnson City, TN
Carter, Robert B., II ... Indianapolis, IN
Carter, Robert Bryson ... Greensboro, NC
Carter, Robert D. ... Oklahoma City, OK
Carter, Robert E. ... Pasadena, CA
Carter, Robert F. ... Woodbridge, CT
Carter, Robert G. ... Fresno, CA
Carter, Robert Guy ... Dallas, TX
Carter, Robert J. ... Greensburg, LA
Carter, Robert J. ... Houston, TX
Carter, Robert L. ... Chicago, IL
Carter, Robert L. ... New York, NY
Carter, Robert L., Jr. ... Washington, DC
Carter, Robert M. ... Golden, CO
Carter, Robert M. ... New Albany, MS
Carter, Robert M. ... Cleveland, OH
Carter, Robert N. ... Abilene, TX
Carter, Robert R. ... Chesapeake, VA
Carter, Robert S. ... Richmond, VA
Carter, Robert T. ... Tullahoma, TN
Carter, Robert T. ... Spokane, WA
Carter, Robert W., Jr. ... Appomattox, VA
Carter, Robin C. ... Tucson, AZ
Carter, Robin C., Attorney-at-Law, P.C. ... Tucson, AZ
Carter, Roch ... Milwaukee, WI
Carter, Rodney T. ... Philadelphia, PA
Carter, Rodney W. ... Milwaukee, WI
Carter, Roger L. ... Sioux City, IA
Carter, Roger R. ... Irvine, CA
Carter, Ronald W. ... Oakland, CA
Carter, Rosette A. ... Columbia, SC
Carter, Ross T. ... Frankfort, KY
Carter, Rowland F. ... Enid, OK
Carter, Roy F. ... Lee's Summit, MO
Carter, Russ ... Aloha, OR
Carter, Russell L. ... Washington, DC
Carter, Russell L. ... Dayton, OH
Carter, Ruth M. ... Sioux City, IA
Carter, S. Booker, Jr. ... Atlanta, GA
Carter, S. Keenan ... Dallas, TX
Carter, Sam A. ... Pikeville, KY
Carter, Samuel H. ... Columbia, SC
Carter, Sandra Jesse ... Boston, MA
Carter, Sandra L. ... Houston, TX
Carter & Sands, P.C. ... Rifle, CO
Carter, Sarah A. ... Bloomington, IN
Carter, Sarah Pitts ... Brookline, MA
Carter, Sasha ... Department of Commerce, Patent and Trademark Office, GV
Carter & Schnedler, P.A. ... Asheville, NC
Carter, Scott ... Asheville, NC
Carter, Scott H. ... Napa, CA
Carter, Scott H. ... Sarasota, FL
Carter, Scott N. ... San Jose, CA
Carter, Scott O. ... Hillsboro, OR
Carter, Sean A. ... Los Angeles, CA
Carter, Sean Patrick ... Philadelphia, PA
Carter & Shands, A Professional Corporation ... Richmond, VA
Carter, Shannan L. ... Albuquerque, NM
Carter, Shelby L. ... San Francisco, CA
Carter, Shelden R. ... Provo, UT
Carter, Sherwood J. ... Hickory, NC
Carter, Sidney ... Bethesda, MD
Carter, Smith, Merriam, Rogers & Traxler, P.A. A Professional Corporation ... Greenville, SC
Greer, SC
Carter, Stacey Lewis ... Raleigh, NC
Carter, Stan ... Wichita Falls, TX
Carter, Stephan W. ... Orlando, FL
Carter, Stephanie E. ... Chicago, IL
Carter, Stephanie Young ... Lynchburg, VA
Carter, Stephen ... Indianapolis, IN
Carter, Stephen A. ... Chicago, IL
Carter, Stephen E. ... Hilton Head Island, SC
Carter, Stephen F. ... Memphis, TN
Carter, Stephen L. ... Rifle, CO
Carter, Stephen L. ... New Haven, CT
Carter, Stephen P., P.A. ... Bentonville, AR
Carter, Steven B. ... Washington, IA
Carter, Steven H. ... Wichita, KS
Carter, Susan K. ... Los Angeles, CA
Carter, Susan Knight ... New Orleans, LA
Carter, Susan W. ... Rockville, MD
Carter, Suzanne M. ... West Hartford, CT
Carter, T. Barton ... Boston, MA
Carter, T. Heyward, Jr. ... Charleston, SC
Carter, T. Wayne ... Baltimore, MD
Carter, Tammy T. ... Oklahoma City, OK
Carter & Tani ... Wheaton, IL
Carter & Taylor ... Metairie, LA
Carter, Terry J. ... Chicago, IL
Carter, Theodore R., III ... Department of Justice, Civil Division, GV
Carter, Theodore U. ... Williamstown, NJ
Carter, Theresa D. ... Mercer Island, WA
Carter, Theresa L. ... Columbus, OH
Carter, Thomas B. ... Dallas, TX
Carter, Thomas C. ... Portland, OR
Carter, Thomas C. ... Alexandria, VA
Carter, Thomas E. ... Treasury Department, Internal Revenue Service, GV
Carter, Thomas E. ... Boston, MA
Carter, Thomas, II ... St. Louis, MO
Carter & Thomas LLP, Law Offices of ... Boca Raton, FL
Carter, Thomas P. ... Los Angeles, CA
Carter, Thomasine B. ... Department Of Health And Human Services, Social Security Administration, GV
Carter, Tia M. ... Washington, DC
Carter, Tom ... Cornelia, GA
Carter, Tracey B. ... Nashville, TN
Carter, Tracy R. ... Nashville, TN
Carter, Travis N. ... Atlanta, GA
Carter, V. Stevens ... Medford Lakes, NJ
Carter, Valerie S. ... Lynnfield, MA
Carter, Van P. ... Cleveland, OH
Carter, Van Rensselaer & Caldwell, A Professional Corporation
Bernardsville, NJ
Clinton, NJ
Plainfield, NJ
New York, NY
Carter, Vereline F. ... Los Angeles, CA
Carter, Victoria H., P.A. ... Orlando, FL
Carter, Vincent G. ... Southfield, MI
Carter, Virginia G. ... Fargo, ND
Carter, Vivian R. ... Melville, NY
Carter, W. Burlette ... Washington, DC
Carter, W. David ... Texarkana, AR
Carter, W. Minor ... Washington, DC
Carter, W. Randolph ... Suffolk, VA
Carter, W. Sanders, Jr. ... Jackson, MS
Carter, W. Thomas, III ... Atlanta, GA
Carter, W. Trav ... Atlanta, GA
Carter, Waco ... Springfield, MO
Carter, Wanda L. ... Columbus, OH
Carter, Warren Randolph, Jr. ... Suffolk, VA
Carter, Weyman C. ... Greenville, SC
Carter, Willard R. ... Danbury, CT
Carter, William A. ... Canton, MS
Carter, William A. ... Albany, NY
Carter, William B. ... Meridian, MS
Carter, William B., Jr. ... Washington, NC
Carter, William B. Mitchell ... Chattanooga, TN
Carter, William C. ... Columbus, GA
Carter, William E. ... Hayesville, NC
Carter, William F. ... Madisonville, TX
Carter, William F. ... Martinsville, VA
Carter, William G. ... Medford, OR
Carter, William H. ... Securities and Exchange Commission, Division of Corporation Finance, GV
Carter, William J. ... Washington, DC
Carter, William L. ... Sacramento, CA
Carter, William M., Jr. ... Washington, DC
Carter, William O. ... Hartwell, GA
Carter, William O., Jr. ... Jackson, MS
Carter, William S., Jr. ... Ruston, LA
Carter, William W. ... Charleston, WV
Carter, Winstol D., Jr. ... Houston, TX
Carter, Wm. E., Jr. ... Richmond, VA
Carter & Young ... Charleston, WV
Clarksburg, WV
Carter, Zachary W. ... New York, NY
Carter Calbassa, Angela ... Tampa, FL
Carter-Galvan, Sheree L. ... New York, NY
Carter-SooHoo, Susan M. ... Rosemead, CA
Carter-White, Kathy ... Tahlequah, OK
Carthel, Mitch D. ... Amarillo, TX
Carthew, Paul A. ... Houston, TX
Carthy, Maria J. ... New York, NY
Cartier, Christopher P. ... Albertson, NY
Cartier & DeMatteo, LLC ... Fairfield, CT
Cartier, Linda C. ... Lutherville, MD
Cartier, Mark A. ... Walnut Creek, CA
Cartier, Michael G. ... Kalamazoo, MI
Cartier, Michael J. ... New Haven, CT
Cartier, Richard M. ... Fresno, CA
Cartier, Rudolph H., Jr. ... Patchogue, NY
Cartier, Susan G. ... Fairfield, CT
Cartier, Vincent J. ... Jersey City, NJ
Cartier Giroux, Lisa C. ... New York, NY
Cartiglia, James R. ... Stamford, CT
Cartiglia, John J. ... Mineola, NY
Cartin, Dan L. ... Denver, CO
Cartin, Jerold A. ... Tucson, AZ
Cartine, Maury ... Roseland, NJ
Cartisano, Linda A. ... Chester, PA
Cartledge, Cynthia Lea ... Anchorage, AK
Cartledge, Glynn Burroughs ... Reno, NV
Cartledge, John D. ... Columbus, GA
Cartledge, Kevin B. ... Winston-Salem, NC
Cartledge, Suzanne Lee ... Stamford, CT
Cartlidge, Blaine E. ... Reno, NV
Cartlidge, Blaine E., Chartered ... Reno, NV
Cartmel, Thomas O. ... Carmel, IN
Cartmell, Nathaniel M., III ... San Francisco, CA
Cartmell, Thomas P. ... Kansas City, MO
Cartner, David W. ... Asheville, NC
Cartner, Holly ... New York, NY
Carto, David D. ... Mansfield, OH
Cartoceti, Robert J. ... Southbury, CT
Cartolano, Frank ... New York, NY
Cartolano, Fredk. J. ... Cincinnati, OH
Cartolano, Mariarosa ... New York, NY
Carton, Arthur B. ... Washington, DC
Carton & Associates ... Middletown, NJ
Carton, Bernard ... Baltimore, MD
Carton, Bruce T. ... Reston, VA
Carton, Catherine Mary ... Ocean Township, NJ
Carton, Christopher R. ... Newark, NJ
Carton, David S. ... Woodbridge, NJ
Carton, Davis & Morris, P.A. ... Brunswick, ME
Carton, E. Anne ... Brunswick, ME
Carton & Faccone ... Avon-By-The-Sea, NJ
Carton, James D., III ... Manasquan, NJ
Carton, James D., IV ... Asbury Park, NJ
Carton, James D., Jr. ... Asbury Park, NJ
Carton, Jeffrey I. ... White Plains, NY
Carton, John C. ... Manasquan, NJ
Carton, Laurence A. ... Chicago, IL
Carton, Lawrence A., III ... Middletown, NJ
Carton, Malcolm V. ... Avon-By-The-Sea, NJ
Carton, Peter C. ... Bakersfield, CA
Carton, Peter J. ... Newark, NJ
Carton, Robert V. ... Asbury Park, NJ
Carton, Robin D. ... Harrison, NY
Carton & Rosoff, Law Offices of,, P.C. ... Harrison, NY
Carton, Ruya ... New York, NY

Carton & Selenkow ... Baltimore, MD
Carton, Sharon ... Fort Lauderdale, FL
Carton, Stephen C. ... **Asbury Park, NJ**
Carton, Thomas A. ... **Chicago, IL**
Munster, IN
Carton, Thomas W., Jr. ... Dublin, OH
Carton, Witt, Arvanitis & Bariscillo, L.L.C.
Asbury Park, NJ
Manasquan, NJ
Cartoni, James E. ... **San Diego, CA**
Cartonia, Colleen P. ... Buffalo, NY
Cartoon, Bernard John
Woodland Hills, CA
Cartoon, Stuart F. ... Tarrytown, NY
Cartotto, Karen L., (P.C.) ... **Boston, MA**
Cartozian, Roger A. ... Folsom, CA
Cartsunis, Lynne Ann ... Dallas, TX
Cartun, Joyce M. ... Cupertino, CA
Cartusciello, Anthony T. ... New York, NY
Cartusciello, Neil S. ... **Florham Park, NJ**
Cartwright & Alexander, LLP, The Law Firm ... **San Francisco, CA**
Cartwright, Allison S. ... Boston, MA
Cartwright, Angela D. ... **Las Vegas, NV**
Cartwright, Angela D., Ltd.
Las Vegas, NV
Cartwright & Armstrong ... Birmingham, AL
Cartwright, Brian G. ... **Los Angeles, CA**
Cartwright, Brian T. ... **Denton, TX**
Cartwright, Bruce D., II ... Merrimack, NH
Cartwright, Charles B. ... Wilmington, NC
Cartwright, Charles E.
West Palm Beach, FL
Cartwright, Charles N. ... Corpus Christi, TX
Cartwright, Christine ... **Princeton, NJ**
Cartwright, Clayton E., Jr.
Richmond, VA
Cartwright, D. Joseph ... **Salt Lake City, UT**
Cartwright, Daniel S. ... Houston, TX
Cartwright, Daniel S., P.C. ... Houston, TX
Cartwright and Darr ... Covington, TN
Cartwright, Darrell L. ... Birmingham, AL
Cartwright, David W. ... **Los Angeles, CA**
Cartwright, Deborah S. ... Elgin, TX
Cartwright, Donald M. ... Corpus Christi, TX
Cartwright, Druker & Ryden
Marshalltown, IA
Cartwright, Fulton & Adams
Santa Cruz, CA
Cartwright, Harold B. ... Santa Cruz, CA
Cartwright, Heather L.
Department of Justice,
Office of Justice Programs, GV
Cartwright, J. Craig ... **Phoenix, AZ**
Cartwright, J. Keith ... **Madisonville, KY**
Cartwright, James Kevin ... Clarksville, TN
Cartwright, James R. ... Portland, OR
Cartwright, Janet L. ... San Jose, CA
Cartwright, Jarold P. ... **Coeur d'Alene, ID**
Spokane, WA
Cartwright, Jas. B. ... Germantown, TN
Cartwright, Jerry G., Jr. ... New Castle, PA
Cartwright, Joan S. ... Oakland, CA
Cartwright, John C. ... Nantucket, MA
Cartwright, John F. ... Orchard Lake, MI
Cartwright, John H., Jr. ... Santa Ana, CA
Cartwright, Kara Kinney ... Gaithersburg, MD
Cartwright, Kelly A. ... Chicago, IL
Cartwright, Kelly-Ann Gibbs ... **Miami, FL**
Cartwright, Lauren S. ... San Diego, CA
Cartwright & Love, PLLC ... Clarksville, TN
Cartwright, Martina E. ... Houston, TX
Cartwright, Mary Ann ... **Grand Rapids, MI**
Cartwright, Matthew A. ... **Scranton, PA**
Wilkes-Barre, PA
Cartwright, Max D. ... Moline, IL
Cartwright, Patrick H. ... **Albany, NY**
Cartwright & Rascati ... Nantucket, MA
Cartwright, Richard D. ... Covington, TN
Cartwright, Robert B. ... **New York, NY**
Cartwright, Robert C. ... Los Angeles, CA
Cartwright, Robert E., Jr.
San Francisco, CA
Cartwright, Thomas C. ... Atlanta, GA
Cartwright, Thomas W. ... **Johnstown, PA**
Cartwright, W. Corey ... Meridian, ID
Cartwright, Wendy A. ... **Bowie, MD**
Cartwright, Wendy A., & Associates, P.C.
Bowie, MD
Lanham, MD
Cartwright, Zachary T., Jr.
Jefferson City, MO
Cartwright-Ladendorf, Rhonda L.
San Diego, CA
Carty, Andrea T. ... Quincy, MA
Carty, Carol D. ... **Costa Mesa, CA**
Carty & Carty ... **Providence, RI**
Carty, Christine E. ... **West Point, PA**
Carty and Dredge, P.A. ... Boise, ID
Carty, James E. ... Woodland, WA
Carty, James E., III ... South Plainfield, NJ
Carty, James E., III, P.C.
South Plainfield, NJ
Carty, James P. ... United States Senate,
Senatorial Assistants, GV
Carty, John P., III ... Modesto, CA
Carty, John P., Jr. ... Sunnyvale, CA
Carty, John T. ... **Princeton, NJ**
Carty, John W. ... Winfield, IA
Carty, Joseph B., Jr. ... **Providence, RI**
Carty, M. Christine ... **New York, NY**
Carty, Mary C. ... **New York, NY**
Carty, Michael A. ... **Santa Barbara, CA**
Carty, Patrick J. ... Birmingham, MI
Carty, Patrick J. ... **New York, NY**
Carty, Paul V., Law Offices of
New Haven, CT
Carty, Peter F. ... Boston, MA
Carty, Robert J., Jr. ... Houston, TX
Carty, Sabina T. ... **Boston, MA**
Carty, Stuart W. ... Boise, ID
Carty, Tate E. ... Knoxville, TN
Carty, Thomas W. ... Dedham, MA
Carty, Thos. F. ... Yonkers, NY
Caruana, Albert G. ... **Miami, FL**
Caruana and Lorenzen, P.A. ... **Miami, FL**
Caruana, Maria A. ... San Francisco, CA
Caruana, Mark V. ... Carlsbad, CA
Carucci, Roderic A. ... Sparks, NV
Carucci, Samuel A. ... Manhasset, NY
Carulas, Anna Moore ... **Cleveland, OH**
Caruncho, Joseph L. ... Coral Gables, FL
Caruncho & Mur, P.A. ... Coral Gables, FL
Caruolo, George D. ... **Boston, MA**
Providence, RI
Caruolo, Thomas H. ... Providence, RI
Carus, Barry R. ... **Syosset, NY**
Carus, Barry R., P.C. ... **Mineola, NY**
Riverhead, NY
Syosset, NY
Carusello and Hunnefeld, P.A.
Coral Gables, FL
Carusello, Kenneth J. ... Coral Gables, FL
Carusillo, Mark G. ... Boca Raton, FL
Carusillo, Thomas M. ... Indianapolis, IN
Caruso, A. Todd ... **Baton Rouge, LA**
Caruso, Aaron Robert ... **Rockville, MD**
Falls Church, VA
Caruso, Albert P. ... **Pittsburgh, PA**
Caruso, Andréa L. ... Cleveland, OH
Caruso, Anthony C. ... Baton Rouge, LA
Caruso, Anthony J. ... West Orange, NJ
Caruso, Anthony J. ... **Cincinnati, OH**
Caruso, Anthony J., Jr. ... **Chicago, IL**
Caruso, Anthony R. ... **Neptune, NJ**
Caruso, Anthony V. ... Rahway, NJ
Caruso, Antonio E. ... **Syracuse, NY**
Caruso, Barbara Gariepy ... La Grange, IL
Caruso & Baxter, P.A. ... Shrewsbury, NJ
Caruso, Burlington, Bohn & Compiani, P.A.
West Palm Beach, FL
Caruso, C. Charles ... Minneapolis, MN
Caruso, Carey ... Beverly Hills, CA
Caruso, Carmen D. ... **Chicago, IL**
Caruso, Carmen D., P.C. ... **Chicago, IL**
Caruso & Caruso, P.C. ... Brooklyn, NY
Caruso, Charles A. ... Rutland, VT
Caruso, Charles M.
Whitehouse Station, NJ
Caruso, Cornelius W., Jr. ... Rahway, NJ
Caruso, Daniel F. ... **Fairfield, CT**
Trumbull, CT
Caruso, Daniel J. ... **New Orleans, LA**
Caruso, David A. ... Schenectady, NY
Caruso, David E., Jr. ... **New Orleans, LA**
Caruso, Deborah A. ... Rochester, NY
Caruso, Deborah J. ... **Indianapolis, IN**
Caruso, Dennis A. ... **Tulsa, OK**
Caruso, Donato ... **New York, NY**
Caruso, Edna L. ... **West Palm Beach, FL**
Caruso, Enrico A. ... Clarkston, MI
Caruso, F. Michael ... Morristown, NJ
Caruso, F. Willis ... Chicago, IL
Caruso, F. Willis, Jr. ... Chicago, IL
Caruso, Francis J., III ... **Lynnfield, MA**
Caruso, Francis J., Jr. ... Crofton, MD
Caruso, Frank A. ... Springfield, MA
Caruso, Frank L. ... Cos Cob, CT
Caruso, Gabrielle Lee ... Bloomfield Hills, MI
Caruso, George R. ... Huntington, IN
Caruso & Georgetti ... **Toledo, OH**
Caruso, Gerald J. ... **Boston, MA**
Caruso, Gerard P. ... New Orleans, LA
Caruso, Ghostlaw, Murray and Brown
Springfield, MA
Caruso, Gina ... **New York, NY**
Caruso, Gina E. ... **Fort Lauderdale, FL**
Caruso, Heather Brooke ... Columbia, SC
Caruso, J. Christine ... San Antonio, TX
Caruso, James D. ... **Toledo, OH**
Caruso, Jane A. ... Falmouth, MA
Caruso, Joanne E. ... **Los Angeles, CA**
Caruso, Joe Teague ... **Merritt Island, FL**
Caruso, John D. ... Syracuse, NY
Caruso, John E. ... **Cherry Hill, NJ**
Philadelphia, PA
Caruso, John F. ... Brooklyn, NY
Caruso, John G. ... **Chicago, IL**
Caruso, John R. ... Farmington, CT
Caruso, Joseph F. ... Kittanning, PA
Caruso, Joseph G. ... Philadelphia, PA
Caruso, Joseph S. ... Oaklyn, NJ
Caruso, Joseph S., P.C. ... Oaklyn, NJ
Caruso, Kathryn M. ... Clarkston, MI
Caruso, Kenneth A. ... **New York, NY**
Caruso Law Offices, P.C. ... Albuquerque, NM
Caruso, Lawrence R. ... Bethesda, MD
Caruso, Leonardo J. ... **Boston, MA**
Caruso, Leroy F. ... Brooklyn, NY
Caruso, Linda A. ... Bethesda, MD
Caruso, Linda R. ... **Los Angeles, CA**
Caruso, Louis J. ... Lansing, MI
Caruso, Margret M. ... **New York, NY**
Caruso, Mark A. ... Bel Air, MD
Caruso, Mark J. ... Albuquerque, NM
Caruso, Mark J. ... Brooklyn, NY
Caruso, Martin I. ... **Detroit, MI**
Caruso, Mary M. ... Cos Cob, CT
Caruso, Matthew T., (P.C.) ... **Wheaton, IL**
Caruso, Michael S. ... **Saratoga Springs, NY**
Caruso, Mike A., Jr. ... Mountain View, OK
Caruso, Nicholas C. ... Morristown, NJ
Caruso, Nicholas D. ... Summit, NJ
Caruso, Patrick F. ... **Hartford, CT**
Caruso, Paul D. ... West Palm Beach, FL
Caruso, Paul F. ... Morris Plains, NJ
Caruso, Paul S. ... **Chicago, IL**
Caruso, Peter J. ... Andover, MA
Caruso, Peter J., Law Offices ... Andover, MA
Caruso, Phillip S. ... Brookfield, WI
Caruso, Ralph A., II ... **Indianapolis, IN**
Caruso, Raymond E. ... Shrewsbury, NJ
Caruso, Richard A. ... Stoneham, MA
Caruso, Samuel H., Jr. ... **Rochester, NY**
Caruso, Spillane, Contrastano & Ulaner, P.C.
New York, NY
Caruso, Stephen ... **Las Vegas, NV**
Caruso, Steven B. ... **New York, NY**
Caruso & Swerbilow, P.A., Law Office of
Merritt Island, FL
Caruso, Thomas C. ... Littleton, CO
Caruso, Thomas R. ... **Slidell, LA**
Caruso, Vincent ... **Menlo Park, CA**
Caruso, Vito ... Los Angeles, CA
Caruso, Vito C. ... Schenectady, NY
Caruso, William J. ... Boston, MA
Carusona, Peter A. ... Ottawa, IL
Carusona, Thomas M. ... Mineola, NY
Carusone & Carusone ... Saratoga Springs, NY
Carusone, John J., Jr. ... Saratoga Springs, NY
Carusone, John S. ... Glens Falls, NY
Caruth, Ben H. ... **Morrilton, AR**
Caruth, Donald T. ... **Bluefield, WV**
Caruthers, C. DeWitt ... Shreveport, LA
Caruthers & Caruthers, P.C. ... Greensburg, PA
Caruthers, D. Michael ... Palm Springs, CA
Caruthers, David W. ... Baltimore, MD
Caruthers, Donald S., Jr. ... **Leesburg, VA**
Caruthers, Donald S., Sr. ... Leesburg, VA
Caruthers, John D., Jr. ... Shreveport, LA
Caruthers, Rachel S. ... Lonedell, MO
Caruthers, W. Philip ... Oakland, CA
Caruthers, William F. ... Greensburg, PA
Caruthers, William F., II ... Greensburg, PA
Carvajal, Arthur G. ... Chicago, IL
Carvajal, Carlos M. ... **New York, NY**
Carvajal, Ian P. ... **San Juan, PR**
Carvajal, Roxane M. ... Long Beach, CA
Carvalho, Amarante M. ... Skokie, IL
Carvalho, Arthur, Jr. ... Woodland Hills, CA
Carvalho, Cristina A. ... **Washington, DC**
Carvalho, Daniel E. ... **Las Vegas, NV**
Carvalho, David N. ... Chicago, IL
Carvalho, Donna Huckabay ... Houston, TX
Carvalho, Jane E. ... New Bedford, MA
Carvalho, John A. ... Woodland Hills, CA
Carvalho, Lisa M. ... **San Francisco, CA**
Carvalho, Matthew A. ... Washington, DC
Carvalho, Michael P. ... **Washington, DC**
Carvalho, Sonia Rubio ... **Riverside, CA**
Carvalko, Joseph R., Jr. ... Bridgewater, CT
Carvel, Shelley Stuart ... Portland, ME
Carvelas, John N. ... Denver, CO
Carvell, D. Wade ... **Dallas, TX**
Carvell, Diane Beckman ... **Philadelphia, PA**
Carvellas, Perry ... **Alexandria, VA**
Carvelli, Paul F. ... **Chatham, NJ**
Toms River, NJ
Carven, A. Frank, III ... Bel Air, MD
Carven, Richard Gerard ... Marshfield, MA
Carver, Alexander H., III ... Westwood, NJ
Carver, Betty Hogue ... Henryville, IN
Carver, Bradford R. ... **Boston, MA**
Carver, C. Mark ... **Nashville, TN**
Carver, C. Paul ... **Minneapolis, MN**
Carver, Carolina L. ... **Phoenix, AZ**
Carver, Charles D. ... Beaumont, TX
Carver, Charles H. ... **Tampa, FL**
Carver, Christine Luba ... **New York, NY**
Carver, Christopher S. ... **Miami, FL**
Carver, Christopher Todd ... **Lubbock, TX**
Carver, Claudia A. ... Los Angeles, CA
Carver, Clyde W. ... Atlanta, GA
Carver, Craig L. ... Amarillo, TX
Carver, Craig R. ... **Denver, CO**
Carver, Darden, Koretzky, Tessier, Finn, Blossman & Areaux, L.L.C.
Metairie, LA
New Orleans, LA
Carver, David Ray ... Salt Lake City, UT
Carver, Elizabeth C. ... **St. Louis, MO**
Carver, Eric Thomas ... **Detroit, MI**
Carver, Fred A. ... Beaumont, TX
Carver, Frederick C. ... **New York, NY**
Carver, George A., Jr.
Department of Justice,
Criminal Division, GV
Carver, George Edwin, Jr. ... **Atlanta, GA**
Carver, George M. ... **Chicago, IL**
Carver, Gordon M., III ... **Houston, TX**
Carver, Harry ... Oklahoma City, OK
Carver, J. Christopher ... Sarasota, FL
Carver, J. Phillip ... **Atlanta, GA**
Carver, James C. ... **Baton Rouge, LA**
Carver, Jerry P. ... **Prescott, AZ**
Carver, Joanne M. ... Albuquerque, NM
Carver, John A., III ... Arlington, VA
Carver, John D. ... **Englewood, CO**
Carver, John L. ... **Belfast, ME**
Unity, ME
Carver, John R. ... Big Flats, NY
Carver, John W. ... **Chicago, IL**
Carver, Kevin S. ... Fort Worth, TX
Carver, Kimball & Baiungo ... **Belfast, ME**
Unity, ME
Carver Law Offices, Ltd. ... Little Rock, AR
Carver, Lesley A. ... Kew Gardens, NY
Carver, Lori S. ... Irvine, CA
Carver, Lyell Henry ... Bartlesville, OK
Carver, M. Hampton ... **New Orleans, LA**
Carver and Mancinelli ... Westwood, NJ
Carver, Mark R. ... **Owatonna, MN**
Carver, Melanie ... San Francisco, CA
Carver, Michael ... Huntingdon Valley, PA
Carver, Michael ... Burlington, VT
Carver, Neil ... Miami, FL
Carver, Neil ... Philadelphia, PA
Carver, Neil, P.A. ... Miami, FL
Carver, Reginald L. ... **Alpharetta, GA**
Carver, Richard ... **Los Angeles, CA**
Carver, Robert Q. ... Scarsdale, NY
Carver, Samuel W. ... **Nogales, AZ**
Brownsville, TX
Carver, Scott A. ... **Princeton, NJ**
Carver, Sheri Wood ... **Fort Payne, AL**
Carver, Spencer ... Dallas, TX
Carver, Stephen D. ... Little Rock, AR
Carver, Susie Taylor ... Tuscaloosa, AL
Carver, Teresa A. ... **Houston, TX**
Carver, Thomas D. ... Springfield, MO
Carver, Todd B. ... **Denver, CO**
Carver, Tracy T. ... San Francisco, CA
Carver, Vincent S. ... **Dallas, TX**
Carver & West, L.L.C. ... Salt Lake City, UT
Carver, William H. ... Oshkosh, WI
Carver, William Matthew ... **Houston, TX**
Carver-Cheney, Kathleen L.
New York, NY
Carveth, Christopher B. ... **Milford, CT**
Carvill, Wynne S. ... **San Francisco, CA**
Carville, Christopher Richard
Cincinnati, OH
Carville, Jules A., III ... La Place, LA
Carvin, Donald H. ... Braintree, MA
Carvin, Joseph W. ... Lakeland, FL
Carvin, Margaret ... Washington, DC
Carvin, Michael A. ... **Washington, DC**
Carvis, Thaddius J. ... **Stamford, CT**
Carvlin, Stephanie M. ... Hartford, CT
Carway & Flipse ... Mineola, NY
Carway, Jacqueline S. ... Mineola, NY
Carwell, Keith M. ... **Bowling Green, KY**
Carwell, Robert M. ... Austin, TX
Carwie, Annette McDermott ... **Mobile, AL**
Carwie, John Gregory ... **Mobile, AL**
Carwile, Dan J. ... Evansville, IN
Carwile, John A. ... **Houston, TX**
Carwile, John J. ... **Tulsa, OK**
Carwile, P. Kevin ... Charlotte, NC
Carwile, Stuart F. ... **Washington, DC**
Carwile, Timothy C. ... Waynesboro, VA
Carwin, Donald R. ... Denver, CO
Cary, Brian Keith ... **Charlotte, NC**
Cary, Carolyn Pollock ... **Saginaw, MI**
Cary, Charles C. ... **Mountain View, CA**
Cary, Charles M. ... **Bolivar, TN**
Cary, David E. ... Fort Myers, FL
Cary, David W. ... Corte Madera, CA
Cary, Dina M. ... **Dayton, OH**
Cary, Donald R. ... San Diego, CA
Cary, Erik E. ... Austin, TX
Cary, Eve ... Brooklyn, NY
Cary, Frederick A. ... Rancho Santa Fe, CA
Cary, G. Keith ... Fort Myers, FL
Cary, George D. ... Washington, DC
Cary, George S. ... **Washington, DC**
Cary & Icaza ... **Elizabeth, NJ**
Newark, NJ
Cary, James E. ... **Hannibal, MO**
Cary, Jean M. ... Buies Creek, NC
Cary, John H. ... **Tulsa, OK**
Cary, John M. ... **Seattle, WA**
Cary, John Sam ... Prospect, KY
Cary, Judith D. ... Cleveland, OH
Cary, Judson D. ... **Englewood, CO**
Cary, Keith A. ... **Kansas City, MO**
Cary, Larry ... **New York, NY**
Cary Law Firm, The ... Rancho Santa Fe, CA
Cary, Marshall T. ... Bangor, ME
Cary, Marticha L. ... **Washington, DC**
Cary, Miles, Jr. ... **Richmond, VA**
Cary, N. Dwight ... **San Francisco, CA**
Cary, Nancy K. ... **Eugene, OR**
Cary, Nelson D. ... **Washington, DC**
Cary, Paul W. ... Shreveport, LA
Cary, Peter George ... **Portland, ME**
Cary R. Alburn III, P.C. ... Laramie, WY
Cary, Reed C. ... **Melbourne, FL**
Miami, FL
Cary, Reed C., P.A. ... Melbourne, FL
Cary, Richard A. ... **Centralia, IL**
Cary, Robert J., Jr. ... **New London, CT**
Cary, Robert M. ... **Washington, DC**
Cary, Robert R. ... **Newark, NJ**
Cary, Robert W. ... Niles, MI
Cary, Stephen T. ... Plantation, FL
Cary, Thomas M. ... Albany, OR
Eugene, OR
Cary, Thomas Wayne ... **Montgomery, AL**
Cary, Timothy E. ... **Ontario, CA**
Cary, Timothy Michael ... Cameron Park, CA
Cary, Tracy W. ... Dothan, AL
Cary, Welch & Hickman, L.L.P.
Hannibal, MO
Palmyra, MO
Cary, William P. H. ... **Greensboro, NC**
Caryl, Michael E. ... **Charleston, WV**
Martinsburg, WV
Caryl, Michael R. ... **Seattle, WA**
Caryl, Michael R., P.S. ... **Seattle, WA**
Caryl, Randall K. ... Flint, MI
Casa, Christine Woodman
Portsmouth, NH
Casab, Alfredo ... Troy, MI
Casabielle, Manuel L. ... Coral Gables, FL
Casablanca, Maria I. ... Miami, FL
Casacca, Ernest A. ... Atascadero, CA
Casacci, Joseph R. ... Fort Lauderdale, FL
Casaccio, Joseph G. ... Omaha, NE
Casaceli, Frank O. ... Rochester, NY
Casad, Benjamin Nathan ... Liberal, KS
Casad, Robert C. ... Lawrence, KS

Casey, Edward C. ....San Francisco, CA
Casey, Edward C., Jr., Law Offices of
San Francisco, CA
Casey, Edward F. ....Attleboro, MA
Casey, Edward J. ....Los Angeles, CA
Casey, Edward J. ....Attleboro, MA
Casey, Edward V., Jr. ....Hanson, MA
Casey, Elizabeth M. ....Needham, MA
Casey, Ellen G. ....Norristown, PA
Casey, Ellen M. ....Trenton, NJ
Casey, Ellen S. ....Santa Fe, NM
Casey, Everett F. ....Silver Spring, MD
Casey, Everett R. ....Orchard Lake, MI
Casey, Francis L., III ....Washington, DC
Casey, Francis Lawton, Jr. ....Washington, DC
Casey, Frederick J. ....Brainerd, MN
Casey, G. Nicholas, Jr. ....Charleston, WV
Casey, Gentz & Sifuentes, L.L.P.
Austin, TX
Casey, George A. ....New York, NY
Casey, George M. ....Waltham, MA
Casey, Gerald J. ....Lake Charles, LA
Casey, Gerald L. ....Port Orchard, WA
Casey, Geraldine Holland ....Sicklerville, NJ
Casey, Gerard W. ....Purchase, NY
Casey, Gerry, Reed & Schenk
San Diego, CA
Casey, Gilson & Williams P.C.
Atlanta, GA
Lawrenceville, GA
Casey Gordon Davis ....Seattle, WA
Bellevue, WA
Casey, Henry D. ....Willits, CA
Casey, Hugh G., Jr. ....Davidson, NC
Casey, J. Robert ....Boston, MA
Casey, Jackson W. ....Newburyport, MA
East Kingston, NH
Casey, Jacqueline J. ....Naperville, IL
Casey, Jama L. ....Tulsa, OK
Casey, James A. ....Durango, CO
Casey, James A. ....Washington, DC
Casey, James A. ....Chicago, IL
Casey, James C. ....Miami, FL
Casey, James D. ....Akron, OH
Casey, James D., Jr. ....Jackson Heights, NY
Casey, James F. ....Ozone Park, NY
Casey, James H. ....St. Louis, MO
Casey, James H. ....Lakewood, NJ
Casey, James J. ....Washington, DC
Casey, James J. ....Chicago, IL
Casey, James J. ....Hyattsville, MD
Casey, James J. ....New York, NY
Casey, James J., Jr. ....Northridge, CA
Casey, James L. ....Washington, DC
Casey, James M. ....Knoxville, TN
Casey, James M. ....Point Pleasant, WV
Casey, James N. ....San Mateo, CA
Casey, James N. ....Sunnyvale, CA
Casey, James Owen ....Lynn, MA
Casey, James P. ....Evansville, IN
Casey, James P. ....Baltimore, MD
Casey, James S. ....Kalamazoo, MI
Casey, James S. ....Cleveland, OH
Casey, Jean M. ....Treasury Department,
Internal Revenue Service, GV
Casey, Jennifer A. ....Albertson, NY
Casey, Jennifer M. ....Los Angeles, CA
Casey, Jennifer Murphy ....Morehead, KY
Casey, John A. ....Milwaukee, WI
Casey, John B. ....Albany, NY
Casey, John C. ....Oakland, CA
Casey, John C. ....Camden, NJ
Casey, John D. ....Attleboro, MA
Casey, John E. ....Brookfield, MO
Casey, John F. ....Roseland, NJ
Casey, John F. ....Columbus, OH
Casey, John F. ....Granville, OH
Hilliard, OH
Lancaster, OH
New Albany, OH
Casey, John J. ....Phoenix, AZ
Casey, John J. ....Chicago, IL
Casey, John J. ....Springfield, IL
Casey, John M. ....Vernon, CT
Casey, John M. ....Portland, OR
Casey, John M. ....Kent, WA
Casey, John P. ....Milwaukee, WI
Casey, John Patrick ....Groton, CT
Casey, John R. ....Bradenton, FL
Casey, John R. ....Albany, NY
Casey, John S. ....Heflin, AL
Casey, John T. ....Chicago, IL
Casey, John T. ....Rensselaer, IN
Casey, John T., Jr. ....Albany, NY
Casey, John W. ....East Hartford, CT
Casey, Johna Howard ....Louisville, KY
Casey, Jones & McKenna ....Tulsa, OK
Casey, Jos. S. ....New Orleans, LA
Casey, Joseph T. ....New Orleans, LA
Casey, Joseph T., Jr. ....Herndon, VA
Casey, Judith Lauth ....Chicago, IL
Casey, Julia K. ....Toledo, OH
Casey, Justine Mary ....Costa Mesa, CA
Casey, Karen A. ....Boise, ID
Casey, Karen Jansen ....Hartford, CT
Casey, Karen S. ....Columbus, OH
Casey, Karen Walker ....Birmingham, AL
Casey, Karie E. ....St. Louis, MO
Casey, Karin G. ....Littleton, CO
Casey, Kathleen E. ....Middleport, NY
Casey, Kathleen L. ....Long Beach, CA
Casey, Kathleen M. ....Estes Park, CO
Casey, Kathleen Molchan
Fort Lauderdale, FL
Casey, Kellie R. ....Atlanta, GA
Casey, Ken C. ....Treasury Department,
Internal Revenue Service, GV
Casey, Kenneth P. ....Madison, WI
Casey, Kerry M. ....Hooksett, NH
Casey, Kevin ....New York, NY
Casey, Kevin A ....Troy, MI
Casey, Kevin G. ....New York, NY
Casey, Kevin P. ....Bellevue, WA
Casey, Kevin R. ....Valley Forge, PA
Casey, Kevin S. ....Albany, NY
Casey, Kim M. ....Rockford, IL
Casey, Kimberly A. ....Denver, CO
Casey & King ....Ithaca, NY
Casey, Klene & Wegs, P.C. ....Denver, CO
Casey, Kristin N. ....St. Helena, CA
Casey, L. Patricia ....Topeka, KS
Casey, Laura Westfall ....Washington, DC
Casey, Laureen Cahill ....Waukegan, IL
Casey, Lauren Catherine ....Annapolis, MD
Casey Law Offices ....Point Pleasant, WV
Casey, Lawrence J. ....Boston, MA
Casey, Lawrence W. ....Greenwich, CT
Casey, Lee A. ....Washington, DC
Casey, Linda J. ....Philadelphia, PA
Casey, Lisa L. ....Denver, CO
Casey, M. Patricia ....Princeton, NJ
Casey, Marc W. ....Dyersville, IA
Casey, Marcia ....Boston, MA
Casey, Margaret O. ....Los Angeles, CA
Casey, Maria T. ....Pottsville, PA
Casey, Martha Lincoln ....Washington, DC
Casey, Martin F. ....New York, NY
Casey, Mary C. ....Shrewsbury, MA
Casey, Mary Linda ....Merrillville, IN
Casey, Mary Louise ....Chicago, IL
Casey, Marylynne B. ....Santa Ana, CA
Casey, Matthew K. ....Sterling Heights, MI
Casey, Matthias E. ....Chicago, IL
Casey, Maureen ....Albertson, NY
Casey, Maureen E. ....Albany, NY
Casey, Maureen T. ....Department of Justice,
Antitrust Division, GV
Casey & Meyerkord, A Prof. Corp.
St. Louis, MO
Casey, Michael ....Albuquerque, NM
Casey, Michael C. ....Rocky Mount, NC
Casey, Michael H. ....San Antonio, TX
Casey, Michael J. ....San Jose, CA
Casey, Michael J. ....Bridgeport, CT
Casey, Michael J. ....Spokane, WA
Casey, Michael P. ....Calumet City, IL
Casey, Michael P. ....St. Louis, MO
Casey, Michael P. ....Montpelier, VT
Casey, Michael R. ....Fort Lauderdale, FL
Casey, Michael V. ....Chicago, IL
Casey, Michael W., III ....Miami, FL
Orlando, FL
Casey, Michelle M. ....San Francisco, CA
Casey, Moira Elizabeth ....Douglaston, NY
Casey and Molchan, Professional Association
Fort Lauderdale, FL
Casey, Morgan A., Jr. ....New York, NY
Casey & Munn ....Palm Springs, CA
Casey, N. Franklyn ....Tulsa, OK
Casey, Nan Elizabeth ....East Lansing, MI
Casey, Neil ....New York, NY
Casey, Neil J., III ....New Brunswick, NJ
Casey, Nellie Maureen ....Los Angeles, CA
Casey, Offa Lunsford ....Laurel, MS
Casey, Orben J. ....Oklahoma City, OK
Casey, Patricia A. ....Washington, DC
Casey, Patricia L ....Houston, TX
Casey, Patrick ....Charleston, WV
Casey, Patrick A. ....Santa Fe, NM
Casey, Patrick A. ....Scranton, PA
Casey, Patrick A., P.A. ....Santa Fe, NM
Casey, Patrick G., (P.C.) ....Lincoln Park, MI
Casey, Patrick J. ....Indian Wells, CA
Casey, Patrick J. ....Denver, CO
Casey, Patrick J. ....Cincinnati, OH
Casey, Patrick J., (P.A.)
West Palm Beach, FL
Casey, Patrick J. J. ....Solon, OH
Casey, Patrick Jon ....Edmond, OK
Casey, Patrick M. ....Department of Justice,
Environment and Natural Resources
Division, GV
Casey, Patrick M. ....Linwood, NJ
Casey, Patrick P. ....Heflin, AL
Casey, Patrick R. ....Scranton, PA
Casey, Patrick S. ....Chicago, IL
Casey, Patrick S. ....Wheeling, WV
Casey, Patrick S. M. ....Monterey, CA
Casey, Paul Brennan ....Chestnut Hill, MA
Casey, Paul G. ....Seattle, WA
Casey, Paul J. ....Boston, MA
Casey, Paul K. ....Washington, DC
Baltimore, MD
Casey, Paula K. ....Olympia, WA
Casey, Paula Kidd ....Wichita, KS
Casey, Paula M. ....Rochester, NY
Casey, Peter J. ....Hartford, CT
Casey, Peter M. ....Boston, MA
Casey, Peter R., III ....Toledo, OH
Casey, Peter S. ....Milford, MA
Casey & Pruzan ....Seattle, WA
Casey, Raymond V. ....New York, NY
Casey, Rebecca A ....Grand Junction, CO
Casey, Regina Ann ....Rockville, MD
Casey, Richard Conway ....New York, NY
Casey, Richard D. ....Denver, CO
Casey, Richard D. ....Sioux Falls, SD
Casey, Richard F. ....Frankfort, KY
Casey, Richard J. ....Chicago, IL
Casey, Richard J. ....Princeton, NJ
Casey, Richard W. ....Salt Lake City, UT
Casey & Richards ....Newport Beach, CA
Casey, Robert ....Skokie, IL
Casey, Robert A. ....Worcester, MA
Casey, Robert E. ....Youngstown, OH
Casey, Robert E. ....Seattle, WA
Casey, Robert E., Jr. ....Atlanta, GA
Casey, Robert F. ....McHenry, IL
Casey, Robert F., Jr. ....Harvard, MA
Casey, Robert F., Jr., P.C. ....Harvard, MA
Casey, Robert F., (P.C.) ....St. Charles, IL
Casey, Robert G. ....Tacoma, WA
Casey, Robert J. ....Washington, DC
Casey, Robert K. ....Costa Mesa, CA
Casey, Robert M. ....Treasury Department,
Internal Revenue Service, GV
Casey, Robert P. ....Chicago, IL
Casey, Robert P. ....Trenton, NJ
Casey, Robert P. ....Blue Bell, PA
Scranton, PA
Casey, Robert P., Jr. ....Harrisburg, PA
Casey, Robert R. ....Baton Rouge, LA
Casey, Robert W. ....Albuquerque, NM
Casey, Robert W., P.C. ....Albuquerque, NM
Casey, Robin A. ....Austin, TX
Casey, Ronald D. ....Indianapolis, IN
Casey & Rossi ....Doylestown, PA
Casey, Roy A. ....New Orleans, LA
Casey, S. Brian ....Evansville, IN
Casey, Samuel A. ....Wisconsin Rapids, WI
Casey, Samuel B. ....Annandale, VA
Casey, Sandra Mulay ....Albany, NY
Casey, Sarah C. ....New York, NY
Casey, Scott C. ....Boone, NC
Casey, Sean A. ....Pittsburgh, PA
Casey, Sean M. ....Dublin, OH
Casey, Sharon Shelfer ....Boston, MA
Casey, Shawn M. ....Jacksonville, FL
Casey, Shawn R. ....Houston, TX
Casey, Sheila Catherine ....Lynn, MA
Casey, Siobhan ....New York, NY
Casey & Slaybod ....Toledo, OH
Casey, Stanley Q. ....New York, NY
Casey, Stephen B. ....Tustin, CA
Casey, Steven F. ....Birmingham, AL
Casey, Steven F. ....Lowell, MA
Casey, Susan A. ....St. Paul, MN
Casey, Susan M. ....Washington, DC
Casey, T. Patrick ....Salt Lake City, UT
Casey, Terry M. ....Fort Worth, TX
Casey, Thomas A. ....Brownsburg, IN
Casey, Thomas A. ....Baton Rouge, LA
Casey, Thomas A., Jr. ....New Orleans, LA
Casey, Thomas Bernard ....Lisle, IL
Casey, Thomas E. ....Mound, MN
Casey, Thomas F. ....Dallas, TX
Casey, Thomas F., III ....Redwood City, CA
Casey, Thomas Francis ....Baltimore, MD
Casey, Thomas H., Law Office of
Costa Mesa, CA
Casey, Thomas J. ....Washington, DC
Casey, Thomas J. ....Lake Forest, IL
Casey, Thomas J. ....St. Louis, MO
Casey, Thomas J. ....Mauston, WI
Casey, Thomas L. ....Laurel, MS
Casey, Thomas P. ....Arvada, CO
Casey, Thomas P. ....Harper Woods, MI
Casey, Thos. A. ....New Orleans, LA
Casey, Timothy A. ....Wilmington, DE
Casey, Timothy F.
Grosse Pointe Woods, MI
Casey, Timothy Guy ....Rockville, MD
Casey, Timothy Guy, P.A. ....Rockville, MD
Casey, Timothy J. ....Phoenix, AZ
Casey, Timothy M. ....Woodbridge, NJ
Casey, Timothy R. ....Chicago, IL
Casey, Valerie ....San Marino, CA
Casey, Veronica ....Minneapolis, MN
Casey, Victoria L. ....Charleston, WV
Casey, Vincent P. ....New York, NY
Casey, W. Robert, Jr. ....Raleigh, NC
Casey, Ward P. ....Fort Worth, TX
Casey, Warren C. ....Raleigh, NC
Casey, Warren J. ....Morristown, NJ
New York, NY
Casey, Wayne J. ....Newport Beach, CA
Casey, Wesley G. ....Tulsa, OK
Casey, William E. ....Laredo, TX
Casey, William F. ....Owings Mills, MD
Casey, William H. R. ....Doylestown, PA
Casey, William J. ....San Francisco, CA
Casey, William M. ....Albuquerque, NM
Casey, William Michael
Colorado Springs, CO
Casey, William S. ....Medford, MA
Casey, William T. ....Chicago, IL
Casey, William T., Jr. ....Marietta, GA
Casey, William Wade ....Dallas, TX
Casey & Young, P.C. ....Lowell, MA
Casey-Herold, Sandra ....Sacramento, CA
Casgar, Timothy R. ....Baltimore, MD
McLean, VA
Cash, Albert D. ....Cincinnati, OH
Cash, Alexander B. ....Charleston, SC
Cash, Andrew B. ....Atlanta, GA
Cash, Arthur L., Jr. ....Chicago, IL
Cash, Barbara M. ....Southfield, MI
Cash, C. B., Jr. ....Shelby, NC
Cash, C. L., Jr. ....Stockbridge, GA
Cash, Clarence W. ....Little Rock, AR
Cash, Clyde R. ....Winston-Salem, NC
Cash, David E. ....Santa Barbara, CA
Cash, Diane R. ....San Francisco, CA
Cash, Donald F. ....Orange, CA
Cash, Gary S. ....Asheville, NC
Cash, Harry R. ....Chattanooga, TN
Cash, J. Jeffrey ....Dallas, TX
Cash, James M. ....Franklinville, NY
Cash, John W. ....Tampa, FL
Cash Jones, L.L.P. ....Houston, TX
Cash, Joseph A., Jr. ....Philadelphia, PA
Cash, Joseph W. ....Houston, TX
Cash, Joshua N. ....Cincinnati, OH
Cash, Julian A. ....Atlanta, GA
Cash, Julian A., P.C. ....Atlanta, GA
Cash, Kelley ....Dallas, TX
Cash, Kevin L. ....Lynchburg, VA
Cash, Larry Lee ....Chattanooga, TN
Cash, Loraine Leach ....Chattanooga, TN
Cash, Lynn ....Tampa, FL
Cash, Mark S. ....New York, NY
Cash, Martin W., Jr. ....Memphis, TN
Cash, Marvin S. ....Charlotte, NC
Cash, Mary McCall ....Decatur, GA
Cash, Matthew E. ....Chicago, IL
Cash, Michael P. ....Houston, TX
Cash, Michelle Hoogendam ....Houston, TX
Cash, Paul F. ....New York, NY
Cash, R. Wyatt ....San Luis Obispo, CA
Cash, Robert B. ....Cincinnati, OH
Cash, Robert J. ....Plainsboro, NJ
Cash, Robert O., Jr. ....Fort Lauderdale, FL
Cash, Roderick W., Jr. ....Washington, DC
Cash, Sharon Christy ....Winder, GA
Cash, Stanley A. ....Birmingham, AL
Cash, Stephanie Trow ....Dallas, TX
Cash, Warren P., III ....Bellaire, TX
Cash, Wilbur F. ....Covington, TN
Cash, W. K. ....Albia, IA
Cashatt, Brent A. ....Des Moines, IA
Cashavelly, Gary ....Dorchester, MA
Cashdan, David R. ....Washington, DC
Cashdan, Golden & Kane, PLLC
Washington, DC
Cashdan, Jeffrey S. ....Atlanta, GA
Cashdan, Russ Alan ....Los Angeles, CA
Cashdan, Spencer W. ....Phoenix, AZ
Cashdollar, Hunter H. ....Dyersburg, TN
Cashdollar, J. Lauson ....Beaver, PA
Cash-Dudley, E.F. ....Modesto, CA
Cashe, Lewis, Moody & Coudrain
Covington, LA
Denham Springs, LA
Greensburg, LA
Hammond, LA
Metairie, LA
New Orleans, LA
Cashe, Rodney C. ....Hammond, LA
Cashel, James D. ....Cherry Hill, NJ
Philadelphia, PA
Cashel, Thomas W. ....New York, NY
Cashen & Cheney ....Montrose, CO
Cashen, Christopher B. ....Norfolk, VA
Cashen, Christopher R. ....Lexington, KY
Cashen, Donald E. ....Montrose, CO
Cashen, Henry C., II ....Washington, DC
Cashen, J. Frank ....Flushing, NY
Cashen, J. Larry ....Louisville, KY
Cashen, James A. ....Hudson, NY
Cashen, John C. ....Troy, MI
Cashen, Raymond, II ....Washington, DC
Cashen, Raymond R. ....Mount Clemens, MI
Cashen & Strehl ....Mount Clemens, MI
Cashen, William K. ....Mount Clemens, MI
Casher, Dana E. ....Boston, MA
Casher, Richard F. ....Hartford, CT
Cashill Law Firm, The, A Professional
Corporation ....Reno, NV
Cashill, William Patterson ....Reno, NV
Cashin, Bonney ....Boston, MA
Cashin, Harry L., Jr. ....Atlanta, GA
Cashin & Hughes ....Prairie Village, KS
Cashin, J. Patrick ....Eden Prairie, MN
Cashin, Julie M. ....Milford, CT
Cashin, Maurice Matthew ....Wadsworth, IL
Cashin, Morton & Mullins ....Atlanta, GA
Cashin, Sheryll D.
Department of Housing and Urban
Development, GV
Cashin, Timothy E. ....Minneapolis, MN
Cashio, Jason R. ....Baton Rouge, LA
Cashio, Randall J. ....Baton Rouge, LA
Cashio, Samuel C. ....Maringouin, LA
Cashiola, Randal G. ....Beaumont, TX
Cashion, Archibald H. ....New York, NY
Cashion, Charles L. ....Oklahoma City, OK
Cashion, David C. ....Pasadena, CA
Cashion, Edw. H. ....Oklahoma City, OK
Cashion, Gregory L. ....Nashville, TN
Cashion, James C. ....Hamilton, AL
Cashion, John Bernard ....Chicago, IL
Cashion, Karen R. ....Atlanta, GA
Cashion, Kelli ....Benton, AR
Cashion, Kelli ....Little Rock, AR
Cashion, Marvin ....Chicago, IL
Cashion, Shelley J. ....Houston, TX
Cashman, Alan M. ....Hanover, PA
Cashman, Charles E. ....Owatonna, MN
Cashman, Cheryl Scott ....Bayonne, NJ
Cashman, Chris Donodeo ....Boston, MA
Cashman, Cornelius T. ....Boston, MA
Cashman, Daniel F. ....Dedham, MA
Cashman, David R. ....Pittsburgh, PA
Cashman, Dennis K. ....Quincy, IL
Cashman, Dennis Ross ....Novato, CA
Cashman, Don A. ....Hiawatha, KS
Cashman, Edward J. ....Essex Junction, VT
Cashman, Erin T. ....Boston, MA
Cashman, George W. ....Boston, MA
Cashman, Gideon ....New York, NY
Cashman, J. Devin ....Quincy, IL
Cashman, James P. ....San Jose, CA
Cashman, James T. ....New York, NY
Cashman, Jeffrey N. ....Seattle, WA
Cashman, John A. ....Chicago, IL
Cashman, John G. ....Chicago, IL
Cashman, John M. ....Manitowoc, WI
Cashman, Judith L. ....Mineola, NY
Cashman, Marie ....Treasury Department,
Internal Revenue Service, GV
Cashman, Michael P. ....Boston, MA
Cashman, Michael R. ....Minneapolis, MN

Cashman, Patricia ... Boston, MA
Cashman, Patricia A. ... Orlando, FL
Cashman, Richard ... New York, NY
Cashman, Robert H. ... San Francisco, CA
Cashman, Scott C. ... Newton, MA
Cashman, Stephen F. ... Hartford, CT
Cashman, Thomas F. ... Chicago, IL
Cashman, William H. ... New Haven, CT
Cashman, William J. ... St. Cloud, MN
Cashman, Wylie P. ... Modesto, CA
Cashman-Kramer, Kathleen A.
San Diego, CA
Cashmere, J. Brian ... McLean, VA
Cashmere, Kirk H. ... Honolulu, HI
Cashmore, Charles R. ... Billings, MT
Cashmore, Linda L. ... Chicago, IL
Cashmore, Timothy C. ... Buffalo, NY
Cashore, Amy C. ... Boston, MA
Cashton, Michael J. ... Boston, MA
Cashwell, Narley L. ... Raleigh, NC
Cashwell, Roseanna C. ... Wilmington, NC
Casi, Paul A., II ... Louisville, KY
Casias, Corinne Martinez ... Pueblo, CO
Casias, Daniel R. ... Pueblo, CO
Casiello, Albert M. ... Chicago, IL
Casiello, Nicholas, Jr. ... Atlantic City, NJ
Casier, David H. ... Burlington, VT
Casilio, William J. ... Williamsville, NY
Casillas, Alfred Michael ... Austin, TX
San Antonio, TX
Casillas, Carol A. ... San Diego, CA
Casillas, Daniel ... San Diego, CA
Casillas, Gaudalupe ... Union City, NJ
Casillas, Juan B. ... Humacao, PR
Casillas, Mark ... San Francisco, CA
Casillas, Olga F. ... Arlington, VA
Casillas, Olga F., P.C. ... Arlington, VA
Casillas, Richard M. ... San Antonio, TX
Casillas, Teresa M. ... Denver, CO
Casillas-Robles, Luis ... San Diego, CA
Casimer, Gregory P. ... Chicago, IL
Casimir, Reginald ... Brooklyn, NY
Casimir-Benoit, Franckline ... Somerset, NJ
Casinghino, Gary ... Manchester, NH
Casini, Christian C. ... Rochester, NY
Casini, Janet M. ... Manalapan, NJ
Casini, Jason M. ... Des Moines, IA
Casini, Victor M. ... Chicago, IL
Casino, Bruce J. ... Washington, DC
Casino, Joseph M. ... New York, NY
Casjens, Carlton B. ... Bell, CA
Casjens, David W. ... Rock Rapids, IA
Casker, Gregory T. ... Danville, VA
Caskey, C. John ... Greensburg, LA
Caskey, David H. ... Rockford, IL
Caskey, Geo. W. ... Atlanta, GA
Caskey, J. Thomas ... Baltimore, MD
Caskey, J. Thomas ... Towson, MD
Caskey, Jack W. ... Lake Charles, LA
Caskey, Jeri Leigh Hibler ... Alton, MO
Caskey, Joseph K. ... Oklahoma City, OK
Caskey, K. Louis ... Kansas City, MO
Caskey, Marshall A. ... Los Angeles, CA
Caskey, Marshall A., Law Offices of
Hollywood, CA
Caskey, Martin Franklin ... Montgomery, AL
Caskey & Pizzolatto ... Lake Charles, LA
Caskey, Priscilla C. ... Baltimore, MD
Caskey, Ray Lee ... Alton, MO
Caskey, Susan ... Blue Bell, PA
Caskey, Wayne F., Jr. ... Dallas, TX
Caskey, Wendy L. ... Troy, MI
Caskey, William J. ... Columbia, SC
Caskie & Frost, A Professional Corporation
Amherst, VA
Bedford, VA
Lynchburg, VA
Rustburg, VA
Caskins, William J., Jr. ... Denver, CO
Caslavka, John R. ... Tulsa, OK
Casler, Gerald J. ... Baton Rouge, LA
Casler, John S. ... Boston, MA
Casler, Joseph C. ... New Orleans, LA
Caslin, Brent L. ... Los Angeles, CA
Caslin, Daniel ... Owensboro, KY
Caslin, John J., Jr. ... New York, NY
Caslin Law Offices, PSC ... Owensboro, KY
Caslione, John A. ... Lake Forest, IL
Caslowitz, Andrew ... East Providence, RI
Casmay, Suzanne R. ... Bridgeton, NJ
Casmere, Vicki L. ... Naperville, IL
Casner, A. James, III
Charlotte Amalie, St. Thomas, VI
Casner, Carol A. ... Wilmington, DE
Casner & Edwards, LLP ... Boston, MA
Casner, Richard K. ... Lubbock, TX
Casner, Truman S. ... Boston, MA
Casnocha, David G. ... San Francisco, CA
Casnoff, Alan E. ... Philadelphia, PA
Caso, Anthony T. ... Sacramento, CA
Caso, Christopher J. ... Dallas, TX
Caso & Egelston ... Dallas, TX
Caso, Gasper, Jr. ... Belmont, MA
Caso, George R., III ... Merrick, NY
Caso, Julio E. ... Coral Gables, FL
Caso, Karen Carter ... Rockville Centre, NY
Caso, Luis S. ... Miami, FL
Caso, Peter John ... Brooklyn, NY
Caso, Ralph G. ... Merrick, NY
Caso, Ronald G. ... Garden City, NY
Caso, Stephen P. ... Philadelphia, PA
Caso, William J. ... Stamford, CT
Casola, Francis H. ... Roanoke, VA
Casolari, Samuel Guy, Jr. ... Cincinnati, OH
Casolaro, Charles John ... New York, NY
Casolaro, John R. ... New York, NY
Cason, Alan C. ... Baltimore, MD
Cason, Anita Y. ... Malvern, PA
Cason, Benny M. ... Corpus Christi, TX
Cason, Christopher M. ... Seattle, WA
Cason, David Raymond ... Monticello, AR
Cason, Edgett, Mahan & Shields, L.L.C.
Clinton, MO
Cason, George M., Jr. ... Eagle Lake, TX
Cason, John C. ... Montgomery, AL
Cason, Kay L. McNabb ... Birmingham, AL
Cason, Laninya A. ... Belleville, IL
Cason, Larissa A. ... New York, NY
Cason, Laura D. ... Walnut Creek, CA
Cason, Len ... Oklahoma City, OK
Cason, Marilynn J. ... Oakbrook Terrace, IL
Cason, Mark ... Dallas, TX
Cason, Selena Mae ... Trussville, AL
Cason, Tiffanie N. ... Chicago, IL
Cason, Warren M. ... Tampa, FL
Cason, William E. ... Houston, TX
Cason, William J. ... Clinton, MO
Cason, William W. "Bill" ... Houston, TX
Cason-Adams, Sharon ... Dublin, OH
Casoni, Dava ... Washington, DC
Casoni, Vito C. ... Buffalo, NY
Casoria, Edward, Jr. ... Winter Park, FL
Casoria & Goff, P.A. ... Fort Lauderdale, FL
Casoria, John B. ... Newport Beach, CA
Casoria, S. M., III ... Fort Lauderdale, FL
Casowitz, Marilyn F. ... Newark, NJ
Casowitz, Paul D. ... New York, NY
Caspar, Bernard J. ... Gaylord, MI
Caspar, Bernard J., P.C. ... Gaylord, MI
Caspar, Frederick J. ... Dayton, OH
Caspar, George J. ... Hartford, CT
Caspar, Robert Lee, Jr. ... Huber Heights, OH
Caspar, Stephen ... West Des Moines, IA
Caspari, Kimberly Peterson
Baltimore, MD
Caspari, William S. ... Alameda, CA
Casparian, Kathryn G. ... New York, NY
Casparian, Thomas W. ... Santa Monica, CA
Caspe, Dennis G. ... Santa Cruz, CA
Casper, Alan H. ... Philadelphia, PA
Casper, Arthur Brandeis ... Middletown, OH
Casper and Casper ... Hamilton, OH
Lebanon, OH
Middletown, OH
Casper, Charles B. ... Cherry Hill, NJ
Philadelphia, PA
Casper, Charles R. ... La Grange, IL
Casper, Charlie Barnes ... Asheboro, NC
Casper, Christopher C.
St. Petersburg, FL
Tampa, FL
Casper, Denise Jefferson ... Boston, MA
Casper & de Toledo LLC ... Greenwich, CT
Norwalk, CT
Stamford, CT
Casper, Donald A. ... San Francisco, CA
Casper, Donald J. ... Springfield, IL
Casper, Donald J., P.C. ... Springfield, IL
Casper, Doris S. ... Margate City, NJ
Casper, Douglas W. ... Middletown, OH
Casper, E. Jeffrey ... Middletown, OH
Casper, Edward A. ... Haddonfield, NJ
Casper & Elias ... Haddonfield, NJ
Casper, Eric M. ... Phoenix, AZ
Casper, Harvey N. ... Brooklyn, NY
Casper, James B. ... Fond du Lac, WI
Casper, Jared ... Las Vegas, NV
Casper, John E. ... Winterset, IA
Casper, Joseph J. ... Wheaton, IL
Casper, Kenneth K. ... Vallejo, CA
Casper, Lawrence A. ... Department of Justice,
Tax Division, GV
Casper, M. Elizabeth ... Louisville, KY
Casper, Marie A. ... Bridgeport, CT
Casper, Mark J. ... Palo Alto, CA
Casper, Martha L. ... Madison, WI
Casper, Meadows & Schwartz, A
Professional Corporation
Walnut Creek, CA
Casper, Michael J. ... Cleveland, OH
Casper, Michael R. ... Gainesville, GA
Casper, Michael R., P.C. ... Gainesville, GA
Casper, Michelle M. ... Des Moines, IA
Casper, Nicholas A. ... Fond du Lac, WI
Casper, Paul W., Jr. ... Cincinnati, OH
Casper, Richard H. ... Salt Lake City, UT
Casper, Richard H. ... Milwaukee, WI
Casper, Richard H, P.C. ... Salt Lake City, UT
Casper, Robert A., Jr ... Oroville, CA
Casper, Robert Y. ... New York, NY
Casper, Robt. L. ... New York, NY
Casper, S. Robert ... West Chester, OH
Casper, Sanford I. ... Middletown, OH
Casper, Seymour A. ... White Plains, NY
Casper, Stan ... Walnut Creek, CA
Casper, Stewart M. ... Stamford, CT
Casper, Susan ... Floral Park, NY
Casper, Thel W. ... Phoenix, AZ
Casper, Thomas D. ... Tampa, FL
Casper, Thomas P. ... Mount Kisco, NY
Casper, Walter F., Jr. ... Carbondale, PA
Caspermeyer, Richard A. ... Prairie Village, KS
Caspers, Christine Jo ... Minneapolis, MN
Caspers, Philip P. ... Minneapolis, MN
Caspers, Stephen C. ... San Antonio, TX
Caspersen, Anna ... New York, NY
Caspersen, Finn M. W. ... Gladstone, NJ
Caspersen, Finn M. W. ... New York, NY
Caspersen, F. W. ... Wheeling, IL
Caspersen, R. Frederick ... St. Helena, CA
San Francisco, CA
Casperson, John E. ... Seattle, WA
Casperson, Patricia ... Philadelphia, PA
Casperson, Timothy A. ... Clear Lake, IA
Caspino, Michael W. ... Orange, CA
Las Vegas, NV
Casriel, Carl ... Deal, NJ
Casriel & Casriel ... Deal, NJ
Casriel, Eric C. ... Deal, NJ
Cass, Alan M., & Associates ... New York, NY
Cass, Bertrand M., Jr. ... New Orleans, LA
Cass, David M. ... Bloomfield, CT
Cass, David S. ... North Kingstown, RI
Cass, Earl B., Jr. ... Pasadena, TX
Cass, Edward B. ... Palm City, FL
Cass, Edward J. ... Cleveland, OH
Cass, Frederick G. ... North Kingstown, RI
Cass, George L. ... Pittsburgh, PA
Cass, Gordon C. ... Abilene, TX
Cass, Harrison E. ... Cumming, IA
Cass, Jennifer C. ... Department of Justice,
Civil Rights Division, GV
Cass, John E. ... Stillwater, MN
Cass, Jonathan A. ... Philadelphia, PA
Cass, Kenneth R. ... Washington, DC
Cass, Kerstin E. ... Denver, CO
Cass Law Associates ... North Kingstown, RI
Cass, Leonard J. ... Memphis, TN
Cass, Marcy ... Brookline, MA
Cass, Nancy J. ... Mount Kisco, NY
Cass, Nathan ... Northridge, CA
Cass, Neil E. ... Chicago, IL
Cass, Paul D. ... Los Angeles, CA
Cass, Paul L. ... Citrus Heights, CA
Cass, Peter J. ... Newark, NJ
Cass, R. Michael ... Barrington, IL
Cass, Raymond M., Jr. ... Holly Hill, FL
Cass, Richard J. ... Dedham, MA
Cass, Richard W. ... Washington, DC
Cass, Robert G. ... Tulsa, OK
Cass, Ronald A. ... Boston, MA
Cass, Rosemary Higgins ... Newark, NJ
Cass, Russell E. ... Chicago, IL
Cass, Stephen W. ... Jamestown, NY
Cass, V. Andrew ... Phoenix, AZ
Las Vegas, NV
Cass, V. Andrew, The Law Office of
Las Vegas, NV
Cass, Walter O. ... Denver, CO
Cass, Willard W. ... Mayville, NY
Cass, William D. ... Metairie, LA
Cass, William E. ... Syracuse, NY
Cass, William J. ... Windsor, CT
Springfield, MA
Cass, William O., Jr. ... Dayton, OH
Cassada, Garland S. ... Charlotte, NC
Cassada, William W. ... Indian Lake, NY
Cassady, Charlotte D. ... Seattle, WA
Cassady, David J. ... Centreville, VA
Cassady, Fuller & Marsh, LLP ... Elba, AL
Enterprise, AL
Geneva, AL
Cassady, G. Edward, III ... Birmingham, AL
Cassady, Joe C. ... Enterprise, AL
Cassady, Joe C., Jr. ... Enterprise, AL
Cassady, John H., III
Department of Transportation,
Federal Aviation Administration, GV
Cassady, John J. ... Oakland, CA
Cassady, Margaret M. ... Syracuse, NY
Cassady, Max ... Evergreen, AL
Cassady, Michael C. ... Cincinnati, OH
Cassady, Peter L. ... Cincinnati, OH
Cassady, Quintin ... Fort Worth, TX
Cassady, Ralph, (P.C.) ... Los Angeles, CA
Cassady, Virginia ... Winter Springs, FL
Cassady, William E. ... Mobile, AL
Cassak, Lance D. ... Treasury Department,
Office of Thrift Supervision, GV
Cassan, Vito J. ... New York, NY
Cassandro, Robert J. ... Jericho, NY
New York, NY
Cassanego, Mark A. ... Burlingame, CA
Cassano, Daniel A. ... Treasury Department,
Internal Revenue Service, GV
Cassano, Lawrence C. ... Chicago, IL
Cassano, Thomas R. ... Buffalo, NY
Cassanos, Arthur P. ... Mechanicsville, VA
Cassanos, Robert ... New York, NY
Cassanova, John D. ... Metairie, LA
Cassar & Fisher, P.C. ... Eastpointe, MI
Cassar, George V., Jr. ... Southfield, MI
Cassar, Hedy E. ... Troy, MI
Cassar, Raymond A. ... Dearborn Heights, MI
Farmington Hills, MI
Cassar, Raymond A. ... Detroit, MI
Cassar, Robert John ... Eastpointe, MI
Cassara, Christopher C. ... Providence, RI
Cassara, William E. ... Baltimore, MD
Cassard, Richard E. ... Grand Rapids, MI
Cassari, Jack R. ... Fairless Hills, PA
Cassarino, Ben J., Jr. ... Rochester, NY
Cassaro, Charles T. ... Cleveland, OH
Cassaro, Michael G. ... Louisville, KY
Cassas, Andrew N. ... Boca Raton, FL
Cassas, Andrew N., P.A. ... Boca Raton, FL
Cassas, Frank ... Reno, NV
Cassas, Nicholas A. ... Coral Springs, FL
Cassat, Kenneth L. ... Clarinda, IA
Cassat, Peter C. ... Washington, DC
Cassatly, Edward, Jr. ... Clifton, NJ
Cassato, Bradley J. ... Chicago, IL
Cassavaugh, George A., Jr. ... Detroit, MI
Cassavechia, Gary R. ... Rochester, NH
Cassavell, Laura Wheeler ... Pennington, NJ
Casscles, J. Stephen ... Albany, NY
Casseb & Casseb ... San Antonio, TX
Casseb, Joseph ... San Antonio, TX
Casseb, Kitty Mullen ... San Antonio, TX
Casseb, Paul Ernest ... San Antonio, TX
Casseb & Pearl, Inc. ... San Antonio, TX
Casseb, R. Michael ... San Antonio, TX
Casseb, Sol, III ... San Antonio, TX
Casseb, Solomon, Jr. ... San Antonio, TX
Cassebaum, McFall, Layman & Jordan, A
Professional Corporation ... Bangor, PA
Cassebaum, William C. ... Bangor, PA
Cassedy, Marshall R. ... Tallahassee, FL
Cassedy, Melissa J. ... Concord, MA
Cassedy, Patrice Rinaldo ... Del Mar, CA
Cassedy, Sherrol L. ... Palo Alto, CA
Cassel, Alan L. ... St. Louis, MO
Cassel, Alvin ... Miami, FL
Cassel & Beeler ... Carey, OH
Cassel, Danielle Meltzer ... Chicago, IL
Cassel, Eugene D. ... Washington, DC
Cassel, F. K. ... Carey, OH
Cassel, James A. ... Philadelphia, PA
Cassel, James S. ... Miami, FL
Cassel, Jamie J. Swenson ... Rockford, IL
Cassel, Jennifer Kathryn ... Annapolis, MD
Cassel, Joel A., (P.C.) ... Los Angeles, CA
Cassel Malm Fagundes LLP
Stockton, CA
Cassel, Marwin S., (P.A.) ... Miami, FL
Cassel, McMahon & Courtney ... Algona, IA
Cassel, Melody J. ... Coventry, RI
Cassel, Natileene W. ... Islamorada, FL
Cassel, P. Gary ... Stockton, CA
Reno, NV
Cassel, Pauline M. ... Perkasie, PA
Cassel, Robert M. ... San Francisco, CA
Cassel, William B. ... Ainsworth, NE
Cassel, William S. ... New Orleans, LA
Casselberry, Robert F. ... Pittsburgh, PA
Casselberry, Russell W. ... Lamesa, TX
Casselberry, Steven ... Newport Beach, CA
Cassell, Barry A. ... New York, NY
Cassell, Deborah ... Plymouth, MA
Cassell, Dennis R. ... Austin, TX
Cassell, Herbert C., Jr. ... Columbia, SC
Cassell, J. Michael ... Charles Town, WV
Cassell, John J. ... Granville, OH
Cassell, Joseph H. ... Wichita, KS
Cassell, Kenneth K. ... Lapeer, MI
Cassell, Lou Ann S. ... Charleston, WV
Cassell & Lower, L.L.C. ... Wichita, KS
Cassell, Martin L. ... Aurora, IL
Cassell, Martin L., Ltd. ... Aurora, IL
Cassell, Martin P. ... San Diego, CA
Cassell, Michael D. ... Uniondale, NY
Cassell, Paul G. ... Salt Lake City, UT
Cassell, Paul R. ... Washington, DC
Cassell, Richard E. ... Alexandria, VA
Cassell, Ruth Naomi ... Rego Park, NY
Cassell, Susan C. ... Newark, NJ
Cassella, David P., Law Office of
Brockton, MA
Cassella, Margaret M. ... Farmington, CT
Cassella, Stefan D. ... Department of Justice,
Criminal Division, GV
Casselle, Dawne Astride ... Allentown, PA
Casselman, Cindy L. ... San Diego, CA
Casselman, Danielle ... Los Angeles, CA
Casselman, David B. ... Tarzana, CA
Casselman, Gary S., Law Offices of
Los Angeles, CA
Casselman, Howard F. ... Morristown, NJ
Casselman, Robert E. ... Scottsdale, AZ
Casselman, Thomas Payne, (P.C.)
Marquette, MI
Casselman, William E., II ... New York, NY
Cassels, Edison Pendleton ... Charlotte, NC
Cassels, Haglund & Clark ... Lufkin, TX
Cassels, Jimmy A. ... Lufkin, TX
Cassels, John D., Jr. ... Okeechobee, FL
Cassels, Kelly M. ... Roswell, NM
Cassels & McCall ... Okeechobee, FL
Cassels, Robert B. ... San Luis Obispo, CA
Cassem, Andrea R. ... Dallas, TX
Cassem, Tierney, Adams, Gotch & Douglas
Omaha, NE
Cassens, Damon Douglas
Colorado Springs, CO
Cassens, Mark A. ... Quincy, IL
Cassens, Tracy R. ... Chicago, IL
Casser, Claudia ... West Paterson, NJ
Casser, Jerry A. ... Roseland, NJ
Casser, Jerry A., P.C. ... Roseland, NJ
Casser, Karen L. ... Washington, DC
Casserly, Brian W. ... Irvine, CA
Casserly, James L. ... Washington, DC
Casserly, James R. ... Minneapolis, MN
Casserly, Janice Rea ... New York, NY
Casserly, John B. ... Minneapolis, MN
Casserly Jones, P.C. ... St. Louis, MO
Casserly, Sarah M. ... Minneapolis, MN
Casserly, Timothy E. ... Albany, NY
Cassese, Anthony P. ... New York, NY
Cassese, Frank V. ... Brooklyn, NY
Cassese, John J. ... Woodbridge, NJ
Cassett, Larry R. ... Murray Hill, NJ
Cassetta, Christine ... Phoenix, AZ
Cassetta, Ralph A. ... New York, NY
Cassetta, Richard P. ... St. Louis, MO
Cassetta, William M. ... Detroit, MI
Cassetty, David R. ... Miami, FL
Cassetty, Michael T. ... Akron, OH
Cassian, William ... Wheaton, IL
Cassiano, Frank A., Jr. ... Greenville, NC
Cassibry, Fred J. ... New Orleans, LA
Cassibry, Reginald E. ... Bossier City, LA
Shreveport, LA
Cassibry, Robert K. ... Houston, TX
Cassiday, Benjamin B., III ... Honolulu, HI
Cassiday, John D, ... Chicago, IL
Waukegan, IL
Cassiday, Schade & Gloor ... Chicago, IL
Elgin, IL
Geneva, IL
Joliet, IL
Rockford, IL

Cassiday, Schade & Gloor—Continued
Waukegan, IL
Wheaton, IL
Woodstock, IL
Cassidy, Alan K. ... Modesto, CA
Cassidy, Alvin M. ... Santa Ana, CA
Cassidy, Andrew D. ... Peoria, IL
Cassidy, Andrew G. ... West Chester, PA
Cassidy, Ann M. ... Indianapolis, IN
Cassidy, Arthur ... Tesuque, NM
Cassidy & Associates ... Washington, DC
Cassidy, Bart E. ... Bala Cynwyd, PA
Cassidy, Bernard James ... Palo Alto, CA
Cassidy, Bernard M. ... Fort Lauderdale, FL
Cassidy, Brian P. ... Gloucester, MA
Cassidy, Bruce G. ... Princeton, NJ
Philadelphia, PA
Cassidy, Bruce G., & Associates, P.A.
Princeton, NJ
Philadelphia, PA
Cassidy, C. Brian ... Austin, TX
Cassidy, Catherine H. ... Fort Pierce, FL
Cassidy, Charles M. ... Bogalusa, LA
Cassidy, Cheatham, Shimko & Dawson, A Professional Corporation
San Francisco, CA
Cassidy, Christine E. ... San Francisco, CA
Cassidy, Christopher F. ... Peoria, IL
Cassidy, Clement J. ... Temple, PA
Cassidy, Colleen A. ... San Francisco, CA
Cassidy, Colleen P. ... New York, NY
Cassidy, Daniel C. ... Los Angeles, CA
Cassidy, Daniel D. ... White Plains, NY
Cassidy, David E. ... Roseland, NJ
New York, NY
Cassidy, David M. ... Uniondale, NY
Cassidy, David R. ... Baton Rouge, LA
Cassidy, David W. ... Newport News, VA
Cassidy, Dennis James ... Kansas City, MO
Cassidy, Donald W. ... San Antonio, TX
Cassidy, Edward Q. ... St. Paul, MN
Cassidy, Edward V., Jr.
Department Of Veterans Affairs, Office of the General Counsel, GV
Cassidy, Elizabeth K. ... Pekin, IL
Cassidy, Foss & San Filippo ... Red Bank, NJ
Cassidy, Francis J., Jr. ... Franklin, ME
Cassidy, Frank J. ... Tucson, AZ
Cassidy, Fred J. ... Gettysburg, PA
Cassidy, Fred M. ... Austin, TX
Cassidy & Gunnell ... Jennings, LA
Cassidy, Hannah K.V. ... Nashville, TN
Cassidy, Harold J. ... Red Bank, NJ
Cassidy, Helen A. ... Houston, TX
Cassidy, J. Peter, Jr. ... Lexington, KY
Cassidy, J. Robert ... Bellingham, WA
Cassidy, James ... New York, NY
Cassidy, James A. ... West Palm Beach, FL
Cassidy, James H. ... Greenville, SC
Greer, SC
Cassidy, James M. ... Washington, DC
Cassidy, James M. ... Attleboro, MA
Cassidy, James P., Jr. ... Lowell, MA
Cassidy, Janice A. ... San Benito, TX
Cassidy, Janice A., P.C. ... San Benito, TX
Cassidy, Jayme Jones ... Miami, FL
Cassidy, Jeremiah J. ... Chicago, IL
Cassidy, J. H. ... Frontenac, MO
Cassidy, Joanne ... Playa Del Rey, CA
Cassidy, John A. ... Phoenix, AZ
Cassidy, John C. ... Chicago, IL
Cassidy, John D. ... Boston, MA
Cassidy, John E., III ... Peoria, IL
Cassidy, John E., Jr. ... Peoria, IL
Cassidy, John F.K. ... Old Greenwich, CT
New York, NY
Cassidy, John H. ... Phoenix, AZ
Cassidy, John H., Jr. ... Waterbury, CT
Cassidy, John J. ... Chicago, IL
Cassidy, John J., Jr. ... Chicago, IL
Cassidy, John Joseph ... Washington, DC
Cassidy, John M. ... Topeka, KS
Cassidy, John P. ... Durango, CO
Cassidy, John S. ... New York, NY
Cassidy, Joseph A., Jr. ... Southold, NY
Cassidy, Joseph J. ... Hartford, CT
Cassidy, Karen Munster ... Roseland, NJ
Cassidy, Kevin H. ... Somers, NY
Cassidy, Kevin P. ... Gooding, ID
Cassidy, Kieran S. ... Fairfield, CT
Cassidy, Kotjarapoglus & Pohland, P.C.
Greensburg, PA
Cassidy, Kristan M. ... Washington, DC
Cassidy, Kristen T. ... Phoenix, AZ
Cassidy, Kyran ... New York, NY
Cassidy, Lee W. ... Washington, DC
Cassidy, Leigh S. ... San Francisco, CA
Cassidy, Leslie Denis, III
Corpus Christi, TX
Cassidy, Lisa N. ... Santa Fe, NM
Cassidy, M. Sharon ... New York, NY
Cassidy, Margaret K. ... Atlanta, GA
Cassidy, Marilyn B. ... Parma Heights, OH
Cassidy, Mark ... Cheney, WA
Cassidy, Marlene Pamela ... Brooklyn, NY
Cassidy, Martha ... Washington, DC
Cassidy, Mary E. ... Washington, DC
Cassidy, Mary Lou ... Midland, TX
Cassidy, Mary Margaret Gorman
Fort Wright, KY
Cassidy, Maryann Cash ... Boston, MA
Cassidy, Mercedes ... Conshohocken, PA
Cassidy, Michael A. ... Pittsburgh, PA
Cassidy, Michael C. ... Jennings, LA
Cassidy, Michael E. ... Burlington, VT
Cassidy, Michael J. ... Orange, CA
Cassidy, Michael J. ... Madison, NC
Cassidy, Michael J. ... Fairfax, VA
Cassidy, Michael M. ... McFarland, WI
Cassidy, Michael P. ... Parma Heights, OH
Cassidy, Michael W. ... Huntingdon Valley, PA
Cassidy, Michele Medlock ... Dallas, TX
Cassidy & Mueller ... Peoria, IL
Cassidy, Myers, Cogan, Voegelin & Tennant, L.C. ... St. Clairsville, OH
Moundsville, WV
Wheeling, WV
Cassidy, Nancy K. ... Providence, RI
Cassidy, Patricia ... Pittsburgh, PA
Cassidy, Patrick J. ... Boston, MA
Cassidy, Patrick M. ... Garden City, NY
Cassidy, Patrick S. ... Wheeling, WV
Cassidy, Paul W. ... Parma Heights, OH
Cassidy, Peter W. ... Boston, MA
Cassidy, R. Michael ... Boston, MA
Cassidy, Reiman & Harbarger
Parma Heights, OH
Cassidy, Richard T. ... Dallas, TX
Cassidy, Richard T. ... Burlington, VT
Cassidy, Richard W., Jr. ... Logansport, IN
Cassidy, Robert C., Jr. ... Washington, DC
Cassidy, Roderick J. ... Englewood Cliffs, NJ
New York, NY
Cassidy, Rory D. ... Chicago, IL
Cassidy, Ryan J. ... Philadelphia, PA
Cassidy, Sean ... Greensburg, PA
Cassidy, Sean ... Pittsburgh, PA
Cassidy, Seán M. ... Tarzana, CA
Cassidy, Stephen H. ... San Francisco, CA
Cassidy, Stephen K. ... San Francisco, CA
Cassidy, Susan Booth ... Washington, DC
Cassidy, Susan F. ... New York, NY
Cassidy, Susan O. ... Madison, CT
Cassidy, Suzanne ... Covington, KY
Cassidy, Terence J. ... Sacramento, CA
Cassidy, Thomas ... Lakeland, FL
Cassidy, Thomas B. ... Lisle, IL
Cassidy, Thomas J. ... New York, NY
Cassidy, Thomas J., Jr. ... Washington, DC
Cassidy, Thomas P. ... Washington, DC
Cassidy, Thomas P., Jr. ... Memphis, TN
Cassidy, Thomas V. ... Marietta, GA
Cassidy, Timothy A. ... Greenville, SC
Cassidy, Timothy J. ... Peoria, IL
Cassidy, Timothy M. ... Jennings, LA
Cassidy, Walter T.
Department of Housing and Urban Development, Office of General Counsel, GV
Cassidy, Warner, Lane & Winstead, A Professional Corporation
Los Angeles, CA
Santa Ana, CA
Cassidy, William A. ... Cleveland, OH
Cassidy, William E., Law Office
Miami, FL
Cassidy, William J., III ... Miami, FL
Cassidy, William J., Jr. ... Ephrata, PA
Lancaster, PA
Cassidybrown, Ruth L ... Kinnelon, NJ
Cassie, Dawn M. ... Chicago, IL
Cassier, Michel Pierre ... Buffalo, NY
Cassil, Donald W. ... Chicago, IL
Cassil & Henson ... Oklahoma City, OK
Cassil, Larry G. ... Oklahoma City, OK
Cassil, Larry G., Jr. ... Dallas, TX
Cassillo, John Christopher ... Deer Park, NY
Cassilly, Joseph I. ... Bel Air, MD
Cassilly, Lisa H. ... Atlanta, GA
Cassilly, Robert G. ... Baltimore, MD
Cassimatis, Anthony E. ... St. Louis, MO
Cassimatis, Emanuel A. ... York, PA
Cassimatis, Gregory E. ... Mechanicsburg, PA
Cassin Cassin & Joseph ... Fort Lee, NJ
Cassin Cassin & Joseph LLP
New York, NY
Cassin Cassin & Joseph, LLP ... Purchase, NY
Cassin, Howard ... Towson, MD
Cassin, Joseph M. ... New York, NY
Purchase, NY
Cassin, Olivia L. ... Brooklyn, NY
Cassin, Stephen J. ... Chicago, IL
Cassin, William F. ... New York, NY
Cassinelli, Denise ... San Francisco, CA
Cassinelli, Tracy A. ... Columbus, OH
Cassingham, John J. ... Hercules, CA
Cassingham, Mary Louise ... New Orleans, LA
Cassini, Joseph C., III ... Newark, NJ
Cassinis, Edward A. ... Aurora, CO
Cassino, Anthony J. ... Bronx, NY
Cassioppi, Gerald A. ... Chicago, IL
Cassirer, Aurora ... New York, NY
Cassis, Bryan M. ... Louisville, KY
Cassis, Charles H. ... Louisville, KY
Cassis, Charles S. ... Louisville, KY
Cassis, Thos. V. ... Spokane, WA
Cassisa, Paul V., Jr. ... Metairie, LA
Oxford, MS
Cassisa, Paul V., Sr. ... Metairie, LA
Cassisi, Frank J. ... Mineola, NY
Cassita, Diane Rocha ... Union, NJ
Cassity, C. Fred ... Pasadena, CA
Cassity, Donn E. ... Salt Lake City, UT
Cassity, G. Kris ... Anchorage, AK
Cassity & Maseda ... Pasadena, CA
Cassity, Michael E. ... Mt. Orab, OH
Cassity, O.A., III ... Carthage, TX
Cassity, Richard E. ... Arlington, TX
Cassling, Donald R. ... Chicago, IL
Cassling, Sally ... Arlington Heights, IL
Cassman, Alan H. ... Los Angeles, CA
Cassman, Frederick S. ... Omaha, NE
Cassman, Joan L. ... San Francisco, CA
Cassman, Ted W. ... Oakland, CA
Casso, David ... McAllen, TX
Casso, James M. ... Montebello, CA
Casso, Raul ... Laredo, TX
Cassody, James B. ... Oklahoma City, OK
Cassol, Robert Y. ... Greensburg, PA
Casson, Andrea C.
United States International Trade Commission, Office of the General Counsel, GV
Casson, Gary ... New York, NY
Casson, George J., Jr. ... Northbrook, IL
Casson, Joseph E. ... Washington, DC
Casson, Joseph Martin, III ... Fairbury, NE
Casson, Luke A. ... Chicago, IL
Casson, Rhonda L. ... Totowa, NJ
Casson, Richard T.
Steamboat Springs, CO
Cassone, John A. ... Stamford, CT
Cassone, Thomas M. ... Stamford, CT
Cassorla, Edward ... Canton, MA
Cassorla, Steven ... San Francisco, CA
Cassou, April K. ... Belvedere-Tiburon, CA
Cassou, Francis A. ... San Diego, CA
Casstevens, Earnest C. ... Austin, TX
Casstevens, Grace Hopkins ... Austin, TX
Casstevens, Hanner, Gunter & Conrad, P.A.
Charlotte, NC
Casstevens, Michael Lee
Corpus Christi, TX
Casstevens, Nelson M., Jr. ... Charlotte, NC
Cassulo, Kim F. ... Santa Monica, CA
Cassun, William C., Jr. ... Denver, CO
Cassuto, Isadore ... Chatham, NY
Cassutt, Hays & Friedman, P.A.
Las Vegas, NM
Santa Fe, NM
Cassutt, Kenneth J. ... Las Vegas, NM
Santa Fe, NM
Cassy, Charles L. ... Ventura, CA
Castafero, Jeanne Crane ... Radnor, PA
Castagliola, Paul ... St. Petersburg, FL
Castagliola, Paul, P.A. ... St. Petersburg, FL
Castagliuolo, Eugene P. ... Clearwater, FL
Castagna, Charles N. ... Clearwater, FL
Castagna, David ... Pearl River, NY
Castagna, Edward C., Jr. ... Charlotte, NC
Castagna, Lynn S. ... Austin, TX
Castagna, Richard P. ... Springfield, MA
Castagna, Robert J. ... Portland, OR
Castagna, William J. ... Tampa, FL
Castagne, Catherine Michelle
Cheboygan, MI
Castagnello, John D. ... New York, NY
Castagnera, James O. ... Philadelphia, PA
Castagnet, Marisa C. ... Irvine, CA
Castagno, Joseph D. ... Laguna Niguel, CA
Castagno, Joseph D.
San Juan Capistrano, CA
Castagno, Philip J. ... Louisville, KY
Castagnola, George J., Jr. ... Petaluma, CA
Castagnoli, Susan G. ... Naperville, IL
Castagnos, Shari D. ... Tampa, FL
Castaing, Edward J., Jr.
New Orleans, LA
Castaldi, Cathrine M. ... Irvine, CA
Castaldi, Frank D., Jr. ... White Plains, NY
Castaldi, Giuseppe ... Simi Valley, CA
Castaldi, Gregory G. ... Chicago, IL
Castaldi, John A. ... Bronx, NY
Castaldi, Leslie J. ... Philadelphia, PA
Castaldi, Terra E. ... Washington, DC
Castaldo, Andrew P. ... New York, NY
Castaldo, Edward A.B. ... Indianapolis, IN
Castaldo, Neil F. ... Concord, NH
Castaldo, Noëlle V. ... Los Angeles, CA
Castaldo, Paula M. ... Newark, NJ
Castañares, Tony ... Los Angeles, CA
Castanares, William Thomas ... Salem, OR
Castaneda, Anthony ... Los Angeles, CA
Castaneda, Carlos E. ... San Diego, CA
Castañeda, Chrysta L. ... Dallas, TX
Castaneda, Daniel F. ... Houston, TX
Castaneda, Janet Kaiser ... Sunnyvale, CA
Castañeda, Janet L. ... Boise, ID
Castaneda, Janet Y. ... Cincinnati, OH
Castañeda, John Anthony ... Chicago, IL
Castañeda, John E. ... Dallas, TX
Castaneda, John J. ... Chicago, IL
Castaneda, Jose O. ... Port Chester, NY
Castañeda, Kirsten M. ... Dallas, TX
Castanes, John C. ... Chicago, IL
Castanes, Theodore J. ... Chicago, IL
Castanias, Gregory A. ... Washington, DC
Castano, David G. ... Houston, TX
Castano, Gregory J. ... Secaucus, NJ
Castano, Gregory J., Jr. ... Secaucus, NJ
Castano, Marianne L. ... Houston, TX
Castano, Robert J. ... New York, NY
Castano, Thomas C. ... Newark, NJ
Castano, Thomas J. ... Parsippany, NJ
Castanon, Isidro O. ... Palacios, TX
San Antonio, TX
Castañón, Myrna ... Novato, CA
Castanon, Paul Alan ... Houston, TX
Castanon, Rhonda M. ... Melbourne, FL
Castanza, Jason D. ... Newberg, OR
Castanzo, Erin Butler ... Scranton, PA
Castator, Alan B. ... La Grange, IL
Castaybert, Andre G. ... New York, NY
Castberg, James P. ... Sheridan, WY
Casteel, Barron ... New Braunfels, TX
Casteel, Carroll K., Jr. ... Washington, DC
Casteel & Carson ... Portland, OR
Casteel, Carter ... New Braunfels, TX
Casteel, Chaelyn W. ... Grafton, WV
Casteel, Charles L. ... Denver, CO
Casteel, Douglas ... Miamisburg, OH
Casteel, Durward D. ... Baton Rouge, LA
Casteel, Elizabeth A. ... Memphis, TN
Casteel, Frederick R. ... Dallas, TX
Casteel, Herbert C. ... Carthage, MO
Casteel, James L. ... Portland, OR
Casteel, John A. ... Eureka Springs, AR
Casteel, John R. ... Vandalia, MO
Casteel, Keith W. ... Arthur, IL
Decatur, IL
Casteel, Kimler G. ... Oxnard, CA
Casteel, Mark Wayne ... Tallahassee, FL
Casteel, Mary M. ... Fort Lauderdale, FL
Casteel, Robert A. ... Lynnwood, WA
Casteel, Wynne M., Jr. ... Fort Lauderdale, FL
Casteen, J. Wesley ... Warsaw, NC
Castegnaro, David R. ... Rockford, IL
Casteix, Barbara Treuting
New Orleans, LA
Casteix, Michael J. ... New Orleans, LA
Castel, Benoit ... Arlington, VA
Castel, P. Kevin ... New York, NY
Castelazo, Thomas A. ... Fresno, CA
Castelblanco, Eric E. ... Beverly Hills, CA
Castelda, Roger A. ... Tonasket, WA
Castele, John T. ... Cleveland, OH
Castellan, C. Patrick ... Florham Park, NJ
Castellana, Margaret ... Naples, FL
Castellanet, Craig David ... Sacramento, CA
Castellani, Anthony P. ... Trenton, NJ
Castellani, David R. ... Atlantic City, NJ
Northfield, NJ
Castellani, Edward J. ... East Lansing, MI
Castellani, Pamela J. ... Pittsburgh, PA
Castellani, Raymond, III ... Wayne, NJ
Castellani, Robert J. ... Decatur, GA
Castellani, Robert J. ... Buffalo, NY
Castellano, Aloysius J. ... Morristown, NJ
Castellano, Andrew ... South Pasadena, CA
Castellano, Anthony J. ... Staten Island, NY
Castellano, Beatrice E. ... Santa Fe, NM
Castellano, Carmela R. ... Sacramento, CA
Castellano, Christine ... Bedford Park, IL
Castellano, Joe C., Jr. ... Santa Fe, NM
Castellano, John A., III ... Falls Church, VA
Castellano, John C. ... Marietta, GA
Castellano, John F. ... Hempstead, NY
Castellano, John M. ... Kew Gardens, NY
Castellano, John S. ... Denver, CO
Castellano, Joseph ... Mount Kisco, NY
Castellano, June M. ... Rochester, NY
Castellano, Lisa M. ... Tampa, FL
Castellano, Lucinda A. ... Denver, CO
Castellano, Nelson T. ... Tampa, FL
Castellano, Patricia J. ... Kansas City, MO
Castellano, Philip, Jr. ... Nesconset, NY
Castellano, Philip T. ... Garden City, NY
Castellano, Randy M. ... Las Cruces, NM
Castellano, Ray ... Verona, NJ
Castellano-Mesa, Christina M. ... Tampa, FL
Castellanos, Alfredo A. ... San Juan, PR
Castellanos, Anita L. ... West Hills, CA
Castellanos, Jesus A. ... San Juan, PR
Castellanos, John J. ... Marysville, CA
Castellanos Law Firm ... San Juan, PR
Castellanos, Maurice ... Miami, FL
Castellanos & Palacios ... New York, NY
Castellanos, Richard H. ... Los Angeles, CA
Castellanos, Robert J. ... Tallahassee, FL
Castellanos, Roland R. ... Marietta, GA
Castellanos del Valle, Laura M.
San Francisco, CA
Castellanos-Perez, Norma ... Visalia, CA
Castellarin, Michael M. ... Nashville, TN
Castellarin, Peter F. ... Homewood, IL
Castellaw, Robert W. ... Spokane, WA
Castelle, George ... Charleston, WV
Castelli, Angelo I. ... Greenbelt, MD
Castelli, Anthony D. ... Cincinnati, OH
Castelli, Beth E. ... Cherry Hill, NJ
Philadelphia, PA
Castelli, Gerard Ignatius ... Eastchester, NY
Castelli, Gregory A. ... Pittsburgh, PA
Castelli, James V. ... San Francisco, CA
Castelli, Jennifer ... Evansville, IN
Castelli, John B. ... Aurora, IL
Castelli, Karen B. ... Harrisburg, PA
Castelli, Laurence E. ... Treasury Department, Office of Regulations and Rulings, GV
Castelli, Mary ... Concord, NH
Castelli, Peter Michael ... Evansville, IN
Castelli, Ralph A., Jr. ... Troy, MI
Castelli, Victor ... New York, NY
Castellini, James H. ... Seattle, WA
Castellini, Richard A. ... Cincinnati, OH
Castellino, Joseph F. ... Pittston, PA
Castellino, Michael J. ... Chicago, IL
Castellino, Samuel J. ... Elmira, NY
Castellitto, Mario ... New York, NY
Castellitto, Paul V. ... Washington, DC
Castello, Brian C. ... Pittsburgh, PA
Castello, David A. ... Omaha, NE
Castello, Geoffrey W. ... Parsippany, NJ
Castello, James E. ... Washington, DC
Castello, Janet M. ... Port Huron, MI
Castello, Joe ... Tampa, FL
Castello, Joe, P.A. ... Tampa, FL
Castello, Raymond R. ... New York, NY
Castello, Raymond V. ... Campbell, CA
Castello, Thomas M. ... Pittsburgh, PA
Castello, Wayne P. ... Gainesville, FL
Castelloe, Paul E. ... Raleigh, NC
Castelloe, Paul E., The Law Office of
Raleigh, NC
Castellon, Elisa ... Milwaukee, WI
Castellon, Michael C. ... Atlanta, GA
Castellon, Ruben A. ... Los Angeles, CA
San Francisco, CA
Castellow, Lester M., (P.C.) ... Moultrie, GA
Castellucci, Philip R. ... Los Banos, CA
Castelluccio, Catherine ... Kansas City, MO
Castelluccio, Peter Michael ... Boston, MA

Castelnuovo, Richard ... Madison, WI
Castelo, Tomas A. ... Santa Barbara, CA
Casten, Kimberley S. ... Toms River, NJ
Casten & Pearce, A Professional Law Corporation ... Shreveport, LA
Casten, Theodore J. ... Shreveport, LA
Castendyck, Robert W. ... Venice, FL
Castengera, Cynthia Barrier ... Columbia, SC
Castenholz, David J. ... Huntington Beach, CA
Caster, Cynthia M. ... Willoughby Hills, OH
Caster, Gary D. ... Imperial Beach, CA
Caster, John M. ... Syracuse, NY
Caster, Kevin J. ... Cedar Rapids, IA
Caster, Lauren J. ... Phoenix, AZ
Caster, Maureen I. Martin ... Flint, MI
Caster, Steven D. ... Aventura, FL
Casterline & Agajanian, LLP
Los Angeles, CA
Casterline, Cecil W. ... Dallas, TX
Casterline, David L. ... Los Angeles, CA
Casterline & Dendinger ... Tipton, IA
Casterline, James F. ... Tipton, IA
Casterline, John E. ... Warren, MI
Buffalo, NY
Casterline, Michael E. ... Asheville, NC
Casterline, Rex L. ... Columbia, SC
Casterline, Weed & Wood ... Dallas, TX
Casterline, William H., Jr. ... Fairfax, VA
Casterton, James S. ... Center City, MN
Casterton, Michael P. ... Gold River, CA
Casterton, Michael P. ... Sacramento, CA
Castete, Herman A. ... Winnfield, LA
Castetter, Alex A. ... Nacogdoches, TX
Castetter, Roy E. ... Detroit, MI
Castex, Jimmy Arthur, Jr. ... Metairie, LA
Castezaz, Kim T. ... Wausau, WI
Castiello, Gerardo ... Miami, FL
Castiello, Thomas R. ... Washington, DC
Castiglia, Ferdinando J., Jr. ... Harrison, NY
Castiglia, Joseph P. ... Hackensack, NJ
Castiglia, Richard P., Jr. ... Washington, DC
Castiglia, V. James, P.C. ... Oak Ridge, NJ
Castigliola, Vincent J., Jr.
Pascagoula, MS
Castiglione, Donna M. ... Tonawanda, NY
Castiglione, Frank P. ... Manhasset, NY
Castiglione, John R. ... Pittsfield, MA
Castiglione, Vincent A. ... Murray Hill, NJ
Castiglioni, Richard E. ... Stamford, CT
Castignoli, Skudlarek & Leo ... Milford, CT
Castignoli, Vito A. ... Milford, CT
Castilian, Christopher James ... Denver, CO
Castilla, Alveno N. ... Jackson, MS
Castilla, Hilliard V. ... Atlanta, GA
Castilla, Sheila M. ... San Ramon, CA
Castille, Ellen M. Cain ... Los Alamos, NM
Castille, Ervin J. ... Austin, TX
Castille, John Murphy, II ... Baton Rouge, LA
Castille, Lenelle C. ... Los Angeles, CA
Castille, M. Angella ... Elkhart, IN
Castille, Preston J., Jr. ... Baton Rouge, LA
Castille, Ronald D. ... Philadelphia, PA
Castille, Traci M. ... Gulfport, MS
Castillo, A. Paul ... Irvine, CA
Castillo, Alan ... Santa Ana, CA
Castillo, Alfred B., Jr. ... Lihue, HI
Castillo, Ana ... Los Angeles, CA
Castillo, Angel F. ... Los Angeles, CA
Castillo, Angel, Jr. ... Miami, FL
Castillo, Avalyn Y. ... Oakland, CA
Castillo, Carlos B. ... Miami, FL
Castillo, Cass M. ... Bartow, FL
Castillo, Celia Foy ... Silver City, NM
Castillo, Christopher J. ... El Paso, TX
Castillo, Daniel L. ... Tampa, FL
Castillo, Daniel T. ... Sugar Land, TX
Castillo, David ... San Francisco, CA
Castillo, Eduardo R. ... San Antonio, TX
Castillo, Eloisa V. ... Union City, NJ
Castillo, Emilia ... Fairfax, VA
Castillo, Emilia, P.C., The Law Office of
Fairfax, VA
Castillo, Emilia R. ... Seattle, WA
Castillo, Emma A. ... Sacramento, CA
Castillo, Epifanio, Jr. ... New York, NY
Castillo, Felipe C. ... Oakland, CA
Castillo, Gale O., (Mr.) ... San Antonio, TX
Castillo, Gaspar M., Jr. ... Albany, NY
Castillo, Gerald E. ... McAllen, TX
Castillo, Guadalupe ... Laredo, TX
Castillo, Hal ... Jacksonville, FL
Castillo, Irene Maree ... Stockton, CA
Castillo, J. C. ... Houston, TX
Castillo, Jesse R. ... San Antonio, TX
Castillo, John M. ... San Antonio, TX
Castillo, Jorge E. ... Denver, CO
Castillo, Jorge E., P.C. ... Denver, CO
Castillo, Jose Mariano ... Los Angeles, CA
Castillo, Justin G. ... Washington, DC
Castillo, Leonard
Research Triangle Park, NC
Castillo, Luis M., Jr. ... Tucson, AZ
Castillo, Lynn M. ... Haddon Heights, NJ
Castillo, Mai-Ling E. ... Miami, FL
Castillo, Marcus A. ... Clearwater, FL
Castillo, Margie ... Los Angeles, CA
Castillo, Mario A., Jr. ... Laredo, TX
Castillo, Marlu S. ... San Jose, CA
Castillo, Martha ... Danbury, CT
Castillo, Martin G. ... Los Angeles, CA
Castillo, Mary Lou ... San Antonio, TX
Castillo, Michelle G. ... Tampa, FL
Castillo, N. Scott ... Sacramento, CA
Castillo, Nestor, Jr., (P.A.) ... Tampa, FL
Castillo, Pedro V. ... Los Angeles, CA
Castillo, Peter P. ... Sacramento, CA
Castillo, Priscila E. ... Los Angeles, CA
Castillo, Priscilla D. ... San Diego, CA
Castillo, Richard R. ... San Diego, CA
Castillo, Robert L. ... Tucson, AZ
Castillo, Ruben ... Chicago, IL
Castillo, Ruth Furman ... Norman, OK
Castillo, Sandra Ann ... Berwyn, IL
Castillo & Siegel ... Albany, NY
Castillo, Sophie A. ... Santa Monica, CA
Castillo, Stacy Tuer ... San Antonio, TX
Castillo, Stafford & Wald ... Miami, FL
Castillo, Victor L. ... San Rafael, CA
Castillo, Walfredo P. ... New York, NY
Castillo, William J. ... Philadelphia, PA
Castillo, Yolanda ... Fall River, MA
Castillo, Yvonne Roselyn ... Denver, CO
Castillón, Alfonso Nevárez
San Antonio, TX
Castillon, Carlos ... Laredo, TX
Castillon, Carlos D. ... Laredo, TX
Castine, Cheney M. ... Athol, MA
Castineyra, Marie T. ... Key West, FL
Castino, Raymond B., Jr. ... New Bedford, MA
Castle, Amii Noelle ... Overland Park, KS
Castle, Amy E. ... Dallas, TX
Castle, Anne Elizabeth ... San Francisco, CA
Castle, Anne J. ... Denver, CO
Castle & Associates, PLC ... Memphis, TN
Castle, Barrett, Daffin & Frappier, LLC
Denver, CO
Castle, Ben T. ... Wilmington, DE
Castle, Billie M. ... Grand Junction, CO
Castle, Bruce E. ... Albuquerque, NM
Castle, Caren Jacobs, (P.C.) ... Denver, CO
Addison, TX
Castle, Charles A. ... Frederick, MD
Castle, Christian L. ... Palo Alto, CA
Castle, Craig F. ... Costa Mesa, CA
Castle, Dale A. ... Santa Ana, CA
Castle, Dana F. ... Akron, OH
Castle, Edwin S. ... Department of the Army, Office of the General Counsel, GV
Castle, F. Guthrie, Jr. ... Memphis, TN
Castle, Gray C. ... Washington, DC
Castle, Gregory F. ... Los Angeles, CA
Castle, Gregory L. ... San Francisco, CA
Castle, James A. ... Denver, CO
Castle, James A., P.C. ... Denver, CO
Castle, Jay Frank ... Atlanta, GA
Castle, John E., Jr. ... Lafayette, LA
Castle, John R., Jr. ... Plano, TX
Castle, John W. ... De Kalb, IL
Castle, Lawrence E. ... Denver, CO
Castle, Leroy R. ... Durham, NC
Castle, Linval B. ... Hayward, CA
Castle, Marilyn C. ... Lafayette, LA
Castle, Mary C. ... Los Angeles, CA
San Francisco, CA
Castle, Mary Keleher ... Albuquerque, NM
Castle, Michael A. ... Herkimer, NY
Castle, Michael M. ... Albany, NY
Castle, Pamela Luckie ... Hattiesburg, MS
Castle, Renée E. ... Memphis, TN
Castle, Richard B. ... Pasadena, CA
Castle, Robert C. ... Minneapolis, MN
Castle, Robert M. ... Redlands, CA
Castle, Roger T. ... Denver, CO
Castle, Roger T., P.C. ... Denver, CO
Castle, Ronald L. ... Washington, DC
Castle, Selena R. ... Rock Island, IL
Castle, Stephen M. ... Atlanta, GA
Castle, Thomas F. ... Palo Alto, CA
Pleasant Hill, CA
Castle, Thomas R. ... Norwich, CT
Castleberry, Arthur D. ... Atlanta, GA
Castleberry, Crystal H. ... Morgantown, WV
Castleberry, D. Leland ... San Francisco, CA
Castleberry, Elizabeth Riley
Oklahoma City, OK
Castleberry, Gene A. ... Oklahoma City, OK
Castleberry, James N., Jr. ... San Antonio, TX
Castleberry, Kenneth H. ... Eureka Springs, AR
Castleberry, Kenneth H., P.A.
Eureka Springs, AR
Castleberry, Patrick M.
Oklahoma City, OK
Castleberry, Robert H. ... Brownsville, TX
Castleberry, Robert W. ... Tustin, CA
Castleberry, Ronald L. ... Everett, WA
Castleberry, Russell D. ... Jacksonville, FL
Castleberry, Virginia H. ... Eureka Springs, AR
Castleberry, W. Lesse ... New York, NY
Castleman, Catherine B. ... Nashville, TN
Castleman, Curtis H., Jr. ... Denver, CO
Castleman, Daniel J. ... New York, NY
Castleman, David A. ... St. Louis, MO
Castleman, Don R. ... Winston-Salem, NC
Castleman & Greene ... Goodlettsville, TN
Castleman, Harry ... Boston, MA
Castleman, Howard J. ... Boston, MA
Castleman, James A. ... Quincy, MA
Castleman, Joseph B. ... Williston Park, NY
Castleman, Lauriston, Jr. ... New York, NY
Castleman Law Firm, The, A Professional Corporation ... Pleasanton, CA
Castleman, Linda M. ... Decatur, IL
Castleman, Lorin ... Pleasanton, CA
Castleman, Penny L. ... San Diego, CA
Castleman, Philip ... Springfield, MA
Castleman, Richard L. ... Pocahontas, AR
Castleman, Toiya D. ... Richmond, VA
Castleman, William D. ... Goodlettsville, TN
Castlen, Joseph W., III ... Owensboro, KY
Castlen, Julie E. ... Los Angeles, CA
Castlen, Thomas O. ... Owensboro, KY
Castlen & Wilkey, P.S.C. ... Owensboro, KY
Castles, Charles C. ... Houston, TX
Castles, Deborah M. ... San Francisco, CA
Castles, Donald E. ... Dania, FL
Castles, James P. ... San Francisco, CA
Castles, Kimberly A. ... Dallas, TX
Castleton, David J. ... Salt Lake City, UT
Castleton, Lowell D. ... Preston, ID
Castleton, Trevor L. ... Pocatello, ID
Castner, Charles F. ... Raleigh, NC
Castner, Daniel E. ... Detroit, MI
Castner, Jane D. ... Bound Brook, NJ
Castner, Jane F. ... Trenton, NJ
Castner, Jeffery P. ... Long Beach, CA
Castner, Karen B. ... Rochester, NY
Castner, Karen R. ... Rochester, NY
Castner, L. John ... South Berwick, ME
Castner, Laura D. ... Los Angeles, CA
Castner, Lawrence V. ... Pittsburgh, PA
Castner, Lynn S., (Mr.) ... Minneapolis, MN
Castner, Michael A. ... Portsmouth, RI
Castner, Milda A. ... Kennebunk, ME
Castner, Sarah L. ... Salem, OR
Castner, Stephen L. ... Grafton, WI
Castner, Susan F. ... Michigan City, IN
Casto, Ann H. ... Columbus, OH
Casto, Brian O. ... Charleston, WV
Casto, Donna L. ... Charlotte, NC
Casto, Edward E., Jr. ... Charleston, WV
Casto, Jamie Ruff ... Columbus, OH
Casto, Jeffrey J. ... Akron, OH
Casto, Keith M. ... San Francisco, CA
San Jose, CA
Casto, Philip M. ... Decatur, GA
Casto, Thomas G. ... Charleston, WV
Casto, William R. ... Oak Ridge, TN
Caston, Harry ... Salt Lake City, UT
Caston, Homer R., Jr. ... Sherman, TX
Whitesboro, TX
Caston, Michael E. ... Irvine, CA
Castonguay, Thomas J. ... El Cajon, CA
Castor, Anthony J. ... Madison, IN
Castor, Bruce L. ... Philadelphia, PA
Castor, Bruce L., Jr. ... Norristown, PA
Castor, Colleen F. ... Atlanta, GA
Castor, Donald F. ... Tampa, FL
Castor, John E. ... Minneapolis, MN
Castor, Katherine ... Tampa, FL
Castor, Klukas, Logren & Padgett, Chartered ... Minneapolis, MN
Castor, Paul G. ... Sunnyvale, CA
Castor, Robert A. ... Laramie, WY
Castor, Robert D. ... West Union, OH
Castor, Stephen E. ... Grand Junction, CO
Castor, Stephen E., PC ... Grand Junction, CO
Castor, William H. ... Tulsa, OK
Castora, Keith A. ... Bloomfield Hills, MI
Castoria, Daniel ... Brooklyn, NY
Castoria, Louis H. ... San Francisco, CA
Castorina, Anthony J. ... Arlington, VA
Castorina, Bryan T. ... Los Angeles, CA
Castoro, Michael W. ... Hollywood, FL
Castoro, Nicholas S. ... Hopewell, NJ
Castranova, James J. ... Santa Monica, CA
Castrataro, Barbara A. ... White Plains, NY
Castree, Samuel J., Jr. ... Rockford, IL
Castrejana, Martha A. ... San Antonio, TX
Castrejon, Rachel ... Novato, CA
Castricone, Andrew D. ... Los Angeles, CA
Castrigano, Charles D. ... Cleveland, OH
Castrillo, Dale Robert ... Idaho Falls, ID
Castro, Ana M. ... Miami, FL
Castro, Anderson ... Miami, FL
Castro, Andréa I. ... Ossining, NY
Castro, Angel ... Brownsville, TX
Castro, Antonio C. ... Miami, FL
Castro, Antonio D. ... Bronx, NY
Castro, Armando ... Palo Alto, CA
Castro, Brian M. ... Harrisburg, PA
Castro, Carlos Alberto ... Miami, FL
Castro, Carmen Iris ... Bridgeport, CT
Castro, Carmine ... San Juan, PR
Castro & Castro ... San Juan, PR
Castro, Chad M. ... Chicago, IL
Castro, Claude ... New York, NY
Castro, Constance M. ... Boston, MA
Castro, Daniel R. ... Austin, TX
Castro, David A. ... Baltimore, MD
Castro, David M. ... Houston, TX
Castro, Deron Robert ... Kew Gardens, NY
Castro, Eduardo M. ... Lemon Grove, CA
Castro, Edward D. ... Los Angeles, CA
Castro, Emma ... Los Angeles, CA
Castro, Eric C. ... Los Angeles, CA
Castro, Erlinda G. ... Berkeley, CA
Castro, Federico ... San Diego, CA
Castro, Fernando ... San Juan, PR
Castro, Gregory A. ... Oklahoma City, OK
Castro, Herminio M. ... Treasury Department, Office of Regulations and Rulings, GV
Castro, Hernan ... Orlando, FL
Castro, Joel B. ... Los Angeles, CA
Castro, John P. ... Mountain View, CA
Castro, Jose E., (P.A.) ... Coral Gables, FL
Castro, Julio Enrique, III ... Tampa, FL
Castro, Kevin D. ... Berlin, NJ
Castro, Leonard E. ... Los Angeles, CA
Castro, Lionel J. ... Houston, TX
Castro, Louis C. ... San Jose, CA
Castro, Luis V. ... Bayamon, PR
Castro, Martin R. ... Chicago, IL
Castro, Melchor E. ... Rochester, NY
Castro, Melissa R. ... Washington, DC
Castro, Michael M. ... Cleveland, OH
Castro, Michelle M. ... San Francisco, CA
Castro, Patricia ... Rock Island, IL
Castro, Rafael A., III ... Miami, FL
Castro, Ramiro R. ... San Francisco, CA
Castro, Ramon ... San Diego, CA
Castro, Raul ... Buena Park, CA
Castro, Raúl H. ... Nogales, AZ
Castro, Raymond S. ... Tampa, FL
Castro, Raymond S., P.A. ... Tampa, FL
Castro, Richard A. ... San Francisco, CA
Castro, Rita Maria ... Walnut Creek, CA
Castro, Robert C. ... Hartland, WI
Castro, Rosalio ... San Bernardino, CA
Castro, Sonia ... Brooklyn, NY
Castro, Stacie M. ... San Francisco, CA
Castro, Stephanie M. ... Salt Lake City, UT
Castro, Tanja H. ... Washington, DC
Castro, Wilton ... San Jose, CA
Castro & Zipf ... Nogales, AZ
Tucson, AZ
Castro-Amy, Francisco ... San Juan, PR
Castro-Blanco, James F. ... Brooklyn, NY
Castro-Colón, María Eugenia
San Juan, PR
Castrodale, Joseph A. ... Cleveland, OH
Castrodale, Robert A. ... Grand Coulee, WA
Castro-Fernandez, Antonio ... San Juan, PR
Castrogiovanni, Cheryl
San Francisco, CA
Castrogiovanni, Jack C. ... New Orleans, LA
Castro-Lang, Rafael F. ... San Juan, PR
Castro-Muriel, Diana Lizzette
San Juan, PR
Castronova, Stephen G. ... Pleasanton, CA
Castronovo, Donna M. ... Riverside, CT
Castronovo, Donna M., P.C. ... Riverside, CT
Castronovo, Tod M. ... Woodland Hills, CA
Castro-Silva, Rodrigo A. ... Los Angeles, CA
Castroverde, Lance ... Honolulu, HI
Castrovinci, Philip John ... Commack, NY
Castro-Woolery, Clemencia ... Tacoma, WA
Castruccio, Constance M.
Santa Barbara, CA
Castruccio, Eugenia L. ... Los Angeles, CA
Castruccio, Louis M., (P.C.)
Los Angeles, CA
Casucci, Michael J. ... Roseland, NJ
Casula, Denise M. ... Washington, DC
Casula, Joseph S. ... Upper Marlboro, MD
Casulli, Robert J. ... New Providence, NJ
Casullo, Francis J. ... Cortland, NY
Casurella, Jeffrey G. ... Marietta, GA
Casuso, Carlos E. ... Miami, FL
Caswall, Edward M. ... Denver, CO
Caswell, A. Gerard ... Eunice, LA
Caswell, A Gerard, A Professional Law Corporation ... Eunice, LA
Caswell & Associates, Ltd. ... St. Paul, MN
Caswell, Bell & Hillison LLP ... Fresno, CA
Caswell, Benson T. ... Chicago, IL
Caswell, Bradford L. ... New York, NY
Caswell, Brandee Lee ... Topeka, KS
Caswell, Christopher K. ... Sarasota, FL
Caswell, Christopher K., P.A. ... Sarasota, FL
Caswell, Dacia E. ... Pasadena, CA
Caswell, Daniel P. ... Chicago, IL
Caswell, Erwin A., Jr. ... New Orleans, LA
Caswell, G. Thomas, Jr. ... Fresno, CA
Caswell, Gary ... San Antonio, TX
Caswell, Gordon G. ... Flint, MI
Caswell, John J. ... Syracuse, NY
Caswell, Kathleen S. ... Glendale, CA
Caswell, Kimberly ... Tampa, FL
Caswell, Mary Elizabeth ... Waldorf, MD
Caswell, Paul P. ... Escanaba, MI
Caswell, Robert M. ... Lakehills, TX
Caswell, Roger L. ... Battle Creek, MI
Caswell, Ronald S. ... Beverly Hills, CA
Caswell, Royal ... Odessa, TX
Caswell, Seldon H. ... St. Paul, MN
Caswell, Stephen J. ... Atlanta, GA
Caswell, Susan P. ... Oklahoma City, OK
Caswell, Thomas A. ... Dallas, TX
Caswell, Thomas B., III ... Minneapolis, MN
Caswell, Viel P., Jr ... Eunice, LA
Caswell Scott, Mary ... Oklahoma City, OK
Cata, Ricardo J. ... Miami, FL
Catafago, Jacques ... New York, NY
Catafago & Lonergan ... New York, NY
Catafago, Nadienne Vincent ... New York, NY
Cátala, Apolo ... Boston, MA
Cátala & Mervis, P.C. ... Boston, MA
Catalan, Cynthia L. ... Atlantic Beach, FL
Catalan, Cynthia L. ... Jacksonville, FL
Cataland, Louis S. ... Atlanta, GA
Catalanello, Gerard S. ... New York, NY
Catalani, Carrie K. ... San Antonio, TX
Catalani, P. Roy ... Honolulu, HI
Catalano, Albert J. ... Washington, DC
Catalano, Anthony ... Brooklyn, NY
Catalano, Anthony A. ... Paterson, NJ
Catalano, Anthony J. ... Naples, FL
Catalano, Benjamin J. ... New York, NY
Catalano, Brian Matthew ... Midland, TX
Catalano, Carol A. ... Clarksville, TN
Catalano, Catherine C. ... Manchester, NH
Catalano, Christopher D. ... New York, NY
Catalano, Cynthia A. ... Highland Heights, OH
Catalano, Douglas P. ... New York, NY
Catalano, Frank A. ... Albany, NY
Catalano, Frank A. ... Albany, NY
Catalano, Frank J. ... Tulsa, OK
Catalano, Frederick J. ... Eustis, FL
Catalano, James Patrick ... Knoxville, TN
Catalano, Jane D. ... Albany, NY
Catalano, Jeffrey N. ... Boston, MA
Catalano, John M. ... Washington, DC
Atlanta, GA
Catalano, Jos. C. ... Westbury, NY
Catalano, Joseph J. ... San Mateo, CA
Catalano, Kim Marie ... Fort Worth, TX
Catalano, Linda A. ... Bismarck, ND
Catalano, Lisa A. ... Weehawken, NJ
Catalano, Louis W. ... North Versailles, PA
Pittsburgh, PA
Catalano, Michael ... Peoria, AZ
Catalano, Michael ... Nashville, TN

Catalano, Michael A. ....Stamford, CT
Catalano, Michael A., (P.A.) ....Miami, FL
Catalano, Michael W. ....Nashville, TN
Catalano, Patrick E. ....San Diego, CA
San Francisco, CA
Catalano, Patrick E., A Prof. Corp., Law Offices of ....San Diego, CA
San Francisco, CA
Catalano, Paul A. ....Pasadena, CA
Catalano, Peter ....Syracuse, NY
Catalano, Ralph A. ....Garden City, NY
Catalano, Ralph (Randy) P. ....Westmont, NJ
Catalano, Randy P. ....Westmont, NJ
Catalano, Richard J. ....North Versailles, PA
Pittsburgh, PA
Catalano, Richard J., P.C.
North Versailles, PA
Pittsburgh, PA
Catalano, Richard S. ....New York, NY
Catalano, Richard T. ....St. Petersburg, FL
Catalano, Robert R. ....Bakersfield, CA
Catalano, Rosanna M. ....Fort Lauderdale, FL
Catalano, Steven L. ....Providence, RI
Catalano, Susan Wondries ....Los Angeles, CA
Catalano, Thomas A. ....New York, NY
Catalano, Thomas C., Jr. ....Jericho, NY
Catalano, Thomas H. ....Fort Worth, TX
Catalano, Victor ....Monroe, CT
Catalano, Vincent J., Jr. ....Poughkeepsie, NY
Catalano, William A. ....Columbus, OH
Catalano, Zingerman & Associates, P.C.
Tulsa, OK
Catalde, Robert J. ....Buffalo, NY
Erie, PA
Cataldi, Donald A. ....Columbus, OH
Cataldi, Lawrence F. ....Buffalo, NY
Cataldi, Richard A. ....Philadelphia, PA
Cataldo, Alexander L. ....Boston, MA
Cataldo, Alexander L., P.C. ....Boston, MA
Cataldo, Carlo J. ....Milwaukee, WI
Cataldo, Ennio ....Medford, MA
Cataldo, Henry J. ....Marshfield, MA
Cataldo, Joseph D. ....Everett, MA
Cataldo, Joseph P. ....Franklin, MA
Cataldo Law Offices, LLP ....Franklin, MA
Wrentham, MA
Cataldo, Mary V.J. ....Carlsbad, CA
Cataldo, Michael A. ....Philadelphia, PA
Cataldo, Paul A. ....Franklin, MA
Cataldo, Paul D. ....Philadelphia, PA
Cataldo, Peter ....Department of Commerce, Patent and Trademark Office, GV
Cataldo, R. Christopher ....Detroit, MI
Cataldo, Sheri B. ....Southfield, MI
Cataldo, Vincent C ....Marlton, NJ
Cataldo, William L. ....Southfield, MI
Cataldo, William L., P.C. ....Southfield, MI
Cataldo-Barile, Annalee J.
Garden City, NY
Cataldo-Cappelletti, Teresa L.
Middlebury, IN
Catalfimo & Catalfimo ....Greenwich, NY
Catalfimo, James A. ....Greenwich, NY
Catalfimo, Michael J. ....Greenwich, NY
Catalfo, Alfred, Jr. ....Dover, NH
Catalfo, Alfred T., III ....Dover, NH
Catalfo, Gail Varney ....Dover, NH
Catalfo Law Firm ....Dover, NH
Catalina, Francesco A. ....Peekskill, NY
Catalina, Frank E. ....Jersey City, NJ
Catalina, Richard A., Jr. ....Woodbridge, NJ
Catalini-Chew, Nancy Ellen ....Groton, MA
Catalino, Cynthia F. ....Long Beach, CA
Catalino, David R. ....San Diego, CA
Catalino, Richard ....Muskegon, MI
Catalinotto, Michael E. ....Albany, NY
Saugerties, NY
Catalinotto, Michael E., Jr. ....Albany, NY
Saugerties, NY
Catallo, George C., Jr. ....Hicksville, NY
Catalona, Alexander P.
San Francisco, CA
Catalona, Janet F. ....Clayton, MO
Catan, Mark A. ....White Plains, NY
Catana, Mark C. ....New York, NY
Catanese, Andrew D. ....Atlantic City, NJ
Catanese, Catherine ....Jamaica, NY
Catanese, David J. ....Phoenix, AZ
Catanese, Joanne F. ....Baltimore, MD
Catanese, John N. ....Lombard, IL
Catanese, Michael J. ....Wildwood Crest, NJ
Catanese, Paul ....Trenton, NJ
Catanese, Santo M. ....Wichita, KS
Catanese, T. Randolph ....Westlake Village, CA
Catangui, Rufino S., Jr. ....Honolulu, HI
Catania, Andrea ....Newark, NJ
Catania, Bruce C. ....Hastings-On-Hudson, NY
Catania, Cally E., P.A. ....Tampa, FL
Catania & Catania, P.A. ....Tampa, FL
Catania, Christina Lee
San Francisco, CA
Catania, David A. ....Washington, DC
Catania, Eugene ....Ellicott City, MD
Catania, Francis J. ....Media, PA
Catania, Francis J. ....Media, PA
Catania, Frank ....North Haledon, NJ
Catania and Harrington ....North Haledon, NJ
Catania, John A. ....New York, NY
Catania, Joseph A., Jr. ....Newburgh, NY
Catania, Joseph V. ....Media, PA
Catania, Matthew J. ....Hackensack, NJ
Catania, Michael A. ....Carlsbad, CA
Buffalo Grove, IL
Catania, Michael J. ....Fort Worth, TX
Catania, Pamela ....Richmond, VA
Catania & Parker ....Media, PA
Catania, Paul B. ....Tampa, FL
Catania, Peter F. ....Tampa, FL
Catania, Richard L. ....Garden City, NY
Catania, Robert F. ....Seal Beach, CA
Catania, Thomas F, Jr.
Benton Harbor, MI
Catania, Vito ....Brooklyn, NY
Catanzano, Raymond A. ....Elmont, NY
Catanzarite, Jeffrey C. ....Pittsburgh, PA
Catanzarite, Kenneth J. ....Anaheim, CA
Catanzarite Law Corporation
Anaheim, CA
Catanzariti, Frank Paul ....Springfield, OH
Catanzaro & Allen ....Ashland, MA
Catanzaro, Angelo P. ....Ashland, MA
Catanzaro, James L., Jr.
Chattanooga, TN
Catanzaro, Jerome D. ....Waverly, OH
Catanzaro, Joseph J. ....New York, NY
Syosset, NY
Catanzaro, Mark W. ....Moorestown, NJ
Philadelphia, PA
Catanzaro, Michael A. ....Springfield, OH
Catanzaro, Michael E., Jr. ....White Plains, NY
Catanzaro & Rosenberger ....Waverly, OH
Catapano, Patricia Sachs ....New York, NY
Catapano, Philip J. ....Garden City, NY
Catapano, Tracy A. ....Kew Gardens, NY
Catapano-Friedman, Robert S.
Newark, NJ
Albany, NY
Catapano-Friedman, Robert S., P.C.
Albany, NY
Cataudella, Mary L. ....Boston, MA
Cataxinos, Edgar R. ....Salt Lake City, UT
Catbagan, Margaret R. ....Marina Del Rey, CA
Catchick, J. Matthew, Jr. ....Torrance, CA
Westland, MI
Catchick, James M. ....Grand Rapids, MI
Catchings, Patricia A. ....Jackson, MS
Catchpole, W. Park ....Jamestown, NY
Catchur, Mark A. ....Tampa, FL
Cate, Alice L. ....San Diego, CA
Cate, Andrew M. ....Nashville, TN
Cate, Beth E. ....Indianapolis, IN
Cate, Charles C. ....Katy, TX
Cate, Clifford C. ....Glendale, CA
Cate, Clifford K., Jr. ....Muskogee, OK
Cate, Dennis M. ....Woodbridge, VA
Cate, Ernest B. ....Springdale, AR
Cate, Fred H. ....Indianapolis, IN
Cate, George H., III ....Nashville, TN
Cate, George H., Jr., Law Office of
Nashville, TN
Cate, James G., Jr. ....Chattanooga, TN
Cate, Jan H. ....Los Angeles, CA
Cate, Jocelyn B. ....Charleston, SC
Cate, John S., Jr. ....Santa Ana, CA
Cate, Kenneth R. ....Sarasota, FL
Cate, Matthew L. ....Sacramento, CA
Cate, Reynolds N. ....San Antonio, TX
Cate, Rodney R. ....Mobile, AL
Cate, Ruth L. ....Spartanburg, SC
Cate, Thomas P. ....Lytle, TX
Cate, William G. ....Salem, OR
Cate, William H. ....Kingsport, TN
Catel, Stephen J. ....Negaunee, MI
Catella, Alvin L. ....St. Charles, IL
Catelli, Frank ....East Meadow, NY
Catelli, Ronald T., Jr. ....Freehold, NJ
Catena, Felix J. ....Amsterdam, NY
Catena, Gene L. ....Fonda, NY
Catena, Gino ....Houston, TX
Catenacci, Henry J. ....Newark, NJ
Catenacci, Richard D. ....Roseland, NJ
Catenaccio, Jos. ....New York, NY
Catenazzo, Suzy B. ....Charlotte, NC
Cater, Charles R. ....La Grande, OR
Cater, Constancio B. ....Tampa, FL
Cater, Gregorio B. ....Washington, DC
Baltimore, MD
Cater, John W. ....Honolulu, HI
Cater, Kathryn A. ....Atlanta, GA
Cater, R. Emmett ....San Antonio, TX
Cater, R. Glenn ....New Orleans, LA
Cater, R. Paul ....Foley, AL
Cater, Richard H. ....Anniston, AL
Cater, Richard H., P.C. ....Anniston, AL
Cater, Rozan E. ....Washington, DC
Cater, Russell E. ....Helena, MT
Cater and Willis, A Professional Law Corporation ....New Orleans, LA
Catera, Joseph P. ....Larchmont, NY
Caterine, Lisa K. Pitner ....Indianapolis, IN
Caterine, Melinda J. ....Portland, ME
Caterini, John R. ....Department of Justice, Justice Management Division, GV
Caterini, Mark ....New York, NY
Caterino, Bartholomew M.
Shaker Heights, OH
Cates, Alan L. ....Chattanooga, TN
Cates, Buford A., Jr. ....Dallas, TX
Cates, C. Thomas ....Memphis, TN
Cates, Charles E. ....Scottsdale, AZ
Cates, Clifton B., III ....Washington, DC
Cates, David G. ....Louisville, KY
Cates, Don T. ....Forney, TX
Cates, Dwane M ....Scottsdale, AZ
Cates & Han ....Irvine, CA
Newport Beach, CA
Cates & Holloway ....Phoenix, AZ
Scottsdale, AZ
Cates, James P. ....Oklahoma City, OK
Cates, Jeffrey ....Phoenix, AZ
Cates, John D., Jr. ....Montgomery, AL
Cates, John L. ....Madison, WI
Cates, John O. ....Huntsville, AL
Cates, Judy L. ....East St. Louis, IL
Cates, Linda B. ....Waco, TX
Cates, Mary Claire Cauley ....Huntsville, AL
Cates, Melissa B. ....New York, NY
Cates, Michelle I. ....Key West, FL
Cates, Michelle I., P.A. ....Key West, FL
Cates, Peter R. ....Macon, GA
Cates, Richard B. ....Los Angeles, CA
Cates, Richard E. ....Los Angeles, CA
Cates, Richard L. ....Madison, WI
Cates, Robert ....Los Lunas, NM
Cates, Robert P. ....Gainesville, FL
Cates, Ronald D. ....Tulsa, OK
Cates, Sidney H., IV (A Professional Law Corporation) ....New Orleans, LA
Cates, T. Bradley ....Waco, TX
Cates, Van A. ....Houston, TX
Cates, Walter Bradsher ....Roxboro, NC
Cates, William L. ....Irvine, CA
Cates, William N. ....Atlanta, GA
Cathcart, Ann N. ....Minneapolis, MN
Cathcart, Camilla R. ....Columbia, SC
Cathcart, Charlene ....Somerdale, NJ
Cathcart, Christopher C. ....Winter Park, FL
Cathcart, Daniel C., (Professional Corporation) ....Los Angeles, CA
Cathcart, David A. ....Los Angeles, CA
Cathcart, David B. ....Cleveland, OH
Cathcart, Frank H. ....Hartford, CT
Cathcart, Gofton & Dooley, A Professional Corporation ....Oklahoma City, OK
Cathcart, James A. ....Tacoma, WA
Cathcart, Patrick A. ....Los Angeles, CA
Cathcart, Peter T., (Professional Corporation) ....Los Angeles, CA
Cathcart, R. Calvin ....Spokane, WA
Cathcart, Ralph H. ....New York, NY
Cathcart, Robert J. ....Los Angeles, CA
Cathcart, Robert J. ....Hartford, CT
Cathcart, Robert S. ....San Francisco, CA
Cathcart, Rodney P. ....Lincoln, NE
Cathcart, Terry L. ....Bountiful, UT
Cathcart, William R. ....Oklahoma City, OK
Cathell, James David, Sr. ....Baltimore, MD
Cather, Carl H., III ....Morgantown, WV
Cather, John S. ....Parkersburg, WV
Cather, Tyler A. ....Morgantown, WV
Cather, William ....Wichita, KS
Cathers, Kimberly F. ....Fort Myers, FL
Cathers, Michael D. ....Albany, NY
Catherwood, Kathryn M. S.
San Diego, CA
Catherwood, Robert K. ....Oxford, NC
Cathey, Dennis T. ....Cornelia, GA
Cathey, G. Wendell ....Durant, OK
Cathey, Imogene L. ....Tampa, FL
Cathey, J. Lee ....Carlsbad, NM
Cathey, John Raymond ....Oklahoma City, OK
Cathey, Karen C. ....McKinney, TX
Cathey, Karen C., P.C. ....McKinney, TX
Cathey, Mark K. ....Roanoke, VA
Cathey, Richard A. ....Toledo, OH
Cathey, Samuel A. ....Statesville, NC
Cathey & Strain ....Cornelia, GA
Cathey, Theodore F.M. ....Staunton, VA
Cathey, William J., III
Hendersonville, NC
Cathlina, Francis W. ....South Milwaukee, WI
Caticchio, Michael J. ....Lyndhurst, OH
Caticchio, Pat ....Cleveland, OH
Catillaz, Margaret Artale ....Rochester, NY
Catina, Janet K. ....Stroudsburg, PA
Catinella, Andrew J. ....Jamaica, NY
Catinello, Don ....Trenton, NJ
Catino, Ann M. ....Hartford, CT
Catino, Theresa M.
Department Of Veterans Affairs, Board of Veterans Appeals, GV
Catino-Nason, Kerri L. ....Providence, RI
Catizone, John ....Baltimore, MD
Catler, Susan L. ....Washington, DC
Catlett, Amy ....Houston, TX
Catlett, Bill ....Dallas, TX
Catlett, Charlotte Wereb ....Dallas, TX
Catlett, George ....Millburn, NJ
White Plains, NY
Catlett, John B., Jr. ....Richmond, VA
Catlett, Larry D. ....Harrodsburg, KY
Catlett, Matthew M. ....Washington, DC
Catlett, Meredith P., (P.A.) ....Little Rock, AR
Catlett, Richard H., Jr. ....Richmond, VA
Catlett, Robert L., Jr. ....Louisville, KY
Catlett, S. Graham ....Little Rock, AR
Catlett, Stanley B., Jr. ....Oklahoma City, OK
Catlett, Steven T. ....Chicago, IL
Catlett, Yancey & Stodola, PLC
Little Rock, AR
Catlin, Ann Blakefield ....El Cajon, CA
Catlin, Catherine M. ....Tampa, FL
Catlin, Edgar S., III ....Brunswick, ME
Catlin, Elizabeth J. ....Washington, DC
Catlin, George B. ....Grosse Pointe Woods, MI
Catlin, George B., P.C.
Grosse Pointe Woods, MI
Catlin, H. James, Jr. ....Miami, FL
Catlin, Hamilton R. ....Tucson, AZ
Catlin, Harold H. ....Jacksonville, FL
Catlin, Harold H., P.A. ....Jacksonville, FL
Catlin, J. Randolph ....Jacksonville, FL
Catlin, Larry A. ....Bryan, TX
Catlin, R. Peter, III ....Atlanta, GA
Catlin, Saxon, Tuttle and Evans, P.A.
Miami, FL
Catliota, Thomas J. ....Washington, DC
Catlos, Katherine S. ....San Francisco, CA
Catlow, James T. ....Los Angeles, CA
Catmull, Janet M. ....Los Angeles, CA
Catmull, K. W. ....Houston, TX
Cato, A. Wallace ....Bainbridge, GA
Cato, Allison D. ....San Diego, CA
Cato, Ann Curry ....Bentonville, AR
Cato, Christopher B. ....San Diego, CA
Cato, Finn R. ....Louisville, KY
Cato, Jima ....Orange, CA
Cato, Lauren J. ....Bingham Farms, MI
Cato, Richard Baylor ....Ocoee, FL
Cato, Robert E. ....London, KY
Cato & Van Arsdale ....Louisville, KY
Cato, Walter L., Jr. ....Louisville, KY
Catoe, Coleman L., Jr. ....Columbia, SC
Catoe, Dennis W. ....Irmo, SC
Catoe, Michael K. ....Washington, DC
Catoe, William M., Jr. ....Greenville, SC
Cato-Miller, Annette ....Mesquite, TX
Cato-Miller, Darensburg & Associates, P.C.
Kaufman, TX
Mesquite, TX
Caton, Betty Ann ....McKinney, TX
Caton, Byron ....Aztec, NM
Caton, Curtis M. ....San Francisco, CA
Caton, Don J. ....Pensacola, FL
Caton, Douglas E. ....Charlottesville, VA
Caton, Edward T. ....Virginia Beach, VA
Caton, Edward T., P.C. ....Virginia Beach, VA
Caton, George W. ....Spokane, WA
Caton, Georgia ....Rochester, NY
Caton, Gilbert C. ....Encino, CA
Caton, James R. ....Seminole, TX
Caton, John E. ....Hutchinson, KS
Caton, Joseph Robert, Jr. ....Milwaukee, WI
Caton, Kevin D. ....Los Angeles, CA
San Francisco, CA
Caton, Matthew R. ....Boston, MA
Caton, Michael R. ....St. Louis, MO
Caton, Ralph W. ....Big Spring, TX
Caton, Richard P. ....St. Petersburg, FL
Caton, Susan Jane ....Cheyenne, WY
Caton, Thomas E. ....Alameda, CA
Catone, Louis J. ....Valley Falls, NY
Catone, Paul J. ....Albany, NY
Catone, Paul J. ....Latham, NY
Catoni-Antonetti, Luis A. ....Miami, FL
Catrambone, Gregory ....Maywood, IL
Catrano, Lauren M. Mikulka ....Charlotte, NC
Catri, Cynthia E. ....Boston, MA
Catri, Holton, Kessler & Kessler, P.A.
Fort Lauderdale, FL
Miami, FL
Catri, Jeffrey Alan ....Dublin, OH
Catri & Kellam Co., L.P.A. ....Sandusky, OH
Catri, Wesley L. ....Fort Lauderdale, FL
Catron, Catron & Sawtell, A Professional Association ....Santa Fe, NM
Catron, Debra A. ....Hazard, KY
Catron, Fletcher R. ....Santa Fe, NM
Catron, Frances E. ....Lexington, KY
Catron, Gary W. ....Oklahoma City, OK
Catron, Gregory W. ....Cincinnati, OH
Catron, J. Gregory ....Louisville, KY
Catron, J. Mark ....St. Paul, MN
Catron, John A. ....Seattle, WA
Catron, John S. ....Santa Fe, NM
Catron, Stephen B. ....Bowling Green, KY
Catron, Thomas B., III ....Santa Fe, NM
Catron, Virginia J. ....Houston, TX
Catsandonis, Paul ....Hackensack, NJ
Catsos, Paul C. ....Portland, ME
Catt, Bradley J. ....Vincennes, IN
Catt, Chas. E. ....Las Vegas, NV
Catt, George L. ....Lawrence, KS
Catt, Lawrence R. ....Springfield, MO
Catt, Malcolm L.
Federal Trade Commission, Bureau of Competition, GV
Cattafesta, Maria L. ....Washington, DC
Cattafesta, Meera Joshi ....New York, NY
Cattalini, Gina ....Washington, DC
Cattalini, Jeff ....Menlo Park, CA
Cattanach, Robert E., Jr.
Minneapolis, MN
Cattanach, Robt. A. ....Houston, TX
Cattaneo, Robert M. ....Baltimore, MD
Easton, MD
Cattani, Kathleen ....Palo Alto, CA
Cattani, Kent E. ....Phoenix, AZ
Cattani, Louis J. ....Wells River, VT
Cattani, Maryellen B. ....Oakland, CA
Cattannach, Sharon ....Houston, TX
Cattano, Janet ....Seattle, WA
Cattano, John P. ....Charlottesville, VA
Cattany, Robert E. ....Tombstone, AZ
Cattarrasa, Frank Josef ....Yonkers, NY
Cattarrasa, Michael L. ....Yonkers, NY
Cattel, Thomas A. ....Bloomfield Hills, MI
Cattel, Tuyn & Rudzewicz, PLLC
Bloomfield Hills, MI
Cattell, Edward V., Jr. ....Philadelphia, PA
Cattell, Joellyn R. ....Cherry Hill, NJ
Cattell, Nancy G. ....Santa Monica, CA
Catterall, Arthur T. ....Vienna, VA
Catterall, Donald P. ....West Des Moines, IA
Catterlin, Charles F. ....Carlsbad, CA
Cattermole, Gregory C. ....Redwood City, CA
Catterson, Cathy A. ....San Francisco, CA
Catterson, James M., Jr. ....Port Jefferson, NY
Catterson, John ....New York, NY
Catterson, John T. ....Hauppauge, NY
Catterton, A. Van, Jr., P.A. ....Melbourne, FL
Catterton, Austin Van, Jr. ....Melbourne, FL
Catterton, Crawford R. ....Fort Worth, TX
Catterton, Judith R. ....Rockville, MD
Catterton, Kemp & Greenberg, P.A.
Rockville, MD
Catterton, William T. ....Fort Worth, TX
Cattie and Fruehauf ....Wilmington, DE
Cattie, Jules R., III ....Baton Rouge, LA
Cattie, William J., III ....Wilmington, DE
Cattier, Jennifer A. ....New York, NY
Cattle, Bradford N. ....Everett, WA

Catto, William H. ... Philadelphia, PA
Catto, William J. ... Inverness, FL
Cattoggio, Joseph V., Jr. ... Revere, MA
Cattran, Christophe Michael ... Visalia, CA
Catts, Austin E. ... Brunswick, GA
Catts, Douglas B. ... Dover, DE
Catts-Tucker, Naomi ... Portland, OR
Catucci, William V. ... Basking Ridge, NJ
Catullo, Anthony G. ... Homewood, IL
Catullo, Kim M. ... Newark, NJ
New York, NY
Catuogno, Karen ... Springfield, MA
Caturia, Charles E. ... Minneapolis, MN
Catuzzi, Jerome P., Jr. ... New York, NY
Catz, Robert S. ... Cleveland, OH
Catz, Sarah L. ... Laguna Beach, CA
Catz, Sheldon P. ... Pittsburgh, PA
Caubarreaux, Brian M. ... Marksville, LA
Cauble, Christopher L. ... Grants Pass, OR
Cauble, Debra L. ... Palo Alto, CA
Cauble, Dianne S. ... Milwaukee, WI
Cauble, John R., Jr. ... Los Angeles, CA
Cauble, Myron L., Jr. ... Milwaukee, WI
Cauble, Richard C. ... Las Cruces, NM
Cauble, Walter L. ... Grants Pass, OR
Cauchon, Robert V. ... Boston, MA
Caucutt, John Allen ... Oconomowoc, WI
Caudal, Andrew H. ... Dallas, TX
Caudell, Alan K. ... Galax, VA
Caudell, B. Chan ... Atlanta, GA
Caudill, April K. ... Cincinnati, OH
Caudill, Burnett ... Indianapolis, IN
Caudill, Carlene A. ... Bloomfield Hills, MI
Caudill, Charles A. ... Louisville, KY
Caudill, D. Michael ... Goochland, VA
Caudill, Dana K ... Ventura, CA
Caudill, Darrell R. ... Marietta, GA
Caudill & Fischer, An Association of Attorneys ... Columbus, IN
Caudill, Franklin T. ... Baltimore, MD
Caudill, J. Gentry ... Charlotte, NC
Caudill, Julia Ann ... Columbus, IN
Caudill, Kathryn Lind ... Northfield, IL
Caudill, Lauren A. ... Richmond, VA
Caudill, L. M. (Mike) ... Whitesburg, KY
Caudill, Loni S. ... Durham, NC
Caudill, Mary Beth ... Dayton, OH
Caudill, Mary Beth ... Xenia, OH
Caudill, Michael E. ... Bowling Green, KY
Caudill, O. Brandt, Jr. ... Tustin, CA
Caudill, Thomas ... San Jose, CA
Caudill, W. Kelly ... Maysville, KY
Caudill, William H. ... Houston, TX
Caudle & Ballato, P.C. ... Richmond, VA
Virginia Beach, VA
Caudle, C. George ... Chattanooga, TN
Caudle, David R. ... Charlotte, NC
Caudle, Dietmar K. H. ... Lawton, OK
Caudle, John P. ... Concord, CA
Caudle, L. Cameron, Jr. ... Charlotte, NC
Caudle, Larry L. ... Anchorage, AK
Caudle, Larry W., Jr. ... Washington, DC
Caudle, Lloyd C. ... Charlotte, NC
Caudle, Rebecca L. ... Albany, NY
Caudle, Robert K., III ... Richmond, VA
Caudle, Robert K., Jr. ... Richmond, VA
Caudle, Sheila R. ... San Francisco, CA
Caudle & Spears, P.A. ... Charlotte, NC
Caudle, Thomas D. ... Dallas, TX
Caudle, W. Robert, II ... Halifax, NC
Caudle, Welch & Umipeg, A Professional Law Corporation ... Concord, CA
Caudry, M. Kendall ... Los Angeles, CA
Cauffield, William G. ... Warren, OH
Cauffman, Linda Bass ... Marble Falls, TX
Caufield, Alicia C. ... Pittsburgh, PA
Caufield, Carolyn R. ... New York, NY
Caufield, Charles F. ... Chicago, IL
Caufield, Frank J. ... Cambridge, MA
Caufield, Jeffery L. ... San Diego, CA
Caufman, Thomas W. ... St. Petersburg, FL
Cauger, A. Scott ... Syracuse, NY
Caugh, Eric ... St. Paul, MN
Caughey, James E. ... Beech Grove, IN
Caughey, Jerold A. ... Ocean Shores, WA
Caughey, Kenneth W. ... Denver, CO
Caughey, Legner & Freehill ... Chenoa, IL
Pontiac, IL
Caughey, Paula F. ... Waterville, ME
Caughey, Robert R. ... Chenoa, IL
Pontiac, IL
Caughey, William C. ... Perrysburg, OH
Caughfield, Lance E. ... Dallas, TX
Caughlan, Deirdre ... Butte, MT
Caughlan, Deirdre, P.C. ... Butte, MT
Caughlin, Keith B. ... Watertown, NY
Caughlin, Mary D. ... Watertown, NY
Caughman, Noël M. ... Richmond, CA
Caughman, Richard B. ... Roswell, GA
Caughman, William L., III
Baton Rouge, LA
Caughran, Kerry B. ... El Paso, TX
Caughran, William H., Jr. ... Blountsville, AL
Caughron & Associates ... Helena, MT
Caughron, R. Clifton ... Helena, MT
Cauhorn, Jay P. ... Cincinnati, OH
Caul, Daniel E. ... San Francisco, CA
Cauldwell, Gerald ... Wichita, KS
Cauldwell, Patricia A. ... Madison, NJ
Cauler, Sandra L. ... Millersville, PA
Cauley, Betty K. ... Warm Springs, VA
Cauley, Bilee K. ... Montgomery, AL
Cauley, E. Paul, Jr. ... Dallas, TX
Cauley, James P., III ... Wilson, NC
Cauley, James R. ... Waukesha, WI
Cauley, Kevin S. ... Cairo, GA
Cauley, Kevin T. ... San Diego, CA

Cauley, Lisa A. ... Cherry Hill, NJ
Philadelphia, PA
Cauley, Mary P. ... Bloomfield Hills, MI
Cauley, Michael A. C. ... Tampa, FL
Cauley, Michael R. ... Erie, PA
Cauley, Michele Elaine ... Macon, GA
Cauley, Michelle H. ... El Dorado, AR
Cauley, Patrick C. ... Northville, MI
Cauley, Richard F. ... San Jose, CA
Cauley, Ronald ... Gardnerville, NV
Cauley, Thomas K., Jr. ... Chicago, IL
Cauley, Wendell ... Montgomery, AL
Caulfield, Alexandra E. ... Portland, ME
Caulfield, Barbara ... San Francisco, CA
Caulfield, Barbara Ann E.
San Francisco, CA
Caulfield, Bryan D. ... Clearwater, FL
Caulfield, Caroline G. ... Kew Gardens, NY
Caulfield, Davies & Donahue
Fairfield, CA
Sacramento, CA
Caulfield, Donald C. ... Fairfield, CT
Caulfield, Donald J. ... Mount Rainier, MD
Caulfield, Eileen F. ... Wilmington, DE
Caulfield, George J. ... West Shokan, NY
Caulfield, Heller & Harris ... New York, NY
Caulfield, James D. ... Newport Beach, CA
Caulfield, James P. ... Waterbury, CT
Caulfield, Jerome J. ... New York, NY
Caulfield, Joseph ... Pepperell, MA
Caulfield, Joseph T. ... Hoboken, NJ
Caulfield, Katherine E. ... Bridgeport, CT
Southport, CT
Stamford, CT
Caulfield, Marianne T. ... Washington, DC
Caulfield, Marilyn Milligan ... Babylon, NY
Caulfield, Martin F. ... Woodbury, NJ
Caulfield, Michael C. ... Cranford, NJ
Caulfield, Michael C., P.C. ... Cranford, NJ
Caulfield, Michael J. ... New York, NY
Caulfield, Michele A. ... Southbury, CT
Caulfield, Patricia K. ... New Buffalo, MI
Caulfield, Patrick J. ... New York, NY
Caulfield, Regina C. ... Elizabeth, NJ
Caulfield, Richard Hyland ... Fairfield, CA
Sacramento, CA
Caulfield, Sharon E. ... Boulder, CO
Caulfield, Thomas W. ... East Quogue, NY
Caulk, David A. ... Rockford, IL
Caulk, Glen Paul ... Columbia, SC
Caulking, John E. ... New Orleans, LA
Caulkins, Cecil L. ... Jefferson City, MO
Caulkins, Charles S., (P.A.)
Fort Lauderdale, FL
Caulkins, D. Stuart, Jr. ... Nashville, TN
Caulkins, Donald S., Sr. ... Franklin, TN
Caulkins, R. Scott ... Alexandria, VA
Arlington, VA
Caulkins, Susan L. ... Port Orchard, WA
Caulum, Steven J. ... Madison, WI
Cauman, Richard ... Washington, DC
Caummisar, Robert L. ... Grayson, KY
Causbie, Michael Edgar
North Andover, MA
Causby, L. Nelsonya ... San Francisco, CA
Causby, W. Thomas ... Columbia, SC
Causeman, Craig J. ... Champaign, IL
Causeman, Sue D. ... Urbana, IL
Causey, B. Joseph, Jr. ... Shallotte, NC
Causey, Brian Lee ... Macon, GA
Causey, C. Dawn ... Washington, DC
Causey, Caywood, Taylor, McManus & Bailey ... Memphis, TN
Causey, Daniel B. ... Darlington, SC
Causey, Gordon E. ... Hammond, LA
Causey, Ingrid M. ... Costa Mesa, CA
Causey, James C., Jr. ... Seattle, WA
Causey, James D. ... Memphis, TN
Causey, Jerry L. ... Atlanta, GA
Causey, John M. ... Conroe, TX
Causey, Joseph F. ... Phoenix, AZ
Causey, J. P., Jr. ... Richmond, VA
Causey Law Firm ... Seattle, WA
Causey, Margaret Cameron
Albuquerque, NM
Causey, Mary Suzanne ... Atlanta, GA
Causey, Omer S. ... Sarasota, FL
Causey, Paul Raymond ... Pasadena, CA
Causey, Travis J., Jr. ... New Orleans, LA
Causey, V. Wayne ... Calera, AL
Causey, Wade R. ... Phoenix, AZ
Causey, William F. ... Washington, DC
Causey, William J., Jr. ... Monroeville, AL
Causing, Jennifer M. ... Aspen, CO
Causseaux, Stephen K., Jr. ... Tacoma, WA
Cautero, John A. ... St. Petersburg, FL
Cauthen, Britt ... Decatur, AL
Cauthen & Cauthen ... Decatur, AL
Cauthen, David B. ... Decatur, AL
Cauthen, David E. ... Tavares, FL
Cauthen, Dawn Hall ... San Diego, CA
Cauthen, Douglas E. ... Lexington, KY
Cauthen & Feldman, P.A. ... Leesburg, FL
Tavares, FL
Cauthen, Florence Mangum
Montgomery, AL
Cauthen, Frank M., Jr. ... Tuscaloosa, AL
Cauthen, George B. ... Columbia, SC
Cauthen, Karen S. ... Beaumont, TX
Cauthen, Kerry T. ... Lexington, KY
Cauthen, Mark D. ... Irmo, SC
Cauthen, Mary Catherin ... Atlanta, GA
Cauthen, Max B., Jr. ... Spartanburg, SC
Cauthen, Oldham & Keough, P.A.
Leesburg, FL
Tavares, FL
Cauthen, Robert H. ... Saint Marys, GA
Cauthen, Robert H., P.C. ... Saint Marys, GA

Cauthen, William H. ... Tavares, FL
Cauthorn, Alison L. ... Marietta, OH
Cauthorn & Associates, A Professional Corporation ... Marietta, GA
Cauthorn Hale Hornberger Fuller Sheehan & Becker, Incorporated
San Antonio, TX
Cauthorn, T. Drew ... San Antonio, TX
Cauthorn, Thomas E., III ... Marietta, GA
Cauthron, Robin J. ... Oklahoma City, OK
Cautiño-Antongiorgi, Beatrice A.
San Juan, PR
Cauvel, Howard L. ... DeLand, FL
Cauvin, Melinda ... Carefree, AZ
Cava, Anita ... Miami, FL
Cava, Christopher F. ... Springfield, MA
Cava, David L. ... Sacramento, CA
Cava, Dennis L. ... Pasadena, CA
Cava, Gregory J. ... Bridgeport, CT
Cava, Robert J. ... East Meadow, NY
Cavacini, Victor F. ... Allentown, PA
Cavada, Viviana Santiago ... Kingsville, TX
Cavadel, Joel H. ... York, PA
Cavage, Lisa M. ... Harrisburg, PA
Cavagnaro, Albert N. ... Wilmington, NC
Cavagnaro, Alfred C. ... San Francisco, CA
Cavagnaro, Carl W. ... Vineland, NJ
Cavagnaro, Charles W., Jr. ... Memphis, TN
Cavagnaro, Jeannine V. ... Vineland, NJ
Cavagnaro, Laura Leak ... Wilmington, NC
Cavagnaro, Patricia Ann ... New York, NY
Cavagnuolo, Frederick T. ... New York, NY
Cavalari, Alfred F. ... New Windsor, NY
Cavalaris, Nicholas C. ... Columbus, OH
Cavaletto, Dean M. ... Phoenix, AZ
Cavalier & Associates, P.C. ... Houston, TX
Cavalier, Carrie ... Dallas, TX
Cavalier, Craig H. ... Houston, TX
Cavalier, Dorothy ... Uniondale, NY
Cavalier, Elisa J. ... Pittsburgh, PA
Cavalier, Gina M. ... Washington, DC
Cavalier, Margot Oliver ... Pittsburgh, PA
Cavalier, Matthew J. ... Rego Park, NY
Cavalier, Michael ... New York, NY
Cavalier, Michael ... Plano, TX
Cavalier, Peter L. ... Bayville, NY
Cavalier, Robert M. ... Philadelphia, PA
Cavalier, Roland M. ... Albany, NY
Cavalier, Thomas F. ... Detroit, MI
Cavaliere, Frank J. ... Beaumont, TX
Cavaliere, Jean M. ... Wayne, NJ
Cavaliere, John V. ... Newark, NJ
Cavaliere, Kevin F. ... White Plains, NY
Cavaliere, Pasquale A. ... Westerly, RI
Cavaliere, Regina Gore ... New York, NY
Cavalieri, Anthony J. ... Lynnfield, MA
Cavalieri, Cristina G. ... Philadelphia, PA
Cavalieri, Nick V. ... Columbus, OH
Cavalieri, Vincent J. ... San Francisco, CA
Cavaliero, Brooke A. ... Stamford, CT
Cavallaro, Alfred ... New York, NY
Cavallaro, Anthony J. ... New York, NY
Cavallaro, Carlo F. ... Elmhurst, IL
Cavallaro, Joseph J. ... Hamden, CT
Cavallaro, Peter I. ... Uniondale, NY
Cavallaro, Richard A. ... New York, NY
Cavallaro, Robert ... New York, NY
Cavallaro, Rosanna ... Boston, MA
Cavallera, Henry W. ... Reno, NV
Cavallero, Robert J. ... Oakland, CA
Cavalletto, George A. ... Goleta, CA
Cavalli, Christopher R. ... Hackensack, NJ
Cavalli, Fred L. ... Atlanta, GA
Cavalli, Fred L. ... Decatur, GA
Cavalli, Gary A. ... North Arlington, NJ
Cavalli, Ronald B. ... Closter, NJ
Cavalli, Steven R. ... Oakland, CA
Cavallo, Christine L. ... Vienna, VA
Cavallo, Ernest J. ... New York, NY
Cavallo, Frank P., Jr. ... Marlton, NJ
Cavallo, Giovanna ... Chicago, IL
Cavallo, Gregory S. ... San Francisco, CA
Cavallo, Joseph G. ... Santa Ana, CA
Cavallo, Krista M. ... Florham Park, NJ
Cavallo, Orlando A. ... Bronx, NY
Cavallo, Robert ... New York, NY
Cavallo, Robert L. ... Hempstead, NY
Cavallo, Victor J. ... Stamford, CT
Cavallo, Vincent A. ... Bronx, NY
Cavallo & Wolf ... New York, NY
Cavallucci, Eugene S. ... Melbourne, FL
Cavalluzzi, Maria ... Los Angeles, CA
Cavalluzzi, Gerard P. ... White Plains, NY
Cavan, Bryan M. ... Atlanta, GA
Cavan, Christopher M. ... Chicago, IL
Cavan, Joe R. ... Buffalo, NY
Cavan, John J., Jr. ... Billings, MT
Cavan, Marc A. ... Chicago, IL
Cavan & Smith ... Billings, MT
Cavan, Stephen E. ... Boston, MA
Cavanagh, Anastasia ... Brooklyn, NY
Cavanagh, Barbara K. ... Austin, TX
Cavanagh, Brian T. ... Fort Lauderdale, FL
Cavanagh, C. Joseph ... Springfield, IL
Cavanagh, Candyce D. ... Atlanta, GA
Cavanagh, Carroll J. ... New York, NY
Cavanagh, Charles C. ... Los Angeles, CA
Cavanagh, Daniel M. ... Pasadena, CA
Cavanagh, Edward D. ... New York, NY
Cavanagh, Elizabeth A. ... Washington, DC
Cavanagh, Harry J. ... Phoenix, AZ
Cavanagh & Hartweger ... St. Louis, MO
Cavanagh, Hubert C. ... San Diego, CA
Cavanagh, James B. ... Wilmington, DE
Cavanagh, James B. ... Omaha, NE
Cavanagh, James G. ... Lansing, MI
Cavanagh, John E. ... Los Angeles, CA
Cavanagh, John J., Jr. ... St. Louis, MO

Cavanagh, Joseph M. ... Sacramento, CA
Cavanagh, Joseph V., Jr. ... Providence, RI
Cavanagh, Julie ... Pennsauken, NJ
Philadelphia, PA
Cavanagh, Karen M. Wade ... Albany, NY
Cavanagh, Kimberly Chase ... St. Louis, MO
Cavanagh, Mark E. ... Seattle, WA
Cavanagh, Mark J. ... Southfield, MI
Cavanagh, Mary E. ... Carlsbad, CA
Cavanagh, Mary V. ... Greenville, NC
New Bern, NC
Cavanagh, Michael A. ... New Bern, NC
Cavanagh, Michael D. ... Troy, MI
Cavanagh, Michael F. ... Lansing, MI
Cavanagh, Michael P. ... Albany, NY
Cavanagh & O'Hara ... Springfield, IL
Cavanagh, Peter C. ... Springfield, IL
Cavanagh, Ralph C. ... San Francisco, CA
Cavanagh, Rita A. ... Treasury Department,
Departmental Offices, GV
Cavanagh, Robert F. ... New Haven, CT
Cavanagh, Roderick A. J. ... Wakefield, RI
Cavanagh, Rosemary ... Department of Justice,
Office of Justice Programs, GV
Cavanagh, Terese A. ... Garden City, NY
Cavanagh, Thomas W., Jr. (P.C.)
West Long Branch, NJ
Cavanagh, Timothy J. ... Chicago, IL
Cavanagh, Timothy J., & Associates, P.C.
Chicago, IL
Cavanagh, Toni Lee ... Springfield, PA
Cavanagh, W. Wallace, Jr. ... Tacoma, WA
Cavanagh, William G. ... New York, NY
Cavanagh, William K., Jr. ... Springfield, IL
Cavanaugh, Amy Moore ... Denver, CO
Cavanaugh, Andrew J. ... New York, NY
Cavanaugh, Bartley W., Jr. ... Sacramento, CA
Cavanaugh & Beauvais, P.C. ... Flint, MI
Cavanaugh, Carol L. ... San Diego, CA
Cavanaugh, Casey M. ... Orlando, FL
Cavanaugh, Colleen A. ... Baltimore, MD
Cavanaugh, Dennis C. ... Hartford, CT
Cavanaugh, Dennis H. ... New York, NY
Cavanaugh, Diana ... Newport Beach, CA
Cavanaugh, Diane Boenig ... Scarborough, NY
Cavanaugh, Earl J. ... Pittsburgh, PA
Cavanaugh, Ellen M. ... Philadelphia, PA
Cavanaugh, Eric M. ... Plainfield, IN
Cavanaugh, Evelyn B. ... Baltimore, MD
Cavanaugh, Frank M. ... Denver, CO
Cavanaugh, George B. ... Orleans, MA
Cavanaugh, Gordon ... Washington, DC
Cavanaugh, Irene D. ... Chicago, IL
Cavanaugh, J. Michael ... Washington, DC
Cavanaugh, Jacquelyn K. ... Greensburg, PA
Cavanaugh, James C. ... Portland, OR
Cavanaugh, James Early ... Long Beach, CA
Cavanaugh, James P. ... Lincoln, NE
Omaha, NE
Cavanaugh, James P., III ... Indianapolis, IN
Cavanaugh, James P. A. ... Marlton, NJ
Cavanaugh, James R. ... Irvine, CA
Cavanaugh, James W. ... Austin, MN
Cavanaugh, Jane M. ... Washington, DC
Cavanaugh, Jerry D. ... Springfield, IL
Cavanaugh, John E. ... Orange, CA
Cavanaugh, John J. ... Chicago, IL
Cavanaugh, John J. ... Omaha, NE
Cavanaugh, John J., Jr. ... Delmar, NY
Cavanaugh, John R. ... Boston, MA
Cavanaugh, Joseph ... Chicago, IL
Cavanaugh, Kathleen ... Parsippany, NJ
Cavanaugh, Kathleen L. ... Springfield, MA
Cavanaugh, Kevin S. ... Kansas City, MO
Cavanaugh, Laurence D. ... Southfield, MI
Cavanaugh Law Offices ... Lincoln, NE
Omaha, NE
Cavanaugh, Lawrence A. ... Hartford, CT
Cavanaugh, Louis N., Jr.
Department of State,
Foreign Service Officers (Overseas), GV
Cavanaugh, Louise Lawler
Cambridge, MA
Cavanaugh, Louise S. ... New York, NY
Cavanaugh, M. Brian ... Denver, CO
Cavanaugh, Margaret A. ... Westfield, MA
Cavanaugh, Mark A. ... Montgomery, AL
Cavanaugh, Mark C. ... Akron, OH
Cavanaugh, Mark C. ... Philadelphia, PA
Cavanaugh, Mark J. ... Denver, CO
Cavanaugh, Mark J. ... Chicago, IL
Cavanaugh, Mary A. ... Cleveland, OH
Cavanaugh, Mary L. ... Chicago, IL
Cavanaugh, Mary L. ... Newark, NJ
Cavanaugh, Matthew E. ... Irvine, CA
Cavanaugh, Merrie Moore ... San Antonio, TX
Cavanaugh, Michael A. ... Wentworth, NC
Cavanaugh, Michael E. ... Lansing, MI
Cavanaugh, Michael E. ... New York, NY
Cavanaugh, Michael E. ... Seattle, WA
Cavanaugh, Michael F. ... Biloxi, MS
Cavanaugh, Michael F. ... Gulfport, MS
Jackson, MS
Cavanaugh, Michael J. ... Denver, CO
Cavanaugh, Michael J. ... Warren, MI
Cavanaugh, Michael K., (P.C.)
Chicago, IL
Cavanaugh, Michaela L. ... Baltimore, MD
Cavanaugh, Patricia M. ... Seattle, WA
Cavanaugh, Patrick ... Baltimore, MD
Cavanaugh, Patrick D. ... Des Moines, IA
Cavanaugh, Patrick J., Jr. ... Norwood, NY
Cavanaugh, Patrick K. ... Pittsburgh, PA
Cavanaugh, Patrick O. ... Washington, DC
Cavanaugh, Paul F. ... Boston, MA
Cavanaugh, Paul F. ... Concord, NH
Cavanaugh, Paul F., II ... Bangor, ME
Cavanaugh, Paul J. ... Malden, MA

Cavanaugh, Paul W. ....Pittsburgh, PA
Cavanaugh, Peter E. ....Philadelphia, PA
Cavanaugh, Peter J. ....Bloomfield Hills, MI
Cavanaugh, Richard E. ....Lowell, MA
Cavanaugh, Robert F. ....Jersey City, NJ
Cavanaugh, Robert L., Jr.
Bridgeport, CT
Westport, CT
Cavanaugh, Stephen E. ....Buffalo, NY
Cavanaugh, Stephen J. ....Houston, TX
Cavanaugh, Stephen W. ....Topeka, KS
Cavanaugh & Stephenson ....Buffalo, NY
Cavanaugh, Susan J. ....Hartford, CT
Cavanaugh, Terrence F. ....Lansing, MI
Cavanaugh, Terrence P. ....Erie, PA
Cavanaugh, Terry C. ....Pittsburgh, PA
Cavanaugh, Thomas G. ....Los Angeles, CA
Cavanaugh, Thomas J. ....Troy, MI
Cavanaugh, Thomas J., P.C. ....Troy, MI
Cavanaugh, Todd A. ....Los Angeles, CA
Cavanaugh, Victor A. ....Atlanta, GA
Cavanaugh, W. Michael ....Englewood, CO
Cavanaugh, William D. ....Dayton, OH
Cavanaugh, William F., Jr. ....New York, NY
Cavanaugh, William J. ....Flint, MI
Cavanaugh, William J. ....Erie, PA
Cavanaugh, William T., Jr. ....Dallas, TX
Cavaneau, Jerry W. ....Little Rock, AR
Cavaness, Ben ....American Falls, ID
Cavanna, Henry D. ....New York, NY
Cavanna-Wilk, Linda ....New York, NY
Cavarello, Daniel T. ....Buffalo, NY
Cavaretta, Laura A. ....San Antonio, TX
Cavarra, Matthew N. ....Omaha, NE
Cavas, Charles P. ....Warwick, RI
Cavasinni, Joseph E. ....Cleveland, OH
Cavataio, Lorraine Kay ....Belleville, IL
Cavataro, Arthur B. ....North Palm Beach, FL
Cavayero, Harvey J. ....Carle Place, NY
Cavazos, Arnaldo N., Jr. ....Corsicana, TX
Dallas, TX
Cavazos, Daniel ....McAllen, TX
Cavazos, Edward A. ....Purchase, NY
Cavazos, Ernesto R. ....Laredo, TX
Cavazos, Hendricks, Poirot & Dewey, P.C.
Dallas, TX
Fort Worth, TX
Cavazos, Jaime ....Dallas, TX
Cavazos, Jesse Y. ....San Antonio, TX
Cavazos, Maricela ....San Antonio, TX
Cavazos, Monica R. ....Houston, TX
Cavazos, Oscar ....Raymondville, TX
Cavazos, Roxella T. ....Houston, TX
Cavazos, Sandra E. ....San Francisco, CA
Cave, Alexander M. ....Ann Arbor, MI
Cave, Allan C., Jr. ....Quincy, MA
Cave, Bradley T., (P.C.) ....Cheyenne, WY
Cave, David ....Dallas, TX
Cave, Deborah A. ....Pasadena, CA
Cave, Donald G. ....Baton Rouge, LA
Cave, Donald G., A Professional Law Corporation ....Baton Rouge, LA
Cave, Edwin B. ....New Providence, NJ
Cave, Gilbert T. ....Painesville, OH
Cave, James W., III ....Joshua Tree, CA
Cave, John M. ....Fulton, MO
Cave, John M., II ....Kansas City, MO
Cave, Kelly D. ....Glenwood Springs, CO
Cave, O. Lee, III ....Louisville, KY
Cave, Philip D. ....Department of the Navy, Office of the Judge Advocate General, GV
Cave, Robert B. ....Washington, DC
Cave, Robert P. ....Greeneville, TN
Cave, Stanton L. ....Lexington, KY
Cave, Thomas H. ....Virginia Beach, VA
Cave, Thomas R. ....San Jose, CA
Cave, Tom ....Fort Worth, TX
Cave, William B. ....Richmond, VA
Cave, William M. ....Rockville, MD
Cave, William R. ....Tallahassee, FL
Caveda, David M. ....Tampa, FL
Caveda, Monica S. ....Boston, MA
Cavedo, Bradley B. ....Richmond, VA
Cavel, Jennifer S. ....Omaha, NE
Cavel, Jo Ann ....Omaha, NE
Cavel, Michael P. ....Omaha, NE
Cavell, Cathleen ....Boston, MA
Cavell, Daniel A. ....Thibodaux, LA
Cavell, Michael C. ....Topeka, KS
Cavell, Rachel L. ....Kingston, NY
Cavell-Howard, Tara J. ....Bentleyville, OH
Cavelli, Grace ....Washington, DC
Cavellier, Gerald P. ....Bloomfield Hills, MI
Cavellini, Stephen ....Santa Rosa, CA
Cavellini, Stephen, A P.C. ....Santa Rosa, CA
Caven, Hubbard S., Jr. ....Houston, TX
Caven, James D. ....Santa Rosa, CA
Caven, Jed W.
Research Triangle Park, NC
Caven, John W., III ....Jacksonville, FL
Caven, John W., Jr. ....Jacksonville, FL
Cavenagh, Teresa N. ....Philadelphia, PA
Cavenagh, Thomas D. ....Naperville, IL
Cavenagh, Timothy J. ....Chicago, IL
Cavenaugh, William F. ....Little Rock, AR
Cavender, Anthony B. ....Houston, TX
Cavender, Bob J. ....Houston, TX
Cavender, C. Paul ....Birmingham, AL
Cavender, Carol J. ....Freeport, TX
Cavender, David L. ....Hinesville, GA
Cavender, David L. ....Morgantown, WV
Cavender, Jeffery W. ....Atlanta, GA
Cavender, J. T. ....Springboro, OH
Cavendish, Jeanne ....Chicago, IL
Cavendish, M. E. ....Greenville, NC
Cavendish, Michael R. ....Jacksonville, FL
Cavendish, Rebecca
West Palm Beach, FL

Caveness, Tracey L. ....Chicago, IL
Wheaton, IL
Caveney, Stuart S. ....Santa Rosa, CA
Caveney, William J. ....Morris Plains, NJ
Caver, Steven B. ....Fort Worth, TX
Cavera, Rose Marie ....New York, NY
Caverlee, John ....Dallas, TX
Caverlee, Samuel W. ....Shreveport, LA
Caverly, Andrew D. ....Andover, MA
Caverly, Joseph L., (P.C.)
New Orleans, LA
Caverly, Kathleen C. ....Los Angeles, CA
Caverly, Kristen E. ....San Diego, CA
Caverly, N. Brian ....Shickshinny, PA
Wilkes-Barre, PA
Cavers, David F., Jr. ....Boston, MA
Cavers, David F., Jr., P.C. ....Boston, MA
Cavert, Harlan M. ....Minnetonka, MN
Cavert, Wm. C. ....Tulsa, OK
Caves & Caves ....Laurel, MS
Caves, Joseph L. ....Carmichael, CA
Caves, Leonard B. ....Laurel, MS
Caves, Terry L. ....Laurel, MS
Cavet, Judy L. ....Newark, NJ
Cavet, Keith J. ....New York, NY
Cavett & Abbott ....Chattanooga, TN
Cavett & Associates ....Mission Viejo, CA
Cavett, Dan ....Tucson, AZ
Cavett, Eldred C. ....Tucson, AZ
Cavett, John C., Jr. ....Chattanooga, TN
Cavett, Jonathan C. ....Mission Viejo, CA
Cavett, Kenneth ....Tyler, TX
Cavett Law Firm, A Professional Corporation ....Tucson, AZ
Cavett, Terry Atkin ....Chattanooga, TN
Cavette, Peter W., Law Offices of
Sierra Madre, CA
Cavey, Nancy L. ....St. Petersburg, FL
Cavey, Patricia M. ....Milwaukee, WI
Cavezza, Edward ....Columbus, OH
Caviale, John L. ....Kenosha, WI
Caviale, Louis A., Jr. ....Glen Ellyn, IL
Caviar & Hill, L.L.C. ....Leawood, KS
Caviar, Nancy M. ....Leawood, KS
Cavic, Paris ....Troy, NY
Cavicchi, Jon R. ....Concord, NH
Cavicchio, John, III ....Erie, PA
Cavicke, David L. ....Hartford, CT
Cavico, Frank J., Jr. ....Fort Lauderdale, FL
Caviedes, Alexander A. ....Tampa, FL
Caviglia, Marco ....Poughkeepsie, NY
Cavilia, James R. ....Carson City, NV
Cavilia, John W. ....Hartford, CT
Cavin, A. Kirby ....McAllen, TX
Cavin, Clark ....Seattle, WA
Cavin, Guyle E. ....Department of State, Foreign Service Officers (Overseas), GV
Cavin, Jeffrey D. ....Downey, CA
Cavin, John A. ....Houston, TX
Cavin, John F. ....San Ramon, CA
Cavin, Lyle C., Jr. ....Oakland, CA
Cavin, Lyle C., Jr., A Professional Corporation ....Oakland, CA
Cavin, Sealy H., Jr. ....Albuquerque, NM
Cavin, S. H. ....Roswell, NM
Cavin, Wylie D., III ....Little Rock, AR
Caviness, Elizabeth J. ....Greensboro, NC
Caviness, James Reece ....Rockingham, NC
Caviness, John P. ....San Rafael, CA
Caviness, Loto Greenlee ....Marion, NC
Caviness, Peter F. ....Opelousas, LA
Caviness, Philip James ....Noblesville, IN
Caviness Wright, Karen ....Shelby, NC
Cavins, Mark K. ....Chicago, IL
Caviola, James Calvin, Jr.
Huntington Beach, CA
Cavise, Paul J., Jr. ....Holmdel, NJ
Caviston, William M. ....Parsippany, NJ
Cavitch, Familo, Durkin & Frutkin Co., L.P.A. ....Cleveland, OH
Cavitch, Matthew P. ....Memphis, TN
Cavitch, Zolman ....Cleveland, OH
Cavitt, Bruce E. ....Kansas City, MO
Cavitt, Janie L. Choice ....Kansas City, MO
Cavitt, Rodney D. ....Elgin, IL
Cavna, Arthur D. ....Los Angeles, CA
Cavness, Charles L. ....Houston, TX
Cavness, Charles L., Jr. ....Denver, CO
Cavness, Marc C. ....Phoenix, AZ
Cavness, Pat E. ....Lampasas, TX
Cavo, Richard C. ....Manchester, CT
Cavoli, Mae A. ....Cleveland, OH
Cavolo, Michael F. ....White Plains, NY
Cavonis, Paul ....Seminole, FL
Cavosie, J. Michael ....Indianapolis, IN
Cavoulas, Shad ....San Diego, CA
Caw, Blythe B. ....Othello, WA
Cawelti, Donald D. ....Westminster, CO
Cawile, Lourdes C. ....Los Angeles, CA
Cawley, Clifford J. ....Providence, RI
Cawley, Daniel R. ....Mastic, NY
Cawley, Donald K. ....Farmington, CT
Cawley, Douglas A. ....Dallas, TX
Cawley, Elaine M. ....Sacramento, CA
Cawley, F. Kelly ....Las Vegas, NV
Cawley, F. Kelly, Law Offices of
Las Vegas, NV
Cawley, Frank G. ....Houston, TX
Cawley, James H. ....Harrisburg, PA
Cawley, James M. ....Mantoloking, NJ
Cawley, James M., Jr. ....Houston, TX
Cawley, Jean M. ....Chicago, IL
Cawley, John A., Jr. ....Elkhart, IN
Cawley, Jonathan P. ....Warren, PA
Cawley, Joseph F., Jr. ....Binghamton, NY
Cawley, Kathleen M. ....Boston, MA
Cawley, Kevin J. ....Chicago, IL
Cawley, M. Terence ....Cleveland, OH

Cawley, Marie ....Santa Clara, CA
Cawley, Mark C. ....Wilmington, DE
Cawley, Mary Ann ....Potsdam, NY
Cawley, Megan R. ....Chicago, IL
Cawley, Michael A. ....Ardmore, OK
Cawley, Michael G. ....Chicago, IL
Cawley, Michael J. ....Philadelphia, PA
Cawley, Michelle ....Kansas City, MO
Cawley, Richard A. ....Bradford, VT
Cawley, Susan ....Wenatchee, WA
Cawley, Thomas A., Jr. ....Chicago, IL
Cawley, Thomas J. ....McLean, VA
Cawley, Thomas J. P., Jr. ....Sarasota, FL
Cawley, Thomas M. ....Cleveland, OH
Cawley, W Allen, JR. ....Waterford, MI
Cawley-McCary, Kimberly A. ....Denton, TX
Cawley-McCary, Kimberly A.
Lewisville, TX
Cawn, Maurice A. ....Greensboro, NC
Cawood, Cathleen M. ....White Oak, PA
Cawood, F. Chris ....Kingston, TN
Cawood, Harry E. ....Mesa, AZ
Cawood, James C., Jr. ....Annapolis, MD
Cawood, Katherine Kelly ....Annapolis, MD
Cawood & Kelly, P.A. ....Annapolis, MD
Cawood & McKindles, P.C. ....Mesa, AZ
Cawood & Nagle, P.S.C. ....Pineville, KY
Cawood, Robert H.B. ....Annapolis, MD
Baltimore, MD
Cawood, Stephen C. ....Lexington, KY
Cawood, Victoria H. ....West River, MD
Cawse & Birmingham ....Staten Island, NY
Cawthon, James David ....Shawnee, OK
Cawthon, Victor M. ....Tallahassee, FL
Cawthorn, Picard & Rowe
Newport News, VA
Richmond, VA
Roanoke, VA
Cawthorn, William R. ....Richmond, VA
Roanoke, VA
Cawthorne, Dennis O. ....Lansing, MI
Cawthorne, Hugh ....Tucson, AZ
Cawthorne, Susan J. ....Stuart, FL
Cawyer, Melissa K. ....Corpus Christi, TX
Cawyer, Russell D. ....Fort Worth, TX
Cay, Metin A. ....Fairfax, VA
Caya, Dale Edward ....Doylestown, PA
Quakertown, PA
Caya, Steven T. ....Milwaukee, WI
Cayatte, Betty Buchman ....Parker, CO
Cayatte, Jean-Michel ....Parker, CO
Cayce, Cheryl Cardoza ....Eden Prairie, MN
Cayce, Christopher C. ....Monterey, CA
Cayce, Graydon K. ....Houston, TX
Cayce, Kameron C. ....Renton, WA
Cayce, Karrollanne K. ....Savannah, GA
Cayce and Ottone ....Monterey, CA
Cayci, Karen L. ....Princeton, NJ
Caye, Woolsey M. ....Louisville, KY
Cayea, Donald J. ....New York, NY
Cayen, Donald ....Fond du Lac, WI
Cayer, Carroll ....Jacksonville, FL
Cayer, Cynthia M. ....Quincy, MA
Cayer, David S. ....Charlotte, NC
Cayer, John Grady ....Boston, MA
Cayer, John J. ....Long Beach, CA
Cayer, Kilstofte & Craton, A Professional Law Corporation ....Long Beach, CA
Cayer, Michael J. ....Waltham, MA
Cayetano, Benjamin J. ....Honolulu, HI
Cayford, Rebecca A. ....Skowhegan, ME
Cayia, Edward de Rosier
Fort Lauderdale, FL
Cayia, Edward de Rosier, P.A.
Fort Lauderdale, FL
Cayia, Robert V. ....East Chicago, IN
Cayley, John S. ....Sherman Oaks, CA
Cayley, Susan N. ....Camarillo, CA
Caylor, David C. ....El Paso, TX
Caylor, Gary M. ....Grass Valley, CA
Caylor, Michele D. ....Los Angeles, CA
Caylor, Steven E. M. ....Lewiston, ID
Caylor, William K. ....Lexington, KY
Cayne, Howard Neil ....Washington, DC
Cayne, Jana M.
Securities and Exchange Commission, Division of Investment Management, GV
Cayne, Jonathan F. ....Washington, DC
Cayne, Jonathan F.
Securities and Exchange Commission, Division of Investment Management, GV
Cayne, Louise E. ....Newark, NJ
Cayne, Richard M. ....New York, NY
Caynon, Jack L., III ....Charleston, SC
Cayo, Richard J. ....Milwaukee, WI
Cayot, Dale L. ....Cincinnati, OH
Caytas & Associates ....New York, NY
Caytas, Ivo G. ....New York, NY
Cayten, Stephanie ....Exeter, NH
Cayten, Thomas E. ....Exeter, NH
Cayton, Alison R. ....Raleigh, NC
Cayton, Darrell B., Jr. ....Washington, NC
Cayton, Howard ....Washington, DC
Caywood, Christopher J.
Hoffman Estates, IL
Caywood, David C. ....Buffalo, NY
Caywood, David E. ....Memphis, TN
Caywood, Kerry W. ....Chickasha, OK
Caywood, Mark James ....Oklahoma City, OK
Caywood, Michael ....Austin, TX
Caywood, Michael J. ....Sturgis, MI
Caywood, Nancy L. ....Washington, DC
Caywood, W. Curtis, IV ....Jacksonville, FL
Caywood, Warren G., Jr. ....New York, NY
Caywood Williams Mullins & McKee
Lexington, KY
Caza, Patricia A. ....Willingboro, NJ
Cazakoff, Martin D. ....Brooklyn, NY

Cazalas, Mary Williams ....New Orleans, LA
Cazalot, James E., Jr. ....New Orleans, LA
Cazares, Carlos A. ....Bonita, CA
Cazares, Craig M. ....Santa Ana, CA
Cazares, David E. ....McAllen, TX
Cazares, Edward A. ....Houston, TX
Cazares, Jorge V. ....Chicago, IL
Cazares, Roy B. ....Chula Vista, CA
Cazaubon, Maurice S., Jr. ....Metairie, LA
Cazayoux, Donald J., Jr. ....New Roads, LA
Cazden, Elizabeth ....Manchester, NH
Cazeau, Rosemarie E. ....Chicago, IL
Cazedessus, Sanders R. ....Baton Rouge, LA
Cazel, Thomas E. ....Fort Lauderdale, FL
Cazel, Thomas E., P.A. ....Fort Lauderdale, FL
Cazenave, Dean Paul ....Baton Rouge, LA
Cazenavette, Joseph E. ....San Antonio, TX
Cazeneuve, Martha L. ....Pasadena, CA
Cazes, Dale B. ....Oklahoma City, OK
Cazes, Mary A. ....Houston, TX
Cazes, Randy Hope ....Philadelphia, PA
Cazier, Allen F. ....San Antonio, TX
Cazier, Edward C., Jr. ....Los Angeles, CA
Cazier, Stanley W., (P.C.) ....Granby, CO
Cazin, Albert ....Tampa, FL
Cazorla, Eugenio ....Dallas, TX
Cazzell, Maryann ....Orange, CA
Cazzell, Richard L. ....Amarillo, TX
Cazzulino, Claude ....Los Angeles, CA
Cea, Anthony E. ....Howard, OH
Cea, Richard J. ....Brooklyn, NY
Melville, NY
Cea, Stephen F. ....Newark, NJ
Cea, William J. ....Winter Haven, FL
Cearley Law Firm, P.A. ....Little Rock, AR
Cearley, Martha Hyde ....Denver, CO
Cearley, Robert M., Jr. ....Little Rock, AR
Ceasar, Mitchell ....Plantation, FL
Ceasar, Mitchell, P.A. ....Plantation, FL
Ceasar, Sharon L. ....Albany, CA
Cease, Allan A., Law Offices of
Sugar Land, TX
Cease, Bruce M. ....Miami, FL
Cease, Jeffrey K. ....Atlanta, GA
Cease, Michael S. ....Miami, FL
Cease, Michael S., P.A. ....Miami, FL
Cease, Richard L. ....Spokane, WA
Ceaser, Paul G. ....Nokomis, FL
Ceballos, Gustavo G. ....Los Angeles, CA
Ceballos, Joanne ....Wilmington, DE
Ceballos, M. Alan ....Jacksonville, FL
Ceballos, M. Alan, P.A. ....Jacksonville, FL
Ceballos, Marta ....Bronx, NY
Ceballos, Richard ....Los Angeles, CA
Cebeci, Brad ....Los Angeles, CA
Cebeci, Rabia A. ....Los Angeles, CA
Cebik, Sarah R. ....New York, NY
Cebuhar, Chas. ....Cedar Rapids, IA
Cebula, Charles S. ....Flossmoor, IL
Cebula, Janet Denise ....Garden City, NY
Cebula, Janice I. ....Kansas City, MO
Cebula, John W. ....Albany, NY
Cebula, John W., Jr. ....Batavia, NY
Cebula, Raymond Adam, III ....Boston, MA
Cebula, T. J. ....Long Beach, CA
Cebulash, Brett H. ....New York, NY
Cebulko, Craig R. ....Kansas City, MO
Cebull, Richard F. ....Great Falls, MT
Cecala, Anthony Michael ....Silver Spring, MD
Cecala, Joseph J., Jr. ....Chicago, IL
Cecala, Robert J. ....New York, NY
Cecava, Kristine R. ....Ogallala, NE
Ceccacci, Diana E. ....New York, NY
Ceccacci, Vincent E., Jr. ....Chicago, IL
Ceccarelli, Edwin M. ....Marietta, GA
Ceccarelli, Joseph J. ....New York, NY
Ceccherini, Andrew R., Jr.
East Hartford, CT
Cecchettini, Horace E. ....Sacramento, CA
Cecchi, Claire C. ....Newark, NJ
Cecchi, Clifford Brian ....Chicago, IL
Cecchi, Donald J. ....Roseland, NJ
Cecchi, Gino P. ....San Francisco, CA
Cecchi, James D., Jr. ....Roseland, NJ
Cecchi, James E. ....Roseland, NJ
Cecchini, Garrett L. ....San Francisco, CA
Cecchini, Pamela M. ....Bloomington, MN
Cecchini, Peter G. ....North Chatham, NY
Cecchini, Robert A. ....Dunmore, PA
Ceccia, Richard M. ....Long Beach, CA
Ceccon, Dorothy B. ....Los Angeles, CA
Ceccon, Robert C. ....Los Angeles, CA
Ceccotti, Babette ....New York, NY
Ceccotti, Eugene B. ....Petaluma, CA
Cece, Frank, Jr. ....Markham, IL
Cece, Robert J. ....Denville, NJ
Cecelic, Jerone C. ....Nashville, TN
Cecere, Andrew C. ....Richmond, IN
Cecere, Dominic J. ....Minneapolis, MN
Cecere, Frank A. ....Albertson, NY
Cecere, I. Barbara ....Teaneck, NJ
Cecere, Jacob J. ....Laytonsville, MD
Cecere, John A. ....Hartford, CT
Cecere, Karen C. ....Cleveland, OH
Cecere, M. Carolyn ....Greenwood, IN
Cecere, Paul M. ....Hackensack, NJ
Cecere, Ralph N ....Melrose, MA
Cecero, Diane M. ....Rochester, NY
Cech, Alan E. ....Wexford, PA
Cech, Richard B. ....New York, NY
Cechini, John B. ....Stockton, CA
Cechini, John Steven, Inc., A Professional Law Corp. ....Stockton, CA
Cechman, John B. ....Fort Myers, FL
Cechony, Gerald J. ....New York, NY
Cech-Vinhais, Viktoria K. ....Greenwich, CT
Stamford, CT
Cecil, Alan V. ....Leonardtown, MD

Cecil, Amy Friedman
Woodland Hills, CA
Cecil, Andrew W. ... Columbus, OH
Cecil, Cameron W. ... Long Beach, CA
Cecil, Cynthia A. ... Columbus, OH
Cecil, Cynthia S. ... Richmond, VA
Cecil, David E. ... Grundy, VA
Cecil, David Lohr ... High Point, NC
Cecil, Elizabeth M. ... Norristown, PA
Cecil, Erik J. ... Washington, DC
Cecil, Gordon B. ... Oklahoma City, OK
Cecil, J. David ... Charleston, WV
Cecil, Jina ... Cordova, TN
Cecil, Joe S.
Federal Judicial Center, GV
Cecil, John L. ... New York, NY
Cecil, Larry G. ... Salem, OH
Cecil, Lee M. ... High Point, NC
Cecil, Leslie J. ... Miami, FL
Cecil, Loretta Arlene ... Dayton, OH
Cecil, Michelle Arnopol ... Columbia, MO
Cecil, Peggy W. ... Rancho Cordova, CA
Cecil, Philip W. ... Chicago, IL
Cecil, Preston S. ... Lexington, KY
Cecil, Robert L. ... High Point, NC
Cecil, Sarah P. ... Swampscott, MA
Cecil, Thomas ... Encino, CA
Cecil, Thomas C. ... Dayton, OH
Cecil, Thomas G. ... Detroit, MI
Cecil, W. Jeffrey ... Naples, FL
Cecile, James H. ... Syracuse, NY
Cecil-Few, Martha L. ... Newark, DE
Ceckowski, Arthur F. ... Gurnee, IL
Ceconi, Lizanne J. ... Summit, NJ
Cedar, Annabelle R. ... Philadelphia, PA
Cedar, David Matthew ... Medford, NJ
Cedar, Philip M. ... New York, NY
Cedar, Strauss & Holt, P.C. ... Selden, NY
Cedarbaum, Bernard ... New York, NY
Cedarbaum, Miriam Goldman
New York, NY
Cedarbaum, Robert D. ... Olympia, WA
Cedarblade, Mary E. ... Sausalito, CA
Cedarburg, Owen L. ... Alexandria, VA
Cedarquist, Wayland B. ... Lombard, IL
Cedars, Chester R. ... Breaux Bridge, LA
Cedarstrand, James T. ... Ridgewood, NJ
Cederbaum, Eugene E. ... Bridgeport, CT
Westport, CT
Cederberg, Cynthia C. ... Boulder, CO
Cederberg, Dan G. ... Missoula, MT
Cederberg, James A. ... Boulder, CO
Denver, CO
Cederberg, Jon C. ... Los Angeles, CA
Cederberg Law Firm, P.C. ... Boulder, CO
Denver, CO
Cederberg, Shott & Smith, P.C.
Hamilton, MT
Missoula, MT
Cederborg, Daniel C. ... Stockton, CA
Cederborg, Mark L. ... Oakland, CA
Cederholm, Eva P. ... Atlanta, GA
Cederholm, Geoffrey H. ... Atlanta, GA
Cederoth, Lisa J. ... Oak Park, IL
Cederoth, Richard A. ... Chicago, IL
Cederquist, Fredrik ... Staten Island, NY
Cederquist, Malin, (Mrs.) ... New York, NY
Cederqvist, Fredrik ... Staten Island, NY
Cederwall, Jennifer Loeb ... Cherry Hill, NJ
Philadelphia, PA
Cedillo, Ricardo G. ... San Antonio, TX
Cedillos, Steve H. ... Honolulu, HI
Cedola & Guerra, P.A. ... Tampa, FL
Cedola, R. Scott ... Tampa, FL
Cedras, Constance L. ... Southlake, TX
Cedro, Alfred M. ... Burbank, CA
Cedrone, Gerard ... Mount Laurel, NJ
Philadelphia, PA
Cedrone, Mark E. ... Philadelphia, PA
Cedzidlo, Martin S. ... Englewood Cliffs, NJ
Cedzidlo, Richard S. ... Wallington, NJ
Ceely, Frederick ... Los Angeles, CA
Ceely, Mary Ellen ... DeLand, FL
Cefali, Anthony J. ... Hobart, IN
Cefali & Cefali, P.A. ... Hobart, IN
Cefali, Jeffrey V. ... Hobart, IN
Cefalo, Albert P. ... Cupertino, CA
Cefalo, Frederick W. ... Boston, MA
Cefalo, Joseph T., Jr. ... Charlestown, MA
Cefalo, Teresa M. ... Dallas, TX
Cefaloni, Andrea M. ... Los Angeles, CA
Cefalu, Maria S. ... San Francisco, CA
Cefola, Richard A. ... Department of Defense,
Defense Legal Services Agency, GV
Cegavske, Johnston & Associates, P.C.
Roseburg, OR
Cegavske, Wallace D. ... Roseburg, OR
Cegelka, W. William ... Lexington, KY
Cegelski, Frank B. ... Rochester, NY
Cegielski, John W. ... Buffalo, NY
Cegla, Kathleen M. ... Salem, OR
Ceglar, Frank J., Jr. ... Los Angeles, CA
Ceglarek, Joseph J., II ... Detroit, MI
Ceglowski, Susan M. ... Rutland, VT
Ceguerra, Cristina Obieta
Santa Rosa, CA
Cehelsky, Kathleen M. ... Roseland, NJ
Ceisler, Antoinette N. ... New York, NY
Ceisler, Robert L. ... Washington, PA
Ceithaml, Lenore A. ... San Diego, CA
Cejas, Helene Christianne ... Miami, FL
Cejas, Peter L. ... Westport, CT
Cejas, Rodolfo, II ... Norfolk, VA
Cejda, Kirk Joseph ... Oklahoma City, OK
Cejka, Oliver J., Jr., P.A. ... Frederick, MD
Cejka, Oliver "John", Jr. ... Frederick, MD
Cejudo, William P. ... Washington, DC
Cekala, Chester, Jr. ... Boston, MA

Cekanski Farrand, Kathleen E.
South Bend, IN
Cekay, Robert A. ... Grand Rapids, MI
Ceko, Daniel D. ... Chicago, IL
Ceko, Maryterese ... Chicago, IL
Ceko, Theresa C. ... Chicago, IL
Cela, Phyllis J.
Commodity Futures Trading Commission,
Division of Enforcement, GV
Celada, M. Cristina ... New York, NY
Celani, Franklin A., Jr. ... Lansing, IL
Celano, Chris E. ... New York, NY
Celano, Josephine M. ... Scarsdale, NY
Celano, Patricia A. ... Newark, NJ
Celaro, Peter J., Jr. ... Woodbury, NJ
Cela-Ureña, Jorge ... San Juan, PR
Celauro, Kathryn Behm ... Nashville, TN
Celauro, Linda B. ... Newark, NJ
Celauro, Steven ... Brooklyn, NY
Celaya, Antonio A. ... San Francisco, CA
Celba & Baird ... Milwaukee, WI
Celba, Steven W. ... Milwaukee, WI
Celebrezze, Anthony J., Jr.
Columbus, OH
Celebrezze, Bruce D. ... Los Angeles, CA
San Diego, CA
San Francisco, CA
Celebrezze, Frank D. ... Cleveland, OH
Celebrezze & Holloway ... Louisville, KY
Celebrezze, James P. ... Cleveland, OH
Celebrezze, Rocco J. ... Louisville, KY
Celebrezze & Wesley ... San Diego, CA
Los Angeles, CA
San Francisco, CA
Celebrezze, William A. ... San Francisco, CA
Celedonia, Baila H. ... New York, NY
Celedonia & Klitsas, P.C. ... Houston, TX
Celedonia, Robert J., III ... Houston, TX
Celedonio, Francisco E. ... New York, NY
Celello, David B. ... Iron Mountain, MI
Celello, Michael P. ... Iron Mountain, MI
Celello, Richard J. ... Iron Mountain, MI
Celentano, James M. ... Hartford, CT
Celentano, Jeffrey ... Orange, CT
Celentano, John A., Jr. ... Clifton, NJ
Celentano, Leslie Z. ... Livingston, NJ
Celentano, Michele R. ... Milford, CT
Celentano, Stadtmauer & Walentowicz
Clifton, NJ
Passaic, NJ
Paterson, NJ
Celentino, Anne Elizabeth ... San Diego, CA
Celentino, Christopher ... San Diego, CA
Celenza, C. Michael ... Concord, NH
Celeski, Nicholas Anthony ... Dearborn, MI
Celeste, Mary A. ... Denver, CO
Celeste, Michael J., Jr.
West Palm Beach, FL
Celeste, Michael J., Jr., P.A.
West Palm Beach, FL
Celeste, Peter J. ... Ventura, CA
Celeste, Peter J., Prof. Law Corp.
Ventura, CA
Celeste, Vincent J. ... Stoneham, MA
Celestin, Joel B. ... Washington, DC
Celestin, Marshall J., Jr. ... Los Angeles, CA
Celestin, Robert A., Law Offices
New York, NY
Celestine, Dionne L. ... New Orleans, LA
Celestini, Stephen D.
Research Triangle Park, NC
Celestre, W. Michael ... Lafayette, CA
Celichowski, Christopher E.
Minneapolis, MN
Celio, Albert D. ... Rockledge, FL
Celio, Albert D., P.A. ... Rockledge, FL
Celio, Christopher M. ... East Hartford, CT
Celio, Michael D. ... Downey, CA
Celio, Michael D. ... Palo Alto, CA
Celio, Richard C. ... Anaheim, CA
Celis, Deborah A. ... Woodstock, VT
Cell, Charles P. ... Oregon, WI
Cella, Ansley Chapman ... Columbia, SC
Cella, Brian L. ... Walnut Creek, CA
Cella, Carl E. ... North Haven, CT
Cella, Catherine A. ... Minneapolis, MN
Cella, Charles H. ... Boston, MA
Cella, Christopher L. ... Walnut Creek, CA
Dallas, TX
Cella, Eugene J. ... Raleigh, NC
Cella, Glen T. ... Farmington, UT
Cella, James D. ... Media, PA
Cella, Joseph J. ... Southold, NY
Cella, Lange & Cella ... Laguna Hills, CA
Walnut Creek, CA
Cella, Mario V. ... Cold Spring Harbor, NY
Cella, Maryann F. ... Walnut Creek, CA
Cella, McKeon & Williams, P.C.
North Haven, CT
Cella, Paul W. ... Powhatan, VA
Cella, Peter R. ... New York, NY
Cella, Richard A. ... Leominster, MA
Cella, Thomas P. ... Hartford, CT
Manchester, CT
Cella-Donovan, Laura J. ... Boston, MA
Cellai, Carlo ... Boston, MA
Cellars, Ray L. ... Geneva, NE
Cellars, J. D. ... Anchorage, AK
Celles, George L., IV ... Natchitoches, LA
Celletti, Madeline M. ... Boston, MA
Celley, Walter J. ... Perrysburg, OH
Celli, Andrea E. ... Albany, NY
Celli, Craig J. ... Stoneham, MA
Celli, Kenneth D., A Professional Corporation
San Rafael, CA
Celli, Kenneth Dana ... San Rafael, CA
Celli and Leto, LLP ... Cherry Hill, NJ
Rosemont, PA

Celli, Marilyn C. ... Hesperia, CA
Celli, Michael G., Jr. ... Long Branch, NJ
Celli, Romy ... Santa Clara, CA
Celli, Rudolph L., Jr. ... Cherry Hill, NJ
Rosemont, PA
Celli, Schlossberg & Diamond, L.L.C.
Morristown, NJ
Celli, Vincent P. ... Morristown, NJ
Cellilli, Thomas H., III ... Omaha, NE
Cellini, Beatrice L. ... Chicago, IL
Cellini, Dando Belmondo, (P.C.)
Department of Justice,
Antitrust Division, GV
Cellini, Dina V. ... Bal Harbour, FL
Cellini, Richard J. ... Boston, MA
Cellini, Robert C. ... Chicago, IL
Cellino, Anna Marie ... Buffalo, NY
Cellino & Barnes, P.C. ... Buffalo, NY
Cellino, Ross M. ... Buffalo, NY
Cellino, Ross M., Jr. ... Buffalo, NY
Cello, Michael M. ... Chicago, IL
Cellon, Connie J. ... Gainesville, FL
Cellucci, Argeo P. ... Hudson, MA
Cellucci, Guy A. ... Philadelphia, PA
Cellucci, John H. ... Liberty Corner, NJ
Cellucci, Laura A. ... Baltimore, MD
Cellucci, Marsha H. ... Naperville, IL
Cellucci & Yacobellis ... Naperville, IL
Cellura, Davin Paul ... Newark, NJ
Cellura, Frank A. ... Grove City, OH
Celmins, Lat J. ... Scottsdale, AZ
Celniker, Craig I. ... San Diego, CA
Celniker, Jonathan R. ... San Francisco, CA
Celniker, Philip ... Buffalo, NY
CeloCruz, Maria T. ... Los Angeles, CA
Celona, Frank P. ... Rush, NY
Celona, John N. ... San Carlos, CA
Celone, David J. ... Thetford Center, VT
Celotti, Janice L. ... Newport Beach, CA
Celotto, Donald W. ... New Haven, CT
Celotto, Donald W., Jr. ... New Haven, CT
Celske, Daniel A. ... McHenry, IL
Celso, Nicholas, III ... Florham Park, NJ
Cemalatin, Iskender (Alex) ... New York, NY
Ceman, Richard E., Jr. ... Wauwatosa, WI
Cembalest, Stanley H. ... New York, NY
Cember, Alicia B. ... Nyack, NY
Cember & Cember, P.C. ... Nyack, NY
Cember, Jonathan P. ... New York, NY
Cember, M. Nathan ... Nyack, NY
Cember, Susan B. ... Kew Gardens, NY
Cember, William ... Nyack, NY
Cemore, Bernadette ... Santa Ana, CA
Cemovich, Robert L. ... McLean, VA
Cena, Celia Mamon ... Deerfield, IL
Cena, David A. ... San Jose, CA
Cena, Thomas A., Jr. ... Tacoma, WA
Cena, Timothy M. ... Chicago, IL
Cenar, Kara Eve Foster ... Chicago, IL
Cenar, Richard G., Jr. ... Chicago, IL
Cenatempo, Roxanne E. ... Roswell, GA
Cenatiempo & Ditta, LLP ... Houston, TX
Cenatiempo, Michael J. ... Houston, TX
Cenci, Cathleen S. ... Albany, NY
Cenci, Eileen ... Boston, MA
Cendali, Dale M. ... New York, NY
Cendejas, Robert E. ... Burbank, CA
Cender, E. Judson ... Mineola, NY
Cender, Joshua F. ... New York, NY
Cendoma, James F. ... Williamsport, PA
Cenerini, Frank J. ... Warwick, RI
Cenesky, Alenik, Stefanski & Pool
Johnson City, NY
Cenesky, John F. ... Johnson City, NY
Ceneviva, Dennis A. ... Meriden, CT
Ceniceros, Joseph F. ... Portland, OR
Ceniceros, Rebecca M. ... Sacramento, CA
Cenis, Michelle Renee ... New York, NY
Cenkus, Richard A. ... Chicago, IL
Cenname, Beverly Caryl ... Washington, DC
Cennamo, Louis W. ... Columbus, OH
Cennamo, Steven G. ... San Antonio, TX
Censoplano, Marie ... New York, NY
Censor, Martin A. ... New York, NY
Censor, Walter S. ... New York, NY
Censullo, Alfred ... Winthrop, MA
Centa, Emil J. ... Cleveland, OH
Centa, Ernest R. ... Cleveland, OH
Centanni, Amy E.
Department Of Veterans Affairs,
Office of the General Counsel, GV
Centanni, Gerald J. ... Verona, NJ
Centanni, Michael A. ... Eastlake, OH
Centano, Candace ... Philadelphia, PA
Centeio, Elena ... New York, NY
Centeio, José ... Boston, MA
Centella, Jill ... Chicago, IL
Centeno, Douglas J. ... Birmingham, AL
Centeno, H. Brian ... Chicago, IL
Centeno, Joseph J. ... Philadelphia, PA
Centeno, Susan D. ... Las Vegas, NV
Centeno-Rossy, Minerva I. ... San Juan, PR
Center, Brian ... Los Angeles, CA
Center, Charles G. ... Madison, WI
Center, Charles N. ... Atlanta, GA
Center, Charles N., P.C. ... Atlanta, GA
Center for Disability Law & Policy
Harrisburg, PA
Philadelphia, PA
Center for Education Law, Inc., The
Oklahoma City, OK
Center for Employment Law, The, P.C.
Roanoke, VA
Center for Family Law, The, P.A.
Pensacola, FL
Center For Professional Legal Services
Orlando, FL
Tampa, FL

Center, Harry B., II ... Saco, ME
Center, John D. ... Madison, WI
Center, Judith A. ... Washington, DC
Center, Lawrence ... Bethlehem, PA
Center, Rosemary F. ... Frankfort, KY
Center, Timothy J. ... Tallahassee, FL
Centers, Donald L. ... Carmel, IN
Indianapolis, IN
Centers, Judith A. ... Whittier, CA
Centers, Louise C. ... Southfield, MI
Centers, Roger D. ... Albertville, AL
Centi, Daniel J. ... Albany, NY
Centifanti, Dina L. ... Rochester Hills, MI
Centinario, Stephen J., Jr. ... Waukesha, WI
Centner, Charles W. ... Grosse Pointe Park, MI
Centner, David W. ... Grand Rapids, MI
Centner, Terence J. ... Athens, GA
Centofanti, Alfred Paul, III
San Diego, CA
Las Vegas, NV
Centofanti, Joseph M. ... Boston, MA
Centofanti, Kelly L. ... Milwaukee, WI
Centola, David D. ... Lantana, FL
Centola, Gary D. ... Uniondale, NY
Centola, Lawrence J., Jr.
New Orleans, LA
Centola, Robert J.
General Accounting Office,
Office of the General Counsel, GV
Centomini, Claudia T. ... Boston, MA
Centone, Anthony J. ... New York, NY
Centore, Christopher J. ... Syracuse, NY
Centorino, Diana Waterous
Fort Lauderdale, FL
Central Wyoming Law Associates, P.C.
Riverton, WY
Centre Business and Estate Planning, Law
Offices, LLP ... Costa Mesa, CA
Centrella, Nicholas M. ... Mount Laurel, NJ
Philadelphia, PA
Centrella, Scott S. ... Stamford, CT
Centrello, Lawrence Joseph ... Yonkers, NY
Centrich, Gary F. ... West Valley, NY
Centrilla-Silvia, JoAnn ... New Britain, CT
Centrone, C. Roland ... Massillon, OH
Centrone, Francis G. ... Canton, OH
Centurelli, Christopher H. ... Boston, MA
Cenzon-Duenas, Maria T. ... Hagåtña, GU
Ceparano, Laurie M. ... Binghamton, NY
Cepeda, Milagros A. ... Parsippany, NJ
Cepeda, Roger N. ... Tysons Corner, VA
Cepeda-Rodriguez, José A. ... San Juan, PR
Cepek, Gretchen ... Chicago, IL
Cepelewicz, Barry B. ... White Plains, NY
Cepenas, Gintaras P. ... Chicago, IL
Ceperley, Tim G. ... Los Angeles, CA
Cepero, Gustavo R. ... Coral Gables, FL
Cephas, Derrick D. ... New York, NY
Cepican, John E. ... Davenport, IA
Cepican, Patricia Rhodes ... Davenport, IA
Cepla, Mary Joan ... Deerfield, IL
Ceplenski, Donald S. ... San Diego, CA
Cepparulo, Albert J. ... New Hope, PA
Ceppi, Dario ... New York, NY
Ceppos, Larry A. ... Rockville, MD
Cepuritis, Talivaldis ... Chicago, IL
Cera, Carol A. ... Chicago, IL
Cera, Kenneth B. ... San Francisco, CA
Newton, MA
Cera, Solomon B. ... San Francisco, CA
Cerabino, Lisa Ann ... New York, NY
Cerabino, Thomas M. ... New York, NY
Cerabino-Hess, John J. ... New York, NY
Ceragioli, Raymond
Rancho Palos Verdes, CA
Ceramella, Michael A. ... Wichita, KS
Cerami, Vincent J. ... Port Orange, FL
Ceran, Allan E. ... Los Angeles, CA
Cerar, Jeffrey O. ... Woodbridge, VA
Cerasani, Denise A. ... New York, NY
Cerasano, Mark E. ... Glens Falls, NY
Cerasano, Stephanie M. ... Phoenix, AZ
Cerasi, Luciano A. ... Garden City, NY
Cerasia, Edward, II ... New York, NY
Cerasia, Lisa ... Weehawken, NJ
Ceraso, Amy Jo ... Pittsburgh, PA
Ceraso, John David ... New Kensington, PA
Ceraso, Jos. W. ... Vandergrift, PA
Ceraso, Louis H. ... New Kensington, PA
Ceraso, Thomas R. ... Greensburg, PA
Cerasoli, Steven J. ... Kaukauna, WI
Cerasuolo, Anthony J. ... New York, NY
Cerasuolo, Gary F. ... Houston, TX
Cerato, Joseph P. ... Charleston, SC
Cerato, Joseph P., P.A. ... Charleston, SC
Cerato, Lori J. ... Stroudsburg, PA
Ceraul, David J. ... Bangor, PA
Ceraulo, Andrew J. ... New York, NY
Ceravolo, Anthony J. ... Northbrook, IL
Ceravolo, Francis J. ... Freeport, NY
Ceravolo, MaryAnn ... Detroit, MI
Cerbins, Susan A. ... Milwaukee, WI
Cerbo, Michael P. ... Denver, CO
Cerbone, Adam P. ... Savannah, GA
Cerbone, Farrell & Joyce ... Mount Kisco, NY
Cerbone, Joseph A. ... Bronx, NY
Cerbone, Joseph J. ... Mount Kisco, NY
Cerbone, Mary E. ... New York, NY
Cerbone, Richard R. ... Florham Park, NJ
Cerbone, Vincent T. ... Mount Kisco, NY
Cercenko, Ariane E. ... Department of Defense,
Defense Legal Services Agency, GV
Cerchiara, Anthony V. ... Mount Vernon, NY
Cerchiara, Vincent F. ... Mount Vernon, NY
Cerchione, Gregory T. ... New York, NY
Cerchione, Richard R. ... Brooklyn, NY
Cerco, Andrew J., Jr. ... Newark, NJ
Cercone, Charles P. ... Lansing, MI

Cercone, David Brian .... Pittsburgh, PA
Cercone, David S. .... Pittsburgh, PA
Cercone, Paul A. .... Buffalo, NY
Cercone, Roland M. .... Buffalo, NY
Cercone, Sue Ann .... Fresno, CA
Cercone, Susan S. .... Aliquippa, PA
Cercone, William F., Jr. .... Pittsburgh, PA
Cercos, Theodore R. .... Los Angeles, CA
San Diego, CA
Temecula, CA
Las Vegas, NV
Cerda, Clarissa .... Chicago, IL
Cerda, David .... Chicago, IL
Cerda, David A. .... Chicago, IL
Cerdá, Elizabeth .... Boston, MA
Cerda, Marc J. .... San Francisco, CA
Cerda, Victor .... Seattle, WA
Cerefice, John W. .... Manahawkin, NJ
Cerefice, Louis R. .... Manahawkin, NJ
Cerefice, Robert L. .... Newark, NJ
Cereghini, Paul G. .... Phoenix, AZ
Cereghino, Jeffrey B. .... Alamo, CA
Cerel, Mark Gordon, Law Office of
Boston, MA
Cerel, Mark Gordon, Law Office of
Medfield, MA
Cerel, Mark Gordon, Law Office of
Walpole, MA
Cereola, Ronald J. .... Candia, NH
Ceres, Monica J. .... Middletown, NJ
Ceresa, John F. .... Ann Arbor, MI
Ceresa, Michele May .... Suffolk, VA
Ceresa, Raymond A. .... Sterling, VA
Ceresa, Raymond A., P.C. .... Sterling, VA
Cerese, Georgiann G.
Department of Justice,
Criminal Division, GV
Cereseto, Michael J. .... Los Angeles, CA
Ceresi, Diana Orantes .... Washington, DC
Ceresi, Frank J. .... Arlington, VA
Ceresia, George B., Jr. .... Troy, NY
Ceresia, Richard D. .... Troy, NY
Ceresia, Singiser & Malone .... Troy, NY
Ceresney, Ian .... New York, NY
Cereste, Saverio V. .... Fort Lee, NJ
Cerezo, Benny Frankie .... San Juan, PR
Cerezo, Francisco J. .... Miami, FL
Cerf, Christopher D. .... Washington, DC
Cergnul, John J. .... South Bend, IN
Cergol, Frank J. .... Cleveland, OH
Cergol, Frank R. .... Gainesville, FL
Cerha, Robert G. .... St. Louis, MO
Ceriani, Gary J. .... Denver, CO
Cerick, M. Richard .... Greenwich, CT
New York, NY
Cerick, Peter A. .... Herndon, VA
Cerick, Peter A., P.C. .... Herndon, VA
Cericola, Ralph J., Jr. .... Media, PA
Ceridan, Mary Zeller Wing
Louisville, KY
Ceridwen, W. Alex .... Sacramento, CA
Ceriello, Lawrence A. .... New York, NY
Cerilli, Benedetto A., Sr. .... Cranston, RI
Cerilli, John M. .... Pittsburgh, PA
Cerilli McGuirl & Bicki .... Providence, RI
Cerilli, Peter J. .... Providence, RI
Cerillo, Patrick J. .... Whitehouse Station, NJ
Cerillo, William A. .... San Francisco, CA
Cerini, Betty .... New York, NY
Cerini, Olga B. .... New York, NY
Cerio, Alexander A. .... Canastota, NY
Cerio, Arthur R. .... Cleveland, OH
Cerio, Arthur R., Co., L.P.A. .... Cleveland, OH
Cerio, Daniel A. .... Falls Church, VA
Cerio, Gary A. .... San Francisco, CA
Cerio, Joseph C., Jr. .... Holly Hill, FL
Cerio, Marian .... Canastota, NY
Cerio, Thomas J. .... Syracuse, NY
Cerio, Timothy M. .... Tampa, FL
Cerisano, Michael J. .... Little Falls, NJ
Cerise, Charles A., Jr. .... New Orleans, LA
Cerise, John P., (P.C.) .... New Orleans, LA
Cerise, Joseph J. .... New York, NY
Cerks, James A. .... Houston, TX
Cerkvenik, Paul D. .... Virginia, MN
Cermack, Thomas F., Jr. .... Ridgewood, NJ
Cermak, Adam Jason .... Alexandria, VA
Cermak, Anthony L. .... Sonoma, CA
Cermak, Bryan .... Troy, MI
Cleveland, OH
Cermak, Geo. R. .... Lakeside, MI
Cermak, John F., Jr. .... Los Angeles, CA
Cermak, Keith D. .... Clinton Township, MI
Cermak, Keith D., P.C.
Clinton Township, MI
Cermak, Thomas A. .... Walnut, CA
Cermanski, Joseph W. .... Conshohocken, PA
Cermelj, Mary R. .... Cleveland, OH
Cermignano, Gregory P. .... Chester, PA
Cerminara, Kathy L. .... Miami, FL
Cerminara, Laura .... De Pere, WI
Cerminaro, Anthony R. .... Pittsburgh, PA
Cerminaro, Deborah A. .... Brandon, FL
St. Petersburg, FL
Cerminaro, Dominic J. .... Highland Park, NJ
Cerminaro Law Office, P.A.
St. Petersburg, FL
Cerna, Catherine J. .... Fresno, CA
Cerna, Sandra M. .... Brooklyn, NY
Cerna, Thomas J. .... Jamaica, NY
Cerna-Fagan, Sarka .... New York, NY
Cernak, Steven J. .... Detroit, MI
Cernava, Leslie C. .... New York, NY
Cerne, Lisa .... Menlo Park, CA
Cerne, Neal W. .... Wheaton, IL
Cerne, Wence F. .... Oak Brook, IL
Cernek, Jeffrey T. .... Chicago, IL
Cernek, Thomas P., & Associates
Chicago, IL
Cernelich, John R. .... Cleveland, OH
Cernero, Joseph Ryan .... Sherman, TX
Cerney, Ann M. .... Stockton, CA
Cerney, J. Timothy .... Chicago, IL
Cerni, Michele G. .... Canfield, OH
Cerni, Terrence S. .... Milwaukee, WI
Cernicharo, Aimee G.
West Palm Beach, FL
Cernicky, Ann Hardman .... Washington, DC
Cerniglia, Nat .... Mineola, NY
Cerniglia, Sam J. .... San Diego, CA
Cerniglia, Sam J. .... Chicago, IL
Cerniglia, Stephen .... New York, NY
Cerniglia, Timothy W. .... New Orleans, LA
Cerniglia-Lowensen, Joan .... Baltimore, MD
Cernigliaro, Frank G. .... Carle Place, NY
Cernigliaro, Michael J. .... Asbury Park, NJ
Cernik, Christopher A. .... Albany, NY
Cernitz, Henry J. .... Garden City, NY
Cernius, Pota A. .... Newport Beach, CA
Cernius, Rimas F. .... Chicago, IL
Cernius, William J. .... Costa Mesa, CA
Cernivivo, Diane .... Chicago, IL
Cernosia, Arthur W. .... Burlington, VT
Cernugel, Joseph M. .... Joliet, IL
Cerny, Edward C., III .... Iselin, NJ
New York, NY
Cerny, Frank J., Jr. .... Schaumburg, IL
Cerny, Judith E. .... San Jose, CA
Cerny, Marilyn-Joy .... New Windsor, NY
Cerny, Milton .... Washington, DC
Cerny, Rebecca A. .... Chicago, IL
Cerny, Robert J. .... Los Angeles, CA
Cerny, Ross A. .... Los Angeles, CA
Cerny, Stephen A.
Department of Housing and Urban
Development,
Office of General Counsel, GV
Cernyar, Eric W. .... San Antonio, TX
Cero, Mark J. .... St. Louis, MO
Cerone, Jack P. .... Chicago, IL
Cerone, Michael A., Jr. .... Clifton, NJ
Cerone, Rudy J. .... New Orleans, LA
Cerow, Darcy Ann .... Phoenix, AZ
Cerow, Stephen P. .... New York, NY
Cerra, James M. .... Newton, NJ
Cerra, Joseph M. .... Rochelle Park, NJ
Cerra, Sharla .... Los Angeles, CA
Cerra, Suzanne M. .... Morristown, NJ
Cerra-Quinones, Hector L. .... San Juan, PR
Cerrato, Anthony J., Jr. .... Yonkers, NY
Cerrato, Dawes, Collins, Saker & Brown, A Professional Corporation .... Freehold, NJ
Cerrato, Dominick A. .... Freehold, NJ
Cerrato, Felix J., Jr. .... Easton, MA
Cerrato, John .... Enfield, CT
Cerrato, Michael A. .... Media, PA
Cerrato, Richard A. .... Bridgeport, CT
Cerrato, Robert Charles .... Yonkers, NY
Cerreta, Nancy G. .... San Francisco, CA
Cerretani, John L. .... Detroit, MI
Cerreto, Aniello D. .... Roseland, NJ
Cerreto, Anthony M. .... Mount Vernon, NY
Cerreto, Joseph D. .... Carmel, NY
Cerrezin, Richard M. .... Cleveland, OH
Cerri, Vincent J. .... Joliet, IL
Cerrillo, Byron M. .... Olathe, KS
Cerrina, Michael H. .... Los Angeles, CA
Cerritelli, E. Gregory .... Derby, CT
Cerrito, Christina M. .... New York, NY
Cerrito, Christopher M. .... Stamford, CT
Cerrito, D. Vincent .... Schenectady, NY
Cerrito, F. Dominic .... New York, NY
Cerro, Kristine R. .... Fresno, CA
Cerrone, Cheryl Ann .... Pittsburgh, PA
Cerrone, Edward D. .... New Orleans, LA
Cerrone, Gary David .... Canton, OH
Cerrone, George J., Jr. .... Denver, CO
Cerrone, Kimberlie L. .... Hillsborough, CA
Cerrone, Stacey C. S. .... New Orleans, LA
Cerrone, Victoria E. .... Orlando, FL
Cerruti & Adams, L.C.
Salt Lake City, UT
Cerruti, Thomas E. K.
Salt Lake City, UT
Cersonsky, M. H. .... Houston, TX
Certa, Cythnia A. .... Phoenix, AZ
Certa, Pellegrino L. .... Seattle, WA
Certain, Gary Todd .... New York, NY
Certain, Harry J. .... Marion, IN
Certilman Balin Adler & Hyman, LLP
East Meadow, NY
Certilman, Morton L. .... East Meadow, NY
Certilman, Steven A. .... Stamford, CT
New York, NY
Certilman, Steven A., P.C., Law Office
Stamford, CT
Certner, David M. .... Washington, DC
Certo, Anthony J. .... Niagara Falls, NY
Certo, Cynthia M. .... Philadelphia, PA
Certo, Peter R. .... Dayton, OH
Cerullo, Alfred Carmine, III
New York, NY
Cerullo, Arthur A. .... Portland, ME
Cerullo, Datte & Wallbillich, P.C.
Pottsville, PA
Cerullo, Joseph P., Jr. .... Yuba City, CA
Cerullo, Martin J. .... Pottsville, PA
Cerullo, Robert J. .... New Carrollton, MD
Rockville, MD
Cerullo, Thomas C. .... Metairie, LA
Cerullo, Thomas C., A Professional Law Corporation .... Metairie, LA
Cerulo, David .... Everett, MA
Cerulo, Gregory A. .... Peoria, IL
Springfield, IL
Cerundolo, Lisa M. .... Boston, MA
Cerundolo, Pat A. .... Boston, MA
Ceruolo, John R. .... Boston, MA
Cerussi, Charles A. .... Middletown, NJ
Cerussi, Michael A., Jr. .... White Plains, NY
Cerussi & Spring, A Professional Corporation .... Greenwich, CT
Stamford, CT
White Plains, NY
Cerussi, Thomas F. .... Greenwich, CT
Cerutti, Dino .... New York, NY
Cerutti, Larry A. .... Costa Mesa, CA
Cerutti, Patrick B. .... Spokane, WA
Ceruzzi, John W. .... Jacksonville, NC
Ceruzzi, Leonard A. .... Washington, DC
Ceruzzi, Louis L., Jr. .... Fairfield, CT
Ceruzzi, Patricia A. .... New York, NY
Cerv, Marleen J. .... La Jolla, CA
Cervantes & Associates .... St. Louis, MO
Cervantes, Carole M. .... Chicago, IL
Cervantes, David .... Modesto, CA
Cervantes, Edward J. .... Bettendorf, IA
Cervantes, Esperanza V. .... Los Angeles, CA
Cervantes, Felipe .... Escondido, CA
Cervantes, Jaime M. .... Los Angeles, CA
Cervantes, Leonard P. .... St. Louis, MO
Cervantes, Lily .... Salinas, CA
Cervantes, Paulina A. .... Miami, FL
Cervantes, Phillip A. .... St. Louis, MO
Cervantez, Eve Hedy .... San Francisco, CA
Cervantez, Thomas J. .... San Francisco, CA
Cervas, Joseph C. .... Palos Hills, IL
Cervase, John .... Newark, NJ
Cervay, Jack A. .... Dayton, OH
Cervelli, Richard I., (P.A.) .... Naples, FL
Cervello, Mark C. .... Girard, OH
Cerven, David .... East Chicago, IN
Merrillville, IN
Cerven, Jennifer M. .... Chicago, IL
Cervenak, James E. .... Washington, DC
Vienna, VA
Cervenka, Alan R. .... Houston, TX
Cervenka, Albert W. .... Findlay, OH
Cervenka, Dan F. .... Hutto, TX
Cervenka, Mark A. .... Houston, TX
Cerveny, David J. .... Boston, MA
Cerveny, John X.
Occupational Safety and Health Review
Commission,
Office of the General Counsel, GV
Cerveny, Joseph F. .... Clarendon Hills, IL
Cerveny, Kathleen L. .... Falls Church, VA
Cerveny, Laurie A. .... Boston, MA
Cervera, D. Robert .... Boston, MA
Cervera, Nicholas J. .... Troy, AL
Cervera & Ralph .... Troy, AL
Cerveris, Steven R. .... Toluca Lake, CA
Cervi, Gregg A. .... Department of the Navy,
Office of the Judge Advocate General, GV
Cervin, Bennett W. .... Dallas, TX
Cervini, Joseph Peter, Jr. .... New York, NY
Cervini, Michael A. .... Jackson Heights, NY
Cervino, Daniele .... Hackensack, NJ
Cervizzi, Laura J. .... Boston, MA
Cervon, Kathryn L. .... Washington, DC
Cervone, Anthony Louis .... Cranston, RI
Cervone, Frank P. .... Philadelphia, PA
Cervone, John B., III .... Waltham, MA
Cervone, Joseph V. .... Poughkeepsie, NY
Cervone Law Firm .... Cranston, RI
Cervone, William P. .... Gainesville, FL
Cervoni, Petra I. .... Springfield, MA
Cervoni, Stephanie K. .... White Plains, NY
Cerwin, Todd R. .... Kings Mountain, NC
Cerwinski, Robert V. .... New York, NY
Ceryak, David V. .... Indianapolis, IN
Cerza, Frank J. .... Hackensack, NJ
New York, NY
Cesani Gonzalez, Roman R. .... Mayaguez, PR
Cesar, Roy R. .... Buffalo, NY
Cesar, Timothy .... Madison, WI
Cesarano, Gregory M. .... Miami, FL
Cesarano, Marilyn J. W., P.A.
Coral Gables, FL
Miami, FL
Cesarano, Marilyn J. W. .... Miami, FL
Cesarano, Michael C. .... Miami, FL
Cesarano, Sheila M. .... Miami, FL
Cesare, Andrew J. .... Solana Beach, CA
Cesare, Carmela M. .... Shepherdstown, WV
Cesare, Christine B. .... New York, NY
Cesare, Lauren Watson .... San Jose, CA
Cesare, Lisa A. .... New York, NY
Cesare, Lucy K. .... Albany, NY
Cesaretti, Alice Good .... Trenton, NJ
Cesaretti, Carol A. .... Oakbrook Terrace, IL
Cesaretti, Jonathan M. .... Chicago, IL
Cesaretti, Marino A. .... Las Vegas, NV
Cesari, D. Ralph .... San Francisco, CA
Cesari, John .... San Rafael, CA
Cesari and McKenna, L.L.P. .... Boston, MA
Cesari, Paul N. .... San Francisco, CA
Cesari, Robert A. .... Boston, MA
Cesari, Werner and Moriarty, A Professional Corporation .... San Francisco, CA
Cesarik, Joseph M. .... Cleveland, OH
Cesarini, Marie .... New York, NY
Cesario, Cheryl D. .... Chicago, IL
Cesario, Deborah R.G. .... Escondido, CA
Cesario, John R. .... Geneva, IL
Cesario, Joseph T., (P.C.) .... Hinsdale, IL
Cesario, Richard L. .... Bloomington, MN
Cesario & Walker .... Hinsdale, IL
Cesario, Wayne V. .... Chicago, IL
Cesena, James H. .... Orange, CA
Cesena & Lee .... Orange, CA
Ceshker, Gregory L. .... Austin, TX
Dallas, TX
Ceshker, Gregory L., P.C. .... Austin, TX
Dallas, TX
Ceshker, T. Alan .... Beaumont, TX
Corpus Christi, TX
Houston, TX
Cesna, Inely Cassia .... McLean, VA
Cesner, Robert E., Jr. .... Worthington, OH
Cespedes, Anthony J. .... Cuyahoga Falls, OH
Cespedes, Carol .... Morristown, NJ
Céspedes, Ernesto .... Fort Lauderdale, FL
Cespedes, Maria E. .... Miami, FL
Cespedes, Maria E., P.A. .... Miami, FL
Céspedes, Samuel T. .... San Juan, PR
Céspedes-Sabater, Samuel T.
San Juan, PR
Cespiva, Brian D. .... Alexandria, LA
Cessac, Christopher .... Hurst, TX
Cessante, Connie M. .... Detroit, MI
Cessante, David M. .... Detroit, MI
Cessar, Robert S. .... Pittsburgh, PA
Cessar, Scott D. .... Pittsburgh, PA
Cessario, Ralph .... Buffalo, NY
Cessna, Stephen W. .... London, KY
Cesso, Stephen .... Boston, MA
Cesta, Kenneth J. .... Short Hills, NJ
Cestare, Thomas W. .... Honolulu, HI
Cestari, Arnold J., Jr. .... Mattapoisett, MA
Cestari, Karen S. .... New York, NY
Cestari, Kenneth C. .... Washington, DC
Cestero, Jorge M. .... West Palm Beach, FL
Cestero, Jose R. .... San Juan, PR
Cestero, Ramon A. .... San Juan, PR
Cestero, Ricardo P. .... Los Angeles, CA
Cestero-Rodriguez, Herman .... San Juan, PR
Cestero Rodriguez, José A. .... San Juan, PR
Cestia, Burton E., Jr. .... New Iberia, LA
Cestone, Joseph J. .... White Plains, NY
Cetina, Hernan O. .... San Diego, CA
Cetina, Michael S. .... Oakbrook Terrace, IL
Cetina & Moreschi, P.C. .... Chicago, IL
Joliet, IL
Oakbrook Terrace, IL
Wheaton, IL
Cetina, Theresa Mary .... New York, NY
Cetkovic, Dragan M. .... Boston, MA
Cetlin, Dana A. .... Natick, MA
Cetlin, Lisa F. .... San Francisco, CA
Cetrone, Michael T. .... Boston, MA
Cetrulo & Capone, LLP .... Boston, MA
New York, NY
Providence, RI
Cetrulo, Lawrence G. .... Boston, MA
New York, NY
Providence, RI
Cetrulo, M. Frances .... Denver, CO
Cetrulo, Robert B. .... Covington, KY
Cetrulo, Robert C. .... Covington, KY
Cetrulo, Robert C., P.S.C. .... Covington, KY
Florence, KY
Independence, KY
Newport, KY
Cetrulo, Susanne M. .... Covington, KY
Cettei, Donna L. .... Haddonfield, NJ
Cettel, Robert W. .... Cincinnati, OH
Cetti, August F.
Federal Mine Safety and Health Review
Commission,
Office of the Administrative Law Judges, GV
Cetti, Charles L. .... Pensacola, FL
Cetti, William E. .... Cartersville, GA
Ceva, Albert J. .... Bronx, NY
Cevallos, Anna P. .... Cherry Hill, NJ
Cevasco, Andrew J. .... Hackensack, NJ
Cevidanes, Maria del Carmen
San Juan, PR
Ceynar, Frank E. .... Burlington, VT
Cezeaux, Andrea M. .... Boston, MA
Cha, Don D. .... Denver, CO
Cha, Eric .... Los Angeles, CA
Cha, Hyunsook Agnes .... Ridgefield Park, NJ
Cha, Jason S. .... Los Angeles, CA
Cha, John S. .... Encino, CA
Cha, Kathryn T. .... Chicago, IL
Cha, Steve Sangchul .... New York, NY
Cha, Yang .... New York, NY
Chaas, Michelle G. .... Buffalo, NY
Chabak, David J. .... Flemington, NJ
Chabal, Matthew, III .... Harrisburg, PA
Chaban, Marvin .... Lombard, IL
Chaban, Mitchell S. .... Chicago, IL
Chabarek, Brian J. .... Plainsboro, NJ
Chabasinski, Theodore .... Berkeley, CA
Chaben, Shelley .... New York, NY
Chaber, Madelyn J. .... San Francisco, CA
Chaberski, Kirk S. .... Nashville, TN
Chaberski, Stephen G. .... Hackensack, NJ
Chabinsky, Steven R. .... Department of Justice,
Federal Bureau of Investigation, GV
Chablais, Jean-Daniel .... Washington, DC
Chabler, Allan J. .... Toledo, OH
Chabner, Brandon S. .... Los Angeles, CA
Boston, MA
Chabner, Howard L. .... San Francisco, CA
Chabon, Gregory M. .... Greensboro, NC
Chabon, Robert S. .... Washington, DC
Chabora, Carolyn .... Palm City, FL
Chabora, Robert A. .... Montville, NJ
Chabot, Daniel T. .... Haverhill, MA
Chabot, David A. .... Hartford, CT
Chabot, David G. .... Hartford, CT
Chabot, Elliot C. .... House of Representatives,
Committee Legal Personnel, GV
Chabot, Herbert L.
United States Tax Court, GV

Chabot, Jo-Ann
Office of Personnel Management, Compensation Division, GV
Chabot, Joseph E. ... Burlingame, CA
Chabot, Kelly Anne ... Rocky Hill, CT
Chabot, Philip L., Jr. ... Washington, DC
Chabot, Philip Vernon ... Hamden, CT
Chabot, Rae Lee ... Detroit, MI
Chabot, Ralph D. ... Ventura, CA
Chabot, Raymond J. ... Danielson, CT
Chabot, Richard R. ... Des Moines, IA
Chabot, Steven J. ... Cincinnati, OH
Chabra, Nicholas J., Jr. ... Arlington, VA
Chabra, Raj P. ... Lafayette, CA
Chabraja, Michael A. ... Chicago, IL
Chabraja, Mitchell P. ... Indianapolis, IN
Chabre, Gustave S. ... Newport Beach, CA
Chabrow, Michael P. ... Bethesda, MD
Fairfax, VA
Chabrow, Penn B. ... Miami, FL
Chabus, Lance P.
Commodity Futures Trading Commission, Division of Enforcement, GV
Chace, Charles E. ... Omaha, NE
Chace, Dean W. ... Edison, NJ
Chace, Diane R. ... New Britain, CT
Chace, N. Jameson ... Portsmouth, RI
Chace, Nathan W. ... Providence, RI
Chace Ruttenberg & Freedman, LLP
Providence, RI
Chace, Stephen D. ... Alexandria, VA
Chach, Kristin ... Stamford, CT
Chachan & Yang ... New York, NY
Chachas, George G. ... La Jolla, CA
Chachas, Gregory J. ... Ely, NV
Chachas, Gregory John, Ltd. ... Ely, NV
Chachère, Matthew J. ... Bronx, NY
Chachere, Ronald L. ... Corpus Christi, TX
Chachere-Compton, Sonya ... Decatur, GA
Chachis, Elizabeth M. ... Philadelphia, PA
Chachkes, Alex V. ... New York, NY
Chachkes, Kari E. ... New York, NY
Chachkin, Joseph
Federal Communications Commission, Office of Administrative Law Judges, GV
Chachkin, Norman J. ... New York, NY
Chachkin, Sherry G. ... Nutley, NJ
Chacker, Edward F. ... Philadelphia, PA
Chacker, Hilarie ... New York, NY
Chackes, Kenneth M. ... St. Louis, MO
Chackman, Steven J. ... Hollywood, FL
Chacko, A. Sheba ... Washington, DC
Chacko, Anna S. ... Hicksville, NY
Chacko, Ray J. ... Boise, ID
Chack-On, Jozette V. ... Tampa, FL
Chacksfield, Roger R. ... Cincinnati, OH
Chaclas, Angelo N. ... Stamford, CT
Chacon, Gerald G., Jr. ... Palo Alto, CA
Chacon, Lawrence E. ... Albuquerque, NM
Chacon, M. David, II ... Albuquerque, NM
Chacon, Matthew L. ... Albuquerque, NM
Chacón, Miguel A. ... San Jose, CA
Chacon, Rene A. ... San Francisco, CA
Chacon, Zacarias R. ... Chicago, IL
Chaconas, Matthew N. ... Chicago, IL
Chad, Nancy A. ... Tampa, FL
Chadakoff, Richard L. ... New York, NY
Chadbourne, Deborah Ann ... Irving, TX
Chadbourne, James D. ... Huntsville, AL
Chadbourne, O'Neill, Thomson, Whalen & Fitzgerald ... Sleepy Hollow, NY
Chadbourne & Parke LLP
Los Angeles, CA
Washington, DC
New York, NY
Chadd, Alan J. ... Charlotte, NC
Chadd, Charles M. ... Chicago, IL
Chadd, Darren C. ... Indianapolis, IN
Chadderdon, James R.
Colorado Springs, CO
Chadderdon, James R., P.C.
Colorado Springs, CO
Chadderdon, Joanne Posey ... Houston, TX
Chadderton, Harry J., Jr. ... Miami, FL
Chaddha, Anil Kumar ... Rochester, NY
Chaddock, Susan Clark ... Minerva, OH
Chadeayne, Burns & Leachman ... Tracy, CA
Chadek, Robert A. ... Milwaukee, WI
Chadha, Jay M. ... New Orleans, LA
Houston, TX
Chadic, Jeffery A. ... San Francisco, CA
Chadick, Earl Buddy, Jr. ... Fayetteville, AR
Chadick, Gary R. ... Woodland Hills, CA
Chadick, Mark Braden ... Pine Bluff, AR
Chadick, Mary Susan
Department of Defense, Defense Legal Services Agency, GV
Chadick, Terrell C. ... Texarkana, TX
Chadick, Terri Dill ... Fayetteville, AR
Chadick, Vincent O. ... Fayetteville, AR
Chadinha, Michael G. ... Brockton, MA
Chadrjian, Nancy ... Bronx, NY
Chadroff, Sy ... Aventura, FL
Chadroff, Terminello & Terminello
Miami, FL
Chadsey, Deborah J. ... Buffalo, NY
Chadsey, Phillip D. ... Portland, OR
Chadurjian, Frank ... Purchase, NY
Chadurjian, Mark F. ... Essex Junction, VT
Chadwell, Ellen T. ... Naples, FL
Chadwell, Greg ... Paoli, IN
Chadwell, James D. ... Springfield, MA
Chadwell, Kenneth M. ... Crossville, TN
Chadwell, Kenneth R. ... Detroit, MI
Chadwell, Robert G. ... Seattle, WA
Chadwell, Steele R. ... Princeton, NJ
Chadwell, Steele R. ... Trenton, NJ
Chadwick & Associates, P.A.
Minneapolis, MN
Chadwick, Bruce M. ... Washington, DC
Chadwick, C. Clifford ... Sylvan Lake, MI
Chadwick, Carol Lee Anderson
New Hartford, NY
Chadwick, Charles M. ... Union Bridge, MD
Chadwick, Charles R. ... Fayetteville, AR
Chadwick, Daniel Linus ... Hamilton, MO
Chadwick, Debra Maller ... St. Petersburg, FL
Chadwick, Donald E. ... Northridge, CA
Chadwick, Douglas A. ... Orange, CA
Chadwick, Eric Hugh ... Minneapolis, MN
Chadwick, G. A. "Jay", IV
Washington, DC
Chadwick, G. A., Jr. ... Boyds, MD
Chadwick, Gary W. ... Wilmington, NC
Chadwick, Geneva C. ... Oberlin, OH
Chadwick, George W., II ... San Jose, CA
Chadwick, Glenn D. ... Glenwood Springs, CO
Chadwick, Harry R., Jr.
St. Petersburg Beach, FL
Chadwick, James C. ... Dallas, TX
Chadwick, James M. ... Palo Alto, CA
Chadwick, Jennifer Lynn ... Rochester, NY
Chadwick, Jon Scot ... Harrisburg, PA
Chadwick, Keith A. ... Chicago, IL
Chadwick, Kenneth Eric ... Fairfax, VA
Richmond, VA
Chadwick, Kyle E. ... Washington, DC
Chadwick, Lauren B. ... Fort Worth, TX
Chadwick, Libbey, Szilagyi & Stone
Bristol, CT
East Hartford, CT
Hartford, CT
Chadwick, Mark Edward ... Tucson, AZ
Chadwick, Marta Philpott
Newburyport, MA
Chadwick, Mary E. ... Waukegan, IL
Chadwick, Megan E. ... Waukegan, IL
Chadwick, Norman L. ... Brewton, AL
Chadwick, Peter ... Hartford, CT
Chadwick, R. O'Neal, Jr. ... New Orleans, LA
Chadwick, Raymond G., Jr. ... Augusta, GA
Chadwick, Richard J. ... Minneapolis, MN
Chadwick, Robert ... Frankfort, KY
Chadwick, Robert G., Jr. ... Addison, TX
Chadwick, Robert J. ... Santa Clara, CA
Chadwick, Robert P. ... Tampa, FL
Chadwick, Robert T. ... Rochelle, IL
Chadwick, Robin A. ... New York, NY
Chadwick, Roger C., Jr. ... Beverly, MA
Chadwick, Ryan ... Houston, TX
Chadwick, Scott R. ... Hartford, CT
Chadwick, Stephen F., Jr.
Bainbridge Island, WA
Chadwick, Sturgis E., III ... Chicago, IL
Chadwick, Taylor & Eisenbraun
Oklahoma City, OK
Addison, TX
Dallas, TX
Chadwick, Vernon H. ... Jackson, MS
Chadwick, Washington, Olters, Moriarty & Lynn, P.C. ... Bethesda, MD
Fairfax, VA
Richmond, VA
Chadwick, Washington & Olters, P.C.
Washington, DC
Chadwick, William G., Jr. ... Oakton, VA
Chadwick, William J. ... Los Angeles, CA
Chadwick Thompson, Lisa ... Fairfield, NJ
Chae, Alexander C. ... Houston, TX
Chae, Don B. ... Dallas, TX
Chae, Helen Heekyong ... Los Angeles, CA
Chae, Meryl K. ... Los Angeles, CA
Chae, Sonia U. ... Chicago, IL
Chae, Susan K. ... Chicago, IL
Chae-Banks, Yunhui ... New York, NY
Chael, Paul R. ... Valparaiso, IN
Chaet, Barry L. ... Milwaukee, WI
Chaet, Louis ... Skokie, IL
Chaet, Tracy M. ... Highland Park, IL
Chafe, Marie Chadeayne ... Boston, MA
Chafee, Gregory D. ... Deerfield, IL
Chafee, John B. "Jody", Jr. ... Seattle, WA
Chafer, Anne E.
Securities and Exchange Commission, Office of the General Counsel, GV
Chafetz, Barry R. ... Chicago, IL
Chafetz, Jay ... Walnut Creek, CA
Chafetz, Marc Edward ... Washington, DC
Chafetz, Samuel D. ... Memphis, TN
Chaff, Sandra L. ... Philadelphia, PA
Chaffe, Maja Dagny ... Seattle, WA
Chaffe, McCall, Phillips, Toler & Sarpy, L.L.P. ... Baton Rouge, LA
New Orleans, LA
Chaffe, Roger L. ... Richmond, VA
Chaffee Alexander, A Professional Corporation
Grosse Pointe, MI
Chaffee, Carol L. ... Spokane, WA
Chaffee, David R. ... Santa Ana, CA
Chaffee, Douglas B. ... Fullerton, CA
Chaffee, Jay Allen ... Houston, TX
Chaffee, John E. ... Greenwich, CT
Chaffee, Kenneth H. ... Shelburne Falls, MA
Chaffee, M. Kate ... Minneapolis, MN
Chaffee & Marshall, A Prof. Corp.
Fullerton, CA
Chaffee, Michele R. ... Chicago, IL
Chaffee, Philip E. ... Grosse Pointe, MI
Chaffetz, Hammond E. ... Chicago, IL
Chaffetz, Peter R. ... Los Angeles, CA
New York, NY
Chaffey, George ... Walnut Creek, CA
Chaffier, Mary ... Philadelphia, PA
Chaffin, Ann ... Houston, TX
Chaffin, Bill M. ... Davis, OK
Chaffin & Chapman-Plumb, P.C.
Tahlequah, OK
Chaffin, Christopher C. ... Houston, TX
Chaffin, David B. ... Boston, MA
Chaffin, Donald J. ... Ardmore, OK
Chaffin, Eric T. ... Pittsburgh, PA
Chaffin, Harvey L. ... Tahlequah, OK
Chaffin & Hurst ... Houston, TX
Chaffin, James E., Jr. ... Columbia, SC
Chaffin, John E. ... Carlsbad, CA
Chaffin, Julie E. ... Jackson, MS
Chaffin, Kevin D. ... Oxnard, CA
Chaffin Law Firm, The, A Professional Corporation ... Houston, TX
Chaffin, Mary D. ... Portland, OR
Chaffin, Michael R. ... Chickasha, OK
Oklahoma City, OK
Chaffin, R. Garry ... Nashville, TN
Chaffin, Randy S. ... Cookeville, TN
Chaffin, Rebecca S. ... Charlotte, NC
Chaffin, Richard E. ... Baton Rouge, LA
Chaffin, Robert A. ... Houston, TX
Chaffin, Robert F. ... Glenwood Springs, CO
Chaffin, Ronald M. ... Omaha, NE
Chaffin, Shelley K. ... Anchorage, AK
Chaffin, Sheri S. ... Yorba Linda, CA
Chaffin, Sidney H. ... Caruthersville, MO
Chaffin, Steven E. ... Marion, OH
Chaffin, Thomas F. ... San Francisco, CA
San Jose, CA
Chaffin, Verner F. ... Athens, GA
Chaffin, W. Ronald ... Miami, FL
Chaffin, William A., Jr. ... Sacramento, CA
Chaffin, William M. ... Clarksdale, MS
Chaffiotte, Francis X. ... Parsippany, NJ
Chaffo, John L. ... Pittsburgh, PA
Chafiian, Liza A. ... New York, NY
Chafin, Andrew K. ... Portsmouth, VA
Chafin, Augustus B., Jr. ... Abingdon, VA
Lebanon, VA
Chafin, Bradley Sean ... Little Rock, AR
Chafin, Chafin & Ely, P.C. ... Abingdon, VA
Lebanon, VA
Chafin, David C. ... Vero Beach, FL
Chafin, Debra V. ... Clarksburg, WV
Chafin, H. Truman ... Williamson, WV
Chafin, J. Scott ... Edinburg, TX
Chafin, James H. ... Albuquerque, NM
Chafin, James Troy, III ... McDonough, GA
Chafin, Janet Douvas ... Houston, TX
Chafin, John T. ... Prestonsburg, KY
Chafin, Lafe C. ... Huntington, WV
Chafin, Matthew Henry ... Columbus, OH
Chafin, Nancy A. ... Houston, TX
Chafin, Robert G. ... Wayne, WV
Chafin, Teresa M. ... Lebanon, VA
Chafitz, Harold N. ... Pearl River, NY
Chafty, Michael D. ... Detroit, MI
Chagal, Deborah Glaser ... Chicago, IL
Chagares, Michael A. ... Newark, NJ
Chagaris, Arthur N. ... Hackensack, NJ
Chagaris, Christopher G. ... Davidson, NC
Chagi, Gary B. ... Palos Verdes Estates, CA
Chagnon, Andre J. ... Northridge, CA
Chagnon, Kathleen A. ... St. Paul, MN
Chagnon, Maurice J. ... Detroit, MI
Chagnon, Roger G. ... Ellsworth, ME
Chagnot, Jeffrey L. ... Youngstown, OH
Chagonjian, Beth Fai ... San Francisco, CA
Chagrin, Susan M. ... Woodbridge, NJ
Chaharbaghi, Stephanie ... Washington, DC
Chahin, Sonia E. ... La Canada Flintridge, CA
Chahine, Steve S. ... Los Angeles, CA
Chahrouri, Katherine ... Atlanta, GA
Chai, Henry K., II ... Salt Lake City, UT
Chai, Huali G. ... San Jose, CA
Chai, Huali G., A Professional Corporation
San Jose, CA
Chaice, Herbert H. ... New York, NY
Chaiet, Clifford P. ... Jericho, NY
Chaiet, David S. ... Hollywood, FL
Chaiet, Donna S. ... New York, NY
Chaiet, Paul F. ... Freehold, NJ
Chaifetz, David H. ... Danbury, CT
Chaifetz, Jill ... New York, NY
Chaifetz, Lawrence B. ... New York, NY
Chaifetz, Malcolm ... New York, NY
Chaifetz, Richard I. ... Columbia, MD
Chaifetz, Stephen K. ... Manhasset, NY
Chaika and Chaika ... Providence, RI
Chaika, Daniel E. ... Providence, RI
Chaika, William Y. ... Providence, RI
Chaikan, Lisa Ann ... Washington, DC
Chaikelson, Steven E. ... New York, NY
Chaiken, Brian W. ... Aventura, FL
Chicago, IL
Chaiken & Chaiken, P.C. ... Dallas, TX
Chaiken, David ... Chicago, IL
Chaiken, Frank D. ... Cincinnati, OH
Chaiken, Fredric ... Atlanta, GA
Chaiken, Joseph ... Philadelphia, PA
Chaiken, Joseph & Associates, P.C.
Philadelphia, PA
Chaiken, Kenneth B. ... Dallas, TX
Chaiken, Mark E. ... New York, NY
Chaiken, Michael J. ... Dallas, TX
Chaiken, Paul W. ... Bangor, ME
Chaiken, Robert L. ... Dallas, TX
Chaiken, Steve ... New York, NY
Chaikin, Adam E. ... Santa Monica, CA
Chaikin, Bonnie Patricia ... Mineola, NY
Chaikin & Chaikin ... New York, NY
Chaikin, Donald J. ... Washington, DC
Rockville, MD
Chaikin, Douglas A. ... Morgan Hill, CA
Chaikin, Ellen R. ... Wilmington, DE
Chaikin, Eric B. ... New York, NY
Chaikin, Lee D. ... New York, NY
Chaikin, Lisa ... Washington, DC
Chaikin & Sherman, P.C.
Washington, DC
Rockville, MD
Falls Church, VA
Chaikin, Stacey ... New York, NY
Chaikovsky, Yar R. ... Los Angeles, CA
Chaille, L. Harold ... El Centro, CA
Chaimov, Gregory A. ... Salem, OR
Chaimowitz, Bruce A.
Fort Lauderdale, FL
Chaimson, Frederic I. ... Chicago, IL
Chaimson & Kanter ... Chicago, IL
Chain, Anne Whatley ... Philadelphia, PA
Chain, Donald J. ... Cincinnati, OH
Chain, Risa Greenberg ... Little Neck, NY
Chain, Younger, Cohn, & Stiles
Bakersfield, CA
Chai-Onn, Robert R. ... Los Angeles, CA
Chaires, Annette ... Austin, TX
Chaires, Gregory A. ... Orlando, FL
Chaires & Maples, P.C. ... Austin, TX
Chaires, Susan C. ... Washington, DC
Chaires, William Michael ... Baltimore, MD
Chairez & Associates ... Irvine, CA
Chairez, Joseph L. ... Irvine, CA
Chairman, Justin W. ... Philadelphia, PA
Chairs, Mary P. ... Lancaster, PA
Chairs, Thomas M. ... Camp Hill, PA
Chais, Richard I. ... Gaithersburg, MD
Chais, Wrenn E. ... Los Angeles, CA
Chaisson, David P. ... Baltimore, MD
Chaisson, Joan M. ... Newton, MA
Chaisson, Joel T. ... Destrehan, LA
Chaisson, John M. ... Sunnyvale, CA
Chaisson, Maria M. ... Destrehan, LA
Chaisson, Robert A. ... Hahnville, LA
Chait, Arnold H. ... Morristown, NJ
Chait, Barry S. ... Newark, NJ
Chait, Bruce H. ... West Orange, NJ
Chait, Charice D. ... Plymouth Meeting, PA
Chait, Cristina M. ... Phoenix, AZ
Chait, Gregory Marshall ... Atlanta, GA
Chait, Jere N. ... Miami, FL
Chait, Leland H. ... Chicago, IL
Chait, Linda R. ... Brooklyn, NY
Chait and Maggio ... Rochester, NY
Chait, Martin J. ... Austin, TX
Chait, Mitchell A. ... Rochester, NY
Chait, Richard E. ... Homestead, FL
Chait, Robert J. ... Los Angeles, CA
Chait, Steven M. ... Pontiac, MI
Chait, Steven M., P.L.L.C. ... Detroit, MI
Pontiac, MI
Chait, Trevor Hilton ... Phoenix, AZ
Chaiten, Lorie A. ... Chicago, IL
Chaitin, Melissa A. ... Los Angeles, CA
Chaitman, Helen Davis ... Somerset, NJ
New York, NY
Chaitovitz, Samuel A.
Federal Labor Relations Authority, Office of the Administrative Law Judges, GV
Chaivoe, Nick ... Portland, OR
Chaix, John E. ... Costa Mesa, CA
Chaiyarachta, Charles R. ... Los Angeles, CA
Chaja, Michael F. ... Chicago, IL
Chajet, Henry ... Washington, DC
Chajson, Howard A. ... Pittsburgh, PA
Chakales, Barbara B. ... Atlanta, GA
Chakan, John M. ... New York, NY
Chakansky, Michael I. ... New York, NY
Chakeres, Andrew A.
United States Postal Service, Mid-Atlantic Office, GV
Chakeres, James G. ... Albuquerque, NM
Chakerian, Gerald H.
Federal Communications Commission, Common Carrier Bureau, GV
Chakhtoura, Raymonda A. ... Melbourne, FL
Chaklos, Jungerheld, Hahn & Washburn, P.C.
Saginaw, MI
Chaklos, Robert G., Jr.
Farmington Hills, MI
Chaklos, Robert G., Sr. ... Saginaw, MI
Chaklos, William D. ... Detroit, MI
Chakmak, John ... Claremont, CA
Newport Beach, CA
Chakmakian, Alice A. ... Charleston, WV
Chakmakian, Edmond C. ... Hauppauge, NY
Chakmakian, Peter L. ... Charles Town, WV
Chakmakian, Peter L., L.C.
Charles Town, WV
Chakmakis, George, Jr. ... Beverly Hills, CA
Chakos, Gus W. ... Chicago, IL
Chakrabart Amoruso, Sreelekha
Quincy, MA
Chakrabarti, Chandrima ... Kensington, MD
Chakrabarty, Lori A. ... Dearborn, MI
Chakrabarty, Prabir ... Towson, MD
Chakravorty, Agnis C. ... Roanoke, VA
Chakravorty, Pinaki ... Palo Alto, CA
Chakwin, Stephen D., Jr. ... New York, NY
Chalabi, Salem ... New York, NY
Chalat, James H. ... Denver, CO
Chalat Law Offices, P.C. ... Denver, CO
Chalat, Linda J. ... Denver, CO
Chale, Christine M. ... Hudson, NY
Poughkeepsie, NY
Chaleff, Daniel R. ... Woodland Hills, CA
Chaleff, Gerald L. ... Los Angeles, CA
Chaleff, Michael David
Department of Justice, Antitrust Division, GV
Chalekian, Suran J. ... Las Cruces, NM
Chalenski, Arthur A., Jr. ... Syracuse, NY
Chaletsky, Lawrence A. ... Billerica, MA
Chalfant, Charles L. ... Boise, ID
Chalfant, Frank E., Jr. ... Boise, ID

Chalfant, Jan L. ... Winchester, IN
Chalfant, Milo W. ... East Lansing, MI
Chalfant, Peter S. ... Morgan Hill, CA
Chalfant, R. Peterson ... Steubenville, OH
Chalfant, William David ... Minneapolis, MN
Chalfant, William Y. ... Hutchinson, KS
Chalfen, Marc J. ... Chicago, IL
Chalfie & Associates ... Chicago, IL
Chalfie, Deborah M. ... Washington, DC
Chalfie, Edward J. ... Chicago, IL
Chalfie, James J. ... Cincinnati, OH
Chalfie, James J., Co., L.P.A. Cincinnati, OH
Chalfie, Samuel L. ... Cincinnati, OH
Chalfin, Robert J. ... Metuchen, NJ
Chalfin, Susan R. ... New York, NY
Chalgian, Doug G. ... Lansing, MI
Chalian, Shant H. ... New York, NY
Chalidze, Lisa L. ... Rutland, VT
Chalif, John L. ... Washington, DC
West Palm Beach, FL
Chalif, John L., J.D., LL.M. Boca Raton, FL
Chalif, Seymour H. ... New York, NY
Chalifoux, James M. ... Troy, MI
Chalifoux, Jennie A. ... Brooklyn, NY
Chalifoux, Richard G. ... Islip, NY
Chalifoux, Richard G., Law Offices of Islip, NY
Chalifoux, Sheila M. ... Rochester, NY
Chalik, John P. ... Oakland, CA
Chalik, Robert M. ... Philadelphia, PA
Chalison, Linda A. ... Pasadena, CA
Chalk, Christina E. Securities and Exchange Commission, Division of Corporation Finance, GV
Chalk, Indra Sehdev ... Washington, DC
Chalk, John A., Jr. ... Fort Worth, TX
Chalk, John Allen, Sr. ... Fort Worth, TX
Chalk, Laura K. ... Charlotte, NC
Chalk, Russell J. ... Austin, TX
Chalk, S. Bradley ... Santa Rosa, CA
Chalk, Wm. David ... Baltimore, MD
Chalker, Bair, P.C. ... Houston, TX
Chalker, Brad A. ... Dayton, OH
Chalker, Charlotte N. ... Tacoma, WA
Chalker, Daniel J., P.E. ... Dallas, TX
Chalker, Howard W. Department Of The Interior, Office of the Solicitor, GV
Chalker, Kenneth L. ... Marietta, GA
Chalker, Richard B. ... Kansas City, MO
Chalker, Ronald F. ... Atlanta, GA
Chalker, Wilton F. ... Houston, TX
Chalkley & Crooke ... Ocala, FL
Chalkley, J. W., III ... Ocala, FL
Chalkley, Ramon E., III ... Ashland, VA
Chalkley, Sheleigh ... Salt Lake City, UT
Chalkley & Witmeyer, L.L.P. ... Ashland, VA
Challa, Dan M. ... Grand Rapids, MI
Challa, Mahalakshmi ... Richmond, VA
Challacombe, Joanna L. ... Schaumburg, IL
Challandes-Angelini, Sophia Department of Energy, Office of the General Counsel, GV
Challas, Christine L. ... McLean, VA
Challed, Richard A. ... Syosset, NY
Challeen, Dennis A. ... Winona, MN
Challen, James J., III ... Memphis, TN
Challenger, Mark L. ... Chicago, IL
Challenger, Patrick M. ... New Orleans, LA
Challgren, Michael L. ... Beverly Hills, CA
Challis, Mark A. ... Englewood, CO
Challis, T. Jack ... St. Louis, MO
Challos, Thomas R., Jr. ... Chicago, IL
Chally, Brian V. ... Las Vegas, NV
Chally, John ... Portland, OR
Chalmers, Arthur S. ... Wichita, KS
Chalmers, Arthur William ... Louisville, KY
Chalmers, C. Paul ... Palo Alto, CA
Chalmers, Carolyn ... Minneapolis, MN
Chalmers, Caryn L. ... Chicago, IL
Chalmers, Charles D. ... San Francisco, CA
Chalmers, Douglas, Jr. ... Atlanta, GA
Chalmers, Douglas M. ... Chicago, IL
Chalmers, Elizabeth C. ... Grand Rapids, MI
Chalmers, Geoffrey T. ... Boston, MA
Chalmers, Henry R. ... Atlanta, GA
Chalmers, Jane H. Overseas Private Investment Corporation, GV
Chalmers, Janis J ... Little Rock, AR
Chalmers, Jean B. ... Rockland, ME
Chalmers, Jeffrey P. ... Kalamazoo, MI
Chalmers, John A. ... Charleston, SC
Chalmers, John R. ... Thatcher, AZ
Chalmers, Richard J. North Miami Beach, FL
Chalmers, Roger A. ... Atlanta, GA
Chalmers, Roy M. ... Sacramento, CA
Chalmers, Tiela M. ... San Francisco, CA
Chalnick, Andrew T. ... New York, NY
Chaloemtiarana, Jennifer W. San Francisco, CA
Chaloemtiarana, Thad ... Chicago, IL
Chaloff, Miriam B. ... Chicago, IL
Chaloff, Rhoda ... New York, NY
Chalom, Joseph A. ... New York, NY
Chalos & Brown, P.C. ... Stamford, CT
New York, NY
Chalos, George M. ... Oyster Bay, NY
Chalos Law Firm ... New York, NY
Oyster Bay, NY
Chalos, Mark P. ... Nashville, TN
Chalos, Michael G. (IBA) ... Oyster Bay, NY
Chaloupka, Maren Lynn ... Scottsbluff, NE
Chaloupka, Robert Paul ... Scottsbluff, NE
Chaloupka, Susan K. ... Boise, ID

Chalphin, Gerald ... Philadelphia, PA
Chalpin, Mitchell A. ... Phoenix, AZ
Chalpin & Tom, Ltd. ... Phoenix, AZ
Chalpin-Shore, Michelle ... New York, NY
Chalsen, Christopher E. ... New York, NY
Chalstrom & Associates ... St. Paul, MN
Chalstrom, Christine ... St. Paul, MN
Chalstrom, Obert F. ... Plano, TX
Chaltraw, William E., Jr. ... Fresno, CA
Chalupa, Dennis F. ... Grinnell, IA
Newton, IA
Sully, IA
Chalupsky, Fred A. ... Chattanooga, TN
Chalverus, Joseph ... Seattle, WA
Chalwick, Jerome T. ... Fort Wayne, IN
Chaly, Ingeborg G. Federal Deposit Insurance Corporation, Trial Litigation Section, GV
Chamberlain, Ann F. ... New York, NY
Chamberlain, Barbara G. ... Denver, CO
Chamberlain, Bart B., Jr. ... Fulton, TX
Chamberlain, B.J. ... Herndon, VA
Chamberlain, Brad A. ... San Francisco, CA
Chamberlain, Bruce A. ... New London, CT
Chamberlain, C. Douglas ... Bellefontaine, OH
Chamberlain, Carole Anne ... Houston, TX
Chamberlain & Chamberlain Springfield, VA
Chamberlain, Chamberlain & Baldo Auburn, CA
Chamberlain, Charles E. ... Washington, DC
Chamberlain, Charles E., Jr. Grand Rapids, MI
Chamberlain, Cheryl D. ... Oak Park, IL
Chamberlain, Claudia E. ... Dayton, OH
Chamberlain, Craig A. ... Greensburg, PA
Chamberlain, Dale R. ... Dallas, TX
Chamberlain D'Amanda Oppenheimer & Greenfield ... Rochester, NY
Chamberlain, Daniel S. ... Indianapolis, IN
Chamberlain, David A. ... Prescott, AZ
Chamberlain, David C., Jr. ... Boston, MA
Chamberlain, David E. ... Austin, TX
San Antonio, TX
Chamberlain, David L. ... Dracut, MA
Chamberlain, David L., P.C. ... Dracut, MA
Chamberlain, David P. ... South Portland, ME
Chamberlain, David P. ... Liberty, MO
Chamberlain, Dennis A. ... Grand Rapids, MI
Chamberlain, Donald E. ... Springfield, VA
Chamberlain, Douglas R. Manchester, NH
Chamberlain, F. Stephen ... Lima, OH
Chamberlain, George M., Jr. Philadelphia, PA
Chamberlain, Gerard A. ... Wilmington, DE
Chamberlain, Hans Q. ... St. George, UT
Chamberlain, Harold A. ... Houston, TX
Chamberlain, Harry W. R., II Los Angeles, CA
Chamberlain, Henry W. ... Cleveland, OH
Chamberlain, Hrdlicka, White, Williams & Martin ... Atlanta, GA
Savannah, GA
Houston, TX
Chamberlain, J. Boatner ... Ross, CA
Chamberlain, James D., Jr. ... Woodbridge, NJ
Chamberlain, James R. ... Minneapolis, MN
Chamberlain, James R. ... Las Vegas, NV
Reno, NV
Chamberlain, James W. ... Lafayette, TN
Chamberlain, Jeanne M. ... Portland, OR
Chamberlain, Jeffrey F. ... Albany, NY
Chamberlain, John ... Garden City, NY
Chamberlain, John A. ... Sterling Heights, MI
Chamberlain, John E. ... Memphis, TN
Chamberlain, John H. ... Palm Beach, FL
Chamberlain, John H. ... Houston, TX
Chamberlain, John P. ... Newport Beach, CA
Chamberlain, Joseph D., Jr. ... Nokomis, FL
Chamberlain & Kaufman ... Albany, NY
Chamberlain, Ken ... Richfield, UT
Chamberlain, Kimberly Hincken Washington, DC
Chamberlain, Kimellen A. ... Chicago, IL
Chamberlain, Linda R. ... Clearwater, FL
Chamberlain, Lois A. ... Patterson, NY
Chamberlain, Lynn R. ... Mount Pleasant, MI
Chamberlain, Margaret A. East Lansing, MI
Chamberlain, Margaret A. ... Greenville, SC
Chamberlain, Merin ... Manchester, NH
Chamberlain, Michael N. ... Studio City, CA
Chamberlain, Michael R. ... Manchester, NH
Chamberlain, Nancy E. Department of Agriculture, Animal and Plant Health Inspection Service, GV
Chamberlain & Neaton PLLP Wayzata, MN
Chamberlain, Park ... Woodside, CA
Chamberlain, Patricia E. ... Seattle, WA
Chamberlain, Paul H. ... Auburn, CA
Chamberlain, Paul H. ... Mount Pleasant, MI
Chamberlain, Paul W. ... Wayzata, MN
Chamberlain, Peter R. ... Portland, OR
Chamberlain, Philetus M. ... Rochester, NY
Chamberlain, Philip H. ... Bloomington, IN
Chamberlain, Rae Balest ... Springfield, VA
Chamberlain, Reca René ... Leesburg, FL
Chamberlain, Richard K. ... Richfield, UT
Chamberlain, Richard M. ... Toledo, OH
Chamberlain, Richard V. Department Of Veterans Affairs, Board of Veterans Appeals, GV
Chamberlain, Rick D. Oklahoma City, OK

Chamberlain, Robert C. ... Barnstable, MA
Yarmouth Port, MA
Chamberlain, Robert D., Jr. ... Harrisburg, PA
Chamberlain, Ronald E. ... Palm Harbor, FL
Chamberlain, Scott B. ... Danbury, CT
Chamberlain, Scott B., P.C., Law Office of Danbury, CT
Chamberlain, Sonya A. ... Tallahassee, FL
Chamberlain, Steven M. ... Gainesville, FL
Chamberlain, Suzanne Viau Newport Beach, CA
Chamberlain, Theodore K. Silver Spring, MD
Chamberlain, Todd A. ... Tarzana, CA
Chamberlain, Todd D. ... Lansing, MI
Chamberlain, Toni I. ... San Antonio, TX
Chamberlain, Valerie R.S. ... San Diego, CA
Chamberlain and Viau, a professional law corporation ... Newport Beach, CA
Chamberlain, W. Clark ... Houston, TX
Chamberlain, W. Dennis ... Greenville, SC
Chamberlain, Willi, Ouchterloney & Watson New York, NY
Chamberlain Simpson, April State College, PA
Chamberland, Alfred P. ... Easthampton, MA
Chamberland, Marc J. ... Fort Lauderdale, FL
Chamberland, Marc. J., P.A. Fort Lauderdale, FL
Chamberlayne, Asa L. ... Treasury Department, Office of the Comptroller of the Currency, GV
Chamberlin, A. Howard ... Lee's Summit, MO
Chamberlin, Andrew S. ... Greensboro, NC
Chamberlin, Carl W. ... Menlo Park, CA
Chamberlin & Chamberlin Highland Park, IL
Chamberlin, Claude A. ... Aberdeen, MS
Chamberlin, Darcy J. ... North Riverside, IL
Oak Brook, IL
Chamberlin, Dwight, P.A. Daytona Beach, FL
Chamberlin, Elizabeth S. ... Pittsburgh, PA
Chamberlin, G. Richard ... Belleview, FL
Chamberlin, Gary A. ... Grand Rapids, MI
Chamberlin, Harvey H. ... Everett, WA
Chamberlin, James ... Norwich, NY
Chamberlin, John B. ... Highland Park, IL
Chamberlin, Joseph E. ... Littleton, CO
Chamberlin, Kirk C. ... Los Angeles, CA
Chamberlin, Lawrence M., Sr. ... Houston, TX
Chamberlin, Leona S. ... New York, NY
Chamberlin, Lydia B. Fort Lauderdale, FL
Chamberlin, M. Lynn ... Houston, TX
Chamberlin, Mary V. ... Bloomfield Hills, MI
Chamberlin, Michael M. ... New York, NY
Chamberlin, Michael S. ... Los Angeles, CA
Chamberlin, Neil Ray ... Little Rock, AR
Chamberlin, Oliver B. ... San Antonio, TX
Chamberlin, Pamela A. ... Miami, FL
Chamberlin, R. Mark ... Boston, MA
Chamberlin, Richard F. ... Riverside, CA
Chamberlin, Robert P. ... Hernando, MS
Southaven, MS
Chamberlin, Susan W. ... Exeter, NH
Chamberlin, Suzanne Q. ... Newark, NJ
Chamberlin, Thomas J. ... Phoenix, AZ
Chambers, Alexander A. ... Atlanta, GA
Chambers, Amy O'Meara Grand Rapids, MI
Chambers, Amy Piro ... New Brunswick, NJ
Chambers, Andrea J. ... Washington, DC
Chambers, Arthur C. ... San Francisco, CA
Chambers & Associates, P.C. Waynesburg, PA
Chambers, Blake L. ... Washington, IN
Chambers, Bradley E. ... Houston, TX
Chambers, Bridget A. ... Des Moines, IA
Chambers, C. Michael ... Cochrane, WI
Chambers, C. Michael, Law Offices, S.C. Cochrane, WI
Chambers, Carlile M. ... Atlanta, GA
Chambers, Carol A. ... Englewood, CO
Chambers, Caroline B. ... Manchester, NH
Chambers, Caryn Ann ... Smithtown, NY
Chambers & Chambers ... Magnolia, AR
Chambers, Chambers & Chambers Atlanta, GA
Chambers, Charles MacKay ... Southfield, MI
Chambers, Charles S. ... Lubbock, TX
Chambers, Coeta ... Santa Clara, CA
Chambers, Craig D. ... Bellingham, WA
Chambers, Dan E. ... Irvine, CA
Chambers, Daniel M. ... La Jolla, CA
Chambers, Darrell ... Baltimore, MD
Chambers, David L. ... Hamburg, AR
Chambers, David L. ... Ann Arbor, MI
Chambers, David L. ... Lincoln, NE
Chambers, David N. ... Las Vegas, NV
Chambers, David R. ... Raleigh, NC
Chambers, Debra Dawn ... Atlanta, GA
Chambers, Dee R. ... Salt Lake City, UT
Chambers, Dorothy J. ... Louisville, KY
Chambers, E. Benson ... Canton, GA
Chambers, E. Evans, III ... Enid, OK
Chambers, Edward G. ... Lighthouse Point, FL
Chambers, Edward L., Jr. ... Yorktown, VA
Chambers, Elizabeth C. ... Seattle, WA
Chambers, Elizabeth J. ... Philadelphia, PA
Chambers, Eugene ... Houston, TX
Chambers, Eugene P., Jr. ... Atlanta, GA
Chambers, Felicia L. ... Department of Justice, Civil Division, GV
Chambers, Franklin J. ... Detroit, MI
Chambers, G. Katherine ... Tampa, FL
Chambers, Garret Wesley ... Dallas, TX
Chambers, Gary L. ... Santa Ana, CA

Chambers, Gene T. ... Orlando, FL
Chambers, Gregory A. ... Fresno, CA
Chambers, Gregory K. ... Denver, CO
Chambers, Guy W. ... San Francisco, CA
Chambers, H. Dudley ... Dallas, TX
Chambers, H. Matthew ... Baton Rouge, LA
Chambers, H. Richard ... Jackson, MI
Chambers, Hayley B. ... Las Vegas, NV
Chambers, Holly A. ... Ruston, LA
Chambers & Insley, P.C. ... Yorktown, VA
Chambers, J. Dennis ... Texarkana, TX
Chambers, J. Drew, (P.C.) ... Clinton, IA
Chambers, J. Michael ... Houston, TX
Chambers, J. Robert ... Cincinnati, OH
Chambers, Jack H. ... Jacksonville, FL
Chambers, Jack P. ... Tazewell, VA
Chambers, James R. ... Oklahoma City, OK
Chambers, Jeffrey B. ... Cary, NC
Chambers, Jeffrey K. ... St. Petersburg, FL
Chambers, Jeffrey W. ... Fort Worth, TX
Chambers, Jerry N. ... Montclair, NJ
Chambers, Joan M. ... Lincoln City, OR
Chambers, John C. ... Washington, DC
Chambers, John C. ... Dayton, OH
Chambers, John C. ... Midland, TX
Chambers, John E. ... Fort Worth, TX
Chambers, John H. ... Portland, OR
Chambers, John H. ... Arlington, TX
Chambers, John J. ... Fairview Park, OH
Chambers, John L. ... Fremont, OH
Chambers, John L. ... Nashville, TN
Chambers, John M. ... Saipan, TT
Chambers, John T. ... New York, NY
Chambers, John W., Jr. ... Atlanta, GA
Chambers, John William, Sr. ... Atlanta, GA
Chambers, Jon Charles ... Los Angeles, CA
Chambers, Jonathan Martin Washington, DC
Chambers, Joseph H. ... St. Petersburg, FL
Chambers, Joseph L. ... Smyrna, GA
Chambers, Joseph M. ... Logan, UT
Chambers, Joseph W. ... St. Petersburg, FL
Chambers, Joy S. ... Washington, DC
Chambers, Joy S. ... Alexandria, VA
Chambers, Judy Nell Branham Columbia, SC
Chambers, Julius LeVonne ... Durham, NC
Chambers, Karen L. Melvin ... Kalamazoo, MI
Chambers, Karl A. ... Denver, CO
Chambers, Kathleen L. ... Memphis, TN
Chambers, Kathleen P. ... Orange, CA
Chambers, Kent ... Beaumont, TX
Jasper, TX
Chambers, Kent B. ... Austin, TX
Chambers, Kevin S. ... Highlands Ranch, CO
Chambers, K. W. Michael ... Mobile, AL
Chambers, Laurie ... San Francisco, CA
Chambers Law Group, Professional Association ... St. Petersburg, FL
Chambers, Lawrence T., Jr. ... Tulsa, OK
Chambers, Leslie R. ... Beaumont, TX
Lufkin, TX
Chambers, Linda M. ... Waynesburg, PA
Chambers, Lloyd L. ... Sun City, AZ
Chambers, Mabry, McClelland & Brooks, LLP ... Atlanta, GA
Decatur, GA
Lawrenceville, GA
Monroe, GA
Chambers, Marc A.R. ... New York, NY
Chambers, Mark C. ... Fort Wayne, IN
Chambers, Mark D., Jr. ... Trophy Club, TX
Chambers, Matthew A. ... Washington, DC
Chambers, Melissa Galvin ... Houston, TX
Chambers, Merle C. ... Denver, CO
Chambers, Michael D. ... Indianapolis, IN
Chambers, Michael L. ... Birmingham, AL
Chambers, Michael L. ... Sun City, AZ
Chambers, Michael R. ... San Francisco, CA
Chambers, Michelle A. ... Los Angeles, CA
Chambers, Milton A. ... White Plains, NY
Chambers, Nathan D. ... Denver, CO
Chambers, Noble M., Jr. ... Crowley, LA
Chambers, Noronha & Lowry Santa Ana, CA
Chambers, Patrick B. ... Webster City, IA
Chambers, Patrick T. ... Peoria, IL
Chambers, Paul T. ... Fresno, CA
Chambers, Phillip A. ... Grand Junction, CO
Chambers, R. Gerald, Jr. ... Beaufort, SC
Chambers, R. Steven ... Salt Lake City, UT
Chambers, R. Steven, A Professional Corporation ... Salt Lake City, UT
Chambers, Randall Lee ... Greenville, SC
Chambers, Rayford G. ... Jackson, MS
Chambers, R. E. ... Wichita Falls, TX
Chambers, Reid Peyton ... Washington, DC
Chambers, Rhonda Pitts Birmingham, AL
Chambers & Rice ... Homerville, GA
Chambers, Richard B. ... Wichita, KS
Chambers, Richard C. ... Lynnfield, MA
Chambers, Robert ... Germantown, MD
Chambers, Robert C. ... Atlanta, GA
Chambers, Robert F. ... Oakland, CA
Chambers, Robert Gordon Philadelphia, PA
Chambers, Robert M. ... Winter Haven, FL
Chambers, Robert M., P.A. Winter Haven, FL
Chambers, Robert Wakefield, III Gainesville, GA
Chambers, Roberta A. ... Corydon, IA
Chambers, Rodney T. ... Magnolia, AR
Chambers, Rolly L. ... Charlotte, NC
Chambers, Rosemary de Juan ... Mobile, AL
Chambers, Rufus A. ... Atlanta, GA
Chambers, Sandra L. ... Morgan Hill, CA

Chambers, Scott A. ....Washington, DC
Chambers, Scott E. ....Dover, DE
Odessa, DE
Chambers Steiner, A Professional Corporation
Detroit, MI
Kalamazoo, MI
Chambers, Stephen C. ....Traverse City, MI
Chambers, Stephen N. ....Charleston, WV
Chambers, Stephen P. ....San Ramon, CA
Chambers, Susan Courtney ....New York, NY
Chambers, Susan K. ....New Orleans, LA
Chambers, Susan Seidler ....New Haven, CT
Chambers, Susan Stevens ....Mankato, MN
Chambers, Suzanne B. ....Indianapolis, IN
Chambers, T. Michael ....Roswell, GA
Chambers Templeton Cashiola, L.L.P.
Beaumont, TX
Jasper, TX
Chambers, Teri L. ....Little Rock, AR
Chambers, Theodore D. ....Hartford, CT
Chambers, Thomas C., III ....Homerville, GA
Chambers, Thomas D. ....Fort Worth, TX
Chambers, Thomas E. ....Homestead, FL
Chambers, Thomas G. ....Yorba Linda, CA
Chambers, Thomas M. ....Detroit, MI
Chambers, Timothy D. ....Atlanta, GA
Chambers, Timothy J. ....Hutchinson, KS
Chambers, Tom J. ....Seattle, WA
Chambers, Victor B. ....Newark, NY
Chambers, Walter R. ....Uniontown, OH
Chambers, Wesley W. ....Dallas, TX
Chambers, Wick R. ....New Haven, CT
Chambers, William D. ....Columbus, IN
Chambers, William R. ....Kansas City, KS
Chambers, William R. ....Reston, VA
Chambers, William S., IV ....Bartow, FL
Chambers, William W. ....Fort Worth, TX
Chambers-Ford, Jeanette T. ....Hartford, CT
Chamble, John ....Brooklyn, NY
Chamblee, Carl E., Jr. ....Birmingham, AL
Chamblee, Carl E., Sr. ....Birmingham, AL
Chamblee, Dana A. ....Springfield, MO
Chamblee, Daryl A. (Sandy)
Washington, DC
Chamblee, Fred G. ....Statesville, NC
Chamblee & Furr, L.L.C. ....Birmingham, AL
Chamblee, Gary D. ....Charlotte, NC
Chamblee, J. Michael ....Alexandria, LA
Chamblee, John J., Jr. ....Tampa, FL
Chamblee, Lawrence W. ......Los Angeles, CA
Chamblee, R.W., Jr. ....South Bend, IN
Chamblee & Ryan ....Dallas, TX
Chamblee, William H. ....Dallas, TX
Chamblee, Wm. H. ....Hickory, NC
Chambless, Andrew R. ....Birmingham, AL
Chambless & Chambless ....Waycross, GA
Chambless, Higdon & Carson
Macon, GA
Chambless, John W., II ....Austin, TX
Chambless, Joseph H. ....Macon, GA
Chambless, Karen P. ....Montgomery, AL
Chambless, Larry ....Cleburne, TX
Chambless, Mark N. ....Montgomery, AL
Chambless, Marla P. ....La Grange, GA
Chambless, Math, Moore & Brown, P.C.
Auburn, AL
Dothan, AL
Mobile, AL
Montgomery, AL
Opelika, AL
Prattville, AL
Tuskegee, AL
Union Springs, AL
Wetumpka, AL
Chambless, R. Martin ....Littleton, CO
Chambless, Ricky T. ....Fayette, AL
Chambless, Thomas S. ....Albany, GA
Chambless, Vernon L. ....Waycross, GA
Chamblin, James H. ....Leesburg, VA
Chamblin, Patricia ....Beaumont, TX
Chamblin and Snyder ....Columbus, OH
Chamblin, Spencer D. ....Alexandria, VA
Chamblis, Alton M. ....Danville, CA
Chamblis, Alvin O., Jr. ....Oxford, MS
Chambliss, Bahner & Stophel, P.C.
Chattanooga, TN
Chambliss, C. Saxby ....Moultrie, GA
Chambliss, Charles D., Jr. ....Richmond, VA
Chambliss, Charles D., Jr., P.C.
Richmond, VA
Chambliss, Denise E. ....Oakland, CA
Chambliss, Frank N. ....West Monroe, LA
Chambliss, Jac ....Chattanooga, TN
Chambliss, James Henry ....Avon, CO
Chambliss, John D. ....Boston, MA
Chambliss, John Jeff ....Santa Maria, CA
Chambliss, Joseph B., Jr. ....Raleigh, NC
Chambliss, Linda ....Fort Lauderdale, FL
Chambliss, Lorenzo E. ....Oakland, CA
Chambliss, Marque C. ....Mountain View, CA
Chambliss, Nancy Griffin ....Richmond, VA
Chambliss, Octavia S. ....Seattle, WA
Chambliss, Prince C., Jr. ....Memphis, TN
Chambliss, Richard E. ....Phoenix, AZ
Chambliss, Samuel M., III ....Atlanta, GA
Chambliss, Wendell J. ....Birmingham, AL
Chambon, Gary Lee, Jr. ....Lansing, MI
Chameides, Steven B. ....Washington, DC
Chameli, David Paul ....St. Paul, MN
Chamelin, Neil C. ....Tallahassee, FL
Chamerlik, Karen A. ....St. Paul, MN
Chames, Deborah S. ....Miami, FL
Chames, Heidi M. ....Wilsonville, OR
Chami, Mardah ....Palo Alto, CA
Chamides, Nancy J. ....Morristown, NJ
New York, NY
Chamie, E. S. ....Tarzana, CA
Chamish, Larry A. ....Newark, NJ
Chamlee, Dubus & Sipple ....Atlanta, GA
Brunswick, GA
Savannah, GA
Chamlee, George H. ....Savannah, GA
Chamlee, Roy Z., III ....Greenville, SC
Chamley, Joseph P. ....Champaign, IL
Chamlin, George M., (P.C.)
West Long Branch, NJ
Chamlin, Kenneth W.
West Long Branch, NJ
Chamlin, Marc ....New York, NY
Chamlin, Rosen, Cavanagh & Uliano, P.A.
West Long Branch, NJ
Chammas, Jihad H. ....Los Angeles, CA
Chammout, Suzanne M. ....Sacramento, CA
Chamness, Christopher L. ....Claremont, CA
Chamness, Jay Nelson ....Nashville, TN
Chamness, Ralph E. ....Salt Lake City, UT
Chamness, Robert P. ....Portland, OR
Chamness, Rodney A., II ....Waco, TX
Chamorro, Kristina K. ....Los Angeles, CA
San Francisco, CA
Chamot, Philip S. ....Buffalo, NY
Lockport, NY
Niagara Falls, NY
Williamsville, NY
Chamoun, Robert A. ....Memphis, TN
Chamousis, Nicholas ....New York, NY
Chamovitz, Richard L. ....Philadelphia, PA
Chamow-Cavayero, Beth ....New York, NY
Chamowitz & Chamowitz, P.C.
Alexandria, VA
Chamowitz, Michael J. ....Alexandria, VA
Chamowitz, Ruth Lankford
Alexandria, VA
Champ, Harry William ....Tulsa, OK
Champ, Michael W. ....Long Beach, CA
Champa, James F. ....Boston, MA
Champa, Ralph F., Jr. ....Cambridge, MA
Champagne & Brumbaugh, P.L.C.
Lafayette, LA
Champagne, Debra S. ....Houston, TX
Champagne, Dorothy ....Baker, LA
Champagne, Frederica M. ....Novato, CA
Champagne, George J., Jr. ....Lafayette, LA
Champagne, Gerard J., Jr. ....Boston, MA
Champagne, Gregory C. ....Luling, LA
Champagne, Jeanne-Marie ....New York, NY
Champagne, Jeffrey F. ....Harrisburg, PA
Champagne, John J. ....Olympia, WA
Champagne, Lloyd P. ....Baton Rouge, LA
Champagne, Louis V. ....Columbia, LA
Champagne, Margot J. ....Washington, DC
Champagne, Melvin H. ....Spokane, WA
Champagne, Norman E. ....Manchester, NH
Champagne, Oliver W. R., Jr.
Chicago, IL
Champagne, Patricia C. ....Gulfport, MS
Champagne, Paula ....San Francisco, CA
Champagne, Randall L. ......Baton Rouge, LA
Champagne, Robert E., III ....Louisville, KY
Champagne, Roger B. ....North Falmouth, MA
Champagne, Stephen E. ....Portland, ME
Champagne, Susan M. ....Manchester, NH
Champagne, Thomas M. ....Washington, DC
Champaneri, Anil R. ....Arlington Heights, IL
Champeaux, Roylene ....Minneapolis, MN
Champeon, Steven R. ....Waltham, MA
Champi, David Lowell ....Plano, TX
Champi, Elaine K.
United States Postal Service,
Law Department, GV
Champi, Stephen R. ....Somerville, NJ
Champine, Martha M. ....Redford, MI
Champion, Barbara Muller ....Phoenix, AZ
Champion, Brian L. ....Bath, ME
Champion, C. Paul, III
Upper Marlboro, MD
Champion, C. Paul, III, P.C.
Upper Marlboro, MD
Champion, Christopher M.
Alexander City, AL
Champion, Daniel E. ....Los Angeles, CA
Blue Springs, MO
Champion, Darrell F. ....Modesto, CA
Champion, David C. ....Detroit, MI
Champion, Edward W. ....Pleasantville, NJ
Champion, F. Lee, III ....Columbus, GA
Champion, Forrest L., Jr. ....Columbus, GA
Champion, Geraldine E.
San Luis Obispo, CA
Champion, Gina S. ....Columbia, SC
Champion, Gregory J. ....Albany, NY
Champion, Jan ....San Jose, CA
Champion, Joe S. ....Albany, GA
Champion, Larry M. ....Houston, TX
Champion, Larry R. ....Indianapolis, IN
Champion, Lee R. ....Honolulu, HI
Champion, Lori A. ....Gorham, ME
Champion, Maxine C. ....Washington, DC
Champion, Peter George ....Visalia, CA
Champion, Ricky Wayne ....Burlington, NC
Champion, Robert A. ....Parchment, MI
Champion, Robert E. ....Helena, MT
Champion, Roger C. ....Tallahassee, FL
Champion, Susan E. ....Wayne, NJ
Champion, Timothy H. ....Akron, OH
Champion, Walker & Niermeyer, A Prof. Law Corp. ....Modesto, CA
Champion, Walter T., Jr. ....Houston, TX
Champion, William J., III ....Troy, MI
Champion, William M. ....University, MS
Champlain, Robert A. ....San Francisco, CA
Champlin, Betty Jane ....Dana Point, CA
Champlin, Blake K. ....Tulsa, OK
Champlin, Calbraith P., III ....Kenmore, NY
Champlin, Harvey L. ....Santa Barbara, CA
Champlin, Judson K. ....Minneapolis, MN
Champlin, Michael J. ....Richmond, VA
Champlin, Nicholas A. ....San Francisco, CA
Champlin, Philip A. ....Napa, CA
Champlin, Richard H. ....Oklahoma City, OK
Champlin, Ronny J. ....Baton Rouge, LA
Champlin, Steven K. ....Minneapolis, MN
Champlin, William H., III ....Hartford, CT
Champnella, Frederic E., II ....Detroit, MI
Champney, Dan E. ....Flint, MI
Champney, Richard K. ....Pulaski, NY
Champney, Richard K., P.C. ....Pulaski, NY
Champon, Into Bo ....Anaheim, CA
Champoux, Barbara E. ....New York, NY
Champoux, David J. ....Portland, ME
Champoux, Ronald E. ....San Rafael, CA
Champy, James A. ....Cambridge, MA
Chan, Ada K. ....Largo, MD
Chan, Alan T. ....New York, NY
Chan, Alashia ....Morristown, NJ
Chan, Albert B. ....San Francisco, CA
Chan, Albert Wai-Kit ....New York, NY
Chan, Alice ....New York, NY
Chan, Alistair K. ....Milwaukee, WI
Chan, Amy ....New York, NY
Chan, Ann C. ....Los Angeles, CA
Chan, Anna M. ....Miami, FL
Chan, Anthony S. ....Honolulu, HI
Chan, Antonia M. ....Santa Monica, CA
Chan, Ashely M. ....Philadelphia, PA
Chan, Ava H. ....San Francisco, CA
Chan, Bennett
Charlotte Amalie, St. Thomas, VI
Chan, Bruce E. ....San Francisco, CA
Chan, Carl ....Framingham, MA
Chan, Caroline E. ....Santa Monica, CA
Chan, Chi-Hung A. ....Redwood City, CA
Chan, Christopher J. ....Atlanta, GA
Chan, Christopher W. ....New York, NY
Chan, Cindy H. ....Chicago, IL
Chan, Clarence ....Stockton, CA
Chan, Clark M. ....San Francisco, CA
Chan, Cyrus W. ....Wailuku, HI
Chan, Dale A. ....Honolulu, HI
Chan, Daniel C. ....Pasadena, CA
Chan, David K. ....New York, NY
Chan, David R. ....Los Angeles, CA
Chan, Deborah ....New York, NY
Chan, Denise M. ....Chicago, IL
Chan, Derek ....Houston, TX
Chan, Diane ....New York, NY
Chan, Doi, Marshall & Leal, LLP
San Francisco, CA
Chan, Dorena J. ....Redwood City, CA
Chan, Douglas S. ....San Francisco, CA
Chan, Edith K. ....Alhambra, CA
Chan, Elaine I.
Federal Emergency Management Agency,
Office of the General Counsel, GV
Chan, Elaine L. ....San Diego, CA
Chan, Estella S. ....Glendale, CA
Chan, Flora W. L. ....Boston, MA
Chan, Frances ....New York, NY
Chan, Gary K. ....Cerritos, CA
Chan, Gayle ....San Francisco, CA
Chan, Gilen ....New York, NY
Chan, Grace L. ....New York, NY
Chan, Hamilton, Jr. ....Los Angeles, CA
Chan, H.C. ....Cupertino, CA
Chan, Hon W. ....San Francisco, CA
Chan, Ida K. ....Richardson, TX
Chan, Jackie ....Danbury, CT
Chan, James A. Wung-Dart
Securities and Exchange Commission,
Office of Compliance Inspections and
Examinations, GV
Chan, Jennifer M. ....Saratoga, CA
Chan, Joanne G. ....Menlo Park, CA
Chan, Joanne M. ....Lafayette, CA
Chan, Joe M. ....San Francisco, CA
Chan, Joseph ....New York, NY
Chan, Joseph W. ....San Francisco, CA
Chan, Karen W. ....San Jose, CA
Chan, Kei-On ....San Francisco, CA
Chan, Kelli Farrand ....Denver, CO
Chan, Kenneth Yuen-Kwan
East Hartford, CT
Chan, Lai Lee ....New York, NY
Chan Law Group LC ....Los Angeles, CA
Chan, Leland L. ....San Jose, CA
Chan, Liza Cheuk May
Bloomfield Hills, MI
Chan, Lorita M. ....Los Angeles, CA
Chan, Marion S. L., (Mr.) ....New York, NY
Chan, Mathew ....Sacramento, CA
Chan, Melinda ....New York, NY
Chan, Melvin D. ....Palo Alto, CA
Chan, Michael ....Dayton, OH
Chan, Min ....Buffalo, NY
Chan, Moon ....Honolulu, HI
Chan, Nelson H. ....Sacramento, CA
Chan & Neri ....San Francisco, CA
Chan, Patricia Yu ....Los Angeles, CA
Chan, Paul H. ....Denver, CO
Chan, Paul S. ....Los Angeles, CA
Chan, Paul T. ....Atlantic City, NJ
Chan, Peter S.P. ....Los Angeles, CA
Chan, Phillip Scott ....San Francisco, CA
Chan, Robert N. ....New York, NY
Chan, Robert Y. ....San Francisco, CA
Chan, Robert Y. P. ....San Francisco, CA
Chan, Ronald ....San Diego, CA
Chan, Sandra J. ....Santa Barbara, CA
Santa Monica, CA
Chan, Sandra J., A Professional Corporation
Santa Barbara, CA
Santa Monica, CA
Chan, Sau Ung Loo ....Honolulu, HI
Chan, Sing ....Pasadena, CA
Chan, Siu Lan ....New City, NY
Chan, Sonia S. ....New York, NY
Chan, Stephen A. ....Houston, TX
Chan, Stephen Y. ....San Diego, CA
Chan, Steven L. ....New York, NY
Chan, Ted W. ....Mountain View, CA
Chan, Teresa Wai Kwan ....New York, NY
Chan, Thomas F. ....San Francisco, CA
Chan, Thomas T. ....Los Angeles, CA
Chan, Wai Y. ....New York, NY
Chan Warner P.C. ....Houston, TX
Chan, Warren ....Seattle, WA
Chan, Wayne H. ....New York, NY
Chan, Wilbert F. ....Napa, CA
Chan, William Y. ....New York, NY
Chan, Yvonne Y. ....New York, NY
Chan, Zesara C. ....San Francisco, CA
Chanak, Adam G. S. ....Seattle, WA
Chanak, Nicholas S. ....Hibbing, MN
Chanales, Sheldon A. ....New York, NY
Chanan, Paul H. ....Chicago, IL
Chananau, Alexander ....Bronx, NY
Chanania, Fredric Davis
Environmental Protection Agency,
Program Office Attorneys, GV
Chananie, Judith W. ....Bronx, NY
Chananie, Steven J. ....Great Neck, NY
Chanay, Jeffrey A. ....Topeka, KS
Chancas, Jeffrey C. ....New York, NY
Chance, Andrew A. ....Austin, TX
Chance, Brian W. ....Lowell, MA
Chance, Calvin E., Jr. ....Augusta, GA
Chance, Calvin E., Jr., P.C. ....Augusta, GA
Chance, Carol E. ....Baltimore, MD
Chance, Chester B. ....Gainesville, FL
Chance, Christa N. ....Dallas, TX
Chance, Donna Y. ....Dallas, TX
Chance, Elizabeth Einstman
Memphis, TN
Chance, Eugene R. ....Tipton, IN
Chance, Hugh E. ....Winfield, KS
Chance, Jeff S. ....Lufkin, TX
Chance, Jonathan G. ....Palo Alto, CA
Chance, Keron D. ....Bridgeton, NJ
Chance, Kimberly A. ....San Francisco, CA
Chance, Lilian C. ....New York, NY
Chance & Maddox ....Calhoun, GA
Chance & McCann ....Bridgeton, NJ
Chance, Michael B. ....Memphis, TN
Chance, Michael W. ....Bannockburn, IL
Chance, Philip C. ....Louisville, KY
Chance, Sandra F. ....Gainesville, FL
Chance, Stephen R. ....Atlanta, GA
Chance, Steven J. ....Bellingham, WA
Chance, Steven K. ....Plymouth Meeting, PA
Chancellor, Bart Alan ....Tulsa, OK
Chancellor, Carl E. ....Bratenahl, OH
Chancellor, David B. ....Montgomery, AL
Chancellor, Eric S.
Christiansted, St. Croix, VI
Chancellor, Sherry ....Pensacola, FL
Chancellor, Thomas H. ....Salt Lake City, UT
Chancey, Joseph C. ....Atlanta, GA
Chancey, Mark E. ....Tampa, FL
Chancey, Matthew ....Waukegan, IL
Chancey, Mike M. ....Norcross, GA
Chancey & Miller, P.C. ....Montgomery, AL
Chancey, Phillip ....Montgomery, AL
Chancey, Richard Lee ....Phenix City, AL
Chancler, Kathleen M. ....Philadelphia, PA
Chanco, Leopoldo Jose ....San Francisco, CA
Chanco, Maria A. ....San Francisco, CA
Chandek, Lynn O'Brien ....Brookfield, WI
Chandek, William J. ....Brookfield, WI
Chandek, William J., Associates
Brookfield, WI
Chandler, A. Lee ....Darlington, SC
Chandler, Alan C. ....Salt Lake City, UT
Chandler, Albert B., III ....Versailles, KY
Chandler, Allison K. ....Dallas, TX
Chandler, Ann K. ....Waukesha, WI
Chandler, Anne Haenel ....Houston, TX
Chandler & Armstrong ....Anaheim, CA
Chandler & Associates ....Riverside, CA
Chandler, Berry M. ....Greenville, MS
Chandler, Beth-Anne ....Cleveland, OH
Chandler, Billy Howard ....Albertville, AL
Chandler, Bo ....Houston, TX
Chandler & Britt, LLC ....Atlanta, GA
Buford, GA
Lawrenceville, GA
Chandler, Brooks W. ....Anchorage, AK
Chandler, Bujold & Chandler ....Detroit, MI
Troy, MI
Chandler, Burton ....Worcester, MA
Chandler, C. Craig ....St. Louis, MO
Chandler, Cameron T. ....Englewood, CO
Chandler, Carl P., II ....Fayetteville, NC
Chandler, Carl P., II ....Lumberton, NC
Raeford, NC
Chandler, Carl R. ....Bridgeport, WV
Chandler, Carol ....Boston, MA
Chandler, Carol ....Bryn Mawr, PA
Chandler, Catherine J. ....Laguna Niguel, CA
Chandler & Chandler ....Dallas, TX
Chandler, Charles ....Tilton, NH
Chandler, Charles W. ....Livonia, MI
Chandler, Cheryl L. ....Detroit, MI
Chandler, Chris L. ....Denver, CO
Chandler, Christian H. ....Boston, MA
Chandler, Christian T. ....Portland, ME
Chandler, Christine Gray ....Los Alamos, NM
Chandler, Christopher R. ....Yuba City, CA
Chandler, Cindi L ....Portland, OR
Chandler, Clarence W., Jr. ....Bowie, TX
Chandler, Clive ....Piedmont, CA
Chandler, Constance S. ....Alexandria, VA
Chandler, Corinne ....Los Angeles, CA

Chandler, D. Daniel .... **Portland, OR**
Vancouver, WA
Chandler, Dan W. .... **Troy, MI**
Chandler, Darlene Kay .... Cincinnati, OH
Chandler, David A. .... Tupelo, MS
Chandler, David M. .... Bristol, PA
Chandler, Dean G. .... Vista, CA
Chandler, Deanna J. .... Omaha, NE
Chandler, Deborah M. .... **Front Royal, VA**
Winchester, VA
Chandler, Deborah Y. .... **Atlanta, GA**
Chandler, Diedre Jana .... Liberal, KS
Chandler, Dori Ray .... Copperas Cove, TX
Chandler, Douglas R. .... **Phoenix, AZ**
Chandler, Drake E. .... **Atlanta, GA**
Chandler, Earl E. .... Evansville, IN
Chandler, Edward G. .... San Francisco, CA
Chandler, Edward J.
Fort Lauderdale, FL
Chandler, Edward J., P.A., Law Office of
Fort Lauderdale, FL
Chandler, Elizabeth A. .... Williamstown, KY
Chandler, Elizabeth Brannen .... **Atlanta, GA**
Chandler, Elizabeth J. .... **Washington, DC**
Chandler, Elsie .... New York, NY
Chandler, Emerson H. .... Berlin, MA
Chandler, Floyd J. .... **Watertown, NY**
Chandler, Frank D. .... Dallas, TX
Chandler, Franklin & O'Bryan
Charlottesville, VA
Fredericksburg, VA
Hampton, VA
Harrisonburg, VA
Norfolk, VA
Chandler, Fred C., Jr. .... **Haddonfield, NJ**
Chandler, Gary R. .... Waltham, MA
Chandler, George E. .... **Lufkin, TX**
Chandler, George F., III .... **Houston, TX**
Chandler, George P. .... Kingsport, TN
Chandler, George W. .... Baytown, TX
Chandler, George Y. .... Parkersburg, WV
Chandler, Gerald R. .... Albemarle, NC
Chandler, Gregory .... **San Francisco, CA**
Chandler, H. Grady .... Garland, TX
Chandler, H. Joseph, Jr. .... Savannah, GA
Chandler, H. Mark .... **Litchfield Beach, SC**
Surfside Beach, SC
Chandler, Harry S. .... **Boise, ID**
Portland, OR
Chandler, Jacqueline M. .... Philadelphia, PA
Chandler, Jacquelyn .... **Dallas, TX**
Chandler, James C. .... **Oklahoma City, OK**
Chandler, James P. .... Washington, DC
Chandler, James R., III .... **Sarasota, FL**
Chandler, James S., Jr. .... Pawleys Island, SC
Chandler, Jayne R. .... Memphis, TN
Chandler, Jeff .... **Myrtle Beach, SC**
Chandler, Jerome J. .... Tempe, AZ
Valrico, FL
Chandler, Jo Bush .... Lafayette, LA
Chandler, Joel R. .... Tuscaloosa, AL
Chandler, John A. .... **Atlanta, GA**
Chandler, John C. .... Kenosha, WI
Chandler, John C., Law Offices of, S.C.
Kenosha, WI
Chandler, John P. .... Meredith, NH
Chandler, John T. .... Fort Pierce, FL
Chandler, John W. .... Irving, TX
Chandler, John W., Jr. .... Treasury Department, Internal Revenue Service, GV
Chandler, John W., Jr. .... **Memphis, TN**
Chandler, John Wyeth .... Memphis, TN
Chandler, Johnny M. .... Cleveland, OH
Chandler, Joseph W. .... Encino, CA
Chandler, Karl D. .... **San Jose, CA**
Chandler, Katherine Mandell
Manhattan Beach, CA
Chandler, Kelly Lynne .... Napa, CA
Chandler, Kenneth .... Shreveport, LA
Chandler, Kent, Jr. .... **Chicago, IL**
Chandler, Kevin M. .... Bloomington, MN
Chandler, Kimberley A. .... **Denver, CO**
Chandler, Lang & Haswell, P.A.
Gainesville, FL
Chandler, Larry W. .... Magnolia, AR
Chandler Law Firm .... **San Jose, CA**
Chandler Law Offices .... **Lufkin, TX**
Chandler, Lawrence .... Calhoun City, MS
Chandler, Lawrence J.
Nuclear Regulatory Commission, Office of the General Counsel, GV
Chandler, Lawrence U.L., & Associates, P.A.
West Palm Beach, FL
Chandler, Lawrence U. L.
West Palm Beach, FL
Chandler, L. B., Jr. .... Charlottesville, VA
Fredericksburg, VA
Harrisonburg, VA
Chandler, Lewis .... Brookline, MA
Chandler, Lewis P., Jr. .... Houston, TX
Chandler, Linda Hart .... Newport Beach, CA
Chandler, Lisa M. .... **Chicago, IL**
Chandler, Lynda Kay .... **San Diego, CA**
Chandler, Lynn F. .... **Charlotte, NC**
Chandler, Lynn Frances .... **Naples, FL**
Chandler, Lynn Frances, P.A. .... **Naples, FL**
Chandler, Madelynne K. .... Indianapolis, IN
Chandler, Malcolm A. .... Chicago, IL
Chandler, Marcus B. .... **Indianapolis, IN**
Chandler, Marion E. .... Dallas, TX
Chandler, Mark .... San Jose, CA
Chandler, Mark D. .... Louisville, KY
Chandler, Mary L. .... Paintsville, KY
Chandler, Mary Titsworth
Indianapolis, IN
Chandler, Mary Z. .... **Phoenix, AZ**
Chandler & Mason, Ltd. .... **St. Paul, MN**

Chandler, Melinda P. .... Department of State, Office of the Legal Adviser, GV
Chandler, Micael Cole .... Oklahoma City, OK
Chandler, Micael Cole, P.C.
Oklahoma City, OK
Chandler, Michael R. .... Greensboro, NC
Chandler, Michael S. .... **Lubbock, TX**
Chandler, Nathalie .... Los Angeles, CA
Chandler, Norbert F. .... Pittsburgh, PA
Chandler, Odra L. .... Anaheim, CA
Chandler, Paul .... **Chicago, IL**
Chandler, Paul W. .... Long Beach, CA
Chandler, Peter L. .... Portland, ME
Chandler, Quinn C. .... Dallas, TX
Chandler, R. Jay .... **Tulsa, OK**
Chandler, R. Joseph .... **Troy, MI**
Chandler, R. Lewis .... Dallas, TX
Chandler, R. Steven .... Denmark, SC
Chandler, R. Wells .... Claremont, NH
Chandler, Ralph W. .... Fort Myers, FL
Chandler, Raman .... Colleyville, TX
Chandler, Ray E. .... **Manning, SC**
Chandler, Reich O'Hara .... **Lufkin, TX**
Chandler, Rhonda R. .... **Houston, TX**
Chandler, Richard .... Marblehead, MA
Chandler, Richard B., Jr. (P.C.)
Buford, GA
Chandler, Richard E., Jr. .... **Houston, TX**
Chandler, Richard G. .... Madison, WI
Chandler, Rick S., Jr. .... Lancaster, SC
Chandler, Rob .... Louisville, KY
Chandler, Robert .... **Boston, MA**
Chandler, Robert C., (P.L.C.) .... Riverside, CA
Chandler, Robert H. .... **St. Paul, MN**
Chandler, Robert L. .... **Gainesville, GA**
Chandler, Robert M., Jr.
Rocky Mount, NC
Chandler, Robin .... Columbia, SC
Chandler, Roger G. .... **Spartanburg, SC**
Chandler, Roscoe D., Jr. .... Memphis, TN
Chandler, Roy W. .... Oklahoma City, OK
Chandler, Samuel P. .... Whitesburg, KY
Chandler, Sarah M. .... Charlotte, MI
Chandler, Sarah M., P.C. .... Charlotte, MI
Chandler, Schiffman, & Associates
Greensboro, NC
Chandler, Seth J. .... Houston, TX
Chandler, Sherry Scott .... **Houston, TX**
Chandler, Stephen G. .... San Leandro, CA
Chandler, Stephen M. .... Oakland, CA
Chandler, Stuart R. .... Fresno, CA
Chandler, Stuart R., A Prof. Corp.
Fresno, CA
Chandler, Susan Kay .... Pacific Palisades, CA
Chandler, Theodore G., Jr. .... **Charlotte, NC**
Chandler, Theodore L., Jr. .... **Richmond, VA**
Chandler, Theodore S. .... Boston, MA
Chandler, Thomas .... **Tucson, AZ**
Chandler, Thomas B. .... **Boise, ID**
Chandler, Thomas E. .... Department of Justice, Civil Rights Division, GV
Chandler, Timothy M. .... Carson City, NV
Chandler, Timothy R. .... **Marietta, GA**
Chandler, Todd R. .... Dallas, TX
Chandler, Tommy W. .... Providence, KY
Chandler, Trina Hill .... **Houston, TX**
Chandler, Troy D. .... **Dallas, TX**
Chandler, Tullar, Udall & Redhair, L.L.P.
Tucson, AZ
Chandler, Tymm .... San Diego, CA
Chandler, Vanessa Y. .... **Washington, DC**
Chandler, Virgil S. .... Kansas City, MO
Chandler, Virgil W. .... Sun Lakes, AZ
Chandler, W. Robert .... **Troy, MI**
Chandler, Walker L. .... Zebulon, GA
Chandler, Walter B. .... Gulf Shores, AL
Chandler, William B., III .... Georgetown, DE
Chandler, William F. .... Albany, NY
Chandler, William H. .... Hemingway, SC
Chandler, William J., Jr. .... Charlotte, NC
Chandler, William R. .... **Montgomery, AL**
Chandler, William W. .... **New York, NY**
Chandler, Wood, Harrington & Maffly LLP
San Francisco, CA
Chandless, Harry H., Jr.
Hasbrouck Heights, NJ
Chandley, Cynthia M. .... Phoenix, AZ
Chandola, M. Varn .... Tucson, AZ
Chandor, Christopher B. .... Doylestown, PA
Chandor, Connolly, Schwartz, Drexler, McCullough & Lyons, A Professional Corporation .... Doylestown, PA
Chandra, Aruna .... **New York, NY**
Chandra, Mona .... **Boston, MA**
Chandra, Rashmi .... **Chicago, IL**
Chandrabose, Bindu .... **Los Angeles, CA**
Chandy, Aney K. .... **Newark, NJ**
Chane, Laurie R. .... Dade City, FL
Chane, Lawrence S. .... **Philadelphia, PA**
Chanel, Lisa D. .... **Springfield, NJ**
Chaneles, Steven B. .... Fort Lauderdale, FL
Chanen, Bruce M. .... **Chicago, IL**
Chanen, Franklin A. .... Chicago, IL
Chanen, Jeanne Y., P.C. .... **Phoenix, AZ**
Chanen, Jeanne Young .... **Phoenix, AZ**
Chanen, Lawrence N. .... **New York, NY**
Chanen, Steven R. .... Phoenix, AZ
Chanen, Stuart J. .... **Chicago, IL**
Chanes, Jeannine W. .... **New York, NY**
Chaney, Albert L., III .... Pasadena, CA
Chaney, Beverly A. .... **New York, NY**
Chaney, Carl J. .... Jackson, MS
Chaney, Carolyn .... St. Petersburg, FL
Chaney, Catherine, Law Office of
Seattle, WA
Chaney & Chaney .... Barnesville, OH
Chaney, Christopher B. .... Salt Lake City, UT
Chaney, Christopher C. .... Glendale, CA

Chaney, Cynthia M. .... Olympia, WA
Chaney, D. Jackson .... **Irving, TX**
Chaney, Dana .... San Jose, CA
Chaney, David A. .... Atlanta, GA
Chaney, David A. .... Germantown, MD
Chaney, Donald E. .... **Springfield, MO**
Chaney, Donald P., Jr. .... **Arkadelphia, AR**
Chaney, Doyle F. .... Birmingham, AL
Chaney, Elaine Marie .... Indianapolis, IN
Chaney, Gary W. .... Sealy, TX
Chaney, Glen E. .... Melbourne, FL
Chaney, Glenn M. .... Pearland, TX
Chaney, James C. .... **Eugene, OR**
Chaney, James M. .... **Oklahoma City, OK**
Chaney, James R., Jr. .... Bristol, TN
Chaney, John F., Jr. .... Corrales, NM
Chaney, Joseph G., Jr. .... Murray, KY
Chaney, Kim James .... Cullman, AL
Chaney, Kristine R. .... Palmdale, CA
Chaney & Lane .... **Dallas, TX**
Fort Worth, TX
Irving, TX
Chaney, Lecia L. .... **Brownsville, TX**
Chaney, Lelia Kathleen .... **Denver, CO**
Chaney, M. James, Jr. .... **Vicksburg, MS**
Chaney & McCurry, LLP
Springfield, MO
Chaney, Michael D. .... Los Angeles, CA
Chaney, Michael T. .... **Charleston, WV**
Chaney, Mitchell C. .... **Brownsville, TX**
Chaney, Pamela Jean Kea .... Eastland, TX
Chaney, Ralph P., Jr. .... Pine Knot, KY
Chaney, Richard G. .... Durham, NC
Chaney, Robert A. .... Chicago, IL
Chaney, Stephen R. .... Fort Worth, TX
Chaney, Victoria Gerrard .... Los Angeles, CA
Chaney, W. Calvin .... Dallas, TX
Chaney, Wayne C. .... Oshkosh, WI
Chaney, Wilbur V. .... Delray Beach, FL
Chaney, William B. .... **Dallas, TX**
Chaney, William E. .... Barnesville, OH
Chanfrau & Associates .... **Naples, FL**
Chanfrau, Chanfrau & Bouck
Daytona Beach, FL
DeLand, FL
New Smyrna Beach, FL
Palm Coast, FL
Sanford, FL
Chanfrau, Chanfrau & Jeffers
Columbus, OH
Chanfrau, Elizabeth R.
Daytona Beach, FL
Chanfrau, Graciela M. .... **Naples, FL**
Chanfrau, Jose M., IV .... **Naples, FL**
Columbus, OH
Chanfrau, Philip J., (P.A.)
Daytona Beach, FL
Chanfrau, W. M., (P.A.)
Daytona Beach, FL
Chang, Adrian Yu-Hoy .... Honolulu, HI
Chang, Ae Kyung .... Greensboro, NC
Chang, Aileen .... **New York, NY**
Chang, Aileen T. .... **San Francisco, CA**
Chang, Alan .... Bristol, CT
Chang, Albert J. C. .... Rowland Heights, CA
Chang, Alec Y. .... **New York, NY**
Chang, Alfred .... Alpharetta, GA
Chang, Alice Pit-Wah .... Daly City, CA
Chang, Allison S.Y. .... **San Francisco, CA**
Chang, Alyssa W. .... **Bethesda, MD**
Chang, Amy T. .... La Puente, CA
Arlington, MA
Chang, Andrew .... **Santa Monica, CA**
Chang, Andrew N. .... San Francisco, CA
Chang, Anthony C. .... **Boston, MA**
Chang, Anthony K. U. .... Honolulu, HI
Chang, Arthur M. .... Riverside, CA
Chang, Barbara Tyler .... Reno, NV
Chang, Betty .... **Austin, TX**
Chang, Beverly .... **Kansas City, MO**
Chang, Carmen I-Hua .... **Palo Alto, CA**
Chang, Caroline J. .... Boston, MA
Chang, Carolyn V. .... **Mount Holly, NJ**
Chang, Catherine S. .... **New York, NY**
Chang, Cecilia V. M. .... New York, NY
Chang, Charles K. C. .... Honolulu, HI
Chang, Ching-Ning Shen .... San Jose, CA
Chang, Ch'iu Lien .... **New York, NY**
Chang, Chris (Chia) K. .... Chicago, IL
Chang, Christine .... **Chicago, IL**
Chang, Christine M. .... **Los Angeles, CA**
Chang, Christopher E., Law Offices of
New York, NY
Chang, Chunmay .... Honolulu, HI
Chang, Connie .... **Los Angeles, CA**
Chang, Corlis J. .... **Honolulu, HI**
Chang, Cynthia L. .... Toledo, OH
Chang, Daniel T. .... Miami, FL
Chang, David S. .... **New York, NY**
Chang, David T. .... **Houston, TX**
Chang, Deborah M. .... **Palo Alto, CA**
Chang, Deborah S. .... **Stamford, CT**
Chang, Dennis W. .... Los Angeles, CA
Chang, Derrick H. .... Los Angeles, CA
Chang, Dexter T. .... **New York, NY**
Chang, Diane .... Grass Valley, CA
Chang, Doris P. .... **New York, NY**
Chang, Douglas K. .... San Jose, CA
Chang, E. Kristine .... Dallas, TX
Chang, Edmond E. .... **Chicago, IL**
Chang, Edward .... New York, NY
Chang, Eileen D. .... **Thousand Oaks, CA**
Chang, Emil C. .... San Jose, CA
Chang, Ernest L. .... Melbourne, FL
Chang, Eugene L. .... **New York, NY**
Chang, Eun-Hee .... **Oakland, CA**
Chang, Eunice .... **San Francisco, CA**
Chang, Frances S. .... **San Francisco, CA**

Chang, Francis H. .... Boston, MA
Chang, Gary W. B. .... Honolulu, HI
Chang, Gene W. .... Costa Mesa, CA
Chang, George P. .... **New York, NY**
Chang, Gerald Y. Y. .... Honolulu, HI
Chang, Gordon G. .... **New York, NY**
Chang, Grace L. .... **Alhambra, CA**
Chang, Grace W. .... Parsippany, NJ
Chang, Hay Kyung .... Huntsville, AL
Chang, Helen Y. .... San Rafael, CA
Chang, Hemmie .... **Boston, MA**
Chang, Henry J. .... Nashville, TN
Chang, Howard F. .... Los Angeles, CA
Chang, Howard T. .... **Honolulu, HI**
Chang, Howard T., A Law Corporation
Honolulu, HI
Chang, Irene Florence .... **Washington, DC**
Chang, Irene S. .... **Arlington, VA**
Chang, J. Laurence .... **New York, NY**
Chang, Jacob D. .... Pasadena, CA
Chang, James A. .... Lebanon, PA
Chang, James H. .... San Jose, CA
Chang, Janie I. .... Pittsford, NY
Chang, Jeffrey C. .... **Gold River, CA**
Chang, Jeffrey J. .... San Francisco, CA
Chang, Jeffrey S. .... **Garden City, NY**
Chang, Jerry C. .... Falls Church, VA
Chang, Jih-Kuei .... New York, NY
Chang, John .... New York, NY
Chang, John O. .... Mount Holly, NJ
Chang, John S. .... Pasadena, CA
Chang, John W. K. .... Honolulu, HI
Chang, Josephine .... **New York, NY**
Chang, Joyce W. .... Windsor, VT
Chang, Julian C. L. .... Los Angeles, CA
Chang, Karen McLaurin .... **Los Angeles, CA**
Chang, Katherine S. .... **New York, NY**
Chang, Katherine Y. .... Vancouver, WA
Chang, Kevin S. C. .... Honolulu, HI
Chang, Kimberly D. .... **Irvine, CA**
Chang, Kristen Y. .... **New York, NY**
Chang, Laban L. B. .... Honolulu, HI
Chang, LaVerne Carol .... Houston, TX
Chang, Lee-Lee .... Flushing, NY
Chang, Leo .... **New York, NY**
Chang, Lily .... **New York, NY**
Chang, Linda C.
Federal Communications Commission, Wireless Telecommunications Bureau, GV
Chang, Linda M. .... **New York, NY**
Chang, Linda S. .... Department of Commerce, Office of the General Counsel, GV
Chang, Lisa E. .... **Atlanta, GA**
Chang, Louis L. C. .... Honolulu, HI
Chang, Lucas S. .... Palo Alto, CA
Chang, Lucy M. .... Department of Commerce, Office of the General Counsel, GV
Chang, Madeline C. .... Alhambra, CA
Chang, Mary .... **New Haven, CT**
Chang, Melissa A. .... **New York, NY**
Chang, Meredith Mantell .... Sacramento, CA
Chang, Michael H. .... Austin, TX
Chang, Michelle S. .... **Seattle, WA**
Chang, Min .... **Irvine, CA**
Chang, Mui & Chock, Attorney at Law, A Law Corporation .... Honolulu, HI
Chang, Nadya .... Cincinnati, OH
Chang, Nat C. .... Maumee, OH
Chang, Neil I. .... **Seattle, WA**
Chang, Nelson C. .... Saugus, MA
Chang, Nelson S. W. .... Honolulu, HI
Chang, Patrick S.
Environmental Protection Agency, Office of the General Counsel, GV
Chang, Peggy .... **Berkeley, CA**
Chang, Peiwen .... **Long Beach, CA**
Chang, Peter, Law Offices of
Santa Cruz, CA
Chang, Peter Y. .... **Mission Viejo, CA**
Chang, Philip W. T. .... Honolulu, HI
Chang, Raymond W. .... **Houston, TX**
Chang, Richard W. .... **Washington, DC**
Chang, Rina W. .... **Houston, TX**
Chang, Robt. H. K. .... Honolulu, HI
Chang, Roy K. S. .... Honolulu, HI
Chang, Ruth Elizabeth .... New Brunswick, NJ
Chang, Ruthenberg & Long, Law Corporation .... **Gold River, CA**
Sacramento, CA
Chang, Sam Hsien-Cheng
Washington, DC
Chang, Samuel B. K. .... Honolulu, HI
Chang, Sara P. .... **Campbell, CA**
Chang, Sarah K. .... **San Francisco, CA**
Chang, Shelleyanne W. L. .... Sacramento, CA
Chang, Stephen H. T. .... New York, NY
Chang, Steve S. .... **Washington, DC**
Chang, Steven Koon-sun .... Honolulu, HI
Chang, Sue J. .... Seattle, WA
Chang, Susan Su-Chi .... San Francisco, CA
Chang, T. Irving .... Honolulu, HI
Chang, Ta-tung J. .... Washington, DC
Chang, Tim T., P.C. .... San Francisco, CA
Chang, Timothy P. .... **Sacramento, CA**
Chang, Tony C. .... **New York, NY**
Chang, Tony C. .... New York, NY
Chang, Vahn .... **Atlanta, GA**
Chang, Valerie W. H. .... Honolulu, HI
Chang, Vicki .... Berkeley, CA
Chang, Victor I. .... **Boston, MA**
Chang, Vincent T. .... **New York, NY**
Chang, W. Gerald .... Martinez, CA
Chang, Wan B. .... Department Of The Interior, Office of the Solicitor, GV
Chang, Wendy Wen Yun
Santa Monica, CA
Chang, Wesley Y. S., Law Offices of
Honolulu, HI

Chang, Williamson B. C. ... Honolulu, HI
Chang, Williana ... Los Angeles, CA
Chang, Won ... Irvine, CA
Chang, Wonkoo ... Los Angeles, CA
Chang, WooJin (Eugene) ... Los Angeles, CA
Chang, Y. Kurt ... Chicago, IL
Chang, Ya-Chiao ... New York, NY
Chang, Yoon H. ... Saipan, TT
Chang, Yvette Y. ... New York, NY
Changaris, Christopher S. ... San Rafael, CA
Changaris, James G. ... Yuba City, CA
Changaris, Michael J. ... San Diego, CA
Changaris, Penelope A. ... Yuba City, CA
Changchien, Lily ... New York, NY
Chang-Lee, Julie C. ... Santa Ana, CA
Chang-Muy, Fernando ... Swarthmore, PA
Changnon, Eugene A., Jr. ... Chicago, IL
Chang-Peshoff, Veronica S.
Overland Park, KS
Chanin, Bernard ... Philadelphia, PA
Chanin, E. David ... Philadelphia, PA
Chanin, Edwin ... Minneapolis, MN
Chanin, Geoffrey E. ... Middletown, NY
Chanin, James B. ... Berkeley, CA
Chanin, Jeffrey R. ... San Francisco, CA
Chanin, Jeffrey T. ... Hartford, CT
Chanin, John A. ... Denver, CO
Chanin, John A., The Law Offices of
Kailua, HI
Chanin, Leah F. ... Washington, DC
Chanin, Leonard N.
Board of Governors Of The Federal Reserve System,
Division of Consumer and Community Affairs, GV
Chanin, Lester ... New York, NY
Chanin, Lloyd K. ... Melville, NY
Chanin, Michael H. ... Washington, DC
Chanin, Robert H. ... Washington, DC
Chanis, Robert J. ... New York, NY
Chanley, Steven M. ... San Luis Obispo, CA
Channel, Robert M. ... San Francisco, CA
Channell, Benjamin L. ... Trussville, AL
Channell, Halbert Bailey, Jr. ... Sonora, CA
Channell, M. Scott ... Beverly, MA
Channell, Wade G. ... New York, NY
Channell, William R. ... Lafayette, CA
Channels, Cedric H. ... Santa Ana, CA
Channels & Giddens ... Santa Ana, CA
Channels, Jon H. ... Orange, CA
Channels, Walter D. ... Santa Ana, CA
Channen, Russell S. ... Haverhill, MA
Channer, David A. ... Boise, ID
Channick, Herbert S. ... Rockford, IL
Channick, Marc ... San Diego, CA
Channick, Susan A. ... San Diego, CA
Channing, Charles E., Jr. ... Lanham, MD
Channing, Melissa S. ... Miami, FL
Channing, Stacey L. ... Concord, MA
Westborough, MA
Channon, Patricia Sugrue
Administrative Office Of The United States Courts, GV
Chanoff, Lisa K. ... San Francisco, CA
Chanon, Bernard L. ... Houston, TX
Chanon, Gregory S. ... Austin, TX
Chanos Escobar Chanos, P.C.
Las Vegas, NV
Chanos, George J. ... Las Vegas, NV
Chanove, Thomas L., Jr. ... New Orleans, LA
Chanover, David E. ... San Diego, CA
Chansky, Edward B. ... Westport, CT
Chansky, Geo. H. ... Beverly, MA
Chansky, Philibosian, Russell, Killmurray & Kinneally, PC ... Freehold, NJ
New Brunswick, NJ
North Brunswick, NJ
Chansky, Thomas F.
North Brunswick, NJ
Chansler, Jeffrey D. ... New York, NY
Chansolme, Beverly W. ... Oklahoma City, OK
Chant, Dale Verfaillie ... Woodbury, NJ
Chant, George H., III ... Riverside, CA
Chant, Paul W. ... Nashua, NH
Chantal, Thomas ... New York, NY
Chanter, Neil ... Springfield, MO
Chanti, Suzanne Bradley ... Eugene, OR
Chantilis, Peter S. ... Dallas, TX
Chantilis, Peter S., A Professional Corporation
Dallas, TX
Chantland, James M. ... Los Angeles, CA
Chanzit, Richard M. ... Denver, CO
Chao, Bernard H. ... San Francisco, CA
Chao, Cedric C. ... San Francisco, CA
Chao, Dorothy Chung ... Deerfield, IL
Chao, Dustin ... New York, NY
Chao, Fei-Fei ... Washington, DC
Chao, Helen T. ... San Diego, CA
Chao, Lisa W. ... Modesto, CA
Chao, Louis R. ... Los Angeles, CA
Chao, Margaret Tze-Ping ... Rockville, MD
Chao, Mark ... Chicago, IL
Chao, Philip L.
Department Of Health And Human Services,
Food & Drug Administration, GV
Rockville, MD
Chao, Stanley ... San Jose, CA
Chao, Theodore T.H. ... New York, NY
Chao, Tina W. ... Palo Alto, CA
Chao, Victor J.
Department of Labor, GV
Chao, Warren ... Palo Alto, CA
Chao, Yuan ... Menlo Park, CA
Chapa, Arthur A. ... Tucson, AZ
Chapa, Ed ... Corpus Christi, TX
Chapa, Fields & Brown, P.L.C. ... Tucson, AZ
Chapa, Jose E., Jr. ... McAllen, TX
Chapa, Lawrence J. ... Chicago, IL

Chapa, Paul D. ... Corpus Christi, TX
Chapa, Ralph C., Jr.
Farmington Hills, MI
Chapa, Ruben R. ... Chicago, IL
Chapa, Teofilo ... Miami, FL
Chapa, Teofilo, A Professional Corporation
Miami, FL
Chapala, Walter P. ... Michigan City, IN
Chapanar, Lawrence E. ... Canton, OH
Chaparro, Eliaser ... Trenton, NJ
Chaparro, Hector Manuel ... Santa Ana, CA
Chaparro, Reynaldo ... Hacienda Heights, CA
Chapas, John W., II ... Pittsburgh, PA
Chapas, William John ... Pittsburgh, PA
Chapdelaine, A. Michael ... Bowie, MD
Chapdelaine, Anita L. ... New York, NY
Chapdelaine & Davis, Chartered
Bowie, MD
Chapdelaine, Rosemarie ... Stamford, CT
Chapekis, A. Frederick ... Chicago, IL
Chapekis, James P. ... Escanaba, MI
Chapekis, Kristina M. ... Chicago, IL
Chapekis, Marcus & Chapekis ... Chicago, IL
Chapekis, Nicholas P. ... Escanaba, MI
Chapel, Charles S. ... Oklahoma City, OK
Chapel, Matthew W. ... Celina, OH
Chapel, Nimrod T., Jr.
Independence, MO
Chapelle, Ellen ... Chicago, IL
Chapelle, Joseph C. ... Indianapolis, IN
Chapello, Margaret E. ... Oak Brook, IL
Chapian, Edward M. ... Flushing, NY
Chapian, Lynne M. ... East Norwich, NY
Chapik, Daniel G. ... Minneapolis, MN
Chapin, Allan M. ... New York, NY
Chapin, Andrew L. ... Greensboro, NC
Chapin, Andrew V.
Commodity Futures Trading Commission,
Division of Trading and Markets, GV
Chapin, Armstrong & Ballerano
Delray Beach, FL
Chapin, Barry W. ... Westborough, MA
Chapin, Bayard S. ... New York, NY
Chapin, Boyd E., Jr. ... Detroit, MI
Chapin, Bruce E., (P.A.) ... Orlando, FL
Chapin & Chapin ... Springfield, IL
Chapin, Charles A. ... Springfield, IL
Chapin, Charles S. ... Casper, WY
Chapin, David C. ... Boston, MA
Chapin, Deborah ... New York, NY
Chapin, Donald E. ... Casper, WY
Chapin, Edward D. ... San Diego, CA
Chapin, Edward W. ... New York, NY
Chapin, Ellen M. ... New Orleans, LA
Chapin, Francis H., Jr. ... Tacoma, WA
Chapin, Henry M. ... Rochester, NY
Chapin & Huang, L.L.C. ... Westborough, MA
Chapin, Hugh A. ... New York, NY
Chapin, James C. ... Rockville, MD
Chapin, James M. ... San Diego, CA
Chapin, James W. ... Greenwich, CT
Chapin, Janice ... Elizabeth, NJ
Chapin, Jennifer H. ... Atlanta, GA
Chapin, Jennifer L. ... New York, NY
Chapin, John K. ... Berkeley, CA
Chapin, John R. ... Springfield, IL
Chapin, Julie K. ... Warren, NJ
Chapin, Lance ... Columbus, OH
Chapin, Loraine Etherington ... San Diego, CA
Chapin, Marilyn Y. ... Okemos, MI
Chapin, Mary Carole ... Washington, DC
Chapin, Mary Patricia (Pat) ... Kansas City, KS
Chapin, Melville ... Boston, MA
Chapin, Nathaniel ... New York, NY
Chapin, Patrick N. ... Las Vegas, NV
Salt Lake City, UT
Chapin, Peter A. ... Washington, DC
Chapin, Richard A. ... Champaign, IL
Chapin, Robert B. ... Brush, CO
Chapin, Robert C. ... Bedminster, NJ
Chapin, Robert D. ... Delray Beach, FL
Chapin, Robert E. ... Casper, WY
Chapin, Scott M. ... New York, NY
Chapin Shea McNitt & Carter, A Professional Corporation
Los Angeles, CA
San Diego, CA
Chapin, Sidney P. ... Bakersfield, CA
Chapin, Thomas P. ... Chicago, IL
Chapin, Timothy R. ... Philadelphia, PA
Chapin, Tuck R. ... San Antonio, TX
Chapin, William D. ... Santa Barbara, CA
Chapin, William L. ... Huntington Beach, CA
Chapkis, James R. ... Woodland Hills, CA
Chapkis, Richard A. ... Thousand Oaks, CA
Chapko, Terry J. ... San Francisco, CA
Chapla, Peter W. ... Scranton, PA
Chapla, Valerie M. ... Pleasant Hill, CA
Chaplan, Scott ... Los Angeles, CA
Chapleau, Alfred D. ... Schenectady, NY
Chapleau, David C. ... South Bend, IN
Chapleau, Edward A. ... South Bend, IN
Chapleau & Kuehl ... South Bend, IN
Chaplick, John S., Jr. ... Toms River, NJ
Chaplick, Trevor J. ... Palo Alto, CA
Chaplik, Ira ... Chicago, IL
Chaplin, Anne Kenney ... Boston, MA
Chaplin, Ansel B. ... Boston, MA
Orleans, MA
Chaplin & Chaplin ... Boston, MA
Orleans, MA
Chaplin, Charles K. ... Falls Church, VA
Chaplin, Denise Carroll
Mount Laurel, NJ
Philadelphia, PA
Chaplin, James B. ... Fort Lauderdale, FL
Chaplin, Papa & Gonet ... Richmond, VA

Chaplin, Peggy ... Washington, DC
Baltimore, MD
Chaplin, Robert P., III ... Ravenel, SC
Chaplin, Ron S. ... Chico, CA
Chaplin, Saxby M. ... Charlotte, NC
Chaplin, Scott D. ... Washington, DC
Chaplin, Stephen A. ... Richmond, VA
Chaplin, Susan Pugh ... Lexington, KY
Chaplin, Wayne E. ... Miami, FL
Chaplin, Wesley A. ... Waterloo, IA
Chaplin, William L. ... West Des Moines, IA
Chapline, Edward S., III ... Dallas, TX
Chapline, Eugene P. ... Sinton, TX
Chaplinski, Randall R. ... Kankakee, IL
Chaplinsky, Margaret M. ... Des Moines, IA
Chaplowe, M. Lewis ... Stratford, CT
Chapman, A. Foster ... Spartanburg, SC
Chapman, A. Michael ... Durango, CO
Chapman, Albert D. ... Tyler, TX
Chapman, Alex D., Jr. ... Ville Platte, LA
Chapman, Alger B., Jr. ... New York, NY
Chapman, Amanda Lee ... Orlando, FL
Chapman, Angela D. ... Newburgh, IN
Chapman, Ann K. ... Portland, OR
Chapman, Anne ... San Francisco, CA
Chapman, Ansel J. ... Iowa City, IA
Chapman, Arnold G. ... Plattsburgh, NY
Chapman, Arthur C. ... Chicago, IL
Chapman, Arthur J. ... Los Angeles, CA
Chapman, Arthur, Jr. ... Cape Elizabeth, ME
Chapman, Arthur R. ... Seattle, WA
Chapman & Associates ... Birmingham, MI
Detroit, MI
Chapman & Associates ... Greensboro, NC
Chapman, Avery S. ... New Haven, CT
Chapman, Barry R. ... Valdosta, GA
Chapman, Basil T. ... Palm Desert, CA
Chapman, Benjamin M. ... Sandusky, OH
Chapman, Beth A.
Department of Commerce,
Patent and Trademark Office, GV
Chapman, BethAnn Boudah ... Juneau, AK
Chapman, Billy K. ... Houston, TX
Chapman, Brad A. ... Amarillo, TX
Chapman, Brainerd ... Chicago, IL
Chapman, Brent A. ... Bethpage, NY
Chapman, Brett Robert ... Burbank, CA
Chapman, Brian E. ... Cincinnati, OH
Chapman, Bruce D. ... Vail, CO
Chapman, Bruce D., Attorneys & Counselors At Law, P.C. ... Vail, CO
Chapman, Bruce G. ... Los Angeles, CA
Chapman, Bryan A. ... Washington, DC
Chapman, Byrholdt & Yon ... Anderson, SC
Walhalla, SC
Chapman, C. Alan ... Greenville, SC
Chapman, C. Davis ... Abilene, TX
Chapman, C. Hayden ... Oklahoma City, OK
Chapman, C. Rodney ... Richmond, VA
Chapman, C. Todd ... Greeneville, TN
Chapman, Carl F. ... Chicago, IL
Chapman, Carlyle H., Jr. ... Dallas, TX
Chapman, Carol R. ... Irvine, CA
Chapman, Carolyn ... Coronado, CA
Chapman, Carye Cole ... Oklahoma City, OK
Chapman, Catherine M. ... Chicago, IL
Chapman & Chapman ... Bismarck, ND
Chapman, Chapman & Chapman
Sarasota, FL
Chapman, Chapman & Hines
Waxahachie, TX
Chapman, Charles L. ... Bismarck, ND
Chapman, Charles L. ... Dallas, TX
Chapman, Charles L. ... Haskell, TX
Chapman, Charles L., P.C. ... Dallas, TX
Chapman, Charles Michael
Laguna Niguel, CA
Chapman, Charles W. ... Edwardsville, IL
Chapman, Charles W. ... New York, NY
Chapman, Chester Randy ... Denver, CO
Chapman, Christine C. ... Charlottesville, VA
Chapman, Christofer R. ... Costa Mesa, CA
Chapman, Christopher W. ... Bryan, TX
Chapman, Christy S. ... Chicago, IL
Chapman, Claire C. ... Macon, GA
Chapman, Colin Daniel ... Menlo Park, CA
Chapman, Colleen D. ... Brownsville, CA
Chapman, Conrad D. ... Troy, MI
Chapman, Cornelius J., Jr. ... Boston, MA
Chapman, Cowherd & Turner, P.C.
Brookfield, MO
Chillicothe, MO
Chapman, Craig E. ... New York, NY
Chapman, Crystal L. ... Orangeburg, SC
Chapman and Cutler ... Phoenix, AZ
Chicago, IL
Salt Lake City, UT
Chapman, Cynthia A. ... Warrenton, VA
Chapman, Cynthia B. ... Houston, TX
Chapman, Dale A. ... St. Paul, MN
Chapman, Daniel D. ... San Antonio, TX
Chapman, Daniel E. ... Troy, MI
Chapman, Daniel G. ... Las Vegas, NV
Chapman, David D. ... Meriden, CT
Chapman, David H. ... La Plata, MD
Chapman, David M. ... Indio, CA
Chapman, David R. ... San Diego, CA
Chapman, Deborah C. ... Greensboro, NC
Chapman, Dennis T. ... Omaha, NE
Chapman, Diane P. ... Cleveland, OH
Chapman, Don L. ... Independence, CA
Chapman, Donald D. ... Arlington, VA
Chapman, Donald L. ... Kansas City, MO
Chapman, Donaldson, Jr. ... Brookfield, MO
Chillicothe, MO
Chapman, Donna L. ... Albuquerque, NM
Chapman, Douglas B. ... Bar Harbor, ME
Chapman, Douglas G., III ... Los Angeles, CA

Chapman, Douglas K. ... Toledo, OH
Chapman, Douglas M. ... Oakland, CA
Chapman, Drew G.L. ... New York, NY
Chapman, Dudley H. ... Washington, DC
Chapman, E. William ... Leesburg, VA
Chapman, Edmund Whyte ... Fairfax, VA
Chapman, Edward J., Jr.
Leavenworth, KS
Chapman, Ernest F. ... Washington, DC
Chapman, Farrel H. ... Dallas, TX
Chapman, Fay L. ... Seattle, WA
Chapman, Floyd B. ... Washington, DC
Chapman, Frank R. ... Casper, WY
Chapman, Frederick S. ... Sierra Vista, AZ
Chapman, Fuller & Bollard ... Irvine, CA
Chapman, G. David, III ... Gulf Shores, AL
Chapman, G. William ... Oconomowoc, WI
Chapman, Gary H. ... Peachtree City, GA
Chapman, Gary L. ... Indianapolis, IN
Chapman, Gena M. ... Minneapolis, MN
Chapman, George B., III ... Cleveland, OH
Chapman, George C. ... Dallas, TX
Chapman, George L. ... Toledo, OH
Chapman, Gerald F. ... Bethesda, MD
Chapman, Gerald F., P.A.
Washington, DC
Bethesda, MD
Chapman, Gerard M. ... Greensboro, NC
Chapman, Glucksman & Dean, A Professional Corporation
Costa Mesa, CA
Los Angeles, CA
Chapman, Gordon M. ... New York, NY
Chapman, Grant M. ... St. Louis, MO
Chapman, Harry A., Jr. ... Greenville, SC
Chapman, Harter & Groves, P.A.
Greenville, SC
Chapman, Heidi G. ... Chapel Hill, NC
Chapman, Henkoff, Kessler, Peduto & Saffer
Newark, NJ
Roseland, NJ
Chapman, Howard L. ... Fort Wayne, IN
Chapman, Howard S. ... Chicago, IL
Chapman, Howard S. ... Bedford Heights, OH
Chapman, Hunter B., III ... Culpeper, VA
Chapman & Intrieri, L.L.P.
San Francisco, CA
San Jose, CA
Chapman, Irwin K. ... Moonachie, NJ
Chapman, J. Milton ... Victoria, TX
Chapman, J. Stanley ... Tallahassee, FL
Chapman, J. Winston, Jr. ... Austin, TX
Chapman, Jack F. ... Omaha, NE
Chapman, Jack T. ... El Paso, TX
Chapman, Jackye L. ... Pascagoula, MS
Chapman, James B. ... Akron, OH
Chapman, James C. ... San Jose, CA
Chapman, James L. ... Washington, DC
Chapman, James L., IV ... Norfolk, VA
Chapman, James P. ... Chicago, IL
Chapman, James P., and Associates, Ltd.
Chicago, IL
Chapman, James R., Jr. ... Spring, TX
Chapman, James R., P.C. ... Spring, TX
Chapman, James S. ... Waxahachie, TX
Chapman, James T. ... Arlington, VA
Chapman, James W. ... Los Angeles, CA
Chapman, James W., Jr.
Department of Justice, Tax Division, GV
Chapman, Janis E. ... Denver, CO
Chapman, Jasmine M.
Environmental Protection Agency,
Office of the General Counsel, GV
Chapman, Jason T. ... El Paso, TX
Chapman, Jay H. ... Denver, CO
Chapman, Jeffrey A. ... Dallas, TX
Chapman, Jeffrey J. ... New York, NY
Chapman & Jenkins ... Charlottesville, VA
Chapman, Jennifer E. ... Austin, TX
Chapman, Jerome I. ... Washington, DC
Chapman, Jill M. ... Chicago, IL
Chapman, John B. ... Houston, TX
Chapman, John D. ... Southfield, MI
Chapman, John D. ... New York, NY
Chapman, John F. ... Stone Mountain, GA
Chapman, John G. ... Dallas, TX
Chapman, John H. ... Seattle, WA
Chapman, John Haven ... New York, NY
Chapman, John S. ... Hailey, ID
Chapman, John S. ... Chicago, IL
Chapman, John S. ... Detroit, MI
Chapman, John S. ... Cleveland, OH
Chapman, John S., Ltd. ... Cleveland, OH
Chapman, John T. ... Minneapolis, MN
Chapman, John W. ... San Francisco, CA
San Jose, CA
Chapman, John W. ... Portland, ME
Chapman, John W. ... Brandon, MS
Chapman, John W. ... Kansas City, MO
Chapman, Joseph F., III ... Panama City, FL
Chapman, Judith A. ... South Barrington, IL
Chapman, Judith A. ... Troy, MI
Chapman, Judson M. ... Tallahassee, FL
Chapman, K. Leigh ... Burbank, CA
Chapman, Karen L. ... Denver, CO
Chapman, Katherine L. ... Dallas, TX
Chapman, Kathleen ... Treasury Department,
Office of Regulations and Rulings, GV
Chapman, Kathleen ... Jaffrey, NH
Chapman, Kathleen A. ... Frederick, MD
Chapman, Kathleen H. ... Cedar Rapids, IA
Chapman, Kathryn Ann ... Rosemont, IL
Chapman, Kenneth D. ... Sarasota, FL
Chapman, Kevin G. ... Princeton, NJ
Chapman, Kevin J. ... Mesa, AZ
Chapman, Kevin J. ... Williston, ND
Chapman, Kevin K. ... Hudsonville, MI
Chapman, Kimberly D. ... Fayetteville, GA

Chapman, Kirk E. ...... New York, NY
Chapman, Klein & Associates, P.C. ...... Denver, CO
Chapman, Kristin L. ...... Rockford, IL
Chapman, Kristine Magnuson ...... Boca Raton, FL
Chapman & Kupferer, Ltd. ...... Rutland, VT
Chapman, L. Peyton, III ...... Montgomery, AL
Chapman, Laura Lindsay ...... San Francisco, CA
Chapman, Laurel I. ...... Dublin, OH
Chapman, Lawrence B. ...... Santa Barbara, CA
Chapman, Lawrence B. ...... Houston, TX
Chapman, Lawrence M. ...... La Jolla, CA
Chapman, Lewis & Swan ...... Clarksdale, MS
Chapman, Linda Ann ...... Charlottesville, VA
Chapman, Linda Rice ...... Miami, FL
Chapman, Lisa Madeline ...... Cupertino, CA
Chapman, Lloyd K. ...... Los Angeles, CA
Chapman, Louis B. ...... Wayne, NJ
Chapman, Lynn Marie ...... Akron, OH
Chapman, Marc D. ...... Orlando, FL
Chapman, Marguerite A. ...... Tulsa, OK
Chapman, Marian C. ...... Oakland, CA
Chapman, Martha ...... Department of Justice, Executive Office for Immigration Review, GV
Chapman, Martin A. ...... Carrollton, OH
Chapman, Marvin S. ...... Glencoe, IL
Chapman, Mary A. ...... Hilton Head Island, SC
Chapman, Mary F. ...... Beverly Hills, CA
Las Vegas, NV
Chapman, Maurice D. ...... New York, NY
Chapman, Melissa A. ...... Granite City, IL
Chapman, Merele David ...... Palm Springs, CA
Chapman, Merrill J. ...... Huntington Station, NY
Chapman, Michael J ...... Washington, DC
Chapman, Michael K. ...... Memphis, TN
Chapman, Michael L. ...... Tampa, FL
Chapman, Michael L. ...... Atlanta, GA
Chapman, Miriam R. ...... Department Of The Interior, Office of the Solicitor, GV
Chapman, Mirla ...... Atlanta, GA
Chapman, Morgan S. ...... Raleigh, NC
Chapman, Morris B. ...... Granite City, IL
St. Louis, MO
Chapman, Morris B., & Associates, Ltd. ...... Granite City, IL
St. Louis, MO
Chapman, Nancy Dwyer ...... Bronxville, NY
Chapman, Neil Byron ...... Evansville, IN
Chapman, Nicholas J. ...... Newburyport, MA
Chapman, Nicholas J., P.C. ...... Newburyport, MA
Chapman, Nolan M., Jr. ...... Chillicothe, MO
Chapman, Patricia G. ...... Portland, OR
Chapman, Patricia Lockary ...... Eugene, OR
Chapman, Paulette E. ...... Washington, DC
Chapman, Philip L. ...... Roseland, NJ
Chapman, Popik & White ...... San Francisco, CA
San Jose, CA
Chapman, R. Donald ...... San Jose, CA
Chapman, Ralph E. ...... Clarksdale, MS
Chapman, Richard D. ...... Spring Valley, CA
Chapman, Richard H. ...... Chicago, IL
Chapman, Richard H. ...... Chicago, IL
Chapman, Richard N. ...... Rochester, NY
Chapman, Richard T. ...... Troy, MI
Chapman, Richard T., Jr. ...... Victoria, TX
Chapman, Richard W. ...... Little Rock, AR
Chapman, Robert A. ...... Chicago, IL
Chapman, Robert A., P.C. ...... Chicago, IL
Chapman, Robert B. ...... Chicago, IL
Chapman, Robert E. ...... Honolulu, HI
Chapman, Robert Gray ...... San Jose, CA
Chapman, Robert L. ...... La Jolla, CA
Chapman, Robert L. ...... New York, NY
Chapman, Robert Lee ...... Brookings, OR
Medford, OR
Chapman, Robert R. ...... Washington, DC
Chapman, Robert S. ...... Los Angeles, CA
Chapman, Robert T. ...... Dallas, TX
Chapman, Robin Belville ...... Baltimore, MD
Bel Air, MD
Chapman & Roin ...... Chicago, IL
Chapman, Ron ...... Dallas, TX
Chapman, Ron, Jr. ...... Dallas, TX
Chapman, Ronald A. ...... Troy, MI
Chapman, Ronald L. ...... Bloomington, IN
Chapman, Ronald L. ...... Charlotte, NC
Chapman, Ronald L. ...... Charleston, WV
Chapman, Ronald S. ...... West Palm Beach, FL
Chapman, Ronald W. ...... Birmingham, MI
Chapman, Rosalyn M. ...... Los Angeles, CA
Chapman, Ross E. ...... Kalamazoo, MI
Chapman, Roy A. ...... Sarasota, FL
Chapman, Roy E. ...... San Bernardino, CA
Chapman, Russell D. ...... Dallas, TX
Chapman, Russell W., Jr. ...... Statesville, NC
Chapman, S. James ...... Phoenix, AZ
Chapman, S. Stacy, III ...... Rutland, VT
Chapman, Sandra M. ...... Wheeling, WV
Chapman, Sarah N. ...... New York, NY
Chapman, Scott B. ...... Boca Raton, FL
Chapman, Scott E. ...... Las Vegas, NV
Chapman, Scott M. ...... Lewiston, ID
Chapman, Scott R. ...... Chelsea, MA
Chapman, Shain V. H. ...... Sherman, TX
Chapman, Sharon L. Gerstman ...... Princeton Junction, NJ
Chapman, Shawn Snider ...... Beverly Hills, CA
Chapman, Shelley C. ...... New York, NY
Chapman, Stacey Stern ...... Denver, CO
Chapman, Stacy ...... Los Angeles, CA
Chapman, Stephen Bruce ...... Topeka, KS
Chapman, Stephen J. ...... Dallas, TX
Chapman, Stephen L. ...... Fort Wayne, IN
Chapman, Stephen S. ...... Plano, TX
Chapman, Steven E. ...... Washington, DC
Chapman, Steven F. ...... Waxahachie, TX
Chapman, Stuart Alan ...... Los Angeles, CA
Chapman, Susan ...... Dallas, TX
Chapman, Susan E. ...... Salinas, CA
Chapman, Susan L. ...... Sarasota, FL
Chapman, Susan M. ...... Yardley, PA
Chapman, Susan R. ...... Aurora, CO
Chapman, Terry G. ...... Chicago, IL
Chapman, Terryence F. ...... Kalamazoo, MI
Chapman, Thomas B. ...... Washington, DC
Chapman, Thomas N. ...... Chillicothe, MO
Chapman, Thomas R. ...... Spokane, WA
Chapman, Thomas W. ...... Granite City, IL
Chapman, Thomas W. ...... St. Louis, MO
Chapman, Tia ...... Boston, MA
Chapman, Todd ...... San Francisco, CA
Chapman, Todd A. ...... Maynard, MA
Chapman, Tyler ...... Boston, MA
Chapman, V. Laniel ...... Anderson, SC
Chapman, V. Standish, III ...... Austin, TX
Chapman, Victor L. ...... Orlando, FL
Chapman, Ward ...... Flint, MI
Chapman, Warren N. ...... Norwalk, CT
Chapman, Warren T. ...... Auburn, WA
Chapman and Waters ...... Leavenworth, KS
Chapman, William B. ...... San Francisco, CA
Chapman, William D. ...... Rancho Santa Margarita, CA
Chapman, William D. ...... Boston, MA
Chapman, William H. ...... Seattle, WA
Chapman, William Justin ...... Houston, TX
Chapman, William L. ...... Concord, NH
Chapman, William Leonard ...... Wilmington, DE
Chapman, William M. ...... Sedalia, MO
Chapman, William N. ...... Lakewood, CA
Chapman, William R. ...... Woodland Hills, CA
Chapman, William T. ...... Lincoln Park, MI
Chapman, William T. ...... Fairlee, VT
Chapman, William T., II ...... Evergreen, AL
Chapman & Younger, Law Office of ...... Brandon, MS
Chapman, Yvette M. ...... St. Petersburg, FL
Chapman, Yvonne K. ...... Germantown, TN
Chapman-Haase, Lisa ...... Southfield, MI
Chapman-Plumb, Susan ...... Tahlequah, OK
Chapnick, Barry E. ...... Fort Lauderdale, FL
Chapnick, Bruce P. ...... Sarasota, FL
Chapnick, David B. ...... New York, NY
Chapnick, Ellen P. ...... New York, NY
Chapnick, Irving ...... New York, NY
Chapnick, Jerrold H. ...... Clayton, MO
Chapnick, Michael A. ...... New York, NY
Chapnick, Michele A. ...... Bingham Farms, MI
Chapnick, Randall B. ...... New Haven, CT
Chapnik, Elaine ...... Blue Bell, PA
Chapo, Richard A. ...... San Diego, CA
Chapot, Suzanne J., (Ms.) ...... Martinez, CA
Chapoton, John E. ...... Washington, DC
Chapoton, John E., Jr. ...... Houston, TX
Chapoton, O. Donaldson ...... Washington, DC
Chapp, Sandra J. ...... Torrance, CA
Westland, MI
Chappano, Perry M. ...... Dublin, OH
Chappano Wood PLL ...... Columbus, OH
Dublin, OH
Chappars, Timothy S. ...... Wilmington, OH
Chappas, James G. ...... Topeka, KS
Chappel, Cynthia C. ...... Nashville, TN
Chappel, David R. ...... Seattle, WA
Chappel, Ernest B. ...... Lakewood, WA
Chappel, Gregory M. ...... Oakhurst, CA
Chappel, Sheila H. ...... Stillwater, MN
Chappelear, Claude K. ...... Plano, TX
Chappelear, Stephen E. ...... Columbus, OH
Chappell, Alan ...... Glendale, CA
Chappell, Alan R. ...... Glendale, CA
Chappell, Amy B. ...... Baltimore, MD
Chappell, Andrew B. ...... Iowa City, IA
Chappell, Benjamin R. ...... San Antonio, TX
Chappell, Bill B. ...... Rockwall, TX
Chappell, Bill G. ...... Bainbridge, IN
Chappell, Bill, Jr. ...... Albuquerque, NM
Chappell, Byron B. ...... Lubbock, TX
Chappell & Chappell ...... Portsmouth, RI
Chappell, Christopher P. ...... Boston, MA
Chappell, Claire D. ...... New York, NY
Chappell, Clifford B. ...... Columbia, SC
Chappell, Clovis G. ...... Midland, TX
Chappell Cohen DiFronzo & Zimmershine LLP ...... Boston, MA
Chappell, Cort B. ...... Portsmouth, RI
Chappell, D. Michael ...... Austin, TX
Chappell, David F. ...... Fort Worth, TX
Chappell, Derek Ralph ...... Ottawa, KS
Chappell, Diane L. ...... Nashville, TN
Chappell, Douglas B. ...... Nashville, TN
Chappell, E. Hugh, Jr. ...... Fort Lauderdale, FL
Chappell, E. Hugh, Jr., P.A. ...... Fort Lauderdale, FL
Chappell, Eric P. ...... Portsmouth, RI
Chappell, Erik Grant ...... Monroe, MI
Toledo, OH
Chappell, Guy D., III ...... Birmingham, AL
Chappell, Harriet Lang ...... Wilmington, DE
Chappell, Henry C., Jr. ...... Montgomery, AL
Chappell, Inajo Davis ...... Cleveland, OH
Chappell, J. David ...... Sussex, VA
Chappell, John B. ...... Dinwiddie, VA
Chappell, John C. ...... Lawrence, KS
Chappell, John C. ...... New York, NY
Chappell, John K. ...... Petersburg, IN
Chappell, John S. ...... Indianapolis, IN
Jasper, IN
Chappell, John Wesley ...... Treasury Department, GV
Chappell, Kirsten A. ...... Chicago, IL
Chappell & Lanehart, P.C. ...... Lubbock, TX
Chappell Law Firm, P.A. ...... Albuquerque, NM
Chappell, Mark D. ...... Columbia, SC
Rock Hill, SC
Chappell, Merrie L. ...... Albuquerque, NM
Chappell, Milton L. ...... Springfield, VA
Chappell, Oliver S. ...... Willimantic, CT
Chappell, Parmelee, Johnson & Hill, P.C. ...... Cleburne, TX
Fort Worth, TX
Chappell, R. Harvey, Jr. ...... Richmond, VA
Chappell, Robert A. ...... Englewood, CO
Chappell, Robert G. ...... Abilene, TX
Chappell, Robert H. ...... Richmond, VA
Chappell, Sam M., III ...... McLean, VA
Chappell & Smith, P.A. ...... Columbia, SC
Rock Hill, SC
Chappell, Stephen C. ...... Plymouth Meeting, PA
Chappell, Stephen R. ...... Lexington, KY
Chappell, Susan G. ...... Albuquerque, NM
Chappell, Thomas T. ...... Montclair, NJ
Chappelle, Allan J. ...... Birmingham, AL
Chappelle, Carlos J. ...... Tulsa, OK
Chappelle, Jeffrey T. ...... Philadelphia, PA
Chappelle, Mary E. ...... Albuquerque, NM
Chappelle, Mary E., P.C. ...... Albuquerque, NM
Chappelle, Ray ...... Dallas, TX
Chapper, Amy Miller ...... Baltimore, MD
Chapper, Bruce R. ...... Baltimore, MD
Chapper, Frank M. ...... Silver Spring, MD
Chapper, Joy A. ...... Washington, DC
Chapple, Evans L. ...... Minneapolis, MN
Chapple, Kevin L. ...... Alexandria, VA
Chapple, Thomas L. ...... Arlington, VA
Chapple, Wayne E. ...... Hartford, CT
Chappo, Leslie Elizabeth ...... Trenton, NJ
Chappuis, Charles W. ...... Rayne, LA
Chappuis, John N. ...... Lafayette, LA
Chappuis, Richard D., Jr. ...... Lafayette, LA
Chapralis, Janice A. ...... El Granada, CA
Chapro, Karen K. ...... San Francisco, CA
White Plains, NY
Chapuis & Ramsaur ...... Oakland, CA
Chapuis Ramsaur, Rose C. ...... Oakland, CA
Chapura, Margaret ...... Camilla, GA
Chapuran, Jeffrey J. ...... Lexington, KY
Chapuran, John E. ...... St. Paul, MN
Chapuran, Ronald F. ...... Rochester, NY
Chapus, David P. ...... Rochester, NY
Chaput, Anna M. ...... Roseville, CA
Chaput, Christopher J. ...... St. Paul, MN
Chaput, Kimberley ...... Portland, OR
Chaput, Nicole M. ...... St. Louis, MO
Chapyak, Mary C. ...... White Plains, NY
Char, Andrew W. ...... Honolulu, HI
Char, C. Jeffrey ...... Scotts Valley, CA
Char, Daniel S. ...... Cambridge, MA
Char Hamilton Campbell & Thom, Attorneys at Law, A Law Corporation ...... Honolulu, HI
Char, Kenneth F. C. ...... Honolulu, HI
Char, Patricia H. ...... Seattle, WA
Char, Peter C. P. ...... Honolulu, HI
Char, Randall Y. Kunn ...... Honolulu, HI
Char, Richard J. ...... San Francisco, CA
Char, Robert L. ...... Honolulu, HI
Char Sakamoto Ishii Lum & Ching ...... Honolulu, HI
Char, Vernon F. L. ...... Honolulu, HI
Charach, Hunt L. ...... Charleston, WV
Charamba, Amelia M. ...... Boston, MA
Charamella, John M. ...... Lansing, MI
Charamella, Philip A. ...... Cherry Hill, NJ
Philadelphia, PA
Charamut, William C. ...... Rocky Hill, CT
Charamza, Walter W. ...... Newport Beach, CA
Charanza, Michelle Wood ...... Lufkin, TX
Charap, Ross J. ...... New York, NY
Charapp, David A. ...... Pittsburgh, PA
Charapp, Deese & Weiss, LLP ...... Washington, DC
Bethesda, MD
Richmond, VA
Vienna, VA
Charapp, Michael G. ...... Washington, DC
Vienna, VA
Charatan, Joni Lacks ...... New York, NY
Charboneau, Jean E. ...... Muskegon, MI
Charboneau, Lynette A. ...... Department of Education, Office of the General Counsel, GV
Charboneau, Robert B. ...... Pasadena, CA
Charboneau, Thomas R., Jr. ...... Bloomfield Hills, MI
Charbonier, Mario J. ...... Tampa, FL
Charbonier, Mario J., P.A. ...... Tampa, FL
Charbonneau, Edward A., IV ...... Augusta, ME
Charbonneau, Edward E. ...... Pittsburg, CA
Charbonneau, Edward V. ...... Washington, DC
Charbonneau, Jacqueline M. ...... West Palm Beach, FL
Charbonneau, Jennifer ...... Boise, ID
Charbonneau, John-Claude ...... Rutland, VT
Charbonneau, Joseph A. ...... Brewster, NY
Charbonneau, Leo B. ...... West Warwick, RI
Charbonneau, Robert P. ...... Hollywood, FL
Charbonneau, Ruth ...... Trenton, NJ
Charbonneau, Thomas E. ...... New York, NY
Charbonnet, Elise D. ...... Washington, DC
Charbonnet, John D. ...... Houston, TX
Charbonnet, John Paul ...... Lafayette, LA
Charbonnet, John W. ...... Metairie, LA
Charbonnet, Robert P. ...... New Orleans, LA
Charbonnet, Stephen G. ...... New Orleans, LA
Charbonnet, Stephen P. ...... Los Angeles, CA
Charbonnier, Peter H. ...... Essex, CT
Charchat, Steve ...... Miami, FL
Charchut, Thomas N. ...... Santa Monica, CA
Chard, Brian A. ...... Detroit, MI
Chard & Lloyd ...... Ann Arbor, MI
Chard, Lynn P. ...... Ann Arbor, MI
Chard, R. David ...... North Charleston, SC
Chard, Robert A. ...... Datil, NM
Chard, Roger ...... Ann Arbor, MI
Chard, Wilbur D. ...... Indian River, MI
Chardavoyne, David G. ...... Detroit, MI
Charde, Luke M., Jr. ...... Warwick, NY
Charek, Nicholas C. ...... Jacksonville, FL
Charen, Jerome M. ...... Philadelphia, PA
Charen, Steven C. ...... New York, NY
Charen, Susan J. ...... Department Of Health And Human Services, Office of the General Counsel, GV
Charendoff, Margaret Loud ...... Philadelphia, PA
Chareq, Adel J. ...... Indianapolis, IN
Charest, Clarence R. ...... Livonia, MI
Charest, Clarence R., Jr. ...... Livonia, MI
Charest, Clarence R., Jr., P.C. ...... Livonia, MI
Charest, Clarence R., P.C. ...... Livonia, MI
Charest, Gregg M. ...... Nashua, NH
Charest, Suzanne J. ...... Newport Beach, CA
Charette, Deborah S. ...... Small Business Administration, Office of the General Counsel, GV
Charfoos & Christensen, P.C. ...... Detroit, MI
Southfield, MI
Charfoos, Lawrence S. ...... Detroit, MI
Charfoos, Myron B. ...... Detroit, MI
Farmington Hills, MI
Charfoos, Reiter, Peterson, Holmquist & Pilchak, P.C. ...... Detroit, MI
Farmington Hills, MI
Flint, MI
Pontiac, MI
Chargar, Richard S. ...... Stamford, CT
Chargin, Ann M. ...... Stockton, CA
Chargin, Anthony J. ...... Stockton, CA
Chargin, John Mark ...... Santa Clara, CA
Chargin, Michael T. ...... Santa Clara, CA
Chargin, Robt. N. ...... Stockton, CA
Chargin, Steven S. ...... San Jose, CA
Chargin, Victor A., Jr. ...... Cupertino, CA
Chargo, Mitchel C. ...... Minneapolis, MN
Chari, Roger S. ...... New York, NY
Charie, Craig S. ...... New York, NY
Chariff, Wayne M. ...... Binghamton, NY
Charipper, Douglas S. ...... Parsippany, NJ
Charish, Michael A. ...... New York, NY
Charisse, Nico ...... Paso Robles, CA
Chariton, Jerry B. ...... Wilkes-Barre, PA
Chariton & Schwager ...... Scranton, PA
Wilkes-Barre, PA
Charity & Associates ...... Chicago, IL
Charity, Elvin E. ...... Chicago, IL
Charkes, Evan J. ...... New York, NY
Charkey, Alan J. ...... Philadelphia, PA
Charkoudian, Stephen G. ...... Boston, MA
Charkovsky, Robert ...... Chicago, IL
Charkow, Andrew B. ...... Newark, NJ
Charkow, Jeffrey B. ...... Chicago, IL
Charkow, Kristen Davey ...... Chicago, IL
Charla, Leonard F. ...... Detroit, MI
Charland, Gary G. ...... Pleasant Hill, CA
Charland, Gerald L. ...... Portage, MI
Charland, John E. ...... Phoenix, AZ
Charland, Robert J. ...... Fitchburg, MA
Charlap, Allan G. ...... Corning, NY
Charle, Edwin G., Jr. ...... Athens, OH
Charlebois, Ronald T. ...... Troy, MI
Charles, Adelbert K. ...... Elyria, OH
Charles, Alan F. ...... Lake Oswego, OR
Charles, Alfred W. ...... New York, NY
Charles, Aliette-Marie ...... Orlando, FL
Charles, Allan E. ...... San Francisco, CA
Charles, Amy Kendall ...... Dresher, PA
Charles, Barry A. ...... Bridgeport, CT
Charles, Bliss L. ...... Huntington, WV
Charles, Bradford H. ...... Lebanon, PA
Charles, Brandie N. ...... Los Angeles, CA
Charles, Bruce ...... Santa Fe, NM
Charles, Bruce H. ...... Irvine, CA
Charles, Carim ...... Vista, CA
Charles, Catherine E. ...... Fairfax, VA
Charles & Charles ...... Bethesda, MD
Charles, Dana F. ...... Miami, FL
Charles, David F. ...... La Jolla, CA
Charles, David J. ...... Washington, DC
Charles, David L. ...... Des Moines, IA
Charles, David M. ...... Pittsburgh, PA
Charles, David R. ...... Chicago, IL
Charles, Deborah St. Lawrence ...... Baltimore, MD
Charles, Debra A. ...... Oklahoma City, OK
Charles, Dennis G. ...... Allentown, PA
Charles, Donald R., Jr. ...... Ocean City, NJ
Charles, Drake H. ...... Olympia, WA
Charles, Edwin B. ...... Johnson City, TN
Charles, Eloise ...... Houston, TX
Charles, Faith L. ...... New York, NY
Charles, Frederick I. ...... Allentown, PA
Charles, Fredrick E. ...... Allentown, PA
Charles & Freebern ...... Glens Falls, NY
Charles, G. Fred, Jr. ...... Ashland, KY
Charles, Gary ...... Irvine, CA
Charles, Gregory J. ...... Covington, LA
Metairie, LA

Charles, Harry ... St. Louis, MO
Charles, Hopkins G. ... Myrtle Beach, SC
Charles, James David ... Buffalo, NY
Charles, James G. ... Bethesda, MD
Charles, James L. ... Nashville, TN
Charles, James N. ... Daytona Beach, FL
DeLand, FL
Charles, James N. ... Ormond Beach, FL
Charles, James N. ... Palm Coast, FL
Charles, Janet Madden ... Indianapolis, IN
Charles, Jeffrey B. ... Holland, OH
Charles, Jerome C. ... Teaneck, NJ
Charles, Jillian E. ... Washington, DC
Charles, John D. ... Clifton Park, NY
Charles, John W., III ... Helena, AL
Charles, Joseph ... Newark, NJ
Charles, Joseph W. ... Glendale, AZ
Charles, Kane & Dye LLP ... Irvine, CA
Charles, Kathy ... Bowie, MD
Charles & Keist, P.C. ... Glendale, AZ
Charles, Kelly N. ... Miami, FL
Charles, Kimberly L. ... Columbus, OH
Charles, Kira ... New York, NY
Charles, Kristin ... Rancho Cordova, CA
Charles & Lance ... Johnson City, TN
Charles L. Carson Law Offices
San Luis Obispo, CA
Charles, Lee D. ... New York, NY
Charles, Lewis W. ... Portage, WI
Charles, Margaret M. ... Washington, DC
Charles, Margaret W. ... Doylestown, PA
Charles, Marianne J. ... Greenwich, CT
Charles, Marina T. ... Washington, DC
Charles, Mark ... Los Angeles, CA
Charles, Mark D. ... Phoenix, AZ
Charles, Mark H. ... New York, NY
Charles, Melissa A. ... Longview, TX
Charles, Paula M. ... Covington, LA
Charles, Rhonda Yvette Pindell
Baltimore, MD
Charles, Rob ... Tucson, AZ
Charles, Robert B. ... Department of Defense,
Defense Legal Services Agency, GV
Charles, Robert H. ... Washington, DC
Charles, Robert L. ... San Antonio, TX
Charles, Robert M. ... Green Bay, WI
Charles, Rosalyn Cary ... West Orange, NJ
Charles, Rosalyn Cary, The Law Offices of
West Orange, NJ
Charles, Scott K. ... New York, NY
Charles, Stephan ... Manchester, KY
Charles, Stephanie ... Woodland Hills, CA
Charles, Steven A. ... Baltimore, MD
Charles, Suzanne H. ... Clifton Park, NY
Charles, Thomas A. ... Pittsburgh, PA
Charles, Warren P. ... Olympia, WA
Charles, William K., III ... Greenwood, SC
Charles, William K., Jr. ... Greenwood, SC
Charles & Woodford, LLC
Baltimore, MD
Charleson & Charleson ... Providence, RI
Charleson, David A. ... Providence, RI
Charleson, Mark A. ... Providence, RI
Charleston, Mark ... Philadelphia, PA
Charleston, R. Jonathan ... Durham, NC
Charleston, Robert D. ... Bala Cynwyd, PA
Charleston, Robin P. ... Chicago, IL
Charlesworth, Denis J. ... Baltimore, MD
Charlesworth, Jacqueline C.
New York, NY
Charlesworth, Timothy D. ... Allentown, PA
Charlesworth, Victoria ... Little Rock, AR
Charley, Frances Woerner ... Pittsburgh, PA
Charlick, Shereen J. ... Los Angeles, CA
Charlier, Patricia A. ... Neenah, WI
Charlier, Scott G. ... Salt Lake City, UT
Charlip, Ari M. ... Bloomfield Hills, MI
Charlip, David H. ... Fort Lauderdale, FL
Charlip, Eliot ... Southfield, MI
Charlip, Steven L. ... Boston, MA
Charlow, Andrea S. ... Des Moines, IA
Charlow, Robin ... Hempstead, NY
Charls, Jerome J. ... Harrison, OH
Charls, Joseph E. ... Cincinnati, OH
Charlse, Sheri Stein ... Boca Raton, FL
Charlson, Alan E. ... St. Louis, MO
Charlson Bredehoft, P.C. ... Reston, VA
Charlson, Curtis L. ... Reston, VA
Charlson, Karen M. ... St. Paul, MN
Charlson, Marben & Jorgenson, P.A.
Thief River Falls, MN
Charlson, Michael L. ... Palo Alto, CA
Charlson, Noah H. ... New York, NY
Charlston, Jeffrey A. ... Los Angeles, CA
Charlston, Revich & Williams LLP
Los Angeles, CA
Charlton, Allan M. ... Trenton, MI
Charlton, C. Brian ... Albuquerque, NM
Charlton, Carla E. ... Pittsburgh, PA
Charlton, Charles P. ... Beverly Hills, CA
Charlton, Clyde H. ... Sausalito, CA
Charlton, David M. ... Baton Rouge, LA
Charlton, Edward J. ... Philadelphia, PA
Charlton, Guy C. ... Milwaukee, WI
Charlton, J. Eric ... Syracuse, NY
Charlton, James M. ... Wheaton, IL
Charlton, Janet Z. ... Wilmington, DE
Charlton, Janna ... Houston, TX
Charlton, Katherine L. ... Milwaukee, WI
Charlton, L. Jane ... Pittsburgh, PA
Charlton Law Firm ... Milwaukee, WI
Charlton, Nykolee A. ... Spokane, WA
Charlton, Paul K. ... Phoenix, AZ
Charlton, Richard ... New York, NY
Charlton, Richard D., Jr. ... Topeka, KS
Charlton, Richard E., III ... Memphis, TN
Charlton, Robert F., Jr. ... Reading, MA
Charlton, Scott ... Tampa, FL
Charlton, Susan H. ... Phoenix, AZ
Charlton, Suzan F. ... Washington, DC
Charlton, William C. ... Houston, TX
Charlton, Wm. Stuart ... Kansas City, MO
Charlton-Perrin, Gawain ... Chicago, IL
Charm, Elizabeth Martha ... Boston, MA
Charmasson, Henri J. A. ... San Diego, CA
Charme, Stephen M. ... Florham Park, NJ
Charmoy, Ira B. ... Fairfield, CT
Charmoy, Ira B., L.L.C., The Law Offices of
Fairfield, CT
Charmoy, Scott M. ... Fairfield, CT
Charmoy, Stanley ... Boston, MA
Charmoy, Stolzberg & Holian ... Boston, MA
Charms, Stephen J. ... Cleveland, OH
Charn, Jeanne ... Jamaica Plain, MA
Charnas, Charles N. ... Palo Alto, CA
Charnas, Douglas W. ... Washington, DC
Charnas, Eileen ... Novi, MI
Charnas, Scott E. ... Boston, MA
Charnas, Stephen ... Albuquerque, NM
Charnas, William Vassilios ... New York, NY
Charnasky, Vincent J. ... Phoenix, MD
Charnay, John B. ... Los Angeles, CA
Charne, David L. ... New York, NY
Charne, Irvin B. ... Milwaukee, WI
Charne, James I. ... Santa Monica, CA
Charnecki, John M. ... St. Louis, MO
Charness, Adam H. ... Washington, DC
Charneski, Carl C.
Environmental Protection Agency,
Office of Administrative Law Judges, GV
Charness, Fred ... West Hills, CA
Charness, Michael R. ... Washington, DC
Charness, Michelle A. ... Los Angeles, CA
Charnetski, Donald J. ... Grinnell, IA
Charnetski, Olson, Lacina & Garland
Grinnell, IA
Charnetsky, Peter P. ... Vestal, NY
Charney, April C. ... Sarasota, FL
Charney, David E. ... Oklahoma City, OK
Dallas, TX
Charney, Dennis M. ... Boise, ID
Charney, Diane F. ... Alexandria, VA
Charney, Elaine H. ... Lansing, MI
Charney, Harold ... Owasso, OK
Charney, Harold S. ... Portland, OR
Charney, Jack G. ... La Jolla, CA
San Diego, CA
Charney, Jeffrey S. ... Linden, NJ
Charney, Jonathan I. ... Nashville, TN
Charney, Leon H. ... New York, NY
Charney, Leonard J. ... New York, NY
Charney, Marc L. ... Oxnard, CA
Charney, Marcia L. ... Kansas City, MO
Charney, Michael D. ... Palo Alto, CA
Charney, Mitchell A. ... Louisville, KY
Charney, Norman M. ... Spokane, WA
Charney, Randee F. ... Owasso, OK
Charney, Richard M. ... Elmhurst, NY
Charney, Scott C. ... Bronx, NY
Charney, Scott J. ... Springfield, MA
Charney, Shawna F. ... Rosemont, IL
Charney, Steven M. ... River Edge, NJ
New York, NY
Charney, Stuart A. ... Chicago, IL
Charney, Wolfe R. ... New York, NY
Charnholm, Rodney A. ... Green Bay, WI
Charnin, Edwin N. ... Garden City, NY
Great Neck, NY
Charnin & Trabucchi ... Garden City, NY
Great Neck, NY
Charnis, Jonathan ... Forest Hills, NY
Charnley, Richard L. ... Santa Monica, CA
Charno, George H., Jr. ... Kansas City, MO
Charno, Steven R. ... San Francisco, CA
Charnock, John N., Jr. ... Charleston, WV
Charnock, Kelly R. ... Charleston, WV
Charnoff, Deborah B. ... Washington, DC
Charnoff, Gerald, (P.C.) ... Washington, DC
Charnoff, Jonathan H. ... Fairfax, VA
Charnoff, Richard W. ... New York, NY
Charnoff, Robert J.
Treasury Department, GV
Charnoff, Samuel K. ... Washington, DC
Charnov, Bruce H. ... Hempstead, NY
Charnovitz, Steve ... Washington, DC
Charns, Mark A. ... Durham, NC
Charnstrom, Andrew C. ... Indianapolis, IN
Charny, Judith S. ... Palmyra, NJ
Charny, Richard B. ... Haddonfield, NJ
Charon, Jay A. ... Merrillville, IN
Charon, Regina L. ... Morgantown, WV
Charone, Sheldon M. ... Chicago, IL
Charonko, John J. ... Charleston, WV
Charos, Augustus, Jr. ... Providence, RI
Charos, Glenn W. ... Del Mar, CA
Charouhis, William N. ... Miami, FL
Charouhis, William N., P.A. ... Miami, FL
Charous, David A. ... Chicago, IL
Charpentier, Kent ... St. Paul, MN
Charpentier & Lange ... Brainerd, MN
Charpentier, Raymond A. ... Brainerd, MN
Charpentier, Rosa Lee ... Poughkeepsie, NY
Charpentier, Stephen G. ... Melbourne, FL
Charpentier, Troy J. ... Baton Rouge, LA
Charpilloz, Sylvia S. ... New York, NY
Charrier, Charles K. ... Alexandria, LA
Charrier & Charrier ... Alexandria, LA
Charrier, John O., Jr. ... Alexandria, LA
Charriez, Gilberto M. ... San Juan, PR
Charron, David W. ... Grand Rapids, MI
Tallmadge, MI
Charron & Hanisch, P.L.C.
Grand Rapids, MI
Tallmadge, MI
Charron, Harold F., Jr. ... Alexandria, VA
Charron, Kenneth G. ... Jacksonville, FL
Charron, Mary Anne Alicia ... Hartford, CT
Charron, Raymond A. ... River Rouge, MI
Charron, Robert Frank ... Hartford, CT
Charron, William ... New York, NY
Charrow, Robert P. ... Washington, DC
Charsinsky, Arthur Z. ... Florham Park, NJ
Chartan, Michael L. ... New York, NY
Charter, Brian H. ... Sacramento, CA
Charter, Janice L. ... Denver, CO
Charter, Joseph M. ... Medford, OR
Charter, Mark C. ... Kalamazoo, MI
Charter, Stephanie A. ... Las Vegas, NV
Charters, A. William ... Norfolk, VA
Charters, Andrea L. ... St. Louis, MO
Charters, Heck, O'Donnell, Petrulis &
Zorza, P.C. ... Detroit, MI
Troy, MI
Charters, John P. ... Troy, MI
Chartier, David S. ... Milwaukee, WI
Chartier, Ogan, Brady, Lukakis, Shute &
Emma ... Chicopee, MA
Holyoke, MA
Chartock, Michael D. ... Chestnut Hill, MA
Chartoff, Laura L. ... New York, NY
Chartoff, Robert ... St. Helena, CA
Charton, Lloyd ... Santa Ana, CA
Santa Ana, CA
Charton, Sandra M. ... Boston, MA
Chartove, Alex ... Washington, DC
Chartrand, Arthur J. ... Olathe, KS
Chartrand & Badgley
Bloomfield Hills, MI
Pontiac, MI
Chartrand, Cory B. ... Modesto, CA
Chartrand, Daniel B. ... Clayton, MO
Chartrand, Douglas ... Bloomfield Hills, MI
Pontiac, MI
Chartrand, G. Lewis, Jr. ... Sacramento, CA
Chartrand, George J. ... Annapolis, MD
Chartrand Law Office ... Olathe, KS
Chartraw, Tina M. ... Reno, NV
Chartz, Jane B. ... Berkeley, CA
Charvat, John L., Jr.
Department of the Army,
Office of the Judge Advocate General, GV
Charvat, Lori J. ... Blaine, WA
Charvat, Marie ... Columbus, OH
Charvat, Richard F. ... Long Beach, CA
Charvet, Ina Christina ... Arlington, VA
Charvet, Josée G. ... New York, NY
Charvet, Kathleen Krail
New Orleans, LA
Charwat, Mark S. ... Garden City, NY
Charwat, Mark S., P.C. ... Garden City, NY
Charwat, Martin A. ... Poughkeepsie, NY
Charyk, William R. ... Washington, DC
Charytan, Lynn R. ... Washington, DC
Chasalow, Irwin ... Los Angeles, CA
Chasalow, Michael A. ... Los Angeles, CA
Chasan, Andrew M. ... Boise, ID
Chasan, Bruce J. ... Philadelphia, PA
Chasan, Jonathan S. ... New York, NY
Chasan, Leon ... Miami, FL
Tampa, FL
Chasan, Leyner, Bariso & Lamparello
Jersey City, NJ
Secaucus, NJ
Chasan, Mark S. ... Woodland Hills, CA
Chasan, Tamara ... Philadelphia, PA
Chasanov, Amy B. ... Washington, DC
Chasanov, William M. ... Georgetown, DE
Chasanow, Deborah K. ... Greenbelt, MD
Chasar, Kathleen Scott ... Trenton, NJ
Chase, A. Scot ... Houston, TX
Chase, Adam W. ... Boulder, CO
Chase, Alan C. ... Red Lodge, MT
Chase, Alan R. ... Miami, FL
Chase, Albert L. ... Lansdale, PA
Chase, Alycia W. ... West Bloomfield, MI
Chase, Amy Fisher ... Chicago, IL
Chase, Ann E. ... Syracuse, NY
Chase, Anthony R. ... Houston, TX
Chase, Arnold ... Suffern, NY
Chase, Barbara B. ... North Miami Beach, FL
Chase, Barry O. ... Miami, FL
Chase, Barry Oliver, P.A. ... Miami, FL
Chase, Berenstein and Murray
Burlingame, CA
Chase, Beverly Fanger ... New York, NY
Chase, Bradley ... Fairfax, VA
Chase, Brian F. ... San Francisco, CA
Chase, Brian N. ... Walnut Creek, CA
Chase, Bruce E. ... Hackensack, NJ
Chase, Bruce H. ... Melbourne, FL
Chase, Bryan E. ... Boston, MA
Chase, Bryce S. ... Princeton, NJ
Trenton, NJ
Chase, Cara M. ... Waco, TX
Chase, Carl C. ... Centerville, TX
Chase, Carol A. ... Malibu, CA
Chase, Carol J. ... Grand Rapids, MI
Chase, Carol L. ... San Francisco, CA
Chase, Carole R. ... Detroit, MI
Chase, Catherine Babics ... Washington, DC
Chase, Celeste ... New York, NY
Chase, Celeste A. ... Philadelphia, PA
Chase, Charles E. ... Burlingame, CA
Chase, Charles E. ... Boston, MA
Chase, Charles H. ... Los Angeles, CA
Chase, Charles R. ... Buffalo, NY
Chase and Chase ... Hackensack, NJ
Chase, Cheryl A. ... Hartford, CT
Chase, Christine D. ... Erie, PA
Chase, Christine L. ... Walnut Creek, CA
Chase, Christine R. ... Chicago, IL
Chase, Christopher ... Santa Monica, CA
Chase, Curt J. ... Kansas City, MO
Chase, Cynthia L. ... Campbell, CA
Chase, Dale H. ... Medina, OH
Chase, D. A. N. ... Overland Park, KS
Chase, Daniel E. ... Hamilton, NJ
Chase, Darrick T. ... San Francisco, CA
Chase, David A., II ... Bangor, ME
Chase, David R. ... Miami, FL
Chase, David W. ... Atlantic, IA
Griswold, IA
Chase, Dennis ... Dallas, TX
Chase, Dennis R. ... Hempstead, NY
Chase, Donald H. ... New York, NY
Chase, Dwight S. ... New York, NY
Chase, Edgar L., III ... New Orleans, LA
Chase, Edward J. ... Cleveland, OH
Chase, Edward T. ... New York, NY
Chase, Edward T., Law Offices of
New York, NY
Chase, Elisha A. ... Denver, CO
Chase, Ellen N. ... Detroit, MI
Chase, Eric A. ... Sherman Oaks, CA
Chase, Eric C. ... Brea, CA
Chase, Eric L. ... Florham Park, NJ
New York, NY
Chase, Eugene A. ... Washington, DC
Chase, F. Brian ... New Orleans, LA
Chase, Francis G. ... Dedham, MA
Chase, Frederick, Jr.
New Port Richey, FL
Chase, G. Thomas ... Columbia, SC
Chase, Gary M. ... United States Senate,
Committee Legal Personnel, GV
Chase, Geoffrey L. ... Allentown, PA
Chase, George ... Waco, TX
Chase, Gerald M. ... Portland, OR
Chase, Geri Lyons ... Greenbelt, MD
Chase & Gilmore ... New Port Richey, FL
Chase, Glenn D. ... Albany, NY
Chase, Gregory W. ... Albuquerque, NM
Chase, Hal, Jr. ... San Francisco, CA
Chase, Harry L. ... Baltimore, MD
Chase, I. William ... Baltimore, MD
Chase, Irving M. ... Costa Mesa, CA
Chase, J. Scott ... Dallas, TX
Chase, James L. ... Pensacola, FL
Chase, James L., & Associates, P.A.
Pensacola, FL
Chase, James M. ... New Haven, CT
Chase, James S. ... Charleston, WV
Chase, Jeffrey A. ... Denver, CO
Chase, Jeffrey L. ... Newark, NJ
New York, NY
Chase, Jeffrey S. ... New York, NY
Chase, Jill M. ... Las Vegas, NV
Chase, Joan Gregory ... Bronxville, NY
Chase, Jodi L. ... Tallahassee, FL
Chase, Joel S. ... Warwick, RI
Chase, John B. ... Greenwich, CT
Chase, John J. ... Fort Garland, CO
Chase, John M., III ... Detroit, MI
Chase, John M., Jr. ... Detroit, MI
Chase, John M., Jr., P.C. ... Detroit, MI
Chase, John R. ... Florence, SC
Chase, Jonathan A. ... Briarcliff Manor, NY
Chase, Jonathan S. ... Oakland, CA
Chase, Joseph F. ... Rochester, MN
Chase, Joseph J. ... West Palm Beach, FL
Chase, Julia Best ... Tampa, FL
Chase, Julius S. ... Lake Worth, FL
Chase, Karla ... Beaver Dam, WI
Mayville, WI
Chase, Kathleen F. ... Vernon, CT
Chase, Kathryn Connolly ... Assinippi, MA
Chase, Kathryn S. ... Eugene, OR
Chase, Kelly R. ... Minden, NV
Chase, Kenneth E. ... Scottsdale, AZ
Chase, Kenneth E., P.C. ... Scottsdale, AZ
Chase, Kenneth H. ... New York, NY
Chase, Kevin K. ... Orlando, FL
Chase Kurshan Suhr Weidenfeld Herzfeld &
Rubin, LLC ... Newark, NJ
Chase, Kyle S. ... Boston, MA
Chase, L. Bryce ... Delano, CA
Chase, Lawrence D. ... Rochester, NY
Chase, Lee James, III ... Memphis, TN
Chase, Leonard E. ... San Juan, TX
Chase, Lester H. ... Glen Cove, NY
Chase, Linda D. ... Medfield, MA
Chase, Linda J. ... Washington, DC
Chase, Lisa ... Tucson, AZ
Chase, Lynn G. ... South Bend, IN
Chase, Marc Alan ... Hackensack, NJ
Chase, Marc J. ... Brooklyn, NY
Chase, Mark K. ... Moorestown, NJ
Chase, Martha M. ... Oakland, CA
Chase, Martha S. ... Nogales, AZ
Chase, Melissa Ann ... Marysville, OH
Chase, Michael B. ... St. Paul, MN
Chase, Michael C. ... Bentonville, AR
Chase, Michael D. ... Tupelo, MS
Chase, Michael E.
Department of Transportation,
Federal Aviation Administration, GV
Chase, Michael E. ... Columbia, SC
Chase, Michael Eric ... Sacramento, CA
Chase, Michael G. ... Cleveland, OH
Chase, Michael P. ... Miami, FL
Chase, Michelle T. ... Aurora, IL
Chase & Myers ... Eureka, KS
Chase, Nicholas J. ... Chevy Chase, MD
Chase, Nicholas W. ... Minneapolis, MN
Chase, Nicole H. ... New York, NY
Chase, Nina Wisznat ... Boca Raton, FL
Chase, Norma ... Pittsburgh, PA
Chase, Norman G. ... Colorado Springs, CO
Chase, Norman K. ... Shelton, CT
Chase, Olsen, Kloet & Gunderson
Oostburg, WI
Chase, Oscar G. ... New York, NY

Chase, Patrick Edward ... Frederick, MD
Chase, Paul J. ... New York, NY
Chase, Peter ... Boston, MA
Chase, Richard Alan ... Jamaica, NY
Chase, Richard D. ... University City, MO
Chase, Richard E. ... Williamson, NY
Chase, Richard S. ... Chicago, IL
Chase, Richard T. ... Minneapolis, MN
Chase, Richard W. ... New York, NY
Chase, Robert D. ... Modesto, CA
Chase, Robert H. ... Metropolis, IL
Chase, Robert L. ... Waterbury, CT
Chase, Robert S. ... Brockton, MA
Chase, Robert S., II ... Washington, DC
Chase & Roberts, P.C. ... Florence, SC
Myrtle Beach, SC
Chase, Rodney A. ... Los Angeles, CA
Chase, Rodney S., Jr. ... New York, NY
Chase, Roger F. ... Spokane, WA
Chase, Roland F. ... Newport, RI
Chase, Rosemary Allyn ... St. Clair Shores, MI
Chase, Rotchford, Drukker & Bogust
Los Angeles, CA
Chase, Sam J. ... Abilene, TX
Chase, Sam J., P.C., Law Offices of
Abilene, TX
Chase, Sandra G. ... Atlanta, GA
Chase, Sarah ... Boston, MA
Chase, Scott T. ... Glendale Heights, IL
Chase, Seymour ... Hackensack, NJ
Chase, Seymour M., P.C.
Snowmass Village, CO
Chase, Shirley I. ... St. Paul, MN
Chase, Stephanie ... Santa Monica, CA
Chase, Stephen M. ... Los Angeles, CA
Chase, Steven A. ... Burlingame, CA
Chase, Steven A. ... Portland, OR
Chase, Steven D. ... Jamaica, NY
Chase, Steven J. ... Sarasota, FL
Chase, Tamara S. ... Middlebury, VT
Chase, Theodore ... Boston, MA
Chase, Thomas C. ... Fort Myers, FL
Chase, Thomas C. ... Boston, MA
Chase, Thomas C., P.A. ... Fort Myers, FL
Chase, Thomas D. ... Elgin, IL
Chase, Thomas E. ... New York, NY
Chase, Thomas G., Jr. ... Waco, TX
Chase, Thomas J. ... Maspeth, NY
Chase, Todd ... Washington, DC
Chase, Tracy L. ... Las Vegas, NV
Reno, NV
Chase, Victoria L. ... Washington, DC
Chase, W. Bradford, Jr. ... Natick, MA
Chase & Weil ... Portland, OR
Chase & Weiss ... Southfield, MI
Chase, William D. ... Department of Justice, Federal Bureau of Investigation, GV
Chase, William E. ... Ashland, WI
Chase & Yakimo, L.C.
Overland Park, KS
Kansas City, MO
Chase-Borden, Mary Ann ... Boston, MA
Chase-Lubitz, Jeffrey F. ... Providence, RI
Chasen, Andrea Nager ... Longmeadow, MA
Chasen, Barry M. ... Greenbelt, MD
Chasen & Chasen ... Washington, DC
Chasen, Harold A. ... Houston, TX
Chasen, Irving L. ... Washington, DC
Chasen, Jeffrey I. ... Chevy Chase, MD
Chasen, Jerry Simon ... Miami Beach, FL
Chasen, Karen T. ... New York, NY
Chasen, Nancy H. ... Bethesda, MD
Chasen, Ronald L. ... Washington, DC
Chaset, Alan J. ... Miami, FL
Chaset, Laurence G. ... San Francisco, CA
Chasey, Jacqueline ... New York, NY
Chasez, Alma L. ... New Orleans, LA
Chasin, Charles ... New York, NY
Chasin, Gail B. ... Greenwich, CT
Chasin, Joseph
Treasury Department, GV
Chasin, Keith ... Miami, FL
Chasin, Milton ... New York, NY
Chasin, Thomas H. ... Beverly Hills, CA
Chasin, Tod S. ... Roseland, NJ
Chaskes, Deborah M. ... Vienna, VA
Chaskes, Robert I. ... Miami, FL
Chaskin, Catherine F. ... Chicago, IL
Chaskin, Jay L. ... Fairfield, CT
Chaskin, Richard M. ... Redondo Beach, CA
Chasle, Dama C. ... Huntington Beach, CA
Chasler and Bowman, P.L.C.
Winchester, VA
Chasler, Thomas J. ... Winchester, VA
Chasman, Herbert ... Laguna Niguel, CA
Chasney, Laura H. ... Baltimore, MD
Chasnis, Dogger & Grierson, P.C.
Saginaw, MI
Chasnis, John A. ... Saginaw, MI
Chasnis, Robert J. ... Saginaw, MI
Chasnoff, Abraham J. ... New Brunswick, NJ
Chasnoff, Barry A. ... San Antonio, TX
Chasnoff, Jack M. ... St. Louis, MO
Chasnoff, Joel ... Washington, DC
Chasnoff, Joel ... Olney, MD
Chasnoff, Jules ... St. Louis, MO
Chasnow, Herman ... Union, NJ
Chasnow, Jeffrey B. ... Washington, DC
Chasnow, Robert M. ... Washington, DC
Chason, Allan R. ... Bay Minette, AL
Chason, Cecil G. ... Foley, AL
Chason & Chason, P.C. ... Bay Minette, AL
Chason, Craig E. ... McLean, VA
Chason, Darryl R. ... Lynbrook, NY
Chason, Eric D. ... Washington, DC
Chason, J. Kevin ... Cairo, GA
Chason, James R. ... Towson, MD
Chason, John Earle ... Bay Minette, AL
Chason, John T. ... Atlanta, GA
Chason & Underwood ... Foley, AL
Chason, W. H. ... Cairo, GA
Chason & Willett ... Cairo, GA
Chass, Mark Irwin ... New York, NY
Reno, NV
Chassaignac, Charles L.
New Orleans, LA
Chassaignac, Charles L., IV
Baton Rouge, LA
Chassaing, J. Patrick ... St. Louis, MO
Chasse, Andrew W. ... Bangor, ME
Chasse, Eric C. ... Raleigh, NC
Chasse, Jeffrey M. ... Sturbridge, MA
Chasse, Mark E. ... Portland, OR
Chasse & Roche, P.C. ... Sturbridge, MA
Chassen, Charles I. ... North Miami Beach, FL
Chassen, Jon C. ... Miami, FL
Chasser, Timothy G. ... Columbus, OH
Chasser, Timothy G. ... Hilliard, OH
Chassin, Richard N. ... New York, NY
Chassman, Mark B. ... Los Angeles, CA
Chassman, Peter J. ... Houston, TX
Chassman, Yang & Seelig, LLP
Los Angeles, CA
Chassman-Smith, Leslie ... Miami, FL
Chasson, Jill J. ... Phoenix, AZ
Chastain, B. Lynn ... Atlanta, GA
Chastain, Bud R. ... Corpus Christi, TX
Chastain, Charles C. ... Oklahoma City, OK
Chastain, David J. ... Birmingham, AL
Chastain, Dixie H., (Mrs.) ... Miami, FL
Chastain, Edward B. ... Chicago, IL
New York, NY
Chastain, Edward E. ... Lago Vista, TX
Chastain, Elizabeth Helen ... Jackson, MO
Chastain, James R., Jr. ... Baton Rouge, LA
Chastain, Jeanne O. ... Corpus Christi, TX
Chastain, Jermaine ... Santa Barbara, CA
Chastain, John L. ... Administrative Office Of The United States Courts, GV
Chastain, Karen M. ... Jacksonville, FL
Chastain, Kimberly J. ... Dallas, TX
Chastain, L. Joel ... Barnwell, SC
Chastain, Lee E. ... Austin, TX
Chastain, Margaret E. ... Williamston, SC
Chastain, Merritt B., III ... Houston, TX
Chastain, Merritt B., Jr., (P.L.C.)
Bossier City, LA
Shreveport, LA
Chastain, Myron N. ... St. Petersburg, FL
Chastain, Parks T. ... Nashville, TN
Chastain, Paul D. ... Kingsport, TN
Chastain, Peter F. ... Greensboro, NC
Chastain, Robert H. ... Atlanta, GA
Chastain, Robert L. ... San Jose, CA
Chastain, Robert R. ... Boise, ID
Chastain, Roy J. ... Sacramento, CA
Chastain, Suzan ... Department of Labor, Office of the Solicitor, GV
Chastain, W. Tyler ... Knoxville, TN
Chastain, Walter E. ... Corpus Christi, TX
Chastain, William W., (P.A.) ... Tampa, FL
Chastaine, Michael L. ... San Jose, CA
Chastang, Charles J. ... Columbus, OH
Chastang, Linda Earley ... South Orange, NJ
Chastang, Richard P. ... Los Angeles, CA
Chastang, Rita C. ... Detroit, MI
Chasteen, Kimberly A.
Newport News, VA
Chasteen, Mark J. ... Minneapolis, MN
Chasteen, Robert W., Jr. ... Fitzgerald, GA
Chasteen, Terry G. ... Greenville, SC
Chastek, Chester ... Spokane, WA
Chasuk, Alfred P. ... Mountain View, CA
Chasuk & Chasuk, A Professional Law Association ... Mountain View, CA
Chasuk, John C. ... Mountain View, CA
Chasworth, Susan D. ... Los Angeles, CA
Chatain, Fabienne ... Washington, DC
Chatburn, Charles R. ... Spokane, WA
Chatburn, Lowell D. ... Wailuku, HI
Chatburn, Stephen P. ... Pennsauken, NJ
Chateau, Francois ... New York, NY
Chateau, Jacqueline Sue ... New York, NY
Chatelain, Barbara G. ... Baton Rouge, LA
Chatelain, David ... Marksville, LA
Chatelain, Edward B., III ... Beaumont, TX
Chatelain, Jill Swearingen ... Beaumont, TX
Chatenever, Robert ... Ventura, CA
Chatfield, Andrea Grilli ... Manchester, NH
Chatfield, Byron G. ... Salem, OR
Chatfield & Chatfield ... Cincinnati, OH
Chatfield, Christopher J. ... New York, NY
Chatfield, Dan ... St. Louis, MO
Chatfield, David Blake ... Oak Park, CA
Chatfield, Elizabeth M. ... Charleston, WV
Chatfield, H. Marshall ... Kansas City, MO
Chatfield, Hedy Schuster ... Cleveland, OH
Chatfield, Lloyd C., II ... Greenwich, CT
Chatfield, Melancthon W. ... Cincinnati, OH
Chatfield, Michelle Bullard ... Memphis, TN
Chatfield, Peter Wilson ... Washington, DC
Chatfield, Scott F. ... Tully, NY
Chatfield, William H. ... Cincinnati, OH
Chatfield-Taylor, Richard F.
Kansas City, MO
Chatham & Babka ... Belleville, IL
Chatham, Gary F. ... Plano, TX
Chatham, Gerald W., Sr. ... Hernando, MS
Chatham, Grey ... Belleville, IL
Chatham, Henry E., Jr. ... Jackson, MS
Chatham, L. Charlyne ... Clearwater, FL
Chatham Law Firm ... Hernando, MS
Tunica, MS
Chatham, M. Brendan ... Superior, CO
Chathas, Alice L. ... Chicago, IL
Chatigny, Robert N. ... Hartford, CT
Chatilovicz, Peter ... Washington, DC
Chatinover, Leah Cohen ... West Hartford, CT
Chatlain, Dean F. ... Greensboro, NC
Chatlin, Kimberly A. ... Las Vegas, NV
Reno, NV
Chatman, Catherine Baker
Jefferson City, MO
Chatman, Charles E. ... McKinney, TX
Chatman, George A. ... Detroit, MI
Chatman, LaTisha O. ... Richmond, VA
Chatman, Linda C. ... Chicago, IL
Chatman, Lorna S. ... Torrance, CA
Chatman-Hendree, Yvonne ... Memphis, TN
Chatmon, Derrel Quantrill ... Jacksonville, FL
Chatoff, Michael A. ... Floral Park, NY
Chatoian, Edward B. ... Fresno, CA
Chatov, Robert ... Amherst, NY
Chatowski, John A. ... Irvine, CA
Chatroo, Arthur J. ... La Jolla, CA
Chatterjea, Maya ... Coral Gables, FL
Chatterjee, Aaron C. ... Washington, DC
Chatterjee, Ella B.
National Labor Relations Board, Office of Board Members, GV
Chatterjee, Ella S. ... Newport Beach, CA
Chatterjee, Neel I. ... Menlo Park, CA
Chatterjee, Somnath Raj ... San Francisco, CA
Chatterjee, Trina ... Berkeley, CA
Chatterji, Shagor Kent ... Washington, DC
Chatterley & Associates, L.L.C.
San Antonio, TX
Chatterley, Brian K. ... San Antonio, TX
Chatterton & Griffith, Law Offices, S.C.
Madison, WI
Chatterton, Mary Lou ... Hackensack, NJ
New York, NY
New York, NY
Chatterton, Patrick L. ... Flint, MI
Chatterton, Robert D. ... Orange, CA
Chatterton, William A. ... Madison, WI
Chattin, Andrew B. ... Charleston, WV
Chattin, R. Mark ... Decatur, AL
Chattin, Ruth Todd ... Bellevue, WA
Chattman, Gaines & Stern
Cleveland, OH
Lorain, OH
Chattman, Gerald B. ... Cleveland, OH
Lorain, OH
Chattman, H. Richard ... Newark, NJ
Chattman, Sanders M. ... Roseland, NJ
Chatton, Tonya ... Houston, TX
Chattoraj, Partha P. ... New York, NY
Chaturvedi, Anjali ... Washington, DC
Chatwin, Kenneth C. ... Phoenix, AZ
Chatz, Barry A. ... Chicago, IL
Lincolnwood, IL
Chatz, James A. ... Chicago, IL
Lincolnwood, IL
Chatz, John K. ... Chicago, IL
Chatzinoff, Barry ... Haddonfield, NJ
Chatzinoff, Howard ... New York, NY
Chatzinoff, Peter R. ... Uniondale, NY
Chatzkel, Larry R. ... Philadelphia, PA
Chatzky and Associates, A Law Corporation
La Jolla, CA
San Jose, CA
Chatzky, John A. ... New York, NY
Chatzky, Michael Gary ... La Jolla, CA
San Jose, CA
Chatzky, Paul, Law Offices of
Northbrook, IL
Chatzky, Paul, Law Offices of ... Skokie, IL
Waukegan, IL
Chatzky, Stephen E. ... La Jolla, CA
San Jose, CA
Chau, Agnes Man Yee ... Orlando, FL
Chau, Andrew E. ... San Francisco, CA
Chau, F., & Associates, LLP
East Meadow, NY
Chau, Frank ... East Meadow, NY
Chau, Lisa ... Santa Fe, NM
Chau, Stanley T. ... New York, NY
Chau, Victoria I. ... Irvine, CA
Chaucer, Bradford J. ... New Haven, CT
Chaucer and Rosado ... New Haven, CT
Chauche, Christine Noelle ... Englewood, CO
Chaudhary, Arslan ... New York, NY
Chaudhry, Alexander Jamil ... Washington, DC
Chaudhry, Rohit ... Washington, DC
Chaudoin, Cheryl L. ... Portland, OR
Chaudoin, Daniel T. ... Washington, DC
Chaudoin, Lauri D. ... Nashville, TN
Chaudoin, Robert C. ... Bowling Green, KY
Chaudoir, Christopher J.
Los Angeles, CA
Chaudoir, E. Patrick, Jr. ... Houston, TX
Chaufty, Ronald M. ... Texarkana, TX
Chauhan, Asha ... New York, NY
Chauhan, Drupti P. ... Charlotte, NC
Chaulk, Jennifer ... Shawnee, KS
Chaumette, David A. ... Houston, TX
Chaumont, Andres P. ... Houston, TX
Chaumont, Lilianne G. ... Calabasas, CA
Chauncey, Harrison K., Jr.
Palm Beach, FL
Chauncey, Harrison K., Jr., P.A., Law Offices of ... Palm Beach, FL
Chauncey, S. David ... Lake Worth, FL
Chauncey, Tom, II ... Phoenix, AZ
Chauppette, Sam J. ... Harvey, LA
Chaurette, Katherine A. ... Boston, MA
Chausow Shafer & Associates, P.C.
Highland Park, IL
Chausow Shafer, Nancy ... Highland Park, IL
Chausse, Paula Mathieu
New Bedford, MA
Chaussee, John B. ... Dallas, TX
Chaussee, Michael D. ... Colorado Springs, CO
Chaut, Alan M. ... New York, NY
Chautin, Joseph C., III ... Metairie, LA
Chauveaux, Tony L. ... Beaumont, TX
Chauvel, Ronald C. ... San Mateo, CA
Chauvin, Arch Cox McKay ... Louisville, KY
Chauvin, Bradley J. ... Metairie, LA
Chauvin, Carl A. ... Golden Meadow, LA
Chauvin, Carroll A. ... New Orleans, LA
Chauvin, Jacqueline ... Louisville, KY
Chauvin, Joan E. ... New Orleans, LA
Chauvin, L. Stanley, III ... Louisville, KY
Chauvin, L. Stanley, Jr. ... Louisville, KY
Chauvin, Michael ... Satellite Beach, FL
Chauvin, Robert J. ... Clifton Park, NY
Chauvin, Suzanne R. ... Houston, TX
Chauza, Roger N. ... Dallas, TX
Chavan, Vivek K. ... Westbury, NY
Chavana, Felipe ... Newark, NJ
Chavana, Hector Antonio ... Houston, TX
Chavanne, Donald E. ... Lake Charles, LA
Chavanne, John H. ... New Orleans, LA
Chávarri, Catherine ... New Orleans, LA
Chavarria, Carlos A., Jr. ... San Diego, CA
Chavarria, Lisa ... Austin, TX
Chavarria, Lisa ReVeal ... Washington, DC
Chavarrie, Cheryl L. ... Elk Grove Village, IL
Chavaux, Paul H. ... St. Louis, MO
Chave, Carolyn M. ... New York, NY
Chaveriat, John W. ... Chicago, IL
Chavern, David C.
Export-Import Bank of The United States, Office of the General Counsel, GV
Chavers, Clayborne E. ... Washington, DC
Chavers, Dane C. ... Columbus, OH
Chavers, Darlene E. ... Columbus, OH
Chavers, Gordon D. ... Cincinnati, OH
Chavers, Herbert Lee ... Riverside, CA
Chavers, Kevin G. ... United States Senate, Committee Legal Personnel, GV
Chavers Law Firm, The, P.C.
Washington, DC
Chavers, Walter G. (Stoney) ... Mobile, AL
Chaves, Carl R. ... Claremore, OK
Chaves, Carla Monteiro ... New York, NY
Chaves, Cristina Maria ... Coral Gables, FL
Chaves, Douglas E. ... Corpus Christi, TX
Chaves, Eric Joseph ... Santa Monica, CA
Chaves, Gonzales & Hoblit, L.L.P.
Corpus Christi, TX
McAllen, TX
Portland, TX
Victoria, TX
Chaves, Herbert H. ... New York, NY
Chaves, Kelly ... Houston, TX
Chaves, Luis F. ... McLean, VA
Chaves, Manuel A. ... Boston, MA
Chaves, Mark A. ... New York, NY
Chaves, Richard R. ... West Palm Beach, FL
Chaves, Robert A. ... Boca Raton, FL
Chaves, Robert L. ... Washington, DC
Chaves, Thomas J. ... New Brunswick, NJ
Chavey, Victoria Woodin ... Hartford, CT
Chavez, AlbertV. ... Albuquerque, NM
Chávez, Andrea Elera ... Menlo Park, CA
Chávez, Anna M.
Department of Transportation, Federal Highway Administration, GV
Chavez, Anthony E. ... Los Angeles, CA
Chavez, Barbara P. ... Bronx, NY
Chavez, Bart A. ... Omaha, NE
Chavez, Bart A., P.C., Attorney At Law
Omaha, NE
Chavez, Bonnie ... Los Angeles, CA
Chavez, Carmela B. ... Albuquerque, NM
Chavez, Charlie W. ... Albuquerque, NM
Chavez, Claudio R. ... Los Angeles, CA
Chavez, D. Mario ... Farmington, NM
Chavez, Daniel ... Bronx, NY
New York, NY
Chavez, David C. ... Los Lunas, NM
Chavez, David L. ... San Ramon, CA
Chavez, Diane Julin ... Studio City, CA
Chavez, Don J. ... Miami, FL
Chavez, Donald E. ... Denver, CO
Chavez, E. Thomas ... Pasadena, CA
Chávez, Edward L. ... Albuquerque, NM
Chavez, Edward M. ... Denver, CO
Chavez, Elaine G. ... Herndon, VA
Chavez, Emilio Gonzalez ... Miami, FL
Chavez, Enrique, Jr. ... El Paso, TX
Chavez, Fernando F. ... San Jose, CA
Chavez, Frank N. ... Las Cruces, NM
Chavez & Gertler LLP ... Mill Valley, CA
San Francisco, CA
Chavez, Harriett E. ... Phoenix, AZ
Chavez, J. Anthony ... Houston, TX
Chavez, Jake J. ... Albuquerque, NM
Chavez, James A. ... Albuquerque, NM
Chavez, James A., P.C. ... Albuquerque, NM
Chavez, James E. ... Kingman, AZ
Chavez, Joan Milkey ... Albuquerque, NM
Chavez, JoAnn ... Dearborn, MI
Chavez, John A. ... Jefferson, WI
Chavez, Joseph H. ... Denver, CO
Chavez, Juanita G. ... San Pedro, CA
Chavez, Kathy Merickel ... Berkeley, CA
Chavez, Leigh Anne ... Albuquerque, NM
Chavez & Lichtenstein ... Bronx, NY
New York, NY
Chavez, Lincoln J. ... Arcadia, CA
Chavez, Lisa A. ... Albuquerque, NM
Chavez, Lisa M. ... Chicago, IL
Chavez, Lorenzo A. ... Albuquerque, NM
Chavez, Luis ... El Paso, TX
Chavez, Luis A. ... Midland, TX
Chavez, Margarita I. ... San Francisco, CA
San Jose, CA
Chavez, Mark A. ... Mill Valley, CA

Chavez, Matthew ... **Washington, DC**
Chavez, Melchor ... Edinburg, TX
Chavez, Morris J. ... Albuquerque, NM
Chavez, N. Michael ... Del City, OK
Chavez, N. Michael, P.C. ... Del City, OK
Chavez, Norma Pedroza ... **Los Angeles, CA**
Chavez, Pablo L. ... **Palo Alto, CA**
Chavez, Patrick I. ... **St. Louis, MO**
Chavez, Richard Anthony
San Francisco, CA
Chavez, Robert J. ... **Long Beach, CA**
Chavez, Ronald A. ... **Costa Mesa, CA**
Chávez, Rosemary Elaine ... Los Angeles, CA
Chavez, Ruben V. ... **Miami, FL**
Chavez, Stephen P. ... **Elyria, OH**
Chavez, Steven A. ... Denver, CO
Chavez, Theodore R. ... **Campbell, CA**
Chavez, Tibo J., Jr. ... Los Lunas, NM
Chavez, Tito D. ... Albuquerque, NM
Chavez, Veronica J. ... Fort Worth, TX
Chavez, Victor E. ... Los Angeles, CA
Chavez, Victoria Marie ... Los Angeles, CA
Chavez, Virginia L. ... **New York, NY**
Chavez, Wilfredo ... Union City, NJ
Chavez, Xavier Vicente ... Long Beach, CA
Chavez de Arnavat, Ghislaine Celsa Madeleine
New York, NY
Chavez-Ochoa, Brian R. ... Valley Springs, CA
Chavez-Pardini, Michele Rae ... Honolulu, HI
Chavez-Ruark, Maria Ellena
Baltimore, MD
Chaviano, Hugo ... **Chicago, IL**
Chavier, Tesha L. ... Boston, MA
Chavies, Michael B. ... Miami, FL
Chavin, Bonnie P. ... Troy, NY
Chavin, Melissa J. ... New York, NY
Chavira, Armando ... Van Nuys, CA
Chavira, Natividad F. ... Brea, CA
Chavis, A. Douglas, III ... Little Rock, AR
Chavis, Adam Joseph ... Reisterstown, MD
Chavis, Clifford W. ... Utica, NY
Chavis, Denise W. ... **Indianapolis, IN**
Chavis, Diane Hernon ... Pittsburgh, PA
Chavis, Ertle Knox ... Lumberton, NC
Chavis, Geraldine L. ... San Francisco, CA
Chavis, Lisa Denese ... Columbia, SC
Chavis, Patrick E., IV ... Indianapolis, IN
Chavis, Robert L. ... Yankton, SD
Chavkin, Jeffrey S. ... **New York, NY**
Chavkin, Peter A. ... **New York, NY**
Chavolla, David J. ... **Boston, MA**
Chavos, Anthony G. ... **Costa Mesa, CA**
Chavos, Melissa Sarris ... Irvine, CA
Chavous, Kevin Pernell ... **Washington, DC**
Chaw, Terisa E. ... San Francisco, CA
Chawaga, Stephen P. ... **Philadelphia, PA**
Chawes, Joseph C. ... Westbrook, ME
Chawla, Kathi W. ... Canton, OH
Chawla, Tarran Paul S. ... Hinsdale, IL
Chawla, Tejpal Singh ... **Washington, DC**
Chay, Eugene F. ... **Cherry Hill, NJ**
Philadelphia, PA
Chaya, Stephen D. ... Irvine, CA
Chayes, Abram ... Cambridge, MA
Chayes, Antonia Handler ... Boston, MA
Chayet, Harvey ... Southfield, MI
Chayet, Julie Min ... **New York, NY**
Chayet, Neil L. ... **Boston, MA**
Chayet, Nikki A. ... Tucson, AZ
Chaykin, Arthur A. ... **Kansas City, MO**
Chaykin, Steven E. ... **Miami, FL**
Chayo, Leslie E. ... Los Angeles, CA
Chayrigues, John R. ... **Boston, MA**
Chayt, Julie I. ... Burlingame, CA
Chayt, Maurice ... **Brooklyn, NY**
Chazan, Michael J. ... **Boston, MA**
Providence, RI
Chazan, Paul M. ... New York, NY
Chazan, Shoshana Y. ... **San Francisco, CA**
Chazankin, Eric ... Boulder, CO
Chaze, Kim T. ... Hattiesburg, MS
Chazen, Bernard ... **Englewood, NJ**
Chazen, Candace S. ... Rockville, MD
Chazen & Chazen ... **Englewood, NJ**
Hackensack, NJ
Chazen, David K. ... **Englewood, NJ**
Chazen & Fox ... **New York, NY**
Richmond, VA
Chazen, Hartley James ... **New York, NY**
Chazen, Joseph B. ... **Riverdale, MD**
Chazen, Leonard ... **New York, NY**
Chazen & Masia ... Freehold, NJ
Chazen, Michael J. ... Freehold, NJ
Chazen, Sandra M. ... **Escondido, CA**
Chazin, Abraham ... Newark, NJ
Chazin & Chazin ... Newark, NJ
Chazin, Daniel D. ... Teaneck, NJ
Chazin, Mark H. ... **Bridgewater, NJ**
Clinton, NJ
Chazin, Martin D. ... **Philadelphia, PA**
Chazin, Meyer ... Newark, NJ
Chazin, Seth P. ... **Santa Monica, CA**
Chazkel, Michael F. ... East Brunswick, NJ
Cheadle, C. Tucker ... **Newport Beach, CA**
Cheadle & Cheadle ... Knoxville, TN
Nashville, TN
Cheadle, Evalina C. ... Knoxville, TN
Nashville, TN
Cheadle & Garrett ... **Newport Beach, CA**
Cheadle, Grant E. ... **Tulsa, OK**
Cheadle, Jason A. ... San Jose, CA
Cheadle, John R., Jr. ... Knoxville, TN
Nashville, TN
Cheadle, L. Shawn ... Lakewood, CO
Cheadle, Lora Plank ... Englewood, CO
Cheadle, Wood & Borochoff ... **Tulsa, OK**
Cheairs, M. Norwood ... **Plano, TX**
Cheal, David D. ... Olympia, WA
Cheaney, Philip N. ... Hendersonville, NC
Cheap, Richard A. ... Columbus, OH
Cheasty, John C. ... Hillsborough, NC
Cheatham, Bruce A. ... **Dallas, TX**
Cheatham, Charles C.
West Bloomfield, MI
Cheatham, Charles E. ... Oklahoma City, OK
Cheatham, D. Denty ... Nashville, TN
Cheatham, David A. ... Bogalusa, LA
Cheatham, Donald T. ... Fairfax, VA
Cheatham, Estes & Hollman, P.C.
Detroit, MI
West Bloomfield, MI
Cheatham, Frank S., Jr. ... Savannah, GA
Cheatham, Gloria J. ... **Atlanta, GA**
Cheatham, James E. ... Aurora, IL
Cheatham, James H., IV ... **Fort Worth, TX**
Cheatham, James T. ... Rocky Mount, NC
Cheatham, Jerry W. ... Tallahassee, FL
Cheatham, John H., III ... Washington, DC
Cheatham & Palermo ... Nashville, TN
Cheatham, Raquel M. ... **Washington, DC**
Cheatham, Richard R. ... **Atlanta, GA**
Cheatham, Richard T. ... Dallas, TX
Cheatham, Robert D. ... Houston, TX
Cheatham, Robert W. ... **San Francisco, CA**
Cheatham, Robin B. ... **New Orleans, LA**
Cheatham, Russell L., III, (P.A.)
St. Petersburg, FL
Cheatham, Stephen V. ... **Cleveland, OH**
Cheatham, Tim A. ... **Little Rock, AR**
Cheatham & Tomlinson ... San Francisco, CA
Cheatham, Vincent T. ... Bessemer, AL
Cheatham, Wiley L. ... Cuero, TX
Cheatham & Womble, P.C.
Oklahoma City, OK
Cheathem, Terrye L. ... Los Angeles, CA
Cheatum, Debra F. ... Olympia, WA
Cheatwood, J. Clifford ... Tampa, FL
Cheatwood, J. Jay ... **Lawrenceburg, TN**
Cheatwood, J. Steven ... **Atlanta, GA**
Cheatwood, Philip H. ... **Fayetteville, NC**
Cheatwood, Roy C. ... **New Orleans, LA**
Cheavens, Joseph D. ... **Houston, TX**
Chebatoris, David V. ... Weeping Water, NE
Chebegia, Jeffrey D. ... San Diego, CA
Chebli, Leslie ... **New York, NY**
Chebot, Jeffrey M. ... Bellmawr, NJ
Philadelphia, PA
Checchio, Isadore H. ... Philadelphia, PA
Checchio, Linda ... Philadelphia, PA
Checchio and Metka ... Philadelphia, PA
Checco, Carole Ann ... Long Beach, CA
Checel, Christina L. ... **Los Angeles, CA**
Chechanover, Michael David ... New York, NY
Chechanover, Victor H. ... New York, NY
Cheche, Pasquale R., (P.C.) ... Phoenix, AZ
Cheche, Pasquale R., and Stanley R. Lerner
Phoenix, AZ
Chechele, T. Samantha ... St. Petersburg, FL
Chechele, T. Samantha, P.A.
St. Petersburg, FL
Chechile, Deanna ... **San Francisco, CA**
Chechitelli, Frank ... Upland, CA
Check, Earl D. ... Boone, IA
Check, Joseph E. ... Shelby Township, MI
Check, Kevin Michael ... Southfield, MI
Check, Kevin Michael, P.C. ... Southfield, MI
Check, Melvin A. ... Port Washington, WI
Check, Merrill A. ... Indianapolis, IN
Check, Nancy D. ... Wayzata, MN
Check, Raymond B. ... **New York, NY**
Checkert, Edward V. ... San Diego, CA
Checkett, J. Kevin ... **Carthage, MO**
Checkett, John J. ... **Phoenix, AZ**
Checkett & Pauly ... **Carthage, MO**
Checketts, Blair H. ... Merced, CA
Checkla, Ira J. ... **New York, NY**
Checkley, James W., Jr. ... **Austin, TX**
Checkman, Neil B. ... **New York, NY**
Checkovich, Paul J. ... Syracuse, NY
Checkoway, Jill A. ... **Auburn, ME**
Checkoway, Robert ... Portland, ME
Checkowsky, Daniel J. ... Bloomfield Hills, MI
Checov, Martin S. ... **San Francisco, CA**
Cheddar, Ann M. ... San Francisco, CA
Chediak, Christopher ... **Sacramento, CA**
Chediak, Janet Z. ... **Sacramento, CA**
Chedid, Maria ... **San Francisco, CA**
Chee, Gregory W. K. ... **Honolulu, HI**
Chee, Herbert C., Jr. ... Houston, TX
Chee, Hon C. ... Honolulu, HI
Chee, Kevin S. W. ... **Honolulu, HI**
Chee, Lyndon Y. ... San Francisco, CA
Chee & Markham ... **Honolulu, HI**
Chee, Oliver K. ... **Palo Alto, CA**
Chee, Russell W. H. ... Honolulu, HI
Chee, William Kam Ming ... Honolulu, HI
Cheek, Allen R. ... Fairbanks, AK
Cheek, Amanda L. ... **New Orleans, LA**
Cheek, Angela J. ... **Portland, OR**
Cheek, Barbara J. ... Indianapolis, IN
Cheek, Ben F., III ... Toccoa, GA
Cheek, Caroline Langley ... Broken Arrow, OK
Cheek, Charles E. ... **Houston, TX**
Cheek, Christy B. ... **Atlanta, GA**
Cheek, Corey L. ... **Dallas, TX**
Cheek, David A. ... **Oklahoma City, OK**
Cheek, Ellen S. ... **Decatur, GA**
Cheek, Emerson, III ... **Columbus, OH**
Cheek, Horace L., Jr. ... Rincon, GA
Cheek, James C., III ... Oklahoma City, OK
Cheek, James Edward, III ... **Orlando, FL**
Cheek, James H., III ... **Nashville, TN**
Cheek, Jennifer Leigh ... **Charleston, SC**
Cheek, John D. ... **Oklahoma City, OK**
Cheek, John J. ... **Peoria, IL**
Cheek Law Firm, The
Oklahoma City, OK
Cheek, Leon B., III ... Orlando, FL
Cheek, Leslie, III ... Blue Hill, ME
Cheek, Lewis A. ... **Durham, NC**
Cheek, Louis E. ... Philadelphia, PA
Cheek, Michael C. ... Belleair, FL
Cheek, Robert C. ... Arlington, VA
Cheek, Roger N. ... Detroit, MI
Cheek, Russell G. ... Toms River, NJ
Cheek, Teresa A. ... **Wilmington, DE**
Cheek, Tim N. ... **Oklahoma City, OK**
Cheek, Tracy Troutman ... Orlando, FL
Cheek, Valoria L. ... Philadelphia, PA
Cheek, Vance W., Jr. ... **Johnson City, TN**
Cheek, Warren M., Jr. ... **Washington, DC**
Cheek and Wheeler, P.L.C.
Johnson City, TN
Cheek, William Tompkins, III
Nashville, TN
Cheek & Zeehandelar, LLP
Columbus, OH
Cheeks, Dansby G. ... Oak Park, IL
Cheeks, James E. ... New York, NY
Cheeley, John P. ... Duluth, GA
Cheeley, Joseph E., Jr. ... Buford, GA
Cheeley, Joseph E., Jr., P.C. ... Buford, GA
Cheeley, Robert D. ... Duluth, GA
Cheeley, Thomas P. ... Colonial Heights, VA
Cheely, Daniel J. ... Chicago, IL
Cheely, Robert A. ... Berwyn, IL
Cheerman, Leonard H. ... Meriden, CT
Cheerva, Michael ... **Indianapolis, IN**
Cheesbrough, Laura A. ... Chicago, IL
Cheeseboro, Edwin ... Wichita, KS
Cheeseboro, Jacqueline P. ... Roosevelt, NY
Cheeseboro, Lois I. ... Wichita, KS
Cheeseman, Candice L. ... **Bethesda, MD**
Cheeseman, Henry R. ... Los Angeles, CA
Cheeseman & Phillips ... Tampa, FL
Cheeseman, Stephen C. ... Tampa, FL
Cheeseman, William J. ... **Boston, MA**
Cheeseman, William Winfield, Sr. ... Troy, MO
Cheeseman-Bak, Kara ... Smithtown, NY
Cheesman, Benbow P., Jr. ... Milwaukee, WI
Cheesman, Mark W. ... Houston, TX
Cheetham, Allin H. ... Fort Benton, MT
Cheetham, Janet Holste ... **Seattle, WA**
Cheetwood, John S. ... **Bowling Green, OH**
Pemberville, OH
Cheetwood Law Office
Bowling Green, OH
Pemberville, OH
Cheever, Alan W. ... Marshfield, VT
Cheever, Charles Augustus ... **Boston, MA**
Cheever, Chas. E., Jr. ... San Antonio, TX
Cheever, Donald G. ... Marshfield, MO
Cheever, Federico ... Denver, CO
Cheever, Gene K. ... **Sacramento, CA**
Cheever, George M. ... **Pittsburgh, PA**
Cheever, Mary M. D. ... Pittsburgh, PA
Cheever, Matthew T. ... **Sacramento, CA**
Cheever, Roger W. ... Superior, WI
Cheever, Sharon A. ... **Newport Beach, CA**
Cheever and Sullivan, P.A. ... Wilton, NH
Cheezem, Jan Carson ... **Miami, FL**
Cheezem, Janis K. ... **Miami, FL**
Chefec, David W. ... **Jericho, NY**
Chefec, David W., P.C. ... **Jericho, NY**
Mineola, NY
Cheffer, M. Brian ... **Fort Myers, FL**
Cheffo, Mark S. ... **New York, NY**
Cheffy, Edward K. ... **Naples, FL**
Cheffy, Jane Yeager ... **Naples, FL**
Cheffy, Louis W. ... **Naples, FL**
Cheffy Passidomo Wilson & Johnson
Naples, FL
Chefitz, Daniel E. ... **Boston, MA**
Chefitz, Joel G. ... **Chicago, IL**
Chefitz, Michael D. ... **Boston, MA**
Providence, RI
Chegwidden, Bryan ... **Boston, MA**
Chegwidden, Irene Boyd ... Des Moines, IA
Chegwidden, Jack L. ... Encino, CA
Chegwidden, Jack L., A Professional
Corporation ... Encino, CA
Cheh, Anthony Y. ... New York, NY
Cheh, Evelyn Y. ... **New York, NY**
Cheh, Kristina ... **Los Angeles, CA**
Cheh, Mary M. ... Washington, DC
Chehanske, George J. ... Howell, NJ
Chehardy, Lawrence A. ... Metairie, LA
Chehardy, Lawrence E., (Professional Law Corporation) ... **Metairie, LA**
Chehardy, Pamela Seeber
Baton Rouge, LA
Chehardy, Sherman, Ellis, Breslin & Murray, L.L.P. ... **Baton Rouge, LA**
Metairie, LA
New Orleans, LA
Chehebar, Anne McMahon
Briarcliff Manor, NY
Chehebar, Charles ... New York, NY
Chehi, Mark S. ... **Wilmington, DE**
Chehock, Donald P. ... Pomona, CA
Chehrazi, Atessa ... **Washington, DC**
Cheifetz & Iannitelli, P.C. ... Phoenix, AZ
Cheifetz, Robert D. ... **Chicago, IL**
Cheifetz, Steven W. ... Phoenix, AZ
Cheiken, Kimberly V. ... Palm Coast, FL
Cheiken, Stanley B. ... Haddonfield, NJ
Cheikes, Robert ... Skillman, NJ
Cheikes, Vicki G. ... **Garden City, NY**
Cheit, David A. ... **Sacramento, CA**
Cheit, Wendy A. ... San Francisco, CA
Cheitlin, Kenneth A. ... Walnut Creek, CA
Chek, Lawrence ... **Dallas, TX**
Chekan, Christopher A. ... Chicago, IL
Detroit, MI
Chekan, Michelle Sage ... Chicago, IL
Chekaway, Fred ... Allen Park, MI
Chekenian, Haig ... Smithtown, NY
Chekian, Michael F. ... Los Angeles, CA
Chekow, Arnold L. ... New York, NY
Chekow & Kisner, P.C. ... New York, NY
Chel, Frederik W. ... Long Beach, CA
Chelak, Gregory H. ... **Milford, PA**
Chelberg, Bruce S. ... Arlington Heights, IL
Chelberg, Kim ... Santa Monica, CA
Cheleden, Charles G. ... Doylestown, PA
Cheleden, Christopher R.
Los Angeles, CA
Cheleden, Robert A. ... Pasadena, CA
Cheleotis, Tassos G. ... Miami, FL
Chelesnik, Steven A. ... **St. Louis, MO**
Cheli, Hess & Brennan, P.L.C.
Detroit, MI
Royal Oak, MI
Cheli, Jacob A. ... Exton, PA
Cheli, Ronald P. ... **Royal Oak, MI**
Chelius, George L. ... Newport Beach, CA
Chelius, Julie Hofmann ... **Philadelphia, PA**
Chelius, Maureen O. ... **Kenilworth, NJ**
Chell, Beverly C. ... **New York, NY**
Chell & Chell, P.A. ... Woodbury, NJ
Chell, Eugene P. ... Woodbury, NJ
Chell, Timothy W. ... Woodbury, NJ
Chellew, Joseph A., III ... Perkasie, PA
Chelli, Angelo F. ... Staten Island, NY
Chelli & Bush ... Staten Island, NY
Chellis & Frampton, P.A.
Summerville, SC
Chellis, James E. ... **Summerville, SC**
Chellis, Michael R. ... **Portland, OR**
Chello, Paul L. ... Branford, CT
Cheloc, Robert S. ... Jersey City, NJ
Chelsea, Susan K. ... San Diego, CA
Cheltenham, Michael Sala ... Alpena, MI
Chelus, Herdzik & Speyer, P.C.
Buffalo, NY
Cheektowaga, NY
Chelus, Michael F. ... **Buffalo, NY**
Chema, Susan R. ... **Dayton, OH**
Chema, Thomas V. ... **Cleveland, OH**
Chemay, Cynthia M. ... **Baton Rouge, LA**
Chembars, Rebecca A. ... Pittsburgh, PA
Chemeleski, John E. ... Long Beach, CA
Chemell, Christine ... San Antonio, TX
Chemerinski, Eliel ... **Los Angeles, CA**
Chemers, Daniel R. ... **Baltimore, MD**
Chemers, Robert Marc ... **Chicago, IL**
Chemides, Bernice F. ... Walnut Creek, CA
Chemino, Stephen S. ... Bunkie, LA
Chemnick, Moen & Greenstreet
Seattle, WA
Chemnick, Paul W. ... **Seattle, WA**
Chemnitz, Gregory R. ... **Painesville, OH**
Chemtob, Nancy Nadel ... **New York, NY**
Chemtob, Stuart M. ... Department of Justice, Antitrust Division, GV
Chen, Alan C. ... Richardson, TX
Chen, Alan Keith ... Chicago, IL
Chen, Albert B. ... **New York, NY**
Chen, Alexander C. ... **Newport Beach, CA**
Chen, Alexander J. ... **Los Angeles, CA**
Chen, Alice F. ... **New York, NY**
Chen, Angeline G. ... **Washington, DC**
Chen, Arthur S., Jr. ... Piedmont, CA
Chen, Audrey W. ... Cupertino, CA
Chen, Belle M. ... Irvine, CA
Chen, Benjamin V. ... Honolulu, HI
Chen, Bernice B. ... San Jose, CA
Chen, Bess L. ... Sacramento, CA
Chen, Betty ... **San Jose, CA**
Chen, Cammie W. ... San Jose, CA
Chen, Carl J. ... Bethesda, MD
Chen, Carlton S. ... Hartford, CT
Chen, Carol ... Camden, ME
Chen, Christianne Chien
San Francisco, CA
Chen, Christina Y., Law Offices of
San Francisco, CA
Chen, Christopher ... Treasury Department, U.S. Customs Service, GV
Chen, Christopher D. ... **San Francisco, CA**
Chen, Christopher S. ... San Francisco, CA
Chen, Chyi G. ... **Costa Mesa, CA**
Chen, Connie C. ... **Los Angeles, CA**
Chen, Connie L. ... Santa Clara, CA
Chen, Dale N. ... San Francisco, CA
Chen, Daniel S. ... **Washington, DC**
Chen, Darin ... Los Angeles, CA
Chen, David ... Southfield, MI
Chen, David ... Kew Gardens, NY
Chen, David C. ... Grover Beach, CA
Chen, David W. ... Walnut Creek, CA
Chen, David Y. ... **San Francisco, CA**
Chen, Deborah ... Los Angeles, CA
Chen, Dennis A. ... Ocoee, FL
Chen, Dennis A., P.A. ... Ocoee, FL
Chen, Destiny Chu-Ling ... Honolulu, HI
Chen, Edward I. ... Bowling Green, OH
Chen, Edward M. ... San Francisco, CA
Chen, Edward W. ... Rockville, MD
Chen, Eric ... San Francisco, CA
Chen, Eric S. ... **Los Angeles, CA**
Chen, Ernest C. ... Pasadena, CA
Chen, Frank W. ... **Los Angeles, CA**
Chen, Gong L. ... **Santa Clara, CA**
Chen, Graeme Hilary ... New York, NY
Chen, Harold H. ... **Greensboro, NC**
Raleigh, NC
Chen, Heidi C. ... New York, NY
Chen, Hollis T. ... **Washington, DC**
Chen, Jackson ... **Menlo Park, CA**

Chen, Jacques C. .... Los Angeles, CA
Chen, James C. .... Washington, DC
Chen, Jaye .... New York, NY
Chen, Jeffrey A. .... San Francisco, CA
Chen, Jennifer C. .... Washington, DC
Chen, Jenny Chyi Ching
Beverly Hills, CA
Chen, John .... Chicago, IL
Chen, John Z. .... Los Angeles, CA
Chen, Judith S.C. .... City of Industry, CA
Chen, Judy H. .... San Mateo, CA
Chen, Julie Y. .... White Plains, NY
Chen, Katharine M. .... New York, NY
Chen, Kemble .... Fresno, CA
Chen, Kent M. .... Costa Mesa, CA
Chen, Kevin M. .... Chicago, IL
Chen, Kurt Michael .... Los Angeles, CA
Chen, Lei Howard .... Dallas, TX
Chen, Leo K. .... New York, NY
Chen, Li .... Dallas, TX
Chen, Lung Chu .... New York, NY
Chen, M. Andrew .... Houston, TX
Chen, Martin Li-te .... Atlanta, GA
Chen, Mary C. .... New York, NY
Chen, Meivile .... New York, NY
Chen, Michael W. .... Bullhead City, AZ
Chen, Micki .... Arlington, VA
Chen, Monica Lee .... Irving, TX
Chen, Nancy .... New York, NY
Chen, Nancy M. .... Menlo Park, CA
Chen, Owen .... New York, NY
Chen, Patricia Jean .... Los Angeles, CA
Chen, Peng .... La Jolla, CA
Chen, Peter G. .... New York, NY
Chen, Peter P. .... Palo Alto, CA
Chen, Po-Chien .... San Gabriel, CA
Chen, Portia .... North Chicago, IL
Chen, Raymond T.
Department of Commerce, Patent and Trademark Office, GV
Chen, Rex .... New York, NY
Chen, Richard L. .... New York, NY
Chen, Richard W. .... Brooklyn, NY
Chen, Ronald K. .... Newark, NJ
Chen, Samuel C. .... Yakima, WA
Chen, Sean T. .... Walnut Creek, CA
Chen, Shereen C. .... Mount Laurel, NJ
Chen, Show-Mao .... New York, NY
Chen, Shun C. .... Irvine, CA
Chen, Siu Ling .... San Francisco, CA
Chen, Sophia Hue .... Washington, DC
Chen, Stella .... Albany, NY
Chen, Stephen .... Los Angeles, CA
Chen, Sylvia .... Libertyville, IL
Chen, Thomas Y. .... Houston, TX
Chen, Tina .... San Francisco, CA
Chen, Tom .... Newport Beach, CA
Chen, Tony .... Red Bank, NJ
Chen, Tony D. .... Encino, CA
Chen, Victor W. .... Houston, TX
Chen, Victoria .... San Diego, CA
Chen, Vincent Joseph .... West Palm Beach, FL
Chen, Vivia J. .... New York, NY
Chen, W. Chelsea .... Los Angeles, CA
Chen, Walsh, Tecler & McCabe, L.L.P.
Rockville, MD
Westminster, MD
Chen, Wan .... New York, NY
Chen, Wei .... New York, NY
Chen, Wesley .... New York, NY
White Plains, NY
Chen, William James, Jr. .... Rockville, MD
Chen, Y. Justin .... San Jose, CA
Chen, Yang .... New York, NY
Chen, Ying .... Los Angeles, CA
Chen, Yoram E. .... New York, NY
Chenail, David L. .... North Adams, MA
Chenail, Lester W. .... Williamstown, MA
Chenal, Carmen A. .... Phoenix, AZ
Chenal, Thomas K. .... Phoenix, AZ
Chenall, David L. .... Williamstown, MA
Chenault, Alanson T., IV
New Orleans, LA
Chenault, D. Larkin .... Lansing, MI
Chenault, H. Lewis .... Richmond, VA
Chenault, H. Robert, Jr. .... Vero Beach, FL
Chenault, Hammond and Hall, P.C.
Decatur, AL
Chenault, James S. .... Richmond, KY
Chenault, Kathryn Cassell
New Rochelle, NY
Chenault, L. McCauley .... Mechanicsville, VA
Chenault, Nadine .... Fayetteville, AR
Chenault, Raymond A.
San Francisco, CA
Chenault, Sally K. .... Ojai, CA
Chenault, Susan L. .... Vero Beach, FL
Chenault, Timothy A.
Department of Transportation, U. S. Coast Guard, GV
Chenault & Trible, PLC .... Mechanicsville, VA
Chenault, William B., III .... San Antonio, TX
Chenault, William L., III .... Decatur, AL
Chen-Carroll, Xiu-Fang .... New York, NY
Chencus, Kendra .... Boston, MA
Cheneler, Al A. .... Winter Park, FL
Cheneler, Al A., P.A. .... Daytona Beach, FL
Winter Park, FL
Chenelle, David Raymond .... Lowell, MA
Chenelle, Kevin A. .... Lowell, MA
Chenen, Arthur R. .... Los Angeles, CA
Chenery, Tina M. .... Woodbury, NY
Chenette, Frank A. .... Cleveland, OH
Chenevert, Christine M. .... Fort Jones, CA
Chenevert, Donald J. .... Atlanta, GA
Chenevert, Matthew P. .... New Orleans, LA
Chenevert, Scott D. .... Washington, DC
Chenevert-Bragg, Irma J. .... Detroit, MI

Cheney, Alton W. .... Prescott, AZ
Cheney, Benjamin I., Jr. .... Washington, GA
Cheney, Brent G. .... Los Angeles, CA
Cheney, Briggs F. .... Albuquerque, NM
Cheney, Brock & Saudek, P.C.
Montpelier, VT
Cheney, Carole A. .... Chicago, IL
Cheney, Caron L. .... Phoenix, AZ
Cheney, Charles David .... Charlotte, NC
Cheney & Cheney, P.C. .... Glennville, GA
Reidsville, GA
Cheney, Courtney M. .... Little Rock, AR
Cheney, Curtis V., Jr. .... Reidsville, GA
Cheney, Cynthia V. .... Phoenix, AZ
Cheney, David A. .... Lima, OH
Cheney, Dupont K. .... Hinesville, GA
Cheney, Elizabeth L. .... Washington, DC
Cheney, Ellen Lech .... Agoura Hills, CA
Cheney, Eva Lu .... Sioux Falls, SD
Cheney, Geoffrey C. .... Miami, FL
Cheney, Glen A. .... Reidsville, GA
Cheney, Glen T. .... Lansing, MI
Cheney, Greg A. .... Rockford, IL
Cheney, Huddie L., III .... Wilmington, DE
Cheney, James S. .... Melbourne, FL
Cheney, Jefferson J.
Glenwood Springs, CO
Cheney, John J., III .... Boston, MA
Cheney, Jonathan Edwin .... Waco, TX
Cheney, Joseph M., Jr. .... Boston, MA
Boston, MA
Cheney, Kimberly B. .... Montpelier, VT
Cheney, M. Lee
Research Triangle Park, NC
Cheney, Marshall C. .... Rancho Mirage, CA
Cheney, Matthew .... Baltimore, MD
Cheney, Matthew S. .... Marion, NC
Cheney & Osborn, P.C. .... Rockford, IL
Cheney, Raymond J., Jr. .... Atlanta, GA
Cheney, Richard E. .... Lima, OH
Cheney, Robert P., Jr. .... Concord, NH
Manchester, NH
Cheney, Roger N. .... Mesa, AZ
Cheney, Ronald L. .... Boston, MA
Cheney, Scott Brian .... Wilmington, DE
Cheney, Scott D. .... Salt Lake City, UT
Cheney, Sharon G. .... Reidsville, GA
Cheney, Stuart F. .... Grand Rapids, MI
Cheney, Terri L. .... Beverly Hills, CA
Cheney, Thomas F., (P.C.) .... Montrose, CO
Cheney, Thomas L. .... Noank, CT
Cheney, Timothy D. .... McMinnville, OR
Cheney, Wallace H. .... Department of Justice, Bureau of Prisons, GV
Cheney, Waters, Gross & Gay, P.C.
Metter, GA
Millen, GA
Reidsville, GA
Cheney, William G., Jr. .... Jackson, MS
Chenfeld, Cliff B. .... New York, NY
Cheng, Adria I. .... San Francisco, CA
Cheng, Andrew A. .... Honolulu, HI
Cheng, Andrew Yuan-sung
San Francisco, CA
Cheng, Angeli K. .... San Francisco, CA
Cheng, Anita Y.
Federal Communications Commission, Common Carrier Bureau, GV
Cheng, Augustine V. .... New York, NY
Cheng, Brian I. .... Los Angeles, CA
Cheng and Campanile .... Dublin, CA
Cheng, Caroline K. .... Chicago, IL
Cheng, Christine H. Tsai .... Savannah, GA
Cheng, Christopher N.
Department of Justice, Civil Rights Division, GV
Cheng, Clement .... Templeton, CA
Cheng, Doris .... San Francisco, CA
Cheng, Edward S. .... Boston, MA
Cheng, Eileen K. .... Chicago, IL
Cheng, Elizabeth C. .... New York, NY
Cheng, Elizabeth N. .... Chicago, IL
Cheng, Eric .... New York, NY
Cheng, Everett Sanru .... New York, NY
Cheng, Hubert H. .... Redwood City, CA
Cheng, J. Weili .... Washington, DC
Cheng, Jeffrey A. .... Menlo Park, CA
Cheng, Jennifer Y. .... Los Angeles, CA
Cheng, Julie J.L. .... Philadelphia, PA
Cheng, Kathryn .... Glendale, CA
Cheng, Kent H. .... New York, NY
Cheng, Lee .... Palo Alto, CA
Cheng, Lee .... Washington, DC
Cheng, Linda Y. H. .... San Francisco, CA
Cheng, Loyti .... New York, NY
Cheng, Michelle M. .... Austin, TX
Cheng, Nolan .... New York, NY
Cheng, Oliver .... Irvine, CA
Cheng, Pai-Pai .... Chicago, IL
Cheng, Patricia Linda .... Menlo Park, CA
Cheng, Patricia M. .... New York, NY
Cheng, Patrick S. .... New York, NY
Cheng, Phyllis Wei-Erh .... Glendale, CA
Cheng, Richard C. .... San Diego, CA
Cheng, Robert .... Buffalo, NY
Cheng, Ronald L. .... Los Angeles, CA
Cheng, Rosalind L. .... New York, NY
Cheng, Rosemeri E. .... Dublin, CA
Cheng, Susie S. .... New York, NY
Cheng, Theodore K. .... New York, NY
Cheng, Theresa Y. .... Rahway, NJ
Cheng, Victor W. .... New York, NY
Cheng, Weili, PhD. .... Sandy, UT
Cheng, Wen-Shin .... Chicago, IL
Chenggis, George G. .... Atlanta, GA
Cheng-Khanna, Vivian .... New York, NY
Chenhall, Teresa R. .... Ketchikan, AK
Chenhall & Treiber .... Ketchikan, AK

Chenier, Maurice L. .... Los Angeles, CA
Chenin, Avery M. .... Cleveland, OH
Chenkin, Calvin .... Livingston, NJ
Chenkin, David A. .... Plantation, FL
Chenkin, David A., P.A.
Fort Lauderdale, FL
Plantation, FL
Chenkin, David B. .... New York, NY
Chen-Langenmayr, Nina .... Philadelphia, PA
Chen Min Juan, Jack .... Las Vegas, NV
Chenn, June-Annette F. .... New York, NY
Chennault, Joe Young .... Decatur, GA
Chennault, Randy .... Chattanooga, TN
Chenot, Charles Frederic, III
New Bloomfield, PA
Chenot, Thomas F. .... Farmington, MI
Chenoweth, Andrew K. .... Portland, OR
Chenoweth, Christopher E.
San Francisco, CA
Chenoweth, Eric P. .... Houston, TX
Chenoweth, Harry W. .... Nutley, NJ
Chenoweth, Isabel E. .... New Haven, CT
Chenoweth, Jan R. .... Indianapolis, IN
Chenoweth, Jenny .... San Diego, CA
Chenoweth, Jenny K. .... San Diego, CA
Chenoweth, John K. .... Fredonia, KS
Chenoweth, Kathryn F. .... Denver, CO
Chenoweth, Laura A. .... New York, NY
Chenoweth Law Office .... Frankfort, KY
Chenoweth, Max .... Dallas, TX
Chenoweth, Michael F. .... Key Largo, FL
Chenoweth, Michael O. .... Indianapolis, IN
Chenoweth, Nicholas .... Orofino, ID
Chenoweth, Priscilla R. .... Newark, NJ
Chenoweth, Richard .... San Pedro, CA
Chenoweth, Richard A. .... Akron, OH
Chenoweth, Robert L. .... Frankfort, KY
Chenoweth, Todd D. .... Arlington, MA
Chenoweth & Whitehead .... Orofino, ID
Chenowith, Susan D. .... Lady Lake, FL
Chensoff, Gary V. .... Winnetka, IL
Cheolas, Steve N. .... Mount Clemens, MI
Cheong & Denove .... Los Angeles, CA
Cheong, Wilkie .... Los Angeles, CA
Cheonis, Ernest G. .... Alamo, CA
Chepaitis, Daniel J. .... Washington, DC
Cheper, Nicholas J. .... New York, NY
Chepiga, Michael J. .... New York, NY
Chepiga, Pamela Rogers .... New York, NY
Chepiga, Stephen F. .... Brooklyn, NY
Cheplin, Gregory M. .... New York, NY
Chepucavage, Peter J. .... New York, NY
Chequer, Nan Budde .... Stamford, CT
Cher, David E. .... Los Angeles, CA
Cher, Ronald A. .... Los Angeles, CA
Cheramie, Carlton J. .... Cut Off, LA
Cheramie, Carlton J., A Prof. Law Corp., Law Office of .... Cut Off, LA
Cheramie & Smith .... Cut Off, LA
Cherande, Michelle .... New York, NY
Cherba, Lawrence M. .... Philadelphia, PA
Cherbini, Martha J. .... Muskogee, OK
Cherbonnier, William G., Jr. .... Harvey, LA
Cherbonnier, Wm. G., Law Offices of, (A PLC)
Harvey, LA
Cherchan, Ralph .... Forest Hills, NY
Cherches, Eric D. .... New York, NY
Cherches, Gisela Blohm .... Houston, TX
Cherdack, Melanie S. .... Miami, FL
Miami, FL
Cherecwich, Paul, Jr. .... Salt Lake City, UT
Cherek, Kristine Susan .... Milwaukee, WI
Cherelle-Caruth, Boni .... Laramie, WY
Cheren, David H. .... Encino, CA
Cherenfant, Guilene .... Bronx, NY
Cherensky, Steven S. .... Menlo Park, CA
Chereskin, James A. .... Orlando, FL
Cheresko, Keith A. .... Dearborn, MI
Cherewka, Michael .... Wormleysburg, PA
Cherewka & Radcliff, LLP
Wormleysburg, PA
Cherf & Greenup, P.C. .... St. Clair Shores, MI
Cherf, Ronald J. .... St. Clair Shores, MI
Cherian, K. T. (Sunny)
San Francisco, CA
Cherian, Limo T. .... Chicago, IL
Cherian, Priya Sara .... Palo Alto, CA
Cherichetti, Joseph J., Jr. .... Pittsburgh, PA
Cherico, Brian M. .... Centreville, VA
Cherico, Cherico & Associates
White Plains, NY
Cherico, John B. .... White Plains, NY
Cherico, Julie A. .... Harrison, NY
Cherico, Louis E. .... White Plains, NY
Cherie, Jules R. .... Chicago, IL
Cherie & Loizzi .... Chicago, IL
Cheriff, Bernard .... New York, NY
Cheriff, Bruce J. .... New York, NY
Cheriff, Frank J. .... Holliston, MA
Cherin, A. Marvin .... Caldwell, ID
Cherin, A. Robert .... Fairfax, VA
Cherin, Alex H. .... Los Angeles, CA
Cherin, Marvin S. .... Los Angeles, CA
Cherin, Richard E. .... Newark, NJ
Cherin, Steven .... Chicago, IL
Cherin, Steven M. .... Pittsburgh, PA
Cherin & Yelsky .... Los Angeles, CA
Cherinchak, Diane .... Wilkes-Barre, PA
Cheris, Howard R. .... Bethesda, MD
Cheris, Samuel David .... Denver, CO
Cherkala, Brian L. .... Cleveland, OH
Cherkas, Corey Shapiro
San Francisco, CA
Cherkas, Vicki M. .... New York, NY
Cherkasky, Clare .... Falls Church, VA
Cherkasky, Michael G. .... New York, NY
Cherken, Harry Sarkis, Jr.
Philadelphia, PA

Cherkin, Jack L. .... Pittsburgh, PA
Cherkin, Rhett P. .... Pittsburgh, PA
Cherkinsky, Edward J. .... Southfield, MI
Cherkinsky & Goutman, P.L.C.
Southfield, MI
Cherkis, Bruce Howard .... Bethesda, MD
Cherkis, Laurence D. .... New York, NY
Cherkos, Russell P. .... Forked River, NJ
Cherkoss, Val .... Amityville, NY
Chermak, Bonnie J. .... Los Angeles, CA
Chermak, Bonnie J. .... Woodland Hills, CA
Chermely, Diane L. .... Youngstown, OH
Chern, Carey C. .... San Francisco, CA
Chern, Cyril .... Long Beach, CA
Chern, Gertrude D. .... Santa Maria, CA
Chern, Marshall M. .... Coral Gables, FL
Chern & Sevin .... Coral Gables, FL
Cherna, David G. .... Carteret, NJ
Cherna, Howard K. .... Weston, FL
Chernack, Virginia Barnett
South Pasadena, CA
Chernak, Frank A. .... Cherry Hill, NJ
Philadelphia, PA
Chernak, John A. .... Cleveland, OH
Chernau, Chaffin & Burnsed, PLLC
Nashville, TN
Chernau, Michael S. J. .... Chesterfield, VA
Chernau, Stanley M. .... Nashville, TN
Chernawsky, Paul M. .... Chicago, IL
Chernay, Gary A. .... North Palm Beach, FL
Cherneff, Peter R. .... White Plains, NY
Chernek, David M. .... Los Angeles, CA
Chernek, Ronald J. .... Cleveland, OH
Chernekoff, Michael A. .... New Orleans, LA
Chernenko, Joyce D. .... Wellsburg, WV
Chernenko, Marc B. .... Wellsburg, WV
Cherner, Abby Strongin .... Washington, DC
Cherner, Jacob C .... Irving, TX
Cherner, Marvin .... Birmingham, AL
Cherner, Norman S. .... Los Angeles, CA
Cherner, Paul Jordan .... Chicago, IL
Cherner, Philip A. .... Denver, CO
Cherner, Shellie R. .... Norcross, GA
Cherner, Susan J. .... Media, PA
Chernesky, Heyman & Kress, P.L.L.
Dayton, OH
Chernesky, Richard J. .... Dayton, OH
Cherness, Harold I. .... Culver City, CA
Chernet, Lori S. .... New York, NY
Chernetsky, James M. .... Boston, MA
Chernett, Robert I. .... Cleveland, OH
Cherney, Andrew K. .... Dayton, OH
Cherney, Burton E. .... Chicago, IL
Cherney, Colburn G. .... Raleigh, NC
Cherney, Colburn T. .... Washington, DC
Cherney, Dana R. .... San Diego, CA
Cherney, David T. .... Chicago, IL
Cherney, Debra L. .... New York, NY
Cherney, Edward .... Woodbury, NY
Cherney, Emanuel S. .... New York, NY
Cherney, James A. .... Chicago, IL
Cherney, Melissa .... Madison, WI
Cherney, Phillip H. .... Visalia, CA
Cherney, Ronald .... New York, NY
Cherniack, Mark E. .... Minnetonka, MN
Cherniak, Edward A. .... Taylor, MI
Cherniak, George A. .... Staten Island, NY
Cherniak, I. David .... Mobile, AL
Cherniak, Leeza R. .... Atlanta, GA
Cherniak, Mark .... Detroit, MI
Cherniak, Samuel A. .... New York, NY
Cherniak, Veronica J. .... Atlanta, GA
Chernich, Scott A. .... Lansing, MI
Chernichaw, Adam .... New York, NY
Chernick, Albert D. .... Jamaica, NY
Chernick, Charles M. .... Chappaqua, NY
Chernick, Clifford Ross, Law Offices of
Menlo Park, CA
Chernick, Dina B. .... Beverly Hills, CA
Chernick, Michael J. .... Springfield, MA
Chernick, Michael J. .... Montpelier, VT
Chernick, Michael K. .... New York, NY
Chernick, Norman M. .... Aventura, FL
Chernick, Richard .... Los Angeles, CA
Chernick, Sharon L. .... New York, NY
Chernick, Vanessa D. .... Washington, DC
Chernick, Wade J. .... Encino, CA
Chernicoff, Richard S. .... Los Angeles, CA
Chernicoff, Robert E. .... Harrisburg, PA
Cherniga, Michael J. .... Tallahassee, FL
Chernigoff, Glenn I.
Commodity Futures Trading Commission, Division of Enforcement, GV
Chernik, Peter R. .... San Francisco, CA
Chernikoff, Robert L. .... Bethesda, MD
Chernin & Gold, LLP .... Binghamton, NY
Hallstead, PA
Chernin, Michael L. .... Milwaukee, WI
Chernin, Norman A. .... Glendale, CA
Chernin, Oliver R. .... New York, NY
Chernin, Russell S. .... Worcester, MA
Chernin, Sanford E. .... Somerville, NJ
Chernis, Michael S. .... New York, NY
Chernis, Paul .... New York, NY
Cherniss, David A. .... Half Moon Bay, CA
Moreno Valley, CA
Chernivec, Gerald F. .... Austin, TX
Cherno, Marc P. .... New York, NY
Chernof, Kenneth L. .... Department of Justice, Office of the Associate Attorney General, GV
Chernof, Stephen L. .... Milwaukee, WI
Chernoff, Carl G. .... Park Ridge, NJ
Chernoff, David S. .... Chicago, IL
Chernoff, George .... Miami, FL
Chernoff, Harry A. .... New York, NY
Chernoff, Holly B. .... Naples, FL
Chernoff, Howard C. .... Union, NJ

Chester, Geraldeen G. ....Department of State, Foreign Service Institute, GV
Chester, Gilbert W. ....Phoenix, AZ
Chester, Ira Sheldon ....Los Angeles, CA
Chester, Jacquie ....Anaheim, CA
Chester, James F. ....Dallas, TX
Chester, James J. ....Columbus, OH
Chester, Jeffrey A. ....Los Angeles, CA
Chester, Jeffrey A. ....New York, NY
Chester, John ....National Science Foundation, Office of the General Counsel, GV
Chester, John J. ....Columbus, OH
Chester, John J., Jr. ....Columbus, OH
Chester, John T. ....Morristown, NJ
Chester, Jonathan S. ....Summit, NJ
Chester, Joseph J. ....Pittsburgh, PA
Chester, Kevin D. ....Corsicana, TX
Chester, Mark D. ....Phoenix, AZ
Chester, Mark L. ....Lanham, MD
Chester, Mark S. ....Phoenixville, PA
Chester, Mark V. ....Chicago, IL
Chester, Mitchell A. ....Fort Lauderdale, FL
Chester, Patricia A. ....Morristown, NJ
Chester, Paula L. ....Albany, NY
Chester, Peter M. ....Oakland, CA
Chester, Ray ....Austin, TX
Chester, Robert H. ....Rutherford, NJ
Chester, Samuel D. ....Hartford, CT
Chester, Stephanie A. ....St. Paul, MN
Chester, Steven E. ....Lansing, MI
Chester, Susan Jane ....Boston, MA
Chester, Suzanne M. ....Raleigh, NC
Chester, Thea M. ....San Francisco, CA
Chester, Theodore A. ....Sierra Madre, CA
Chester, Theodore A., Jr. ....Los Angeles, CA
Chester, Thomas ....Providence, RI
Chester & Vestal ....Portland, ME
Chester, Victoria L. ....Cincinnati, OH
Chester, Willard H. ....Elkhart, IN
Chester, Willcox and Saxbe LLP
Columbus, OH
Delaware, OH
Chester, William K. ....West Palm Beach, FL
Chester, Yvonne E. ....Los Angeles, CA
Chesterman, John A. ....Albert Lea, MN
Chesterman, Melany S. ....Omaha, NE
Chesterman, Tracie R. ....Tampa, FL
Chesters, Frank C. ....Lancaster, PA
Chesters & Miller LLP ....Lancaster, PA
Chesterton, Paul D. ....St. Louis, MO
Chestler, Stuart ....Portland, OR
Chestney, Robert W. ....Atlanta, GA
Chestney-Hawkins Law Firm, The
Atlanta, GA
Decatur, GA
Lawrenceville, GA
Marietta, GA
Chestnut, Brian W. ....Seattle, WA
Chestnut & Cambronne, Professional Association ....Minneapolis, MN
St. Paul, MN
White Bear Lake, MN
Chestnut, Gayle B. ....Kansas City, MO
Chestnut, Geneviève ....San Diego, CA
Chestnut, Herbert J. ....Marietta, GA
Chestnut, Herbert J., P.C. ....Marietta, GA
Chestnut, Jack L. ....Minneapolis, MN
Chestnut, J. L., Jr. ....Selma, AL
Chestnut, John W. ....Chicago, IL
Chestnut, Kathi L. ....St. Louis, MO
Chestnut, Kelly D. ....Independence, MO
Chestnut, L. McNeil ....Raleigh, NC
Chestnut Law Offices ....Albuquerque, NM
Chestnut, Lee ....Springfield, MO
Chestnut, Marlane R. ....Philadelphia, PA
Chestnut, Michael D. ....Washington, IN
Chestnut, Peter C. ....Albuquerque, NM
Chestnut, Steven H. ....Seattle, WA
Chestnut, William A., Jr. ....San Jose, CA
Chestnut, Ellen J. Ziemann
Colorado Springs, CO
Chestnutt, Mark D.
Department Of Veterans Affairs, Board of Veterans Appeals, GV
Cheston, E. Calvert ....Gladwyne, PA
Cheston, Frank C., Jr. ....Chatham, NJ
Cheston, George M. ....Philadelphia, PA
Cheston, Morris, Jr. ....Philadelphia, PA
Cheston, Sheila C. ....Washington, DC
Chestovich, Milan J. ....Mishawaka, IN
Chesworth, Donald O. ....Rochester, NY
Chetkof, Michael ....Garden City, NY
Chetlin, Susan E. ....Englewood, CO
Chetney, Jean S. ....Vineland, NJ
Chetrick, Harold ....New York, NY
Chetrick, Harold, P.C. ....New York, NY
Chetta, Philip J. ....Kew Gardens, NY
Chetta, Rosario ....New York, NY
Chettih, Mindy H. ....New York, NY
Chettle, A. B., Jr. ....Manhattan Beach, CA
Chettle, Arthur W. ....San Diego, CA
Chettle, John H. ....Washington, DC
Chettle, Karen S. ....San Diego, CA
Chettle, Leslie R. ....Oakland, CA
Chetwynd, Frances J. ....Washington, DC
Cheugh, Robert W., II ....Columbus, OH
Cheuk, Lydia L. ....New York, NY
Cheung, Andrew J. ....New York, NY
Cheung, Angela ....Santa Monica, CA
Cheung, David ....Brooklyn, NY
Cheung, Denise ....Department of Justice, Antitrust Division, GV
Cheung, Elinor Lee ....St. Paul, MN
Cheung, Katherine Y.K. ....Washington, DC
Cheung, Keith K. ....St. Louis, MO
Cheung, Mark H. ....Irvine, CA
Cheung, Noland Jin-Poh ....Pittsburgh, PA
Cheung, Rosita ....New York, NY
Cheung, Sheri T. ....Los Angeles, CA
Cheung, Shirley M. ....Honolulu, HI
Cheung, TanYee ....New York, NY
Cheung, Vanita S. ....Lowell, MA
Cheung, Virginia L. ....Rockville, MD
Cheung, Yak-Fa ....Princeton, NJ
Cheung-Truslow, Marie ....Quincy, MA
Cheuvront, F. Bryan, III ....Phoenix, AZ
Cheuvront, Jeffre P. ....Lincoln, NE
Cheuvront, Steven M. ....Morganton, NC
Chevaillier, William C., Jr. ....Tulsa, OK
Chevalier, Alisa M. ....Los Angeles, CA
Chevalier, Allen & Lichman, LLP
Irvine, CA
Chevalier, Carol Lee ....New York, NY
Chevalier, Corlis ....Pasadena, CA
Chevalier, Fred L. ....Baton Rouge, LA
Chevalier, James L. ....Central Valley, NY
Chevalier, Jas. F. ....Maplewood, MN
Chevalier, John, Jr.
Palos Verdes Estates, CA
Chevallier, Edward P., Jr. ....Many, LA
Chevallier, J. Mark ....Dallas, TX
Chevarley, Jos. W. ....Newton, MA
Chevat, Alan ....Brooklyn, NY
Chevat, Benjamin ....Bayside, NY
Cheven, Barbara Ann ....New York, NY
Chévere, Francisco ....San Juan, PR
Chevere, Gloria ....Chicago, IL
Cheverie, Robert M. ....East Hartford, CT
Cheverine, Carolyn E. ....Cleveland, OH
Cheverine, Vincent L. ....Cleveland, OH
Cheverton, Paul, Law Offices of
San Diego, CA
Cheves, Cecil M. ....Columbus, GA
Cheves, Charles J. ....Venice, FL
Cheves, Langdon, III ....Greenville, SC
Chevigny, John E. ....Hammond, IN
Chevigny, Paul G. ....New York, NY
Chevillat, Terry ....Redondo Beach, CA
Chevillon, David H. ....San Diego, CA
Chevion, Ruth S. ....Concord, NH
Chevis, Cheryl A., (P.C.) ....Portland, OR
Chevis, John C., Jr. ....Bay St. Louis, MS
Chevis, Ronald A. ....Metairie, LA
Chevlen, Alden B. ....Youngstown, OH
Chevlen, S. Jack ....San Jose, CA
Chevlin, Paul J. ....Chicago, IL
Chevlin, Sanford Z. ....Hallandale Beach, FL
Chevlowe, Roberta K. ....New York, NY
Chevoor, Amy Burnham ....Peabody, MA
Chevrier, John A. ....Waterville, ME
Chew, Alberta C. ....Fairfield, CA
Chew, Belinda W. ....New York, NY
Chew, Benjamin G. ....Washington, DC
Chew, Deborah S. ....San Francisco, CA
Chew, Denley Y.S. ....New York, NY
Chew, Doris S. ....New York, NY
Chew, Edward M. ....Bartow, FL
Chew, Elizabeth C. ....Farmington, CT
Chew, Eric M. ....Albany, NY
Chew, H. Richard ....Arlington, VA
Chew, Hanley ....Palo Alto, CA
Chew, Hon ....Walnut Creek, CA
Chew, J. Alan, Jr. ....Marblehead, MA
Chew, John C. ....Daytona Beach, FL
Chew, Katherine H. ....Los Angeles, CA
Chew, Lawrence M. ....San Francisco, CA
Chew, Linda Yee ....El Paso, TX
Chew, Pat K. ....Pittsburgh, PA
Chew, Randall E. ....Pelham, GA
Chew, Thomas G. ....Fairfax, VA
Chew, Wayne G. ....Albuquerque, NM
Chew, Wayne G., P.C. ....Albuquerque, NM
Chewcaskie, Brian M. ....Fort Lee, NJ
Chew-Crawford, Debra C.
Department Of Health And Human Services, Office of the General Counsel, GV
Atlanta, GA
Chewkanes, Lori L. ....Philadelphia, PA
Chewning & Chewning ....Hopkinsville, KY
Chewning, John B. ....Cincinnati, OH
Chewning, John J. ....Hopkinsville, KY
Chewning, Maria K.
Upper Marlboro, MD
Chewning, Martha F. M. ....Hamilton, GA
Chewning, Richard L. ....Treasury Department, Internal Revenue Service, GV
Chewning, Richard W., III ....Lexington, SC
Chewning, Sands M. ....Hopkinsville, KY
Chey, Jean H. ....Philadelphia, PA
Cheyette, Daniel L. ....Nome, AK
Cheyne, Jeffrey M. ....Beaverton, OR
Cheyney, Curtis P., III ....Philadelphia, PA
Cheyney, Elizabeth R. ....Falls Church, VA
Cheyney, Karen ....Richardson, TX
Chez, Lawrence A. ....Chicago, IL
Chez, Steve P. ....Aurora, OR
Chezek, Denise D. ....New York, NY
Chezem, David Michael ....Tucson, AZ
Chezem, Linda L. ....Indianapolis, IN
Chezem, Serall ....O'Fallon, MO
Chhablani, Sanjay K. ....Chicago, IL
Chhabra, Ashwini K. ....New York, NY
Chhabra, Bhupinderpal S.
Washington, DC
Chi, Anthony ....Baytown, TX
Chi, Christina W. ....San Francisco, CA
Chi, Emily Catherine ....Cambridge, MA
Chi, Emily Chang ....Honolulu, HI
Chi, Joseph H. ....Irvine, CA
Chi, K. Conly ....New York, NY
Chi, Patrick C. ....Washington, DC
Chi, Taylor B. ....Palo Alto, CA
Chi, Willard H. ....Salem, OR
Chi, William ....Alhambra, CA
Chiacchia, Daniel J. ....Buffalo, NY
Chiacchiaro, Suanne Linder ....Manhasset, NY
Chiacchio, Thomas H., Jr. ....Pittsburgh, PA
Chiaf, John ....Oklahoma City, OK
Chiaf, Joseph D. ....Oklahoma City, OK
Chiaf, Law Offices, P.C.
Oklahoma City, OK
Chiafullo, James D. ....Pittsburgh, PA
Chiafullo, Louis A. ....Newark, NJ
Chiaia, Nicholas J. ....Brooklyn, NY
Chiakulas, James Newport ....Niles, IL
Chiakulas, Stacey L. ....Chicago, IL
Chialtas, George T. ....San Diego, CA
Chiama, Bernard A. ....Salem, SC
Chiamp & Associates, P.C. ....Detroit, MI
Chiamp, Carole L. ....Detroit, MI
Chianchiano, Dolph ....New York, NY
Chianco, David B. ....Crystal Beach, FL
Chianelli, Eugene W., Jr. ....St. Louis, MO
Chianese, Albert W. ....East Rockaway, NY
Chiang, Antony E. ....Cupertino, CA
Chiang, Chun-I ....Department of Justice, Civil Division, GV
Chiang, Darryl D. ....Hercules, CA
Chiang, Dean T. ....Gaithersburg, MD
Chiang, Eilin Jiunru ....Bellaire, TX
Chiang, Hsingkan ....Topeka, KS
Chiang, Joyce C. ....Los Angeles, CA
Chiang, Max C. ....Cerritos, CA
Chiang, Peter T. ....San Francisco, CA
Chiang, Ruguei Ruby ....Des Moines, IA
Chiang, W. Alexa ....Denver, CO
Chiang, Yung F. ....New York, NY
Chiang, Yung Frank ....New York, NY
Chiantelli, Alfred G. ....San Francisco, CA
Chiantera, Dominic J. ....Durham, NC
Chiaparas, E. Michael
Department of Justice, Civil Division, GV
Chiapella, John André, (P.C.)
Memphis, TN
Chiapete, W. Richard ....Racine, WI
Chiapetta, James R. ....Minneapolis, MN
Chiappa, Carl J. ....New York, NY
Chiapparelli, Charles A. ....Baltimore, MD
Chiappari, Ted J. ....New York, NY
Chiappe, Laura K. ....San Jose, CA
Chiappetta, David P. ....San Francisco, CA
Chiappetta, Dennis F., Jr.
Department Of Veterans Affairs, Board of Veterans Appeals, GV
Chiappetta, John ....Pittsburgh, PA
Chiappetta, Lisa A. ....New York, NY
Chiappetta, Vincent F. ....Salem, OR
Chiappinelli, John A. ....Rochester, NY
Chiappone, Philip M. ....New York, NY
Chiapuzio, Douglas S. ....Portland, OR
Chiapuzio, Douglas S., P.C. ....Portland, OR
Chiara, Frank J., Jr. ....Arlington, MA
Chiara, Gerard J. ....Jersey City, NJ
Chiara, Keith H. ....Price, UT
Chiara, Margaret M. ....Cassopolis, MI
Chiaramonte, Celeste M. ....Hyde Park, NY
Chiaramonte, Christina ....New York, NY
Chiaramonte, Paul S. ....Paterson, NJ
Chiaramonte, Philip G. ....New York, NY
Chiaravalli, Robert L. ....Detroit, MI
Chiaravalloti, Mariangela ....Saddle River, NJ
Chiaravalloti, Paul A. ....Buffalo, NY
Chiarchiaro, Frank J. ....New York, NY
Chiarella, Michael T. ....New London, NH
Chiarelli, Eugene J. ....San Francisco, CA
Chiarelli, Joseph M. ....Lee's Summit, MO
Chiarelli, Lawrence ....New York, NY
Chiarelli, Linda ....Brooklyn, NY
Chiarelli, Luke J. ....Milwaukee, WI
Chiarello, Donald F. ....Baltimore, MD
Chiarello, Gustav ....Washington, DC
Chiarello, Kenneth M. ....Boston, MA
Chiarello, Kevin R. ....Irvine, CA
Chiarello, Robert V. ....Elizabeth, NJ
Chiarello, Vincent J. ....San Francisco, CA
Chiari, Donald P. ....Buffalo, NY
Chiari, Gerald ....Buffalo, NY
Chiariello, Dominic L. ....Forest Hills, NY
Chiariello, Lana R. ....Tampa, FL
Chiariello, Richard J. ....Greer, SC
Chiariello, Susan A. ....Warwick, RI
Chiarmonte, Christina ....New York, NY
Chiaro, Cynthia M. ....Cincinnati, OH
Chiaro, Maria J. ....Naples, FL
Chiarolanza and DeAngelis ....Madison, NJ
Chiarolanza, Louis A. ....Madison, NJ
Chiartas, Gregory B. ....Charleston, WV
Chiarucci, Regina L. ....Cleveland, OH
Chiarulli, Eugene E., Jr. ....Lafayette, LA
Chiaruttini, James E. ....York, PA
Chiasson, Jennifer L. ....Boston, MA
Chiasson, Remy ....Thibodaux, LA
Chiasson, Roger E., II ....Bristol, CT
Chiasson, Stephen J. ....Los Angeles, CA
Chiat, Larry J. ....Minneapolis, MN
Chiatalas, John R. ....Neenah, WI
Chiate, Kenneth R. ....Los Angeles, CA
Chiatti, Remo ....Blue Bell, PA
Chiavarini, Kenneth B. ....Providence, RI
Chiaviello, Philip S. ....Chicago, IL
Chiaviello, Robert M., Jr. ....Dallas, TX
Chibib, Kristi Taylor ....Dallas, TX
Chibib, Michael ....Austin, TX
Chibos, Bradley R. ....San Jose, CA
Chiboucas, James ....Newport Beach, CA
Chibundu, Maxwell O. ....Baltimore, MD
Chicarelli, David A. ....Franklin, OH
Chiccarelli, Stephen F. ....Baton Rouge, LA
Chicchelly, Mary Elizabeth ....Marion, IA
Chicco, Giuliano J. ....St. Louis, MO
Chicco, Joseph ....Philadelphia, PA
Chicco, Robert ....Jericho, NY
Chicha, Andree R. ....Bellevue, WA
Chichester, Daniel M. ....Stafford, VA
Chichester, Gilbert W. ....Littleton, NC
Chichester, Robert S. ....Boulder, CO
Chichester, Ronald L. ....Houston, TX
Chichi, C. Drue ....Wilmington, DE
Chichoni, Héctor A. S. ....Plano, TX
Chick, Catherine Irene ....Cincinnati, OH
Chick, John E., Jr. ....Kansas City, MO
Chick, Marshall J. ....New York, NY
Chick, Patricia G. ....Department of Justice, Antitrust Division, GV
Chick, Robert S. ....Hernando, MS
Chick, Warren H. ....Oakland, CA
Chick, William S. ....Phoenix, AZ
Chick, William S., P.C. ....Phoenix, AZ
Chicka, Douglas W. ....Madison, TN
Chicka, Ronald L. ....Greensburg, PA
Chickedantz, C. Erik ....Fort Wayne, IN
Chickering, Chet R. ....Winterset, IA
Chickering, Frances P. ....St. Joseph, MI
Chickering & Gregory, A Professional Corporation ....San Francisco, CA
Chickering, John B. ....Tucson, AZ
Chickering, Robert B. ....San Francisco, CA
Chickering, Sharon R. ....Roanoke, VA
Chickering, William John
Benton Harbor, MI
Chickerneo, Carey Laurence
Mount Prospect, IL
Chickerneo & Fosco ....Mount Prospect, IL
Chickinell, Rockne J. .....Department of Justice, U. S. Parole Commission, GV
Chicknavorian, Elizabeth D. ....Rochester, NH
Chickos, Sarah Janette ....St. Louis, MO
Chickris, Greg G. ....East Moline, IL
Chiclana, Jose A. ....Union City, NJ
Chiclana, Maria I. ....New York, NY
Chico, Gery J. ....Chicago, IL
Chico, Julia M. ....Morgantown, WV
Chicoine, Caroline G. ....St. Louis, MO
Chicoine, Denise A. ....Newton, MA
Chicoine & Hallett, P.S. ....Seattle, WA
Chicoine, Jeffrey P. ....Portland, OR
Chicoine, Jerry L. ....Des Moines, IA
Chicoine, Julie E. ....Albuquerque, NM
Chicoine, Patricia Hendrix ....Houston, TX
Chicoine, Robert J. ....Seattle, WA
Chida, Junaid H. ....New York, NY
Chidakel, Susan Shirley
Nuclear Regulatory Commission, Office of the General Counsel, GV
Chidekel, David H. ....New York, NY
Chidekel, David M. ....New York, NY
Chidester, Alfred C. ....Denver, CO
Chidester, Glen A. ....Baton Rouge, LA
Chidester, Margaret A., (P.C.) ......Tustin, CA
Chidester, Richard L. ....Pearisburg, VA
Chidester, Robert G. ....Salem, OR
Chidester, Steven J. ....Rancho Santa Fe, CA
Chidester, Steven Russell ....Santa Ana, CA
Chidester, Walter S. ....Richmond, IN
Chidi, Elizabeth M. ....Los Angeles, CA
Chidiac, Norman J. ....Clifton, NJ
Chidichimo, Rose Marie J. ....Chicago, IL
Chidlaw, Ben E. ....Boulder, CO
Chidlaw, David B. ....San Diego, CA
Chidlaw, Edward H. ....San Luis Obispo, CA
Chidlaw, Keith D. ....Sacramento, CA
Chidlaw, Mariam E. ....El Cajon, CA
Chidnese, Patrick N. ....Asheville, NC
Chidsey, John W., III ....New York, NY
Chidsey, William R., Jr. ....Los Angeles, CA
Chiechi, Carolyn P.
United States Tax Court, GV
Chieco, Michael J. ....Springfield, MA
Chiefa, Cynthia I. ....Miami, FL
Chiefetz, Cary B. ....Livingston, NJ
Chieffo, Dominic J. ....Golden Gate, FL
Chieffo, Vincent H. ....Los Angeles, CA
Chiel, Jonathan, (P.C.) ....Boston, MA
Chiella, Karen A ....Los Angeles, CA
Chielpegian, Elliott D. ....Fresno, CA
Chielpegian, Elliott D., A Prof. Corp., Law Offices of ....Fresno, CA
Chielpegian, Mark E. ....Fresno, CA
Chielpegian, Michael S. ....Fresno, CA
Chien, Benny ....La Jolla, CA
Chien, Christine Y. ....Santa Ana, CA
Chien, David S. ....Burlington, VT
Chien, Julie C. ....Los Angeles, CA
Chien, Katherine ....Riverwoods, IL
Chien, Nadine Carol ....Fort Collins, CO
Chien, Peter W. ....Los Angeles, CA
Chien, Vanessa ....New York, NY
Chien-Hale, Elizabeth ....Menlo Park, CA
Chiepalich, Christopher S. ....Mobile, AL
Chiera & Brady ....New York, NY
Chiera, Randall J. ....New York, NY
Chierichella, John W. ....Los Angeles, CA
Washington, DC
Chierici, Chierici & Smith, A Professional Corporation ....Camden, NJ
Moorestown, NJ
Mount Holly, NJ
Chierici, Donald R., III ....Moorestown, NJ
Chierici, Donald R., Jr. ....Moorestown, NJ
Chierici, Elizabeth Coleman
Moorestown, NJ
Chierici, Wendy ....Haddonfield, NJ
Philadelphia, PA
Chiericozzi, Amy M. ....Charleston, WV
Chiert, Donald A. ....Bayside, NY
Chiesa, Debra Christine ....West Orange, NJ
Chiesa, Douglas D. ....Trenton, NJ
Chiesa, Jeffrey S. ....Cranford, NJ
Chiesa, Joseph F. ....Detroit, MI
Chiesa, Lisa A. ....Pittsburgh, PA
Chiesa, Mark Gerard
Farmington Hills, MI
Chiesa, Peter R. ....Manchester, NH

Chiesa, Robert L. ... Manchester, NH
Chiet, Arnold ... Bethesda, MD
Chiew, Elaine P. ... New York, NY
Chiga, Ann ... Boston, MA
Chiga, George C. ... Tulsa, OK
Chiganos, Terry C. ... Chicago, IL
Chigbu, John N. ... San Francisco, CA
Chiglo, Terry Allen ... Houston, MN
Chignell, Kevin L. ... Raleigh, NC
Chignola, William L., Jr. ... Framingham, MA
Chihak, Cynthia R. ... San Diego, CA
Chihak, John J., Jr. ... Seattle, WA
Chihara, Ted Akira ... Lihue, HI
Chikamoto, Oren T. ... Honolulu, HI
Chikamoto, Roy T. ... Honolulu, HI
Chikasuye, C. William ... Hilo, HI
Chikasuye, Clesson Y. ... Honolulu, HI
Chikezie, Charles C. ... Irvington, NJ
Chikofsky, Edward M. ... New York, NY
Chikovsky, Ben & Schafer ... Hollywood, FL
Chikovsky, Diane ... Hollywood, FL
Chikovsky, Fred ... Hollywood, FL
Chikovsky, Sara Lee ... Hollywood, FL
Chikowski, Brian T. ... Fairfield, CA
Chikowski, Eugene J. ... Malvern, PA
Chilcoat, David L. ... Columbus, OH
Chilcoat, Jeffrey R. ... Columbus, OH
Chilcote, Damon S. ... Beaver, PA
Chilcote, Karen E. ... Pittsburgh, PA
Chilcote, Lee A. ... Cleveland, OH
Chilcote, Max K. ... Boynton Beach, FL
Chilcote, Randall L. ... Indianapolis, IN
Chilcott, Stephen E. ... Sacramento, CA
Chilcott, Thomas E. ... Fairfax, VA
Chilcutt, Ben J. ... San Antonio, TX
Child, Barbara ... Berkeley, CA
Child, Bradford T. ... Los Angeles, CA
Child, Carey G. ... Washington, DC
Child, Charles H. ... Knoxville, TN
Child, Colleen ... San Mateo, CA
Child, Curtis L. ... Sacramento, CA
Child, Erik E. ... Sacramento, CA
Child & Fisher ... Coeur d'Alene, ID
Child, G. S., Jr. ... Knoxville, TN
Child, James K., Jr. ... Jackson, MS
Child, James W. ... Bowling Green, OH
Child, Jeffrey A. ... Coeur d'Alene, ID
Child, John L. ... Los Angeles, CA
Child, John S., Jr. ... Philadelphia, PA
Child, Martha ... Nashville, TN
Child, Michael Scott ... Department of the Army, U.S. Army Legal Services Agency, GV
Child, Nicole L. ... Foster City, CA
Child, Ralph A. ... Boston, MA
Child, Richard B. ... Boston, MA
Child, Richard L. ... Haines City, FL
Child, Robert M. ... Knoxville, TN
Childers, Ben W. ... Richmond, TX
Childers, B. M. Miller ... Selma, AL
Childers, Bradley P. ... Los Angeles, CA
Childers, Bruce ... Pensacola, FL
Childers, Bruce K. ... Scottsdale, AZ
Childers, Bruce K., Ltd. ... Scottsdale, AZ
Childers, C. Andrew ... Lawrenceville, GA
Childers, Carol ... New York, NY
Childers, Charlotte A. ... Chicago, IL
Childers, D. Bradley ... Los Angeles, CA
Childers, Dan ... Cedar Rapids, IA
Childers, Dana Anderson ... Los Angeles, CA
Childers, David A. ... Springfield, MO
Childers, David C. ... Mount Holly, NC
Childers, Emmett D. ... Omaha, NE
Childers, Fowler & Childers, P.A. ... Mount Holly, NC
Childers, Frances S. ... Palatka, FL
Childers, Frank G. ... Clarksville, TN
Childers, Howard D. ... Tustin, CA
Childers, J. Gilmore ... New York, NY
Childers, J. Michael ... Atlanta, GA
Childers, J. Richard ... Chicago, IL
Childers, Jack Alford, Jr. ... Memphis, TN
Childers, Jack D. ... Houston, TX
Childers, James G. ... Frankfort, KY
Childers, James H. ... Frankfort, KY
Childers, Jesse L. ... Mission Hills, KS
Childers, Jim Joseph ... Sacramento, CA
Childers, Joe F. ... Lexington, KY
Childers, John A. ... Chicago, IL
Childers, John C. ... Carrollton, OH
Childers, Karen Adell ... Lake Worth, FL
Childers, Keith T. ... Oklahoma City, OK
Childers, Kevin Paul ... Manassas, VA
Childers, Kevin Paul, P.C. ... Manassas, VA
Childers, Linda E. ... Tulsa, OK
Childers, Margaret Scholten ... Montgomery, AL
Childers, Mark L. ... Mooresville, NC
Childers, Martha D. ... Taylorsville, NC
Childers, Marvin L. ... Blytheville, AR
Childers, Masten, II ... Richmond, KY
Childers, Max L. ... Mount Holly, NC
Childers, Michael A. ... Chicago, IL
Childers, Michael J. ... Phoenix, AZ
Childers, Michelle A. ... San Francisco, CA
Childers & Murray ... Sacramento, CA
Childers, Nancy L. ... Oklahoma City, OK
Childers, Neal B. ... Atlanta, GA
Childers, Robert B. ... Jackson, MS
Childers, Robert D. ... New Albany, MS
Childers, Robert J. ... Tulsa, OK
Childers, Robert L. ... Memphis, TN
Childers, Robert T. J. ... Montgomery, AL
Childers, S. David ... Phoenix, AZ
Childers & Smith ... Carrollton, OH
Childers, Staton M. ... Houston, TX
Childers, Susan N. ... Little Rock, AR
Childers, Suzanne Smith ... Birmingham, AL
Childers, Thomas H. ... Prescott, AZ
Childers, Todd K. ... Lexington, KY
Childers, Valerie N. ... Chicago, IL
Childers, William R., Jr. ... Monroe, GA
Childers, William R., Jr., P.C. ... Monroe, GA
Childers, Williams & Windham ... Chicago, IL
Childers, Wm. Michael ... Kerrville, TX
Childers, Wm. Michael ... San Marcos, TX
Childerston, H. James ... Wilmington, DE
Childre, Aubrey M. ... Pearl, MS
Childres, Victoria S. ... Chattanooga, TN
Childress, Albert Franklin ... Lexington, MA
Childress, Alvin Roch, III ... New Orleans, LA
Childress, Andrew W. ... Clintwood, VA
Childress, Austin B. ... Spencer, IN
Childress, Calvin H. ... Virginia Beach, VA
Childress, Charles G. ... Austin, TX
Childress & Charpentier, P.A. ... Cocoa, FL; Melbourne, FL; Titusville, FL
Childress, D. Wayne ... Tuscaloosa, AL
Childress, David R. ... Fort Worth, TX
Childress, David W. ... Houston, TX
Childress, E. Franklin, Jr. ... Memphis, TN
Childress, Edward H. ... Charlottesville, VA
Childress, Elizabeth A.H. ... Mansfield, OH
Childress, George H. ... Rochester, NY
Childress, Georgia H. ... Charlottesville, VA
Childress, Hubert C., Jr. ... Melbourne, FL
Childress, Hubert M. ... Palm Desert, CA
Childress, James A. ... San Saba, TX
Childress, James L. ... Mansfield, OH
Childress, James W. ... St. Louis, MO
Childress, Jennifer A. ... Austin, TX
Childress, John A. ... Whittier, CA
Childress, John E. ... Springfield, IL
Childress, Josefina R. ... Boston, MA
Childress, Lewis E. ... Marshfield, MO
Childress, Lori Ann ... Detroit, MI
Childress, Louis W., Jr. ... East Orange, NJ
Childress, M. Lindsay ... New York, NY
Childress, Michael ... Chicago, IL
Childress, R. Paul, Jr. ... Richmond, VA
Childress, Randall W. ... Santa Fe, NM
Childress, Raymond S. ... Covington, LA
Childress, Raymond S., P.L.C. ... Covington, LA
Childress, Richard H. ... Bonita Springs, FL
Childress, Robert E. ... Springfield, MO
Childress, Ronald J. ... Albuquerque, NM
Childress, Ronald M. ... Columbia, SC
Childress, S. Alan ... New Orleans, LA
Childress, Scott Nelson Grimshaw ... Roswell, GA
Childress, Selena M. ... Charlotte, NC
Childress, Steven H. ... Bellingham, WA
Childress, Suzanne M. ... Environmental Protection Agency, Program Office Attorneys, GV
Childress, Tyrone R. ... Los Angeles, CA
Childress, Vincent D., Jr. ... Asheville, NC
Childress, Walter M. ... Jackson, MS
Childress, William A. ... Old Saybrook, CT
Childress, Yolanda ... New York, NY
Childress & Zdeb, Ltd. ... Chicago, IL
Childs, Alan D. ... Ocean Ridge, FL
Childs, Allyson ... Securities and Exchange Commission, Division of Market Regulation, GV
Childs, Benjamin B. ... Las Vegas, NV
Childs Bishop & White, P.C. ... Odessa, TX
Childs, Callis L. ... Conway, AR
Childs, Carol I. ... McLean, VA
Childs, Cathie A. ... San Diego, CA
Childs, Charles W., Jr. ... Newton, NC
Childs, Clayton Fisher ... Albuquerque, NM
Childs, Craig M. ... Macon, GA
Childs, Dana W. ... Portland, ME
Childs, Daniel Gilpin ... Philadelphia, PA
Childs, Deborah L. ... Los Angeles, CA
Childs, Dennis ... San Diego, CA
Childs, Donald G. ... Marco Island, FL
Childs, Emerson, Rundlett, Fifield & Childs ... Portland, ME
Childs, F. Carter ... Williamsburg, VA
Childs, Frank H., Jr. ... Macon, GA
Childs, George C., Jr. ... Marietta, GA
Childs, George L., III ... New York, NY
Childs, George N. ... Grand Island, FL
Childs & Halligan, P.A. ... Columbia, SC
Childs & Hilmer ... Three Oaks, MI
Childs, Homer A. ... Bloomington, MN
Childs, Howard R. ... Pittsburgh, PA
Childs, Ishmael C. ... Cleveland, OH
Childs, J. Mark ... Los Angeles, CA
Childs, J. Michelle ... Columbia, SC
Childs, James F., Jr. ... Los Angeles, CA
Childs, James M., Jr. ... Chicago, IL
Childs, James W. ... Akron, OH
Childs, James W., Jr. ... Birmingham, AL
Childs, Jennifer ... Los Angeles, CA
Childs, Jennifer A. ... Houston, TX
Childs, Jerry P. ... Odessa, TX
Childs, John C. ... Chicago, IL
Childs, John N. ... Akron, OH
Childs, Julie ... Atlanta, GA
Childs, Kathryn ... Boston, MA
Childs, Kenneth H. ... Grand Rapids, MI
Childs, Kenneth L. ... Columbia, SC
Childs, Kenneth P. ... Portland, OR
Childs, Kim B. ... Denver, CO
Childs & Knight ... Marietta, GA
Childs, Kristen ... San Francisco, CA
Childs, Larry B. ... Birmingham, AL
Childs, Leonard W., Jr. ... Savannah, GA
Childs, Leonard W., Jr., Law Offices of ... Savannah, GA
Childs, Linton J. ... Chicago, IL
Childs, Lisa C. ... Chicago, IL
Childs, Mary ... Claremont, CA
Childs, Matt W. ... Houston, TX
Childs, Matthew M., (P.A.) ... Tallahassee, FL
Childs, Michael A. ... Kansas City, MO
Childs, Michael C. ... Houston, TX
Childs, Michael P. ... Elk Horn, IA; Harlan, IA
Childs, Miller & Associates, LPA ... Cleveland, OH; Westlake, OH
Childs, Mobley F. ... Decatur, GA
Childs, Ozro William ... Santa Rosa, CA
Childs, Patrick J. ... Lihue, HI
Childs, R. Michael ... Charlotte, NC
Childs, Richard A. ... Columbus, GA
Childs, Robert C., III ... Greenville, SC
Childs, Robert F., Jr. ... Birmingham, AL
Childs, Roland A. ... Beverly Hills, CA
Childs, Ronald C. ... White Plains, NY
Childs, Ross Ann Clark ... Spokane, WA
Childs, Samuel L., Sr. ... Houston, TX
Childs, Sandra J. ... Portland, OR
Childs, Scott Ellis ... Dothan, AL
Childs & Shannonhouse ... Charlotte, NC
Childs & Silfani, LLP ... Akron, OH; Bath, OH
Childs, Stephanie ... Washington, DC
Childs, Stuart R. ... Charlotte, NC
Childs, T. Allen, Jr. ... Augusta, GA
Childs, Theron D., Jr. ... Three Oaks, MI
Childs, Thomas E., Jr. ... Fulton, MS
Childs, W. Boswell ... Silver Spring, MD
Childs, W. Douglas ... Jacksonville, FL
Childs, Walter S. B. ... Annapolis, MD
Childs, W. H., Jr. ... Lincolnton, NC
Childs, William H. ... Portland, ME
Childs-Swift, Linda ... Newark, NJ
Chilen, Joseph F. ... Fairbury, NE
Chiles, Charles M. ... Carrollton, TX
Chiles, Christopher D. ... Huntington, WV
Chiles, E. B., IV ... Little Rock, AR
Chiles, Emmett B., IV ... Little Rock, AR
Chiles, Gene T. ... Austin, TX
Chiles, Harry Frazier ... Tallahassee, FL
Chiles, Harry Ray, Jr. ... Wheaton, IL
Chiles, John P. ... Kingsport, TN
Chiles, John R. ... Birmingham, AL
Chiles, Lawton M. ... Tallahassee, FL
Chiles, Leigh M. ... Fort Smith, AR
Chiles, Lewis & Royer, Inc., A P.C. ... Oklahoma City, OK
Chiles, Robert C. ... San Francisco, CA
Chiles, Robert K. ... Oklahoma City, OK
Chiles, Stephen M. ... Chicago, IL
Chiles, William David ... Silver Spring, MD
Chilewich, Daniel S. ... New York, NY
Chilgren, Delia M. ... Rancho Cordova, CA
Chilian, Steven A. ... Boston, MA
Chilimigras, James C. ... Senatobia, MS
Chilingirian, Jack ... St. Clair Shores, MI
Chilivis, Cochran, Larkins & Bever LLP ... Atlanta, GA
Chilivis, Nickolas P. ... Atlanta, GA
Chill, Adam J. ... New York, NY
Chill, Bernard W. N., Jr. ... Jackson, MS
Chill, C. Daniel ... New York, NY
Chill & Chill ... Jackson, MS
Chill, Chill & Radtke, P.C. ... Chicago, IL
Chill, Ilana B. ... New York, NY
Chill, Marlane Elizabeth ... Greenwood, MS; **Jackson, MS**
Chill, Max ... Chicago, IL
Chill, Paul ... Hartford, CT
Chill, Steven G. ... New York, NY
Chillag, Nancy A. ... Menlo Park, CA
Chillas, Dayna C. ... San Diego, CA
Chillas, William E. ... Lancaster, PA
Chillemi, Clifford L. ... Broomfield, CO
Chillemi, Francine M. ... New York, NY
Chilleri, Gino A. ... Los Angeles, CA
Chillingworth, Charles C. ... West Palm Beach, FL
Chillingworth, William S. ... Hilo, HI
Chillinsky, Joseph J. ... Dayton, OH
Chilman, David M. ... Atlanta, GA
Chilman, W. Scott ... Ishpeming, MI
Chilnick, Andrea J. ... Philadelphia, PA
Chilson, Christopher A. ... Clayton, CA
Chilson, John H. ... Loveland, CO
Chilson, Mark R. ... Dayton, OH
Chilstrom, Christopher P. ... Minneapolis, MN
Chilstrom, Robert M. ... New York, NY
Chilton, Andrew S. ... Portland, OR
Chilton, Brian S. ... Washington, DC
Chilton, Charles R. ... Winter Haven, FL
Chilton, Douglas H. ... Texas City, TX
Chilton, Elizabeth G. ... Los Angeles, CA
Chilton, Frederick R., Jr. ... Palo Alto, CA
Chilton, Gary S. ... Oklahoma City, OK
Chilton, Gregory M. ... Salinas, CA
Chilton, Jan T. ... San Francisco, CA
Chilton, Jeffrey H. ... Grosse Pointe, MI
Chilton, Katherine ... Burbank, CA
Chilton, Larry J. ... Chicago, IL
Chilton, Michael G. ... Eureka, MT
Chilton, Ralph H. ... Hartford, CT
Chilton, Sarah ... Phoenix, AZ
Chilton, Stephanie L. ... Phoenix, AZ
Chilton, T. Gerald, Jr. ... Mesa, AZ
Chilton, T. Gerald, Jr., P.C., Law Offices of ... Mesa, AZ
Chilvers, Robert M. ... Emeryville, CA
Chilvers & Taylor, PC ... Emeryville, CA
Chima, Ron S. ... Cherry Hill, NJ; Harrisburg, PA; King Of Prussia, PA
Chimarusti, Wayne S. ... Carson City, NV
Chimel Dorado ... New York, NY
Chimel, Rita A. ... New York, NY
Chimenti, Norman V. ... Oak Brook, IL
Chimento, George L. ... Boston, MA
Chimento, Peter J. ... Huntington Station, NY
Chimera, Cathy ... Delray Beach, FL
Chimera, Thomas F. ... Bowling Green, KY
Chimeri, William F. ... Freeport, NY
Chimerine, Julie Anne ... West Palm Beach, FL
Chimes, Lewis H. ... New Haven, CT
Chimicles, Nicholas E. ... Haverford, PA
Chimicles & Tikellis LLP ... Wilmington, DE; Haverford, PA
Chimienti, Antonio ... Miami, FL
Chimileski, Robert B. ... Newport, VT
Chimileski, Robert B., P.C. ... Newport, VT
Chiminello, Phillip D. ... San Antonio, TX
Chimitris, Michael ... Chicago, IL
Chimko, Darryl J. ... Detroit, MI; Rochester Hills, MI
Chimos, Bill P. ... New York, NY
Chimovitz, Jeffrey A. ... Owosso, MI
Chimovitz, Robert M. ... Flint, MI
Chimples, Constantine G. ... Parma, OH
Chimples, George ... Philadelphia, PA
Chimpoulis, Jay P. ... Fort Lauderdale, FL; Miami, FL
Chin, Alice ... Oakland, CA
Chin, Alvin R. ... New York, NY
Chin, Archie ... Los Angeles, CA
Chin, Barbara ... Boston, MA
Chin, Benjamin M. ... Denver, CO
Chin, Beverly A. ... San Clemente, CA
Chin & Chin ... New York, NY
Chin, Ching Wah ... New York, NY
Chin, Christopher ... New York, NY
Chin, Christopher L. ... Mountain View, CA
Chin, Christopher L. ... New York, NY
Chin, Clifford F. ... Chicago, IL
Chin, Daniel Yit ... Austin, TX
Chin, David T. ... New York, NY
Chin, Davis ... Chicago, IL
Chin, Debra Kay ... New York, NY
Chin, Debra Kay, P.C. ... New York, NY
Chin, Denny ... New York, NY
Chin, Dickson ... New York, NY
Chin, Donna C. ... Livingston, NJ
Chin, Edward ... Dallas, TX
Chin, Edward G. H. ... New York, NY
Chin, Elleanor H. ... Cleveland, OH
Chin, Eugene T. ... San Francisco, CA
Chin, Francis Edwin ... Boston, MA
Chin, Francis F. ... Oakland, CA
Chin, Gabriel J. ... Cincinnati, OH
Chin, Gay ... Bethesda, MD
Chin, Geoffrey D. ... Los Angeles, CA
Chin, Gordon C. F. ... Charleston, WV
Chin, Gregory ... Palo Alto, CA
Chin, Hazel F. ... New York, NY
Chin, Helen H. ... New York, NY
Chin, James ... Sacramento, CA
Chin, James ... Cleveland, OH
Chin, James V. ... Athens, GA
Chin, James Y. ... New York, NY
Chin, Jason Wai-Yuen ... San Francisco, CA
Chin, Jean S. ... New York, NY
Chin, Jim L. ... Williamsburg, VA
Chin, John Q. ... South Miami, FL
Chin, Julia H. ... Houston, TX
Chin, Kathryn J. ... Woodbury, NY
Chin, Kathy Hirata ... New York, NY
Chin, Ken C. ... Houston, TX
Chin, Ken J. ... St. Petersburg, FL
Chin, Kena B. ... Los Angeles, CA
Chin, Kenneth ... New York, NY
Chin, Kirby ... New York, NY
Chin, Lily ... New York, NY
Chin, Linda T. ... New York, NY
Chin, Linda Y. ... Concord, MA
Chin, Llewellyn P. ... Los Angeles, CA
Chin, Lorelle J. ... Menlo Park, CA
Chin, May ... New York, NY
Chin, Ming W. ... San Francisco, CA
Chin, Nee Fong ... Cincinnati, OH
Chin, Owen H. ... Miami, FL
Chin, Pamela G. ... Pasadena, CA
Chin & Patrick, LLP ... Austin, TX
Chin, Paul A. ... Baltimore, MD
Chin, Ralph ... Hartford, CT
Chin, Robert V. ... San Rafael, CA
Chin, Rockwell J. ... New York, NY
Chin, Roderick W. ... New York, NY
Chin, Roger J. ... Palo Alto, CA
Chin, Ronald J. ... Coronado, CA
Chin, Ronald Patrick ... Houston, TX
Chin, Russell L. ... Boston, MA
Chin, Sherry ... Ann Arbor, MI
Chin, Stanley L. ... New York, NY
Chin, Stephanie Anne ... Honolulu, HI
Chin, Stephen C. ... Washington, DC
Chin, Stephen M. ... New York, NY
Chin, Steven D. ... New York, NY
Chin, Susan L. ... New York, NY
Chin, Susan Y. ... Dallas, TX
Chin, Sylvia Fung ... New York, NY
Chin, Sylvia Jean ... Gillette, NJ
Chin, Victoria ... San Francisco, CA
Chin, Vina ... Los Angeles, CA
Chin, William D. ... Boston, MA
Chin, Wright & Branson, P.C. ... Boston, MA
Chin, Yee Wah ... New York, NY
China, Chris Chitose ... Honolulu, HI

China, Daniel William ....Towson, MD
Chinaris, Timothy P. ....Tallahassee, FL
Chin-Bow, Eileen ....Plantation, FL
Chinbuah, Kwesi B. ....Menlo Park, CA
Chin-Caplan, Sylvia ....Boston, MA
Chincheck, Julia A. ....Charleston, WV
Chinchilla, George ....Whittier, CA
Chinchilla, Hector J. ....San Francisco, CA
Chin-Chuan Cha, Eugene ....New York, NY
Chindlund, Hugh P. ....San Diego, CA
Chindlund, John S. ....Salt Lake City, UT
Chine, Jeffrey A. ....San Diego, CA
Chinen, Marshall D. ....Honolulu, HI
Chinen, Richard L. ....Pasadena, CA
Chinen, Tracy G. ....Honolulu, HI
Ching, Alexander B. ....Dallas, TX
Ching, Amy W. ....Los Angeles, CA
Ching, Andrew B. ....Tempe, AZ
Ching, Angela ....San Francisco, CA
Ching, Anthony B. ....Tempe, AZ
Ching, Anthony C. ....Camas, WA
Ching, Armima ....Honolulu, HI
Ching & Associates, A Law Corp. Tustin, CA
Ching, Calleen J. ....Honolulu, HI
Ching, Cara M. K. ....Honolulu, HI
Ching, Charles R. ....Honolulu, HI
Ching Civille Calvo & Tang, A Professional Corporation ....Hagåtña, GU
Ching, Clarence F. T. ....Honolulu, HI
Ching, Clinton K. L. ....Honolulu, HI
Ching, Curtis B. ....Honolulu, HI
Ching, Cynthia K., (A Law Corporation) Honolulu, HI
Ching, Darwin L. D. ....Honolulu, HI
Ching, Deborah A. ....San Francisco, CA
Ching, Earl M. ....Honolulu, HI
Ching, Edric M. ....Honolulu, HI
Ching, Edwin K. W. ....Hagåtña, GU
Ching, Elizabeth T. ....Carrollton, TX
Ching, Ernest F., Jr. ....Tustin, CA
Ching, Fawn Y.J. ....Honolulu, HI
Ching, Gale L. F. ....Honolulu, HI
Ching, Glenn K.C., (A Law Corporation) Honolulu, HI
Ching, Han P. ....Honolulu, HI
Ching, Jade Lynne ....Honolulu, HI
Ching, Jennifer L. ....Honolulu, HI
Ching, Joseph E. ....New Orleans, LA
Ching, Keith S. K. ....Reno, NV
Ching, Kristine L. ....Palo Alto, CA
Ching & Lee ....Honolulu, HI
Ching, Les K. S. ....Olympia, WA
Ching, Leslie D. ....Brooklyn, NY
Ching, Melinda Yaki ....Honolulu, HI
Ching, Pamela K.S. ....Department of Justice, Executive Office for Immigration Review, GV
Ching, Randall K. H. ....San Francisco, CA
Ching, Randall Y. C. ....Honolulu, HI
Ching, Richard Michael ....Reston, VA
Ching, Rodney K. F. ....Honolulu, HI
Ching, Russell L. ....Honolulu, HI
Ching, Stanley L. ....Honolulu, HI
Ching, Stephen W.W., Jr. Philadelphia, PA
Ching, Steven L. ....Honolulu, HI
Ching & Thompson ....San Francisco, CA
Ching, Walter D. H. ....Madison, WI
Ching, Wesley H. H. ....Honolulu, HI
Ching, William J. ....Atlanta, GA
Ching, Yuen & Morikawa ....Honolulu, HI
Chingas, George L., Jr. ....Provo, UT
Chinian, John S. ....Worcester, MA
Chiniara, Ellen V. ....Avon, CT
Chinichian, Ginette M. ....Phoenix, AZ
Chinigo, Dario Anthony ....Bronx, NY
Chinigo, Paul F. ....Norwich, CT
Chiniquy, Sean-Paul ....San Francisco, CA
Chinitz, Gilbert M. ....Southfield, MI
Chinitz, Mark Ira ....New York, NY
Chinitz, Michael L. ....Boston, MA
Chinitz, Ross M. ....Stamford, CT
Chinitz, Stanley A. ....New York, NY
Chinitz, Stephen S., & Associates Bloomfield, CT
Chinitz, Stephen S., & Associates Hartford, CT
Chin-Kee-Fatt, Camille R. ....Brooklyn, NY
Chin-Lenn, Natalie C. ....West Palm Beach, FL
Chinlund, Gregory J. ....Chicago, IL
Chinn, Adam D. ....New York, NY
Chinn, Alison J. ....Vancouver, WA
Chinn, Alison K. ....Seattle, WA
Chinn, Anthony Scott ....Indianapolis, IN
Chinn & Associates, PLLC ....Jackson, MS
Chinn, C. Bradley ....Spokane, WA
Chinn, Cathryn S. ....Menlo Park, CA
Chinn, Claire W. S. ....Honolulu, HI
Chinn, Clayton D. ....Oakland, CA
Chinn, David P. ....Jeffersonville, IN
Louisville, KY
Chinn, Geoffrey M. ....New York, NY
Chinn, Julie C. ....Memphis, TN
Chinn, Kenneth O. ....Santa Ana, CA
Chinn, Linda M. ....Lexington, MA
Chinn, Lloyd B. ....New York, NY
Chinn, Mark A. ....Jackson, MS
Chinn, Nancy Jean ....Stevens Point, WI
Chinn, Richard L. ....Arlington, VA
Chinn, Sicilia S. Commission on Civil Rights, Office of the General Counsel, GV
Chinn, Stephen P. ....Kansas City, MO
Chinn, Steven C. ....New York, NY
Chinn, Timothy James ....Honolulu, HI
Chinnaswamy, Elizabeth Ann Westminster, MA
Chinnery, Carl, & Associates, P.C. Lee's Summit, MO
Chinnery, Carl L. ....Lee's Summit, MO
Chinni, Benjamin T. ....Cleveland, OH
Chinni, Christine L. ....Hartford, CT
Chinnis, C. Cabell, Jr. ....Washington, DC
Chin-Nobile, Lorna Lorraine New York, NY
Chino, Mitsuru Claire ....San Francisco, CA
Chinoy, Kathy G. ....Ponte Vedra Beach, FL
Chinquee, Anthony L. ....Brooklyn, NY
Chinquist, C. Charles ....Fargo, ND
Chinski, Arthur ....Los Angeles, CA
Chinski, Tobi J., Law Offices of Los Angeles, CA
Chinuntdet, John S. ....Charlotte, NC
Chiocca, John A. ....Tallahassee, FL
Chiocca, Michele L. ....Richmond, VA
Chiocca, Randal C. ....Parsippany, NJ
Chiocchi, Adriana Guevara ....San Jose, CA
Chiodi, Maria ....New York, NY
Chiodini, James J. ....Okemos, MI
Chiodo, Ernest P. ....Harrison Township, MI
Chiodo, Julie E. ....Willoughby, OH
Chiofalo, Anthony ....New York, NY
Chiofalo, Maureen C. ....Bradenton, FL
Chioffi, Joseph ....Hartford, CT
Chioffi, Mark P. ....Stamford, CT
Chioffi, Monica Copertino ....Norwalk, CT
Chioini, Carl E. ....Mount Clemens, MI
Chiola, Thomas R. ....Chicago, IL
Chion, Antonia Securities and Exchange Commission, Division of Enforcement, GV
Chionchio, Debra A. ....Boston, MA
Chionchio, John A. ....Philadelphia, PA
Chionopoulos, Debra L. Oklahoma City, OK
Chionopoulos, Michael E. Oklahoma City, OK
Chionos, Tom ....Dearborn, MI
Chionuma and Associates, P.C. Overland Park, KS
Kansas City, MO
Chionuma, Bettye Y. Mims ....Little Rock, AR
Chionuma, Chukwuemeka (Chuck) N. Kansas City, MO
Chiosso, James R. ....Oakland, CA
Chiou, Anson David ....Boston, MA
Chiozza, Louis P., Jr. ....Memphis, TN
Chip, William W. ....Washington, DC
Chipchase, Calvert G., III ....Honolulu, HI
Chiperfield, Robert N., Jr. ....New York, NY
Chiphe, Imani ....Chicago, IL
Chipinski, Elizabeth Martinez Houston, TX
Chipinski, Robert L. ....Minneapolis, MN
Chipkin, Joel M. ....Atlantic City, NJ
Chipkin, Leonard B. ....Mineola, NY
Chiple, Rosana I. ....West Chester, PA
Chiplin, Alfred J., Jr. ....Washington, DC
Chipman, Alan D. ....Boston, MA
Chipman, Brent R. ....Salt Lake City, UT
Chipman, Christine L. ....Danbury, CT
Chipman, Curtis M. ....Mesa, AZ
Chipman, David R. ....Danbury, CT
Chipman, David S. ....Denver, CO
Chipman, E. Nelson, Jr. ....Plymouth, IN
Chipman, Eugene N. ....Plymouth, IN
Chipman, James W. ....Springfield, IL
Chipman, James Wayne ....Springfield, MO
Chipman, Jayne Benz ....San Francisco, CA
Chipman, John M. ....Salt Lake City, UT
Chipman, Kerry D. ....Portland, OR
Chipman, Larry G. ....Independence, MO
Chipman Law Offices ....Plymouth, IN
Chipman, Marion W. ....Olathe, KS
Chipman, Mazzucco, Land & Pennarola, LLC ....Danbury, CT
Chipman, Nolan P. ....Miami, FL
Chipok, Paul H. ....Orlando, FL
Chipokas, Mark L. ....Cedar Rapids, IA
Chippas, Stephen J. ....Chicago, IL
Chipperfield, Alan ....Jacksonville, FL
Chipperfield, Lynn ....St. Louis, MO
Chippey, Rollin B., II ....San Francisco, CA
Chipser, Brett S. ....Montgomery, AL
Chiquoine, Molberg & Natwick, S.C. Reedsburg, WI
Chiquoine, Stephen D. ....Reedsburg, WI
Chira, Robert, & Associates ....New York, NY
Chirafis, Johnny M. ....Corsicana, TX
Chiras, David L. ....Fort Lauderdale, FL
Chirba-Martin, Mary Ann ....Medfield, MA
Chirchick, Lisa ....Newton, NJ
Chirco, Herrinton, Runstadler & Thomas, L.L.P. ....Troy, MI
Chirco, Norman J. ....Auburn, NY
Chircop, Manuel J. ....Detroit, MI
Chircus, Eugene V. ....Baltimore, MD
Chirelstein, Marvin A. ....New York, NY
Chirgott, Paul S. ....Pittsburgh, PA
Chirhart, Timothy H. ....St. Cloud, MN
Chiriatti, Karyn Meredith ....Reno, NV
Chiriatti, Michael, Jr. ....Reno, NV
Chirich, Elizabeth Girafalco ....Houston, TX
Chirichella, Thomas J., Jr. ....Somerville, NJ
Chirico, Carol Huggins ....Boston, MA
Chirico, Guy W. ....Tannersville, NY
Chirico, R. R. ....Garfield, NJ
Chirico, Vincent ....Millburn, NJ
New York, NY
Chirigotis, Frederick ....Falmouth, MA
Chirinian, Guy ....Brea, CA
Chirite, Norman D. ....New York, NY
Chirlin, Judith C. ....Los Angeles, CA
Chirls, Andrea B. ....Fort Lauderdale, FL
Chirls, Andrew A. ....Philadelphia, PA
Chirls, Richard ....New York, NY
Chiro, Ned J. ....Jefferson, LA
Chirokas, Thomas J. ....Roslindale, MA
Chiron, Linda J. ....Riverwoods, IL
Chiron, Stuart Z. ....McLean, VA
Chirra, Joseph ....Vista, CA
Chirumbole, Stephen ....Gaithersburg, MD
Chirwa, Dawn Executive Office Of The President, GV
Chisari, Thomas V. ....Holtsville, NY
Chiscano, Steve Alfonso ....San Antonio, TX
Chisenhall, Lawrence E., Jr. Little Rock, AR
Chisenhall, Nestrud & Julian, P.A. Little Rock, AR
Chisholm, Allan D. ....Mount Clemens, MI
Chisholm, Anne Winthrop ....Boston, MA
Chisholm, Chisholm & Kilpatrick Providence, RI
Chisholm, David R. ....Billings, MT
Chisholm, Dean D. ....Columbia Falls, MT
Chisholm, Dolly ....Savannah, GA
Chisholm, Donald H. ....Kansas City, MO
Chisholm, Donald J. ....Burley, ID
Chisholm, Donald R. ....Royal Oak, MI
Chisholm, Karen L. ....Houston, TX
Chisholm, Lawrence F. ....Metairie, LA
Chisholm, Malcolm J., Jr. ....Lee, MA
Chisholm, Maria P. ....Buffalo, NY
Chisholm, Mary Ellen ....Troy, MI
Chisholm, Michael H. ....Jackson, CA
Chisholm, Patricia L. ....Lexington, MA
Chisholm, Penni L. ....Great Falls, MT
Chisholm, Richard ....Menlo Park, CA
Chisholm, Richard A. ....Palos Park, IL
Chisholm, Richard S. ....Bethesda, MD
Chisholm, Robert F. ....Parsippany, NJ
Chisholm, Robert V. ....Providence, RI
Chisholm, Sarah T. ....Troy, MI
Chisholm, Tommy ....Atlanta, GA
Chisholm, Valerie W. ....Houston, TX
Chisholm, Vincent J. ....Providence, RI
Chisholm, William M. ....Peekskill, NY
Chishti, Muzaffar A. ....New York, NY
Chisling, Brian E. ....Columbus, OH
Chism, Brent L. ....Lake Charles, LA
Chism, Dawn Renee ....Philadelphia, PA
Chism, Edna M. ....Los Angeles, CA
Chism, Geoffrey P. ....Seattle, WA
Chism, J Roger ....Houston, TX
Chism, Kerry D. ....Mountain Home, AR
Chism, Randy N. ....Union City, TN
Chism, Thomas E. ....Albuquerque, NM
Chism, Timothy K., Jr. ....Bowling Green, KY
Chismire, Lisa E. ....Wilmington, DE
Chisnell, Brian J. ....Mansfield, OH
Chisnell, Janice Hoffman ....Pittsburgh, PA
Chisolm, Bentina D. ....Raleigh, NC
Chisolm, John H. ....Covington, TN
Chisolm, Laura Brown ....Cleveland, OH
Chisolm, Laurie K. ....Shaftsbury, VT
Chisolm, Page A. ....New York, NY
Chissell, Robert ....Baltimore, MD
Chisum, Donald ....Palo Alto, CA
Chisum, William T. ....Sacramento, CA
Chisvin, Craig L. ....Los Angeles, CA
Chitkowski, John J. ....Glen Ellyn, IL
Chitkowski, John J., Ltd. ....Chicago, IL
Glen Ellyn, IL
Chitlik, Edward ....Cleveland, OH
Chitlik, Glenn D. ....Atlanta, GA
Chitre, Nanda S. Executive Office Of The President, GV
Chitsey, Allison L. ....San Angelo, TX
Chittem Hartnett, Allison ....Miami, FL
Chittenden, Ann ....Tallahassee, FL
Chittenden, Russell W. ....Los Angeles, CA
Chittenden, Thomas S. ....New York, NY
Chittenden, William A., III ....Chicago, IL
Chittero, Frank S. ....Wauwatosa, WI
Chittick, David O. ....Monroe, CT
Chittick, Hilary A. ....Fresno, CA
Chittick, Michael D. ....Providence, RI
Chittle, Thomas E. ....Flint, MI
Chittom, Michael B. ....Jackson, MS
Chittum, Robert A. ....Rochester, NY
Chittum, Roger D. ....Atlanta, GA
Chittur, Krishnan, Law Office of New York, NY
Chitty, B. Michael ....Terrell, TX
Chitty, Robert A. ....Miami, FL
Chitwood, Carey J. ....Birmingham, AL
Chitwood & Harley ....Atlanta, GA
Chitwood, Howard Lee ....Wytheville, VA
Chitwood, Martin D. ....Atlanta, GA
Chitwood, Stephen R. ....Alexandria, VA
Chiu, Agnes Sau-Chun ....Alhambra, CA
Chiu, Alexis S. M. ....San Francisco, CA
Chiu, Andrew ....Phoenix, AZ
Chiu, Armando Sung ....Dallas, TX
Chiu, Bruce H. ....Pittsburgh, PA
Chiu, Charmaine T.M. ....Jacksonville, FL
Chiu, Colin K. W. ....Los Angeles, CA
Chiu, Conrad K. ....New York, NY
Chiu, Daina C. ....San Francisco, CA
Chiu, Daniel ....New York, NY
Chiu, Dennis W. ....San Jose, CA
Chiu, Grace R. ....Washington, DC
Chiu, Jerrie L. ....Boston, MA
Chiu, John C. ....Washington, DC
Chiu, Julie C. ....Charlotte, NC
Chiu, Karen V. ....Seattle, WA
Chiu, Kit Wan ....New York, NY
Chiu, Lily R. Securities and Exchange Commission, Division of Investment Management, GV
Chiu, Louise L. ....Oakland, CA
Chiu, Lucy C. ....Fairfax, VA
Chiu, Maria J. ....Jamaica, NY
Chiu, Nancy K. ....Oakland, CA
Chiu, Ning ....New York, NY
Chiu, Peggy Pei-Ru ....Denver, CO
Chiu, Richard M. ....Houston, TX
Chiu, Victor Tai Wung ....Garden City, NY
Chiu, Vivien M. ....Irvine, CA
Chiu, Wei-Wei ....West Chester, PA
Chiu, Wing K. ....New York, NY
Chiulli, E. Antoinette ....Haddonfield, NJ
Chiulos, Ellen D. ....San Francisco, CA
Chiumenti, Stephen ....Boston, MA
Chiumento, Braunstein, Guntharp & Emery, P.A. ....Palm Coast, FL
Chiumento, Gary C. ....Cherry Hill, NJ
Chiumento, Michael D., III Winter Park, FL
Chiumento, Michael D., Jr. ....Palm Coast, FL
Chiuminatto, Martin J., Jr. ....Kingsville, TX
Chiungos, John C. ....Chelmsford, MA
Chiurazzi, Richard J. ....Sacramento, CA
Chiurazzi, Wayne M. ....Pittsburgh, PA
Chiusano, Peter Vincent ....Norfolk, VA
Chivaro, Richard John ....Sacramento, CA
Chivell, Michael A. ....Belleville, IL
St. Louis, MO
Chivers, David K. ....Springfield, MA
Chivers, James L. ....Binghamton, NY
Chivers, Joseph H. ....Pittsburgh, PA
Chivetta, A. J. ....St. Louis, MO
Chivily, Nicholas J. ....White Plains, NY
Chivukula, Padmaja ....Pittsburgh, PA
Chizek, Martin S. ....Brunswick, ME
Chizever, Gerald M. ....Beverly Hills, CA
Chizewer, David J. ....Chicago, IL
Chizik, Joseph S. ....Mount Laurel, NJ
Chizmadia, Gerald P. ....Milltown, NJ
Chizmar, Gregory A. ....Parma Heights, OH
Chizmar, R. Erick ....Philadelphia, PA
Chlad, Michele M. ....San Diego, CA
Chlan, Charles E. ....Baltimore, MD
Chlan, William P., Jr. ....Towson, MD
Chlapowski, Francis S. ....New York, NY
Chlappetta, Donald D. ....Muncie, IN
Chlarson, Kerry L. ....Sandy, UT
Chlastawa, Allan F. ....Wynantskill, NY
Chleborad, Kenneth L. ....Rapid City, SD
Chleboski, Ronald J., Jr. ....Pittsburgh, PA
Chlebus, Andrew J. ....Providence, RI
Chlopecka, Elzbieta ....Washington, DC
Chlopecki, Mary ....Washington, DC
Chlouber, Steven E. ....Tulsa, OK
Chloupek, Carol E. ....Miami, FL
Chloupek, Carol E., & Associates, P.A. Miami, FL
Chloupek, Joseph R. ....West Palm Beach, FL
Chloupek, Mark M. ....Dallas, TX
Chlysta, John R. ....Akron, OH
Chmar, Linda D. ....Atlanta, GA
Chmara, Theresa ....Washington, DC
Chmelik, Frank J. ....Bellingham, WA
Chmelik Sitkin & Davis, P.S. Bellingham, WA
Chmelka, Dayna Lyn ....Los Angeles, CA
San Diego, CA
Chmiel, Arthur J. ....Fairmont, WV
Chmiel, Michael A. ....Anoka, MN
Chmiel, Michael J. ....Crystal Lake, IL
Chmielarski, Mark J. ....Casselberry, FL
Chmielarski, Mark J., P.A. ....Casselberry, FL
Chmielarz, Melinda L. Fort Lauderdale, FL
Chmielecki, Maureen A. ....Hartford, CT
Chmielewski, Christine A. ....Ridgewood, NJ
Chmielewski, Cynthia M. Washington, DC
Chmielewski, Deborah A. ....Portland, ME
Chmielewski, Paul ....Pinellas Park, FL
Chmielewski, Stefan V. Bloomfield Hills, MI
Chmielewski, Terry J. ....Denver, CO
Chmielinski, Henry H., Jr. ....Boston, MA
Chmielinski, Richard G. ....Newton, MA
Chmielinski, Robert W. ....Wellesley, MA
Chmielinski, Wilchins & Witman, A Professional Association ....Wellesley, MA
Chmura, Donna Ray ....Creedmoor, NC
Durham, NC
Greensboro, NC
Raleigh, NC
Chmura, Eugene ....Long Island City, NY
Chmura, Jennifer A. ....Los Angeles, CA
Chmura, John M. ....Warren, MI
Chmura, Martin W. ....Oak Brook, IL
Cho, Anthony P. ....Bloomfield Hills, MI
Cho & Brown, Law Offices of ....Ventura, CA
Cho, Cynthia S. ....Fremont, CA
Cho, Daniel D. ....Los Angeles, CA
Cho, Daniel H. ....Costa Mesa, CA
Cho, David J. ....Washington, DC
Cho, Dean T. ....New York, NY
Cho, Dennis Hohn ....Los Angeles, CA
Cho, Douglas A. ....Hartford, CT
Cho, Ellen I. ....Miami, FL
Cho, Erin K. ....New York, NY
Cho, George ....Oakton, VA
Cho, Hee ....New York, NY
Cho, Howard ....Ventura, CA
Cho, Ines M. ....Los Angeles, CA
Cho, Jenny ....New York, NY
Cho, JoAn H. ....Los Angeles, CA
Cho, John ....Rockville, MD
Cho, Johnna C. ....Burbank, CA
Cho, Joseph ....Los Angeles, CA
Cho, Julie M. ....Chicago, IL
Cho, Justine H. ....Cliffside Park, NJ
Cho, Kenneth Kunho ....New York, NY
Cho, Laura Scanlan ....Austin, TX

Cho, Lawrence H. ... Los Angeles, CA
Cho, Lawrence M. ... Lisle, IL
Cho, Lisa M. ... Palo Alto, CA
Cho, Louise M. ... North Brunswick, NJ
Cho, Mark M. ... Miami, FL
Cho, Michael Sanghun ... San Antonio, TX
Cho, Peter M. ... New York, NY
Cho, RoseAnn Younghee ... New York, NY
Cho, Shirley S. ... Los Angeles, CA
Cho, Steve Y. ... Menlo Park, CA
Cho, Sukjin ... New York, NY
Cho, Susan M. ... St. Louis, MO
Cho, Teresa ... Los Angeles, CA
Cho, Theresa ... San Francisco, CA
Cho, Tilda L. ... Los Angeles, CA
Cho, Woo Jung A. ... New York, NY
Choal, Timothy ... St. Paul, MN
Choat, Lindell ... Eddyville, KY
Choate, Alan G. ... Baltimore, MD
Choate, Allison ... New York, NY
Choate, Andrew B. ... Lewiston, ME
Choate, Arthur B. ... Miami, FL
Choate, Ben P., Jr. ... Muskogee, OK
Choate, Charles F. ... Manchester, MA
Choate and Choate ... Los Angeles, CA
Choate & Choate, P.C. ... Seminole, OK
Choate, Chris A. ... Fort Worth, TX
Choate, Cortlandt C., Jr. ... Morristown, NJ
Choate, Craig A. ... Houston, TX
Choate, Cynthia L. ... Tucson, AZ
Choate, D. Jeff ... Albany, KY
Choate, David L. ... Worth, IL
Choate, David R. ... Albany, KY
Choate, David R. ... Monticello, KY
Choate, Dena G. ... Arlington, TX
Choate, Dennis S. ... Santa Ana, CA
Choate, Edward L. ... Hamden, CT
Choate, G. Wayne ... San Antonio, TX
Choate, Guinn & Springmeyer, L.L.P.
Carmel, CA
San Diego, CA
Choate, Guy D. ... San Angelo, TX
Choate, Hall & Stewart ... Boston, MA
Manchester, NH
Choate, Harold J., III ... Calhoun, GA
Cartersville, GA
Choate, J. Samuel, Jr. ... Cleveland, TN
Choate, Jim K. ... Dallas, TX
Choate, John I. ... Stamford, CT
Choate, John I.M. ... Seminole, OK
Choate, John L. ... Atlanta, GA
Choate, John S. ... Arkadelphia, AR
Choate, Joseph, Jr. ... Los Angeles, CA
Choate, K.J. ... Saginaw, MI
Choate, Leon, Jr. ... Iselin, NJ
New York, NY
Choate, Leonard E. ... San Antonio, TX
Choate, Lile S. ... Little Rock, AR
Choate & Lilly, A Professional Corporation
Dallas, TX
Choate, Mark Clayton ... San Diego, CA
Choate, Michael J. ... Chicago, IL
Choate, Mitchell, Baker & Nelson
New York, NY
Choate, Nancy L. ... Jackson, TN
Choate, Natalie B. ... Boston, MA
Choate, Paul A. ... Auburn, ME
Choate, Robert J. ... Jasper, TX
Choate, Scott M. ... Bellingham, WA
Choate, Stephen ... Heber Springs, AR
Choate, Thomas W. ... Abilene, TX
Choate, W. Lee ... Austin, TX
Choate, William Rufus ... Houston, TX
Choate, William W. ... Seminole, OK
Choban, Irving ... Brooklyn, NY
Choban, Steven L. ... Portland, OR
Chobor, Jennifer L. ... Hartford, CT
Chobot, Daniel L. ... Niles, IL
Chocallo, Wanda P. ... Drexel Hill, PA
Chochrek, Nancy Shaw ... Chicago, IL
Chociey, Edwin F., Jr. ... Morristown, NJ
Chock, Allan S. ... Honolulu, HI
Chock, Annette Y. W. ... Honolulu, HI
Chock, Jay R. ... Portland, OR
Chock, Nolan K. C. ... Captain Cook, HI
Chock, Patricia N. ... Los Angeles, CA
Chocklett, Gregory P., Law Offices of
Cary, NC
Chocklett, Gregory P., Law Offices of
Raleigh, NC
Chocklett, Gregory P., Law Offices of
Research Triangle Park, NC
Chockley, F. Wilson, Jr. ... Cleveland, OH
Chockley, Frederick W., III
Washington, DC
Chod, Edward A. ... St. Louis, MO
Chod, Jeffrey E. ... St. Louis, MO
Chodak, Murray J. ... Farmington Hills, MI
Chodash, Louis ... Englewood, NJ
Choderker, Dorie G. ... Los Angeles, CA
Chodil, Mary Beth ... Lafayette, CO
Chodoff, Louis L. ... Haddonfield, NJ
Chodorow, Adam S. ... San Francisco, CA
Chodorow, Gary ... Chicago, IL
Chodorow, Hilton I. ... Los Angeles, CA
Chodorow, Jordan ... Los Angeles, CA
Chodos, David M. ... Los Angeles, CA
Chodos, Deborah ... Los Angeles, CA
Chodos, Hillel ... Los Angeles, CA
Chodos, Jonathan P. ... Los Angeles, CA
Chodos, Julie C. ... New York, NY
Chodos, Linda W. ... Kenmore, NY
Chodos, Michael A.
Palos Verdes Estates, CA
Chodos, Rafael ... Woodland Hills, CA
Chodosh, Bernard ... New York, NY
Chodosh & Chodosh ... Columbus, OH
Chodosh, Hiram E. ... Cleveland, OH
Chodosh, Leonard ... Jamaica, NY
Chodosh, Loren ... New York, NY
Chodosh, Loren, P.C. ... New York, NY
Chodosh, Louis J. ... Columbus, OH
Chodosh, Sheila R. ... Columbus, OH
Chodsky, Valery V. ... Walnut Creek, CA
Chodun, Eric ... Dallas, TX
Chodzko, James E. ... San Diego, CA
Choe, Anna H. ... New York, NY
Choe, Catherine ... Washington, DC
Choe, Chong U. ... Riverside, CA
Choe, Gene W., Law Offices of
Los Angeles, CA
Choe, Iva Y. ... Cleveland, OH
Choe, J. Tiffani ... New York, NY
Choe, Jae-Ung ... New York, NY
Choe, Jennifer ... Roseland, NJ
Choe, Jennifer D. ... New York, NY
Choe, Jiyon ... San Francisco, CA
Choe, Julie H. ... Boston, MA
Choe, Melissa M. ... New York, NY
Choe, Sandy Minah ... Cherry Hill, NJ
Choe, U-Jung ... Chicago, IL
Choe, William W. ... Palo Alto, CA
Choe, Young J. ... Livingston, NJ
Chofnas, Lori S. ... Norristown, PA
Chohan, Kiren K. ... Los Angeles, CA
Choharis, Peter C. ... Washington, DC
Choi, Albert B. ... Los Angeles, CA
Choi, Alexander P. ... Department of Education,
Office for Civil Rights, GV
Choi, Alice H. ... Sacramento, CA
Choi, Austin ... Palo Alto, CA
Choi, Barbara H. ... San Jose, CA
Choi, Benjamin B. ... Secaucus, NJ
Choi, Byung W. ... Boston, MA
Choi, Carolyn, Law Offices of
San Jose, CA
Choi, Carolyn, Law Offices of
Santa Clara, CA
Choi, Catherine K. ... Columbus, OH
Choi, Cedric ... Honolulu, HI
Choi, Chuck C. ... Honolulu, HI
Choi, Chung-In Anthony ... New York, NY
Choi, Dana L. ... Miami, FL
Choi, Frank I. ... Department of Commerce,
Patent and Trademark Office, GV
Choi, Gavin M. ... New York, NY
Choi, George Y. ... Orinda, CA
Choi, Glen B. ... San Jose, CA
Choi, H. Sunny ... Washington, DC
Choi, Han C. ... Atlanta, GA
Choi, Hunt K. ... Raleigh, NC
Choi, Hye-Won ... New York, NY
Choi, Hyungmoo ... Flushing, NY
Choi, IL Young ... Miami, FL
Choi, Jane J. ... Chicago, IL
Choi, Janine M., Law Offices of
Redondo Beach, CA
Choi, Jay J. ... Denver, CO
Choi, Jeffrey ... Hilo, HI
Choi, Jennifer S.
Securities and Exchange Commission,
Division of Market Regulation, GV
Choi, Jin S. ... Pasadena, CA
Choi, John H. ... Los Angeles, CA
Choi, John J. ... Minneapolis, MN
Choi, John W. ... New York, NY
Choi, Jung-Won ... Upper Marlboro, MD
Choi, Karen J. ... Liberty Corner, NJ
Choi, Kathleen L. ... San Francisco, CA
Choi, Kenneth J. ... New York, NY
Choi, Kerry Paul ... Boston, MA
Choi, Kiwon ... New York, NY
Choi, Lisa C.
Federal Communications Commission,
Common Carrier Bureau, GV
Choi, Madelyn ... San Jose, CA
Choi, Margaret S. ... Denver, CO
Choi, Melissa J. ... New York, NY
Choi, Michael S. ... Los Angeles, CA
Choi, Monica H. ... Chicago, IL
Choi, Paul L. ... Chicago, IL
Choi, Rebecca J. ... Alexandria, VA
Choi, Richard T. ... Washington, DC
Choi, S.J. Robin ... Chicago, IL
Choi, Steven S. ... Los Angeles, CA
Choi, Sue J. ... Washington, DC
Choi, Susan Ser ... Los Angeles, CA
Choi, Wendy A. ... Philadelphia, PA
Choi, William C. ... Los Angeles, CA
Choi, Yong S. ... Los Angeles, CA
Choi, Yun Y. ... Los Angeles, CA
Choi, Zenas J. ... Washington, DC
Choice, Bennett E. ... Milwaukee, WI
Choiniere, Lori R. ... Burlington, VT
Choiniere, Monique ... Washington, DC
Choisser, Dale F. ... Vandalia, IL
Choi-Wolff, Jeannie ... Santa Monica, CA
Chojnacki, Roman A. ... Waukesha, WI
Chojnowski, Edmund F.
Sterling Junction, MA
Chojnowski, Michael L. ... Kalamazoo, MI
Choka, Allen D. ... Tucson, AZ
Choka, Byron S. ... Toledo, OH
Chokey, James A. ... St. Francis, WI
Chokshi, Samir D. ... New York, NY
Cholack, Eric W. ... Troy, MI
Cholakian, Kevin K. ... San Francisco, CA
Cholakis, George N. ... Albany, NY
Cholakis, Gregory D. ... Troy, NY
Cholakis, Nia C. ... Albany, NY
Cholden, Pamela J. ... Media, PA
Cholden, Steven P. ... Philadelphia, PA
Cholette, Perkins & Buchanan
Grand Rapids, MI
Cholette, Robert L. ... Rochester, NY
Cholewa, Matthew J. ... Cromwell, CT
Cholewka, Jerry A. ... New Brunswick, NJ
Cholis, Alexis T. ... South Bend, IN
Cholis and Cholis ... South Bend, IN
Cholis, Paul T. ... South Bend, IN
Cholis, Thomas J. ... Washington, DC
Cholmondeley, M. Maxine ... Richmond, VA
Cholobel, Michael ... Miami, FL
Cholobel, Michael, P.A. ... Miami, FL
Cholodenko, Michael A. ... Beverly Hills, CA
Cholodofsky, Arthur ... Hollywood, FL
Cholowski, Mark S. ... Sayreville, NJ
Cholst, Betty ... Fort Lauderdale, FL
Cholst, Betty, P.A. ... Fort Lauderdale, FL
Cholst, Bruce A. ... New York, NY
Cholst, David J. ... Chicago, IL
Choly, Deborah ... Detroit, MI
Choma, Adrienne ... Nutley, NJ
Choma, Roman I ... Baltimore, MD
Chomas, J. Louis ... Elizabeth, PA
Chomeau, Douglas B. ... St. Louis, MO
Chomel, Marc Alain ... Long Beach, CA
Chomel, Michael J. ... Frederick, MD
Chomet, Charles H. ... Detroit, MI
Chomiak, Robert J., Jr. ... Cheshire, CT
Chomicz, Thomas E. ... Chicago, IL
Cho-Miller, Kyung
Board of Governors Of The Federal Reserve
System,
Division of Consumer and Community
Affairs, GV
Chomsky, Eric ... Santa Monica, CA
Chomsky, Judith Brown ... Edison, NJ
Nutley, NJ
Chomsky, Maryellen ... New York, NY
Chon, Jung S. ... Orange, CA
Chon, Sam Y. ... Fresno, CA
Chon, Su J. ... Salt Lake City, UT
Chone & Mauprivez, PLLC
Washington, DC
Chone, Pierre ... Washington, DC
Chong, Alice S. ... Lanham, MD
Chong, Arthur ... San Francisco, CA
Chong, Bradley R. ... Honolulu, HI
Chong, Chang-Sop ... Chamblee, GA
Chong, Charles K.H. ... Las Vegas, NV
Chong & Chong ... Hilo, HI
Chong, Clayton E. ... Hilo, HI
Chong, Curtis E. ... Hilo, HI
Chong, Debra A. ... San Francisco, CA
Chong, Ginger G.U. ... Honolulu, HI
Chong, Irene K. ... San Francisco, CA
Chong, Jerry L. ... Sacramento, CA
Chong, Kristin L. ... Minneapolis, MN
Chong, Leighton K. ... Honolulu, HI
Chong, Martin D. ... San Francisco, CA
Chong, Nicole Raymond ... Lancaster, PA
Chong, Norman L. ... San Francisco, CA
Chong, Oy-Lene ... Oakland, CA
Chong, Paula W. ... Honolulu, HI
Chong, Polly ... Newport News, VA
Chong, R. Dennis ... Honolulu, HI
Chong, Rachelle B. ... Palo Alto, CA
San Francisco, CA
Chong, Robert A. ... Honolulu, HI
Chong, Stanley Kwock-Wen ... Honolulu, HI
Chong, Stephen C. L. ... Orlando, FL
Chong, Sue Lin ... Washington, DC
Chong, Suet M. ... Washington, DC
Chong, Tiffany C. ... New Brunswick, NJ
Chong Kee, Dennis W. ... Honolulu, HI
Chonin, Neil ... Miami, FL
Chonin, Sher & Navarrete, P.A. ... Miami, FL
Chonoles, Andrew M. ... New York, NY
Chonoles, Stephen J. ... Long Beach, CA
Chontos, Joseph E. ... Falls Church, VA
Chontos, Leslie Peter ... Lynnwood, WA
Choo, Katherine M. ... New York, NY
Choo, Rodney ... Federal Trade Commission,
Bureau of Competition, GV
Choo, Tai-Sam ... Midland, MI
Chooljian, Jacqueline ... Los Angeles, CA
Choos, S. Scott ... Homestead, FL
Chopak, William I. ... Costa Mesa, CA
Chopek, Anna ... Los Alamos, NM
Chopelas, Thomas ... Malden, MA
Chopelas, Timothy W. ... Melrose, MA
Choper, Jessica E. ... Trenton, NJ
Chopin & Chopin ... West Palm Beach, FL
Chopin, L. Frank ... Palm Beach, FL
Chopin & Miller ... Palm Beach, FL
West Palm Beach, FL
Chopin, Paul Dean ... Malibu, CA
Chopin, Philip M. ... West Palm Beach, FL
Chopin, Richard A., (P.L.C.) ... Metairie, LA
Chopin, Susan Gardiner
West Palm Beach, FL
Chopin, Wagar, Cole, Richard, Reboul &
Kutcher, LLP ... Baton Rouge, LA
Covington, LA
Mandeville, LA
Metairie, LA
New Orleans, LA
Chopko, David A. ... Wilmington, DE
Chopko, Mark E. ... Washington, DC
Choplin, John M., II ... Indianapolis, IN
Chopnick, Max ... New York, NY
Chopnick, Stephen D. ... Philadelphia, PA
Chopp, Gary R. ... Bingham Farms, MI
Chopp, Harold ... Miami, FL
Chopp, Harold, A Professional Association
Miami, FL
Chopp, Joseph H., Jr. ... McLean, VA
Choppelas, George T. ... San Francisco, CA
Choppin, Timothy J. ... Washington, DC
Chopra, Apalla U. ... Los Angeles, CA
Chopra, Krishan S. ... Riverside, CA
Chopra, Kunoor ... Los Angeles, CA
Chopra, Marie ... Washington, DC
Chopra, Mira Bhushan ... Cleveland, OH
Chopskie, Gregory A. ... Washington, DC
Choquette, Denise E. ... Boston, MA
Choquette, Ernest J. ... Reading, PA
Choquette, Joseph E. ... Trenton, NJ
Choquette, Paul J., Jr. ... Providence, RI
Choquette, Steven C. ... Denver, CO
Choquette, William L. ... Anchorage, AK
Chor, Patricia ... Portland, OR
Chorazy, Michael W. ... Altoona, PA
Chorba, Dennis M. ... Portland, OR
Chorba, Timothy A. ... Washington, DC
Chorbajian, Beverly B. ... Worcester, MA
Chorbajian, Vatche ... Glendale, CA
Chorches, Martin ... Wethersfield, CT
Chorches & Novak, P.C. ... Hartford, CT
Wethersfield, CT
Chorches, Ronald I. ... Hartford, CT
Chorches, Samuel H. ... Chester, CT
Chorey, Taylor & Feil, A Professional
Corporation ... Atlanta, GA
Chorey, Thomas V., Jr. ... Atlanta, GA
Chorle, Erhard ... Chicago, IL
Chorlian, Jonathan A. ... Concord, NH
Chorlins, Stanley H. ... St. Louis, MO
Chorman, James R. ... Georgetown, DE
Chormanski, Joanne M. ... New York, NY
Chorne, Alan R. ... New York, NY
Chornenky, O. Joseph ... Phoenix, AZ
Chornenky, O. Joseph, P.C. ... Phoenix, AZ
Chorney, Alan D. ... Hauppauge, NY
Chorney, Alvin J. ... Brooklyn, NY
Chorney & Associates, LLC ... Denver, CO
Englewood, CO
Chorney, Christine A. ... Oakland, CA
Chorney, Jacqueline ...
Federal Communications Commission, GV
Chorney, Marc A. ... Englewood, CO
Chorny, Dennis Terence ... New York, NY
Chorny, Stephen ... Grosse Pointe Woods, MI
Choroski, Edmund P. ... Deerfield, IL
Chorost, Howard Alan ... Tucson, AZ
Choroszej, Walter R. ... Boston, MA
Choroszucha, Lech ... New York, NY
Chorowski & Greenhart
Fort Lauderdale, FL
Chorowski, Rae ... Fort Lauderdale, FL
Chorpening, Paul L. ... Ashland, OH
Chortek, Irving L. ... Milwaukee, WI
Chortek, Kimberly A. ... San Jose, CA
Chortek, Robert L. ... San Jose, CA
Chorvat, Timothy J. ... Chicago, IL
Chory, John H. ... Boston, MA
Chorzempa, David J. ... Chicago, IL
Chorzempa, Janelle E. ... Portland, OR
Choset, Malcolm B. ... East Islip, NY
Choset, Seth M. ... Garden City, NY
Chosid, Matthew A. ... Ann Arbor, MI
Chosid, Richard G. ... Fort Lauderdale, FL
Troy, MI
Chosid, Robin S. ... Washington, DC
Chosnek, Edward ... Lafayette, IN
Chostner, Chester R., Jr. ... Rockford, IL
Chostner, Chester R., Jr., P.C. ... Rockford, IL
Chosy, James L. ... Minneapolis, MN
Chosy, John A. ... Madison, WI
Chosy, John E. ... Brownsville, TX
Chotalia, Tushar ... Chicago, IL
Chotard, Richard, Jr. ... Jackson, MS
Chotas, Elias N. ... Orlando, FL
Chote, James B. ... Austin, TX
Chote, Richard W. ... Austin, TX
Chotena, Thomas L. ... Phoenix, AZ
Chotiner, Adam S. ... Hollywood, FL
Chotiner, Kenneth Lee ... Los Angeles, CA
Chotiner, Lori ... Los Angeles, CA
Chotiner, Renee D. ... Branford, CT
Chotiner, Seymour ... Live Oak, FL
Chotkowski, Kimberly S. ... Stamford, CT
Chotlos, Elaine A. ... Cleveland, OH
Chott, John W., Jr.
Department of Agriculture,
Farm Service Agency, GV
Chou, Anne ... New York, NY
Chou, Catherine L. ... Redwood City, CA
Chou, Chien (Chris) W. ... Palo Alto, CA
Chou, Danny ... San Francisco, CA
Chou, Donald ... Mission Viejo, CA
Chou, Elaine N. ... Red Bank, NJ
New York, NY
Chou, James P. ... New York, NY
Chou, John G. ... Houston, TX
Chou, John S. ... Monterey Park, CA
Chou, Kevin Shih-Chun ... Palo Alto, CA
Chou, May-Wong ... St. Petersburg, FL
Chou, May-Wong, P.A. ... Clearwater, FL
St. Petersburg, FL
Tampa, FL
Chou, Michael W. ... Los Angeles, CA
Chou, Shawn C. H. ... Alhambra, CA
Chou, Sychi Albert ... San Francisco, CA
Chou, Thomas Tze-Hun
San Francisco, CA
Chou, Y. Vicky ... Palo Alto, CA
Chou, Yu-Feng (Frances)
Santa Monica, CA
Chou, Yung Ming ... Fremont, CA
Chouai, Kathleen ... Washington, DC
Chouake, Abe S. ... Little Neck, NY
Choudhary, Ajay ... Houston, TX
Choudhary, Nargis ... Brea, CA
Choudhry, Ray ... Moline, IL
Choudhry, Sabina R. ... Dallas, TX
Choudhury, H. Taufiq ... New York, NY
Choudhury, H. Taufiq, P.C.
New York, NY
Choueke, Ary ... Miami, FL
Chouest, Stephen M. ... Metairie, LA

Chouest, Stephen M., and Associates, A Prof. Law Corp. ... Metairie, LA
Chouinard, Joseph W. ... Morristown, NJ
Choukas-Bradley, James R. ... Washington, DC
Choulas, James G. ... Kensington, MD
Choulos, Alexander V. ... San Francisco, CA
Choulos, Choulos & Wyle ... San Francisco, CA
Choulos, George V. ... San Francisco, CA
Choulos, James V. ... San Francisco, CA
Choulos, Stephan V. ... San Francisco, CA
Choulos, Vasilios B. ... San Francisco, CA
Choumbakos, Cheryl McMurry ... Livingston, NJ
Choundas, George P. ... Tampa, FL
Choundas, Marina A. ... Tampa, FL
Chouteau, Mark D. ... Austin, TX
Chouteau, Rene Auguste ... Santa Rosa, CA
Chovan-Anderson, Darlene Ann ... Spokane, WA
Chovanec, Albin E. ... Universal City, TX
Chovanec, James E. ... Huntington, IN
Chovanec, Michael A. ... San Antonio, TX
Chovanec, Michael A., P.C. ... San Antonio, TX
Chovanec, Robert J. ... Grand Rapids, MI
Chovanec, Timothy G. ... Fort Worth, TX
Chovanec, Timothy G., P.C. ... Fort Worth, TX
Chovanec & Truitt ... Huntington, IN
Chovanes, Eugene ... Bala Cynwyd, PA
Chovanes, Eugene ... Philadelphia, PA
Chovanes, Joseph E. ... Philadelphia, PA
Chovanes, Martha Baskett ... Ardmore, PA
Chovev, Susie ... New York, NY
Chovitz, Eli S. ... Norfolk, VA
Chow, Andrew K. ... New York, NY
Chow, Camila Andrea ... South San Francisco, CA
Chow, Carol ... Los Angeles, CA
Chow, Christopher W. ... Honolulu, HI
Chow, David ... Palo Alto, CA
Chow, Frank S. ... Carlsbad, CA
Chow, Gary T. ... Irvine, CA
Chow, Gon Ling ... New York, NY
Chow, Hallam ... New York, NY
Chow, Hannah Lai ... Houston, TX
Chow, Henry G. ... San Francisco, CA
Chow, Jennifer M. ... New York, NY
Chow, John J. ... Sierra Madre, CA
Chow, John K. ... Stockton, CA
Chow, Josephine M. ... Riverside, CA
Chow, Joyce C. ... Cupertino, CA
Chow, Lily ... Irvine, CA
Chow, Lisa V. ... New York, NY
Chow, Martin Caling ... Flushing, NY
Chow, Martin W. ... New York, NY
Chow, Peter ... Monterey Park, CA
Chow, Robert Y. ... Boston, MA
Chow, Robin D. ... Beverly Hills, CA
Chow, Rose Tseng ... New York, NY
Chow, Stanley M. ... Honolulu, HI
Chow, Stephen Y. ... Boston, MA
Chow, Steven J. T. ... Honolulu, HI
Chow, Wade Kuowei ... San Francisco, CA
Chow, Walter F. ... San Juan, PR
Chow, Warren E. ... Mountain View, CA
Chow, Wendy ... San Francisco, CA
Chowdry, Frank K.N. ... Augusta, ME
Chowes, Helene ... New York, NY
Chowhan, Amera Z. ... New York, NY
Chowins, David W. ... Chicago, IL
Chown, Norman R. ... Santa Rosa, CA
Chowning, John C. ... Grand Blanc, MI
Chowning, John S., (P.A.) ... Miami, FL
Chowning, Robert E. ... Little Rock, AR
Chowning, Thomas J. ... Terre Haute, IN
Choy, Albert F. ... Boston, MA
Choy, Brian G. S. ... Glenwood Springs, CO; Honolulu, HI
Choy, Bruce A. ... Milpitas, CA
Choy, Cheryl Y. K. ... Oakland, CA
Choy, Claudia J. ... San Francisco, CA
Choy, Darryl Y. C. ... Honolulu, HI
Choy, Dean ... Honolulu, HI
Choy, Eliot S. ... Newark, NJ
Choy, Glenn D. ... Honolulu, HI
Choy, Herbert Y. C. ... Honolulu, HI
Choy, Ivette Santaella ... Newport Beach, CA
Choy, Kathleen Barrett ... New York, NY
Choy, L. Lelanne ... Walnut Creek, CA
Choy, Lana ... New York, NY
Choy, Mallory M. ... Honolulu, HI
Choy, Michael K. K. ... Birmingham, AL
Choy, Milton W. B. ... Honolulu, HI
Choy, Myla Calhoun ... Birmingham, AL
Choy, Peter M. C. ... Palo Alto, CA
Choy, Randall P. ... San Francisco, CA
Choy, Samuel S. ... Key West, FL; Greeneville, TN; Kingsport, TN
Choy, Stephanie L. ... San Francisco, CA
Choy, Sun S. ... Louisville, KY
Choy, Tracy M.Y. ... Los Angeles, CA
Choy, Victoria ... Washington, DC
Choy, Wendell J.H. ... Honolulu, HI
Choy, William S. ... San Francisco, CA
Choy-Cavanaugh, Albert F. ... Boston, MA
Choyce, Charles V. ... Orlando, FL
Choyce, Philip A. ... Houston, TX
Choyce, Thomas F. ... Atlanta, GA
Choyke, Amy Brown ... Houston, TX
Choyke, Michael A. ... Houston, TX
Chozen, Michael J. ... Spirit Lake, IA
Chozen, Richard A. ... Lake Charles, LA
Chozen & Saunders ... Spirit Lake, IA
Chozick, H. Edw. ... Chevy Chase, MD
Chozick, Jason W. ... San Antonio, TX
Chozick, Robert H. ... Richardson, TX
Chraghchian, Milene ... Los Angeles, CA
Chrastil, Rockford R. ... Minneapolis, MN
Chrastil, Steinberg & Sarnoski, P.L.L.P. ... Minneapolis, MN
Chrein, Aaron S. ... Brooklyn, NY
Chrein, Molly C. ... Upper Marlboro, MD
Chrestionson, Keith I. ... San Francisco, CA
Chrestman, Don M. ... Weatherford, TX
Chrestman, Keith L. ... Maumelle, AR
Chretien, Justin L. ... Department of Justice, Civil Division, GV
Chrétien, Paul-Noël ... McLean, VA
Chretien-Dar, Barbara C. ... Securities and Exchange Commission, Division of Investment Management, GV
Chrey, Gary T. ... Port Orchard, WA
Chrimes, Shari Greenberg ... Albany, NY
Chris, William G. ... Akron, OH
Chrisafis, Jerry ... Flushing, NY
Chrisbens, F. Christopher ... Boulder, CO
Chriscoe, Johnny C., Jr. ... Lillington, NC
Chrishon, James Roy ... Shreveport, LA
Chriske, Tracey A. ... Cincinnati, OH
Chrisler, Thomas E. ... Chicago, IL
Chrislip, Ronald W. ... Santa Ana, CA
Chrisman, Bynum & Johnson, P.C. ... Boulder, CO
Chrisman, Byron R. ... Boulder, CO
Chrisman, Carol J. ... Orlando, FL
Chrisman, Christine A. ... Los Angeles, CA
Chrisman, James J. ... Sidney, OH
Chrisman, James P. ... Las Vegas, NV
Chrisman, John R. ... Baltimore, MD
Chrisman, Joseph C. ... Ventura, CA
Chrisman, Mark A. ... Denver, CO
Chrisman, Paul J. ... Sacramento, CA
Chrisman, Perry Oswin, (P.C.) ... Dallas, TX
Chrisman, Robert A. ... Covina, CA
Chrisman, Sue ... Springfield, MO
Chrismer, Charles R. ... Tigard, OR
Chrismon, Randolph L. ... Bedminster, NJ
Chrisomalis, Jack S. ... Brooklyn, NY
Chrisos, Nicholas S. ... Santa Ana, CA
Chrispell, David Jack ... Jamestown, NY
Chriss, Evan Alevizatos ... Baltimore, MD
Chriss, Margaret J. ... Washington, DC
Chriss, Sherry L. ... House of Representatives, Office of Legislative Counsel, GV
Chriss, Timothy D. A. ... Baltimore, MD
Chriss, William J. ... Corpus Christi, TX
Chriss, William J., P.C., Law Offices of ... Corpus Christi, TX
Chrissinger & Baumberger ... Wilmington, DE
Chrissinger, Nancy E. ... Wilmington, DE
Christ, Chris S. ... Birmingham, AL
Christ, Chris T. ... Battle Creek, MI; Coldwater, MI
Christ, Cindy ... Charlotte, NC
Christ, Donald C. ... New York, NY
Christ, Gustav W. ... Campbellsport, WI
Christ, Hadler & Brothers ... Indianapolis, IN
Christ, Joanne ... Minneapolis, MN
Christ, John C. ... Indianapolis, IN
Christ, Keri A. ... New York, NY
Christ, Kristin L. ... Bloomfield Hills, MI
Christ, LeeAnn Solomon ... Waltham, MA
Christ, Marcus H. ... Rockville, MD
Christ, P. Daniel ... Bloomfield Hills, MI
Christ, Paula B. ... Cleveland, OH
Christ, Robt. M. ... Wilsonville, OR
Christ, Roxanne E. ... Los Angeles, CA
Christ, Thomas M. ... Portland, OR
Christ, William D. ... Buffalo, NY
Christa & Jackson ... Los Angeles, CA
Christa, Laura K. ... Los Angeles, CA
Christakis, Anna-Katrina S. ... Chicago, IL
Christakis, Charles ... Phoenix, AZ
Christakos, Nicholas T. ... Washington, DC
Christal, Mark D. ... Rye, NY
Christaldi, Brian ... Overseas Private Investment Corporation, GV
Christaldi, Ronald Anthony ... Tampa, FL
Christe, Ralf ... Sacramento, CA
Christean, Arthur G. ... Sandy, UT
Christel, David W. ... Vancouver, WA
Christel, Diane J. ... Wexford, PA
Christel, Peter M. ... Westport, CT; Princeton Junction, NJ
Christelis, Deena F. ... Boston, MA
Christelis, Gary C. ... Waltham, MA
Christen, Amy M. ... Detroit, MI
Christen, Cynthia K. ... Tallahassee, FL
Christen, Daniel R. ... Austin, TX
Christen, Darryl K. ... Houma, LA
Christen, Frederick C. ... Toledo, OH
Christen, Lee A. ... Washington, DC
Christen, Morgan ... Anchorage, AK
Christen & Pigeon ... Kansas City, MO
Christen, Tracy E. ... New York, NY
Christen, W. Ernest ... Kansas City, MO
Christen, William D. ... Indianapolis, IN
Christenberry, Andrew C. ... Metairie, LA
Christenberry & Associates, A Professional Law Corporation ... Metairie, LA
Christenberry, Dexter A. ... Knoxville, TN
Christenberry, Herbert W., Jr. ... Metairie, LA
Christenberry, J. G. ... Seymour, TN
Christenberry, Susan L. ... United States Court Of Appeals For The Federal Circuit, GV
Christenbury, Edward S. ... Knoxville, TN
Christenbury, Lynne M. ... Wilmington, DE
Christenbury, Sharon Len ... Miami, FL
Christenbury, T. Daniel ... Philadelphia, PA
Christenfeld, Alan M. ... New York, NY
Christenfeld, Stuart H. ... Beverly Hills, CA
Christensen, A. Thomas ... Toledo, OH
Christensen, Aaron M. ... Charlotte, NC
Christensen, Allen C. ... Eagle, CO; Minturn, CO
Christensen, Allen C., P.C. ... Eagle, CO
Christensen, Alphus R. ... Tucson, AZ
Christensen, Amy D. ... Helena, MT
Christensen, Amy Laurel ... Des Moines, IA
Christensen, Andrea Croak ... Sacramento, CA
Christensen, Andrea S. ... New York, NY
Christensen, Arlene M. ... Auburn, WA
Christensen & Ashleman, A Professional Corporation ... Las Vegas, NV
Christensen & Associates ... Mount Pleasant, SC
Christensen & Auer ... Los Angeles, CA; Pasadena, CA
Christensen, Bacigalupi & Barrus ... Roseville, CA
Christensen, Barbara B. ... Los Altos, CA
Christensen, Becky V. ... Malibu, CA
Christensen, Birgitte M. ... Boston, MA
Christensen & Boggess, Chartered ... Las Vegas, NV
Christensen, Brain D. ... Casper, WY
Christensen, Brent ... Salt Lake City, UT
Christensen, Brian J. ... Wichita, KS
Christensen, Bruce A. ... Miami, FL
Christensen, Bruce Hans, Jr. ... Akron, OH
Christensen, C. Brophy, Jr. ... San Francisco, CA
Christensen, C. John ... Maitland, FL
Christensen, Carl J. ... Las Vegas, NV
Christensen, Carlie ... Salt Lake City, UT
Christensen, Carma ... Bismarck, ND
Christensen, Catherine M. ... Miami, FL
Christensen, Catherine M. ... Westbury, NY
Christensen, Cathy M. ... Oklahoma City, OK
Christensen, Charles B. ... San Diego, CA
Christensen, Charles S., III ... Anchorage, AK
Christensen, Cherie ... San Jose, CA
Christensen, Chris P. ... Conrad, MT
Christensen, Christopher R. ... New York, NY
Christensen, Colleen A. ... Seattle, WA
Christensen, Craig A. ... Denver, CO
Christensen, Craig A. ... Appleton, WI
Christensen, Craig G. ... Roseville, CA
Christensen, Craig H. ... Orem, UT
Christensen, Craig W. ... Los Angeles, CA
Christensen, Craig W. ... Pocatello, ID
Christensen, Craig W., Chartered ... Pocatello, ID
Christensen, Curtis L. ... Omaha, NE
Christensen, D. Gary ... Portland, OR
Christensen, D. Wade ... Oklahoma City, OK
Christensen, Dale C., Jr. ... New York, NY
Christensen, Dana L. ... Kalispell, MT
Christensen, Daniel J. ... Austin, TX; Georgetown, TX; Killeen, TX; Round Rock, TX
Christensen, Daniel Krege ... Salt Lake City, UT
Christensen, Darin ... Portland, OR
Christensen, David A. ... Omaha, NE
Christensen, David C. ... Morristown, NJ
Christensen, David E. ... San Diego, CA
Christensen, David E. ... Southfield, MI
Christensen, David E. ... Pipestone, MN
Christensen, David L. ... Lenox, IA
Christensen, David L., P.C. ... Chandler, AZ
Christensen, David S. ... Department of Justice, Environment and Natural Resources Division, GV
Christensen, David W. ... Detroit, MI; Southfield, MI
Christensen, Deanna ... Orem, UT
Christensen, Del S. ... Houston, TX
Christensen, Dennis J. ... Mount Pleasant, SC
Christensen, Deverie J. ... Las Vegas, NV
Christensen, Diane ... Stoughton, MA
Christensen, Dirk G. ... Atlanta, GA
Christensen, Donald J. ... Tucson, AZ
Christensen, Donald L. ... Reno, NV
Christensen, Donn Wayne ... Los Angeles, CA
Christensen, Douglas A. ... Grand Forks, ND
Christensen, Douglas J. ... Minneapolis, MN
Christensen, Douglas R. ... Minneapolis, MN
Christensen, Drew R. ... Las Vegas, NV
Christensen, Earl ... Bear, DE
Christensen, E. D. ... Houston, TX
Christensen, Edgar A. ... Christiansted, St. Croix, VI
Christensen, Edward A. ... Oyster Bay, NY
Christensen & Ehret ... Chicago, IL
Christensen, Einer ... Racine, WI
Christensen, Elizabeth Wiese ... Peoria, IL
Christensen, Eric C. ... Fresno, CA
Christensen, Eric C. ... Albuquerque, NM
Christensen, Eric L. ... Rossmoor, CA
Christensen, Eric L. ... Everett, WA
Christensen, Ethan ... San Diego, CA
Christensen, F. LaVar ... Draper, UT
Christensen, Fleur A. ... Austin, TX
Christensen & Frederickson Law Offices ... Deadwood, SD; Spearfish, SD; Sturgis, SD
Christensen, Gary L. ... Arlington, VA
Christensen, Gary R. ... St. Paul, MN
Christensen, Gene Craig ... Minneapolis, MN
Christensen, George ... Alameda, CA
Christensen, George ... Santa Monica, CA
Christensen, George A. ... Rocky River, OH
Christensen, Gerald D. ... Billings, MT
Christensen, Gerald L. ... Sausalito, CA
Christensen, Gerald M. ... Santa Cruz, CA
Christensen, Glenna M. ... Boise, ID
Christensen, Gregory J. ... Corvallis, OR
Christensen, Hal M. ... Chevy Chase, MD
Christensen, Harold G. ... Salt Lake City, UT
Christensen, Harry C., Jr. ... Marblehead, MA; Salem, MA
Christensen, Helen ... Platte, SD
Christensen, Henry, III ... New York, NY
Christensen, Henry N., Jr. ... Rochelle Park, NJ; Goshen, NY
Christensen, J. Clay ... Oklahoma City, OK
Christensen, James B. ... Raytown, MO
Christensen, James G. ... Reno, NV
Christensen, James L. ... Salt Lake City, UT
Christensen, James R. ... Las Vegas, NV
Christensen, Jan ... Washington, DC
Christensen, Janelle K. ... Waukegan, IL
Christensen, Jay D. ... Pasadena, CA
Christensen, Jean W. ... Salem, OR
Christensen, Jeanne-Marie ... Garden City, NY
Christensen, Jeanne-Marie ... New York, NY
Christensen, Jeannette L. ... Seal Beach, CA
Christensen & Jensen, A Professional Corporation ... Salt Lake City, UT
Christensen, Jo Ippolito ... Alexandria, VA
Christensen, Joanna L. ... Ware, MA
Christensen, John A. ... Soda Springs, ID
Christensen, John E. ... Topeka, KS
Christensen, John F. ... San Francisco, CA
Christensen, John M. ... Grand Rapids, MI
Christensen, John R. ... Lewistown, MT
Christensen, John R. ... Tacoma, WA
Christensen, John W. ... Columbus, OH
Christensen, Johnston & Eisenhauer ... Medicine Lodge, KS; Pratt, KS
Christensen, Jon A. ... Columbus, OH
Christensen, Jon P. ... Chicago, IL
Christensen, Joseph J. ... Minneapolis, MN
Christensen, Julie M. ... Fort Worth, TX
Christensen, Julius G. ... Newport Beach, CA
Christensen, Karen A. ... Quincy, MA
Christensen, Katherine M. ... Chicago, IL
Christensen, Kay M. ... Pocatello, ID
Christensen, Keith S. ... Salt Lake City, UT
Christensen & Kenney ... Madison, WI
Christensen, Kevin A. ... Milwaukee, WI
Christensen, Kevin B. ... Las Vegas, NV
Christensen, Kevin J. ... New Orleans, LA
Christensen, Kevin M. (Casey) ... San Francisco, CA
Christensen, Kory ... Salt Lake City, UT
Christensen, Kristine ... Haddonfield, NJ; Philadelphia, PA
Christensen, Laurence L. ... Marietta, GA
Christensen, Laurence L., P.C. ... Marietta, GA
Christensen Law Offices, Chartered ... Las Vegas, NV
Christensen, Leah M. ... Madison, WI
Christensen, Linda Ann ... New York, NY
Christensen, Linda M. ... Department of the Navy, GV
Christensen, Louis David ... Denver, CO
Christensen, M. Jane ... Hartford, CT
Christensen, M. Kay ... Midvale, UT
Christensen, Maren J. ... Granite Bay, CA
Christensen, Maren J. ... Universal City, CA
Christensen, Mark A. ... Lincoln, NE
Christensen, Mark D. ... Palmer, AK
Christensen, Mark E. ... Chicago, IL
Christensen, Mark John ... Andalusia, AL
Christensen, Mark R. ... Tucson, AZ
Christensen, Mary W. ... Columbus, OH
Christensen, Matthew T. ... Fitchburg, MA
Christensen, Michael J. ... Salt Lake City, UT
Christensen, Mike ... Des Moines, IA
Christensen, Miller, Fink, Jacobs, Glaser, Weil and Shapiro, LLP ... Los Angeles, CA
Christensen, Milt, P.C. ... Portland, OR
Christensen, Moore, Cockrell & Cummings, P.C. ... Kalispell, MT
Christensen, Nels A. ... Chico, CA
Christensen, O'Connor, Johnson & Kindness, PLLC ... Seattle, WA
Christensen, Patricia W. ... Salt Lake City, UT
Christensen, Patti A. ... St. Augustine, FL
Christensen, Patti A., P.A. ... St. Augustine, FL
Christensen, Pattie S. ... Salt Lake City, UT
Christensen, Peter H. ... Salt Lake City, UT
Christensen, Peter T. ... Newport Beach, CA
Christensen, Quinton D. ... Everett, WA
Christensen, Ralph C. ... Clairton, PA
Christensen, Ray R. ... Salt Lake City, UT
Christensen, Renee H. ... Sioux Falls, SD
Christensen, Rex A. ... Tempe, AZ
Christensen, Richard S. ... St. Maries, ID
Christensen, Robert Anker ... Madison, WI
Christensen, Robert C. ... San Rafael, CA
Christensen, Robert H. ... Fort Myers, FL
Christensen, Robert H., Law Offices of ... San Jose, CA
Christensen, Robert M. ... Glenwood, MN
Christensen, Robert N. ... Brea, CA
Christensen, Robert P., (P.A.) ... Minneapolis, MN
Christensen, Robert W. ... Medicine Lodge, KS; Pratt, KS
Christensen, Roberta J. ... Omaha, NE

Christensen, Roger P. ....**Salt Lake City, UT**
Christensen, Ronald E. ....Norman, OK
Christensen, Ronald M. ....Hartford, CT
Christensen, Ronald R. ....Gaithersburg, MD
Christensen, Sarah ....Colorado Springs, CO
Christensen & Schwarz, LLP ....**Chico, CA**
Christensen, Scott E. ....Santa Ana, CA
Christensen, Scott H. ....Flint, MI
Christensen, Scott W. ....**Salt Lake City, UT**
Christensen, Shaun A. ....**Denver, CO**
Christensen, Sherie Ann ....Santa Ana, CA
Christensen, Shoemaker & Winkler
Columbus, OH
Christensen, Stanley B. ....Fullerton, CA
Christensen, Stephanie Cooper
Las Vegas, NV
Christensen, Stephen K. ....Salt Lake City, UT
Christensen, Steven L. ....**Portland, OR**
Christensen, Steven M. ....**Deadwood, SD**
Christensen & Stout ....Brea, CA
Christensen, Susan Larson ....Harlan, IA
Christensen, Susan M. ....Omaha, NE
Christensen, Terry N. ....**Los Angeles, CA**
Christensen, Theodore J. ....Alexandria, VA
Christensen, Thomas ....**Las Vegas, NV**
Christensen, Thomas A. ....**Chicago, IL**
Christensen, Thomas E.
Corona Del Mar, CA
Christensen, Thomas, Jr.
Salt Lake City, UT
Christensen & Thompson ....Bismarck, ND
Christensen, Timothy J. ....Detroit, MI
Christensen, Val John ....Salt Lake City, UT
Christensen, Wallace A. ....**Washington, DC**
Christensen, Wayne W. ....Worthing, SD
Christensen & Will ....Houston, TX
Christensen, William B. ....Minneapolis, MN
Christensen, William H.
Salt Lake City, UT
Christensen, William J. ....**Columbus, OH**
Christensen-Mores, Donna ....Harlan, IA
Christenson, Arlen C. ....Madison, WI
Christenson, Barbara B. ....**Sun Prairie, WI**
Christenson, Bruce J. ....Los Gatos, CA
Christenson, Bruce J., Inc., Law Offices of
Los Gatos, CA
Christenson, Carol J. ....Minneapolis, MN
Christenson, Cass Walker
Washington, DC
Christenson, Christopher R.
Minneapolis, MN
Christenson, David M. ....Calabasas, CA
Christenson, Don G. ....Porterville, CA
Christenson, G. Scott ....**San Jose, CA**
Christenson, Gordon A. ....Cincinnati, OH
Christenson, Heather T. ....**Seattle, WA**
Christenson, James A. ....Porterville, CA
Christenson, James A. ....Holden, MO
Independence, MO
Christenson, James E. ....Zeeland, MI
Christenson, James M. ....**Minneapolis, MN**
Christenson, Jeffrey R. ....Boise, ID
Christenson, Jim ....Des Moines, IA
Christenson, Jimmy S. ....Madison, WI
Christenson, John M. ....**Madison, WI**
Christenson, Karen E. ....Wauwatosa, WI
Christenson, Keith A. ....Eagle River, AK
Christenson, Kelli L. ....**Chicago, IL**
Christenson Law Firm ....Porterville, CA
Christenson, Lesa ....**San Diego, CA**
Christenson, Linda E. ....Reston, VA
Christenson, Mary E. ....**Minneapolis, MN**
Christenson, Pamela Keithley ....Seattle, WA
Christenson, Paul ....Murphysboro, IL
Christenson, Richard L. ....Porterville, CA
Christenson, Robert C. ....**Atlanta, GA**
Christenson, Robert D. ....Porterville, CA
Christenson, Scott R. L. ....St. James, MN
Christenson, Stephen K. ....Fairfax, VA
Christenson, Stephen K., P.C. ....Fairfax, VA
Christenson, Steven M. ....**St. Paul, MN**
Christenson, Terrance P. ....**Albany, NY**
Christenson, Thomas D.
Woodland Hills, CA
Christenson, Thomas J. ....**Rochester, MN**
Christenson, Thomas R. ....Milwaukee, WI
Christerson, Blanche Lark ....New York, NY
Christerson, John A. ....Aptos, CA
Christerson, Mark M. ....Chicago, IL
Christesen, Scott ....Hauppauge, NY
Christey, Clyde N. ....Topeka, KS
Christhilf, Anthony F. ....Annapolis, MD
Christhilf, George H. ....Canton, OH
Christhilf & Swope ....Canton, OH
Christian, Adam G.
Charlotte Amalie, St. Thomas, VI
Christian, Alan C. ....**Mobile, AL**
Christian, Alexandra ....**Dallas, TX**
Christian, Allan A.
Frederiksted, St. Croix, VI
Christian, Almeric L.
Charlotte Amalie, St. Thomas, VI
Christian, Alphonso A., II
Washington, DC
Christian, Amy C. ....East Lansing, MI
Christian & Barton, L.L.P.
Richmond, VA
Christian, Bertrand E. ....**Los Angeles, CA**
Christian, Betty Jo ....**Washington, DC**
Christian, Brent ....**Le Center, MN**
Christian, C. Lynch, III ....Lynchburg, VA
Christian, Calvin T. ....**Missoula, MT**
Christian, Carole Douglas ....**Louisville, KY**
Christian, Carolyn M. ....Taylor, MI
Christian, Casey J. ....Owatonna, MN
Christian, Catherine A. ....New York, NY
Christian, Cathy ....**Sacramento, CA**
San Francisco, CA

Christian, Charles E. ....**Lexington, KY**
Lexington, KY
Christian, Christopher P. ....**Wichita, KS**
Christian, Claudette M. ....**Washington, DC**
Christian, Clyde A. ....Omaha, NE
Christian, Craig W. ....Ellicott City, MD
Christian, Craig W., P.C. ....Ellicott City, MD
Christian, Cynthia J. ....Irvine, CA
Christian, D. Gary ....**Salt Lake City, UT**
Christian, Dana C. ....Livingston, MT
Christian, Daniel G. ....Hickory, NC
Christian, David B. ....**Woodward, OK**
Christian, David B. ....Meridian, TX
Christian, David C. ....Kansas City, MO
Christian, David C., II ....**Kansas City, MO**
Christian, David L. ....Green Bay, WI
Christian, David R. ....Houston, TX
Christian & Davis ....Greenville, SC
Christian, Douglas J. ....**Le Center, MN**
Christian, Douglas L. ....**Phoenix, AZ**
Las Vegas, NV
Christian, Douglas Y. ....**Philadelphia, PA**
Christian, E. Ann ....Raleigh, NC
Christian, Eddie N. ....Fort Smith, AR
Christian, Edward M. ....Minneapolis, MN
Christian, Edward P. ....**San Diego, CA**
Christian, Edward R. ....**Birmingham, AL**
Christian, Edward T. ....Albert Lea, MN
Christian, Eileen ....Kansas City, MO
Christian, Eileen M. ....Philadelphia, PA
Christian, Elizabeth Hellmers
Middletown, NJ
Christian, Ernest S., Jr. ....Washington, DC
Christian, Floyd H., Jr. ....Angleton, TX
Christian, Frank L.
Department Of Veterans Affairs,
Board of Veterans Appeals, GV
Christian, Frederick W. ....Little Rock, AR
Christian, Freya L. ....**Los Angeles, CA**
Christian, Gabriel J., & Associates
Bowie, MD
Christian, Gary C. ....Washington, DC
Christian, Gary I. ....**Jacksonville, FL**
Christian, Geoffrey M. ....**McLean, VA**
Christian, George ....Albany, NY
Christian, George Robert ....Macon, GA
Christian, George S. ....Austin, TX
Christian, Guy E. ....Jackson, MI
Christian, Harry F. ....**Le Center, MN**
Christian, Helen E. ....**Salt Lake City, UT**
Christian, Hurschell D. ....Covina, CA
Christian, J. Eddie ....Fort Smith, AR
Christian, James B., Jr. ....**Washington, DC**
Christian, James W., P.C. ....Houston, TX
Christian, Janelle T. ....Wrangell, AK
Christian, Jo Anne M. ....Austin, TX
Christian, John C., (P.C.)
New Orleans, LA
Christian, John D. ....**Austin, TX**
Christian, John M. ....**Chicago, IL**
Christian, John M. ....**New York, NY**
Christian, John P. ....**San Francisco, CA**
Christian, John R. ....Birmingham, AL
Christian, John R. ....**Phoenix, AZ**
Christian, Joseph J. ....**Boston, MA**
Christian, Juanita L. ....Ann Arbor, MI
Christian, Kaare G. ....Towson, MD
Christian, Karin V.
Department of Transportation,
Research and Special Programs
Administration, GV
Christian, Kaye K. ....Washington, DC
Christian, Kirby S. ....**Missoula, MT**
Christian, Kristin Lynn ....Albany, GA
Christian, Lamar M. ....Rossville, GA
Christian, Lee E. ....Fort Collins, CO
Christian, Lee E., P.C. ....Fort Collins, CO
Christian, Lisa A. ....Los Angeles, CA
Christian, Lynda G. ....Newton, MA
Christian, Madison M. ....**Oxnard, CA**
Christian, Malcolm M. ....**Richmond, VA**
Christian, Marcus Antony
United States Court Of Appeals For The
Federal Circuit, GV
Christian, Margaret A. ....**El Paso, TX**
Christian, Melva D. ....Houston, TX
Christian, Michael ....**Phoenix, AZ**
Christian, Michael A. ....Boston, MA
Christian, Michael J. ....**Sacramento, CA**
Christian, Paul S. ....College Park, MD
Christian & Peterson, P.A.
Albert Lea, MN
Ellendale, MN
Kiester, MN
Christian, Ralph B., II ....Nashville, TN
Christian, Randall L. ....**Austin, TX**
Christian, Raymond M.
Palm Beach Gardens, FL
Christian, Rebecca T. ....**Atlanta, GA**
Christian, Renee E. ....**Denver, CO**
Christian, Richd. C. ....Waukegan, IL
Christian, Robert E. ....Duncan, OK
Christian, Robert F. ....Peachtree City, GA
Christian, Robert J. ....Youngstown, OH
Christian, Ronald C. ....**Cincinnati, OH**
Christian, Samson & Jones, P.C.
Deer Lodge, MT
Missoula, MT
Polson, MT
Christian, Sarah A. ....Susanville, CA
Christian, Scott T. ....**Delavan, WI**
Christian, Shirley J. ....**Youngstown, OH**
Christian & Smith, L.L.P. ....Houston, TX
Christian, Spartz, Keogh & Christian
Le Center, MN
Christian, Stephen L. ....**Laguna Hills, CA**
Christian, Stephen M. ....Denver, CO
Christian, Stephen R. ....Duncan, OK

Christian, Steven L. ....Sugar Land, TX
Christian, Stewart A. ....Howell, MI
Christian, Susan B. ....San Francisco, CA
Christian, Susan D. ....**Sacramento, CA**
Christian, T. Michael ....Lancaster, OH
Christian, Terry Clifton ....**Tampa, FL**
Christian, Terry Clifton, P.A. ....**Tampa, FL**
Christian, Thomas W. ....**Birmingham, AL**
Christian, Valda Clark ....Jacksonville, FL
Christian, Victoria Anne ....Cleveland, OH
Christian Wadsworth & Smith
Washington, DC
New York, NY
Christian, Warren H., Jr. ....Greenville, SC
Christian, Wayne A., II ....San Antonio, TX
Christian, William ....**Austin, TX**
Christian, William A. ....Sanford, NC
Christian, William G., Jr. ....Houston, TX
Christian, William N. ....Oklahoma City, OK
Christian, William R. ....**Los Angeles, CA**
Christian, William T. ....Los Angeles, CA
Christian, Wm. P. ....Amsterdam, NY
Christian, Zane Dale ....Bluefield, VA
Christiana Legal Associates, P.A.
Newark, DE
Christiana, Mary Lou P. ....**Ellenville, NY**
Christiana, Timothy F. ....Chicago, IL
Christian-Bingham, Teresa ......Kansas City, MO
Christiani, Toni Lorilee ....Riverside, CA
San Diego, CA
Christiano, Albert R. ....Rochester, NY
Christiano & Brennan ....Rochester, NY
Christiano, Gary A. ....Rochester, NY
Christiano, Lawrence A. ....Stamford, CT
Christiano, Maureen E. ....Roseland, NJ
Christiano, Samuel A. ....West Orange, NJ
Christiano, Stephen J. ....West Orange, NJ
Christians, Elizabeth Ayer ....Dayton, OH
Christians, Fred C. ....Grosse Pointe Park, MI
Christians, Julia A. ....**Minneapolis, MN**
Christians, Robert J. ....**Grand Rapids, MI**
Christiansen, Axel E. ....Fresno, CA
Christiansen, Barbara Kay ....Shawnee, OK
Christiansen, Barbara L.
Granite Bay, CA
Christiansen, Becky J. ....**Las Vegas, NV**
Christiansen, Carol A. ....**Syracuse, NY**
Christiansen, Catherine E. ....Tustin, CA
Christiansen, Cathy D. ....**Woodbridge, VA**
Christiansen, Clarence H. ....Davenport, IA
Christiansen, Dana A. ....La Junta, CO
Christiansen, David A. ....**Wyomissing, PA**
Christiansen & Dehner, P.A. ....Sarasota, FL
Christiansen, Edward J., Jr. ....Boston, MA
Christiansen, Erik A. ....**Salt Lake City, UT**
Christiansen, Gary R., (P.C.)
Kalispell, MT
Christiansen, George G. ....Brighton, CO
Christiansen & Jacknin
West Palm Beach, FL
Christiansen, James H. ....Fresno, CA
Christiansen, James R.
Santa Barbara, CA
Christiansen, Jan Peter ....**Monroe, LA**
Christiansen, Jay D. ....**Minneapolis, MN**
Christiansen, John Adams
Blue Springs, MO
Christiansen, John Adams, L.C.
Blue Springs, MO
Christiansen, John O. ....Beaver, UT
Christiansen, John R. ....**Seattle, WA**
Christiansen, John T.
West Palm Beach, FL
Christiansen, Jon C. ....**Salt Lake City, UT**
Christiansen, Jon P. ....**Milwaukee, WI**
Christiansen, Jube & Keegan, A Professional Corporation ....**Shrewsbury, NJ**
Christiansen, Karie L. ....Bartow, FL
Christiansen, Karl H. ....**San Francisco, CA**
Christiansen, Keith A. ....**Milwaukee, WI**
Christiansen, Larry A. ....San Diego, CA
Christiansen, Mark D.
Oklahoma City, OK
Christiansen, Mark Lewis ....Granite Bay, CA
Christiansen, Marvin J. ....Ben Lomond, CA
Christiansen, Marybeth Stanton
Philadelphia, PA
Christiansen, Michael Eric
Fort Lauderdale, FL
Christiansen, Nelson John
Oklahoma City, OK
Christiansen, Patricia M.
West Palm Beach, FL
Christiansen, Patrick T. ....**Orlando, FL**
Christiansen, Peter J. ....Las Vegas, NV
Christiansen, Peter S. ....Las Vegas, NV
Christiansen, Randy J. ....Provo, UT
Christiansen, Richd. M. ....Mansfield, OH
Christiansen, Robert E. ......New Brunswick, NJ
Christiansen, Robert G. ....Toledo, OH
Christiansen, Roy H. ....**Detroit, MI**
Christiansen, Scott A. ....**Dallas, TX**
Christiansen, Scott R. ....Sarasota, FL
Christiansen, Sharilyn E. ....Yuba City, CA
Christiansen, Stephen C.
Cape Girardeau, MO
Christiansen, Stephen K.
Salt Lake City, UT
Christiansen, Steven A. ....**Kansas City, MO**
Christiansen, Steven A. ....Meeteetse, WY
Christiansen, Steven J.
Salt Lake City, UT
Christiansen, Susan L. ....Winston-Salem, NC
Christiansen, Suzanne Prevot
Los Angeles, CA
Christiansen, T. Wade ....Houston, TX
Christiansen, Terry L. ....Coalville, UT
Park City, UT

Christiansen, Vicky M. ....Newark, OH
Christiansen, William T., II ....**Seattle, WA**
Christiansen, Wm. L. ....Tiburon, CA
Christianson, Bernard C. ......**New Haven, CT**
Christianson, Brian O. ....**Coral Gables, FL**
Christianson, Bryce T. ....Des Moines, IA
Christianson, Cabot, (P.C.)
Anchorage, AK
Christianson, Carlye ....San Diego, CA
Christianson, Carol A. ....Des Moines, IA
Christianson, Charles A.P. ....Baltimore, MD
Christianson, Clay J. ....**Santa Rosa, CA**
Christianson, Colleen M.
Minneapolis, MN
St. Cloud, MN
Christianson, Cynthia Pickering
Anchorage, AK
Christianson, Dave R.
Bainbridge Island, WA
Christianson, David L. ....**Minneapolis, MN**
Christianson, David P. ....Newport Beach, CA
Christianson, Dean L. ....Belleville, IL
St. Louis, MO
Christianson, George E. ....**Lebanon, PA**
Christianson, Greg A. ....**Los Angeles, CA**
Christianson, Harry W. ....**Rapid City, SD**
Christianson, James J. ....Sacramento, CA
Christianson, Jeffrey A. ....Seattle, WA
Christianson, Jim ....Austin, TX
Christianson, Jonathan E. ....Sacramento, CA
Christianson, Karen M. ....**West Bend, WI**
Christianson, Marc T. ....**Tacoma, WA**
Christianson, Marcus J. ....Cottonwood, MN
Marshall, MN
Minneota, MN
Christianson, Melvin ....Devils Lake, ND
Christianson Meyer ....**Lebanon, PA**
Christianson, Michael J.
Newport Beach, CA
Christianson, Peter C. ....**Madison, WI**
Milwaukee, WI
Christianson, Robert A. ....Harrisburg, PA
Christianson, Robert J., Jr.
Minneapolis, MN
Christianson, Roger A. ....St. Paul, MN
Christianson, Ronald M.
San Bernardino, CA
Christianson, Sandra S. ....Harrisburg, PA
Christianson, Shawn M.
San Francisco, CA
Christianson, Stephen G. ....Fairfax, VA
Christianson, Steven M. ....Lancaster, WI
Christianson, Stoneberg, Giles & Stroup, P.A. ....Cottonwood, MN
Marshall, MN
Minneota, MN
Christianson, Tim O. ....Milwaukee, WI
Christianson, Warren C. ....Sitka, AK
Christianson, William L. ....Red Wing, MN
Christianssen, Kenneth G. ....**Denver, CO**
Christidis, Aurora ....New York, NY
Christie, Arthur N. ....Chicago, IL
Christie, Barbara L. ....Harrisburg, PA
Christie, Carrie L. ....Atlanta, GA
Christie, Carter B. ....Beaumont, TX
Christie, Chester C. ....Columbus, OH
Christie, Chris A. ....**Virginia Beach, VA**
Christie, Chris J. ....Laurel, MD
Christie & Christie ....McConnelsville, OH
Christie, Christie A. Linskens
Milwaukee, WI
Christie, Christopher J. ....**Cranford, NJ**
Christie, David A., Jr. ....**Haddonfield, NJ**
Christie, David M. ....Seattle, WA
Christie, Deborah C. ....Durham, NC
Christie, Donald J. ....Las Vegas, NV
Christie, Edward C. ....Cleveland, OH
Christie, F. James, III ....Penfield, NY
Christie, Francis J. ....Miami, FL
Christie & Frazee ....**Springfield, MA**
Christie, Frederick W. ....**Richmond, VA**
Christie, George A. ....**Virginia Beach, VA**
Christie, George C. ....Durham, NC
Christie, George F. ....**Fort Worth, TX**
Christie, Heather J. ....**Chicago, IL**
Christie, James D. ....**Allentown, PA**
Christie, James S., Jr. ....**Birmingham, AL**
Christie, James W. ....**New York, NY**
Philadelphia, PA
Christie, JoAnna N. ....Columbus, OH
Christie, Joanne F. ....Stamford, CT
Christie, Joe W. ....El Paso, TX
Christie, Joel A. ....**Washington, DC**
Christie, John C., Jr. ....**Washington, DC**
Christie, John R. ....**Cleveland, OH**
Christie, John V. ....Hobe Sound, FL
Christie, John W. ....Shrewsbury, NJ
Christie, John W., P.A. ....Shrewsbury, NJ
Christie, Joyce E. ....Miami, FL
Christie & Kantor, P.C. ....**Chesapeake, VA**
Norfolk, VA
Virginia Beach, VA
Christie, Kasey C. ....**Portland, OR**
Christie, Kathryn McLean
Research Triangle Park, NC
Christie, Keith A. ....Billings, MT
Christie, Kenneth A. ....White Plains, NY
Christie, Lee C. ....**Indianapolis, IN**
Christie, Lee F. ....**Fort Worth, TX**
Christie, Margaret A. ....**Chicago, IL**
Christie, Mark C. ....**Richmond, VA**
Christie, Mary Lu ....San Francisco, CA
Christie, Monica C. ....Cambridge, MA
Christie, Pabarue, Mortensen and Young, A Professional Corporation ....**Boston, MA**
Cherry Hill, NJ
New York, NY
Philadelphia, PA

Christie, Pabarue, Mortensen and Young, A Professional Corporation—Continued
Radnor, PA
Christie, Parker & Hale, LLP ....Irvine, CA
Los Angeles, CA
Pasadena, CA
Christie, Philip A. ....Rockport, ME
Christie, R. Lee ....Chicago, IL
Christie, Reginald J., Jr. ....Anchorage, AK
Christie, Robert ....Chicago, IL
Christie, Robert C. ....Silver Spring, MD
Christie, Robert J. ....McConnelsville, OH
Christie, Robert L. ....Seattle, WA
Christie, Sandra M. ....New York, NY
Christie, Sarah B. ....Worcester, MA
Christie, Scott S. ....Newark, NJ
Christie, Sharon A. ....Baltimore, MD
Christie, Sheila K. ....Cincinnati, OH
Christie, Stephen Douglas
Birmingham, AL
Christie, Wayne I. ....Red Bank, NJ
Christie, William B. ....Seattle, WA
Christie, William E. ....Concord, NH
Christie, William J., II ....Falls Church, VA
Christie, William P. ....Irvine, CA
Christie, William Y. ....Springfield, MA
Christie-Miner, Tara A. ....New York, NY
Christilles, Arlene R. ....LaCoste, TX
Christin, Barbara K.
Federal Energy Regulatory Commission, Office of the General Counsel, GV
Christin, Claudia D. ....Houston, TX
Christin, Nicholas E. ....Miami, FL
Christin, Robert F.
Federal Energy Regulatory Commission, Office of the General Counsel, GV
Christin, S. Link ....Pittsburgh, PA
Christina, Joe W., Jr. ....Corpus Christi, TX
Christina, Murphy S. ....New Orleans, LA
Christina, Thomas M. ....Greenville, SC
Christine, Alexander R., Jr.
St. Augustine, FL
Christine, Anthony P. ....Warren, OH
Christine, Bobby Lee ....Augusta, GA
Christine & Christine ....East Stroudsburg, PA
Christine, E. David, Jr.
East Stroudsburg, PA
Christine, Elmer D., Sr.
East Stroudsburg, PA
Christine, Frank, III ....Sherman Oaks, CA
Christine, Joanne Book ....Harrisburg, PA
Christinidis, Jon P. ....Detroit, MI
Christison, Kenneth M.
Belvedere-Tiburon, CA
Christison, Kent F. ....Raleigh, NC
Christison, Perry T. ....San Diego, CA
Christison, Randall B. ....San Diego, CA
Christison, Robert A. ....Fair Oaks, CA
Christison, William H. ....Peoria, IL
Christl, Donald J. ....Milwaukee, WI
Christl, Frank C. ....Los Angeles, CA
Christley, Herington & Pierce ....Aurora, OH
Christley, Judith A. ....Warren, OH
Christley, Judith J. ....Cleveland, OH
Christley, Norman L. ....Aurora, OH
Christlieb, Jon C. ....Overland Park, KS
Christlieb, Terry J. ....Trophy Club, TX
Christman, Allyson M. ....Topeka, KS
Christman, Anne ....Cambridge, MA
Christman, Anne Clark ....Washington, DC
Christman, Beth H. ....Wilmington, DE
Christman, Bruce L. ....Falls Church, VA
Christman and Chrisman ....Sidney, OH
Christman, David A. ....Stamford, CT
Christman, Douglas L. ....Boulder, CO
Christman, Eileen H. ....Pittsburgh, PA
Christman, Harold E. ....Sidney, OH
Christman, Henry C. ....Yakima, WA
Christman, James A. ....Chicago, IL
Christman, James N. ....Richmond, VA
Christman, Jason Zac ....East Stroudsburg, PA
Christman, Jean M. ....Denver, CO
Christman, Judith H. ....Perrysburg, OH
Christman, Kenneth P. ....Pittsburgh, PA
Christman, Kenneth P., Jr.
Treasury Department, Internal Revenue Service, GV
Christman, Kenneth W. ....Pittsburgh, PA
Christman, Laura Jean ....Denver, CO
Christman, Leif ....Cleveland, OH
Christman, Mark H. ....Wilmington, DE
Christman, Mark J. ....Pittsburgh, PA
Christman, Stacia A. ....Pittsburgh, PA
Christman, Steven M. ....Albertson, NY
Christman, Susan ....Charlotte, NC
Christmann, Guinevere M. ....Houston, TX
Christmann, Kathryn A. ....Miami, FL
Christmas, Angela ....New York, NY
Christmas & Associates, P.A.
Tallahassee, FL
Christmas, John D. ....Philadelphia, PA
Christmas, Patrick J. ....Washington, DC
Christmas, Patrick J., & Associates, P.C.
Washington, DC
Christmas, Patrick J., II ....Washington, DC
Christmas, Robert N. H. ....New York, NY
Christmas, Sandra R. ....Ormond Beach, FL
Christmas, Sheryl Klemme
Washington, DC
Christmas, Stuart A. ....Tallahassee, FL
Christnacht, George W. ....Tacoma, WA
Christnacht, James F. ....Tacoma, WA
Christner, Barbara J. ....Greensburg, PA
Christner, John F. ....Abilene, KS
Christner, Richard S. ....Pittsburgh, PA
Christner, Wallace E. ....Washington, DC
Baltimore, MD
Christnot, Kate A. ....Green Bay, WI

Christo, James D. ....New York, NY
Christo, Robert ....Springfield, MA
Christo, Thomas K. ....Boston, MA
Christodoulo, George E. ....Boston, MA
Christof, Joseph S. D., II ....Pittsburgh, PA
Wheeling, WV
Christofeno, Michael A. ....Elkhart, IN
Christoff, BiBi L. ....Carpinteria, CA
Christoff, Carl C. ....Dallas, TX
Christoff, Catherine S. ....Fort Wayne, IN
Christoff & Christoff ....Fort Wayne, IN
Christoff, Danziger Patricia
Toms River, NJ
Christoff, Haskins, Fiocca & Morris
Akron, OH
Christoff, James D. ....St. Paul, MN
Christoff, John P. ....Ada, OH
Christoff, Joseph ....Fort Wayne, IN
Christoff, Joseph A. ....Fort Wayne, IN
Christoff, Mark S. ....Danville, IL
Christoff, Patrick G. ....Las Vegas, NV
Christoff, Paul K. ....Akron, OH
Christoff, Richard W. ....Chicago, IL
Christoff, William Z. ....Massillon, OH
Christoffel, Dean C. ....Tucson, AZ
Christoffel & Elliott, P.A.
Minneapolis, MN
St. Paul, MN
Christoffel, Gregory J. ....St. Louis, MO
Christoffel, James F. ....St. Paul, MN
Christoffersen, Craig J. ....Minneapolis, MN
Christoffersen, Dawn T. ....St. Louis, MO
Christoffersen, Harold ....Lawrenceville, NJ
Christoffersen & Knierim, P.C.
Glasgow, MT
Christoffersen, Steven E. ....Denver, CO
Christoffersen, Svein-Erik M.
New York, NY
Christofferson, Carla J. ....Los Angeles, CA
Christofferson, Clyde R ....Oakton, VA
Reston, VA
Christofferson, David B. ....Tulsa, OK
Christofferson, Lee A. ....Devils Lake, ND
Christofferson, P. Chris ....New Orleans, LA
Christofferson, Philip J. ....St. Louis, MO
Christoff-Fox, D. Kathleen
Casselberry, FL
Christofides, Chris ....New York, NY
Christofilis, Charles A ....Brooklyn, NY
Christofolo, Rosemarie ....Phoenix, AZ
Christoforatos, Kate D.
Long Island City, NY
Christoforo, William G. ....Cockeysville, MD
Christoforo, William G., Jr. ....Bel Air, MD
Christol, Carl Q. ....Pacific Palisades, CA
Christol, E. W. ....Rapid City, SD
Christon, James T. ....Elm Grove, WI
Christon, Lisa M. ....Pocatello, ID
Christoph, Carl S. ....West Bloomfield, MI
Christoph, James R. ....Boulder, CO
Christoph, Joel ....New York, NY
Christoph, William R. ....Vista, CA
Christopher, A. Mark ....McLean, VA
Christopher, Alissa K. ....Dallas, TX
Christopher, Angela R.
Oklahoma City, OK
Christopher, BK ....Kansas City, MO
Christopher, Brent E. ....Dallas, TX
Christopher & Byers, PLLC ....Tupelo, MS
Christopher, Charles B.
Treasury Department, Internal Revenue Service, GV
Christopher, Charles D. ....San Diego, CA
Christopher, Christopher ....Worcester, MA
Christopher, Craig ....San Antonio, TX
Christopher, Daniel G. ....Los Angeles, CA
Christopher, Daniel R. ....Denver, CO
Christopher, Darla J. ....Starke, FL
Christopher, Deborah Kim ....Polson, MT
Christopher, Donald E. ....Orlando, FL
Christopher, Edward F. ....Red Bank, NJ
Christopher, Gary W. ....Annapolis, MD
Christopher, George E., Jr. ....Rockville, MD
Christopher, George L. ....Washington, DC
Christopher, Gina M. ....Palo Alto, CA
Christopher, Gregory M.
Federal Communications Commission, Office of the General Counsel, GV
Christopher, Hays, Wojcik & Mavricos
Boston, MA
Worcester, MA
Christopher, Henry W., Jr.
San Antonio, TX
Christopher, J. Michael ....Phoenix, AZ
Christopher, James M. ....San Antonio, TX
Christopher, Jeffrey P. ....Westlake Village, CA
Christopher, John ....Boston, MA
Christopher, John A. ....Danvers, MA
Christopher, John D. "Jack", Jr.
Lexington, KY
Christopher, John E., Jr. ....Cincinnati, OH
Christopher, John J. ....Buffalo, NY
Christopher, John S. ....Los Angeles, CA
Christopher, John W. ....Chicago, IL
Christopher, John W. ....Ridgeland, MS
Christopher, Joseph D. ....Newport Beach, CA
Christopher, Judith E. ....Columbus, OH
Christopher, Kenneth J. ....San Francisco, CA
Christopher, Kristi Lee ....Oklahoma City, OK
Christopher, Laurence G. ....St. Louis, MO
Christopher Law Offices, S.C. ....Madison, WI
Christopher, Linda ....Nyack, NY
Christopher, Linda, P.C. ....New City, NY
Nyack, NY
Christopher, Lynne ....Tupelo, MS
Christopher, M. Ronald ....Frankfort, KY
Christopher, Margaret D. ....Seattle, WA
Christopher, Mark M. ....Boston, MA

Christopher, Megan Hyde ....Framingham, MA
Christopher, Michael R. ....Madison, WI
Christopher, Milena C. ....Fort Lauderdale, FL
Christopher, M. Ronald, P.S.C., Law Offices of
Frankfort, KY
Christopher, Nancy D.
Department of Housing and Urban Development, Office of General Counsel, GV
Christopher, Nathan H., Jr. ....Salisbury, MD
Christopher, Richard A. ....Chicago, IL
Christopher, Richard L. ....Fowler, IN
Indianapolis, IN
Christopher, Rita G. ....Old Lyme, CT
Christopher, Robert A. ....San Jose, CA
Christopher, Robert B. ....Monticello, IN
Christopher, Robert J. ....Hackensack, NJ
Christopher, Ronald J. ....Houston, TX
Christopher, S. Paige ....Cleveland, OH
Christopher, Sharon B. ....Raleigh, NC
Christopher, Shawn ....Henderson, NV
Christopher, Stanley ....Cleveland, OH
Christopher, Steven D. ....Findlay, OH
Kenton, OH
Christopher & Taylor ....Fowler, IN
Indianapolis, IN
Christopher, Thomas ....Pebble Beach, CA
Christopher, Thomas H. ....Atlanta, GA
Christopher, Thomas P. ....Los Angeles, CA
Christopher, Thomas V.
San Francisco, CA
Christopher, Thomas W. ....New York, NY
Christopher, Thomas W. ....Greenville, SC
Christopher, Tracy Kee ....Houston, TX
Christopher, Vance ....Houston, TX
Christopher, Walter A. ....Oak Park, IL
Christopher, Warren ....Los Angeles, CA
Washington, DC
Christopher, William G. ....Sarasota, FL
Christopher, William L.
Research Triangle Park, NC
Christopher, William R. ....Butler, AL
Christopher, William S. ....New Canaan, CT
Christophersen, Amy S. ....Seattle, WA
Christophersen, C. Eric ....Geneva, IL
Christophersen, Steven J.S. ....Seattle, WA
Christopherson & Alexander
Walnut Creek, CA
Christopherson, Bailin & Anderson
Hartford, SD
Sioux Falls, SD
Christopherson, Bruce ....Granite Falls, MN
Christopherson, Dean Allen
Walnut Creek, CA
Christopherson, Donna M. ....El Paso, TX
Christopherson, Gary ....Stockton, CA
Christopherson, George W., II ....Houston, TX
Christopherson, Ian ....Las Vegas, NV
Christopherson, James A.
Traverse City, MI
Christopherson, John A. ....Mount Vernon, WA
Christopherson, M. Kent ....St. George, UT
Christopherson, Mark D.
Minneapolis, MN
Christopherson, M. Kent, P.C.
St. George, UT
Christopherson, Norman J. ....Flint, MI
Christophillis, Catherine C. ....Greenville, SC
Christophillis, Constantine Sotiros, Jr.
Greenville, SC
Christophorou, Penelope L.
New York, NY
Christopoulos, Dimitrios G. ....Chicago, IL
Christopoulos, George J. ....Detroit, MI
Christopoulos, James P.
Executive Office Of The President, Office of Management and Budget, GV
Christou, Peter A. ....San Francisco, CA
Christou, William M. ....Oak Brook, IL
Christovich, Alvin R., Jr.
New Orleans, LA
Christovich, Jeffrey J. ....Los Angeles, CA
Christovich and Kearney, L.L.P.
New Orleans, LA
Christovich, Michael M.
New Orleans, LA
Christovich, Richard K. ....New Orleans, LA
Christovich, William K. ....New Orleans, LA
Christrup, G. Kenneth ....Stamford, CT
Christu, Eric C. ....Boca Raton, FL
Christu, Maria C. ....St. Paul, MN
Christus, Daniel N. ....Chicago, IL
Christy, Alex ....Portland, OR
Christy, Allen E., Jr. ....Minneapolis, MN
Christy, Allen R. ....Littleton, CO
Christy, Angela Mulkerin
Minneapolis, MN
Christy, Arthur H. ....New York, NY
Christy, Barbara R. ....Greensboro, NC
Christy, Bradley S. ....Covington, KY
Christy, Cynthia Ullem ....Denver, CO
Christy, David M. ....Niagara Falls, NY
Christy, David S., Jr. ....Washington, DC
Christy, Dennis D. ....Victorville, CA
Christy, Frank J., Jr. ....San Rafael, CA
Christy, Gary C. ....Cordele, GA
Christy, H. Chris ....North Little Rock, AR
Christy, J. Gordon ....Dearborn, MI
Christy, James O. ....Libertyville, IL
Christy, Jeannette ....Los Angeles, CA
Christy, Jennifer Neviaser ....Chicago, IL
Christy, John A. ....Atlanta, GA
Christy, John C. ....Newport Beach, CA
Christy, John D. ....Perry, GA
Christy, John W. ....Chicago, IL
Christy, Kaign N. ....Cottonwood, AZ
Flagstaff, AZ
Sedona, AZ

Christy, Katherine A. ....Heathrow, FL
Christy, Katherine A., P.A. ....Heathrow, FL
Christy, Nancy J. ....North Syracuse, NY
Christy, R. David ....Atlanta, GA
Christy, Robert ....Manchester, NH
Christy, Roland J. ....Spring House, PA
Christy & Tessier ....Manchester, NH
Christy, Thomas ....San Diego, CA
Christy, Thomas P. ....Westland, MI
Christy & Viener ....New York, NY
Christy, Walter R. ....Canton, NY
Christy, Walter W. ....New Orleans, LA
Christy, William R. ....Santa Clara, CA
Christy, Wm. P., Jr. ....North Syracuse, NY
Christy-Cirillo, Curtis F. ....San Francisco, CA
Chriszt, James R. ....Cleveland, OH
Chritton, Charles P. ....Lakeland, FL
Chritton, J. Kirby ....Jacksonville, FL
Chritton, Phillip William ....New York, NY
Chritton, Rand L. ....Walnut Creek, CA
Chritton, Robert E. ....Madison, WI
Stoughton, WI
Chritton, Valerie C. ....Jacksonville, FL
Chritton, William E. ....Stoughton, WI
Chroman, Melissa B. ....Chicago, IL
Chroman, Nathan L. ....Beverly Hills, CA
Chroman, Stacie E. ....Los Angeles, CA
Chromek, Paul G. ....Chicago, IL
Chromey, Barry J. ....Pittston, PA
Chromow, Charles E. ....New York, NY
Chromow, Sheri P. ....New York, NY
Chromulak, Cathy Ann ....Pittsburgh, PA
Chron, Tony J. ....Fort Worth, TX
Chronis & Kreher ....San Francisco, CA
Chronis, Paul E. ....Chicago, IL
Chronis, Penelope Ann ....Oakland, CA
San Francisco, CA
Chronis, Phillip ....Beverly Hills, CA
Chronister, Allen B. ....Helena, MT
Chronister, Carl F. ....Harrisburg, PA
Chronister, John ....Tulsa, OK
Chronister, John H. ....York, PA
Chronister, Moreen & Larson, P.C.
Helena, MT
Chronister, Rex W. ....Fort Smith, AR
Chronister, Rex W., P.A. ....Fort Smith, AR
Chronister, Wendy L. ....Chicago, IL
Chronos, William J. ....Tulsa, OK
Chronus, Peter J. ....Milwaukee, WI
Chroust, David J. ....Lisle, IL
Chrusch, Michael J. ....Miami, FL
Chrusciel, Jerilynn Kay ....Angleton, TX
Chrusciel, Sophia E. ....Seattle, WA
Chrysanthem, Nicholas P. ....New York, NY
Chrysanthis, Alexandra C. ....Las Vegas, NV
Chrysler, Denise ....Lansing, MI
Chryssikos, Telemac N. ....Washington, DC
Chryssos, Dean ....Old Bethpage, NY
Chryst, Roberto D. ....Syracuse, NY
Chrystal, John J. ....Chicago, IL
Chrystal, Lisa F. ....Westfield, NJ
Chrystal, Margot C. ....Larchmont, NY
Chrystal, Neil R. ....Miami, FL
Naples, FL
Palm Beach, FL
Chrystie, Richard J. ....Whittier, CA
Chrystler, Gary L. ....Provo, UT
Chrzan, Linda Peters ....Fort Wayne, IN
Chrzanowski, Eugene L. ....Irvine, CA
Chrzanowski, Mary A. ....Mount Clemens, MI
Chrzastek, Myron J. ....Alexandria, VA
Chu, Adam ....Boston, MA
Chu, Alain ....Culver City, CA
Chu, Albert S. ....Seattle, WA
Chu, Anthony ....San Diego, CA
Philadelphia, PA
Chu, Brian T. ....Monterey Park, CA
Chu, Carl S. ....Fishkill, NY
Chu, Clifford J. ....Great Neck, NY
Chu, Dennis Y. S. ....Honolulu, HI
Chu, Elise ....San Francisco, CA
Chu, Eric S. H. ....New York, NY
Chu, Euclid ....Bethesda, MD
Chu, Eugenia ....Miami, FL
Chu, Flora Y. F. ....San Jose, CA
Chu, Forrest ....San Diego, CA
Chu, Frank S.C. ....Redwood City, CA
Chu, Frankie ....New York, NY
Chu, Gracie W. ....Alhambra, CA
Chu, Harold ....Honolulu, HI
Chu, Harold, Attorney at Law, A Law Corporation ....Honolulu, HI
Chu, Howard ....New York, NY
Chu, Ileana ....Charlotte, NC
Chu, Jeffrey M. ....San Francisco, CA
Chu, John ....San Francisco, CA
Chu, John H. ....Boston, MA
Chu, John Ya-Ou ....Solvang, CA
Chu, Joseph S. ....Cleveland, OH
Chu, Justin ....New York, NY
Chu, Kevin M. ....Philadelphia, PA
Chu, Lawrence M. ....New York, NY
Chu, Lynn T. ....New York, NY
Chu, Mable ....Washington, DC
Chu, Mary H. ....Los Angeles, CA
Chu, Michael P. ....Chicago, IL
Chu, Morgan ....Los Angeles, CA
Chu, Nancy Y. ....Chicago, IL
Chu, Newton J. ....Hilo, HI
Chu, Norbert ....Oakland, CA
Chu, Paul C. Y. ....White Plains, NY
Chu, Phyllis ....Brooklyn, NY
Chu, Rai Saint ....Honolulu, HI
Chu, Regina M. ....Minneapolis, MN
Chu, Ring & Hazel, LLP ....Boston, MA
Chu, Sylvia ....Boston, MA
Chu, Terence ....Charlotte, NC
Chu, Thomas S. ....Los Angeles, CA

Chu, Timothy ... Menlo Park, CA
Chu, Vernon G. ... New York, NY
Chu, Wilson (IBA) **... Dallas, TX**
Chu, Yen D. ... New York, NY
Chu, Yueh-Ru ... New York, NY
Chua, Alvin ... Denver, CO
Chua, Amy L. ... Durham, NC
Chua, Barbara C. ... Chicago, IL
Chua, Christine S. ... Palo Alto, CA
Chua, Frances M. ... Chicago, IL
Chua, Poh C. ... Washington, DC
Chuang, Annie Y. S. ... San Francisco, CA
Chuang, Deborah J. ... Los Angeles, CA
Chuang, Diana K. ... Los Angeles, CA
Chuang, Enna ... Fort Lee, NJ
Chuang, George ... Los Angeles, CA
Chuang, George, & Associates, P.C.
Los Angeles, CA
Chuang, Samuel J. ... New York, NY
Chuang, Theodore D. ... Boston, MA
Chuang, Thomas ... San Francisco, CA
Chuang, William Wei-Li ... Palo Alto, CA
Chua-Rocco, Caroline S. ... New York, NY
Chubaty, Andrew R. ... St. Petersburg, FL
Chubb, Diane M. ... Los Angeles, CA
Chubb, Heather R. ... Sacramento, CA
Chubb, James J. ... Ferguson, MO
Chubb, Janet A. ... Topeka, KS
Chubb, Janet L. ... Reno, NV
Chubb, Jeffrey A. ... Independence, KS
Chubb, Kathryn A. ... Columbus, OH
Chubb, Larry L., Law Office of
Chesterton, IN
Chubb, Nita Colgate ... Brooklyn, NY
Chubb, Philip S. ... Charlotte, NC
Chubb, Robert A. ... Atlanta, GA
Chubb, Russell P. ... Thomasville, GA
Chubb, T. Spence
United States International Trade Commission,
Office of Unfair Import Investigations, GV
Chubb, Thomas Caldecot, III
Atlanta, GA
Chubb, William St. John ... Springfield, VA
Chubbuck, Gary Mitchell
Oklahoma City, OK
Chubbuck, June L. ... Oklahoma City, OK
Chubbuck Smith & Rhodes, A Professional Corporation ... Oklahoma City, OK
Chuberka, Susan M. ... San Francisco, CA
Chubin, Ellen L. ... Department of Justice, Criminal Division, GV
Chubinsky, James H. ... Bronx, NY
Chubinsky, Leonard I. ... Armonk, NY
Chubre, Steve ... Richmond, CA
Chubrich & Harrigan, P.A. ... Portsmouth, NH
Chubrich, Michael E. ... Portsmouth, NH
Chucala, Steven ... Dale City, VA
Chucas, Terence M. ... San Diego, CA
Chuck, Catherine Endo ... Los Angeles, CA
Chuck, Evan Y. ... Los Angeles, CA
Chuck, Jamie A. ... Honolulu, HI
Chuck, Jamie A., Attorney At Law, A Law Corporation ... Honolulu, HI
Chuck Jones & MacLaren, Attorneys at Law, A Law Corporation ... Honolulu, HI
Chuck, Samuel A. ... San Jose, CA
Chuck, Stephen C. ... Pasadena, CA
Chuck, W. Gregory ... Honolulu, HI
Chuck, Walter G. ... Honolulu, HI
Chuck, Walter G., Attorney at Law, A Law Corporation ... Honolulu, HI
Chucka, Patricia Ann ... Sheboygan, WI
Chucker, G. Barton ... Richmond, VA
Chucker & Reibach ... Richmond, VA
Chudacoff, Bruce ... Appleton, WI
Chudacoff, Gregory S. ... Los Angeles, CA
Chudacoff & Liebzeit ... Appleton, WI
Chudacoff, Mark R. ... Chicago, IL
Chudacoff, Nancy Fisher ... Pawtucket, RI
Chudada, Robert F. ... Chicago Heights, IL
Chudakoff, Reneé F. ... Cleveland Heights, OH
Chudakoff, Robert E. ... Cleveland, OH
Chudd, Reeve E. ... Beverly Hills, CA
Chudgar, Praful S. ... Fremont, CA
Chudler, Brett S. ... Pontiac, MI
Chudler, Kevin M. ... Bloomfield Hills, MI
Chudnoff, Jonathan P. ... Rockville, MD
Chudnovsky, Christine Pardo
New York, NY
Chudnow, Avrum M. ... Milwaukee, WI
Chudnow, Daniel M. ... Milwaukee, WI
Chudnow, David ... Los Angeles, CA
Chudnow Law Offices ... Milwaukee, WI
Chudnow, Meyer ... Oak Park, MI
Chudnow, Saul S. ... Oak Park, MI
Chudnow, Steven L. ... New York, NY
Chudwick, Bruce A. ... Hartford, CT
Chudy, Brendan F. ... Albany, NY
Chudy, James T. ... New York, NY
Chudyk, Peter ... Hudson, OH
Chudzicki, Pawel ... Chicago, IL
Chudzik, Helene Paterra ... Trenton, NJ
Chudzik, Henry, Jr. ... East Brunswick, NJ
Chudzik, John S. ... Baltimore, MD
Chudzinski, Anthony A. ... Fremont, OH
Chudzinski, Mark A. ... Chicago, IL
Chuey, Paul ... Seattle, WA
Chuff, David F. ... Scranton, PA
Chuff, Patricia Moran ... Wilmington, DE
Chu Fong, Fay ... Denver, CO
Chuh, Charles S. ... Woodland Hills, CA
Chuh, Patricia M. ... Washington, DC
Chuh, Teresa D. ... Emeryville, CA
Chuha, Edward F. ... Columbus, OH
Chuhak & Tecson, P.C. ... Chicago, IL
Chuhinka, Michael S. ... Philadelphia, PA
Chuhran, Thomas P. ... Detroit, MI
Chukas, Jason P. ... St. Louis, MO
Chukla, Joseph, Jr. ... Hagerstown, MD
Chulak, Michael J. ... Union City, NJ
Chulick, Andrew ... Wilton, CT
Chulick, Mark R. ... Cleveland, OH
Chulick, Peter ... St. Louis, MO
Chullen, John L. ... Benton, IL
Chulock, Larry R. ... Bradenton, FL
Chulock, Robert Y. ... Coral Gables, FL
Chulock, Vicki Wood ... Coral Gables, FL
Chulos, Nicholas J. ... Indianapolis, IN
Chuman, Frank F. ... Los Angeles, CA
Chuman, Paul R. ... Los Angeles, CA
Chumbler, Martha Harrell
Tallahassee, FL
Chumbley, Douglas J. ... Miami, FL
Chumbley, Joseph H. ... St. Petersburg, FL
Chumbley, William D., Jr.
San Antonio, TX
Chumbris, Peter N. ... United States Senate, Committee Legal Personnel, GV
Chumbris, Stephen C. ... St. Petersburg, FL
Chumlea, Joseph G. ... Dallas, TX
Chumlea, Kevin L. ... Akron, OH
Chumley, Donald C.
Securities and Exchange Commission, Division of Enforcement, GV
Chumley, Loren L. ... Nashville, TN
Chumley, Mark J. ... Cincinnati, OH
Chumnanvech, Alyssa ... Washington, DC
Chumney, Carolyn J. ... Memphis, TN
Chumney, Wm. T., Jr. ... San Antonio, TX
Chumrau, Gary B. ... Missoula, MT
Chun, A. Marisa ... San Francisco, CA
Chun, Alan G. ... North Highlands, CA
Chun, Alexandra Sun Young
New York, NY
Chun, Barbara Y. K.
Commodity Futures Trading Commission, Division of Enforcement, GV
Chun, Benedict W. ... New York, NY
Chun, Benjamin L. ... Palo Alto, CA
Chun, Carlton W. T. ... Honolulu, HI
Chun Chipchase Takayama Nagatani
Honolulu, HI
Chun, Christine S.Y. ... Honolulu, HI
Chun, Christopher W. ... Los Angeles, CA
Chun, Connie C. ... Honolulu, HI
Chun, Darrell J. ... Glendale, CA
Chun, David J. ... San Jose, CA
Chun, David Y. ... San Jose, CA
Chun, Deborah Macer ... Honolulu, HI
Chun, Edward Y. C. ... Honolulu, HI
Chun, Eunu ... New York, NY
Chun, Gaye Lynne ... Honolulu, HI
Chun, Grant Y. M. ... Wailuku, HI
Chun, Henry ... San Francisco, CA
Chun, Hoon ... Los Angeles, CA
Chun, Jason Y. ... Santa Ana, CA
Chun, Jennifer J. ... Roseland, NJ
Chun, Jennifer K. ... Los Angeles, CA
Chun, Jennifer Miseong ... Chapel Hill, NC
Chun, Jerrold Y. ... Honolulu, HI
Chun, Jinny ... Washington, DC
Chun, Joanne J. ... Chicago, IL
Chun, John H. ... Seattle, WA
Chun, Jonathan J. ... Lihue, HI
Chun, Julianne L. ... Los Angeles, CA
Chun, Keith ... Honolulu, HI
Chun, Kerr, Dodd, Beaman & Wong
Honolulu, HI
Chun, Lisa Ann ... Honolulu, HI
Chun, Madeline ... San Francisco, CA
Chun, Marylene O. S. ... Honolulu, HI
Chun, Michael L. ... Honolulu, HI
Chun, Nelson N. S. ... Honolulu, HI
Chun, Richard ... New York, NY
Chun, Richard C. F. ... Honolulu, HI
Chun, Robert T. ... Chicago, IL
Chun, Robyn B. ... Honolulu, HI
Chun, Ron S. ... Los Angeles, CA
Chun, Ronald ... San Francisco, CA
Chun, Sang-Ah Deborah ... Los Angeles, CA
Chun, Sun Young ... New York, NY
Chun, Susan ... New York, NY
Chun, Susan Y. W. ... Lexington, KY
Chun, Thomas W. N. ... Honolulu, HI
Chun, Tobias D. ... Palo Alto, CA
Chun, Tom S. ... Irvine, CA
Chunderlik, Frank J., III ... Indianapolis, IN
Chung, Aaron S. Y. ... Hilo, HI
Chung, Amy Teresa ... San Francisco, CA
Chung, Ann L.K. ... Santa Rosa, CA
Chung, April M. ... New York, NY
Chung, Barry ... Honolulu, HI
Chung, Cecil S. ... Washington, DC
Chung, Chanmaly Kendie
Santa Monica, CA
Chung, Chul ... New York, NY
Chung, Clairmont M. ... Newark, NJ
Chung, D. James ... Los Angeles, CA
Chung, Daniel ... New York, NY
Chung, Daniel C. ... New York, NY
Chung, David H. ... New York, NY
Chung, David S. ... Washington, DC
Chung, Edward J. H. ... New York, NY
Chung, Elizabeth Holmes ... Cleveland, OH
Chung, Eric C. ... St. Louis, MO
Chung, Ernest W. ... New York, NY
Chung, Frederick S. ... San Francisco, CA
Chung, George ... New York, NY
Chung, Ginny Y. ... Treasury Department, Internal Revenue Service, GV
Chung, Grace ... La Jolla, CA
San Jose, CA
Chung, H. Helen ... New York, NY
Chung, Harrison P., Law Office of
Honolulu, HI
Chung, Henry H. ... New York, NY
Chung, Howard N. ... San Francisco, CA
Chung, Huhnsik ... New York, NY
Chung, Hyun ... New York, NY
Chung, Jae Won ... New York, NY
Chung, Jae-Bum ... Portland, OR
Chung, Jaehoon ... New York, NY
Chung, James ... New York, NY
Chung, Jamie E. ... San Francisco, CA
Chung, Janet S. ... Seattle, WA
Chung, Jason N. ... Los Angeles, CA
Chung, Jay J. ... Los Angeles, CA
Chung, Jennifer ... Washington, DC
Chung, Jo Ann ... Anchorage, AK
Chung, Jock K. ... Federal Trade Commission, Bureau of Consumer Protection, GV
Chung, John J. ... Los Angeles, CA
Chung, Judy Y. ... New York, NY
Chung, Julian S.H. ... New York, NY
Chung, Kenneth W. ... Irvine, CA
Chung, Kerwin ... Washington, DC
Chung, Kevin F. ... Palo Alto, CA
Chung, Kristina H. ... Redwood City, CA
Chung, Kwang Mo ... McLean, VA
Chung, Linda ... New York, NY
Chung, Linda A. ... Walnut Creek, CA
Chung, Lisa M. ... Los Angeles, CA
Chung, Lynda I. ... Los Angeles, CA
Chung, Megan Sue-Anne ... Greenbelt, MD
Chung, Melvin L. ... Los Angeles, CA
Chung, Nancy ... New York, NY
Chung, Nicholas S. ... Los Angeles, CA
Chung, Patrick S. ... Palo Alto, CA
Chung, Paul W. ... Houston, TX
Chung, Peter J. ... Kansas City, MO
Chung, Philip K. ... McLean, VA
Chung & Press, P.C. ... McLean, VA
Chung, Racquel-Ann Leialoha
Las Vegas, NV
Chung, Randall Y. S. ... Honolulu, HI
Chung, Ricky ... New York, NY
Chung, Robert ... New York, NY
Chung & Romano ... San Jose, CA
Chung, Samuel S. ... Seattle, WA
Chung, Stephen P. ... Houston, TX
Chung, Steven K. S. ... Honolulu, HI
Chung, Suey K. ... Jersey City, NJ
New York, NY
Chung, Sun H. ... Los Angeles, CA
Chung, Susan Myung-Sook ... San Jose, CA
Chung, Theodore T. ... Chicago, IL
Chung, Timothy J. ... Los Angeles, CA
Chung, Unbo ... Chicago, IL
Chung, Walter C. ... San Diego, CA
Chung-A-Fung, Ronald A.
Treasury Department, Community Development Financial Institutions, GV
Chung-Han, Ariana M. ... Palo Alto, CA
Chung Ushijima, Marilyn ... Honolulu, HI
Chun-Hoon, Lowell K. Y. ... Honolulu, HI
Chunka, Gary G. ... Lincoln, NE
Chunko, Daniel L. ... Washington, PA
Chunn, Douglas D. ... Jacksonville, FL
Chunn, Douglas D., P.A. ... Jacksonville, FL
Chunn, E. Keith, Jr. ... Houston, TX
Chunn, John C. ... New Braunfels, TX
Chunn, L. Brian ... Bay Minette, AL
Daphne, AL
Foley, AL
Chunn, Lonnie E. ... San Antonio, TX
Chuoarkoff, David F. ... Youngstown, OH
Chupa & Alberti, P.C. ... Farmington Hills, MI
Chupa, John Gerard ... Farmington Hills, MI
Chupa, Michael Charles ... Warren, MI
Chupack, Edward A. ... Chicago, IL
Chupack, Mitchell M. ... Los Angeles, CA
Chuparkoff & Chuparkoff ... Youngstown, OH
Chuparkoff, George A. ... Youngstown, OH
Chuparkoff, Karen M. ... Akron, OH
Chuparkoff, Stephen J. ... Youngstown, OH
Chuparkoff, Theodore ... Akron, OH
Chupein, Joseph W., Jr. ... Media, PA
Chupik, Phillip B. ... Galveston, TX
Chupp, Frank M. ... Binghamton, NY
Chupp, John Parrish ... Arlington, TX
Chuppa, Norbert A. ... Grafton, WI
Chuppe, Frank F., Jr. ... Louisville, KY
Chuprinski, David M. ... Muncy, PA
Williamsport, PA
Chuquimia, Ruben K. ... St. Louis, MO
Chur, Daniel E. ... Honolulu, HI
Churak, Gary ... San Antonio, TX
Churay, Daniel John ... Houston, TX
Churbuck, Lewis M. ... Charles City, IA
Cresco, IA
New Hampton, IA
Churbuck, Robert B. ... Rockville Centre, NY
Church, Allen ... San Antonio, TX
Church, Allen, P.C. ... San Antonio, TX
Church, Arthur C., (Co., L.P.A.)
Cincinnati, OH
Church, Beresford L., Jr.
North Little Rock, AR
Church, Bert Edward ... Wellington, KS
Church, Billy L. ... Pell City, AL
Church, Brenda K. ... Scottsdale, AZ
Sun City, AZ
Church, Charles F. ... Portage, WI
Church, Charles R. ... Roseland, NJ
Church, Chas. ... Akron, OH
Church and Church ... Branford, CT
New Haven, CT
Church & Church ... Albion, NY
Church, Church, Hittle & Antrim
Carmel, IN
Indianapolis, IN
Noblesville, IN
Church, Craig W. ... Chicago, IL
Church, Dale W. ... Washington, DC
Church, Daniel F. ... Lenexa, KS
Church, David L. ... Salt Lake City, UT
Church, Debra A. ... Wilmington, NC
Church, Denise Lynn ... Chicago, IL
Springfield, IL
Church, Diane K. ... Buffalo, NY
Church, Donald ... Tulsa, OK
Church, Donald E. ... Norwood, MA
Church, Douglas D. ... Noblesville, IN
Church, Edgar L. ... Lansing, MI
Church, Edgar L., Jr. ... Lansing, MI
Church, Gary L. ... Overland Park, KS
Church, Geoffrey K. ... Elkhart, IN
Church, George K. (Nick), Jr. ... Lilburn, GA
Church, George M. ... Baltimore, MD
Towson, MD
Church, Glenn J. ... Cocoa Beach, FL
Church, H. Collyer ... San Francisco, CA
Church, Harris, Johnson & Williams, P.C.
Great Falls, MT
Missoula, MT
Church, Harrison A. ... Jensen Beach, FL
Church, Harrison L. ... Lebanon, IL
Church & Houff, P.A. ... Washington, DC
Baltimore, MD
Towson, MD
Church, J. Jeffrey ... Solon, OH
Church, J. Thomas ... St. Paul, MN
Church, James D. ... Portland, OR
Church, Jeffrey E. ... South Padre Island, TX
Church, John A. ... Lewiston, ID
Church, John D. ... Shelby, NC
Church, John V. ... Baltimore, MD
Church, Jordan D. ... Noblesville, IN
Church, Judith L. ... New York, NY
Church, Katrina J. ... Palo Alto, CA
Church, Keith D. ... Bend, OR
Church, Kim ... Raleigh, NC
Church, Kritselis & Wyble, P.C.
Lansing, MI
Church, Larry R. ... New Albany, IN
Church, Laura ... Davie, FL
Church, Lawrence D. ... Norwalk, CT
Church, Linda A. ... Miami, FL
Church, Lindell R. ... Springfield, MO
Church, Lisa-Michele ... Salt Lake City, UT
Church, Manson E. ... Noblesville, IN
Church, Margaret Kezer ... New Haven, CT
Church, Mark M., & Associates
Millbrae, CA
Church, Michael H. ... Spokane, WA
Church, Michael S. ... Columbia, SC
Church, Norbert W., Jr. ... New Haven, CT
Church, Paksoy & Wray ... Shelby, NC
Church, Pamela T. ... New York, NY
Church, Peter W. ... Rock Island, IL
Church, R. Dean, Jr. ... New Orleans, LA
Church, Ralph E., Jr. ... Vero Beach, FL
Church, Randolph W. ... McLean, VA
Church, Rayma ... Fresno, CA
Church, Robert F. ... Rockville, MD
Church, Robert Frederick ... Naples, FL
Church, Robert R. ... Harrisburg, PA
Church, Roberta Sue ... Elbe, WA
Church, Russel A. ... Clarksville, TN
Church, Sanford A. ... Albion, NY
Church, Sanford L. ... Albion, NY
Church, Sarah L. ... Pittsburgh, PA
Church & Seay, P.C. ... Pell City, AL
Talladega, AL
Church, Shirley L. ... San Jose, CA
Church, Stanley R. ... Warrenton, OR
Church, Steven A. ... Indianapolis, IN
Church, Terry W. ... Olympia, WA
Church, Thomas L. ... Philadelphia, PA
Church, Walter W., Law Offices of
San Antonio, TX
Church, William B., III ... Cincinnati, OH
Church, William H., Jr. ... Dallas, TX
Church, William L. ... Madison, WI
Church, Wm. H. ... Metairie, LA
Church, Wm. Scott ... Fairview, OK
Churchill, Allen D. ... Belleville, IL
Churchill, Amy C. ... Des Moines, IA
Churchill, Baumgartner & Quinn, Ltd.
Grayslake, IL
Churchill & Boskovich ... Long Beach, CA
Churchill, Bruce W., (P.C.) ... Washington, DC
Churchill, Bryan K. ... Albany, OR
Churchill, Carol A. ... Long Beach, CA
Churchill, Christopher J. ... Philadelphia, PA
Churchill & Churchill ... Moline, IL
Rock Island, IL
Churchill, Cynthia T. ... Portland, ME
Churchill, Cyrus ... Moline, IL
Churchill, Daniel ... Moline, IL
Churchill, David A. ... Washington, DC
Churchill, David B. ... Poway, CA
Churchill, David J. ... Lapeer, MI
Churchill, David L. ... Greensboro, NC
Churchill, Diann J. ... Towson, MD
Churchill, Glenn E. ... Marshfield, MA
Churchill, Glenn Patchin
North Charleston, SC
Churchill, Gordon S. ... San Diego, CA
Churchill, Howard L. ... Walnut Creek, CA
Churchill, James A. ... City of Industry, CA
Churchill, James E., Jr. ... Metairie, LA
Churchill, James M. ... Austin, TX
Churchill, James P. ... Good Hart, MI
Churchill, John A. ... Calais, ME
Churchill, John C. ... Parker, AZ
Churchill, Jonathan H. ... New York, NY
Churchill, Joseph L. ... Atlanta, GA
Churchill, Joseph L. & Co., P.C.
Atlanta, GA

Churchill, Kimberly J. ....Milwaukee, WI
Churchill, Kristen L. ....San Diego, CA
Churchill & Krueger ....Parker, AZ
Churchill, Lance D. ....Boise, ID
Churchill Law Offices, P.C. ....Boise, ID
Churchill Law Offices, S.C. ....Saukville, WI
Churchill, Leonard, Brown, Lodine & Hendrie ....Portland, OR
Salem, OR
Churchill, M. Susan ....Saukville, WI
Churchill, Manolis, Freeman, Kludt & Shelton ....Huron, SD
Churchill, Mark H. ....Washington, DC
Churchill, Martha A. ....Roswell, NM
Churchill, Matthew S. ....Charlotte, NC
Churchill, Michael ....Philadelphia, PA
Churchill, Michael A. ....Solana Beach, CA
Churchill, Paul ....San Francisco, CA
Churchill, Phillip David, Jr. ....Lansing, MI
Churchill, Phyllis E. ....Acton, MA
Churchill, Ralph D. ....Dallas, TX
Churchill, Randall J. ....Los Angeles, CA
Churchill, Raymond F. ....Fremont, CA
Churchill, Robert S. ....New York, NY
Churchill, Robert W. ....Grayslake, IL
Churchill, Sharon P. ....Hartford, CT
Churchill, Stephen S. ....Boston, MA
Churchill, Thomas A. ....Milwaukee, WI
Churchill, Thomas W. ....Salem, OR
Churchill, Timothy D. ....Temperance, MI
Churchill, Vickie I. ....Oak Harbor, WA
Churchill, Violet M. ....Dublin, CA
Churchill, W. Stanley ....Wichita, KS
Churchill, William A. ....Grayslake, IL
Churchill, William B. ....Garland, TX
Churchill, William O. ....Tampa, FL
Churchill, William O., Jr. ....Dallas, TX
Churchill, William P., III ....Atlanta, GA
Churchill, Winston H. ....Boise, ID
Churchill, Winston T., II
St. Petersburg, FL
Churchmack, Allan G. ....Cleveland, OH
Churchman, Glenn E. ....Camarillo, CA
Churchman, John P. ....Council Bluffs, IA
Churchville, John E. ....Philadelphia, PA
Churchwell, Elizabeth L. ....Chicago, IL
Churchwell, H. Richard ....Rapid City, SD
Churchwell, Steven G. ....Sacramento, CA
Churchwell, Thomas L. ....Winnetka, IL
Churchwell, Timothy M. ....Long Prairie, MN
Churchya, Nicole M. ....Hollywood, FL
Churella, Robert M. ....Los Angeles, CA
Churgin, Ira ....Chicago, IL
Churgin, Joseph A. ....New York, NY
Churgin, Michael J. ....Austin, TX
Churilla, Donald M. ....Sterling Heights, MI
Churilla, Lisa Renee ....Southfield, MI
Churilla, Scott Alan ....Boston, MA
Churin, Kenneth S. ....New York, NY
Churm, Arthur A. ....Argonne, IL
Churm, Catherine E. ....Chicago, IL
Churm, James W. ....New York, NY
Churney, Bonita L. ....Santa Monica, CA
Churney, Liane L. ....Kalamazoo, MI
Churnside, Donald J. ....Eugene, OR
Churovich, Douglas D. ....St. Louis, MO
Chused, David J. ....Boston, MA
Chused, Joseph ....St. Louis, MO
Chused, Richard H. ....Washington, DC
Chused, Wesley S. ....Boston, MA
Chusid, Ann L. ....New York, NY
Chusid, Bruce G. ....Los Angeles, CA
San Francisco, CA
Chusid, Joanna ....Alexandria, VA
Chusid, Jodie L. ....Los Angeles, CA
Chusid, Lawrence A. ....Los Angeles, CA
Chusid, Mitchel ....Boca Raton, FL
Chustz, J. Steve ....Jackson, MS
Chustz, Ralph B. ....New Roads, LA
Chut & Chut, P.A. ....Greensboro, NC
Chut, Frank J. ....Liberty Corner, NJ
Chut, Frank J., Jr. ....Greensboro, NC
Chut, Mercedes Oglukian ....Greensboro, NC
Chute, Alan D. ....Pittsburgh, PA
Chute & Associates ....South Casco, ME
Chute, Christine A. ....Salem, OR
Chute, David M. ....Irvine, CA
Chute, J. Thomas ....Chicago, IL
Chute, James C. ....Portland, ME
Chute, Pamela D. ....Bangor, ME
Chute, Richard S. ....Boston, MA
Chute, Stephen C. ....South Casco, ME
Chuzi, George M. ....Washington, DC
Chval, Craig J. ....Wheaton, IL
Chvala, Janet L. Krotter ....O'Neill, NE
Chvala, Joseph F. ....Madison, WI
Chvany, Barbara ....Orinda, CA
Chvany, Silbert & Knowlton, L.L.P.
Orinda, CA
Chvatal, Patricia J. ....Richland, WA
Chvisuk, Gregor S. ....Framingham, MA
Chwalek, Bernadine (Bonnie) E.
Newport Beach, CA
Chwalek, John P. ....Syracuse, NY
Chwalibog, Andrew J. ....Huntington, WV
Chwaliszewski, Robert J. ....Palo Alto, CA
Andover, MA
Chwasky, Milton ....New York, NY
Chwat, Anne E. ....New York, NY
Chwialkowski, Keith ....St. Paul, MN
Chwirka, Zigmund ....Sioux City, IA
Chyatte, Scott G. ....Duluth, GA
Chybinski, Nicholas C. ....Alexandria, VA
Chyette, Mitchell, Law Offices of
San Francisco, CA
Chyette, Richard ....Bingham Farms, MI
Chylack, Theodore J. ....Philadelphia, PA
Chylinski, James R. ....Detroit, MI
Chylinski, Joseph L. ....Detroit, MI
Chynoweth, B. Kate ....Houston, TX
Chynoweth, Graham ....Concord, NH
Chynoweth, W. Edward ....Sanger, CA
Chyr, Charlotte ....Treasury Department, Internal Revenue Service, GV
Chyten, David M. ....Framingham, MA
Chyten, Kenneth E. ....Los Angeles, CA
Chytilo, Marc S. ....Santa Barbara, CA
Chytla, Anna ....Washington, DC
Chytraus, Brett R. ....Albany, OR
Chytraus, Kimberly Kesler
Los Angeles, CA
Chyun, Mary Schneider ....Washington, DC
Rockville, MD
Chyung, Chie-Young ....Miami, FL
Chyz, Laurie Lootens ....Seattle, WA
Ciabarra, Laura Gonzalez ....New York, NY
Ciabattari, John C. ....Paterson, NJ
Ciabattari, Mary A. ....Ardsley, NY
Ciacchi, Betty L. ....New York, NY
Ciacci, Richard S. ....New York, NY
Ciacci, Walter F. ....White Plains, NY
Ciaccio, Arnold F. ....Rochester, NY
Ciaccio, Carl J. ....Metairie, LA
Ciaccio, Charles P. ....New Orleans, LA
Ciaccio, Christopher S. ....Rochester, NY
Ciaccio, Franklin ....New York, NY
Ciaccio, Joseph ....Springfield, IL
Ciaccio, Joseph J., Sr. ....Springfield, IL
Ciaccio, Michael G. ....Tucson, AZ
Ciaccio, Philip C. ....New Orleans, LA
Ciaccio, Richard T. ....Rochester, NY
Ciaccio, Robert David ....Torrance, CA
Ciaccio, Salvatore T. ....Hempstead, NY
Ciaccio, Suzanne M. ....Metairie, LA
Ciaffa, Michael A. ....Mineola, NY
Ciaffa, Robert ....Miami, FL
Ciaffone, Leisa Kube ....Roanoke, VA
Ciafone, Frank C., Jr. ....Los Angeles, CA
Ciafullo, Mark A. ....Newark, NJ
Ciaglia, Stephen V. ....Miami, FL
Cialella, Paula J. ....New Castle, PA
Cialeo, Anthony J. ....San Francisco, CA
Cialino, Carmen P., Jr. ....Philadelphia, PA
Ciallella, Sandra ....Del Mar, CA
Ciallella, Susan Stranahan ....Mount Laurel, NJ
Cialone, Anthony P. ....Ridgefield, NJ
Cialone, Frank A. ....San Francisco, CA
Cialone, Joseph A., II ....Houston, TX
Ciambella, Cory J. ....West Seneca, NY
Ciambotti, Anna Marie ....Canfield, OH
Ciambotti, Peter A. ....Lake Charles, LA
Ciambrone, Angelo A. ....Chicago Heights, IL
Ciambrone, Richard A. ....Dayton, OH
Ciambrone, Rosanne ....Chicago, IL
Ciampa, Donna A. ....Huntington, NY
Ciampa, Elizabeth R. ....Salem, MA
Ciampa, Gary L. ....Huntington Woods, MI
Ciampa, George R. ....Hartford, CT
Ciampa, James D. ....Pasadena, CA
Ciampa, Jeffrey Nelson
Farmington Hills, MI
Ciampa, Maria Elisa ....Cambridge, MA
Ciampa, Nancy Carolyn ....Miami, FL
Ciampa, Thomas M. ....Boston, MA
Ciampi, Arthur J. ....New York, NY
Ciampi, Richard J., Jr. ....New York, NY
Ciampitti, Denise A. ....King Of Prussia, PA
Ciampitti, Robert, Jr. ....Boston, MA
Ciampitti, Robert, Jr., P.C. ....Boston, MA
Ciampoli, John ....Mineola, NY
Ciamporcero, Audley A., Jr.
New Brunswick, NJ
Cianca, Marc A. ....Stuart, FL
Cianci, Donald P. ....Columbia, CT
Cianci, Joy ....Philadelphia, PA
Cianci, Peter F. ....Reading, PA
Cianci, Peter J. ....Bryn Mawr, PA
Ciancia, James J. ....Camden, NJ
Ciancia, Peter D. ....Englewood, NJ
Cianciarulo, Marisa S. ....Falls Church, VA
Ciancimino, Albert F. ....Neponsit, NY
Ciancio, Cynthia M. ....Westminster, CO
Ciancio, Donna D. ....Chicago, IL
Waukegan, IL
Ciancio, Gene A. ....Westminster, CO
Ciancio & Jonsen, P.C. ....Denver, CO
Westminster, CO
Ciancio, Lisa A. ....Huntington Beach, CA
Ciancio, Ronald J. ....Chicago, IL
Cianciola, Jill E. ....Rockville, CT
Cianciolo, Jeffrey B. ....Providence, RI
Cianciolo, Lawrence J. ....New Hartford, CT
Cianciolo, Linda ....San Diego, CA
Cianciolo, Marylu ....Chicago, IL
Cianciolo, Michael W. ....Detroit, MI
Cianciosi, Lawrence David ....Flint, MI
Cianciosi, Leo A. ....Binghamton, NY
Cianciulli, Emil V. ....Uniondale, NY
Cianciulli, Lori A. ....Beverly, MA
Cianciulli & Meng, P.C. ....Uniondale, NY
Cianciulli & Ouellette, P.A. ....Beverly, MA
Cianciulli, Robert D. ....Livingston, NJ
Ciancola, Robert E. ....Phoenix, AZ
Ciancuillo, David A. ....Chicago, IL
Ciandella, Robert D. ....Exeter, NH
Cianelli, Paul R. ....Braintree, MA
Cianflone & Cianflone, P.C. ....Pittsfield, MA
Cianflone, David R. ....Pittsfield, MA
Cianflone, Kristin G. ....Hartford, CT
Cianflone, Ralph, Jr. ....Pittsfield, MA
Cianforani, Chester D. ....Eastpointe, MI
Cianfrani, Joseph S. ....Newport Beach, CA
Cianfrani, Karen Sawyer ....Santa Ana, CA
Cianfrini, Raymond F. ....Oakfield, NY
Cianfrogna, Louis V. ....Melbourne, FL
Cianfrogna, Telfer, Reda, Faherty & Anderson, P.A. ....Cocoa, FL
Melbourne, FL
Titusville, FL
Cianfrone, Joseph R. ....Dunedin, FL
Ciani, George J. ....Lincoln, NE
Ciani, Judith Elaine ....Inverness, CA
Cianni Law Offices ....Buhl, MN
Chisholm, MN
Hibbing, MN
Cianni, Louis J. ....Chisholm, MN
Ciano, Cheri R. ....East Brunswick, NJ
Ciano, Frank J. ....Cambridge, MA
Ciano, Frank J. ....White Plains, NY
Ciano, Karin M. ....New York, NY
Ciano, Mario C. ....Cleveland, OH
Ciano, Peter J. ....Jupiter, FL
Ciano, Phillip A. ....Cleveland, OH
Ciantra, Thomas N. ....New York, NY
Ciapas, John C. ....Chicago, IL
Ciapciak, James J. ....East Hartford, CT
Boston, MA
Norwood, MA
Providence, RI
Ciaramella, Joanne T. ....White Plains, NY
Ciaramitaro, Jerome P. ....Mount Clemens, MI
Ciaramitaro, Joseph P., Jr. ....Clinton, MI
Ciaramitaro, Joseph P., Jr., P.C. ....Clinton, MI
Ciaramitaro, Leo J. ....Greensburg, PA
Ciaramitaro, Salvatore A., Jr. ....Detroit, MI
Ciaravella, Mark W. ....Tampa, FL
Ciaravella, Mark W., P.A. ....Tampa, FL
Ciaravino, Anthony S. ....Detroit, MI
Ciaravino, Benedict P. ....Freeport, NY
Ciaravino, Jackson and Tedeschi
Freeport, NY
Ciaravino, James R. ....Orlando, FL
Ciaravino, William J. ....Endicott, NY
Ciarciaglino & Coyle, P.A.
St. Petersburg, FL
Ciarciaglino, Joseph M.
St. Petersburg, FL
Ciardi, Albert A., III ....Cherry Hill, NJ
Philadelphia, PA
Ciardi, Albert A., Jr. ....Philadelphia, PA
Ciardi, John L. ....Boston, MA
Ciardi, Maschmeyer & Karalis, P.C.
Cherry Hill, NJ
Philadelphia, PA
Ciardi, Valerie Noel ....Boston, MA
Ciardiello, Ronald J. ....Middleton, MA
Ciardiello, Rosanne ....Boston, MA
Ciardiello, Steven P. ....Hamden, CT
Ciardullo, Frances A. ....Syracuse, NY
Ciarelli & Dempsey ....Melville, NY
Riverhead, NY
Ciarelli, John L. ....Melville, NY
Ciarimboli, Dina M. ....Boston, MA
Ciarimboli, Dominic ....Harrisburg, PA
Ciarlo, Michael ....New York, NY
Ciarochi, Jason C. ....Dallas, TX
Ciarrocca & Ciarrocca ....Union, NJ
Ciarrocca, Mark P. ....Union, NJ
Ciarrocchi, Christine C. ....Philadelphia, PA
Ciarrocchi, Pamela M. ....Chicago, IL
Ciasulli, Anthony ....Los Angeles, CA
Ciasulli, Joseph ....Los Angeles, CA
Ciatti, Michael J. ....Washington, DC
Ciatto, Frank A. ....Washington, DC
Ciavarella, Angelo ....New York, NY
Ciavarella, Nick E. ....Seven Hills, OH
Ciavarra, J. Kevin ....Dallas, TX
Ciavarra, Louis M. ....Worcester, MA
Ciavola, Robert P. ....Cambridge, MA
Cibak, Craig M. ....Washington, DC
Cibak, Harry ....Short Hills, NJ
Cibbarelli, Edward A. ....Kew Gardens, NY
Cibella, Mary L. ....Cleveland, OH
Cibella, Rosario ....Chicago, IL
Cibelli, Peter A. ....Selden, NY
Cibener, Joel A. ....Beverly Hills, CA
Cibener, Richard Michael ....Los Angeles, CA
Cibik & Cataldo ....Philadelphia, PA
Cibik, Melanie S. ....Pittsburgh, PA
Cibik, Michael A. ....Philadelphia, PA
Cibinic, John, Jr. ....Washington, DC
Cibinic-Ondreyka, Amy A. ....New York, NY
Cibor, Edward J. ....Pontiac, MI
Cibrario, John J. ....Westland, MI
Cibrian, David J. ....San Antonio, TX
Cibula, Elizabeth E. ....Chicago, IL
Cibula, Frank G., Jr. ....West Palm Beach, FL
Cibula, Franklin S. ....Redding, CA
Cibula, Mark Hanbury ....Redding, CA
Cibulay, Edward J. ....Larchmont, NY
Cicack, Walter J. ....Houston, TX
Cicala, Angele K. ....San Francisco, CA
Cicala, Conte C. ....San Francisco, CA
Cicala, Joanne M. ....New York, NY
Cicala, Karen R. ....Memphis, TN
Cicala, Peter A. ....Westfield, NJ
Cicalese, Carmen V., Jr. ....West Caldwell, NJ
Cicalese, Heather A. ....Philadelphia, PA
Cicalese, Patrick ....Tequesta, FL
Cicardo, Eugene P., Jr. ....Alexandria, LA
Cicardo, Eugene P., Sr. ....Alexandria, LA
Cicarella, Thomas A. ....Cleveland, OH
Cicatelli & Cicatelli ....Stoneham, MA
Cicatelli, Martin J. ....Stoneham, MA
Cicatelli, Steven L. ....Stoneham, MA
Cicatiello, Judith L. ....Youngstown, OH
Ciccarelli, Ferdinand J. ....Snyder, NY
Ciccarelli, John K. ....Beverly Hills, CA
Ciccarelli, Lee A. ....Philadelphia, PA
Ciccarelli, Mark A. ....East Liverpool, OH
Ciccarelli, Massimo "Max"
Fort Worth, TX
Ciccarelli, Michelle M. ....Louisville, KY
Ciccarelli, Patricia S. ....Buffalo, NY
Ciccarelli, Arthur T. ....Charleston, WV
Ciccarello, Del Giudice & LaFon
Charleston, WV
Ciccarello, Louis S. ....Norwalk, CT
Ciccariello, Daniel J. ....Hull, MA
Ciccarillo, Dennis G. ....New Britain, CT
Ciccarone, John A. ....Wilmington, DE
Ciccarone, Michael J. ....Fort Myers, FL
Cicchelli, Anthony J. ....Frankfort, MI
Cicchetti, Albert A. ....Burlington, VT
Cicchetti, Anthony N. ....Simsbury, CT
Cicchetti, Carl R. ....Waterbury, CT
Cicchetti, Josephine ....Washington, DC
Miami, FL
Cicchetti Law Firm, The ....Tallahassee, FL
Cicchetti, Michael H. ....Waterbury, CT
Cicchetti, Paul W. ....New York, NY
Cicchetti, Richard D. ....Uniontown, PA
Cicchetti & Tansley ....New Haven, CT
Waterbury, CT
Cicchiello, Angelo ....Hartford, CT
Cicchillo, Richard, Jr. ....Atlanta, GA
Cicchino, Anthony T. ....Pittsburgh, PA
Cicchino, John ....Roseland, NJ
Cicci, Raymond J. ....Springfield, IL
Cicci, Stephen A. ....Syracuse, NY
Ciccia, S. Joseph ....Springfield, MA
Ciccio, Jacqueline ....Denver, CO
Cicitto, Joseph A. ....Collegeville, PA
Ciccodicola, Liliana A. ....Southfield, MI
Ciccodicola, Pasquale ....Detroit, MI
Ciccolella, John B. ....Colorado Springs, CO
Ciccolella, John B., P.C., The Law Offices of
Colorado Springs, CO
Ciccolella, M. E. ....Stockton, CA
Ciccolini, Elio ....Akron, OH
Ciccolini, James F. ....Medina, OH
Ciccolini, Michael E. ....Akron, OH
Ciccolini, Thomas A. ....Akron, OH
Ciccolini, Vincent N. ....Akron, OH
Ciccolo, Angela ....Washington, DC
Ciccolo, Kris A. ....Denver, CO
Ciccone, Anthony J., Jr.
Department of Justice, Executive Office for United States Trustees, GV
Ciccone, Cynthia N. ....Allentown, PA
Ciccone, Diane ....New York, NY
Ciccone, Edward L. ....Corpus Christi, TX
Ciccone, F. Emmet ....Havertown, PA
Philadelphia, PA
Ciccone, Gina Marie ....Albany, NY
Ciccone, J. Gary ....Fayetteville, NC
Ciccone, James
Department of Labor, GV
Ciccone, James J. ....Los Angeles, CA
Ciccone, Karen Palladino
Los Angeles, CA
Ciccone, Louis M. ....New York, NY
Ciccone & Pollock ....Havertown, PA
Ciccone and Pollock ....Philadelphia, PA
Ciccone, Richard A. ....Providence, RI
Ciccone, Yolanda ....New Brunswick, NJ
Ciccone-Fiorentino, Maria D.
Gaithersburg, MD
Cicconetti, Frank ....Wooster, OH
Cicconetti, Michael A. ....Painesville, OH
Cicconi, Anthony J. ....Charleston, WV
Cicconi, Chad A. ....Pittsburgh, PA
Cicconi, Christopher M. ....Harrisburg, PA
Cicconi, Drew A. ....Santa Monica, CA
Cicconi, Ernest J. ....Livingston, NJ
Cicconi, James W. ....Washington, DC
Cicconi, Philip C. ....Santa Monica, CA
Cicconi, Ricardo J. ....Uniontown, PA
Cicotelli, Teresa T. ....Malvern, PA
Cicotta, Reno J. ....Philadelphia, PA
Cicerchi, Kent B. ....Cleveland, OH
Cicerelli, Anthony J., (P.C.) ....Denver, CO
Ciceric, Richard S. ....San Diego, CA
Cicero, Anita J. ....Washington, DC
Cicero, David C. ....Birmingham, AL
Cicero, Deborah R. ....Malden, MA
Cicero & France ....Rockford, IL
Cicero, Frank, Jr., (P.C.) ....Chicago, IL
Cicero, Frederick J. ....Malden, MA
Cicero, Jill M. ....Rochester, NY
Cicero, Jill M., & Associates ....Rochester, NY
Cicero, John E., II ....Redmond, WA
Cicero, Joseph B. ....Chicago, IL
Cicero, Joseph R. ....Tacoma, WA
Cicero, Lisa Connor ....Miami Lakes, FL
Cicero, Mathew P. ....Rockford, IL
Cicero, Michael A. ....Atlanta, GA
Cicero, Michael E. ....Cleveland, OH
Cicero, Michael J. ....Washington, DC
Cicero, Paul R. ....Rockford, IL
Cicero, Robert ....New York, NY
Cices, Simon D. ....New York, NY
Cicet, Donald J. ....La Place, LA
Cich, Brian C. ....Canton, OH
Cich, Frank A. ....Akron, OH
Cich, Joel A. ....Mankato, MN
Cichanowicz, Callan, Keane, Vengrow & Textor, LLP ....New York, NY
Cichanowicz, Lawrence V. ....New York, NY
Cichelero, John M. ....St. Louis, MO
Cichello, Anthony J. ....Boston, MA
Cichetti, Kevin P.
Executive Office Of The President, Office of National Drug Control Policy, GV
Cichocki, Bruce M. ....Parma, OH
Cichocki, Charles F. ....Twinsburg, OH
Cichocki, Robert T. ....Chicago, IL
Cichon, Dennis E. ....Lansing, MI
Cichon, Gary J. ....Hillside, IL
Cichon, Pamela D. ....St. Petersburg, FL

Cichon, Scott W. ... **Daytona Beach, FL**
Cichon, Steven E. ... Sarasota, FL
Cichorski, Arthur F. ... **Chicago, IL**
Cichoski, Mark D. ... Las Vegas, NV
Cichowski, Carol A. ... Washington, DC
Cichowski, Curtis W. ... Valparaiso, IN
Cichowski, M. Michael ... Port Arthur, TX
Cichowski, M. Steve ... **San Antonio, TX**
Cichy, Joseph J. ... Bismarck, ND
Cichy, Marvin J. ... El Monte, CA
Cicileo, Joseph N. ... Hillsdale, NY
Cicilline, David N. ... Providence, RI
Cicilline, John F. ... Providence, RI
Cicilline, Stephen E. ... Providence, RI
Cicinelli, Peter F. ... East Tawas, MI
Cicio, Anthony L. ... Birmingham, AL
Cicio, Anthony L., Jr. ... Birmingham, AL
Cicio & Cicio, P.C. ... Birmingham, AL
Cicione, Douglas D. ... **Irvine, CA**
Manhattan Beach, CA
Cicione, Douglas D., A Professional Corporation ... **Irvine, CA**
Manhattan Beach, CA
Cicione, Giovanni Daniel ... Providence, RI
Cicirelli, Sandra A. Ference ... Westland, MI
Cicka, Markus P. ... **St. Louis, MO**
Ciclet, Donna R. ... **Cincinnati, OH**
Cicone, Frank E. ... Lutherville, MD
Cicone, Frank J. ... Bakersfield, CA
Cicone, Frank J., Law Corporation
Bakersfield, CA
Cicone, Vincent P. ... Los Angeles, CA
Ciconte, Edward T. ... **Wilmington, DE**
Ciconte, Roseman & Wasserman
Wilmington, DE
Cicoria, Eva A. ... Pasadena, CA
Cicoria, Ronald A. ... Geneseo, NY
Cicotte, George F. ... Denver, CO
Washington, DC
Cicotte, Roy B. ... Lincoln Park, MI
Cicurel, Mitchell J. ... Southfield, MI
Ciechanover, Joseph ... New York, NY
Ciechanowski, Craig A. ... **Franklin, MA**
Ciechanowski, Thomas J. ... Chicago, IL
Ciechon, Edward J., Jr. ... **Philadelphia, PA**
Ciecimirski, L.S. John ... **New York, NY**
Ciecka, Vincent J. ... Pennsauken, NJ
Ciecko, Thomas L. ... Oak Brook, IL
Ciejka, Gerald P. ... Springfield, MA
Cielak, Marianne H. ... **Chicago, IL**
Cielinski, Michael P. ... **Columbus, GA**
Cielo, Neda N. Dal ... **San Jose, CA**
Ciembroniewicz, Julius ... Augusta, ME
Ciemniecki, Edward L. ... **Haddonfield, NJ**
Philadelphia, PA
Cienava, AnnMarie ... **Middletown, CT**
Cienava, Edmund J. ... **Stamford, CT**
Ciener, Daniel S. ... Merritt Island, FL
Cieniawski, Brian E. ... **Phoenix, AZ**
Cieply, Kevin Michael
Department of the Army, U.S. Army Legal Services Agency, GV
Cier, Ronald J. ... **Fairfax, VA**
Cieri, Dennis Victor ... Carlstadt, NJ
Cieri, George J. ... Long Branch, NJ
Cieri, Richard M. ... **Cleveland, OH**
Ciervo, George A. ... Willingboro, NJ
Ciervo, John J. ... Schenectady, NY
Ciervo & Strozyk-Ciervo ... Willingboro, NJ
Cierzniak, Elizabeth Kelley
Indianapolis, IN
Ciesar, William W., Jr. ... Whiting, IN
Ciesiel, Ronald W. ... Little Rock, AR
Ciesielski, Alexander K. ... McLean, VA
Ciesielski, Robert M. ... Cheektowaga, NY
Ciesinski, Kim Marie ... Melville, NY
Ciesla, Felicia A. ... Baltimore, MD
Ciesla, Frank R. ... **Middletown, NJ**
Ciesla, Kathryn L. ... Evanston, IL
Ciesla, Larry E., Law Office of
Gainesville, FL
Ciesla, M. Frances ... **Newark, NJ**
Ciesla, Robert S. ... Kew Gardens, NY
Cieslak, James L. ... Parma, OH
Cieslak, Jon C. ... Apple Valley, MN
Cieslak, Lee J. ... Clearwater, FL
Cieslewicz, Mark M. ... Camden, NJ
Cieslewicz, Michael J. ... **Milwaukee, WI**
Cieslik, Karlene L. ... Niagara Falls, NY
Cieslik, Paul J. ... **Buffalo, NY**
Cieslik, Robert ... Dearborn Heights, MI
Cieslik, Vincent T. ... **Haddonfield, NJ**
Cieszeski, Charles H. ... Fulton, NY
Cieutat, Becky R. ... **Chalmette, LA**
Cifaldi, Angelo J. ... **Woodbridge, NJ**
New York, NY
Cifarelli Law Firm, The ... **Santa Ana, CA**
Cifarelli, Philip C. ... Santa Ana, CA
Cifarelli, Philip S. ... **Santa Ana, CA**
Cifarelli, Thomas A. ... Santa Ana, CA
Cifelli, Albert J. ... Harrison, NJ
Cifelli, Alfonse J. ... Totowa, NJ
Cifelli, Angelo, Jr. ... Nutley, NJ
Cifelli, Armand ... Southport, CT
Cifelli, August G. ... **Seattle, WA**
Cifelli, David J. ... Chicago Heights, IL
Cifelli & Davie ... Harrison, NJ
Cifelli, James Craig ... **Atlanta, GA**
Cifelli, John L. ... Chicago Heights, IL
Cifelli, Michael A. ... **Springfield, NJ**
Cifelli, Thomas H. ... Gillette, NJ
Cifelli, Thomas, Jr. ... Short Hills, NJ
Ciferni, Leon P. ... Jersey City, NJ
Cifone, Nancy ... Hempstead, NY
Cifrese, Scott C. ... **Coeur d'Alene, ID**
Spokane, WA
Cifrino, David A. ... **Boston, MA**

Cifrino, Michael J. ... Department of Defense, Defense Legal Services Agency, GV
Cifu, Douglas A. ... **New York, NY**
Cifuentes de Castro, Alvaro
Washington, DC
Cigan, Joseph ... Wilkes-Barre, PA
Ciganek, Carrie A. ... New City, NY
Ciganek, Thomas A. ... Tappan, NY
Cigarroa, Maria-Elena ... Austin, TX
Cigarroa Dellano, Martha ... **Laredo, TX**
Cige, Brian M. ... Somerville, NJ
Cigel, Rick A. ... **Los Angeles, CA**
Cigelnik, Patricia A. ... Chicago, IL
Cigelnik, Randi Lyn ... Chicago, IL
Cigelske, Bryan N. ... **Mobile, AL**
Cigoy, Penny L. ... Phoenix, AZ
Cihak, Don W. ... Tucumcari, NM
Cihak, Jerome E. ... Chicago, IL
Cihak, Kelly Daly ... St. Petersburg, FL
La Grange, IL
Cihak, Kristin L. ... **Sacramento, CA**
Cihak, Raymond M. ... Corvallis, OR
Cihal, Stephen A. ... Victoria, TX
Cihan, Beverly J. ... **Tysons Corner, VA**
Cihigoyenetche, Grossberg & Clouse
Ontario, CA
Cihigoyenetche, Jean ... Ontario, CA
Cihlar, Frank P. ... Department of Justice, Tax Division, GV
Cihon, Christopher M. ... **Washington, DC**
Cihon, Jennifer L. ... Cleveland, OH
Cikanek, Terry L. ... Stockton, KS
Ciklin, Alan J., (P.A.)
West Palm Beach, FL
Ciklin, Cory J. ... West Palm Beach, FL
Ciko, Christopher N. ... Pittsburgh, PA
Ciko, Eva M. ... **New York, NY**
Ciko, John, Jr. ... Pittsburgh, PA
Cikut, Barbara B. ... **Houston, TX**
Cikut, John J. ... Houston, TX
Cil, Jose E. ... **Miami, FL**
Cil, Marta M. ... **Miami, FL**
Cilea, Anthony J. ... **Boston, MA**
Cilek, Thomas J. ... Hills, IA
Cilenti, Maria ... **New York, NY**
Cilenti, Sheryl Bernstein ... Lyndhurst, NJ
Cilenti, Steven ... **Jackson, CA**
Cilfone, Charlie J. ... **Harlingen, TX**
Cilfone, Patricia L. ... Chicago, IL
Ciliberti, Judi B. ... Prospect, KY
Cilingin, William G. ... **Philadelphia, PA**
Cilke, Kimberly J. ... **Phoenix, AZ**
Cilley, Arthur B. ... Irving, TX
Cilley, Bernice H. ... **Richmond, VA**
Cilley, James P. ... **Campbell, CA**
Cilley, John H., IV ... **Newton, NC**
Cilley, Robert S. ... Brevard, NC
Cilli, Gabriel P. ... New Castle, PA
Cilli, Gregory S. ... Julian, CA
Cillick, Edward W. ... Hackensack, NJ
Cillick, Martin P. ... Bloomington, IL
Cillick & Sprague ... Hackensack, NJ
Cillo, Anthony ... **Pittsburgh, PA**
Cillo, Daniel P. ... **Pittsburgh, PA**
Cillo, Michael P. ... **Denver, CO**
Cilluffo, Anthony F. ... Smithtown, NY
Cilluffo, Joseph A. ... **New York, NY**
Cilluffo, William A. ... Farmington Hills, MI
Cilmi & Associates PLLC ... Westfield, NJ
New York, NY
Staten Island, NY
Cilmi, John M. ... Westfield, NJ
New York, NY
Staten Island, NY
Cilo, Leah-Beth ... **Philadelphia, PA**
Cilo, Stuart A. ... Lewistown, PA
Cilz, Douglas A. ... Grand Forks, ND
Cima, Kathryn J. ... **Minneapolis, MN**
Cima, Lyn ... Waukegan, IL
Cima, Ronald P. ... **New York, NY**
Cimbal, Marc A. ... Yonkers, NY
Cimbala, Michele A. ... **Washington, DC**
Cimbalo, Janice L. ... Los Angeles, CA
Cimbalo, Jeffrey L. ... New York, NY
Cimbaluk, John ... San Bernardino, CA
Cimbaluk, Julian ... Santa Ana, CA
Ciment, Ivan S. ... **New York, NY**
Ciment, Melvyn ... Silver Spring, MD
Ciment, Norman ... Miami Beach, FL
Cimerman, Adrian P. ... Toledo, OH
Cimicata, Thomas J. ... Dumont, NJ
Cimildora, H. Fred, Jr. ... **Towson, MD**
Cimiluca, Andrew M. ... Clifton, NJ
Cimiluca & Frank ... Clifton, NJ
Ciminelli, Daniel ... Buffalo, NY
Ciminelli, James A. ... Buffalo, NY
Ciminelli, Michael L. ... Washington, DC
Ciminelli, Paul V. ... Rochester, NY
Ciminesi, David J. ... **New York, NY**
Cimini, Albert J. ... Pittsfield, MA
Cimini, Christine N. ... Hillsboro, OR
Cimini, Eugene P., Jr. ... **Jericho, NY**
Cimini, Frank W. ... Pittsfield, MA
Cimini, Joseph F. ... Scranton, PA
Cimini, Louis A. ... Scranton, PA
Cimini, Sally Griffith ... **Pittsburgh, PA**
Cimini, Vincent S. ... **Scranton, PA**
Cimino, Andrew S., Jr. ... Springfield, NJ
Cimino, Audrey S. ... Westminster, MD
Cimino, Diana S. ... **Lake Forest, CA**
Cimino, Elizabeth S. ... **Charleston, WV**
Cimino, Frank C., Jr. ... **Washington, DC**
Cimino, Frank J. ... Ravenna, OH
Cimino, Gregory P., II ... **Providence, RI**
Cimino, John A. ... Colorado Springs, CO
Denver, CO
Cimino, John A., P.C. ... Colorado Springs, CO
Denver, CO

Cimino, Margaret M. ... New York, NY
Cimino, Michael T. ... **Charleston, WV**
Cimino, Paul M. ... **Boston, MA**
Cimino, Peter ... **New York, NY**
Cimino, Richard D. ... Naples, FL
Cimino, Robert J. ... Hauppauge, NY
Cimino, Robt. R. ... San Jose, CA
Cimino, Ronald A. ... Department of Justice, Tax Division, GV
Cimino, Stephen Lance ... Syracuse, NY
Cimino, Thomas P., Jr. ... **Chicago, IL**
Cimko, John, Jr. ... **Washington, DC**
Cimkowski, Carol A. ... Tavernier, FL
New York, NY
Cimmet, Jerry K. ... San Francisco, CA
Cimmet, Sidney L.
Securities and Exchange Commission, Division of Investment Management, GV
Cimmino, Kelli A. ... **Coshocton, OH**
Cimmino, Nicholas J. ... New Haven, CT
Cimo, Craig J. ... Gretna, LA
Cimo, David C. ... **Miami, FL**
Cimokowski, Edwin W. ... Hyattsville, MD
Cimons, Wayne A. ... New York, NY
Cimorell, Bret J. ... Ashtabula, OH
Cimperman, Anthony J. ... Westerville, OH
Cimpl, Dennis R. ... Milwaukee, WI
Cimpl, Richard F. ... Milwaukee, WI
Cin, Bennett D. ... Chicago, IL
Cin, Elliott M. ... Houston, TX
Cin & Wagner ... Chicago, IL
Cina, Anne ... La Crosse, WI
Cinabro, Robert H. ... Kalamazoo, MI
Cinaglia, Leonard A. ... Collingswood, NJ
Cinamon, Aliza R. ... **New York, NY**
Cinamon, Jay S. ... **New York, NY**
Cinamon, Samuel B. ... Perkasie, PA
Cinardo, Claudia L. ... New York, NY
Cincione, Alphonse P. ... Columbus, OH
Cincione, Karen A. ... Columbus, OH
Cincione, Matthew P. ... Columbus, OH
Cinciotta, Linda A. ... Department of Justice, Office of Attorney Personnel Management, GV
Cinclair, J. Praba ... Dallas, TX
Cinclair, Richard J., Jr. ... **Dallas, TX**
Cincone, Gia L. ... **Emeryville, CA**
Cincore, Lydia V. ... Los Angeles, CA
Cincotta, Anthony J. ... Morristown, NJ
Cincotta, Anthony J. ... Woodbury, NY
Cincotta, Antone G., Jr. ... Novato, CA
Cincotta, Barbara J. ... Framingham, MA
Cincotta, David P. ... **San Francisco, CA**
Cincotta, Dominick A. ... Ridgewood, NY
Cincotta, Felix E. ... Waltham, MA
Cincotta, Joseph M. ... **Haddonfield, NJ**
Philadelphia, PA
Cincotta, Joseph R. ... Milwaukee, WI
Cindea, Nicholas M. ... Roselle Park, NJ
Cindric, David T. ... **Houston, TX**
Cindrich, Ralph E. ... Pittsburgh, PA
Cindrich, Robert J. ... Pittsburgh, PA
Cinelli, Giovanna M. ... **McLean, VA**
Cinelli, Jean M. ... Bedford Hills, NY
Cinelli, Ronald M. ... Buffalo, NY
Cingolani, Armand R., Jr. ... Butler, PA
Cini, Dale A. ... Charleston, IL
Cinnamon, Casterton & Hagedorn
Sacramento, CA
Cinnamon, Christopher C. ... **Chicago, IL**
Cinnamon, Gregory K. ... **Atlanta, GA**
Cinnamon, John B. ... Sacramento, CA
Cinnamon, John B., Inc., A Law Corporation
Sacramento, CA
Cinnamon, Michael M. ... Sacramento, CA
Cinnamon, Michael S. ... **Gold River, CA**
Cinnamon, Michael S. ... **Sacramento, CA**
Cinnamon, Scott C. ... **Washington, DC**
Cinnamond, Clyde A. ... Cleveland, OH
Cinnamond, Teresa M. ... **New York, NY**
Cinnamond, Thomas E. ... **Baltimore, MD**
Cinnater, C. Bradley ... Houma, LA
Cinniger, Ronald E. ... Portland, OR
Cinniger, Ruth M. ... Portland, OR
Cino, Charles J. ... Ormond Beach, FL
Cino, Richard J. ... **Westfield, NJ**
Cino, Vincent A. ... **Morristown, NJ**
Cinocca, Hillary E. ... **Tulsa, OK**
Cinocca, Holly Ann ... Tulsa, OK
Cinocca, James Edward, Jr. ... **Tulsa, OK**
Cinocca, Jonathan M. ... **Tulsa, OK**
Cinocca, Tracy A. ... **Oklahoma City, OK**
Cinotti, Carol A. ... **Radnor, PA**
Cinotto, James V. ... Springfield, IL
Cinpinski, Robert A. ... Kittanning, PA
Cinq-Mars, Eli G. ... Keene, NH
Cinque & Cinque, P.C. ... New York, NY
Cinque, James P. ... New York, NY
Cinque, John F. ... **Princeton, NJ**
New York, NY
Cinque, Katherine L. ... **Houston, TX**
Cinque, Marie ... Secaucus, NJ
Cinque, Robert W. ... New York, NY
Cinquegrana, Ralph J. ... **Boston, MA**
Cinquegrani, Peter J. ... **Washington, DC**
Cinquemani, Leo S. ... Astoria, NY
Cinquemani, Rosemary A. ... **Mineola, NY**
Cinquina, Frank R. ... **Montclair, NJ**
Cinquino, Celeste P. ... **Chicago, IL**
Cinquino, Leo N. ... **Chicago, IL**
Cinti, John M. ... **Trenton, NJ**
Cinti, Thomas A. ... Haddonfield, NJ
Cintolo, William J. ... **Boston, MA**
Cintron, Ivan ... Dallas, TX
Cintron, Lisa ... **New York, NY**
Cintron, Michael A. ... New York, NY
Cintron, Robert, Jr. ... **Tallahassee, FL**

Cintron-Silva, Maria I.
Environmental Protection Agency, Office of Enforcement and Compliance Assurance, GV
Cintz, Benjamin ... Palo Alto, CA
San Francisco, CA
Ciocca, Alexander J., III ... Pittsburgh, PA
Ciocca, Henry G. ... Stamford, CT
Ciocca, Stephan C. ... Pittsburgh, PA
Ciocco, Mary Beth ... Rocky River, OH
Ciocco, Scott J. ... **Cherry Hill, NJ**
Cioce, Joseph ... Belle Mead, NJ
Ciochina & Lorey ... Clearwater, FL
Ciochina, Michael E. ... Clearwater, FL
Ciochon, Carl D. ... **San Francisco, CA**
Cioci, Geralo S. ... East Brunswick, NJ
Ciociola, Gabriel Daniel Martin
Boston, MA
Ciociola, Robert L. ... **Manchester, CT**
Somerville, MA
Cioffero, Erica G. ... Central Islip, NY
Cioffi, Andrew P. ... Raleigh, NC
Cioffi, Antonio R. ... Cherry Hill, NJ
Cioffi, Cristine ... Niskayuna, NY
Cioffi, Eric R. ... **Manchester, NH**
Cioffi, Greg B. ... **New York, NY**
Cioffi, Gregory J. ... Branford, CT
Cioffi, James A. ... **Tequesta, FL**
Cioffi, John J. ... Scarsdale, NY
Cioffi, Joseph ... **New York, NY**
Cioffi, Michael A. ... Boston, MA
Cioffi, Michael L. ... **Cincinnati, OH**
Cioffi, Nicholas A. ... Hartford, CT
Cioffi, Thomas R. ... Troy, NY
Ciol, John ... Everett, MA
Ciolek, Douglas F. ... **Hackensack, NJ**
Ciolek, Robert C. ... **Florham Park, NJ**
Ciolek, Robert J. ... Charlestown, MA
Ciolfi, Mary Lou ... Brunswick, ME
Ciolino, Barbara ... Altadena, CA
Ciolino, Dane S. ... New Orleans, LA
Ciolino, Lisa E. ... **New Orleans, LA**
Ciolino, Peter ... **Hackensack, NJ**
Ciolino, Wendy D. ... New Orleans, LA
Ciolli, David E. ... West Chicago, IL
Ciombor, Roderick C. ... Chicago, IL
Ciompi, N. A. ... Durham, NC
Cion, Judith A. ... New Orleans, LA
Cion, Richard M. ... Fairfield, CT
Cione, Anthony L. ... **Los Angeles, CA**
Cione, Denise L. ... Hauppauge, NY
Cione, John P. ... **Basking Ridge, NJ**
Ciongoli, Adam G. ... Washington, DC
Ciorciari, John D. ... **New York, NY**
Ciordia, Angel M. ... Vega Baja, PR
Ciota, Andrea L. ... **Bethesda, MD**
Ciota, Jos. G. ... Lynn, MA
Ciota, Michael J. ... **Fitchburg, MA**
Ciota, Starr & Vander Linden, LLP
Fitchburg, MA
Worcester, MA
Cioth, Marie A. ... **Cerritos, CA**
Ciotola, Anthony J. ... Conyngham, PA
Hazleton, PA
Ciotola, Joseph A. ... Baltimore, MD
Ciotola, Robert Ascenzo, Co., L.P.A.
Youngstown, OH
Ciotola, Robert Ascenzo, (Co., L.P.A.)
Youngstown, OH
Ciotoli, Eugene L. ... **North Palm Beach, FL**
Ciotti, Christine C. ... **Cambridge, MA**
Ciotti, Glenn ... Boston, MA
Ciotti, Jane S. ... Malvern, PA
Ciotti, Karan C. ... **Houston, TX**
Ciotti, Lisa M. ... Reading, PA
Ciotti, Martin J. ... **Chicago, IL**
Ciotti, Robert L. ... **Tampa, FL**
Ciotti, Ronald D. ... **Manchester, NH**
Ciotti, Thomas E. ... **Palo Alto, CA**
Ciottone, Richard T. ... **Jefferson City, MO**
Ciovacco, Robert J. ... **East Meadow, NY**
Ciparick, Carmen Beauchamp, (Ms.)
New York, NY
Cipes, Andrew P. ... **Los Angeles, CA**
Cipinko, Sanford M. ... San Francisco, CA
Cipinko, Scott J. ... Rosemont, IL
Cipiti, Anthony, Jr. ... **Washington, DC**
Cipiti, Nicholas A. ... **Orange, CA**
Cipoletta, James J. ... Revere, MA
Cipoletti, Christopher
Colorado Springs, CO
Cipolla, Carl J. ... Chicago, IL
Cipolla, Charles ... Jamaica, NY
Cipolla, Charles W. ... Englewood Cliffs, NJ
Cipolla, James M. ... **Fresno, CA**
Cipolla, John S. ... **Cleveland, OH**
Cipolla, Jos. S. ... Quincy, MA
Cipolla, Loretta ... **Los Angeles, CA**
Cipolla, Otto P., Jr. ... Agoura Hills, CA
Cipolla, Patrick W. ... **Tulsa, OK**
Cipolla, Richard J., Jr. ... **Tulsa, OK**
Cipolla, Robert M. ... **Richmond, VA**
Cipolla, Stephen J. ... **West Point, PA**
Cipolla, Thomas A. ... St. Louis, MO
Cipolla, Toni D. ... Kansas City, MO
Cipolla, Vincent C. ... Arlington Heights, IL
Cipollone, Anthony D. ... **Hackensack, NJ**
Cipollone, Diane Welling ... Severna Park, MD
Cipollone, Pat A. ... **New Haven, CT**
Cipollone, Thomas J. ... Dearborn, MI
Cipparone, Joseph A. ... **New London, CT**
Cipparone, Rocco C., Jr.
Haddon Heights, NJ
Cipparulo, Peter, III ... Morristown, NJ
Cipperman, Todd B. ... Oaks, PA
Cipponeri, Terri L. ... **Modesto, CA**
Cipra, Richard R. ... **Beverly Hills, CA**
Cipressi, June C. ... Philadelphia, PA

Ciprian, John H., Jr. ... Chicago, IL
Ciprian, Muriel ... New York, NY
Cipriani, Anthony ... Boston, MA
Cipriani, Cindy M. ... San Diego, CA
Cipriani, Eugene N. ... Philadelphia, PA
Cipriani, Gerard J. ... Pittsburgh, PA
Cipriani, Karen L. ... Washington, DC
Cipriani, Linda M. ... Del Mar, CA
Cipriani, Nicholas A. ... Philadelphia, PA
Cipriani, Patricia M. ... Buffalo, NY
Cipriani & Paull, L.C. ... Wellsburg, WV
Cipriani, Ralph A. ... Suffern, NY
Cipriani, Terry ... Islandia, NY
Cipriani and Werner, P.C.
Harrisburg, PA
Lemoyne, PA
Pittsburgh, PA
Cipriani, William ... Wellsburg, WV
Cipriano, Aldo ... Marlborough, MA
Cipriano, Anthony P., Jr. ... Cheshire, CT
Cipriano, Anthony W. ... St. Louis, MO
Cipriano & Brown, P.C.
Rockville Centre, NY
Cipriano, Dennis A. ... West Orange, NJ
Cipriano & Donadio, P.C. ... Montclair, NJ
Cipriano, Douglas A. ... Chicago, IL
Cipriano, Edwinna G. ... Austin, TX
Cipriano, Francis P. ... Hamden, CT
Cipriano, Frank J. ... Rockville Centre, NY
Cipriano, Gayle ... Austin, TX
Cipriano, Gene R., Jr. ... Fort Myers, FL
Cipriano, Gene R., Jr., P.A. ... Fort Myers, FL
Cipriano, Gregory J. ... Montclair, NJ
Cipriano, John E. ... Mount Prospect, IL
Cipriano, John L., Jr. ... Hamden, CT
Cipriano, Lisa M. ... Chicago, IL
Cipriano, Renee ... Chicago, IL
Cipriano, Robert F. ... Burbank, CA
Cipriano-Marciano, E. Gioia
West Orange, NJ
Ciprich, Paula M. ... Buffalo, NY
Cipriettì, Philip T. ... Marlton, NJ
Cira, Carl A., Jr.
Agency for International Development, Other Offices of A.I.D., GV
Cirabisi, Leonard F. ... Malverne, NY
Cirac, Michael E. ... Reno, NV
Cirafesi, Robert J. ... Woodbridge, NJ
Cirafici, Joseph F. ... Princeton Junction, NJ
Ciraldo, John A. ... Portland, ME
Cirame, John D. ... Boston, MA
Cirando, D. J. & J. A. ... Syracuse, NY
Cirando, John A. ... Syracuse, NY
Cirangle, Ellen A. ... Denver, CO
Ciranni, Eugene H. ... San Francisco, CA
Ciraolo, Caroline DeLisle ... Baltimore, MD
Cirasuolo, Anne T. ... Miami, FL
Ciravolo, Benedict G. ... Morristown, NJ
Ciravolo & Ciravolo ... Morristown, NJ
Newark, NJ
Ciravolo, Kate Lommel ... Morristown, NJ
Ciravolo, Rick G. ... Fort Lauderdale, FL
Cirba, Ronald E. ... Reading, PA
Cirba, Sapira & Nice, P.C. ... Reading, PA
Circeo, Lisa E. ... Memphis, TN
Circeo, Richard E. ... Memphis, TN
Circio, Julie ... Charlotte, NC
Circle, Brent L. ... New Castle, PA
Circo, Carl J. ... Leawood, KS
Circuit, McKellogg, Kinney & Ross LLP
La Jolla, CA
San Diego, CA
Circuit, Richard K. ... La Jolla, CA
Cire, George E. (Buck), Jr. ... Houston, TX
Cirel, Paul R. ... Boston, MA
Cirella, Phillip M. ... Cedar Grove, NJ
Cirelli, Cory John ... Pittsburgh, PA
Cirelli, Dominick, Jr. ... Newark, NJ
Cirelli, Lawrence M. ... San Francisco, CA
Cirelli, Monique K. ... Detroit, MI
Cirenza, Bartholomew
Department of Justice, Tax Division, GV
Cires, Adriana S. ... New York, NY
Ciresi, Helen S. ... West Haven, CT
Ciresi, Jerome D. ... St. Paul, MN
Ciresi & Mass ... West Haven, CT
Ciresi, Michael V. ... Minneapolis, MN
Ciresi, Robert S. ... North Providence, RI
Ciriaco, Anthony C. ... Columbus, OH
Ciriano, Daniella Caputo ... Staten Island, NY
Ciriano, Joy Ammons ... Graham, NC
Ciriello, Leonard P. ... New York, NY
Ciriello, Nicholas G. ... Los Angeles, CA
Cirigliano, Caesar D. ... Brooklyn, NY
Cirigliano, Joseph E. ... Milwaukee, WI
Cirignani, Mario F. ... Chicago, IL
Cirignani, Thomas R. ... Chicago, IL
Cirignani, Thomas R., & Associates
Chicago, IL
Cirignani, William A. ... Chicago, IL
Cirilano, James ... McKees Rocks, PA
Cirilano, Joseph J. ... Pittsburgh, PA
Cirilli, Gary S. ... Rhinelander, WI
Cirilli, Gondik, Moldenhauer & Zuber
Superior, WI
Cirilli, James L. ... Superior, WI
Cirilli, John M. ... Rhinelander, WI
Cirilli Law Offices, S.C. ... Rhinelander, WI
Cirilli, Robert Richard, Jr. ... Jackson, MS
Cirilli, Scott A. ... Rhinelander, WI
Cirillo, Frank L. ... New Haven, CT
Cirillo, Gregory F. ... Philadelphia, PA
Cirillo, Gregory P. ... Washington, DC
Cirillo, Henry A. ... San Francisco, CA
Cirillo, James F., Jr. ... New Haven, CT
Cirillo, Joan E. ... Boston, MA
Cirillo, Marianne Christopher ... Darien, CT
Cirillo, Patricia N. ... New York, NY
Cirillo, Richard A. ... New York, NY
Cirillo, Stephen J. ... Trenton, NJ
Cirillo, Vincent A. ... Bala Cynwyd, PA
Cirillo, Vincent A., Jr. ... Norristown, PA
Cirincion, John C. ... New York, NY
Cirincion, Regina M. ... Baltimore, MD
Cirincione, Martin J. ... Albany, NY
Cirincione, Richard D. ... Albany, NY
Cirincione-Vanzant, Lisa ... Denver, CO
Cirino, Gloria A. ... Corona, NY
Cirino, Nicholas A. ... Detroit, MI
Cirino, Paul ... New York, NY
Cirisan, Kenneth P. ... San Luis Obispo, CA
Cirisano, Daria M. ... Durham, NC
Cirkal, Thomas E. ... Denver, CO
Cirkiel & Associates, P.C.
Round Rock, TX
Cirkiel, Martin J. ... Round Rock, TX
Cirlin, Vincent J. ... Livingston, NJ
Cirome, Alfred J. ... Haverhill, MA
Cirome & Harb ... Haverhill, MA
Cirone, Albert J., Jr. ... Lebanon, NH
Cirone, Albert J., Jr., P.C. ... Lebanon, NH
Cirone, Thomas J. ... New York, NY
Cirricione, John F. ... Joliet, IL
Cirrilla, Louis John ... Hackensack, NJ
Cirrincione, James F. ... Bronx, NY
Cirrincione, Kathleen K. ... Chicago, IL
Cirrito, Mary Ellen ... Hempstead, NY
Cirrito, Michael L. ... Hempstead, NY
Cirullo, Michael D., Jr.
Fort Lauderdale, FL
Cirulnick, Arthur E. ... Washington, DC
Cisa, Frank M. ... Mount Pleasant, SC
Cisan, Heidi M. ... Chardon, OH
Cisar, David I. ... Milwaukee, WI
Cisar, Elizabeth J. ... Chicago, IL
Cisar, Thomas J. ... Oak Brook, IL
Cisar, Timothy R. ... Jefferson City, MO
Lake Ozark, MO
Cisarik, Michael J. ... Culver City, CA
Cischke, Gino A. ... Dallas, TX
Cischke, Steven M. ... Torrance, CA
Cisco, Ann M. ... Cedar Rapids, IA
Cisco, Raymond P. ... Oak Brook, IL
Cisek, Donald J. ... Kansas City, MO
Cisel & Kopp ... Windsor, MO
Cisler, Timothy A. ... Green Bay, WI
Cislo, Daniel M. ... Santa Monica, CA
Cislo, Donald M. ... Santa Monica, CA
Cislo & Thomas LLP ... Los Angeles, CA
Santa Monica, CA
Cisne, Jenny L. ... Jacksonville, FL
Cisneros, Arturo ... McAllen, TX
Cisneros, Arturo M. ... Irvine, CA
Riverside, CA
Cisneros, Cisneros & Cisneros, Law Offices of ... McAllen, TX
Cisneros, David C. ... Denver, CO
Cisneros, Edna E. ... Raymondville, TX
Cisneros, Ernesto L. ... El Paso, TX
Cisneros, Hector J. ... Chula Vista, CA
Cisneros, Joe A. ... McAllen, TX
Cisneros, Johnny E. ... San Antonio, TX
Cisneros, Jude A. ... Albuquerque, NM
Cisneros, Mario E. ... San Antonio, TX
Cisneros, Mario H. ... Detroit, MI
Cisneros, Mary Elizabeth C.
New York, NY
Cisneros, Michael A. ... Glendale, CA
Cisneros, Michael J. ... McAllen, TX
Cisneros, Norberto J., Law Office of
San Diego, CA
Cisneros, Pedro L. ... Austin, TX
Fort Worth, TX
Houston, TX
Cisneros, Ramiro P. ... Los Angeles, CA
Cisneros, Roger ... Denver, CO
Cisneros, Teresa ... Los Angeles, CA
Cisneros, Theresa M. ... Colorado Springs, CO
Cisney & Cisney ... Greenville, KY
Cisney, L. Wayne, Jr. ... Greenville, KY
Cisney, Lucien T. ... Greenville, KY
Cissel, Robert F. ... Department of Commerce, Patent and Trademark Office, GV
Cissell, Clarissa M. ... Memphis, TN
Cissell, James C. ... Cincinnati, OH
Cissik, Pamela J. ... Morristown, NJ
Cissna, Bruce E. ... Dale, IN
Cissna, L. Francis ... Washington, DC
Cissna, Robert L. ... Los Angeles, CA
Cissna, Timothy P. ... Eureka, CA
Cisternino, Andrew L. ... Lake Success, NY
Cisternino, Denise Laura ... New York, NY
Cistrelli, Henry J. ... Elizabeth, NJ
Newark, NJ
Cistrelli, Lawrence ... Indianapolis, IN
Cistulli, Joseph P. ... Danbury, CT
Cisz, Louis J., III ... San Francisco, CA
Ciszak, George ... Trenton, NJ
Ciszczon, William J. ... Westlake, OH
Ciszek, Judith Karns ... Greensburg, PA
Ciszewski, Steven J. ... Chicago, IL
Citak, Burton ... New York, NY
Citak & Citak ... New York, NY
Citak, Daniel F. ... Titusville, FL
Citak, Donald L. ... New York, NY
Citardi, Paul T. ... Boston, MA
Citek, Scott T. ... Houston, TX
Citera, Francis A. ... Chicago, IL
Citera, Gerard S. ... New York, NY
Citera, Kathleen M. ... New York, NY
Citera, Michael G. ... Chicago, IL
Citera, Toni-Ann ... Chicago, IL
Citko, Christopher A. ... Sacramento, CA
Citkowski, Ronald W. ... Birmingham, MI
Citrano, Frank J., Jr. ... New York, NY
Citren, Michael D. ... Silver Spring, MD
Citrin, Andrew T. ... Daphne, AL
Citrin, Andrew T., P.C. ... Daphne, AL
Citrin, Caryn B. ... Suffern, NY
Citrin, Charles A. ... Miami Beach, FL
Citrin, David A. ... Marietta, GA
Citrin, David A., P.C. ... Marietta, GA
Citrin, Ilene Fisher
Securities and Exchange Commission, Office of the General Counsel, GV
Citrin, Josephine L. ... Thomasville, NC
Citrin, Josephine L., P.A. ... Thomasville, NC
Citrin, Marc D. ... Suffern, NY
Citrin, Marc J. ... Lake Success, NY
Citrin, Mark ... Miami, FL
Citrin, Nathan J., (P.C.) ... Atlanta, GA
Citrin, Phillip M. ... Santa Fe, NM
Citrin, Robert M. ... Southfield, MI
Citrin, Toby ... Ann Arbor, MI
Citrin, Yale ... Scarsdale, NY
Citrino, Diane E. ... Cleveland, OH
Citrino, Harry C., Jr. ... Philadelphia, PA
Citrino, Vicki A. ... Livingston, NJ
Citro, Lawrence F. ... Fairfield, NJ
Citro, Marvin H. ... Northbrook, IL
Citron & Alex PC ... Pittsburgh, PA
Citron, Andrew ... New York, NY
Citron, Beatrice S. ... Miami, FL
Citron, Bernard I. ... Chicago, IL
Citron, Bill E. ... Bloomfield Hills, MI
Citron, Brad D. ... Los Angeles, CA
Citron, Carl D. ... Pittsburgh, PA
Citron, Christiane Hyde ... Denver, CO
Citron & Deutsch, A Law Corporation
Los Angeles, CA
Citron, Diane ... New York, NY
Citron, Jeffrey I. ... New York, NY
Citron, Jeremy Emanuel ... Atlanta, GA
Citron, Jerome D. ... Chicago, IL
Citron, Jill S. ... New York, NY
Citron, Joel F. ... Santa Monica, CA
Citron, Joseph ... Atlanta, GA
Citron, Kenneth E. ... Boston, MA
Citron, Lowell A. ... New York, NY
Citron, Marc A. ... Princeton, NJ
New York, NY
Citron, Nadine G. ... Long Beach, NY
Citron, Richard K. ... Los Angeles, CA
Citron, Rodger D. ... Department of Justice, Civil Division, GV
Citron, Stacey J. ... Old Bridge, NJ
Citron, Stanley R. ... Department of the Army, Army Materiel Command, GV
Citron, Thomas H. ... Santa Monica, CA
Citron, Wendy W. ... Minneapolis, MN
Citronberg, David L. ... Bridgeport, CT
Citronberg, Robert H. ... Atlanta, GA
Citrynell, Edward ... Garden City, NY
Citrynell, Kyle Anne ... Louisville, KY
Citta, Anthony L. ... Clearwater, FL
Citta, Joseph A. ... Toms River, NJ
Cittadine, Jack P. ... Elkhart, IN
Cittadino, Benjamin N. ... Trenton, NJ
Citti & Associates ... Galveston, TX
Houston, TX
Citti, Ross ... Houston, TX
Citti, Steven M. ... Fremont, CA
City, Hayes, Meagher & Dissette, P.C.
Boston, MA
City, Robert D. ... Boston, MA
Ciucci, Joseph A. ... Atlanta, GA
Ciuffa, Barbara Joan Paul ... Kalamazoo, MI
Ciuffa, Robert A. ... St. Louis, MO
Ciuffani, Frank M. ... Woodbridge, NJ
Ciuffo, John M. ... Stamford, CT
Ciuffreda, Leonard J. ... Woodbridge, NJ
Ciulla, Ann H. ... Apex, NC
Ciulla, Anthony ... Las Vegas, NV
Ciulla & Donofrio, LLP ... New Haven, CT
North Haven, CT
Ciulla, Jay L. ... Phoenix, AZ
Ciulla, John H., Jr. ... Mechanicville, NY
Ciulla, John S. ... Mineola, NY
Ciulla, Joseph F. ... Cleveland, OH
Ciulla, Kristin Bekkum ... Phoenix, AZ
Ciulla, Robert K. ... North Haven, CT
Ciullo, Albert R. ... Tiverton, RI
Ciullo, Sandra A. ... New York, NY
Ciumei, Laura ... Staten Island, NY
Ciummo, Richard A. ... Madera, CA
Ciupak, Susan Marie ... Phoenix, AZ
Ciura, Bruce F. ... Palatine, IL
Ciurczak, Diane ... Buffalo, NY
Civale, Kevin M. ... Los Angeles, CA
Civan, Ethan D. ... Philadelphia, PA
Civardi, Stephen ... Mineola, NY
Civerolo, Gralow & Hill, A Professional Association ... Albuquerque, NM
Civerolo, Paul L. ... Albuquerque, NM
Civerolo, Richard C. ... Albuquerque, NM
Civetta, Margaret ... New York, NY
Cividanes, Emilio W. ... Washington, DC
Cividanes, Maria Del Carmen ... San Juan, PR
Civilette, David M. ... Dunkirk, NY
Civiletti, Andrew S. ... Newark, DE
Civiletti, Benjamin R., (P.C.)
Washington, DC
Baltimore, MD
Towson, MD
Civiletti, Denise ... Riverhead, NY
Civiletto, Samuel J. ... Niagara Falls, NY
Civille, George Patrick ... Hagåtña, GU
Civils, John S., Jr. ... Birmingham, AL
Civinelli & Casale ... Bloomingdale, IL
Civinelli, Ronald R. ... Bloomingdale, IL
Civins, Jeff ... Austin, TX
Civins, Kathleen M. ... Austin, TX
Civitello, Donna ... Woodbridge, CT
Civitello, Maryann ... Boston, MA
Civitello, Therese M. ... Lake Success, NY
Civitts, Glen A. ... Nashville, TN
Ciyou, Bryan Lee ... Indianapolis, IN
Cizek, Margaret ... Washington, DC
Cizek, Mart S. ... Clinton, TN
Cizmarik, Andre K. ... New York, NY
Claassen, Ann ... Washington, DC
Claassen, Anne-Kathryn
United States Senate, Senatorial Assistants, GV
Claassen, Robert ... Palo Alto, CA
Claassen, Sarah (Sally) D., P.C.
Steamboat Springs, CO
Claassen, Sarah (Sally) D.
Steamboat Springs, CO
Claassen, Sharon E. ... Carson City, NV
Claassen, Terry L. ... Washington, DC
Clabaugh, E. E., Jr., A Professional Corporation
Los Osos, CA
Clabaugh, E. E., Jr. ... Los Osos, CA
Clabaugh, Frank H. ... Hilton Head Island, SC
Clabaugh, Jon T. ... Columbia, SC
Clabaugh Law Offices, A Professional Association ... Hilton Head Island, SC
Clabault, James M. ... Mukwonago, WI
Clabault, William T. ... Department of Justice, Criminal Division, GV
Clabby, John J. ... Flushing, NY
Clabby, Rick ... Lemon Grove, CA
Clabo, Paul C. ... Minneapolis, MN
Claborne, John L. ... Phoenix, AZ
Clabuesch, David L. ... Pigeon, MI
Clabuesch, Werner ... Pigeon, MI
Clack, Cynthia L. ... Odessa, TX
Clack, Gene ... Crane, TX
Clack, James D. ... Seattle, WA
Clack, James H. ... Andrews, TX
Clack, Jeanette L.
Department of Justice, GV
Clack, Lane A. ... Saginaw, MI
Clack, Rex M. ... San Francisco, CA
Clack, Richard A. ... Buffalo, NY
Clack, Steven L. ... Kerrville, TX
Clade, Susan F. ... New Orleans, LA
Cladis, Mark D. ... New Lenox, IL
Cladouhos, Harry W. ... Washington, DC
Clady, Susan E. ... Cleveland, OH
Claeboe, Bertram F. ... Palm Coast, FL
Claerhout, William A. ... Phoenix, AZ
Claes, Kelli C. ... Detroit, MI
Claes & Partners ... New York, NY
Claes, Robert M. ... Darien, IL
Claesgens, Charles A. ... Napa, CA
Claeson, Louis W. ... St. Paul, MN
Claeson, Robert W. ... New York, NY
Claessens, R. Dennis ... Emeryville, CA
Claeys, Carla L. ... Santa Rosa, CA
Claeys, Charles F., (P.C.) ... Boston, MA
Claeys, Eric R. ... Washington, DC
Claeys, John P. ... Augusta, GA
Claeys, Joseph V. ... Schenectady, NY
Claeys, Ronald P. ... Denver, CO
Claeys, Sally J. ... Excelsior, MN
Claeys, Stephen J. ... Washington, DC
Claff, Warren L. ... Hull, MA
Claffey, James H. ... Santa Rosa, CA
Claffey, John Michael ... Springfield, MA
Claffey, Kevin J. ... Springfield, MA
Claffey, Kevin P. ... New York, NY
Claffey, Stephen A. ... Indianapolis, IN
Claffie, Richard F. ... Dalton, MA
Claffy, Joseph F. ... West Chester, PA
Claflin, Arthur C. ... Seattle, WA
Claflin, Beecher N. ... Cleveland, OH
Claflin & Christensen LLP ... Seattle, WA
Claflin, David ... Austin, TX
Claflin, Deborah A. ... Chicago, IL
Claflin, Jeffrey D. ... Indianapolis, IN
Claflin, Mark J. ... Hartford, CT
Claflin, O. Q., III ... Kansas City, KS
Clagett, A. C. Brooke ... Washington, DC
Clagett, Brice M. ... Washington, DC
Clagett & Gorey ... Fairmont, WV
Clagett, Hal C. B. ... Upper Marlboro, MD
Clagett, Hal C. B., III
Upper Marlboro, MD
Clagett, Michael G. ... Fairmont, WV
Clagett, Robert Y. ... Upper Marlboro, MD
Clagett, Stephen L. ... Prince Frederick, MD
Clagett, Tucker V. ... Waldorf, MD
Clagg, Therll Willard ... Sun City, AZ
Clagg, Thomas L. ... Fort Wayne, IN
Claggett, Daniel E. ... St. Louis, MO
Claggett, Dave L. ... Spearfish, SD
Claggett, David L., P.C. ... Spearfish, SD
Claggett, Edward R. ... Columbus, OH
Claggett, W. Stephen ... Springfield, IL
Claggett, Walter W. ... Baltimore, MD
Claghorn, Holly ... Austin, TX
Clague, Holly W. ... Chicago, IL
Clague, Michael W ... Butte, MT
Clague, William ... Bethesda, MD
Clague, William E. ... Orlando, FL
Claiborn, Holley L. ... Stamford, CT
Claiborne, Anthony B. ... San Diego, CA
Claiborne, Anthony B. ... Niwot, CO
Claiborne, Charles A. ... Austin, TX
Claiborne, Dan L. ... Carrollton, TX
Claiborne, Davis, Buuck & Hurley
Knoxville, TN
Claiborne, G. Battle ... Nashville, TN
Claiborne, Glen R., (P.C.) ... Knoxville, TN
Claiborne, Herbert A., III ... Richmond, VA
Claiborne, Ian W. ... Port Allen, LA
Claiborne, J. Patrick ... Augusta, GA
Claiborne, J. Patrick, P.C. ... Appling, GA
Augusta, GA
Claiborne, Jonathan E. ... Towson, MD

Clark, Bruce F. .... **Frankfort, KY**
Clark, Bruce G., & Associates **New York, NY**
Clark, Bruce H. .... **Austin, TX**
Clark, Bruce J. .... **Topeka, KS**
Clark, Bruce N. .... Oswego, NY
Clark, Bruce P., & Associates .... Munster, IN
Clark, Bruce T. .... **Culpeper, VA**
Clark, Bruce T. .... Seattle, WA
Clark, Bruce W. .... Department of State, GV
Clark, Bruce W. .... **Princeton, NJ**
Clark, Bryan R. .... **Las Vegas, NV** **Reno, NV**
Clark, Bryant George .... Congers, NY
Clark, B. S. .... **Little Rock, AR**
Clark, Burney P. .... Department of Justice, Antitrust Division, GV
Clark, Butler, Walsh & Hamann **Waterloo, IA**
Clark & Byarlay .... Little Rock, AR
Clark, C. Scott .... Little Rock, AR
Clark, C. William .... **Towson, MD**
Clark, Cali & Negranti, L.L.P. Paso Robles, CA San Luis Obispo, CA
Clark, Calvin E. .... Salt Lake City, UT
Clark, Cameron .... New York, NY
Clark, Cameron F. .... **Indianapolis, IN**
Clark & Campbell, P.A. .... **Lakeland, FL**
Clark, Candace A. .... **Bloomfield, CT**
Clark, Candee & Wickler .... San Jose, CA
Clark, Carl R. .... Overland Park, KS
Clark, Carl S. .... **Grand Rapids, MI**
Clark, Carla E. .... United States Senate, Senatorial Assistants, GV
Clark, Carleen T. .... **Denver, CO**
Clark, Carlton E. .... Elwood, NE
Clark, Carlton S. .... Philadelphia, PA
Clark, Carol A. .... **Detroit, MI**
Clark, Carol C. .... **Austin, TX**
Clark, Carol L. .... **Charleston, SC**
Clark, Carol S. .... **Overland Park, KS**
Clark, Carol T. .... **St. Louis, MO**
Clark, Carol V. .... **Atlanta, GA**
Clark, Carole W. .... Tyler, TX
Clark, Caroline R. .... **New York, NY**
Clark, Carolyn .... **Boston, MA**
Clark, Carolyn .... Oklahoma City, OK
Clark, Carolyn C. .... **New York, NY**
Clark, Carrie H. .... **Chicago, IL**
Clark, Carrie L. .... **Memphis, TN**
Clark, Carroll D. .... Spring Valley, CA
Clark, Cary P. .... Hanover, NH
Clark, Catherine C. .... **Seattle, WA**
Clark, Catherine E. .... Burlington, VT
Clark, Catherine Gray .... Nashville, TN
Clark, Catherine Lynn .... Houston, TX
Clark, Catherine M. .... Fort Collins, CO
Clark, Catherine S. ("Sue") **West Chester, PA**
Clark, Celia R. .... **New York, NY**
Clark, Chaney L. .... Jasper, AL
Clark, Chapin D. .... Eugene, OR
Clark, Charles .... **Jackson, MS**
Clark, Charles A., (L.C.) .... Huntington, WV
Clark, Charles B. .... Cleveland, OH
Clark, Charles B., Jr. .... San Antonio, TX
Clark, Charles E. .... Marietta, GA
Clark, Charles E. .... Overland Park, KS
Clark, Charles Edward .... **Pasadena, CA**
Clark, Charles F. .... Tampa, FL
Clark, Charles H. .... Gloucester, MA
Clark, Charles H. .... Canajoharie, NY
Clark, Charles H. .... Tyler, TX
Clark, Charles H., Jr. .... **Birmingham, AL**
Clark, Charles, III .... **Savannah, GA**
Clark, Charles L. .... Prentiss, MS
Clark, Charles M. .... Canajoharie, NY
Clark, Charles R. .... **Boise, ID**
Clark, Charles R. .... **Muncie, IN**
Clark, Charles T. .... **Dallas, TX**
Clark, Charles Tyler .... **Birmingham, AL**
Clark, Charles Tyler, P.C. **Birmingham, AL**
Clark, Charles W. .... Crystal Lake, IL
Clark, Charles W. .... Cheney, WA
Clark, Charles W., Jr. .... Nashua, NH
Clark, Charlotte K. .... **Atlanta, GA**
Clark, Charlton .... **Savannah, GA**
Clark, Charlton, Martino & Borders, P.A. **Tampa, FL**
Clark, Charmaine L. .... **Las Vegas, NV**
Clark, Cheri .... Ardmore, OK
Clark, Chris D. .... El Paso, TX
Clark, Chris W. .... North Falmouth, MA
Clark, Christina L. .... St. Paul, MN
Clark, Christine A. .... **Jacksonville, FL**
Clark, Christopher .... **Boston, MA**
Clark, Christopher B. .... **Tampa, FL**
Clark, Christopher D. .... **Troy, OH**
Clark, Christopher E. .... **Indianapolis, IN**
Clark, Christopher I. .... **Dallas, TX**
Clark, Christopher J. .... Kennett Square, PA Malvern, PA
Clark, Christopher L. .... Porterville, CA
Clark, Christopher R. **Newport Beach, CA**
Clark, Christopher R. .... **Chicago, IL**
Clark, Christopher S. .... Toledo, OH
Clark, Christopher W. .... Boise, ID
Clark, Cindy .... Manchester, NH
Clark, C. L. .... **Salina, KS**
Clark & Clark .... Bentonville, AR
Clark and Clark .... **San Jose, CA**
Clark & Clark .... **Savannah, GA**
Clark & Clark .... **New Rochelle, NY**
Clark & Clark .... East Liverpool, OH
Clark and Clark .... Ridley Park, PA
Clark & Clark .... Tyler, TX
Clark & Clark .... Waco, TX
Clark & Clark .... Salt Lake City, UT
Clark & Clark .... **Ashland, WI**
Clark & Clark, A Legal Professional Association .... Cincinnati, OH
Clark & Clark, L.L.P. .... Iola, KS
Clark and Clark, P.A. .... Hattiesburg, MS
Clark & Clark, P.C. .... Bad Axe, MI
Clark, Clayton A. .... **Houston, TX**
Clark, Clifford H. .... Grover Beach, CA
Clark, Clifford P., Jr. .... Floral City, FL
Clark, Clifton B. .... **Lexington, KY**
Clark, Cloyd .... McCook, NE
Clark, Colleen .... Santa Rosa, CA
Clark, Collen A. .... **Tyler, TX**
Clark, Connie .... Orlando, FL
Clark, Connie J. .... Osage Beach, MO
Clark, Conrad J. .... **Washington, DC**
Clark, Conrad R. .... Diamond Bar, CA
Clark, Constance G. .... **Fayetteville, AR**
Clark, Corinne D. .... San Diego, CA
Clark, Cornelia A. .... Franklin, TN
Clark, Cornelia M. .... Tukwila, WA
Clark, Cornelius E., Jr. .... Nokomis, FL
Clark, Craig E. .... **Birmingham, MI**
Clark, Craig O. .... **Waterloo, IA**
Clark, Craig T. .... Treasury Department, Office of Regulations and Rulings, GV
Clark, Curtis L. .... Atascadero, CA
Clark, Curtis M. .... Shrewsbury, MA
Clark, Cynthia .... San Francisco, CA
Clark, Cynthia A. .... **San Francisco, CA**
Clark, Cynthia A. .... **Philadelphia, PA**
Clark, Cynthia C. .... Orlando, FL Crossville, TN
Clark, Cynthia H. .... **Washington, DC**
Clark, Cynthia Jackman .... Fitchburg, MA
Clark, Cynthia L. .... Hygiene, CO
Clark, Cynthia Ruth .... **Hicksville, NY**
Clark, Cynthia S. .... Evanston, IL
Clark, D. Blair .... Boise, ID
Clark, D. Graham C., Jr. .... St. Paul, MN
Clark, D. Jeffrey .... St. Louis, MO
Clark, D. Lewis, Jr. .... **Columbus, OH**
Clark, D. Shawn .... Hickory, NC
Clark, Dale J. .... Elgin, IL
Clark, Dale J. .... Bath, NY
Clark, Dale R. .... **Ashland, WI**
Clark, Dallas, Jr. .... **Greenville, NC**
Clark, Dallas, Jr., P.A. .... **Greenville, NC**
Clark, Dan W. .... **Roseburg, OR**
Clark, Dana C. .... Orange, CA
Clark, Daniel .... **San Jose, CA**
Clark, Daniel Allen .... Houston, TX
Clark, Daniel B. .... Alexandria, VA
Clark, Daniel E. .... Saginaw, MI
Clark, Daniel F. .... Mifflintown, PA
Clark, Daniel M. .... Detroit, MI
Clark, Daniel N. .... Walla Walla, WA
Clark, Daniel P. .... Dallas, TX
Clark, Daniel S. .... Fairfax, CA
Clark, Daniel T. .... **Boston, MA**
Clark, Daniel W. .... **Raleigh, NC**
Clark, Daniel William .... Pensacola, FL
Clark, Darcel D. .... Bronx, NY
Clark, Darrell W. .... **Washington, DC**
Clark, David .... Los Angeles, CA
Clark, David A. .... Columbus, GA
Clark, David A. .... Iola, KS
Clark, David A. .... **Las Vegas, NV**
Clark, David A. .... **Teaneck, NJ**
Clark, David A. .... **Houston, TX**
Clark, David A. .... **Alexandria, VA**
Clark, David B. .... **Minneapolis, MN**
Clark, David B. .... Florence, MS
Clark, David Bert .... Flint, MI
Clark, David C. .... Delray Beach, FL
Clark, David C. .... Columbia, SC
Clark, David C. .... Rawlins, WY
Clark, David D. .... Anchorage, AK
Clark, David E. .... **Lawrenceville, GA**
Clark, David G. .... Lansing, IL
Clark, David J. .... **Wilmington, DE**
Clark, David J. .... Traverse City, MI
Clark, David J. .... **New York, NY**
Clark, David K. .... Fredonia, KS
Clark, David K. .... Dallas, TX
Clark, David K., P.A. .... Fredonia, KS
Clark, David L. .... **Palo Alto, CA**
Clark, David L. .... Chicago, IL
Clark, David L. .... **Evansville, IN**
Clark, David L. .... Florence, OR
Clark, David L., P.C. .... Florence, OR
Clark, David Lewis .... Amity, AR
Clark, David Lewis, P.A. .... Amity, AR
Clark, David M. .... Conway, AR
Clark, David M. .... **San Diego, CA**
Clark, David M. .... Lansing, MI
Clark, David M. .... **Greensboro, NC**
Clark, David R. .... **San Diego, CA**
Clark, David R. .... **San Diego, CA**
Clark, David Reid .... Monmouth, IL
Clark, David S. .... Oak Ridge, TN
Clark, David V. .... **Kansas City, MO**
Clark, David W. .... **West Palm Beach, FL**
Clark, David W. .... **Wheaton, IL**
Clark, David W. .... **Lake Charles, LA**
Clark, David W. .... **Jackson, MS**
Clark, Davis & Belk, P.A. .... **Indianola, MS**
Clark, Dawn D. .... **Columbia, SC**
Clark, D.D. Cameron .... Lenexa, KS
Clark, Deborah G. .... **Austin, TX**
Clark, Deborah J. .... Lake Stevens, WA
Clark, Deborah Y. .... Treasury Department, Internal Revenue Service, GV
Clark, Debra S. .... **Chicago, IL**
Clark, Deen & Copeland, P.C. **Mobile, AL**
Clark & DeGrand .... **Chicago, IL**
Clark, Delia A. .... **Wilmington, DE**
Clark, Denise Atkinson .... Annapolis, MD
Clark, Denise M. .... **Washington, DC**
Clark, Denise M. .... **New York, NY**
Clark, Dennis B. .... Baltimore, MD
Clark, Dennis D. .... Washington, DC
Clark, Dennis J. .... **Detroit, MI** **Pittsburgh, PA**
Clark Depew & Siess, LLP .... **Houston, TX**
Clark, Diana C. .... Harrisburg, PA
Clark, Diana D. .... Department of Energy, Office of the General Counsel, GV
Clark, Diane E. .... New Castle, PA
Clark, Diddo .... Lafayette, CA
Clark, Don J. .... Pasco, WA
Clark, Donald B. .... Green Valley, AZ
Clark, Donald B. .... Wichita, KS
Clark, Donald B. .... **Charleston, SC**
Clark, Donald C., Jr. .... **Chicago, IL**
Clark, Donald D. .... **Sarasota, FL**
Clark, Donald E. .... Methuen, MA
Clark, Donald E., Jr. .... **Washington, DC**
Clark, Donald E., Jr. .... Goldsboro, NC
Clark, Donald H. .... **Virginia Beach, VA**
Clark, Donald H., Jr. .... Hudson Falls, NY
Clark, Donald J. .... Bad Axe, MI
Clark, Donald, Jr. .... **Jackson, MS**
Clark, Donald L. .... San Jose, CA
Clark, Donald Leland .... Barstow, CA
Clark, Donald O. .... **Washington, DC**
Clark, Donald P. .... **Los Angeles, CA**
Clark, Donald R. .... Davenport, IA
Clark, Donald S. Federal Trade Commission, Office of the Secretary, GV
Clark, Donna M. J. .... **Harrisburg, PA**
Clark, Donna Schewel .... Lynchburg, VA
Clark, Donna Schmerin .... **Houston, TX**
Clark, Dougald N., Jr. .... Fayetteville, NC
Clark, Douglas .... Peoria, AZ
Clark, Douglas B. .... **Madison, WI**
Clark, Douglas H., Jr. .... Tucson, AZ
Clark, Douglas J. .... **Palo Alto, CA**
Clark, Douglas R. .... Hamburg, NJ
Clark, Duncan W. .... Newburgh, NY
Clark, Dwayne L. .... Jacksonville, FL
Clark, E. Fielding, II .... **Hickory, NC**
Clark, E. Payson, Jr. .... New York, NY
Clark, E. Sharon .... **Ann Arbor, MI**
Clark, E. Sharon, PLLC .... **Ann Arbor, MI**
Clark, E. Spaulding .... Ann Arbor, MI
Clark, Eben P. .... **Denver, CO**
Clark, Eddie Lee, III .... Philadelphia, PA
Clark, Edith Lee Anne .... Los Angeles, CA
Clark, Edmund B. .... Bethesda, MD
Clark, Edward B. .... Raleigh, NC
Clark, Edward F. .... Delphos, OH
Clark, Edward K. .... **Fort Worth, TX**
Clark, Edward L. .... Louisville, KY
Clark, Edward L. .... **Columbus, OH**
Clark, Edward P. .... Fairfax, VA
Clark, Edwin H. .... Frankfort, KY
Clark, Edwin M., Jr. .... Indiana, PA
Clark, Edwin S. .... Ventura, CA
Clark, Eileen Coyne .... Malvern, PA
Clark, Eileen M. .... Roseland, NJ
Clark, Elaine M. .... Beverly, MA
Clark & Elbing, LLP .... **Boston, MA**
Clark, Elford H. .... Los Angeles, CA
Clark, Eli D. .... **New York, NY**
Clark, Elias .... New Haven, CT
Clark, Elizabeth A. .... **Washington, DC**
Clark, Elizabeth A. .... Wilsonville, OR
Clark, Elizabeth A. **Charlotte Amalie, St. Thomas, VI**
Clark, Elizabeth Ann .... Nashville, TN
Clark, Elizabeth D. .... Cincinnati, OH
Clark, Elizabeth G. .... **Buffalo, NY**
Clark, Elizabeth L. .... Lexington, GA
Clark, Elizabeth L. .... **Chicago, IL**
Clark, Elizabeth Lundberg .... Kalamazoo, MI
Clark, Elizabeth M. .... **Morristown, NJ** **New York, NY**
Clark, Elizabeth T. .... Baltimore, MD
Clark, Ellen H. (IBA) .... **New York, NY**
Clark, Elliot .... **Houston, TX**
Clark, Elliot J., Jr. .... Department of Defense, Defense Commissary Agency, GV
Clark, Emory W. .... **Lapeer, MI**
Clark, Eric H. .... Redford, MI
Clark, Erin B. .... **Plano, TX**
Clark, Ernest M., Jr. .... **Los Angeles, CA**
Clark, Etta Ryan .... **Kingsport, TN**
Clark, Eugene T. .... Marietta, GA
Clark, Eugene V. .... **New York, NY**
Clark, Eugene V. .... **Bennington, VT**
Clark, Ezra T., III .... Mesa, AZ
Clark, Ezra Tom, Jr. .... Mesa, AZ
Clark, F. Lee .... Pasadena, TX
Clark, F. E. .... Franklin, VA
Clark and Feeney .... **Lewiston, ID** **Clarkston, WA**
Clark, Florine L. .... **Torrance, CA**
Clark, Forest E., Jr. .... Denver, CO
Clark, Francis C. .... Charlotte, NC
Clark, Francis X. .... **Wayne, PA**
Clark, Frank A. .... Syracuse, NY
Clark, Frank I. .... Columbia, MO
Clark, Frank I., P.C. .... Columbia, MO
Clark, Frank J., III .... Buffalo, NY
Clark, Frank P. .... **Hershey, PA**
Clark, Frank R., Jr. .... Nashville, TN
Clark, Frank W., Jr. .... **Los Angeles, CA**
Clark, Fred .... New Braunfels, TX
Clark, Fred J. .... House of Representatives, Committee Legal Personnel, GV
Clark, Fred S. .... **Savannah, GA**
Clark, Frederic W. .... **Philadelphia, PA**
Clark, Frederick A. .... **Los Angeles, CA**
Clark, Frederick B., III .... San Diego, CA
Clark, Frederick H. .... Detroit, MI
Clark, Frederick P. .... Hartford, CT
Clark, Freeda .... Louisville, KY
Clark, G. A., & Associates .... Akron, OH
Clark, G. Bert, Jr. .... Atlanta, GA
Clark, G. Blane, Jr. .... **Baton Rouge, LA**
Clark, G. Peter .... **New York, NY**
Clark, G. Russell .... La Jolla, CA
Clark, Gagliardi & Miller, P.C. **New York, NY** **White Plains, NY**
Clark, Gail Prebil .... **Oakland, CA** **Walnut Creek, CA**
Clark, Gary A. .... **Los Angeles, CA**
Clark, Gary B. .... **Dallas, TX**
Clark, Gary C. .... **Tulsa, OK**
Clark, Gary L. .... Peoria, IL
Clark, Gary R. .... **Chicago, IL**
Clark, Gayle Dauscher .... Warwick, RI
Clark, Gaylon L. .... Evansville, IN
Clark, Gene .... Manchester, KY McKee, KY
Clark, George A. .... Akron, OH
Clark, George E., Jr. .... **Scranton, PA**
Clark, George H., Jr. .... Ames, IA
Clark, George M., Jr. .... Huntsville, AL
Clark, George N. .... Montgomery, AL
Clark, George P. .... Covington, LA
Clark, George R. .... **Washington, DC**
Clark, George S. .... Bloomfield Hills, MI Troy, MI
Clark, George T., Jr. .... **Wilmington, NC**
Clark, George W. .... **Boston, MA**
Clark, George W. .... Cincinnati, OH
Clark, George W., Jr. .... Newburyport, MA
Clark, Gerald F. .... New York, NY
Clark, Gerald H. .... **New York, NY**
Clark, Gerald T. .... Philadelphia, PA
Clark, Gerard A. .... **Washington, DC**
Clark, Gertrude Lumpkin .... Miami, FL
Clark, Giles R. .... Elizabethtown, NC
Clark, Glen E. .... Salt Lake City, UT
Clark, Glen W., Jr. .... **Douglasville, GA**
Clark, Glenn A. .... Broken Bow, NE
Clark, Glenn A. .... **Morristown, NJ**
Clark, Glenn H. .... Orange, CA
Clark, Glenn M. .... Berkeley, CA
Clark, Glenn W. .... McLean, VA
Clark & Gonzales .... San Antonio, TX
Clark, Gordon T. .... Portland, OR
Clark, Gorham S. (Rory) .... **McLean, VA**
Clark, Graham G. .... Treasury Department, Internal Revenue Service, GV
Clark, Greene & Associates, Ltd. **Las Vegas, NV**
Clark, Greg .... Phoenix, AZ
Clark, Gregory .... **Newport Beach, CA**
Clark, Gregory A. .... **Albany, GA**
Clark, Gregory A. .... Fort Wayne, IN
Clark, Gregory D. .... Clearwater, FL
Clark, Gregory G. .... Los Angeles, CA
Clark, Gregory H. .... Rockford, IL
Clark, Gregory M. .... **Houston, TX**
Clark, Gregory S. .... Solvang, CA
Clark, Grenville, III .... **Manchester, NH**
Clark, Grenville, Jr. .... Chestnut Hill, MA
Clark, Griffin & McCollum .... Monroe, NC
Clark, Grover C. .... Jackson, MS
Clark, Guy P. .... **Ponca City, OK**
Clark, H. Andrew .... **Eugene, OR**
Clark, H. Christopher .... Boulder, CO
Clark, H. David, II .... Forest, MS
Clark, H. Douglas .... Las Vegas, NV
Clark, H. Sol .... **Savannah, GA**
Clark, H. Thomas .... Little Rock, AR
Clark, H. Westley .... United States Senate, Committee Legal Personnel, GV
Clark, Hall Barton, Jr. .... **Houston, TX**
Clark, Harley R., Jr. .... Austin, TX
Clark, Harman R., Jr. .... Green Brook, NJ
Clark, Harold G., Jr. .... Dallas, TX
Clark, Harold O. .... Waco, TX
Clark, Harold R. .... **Binghamton, NY**
Clark, Harry E. .... Easton, MD
Clark, Harry Lewis .... **Washington, DC**
Clark, Harvey L. .... Brandon, MS
Clark & Hastings .... Ames, IA
Clark & Hedien .... Columbus, OH
Clark, Hedley A. .... **Baltimore, MD**
Clark, Heman R. .... Raleigh, NC
Clark, Henry C. .... **Harrisonburg, VA**
Clark, Henry James, Jr. .... Flint, MI
Clark, Henry W. .... **Cambridge, MA**
Clark Hill PLC .... **Birmingham, MI** **Detroit, MI** **Lansing, MI** **Okemos, MI**
Clark, H. L., III .... Indian Harbour Beach, FL
Clark, Homer H., Jr. .... Boulder, CO
Clark, Horace G. Department Of The Interior, Office of the Solicitor, GV
Clark, Howard E. .... Jackson, MI
Clark, Howard F. G., Jr. North Syracuse, NY
Clark & Howell .... Fort Worth, TX
Clark, Hugh C. .... Philadelphia, PA
Clark, Hunt & Embry .... **Boston, MA** **Cambridge, MA** **Providence, RI**
Clark, Hunter R. .... Des Moines, IA
Clark, Ilisa S. .... Chestnut Hill, MA

Clark, Maryann K. ..... Sudbury, MA
Clark, Mary-Ellen Barrett ..... San Diego, CA
Clark, Matthew J. ..... Washington, DC
Clark, Matthew J. ..... Rochester, NY
Clark, Matthew L. ..... Point Pleasant, WV
Clark, Matthew M. ..... Louisville, KY
Clark, Matthew M. ..... Grass Lake, MI
Clark, Matthew R. ..... Indianapolis, IN
Clark, Maureen E. ..... Santa Barbara, CA
Clark, Maurice C. ..... Seattle, WA
Clark, Maurice E., Jr. ..... New Orleans, LA
Clark, McGill, Newkirk & Seay
Philadelphia, PA
Clark & McPherson ..... Mifflintown, PA
Clark, Megan E. ..... Cincinnati, OH
Clark, Melanie Hite ..... Greenville, NC
Clark, Melissa A. ..... Noblesville, IN
Clark, Melissa Kay ..... Covington, TN
Clark, Melvin E., Jr. ..... Washington, DC
Clark, Merle C. ..... Danville, KY
Clark, Merlyn W. ..... Boise, ID
Clark, Merrell E., Jr. ..... New York, NY
Clark, Merrill J. ..... New York, NY
Clark, Michael ..... Brooksville, KY
Clark, Michael ..... Garden City, NY
Clark, Michael A. ..... Chicago, IL
Clark, Michael C. ..... Lawrenceville, GA
Clark, Michael D. ..... Belleville, IL
Clark, Michael D. ..... Dallas, TX
Clark, Michael E. ..... Houston, TX
Clark, Michael J. ..... Menlo Park, CA
Clark, Michael J. ..... Austin, TX
Clark, Michael N. ..... Washington, DC
Clark, Michael O. ..... Torrance, CA
Clark, Michael P. ..... Walnut Creek, CA
Clark, Michael Scott ..... Jackson, MS
Clark, Michael T. ..... Westlake Village, CA
Clark, Michael Thomas ..... Indiana, PA
Clark, Michael Wade ..... Washington, MO
Clark, Michael Wood ..... Raleigh, NC
Clark, Michele M. ..... Sacramento, CA
Clark, Michelle M. ..... San Diego, CA
Clark, Michelle Y. ..... Seattle, WA
Clark, Millard W. ..... Naugatuck, CT
Clark, Miriam F. ..... New York, NY
Clark & Mitchell, P.C.
Oklahoma City, OK
Clark, Mize & Linville, Chartered
Lindsborg, KS
Salina, KS
Clark, Molly Kendall ..... Department of Justice, Executive Office for Immigration Review, GV
Clark, Mona W. ..... Louisville, CO
Clark, Monica L. ..... Minneapolis, MN
Clark, Morton H. ..... Norfolk, VA
Clark, Myron A. ..... Castle Rock, CO
Clark, Myron A., P.C. ..... Castle Rock, CO
Clark, N. Chapin, Jr. ..... Wayne, PA
Clark, Nancy Carol Laha ..... Houston, TX
Clark, Nancy J. ..... Redwood City, CA
Clark, Nancy M. ..... New Britain, CT
Clark, Nathan D. ..... Miami, FL
Clark, Nathan E. ..... Tulsa, OK
Clark, Neil A. ..... Providence, RI
Clark & Nelson ..... Colusa, CA
Clark, Newton A., Jr. ..... West Hartford, CT
Clark, Newton & Hinson, P.A.
Wilmington, NC
Clark, Nicholas J. ..... Delphos, OH
Clark, Nicholas W. ..... Washington, DC
Clark, Nicole E. ..... New York, NY
Clark, Nikki A. ..... Tallahassee, FL
Clark, Nikole C. ..... Dallas, TX
Clark, Norman Clifford ..... Detroit, MI
Clark, Norman K. ..... Newtown Square, PA
Clark and Odenwald ..... New Orleans, LA
Clark, Owen S. ..... Palmer, MA
Clark, Pamela ..... Charlottesville, VA
Clark, Pamela Anne ..... Houston, TX
Clark, Partington, Hart, Larry, Bond, Stackhouse & Stone ..... Destin, FL
Pensacola, FL
Clark, Pat E. ..... Houston, TX
Clark, Patricia A. ..... New York, NY
Clark, Patricia Ann ..... Denver, CO
Clark, Patricia Jean ..... Greensburg, PA
Clark, Patricia Snapp ..... Beaumont, TX
Clark, Patrick A. ..... Orange, TX
Clark, Patrick F. ..... Atlanta, GA
Clark, Paul A. ..... Lufkin, TX
Clark, Paul Curtis ..... Seal Beach, CA
Clark, Paul E. ..... Paso Robles, CA
San Luis Obispo, CA
Clark, Paul F. ..... Westfield, NJ
New York, NY
Clark, Paul H. ..... Alcoa, TN
Clark, Paul S. ..... Laguna Beach, CA
Clark, Paul T. ..... Washington, DC
Clark, Paul T. ..... Lewiston, ID
Clark, Paul T. ..... Boston, MA
Clark, Paul W. ..... Wichita, KS
Clark & Peelor ..... Pittsburgh, PA
Clark, Perdue, Roberts & Scott Co., L.P.A.
Columbus, OH
Clark, Perry R. ..... Menlo Park, CA
Clark, Peter A. ..... New Haven, CT
Clark, Peter A. ..... Chicago, IL
Clark, Peter B. ..... Department of Justice, Criminal Division, GV
Clark, Peter D. ..... Shelton, CT
Clark, Peter D. ..... Fredonia, NY
Clark, Peter D. ..... New York, NY
Clark, Peter F. ..... Wilmington, DE
Clark, Peter L., (P.C.) ..... St. Louis, MO
Clark, Peter M. ..... Woodbury, CT
Clark, Peter N. ..... Chicago, IL
Clark, Peter S. ..... Philadelphia, PA
Clark, Philip D. ..... San Antonio, TX
Clark, Philip W. ..... New York, NY
Clark, Phillip L., Jr. ..... New Castle, PA
Clark, Phillip R. ..... Denver, CO
Clark, Pinkie Lue ..... Cleveland, OH
Clark, Platte E. ..... Department Of The Interior, Minerals Management Service, GV
Clark & Prager ..... New York, NY
Clark & Prebich ..... Hibbing, MN
Clark, Quinn Beaumont ..... Gretna, LA
Clark, Quinn, Moses & Clark
Indianapolis, IN
Clark, R. Bradbury ..... Los Angeles, CA
Clark, R. Christopher ..... San Antonio, TX
Clark, R. Craig, Jr. ..... San Diego, CA
Clark, R. David ..... Lexington, KY
Clark, R. Gary ..... Providence, RI
Clark, R. Hix ..... Nashville, TN
Clark, R. John ..... Syracuse, NY
Clark, R. Michael ..... Columbus, OH
Clark, R. Scott ..... Birmingham, AL
Clark, R. Theodore, Jr. ..... Chicago, IL
Clark, R. Yvette ..... Nacogdoches, TX
Clark, Rae A. ..... Pittsford, NY
Rochester, NY
Clark, Rae A., Jr. ..... Pittsford, NY
Clark, Ralph M. ..... Denver, CO
Clark, Ralph M. ..... Gardiner, ME
Clark, Ramsey ..... New York, NY
Clark, Randa Bobette ..... Butler, PA
Clark, Randall F. ..... Chicago, IL
Clark, Randall Lee ..... San Diego, CA
Clark, Randall M. ..... Brunswick, GA
Clark, Randy G. ..... Pikeville, KY
Clark, Randy Keith ..... Roswell, NM
Clark, Ravert Jerome ..... Cincinnati, OH
Clark, Ray C. ..... Dallas, TX
Clark, Ray G. ..... Los Angeles, CA
Clark, Raymond D. ..... Jacksonville, FL
Clark, Raymond E. ..... Columbia, SC
Clark, Raymond H. ..... Cincinnati, OH
Clark, Raymond M. ..... Milwaukee, WI
Clark, R. E., Jr. ..... Denver, CO
Clark, Rea S. ..... Lafayette, AL
Clark, Reed E. ..... Lincoln, NE
Clark, Reginald J. ..... Atlanta, GA
Clark, Rehberg & McArdle, P.C.
Crystal Lake, IL
Clark, Reuben G., III ..... Raleigh, NC
Clark, Richard ..... Pasadena, CA
Clark, Richard ..... Plains, TX
Clark, Richard A. ..... Los Angeles, CA
Clark, Richard A. ..... Fort Wayne, IN
Clark, Richard A. ..... Pittsburgh, PA
Clark, Richard A. ..... Seattle, WA
Clark, Richard C. ..... Chicago, IL
Clark, Richard C. ..... Escanaba, MI
Clark, Richard E. ..... Phoenix, AZ
Clark, Richard E. ..... North Palm Beach, FL
Clark, Richard E., P.A.
North Palm Beach, FL
Clark, Richard I. ..... Sparta, NJ
Clark, Richard K. ..... Denver, CO
Clark, Richard L. ..... Waco, TX
Clark, Richard L. ..... Herndon, VA
Clark, Richard M. ..... Sacramento, CA
Clark, Richard M. ..... Chicago, IL
Waukegan, IL
Clark, Richard M. ..... Kalamazoo, MI
Clark, Richard M. ..... Delmar, NY
Clark, Richard M. ..... Houston, TX
Clark, Richard O. ..... Iuka, MS
Clark, Richard P., II ..... Conway, AR
Clark, Richard R. ..... Washington, DC
Clark, Richard S. ..... Wayne, MI
Clark, Richard S. ..... New York, NY
Clark, Richard S. ..... Monroe, NC
Clark, Richard W. ..... Phoenix, AZ
Clark, Richard W. ..... Eugene, OR
Clark, Richd. J. ..... East Liverpool, OH
Clark, Rita S. ..... Rancho Santa Fe, CA
Clark, Robert A. ..... Minerva, OH
Clark, Robert B. ..... Stamford, CT
Clark, Robert B. ..... Madison, NJ
Clark, Robert C. ..... Glendale, CA
Clark, Robert C. ..... Vero Beach, FL
Clark, Robert C. ..... Cambridge, MA
Clark, Robert C., Jr.
Department of Commerce, Patent and Trademark Office, GV
Clark, Robert D. ..... Colusa, CA
Clark, Robert D. ..... Denver, CO
Clark, Robert D. ..... New Canaan, CT
Clark, Robert D. ..... Atlanta, GA
Clark, Robert D. ..... Gaithersburg, MD
Clark, Robert D. ..... New York, NY
Clark, Robert D. ..... New Wilmington, PA
Clark, Robert E. ..... Vidalia, LA
Clark, Robert E., (P.C.) ..... Las Vegas, NV
Clark, Robert F. ..... Mobile, AL
Clark, Robert F. ..... Bloomfield, CT
Clark, Robert F. ..... Melbourne, FL
Clark, Robert F. ..... Danvers, MA
Clark, Robert F. ..... Staten Island, NY
Clark, Robert G. ..... Tucson, AZ
Clark, Robert G.
Federal Deposit Insurance Corporation, Trial Litigation Section, GV
Clark, Robert G. ..... Abilene, TX
Clark, Robert G., III ..... Bridgewater, MA
Brockton, MA
Clark, Robert G., Jr., Law Offices of
Bridgewater, MA
Clark, Robert H. ..... Rockford, IL
Clark, Robert H. ..... Marquette, MI
Clark, Robert H. ..... Albuquerque, NM
Clark, Robert J. ..... Wichita, KS
Clark, Robert J. ..... Trenton, NJ
Clark, Robert J. ..... Akron, OH
Clark, Robert L. ..... Sarasota, FL
Clark, Robert L. ..... Valparaiso, IN
Clark, Robert L. ..... Orchard Lake, MI
Clark, Robert L. ..... Dayton, OH
Clark, Robert L., Jr. ..... Toledo, OH
Clark, Robert M. ..... Treasury Department, Office of the Comptroller of the Currency, GV
Clark, Robert M. ..... Dallas, TX
Clark, Robert M. ..... Fairfax, VA
Clark, Robert M., Jr. ..... Dallas, TX
Clark, Robert Michael ..... Addison, TX
Clark, Robert N. ..... San Diego, CA
Clark, Robert P. ..... Sea Girt, NJ
Clark, Robert R. ..... Indianapolis, IN
Clark, Robert S. ..... Atlanta, GA
Clark, Robert S. ..... Houston, TX
Clark, Robert S. ..... Salt Lake City, UT
Clark, Robert S., P.C., Law Office of
Houston, TX
Clark, Robert W. ..... Phoenix, AZ
Clark, Robert W. ..... Hartford, CT
Clark, Robert W. ..... Norwich, CT
Clark, Robert W. ..... Washington, DC
Clark, Robert W. ..... Tampa, FL
Clark, Robert W. ..... New Orleans, LA
Clark, Robert W. ..... Albuquerque, NM
Clark, Robin A. ..... Washington, DC
Clark, Robin E. ..... Omaha, NE
Clark, Robin Frazer ..... Atlanta, GA
Clark, Rodney G ..... Carthage, IL
Clark, Roger A. ..... Washington, DC
Clark, Roger E. ..... Loveland, CO
Clark, Roger E. ..... Harrisburg, PA
Clark, Roger L. ..... Portsmouth, OH
Clark, Roger Lee ..... Eugene, OR
Clark, Roger M. ..... Grand Rapids, MI
Clark, Roger N. ..... Toledo, OH
Clark, Roger T. ..... Gulfport, MS
Hattiesburg, MS
Clark, Roger W. ..... Santa Monica, CA
Clark, Roger W. ..... Neenah, WI
Clark, Romano ..... Salinas, CA
Clark & Romano, P.A. ..... Orlando, FL
Clark, Ronald E. ..... Bunnell, FL
Palatka, FL
St. Augustine, FL
Clark, Ronald H. ..... Washington, DC
Clark, Ronald H. ..... Sherman, TX
Clark, Ronald H. ..... Seattle, WA
Clark, Ronald J. ..... Phoenix, AZ
Clark, Ronald J. ..... Chicago, IL
Clark, Ronald J. ..... Grand Rapids, MI
Clark, Ronald J. ..... Portland, OR
Clark, Ronald L. ..... Lakeland, FL
Clark, Ronald M. ..... Little Rock, AR
Clark, Ronald R. ..... Kansas City, MO
Clark, Ronetta S. ..... Reno, NV
Clark, Ross B., II ..... Memphis, TN
Clark, Ross T. ..... Jacksonville, FL
Clark, Rowand H. ..... Scotch Plains, NJ
Clark, Roy Thomas ..... Pittsburgh, PA
Clark, Russell B. ..... Decatur, GA
Clark, Russell G. ..... Springfield, MO
Clark, Russell L. ..... Alamo, GA
Clark, Russell R. ..... Alexandria, VA
Clark, Ryan ..... Commerce City, CO
Clark, Sallye A. ..... Washington, DC
Clark, Samantha Gibbs ..... Spartanburg, SC
Clark, Samuel Earle ..... Omaha, NE
Clark, Sandra F. ..... Beaumont, TX
Clark, Sandra J. ..... Redding, CA
Clark, Sandra L. ..... Los Angeles, CA
Clark, Sandra M. ..... Raleigh, NC
Clark, Sanford L. ..... Buffalo, NY
Clark, Sara A. ..... Sacramento, CA
Clark, Sara Dominick ..... Birmingham, AL
Clark, Sara J. ..... Boulder, CO
Clark, Sara R. ..... Trumbull, CT
Clark, Sarah E. ..... Manhattan Beach, CA
Clark, Sarah E. ..... Dallas, TX
Clark, Sarah J. ..... Dallas, TX
Clark & Scholnik ..... Fort Lauderdale, FL
Clark, Scot L. ..... Palm Springs, CA
Clark, Scott Andrew ..... Denver, CO
Clark, Scott B. ..... Stamford, CT
Clark, Scott B. ..... Broadview, IL
Clark, Scott D. ..... Winter Park, FL
Clark, Scott H. ..... Seattle, WA
Clark, Scott Hancock ..... Salt Lake City, UT
Clark, Scott M. ..... Scottsdale, AZ
Clark & Scott, P.C. ..... Birmingham, AL
Clark, Scott & Streetman, P.A.
Jackson, MS
Clark, Scott & Sullivan, P.C. ..... Mobile, AL
Clark, Scott W. ..... Houston, TX
Clark, Scott W. ..... Ashland, WI
Clark, Sean P. ..... Wethersfield, CT
Clark & Seay, P.L.L.C. ..... Dallas, TX
Clark, Seymour G. ..... Pittsburgh, PA
Clark, Shannon L. ..... Honolulu, HI
Clark, Shannon L. ..... Chattanooga, TN
Clark, Shannon R. ..... Washington, DC
Clark, Shannon Renell Sims ..... Enterprise, AL
Clark, Sharon C. ..... Anderson, IN
Clark, Sharon L. ..... Roseville, CA
Clark, Shaun C. ..... Los Angeles, CA
Clark & Shaw, L.L.P. ..... Fayetteville, NC
Clark, Sheila ..... Columbus, OH
Clark, Sheila A. ..... Dulles, VA
Clark, Sheila J. ..... Los Angeles, CA
Clark, Shelby L. ..... Menlo Park, CA
Clark, Shelley Hickman ..... Lawrence, KS
Clark, Shelton & Pratt, P.A. ..... Hill City, KS
Clark, Sherman J. ..... Washington, DC
Clark, Sherry A. ..... Kotzebue, AK
Clark, Sherry Walker ..... Walnut Creek, CA
Clark, Sidney D. ..... Hilton Head Island, SC
Clark & Smith ..... Glendale, CA
Clark, Stakem, Wood & Douglas, P.C.
Norman, OK
Oklahoma City, OK
Clark, Stan D. ..... Portsmouth, VA
Clark, Stanley E. ..... Redmond, OR
Clark, Stanley H., Jr. ..... Bloomington, IL
Clark, Stanley M. ..... Brecksville, OH
Clark & Stant, P.C. ..... Newport News, VA
Virginia Beach, VA
Clark, Stephen B. ..... East St. Louis, IL
Clark, Stephen C. ..... San Diego, CA
Clark, Stephen C. ..... Utica, NY
Clark, Stephen E. ..... San Francisco, CA
Clark, Stephen J. ..... Rigby, ID
Clark, Stephen P. ..... San Diego, CA
Clark, Stephen P. ..... Santa Monica, CA
Clark, Stephen R. ..... Belleville, IL
Clark, Stephen R. ..... Fremont, MI
Clark, Stephen R. ..... St. Louis, MO
Clark, Stephen S. ..... Cambridge, MA
Clark, Stephen Wells ..... New York, NY
Clark, Steven ..... San Jose, CA
Clark, Steven A. ..... Cambridge, MA
Clark, Steven A. ..... Londonderry, NH
Clark, Steven E. ..... Oklahoma City, OK
Clark, Steven E. ..... Dallas, TX
Clark, Steven J. ..... Clayton, MO
Clark, Steven J. ..... Peralta, NM
Clark, Steven J. ..... Goldsboro, NC
Clark, Steven L. ..... Chicago, IL
Clark, Steven Lee ..... Chicago, IL
Clark, Steven P. ..... Topeka, KS
Clark, Steven R. ..... Melbourne, FL
Clark, Steven Scott ..... Ventura, CA
Clark, Steven W. ..... Muskegon, MI
Clark, Stuart C. ..... Palo Alto, CA
Clark and Sturgeon ..... Belleville, IL
Clark, Susan A. ..... Los Angeles, CA
Clark, Susan E. ..... Lancaster, CA
Clark, Susan J. ..... Portland, ME
Clark, Susan Leslie Forbes ..... Tallahassee, FL
Clark, Susan M. ..... Boise, ID
Clark, Susan M. ..... Cleveland, OH
Clark, Susan M. ..... Memphis, TN
Clark, Suzan L. ..... Vancouver, WA
Clark, Suzanne Krumholz ..... Okemos, MI
Clark, Suzanne M. ..... New York, NY
Clark, Tammy Sue ..... Lansing, MI
Clark, Taylor L. ..... Malibu, CA
Clark, Terence G. ..... Atlanta, GA
Clark, Terence J. ..... Cleveland, OH
Clark, Teresa L. ..... Kansas City, MO
Clark, Teresa P. ..... Newport Beach, CA
Clark, Terry A. ..... Winston-Salem, NC
Clark, Terry F. ..... Spartanburg, SC
Clark, Terry L. ..... Saginaw, MI
Clark, Terry L. ..... Falls Church, VA
Clark, Thad ..... Jamestown, NY
Clark, Theodosia D. ..... Nashville, TN
Clark, Thomas A. ..... Atlanta, GA
Clark, Thomas A. ..... Perth Amboy, NJ
Clark, Thomas A., III ..... Mount Laurel, NJ
Clark, Thomas C. ..... Fairfield, CA
Clark, Thomas C. ..... Wheat Ridge, CO
Clark, Thomas C. ..... Hartford, CT
Clark, Thomas C. ..... Kansas City, MO
Clark, Thomas C. ..... Delaware, OH
Clark, Thomas C. ..... Middleburg, PA
Clark, Thomas C. ..... Dallas, TX
Clark, Thomas C. ..... Houston, TX
Clark, Thomas C., II ..... Delaware, OH
Clark, Thomas C., III ..... Birmingham, AL
Clark, Thomas C., P.C. ..... Middleburg, PA
Clark, Thomas Charles, II ..... St. Louis, MO
Clark, Thomas D. ..... Oakland, CA
Clark, Thomas Gene, Law Offices of
Laurel, MS
Clark, Thomas Gerard ..... Ridgewood, NJ
Clark, Thomas H.
National Labor Relations Board, Office of Board Members, GV
Clark, Thomas H. ..... Baltimore, MD
Clark, Thomas H. ..... Marquette, MI
Clark, Thomas H. ..... Cincinnati, OH
Clark, Thomas J. ..... Department of Justice, Tax Division, GV
Clark, Thomas J. ..... Chicago, IL
Clark, Thomas J. ..... Newton, NJ
Clark, Thomas L. ..... Wilmington, DE
Clark, Thomas L. ..... Lexington, KY
Clark, Thomas M. ..... Santa Fe, NM
Clark, Thomas M. ..... San Antonio, TX
Clark, Thomas M., (P.A.)
Fort Lauderdale, FL
Clark, Thomas Mahlon ..... Jacksonville, FL
Clark, Thomas P. ..... Fort Myers, FL
Clark, Thomas P., Jr. ..... Newport Beach, CA
Clark, Thomas R. ..... Grove City, OH
Clark, Thomas S. ..... Bakersfield, CA
Clark, Thomas S. ..... Simsbury, CT
Clark, Thomas T., III ..... Las Cruces, NM
Clark, Thomas W. ..... Pocatello, ID
Clark, Thomas W. ..... Alma, WI
Clark, Thomas & Winters, A Professional Corporation ..... Austin, TX
Clark, Tim A. ..... Norwich, VT
Clark, Timothy ..... Plantation, FL
Clark, Timothy A. ..... Joliet, IL
Clark, Timothy A. ..... Lowell, MA
Clark, Timothy J. ..... New York, NY
Clark, Timothy M. ..... New York, NY
Clark, Timothy S. ..... Elm Grove, WI
Clark, Tina S. ..... New Orleans, LA
Clark, Tobin K. ..... Dallas, TX
Clark, Toki Michelle ..... Columbus, OH
Clark, Tom R. ..... Tucson, AZ

Clarkson, Elinor W. .... **Winnsboro, SC**
Clarkson, Ellen R. .... **Metuchen, NJ**
Clarkson, Erin L. Markey .... Oneida, NY
Clarkson, Fortson, Walsh & Rheney, P.A.
Greenville, SC
Clarkson, Gordon N. .... Newberry, SC
Clarkson Gore & Marsella .... **Irvine, CA**
Los Angeles, CA
Torrance, CA
Clarkson, J. Brainerd .... Minneapolis, MN
Clarkson, James A.
Securities and Exchange Commission, Division of Enforcement, GV
Clarkson, James E. .... Maysville, KY
Clarkson, Jeffrey L. .... Houston, TX
Clarkson, John B.
Department of the Navy, GV
Clarkson, John E. .... Norfolk, VA
Clarkson, John M., III
Department Of Veterans Affairs, Board of Veterans Appeals, GV
Clarkson, John P. .... **Middletown, CT**
Clarkson, John R. .... Reno, NV
Clarkson, June M. .... Hollywood, FL
Clarkson, June M., P.A. .... Hollywood, FL
Clarkson, Kenneth J. .... **Boca Raton, FL**
Clarkson, Kevin G. .... **Anchorage, AK**
Clarkson Law Offices .... **Connersville, IN**
Rushville, IN
Clarkson, Law Office, Ltd. .... Reno, NV
Clarkson, Lisa J. .... **Oklahoma City, OK**
Clarkson, Lynn .... Cerro Gordo, IL
Clarkson, Mary P. .... Omaha, NE
Clarkson, N. Heyward, III .... **Greenville, SC**
Clarkson, N. Heyward, Jr. .... Columbia, SC
Clarkson, Nancy M. .... Williamsburg, VA
Clarkson, Patricia H. .... Jacksonville, FL
Clarkson, Philip .... **Boston, MA**
Clarkson, Philip R. .... San Luis Obispo, CA
Clarkson, R. Westmoreland
Winnsboro, SC
Clarkson, Richard J. .... **Beaumont, TX**
Clarkson, Richard S., Jr. .... Woodlyn, PA
Clarkson, Robert L. .... **Los Angeles, CA**
Clarkson, Robert T. .... Cupertino, CA
Clarkson & Rochna .... Houston, TX
Clarkson, S. James .... Detroit, MI
Clarkson, Scott C. .... **Torrance, CA**
Clarkson, Stephen B. .... **Newport News, VA**
Clarkson, Ted H. .... **Augusta, GA**
Clarkson, Thomas C. .... Wichita, KS
Clarkson, William B. .... Houston, TX
Clarkson, William J. .... Poplar Bluff, MO
Clark-Weintraub, Deborah
New York, NY
Claro, John Anthony .... Oklahoma City, OK
Claro, Joseph A. .... Oklahoma City, OK
Claro, Karen Au .... Woodbury, NY
Claroni, Geoffrey P. .... White Plains, NY
Clarry, Melissa .... **Washington, DC**
Clarvit, Richard N. .... North Miami, FL
Clarvit, Richard N., P.A. .... North Miami, FL
Clary, Albert Dale .... **Baton Rouge, LA**
Clary, Ann E. .... Pasadena, CA
Clary, Betty J. .... Treasury Department, Internal Revenue Service, GV
Clary, Bradley G. .... **Minneapolis, MN**
Clary, Brent E .... **Lafayette, IN**
Clary, Bruce E. .... Hot Springs, NC
Clary, Claudia S. .... Gainesville, FL
Clary & Clements, Inc. .... Bridgeport, TX
Clary, David Temple .... Santa Maria, CA
Clary, Dennis A. .... Lewiston, NY
Clary, Donald M. .... **Los Angeles, CA**
Clary, Everett B. .... Los Angeles, CA
Clary, Gary E. .... Gaffney, SC
Clary, Harold F. .... Department of Defense, Office of the General Counsel, GV
Clary, Jack C. .... **Grand Rapids, MI**
Clary, Jack R. .... **Grand Rapids, MI**
Clary, James M., III .... Newton, MA
Clary, James R., Jr. .... Baton Rouge, LA
Clary, John .... **Woodcliff Lake, NJ**
Clary, John Carter .... Las Cruces, NM
Clary, John T., Jr. .... **Scranton, PA**
Clary, Lee .... Watertown, NY
Clary, Lori A. .... **Columbus, OH**
Clary, Mary Beth .... **Naples, FL**
Clary, Matthew A., III .... **Falls Church, VA**
Clary, Matthew A., Jr. .... Fairfax, VA
Clary, Michael D. .... Danville, IL
Clary, Patricia A. .... Clovis, NM
Clary, Patrick C. .... **Las Vegas, NV**
Reno, NV
Clary, Patrick C., Chartered
Las Vegas, NV
Reno, NV
Clary, Raymond F. .... **Spokane, WA**
Clary, Rhoda .... New York, NY
Clary, Richard W. .... **New York, NY**
Clary, Robert Clinton, Jr. .... Lawrenceville, VA
Clary, Robert F., Jr. .... Great Falls, MT
Clary, Robert J. .... **Dallas, TX**
Clary, Ronald B. .... Canoga Park, CA
Clary, Susan Stokley .... Frankfort, KY
Clary, Tammy Lynn .... **Dallas, TX**
Clary, William J. .... North Scituate, MA
Clary, William K. .... Bridgeport, TX
Clary, William M., Jr. .... Jeffersonville, IN
Clary-Cooke, Kathleen .... Miamisburg, OH
Clasby, Sarah Becket .... **Miami, FL**
Clase, Stephen D. .... Anderson, IN
Claseman, George J. .... **Las Vegas, NV**
Clasen, D. Michael .... Reno, NV
Clasen, Jeanine K. .... **Oakland, CA**
Clasen, Joseph L. .... **Stamford, CT**
New York, NY

Clasen, Marc T.
Department of Transportation, Office of the Secretary, GV
Clasen, Robert L. .... Los Angeles, CA
Clasgens, Joseph H., III .... Menlo Park, CA
Clasing, Alfred E., III .... Baltimore, MD
Clasing, Kevin A. .... Baltimore, MD
Clason, Jeffrey D. .... Roseville, CA
Clason, Jenifer Ward .... Homer, LA
Class, Edgar .... Washington, DC
Class, Jamie N. .... **Boston, MA**
Class, Maribeth .... Cincinnati, OH
Classe, John G. .... Birmingham, AL
Classen, H. Ward .... **Bethesda, MD**
Classen, R. Derek .... **Long Beach, CA**
Classens, Michael J. .... **Statesboro, GA**
Classetti, Peter J. .... Newtown, PA
Class Matthews, Virginia .... Newark, NJ
Classon, Gregory B. .... New York, NY
Claster, Mark L. .... New York, NY
Claster, William D. .... **Irvine, CA**
Clateman, Michael G. .... New York, NY
Claton, Denise R. .... **Des Moines, IA**
Clattenburg, Theodore, Jr. .... Philadelphia, PA
Clatterbuck, Gary N. .... **Omaha, NE**
Claud, R. Daniel, Jr. .... Wheaton, IL
Claude, Robert W. .... **Houston, TX**
Clauder, J. Martin .... Houston, TX
Claudet, Michel H. .... Houma, LA
Claudio, Brenda L. .... Kankakee, IL
Claudio, Carmen-Delia .... Phoenix, AZ
Claudio Vazquez, Flor D. .... San Juan, PR
Claudon, Chester J. .... Canton, IL
Claudon, Kost, Barnhart & Beal, Ltd.
Canton, IL
Claudon, Roger K. .... Frankfort, IN
Clauer, George L., III .... **Baton Rouge, LA**
Clauer, Laurel B. .... **Baton Rouge, LA**
Claughton, Calvin E. .... Kent, WA
Claughton, Edward N., Jr. .... Miami, FL
Claugus, Bruce A. .... New York, NY
Claugus & Mitchell .... New York, NY
Claunch, Beverly C. .... Heber Springs, AR
Claunch, Charles C. .... **Austin, TX**
Claunch, Jim .... Cleburne, TX
Fort Worth, TX
Claunch, Kirk M. .... Cleburne, TX
Fort Worth, TX
Claunch, Kyle .... Cleburne, TX
Fort Worth, TX
Claunch Law Firm .... Cleburne, TX
Fort Worth, TX
Claus, Ambrose J. .... Needham, MA
Claus, Curry, Schuster & Schwartzman
Rochester, NY
Claus, Lawrence N. .... Pittsburgh, PA
Claus, Marcie R. .... Chicago, IL
Claus, Mary Beth .... **Indianapolis, IN**
Claus, R. Charles, Jr. .... Pontiac, MI
Claus, Rachel .... **Stanford, CA**
Claus, Robert C. .... Chicago, IL
Claus, Scot L. .... **Phoenix, AZ**
Claus, Steve A. .... Lubbock, TX
Claus, Tracy E. .... **New York, NY**
Clause, C. Russell .... **Washington, DC**
Clause, Carlyn .... **Palo Alto, CA**
Clause, George E. .... **San Jose, CA**
Clause, Herman C. .... Lafayette, LA
Clause, Loretta J. .... Costa Mesa, CA
Clause, Tammy Lee .... Newfoundland, PA
Clause, Ted Gamble .... Honolulu, HI
Clausel, Clinton P. .... Pasadena, TX
Clausen, Alan G. .... Dillon, CO
Littleton, CO
Clausen, Andrew C. .... **Mobile, AL**
Clausen, Brian H. .... **Santa Barbara, CA**
Clausen, Brian J. .... St. Paul, MN
Clausen, Charles D. .... Milwaukee, WI
Clausen, Christopher .... Marshalltown, IA
Clausen, Christopher N. .... **New York, NY**
Clausen, Doris .... **Boston, MA**
Clausen, Edward C. .... **Jefferson City, MO**
Clausen, Fred .... Boulder, CO
Clausen, Gerald A. .... **San Francisco, CA**
Clausen, Glenn R. .... Northbrook, IL
Clausen, Keith .... **Washington, DC**
Clausen, Mark A. .... Seattle, WA
Clausen Miller P.C. .... Newport Beach, CA
Chicago, IL
Wheaton, IL
Newark, NJ
New York, NY
White Plains, NY
Clausen, Monte C. .... Tucson, AZ
Clausen, Paul A. .... **Spokane, WA**
Clausen, Paul F. .... Somerset, NJ
Clausen, Rebecca L. .... New Orleans, LA
Clausen, Robert J. .... Altadena, CA
Clausen, Ronald K. .... **San Francisco, CA**
Clausen, Shellie L. .... **Kansas City, MO**
Clausen, Steven J. .... **Houston, TX**
Clausen, Timothy A. .... **Sioux City, IA**
Clauser, David C. .... Topeka, KS
Clausing, Kurt F. .... Wichita, KS
Clausing, Marilee .... **Chicago, IL**
Clausing, Richard B. .... Wichita, KS
Clausing, Vivian Metzger
Mountain View, CA
Clausing, W. Kirk .... **Tulsa, OK**
Clauson & Atwood .... Hanover, NH
Clauson, Eric L. .... Seattle, WA
Clauson, Heather L. .... **Atlanta, GA**
Clauson, K. William .... Hanover, NH
Clauss, Amy C. .... **New York, NY**
Clauss, Andrew B. .... **Philadelphia, PA**
Clauss, C. David .... **Jackson, WY**
Clauss & Chakwin .... **New York, NY**
Clauss, D. Michael .... **Costa Mesa, CA**

Clauss, Eliot R. .... **New York, NY**
Clauss, Paul C. .... **Sacramento, CA**
Clauss, Peter O. .... **Philadelphia, PA**
Clauss, Thomas F., Jr. .... **Stamford, CT**
New York, NY
Clauss, Victoria J. .... **Doylestown, PA**
Claussen, Anne W. .... Tallahassee, FL
Claussen, Frederic P. .... Barnstable, MA
Claussen, John H. .... Windsor, CT
Claussen, Kenneth F. .... Miami, FL
Claussen, Nicole L. .... **Cedar Rapids, IA**
Claussen, Peter R. .... Phoenix, AZ
Claussen, Steven M. .... **Portland, OR**
Claussen, Warren Kim .... Pocatello, ID
Clausz, Daniel R. .... **Appleton, WI**
Clavell, Adam S. .... **Providence, RI**
Clavelli, Carl P. .... Chicago, IL
Claveloux, Ronald L. .... San Francisco, CA
Claveran-Lopez, Laura E. .... Long Beach, CA
Clavere, Armand J. .... Sacramento, CA
Clavere, Eilleen M. .... Oakland, CA
Claverie, Louis B. .... New Orleans, LA
Claverie, Maumus F., Jr. .... New Orleans, LA
Claverie, Philip deV. .... **New Orleans, LA**
Clavin, Donald X. .... Valley Stream, NY
Clavin, Virginia A. .... Hempstead, NY
Clavio, John C. .... **Oak Brook, IL**
Clawater, Wayne .... **Houston, TX**
Clawges, Timothy L. .... Carlisle, PA
Clawson, Bruce A. .... Omaha, NE
Clawson, Byde W. .... **Palo Alto, CA**
Clawson, Carol .... **Salt Lake City, UT**
Clawson, Charles E., Jr. .... Conway, AR
Clawson, Craig S. .... Omaha, NE
Clawson, Debra A. .... **Benton Harbor, MI**
Clawson, Helen E. .... Charleston, SC
Clawson, Kurt E. .... Philadelphia, PA
Clawson, Mark A. .... Palo Alto, CA
Clawson, Michael Millen .... Aurora, CO
Clawson, Michael S. .... **Birmingham, MI**
Clawson, Millen C. .... Colorado Springs, CO
Clawson, Nancy J. .... Chicago, IL
Clawson, Potter & Gardner, P.C.
Colorado Springs, CO
Clawson, Richard L. .... Camden, ME
Clawson, Robert C. .... Irmo, SC
Clawson, Robert E. .... Plant City, FL
Clawson, Robert G., Jr. .... **Charleston, SC**
Clawson, Robin Burnham
Hoffman Estates, IL
Clawson, Samuel R. .... **Charlotte, NC**
Charleston, SC
Clawson & Staubes, L.L.C. .... **Charlotte, NC**
Charleston, SC
Clawson, Steven R. .... Fairfield, CA
Clawson, Suzanne Hulst .... **Columbia, SC**
Clawson, Thomas G. .... Greensboro, NC
Clawson, Thomas W. .... **Salt Lake City, UT**
Clawson, Tony Charles .... Cambridge, MA
Clawson, W. Andrew .... Victor, NY
Clawson, Walter F. .... **Shreveport, LA**
Claxon, Colin C. .... **San Rafael, CA**
Claxton, Anthony R. .... Atlanta, GA
Claxton, Charles R. (Rick)
Washington, DC
Claxton & Claxton, LLC .... **Atlanta, GA**
Claxton, Douglas A. .... Asheville, NC
Claxton, Edward B., III .... **Dublin, GA**
Claxton & Hill, PLLC .... **Dallas, TX**
Claxton, Joseph E. .... Macon, GA
Claxton, Kimberle Kennedy
Kansas City, MO
Claxton Law Firm, P.C. .... Asheville, NC
Claxton, Leslie H. .... **Atlanta, GA**
Claxton, Linda K. .... **Los Angeles, CA**
Memphis, TN
Claxton, Lisa R. .... **Greenville, SC**
Claxton, Michael A. .... **Longview, WA**
Claxton, Philander P., Jr. .... Bethesda, MD
Claxton, Richard Allen .... Hanover, PA
Claxton, Roger F. .... **Dallas, TX**
Claxton, Sale & Quinn, Professional Corporation .... **Washington, DC**
Claxton, Thomas L. .... Gainesville, TX
Claxton, Timothy L. .... **Fort Wayne, IN**
Claxton, William H. .... Morristown, NJ
Claxton, William P. .... **Atlanta, GA**
Clay, A. Bruce .... Research Triangle Park, NC
Clay, A. Stephens .... **Atlanta, GA**
Clay, Aaron R. .... Delta, CO
Clay, Alexander S., V .... **Atlanta, GA**
Clay, Alexandra N. .... San Francisco, CA
Clay, Alonzo W. .... Pontiac, IL
Clay, Andrea L. .... **San Francisco, CA**
Clay, Atreus M. .... Houston, TX
Clay, Barbara .... Dallas, TX
Clay, Barbara Ann .... **Armonk, NY**
Clay, Beth C. .... **Jackson, MS**
Clay, Bill, P.A., II .... **Miami, FL**
Clay, C. Lloyd .... Clayton, GA
Clay, C. Lloyd, P.C. .... Clayton, GA
Clay, Candace W. .... **Lexington, KY**
Clay, Carol A.
Department of Justice, GV
Clay, Charles C. .... **Marietta, GA**
Clay, Charles G. .... Catskill, NY
Clay, Charles G. .... Dallas, TX
Clay, Charles H. .... **Minneapolis, MN**
Clay, Charles Q., III .... Los Angeles, CA
Clay, Clarence H., Jr. .... Macon, GA
Clay & Clay .... **Danville, KY**
Clay & Clay .... **Lexington, KY**
Clay, Connie R. .... Jacksonville, FL
Clay, Curtis L. .... **Denver, CO**
Clay, Darrell A. .... **Cleveland, OH**

Clay, David K.
Environmental Protection Agency, Office of Enforcement and Compliance Assurance, GV
Clay and Dodson, P.C. .... Delta, CO
Clay, Edward S. .... Towson, MD
Clay, Emily M. .... **Philadelphia, PA**
Clay, Eric Lee .... Detroit, MI
Clay, Gerald S. .... Honolulu, HI
Clay, Gordon M. .... **Washington, DC**
Clay, H. Gerrard .... Mobile, AL
Clay, Helen P., (Mrs.) .... Oakhurst, CA
Clay, Henry A. .... Detroit, MI
Clay, Henry Bernard, III .... Detroit, MI
Clay, Henry E., Jr. .... Boxford, MA
Clay, Henry J., Jr. .... **New York, NY**
Clay, Herbert C. .... Marion, VA
Clay, J. Calvin .... Mobile, AL
Clay, James C. .... Kailua-Kona, HI
Clay, James Crayton .... **Lexington, KY**
Clay, James F. .... **Danville, KY**
Clay, James M. .... **Minneapolis, MN**
Clay, James N., III .... Memphis, TN
Clay, James W. .... Winchester, KY
Clay, Janis M. .... **Minneapolis, MN**
Clay, Jeffrey B. .... Harrisburg, PA
Clay, John E. .... Oakhurst, CA
Clay, John E. .... Chicago, IL
Clay, John W. .... Houston, TX
Clay, Jonathan Buckley .... **Lexington, KY**
Clay, Jordan E. .... Bloomington, IL
Wichita, KS
Clay, Karen L. .... San Francisco, CA
Clay, Kendall O. .... Independence, VA
Radford, VA
Clay, Kendall O., Attorney at Law, P.C.
Independence, VA
Radford, VA
Clay, L. Kent .... **Fort Worth, TX**
Clay, Leslie L. .... Columbia, MO
Clay, Lisa A. Coughlin .... San Francisco, CA
Clay, Lyell B. .... Charleston, WV
Clay, Martin M., Jr. .... **St. Louis, MO**
Clay, Massey & Gale, P.C. .... Mobile, AL
Clay, Michael D. .... **Tulsa, OK**
Clay, Michelle C. .... Washington, DC
Silver Spring, MD
Clay, Michelle Cochran .... **Dallas, TX**
Clay, Neil C. .... Bessemer, AL
Birmingham, AL
Clay, Pam .... **Lexington, KY**
Clay, Pamela S. .... Cleveland, OH
Clay, Patrick N. .... Bellaire, TX
Clay, Paul E. .... **Spokane, WA**
Clay, Paul O., Jr. .... **Fayetteville, WV**
Clay, Peggy L. .... **Doylestown, PA**
Clay, Philip M.
Hot Springs National Park, AR
Clay, R. Kent .... **San Francisco, CA**
Clay, Raymond C., Jr. .... Pensacola Beach, FL
Clay, Richard .... **Danville, KY**
Clay, Richard H. C. .... **Louisville, KY**
Clay, Robert A. .... Greenville, SC
Clay, Robert M. .... **Raleigh, NC**
Clay, Roger A., Jr. .... New York, NY
Clay, Ronnie L. .... Fincastle, VA
Clay, Scott D. .... **Tampa, FL**
Clay, Stan .... Columbia, MO
Clay, Steven C. .... **Minneapolis, MN**
Clay, Sulee J. .... **Washington, DC**
Clay, Thomas E. .... Louisville, KY
Clay, Thomas E., P.S.C. .... Louisville, KY
Clay, Tracy-Elizabeth .... **Washington, DC**
Clay, Ursula .... **Florham Park, NJ**
New York, NY
Clay, W. Dane .... **Little Rock, AR**
Clay, W. Howard .... Louisville, KY
Clay, W. Michael .... Irving, TX
Clay, Ward S. .... San Diego, CA
Clay, William "Bill" .... **Miami, FL**
Clay, William J. .... **Dallas, TX**
Clay, Williamson and Lane .... Lexington, KY
Claybon, Stanley .... Cincinnati, OH
Clayborn, Ulysses M. .... Kansas City, MO
Clayborne, Courtney R. .... **Rapid City, SD**
Clayborne, James F., Jr. .... **Belleville, IL**
Clayborne, Karen McLaurin
Memphis, TN
Clayborne, Mark A. .... Oklahoma City, OK
Claybourne, Frank .... St. Paul, MN
Claybrook, Frederick W., Jr.
Washington, DC
Claybrook, John D. .... **Nashville, TN**
Claybrook, Richard A., Jr. .... Harrisonburg, VA
Claybrook, Terri W. .... Cherry Hill, NJ
Clayburgh, Richard (Rick) S. .... Bismarck, ND
Clay-Clark, LaGuina .... Chicago, IL
Claycomb, David M. .... Kansas City, MO
Claycomb, Gregory J. .... Cincinnati, OH
Claycomb, H. Murray, (P.A.) .... **Warren, AR**
Claycomb, Lawrence W. .... Louisville, KY
Claycomb, Robert K. .... Hodgenville, KY
Claycombe, Bruce W. .... **Dallas, TX**
Claycombe, John R. .... Indianapolis, IN
Claycombe, Robert A. .... **Indianapolis, IN**
Clay-Conti, Donna P. .... Oakland, CA
Claydon, John M., Jr. .... Fairfield, CT
Claydon, June Ellen .... Allentown, PA
Claydon, Sevilla CP .... Seattle, WA
Clay-Jackson, Lydia .... Conroe, TX
Clayman, Amanda B. .... **Chicago, IL**
Clayman, Carol Heineman .... St. Louis, MO
Clayman, Caryn J. .... Boca Raton, FL
Clayman, Charles E. .... **New York, NY**
Clayman, Edward P. .... Philadelphia, PA
Clayman, Eric J. .... Haddon Heights, NJ
Clayman, Joel A. .... Niles, OH
Clayman, John D. .... **Tulsa, OK**

Clayman, Kenneth I. ....Ventura, CA
Clayman, Kenneth J. ....Atlanta, GA
Clayman, Landon K. ....Miami, FL
Clayman, Markowitz, Pinney and Baram, L.L.C. ....Bloomfield, CT
Hartford, CT
Clayman, Martin A. ....Bloomfield, CT
Clayman, Michael D. ....Kansas City, MO
Clayman, Paul F. ....Department of State, Office of the Legal Adviser, GV
Clayman, Raymond ....Dayton, OH
Clayman, Robert S. ....Washington, DC
Clayman & Rosenberg ....New York, NY
Claymon, Allan W. ....Cincinnati, OH
Claymon, Jennifer B. ....Austin, TX
Claypool, Allan J. ....Lansing, MI
Claypool, Brian E. ....Los Angeles, CA
Claypool, Charles A. ....Dayton, OH
Claypool & Claypool ....Williamsburg, IA
Claypool, David L. ....Des Moines, IA
Claypool, Forrest E. ....Chicago, IL
Claypool, James E. ....Williamsburg, IA
Claypool, James R. ....Phoenix, AZ
Claypool, John D. ....Appleton, WI
Claypool, Joseph L. ....Indianapolis, IN
Claypool Law Firm, The ....Los Angeles, CA
Claypool, Mark G. ....Erie, PA
Claypool, Megan Templeton
Des Moines, IA
Claypool, Ralph L., Jr. ....St. Louis, MO
Claypool, Rebecca L. ....Williamsburg, IA
Claypool, Thomas H. ....Williamsburg, IA
Claypoole, Erin Leigh ....Dayton, OH
Claypoole, Howard F. ....Dayton, OH
Claypoole, J. Stanley ....Charleston, SC
Claypoole, Susan L. ....Medford, NJ
Claypoole, Theodore F. ....Charlotte, NC
Clayson, David R. ....Las Vegas, NV
Clayson, Mann, Yaeger & Hansen, A Professional Law Corporation
Corona, CA
Clayton, Alfred, Jr. ....Anchorage, AK
Clayton, Ann Clarissa ....Pittsburgh, PA
Clayton, Archie P., III ....Austin, TX
Clayton, Ben E. ....Pearl River, LA
Clayton, Benjamin C. ....Newton, IA
Clayton, Benjamin W. ....San Angelo, TX
Clayton, Boyce G. ....Paducah, KY
Clayton, Brenda L. ....Austin, TX
Clayton, Carl J. ....Bel Air, MD
Clayton, Carol ....Washington, DC
Clayton, Carolyn Doozan
Washington, DC
Clayton, Catherine B. ....Jackson, TN
Clayton, Charles ....Minneapolis, MN
Clayton, Charles G., IV ....Baton Rouge, LA
Clayton, Charlotte Railey ....Birmingham, AL
Clayton, Cheryl Ann ....Noble, OK
Clayton, Christina E. ....Stamford, CT
Clayton, Claude F., Jr. ....Columbus, MS
Tupelo, MS
Clayton & Clayton ....Eufaula, AL
Clayton and Clayton, P.A. ....Warrenton, NC
Clayton, Cleo G., Jr. ....Amarillo, TX
Clayton, D. Michael ....Denver, CO
Clayton, Dale M. ....Hartford, CT
Clayton, Dan L. ....Indianapolis, IN
Clayton, Dana A. ....Miami, FL
Clayton, Daniel D. ....Beaumont, TX
Clayton, Daniel L. ....Nashville, TN
Clayton, Darcia ....Rockville, MD
Clayton, David I. ....San Francisco, CA
Clayton, David N. ....Cold Spring, KY
Clayton, David W. ....Hauppauge, NY
Clayton, Dawn A. ....Vienna, MO
Clayton, Dennis W. ....Spokane, WA
Clayton, Dennis W., P.S. ....Spokane, WA
Clayton, Donna L. ....Syracuse, NY
Clayton, Doug W. ....Dallas, TX
Clayton, E. Steele, IV ....Nashville, TN
Clayton, Elizabeth T. ....Sacramento, CA
Clayton, Ellery W. ....East Troy, WI
Clayton, Everett McCord
Philadelphia, PA
Clayton, F. Brittin, III ....Boulder, CO
Clayton, Fay ....Chicago, IL
Clayton, Fred B. ....Orlando, FL
Clayton, Gail P. ....Charles City, VA
Clayton, Glenn L., II ....Springfield, VA
Clayton, Grant R. ....Sandy, UT
Clayton, Gregory D. ....Nashville, TN
Clayton, Gregory S. ....Littleton, NH
Clayton, Gretchen Butler ....New York, NY
Clayton, H. James ....Niagara Falls, NY
Clayton, Harold R. ....Beaumont, TX
Clayton, Howard D. ....Albany, NY
Slingerlands, NY
Clayton, Howarth & Cannon, P.C.
Salt Lake City, UT
Sandy, UT
Clayton, Jalynn M. ....Albuquerque, NM
Clayton, James A., Jr. ....Lexington, MA
Clayton, James B. ....De Leon Springs, FL
Clayton, James E. ....Gainesville, FL
Clayton, James H. ....Brielle, NJ
Clayton, James K., Jr. ....Murfreesboro, TN
Clayton, James N., III ....Plano, TX
Clayton, James R. ....DeLand, FL
Orange City, FL
Clayton, Jane S.E. ....Bangor, ME
Clayton, J. D. ....New York, NY
Clayton, Jeffrey N. ....Salt Lake City, UT
Clayton, Jerry B. ....Durham, NC
Clayton, Jill E. ....New York, NY
Clayton, Joe D. ....Tyler, TX
Clayton, John A. ....Vienna, MO
Clayton, John B. ....Detroit, MI
Raleigh, NC
Clayton, John F. ....Sacramento, CA
Clayton, John H., Jr. ....Marion, IL
Clayton, John R. ....Houston, TX
Clayton, Johnston, Quincey, Ireland, Felder, Gadd & Roundtree, P.A. ....Gainesville, FL
Clayton, Joseph M., Jr. ....Princeton, NJ
Clayton, Joye M. ....Gainesville, FL
Clayton, Kenneth M. ....Maitland, FL
Clayton, Kent M. ....Costa Mesa, CA
Clayton, Kevin C. ....Washington, DC
Clayton, L. Craig ....Casper, WY
Clayton, L. Whitney, III
Newport Beach, CA
Clayton, Larinzo D. ....Uniondale, NY
Clayton, Laura A. ....Palo Alto, CA
Clayton, Laura Lee ....Indianapolis, IN
Clayton Law Firm, The, P.A.
Sarasota, FL
Clayton, L. Craig, P.C. ....Casper, WY
Clayton, Lea W., Jr. ....St. Louis, MO
Clayton, Lewis R. ....New York, NY
Clayton, Lisa Wilson ....Las Vegas, NV
Clayton, Mack ....Alexander City, AL
Clayton, Mark A. ....Las Vegas, NV
Clayton, Mark A. ....McAlester, OK
Clayton, Matthew D. ....Philadelphia, PA
Clayton & McCulloh ....Maitland, FL
Clayton & McEvoy, A P.C. ....San Jose, CA
Clayton, Melodie H. ....Marietta, GA
Clayton, Meryl Conte ....Sarasota, FL
Clayton, Michael B. ....Santa Maria, CA
Clayton, Michael E. ....Cleveland, OH
Clayton, Michael F. ....Washington, DC
Clayton, Myrick, McClanahan & Coulter
Durham, NC
Clayton, Nicole Bandy ....Nashville, TN
Clayton, Paul D. ....Albany, NY
Clayton, Paul D. ....Eugene, OR
Clayton, Paula J. ....Chicago, IL
Clayton, Preston C. ....Eufaula, AL
Clayton, Preston C., Jr. ....Eufaula, AL
Clayton, Ralph R. ....Balsam Grove, NC
Clayton, Raymond C.
Thousand Oaks, CA
Clayton, Rebecca E. ....Philadelphia, PA
Clayton, Richard A. ....North Plainfield, NJ
Clayton, Richard D. ....Salt Lake City, UT
Clayton, Riley A. ....Las Vegas, NV
Clayton, Robert B. ....Los Angeles, CA
Clayton, Robert B. ....Eaton, OH
Clayton, Robert G., Jr. ....Toledo, OH
Clayton, Robert H. ....Hyannis, MA
Clayton, Robert L., (P.C.)
New Orleans, LA
Clayton, Robert M., II ....Hannibal, MO
Clayton, Robert M., III ....Hannibal, MO
Clayton, Roger R. ....Peoria, IL
Clayton, Ronald A. ....New York, NY
Clayton, Sally J. ....Lebanon, IL
Clayton, Stephen M. ....New York, NY
Clayton, Sterling S. ....Long Beach, CA
Clayton, Steven E. ....Ketchum, ID
Clayton and Stone, L.L.C. ....Boulder, CO
Clayton, Stuart F., Jr. ....Atlanta, GA
Clayton, Tacey Clark ....Corinth, MS
Tupelo, MS
Clayton, Tamela Gay ....Rockingham, NC
Clayton & Teal, P.A. ....Daytona Beach, FL
DeLand, FL
Deltona, FL
Orange City, FL
Clayton, Theaoseus T., Sr. ....Warrenton, NC
Clayton, Thomas A. ....Santa Fe, NM
Clayton, Thomas M. ....Jacksonville, FL
Clayton, Thomas W. ....Sioux Falls, SD
Clayton, Tom ....Arlington, TX
Clayton, Tom ....Fort Worth, TX
Clayton, Vicki A. ....San Francisco, CA
Clayton, W. Andrew, Jr. ....Sarasota, FL
Clayton, Walter G., III ....Seattle, WA
Clayton, Walter J., III ....New York, NY
Clayton, Wendy Schnipper ....Wellesley, MA
Clayton, Wesley A. ....Jackson, TN
Clayton, Wesley G. ....Canyon, TX
Clayton, William B., Jr. ....San Jose, CA
Clayton, William F. ....Sioux Falls, SD
Clayton, William J. ....Los Angeles, CA
Clayton, William J. ....Batesville, MS
Clayton, William R. ....Miami, FL
Clayton, Yvonne Lee ....Cherry Hill, NJ
Philadelphia, PA
Claytor, Hugh M. ....Florence, SC
Claytor, James D. ....Lafayette, CA
Claytor, Janice L. ....Knoxville, TN
Claytor, John M. ....Richmond, VA
Claytor, Michael A. ....Indianapolis, IN
Claytor, William G. ....Cincinnati, OH
Claytor, William M. ....Charlotte, NC
Cleage, Henry ....Idlewild, MI
Cleal, Scott C. ....Wheaton, IL
Clear & Clear, PA ....Albuquerque, NM
Clear, Colleen M. ....Albuquerque, NM
Clear, James J. ....Department of Justice, Environment and Natural Resources Division, GV
Clear, John Michael ....St. Louis, MO
Clear, Michael Gene, Law Offices of
Greenwich, CT
Clear, Michael Gene, Law Offices of
Stamford, CT
Clear, Michael Gene, Law Offices of
Westport, CT
Clear, Rory T. ....Cincinnati, OH
Clear, Thomas J., III ....Albuquerque, NM
Clear, Thomas J., Jr. ....Albuquerque, NM
Clearfield, Daniel ....Harrisburg, PA
Clearfield & Feinman, P.C. ....Cherry Hill, NJ
Philadelphia, PA
Clearfield, Kathryn E. ....Albany, NY
Clearfield, Ronald A. ....Philadelphia, PA
Clearman, Danny K. ....Decatur, MS
Clearman, Jennifer Witten ....Houston, TX
Clearman, Scott M. ....Houston, TX
Clearwater, Christina Eads
Federal Communications Commission, Wireless Telecommunications Bureau, GV
Clearwater Law Offices ....Lewiston, ID
Clearwater, Scott William ....Fairfax, VA
Clearwater, Susan B. ....New York, NY
Clearwaters, Lon R. ....Los Angeles, CA
Cleary, Alyson Greenlaw ....North Haven, CT
Cleary, Amy M. ....Philadelphia, PA
Cleary, Andrea Davis ....Orlando, FL
Cleary, Annemarie DiNardo
Falls Church, VA
Cleary & Associates ....Cleveland, OH
Hudson, OH
Independence, OH
Cleary, Brian P. ....Buffalo, NY
Cleary, Catherine B. ....Milwaukee, WI
Cleary, Charles F. ....Manchester, NH
Cleary, Christine L. ....San Francisco, CA
Cleary, Claudia Tenney ....Clinton, NY
Cleary, Daintry E. ....Tampa, FL
Cleary, David D. ....Chicago, IL
Cleary, David L. ....Rutland, VT
Cleary, David M. ....Memphis, TN
Cleary, Dennis H. ....Carlsbad, CA
Cleary, Dennis P. ....Buffalo, NY
Cleary, Douglas A. ....San Diego, CA
Cleary, E. Garrett ....Rochester, NY
Cleary, Edward J. ....St. Paul, MN
Cleary, Edward L., Jr. ....Bridgeport, CT
Cleary, Edward P. ....Marshall, MO
Cleary, Francis C., Jr. ....Boston, MA
Cleary, Frank B. ....Bridgeport, CT
Cleary, Gail Patrick ....New York, NY
Cleary, Gerald P. ....Chicago, IL
Cleary, Gerald V., III ....Chicago, IL
Cleary, Gordon P. ....Providence, RI
Cleary, Gottlieb, Steen & Hamilton
Washington, DC
New York, NY
Cleary, Helen Curtin ....Louisville, KY
Cleary, Henry V. ....Palm Desert, CA
Cleary, J. Dinnen ....Tacoma, WA
Cleary, J. Michael ....Washington, DC
Cleary, Jacqueline P. ....Washington, DC
Cleary, James C. ....Rochester, NY
Cleary, James H. ....Rutherford, NJ
Cleary, James H., P.A. ....Rutherford, NJ
Cleary, James J. ....Birmingham, AL
Cleary, James J. ....Matawan, NJ
Cleary, James J. ....Massapequa, NY
Cleary, James J., Jr. ....New York, NY
Cleary, James M., Jr. ....Houston, TX
Cleary, James Michael ....Jenkintown, PA
Cleary, James P. ....San Francisco, CA
Cleary, James P., III ....Haverhill, MA
Cleary, James R. ....Huntsville, AL
Cleary, Janet Walters ....Corning, NY
Cleary, Janice L. ....Chicago, IL
Cleary, Jas. F. ....Troy, NY
Cleary, Jean K. ....Albany, NY
Cleary, Jeffrey L. ....Chattanooga, TN
Cleary, Jeffrey T. ....San Francisco, CA
Cleary, Jennifer A. ....Saratoga Springs, NY
Cleary, Jill E. ....San Diego, CA
Cleary, Joan M. ....Evergreen Park, IL
Cleary, John ....Waukegan, IL
Cleary, John C. ....Pittsburgh, PA
Cleary, John E. ....Omaha, NE
Cleary, John F. ....Merrill, WI
Cleary, John G. ....Haverhill, MA
Cleary, John J. ....San Diego, CA
Cleary, John J. ....New Canaan, CT
Cleary, John J. ....New York, NY
Cleary, John J., (P.C.) ....Boston, MA
Cleary, John L. ....New York, NY
Cleary, John L. ....Spencer, TN
Cleary, John P. ....San Diego, CA
Cleary, John P. ....Uniondale, NY
Cleary, John R. ....Kansas City, MO
Cleary, Josele ....Lancaster, PA
Cleary & Josem, LLP ....Philadelphia, PA
Cleary, Joseph A. ....Haverhill, MA
Cleary, Joseph F. ....Eastham, MA
Cleary, Joseph N.
Equal Employment Opportunity Commission, Office of Legal Counsel, GV
Cleary, Joseph T. ....Philadelphia, PA
Cleary, Kathleen Anne ....Pittsburgh, PA
Cleary, Kenneth W. ....Bradenton, FL
Cleary, Kevan ....Brooklyn, NY
Cleary, Kevin P. ....Lake Orion, MI
Cleary & Komen, LLP ....Washington, DC
Cleary, Kristine H. ....Milwaukee, WI
Cleary, Lara A. ....Chicago, IL
Cleary, Lauren A ....Adams, MA
Cleary, Lauri E. ....Bethesda, MD
Fairfax, VA
Cleary Law Offices, P.C. ....Haverhill, MA
Cleary, Lisa E. ....New York, NY
Cleary & Lockett, P.C. ....Chattanooga, TN
Cleary, Lora H. ....Columbus, OH
Cleary, Loretta ....Los Angeles, CA
Cleary, Lori L. ....Omaha, NE
Cleary, M. Blake ....Wilmington, DE
Cleary, Mansfield R. ....Cave Junction, OR
Cleary, Mark A. ....Augusta, GA
Cleary, Mark A., P.C. ....Augusta, GA
Cleary, Mary Jane ....Denver, CO
Cleary, Maureen E. ....Philadelphia, PA
Cleary, Maureen L. ....Salt Lake City, UT
Cleary & McCrystal ....Massapequa, NY
Cleary, Michael A. ....Roanoke, VA
Cleary, Michael E. ....Wichita, KS
Cleary, Michael J. ....Rockford, IL
Cleary, Michael P. ....Columbus, OH
Cleary, Patricia A. ....Cleveland, OH
Cleary, Patricia DelBueno ....Freehold, NJ
Cleary, Patricia L. ....Escondido, CA
Cleary, Paul G. ....Clarence, NY
Cleary, Paul J. ....Tulsa, OK
Cleary, Richard C. ....Houlton, ME
Cleary, Richard C., P.A. ....Houlton, ME
Cleary, Richard D. ....Los Angeles, CA
Cleary, Richard M. ....Los Angeles, CA
Cleary, Richard M.J. ....Riverside, CA
Cleary, Richard S. ....Louisville, KY
Cleary, Robert F. ....Chicago, IL
Cleary, Robert J. ....Newark, NJ
Cleary, Robert R. ....Detroit, MI
Cleary, Ruth M. ....Bloomington, MN
Cleary, Scott A. ....Jacksonville, FL
Cleary, Sean M. ....Miami, FL
Cleary & Sevilla ....San Diego, CA
Cleary Shahi Associates, A Professional Corporation ....Brattleboro, VT
Burlington, VT
Rutland, VT
Cleary, Stephen L. ....Chicago, IL
Cleary, Stephen M. ....Albany, NY
Cleary, Stephen R. ....Treasury Department, Internal Revenue Service, GV
Cleary, Terese ....Chicago, IL
Cleary, Therese M. ....Woodside, CA
Cleary, Thomas M. ....Los Angeles, CA
Cleary, Thomas M. ....Chicago, IL
Cleary, Thomas P. ....Buffalo, NY
Cleary, Thomas Patrick ....Portland, OR
Cleary, Timothy B. ....Kenilworth, NJ
Cleary, Timothy G. ....Santa Cruz, CA
Cleary, Timothy R. ....Cleveland, OH
Cleary, Todd ....Milwaukee, WI
Cleary, Ward Frank ....Stamford, CT
Cleary, William J. ....Great Neck, NY
Cleary, William J. ....New York, NY
Cleary, William J., Jr. ....Los Angeles, CA
Cleary, William W. ....Keene, NH
Cleasby, Donald S. ....Des Plaines, IL
Cleave, Scott W., Jr. ....Decatur, IL
Cleaveland, Jack M., Jr. ....Dallas, TX
Cleaveland, John A. ....San Francisco, CA
Cleaveland, John M. ....Columbia, MO
Cleaveland, Kathleen S. ....Dallas, TX
Cleaveland, Lloyd A. ....Chillicothe, MO
Cleaveland, Macoubrie, Cox, Elliott and Macoubrie, L.L.C. ....Chillicothe, MO
Cleaveland, Michael R. ....Jacksonville, FL
Cleaveland, Patricia A. ....Baltimore, MD
Cleaveland, William D. ....Phoenix, AZ
Cleaveland, William H. ....Roanoke, VA
Cleavenger, John D. ....Des Moines, IA
Cleavenger, Paul T. ....Kingston, NC
Cleaver & Cleaver ....Boulder, CO
Cleaver, David C. ....Chambersburg, PA
Cleaver, David C., & Associates, P.C.
Chambersburg, PA
Cleaver, James A. ....Annapolis, MD
Fort Washington, MD
Waldorf, MD
Cleaver, Kenneth ....Las Vegas, NV
Cleaver, Lauren (Von Helbig) ....Boulder, CO
Cleaver, Mary Jo ....Omaha, NE
Cleaver, Paul D. ....Upper Marlboro, MD
Cleaver, Sandra Watkins ....Canton, OH
Cleaver, Thoburn G. ....Boulder, CO
Cleaver, William A. ....Olathe, KS
Cleaver, William D. ....Glen Ellyn, IL
Cleaver, William L. ....Moline, IL
Cleaver-Bascombe, Karen P.
Washington, DC
Cleaves, Dana A. ....Portland, ME
Cleaves, Mark Andrew ....Reston, VA
Cleaves, Matthew J. ....Dallas, TX
Cleaves, Robert E., IV ....Portland, ME
Cleaves, Robert N. ....Los Angeles, CA
Cleavinger, Diane ....Tallahassee, FL
Cleavinger, Janice J. ....Houston, TX
Cleavinger, Marc D. ....Carlsbad, CA
Clebowicz, Francine E. ....Los Angeles, CA
Clebowicz, Walter A. ....New Britain, CT
Cleckler, Michael H. ....Birmingham, AL
Cleckley, Franklin D. ....Morgantown, WV
Cleckner and Fearen ....Harrisburg, PA
Cleckner, Paul E. ....Memphis, TN
Cleckner, Richard W. ....Harrisburg, PA
Clee, Susan M. ....New York, NY
Cleek, Amy ....Dallas, TX
Cleek, Elizabeth M. Dilloway ....Media, PA
Cleek, Robert J. ....Novato, CA
Cleek, Ronald G. ....Springfield, MO
Cleek, W. Todd ....Portland, OR
Cleeland, Anne B. ....Santa Ana, CA
Cleeland, Bruce L. ....Santa Ana, CA
Cleeman, Raymond ....Mount Vernon, NY
Cleere, Brian P. ....Wynnewood, PA
Cleere, Carole A. ....Wynnewood, PA
Cleere, Gerard R. ....Phoenix, AZ
Cleere, Robert F. ....Phoenix, AZ
Cleereman, Jason Try ....Milwaukee, WI
Clees, Joseph T. ....Phoenix, AZ
Cleesattle, Jodi L. ....Washington, DC
Cleeton, Bruce Cameron ....Portland, OR
Clefisch, Kevin H. ....Garnavillo, IA
Clefisch & Saunders ....Elkader, IA
Garnavillo, IA
Clegg, Alicia J. ....Stonington, CT
Clegg, Barry F. ....Minneapolis, MN
Clegg, C. Bailey ....Kent, OH
Clegg, Carolyn J. ....Magnolia, AR
Clegg, Christopher R. ....Richfield, OH

Clegg, David B. ... San Rafael, CA
Clegg, David L. ... Bolivia, NC
Clegg, Elliott L. ... Magnolia, AR
Clegg, Georgette B. ... Austin, TX
Clegg, H. James ... Salt Lake City, UT
Clegg, James L. ... Augusta, GA
Clegg, Jennie L. ... Portland, ME
Clegg, John H. ... New Orleans, LA
Clegg, Karen K. ... Kansas City, MO
Clegg, Karen W.
Department Of Veterans Affairs, Office of the General Counsel, GV
Clegg, Kenneth R. ... Sanford, ME
Clegg Law Offices, The, P.S. ... Tukwila, WA
Clegg, Marcia L. ... Lansing, IL
Clegg, Marvin F. ... Holly Hill, FL
Clegg, Michael V. ... Baton Rouge, LA
Clegg, Perry S. ... Washington, DC
Clegg, Richard A. ... San Diego, CA
Atlanta, GA
Clegg, Robert M. ... Tukwila, WA
Clegg, Roger ... Washington, DC
Clegg, Thomas S. ... Decatur, GA
Clegg, Trevor C. ... Fresno, CA
Clegg, Whitney G. ... New Martinsville, WV
Clegg, William J., III (IBA) ... Providence, RI
Cleghorn, Kathleen M. ... Putney, VT
Cleghorn, Megan E. ... Philadelphia, PA
Clein, A. Michael ... Las Vegas, NV
Clein, Carrie H. ... Denver, CO
Clein, Harvey A. ... Atlanta, GA
Clein, Scott R. ... Miami, FL
Clekis Law Firm, The, P.A.
Charleston, SC
Hollywood, SC
Moncks Corner, SC
Summerville, SC
Clekis, Nicholas J. ... Charleston, SC
Cleland, A. Craig ... Atlanta, GA
Cleland, Andrea L. ... Columbus, OH
Cleland, Bartlett D. ... United States Senate, Senatorial Assistants, GV
Cleland, Charles N., Jr. ... Sarasota, FL
Cleland, Christopher T. ... Sacramento, CA
Cleland, E. Gordon ... New York, NY
Cleland, George M. ... Winston-Salem, NC
Cleland, George M., IV ... Winston-Salem, NC
Cleland, Jack H. ... Corning, NY
Cleland, James A. ... Durango, CO
Cleland, James K. ... Chicago, IL
Cleland, Jennifer J. ... Raleigh, NC
Cleland, John D. ... Houston, TX
Cleland, John M. ... Smethport, PA
Cleland, Kelly ... Chicago, IL
Cleland, Lianna L. ... New York, NY
Cleland, Michael J. ... Grosse Pointe, MI
Troy, MI
Cleland, Richard L.
Federal Trade Commission, Bureau of Consumer Protection, GV
Cleland, Robert H. ... Bay City, MI
Cleland, Sean S. ... Mount Clemens, MI
Cleland, Terri J. ... Upland, CA
Cleland-Hamnett, Wendy
Environmental Protection Agency, Program Office Attorneys, GV
Clelland, Robert T., Jr. ... Seattle, WA
Clelland, Wilfred Shawn
Chattanooga, TN
Clelland, William G. ... Minneapolis, MN
Clem, A. Winfield, IV ... Paris, TX
Clem, Alexander M. ... Orlando, FL
Clem, Carmon D. ... Port Orchard, WA
Clem, Carol A. ... Los Angeles, CA
Clem, Charles Edward ... Henderson, KY
Clem, Chester, (P.A.) ... Vero Beach, FL
Clem, Christopher ... Cleveland, OH
Clem, Harry Earl ... Urbana, IL
Clem, J. Christopher ... Chattanooga, TN
Clem, James Steven ... Birmingham, AL
Clem, Marvin E. ... Lexington, KY
Clem, Polackwich & Vocelle
Vero Beach, FL
Clem, R. Garry ... Birmingham, AL
Clem, Richard A. ... Indianapolis, IN
Clem, Richard P. ... Minneapolis, MN
Clem, Robert C. ... Sioux City, IA
Clem, Susan C. ... Covina, CA
Clem, Terrance A. ... Lansing, MI
Clem, Thomas L. ... Anderson, IN
Clem, Vanessa M. ... Houston, TX
Clemans, Melvin S. ... Bridgeport, WV
Clemans, Warren M. ... Seattle, WA
Clemen, John D. ... Morristown, NJ
Clemen, Mary E. ... Minneapolis, MN
Clemenceau, Paul B. ... Houston, TX
Clemency, John R. ... Phoenix, AZ
Clemency, Robert E. ... Milwaukee, WI
Clemens, Barbara A. ... Joliet, IL
Clemens, Barton E., Jr.
Santa Barbara, CA
Clemens, Bruce A., (A Professional Corporation) ... Beverly Hills, CA
Clemens, Charles A. ... Cleveland, OH
Clemens, Charles W. ... Somerville, NJ
Clemens, Cindy B. ... San Luis Obispo, CA
Clemens, Cynthia J. ... San Diego, CA
Clemens, David A. ... Buffalo, NY
Clemens, David L. ... Dubuque, IA
Clemens, David R. ... Glastonbury, CT
Clemens, Erwin L. ... Defiance, OH
Hicksville, OH
Clemens, Frank J., Jr. ... White Plains, NY
Clemens, Gerald O. ... Salem, VA
Clemens, J. Christopher ... Roanoke, VA
Clemens, Jane F. ... Buffalo, NY
Clemens, Jay C. ... San Jose, CA
Clemens, Jeanne Ress ... Louisville, KY
Clemens, Jennifer A. ... Dubuque, IA
Clemens, Jeptha C. ... Oxford, MS
Clemens, Kathleen L. ... Los Angeles, CA
Clemens, Keith M. ... Los Angeles, CA
Clemens, Korhn, Liming & Warncke
Defiance, OH
Hicksville, OH
Clemens, Loretta Lee, P.C. ... Dallas, TX
Clemens, Loretta Lee, (P.C.) ... Dallas, TX
Clemens, Margaret A. ... Rochester, NY
Clemens, Mark W. ... Austin, TX
Clemens, Mary Etcheverry ... Moss Beach, CA
Clemens, Melissa ... Los Angeles, CA
Clemens, Michael J. ... Beverly Hills, CA
Clemens, Michael P. ... Albuquerque, NM
Clemens, Nulty & Gifford ... Souderton, PA
Clemens, Patricia A. ... Los Angeles, CA
Clemens, Paul Philip ... Louisville, KY
Clemens, R. Wayne ... Souderton, PA
Clemens, Radley E. ... Omaha, NE
Clemens, Randy W. ... Decatur, IL
Clemens, Richard G. ... Chicago, IL
Clemens, Robert B. ... Indianapolis, IN
Clemens, Robert Lyle ... Oklahoma City, OK
Clemens, Scott E. ... Kewanee, IL
Clemens & Spencer, A Professional Corporation ... San Antonio, TX
Clemens, Steven E. ... New York, NY
Clemens, Thomas J. ... Boston, MA
Clemens, Tim A. ... Antwerp, OH
Clemens, Travis G., Jr. ... Phoenix, AZ
Clemens, William J. ... Livonia, MI
Clemens, William J. ... Philadelphia, PA
Clemenson, Christina E. ... Clearwater, FL
Clemenson, Christopher S. ... Seattle, WA
Clement, Alan B. ... New York, NY
Clement, Alden A., Jr. ... Baton Rouge, LA
Clement, Andrew Payne ... Kannapolis, NC
Clement, Arthur J., III ... Durham, NC
Clement & Associates ... Sacramento, CA
Clement, Barbara H. ... San Francisco, CA
Clement, Bret S. ... Fishers, IN
Indianapolis, IN
Clement, Bruce ... Federal Way, WA
Clement, Candice J. ... Albany, NY
Clement, Catherine ... Newton, MA
Clement, Charles E. ... Boone, NC
Clement, Clayton E. ... Santa Rosa, CA
Clement, Colin C. ... Itasca, IL
Clement, Daniel E. ... New York, NY
New York, NY
Clement, Daniel G. ... San Diego, CA
Clement, Daniel J. ... Lewisburg, PA
Clement, David C. ... New Orleans, LA
Clement, David J. ... Horse Cave, KY
Clement, Debra A. ... Mineola, NY
Clement, Edith Brown ... New Orleans, LA
Clement, Edward H. ... Richmond, VA
Clement, Fitzpatrick & Kenworthy, Incorporated ... St. Helena, CA
Santa Rosa, CA
Clement, Frances R. ... Montgomery, AL
Clement, Frank G., Jr. ... Nashville, TN
Clement, Fredrick E. ... Redding, CA
Clement, G. Edward ... Mount Dora, FL
Clement & Gates, LLC ... New Orleans, LA
Clement, Geoffrey P. ... Metairie, LA
Clement, Gloria Griffin ... Topeka, KS
Clement, Gregory M. ... Pomona, CA
Clement, Holly Harmuth
Department Of The Interior, Office of Hearings & Appeals, GV
Clement, Irma C. ... Teaneck, NJ
Clement, J. Michael ... Clinton, TN
Clement, James A. ... Hettinger, ND
Clement, James G. ... Irving, TX
Clement, James L. ... Crown Point, IN
Clement, James L., Jr. ... Valparaiso, IN
Clement, James W. ... Chicago, IL
Clement, Janice T. ... Naples, FL
Clement, Jessica J. ... Boulder, CO
Clement, Jill Habenicht ... Bellaire, TX
Clement, J. M., Jr. ... Dickson, TN
Clement, John A. ... Chicago, IL
Clement, John D., Jr. ... Tuscumbia, AL
Clement, John D., Jr. LLC ... Florence, AL
Tuscumbia, AL
Clement, John M. ... Dallas, TX
Clement, Kelly A. ... Washington, DC
Clement, Kimberly R. ... Santa Rosa, CA
Clement, Kori L. ... Birmingham, AL
Clement, Laurence A., Jr. ... Manhattan, KS
Clement Law Center ... Federal Way, WA
Clement, Lesley Ann ... Sacramento, CA
Clement, Leslie J., Jr., A Prof. Law Corp.
Thibodaux, LA
Clement, Lisa Frisina ... Abingdon, VA
Richmond, VA
Clement, L. K., Jr. ... New Orleans, LA
Clement & Lobdell ... Honolulu, HI
Clement, Mark ... Pittsburgh, PA
Clement, Mark D. ... Honolulu, HI
Clement, Mark N. ... Flint, MI
Clement, Martha B. ... Houston, TX
Clement, Matthew A. ... Jefferson City, MO
Clement, Michael J. ... Blue Bell, PA
Clement, Nathaniel E. ... Chapel Hill, NC
Clement, Neal ... Jackson, MS
Clement, Neil Richard ... Birmingham, AL
Clement, Norman M. ... Boston, MA
Clement, Paul D. ... Washington, DC
Clement, Randall C. ... Lakeland, FL
Orlando, FL
Clement, Randall J. ... Costa Mesa, CA
Clement, Ray S., Jr. ... Kenner, LA
Clement, Rebecca J. ... Haverford, PA
Clement, Robert E. ... Victoria, VA
Clement, Robert L., Jr. ... Charleston, SC
Clement, Robyn L. ... Friendswood, TX
Clement, Roger A., Jr. ... Portland, ME
Clement, Ronald S. ... Greenville, SC
Clement, Rutledge C., Jr.
New Orleans, LA
Clement, Sanford ... Vancouver, WA
Clement, Sarah Preston
Merit Systems Protection Board, Washington, D.C. Regional Office, GV
Clement, Susan J. ... New York, NY
Clement, Tanya Taylor ... Little Rock, AR
Clement, Thomas E. ... Rochester, NY
Clement, Todd ... Dallas, TX
Clement, W. Rodney, Jr. ... Jackson, MS
Clement, W. Scott ... Seattle, WA
Clement & Wheatley, A Professional Corporation ... Danville, VA
Clement, Whittington W. ... Danville, VA
Clement, William D. ... Junction City, KS
Clement & Yates ... Boone, NC
Clement, Zack A. ... Houston, TX
Clemente, Anthony D. ... Endicott, NY
Clemente, C. Daniel ... Vienna, VA
Clemente, Coleen A. S. ... Westminster, MD
Clemente, Constantine L. ... New York, NY
Clemente, Dickson & Mueller, P.A.
Morristown, NJ
Clemente, Ellen L. ... Washington, DC
Clemente, Frances S. ... Beach Lake, PA
Clemente & Gesicki ... Roseland, NJ
Clemente, Jonathan D. ... Morristown, NJ
Clemente, Josephine ... Newburgh, NY
Clemente, Laurence A. ... Goshen, NY
Clemente, Laurence A., P.C. ... Goshen, NY
Clemente, Luke D. ... Latham, NY
Clemente, Mark A. ... Roseland, NJ
Clemente, Matthew A. ... Chicago, IL
Clemente, Michael C. ... Struthers, OH
Clemente, Nicholas A. ... Brooklyn, NY
Clemente, Nicholas A. ... Philadelphia, PA
Clemente, Paul R. ... Waterbury, VT
Clemente, Paul S. ... Brooklyn, NY
Clemente, Peter C. ... Jersey City, NJ
Clemente, Robert A. ... Troy, MI
Clemente, Robert G. ... Hartford, CT
Clemente, Robert P. ... Holtsville, NY
Clemente, Robert S. ... New York, NY
Clemente, Salvatore A. ... Philadelphia, PA
Clemente & Wagner Co., L.P.A.
Struthers, OH
Clementi, John R. ... Leominster, MA
Clementi, Paul J. ... Chicago, IL
Clementi, Robert S. ... Park Ridge, IL
Clementi, Vito A.
Department Of Veterans Affairs, Board of Veterans Appeals, GV
Clementino, Barbara J. ... Sonoma, CA
Clementino, Debra Ann ... Lansing, MI
Clementino, Valentino D. ... West Hartford, CT
Clements, Alan B. ... San Diego, CA
Clements, Allen, Fishman, Woods & Walsh
Addison, TX
Clements, Allen, Jr. ... Lady Lake, FL
Clements, Ann Carol ... Norwalk, CT
Clements, Anna C. ... Clinton, MS
Clements, Arthur L. (Tim), III
Cleveland, OH
Clements, Barbara Webb ... Indianapolis, IN
Clements, Bernadine Morielli
Glens Falls, NY
Clements, Betty J. ... Atlanta, GA
Clements, Brown & McNichols, P.A.
Lewiston, ID
Clements, Bruce W. ... Trenton, MI
Clements, Bruce W. ... San Antonio, TX
Clements, Catherine A.
San Francisco, CA
Clements, Cathleen A. ... New York, NY
Clements, Charles, Jr. ... La Fayette, GA
Clements, Chris A. ... Wichita, KS
Clements, Christopher J. ... Harrisburg, PA
Clements, Christopher M. ... Dalton, GA
Clements & Clements ... Dallas, TX
Clements, Curtis D. ... Bentonville, AR
Clements, Daniel M. ... Baltimore, MD
Clements, Daniel O. ... Cincinnati, OH
Clements, Darrell L. ... Dallas, TX
Clements, Dawn Ferrell ... San Antonio, TX
Clements, Deborah Bradley
Washington, DC
Clements, Don W. ... Brownwood, TX
Clements, Donald A. ... Department of Justice, Drug Enforcement Administration, GV
Clements and Drevo ... Elmwood, NE
Lincoln, NE
Clements & Ducharme, P.C. ... Canton, NY
Clements, Durant F. ... Bridgeport, TX
Clements, Dwight L. ... Elmwood, NE
Clements, Elaine F. ... Metairie, LA
Clements Firm, The ... Glens Falls, NY
Clements, Frank J. ... Pittsburgh, PA
Clements, George E. ... Baltimore, MD
Clements, Gregory Neil ... Charlotte, NC
Clements, Hal F. S. ... Chattanooga, TN
Clements, Hanna R. ... Chicago, IL
New York, NY
Clements, Howell Dean ... Chattanooga, TN
Clements, Howell G. ... Chattanooga, TN
Clements, Ivan K., Jr. ... Daytona Beach, FL
Clements, Ivan K., Jr. ... DeLand, FL
Clements, Jacqueline M. ... New York, NY
Clements, James Bryson ... Davenport, IA
Clements, James G. ... New York, NY
Clements, James W., III ... Chattanooga, TN
Clements, Jamie H. ... Temple, TX
Clements, Janine M. ... Indianapolis, IN
Clements, Janis E. ... Austin, TX
Clements, Jean Harrison ... Leesburg, VA
Clements, Jeffrey D. ... Boston, MA
Clements, Jeffrey E. ... West Union, IA
Clements, Jennifer ... Milwaukee, WI
Clements, Jerry K. ... Dallas, TX
Clements, Jim O. ... Sherman, TX
Clements, John D. ... Birmingham, AL
Clements, John H.
Federal Energy Regulatory Commission, Office of the General Counsel, GV
Clements, Jordan W. ... Burlingame, CA
Clements, Joseph T., Jr. ... Little Rock, AR
Clements, Kara K. ... Atlanta, GA
Clements, Kelly R. ... Dallas, TX
Clements, L. Thomas ... Atlanta, GA
Clements Law Firm ... Oskaloosa, IA
What Cheer, IA
Clements, Lori A. ... Franklin, MA
Clements, Lynn A. ... Washington, DC
Clements, M. Jeannine ... Louisville, KY
Clements, Mahin & Cohen ... Blue Ash, OH
Cincinnati, OH
Clements, Mahlon T. ... Glens Falls, NY
Clements, Marc P. ... Wichita, KS
Clements, Mark C. ... Addison, TX
Clements, Mark E. ... Lakeland, FL
Clements, Mark E., P.A. ... Lakeland, FL
Clements, Mark R. ... Salt Lake City, UT
Clements, Martin E. ... Lapeer, MI
Clements, Merritt M. ... San Antonio, TX
Clements, Michael K. ... New York, NY
Clements, Miles P. ... New Orleans, LA
Clements & Nutt ... Baltimore, MD
Clements, O'Neill, Pierce Nickens & Wilson, L.L.P. ... Dallas, TX
Houston, TX
Clements, Owen J. ... San Francisco, CA
Clements, Paul R.
Department of the Air Force, Office of the Judge Advocate General, GV
Spartanburg, SC
Clements, Philip W. ... Seattle, WA
Clements, Ralph M. ... Sebring, FL
Clements, Reed ... Lewiston, ID
Clements, Richard L. ... Elmwood, NE
Clements, Richard R. ... Signal Hill, CA
Clements, Richard R., A Professional Corporation ... Signal Hill, CA
Clements, Robert D., Jr. ... Alvin, TX
Clements, Robert G. ... Orlando, FL
Clements, Robert G. ... Virginia Beach, VA
Clements, Robert K. ... Oskaloosa, IA
Clements, Robert L. ... Dallas, TX
Clements, Robert W. ... Lake Charles, LA
Clements, Robt H. ... Chicago, IL
Clements, Robt. S. ... Arlington, VA
Clements, Roxanne S. ... Washington, DC
Clements, Rush M. ... Rolling Fork, MS
Clements, Ruth P. ... West Palm Beach, FL
Clements, Scott D. ... Pittsburgh, PA
Wheeling, WV
Clements, Scott M. ... Orlando, FL
Clements, Shonagh ... St. Louis, MO
Clements, Stephen E., P.C. ... Mobile, AL
Clements, Thomas A. ... Hammond, IN
Clements, Thomas G. ... Glens Falls, NY
Clements, Thomas H. ... Fayetteville, NC
Clements, Thomas V. ... Orange, CA
San Diego, CA
Walnut Creek, CA
Clements, Tracy M. ... San Francisco, CA
Clements, William E. ... Cincinnati, OH
Clements, William L. ... Washington, DC
Clements, William W. ... Scottsdale, AZ
Clemenz, Robert ... New Orleans, LA
Clemer, Jack M. ... Kerrville, TX
Clemer, Mark C. ... Houston, TX
Clemetson, Tilman O. ... St. Paul, MN
Cleminshaw, Charles H. ... Cleveland, OH
Clemm, Mark C. ... Plymouth Meeting, PA
Clemmens, John C. ... Reading, PA
Clemmensen, Fritz J. ... Crosslake, MN
Clemmer, Brent S. ... Tustin, CA
Clemmer, Michael J. ... Birmingham, AL
Clemmer, Robert W. ... Orange, CA
Clemmer, Robert W., P.C. ... Orange, CA
Clemmer, Stephen B. ... Long Beach, CA
Clemmer, Wynn R. ... Lincoln, NE
Clemmons, Alan D. ... Myrtle Beach, SC
Clemmons, Amy C. ... Coeur d'Alene, ID
Spokane, WA
Clemmons, Brian E. ... Raleigh, NC
Clemmons, Denise L. ... Troy, MI
Clemmons, Gary H. ... New Bern, NC
Clemmons, John H. ... Fairfield, OH
Clemmons, Lauren Murphy ... Raleigh, NC
Clemmons, Melanie A. ... Houston, TX
Clemmons, Penny ... Santa Barbara, CA
Clemmons, William B., Jr. ... Memphis, TN
Clemo, George J. A. ... Roanoke, VA
Clemon, U. W. ... Birmingham, AL
Clemons, A. O., Jr. ... Vancouver, WA
Clemons, Bill ... Hardshell, KY
Clemons, E. Steven ... Hazard, KY
Clemons, Elgin ... New York, NY
Clemons, Holly Fujiye ... Urbana, IL
Clemons & Hood ... Carbondale, IL
Clemons, Howard L. ... McLean, VA
Clemons, Jack N. ... Memphis, TN
Clemons, James E. ... Los Angeles, CA
Clemons, James E. ... Montpelier, VT
St. Johnsbury, VT
Clemons, John R. ... Carbondale, IL
Clemons, Keefe Bryant ... Boston, MA
Clemons & Klimpl ... Doylestown, PA
Clemons, Lamar G. ... Corpus Christi, TX
Clemons, M. LaMarr ... Amite, LA
Clemons, Martha ... Chicago, IL
Clemons, Mary ... Nashville, TN

Clemons, Michelle L. ....**Cincinnati, OH**
Clemons, Scott W. ....Panama City, FL
Clemons, Steven H. ....**Dallas, TX**
Clemons & Taube ....Memphis, TN
Clemons, Terry W. ....Doylestown, PA
Clemons, Thomas M., Jr. ....Algonac, MI
Clemons, Timothy C. ....Folsom, CA
Clemons, Ursula L. ....Sacramento, CA
Clemons, William E. ....Jackson, MS
Clemons, William T., III ......**Los Angeles, CA**
Clemons, Willis J. ....Santa Ana, CA
Clemow, Brian ....**Hartford, CT**
Clendenen, Patrick T. ....**Boston, MA**
Clendenen, William H., Jr.
New Haven, CT
Clendenen, William H., Jr., A Professional Corporation ....**Madison, CT**
New Haven, CT
Clendenen, Charles E. ....New Richmond, OH
Clendenin, Craig H. ....**Houston, TX**
Clendenin, Harry H., III ......**Greensboro, NC**
Clendenin, J. Gregg ....Lexington, KY
Clendenin, Jennifer A. ....**Des Moines, IA**
Clendenin, John F. ....Sparta, IL
Clendenin, John T. ....**Des Moines, IA**
Clendening, Gary J. ....**Bloomington, IN**
Clendening, Warren E. ....Santa Monica, CA
Clendening, Wendy Olin ....Los Angeles, CA
Clendenny, Gerald ....Wayne, NJ
Clendenon, Donn A. ....Sioux Falls, SD
Clendinen, Craig P. ....Tampa, FL
Clendinen, Harry H., III ....Greensboro, NC
Clennan, John F. ....Ronkonkoma, NY
Clennan, John J. ....Stafford, TX
Clenney, Kathryn S. ....Escondido, CA
Clenney, R. Eugene, Jr. ....**Dothan, AL**
Clennon, Cary ....Washington, DC
Cleous, Cindy L. ....**Wichita, KS**
Clephane, Debra Auerbach ....**Detroit, MI**
Clepper, Michael H. ....Riverside, CA
Clerc, Marc Raymond ....Arlington, MA
Clerge, Sabrina ....Morris Plains, NJ
Clerici, John M. ....**Washington, DC**
Clerissi, Vivienne M. ....**Hoboken, NJ**
New York, NY
Clerke, W. Henry, IV ....Atlanta, GA
Clerkin, James C. ....**Mineola, NY**
New York, NY
Smithtown, NY
Clerkin, John J. ....Chicago, IL
Clerkin, John J. ....White Plains, NY
Clerkin, John R. ....Macomb, IL
Clerkin, Mary Ellen ....Albany, NY
Clerkin, Robert J. ....New York, NY
Clermont, Adam P. ....**Pittsfield, MA**
Clermont, Fabienne M. ....**Washington, DC**
Clermont, Joseph C. ....Dracut, MA
Clermont, Kevin M. ....Ithaca, NY
Clermont, Pamela A. ....Ithaca, NY
Clery & Clery ....Schaumburg, IL
Clery, Jeffrey M. ....Schaumburg, IL
Clery, John T. ....Schaumburg, IL
Clesi, Anthony J., Jr. ....**New Orleans, LA**
Clessuras, James G. ....**Chicago, IL**
Cleva, Richard H. ....Treasury Department, Office of the Comptroller of the Currency, GV
Cleva, Vern J. ....Santa Monica, CA
Cleve, Mary Alice ....**Philadelphia, PA**
Cleveland, A. Gus ....**Atlanta, GA**
Cleveland, Alan P. ....**Manchester, NH**
Cleveland, Alfred E. ....**Fayetteville, NC**
Cleveland, Allen L. ....Houston, TX
Cleveland, Anna Marie ....Hattiesburg, MS
Cleveland, Arlene Austin ....Sweetwater, TN
Cleveland & Bartkus, P.C. ....Denver, CO
Cleveland, Blair K. ....**Macon, GA**
Cleveland, Bryan R. ....**Miami, FL**
Cleveland, C. Anthony ....**Tallahassee, FL**
Cleveland, C. Wade ....Greenville, SC
Cleveland, Carl W. ....New Orleans, LA
Cleveland, Carl W., & Associates LLP
New Orleans, LA
Cleveland, Caroline Wrenn ......**Columbia, SC**
Cleveland, Catherine A.
Newport Beach, CA
Cleveland, Charles ....Birmingham, AL
Cleveland, Charles A. ....Spokane, WA
Cleveland, Charles R. ....Tulsa, OK
Cleveland, Christopher C.
Minneapolis, MN
Cleveland & Cleveland ....Birmingham, AL
Cleveland & Cleveland, A Professional Corporation ....Sweetwater, TN
Cleveland, Clifford W. ....Prattville, AL
Cleveland, Clifford W., II ....Prattville, AL
Cleveland, Constance L. ....Fargo, ND
Cleveland, Dan, Jr. ....**Boulder, CO**
Cleveland, David ....Palo Pinto, TX
Cleveland, David C. ....**Charleston, SC**
Cleveland, David G. ....**Atlanta, GA**
Cleveland, David L. ....Washington, DC
Cleveland, David R. ....**St. Paul, MN**
Cleveland, Deborah G. ....Fort Worth, TX
Cleveland, Donald R. ....West Point, GA
Cleveland, Edward D.
Colorado Springs, CO
Cleveland, Edward D., P.C.
Colorado Springs, CO
Cleveland, Frank C. ....Point Pleasant, WV
Cleveland, Frederick G. ....**Montpelier, VT**
Cleveland, Gabriela F. ....**Chicago, IL**
Cleveland, Gaines H. ....New York, NY
Cleveland, Greggory D. ....**Dallas, TX**
Cleveland, Gregory P. ....Stockton, CA
Cleveland, Grover E. ....**Seattle, WA**
Cleveland, Henry C., III ....**Denver, CO**
Cleveland, Herbert E. ....Chicago, IL
Cleveland, Herschel W. ....**Paris, AR**
Cleveland, Howard L., IV ....**Memphis, TN**
Cleveland, James E., III ....**Ashland, KY**
Cleveland, Janice S. ....Riverside, CA
Cleveland, Jean G. ....**Chicago, IL**
Cleveland, Jesse Marvin ....Conyers, GA
Cleveland, Joan B. ....Stamford, CT
Cleveland, John R. ....Gainesville, GA
Cleveland, John W. ....Sweetwater, TN
Cleveland, Jonathan B. ....Minneapolis, MN
Cleveland, Joseph F. ....**Fort Worth, TX**
Cleveland, Joseph H. ....Irving, TX
Cleveland, Kenneth Lee ....Birmingham, AL
Cleveland, King D. ....Atlanta, GA
Cleveland, Larry W. ....Frankfort, KY
Cleveland, Lynn A. ....**Denver, CO**
Cleveland, Mack N., Jr. ....**Sanford, FL**
Cleveland, Mae Elizabeth ....**Valdosta, GA**
Cleveland, Marcia J. ....Topsham, ME
Cleveland, Maria T. ....**Las Vegas, NV**
Cleveland, Marilyn J. ....**San Francisco, CA**
Cleveland, Matthew J. ....**Chicago, IL**
Cleveland, Melford O. ....Birmingham, AL
Cleveland, Michael G. ....**Chicago, IL**
Cleveland, Nancy S. ....**New York, NY**
Philadelphia, PA
Cleveland, Paul B. ....San Francisco, CA
Cleveland, Peter D. ....**Indianapolis, IN**
Cleveland, Peter D., P.C., A Professional Corporation ....**Indianapolis, IN**
Cleveland, Peter M. ....Shelburne, VT
Cleveland, Peter W. ....Gulfport, MS
Cleveland, Phyllis E. ....Cleveland, OH
Cleveland, Richard L., (P.S.) ....**Seattle, WA**
Cleveland, Richard W. ....Eugene, OR
Cleveland, Robert W. ....**Philadelphia, PA**
Cleveland & Robinette ....Eugene, OR
Cleveland, S. Jan ....Denver, CO
Cleveland and Shaaber ....Jacksonville, FL
Cleveland, Sherwood M. ....**Columbia, SC**
Cleveland, Theron C., Jr. ....Greenville, SC
Cleveland, Timothy L. ....Spartanburg, SC
Cleveland, Troy Edward ....San Antonio, TX
Cleveland, Waters and Bass, P.A.
Concord, NH
Wolfeboro, NH
Cleveland, William A. ....**Auburn, AL**
Cleveland, William C. ....**Charleston, SC**
Cleveland, William Joseph
Baton Rouge, LA
Slaughter, LA
Cleven, Dane H. ....Chicago, IL
Cleven, Jeffrey P. ....**Boston, MA**
Cleven, Kern W. ....Seattle, WA
Clevenger, Angel & Miller, P.L.L.C.
Little Rock, AR
Clevenger, Ann Bogorowski ....Medford, NJ
Clevenger, Catherine M.
Merit Systems Protection Board, Office of Appeals Counsel, GV
Clevenger, Daniel E., II ....**Akron, OH**
Clevenger, Don J. ....**Dallas, TX**
Clevenger, James E. ....San Diego, CA
Clevenger, James H. ....**Visalia, CA**
Clevenger, James N. ....**Plymouth, IN**
Clevenger, Jenny J. ....Phoenix, AZ
Clevenger, Kimberly S. ....**Riverside, CA**
San Diego, CA
Clevenger, Linda A. ....Sacramento, CA
Clevenger, Mark B. ....St. Charles, MO
Clevenger, Mark Wheeler ....Louisa, KY
Clevenger, Marsha Wardlaw
Little Rock, AR
Clevenger, Raymond C., III
United States Court Of Appeals For The Federal Circuit, GV
Clevenger, Raymond F. ....Ann Arbor, MI
Clevenger, Raymond F., P.C. ....Ann Arbor, MI
Clevenger, Robert B. ....San Francisco, CA
Clevenger, Robert V. ....Pekin, IL
Clevenger, Sherman Gary
Independence, OH
Clevenger, T. Scott ....**Little Rock, AR**
Clevenger, Ted B. ....**Columbus, OH**
Clevenger, William C. ....Los Angeles, CA
Clever, Alan R. ....**Overland Park, KS**
Clever, Kathleen K. ....**Kansas City, MO**
Clever, Ronald L. ....Allentown, PA
Cleverdon, Edwin B. ....Treasury Department, Internal Revenue Service, GV
Cleverdon, Richard ....**Tulsa, OK**
Cleveringa, Brad W. ....**Los Angeles, CA**
Cleverley, James W., Jr. ....Newton, IA
Cleverley Law Office ....Idaho Falls, ID
Cleverley, Matthew R. ....Idaho Falls, ID
Cleversey, Philip R. ....Beverly, MA
Clevert, Charles N., Jr. ....Milwaukee, WI
Cleves, Cynthia M. ....Covington, KY
Cleves, Joseph A., Jr. ....**Covington, KY**
Clew, Cary W. ....Long Beach, CA
Clewell, Robert H. ....Boston, MA
Clewell, Robert S. ....Elkins Park, PA
Clewis, Monroe Thomas ....Alhambra, CA
Click, Clyde E. ....**Atlanta, GA**
Click, David F. ....**Jupiter, FL**
Click, David L. ....Treasury Department, Internal Revenue Service, GV
Click, Grady H., Jr. ....Austin, TX
Click, John H., Jr. ....**Richmond, VA**
Click, Joseph O. ....**Washington, DC**
Click, Kimberly Hook ....Lexington, KY
Click, Myron E. ....Naples, FL
Click, Myron E., P.A. ....Naples, FL
Click, Tammy Bruch ....San Antonio, TX
Clickner, M. Jean ....Pittsburgh, PA
Cliett, Mark A. ....**West Point, MS**
Cliett & McRae, PLLC ....**Starkville, MS**
West Point, MS
Cliff, Carolyn ....Langley, WA
Cliff, Cary Alan ....**Naples, FL**
Cliff, Frank ....San Jose, CA
Cliff, John W., Jr. ....Odessa, TX
Cliff, Nancy J. ....Miami, FL
Cliff, Patricia Warburg ....New York, NY
Cliff, Paul ....**Riverside, CA**
Cliff, Scott Talmage ....**Portland, OR**
Cliff, Thomas V. ....Grosse Pointe, MI
Cliff, Walter C., (P.C.) ....**New York, NY**
Cliffe, Daniel L. ....**De Kalb, IL**
Cliffe, David W. ....**Findlay, OH**
Cliffe, Foster, Corneille & Buick
De Kalb, IL
Hinckley, IL
Shabbona, IL
Waterman, IL
Cliffe, Jason R. ....**San Antonio, TX**
Cliffe, Lori M. ....San Antonio, TX
Cliffel, Susan K. ....**Columbus, OH**
Clifford, Alice E. ....Portland, ME
Clifford, Brendan M. ....**Boston, MA**
Clifford, Brian C. ....**Hartford, CT**
Clifford & Brown, A Professional Corporation ....**Bakersfield, CA**
Clifford, Carol ....Washington, DC
Clifford, Carol A. ....**Santa Fe, NM**
Clifford, Carolyn Welch ....Barrington, IL
Clifford Chance Rogers & Wells LLP
Washington, DC
Clifford Chance Rogers & Wells LLP
New York, NY
Clifford, Charles G. ....Pelahatchie, MS
Clifford, Charles H. ....**San Francisco, CA**
Clifford, Charles M. ....Maryville, TN
Clifford, Christopher J.
San Francisco, CA
Clifford Clendenin O'Hale & Jones, L.L.P.
Greensboro, NC
High Point, NC
Clifford & Clifford ....Worcester, MA
Clifford, Clifford & Stone ....Lewiston, ME
Clifford, D. Shane ....**Las Vegas, NV**
Clifford, Daniel H. ....**Newport Beach, CA**
Clifford, Daniel J. ....**Norristown, PA**
Clifford, Danl. J. ....East Orland, ME
Clifford, Dawn Colleen ....Columbus, OH
Clifford, Denis J. ....Berkeley, CA
Clifford, Donald F., Jr. ....Chapel Hill, NC
Clifford, Donald R., (P.C.) ....Fort Wayne, IN
Clifford, Donna M. ....Mount Clemens, MI
Clifford & Duke, P.C. ....Richmond, VA
Clifford, Edward T. ....**Sacramento, CA**
Clifford, Eileen M. ....Boston, MA
Clifford, Eric S. ....Paris, TX
Clifford, Eugene T. ....Rochester, NY
Clifford, Field, Krier, Manning, Stone & Wilkerson, P.C. ....**Lubbock, TX**
Clifford, Francis V. ....San Francisco, CA
Clifford, Gary ....Osage Beach, MO
Clifford, Gary J. ....Hollister, CA
Clifford, Gelband, Purves & Constabile
Larchmont, NY
Clifford & Golden, P.A. ....Lisbon Falls, ME
Clifford, Gregory F. ....Cleveland, OH
Clifford, Harry F., Jr. ....San Francisco, CA
Clifford, J. Stephen ....Atlanta, GA
Clifford, Jack F., and Associates, Ltd.
Chicago, IL
Clifford, James A. ....**Portland, ME**
Clifford, James E. ....**New Haven, CT**
Clifford, James L. ....Worcester, MA
Clifford, James R. ....Pine City, MN
Clifford, James R., Sr. ......**Gaithersburg, MD**
Clifford, Jeffrey K. ....Boston, MA
Clifford, Jere R. ....Lewiston, ME
Clifford, Joan ....**Boulder, CO**
Clifford, John A. ....**Minneapolis, MN**
Clifford, John A. ....Long Beach, NY
Clifford, John D., III ....Lisbon Falls, ME
Clifford, John D., IV ....Lisbon Falls, ME
Clifford, John F. ....East Hartford, CT
Clifford, John G. ....Charlotte, NC
Clifford, John J. ....East Bridgewater, MA
Clifford, John M. ....**Washington, DC**
Clifford, John N. ....Richmond, VA
Clifford, John P. ....**Minneapolis, MN**
Clifford, John P., Jr. ....**Hartford, CT**
Clifford, John R. ....**San Diego, CA**
Clifford, John S. ....**Santa Ana, CA**
Clifford, John S. ....**Eden Prairie, MN**
Clifford, John Stuart Gavin ....Lebanon, NH
Clifford, John W. ....Chicago, IL
Clifford, Joseph E., III ....Phoenix, AZ
Clifford, Joseph P. ....Larchmont, NY
Clifford, Joyce E. ....**San Francisco, CA**
Clifford, Julie M. ....Alexandria, VA
Clifford, Karl N. ....**Lubbock, TX**
Clifford, Keith R. ....Madison, WI
Clifford, Kharma S. ....**Yakima, WA**
Clifford, Larmore, Nakos & Tutwiler
Fort Wayne, IN
Clifford Law Offices, P.C. ....**Chicago, IL**
Clifford, Lawrence J. ....South Bend, IN
Clifford, Leo J. ....Valparaiso, IN
Clifford, Linda M. ....**Madison, WI**
Clifford, Locke T. ....**Greensboro, NC**
Clifford, Lori W. ....**Fort Myers, FL**
Clifford, Lyons & Garde ....**Washington, DC**
Clifford, Mann & Swisher, L.C.
Charleston, WV
Dunbar, WV
Clifford, Marcia L. ....Deerfield, IL
Clifford, Margaret Joan ....Boulder, CO
Clifford, Maryann ....Hudson, FL
Clifford, Matthew O. ....**Missoula, MT**
Clifford, Michael T. ....Riverhead, NY
Clifford, Michael T. ....Charleston, WV
Clifford, Michael T., & Associates
Riverhead, NY
Clifford, Nicholas B., Jr. ....**St. Louis, MO**
Clifford, Patrick J. ....New Haven, CT
Clifford, Paul ....**Lafayette, CA**
Clifford, Paul E. ....**Boston, MA**
Clifford, Paula J. ....New Bedford, MA
Clifford, Peter ....**Kennebunk, ME**
Clifford, Peter B. ....Worcester, MA
Clifford, Ralph D. ....Lexington, MA
Clifford & Reuter, S.C. ....Madison, WI
Clifford, Richard B., Jr. ....**Washington, DC**
Clifford, Richard C. ....New York, NY
Clifford, Richard R., A P.C.
North Hollywood, CA
Clifford, Robert A. ....**Chicago, IL**
Clifford, Robert B. ....Arlington, MA
Clifford, Robert C. ....Carmel, CA
Clifford, Robert J. ....Markham, IL
Clifford, Robert L. ....**Morristown, NJ**
Clifford, Robert Scot ....**Pasadena, CA**
Clifford, Robert W. ....Auburn, ME
Clifford, Roger L. ....Chicago, IL
Clifford, Sandra E. ....Baltimore, MD
Clifford, Scott James ....Holbrook, MA
Clifford, Shawn P. ....**Chicago, IL**
Clifford, Sidney, Jr. ....Pawtucket, RI
Clifford, Standifer & McDowell ....Paris, TX
Clifford, Stephen C. ....**Westlake Village, CA**
Clifford, Stephen T. ....**Bakersfield, CA**
Clifford, Thomas D. ....Bloomfield, CT
Clifford, Thomas G. ....Salem, OR
Clifford, Thomas J. ....Grand Forks, ND
Clifford, Thomas N. ....Ellicott City, MD
Clifford, Thomas T. ....**Tampa, FL**
Clifford, Timothy J. ....**Troy, MI**
Clifford, W. Michael ....**Orlando, FL**
Clifford, Walter G. ....Chicago, IL
Clifford, William A. ....Lubbock, TX
Clifford, William C. ....Wakefield, MA
Clifford, William D. ....**Pittsburgh, PA**
Clifford, William H., Jr. ....Lewiston, ME
Clifford, William J. ....Charleston, SC
Clifford, William R. ....Anderson, IN
Clift, Gregory Michael ....**Dallas, TX**
Clift, Jean D. ....Denver, CO
Clift, Michael E. ....**Cookeville, TN**
Clift, Michael E. ....Shelton, WA
Clift, Orville C. ....Fort Smith, AR
Clift, Raymond S., Jr. ....Memphis, TN
Clift, Rhea ....Memphis, TN
Clift, Wyland Dale ....Bristol, CT
Clifthorne, Lucy Russell ....**Tacoma, WA**
Clifton and Associates ....**Providence, RI**
Clifton, Benjamin F., Jr. ....**Raleigh, NC**
Clifton, Benjamin J.
Hot Springs National Park, AR
Clifton, Bill C. ....Memphis, TN
Clifton, Bill C., P.C. ....Memphis, TN
Clifton Budd & DeMaria, LLP
Fort Lee, NJ
New York, NY
Clifton, Cara Lousia Epps
Oklahoma City, OK
Clifton, Cecil L., Jr. ....**Toccoa, GA**
Clifton, Daniel W. ....Louisville, KY
Clifton, George M. ....Tomball, TX
Clifton, Gregory A. ....**Detroit, MI**
Clifton, Hook & Bovarnick, P.C.
Denver, CO
Grand Junction, CO
Clifton, Jacob K., Jr. ....**Eugene, OR**
Clifton, James R. ....**Andalusia, AL**
Clifton, James R. ....**Denver, CO**
Grand Junction, CO
Clifton, Jeffrey James ....Birmingham, AL
Washington, DC
Clifton, Jill S. ....Collbran, CO
Clifton, John H. ....Carlisle, PA
Clifton, John L., IV ....Norman, OK
Clifton, John M., Jr. ....**Fort Wayne, IN**
Clifton, K. Nicole ....**Atlanta, GA**
Clifton, Kenneth D. ....Englewood, CO
Clifton, Larry D. ....Birmingham, AL
Clifton, Leo W. ....Austell, GA
Clifton, Lowell E. ....Oklahoma City, OK
Clifton, Michelle B. ....**Winston-Salem, NC**
Clifton, Philip K. ....New Iberia, LA
Clifton, R. Brent ....**Dallas, TX**
Clifton, Ralph M. ....Brinkley, AR
Clifton, Richard R. ....**Honolulu, HI**
Clifton, Sanders & Smith, P.C.
Toccoa, GA
Clifton & Singer, L.L.P. ....**Raleigh, NC**
Clifton, Stephen P. ....Traverse City, MI
Clifton, Steven E. ....Nashville, TN
Clifton, Stewart ....Nashville, TN
Clifton, Thomas B., Jr. ....Brunswick, GA
Clifton, Thomas S. ....**San Francisco, CA**
Clifton, William C. ....**Providence, RI**
Clifton, William C. ....**Dallas, TX**
Clifton, William D. ....**Louisville, KY**
Clifton, William M., III ....**Macon, GA**
Clifton, William O. ....Trenton, FL
Clifton, William R. ....Melbourne, FL
Clifton, William W., Jr. ....**Midland, TX**
Cliggett & Associates, A Professional Corporation ....**Crested Butte, CO**
Gunnison, CO
Cliggett, Charles F. ....**Gunnison, CO**
Cliggett, Terrie Zenoff ....Phoenix, AZ
Clikeman, John M. ....**Denver, CO**
Climaco, John R. ....Washington, DC
Cleveland, OH
Columbus, OH

Climaco, Lefkowitz, Peca, Wilcox & Garofoli Co., L.P.A. ....Washington, DC
Cleveland, OH
Columbus, OH
Climaco, Michael L. ....Cleveland, OH
Climan, Richard E. ....Palo Alto, CA
Climenko, Jesse ....New York, NY
Climenson, Peggy Ann ....Wayne, NJ
Climer, James A. ....Cleveland, OH
Climpson, Jeffrey Thomas ....Trenton, NJ
Clinage, Russell E. ....Arlington, TX
Clinard, Aaron Neal ....High Point, NC
Clinard, Christine H. ....Portland, OR
Clinard, Forrest K. ....Atlanta, GA
Clinard, Forrest K. ....Roswell, GA
Clinard, Keith A. ....Winston-Salem, NC
Clinard, R. Noel ....Richmond, VA
Clinard, Robert A. ....Uniondale, NY
Clinch, Francis X. ....Great Falls, MT
Clinch, H. Carleton ....Hackensack, NJ
Clinch, H. Carleton ....Ridgewood, NJ
Clinch, James J. ....New York, NY
Clinch, Nanci G. ....Nevada City, CA
Clinch, Nanci G., A Professional Corporation ....Grass Valley, CA
Nevada City, CA
Clinch, Nanette Cleri ....Hackensack, NJ
Clinch, Nicholas B. ....Palo Alto, CA
Clinco, Peter L. ....Los Angeles, CA
Clincy, Robert A. ....Santa Monica, CA
Cline, Adkins & Cline ....Norton, VA
Cline, Alanna G. ....Brighton, MA
Cline, Andrew H. ....Harrisburg, PA
Cline, Andy ....San Antonio, TX
Cline, Arthur L. ....Arlington, VA
Cline, Barry B. ....Prescott, AZ
Cline, Bill, Jr. ....Austin, TX
Cline, Bruce C. ....Sacramento, CA
Cline, Carl A. ....Merriam, KS
Cline, Channing H. ....Atlanta, GA
Cline, Charles M. ....Wichita, KS
Cline, Charles P. ....Alameda, CA
Cline, Christina L. ....San Francisco, CA
Cline, Christopher P. ....Portland, OR
Cline, Christopher T. ....Dublin, OH
Cline & Cline ....Dayton, OH
Cline, Cline & Griffin ....Flint, MI
Grand Blanc, MI
Cline, Cook & Weisenburger Co., L.P.A.
Toledo, OH
Cline, Craig L. ....Oklahoma City, OK
Cline, Cristen ....Houston, TX
Cline, Cullen ....Columbia, MO
Cline, Daniel J. ....Midland, MI
Cline, Danny O. ....Sutton, WV
Cline, David M. ....Manchester, NH
Cline, David P. ....Wilmington, DE
Cline, David P., P.A. ....Wilmington, DE
Cline, Debra Leigh ....Lakeland, FL
Lake Wales, FL
Winter Haven, FL
Cline, Debra S. ....Atlanta, GA
Cline, Della M. ....Williamson, WV
Cline, Denise Smith ....Raleigh, NC
Cline, Dennis N. ....Los Angeles, CA
Cline, Donald E., Jr. ....Saginaw, MI
Tawas City, MI
Cline, Donald G. ....San Diego, CA
Cline, Donald R. ....Dallas, TX
Cline, E. Roderick ....Gualala, CA
Cline, Earl J. ....Flint, MI
Cline, Elizabeth M. ....Portland, OR
Cline, Eugene ....Marietta, GA
Cline Farrell Christie & Lee
Indianapolis, IN
Cline & Fox ....San Diego, CA
Cline, Gary L. ....Springfield, IL
Cline, Gerald L. ....Woodland Hills, CA
Cline, Guy G. ....Circleville, OH
Cline, Harry S. ....Clearwater, FL
Cline, Heather M. ....Oklahoma City, OK
Cline, Howard D., Jr. ....Flint, MI
Grand Blanc, MI
Cline, Hugh P. ....Norton, VA
Cline, Hugh P., Jr. ....Norton, VA
Cline, J. Timothy, Jr. ....Dayton, OH
Cline, Jack E. ....Atlanta, GA
Cline, Jack W. ....Mercer, PA
Cline, James A. ....Wichita, KS
Cline, James A. ....Dallas, TX
Cline, James E. ....Raleigh, NC
Cline, James L., Jr. ....Eatonton, GA
Cline, Jean M. ....Rapid City, SD
Cline, Jeffrey L. ....Oklahoma City, OK
Cline, Jerome Z. ....Lynbrook, NY
Cline, Joanna J. ....Philadelphia, PA
Cline, John B. ....Falls Church, VA
Cline, John D. ....Albuquerque, NM
Cline, John O. ....Danville, CA
Cline, John R. ....Richmond, VA
Cline, John Warren, II ....Huntington, WV
Cline, Jon J. ....Fergus Falls, MN
Cline, J. P., III ....Middlesboro, KY
Cline, K. Wade ....Houston, TX
Cline, Karen J. ....El Verano, CA
Cline, Kenneth S. ....Bar Harbor, ME
Cline, King & King, P.C. ....Columbus, IN
Cline, Lance D. ....Indianapolis, IN
Cline, Larry R. ....Denver, CO
Cline Law Offices ....Oklahoma City, OK
Cline, Lawrence A. ....Los Angeles, CA
Cline, Leonard J. ....Metairie, LA
Cline, Mary G. ....Ellsworth, ME
Portland, OR
Cline, Max ....Oakland, CA
Cline, Michael A. ....Columbus, OH
Cline, Michael R., Law Offices
Charleston, WV

Cline & Migner, P.C. ....Marlborough, MA
Worcester, MA
Cline, Miller & Richard ....Rayne, LA
Cline, Peter ....Concord, NH
Cline, R. Alan ....Forrest City, AR
Cline, Rebecca E. ....Milwaukee, WI
Cline, Richard A. ....Columbus, OH
Cline, Richard G. ....Vista, CA
Cline, Richard L. ....Naperville, IL
Cline, Richard W. ....Columbus, OH
Cline, Robert D., Jr. ....Charleston, WV
Cline, Robert T. ....Rayne, LA
Cline, Roger F. ....Placerville, CA
Cline, Ronald L. ....Stow, OH
Cline, Russell A. ....Salt Lake City, UT
Cline, Russell C. ....Denver, CO
Cline, Scott F. ....San Antonio, TX
Cline, Sherrill P. ....Marlborough, MA
Worcester, MA
Cline, Stephen R. ....Grand Junction, CO
Cline, Stephen R. ....Essex, CT
Cline, Susan D. ....West Palm Beach, FL
Cline, Susan E. ....Indianapolis, IN
Cline, Theresa R. ....Boston, MA
Cline, Thomas G. ....Evanston, IL
Cline, Thomas W. ....Gainesville, MO
Cline, Todd W. ....Greensboro, NC
Cline, Tracy R. ....Franklin, KY
Cline, Troice G. ....Fort Worth, TX
Cline, Van H. ....San Francisco, CA
Cline, Victoria S. ....Sacramento, CA
Cline, Vivian M. ....Houston, TX
Cline, William A. ....Mendham, NJ
Cline, William S. ....Canton, OH
Cline, William T. ....Somerset, PA
Cline, Williams, Wright, Johnson & Oldfather ....Lincoln, NE
Omaha, NE
Cline, Wilson E. ....Oakland, CA
Clinebell, Donald R. ....Inverness, CA
Clinebell, James E. ....Houston, TX
Clinebell, Law Corporation ....Inverness, CA
Clineburg, Lauren A. ....Fairfax, VA
Clineburg, Stephen R. ....Washington, DC
Clineburg, Susan Elliot ....Atlanta, GA
Clineburg, William A., Jr. ....Atlanta, GA
Clines, Peter James ....New York, NY
Clines, Robert P. ....Bedford, TX
Cline-Silverstein, Judith ....Bel Air, MD
Havre de Grace, MD
Cling, B.J. ....New York, NY
Cling, Michael D. ....Salinas, CA
Clingan, James L., Jr. ....Austin, TX
Clingan, Lauren ....Martinsburg, WV
Clingen, Kenneth W. ....Wheaton, IL
Clinger, David S. ....Bentonville, AR
Clinger, Guy K. ....Denver, CO
Clinger, James H. ....Washington, DC
Clinger, Lynda F. ....Wichita, KS
Clinger, William F., Jr. ....Warren, PA
Clingerman, Aaron E. ....Salem, OR
Clingham, James H. ....Princeton, NJ
Clingman, David W. ....San Diego, CA
Clingman, Gary ....Lovington, NM
Clingman, Nan B. ....Canton, NY
Clingman, Sarah Linley ....Columbia, SC
Clingman, Teresa Jane ....Midland, TX
Clingman, Wm. Edward, Jr. ....Richmond, VA
Clinite, Barbara J. ....Chicago, IL
Clinkenbeard, David B. ....Bedford, TX
Clinkenbeard, Neil E. ....Killeen, TX
Clinkenbeard, Thomas ....Kansas City, MO
Clinkenbeard, Tommy E. ....Sacramento, CA
Clinkenbeard, William
Santa Barbara, CA
Clinkinbeard, Karl ....Newport, OR
Clinkscale, Brent O. E. ....Greenville, SC
Clinkscale, Debra Lynnette ....Columbus, OH
Clinkscales, Barbara J. ....Hays, KS
Clinkscales & Clinkscales ....Hays, KS
Clinkscales, J. Randall ....Hays, KS
Clinnin & Clinnin ....Pasadena, CA
Clinnin, David F. ....Baltimore, MD
Clinnin, John A. ....Venice, CA
Clinnin, Mark G. ....Pasadena, CA
Clinnin, Robert G., (A Professional Corporation) ....Pasadena, CA
Clinton, Bill
Executive Office Of The President, The White House Office, GV
Clinton, Cleveland G. ....Dallas, TX
Clinton, Clinton, Wisner & Chern
Long Beach, CA
Los Angeles, CA
Clinton, David A. ....Long Beach, CA
Clinton, David J. ....Cooperstown, NY
Clinton, David W. ....Belleville, IL
Clinton, DeWitt W. ....Long Beach, CA
Clinton, Edward J., Jr. ....Drexel Hill, PA
Clinton, Edward X. ....Chicago, IL
Clinton, Edward X., Jr. ....Chicago, IL
Clinton, Edward X., P.C. ....Chicago, IL
Clinton, Gordon S. ....Seattle, WA
Clinton, Henry Michael ....Philadelphia, PA
Clinton, Hillary Rodham ....Washington, DC
Clinton, J. Paul ....Mobile, AL
Clinton, J. Warren ....Estes Park, CO
Clinton, Jack W. ....Hastings, MN
Clinton, Janet ....Alameda, CA
Clinton, Janet ....Oakland, CA
Clinton, John P. ....Jamesville, NY
Clinton, Lawrence M. ....Lincoln, NE
Clinton, L. G., III ....Houston, TX
Clinton, L.G., Jr. ....Houston, TX
Clinton, Lloyd Eugene, Jr. ....Glen Burnie, MD
Clinton, Mary F. ....Ann Arbor, MI
Clinton & McKain ....Philadelphia, PA
Clinton, Michael H. ....Glastonbury, CT

Clinton, Michael W. ....Philadelphia, PA
Clinton & Muzyka, P.C. ....Boston, MA
Clinton, Olabisi L. ....Mountain View, CA
Clinton, Richard M. ....Seattle, WA
Clinton, Robert L. ....Littleton, CO
Clinton, Robert M. ....Noble, OK
Clinton, Robert N. ....Iowa City, IA
Clinton, Rosemary ....Tulsa, OK
Clinton, Sam Houston ....Austin, TX
Clinton, Sandra J. ....Albuquerque, NM
Clinton, Stanford, Sr. ....Miami Beach, FL
Clinton, Thomas E. ....Boston, MA
Clinton, Thomas F., Jr. ....Columbia, MD
Clinton, Thomas J. ....Pittsburgh, PA
Clinton, Thomas R. ....Denver, CO
Clinton, Thos. L. ....Peotone, IL
Clinton, Tongren & Knuth ....Peotone, IL
Clinton, W. Daniel ....San Francisco, CA
Clinton, W. Philip ....New Orleans, LA
Clinton, William J. ....Washington, DC
Clippard, Richard Fox ....Nashville, TN
Clipper, David C. ....Harrisburg, PA
Clippert, Charles F. ....Bloomfield Hills, MI
Clippinger, James R. ....Harrisburg, PA
Clippinger, Scott J. ....Norwich, NY
Clisbee, John F. ....Kansas City, MO
Clisby, Barrett J. ....Oxford, MS
Clise, Timothy B. ....Kalamazoo, MI
Clisham, David P. ....San Francisco, CA
Clisham, Patricia Jean ....Denver, CO
Clisham, Sharon L. ....San Francisco, CA
Clissold, David B. ....Washington, DC
Clithero, Michael A. ....St. Louis, MO
Clithero, Monte P. ....Springfield, MO
Clivner, Daniel ....Palo Alto, CA
Universal City, CA
Clo, John Norman ....Amsterdam, NY
Cload, Lisbeth W. ....Ridgewood, NJ
Cloar & Kincannon ....Fort Smith, AR
Cloar, Ralph M., Jr. ....Little Rock, AR
Cloar, Robert R. ....Fort Smith, AR
Clobes, Bryan L. ....Philadelphia, PA
Clobridge, Kurt D. ....West Sand Lake, NY
Clobridge, Robert R. ....Binghamton, NY
Clock, Nancy M. ....San Francisco, CA
Clocksin, Don ....Olympia, WA
Clodfelder, Wiley H. ....Columbus, OH
Clodfelter, Daniel G. ....Charlotte, NC
Clodfelter, David C. ....Cincinnati, OH
Clodfelter, Jas. A. ....Nashville, TN
Clodfelter, Nancy Andreas ....Denver, CO
Clodfelter, Robert F. ....Winston-Salem, NC
Clodfelter, Scott E. ....Tallahassee, FL
Clodfelter, T. Lynn ....Wadesboro, NC
Clodig, John B. ....Fallbrook, CA
Clodig, John B., Inc., A Prof. Corp.
Fallbrook, CA
Cloe, Rafe H. ....Birmingham, AL
Cloer, John W. ....Springdale, AR
Cloern, Boyd Tristan ....Frankfort, KY
Lexington, KY
Clofine, Robert ....York, PA
Clogg, Hollis & Moffett ....Rockville, MD
Clogg, Milton F. ....Rockville, MD
Clogg, Richard B. ....Indianola, IA
Clogston, Madeline Moriyama
San Diego, CA
Clohan, Frank E. ....Palo Alto, CA
Cloherty, Alexander Paul ....Jamaica Plain, MA
Cloherty, Daniel J. ....Boston, MA
Cloherty, Kevin J. ....Boston, MA
Cloherty, Monica K. ....Boston, MA
Cloherty, Thomas M. ....Hartford, CT
Clohessy, Michael Patrick ....Buffalo, NY
Clohosey, Thomas W. ....Bloomfield, NJ
Cloke, Kenneth ....Santa Monica, CA
Clokey, Jane F. ....Madison, WI
Clokey, Kathryn A. ....New Brunswick, NJ
Clolery, Denise M. ....Los Angeles, CA
New York, NY
Clomiro, Richard T. ....Fairfield, CT
Clonce, Robin Kay ....Norman, OK
Clonch, Richard W. ....Charleston, WV
Cloney, Christopher C. ....Fort Lauderdale, FL
Cloney, Christopher C., P.A.
Fort Lauderdale, FL
Cloney, John E. ....Park Ridge, IL
Cloney, Terence J. ....Chicago, IL
Cloninger, Alan G. ....Dallas, NC
Cloninger, Coite E. ....Boise, ID
Cloninger, E. Scott ....Kings Mountain, NC
Cloninger, Evelyn W. ....Oviedo, FL
Cloninger, James P. ....Ventura, CA
Cloninger, John C. ....Asheville, NC
Cloninger, Lindsay, Hensley, Searson & Arcuri, P.L.L.C. ....Asheville, NC
Cloninger, M. Charles ....Asheville, NC
Cloninger & Neisler ....Kings Mountain, NC
Cloninger-Kojis, Cathryn ....Baton Rouge, LA
Clonts, David R. ....Houston, TX
Clontz, Carl R. ....Mount Vernon, KY
Clontz, Clontz & Hunter, P.L.L.C.
Charlotte, NC
Clontz & Cox ....Mount Vernon, KY
Somerset, KY
Stanford, KY
Clontz, Donna ....Camarillo, CA
Clontz, J. Stewart ....Greensboro, NC
Clontz, Jeffrey N. ....Laughlin, NV
Clontz, John E. ....Mount Vernon, KY
Clontz, J. W. ....High Point, NC
Clontz, Ralph C., III ....Charlotte, NC
Clontz, Ralph C., Jr. ....Charlotte, NC
Clontz, Stanford K. ....Asheville, NC
Clontz, Wayne O. ....Morganton, NC
Cloon, Bennett & Ronan ....Overland Park, KS
Cloon, Bryson R. ....Overland Park, KS
Cloon, Russell B. ....Baldwin City, KS

Cloon, William G., Jr. ....Ironwood, MI
Cloonan, Joan M. ....Boise, ID
Cloonan, Joseph E. ....Boston, MA
Cloonan, Karen L. ....Omaha, NE
Cloonan, Terrence F. ....Youngstown, OH
Cloonan, William N. ....Kingston, NY
Cloonan, William P. ....Cleveland, OH
Clooney & Anderson ....St. Louis, MO
Clooney, Andrew N. ....Louisville, KY
Clooney, Donald H. ....St. Louis, MO
Clooney, Raymond M. ....Louisville, KY
Clopeck, Jeffrey A. ....Boston, MA
Clopine, Richard W. ....Redding, CA
Cloppert, Frederick G., Jr. ....Columbus, OH
Cloppert, Portman, Sauter, Latanick & Foley
Columbus, OH
Clopton, James Roby, (Attorney at Law, Inc.)
McAllen, TX
Clopton, Karen Valentia
San Francisco, CA
Clopton, Penny & Brenner, A P.C.
Los Angeles, CA
Clopton, William H. ....San Jose, CA
Clor, Penelope ....Breckenridge, CO
Englewood, CO
Cloran, William F. ....Salem, OR
Clore & Blakeney, L.L.P. ....Houston, TX
Clore, Duncan L., (P.C.) ....Dallas, TX
Clore, Gregory S. ....San Francisco, CA
Clore, Lawrence H. ....Houston, TX
Clore, Mark D. ....Houston, TX
Clore, William E. ....Crestview Hills, KY
Clorfeine, Joshua E. ....Los Angeles, CA
Clorite, Michael T. ....Hartford, CT
Clos, Charles E. ....Torrance, CA
Westland, MI
Close, A. L., Jr. ....Youngstown, OH
Close, Albert P. ....Churchville, MD
Close Associates ....Truckee, CA
Close, Bertrand J. ....Portland, OR
Close, C. Ed. ....Syracuse, NY
Close, Cary Elizabeth ....Raleigh, NC
Close, Chas. B. & C. Ed. ....Syracuse, NY
Close, Craig Bradford ....Truckee, CA
Close, Dale H. ....Springfield, MO
Close, David P. ....Washington, DC
Close, Deirdre Ann ....Chicago, IL
Close, Henry J. ....Rockford, IL
Close, Howard L. ....Beaumont, TX
Close, James A. ....Bel Air, MD
Close, James A., P.A. ....Bel Air, MD
Close, Jeffrey G. ....Chicago, IL
Close, Jimmie H. ....Edmonds, WA
Close, John M. ....Wayne, PA
Close, Julia A. ....Midland, MI
Close, Julie P. ....Ann Arbor, MI
Close, Larry B. ....Long Beach, CA
Close, Louis G., III ....Towson, MD
Close, Louis G., III, P.A. ....Baltimore, MD
Towson, MD
Close, Louis G., Jr. ....Baltimore, MD
Close, M. Douglas ....Los Angeles, CA
Close, Matthew W. ....Los Angeles, CA
Close, Maurice S. ....Andover, MA
Close, Melvin D., Jr. ....Las Vegas, NV
Close, Michael J. ....Sarasota, FL
Close, Michael L. ....Columbus, OH
Close, Nalini V. ....Department of Labor, Pension and Welfare Benefits, GV
Close, Peter D. ....New York, NY
Close, Polly Kim ....Seattle, WA
Close, Richard H. ....Santa Monica, CA
Close, Sean H. ....New York, NY
Close, Thomas H. ....Rochester, NY
Close, Thomas M. ....Cherry Hill, NJ
Paoli, PA
Philadelphia, PA
Close, Thomas V. ....Wellington, FL
Closen, Michael L. ....Chicago, IL
Closky, Stephen Andrew ....Boulder, CO
Closs, John D. ....Placerville, CA
Closs, Louise Toby ....Bakersfield, CA
Closser, Ann S. ....Boulder, CO
Closser, Arleigh V. ....Washington, DC
Closser, Daniel P., Jr. ....San Diego, CA
Closser, Ernest R., III ....Morrisville, PA
Clossey, David F. ....New York, NY
Clossin, J. David ....Indianapolis, IN
Closson & Bass ....Valdosta, GA
Closson, Luke E., Jr. ....Valdosta, GA
Closson, Patrick C. ....Manchester, NH
Closson, Robert V. ....San Diego, CA
Closson, Thomas M. ....Exeter, NH
Closson, Walter F. ....Ellicott City, MD
Clostermann, Adelbert G. ....Portland, OR
Closuit, Alicemary L. ....Fairbanks, AK
Closz, Harold F., III ....Muskegon, MI
Clote, Paul D. ....Houston, TX
Clotfelter, Cortland, Law Offices of
Wichita, KS
Clotfelter, Patricia ....Birmingham, AL
Clothier, Birchard T. ....Philadelphia, PA
Clothier, Daniel G. ....Wichita, KS
Clothier, Isaac H., IV ....Philadelphia, PA
Clothier, Jeffrey E. ....Flint, MI
Clothier, Louis M. ....Leavenworth, KS
Clothier, R. Robert
Colorado Springs, CO
Clothier, R. Robert, P.C.
Colorado Springs, CO
Clothier, Robert C., III ....Philadelphia, PA
Clothier, Steffanie E. ....Denver, CO
Clotiaux, Patricia McKay
New Orleans, LA
Clott, Abraham L. ....Brooklyn, NY
Clott, Gail R. ....New York, NY
Clott, Jeffrey H. ....Roseland, NJ
Clotworthy, Robert C. ....New Orleans, LA

Clouatre, Mark T. ... Denver, CO
Clouatre, Stephanie M. ... Denver, CO
Cloud, A. Doyle, Jr. ... Memphis, TN
Cloud, A. Kelley E. ... Atlanta, GA
Cloud, A. Morgan, III ... Atlanta, GA
Cloud, Bradley G.A. ... Tucson, AZ
Cloud, Christopher H. ... New York, NY
Cloud, Clifford R. ... Columbus, OH
Cloud and Cloud ... Huntsville, AL
Cloud, D. Wade, Jr. ... Addison, TX
Cloud, David Luke ... Lansing, MI
Cloud, Douglas E. ... Atlanta, GA
Cloud, Earl E. ... Huntsville, AL
Cloud, Earl E., Jr. ... Huntsville, AL
Cloud, Ian P. ... Houston, TX
Cloud, Jared Ryckoff ... Chicago, IL
Cloud, Jay ... Nashville, TN
Cloud, John M. ... Dayton, OH
Cloud, Joseph M. ... Huntsville, AL
Cloud, Katharine R. ... Nashville, TN
Cloud, Linda Crawford ... Columbus, OH
Cloud, Mio E. ... New York, NY
Cloud & Olsen ... Long Beach, CA
Los Angeles, CA
Cloud, Priscilla ... Santa Ana, CA
Cloud, Robert L. ... Cincinnati, OH
Cloud, Roger Allen ... Scotts Valley, CA
Cloud, Scott B. ... Long Beach, CA
Cloud, Stephen R. ... Fresno, CA
Cloud, Susan L. ... Huntsville, AL
Cloud, Thomas A. ... Orlando, FL
Cloud, W. Dean ... Irvine, CA
Cloud, William M. ... Oklahoma City, OK
Cloud, William M., Jr. ... Clarksville, TN
Cloudt, Jim B. ... Austin, TX
Cloudt, Jim B. ... Rocksprings, TX
Cloudy, Charles L. ... Ketchikan, AK
Clouette, James P. ... Little Rock, AR
Clough & Associates, P.C. ... Juneau, AK
Clough, David A. ... Southbury, CT
Clough, David W. ... Chicago, IL
Clough, Frederick W. ... Santa Barbara, CA
Clough, George E. ... North Platte, NE
Clough, Hobart C. ... Arlington, VA
Clough, James O. ... Harrisonburg, VA
Clough, James P. ... San Francisco, CA
Clough, Jay S. ... Ossipee, NH
Clough, John A., III ... Cleveland, OH
Clough, John E. ... Denver, CO
Clough, John E. ... Springfield, OH
Clough, John F., III ... Juneau, AK
Clough, John H. ... Denver, CO
Clough, Joyce F. ... Chicago, IL
Clough, Julie V. ... Grand Rapids, MI
Clough, Lawrence R. ... Portland, ME
Clough, Linda F. ... New Britain, CT
Clough, Paul H. ... Boston, MA
Clough, Richard F. ... Carrollton, IL
Clough, Roger L. ... Culver City, CA
Clough, Ruth E. ... Bethel, VT
Clough, Steven M. ... Monroe, WA
Clough, Thomas E. ... Chadds Ford, PA
Clough, William J. ... Pleasanton, CA
Clough, William R. ... Flemington, NJ
Clougher, Jeanne ... Tampa, FL
Clougher, Marie C. ... Sandwich, MA
Clougherty, Thomas P. ... Worcester, MA
Clous, A. Alysha ... Columbus, OH
Clouse, Gary R. ... Santa Monica, CA
Clouse, Gerard J. ... Columbus, OH
Clouse, James R., Jr. ... Evansville, IN
Clouse, Joanne M. ... Columbus, OH
Clouse, John D. ... Evansville, IN
Clouse, Jordan L ... Painesville, OH
Clouse, Karen L. ... Columbus, OH
Clouse, Keith A. ... Dallas, TX
Clouse, Kenneth A. ... Media, PA
Clouse, Mark K. ... East Lansing, MI
Clouse, Peter T. ... Albany, NY
Clouse, Richard R. ... Ontario, CA
Clouse, Roger R. ... Ashville, NY
Clouser, Bruce E. ... Philadelphia, PA
Clouser, Glenn A. ... New York, NY
Clouser, Lynn A. ... Berwyn, PA
Clouser, Mark E. ... Harrisburg, PA
Clouser, Michael A. ... Harrisburg, PA
Clouser, Paul D. ... Lancaster, PA
Clouser, Robbin R. ... Pittsburgh, PA
Clouser, Stephen R. ... Tulsa, OK
Clousson & Butz ... Chicago, IL
Clousson, Jerry P. ... Chicago, IL
Clouston, David R. ... Dallas, TX
Cloutier, Alison Mills ... Boston, MA
Cloutier, Andrew J. ... Roswell, NM
Cloutier, Barrett, Cloutier & Conley
Portland, ME
Cloutier & Briggs, P.A. ... Rockport, ME
Cloutier, C. Edgar ... New Orleans, LA
Cloutier, Claudine A. ... Taunton, MA
Cloutier & Cloutier ... Minneapolis, MN
Cloutier, Cortlen G. ... Minneapolis, MN
Cloutier, Darquise ... Vancouver, WA
Cloutier, David A. ... Augusta, ME
Cloutier, Denise M. ... Litchfield, CT
Cloutier, Domnarski & Eddy
Old Saybrook, CT
Cloutier, Ernest W. ... Boston, MA
Cloutier, Gary R. ... San Francisco, CA
Cloutier, James F. ... Portland, ME
Cloutier, Joseph M. ... Rockport, ME
Cloutier, Leslie J. ... Washington, DC
Cloutier, Margaret ... Jacksonville, NC
Cloutier, Mark A. ... Portland, ME
Cloutier, Monique Legendre ... Lafayette, LA
Cloutier, Philip D. ... Wilmington, DE
Cloutier, Philip R. ... Bowling Green, KY
Cloutier, Raymond A. ... Manchester, NH
Cloutier, Raymond A. ... Nashua, NH
Cloutier, Teresa M. ... Portland, ME
Cloutier, Thomas A. ... Old Saybrook, CT
Cloutier, Thomas W. ... Portland, ME
Cloutier, Valerie V. ... Baltimore, MD
Cloutman, Edward B., III ... Dallas, TX
Clover, Carl E., Jr., (P.C.) ... Sealy, TX
Clover, Frank H. ... Department of Agriculture, Office of the General Counsel, GV
Clover, Glen E., P.C. ... Sugar Land, TX
Clover, Joan M. ... Anchorage, AK
Clover, Kathleen ... Pittsburgh, PA
Clover, Michael D. ... Shawnee, OK
Clover, Suzette ... Los Angeles, CA
Clover, Timothy D. ... Chanute, KS
Clovis, Albert L. ... Columbus, OH
Clovis, David C. ... Clarksburg, WV
Clovis, Debora L.
Environmental Protection Agency, Program Office Attorneys, GV
Clow, Casey S. ... San Francisco, CA
Clow, Janet ... Santa Fe, NM
Clow, Thomas D. ... Bakersfield, CA
Clow, Timothy J. ... Dallas, TX
Clowdus, Gloyd T. ... Sacramento, CA
Clowdus, Kenneth W. ... Glendora, CA
Clowdus, Patricia Lester ... Denver, CO
Clowdus, W. Michael ... Denver, CO
Clowe, Olney H. ... Buffalo, NY
Clower, David M. ... Daytona Beach, FL
Clower, Dennis S. ... Elkton, MD
Clower, Donald A. ... Elkton, MD
Clower, Elizabeth ... Fort Worth, TX
Clower, Gary M. ... Tacoma, WA
Clower, James G. ... Troy, AL
Clower, Laura D. ... Champaign, IL
Clower, Margot Ames ... Winchester, MA
Clower, Parrack & Seaman ... Elkton, MD
Clower, Robert P., III ... Boston, MA
Clower, Ronald L. ... Fort Worth, TX
Clower, Sarah Mullaney ... Dallas, TX
Clowes, Elise ... Burlingame, CA
Clowes, Jefferson J. ... St. Paul, MN
Clowes, John Howard ... San Francisco, CA
Clowney, Frank S., III ... San Diego, CA
Clowney, Patricia L. ... San Diego, CA
Cloy & Ellis ... McDonough, GA
Cloy, Gary B. ... McDonough, GA
Cloyd, Alison Paddock ... Lexington, KY
Cloyd, Casey D. ... Muncie, IN
Cloyd, Leslie Gern ... West Palm Beach, FL
Cloyd, Preston D. ... Lafayette, LA
Cloyd, Sally F. ... Columbus, IN
Clubb, Bruce E. ... Washington, DC
Clubok, Andrew B. ... Washington, DC
Clucas, Lloyd L. ... Tucson, AZ
Cluchey, David P. ... Portland, ME
Cluck, Allen B. ... Houston, TX
Cluck, Damon N. ... Killeen, TX
Cluck, David O. ... Houston, TX
Cluck, Jonathan B. ... San Antonio, TX
Cluck, Roxie Williams ... Canton, TX
Cluck, Sharail L. ... Tulsa, OK
Cluck, William J. ... Harrisburg, PA
Cluff, Jeffrey H. ... Lubbock, TX
Cluff, Jerry D. ... San Diego, CA
Cluff, Rex Aaron ... Woodland, CA
Cluff, Tanya ... Boston, MA
Clugg, Lorraine S. ... Edina, MN
Clugston, Scott ... Greeley, CO
Clugston, William H. ... Riverwoods, IL
Clukay-Whittier, Ann E. ... New Salem, MA
Clukey, Beth A. ... Chicago, IL
Clukey, Nathan Elliott ... Washington, DC
Clulo, Paul J. ... Midland, MI
Clulo, Timothy J. ... Traverse City, MI
Clum, Anthony D. ... Topeka, KS
Clum, John P. ... Three Rivers, CA
Clum, Lewis L. ... Cincinnati, OH
Clump, Jennifer A. ... St. Louis, MO
Clumpner, William M. ... Bellevue, WA
Clunan, Amy M. ... Memphis, TN
Clune, Albert E. ... Sidney, NY
Unadilla, NY
Clune, Hayes & Lo Presti, P.C.
Harrison, NY
Clune, James R. ... Chicago, IL
Clune, John C. ... Eagle, CO
Clune, John O. ... San Diego, CA
Clune, Jonathan E. ... New Haven, CT
Clune, Kevin P. ... Harrison, NY
Clune, Leslie L.
Department Of Health And Human Services, GV
Clune, Mary Beth ... Independence, MO
Clune, Robert J. ... Ithaca, NY
Clune, William H., III ... Madison, WI
Clunies, Jonathan P. ... Pittsburgh, PA
Clunk, Dennis R. ... Alliance, OH
Clunk Law Office ... Alliance, OH
Clunk, R. R. Denny ... Canton, OH
Clure Eaton Butler, P.A. ... Duluth, MN
Clure, Thomas A. ... Duluth, MN
Clurman, Barbara Baker ... Wellesley, MA
Clurman, David ... New York, NY
Clurman, Herman ... New York, NY
Clusserath, Thomas M. ... Fort Myers, FL
Cluster, Darryl W. ... Los Angeles, CA
Cluster, Edwin C. ... Ocala, FL
Cluster, H. Raymond ... Baltimore, MD
Clute, Clute & Thompson ... Plattsburgh, NY
Clute, James W. ... Plattsburgh, NY
Clute, John E. ... Plattsburgh, NY
Clute, John E. ... Spokane, WA
Clute, Karen L. ... New Haven, CT
Clute, Penelope D. ... Plattsburgh, NY
Clute, Robert E., Jr. ... Mobile, AL
Clute, Sylvia ... Richmond, VA
Clute, Wyncia ... Jamesville, NY
Clutter, Hinkel & Aadalen, LLP
Topeka, KS
Clutter, Michael ... Atlanta, GA
Clutter, Michael Lee ... Topeka, KS
Clutter, Robert V. ... Indianapolis, IN
Clutter, Roderick W., Jr. ... Evansville, IN
Clutterbuck, Jeffrey L. ... Ridgewood, NJ
Clutterbuck, John B. ... Houston, TX
Clutts, Raymond E. ... Des Plaines, IL
Clutts, Raymond E., P.C. ... Chicago, IL
Des Plaines, IL
Waukegan, IL
Wheaton, IL
Clutts, Rodney A. ... Jonesboro, IL
Cluverius, James K. ... Richmond, VA
Cluxton-Kremer, Diane G. ... Denver, CO
Clyatt, Clyatt & DeVaughn, P.C.
Valdosta, GA
Clyatt, Melissa M. ... Valdosta, GA
Clyatt, Rhonda S. ... Panama City, FL
Clyatt & Richardson, P.A.
West Palm Beach, FL
Clyatt, Robert M. ... Valdosta, GA
Clyatt, Shelton, Jr. ... West Palm Beach, FL
Clyborne, William L., Jr. ... San Antonio, TX
Clyburn, James Albert ... Wilmington, NC
Clyburn, Jill Graves ... Memphis, TN
Clyburn, Thomas M., Jr. ... Cleveland, GA
Clyde, David N. ... Hereford, TX
Clyde, Dennis M. ... Overland Park, KS
Clyde, H. Michael ... Phoenix, AZ
Clyde, Hunter Brooke ... Santa Rosa, CA
Clyde, Kristin Ramsey ... Atlanta, GA
Clyde, Robert M., Jr. ... Columbus, OH
Clyde Snow Sessions & Swenson, PC
Salt Lake City, UT
Clyde, Steven E. ... Salt Lake City, UT
Clyde, Thomas E. ... Kamas, UT
Clyde, Thomas M. ... Atlanta, GA
Clyde, William M. ... Media, PA
Clyde & Wood, L.L.C. ... Kansas City, KS
Overland Park, KS
Clydesdale, Nan L. ... Denver, CO
Clydesdale, Thomas R. ... Ottawa, IL
Clydesdale, William L. ... New York, NY
Clyman, Barry J. ... Lake Mary, FL
Clyman, Howard ... Brooklyn, NY
Clyman, Jeffrey M. ... Lake Worth, FL
Clyman, Jeffrey M. ... New York, NY
Clymer, Brian ... Tucson, AZ
Clymer, Charles C. ... Dallas, TX
Clymer, James G. ... Columbus, OH
Clymer, James N. ... Intercourse, PA
Lancaster, PA
Clymer, Jeffrey W. ... Valparaiso, IN
Clymer, John H. ... Boston, MA
Clymer, Lewis W. ... Kansas City, MO
Clymer & Musser, P.C. ... Intercourse, PA
Lancaster, PA
Clymer, Steven ... Boulder, CO
Clymer, Steven David ... Ithaca, NY
Clymer, Steven, P.C. ... Boulder, CO
Clymo, Kevin D. ... Sacramento, CA
Clynch, Cecilia Marie ... Olympia, WA
Clyne, Dana P. ... Los Angeles, CA
Clyne, Dennis ... Port Huron, MI
Clyne, Elizabeth K. ... Albany, NY
Clyne, James D. ... Toms River, NJ
Clyne, James W. ... Albany, NY
Clyne, John J. ... Delmar, NY
Clyne, John M., Jr. ... Cedar Knolls, NJ
Clyne, John M., Jr., A Professional Corporation
Cedar Knolls, NJ
Clyne, Joseph F. ... New York, NY
Clyne, Matthew J. ... Albany, NY
Clyne, Reginald J. ... Miami, FL
Port St. Lucie, FL
Clyne, Robert C. ... New York, NY
Clyne, Robert G. ... Jersey City, NJ
New York, NY
Clyne, Susan M. ... Lindenhurst, NY
Clyne, V. Shannon ... Los Angeles, CA
Clynes, James J., Jr. ... Ithaca, NY
Cmejrek, James R. ... Ann Arbor, MI
Cmejrek & Lipnik ... Ann Arbor, MI
Cmelik, Dennis ... Hartley, IA
C'Miel, Carol A. ... Springfield, MA
CNA Insurance Companies, Professional Liability Loss ... Chicago, IL
Co, Adamson ... Covina, CA
Coachys, James K. ... Franklin, IN
Coad, Brian D. ... New York, NY
Coad, Michael R. ... Beaverton, OR
Coad, Michele ... Seattle, WA
Coady, Edward P. ... Winchester, MA
Coady, James M. ... Los Angeles, CA
Coady, Janet F. ... Malvern, PA
Coady, John P. ... Taylorville, IL
Coady, John Tingle ... St. Michaels, MD
Coady, Larry T. ... Portland, OR
Coady, Martin E. ... Covington, LA
Coady, Michael F. ... Columbus, OH
Coady, Orville L. ... Hebron, NE
Coady, Paul J. ... Los Angeles, CA
Coady, Thomas C. ... Columbus, OH
Coakley, Albert J., Jr.
Palos Verdes Estates, CA
Coakley, Brett L.
Department of the Air Force, Office of the Judge Advocate General, GV
Coakley, Bryan J. ... New York, NY
Coakley, Christopher ... Milwaukee, WI
Coakley, George S. ... Cleveland, OH
Coakley, Gerald M. ... Westwood, MA
Coakley, John P. ... Boston, MA
Coakley, Joseph A. ... Worth, IL
Coakley, Kevin J. ... Roseland, NJ
Coakley, Lisabeth H. ... Troy, MI
Coakley, Martha ... Cambridge, MA
Coakley, Michael P. ... Detroit, MI
Coakley, Michelle L. ... Detroit, MI
Coakley, Mike B. ... Highlands Ranch, CO
Coakley, Monica M. ... New York, NY
Coakley, Robert J. ... Gloucester, MA
Coakley, Rosemarie ... San Diego, CA
Coakley, Sheila M. ... Quincy, MA
Coakley, Susan M. ... Brookline, MA
Coakley, Walter J. ... New York, NY
Coale, Cooley, Lietz, McInerny & Broadus
Bethesda, MD
Washington, DC
Coale, D. Jeffrey ... Abingdon, VA
Coale, David S. ... Dallas, TX
Coale, Dukes & Kirkpatrick, P.C.
Mobile, AL
Coale, Elizabeth Chase ... Charlotte, NC
Coale, Harwell E., Jr. ... Mobile, AL
Coale, James A. ... Decatur, IL
Coale, James Eric ... Brewton, AL
Coale, John P., (A Professional Corporation)
Washington, DC
Coale, Joseph ... Washington, DC
Coale, Michael L. ... San Francisco, CA
Coalson, Clay E. ... Corpus Christi, TX
Coalson, John L., Jr. ... Atlanta, GA
Coalson, William L. ... Jacksonville, FL
Coalwell, Bruce R. ... Roseburg, OR
Coalwell, James D. ... Ventura, CA
Coamey, Lisa Marie ... Orlando, FL
Coan, Alison M. ... Albany, NY
Coan, Carl A. S., III ... Washington, DC
Coan, Carl A. S., Jr. ... Washington, DC
Coan, Craig S. ... Highland Park, IL
Coan, Elizabeth C. ... Trenton, NJ
Coan & Elliott, L.L.P. ... Stephenville, TX
Coan, G. Brent ... Greeley, CO
Coan, Geoffrey M. ... Boston, MA
Coan, George R. ... San Francisco, CA
Coan, J. Paul ... Fairfield, CA
Coan, Jill C. ... Atlanta, GA
Coan, L. Frank, Jr. ... Atlanta, GA
Coan, Lewendon, Royston & Gulliver, LLC
New Haven, CT
Coan & Lyons ... Washington, DC
Coan, Marvin L. ... Louisville, KY
Coan, Mary Alice ... Madison, WI
Coan, Nancy S. ... San Francisco, CA
Coan, Patricia A. ... Denver, CO
Coan, Rachel B. ... New York, NY
Coan, Richard D. ... Stephenville, TX
Coan, Richard M. ... New Haven, CT
Coan, Robert J. ... Schenectady, NY
Coan, Robert Patrick ... Schenectady, NY
Coan, Thomas K. ... Portland, OR
Coan, Tracey Banks ... Greensboro, NC
Coane, Bruce A. ... Houston, TX
Coant, Charles I. ... Vineland, NJ
Coape-Arnold, Karen ... Scarsdale, NY
Coapman, Carl A. ... Spencerport, NY
Coar, David H. ... Chicago, IL
Coard, Lynn McMiller ... McLean, VA
Coartney, Michael J. ... Coral Springs, FL
Coarts, William J. ... Eldora, IA
Coash, Michael G. ... El Dorado, KS
Coassin, Lawrence P. ... Hartford, CT
Coate, Alfred B. ... Forsyth, MT
Coate, Brian R. ... Cleveland, OH
Coate, Charles M. ... Beverly Hills, CA
Coate, James M. ... Malvern, PA
Coate, Robert H. ... Denver, CO
Coates, Amy E. ... New York, NY
Coates, B. Randall ... Berlin, MD
Ocean City, MD
Snow Hill, MD
Coates, Bradley A. ... Honolulu, HI
Coates, Cathi V. ... Ocean City, MD
Coates, Charles E., III ... Greenwich, CT
Coates, Christine A. ... Boulder, CO
Coates, Coates & Coates, P.A. ... Berlin, MD
Ocean City, MD
Snow Hill, MD
Coates, Cynthia A. ... Phoenix, AZ
Coates & Davenport ... Richmond, VA
Coates, David H. ... Hightstown, NJ
Coates, David J. ... San Antonio, TX
Coates, Dolores Ann ... Southfield, MI
Coates, Eric S. ... Oxford, PA
Coates, F. Ramsey ... Pittsburgh, PA
Coates, Frank M., Jr. ... Baton Rouge, LA
Coates, Frederick R. ... Madison, VA
Coates & Frey ... Honolulu, HI
Coates, Gary M. ... Lynchburg, VA
Coates, Glenn R. ... Racine, WI
Coates, Greg A. ... San Luis Obispo, CA
Coates, Greig W. ... Austin, TX
Houston, TX
Coates, Hatfield, Calkins & Wellnitz
Indianapolis, IN
Coates, Henry G. P. ... Hightstown, NJ
Coates, Howard K., Jr. ... Boca Raton, FL
Coates, J. Keith, Jr. ... Atlanta, GA
Coates, Jennifer ... New York, NY
Coates, Jo Ann L. ... Vista, CA
Coates, John ... Austin, TX
Coates, John A. ... Tulsa, OK
Coates, John J. ... Denver, CO
Coates, John J., III ... Oklahoma City, OK
Coates, John J., Jr. ... Oklahoma City, OK
Coates, Joseph A. ... Fairborn, OH
Coates, Joseph C., III (P.A.)
West Palm Beach, FL
Coates, Karen S. ... Bethlehem, PA
Harrisburg, PA
Coates, Kevin Michael ... Brighton, CO
Coates, Leonard J. ... Hightstown, NJ

Coates, Leslie Noftsinger ... Berlin, MD
Ocean City, MD
Snow Hill, MD
Coates, Linda Jane ... Topeka, KS
Coates, Lisa L. ... Cleveland, OH
Coates, Margaret L. ... San Diego, CA
Coates, Marsden S. ... Baltimore, MD
Coates, Melanie D. ... Washington, DC
Coates, Michael L. ... Orange, CA
Coates, Patricia S. ... Philadelphia, PA
Coates, Paul D. ... Greensboro, NC
Coates, Raymond ... Burlingame, CA
Coates, Raymond D., Jr. ... Berlin, MD
Ocean City, MD
Snow Hill, MD
Coates, Raymond D., Sr. ... Berlin, MD
Ocean City, MD
Coates, Raymond G. ... Seattle, WA
Coates, Richard E. ... Tallahassee, FL
Coates, Richard W. ... Denver, CO
Coates, Robert C. ... San Diego, CA
Coates, Robert W. ... Seattle, WA
Coates, Roberta A. ... Cheyenne, WY
Coates, Stephen Michael ... Tulsa, OK
Coates, Theodore P. ... Englewood, CO
Coates, Thomas F., III ... Richmond, VA
Coates, Thomas K. ... Berlin, MD
Ocean City, MD
Snow Hill, MD
Coates, Timothy T. ... Beverly Hills, CA
Coates, Townes C. ... Richmond, VA
Coates, Tracy E. ... Kansas City, MO
Coates, W. Shelby, Jr. ... Oyster Bay, NY
Coates, Wade S. ... Tazewell, VA
Coates, Walton ... Norristown, PA
Coates, Will ... Austin, TX
Coates, William A. ... Greenville, SC
Coates, William H. ... Omaha, NE
Coates, William P., Jr. ... Prairie Village, KS
Coatney, Doyle L. ... San Antonio, TX
Coats, Andrew M. ... Oklahoma City, OK
Coats, Arthur W., Jr. ... Santa Barbara, CA
Coats, Benjamin F., Jr. ... Ventura, CA
Coats & Bennett, PLLC ... Cary, NC
Raleigh, NC
Coats, Christopher D. ... Smyrna, TN
Coats, Daniel R. ... Washington, DC
Coats, David S. ... Raleigh, NC
Coats, Donald F. ... Marion, NC
Coats, Doyle L. ... Gulfport, MS
Coats, Eric S. ... Amarillo, TX
Coats & Evans ... Houston, TX
The Woodlands, TX
Coats, Evelyn H. ... Atlanta, GA
Coats, Francis E. ... Sacramento, CA
Coats, George Andrew (Drew)
The Woodlands, TX
Coats, J. Thomas ... The Dalles, OR
Coats, James D. ... New York, NY
Coats, John D. ... Austin, TX
Coats, Kimberly Flanery ... Fayetteville, AR
Coats, Larry L. ... Cary, NC
Coats, Linda F. ... Huntsville, AL
Coats, Monica A. ... Fresno, CA
Coats, Nancy L. ... Oklahoma City, OK
Coats, Nathan Ben ... Denver, CO
Coats, Richard D. ... Los Angeles, CA
Coats, Robert D. ... Decatur, GA
Coats, Robert G. ... Anchorage, AK
Coats, Robert K. ... Richmond, VA
Coats, Robert T., Jr. ... Chicago, IL
Coats, Rose, Yale, Ryman & Lee, A Professional Corporation ... Houston, TX
Coats, Sanford C. ... Oklahoma City, OK
Coats, Sarah J. ... Olympia, WA
Coats & Spinks ... Tyler, TX
Coats, Stephen S. ... Houston, TX
Coats, Susan Stephens ... San Francisco, CA
Coats, W. Fred ... Tyler, TX
Coats, Wallace J. ... Sacramento, CA
Coats, William A. ... Tacoma, WA
Coats, William D. ... Tracy, CA
Coats, William M. ... Houston, TX
Coats, William Sloan ... Menlo Park, CA
Coats-Siercks, Charlotte A.
Garden Grove, CA
Coats-Thomas, Marilyn ... Hackensack, NJ
Coatsworth, Karen T. ... Hartford, CT
Coaty, John D. ... Bailey, CO
Coaty, Michael P. ... Minneapolis, MN
Coaty, Steven J. ... Middletown, RI
Coaty, Thomas J. ... Madison, WI
Coaxum, David Samuel ... Greenbelt, MD
Coaxum, Donna M. Bunch ... Northfield, IL
Coaxum, Edward C., Jr. ... Cleveland, OH
Coaxum, Ghunise L. ... Orlando, FL
Coaxum, Richard, Jr. ... Orlando, FL
Cobau, Charles D., Jr. ... Perrysburg, OH
Cobau, John R. ... Grosse Pointe Woods, MI
Cobau, Prephan & Walsh ... Perrysburg, OH
Cobb, A. Thomas ... Indianapolis, IN
Cobb, Alan E. ... Wichita, KS
Cobb, Alexander B. T. ... Los Angeles, CA
Cobb, Alexander P. ... Belfair, WA
Cobb, Angela L. ... Indianapolis, IN
Cobb, Anita D. ... New Britain, CT
Cobb, Antoine P. ... Washington, DC
Cobb, Arthur ... Baton Rouge, LA
Cobb, Arthur L. ... Cleveland, OH
Cobb, Barry S. ... Raleigh, NC
Cobb, Betty J. Gambrell ... Columbia, SC
Cobb, Billy D. ... Big Rock, TN
Cobb, Bobby L. ... Norcross, GA
Cobb, Bradley L. ... Detroit, MI
Cobb, C. Houston ... Memphis, TN
Cobb, Calvin H., III ... Washington, DC
Cobb, Calvin H., Jr. ... Washington, DC
Cobb, Carroll ... Houston, TX
Cobb, Catherine Christine ... **Houston, TX**
Cobb, Charles A. ... Oakland, CA
Cobb, Charles K., Jr. ... Atlanta, GA
Cobb, Charles K., Jr. ... Boston, MA
Cobb, Charles L. ... Lubbock, TX
Cobb, Charles M. ... Austin, TX
Cobb, Charles Pittman ... Memphis, TN
Cobb, Charles W. ... Newton, MA
Cobb, Cheryl D. ... Birmingham, AL
Cobb, Chester L. ... New York, NY
Cobb, Christine S. ... Ridgewood, NJ
Cobb, Christopher C. ... Hartford, CT
Cobb & Cobb ... Tuxedo, NY
Cobb & Cobb, A Law Corporation
Baton Rouge, LA
Cobb Cole & Bell ... Daytona Beach, FL
Cobb, Cristina ... New York, NY
Cobb, Dale T., Jr. ... Charleston, SC
Cobb, Dana B. ... Montvale, NJ
Cobb, Dana Livingston ... Austin, TX
Cobb, David L. ... Gulfport, MS
Cobb, David L. ... Brownsville, TN
Cobb, David R. ... Lubbock, TX
Cobb, David S. ... Charleston, SC
Cobb, David T., Law Offices of
Jackson, MS
Cobb, Deborah Crouse ... Edwardsville, IL
Cobb, Dennis L. ... Beloit, KS
Cobb, Dianne Campbell ... Bethesda, MD
Cobb, Douglas E. ... Atlanta, GA
Cobb, Earle, Jr. ... San Antonio, TX
Cobb & Ebin, P.A. ... Miami, FL
Cobb & Eisenberg LLC ... Westport, CT
Cobb, Elizabeth H. ... Minneapolis, MN
Cobb, Ellen Pinkos ... Newton, MA
Cobb, Francis H. ... St. Augustine, FL
Cobb, Frank R. ... Wichita, KS
Cobb, G. Elliott, Jr. ... Franklin, VA
Cobb, Gene S. ... Lubbock, TX
Cobb, George L. ... Catskill, NY
Cobb, George S. ... Thiells, NY
Cobb, Gerald W. ... Denton, TX
Cobb, Gregory J. ... San Diego, CA
Cobb, Grover B., Jr. ... Houston, TX
Cobb, H. Clifton ... Atlanta, GA
Cobb & Hallinan, P.C. ... Lincoln, NE
Cobb, Helene O. ... Chevy Chase, MD
Cobb, Herman W. ... Dothan, AL
Cobb, Howard, Hayes & Windsor
Washington, DC
Cobb, Howell ... Beaumont, TX
Cobb, Howell, III ... El Paso, TX
Cobb & Hyre ... Atlanta, GA
Cobb, Ike W. ... Atlanta, GA
Cobb, J. Glenn, Jr. ... Mobile, AL
Cobb, James A., Jr. ... New Orleans, LA
Cobb, James Abernethy, Jr.
Fort Lauderdale, FL
Cobb James C., P.C. ... Detroit, MI
Cobb, James Clark, Jr. ... Detroit, MI
Cobb, James E. ... Jacksonville, FL
Ocala, FL
Cobb, James F., Jr. ... Salt Lake City, UT
Cobb, James L., Jr. ... Covington, KY
Cobb, James L.S. ... Raleigh, NC
Cobb, James O. ... Charlotte, NC
Cobb, Jeffrey B. ... Westport, CT
Cobb, Jennifer Dunn ... Seattle, WA
Cobb, Jennifer E. ... Columbus, GA
Cobb, Jmaes K. ... Santa Rosa, CA
Cobb, Joanne S. ... Clinton, NJ
Cobb, Joey M. ... Iuka, MS
Cobb, John B. ... Newport Beach, CA
Cobb, John F. ... Los Angeles, CA
Cobb, John H. ... Charlotte, NC
Cobb, John H., Jr. ... New York, NY
Cobb, John Richardson ... Augusta, MT
Cobb, John S. ... Decatur, IL
Cobb, John S. ... Towson, MD
Cobb, John W. ... Boulder, CO
Cobb, John W. ... Cambridge, MA
Cobb, John W. ... Tuxedo, NY
Cobb, Juan A. Cuyar ... San Juan, PR
Cobb, Katherine M. ... Melbourne, FL
Cobb, Kay B. ... University, MS
Cobb, Kenneth ... Lincoln, NE
Cobb, Kenneth A. ... Winthrop, ME
Cobb, Kenneth A. ... Kansas City, MO
Cobb, Kent C. ... Plantation, FL
Tulsa, OK
Cobb, Kevin W. ... Detroit, MI
Cobb, Kolleen O. Pasternack ... Miami, FL
Cobb, Kristi L. ... Thousand Oaks, CA
Cobb, L. Dean ... Austin, TX
Cobb, Laurence A. ... Raleigh, NC
Cobb, Laurie C. ... Houston, TX
Cobb, LaVerne B. ... Houston, TX
Cobb, Lawrence P., Jr. ... Atlanta, GA
Cobb, Leonard B. ... Meridian, MS
Cobb, LeRoy Alan ... Anniston, AL
Cobb, Lewis L., Jr. ... Jackson, TN
Cobb, Lisa M. ... New York, NY
Cobb, M. Anderson, Jr. ... Memphis, TN
Cobb, Marck R. ... Galva, KS
Cobb, Maria M. ... Biloxi, MS
Cobb, Mark R. ... Owenton, KY
Cobb, Michael D. ... Newport Beach, CA
Cobb, Montgomery W. ... Portland, OR
Cobb, Morris G. ... Amarillo, TX
Cobb & Oldfield ... Covington, KY
Cobb, Owens T., Jr. ... Columbia, SC
Cobb, Patricia A. ... Carbondale, PA
Cobb, Paul W. "Whit", Jr.
Washington, DC
Cobb, Paula K. ... Baton Rouge, LA
Cobb, Peter V. Z. ... Washington, DC
New York, NY
Cobb, Philip G. ... Portland, OR
Cobb, Priscilla L. ... Boston, MA
Cobb, Ralph F. ... Eugene, OR
Cobb, Raymond W. ... Wilmington, DE
Cobb, Regina Liudzius ... Los Angeles, CA
Cobb, Renee M. ... Alexandria, VA
Cobb, Richard A. ... Chicago, IL
Cobb, Richard L. ... Phoenix, AZ
Cobb, Richard S. ... Wilmington, DE
Cobb, Richard W. ... Orange Park, FL
Cobb, Rita Batz ... Hillsboro, OR
Cobb, Robert E. ... Fort Lauderdale, FL
Cobb, Robert W.
Office of Government Ethics, Office of General Counsel and Legal Policy, GV
Cobb, Rodney A. ... Atlanta, GA
Cobb, Ronald W., Jr. ... Chicago, IL
Cobb, Roy C., Jr. ... Clayton, MO
Cobb, Russell, III ... Tulsa, OK
Cobb, Sam B., Jr. ... Tyler, TX
Cobb & Shealy, P.A. ... Abbeville, AL
Dothan, AL
Enterprise, AL
Geneva, AL
Ozark, AL
Cobb, Stanton L. ... Orlando, FL
Cobb, Stanton L., P.A., Law Firm of
Orlando, FL
Cobb, Steve ... Nashville, TN
Cobb, Steven L. ... Edmonds, WA
Cobb, Sue Bell ... Montgomery, AL
Cobb, Susan A. ... Washington, DC
Cobb, Susan D. ... Boston, MA
Cobb, Susan F. ... Houston, TX
Cobb, Susan M. ... Columbia, SC
Cobb, Suzanne R. ... Phoenix, AZ
Cobb, T. Keller ... Atlanta, GA
Cobb, Teresa Gaba ... Jackson, TN
Cobb, Terry ... Topeka, KS
Cobb, Terry West ... St. Petersburg, FL
Cobb, Theodore A. ... Sacramento, CA
Cobb, Thomas C. ... Miami, FL
Cobb, Thomas R. ... New Albany, MS
Cobb, Thomas T. ... Daytona Beach, FL
Cobb, Tiffany Strelow ... Columbus, OH
Cobb, Timothy F. S. ... Atlanta, GA
Cobb, Ty ... Denver, CO
Washington, DC
Cobb, Tyrus H. ... Shelbyville, TN
Cobb, Verna W. ... Tuxedo, NY
Cobb, Virginia ... Dallas Center, IA
Cobb, W. Allen ... Wrightsville Beach, NC
Cobb, W. Allen, Jr. ... Wilmington, NC
Cobb & Walton, P.C. ... Norcross, GA
Cobb, Warren H. ... Daytona Beach, FL
Cobb, Wayne H., Jr. ... Dallas, TX
Cobb, Wayne L. ... Dade City, FL
Cobb, William Allen ... Wilmington, NC
Cobb, William C. ... Atlanta, GA
Cobb, William D., Jr. ... Dallas, TX
Cobb, William G. ... Reno, NV
Cobb, William J. ... Decatur, GA
Cobb, William J., III ... Austin, TX
Cobb, William M. ... Wichita, KS
Cobb, William P., II ... Montgomery, AL
Cobb & Woodworth, LLP ... Portland, OR
Cobbe, Charles M. ... Dallas, TX
Cobble, Dean P. ... Gary, IN
Cobble, Jeffrey A. ... Harrisburg, PA
Greeneville, TN
Cobble, Wm. E., Jr. ... Atlanta, GA
Cobbs, Cabell F. ... Staunton, VA
Cobbs, Louise B. ... Washington, DC
Cobbs, Michael ... Sodus, NY
Cobbs, Nicholas H. ... Washington, DC
Cobbs, Nicholas H., Jr. ... Greensboro, AL
Cobbs, Peter P. ... Detroit, MI
Cobb-Zahour, Nancy E.C. ... Freeland, MI
Cobden, Cynthia G. ... New York, NY
Cobden, Sandra ... New York, NY
Cobeaga, J. Mitchell ... Las Vegas, NV
Cobean & Renn ... Wellington, KS
Coben, Gregory ... Ocean City, NJ
Coben, Gregory M. ... Santa Cruz, CA
Coben, James R. ... St. Paul, MN
Coben, Jerome L. ... Los Angeles, CA
Coben, Larry E. ... Scottsdale, AZ
CoBen, Melvyn J. ... Sacramento, CA
Coben, Scott A. ... Sacramento, CA
Coben, William A. ... Malibu, CA
Coberly & Brown ... Overland Park, KS
Coberly, E. Clark ... Sierra Madre, CA
Coberly, Jennifer Rae ... Miami, FL
Coberly, Mark T. ... Norfolk, VA
Coberly, Robert G. ... Washington, DC
Coberly, Sharon A. ... Overland Park, KS
Coberly, Steven ... Washington, DC
Coberly, Susan F. ... Fresno, CA
Cobert, Eugene O. ... Somers, NY
Cobert, Harriette I. ... Beverly Hills, CA
Cobert, Joseph M., A Professional Corporation
Encino, CA
Cobert, Joseph Maxwell, (A Professional Corporation) ... Encino, CA
Cobert, Milton L. ... Cranbury, NJ
Cobert, Mitchell H. ... Morristown, NJ
Cobert, Ronald N. ... Washington, DC
Cobert-Alvarez, Jill ... New York, NY
Cobery, James E. ... Boston, MA
Cobetto, Jack B. ... Pittsburgh, PA
Cobey, Alexander D. ... McLean, VA
Cobey, Christopher E. ... San Jose, CA
Cobey, Donald E. ... New Haven, CT
Cobey, Elizabeth R. ... San Francisco, CA
Cobey, John G. ... Cincinnati, OH
Cobey, Penny P. ... Los Angeles, CA
Cobham, Denise A. ... Plainfield, NJ
Cobian, Darlene M. ... St. Paul, MN
Cobian, Francisco J. ... San Juan, PR
Cobian, Michael G. ... River Falls, WI
Cobian & Valls ... San Juan, PR
Cobián Guzmán, Magali ... San Juan, PR
Cobin, David M. ... St. Paul, MN
Cobine, Craig J. ... Naperville, IL
Cobitz, Thomas A. ... Hialeah, FL
Coble, Charles E. ... Greensboro, NC
Raleigh, NC
Coble, Debra H. ... Florence, AL
Coble, Edgar O., Jr. ... Fort Worth, TX
Coble, Eugene J. ... Denver, CO
Coble, George R. (Ran), Jr. ... Raleigh, NC
Coble, J. Howard ... Greensboro, NC
Coble, J. Kermit, (P.A.)
Daytona Beach, FL
Coble, John A. ... Fremont, OH
Toledo, OH
Coble, John L. ... Wilmington, NC
Coble, John P. ... Florence, AL
Coble, Karin Dale ... Nashville, TN
Coble, Kathleen ... Seattle, WA
Coble & Milone ... Flora, IL
Coble, Odom & Mabry ... Albemarle, NC
Coble, Paul R. ... Los Angeles, CA
Coble, Richard A. ... Perrysburg, OH
Coble, Robert D. ... Columbia, SC
Coble, Robert G. ... Flora, IL
Coble, Robert R. ... Gainesville, TX
Coble, Ronald W. ... Bellevue, WA
Coble & Simpson ... Daytona Beach, FL
Coble, Terry A. ... Miami, FL
Coble, Warren L. ... Albemarle, NC
Cobleigh, Gerard P. ... Warwick, RI
Cobleigh, Kenneth W. ... Baltimore, MD
Cobleigh, Lisa ... Boston, MA
Cobleigh, Sprague & Giacobbe ... Warwick, RI
Coblence, Alain ... New York, NY
Coblence & Warner ... New York, NY
Coblens, Douglas A. ... Oyster Bay, NY
Coblens, Robert P. ... Milton-Freewater, OR
Coblens, Robert P., P.C.
Milton-Freewater, OR
Coblentz, Donald R. ... Worcester, MA
Coblentz, J. Wendell ... Reading, PA
Coblentz, Patch, Duffy & Bass, LLP
San Francisco, CA
Coblentz, Peter D. ... Chicago, IL
Coblentz, William K. ... San Francisco, CA
Coblenz, Michael L. ... Houston, TX
Coblin, James A. ... Atlanta, GA
Coblitz, Don & Willis ... Chicago, IL
Coblitz, Marta ... Chicago, IL
Cobos, Antonio A. ... Austin, TX
Cobourn, Sean C. ... Charlotte, NC
Cobrin & Gittes ... New York, NY
Cobrin, Jill A. ... New York, NY
Cobrin, Peter T. ... New York, NY
Cobrinik, Daniel ... New York, NY
Coburn, Andrew B. ... Greenville, SC
Coburn, Arthur R. ... Seattle, WA
Coburn, Barry ... Washington, DC
Coburn, Beneta D. ... Duluth, GA
Coburn, C. Gregory ... Ocean City, MD
Coburn, Christopher T. ... Stamford, CT
Coburn, Corbett B., III ... Duluth, GA
Coburn, Craig C. ... Salt Lake City, UT
Coburn & Croft ... Belleville, IL
St. Louis, MO
Coburn, Daniel J. ... Treasury Department, Internal Revenue Service, GV
Coburn, Daniel R. ... Morristown, NJ
Coburn, David H. ... Washington, DC
Coburn & Di Sesa, P.A. ... Leominster, MA
Coburn, Donald S. ... Newark, NJ
Coburn, Evelyn ... Washington, DC
Coburn, G. Lance ... Las Vegas, NV
Coburn, George M. ... Washington, DC
Coburn, H. Christopher ... Irvine, CA
Coburn, Hayward H. ... Southington, CT
Coburn, Howard E. ... Cleveland, OH
Coburn, John F., III ... Beaverton, OR
Coburn, John H. ... Winnetka, IL
Coburn, John T. ... Glen Ellyn, IL
Coburn, Joseph W., IV ... Pine Bush, NY
Coburn, Judith M. ... Portland, ME
Coburn, Kathryn R. ... Woodland Hills, CA
Coburn, Lee L. ... Bellevue, WA
Coburn, Maren ... Hackensack, NJ
New York, NY
Coburn, Mary Beth ... San Diego, CA
Coburn, Marykate ... Leominster, MA
Coburn, Michelle D. ... Atlanta, GA
Coburn, Michelle E. ... Dallas, TX
Coburn, Natalie G. ... Washington, DC
Coburn, Patricia A. ... Dublin, OH
Coburn, Paul J. ... Atlanta, GA
Coburn, Raymond E. ... Simsbury, CT
Coburn, Richard J. ... New York, NY
Coburn, Robert L. ... Mount Clemens, MI
Coburn & Schertler ... Washington, DC
Coburn, Stanley A. ... Atlanta, GA
Coburn, Violet M. ... Oak Park, IL
Coburn, William H. ... Alexandria, VA
Coburn, Wm. H., Jr. ... Moraga, CA
Cobuzio, Joseph K. ... Newark, NJ
Coby, Mark S. ... San Francisco, CA
Coca, Denise A. ... Department of Education, Office for Civil Rights, GV
Coca, T. Rao ... Hopewell Junction, NY
Cocalis, Alexander ... Fort Lauderdale, FL
Cocalis, James S. ... Westfield, NJ
Cocalis, Kimberly W. ... Fort Lauderdale, FL
Cocalis, Patricia W. ... Fort Lauderdale, FL
Cocalis, Reid A., (P.A.)
Fort Lauderdale, FL
Cocanougher, Elizabeth L. ... Louisville, KY
Cocanougher, Tim ... Springfield, KY

Cocanower, David L. ....Phoenix, AZ
Cocanower, Liana C. ....Los Angeles, CA
Cocanower & Robbins ....Fort Worth, TX
Cocanower, S. C. ....Fort Worth, TX
Cocas, Donovan ....Los Angeles, CA
Cocca, Matthew C. ....New York, NY
Cocca & Pepe ....New York, NY
Cocchia, Robert A. ....Los Angeles, CA
Cocchia, Timothy L. ....Phoenix, AZ
Cocchiarella, Alfonse J. ....Oakdale, MN
Cocchiarella, John C. ....New York, NY
Cocchiarella, Joseph A. ....Orlando, FL
Cocchiola, Carol A. ....Binghamton, NY
Cocchiola & Garelick, P.C. ....Lebanon, NJ
Morristown, NJ
Cocchiola, Gina ....Hartford, CT
Cocchiola, Glenn J. ....Lebanon, NJ
Cocci, Meghan ....Tucson, AZ
Coccia, Michel A. ....Phelps, WI
Cocco, Leonard M. ....Bridgeport, CT
Cocco, Maria Carol ....Philadelphia, PA
Cocco, Robert P. ....Philadelphia, PA
Cocco, Robert P., P.C. ....Philadelphia, PA
Coccodrilli, Fred J. ....Portland, OR
Coccoma, Ellen Leary ....Cooperstown, NY
Coccoma, Michael V. ....Cooperstown, NY
Coccomo, Cynthia J. ....West Hartford, CT
Cocek, Carol ....Reseda, CA
Coch, Deborah Lucas ....Caledonia, MI
Coch, Liora R. ....Roosevelt, NY
Coch, Nicholas L. ....New York, NY
Cochell, Stephen R. ....Memphis, TN
Cochener, Donna M. ....Seattle, WA
Cochenour, Charles G. ....Pittsburgh, PA
Cochenour, Craig G. ....Pittsburgh, PA
Cochenour, Pamela G. ....Pittsburgh, PA
Cocheo, John F. ....New London, CT
Cocheres, Carol Porell ....Harrisburg, PA
Cocheres, Louis G. ....Harrisburg, PA
Cochet, Laura A. ....Haddonfield, NJ
Cochi, Carl J. ....Utica, NY
Cochi, Stephen J. ....Union City, NJ
Bronx, NY
Cochilla, Stephen J. ....Washington, DC
Cochis, Alexander Joseph ....Quincy, MA
Cochnauer, Amé Q. ....Lewiston, ID
Cochonour, Robert B. ....Casey, IL
Cochran, A. Andrew ....Annapolis, MD
Cochran, Adam ....San Dimas, CA
Cochran, Andrew R. ....Washington, DC
Cochran, Anthony L. ....Atlanta, GA
Cochran, Barbara G. ....Houston, TX
Cochran, Brian ....San Diego, CA
Cochran, Brian D. ....Los Angeles, CA
Cochran, Bruce W. ....Los Angeles, CA
Cochran, Bryan M. ....Wilmington, DE
Cochran, Calloway ....Dallas, TX
Cochran, Camp & Snipes ....Marietta, GA
Smyrna, GA
Cochran, Charles D. ....Santa Rosa, CA
Cochran, Charles J., Jr. ....Suffield, OH
Cochran, Charles Malcolm, IV
Wilmington, DE
Cochran, Charles W., III ....Florence, AL
Cochran, Cherry, Givens & Smith, P.C.
Dothan, AL
Mobile, AL
Cochran, Chudleigh B. ....Houston, TX
Cochran, Clark J., Jr.
Fort Lauderdale, FL
Tampa, FL
West Palm Beach, FL
Cochran, Clifton S. ....Kennesaw, GA
Cochran & Cochran ....Houston, TX
Cochran & Cochran, P.C. ....Dallas, TX
Cochran, D. Bruce ....Dallas, TX
Killeen, TX
Cochran & Dahl, P.C. ....Phoenix, AZ
Cochran, Darrell L. ....Tacoma, WA
Cochran, David ....Stateline, NV
Cochran, David B. ....Cleveland, OH
Cochran, David L. ....Albany, NY
Cochran, David R. ....Stateline, NV
Cochran, David S. ....Downers Grove, IL
Cochran, Deborah Donick ....McLean, VA
Cochran, Diane Zaar ....Newton, MA
Cochran, Don R. ....Hampton, VA
Cochran, Donald E. ....Westville, IN
Cochran, Douglas J. ....Baton Rouge, LA
Cochran, Edward W. ....Shaker Heights, OH
Cochran, Eileen K. ....Annapolis, MD
Cochran, Eric L. ....New York, NY
Cochran, Fielding B., III ....Houston, TX
Cochran, Fletcher W. ....Slidell, LA
Cochran, Foley & Associates, P.C.
Detroit, MI
Flint, MI
Livonia, MI
Cochran Follett & Yarbrough
Crescent City, CA
Cochran, Frank B. ....New Haven, CT
Cochran, Franklin D. ....Nashville, TN
Cochran, Gaye E. ....Phoenix, AZ
Cochran, Gene ....Bristol, VA
Cochran, Gene, A Professional Corporation
Bristol, VA
Cochran, George C. ....University, MS
Cochran, George M. ....Staunton, VA
Cochran, George R. ....Oklahoma City, OK
Cochran, George W., Jr. ....Streetsboro, OH
Cochran, Gill ....Annapolis, MD
Cochran, Glenda G. ....Birmingham, AL
Cochran, Glenn R. ....Princeton, NJ
Cochran, Gregory L. ....Chicago, IL
Cochran, Gregory P. ....Lynchburg, VA
Cochran, H. Esther ....Dallas, TX
Cochran, Harry M., Jr. ....Institute, WV
Cochran, Heather Fleniken ....Houston, TX
Cochran, Hunter K. ....Memphis, TN
Cochran, J. Al ....Smyrna, GA
Cochran, J. Chris ....Birmingham, AL
Cochran, J. Michael ....Pasadena, CA
Cochran, J. Wesley ....Lubbock, TX
Cochran, Jack ....Blue Springs, MO
Cochran, James C. ....Cleveland, OH
Cochran, James Daniel ....Huntsville, AL
Cochran, James S. ....Los Angeles, CA
Cochran, Janette Freeman ....Pasadena, CA
Cochran, Janine G. ....Cincinnati, OH
Cochran, Jeanne M. ....St. Paul, MN
Cochran, Jeffery D. ....Berlin, CT
Cochran, Jeffrey W. ....Arlington, TX
Cochran, Jerald R. ....Pasadena, CA
Cochran, Jerome ....Pittsburgh, PA
Cochran, Jerry L. ....Phoenix, AZ
Cochran, Jill Beckett ....Austin, TX
Cochran, Joan E. ....Los Angeles, CA
Cochran, Joe ....Houston, TX
Cochran, John B. ....Boston, MA
Cochran, John D. ....Indianapolis, IN
Cochran, John D., Jr. ....Indianapolis, IN
Cochran, John E., Jr. ....Auburn, AL
Cochran, John H. ....Dallas, TX
Cochran, John L. ....Sacramento, CA
Cochran, John R. ....Olathe, KS
Cochran, John R., Jr. ....Houston, TX
Cochran, John W. ....Minneapolis, MN
Cochran, Johnnie L., Jr. ....Los Angeles, CA
Washington, DC
Cochran, Johnnie L., Jr. A Prof. Corp., Law Offices of ....Los Angeles, CA
Cochran, Johnnie L., Jr., Jr. A Prof. Corp., Law Offices of ....Washington, DC
Cochran, Joseph M. ....Charlottesville, VA
Cochran & Kakac ....Fairfield, IL
Cochran, Kathleen F. ....Seattle, WA
Cochran, Kathryn M. ....Chicago, IL
Cochran, Kathy A. ....Seattle, WA
Cochran, Keith C. ....Seattle, WA
Cochran, Kenneth L. ....Somers, NY
Cochran, Kent W. ....Nashville, TN
Cochran, Lance W. ....Salina, KS
Cochran, Les ....Houston, TX
Cochran, Lisa L. ....San Diego, CA
Cochran, Marc H. ....Tacoma, WA
Cochran, Marie ....Washington, DC
Cochran, Marilyn M. ....New York, NY
Cochran, Mark D. ....San Mateo, CA
Cochran, Mark S. ....Arlington, TX
Cochran, Mark W. ....San Antonio, TX
Cochran, Mark Wright ....San Antonio, TX
Cochran, Martha ....La Jolla, CA
Cochran, Martha L. ....Washington, DC
Cochran, Martha L. ....Knoxville, TN
Cochran, Michael A. ....Gnadenhutten, OH
Cochran, Michael E. ....Port Neches, TX
Cochran, Michael H. ....Columbus, OH
Cochran, Michael T. ....Tallahassee, FL
Cochran, Oswald, McDonald, Roam & Moore, P.C. ....Blue Springs, MO
Cochran, Patricia A. ....Philadelphia, PA
Cochran, Philip B. ....Columbus, OH
Cochran & Phillips, L.L.P. ....Arlington, TX
Fort Worth, TX
Cochran & Pirtle ....Los Angeles, CA
Cochran, Rebecca A. ....Dayton, OH
Cochran, Richard A., Jr. ....Marietta, OK
Cochran, Richard C. ....Fairfield, IL
Cochran, Richard H. ....Visalia, CA
Cochran, Richard J. ....Chicago, IL
Cochran, Richard R. ....Miami, FL
Cochran, Robert B. ....Pompano Beach, FL
Cochran, Robert F. ....Crescent City, CA
Cochran, Robert F., Jr. ....Malibu, CA
Cochran, Robert G. ....Tampa, FL
Cochran, Robert H. ....Auburn, AL
Cochran, Robert J. ....Columbus, OH
Cochran, Robert P. ....New York, NY
Cochran, Robert R. ....Tulsa, OK
Austin, TX
Cochran, Robin C. ....San Bernardino, CA
Cochran, Ronald S. ....Biloxi, MS
Cochran, Sarah W. ....Fairfield, IA
Cochran & Schultz ....Kingston, NJ
Princeton, NJ
Cochran, Scott A. ....Smyrna, GA
Cochran, Sharon K. ....Aurora, CO
Cochran, Sherry L. ....Farmington Hills, MI
Cochran, Shirley A. ....Columbus, OH
Cochran, Sidney A., Jr. ....Tyler, TX
Cochran, Steffani A. ....isleta, NM
Cochran, Stephen G. ....San Antonio, TX
Cochran, Stephen G. ....Harrisonburg, VA
McLean, VA
Cochran, Steve ....Los Angeles, CA
Cochran, Steven K. ....Dallas, TX
Cochran, Suzanne ....Dallas, TX
Cochran, T. Kent ....Brentwood, TN
Cochran, Tamra Lee McMillian ....Rogers, AR
Cochran, Tara Blakewood ....Marksville, LA
Cochran, Terry L. ....Livonia, MI
Cochran, Theron G. ....Greenville, SC
Cochran, Thia M. ....Newport Beach, CA
Cochran, Thomas C., Jr. ....Pittsburgh, PA
Cochran, Thomas D. ....Spokane, WA
Cochran & Thomas, P.L.L. ....Cleveland, OH
Cochran, Thomas R. ....Oklahoma City, OK
Cochran, Tod A. ....San Francisco, CA
Cochran, Tommie Douglas ....Columbia, SC
Cochran, Uhlmann, Abney, Duck & Wright
Memphis, TN
Cochran, Vicki Arroyo ....Washington, DC
Cochran, Vickie J. ....St. Louis, MO
Cochran, Victoria Kay Hoffman ....Rogers, AR
Cochran, Virginia E. ....Helena, MT
Cochran, Virginia L. ....Virginia Beach, VA
Cochran, W. Thad ....Jackson, MS
Cochran, Wanda J. ....Mobile, AL
Cochran, Wilbur P., III ....Hinsdale, IL
Cochran, William D., IV ....Jacksonville, FL
Cochran, William W., II ....Denver, CO
Cochran, Winston E., Jr. ....Houston, TX
Cochran-Becchina, Ann M.
New York, NY
Cochran-Bond & Connon LLP
Los Angeles, CA
Cochran-Bond, Walter ....Los Angeles, CA
Cochrane & Bresnahan, P.A. ....St. Paul, MN
Cochrane, Carl L. ....Kansas City, MO
Cochrane, Charles M. ....Roseville, MN
Cochrane, Darryl R. ....Muskegon, MI
Cochrane, Dennis O. ....Superior, WI
Cochrane, Don ....Tulsa, OK
Cochrane, Drew J. ....Milwaukee, WI
Cochrane, Edward G., II ....Greenville, SC
Cochrane, Gordon A. ....Olympia Fields, IL
Cochrane, J. Michael ....Sacramento, CA
Cochrane, James A., III
Cape Girardeau, MO
Cochrane, John A. ....St. Paul, MN
Cochrane, John E. ....Washington, DC
Cochrane, John W. ....Irvine, CA
Cochrane, Julia L. ....Santa Clara, CA
Cochrane, Kenneth C. ....Modesto, CA
Cochrane Law Office, P.A. ....Roseville, MN
Cochrane, Michael J. ....Danville, CA
Cochrane, R. Scott ....Federal Way, WA
Cochrane, Robert V. ....Albuquerque, NM
Cochrane, Stephen R. ....Buffalo, NY
Cochrane, Steven Andrew ....Clifton, NJ
Cochrane, Stuart J. ....Fort Dodge, IA
Cochrane, Susan M. ....St. Paul, MN
Cochrane, Thomas B. ....Muskegon, MI
Cochrane, Thomas H. ....Las Vegas, NV
Cochrane, William, Jr. ....Canton, OH
Cochrane, William M. ....Washington, DC
Cochrane, William M. ....United States Senate, Senatorial Assistants, GV
Cochran-May, Tamara L. ....San Antonio, TX
Cochrun, Julia Truesdell
Birmingham, AL
Cochrun, Steven Lee ....Augusta, GA
Cock, Lawrence R. ....Seattle, WA
Cockburn, Christina R. ....Houston, TX
Cockburn, Joscelyn G. ....Raleigh, NC
Cockburn, Juan S.
United States International Trade Commission, Office of Unfair Import Investigations, GV
Cockburn, Ross E. ....Houston, TX
Cockburn, Ruth B. ....River Ridge, LA
Cockburn, Thomas N. ....Austin, TX
Cockcroft, Irene C. ....San Diego, CA
Cockcroft, John Van V., Jr.
Yorktown Heights, NY
Cocke, Beth ....Memphis, TN
Cocke, Charles P. ....Vienna, VA
Cocke, David J. ....Memphis, TN
Cocke, Jas. W., Jr. ....Jackson, MS
Cocke, Joe N. ....Macon, TN
Cocke, John H. ....Clarksdale, MS
Cocke, Richard ....Richmond, VA
Cocke, Thomas B., Jr. ....Madisonville, LA
Cocke, William B., Jr. ....Newland, NC
Cockerell, Perry J. ....Fort Worth, TX
Cockerham, Judy Kay ....New Orleans, LA
Cockerham, Kristi K. ....Dallas, TX
Cockerham, Robert W. ....St. Louis, MO
Cockerham, W. Stephen ....Dallas, TX
Cockerill, Christine C. ....Woodbury, NJ
Cockerill, H. Richd. ....Cincinnati, OH
Arlington, TX
Cockerill, Heike ....Hammond, IN
Cockerill, Leonard J. ....San Antonio, TX
Cockerill, Thomas M. ....Winchester, IN
Cockerille, Monica G. ....Boise, ID
Cockerille, Philip R., (P.C.) ....Denver, CO
Cockerille, Roger E. ....Boise, ID
Cockett, William J. ....Mountain City, TN
Cockey, Brennan & Maloney, P.C.
Ocean City, MD
Salisbury, MD
Cockey, Preston O., Jr. ....Tampa, FL
Cockey, Robin R. ....Salisbury, MD
Cockey, Sharon ....New York, NY
Cockfield, J. Gavin ....Boston, MA
Cockfield, James E. ....Boston, MA
Cockfield, Susan Cary ....New York, NY
Cockle, John R. ....Kansas City, MO
Cockle, John R. ....Portland, OR
Cockle, Lynn Deal ....Kansas City, MO
Cocklereece, John A., Jr.
Winston-Salem, NC
Cockley, Heather M. ....Mansfield, OH
Cockley, Stephen ....Mansfield, OH
Cockman, David R. ....Raleigh, NC
Cockman, Madison H., Jr.
Fort Lauderdale, FL
Cockram, R. Yvonne ....Martinsville, VA
Cockram, Ruby Yvonne ....Dallas, TX
Cockrel, Paul R. ....Denver, CO
Cockrell, Arthur E. ....Plymouth, NC
Cockrell, Barry K. ....Jackson, MS
Cockrell, Bobby Hill, Jr. ....Tuscaloosa, AL
Cockrell, Christopher L., Sr.
San Bernardino, CA
Cockrell & Cockrell ....Tuscaloosa, AL
Cockrell, D. Michael ....Laurel, MS
Cockrell, Dale R. ....Kalispell, MT
Cockrell, Geoffrey ....Chicago, IL
Cockrell, Ginger Dickerson ....Tuscaloosa, AL
Cockrell, James R. ....Leeds, AL
Cockrell, Joel M.
Federal Energy Regulatory Commission, Office of the General Counsel, GV
Cockrell, Kerry W. ....Gonzales, LA
Cockrell, Kevin Clay ....Mount Sterling, KY
Cockrell, Matthew W. ....Chicago, IL
Cockrell, Melody Lynn ....Norfolk, VA
Cockrell, M. W., Jr. ....Fort Worth, TX
Cockrell, Phillip N. ....Texarkana, TX
Cockrell, Quinn & Creighton ....Denver, CO
Flagler, CO
Cockrell, Richard C. ....Denver, CO
Cockrell, William Patrick, II
Birmingham, AL
Cockren, Robert W. ....Short Hills, NJ
New York, NY
Cockriel, Stephen E. ....Long Beach, CA
Cockriel, Stephen E. ....Los Angeles, CA
Newport Beach, CA
Cockriel, Steven M. ....St. Louis, MO
Cockriel, Steven M., L.L.C., Law Offices of
St. Louis, MO
Cockrill, Ann T. ....Seattle, WA
Cockrill, Donald A. ....Greenville, SC
Cockrill, Howard ....Little Rock, AR
Cockrill, Leonard M. ....Yakima, WA
Cockrill, Patrick R. ....Yakima, WA
Cockrill, Rogers ....Little Rock, AR
Cockrill, Todd G. ....Little Rock, AR
Cockrill & Weaver, P.S. ....Yakima, WA
Cockrill, William C. ....Springfield, MO
Cockrill, William G. ....Huntsville, AL
Cockrum, Carlynne S. ....Washington, DC
Cockrum, James Douglas ....Louisville, KY
Cockrum, Jesse C. ....Goldthwaite, TX
Cockrum, Robert B. ....Fort Wayne, IN
Cockrum, Scott B. ....Hammond, IN
Cockrum, William G. ....Columbus, OH
Cockshoot, Bruce J. ....Swansboro, NC
Cockson, Michael F. ....Minneapolis, MN
Coclin, Andrew C. ....North Easton, MA
Coco, Alfred J. ....Denver, CO
Coco, Amanda M. ....Chicago, IL
Coco, Amy J. ....Pittsburgh, PA
Coco, Ann C. ....Baton Rouge, LA
Coco, Anthony J. ....Santa Ana, CA
Coco, Chester J. ....Marksville, LA
Coco, Christopher T. ....Beaumont, TX
Coco, Elvira, (Mrs.) ....Hicksville, NY
Coco, Joseph A. ....New York, NY
Coco, Mark S. ....Columbus, OH
Coco, Matthew J. ....Seattle, WA
Coco, Michael ....Glen Cove, NY
Coco, Nathan F. ....Chicago, IL
Coco, Robert Anthony ....Rosemont, IL
Coco, Robert L. ....Baton Rouge, LA
Coco, Salvatore ....Alhambra, CA
Coco, Stephen L. ....Boston, MA
Coco, Stephen P. ....Jennings, LA
Coco, Susan ....Hattiesburg, MS
Cococcia, Amy C. ....New York, NY
Coco-Ewing, Celeste R. ....New Orleans, LA
Cocola, John F. ....Holmes, NY
Cocoma, Christopher J. ....Rockford, IL
Coconis, Tasha ....Bethesda, MD
Coconis, Thomas C. ....Chelmsford, MA
Cocoros, George J. ....Baltimore, MD
Cocoros, Paul ....Baltimore, MD
Cocotas, Vivian P. ....Orlando, FL
Cocoves, Spiros P. ....Toledo, OH
Cocoziello, J. Barry ....Newark, NJ
Cocozza, Frank P. ....Yonkers, NY
Cocozza, Paul F. ....Yonkers, NY
Cocozziello, Victor A. ....New York, NY
Cocquyt, Donald A. ....Ventura, CA
Cocquyt, Ronald A. ....Rochester, NY
Coday, Roderick M. ....St. Louis, MO
Codd, Bernard P. ....Reisterstown, MD
Codd & Codd ....Severna Park, MD
Codd, Downie D. ....Severna Park, MD
Codd, John M. ....Edison, NJ
Codd, Norman L. ....Los Angeles, CA
Codd, Paul J. ....Seattle, WA
Codd, Thomas Christopher
Severna Park, MD
Codd, Timothy J. ....Baltimore, MD
Codde, Diane L. ....Fresno, CA
Codding, Charles A. ....Oklahoma City, OK
Codding & Codding ....Fairfax, VA
Codding, Donald W. ....Albuquerque, NM
Codding, F. Hayden ....Fairfax, VA
Codding, Fred H. ....Fairfax, VA
Codding, George A., III ....Boulder, CO
Codding, Richard J. ....Los Angeles, CA
Coddington, Clinton H.
Redwood City, CA
Coddington, David Eric ....Hornell, NY
Coddington, Hicks & Danforth, A Professional Corporation
Menlo Park, CA
Redwood City, CA
Coddington, James W. ....Bella Vista, AR
Coddington, Kipp A. ....Washington, DC
Coddington, Michael K. ....Minneapolis, MN
Coddington, Peter D. ....New York, NY
Coddon, Eve Mary ....Los Angeles, CA
Coddon, Louis D., II ....Atlanta, GA
Coddou & Coddou ....Houston, TX
Coddou, Elizabeth S. ....Houston, TX
Coddou, Wesley S. ....Houston, TX
Code, Howard T. ....Briarcliff Manor, NY
Code Law Firm, The, P.A. ....Greenville, SC
Code, Merl F. ....Greenville, SC
Code, Michael A. ....Chicago, IL
Code, Ralph J., III ....Rochester, NY
Code, Thomas J. ....San Juan, PR
Codeanne, Sharon Lynn ....Hartford, CT
Codega, Joseph M. ....Cranston, RI

Codekas, Katherine ... Sacramento, CA
Codel, Alissa H. ... Atlanta, GA
Codell, David C. ... Los Angeles, CA
Codella, James V. ... Lewistown, PA
Coden, Andrew M. ... Southfield, MI
Coder, G. Norman ... Fort Worth, TX
Coder, H. William ... Great Falls, MT
Coderre, John P. ... Hadley, MA
Coderre, Nancy J. ... Southbridge, MA
Codevilla, David A. ... Washington, DC
Codey, Colleen M. ... New York, NY
Codias, Julio C. ... Miami, FL
Codiga, Douglas A. ... Honolulu, HI
Codiga, Gayle Godfrey, (Mrs.)
Alameda, CA
Codikow, Carroll, Guido & Groffman, LLP
Beverly Hills, CA
Los Angeles, CA
New York, NY
Codikow, David ... Los Angeles, CA
Codilis, Ernest J., Jr. ... Englewood, CO
Houston, TX
Codilis & Stawiarski ... Houston, TX
Englewood, CO
Codinach, Maria J. ... Cleveland, OH
Codington, Stacy L. ... West Linn, OR
Codinha, J. William, (P.C.)
Washington, DC
Boston, MA
Codispoti, Bruno F. ... New York, NY
Codispoti, Joseph S. ... Iselin, NJ
Codispoti, Kelly Gilmore ... Logan, WV
Codispoti, Lawrence A. ... Waldwick, NJ
Suffern, NY
Codlin, Craig J. ... New York, NY
Codlin, Dennis E. ... East Rutherford, NJ
Codner, Susan T. ... Randolph, MA
Codo, Bonds, Zumstein & Konzelman, A Professional Corporation ... Joliet, IL
Codo, Norman F. ... Boca Raton, FL
Codon, Dennis P. ... El Segundo, CA
Codrea, Cathy L. ... Reading, PA
Codrea, John Eli ... Akron, OH
Codron, Keith ... Irvine, CA
Coduti, Leonard L. ... Kingsburg, CA
Cody, Art C. ... New York, NY
Cody, Bernard C. ... Department of Commerce, National Oceanic and Atmospheric Administration, GV
Cody, Brendan John ... St. Paul, MN
Cody, Chapin Cimino ... Philadelphia, PA
Cody, Christopher M. ... Milford, CT
Cody, Christopher T. ... Oakland, CA
Cody, Daniel A. ... Washington, DC
Cody, Daniel J. ... St. Louis, MO
Cody, Daniel S. ... Akron, OH
Cody, David A. ... Bowling Green, OH
Cody, Dolores L. ... Columbia, MD
Cody, Donna K. ... Robbinsville, NC
Cody, Douglas H. ... Lancaster, PA
Cody, Edward C. ... St. Louis, MO
Cody, George W. ... Lynnwood, WA
Cody & Gonillo, LLP ... Milford, CT
Cody, Gregory L. ... Seattle, WA
Cody, Harriett M. ... Seattle, WA
Cody, Harvey H., III ... Houston, TX
Cody, Hatch & Blanchard ... Lynnwood, WA
Cody, J. Derrill ... Oklahoma City, OK
Cody, J. Terrence ... New Albany, IN
Cody, James R. ... Burlingame, CA
Cody, Jamie Nadeau ... Quincy, MA
Cody, Jeffery A. ... Dallas, TX
Cody, Jennifer A. ... Brookline, MA
Cody, Jennifer Purtle
Palos Verdes Estates, CA
Cody, Jeremy A. ... San Francisco, CA
Cody, John A., Jr. ... New Albany, IN
Cody, John C. ... Delmar, NY
Cody, Justine D'Isidori ... Chicago, IL
Cody, Kathleen
Securities and Exchange Commission, Office of the General Counsel, GV
Cody, Kevin P. ... San Jose, CA
Cody, Lynne P. ... Rochester, NY
Cody, Mark A. ... Chicago, IL
Cody, Mark A. ... Lansing, MI
Cody, Mary Bennett ... St. Louis, MO
Cody, Mary Dell ... Yankton, SD
Cody, Matthew J., Jr. (P.C.) ... Lebanon, VA
Cody, Michael T. ... Braintree, MA
Cody, Nancy C. ... Highland Heights, OH
Cody and Neely ... New Albany, IN
Cody, P. Gerald ... Cornelia, GA
Cody, Patricia A. ... New York, NY
Cody, Paul J. ... Philadelphia, PA
Cody, Philip F. ... New York, NY
Cody, Raphael J. ... Boston, MA
Cody, Raymond J. ... Arvada, CO
Cody, Richard ... Hartford, CT
Cody, Richard A. ... Cambridge, MA
Cody, Robert F. ... Rochester, NY
Cody, Robert J. ... Philadelphia, PA
Cody, Robert M. ... Columbus, OH
Cody, Ronald H. ... Southampton, MA
Cody, Sharon Greelish ... Lancaster, PA
Cody, Sharon Greelish, P.C.
Lancaster, PA
Cody, Stephen M. ... Miami, FL
Cody, Stephen W. ... Lancaster, PA
Cody, Tari Lynn ... Westlake Village, CA
Cody, T. H., Jr. ... Houston, TX
Cody, Thalia Mary ... New York, NY
Cody, Theodore J. ... Newport Beach, CA
Cody, Thomas G. ... Cincinnati, OH
Cody, Thomas J. ... New City, NY
Cody, Thomas P. ... Hartford, CT
Cody, Tracey Wallace ... Chelmsford, MA
Cody, William J. ... Brockport, NY
Cody, William W. ... St. Louis, MO
Cody, W. J. Michael ... Memphis, TN
Coe, A. Marshall ... San Antonio, TX
Coe, A. Renee ... Library of Congress, Copyright Office, GV
Coe, Allen B. ... Oklahoma City, OK
Coe, Anthony C. ... United States Senate, Office of the Legislative Counsel, GV
Coe, Anthony C. ... Lincoln, NE
Coe and Broberg, LLP ... Palm Beach, FL
Coe, Carl C., Jr. ... Glen Allen, VA
Coe, Charles W. ... Anchorage, AK
Coe, Cheryl Miller ... Washington, DC
Coe, Colin Ashley ... Austin, TX
Coe, Dalrymple, Coe & Zabel, S.C.
Rice Lake, WI
Coe, Diane M. ... Oxnard, CA
Coe, Edward J. ... Rice Lake, WI
Coe, George R. ... Denver, CO
Coe, Gerald L. ... Portland, OR
Coe, Glenn E. ... Hartford, CT
Coe, Harold B. ... Seattle, WA
Coe, Harry L., III ... Tampa, FL
Coe, Harry Lee, IV ... Tampa, FL
Coe, Helen M. ... Maumee, OH
Coe, Henry A., III ... Kountze, TX
Coe, Henry A., Jr ... Kountze, TX
Coe, Ilse G. ... Brooklyn, NY
Coe, Jack Brooks ... Houston, TX
Coe, Jack J., Jr. ... Malibu, CA
Coe, Jack Martin, Law Offices of
Miami, FL
Coe, James R. ... Omaha, NE
Coe, John A. ... Seattle, WA
Coe, John C. ... Steamboat Springs, CO
Coe, John R. ... Houston, TX
Coe, Jonathan R. ... Atlanta, GA
Coe, Karen C. ... Washington, DC
Coe, Keeva G. ... Sacramento, CA
Coe, Kenneth S. ... Charlotte, NC
Coe, Larry M. ... Wilmington, NC
Coe, Laura J. ... Houston, TX
Coe, Lewis Burton ... Cranford, NJ
Coe, Linda B. ... Washington, DC
Coe, Lisa Anne ... Torrance, CA
Coe, Lynn Leland ... Chicago, IL
Coe, Mark E. ... Rice Lake, WI
Coe, Matthew J. ... White Plains, NY
Coe, Michael E.
Securities and Exchange Commission, Division of Enforcement, GV
Coe, Michael I. ... Washington, DC
Coe, Pamela L. ... Englewood, CO
Coe, Patricia M. ... Bingham Farms, MI
Coe, Philip S. ... Atlanta, GA
Coe, Philip S. ... Fayetteville, GA
Coe, Rachel M. ... Woodbridge, NJ
Coe, Richard P., Jr. ... Philadelphia, PA
Coe, Richard T. ... Troy, MI
Coe, Robert ... White Plains, NY
Coe, Robert A. ... Northbrook, IL
Coe, Robert A., Ltd. & Assoc.
Northbrook, IL
Coe, Rocky L. ... Peoria, IL
Coe, Roger A. ... Millburn, NJ
Coe, Roger N. ... Elkhart, IN
Coe, R. S. ... Kountze, TX
Coe & Sanders, PLLC ... Seattle, WA
Coe, Sara M. ... Treasury Department, Internal Revenue Service, GV
Coe, Shelley Kathleen, (P.C.)
Walled Lake, MI
Coe, Suzanne E. ... Greenville, SC
Coe, Thomas H. ... Salem, OH
Coe, Ward B., III ... Baltimore, MD
Coe, William ... Austin, TX
Coe, William H. ... Milwaukee, WI
Coe-Barbee, Delores N. ... Lincoln, NE
Coebergh, Bastiaan K.
Salt Lake City, UT
Coebergh, Philip ... Grand Junction, CO
Coe-Hauskins, Carole V. ... Seattle, WA
Coel, Mark A. ... Hollywood, FL
Coel, Mark A., P.A. ... Hollywood, FL
Coelho, Helder ... New York, NY
Coelho, James R. Barlow
Los Angeles, CA
Coelho, Jean E. ... Middlesex, NJ
Coelho, Robert M. ... San Jose, CA
Coen, Alvin M. ... Huntington Beach, CA
Coen, Barbara J. ... Farmers Branch, TX
Coen, Barbara Novak
Department Of The Interior, Office of the Solicitor, GV
Coen, Beverly J. ... Westlake, OH
Coen, Cary J. ... Providence, RI
Coen, Frank Steven ... Wichita, KS
Coen, Frederick J. ... Manhasset, NY
Coen & Geoghan, P.C. ... Brooklyn, NY
Coen, Geri A. ... Elizabethtown, KY
Coen, Holly A. ... Wooster, OH
Coen, John P. ... Port Jefferson Station, NY
Coen, M. Lisbeth ... Washington, DC
Coen, Martin J., III ... Santa Maria, CA
Coen, Maureen R. ... New York, NY
Coen, Patrick D. ... Crystal Lake, IL
Coen, Richard L. ... Chicago, IL
Coen, Richard M. ... Providence, RI
Coen, Ronald S. ... Los Angeles, CA
Coen, Seth E. ... Brooklyn, NY
Coen, Shannon A. ... Fairfax, VA
Coen, Stephen C. ... Arlington, TX
Coen, Timothy F. ... Atlanta, GA
Coen, Victor A. ... Southfield, MI
Coen, W. Edward, Jr. ... Kansas City, MO
Coen, William R. ... Kettering, OH
Coenen & Berry ... Rayville, LA
Coenen, Kevin J. ... Chicago, IL
Coenen, Richard J. ... Omaha, NE
Coenen, Theo J., III ... Rayville, LA
Coenen, William R., Jr. ... Rayville, LA
Coenen, William R., Law Offices of
Monroe, LA
Rayville, LA
Coerdt, R. Timothy ... Cleveland, OH
Coerdt, Thomas R. ... Livonia, MI
Coerper, Milo G. ... Washington, DC
Coers-Mitchell, Christine ... Portland, OR
Coerver, Joe F. ... Dallas, TX
Coes, Kendal M. ... Cincinnati, OH
Coester, Thomas M. ... Los Angeles, CA
Coester, William E. ... Milbank, SD
Coey, Bennett & Carlson Co., L.P.A.
Elyria, OH
Coey, David C. ... Lansing, MI
Coey, G. Edward ... Birmingham, AL
Coey, Larry E. ... Elyria, OH
Cofano, Russell G. ... Bellevue, WA
Cofar, Lawrence J. ... Fort Lauderdale, FL
CoFell, Ann C. ... St. Cloud, MN
Cofer, Beauchamp, Stradley & Hicks, LLP
Atlanta, GA
Cofer, Carl H. ... Atlanta, GA
Cofer, Charles G. ... Jacksonville, FL
Cofer, D. Brooks ... Bryan, TX
Cofer, David T. ... Latrobe, PA
Cofer, Edwin T. ... Grenada, MS
Cofer, Hume ... Austin, TX
Cofer, John I., III ... Richmond, VA
Cofer, Patricia K. ... Fullerton, CA
Cofer, Robert H., II ... Thomson, GA
Cofer, Scott E. ... Sacramento, CA
Cofer, Walter L. ... Kansas City, MO
Cofer, Wesley R., Jr. ... Grafton, VA
Cofer, William L. ... Winston-Salem, NC
Cofer, William L., P.A.
Winston-Salem, NC
Coff, Harry E., Jr. ... Grand Junction, CO
Coff, Jerrold A. ... Hollywood, FL
Coff, Jerrold A., P.A. ... Hollywood, FL
Coff, L. Dean ... Austin, TX
Coffaro, Joseph M. ... Cincinnati, OH
Coffaro, Katrina L. Trimble
Cincinnati, OH
Coffaro, Steven C. ... Cincinnati, OH
Coffas, James ... Columbia, SC
Coffee, Anna M. ... Beaumont, TX
Coffee, Brett B. ... New York, NY
Coffee, Charles C. ... New Orleans, LA
Coffee & Coffee ... Dallas, TX
Coffee, Cynthia L. ... Louisville, KY
Coffee, David ... Paramus, NJ
Coffee, Gordon Alan ... Washington, DC
Coffee, James D. ... San Antonio, TX
Coffee, James R. ... Los Angeles, CA
Coffee, John C., Jr. ... New York, NY
Coffee, Jon N. ... Bloomfield Hills, MI
Coffee, K. Blake ... San Antonio, TX
Coffee, Linda N. ... Dallas, TX
Coffee, Mary Lynn K. ... Newport Beach, CA
Coffee, Melvin ... Denver, CO
Coffee, Melvin, P.C. ... Denver, CO
Coffee, Michael S. ... Department of State, Office of the Legal Adviser, GV
Coffee, Paul H. ... Ventura, CA
Coffee, Paula R. ... Saginaw, MI
Coffee, Richard J., II ... Waterloo, IL
Coffee, Richard P., Sr. ... Portage, IN
Coffee, Ronald M. ... Denver, CO
Coffee, Roy C., III ... Washington, DC
Coffee, Roy C., Jr. ... Dallas, TX
Coffee, Sandra E. ... Palmdale, CA
Coffee, Stacey Todd ... Anderson, SC
Coffee, Steven C. ... Saginaw, MI
Coffee, Thomas P. ... Columbus, OH
Coffee, V. Glenn ... Edmond, OK
Coffee, Wendell ... Lubbock, TX
Coffee, William D. ... Irvine, CA
Coffeen, Debra Burchard
Los Angeles, CA
Coffel, Ron D. ... Benton, IL
Coffelt, Burrow and Sawyer
Bentonville, AR
Coffelt & Coffelt, P.C. ... St. Louis, MO
Coffelt, George Q. ... St. Louis, MO
Coffelt, Guy D. ... Allentown, PA
Coffelt, Kemper R. ... St. Louis, MO
Coffelt, Richard D. ... Hays, KS
Coffelt, Terry P. ... Colorado Springs, CO
Coffelt, Wayne P. ... Bloomington, IL
Coffer & Atkinson ... Fairfield, CA
Coffer, John M. ... Fairfield, CA
Coffey, A. Tracy ... Houston, TX
Coffey, Alan F., Jr. ... Washington, DC
Coffey, Antonina P. ... Mount Laurel, NJ
Coffey, Arthur G. ... Boston, MA
Coffey, Barbara L. ... Brockton, MA
Coffey, Bill ... Beaumont, TX
Houston, TX
Coffey, Brian J. ... San Diego, CA
Coffey, Bruce A. ... Seattle, WA
Coffey, C. David ... Gainesville, FL
Coffey, Carolyn ... Washington, DC
Coffey, Catherine ... Detroit, MI
Coffey, Catherine B. ... Knoxville, TN
Coffey, Chandler, Johnson & McKenzie, P.A.
Manning, SC
Coffey, Christine A. ... Phoenix, AZ
Coffey, Christopher ... Brooklyn, NY
Coffey, Colin J. ... Richmond, CA
Coffey, Craig J. ... Needham, MA
Coffey, Dan C. ... Denton, TX
Coffey, Dan K. ... Anchorage, AK
Coffey, Daniel J. ... Indianapolis, IN
Coffey, Daniel W. ... San Diego, CA
Coffey, Daniel W. ... Albany, NY
Coffey, Daryl R. ... Fort Worth, TX
Coffey, David J. ... Boston, MA
Coffey, David M. ... Buffalo, NY
Coffey, David M. ... Cleveland, OH
Coffey, David M. ... Austin, TX
Coffey, Dennis P. ... Milwaukee, WI
Coffey, Diane Marie ... Wilmington, DE
Coffey, Diaz & O'Naghten, L.L.P.
Miami, FL
Coffey, Dixie L. ... Oklahoma City, OK
Coffey, Donald J. ... Atlanta, GA
Coffey, Donald J., P.C. ... Atlanta, GA
Coffey, Donald R. ... Knoxville, TN
Coffey, Edward C. ... Boulder, CO
Coffey, Edward J. ... San Antonio, TX
Coffey, Edward John, Jr. ... Northwood, NH
Coffey, Ellen S. ... Harrisburg, PA
Coffey, Eugene ... Corpus Christi, TX
Coffey, Frank D. ... Fort Worth, TX
Coffey, Fred L., Jr. ... Huntsville, AL
Coffey, Gambol & DiPalma ... Mentor, OH
Coffey, Gary R. ... Edwardsville, IL
Coffey, George V., Jr. ... Tucson, AZ
Coffey, Glenn S. ... Hackensack, NJ
Coffey, Gregg Alan ... Upper Nyack, NY
Coffey, Gregory J. ... Morristown, NJ
Coffey, Gregory R. ... Lincoln, NE
Coffey, Gregory W. ... Edwardsville, IL
Coffey & Griesbach ... St. Louis, MO
Coffey, J. Bradford ... Bangor, ME
Coffey, J. Randall ... Kansas City, MO
Coffey, James C. ... North Bend, OR
Coffey, James F. ... Boston, MA
Coffey, James J. ... Plattsburgh, NY
Coffey, Jane Demlow ... Paoli, PA
Coffey, Jas. J. ... Springfield, MA
Coffey, Jerry F. ... Kansas City, MO
Coffey, John E. ... Downers Grove, IL
Coffey, John E. ... Philadelphia, PA
Coffey, John E. ... Falls Church, VA
Coffey, John F. ... Ancram, NY
Coffey, John F.K. ... Malverne, NY
Coffey, John G. ... Providence, RI
Coffey, John G., Jr. ... Newport, RI
Coffey, John J. ... Norristown, PA
Coffey, John J., III ... Chicago, IL
Coffey, John L. ... San Diego, CA
Coffey, John L. ... Milwaukee, WI
Coffey, John M. ... Oklahoma City, OK
Coffey, John P. ... New York, NY
Coffey, John W. ... McLean, VA
Coffey, Joni Armstrong ... Miami, FL
Coffey, Joseph A., Jr. ... Bala Cynwyd, PA
Coffey, Joseph E. ... Boston, MA
Coffey, Karen P. ... Austin, TX
Coffey, Kathleen E. ... Boston, MA
Coffey & Kaye ... Bala Cynwyd, PA
Philadelphia, PA
Coffey, Kendall ... Miami, FL
Coffey, Kevin M. ... Oklahoma City, OK
Coffey, Larry B. ... Winston-Salem, NC
Coffey, Lawrence A. ... Corpus Christi, TX
Coffey, Linda M. ... Mineola, NY
Coffey, Lois M. ... Salem, OR
Coffey, Louis ... Philadelphia, PA
Coffey, M. Christopher ... Knoxville, TN
Coffey, Mark J. ... San Francisco, CA
Coffey, Mark S. ... Columbus, OH
Coffey, Martin E. ... Brooklyn, NY
Coffey, Mary ... St. Louis, MO
Coffey, Mary LeBeau ... Cleveland, OH
Coffey, Matthew J. ... Saginaw, MI
Coffey, Meldon R. ... Portland, OR
Coffey, Michael A. ... Georgetown, TX
Coffey, Michael D. ... Mentor, OH
Coffey, Michael P. ... Chicago, IL
Coffey, Monica A. ... Malverne, NY
Coffey, Patricia Christo ... Concord, NH
Coffey, Patricia J. ... Wichita, KS
Coffey, Patrick J. ... Appleton, WI
Coffey, Patrick Lenane ... McLean, VA
Coffey, Patrick S. ... Chicago, IL
Coffey, Paul B. ... Dearborn, MI
Coffey, Paul H., Jr. ... Lynchburg, VA
Coffey, Pegeen A. ... Whitefish Bay, WI
Coffey, Peggy R. ... Richmond, CA
Coffey, Peter L. ... Milwaukee, WI
Coffey, Peter V. ... Schenectady, NY
Coffey, Randy ... Angola, IN
Coffey, Richard J. ... Fishkill, NY
Coffey, Robert D. ... Hartford, CT
Coffey, Robert P., Jr. ... Tulsa, OK
Coffey, Ronald J. ... Cleveland, OH
Coffey, Rory J. ... Sacramento, CA
Coffey, Samuel Aaron
Fort Lauderdale, FL
Coffey, Samuel Raymond
San Francisco, CA
Coffey, Scott ... Pittsburgh, PA
Coffey, Scott M. ... West Palm Beach, FL
Coffey, Sean O. ... Providence, RI
Coffey, Shirley A. ... Cincinnati, OH
Coffey, Stephen R. ... Albany, NY
Coffey & Sullivan ... Morristown, NJ
Coffey, Tamura D. ... Winston-Salem, NC
Coffey, Thomas B., Jr. ... Cranston, RI
Coffey, Thomas E. ... San Diego, CA
Coffey, Thomas P. ... Chicago, IL
Coffey, Thomas W. ... Cincinnati, OH
Coffey, Tillman, Kalishman & Owens, P.A.
Gainesville, FL
Coffey, Tillman Y. ... Atlanta, GA
Coffey, Timothy F. ... Philadelphia, PA
Coffey, Timothy J. ... Chicago, IL
Coffey, Timothy V. ... El Paso, TX
Coffey, Vincent R. ... Mamaroneck, NY
New York, NY
Coffey, William C. ... Boston, MA

Cohan, William A. .... San Diego, CA
Cohan, William A., P.C. .... San Diego, CA
Cohan, William D. .... Detroit, MI
Cohane, Jennifer R .... New York, NY
Cohane, John K. .... Fairfield, CT
Cohane, William J. .... New York, NY
Cohanim, Modjgan .... Mineola, NY
Cohar, Alvin J. .... Eastchester, NY
Cohea, Maryann S. .... Baltimore, MD
Cohee, H. Lee, II .... Tallahassee, FL
Cohee, Jason C. .... Dover, DE
Cohee, Lynne M. .... Seattle, WA
Cohelan & Khoury .... San Diego, CA
Cohelan, Timothy .... San Diego, CA
Cohelan, A. Stephen .... Hollidaysburg, PA
Cohen, Aaron .... Chicago, IL
Cohen, Aaron B. .... Westbury, NY
Cohen, Aaron M. .... New York, NY
Cohen, Aaron M. .... New York, NY
Cohen, Aaron R. .... Jacksonville, FL
Cohen, Abate & Cohen, L.C.
Fairmont, WV
Morgantown, WV
Cohen, Abbi L. .... Philadelphia, PA
Cohen, Abe .... Oklahoma City, OK
Cohen, Abigail Faye .... Baltimore, MD
Cohen, Abigail M. .... Redondo Beach, CA
Cohen and Acampora .... East Haven, CT
New Haven, CT
North Haven, CT
Cohen, Adam .... Washington, DC
Cohen, Adam .... Mount Vernon, NY
Cohen, Adam B. .... New York, NY
Cohen, Adam G. .... Boston, MA
Cohen, Adam J. .... Bridgeport, CT
Cohen, Adam M. .... Los Angeles, CA
Cohen, Adam M. .... New York, NY
Cohen, Adam Noah .... Memphis, TN
Cohen, Adam S. .... Baltimore, MD
Cohen, Adam S. .... New York, NY
Cohen, Adam W. .... Department of Justice, Executive Office for United States Attorneys, GV
Cohen, Adele H. .... New York, NY
Cohen, Adrian N. .... Milwaukee, WI
Cohen, Adrienne D. .... Santa Ana, CA
Cohen, Aileen E. .... Las Vegas, NV
Cohen, Alan .... Bensenville, IL
Cohen, Alan B. .... Federal Deposit Insurance Corporation, GV
Cohen, Alan C. .... Treasury Department, Office of Regulations and Rulings, GV
Cohen, Alan Curtis .... Hartford, CT
Cohen, Alan E. .... Atlanta, GA
Cohen, Alan F. .... Torrance, CA
Cohen, Alan G., (A Professional Corporation) .... Los Angeles, CA
Cohen, Alan H. .... Indianapolis, IN
Cohen, Alan J. .... Atlantic City, NJ
Cohen, Alan Jay .... Los Angeles, CA
Cohen, Alan L. .... San Francisco, CA
Cohen, Alan L. .... Baltimore, MD
Cohen, Alan L. .... Arlington, VA
Cohen, Alan M. .... Walnut Creek, CA
Cohen, Alan M. .... New York, NY
Cohen, Alan M., Law Offices of
Framingham, MA
Cohen, Alan S. .... New York, NY
Cohen, Alan S. .... New York, NY
Cohen, Albert .... Denver, CO
Cohen, Albert J. .... North Woodmere, NY
Cohen, Albert M. .... Los Angeles, CA
Cohen, Albert N. .... Miami, FL
Cohen, Alexander .... Newark, NJ
Cohen, Alexander & Clayton, A Professional Corporation .... Los Angeles, CA
Thousand Oaks, CA
Ventura, CA
Cohen, Alfred M. .... Cincinnati, OH
Cohen, Alisa G. .... Indianapolis, IN
Cohen, Allan G. .... Miami, FL
Cohen, Allan H. .... Garden City, NY
Cohen, Allan H. .... Pittsburgh, PA
Cohen, Allan M. .... New York, NY
Cohen, Allen A. .... Great Neck, NY
Cohen, Allen Louis .... Richmond, VA
Cohen, Allen Lynn .... Wyncote, PA
Cohen, Allen W. .... Annapolis, MD
Cohen, Alpert & Forman .... Baltimore, MD
Cohen, Alvin M. .... Denver, CO
Cohen, Alys I. .... Federal Trade Commission, Bureau of Consumer Protection, GV
Cohen, Alyssa M. .... New York, NY
Cohen, Amy B. .... Springfield, MA
Cohen, Amy B. .... Philadelphia, PA
Cohen, Amy S. .... Wilmington, DE
Cohen, Amy S. .... New York, NY
Cohen, Andréa D. .... Los Angeles, CA
Cohen, Andrea G. .... Department of Justice, Civil Division, GV
Cohen, Andrea Harris .... New York, NY
Cohen, Andrea L. .... New York, NY
Cohen, Andrea R. .... Palo Alto, CA
Cohen, Andrea R. .... New York, NY
Cohen, Andrea S. .... New York, NY
Cohen, Andrew A. .... New Haven, CT
Cohen, Andrew B. .... Haddonfield, NJ
Cohen, Andrew B. .... New York, NY
Cohen, Andrew B. .... New York, NY
Cohen, Andrew B. .... Durham, NC
Cohen, Andrew D. .... Denver, CO
Cohen, Andrew H. .... Boston, MA
Cohen, Andrew I. .... New York, NY
Cohen, Andrew J. .... Chicago, IL
Cohen, Andrew J. .... Springfield, MA
Cohen, Andrew M. .... Hopkinton, MA
Cohen, Andrew R. .... San Francisco, CA
Cohen, Andrew S. .... San Antonio, TX
Cohen, Andrew W. .... Washington, DC
Cohen, Ann E. .... St. Paul, MN
Cohen, Ann F. .... Herndon, VA
Cohen, Anne E. .... New York, NY
Cohen, Anne M. .... Boston, MA
Cohen, Anthony .... Santa Rosa, CA
Cohen, Arlan A. .... Pasadena, CA
Cohen, Arnold .... Boca Raton, FL
Westbury, NY
Cohen, Arnold .... Albertson, NY
Cohen, Arnold B. .... Villanova, PA
Cohen, Arnold B. .... Madison, WI
Cohen, Arnold E. .... Boston, MA
Cohen, Arnold E. .... Philadelphia, PA
Cohen, Arnold G. .... Knoxville, TN
Cohen, Arnold L. .... Cedar Grove, NJ
Cohen, Arnold P. .... Boston, MA
Cohen, Arnold S. .... Wanaque, NJ
Cohen, Arnold S. .... New York, NY
Cohen, Arnold Shep .... Newark, NJ
Cohen, Arthur A. .... Washington, DC
Cohen, Arthur A. .... Miami, FL
Cohen, Arthur A. .... Newport, RI
Cohen, Arthur D. .... Los Angeles, CA
Cohen, Arthur D. .... San Diego, CA
Cohen, Arthur D. .... Penfield, NY
Cohen, Arthur G. .... New York, NY
Cohen, Arthur J. .... Fullerton, CA
Cohen, Arthur J. .... Bradenton, FL
Cohen, Arthur J. .... Marlton, NJ
Cohen, Arthur L. .... Sunnyvale, CA
Cohen, Arthur M. .... New York, NY
Cohen, Arthur N. .... North Miami Beach, FL
Cohen, Arthur W. .... Milwaukee, WI
Cohen & Associates .... Juneau, AK
Cohen & Associates .... Newton, MA
Cohen, Audra D. .... New York, NY
Cohen, Audrey G. .... Trenton, NJ
Cohen, Audrey P. .... Phoenix, AZ
Cohen, Austin B. .... Philadelphia, PA
Cohen, Avery S. .... Cleveland, OH
Cohen, Avram N. .... Providence, RI
Cohen & Axinn .... Hollidaysburg, PA
Cohen, B. Robertson .... West Palm Beach, FL
Cohen & Baldinger .... Rockville, MD
Cohen, Barbara .... New York, NY
Cohen, Barbara E. .... Chicago, IL
Cohen, Barbara Gratch .... New York, NY
Cohen, Barbara M. .... Oakland, CA
Cohen, Barbara S. .... Providence, RI
Cohen, Barney I. .... Chicago, IL
Cohen, Barry A. .... Tampa, FL
Cohen, Barry A. .... Bangor, ME
Cohen, Barry A. .... Elmwood Park, NJ
Cohen, Barry C. .... New York, NY
Cohen, Barry D. .... Northfield, NJ
Cohen, Barry E. .... Washington, DC
Cohen, Barry J. .... Waldwick, NJ
Cohen, Barry J. .... Stroudsburg, PA
Cohen, Barry L. .... Los Angeles, CA
Cohen, Barry L. .... Philadelphia, PA
Cohen, Barry Lee .... Northport, NY
Cohen, Barry Lee, P.C. .... Northport, NY
Cohen, Barry M. .... Delray Beach, FL
Cohen, Barry M. .... West Palm Beach, FL
Cohen, Barry M. .... Baltimore, MD
Cohen, Barry R. .... Miami, FL
Cohen, Barry R. .... Buffalo, NY
Cohen, Barry S. .... Berkley, MI
Cohen, Barry S. .... Melville, NY
Cohen, Barry S. .... Elkhart Lake, WI
Cohen, Barry S., (P.C.) .... New York, NY
Cohen, Barry S., S.C. .... Elkhart Lake, WI
Cohen, Bart D. .... Philadelphia, PA
Cohen, Barton P. .... Overland Park, KS
Cohen, Ben S. .... Louisville, KY
Cohen, Benjamin H. .... Chicago, IL
Cohen, Benjamin J. .... New York, NY
Cohen, Benjamin Ryan .... Baltimore, MD
Cohen, Benjamin S. .... Pasadena, CA
Cohen, Bennett L. .... Denver, CO
Cohen, Bennett L. .... Northbrook, IL
Cohen, Berke, Bernstein, Brodie & Kondell, P.A. .... Miami, FL
Cohen, Bernard .... Hollywood, FL
Cohen, Bernard .... Columbus, OH
Cohen, Bernard B. .... New York, NY
Cohen, Bernard D. .... Chattanooga, TN
Cohen, Bernard H. .... Floral Park, NY
Cohen, Bernard, Inc., Law Offices of .... Brockton, MA
Cohen, Bernard M. .... Bloomfield Hills, MI
Cohen, Bernard S. .... Alexandria, VA
Cohen, Bert H. .... Beverly Hills, CA
Cohen, Beryl W. .... Boston, MA
Cohen, Beth R. .... New York, NY
Cohen, Betsy D. .... Cambridge, MA
Cohen, Betsy Z. .... Philadelphia, PA
Cohen, Beverly .... Albany, NY
Cohen, Beverly L. .... Roswell, GA
Cohen, Beverly S. .... New York, NY
Cohen, Bob .... Albany, NY
Cohen, Bonnie R. .... San Francisco, CA
Cohen, Bonnie R. .... Kew Gardens, NY
Cohen, Brad .... Atlanta, GA
Cohen, Bradford S. .... Los Angeles, CA
Cohen, Bradley H. .... Indianapolis, IN
Cohen, Brenda L. .... New York, NY
Cohen, Brent M. .... San Francisco, CA
Cohen, Brent R. .... Denver, CO
Cheyenne, WY
Cohen, Bret A. .... Boston, MA
Cohen, Brett Evan .... Bethesda, MD
Cohen, Brett J. .... Los Angeles, CA
Cohen, Brian .... Washington, DC
Cohen, Brian Jeffrey .... Boynton Beach, FL
Cohen, Brian M. .... New York, NY
Cohen, Brian Scott .... Atlanta, GA
Cohen, Brian T. .... New York, NY
Cohen, Bruce .... New York, NY
Cohen, Bruce A. .... Palo Alto, CA
Cohen, Bruce A. .... Washington, DC
Rockville, MD
Vienna, VA
Cohen, Bruce A. .... Department of Labor, Office of the Solicitor, GV
Cohen, Bruce A. .... Huntingdon Valley, PA
Cohen, Bruce C. .... Clayton, MO
Cohen, Bruce D. .... Atlanta, GA
Irving, TX
Cohen, Bruce E. .... Rockville Centre, NY
Cohen, Bruce F. .... Greenwich, CT
Cohen, Bruce H. .... Sharon, MA
Cohen, Bruce I. .... San Francisco, CA
Cohen, Bruce J. .... Bellmore, NY
Cohen, Bruce K. .... New York, NY
Philadelphia, PA
Cohen, Bruce M. .... Los Angeles, CA
Cohen, Bruce M. .... New York, NY
Cohen, Bruce P. .... Atlanta, GA
Cohen, Bruce R. .... Phoenix, AZ
Cohen, Bryan .... Cherry Hill, NJ
Cohen, Bryna .... Scarsdale, NY
Cohen & Buckley, LLP .... Encinitas, CA
Baltimore, MD
Cohen, Burton .... New York, NY
Cohen, Burton B. .... Hartford, CT
Cohen, Burton D. .... Oak Brook, IL
Cohen, Burton I. .... El Paso, TX
Cohen, Burton T. .... Scottsdale, AZ
Cohen, Byron .... Clayton, MO
Cohen, Candice H. .... Indio, CA
Cohen, Carl A. .... Pittsburgh, PA
Cohen, Carl D. .... Omaha, NE
Cohen, Carl G. .... Carle Place, NY
Cohen, Carla L. .... Cheshire, CT
Cohen, Carol A. .... Warren, NJ
Cohen, Carol Indursky .... Westfield, NJ
Cohen, Carol Nakhuda .... Washington, DC
Cohen, Carol Ruffee .... Boston, MA
Cohen, Carole H. .... Beverly Hills, CA
Cohen, Carolyn F. .... Chappaqua, NY
Cohen, Carrie H. .... New York, NY
Cohen, Caryl W. .... Atlanta, GA
Cohen, Cathryn A. .... New York, NY
Cohen, Cathryn G. .... Pacific Grove, CA
Cohen, Charles .... Trumbull, CT
Cohen, Charles A. .... Indianapolis, IN
Cohen, Charles C. .... Pittsburgh, PA
Cohen, Charles E. .... St. Louis, MO
Cohen, Charles H. .... Fort Lauderdale, FL
Cohen, Charles H. .... Long Island City, NY
Cohen, Charles I. .... Washington, DC
Cohen, Charles I. .... Boca Raton, FL
Cohen, Charles M. .... Augusta, ME
Cohen, Charles P. .... Verona, NJ
Cohen, Charles R. .... Denver, CO
Cohen, Charles S. .... Lisle, IL
Cohen, Charles S. .... Springfield, MA
Cohen, Charles S. .... Newark, NJ
Cohen, Charles S. .... New York, NY
Cohen, Charles W. .... Juneau, AK
Cohen, Charles W. .... Thousand Oaks, CA
Cohen, Charles W. .... New York, NY
Cohen, Chase & Hoffman, P.A.
Miami, FL
Cohen, Cheryl F. .... New York, NY
Cohen, Cheryl Hendler .... Camden, NJ
Cohen, Christopher B. .... Chicago, IL
Cohen, Cindi E. .... Bethesda, MD
Cohen, Claudia .... New York, NY
Cohen, Clifford A. .... Leawood, KS
Kansas City, MO
Cohen, Clifford R. .... Glendale, CA
Cohen, Clifford R. .... Boston, MA
Providence, RI
Cohen, C. N. Coby .... San Francisco, CA
Cohen and Cohen .... Los Angeles, CA
Cohen & Cohen .... Washington, DC
Cohen & Cohen .... Louisville, KY
Cohen & Cohen .... Portland, ME
Cohen & Cohen .... Santa Fe, NM
Cohen and Cohen, A Law Corporation .... Camarillo, CA
Cohen & Cohen, P.A. .... Bangor, ME
Cohen & Cohen, P.C. .... Boulder, CO
Cohen and Cohen, P.C. .... Stroudsburg, PA
Cohen, Cohen & Salk, P.C. .... Northbrook, IL
Cohen, Conway, Copeland & Paiva, P.A.
Stuart, FL
Cohen, Craig A. .... Philadelphia, PA
Cohen, Craig H. .... New York, NY
Cohen, Craig L. .... New York, NY
Cohen, Cynthia J. .... Boston, MA
Cohen, Cynthia M. .... Los Angeles, CA
Cohen, D. David .... Jericho, NY
Cohen, D. Jay .... St. Louis, MO
Cohen, D. Stephen .... North Andover, MA
Cohen, Dale M. .... Chicago, IL
Cohen, Dale T. .... New York, NY
Cohen, Dan R. .... Denver, CO
Cohen, Dana S. .... Philadelphia, PA
Cohen, Daniel .... Washington, DC
Cohen, Daniel .... Department of Commerce, Office of the General Counsel, GV
Cohen, Daniel .... Baltimore, MD
Cohen, Daniel .... Staten Island, NY
Cohen, Daniel A. .... New York, NY
Cohen, Daniel A. .... New York, NY
Cohen, Daniel C. .... Savannah, GA
Cohen, Daniel C. .... Philadelphia, PA
Cohen, Daniel E. .... Washington, DC
Cohen, Daniel E. .... Atlanta, GA
Cohen, Daniel E. .... New York, NY
Cohen, Daniel E. .... Easton, PA
Cohen, Daniel G. .... Detroit, MI
Farmington Hills, MI
Cohen, Daniel I. .... Silver Spring, MD
Cohen, Daniel I. A. .... New York, NY
Cohen, Daniel J. .... Morristown, NJ
Cohen, Daniel L. .... Somers Point, NJ
Cohen, Daniel L. .... Houston, TX
Cohen, Daniel M. .... New York, NY
Cohen, Daniel M. .... Philadelphia, PA
Cohen, Daniel S. .... Sacramento, CA
Cohen, Daniel S. .... Utica, NY
Cohen, Daniel S. .... Pittsburgh, PA
Cohen, Darcy Mitchell .... San Diego, CA
Cohen, Darlene .... Baltimore, MD
Cohen Darnell & Cohen .... Oklahoma City, OK
Dallas, TX
El Paso, TX
Cohen, Darren .... New York, NY
Cohen, Darryl B. .... Atlanta, GA
Cohen, David .... Palo Alto, CA
Cohen, David .... Seal Beach, CA
Cohen, David .... Jacksonville, FL
Cohen, David .... New York, NY
Cohen, David .... New York, NY
Cohen, David .... Bensalem, PA
Cohen, David .... Philadelphia, PA
Cohen, David A. .... Walnut Creek, CA
Cohen, David A. .... Washington, DC
Cohen, David A. .... Washington, DC
Cohen, David A. .... Newark, NJ
Cohen, David A. .... New York, NY
Cohen, David A. .... Syosset, NY
Cohen, David Alan .... New York, NY
Cohen, David B. .... Los Angeles, CA
Cohen, David B. .... Washington, DC
Cohen, David Carlin .... Las Vegas, NV
Cohen, David E. .... Washington, DC
Cohen, David G. .... Springfield, MA
Cohen, David G. .... Rochester, NY
Cohen, David H. .... Baltimore, MD
Cohen, David H. .... Brooklyn, NY
Cohen, David H. .... Garden City, NY
Cohen, David Howard .... Rockville, MD
Cohen, David I. .... Pittsburgh, PA
Cohen, David Ira .... Lynn, MA
Cohen, David J. .... Marina Del Rey, CA
Cohen, David J. .... San Francisco, CA
Cohen, David J. .... Avon, CT
Cohen, David J. .... Washington, DC
Cohen, David J. .... Philadelphia, PA
Cohen, David L. .... Los Angeles, CA
Cohen, David L. .... Sacramento, CA
Cohen, David L. .... Department of the Army, Office, Chief of Engineers/Headquarters, U.S. Army Corps of Engineers, GV
Cohen, David L. .... Kew Gardens, NY
Cohen, David L. .... New York, NY
Cohen, David L. .... Philadelphia, PA
Cohen, David, Law Office of .... Austin, TX
Cohen, David M. .... Santa Monica, CA
Cohen, David M. .... Stamford, CT
Cohen, David M. .... Department of Justice, Civil Division, GV
Cohen, David M. .... Portland, ME
Cohen, David M. .... Silver Spring, MD
Cohen, David M. .... Verona, NJ
Cohen, David M. .... Jamaica, NY
Cohen, David M. .... Melville, NY
Cohen, David M. .... New York, NY
Cohen, David M. .... New York, NY
Cohen, David M. .... New York, NY
Cohen, David M. .... Lancaster, OH
Cohen, David M., L.L.C. .... Verona, NJ
Cohen, David N. .... Short Hills, NJ
Cohen, David P. .... Chicago, IL
Cohen, David P. .... Flushing, NY
Cohen, David R. .... Tucson, AZ
Cohen, David R. .... Lake Worth, FL
Cohen, David R. .... Princeton, NJ
Cohen, David R. .... Cleveland, OH
Cohen, David R. .... Pittsburgh, PA
Cohen, David S. .... Phoenix, AZ
Cohen, David S. .... Denver, CO
Cohen, David S. .... Washington, DC
Cohen, David S. .... Washington, DC
Cohen, David S. .... Washington, DC
Cohen, David S. .... Orlando, FL
Cohen, David S. .... Santa Fe, NM
Cohen, David S. .... Philadelphia, PA
Cohen, David S., P.C. .... Denver, CO
Cohen, David T. .... Department of Justice, Civil Division, GV
Cohen, David T. .... Fort Worth, TX
Cohen, David W. .... Baltimore, MD
Cohen, Davis .... Savannah, GA
Cohen, Dax & Koenig, P.C. .... Albany, NY
Cohen, Debbi M. .... Washington, DC
Cohen, Deborah Fuchs .... Philadelphia, PA
Cohen, Deborah L. .... New York, NY
Cohen, Deborah S. .... Boston, MA
Cohen, Debra E. .... Coral Gables, FL
Cohen, Debra J. .... New York, NY
Cohen, Debra Mann
West Palm Beach, FL
Cohen, Deidre F. .... Orange, CA
Cohen, Dena .... Jericho, NY
Cohen, Denis P. .... Philadelphia, PA
Cohen, Dennis A. .... Culver City, CA
Cohen, Dennis D. .... Rock Island, IL
Cohen, Dennis L. .... Philadelphia, PA
Cohen, Dennis S. .... Caledonia, NY
Cohen, Derek A. .... Washington, DC
Cohen, Devin P. .... New York, NY
Cohen, Diane B. .... Haddonfield, NJ
Cohen, Diane R. .... New York, NY
Cohen, DiPaul & Haber, P.C. .... Philadelphia, PA
Cohen, Donald B. .... New York, NY

Cohen, Jeri B. ... Miami, FL
Cohen, Jerilyn ... Pasadena, CA
Cohen, Jerilyn M. ... St. Louis, MO
Cohen, Jerilyn S. ... Chicago, IL
Cohen, Jerold D. ... General Accounting Office, Office of the General Counsel, GV
Cohen, Jerome Alan ... New York, NY
Cohen, Jerome B. ... San Antonio, TX
Cohen, Jerome J. ... Beverly Hills, CA
Cohen, Jerome J. ... North Miami, FL
Cohen, Jerome J. ... New York, NY
Cohen, Jerome L. ... Wilkes-Barre, PA
Cohen, Jerome O. ... Seattle, WA
Cohen, Jerome S. ... Long Beach, CA
Cohen, Jerome S. ... Los Angeles, CA
Cohen, Jerome S. ... Port Jervis, NY
Cohen, Jerrold ... Jericho, NY
Cohen, Jerry L. ... Bensalem, PA
Cohen, Jerry, (P.C.) ... Boston, MA
Cohen, Jeryll S. ... Los Angeles, CA
Cohen, Jess B. ... Edina, MN
Cohen, Jessica N. ... Department of Justice, Antitrust Division, GV
Cohen, Jill A. ... New York, NY
Cohen, Jill F. ... Washington, DC
Cohen, Jill R. ... Los Angeles, CA
Cohen, Jill R., Law Offices of
Los Angeles, CA
Cohen, Joan Blatcher ... Philadelphia, PA
Cohen, Joan L. ... New York, NY
Cohen, Joan Z. ... St. Louis, MO
Cohen, JoAnne ... Worcester, MA
Cohen, Joanne Polvy ... Los Angeles, CA
Cohen, Jodi B. ... Washington, DC
Cohen, Jodi L. ... Linwood, NJ
Cohen, Jodi S. ... Long Beach, CA
Cohen, Joel ... New York, NY
Cohen, Joel ... New York, NY
Cohen, Joel ... New York, NY
Cohen, Joel E. ... New York, NY
Cohen, Joel Grant ... Warren, NJ
Cohen, Joel J. ... New York, NY
Cohen, Joel M. ... Pensacola, FL
Cohen, Joel M. ... New York, NY
Cohen, John A. ... Washington, DC
Cohen, John D. ... New York, NY
Cohen, John J. ... Pittsburgh, PA
Cohen, Johnson, Day & Clayson, A Professional Corporation ... Las Vegas, NV
Cohen, Jon D. ... Chicago, IL
Cohen, Jon S. ... Phoenix, AZ
Cohen, Jonathan ... Miami, FL
Cohen, Jonathan A. ... Washington, DC
Cohen, Jonathan A. ... Chicago, IL
Cohen, Jonathan D. ... Boston, MA
Cohen, Jonathan E. ... Albany, NY
Cohen, Jonathan E. ... Tappan, NY
Cohen, Jonathan E. ... Portland, OR
Cohen, Jonathan G. ... Hartford, CT
Cohen, Jonathan M. ... San Francisco, CA
Cohen, Jonathan M. ... Washington, DC
Cohen, Jonathan M. ... Washington, DC
Cohen, Jonathan M. ... Spring Valley, NY
White Plains, NY
Cohen, Jonathan M. ... Philadelphia, PA
Cohen, Jonathan R. ... Gainesville, FL
Cohen, Jonathan S. ... Department of Justice, Tax Division, GV
Cohen, Jonathan T.K. ... Roseland, NJ
Cohen, Jonathan V. ... Washington, DC
Cohen, Jordan M. ... San Diego, CA
Cohen, Jordan S. ... Los Angeles, CA
Cohen, Jos. A. ... New York, NY
Cohen, Jos. M. ... Brookline, MA
Cohen, Joseph ... Bronx, NY
Cohen, Joseph B. ... New York, NY
Cohen, Joseph C. ... Littleton, CO
Cohen, Joseph C., P.C., Law Office of
Denver, CO
Littleton, CO
Cohen, Joseph D. ... Portland, OR
Cohen, Joseph D. ... Dallas, TX
Cohen, Joseph H. ... Louisville, KY
Cohen, Joseph H., Jr. ... Newton, MA
Cohen, Joseph L. ... Albany, NY
Cohen, Joseph M. ... Weehawken, NJ
Cohen, Joseph S. ... Houston, TX
Cohen, Joseph T. ... Schenectady, NY
Cohen, Joshua Albert ... Los Angeles, CA
Cohen, Joshua D. ... Walnut Creek, CA
Cohen, Joshua D. ... Lancaster, PA
Cohen, Joshua L. ... Maywood, NJ
Cohen, Joshua L. ... Valley Forge, PA
Cohen, Joshua R. ... New York, NY
Cohen, Joshua R. ... Cleveland, OH
Cohen, Joshua W. ... Stamford, CT
Cohen, J. S. Lee ... Teaneck, NJ
Cohen, Judah Z. ... New York, NY
Cohen, Judd ... Lake Success, NY
Cohen, Judd H. ... New York, NY
Cohen, Judith Ann ... Oakland, CA
Cohen, Judith Cavell ... Treasury Department, Internal Revenue Service, GV
Cohen, Judith D. ... Boston, MA
Cohen, Judith H. ... Oceanside, NY
Cohen, Judith H. B. ... Corte Madera, CA
Cohen, Judith L. ... Washington, PA
Cohen, Judith R. ... New York, NY
Cohen, Judson Lee ... Miami, FL
Cohen, Jules S. ... Orlando, FL
Cohen, Julia R. ... New York, NY
Cohen, Julian ... Cleveland, OH
Cohen, Julian H. ... New York, NY
Cohen, Julie A. ... Detroit, MI
Cohen, Julius ... Newark, NJ
Cohen & Kandell ... Miami, FL
Cohen, Karen B. ... Miami Beach, FL
Cohen, Karen L. ... Washington, DC
Cohen, Karen Lynn ... Woodland Hills, CA
Cohen, Karla A. ... New York, NY
Cohen, Katherine Meyers ... Atlanta, GA
Cohen, Kay Chopard ... Washington, DC
Des Moines, IA
Cohen, KC ... Fishers, IN
Cohen, Keith (Casey) D. ... Prairie Village, KS
Cohen and Keith-Miller, A Professional Service Corporation ... Seattle, WA
Cohen & Kendziorra, P.A. ... Cape Coral, FL
Cohen Kennedy Dowd & Quigley, P.C.
Phoenix, AZ
Cohen, Kenneth ... New York, NY
Cohen, Kenneth A. ... Buffalo, NY
Cohen, Kenneth A., (P.C.) ... Boston, MA
Cohen, Kenneth E.
Department of Agriculture, Office of the General Counsel, GV
Cohen, Kenneth E. ... Treasury Department, Internal Revenue Service, GV
Cohen, Kenneth E. ... Miami, FL
Cohen, Kenneth F. ... Abington, PA
Cohen, Kenneth J. ... San Francisco, CA
Cohen, Kenneth J. ... Niles, IL
Cohen, Kenneth L. ... Beverly Hills, CA
Cohen, Kenneth P. ... Washington, DC
Cohen, Kenneth P. ... Houston, TX
Cohen, Kenneth R. ... Florham Park, NJ
Cohen, Kenneth S. ... Springfield, MA
Cohen, Kenneth S. ... New York, NY
Cohen, Kenneth S. ... Cleveland, OH
Cohen, Kenneth S. ... Jackson, WY
Cohen & Kessler ... New Milford, CT
Cohen, Kevin H. ... Morristown, NJ
New York, NY
Cohen and Khani ... New York, NY
Cohen, Kimberly E. ... Boston, MA
Cohen, Kipp B. ... Philadelphia, PA
Cohen & Kyres ... St. Petersburg, FL
Cohen, L. Michael ... San Antonio, TX
Cohen, Lance P. ... Jacksonville, FL
Cohen, Lane N. ... Cincinnati, OH
Cohen, Larry D. ... Chicago, IL
Cohen, Larry D. ... Charleston, SC
Cohen, Larry D., LLC ... Charleston, SC
Cohen, Larry H. ... Chicago, IL
Cohen, Larry J. ... Phoenix, AZ
Cohen, Laura ... Monroeville, PA
Cohen, Laura E. ... Long Grove, IL
Cohen, Laura G. ... Los Angeles, CA
Cohen, Laura R. ... Los Angeles, CA
Cohen, Laura S. ... Indianapolis, IN
Cohen, Lauren A. ... Fort Lauderdale, FL
Cohen, Lauren B. ... Wayne, NJ
Cohen, Laurence Ian ... Syosset, NY
Cohen, Laurence J. ... Washington, DC
Cohen, Laurence W. ... New York, NY
Cohen, Lauri ... New York, NY
Cohen, Laurie ... New York, NY
Cohen, Laurie A. ... Los Angeles, CA
Cohen, Laurie J. ... Rockford, IL
Cohen, Laurie Schack ... Fort Lauderdale, FL
Cohen, Laurie Stilwell
West Palm Beach, FL
Cohen Law Firm ... San Francisco, CA
Cohen Law Firm ... Green Bay, WI
Cohen Law Offices ... Los Angeles, CA
Ontario, CA
Cohen Law Offices, P.C.
North Andover, MA
Cohen, Lawr. A. ... New York, NY
Cohen, Lawrence ... Newark, NJ
Cohen, Lawrence B. ... Boston, MA
Cohen, Lawrence D. ... St. Paul, MN
Cohen, Lawrence E. ... Worcester, MA
Cohen, Lawrence G. ... Norfolk, VA
Cohen, Lawrence H. ... Basking Ridge, NJ
Cohen, Lawrence H. ... Dublin, OH
Cohen, Lawrence J. ... Boston, MA
Cohen, Lawrence J. ... New York, NY
Cohen, Lawrence M. ... San Francisco, CA
Cohen, Lawrence M. ... Chicago, IL
Cohen, Lawrence P. ... Boston, MA
Cohen, Lawrence P. ... Chestnut Hill, MA
Cohen, Lawrence P. ... Hackettstown, NJ
Morristown, NJ
Trenton, NJ
Cohen, Lawrence R. ... Honolulu, HI
Cohen, Lawrence S. ... Los Angeles, CA
Cohen, Leah Willner ... LaGrangeville, NY
Poughkeepsie, NY
Cohen, Leatrice L. ... Pacific Palisades, CA
Cohen, Leavitt, Leavitt & Cohen
New York, NY
Cohen, Lee A. ... Atlanta, GA
Cohen, Lee S. ... Department of Commerce, Patent and Trademark Office, GV
Cohen, Leigh B. ... Harrisburg, PA
Cohen, Leighton ... Allentown, PA
Cohen, Lenard A. ... Philadelphia, PA
Cohen, Leonard
Treasury Department, GV
Cohen, Leonard E. ... Baltimore, MD
Cohen, Leonard H. ... Pittsfield, MA
Cohen, Leonard Mark ... Vienna, VA
Cohen, Lerner & Rabinovitz, P.C.
Bloomfield Hills, MI
Cohen, Leslee Moss ... Chicago, IL
Cohen, Leslie ... Cambridge, MA
Cohen, Leslie A. ... Los Angeles, CA
Cohen, Leslie B. ... McLean, VA
Cohen, Leslie D. ... Miami, FL
Cohen, Leslie H. ... East Syracuse, NY
Cohen, Leslie I. ... Verona, PA
Cohen, Leslie J. ... Tucson, AZ
Cohen, Leslie R. ... Washington, DC
Cohen, Lester ... San Diego, CA
Cohen, Lester H. ... Indianapolis, IN
Cohen, Lester H. ... Philadelphia, PA
Cohen, Lewis F. ... Miami, FL
Cohen, Lewis H. ... Hollywood, FL
Cohen, Lewis R. ... Miami, FL
Cohen, Lewis R., P.A. ... Miami, FL
Cohen, Lewis Rinaudo ... New York, NY
Cohen, Lillian M. ... New Orleans, LA
Cohen, Lillian Z. ... New York, NY
Cohen, Linda D. ... East Haven, CT
Cohen, Linda J. ... Portland, ME
Cohen, Linda J. ... Albany, NY
Cohen, Linda M. ... Columbus, OH
Cohen, Linda M. ... Providence, RI
Cohen and Lippman, LLP ... New York, NY
Cohen, Lisa Ann ... Santa Monica, CA
Cohen, Lisa Beth ... New City, NY
Cohen, Lisa C. ... Gainesville, FL
Cohen, Lisa C. ... New York, NY
Cohen, Lisa G. ... New York, NY
Cohen, Lisa S. ... Atlanta, GA
Cohen, Lita I. ... Philadelphia, PA
Cohen, Lloyd D. ... Columbus, OH
Cohen, Lloyd R. ... Arlington, VA
Cohen, Lois J. ... Washington, DC
Cohen & Lombardo, P.C. ... Buffalo, NY
Cohen & Lord, P.C. ... Los Angeles, CA
Cohen, Loren H. ... Miami, FL
Cohen, Loris L. ... Bridgeport, CT
Cohen, Lottie ... Santa Monica, CA
Cohen, Louis ... Louisville, KY
Cohen, Louis ... Silver Spring, MD
Cohen, Louis B. ... Bethany, CT
Cohen, Louis H. ... Silver Spring, MD
Cohen, Louis H. ... Springfield, MA
Cohen, Louis H. ... New York, NY
Cohen, Louis R. ... Washington, DC
Cohen, Louis S. ... Chicago, IL
Cohen, Louise B.
Environmental Protection Agency, Office of Congressional and Legislative Affairs, GV
Cohen, Louise E. ... New York, NY
Cohen, Lyle S. ... Chicago, IL
Cohen, Lynn A. ... Skokie, IL
Cohen, Madeline S. ... Denver, CO
Cohen, Maileen S. ... Norristown, PA
Cohen & Malad, P.C. ... Fishers, IN
Indianapolis, IN
Cohen, Malcolm A. ... Boynton Beach, FL
Cohen, Malcolm S. ... Kew Gardens, NY
Cohen, Mandy S. ...
Securities and Exchange Commission, GV
Cohen, Manni & Theune
Oak Harbor, WA
Cohen, Marc B. ... Oakland, CA
Cohen, Marc B. ... Stuart, FL
Cohen, Marc E. ... Albany, NY
Cohen, Marc E., P.C. ... Albany, NY
Cohen, Marc H. ... Los Angeles, CA
Cohen, Marc K. ... Baltimore, MD
Cohen, Marc L. ... Short Hills, NJ
Cohen, Marc M. ... Fort Lauderdale, FL
Cohen, Marc R. ... Washington, DC
Cohen, Marc S. ... Los Angeles, CA
Cohen, Marcella ... Miami, FL
Cohen, Marcia S. ... St. Petersburg, FL
Cohen, Marcia Smithen ... Chappaqua, NY
Cohen, Marcy Sharon ... New York, NY
Cohen, Mardi Levey ... Fort Lauderdale, FL
Cohen, Margaret L. ... Washington, DC
Cohen, Margaret Ruth ... Boston, MA
Cohen, Marilyn ... Eugene, OR
Cohen, Marilyn R. ... Metairie, LA
Cohen, Marina ... New York, NY
Cohen, Marjorie Fay ... Washington, DC
Cohen, Marjorie L. ... New York, NY
Cohen, Marjory B. ... Detroit, MI
Cohen, Mark ... Meredith, NH
Portsmouth, NH
Cohen, Mark ... Austin, TX
Cohen, Mark ... Houston, TX
Cohen, Mark A. ... Washington, DC
Cohen, Mark A. ... Washington, DC
Cohen, Mark A. ... Baltimore, MD
Cohen, Mark A. ... New York, NY
Cohen, Mark A. (IBA) ... Dallas, TX
Cohen, Mark C. ... New York, NY
Cohen, Mark D. ... Hollywood, FL
Cohen, Mark D. ... Riverhead, NY
Cohen, Mark E. ... Boston, MA
New York, NY
Cohen, Mark E. ... Brooklyn, NY
Cohen, Mark H. ... Atlanta, GA
Cohen, Mark I. ... Westfield, MA
Cohen, Mark I. ... New York, NY
Cohen, Mark J. ... Garden City, NY
Cohen, Mark N. ... Philadelphia, PA
Cohen, Mark P. ... Fremont, CA
Cohen, Mark P. ... Oak Brook, IL
Cohen, Mark P. ... Baltimore, MD
Cohen, Mark P. ... Takoma Park, MD
Cohen, Mark S. ... Nederland, CO
Omaha, NE
Cohen, Mark S. ... Baltimore, MD
Cohen, Mark S. ... New York, NY
Cohen, Mark S. ... New York, NY
Cohen, Mark S. ... Philadelphia, PA
Cohen & Marks ... Great Neck, NY
Cohen, Marla Chernof ... Chicago, IL
Cohen, Marsha I. ... Philadelphia, PA
Cohen, Marsha N. ... San Francisco, CA
Cohen, Marshall J. ... New York, NY
Cohen, Marshall L. ... Fort Myers, FL
Cohen, Marshall L. ... Atlanta, GA
Cohen, Marshall L., P.A. ... Fort Myers, FL
Cohen, Martin ... Los Angeles, CA
Cohen, Martin ... Philadelphia, PA
Cohen, Martin B. ... Boston, MA
Cohen, Martin D. ... Easton, PA
Cohen, Martin H. ... Fort Lauderdale, FL
Cohen, Martin I. ... New York, NY
Cohen, Martin J. ... Newark, NJ
Cohen, Martin J. ... Armonk, NY
New York, NY
Cohen, Martin L., (P.C.) ... Dix Hills, NY
Cohen, Martin M. ... Irvine, CA
Cohen, Martin M. ... New York, NY
Cohen, Martin P. ... Rockville Centre, NY
Cohen, Martin R. ... Department of the Army, Office, Chief of Engineers/Headquarters, U.S. Army Corps of Engineers, GV
Cohen, Martin S. ... Miami, FL
Cohen, Martin S. ... New York, NY
Cohen, Martin W. ... Boston, MA
Cohen, Marvin G. ... Van Nuys, CA
Cohen, Marvin H. ... New York, NY
Cohen, Marvin M. ... Suffern, NY
Cohen, Marvin S. ... Scottsdale, AZ
Cohen, Mary Ann ...
United States Tax Court, GV
Cohen, Mary Louise ... Washington, DC
Cohen, Maryjo ... Eau Claire, WI
Cohen, Matthew ... Englewood, NJ
New York, NY
Cohen, Matthew ... Seattle, WA
Cohen, Matthew A. ... Kenilworth, NJ
Cohen, Matthew B.
Federal Labor Relations Authority, Washington Regional Office, GV
Cohen, Matthew B. ... Minneapolis, MN
Cohen, Matthew B. ... Brooklyn, NY
Cohen, Matthew E. ... Albuquerque, NM
Cohen, Matthew E., P.C. ... Albuquerque, NM
Cohen, Matthew J. ... San Francisco, CA
Cohen, Matthew J. ... Boston, MA
Cohen, Matthew L. ... Applegate, CA
Cohen, Matthew P. ... Washington, DC
Cohen, Matthew R. ... Washington, DC
Cohen, Matthew S. ... New York, NY
Cohen, Maurice S. ... Seaford, NY
Cohen, Max ... Merrillville, IN
Cohen, Max ... Canandaigua, NY
Cohen, Max ... New York, NY
Cohen, Max J. ... New Orleans, LA
Cohen, Maxwell H. ... Stroudsburg, PA
Cohen McNeile Pappas & Shuttleworth P.C.
Leawood, KS
Overland Park, KS
Kansas City, MO
Cohen, Melanie Rovner ... Chicago, IL
Cohen, Melissa Beth ... Merrillville, IN
Cohen, Melissa E. ... Oxnard, CA
Cohen, Melvin ... Greenbrae, CA
Cohen, Melvin C. ... Tucson, AZ
Cohen, Melvin F. ... San Juan Capistrano, CA
Cohen, Melvin S. ... Eau Claire, WI
Cohen, Melvyn D. ... Brockton, MA
Cohen, Meredith J. ... Daytona Beach, FL
Maitland, FL
Oviedo, FL
Cohen, Meredith J., P.A., Law Offices of
Oviedo, FL
Cohen, Meredith Siegel ... Haddonfield, NJ
Cohen, Merrill ... Rockville, MD
Cohen, Mia F. ... Washington, DC
Cohen, Michael ... San Francisco, CA
Cohen, Michael ... New York, NY
Cohen, Michael A. ... Los Angeles, CA
Cohen, Michael A. ... Lakewood, CO
Cohen, Michael A. ... Miami, FL
Cohen, Michael A. ... Great Neck, NY
Cohen, Michael A. ... Portland, OR
Cohen, Michael A. ... Pittsburgh, PA
Cohen, Michael B. ... Miami, FL
Cohen, Michael B. ... Chicago, IL
Cohen, Michael B. ... Newton, MA
Cohen, Michael B. ... Dallas, TX
Cohen, Michael C. ... Los Angeles, CA
Cohen, Michael C. ... Los Angeles, CA
Cohen, Michael E. ... Roseville, CA
Cohen, Michael F. ... Smithtown, NY
Cohen, Michael H. ... Livingston, NJ
Cohen, Michael I. ... Duluth, MN
Cohen, Michael J. ... Phoenix, AZ
Cohen, Michael J. ... Fort Lauderdale, FL
Cohen, Michael J. ... Miami, FL
Cohen, Michael J. ... Atlanta, GA
Cohen, Michael J. ... Chicago, IL
Cohen, Michael J. ... Hyattsville, MD
Cohen, Michael J. ... Milwaukee, WI
Cohen, Michael J., Ltd. ... Chicago, IL
Northbrook, IL
Cohen, Michael J., P.A.
Fort Lauderdale, FL
Cohen, Michael L. ... Encinitas, CA
Baltimore, MD
Cohen, Michael L. ... West Palm Beach, FL
Cohen, Michael L. ... Metairie, LA
Cohen, Michael L. ... Seattle, WA
Cohen, Michael, Law Office of
El Paso, TX
Cohen, Michael Lee ... Dallas, TX
Cohen, Michael M. ... Bayside, NY
Cohen, Michael Marks ... New York, NY
Cohen, Michael N. ... Canoga Park, CA
Cohen, Michael P. ... Chicago, IL
Cohen, Michael Paul Austern
Washington, DC
Cohen, Michael R. ... Minneapolis, MN
Cohen, Michael R. ... Eau Claire, WI
Cohen, Michael S. ... Chicago, IL
Lake Forest, IL
Cohen, Michael S. ... Garden City, NY
Cohen, Michael S. ... Philadelphia, PA
Cohen, Michael Scott ... Cumberland, MD
Cohen, Michael Seth ... Coral Gables, FL

Cohen, Stanley B. ....Washington, DC
Cohen, Stanley D. ....Redondo Beach, CA
Cohen, Stanley D. ....Lincoln, NE
Cohen, Stanley H. ....Philadelphia, PA
Cohen, Stanley I. ....Brooklyn, NY
Cohen, Stanley J. ....Dayton, OH
Cohen, Stanley L. ....Bronx, NY
Cohen, Stanley L. ....New York, NY
Cohen, Stanley M. ....Boston, MA
Cohen, Stanley S. ....Philadelphia, PA
Cohen & Steinberg ....Cleveland, OH
Cohen, Stephan L. ....Miami Beach, FL
Cohen, Stephanie J. ....Newark, NJ
Cohen, Stephen ....Cincinnati, OH
Cohen, Stephen A. ....Chicago, IL
Cohen, Stephen A. ....New York, NY
Cohen, Stephen B. ....Washington, DC
Cohen, Stephen B. ....Northbrook, IL
East Chicago, IN
Cohen, Stephen B., P.C. ....Chicago, IL
Northbrook, IL
East Chicago, IN
Cohen, Stephen E. ....Mount Prospect, IL
Garden City, NY
Cohen, Stephen H. ....New York, NY
Cohen, Stephen H. ....Syracuse, NY
Cohen, Stephen I. ....Orange, CA
Cohen, Stephen I. ....Memphis, TN
Cohen, Stephen J. ....Fort Lauderdale, FL
Cohen, Stephen L. ....Washington, DC
Cohen, Stephen L.
Federal Trade Commission,
Bureau of Consumer Protection, GV
Cohen, Stephen L. ....Miami, FL
Cohen, Stephen L. ....New York, NY
Cohen, Stephen M. ....Ontario, CA
Cohen, Stephen M. ....Delray Beach, FL
Cohen, Stephen M. ....West Palm Beach, FL
Cohen, Stephen M. ....Metairie, LA
Cohen, Stephen M. ....New Hyde Park, NY
Cohen, Stephen M. ....New York, NY
Cohen, Stephen M. ....Philadelphia, PA
Cohen, Stephen M. L., (P.C.) ....Boston, MA
Cohen, Stephen P. ....Hopkins, MN
Cohen, Stephen R. ....Torrance, CA
Cohen, Steven ....Palm Beach, FL
Cohen, Steven ....Manchester, NH
Cohen, Steven ....Hackensack, NJ
New York, NY
Cohen, Steven A. ....Phoenix, AZ
Cohen, Steven A. ....Denver, CO
Cohen, Steven A. ....Washington, DC
Cohen, Steven A. ....Owings Mills, MD
Cohen, Steven A. ....Cambridge, MA
Cohen, Steven A. ....New York, NY
Cohen, Steven A. ....New York, NY
Cohen, Steven A. ....Media, PA
Cohen, Steven B. ....Las Vegas, NV
Cohen, Steven D. ....New York, NY
Cohen, Steven E. ....Fort Lauderdale, FL
Cohen, Steven E. ....Manalapan, NJ
New York, NY
Cohen, Steven E. ....Garden City, NY
Cohen, Steven E. ....New York, NY
Cohen, Steven Elliot ....Hempstead, NY
Cohen, Steven Elliott ....Sacramento, CA
Cohen, Steven G. ....Palo Alto, CA
Cohen, Steven G. ....Farmington Hills, MI
Cohen, Steven H. ....Chicago, IL
Cohen, Steven H. ....Long Beach, NY
Cohen, Steven H. ....Newburgh, NY
Cohen, Steven H. ....New York, NY
Cohen, Steven I. ....Green Bay, WI
Cohen, Steven J. ....Miami, FL
Cohen, Steven J. ....Indianapolis, IN
Cohen, Steven J. ....Southfield, MI
Cohen, Steven J. ....New York, NY
Cohen, Steven J., & Associates, P.A.
Miami, FL
Cohen, Steven Jay ....New York, NY
Cohen, Steven L. ....Los Angeles, CA
Cohen, Steven M. ....Denver, CO
Cohen, Steven M. ....Boston, MA
Cohen, Steven M. ....St. Louis, MO
Cohen, Steven M. ....Princeton, NJ
Cohen, Steven M. ....Buffalo, NY
Cohen, Steven M. ....New York, NY
Cohen, Steven Mark ....Manchester, MO
Cohen, Steven N. ....New York, NY
Charlotte, NC
Cohen, Steven P. ....Prides Crossing, MA
Cohen, Steven R. ....Sacramento, CA
Cohen, Steven R. ....Pembroke Pines, FL
Cohen, Steven R. ....Frederick, MD
Cohen, Steven R. ....Mount Laurel, NJ
Cohen, Steven Reed, P.A.
Pembroke Pines, FL
Cohen, Steven Z. ....Bloomfield Hills, MI
Cohen, Stewart I. ....Orlando, FL
Cohen, Stewart L. ....Philadelphia, PA
Cohen & Stimpert ....Los Angeles, CA
Cohen, Stuart A. ....Pembroke Pines, FL
Cohen, Stuart A. ....Seattle, WA
Cohen, Stuart C. ....New York, NY
Cohen, Stuart D. ....Moline, IL
Cohen, Stuart Foster ....Hollywood, FL
Cohen, Stuart I. ....Peoria, IL
St. Louis, MO
Cohen, Stuart K. ....Portland, OR
Cohen, Stuart L. ....Miami, FL
Cohen, Stuart M. ....Bangor, ME
Cohen, Stuart M. ....Brooklyn, NY
Cohen, Stuart M. ....New York, NY
Cohen, Stuart N. ....King Of Prussia, PA
Cohen, Stuart R. ....Tampa, FL
Cohen, Stuart R. ....Baltimore, MD
Cohen, Stuart R. ....Detroit, MI
Cohen, Susan ....Baltimore, MD
Cohen, Susan ....New York, NY
Cohen, Susan ....New York, NY
Cohen, Susan ....New York, NY
Cohen, Susan A. ....Columbus, OH
Cohen, Susan B. ....San Rafael, CA
Cohen, Susan D. ....Baltimore, MD
Cohen, Susan E. ....Boston, MA
Cohen, Susan E. ....Bloomfield Hills, MI
Bloomfield Hills, MI
Cohen, Susan E. ....Woodbury, NJ
Cohen, Susan J. ....Boston, MA
Cohen, Susan Jeanblanc ......Washington, DC
Cohen, Susan L. ....Rockville, MD
Cohen, Susan L. ....New York, NY
Cohen, Susan Michelle ....New York, NY
Cohen, Susan N. ....Portland, OR
Cohen, Susan R. ....Miami, FL
Cohen Swados Wright Hanifin Bradford & Brett, LLP ....Buffalo, NY
Niagara Falls, NY
Cohen, Sy R. ....Los Angeles, CA
Cohen, Sylvan M. ....Philadelphia, PA
Cohen, Terese R. ....New York, NY
Cohen, Terri B. ....Denver, CO
Cohen, Thelma S. ....Pasadena, CA
Cohen, Theodore A. ....Los Angeles, CA
Cohen, Theodore J. ....Santa Monica, CA
Cohen, Theodore J. ....Inwood, NY
Cohen, Theodore P. ....New York, NY
Cohen & Thiros, P.C. ....Merrillville, IN
Cohen & Thomas ....Ansonia, CT
Bridgeport, CT
Derby, CT
Litchfield, CT
New Haven, CT
Waterbury, CT
Cohen, Thomas A. ....San Francisco, CA
Cohen, Thomas F. ....South Bend, IN
Cohen, Thomas L. ....Atlanta, GA
Cohen, Thomas M. ....Overland Park, KS
Cohen, Thomas S. ....Thousand Oaks, CA
Cohen & Thurston, P.A. ....Jacksonville, FL
Cohen, Todd A. ....Lakewood, NJ
Cohen, Todd, Kite & Stanford, LLC
Covington, KY
Florence, KY
Newport, KY
Cincinnati, OH
Fairfax, OH
Cohen, Todd S. ....New York, NY
Cohen, Tracey H. ....Washington, DC
Cohen, Tricia R. ....New York, NY
Cohen & Tucker ....New York, NY
Cohen, V. Stephen ....Tampa, FL
Cohen Vacanti Higgins ....Lincoln, NE
Omaha, NE
Cohen, Valerie A. ....Burbank, CA
Cohen, Vicki ....Barrington, IL
Cohen, Victor ....New York, NY
Cohen, Victor A.
Farm Credit Administration,
Regulatory Enforcement Division, GV
Cohen, Victor A. ....Somers, NY
Cohen, Victor A. ....Westbury, NY
Cohen, Victor C. ....Toluca Lake, CA
Cohen, Victor L. ....Washington, DC
Cohen, Vincent H. ....Washington, DC
Cohen, Walter ....New York, NY
Cohen, Walter N. ....Atlanta, GA
Cohen, Walter W. ....Harrisburg, PA
Cohen, Wanda M. ....Houston, TX
Cohen, Warren H. ....Costa Mesa, CA
Cohen, Warren L. ....Tuckahoe, NY
Cohen & Warren, P.C. ......Farmington Hills, MI
Smithtown, NY
Cohen, Wayne R. ....Washington, DC
Cohen, Weiss and Simon ....New York, NY
Cohen, William ....Palo Alto, CA
Cohen, William ....Troy, MI
Cohen, William D. ....Burlington, VT
Cohen, William D. ....Rutland, VT
Cohen, William E.
Federal Trade Commission,
Policy Planning, GV
Cohen, William G. ....Chicago, IL
Cohen, William G. ....New Castle, PA
Cohen, William I. ....Palo Alto, CA
Cohen, William J. ....Atlanta, GA
Cohen, William J. ....Elkhart, IN
Cohen, William M. ....Boulder, CO
Cohen, William M. ....Department of Justice,
Environment and Natural Resources
Division, GV
Cohen, William M. ....Nashville, TN
Cohen, William N. ....Calabasas, CA
Cohen, William R. ....Troy, MI
Cohen, William S. ....Beverly Hills, CA
Cohen, William S. ....Bangor, ME
Cohen, William S., (P.C.) ....Indianapolis, IN
Cohen and Wolf, P.C. ....Bridgeport, CT
Danbury, CT
Stamford, CT
Westport, CT
Cohen, Y. Jerry, & Associates
New York, NY
Cohen, Yocheved ....New York, NY
Cohen, Yoram Jerry ....New York, NY
Cohen, Zoe Allison ....Falls Church, VA
Cohen and Zwerner ....Dallas, TX
Cohen/David & Associates, P.C.
Atlanta, GA
Roswell, GA
Cohen-Cutler, Olivia J. ....Los Angeles, CA
Cohen-Davidson, Robin ....Millburn, NJ
New York, NY
Cohen-Kutzenco, Martine ....Trenton, NJ
Cohen-Milch, Janis ....Los Angeles, CA
Cohenour, Cynthia ....Oklahoma City, OK
Cohenour, John H. ....Sacramento, CA
Cohen-Soyer, Romy ....Deerfield, IL
Cohernour, David C. ....Denville, NJ
Cohernour, Elizabeth N. ....Short Hills, NJ
Cohick, Cameron ....Washington, DC
Cohill, Maurice B., Jr. ....Pittsburgh, PA
Cohill, Stephen E. ....Timonium, MD
Cohl, Peter A. ....Lansing, MI
Cohl, Stoker & Toskey, P.C. ....Lansing, MI
Cohlan, Richard M. ....White Plains, NY
Cohler, Charles B. ....San Francisco, CA
Cohler, Richard D. ....Chicago, IL
Cohn, A. Richard ....Sudbury, MA
Waltham, MA
Cohn, Aaron ....Columbus, GA
Cohn, Adam G. ....Federal Trade Commission,
Bureau of Consumer Protection, GV
Cohn, Alan ....Washington, DC
Cohn, Alan B. ....Hollywood, FL
Cohn, Alan W. ....Pembroke Pines, FL
Cohn, Albert L. ....Saddle Brook, NJ
Cohn, Alexandra C. ....New York, NY
Cohn, Allan C. ....Jericho, NY
Cohn, Andrew B. ....Marlton, NJ
Philadelphia, PA
Plymouth Meeting, PA
Cohn, Andrew H. ....Boston, MA
Cohn, Andrew S. ....Berkeley, CA
Cohn, Arnold S. ....Houston, TX
Cohn, Arthur B. ....Fairfield, VT
Cohn, Arthur J. ....St. Davids, PA
Cohn & Associates ....Philadelphia, PA
Cohn, Avern ....Detroit, MI
Cohn, B. Renee Sanderlin ....Atlanta, GA
Cohn, Barbara L. ....Waterbury, CT
Cohn, Bennett S. ....Tesuque, NM
Cohn, Beth S. ....Phoenix, AZ
Cohn Birnbaum & Shea P.C.
Hartford, CT
Stamford, CT
Westport, CT
New York, NY
Cohn, Bracaglia & Gropper, P.C.
Somerville, NJ
Cohn, Bradley L. ....Chicago, IL
Cohn, Bradley M. ....Mount Prospect, IL
Cohn, Bruce M. ....Mineola, NY
Riverhead, NY
Cohn & Burger ....Palisades Park, NJ
Cohn, Carol Kunkis ....Newport Beach, CA
Cohn, Carolyn J. ....Tustin, CA
Cohn, Casstevens & Bircher, P.C.
Corpus Christi, TX
Cohn, Celia ....North Hollywood, CA
Cohn, Charles ....San Luis Obispo, CA
Cohn, Charles A. ....Chicago, IL
Cohn, Christine Covert ....Los Angeles, CA
Cohn, Cindy A. ....San Mateo, CA
Cohn, Clifford B. ....Philadelphia, PA
Cohn & Cohn ....Chicago, IL
Cohn & Cohn ....South Orange, NJ
Cohn & Cohn ....Cleveland, TX
Cohn, Cohn, Bianco & Hendrix, P.A.
Tampa, FL
Cohn & Cohn, P.C. ....Waterbury, CT
Cohn & Cohn, P.C. ....Columbus, GA
Cohn, Constance J. ....Albuquerque, NM
Cohn, Creighton J. ....St. Louis, MO
Cohn, Daniel C. ....Boston, MA
Cohn, Daniel E. ....St. Helena, CA
San Francisco, CA
Cohn, David A. ....Encino, CA
Cohn, David K. ....Bakersfield, CA
Cohn, David M. ....Santa Ana, CA
Cohn, David M. ....Baton Rouge, LA
Cohn, David M. ....New York, NY
Cohn, David S. ....San Bernardino, CA
Cohn, David S. ....Richmond, VA
Cohn, Deborah A. ....Bethesda, MD
Cohn, Deborah S. ....Detroit, MI
Cohn, Deborah Schaffer
Department of Commerce,
Patent and Trademark Office, GV
Cohn, Devora B. ....Brooklyn, NY
Cohn, Diane B. ....Philadelphia, PA
Cohn, Don S., (P.A.) ....Miami, FL
Cohn, Dona E. ....San Francisco, CA
Cohn, Donald A. ....Wilmington, DE
Cohn, Donald J. ....New York, NY
Cohn, Donna E. ....Hollywood, FL
Cohn, Douglas R. ....Brooklyn, NY
Cohn & Dussi, LLC ....Boston, MA
Cohn, Edward ....New York, NY
Cohn, Edward H. ....Brooklyn, NY
Cohn, Edward S. ....Silver Spring, MD
Towson, MD
Cohn, Eileen M. ....Los Angeles, CA
Cohn, Eli Saul ....New York, NY
Cohn, Emory F. ....Miami Beach, FL
Cohn, Eric A. ....Philadelphia, PA
Cohn, Erwin ....Chicago, IL
Cohn, Frederick F., (Ltd.) ....Chicago, IL
Cohn, Frederick H. ....New York, NY
Cohn, Gail Rudie ....Baltimore, MD
Cohn, Gary C. ....Kirkland, WA
Cohn, George G. ....Boca Raton, FL
Cohn, George L. ....Los Angeles, CA
Cohn, George L. ....Redondo Beach, CA
Cohn, Gerald ....New York, NY
Cohn, Gerald A. ....Orinda, CA
Cohn, Gerald B. ....East St. Louis, IL
Cohn, Goldberg & Deutsch, LLC
Baltimore, MD
Silver Spring, MD
Towson, MD
Cohn, Guenter S. ....San Diego, CA
Cohn, Halli D. ....Atlanta, GA
Cohn, Hanna S. ....Rochester, NY
Cohn, Harold B. ....Rancho Mirage, CA
Cohn, Harold Jonas ....Los Angeles, CA
Cohn, Harry Edward ....Richmond, VA
Cohn, Harry L. ....Richmond, VA
Cohn, Helen Fein ....Bellaire, TX
Cohn, Henry A.
Department Of Veterans Affairs,
Office of the General Counsel, GV
Cohn, Henry G. ....Albany, NY
Cohn, Henry M. ....New York, NY
Cohn, Henry S. ....Hartford, CT
Cohn, Herbert B. ....Washington, DC
Cohn, Hillel T. ....Los Angeles, CA
Cohn, Howard L. ....Baltimore, MD
Cohn, Howard M. ....Cleveland, OH
Cohn, Ina S. ....Santa Monica, CA
Cohn, Irene P. ....Berkeley, CA
Cohn, Irving A. ....Woodbury, NY
Cohn, Irving F. ....Baltimore, MD
Cohn, J. Bradley ....Roslyn, NY
Cohn, Jacob ....Huntington Station, NY
Cohn, Jacob C. ....Philadelphia, PA
Cohn, James I. ....Fort Lauderdale, FL
Cohn, Jason D. ....Santa Ana, CA
Cohn, Jean A. ....Hartford, CT
Cohn, Jeffrey B. ....Scottsdale, AZ
Cohn, Jeffrey B., P.C., Law Offices of
Scottsdale, AZ
Cohn, Jeffrey R. ....Mineola, NY
Cohn, Jennifer A.
Farm Credit Administration,
Legal Counsel Division, GV
Cohn, Jennifer S. ....San Francisco, CA
Cohn, Jerald S. ....Washington, DC
Cohn, Jerold S. ....Van Nuys, CA
Cohn, Jerry ....New York, NY
Cohn, Joel M., (P.C.) ....Washington, DC
Cohn, Joel S. ....Washington, DC
Cohn, Johann ....Lakewood, CO
Cohn, John R. ....Dallas, TX
Cohn, John W. ....Los Angeles, CA
Cohn, Jonathan D. ....New York, NY
Cohn, Jonathan F. ....New York, NY
Cohn, Jonathan K. ....New York, NY
Cohn, Jonathon E. ....Los Angeles, CA
Cohn, Jordan ....Jackson Heights, NY
Cohn, Joseph ....St. Louis, MO
Cohn, Joseph A., Jr. ....Corpus Christi, TX
Cohn, Joseph H. ....Houston, TX
Cohn, Joseph S. ....New York, NY
Cohn, Joshua D. ....New York, NY
Cohn, Joshua P. ....Saddle Brook, NJ
Cohn, Judith E. ....Houston, TX
Cohn, Judy C. ....Atlanta, GA
Cohn, Julius W. ....White Plains, NY
Cohn & Kelakos LLP ....Boston, MA
Cohn, Kenneth ....Kansas City, MO
Cohn, Lambert, Ryan and Schneider, Ltd.
Chicago, IL
Cohn, Lauren Weiner ....Cincinnati, OH
Cohn Law Firm, The ....Memphis, TN
Cohn, Lawrence B. ....Newport Beach, CA
Cohn, Lawrence H. ....Chester, PA
Cohn, Lawrence H., P.C. ....Chester, PA
Cohn, Lawrence J. ....Chicago, IL
Cohn, Lawrence N. ....Washington, DC
Cohn, Lawrence W. ....Kailua-Kona, HI
Cohn, Lawrence W., A Law Corporation
Kailua-Kona, HI
Cohn, Leonard M. ....Hellertown, PA
Cohn, Leslie L. ....Columbus, GA
Cohn, Leslie S. ....Philadelphia, PA
Cohn, Lewis B. ....Short Hills, NJ
Cohn, Lewis J. ....Boston, MA
Cohn Lifland Pearlman Herrmann & Knopf LLP ....Hackensack, NJ
Paterson, NJ
Saddle Brook, NJ
Cohn, Linda A. ....Hartford, CT
Cohn, Linda F. ....Englewood, CO
Cohn, Lisa Reckler ....Denver, CO
Cohn, Louis A. ....Kansas City, MO
Cohn, Louis H. ....Norfolk, VA
Cohn, Louis J. ....Chicago, IL
Cohn, Malcolm ....Cleveland, TX
Cohn, Marc A. ....New York, NY
Cohn, Marcus ....Washington, DC
Cohn, Marcus E., (P.C.) ....Boston, MA
Cohn, Marjorie ....San Diego, CA
Cohn, Mark B. ....Cleveland, OH
Cohn, Mark S. ....Southfield, MI
Cohn and Marks ....Washington, DC
Cohn, Martin ....Los Angeles, CA
Cohn, Martin ....Chicago, IL
Cohn, Martin D. ....Hazleton, PA
Cohn, Martin P. ....Santa Barbara, CA
Cohn, Marvin ....Chicago, IL
Cohn, Mary P. ....Boston, MA
Cohn, Mary Saur ....Grand Rapids, MI
Cohn, Matt ....Denver, CO
Cohn, Melvin E. ....San Carlos, CA
Cohn, Melvin S., (P.C.) ....Houston, TX
Cohn, Merle D. ....Seattle, WA
Cohn, Merle D., Inc., Inc., P.S. ....Seattle, WA
Cohn, Michael A. ....Clearwater, FL
Cohn, Michael A. ....New York, NY
Cohn, Michael H. ....Mineola, NY
Cohn, Michael J. ....Milwaukee, WI
Cohn, Michelle J. ....Stamford, CT
Cohn, Milton L. ....Bridgeport, CT
Cohn, Morris ....Jamaica, NY
Cohn, Morris Marshall ....Schenectady, NY
Cohn, Morton R., Sr. ....Monroe, MI
Cohn, Myron G. ....Tustin, CA
Cohn, Nancy E. ....New York, NY
Cohn, Ned M. ....Somerville, NJ
Cohn, Otis Malcolm ....Cleveland, TX
Cohn, Paul T. ....New York, NY

Cohn, Pauletta Palasota ... Houston, TX
Cohn, Peter ... Menlo Park, CA
Cohn, Powell and Hind, P.C.
St. Charles, MO
St. Louis, MO
Cohn, Reuven Z. ... Newton, MA
Cohn, Richard ... Washington, DC
Cohn, Richard A. ... Beverly Hills, CA
Cohn, Richard A. ... Santa Ana, CA
Cohn, Richard A. ... Washington, DC
Cohn, Richard B. ... Westmont, NJ
Philadelphia, PA
Cohn, Richard J. ... Birmingham, AL
Cohn, Richard L. ... New York, NY
Cohn, Richard P. R. ... Denver, CO
Cohn, Robert A. ... St. Louis, MO
Cohn, Robert E. ... Hartford, CT
Cohn, Robert E. ... Washington, DC
Cohn, Robert F. ... New Haven, CT
Cohn, Robert I. ... Colorado Springs, CO
Denver, CO
Cohn, Robert L. ... New York, NY
Cohn, Robin E. ... Carrollton, GA
Cohn, Robin F. ... Washington, DC
Cohn, Ronald B. ... Tampa, FL
Cohn, Ronald G. ... Casnovia, MI
Cohn, Ronald R. ... Los Angeles, CA
Cohn, Roy W. ... Tampa, FL
Cohn, S. Alan ... Norcross, GA
Cohn, Samuel C. ... New York, NY
Cohn, Sanford A. ... Atlanta, GA
Cohn, Scott A. ... New York, NY
Cohn, Scott E. ... Fort Lauderdale, FL
Cohn, Sharon Beth ... Washington, DC
Cohn, Sheldon J. ... Los Angeles, CA
Cohn, Sherman L. ... Washington, DC
Cohn, Sidney L. ... Birmingham, MI
Cohn, Stacee P. ... Kansas City, MO
Cohn, Stanley A. ... Clearwater, FL
Cohn, Stanley J. ... New Orleans, LA
Cohn, Stephan S. ... Irvine, CA
Cohn, Steven ... Carle Place, NY
Cohn, Steven D. ... Brooklyn, NY
Cohn, Steven L.
Department Of Veterans Affairs, Board of Veterans Appeals, GV
Cohn, Steven M. ... Sacramento, CA
Cohn, Steven P. ... San Jose, CA
Cohn, Steven P. ... Oak Brook, IL
Cohn, Stuart A. ... Deerfield, IL
Cohn, Stuart R. ... Gainesville, FL
Cohn, Susan Clark ... Pembroke Pines, FL
Cohn, Sylvia J. ... Saddle Brook, NJ
Cohn, Teri A. ... New York, NY
Cohn, Terri E., Law Office
Beverly Hills, CA
Cohn, Terri P. ... Atlanta, GA
Cohn, Theodore R. ... Livingston, NJ
Cohn, Thomas A.
Federal Trade Commission, Bureau of Consumer Protection, GV
Cohn, Thomas E. ... Roseland, NJ
Cohn, Turpen & Anderson ... Atlanta, GA
Roswell, GA
Snellville, GA
Cohn, Vanessa Negrón ... Tampa, FL
Cohn, Walter R. ... South Orange, NJ
Cohn, William A. ... Memphis, TN
Cohn, William L. ... Springfield, MA
Cohn, William S. ... Melville, NY
Mineola, NY
Cohn-Connor, Jeanne T. ... Portland, ME
Cohne, Bruce G. ... Salt Lake City, UT
Cohne, Rappaport & Segal, P.C.
Salt Lake City, UT
Cohn-Lee, Richard G. ... Portland, OR
Cohn-Mintz, Beth A. ... Palo Alto, CA
Cohn-Postar Law Offices, The
Berkeley, CA
Oakland, CA
San Jose, CA
Cohn-Postar, Robert ... Berkeley, CA
Cohn-Postar, Susan ... Berkeley, CA
Cohnstaedt, William ... Corvallis, OR
Coho, Frank E. ... Pittsburgh, PA
Coho, Kenneth F. ... Copperopolis, CA
Cohoe, Bruce W. ... Tacoma, WA
Cohoes, David William ... Minneapolis, MN
Coholan, Ann M. ... Pittsburgh, PA
Coholan, William D. ... Pittsburgh, PA
Cohon, Bennett B. ... Los Angeles, CA
Cohon & Gardner, P.C. ... Los Angeles, CA
Cohon, Jeffrey M. ... Los Angeles, CA
Cohon, Keith E.
Environmental Protection Agency, Office of Enforcement and Compliance Assurance, GV
Cohon, Maureen B. ... Pittsburgh, PA
Cohon, Morton H. ... Chicago, IL
Cohon, Peter L. ... San Francisco, CA
Cohon, Raizes & Regal ... Chicago, IL
Cohon, Robert M. ... Bellevue, WA
Cohoon, James B. ... Torrance, CA
Cohorn, Cheryl S. ... Houston, TX
Cohron, Peter Pruitt ... Lexington, KY
Cohrs, Denis A. ... Clearwater, FL
Cohrs, Denis A., P.A. ... Clearwater, FL
Cohrs, Robert D. ... Alexandria, VA
Cohrs, William R. ... Irving, TX
Cohrt, Larry J. ... Waterloo, IA
Coia, Arthur A. ... Providence, RI
Coia, Gladys L. ... North Miami Beach, FL
Coia & Lepore, Ltd. ... Providence, RI
Coia, Raymond C. ... Providence, RI
Coia, Richard ... Rochester, NY
Coia-Custer, Marilyn ... Dayton, OH
Coican, Gregory G. ... Fort Lauderdale, FL
Coie, Allan Lee ... Los Angeles, CA
Coil, James D. ... Waterloo, IA
Coil, James H., III ... Atlanta, GA
Coil, Michael C. ... Bozeman, MT
Coil, Roger Marlow ... Oklahoma City, OK
Coile, Carol A. ... Fairfax, VA
Coile, Kristin Murphy ... Nashville, TN
Coilparampil, Meera S. ... Newark, NJ
Coin, Angela M. ... Chicago, IL
Coiner, Andrew T. ... Paducah, KY
Coiner, Francis M., Law Offices of
Hendersonville, NC
Coiner, R. H., Jr. ... Miami, OK
Coira, Charles F., Jr. ... Laurel Park, NC
Coiro, Joseph ... New York, NY
Coiro, Joseph W. ... Somerset, NJ
Coit, George S., Jr. ... St. Petersburg, FL
Coit, Kent A. ... Boston, MA
Coit, Laurence ... Palo Alto, CA
Coit, Lynde H. ... New York, NY
Coit, Robert ... Department of the Air Force, Office of the Judge Advocate General, GV
Coit, Robert D. ... Chunky, MS
Coit, Robert Lamont ... Camarillo, CA
Ventura, CA
Coit, Robert Lamont, A Professional Law Corporation ... Camarillo, CA
Ventura, CA
Coit, Rosanne J. ... Oak View, CA
Coit, Stephen R. ... Norwich, CT
Cojocar, Jeffery Alexander
Sterling Heights, MI
Cok, Michael D. ... Bozeman, MT
Cok, Wheat, Brown & McGarry, PLLP
Bozeman, MT
Coke, Bruce E. ... Salt Lake City, UT
Coke, Carrie-Lee ... Sacramento, CA
Coke, Catherine J. ... Altus, OK
Coke, Elizabeth ... Fort Pierce, FL
West Palm Beach, FL
Coke, Jack L., Jr. ... Dallas, TX
Coke, Jennifer A. ... St. Louis, MO
Coke, Laurel D. ... Alameda, CA
Coke, Mark T. ... Altus, OK
Coke, Mark T. ... Altus, OK
Coke, Michael E. ... Alameda, CA
Coke, Michael E. ... New York, NY
Coke, Randy B., (P.C.)
Salt Lake City, UT
Coke, Stephen A. ... Dallas, TX
Cokeley, Bryan R. ... Charleston, WV
Coker, Billy F. ... Dallas, TX
Coker & Coker ... Jacksboro, TN
Coker, Curtis E. ... Jackson, MS
Coker, Cynthia A. ... Columbia, SC
Coker, D. Gerald ... Atlanta, GA
Coker, Darby T. ... Atlanta, GA
Coker, David L. ... Atlanta, GA
Coker, Derrick W. ... Philadelphia, PA
Coker, Duane L. ... Denton, TX
Coker, Edward C., III ... Jacksonville, FL
Coker, Elizabeth E. ... Crockett, TX
Coker, Ernest, Jr. ... Conroe, TX
Coker, Ernest, P.C. ... Conroe, TX
Coker, Gary W. ... Beaumont, TX
Coker, Gene V. ... Atlanta, GA
Coker, H. Jeffrey ... Flagstaff, AZ
Coker, Howard C. ... Jacksonville, FL
Coker, J. Edward ... Silverado, CA
Coker, James E. ... Bakersfield, CA
Coker, Jean C. ... Jacksonville, FL
Coker, Jean C., P.A.
Fernandina Beach, FL
Jacksonville, FL
Ponte Vedra Beach, FL
St. Augustine, FL
Coker, John Diaz ... Pittsburg, CA
Coker, Joseph G. ... Jacksboro, TN
Coker, Joseph L. ... Birmingham, AL
Coker, Judith E. ... San Diego, CA
Coker, Keith D. ... Russellville, AR
Coker Law Firm, P.A. ... Russellville, AR
Coker, Mary Day ... Gainesville, FL
Coker, Michael C. ... Tyler, TX
Coker, Michael G. ... Oklahoma City, OK
Coker, Mina Cathryn ... Prattville, AL
Coker, Myers, Schickel, Sorenson, Higginbotham & Green, P.A.
Jacksonville, FL
Coker, Phillip H. ... West Sacramento, CA
Coker, Richard C. ... Jackson, MS
Coker, Richard G., Jr. ... Fort Lauderdale, FL
Coker, Robert C., (P.A.) ... Bradenton, FL
Coker, Robert E. ... La Fayette, GA
Coker, Ronald L., Jr. ... Houston, TX
Coker, Shirley L. ... Philadelphia, PA
Coker, Stanley C. ... Atlanta, GA
Coker, Tammy Grubb ... Kansas City, MO
Coker, Thomas D. ... Los Angeles, CA
Coker, Thomas H., Jr. ... Greenville, SC
Coker, Thomas M., Jr. ... Plantation, FL
Coker, Todd A. ... Jackson, MS
Coker-Creque, Yvonne ... Kew Gardens, NY
Cokinos, Bosien & Young, A Professional Corporation ... Beaumont, TX
Corpus Christi, TX
Houston, TX
Cokinos, Gregory M. ... Beaumont, TX
Corpus Christi, TX
Houston, TX
Col, Sonia Valeria ... New York, NY
Cola, Catherine M. ... Columbus, OH
Cola, Neil R. ... Chelsea, MA
Colabella, Chris H. ... Hackettstown, NJ
Hopatcong, NJ
Newton, NJ
Colabella, Mark R. ... Providence, RI
Colabella, Nicholas ... White Plains, NY
Colabianchi, Nicholas A. ... Cleveland, OH
Colachico, Jeanne M. ... Boston, MA
Colacino, Antonio ... Des Moines, IA
Colacino, William C., Jr. ... Garfield, NJ
Coladarci, Anne Margaret ... Chicago, IL
Coladarci, Peter R. ... Chicago, IL
Colagiovanni, Frank D. ... Hyde Park, MA
Colagiovanni, Joseph A., Jr.
St. Louis, MO
Colagiovanni, Robert V. ... Warwick, RI
Colagreco, Louis J., Jr. ... Paoli, PA
Colaguori, Louis A. ... Burlington, NJ
Colaguori, Louis A., P.C. ... Burlington, NJ
Colahan, Timothy J. ... Burns, OR
Colaianne, Joseph W. ... Chicago, IL
Colaianni, Cary B. ... Boise, ID
Colaianni, Joseph V. ... Washington, DC
Colaianni, Joseph V., Jr. ... Washington, DC
Colaiano, Joseph M. ... Omaha, NE
Colaizzi, Roger A. ... Washington, DC
Colalillo, Mary Eva ... Camden, NJ
Colaluca, Kenneth A. ... East Greenwich, RI
Colaluca, Kenneth A., Jr. ... New York, NY
Colaluca, Thomas L. ... Cleveland, OH
Colamaria, Andrew T. ... Wellesley Hills, MA
Colamarino, Katrin B. ... New York, NY
Colamarino, Leonard J. ... New York, NY
Colamarino & Sohns, LLP ... New York, NY
Colameo, Thomas J. ... New York, NY
Colan, Bruce Jay ... Miami, FL
Colan, John G. ... Richmond, VA
Colan, Jonathan D. ... Miami, FL
Colan, Lonnie L. ... Miami, FL
Colan, Owen R. ... South Charleston, WV
Colan, Robert ... New York, NY
Colananni, Ann K. ... New York, NY
Colando, Andrew C., Jr. ... Mount Dora, FL
Colaner, Deborah E. ... Irvine, CA
Colaneri, Christopher Heintz ... Darien, CT
Colaneri, Elizabeth Thomas ... Linwood, NJ
Colaneri, Janet K. ... Arlington, TX
Colaneri, Marie E. ... Glendale, CA
Colaneri, Massad, Haman & Reilly, P.C.
Arlington, TX
Dallas, TX
Fort Worth, TX
Colaneri, Rockwell D. ... Central Islip, NY
Colanero, Alfred J. ... Summerfield, NC
Colangelo, Anthony T. ... Pittsburgh, PA
Colangelo, Carolyn Gentile ... Norwalk, CT
Colangelo, David A.
National Labor Relations Board, Office of the General Counsel, GV
Colangelo & Goldenberg, LLP
New York, NY
White Plains, NY
Colangelo, John B. ... Rye Brook, NY
Colangelo, John P. ... New York, NY
White Plains, NY
Colangelo, Kevin E. ... New York, NY
Colangelo, Kristian James ... Boston, MA
Colangelo, Louis J., Jr. ... Norwalk, CT
Colangelo, Nicholas L. ... Cranston, RI
Colangelo, Paul D. ... Vineland, NJ
Colangelo, Stephen M. ... McLean, VA
Colannino, John G. ... Monmouth Beach, NJ
Colantonio, Mark A. ... Weirton, WV
Wheeling, WV
Colantuno, Joseph F. ... Englewood, CO
Colantuono, Joseph R. ... Leawood, KS
Colantuono, Michael G. ... Los Angeles, CA
Colantuono, Thomas P. ... Derry, NH
Colao, Andrew ... New York, NY
Colao, Brian A. ... Dallas, TX
Colao, Gregory J. ... New York, NY
Colao, Ivan A. ... Jacksonville, FL
Colao, Jennifer Nelsen ... New York, NY
Colao, Joseph G. ... New York, NY
Colao, Joseph J., Jr. ... Asbury Park, NJ
Colapietro, Bruno ... Binghamton, NY
Colapinto, David K. ... Washington, DC
Colaprete, Zuzana ... San Diego, CA
Colaprico, James M. ... Kingston, NJ
Colaresi, Richard T. ... Bowie, MD
Colaric, Douglas A. ... Grand Junction, CO
Colaric, Jack A. ... Phoenix, AZ
Colarich, Paul W., Jr. ... Holbrook, AZ
Colarte, Antoinette M. ... New York, NY
Colarulli, Paul F. ... Washington, DC
Colarusso, Joseph J. ... White Plains, NY
Colarusso, Michael J. ... Pittsburgh, PA
Colarusso, Sam A. ... Morristown, NJ
Colas, Arthur H., Jr. ... San Francisco, CA
Colas, Leon S. ... Forest Grove, OR
Colasanti, Anthony T. ... West Caldwell, NJ
Colasanti, Ermel & Casale
West Caldwell, NJ
Colasanti, Ralph A. ... Bloomfield, NJ
Colasuonno, Ralph ... Sterling Heights, MI
Colasurd, Christopher P. ... Columbus, OH
Colasurd, Donald M. ... Columbus, OH
Colasurd, Michael D. ... Columbus, OH
Colasurd, Michael D., Co., L.P.A.
Columbus, OH
Colasurd, Richard M. ... Rochester, NY
Colasurdo, Anthony L. ... Nutley, NJ
Colasurdo, Joseph T. ... White Plains, NY
Colatosti, Sandra M. ... Albany, NY
Colatriano, Vincent J. ... Washington, DC
Colatsky, Susan Dignam ... Philadelphia, PA
Colautti, Lisa M. ... Pittsburgh, PA
Colavecchi, Joseph ... Clearfield, PA
Colavecchi & Ryan ... Clearfield, PA
Colavecchio, Michael T. ... Melville, NY
Colavecchio, Paul V. ... Macedonia, OH
Colavincenzo, John P. ... Beaver, PA
Colavincenzo, Martin G. ... Pittsburgh, PA
Colavita, Anthony J. ... Eastchester, NY
Colavita, Anthony J., P.C. ... Eastchester, NY
Colavita, Anthony P. ... Garden City, NY
Colavita, Lynne A. ... Eastchester, NY
Colavita, Pasquale J. ... Glendora, NJ
Philadelphia, PA
Colavito, James S. ... Livingston, NJ
Colavito, William A. ... White Plains, NY
Colavito, William J. ... Somers, NY
Colavolpe, William A. ... Brooklyn, NY
Colaw & Augustine ... Modesto, CA
Colaw, Curtis D. ... Modesto, CA
Colaw, Frank D. ... Huntington Beach, CA
Colaw, Thierry Patrick ... Santa Ana, CA
Colazzo, Rosemary ... Paterson, NJ
Colb, Valerie H. ... La Canada Flintridge, CA
Colbassani, Joseph S. ... Scranton, PA
Colbath, Bruce A. ... New York, NY
Colbath, Gary G. ... Rapid City, SD
Colbath, Gary G., Jr. ... Rapid City, SD
Colbath, Jeffrey J. ... West Palm Beach, FL
Colbath, Joe D. ... Pleasant Hill, CA
Colbath, Paula K. ... New York, NY
Colbath, Walter N., Jr.
West Palm Beach, FL
Colbeck, J. Richard ... Coldwater, MI
Colbeck, McAlhany & Stewart ... Angola, IN
Coldwater, MI
Colber, Douglas W. ... Downers Grove, IL
Colberg, Chi C. ... Atlanta, GA
Colberg, Herman W. ... San Juan, PR
Colberg, Talis J. ... Palmer, AK
Colberg-Guerra, Herman G.
San Juan, PR
Colbert, Albert ... Potomac, MD
Colbert & Associates ... Fort Worth, TX
Colbert, B. James ... Chippewa Falls, WI
Colbert, Bradford W. ... St. Paul, MN
Colbert, Brian L. ... New York, NY
Colbert, Celia A. ... Whitehouse Station, NJ
Colbert, Christina M. ... Darien, CT
New York, NY
Colbert, Clarence, Jr. ... Memphis, TN
Colbert, D. Scott ... Sulphur, OK
Colbert, David M. ... United States Senate, Senatorial Assistants, GV
Colbert, Douglas L ... Baltimore, MD
Colbert, Douglas M. ... New York, NY
Colbert & Duck ... Sulphur, OK
Colbert, Edward T. ... Washington, DC
Colbert, Edward V., III ... Boston, MA
Colbert, Freeman & Stribling ... Austin, TX
Colbert, James P. ... Rochester, MI
Colbert, James W., III ... Los Angeles, CA
Colbert, Joe ... Austin, TX
Colbert, John
Department of Labor, GV
Colbert, John D., & Associates ... Chicago, IL
Colbert, John P. ... Cincinnati, OH
Colbert, John R. ... Ardmore, OK
Colbert, John W. ... New Orleans, LA
Colbert, Joseph G. ... New York, NY
Colbert, Judith A. ... Houston, TX
Colbert, Kathleen M. ... Boston, MA
Colbert, Kathryn H. ... Irving, TX
Colbert, Kevin Coyle ... Miami, FL
Colbert, Kevin L. ... Houston, TX
Colbert Law Firm ... Ardmore, OK
Colbert, Lawr. L. ... Washington, DC
Colbert, Lois Wagman ... Raleigh, NC
Colbert, Lori Ann ... Anchorage, AK
Colbert, Marc H. ... Chicago, IL
Colbert, Mark A. ... Pine Bluff, AR
Colbert, Mark H. ... Ardmore, OK
Colbert, Nicole J. ... St. Louis, MO
Colbert, Pamela Felkins ... Birmingham, AL
Colbert, Pamela K. ... Milwaukee, WI
Colbert, Paul A. ... Scituate, MA
Colbert, Renee ... Oklahoma City, OK
Colbert, Richard
Environmental Protection Agency, Office of Enforcement and Compliance Assurance, GV
Colbert, Richard L. ... Kansas City, MO
Colbert, Richard L. ... Nashville, TN
Colbert, Richard M. ... Pensacola, FL
Colbert, Richard P. ... Stamford, CT
Colbert, Roger U. ... Paragould, AR
Colbert, Sally ... Austin, TX
Colbert, Shepard & Sadowski ... Rochester, MI
Colbert, Stephen D. ... Lewisville, TX
Colbert, Thomas F. ... Chicago, IL
Colbert, Timothy K. ... Sulphur, OK
Colbert, Trang H. ... Gig Harbor, WA
Colbert, W. A. ... San Francisco, CA
Colbert, William H., III ... Houston, TX
Colbert, William L. ... Sanford, FL
Colbert, William L., Jr. ... Jackson, MS
Colbert, Winfred T. ... Fort Worth, TX
Colbo, Kimberlee A. ... Anchorage, AK
Colborn, G. Diane ... Sacramento, CA
Colborn, James W. ... Tacoma, WA
Colborn, John A. ... Lincoln, NE
Colborn, Paul P. ... Department of Justice, Office of Legal Counsel, GV
Colborn, Robert J. ... Annapolis, MD
Colbourn, Elinor L. ... Department of Justice, Environment and Natural Resources Division, GV
Colbourn, Frank E. ... Massapequa, NY
Colbran, Philip Leonard ... New York, NY
Colbrunn, Charles R. ... Winter Springs, FL
Colburn, Anthony J. ... Toledo, OH
Colburn, B. G. ... Jacksonville, IL
Colburn, Charles M. ... Jacksonville, IL
Colburn, Craig P., Jr. ... Atlanta, GA
Colburn, Donald D. ... Phoenix, AZ
Colburn, Donald F. ... Hadley, MA
Colburn, F. William ... Houston, TX
Colburn, Guy B., Jr. ... San Francisco, CA

Colburn, Harry S., Jr. ... Jupiter, FL
Stuart, FL
Vero Beach, FL
Colburn, James Allan ... Huntington, WV
Colburn, John V. ... Boston, MA
Colburn, Joseph L., Jr. ... Columbus, OH
Colburn, Karen ... Denver, CO
Colburn, Kathryn R. ... Washington, DC
Colburn, Kurt B. ... Denver, CO
Colburn Law Offices, P.C. ... Phoenix, AZ
Colburn, Mitchell D. ... Tupelo, MS
Colburn, Philmore H., II ... Windsor, CT
Springfield, MA
Colburn, Stuart ... Austin, TX
Colburn, Susan F. ... Springfield, MO
Colburn, Virginia C. ... Huntington, WV
Colburn-O'Neill, Mary F. ... Malden, MA
Colby, A. Robert ... New York, NY
Colby, Alfred A. ... Tampa, FL
Colby, Andrea Loshin ... New Brunswick, NJ
Colby, Ann E. ... Owego, NY
Colby, Bernard G. ... Chicago, IL
Colby, Charles C., II ... Chicago, IL
Colby, David H., (P.C.) ... Phoenix, AZ
Colby, Dennis C. ... Orlando, FL
Colby, Deron Matthew
Newport Beach, CA
Colby, Douglas A. ... Chicago, IL
Colby, Drew W. ... Boston, MA
Colby, Edwin A. ... Boston, MA
Colby, Fred W. ... Fargo, ND
Colby, Gary D. ... Philadelphia, PA
Colby, Gregory G. ... Northfield, MN
Colby, Jamie Nell ... New York, NY
Colby, Jeanne M. ... San Francisco, CA
Colby, Jeffery A. ... Burbank, CA
Colby, John D. ... Portland, OR
Colby, Jonathan Elbridge ... New York, NY
Colby, Jonathan T. ... Miami, FL
Orlando, FL
Colby, Lauren A. ... Frederick, MD
Colby, Lawrence A. ... Miami, FL
Colby, Lisa A. ... Metairie, LA
Colby, Marc W. ... Wichita, KS
Colby, Maxwell X. ... Oakhurst, NJ
Colby, Michael Kittridge ... Washington, DC
Colby, Paul L. ... Department of Justice, Office of Professional Responsibility, GV
Colby, Peter W. ... San Francisco, CA
Colby, Raquel S. ... Concord, NH
Colby, Richard D. ... Columbus, OH
Colby, Robert
Securities and Exchange Commission, Division of Market Regulation, GV
Colby, Robert F. ... Purchase, NY
Colby, Ronald E., III ... Augusta, ME
Colby, Stephen A. ... Newport Beach, CA
Colby, Thomas B. ... Washington, DC
Colby, Walter I. ... San Diego, CA
Colby, William E. ... New York, NY
Colby, William F., Jr. ... Birdsboro, PA
Morgantown, PA
Reading, PA
Colby, William H. ... Kansas City, MO
Colby, William M. ... Buffalo, NY
Rochester, NY
Colby-Clements, Paula M. ... Andover, MA
Colca, Laura A. ... Buffalo, NY
Colca, Vicki D.C. ... New York, NY
Colchagoff, Cassandra C. ... Tulsa, OK
Colchamiro, Arthur ... Port Washington, NY
Colchamiro, Eric D. ... New York, NY
Colclaser, H. Alberta ... Wooster, OH
Colclazier, Amie Rose ... Seminole, OK
Colclazier, Jerry L. ... Seminole, OK
Colclough, Jacqueline T. ... Washington, DC
Colclough, Thomas W. ... Redlands, CA
Colcord, Bradford P. ... New York, NY
Colcord, Debra Hayes ... Wausau, WI
Cold, Kathleen Holbrook ... Jacksonville, FL
Coldagelli, Gordon P. ... Virginia, MN
Coldebella, Gus P. ... Boston, MA
Colden, David ... Beverly Hills, CA
Colden, Herbert ... Santa Monica, CA
Colden & McKuin, LLP ... Beverly Hills, CA
Colden, Richard L., Jr. ... Drexel Hill, PA
Colden, Tracy M.J. ... Bethesda, MD
Coldiron, Bradley D. ... Denver, CO
Coldiron, Brent D. ... Oklahoma City, OK
Coldiron, Cindy Ann
Environmental Protection Agency, Office of Enforcement and Compliance Assurance, GV
Coldiron, Hecker & Howell, LLC.
Denver, CO
Coldiron, Holly Ann ... Raleigh, NC
Coldiron, Mark D. ... Oklahoma City, OK
Coldiron, William H. ... Helena, MT
Coldren Adams ... Greensburg, PA
Uniontown, PA
Coldren & Frantz ... Portland, IN
Coldren, Ira B., Jr. ... Greensburg, PA
Uniontown, PA
Coldren, John E. ... Portland, IN
Coldren, John I. ... Department of Defense, Armed Services Board of Contract Appeals, GV
Coldren, Robert H. ... Delaware, OH
Coldren, Robert S. ... Santa Ana, CA
Coldsnow, Robert A. ... Topeka, KS
Coldwell, Bradley M. ... Austin, TX
Coldwell, Colbert ... El Paso, TX
Coldwell, Colbert N. ... El Paso, TX
Coldwell, Deborah S. ... Dallas, TX
Coldwell & Dow ... Austin, TX
Coldwell, Frederic L. ... Denver, CO
Coldwell, Mark F. ... Purchase, NY

Cole, A. Thomas, The Law Offices of
Casa Grande, AZ
Cole, A. Thomas, The Law Offices of
Florence, AZ
Cole Acton Harmon Dunn, A Legal Professional Association ... Springfield, OH
Urbana, OH
Cole, Adam D. ... New York, NY
Cole, Adam M. ... San Francisco, CA
Cole, Alan C. ... Arvada, CO
Cole, Alden Brewer ... Greenville, NC
Cole, Alexandra R. ... Chicago, IL
Cole, Allison Doyle ... Savannah, GA
Cole & Amestoy ... Malta, MT
Cole, Angela D. ... Tampa, FL
Cole, Ann Catherine ... Media, PA
Cole, Ann L.R. ... Dallas, TX
Cole, Arlton G. ... Lawrenceville, GA
Cole, Arthur J. ... Southfield, MI
Cole, Arthur N. ... Boston, MA
Cole, Avis LeAnn ... Atlantic City, NJ
Cole, Barbara S. ... Denver, CO
Cole & Barbee, Inc., P.S. ... Bellevue, WA
Cole, Barry L. ... Mancelona, MI
Cole, Bartlett F. ... Portland, OR
Cole, Basil ... Washington, DC
Cole, Ben Thomas, II ... West Memphis, AR
Cole, Benjamin S., Jr. ... Holbrook, AZ
Cole, Bernadette ... Milwaukee, WI
Milwaukee, WI
Cole, Bernard ... Newton, MA
Cole, Bernard E. ... Cheyenne, WY
Cole, Beth G. ... Philadelphia, PA
Cole, Beth Lincow ... Cherry Hill, NJ
Cole, Betty Shelton ... Muncie, IN
Cole, Bradley S. ... Tampa, FL
Alexandria, VA
Cole, Bradley W. ... Houston, TX
Cole, Brenda H. ... Atlanta, GA
Cole, Brent R. ... Anchorage, AK
Cole, Brian E. ... Irvine, CA
Cole, Brian H. ... Dallas, TX
Cole, Brian K. ... Searcy, AR
Cole, Brian M. ... Syracuse, NY
Cole, Brown & Fesmier ... Mansfield, OH
Cole, Bruce A. ... Beverly Hills, CA
Cole, C. Craig, & Associates
Oklahoma City, OK
Cole, C. Mark ... Pittsburg, KS
Cole, C. Richard ... Rochester, NY
Cole, C. Wharton ... Gainesville, FL
Cole, Candace R. ... Harrisonville, MO
Cole, Carla J. ... New York, NY
Cole, Casey J. ... Pasadena, CA
Cole, Catherine M. ... New York, NY
Cole, Charles A., Jr. ... Smyrna, GA
Cole, Charles D. ... Birmingham, AL
Cole, Charles D. ... Lexington, KY
Cole, Charles Dewey, Jr. ... New York, NY
Cole, Charles E. ... Fairbanks, AK
Cole, Charles E., Jr. ... Wichita, KS
Cole, Charles F. ... Boise, ID
Cole, Charles G. ... Washington, DC
Cole, Charles G. ... Barbourville, KY
Cole, Charles H. ... Chicago, IL
Cole, Charles J. ... Hartford, CT
Cole, Charles J. ... Atlanta, GA
Cole, Charles L. ... Victoria, TX
Cole, Charles M. ... Washington, DC
Cole, Charles M. ... Charleston, SC
Cole, Charles R. ... Grand Junction, CO
Cole, Charles T. ... Tucson, AZ
Cole, Charles T. ... Dallas, TX
Cole, Charles T. ... Stanwood, WA
Cole, Christine ... New York, NY
Cole, Christopher ... Manchester, NH
Portsmouth, NH
Cole, Christopher A. ... Washington, DC
Cole, Christopher J. ... Honolulu, HI
Cole, Christopher M. ... Falls Church, VA
Cole, Christopher S., L.L.M.
The Woodlands, TX
Cole, Christopher Scott ... Wichita, KS
Cole, Claire Pierce ... Charlotte, NC
Cole, Clark H. ... Belleville, IL
St. Louis, MO
Cole, Claudèrick A. ... Brooklyn, NY
Cole, Clifford M. ... Memphis, TN
Cole, Clinton M. ... Colorado Springs, CO
Cole Co., L.P.A. ... Akron, OH
Cole & Cole ... Hartford, CT
Cole & Cole ... Jersey City, NJ
Cole & Cole ... Cheyenne, WY
Cole, Cole & Anderson ... Barbourville, KY
Cole, Cole, & Easley, P.C. ... Victoria, TX
Cole and Cole, P.C. ... Brigantine, NJ
Cole, Constance W. ... Chicago, IL
Cole Corette & Abrutyn, A Prof. Corp.
Washington, DC
Cole & Cox, LLP ... Macon, GA
Warner Robins, GA
Cole, Craig E. ... Garnett, KS
Cole, Curtis A. ... Fresno, CA
Cole, Curtis A. ... Los Angeles, CA
Cole, Dale Sondel ... Alamo, CA
Cole, Dallas J. ... Modesto, CA
Cole, Dana M. ... Los Angeles, CA
Cole, Daniel C. ... Chicago, IL
Cole, Daniel H. ... Indianapolis, IN
Cole, Daniel J., Jr. ... St. Paul, MN
Cole, Daniel Randolph, Jr.
Washington, DC
Cole, Dargan Scott ... Atlanta, GA
Cole, David A. ... Pueblo, CO
Cole, David A. ... Cassville, MO
Cole, David A. ... Holland, OH
Cole, David Bruce ... Hyannis, MA
Cole, David C. ... Atlanta, GA

Cole, David C., P.C. ... Atlanta, GA
Cole, David D. ... Washington, DC
Cole, David G. ... Cleveland, OH
Cole, David H. ... Baltimore, MD
Cole, David H. ... Oklahoma City, OK
Cole, David J. ... Cambridge, MA
Cole, David L., Jr. ... Baltimore, MD
Cole, David N., Law Office of ... Hanover, NH
Cole, David S. ... Washington, DC
Cole, David W. ... Tulsa, OK
Cole, Dawn H. ... Sacramento, CA
Cole, Dayton T. ... Boone, NC
Cole, Dean Anderson, (P.C.)
Lafayette, LA
Cole, Deborah G. ... Chicago, IL
Cole, Deborah Y. ... San Jose, CA
Cole, Debra A. ... Los Angeles, CA
Cole, Debra A. ... Oviedo, FL
Cole, Denis E. ... Garden City, NY
Cole, Denise A. ... San Jose, CA
Cole, Dennis G. ... Rancho Cucamonga, CA
Cole, Derek P. ... Sacramento, CA
Cole, Dezzie R. ... Newark, DE
Cole, Diana L. ... Beverly Hills, CA
Cole, Don ... Santa Ana, CA
Cole, Donald A. ... Cheyenne, WY
Cole, Donald A., Jr. ... Westwood, MA
Cole, Donald D. ... Malta, MT
Cole, Donald D. ... Elmira, NY
Cole, Dorothy A. ... Escondido, CA
Cole, Dorothy A. ... San Diego, CA
Cole & Dougherty ... Houston, TX
Cole, Douglas G. ... Cincinnati, OH
Cole, Douglas R. ... Columbus, OH
Cole, Duane A. ... Fort Collins, CO
Cole, Dwight E. ... St. Louis, MO
Cole, Eddie M., (Co., L.P.A.) ... Toledo, OH
Cole, Edward B. ... Clearwater, FL
Cole, Edward H. ... Syracuse, NY
Cole, Edward R. ... Spartanburg, SC
Cole, Eileen M. ... New York, NY
Cole, Elaine Zipp ... Rochester, NY
Cole, Ellerbe P. ... Augusta, ME
Cole, Elliot H. ... Washington, DC
Cole, Elsa Kircher ... Ann Arbor, MI
Cole, Emily ... Chicago, IL
Cole, Emmett, Jr. ... Victoria, TX
Cole, Emried D., Jr. ... Baltimore, MD
Cole, Enser W., Jr. ... Arlington, VA
Cole, Ernest G. ... New Port Richey, FL
Cole, Erwin J. ... Bridgeport, CT
Cole, Fisher, Bosquez-Flores & Cole, A Prof. Corp. ... Fresno, CA
Cole, Ford R. ... Department of Justice, Federal Bureau of Investigation, GV
Cole, Frances ... San Francisco, CA
Cole, Francine R. ... Cleveland, OH
Cole, Frank E. ... Savannah, GA
Cole, Frank H., Jr. ... Jacksonville, FL
Cole, Franklin A. ... Chicago, IL
Cole, G. Mark ... Atlanta, GA
Cole, G. Severe ... Oak Park, IL
Cole, Garrick F. ... Boston, MA
Cole, Gary ... Carmel, IN
Cole, Gary D. ... Portland, OR
Cole, Gary H. ... Chicago, IL
Cole, Gary L. ... Chicago, IL
Cole, Gary M. ... Akron, OH
Cole, Gary Severe, & Associates, P.C.
Oak Park, IL
Cole, George F. ... Astoria, OR
Cole, George H., Jr. ... Burlingame, CA
San Jose, CA
Cole, George S. ... Menlo Park, CA
Cole, George T. ... Phoenix, AZ
Cole, George W. ... Chicago, IL
Cole, Gerald R. ... Albuquerque, NM
Cole, Glenn, III ... Charlotte, NC
Cole, Gloria ... Weston, MA
Cole, Gregory A. ... Tulsa, OK
Cole, Gregory Martin ... Fort Wayne, IN
Cole, Gretchen ... Salt Lake City, UT
Cole, H. Buckley ... Nashville, TN
Cole, H. Lamar ... Valdosta, GA
Cole, Harold E. ... Rochester, NY
Cole, Harold H. ... White House, TN
Cole, Harry ... Montgomery, AL
Cole, Harry F. ... Washington, DC
Cole & Hart ... Elmira, NY
Cole, Herman A., Jr. ... Manteo, NC
Cole, Howard A. ... Ann Arbor, MI
Cole, Howard E. ... Las Vegas, NV
Cole, Hoyt M. ... Anchorage, AK
Cole, Hoyt M., P.C. ... Anchorage, AK
Cole, Hugh K., Jr. ... Eugene, OR
Cole, Ian A. ... Derby, CT
Cole, J. Chase ... Nashville, TN
Cole, J. Clay ... Memphis, TN
Cole, J. Derham ... Spartanburg, SC
Cole, J. Tipton ... Austin, TX
Cole, J. William ... Birmingham, AL
Cole, Jack Donald ... Atlanta, GA
Cole, Jack E., Jr. ... Dallas, TX
Cole, Jacqueline A.
Department of Commerce, Patent and Trademark Office, GV
Cole, James A. ... Baltimore, MD
Cole, James A. ... Greenbelt, MD
Cole, James A., Jr. ... Durham, NC
Cole, James B. ... Ventura, CA
Cole, James B. ... Pittsburgh, PA
Cole, James D. ... Dayton, OH
Cole, James H. ... Atlanta, GA
Cole, James Henry ... Atlanta, GA
Cole, James, Jr. ... New York, NY
Cole, James L. ... Kansas City, MO
Cole, James L. ... Akron, OH
Cole, James M. ... Washington, DC

Cole, James M. ... North Miami, FL
Cole, James O. ... Fort Lauderdale, FL
Cole, James O. ... Peru, IN
Cole, James R. ... Madison, WI
Cole, James S., Jr. ... St. Louis, MO
Cole, James V., II ... Washington, DC
Cole, James W. ... Victoria, TX
Cole, Jamie A. ... Fort Lauderdale, FL
Miami, FL
Cole, Janet B. ... Abington, MA
Cole, Janice M. ... Raleigh, NC
Cole, Jas. E. ... Jackson, MS
Cole, Jeanette L. ... Baltimore, MD
Cole, Jeanne M. ... Chicago, IL
Cole, Jeannie B. ... Huntsville, AL
Cole, Jeffrey ... Chicago, IL
Cole, Jeffrey A. ... Parker, SD
Cole, Jeffrey J. ... San Francisco, CA
Cole, Jeffrey J. ... Erie, PA
Cole, Jeffrey M. ... Lake Charles, LA
Cole, Jeffrey M. ... New York, NY
Cole, Jesse, Jr. ... Waverly, OH
Cole, Joanne F. ... Portland, ME
Cole, Joel C. ... North Little Rock, AR
Cole, John A. ... New York, NY
Cole, John B. ... Auburn, ME
Cole, John D. ... Baltimore, MD
Cole, John D. ... Charlotte, NC
Cole, John David ... Bowling Green, KY
Cole, John David, Jr. ... Bowling Green, KY
Cole, John H. W. ... Shelburne, VT
Cole, John J., (P.C.) ... St. Louis, MO
Cole, John L. ... Birmingham, AL
Cole, John N. ... Newport, RI
Cole, John O. ... Macon, GA
Cole, John P. ... Jacksonville, FL
Cole, John P. ... Macon, GA
Cole, John P., Jr. ... Washington, DC
Cole, John W. ... Malvern, AR
Cole, John W. ... Ottawa, KS
Cole, Jonathan ... Orlando, FL
Cole, Jonathan ... Nashville, TN
Cole, Jonathan B. ... Sherman Oaks, CA
Cole, Jonathan E. ... Palm Beach, FL
Cole, Jonathan S.
Environmental Protection Agency, Office of Enforcement and Compliance Assurance, GV
Cole, Jonathan W. ... New York, NY
Cole, Joseph J. ... Chicago, IL
Cole, Joseph L. ... Santa Barbara, CA
Cole, Judith A. ... Federal Trade Commission, Bureau of Competition, GV
Cole, Judith K. ... Department of State, Office of the Legal Adviser, GV
Cole, Julie L. ... St. Joseph, MO
Cole, Karen K. ... Jacksonville, FL
Cole, Karen Rae ... Minneapolis, MN
Cole, Kathleen L. ... Palatine, IL
Cole, Kathryn B. ... Durham, NC
Cole, Kathryn M. ... Washington, DC
Cole, Kecia Khae ... Oklahoma City, OK
Cole, Keith H., Jr. ... Dallas, TX
Cole, Keith N. ... Washington, DC
Cole, Kelli C. ... Birmingham, AL
Cole, Kendall M. ... Naples, FL
Cole, Kenneth B., Jr. ... Huntsville, AL
Cole, Kenneth G. ... Cleveland, OH
Cole, Kenneth G. ... Oklahoma City, OK
Cole, Kenneth H. ... Hyattsville, MD
Cole, Kenneth L. ... Russell, KS
Cole, Kenneth M., III ... Portland, ME
Cole, Kenneth M., Jr. ... Dallas, TX
Cole, Kenneth W. ... Washington, DC
Cole, Kevin L. ... San Diego, CA
Cole, Kevin L. ... Mandeville, LA
Metairie, LA
Cole, Kevin P. ... Cleveland, OH
Cole, Kevin T. ... Portland, ME
Cole, Kevin W. ... Jonesboro, AR
Cole, Kevin Wayne ... Austin, TX
Cole, Kimberly ... Auburn, CA
Cole, L. David ... Beverly Hills, CA
Cole, Larry M. ... Jersey City, NJ
Cole, Larry P. ... Memphis, TN
Cole, Larry R. ... Spearfish, SD
Cole, Laura A. ... Alton, IL
Cole, Laura J. ... Chicago, IL
Cole, Laura Richmond ... San Antonio, TX
Cole Law Offices, P.C. ... Bath, NY
Hammondsport, NY
Cole, L. David, A Law Corporation
Beverly Hills, CA
Cole, Leah R. ... Fresno, CA
Cole, Leigh Polk ... Burlington, VT
Cole, Leland D. ... Akron, OH
Cole, Leslie M. B. ... Los Angeles, CA
Cole & Lewis ... Gallipolis, OH
Jackson, OH
McArthur, OH
Pomeroy, OH
Waverly, OH
Cole, Lewis G. ... New York, NY
Cole, Lewis N. ... Ramona, CA
Cole, Linda J. ... Houston, TX
Cole, Lisa R. ... Nashville, TN
Cole, Liz Ryan ... South Royalton, VT
Cole, Lloyd E., Jr. ... Stilwell, OK
Cole & Loeterman ... Los Angeles, CA
Cole, Lois J. ... Cleveland, OH
Cole, Louis I. ... Dallas, TX
Cole, Luther F. ... Baton Rouge, LA
Cole, Lynda L. ... Moraga, CA
Cole, Lynn H. ... Tampa, FL
Cole, Lynn Hamilton, P.A., Law Offices of
Tampa, FL
Cole, M. Susan ... Americus, GA
Seattle, WA

Cole, Madeleine Birmingham ... St. Louis, MO
Cole, Marjorie F. ... Treasury Department, Office of Regulations and Rulings, GV
Cole, Mark D. ... New York, NY
Cole, Mark J. ... Houston, TX
Cole, Mark S. ... Seattle, WA
Cole, Martin A. ... St. Paul, MN
Cole, Martin S. ... New York, NY
Cole, Marvin F. ... Richmond, VA
Cole, Mary A. Securities and Exchange Commission, Division of Investment Management, GV
Cole, Maryland Hartge ... Catonsville, MD
Cole, Matthew A. ... New York, NY
Cole, Maurice Y., Jr. ... Brigantine, NJ
Cole, Melissa A. ... New York, NY
Cole, Melvin C. ... Rochester, NY
Cole, Melvin J. ... Chicago, IL
Cole, Merritt A. ... Philadelphia, PA
Cole, Michael A. ... Houston, TX
Cole, Michael D. ... Kansas City, MO
Cole, Michael E. ... Hartford, CT
Cole, Michael F. ... Washington, DC
Cole, Michael P. ... Berkeley, CA
Cole, Michael P. ... Lynn, MA
Cole, Michael R. ... Troy, MI
Cole, Michael R. ... Teaneck, NJ
Cole, Michael S. ... Small Business Administration, GV
Cole, Michael T. ... Charleston, SC
Cole, Michele T. ... Pittsburgh, PA
Cole, Michelle Jerusalem ... Atlanta, GA
Cole, Miriam T. ... Chicago, IL
Cole, Mitzi G. ... St. Davids, PA
Cole, Montgomery ... Long Beach, CA
Cole, Montina M. ... Washington, DC
Cole, Moore & Baker ... Bowling Green, KY
Cole, Morrill J. ... Hackensack, NJ
Cole, Morry S. ... St. Louis, MO
Cole, Morton E. ... Hartford, CT
Cole, Murray L. ... Wayne, NJ
Cole, Nancy A. ... Medford, MA
Cole, Nancy Long ... Cerritos, CA
Cole, Nathan, Jr. ... Louisburg, NC
Cole, Neil ... Purchase, NY
Cole, Neil A. ... Portland, OR
Cole, Norman D. ... Salem, OR
Cole, Orville J. ... Garnett, KS
Cole, P. Michael ... Athens, AL
Cole, Pamela ... San Francisco, CA
Cole, Pamela Patrick ... Greenville, SC
Cole, Patricia C. ... Oberlin, LA
Cole, Patricia Cash ... Birmingham, AL
Cole, Patricia E. ... Mountain View, CA
Cole, Patrick B. ... Fairbanks, AK
Cole, Paul Charles ... San Jose, CA
Cole, Paul K. ... Fairfax, VA
Cole, Paul R. ... Champaign, IL
Cole, Paula L. ... Detroit, MI
Cole, Peggy S. ... Northridge, CA
Cole, Peter D. ... Boston, MA
Cole, Peter M. ... Ossipee, NH
Cole, Philip G. ... Vero Beach, FL
Cole, Philip J. ... Miami, FL
Cole, Philip T. ... El Paso, TX
Cole, Phillip A. ... Minneapolis, MN
Cole, R. Guy, Jr. ... Columbus, OH
Cole, R. John, II ... Sarasota, FL
Cole, R. John, II, P.A. ... Sarasota, FL
Cole, R. Michael ... Cleveland, OH
Cole, R. Michael ... Tulsa, OK
Cole, R. Rosser ... Glendale, CA
Cole, Ralph C. ... Chevy Chase, MD
Cole, Ralph D., Jr. ... Findlay, OH
Cole, Randal Ray ... Troy, MI
Cole, Randall A. ... Cleveland, OH
Cole, Randall L. ... Fort Payne, AL
Cole, Raymond L. ... Bay City, TX
Cole, Raywid & Braverman, L.L.P. Washington, DC; Fairfax, VA
Cole, Rebecca J. ... Houston, TX
Cole, Richard ... Edmonds, WA
Cole, Richard A. ... Seattle, WA
Cole, Richard A., P.S., The Law Firm of Seattle, WA
Cole, Richard B. ... Albuquerque, NM
Cole, Richard G. ... Forestville, CA
Cole, Richard G. ... Department of Commerce, Patent and Trademark Office, GV
Cole, Richard H. ... Buffalo, NY
Cole, Richard L., Jr. ... Norristown, PA
Cole, Richard M., III ... Houston, TX
Cole, Richard P. ... Springfield, MA
Cole, Richard P., (P.A.) ... Miami, FL
Cole, Richard R. ... Anchorage, AK
Cole, Richard T. ... Springfield, OH
Cole, Richard T., (P.S.) ... Ellensburg, WA
Cole, Richard W. ... Boston, MA
Cole, Richard W. ... Buffalo, NY
Cole, Robert A. ... Jacksonville, FL
Cole, Robert A. ... Battle Creek, MI
Cole, Robert A. ... Knoxville, TN
Cole, Robert D., Jr. ... Baltimore, MD
Cole, Robert E. ... Philadelphia, PA
Cole, Robert Eugene ... Mesa, AZ
Cole, Robert G. ... Denver, CO
Cole, Robert H. ... Berkeley, CA
Cole, Robert H. ... Bath, NY; Hammondsport, NY
Cole, Robert H., Jr. ... Corning, NY
Cole, Robert J. ... Niles, IL
Cole, Robert J. ... New York, NY
Cole, Robert Jeffery ... Dallas, TX
Cole, Robert L. ... Decatur, IL
Cole, Robert L. ... Lafayette, LA
Cole, Robert L. ... Las Cruces, NM
Cole, Robert L., Jr. ... Bryan, TX
Cole, Robert M. ... Davis, CA
Cole, Robert P. ... Dade City, FL
Cole, Robert P. ... Huntley, IL
Cole, Robert R. ... Dallas, TX
Cole, Robert R. ... Stanwood, WA
Cole, Robert R., Jr. ... Dallas, TX
Cole, Robert T. ... Washington, DC
Cole, Robert W. ... Oklahoma City, OK
Cole, Robt. W. ... Sacramento, CA
Cole, Rodger ... Palo Alto, CA
Cole, Roger E. ... Mobile, AL
Cole, Roger E. ... Winston-Salem, NC
Cole, Roland A. ... Portland, ME
Cole, Roland J. ... Kansas City, MO
Cole, Rollin W. ... Shreveport, LA
Cole, Ronald C. ... Baltimore, MD; Glen Burnie, MD
Cole, Ronald H. ... Lake City, FL
Cole, Ronald J. ... Indianapolis, IN
Cole, Ronald M. ... Irvine, CA
Cole, Ronald T. ... San Diego, CA
Cole, Ronald V. ... Elkins Park, PA
Cole, Ronnie M. ... Anderson, SC
Cole, Roy E. ... Farmington Hills, MI
Cole, Roy L. ... Garnett, KS
Cole, Russell A., Jr. ... Bonifay, FL
Cole, Russell J. ... Los Angeles, CA
Cole, Ryan G. ... Tulsa, OK
Cole, S. Michael ... Woodland Hills, CA
Cole, Sam F., Jr. ... Memphis, TN
Cole, Samuel D. ... Walnut Creek, CA
Cole, Sandra Lefler ... Tulsa, OK
Cole, Sarah Rudolph ... Chicago, IL
Cole, Schotz, Meisel, Forman & Leonard, P.A., A Professional Corporation Hackensack, NJ
Cole, Scott ... La Mesa, CA
Cole, Scott A. ... Miami, FL
Cole, Scott C. ... Indianapolis, IN
Cole, Scott C., P.C. ... Indianapolis, IN
Cole, Scott L. ... Dallas, TX
Cole, Sean A.B. ... Raleigh, NC
Cole, Sharon L. ... Oklahoma City, OK
Cole, Shawn Junkins ... Montgomery, AL
Cole, Shelley A. ... Owings Mills, MD
Cole, Shirley H. ... Palm Springs, CA
Cole, Sonya E. ... Durham, NC
Cole, Sorrentino, Hurley & Hewner, P.C. Buffalo, NY
Cole, Stacey L. ... Orlando, FL
Cole & Staes, Ltd. ... Chicago, IL
Cole, Stanley G. ... Rupert, ID
Cole, Stanley Z. ... Los Altos Hills, CA
Cole, Stephanie J. ... Anchorage, AK
Cole, Stephen E. ... Yellowstone Park, WY
Cole, Stephen Lawrence ... Miami, FL
Cole, Stephen M. ... Kansas City, MO
Cole, Stephen N. ... West Sacramento, CA
Cole, Stephen N. & Associates, Law Office Of West Sacramento, CA
Cole, Stephen O. ... Clearwater, FL
Cole, Stephen T. ... Los Angeles, CA
Cole, Steve W. ... Kodiak, AK
Cole, Steven E. ... Rochester, NY
Cole, Steven J. ... Arlington, VA
Cole, Steven P. ... Oklahoma City, OK
Cole, Steven R. ... Troy, MI
Cole, Steven W. ... Wichita, KS
Cole, Steven Warren ... Marietta, GA
Cole, Steven Warren, P.C. ... Marietta, GA
Cole, Stone, Stoudemire, Morgan & Dore, P.A. ... Jacksonville, FL
Cole, Stuart A. ... Columbus, OH
Cole, Susan ... Pasadena, CA
Cole, Susan J. ... Miami, FL
Cole, Susan J. ... Boston, MA
Cole, Susan S. ... Macon, GA
Cole, T. David ... Chicago, IL
Cole, T. Edward ... Knoxville, TN
Cole, Teresa S. ... Culpeper, VA
Cole, Terry ... Tallahassee, FL
Cole, Terry K. ... Modesto, CA
Cole, Theron J. ... Sitka, AK
Cole, Thomas A. ... Marietta, GA
Cole, Thomas A. ... Chicago, IL
Cole, Thomas Charles ... Fort Collins, CO
Cole, Thomas J., Jr. ... Philadelphia, PA
Cole, Thomas L. ... Savannah, GA
Cole, Thomas L. ... Mansfield, OH
Cole, Thomas M. ... Gainesville, GA
Cole, Thomas M. ... Knoxville, TN
Cole, Thomas P. ... Roseland, NJ
Cole, Thomas P., II ... Greensburg, PA
Cole, Thomas R. ... Wailuku, HI
Cole, Thomas T. ... Lebanon, OH
Cole, Thomas W. ... McLean, VA
Cole, Timothy S. ... Paoli, PA
Cole, Tobias A. ... Houston, TX
Cole, Todd Aeron ... Tulsa, OK
Cole, Tom C. ... Yuma, AZ
Cole, Tom Hunt, Jr. ... Jackson, MS
Cole, Tracy Applegate ... Hutchinson, KS
Cole, Troy J. ... Indianapolis, IN
Cole, Vincent J. ... Lexington, KY
Cole, W. Scott ... Gainesville, FL
Cole, W. Warren, Jr. ... Daytona Beach, FL
Cole, Walter G., Jr. ... Maryville, TN
Cole, Walter J. ... Madison, WI
Cole, Walter W., Jr. ... Tustin, CA
Cole, Warren ... Houston, TX
Cole, Warren B. Christiansted, St. Croix, VI
Cole, Wayne L. ... Denver, CO
Cole, White & Billbrough, P.A. Miami, FL; West Palm Beach, FL
Cole, Whitney L. ... New Orleans, LA
Cole, William A. ... Billings, MT
Cole, William Allen ... New York, NY
Cole, William B., Jr. ... Stateline, NV
Cole, William C. ... Kulpmont, PA
Cole, William C. ... Millington, TN
Cole, William F. ... Dallas, TX
Cole, William G. ... Department of Justice, Civil Division, GV
Cole, William J. ... Muskegon, MI
Cole, William J., III ... Jackson, MS
Cole, William K. ... Hartford, CT
Cole, William L. ... St. Louis, MO
Cole, William L., (A Professional Corporation) ... Los Angeles, CA
Cole, William Miles ... Annapolis, MD
Cole, William P. ... Oakland, CA
Cole, William P. ... San Diego, CA
Cole, William R., M.D. ... Dallas, TX
Cole, William S. ... Jackson, OH
Cole, William S. ... Madison, WI
Cole, Yadira Rodriguez ... Miami, FL
Cole-Alston, Brenda ... New York, NY
Cole-Brulé, Donna G. ... Burbank, CA
Coleburn, Lila A. ... New York, NY
Colecchi, Stephen ... Ravenna, OH
Colecchia, Theresa J. ... Pittsburgh, PA
Cole-Chu & Cipparone, L.L.C. New London, CT
Cole-Chu, Leeland J. ... New London, CT
Cole-Chu, Ruth A. ... New London, CT
Cole-Durst, Carolyn ... New York, NY
Colee, Donald L., Jr. ... Birmingham, AL
Colee & Tucker ... Birmingham, AL
Cole-Frieman, Karl A. ... San Francisco, CA
Colegrove, Bruce D. ... Montague, MA
Colegrove, Sarah W. ... Detroit, MI
Colella, A. Vince ... Southfield, MI
Colella, Benedetto ... Los Angeles, CA
Colella, Donald P. ... Syracuse, NY
Colella, Frank G. ... New York, NY
Colella, James A. ... Pittsburgh, PA
Colella, Jeanette M. ... Grand Haven, MI
Colella, Joseph M. ... River Edge, NJ
Colella & Kolczun, P.L.L. ... Lorain, OH
Colella, Laura E. ... Boston, MA
Colella, Louis J. ... Dansville, NY
Colella, Paul T. ... Middletown, NJ
Colella, Richard ... Lorain, OH
Colella, Richard J. ... Lorain, OH
Colella, Stephen A. ... Boston, MA
Colella, Ugo ... Department of Justice, Civil Division, GV
Colelli, Vincent P. ... Pittsburgh, PA
Colello, Emil ... Whiting, NJ
Colello, John J. ... Rocky Hill, CT
Coleman, A. J. ... Decatur, AL
Coleman, Alex ... Brookline, MA
Coleman, Alonzo B., Jr. ... Hillsborough, NC
Coleman, Andrew ... Chicago, IL
Coleman, Andrew D. ... Cheshire, CT
Coleman, Andrew W. ... Chicago, IL
Coleman, Anne Marie ... Kingston, RI
Coleman, Anthony G., Jr. ... Boca Raton, FL
Coleman, Anthony G., Jr., P.A. Boca Raton, FL
Coleman, Arlene L. ... Atlanta, GA
Coleman, Arthur H. ... San Francisco, CA
Coleman, Arthur H. ... Austin, TX
Coleman, Arthur H., P.C. ... Austin, TX
Coleman, Arthur L. Department of Education, Office for Civil Rights, GV
Coleman, Ashlyn A. ... Houston, TX
Coleman & Associates ... Los Angeles, CA
Coleman & Associates, P.A. ... Miami, FL
Coleman, Aubrey L., Jr. ... Atlanta, GA
Coleman, Bartlett & Associates, A Professional Corporation ... Houston, TX
Coleman, Bebette G. ... Arcadia, CA
Coleman, Ben E. ... Shreveport, LA
Coleman, Bert William ... Kansas City, MO
Coleman, Beth M. ... Clearwater, FL
Coleman, Beth M., P.A. ... Clearwater, FL
Coleman, Bevelyn A. ... Philadelphia, PA
Coleman, Beverly M. ... Burbank, CA
Coleman and Bianco ... Steubenville, OH
Coleman, Billy C. ... Lexington, SC; Saluda, SC
Coleman, Bonita ... Chicago, IL
Coleman, Bonnie C. ... Merrillville, IN; Portage, IN
Coleman, Bradley C. ... Chicago, IL
Coleman, Brian A. ... Washington, DC
Coleman, Brian A. ... Salt Lake City, UT
Coleman, Brian R. ... Palo Alto, CA
Coleman, Brittin Turner ... Birmingham, AL
Coleman, Bruce R. ... Dallas, TX
Coleman, Bruce S. ... New York, NY
Coleman, C. Caren ... Jacksonville, FL
Coleman, C. Joseph, Jr. ... Fort Dodge, IA
Coleman, C. Michelle ... Jefferson City, MO
Coleman, C. Payson, Jr. ... New York, NY
Coleman, C. Randolph ... Jacksonville, FL
Coleman, C. Randolph, P.A., Law Office of Jacksonville, FL
Coleman, Carl H. ... New York, NY
Coleman, Carl Joseph ... Fort Myers, FL
Coleman, Carlo B. ... Jeffersonville, IN
Coleman, Carolyn M. ... Indianapolis, IN
Coleman, Catherine H. ... Los Angeles, CA
Coleman, Cece Lynn Goodrich Oklahoma City, OK
Coleman, Chad E. ... Sacramento, CA
Coleman & Chambers ... Gainesville, GA
Coleman, Charles B. ... Reading, PA
Coleman, Charles Boyd, Jr. ... Jasper, TN
Coleman, Charles D. ... Richardson, TX
Coleman, Charles J. ... Rockville Centre, NY
Coleman, Charles L., III San Francisco, CA
Coleman, Charles M. ... Tuscaloosa, AL
Coleman, Charles S., II ... Indianapolis, IN
Coleman, Charles T. ... Little Rock, AR
Coleman, Chas. E. ... Tyler, TX
Coleman, Christopher C. ... Ocala, FL
Coleman, Christopher J. ... Rockledge, FL
Coleman, Christopher S. ... Phoenix, AZ
Coleman, Christopher S. Poughkeepsie, NY
Coleman, Claude S. ... Chester, SC
Coleman, Clayton A. ... Baton Rouge, LA
Coleman & Coleman ... Fort Myers, FL
Coleman, Coleman & Coleman West Point, MS
Coleman, Colin A., & Associates Boston, MA
Coleman, Colin A., & Associates Needham, MA
Coleman, Craig E. ... Pittsburgh, PA
Coleman, Craig J. ... Los Angeles, CA
Coleman, Creighton B. ... Columbia, SC; Winnsboro, SC
Coleman, Curtin R., II ... Charlottesville, VA
Coleman, Curtis C., III ... Greenville, NC
Coleman, Cynthia ... Columbus, OH
Coleman, Cynthia Lee ... Atlanta, GA
Coleman, D. Kevin ... Wheeling, WV
Coleman, Daniel H. ... Woodland Hills, CA
Coleman, Daniel T. ... Raleigh, NC
Coleman, Daren F. ... Mesa, AZ
Coleman, Darren Keith ... Longview, TX
Coleman, David ... Brentwood, TN
Coleman, David A. ... Twin Falls, ID
Coleman, David A. ... Indianapolis, IN
Coleman, David C. ... Fort Lauderdale, FL
Coleman, David G. ... Lansing, MI
Coleman, David G. ... Columbus, OH
Coleman, David H. ... Danville, IN
Coleman, David L. ... Corinth, MS
Coleman, David L. ... Philadelphia, PA
Coleman, David, Law Office of Sherman Oaks, CA
Coleman, David S. ... New York, NY
Coleman, David S. ... Brentwood, TN
Coleman, David W. ... New Fairfield, CT
Coleman, Deborah A. ... Cleveland, OH
Coleman, Deborah J. ... Boston, MA
Coleman, Deborah R. ... Washington, DC
Coleman & Dempsey ... Atlanta, GA
Coleman, Dennis M. ... Providence, RI
Coleman, Derrell A. ... Austin, TX
Coleman, Derrick ... Los Angeles, CA
Coleman, Donald ... Chicago, IL
Coleman, Donald D. ... Sun City, AZ
Coleman, Donald D. ... Ventura, CA
Coleman, Donald Ray, Jr. Jacksonville, FL
Coleman, Donna M. ... St. Louis, MO
Coleman, Donnie Jeanne ... Junction, TX
Coleman, Dorothy Burke ... Washington, DC
Coleman, Douglas ... Lyndhurst, NJ
Coleman, Douglas M. ... Washington, DC; Alexandria, VA
Coleman, Duane L. ... St. Louis, MO
Coleman, Earl B. ... Indianapolis, IN
Coleman, Easton, Lochmiller & Hall Elizabethtown, KY
Coleman, Edward D. ... Washington, DC
Coleman, Edward E. ... Anoka, MN
Coleman, Edward G. ... Springfield, IL
Coleman, Edward J., III ... Augusta, GA
Coleman, Edward S. ... Las Vegas, NV
Coleman, Edward S., A Prof. Law Corp. Las Vegas, NV
Coleman, Elaine B. ... West Hartford, CT
Coleman, Elizabeth Abbene ... Chicago, IL
Coleman, Elizabeth Fitch ... Memphis, TN
Coleman, Emanuel A. ... Huntsville, AL
Coleman and Enke ... Fort Dodge, IA
Coleman, Erin C. ... Atlanta, GA
Coleman & Eufinger ... Marysville, OH
Coleman, F. Woodrow ... Tampa, FL
Coleman, F.J. Hank ... Houston, TX
Coleman, Francis D. R. ... Victor, NY
Coleman, Francis Thomas Washington, DC
Coleman, Frank D. ... Westminster, MD
Coleman, Franklin M. ... Meridian, MS
Coleman & Friday ... Birmingham, AL
Coleman, G. Edward, III ... Memphis, TN
Coleman, Gabriella Morris ... Newark, NJ
Coleman, Gail S. Equal Employment Opportunity Commission, Office of the General Counsel, GV
Coleman, Gail V. ... Department of Labor, Office of the Solicitor, GV
Coleman, Gayle ... Boca Raton, FL
Coleman, George F., Jr. ... Winnsboro, SC
Coleman, George J., III ... Phoenix, AZ
Coleman, George T. ... Newark, NJ
Coleman, George W. ... Los Angeles, CA
Coleman, George W. ... Dallas, TX
Coleman, Gerald A. ... West Memphis, AR
Coleman, Gerald C. ... Laguna Niguel, CA
Coleman, Gerald P. ... Grundy, VA
Coleman, Gerry Curtis Rancho Santa Fe, CA
Coleman, Gledhill & Hargrave, P.C. Chapel Hill, NC; Durham, NC; Hillsborough, NC; Raleigh, NC
Coleman, Glenn B. ... New York, NY
Coleman, Gould H. ... Gardner, MA
Coleman, Granetta M. ... Washington, DC

Coleman, Gregory F. ... **Knoxville, TN**
Coleman, Gregory S. ... **Houston, TX**
Coleman, Gregory William
North Palm Beach, FL
Coleman, Gwen L. ... **Newark, NJ**
New York, NY
Coleman, H. Edmunds, III ... Winchester, VA
Coleman, H. Tobias ... Jackson, MO
Coleman, H. Yvonne, Law Offices of
Chicago, IL
Coleman, Harold D. ... Lawrenceville, NJ
Coleman, Harold, Jr. ... San Diego, CA
Coleman, Harriette R. ... **Memphis, TN**
Coleman, Harry J. ... Millburn, NJ
Coleman, Harry T. ... **Scranton, PA**
Coleman, Harvey Dennis
Virginia Beach, VA
Coleman, Harvey Dennis, & Associates, P.C.
Norfolk, VA
Virginia Beach, VA
Coleman, Hayden A. ... **New York, NY**
Coleman, Heather K. ... Charleston, SC
Coleman, Heidi Lewis
Department of Transportation,
National Highway Traffic Safety
Administration, GV
Coleman, Henry D. ... **New York, NY**
Coleman, Henry T. ... Jackson, MS
Coleman, Herbert J. ... Houston, TX
Coleman, Hillary H. ... **St. Petersburg, FL**
Coleman & Horowitt LLP ... **Fresno, CA**
Coleman, Howard A. ... Bellevue, WA
Coleman, Howard D. ... **Los Angeles, CA**
Coleman, H. S. ... Tigard, OR
Coleman, Hull & van Vliet, P.L.L.P.
Minneapolis, MN
Coleman, Hume F. ... **Tallahassee, FL**
Coleman, Ira J. ... **Miami, FL**
Coleman, Irving W. ... Allentown, PA
Coleman, J. Grant ... **New Orleans, LA**
Coleman, J. Leon ... Hollywood, FL
Coleman, J. Marshall ... McLean, VA
Coleman, J. Michael ... **Naples, FL**
Coleman, J. Michael ... **Denton, TX**
Coleman, J. Patrick ... Montrose, CO
Coleman, J. Paul ... **Johnson City, TN**
Coleman, J. Price ... **Jackson, MS**
Coleman, J. Robert ... Atlanta, GA
Coleman, J. Walker, IV ... **Charleston, SC**
Coleman, Jacqueline E. ... **Washington, DC**
Coleman, James A. ... **Santa Rosa, CA**
Coleman, James A. ... **Orlando, FL**
Coleman, James D. ... **Philadelphia, PA**
Coleman, James E., Jr. ... Durham, NC
Coleman, James E., Jr. ... **Dallas, TX**
Coleman, James H., Jr. ... Springfield, NJ
Coleman, James Julian ... **New Orleans, LA**
Coleman, James Julian, Jr.
New Orleans, LA
Coleman, James M. ... **Portland, OR**
Coleman, James M. ... **Arlington, VA**
Coleman, James M., Jr. ... Asbury Park, NJ
Coleman, James P. ... Watkins Glen, NY
Coleman, James R. ... Minneapolis, MN
Coleman, Janet ... Minneapolis, MN
Coleman, Janet K. ... Baltimore, MD
Coleman, Jean L. ... Minneapolis, MN
Coleman, Jeanne Laurie ... **Tampa, FL**
Coleman, Jeanne M. ... **Denver, CO**
Coleman, Jeff ... Ithaca, NY
Coleman, Jeffery T. ... **Atlanta, GA**
Coleman, Jeffrey P. ... **Clearwater, FL**
Coleman, Jeffrey R. ... **New York, NY**
Coleman, Jeffrey W. ... **Minneapolis, MN**
Coleman, Jennifer A., Law Office of
Buffalo, NY
Coleman, Jerome C. ... **Clayton, MO**
Coleman, Jerome F. ... Belmont, CA
Coleman, Jerome P. ... **New York, NY**
Coleman, Jerry M. ... **Elizabethtown, KY**
Coleman, Jerry M. ... El Paso, TX
Coleman, Jerry P. ... San Francisco, CA
Coleman, Jesse L. ... Indianapolis, IN
Coleman, Jill Ann ... **Chicago, IL**
Coleman, Jill E. ... Federal Trade Commission,
Office of the General Counsel, GV
Coleman, Jill L. ... Hollywood, FL
Coleman, Jo Ann ... Shasta, CA
Coleman, Joe E., (P.C.) ... **Houston, TX**
Coleman, Joe W. ... **Kansas City, MO**
Coleman, John A., Jr. ... **New York, NY**
Coleman, John B. ... Abingdon, VA
Coleman, John B. ... **Abingdon, VA**
Coleman, John B., II ... Columbia, TN
Coleman, John Charles ... **Midland City, AL**
Coleman, John Charles ... Fort Myers, FL
Coleman, John E. ... East Walpole, MA
Coleman, John E. ... Dayton, OH
Coleman, John E., Jr. ... **Franklin, LA**
Morgan City, LA
Coleman, John J., III ... **Birmingham, AL**
Coleman, John James, Jr.
Birmingham, AL
Coleman, John K. ... **Burke, VA**
Coleman, John L. ... Indianapolis, IN
Coleman, John M. ... Los Angeles, CA
Coleman, John M. ... Chicago, IL
Coleman, John Michael ... New York, NY
Coleman, John P. ... **Sacramento, CA**
Coleman, John P. ... Las Vegas, NV
Coleman, John P., Jr. ... Knoxville, TN
Coleman, John Philip ... Stamford, CT
Coleman, John R. ... **Twin Falls, ID**
Coleman, John R., Jr. ... **Gainesville, GA**
Coleman, John T. ... **Chicago, IL**
Coleman, John W. ... **Mobile, AL**
Coleman, John W. ... Talladega, AL

Coleman, Johnson & Artigues, L.L.C.
New Orleans, LA
Coleman, Jon R. ... **Jonesboro, AR**
Coleman, Jonathan M.
Department of Justice, Civil Division, GV
Coleman, Jonathan Strickland
Tampa, FL
Coleman, Joseph C. ... Grand Junction, CO
Coleman, Joseph C. ... **Columbia, SC**
Coleman, Joseph, Jr. ... Fort Dodge, IA
Coleman, Joseph L. ... Newport Beach, CA
Coleman, Joseph M. ... **Dallas, TX**
Coleman, Jouflas & Williams, LLC
Grand Junction, CO
Coleman, Joyce M. ... Lynchburg, VA
Coleman, Julianne M. Cole
Richmond, VA
Coleman, Julie Ann ... **Phoenix, AZ**
Coleman, Julie Burbank
San Francisco, CA
Coleman, June D. ... **Sacramento, CA**
Coleman, K. Brooke ... Phoenix, AZ
Coleman, Kaleonani Chang ... Honolulu, HI
Coleman, Karen D. ... Little Rock, AR
Coleman, Katherine "Kacey" M.
Richmond, KY
Coleman, Katherine M. ... **Denver, CO**
Coleman, Kathleen M. ... Groton, CT
Coleman, Kathleen M.
Environmental Protection Agency,
Office of the General Counsel, GV
Coleman, Kathleen N.
Department of Justice,
Criminal Division, GV
Coleman, Kathleen Yocca
Laguna Niguel, CA
Coleman, Kathryn Anne
San Francisco, CA
Coleman, Keith B. ... Philadelphia, PA
Coleman, Keith Chenney ... Brighton, CO
Coleman, Kelly Ann ... **Los Angeles, CA**
Coleman, Kenneth E. ... Findlay, OH
Coleman, Kenneth P. ... **New York, NY**
Coleman, Kerriann P. ... **Troy, NY**
Coleman, Kevin C. ... Larkspur, CA
Coleman, Kevin G. ... **Naples, FL**
Coleman, Kevin M. ... New York, NY
Coleman, Kevin W. ... **San Francisco, CA**
San Jose, CA
Coleman, Kimberlee R. ... Boston, MA
Coleman, Kimberly A. ... Cincinnati, OH
Coleman, L. Kevin ... New Orleans, LA
Coleman, L. Royce ... Dallas, TX
Coleman, Lara Ashley ... **Jackson, MS**
Coleman, Larry D. ... Kansas City, MO
Coleman, Larry K. ... **Bradenton, FL**
Coleman, Laura J. ... Alpharetta, GA
Coleman, Lauren Gay ... Alexandria, LA
Coleman Law Firm ... Jacksonville, NC
Coleman, Lawrence J. ... Dallas, TX
Coleman, Lee ... Downers Grove, IL
Coleman, Lee A. ... West Covina, CA
Coleman, Lee L. ... Bowling Green, KY
Coleman, Lee, P.C., Law Office of
Downers Grove, IL
Coleman, Lee S. ... West Point, MS
Coleman, Leighton H. ... New York, NY
Coleman, Leonard S. ... **Charleston, WV**
Coleman, Leslie Gattas ... **Memphis, TN**
Coleman, Lester L. ... **Dallas, TX**
Coleman, LeVawn D. ... Columbus, OH
Coleman, Lex Alan ... Chattanooga, TN
Coleman, Lisa K. ... **Washington, DC**
Coleman, Lisa K. ... Frazer, PA
Coleman, Lisa L. ... Los Angeles, CA
Coleman, Lisandré S. ... White Plains, NY
Coleman, Lonnie ... **Jericho, NY**
Coleman, Louis K. ... Baltimore, MD
Coleman, Lourdes Neely ... **Augusta, GA**
Coleman, Lovida H., Jr. ... **Washington, DC**
Coleman, Lynn E. ... **McAllen, TX**
Coleman, Lynn R. ... **Washington, DC**
Coleman, M. Graham, 2d ... **New York, NY**
Coleman, M. Wallace ... **Lawrenceburg, TN**
Nashville, TN
Coleman, Major G. ... Warren, MI
Coleman, March ... **Washington, DC**
Coleman, March Dolan ... **Richmond, VA**
Coleman, Marjorie Thalheimer
Brooklyn, NY
Coleman, Mark J. ... **San Francisco, CA**
Coleman, Mark W. ... **Fresno, CA**
Coleman, Mark Warren, Law Offices of
Valparaiso, IN
Coleman, Martha Crandall ... Dallas, TX
Coleman, Martha S. ... Wichita, KS
Coleman, Martin S. ... **Philadelphia, PA**
Coleman, Mary Ann ... Talihina, OK
Coleman, Mary Kathleen ... **Pittsburgh, PA**
Coleman, Mary Lynch ... Oak Park, IL
Coleman, Mary MacIsaac
Los Angeles, CA
Coleman & Massey, P.C. ... **Roanoke, VA**
Coleman, Matthew E. ... Los Altos, CA
Coleman, Maureen A. ... **Chicago, IL**
Coleman, Maureen A. ... **Albany, NY**
Coleman, Maureen N. ... New York, NY
Coleman & Mayo ... **Shreveport, LA**
Coleman, Michael A. ... **Columbus, OH**
Coleman, Michael Bennett ... Columbus, OH
Coleman, Michael D. ... Oklahoma City, OK
Coleman, Michael D. ... **Cranston, RI**
Coleman, Michael J. ... **San Francisco, CA**
Coleman, Michael J. ... Chicago, IL
Coleman, Michael J. ... High Ridge, MO
Coleman, Michael, Jr. ... New York, NY
Coleman, Michael L. ... **Chicago, IL**
Coleman, Michael M. ... Philadelphia, PA

Coleman, Michael S. ... San Anselmo, CA
Coleman, Michael V. ... **Atlanta, GA**
Coleman, Michael W. ... Franklin, TN
Coleman, Myron ... Steubenville, OH
Coleman, Nan Lou ... **Roanoke, VA**
Coleman, Nicholas P. ... **Washington, DC**
Coleman, N. R., Jr. ... **Greeneville, TN**
Coleman & O'Halloran, Ltd. ... Chicago, IL
Coleman, Pariss M., II ... **Toledo, OH**
Coleman, Patrice Baker ... Dearborn, MI
Coleman, Patricia A. ... Los Altos, CA
Coleman, Patricia M. ... **Los Angeles, CA**
Coleman, Patrick D. ... **Jacksonville, FL**
Coleman, Patrick N. ... Dunmore, PA
Coleman, Paul D. ... **Washington, DC**
Coleman, Paul H. ... Columbus, OH
Coleman, Paul T. ... Knoxville, TN
Coleman, Paula W. ... Department of Labor,
Office of the Solicitor, GV
Coleman & Perez ... Greenville, NC
Coleman, Peter C. ... **San Francisco, CA**
Coleman, Peter D. ... **New Orleans, LA**
Coleman, Peter Jon ... Houston, TX
Coleman, Peter S. ... Cary, NC
Coleman, Philip W. ... Bronx, NY
Coleman, Philippe C. ... Laguna Niguel, CA
Coleman, Phyllis G. ... Fort Lauderdale, FL
Coleman, R. Kenneth ... New Albany, MS
Coleman, R. Lynn ... Jacksonville, NC
Coleman, Ralph E. ... Birmingham, AL
Coleman, Ralph E. ... **Syracuse, NY**
Coleman, Randall C., III ... **Houston, TX**
Coleman, Randy ... Little Rock, AR
Coleman, Ransome A. ... **Spartanburg, SC**
Coleman, Ray J. ... Lake San Marcos, CA
Coleman, Reford H. ... **Elizabethtown, KY**
Coleman, Regina T. ... **Los Angeles, CA**
Coleman, Rhine & Goodwin LLP
New York, NY
Coleman, Richard H.
North Massapequa, NY
Coleman, Richard J. ... **West St. Paul, MN**
Coleman, Richard L. ... **Valdosta, GA**
Coleman, Richard M. ... **Los Angeles, CA**
Coleman, Richard W. ... Boston, MA
Coleman & Richards, A Professional Corporation ... **Los Angeles, CA**
Coleman, Ritchie & Robertson
Twin Falls, ID
Coleman, Robert B., Jr. ... Afton, OK
Coleman, Robert Emmet ... New York, NY
Coleman, Robert F. ... **West Covina, CA**
Coleman, Robert F., & Associates
Chicago, IL
Coleman, Robert J. ... Fort Myers, FL
Coleman, Robert J. ... **Philadelphia, PA**
Coleman, Robert L. ... Oakland, CA
Coleman, Robert L. ... Peotone, IL
Coleman, Robert L. ... Kansas City, MO
Coleman, Robert Lynn ... **Blytheville, AR**
Coleman, Robert P. ... **Philadelphia, PA**
Coleman, Robert P. ... **Manassas, VA**
Coleman, Robert R. ... Tuscaloosa, AL
Coleman, Robert S., Jr. ... Little Rock, AR
Coleman, Robert T., III ... **Greenville, SC**
Coleman, Robert W., (P.C.) ... **Dallas, TX**
Coleman, Roderick F. ... Miami, FL
Coleman, Rodney V. ... Cleveland, OH
Coleman, Roe Ellen ... Nashville, TN
Coleman, Roland L., Jr. ... **Los Angeles, CA**
Coleman, Ronald D. ... **Morristown, NJ**
Coleman, Ronald D. ... El Paso, TX
Coleman, Ronald G. ... San Jose, CA
Coleman, Ronald L. ... **Tacoma, WA**
Coleman, Ronald R., Jr. ... Sandy Springs, GA
Coleman, Ronald Ray, Jr. ... **Atlanta, GA**
Coleman, Ronald T., Jr. ... **Atlanta, GA**
Coleman, Ronnae Lee, (Mr.)
Kansas City, MO
Coleman, Rudy B. ... Newark, NJ
Coleman, Russell F. ... **Dallas, TX**
Coleman, Ryan Reese ... Philadelphia, PA
Coleman, S.J. & Associates ... Santa Ana, CA
Coleman, S. Walt, IV ... **Charlotte, NC**
Coleman & St. Martin ... Gate City, VA
Coleman, Samuel E ... **Hillsborough, NC**
Coleman, Samuel Melville ... Charleston, SC
Summerville, SC
Coleman, Samuel W., III ... Richmond, VA
Coleman, Sana D. ... **Washington, DC**
Coleman, Sandra J. ... Santa Ana, CA
Coleman, Sanford D. ... Boulder, CO
Coleman, Scott A. ... **Minneapolis, MN**
Coleman, Scott R. ... New York, NY
Coleman, Sean J. ... **Atlanta, GA**
Coleman, Sean J. ... Fairfax, VA
Coleman, Sean L. ... Annapolis, MD
Coleman & Sedlak ... **Decatur, AL**
Coleman & Seife ... White Plains, NY
Coleman, Selwyn ... Roselle, IL
Coleman, Shane P. ... **Billings, MT**
Coleman, Sharon A. ... Millbrae, CA
Coleman, Sharon K. ... Scottsdale, AZ
Coleman, Shelbonnie Larnail ... Opelika, AL
Coleman, Shelley W. ... **Charlotte, NC**
Coleman, Sherwood S. (Flip)
Clearwater, FL
Coleman, Staci D. ... **Washington, DC**
Coleman, Stan, (P.C.) ... **Beverly Hills, CA**
Coleman, Stephanie L. ... Lansing, MI
Coleman, Stephen A., P.C.
Oklahoma City, OK
Coleman, Stephen G. ... Marysville, OH
Coleman, Stephen M. ... Lake Jackson, TX
Coleman, Stephen P. ... Clearwater, FL
Coleman, Steven E. ... Cleveland, OH
Coleman, Steven F. ... Minneapolis, MN
Coleman, Steven F. ... St. Paul, MN

Coleman, Stuart H. ... **New York, NY**
Coleman Sudol, LLP ... **New York, NY**
Coleman, Susan E. ... **Fort Worth, TX**
Coleman, Susan W. ... Garrison, NY
Coleman, Talley, Newbern, Kurrie, Preston & Holland, LLP ... **Valdosta, GA**
Coleman, Ted P. ... Kissimmee, FL
Coleman, Terrence J. ... **San Francisco, CA**
Coleman, Terri-Lynn ... **Fairbanks, AK**
Coleman, Terry ... **Washington, DC**
Coleman, Thomas ... Birmingham, AL
Coleman, Thomas A. ... Jackson, MS
Coleman, Thomas A. ... Portland, OR
Coleman, Thomas B. ... Live Oak, FL
Coleman, Thomas C., Jr. ... Jamestown, TN
Coleman, Thomas F. ... Los Angeles, CA
Coleman, Thomas F. ... **Minneapolis, MN**
Coleman, Thomas H., Jr. ... Midland, TX
Coleman, Thomas Henry
Los Angeles, CA
Coleman, Thomas J. ... Los Angeles, CA
Coleman, Thomas J. ... Shreve, OH
Coleman, Thomas J., III ... **Cherry Hill, NJ**
Coleman, Thomas, Jr. ... **Birmingham, AL**
Coleman, Thomas Y. ... **San Francisco, CA**
Coleman, Timothy J. ... New York, NY
Coleman, Timothy J. ... **Portland, OR**
Coleman, Timothy Ray ... Lexington, KY
Coleman, Todd C. ... Omaha, NE
Coleman, Tom F. ... Houston, TX
Coleman, Tom G., Jr. ... Brentwood, TN
Coleman, Tommy ... **Albany, GA**
Coleman, Tony C. ... **Louisville, KY**
Coleman, Tucker S. ... Gate City, VA
Coleman, Veronica F. ... Memphis, TN
Coleman, Vicki Gregory ... Washington, NC
Coleman, Victoria Ann
West Palm Beach, FL
Coleman, Virginia F. ... **Boston, MA**
Coleman, W. Brad, P.C., & Associates
Salem, OR
Coleman, W. Bradley ... Salem, OR
Coleman, W. Chris ... **Oklahoma City, OK**
Coleman, W. Harrison, Jr. ... **Atlanta, GA**
Coleman, W. Jackson
Department Of The Interior,
Office of the Solicitor, GV
Coleman, W. Kent ... Murfreesboro, TN
Coleman, W. Robert ... **Jackson, MS**
Coleman, W. Stephen ... Richmond, VA
Coleman, W. Todd ... **Phoenix, AZ**
Coleman, Wade H. ... **Valdosta, GA**
Coleman & Wallace ... Buckhannon, WV
Coleman, Wendy Theophilos
Palo Alto, CA
Coleman, Wilby C. ... Valdosta, GA
Coleman, William D. ... **Montgomery, AL**
Coleman, William D. ... Jackson, MS
Coleman, William F. ... Jackson, MS
Coleman, William F., Jr. ... Fairfax, VA
Coleman, William G. ... Tonawanda, NY
Coleman, William H. ... **Fresno, CA**
Coleman, William R. ... Richmond, VA
Coleman, William R., Jr. ... Evans, GA
Coleman, William S., Jr. ... Columbia, SC
Coleman, William T. ... **Fort Lauderdale, FL**
Coleman, William T. ... Chicago, IL
Coleman, William T., III
Department of the Army,
Office of the General Counsel, GV
Coleman, William T., Jr. ... **Washington, DC**
Coleman, William T., Jr. ... Huntsville, TX
Coleman, William V. ... **Philadelphia, PA**
Coleman, Wm. H., Jr. ... Washington, DC
Coleman & Wood, A Professional Corporation
Fairfax, VA
Coleman-Irwin, C. ... Westerville, OH
Coleman James, Patricia ... San Francisco, CA
Coleman-Lee, Genia ... Lake Charles, LA
Colen, Alyse Ghee ... Gladwyne, PA
Colen, Frederick H. ... **Pittsburgh, PA**
Colen, Gerald R. ... **Largo, FL**
Colen, Jeffrey A. ... Norristown, PA
Colen, Marc Steven ... Woodland Hills, CA
Colen, Stephanie R. ... Clearwater, FL
Colender, Andrea E. ... Annapolis, MD
Cole-Palmer, Karlene Marie
Fort Lauderdale, FL
Coler, Susan M. ... **Minneapolis, MN**
Colerick, Jeffrey J. ... **Colorado Springs, CO**
Coles, Anthony C. ... **New York, NY**
Coles, Barbara Carrington
General Accounting Office,
Office of the General Counsel, GV
Coles, Carl E. ... Hilliard, OH
Coles, D. Bruce ... **Denver, CO**
Coles, George M., Jr. ... Charlottesville, VA
Coles, James A. ... **Indianapolis, IN**
Coles, John M.
Federal Communications Commission,
International Bureau, GV
Coles, Kathleen L. ... De Kalb, IL
Coles, Kevin ... **Memphis, TN**
Coles, Kevin A. ... Fairfield, CT
Coles, Lawrence A., Jr. ... **Chicago, IL**
Coles, Matthew A. ... San Francisco, CA
Coles, Matthew S. ... **Atlanta, GA**
Coles, Melinda J. ... Vacaville, CA
Coles, Michael E. ... **Dallas, TX**
Coles, Michael F. ... **Bloomington, IL**
Coles, O'Connell, Dolan & McDonald, P.C.
Bridgeport, CT
Coles, Robert L. ... Moorestown, NJ
Coles, Ronald R. ... **Kennebunk, ME**
Coles, Stephen W. ... **Lexington, NC**
Coles, Terence A. ... Washington, DC
Coles, Terence E. ... **Boston, MA**

Coles & Thompson, LLC
Kennebunk, ME
Coles, Todd R. .... **Washington, DC**
Coles, Truman E. .... Riverdale, GA
Coles, Virginia R. .... Mountain View, CA
Colesanti, Anthony .... **Philadelphia, PA**
Colesanti, J. Scott .... New York, NY
Coleson, Janet E. .... **San Francisco, CA**
Coleson, Richard E. .... **Terre Haute, IN**
Colessides, Nick J. .... **Salt Lake City, UT**
Coles-Stewart, Sharon A.
Newport News, VA
Colestock, Robert D. .... Clearwater, FL
Fort Wayne, IN
Coleston, Howard J., Jr. .... Berkeley, CA
Colett, Charles D. .... Portland, OR
Colett, Rose Sahlberg .... Lake Oswego, OR
Coletta, Andria .... **Boston, MA**
Providence, RI
Coletta, Cristina V. .... **Boston, MA**
Coletta, Edmond R. .... Warwick, RI
Coletta, James P. .... Carnegie, PA
Coletta, John .... **New York, NY**
Coletta, Joseph Michael .... Highland Park, IL
Coletta, Karen A. .... Norristown, PA
Coletta, Michael A. .... Menlo Park, CA
Coletta, Phyllis .... Atlantic City, NJ
Pleasantville, NJ
Coletta, Ralph J. .... Peoria, IL
Coletta, Raymond R. .... Sacramento, CA
Coletta, Robert J. .... **Peoria, IL**
Colette, John M. .... **Jackson, MS**
Colette, John M., & Associates, P.A.
Jackson, MS
Coletti, Alterio A. .... New York, NY
Coletti, Carroll D. .... Easton, MA
Coletti, David L. .... Rego Park, NY
Coletti, David R. .... Rochester, NY
Coletti, John M. .... **Portland, OR**
Coletti, Julie A. .... **Pittsburgh, PA**
Coletti, Michael A. .... **Los Angeles, CA**
Coletti, Paul A. .... New Brunswick, NJ
Coletti, Robert E. .... **Cincinnati, OH**
Coletti, Robert J., Jr. .... Hauppauge, NY
Coley, Christopher R. .... **Reno, NV**
Coley, Darnell D. .... **Montgomery, AL**
Coley, David R., III .... **Mobile, AL**
Coley, Edward .... Fairhope, AL
Coley, Elizabeth A. .... **New York, NY**
Coley, F. Luke, Jr. .... **Mobile, AL**
Coley, J. William .... **Knoxville, TN**
Coley, John E., Jr. .... **Warren, NJ**
Coley, Julia Smartt .... Los Angeles, CA
Coley, Maurita K. .... **Washington, DC**
Coley, Mickey C. .... Oklahoma City, OK
Coley, Randolph C. .... **Houston, TX**
Coley, Robert L. .... Atlanta, GA
Coley, Roger D. .... Bakersfield, CA
Coley, Roger D., A Professional Corporation
Bakersfield, CA
Coley, William C., III .... Kinston, NC
Coley, William P., II .... Cincinnati, OH
Colfer, Gerald F. .... Silver Spring, MD
Colfer, James W. .... **Los Angeles, CA**
Colfer, Thomas F. .... **McCook, NE**
Colfer, Wood, Lyons & Wood
McCook, NE
Colfin, Bruce E. .... **New York, NY**
Colflesh, Ralph H., Jr. .... **Cherry Hill, NJ**
Philadelphia, PA
Colgan, Allison B. .... **Baltimore, MD**
Colgan, Charles T. .... Elkton, MD
Colgan, David L. .... **Irvine, CA**
Colgan, James P. .... Kansas City, KS
Colgan, James R. .... **San Francisco, CA**
Colgan, Mark .... Indianapolis, IN
Colgan, Michael B. .... **Tampa, FL**
Colgan, Michael J. .... La Crosse, WI
Colgan, Patricia Margaret .... Carle Place, NY
Colgan, Richard J. .... Virginia Beach, VA
Colgan, Timothy J. .... **Dillsburg, PA**
Colgate, Jessie M. .... Washington, DC
Colgate, Kimberly Adams .... Sarasota, FL
Colgin, Deborah L. Lowham .... McLean, VA
Colgin, Lisa Rey .... **Houston, TX**
Colgin, William F., Jr. .... **Palo Alto, CA**
Colgin, William M., IV .... Richmond, TX
Colglazier, Jerry L. .... Surprise, AZ
Colglazier, Michael D. .... **Baltimore, MD**
Colglazier, Raymond E., Jr.
Saint Simons Island, GA
Colgo, Joseph J., Jr. .... West Long Branch, NJ
Colgrove, Peter B. .... **Melville, NY**
Colhour, Sandra J. .... **Columbia, MO**
Coli, Gerald A. .... Coventry, RI
Coli, Robert J. .... Los Angeles, CA
Las Vegas, NV
Colia, Milton C. .... **El Paso, TX**
Coliane, Norman A. .... Wexford, PA
Colianni, Vincent .... **Palo Alto, CA**
Colianni, Vincent A.
Christiansted, St. Croix, VI
Colicchio, Philip M. .... **Princeton, NJ**
Plymouth Meeting, PA
Colicchio, Roy E. .... **Rochester, NY**
Colihan, Hugh J. .... Philadelphia, PA
Colihan, James C. .... **New York, NY**
Colihan, Jennifer Lee .... **Baltimore, MD**
Colihan, Michael .... Brooklyn, NY
Colin, Andrew .... Irvington, NY
Colin, Charles R. .... Brooklyn, NY
Colin, John A. .... Ashtabula, OH
Colin, Lisa .... **Pearl River, NY**
Colin, Marc F. .... Denver, CO
Colin, Martin H. .... Lake Worth, FL
Colin, Samuel A. .... New York, NY
Colin, Stevan .... Torrance, CA
Colin, Thomas D. .... **Greenwich, CT**
Colingo, Joe R. .... **Pascagoula, MS**
Colingo, Williams, Heidelberg, Steinberger & McElhaney, P.A. .... **Biloxi, MS**
Gulfport, MS
Hattiesburg, MS
Jackson, MS
Lucedale, MS
Natchez, MS
Ocean Springs, MS
Pascagoula, MS
Colins, James Gardner .... Philadelphia, PA
Colins, Mary D. .... Philadelphia, PA
Colinvaux, Catherine M. .... **Waltham, MA**
Colinvaux, Roger P. .... **Washington, DC**
Colip, Greg R. .... Houston, TX
Colip, John R. .... **Buchanan, MI**
Colis, Thomas D. .... **Detroit, MI**
Colish, Faith .... New York, NY
Colish, Faith, A Prof. Corp. .... New York, NY
Colista, F. Philip .... Ann Arbor, MI
Colistro, Donald J. .... Spokane, WA
Colitz, Michael J., III .... **Largo, FL**
Colitz, Michael J., Jr., Law Office of
Largo, FL
Coliver, Norman .... San Francisco, CA
Colker, David .... **Palo Alto, CA**
Colker, David .... Evanston, IL
Colker, Pamela B.
Department of Labor, GV
Colkitt, Benjamin E., III .... Englewood, CO
Colkitt, Marcy L. .... **Indiana, PA**
Colkitt, Marcy L., & Associates, P.C.
Indiana, PA
Colky, Scott C. .... **Chicago, IL**
Colky, Scott C., & Associates, Ltd.
Chicago, IL
Coll, Alexis S. .... **New York, NY**
Coll, Charles H. .... **Roswell, NM**
Coll, Clarke C. .... **Roswell, NM**
Coll, Cristina S. .... Miami, FL
Coll Davidson Smith Salter & Barkett, P.A.
Miami, FL
Coll, Dennis M. .... Cheyenne, WY
Coll, Eric J. .... **Roswell, NM**
Coll, Geoffrey H. .... **New York, NY**
Coll, J. Peter, Jr. .... **New York, NY**
Coll, John R. .... **Phoenix, AZ**
Coll, Lauren C. .... Coral Gables, FL
Coll, Lynne A. .... Norwalk, CT
Coll, Max .... Santa Fe, NM
Coll, Norman A. .... **Miami, FL**
Coll, Patrick P. .... **Jacksonville, FL**
Coll, Pelayo .... **Washington, DC**
Coll, Richard J. .... **New York, NY**
Coll, Robert W. .... Washington, DC
Coll, Thomas A. .... **San Diego, CA**
Colla, Raymond A., Jr. .... **Hartford, CT**
Colladay, Coralyn
Department Of Health And Human Services, GV
Colladay, Sharli .... **Los Angeles, CA**
Collado, Ana Margarita .... Coral Gables, FL
Collado & Collado .... Brentwood, NY
Collado, John J. .... Brentwood, NY
Collado, Victoria R. .... **Chicago, IL**
Collado, William J. .... Brentwood, NY
Collaer, Phillip J. .... **Boise, ID**
Collander, Dan M. .... Naperville, IL
Collander, Deborah H. .... Naperville, IL
Collanton, Roger E. .... **Walnut Creek, CA**
Collanton, Valerie E. .... Fremont, CA
Collar, John Lind, Jr. .... **Atlanta, GA**
Collar, Melissa Nestico .... **Grand Rapids, MI**
Collard, Allison C. .... **Roslyn, NY**
Collard, Carol D. .... **Buffalo, NY**
Collard, Clifford G. .... Newport, OR
Collard, E. Bert, Jr. .... Leavenworth, KS
Collard, Gregory A. .... **Newport Beach, CA**
Collard, Kathryn .... Salt Lake City, UT
Collard, Kathryn, L.C., The Law Firm of
Salt Lake City, UT
Collard, Peter M. .... **Buffalo, NY**
Collard, Richard T. .... Chandler, TX
Collard & Roe, P.C. .... **Roslyn, NY**
Collard, Stacey L. .... **Orlando, FL**
Collard, William .... **Roslyn, NY**
Collard, William Edwin .... Houston, TX
Collard, William H. .... **Sacramento, CA**
Collari, Dennis L. .... Plymouth, MA
Collari, Richard L., Jr.
Walnut Creek, CA
Collarile, Paul J. .... Yonkers, NY
Collaros, Sophia S. .... Santa Fe, NM
Collatos, Theodore S. .... Beverly, MA
Collazo, Agustin, Law Office .... San Juan, PR
Collazo Carling & Mish LLP
New York, NY
Collazo, Cynthia Hawkins .... Orlando, FL
Collazo, Erik D. .... New Brunswick, NJ
Collazo, Ernest J. .... **New York, NY**
Collazo, Jesus A. .... Brick, NJ
Neptune, NJ
Collazo, Ramira .... Indianapolis, IN
Collazo, Salvador .... Bronx, NY
Collazo, Sharon Kay .... Bronx, NY
Collazo-Bougeois, Alys M. .... **Ponce, PR**
Collazo Correa, Sylma I. .... San Juan, PR
Collazo-Lizardi, Francisco .... San Juan, PR
Collazo Mejía, Agustín .... San Juan, PR
Collazo Mojica, Agustín .... San Juan, PR
Collazo-Rivera, Ivelisse .... **San Juan, PR**
Collazo Salazar, Baldomero .... **San Juan, PR**
Collazo Torres, Baldomero .... **San Juan, PR**
Collazo-Valencia, Gladys O.
Equal Employment Opportunity Commission,
Office of the General Counsel, GV
Coll De Pestana, Ivette .... San Juan, PR
Colle, Britt .... McPherson, KS
Colleary, Kathleen .... Boston, MA
Colleli, Ralph .... Washington, DC
Colleluori, Anthony J. .... **Farmingdale, NY**
Garden City, NY
Colleluori, Donald .... **Dallas, TX**
Collen, Jerry T. .... **St. Louis, MO**
Collen, John .... **Chicago, IL**
Collen, Sheldon O. .... Chicago, IL
Collen, Sheldon O., P.C. .... Chicago, IL
Collender, Richard A. .... Orange, CA
Collens, Lewis M. .... Chicago, IL
Collentine, John R. .... Whitefish Bay, WI
Coller, Edmond M. .... **New York, NY**
Coller, Garth C. .... Marathon, FL
Coller, Mark D.
Securities and Exchange Commission,
Division of Corporation Finance, GV
Coller, Philip L. .... Miami, FL
Coller & Rockman .... Miami, FL
Colleran, David B. .... **Boston, MA**
Colleran, Francis T. .... **Philadelphia, PA**
Colleran, James E., Jr. .... **Philadelphia, PA**
Colleran, James E., Law Offices of
Philadelphia, PA
Colleran, John W. .... **New Haven, CT**
Colleran, John W., P.C., Law Offices of
New Haven, CT
Colleran, Kevin .... **Lincoln, NE**
Colleran, Mary T. .... **Philadelphia, PA**
Colleran, Matthew G. .... Salem, MA
Colleran, Michael J. .... **Harrisburg, PA**
Philadelphia, PA
Colleran, Neil Francis .... Lexington, MA
Colleran, O'Hara & Mills
Garden City, NY
Mineola, NY
New York, NY
Colleran, Paul .... Boston, MA
Colleran, Ray, Jr. .... Norcross, GA
Colleran, Robert T. .... **New York, NY**
Colleran-McKenry, Clare C.
Coral Gables, FL
Colleran Quinn, Teresa .... **Philadelphia, PA**
Collery, Elizabeth D. .... Washington, DC
Collesano, Charles S. .... Fredonia, NY
Collesano, Mark A. .... **New York, NY**
Collesano, Stanley F. .... **Indianapolis, IN**
Collet, Charles J. .... Indianapolis, IN
Collet, Elizabeth N. .... Portland, ME
Colleton, Donald P. .... **Chicago, IL**
Colleton, Larry H. .... Orlando, FL
Colleton, Thomas E., Jr. .... Madison, NJ
Collett & Amacker .... Bogalusa, LA
Collett, Charles W. .... Annapolis, MD
Collett, Darrell D. .... **Denver, CO**
Collett, Edmond .... Hyden, KY
Collett, Gregory S.
Commodity Futures Trading Commission,
Division of Trading and Markets, GV
Collett, James William .... **Pasadena, CA**
Collett, Julie J. .... **Denver, CO**
Collett, Keith .... Marion, KS
Collett, Keith W. .... **Fairfield, OH**
Collett, Lucy A. .... **New York, NY**
Collett, Mary Ruffin .... Morganton, NC
Collett, Phillip R. .... Ottumwa, IA
Collett, Ronald E. .... Santa Clara, CA
Collett, Ronald W. .... **Phoenix, AZ**
Collett, Sam J., Jr. .... Bogalusa, LA
Collett, Thomas E. .... Cincinnati, OH
Colletta, Anthony J. .... **New York, NY**
Colletta, Dominic G. .... **Portland, OR**
Collette, Angela .... Southfield, MI
Collette, Charles T. "Chip" .... Tallahassee, FL
Collette, Curtis D. .... **Houston, TX**
Collette & Erickson LLP
San Francisco, CA
Collette, Frances M. .... Miami, FL
Collette, John M. .... **San Francisco, CA**
Collette, Kevin J. .... **Seattle, WA**
Collette, Matthew M.
Department of Justice, Civil Division, GV
Collette, Randolph P. .... Tallahassee, FL
Collette, Stephen P. .... Washington, DC
Collette, William E. .... Lansing, MI
Colletti, Anthony .... Northport, NY
Colletti, Anthony C. .... **Ardmore, PA**
Colletti, Anthony J. .... Sag Harbor, NY
Colletti, Debra Ann .... Los Angeles, CA
Colletti, Debra Jane .... Grand Rapids, MI
Colletti & Mobilia, P.C. .... Grand Rapids, MI
Colletti, Robert E. .... **New York, NY**
Colletti, Salvatore .... New York, NY
Colletti, Tony S. .... Libertyville, IL
Colley, A. Gordon, Jr. .... Shelby, NC
Colley, Adrian A. .... **San Francisco, CA**
Colley, Brian O. .... New York, NY
Colley, Christine .... Boston, MA
Colley, Dan J. .... Atlanta, GA
Colley, D'Ann Parker .... Mount Pleasant, TX
Colley, David .... Mount Pleasant, TX
Colley, David A. .... Columbus, OH
Colley, David C. .... **Dallas, TX**
Colley, Donna S. .... **Omaha, NE**
Colley, Drake A. .... New York, NY
Colley, Gary L. .... St. Louis, MO
Colley, Gary R. .... **Port Angeles, WA**
Colley, Kimberly E. .... **Paintsville, KY**
Colley, Kristopher Maurice .... Denver, CO
Colley, Louis C. .... Prattville, AL
Colley, Mark D. .... **Washington, DC**
Colley, Mary Durr .... Nashville, TN
Colley, Michael F. .... **Columbus, OH**
Colley, Paul S., Jr. .... **Tyler, TX**
Colley, Sarah B. .... **Washington, DC**
Colley Shroyer & Abraham, Co., L.P.A.
Columbus, OH
Colley, Stephen A. .... **San Diego, CA**
Colley, Susan J. .... **Tyler, TX**
Colley, William E. .... Fort Payne, AL
Colley, William H., Jr. .... Nashville, TN
Colleye, Beth Hilliard .... **Washington, DC**
Colli, Bart J. .... **Newark, NJ**
Colli, Peter T. .... Woburn, MA
Colliander, John D. .... **Manchester, NH**
Collias, Gary A. .... Charleston, WV
Collias, George N. .... **Burlington, VT**
Collias, Gina R. .... Shelby, NC
Collias, Peter G. .... **Fall River, MA**
Collias, Philip J. .... Irvine, CA
Collias, Philip J., Jr. .... Chicago, IL
Collias, Shari Lynne .... **Charleston, WV**
Colliau, Michael T. .... Los Angeles, CA
Collica, Raymond C., II .... Cadiz, OH
Collica, Christine Corinne .... Dallas, TX
Collie, Christopher Page
Hendersonville, NC
Collie, Cynthia E. .... Sullivan's Island, SC
Collie, Dan L. .... Beaumont, TX
Collie, James T., Jr. .... Pittsburgh, PA
Collie, K. Kaye .... Orlando, FL
Collie, Key .... Austin, TX
Collie & Pollard .... Austin, TX
Collie, Robert M., Jr. .... **Houston, TX**
Collie, Roberts & Collie .... Dallas, TX
Collie, Suzanne C. .... Dallas, TX
Collie, Waller M., Jr. .... Dallas, TX
Collier, Adam S. .... **Portland, OR**
Collier, A. E. .... Stamford, CT
Collier, Alan H. .... **Los Angeles, CA**
Collier, Angela C. .... Edinburg, TX
Collier, Anne E. .... **Washington, DC**
Collier and Associates, P.C. .... Lubbock, TX
Collier, Bayard V. .... **Prestonsburg, KY**
Collier, Benjamin Raye .... Rockwall, TX
Collier, Beth Ann .... **New York, NY**
Collier, Boyd F. .... **Richmond, VA**
Collier, Brandon S. .... **New York, NY**
Collier, Brenda H. .... **Dallas, TX**
Collier, Bruce J. .... **Ketchum, ID**
Collier, Byron S. .... Detroit, MI
Collier, C. Clark .... **Birmingham, AL**
Collier, Caitlin F. .... **Vermillion, SD**
Collier, Calvin J. .... **Northfield, IL**
Collier, Carl M. .... **Lake Worth, FL**
Collier, Carol A. .... Marietta, GA
Collier, Carole K. .... **Virginia Beach, VA**
Collier, Charles A., Jr. .... **Los Angeles, CA**
Collier, Charles B. .... Douglasville, GA
Collier, Charles W. .... Bradford, VT
Collier, Christopher J. .... Medina, OH
Collier, Christopher M. .... Statesville, NC
Collier, Clay Allen .... **Wilmington, NC**
Collier, Clinton D. .... Leawood, KS
Kansas City, MO
Collier & Collier .... Ironton, OH
Collier, Curtis .... Chattanooga, TN
Collier, D. Brian .... Ocala, FL
Collier, Danny J., Jr. .... **Mobile, AL**
Collier, Darin W. .... **Atlanta, GA**
Collier, Diane K. .... Kalispell, MT
Collier, Donovan C. .... **Riverside, CA**
San Bernardino, CA
Collier, Dorsey, Carter & Williams, L.L.C.
St. Louis, MO
Collier, Douglas A. .... Indianapolis, IN
Collier, Douglas M. .... Brenham, TX
Collier, Earl M., Jr. .... Washington, DC
Collier, Edmond J., II .... Philadelphia, PA
Collier, Edmund Q. .... Milford, CT
Norwalk, CT
Collier, Edward R. .... **Dawson, GA**
Collier, Edwin .... Rockville, MD
Collier, Elizabeth A. .... **San Francisco, CA**
Collier, Frances .... Washington, DC
Collier, G. Robert, Jr. .... **Monroe, LA**
Collier & Gamble .... **Albany, GA**
Dawson, GA
Collier, George P., Jr. .... Memphis, TN
Collier, Gerald A. .... Agoura Hills, CA
Collier, Glay H., II .... Alexandria, LA
Collier, Glenn H. .... Peoria, IL
Collier, Glenn W. .... **Springfield, OH**
Collier, H. Guy .... **Washington, DC**
Collier, Heidi D. .... **San Diego, CA**
Collier, Homann & Siamas
Crawfordsville, IN
Collier, Hurlie H. .... **Houston, TX**
Collier, Jack W. .... Houston, TX
Collier, Jacob & Mills .... **Newark, NJ**
New Brunswick, NJ
Princeton, NJ
Somerset, NJ
Somerville, NJ
Trenton, NJ
Collier, Jake .... Lewisville, TX
Collier, James D. .... Crawfordsville, IN
Collier, James D. .... Vienna, VA
Collier, James I., Jr. .... Springfield, VA
Collier, James M. .... **Dawson, GA**
Collier, James M. .... Elizabethtown, KY
Collier, James W. .... **Detroit, MI**
Collier, James W. .... Azle, TX
Collier, Jason S. .... Santa Ana, CA
Collier, J. B. .... Ironton, OH
Collier, J. B., Jr. .... Ironton, OH
Collier, Jean C. .... Frankfort, KY
Collier, Jeffrey W. .... **Jackson, MS**
Collier & Jennings .... **Harrisburg, AR**
Collier, Jo Ann .... **Houston, TX**
Collier, John .... Lubbock, TX
Collier, John A. .... **Reno, NV**
Collier, John S. .... Deshler, OH
Collier, John W. .... Macon, GA
Collier, Judith L. .... **Troy, MI**

Collier, Judson W., Jr. ....Richmond, VA
Collier, Judson W., Jr., P.C., Law Offices of Richmond, VA
Collier, Julie Montgomery ......Birmingham, AL
Collier, Kathleen A. ....Birmingham, AL
Collier, Katrida ....Atlanta, GA
Collier, Keith M. ....Florence, AL
Collier, Kelley W. ....Bartow, FL
Collier, Kendra S. ....Chicago, IL
Collier, Lelia Anne ....Lafayette, LA
Collier, Linda J. ....Broomall, PA
Collier, Linda M. ....Kansas City, MO
Collier, Linda P. ....Conway, AR
Collier, Lizabeth Cooper
Winston-Salem, NC
Collier, Lloyd D.
Federal Communications Commission, Common Carrier Bureau, GV
Collier, Lori S. ....Dothan, AL
Collier, Louie K. ....Harrisburg, AR
Collier, Marc B. ....Austin, TX
Collier, Mark S. ....Los Angeles, CA
Collier, Mary M. ....Nashville, TN
Collier, Nathan S. ....Gainesville, FL
Collier, Orla Ellis, III ....Columbus, OH
Collier, Paul, III ....Cambridge, MA
Collier, Peter D. ....Paterson, NJ
Collier, Philip W. ....Louisville, KY
Collier, Richard F., Jr. ....Somerset, NJ
Collier, Richard J. ....San Francisco, CA
Collier, Richard L. ....Griffin, GA
Collier, Richard T. ....Bridgewater, NJ
Collier, Robert Don ....Dallas, TX
Collier, Robert E., II
Fort Lauderdale, FL
Miami, FL
Collier, Robert W. ....Taloga, OK
Collier, Ronald L. ....Sarasota, FL
Collier, Ronald V. ....Oklahoma City, OK
Collier, Ryan W. ....Seattle, WA
Collier, Scott A. ....Vancouver, WA
Collier, Shannon, Rill & Scott, PLLC
Washington, DC
Collier, Shapiro and McCutcheon
Cambridge, MA
Collier, Sharon Cohen ......Walnut Creek, CA
Collier, Stephen H. ....Surry, ME
Collier, Stephen L. ....San Francisco, CA
Collier, Steven ....Hurst, TX
Collier, Steven D. ....Atlanta, GA
Collier, Steven P. ....Toledo, OH
Collier, Stuart R. ....Wichita, KS
Collier, Susan A. ....Roseville, CA
Collier, T. Harris, III ....Jackson, MS
Collier, Theresa J. ....Denver, CO
Collier, Thomas B. ....Beverly Hills, CA
Collier, Thomas C., Jr. ....Washington, DC
Collier, Thomas C., Jr. ....Indianapolis, IN
Collier, Timothy W. ....Augusta, ME
Collier, Travis R. ....Albuquerque, NM
Collier, Tyree C. ....Dallas, TX
Collier, Wayne F. ....Lexington, KY
Collier, William B. ....Baton Rouge, LA
Collier, William C. ....Chardon, OH
Collier, William H. ....Jennings, LA
Lafayette, LA
Collier, William H. ....Cary, NC
Collier, William H., III ....Accord, NY
Ellenville, NY
Collier, William H., Jr. ....Long Beach, CA
Collier, William J. ....San Diego, CA
Collier, William J., Jr. ....Stamford, CT
New York, NY
White Plains, NY
Collier, Willyerd R. ....Fayetteville, GA
Collier-Magar, Kenneth ....Indianapolis, IN
Collier-Magar, P.C., Law Offices of
Indianapolis, IN
Collier-Nix, Tracy L. ....Flint, MI
Collier-Pittman, E. Kay ....Pigeon Forge, TN
Colliers, Denise D. ....Philadelphia, PA
Collier-Williams, Cassandra ....Cleveland, OH
Colliflower, Michael A. ....Carmel, IN
Colligan, Brian M. ....Beverly Hills, CA
Colligan, David J. ....Buffalo, NY
Colligan, Edward A. ....Newark, NJ
Colligan, Edward M. ....Newark, NJ
Colligan, Jerome A. ....Traverse City, MI
Colligan, Linda A. ....Secaucus, NJ
Colligan, Michael F. ....Pittsburgh, PA
Colligan, Owen M. ....New York, NY
Colligan, Sean W. ....Kansas City, MO
Collignon, David V. ....Ozark, MO
Collignon, Thomas D. ....Indianapolis, IN
Collimore and Collimore ....Fairfield, CT
Collimore, Donal C. ....Fairfield, CT
Collimore, Kevin G. ....Manchester, NH
Collin, Donald V. ....Sacramento, CA
Collin, Dwight R. ....Rochester, NY
Collin, Francis J., Jr. ....Napa, CA
Collin, Robert ....New Orleans, LA
Collin, Sean L. ....San Diego, CA
Collin, Thomas J. ....Cleveland, OH
Collina, Mary Robbins ....Deerfield, IL
Colling, J. Kirby ....Arcade, NY
Colling, J. Kirby, P.C. ....Arcade, NY
Colling, Jay S. ....Orlando, FL
Colling, Lee Jay ....Maitland, FL
Colling, Lee Jay, & Associates, P.A.
Maitland, FL
Colling, Lisa D. ....Chicago, IL
Colling, Ronald E. ....Osceola, NE
Colling, Stewart L. ....Orlando, FL
Collinge, Jared E. ....Muskegon, MI
Collingon, Jennifer M. ....Madison, WI
Collings, Chadwick W. ....New Orleans, LA
Collings & Collings, A Professional Law Corporation ....Lake Charles, LA
Collings, Gary L. ....Oakhurst, CA
Collings, Katherine M. ....Port Orchard, WA
Collings, R. William ....Lake Charles, LA
Collings, Robert B. ....Boston, MA
Collings, Robert L. ....Lake Charles, LA
Collings, Robert L. ....Philadelphia, PA
Collings, Susan G. ....Philadelphia, PA
Collings, William N. ....Chicago, IL
Collingsworth, Connie R. ....Seattle, WA
Collingsworth, Grant W. ....Atlanta, GA
Collingsworth, Terrence P. ......Los Angeles, CA
Collingsworth, William J. ....Tulsa, OK
Collingwood, Susan B. ....Gainesville, FL
Collini, Charles Weaver ....Wadesboro, NC
Collini, Robert ....Brooklyn, NY
Collins, Adrian A. ....New York, NY
Collins, Adrian Anthony, P.C.
New York, NY
Collins, Alice V. ....San Francisco, CA
Collins, Alicia ....Crystal City, MD
Collins, Allen H. ....Collinsville, IL
Collins, Allen & McFarland
Salyersville, KY
Collins, Alphonso A. ....New York, NY
Collins, Alysan Boothe ......Albuquerque, NM
Collins, Amy ....Tulsa, OK
Collins, Amy L. Tsui ....Emeryville, CA
Collins, Andrea J. ....Los Angeles, CA
Collins, Andrew J. ....San Francisco, CA
Collins, Andrew J., Jr. ....Sherwood, AR
Collins, Andrew M. ....Temecula, CA
Collins, Ann Finley ....Chicago, IL
Collins, Ann M. ....Boston, MA
Collins, Ann Marie ....Newark, NJ
New York, NY
Collins, Anne J. ....Lexington, MA
Collins, Anne L. ....Boston, MA
Collins, April D. ....Dover, DE
Collins, Arthur R. ....Merced, CA
Collins, Arvil Lee ....Kernersville, NC
Collins & Associates ....Santa Barbara, CA
Collins, Audrey B. ....Los Angeles, CA
Collins, B. Craig ....Columbia, SC
Collins, Barbara B. ....Springfield, IL
Collins, Barbara J. ....Hartford, CT
Collins, Barbara J. ....Minneapolis, MN
Collins & Bargione ....Chicago, IL
Collins, Barry G. ....Chicago, IL
Collins & Beeson, An Assn. ....Oakland, CA
Collins & Bellenghi, LLP ....Irvine, CA
Collins, Betsy Palmer ....Birmingham, AL
Collins, Betty Toon ....Jackson, MS
Collins, Billy F. ....Houston, TX
Collins, Blaha & Slatkin ....Southfield, MI
Collins, Blomeley & Woody, PLLC
Hayesville, NC
Murphy, NC
Collins, Brant S., (P.A.) ....Brick, NJ
Collins, Brendan ....Department of Justice, Civil Division, GV
Collins, Brendan K. ....Philadelphia, PA
Collins, Brian F. ....Columbus, OH
Collins, Brian J. ....Allentown, PA
Bethlehem, PA
Jim Thorpe, PA
Collins, Brian M. ....San Francisco, CA
Collins, Brian M. ....Chicago, IL
Collins, Brian William ....San Bernardino, CA
Collins, Brown, Caldwell, Barkett & Garavaglia, Chartered ......Vero Beach, FL
Collins, Bruce D. ....Lakeport, CA
Collins, Bruce Dennis ....Washington, DC
Collins, Bruce L., III ....Corpus Christi, TX
Dallas, TX
Collins, Bruce M. ....Princeton, NJ
Collins, Bruce S. ....Irvine, CA
Collins, Bruce W. ....Dallas, TX
Collins, Brunella B. ....League City, TX
Collins, Bryan C. ....Dallas, TX
Collins, Bryan J. ....Indianapolis, IN
Collins, Bryan Patrick ....Washington, DC
Collins, Bryant M. ....Three Rivers, TX
Collins, Bryn K. ....San Diego, CA
Collins, Bryson Kyle ....Montgomery, AL
Collins, Buckley, Sauntry and Haugh, P.L.L.P. ....Minneapolis, MN
St. Paul, MN
Collins, C. Daniel ....Chattanooga, TN
Collins, C. Guerry ....Los Angeles, CA
Collins, C. Leon, Jr. ....Byron, GA
Collins, C. Lewis ....Boston, MA
Collins, C. Richard ....Evansville, IN
Collins, C. Robert ....Phoenix, AZ
Collins, Calvin W. ....Portland, OR
Collins, Camden L. ....San Francisco, CA
Collins, Candice J. ....Los Angeles, CA
Collins, Caprice L. ....Inglewood, CA
Collins, Carl W. ....Modesto, CA
Collins, Carol M. ....San Francisco, CA
Collins, Carol Warren ....Indianapolis, IN
Collins, Carolyn ....San Francisco, CA
Collins, Carolyn Alexander
Greenwich, CT
Collins, Carroll J., III ......San Francisco, CA
Collins, Carville B. ....Baltimore, MD
Collins, Cary J. ....Hoffman Estates, IL
Collins, Cassandra C. ....Richmond, VA
Collins, Catherine C.
Upper Marlboro, MD
Collins, Catherine Catlett
Colorado Springs, CO
Collins, Catherine S. ....Grand Rapids, MI
Collins, Catherine Z. ....Worcester, MA
Collins, Cathleen ....Los Angeles, CA
Collins, Catriona M. ....New York, NY
Collins, Celia J. ....Mobile, AL
Collins, Charles A. ....Brewster, MA
Collins, Charles A. ....St. Paul, MN
Collins, Charles A., Jr. ....White Plains, NY
Collins, Charles A., P.A. ....St. Paul, MN
Collins, Charles C., Jr. ....Ridgewood, NJ
Collins, Charles E., Jr. ....Fairfax, VA
Collins, Charles F. ....Bakersfield, CA
Collins, Charles J., Jr. ....Orlando, FL
Collins, Charles K. ....Los Angeles, CA
Collins, Charles M. ....San Francisco, CA
Collins, Charles P. ....Gainesville, FL
Collins, Charles R. ....San Francisco, CA
Collins, Charles Thomas ....Earlysville, VA
Collins, Charles W. ....Milwaukee, WI
Collins, Charlotte ....Washington, DC
Collins, Christa L. ....St. Petersburg, FL
Tampa, FL
Collins, Christina ....Topeka, KS
Collins, Christine M. ....Rockville, MD
Collins, Christine R. ....Boston, MA
Collins, Christine Smith ....Worcester, MA
Collins, Christopher H. ....Washington, DC
Bethesda, MD
Collins, Christopher J. ....New York, NY
Collins, Christopher J.
Oklahoma City, OK
Collins, Christopher M. ....Washington, DC
McLean, VA
Collins, Christopher R. ....Auburn, CA
Collins, Christopher M., P.C. ....McLean, VA
Collins, Christopher S. ....Houston, TX
Collins, Clifton W. ....Ephrata, WA
Collins, Clinton, & Associates, P.A.
Minneapolis, MN
Collins, Clinton C., Jr. ....Minneapolis, MN
Collins, Clyde H. ....New Lexington, OH
Collins, Clyde M., Jr. ....Jacksonville, FL
Collins and Cockrel, P.C. ....Denver, CO
Lakewood, CO
Collins & Collins ....Phoenix, AZ
Collins & Collins ....Chicago, IL
Collins & Collins ....Wichita, KS
Collins & Collins ....Quincy, MA
Collins & Collins ....Pendleton, OR
Collins & Collins, Inc. ....Ardmore, OK
Collins, Collins, Kantor and Maxwell
Buffalo, NY
Hamburg, NY
Collins, Collins, Muir & Traver LLP
Los Angeles, CA
Newport Beach, CA
Pasadena, CA
Santa Ana, CA
Collins, Connie L. ....Cape Coral, FL
Collins, Cooper W. ....Santa Ana, CA
Collins, Corey ....Miami, FL
Collins, Corinne C. ....Chalfont, PA
Collins, Cornelius F. ....Buffalo, NY
Collins, Cornell ....Gary, IN
Collins, Courtney Helen ....Washington, DC
Collins & Courtright ....Charleston, WV
Collins, Craig E. ....Sun City, AZ
Collins, Craig Harris ....San Mateo, CA
Collins, Craig M. ....Santa Monica, CA
Collins, Craig S. ....Dallas, TX
Collins, Cynthia G. ....Matunuck, RI
Collins, Cynthia J. ....Memphis, TN
Collins, Cynthia L. ....Los Angeles, CA
Collins, Cynthia S. ....Wilmington, DE
Collins, D. Mark ....Sioux Falls, SD
Collins, Daisy G. ....Cleveland, OH
Collins, Dan A. ....Greenville, SC
Collins, Dan A., & Associates, P.A.
Greenville, SC
Collins, Dana L. ....Louisville, KY
Collins, Daniel ....New York, NY
Collins, Daniel E. ....Southfield, MI
Collins, Daniel E. ....Cleveland, OH
Collins, Daniel F. ....Washington, DC
Collins, Daniel G. ....Bridgehampton, NY
Collins, Daniel J. ....Chicago, IL
Collins, Daniel J. ....Janesville, WI
Collins, Daniel L. ....Chicago, IL
Collins, Daniel L. ....Oak Lawn, IL
Collins, Daniel Leo ....Chicago, IL
Collins, Daniel P. ....Phoenix, AZ
Collins, Daniel P. ....Los Angeles, CA
Collins, Daniel W. ....Indianapolis, IN
Collins, Danny R. ....Columbia, SC
Collins, Dara J. ....Miami, FL
Collins, Darren W. ....Dallas, TX
Collins, David ....San Francisco, CA
Collins, David A. ....Orlando, FL
Collins, David A. ....Bloomington, IN
Collins, David A. ....Flemingsburg, KY
Collins, David A. ....Detroit, MI
Springhill, TN
Collins, David A. ....New York, NY
Collins, David A. ....Dayton, OH
Collins, David Andrew ....Springfield, MO
Collins, David B., Jr. ....Wilmington, NC
Collins, David Blair ....Peoria, IL
Collins, David M. ....Enid, OK
Collins, David M. ....Charleston, SC
Collins, David R., Law Office of
Seattle, WA
Collins, David T. ....Lancaster, CA
Collins, David W. ....Tucson, AZ
Collins, David W. ....Monticello, FL
Collins, David Y. ....Beloit, WI
Collins, Davidson & Jensen, L.L.C.
Mobile, AL
Collins, Dawn T. ....Los Angeles, CA
Collins, Deborah F. ....Detroit, MI
Collins, Deborah M. ....New York, NY
Collins, Dennis ....Port Jefferson, NY
Collins, Dennis A. ....West Long Branch, NJ
Collins, Dennis B.
Federal Labor Relations Authority, Authority Member Staff, GV
Collins, Dennis G. ....St. Louis, MO
Collins, Dennis W. ....Norfolk, NE
Collins, Desmond J. ....Newport Beach, CA
Collins, Diana G. ....Chicago, IL
Collins, Diane M. ....Farmingdale, NY
Collins, Djenaba ....Vallejo, CA
Collins, Don Cary ....Belleville, IL
Collins, Donald B. ....Dallas, TX
Collins, Donald M. ....Columbus, OH
Collins, Donald M. ....Philadelphia, PA
Collins, Donald O. ....New Orleans, LA
Collins, Donald P. ....Milton, MA
Collins, Donald R. ....Seattle, WA
Collins, Donna Marie ....Fort Myers, FL
Collins, Donnell J. ....Atlanta, GA
Collins, Douglas J. ....Baytown, TX
Collins, Douglas L. ....Irvine, CA
Collins, E. Michael ....Boston, MA
Collins, E. Scott ....Ocean City, MD
Collins, E. Scott, P.A. ....Ocean City, MD
Collins and Eddings ....Calhoun, GA
Collins, Edmond A. ....Warren, NJ
Collins, Edward B. ....San Francisco, CA
Collins, Edward J. ....Cincinnati, OH
Collins, Edward J., Jr. ....Cambridge, MA
Collins, Edward M. ....Rockland, ME
Collins, Edward M., III ....Reading, PA
Collins, Edward R. ....San Diego, CA
Collins, Edward T. ....Northbrook, IL
Collins, Edwin M. ....New York, NY
Collins, Eileen P. ....New York, NY
Collins, Einhorn, Farrell & Ulanoff, A Professional Corporation ....Detroit, MI
Southfield, MI
Collins, Elise D. ....Morristown, NJ
Collins, Elizabeth C. ....Washington, DC
Collins, Elizabeth F. ....East Hartford, CT
Collins, Elizabeth L. ....Springfield, IL
Collins, Elizabeth Tansil ....Memphis, TN
Collins, Ellen K. ....Park Ridge, IL
Collins, Ellen M. ....New York, NY
Collins, Elwood F., Jr. ....New York, NY
Collins, Eric A. ....Beckley, WV
Collins, Erika C. ....Palo Alto, CA
Collins, Ernest, Jr. ....Phoenix, AZ
Collins, Ernest Terrell ....Weldon, NC
Collins, Etta Katherine Simons
Charleston, SC
Collins, Eugene N. ....Chattanooga, TN
Collins & Everett, LLP ....Santa Monica, CA
Collins, F. Stephen ....Denver, CO
Collins, Forrest L. ....Wickliffe, OH
Collins, Foster Clay ....Kansas City, MO
Collins, Francis E., P.C. ....Northampton, MA
Collins, Francis J. ....Danbury, CT
Collins, Francis J. ....Baltimore, MD
Collins, Francis L. ....Fall River, MA
Collins, Francis M. ....Feeding Hills, MA
Collins, Francis P. ....Hackensack, NJ
Collins, Francis X. ....Quincy, MA
Collins, Frank A. ....Pittsburgh, PA
Collins, Frank C., Jr. ....Houston, TX
Collins, Frank F. ....Phoenix, AZ
Collins, Frank M. ....Media, PA
Collins, Fred ....Milan, TN
Collins, Fred G. ....Mobile, AL
Collins, Frederick H., Law Offices of
Annapolis, MD
Collins, Freida Gunn ....Ellisville, MS
Collins, G. Bryan, Jr. ....Raleigh, NC
Collins, G. Patrick ....Dallas, TX
Collins, G. Richard ....Suitland, MD
Collins, Gale Forman ....Asheville, NC
Collins, Gary ....New York, NY
Collins, Gary J. ....Sterling Heights, MI
Collins, Gary M. ....Fenton, MI
Collins, Gary W. ....Excelsior Springs, MO
Collins & Gascoyne, L.L.P. ....Houston, TX
Collins, Geneva A. ....Los Angeles, CA
Collins, Genevieve J.
Department of Justice, Tax Division, GV
Collins, George A. ....Concord, NH
Collins, George B. ....Chicago, IL
Collins, George C. ....Burlingame, CA
Collins, George G., Jr. ....Vero Beach, FL
Collins, George J., Jr. ....East Milton, MA
Collins, George L. ....Jacksonville, NC
Collins, George V., III ....Albany, NY
Collins, George W. ....Santa Monica, CA
Collins, George W., Jr. ....Buffalo, NY
Collins, Gerald J. ....Chicago, IL
Collins, Gerald L. ....Rio Rancho, NM
Collins, Gerald M. ....Vermillion, SD
Collins, Gerald R., Jr. ....Hayesville, NC
Murphy, NC
Collins, Gerard S. ....Springfield, MA
Collins, Glenn ....Chicago, IL
Collins, Glenn ....Tyler, TX
Collins, Granville E. ....Fulton, MO
Collins, Gregory C. ....Madison, WI
Collins, Gregory H. ....Akron, OH
Cleveland, OH
Collins, Gregory J. ....Minneapolis, MN
Collins, Gregory S. ....Pittsburgh, PA
Collins, Guzin N. ....Virginia Beach, VA
Collins, H. Clay ....Fairburn, GA
Collins, H. Richard ....Wilmette, IL
Collins, H. William ....San Diego, CA
Collins, Hallett & Ford ....St. Petersburg, FL
Collins, Halsey B. ....Boston, MA
Collins, Hannafin, Garamella, Jaber & Tuozzolo, Professional Corporation
Bridgeport, CT
Danbury, CT
Ridgefield, CT
Collins, Harold E. ....Chicago, IL
Collins, Harold L. ....Mira Loma, CA
Collins, Harold R., Jr. ....Los Angeles, CA

Collins, Harry M. .... Houston, TX
Collins, Harry Prim Gerard .... York, SC
Collins, Hedgepath, Lee & Young
Nashville, TN
Collins, Helen Dalton .... Hackensack, NJ
Collins & Henderson .... Beloit, WI
Collins, Henry C. .... Schenectady, NY
Collins, Henry W. .... Miami Lakes, FL
Collins & Hensley, P.A. .... Franklin, NC
Collins, Howard W. .... Salem, OR
Collins, Howard W., & Associates
Salem, OR
Collins, Hugh B. .... Medford, OR
Collins, J. Barclay, II .... New York, NY
Collins, J. Barclay, III .... Washington, DC
Collins, J. Charles, Jr. .... New Orleans, LA
Collins, J. Christopher .... Worcester, MA
Collins, J. Ernest .... Panama City, FL
Collins, J. Gregg .... Metairie, LA
Collins, J. Kevin .... Virginia Beach, VA
Collins, J. Michael .... Alexandria, VA
Collins, J. O'Neill
Research Triangle Park, NC
Collins, J. Peter .... Carmel, NY
Collins, J. Richard .... Ocean City, MD
Collins, Jack G. .... Portland, OR
Collins, Jacquelin .... Lubbock, TX
Collins, James .... Lubbock, TX
Collins, James A. .... Denver, CO
Collins, James A. .... Milwaukee, WI
Collins, James B. .... Farmington, NM
Collins, James Brian .... Mill Valley, CA
Collins, James C. .... San Francisco, CA
Collins, James C. .... Whitney Point, NY
Collins, James Daly .... Yarmouth Port, MA
Collins, James E. .... Ocala, FL
Collins, James E. .... Freehold, NJ
Collins, James F. .... Hartford, CT
Collins, James F., III .... San Diego, CA
Collins, James Francis .... Louisville, KY
Collins, James Francis .... Freehold, NJ
Collins, James G. .... Amherst, MA
Collins, James H. .... Frankfort, MI
Collins, James H., Jr. .... Detroit, MI
Collins, James I. .... Stockton, CA
Collins, James Irvin, Jr. .... La Fayette, GA
Collins, James J. .... Quincy, MA
Collins, James J. .... Mineola, NY
Collins, James L. .... Portland, OR
Collins, James M. .... Marquette, MI
Collins, James M. .... Woodbridge, VA
Collins, James P. .... Glendale, CA
Collins, James P. .... Menlo Park, CA
Collins, James P. .... San Francisco, CA
Collins, James P. .... Denver, CO
Collins, James P. .... Kankakee, IL
Collins, James P., Jr. .... Santa Ana, CA
Collins, James P., Sr. .... Wilmington, DE
Collins, James R. .... Amarillo, TX
Collins, James S., II .... St. Louis, MO
Collins, James T. .... Birmingham, AL
Collins, James T. .... Chicago, IL
Collins, James V. .... Oklahoma City, OK
Collins, James W. .... Chicago, IL
Collins, James W. .... Farmington Hills, MI
Collins, James W. .... Austin, TX
Collins, Jane L. .... Woodstock, IL
Collins, Janet M. .... Brockton, MA
Collins, Jas. F. .... Herkimer, NY
Collins, Jeanne C. .... El Paso, TX
Collins, Jefferson T. .... Phoenix, AZ
Collins, Jeffrey C. .... Colorado Springs, CO
Collins, Jeffrey D. .... Boston, MA
Collins, Jeffrey M. .... Tampa, FL
Collins, Jeffrey T. .... Concord, NH
Collins, Jennifer Long .... Raleigh, NC
Collins, Jennifer Tankersley .... Tallahassee, FL
Collins, Jeremiah A. .... Washington, DC
Collins, Jeremiah C. .... Washington, DC
Collins, Jerri Lynn .... Longwood, FL
Collins, Jessica .... La Plata, MD
Collins, Jill H. .... Detroit, MI
Collins, Jody E. .... Fort Lauderdale, FL
Collins, Joe .... Stockton, MO
Collins, Joel W., Jr. .... Columbia, SC
Collins, Joelle G. .... Manchester, NH
Collins, John A. .... Department of State, Director General—Foreign Service, GV
Collins, John A. .... Buffalo, NY
Collins, John A., III .... New London, CT
Collins, John B. .... Ypsilanti, MI
Collins, John B. .... Denville, NJ
Collins, John C. .... Salyersville, KY
Collins, John C. .... Wilmington, NC
Collins, John C. .... Alliance, OH
Collins, John D. .... San Diego, CA
Collins, John D. .... Macon, MO
Collins, John E. .... Lawrenceville, NJ
Collins, John E. .... Sand Springs, OK
Collins, John E. .... Dallas, TX
Collins, John F. .... Gulfport, FL
Collins, John F. .... Falmouth, MA
Collins, John F. .... Atlantic City, NJ
Collins, John F. .... Buffalo, NY
Collins, John F. .... New York, NY
Collins, John J. .... Newport Beach, CA
Pasadena, CA
Collins, John J. .... Chicago, IL
Collins, John J. .... Davenport, IA
Collins, John J. .... Clayton, MO
Collins, John J. .... Fairless Hills, PA
Collins, John J. .... Burlington, VT
Collins, John J. .... Alexandria, VA
Collins, John J. .... Alexandria, VA
Collins, John J., Jr. .... Auburn Hills, MI
Collins, John K. .... New York, NY
Collins, John L. .... New Bedford, MA
Collins, John L. .... Lansing, MI
Collins, John L. .... Staten Island, NY
Collins, John L. .... McMinnville, OR
Collins, John L. .... Houston, TX
Collins, John M. .... Washington, DC
Collins, John M. .... Pensacola, FL
Collins, John M. .... Shrewsbury, MA
Collins, John M. .... Dallas, TX
Collins, John M., Jr. .... Chicago, IL
Collins, John M., (P.C.) .... Kansas City, MO
Collins, John Marshall .... San Jose, CA
Collins, John P. .... Chicago, IL
Collins, John P. .... Bronx, NY
Collins, John P., Jr. .... Lakeland, FL
Collins, John R. .... Midland, TX
Collins, John Steven .... Knoxville, TN
Collins, John T. .... Washington, DC
Collins, John T. .... Boston, MA
Collins, John W., Jr. .... Dallas, TX
Collins, Johnson & Markey .... Media, PA
Collins & Johnson, P.C. .... Lewistown, IL
Collins, Johnson & Volk .... New Orleans, LA
Collins, Joseph A. .... Hamburg, NY
Collins, Joseph B. .... Springfield, MA
Collins, Joseph B. .... Pittsburgh, PA
Collins, Joseph E. .... Phoenix, AZ
Collins, Joseph E. .... Chicago, IL
Collins, Joseph F. .... Topsfield, MA
Collins, Joseph M. .... Franklin, NC
Collins, Joseph O., Jr. .... Dallas, TX
Collins, Joseph P. .... Los Angeles, CA
Collins, Joseph P. .... Chicago, IL
Collins, Josiah W. .... Macomb, IL
Collins, Joyce M. .... Hyannis, MA
Collins, Judith E. .... Paramus, NJ
Collins, Judith P. .... Madison, WI
Collins, Judy R. .... Gainesville, FL
Collins, Julien H., III .... Arlington Heights, IL
Collins, Justin .... White Plains, NY
Collins, Karen .... Newburgh, NY
Collins, Katharine Marie .... Overland Park, KS
Collins, Kathleen
Federal Communications Commission, International Bureau, GV
Collins, Kathleen A. .... Galveston, TX
Collins, Kathleen D. .... Phoenix, AZ
Collins, Kathleen E. .... Los Angeles, CA
Collins, Kathleen M. .... Santa Ana, CA
Collins, Kathleen M. .... Torrance, CA
Collins, Kathleen M. .... New York, NY
Collins, Kathleen M. .... Allentown, PA
Collins, Kathleen Wooley
Washington, DC
Collins, Kathryn Shaw .... Chicago, IL
Collins, Kathy Lepesha
St. Petersburg, FL
Collins, Kay L. .... Fort Collins, CO
Collins, Keith D. .... Waverly, IA
Collins, Kelliss Ann .... Portland, OR
Collins, Kelly A. .... Waukegan, IL
Collins, Kelly K. .... Topeka, KS
Collins, Kendall D. .... Oakland, CA
Collins, Kenneth J. .... Kneeland, CA
Collins, Kenneth K. .... Walnut Creek, CA
Collins, Kent H. .... Salt Lake City, UT
Collins, Kent J. .... Wichita, KS
Collins, Kevin B. .... Baltimore, MD
Rockville, MD
Collins, Kevin H. .... Cedar Rapids, IA
Collins, Kevin J. .... Tampa, FL
Collins, Kevin J. .... De Pere, WI
Collins, Kevin L. .... San Antonio, TX
Collins, Kevin L., P.C. .... San Antonio, TX
Collins, Kevin P. .... Marion, OH
Collins, Kevin Sherrill .... Los Angeles, CA
Collins, Kevin T. .... Riverside, CA
Collins, Kevin T. .... New York, NY
Collins, Kim H. .... Sacramento, CA
Collins, Kimberly A. .... Pittsburgh, PA
Collins, Kimberly M. .... Boston, MA
Collins, Kirk L. .... Fremont, CA
Collins, Kourtney .... Sacramento, CA
Collins, Kristen M. .... Washington, DC
Collins, Kristine Freyleue .... Philadelphia, PA
Collins, Kyle B. .... Austin, TX
Collins, L Dennis .... Chesterfield, VA
Collins, L Fred .... Ardmore, OK
Collins, L. Joel .... Phenix City, AL
Collins & Lacy, P.C. .... Columbia, SC
Collins, Lance B. .... Englewood, NJ
Collins, LaNell W. .... Phoenix, AZ
Collins, Lani Meanley .... Santa Barbara, CA
Collins, Larry .... Phenix City, AL
Collins, Larry .... Ocala, FL
Collins, Larry .... Waseca, MN
Collins Law Firm .... Janesville, WI
Collins Law Firm, P.C. .... Manchester, CT
Collins Law Firm, The, P.C. .... Naperville, IL
Collins Law Office .... Jackson, MS
Collins, Lawrence C. .... Byron, GA
Collins, Lawrence T. .... Winona, MN
Collins, Lee A. .... Houston, TX
Collins, Leo R. .... Mentor, OH
Collins, Leonard C. .... Washington, DC
Collins, Leslie A. .... New Orleans, LA
Collins, Leslie G. .... Mechanicsburg, PA
Collins, Lewis F., Jr. .... Tampa, FL
Collins, L. Fred, P.C. .... Ardmore, OK
Collins, Lisa L. .... Chicago, IL
Collins, Lisa L. .... Nashville, TN
Collins, L. Joel, P.C. .... Phenix City, AL
Collins, Lonnie D. .... Madison, IN
Collins, Loreen P. .... Escondido, CA
Collins, Loren W. .... Salem, OR
Collins, Lorenzo T. .... Ardmore, OK
Collins, Lori J. .... Dayton, OH
Collins, Louisa Ann .... Dallas, TX
Collins, Lynn A. .... Philadelphia, PA
Collins, Lynn M., Jr. .... Dallas, TX
Collins, Lynn R. .... Salt Lake City, UT
Collins, Lynn Toney .... Boston, MA
Collins, Lynne Ann .... Sheridan, WY
Collins, M. Charles .... Toledo, OH
Collins, M. Kelly .... Yazoo City, MS
Collins, M. Wyatt, Jr. .... Ellisville, MS
Collins, Marcus L. .... Cincinnati, OH
Collins, Margaret A. .... Roswell, GA
Collins, Margaret C. .... Flushing, NY
Collins, Margaret E. G. .... Universal City, CA
Collins, Margaret (Meg) Antley
West Columbia, SC
Collins, Marie E., Law Offices of
Deer Park, TX
Collins, Mark A. .... Washington, DC
Collins, Mark B. .... Houston, TX
Collins, Mark D. .... Wilmington, DE
Collins, Mark Douglas .... Hopkinsville, KY
Collins, Mark E. .... New York, NY
Collins, Mark L. .... Tucson, AZ
Collins, Mark L. .... Grand Rapids, MI
Collins, Mark Scott, (Inc.) .... San Jose, CA
Collins, Mark Warner .... Titusville, FL
Collins, Marshall R. .... Glastonbury, CT
Collins, Martin C. .... Syracuse, NY
Collins, Martin G. .... Milwaukee, WI
Collins, Martin J. .... New York, NY
Collins, Martin J. .... San Antonio, TX
Collins, Mary A. .... San Francisco, CA
Collins, Mary Ann .... Auburn, CA
Collins, Mary Ann W. .... Bridgewater, NJ
Collins, Mary E. .... Treasury Department, Internal Revenue Service, GV
Collins, Mary Elizabeth
San Luis Obispo, CA
Collins, Mary L. .... Downers Grove, IL
Collins, Mary M. .... Dedham, MA
Collins, Maryann .... Wayland, MA
Collins, Matthew D. .... Denver, CO
Collins, Matthew M. .... Roseland, NJ
Collins, Matthew P. .... Norcross, GA
Collins, Matthew W. .... Lansing, MI
Collins & Mau .... Oakland, CA
Collins, McDonald & Gann
Carle Place, NY
Collins, Melissa B. .... Birmingham, AL
Collins, Michael .... Los Osos, CA
Collins, Michael .... San Luis Obispo, CA
Collins, Michael B. .... Pendleton, OR
Collins, Michael D. .... Stroudsburg, PA
Collins, Michael E. .... Garden City, KS
Collins, Michael F. .... Lansdale, PA
Collins, Michael G. .... New Orleans, LA
Collins, Michael H. .... Williamsport, PA
Collins, Michael H. .... Dallas, TX
Collins, Michael J. .... Encino, CA
Collins, Michael J. .... Irvine, CA
Collins, Michael J. .... Washington, DC
Collins, Michael J. .... Baltimore, MD
Collins, Michael J. .... Columbus, OH
Collins, Michael J. .... Wilkes-Barre, PA
Collins, Michael J. .... Dallas, TX
Collins, Michael J. .... Dallas, TX
Collins, Michael J. .... Houston, TX
Collins, Michael Joseph .... San Antonio, TX
Collins, Michael K. .... Los Angeles, CA
Collins, Michael McHale .... Covington, VA
Collins, Michael P. .... Biloxi, MS
Collins, Michael P. .... New York, NY
Collins, Michael P. .... New York, NY
Collins, Michael R. .... Chicago, IL
Collins, Michael R. .... Ponca City, OK
Collins, Michael T. .... Bethesda, MD
McLean, VA
Collins, Michael T. .... Manahawkin, NJ
Collins, Michael W. .... Evergreen Park, IL
Collins, Michele D. .... Nashville, TN
Collins, Michelle Louise .... Pittsburgh, PA
Collins, Mildred L. .... Los Angeles, CA
Collins, Mildred S. .... Cleveland, OH
Collins & Mitchell .... Cherokee, OK
Collins, Mitzi R. .... Salt Lake City, UT
Collins and Moore .... Jacksonville, NC
Collins, Morgan .... Yakima, WA
Collins, Morris L. .... San Antonio, TX
Collins, Morton H. .... Southfield, MI
Collins, N. Brock .... Frankfort, KY
Collins, N. Quinn .... Brunswick, ME
Collins, Nancy C. .... Atlanta, GA
Collins, Nancy G. .... New Orleans, LA
Collins, Nancy M. .... Hazard, KY
Collins, Natalyn A. .... Lubbock, TX
Collins, Nathan C. .... St. Louis, MO
Collins, Nina Suzanne Welborn
Fort Worth, TX
Collins, Norman & Basinger, P.C.
Dallas, TX
Collins, O. Clark, Jr. .... Ironton, OH
Collins, Ollie .... Washington, DC
Collins, P. Clarkson, Jr. .... Wilmington, DE
Collins, Paige Miles .... Morristown, TN
Collins, Palmer W. .... Indialantic, FL
Collins, Parrish .... Albuquerque, NM
Collins, Patricia .... Brooklyn, NY
Collins, Patricia A. .... Ketchikan, AK
Collins, Patricia A. .... Chicago, IL
Collins, Patricia A. .... Charleston, WV
Collins, Patricia C. .... Blue Bell, PA
Collins, Patricia D. .... Mineola, NY
Collins, Patricia H. .... Madison, WI
Collins, Patricia L. .... Santa Monica, CA
Collins, Patricia M. .... Fairfield, NJ
Collins, Patricia S. .... Seattle, WA
Collins, Patrick .... Dallas, TX
Collins, Patrick B. .... Mobile, AL
Collins, Patrick H. .... Hendersonville, NC
Collins, Patrick J. .... Denver, CO
Collins, Patrick M. .... Chicago, IL
Collins, Patrick M. .... New York, NY
Collins, Patrick S. .... Fullerton, CA
Collins, Patrick S. .... Cleveland, OH
Collins, Patrick T. .... Livingston, NJ
Collins, Patrick T. .... Somerville, NJ
Collins, Patrick T. .... Uniondale, NY
Collins, Patrick V. .... Boise, ID
Collins, Paul C. .... Albuquerque, NM
Collins, Paul E. .... Denver, CO
Collins, Paul J. .... Palo Alto, CA
Collins, Paul J. .... New York, NY
Collins, Paul M. .... Albany, NY
Collins, Paul R. .... Hazard, KY
Collins, Paul R. .... McLean, VA
Collins, Paul W. .... Glastonbury, CT
Collins, Paula M. .... New York, NY
Collins, Peggi, Law Offices of
Los Angeles, CA
Collins, Peggi, Law Offices of
Torrance, CA
Collins, Peggy L. .... Charleston, WV
Collins, Percy H., Jr. .... Belleville, KS
Collins, Peter B. .... Waltham, MA
Collins, Peter C. .... Salt Lake City, UT
Collins, Peter G. .... Wichita, KS
Collins, Peter H. .... Quincy, MA
Collins, Peter H. B. .... Mentor, OH
Collins, Peter J. .... Ann Arbor, MI
Collins, Peter, Jr. .... Tucson, AZ
Collins, Peter M. .... New York, NY
Collins, Peter M. .... Burlington, VT
Collins, Philip .... Canton, MA
Collins, Philip D. .... Dallas, TX
Collins, Philip D., & Associates, P.C.
Dallas, TX
Collins, Philip J. .... Bethesda, MD
Collins, Philip R. .... Birmingham, AL
Collins, Philip Reilly .... Arlington, VA
Collins, Phyllis .... Fresno, CA
Collins, Price J. .... Dallas, TX
Collins & Pringle .... Denver, CO
Collins, Quillin & Knothe, Ltd.
La Crosse, WI
Collins, R. Earl .... Wauchula, FL
Collins, R. Scott .... Sarasota, FL
Collins, Ralph E., Jr. .... Montgomery, AL
Collins, Ralph O., III .... St. Louis, MO
Collins, Ralph T., III .... Redding, CA
Collins, Randall D. .... Lake Charles, LA
Beaumont, TX
Collins, Randolph M. .... Washington, DC
Collins, Raner C. .... Tucson, AZ
Collins, Ray A. .... Larose, LA
Collins, Raymond L. .... Treasury Department, Internal Revenue Service, GV
Collins, Raymond M. .... Los Angeles, CA
Collins, Rebecca Kozloff .... Phoenix, AZ
Collins, Rebecca L. .... Decatur, GA
Collins, Reuben B., II .... Washington, DC
Collins, Rhonda L. .... Ponte Vedra Beach, FL
Cincinnati, OH
Collins, Richard B. .... Anchorage, AK
Collins, Richard B. .... Boulder, CO
Collins, Richard B. .... Panama City, FL
Tallahassee, FL
Collins, Richard D. .... Carle Place, NY
Collins, Richard G. .... Fort Lauderdale, FL
Collins, Richard G. .... Buffalo, NY
Collins, Richard J. .... Joplin, MO
Collins, Richard J., Jr. .... St. Louis, MO
Collins, Richard Jay .... Temecula, CA
Collins, Richard L. .... Cullman, AL
Collins, Richard L., Jr. .... Painesville, OH
Collins, Richard S. .... New York, NY
Collins, Richard T. .... Orange, CA
Collins, Richard W. .... Vero Beach, FL
Collins, Richard W. .... Overland Park, KS
Collins, Richard W. .... Ponca City, OK
Collins, Robert A. .... Fort Lauderdale, FL
Collins, Robert B. .... Albuquerque, NM
Collins, Robert C. .... Troy, MI
Collins, Robert C., Jr. .... Calumet City, IL
Collins, Robert D. .... Phoenix, AZ
Collins, Robert D. .... Sacramento, CA
Collins, Robert E. .... Boston, MA
Cranston, RI
Collins, Robert E. .... Janesville, WI
Collins, Robert E., (P.A.) .... Graham, NC
Collins, Robert F. .... Minneapolis, MN
Collins, Robert F. The Law Firm, Professional Association .... Minneapolis, MN
Collins, Robert G. .... Helena, MT
Collins, Robert H. .... Forest Lake, MN
Collins, Robert J. .... Baton Rouge, LA
Collins, Robert J. .... Houston, TX
Collins, Robert K. .... San Jose, CA
Collins, Robert K. .... New York, NY
Collins, Robert L. .... Sacramento, CA
Collins, Robert L. .... Westford, MA
Collins, Robert L. .... Minneapolis, MN
Collins, Robert L. .... Houston, TX
Collins, Robert L., Jr. .... Calhoun, GA
Collins, Robert M. .... Birmingham, AL
Collins, Robert M. .... Chicago, IL
Collins, Robert M. .... Wichita, KS
Collins, Robert O., (P.A.)
Fort Lauderdale, FL
Collins, Robert R. .... Breckenridge, CO
Collins, Robert R., III .... Dallas, TX
Collins, Robert R., P.C. .... Breckenridge, CO
Collins, Robert S. .... Chicago, IL
Collins, Robert Scott .... Sarasota, FL
Collins, Robert T. .... San Juan, PR
Collins, Robert V., Jr. .... Quincy, MA
Collins, Robert W. .... Pendleton, OR
Collins, Robert W., Jr. .... Pendleton, OR
Collins, Robin .... El Paso, TX
Collins, Robin L. .... Dayton, OH

Collins, Rodney J. .... Naples, FL
Collins, Ronald B. .... El Campo, TX
Collins, Ronald D. .... Jackson, MS
Collins, Ronald G. .... Ridgewood, NJ
Collins, Ronald L. .... Clearfield, PA
Collins, Ronald S., Jr. .... Cherry Hill, NJ
Collins, Roy G. .... London, KY
Collins, Russell J. .... Houston, TX
Collins, Russell Lewis .... Oakland, CA
Collins, Russell S. .... Portland, OR
Collins, S. Keith .... Chicago, IL
Collins, Sally C. .... Morgantown, WV
Collins, Samuel B. .... Houston, TX
Collins, Sara E. .... Tampa, FL
Collins & Scanlon LLP .... Cleveland, OH
Collins & Schlothauer .... San Jose, CA
Collins & Schwartz, P.C. .... Walnut Creek, CA
Collins, Scott C. .... Boston, MA
Collins, Scott D. .... Los Angeles, CA
Collins, Scott E. .... Seattle, WA
Collins, Scott G. .... Moorhead, MN
Collins, Scott M. .... Seattle, WA
Collins, Scott P. .... Richmond, VA
Collins, Shaela McNulty .... Boston, MA
Collins, Sharlene N. .... Austin, TX
Collins, Sharon D. .... Elk Grove, CA
Collins, Shawn M. .... Naperville, IL
Collins, Shawna Davis .... Beaufort, SC
Collins, Sheila Day .... Laurel, MD
Collins, Sherri L. .... Marathon, FL
Collins, Sheryl A. .... Wyandotte, MI
Collins, Sigmund J. .... New York, NY
Collins, Simon R. .... Spokane, WA
Collins, Stanley J. .... Cincinnati, OH
Collins, Stanton J., Jr. .... Boston, MA
Collins, Stephan A. .... Anchorage, AK
Collins, Stephan B. .... Medina, OH
Collins, Stephanie A. .... Los Angeles, CA
Collins, Stephen A. .... Albertson, NY
Collins, Stephen C. .... Cooperstown, NY
Collins, Stephen C. .... Springfield, OH
Collins, Stephen G. .... Birmingham, AL
Collins, Stephen T. .... Northbrook, IL
Collins, Stephen T. .... Shreveport, LA
Collins, Steven M. .... Atlanta, GA
Collins, Steven R. .... Austin, TX
Collins, Steven W. .... Dallas, TX
Collins, Sue L. .... Irvine, CA
Collins, Susan B. .... West Seneca, NY
Collins, Susan B. .... Martin, TN
Collins, Susan E. .... Houston, TX
Collins, Susan L. .... Crown Point, IN
Collins, Susan L. .... Madison, WI
Collins, Susan M. .... Danvers, MA
Collins, Susan Porter .... Warren, OH
Collins, Suzanne Edgett .... Tampa, FL
Collins, Sven .... Denver, CO
Collins, T. Frank .... Jackson, MS
Collins, T. Fred .... Ardmore, OK
Collins, Tamara Jo .... Wichita, KS
Collins, Tarren .... Atascadero, CA
Collins, Ted F. .... Highland, KS
Collins, Ted G. .... Lewistown, IL
Collins, Terence R. .... La Crosse, WI
Collins, Terri Maderson .... Baton Rouge, LA
Collins, Terry Alexis .... Atlanta, GA
Collins, Terry G. .... Houston, TX
Collins, Terry P. .... Morris, MN
Collins, Thad J. .... Cedar Rapids, IA
Collins, Theda J. .... Fort Lauderdale, FL
Collins, Theodore J. .... St. Paul, MN
Collins, Theodore J. .... Seattle, WA
Collins, Thomas A. .... Orange, CA
Collins, Thomas A. .... Lexington, KY
Collins, Thomas A. .... Reno, NV
Collins, Thomas A. .... Austin, TX
Collins, Thomas Abell, II .... Naples, FL
Collins, Thomas D. .... Frankfort, KY
Collins, Thomas D., III .... Honolulu, HI
Collins, Thomas E. .... McLean, VA
Collins, Thomas F. .... Plainview, NY
Collins, Thomas F., Jr. .... Morristown, NJ
Collins, Thomas G. .... Boston, MA
Collins, Thomas G. .... Rochester, NY
Collins, Thomas G. .... Harrisburg, PA
Collins, Thomas J. .... New York, NY
Collins, Thomas J. .... Seattle, WA
Collins, Thomas M. .... Pasadena, CA
Collins, Thomas M. .... Cedar Rapids, IA
Collins, Thomas M., Jr. .... Camarillo, CA
Collins, Thomas P. .... Wilmington, DE
Collins, Thomas P. .... Richmond, VA
Collins, Thomas R. .... Everett, WA
Collins, Thomas S. .... Dubuque, IA
Collins, Thomas W. .... West Hartford, CT
Collins, Thomas W., III .... Kansas City, MO
Collins, Thos. B. .... United States Senate, Committee Legal Personnel, GV
Collins, Tim L. .... Cleveland, OH
Collins, Timothy M. .... Baker City, OR
Collins, Timothy R., Jr. .... Burbank, CA
Collins, Todd C. .... Houston, TX
Collins, Todd S. .... Philadelphia, PA
Collins, Toner & Rusen .... Florham Park, NJ
Collins, Tracy A. .... Oak Park, CA
Collins, Tracy M. .... New London, CT
Collins & Truett .... Destin, FL
Panama City, FL
Tallahassee, FL
Collins, Valerie A. .... Jacksonville, FL
Collins, Van A. .... Auburn, WA
Collins, Vernon J. .... Cherokee, OK
Collins, Vincent A. .... Clarksburg, WV
Collins, Virginia C. .... White Plains, NY
Collins, W. Douglas .... Morristown, TN
Collins, W. Eric .... Lafayette, CA
Collins, W. Scott .... Columbus, MS
Tupelo, MS

Collins, W. Thomas .... Indianapolis, IN
Collins, Wallace C., Jr. .... Alexandria, VA
Collins, Wallace E. J., III .... New York, NY
Collins, Walter J. .... Malverne, NY
Collins, Warren L. (Rip), Jr. .... Austin, TX
Collins, Wascha & McNally, P.C. .... Flint, MI
Collins, Wayne C. .... Cedar Rapids, IA
Collins, Wayne Dale .... New York, NY
Collins, Wayne M. .... Oakland, CA
Santa Rosa, CA
Collins, W. E. (Gene) .... Le Mars, IA
Collins, Webster & Krause, P.A.
Longwood, FL
Collins, Webster and Rouse, A Professional Corporation .... Joplin, MO
Collins, Wendy S. .... Montpelier, VT
Collins, Whitfield J. .... Fort Worth, TX
Collins, Wilbur L. .... Cincinnati, OH
Collins, William B. .... Manchester, CT
Collins, William B. .... Harrisonville, MO
Collins, William B. .... Buffalo, NY
Collins, William C. .... Midland, MI
Collins, William C. .... El Paso, TX
Collins, William C., Jr. .... Atlanta, GA
Collins, William C., Jr. .... Olympia, WA
Collins, William D. .... Boise, ID
Collins, William E. .... Encino, CA
Collins, William E. .... Rockford, IL
Collins, William E. .... Dallas, TX
Collins, William F. .... Glenmont, NY
Collins, William F. .... Pittsboro, NC
Collins, William G., II .... Vero Beach, FL
Collins, William G., Jr. .... Houston, TX
Collins, William J. .... San Diego, CA
Collins, William J.
Federal Energy Regulatory Commission, Office of the General Counsel, GV
Collins, William J. .... St. Paul, MN
Collins, William J., III .... Houston, TX
Collins, William Lewis .... Frankfort, KY
Collins, William Martin .... Youngstown, OH
Collins, William Ovid, Jr. .... Nashville, TN
Collins, William R. .... Canton, MS
Jackson, MS
Collins, William R. .... New York, NY
Collins, William S. .... New Orleans, LA
Collins, Willis B., Jr. .... Washington, DC
Collins, Wm. W., Jr. .... Fort Worth, TX
Collins & Workowski .... Covington, VA
Collins, Wynn L. .... Long Beach, CA
Collins, Wynter Reneaux .... Louisville, KY
Collins, Zorn, Jones & Wagner, P.C.
Oklahoma City, OK
Collins Berger, Susan M. .... Canton, OH
Collins-Cutter, Janet .... Lafayette, IN
Collinson, Brent P., Law Offices of
Truckee, CA
Collinson, Dale S. .... New York, NY
Collinson & Goldman, P.C.
Upper Marlboro, MD
Collinson, Joseph F., III
Upper Marlboro, MD
Collinson, Kenneth M. .... Milan, IL
Collinson, Lisa D. .... Los Angeles, CA
Collinson, Stephen A. .... Tulsa, OK
Collinson Vincent, Brenda J.
Oklahoma City, OK
Collins-Tremblay, Loretta .... Marlborough, MA
Collinsworth, Coy Mark .... Midland, TX
Collinsworth, Dawn M. .... Juneau, AK
Collinsworth, John D. .... Shreveport, LA
Collinsworth, John L. .... Oklahoma City, OK
Collinsworth, Kelly Estes .... Morehead, KY
Collinsworth, Mark T. .... San Diego, CA
Collinsworth, Vickie Lynn Howard
Paintsville, KY
Collis, Christian P. .... Farmington Hills, MI
Collis, Conway H. .... United States Senate, Committee Legal Personnel, GV
Collis, Elizabeth Yaghooti .... Columbus, OH
Collis, Eric R. .... Louisville, KY
Collis, Gary A. .... Los Angeles, CA
Collis and Kuhlman, Ltd. .... Hinsdale, IL
Collis, Michael T. .... Pittsburgh, PA
Collis, Pamela V. .... Pittsburgh, PA
Collis, Stuart M. .... Southfield, MI
Collis, Todd William .... Columbus, OH
Collishaw, William C.
Federal Deposit Insurance Corporation, GV
Collison, Bert A. .... New York, NY
Collison, Charles C. .... Saginaw, MI
Collison, Charles C., Jr. .... Saginaw, MI
Collison, Charles H. .... Endicott, NY
Collison, Charles H. .... Endwell, NY
Collison & Collison, P.C. .... Saginaw, MI
Collison, Daniel G. .... Saginaw, MI
Collison, Douglas A. .... Easton, MD
Collison, Edgar K., III .... Elgin, IL
Northbrook, IL
Collison, Gary H .... Syracuse, NY
Collison, Gregory .... Solvang, CA
Collison, Jack L. .... Solvang, CA
Collison, Jack L., A Professional Law Corporation .... Solvang, CA
Collison, Jeffrey C. .... Saginaw, MI
Collison, Joseph T. .... Saginaw, MI
Collison, Madeline A. .... Denver, CO
Collison, Patrick K .... Saginaw, MI
Collisson, Peter D. .... Newport Beach, CA
Collister, Edward G., Jr. .... Lawrence, KS
Collister and Kampschroeder
Lawrence, KS
Collister, Lawrence C. .... Denton, TX
Collister, William B. .... Denver, CO
Colliton, Edward O. .... Springfield, IL
Colliton, James P. .... New York, NY
Colliton, James W. .... Chicago, IL

Colliton, Janet M., Assessment Law Center
West Chester, PA
Collman, Richard A. .... Sanibel, FL
Collman-Brown, Victoria .... Palo Alto, CA
Collmer, June E. .... Charlottesville, VA
Collmer, Mark W. .... Houston, TX
Collmer, Stephen A. .... Dallas, TX
Collmeyer, Michael K .... Portland, OR
Colloca, Richard C. .... Denville, NJ
Collodel, Douglas J. .... Los Angeles, CA
Colloff, Margery A. .... New York, NY
Collom, Douglas H. .... Palo Alto, CA
Colloms, Carl E. .... Cleveland, TN
Collon, Thomas P. .... Bad Axe, MI
Collopy, Alice F., Law Offices of
Great Neck, NY
Collopy, Daniel F.
National Labor Relations Board, Office of the General Counsel, GV
Collopy, Daniel R. .... Boynton Beach, FL
Collopy, Jeanne F. .... Denver, CO
Collopy, Michael John .... Hobbs, NM
Collora, Michael A. .... Boston, MA
Collora, Philip J. .... Chicago, IL
Colloton, Annette Ballentine
East Greenbush, NY
Colloton, J. Michael .... Minneapolis, MN
Colloton, Patricia N. .... Leawood, KS
Collotta, Michael A. .... East Hartford, CT
Collum, Curtis W. .... Vidor, TX
Collum, Hugh H. .... Oklahoma City, OK
Collum, Leslie Anne .... Oklahoma City, OK
Collum, William R. .... Rohnert Park, CA
Collum-Butler, Sherry .... Florence, AL
Collums, Haley D. .... Department of State, Office of the Legal Adviser, GV
Collums, Lisa D. .... Gulfport, MS
Collura, Anthony M. .... New York, NY
Collura, Brenda K. .... Atlanta, GA
Collura, Frank J. .... Houston, TX
Collura, James A., Jr. .... Atlanta, GA
Collura, Thomas J. .... Albany, NY
Syracuse, NY
Collver, Gary A. .... Tulsa, OK
Collver, Kevin M. .... Miami, FL
Collyar, Daniel J. .... Denver, CO
Collyer, Gerald F. .... New York, NY
Collyer, Glen B. .... Los Angeles, CA
Collyer, Jeanne G. .... Oceanport, NJ
Collyer, Keith E. .... Satsuma, FL
Collyer, Macon .... Sarasota, FL
Collyer, Macon, P.A. .... Sarasota, FL
Collyer, Michael .... New York, NY
Collyer, Rosemary M. .... Washington, DC
Colm, Mark E. .... New York, NY
Colman, Abraham J. .... Los Angeles, CA
Colman, Albert M. .... Bloomfield Hills, MI
Colman, Albert M., P.C.
Bloomfield Hills, MI
Colman, Ariella M. .... New York, NY
Colman, Arlene A. .... Los Angeles, CA
Colman, Charles L. .... New York, NY
Colman, Christopher S. .... Woodbridge, NJ
Colman, David J. .... Bloomington, IN
Colman, Fred B. .... Milwaukee, WI
Colman, George .... Westlake Village, CA
Colman & Goodman, P.C.
Sterling Heights, MI
Colman, Jeffrey D. .... Chicago, IL
Colman, Jeffrey W. .... Newton, MA
Colman, Jonathan H. .... Paoli, PA
Colman, Jonathan H. .... Philadelphia, PA
Colman, Laurie M. .... Seattle, WA
Colman Law Offices .... Bloomington, IN
Colman, Mark S. .... Bayside, NY
Colman, Nancy Berz
West Palm Beach, FL
Colman, Neil M. .... Sterling Heights, MI
Colman, Peter A. .... Fayetteville, NY
Colman, Peter J. .... San Francisco, CA
Colman, Philip .... Weston, MA
Colman, Phyllis R. .... Los Angeles, CA
Colman, Richard Keith .... Carlisle, MA
Colman, Richard T. .... Washington, DC
Colman, Stephen J. .... North Quincy, MA
Colman, Susan E. .... Washington, DC
Colman, Tina L. .... Philadelphia, PA
Colman-Schwimmer, Arlene
Beverly Hills, CA
Colman-Schwimmer & Warren, A Professional Law Corporation
Beverly Hills, CA
Los Angeles, CA
Colmant, Andrew R. .... Keyport, NJ
Colmar, Craig P. .... Chicago, IL
Colmar, John L. .... Chicago, IL
Colmar, Joyce D. .... Atlanta, GA
Colmenares, Michael H. .... Gardena, CA
Colmenero, David E. .... Dallas, TX
Colmenero, Rudy R. .... Austin, TX
Colmenero, Valentin P. .... Alice, TX
Colmer, James H., Jr. .... Pascagoula, MS
Colmer, James H., Sr. .... Pascagoula, MS
Colmerauer, Michael J. .... Getzville, NY
Colmery, Mary Elizabeth .... Marietta, PA
Colmery, William R. .... Lancaster, PA
Colmey, Marie E. .... Los Angeles, CA
Colnar, Mary-Lynn R. .... Chicago, IL
Colner, Daniel .... Santa Monica, CA
Colner, James D. .... Columbus, OH
Colñn-Navarro, Fernando .... Chicago, IL
Colo, Michael S. .... Rocky Mount, NC
Coloca, Caterina .... Miami, FL
Colocotronis, Andrew L. .... Knoxville, TN
Colocotronis, Catherine Lane
Knoxville, TN
Colodne, Mark R. .... Boca Raton, FL
Colodner, Barbara Maltz .... Mineola, NY

Colodner, Michael .... New York, NY
Colodner, Warren H. .... New York, NY
Colodny, David A. .... Washington, DC
Colodny, Edwin I. .... Washington, DC
Colodny, Fass & Talenfeld, P.A.
Fort Lauderdale, FL
Colodny, Mark M. .... New York, NY
Colodny, Michael .... Fort Lauderdale, FL
Cologne, Gordon .... Sacramento, CA
Cologne, Knox M. .... Los Angeles, CA
Cologne, Steven J. .... San Diego, CA
Colognesi, Michael J. .... Southbridge, MA
Colom Law Firm, The, P.A. .... Columbus, MS
Colom, Wilbur O. .... Columbus, MS
Coloma-Agaran, Gilbert S. .... Wailuku, HI
Coloma-Gaines, Iris E. .... Philadelphia, PA
Colomb, Bartley J. .... New Albany, IN
Colomb, Michael A. .... Baton Rouge, LA
Colomb, P. Kevin .... New Orleans, LA
Colomb, Patrick L. .... Lafayette, LA
Colomb, Thomas W. .... Quincy, MA
Colomb, William F., Sr. .... Metairie, LA
Colombatto, P. Richard
San Francisco, CA
Colombe, Leroy E. .... Honolulu, HI
Colombe, Robt. N. .... Tonkawa, OK
Colombell, William E. .... Fairfax Station, VA
Colombik, Richard M. .... Schaumburg, IL
Colombik, Richard M., & Associates, P.C.
Schaumburg, IL
Colombo, Andrew G. .... Kansas City, MO
Colombo, Armond C., Jr. .... Boston, MA
Colombo, Barrett L. .... St. Cloud, MN
Colombo & Bonacci, P.C. .... Phoenix, AZ
Colombo, Carlos M. .... Orlando, FL
Colombo, Carol A. .... Phoenix, AZ
Colombo and Colombo, P.C.
Bloomfield Hills, MI
Detroit, MI
Mount Clemens, MI
Pontiac, MI
Colombo, Dennis P. .... Kansas City, MO
Colombo, Frederick .... Bloomfield Hills, MI
Colombo & Heavey, P.C. .... Papillion, NE
Colombo, Janice M. .... Stockton, CA
Colombo, Jeanne M. .... Rochester, NY
Colombo, Joseph G. .... Melbourne, FL
Colombo, Kevin M. .... Danville, IL
Colombo, Kitchin, Johnson, Dunn & Ball, L.L.P. .... Greenville, NC
Colombo, Leonard K. .... Los Angeles, CA
Colombo, Liana M. .... Portland, OR
Colombo, Louis A. .... Cleveland, OH
Colombo, Michael A. .... Greenville, NC
Colombo, Robert J. .... Detroit, MI
Colombo, Robert J., Jr. .... Detroit, MI
Colombo, Ronald J. .... New York, NY
Colombo, Sherril M. .... Miami, FL
Colombo, Steven J. .... Charlotte, NC
Colombo, Teresa J. .... Papillion, NE
Colombo, Virgil .... Portland, OR
Colon, Adrian A., Jr. .... Belle Chasse, LA
Colon, Agnes .... Dorchester, MA
Colon, Andres .... Department of Justice, Civil Division, GV
Colón, Colón & Martínez .... San Juan, PR
Colon, Cristobal .... San Juan, PR
Colon, Dan A. .... Honolulu, HI
Colon, Eduardo N. .... Fort Lauderdale, FL
Colon, Flor M. .... Rochester, NY
Colon, Francisco J. .... San Juan, PR
Colón, Francisco, Jr. .... Maitland, FL
Colón, Francisco, Jr., P.A., Law Offices of, The .... Maitland, FL
Colón, Georgiana S. .... San Juan, PR
Colon, Gil, Jr .... Lakeland, FL
Colon, Gloria Esther .... New York, NY
Colon, Gustavo Eugenio .... New Orleans, LA
Colón, Ida I. .... Hartford, CT
Colón, Jeffrey M. .... New York, NY
Colón, Jeffrey M. .... New York, NY
Colon, Jose .... Commerce, CA
Colon, Jose A. .... Phoenix, AZ
Colón, Karl F. .... Cincinnati, OH
Colón, Kenneth .... San Juan, PR
Colón, Louis N. .... Albuquerque, NM
Colon, Mark J. .... Grand Rapids, MI
Colon, Michael A. .... Humacao, PR
Colón, Nairda T. Lesa .... New Orleans, LA
Colon, Pedro A. .... Milwaukee, WI
Colon, Raymond L. .... New York, NY
Colón, Robert A. .... Rochester, NY
Colon, Sonia .... San Juan, PR
Colona, Michael J. .... St. Louis, MO
Colón-Acevedo, Sara E. .... San Juan, PR
Colón Arrarás, Edgardo .... San Juan, PR
Colón-Conde, Luis F. .... San Juan, PR
Colon-Cruz, Francisco A. .... San Juan, PR
Colon de Ducret, Ada .... San Juan, PR
Colonello, Donald A. .... New York, NY
Colonese, Michael D. .... Norwich, CT
Colon-Ferenczi, Giselle .... San Juan, PR
Colon-Garcia, Ennio M. .... San Juan, PR
Colon-Marchand, Carlos .... San Juan, PR
Colon-Martinez, Balbino .... San Juan, PR
Colon-Martinez, Noel .... San Juan, PR
Colon Morales, Ivan A. .... San Juan, PR
Colon-Morales, Ruben .... San Juan, PR
Colonna, Jas. J. .... Bronx, NY
Colonna, John A. .... Forest Hills, NY
Colonna, Leonard A. .... Greensboro, NC
Colonna, Maria .... Staten Island, NY
Colonna, Thomas F. .... Medford, MA
Colonna, William N., III .... Baltimore, MD
Colon-Navarro, Fernando .... Houston, TX
Colón-Pagán, Francisco J. .... San Juan, PR
Colon Ramery, Luis E. .... Ponce, PR

Colón-Ramirez, Francisco E. ... San Juan, PR
Colon Ramirez, Jose L. ... Caguas, PR
Colon-Rivera, Frances R. ... San Juan, PR
Colón-Rodriguez, José E. ... San Juan, PR
Colopy, Conchita M. ... Akron, OH
Colopy, Hugh M. ... Akron, OH
Colopy, James H. ... San Francisco, CA
Colopy, Katie J. ... Dallas, TX
Colopy, Robert H. ... Akron, OH
Colorado, Gabriel ... Los Angeles, CA
Colorado-Laguna, Antonio J. ... Washington, DC
Colosey, Elise M. ... Eden Prairie, MN
Colosi, Darryl J. ... Buffalo, NY
Colosi, Joseph A. ... Rocky Gap, VA
Colosi, Michael F. ... New York, NY
Colosi, Robert A. ... Phoenix, AZ
Colosimo, John M. ... Virginia, MN
Colosimo, Kevin L. ... Erie, PA
Colosimo, Louis A. ... Westport, CT
Colosimo, Patchin, Aronson & Kearney, Ltd. ... Virginia, MN
Colosimo, Richard J. ... Palo Alto, CA
Colosky, Douglas S. ... Simsbury, CT
Colosky, James M. ... Grand Junction, CO
Colovas, Dean A. ... Cleveland, OH
Colovic, Mary Anne ... Minneapolis, MN
Colovos, Bill ... Southgate, MI
Colowich, John F. ... Fort Pierce, FL
Colowich, John F. ... Vero Beach, FL
Colowick, Maryda S. ... Nashville, TN
Colozzi, Arthur L. ... Garden City, NY
Colozzi, Gaetano L. ... Syracuse, NY
Colpean & Associates, P.C. ... Lansing, MI
Colpean, John C. ... Lansing, MI
Colpitts, Donald R. ... New Orleans, LA
Colpoys, Francis L., Jr. ... Braintree, MA
Colpoys, J. Michael, (P.C.) ... Dallas, TX
Colquett, Donald F. ... Opp, AL
Colquett, P. Ted ... Birmingham, AL
Colquhoun & Colquhoun, A Professional Corporation ... Morristown, NJ
Colquhoun, Kevin F. ... Morristown, NJ
Colquhoun, Moira E. ... Morristown, NJ
Colquhoun, Robert F. ... Morristown, NJ
Colquhoun, Robert F., II ... Morristown, NJ
Colquhoun, Sean F. ... Morristown, NJ
Colquitt, John D. ... Tucker, GA
Colquitt, Joseph A. ... Tuscaloosa, AL
Colquitt & Knudson, P.C. ... Las Vegas, NV
Colquitt, Michael G. ... Marietta, GA
Colquitt, Richard P. ... Houston, TX
Colquitt, Ronald A. ... Las Vegas, NV
Colrick, Edward F., Jr. ... Spring Lake, NJ
Colsky, Andrew E. ... Fort Lauderdale, FL
Colsky, Steven A. ... Miami, FL
Colsky, Susan Craft ... Sausalito, CA
Colson, Bill ... Miami, FL
Colson, Brian M. ... Washington, DC
Colson, Christopher D. ... Santa Ana, CA
Colson, David A. ... Washington, DC
Colson, David L. ... Farmington, MO
Colson, Dean C. ... Miami, FL
Colson, Dennis C. ... Moscow, ID
Colson, Earl M. ... Washington, DC
Colson, Enid M. ... Los Angeles, CA
Colson, Faith ... Treasury Department, Internal Revenue Service, GV
Colson, G. Wallace ... Stone Mountain, GA
Colson, George L. ... Park Forest, IL
Colson, Guy R. ... Lexington, KY
Colson, Hicks, Eidson, Colson, Matthews, Martinez & Mendoza ... Miami, FL
Colson, Jacqueline F. ... Burnsville, NC
Colson, Joyce E. ... Boulder, CO
Colson, Kerry Anne ... South Easton, MA
Colson, O. Kirby, III ... St. Louis, MO
Colson, R. Scott, III ... Birmingham, AL
Colson, Randall E. ... Dallas, TX
Colson, Stephen R. ... Gulfport, MS
Colson, Stephen R. ... Jackson, MS
Colson, Sybil Kay ... Paris, TX
Colson, Wagner & Ray ... Farmington, MO
Colson, William P. ... Chicago, IL
Colson, Wm. G. ... Louisville, KY
Colson-Burns, Mary Jo ... Minneapolis, MN
Colson-Quinn ... Boulder, CO
Colston, Cheryl J. ... Chicago, IL
Colston, Fred ... Washington, DC
Colston, Gregory A. ... Cincinnati, OH
Colston, Harold D. ... Rocky Mount, NC
Colston, Harold D., P.A. ... Rocky Mount, NC
Colston, J. Gregory ... Kansas City, MO
Colston, Kristen M. ... Washington, DC
Colston, Larry A. ... Philadelphia, PA
Colston, Sean Dewayne ... Fort Worth, TX
Colston, Tambra P. ... Rome, GA
Colt, Charlene ... Belmont, MA
Colt, Cynthia ... New York, NY
Colt, David G. ... Pittsfield, MA
Williamstown, MA
Colt, Edward S. ... Colorado Springs, CO
Colt, Elizabeth ... Warwick, RI
Colt, James D. ... Beverly, MA
Boston, MA
Colt Knutson ... Manhattan, KS
Colt, Mack V. ... Manhattan, KS
Colt, Suzanne K. ... New York, NY
Colteaux, John H. ... San Anselmo, CA
Coltellino, Brian James ... Bethpage, NY
Colten, Richard J. ... Fairfax, VA
Colter, Gretchen Ann ... Detroit, MI
Colter, Martha ... Denver, CO
Colter, Michael P. ... San Diego, CA
Coltharp, L. H., Jr. ... De Ridder, LA
Colthurst, Eric ... Plymouth, MI
Colthurst, Wallace G. ... Larkspur, CA
Coltin, Mark J. ... Boston, MA
Coltin, Mark J., P.C. ... Boston, MA
Coltin, Robert E. ... Scottsdale, AZ
Coltman, Thomas J. ... Fairview Park, OH
Coltman & Valore, Co., L.P.A. ... Fairview Park, OH
Colton, Alison Eckstein ... St. Paul, MN
Colton, Barnum L., Jr. ... Washington, DC
Colton, Bruce E. ... Springfield, MA
Colton, Bruce H. ... Fort Pierce, FL
Colton, Bruce L. ... Detroit, MI
Colton, Carolyn ... Washington, DC
Colton, Carrie A. ... San Rafael, CA
Colton, Christopher K. ... Clarklake, MI
Colton, David S. ... Washington, DC
Colton, Donne L., Jr. ... Alexandria, VA
Colton, Edward A. ... Los Angeles, CA
Colton, Eldon L. ... Cedar Rapids, IA
Colton, Gary S., Jr., ... Chicago, IL
Colton, Glenn C. ... New York, NY
Colton, Gregory S. ... Indianapolis, IN
Colton, Henry E. ... Asheville, NC
Colton, Howard Eric ... Freeport, NY
Colton, I. Daniel ... Minneapolis, MN
Colton, Jacqueline Rackow ... Woodbury, NY
Colton, Jayson Matthew ... Farmington Hills, MI
Colton, Jennifer Williams ... Atlanta, GA
Colton, Jerome G. ... Long Beach, CA
Colton, Jerrold D. ... Voorhees, NJ
Colton, John A. ... Sarasota, FL
Colton, John P., Jr. ... Memphis, TN
Colton, Joseph R. ... San Francisco, CA
Colton, Kendrew H. ... Washington, DC
Colton, Kevin M. ... Torrance, CA
Colton, Kim S ... Salt Lake City, UT
Colton, Kimberly H. ... House of Representatives, Congressional Assistants, GV
Colton, Kimberly J. ... Philadelphia, PA
Colton, Larisa Murphy ... Dallas, TX
Colton, Laurence P. ... Atlanta, GA
Colton, Lee F. ... Los Angeles, CA
Colton Mann Partnership ... Los Angeles, CA
Colton, Marvin V. ... Albia, IA
Colton, Michael A. ... Santa Barbara, CA
Colton, Michael W. ... Farmington Hills, MI
Colton, Michelle McQuarrie ... St. Paul, MN
Colton, Milo L. ... Winnebago, NE
Colton, Neal D. ... Philadelphia, PA
Colton, Paul D. ... Las Vegas, NV
Colton, Philip T. ... Minneapolis, MN
Colton, R. Douglas ... Nashville, TN
Colton, Richard I. ... Houston, TX
Colton, Robert C. ... Los Angeles, CA
Colton, Roberta A. ... Tampa, FL
Colton, Roger B. ... West Palm Beach, FL
Colton, S. David ... Phoenix, AZ
Colton, Seth M. ... Minneapolis, MN
Colton, Shane D. ... Billings, MT
Colton, Stein & Zamost ... Voorhees, NJ
Colton, Susan Sudick ... Philadelphia, PA
Colton, Sylvia ... Midvale, UT
Colton, William A. ... Brooklyn, NY
Coltrain, Keith E. ... Raleigh, NC
Coltrane and Alford ... Beaufort, SC
Charleston, SC
Hilton Head Island, SC
Ridgeland, SC
Coltrane, Charles W. ... Greensboro, NC
Coltrane, Curtis L. ... Hilton Head Island, SC
Coltrane, James E. ... Greensboro, NC
Coltrane, Joseph M., Jr. ... Kernersville, NC
Coltun, Harry ... Boston, MA
Coltzer, Robert G. ... Galveston, TX
Colucci, Anne A. ... Mount Kisco, NY
Colucci, Anthony J., III ... Buffalo, NY
Colucci, Anthony J., Jr. ... Jupiter, FL
Buffalo, NY
Colucci & Associates, P.C. ... Beverly, MA
Colucci, Carmine J. ... Las Vegas, NV
Colucci, Cecilia C. ... Atlanta, GA
Colucci & Colucci, P.C. ... Dedham, MA
Milton, MA
Colucci, Darin Michael ... Milton, MA
Colucci, Dean M. ... New York, NY
Colucci, Dino Matthew ... Milton, MA
Colucci, Donald J. ... San Francisco, CA
Colucci, Frank J. ... New York, NY
Scarsdale, NY
Colucci, Gregory J. ... Scarsdale, NY
Colucci, John ... New York, NY
Colucci, John D. ... Beverly, MA
Colucci, John N. ... Livonia, MI
Colucci, Mark ... Indianapolis, IN
Colucci, Marlene M. ... Washington, DC
Colucci, Michael J. ... Warwick, RI
Colucci, Michele A. ... Los Angeles, CA
Colucci, Paul J. ... New York, NY
Colucci, Thomas J. ... Arlington, VA
Colucci & Umans ... New York, NY
Scarsdale, NY
Colucci, Vito A. ... Addison, IL
Colucci, William R. ... San Jose, CA
Coluccio, Bryan P. ... Seattle, WA
Coluccio, Christopher A. ... Tukwila, WA
Coluccio, Kevin ... Seattle, WA
Colucy, Barbara Lynn ... Boston, MA
Columbia, Sarah Chapin, (P.C.) ... Boston, MA
Columbia, Vincent J., Jr. ... Baltimore, MD
Frederick, MD
Columbine, Linda ... Center Harbor, NH
Columbo, Elizabeth Mihalyak ... New York, NY
Columbro, Elaine J. ... Westlake, OH
Columbus, R. Timothy ... Washington, DC
Columbus, Stephen ... Stoneham, MA
Columbus, Thomas B. ... Surfside, FL
Colunga, Rogelio ... San Antonio, TX
Colussi, Joseph A. ... Madison, IN
Colussi Law Office ... Madison, IN
Colussi, Louis Andrew ... Erie, PA
Colussy, Susan Eileen Hillick ... Atlanta, GA
Coluzza, Michael Anthony ... Utica, NY
Coluzzi, Anthony C. ... Hempstead, NY
Coluzzi, Samuel C. ... New York, NY
Colvard, Howard C., Jr. ... North Wilkesboro, NC
Colvard, Judith Armstrong ... Delray Beach, FL
Colvard, Judith Armstrong, P.A. ... Delray Beach, FL
Colvard, Landon, Jr. ... Crossville, TN
Colvard, Michael G. ... San Antonio, TX
Colvard, Todd H. ... Houston, TX
Colven, Bruce R. ... Vancouver, WA
Colven, Thomas J., III ... Dallas, TX
Colver, David O. ... Holyoke, CO
Colver, John W. ... Anchorage, AK
Colvert, Christopher A. ... Houston, TX
Colvert, Ramon P. ... Denver, CO
Colvig, Anne J. ... Sawyers Bar, CA
Colvig, Timothy A. ... Oakland, CA
Colville, Carolyn June ... Alexandria, VA
Colville, Dianne Kremen ... Walnut Creek, CA
Colville, Douglas W. ... Denver, CO
Colville, Mary Dauer ... Pittsburgh, PA
Colville, Michael C. ... Pittsburgh, PA
Colville, Robert J. ... Pittsburgh, PA
Colville, Sam L. ... Prairie Village, KS
Kansas City, MO
Colville, Stephen E. ... Sacramento, CA
Colville, William W. ... Toledo, OH
Colvin, A. Elizabeth ... Austin, TX
Colvin, Amy L. ... Halesite, NY
Colvin, Andrew M. ... Oakland, CA
Colvin, Arlene D. ... Gary, IN
Colvin, Arthur B., (P.C.) ... New York, NY
Colvin, Barbara Jean ... Carbondale, IL
Colvin, Barnett Jay ... Detroit, MI
Colvin, Bruce E. ... Winston-Salem, NC
Colvin, C. Richard ... Newport, KY
Colvin, Charles B. ... New Orleans, LA
Colvin, Christopher A. ... New Orleans, LA
Colvin, Clark T. ... Jackson, MS
Colvin, David L. ... Gretna, LA
Colvin, Dean A. ... Plymouth, IN
Colvin, Diane T. ... Bainbridge Island, WA
Colvin, Emmett ... Dallas, TX
Colvin, F. Neal, Jr. ... Fort Lauderdale, FL
Colvin & Foster, P.A. ... Gaffney, SC
Spartanburg, SC
Union, SC
Colvin, Geoffrey J. ... Secaucus, NJ
Colvin, Gerald D., Jr. ... Birmingham, AL
Colvin, Gerald DeWitt (Whit), III ... Birmingham, AL
Colvin, Greene B. (Bing), III ... Dermott, AR
Colvin, Gregory L. ... San Francisco, CA
Colvin, Gregory P. ... Redmond, OR
Colvin, Gus, Jr. ... Anniston, AL
Colvin, Ira B. ... Reform, AL
Colvin, James G., II ... Colorado Springs, CO
Colvin, James H., Jr. ... Homer, LA
Colvin, Jeremy M. ... West Palm Beach, FL
Colvin, Joe E. ... Reno, NV
Colvin, Joe E., A P.C., Law Offices of ... Reno, NV
Colvin, John M. ... Seattle, WA
Colvin, John O. ... United States Tax Court, GV
Colvin, John R. ... Winchester, TN
Colvin, John V. ... Orlando, FL
Colvin, Joseph W. ... Fort Worth, TX
Colvin, K. Denny ... Yakima, WA
Colvin, Kathy D. ... Longview, TX
Colvin, Michael D. ... Dallas, TX
Colvin, Michael H. ... Lafayette, LA
Colvin, Michael P. ... Baton Rouge, LA
Colvin, Michael S. ... Dallas, TX
Colvin, Michael V. ... Florham Park, NJ
Colvin, Morton R. ... Windsor, CA
Colvin, Norton A., Jr. ... Brownsville, TX
Colvin, Paul ... Dover, NJ
Colvin, R. Keith ... New Orleans, LA
Colvin, Rick F. ... Rochester, MN
Colvin, Robert D. ... Houston, TX
Colvin, Roger A. ... Montebello, CA
Colvin, Ronald H. ... Spartanburg, SC
Colvin, Sandra Pauline ... Southfield, MI
Colvin, Shannon O. ... Towson, MD
Colvin, Sherrill Wm. ... Fort Wayne, IN
Colvin, Stanley S. ... United States Information Agency, Office of the General Counsel, GV
Colvin, Sterling W. ... Cincinnati, OH
Colvin & Stout, P.C. ... Ennis, TX
Colvin, Terra L. ... Columbus, OH
Colvin, Timothy K. ... Austin, TX
Colvin, William ... Greensburg, KY
Colvin, William Given ... Chattanooga, TN
Colvin, William L. ... Canton, GA
Colway, Mary H. ... Mineola, NY
Colwell, Amie ... New York, NY
Colwell, Angelica M. ... Toledo, OH
Colwell, Carl T. ... Wyandotte, MI
Colwell, Christian ... Andover, MA
Colwell, David K. ... South Padre Island, TX
Colwell, Dennis R. ... Aberdeen, WA
Colwell, John C. ... San Diego, CA
Colwell, John F. ... Department of Labor, GV
Colwell, Joy L. ... Munster, IN
Colwell, Kathleen Bradley ... North Andover, MA
Colwell, Kimberly E. ... San Francisco, CA
Colwell, Marcus R. ... New York, NY
Colwell, Michael J. ... Aurora, IL
Colwell, Misty L. ... Long Beach, CA
Colwell, Neil A. ... Woodland, CA
Colwell, Paul M. ... Roseland, NJ
Colwell, Robbie E. ... Blairsville, GA
Colwell, Robert C. ... Palo Alto, CA
Colwell, Stephen D. ... Berkeley, CA
Colwell, Teresa M. ... Berkeley, CA
Colwell, Tina M. ... Grand Prairie, TX
Colwell, Vicki L. ... Omaha, NE
Colwell, William F. ... Pawnee City, NE
Colwell, William S. ... New Haven, CT
North Haven, CT
Colwell, William S. ... Fairfax, VA
Springfield, VA
Colwick, Elizabeth Faxon ... Tuscaloosa, AL
Colwill, Gary F. ... Sioux Falls, SD
Colwin, David J. ... Fond du Lac, WI
Colwin, Mercedes ... Garden City, NY
Colyar, Robert C. ... San Jose, CA
Colyer, Bruce E., (P.C.) ... Osage Beach, MO
Colyer, Catherine ... Washington, DC
Colyer, Jeffrey G. ... Minneapolis, MN
Colyer, Jennifer L. ... New York, NY
Colyer, Scott I. ... Denver, CO
Colyer, Terence F. ... San Rafael, CA
Coman, Daniel G. ... Naperville, IL
Coman, Evelyn M. ... Durham, NC
Coman, Francis X. ... Charlotte, NC
Coman, J. Michael ... Pasadena, TX
Coman, James J. ... Raleigh, NC
Coman, John B. ... Beverly Hills, CA
Coman, John C. ... Westlake, OH
Coman, John M., Jr. ... New Orleans, LA
Coman, Matthew ... New Orleans, LA
Comander, James F. ... Miami, FL
Comander, James F., P.A. ... Miami, FL
Comanor, Lawrence B. ... Akron, OH
Comar, Peter L. ... Alamosa, CO
Comarow, David ... Las Vegas, NV
Comarow, Murray ... Bethesda, MD
Comart, Jack ... Augusta, ME
Comart, Kim, (Mr.) ... Boston, MA
Comas, Christine M. ... New York, NY
Comas, Waldemar A. ... Valhalla, NY
Comas-Rodon, Arsenio ... San Juan, PR
Comatos, Gerard J. ... Poughkeepsie, NY
Comay, Estelle F. ... Pittsburgh, PA
Comba, Alan R. ... Princeton, IL
Comba, Allen P. ... Woodbridge, NJ
Combaluzier, George L. ... Coral Gables, FL
Combe, Daniela K. ... Hopewell Junction, NY
Combe, David A. ... Metairie, LA
Combe, John C., Jr. ... New Orleans, LA
Combellack, David W. ... Placerville, CA
Combellack & Driscoll ... Placerville, CA
Comberiati, Vicki K. ... Greenwich, CT
Combes, Jeffrey E. ... New Orleans, LA
Combest, Christopher ... Chicago, IL
Combest, Christopher E. ... Overland Park, KS
Combest, Ronald R. ... Covelo, CA
Combo, James F. ... Coeur d'Alene, ID
Combo, John M. ... Chandler, AZ
Combo, John X. ... Idaho Falls, ID
Combo, Mary Ellen ... Olympia, WA
Combo, William P. ... Idaho Falls, ID
Combos & Associates, P.C. ... Nashville, TN
Combos, Jeffrey W. ... Nashville, TN
Combothekras, Eoanna ... Flushing, NY
Combre, Charlotte A. ... Atlanta, GA
Combs, A. Bennett ... Laguna Niguel, CA
Combs, A. Bennett, A Professional Corporation ... Laguna Niguel, CA
Combs, Ann Laine ... Washington, DC
Combs, Ann Ruley ... Cincinnati, OH
Combs & Associates, P.C. ... Phoenix, AZ
Combs, Barbara Harris ... Dayton, OH
Combs, Ben M. ... Lexington, KY
Combs, Bert L. ... Tallahassee, FL
Combs, Beth A. ... Pasadena, CA
Combs, Brenda M. ... Tampa, FL
Combs, Brian G. ... Milledgeville, GA
Combs, C. Bruce ... Bozeman, MT
Combs, C. Edward ... Middletown, OH
Combs, C. Kilmer ... Lexington, KY
Combs, Carl E. ... Modesto, CA
Oakdale, CA
Combs, Carl H. ... Hilton Head Island, SC
Combs, Cathleen M. ... Chicago, IL
Combs, Charles H. ... Oregon City, OR
Combs, Charles W. ... Lake Oswego, OR
Combs, Christopher A. ... Phoenix, AZ
Combs, Christopher W. ... Los Angeles, CA
Combs, Claire Grandpré ... Cincinnati, OH
Combs & Combs, P.S.C. ... Pikeville, KY
Prestonsburg, KY
Combs, Craig S. ... Morristown, NJ
Combs, Donald Howard ... Pikeville, KY
Combs, Doris J. ... Puyallup, WA
Combs, Douglas Clinton, Jr. ... Hazard, KY
Combs, Douglas G. ... Vancouver, WA
Combs, Douglas L. ... Shawnee, OK
Combs, Elaine J. ... New York, NY
Combs, Eric K. ... Cincinnati, OH
Combs, Eva B. ... Schaumburg, IL
Combs, Frederick H., II ... Tazewell, VA
Combs, Gene D. ... Collinsville, OK
Combs & Greene, P.A. ... Jacksonville, FL
Combs, Gregory N. ... Tahlequah, OK
Combs, Gregory S. ... Mobile, AL
Combs, Gwendolyn Gregory ... Jackson, MS
Combs, Heather ... Stanton, KY
Combs, Herbert C., Jr. ... Shelby, NC

Combs & Hoffman ....Versailles, KY
Combs and Isaac ....Prestonsburg, KY
Combs, J. Michael ....Nashville, TN
Combs, Jack B. ....Grand Rapids, MI
Combs, Jack L., Jr. ....Blountville, TN
Combs, James A. ....Prestonsburg, KY
Combs, James M. ....West Lawn, PA
Combs, Jameson D. ....Hazard, KY
Combs, Jan J. ....Austin, TX
Combs, Jeanne ....Rapid City, SD
Combs, Jo Ann E. ....Kaufman, TX
Combs, John Allan ....Lexington, KY
Combs, John B. ....Grand Rapids, MI
Combs, John Byron ....Oklahoma City, OK
Combs, John M., Jr. ....Jackson, MS
Combs, Katherine K. ....Philadelphia, PA
Combs, Keith R. ....Englewood, CO
Combs, Kenneth H. ....Newport Beach, CA
Combs, Kenneth L. ....St. George, UT
Combs, Kevin Clark ....Memphis, TN
Combs, Lamar G. ....Beaumont, TX
Combs, Lanny ....Hazard, KY
Combs, Larry D. ....Sarasota, FL
Combs, Laurence A. ....La Grange, IL
Combs, Lee R. ....Denver, CO
Combs, Leigh Taylor ......**Newport Beach, CA**
Combs, Leslie ....**Fort Worth, TX**
Combs, Lewis A., Jr. ....Knoxville, TN
Combs, Loren D. ....Tacoma, WA
Combs, Lori ....Oklahoma City, OK
Combs, Lou Ellen ....Orlando, FL
Combs, Mark E. ....Cincinnati, OH
Combs, Megan A ....Castle Rock, CO
Combs, Melvin, Jr. ....Oklahoma City, OK
Combs, Michael D. ....Chandler, AZ
Combs & Miner, P.C. ....Castle Rock, CO
Combs, Nancy ....Cedar Rapids, IA
Combs, Nelson Brown ....San Francisco, CA
Combs, Paul C. ....Prestonsburg, KY
Combs, Philip J. ....Charleston, WV
Combs, Ralph K. ....Versailles, KY
Combs, Randall R. ....Concord, NC
Combs, Rania S. ....Houston, TX
Combs, Reginald F. ....Winston-Salem, NC
Combs, Richard H. ....Quincy, FL
Combs, Robert P. ....Pikeville, KY
Combs, Robert V.
Department of the Air Force, Office of the Judge Advocate General, GV
Combs, Roger E. ....Albany, MO
Combs, Roland V., III ....Oklahoma City, OK
Combs, Ronald D. ....Gainesville, FL
Combs, Ronald G. ....Hazard, KY
Combs, Roy A. ....Oakland, CA
Combs, Sara Walter ....Stanton, KY
Combs & Schaefer ....Middletown, OH
Combs & Schaertel ....Claremont, CA
San Francisco, CA
Combs, Scott ....Southfield, MI
Combs, Stephen Benjamin
Jacksonville, FL
Combs, Steven Daniel ....Pikeville, KY
Combs, Steven E. ....Pittsfield, MA
Combs, Steven P. ....Jacksonville, FL
Combs and Stirn ....Fort Collins, CO
Combs, Su-Lyn ....Colorado Springs, CO
Combs, Susan ....Austin, TX
Combs, T. Neal ....Austin, TX
Combs, Tammy Owens ....Chattanooga, TN
Combs, Terri L. ....Des Moines, IA
Combs, Thomas H. ....Davie, FL
Combs, Tina W. ....San Francisco, CA
Combs, Todd J. ....Charlotte, NC
Combs, Tom ....New York, NY
Combs, Travis, Jr. ....La Grange, KY
Combs, Virginia M. ....Hattiesburg, MS
Combs, W. Henry, III ....Casper, WY
Combs, Wesley E. ....Miami, OK
Combs, William B. ....Evansville, IN
Combs, William L. ....Evanston, WY
Combs, William R. ....Fort Collins, CO
Comden, Anthony R. ....Grand Rapids, MI
Comden, Leonard J. ....Tarzana, CA
Come, Norton J.
National Labor Relations Board, Office of the General Counsel, GV
Comeau, David J. ....Chicago, IL
Comeau, Irene R. ....Boston, MA
Comeau, John J. ....Treasury Department, Internal Revenue Service, GV
Comeau, Lisa M. ....New York, NY
Comeau, Louis P. ....Elizabethtown, NY
Essex, NY
Comeau, Maldegen, Templeman & Indall, L.L.P. ....Santa Fe, NM
Comeau, Michael R. ....Santa Fe, NM
Comeau, Paul R. ....Boca Raton, FL
Buffalo, NY
New York, NY
Comeau, Robert F.
United States Court Of Veterans Appeals, GV
Comeaux, Craig S. ....Austin, TX
Comeaux, David J.
Charlotte Amalie, St. Thomas, VI
Comeaux and Grace ....Baton Rouge, LA
Comeaux, James ....Columbus, OH
Comeaux, Jeanne C. ....Baton Rouge, LA
Comeaux, Keith R. ....New Iberia, LA
Comeaux, Norman E. ....New Orleans, LA
Comeaux, Paul E. ....Dallas, TX
Comeaux, Robert J., Jr. ....Metairie, LA
Comeaux, Todd C. ....Baton Rouge, LA
Comeaux, Walter L. ....Baton Rouge, LA
Comegno, John B., II ....Haddonfield, NJ
Comegys, Walker B. ....Boston, MA
Comegys, William M., III ......Shreveport, LA
Comegys, William M., III, A Professional Law Corp. ....Shreveport, LA
Comella, Ignatius A. ....Shaker Heights, OH
Comella, Philip L. ....Chicago, IL
Comellas, Donna K. ....Orlando, FL
Comen, Steven J. ....Boston, MA
Comens, Leslie E. ....Bayside, NY
Comenzo, Richard F. ....Brookline, MA
Comenzo, Susan A. ....Albany, NY
Comer, Amy Beth ....Washington, DC
Comer, Ann K. ....Milwaukee, WI
Comer, Carol S. ....Indianapolis, IN
Comer, Cheryl A. ....Tacoma, WA
Comer, Dale A. ....Lincoln, NE
Comer, David L. ....Lawrenceburg, TN
Comer, Donald M., II ....Jonesboro, GA
Comer, Edward H. ....Washington, DC
Comer, Harold L. ....Pampa, TX
Comer, Jerome E. ....Indianapolis, IN
Comer, Jess L. ....Nashville, TN
Comer, John D. ....Macon, GA
Comer, John F. ....Greensboro, NC
Comer, John M. ....Dakota City, NE
Comer, Katherine M. ....Boston, MA
Comer, Kristin L. ....Rancho Cordova, CA
Comer, Lee T. ....Danville, IN
Comer, Linda S. ....Denver, CO
Comer, Lisa E.
Environmental Protection Agency, Office of Enforcement and Compliance Assurance, GV
Comer, Lori K. ....Norristown, PA
Comer, Marc J. ....Asbury Park, NJ
Comer, Mary Lee ....Danville, IN
Comer, Neal S. ....White Plains, NY
Comer, Neil R. ....Osgood, IN
Comer, Neil R., A Prof. Corp., Law Offices of
Osgood, IN
Comer, Patricia Ann York ....Birmingham, AL
Comer, R.J. ....Los Angeles, CA
Comer, Robert D. ....Denver, CO
Comer, Roy L. ....Newport Beach, CA
Comer, Steven E. ....San Diego, CA
Comer, Thomas H., Jr. ....Booneville, MS
Comer, Thomas M. ....Hazlet, NJ
Comer, Timothy S. ....Houston, TX
Comer, Walter W. ....Bethesda, MD
Comeras, Leonard A. ....Columbus, OH
Comerford, Anita J. ....Norwell, MA
Comerford, Barbara B. ....Midland Park, NJ
Comerford, Brian E. ....Brooklyn, NY
Comerford, Brian J. ....Hartford, CT
Comerford & Britt, L.L.P.
Winston-Salem, NC
Comerford, Carolyn A. ....Stamford, CT
Comerford, Ciara M. ....Detroit, MI
Comerford, David L. ....Philadelphia, PA
Comerford & Doliner ....Midland Park, NJ
Comerford, Gregory A. ....New York, NY
Comerford, Harry G. ....Chicago, IL
Comerford, James D. ....Atlanta, GA
Comerford, John ....Madison, WI
Comerford, John Patrick ....Buffalo, NY
Comerford, Mary Guerin
New Rochelle, NY
Comerford, Michael J. ....Garden City, NY
Comerford, Michael J., P.C., Law Offices of
Garden City, NY
Comerford, Patrick J. ....New York, NY
Comerford, Peter Flynn ....Niagara Falls, NY
Comerford, Peter J. ....Providence, RI
Comerford, Richard F., Jr. ....Stamford, CT
Comerford, Thomas M. ....Plano, TX
Comerford, Thomas P. ....Scranton, PA
Comerford, W. Thompson, Jr.
Winston-Salem, NC
Comerio, D. Ann ....San Antonio, TX
Comes, Ronald L. ....Omaha, NE
Comess, Alan B. ....Virginia Beach, VA
Comess, Barry S. ....Richmond, VA
Comess, Faye K. ....Washington, DC
Comet, Howard B. ....New York, NY
Cometa, Angelo T. ....New York, NY
Cometa, Thomas J. ....Newtown Square, PA
Cometa, Thomas S. ....Kingston, PA
Cometti, Joseph C. ....Charleston, WV
Cometti, Mario D. ....Albany, NY
Comey Boyd & Luskin ....Washington, DC
Comey, Eugene J. ....Washington, DC
Comey, Margaret Walker ....Cincinnati, OH
Comfort, Brian T. ....Tacoma, WA
Comfort, Cameron G. ....Olympia, WA
Comfort, Davies & Comfort ....Tacoma, WA
Comfort, E. Ronald ....Westminster, MD
Comfort, Frank B. ....Des Moines, IA
Comfort, James T. ....Dallas, TX
Comfort, Jennifer Adair ....Terrace Park, OH
Comfort, Julie P. ....Peoria, IL
Comfort, Kathryn C. ....Tacoma, WA
Comfort, Kim W., (Mr.) ....Tacoma, WA
Comfort Law Firm ....Gainesville, FL
Comfort, Mary Wild Ennis
Department of State, Office of the Legal Adviser, GV
Comfort, Michael G. ....Burlingame, CA
Comfort, Patricia E. ....Boston, MA
Comfort, Patrick C. ....Tacoma, WA
Comfort, Paul W. ....Sudlersville, MD
Comfort, R. Dennis ....Gainesville, FL
Comfort, Richard E. ....Tulsa, OK
Comfort, Richard E., A Professional Corporation ....Tulsa, OK
Comfort, Robert A. ....Valley Center, CA
Comfort, Robert D. ....Philadelphia, PA
Comfort, Robert J. ....Chicago, IL
Comfort & Smith ....Tacoma, WA
Comfort, William T., Jr. ....New York, NY
Comforti, Lori M. ....Norwich, CT
Comfort-Small, Debra M. ....Boston, MA
Comfrey, Kathleen M. ....New York, NY
Comi, Diane M. ....Santa Monica, CA
Comiano, Philip A. ....Carol Stream, IL
Comin, Barry A. ....Chicago, IL
Comin, Janet L. ....Seattle, WA
Comin, Sally A. ....Chicago, IL
Comingdeer, Ronald ....Oklahoma City, OK
Comingore, Richard F. ....Rensselaer, IN
Comings, Ronda K. ....Fort Collins, CO
Cominos, Dion N. ....San Francisco, CA
Cominos, Theodore H., Law Office of
Salinas, CA
Comins & Newbury ....Boston, MA
Comins, Randy Joan ....Stone Mountain, GA
Cominsky, Michael D. ....Utica, NY
Cominsky, Roger F. ....Buffalo, NY
Cominsky, Sidney P. ....Syracuse, NY
Cominsky, Sidney P., P.C. ....Syracuse, NY
Comis, Stuart A. ....Oxnard, CA
Comisar, H. Paul ....Rochester, NY
Comisford & Port ....Columbus, OH
Comisford, Tracy S. ....Columbus, OH
Comiskey, Catherine A.
Export-Import Bank of The United States, Office of the General Counsel, GV
Comiskey, Edwin Joseph ....Des Plaines, IL
Comiskey & Hunt ....Washington, DC
Arlington, VA
Fairfax, VA
McLean, VA
Comiskey, James A. ....New Orleans, LA
Comiskey, Joan ....Chicago, IL
Comiskey, Michael P. ....Chicago, IL
Comiskey, Raymond R., Jr. ....Troy, MI
Comiskey, Richard J. ....Albany, NY
Comiskey, Stephen W. ....McLean, VA
Comiskey, Warren C. ....Jacksonville, FL
Comisky, Clifford C. ....Cannon Beach, OR
Comisky, Hope A. ....Philadelphia, PA
Comisky, Hugh E., Jr. ....Alturas, CA
Comisky, Ian M. ....Boca Raton, FL
Philadelphia, PA
Comisky, Marvin ....Philadelphia, PA
Comisky, Matthew James
Boca Raton, FL
Philadelphia, PA
Comisky, Maxine Lechter ......Norristown, PA
Comiter, Donald ....Pompano Beach, FL
Comiter, Law Offices of, P.A.
Deerfield Beach, FL
Comiter, Lloyd A. ....Deerfield Beach, FL
Comiter, Richard B. ....Aventura, FL
West Palm Beach, FL
Comiter, Richard B., & Associates, P.A.
West Palm Beach, FL
Comito, Cecelia M. ....Chicago, IL
Comito, Frank A. ....Des Moines, IA
Comito, Frank J. ....Carroll, IA
Comitz, Edward O. ....Tucson, AZ
Comizio, V. Gerard ....Washington, DC
Comjean, Marc G. ....Boston, MA
Comley, Frederick L. ....Bridgeport, CT
Comley, Mark W. ....Jefferson City, MO
Comly, Barbara J. ....Princeton, NJ
Commander, Bettye Stephanie
Charlottesville, VA
Commander, Charles E., III
Jacksonville, FL
Commander, Christopher G.
Jacksonville, FL
Commander, Eugene R. ....Denver, CO
Commander, Jonathan D.
West Palm Beach, FL
Commander, Jonathan D., P.A.
West Palm Beach, FL
Commander, Kathleen Sarah
New York, NY
Commander, Mary G. ....Norfolk, VA
Commander, Scott C. ....Decatur, GA
Commender, David G. ....New York, NY
Commer, Eric A. ....Wichita, KS
Commerce Law Group ....San Francisco, CA
Commercial Litigation Group ....Tulsa, OK
Commerford, Cheryl B. ....Washington, DC
Commers, Frank G. ....Golden Valley, MN
Commers, Lawrence R. ......Minneapolis, MN
Commerton, Mary C. ....Parsippany, NJ
New York, NY
Commette, Peter M. ......Fort Lauderdale, FL
Commette, Peter M., P.A.
Fort Lauderdale, FL
Commins, David H. S. ......San Francisco, CA
Commins, Gregory J., Jr.
Washington, DC
Commins, Mark A. ....West Islip, NY
Commins, Robert E. ....Vista, CA
Commins, Stephen D. ....Albany, NY
Commins, Susan Daly ....San Francisco, CA
Commisa & Campanile ....Livingston, NJ
Commisa, Vincent D. ....Livingston, NJ
Commisa, Vincent J. ....Newark, NJ
Commissaris, Anton Theodore
Palo Alto, CA
Commisso, Jeffrey V. ....San Francisco, CA
Committe, Bruce E. ....Pensacola, FL
Commodore, Wilbur E. ....Boston, MA
Commons, Carolyn D. ....Philadelphia, PA
Commons & Commons LLP
Philadelphia, PA
Commons, David B. ....Santa Barbara, CA
Commons, Donald W. ....Toledo, OH
Commons, Geoffrey ....Montpelier, VT
Commons, Glenn D. ....Gary, IN
Commons, Harold T., Jr. .....Philadelphia, PA
Commons, James W. ....Indianapolis, IN
Commons, John V. ....Indianapolis, IN
Commons, Mark D. ....Indianapolis, IN
Communiello, Anthony M., Jr.
Kew Gardens, NY
Comnas, Aspasia G. ....Bridgehampton, NY
Comnenos, Caroline Johnson ....Archer, FL
Comninel, John ....Andes, NY
Como, Christopher T. ....Monroeville, PA
Como, Frank M. ....Waverly, NY
Como, Greg S. ....Phoenix, AZ
Como, Michael M. ....Pueblo, CO
Como, Robert Michael ....Berwyn, IL
Comodeca, James A. ....Cincinnati, OH
Comodeca, Peter J. ....Cleveland, OH
Comoglio, Rick F. ....Fort Lauderdale, FL
Comolli, George A. ....Westerly, RI
Comolli, John M. ....Athens, GA
Comolli, Víctor M. ....San Juan, PR
Comollo, Bruce J. ....Manchester, CT
Comp, Heinrich O., Jr. ....Greenville, SC
Compa, Gary P. ....Portland, OR
Compagni, Frank W. ....Salt Lake City, UT
Compagni, Michael J. ....Syracuse, NY
Compagno, John Matthew
San Francisco, CA
Compagno, Michael J.
West Palm Beach, FL
Compagno, Peter J. ....New Orleans, LA
Compagnone, David ....Joplin, MO
Compaine, Bruce C., (P.A.)
Haddon Heights, NJ
Compall, Thaddeus J. ....Chicago, IL
Companey, Roy T. ....Fairview Park, OH
Companion, Christine L. ....Charleston, SC
Companion, James F. ....Wheeling, WV
Companioni, Jose M. ....Miami, FL
Comparato, Susan ....New York, NY
Comparet, Thomas M. ....Los Angeles, CA
Comparetto, Anthony J. ....St. Petersburg, FL
Comparetto, Frank, Jr. ....Lakeland, FL
Compasso, Jeffrey A. ....Orange, CA
Compatore, E. John ....Seattle, WA
Compatore, E. John, P.S. ....Seattle, WA
Compau, J. Parker ....Spokane, WA
Compeán, Efren A. ....Pasadena, CA
Compean, Michael D. ....Los Angeles, CA
Compere, John ....San Antonio, TX
Compere, Richard A. ....Jackson, MS
Compernolle, Paul J. ....Chicago, IL
Competiello, Mark A. ....New York, NY
Competiello, Shari T. ....Secaucus, NJ
Competition Law Group LLC
Chicago, IL
Compiani, Barbara J.
West Palm Beach, FL
Compitello, Jeanne A. ....Stony Brook, NY
Compoli, Craig J., Jr. ....Morristown, NJ
Componovo, W. Christopher
Wilmington, DE
Composto, Dennis V. ....Lincolnshire, IL
Composto, Frank A. ....Brooklyn, NY
Composto, Joseph ....Department of the Navy, Office of the Judge Advocate General, GV
Compretta, J. P. ....Bay St. Louis, MS
Compson, Geo. A. ....Columbus, OH
Compson, John E. ....Findlay, OH
Compson, Richard G. ....Utica, NY
Compson, Richard G., P.C. ....Utica, NY
Compter, Herman E. ....East Amherst, NY
Compton, A. Christian ....Richmond, VA
Compton, Allen T. ....Anchorage, AK
Compton, Brooks A. ....Dayton, OH
Compton, C. Eugene ....Lebanon, VA
Compton, C. Lacey, Jr. ....Woodbridge, VA
Compton, Cathleen V. ....Little Rock, AR
Compton, Charles A. ....Grass Valley, CA
Compton, Charles A. ....Evansville, IN
Compton, Charles L. ....Laurens, SC
Compton, Charles N. ....Kansas City, MO
Compton, Charles T. C. ....Palo Alto, CA
Compton, Claude T. ....Manassas, VA
Compton, Clyde D. ....Merrillville, IN
Portage, IN
Compton, Crowell and Hewitt, P.L.L.C.
Bay St. Louis, MS
Biloxi, MS
Gulfport, MS
Hattiesburg, MS
Jackson, MS
Ocean Springs, MS
Pascagoula, MS
Compton, Daisy N. ....Dungannon, VA
Compton, Daniel Ervin ....Elgin, IL
Compton, Dave E. ....Chicago, IL
Compton, David S. ....Seattle, WA
Compton, Dollie M. ....Lebanon, VA
Compton, Donald M. ....Dayton, OH
Compton & Duling, L.C. ....Woodbridge, VA
Compton, Dwight Edward ....Hillsville, VA
Compton, Edward L., Jr. ....Carlsbad, CA
Compton, G. Frederick, Jr. ....Akron, OH
Compton, Gary D. ....Austin, TX
Compton, Gary L. ....Las Vegas, NV
Compton, Gary L. ....Spartanburg, SC
Compton, Gene ....Borger, TX
Compton, Gregory A. ....Louisville, KY
Compton, J. Douglas ....Albuquerque, NM
Compton, J. Paul, Jr. ....Birmingham, AL
Compton, James C. ....Albuquerque, NM
Compton, James L. ....Bakersfield, CA
Compton, James N. ....Biloxi, MS
Compton, Jeffrey K. ....Los Angeles, CA
Compton, Jeffrey Paul ....Columbus, OH
Compton, Jennifer Brynn ....Little Rock, AR
Compton, Jenny B. ....Tuscaloosa, AL
Compton, John C. ....Strawberry Point, IA
Compton, John D. ....Springfield, MO
Compton, John DeVore, III ....Greenwood, SC
Compton, John G. ....Meridian, MS
Compton, John H. ....San Francisco, CA

Condon, Timothy S. ....Tampa, FL
Condon, Wilhemina M. ....Seattle, WA
Condon, William E., Jr. ....Greeley, CO
Condon, William J. ....New York, NY
Condon, Wilson L. ....Juneau, AK
Condos, Barbara Moir ....Washington, DC
Condos, Basil ....Chevy Chase, MD
Condos, Laurie J. ....Boston, MA
Condos, Leonidas G. ....Indianapolis, IN
Terre Haute, IN
Condos, Leonidas G., P.C. ....Indianapolis, IN
Terre Haute, IN
Condos, Mitchell G. ....West Orange, NJ
Condotti, Anthony P. ....Santa Cruz, CA
Condra, Allen L. ....Madisonville, KY
Condra, Darlene P. ....Troy, MI
Condra, David Thomas ....Los Angeles, CA
Condra, Gary D. ....Lubbock, TX
Condra, Philip A. ....Jasper, TN
Condra, Shirley Harden ....San Diego, CA
Condray, John C.
Office of Government Ethics, Office of General Counsel and Legal Policy, GV
Condray, Mattie Cohan ....Washington, DC
Condray, Scott R. ....Concordia, KS
Condrell, Paul K. ....Alexandria, VA
Condrell, William K. ....Washington, DC
Condren, Alan D. ....Santa Barbara, CA
Condren, James L. ....New York, NY
Condren, John Christopher
Oklahoma City, OK
Condren, John R. ....Buffalo, NY
Condren, Sheila A. ....Tulsa, OK
Condren, William J. ....New York, NY
Condren, Willis D. ....Carmel, CA
Condrey, John L. ....San Francisco, CA
Condrey, Lisa A. ....New Orleans, LA
Condrey, William V. ....Houston, TX
Condrey, William V., P.C. ....Houston, TX
Condrige, John J. ....Harrisburg, PA
Condrin, Stephen C. ....Chicago, IL
Condro, Charles J.
Department of Commerce, Patent and Trademark Office, GV
Condron, Linda Ruth ....San Jose, CA
Condron, Michael J. ....Washington, DC
Condron, Nancy Kablach ....Marietta, GA
Condron, Peter C. ....Washington, DC
Condron, Sean Mannon ....Mililani Town, HI
Condron, William J. ....Prineville, OR
Condry, James B. ....Springfield, MO
Condry, Michael Lee ....Sanger, CA
Condry, W. James, II ....Orlando, FL
Conduzio, Arthur L. ....Albany, NY
Condy, Jennifer L. ....Laguna Beach, CA
Condy, Shawn W. ....Laguna Beach, CA
Condyles, Michael A. ....Richmond, VA
Condzal, Paul F. ....New York, NY
Cone, A. Clark ....West Palm Beach, FL
Cone, A. Read, III ....Troy, MI
Cone, Al J. ....Ocala, FL
West Palm Beach, FL
Cone, Allan E. ....Mendocino, CA
Cone, Anne D. ....Palo Alto, CA
Cone, C. Thomas ....Greenfield, IN
Cone, Carl Timothy ....Lexington, KY
Cone, Chairez & Kassel
Newport Beach, CA
Cone, Charles T. ....Tampa, FL
Cone, Charles W. ....Wenatchee, WA
Cone, Cleary S. ....Ellensburg, WA
Moses Lake, WA
Cone & Cone ....West Palm Beach, FL
Cone, Dominique D.Y. ....Cheyenne, WY
Cone, Fred M., Jr. ....Jacksonville, FL
Cone, G. Alan ....Dallas, TX
Cone, George E. ....Somers, NY
Cone, George W. ....Edisto Island, SC
Walterboro, SC
Cone, Gilreath, Ellis, Cole & Anderson
Cle Elum, WA
Ellensburg, WA
Cone, Gregory A. ....Albuquerque, NM
Cone, H. Maria ....Hartford, CT
Cone, Hope S. ....Morristown, NJ
Cone, Hutchinson I., Jr.
Jacksonville Beach, FL
Cone, James C. ....Knoxville, TN
Cone, Jared R., Jr. ....Jefferson City, MO
Cone, Jessica N. ....Philadelphia, PA
Cone, Joe J. ....Houston, TX
Cone, Joe J., & Associates, P.C.
Houston, TX
Cone, John A., Jr. ....Newport Beach, CA
Cone, John E., Jr. ....Mount Kisco, NY
Cone, John M. ....Dallas, TX
Cone, Michael T. ....New York, NY
Cone, Mike ....Jonesboro, AR
Cone, Neal ....New Haven, CT
Cone, Norman F. ....Waukegan, IL
Cone, Pamela L. ....St. Joseph, MO
Cone, Pamela L., P.C. ....St. Joseph, MO
Cone, Paul J., II ....Barnwell, SC
Cone, Perry Ian ....Miami, FL
Cone, Robert C. ....Greensboro, NC
Cone, Robert W. ....Greenwood, SC
Cone, Rush E. ....San Antonio, TX
Cone, Sally B. ....Greensboro, NC
Cone, Sanford A. ....Shaker Heights, OH
Cone, Sherman H. ....Kentwood, MI
Cone, Steve M. ....Addison, TX
Cone, Steven J. ....Palo Alto, CA
Cone, Sydney M., III ....New York, NY
Cone, Thomas E. ....Greensboro, NC
Cone, Thomas E., Jr. ....Lutz, FL
Cone, Thomas E., Jr., P.A. ....Lutz, FL
Cone, Thomas F. ....Nashville, TN

Cone, Timothy ....Miami, FL
Cone, Timothy C. ....Gilmer, TX
Cone, Trista ....Danvers, MA
Cone, Virginia B. ....Minneapolis, MN
Cone, W. Mitchell ....Nashville, TN
Cone, Yong, Stewart & Houston, P.A.
Jacksonville, FL
Conell, Kenneth H. ....Lake Geneva, WI
Conell & Wilson ....Lake Geneva, WI
Conely & Conely, P.A. ....Okeechobee, FL
Conely, Thomas W., III ....Okeechobee, FL
Conen, Gerald E. ....Milwaukee, WI
Conen, Jeffrey A. ....Milwaukee, WI
Conenello, Gail Howie ....Morristown, NJ
Conerly, Charles S. ....Atlanta, GA
Conerly, Edward O. ....Birmingham, AL
Conerly, Lamar A., Jr. ....Destin, FL
Conery, John E. ....Franklin, LA
Conery, John E., A Professional Law Corporation ....Franklin, LA
Conery, John Edward, Jr. ....Houston, TX
Cones, George E., Jr. ....Houston, TX
Cones, John W. ....Los Angeles, CA
Conese, Michael S. ....Hamilton, OH
Conetta, Tami F. ....Sarasota, FL
Coney, Aims C., Jr. ....Pittsburgh, PA
Coney, Byron D. ....Seattle, WA
Coney, Gail ....Oakland, CA
Coney, Karen T. ....Naples, FL
Coney, Michael E. ....Houston, TX
Coney, Steven Edward ....Fayetteville, AR
Coneys, Michael P. ....Brooklyn, NY
Confair, Susan H. ....Camp Hill, PA
Confalone, Perry W. ....Honolulu, HI
Confalone, William F. ....Yonkers, NY
Confer, Carolyn E. ....Riverside, CA
Confer, Chester P. ....Pawleys Island, SC
Confer, Chester P., A Prof. Corp., Law Offices of ....Pawleys Island, SC
Confer, Roan J., Jr ....Williamsport, PA
Confer, Rodney M. ....Lincoln, NE
Confer, Scott M. ....Ann Arbor, MI
Conflenti, Deborah ....West Mifflin, PA
Conflenti, Jack F. ....Pittsburgh, PA
Conflitti, Robert J. ....Middletown, NY
Conforti, Anthony T. ....Hauppauge, NY
Conforti, David A. ....Washington, DC
Conforti, E. John ....Wauwatosa, WI
Conforti, Frank A.
Department Of The Interior, Office of the Solicitor, GV
Conforti, Gregory D. ....Chicago, IL
Conforti, Joe ....Chicago, IL
Conforti, Mark W. ....Tacoma, WA
Conforti, Michael Patrick ....Alexandria, VA
Conforti, N. Peter ....Newton, NJ
Conforti, Robert A. ....Spring Lake, NJ
Conforti, Vitaliana G. ....Chicago, IL
Conforti, Waller & Kaplowitz, LLP
Hauppauge, NY
New York, NY
Confoy, Karen A. ....Trenton, NJ
Congalton, Christopher W. ....Schiller Park, IL
Congalton, John S. ....Mercer Island, WA
Congalton, John S. ....Seattle, WA
Congar, Wayne W., & Associates ....Media, PA
West Chester, PA
Congdon, Byron E. ....San Bernardino, CA
Congdon, Charles B. ....Philadelphia, PA
Congdon, Douglas E. ....Fairfax, VA
Congdon, Flaherty, O'Callaghan, Reid, Donlon, Travis & Fishlinger
Garden City, NY
New York, NY
Congdon, James E. ....Missoula, MT
Congdon, James W. ....Houston, TX
Congdon, Jeannette Griffith ....Angier, NC
Congdon, John P. ....Denver, CO
Congdon, Michael S. ....Garden City, NY
Congdon, Perreault, Dohl & Rickert
Salamanca, NY
Congdon, Rick ....Waukesha, WI
Congdon, Robert E. ....Anchorage, AK
Congdon, Ward and Walden, S.C.
Waukesha, WI
Congdon, William S. ....Attleboro, MA
Conge, Allan R. ....Houston, TX
Congel, Alexandra Dowling
Skaneateles, NY
Congelio, Louis T. ....Latrobe, PA
Conger, B. Thomas ....Bainbridge, GA
Conger, Basil D. ....Alta Loma, CA
Conger, Dawn P. ....Greenville, NC
Conger, Dwight G. ....Detroit, MI
Conger, E. Richard ....Paso Robles, CA
Conger, Edwin H. ....Chicago, IL
Conger & Elliott, Prof. Corp. ....Carmi, IL
Conger, Heather M. ....Orlando, FL
Conger, J. Hilton ....Smithville, TN
Conger, J. William ....Oklahoma City, OK
Conger, James W., Jr. ....Bainbridge, GA
Conger, John C. ....Des Moines, IA
Conger, John Gray ....Columbus, GA
Conger, John H. ....Owosso, MI
Conger, John R. ....Sacramento, CA
Conger, Julie Mendlow ....Oakland, CA
Conger, Michael A. ....San Diego, CA
Conger, Michael M. ....Salt Lake City, UT
Conger, Michael V. ....Kansas City, MO
Conger, N. Scott ....Wheaton, IL
Conger, Neal A. ....Elyria, OH
Conger, Pamela Alice ....Columbus, OH
Conger, Paul S., Jr. ....Tuscaloosa, AL
Conger, Susan B. ....Chadds Ford, PA
Conger, Suzanne X. ....Danville, IN
Conger, W. Mark ....Winston-Salem, NC
Conger, William G. ....Southfield, MI
Congero, Kathleen M. ....Avon, CT

Congett, Horacio R. ....Kearny, NJ
Congleton, Joseph P. ....Knoxville, TN
Congleton, R. Michael ....Indianapolis, IN
Congleton, William G. ....Essex Junction, VT
Congress, Donald D. ....New York, NY
Congress, Jerome M. ....New York, NY
Congreve, William, III ....Washington, NH
Conheim, Robert F. ....Sacramento, CA
Conheim, Susan ....New York, NY
Coniam, Robert T. ....Cleveland, OH
Coniaris, Jeffrey J. ....Houston, TX
Coniaris, William ....Salem, MA
Conick & Conick ....Wheaton, IL
Conick, Harold W. ....Wheaton, IL
Conick, Marshall W. ....Wheaton, IL
Conifrey, Regan ....Redondo Beach, CA
Conigland, LeRoy ....New York, NY
Conigliaro, Matthew J.
St. Petersburg, FL
Coniglio, C. John ....Wildwood, FL
Coniglio, George ....Chicago Heights, IL
Coniglio, James A. ....Rochester, NY
Coniglio, Jonann E., (P.A.)
Little Rock, AR
Coniglio, Joseph F. ....Dallas, TX
Coniglio, Michael J. ....Tallahassee, FL
Coniglio, Michael J., Professional Association
Tallahassee, FL
Coniglio, Peter J. ....Monterey, CA
Coniglio, Peter J. ....Department of Justice, Executive Office for United States Attorneys, GV
Coniglio, Philip J. ....North Miami, FL
Coniglio, Shirley J. ....Canfield, OH
Coniglio, Terry John ....Long Beach, CA
Coniglio & Uthoff, A Professional Law Corporation ....Long Beach, CA
Los Angeles, CA
Conilogue, Alan P. ....Boise, ID
Conine, Casey ....Fort Worth, TX
Cônine, John Clifton ....Natchitoches, LA
Conine, Kashous E. ....Tampa, FL
Conine, Nancy L. ....Boulder, CO
Coningsby, Donna Jo ....Portland, OR
Conino, Joseph A. ....Jefferson, LA
Conis, Stephanie S. ....Chicago, IL
Conis, Thomas G. ....Milwaukee, WI
Conison, Jay ....Oklahoma City, OK
Conison, Nancy Jo ....Oklahoma City, OK
Conits, George J. ....Greenville, SC
Conk, George W. ....South Orange, NJ
Conkel, Jeanne M.V. ....Glencoe, MN
Conkel, Robert D. ....Richardson, TX
Conkel, Terrence E. ....Glencoe, MN
Conkey, George R. ....Dallas, TX
Conkey, Howard N. ....Detroit, MI
Conkey, Kathleen ....New York, NY
Conkey, Patrick B. ....Escondido, CA
Conkin, Elizabeth ....Cincinnati, OH
Conkin, Joel A. ....Kingsport, TN
Conkin, Robert L. ....Van Nuys, CA
Conkin, William K. ....Philadelphia, PA
Conkle, Allan J. ....Toledo, OH
Conkle, Clifford L. ....Sacramento, CA
Conkle, Daniel O. ....Bloomington, IN
Conkle, John A. ....Santa Monica, CA
Conkle, Louis B. ....Marion, OH
Conkle & Olesten, Professional Law Corporation ....Los Angeles, CA
Santa Monica, CA
Conkle, Thomas J. ....Columbus, OH
Conkle, William C. ....Santa Monica, CA
Conklin, Aaron J. ....Smyrna, TN
Conklin, Alfred R., III ....Sonoma, CA
Conklin, Barbara L. ....Trenton, NJ
Conklin, Barron T. ....Mesa, AZ
Conklin, Benham, Ducey, Listman & Chuhran, P.C. ....Detroit, MI
Traverse City, MI
Conklin, Benjamin P. ....Lighthouse Point, FL
Conklin, Carol M. ....Detroit, MI
Conklin, Charles C. ....Bloomfield Hills, MI
Conklin, Charles R.
Joint Committees And Commissions, GV
Conklin, Daniel L. ....Kalamazoo, MI
Conklin, Daral G. ....Kailua, HI
Conklin, Darin M. ....Topeka, KS
Conklin, David L. ....Grand Rapids, MI
Conklin, David L., P.C. ....Grand Rapids, MI
Conklin, David S. ....Albertson, NY
Conklin, Deborah Duchardt
Kansas City, MO
Conklin, Denise E. ....Chicago, IL
Conklin, Dennis J. ....Trenton, NJ
Conklin, El Marie ....Grand Forks, ND
Conklin, Francis J. ....Spokane, WA
Conklin, Frederick, Jr. ....Kingsport, TN
Conklin, Gary F. ....Westmoreland, KS
Conklin, Gary W. ....Sioux Falls, SD
Conklin, George J. ....Toledo, OH
Conklin, Gregory J. ....San Francisco, CA
Conklin, Harry E. ....Great Barrington, MA
Conklin, Howard L. ....Fort Lauderdale, FL
Conklin, J. Dan ....Springfield, MO
Conklin, James H. W., II ....Bucksport, ME
Conklin, James Lance
South San Francisco, CA
Conklin, Jeffrey J. ....Albany, NY
Conklin, John B. ....Chicago, IL
Conklin, John L. ....Denver, CO
Conklin, Joseph J. ....Otsego, MI
Conklin, Joseph J. ....Hauppauge, NY
Conklin, Katherine ....New Orleans, LA
Conklin, Kathleen M. ....Madison, WI
Conklin, Kelly ....Houston, TX
Conklin, Kevin Thomas ......White Plains, NY
Conklin, Leslie M. ....Clearwater, FL
Conklin, Lorianne G. ....Kansas City, MO

Conklin, Lucianne A. ....Kalamazoo, MI
Conklin, Mara E. ....Columbus, OH
Conklin, Margaret A. ....New York, NY
Conklin, Marianne S. ....Garden City, NY
Conklin, Marilyn J. ....Minneapolis, MN
Conklin, Mark A. ....Orangeburg, NY
Conklin, Mary M. ....East Lansing, MI
Conklin, Michael D. ....Tulsa, OK
Conklin, Michael F. ....Woodstock, NH
Conklin, Nybo, LeVeque & Lanning, P.C.
Great Falls, MT
Conklin, Randall R. ....Houston, TX
Conklin, Raymond C. ....Tallahassee, FL
Conklin, Raymond J. ....Moline, IL
Conklin, Richard C. ....Rolling Meadows, IL
Conklin, Robert B. ....Buffalo, NY
Conklin, Robert B. ....Portland, OR
Conklin, Robert C. ....Albuquerque, NM
Conklin, Robert V. ....Suffern, NY
Conklin, Stanley & Probst, Professional Association ....Clearwater, FL
Conklin, Susan ....Monticello, NY
Conklin, Thomas, Jr. ....Chicago, IL
Conklin, Thomas R. ....Topeka, KS
Conklin, Thomas W. ....Chicago, IL
Conklin, Warren C. ....Corte Madera, CA
Conklin, William ....Great Falls, MT
Conklin, William M. ....Traverse City, MI
Conklin, William M., P.C. ....Traverse City, MI
Conklin, William R., (P.C.)
Redwood City, CA
Conkling, Carolyn W. ....Washington, DC
Conkling, Christopher A. ....Pittsburg, CA
Conkling, Daniel C. ....Glen Burnie, MD
Conkling, Raymond Francis ....Arlington, VA
Conkling, Robert H. ....Skowhegan, ME
Conkling, Robert L. ....White Plains, NY
Conkling, Rowena H.
Department of Transportation, Research and Special Programs Administration, GV
Conko, Bernard A.
North Palm Beach, FL
Conkright, James D. ....Kansas City, MO
Conkwright, Lisa A. ....Fort Worth, TX
Conlan, James F. ....Chicago, IL
Conlan, Michael J. ....Sacramento, CA
Conlan, Michael J. ....Princeton, NJ
Conlan, Michael J. ....Milwaukee, WI
Conlan, Rebecca S. ....Tallahassee, FL
Conlan, Robert J., Jr. ....Washington, DC
Conlan, Russell S.
Department of Housing and Urban Development, Washington, D. C. Office, GV
Conlay, Bruce R. ....New Orleans, LA
Conlay & Conlay ....New Orleans, LA
Conlay, Donald P. ....New Orleans, LA
Conlay, Gary L. ....Natchitoches, LA
Conlee, John T. ....Wichita, KS
Conley, A. Byrne ....Walnut Creek, CA
Conley, B. Harrison ....Salem, OR
Conley, Brian Scott ....Lexington, KY
Conley, Bruce ....Union City, TN
Conley, Bruce S. (Steve), Jr.
Union City, TN
Conley, Cale H. ....Atlanta, GA
Columbus, GA
Conley, Campbell, Moss and Smith
Union City, TN
Conley, Carl C. ....Raymondville, TX
Conley, Carol Nevits ....Denver, CO
Conley, Cathleen Grady ....Tullahoma, TN
Conley, Charles A. ....Havertown, PA
Conley, Charles S. ....Montgomery, AL
Conley, Christine A. ....Boston, MA
Conley, Christopher A. ....Ashland, KY
Conley, Christopher G. ....Athens, GA
Conley, Cindy Sebastian ....Harrisburg, PA
Conley & Cleary ....Bradenton, FL
Conley, Clive D. ....New York, NY
Conley and Conley ....Carlisle, KY
Conley, Craig T. ....Canton, OH
Conley, Cristin A. ....Gainesville, FL
Conley, Cynthia A. ....Boston, MA
Conley, Daniel C. ....Galveston, TX
Conley, Daniel E. ....Milwaukee, WI
Conley, David C. ....Colorado Springs, CO
Conley, David C., P.C.
Colorado Springs, CO
Woodland Park, CO
Conley, David F. ....Concord, NH
Conley, David T. ....Raleigh, NC
Conley, Deborah Cooper ....Charleston, SC
Conley, Donald E. ....Bloomfield Hills, MI
Conley, Donald W. ....Chicago, IL
Conley, Donald W. ....Columbus, OH
Conley, Donald W., P.C. ....Chicago, IL
Conley, Donna L. ....Medford, MA
Conley, Edward J. ....Hillside, IL
Conley, Edward, Law Office of
Houston, TX
Conley, Elizabeth S. ....Salt Lake City, UT
Conley, Elnora Destin ....Houston, TX
Conley, Erminie Lane ....New Brunswick, NJ
Conley & Foote ....Middlebury, VT
Conley, Frank ....Columbia, MO
Conley, Gary I. ....Hazard, KY
Conley, George W. ....Medford, NJ
Conley, Gerald C. ....Dallas, TX
Conley, Gerald M. ....Livonia, MI
Conley, Gerard P., Jr. ....Portland, ME
Conley, Gregory A. ....Rosemont, IL
Conley, Guyanne E. ....Dallas, TX
Conley, Henry Q. ....New York, NY
Conley, J. Michael ....Bath, ME
Saco, ME

Conley, J. Michael, P.A., Law Offices of ... Bath, ME
Conley, James B. ... Washington, DC
Conley, James E., Jr. ... Memphis, TN
Conley, James F. ... Tullahoma, TN
Conley, James H. ... Salem, OR
Conley, James L. ... Detroit, MI
Conley, James M. ... Camden, NJ
Conley, James M. ... Massillon, OH
Conley, James O., Jr. ... Marietta, GA
Conley, James R., Jr. ... Carmi, IL
Conley, Jane Harris ... Indianapolis, IN
Conley, Jay N. ... Oconto, WI
Conley, Jeffrey D. ... Littleton, CO
Conley, Jeffrey, P.C. ... Littleton, CO
Conley, Jessica R. ... Media, PA
Conley, Jessie A. ... Statesville, NC
Conley, John A. ... Yonkers, NY
Conley, John D. ... Santa Ana, CA
Conley, John E. ... Clearwater, FL
Conley, John F. ... Norfolk, VA
Conley, John M. ... Charlotte, NC
Conley, Joseph E. ... Treasury Department, Internal Revenue Service, GV
Conley, Joseph E., Jr. ... Covington, KY
Conley, Joseph H. ... Carlisle, KY
Conley, Joseph M. ... Itasca, IL
Conley, Kenna Noelle ... Boston, MA
Conley, Kevin M. ... Cedar Rapids, IA
Conley, Larry E. ... Corbin, KY
Conley, Laura Marie ... Department of Justice, Tax Division, GV
Conley, Lawrence E. ... Rockville, MD
Conley, Lena A. ... St. Louis, MO
Conley, Luke G., III ... Elk Grove, CA
Conley, Marc F. ... Tulsa, OK
Conley, Marc F., P.C. ... Tulsa, OK
Conley, Mark A. ... Los Angeles, CA
Conley, Martha R. ... Pittsburgh, PA
Conley, Martin J. ... Mokena, IL
Conley, Mary G. ... St. Paul, MN
Conley, Michael ... Philadelphia, PA
Conley, Michael A. ... Washington, DC
Conley, Ned L. ... Houston, TX
Conley, Patricia A. ... Lansing, MI
Conley, Paul A., Jr. ... Omaha, NE
Conley, Paul B. ... Boston, MA
Conley, Paul M. ... Lincoln, NE
Conley, Peter James ... Clarksburg, WV
Conley, Peter S. ... Boston, MA
Conley, Phillip J. ... Addison, TX
Conley, R. Michael ... Birmingham, AL
Conley, Reginald G. ... Forest, VA
Conley, Richard G. ... Charleston, WV
Conley, Richard M. ... Princeton, NJ
Conley, Robert ... Chandlersville, OH
Conley, Robert B. ... Washington, DC
Conley, Robert B. ... Ashland, KY
Conley, Robert E. ... Des Moines, IA
Conley, Robert G. ... Cambridge, MA
Conley, Robert J. ... Marshall, MI
Conley, Robt. M. ... Chicago, IL
Conley, Robt. W. ... Bellevue, WA
Conley, Roger P. ... Bradenton, FL
Conley, Ronald W. ... Chicago, IL
Conley Rose & Tayon, P.C. ... Austin, TX
Houston, TX
Conley & Rosenberg, P.C. ... Addison, TX
Dallas, TX
Conley, Sarah S. ... Portland, OR
Conley, Sean ... Walnut Creek, CA
Conley, Shea W. ... Lexington, KY
Conley, Stephanie I. ... Fort Lauderdale, FL
Conley, Stephanie M. ... Merit Systems Protection Board, Office of the General Counsel, GV
Conley, Stephen D. ... Lansing, MI
Conley, Stephen E. ... Buffalo, NY
Conley, Thomas J. ... Minneapolis, MN
Conley, Thomas K. ... Butler, PA
Conley, Thomas P. ... Chicago, IL
Conley, Timothy C. ... Cape Canaveral, FL
Tampa, FL
Conley, Timothy J. ... Irvine, CA
Conley, Tracey Coleman ... Dallas, TX
Conley, Virginia A. ... Parkersburg, WV
Conley, William D. ... Gallipolis, OH
Conley, William H. ... Beaumont, TX
Conley, William H. ... El Paso, TX
Conley, William J., Jr. ... East Providence, RI
Conley, William M. ... Madison, WI
Conley, William V. ... New York, NY
Pittsburgh, PA
Conley-Pitchell, M. Anne ... Warren, NJ
Conliff, Charles M. ... Fairfield, OH
Conliffe, F. Kenneth ... Louisville, KY
Conliffe, Leza ... Washington, DC
Conliffe, Michael E. ... Louisville, KY
Conliffe, Sandmann & Sullivan
New Albany, IN
Louisville, KY
Conlin, Anne ... Cottonwood, AZ
Conlin, Ariel V. ... Atlanta, GA
Conlin, Bernard J. ... Worcester, MA
Conlin, Christina ... Chicago, IL
Conlin, Colleen L. ... Department of Justice, Civil Division, GV
Conlin, David G., (P.C.) ... Boston, MA
Conlin, Elizabeth E. ... Rockville Centre, NY
Conlin, Ellen S. ... Springfield, MA
Conlin, James ... Seattle, WA
Conlin, James M., Jr. ... Akron, OH
Conlin, Jan M. ... Minneapolis, MN
Conlin, John W. ... Marathon, FL
Ann Arbor, MI
Conlin, John W., P.A. ... Marathon, FL
Conlin, Joseph S. ... Tallahassee, FL
Conlin, Marcia L. ... Baltimore, MD
Conlin, Mark J. ... Spokane, WA
Conlin, Mark J., P.S. ... Spokane, WA
Conlin, McKenney & Philbrick, P.C.
Ann Arbor, MI
Conlin, Nancy L. ... Boston, MA
Conlin, Patrick J., Jr. ... Chelsea, MI
Conlin, R. Dean ... Chicago, IL
Conlin, Richard E. ... Chelsea, MI
Conlin, Robert J. ... Baraboo, WI
Conlin, Roxanne B. ... Des Moines, IA
Conlin, Roxanne B., and Associates, P.C.
Des Moines, IA
Conlin, S. Elizabeth ... Marietta, GA
Conlin, Stephen G. ... Orlando, FL
Conlin, Stephen R. ... Lexington, MA
Conlin, Terrance P. ... Ann Arbor, MI
Conlin, Thomas J. ... Minneapolis, MN
Conlin, Thomas M. ... St. Paul, MN
Conlin, Thomas W. ... Bristol, CT
Conlin, William J. ... Ann Arbor, MI
Conlisk, D. Dawn ... St. Louis, MO
Conlisk, Daniel V. ... St. Louis, MO
Conlogue, James L. ... Bisbee, AZ
Conlon, Benjamin A. ... Scotia, NY
Conlon, Christopher M. ... Garden City, NY
Conlon & Conlon ... Union, NJ
Conlon, David M. ... Okeechobee, FL
Conlon, Debera Frick ... Norfolk, VA
Conlon, Denis J. ... Chicago, IL
Conlon, Elizabeth D. ... Knoxville, TN
Conlon, Erica J. ... Chicago, IL
Conlon, Frantz, Phelan & Pires, LLP
Washington, DC
Conlon, Harry B., Jr. ... Green Bay, WI
Conlon, Heather E. ... Gettysburg, PA
Conlon, J. Scott ... Phoenix, AZ
Conlon, Jacquelyn A. ... Stamford, CT
Conlon, James C. ... Union, NJ
Conlon, James E. ... Broadview Heights, OH
Conlon, James F. ... Bear Mountain, NY
Conlon, James J. ... Chicago, IL
Conlon, James T. ... New York, NY
Conlon, Jerome W. ... Park Ridge, IL
Conlon, John J. ... Portage, MI
Conlon, John L. ... Chicago, IL
Conlon, John M. ... New York, NY
Conlon, Kathleen Ann ... San Francisco, CA
Conlon, Kathleen M. ... Boston, MA
Conlon, Kevin J. ... Itasca, IL
Conlon, Kieran J. ... New York, NY
Conlon, Lisa Plunkett ... Chicago, IL
Conlon, Mariann Doherty ... Hauppauge, NY
Conlon, Michael I. ... Traverse City, MI
Conlon, Michael J. ... Washington, DC
Conlon, Michael W. ... Houston, TX
Conlon, Patrick J. ... Houston, TX
Conlon, Raymond J. ... Pittsburgh, PA
Conlon, Robert C. ... Redwood City, CA
Conlon, Robert P. ... Chicago, IL
Conlon, Stephen P. ... Melville, NY
Conlon, Steven D. ... Chicago, IL
Conlon, Susan C. ... Huntsville, AL
Conlon, Suzanne B. ... Chicago, IL
Conlon, Thomas A., Jr. ... Binghamton, NY
Conlon, Timothy J. ... Providence, RI
Conlon, Walter J. ... Muscatine, IA
Conlon, Walter Maclyn ... Hauppauge, NY
Conlon, Wilfred ... Chicopee, MA
Conlon, William F. ... Chicago, IL
Conly, John James ... Wilmington, DE
Conly, William G. ... Lafayette, LA
Conmey, Edwin W. ... Oconomowoc, WI
Conmey, Larry J. ... Anamosa, IA
Conmy, E. Thomas, III ... Fargo, ND
Conmy, E. T., Jr. ... Fargo, ND
Conmy, Feste, Hubbard, Corwin & Brust, Ltd. ... Moorhead, MN
Fargo, ND
Conmy, James F. ... Philadelphia, PA
Conmy, Patrick A. ... Bismarck, ND
Conn, Bernice ... Los Angeles, CA
Conn, Blythe C. ... Des Moines, IA
Conn, Charles L. ... Toledo, OH
Conn and Christine, P.A. ... St. Augustine, FL
Conn, Clendenin & Norton ... Marissa, IL
Sparta, IL
Conn, ClydeL. ... Stow, OH
Conn, David F. ... Federal Trade Commission, Bureau of Competition, GV
Conn, David F ... Philadelphia, PA
Conn, David G. ... St. Augustine, FL
Conn, David L. ... Department of the Army, U.S. Army Legal Services Agency, GV
Conn, David L. ... Pittsburgh, PA
Conn, David P. ... Los Angeles, CA
Conn, David R. ... Des Moines, IA
Conn, Deanna ... Tucson, AZ
Conn, Donald D. ... Clearwater, FL
Conn, Donald L., Jr. ... Medford, MA
Conn, Franklin C. ... Roswell, GA
Conn, Gary E. ... Sandy Hook, KY
Conn, Gene E. ... Warsaw, IN
Conn, Gordon B., Jr. ... Minneapolis, MN
Conn, Harry R. ... Lisbon, OH
Conn, James J. ... Baltimore, MD
Conn, Jeffrey J. ... Pittsburgh, PA
Conn, Jennie S. ... Atlanta, GA
Conn, Joffrey B. ... Philadelphia, PA
Conn, Kavanaugh, Rosenthal, Peisch & Ford, L.L.P. ... Boston, MA
Conn, Kenneth E. ... Visalia, CA
Conn, Kim Ornelas ... Dulles, VA
Conn, Kraig A. ... Tallahassee, FL
Conn, Laurence D. ... Memphis, TN
Conn, Lawrence C. ... Los Angeles, CA
Conn, Lawrence S. ... Baltimore, MD
Conn, Lisa M. ... Hoboken, NJ
Conn, Martin A. ... Richmond, VA
Conn, Mary Chmura ... Washington, PA
Conn, Mary E. ... Houston, TX
Conn, Michael C. ... Minneapolis, MN
Conn, Natalie R. ... Marion, IN
Conn, Norman E. ... West Bloomfield, MI
Conn, Richard A., Jr. ... Washington, DC
Conn, Richard S. ... Los Angeles, CA
Conn, Robert E. ... Washington, DC
Conn, Robert F. ... Kirbyville, TX
Conn, Robert I. ... Sausalito, CA
Conn, Robert L. ... Newport Beach, CA
Conn, Roy, III ... Department of Justice, Civil Rights Division, GV
Conn, Russell F. ... Boston, MA
Conn, Stephen ... Las Cruces, NM
Conn, Steven ... Kingman, AZ
Conn, Susan Vawter ... Des Moines, IA
Conn, Thomas L. ... Lexington, KY
Conn, Todd R. ... Livingston, NJ
Conn, Walton T. ... Nashville, TN
Conn, William A. ... Department of Commerce, Patent and Trademark Office, GV
Conn, William B. ... Petoskey, MI
Connaghan, Patrick J. ... St. Louis, MO
Connaghan, Paul R. ... Las Vegas, NV
Connah, Douglas D., Jr. ... Baltimore, MD
Connair, Thomas P. ... Claremont, NH
Connall, Desmond D. ... Portland, OR
Connall, Desmond D., Jr.
Washington, DC
Connally, Alexis R. ... Dallas, TX
Connally, Andrew D. ... Tallahassee, FL
Connally, C. Ellen ... Cleveland, OH
Connally, Dan Michael ... Oklahoma City, OK
Connally, Don M. ... Abilene, TX
Connally, Gary E. ... Abilene, TX
Connally, Joel ... Birmingham, AL
Connally, John B., IV ... Houston, TX
Connally, Joseph ... Odessa, TX
Connally, Kent B. ... Denver, CO
Connally, Michael W. ... Costa Mesa, CA
Connally, N. Thomas, III ... McLean, VA
Connally, Patricia M. ... Washington, DC
Connally, Sarah Thiemann ... Boston, MA
Connarn, John P. ... Northfield, VT
Connarton, John B., Jr. ... Boston, MA
Connarton, Wood & Callahan
Boston, MA
Connaughton, Anne Q. ... Department of Commerce, Office of the General Counsel, GV
Connaughton, Barney ... San Diego, CA
Connaughton, Blaine T. ... Yakima, WA
Connaughton, Clare B. ... Smithtown, NY
Connaughton, E. Joseph ... San Diego, CA
Connaughton, Gary M ... Oakland, CA
Connaughton, James L. ... Washington, DC
Connaughton, Jeffrey J. ... Washington, DC
Connaughton, John B. (J.B.) ... Hamilton, OH
Connaughton, Joseph J. ... Cincinnati, OH
Connaughton, Kimberly A. ... Baltimore, MD
Connaughton, Martin ... Dublin, OH
Connaughton, Maureen B.
Bloomfield Hills, MI
Connaughton, Michael O. ... Annapolis, MD
Connaughton, Michele A. ... New York, NY
Connaughton, Robert J., Jr. ... Manchester, NH
Connaughton, Rory O. ... Lancaster, PA
Connaughton, Sean T. ... Washington, DC
Connaughton, Thomas A.
Washington, DC
Connaway, Nancy I. ... Arlington, TX
Connealy, Cathleen ... Kansas City, MO
Connealy, Michalene ... Blytheville, AR
Connealy, Patrick M. ... Chadron, NE
Connealy, Ross L. ... Department of Justice, Environment and Natural Resources Division, GV
Connealy, Sandra J. ... Stillwater, MN
Connealy, William P. ... Phoenix, AZ
Conneely, Brian S. ... Mineola, NY
Conneely, John J. ... San Mateo, CA
Conneely, Kevin D. ... Minneapolis, MN
Conneely, Mary Grace Daguano ... Monticello, NY
Conneely, Maureen A. ... Danville, CA
Conneely, Thomas F. ... Sacramento, CA
Conneen, Daniel P. ... New York, NY
Conneen, James T. ... Ridgewood, NJ
Connell, Alan W. ... Thomaston, GA
Connell, Andrew S. ... Miami, FL
Connell, Andrew S., Jr. ... Miami, FL
Connell & Associates ... Medford, MA
Connell, Brian J. ... Medford, MA
Connell, Bruce A. ... Houston, TX
Connell, Byron L., Jr. ... Cape Girardeau, MO
Connell, C. Willis, Jr. ... Clarksdale, MS
Connell, Carolyn S. ... Paris, KY
Connell, Charles J. ... Greeley, CO
Connell, Christian Lee
Virginia Beach, VA
Connell, Christopher J.
Walnut Creek, CA
Connell, Christopher S. ... Malvern, PA
Connell, Colleen K. ... Chicago, IL
Connell & Connell ... El Dorado, KS
Connell & Connell ... Lowell, MA
Connell & Connell ... Manasquan, NJ
Connell, Corwin C. ... Edinburg, TX
Connell, Craig ... New York, NY
Connell, Dan ... Storm Lake, IA
Connell, Dan, P.C. ... Storm Lake, IA
Connell, Dana S. ... Chicago, IL
Connell, Daniel D. ... Westford, MA
Connell, David B. ... Corvallis, OR
Connell, David R. ... Londonderry, NH
Connell, Deirdre E. ... Chicago, IL
Connell, Edward P. ... Clarksdale, MS
Connell, Edward (Ted) P., Jr.
Clarksdale, MS
Connell, Eugene F. ... Chicago, IL
Connell, Foley & Geiser LLP
Roseland, NJ
Connell, Frances J. ... Pittsburgh, PA
Connell, Francis J., III ... Philadelphia, PA
Connell, G. Mason, Jr. ... Richmond, VA
Connell, Gary J. ... Denver, CO
Connell, Gene M., Jr. ... Surfside Beach, SC
Connell, George H. ... Atlanta, GA
Connell, George W. ... Roseland, NJ
Connell, Gerald A. ... Washington, DC
Connell, Jack ... Wichita Falls, TX
Connell, James B. ... Wausau, WI
Connell, James M. ... Dayton, OH
Connell, James M. ... Bethlehem, PA
Connell, James R. ... Montclair, NJ
Connell, Janice T. ... Pittsburgh, PA
Connell, Janine ... Philadelphia, PA
Connell, Jerome F., Jr. ... Atlanta, GA
Connell, Jerry C. ... Littleton, CO
Connell, Jimmy O. ... Houston, TX
Connell, John A. ... Amarillo, TX
Connell, John C. ... Haddonfield, NJ
Connell, John F. ... New York, NY
Connell, John H. ... Raleigh, NC
Connell, John J. ... Rochester, NY
Connell, John L., Jr. ... Lowell, MA
Connell, John M. ... Denver, CO
Connell, John N. ... Bellingham, WA
Connell, John P. ... Chicago, IL
Connell, Joseph J. ... La Crosse, WI
Connell, Joseph N. ... Camden, SC
Connell, Karl ... Claryville, NY
Connell, Kathleen L. ... San Diego, CA
Connell, Kevin C. ... Dayton, OH
Connell, Kevin J. ... Newark, NJ
Connell, L. David ... Portland, OR
Connell, Laura Lembo ... Manasquan, NJ
Connell Law Firm ... Missoula, MT
Connell Law Office ... Seattle, WA
Connell, Lawrence J. ... Wilmington, DE
Connell, Linda Crandall ... Manchester, NH
Connell, Linda H. ... Lombard, IL
Connell, Lisa M. ... Ormond Beach, FL
Connell, Mark S. ... Missoula, MT
Connell, Mark T. ... Toms River, NJ
Connell, Mary C. ... Lowell, MA
Connell, Mary Jane ... Honolulu, HI
Connell, Mary Patricia ... Columbia, SC
Connell, Matthew Seth ... Brighton, CO
Connell, Melanie M. ... Bridgeville, PA
Connell, Melissa A. ... Chicago, IL
Connell, Michael J. ... Los Angeles, CA
Connell, Michael T. ... San Francisco, CA
Connell, Noah ... Department of Labor, Office of the Solicitor, GV
Connell, O. J., Jr. ... El Dorado, KS
Connell, Patrice M. ... Trenton, NJ
Connell, Patricia A. ... New York, NY
Connell, Patrick Daniel ... Chelmsford, MA
Connell, Paul J. ... Atlanta, GA
Connell, R. Campbell ... Washington, DC
Connell, R. Peter ... Manasquan, NJ
Connell, R. Walter ... Bozeman, MT
Connell, Randy E. ... Newnan, GA
Connell, Raymond A. ... Seattle, WA
Connell, Raymond L. ... El Dorado, KS
Connell, Raymond R. ... Fairfield, NJ
Connell, Richard E. ... Harrisburg, PA
Connell, Robert A. ... Jackson, LA
Connell, Robert W. ... Newport, OR
Connell, Robert W. ... Brookfield, WI
Connell, Thomas ... New Orleans, LA
Connell, Thomas F. ... Washington, DC
Connell, Thomas H. ... Hartford, CT
Connell, Tim ... El Dorado, KS
Connell, Timothy K. ... Luverne, MN
Connell, Todd M. ... Wichita, KS
Connell & Wiener LLP ... New York, NY
Connell, William C. ... Eureka, CA
Connell, William D. ... Mountain View, CA
Connell, William F. ... New York, NY
Connell, William J. ... Elmwood Park, IL
Connell, William T. ... Fairfield, NJ
Connella, E. Conrad ... Oakland, CA
Connella, Susan R. ... Washington, DC
Connellan, Elizabeth ... Portland, ME
Connelley, Gary M. ... Billings, MT
Connelli, Lawrence L. ... Hartford, CT
Connelly, A. Kristina Cook ... Summerville, GA
Connelly, Alan F. ... Philadelphia, PA
Connelly, Alan M. ... Massillon, OH
Connelly, Alan M., Co., L.P.A. ... Massillon, OH
Connelly, Alisa K. ... Kansas City, MO
Connelly, Allison I. ... Frankfort, KY
Connelly, Andrew J. ... Wilton, CT
Connelly, Anne E. ... Sacramento, CA
Connelly, Arthur M. ... Manchester, NH
Connelly, Barry J. ... Boston, MA
Connelly, Blair G. ... New York, NY
Connelly, Brian F. ... Wayne, NJ
Connelly, Brian J. ... Vero Beach, FL
Connelly, Brian P. ... Auburn, CA
Connelly, Carol M. ... Treasury Department, Office of the Comptroller of the Currency, GV
Connelly, Catherine ... Kansas City, MO
Connelly, Charles W., Jr. ... Charlotte, NC
Connelly, Cheryl Lynne ... Huntington, WV
Connelly, Christine E. ... Washington, DC
Connelly, Christopher A. ... Charlotte, NC
Connelly, Claudia Ausdal ... Springfield, IL
Connelly, Colin, & Associate ... Chester, VA
Connelly & Connelly, P.S. ... Spokane, WA

Connelly, Crowley, Groth and Seglund
Walled Lake, MI
Connelly, David B. ....Los Angeles, CA
Connelly, David J. ....Brick, NJ
Connelly, David Martin ....Washington, DC
Connelly, Francis S. Michael
Indianapolis, IN
Connelly, Frank H., Jr. .....New Rochelle, NY
Connelly, Frederick E., Jr. ....Boston, MA
Connelly, Gary P. ....Pittsburgh, PA
Connelly, George W., (P.C.) ....Houston, TX
Connelly, Hugh H. ....Fairbanks, AK
Connelly, J. Dan ....Alto, TX
Connelly, James A., II ....Rochester, NY
Connelly, James E. ....New York, NY
Connelly, James J. ....Youngstown, OH
Connelly, James M. ....Philadelphia, PA
Connelly, James P. ....Skokie, IL
Connelly, James P. ....Detroit, MI
Connelly, James P. ....Spokane, WA
Connelly, James P. ....Milwaukee, WI
Connelly, James Thomas ....Hingham, MA
Connelly, Jeanne K. ....Washington, DC
Connelly, Joe ....Eugene, OR
Connelly, John C. ....United States Senate,
Senatorial Assistants, GV
Connelly, John C. ....Edina, MN
Connelly, John C., Jr. ....Chicago, IL
Connelly, John Edward ......Minneapolis, MN
Connelly, John J. ....Washington, DC
Connelly, John J., Jr. ....Harrisburg, PA
Hershey, PA
Connelly, John Joseph ....Mineola, NY
Connelly, John L. ....Jackson, MS
Connelly, John M. ....Overland Park, KS
Connelly, John P. ....Boston, MA
Connelly, John R., Jr. ....Red Bank, NJ
Connelly, John R., Jr. ....Tacoma, WA
Connelly, Jos. F. ....Dayton, OH
Connelly, Joseph M. ....Chicago, IL
Connelly, Joseph R. ....Buffalo, NY
Connelly & Kaercher ....Fairdale, KY
Connelly, Karen N. ....Harrisburg, PA
Connelly, Kathleen A. ....New Brighton, MN
Connelly, Kathleen M. ....Andover, MA
Connelly, Kathleen M. ....Westfield, NJ
Connelly, Kathryn L. ....Philadelphia, PA
Connelly, Kenneth A., Jr. ....Louisville, KY
Connelly, Kevin B. ....Treasury Department,
Internal Revenue Service, GV
Connelly, Kevin M. ....Eagan, MN
Connelly, Kevin P. ....Washington, DC
Connelly, Kevin R. ....Boston, MA
Connelly, Kimberly A. ....Dearborn, MI
Connelly, Kristen A. ....Toledo, OH
Connelly, L. Branch S. ....Summerville, GA
Connelly, Laurie Flinn ....Spokane, WA
Connelly Law Firm ....Kansas City, MO
Connelly, Leo B. ....Elmhurst, NY
Connelly, Lloyd G. ....Sacramento, CA
Connelly, M. Coy ....Houston, TX
Connelly & Manfredi, L.L.C.
Bedminster, NJ
New York, NY
Connelly, Mark E. ....Contoocook, NH
Connelly, Mary T. ....Washington, DC
Connelly, Maryann T. ....Philadelphia, PA
Connelly, Matthew J. ....Fort Wayne, IN
Connelly, Matthew L. ....Albuquerque, NM
Connelly, Matthew Patrick ....Chicago, IL
Connelly, Maurice H. ....Bayonne, NJ
Connelly, Michael ....Bridgeport, CT
Connelly, Michael C. ....Springfield, IL
Connelly, Michael E.
Department of Transportation,
Federal Transit Administration, GV
Connelly, Michael E. ....Chicago, IL
Connelly, Michael E. ....East Chicago, IN
Connelly, Michael F. ....Spokane, WA
Connelly, Michael G. ....Pittsburgh, PA
Connelly, Michael J. ....New York, NY
Connelly, Michael O. ....Houston, TX
Connelly, Michael P. ....Chicago, IL
Connelly, Michael R. ....Baton Rouge, LA
Connelly, Michael T. ....Fairdale, KY
Connelly, Mindi B. ....Boston, MA
Connelly, Mindy R. ....New York, NY
Connelly & Norton, P.C. ....Boston, MA
Connelly, P. Kevin ....Chicago, IL
Connelly, Padmini Balakrishnan
Boston, MA
Connelly, Pamela Wilkins ....Pittsburgh, PA
Connelly, Patrick ....Syracuse, NY
Connelly, Patrick E. ....Spokane, WA
Connelly, Patrick M. ....Rockville, MD
Connelly, Patrick M. ....Pittsburgh, PA
Connelly, Patrick P. ....Hamilton, OH
Connelly, Paula J.
Pension Benefit Guaranty Corporation,
Office of the General Counsel, GV
Connelly, Paula M. ....Denver, CO
Connelly, Paula M. ....Burlington, MA
Connelly, Peter R. ....North Babylon, NY
Connelly, Randal E. ....Rapid City, SD
Connelly, Rebecca B. ....Lexington, VA
Connelly, Rebecca Lynn
Winston-Salem, NC
Connelly, Reid & Spade ....Harrisburg, PA
Connelly, Richard F., Jr. ....Athens, GA
Connelly, Richard M. ....Norristown, PA
Connelly, Riley W. ....Parker, SD
Connelly, Robert F. ....Springfield, MA
Connelly, Robert J. ....Kalamazoo, MI
Connelly, Robert J., Jr. ....Lincoln, RI
Connelly, Robert L., Jr. ....Denver, CO
Connelly, Robert W. ....Centerville, MA
Connelly & Schroeder ....Chicago, IL
Geneva, IL

Connelly, Sean ....Tucson, AZ
Connelly, Shannon M. ....Portland, OR
Connelly Sheehan Moran ....Chicago, IL
Connelly, Sheri L. ....Bakersfield, CA
Connelly, Soutar & Jackson ....Toledo, OH
Connelly, Stephen ....Vero Beach, FL
Connelly, Steven L. ....Berea, KY
Connelly, Teresa M. ....New York, NY
Connelly, Terrence R. ....New York, NY
Connelly, Thomas A., (P.C.) ....St. Louis, MO
Connelly, Thomas J. ....Walled Lake, MI
Connelly, Thomas J. ....North Babylon, NY
Connelly, Thomas J. ....Neenah, WI
Connelly, Thomas P., III ....Buffalo, NY
Connelly, Thomas V. ....St. Louis, MO
Connelly, Vincent J. ....Chicago, IL
Connelly, W. Mowry ....Cleveland, OH
Connelly, Walter J. ....Boston, MA
Connelly, Warren E. ....Washington, DC
Connelly, William C. ....Morristown, NJ
Connelly, William J. ....Chicago, IL
Connelly, William J., III ....Tinton Falls, NJ
Connelly, William M. ....Toledo, OH
Connelly, William M. ....Barnwell, SC
Charleston, SC
Connelly, William R. ....Bedminster, NJ
Connelly-Warren, Catherine ....Chicago, IL
Connely, Dwight W. ....Tucson, AZ
Connely, Edmund J. ....Houma, LA
Connely, Mark B. ....San Luis Obispo, CA
Conner, A. Jay ....San Rafael, CA
Conner, Andrew J. ....Erie, PA
Conner, Bentley E. ....Canton, MS
Conner, Bren C. ....Manhattan Beach, CA
Conner, Brenda Renee ....Fincastle, VA
Conner, Burton C. ....Okeechobee, FL
Conner, C. Diane ....Missoula, MT
Conner, Cantey & Clover ....Brenham, TX
Sealy, TX
Conner, Catherine ....Phoenix, AZ
Conner, Catherine A. ....Santa Rosa, CA
Conner, Charlotte Jean ....Valley, NE
Conner, Cheryl L. ....Boston, MA
Conner & Chopnick ....New York, NY
Conner, Christopher B. ....Los Angeles, CA
San Francisco, CA
Conner, Christopher C. ....Harrisburg, PA
Conner, Christopher W. ....Knoxville, TN
Conner, Clarence M., Jr. ....Richmond, VA
Conner, Claudia Cole ....Oklahoma City, OK
Conner, Coye, Jr. ....Tyler, TX
Conner, Coye, Law Office of ....Tyler, TX
Conner, D. Michael ....Savannah, GA
Conner, Dabney L. ....Bartow, FL
Conner, Daniel ....Philadelphia, PA
Conner, Daniel K. ....Eugene, OR
Conner, David J. ....Bay Minette, AL
Conner, David M. ....Denver, CO
Conner, Dennis P. ....Great Falls, MT
Conner, Douglas H., III ....Irving, TX
Conner, Douglas W., (Ltd., P.C.)
Richmond, VA
Conner, Edward J. ....San Francisco, CA
Conner, Ernest L., Jr. ....Greenville, NC
Conner, Francis D., P.C. ....Belleville, IL
Conner, Frank A. ....Aliso Viejo, CA
Conner, Frank M., III ....Washington, DC
Conner, Fred L. ....Great Bend, KS
Conner, Gary L. ....Washington, DC
Conner, Gary L. ....Bethesda, MD
Conner, George E., Jr. ....New Orleans, LA
Conner, George M., III ....Tyler, TX
Conner, Gordon S. ....Dallas, TX
Conner Gwyn Schenck PLLC
Greensboro, NC
Raleigh, NC
Conner, Herbert Bennett ....Pittsburgh, PA
Conner, J., and Associates ....Durham, NC
Conner, J. Yost, Jr. ....Washington, DC
Conner, Jack ....Dallas, TX
Conner, James C., Jr. ....Bristol, FL
Tallahassee, FL
Conner, James L., II ....Durham, NC
Conner, James P. ....Covington, LA
Conner, James R. ....Northbrook, IL
Conner, James S. ....Mandeville, LA
Conner, James W. ....Akron, OH
Conner, Jay R. ....Houston, TX
Conner, Jeff R. ....Bentonville, AR
Conner, Jeffrey A. ....Jacksonville, FL
Conner, Jeffrey B. ....Los Angeles, CA
Conner, Jeffrey S. ....Newport Beach, CA
Conner, Jerry Ann ....Newnan, GA
Conner, Jerry D. ....Houston, TX
Conner, Jerry E. ....Harlem, GA
Conner, Joe A. ....Chattanooga, TN
Conner, John D. ....Washington, DC
Conner, John D., Jr. ....Washington, DC
Conner, John K. ....Cherry Hill, NJ
Jenkintown, PA
Conner, John S. ....Kansas City, MO
Conner, John T. ....Pittsburgh, PA
Conner, Jon C. ....Scottsdale, AZ
Conner, Julie ....San Francisco, CA
Conner, Katherene E. Holtzinger
Mechanicsburg, PA
Conner, Kevin D. ....Buras, LA
Conner, Kevin W. ....Mobridge, SD
Conner, Kobie B. ....Los Angeles, CA
Conner, Larry W., II ....Cleveland, OH
Conner, Lawrence, Rodney & Gurney
Santa Rosa, CA
Conner, Lea ....Houston, TX
Conner, Leslie L., Jr. ....Oklahoma City, OK
Conner, Leslie L., Jr., P.C.
Oklahoma City, OK
Conner, Lew ....Nashville, TN
Conner, Linda ....Houston, TX

Conner & Lindamood, P.C. ....Houston, TX
Conner, Lindsay ....Los Angeles, CA
Conner, Lisa Marie ....San Diego, CA
Conner, Luther C., Jr. ....Albany, KY
Conner, M. Timothy
Department of Commerce,
Office of the General Counsel, GV
Conner, Marjorie K. ....Washington, DC
Conner, Marjorie L. ....Kent, OH
Conner, Mark H. ....Newark, DE
Conner, Matthew W. ....Indianapolis, IN
Conner, Michael D. ....Marion, IN
Conner, Michael D. ....Houston, TX
Conner, Michael R. ....Indianapolis, IN
Conner, Neal L., Jr. ....Waycross, GA
Conner, Neal P. ....Decatur, AL
Conner, Neal P., & Associates, P.C.
Decatur, AL
Conner & Nitsche, P.C. ....Phoenix, AZ
Conner, Pat D. ....Ann Arbor, MI
Conner, Patrick D. ....Atlanta, GA
Conner, Patrick W. ....Cherry Hill, NJ
Conner, Paul A. ....Fort Worth, TX
Conner, Phillip Lee ....Atlanta, GA
Greenville, SC
Conner, R. Kelton ....Granbury, TX
Conner, Randall ......Federal Trade Commission,
Bureau of Competition, GV
Conner, Randy Patrick ....Oklahoma City, OK
Conner, Richard D. ....Greensboro, NC
Conner, Richard E. ....Fort Lauderdale, FL
Conner, Richard J. ....Milton, MA
Conner & Riley ....Erie, PA
Conner, Robert H. ....McCook, NE
Conner, Robin H. ....St. Augustine, FL
Conner, Ronald Clyde ....Atlanta, GA
Conner, Scot A. ....Oklahoma City, OK
Conner, Stephanie Bass ....Chicago, IL
Conner, Stewart E. ....Lexington, KY
Louisville, KY
Conner, Stuart W. ....Billings, MT
Conner, Susan E. Seiwert ....Chicago, IL
Conner, Terrence P. ....Palo Alto, CA
Conner, Terry W. ....Dallas, TX
Conner, Thomas R. ....Houston, TX
Conner, Timothy J. ....Jacksonville, FL
Conner, Timothy J. ....Palm Coast, FL
Conner, Timothy W. ....Knoxville, TN
Conner, Tommy A. ....San Francisco, CA
Conner, Tonya S. ....Lexington, KY
Conner, Tracey E. ....Davenport, IA
Conner, Tracy E. ....Santa Fe, NM
Conner, Tracy E., P.C. ....Santa Fe, NM
Conner, Troy B., Jr. ....Potomac, MD
Conner, W. Ted ....Orlando, FL
Conner, W. Thomas ....Washington, DC
Conner, Warren Wesley, (P.C.) ....Sealy, TX
Conner, William C. ....White Plains, NY
Conner, William David ....Greenville, SC
Conner, William H. ....Cleveland, OH
Conner, William H., Jr. ....Florence, SC
Conner, William R. ....Rio Rancho, NM
Conner, William S. ....Columbus, IN
Conner & Winters, A Professional
Corporation ....Washington, DC
Oklahoma City, OK
Tulsa, OK
Fayetteville, AR
Conneran, Michael N. ......San Francisco, CA
Connerat, Jean H. ....Carrboro, NC
Connerat, W. Spencer, Jr. ....Savannah, GA
Connerly, Tricia Hwang ....Boston, MA
Conners, Cynthia Swarthout
San Francisco, CA
Conners, Edward A. ....Austin, TX
Conners, Jack E. ....Cincinnati, OH
Conners, John D. ....Oswego, NY
Conners, John T., Jr. ....Nashville, TN
Conners, Kerry B. ....Paramus, NJ
Conners, Mary E. ....Belmont, MI
Conners, Nelissa Saenz ....Austin, TX
Conners, Patricia A ....Tallahassee, FL
Conners, Richard J. ....Warren, NJ
Conners, Stephanie G. ....New York, NY
Conners, Stephen ....Ballston Spa, NY
Conners, Thos. J. ....Cincinnati, OH
Conners, Tony ....Austin, TX
Conners, William B. ....Monterey, CA
Conners, Wm. A., Jr. ....Houston, TX
Connerton, John J. ....Binghamton, NY
Connerton, Kathryn ....Binghamton, NY
Connerton, Kelly C. ....Atlanta, GA
Connerton, Mary Rita ....Binghamton, NY
Connerton & Ray ....Washington, DC
Connerton, Robert J. ....Washington, DC
Connerton, Tèrese M. ....Washington, DC
Conner-Wolfe, Jennifer ....Tallahassee, FL
Connery, Charles J. ....Cherry Hill, NJ
Connery, James G. ....Ventura, CA
Connery, John C., Jr. ....Chicago, IL
Connery, John M. ....Glenview, IL
Connery, Lynne R. ....Birmingham, AL
Connery, Michael G. ....Omaha, NE
Connery, Michael M. ....New York, NY
Connery, Nancy Ann ....New York, NY
Connery, Robert T. ....Denver, CO
Connery, Terry John ....Santa Barbara, CA
Connery, Thomas F., Jr. ....Camden, NJ
Westmont, NJ
Connery, Walter P. ....Centerport, NY
Conness, John W. ....Fort Lauderdale, FL
Conness, John W., P.A.
Fort Lauderdale, FL
Connet, L. Rae ....Redondo Beach, CA
Connett, Frank D., Jr. ....St. Joseph, MO
Connett, Robert H. ....Sacramento, CA
Connett, William C., IV ....Ocean Ridge, FL
Connette, Edward G., III ....Charlotte, NC

Conney, Carl M. ....St. Paul, MN
Connich, Michael J. ....Fremont, CA
Connick, A. Thomas, (P.A.)
Deerfield Beach, FL
Connick, Andrew J. ....New York, NY
Connick, Harry ....New Orleans, LA
Connick, J. Patrick ....Metairie, LA
Connick, Lentini, Wimberly & deLaup
Metairie, LA
New Orleans, LA
Connick & Liljeberg, L.L.C.
Metairie, LA
New Orleans, LA
Connick, Michael J. ....Cleveland, OH
Connick, Nancy ....Denver, CO
Connick, Paul D., Jr. ....Metairie, LA
Connick, Thomas J. ....Cleveland, OH
Connick, Timothy ....Albany, NY
Connick, William P. ....Metairie, LA
Conniff, Anthony J. ....Oak Brook, IL
Conniff, Christopher ....New York, NY
Conniff, Dennis J. ....Louisville, KY
Conniff, Desa Gese ....Tacoma, WA
Conniff, John S. ....Olympia, WA
Conniff, Lyn C. ....Oak Park, IL
Conniff, Lyn C., P.C. ....Oak Park, IL
Conniff, Martin F. ....New York, NY
Conniff, Raymond F. ....New York, NY
Conniff, Thomas A. ....New York, NY
Conniff, Thomas C. ....Newark, NJ
Connly, Jacklyn M. ....Northampton, MA
Connole, James W. ....Escondido, CA
Connole, Jennifer A. ....Salt Lake City, UT
Connolly, A. Joan ....Mobile, AL
Connolly, Andrew J. ....Philadelphia, PA
Connolly, Anne E. ....Wilmington, DE
Connolly, Annemargaret ......Washington, DC
Connolly, Arthur G. ....Wilmington, DE
Connolly, Arthur G., III ....Wilmington, DE
Connolly, Arthur G., Jr. ....Wilmington, DE
Connolly, Arthur H., Jr. ....Santa Cruz, CA
Connolly, Barbara M. ....Detroit, MI
Connolly, Beverley Burge ....Middletown, DE
Connolly Bove Lodge & Hutz, LLP
Dover, DE
Connolly Bove Lodge & Hutz LLP
Wilmington, DE
Connolly, Brendan J. ....Jamesburg, NJ
Connolly, Brian P. ....Boston, MA
Connolly, Bridget ....New York, NY
Connolly, C. Lawrence, III ....Lincolnshire, IL
Connolly & Callahan, LLC
West Hartford, CT
Connolly, Carla Garcia ....Austin, TX
Connolly, Carol A. ....Boston, MA
Connolly, Charles F. ....Washington, DC
Connolly, Charles P. ....Longview, TX
Connolly, Christopher ....New York, NY
Connolly, Christopher E. ....Florence, AL
Connolly, Christopher F. ....Boston, MA
Connolly, Christopher J. ....San Diego, CA
Connolly, Christopher J. ....Boston, MA
Connolly, Christopher J. ....Wayne, NE
Connolly, Coleman M. ....Denver, CO
Connolly, Colm F. ....Wilmington, DE
Connolly & Connolly ....Lexington, MA
Connolly & Connolly ....Newburyport, MA
Connolly & Connolly ....Bloomfield, NJ
Connolly, D. Hugh ....Augusta, GA
Connolly, Damon M. ....Oakland, CA
Connolly, Daniel J. ....Minneapolis, MN
Connolly, Daniel J. ....Concord, NH
Connolly, David ....Rockford, IL
Connolly, David A., Jr. ....Washington, DC
Bowie, MD
Connolly, David Barry ....Boston, MA
Providence, RI
Connolly, David H., Jr. ....Athens, GA
Connolly, David J. ....Bolton, MA
Connolly, David J., Jr. ....Morristown, NJ
Connolly, Deborah Miaskowski
New York, NY
Connolly, Dennis F. ....Milwaukee, WI
Connolly, Dennis J. ....Atlanta, GA
Connolly, Dennis Michael ....Rochester, NY
Connolly, Dennis R. ....New York, NY
Connolly, Diane M. ....Louisville, CO
Connolly, Dorothy K. ....Jersey City, NJ
Connolly, Edward C. ....Warminster, PA
Connolly, Edward W. ....Livingston, NJ
Connolly, Eileen Mary ....Falls Church, VA
Connolly, Elizabeth A. ....Minneapolis, MN
Connolly Epstein Chicco Foxman Oxholm & Ewing ....Philadelphia, PA
Connolly, Francesca E. ....White Plains, NY
Connolly, Francis J. ....Minneapolis, MN
Connolly, Francis M. ....Cockeysville, MD
Connolly, Francis W. ....Baltimore, MD
Reston, VA
Connolly, Francis X. ....Bloomfield, NJ
Connolly, Frey, Eschmann & LaPasta
Floral Park, NY
Connolly, George C., Jr. ....New Orleans, LA
Connolly, George M. ....Denver, CO
Connolly, Gerald E. ....Clintonville, WI
Connolly, Gerald E. ....Milwaukee, WI
Connolly, Gerard A. ....Mineola, NY
Connolly, Gerard A., Jr. ....New York, NY
Connolly, Grace Gonzalez
Newburyport, MA
Connolly, Gwendolyn G. ....Milwaukee, WI
Connolly, Heather H. ....Charleston, WV
Connolly, Hillyer & Welch ....Uhrichsville, OH
Connolly, Holm, Tacon & Meserve, A Professional Service Corporation
Olympia, WA
Connolly, Hugh F. ....San Mateo, CA
Connolly, Hugh J. ....Miami, FL

Connolly, J. Joseph ... **Santa Monica, CA**
Connolly, J. Wray, Jr. ... Pittsburgh, PA
Connolly, Jacqueline O. ... Department Of Veterans Affairs, Board of Veterans Appeals, GV
Connolly, James A. ... **Olympia, WA**
Connolly, James D. ... Richardson, TX
Connolly, James J. ... Racine, WI
Connolly, James M. ... Stratford, CT
Connolly, James Michael ... Elkridge, MD
Connolly, James P. ... West Hartford, CT
Connolly, James P. ... **Boston, MA**
Connolly, James P. ... Livonia, MI
Connolly, James T., Jr. ... **Newburyport, MA**
Connolly, Janet Frances ... Portland, OR
Connolly, Janet M. ... **Rockville Centre, NY**
Connolly, Jay W. ... **San Francisco, CA**
Connolly, Jean E. ... **Omaha, NE**
Connolly, Jeremiah P. ... **Chicago, IL**
Connolly, Joanna B. ... Boston, MA
Connolly, John C. ... **Mission Viejo, CA**; **San Francisco, CA**
Connolly, John C., III ... **Northbrook, IL**
Connolly, John E., Jr. ... Boston, MA
Connolly, John F. ... Treasury Department, Departmental Offices, GV
Connolly, John F., Jr. ... Conway, NH
Connolly, John G. ... **Los Angeles, CA**
Connolly, John, IV ... Corte Madera, CA
Connolly, John J. ... San Jose, CA
Connolly, John J. ... **Baltimore, MD**
Connolly, John, Jr. ... Wakefield, MA
Connolly, John M. ... **Boston, MA**
Connolly, John M. ... Falmouth, MA
Connolly, John P. ... **Washington, DC**
Connolly, John P. ... Boise, ID
Connolly, John P. ... **Chicago, IL**
Connolly, John P. ... Boston, MA
Connolly, John P. ... Royal Oak, MI
Connolly, John P. ... East Meadow, NY
Connolly, John P. ... **Alexandria, VA**
Connolly, John S. ... St. Paul, MN
Connolly, John T. ... Lapeer, MI
Connolly, Joseph A. ... Asheville, NC
Connolly, Joseph E. ... Livingston, NJ
Connolly, Joseph E., Jr. ... Livingston, NJ
Connolly, Joseph G., Jr. ... **Washington, DC**
Connolly, Joseph G. J. ... **Philadelphia, PA**
Connolly, Joseph J. ... Marlborough, MA
Connolly, Joseph P. ... San Pablo, CA
Connolly, Julie Kielty ... Concord, NH
Connolly, K. Thomas ... **Spokane, WA**
Connolly, Karen A. ... Las Vegas, NV
Connolly, Kathleen Elisabeth ... **Boston, MA**
Connolly, Kathleen M. ... Austin, TX
Connolly, Kerry E. ... **New York, NY**
Connolly, Kevin J. ... **New York, NY**
Connolly, Kevin P. ... Department of Justice, Criminal Division, GV
Connolly, Kevin S. ... Albany, NY
Connolly, L. William ... Milwaukee, WI
Connolly Law Office ... Clintonville, WI
Connolly, Leonard J. ... **New York, NY**
Connolly, Lincoln J. ... **Miami, FL**
Connolly, Linda K. ... **Morristown, NJ**
Connolly, Lisa Ann ... Akron, OH
Connolly, M. Jean ... **New York, NY**; Pittsburgh, PA
Connolly, Marcia E. ... **New York, NY**
Connolly, Marie-Therese ... Department of Justice, Civil Division, GV
Connolly, Mark A. ... **Tampa, FL**
Connolly, Mark John ... **New York, NY**
Connolly, Mark L. ... Sewickley, PA
Connolly, Mark V. ... Tracy, CA
Connolly, Mark V. ... **Hartford, CT**
Connolly, Martha A. ... **Rochester, NY**
Connolly, Martin F. ... **Boston, MA**
Connolly, Mary C. ... Brookline, MA
Connolly, Mary H. ... Metairie, LA
Connolly, Mary K. ... **Rosemont, IL**
Connolly, Mary Lou ... Plymouth, IN
Connolly, Mary Margaret ... Boston, MA
Connolly, Mary S. ... Chicago, IL
Connolly, Mary-Elise ... **Boston, MA**
Connolly, Matthew J. ... Tracy, CA
Connolly, Matthew T. ... **Boston, MA**
Connolly, Matthew T. ... Dedham, MA
Connolly, Maureen ... **Cleveland, OH**
Connolly, Michael ... **New York, NY**
Connolly, Michael A. ... Littleton, CO
Connolly, Michael A. ... **Sarasota, FL**
Connolly, Michael F. ... **Boston, MA**
Connolly, Michael J. ... **Washington, DC**; **Detroit, MI**; **Harbor Springs, MI**
Connolly, Michael J. ... **Boston, MA**; **Providence, RI**
Connolly, Michael J. ... Waltham, MA
Connolly, Michael J. ... **Florham Park, NJ**
Connolly, Michael J. ... **Morristown, NJ**
Connolly, Michael J. ... **Doylestown, PA**
Connolly, Michael P. ... **Boston, MA**
Connolly, Michael V. ... Chicago, IL
Connolly, N. Neil ... Lexington, MA
Connolly, Nancy M. ... San Jose, CA
Connolly, Noreen P. ... **Chicago, IL**
Connolly, Norma C. ... New York, NY
Connolly, Norman N. ... Lexington, MA
Connolly, O'Malley, Lillis, Hansen & Olson, L.L.P. ... **Des Moines, IA**
Connolly, Owen D., Jr. ... Troy, NY
Connolly, Patricia J. ... **Burbank, CA**
Connolly, Patricia L. ... San Rafael, CA
Connolly, Patricia M. ... Spokane, WA
Connolly, Patrick A., III ... **Los Angeles, CA**
Connolly, Patrick E. ... Compton, CA
Connolly, Patrick J. ... **Boston, MA**
Connolly, Patrick J. ... **New York, NY**
Connolly, Patrick M. ... **Atlanta, GA**
Connolly, Paul A. ... Los Angeles, CA
Connolly, Paul K., Jr. ... **Boston, MA**
Connolly, Paul R. J. ... Salem, OR
Connolly, Paul S. ... Milwaukee, WI
Connolly, Peter D. ... Chicago, IL
Connolly, Peter M. ... **Washington, DC**
Connolly, Rebecca A. ... **Boston, MA**
Connolly, Richard E. ... **Boston, MA**
Connolly, Robert ... **Mineola, NY**
Connolly, Robert E. ... Fort Wayne, IN
Connolly, Robert J. ... Mascoutah, IL
Connolly, Robert M. ... **Louisville, KY**
Connolly, Robert P. ... New York, NY
Connolly, Robert W. ... **Syracuse, NY**
Connolly and Rodriguez ... Metairie, LA
Connolly, Rosemary ... Boston, MA
Connolly, Scott B. ... **Philadelphia, PA**
Connolly, Sean F. ... San Francisco, CA
Connolly, Shanda W. ... **Los Angeles, CA**
Connolly, Shannon Eileen ... Boston, MA
Connolly & Smyser, Chartered ... Boise, ID; Parma, ID
Connolly, Stephen J. ... Hinsdale, IL
Connolly, Stephen J. ... **Portland, OR**
Connolly, Stephen M. ... Oak Park, IL
Connolly, Steven M. ... **Albany, NY**
Connolly, Steven M. ... Garden City, NY
Connolly, Susan M. ... **Niantic, CT**
Connolly, Susanne Marie ... **New York, NY**
Connolly, Suzanne M. ... **New York, NY**
Connolly, Terrence J. ... **New York, NY**
Connolly, Theresa M. ... **Baltimore, MD**
Connolly, Theresa M. ... San Antonio, TX
Connolly, Thomas A. ... **Flint, MI**
Connolly, Thomas A., P.C., Law Office of ... **Flint, MI**; **Saginaw, MI**
Connolly, Thomas E. ... Boston, MA
Connolly, Thomas G. ... **New York, NY**
Connolly, Thomas J. ... Portland, ME
Connolly, Thomas P. ... **Albany, NY**
Connolly, Thomas P., III ... **Sacramento, CA**
Connolly, Timothy W. ... Adelphi, MD
Connolly, Tom H. ... Denver, CO
Connolly, Vera I. ... Department of Energy, Office of the General Counsel, GV
Connolly, Vreeland & Connolly, A Professional Corporation ... Livingston, NJ
Connolly, Walter B. ... Stuart, FL
Connolly, Walter Briggs, Jr. ... **Detroit, MI**
Connolly, Ward S. ... **Palo Alto, CA**
Connolly, William G. ... **Morristown, NJ**
Connolly, William J. ... Mineola, NY
Connolly, William J. ... **Richmond, VA**
Connolly, William J., III ... **Boston, MA**
Connolly, William J., Jr. ... Miramar, FL; Des Plaines, IL
Connolly, William M. ... Camarillo, CA
Connolly, William M. ... Lincoln, NE
Connolly, William M. ... **Philadelphia, PA**
Connolly, William R. ... Troy, MI
Connolly, William S. ... Clearwater, FL
Connon, Charles J ... Boston, MA
Connon, John ... **New York, NY**
Connon, Kathleen A. ... Department of Transportation, Federal Aviation Administration, GV
Connon, Matthew R. ... Boston, MA
Connon, Nicholas P. ... Los Angeles, CA
Connon, Richard F. ... South Yarmouth, MA
Connon, William R. ... Hartford, CT
Connoni, Stephen R. ... **New York, NY**
Connop, Thomas A. ... **Dallas, TX**
Connor, Andrew F. ... Commack, NY
Connor, Andrew H. ... **Chicago, IL**
Connor & Behal ... **Columbus, OH**
Connor & Bishop ... San Francisco, CA
Connor, Bunn, Rogerson & Woodard, P.L.L.C. ... **Nashville, NC**; **Smithfield, NC**; **Wilson, NC**
Connor, Carla E. ... **Norristown, PA**
Connor, Carol ... Columbia, SC
Connor, Carol A. ... Albuquerque, NM
Connor, Charles D. ... Arlington, VA
Connor, Clare E. ... **Chicago, IL**
Connor, Colin M. ... Boston, MA
Connor, Colleen H. ... **Fairfield, CT**
Connor & Connor ... Hudson, NY
Connor, Culver, Blake & Griffin LLP ... **Irvine, CA**
Connor, Curran & Schram, P.C. ... **Chatham, NY**; **Hudson, NY**
Connor, Daniel D. ... **Columbus, OH**
Connor, David A. ... Columbus, OH
Connor, David Forrester ... Philadelphia, PA
Connor, David P. ... Agawam, MA
Connor, Deborah L. ... Department of Justice, Antitrust Division, GV
Connor, Dennis S. ... New York, NY
Connor, Doreen F. ... **Manchester, NH**
Connor, Douglas P. ... Mount Olive, NC
Connor, Douglas S. ... Bartow, FL
Connor, Earl M., Jr. ... Columbus, TX
Connor, Edmond M. ... **Irvine, CA**
Connor, Edward J. ... State College, PA
Connor, Edward J., Jr. ... Carmichael, CA
Connor, Eugene B., Jr. ... Baltimore, MD
Connor, Eugene J. ... **Chicago, IL**
Connor, F. Gale ... **San Francisco, CA**
Connor, Faith L. ... **West Palm Beach, FL**
Connor, Francis A., III ... **Boston, MA**; **Providence, RI**
Connor, Francis T. ... Warwick, RI
Connor, G. Brent ... **Washington, DC**
Connor, Geoffrey M. ... **Princeton, NJ**
Connor, Geoffrey Scott ... **Austin, TX**
Connor, George X. ... Minnetonka, MN
Connor, Gerald D. ... San Francisco, CA
Connor, Gilbert D. ... St. Louis, MO
Connor, Glen M. ... **Birmingham, AL**
Connor, Gregory s. ... Chapel Hill, NC
Connor, Haldan E., Jr. ... Cos Cob, CT
Connor, Harry D. ... Chicago, IL
Connor & Hilliard, P.C. ... Walpole, MA
Connor, Hugh G., II ... **Fort Worth, TX**
Connor, J. Davis ... **Lakeland, FL**; **Lake Wales, FL**; **Winter Haven, FL**
Connor, J. Parker ... Washington, DC
Connor, J. Robert ... Wellesley, MA
Connor, Jack A. ... Owensboro, KY
Connor, Jack W. ... Uniontown, PA
Connor, Jacqueline A. ... Los Angeles, CA
Connor, James A. ... Manchester, NH
Connor, James B. ... **Phoenix, AZ**
Connor, James E. ... Omaha, NE
Connor, James Lewis, III ... **Houston, TX**
Connor, James M. ... **Hartford, CT**
Connor, James M. ... Kingstree, SC
Connor, James W. ... Hudson, NY
Connor, James W. ... **Bartlesville, OK**
Connor, James W., Jr. ... **Tulsa, OK**
Connor, Jan Allen ... **Los Angeles, CA**
Connor, Jeff J. ... **Chattanooga, TN**
Connor, Jerome F. ... Winston-Salem, NC
Connor, Joan Webster ... Chicago, IL
Connor, John A. ... Columbus, OH
Connor, John B. ... **Alexandria, VA**
Connor, John B. ... **Fairfax, VA**
Connor, John D. ... **Indianapolis, IN**
Connor, John G. ... Portland, ME
Connor, John G. ... Hudson, NY
Connor, John J. ... **Kansas City, MO**
Connor, John, Jr. ... Hudson, NY
Connor, John P. ... Lenexa, KS
Connor, John P. ... Agawam, MA
Connor, John P. ... Cody, WY
Connor, John P., Jr. ... Walpole, MA
Connor, John P., Jr. ... Helena, MT
Connor, John T. ... North Palm Beach, FL
Connor, Jonathan S. ... **Austin, TX**
Connor, Joseph P., III ... Cherry Hill, NJ; **Paoli, PA**; **Philadelphia, PA**
Connor, Justin A. ... Washington, DC
Connor, Kenneth L. ... Tallahassee, FL
Connor, Kevin H. ... Columbus, OH
Connor, Kevin J. ... Chicago, IL
Connor, Kevin J. ... Gaithersburg, MD
Connor, Kevin M. ... **Kansas City, MO**
Connor & Kitchen ... **Laconia, NH**; **Manchester, NH**
Connor, Kristin R. ... **Atlanta, GA**
Connor, Kyran ... Cape May Court House, NJ
Connor, L. Sidney, IV ... **Surfside Beach, SC**
Connor, Laurence D. ... **Detroit, MI**
Connor Law Firm, The, PLLC ... Chapel Hill, NC
Connor, Leila G. ... **Laconia, NH**; **Manchester, NH**
Connor, Linda Dukes ... Birmingham, AL
Connor, Lisa G. ... **New York, NY**
Connor, Louis G., Jr. ... Baltimore, MD
Connor, M. Colleen ... Phoenix, AZ
Connor, Mairead E. ... Syracuse, NY
Connor, Margaret ... Department of Agriculture, Agricultural Research Service, GV
Connor, Margaret E. ... Brooklyn, NY
Connor, Margaret M. ... New York, NY
Connor, Margery C. ... Manlius, NY
Connor, Mark J. ... West Chester, PA
Connor, Martin E. ... Brooklyn, NY
Connor, Martin F., III ... Arlington, VA
Connor, Maryellen ... **Washington, DC**
Connor, Maureen S. ... **Gainesville, GA**
Connor, Michael A. ... **Irvine, CA**
Connor, Michael J. ... **Detroit, MI**
Connor, Michael L. ... Albuquerque, NM
Connor, Michael R. ... Mays Landing, NJ
Connor, Michael S. ... **Charlotte, NC**
Connor, Michael S. ... Philadelphia, PA
Connor, Miriam E. ... Westminster, CO
Connor, Neal, Stevenson & Mitchell, LLP ... Owensboro, KY
Connor, Noelle Anne ... Mount Laurel, NJ
Connor, P. Phillips ... Chicago, IL
Connor, Patricia C. ... Chatham, NJ
Connor, Patrick J. ... Minneapolis, MN
Connor, Patrick J. ... New York, NY
Connor, Patrick T. ... **Los Angeles, CA**
Connor, Peter C. ... **Holyoke, MA**
Connor and Price, P.C. ... Norfolk, VA
Connor, Richard D., Jr. ... **Winter Park, FL**
Connor, Richard D., Jr., P.A. ... **Orlando, FL**; **Winter Park, FL**
Connor, Richard E. ... Securities and Exchange Commission, Office of the General Counsel, GV
Connor, Robert C., Jr. ... Port Gibson, MS
Connor, Robert J. ... Chicago, IL
Connor, Robert T. ... **Philadelphia, PA**
Connor, Robert W., Jr. ... Sheridan, WY
Connor, Robin B. ... **Fort Worth, TX**
Connor, Sandman & Weisser ... Agawam, MA
Connor, Sean C. ... **Providence, RI**
Connor, Sean P. ... Chicago, IL
Connor, Sheila Brennan ... St. Davids, PA
Connor, Stephen E. ... **Denver, CO**
Connor, Stephen P. ... **Seattle, WA**
Connor, Stephen R. ... **Aspen, CO**; Snowmass Village, CO
Connor, Stephen R., P.C. ... **Aspen, CO**; Snowmass Village, CO
Connor, Sydell B. ... Studio City, CA
Connor, Tamara E. ... Reston, VA
Connor, Ted A. ... **Irvine, CA**
Connor, Terence G. ... **Miami, FL**
Connor, Terrence E. ... Reading, PA
Connor, Thomas A. ... Norfolk, VA
Connor, Thomas S. ... Cleveland, OH
Connor, Thomas W. ... Columbus, OH
Connor, Timothy J. ... Fort Wayne, IN
Connor, Timothy M. ... San Diego, CA
Connor, W. H. ... **Georgetown, TX**
Connor, Wayne M. ... Nashua, NH
Connor, Weber & Oberlies ... Cherry Hill, NJ; **Paoli, PA**; **Philadelphia, PA**
Connor, William C. ... **Peoria, IL**
Connor, William C. ... **Greensboro, NC**
Connor, William H. ... **Georgetown, TX**
Connor, William J. ... Springfield, IL
Connor, William J. ... **Kennewick, WA**
Connor, William M. ... **Philadelphia, PA**
Connor, William R., III ... **New York, NY**
Connor, Winston H., II ... Jay, OK
Connor-Heath, Sheila ... **Bloomfield Hills, MI**
Connors, Arlene D. ... Greendale, WI
Connors, Bliss & Courville ... Boston, MA
Connors, Brendan M. ... Waltham, MA
Connors, Brian F. ... San Francisco, CA
Connors, Brian R. ... Chicago, IL
Connors, Bruce H. ... **Greensboro, NC**
Connors, Carolyn Gates ... Wilmington, DE
Connors, Catherine R. ... **Portland, ME**
Connors, Charles C. ... **Atlanta, GA**
Connors, Charles W. B. ... Addison, IL
Connors, Christopher E. ... Ridgewood, NJ
Connors, Christopher J. ... Utica, NY
Connors, Claire T. ... Houston, TX
Connors, Clifford P. ... Orange, CA
Connors & Connors, LLP ... **Boston, MA**; **Waltham, MA**
Connors & Connors, P.C. ... **Staten Island, NY**
Connors & Corcoran, L.L.P. ... **Rochester, NY**
Connors, Curtis A. ... Lexington, MA
Connors, Daniel C. ... Williamson, NY
Connors, Daniel J. ... Bethesda, MD
Connors, Daniel L. ... Rutherford, NJ
Connors, David M. ... **Salt Lake City, UT**
Connors, Donald F. ... Vero Beach, FL
Connors, Donald L. ... Boston, MA
Connors, Donald R. ... Bethel Park, PA
Connors, E. Michael ... **Portland, OR**
Connors, Edward T. ... Venice, FL
Connors, Eugene K. ... **Pittsburgh, PA**
Connors & Farrell ... **Boston, MA**; **South Chatham, MA**
Connors, Francis P. ... Media, PA
Connors, Frank J. ... Cambridge, MA
Connors, G. Patrick, III ... **Rancho Santa Fe, CA**
Connors, Henry L. ... Hartsdale, NY
Connors, Hollis Gay ... Milwaukie, OR
Connors, James E. ... New York, NY
Connors, James F., Law Offices of ... Fitchburg, MA; Worcester, MA
Connors, James H. ... Madison, WI
Connors, James M. ... Melrose, MA
Connors, James P. ... **Mineola, NY**; **New York, NY**; White Plains, NY
Connors, James P. ... **New York, NY**
Connors, James P. ... **Columbus, OH**
Connors, James P., Jr. ... **White Plains, NY**
Connors, John E. ... Bronxville, NY
Connors, John J. ... Fairbanks, AK
Connors, John J. ... Newport Beach, CA
Connors, John J. ... Department of Justice, Office of Intelligence Policy and Review, GV
Connors, John J. ... Fall River, MA
Connors, John J. ... Portland, OR
Connors, John J., Jr. ... Southampton, PA
Connors, John M. ... Covina, CA
Connors, John M. ... Salem, MA
Connors, John P. ... Washington, DC
Connors, John P. ... **Staten Island, NY**
Connors, John P., Jr. ... **Staten Island, NY**
Connors, John Patrick ... **Cherry Hill, NJ**
Connors, John T. ... **Stamford, CT**
Connors, John W. ... Worcester, MA
Connors, Joseph A., III ... **McAllen, TX**
Connors, Joseph C. ... **Madison, NJ**
Connors, Joseph C., Jr. ... Anaconda, MT
Connors, Joseph C., Sr. ... Anaconda, MT
Connors, Joseph M., Jr. ... **Waltham, MA**
Connors, Joseph P. ... **Greenwich, CT**
Connors, Joseph P. ... New York, NY
Connors, Julia K. ... **Tucson, AZ**
Connors, Karen M. ... **Wellesley, MA**
Connors, Karen Marie ... Wellesley, MA
Connors, Kathryn I. ... **Brentwood, TN**
Connors, Kathryn Young ... Beachwood, OH
Connors, Kevin C. ... **Willimantic, CT**
Connors, Kevin J. ... **Wilmington, DE**
Connors, Kimberly A. ... San Jose, CA
Connors, Kristin ... **Waterbury, CT**
Connors, Lauretta L. ... Bronx, NY
Connors, Leonard J. ... Plant City, FL
Connors, Linda K. ... Fort Collins, CO
Connors, Manning A., III ... **Greensboro, NC**
Connors, Mariangeles Marquez ... Brooklyn, NY

Connors, Marissa G. .... Atlanta, GA
Connors, Mark G. .... Nashua, NH
Connors, Mary Ann .... Bridgeport, CT
Connors, Mary McAuley .... Rochester, NY
Connors, Mary Van .... Denver, CO
Connors, Matthew E. .... Boston, MA
Connors, Maureen E. .... Chicago, IL
Connors, Maureen L. .... Albany, NY
Connors, Michael N. .... Bayside, NY
Brooklyn, NY
New York, NY
Connors, Michael P. .... Hauppauge, NY
Connors, Michael W.
West Palm Beach, FL
Connors, Neal A. .... Belleville, IL
Connors, Patricia A. .... Boston, MA
Connors, Patricia L. .... Sacramento, CA
Connors, Patricia Lee, Law Office of
Sacramento, CA
Connors, Patrick J. .... Media, PA
Connors, Patrick M. .... Syracuse, NY
Connors, Patrick T. .... Washington, DC
Connors, Paul J. .... Washington, DC
Connors, Peter J. .... New York, NY
Connors, Richard D. .... Bloomfield Hills, MI
Connors, Richard F. .... North Haven, CT
Connors, Richard F. .... Jersey City, NJ
Connors, Richard F., Jr. .... Newark, NJ
Connors, Richard F., P.C.
North Haven, CT
Connors, Richard H. .... Rochester, NY
Connors, Richard J., Jr. .... St. Louis, MO
Connors, Richard L. .... Leawood, KS
Connors, Richard S. .... Chicago, IL
Connors, Richard T. .... Lynn, MA
Connors, Richard X. .... Boston, MA
Connors, Robert A. .... Western Springs, IL
Connors, Robert E., Jr. .... Waltham, MA
Connors, Robert T. .... Media, PA
Connors, Rose .... Boston, MA
Connors, Sandra L.
Environmental Protection Agency, Office of Enforcement and Compliance Assurance, GV
Connors, Sean C. .... New Haven, CT
Connors, Sean C. .... Washington, DC
McLean, VA
Connors, Sharon A. .... Westmont, NJ
Connors, Steven P. .... Cumberland, RI
Connors and Sullivan, P.C. .... Bayside, NY
Brooklyn, NY
New York, NY
Connors, Susan A. .... West Hartford, CT
Connors, Susan Fetten .... Livingston, NJ
Connors, Terrence M. .... Buffalo, NY
Connors, Thomas H. .... Miami, FL
Connors, Thomas H. .... Boston, MA
Connors, Thomas W. .... Canton, OH
Connors, Tim .... Beverly Hills, CA
Connors, Timothy D. .... Toledo, OH
Connors, Timothy J. .... Cleveland, OH
Connors, Timothy P. .... Ann Arbor, MI
Connors & Vilardo, LLP .... Buffalo, NY
Connors, Virginia Gandy .... Memphis, TN
Connors, William E. .... Minneapolis, MN
Connors, William F. .... Braintree, MA
Connors, William R. .... Seattle, WA
Connorton, John V., Jr. .... New York, NY
Connot, Mark J. .... Rapid City, SD
Connoyer, Barbara S. .... St. Charles, MO
Connuck, Eric S. .... New York, NY
Connuck, Paul D. .... New York, NY
Connuck, Wendy E. .... Mamaroneck, NY
Conod, Marianne .... Green Village, NJ
Conohan, James R. .... Madison, WI
Conole, Wendy M. .... Los Angeles, CA
Conoley, Clarence A. .... Leawood, KS
Conoley, Robert O. .... Bainbridge Island, WA
Conolly, Dawn A. .... Galesburg, IL
Conolly, Henry Neal .... New York, NY
Conoly, David Z. .... Corpus Christi, TX
Conoly, David Z., P.C.
Corpus Christi, TX
Conom, Tom P. .... Edmonds, WA
Conomos, Christopher W. .... Orlando, FL
Cononico, Vincent E. .... Warren, OH
Conormon, Todd Clark .... Fayetteville, NC
Conoshenti, Donna M. .... Ocean Gate, NJ
Conour • Doehrman • Starkey
Indianapolis, IN
Conour, Elizabeth A. .... Del Norte, CO
Conour, Kenneth P. .... San Francisco, CA
Conour, Melissa Newel
San Francisco, CA
Conour, William F. .... Indianapolis, IN
Conover, Alison C. .... Denver, CO
Conover, Arthur L. .... Jefferson City, MO
Conover & Associates .... Torrance, CA
Conover, Bradford D. .... New York, NY
Conover, Brooks William, III .... Austin, TX
Conover, Carla .... Department of Defense, Defense Legal Services Agency, GV
Conover, Christopher J. .... New York, NY
Conover, David W. .... Washington, DC
Conover, Douglas .... Chicago, IL
Conover, Duane H. .... Torrance, CA
Conover, E. Scott .... Columbia, MD
Conover, Frederic K., II .... Denver, CO
Conover, Garrett V. .... Crown Point, IN
Conover, George H., Jr. .... Edison, NJ
Conover, John G. .... Charlottesville, VA
Conover, John L. .... Davison, MI
Conover, John L. .... Newark, NJ
Conover, John R. .... Grand Prairie, TX
Conover, Julia A. .... Philadelphia, PA
Conover, Lee M. .... Sarasota, FL
Conover, Leslie A.
Federal Deposit Insurance Corporation, Professional Liability Section, GV
Conover, Michael .... Harrodsburg, KY
Conover, Nelson G. .... Talladega, AL
Conover, Pamela M. .... Baltimore, MD
Conover, Patricia Allen .... Montgomery, AL
Conover, Paul N. .... Newport Beach, CA
Conover, Richard C. .... Bozeman, MT
Conover, Robert C. .... Eugene, OR
Conover, Robert D. .... Buena Vista, CO
Conover, Robert V. .... Elkhorn, WI
Conover, Ron, Law Office Of
Grand Prairie, TX
Conover, Scott .... Washington, DC
Conover, Scott R. .... Freehold, NJ
Conover, Stephen J. .... Norwalk, CT
Conover, Suzanne D. S. .... Sarasota, FL
Conover, Todd M. .... Crown Point, IN
Conover, William G. .... Indianapolis, IN
Conover, Wm. V., II .... Houston, TX
Conover & Zayas, LLP
West New York, NJ
New York, NY
Conque, Durwood W. .... Abbeville, LA
Conques, Lawrence .... New Braunfels, TX
Conrad, Albert H., Jr. .... Atlanta, GA
Conrad, Allan D. .... Jamesburg, NJ
Conrad, Amy Elizabeth .... Gaithersburg, MD
Conrad, Andrew J. .... Washington, DC
Conrad, Anita M. .... Winston-Salem, NC
Conrad, Anne McGrew .... Memphis, TN
Conrad & Barlar .... Mobile, AL
Conrad, Bette Kester .... Vero Beach, FL
West Palm Beach, FL
Conrad & Boutillier .... Montclair, NJ
Conrad, Bruce R. .... Akron, OH
Conrad, Carl .... Nokomis, FL
Conrad, Carl T. .... Houma, LA
Conrad, Carol C. .... Rockville, MD
Conrad, Carsten .... Atlanta, GA
Conrad, Catherine .... Salem, OR
Conrad, Cathryn A. .... St. Louis, MO
Conrad, Charles T. .... Spokane, WA
Conrad, Christopher J. .... Brookfield, WI
Conrad, Christy D. .... Fort Worth, TX
Conrad, Clay S. .... Austin, TX
Conrad, Daniel A., Law Offices of
San Francisco, CA
Conrad, Daniel T. .... Dallas, TX
Conrad, David K. .... Columbus, OH
Conrad, David L. .... Los Angeles, CA
Conrad, David S. .... Mobile, AL
Conrad, David W. .... Montclair, NJ
Conrad, Deborah I. .... St. Louis, MO
Conrad, Debra Peterson .... Madison, WI
Conrad, Denise C. .... Los Angeles, CA
Conrad, Dennis M. .... Fort Worth, TX
Conrad, Diane W. .... Dallas, TX
Conrad, Donald E. .... Phoenix, AZ
Conrad, Donald Michael .... Littleton, CO
Conrad, Donald R. .... Sun City, AZ
Conrad, Donald R. .... Westland, MI
Conrad, Earl W. .... Berea, OH
Conrad, Edward M. .... Sigourney, IA
Conrad, Ellen Rouse .... New York, NY
Conrad, Erwin L. .... Fayetteville, WV
Conrad, Eugene B. .... Canton, OH
Conrad, F. Walter, Jr. .... Houston, TX
Conrad, Francis B. .... New York, NY
Conrad, Frank .... Rutland, VT
Conrad, Frank P. .... Boston, MA
Conrad, Frantz C., Jr. .... Enid, OK
Conrad, Frederick L., Jr. .... Knoxville, TN
Conrad, Frederick M. .... Tallahassee, FL
Conrad, G. Coleman .... San Diego, CA
Conrad, George D. .... Coeur d'Alene, ID
Conrad, George W. .... Silver Spring, MD
Conrad, Glen E. .... Roanoke, VA
Conrad, H. Clifton, Jr. .... Canton, GA
Conrad, Hugh V. .... Huntsville, AL
Conrad & Huyett .... Martinsburg, WV
Conrad, Ira L. .... Peterborough, NH
Conrad, J. Christian .... Aliso Viejo, CA
Conrad, J. Marshall .... Tallahassee, FL
Conrad, James E. .... Dearborn, MI
Conrad, James P. .... Warren, MI
Conrad, James W., Jr. .... Arlington, VA
Conrad, Jane A. .... Rochester, NY
Conrad, Janice M. .... Flint, MI
Saginaw, MI
Conrad, Jeffrey C. .... Anchorage, AK
Conrad, Jeffrey T. .... Indianapolis, IN
Conrad, Jodee K. .... Portland, OR
Conrad, John A. .... Richmond, VA
Conrad, John H. .... Gaithersburg, MD
Conrad, John N. .... Tampa, FL
Conrad, John N., P.A. .... Tampa, FL
Conrad, John R. .... Jupiter, FL
Conrad, Josef A. .... Bingham Farms, MI
Conrad, Julie Meredith .... Indianapolis, IN
Conrad, K. Robert .... Philadelphia, PA
Conrad, Karen Ann .... Louisville, KY
Conrad, Keith R. .... New Albany, IN
Conrad, Kyle D. .... Oklahoma City, OK
Conrad Law Offices .... Fayetteville, WV
Conrad, Lee A. .... Allentown, PA
Conrad, Lillian .... Plantation, FL
Conrad, Linda W. .... Lexington, MA
Conrad, Loral R. .... Dallas, TX
Conrad, Lynn R. .... Wheaton, IL
Conrad, Marc H. .... Metairie, LA
Conrad, Marcel E., III .... San Francisco, CA
Conrad, Marcia .... Annapolis, MD
Conrad, Marcia and Paul M. Kirby, LLC
Annapolis, MD
Conrad, Mark A. .... New York, NY
Conrad, Martin L. .... New York, NY
Conrad, Mickey N. .... Madison, WI
Conrad, Monica J. .... Chicago, IL
Conrad, Nancy .... Allentown, PA
Conrad, Norman L. .... Carlyle, IL
Conrad O'Brien Gellman & Rohn, P.C.
Mount Laurel, NJ
Philadelphia, PA
West Chester, PA
Conrad, Paul R. .... Tacoma, WA
Conrad, Peter D. .... New York, NY
Conrad, Philip L. .... Boston, MA
Conrad, Phillip G. .... Allentown, PA
Conrad, Ralph D. .... Greensburg, PA
Conrad, Ralph J. .... Cincinnati, OH
Conrad, Randall R., II .... Martinsburg, WV
Conrad, Ray C., Jr. .... Kansas City, MO
Conrad, Rebecca L. .... Dallas, TX
Conrad, Renee .... Walnut Creek, CA
Conrad, Rex .... Fort Lauderdale, FL
Conrad, Richard F. .... Orlando, FL
Conrad, Richard P. .... Dearborn, MI
Conrad, Richard T., III .... Alexandria, LA
Conrad, Robert .... New York, NY
Conrad, Robert Allen .... Indianapolis, IN
Conrad, Robert J. .... New Orleans, LA
Conrad, Robert J., Jr. .... New Orleans, LA
Conrad, Robert N. .... Los Angeles, CA
Conrad, Robert Nolan, A Law Corporation
Los Angeles, CA
Conrad, Robert P. .... Crownsville, MD
Conrad, Robert P., P.A. .... Crownsville, MD
Conrad, Robert W. .... Knoxville, IA
Conrad, Robin S. .... Washington, DC
Conrad & Scherer .... Fort Lauderdale, FL
Miami, FL
Conrad, Scott D. .... Newton, NC
Conrad, Scott J. .... Dallas, TX
Conrad, Shelby R. .... Huntington, WV
Conrad, Sherri J., Law Offices of
San Francisco, CA
Conrad & Shuman .... Dallas, TX
Conrad & Smith .... Scarsdale, NY
Conrad, Stuart W. .... Kansas City, MO
Conrad, Susan Dennehy .... Oklahoma City, OK
Conrad, T. Scott .... Tampa, FL
Conrad, Teresa L. .... Charlotte, NC
Conrad, Thomas A. .... Hollywood, FL
Conrad, Trosch & Kemmy .... Charlotte, NC
Conrad, Vivienne .... Los Angeles, CA
Conrad, W. Christopher .... Pittsburgh, PA
Conrad, Warren T. .... Wilmette, IL
Conrad, William .... Treasury Department, Office of Regulations and Rulings, GV
Conrad, William J. .... New Orleans, LA
Conrad, Winthrop B., Jr. .... New York, NY
Conrad-Bayer, Cynthia K. .... Houston, TX
Conrades, Stanley A., Jr.
Upper Marlboro, MD
Conradi, Charles R. .... San Francisco, CA
Conradi, Gerald A. .... San Diego, CA
Conradi, Lesley M. .... Milford, OH
Conradi, Rebecca .... Oakland, CA
Conradregan, Terri J. .... Albany, NY
Conrad-Sandoval, Rosemary J.
Brownsville, TX
McAllen, TX
Conradt, Louis W., Jr. .... Terrell, TX
Conrady, Michael H. .... Charleston, SC
Conragan, Aram K., Jr. .... Cambridge, MA
Conran, Joseph P. .... St. Louis, MO
Conran, Sharon A. .... Dearborn, MI
Conran, Thomas C. .... Fairfax, VA
Conrath, Craig W. .... Department of Justice, Antitrust Division, GV
Conratt, Linda .... Portland, OR
Conratt, Robert C. .... Portland, OR
Conrey, Charles Kevin .... Louisville, KY
Conrey, Martin E.
Small Business Administration, Office of the General Counsel, GV
Conrod, Richard J., Sr. .... Virginia Beach, VA
Conrod, RichardJ., Sr., P.C.
Virginia Beach, VA
Conron, Michael W. .... Baltimore, MD
Conrow, Mary L. .... Binghamton, NY
Conroy, Annemarie .... San Francisco, CA
Conroy, Anthony J. .... Palo Alto, CA
Conroy, Ballman & Dameron, Chartered
Bethesda, MD
Bowie, MD
Gaithersburg, MD
Rockville, MD
Conroy, C. Michael .... Knoxville, TN
Conroy, Carl S. .... Syracuse, NY
Conroy, Catherine E. (Liza) .... Henderson, NV
Conroy, Charles J. .... New York, NY
Conroy, Christopher A. .... Montclair, NJ
Conroy, Cynthia P. .... Metairie, LA
Conroy, Daniel H. .... Boston, MA
Conroy, David J. .... Asheville, NC
Conroy, David, (P.C.) .... New Orleans, LA
Conroy, David S. .... Wheaton, IL
Conroy, Deann Marie .... Denver, CO
Conroy, Delfido R. .... Los Lunas, NM
Conroy, Dennis J. .... Salt Lake City, UT
Conroy, Douglas C. .... Stamford, CT
Conroy, Edmund J. .... St. Louis, MO
Conroy, Edward A., Jr. .... Stamford, CT
Conroy, Edward C. .... Stamford, CT
Conroy, Edward Gerard .... West Chester, PA
Conroy, Frederick J. .... Lexington, MA
Conroy, Gerald P. .... New York, NY
Conroy, Harold W. .... Honolulu, HI
Conroy, Helen Leah .... San Francisco, CA
Conroy, Hugh C., Jr. .... New York, NY
Conroy, J. Britton .... Corvallis, OR
Conroy, J. Michael, Jr. .... Bowie, MD
Gaithersburg, MD
Conroy, J. Thomas, III .... Naples, FL
Conroy, James B. .... Boston, MA
Conroy, James J., III .... Fairfax, VA
Conroy, James P. .... New York, NY
Conroy, James P. .... Cleveland, OH
Conroy, Janet E. .... Rocky Point, NY
Conroy, Jayne .... New York, NY
Conroy, Jeanne S. .... Boston, MA
Conroy, Jim W. .... Seattle, WA
Conroy, John D. .... Doylestown, PA
Conroy, John F. .... Washington, DC
Conroy, John J., Jr. .... Chicago, IL
Conroy, John L., Jr. .... Camden, NJ
Conroy, John M. .... Mineola, NY
Conroy, John P. .... New York, NY
Conroy, John S., IV .... Burlington, NJ
Conroy, John T. .... Dolton, IL
Conroy, John T. .... Oak Lawn, IL
Conroy, John T. .... Columbus, OH
Conroy, John T., P.C. .... Dolton, IL
Conroy, John Thomas .... Grand Rapids, MI
Conroy, John W. .... Milford, CT
Conroy, Joseph W. .... Reston, VA
Conroy, Jude D. .... Philadelphia, PA
Conroy, Katharine Wilson
White Plains, NY
Conroy, Kevin T. .... Chicago, IL
Conroy, Kim .... Washington, DC
Conroy, Kristin M. .... Tallahassee, FL
Conroy, Kristin McQueen .... Burbank, CA
Conroy, Lynn M. .... Rockford, MI
Conroy, Mark L. .... Santa Monica, CA
Conroy, Martin J. .... Princeton, NJ
Conroy, Maryellen T. .... Philadelphia, PA
Conroy, Michael C. .... Rutland, VT
Conroy, Michael D. .... Covington, LA
Conroy, Michael E. .... Miami, FL
Conroy, Michael F. .... San Diego, CA
Conroy, Michael G. .... Philadelphia, PA
Conroy, Michael J., Jr. .... Philadelphia, PA
Conroy & Murphy, L.L.C. .... Covington, LA
Conroy, Nancy A. .... Los Angeles, CA
Conroy, Nora E. .... Honolulu, HI
Conroy, Patricia A. .... Yreka, CA
Conroy, Patrick K. .... Chicago, IL
Conroy, Patrick T. .... Clayton, MO
Conroy, Paul A. .... Irving, TX
Conroy, Richard J. .... Crown Point, IN
Conroy, Rita N. .... Chicago, IL
Conroy, Robert Anthony .... Pittsburgh, PA
Conroy, Robert J. .... Bridgewater, NJ
Conroy, Roberta A. .... Los Angeles, CA
Conroy, S. Michael .... Acme, MI
Conroy, Sandra L. .... Minneapolis, MN
Conroy, Sheila M. .... Chicago, IL
Conroy, Simberg & Ganon, P.A.
Fort Myers, FL
Hollywood, FL
Miami, FL
Orlando, FL
Pensacola, FL
West Palm Beach, FL
Conroy, Stephen K., & Associates
Metairie, LA
Conroy, Stephen K., & Associates
New Orleans, LA
Conroy, Stephen L. .... Lynnwood, WA
Conroy, Theresa A. .... Brockport, NY
Conroy, Thomas .... Bloomington, IL
Conroy, Thomas C. .... St. Louis, MO
Conroy, Thomas H. .... Beloit, KS
Conroy, Thomas J. .... Cambridge, MA
Conroy, Thomas M. .... Madison, CT
Conroy, Thomas W. .... Hollywood, FL
Pensacola, FL
Conroy, Timothy J. .... Grand Rapids, MI
Conroy, Walter I. .... New York, NY
Conroy, William F. .... Washington, DC
Conroy, William J. .... Philadelphia, PA
Conroy, William T., Jr. .... Goshen, NY
Conroyd, Cinda M. .... Salem, OR
Conroyd, Michael F. .... Salem, OR
Conroyd, Walter F. .... Chicago, IL
Conry, Colleen A. .... Department of Justice, Civil Division, GV
Conry, Dennis J. .... Wareham, MA
Conry, Leonard M. .... Eureka, CA
Conry, Martin J. .... Amherst, OH
Consadene, Jonathan Davis
Fort Lauderdale, FL
Consagra, Charles L. .... Scranton, PA
Consales, Leon A. .... Totowa, NJ
Consalo, Marc Anthony .... Orlando, FL
Consalus, Charles E. .... East Lansing, MI
Consalvi, Mary S. .... La Jolla, CA
Consalvo, Gennaro J. .... Ventnor City, NJ
Consedine, Megan L. .... Harrisburg, PA
Consedine, Michael F. .... Harrisburg, PA
Conselatore, Louis D. .... Brooklyn, NY
Consentino, Lynn P. .... New York, NY
Conser, Janet A. .... Wilkes-Barre, PA
Conser, Lee C. .... Orlando, FL
Conser, Richard E. .... Des Plaines, IL
Consevage, John B. .... Harrisburg, PA
Considine, Brian J. .... Torrance, CA
Westland, MI
Considine, Christopher A. .... New York, NY
Considine, Daniel V. .... Chicago, IL
Considine, Eileen M. .... Washington, DC
Albany, NY
Considine, J. Michael, Jr. .... West Chester, PA
Considine, James C. .... Midland, TX
Considine, John J., III .... West Palm Beach, FL
Considine, John J., Jr. .... Rochester, NY
Considine, Joseph M. .... West Palm Beach, FL
Considine, Kevin M. .... Boston, MA
Considine, Michael G. .... Stamford, CT
Considine, Michael J. .... Lee, MA

Considine, Michael J. ....Lenox, MA
Considine, Michael M.
South Lake Tahoe, CA
Considine, Richard J. ....Worcester, MA
Considine, Sheila E. ....Chicago, IL
Considine, Thomas B. ....New York, NY
Considine, Thomas V. ....Buffalo, NY
Considine, Timothy P. ....Rockford, IL
Considine, Tracy Joseph ....Miami, FL
Considine, William M. ....New York, NY
Consigli, Aldo B., Jr. ....Milford, MA
Consigli and Brucato, P.C. ....Milford, MA
Consiglio, Charles J. ....Cleveland, OH
Consiglio, Christine DeMichele
Harrisburg, PA
Philadelphia, PA
Consiglio, Joseph O. ....Mercerville, NJ
Consiglio, Michael E. ....Northridge, CA
Consiglio, Richard ....Hollidaysburg, PA
Consigny, Andrews, Hemming & Grant, S.C.
Brodhead, WI
Janesville, WI
Madison, WI
Consigny, Robert H. ....**Janesville, WI**
Madison, WI
Consilvio, Felix J., Jr. ....Medford, MA
Consoer, George L., Jr. ....**Fort Myers, FL**
Consolazio, Joseph O. ....Coconut Creek, FL
Consoldane, Anthony V. ....Warren, OH
Console, Dale E. ....Skillman, NJ
Console, Raymond G. ....**Cherry Hill, NJ**
Console, Stephen G., Law Offices of
Haddon Heights, NJ
Philadelphia, PA
Consoli, Carla A. ....**Phoenix, AZ**
Consoli, Richard P. ....**North Andover, MA**
Consoli, Scott P. ....**Hartford, CT**
Consolino, Lisa S. ....**New York, NY**
Consolo, Jeffrey P. ....**Cleveland, OH**
Consolo, Linda S. ....Chicago, IL
Consolo, Patricia Daley ....Cleveland, OH
Consolver, Carol A. ....**San Diego, CA**
Consolver, Kay Ellen ....Boston, MA
Consolvo, Charles W.
Charlotte Amalie, St. Thomas, VI
Consolvo, Ernest C. ....Virginia Beach, VA
Consolvo, George L. ....**Norfolk, VA**
Consolvo, Markowitz & Webb
Virginia Beach, VA
Consor, Jeannette E. ....Dallas, TX
Consovoy, Andrew B. ....Mount Holly, NJ
Consovoy & Demko ....Mount Holly, NJ
Constabile, Thomas R., Jr.
Larchmont, NY
Constable, Gary E. ....**New York, NY**
Constable, George ....Seattle, WA
Constable, George W. ....**Baltimore, MD**
Constable, James W. ....**Baltimore, MD**
Constable, Linda K. ....**Wichita, KS**
Constable, Richard E., III ....**New York, NY**
Constable, Robert L., (Chtd.) ....Salina, KS
Constable, Sean P. ....**New York, NY**
Constan, Katherine Mitchell ....New York, NY
Constan, Katherine W. ....**New York, NY**
Constance, Bradley A. ......**Independence, MO**
Constance, Byron ....**Independence, MO**
Constance, George Gregory ....Warren, MI
Constance, Michael B. ....Belleville, IL
Constance, Richard L. ....St. Louis, MO
Constance, Thomas E. ....**New York, NY**
Constangy, Brooks & Smith, LLC
Birmingham, AL
Washington, DC
Atlanta, GA
Macon, GA
Winston-Salem, NC
Columbia, SC
Nashville, TN
Arlington, VA
Constangy, H. William (Bill) ....Charlotte, NC
Constant, Dennis R. ....La Habra, CA
Constant, Donald M. ....New Bedford, MA
Constant, Donald M., P.C.
New Bedford, MA
Constant, Gary D. ....Bristol, CT
Constant, George C. ....Winchester, MA
Constant, Irving, (P.C.) ....**New York, NY**
Constant, Mary J. ....**New York, NY**
Constant, Patricia Reed
Corpus Christi, TX
Constant, Richard E. ....Middleburg, PA
Constant, Terry L. ....Kenosha, WI
Constant, Thomas ....Hauppauge, NY
Constantakes, Peter ....Arlington, MA
Constantakis, Clarence R. ....Dearborn, MI
Constantikes, George D. ....**Westport, CT**
Constantikes, John J. ....McAlester, OK
Constantine, Amy ....Grand Rapids, MI
Constantine Anderson & O'Brien, P.C.
Littleton, CO
Constantine & Associates, P.C.
Atlanta, GA
Constantine & Associates, P.C.
Albuquerque, NM
Constantine, Benjamin P. ....Eveleth, MN
Constantine, Christine A. F. ....Rochester, NY
Constantine, Constantine ....Glastonbury, CT
Constantine, Costa ....New York, NY
Constantine, Dean ....**Livingston, NJ**
Constantine, Dean G. ....**Albuquerque, NM**
Constantine, Eleni M. ......Treasury Department,
Office of the General Counsel, GV
Constantine, George Anthony
Garden City, NY
Constantine, George C. ....Northville, MI
Constantine, James Dow ....Seattle, WA
Constantine, Jan F. ....**New York, NY**

Constantine, Katherine A.
Minneapolis, MN
Constantine, Lloyd ....**New York, NY**
Constantine, Mark Edmond ....Brooklyn, NY
Constantine & Partners ....**New York, NY**
Constantine, Peter John
Federal Labor Relations Authority,
Office of the Chair, GV
Constantine, Phillip S. ....Medford, MA
Constantine, Randall A. ....**Atlanta, GA**
Constantine, Richard M. ....**New York, NY**
Constantine, Robert P., Jr. ....**Atlanta, GA**
Constantine, Robert W. ....**Buffalo, NY**
Constantine, Robert W. ......**Williamsville, NY**
Constantine, Thomas B. ....**Jacksonville, FL**
Constantine, Thomas J. ....**Littleton, CO**
Constantine, Walter E., Jr. ....Buffalo, NY
Constantine, William James ....Santa Cruz, CA
Constantine, Zinder & Pallis ....Chicago, IL
Constantinides, Catherine Pozos
San Jose, CA
Constantinides, Charles ....San Jose, CA
Constantinides, John S. ....Baltimore, MD
Constantinides, Panos P. ....Atlanta, GA
Constantinides, Platon P. ....Atlanta, GA
Constantino, Alexander L. ....**Auburn, CA**
Constantino, Cynthia A. ....**Rochester, NY**
Constantino, Gregory J. ....Oak Brook, IL
Constantino, Gregory M., Law Office of
Salt Lake City, UT
Constantino, Jacqueline A. ......**Rochester, NY**
Constantino, James P. ....**Poughkeepsie, NY**
Constantino, Mary C. ....Wheaton, IL
Constantino, Michael A. ....Lynnfield, MA
Constantino, Paul C. ....Leominster, MA
Constantino, Paul J. ....Burlingame, CA
Constantino, Paul R. ....Brookline, MA
Constantinople, George R.
National Labor Relations Board,
Office of Board Members, GV
Constantinou, Clay ....**Woodbridge, NJ**
Constants, Alfred C., III ....Roseland, NJ
Constantz, Virginia A. ....Hillsboro, MO
Constas, Dorothea ....New York, NY
Constas, Michael ....Torrance, CA
Constine, David E., III ....**Richmond, VA**
Constine, Donald B. ....San Francisco, CA
Constine, Jonathan A. ....**Washington, DC**
Constitutional Litigation Associates, P.C.
Detroit, MI
Conston, Henry S. ....**New York, NY**
Conston, Stuart F. ....Narberth, PA
Construction Law Group, The
San Francisco, CA
Construction Legal Services, P.C.
Wyandotte, MI
Consuegra, Daniel C. ....Tampa, FL
Consuegra, Luis A. ....Miami, FL
Consuegra, Maria E. ....Miami, FL
Consul, Vincent A. ....**Las Vegas, NV**
Consumano, Dennis ....**New York, NY**
Cont, Patrick L. ....**Spartanburg, SC**
Conta, Jeffrey J. P. ....**Milwaukee, WI**
Conta, Lee Anne N. ....**Milwaukee, WI**
Contaldi, Joseph R. ....Hackensack, NJ
Contant, Elaine L. ....Cambridge, MA
Contant, Philip A. ....Westfield, MA
Contant, Richard J. ....**Hackensack, NJ**
Contant, Scherby & Atkins
Hackensack, NJ
Jersey City, NJ
Newark, NJ
Paterson, NJ
Contarino, Alfred V. ....**Los Angeles, CA**
Contas, Charles J. ....Keene, NH
Conte, Anthony R. ....Newton, MA
Conte, Catherine E. ....Grafton, MA
Conte, Christine W. ....**Detroit, MI**
Conte, Christopher A. ....**Washington, DC**
Silver Spring, MD
Conte, Christopher R.
Securities and Exchange Commission,
Division of Enforcement, GV
Conte, Donald A. ....Worcester, MA
Conte, Francis L. ....Swampscott, MA
Conte, Frank A. ....Washington, PA
Conte, Frank A., P.C. ....Washington, PA
Conte, Frederick P. ....Johnson City, NY
Conte, Gregory Michael ....Bridgeport, CT
Conte, James B. ....**Chicago, IL**
Conte, James J. ....**Latrobe, PA**
Conte, John A. ....Hackensack, NJ
Conte, John A., Jr. ....Saddle Brook, NJ
Conte, John Alan ....**Conway, PA**
Conte, Joseph A.
Department of Transportation,
Federal Aviation Administration, GV
Conte, Joseph R. ....**Washington, DC**
Conte, Joseph R. ....**Clawson, MI**
Plymouth, MI
Conte, Joseph R. ....Huntington, NY
Conte, Lisa ....**White Plains, NY**
Conte, Melton & D'Antonio ....**Beaver, PA**
Butler, PA
Conway, PA
New Castle, PA
Pittsburgh, PA
Conte, Michele F. ....**Cherry Hill, NJ**
Harrisburg, PA
King Of Prussia, PA
Conte, Nicholas C. ....**Roanoke, VA**
Conte, Richard J. ....**Hackensack, NJ**
Conte, Richard M. ....Willoughby, OH
Conte, Richard M. ....Jeannette, PA
Conte, Robert F. I. ....**Chicago, IL**
Conte, Rocco ....**White Plains, NY**
Conte, Salvatore R.
Research Triangle Park, NC

Conte, Samuel ....**Kenilworth, NJ**
Conte, Stephen C. ....**Richmond, VA**
Conte, Stephen P. ....New York, NY
Conte, Thomas J. ....**Worcester, MA**
Conte, William W. ....Bangor, ME
Conte, Wm. P. ....Edison, NJ
Content, Arthur L. ....Washington, DC
Contente, Eve T. ....Albany, CA
Contente, William ....**Boston, MA**
Contento, Denise P. ......Department of Defense,
Defense Legal Services Agency, GV
Contento, Mark M. ....Tucson, AZ
Conter, Belinda A. ....Colorado Springs, CO
Conter, C. Michael ....Tampa, FL
Conter, C. Michael, P.A. ....Tampa, FL
Conter, Edward N. ....Tempe, AZ
Contes, Constance Coin ....Tempe, AZ
Conti, Adam J. ....**Atlanta, GA**
Conti, Adam J., LLC ....**Atlanta, GA**
Conti, Albert B. ....Stoneham, MA
Conti, Alexander L. ....**Irvine, CA**
Conti, Anthony J. ....New York, NY
Conti, Caterina A. ....New York, NY
Conti, Christopher J. ....**Cleveland, OH**
Conti, Daniel A. ....**Hempstead, NY**
Conti, David V., Jr. ....Union, NJ
Conti, Elizabeth Katherine ....Placerville, CA
Conti, Frederic L. ....Glenside, PA
Conti, George A., Jr. ....Greensburg, PA
Conti, Henry H. ....Waupun, WI
Conti, Jason Schian ....**Detroit, MI**
Conti, Jill A. ....Gainesville, FL
Conti, John C. ....**Pittsburgh, PA**
Conti, John W. ....Bangor, ME
Conti, Jonathan M. ....**Milwaukee, WI**
Conti, Joseph P. ....Erie, PA
Conti, Joseph S. ....Niagara Falls, NY
Conti, Joy Flowers ....**Pittsburgh, PA**
Conti, Judith M. ....**Washington, DC**
Conti, Karen ....**Chicago, IL**
Conti, Kevin A. ....**Teaneck, NJ**
Conti, Laura G. ....Los Angeles, CA
Conti, Lee Ann ....**Woodridge, IL**
Conti, Louis T. M. ....**Orlando, FL**
Conti and Mallozzi ....Union, NJ
Conti, Matthew J. ....Chicago, IL
Conti, Michael J. ....Chicago, IL
Conti, Pat S. ....**Washington, DC**
Conti, Philip O. ....Portland, OR
Conti, Richard J. ....**Danville, CA**
Conti, Richard S. ....**Manchester, CT**
Conti, Robert Joseph ....Huntington, NY
Conti, Robert W. ....Sherman Oaks, CA
Conti, Samuel ....San Francisco, CA
Conti, Samuel D. ....North Andover, MA
Conti, Sara A. ....Chapel Hill, NC
Conti, Victor J. ....**Danville, CA**
Conti, William A. ....Torrington, CT
Conti, William J. ....**Washington, DC**
Conti, William L. ....Oceanside, CA
Conticello, Anthony L. ....**Stuart, FL**
Contie, Leroy J., Jr. ....Akron, OH
Contiguglia, Andrew John ....Denver, CO
Contiguglia, David A. ....**Auburn, NY**
Contiguglia & Giacona ....**Auburn, NY**
Syracuse, NY
Contiguglia, Joseph ....Little Neck, NY
Contiguglia, Louis P. ....**Auburn, NY**
Contiguglia, Robert A. ....Auburn, NY
Contillo, Robert P. ....Paramus, NJ
Contini, Jennifer M. ....Santa Ana, CA
Contini, John Patrick
Fort Lauderdale, FL
Contini, John Patrick, P.A., Law Office of
Fort Lauderdale, FL
Contini, Peter L. ....**Garden City, NY**
Contini, Stephen A. ....Columbus, OH
Contini II, James F. ....**Canton, OH**
New Philadelphia, OH
Salem, OH
Contino, James J. ....**Buffalo, NY**
Contino, John ....Harrisburg, PA
Contino, Peter C. ....**Uniondale, NY**
Contino, Victoria ....**Albany, NY**
Contis, David J. ....Chicago, IL
Contis, George A. ....**Sterling Heights, MI**
Contois, Kathie M. ....**Chicago, IL**
Contois, Robert M., Jr. ....New Orleans, LA
Contois, Thomas M. ....**Washington, DC**
Contole, William L. ....North Palm Beach, FL
Contopoulos, Andrew N.
Walnut Creek, CA
Contopulos, Stephen G. ....Los Angeles, CA
Contor, Maurice D. ....Upperville, VA
Contorer, Jay ....Chicago, IL
Contorno, Michael ....Houston, TX
Contos & Bunch ....**Westlake Village, CA**
Contos, Harry, Jr. ....**Kalamazoo, MI**
Contos, Helen ....**Lisle, IL**
Contos, John R. ....**Westlake Village, CA**
Contract, Victor A. ....**Washington, DC**
Contractor, Ratna M. ....Ocoee, FL
Contrada & Associates ....**Findlay, OH**
Tiffin, OH
Toledo, OH
Contrada, Carol A. ....**Toledo, OH**
Contrada, Charles V. ....**Toledo, OH**
Contrastano, Mauro A. ....New York, NY
Contratto, Anthony M. ....Redondo Beach, CA
Contratto, Dana C. ....**Washington, DC**
Contreni, Rachel A. ....Lincolnshire, IL
Contrera, Joseph G. ....**Alexandria, VA**
Contreras, Alejandro ....San Jose, CA
Contreras, Andrew M. ....**Morristown, NJ**
Contreras, Carlos J., III ....Austin, TX
Contreras, Celestina Lopez ....Austin, TX
Contreras, Colleen M. Danaher
Chicago, IL

Contreras, Dorothea H. (Dee)
Sacramento, CA
Contreras, Duarte, Jr. ....New Brunswick, NJ
Contreras, Gilberto A. ....Coral Gables, FL
Contreras & Gomez ....**Chula Vista, CA**
Contreras, Jeffrey H. ....Oklahoma City, OK
Contreras, Jesse J. ....**Los Angeles, CA**
Contreras, Jesús, Law Offices of
Mercedes, TX
Contreras, Jesús, Law Offices of
Weslaco, TX
Contreras, Joe W. ....Phoenix, AZ
Contreras, Jorge L., Jr. ....**Boston, MA**
Contreras, Juan M. ....Houston, TX
Contreras, Maria Luisa ....**San Juan, PR**
Contreras, Matias R. ....El Centro, CA
Contreras, Raul C. ....Van Nuys, CA
Contreras, Raymond M. ....**Chula Vista, CA**
Contreras, Ricardo Mendoza
Albuquerque, NM
Contreras, Richard ....El Paso, TX
Contreras, Robert A. ....**Chicago, IL**
Contreras, Robert A. ....**Kenner, LA**
Contreras, Roger H. ....**Tucson, AZ**
Contreras, Rudolph ....Washington, DC
Contreras, Sean D. ....Spotsylvania, VA
Contreras-Gómez, Fermín M. ....San Juan, PR
Contreras-Gomez, Mariana M.
San Juan, PR
Contreras-Hendler, Lisa J. ....Lakewood, CO
Contris, Lisa ....Tacoma, WA
Contrivo, Frank J. ....**Asheville, NC**
Contrivo, Frank J., P.A. ....**Asheville, NC**
Contrubis, John ....Library of Congress,
Congressional Research Service, GV
Contrucci, Joseph J. ....Gainesville, VA
Contrucci, Robt. L. ....Milwaukee, WI
Conturo, Mary K. ....**Pittsburgh, PA**
Conturso, Charles J. ....Morrisville, PA
Contuzzi, Peter ....Northampton, MA
Conver, David W. ....**Lansdale, PA**
Conver, Neil L. ....**Lansdale, PA**
Converse, Daniel K. ....Dearborn, MI
Converse, Jane S.
Federal Housing Finance Board,
Office of General Counsel, GV
Converse, Jerome M. ....Springfield, TN
Converse, John R. ....Lafayette, CA
Converse, Kari ....Albuquerque, NM
Converse, Mark E. ....Green Bay, WI
Converse, Michael L. ....**Washington, DC**
Converse, Mitchell W. ....**St. Paul, MN**
Converse, Morell & Hughes ....Palmyra, NY
Converse, P. Bruce ....**Phoenix, AZ**
Converse, Philip M. ....Seattle, WA
Converse, Philip R. ....Memphis, TN
Converse, Robert E., Jr. ....**Washington, DC**
Converse, Robert G. ....**Austin, TX**
Converse, Willard L. ....**St. Paul, MN**
Convertito, John J. ....**Fairfield, CT**
Convery, Brian J. ....**Newark, NJ**
Convery, Clark W. ....Metuchen, NJ
Convery, J. Ferd, III ....**Princeton, NJ**
Convery, J. Ferd, III ....Westfield, NJ
Convery, James B. ....Newark, NJ
Convery, James J. ....**Chicago, IL**
Convery, James V., III ....Fair Lawn, NJ
Convery, Jerome J. ....Old Bridge, NJ
Convery, John A. ....San Antonio, TX
Convery, John J. ....Paterson, NJ
Convery, Martin P. ....Edison, NJ
Convery, Maureen A. ....**St. Paul, MN**
Convery, Neil P. ....St. Paul, MN
Convery, Patrick S. ....**Middletown, NJ**
Convery, Susannah J. ....Walnut Creek, CA
Convery, Thomas V. ....**Woodbridge, NJ**
Staten Island, NY
Convery, Vincent J. ....Trenton, NJ
Convery, Vincent J., Jr.
Federal Election Commission,
Office of the General Counsel, GV
Convey, Michael J. ....Sherman Oaks, CA
Convicer, Richard G. ....**Glastonbury, CT**
Convicer, Richard G., LLC
Glastonbury, CT
Convis, Charles L. ....Stockton, CA
Conviser, Daniel ....Albany, NY
Conviser, Richard J. ....Chicago, IL
Convissar, Robert N. ....**Buffalo, NY**
Convisser, Ellen ....Boston, MA
Convisser, Theodora S. ....Boston, MA
Conway, Alice E. ....**St. Louis, MO**
Conway, Amy Jeanne ....Washington, DC
Conway, Andrew S. ....**Bloomfield Hills, MI**
Conway, Andrew W. ....Rochester, NY
Conway, Ann Maloney ....**Albuquerque, NM**
Santa Fe, NM
Conway, Anne C. ....Orlando, FL
Conway, Audrey M. ....Las Vegas, NV
Conway, A. V., II ....**Abingdon, VA**
Conway, Bernard J. ....Chicago, IL
Conway, Bernard J. ....Chicago, IL
Conway, B. L., II ....**Abingdon, VA**
Conway & Blanck ....Boonville, MO
Conway, Bradley A. ....**Orlando, FL**
Conway, Brendan T. ....**Philadelphia, PA**
Conway, Brian J. ....White Plains, NY
Conway, Brian P. ....**Pittsburgh, PA**
Conway, Brian T. ....Holyoke, MA
Conway, Bryant W. ....Baker, LA
Conway, Camille B. ....Chicago, IL
Conway, Carole Friend ....**Pikeville, KY**
Conway, Caroline E. ....Washington, DC
Conway, Carolyn M. ....**Boston, MA**
Conway, Catherine A. ....**Los Angeles, CA**
Conway, Catherine F. ....**Milwaukee, WI**
Conway, Charles J., Jr. ....**Oxnard, CA**
Conway, Charles M., Jr. ....Jacksonville, FL

Conway & Chiaviello, Ltd. ....Chicago, IL
Conway, Chris R. ....Norwalk, CA
Conway, Colleen M. ....Chicago, IL
Conway, Connolly and Pauley, P.C.
Hastings, NE
Conway & Conway ....New York, NY
Conway & Conway, L.L.C. ....Bristol, TN
Abingdon, VA
Conway, Cotter C. ....Incline Village, NV
Conway Crowley & Homer, P.C.
Boston, MA
Conway, Daniel C. ....Milwaukee, WI
Conway, Daniel R. ....Columbus, OH
Conway, Darrell J. ....Melville, NY
Conway, David S. ....Wilmington, DE
Conway, Dennis D. ....Wisconsin Rapids, WI
Conway, Dianne K. ....Tacoma, WA
Conway, Donald L. ....West Palm Beach, FL
Conway, Donald P. ....Agawam, MA
Conway, Douglas E. ....Bridgeport, CT
Conway & Duley ....Upper Marlboro, MD
Conway, E. Virgil ....Bronxville, NY
Conway, Edna M. ....Nashua, NH
Conway, Edward D. ....Philadelphia, PA
Conway, Edward S. ....Delmar, NY
Conway, Elizabeth ....Norwich, CT
Conway, Ellen A. ....Springfield, MA
Conway, Ellen Nolan ....Chicago, IL
Conway, F. Thomas ....Louisville, KY
Conway, F. Thomas, P.S.C. ....Louisville, KY
Conway, Farrell, Curtin & Kelly, P.C.
New York, NY
Conway, F. H. ....Danville, VA
Conway, Francis D. ....San Francisco, CA
Conway, Francis P. ....New York, NY
Conway, Frederic L., III
Department Of Veterans Affairs, Office of the General Counsel, GV
Conway, Gene D. ....Kew Gardens, NY
Conway, George F. ....Cazenovia, NY
Conway, George M., III ....Cherry Hill, NJ
Conway, George T., III ....New York, NY
Conway, Gerald W. ....Morristown, NJ
Conway, Gerard L. ....Albany, NY
Conway, Gerard L., Jr. ....Albany, NY
Conway, Glenn M. ....New Haven, CT
Conway, Gregory B. ....Green Bay, WI
Conway, Gregory K. ....Washington, DC
Conway, H. Vincent, Jr. ....Newport News, VA
Conway & Hall, A Legal Professional Association ....Dayton, OH
Conway, Holly B. ....Scranton, PA
Conway, J. Michael ....Boonville, MO
Conway, Jack K. ....Los Angeles, CA
Conway, Jack K. ....San Marino, CA
Conway, Jacqueline R. ....Manly, IA
Mason City, IA
Conway, James A. ....Stuart, FL
Conway, James E. ....Washington, DC
Conway, James E. ....Paramus, NJ
Conway, James E. ....Albany, NY
Conway, James E. ....Albany, NY
Conway, James F. ....Towson, MD
Conway, James G. ....El Cajon, CA
Conway, James J. ....Cleveland, OH
Conway, James M. ....San Francisco, CA
Conway, James M. ....Chicago, IL
Conway, James M. ....Manchester, MA
Conway, James O. ....Sheboygan, WI
Conway, James P. ....Cleveland, OH
Conway, James R., III ....New Orleans, LA
Conway, James S. ....New York, NY
Conway, James W. ....Shepherdsville, KY
Conway, James W. ....Kenosha, WI
Conway, Jane E. ....Smithtown, NY
Conway, Jeanne Odom
West Palm Beach, FL
Conway, Jeffrey D. ....Las Vegas, NV
Conway, John A. ....Dallas, TX
Conway, John B. ....New York, NY
Conway, John C. ....Los Angeles, CA
Conway, John C. ....Beverly, MA
Conway, John E. ....Albuquerque, NM
Conway, John F. ....New Haven, CT
Conway, John F. ....Cleveland, OH
Conway, John H. ....Sunnyvale, CA
Conway, John H.
Federal Energy Regulatory Commission, Office of the General Counsel, GV
Conway, John H., Jr. ....Tulsa, OK
Conway, John J. ....San Francisco, CA
Conway, John J. ....San Mateo, CA
Conway, John J. ....Denver, CO
Conway, John J. ....Oak Brook, IL
Conway, John J. ....Troy, MI
Conway, John J. ....Cleveland, OH
Conway, John J., III ....Albany, NY
Conway, John J., Jr. ....Rochester, NY
Conway, John M. ....Anchorage, AK
Conway, John M. ....Troy, MI
Conway, John W. ....Auburn, ME
Conway, John W. ....Philadelphia, PA
Conway, Joseph P. ....New York, NY
Conway, Joseph R. ....Garden City, NY
Conway, Joseph W. ....Framingham, MA
Conway, Joseph Wm. ....Pittsburgh, PA
Conway, Joyce A. ....Boca Raton, FL
West Palm Beach, FL
Conway, J. W. ....Muscatine, IA
Conway, Karen L. ....Dallas, TX
Conway, Karen P. ....Hartford, CT
Conway, Karla Barz ....Albany, NY
Conway, Kathleen M. ....New Haven, CT
Conway, Kathleen O'Brien ....Richmond, VA
Conway, Kathryn M. ....Menlo Park, CA
Conway, Keith J. ....Woodbury, NY
Conway, Kenneth H. ....Baraboo, WI
Conway, Kerry Brian ....Pasadena, CA

Conway, Kevin A. ....Catskill, NY
Conway, Kevin J. ....Chicago, IL
Conway, Kevin P. ....Boston, MA
Conway, Kevin P. ....New York, NY
Conway, Kevin T. ....Pearl River, NY
Conway, Kevin W. ....Mystic, CT
New London, CT
Conway, Kristine E. ....Fairfax, VA
Conway, LaDawn Horn ....Dallas, TX
Conway, Laura C. ....Morristown, NJ
Conway Lavelle & Finn, LLP ....Albany, NY
Conway, Leonard B. ....Westfield, MA
Conway, Leonard F., Jr. ....Marblehead, MA
Conway, Leonard T.
Westhampton Beach, NY
Conway, Linda S. ....Orange, CA
Conway, Lisa D. ....Kansas City, MO
Conway & Londregan, P.C. ....Mystic, CT
New London, CT
Conway, Louis E. ....Ormond Beach, FL
Conway, Louise G. ....Brooklyn, NY
Conway, Mara Eleina ....San Francisco, CA
Conway, Margaret T. ....Chicago, IL
Conway, Maria ....New York, NY
Conway, Maribeth ....Seattle, WA
Conway, Mark A. ....Dayton, OH
Conway, Mark F. ....Waterloo, IA
Conway, Mark J. ....Scranton, PA
Conway, Marken, Wyner, Kurant & Kern Co., L.P.A. ....Beachwood, OH
Cleveland, OH
Pepper Pike, OH
Solon, OH
Conway, Martin C. ....McLean, VA
Conway, Martin E. ....Minneapolis, MN
Conway, Martin E., Jr. ....Rock Island, IL
Conway, Mary B. ....New York, NY
Conway, Mary J. ....Seattle, WA
Conway, Maryann ....Pottsville, PA
Conway, Maryann, & Associates, P.C.
Pottsville, PA
Conway, Matthew G. ....Hartford, CT
Conway, Megan Ann ....Richmond, VA
Conway, Michael C. ....Upper Marlboro, MD
Conway, Michael C. ....Albany, NY
Conway, Michael F. ....Chicago, IL
Conway, Michael F. ....Boston, MA
Conway, Michael J. ....Beverly Hills, CA
Conway, Michael J. ....Waukegan, IL
Conway, Michael J. ....New York, NY
Conway, Michael K. ....Albany, NY
Conway, Michael M. ....Chicago, IL
Conway, Michael P. ....Chicago, IL
Conway, Michael R., Jr. ....Chicago, IL
Conway, Michael T. ....Indianapolis, IN
Conway, Michael T. ....New York, NY
Conway, Michaela E. (Micki) ....Irving, TX
Conway, Neil J. ....Cleveland, OH
Conway, Neil J. ....Mentor, OH
Conway, Neil J. ....Painesville, OH
Conway, Neil L. ....Allentown, PA
Conway, Neil M. ....Dresbach, MN
Conway, Noel G. ....Signal Hill, CA
Conway, Patricia J ....Huntington, CT
Conway, Patrick J. ....Cincinnati, OH
Conway, Patton, Bouhall & Reichard
Cleveland, OH
Conway, Peter L. ....Lapeer, MI
Conway, Richard A. ....Boston, MA
Conway, Richard A. ....Richmond, VA
Conway, Richard C. ....Hanford, CA
Conway, Richard E. ....Long Beach, CA
Conway, Richard J. ....Washington, DC
Conway, Richard J., Jr. ....Morristown, NJ
Conway, Richard T. ....Washington, DC
Conway, Richard W., Jr. ....Tulsa, OK
Conway, Robert G. ....Delmar, NY
Conway, Robert G., Jr. ....Albany, NY
Conway, Robert H., Sr. ....Panama City, FL
Conway, Robert J. ....New York, NY
Conway, Robert J. ....Honesdale, PA
Conway, Robert M. ....Basking Ridge, NJ
Conway, Robert S. ....Washington, DC
Conway, Robert T. ....Lexington, MA
Conway, Ronald A. ....Springfield, MO
Conway, Sean ....Orlando, FL
Conway, Sean J. ....Hauppauge, NY
Conway, Seefeld & Varner, S.C.
Baraboo, WI
Conway, Shannon W. ....Washington, DC
Conway, Sharon E. ....Houston, TX
Conway, Sue O. ....Grand Rapids, MI
Conway, Susan G. ....Austin, TX
Conway, Teresa M. ....Chicago, IL
Conway, Thomas A. ....Albany, NY
Conway, Thomas B. ....Modesto, CA
Conway, Thomas B. ....Oxon Hill, MD
Conway, Thomas D. ....New York, NY
Conway, Thomas V.
Department of Agriculture, Office of the General Counsel, GV
Conway, Timothy J. ....Portland, OR
Conway, Timothy R. ....Chicago, IL
Conway, Vaughan ....Baraboo, WI
Conway, Vaughn B. ....Oklahoma City, OK
Conway, W. Gregory ....Nashville, TN
Conway, W. Michael ....Dayton, OH
Conway, Warren L. ....Gulfport, MS
Conway, Wendy H. ....Portland, OR
Conway, William A. ....McLean, VA
Conway, William B., Jr. ....Decatur, IL
Conway, William C. ....Fort Lauderdale, FL
Conway, William Carter ....Franklin, TN
Conway, William F. ....Albany, NY
Conway, William F., IV ....Albany, NY
Conway, William J., III ....Saddle River, NJ
Conway, William M. ....Tucson, AZ
Conway, William M. ....Boston, MA

Conwell, Bruce B. ....Cape May, NJ
Conwell, Chad C. ....Los Angeles, CA
Conwell, Chrystale B. ....Philadelphia, PA
Conwell, Edward L., III
United States Senate, Senatorial Assistants, GV
Conwell, G. Donovan, Jr. ....Tampa, FL
Conwell, Gary L. ....Topeka, KS
Conwell, J. Thomas, Jr. ....Huntsville, AL
Conwell, James E. ....Great Falls, MT
Conwell, Lewis J. ....Tampa, FL
Conwell, Robert F. ....Mesquite, NV
Conwell, Roberta C. ....Rosemont, IL
Conwell, Susan ....Milwaukee, WI
Conwell, William M. ....Pittsburgh, PA
Conwell, William W. ....Birmingham, AL
Conwell, William Y. ....Portland, OR
Conwick, G. Kevin ....Denver, CO
Conwill, Hewitt L. (Sonny)
Columbiana, AL
Conwill & Justice, P.C. ....Columbiana, AL
Conybeare, Barry R. ....St. Joseph, MI
Conybeare, Bruce C. ....St. Joseph, MI
Conybeare, Bruce C., Jr. ....St. Joseph, MI
Conybeare Law Office, P.C.
St. Joseph, MI
Conyers & Conyers ....Tulsa, OK
Conyers, Henry W., Jr. ....Tulsa, OK
Conyers, Howard W. ....Oklahoma City, OK
Conyers, John ....Detroit, MI
Conyers, John F., Jr. ....Boerne, TX
Conyers, Laura J. ....Valparaiso, IN
Conyers, Susan Witt ....Oklahoma City, OK
Conyngham, Kevin J. ....Saddle Brook, NJ
Conyngham, Monica E. ....Boston, MA
Conyngham, William J., Jr.
Washington, DC
Conza, Michael A. ....Boston, MA
Conza, Richard V. ....New York, NY
Conza, Teresa V. ....New York, NY
Conzelman, Murray R. ....Lake Forest, IL
Conzelman, Nancy C. ....Southfield, MI
Conzett & O'Brien ....Dubuque, IA
Conzett, William A. ....Dubuque, IA
Conzo, Valerie A. ....Miami, FL
Coo, Alida M. ....Boston, MA
Coo, Gabriela W. ....Santa Ana, CA
Coobs, Evan D. ....Champaign, IL
Cooch, Edward W., Jr. ....Newark, DE
Wilmington, DE
Cooch, Richard R. ....Wilmington, DE
Cooch and Taylor ....Newark, DE
Wilmington, DE
Kennett Square, PA
Coode, Timothy P. ....Knoxville, TN
Coody, Brian L. ....Lake Charles, LA
Coody, Charles S. ....Montgomery, AL
Coody, Lisa R. ....Warner Robins, GA
Coogan, Alan D. ....Portland, OR
Coogan, Bernard J. ....Wentzville, MO
Coogan, Daniel J. ....Nogales, AZ
Coogan, David L. ....Lincoln, IL
Coogan, Donald M. ....Fairhope, AL
Coogan, Edmond G. ....Vineyard Haven, MA
Coogan, Fred, III ....Austin, TX
Coogan, J. Jerome ....Attleboro, MA
Coogan, J. Russell, Jr. ....Stoughton, MA
Coogan, James H. ....Cincinnati, OH
Coogan, James M. ....Bronxville, NY
Coogan, Jill Robin ....Washington, DC
Coogan, John M., Jr. ....Philadelphia, PA
Coogan, John P. ....Garden City, NY
Coogan, Kelly O'Malley ....Atlanta, GA
Coogan, Lawrence J. ....Allen Park, MI
Coogan, Mary E. ....Newark, NJ
Coogan, Megan A. ....Baton Rouge, LA
Coogan, Michael F. ....Atlanta, GA
Coogan, Patrick D. ....Tacoma, WA
Coogan, Peter W. ....Boston, MA
Coogan, Robert F. ....New York, NY
Coogan, Russell D. ....Lockport, NY
Coogan, Smith, Bennett, McGahan, Lorincz & Jacobi, LLP ....Attleboro, MA
Taunton, MA
Coogan, Thomas D. ....Arlington, VA
Coogan, Timothy P. ....Tacoma, WA
Coogan, William H. ....Portland, ME
Coogan, William H. ....Vineyard Haven, MA
Coogle, Andrew B. ....Columbus, OH
Coogle, Jon L. ....Oglethorpe, GA
Coogle, Jon L., P.C. ....Oglethorpe, GA
Coogle, Matthew F. ....Paducah, KY
Coogler, Gil M. ....New York, NY
Coogler, Kindy K. ....Fort Lauderdale, FL
Coogler, L. Scott ....Tuscaloosa, AL
Coogler, Monroe A., Jr. ....Inverness, FL
Cook, A. David ....Wauwatosa, WI
Cook, A. Ronald ....Griffin, GA
Cook, A. Samuel, (P.C.) ....Towson, MD
Cook, Aaron L. ....Harrisonburg, VA
Cook, Adam N. ....Crawfordsville, IN
Cook, Adrienne ....Chicago, IL
Cook, Aimee M. ....San Francisco, CA
Cook, A. J. ....Memphis, TN
Cook, Alan A. ....Monroe, GA
Cook, Alan J. ....Chicago, IL
Cook, Alan W. ....Northfield, VT
Cook, Albert R. ....Casselberry, FL
Cook, Alex, McFarron, Manzo, Cummings & Mehler ....Chicago, IL
Cook, Alexander B. ....Wilmington, NC
Cook, Allan K. ....Amherst, MA
Cook, Allen E. ....Andalusia, AL
Cook, Allyson True ....Florence, KY
Cincinnati, OH
Cook, Alvaro I. ....North Aurora, IL
Cook, Amanda Lydia ....New York, NY
Cook, Amy Berlin ....Braintree, MA

Cook, Amy Decker ....Washington, DC
Cook, Andrea L. ....Long Beach, CA
Cook, Andrew D. ....San Diego, CA
Cook, Andrew J. ....New York, NY
Cook, Andrew N. ....Washington, DC
Cook, Ann W. ....Silverdale, WA
Cook, Ann Z.
Occupational Safety and Health Review Commission, Administrative Law Judges, GV
Cook, Anne L. ....Dallas, TX
Cook, Anne Marie ....Cambridge, MA
Cook, Annette J. ....Chicago, IL
Cook, Anthony E. ....Gainesville, FL
Cook, Arthur B., II, (P.C.)
Los Angeles, CA
Cook and Associates, P.C. ....Laramie, WY
Cook, B. Thomas ....Houston, TX
Cook, B. Thomas, Jr. ....Atlanta, GA
Cook, B. Thomas, Jr., P.C. ....Atlanta, GA
Cook, Barbara A. ....Lake Forest, IL
Cook, Barbara Ann ....New York, NY
Cook, Barbara Pollak ....Farmington Hills, MI
Cook, Barry A. ....Charlotte, NC
Cook and Batista Co., L.P.A. ....Lorain, OH
Cook & Bell ....Melrose, MA
Cook Bell & MacDonald Mediation Group
Tampa, FL
Cook, Bennett G., III ....Lubbock, TX
Cook, Bernard A. ....Baltimore, MD
Cook, Berryhill, Edwards & Miller
Santa Barbara, CA
Cook, Berst, Landeen & Butler ....Seattle, WA
Cook, Bert ....Orange, CA
Cook, Bert J. ....Orange, CA
Cook, Beth E. ....Department of Justice, Civil Division, GV
Cook, Bethany A. ....Los Angeles, CA
Cook, Betty ....Plainview, NY
Cook, Billie ....New York, NY
Cook, Billy Earl ....Brewton, AL
Cook, Billy Earl, Jr. ....Decatur, AL
Cook, Blanche B. ....Detroit, MI
Cook, Bobby Lee ....Summerville, GA
Nashville, TN
Cook, Bradford E. ....Concord, NH
Manchester, NH
Cook, Bradley R. ....Boston, MA
Cook, Bratten Hale, II ....Smithville, TN
Cook, Brendan D. ....Houston, TX
Cook, Bret D. ....Fairbanks, AK
Cook, Brian ....Kimball, NE
Cook, Brian D. ....Kansas City, MO
Cook, Brian J. ....Chicago, IL
Cook, Brian P. ....Buffalo, NY
Cook, Bridget L. ....Lancaster, CA
Cook & Brown, P.L.C. ....Clive, IA
Des Moines, IA
Cook, Brown & Prager, LLP
Sacramento, CA
Salinas, CA
Santa Ana, CA
Cook, Bruce A. ....Garden City, NY
Cook, Bruce L. ....Chicago, IL
Cook, Bruce L. ....Clive, IA
Cook, Bruce M. ....San Luis Obispo, CA
Cook, Bruce N. ....Belleville, IL
Cook, Bruce V., P.C. ....Newport Beach, CA
Cook, Bryson L., (P.C.) ....Washington, DC
Baltimore, MD
Cook, Byron Ann ....New Orleans, LA
Cook, C. Brant ....Dayton, OH
Cook, C. Jeffrey ....Pittsfield, MA
Cook, C. Randall, Law Offices of
Morro Bay, CA
Cook, C. Randall, Law Offices of
San Luis Obispo, CA
Santa Maria, CA
Cook, Camille W. ....Tuscaloosa, AL
Cook, Cantacuzene, Higdon, P.C.
Midland, TX
Cook, Caren M. ....Rochester, NY
Cook, Carmen C. ....San Jose, CA
Cook, Carmen L. ....Seattle, WA
Cook, Carmol D. ....Beaver Dam, KY
Cook, Carrie A. ....Seattle, WA
Cook, Cassandra J. ....Decatur, GA
Cook, Catherine A. ....Chicago, IL
Cook, Catherine C. ....Chicago, IL
Cook, Cathy R. ....Cincinnati, OH
Cook, Charles A. ....Boston, MA
Cook, Charles D. ....Bronxville, NY
Cook, Charles E. ....Chicago, IL
Cook, Charles H. ....Columbia, SC
Cook, Charles L. ....West Monroe, LA
Cook, Charles T. ....Las Vegas, NV
Cook, Charles W. ....Vidalia, GA
Cook, Charles W. ....Bruce, MS
Cook, Charles W., III ....Nashville, TN
Cook, Charles W., Jr. ....Kansas City, MO
Cook, Charles W., P.C. ....Vidalia, GA
Cook, Cheryl A. ....Philadelphia, PA
Cook, Cheryl Brienza ....Norwalk, CT
Cook, Cheryl D. ....Ann Arbor, MI
Cook, Christine M. ....Geneva, NY
Cook, Christopher A.
Department of Transportation, GV
Cook, Christopher H.
Palm Beach Gardens, FL
West Palm Beach, FL
Cook, Christopher J. ....Washington, DC
Cook, Christopher L. ....Wheaton, IL
Cook, Christopher N. ....Boston, MA
Cook, Claib L. ....Detroit, MI
Cook, Clarissa W. ....Minneapolis, MN
Cook, Claudia Lemon ....Longwood, FL
Cook, Clinton W. ....Lubbock, TX
Cook, Colleen C. ....Boston, MA

Cook, Colleen E. ..... Marietta, OH
Cook, Collins B. ..... San Antonio, TX
Cook & Connelly ..... La Fayette, GA
Summerville, GA
Cook, Constance E. ..... Ithaca, NY
Cook & Cook ..... Madison, WV
Cook, Craig ..... Anchorage, AK
Cook, Craig A. ..... Somers, NY
Cook, Craig L. ..... Fort Smith, AR
Paris, AR
Cook, Craig S. ..... Salt Lake City, UT
Cook, Curtis C. ..... Hamilton, MT
Cook, Cynthia A. ..... Kansas City, MO
Cook, Cynthia A. ..... Fort Worth, TX
Cook, Cynthia D. ..... Knoxville, TN
Cook, Cynthia G. ..... New York, NY
Cook, Cynthia R. ..... McLean, VA
Cook, D. Duane ..... Stamping Ground, KY
Cook, D. Durand ..... Beverly Hills, CA
Cook, D. Martin ..... Anaheim, CA
Cook, D. Max ..... Sapulpa, OK
Cook, Dale D. ..... Columbus, OH
Cook, Dale R. ..... Austin, TX
Cook, Daniel A. ..... Lorain, OH
Cook, Daniel E. ..... Martinez, CA
Cook, Daniel F. ..... San Francisco, CA
Cook, Daniel J. ..... Milwaukee, WI
Cook, Daniel R. ..... Palo Alto, CA
Cook, Daniel W. ..... Ashland City, TN
Cook, Danna L., (A Professional Corporation) ..... Los Angeles, CA
Cook, Danny J. ..... Texarkana, TX
Cook, Darold ..... Arroyo Grande, CA
Cook, Darrell F. ..... Department of Defense, Defense Legal Services Agency, GV
Cook, Darren R. ..... Oklahoma City, OK
Cook, Dave J. ..... Manly, IA
Cook, David B. ..... Washington, DC
Cook, David B. ..... Webster, NY
Cook, David C. ..... Oakland, CA
Cook, David C. ..... Jacksonville, FL
Cook, David C. ..... New York, NY
Cook, David E. ..... Galveston, TX
Cook, David H. ..... Independence, MO
Cook, David J. ..... San Francisco, CA
Cook, David J. ..... Boulder, CO
Cook, David J. ..... Cleveland, OH
Cook, David L. ..... Bonita Springs, FL
Cook, David L. ..... Buffalo, NY
Rochester, NY
Cook, David L. ..... New York, NY
Cook, David L. ..... Butler, PA
Cook, David L. ..... Arlington, TX
Cook, David L., Jr. ..... Houston, TX
Cook, David M. ..... Denver, CO
Cook, David M. ..... Cincinnati, OH
Cook, David M. ..... Edmond, OK
Cook, David R. ..... Cleveland, OH
Cook, David S. ..... Lafayette, LA
Cook, David S. ..... Houston, TX
Cook, David S. ..... Bountiful, UT
Cook, David S., A Professional Law Corporation ..... Lafayette, LA
Cook, David T. ..... Oklahoma City, OK
Cook, David W. ..... Columbus, OH
Cook, David W. ..... Greensburg, PA
Cook, D. Durand, Law Offices of ..... Beverly Hills, CA
Cook, Deanna D. ..... Richmond, VA
Cook, Deborah J. ..... South Sioux City, NE
Cook, Deborah L. ..... Columbus, OH
Cook, Debra Williams ..... New York, NY
Cook, Denise A. ..... Lone Tree, CO
Cook, Denise Lyles ..... Temple Terrace, FL
Cook, Dennis B. ..... Sacramento, CA
Cook, Dennis C. ..... Laramie, WY
Cook, Dennis E. "Skip" ..... Fairbanks, AK
Cook, Dennis L. ..... Tampa, FL
Cook, Dennis M. ..... Milwaukee, WI
Cook, Diane M. ..... Philadelphia, PA
Cook, Dianne ..... Dalton, GA
Cook, Donald, & Associates, Law Offices of ..... Los Angeles, CA
Cook, Donald C. ..... Los Angeles, CA
Cook, Donald D. ..... Harper Woods, MI
Cook, Donald D. ..... Powell, OH
Cook, Donald L. ..... Denver, CO
Cook, Donald L., Jr. ..... Atlanta, GA
Cook, Donald T. ..... Buffalo, NY
Cook, Donald T., P.C. ..... Buffalo, NY
Cook, Douglas E. ..... Jewell, IA
Story City, IA
Cook, Douglas E. ..... Drexel Hill, PA
Cook, Douglas G. ..... New York, NY
Cook, Douglas H. ..... Virginia Beach, VA
Cook, Douglas K. ..... Mesa, AZ
Cook, Douglas K. ..... Phoenix, AZ
Cook, Doyle & Bradshaw, L.L.P. ..... Houston, TX
Cook, Dudley & Associates, P.C. ..... Corpus Christi, TX
Cook, E. Michael ..... Rochester, NY
Cook, Edward A., III ..... Lexington, NE
Cook, Edward F. ..... Lansing, MI
Cook, Edward L. ..... Charleston, SC
Cook, Edward M., III ..... Los Angeles, CA
Cook, Edward Shuff ..... Atlanta, GA
Cook, Edward Shuff, P.C. ..... Atlanta, GA
Cook, Edwin J. ..... Edinburg, TX
Cook, Elaine ..... New York, NY
Cook, Elise A. ..... Charlotte, NC
Cook, Elizabeth A. ..... Houston, TX
Cook, Elizabeth Lane ..... Columbia, SC
Cook, Elizabeth Raines ..... Atlanta, GA
Cook, Elizabeth W. ..... Reston, VA
Cook, Elliot J. ..... New York, NY
Cook, Eric D. ..... Minneapolis, MN
Cook, Eric D. ..... Durham, NH
Cook, Erwin A. ..... Hot Springs National Park, AR
Cook, Eugene A. ..... Houston, TX
Cook, Faye Alston ..... Winston-Salem, NC
Cook Fitch & Hames ..... Phoenix, AZ
Englewood, CO
Cook, Forest D., Law Offices of ..... Austin, TX
Cook, Forrest E. ..... Boulder, CO
Cook, Forrest E. ..... Whitesburg, KY
Cook, Francis X. ..... Cleveland, OH
Cook, Frank M. ..... Indianapolis, IN
Cook, Frank S. ..... Rome, NY
Cook & Franke S.C. ..... Milwaukee, WI
Cook, Franklin C. ..... Freeport, IL
Cook, G. Bradford ..... New York, NY
Cook, G. Mark ..... Washington, DC
Cook, G. Roger ..... Farmington, MN
Cook, Gary ..... Cleveland, OH
Cook, Gary G. ..... Toledo, OH
Cook, Gary S. ..... Richmond, VA
Cook, Gavin A. ..... Albany, NY
Cook, Gayle Freeman ..... Oklahoma City, OK
Cook, Geoffrey C. ..... Washington, DC
Cook, George P. ..... New York, NY
Cook, George R., Law Offices of ..... Monterey, CA
Cook, George S. ..... Seattle, WA
Cook, George T. ..... Lancaster, PA
Cook, George V. ..... Baldwinsville, NY
Cook, George V. ..... Garden City, NY
Cook, George V., P.C. ..... Baldwinsville, NY
Cook, George W. F. ..... Rutland, VT
Cook, Gerald C. J. ..... Melrose, MA
Cook, Gerald S. ..... Detroit, MI
Cook, Geralyn Mary ..... Providence, RI
Cook, Gerard W. ..... Northbrook, IL
Cook, Glen ..... Salt Lake City, UT
Cook, Glenda S. ..... Atlanta, GA
Cook, Glyn M. ..... Houston, TX
Cook, Goetz, Rogers & Lukey, P.C. ..... Bloomfield Hills, MI
Detroit, MI
Pontiac, MI
Cook, Granger, Jr. ..... Chicago, IL
Cook, Grant, (P.C.) ..... Houston, TX
Cook, Gregory ..... Fort Lauderdale, FL
Cook, Gregory Carl ..... Birmingham, AL
Cook, Gregory D. ..... West Palm Beach, FL
Cook, Gregory F. ..... Douglas, AK
Cook, Gregory J. ..... Milwaukee, WI
Cook, Guy R. ..... Des Moines, IA
Cook, Guy S., Jr. ..... Lamarque, TX
Cook, Gwendolyn Alicia ..... Columbus, OH
Cook, H. Clayton, Jr. ..... Washington, DC
Cook, H. Dale ..... Tulsa, OK
Cook, H. Fred ..... Houston, TX
Cook, H. Lee ..... Portland, OR
Cook, H. Neal ..... Double Springs, AL
Cook, H. Pratt, III ..... Richmond, VA
Cook, Harold J. ..... Mishawaka, IN
Cook, Harry E., Jr. ..... Ridgway, CO
Cook, Harry J. ..... Mount Horeb, WI
Cook, Harry O. ..... San Juan, PR
Cook, Harvey W. ..... Hammond, LA
Cook and Haviza ..... Winchester, IN
Cook, Heather A. ..... Los Angeles, CA
Cook, Heather L. ..... Charlotte, NC
Cook, Henry D. ..... Jackson, MS
Cook, Henry J., III ..... Bay St. Louis, MS
Cook, Herbert J. ..... Faribault, MN
Cook, Holly M. ..... Department of Transportation, Federal Highway Administration, GV
Cook, Howard, Downes & Tracy ..... Towson, MD
Cook, Howard E. ..... Lawrenceville, GA
Cook, Ivarsson & Shober ..... Fayetteville, NC
Cook, J. Aaron ..... Kansas City, MO
Cook, J. Allen ..... Andalusia, AL
Cook, J. Bradley ..... Noblesville, IN
Cook, J. Christopher ..... Sioux City, IA
Cook, J. David ..... Thorntown, IN
Cook, J. Gordon ..... Phoenix, AZ
Cook, J. Harris ..... Port Richey, FL
Cook, J. Hilary ..... Markleeville, CA
Cook, J. Kendal "Ken" ..... Little Rock, AR
Cook, J. Rowland ..... Austin, TX
Cook, J. Sydney, III ..... Tuscaloosa, AL
Cook, J. Sydney, Jr. ..... Carrollton, GA
Cook, J. Vincent ..... Athens, GA
Cook, J. William ..... New York, NY
Cook, Jack F., Jr. ..... Austin, TX
Cook, Jack H. ..... West Palm Beach, FL
Cook, Jack R. ..... Rockton, IL
Cook, Jack R., Jr. ..... Rockton, IL
Cook, Jacqueline A. ..... Kansas City, MO
Cook, Jacques J. ..... Rockville, MD
Cook, Jake C. ..... Fort Worth, TX
Cook, James ..... Fullerton, CA
Cook, James A. ..... Boise, ID
Cook, James A., Jr. ..... Hattiesburg, MS
Cook, James C. ..... Belleville, IL
Cook, James C. ..... Winston-Salem, NC
Cook, James C. ..... Columbia, SC
Cook, James E. ..... Wichita Falls, TX
Cook, James F. ..... Lexington, KY
Cook, James G. ..... Manchester, NH
Cook, James H. ..... Waterloo, IA
Cook, James H., (P.C.) ..... Harrisville, MI
Cook, James J. ..... Monterey, CA
Cook, James J. ..... San Marino, CA
Cook, James J. ..... St. Louis, MO
Cook, James J. ..... Cherry Hill, NJ
Cook, James K. ..... St. Louis, MO
Cook, James R. ..... West Des Moines, IA
Cook, James R. ..... Lincoln, NE
Cook, James T. ..... Kansas City, MO
Cook, James W. ..... Toms River, NJ
Cook, James W. ..... Memphis, TN
Cook, Jan Myers ..... New York, NY
Cook, Janice J. ..... Adams, MA
Cook, Janine ..... Washington, DC
Cook, Jason L. ..... Elmira, NY
Cook, Jay ..... Muskogee, OK
Cook, Jay D., III ..... Winchester, VA
Cook, Jay F. ..... Minneapolis, MN
Cook, Jeffrey A. ..... Hagåtña, GU
Cook, Jeffrey E. ..... Dallas, TX
Cook, Jeffrey G. ..... Baltimore, MD
Cook, Jeffrey S. ..... New York, NY
Cook, Jeffrey W. ..... Minneapolis, MN
Cook, Jeffrey W. ..... Bandon, OR
Cook, Jennifer E. ..... St. Louis, MO
Cook, Jennifer N. ..... Dallas, TX
Cook, Jennifer Reilly ..... New Orleans, LA
Cook, Jeremy C., Jr. ..... Modesto, CA
Cook, Jeremy L. ..... Charleston, SC
Greenville, SC
Cook, Jerold S. ..... Chesterland, OH
Cook, Jerome W. ..... Cleveland, OH
Cook, Jerry D. ..... Glendive, MT
Cook, Jerry D., P.C. ..... Glendive, MT
Cook, Jerry W. ..... Madison, WV
Cook, Jessica Suzanne ..... Durham, NC
Cook, Jessie A. ..... Terre Haute, IN
Cook, Joan E. ..... Great Falls, MT
Cook, Joan LaBrique ..... Kennebunk, ME
Cook, Joe E. ..... Birmingham, AL
Cook, Joe Mark ..... Northampton, MA
Cook, Joe W. ..... Stone Mountain, GA
Cook, John ..... Sacramento, CA
Cook, John A. ..... Chicago, IL
Cook, John A. ..... Bloomfield Hills, MI
Cook, John August, P.C. ..... Chicago, IL
Cook, John C. ..... San Francisco, CA
Cook, John C. ..... Chattanooga, TN
Cook, John C. ..... Austin, TX
Cook, John C. ..... Reston, VA
Cook, John D. ..... Eureka, CA
Cook, John E. ..... Edinburg, TX
Cook, John F. ..... Aurora, CO
Cook, John F. ..... Sarasota, FL
Cook, John F. ..... Minneapolis, MN
Cook, John F., II ..... Germantown, TN
Cook, John H., IV ..... Midland, TX
Cook, John H., Jr. ..... Cherokee, IA
Cook, John J. ..... Kingston, NY
Cook, John J. ..... Memphis, TN
Cook, John J., Jr. ..... Fairless Hills, PA
Cook, John K. ..... Wake Forest, NC
Cook, John L. ..... Napa, CA
Cook, John L. ..... Oakland, CA
Cook, John L. ..... Cape Girardeau, MO
Cook, John L. ..... Houston, TX
Cook, John Marshall ..... Vienna, VA
Cook, John P. ..... Seattle, WA
Cook, John R. ..... San Diego, CA
Cook, John R. ..... Okeechobee, FL
Cook, John R. ..... Kalamazoo, MI
Cook, John R. ..... Pittsburgh, PA
Cook, John R. ..... Breckenridge, TX
Cook, John R., & Associates ..... Pittsburgh, PA
Cook, John R., P.A. ..... Okeechobee, FL
Cook, John T. ..... St. Petersburg, FL
Cook, John T. ..... Winchester, IN
Cook, John T. ..... Nashville, TN
Cook, John T. ..... Lynchburg, VA
Cook, John T., P.A. ..... St. Petersburg, FL
Cook, John T., P.C. ..... Nashville, TN
Cook, John W. ..... Colorado Springs, CO
Cook, John W. ..... Columbus, OH
Cook, John W., III ..... Columbus, OH
Cook, Jonathan K. ..... Englewood, CO
Cook, Jonathan R. ..... New Orleans, LA
Cook, Joseph E. ..... Castle Rock, CO
Cook, Joseph F. ..... Brattleboro, VT
Cook, Joseph F., Jr. ..... Akron, OH
Cook, Joseph J., II ..... San Francisco, CA
Cook, Joseph L. ..... Roseland, NJ
Cook, Joseph L. ..... Waukesha, WI
Cook, Joseph Michael ..... Memphis, TN
Cook, Joseph R. ..... Boca Raton, FL
Cook, Joseph R. ..... Columbus, OH
Cook, Joseph T. ..... Irvine, CA
Cook, Judith A. ..... Farmington, MI
Cook, Julia A. ..... Houston, TX
Cook, Julian A., Jr. ..... Detroit, MI
Cook, K. Marshall ..... Richmond, VA
Cook, Kamil Poorman ..... Export-Import Bank of The United States, Office of the General Counsel, GV
Cook, Kara L. ..... Park Ridge, IL
Cook, Karen A. ..... San Francisco, CA
Cook, Karen H. ..... Reading, PA
Cook, Katharine A. ..... Albuquerque, NM
Cook, Katherine M. ..... Rockville, MD
Cook, Kathleen A. ..... Omaha, NE
Cook, Kathleen F. ..... Marshall, MI
Cook, Kathleen S. ..... Montvale, NJ
Cook, Kathryn J. ..... Frankfort, IN
Cook, Kathryn M. ..... Myrtle Beach, SC
Cook, Kathy S. ..... Gainesville, FL
Cook, Kathy W. ..... Phoenix, AZ
Cook, Kay-Ann ..... Rockville, MD
Cook, Keith H. ..... Tucker, GA
Cook, Kenneth R. ..... Omaha, NE
Cook, Kenneth T. ..... Denver, CO
Cook, Kevin C. ..... Cheyenne, WY
Cook, Kevin F. ..... New York, NY
Cook, Kevin J. ..... Dallas, TX
Cook, Kimberly A. ..... Miami, FL
Cook, Kimberly L. ..... Washington, DC
Cook, Kimble R. ..... San Mateo, CA
Cook & Koch, P.A. ..... Tampa, FL
Cook, Kristen E. ..... Tulsa, OK
Cook, Krystil Borrouso ..... New Orleans, LA
Cook, Larry E. ..... Walnut Creek, CA
Cook, Larry E. ..... Prospect, KY
Cook, Larry K. ..... Cabot, AR
Cook, Larry L. ..... Miami, FL
Cook, Larry W. ..... Russellville, KY
Cook, LaRue E. ..... Washington, DC
Cook, Laura A. ..... Houston, TX
Cook Law Offices ..... Whitesburg, KY
Cook Law Offices, P.C. ..... Texarkana, TX
Cook, Lawrence J. ..... Akron, OH
Cook & Lee, P.C. ..... Boulder, CO
Denver, CO
Cook, Lee W. ..... Oklahoma City, OK
Cook, Leila Holmes ..... Environmental Protection Agency, Program Office Attorneys, GV
Cook, Leland G. ..... Atlanta, GA
Cook, Leo K. ..... St. Joseph, MI
Cook, Leonard J. ..... Philadelphia, PA
Cook, Leslie A. ..... Marietta, GA
Cook, Leslie C. ..... Dallas, TX
Cook, Leslie M. ..... Houston, TX
Cook, Lew R. ..... Phoenix, AZ
Cook, Linda J. ..... Idaho Falls, ID
Cook, Linda M. ..... Baldwinsville, NY
Cook, Linda S. ..... Coral Gables, FL
Cook, Lindsey L. ..... Atlanta, GA
Cook, Lisa Jo ..... Rockville, MD
Cook, Little, Rosenblatt & Manson, P.L.L.C. ..... Concord, NH
Manchester, NH
Cook, Loring A., III ..... Boston, MA
Cook, Lyle W. ..... Sacramento, CA
Cook, Lynda ..... Salt Lake City, UT
Cook, Lynda G. ..... Cheyenne, WY
Cook, M. Jeffrey ..... Davenport, IA
Cook, M. Kristi ..... Jenkintown, PA
Cook, Marc P. ..... Las Vegas, NV
Cook, Marcia A. ..... Gainesville, GA
Cook, Marcia S. ..... Overland Park, KS
Cook, Marguerite D. ..... Lincolnshire, IL
Cook, Marianna M. ..... Roseburg, OR
Cook, Mark G. ..... Woodstock, IL
Cook, Mark J. ..... Northampton, MA
Cook, Martha J. ..... Tampa, FL
Cook, Martha Reeves ..... Birmingham, AL
Cook, Marvin L. ..... San Antonio, TX
Cook, Marvin R. ..... Wichita, KS
Cook, Marvin V. ..... Denver, CO
Cook, Mary ..... Houston, TX
Cook, Mary B. ..... Milwaukee, WI
Cook, Mary Rose E. ..... Owings Mills, MD
Cook, Mary S. ..... Haddonfield, NJ
Cook, Matthew M. ..... Durham, NC
Cook, Matthew P. ..... Bowling Green, KY
Cook, Maura Rhea ..... Southfield, MI
Cook, Maurice E. ..... Bismarck, ND
Cook, Max ..... Lawton, OK
Cook & Meharry ..... Kansas City, MO
Cook, Melanie B. ..... New York, NY
Cook, Melanie K. ..... Beverly Hills, CA
Cook, Melissa ..... Brooklyn, NY
Cook, Melissa W. ..... Del Mar, CA
Cook, Melynda W. ..... Cincinnati, OH
Cook, Mercer ..... Chicago, IL
Cook, Meredith P. ..... Manchester, NH
Cook, Michael ..... Syosset, NY
Cook, Michael C. ..... Colorado Springs, CO
Cook, Michael C. ..... Chicago, IL
Cook, Michael C. ..... Indianapolis, IN
Cook, Michael D. ..... Plymouth, IN
Cook, Michael E. ..... Warsaw, IN
Cook, Michael H. ..... Washington, DC
Cook, Michael J. ..... Sacramento, CA
Cook, Michael J. ..... Denver, CO
Cook, Michael J. ..... Troy, MI
Cook, Michael James ..... Denver, CO
Cook, Michael K. ..... Quincy, MA
Cook, Michael K. ..... St. Joseph, MI
Cook, Michael K., P.C. ..... Quincy, MA
Cook, Michael L. ..... New York, NY
Cook, Michael L. ..... Austin, TX
Cook, Michael R. ..... Woodstock, VA
Cook, Michael T. ..... Kingston, NY
Cook, Mitchell E. ..... Fort Lauderdale, FL
Cook, Mitchell W. ..... Key West, FL
Cook & Molan, P.A. ..... Concord, NH
Manchester, NH
Cook, Murline Vivit ..... Rockledge, FL
Cook, Nancy Douglas ..... Richmond, VA
Cook, Nancy E. ..... North Bend, OR
Cook, Nancy G. ..... Atlanta, GA
Cook, Nancy L. ..... Ithaca, NY
Cook, Neil A. ..... Walnut Creek, CA
Cook, Nena ..... Portland, OR
Cook, Nevada Brooks ..... Pacific Palisades, CA
Cook, Newell ..... Boston, MA
Cook, Nicholas J. ..... Uniontown, PA
Cook, Nicholas John ..... Atlanta, GA
Cook & Niven ..... Harrisburg, PA
Cook, Noel M. ..... San Francisco, CA
Cook, Noell, Tolley, Bates & Michael, LLP ..... Athens, GA
Cook, Noelle S. ..... Hanford, CA
Cook, Norman D. ..... Antioch, TN
Cook, Norman E. ..... Paulding, OH
Payne, OH
Cook, O. Jackson ..... Atlanta, GA
Cook, O'Bannon M. ..... Tallahassee, FL
Cook, Oliver T. ..... Peabody, MA
Cook, Oscar T., Jr. ..... Boston, GA
Cook, Owen W. ..... Fayetteville, NC
Cook, P. Neal ..... Charlotte, NC
Cook Partners Law Offices, Ltd. ..... Chicago, IL
Cook, Patricia Cronin ..... Chicago, IL

Cook, Paul C. .... Los Angeles, CA
Cook, Paul J. .... Madison, WI
Cook, Paul K. .... Dublin, GA
Vidalia, GA
Cook, Paul W. .... Cranford, NJ
Cook, Paula Ann .... Santa Fe, NM
Cook, Peggy R. .... Taylor, MI
Cook, Perkiss & Lew, A Professional Law Corporation .... San Francisco, CA
Cook, Peter D., (P.C.) .... Buffalo, NY
Cook, Peter G. .... Cambridge, MA
Cook, Peter H. .... Edison, NJ
Cook, Philip .... Miami, FL
Cook, Philip C. .... Washington, DC
Atlanta, GA
Cook, Philip E. .... Los Angeles, CA
Cook, Philip E. .... Pittsburgh, PA
Cook, Prentis, Jr. .... Department of Energy, Office of the General Counsel, GV
Cook, Quentin L. .... Burlingame, CA
Cook, R. Christopher .... Chicago, IL
Cook, Rafael L. .... Chicago, IL
Cook, Raili S. .... San Diego, CA
Cook, Ralph J. .... Merced, CA
Cook, Rand L. .... Salt Lake City, UT
Cook, Randall J. .... Tyler, TX
Cook, Randall W. .... Salem, OR
Cook, Ransom S. .... San Francisco, CA
Cook, Rebecca H. .... Akron, OH
Cook, Rebecca McDowell
Cape Girardeau, MO
Cook, Reuben Wright .... Tuscaloosa, AL
Cook, Richard A. .... Indianapolis, IN
Cook, Richard Ary .... Cherokee, IA
Cook, Richard F., Jr. .... Stamford, CT
Cook, Richard F., Jr. .... Richmond, VA
Cook, Richard G., Jr. .... Macomb, IL
Cook, Richard R. .... DeLand, FL
Cook, Richard W. .... Syracuse, NY
Cook, Roach & Lawless, L.L.P.
Austin, TX
Houston, TX
Cook, Rob .... Los Angeles, CA
Cook, Robert A. .... Santa Fe Springs, CA
Cook, Robert A. .... Crofton, MD
Cook, Robert B. .... North Palm Beach, FL
Cook, Robert B., Jr. .... Dallas, TX
Cook, Robert C. .... Sacramento, CA
Cook, Robert C. .... Jefferson City, MO
Cook, Robert D. .... Grand Rapids, MI
Cook, Robert D. .... Kingston, NY
Cook, Robert E.
Board of Governors Of The Federal Reserve System, Division of Consumer and Community Affairs, GV
Cook, Robert E. .... New York, NY
Cook, Robert E. .... Milwaukee, WI
Cook, Robert F. .... Atlanta, GA
Cook, Robert G. .... Winchester, IN
Cook, Robert J. .... Marysville, CA
Cook, Robert M. .... Yuma, AZ
Cook, Robert M. .... Edison, NJ
Cook, Robert M., II .... Columbia, SC
Cook, Robert N. .... Washington, DC
Cook, Robert P., III .... Springfield, MA
Cook, Robert R. .... Thousand Oaks, CA
Cook, Robert R. .... Saginaw, MI
Cook, Robert S., Jr. .... New York, NY
Cook, Robert W. .... Washington, DC
Cook, Robert W. .... Carthage, IL
Cook, Robert W. .... Quincy, IL
Cook, Roberta L.
Federal Communications Commission, Office of the General Counsel, GV
Cook, Rodman L. .... Woodbury, NJ
Cook, Rodney L. .... Oklahoma City, OK
Cook, Rodney L. .... Oklahoma City, OK
Cook, Roger .... Detroit, MI
Cook, Roger L. .... San Francisco, CA
Cook, Ronald D. .... Tampa, FL
Cook, Ronald E. .... Concord, NH
Cook, Ronald E. .... Erie, PA
Cook, Ronald E. .... Houston, TX
Cook, Ronald J. .... San Jose, CA
Cook, Ronald K. .... Monroe, LA
Cook, Ronald R. .... Bloomfield Hills, MI
Cook, Ronald W. .... Santa Barbara, CA
Cook & Roos, PLC .... San Francisco, CA
Cook, Roxana E. .... Milwaukee, WI
Cook, Roy C. .... Washington, DC
Cook, Rufus L. .... Chicago, IL
Cook, Russell Austin .... Oklahoma City, OK
Cook, Russell D. .... Fresno, CA
Cook, Russell L., Jr. .... Houston, TX
Cook, Russell T. .... Brentwood, TN
Cook, Russell W. .... Springfield, MO
Cook, S. Alan .... Phoenix, AZ
Cook, S. Alan, P.C. .... Phoenix, AZ
Cook, S. Matthew .... Houston, TX
Cook, S. Ronald, Jr. .... Columbus, OH
Cook, Sally A. .... Indianapolis, IN
Cook, Sara E. .... Woodstock, IL
Cook Schuhmann & Groseclose, Inc.
Fairbanks, AK
Cook, Schuyler Mouser .... Cleveland, OH
Cook, Scott R. .... Englewood, CO
Cook, Scott T. .... Corpus Christi, TX
Cook, Sean H. .... Southfield, MI
Cook, Shannon E. .... Jefferson City, MO
Cook, Shannon J .... Cincinnati, OH
Cook, Shawn P. .... Los Angeles, CA
Cook, Sherwood N. .... Las Vegas, NV
Cook, Shevlin, Ysursa, Brauer & Bartholomew, Ltd. .... Belleville, IL
Cook, Sidney A. .... Dallas, TX
Cook, Sidney E., Jr. .... Shreveport, LA
Cook, Smith & Schwartz .... Cleveland, OH
Cook, Stacy L. .... Topeka, KS
Cook, Stacy S. .... Denver, CO
Cook, Stanley C. .... Cincinnati, OH
Cook, Stanley J. .... San Francisco, CA
Cook and Steen .... Hattiesburg, MS
Cook, Stephen E. .... Orlando, FL
Cook, Stephen F. .... Portland, OR
Cook, Stephen H. .... Boulder, CO
Cook, Stephen H. .... Columbia, SC
Cook, Stephen L. .... Palm Beach Gardens, FL
Cook, Stephen W. .... Salt Lake City, UT
Cook, Steven D. .... Houston, TX
Cook, Steven H. .... Knoxville, TN
Cook, Steven M. .... Hoffman Estates, IL
Cook, Steven T. .... Huntington, WV
Cook, Steven W. .... Alexandria, LA
Cook, Stuart M. .... Rochester, NY
Cook, Susan E. .... East Hampton, NY
Cook, Susan L. .... Washington, NJ
Cook, Susan Louise
Equal Employment Opportunity Commission, Office of Federal Operations, GV
Cook, Susan M. .... Washington, DC
Cook, Susan M. .... Bay City, MI
Cook, Susan M. .... Fruitport, MI
Cook, Susan M. .... Omaha, NE
Cook, Susan P. .... Salem, OR
Cook, Susan V. .... Department of Justice, Environment and Natural Resources Division, GV
Cook, Suzanne Sweet .... Johnson City, TN
Kingsport, TN
Cook, T. Robert .... St. Louis, MO
Cook, Tamara Brandt .... Juneau, AK
Cook, Tania Yamamoto .... Torrance, CA
Cook, Tark .... Perryton, TX
Cook, Terrence Shea .... Abingdon, VA
Cook, Terri L. .... Raleigh, NC
Cook, Terry L. .... Ontario, CA
Cook, Theresa A. .... Boston, MA
Cook, Thomas A. .... Jackson, MS
Cook, Thomas A. A. .... St. Louis, MO
Cook, Thomas Christopher .... Carson City, NV
Cook, Thomas D. .... Pittsford, NY
Cook, Thomas E. .... Honolulu, HI
Cook, Thomas H., Jr. .... Raleigh, NC
Cook, Thomas H., Jr. .... Dallas, TX
Cook, Thomas J. .... Somerset, PA
Cook, Thomas, Law Office
San Francisco, CA
Cook, Thomas, Law Office .... Sausalito, CA
Cook, Thomas P. .... Princeton, NJ
Cook, Thomas R. .... Oklahoma City, OK
Cook, Thomas S. .... Harrisburg, PA
Cook, Thomas W. .... San Antonio, TX
Cook, Tim .... Houston, TX
Houston, TX
San Antonio, TX
Cook, Timothy A. .... Aberdeen, MD
Cook, Timothy C. .... Minneapolis, MN
Cook, Todd A. .... Columbus, OH
Cook, Tom .... Bartlesville, OK
Cook, Tom A. .... Salt Lake City, UT
Cook, Tony M. .... Olympia, WA
Cook, Tonya K. .... Austin, TX
Cook, Tracy Bennington .... Cincinnati, OH
Cook, Troth & Burkard, Ltd.
Paulding, OH
Payne, OH
Cook, Tucker, Netter & Cloonan, P.C.
Kingston, NY
Cook, V. Susanne .... Pittsburgh, PA
Cook, Valeria L. .... Vinton, VA
Cook, Valta A., Law Offices of .... Hilo, HI
Cook, Valta Albert .... Hilo, HI
Cook, Vance W. .... Princeton, KY
Cook, Vernon .... Gresham, OR
Cook, Vetter, Doerhoff and Landwehr, A Professional Corporation
Jefferson City, MO
Cook, Vicki S.
Hot Springs National Park, AR
Cook, Victor V. .... Sun City West, AZ
Cook, Victoria A. Shane .... New York, NY
Cook, Vincent P. .... Chicago, IL
Cook, Vincent S. .... Aurora, IL
Cook, Vinson L. .... Oklahoma City, OK
Cook, Virgil G. .... Avalon, MS
Cook, Virginia I. .... Pittsburgh, PA
Cook, Virginia Parker .... Northport, AL
Cook & Voegele, P.A. .... Faribault, MN
Cook, W. Rand .... Mechanicsville, VA
Cook & Wagner .... Mount Horeb, WI
Cook, Walter G. .... Fort Worth, TX
Cook, Walter M., Jr. .... Mobile, AL
Cook, Ware, Lonnes & Heyward, A Professional Corporation .... Richmond, VA
Cook, Wayne P. .... Lexington, KY
Cook, Webster .... Glen Arbor, MI
Cook, Wendell H., Jr. .... Jackson, MS
Cook, Whit M., II .... Baton Rouge, LA
Cook, Wightman & Doyle .... Gothenburg, NE
Lexington, NE
Cook, Willard E. .... Ridgeland, MS
Cook, William C. .... Oklahoma City, OK
Cook, William D. .... Eagle River, AK
Cook, William D. .... Cherokee, IA
Cook, William E. .... Terre Haute, IN
Cook, William Edro, Jr. .... Washington, DC
Cook, William H. ....
United States Court Of Appeals For The Armed Forces, GV
Cook, William H., Jr. .... Shreveport, LA
Cook, William J. .... Tampa, FL
Cook, William J. .... Chicago, IL
Cook, William J. .... Chicago, IL
Cook, William J. .... Camden, NJ
Cook, William J. .... Barnwell, SC
Cook, William J., III .... Bridgeport, CT
Cook, William L., Jr. .... Batesville, MS
Cook, William L., Jr., P.A. .... Batesville, MS
Cook, William M. .... Austin, TX
Cook, William P. .... Washington, DC
Cook, William R. .... Findlay, OH
Cook, William R. .... Salem, OR
Cook, William R., II .... Oklahoma City, OK
Cook, William W. .... Springfield, MO
Cook, Wm. Bailey, III .... Ada, OK
Cook, Woodrow W. .... Oceana, WV
Cook, Yancey, King & Galloway, A Professional Law Corporation
Bossier City, LA
Shreveport, LA
Cook, Youndy C. .... Tampa, FL
Cook-Delvilbis, Gail W. .... Radford, VA
Cooke, A. Hamilton .... Jacksonville, FL
Cooke, A. Hamilton, P.A., Law Offices of
Jacksonville, FL
Cooke, A. Wayland .... Greensboro, NC
Cooke, Alan Jay .... Boston, MA
Cooke, Andrew .... Battle Creek, MI
Cooke, Andrew B. .... Charleston, WV
Cooke, Andrew P. .... Columbus, OH
Cooke, Anthony M. .... Philadelphia, PA
Cooke, Arthur Campbell .... Tulsa, OK
Cooke, Arthur R. .... Parsippany, NJ
Cooke, Barden W. .... Greensboro, NC
Cooke, Benjamin H. .... Union Level, VA
Cooke, Bradford .... New York, NY
Cooke, Brian J. .... West Palm Beach, FL
Cooke, Bruce J. .... Plainsboro, NJ
Cooke, Carol A. .... Reno, NV
Cooke, C.C. "Kit", III .... Cleburne, TX
Cooke, Christine A. .... Hardin, MT
Cooke, Christopher .... Cleburne, TX
Cooke, Christopher K. .... Grand Rapids, MI
Cooke, Christopher R. .... Bethel, AK
Cooke, Clancy & Gruenthal, LLP
Boston, MA
Cooke, Claude E., Jr. .... Houston, TX
Cooke & Cooke .... Greensboro, NC
Cooke and Cooke Law Firm
Sacramento, CA
Cooke, Courtney B. .... Chicago, IL
Cooke, Craig R. .... Selden, NY
Cooke, Cynthia L. .... Asheville, NC
Cooke, David D. .... San Francisco, CA
Cooke, David P. .... Morristown, NJ
Cooke & Davis .... Monticello, NY
Cooke & Davis, A Prtnshp incl. A P.C.
Eldred, NY
Cooke, Deane M. .... Cambridge, NY
Cooke, Deborah M. .... Sacramento, CA
Cooke, Deborah M. .... Sacramento, CA
Cooke, Don .... Edmond, OK
Cooke, Donald J. .... Fargo, ND
Cooke, Donna Libretti .... Roseland, NJ
Cooke, Edmund D., Jr. .... Washington, DC
Cooke, Edward J., III .... New York, NY
Cooke, Edward J., Jr. .... West Chester, PA
Cooke, Edward M. .... Eldred, NY
Monticello, NY
Cooke, Elizabeth C. .... Raleigh, NC
Cooke, Elizabeth Ilgen .... Columbus, OH
Cooke, Fletcher A. .... Richmond, VA
Cooke, Frank D., Jr. .... West Covina, CA
Cooke, Frederick D., Jr. .... Washington, DC
Cooke, Gary C. .... North Brunswick, NJ
Cooke, Gary E., II .... Chicago, IL
Cooke, George A., Jr. .... New York, NY
Cooke, Gregory M.
Federal Communications Commission, Common Carrier Bureau, GV
Cooke, Ira C. .... Baltimore, MD
Towson, MD
Cooke, J. Aaron .... Lafayette, IN
Cooke, J. Jeffrey .... Louisville, KY
Cooke, Jack W., Jr. .... Jackson, MS
Cooke, James A., P.C. .... Boulder, CO
Cooke, James F. .... St. Charles, IL
Cooke, James H., Jr. .... Fayetteville, NC
Cooke, James M. .... Chico, CA
Cooke, James P. .... Washington, DC
Cooke, James R. .... Washington, DC
Cooke, James R., Jr. .... Charlottesville, VA
Cooke, James W. .... Garden City, NY
Cooke, Jay C. .... New York, NY
Cooke, Jeffrey A. .... Lafayette, IN
Cooke, Jodi H. .... San Diego, CA
Cooke, John C. .... Raleigh, NC
Cooke, John F. .... Emeryville, CA
Cooke, John Francis .... New York, NY
Cooke, John H. .... Orchard Park, NY
Cooke, Joseph A. .... Falls Church, VA
Cooke, Joseph J. .... Morristown, NJ
New York, NY
Cooke, Kenneth M. .... San Diego, CA
Cooke, Kevann M. .... Chicago, IL
Cooke, Kim Daniel .... Cary, NC
Cooke, L. Susan .... Washington, NJ
Cooke, Lamanna, Smith, Cogswell & Elliott, Chartered .... Priest River, ID
Sandpoint, ID
Cooke, Larry H. .... Greenville, SC
Cooke, Laura J. .... Oklahoma City, OK
Cooke Law Office, The .... Lafayette, IN
Cooke, Lawrence H. .... Albany, NY
Cooke, Lawrence H., II .... New York, NY
Cooke, Leon R. .... Chicago, IL
Cooke, Lewis & Lapat .... Chicago, IL
Cooke, Lot H. .... Department of Energy, Office of the General Counsel, GV
Cooke, M. Colette .... Cambridge, MA
Cooke, M. Dawes, Jr. .... Charleston, SC
Cooke, Marcia G. .... Miami, FL
Cooke, Marie Fischer .... Owings Mills, MD
Cooke, Marjorie Sommer .... Boston, MA
Cooke, Marvin Allen .... Detroit, MI
Cooke, Michael D. .... Iuka, MS
Cooke, Michael D. .... Tulsa, OK
Cooke, Michael G. .... Tampa, FL
Cooke, Michael T. .... Fort Worth, TX
Cooke, Michelle A. .... Los Angeles, CA
Cooke & Miller .... Rochester, NY
Cooke, Pamela S. .... Los Angeles, CA
Cooke, Patrick G. .... Chicago, IL
Cooke, Paul M. .... Shreveport, LA
Cooke, Peter A. .... West Palm Beach, FL
Cooke, Phillip A. .... Yuba City, CA
Cooke, R. Cameron .... Greensboro, NC
Cooke, Randolph .... Sacramento, CA
Cooke, Raymond C. .... La Grange, IL
Cooke, Reggie .... Columbus, OH
Cooke, Richard C. .... Chicago, IL
Cooke, Richard T. .... Alden, NY
Cooke, Robert Joseph .... Kingston, NY
Cooke, Roberts and Reese, Ltd.
Reno, NV
Cooke, Roger A. .... Portland, OR
Cooke, Ronald J. .... Los Angeles, CA
Cooke, Ronald Lee .... Aurora, CO
Cooke, Samuel Jay .... Philadelphia, PA
Cooke & Steffan .... Alden, NY
Cooke, Stephen D. .... Costa Mesa, CA
Cooke, Stephen D. .... New York, NY
Cooke, Steven D. .... Richland, WA
Cooke, Susan M. .... Boston, MA
Cooke, Suzanne H. .... Marianna, FL
Cooke, Terence S. .... Washington, DC
Cooke, Theodore .... Novato, CA
Cooke, Theodore K. .... La Grange, IL
Cooke, Thomas B. .... Washington, DC
Cooke, Thomas E. .... Priest River, ID
Sandpoint, ID
Cooke, Thomas F., II .... Hoffman Estates, IL
Cooke, Thomas J. .... Citrus Heights, CA
Cooke, Thomas V. .... Long Island City, NY
Cooke, Valerie P. .... Reno, NV
Cooke, Vinyard V., III .... Washington, DC
Cooke, W. Stanley, Law Offices of
Pittsfield, MA
Cooke, Walter Clay .... The Woodlands, TX
Cooke, Warren F. .... New York, NY
Cooke, Wendell S., Jr. .... Nashville, TN
Cooke & Whitcomb .... Chicago, IL
Cooke, William .... Canterbury, CT
Cooke, William L. .... Windsor, NC
Cooke, William O., Jr. .... Greensboro, NC
Cooke, William Owen .... Greensboro, NC
Cook-Edwards, Jill A. .... Miami, FL
Cookerly & Barroll, LLC
Centreville, MD
Chestertown, MD
Cookerly, Ernest S. .... Chestertown, MD
Cookerly, Jacqueline A. .... Los Angeles, CA
Cookerly, Richard O. .... Chestertown, MD
Cookingham, Jay Howard .... Spring, TX
Cookler, Jonathan N. .... Tarzana, CA
Cookman, Donald H. .... Romney, WV
Cookman, Donald P. .... Romney, WV
Cookney, Leonard E. .... Stamford, CT
Cooks, Herbert .... Rockville Centre, NY
Cooks, James E.
Equal Employment Opportunity Commission, Office of Legal Counsel, GV
Cooksey, Byron T. .... Vero Beach, FL
Cooksey, Charlotte M. .... Baltimore, MD
Cooksey & Cooksey, P.A.
Riviera Beach, FL
Denver, CO
Cooksey, Curry L. .... Beaumont, TX
Cooksey, David R. .... Costa Mesa, CA
Cooksey, Don C. .... Texarkana, TX
Cooksey, Frank C. .... Austin, TX
Cooksey, Howard, Martin & Toolen, A Professional Corporation
Costa Mesa, CA
Cooksey, James M. .... Moberly, MO
Cooksey, James P. .... Denver, CO
Riviera Beach, FL
Cooksey, Kenneth E. .... Monticello, FL
Cooksey, Lynn .... Texarkana, TX
Cooksey, Michael G. .... Denver, CO
Riviera Beach, FL
Cooksey, Neil C. .... Charlotte, NC
Cooksey, Paul H. .... Washington, DC
Cooksey, Taylor V. .... Houston, TX
Cooksey, William J. .... Albuquerque, NM
Cookson, Eloise Gries .... Columbus, OH
Cookson, Gail M. .... Newark, NJ
Cookson, J. Thomas .... Miami, FL
Cookson, John P. .... New York, NY
Cookson, Kenneth R. .... Columbus, OH
Cookson, Kirk S. .... Lake Havasu City, AZ
Cookson, Patricia K. .... El Cajon, CA
Cookson, Scott A. .... Orlando, FL
Cookson, W. William .... Ellicott City, MD
Cookston, Steven C. .... Greenwood, MS
Cool, Dwight I. .... Winter Park, FL
Cool, John F. .... Saipan, TT
Cool, Kenneth J. .... Omaha, NE
Cool, Stephen N. .... Arroyo Grande, CA
Coolahan, James M. .... West Long Branch, NJ
Coolahan, Patrick M. .... Wheaton, IL
Coolbaugh, Colette A. .... Lawrenceville, NJ
Coolbroth, Frederick J. .... Manchester, NH
Coole, Arthur J. .... Troy, MI
Coole, William R. .... Rockford, IL
Cooledge & Lauro .... Springfield, MA
Cooledge, Richard Calvin .... Phoenix, AZ
Cooledge, Theodore E. .... Springfield, MA

Cooleen, John J. ... **Washington, DC**
Arlington, VA
Cooley, Andrew C. ... **Seattle, WA**
Cooley, Anne S. Duncan ... **Hanover, NH**
Norwich, VT
Cooley, Brent D. ... Greenbelt, MD
Cooley, Carolyn J. ... Utica, NY
Cooley, Carolyn J., & Richard P. Ferris, Law Offices of ... Utica, NY
Cooley, Colin S. ... St. Louis, MO
Cooley & Compton ... **Hillsville, VA**
Wytheville, VA
Cooley, Cooley & Agee ... Kingston, TN
Rockwood, TN
Cooley, Craig S. ... Richmond, VA
Cooley, Dana W. ... Snyder, TX
Cooley, Daniel F. ... **San Francisco, CA**
Cooley, David E., Jr. ... Baton Rouge, LA
Cooley, Dennis M. ... Chicago, IL
Cooley, Diane E. ... **Washington, DC**
Cooley, Donald C. ... Hazlehurst, MS
Cooley, Earle C. ... **Boston, MA**
Cooley, Edward C. ... Quincy, MA
Cooley, Edward L. ... Lexington, KY
Cooley, Frank G. ... **Meeker, CO**
Cooley, Frank G., Professional Corporation
Meeker, CO
Cooley, Frank J. ... **Rosemead, CA**
Cooley, George B., Jr. ... Hillsville, VA
Cooley, George C. ... Albany, NY
Cooley, George H., III ... Galveston, TX
Cooley, Gerald L. ... Phoenix, AZ
Cooley, Gerald L. ... **Lawrence, KS**
Cooley Godward LLP ... **Menlo Park, CA**
Palo Alto, CA
San Diego, CA
San Francisco, CA
Boulder, CO
Denver, CO
Reston, VA
Kirkland, WA
Cooley, Gordon M. ... Frederick, MD
Cooley, J. Polk ... Rockwood, TN
Cooley, J. Sid ... Humansville, MO
Cooley, James M. ... St. Albans, VT
Cooley, Jeremy P. ... **Trenton, NJ**
Cooley, Jim D. ... **Charlotte, NC**
Cooley, John L. ... **Roanoke, VA**
Cooley, John M. ... Joplin, MO
Cooley, John Mark ... **Roanoke, VA**
Cooley, John P. ... **San Diego, CA**
Cooley, John W. ... **Evanston, IL**
Cooley, Joseph D., III ... **Gainesville, GA**
Cooley, K. Michael ... **Milwaukee, WI**
Cooley, Kenneth Keith ... Bakersfield, CA
Cooley, Kenneth W. ... Sacramento, CA
Cooley, Kerry L. ... Baton Rouge, LA
Cooley, Lawrence F. ... Eugene, OR
Cooley, L. E. ... Kansas City, MO
Cooley, Linda J. ... **Indianapolis, IN**
Cooley, Lydia Y. ... Cedarburg, WI
Cooley Manion Jones LLP ... **Boston, MA**
Cooley, Mark A. ... Lansing, MI
Cooley, Matthew R. ... **New York, NY**
Cooley, Melissa ... Cary, NC
Cooley, Miles ... **San Francisco, CA**
Cooley, Norman I. ... Wichita, KS
Cooley, Norman Michael ... San Diego, CA
Cooley, Patricia Handy ... **Doylestown, PA**
Cooley, Patrick C. ... Kingston, TN
Cooley, Paul N. ... Missoula, MT
Cooley, Peter W. ... Philadelphia, PA
Cooley, R. Craig ... Orlando, FL
Cooley, R. Craig ... Leoti, KS
Cooley, R. Craig, P.A. ... Leoti, KS
Cooley, R. Edward ... Longwood, FL
Cooley, Raleigh M. ... **Hillsville, VA**
Cooley, Richard A., Jr. ... Port Huron, MI
Cooley, Richard E. ... **Flint, MI**
Cooley & Robbins, L.L.C. ... **Phoenix, AZ**
Sun City, AZ
Cooley, Robert A. ... **Owensboro, KY**
Cooley, Ronald G. ... **Sun City, AZ**
Cooley, Scott J. ... Phoenix, AZ
Cooley, Scott S. ... **Austin, TX**
Cooley, Seth v.d.H. ... **Philadelphia, PA**
Cooley, Sheila M. ... East Greenwich, RI
Cooley, Sheila P. ... **Cleveland, OH**
Cooley, Shrair, P.C. ... **Springfield, MA**
Cooley, Stephen L. ... Los Angeles, CA
Cooley, Steve ... Birmingham, AL
Cooley, Susan C. ... **Dallas, TX**
Cooley, Susan J. ... **Los Angeles, CA**
Cooley, Susan McKinney ... Topeka, KS
Cooley, Susannah Ross ... **New Orleans, LA**
Gulfport, MS
Cooley, Talmage N. ... Waynesboro, VA
Cooley, Tenal S., III ... **Oklahoma City, OK**
Cooley, Tenal S., Jr. ... Oklahoma City, OK
Cooley, Wendy ... Detroit, MI
Cooley, Winchester, III ... Denver, CO
Cooleybeck, Sarah ... **Boston, MA**
Coolidge, Bruce E. ... **Washington, DC**
Coolidge, Clyde R. ... Somersworth, NH
Coolidge, Daniel S. ... **Manchester, NH**
Coolidge, David Gregory ... **Washington, DC**
Coolidge, Donn M. ... Kingman, AZ
Coolidge, Edwin Channing, Jr.
DeLand, FL
Coolidge, Francis L. ... **Boston, MA**
Coolidge & Gisi, A Professional Corporation
Yuba City, CA
Coolidge, H. Calvin ... Glen Ellyn, IL
Coolidge, Harry C. ... Capitola, CA
Coolidge, Herman W. ... **Savannah, GA**
Coolidge, Hermann W., Jr. ... **Savannah, GA**
Coolidge, Joel B. ... Houston, TX
Coolidge, Katherine A. ... Fresno, CA
Coolidge, Katherine K. ... Springfield, MA
Coolidge, Laura J. ... New York, NY
Coolidge, Lowell ... Wellsboro, PA
Coolidge, Nicholas J. ... New York, NY
Coolidge, Philip W. ... Boston, MA
Coolidge Professional Association
Somersworth, NH
Coolidge, Richard T. ... Tucson, AZ
Coolidge, Stanley A., Jr. ... Yuba City, CA
Coolidge, Todd Kevin ... **Tempe, AZ**
Coolidge, Wall, Womsley & Lombard
Dayton, OH
Coolidge, William M., III ... Lilburn, GA
Cooling & Herbers, P.C. ... **Boulder, CO**
Merriam, KS
Kansas City, MO
Cooling, James E. ... **Kansas City, MO**
Cooling, Norman C. ... Canon City, CO
Coolley, Ronald B. ... **Chicago, IL**
Cooluris, John G. ... **Sacramento, CA**
Cooman, Kevin S. ... **Rochester, NY**
Coomaraswamy, Bernadette M.
Greenwich, CT
Coombe, George W., Jr. ... San Francisco, CA
Coombe, James M. ... Cincinnati, OH
Coombe, John D. ... Denver, CO
Coombe, Owen L. ... Yakima, WA
Coomber, Skip R., III ... **Los Angeles, CA**
Rancho Santa Fe, CA
Coombes, Kevin W. ... Hartford, CT
Coombes, Robert R. ... Lake Worth, FL
Coombs, Abel R. ... **New York, NY**
Coombs, Chad Chase ... **Los Angeles, CA**
Coombs & Coombs ... **Culver City, CA**
Coombs, Craig E. ... Bellevue, WA
Coombs, Cyril F. ... Richmond, VA
Coombs, Damon E. ... **Salt Lake City, UT**
Coombs, David L. ... **Boston, MA**
Coombs, Dianne C. ... **Washington, DC**
Coombs, Douglas M. ... Wilmington, DE
Coombs & Dunlap, LLP ... **Napa, CA**
St. Helena, CA
Coombs and Durrett, Chartered
Wichita, KS
Coombs, Eugene G. ... **Wichita, KS**
Coombs, Eugene G., Jr. ... **Boston, MA**
Coombs, Fred G. ... New London, NH
Coombs, Frederick S., III
Youngstown, OH
Coombs, Frederick W. ... Williston, VT
Coombs, Harold M., Jr. ... Columbia, SC
Coombs, Henry M. ... Madison, IN
Coombs, J. Andrew ... **Burbank, CA**
Coombs, James E. ... Poughkeepsie, NY
Coombs, James R. ... Folsom, CA
Coombs, Jennifer L. ... Everett, WA
Coombs, John Michael ... Salt Lake City, UT
Coombs, Karen D. ... **New York, NY**
Coombs, Linn K. ... **Danville, CA**
Coombs & Lissor ... Williston, VT
Coombs, Renate A. ... Oakland, CA
Coombs, Richard E. ... **Sacramento, CA**
Coombs, Richard E., A Prof. Corp., Law Offices of ... **Sacramento, CA**
Coombs, Richard H., Jr. ... Lake Forest, CA
Coombs, Roger A. ... Spokane, WA
Coombs, Ronald E. ... **Culver City, CA**
Coombs, Ronald L. ... Louisville, KY
Coombs, Russell M. ... Camden, NJ
Coombs, Scott H. ... Phoenix, AZ
Coombs, W. Dick ... Akron, OH
Coombs, William D. ... Chanute, KS
Coomer, Bryan N. ... Louisville, KY
Coomer, C. Edward ... Nashville, TN
Coomer, Jason S. ... **Austin, TX**
Coomer, Jason S. ... **San Antonio, TX**
Coomer & Jenkins ... Nashville, TN
Coomer, Nancy M. ... Tucson, AZ
Coomes, A. Joseph ... **Atlanta, GA**
Coomes, Ben P. ... New Castle, KY
Coomes, C. Andrew ... Orlando, FL
Coomes, Coomes & Coomes
New Castle, KY
Coomes, James J. ... **Birmingham, AL**
Coomes, John W. ... New Castle, KY
Coomes, John W., II ... New Castle, KY
Coomes, Joseph E., Jr. ... **Sacramento, CA**
Coomes, Sarretta C. ... **Los Angeles, CA**
Coomes, Scott F. ... Thousand Oaks, CA
Cooms, Robert S., Jr. ... Houston, TX
Coon, Alan R. ... **Stockton, CA**
Coon, Allan E. ... **Olathe, KS**
Coon, Allan H. ... Grants Pass, OR
Coon, Allen H. ... Monroe, LA
Coon, Arthur F. ... **Walnut Creek, CA**
Coon, Brent W. ... **Beaumont, TX**
Coon, Carol A. ... Wheaton, IL
Coon, Cheryl F. ... Portland, OR
Coon, Curtis E. ... **Baltimore, MD**
Coon, David G. ... **Providence, RI**
Coon, Dean M. ... Saratoga Springs, NY
Coon, Donald M. ... Palm City, FL
Coon, E. Ralph, Jr. ... **Manassas, VA**
Coon, Earl F. ... Antioch, CA
Coon, Ellen L. ... **Bingham Farms, MI**
Coon, Fred A., Jr. ... Monroe, LA
Coon, Gerald L. ... Danbury, CT
Coon, James S. ... **Portland, OR**
Coon, Jeffroy C., (P.A.) ... Tampa, FL
Coon, John R. ... **Portland, ME**
Coon & Johnston ... **Manassas, VA**
Coon, Karen E. ... Northville, MI
Coon, Lawrence K. ... **Milwaukee, WI**
Coon, Linda S. ... Chicago, IL
Coon, Liston F. ... Watkins Glen, NY
Coon, Lois Reynolds ... Rockville, MD
Coon, Lorinda S. ... **Hartford, CT**
Coon, Mark S. ... **Walnut Creek, CA**
Coon, Miles A. ... Great Neck, NY
Coon, Nancy C. ... Eden Prairie, MN
Coon, O. Wayne ... **Dallas, TX**
Coon, Robert C. ... Springfield, VA
Coon, Robert D. ... Flint, MI
Coon, Robert D. ... **Omaha, NE**
Coon, Robert E. ... McGregor, IA
Coon, Robert Morell, Jr. ... **New York, NY**
Coon, Scott T. ... Bowling Green, OH
Coon & Shach, LLC ... **Washington, DC**
Baltimore, MD
Towson, MD
Coon, Steven J. ... Denver, CO
Coon, Thomas T., Jr.
Fort Lauderdale, FL
Coon, Timothy ... Valrico, FL
Coon, Timothy P. ... **White Plains, NY**
Coon, Timothy S. ... **Pittsburgh, PA**
Coon, William G. ... **Troy, MI**
Coonan, James M. ... **Chicago, IL**
Coonan, Liam S. ... San Antonio, TX
Coonan, Scott J. ... College Park, MD
Coonan, William Edward
Fairview Heights, IL
Coonelly, Colleen F. ... **Philadelphia, PA**
Coonelly, Francis X. ... Washington, DC
Coonen, Martin J. ... Crystal Lake, IL
Coonen & Roth, Ltd. ... Crystal Lake, IL
Cooner, Angela L. ... **Montgomery, AL**
Cooner, David J. ... **Newark, NJ**
Cooner, Jonathan H. ... Montgomery, AL
Coonerty, Sean E. ... **New York, NY**
Cooney, Anne Tennant ... **San Francisco, CA**
Cooney, Bernard J. ... Silver Spring, MD
Cooney, C. Hayes ... **Nashville, TN**
Cooney, C. Michael ... **Santa Barbara, CA**
Cooney, Charles E. ... Santa Fe, NM
Cooney, Colleen Conway ... Cleveland, OH
Cooney and Conway ... Chicago, IL
Cooney & Crew, P.C. ... **Portland, OR**
Cooney, D. Jay ... Detroit, MI
Cooney, Daniel P. ... Chicago, IL
Cooney, David F. ... **Fort Lauderdale, FL**
Cooney, David W. ... **Hartford, CT**
Cooney, Dee Ann G. ... Helena, MT
Cooney, Dennis ... Bayville, NY
Cooney, Donald L. ... Le Roy, NY
Cooney, Douglas Paul ... Palm Beach, FL
Cooney, Edmond P. ... Pasadena, CA
Cooney, Elizabeth A. ... **New York, NY**
Cooney, Eugene A. ... **Hartford, CT**
Cooney, Gary J. ... **Tavares, FL**
Cooney, Gary J., P.A. ... **Tavares, FL**
Cooney, George A., Jr.
Bloomfield Hills, MI
Farmington Hills, MI
Cooney, George A., P.C., Law Offices of
Bloomfield Hills, MI
Cooney, Henry B. ... **Detroit, MI**
Cooney & Humphrey ... Le Roy, NY
Cooney, J. Gordon, Jr. ... **Philadelphia, PA**
Cooney, J. Mark ... **Southfield, MI**
Cooney, J. Michael ... **Cincinnati, OH**
Cooney, Jack R., Jr. ... Pleasanton, CA
Cooney, Jack R., Jr. Inc. ... Pleasanton, CA
Cooney, James B. ... **Albuquerque, NM**
Cooney, James E. ... Hamilton, OH
Cooney, James Evans ... Des Moines, IA
Cooney, James J. ... **Palm Beach, FL**
Cooney, James L. ... Spokane, WA
Cooney, James M. ... Somerset, NJ
Cooney, James P., III ... **Charlotte, NC**
Cooney, James Patrick ... **Houston, TX**
Cooney, James R. ... **Sarasota, FL**
Cooney, Jane E. Hewett ... **New York, NY**
Cooney, John A. ... **Minneapolis, MN**
Cooney, John, & Associates, P.S.
Spokane, WA
Cooney, John C. ... Spokane, WA
Cooney, John D. ... Chicago, IL
Cooney, John F. ... **Washington, DC**
Cooney, John F. ... **St. Louis, MO**
Cooney, John Francis, Jr.
San Francisco, CA
Cooney, John G. ... Cleveland, OH
Cooney, John M. ... **Aventura, FL**
Cooney, John P., Jr. ... **New York, NY**
Cooney, John R. ... **Albuquerque, NM**
Cooney, John W. ... Manchester, CT
Cooney, John W. ... Salt Lake City, UT
Cooney, Joseph K. ... **Oakhurst, NJ**
Cooney, Joseph M., (P.S.) ... Spokane, WA
Cooney, Kathryn P., Law Offices of
Vista, CA
Cooney, Kevin L. ... **Cincinnati, OH**
Cooney, Leslie Larkin ... Fort Lauderdale, FL
Cooney, Lisa Ann ... **Philadelphia, PA**
Cooney, Loretta Weber ... Chicago, IL
Cooney, Mary Carole ... Atlanta, GA
Cooney, Mattson, Lance, Blackburn, Richards & O'Connor, P.A.
Fort Lauderdale, FL
Miami, FL
Orlando, FL
West Palm Beach, FL
Cooney, Maureen C. ... Treasury Department, Office of the Comptroller of the Currency, GV
Cooney, Melissa J. ... **Crystal Lake, IL**
Cooney, Michael J. ... **New York, NY**
Rochester, NY
Cooney, Michael M. ... Kansas City, MO
Cooney, Michael P. ... **Detroit, MI**
Cooney, Michael T. ... Elizabeth, NJ
Cooney, Nicholas J. ... New York, NY
Cooney, Patricia J. ... **Chatham, NJ**
Cooney, Patricia J. ... Philadelphia, PA
Cooney, Patricia N. ... Berkeley, CA
Cooney, Patrick J. ... **Albertson, NY**
Cooney, Patrick J., III ... **Cleveland, OH**
Cooney, Paul A. ... **Portland, OR**
Cooney, Paul E. ... **Washington, DC**
Cooney, Paul K. ... Spokane, WA
Cooney, Peter F. ... Ventura, CA
Cooney, Philip A. ... Washington, DC
Cooney, Raymond P. ... Central Falls, RI
Cooney, Richard W. ... **Sarasota, FL**
Cooney, Rita M. ... Spokane, WA
Cooney, Robert J. ... Cameron Park, CA
Cooney, Robert J. ... **Bridgeport, CT**
Cooney, Robert J. ... Indianapolis, IN
Cooney, Robert J., Jr. ... Chicago, IL
Cooney, Robert L., Jr. ... **Philadelphia, PA**
Cooney, Rosemary ... **West Palm Beach, FL**
Cooney, Scully and Dowling
Hartford, CT
Cooney, Stephen M. ... **Springfield, OR**
Cooney, Stuart B. ... Clarkston, MI
Cooney, Theresa ... Department of Justice, Antitrust Division, GV
Cooney, Thomas E. ... **Portland, OR**
Cooney, Thomas E. ... Spokane, WA
Cooney, Thomas F., III ... **Washington, DC**
Cooney, Thomas J., Jr. ... **Houston, TX**
Cooney, Thomas M. ... Brooklyn, NY
Cooney, Thomas M. ... **Portland, OR**
Cooney, Thomas O. ... Moline, IL
Cooney, Timothy J. ... **Washington, DC**
Cooney, Tom ... Houston, TX
Cooney, Valerie J. ... **Carson City, NV**
Cooney, Wallace P. ... Philadelphia, PA
Cooney, Walter E. ... Roseville, MN
Cooney, William A. ... **New York, NY**
Cooney, William F. ... **Schenectady, NY**
Cooney, William H. ... Springfield, MA
Cooney, William J. ... Augusta, GA
Cooney, William J. ... **Chicago, IL**
Cooney, William J., P.C. ... Augusta, GA
Cooney, William N. ... **Los Angeles, CA**
Cooney-Mueller, Helen E. ... Wayne, NJ
Cooney-Porter, Kathleen ... **Arlington, VA**
Coonin, Robert Burton ... Wilmington, DE
Coonley, Ann P. ... New Haven, CT
Coonley & Coonley ... Hampton, IA
Coonley, James E. ... Hampton, IA
Coonley, John E. ... Hampton, IA
Coonrad, Douglas V. ... Hudson, IA
Coonrod, Brett C. ... **Prairie Village, KS**
Kansas City, MO
Coonrod, C. Kevin ... Seattle, WA
Coonrod, Doris A. ... Tacoma, WA
Coonrod, John ... Winchester, IL
Coonrod, R. Stephen ... **Tallahassee, FL**
Coonrod, Stephan H. ... **Seattle, WA**
Coons, Albert H., Jr. ... Montpelier, VT
Coons, Allan H. ... Eugene, OR
Coons, Ann McCallister ... Irwindale, CA
Coons, Arnold A., Jr. ... Portage, IN
Coons, Cole, Cary & Wing, P.C.
Albany, OR
Eugene, OR
Coons, Curtis H. ... Bremerton, WA
Coons, David W. ... **St. Louis, MO**
Coons, Gordon R. ... **Chicago, IL**
Coons, Harold M. ... New Albany, IN
Coons, James K. ... **Eugene, OR**
Coons, Michael H. ... **Los Angeles, CA**
Coons, Shane M. Emerson
Los Angeles, CA
Coons, Sherie L. ... **Tacoma, WA**
Coons, Stephen M. ... Indianapolis, IN
Coons, Thomas W. ... **Baltimore, MD**
Coonts, Gilbert Gray ... Buckhannon, WV
Coonts, Stephen P. ... New Orleans, LA
Coontz, J. Greg ... Burleson, TX
Coontz, M. Stephen
San Juan Capistrano, CA
Coontz & Matthews, LLP
San Juan Capistrano, CA
Coony, Kacey ... San Diego, CA
Coony, Thomas E. ... **Washington, DC**
Coop, Jeffrey A ... **Billings, MT**
Coope, Dara A. Levy ... **Melville, NY**
Coope, Erica ... **New York, NY**
Coope, Fred ... Canfield, OH
Cooper, Abbott ... **New York, NY**
Cooper, Abner T. ... West Palm Beach, FL
Cooper, Ada S. ... Chicago, IL
Cooper, Adam Philip ... Jamaica, NY
Cooper, Adam R. ... **New York, NY**
Cooper, A. J., Jr. ... Washington, DC
Cooper, Alan ... **Hawley, PA**
Cooper, Alan H. ... Rochelle, IL
Cooper, Alan H. ... Richmond, VA
Cooper, Alan J. ... Jupiter, FL
Cooper, Alan J., P.A. ... Jupiter, FL
Cooper, Alan K. ... Tampa, FL
Cooper, Alan N. ... Wilmington, DE
Cooper, Alan S. ... **Washington, DC**
Cooper, Albert B. ... New York, NY
Cooper, Albert, III ... Trenton, NJ
Cooper, Albert T., III ... Clearwater, FL
Cooper, Alexander M. ... **New York, NY**
Cooper, Alfred D., Sr. ... New York, NY
Cooper, Alfred J. ... Fremont, OH
Cooper, Allan B. ... **Beverly Hills, CA**
Cooper, Allison Lane ... **San Francisco, CA**
Cooper, Amy Starr ... **New York, NY**
Cooper, Andrea L. ... **Nashville, TN**
Cooper, Andrea L. ... Milwaukee, WI
Cooper, Andrew C. ... **Washington, DC**
Cooper, Andrew C. ... **Baltimore, MD**
Cooper, Andrew Paul ... **Brooklyn, NY**
Mineola, NY
Cooper, Andrew R. ... New York, NY
Cooper, Angela M. ... **Washington, DC**

Cooper, Angela T. ... Akron, OH
Cooper, Anita G. ... Jerseyville, IL
Cooper, Ann M. ... Grand Rapids, MI
Cooper, Anne L. ... Lancaster, PA
Cooper, Annjanette M. ... Seattle, WA
Cooper, Arguedas & Cassman ... Oakland, CA
Cooper, Arthur L. ... Savannah, GA
Cooper, Arthur M. ... Buffalo, NY
Cooper, Arthur R. ... Baton Rouge, LA
Cooper, Ashton A., Jr. ... Compton, CA
Cooper and Associates, P.C.
Washington, DC
New York, NY
Cooper, A. T., Jr. ... Clearwater, FL
Cooper & Avery ... Duluth, GA
Cooper, Avery M. ... Santa Monica, CA
Cooper, Avery M., A Professional Corporation ... Santa Monica, CA
Cooper, Barbara A. ... Hesperia, CA
Cooper, Bari Barton ... Rockville, MD
Cooper, Bari J. ... Beverly Hills, CA
Cooper, Barry A. ... New York, NY
Cooper, Barry N. ... New York, NY
Cooper, Ben D. ... San Diego, CA
Cooper, Bennett Evan ... Phoenix, AZ
Cooper, Bennett M. ... Breckenridge, CO
Cooper, Bernard ... Glendale, CA
Cooper, Bertram ... St. Louis, MO
Cooper, Bertram, P.C. ... St. Louis, MO
Cooper, Bertrand M. ... Los Angeles, CA
Cooper, Beth H. ... Department of State,
Bureau of Consular Affairs, GV
Cooper, Billy J. ... Clinton, NJ
Cooper, B. J., Law Offices of
Oklahoma City, OK
Cooper, Bonnie Lee ... Key Biscayne, FL
Cooper, Brad ... Philadelphia, PA
Cooper, Brad ... The Woodlands, TX
Cooper, Bradley D. ... Franklin, IN
Cooper, Bradley H.K. ... Philadelphia, PA
Cooper, Bradley L. ... Atlanta, GA
Cooper, Brand L. ... Pasadena, CA
Cooper, Brenda A. ... New York, NY
Cooper, Brett E. ... San Francisco, CA
Cooper, Brian ... Dallas, TX
Cooper, Brian E. ... Los Angeles, CA
Cooper, Bridgette M. ... Atlanta, GA
Cooper & Bringhurst, L.C.
Salt Lake City, UT
Cooper & Brown ... Baldwinsville, NY
Cooper, Brown & Behrle, P.C.
New York, NY
Cooper, Bruce J. ... New York, NY
Cooper, Bruce M. ... Washington, DC
Cooper, Byrne, Blue & Schwartz, LLC
Perry, FL
Tallahassee, FL
Cooper, Byron W. ... Palo Alto, CA
Cooper, C. James ... Denver, CO
Cooper, C.S. Law Firm, Ltd.
Farmington, MN
Cooper, C. Wade ... Austin, TX
Cooper, Camille S. ... Armonk, NY
Cooper, Candace Cohen ... Toledo, OH
Cooper, Candace D. ... Los Angeles, CA
Cooper, Candide C. ... Potosi, MO
Cooper, Carey L. ... San Diego, CA
Cooper, Carl M. ... Treasury Department,
Internal Revenue Service, GV
Cooper, Carol ... New Providence, NJ
Summit, NJ
Cooper, Carol J. ... Tallahassee, FL
Cooper, Carol J. ... Tacoma, WA
Cooper, Carol Sheppard ... Farmington, MN
Cooper, Caroline S. ... Bethesda, MD
Cooper Carvin & Rosenthal, PLLC
Washington, DC
Cooper, Cary Rodman ... Ann Arbor, MI
Findlay, OH
Toledo, OH
Cooper, Catherine C. ... St. Paul, MN
Cooper, Catherine Chauvin
New Orleans, LA
Cooper, Cathy L. ... Denver, CO
Cooper, Cecilia M. ... Americus, GA
Cooper, Charles ... Ironton, OH
Cooper, Charles A. ... New York, NY
Cooper, Charles B. ... Waco, TX
Cooper, Charles D. ... Philadelphia, PA
Cooper, Charles F., II ... Columbia, SC
Cooper, Charles H., Jr. ... Columbus, OH
Cooper, Charles J. ... Washington, DC
Cooper, Charles J. ... Ashland, VA
Cooper, Charles L., Jr. ... Tallahassee, FL
Cooper, Charles N. ... Norfolk, VA
Cooper, Charles R., Jr. ... Lancaster, PA
Cooper, Charles S. ... Audubon, NJ
Bala Cynwyd, PA
Philadelphia, PA
Cooper, Charles W. ... Madison, IN
Cooper, Charles Y. ... Royal Oak, MI
Cooper, Cheryl L. ... Tulsa, OK
Cooper, Chris P. ... Washington, DC
Cooper, Christine G. ... Chicago, IL
Cooper, Christopher ... New York, NY
Cooper, Christopher C. ... Boston, MA
Cooper, Christopher M. ... Columbus, OH
Cooper, Christopher R. ... Washington, DC
Cooper, Clarence P. ... Laguna Hills, CA
Cooper, Clark A. ... Birmingham, AL
Cooper, Clark R. ... Medina, OH
Cooper, Clayton E. ... Los Angeles, CA
Cooper, Clement T. ... Washington, DC
Cooper, Clifton C., Jr. ... San Francisco, CA
Cooper & Clough, P.C. ... Denver, CO
Cooper, Coffas, Moore & Gray, P.A.
Columbia, SC
Cooper, Colin R. ... Oakland, CA

Cooper and Collins ... Chalfont, PA
Cooper & Cooper ... Montgomery, AL
Cooper and Cooper ... Clearwater, FL
Cooper & Cooper ... Nassau, NY
Cooper and Cooper ... Corpus Christi, TX
Cooper & Cooper ... Houston, TX
Cooper & Cooper, LLP ... Mineola, NY
Cooper, Coppins & Monroe, P.A.
Panama City, FL
Pensacola, FL
Tallahassee, FL
Cooper, Corinne ... Kansas City, MO
Cooper, Cornelia R. ... San Francisco, CA
Cooper, Coy M. ... Birmingham, AL
Cooper, Craig B. ... Los Angeles, CA
Cooper, Cristina Mireles ... Austin, TX
Cooper, Curt D. ... Columbus, OH
Cooper, Cynthia A. ... Columbus, OH
Cooper, Cynthia B. ... Columbia, SC
Cooper, Cynthia Penney ... Concord, NC
Cooper, Dale E. ... Brighton, MI
Cooper, Dale H. ... Wichita, KS
Cooper, Dale Stuart ... Forest Hills, NY
Cooper, Dan H. ... Tucson, AZ
Cooper, Daniel C. ... Clarksburg, WV
Cooper, Daniel E. ... Eureka, CA
Cooper, Daniel J. ... Laguna Hills, CA
Cooper, Daniel J. ... Los Angeles, CA
Cooper, Daniel James ... New York, NY
Cooper, Daniel P ... Milwaukee, WI
Cooper, Daniel R., Jr. ... Anchorage, AK
Cooper, Daniel S. ... Farmington Hills, MI
Cooper, Daniel W. ... Pittsburgh, PA
Cooper & Daniele ... White Plains, NY
Cooper, Danielle R. ... New York, NY
Cooper, Davalene ... Boston, MA
Cooper, David A. ... Providence, RI
Cooper, David C. ... Topeka, KS
Cooper, David F. ... Yuma, AZ
Cooper, David F. ... Atlanta, GA
Cooper, David F. ... Toledo, OH
Cooper, David F. ... Vashon, WA
Cooper, David H. ... Louisville, KY
Cooper, David J. ... Bakersfield, CA
Cooper, David J. ... Tecumseh, MI
Cooper, David J. ... West Bloomfield, MI
Cooper, David J., A Prof. Corp., Law Offices of ... Detroit, MI
West Bloomfield, MI
Cooper, David Jackson, Jr. ... Columbia, SC
Cooper, David, Jr. ... Columbus, OH
Cooper, David L. ... Liberty, MO
Cooper, David L. ... Nashville, TN
Cooper, David L., (P.C.) ... Palo Alto, CA
Cooper, David L., P.C., Law Office of
Nashville, TN
Cooper, David P. ... Boise, ID
Portland, OR
Cooper, David R.
Department of Housing and Urban Development,
Office of General Counsel, GV
Cooper, David R. ... Topeka, KS
Cooper, David Rodman ... Ann Arbor, MI
Findlay, OH
Toledo, OH
Cooper, David S. ... Santa Rosa, CA
Cooper, David S. ... Alpharetta, GA
Cooper, David S. ... Worthington, OH
Cooper, David Samuel ... Pittsboro, NC
Cooper, Davis & Cooper ... Fayetteville, NC
Hope Mills, NC
Cooper, Dean F. ... Modesto, CA
Cooper, Dean L. ... Jefferson City, MO
Cooper, Dean S. ... McLean, VA
Cooper, Deans & Cargill, P.A.
North Conway, NH
Cooper, Deborah A. ... Denver, CO
Cooper, Deborah Jones ... Lebanon, NH
Cooper, Debra D. ... Pensacola, FL
Cooper, Denise D. ... White Plains, NY
Cooper, Denise M. ... Las Vegas, NV
Cooper, Dennis J. ... Fresno, CA
Cooper, Diana L. ... Boston, MA
Cooper, Diane M. ... Dallas, TX
Cooper, Dionne ... East Hartford, CT
Cooper, Dixie W. ... Nashville, TN
Cooper, Dolores J. ... Colfax, WA
Cooper, Don W. ... Bristol, TN
Cooper, Donald D. ... Boston, MA
Cooper, Donald Joseph ... Topeka, KS
Cooper, Donald L. ... Oklahoma City, OK
Cooper, Donnette A. ... Arlington, VA
Cooper, Donnie A. ... Knoxville, TN
Cooper, Douglas A. ... Mineola, NY
New Rochelle, NY
Cooper, Douglas Collins
Federal Communications Commission,
Common Carrier Bureau, GV
Cooper, Douglas K. ... Southfield, MI
Cooper, Douglas O. ... Cleveland, OH
Cooper, Drew Avon ... Ocala, FL
Cooper, Duncan B., III ... Peoria, IL
Cooper & Dunham LLP ... New York, NY
Cooper, Dwayne Emery ... Indianapolis, IN
Cooper, E. Shannon ... New Orleans, LA
Cooper, Earle N. ... Nassau, NY
Cooper, Edward ... Buffalo, NY
Cooper, Edward H. ... Ann Arbor, MI
Cooper, Edward L. ... Chicago, IL
Waukegan, IL
Cooper, Edward S. ... Carteret, NJ
Cooper, Edwin D. ... West Memphis, AR
Cooper, Edwin H., III ... Charleston, SC
Cooper, Edwin H., Jr. ... Columbia, SC
Cooper, Elbert M., Jr. ... Clinton, TN
Cooper, Elizabeth A. ... Kirkland, WA
Cooper, Elizabeth B. ... New York, NY

Cooper, Elizabeth Kluger ... Washington, DC
Cooper, Elizabeth M. ... Austin, TX
Cooper, Ellen Marie ... Wilmington, DE
Cooper, Ellen S. ... Baltimore, MD
Cooper, Elliott E. ... Forest City, IA
Cooper, Emily K. ... Toledo, OH
Cooper, Eric L. ... New York, NY
Cooper, Eric P. ... Chicago, IL
Cooper, Erica F. ...
Department Of Health And Human Services, GV
Cooper, Errol ... Lexington, KY
Cooper, Erving, Savage, Nolan & Heller, LLP ... Albany, NY
Cooper, Erwin E. ... Needham, MA
Cooper, Ethan S. K. K. ... Alexandria, VA
Cooper, Ethna B. ... Cincinnati, OH
Cooper, Eugene H. ... Palmdale, CA
Cooper, Florence Marie ... Los Angeles, CA
Cooper, Flowers, Davis, Fraser & Derryberry, L.L.P. ... Tyler, TX
Cooper & Forbes ... Chardon, OH
Mentor, OH
Painesville, OH
Cooper, Frank G. ... Philadelphia, PA
Cooper, Frank V. ... Tulsa, OK
Cooper, Fred L. ... Columbia, MS
Cooper, Frederic J. ... New York, NY
Cooper, Frederick L., III ... Atlanta, GA
Cooper, G. Robert ... Pittsburgh, PA
Cooper, G. Shane ... Lafayette, AL
Cooper, G. Thomas, Jr. ... Camden, SC
Cooper, Gail B. ... San Francisco, CA
Cooper, Gail G. ... Towson, MD
Cooper & Gardener ... Sacramento, CA
Cooper, Gary A. ... Chattanooga, TN
Cooper, Gary C. ... Oakland, CA
Cooper, Gary E. ... Colby, KS
Cooper, Gary G. ... New Haven, CT
Cooper, Gary G. ... Elmsford, NY
New York, NY
Cooper, Gary G. ... Akron, OH
Cooper, Gary L. ... Pocatello, ID
Cooper, Gary L. ... St. Louis, MO
Cooper, Gary M. ... Duluth, GA
Cooper, Gary M. ... Baton Rouge, LA
Cooper, Gary M. ... Houston, TX
Cooper, Gary S. ... Boston, MA
Cooper & Genetin ... Kew Gardens, NY
Cooper, Geoffrey K.
Environmental Protection Agency,
Office of the General Counsel, GV
Cooper, George ... San Antonio, TX
Cooper, George J. ... Portland, OR
Cooper, George M. ... Arlington, VA
Cooper, George M. ... Sutton, WV
Cooper, George W. (IBA) ... **Stamford, CT**
Cooper, Gerald A. ... Columbus, OH
Cooper, Gerald F. ... Cleveland, OH
Cooper, Gerald F., Jr. ... Chicago, IL
Cooper, Gerald H. ... New Haven, CT
Cooper, Gerald H. ... Baltimore, MD
Cooper, Gerald R. ... New Orleans, LA
Cooper, Gerry B. ... Garland, TX
Cooper & Gibson, LLC ... Alpharetta, GA
Cooper, Gladys B. ... Newark, NJ
Cooper Glasgow Kupchynsky & Kittelson, L.L.P. ... Dallas, TX
Cooper & Glass ... Charleston, WV
Cooper, Glenn M. ... Miami, FL
Cooper, Glenn M. ... Bethesda, MD
Cooper, Gordon G. ... Spartanburg, SC
Cooper, Gordon R. ... Pueblo, CO
Cooper, Gordon R., II ... Houston, TX
Cooper, Gregory ... Department of Agriculture,
Office of the General Counsel, GV
Cooper, Gregory E. ... Brooklyn, NY
Cooper, Gregory H. ... Los Angeles, CA
Cooper, Gregory S. ... Fort Wayne, IN
Cooper, Grover C. ... Washington, DC
Cooper, H. Laurence, Jr.
West Palm Beach, FL
Cooper, H. Wayne ... Tulsa, OK
Cooper, Hal D. ... Cleveland, OH
Cooper, Hall, Whittum and Shillaber, P.C.
Concord, NH
Rochester, NH
Cooper, Harold J. ... Dallas, TX
Cooper, Harris ... Naples, FL
Cooper, Harry J. ... Chalfont, PA
Cooper, Harry L. ... Atlanta, GA
Cooper, Harvey B. ... Omaha, NE
Cooper & Hays ... Tucson, AZ
Cooper, H. C. ... Oklahoma City, OK
Cooper, Heather A. ... Fairfax, VA
Cooper, Helen L. ... Salem, OR
Cooper & Hemar ... Santa Monica, CA
Cooper, Herbert E. ... El Paso, TX
Cooper, Herbert J. ... Boston, MA
Cooper, Herbert Warren, IV ... Wellesley, MA
Cooper, Herman ... Los Osos, CA
Cooper, Hope G.
Federal Communications Commission,
Mass Media Bureau, GV
Cooper, Hope L. ... New York, NY
Cooper & Hoppe ... Fresno, CA
Monterey, CA
Cooper, Howard A. ... Washington, DC
Cooper, Howard Kent ... Jamestown, KY
Cooper, Howard M. ... Boston, MA
Cooper, Howard S.
Small Business Administration,
Office of the General Counsel, GV
Cooper, Hylan ... New York, NY
Cooper, Ian M. ... San Francisco, CA
Cooper, Ian P. ... St. Louis, MO
Cooper, Ilene S. ... Uniondale, NY
Cooper, Iles ... Pottsville, PA

Cooper, Ira ... Rockville Centre, NY
Cooper, Ira G. ... Kew Gardens, NY
Cooper, Ira S. ... Pomona, NY
Cooper, Irving L. (Buddy) ... St. Louis, MO
Cooper, Irving T.J. ... North Wales, PA
Cooper, Isaiah D. ... Hartford, CT
Cooper, Ivan B. ... Birmingham, AL
Cooper, Iver P. ... Washington, DC
Cooper, J. Allen, Jr. ... Shreveport, LA
Cooper, J. Fenimore, Jr. ... Orlando, FL
Cooper, J. James ... Houston, TX
Cooper, J. Kent ... Deming, NM
Cooper, J. Michael ... Birmingham, AL
Cooper, J. Robert ... Atlanta, GA
Cooper, J. Robert ... Taylorville, IL
Cooper, J. Stephen ... Dallas, TX
Cooper, J. Ward ... Gardners, PA
Cooper, Jack B. ... Canton, OH
Cooper, Jack D. ... Overland Park, KS
Cooper, Jack L. ... Augusta, GA
Cooper, Jack R. ... Ellicott City, MD
Cooper, Jacqueline Gerson
Washington, DC
Cooper, Jacqueline S. ... Akron, OH
Cooper, James B. ... Lexington, KY
Cooper, James D. ... New York, NY
Cooper, James D., Jr. ... Columbia, SC
Cooper, James E., Jr. ... Washington, DC
Cooper, James H. ... Kansas City, MO
Cooper, James H. ... Montvale, NJ
Cooper, James L. ... Washington, DC
Cooper, James L. ... Northfield, NJ
Cooper, James M. ... Fayetteville, NC
Cooper, James M. ... Bellville, TX
Cooper, James P., III ... Los Angeles, CA
Cooper, James R. ... Newark, OH
Cooper, James R., Jr. ... Montgomery, AL
Cooper, James S. ... Boston, MA
Cooper, James Sherman
Woodland Hills, CA
Cooper, James T. ... Charleston, WV
Cooper, James W. ... United States Senate,
Committee Legal Personnel, GV
Cooper, James W. ... Warrensburg, NY
Cooper, Jane E. ... San Jose, CA
Cooper, Janet K. ... Dayton, OH
Cooper, Jarrett Evan ... Boca Raton, FL
Cooper, Jas. C. ... Albany, NY
Cooper, Jason Allen ... Atlanta, GA
Cooper, Jason P. ... Charlotte, NC
Cooper, Jay ... Naples, FL
Port Charlotte, FL
Weston, FL
Cooper, Jay L. ... Los Angeles, CA
Cooper, Jay P. ... Corona Del Mar, CA
Cooper, Jay P. ... Lebanon, NH
Cooper, Jean A. ... Los Angeles, CA
Cooper, Jean S.
Department of Housing and Urban Development,
Board of Contract Appeals, GV
Cooper, Jeff K. ... Topeka, KS
Cooper, Jeffery M. ... Houston, TX
Cooper, Jeffrey ... Philadelphia, PA
Cooper, Jeffrey A. ... Greenwich, CT
Cooper, Jeffrey A. ... Roseland, NJ
Cooper, Jeffrey A. ... Milwaukee, WI
Cooper, Jeffrey D. ... Langhorne, PA
Cooper, Jeffrey H. ... New York, NY
Cooper, Jeffrey M. ... New York, NY
Cooper, Jeffrey M. ... Oklahoma City, OK
Cooper, Jeffrey M. ... Philadelphia, PA
Upper Darby, PA
Cooper, Jeffrey O. ... Indianapolis, IN
Cooper, Jeffrey R. ... Cincinnati, OH
Cooper, Jennie M. ... Rochester, NY
Cooper, Jennifer Grandoff ... Atlanta, GA
Cooper, Jennifer L. ... New York, NY
Cooper, Jennifer L. ... Knoxville, TN
Cooper, Jerome ... Lynbrook, NY
Cooper, Jerome A. ... Birmingham, AL
Cooper, Jerome S. ... Portland, OR
Cooper, Jesse Jay ... Harrisburg, PA
Cooper, Jessica B. ... New York, NY
Cooper, Jessica R. C. ... Pontiac, MI
Cooper, Jill F. ... Denver, CO
Cooper, Jill F. ... Los Angeles, CA
Cooper, Jill Z. ... Santa Fe, NM
Cooper, Joan Lloyd ... Louisville, KY
Cooper, Joanne B. ... Warner Robins, GA
Cooper, Jodi Lin ... Washington, DC
Cooper, Joel B. ... Norfolk, VA
Cooper, Joel T. ... Chicago, IL
Cooper, John A. ... Bentonville, AR
Cooper, John B. ... Duncan, OK
Cooper, John C. ... Tallahassee, FL
Cooper, John C., III ... Santa Fe, NM
Cooper, John C., III ... Milwaukee, WI
Cooper, John D. ... San Francisco, CA
Cooper, John D. ... Tulsa, OK
Cooper, John E. ... Chicago, IL
Cooper, John E. ... Erie, PA
Cooper, John F. ... St. Petersburg, FL
Cooper, John G. ... Seattle, WA
Cooper, John H. ... Birmingham, AL
Cooper, John Hughes ... Sullivan's Island, SC
Cooper, John Hughes, P.C.
Sullivan's Island, SC
Cooper, John J. ... Royal Oak, MI
Cooper, John K., Jr. ... Grand Rapids, MI
Cooper, John Kennedy ... Roseland, NJ
Cooper, John L. ... San Francisco, CA
Cooper, John M. ... Roseboro, NC
Cooper, John M. ... Virginia Beach, VA
Cooper, John M. ... Bainbridge Island, WA
Cooper, John Michael ... Washington, DC
Cooper, John N. ... New York, NY
Cooper, John N., II ... Kalamazoo, MI

Cooper, John S. ... Moraga, CA
Cooper, John T. ... Atlanta, GA
Cooper, John W. ... Birmingham, AL
Cooper, John W. ... Summit, NJ
Cooper, John W. ... Parsons, WV
Cooper, John W., Jr. ... Eureka, CA
Cooper, Johnetta ... Houston, TX
Cooper, Jon D. ... Lansing, MI
Cooper, Jon R. ... Tucson, AZ
Cooper, Jonathan D. ... Knoxville, TN
Cooper, Jonathan M. ... Chicago, IL
Cooper, Jonathan R. ... Cleveland, OH
Cooper & Jones, LLP ... Marietta, GA
Cooper, Jordan D. ... Nutley, NJ
Cooper, Jordana ... Cherry Hill, NJ
Cooper, Josef D. ... San Francisco, CA
Cooper, Joseph ... Sacramento, CA
Cooper, Joseph D. ... Fresno, CA
Monterey, CA
Cooper, Joseph E. ... Albuquerque, NM
Cooper, Joseph J. ... Trenton, NJ
Cooper, Joseph, Personal Injury Law Office
Sacramento, CA
Cooper, Joseph W. C. ... East Liverpool, OH
Cooper, Judith Diane
La Canada Flintridge, CA
Cooper, Judith Diane ... Clayton, NM
Cooper, Judith G. ... Houston, TX
Cooper, Judith G., P.C. ... Houston, TX
Cooper, Julia Boaz ... Birmingham, AL
Cooper, Justin L. ... Deer Park, NY
Cooper, J. W., Jr. ... Corpus Christi, TX
Cooper Kardaras & Kelleher L.L.P.
Pasadena, CA
New York, NY
Cooper, Karen E. ... Atlanta, GA
Cooper, Karen Foytlin ... Philadelphia, PA
Cooper, Karen J. ... Garden City, NY
Cooper, Karl D.
Commodity Futures Trading Commission, Division of Enforcement, GV
Cooper, Karl D. ... Lansdale, PA
Cooper, Katherine ... Manchester, NH
Cooper, Katherine M. ... Phoenix, AZ
Cooper, Kathleen A. ... Houston, TX
Cooper, Kathleen J. ... Fort Lauderdale, FL
Cooper, Kathryn Jones ... Raleigh, NC
Cooper, Kathryn Renee ... Baton Rouge, LA
Cooper, Kathy L. ... Washington, DC
Cooper, Katie ... Santa Monica, CA
Cooper, Keith D. ... Pensacola, FL
Cooper, Keith E. ... Beverly Hills, CA
Cooper, Keith L. ... Santa Monica, CA
Cooper, Kenneth B. ... Santa Monica, CA
Cooper, Kenneth D. ... Santa Monica, CA
Cooper, Kenneth D. ... Fort Lauderdale, FL
Cooper, Kenneth D., P.A.
Fort Lauderdale, FL
Cooper, Kenneth G. ... Charleston, SC
Summerville, SC
Cooper, Kenneth J.
Pension Benefit Guaranty Corporation, Office of the General Counsel, GV
Cooper, Kenneth J. ... Auburn, WA
Cooper, Kenneth L. ... Buffalo, NY
Cooper, Kenneth R. ... San Antonio, TX
Cooper, Kenneth S. ... Philadelphia, PA
Cooper, Kevin D. ... Naples, FL
Cooper, Kevin D. ... Salem, MA
Cooper, Kevin J. ... New York, NY
Cooper, Kim A. ... Houston, TX
Cooper, Kim Martens ... Cupertino, CA
Cooper & Kirkham, A Professional Corporation ... San Francisco, CA
Cooper, Kitt C. ... Columbus, OH
Cooper, Kretek and Associates ... Deming, NM
Cooper, Kristin B. ... Rocky Mount, NC
Cooper, Kyle A. ... Clarksville, IN
Louisville, KY
Cooper, L. Andrew ... Denver, CO
Cooper, L. Cole ... Tulsa, OK
Cooper, Lance A. ... Marietta, GA
Cooper, Langdon M. ... Gastonia, NC
Cooper, Larry G., Jr. ... Auburn, AL
Cooper & Larsen ... Pocatello, ID
Cooper, Laura M. Craska ... Bend, OR
Portland, OR
Cooper, Laurie A. ... Memphis, TN
Cooper Law Firm, P.A.
Mountain Home, AR
Cooper Law Firm, The, Chartered
Minneapolis, MN
Cooper, Lawrence ... Millburn, NJ
Cooper, Lawrence A. ... Atlanta, GA
Cooper, Lawrence D. ... Cleveland, OH
Cooper, Lawrence R. ... Bronx, NY
Cooper, Lea C. ... Boise, ID
Cooper, Lee C. ... Oakland, CA
Cooper, Lee E., Jr. ... Mammoth Lakes, CA
Cooper, Lenox G., II ... Bethesda, MD
Cooper, Leon M. ... Los Angeles, CA
Cooper, Leonard B. ... Uniondale, NY
Cooper, Leonard J. ... Philadelphia, PA
Cooper, Leonard M. ... Denver, CO
Cooper, Leonard, (P.C.) ... Deer Park, NY
Cooper, Lesley B. ... McLean, VA
Cooper, Leslie ... New York, NY
Cooper, Leslie A. ... Mendham, NJ
Cooper, Leslie Kyman ... Phoenix, AZ
Cooper, Leslie R. ... Everett, WA
Cooper, Lester ... Melville, NY
Mineola, NY
Cooper, Linda D. ... Painesville, OH
Cooper, Linda S. ... Bloomington, IL
Cooper, Lisa I. ... Raleigh, NC
Cooper, Loren Gail ... Philadelphia, PA
Cooper, Louisa Dawn ... Andalusia, AL
Cooper, Lucius A. ... San Ramon, CA
Cooper, M. Armon ... San Francisco, CA
Cooper, M. Scott ... Los Angeles, CA
Cooper, Maddon L. ... Long Beach, CA
Cooper, Marc ... Miami, FL
Cooper, Marc J. ... Boston, MA
Cooper, Marcia L. ... Pittsburgh, PA
Cooper, Marcus Duran ... Las Vegas, NV
Cooper, Margaret A. ... Austin, TX
Cooper, Margaret L.
West Palm Beach, FL
Cooper, Margaret R. ... Dover, DE
Cooper, Marie A. ... Walnut Creek, CA
Cooper, Mario M. ... Washington, DC
New York, NY
Cooper, Marion S. ... Richmond, VA
Cooper, Mark A. ... Punta Gorda, FL
Cooper, Mark F. ... Mountain Home, AR
Cooper, Mark G. ... Royal Oak, MI
Cooper, Mark J. ... New York, NY
Cooper, Mark O., (P.A.) ... Orlando, FL
Cooper, Mark S. ... Oklahoma City, OK
Cooper, Mark Stephen ... Tumwater, WA
Cooper, Markita Darolyn ... San Francisco, CA
Cooper, Marlene S. ... Los Angeles, CA
Cooper, Marsha Andrade ... Torrance, CA
Cooper, Martin, Chojnowski & Beck, P.C.
Kalamazoo, MI
Cooper, Martin S. ... New York, NY
Cooper, Marvin A. ... White Plains, NY
Cooper, Marvin A., P.C.
Mount Vernon, NY
Scarsdale, NY
White Plains, NY
Cooper, Marvin B. ... Baltimore, MD
Cooper, Mary A. ... Danville, IN
Cooper, Mary B. ... Pasadena, CA
Cooper, Mary Jane R. ... Skillman, NJ
Cooper, Mary Little ... Trenton, NJ
Cooper, Mary M. ... Washington, DC
Cooper, Mary P. ... Rockville, MD
Cooper, Matt ... Long Beach, CA
Cooper, Matthew B. ... Baltimore, MD
Cooper, Matthew F. ... New York, NY
Cooper, Matthew R. ... Paw Paw, MI
Cooper, Matthew W. ... Birmingham, AL
Cooper, Maureen "Mike" K.
Huntsville, AL
Cooper & McAlister, A Professional Corporation ... Oklahoma City, OK
Cooper & McCann, LLP ... Stamford, CT
Elmsford, NY
New York, NY
Cooper & McCauslin ... Southfield, MI
Cooper, Melinda S. ... Xenia, OH
Cooper, Melodie Dawn Edwards
Baltimore, MD
Cooper, Melody H. ... Corpus Christi, TX
Cooper, Melvin ... Biloxi, MS
Cooper, Melvin E. ... Columbus, GA
Cooper, Melvin G., P.A. ... Biloxi, MS
Cooper, Michael A. ... New York, NY
Cooper, Michael C. ... San Francisco, CA
Cooper, Michael D. ... Oakland, CA
Cooper, Michael D. ... Westbrook, ME
Cooper, Michael E. ... Ellensburg, WA
Cooper, Michael H. ... Bronx, NY
Cooper, Michael H. ... Dallas, TX
Cooper, Michael J. ... Denver, CO
Cooper, Michael J. ... Washington, DC
Cooper, Michael J. ... Ocala, FL
Cooper, Michael J. ... Buffalo, NY
Cooper, Michael J. ... Salt Lake City, UT
Cooper, Michael K. ... Gaylord, MI
Cooper, Michael L. ... Eugene, OR
Cooper, Michael R. ... Jackson, MS
Cooper, Michael R. ... New York, NY
Cooper, Michael R. ... Dallas, TX
Cooper, Michael T. ... Louisville, KY
Cooper, Michael W. ... Fairfield, CA
Cooper, Michael W. ... Houston, TX
Cooper, Michelle ... Beverly Hills, CA
Cooper, Milburn N. ... Phoenix, AZ
Cooper, Miles Hall ... Corpus Christi, TX
Cooper, Milton ... Waltham, MA
Cooper, Milton ... New Hyde Park, NY
Cooper, Milton ... New York, NY
Cooper, Mimi Raffel ... Baltimore, MD
Cooper, Mitchell Eben ... Madison, WI
Cooper, Mitchell J. ... Washington, DC
Cooper, Mitchell J. ... Mineola, NY
Cooper, Monika ... Fort Worth, TX
Cooper, Monte ... Menlo Park, CA
Cooper & Morris, A Professional Law Corporation ... Fairfield, CA
Cooper, N. Lee ... Birmingham, AL
Cooper, Nancy G. ... San Antonio, TX
Cooper, Nancy M. ... Portland, OR
Cooper, Nancy W. ... Tarrytown, NY
Cooper, Natasha S. ... Los Angeles, CA
Cooper, Nathan ... New York, NY
Cooper, Neal A. ... Chicago, IL
Cooper, Neil A. ... Lynnfield, MA
Cooper, Neil J. ... Roslyn Heights, NY
Cooper, Nicholas C. ... Brooklyn, NY
Cooper, Nicole C. ... San Diego, CA
Cooper, Noel D. ... San Angelo, TX
Cooper, Noelle E. ... Seattle, WA
Cooper, Norman G.
Department of Agriculture, GV
Cooper, Owen B. ... Department of Justice, Immigration and Naturalization Service, GV
Cooper, P. Ronald ... Pittsburgh, PA
Cooper & Pachell ... Akron, OH
Cooper, Pamela C. ... Washington, DC
Cooper, Pamela L. ... Tallahassee, FL
Cooper, Patricia A. ... Chardon, OH
Cooper, Patricia E. ... Benson, AZ
Cooper, Patrick C. ... Birmingham, AL
Cooper, Patrick M. ... Milwaukee, WI
Cooper, Patrick R. ... Tacoma, WA
Cooper, Patsy McDowell ... Baton Rouge, LA
Cooper, Patsy McDowell, Ltd.
Baton Rouge, LA
Cooper, Paul ... Lynbrook, NY
Cooper, Paul D. ... Denver, CO
Cooper, Paul R. ... Montgomery, AL
Cooper and Pautz ... Horseheads, NY
Cooper, Pell C. ... Nashville, NC
Cooper, Penelope M. ... Oakland, CA
Cooper Perskie April Niedelman Wagenheim & Levenson, A Professional Association
Atlantic City, NJ
Cape May Court House, NJ
Cherry Hill, NJ
Northfield, NJ
Cooper, Peter A. ... New York, NY
Cooper, Peter B. ... New Haven, CT
Cooper, Peter B. ... Newark, NJ
Cooper, Peter D. ... Erlanger, KY
Cooper, Peter E. ... Chicago, IL
Cooper, Peter L. ... Minneapolis, MN
Cooper, Peter M. ... Southfield, MI
Cooper, Philip A. ... Atlanta, GA
Cooper, Philip G. ... Huntingdon Valley, PA
Cooper, Philip Joseph ... Memphis, TN
Cooper, Philip S. ... Anderson, IN
Cooper, Phyllis N. ... North Hollywood, CA
Cooper & Pierson ... Baton Rouge, LA
Cooper & Preston ... Elkins, WV
Parsons, WV
Cooper, R. Brent ... Dallas, TX
Cooper, R. Casey ... Tulsa, OK
Cooper, R. Fred ... Idaho Falls, ID
Cooper, R. John ... New York, NY
Cooper, R. Maurice ... Spokane, WA
Cooper, R. Thompson ... Oklahoma City, OK
Cooper, Randall F. ... North Conway, NH
Cooper, Raymond F., Jr. ... Denver, CO
Cooper, Rebecca ... Jacksonville, FL
Cooper, Rebecca Anne ... Canton, TX
Cooper, Rebecca Y. ... New Orleans, LA
Cooper, Reinette W. ... Wailuku, HI
Cooper, Renata Kendrick ... Washington, DC
Cooper, Rhonda C. ... Jackson, MS
Cooper, Richard ... Louisville, KY
Cooper, Richard A. ... La Plata, MD
Cooper, Richard A. ... Cleveland, OH
Cooper, Richard A. ... Houston, TX
Cooper, Richard Alan ... St. Louis, MO
Cooper, Richard B. ... New York, NY
Cooper, Richard C. ... Red Bud, IL
Cooper, Richard C. ... Grand Rapids, MI
Cooper, Richard C. ... Newark, NJ
Cooper, Richard F. ... Fort Smith, AR
Cooper, Richard H. ... Beverly Hills, CA
Cooper, Richard H. ... Orlando, FL
Cooper, Richard I. ... Ludington, MI
Cooper, Richard J. ... New York, NY
Cooper, Richard L. ... Geneva, IL
Cooper, Richard M. ... Washington, DC
Cooper, Richard P. ... Rockaway Park, NY
Cooper, Richard, P.S.C. ... Louisville, KY
Cooper, Richard S. ... Cleveland, OH
Cooper, Richard T.
United States Postal Service, Law Department, GV
Cooper, Ridge & Beale, P.A.
Jacksonville, FL
Cooper, Robert A. ... Northfield, NJ
Cooper, Robert C. ... Eustis, FL
Cooper, Robert Clayton ... Washington, DC
Baltimore, MD
Rockville, MD
Cooper, Robert D. ... Los Angeles, CA
Cooper, Robert Darryl
Federal Communications Commission, Cable Services Bureau, GV
Cooper, Robert E. ... Birmingham, AL
Cooper, Robert E. ... Los Angeles, CA
Cooper, Robert E., Jr. ... Nashville, TN
Cooper, Robert F., Jr. ... Jackson, MS
Cooper, Robert G. ... Columbia, SC
Cooper, Robert H. ... Metairie, LA
New Orleans, LA
Cooper, Robert I. ... Torrance, CA
Cooper, Robert I., A Professional Corporation
Torrance, CA
Cooper, Robert James ... Camden, NJ
Cooper, Robert L. ... Englewood, CO
Cooper, Robert L. ... Ypsilanti, MI
Cooper, Robert L. ... New York, NY
Cooper, Robert L. ... Fayetteville, NC
Cooper, Robert M. ... Broomfield, CO
Cooper, Robert M. ... Washington, DC
Cooper, Robert O. ... Houston, TX
Cooper, Robert P. ... Forest City, IA
Cooper, Robert P. ... Grand Rapids, MI
Cooper, Robert P. ... Grand Rapids, MI
Cooper, Robert S. ... Beverly Hills, CA
Cooper, Robert S. ... Los Angeles, CA
Cooper, Robert S. ... Bridgeport, CT
Cooper, Robert S. ... Bruce, MS
Cooper, Robert S. ... Rochester, NY
Cooper, Robt. E. ... Signal Mountain, TN
Cooper, Rochelle L.
Kennedy Space Center, FL
Cooper, Rodney A. ... Dallas, TX
Cooper, Roger Alan ... Owensboro, KY
Cooper, Roger B. ... Arlington, VA
Cooper, Roger R. ... Horseheads, NY
Cooper, Ronald H. ... Upper Marlboro, MD
Cooper, Ronald S. ... Costa Mesa, CA
Cooper, Ronald S. ... Washington, DC
Cooper, Rosalie B. ... Toms River, NJ
Cooper Rose & English, LLP ... Rumson, NJ
Summit, NJ
Cooper, Rose Russell ... Louisville, KY
Cooper, Rosemary J. ... Springfield, MA
Cooper, Ross D. ... Washington, DC
Cooper, Ross M. ... Phoenix, AZ
Cooper, Roy A., III ... Rocky Mount, NC
Cooper, Roy A., Jr. ... Nashville, NC
Cooper, Roy G. ... Manchester, MO
Cooper, Roy P. ... Louisville, KY
Cooper, Russell Wade ... Tyler, TX
Cooper, S. Michael ... New Orleans, LA
Cooper, Sally Anne ... Portland, OR
Cooper, Sam ... Tulsa, OK
Cooper, Samara J. ... Palm Beach, FL
Cooper, Saml. ... Baltimore, MD
Cooper, Samuel T., III ... Harrisburg, PA
Cooper, Samuel V. ... Omaha, NE
Cooper, Samuel W. ... Omaha, NE
Cooper, Samuel W. ... Houston, TX
Cooper, Sarah ... Houston, TX
Cooper, Scott A. ... Gaithersburg, MD
Cooper, Scott B. ... Harrisburg, PA
Cooper, Scott D. ... Department of Justice, Justice Management Division, GV
Cooper, Scott E. ... Boston, MA
Providence, RI
Cooper, Scott F. ... Troy, MI
Cooper, Scott F. ... Cherry Hill, NJ
Philadelphia, PA
Cooper, Scott P. ... Los Angeles, CA
Cooper & Scully, P.C. ... Dallas, TX
Sherman, TX
Cooper, Seth L. ... Southport, CT
Cooper, Seward M. ... Silver Spring, MD
Cooper, Sharon K. ... New York, NY
Cooper, Sharon M. ... Dallas, TX
Cooper, Sheila O'Connell ... Plano, TX
Cooper, Shelley Ann ... Grand Prairie, TX
Cooper, Shifman, Gabe, Quinn & Seymour
Detroit, MI
Novi, MI
Royal Oak, MI
Cooper, Silas B., Jr. ... Abbeville, LA
Cooper, Sonja J. M. ... New York, NY
Cooper, Sonja K. P. ... Marietta, GA
Cooper, Sophie ... Albuquerque, NM
Cooper, Spector & Weil Co., L.P.A.
Cleveland, OH
Cooper, Spong & Davis, P.C. ... Norfolk, VA
Portsmouth, VA
Cooper, Stacey M. ... New York, NY
Cooper, Stanley H. ... Allston, MA
Cooper, Stefanie L. ... Dallas, TX
Cooper, Stephanie R. ... New York, NY
Cooper, Stephen ... Fairbanks, AK
Cooper, Stephen Alan ... St. Louis, MO
Cooper, Stephen B. ... Pottstown, PA
Cooper, Stephen C. ... Southfield, MI
Cooper, Stephen C. ... New York, NY
Cooper, Stephen E. ... Nassau, NY
Cooper, Stephen H. ... New York, NY
Cooper, Stephen L. ... Los Angeles, CA
Cooper, Stephen M. ... Geneva, IL
Cooper, Stephen M. ... Tyler, TX
Cooper, Stephen R. ... Casa Grande, AZ
Cooper, Stephen W. ... Minneapolis, MN
Cooper, Steven ... New York, NY
Cooper, Steven A. ... San Francisco, CA
Cooper, Steven D. ... Atlanta, GA
Cooper, Steven G. ... Bartlesville, OK
Cooper, Steven M. ... Los Angeles, CA
Cooper, Steven M. ... Silver Spring, MD
Cooper & Stieler ... Newark, NJ
New Providence, NJ
Parsippany, NJ
Summit, NJ
Cooper & Storm ... Geneva, IL
Cooper, Stuart K. ... Baldwin, NY
Cooper, Stuart Thornton ... Charleston, WV
Cooper, Subrina L. ... Hattiesburg, MS
Cooper, Susan C. ... Wellesley, MA
Cooper, Susan Hager ... Charlotte, NC
Cooper, Susan L. ... Springfield, MA
Cooper, Susan M. ... Dallas, TX
Cooper, Susan Starbuck ... Highland, CA
Cooper, Susan T. ... St. Louis, MO
Cooper, Suzanne M. ... Philadelphia, PA
Cooper, T. Hatfield ... Laguna Beach, CA
Cooper, Tamela K. ... Houston, TX
Cooper & Tanis, P.C. ... Broomfield, CO
Cooper, Tanya Adair ... Fort Worth, TX
Cooper, Terence M. ... Houston, TX
Cooper, Teresa ... Richardson, TX
Cooper, Teresa Lee ... Oklahoma City, OK
Cooper, Thaxter A. ... Tampa, FL
Cooper, Thom L, Co., LPA
Centerburg, OH
Cooper, Thom Loyal ... Centerburg, OH
Cooper, Thomas A., P.C. ... Richmond, VA
Cooper, Thomas E. ... San Francisco, CA
Cooper, Thomas E. ... Elizabethtown, KY
Cooper, Thomas G. ... Boston, MA
Cooper, Thomas G. ... Concord, NH
Cooper, Thomas J. ... Washington, DC
Cooper, Thomas L. ... Petoskey, MI
Cooper, Thomas L. ... Pittsburgh, PA
Cooper, Thomas L. ... Everett, WA
Cooper, Thomas M. ... Lexington, KY
Cooper, Thomas M. ... New York, NY
Cooper, Thomas N. ... Sacramento, CA
Cooper, Thomas N. ... Myerstown, PA
Cooper, Thomas R. ... Houston, TX
Cooper, Thomas R. ... Milwaukee, WI
Cooper, Thomas R., Jr.
Department of the Army, Office, Chief of Engineers/Headquarters, U.S. Army Corps of Engineers, GV

Cooper, Thomas W., Jr. ....Manning, SC
Cooper, Timothy J. ....Hamburg, NY
Cooper, Timothy M. ....Newark, OH
Cooper, Tink D. ....Department of Justice, Civil Rights Division, GV
Cooper, Todd A. ....Los Angeles, CA
Cooper, Todd L. ....Cincinnati, OH
Cooper and Todd, L.L.P. ....Camden, SC
Cooper, Tom ....Ashdown, AR
Cooper, Trisha Leigh ....Atlanta, GA
Cooper, Troy Asao Kaleolani
Philadelphia, PA
Cooper & Tuerk, LLP ....Annapolis, MD
Baltimore, MD
Towson, MD
Cooper, Tyrone E. ....Beaumont, TX
Cooper & VanAntwerp ....Ironton, OH
Cooper, Vanessa Olivia ....Columbia, SC
Cooper, Victor G. ....Los Angeles, CA
Cooper, W. Austin ....Sacramento, CA
Cooper, W. Jack ....Baltimore, MD
Cooper, W. Lee, Jr. ....Lexington, SC
Cooper, W. Ronald ....Chicago, IL
Cooper, W. Scott ....Charlotte, NC
Cooper & Wade, P.A. ....Lebanon, NH
Cooper, Walinski & Cramer, A Legal Professional Association ....Ann Arbor, MI
Findlay, OH
Port Clinton, OH
Toledo, OH
Cooper, Walter E. & Walter M. ....Cranford, NJ
Cooper, Walter M. ....Cranford, NJ
Cooper, Ward R. ....Washington, DC
Cooper, Wayne A. ....Chicago, IL
Cooper, Wayne B. ....San Francisco, CA
Cooper, Wendy E. ....New York, NY
Cooper, Wendy Fein ....Philadelphia, PA
Cooper, Wetzel, Avery & Lee, Attorneys at Law, P.A. ....Idaho Falls, ID
Cooper, White & Cooper LLP
San Francisco, CA
Walnut Creek, CA
Cooper, Whitney, Cochran & Francois
New Haven, CT
Cooper, William A., Jr. ....Panama City, FL
Cooper, William Bennett, III ....Exton, PA
Cooper, William C. ....Martinez, CA
Cooper, William C. ....Denver, CO
Cooper, William D. ....Roswell, GA
Cooper, William D. ....Rockville Centre, NY
Cooper, William E. ....St. Louis, MO
Cooper, William E. ....Las Vegas, NV
Cooper, William F. ....Honolulu, HI
Cooper, William F. ....Mentor, OH
Cooper, William G. ....Jacksonville, FL
Cooper, William H. ....White Plains, NY
Cooper, William H. ....Greenville, OH
Cooper, William H. ....Dallas, TX
Cooper, William H., Jr. ....Hapeville, GA
Cooper, William H., Jr. ......Baton Rouge, LA
Cooper, William J. ....Akron, OH
Cooper, William J. ....Houston, TX
Cooper, William J., Jr. ....Louisville, KY
Cooper, William Jay ....Charleston, WV
Cooper, William L. ....San Francisco, CA
Cooper, William L. ....Williamsburg, VA
Cooper, William L., III ....Cincinnati, OH
Cooper, William M. ....Spartanburg, SC
Cooper, William Marion ....Pittsburgh, PA
Cooper, William P., III ....Los Angeles, CA
Cooper, William R. ....Charlotte, NC
Cooper, William S. ....Elizabethtown, KY
Cooper, William S. ....Baltimore, MD
Cooper, William S., III ....Oneida, TN
Cooper, William T. ....Columbus, MS
Cooper, William T. ....Somerville, NJ
Cooper, William Thomas, III ......Somerville, NJ
Cooper, Wm. R. ....Glenside, PA
Lansdale, PA
Cooper & Wolfe, P.A. ....Miami, FL
Cooper & Wolowski, A Prtnrshp. incl. A Prof. Corp. ....Laguna Hills, CA
Cooper & Woodruff, A Law Corporation
Abbeville, LA
Cooperberg, Barry ....Lansdale, PA
Cooperberg, Douglas M. ......Philadelphia, PA
Cooper-Boggs, Karla ....Indianapolis, IN
Cooper-Finkle, Andrea ....Chicago, IL
Cooper-Folb, Gail S. ....Los Angeles, CA
Cooper-Hill, James ....Corpus Christi, TX
Rockport, TX
Cooper-Hill, James, P.C. Corpus Christi, TX
Rockport, TX
Cooperider, Dan W. ....Palo Alto, CA
Cooperman & Allen, P.C. ....Yonkers, NY
Cooperman, Amanda ....Philadelphia, PA
Cooperman, Arnold L. ....Tallahassee, FL
Cooperman, Barnet M. ....Los Angeles, CA
Cooperman, Bruce E. ....Los Angeles, CA
Cooperman, Cindy Beth ....Yonkers, NY
Cooperman, Daniel ....Redwood City, CA
Cooperman, Don A. ....New York, NY
Cooperman, Harding, & Moore
Kew Gardens, NY
Cooperman, Harriet E. ....Baltimore, MD
Cooperman, Joelle ....Boca Raton, FL
Cooperman, Jonathan K. ....New York, NY
Cooperman, Jonathan L. ....Philadelphia, PA
Cooperman, Jonathan M. ....Akron, OH
Cooperman, Joshua G. ....Hillsborough, CA
Cooperman, Kathryn ....New York, NY
Cooperman, Larry F. ....Minneapolis, MN
Cooperman, Lee ....Los Angeles, CA
Cooperman, Leonard J. ....Miami Shores, FL
Cooperman Levitt Winikoff Lester & Newman, P.C. ....Manhasset, NY
New York, NY
Cooperman, M. James ....New York, NY
Cooperman, Marc S. ....Chicago, IL
Cooperman, Marlene S. ....Philadelphia, PA
Cooperman, Miles R. ....Encino, CA
Cooperman, Peter R. ....Kew Gardens, NY
Cooperman, Robert B. ....Denville, NJ
Cooperman, Robert N. ....Manhasset, NY
New York, NY
Cooperman, Ronald ....Calabasas, CA
Cooperman, Ronald M. ....Toledo, OH
Cooperrider, Carl D. ....Quincy, MA
Cooperrider, Luke K. ....Sun City West, AZ
Cooper Roy, Jennifer ....Alexandria, VA
Coopersmith & Coopersmith ......New York, NY
Coopersmith, Douglas P. ....Philadelphia, PA
Coopersmith, Henry J.
Newport Beach, CA
Coopersmith, Irving ....New York, NY
Coopersmith, Jack W. ....Media, PA
Coopersmith, Jeffrey ....Seattle, WA
Coopersmith, Richard D. ....New York, NY
Coopersmith, Stephen ....Beverly Hills, CA
Coopersmith, Wendy Anne ....Media, PA
Cooperson, Solis ....Los Angeles, CA
Cooperson, Solis ....Santa Monica, CA
Cooperstein, Edward ....Taunton, MA
Cooperstein, Eric T. ....Minneapolis, MN
Cooperstein, Foster Jay ....Newton, MA
Cooperstein, Gary P. ....New York, NY
Cooperstein, Jamie ....Santa Monica, CA
Cooperstein, Kenneth ....Centerport, NY
Cooperstein, Robert L. ....Taunton, MA
Cooperstein, Steven J. ....Philadelphia, PA
Cooperstein, Theodore M.
Washington, DC
Cooperstein, Theodore M., P.C.
Washington, DC
Cooperstein, Walter M. ....Boca Raton, FL
Coopman, Amy L. ....Kansas City, MO
Coopman, Robert J. ....Duluth, GA
Coop-Ullman, Virginia ....Bellevue, WA
Coopwood, Robin Wilkes ....Austin, TX
Coordes, Duane A. ....Moline, IL
Coorlas, Peter S. ....Chicago, IL
Coors, Darden Kistler ....Golden, CO
Coorssen, James L. ....Louisville, KY
Coote, Peter J. ....Philadelphia, PA
Cooter, Dale A. ....Washington, DC
Cooter, Harriet H. ....Knoxville, TN
Cooter, Mangold, Tompert & Wayson, L.L.C. ....Annapolis, MD
Washington, DC
Cooter, Paul A. ....Albuquerque, NM
Coots, Brandon S. ....Troy, AL
Coots, Daniel E. ....Carmel, IN
Coots, E. Davis ....Carmel, IN
Coots, Henke & Wheeler, Professional Corporation ....Carmel, IN
Indianapolis, IN
Coots, James D. ....Marietta, GA
Coots, John C. ....Washington, DC
Coots, Robert M. ....Taylorsville, KY
Coover, Ann E. ....Corpus Christi, TX
Coover, Bradley J. ....Brighton, CO
Coover & Coover ....Corpus Christi, TX
Coover, David M., Jr. ......Corpus Christi, TX
Coover, Fred L. ....Columbia, MD
Coover, Fred L., P.C. ....Columbia, MD
Coover, Lewis Bryan, III ....Milwaukie, OR
Coover, Stephen H. ....Sanford, FL
Copa, Joseph C. ....Madison, WI
Copaken, Richard D. ....Washington, DC
Copani, Anthony F. ....Syracuse, NY
Copas, David N., Jr. ....Baltimore, MD
Copas, Gary D. ....Madison, TN
Copat, Giovanna Jill ....Terre Haute, IN
Cope, Alicia Lee ....Virginia, MN
Cope, Allen D. ....Birmingham, AL
Cope, Barry C. ....Indianapolis, IN
Cope, Bradley N. ....Irving, TX
Cope, Carol Soret ....Miami, FL
Cope, Carrie E. ....Chicago, IL
Cope, Charles L., II
Federal Deposit Insurance Corporation, Trial Litigation Section, GV
Cope, Charles W., IV ....Clearwater, FL
Cope and Cope, P.A. ....Portland, ME
Cope, Donald E. ....Redwood City, CA
Cope, Gerald B., Jr. ....Miami, FL
Cope, Gerald S. ....Portland, ME
Cope & Guerra ....Reno, NV
Cope, H. Brooks ....Anaheim, CA
Cope, James C. ....Murfreesboro, TN
Cope, James L. ....Yankton, SD
Cope, James M. ....Salt Lake City, UT
Cope, James R. ....Ely, MN
Virginia, MN
Cope, James R. ....Kansas City, MO
Cope, Joe L. ....Abilene, TX
Cope, Joel R. ....Atlanta, GA
Cope, John C. ....Martinez, CA
Cope, John F. ....Ely, MN
Virginia, MN
Cope, John R. ....Washington, DC
Cope, Johnny C. ....Newport News, VA
Cope, Jon M. ....Columbus, OH
Cope, Jonathan D. ....Sedalia, MO
Cope, Jonathan I. ....Chicago, IL
Cope, Jonathan M. ....Columbus, OH
Cope, Joseph Adams ....Boulder, CO
Cope, Larry R. ....Rosemead, CA
Cope Law Firm, The ....Sedalia, MO
Cope, Lee Deer ....Johns Island, SC
Cope, Leland H. ....North Canton, OH
Cope, Monette ....London, OH
Cope & Peterson, Professional Association
Ely, MN
Virginia, MN
Cope, Phillip Scott ....Jacksonville, FL
Cope, R. E. L., III ....Montgomery, AL
Cope, Robert DeN. ....Boston, MA
Cope, Robert L. ....Washington, DC
Cope, Ronald S. ....Chicago, IL
Cope, S. Gregory ....Nashville, TN
Cope, Stephen L. ....Los Angeles, CA
Cope, Steven A. ....House of Representatives, Office of Legislative Counsel, GV
Cope, Steven E. ....Portland, ME
Cope, Tara A. ....Chicago, IL
Cope, Thom K. ....Lincoln, NE
Cope, Thomas F. ....Denver, CO
Cope, Timothy A. ....Manassas, VA
Cope, W. Robert ....Poplar Bluff, MO
Cope, Walter B., Jr. ....Indiana, PA
Cope, William D. ....Reno, NV
Cope-Flanagan, John ....Cambridge, MA
Copelan, Dean C. ....Atlanta, GA
Copelan, Dean C. ....Macon, GA
Copelan, Jesse T., Jr. ....Eatonton, GA
Copelan, John J., Jr.
Fort Lauderdale, FL
Copelan, Jos. B. ....Sherman Oaks, CA
Copeland, Amy F. ....Madison, WI
Copeland, Amy Lee ....Savannah, GA
Copeland, Audrey Jacobsen
Philadelphia, PA
Copeland, Barry L. ....Fort Worth, TX
Copeland, Bradley S. ....Eugene, OR
Copeland, Brian Keith ....Gadsden, AL
Copeland & Brown Co., L.P.A.
Cincinnati, OH
Copeland, Bruce A. ....Joplin, MO
Copeland, Bruce E. ....San Francisco, CA
Copeland, Buford L. ....Gadsden, AL
Copeland, Buxton S. ....Raleigh, NC
Copeland, C. Michael ....Tulsa, OK
Copeland, Cary H. ....Dallas, TX
Copeland & Chambliss, P.A.
Fort Lauderdale, FL
Copeland, Charlene C. ....New Lenox, IL
Copeland, Charles G. ....Jackson, MS
Ridgeland, MS
Copeland, Christopher Charles
West Palm Beach, FL
Copeland, Clay A. ....Louisville, KY
Copeland, Clyde Xenophon, III
Jackson, MS
Copeland, Conley & Hazard ......Tullahoma, TN
Copeland Cook Taylor & Bush, A Professional Association ....Jackson, MS
Ridgeland, MS
Copeland & Copeland ....Gadsden, AL
Copeland & Copeland, LLP ......Norristown, PA
Copeland, David A. ....Cincinnati, OH
Copeland, David S. ....New York, NY
Copeland, Donald F. ....Norristown, PA
Copeland, Donald F. Jr ....Norristown, PA
Copeland, Donna M. ....Fort Smith, AR
Copeland, Douglas A. ....St. Louis, MO
Copeland, Edward ....New York, NY
Copeland, Edward J. ....Chicago, IL
Copeland, Edward M., IV ....Tampa, FL
Copeland, Elizabeth A. ....San Antonio, TX
Copeland, Ellyn M. ....Chicago, IL
Copeland, Emily R. ....Raleigh, NC
Copeland, Erin M. ....Los Angeles, CA
Copeland, Eugene L. ....Denver, CO
Copeland, F. Dean ....Chattanooga, TN
Copeland, Franco, Screws & Gill, P.A.
Montgomery, AL
Copeland, Fred W. ....New Madrid, MO
Copeland, Glenn R. ....Chattanooga, TN
Copeland & Haugabrook ....Valdosta, GA
Copeland, Henry C. ....Overland Park, KS
Copeland, Howard E. ....Norfolk, VA
Copeland, Hyman Z. ....Lawton, OK
Copeland, James E.
Palm Beach Gardens, FL
Copeland, James E., P.A.
Palm Beach Gardens, FL
Copeland, James L. ....San Francisco, CA
Copeland, James M. ....Gadsden, AL
Copeland, James W. ....Atlanta, GA
Copeland, James W., Jr. ....Goldsboro, NC
Copeland, Jami I. ....Los Angeles, CA
Copeland, Jefferson Gregory
Houston, TX
Copeland, Johanna E. ....New York, NY
Copeland, John D. ....Springdale, AR
Copeland, John E. ....Myrtle Beach, SC
Copeland, John K. ....Stuart, FL
Copeland, Judith M. ....San Diego, CA
Copeland, Julius A. ....New York, NY
Copeland, Karen ....New York, NY
Copeland, Kenneth Edward
Kankakee, IL
Copeland, Kimberly L., & Associates
Jesup, GA
Copeland, Landye, Bennett and Wolf, LLP
Anchorage, AK
Portland, OR
Vancouver, WA
Copeland, Lee H. ....Montgomery, AL
Copeland, L. G. ....Columbia, MO
Copeland, Lisa Ann ....Birmingham, AL
Copeland, Marian B. ....Princeton, NJ
Copeland, Mark G. ....Anchorage, AK
Copeland, Martha Farmer ....Corbin, KY
Copeland, Mary ....Fort Lauderdale, FL
Copeland, Mary D. ....Oak Ridge, TN
Copeland, Melissa J. ....Columbia, SC
Copeland, Michelle M. ....San Antonio, TX
Copeland, Milton ....Fayetteville, AR
Copeland, Molinary & Bieger, P.C.
Abingdon, VA
Copeland, Morgan L. ....Houston, TX
Copeland, Morgan Lee, Jr. ....Houston, TX
Copeland, Patricia G. ....Palo Alto, CA
Copeland, Paul R., III ....Brunswick, ME
Copeland, Paul W. ....Montgomery, AL
Copeland, Peter A. ....Kalamazoo, MI
Copeland, Peter D. ....Atlanta, GA
Copeland, Ralph C. ....Wellesley, MA
Copeland, Randolph G. ....DeLand, FL
Copeland, Rebecca S. ....Anchorage, AK
Copeland, Reese B. ....Bartlesville, OK
Copeland, Reggie, Jr. ....Mobile, AL
Copeland, Richard B. ....San Antonio, TX
Copeland, Richard Stanfill ....Memphis, TN
Copeland, Richard W.
Altamonte Springs, FL
Copeland, Richard Z. ....Chicago, IL
Copeland, Robert ....San Francisco, CA
Copeland, Robert G. ....San Diego, CA
Copeland, Robert M. ....Detroit, MI
Copeland, Robert T. ....Abingdon, VA
Copeland, Rod W. ....Prophetstown, IL
Copeland, Roy W. ....Valdosta, GA
Copeland, Sally C. ....Greenville, SC
Copeland, Scot B. ....Tallahassee, FL
Copeland & Scott ....Joplin, MO
Copeland, Shawn A. ....Richmond, VA
Copeland, Sheldon I. ....Chicago, IL
Copeland, Stanley D. ....Myrtle Beach, SC
Copeland, Stephen Russell ....Butler, AL
Mobile, AL
Copeland, Steven B. ....Los Angeles, CA
Copeland, Susan G. ....Montgomery, AL
Copeland, Susan Lawton ....Stuart, FL
Copeland, Thomas H. ....Tullahoma, TN
Copeland, Thompson & Farris, P.C.
St. Louis, MO
Copeland & Tierman ....San Diego, CA
Copeland, Tim B. ....Abilene, TX
Copeland, Timothy E., Jr. ... Brattleboro, VT
Copeland, Todd E. ....Orlando, FL
Copeland, Tom L. ....Alachua, FL
Copeland, Trent B. ....Los Angeles, CA
Copeland, Vicki R. ....Carroll, IA
Jefferson, IA
Copeland, Victor G. ....Palatine, IL
Copeland, W. Lloyd ....Mobile, AL
Copeland, Wade K., (P.C.) ....Atlanta, GA
Copeland, Wayne ....Gadsden, AL
Copeland, Weldon S. ....El Paso, TX
Copeland, Weldon S. ....McKinney, TX
Copeland & Whittenburg ... Chattanooga, TN
Copeland, William Bobo ....McMinnville, TN
Copeland, William H. ....St. Louis, MO
Copeland, William J. ....Pittsburgh, PA
Copeland, William M. ....Cincinnati, OH
Copeland, William R. ....El Paso, TX
Copeland, William T. ....Gadsden, AL
Copeland, Wilson A., II ....Detroit, MI
Copeland, Yolanda ....Los Angeles, CA
Copeland-Lopez, Francisca ....Miami, FL
Copeley, Leto ....Raleigh, NC
Copelin, David ....Piggott, AR
Copelin, Staci ....Austin, TX
Copelon, Rhonda ....Flushing, NY
Copeman, Frederick H. ....Boston, MA
Copen, Noel P. ....Charleston, WV
Huntington, WV
Copen, Robert A. ....New York, NY
Copenbarger & Associates ....Santa Ana, CA
Copenbarger, Lloyd G. ....Newport Beach, CA
Copenbarger, Paul D. ....Santa Ana, CA
Copenhagen, Margaret A. Redwood City, CA
Copenhaver, Bradley S.
Fort Lauderdale, FL
Copenhaver, Brent P. ....Morgantown, WV
Copenhaver, Charles L., III ....Boulder, CO
Copenhaver, David B. ....Santa Rosa, CA
Copenhaver, David L. ....New Castle, IN
Copenhaver, Ellett, Cornelison & Derrico
Roanoke, VA
Copenhaver, Harris D., Jr. ......Baton Rouge, LA
Copenhaver, James M. ....Elko, NV
Copenhaver, James M., P.C. ....Elko, NV
Copenhaver, James S. ....Richmond, VA
Copenhaver, John D. ....Roanoke, VA
Copenhaver, John M. ....Bend, OR
Copenhaver, John T., Jr. ....Charleston, WV
Copenhaver, Karen Faulds ....Boston, MA
Copenhaver, Kath and Kitchen, LLC
Powell, WY
Copenhaver, Lisa C. ....Augusta, ME
Copenhaver, Ronald D. ....Laramie, WY
Copenhaver, Steven C. ....Georgetown, TX
Copenhaver, Tracy J., (A Professional Corporation) ....Powell, WY
Copenhaver, W. Andrew ......Washington, DC
Winston-Salem, NC
Copenhaver, William D. ....Bellville, TX
Copenhefer, Lea Anne ....Boston, MA
Copening, Frank L., Jr. ....Columbus, OH
Copernoll, Margaret J. ....Sterling, VA
Copersino, Albert J. ....Westport, CT
Copertino, Alan J. ....Melville, NY
Melville, NY
Tarrytown, NY
Copertino, Anthony P., Jr. ....Bridgeport, CT
Copertino, Carl J. ....Hempstead, NY
Copertino, John ....Stony Brook, NY
Copertino, Mark F. ....Denver, CO
Copes, John F.
Federal Communications Commission, International Bureau, GV

Copes, LaVerne B. ... New York, NY
Copes, Wilson B. ... Toluca Lake, CA
Copetas, Chris G. ... Pittsburgh, PA
Copetas, Stephen A. ... Pittsburgh, PA
Copetas, Theodore C. ... Dayton, OH
Copetas, William P. ... Pittsburgh, PA
Copier, Robert H. ... Salt Lake City, UT
Copilevitz & Canter, P.C. ... Washington, DC
Kansas City, MO
Copilevitz, Errol ... Kansas City, MO
Copilow, Barry Lee ... Los Angeles, CA
Coplan, Dale J. ... Englewood, CO
Coplan, Daniel J. ... Pasadena, CA
Coplan, Gregory F. ... Rockford, IL
Coplan, Jennifer B. ... New York, NY
Coplan, Karl S. ... New York, NY
Coplan, Larry M., (P.C.) ... Washington, DC
Coplan, Norman A. ... New York, NY
Coplan, Patricia W. ... Tyler, TX
Coplan, Robert C. ... Cleveland, OH
Coplan, Robert G. ... Rockford, IL
Coplan, Ronald F. ... Morrison, IL
Copland and Brenner ... Latham, NY
Copland, David A. ... Chicago, IL
Copland, Eric K. ... Latham, NY
Copland, Gloria A. ... Albany, NY
Copland, Gordon H. ... Clarksburg, WV
Copland, Laura ... Tarrytown, NY
Copland, Lisa A. ... Chicago, IL
Copland & Micheau ... Aberdeen, WA
Copland, Richard M. ... Bronx, NY
Copland, Thomas A. ... Aberdeen, WA
Coplans, Gregory M. ... Santa Clara, CA
Cople, William J., III ... Washington, DC
Coplein, Allison P. ... Atlanta, GA
Coplein, Gail E. ... Princeton, NJ
Yardley, PA
Coplein, Gordon D. ... New York, NY
Coplen, Bruce A. ... Houston, TX
Coplen, Joel ... Binford, ND
Coplen, Lisa Marie Le Nay
Los Angeles, CA
Coplen, R. Bruce ... Los Angeles, CA
Coplen, Robert M. ... Tampa, FL
Copley, Alison B., Law Offices of
Sebring, FL
Copley, Alison B., Law Offices of
Wauchula, FL
Copley, Ann G. ... Seattle, WA
Copley, Brandy L. ... Houston, TX
Copley, C. Douglas ... Dayton, OH
Copley, Dawn R. ... Detroit, MI
Copley, Edward A., (P.C.) ... Dallas, TX
Copley, James O. ... Newark, NJ
Copley, Jan ... Pasadena, CA
Copley, Jason A. ... Philadelphia, PA
Copley, John R. ... Washington, DC
Copley, Kara Lee ... Washington, DC
Copley, Michael F. ... Columbus, OH
Copley, Ralph D., Jr. ... Carlsbad, CA
Copley, Rhonda M. ... Elizabethtown, KY
Copley, Rocky K. ... San Diego, CA
Copley, Steven W. ... New Orleans, LA
Copley, T. David ... Seattle, WA
Copley, Wanda Milligan ... Wilmington, NC
Copley, William E., III ... Washington, DC
Coplin, Barry E., (P.A.) ... Little Rock, AR
Coplin, Holly L. ... Corte Madera, CA
Coplin, Mark D. ... Baltimore, MD
Coplin, Susan J. ... McLean, VA
Coplin, William T., Jr. ... Demopolis, AL
Coplit, James G. ... Stamford, CT
Coploff, Anne J. ... New York, NY
Coploff, Larry E. ... Lock Haven, PA
Coploff, Ryan & Welch ... Lock Haven, PA
Coploff, Steven A. ... White Plains, NY
Coplon, Richard K. ... Newark, NJ
Copous, Sandy R. ... Nashville, TN
Copp, Belton A. ... Hartford, CT
Copp & Berall, LLP ... Hartford, CT
Copp, Catherine L. ... Rockville, MD
Copp, Gary T. ... Markham, IL
Copp, Kimberly M. ... Chicago, IL
Copp, Matthew R. ... Columbus, OH
Copp, Maurice D. ... Wichita, KS
Copp, Webster T. ... Mystic, CT
Coppa, Carlo J. ... West Paterson, NJ
Coppa, Francis T. ... Rensselaer, NY
Coppa, Peter J. ... Chicago Heights, IL
Coppage, Charles D. ... Kill Devil Hills, NC
Coppage, James R. ... Darien, GA
Coppage, Jeffrey B. ... Hartford, CT
Coppage, Kenton J. ... Atlanta, GA
Coppage Law Firm, P.A., The
Kill Devil Hills, NC
Coppage, Robert B. ... New Britain, CT
Coppala, Lynne E. ... Charleston, WV
Coppede, John A. ... Cheyenne, WY
Coppedge, Bradley R. ... Columbus, GA
Coppedge, Jack W., II ... Tishomingo, OK
Coppedge, Jim ... Houston, TX
Coppedge, L. Joe ... Las Vegas, NV
Coppedge & Leman, P.C. ... Calhoun, GA
Chatsworth, GA
Dalton, GA
La Fayette, GA
Ringgold, GA
Coppedge, Lewis ... Amarillo, TX
Coppedge, Michael E. ... Crystal Lake, IL
Coppedge, Susan ... Department of Justice,
Environment and Natural Resources
Division, GV
Coppedge, T. Louis ... Birmingham, AL
Coppedge, Warren N., Jr. ... Dalton, GA
Coppedge, William W. ... Raleigh, NC
Coppejans, Elroy A. ... Daphne, AL
Coppel, Lawrence D. ... Baltimore, MD
Coppel, Patricia C. ... Chester, NJ

Coppel, Paul S. ... Columbus, OH
Coppel, William R. ... Flint, MI
Coppel, William R., P.C. ... Flint, MI
Coppeler, John A. ... Port Clinton, OH
Sandusky, OH
Coppelman, Peter D. ... Department of Justice,
Environment and Natural Resources
Division, GV
Coppenrath, Walter G., Jr.
Los Angeles, CA
Copper, Mary E. ... Wilmington, DE
Copperman, Amy E. ... Boston, MA
Copperman, Samuel H. ... Youngstown, OH
Coppersmith Gordon Schermer Owens &
Nelson P.L.C. ... Phoenix, AZ
Coppersmith, Robert ... New York, NY
Coppersmith, Samuel G. ... Phoenix, AZ
Coppersmith, William E.
Treasury Department,
Internal Revenue Service, GV
Copperstone, Jeanine ... Tempe, AZ
Copperthite, Albert D. ... Baltimore, MD
Copperthite, Charlotte Howell
Newark, NJ
Copperthwaite, Nancy A. ... Miami, FL
Coppess, Michael J. ... Pasadena, CA
Coppeto, Barbara A. ... Milford, CT
Coppeto, Scott J. ... Florham Park, NJ
Coppiellie, Raymond Lawrence
Dearborn, MI
Coppin, Christopher D. ... Albuquerque, NM
Coppin, Darrell G. ... Oak Brook, IL
Coppin, Dennis Bowen ... Bayside, NY
Coppin, Michael D. ... Chicago, IL
Coppinger, Carter, Schrempf & Blaine, Ltd.
Alton, IL
Coppinger, David J. ... Waukee, IA
Coppinger, Francis X. ... Boston, MA
Coppinger, John J. ... Oakland, CA
Coppinger, Linda W. ... Hampton, VA
Coppinger, Peter M. ... Boston, MA
Coppinger, Stanley K. ... Austin, TX
Coppins, Cray J., Jr. ... New Orleans, LA
Coppins, Cray J., Jr., Co., L.P.A.
New Orleans, LA
Coppins, Kent G. ... Milwaukee, WI
Coppins, Michael F. ... Tallahassee, FL
Copple, Brandon J. ... Topeka, KS
Copple, Brian W. ... Roswell, NM
Copple, Chamberlin, Boehm & Murphy, P.C.
Phoenix, AZ
Tucson, AZ
Copple, David E. ... Norfolk, NE
Copple, Dwayne E. ... Seattle, WA
Copple, E. Don ... Boise, ID
Copple, George E., Jr. ... Nashville, TN
Copple, Kenneth & Associates, P.C.
Fort Collins, CO
Copple, Kenneth S. ... Fort Collins, CO
Copple, Leonard W., (P.C.) ... Tempe, AZ
Copple, Robert F. ... Scottsdale, AZ
Copple & Rockey P.C. ... Norfolk, NE
Copple, Roger L. ... Albuquerque, NM
Copple, Ryan S. ... West Palm Beach, FL
Copple, S. Christopher ... Phoenix, AZ
Copple, Steven D. ... Phoenix, AZ
Tucson, AZ
Copple, Terry C. ... Boise, ID
Copple, William P. ... Phoenix, AZ
Coppler, Frank R. ... Santa Fe, NM
Coppler, Gerald A. ... Santa Fe, NM
Coppler, Kati ... Santa Fe, NM
Coppler & Mannick, P.C. ... Santa Fe, NM
Coppo, Carlo ... San Diego, CA
Coppock, E. Allen ... Houston, TX
Coppock, Lance A. ... Des Moines, IA
Coppock, Lee A. ... Orlando, FL
Coppock, Mark L. ... Cedar Rapids, IA
Coppock, Michael R. ... Boston, MA
Coppock, Paul C. ... Camp Hill, PA
Coppock, Renee L. ... Billings, MT
Coppock, S. Dawn ... Strawberry Plains, TN
Coppola, Anthony ... Secaucus, NJ
Coppola, Anthony A. ... New York, NY
Coppola, Arthur M. ... Santa Monica, CA
Coppola, Carol L. ... Des Moines, IA
Coppola, Charles A. ... West Des Moines, IA
Coppola, Clifford A. ... Virginia Beach, VA
Coppola, Donald P. ... Buffalo, NY
Coppola, Donna M. ... North Reading, MA
Coppola, Douglas S. ... Buffalo, NY
Coppola, Frank ... Yonkers, NY
Coppola, Frank W. ... Denver, CO
Coppola, Heidi S. ... New York, NY
Coppola, James E., Jr. ... Marblehead, MA
Coppola, Jas. E. ... Marblehead, MA
Coppola, John M. ... Vienna, VA
Coppola, Jos. M. ... Des Moines, IA
Coppola, Joseph A. ... Rahway, NJ
Coppola, Joseph John ... Boston, MA
Coppola, Joseph L. ... Greenwood Village, CO
Coppola, Joseph M. ... New York, NY
Coppola, Joseph T. ... Branford, CT
Coppola, Joseph V. ... Ridgewood, NY
Coppola, Joseph V., Sr.
Bloomfield Hills, MI
Coppola, Leibert F. ... Buffalo, NY
Coppola, Lisa A. ... Buffalo, NY
Coppola, Matthew F. ... White Plains, NY
Coppola, Michael V. ... Kearny, NJ
Coppola, Michelle S. ... New York, NY
Coppola, Robert E. ... Long Beach, CA
Coppola, Sandre & McConville, A Professional
Corporation ... West Des Moines, IA
Coppola, Steven A. ... Mount Olive, NJ
Coppola, Thomas ... New York, NY
Coppola, Thomas A. ... New York, NY
Coppola, Trout & Taha ... West Des Moines, IA

Coppola, William C. ... Newark, NJ
Coppolecchia, Pasquale J. ... White Plains, NY
Coppolino, Anthony J.
Department of Justice, Civil Division, GV
Coppolino, Louis S. ... North Kingstown, RI
Coppolo, Alvin B. ... St. Marys, PA
Coppolo & Coppolo ... St. Marys, PA
Coppolo, Lisa C. ... St. Marys, PA
Coppolo, Thomas G.G. ... St. Marys, PA
Copps, Anne Reynolds ... Albany, NY
Copps, Carl D. ... Albany, NY
Copps, Lonnie J. ... Fort Worth, TX
Copps, Robert E. ... Atlanta, GA
Coppula, Christopher A. ... Pittsburgh, PA
Coprich, Dorothy Webb ... Decatur, GA
Cops, Kevin ... Los Angeles, CA
Copsey, Carol C. ... San Francisco, CA
Copsey, Cheri C. ... Boise, ID
Copulos, Hoffman & Yoshimura
Honolulu, HI
Copulos, William ... Honolulu, HI
Copus, David A. ... Washington, DC
Coquillette, Daniel R. ... Newton, MA
Coquillette, William H. ... Cleveland, OH
Corabi & Corabi ... Steubenville, OH
Corabi, Joseph M. ... Steubenville, OH
Corabi, Mary F. ... Steubenville, OH
Coral Ortenberg Zeck & Codispoti, P.C.
Waldwick, NJ
Suffern, NY
Coral Reef Law Offs., P.A. ... Miami, FL
Corallo, Gerald A., Jr. ... Garden City, NY
Corallo, Karen C. ... Dallas, TX
Corallo, Laurie Ann ... Jericho, NY
Coran, Kimberly Dean ... Simsbury, CT
Coran, Michael K. ... Philadelphia, PA
Coran, Paul M. ... Department of State,
Office of the Secretary, GV
Coran, Stephen E. ... Washington, DC
Cora-Ramsey, Elvira ... Bayamon, PR
Corasanti, Joseph J. ... Utica, NY
Corash, Michèle B. ... Los Angeles, CA
San Francisco, CA
Corash, Richard ... Staten Island, NY
Corash, Robert A. ... Northampton, MA
Corash & Zurn, LLP ... Amherst, MA
Northampton, MA
Coravos, Martha A. ... Boston, MA
Coravos, Pamela ... Boston, MA
Coraz, Gerald A. ... Indianapolis, IN
Corazzelli, Frank G. ... New York, NY
Corazzin, Janette W. ... Topeka, KS
Corazzini, Robert F. ... Washington, DC
Corba, Alice T. K. ... Berwick, PA
Corbacio, Vincent G. ... Syracuse, NY
Corbalis, Fred F., III ... Redondo Beach, CA
Corbally, Gartland and Rappleyea, LLP
Clearwater, FL
Millbrook, NY
Poughkeepsie, NY
Rhinebeck, NY
Corbally, Richard V. ... Poughkeepsie, NY
Corban & Corban ... Fayette, MS
Corban, David Wilks ... Houston, TX
Corban & Gunn ... Biloxi, MS
Gulfport, MS
Jackson, MS
Ocean Springs, MS
Pascagoula, MS
Corban, Harry L. ... Fayette, MS
Corban, Lawrence C., Jr. ... Biloxi, MS
Corban, Stephen M. ... Tupelo, MS
Corban, William V. ... Pataskala, OH
Corbat, Sara S. ... Fort Wayne, IN
Corbe, Bernard M. ... Honolulu, HI
Corbeil, Lynn Marie ... Omaha, NE
Corbeil, Stephen R. ... Manchester, CT
Corbell, Brian J. ... Santa Monica, CA
Corbell, Gretchen W. ... Los Angeles, CA
Corbell, Martin J. ... Vandalia, IL
Corbelli, James J. ... San Francisco, CA
Corbelli, James V. ... Pittsburgh, PA
Corbelli, Linda C.
Supreme Court Of The United States, GV
Corbello, Brenda F. ... Houston, TX
Corber, Billy G. ... Los Angeles, CA
Corber, Brian Lee ... Panorama City, CA
Corber, Robert J. ... Washington, DC
Corbera, Michael J. ... San Francisco, CA
Corbert, Richard A. ... Springfield, MA
Corbet, Daniel R. ... Detroit, MI
Corbet, James L. ... Wickenburg, AZ
Corbet, Jennifer A. ... New York, NY
Corbet, Leo F., Jr. ... Phoenix, AZ
Corbett, Albert A., Jr. ... Smithfield, NC
Corbett, Alfred H. ... Bend, OR
Corbett, Amy Lind ... Burlington, MA
Corbett, Anderson, Corbett, Poulson, Flom
& Vellinga ... Sioux City, IA
South Sioux City, NE
Dakota Dunes, SD
Corbett, Anthony S. ... Austin, TX
Corbett, Bernard R. ... McHenry, MD
Alexandria, VA
Corbett, Bradley P. ... Stevens Point, WI
Corbett, Brian T. ... Radnor, PA
Corbett & Brinks ... Stuart, VA
Corbett, Bruce R. ... Irvine, CA
Corbett, Bryan ... Washington, DC
Corbett, C. Anthony ... Raleigh, NC
Corbett, Cecelia L. ... Sioux City, IA
Corbett, Charles L. ... Sioux City, IA
Corbett, Christopher A. ... Stuart, VA
Corbett, Christopher J. ... New York, NY
Corbett, Conrad M., Law Offices of
San Francisco, CA
Corbett, Craig ... Orlando, FL

Corbett Crockett & Leckrone
Nashville, TN
Corbett, Daniel K. ... Juno Beach, FL
Corbett, David J. ... Palatine, IL
Corbett, Denis J. ... Toms River, NJ
Corbett, Dennis P. ... Washington, DC
Corbett, Diane K. ... Chicago, IL
Corbett, Donald A. ... New York, NY
Corbett, Donald J., Jr. ... Rochester, NY
Corbett, Donald S. ... Somers, NY
Corbett, Dorothy K. ... Cincinnati, OH
Corbett, Duncan ... Richmond, TX
Corbett, Edward H. ... Akron, OH
Corbett, Ellen M. ... San Leandro, CA
Corbett & Fisler ... Burgaw, NC
Corbett, Francis E. ... Pittsburgh, PA
Corbett, Gail M. ... Springfield, MA
Corbett, George K. ... Hays, KS
Corbett, Glenn F. ... Newark, NJ
Corbett Gordon & Associates, P.C.
Portland, OR
Corbett, Grafton J., III ... Boston, MA
Corbett, Haultain E. ... Sheridan, WY
Corbett, Hugh Timothy ... Waterville, ME
Corbett, James E. ... Springfield, MO
Corbett, James J. ... Concord, OH
Corbett, James J. ... Columbia, SC
Corbett, James M. ... Edison, NJ
Corbett, James M. ... Houston, TX
Corbett, James R. ... Newport News, VA
Corbett, James S. ... Westwood, MA
Corbett, J. J. ... Tinley Park, IL
Corbett, John ... West Palm Beach, FL
Corbett, John E. ... Atco, NJ
Corbett, John F. ... Watertown, MA
Corbett, John H., Jr. ... Pittsburgh, PA
Corbett, John J. ... Chicago, IL
Corbett, John J., Jr. ... Washington, DC
Corbett, John J., (Ltd.)
New Port Richey, FL
Corbett, John K. ... Revere, MA
Corbett, Julia Ketcham ... Mankato, MN
Corbett, Karen ... New York, NY
Corbett, Kathleen A.
Saratoga Springs, NY
Corbett, Kelly M. ... Boston, MA
Corbett, Kenneth C. ... St. Paul, MN
Corbett, Kenneth S. ... Myrtle Beach, SC
Corbett, Kenneth S., P.A.
Myrtle Beach, SC
Corbett, Kevin A. ... Los Angeles, CA
Corbett, Kevin M. ... San Francisco, CA
Corbett, Kevin M. ... San Francisco, CA
Corbett, Kevin Michael ... San Leandro, CA
Corbett, Krystilyn ... Palo Alto, CA
Corbett & Larson ... Springfield, MO
Corbett, Laurence P. ... Oakland, CA
Corbett, Lawrence E., Jr. ... Glens Falls, NY
Corbett, Leon H. ... Burgaw, NC
Corbett, Leon H., Jr. ... Winston-Salem, NC
Corbett, Lisa Granberry ... Goldsboro, NC
Corbett, Luke R. ... San Diego, CA
Corbett, Margarita Manzano
Laguna Vista, TX
Corbett, Mary ... Topeka, KS
Corbett, Mary E. ... Boston, MA
Corbett and Mathews ... Chicago, IL
Corbett, Michael L. ... New Rochelle, NY
Corbett, Mitchell B. ... Medford, MA
Corbett, Nancy Hamilton ... Brandon, FL
Corbett, Nancy Hasley ... New York, NY
Corbett, Patricia ... Scranton, PA
Corbett, Patricia M. ... Philadelphia, PA
Corbett, Patrick J. ... New York, NY
Corbett, Peter D. ... Boston, MA
Corbett, Peter G. ... Dallas, TX
Corbett Professional Corporation
San Leandro, CA
Corbett, Richard T. ... Boston, MA
Corbett, Robert H. ... Burgaw, NC
Corbett, Robert V. ... New York, NY
Corbett, Robt. G. ... Arlington Heights, IL
Corbett, Robt. M. ... Topeka, KS
Corbett, Roger ... Berkeley, CA
Corbett, Rose M. ... New York, NY
Corbett, Scott R. ... Orlando, FL
Corbett, Sherrill A. ... Portland, OR
Corbett, Stanley M. ... Sioux City, IA
Corbett & Steelman, A Professional Law
Corporation ... Irvine, CA
Corbett, Sue ... Oklahoma City, OK
Corbett, Terry L. ... Phoenix, AZ
Corbett, Thomas R. ... St. Louis, MO
Corbett, Thomas W., Jr. ... Pittsburgh, PA
Corbett, Timothy J. ... Boston, MA
Corbett, Victor M. ... Chico, CA
Corbett, W. Jason ... Summerton, SC
Corbett, W. Jason, P.A. ... Summerton, SC
Corbett, W. Lee, (P.C.) ... Nashville, TN
Corbett, William D. ... San Leandro, CA
Corbett, William J. ... Las Cruces, NM
Corbett, William J. ... Floral Park, NY
Corbett, William L. ... United States Senate,
Senatorial Assistants, GV
Corbett, William P., Jr. ... Boston, MA
Corbett, William T. ... Boston, MA
Corbett, William T., Jr.
Florham Park, NJ
Corbett, William T., Jr. ... Greensboro, NC
Corbett, William V. ... Louisville, KY
Corbetta, Richard L. ... Denver, CO
Corbett-Rivielle, Michelle M.
Los Angeles, CA
Corbin, Amber A. ... Pittsboro, NC
Corbin, Arthur L. ... Department of Commerce,
Patent and Trademark Office, GV
Corbin, Barbara F. ... Kansas City, MO
Corbin, Camille A. ... Cleveland, OH

Corbin, Catherine Mary ....New York, NY
Corbin, Charles T. ....Mansfield, TX
Corbin, Christopher L. ....Summerville, GA
Corbin, Daniel Austin ....Killeen, TX
Corbin, David Gregory ....Avon, CO
Corbin, Diana C. ....Boston, MA
Corbin, Donald K. ....Fort Lauderdale, FL
Corbin, Donald L. ....Little Rock, AR
Corbin, Dorcy Kyle ....Little Rock, AR
Corbin, Douglas T. ....Richmond, CA
Corbin & Duvall ....Jacksonville, FL
Corbin, Elwood M. ....Marlton, NJ
Corbin & Fitzgerald, LLP
Los Angeles, CA
Corbin, Fred E. ....San Diego, CA
Corbin, Gary M. ....Romeo, MI
Corbin, Gregory J. ....Dayton, OH
Corbin, Harold K. ....Atlanta, GA
Corbin, J. Dennis ....Miles City, MT
Corbin, Jerry W., P.C. ....Denver City, TX
Corbin, Karen A. ....Santa Barbara, CA
Corbin, Kathleen W. ....San Diego, CA
Corbin, Kathy J. ....Downers Grove, IL
Corbin, Keith S. ....Schiller Park, IL
Corbin, Laura J. ....Ada, OK
Tishomingo, OK
Corbin, Lee Harrison ....White Plains, NY
Corbin, Lorrie A. ....Oklahoma City, OK
Corbin, Louis C. ....Jacksonville, FL
Corbin, Michael A. ....Dalton, GA
Corbin, Norman L. ....Orlando, FL
Corbin, Peter Reed ....Jacksonville, FL
Corbin, Robert A. ....Georgetown, OH
Corbin, Robert D. ....Calabash, NC
Corbin, Robert H. ....North Brunswick, NJ
Corbin, Robert K. ....Phoenix, AZ
Corbin, Robert L. ....Los Angeles, CA
Corbin, Robert M. ....Crown Point, IN
Corbin, Robert P. ....Philadelphia, PA
Corbin, Schaffer & Aviles, Chartered
Annapolis, MD
Severna Park, MD
Corbin Silverman & Sanseverino LLP
New York, NY
Corbin, Sol Neil ....New York, NY
Corbin, Suzanne L. ....New York, NY
Corbin, Teresa M. ....Menlo Park, CA
Corbin, Thomas J., and Associates
Lancaster, OH
Corbin, Valinda Spaulding ....Cambridge, MA
Corbin, William E., Jr. ....Chicago, IL
Corbin, William L. ....Severna Park, MD
Corbishley, Deborah Sampieri ......Miami, FL
Corbit, Frederick P. ....Seattle, WA
Corbitt, Aubria D. ....Washington, DC
Corbitt, Christy L. ....Marianna, FL
Corbitt, Craig C. ....San Francisco, CA
Corbitt, David E. ....Chicago, IL
Corbitt, Earl A. ....Austin, TX
Corbitt, Jack ....Ozark, AL
Corbitt, Jack, P.C. ....Ozark, AL
Corbitt, James W., Jr. ....Treasury Department,
Internal Revenue Service, GV
Corbitt & Johnson, P.C. ....Tulsa, OK
Corbitt, Marlin H. ....El Cajon, CA
Corbitt, R. Steven ....Orinda, CA
Corbitt, Richard J. ....Dallas, TX
Corbitt, Scott M. ....Missoula, MT
Corbitt, Sharon L. ....Tulsa, OK
Corbley, John J. ....Baltimore, MD
Corbley, Wm. H. ....Orlando, FL
Corbly, Mark T. ....Windsor, CT
Corbman, Scott K. ....Philadelphia, PA
Corbo, Cara M. ....Jersey City, NJ
Millburn, NJ
Corbo, Cristina A. ....Dallas, TX
Corbo, Dana ....Las Vegas, NV
Corbo, Ellen Nunno ....Newark, NJ
Corbo, Gregg J. ....Boston, MA
Corbo, Joseph A., Jr. ....Las Vegas, NV
Corbo, Paschal A. ....Staten Island, NY
Corbo, Richard Joseph, Jr. ....Sacramento, CA
Corbo, Todd A. ....St. Paul, MN
Corbo, Victor ....New York, NY
Corbosie, Edward L. ....Natick, MA
Corbosiero, Edward L. ....Natick, MA
Corboy, Allison L. ....Cherry Hill, NJ
Jenkintown, PA
Corboy & Demetrio, P.C. ....Chicago, IL
Corboy, John G. ....Leesburg, VA
Corboy, Philip H. ....Chicago, IL
Corboy, Philip Harnett, Jr. ....Chicago, IL
Corbridge, Baird & Christensen
Salt Lake City, UT
Corbridge, Clark ....Pinedale, WY
Corbridge, James N., Jr. ....Boulder, CO
Corbridge, John ....Englewood, CO
Corbridge, Lawrence E.
Salt Lake City, UT
Corbridge, Richard M. ....Tulsa, OK
Corbusier, William H., III ....Fort Worth, TX
Corby, Francis M. ....Chicago, IL
Corby, Karen L. ....San Antonio, TX
Corbyn, George S., Jr.
Oklahoma City, OK
Corbyn & Hampton, A Professional Corporation ....Oklahoma City, OK
Corcelius, A. Lynn ....Huntingdon, PA
Corces, Charles, Jr. ....Tampa, FL
Corces, Joan Elizabeth ....Tampa, FL
Corchia, Vanessa M. ....New York, NY
Corchin, Mark A. ....Valley Forge, PA
Corchin & Rosato, P.C. ....Valley Forge, PA
Corchine, Robert A. ....Albuquerque, NM
Corchnoy, Jonathan S. ....Philadelphia, PA
Corcino, Melissa A. ....Altoona, PA
Corcoran, Alayne R. ....Metairie, LA
Corcoran, Andrea M.
Securities and Exchange Commission,
Office of International Affairs, GV
Corcoran, Andrew P., Jr. ....Norfolk, VA
Corcoran, Ann Pfeiffer ....Tampa, FL
Corcoran, Anne L. ....Baker City, OR
Corcoran & Brady, P.C.
Hastings-On-Hudson, NY
Corcoran, Brian H. ....Washington, DC
Corcoran, Bryan C. ....Centerville, OH
Corcoran, C. Timothy, III ....Tampa, FL
Corcoran, Carole ....New York, NY
Corcoran, Charles F., III ......New Haven, CT
Corcoran, Christopher H. ....Rochester, NY
Corcoran, Claire M. ....Los Osos, CA
San Luis Obispo, CA
Corcoran, Collene K.
Bingham Farms, MI
Corcoran & Corcoran, Professional Corporation
Chicago, IL
Evanston, IL
Corcoran, Cynthia A. ....Houston, TX
Corcoran, Dan'l R. ....Chagrin Falls, OH
Corcoran, Deborah Louise
Fort Lauderdale, FL
Corcoran, Donna R. ....Boston, MA
Corcoran, Edmund C., Jr. ....Whitman, MA
Corcoran, Edward A. ....Madison, WI
Corcoran, Edward B. ....Newport, RI
Corcoran, Elizabeth Ann ....Columbus, OH
Corcoran, Finigan & Hennessy, LLP
Boston, MA
Corcoran, George J. ....Stone Mountain, GA
Corcoran, George W. ....Kansas City, KS
Corcoran, Gerald J. ....Atlantic City, NJ
Pleasantville, NJ
Corcoran, Helen M. ....New York, NY
Corcoran, Howard F.
Environmental Protection Agency,
Office of the General Counsel, GV
Corcoran, Irene M. ....Los Angeles, CA
Corcoran, J. Walter ....New York, NY
Corcoran, James F. ....New York, NY
Corcoran, James I. W. ....Cleveland, OH
Corcoran, James M., Jr. ....Chicago, IL
Evanston, IL
Corcoran, James P. ....New York, NY
Corcoran, Jane D. ....Sebring, OH
Corcoran, Janet C. ....New York, NY
Corcoran, Janet L. ....Madison, WI
Corcoran, Jennifer J. ....Albany, NY
Corcoran, Joan M. ....Washington, DC
Corcoran, John C. ....San Francisco, CA
Corcoran, John F. ....Tucson, AZ
Corcoran, John F. ....Syracuse, NY
Corcoran, John F. ....Roanoke, VA
Corcoran, John J. ....Lakewood, NJ
Corcoran, John M. ....Philadelphia, PA
Corcoran, John P., Jr. ....Tampa, FL
Corcoran, John P., Jr ....Pittsburgh, PA
Corcoran, John R.
Department Of Health And Human Services,
Social Security Administration, GV
Corcoran, Joseph P., III ....Philadelphia, PA
Corcoran, Justin O. ....Albany, NY
Corcoran, Karen A. ....New York, NY
Corcoran, Karen C. ....Boston, MA
Corcoran, Karla W. ....Bowie, MD
Corcoran, Kathleen ....Iowa City, IA
Corcoran, Kevin ....Cleveland, OH
Corcoran, Kevin A. ....Treasury Department,
Office of Thrift Supervision, GV
Corcoran, Kieran M. ....New York, NY
Corcoran, Kimberly ....Santa Rosa, CA
Corcoran, Larry M. ....Department of Justice,
Environment and Natural Resources
Division, GV
Corcoran, Lawrence E. ....Arlington, MA
Corcoran, Loretta C. ....East Northport, NY
Corcoran, Lucy I. ....Bensalem, PA
Corcoran, Margaret M. ....Buffalo, NY
Corcoran, Matthew E.
House of Representatives,
Congressional Assistants, GV
Corcoran, Maureen A. ....Millersburg, OH
Corcoran, Maureen E. ......San Francisco, CA
Corcoran, Maurice W. ....Wichita, KS
Corcoran, Melanie S. ....Cleveland, OH
Corcoran, Michael Charles
Philadelphia, PA
Corcoran, Michael J. ....Charlevoix, MI
Corcoran, Michael M. ....Waukesha, WI
Corcoran, Michael M., S.C., Law Offices of
Waukesha, WI
Corcoran, Michael P. ....Traverse City, MI
Corcoran, Michael P. ....Phillipsburg, NJ
Corcoran, Patrick J. ....New Haven, CT
Corcoran, Paul F. ....New York, NY
Corcoran, Peckham & Hayes, P.C.
Newport, RI
Corcoran, Peter ....Indianapolis, IN
Corcoran, Peter J. ....Washington, DC
Corcoran, R. Brian ....Washington, DC
Corcoran, Richard D. ....Kensington, MD
Corcoran, Richard J. ....Mankato, MN
Corcoran, Richard J. ....Sioux Falls, SD
Corcoran, Robert E. ....Springfield, NJ
Corcoran, Robert J. ....Phoenix, AZ
Corcoran, Robert J.
Department of Commerce,
Patent and Trademark Office, GV
Corcoran, Robert P. ....Boston, MA
Corcoran, Robert T. ....Hackensack, NJ
Corcoran, Robert T., P.C.
Hackensack, NJ
Corcoran, Robert W. ....Oyster Bay, NY
Corcoran, Sean J. ....Waltham, MA
Corcoran, Sean P. ....Bloomfield Hills, MI
Corcoran, Sheila M. ....Evansville, IN
Corcoran, Stephen J. ....Haverhill, MA
Corcoran, Susan C. ....White Plains, NY
Corcoran, Susan M. ....White Plains, NY
Corcoran, T. Jeffrey ....Cincinnati, OH
Corcoran, T. Stephen ....Los Angeles, CA
Corcoran, Thomas Frank ....Baltimore, MD
Corcoran, Thomas G., Jr.
Washington, DC
Corcoran, Thomas J. ....Londonderry, NH
Corcoran, Thomas J., Jr. ....Irving, TX
Corcoran, Timothy J. ....Redlands, CA
Corcoran, Timothy J. ....Riverside, CA
San Bernardino, CA
Corcoran, Timothy M. ....Boston, MA
Corcoran, Timothy Patrick ....Lincoln, MA
Corcoran, Victor F. ....Rochester, NY
Corcoran, Walter J. ....Waltham, MA
Corcoran, William E. ....McAllen, TX
Corcoran, William J. ....Department of Justice,
Criminal Division, GV
Corcoran, William J. ....Chicago, IL
Corcoran, William J. ....Boston, MA
Corcoran, William J. ....Newport, RI
Corcoran, William W. ....Durham, NH
Corcoran, William W. ....Newport, RI
Corcos, Christine ....Baton Rouge, LA
Corcovelos & Forry ....Manhattan Beach, CA
Corcovelos, Thomas C.
Manhattan Beach, CA
Cord, C. Michael ....Kokomo, IN
Cord, Edward Joseph ......Colorado Springs, CO
Cord, G. Mark ....Scottsdale, AZ
Cord, Janet I. ....New York, NY
Cord, Kathleen ....Indianapolis, IN
Cord & Shoush ....Scottsdale, AZ
Corda, Cathy ....Clearwater, FL
Corda, William J. ....Lakeland, FL
Cordano, James J. ....Sacramento, CA
Cordano, Kathleena J. ....Los Angeles, CA
Cordara, Carl ....Woodlawn, MD
Cordaro, Linda R. ....Connellsville, PA
Cordaro, Robert C. ....Dunmore, PA
Cordaro, Stephen G. ....New York, NY
Cordaro, Thomas J. ....Pittsburgh, PA
Cordas, Cynthia A. ....Phoenix, AZ
Corday, Amy B. ....Chicago, IL
Corday, Chrissa N. ....San Diego, CA
Corday & Hartney ....San Diego, CA
Corday, Jacquelyn M. ....Florence, MT
Corday, Lane Allan ....Chicago, IL
Corddry, Charles W., III ....Houston, TX
Corde, Daniel S. ....New York, NY
Corde, Lorraine K. ....Napoleonville, LA
Corde, Richard G. ....White Plains, NY
Cordeiro, Anthony J. ....Warwick, RI
Cordeiro, Leonard M. ....East Providence, RI
Cordell, Brent M. ....Houston, TX
Cordell & Cordell, P.C. ....St. Louis, MO
Cordell, David O. ....Tulsa, OK
Cordell, David R. ....Tulsa, OK
Cordell, Dolores ....Los Angeles, CA
Oakland, CA
San Francisco, CA
Cordell, Don J. J. ....Wellesley, MA
Cordell, F. Thomas, Jr. ....Chickasha, OK
Oklahoma City, OK
Cordell, Franklin D. ....Seattle, WA
Cordell, H. William, Jr. ....Englewood, CO
Cordell, Helen S. ....Argonne, IL
Cordell, Jenny R. ....Austin, TX
Cordell, Joseph B. ....Martinsburg, WV
Cordell, Joseph E. ....St. Louis, MO
Cordell, Julius S. ....Lauderdale Lakes, FL
Cordell, LaDoris H. ....San Jose, CA
Cordell, Leslie A. ....New Orleans, LA
Cordell, Martin D. ....Olympia, WA
Cordell, Martin L. ....Orlando, FL
Cordell, Robert L., II ....New York, NY
Cordell, Ruffin B. ....Washington, DC
Cordell, S. Gay ....Wenatchee, WA
Cordell, S. Gay, P.S. ....Wenatchee, WA
Cordell, Sherie Y. ....Raleigh, NC
Cordell, Stephen L. ....Charlotte, NC
Cordell, Stuart W. ....Ashtabula, OH
Cordell, Thomas Drury ....Houston, TX
Corden, James T. ....Port Huron, MI
Corden, Nicholas D.
Farmington Hills, MI
Corder, Floyd D. ....Great Falls, MT
Corder, James M., Jr. ....Athens, AL
Corder, M. Brice ....Titusville, FL
Corder, Mark A. ....Olathe, KS
Corderman, John P. ....Koror, TT
Cordero, Ana Diaz ....Miami, FL
Cordero, C. Darryl ....Los Angeles, CA
Cordero, Charles A. ....San Juan, PR
Cordero, David ....Woodcliff Lake, NJ
Cordero, Ernest, Jr. ....San Diego, CA
Cordero, Jeannine M. ....Chicago, IL
Cordero, L. Frank ....Miami, FL
Cordero, Luis A. ....Miami, FL
Cordero, Mario ....Encino, CA
Cordero, Mark A. ....Miami Lakes, FL
Cordero, Mark A., P.A. ....Miami Lakes, FL
Cordero, Michael J. ....San Francisco, CA
Cordero, Patrick H. ....Midland, TX
Cordero, Patrick L. ....Miami, FL
Cordero, Yesef Yair ....San Juan, PR
Cordero-Acabá, Brenda L. ....San Juan, PR
Cordero-Osorio, Santiago ....San Juan, PR
Cordery, Angela E. ....Louisville, KY
Cordery, F.W., P.C. ....Montgomery, AL
Cordery, Franklin W. ....Montgomery, AL
Cordery, Suzanne D. ....Louisville, KY
Cordery, Theodore T. ....San Francisco, CA
Cordes, Alexander C. ....Buffalo, NY
Cordes Brandt, PLLC ....Olympia, WA
Cordes, Chris ....Greenville, NC
Cordes, Christen B. ....Kansas City, MO
Cordes, Christine M. ....Olympia, WA
Cordes, Clifford F., III ....Olympia, WA
Cordes, David C. ....Charlotte, NC
Cordes, Diane Mcdonnell ......Sunset Beach, CA
Cordes, Donald L. ....Wichita, KS
Cordes, Elizabeth S. ....New Orleans, LA
Cordes, Gary W. ....De Kalb, IL
Cordes & Hess ....Meade, KS
Cordes, Jack R., Jr. ....Department of Justice,
Federal Bureau of Investigation, GV
Cordes, James H. ....Santa Barbara, CA
Cordes, John F., Jr.
Nuclear Regulatory Commission,
Office of the General Counsel, GV
Cordes & King, L.L.P. ....New Hope, PA
Newtown, PA
Cordes, Mark A. ....St. Louis, MO
Cordes, Michael G. ....New Orleans, LA
Cordes, Paul D., Jr. ....New Orleans, LA
Cordes, Richard J. ....Redondo Beach, CA
Cordes, Roy L., Jr. ....Sugar Land, TX
Cordes, Samuel J. ....Pittsburgh, PA
Cordes, Scott R. ....Dallas, TX
Cordes, Stacy C. ....Charlotte, NC
Cordes, Steven W. ....St. Petersburg, FL
Cordes, Terry E. ....Meade, KS
Cordes, Wayne N. ....Newtown, PA
Cordes, William H. ....Cincinnati, OH
Cordi, C. Joseph, Jr. ....Little Rock, AR
Cordi, James M. ....Los Angeles, CA
Cordi, Stephen M. ....Annapolis, MD
Cordiano, Dean M. ....Hartford, CT
Cordi-Bejarano, Elizabeth ....Auburn, WA
Cordier, Danielle C. ....Margaretville, NY
Cordier, Marianne C. ....Rockville, MD
Cordier, Michael A. ....Phoenix, AZ
Cordileone, Joe B. ....San Diego, CA
Billings, MT
Cordill, Joe B., Jr. ....Shreveport, LA
Cordill, Stephen R. ....Chicago, IL
Cording, Colleen Creevy ....Putnam, CT
Cording, David E. ....Hebron, NE
Cordingley, Bruce A. ....Indianapolis, IN
Cordingly, David W. ....Gig Harbor, WA
Cordis, Kerry R. ....Princeville, IL
Cordis, Kerry R., Ltd. ....Princeville, IL
Cordisco, John F. ....Bristol, PA
Cordisco, Kari Lepori ....Reno, NV
Cordish and Cordish ....Baltimore, MD
Cordish, David S. ....Baltimore, MD
Cordish, Melissa F. ....Baltimore, MD
Cordish, Paul L. ....Baltimore, MD
Cordish, Stuart J. ....Baltimore, MD
Cordle, Robert B. ....Charlotte, NC
Cordner, Andrew J. ....Boston, MA
Cordner, Terence A., Jr. ....Tarrytown, NY
Cordo, Jane B. ....Lakehurst, NJ
Cordo and Murphy ....Lakehurst, NJ
Toms River, NJ
Cordon, Bruce W. ....Portland, OR
Cordon, Michael ....Walnut Creek, CA
Cordone, James A. ....Stamford, CT
Cordone, Laura ....White Plains, NY
Cordone, Michael J. ....Philadelphia, PA
Cordonnier, Justin C. ....St. Louis, MO
Cordonnier, Michael J. ....Springfield, MO
Cordova, Adolfo E. ....San Benito, TX
Cordova, Albert E. ....San Rafael, CA
Cordova, Albert E., A P.L.C.
San Rafael, CA
Cordova, Carlos A. ....Perrysburg, OH
Cordova, Cindy J. ....Santa Fe, NM
Cordova, Donald E. ....Denver, CO
Cordova, Douglas Paul ....Albuquerque, NM
Cordova, Gloria Dale ....Diamond Bar, CA
Cordova, Holly Traube ....San Diego, CA
Cordova, Irma P. ....Santa Rosa, CA
Córdova, Janet Wilson ....Santa Fe, NM
Córdova, Jorge L., Jr. ....San Juan, PR
Cordova, Marion T.
Department of Agriculture,
Office of the General Counsel, GV
Cordova, Michelle L. ....Canton, OH
Cordova, Pete ....Salida, CO
Cordova, Pete, P.C., Law Office of
Salida, CO
Cordova, Ralph, Jr. ....El Centro, CA
Cordova, Raul F. ......Department of Commerce,
Patent and Trademark Office, GV
Cordova & Reiser ....Diamond Bar, CA
Cordova, Ricardo ....Modesto, CA
Cordova, Ron ....Newport Beach, CA
Cordova-Lopez, Eunice ....Chicago, IL
Cordovani, Stephen V. ....Tonawanda, NY
Cordovano, Peter Mariano ....Marlboro, NY
Cordova Pelegrina, Pedro J.
San Juan, PR
Cordova Velez, Carlos J. ....San German, PR
Cordover, Sara K. ....Brooklyn, NY
Cordoza, Christina G. ......San Francisco, CA
Cordray & Goodrich, Professional Corporation ....Houston, TX
Cordray, Howard F., Jr. ....Houston, TX
Cordray, Margaret Meriwether
Columbus, OH
Cordray, Monique L.
Thousand Oaks, CA
Cordrey & Clark, P.A. ....Georgetown, DE
Cordrey, David M. ....Beverly Hills, CA
Cordrey, Gregory S. ....Los Angeles, CA
Cordrey, John H. ....Georgetown, DE
Cordrey, Matthew M. ....New York, NY
Cords, Manuel ....Colebrook, CT
Cordts, April L. ....Bethlehem, PA
Cordts, Arthur ....Massapequa Park, NY
Cordts, Colleen Cordts ....Conroe, TX

Cordts, Julianne ... Lombard, IL
Cordua, Jennifer L. ... Stockton, CA
Cordutsky, Joan L. ... Denver, CO
Cordy, Gary M. ... Salem, OR
Cordy, Robert J. ... Boston, MA
Core, Anthony E. ... Bellefontaine, OH
Core, Ben ... Fort Smith, AR
Core, Daniel H., Jr. ... Duluth, MN
Core, David A. ... West Palm Beach, FL
Core, David L. ... Elkins, WV
Core, Eric M. ... Bethesda, MD
Core, M. Allen ... Tulsa, OK
Core, Philip K. ... Pittsburgh, PA
Core, R. Sue ... Elkins, WV
Core, Suzanne Doty ... Brighton, CO
Corea, Thomas M. ... Phoenix, AZ
Coreil, C. Brent ... Ville Platte, LA
Coreil, C. Brent, Ltd. ... Ville Platte, LA
Coreil, Joseph E. ... Ville Platte, LA
Corelli, Julia D. ... Philadelphia, PA
Corello, Sara A. ... New York, NY
Coren, A. M. ... Denver, CO
Coren, Arthur A. ... Los Angeles, CA
Coren, Kenneth A. ... Mill Valley, CA
Coren, Lewis ... Philadelphia, PA
Coren, Meyer H. ... Omaha, NE
Coren, Michael ... Cherry Hill, NJ
Philadelphia, PA
Coren, Paul H. ... San Jose, CA
Coren, Richard A. ... Aventura, FL
Coren, Steven M. ... Philadelphia, PA
Corenblum, Caryn L. ... Birmingham, AL
Corenblum, Steven B. ... Birmingham, AL
Corenevsky, Angela C. ... Raleigh, NC
Corenswet, Ellen B. ... New York, NY
Corenswet, Jay, (P.C.) ... New Orleans, LA
Corenthal, Norman T. ... Jamaica, NY
Corenthal, Richard S. ... Mineola, NY
Corenthal, Seymour F. ... New York, NY
Coreson, Latricia K. ... Portland, OR
Corette, John E., III ... Washington, DC
Corette Pohlman & Kebe, A Professional Corporation ... Butte, MT
Dillon, MT
Corette, R. D. ... Butte, MT
Corey, Alfred E. ... Meridian, MS
Corey, Angela B. ... Jacksonville, FL
Corey, Arthur R. ... Clinton Township, MI
Corey, Barry M. ... Tucson, AZ
Corey, Benjamin W. ... Cambridge, MA
Corey, Brian F. ... St. Paul, MN
Corey, Brian R. ... Fall River, MA
Corey, Byler, Rew, Lorenzen & Hojem, L.L.P. ... Baker City, OR
La Grande, OR
Pendleton, OR
Corey, Carl W. ... West Roxbury, MA
Corey, Carol S. ... Fresno, CA
Corey & Carolan, P.C. ... Royal Oak, MI
Corey, Cecilia M. ... Broomall, PA
Corey, Dana R. ... Calabasas, CA
Corey, Daniel A. ... Atlantic City, NJ
Corey, Edgar ... New Orleans, LA
Corey, Edward E. ... Los Angeles, CA
Corey, Edward J., Jr. ... Sacramento, CA
Corey, Elaine ... Denver, CO
Corey, Elizabeth H. ... Treasury Department, Office of the Comptroller of the Currency, GV
Corey, Elizabeth L. ... Chicago, IL
Corey, Ethan D. ... Washington, DC
Corey, Farrell, Kime & Bromiel, P.C.
Tucson, AZ
Corey, Fred M., (P.A.) ... St. Augustine, FL
Corey, George C. ... Gardner, MA
Corey, George D. ... Newton, MA
Corey, George H. ... Pendleton, OR
Corey, George N. ... Columbus, OH
Corey, George R. ... Millbrae, CA
Corey, George S. ...
Small Business Administration, GV
Corey, H. Allen ... Chattanooga, TN
Corey, Harold ... Chicago, IL
Corey, Henry ... Oak Bluffs, MA
Corey, Jason R ... The Dalles, OR
Corey, Jennifer M. ... Tallahassee, FL
Corey, Jon D. ... Los Angeles, CA
Corey, Joseph P. ... San Francisco, CA
Corey, Kathleen Brown ... Tucson, AZ
Corey, Laurie Brooke Rasmussen
Clinton, MI
Corey, Louis G. ... Royal Oak, MI
Corey, Luzaich, Manos & Pliska LLP
Millbrae, CA
Corey, Marian F. ... McLean, VA
Corey, Mary L. ... Louisville, KY
Corey, Michael D., (P.C.) ... Anchorage, AK
Corey, Michael J. ... Hastings, MI
Corey, Michael R. ... Dallas, TX
Corey & Patzakis ... Los Angeles, CA
Corey, Richard G. ... Quogue, NY
Corey, Robert W. ... Minneapolis, MN
Corey, Steven H. ... Pendleton, OR
Corey, Timothy T. ... Hartford, CT
Corey, Todd S. ... New York, NY
Corey, Walter E., III ... Portland, ME
Corey, William S. ... Washington, DC
Corey-Edstrom, Kenneth
Minneapolis, MN
Corey-Mongue, Heather A.
Clifton Park, NY
Corfee, Catherine M. ... Sacramento, CA
Corfield, Keri Flynn ... Irvine, CA
Corfield, Michael A. ... Laguna Beach, CA
Corfield & Rovell ... Carlsbad, CA
Laguna Beach, CA
Corgan, Anne C. ... Pittsburgh, PA
Corgan, Brian G. ... Atlanta, GA
Corgan, Cleone S. ... Sedona, AZ
Corgan, John J. ... New York, NY
Corgan, Lloyd P. ... Seattle, WA
Corgan, Lynn L. ... Petoskey, MI
Corgill, Dennis S. ... Harrisburg, PA
Corhan, Kenneth P. ... Upland, CA
Corhouse, Debra M. ... St. Paul, MN
Cori, Belle A. ... St. Louis, MO
Cori, Frank Robert ... Orwigsburg, PA
Coric, Drzislav (Dado) ... New London, CT
Coriden, David T. ... Eau Claire, WI
Coriden, G. Terrence ... Columbus, IN
Coriden, James A. ... Washington, DC
Coriden, Kathleen Tighe ... Columbus, IN
Coriden, Michael W. ... Evergreen, CO
Coriden, Michael W., P.C. ... Evergreen, CO
Corie, Florin Alin ... Sunnyvale, CA
Corie, Joseph ... Huntington Beach, CA
Coriell, Karen Bond ... Reynoldsburg, OH
Corigliano, Agnes-Theresa Scully
Stamford, CT
Corigliano, Jean ... Troy, NY
Corin, Michael M. ... Tallahassee, FL
Corina, Errante ... Birmingham, AL
Corinblit, Jack, A Law Corporation
Los Angeles, CA
Corini, Robert O. ... New Rochelle, NY
Corino, Doreen Y. ... Wildwood, NJ
Corino & Dwyer ... Wildwood, NJ
Corino, John ... Wildwood, NJ
Corirossi, Robert G., (P.A.) ... Miami, FL
Corish, Joseph P. ... Arlington, VA
Corish, Robert S. ... Falls Church, VA
Coritsidis, Demetrios ... Astoria, NY
Coritsidis, Michael N. ... New York, NY
Coritsidis, Sotirakis & Saketos ... Astoria, NY
Corizzi, Anthony J. ... Manassas, VA
Cork, Charles M., III ... Atlanta, GA
Macon, GA
Cork, Charles M., Jr. ... Macon, GA
Cork & Cork ... Valdosta, GA
Cork, Gregory M. ... Washington, DC
Cork, Jamie L. ... Minneapolis, MN
Cork, Jill Chessen ... Washington, DC
Cork, John C. ... Macon, GA
Cork, Michael J. ... Indianapolis, IN
Cork, Patrick C. ... Valdosta, GA
Cork, Robert L. ... Valdosta, GA
Cork, Steven E. ... Tupelo, MS
Corke, Robert G. ... White Plains, NY
Corken, Heather M. ... Houston, TX
Corker, Alice K. ... Johnson City, TN
Corker, Bruce D. ... Seattle, WA
Corker, Charles E. ... Seattle, WA
Corker, Clifton L. ... Johnson City, TN
Corker, Robert S. ... Cincinnati, OH
Corker, W. Russell ... Mineola, NY
Corkern & Crews, L.L.C.
Natchitoches, LA
Corkern, Ronald E., Jr. ... Natchitoches, LA
Corkery, Alice ... Westfield, NJ
Corkery, Deidre E. ... Boston, MA
Corkery, Ellen M. ... New York, NY
Corkery, F Daniel ... New York, NY
Corkery, Grace Cashman ... Winchester, MA
Corkery, John E. ... Chicago, IL
Corkery, Joseph J., II ... Rochester, NH
Corkery, Ronald E. ... Allentown, PA
Corkhill, Douglas W. ... Raleigh, NC
Corkhill, Jamie L. ... Topeka, KS
Corkill, Richard R. ... La Grange, TX
Corkins, Kathleen K. ... Denver, CO
Corkland, Alvin Murray ... Mill Valley, CA
Corkran, Christopher T. ... Hollywood, FL
Corkran, M. Blair, Jr.
Securities and Exchange Commission, Division of Market Regulation, GV
Corkran, Thomas D. ... Lynchburg, VA
Corkrey, Barbara ... Los Angeles, CA
Corkrum, Lee ... Seattle, WA
Corl, Christina L. ... Columbus, OH
Corl, Robert D., Jr. ... Corvallis, OR
Corle, James T. ... Wilmington, DE
Corle, Susan M. ... Grand Junction, CO
Corle, Wesley D. ... Charlotte, NC
Corless, Carlos L. ... Atlanta, GA
Corless, Peter F. ... Boston, MA
Corless, Theodore A. ... Tampa, FL
Corless, Thomas C. ... Los Angeles, CA
Corless & Webster, P.C. ... Atlanta, GA
Corleto, Ackerman & Hearn, LLP
Encino, CA
Corleto, Anthony B. ... Danbury, CT
Corleto & Associates, P.C. ... Danbury, CT
Corleto, Raymond A. ... Garden City, NY
Corleto, Richard A. ... Encino, CA
Corlett, Deborah G. ... Santa Rosa, CA
Corlett, Edward S., III ... Miami, FL
Corlett, Jere C. ... Santa Fe, NM
Corlett, Karyn E. ... New York, NY
Corlett Killian, A Professional Association
Miami, FL
Corlett, Robert E. ... Cheney, WA
Corlett, Robert W. ... San Rafael, CA
Corletta, Thomas A. ... Farmington, NY
Rochester, NY
Corlew, Donald L. ... Nashville, TN
Corlew, Gary L. ... Joliet, IL
Corlew, Harold D. ... Atlanta, GA
Corlew, Harold D., P.C. ... Atlanta, GA
Corlew, John G. ... Jackson, MS
Corlew, Reginald R. ... Miami, FL
Corlew, Robert E., III ... Murfreesboro, TN
Corlew, Scott ... Pascagoula, MS
Corlew, Scott ... Pascagoula, MS
Corley, B. Wayne, II ... Dallas, TX
Corley, Bobbie S. ... Columbus, OH
Corley, Dewey W. ... Shreveport, LA
Corley, Donald G. ... Tryon, NC
Corley, Duane T. ... Conroe, TX
Corley, E. Terrill ... Tulsa, OK
Corley, E. Todd ... Alamo, CA
Corley, Elizabeth A. ... Watkins Glen, NY
Corley, Emery L. ... St. Louis, MO
Corley, Frederick M. ... Beaufort, SC
Corley & Ganem ... Tulsa, OK
Corley, Gary D. ... Sherman, TX
Corley, Gayla S. ... San Antonio, TX
Corley, Jacqueline Scott ... San Francisco, CA
Corley, James W. ... Columbia, SC
Corley, Jas. R. ... Mansfield, OH
Corley, John P. ... Pleasanton, CA
Corley, Judith L. ... Washington, DC
Corley, Julie Jones ... Oklahoma City, OK
Corley, Katherine L. ... Birmingham, AL
Corley, Leland H. ... Kansas City, MO
Corley, M. Corinne ... Kansas City, MO
Corley, M. Gayle, (P.A.) ... Little Rock, AR
Corley, Mark W. ... Fayetteville, AR
Corley, Max L., III ... Huntington, WV
Corley, Melly N. ... Vero Beach, FL
Corley, Melvin E. ... Georgetown, TX
Corley, Michael H. ... Austin, TX
Corley, Moncus & Ward, P.C.
Birmingham, AL
Corley, Nancy Krider ... Nashville, TN
Corley, Nolly Elisabeth ... Boston, MA
Corley, O. Paul, Jr. ... Dallas, TX
Corley, O. Wayne ... Columbia, SC
Corley, Patricia E. ... Forsyth, GA
Corley, Phillip Craig ... Stillwater, OK
Corley, Phillip Dale, Jr. ... Birmingham, AL
Corley, Robert H. ... Mullins, SC
Corley, Ronald E. ... Duncan, OK
Corley, Timothy K. ... Florence, AL
Corley, Timothy K., P.C. ... Florence, AL
Corley, W. Michael ... Smithville, TN
Corley, W. Michael ... Woodbury, TN
Corley, William E., III ... Stuart, FL
Corley, William E., III, P.A. ... Stuart, FL
Corley, William M. ... Jacksonville, FL
Corliss, Cynthia L. ... Wilmington, DE
Corliss, Deane K. ... Birmingham, AL
Corliss, Donald M., Jr. ... Santa Monica, CA
Corliss, George F. ... New York, NY
Corliss & Geringer, A Law Corp.
Santa Monica, CA
Corliss, Kevin G. ... Corning, NY
Corliss, Marie A. ... Bronx, NY
Corliss, Patrick Anthony ... Northampton, MA
Corliss, Robert F. ... Boston, MA
Cormack, Caroline Ann ... Albany, GA
Corman and Barefield ... Minneapolis, KS
Corman, Bernice I. ... Department of Justice, Environment and Natural Resources Division, GV
Corman, Calvin W. ... Camden, NJ
Corman, Craig A. ... Beverly Hills, CA
Corman, Evan ... Minneapolis, KS
Corman, Gerald W. ... Merced, CA
Corman, Jack ... Dallas, TX
Corman, James C. ... Washington, DC
Corman, Karen L. ... Los Angeles, CA
Corman, Larry, (P.A.) ... Boca Raton, FL
Corman, Lawrence W. ... Cleveland, OH
Corman, Marc H. ... Los Angeles, CA
Corman, Michael L. ... Santa Cruz, CA
Corman, Michael L., A Professional Corporation ... Santa Cruz, CA
Corman, Michael R. ... Farmington Hills, MI
Corman, Richard W. ... Arlington, VA
Corman, Robert P. ... New Brunswick, NJ
Corman, William ... San Francisco, CA
Cormaney, D. Michael ... Washington, DC
Cormany, Carl E. ... Cleveland, OH
Cormany, Cynthia M. ... Indianapolis, IN
Cormany, J. Barry ... Arlington, VA
Cormany, Jon K. ... Charleston, WV
Cormany, Ralph L. ... Oxnard, CA
Cormell, Shaffer T. ... Blythe, CA
Cormey, Steven P. ... Worcester, MA
Cormicle, Bruce ... Santa Monica, CA
Cormie, Nathan A. ... Lake Charles, LA
Cormier, Alan R. ... Billerica, MA
Cormier, Anthony O. ... Woodland Hills, CA
Cormier, B. Michael ... Portsmouth, NH
Cormier, Bruce M. ... Washington, DC
Cormier, Carolyn H. ... Houston, TX
Cormier, Claire T. ... Palo Alto, CA
Cormier and Cormier ... Bennington, VT
Cormier, Errol L. ... Lafayette, LA
Cormier, James J. ("Jake"), III
Bennington, VT
Cormier, James J., Jr. ... Bennington, VT
Cormier, Jennifer A. ... San Francisco, CA
Cormier, Mary Patricia ... Boston, MA
Cormier, Monique ... Boston, MA
Cormier, Paul E.
Department of the Air Force, Office of the Judge Advocate General, GV
Cormier, Paul W. ... Pittsfield, MA
Cormier, Philip G. ... Boston, MA
Cormier, Roland A. ... Natick, MA
Cormier, Rufus, Jr. ... Houston, TX
Cormier, Shawn A. ... Cleveland, OH
Cormier, Susan M. ... Hartford, CT
Corn, Alan R. ... Hempstead, NY
Corn, Albert A. ... Chicago, IL
Corn, Amy C. ... Stamford, CT
Corn, Barry F. ... Wayne, NJ
Corn, Burton N. ... Tulsa, OK
Corn, Charles M. ... Cleveland, TN
Corn, Diane R. ... Honolulu, HI
Corn, Gavin Alexander
Department of Justice, Criminal Division, GV
Corn, George H. ... Hamilton, MT
Corn, Gregory D. ... Elko, NV
Corn, Harvey E. ... New York, NY
Corn, James P. ... Sacramento, CA
San Francisco, CA
Corn, John M. ... Los Angeles, CA
Corn, John P. ... Little Rock, AR
Corn, Jonathan C. ... Solana Beach, CA
Corn, Martin J. ... Cary, IL
Corn, Michael A. ... Kent, WA
Corn, Peggy W. ... Columbus, OH
Corn, Philip M. ... Treasury Department, Internal Revenue Service, GV
Corn, R. Todd ... Bloomfield, IN
Corn, Robert C. ... Omaha, NE
Corn, Robert M. ... Houston, TX
Corn, Robert O. ... Denver, CO
Corn, Stephen L. ... Mattoon, IL
Corna, Maryellen ... Columbus, OH
Cornaby, K. S. ... Salt Lake City, UT
Cornacchia, Michael T. ... Garden City, NY
Cornacchia, P. Steve ... Eugene, OR
Cornacchio, Elizabeth ... Stamford, CT
New York, NY
Cornacchio, Susan R ... Topsfield, MA
Cornachio, Albert W. ... Yonkers, NY
Cornachio, Albert W., P.C. ... Yonkers, NY
Cornachio, Anthony W. ... Mineola, NY
Cornachio, Julia D. ... Bronx, NY
Cornachio, William ... Melville, NY
Cornaghie, Chris A. ... Memphis, TN
Cornaghie, Janice Esposito ... Memphis, TN
Cornaire, Cynthia J. ... Garden City, NY
Troy, NY
Cornay, Shannon A. ... Los Angeles, CA
Cornblath, Glen R. ... Chicago, IL
Cornblatt, Alan J. ... Brick, NJ
Cornblatt, Alan J., P.A. ... Brick, NJ
Cornblatt, Bennett, Penhallegon & Roberson, P.A. ... Baltimore, MD
Cornblatt, James L. ... Newton, MA
Cornblatt, Marc S. ... Philadelphia, PA
Cornblatt, Theodore B. ... Baltimore, MD
Cornblum, Bruce ... San Diego, CA
Cornblum, Bruce, A Professional Corporation
San Diego, CA
Cornbrooks, Ernest I., III ... Salisbury, MD
Corne, Corne & Grant, P.A. ... Newton, NC
Corne, John R. ... Raleigh, NC
Corne, Louis M. ... Lafayette, LA
Corne, Ray Garrison ... Newton, NC
Corne, Stanley J. ... Newton, NC
Corneal, David B. ... State College, PA
Corneau, Barbara L. ... Denver, CO
Corneau, Ellen M. Flynn ... Providence, RI
Corneck, Lawrence J. ... New York, NY
Corneel, Frederic G. ... Boston, MA
Corneglio, Donald L., Jr. ... Indianapolis, IN
Kalamazoo, MI
Corneille, Barrett J. ... Madison, WI
Corneille, John R., II ... De Kalb, IL
Hinckley, IL
Corneille Law Group, L.L.C.
Madison, WI
Corneille, Margaret Fuller ... St. Paul, MN
Cornejo, Adrienne Fauz ... Boca Raton, FL
Cornejo, Gonzalo M. ... Philadelphia, PA
Cornejo, Juan ... San Francisco, CA
Cornejo-Lopez, Elia L. ... Brownsville, TX
Cornelio, Albert C. ... Pittsfield, MA
Cornelio, Carmine ... Tucson, AZ
Cornelio, Charles C. ... Concord, NH
Cornelio, James P. ... New York, NY
Cornelison, Bert, Jr. ... Houston, TX
Cornelison, Charles O. ... Roanoke, VA
Cornelison, Daniel ... West Des Moines, IA
Cornelison, Kari L. ... Chicago, IL
Cornelison, Michael J. ... Chantilly, VA
Cornelison, Rex P., III ... Roswell, GA
Cornelison, Rex P., III, P.C. ... Roswell, GA
Cornelison, Stephen K. ... Richmond, CA
Cornelison, Steven A. ... Gainesville, GA
Cornelius, Alexandre Ian
Los Angeles, CA
Cornelius, Alice C., (Mrs.) ... Wilmette, IL
Cornelius, Allen R., III
Securities and Exchange Commission, Office of Compliance Inspections and Examinations, GV
Cornelius, Allen R., Jr. ... Nashville, TN
Cornelius, Barbara L. ... Torrance, CA
Cornelius, Benjamin F. ... Sewickley, PA
Cornelius, Bruce A. ... Lafayette, CA
Cornelius, Byron G., Law Office of
Palm Springs, CA
Cornelius, C. Richard ... Berwyn, PA
Cornelius, Charles B. R. ... San Jose, CA
Cornelius, Charles G. ... Nashville, TN
Cornelius, Charles L., Jr. ... Nashville, TN
Cornelius, Charles R. ... Youngstown, OH
Cornelius & Collins, LLP ... Nashville, TN
Cornelius, Darrell L. ... Portland, OR
Cornelius, Dominic J. ... Catskill, NY
Cornelius, Douglas A. ... Clarksburg, WV
Cornelius, Douglas E. ... Boston, MA
Cornelius, Durham & Horan ... Houston, TX
Cornelius, E. E., Jr. ... Tyler, TX
Cornelius, Ellen Audrey ... Northville, MI
Cornelius, Frank S. ... Rockville, MD
Cornelius, Gary E. ... Towson, MD
Cornelius, George E. ... Philadelphia, PA
Cornelius, H. Lloyd ... Wooster, OH
Cornelius, Henry B., Jr. ... Birmingham, AL
Cornelius, James A. ... Bronson, FL
Cornelius, James M. ... New Braunfels, TX
Cornelius, James M., Jr. ... Knoxville, TN
Cornelius, James R. ... Lufkin, TX
Cornelius, James Russell ... Houston, TX

Cornelius, Karen L. ... New York, NY
Cornelius, Kelley L. ... Oklahoma City, OK
Cornelius, Kelley L., P.C.
Oklahoma City, OK
Cornelius, Linda S. ... Oak Park, IL
Cornelius, Lon S., Jr. ... Orlando, FL
Cornelius, Marcus M., & Assocs., P.A.
St. Augustine, FL
Cornelius, Marcus M., III ... St. Augustine, FL
Cornelius, Mark A. ... Orlando, FL
Cornelius, Mark S. ... Pleasant Hill, CA
Cornelius, Nicolas J. ... Phoenix, AZ
Cornelius, O. Ray ... New Orleans, LA
Cornelius, Patrick ... Columbus, OH
Cornelius & Powell ... New Braunfels, TX
Cornelius, Quincy B. ... Escondido, CA
Cornelius, Raymond E. ... Rochester, NY
Cornelius, Richard M. ... Charlottesville, VA
Cornelius, Robert S. ... Santa Ana, CA
Cornelius, Robert T. ... Water Valley, MS
Cornelius, R. P. (Skip) ... Houston, TX
Cornelius, Russell M. ... New Orleans, LA
Cornelius and Salhab ... Houston, TX
Cornelius, Sartin & Murphy
New Orleans, LA
Cornelius, Simon C. ... Victoria, TX
Cornelius, Stephen M. ... La Grange, IL
Cornelius, Terry ... Houston, TX
Cornelius, Terry L. ... Fort Wayne, IN
Cornelius, Timothy Lynn ... Hope, AR
Cornelius, U. Sidney, Jr. ... Dallas, TX
Cornelius, Vincent F. ... Wheaton, IL
Cornelius, Walter ... Birmingham, AL
Cornelius, Weingartner & Polley
Fort Wayne, IN
Cornelius, William ... Tyler, TX
Cornelius, William J. ... Texarkana, TX
Cornelius, William T. ... Houston, TX
Cornell, Angela B. ... Albuquerque, NM
Cornell, Anne Collett ... Syracuse, NY
Cornell, Arthur B., Jr. ... Springfield, IL
Cornell, Athina Lekas ... Westfield, NJ
Cornell, Bradley L. ... Los Angeles, CA
Cornell, Bruce E. ... Fort Dodge, IA
Cornell, Bruce G. ... Gulfport, MS
Cornell, Chadwick M. ... Chicago, IL
Cornell, Cheri Y. ... Seattle, WA
Cornell, Connie ... Austin, TX
Cornell, Creighton ... Tucson, AZ
Cornell, Dalzell, Fette & Ramey
Kalamazoo, MI
Cornell, Daniel Stephen ... Palo Alto, CA
Cornell, Danny L. ... Des Moines, IA
Cornell, David A. ... Gainesville, FL
Cornell, David D., Jr. ... Kalamazoo, MI
Cornell, David P. ... Honolulu, HI
Cornell, Diane J.
Federal Communications Commission,
Wireless Telecommunications Bureau, GV
Cornell, Diane M. ... St. Paul, MN
Cornell, Errol S. ... Palm City, FL
Cornell, F. Duncan ... Baltimore, MD
Cornell, G. Ware, Jr.
Fort Lauderdale, FL
Cornell, G. Ware, Jr., P.A.
Fort Lauderdale, FL
Cornell, George V., III
Palm Beach Gardens, FL
Cornell & Gollub ... Boston, MA
Wakefield, RI
Cornell, Hansen, Bugni & McConnell, P.S.
Seattle, WA
Cornell, Harold D., Jr. ... San Diego, CA
Cornell, Heather M. ... Binghamton, NY
Cornell, Helen Loftin ... Nashville, TN
Cornell, Henry ... New York, NY
Cornell, Henry W., III ... Buffalo, NY
Cornell, Hilary S. ... Philadelphia, PA
Cornell, J. Martin ... New City, NY
Cornell, James H. ... Danbury, CT
Cornell, James L., Jr. ... Houston, TX
Cornell, Janet O'Connor ... New York, NY
Cornell, John E.
General Services Administration,
Office of the General Counsel, GV
Cornell, John H., III ... Boston, MA
Cornell, John R. ... Atlanta, GA
Cornell, John W. ... Chicago, IL
Cornell, Karen Holley ... Dallas, TX
Cornell, Keith J. ... New City, NY
Cornell, Kendal E. ... Chico, CA
Cornell, Kenneth L. ... Seattle, WA
Cornell, Lange & Peters ... San Francisco, CA
Cornell, Lesley F. ... Portsmouth, NH
Cornell, Lila J. ... Indianapolis, IN
Cornell, Lois Dehls ... Waltham, MA
Cornell & Merkin LLP ... Philadelphia, PA
Cornell, Patricia L. ... Miami, FL
Cornell, Patrick T. ... Clinton, OK
Cornell, Paul Lincoln, Jr.
Washington Depot, CT
Cornell, Philip S. ... East Lansing, MI
Cornell, Richard ... Encinitas, CA
Cornell, Richard D., Jr. ... Muskegon, MI
Cornell, Richard F., Law Offices of
Reno, NV
Cornell, Robert B. ... Fort Lauderdale, FL
Cornell, Robert H. ... San Francisco, CA
Cornell, Robin M. L. ... Melbourne, FL
Cornell, Ronald L., Jr. ... Southfield, MI
Cornell, Ronald S. ... Needham, MA
Cornell, Ross H. ... McLean, VA
Cornell, Russell ... Sterling Heights, MI
Cornell, Susan R. ...
Commodity Futures Trading Commission,
GV
Cornell, T. H. Maher ... Philadelphia, PA
Cornell, Theodore E., III ... Chicago, IL
Cornell, Theodore E., Jr. ... Highland Park, IL
Cornell, Trent P. ... Chicago, IL
Cornell, W. Glenn ... Los Angeles, CA
Cornell, William A. ... Crescent City, CA
Cornell, William E. ... Bloomfield Hills, MI
Cornell, Winston R. ... Everett, WA
Cornella, Dominic J., Associates, P.C.
Mineola, NY
New York, NY
Cornellier, J. Roger ... Fairfax, VA
Cornely, C. Michael ... Miami, FL
Cornely, Francis J. ... Charleston, SC
Cornely, John P. ... Cleveland, OH
Corner, Barbara S. ... Columbus, OH
Corner, Bernice M. ... Blackduck, MN
Corner, Finn, Nicholson & Charles
Brooklyn, NY
Garden City, NY
Corner, Mark W. ... Boston, MA
Cornet, Stephen H., A Professional Corporation
Oakland, CA
Cornetet, John B. ... Cincinnati, OH
Cornett, Beverley S. ... Knoxville, TN
Cornett, Bill ... Amarillo, TX
Cornett, Bradley Williams ... Gadsden, AL
Cornett, Calvin Mack, Jr. ... Harrisonburg, VA
Cornett, Candie Lynn ... Hamilton, OH
Cornett, Clay A. ... Houston, TX
Cornett, Clydine ... Oklahoma City, OK
Cornett, Curtis L. ... Cincinnati, OH
Cornett, Dan B. ... Jena, LA
Cornett, Earl M. ... Charleston, WV
Cornett, Galen L. ... Terrell, TX
Cornett, Googe, Ross & Earle, P.A.
Stuart, FL
Cornett, Harry D., Jr. ... Cleveland, OH
Cornett, Homer W. ... Phenix City, AL
Cornett & Ivins ... Phenix City, AL
Cornett, Jack ... Columbus, OH
Cornett, Jane L. ... Stuart, FL
Cornett, John Gregory ... Louisville, KY
Cornett, John T., Jr. ... Richmond, VA
Cornett, Judy M. ... Knoxville, TN
Cornett, Leighton ... Paris, TX
Cornett, Marion W., Jr. ... Atlanta, GA
Cornett, Marvin ... Stanford, KY
Cornett, Pamla Kehn ... Tulsa, OK
Cornett, Patti P. ... Gainesville, GA
Cornett, Paul M. ... Little Chute, WI
Cornett, Tess ... Atlanta, GA
Cornett, Wendy ... Birmingham, AL
Cornetta, Robert A. ... Saugus, MA
Cornette, Dan ... Greenville, KY
Cornette, Daniel C. ... Washington, DC
Cornette, T. Robin ... Lexington, KY
Cornetti, Timothy J. ... Pittsburgh, PA
Cornez, Debra M. ... Sacramento, CA
Cornfeld, Arthur B. ... New York, NY
Cornfeld, Dave L. ... St. Louis, MO
Cornfeld, Richard S. ... St. Louis, MO
Cornfeld, Ruth E. ... Boulder, CO
Cornfeld-Urfirer, Leslie ... Brooklyn, NY
Cornfield and Feldman ... Chicago, IL
Cornfield, Gilbert A. ... Chicago, IL
Cornfield, Melvin ... New York, NY
Cornfield, Michael J. ... Chicago, IL
Cornfield, Richard ... Washington, DC
Cornforth, Theodore W. ... Santa Ana, CA
Corngold, Eric ... Brooklyn, NY
Cornicelli, Anthony M. ... Warren, OH
Cornicelli, Michael F. ... Chicago, IL
Cornicello, Anthony J. ... New York, NY
Cornick, Christine L. ... San Diego, CA
Cornick, Gary Ben ... Burlington, VT
Cornick, Gerald A. ... Fort Worth, TX
Cornick, Matthew S. ... Atlanta, GA
Cornilles, Fredrick R. ... Beaverton, OR
Cornillie, Janet A. ... Detroit, MI
Corning, Jane A. ... San Francisco, CA
Corning, Nicholas F. ... Seattle, WA
Corning, Peter E. ... Auburn, NY
Corning, Robert E. ... Woodinville, WA
Corning, Roland S. ... Columbia, SC
Cornish, B. C. ... Fort Worth, TX
Cornish, Cornell D.M. Judge
Washington, DC
Cornish, Craig M. ... Colorado Springs, CO
Cornish, David R. ... Fairborn, OH
Cornish & Dell'Olio ... Colorado Springs, CO
Cornish, Eleanor R. ... Boston, MA
Cornish, Filbert ... Broken Bow, NE
Cornish, Handley M. ... Hemet, CA
Cornish, Harry L. ... Paterson, NJ
Cornish, Irene L. ... Vernon, CT
Cornish, Jane D. ... Hemet, CA
Cornish, John C. ... Phillipsburg, NJ
Cornish, John C., P.C. ... Phillipsburg, NJ
Cornish, John M., (P.C.) ... Boston, MA
Cornish, Kelley A. ... New York, NY
Cornish, Margaret Mcmanus
Dorchester, MA
Cornish, Mark T. ... Albert City, IA
Storm Lake, IA
Cornish, Richard C. ... Englewood, CO
Cornish, Richard P. ... McAlester, OK
Cornish, Robert Vaughan, Jr.
Santa Monica, CA
Cornish, Thomas G. ... Albuquerque, NM
Cornish, Thomas G., Jr. ... Las Cruces, NM
Cornish, Timothy W. ... Santa Fe, NM
Cornish, Tom R. ... Okmulgee, OK
Cornman, Jack T. ... Irvine, CA
Cornman, Michael A. ... New York, NY
Cornman, Susan B. ... San Jose, CA
Cornman & Swartz ... Irvine, CA
Cornn, Thomas L. ... Athens, OH
Cornnell, Frederick L., Jr.
National Labor Relations Board,
Office of the General Counsel, GV
Cornog, E. Carr ... Lebanon, NJ
Cornog, Robert A., Jr. ... New York, NY
Corn-Revere, Robert L. ... Washington, DC
Cornrich, Katz & Cornrich, Co., L.P.A.
Cleveland, OH
Cornrich, Neil M. ... Cleveland, OH
Cornrich, Sidney M. ... Cleveland, OH
Corns, Autumn Faith ... Frankfort, KY
Corns, Carole A. ... Chicago, IL
Corns, Frederick S. ... Akron, OH
Corns, Ray ... Frankfort, KY
Cornuaud, Scott Allan ... Quinlan, TX
Cornwall, Avery, Bjornstad & Scott
Spencer, IA
Cornwall, Carol V. ... El Paso, TX
Cornwall, Cedric S. ... Milwaukee, WI
Cornwall, Christopher A. ... Detroit, MI
Cornwall, Gary A. ... Walnut Creek, CA
Cornwall, Joseph C. ... Short Hills, NJ
Cornwall, Rhiel & Yamahiro
Milwaukee, WI
Cornwall, Tom W. ... Spencer, IA
Cornwell, A. Milton ... Wadesboro, NC
Cornwell, Allison ... Little Rock, AR
Cornwell, Barbara E. L. ... Chicago, IL
Cornwell, Carl E. ... Overland Park, KS
Cornwell, Caroline Cole ... Providence, RI
Cornwell, Clark L., III ... Wayne, NJ
Cornwell, Daphne H. ... Maryville, TN
Cornwell, David D. ... Syracuse, IN
Cornwell, David K.S. ... Washington, DC
Cornwell, David W. ... Torrance, CA
Cornwell, DNK, P.C. ... Newport Beach, CA
Cornwell, Donald L. ... Los Angeles, CA
Cornwell, Foster B. ... Athens, OH
Cornwell, Gary T. ... Beaumont, TX
Cornwell, James E., Jr. ... Toccoa, GA
Cornwell, James E., Jr. ... Radford, VA
Cornwell, Joel R. ... Chicago, IL
Cornwell, John Kip ... South Orange, NJ
Cornwell, Julie M. ... Omaha, NE
Cornwell, Kevin C. ... Duluth, MN
Cornwell, Kimberly H. ... Irvine, CA
Cornwell, Mary L. ... Costa Mesa, CA
Cornwell, Michael C. ... Tuscaloosa, AL
Cornwell, Mitchell J. ... Easton, MD
Cornwell, Rick ... High Point, NC
Cornwell, Robert T., Law Offices of
Wichita, KS
Cornwell, Stephen R. ... Fresno, CA
Cornwell, Ted E. ... Columbus, OH
Lima, OH
Cornwell, William J. ... Atlanta, GA
Cornwell, Wm. David ... Carlsbad, CA
Cornwell, Wm. David, Sr.
Newport Beach, CA
Cornwell-Williams, V. Claire ... Savannah, GA
Cornyn, Christopher J. ... Springboro, OH
Cornyn, Christopher J., Co., L.P.A.
Springboro, OH
Cornyn, Erin T. ... New York, NY
Cornyn, Frank P. ... Staten Island, NY
Cornyn, John, III ... Dallas, TX
Cornyn, Michael R. ... Champaign, IL
Coroa, John G. ... Tiverton, RI
Corodemus & Corodemus ... Metuchen, NJ
Corodemus, Marina ... Metuchen, NJ
Corodemus, Steven J. ... Metuchen, NJ
Corogin, Thomas L. ... Port Clinton, OH
Corona, Adolfo M. ... Fresno, CA
Corona, Amador L. ... Corona, CA
Corona Firm, The, LLP ... San Diego, CA
Corona, Jennifer K. ... Albany, NY
Corona, John A., P.C. ... Middlefield, CT
Corona, Johnny C. ... Oklahoma City, OK
Corona, Joseph P. ... Salem, MA
Corona, Luis J. ... Corpus Christi, TX
Corona, Maria L. ... East Chicago, IN
Corona, Michael S ... San Juan, PR
Corona, Nicholas, Jr. ... Forest Hills, NY
Corona, Richard D., (A Professional
Corporation) ... San Diego, CA
Corona, Sharon Ingram ... Kenner, LA
Coronado, Baltasar ... Raymondville, TX
Coronado, J. Ramiro ... Las Cruces, NM
Coronado, Jim ... Austin, TX
Coronado, Maria Teresa ... Edinburg, TX
Coronado, Robert P.
Environmental Protection Agency,
Office of Congressional and Legislative
Affairs, GV
Coronado, Sergio ... El Paso, TX
Coronado, Steven F. ... Leawood, KS
Kansas City, MO
Coronado, Susana J. ... St. Louis, MO
Coronado-de Anda, Hector ... McAllen, TX
Corona-Perez, Alba C. ... Chelsea, MA
Coronato, Joseph D. ... Toms River, NJ
Coronato, Wilfred P. ... Springfield, NJ
Coronel, Kenneth H. ... Los Angeles, CA
Coroneos and Rubenstein, P.C.
Washington, DC
Rockville, MD
Coroneos, Tas S. G. ... Rockville, MD
Coronios, Andrew C. ... New York, NY
Coronna, David M. ... Chicago, IL
Corontzos, Ted ... Great Falls, MT
Cororve, Brian D. ... Houston, TX
Corozzo, Joseph R., Jr. ... New York, NY
Corp, Michael L. ... Syracuse, NY
Corpas, Constantine L. ... Cleveland, OH
Corpas & Pahys ... Cleveland, OH
Corpening, Gregory S. ... Kemmerer, WY
Corpening, J. H., II ... Wilmington, NC
Corpening, Lloyd M. ... Houston, TX
Corpening, Robert B. ... Los Angeles, CA
Corpina, Joseph B. ... New York, NY
Corpina & Overzat ... New York, NY
Corpora, Corine ... Cleveland, OH
Corpora, Joseph A., III ... Easton, PA
Corpora, L. Elizabeth ... Lone Pine, CA
Corpora-Buck, Maria ... Elkins Park, PA
Corporate Advisory Law Group
Los Altos, CA
Palo Alto, CA
Corporate Counsel Group, LLP
Kansas City, MO
Corporate Counsel Law Group, LLP
San Francisco, CA
Corporate Law Group, The
Burlingame, CA
Corporon, Eyler & Katz, LLC
Denver, CO
Corporon, James Scott ... Dalton, GA
Corporon, Jeffrey Scott ... Denver, CO
Corporon, Mary C. ... Salt Lake City, UT
Corporon, Vern R. ... Denver, CO
Corporon & Williams, A Professional
Corporation ... Salt Lake City, UT
Corprew, Barbara A. ... Department of Justice,
Criminal Division, GV
Corprew, Kaye C. ... Houston, TX
Corpus, Karla M. ... Syracuse, NY
Corpuz, Marcelo N., III ... Chicago, IL
Corpuz, Victor N. ... Dallas, TX
Corr, Christopher F. ... Washington, DC
Corr Cronin LLP ... Seattle, WA
Corr, James V. ... Atlanta, GA
Corr, Janice K. ... Albany, NY
Corr, Jeanine M. ... Palo Alto, CA
Corr, John A. ... Philadelphia, PA
Corr, John B. ... Williamsburg, VA
Corr, Jonathan A. ... Sacramento, CA
Corr, Kelly P. ... Seattle, WA
Corr, Kevin M. ... Boston, MA
Corr, Kevin R. ... Springfield, IL
Corr, Larry E. ... Elgin, IL
Corr, Marianne ... Providence, RI
Corr, Martin J. ... Warminster, PA
Corr, Mathew E. ... Milwaukee, WI
Corr, Michael N. ... Warminster, PA
Corr, Richard C., Jr. ... Oneonta, AL
Corr, Richard M. ... Rocky Hill, CT
Corr, Sean M. ... Warminster, PA
Corr, Stevens & Fenningham ... Marlton, NJ
Trevose, PA
Warminster, PA
Corr, Thomas Nathan ... Albany, OR
Corr, Thomas P. ... Berkeley, CA
Corrada, Theresa L. ... Denver, CO
Corrada-Mejiá, Margarita ... San Juan, PR
Corradini, Paul R. ... Elmira, NY
Corradini, Stefano D. ... Tucson, AZ
Corradino, Elizabeth A. ... New York, NY
Corradino, G. Dolph ... Little Falls, NJ
Corradino, Jeffrey J. ... Morristown, NJ
Corradino, Thomas J. ... Branford, CT
Corrado, Angelo Ralph ... Fresh Meadows, NY
Corrado, Bernadette M. ... Chelsea, MA
Corrado & Cifone ... Hempstead, NY
Corrado Counsellors At Law
New York, NY
Corrado, David Allan ... Cleveland, OH
Corrado, Frank L. ... Wildwood, NJ
Corrado, Frank L. ... Forest Hills, NY
Corrado, Geraldine M. ... Quincy, MA
Corrado, Giacomo ... New York, NY
Corrado, Jason R. ... New York, NY
Corrado, Jeanne Marie
Federal Labor Relations Authority,
Office of the General Counsel, GV
Corrado, John P. ... Washington, DC
Corrado, Kristin Mari ... Totowa, NJ
Corrado, Marie A. ... Albany, NY
Corrado, Melissa P. ... Hempstead, NY
Corrado, Michael L. ... Chapel Hill, NC
Corrado, Nicholas P. ... Bloomfield, NJ
Corrado, Paul J. ... Cleveland, OH
Corrado, Pearl B. ... Kew Gardens, NY
Corrado, Philip C., Jr. ... Chicago, IL
Corrado, Regine W. ... Chicago, IL
Corrado, Robert E. ... Totowa, NJ
Corrado, Thomas A. ... Washington, DC
Corrado, Victoria F. ... Irvine, CA
Corral, Francis S. ... Tulsa, OK
Corral, George, Jr. ... Lake Elsinore, CA
Corral, Jaime R. ... Alhambra, CA
Corral, John ... Orange, CA
Corral, Xiomara ... Boston, MA
Corrales, Arthur S., (P.A.) ... Tampa, FL
Corrales, Carmen Amalia ... New York, NY
Corrales, M. Rito ... Santa Ana, CA
Corrales, Manuel, Jr. ... San Diego, CA
Corrales, Michael J. ... Lawton, OK
Corral L., Dalila ... Los Angeles, CA
Corrallo, Carl A. ... Houston, TX
Corrallo, Mark L. ... Rockville, MD
Corrallo, Peter P. ... Lockport, NY
Corran, Patricia L. ... St. Louis, MO
Corrao, Darren J. ... New York, NY
Corrao, Edward W. ... South Weymouth, MA
Corrao, Joseph F. ... Alexandria, VA
Corrao, Laura S. ... New York, NY
Corrao, Miller, Rush & Wiesenthal
New York, NY
Corrarino, Mary ... New York, NY
Corraro, Anne Marie ... Cambridge, MA
Correa, A. Carlos ... Treasury Department,
Departmental Offices, GV
Correa, Collazo, Herrero, Jimenez &
Fortuño ... San Juan, PR
Correa, Danny ... Miami, FL
Correa, David ... Bronx, NY

Correa, Donald J. ..... Plymouth, MA
Correa, Edward L., Jr. ..... Honolulu, HI
Correa, Glenn E. ..... La Quinta, CA
Correa, Haydee ..... Bronx, NY
Correa, J. Gerard ..... St. Petersburg, FL
Correa, Louis W. ..... San Antonio, TX
Correa, Mario ..... Naperville, IL
Correa, Murrey Aran ..... Los Angeles, CA
Correa, René ..... Weslaco, TX
Correa, Richard A. ..... Niskayuna, NY
Correa, Sylvia I.
Environmental Protection Agency, Program Office Attorneys, GV
Correa-Avilés, Maggie ..... San Juan, PR
Correa-Calzada, Manuel ..... San Juan, PR
Correa-Cestero, Mariacté ..... San Juan, PR
Correale, Andre Joseph ..... New York, NY
Correale, Jennifer D. ..... New York, NY
Correale, Michael G. ..... Fairview Heights, IL
Correale, Robert D. ..... Succasunna, NJ
Correales, Robert I. ..... Madison, WI
Correa Marquez, Manuel Luis
San Juan, PR
Correa-Noa, Johnny ..... San Juan, PR
Corredor, Livia M. ..... New York, NY
Corredor, Maria E. ..... Hollywood, FL
Correia, Catherine Booth ..... Wakefield, MA
Correia, Charles A. ..... Costa Mesa, CA
Correia, Cristina ..... Atlanta, GA
Correia, Kimberly A. ..... Hyannis, MA
Correia, Linda M. ..... Washington, DC
Correia, Lisa M. ..... Exeter, NH
Correia, Manuel A. ..... Hackensack, NJ
Correia, Nancy C. ..... East Dennis, MA
Correia, Sharon Hague ..... Fall River, MA
Correia-Champa, Susan ..... Boston, MA
Correira, David J. ..... Swansea, MA
Correira, Jon-Paul ..... Providence, RI
Correl, Theodore ..... San Francisco, CA
Correll, Alston D., III ..... Atlanta, GA
Correll, Charles C., Jr. ..... Houston, TX
Correll, Craig O. ..... Carlsbad, CA
Correll, David H. ..... Cedar Falls, IA
Correll, David M. ..... Robinson, IL
Correll, Donna E. ..... New York, NY
Correll, E. K. ..... Tyler, TX
Correll, Francis M., Jr. ..... Philadelphia, PA
Correll, James Michael ..... Lenoir, NC
Correll, Joanna R. ..... Weaverville, CA
Correll, Julie A. ..... Chicago, IL
Correll, Kathleen J. ..... Eugene, OR
Correll, Linda R. ..... Dallas, TX
Correll, Merlen E. ..... Des Moines, IA
Correll, Philip Kent ..... New York, NY
Correll, Philip R. ..... Carmel, IN
Correll, Raymond A. ..... Farmington Hills, MI
Correll, Raymond A., P.C.
Farmington Hills, MI
Correll & Sheerer ..... Cedar Falls, IA
Correll, Thomas M. ..... San Diego, CA
Correll, Tim ..... Denver, CO
Correlli, John M. ..... Woodland Hills, CA
Correll Wofford, Penny ..... Spartanburg, SC
Corren, Adam Blair ..... Stockton, CA
Corren, Craig L. ..... Stockton, CA
Corren, Denise H. ..... Tarzana, CA
Corren, Edye ..... San Francisco, CA
Corren, Irving M. ..... Stockton, CA
Corren, Todd R. ..... Stockton, CA
Corrente, Carmen F. ..... Daytona Beach, FL
Corrente, Darren F. ..... Providence, RI
Corrente, Gail A. ..... Cranston, RI
Corrente, Michael F. ..... Providence, RI
Corrente, Robert ..... Boston, MA
Providence, RI
Corrente, Susan ..... Augusta, ME
Correnti, Christopher F. ..... Kingsport, TN
Correnti, John G. ..... Los Angeles, CA
Correnti, Joseph C. ..... Salem, MA
Correnti, Peter James
Altamonte Springs, FL
Correri, Anthony F. ..... Hicksville, NY
Correro, Anthony J., III
New Orleans, LA
Correro Fishman Haygood Phelps Walmsley & Casteix, L.L.P. ..... New Orleans, LA
Correro, Margaret O. ..... New Orleans, LA
Corretjer-Piquer, Antonio L. ..... San Juan, PR
Corretore, David Timothy ..... Webster, NY
Corretti, Douglas P. ..... Birmingham, AL
Corretti, Newsom & Hawkins
Birmingham, AL
Tuscaloosa, AL
Corricello, Julie A. ..... Boulder, CO
Corrick, Dennis G. ..... Lakeland, FL
Lake Wales, FL
Winter Haven, FL
Corrick, Max Edward, II ..... Las Vegas, NV
Corrick, W. David ..... Sacramento, CA
Corrick, William J. ..... Minneapolis, MN
Corridan, John M. ..... Springfield, MA
Corridon, Laura A. ..... Deerfield, IL
Corrie, Clint A. ..... Dallas, TX
Corrie, Pamela B. ..... Ridgefield, CT
Corrie, Quentin R. ..... Fairfax, VA
Corriere, Alfred N. ..... Albany, GA
Corriere, Donald B. ..... Bethlehem, PA
Corriere, Michael F. ..... Bethlehem, PA
Corriero, Michael A. ..... New York, NY
Corrigall, John A. ..... Wisconsin Rapids, WI
Corrigall, Kevin ..... Kenosha, WI
Corrigall, Malcolm J. ..... Coos Bay, OR
Corrigan, Alfred E. ..... Cambridge, MA
Corrigan, Amy ..... Chicago, IL
Corrigan, Ann Phillips ..... St. Louis, MO
Corrigan, Anne T. ..... Cleveland, OH
Corrigan, Annette Kraus ..... Naperville, IL
Corrigan, Bradford D., Jr. ..... Dallas, TX
Corrigan, Brian J. ..... Cleveland, OH
Corrigan, Brian N. ..... Baldwin, NY
Corrigan, Brian T. ..... Los Angeles, CA
Corrigan, Brian T. ..... San Antonio, TX
Corrigan, Brian Thomas ..... Winchester, MA
Corrigan, Bruce J., Jr. ..... Westport, CT
Corrigan, Carol A. ..... San Francisco, CA
Corrigan, Charles E. ..... Portland, OR
Corrigan, Charles J. ..... Naperville, IL
Corrigan, Christopher D. ..... Lafayette, IN
Corrigan, Daniel P. ..... Solon, OH
Corrigan, Dara A.
Department Of Health And Human Services, Office of the General Counsel, GV
Corrigan, David F. ..... Little Silver, NJ
Corrigan, David P. ..... Middletown, NJ
Toms River, NJ
Corrigan, David P. ..... Richmond, VA
Corrigan, Donald W.
Department of Commerce, GV
Corrigan, Eddie ..... Cleveland, OH
Corrigan, Edmund J. ..... Toms River, NJ
Corrigan, Edward R. ..... Boonton, NJ
Corrigan, Edward T. ..... Worcester, MA
Corrigan, Eugene Patrick, III
Charleston, SC
Corrigan, George R. ..... Madison, WI
Corrigan, Hugh, IV ..... Dallas, TX
Corrigan, J. Michael, Jr. ..... Meridian, MS
Corrigan, James ..... Cleveland, OH
Corrigan, James A. ..... Chicago, IL
Corrigan, James A., Ltd. ..... Chicago, IL
Corrigan, James B., Jr. ..... Westmont, NJ
Philadelphia, PA
Corrigan, James J. ..... Cleveland, OH
Corrigan, James M. ..... Pensacola, FL
Corrigan, James T. ..... St. Louis, MO
Corrigan, James W., III ..... Lindenhurst, NY
Corrigan, Jeffrey J. ..... New York, NY
Corrigan, Jodi L. ..... Tampa, FL
Corrigan, John C. ..... Chicago, IL
Corrigan, John C., Jr. ..... Boston, MA
Fall River, MA
Corrigan, John D., Jr. ..... Boston, MA
Corrigan, John E. ..... Cleveland, OH
Corrigan, John F. ..... Jacksonville Beach, FL
Corrigan, John F. ..... Boston, MA
Providence, RI
Corrigan, John F. ..... Riverhead, NY
Corrigan, John F. ..... Cleveland, OH
Corrigan, John J. ..... San Francisco, CA
Corrigan, John J., Jr. ..... Dedham, MA
Corrigan, John V. ..... Cleveland, OH
Corrigan, Johnson & Tutor, P.A.
Boston, MA
Fall River, MA
Corrigan, Karen B. ..... New York, NY
Corrigan, Karen J. ..... Cleveland, OH
Corrigan, Katherine T. ..... Orange, CA
Corrigan, Kevin H. ..... Kirkland, WA
Corrigan, Lawrence J. ..... Omaha, NE
Corrigan, Lorna S. ..... Everett, WA
Corrigan, Margaret A. ..... Cohasset, MA
Corrigan, Margaret E. ..... Glastonbury, CT
Corrigan, Mark R. ..... Harrisburg, PA
Corrigan, Mary A. ..... Peoria, IL
Corrigan, Mary Beth ..... Medina, OH
Corrigan, Mary Louise ..... Schenectady, NY
Corrigan, Maura D. ..... Detroit, MI
Corrigan, Michael ..... Wichita, KS
Corrigan, Michael J. ..... Cleveland, OH
Corrigan, Michael P. ..... St. Louis, MO
Corrigan, Michael S. ..... Wilmington, DE
Corrigan, Michael V. ..... New York, NY
Corrigan, Michelle L. ..... New Orleans, LA
Corrigan, Nancy Denardo ..... New York, NY
Corrigan, Patrick S. ..... Cleveland, OH
Corrigan, Peter J. ..... Albany, NY
Corrigan, Peter J. ..... Cleveland, OH
Corrigan, Peter M. ..... Princeton, NJ
New York, NY
Corrigan, Richard E. ..... Mobile, AL
Corrigan, Richard P. ..... San Antonio, TX
Corrigan, Robert F., Jr. ..... Houston, TX
Corrigan, Robert N., Jr. ..... Corpus Christi, TX
Corrigan, Robert P. ..... Providence, RI
Corrigan, Sarah D. ..... Boston, MA
Corrigan, Scott ..... New York, NY
Corrigan, Sean F. ..... New York, NY
Corrigan, Stephen G. ..... Framingham, MA
Corrigan, Terence J. ..... Springfield, IL
Corrigan, Terence J. ..... New York, NY
Corrigan, Thomas D. ..... Cleveland, OH
Corrigan, Thomas H. ..... Hartford, CT
Corrigan, Thomas J., Jr.
Washington Crossing, PA
Corrigan, Thomas J., Jr. ..... Providence, RI
Corrigan, Timothy F. ..... Boston, MA
Corrigan, Timothy J. ..... Jacksonville, FL
Corrigan, Timothy J. ..... Springfield, MO
Corrigan, Timothy W. ..... Charlotte, NC
Corrigan, William F. ..... Hartford, CT
Corrigan, William J. ..... San Francisco, CA
Corrigan, William J. ..... Milwaukee, WI
Corrigan, William M. ..... Ballwin, MO
Corrigan, William M., Jr. ..... St. Louis, MO
Corrigan, William S., Jr.
Colorado Springs, CO
Corriher, Dooley & Locklear ..... Landis, NC
Salisbury, NC
Corriher, James A. ..... Landis, NC
Salisbury, NC
Corrin, Dwight A. ..... Wichita, KS
Corrin, Dwight A., Chartered
Wichita, KS
Corrington, Kevin M. ..... Sacramento, CA
Corrington Law Firm, The
New Orleans, LA
Corrington, Thomas ..... New Orleans, LA
Corris, Robert B. ..... Milwaukee, WI
Corris, Robert B., S.C. ..... Milwaukee, WI
Corris, Steve ..... Irvine, CA
Corriss, John P. ..... Miami Beach, FL
Corriss, Stephen C. ..... New York, NY
Corriston, E. Carter ..... Hackensack, NJ
Corriston, E. Carter, Jr. ..... Hackensack, NJ
Corriston, Kevin C. ..... Hackensack, NJ
Corriston, Lina Papalia ..... Hackensack, NJ
Corriston, Terrence J. ..... Hackensack, NJ
Corriston, Timothy E. ..... Roseland, NJ
Corriveau, Richard J. ..... Northville, MI
Corrodi, James A. ..... Wilmington, DE
Corrons-Hickey & Hickey ..... Santa Ana, CA
Corrons-Hickey, Jacqueline ..... Santa Ana, CA
Corroon, Hugh ..... Wilmington, DE
Corroto, Gary A. ..... Canton, OH
Corroto, Thos. L., Jr. ..... Youngstown, OH
Corrou, Vincent R., Jr. ..... Utica, NY
Corry, Carolyn M. ..... Pittsburgh, PA
Corry, Charles A. ..... Pittsburgh, PA
Corry, Clayward C., Jr.
Kings Mountain, NC
Corry, Clinton B. ..... Richmond, VA
Corry, Clinton B., Jr. ..... Richmond, VA
Corry & Corry, P.C. ..... Richmond, VA
Corry, David M. ..... Tampa, FL
Corry, Jill Mataya ..... Des Moines, IA
Corry, Jody Jenkins ..... Athens, GA
Corry, John A. ..... New York, NY
Corry, Lawrence H. ..... Fairfax, VA
Corry, Michael P. ..... Lafayette, LA
Corry, Robert E., Jr. ..... Atlanta, GA
Corry, Robert John
House of Representatives, Committee Legal Personnel, GV
Corry, W. Kent ..... Cedar City, UT
Corry, W. Kent, P.C. ..... Cedar City, UT
Corry, William W. ..... Tallahassee, FL
Corry, William W., P.A., Law Offices of
Tallahassee, FL
Corryn-Blessing, Tracey K.
Upper Marlboro, MD
Cors & Bassett ..... Fort Wright, KY
Cincinnati, OH
Cors, Dylan ..... Washington, DC
Cors, L. Barry ..... Cincinnati, OH
Corsa, LeRoy S. ..... New York, NY
Corsac, Christina M. ..... Philadelphia, PA
Corsair, Bradley J. ..... Kew Gardens, NY
Corsair, Todd Everett ..... New York, NY
Corsale, Joseph N., Jr.
Saratoga Springs, NY
Corsano, Anthony J. ..... New York, NY
Corsano, Bonnie M. ..... New York, NY
Corsaro, Amy M. ..... Indianapolis, IN
Corsaro, Carmen R. ..... Methuen, MA
Corsaro, Daniel S. ..... Indianapolis, IN
Corsaro, Gregory P. ..... Indianapolis, IN
Corsaro, Paul J. ..... Indianapolis, IN
Corsbie, Bill, P.C. ..... Austin, TX
Corsbie, William (Bill) Lance, Jr.
Austin, TX
Corscadden, Henry James, III ..... Seattle, WA
Corse, Bell & Miller, P.A. ..... Jacksonville, FL
Corse, Chester C., Jr. ..... Pottsville, PA
Corse, John D. ..... Baltimore, MD
Corse, John D. ..... Charlottesville, VA
Corse, Robert L. ..... Jacksonville, FL
Corse, Stephen M. ..... Miami, FL
Corsell, Laura Anne ..... Philadelphia, PA
Corselli, Andrew ..... New York, NY
Corsello, Bradley S. ..... New York, NY
Corsello, Joyce M. V. ..... Port Washington, NY
Corsello, Kenneth R. ..... Washington, DC
Corsello, Michael R. ..... Norwalk, CT
Corsello, Philip F. ..... Newark, NJ
Corsello, T. Dominic ..... Des Moines, IA
Corsentino, Anthony P. ..... Peoria, IL
Corsentino, Anthony P., Ltd. ..... Peoria, IL
Corsetti, George L. ..... Detroit, MI
Corsetti, Mary Jo ..... Pittsburgh, PA
Corsetti, Nicholas V. ..... Cheswick, PA
Corsetti, Rosemary L. ..... Pittsburgh, PA
Corsetti, Vincent B. ..... Philadelphia, PA
Corsetto, Richard Francis ..... New York, NY
Corshen, Nancy L. ..... Burbank, CA
Corsi, Alfred R., Jr. ..... Pittsburgh, PA
Corsi, David P. ..... Novato, CA
Corsi, Ennio J. ..... Albany, NY
Corsi, Louis G. ..... New York, NY
Corsi, Mario D. ..... Dover, OH
Corsi, Megan J. ..... Cleveland, OH
Corsi, Michelle A. ..... Seattle, WA
Corsi, Q. Albert ..... Columbus, OH
Corsi, Thomas M.
Board of Governors Of The Federal Reserve System, Office of the General Counsel, GV
Corsiglia, Bradley M. ..... San Jose, CA
Corsiglia, Christina Karcher ..... Chicago, IL
Corsiglia, George R. ..... Allegan, MI
Corsiglia, Thomas ..... Bettendorf, IA
Corsilles, Angela ..... Palo Alto, CA
Corsini, Anthony P.
North Palm Beach, FL
Corsini, Gerard A. ..... New York, NY
Corsino, Janice M. ..... Pasadena, CA
Corsino, Joseph C. ..... Markham, IL
Corsmeier, Arnold B. ..... Tampa, FL
Corsmeier, Joseph A. ..... Clearwater, FL
Corsmeier, Kathryn M. ..... Los Angeles, CA
Corso, Ann Fortenberry ..... Jackson, MS
Corso, Anthony R. ..... Fairfax, VA
Corso, Arturo ..... Cambridge, MA
Corso, David A. ..... Orlando, FL
Corso, David J., Jr. ..... North Haven, CT
Corso, Frank C. ..... Boston, MA
Corso, Frank Mitchell ..... Westbury, NY
Corso, Frank Mitchell, P.C. ..... Westbury, NY
Corso, Gregg W.
Securities and Exchange Commission, Executive Staff, GV
Corso, Jennifer A. ..... Cleveland, OH
Corso, John B. ..... Chicago, IL
Corso, John R. ..... Juneau, AK
Corso, Joseph J. ..... Cleveland, OH
Corso, Joseph J. ..... Rocky River, OH
Corso, Judith A. Salamandra ..... Danville, VT
Corso, Kenneth F. ..... Perkasie, PA
Corso, Mary Donna ..... Houston, TX
Corso, Matthew T. ..... Plymouth Meeting, PA
Corso, Michael C. ..... Jackson, MS
Corso, Michael J. ..... Fort Myers, FL
Corso, S. Gerald ..... Norristown, PA
Corso, Trevor R. ..... Secaucus, NJ
Corson, Barry A. ..... Burlington, IA
Corson, Brett A. ..... Preston, MN
Stewartville, MN
Corson, Christopher T.
Upper Marlboro, MD
Corson, Dan W. ..... Denver, CO
Corson, Don ..... Eugene, OR
Corson, George C., Jr.
Fort Washington, PA
Corson, George E., IV ..... Costa Mesa, CA
Corson, Getson & Schatz ..... Philadelphia, PA
Corson, J. Jay, IV ..... McLean, VA
Corson, Jas. P. ..... St. Paul, MN
Corson, John R., Jr. ..... Mays Landing, NJ
Corson, Kenneth S. ..... New York, NY
Corson, Laurie A. ..... Camden, NJ
Corson Law Offices ..... Preston, MN
Stewartville, MN
Corson, Lawrence ..... Philadelphia, PA
Corson, Neal C. ..... Madison, ME
Corson, Niles S. ..... Kansas City, MO
Corson, Peter L. ..... Jackson, MS
Corson, Peter L. ..... Madison, MS
Corson, Robt. M. ..... Carmel, CA
Corson, Rochelle ..... New York, NY
Corson, Rodney E. ..... Indianapolis, IN
Corson, Samantha R. ..... Philadelphia, PA
Corson, Steven ..... Preston, MN
Stewartville, MN
Corson, Theresa Sweeney ..... Cherry Hill, NJ
Philadelphia, PA
Corsones, Christopher T. ..... Rutland, VT
Corsones & Corsones ..... Rutland, VT
Corsones, Cortland T. ..... Rutland, VT
Corsones, Nancy S. ..... Rutland, VT
Corsones, Theodore ..... Tampa, FL
Corsones, Therese M. ..... Rutland, VT
Corsun, Lori A. ..... New York, NY
Corsun, Robert B. ..... Sherman Oaks, CA
Corsun, Robert B., A Professional Corporation
Sherman Oaks, CA
Corsuti, Carlo S. ..... New York, NY
Cort, Daniel G. ..... New York, NY
Cort, Julia A. ..... New York, NY
Cort, Kenneth M. ..... Painesville, OH
Cort, Nicholas ..... Concord, NH
Cort, Paul R.
Environmental Protection Agency, Office of the General Counsel, GV
Cort, Robert J. ..... San Francisco, CA
Cort, William G. ..... Woodland Hills, CA
Cortada, Luis A. Armstrong, Jr.
Ponce, PR
Cortazzo, Arna D. ..... Cocoa, FL
Cortazzo, James ..... Mineola, NY
Cortazzo, Thomas J. ..... New Orleans, LA
Corte, Lawrence J. ..... Phoenix, AZ
Lakewood, CO
Cortegiano, Mark L. ..... Middle Village, NY
Corteguera, Joseph R. ..... Houston, TX
Cortell, Mark N. ..... Los Angeles, CA
Cortell, Nina ..... Dallas, TX
Cortellessa, Gary R. ..... McLean, VA
Cortellini, Joseph F. ..... Boston, MA
Cortés, Antonio L. ..... Hagåtña, GU
Cortes, Bertha A. ..... Los Angeles, CA
Cortes, David J. ..... Raleigh, NC
Cortes, Geary D. ..... San Diego, CA
Cortes, Isaac, Jr. ..... Clinton, NC
Cortes, Rita M. ..... Kansas City, MO
Cortes, Roland B. ..... Mountain View, CA
Cortes, Wendy M. ..... New York, NY
Cortes, William Patrick ..... Denver, CO
Cortes, Yolanda ..... Temple, TX
Cortes-Bridgwater, Kerri C ..... Houston, TX
Cortés-Dapena, Rafael ..... San Juan, PR
Cortese, Anthony V. ..... Tampa, FL
Cortese, David D. ..... San Jose, CA
Cortese, Diane Caniglia ..... Des Moines, IA
Cortese, Eugene B., Jr. ..... Jenkintown, PA
Cortese, Gregory T. ..... New Hartford, NY
Cortese, Joseph R. ..... Cleveland, OH
Cortese, Joseph S., II ..... Des Moines, IA
Cortese, Kathleen A. ..... Broomall, PA
Cortese, Maria T. ..... Bronx, NY
Cortese, Philip V. ..... Amsterdam, NY
Cortese, Richard S. ..... Montpelier, VT
Cortese, Shari N. ..... Tampa, FL
Cortese-Costa, Loraine ..... Bridgeport, CT
Corteselli, Karen P. ..... Garden City, NY
Cortesi, Henry B., Law Office of
New York, NY
Cortesi, Kenneth J. ..... Chicago, IL
Cortesio, John C., Jr. ..... Des Moines, IA
Cortés-Rexach, Paul R. ..... San Juan, PR
Cortes-Sykes, Carmen ..... Paterson, NJ
Cortez, Antonio ..... El Paso, TX
Cortez, Carlos R. ..... Dallas, TX
Cortez, Daniel E. ..... Nashville, TN

Cortez, Dawn C. ....Spokane, WA
Cortez, Elizabeth M. ....Los Angeles, CA
Cortez, Esther ....Houston, TX
Cortez, Ezekiel E. ....San Diego, CA
Cortez, H. Glenn ....Austin, TX
Cortez, Jesse, Jr. ....Los Angeles, CA
Cortez Macaulay Bernhardt & Schuetze LLC ....Denver, CO
Cortez, Michael ....Dallas, TX
Cortez, Miguel J. ....Atlanta, GA
Cortez, Miles ....Denver, CO
Cortez, Priscilla J. ....San Francisco, CA
Cortez, R. Michael ....Altoona, PA
Cortez, Ray ....Houston, TX
Cortez, Richard, Jr. ....Dallas, TX
Cortez, RosaMaria R. ....Granger, WA
Corthell, Jon R. ....Somers, NY
Corthell and King, P.C. ....Laramie, WY
Corthell, Pauline ....Olympia, WA
Corti and Aleksy ....Chicago, IL
Corti, Anna M. ....Framingham, MA
Corti, Peter D. ....Chicago, IL
Cortigene, Seth ....Houston, TX
Cortina, A. Jose ....Raleigh, NC
Cortina, Armando ....Coral Gables, FL
Cortina, Frank J., Jr. ....Coal City, IL
Cortina, Jana Ranieri
Fort Lauderdale, FL
Cortina, Mueller and Garretson
Coal City, IL
Morris, IL
Cortiñas, Angel A. ....Miami, FL
Cortinez Law Firm, The, PLLC
Hot Springs National Park, AR
Little Rock, AR
Pine Bluff, AR
Cortinez, Robert R.
Hot Springs National Park, AR
Little Rock, AR
Cortinez, Robert R., II ....Little Rock, AR
Cortinovis, Stephen P. ....St. Louis, MO
Cortis, Donald E., Jr. ....Anchorage, AK
Cortman, David A. ....Virginia Beach, VA
Cortner, Claire L. ....San Francisco, CA
Cortopassi, Gary E. ....Fresno, CA
Cortopassi, Santiago J., III ....Indianapolis, IN
Cortright, Edward G., Jr. ....Yazoo City, MS
Cortright, Shane K. ....Sunnyvale, CA
Cortright, Stephen P. ....Tulsa, OK
Cortrite, Alicia W. ....Santa Monica, CA
Corts, Thomas C. ....Nashville, TN
Cortson, Michael D. ....Pasadena, CA
Corujo, David C. ....Media, PA
Corum, Allison Smith ....Raleigh, NC
Corum, Gary D. ....Little Rock, AR
Corum, Jesse M., IV ....Brattleboro, VT
Corum, Lee L. ....Durham, NC
Corum, William E. ....Overland Park, KS
Corum, William R. ....Oklahoma City, OK
Coruzzi, Laura A. ....New York, NY
Corveleyn, Daniel M. ....Stroudsburg, PA
Corvette, Ted E. ....Charlotte, NC
Corvette, Theo. ....Roswell, GA
Corvette, Theodore E., Jr. ....Charlotte, NC
Corvi, Paul J. ....San Francisco, CA
Corvin, Carl D. ....Bartlesville, OK
Corvino, Beth Byster ....Horsham, PA
Corvino, John P. ....Bannockburn, IL
Corvino, Sheila G. ....New York, NY
Corvino, Thomas R. ....New York, NY
Corvo, Tara M. ....Washington, DC
Corwin, Alexandra ....Albuquerque, NM
Corwin, Andrew M. ....Braintree, MA
Corwin, Brent E. ....Scottsdale, AZ
Corwin, Brent E., P.C. ....Scottsdale, AZ
Corwin, Carolyn F. ....Washington, DC
Corwin, Charles D. ....Cadillac, MI
Corwin, Corwin & Fisher, L.L.C.
Waco, TX
Corwin & Corwin LLP ....Boston, MA
Corwin, David M. ....Los Angeles, CA
Corwin, David S. ....St. Louis, MO
Corwin, Diane M. ....Altadena, CA
Corwin, Edward J. ....Honolulu, HI
Corwin, Erik H. ....Washington, DC
Corwin, Erwin L. ....New York, NY
Corwin, Frances ....Chicago, IL
Corwin, G. Lester, II ....South Royalton, VT
Corwin, Garrison R., Jr. ....Mamaroneck, NY
Corwin & Greenberg ....New York, NY
Corwin, Gregg M., & Associates
Minneapolis, MN
Corwin, Joel S., Law Offices of
Chicago, IL
Corwin, John T. ....Calhoun, GA
Cartersville, GA
Corwin, Joseph M. ....Boston, MA
Corwin, Jules A. ....New York, NY
Corwin, Julie Ann ....San Antonio, TX
Corwin, Laura J. ....New York, NY
Corwin, Leonard S. ....White Plains, NY
Corwin, Leslie D. ....New York, NY
Corwin, Linda K. ....Thousand Oaks, CA
Corwin, Lisa R. ....Bloomington, IL
Corwin, Manal S. ....Treasury Department,
Departmental Offices, GV
Corwin, Marjorie A. ....Baltimore, MD
Corwin, Mary J. ....Hillsboro, OR
Corwin & Matthews ....Huntington, NY
Corwin, Melanie S. ....Cincinnati, OH
Corwin, Nathaniel L. ....Mineola, NY
Corwin, Neil M. ....New York, NY
Corwin, Paul M. ....New York, NY
Corwin, Philip S. ....Washington, DC
Corwin, Rachel G. ....Kalamazoo, MI
Corwin, Richard A. ....New York, NY
Corwin, Robert L. ....Huntington, NY
Corwin, Sally A., (Mrs.) ....Boston, MA
Corwin, Scott J. ....Los Angeles, CA
Corwin, Seth D. ....New York, NY
Corwin, Sherman P. ....Chicago, IL
Corwin, Solomon & Tenenbaum, P.C.
New York, NY
Corwin, Stephen C. ....Muskegon, MI
Corwin, Thomas K. ....Waco, TX
Corwin, Tilley, Deems & Brumlow, P.C.
Calhoun, GA
Cartersville, GA
Rome, GA
Corwin, Timon Jon ....Kalamazoo, MI
Corwin, Timothy S. ....Waco, TX
Corwin, Wickham ....Fargo, ND
Corwin, William F. ....Durango, CO
Corwin, William J. ....Menlo Park, CA
Corwine, David B. ....Flossmoor, IL
Cory, Alec L. ....San Diego, CA
Cory, Barbara E. ....Burlington, VT
Cory, C. Ray ....Bellevue, WA
Cory, Charles F. ....Denver, CO
Cory, Charles F. ....Hiawassee, GA
Cory, Charles J. ....San Jose, CA
Cory, Charles R. ....New York, NY
Cory & Cory ....Bucyrus, OH
Cory, David R. ....Bucyrus, OH
Cory, Donald W. ....Des Plaines, IL
Cory, Ernest ....Birmingham, AL
Cory, Ernest N., Jr. ....Harwood, MD
Cory, Frank B. ....Lima, OH
Cory, Frederick W. ....Washington, DC
Cory, G. Lee, Jr. ....Charlotte, NC
Cory, George L. ....Sacramento, CA
Cory, Gerald A. ....Waterford, CT
Cory, Janet B. ....Chicago, IL
Cory, Jennifer Lee ....Orlando, FL
Cory, John A. ....Atlanta, GA
Cory, John A., P.C. ....Atlanta, GA
Cory, Kenneth C. ....Las Vegas, NV
Cory, Kenneth C., A Professional Corporation ....Las Vegas, NV
Cory, Larry D. ....Los Angeles, CA
Cory, Lee Troutman ....Louisville, KY
Cory, Meredith, Witter, Roush & Cheney, A Legal Professional Association ....Lima, OH
Cory, Michael J. ....Mount Clemens, MI
Cory, Michael V., Jr. ....Jackson, MS
Cory, Nancy P. ....Great Falls, MT
Cory, R. Mark ....Des Moines, IA
Cory, Richard H. ....Austin, TX
Cory, Richard J., P.A. ....Fort Lauderdale, FL
Cory, Richard L. ....Bucyrus, OH
Cory, Rick A. ....Evansville, IN
Cory, Thomas J. ....Troy, MI
Cory, Timothy S., & Associates, Law Offices of ....Las Vegas, NV
Cory, Walter J., Jr. ....Roanoke, VA
Cory, Watson, Crowder & DeGaris
Birmingham, AL
Coryea, W. Gordon ....Marion, IN
Coryell, Cornelius E., II ....Louisville, KY
Coryell, Frank ....Louisville, KY
Coryell, James R. ....Decatur, IL
Coryell, Jeffrey Alan ....Austin, TX
Coryell, Kenneth M. ....Atlanta, GA
Coryell, Marshall K. ....Anchorage, AK
Coryer, Amy L. ....Harrisburg, PA
Coryn, James J. ....Rock Island, IL
Coryn, Walker and Meehan ....Rock Island, IL
Corzatt, Jeffrey C.
Department of Labor, GV
Corzilius, Daniel ....Quincy, MA
Corzin, Fiocca, Sanislo & Ufholz
Akron, OH
Corzin, Harold A. ....Akron, OH
Corzine, Darrell Wayne ....Odessa, TX
Corzine, Jeffrey L. ....Sacramento, CA
Corzine, John A. ....Sacramento, CA
Corzine, R. Allen ....Waterloo, IA
Corzine, William J., III ....Chillicothe, OH
Cosantino, Joseph A. ....Copiague, NY
Cosbey, Roger B. ....Fort Wayne, IN
Cosby & Bell, P.C. ....Chicago, IL
Cosby, Brian P., P.A. ....Ocean City, MD
Cosby, Brian Peter ....Ocean City, MD
Cosby, Cameron N. ....Richmond, VA
Cosby, Catherine Czufin ....Jacksonville, FL
Cosby, Charles C., Jr. ....Richmond, VA
Cosby, Fielding Pentecost ....Indianapolis, IN
Cosby, James C. ....Richmond, VA
Cosby, James G. ....Roanoke, VA
Cosby, Jeffrey C. ....West Palm Beach, FL
Cosby, Joseph G. ....Arlington, VA
Cosby, M. Ann Neil ....Richmond, VA
Cosby, Megan K. ....Los Angeles, CA
Cosby, Michael G. ....Waco, TX
Cosby, Richard W. ....Chicago, IL
Cosby, Robert E. ....Jacksonville, FL
Cosby, Robert W. ....San Francisco, CA
Cosby, Sandra E. ....Harrogate, TN
Cosby, Sandra Kaye ....Metairie, LA
Coscarelli, Dianne S. ....Cleveland, OH
Coschignano, Christopher J. ....Syosset, NY
Coscia, Anthony R. ....New Brunswick, NJ
New York, NY
Coscia, Claudia V. ....Fort Worth, TX
Coscia, Frank M. ....Hackensack, NJ
Coscia, John B. ....Staten Island, NY
Coscia, Monica A. ....Chicago, IL
Coscia, Thomas P. ....Hartford, CT
Coscino, Vincent M. ....Irvine, CA
Cosco, Anne M. ....Lowell, MA
Cosco, Jonathan M. ....Boston, MA
Cosculluela, Alex E. ....Houston, TX
Cosden, Christopher E. ....Sarasota, FL
Cosden, Edward D., Jr. ....Greenwich, CT
Cosden, William E., Jr. ....Orinda, CA
Cosdon, L. C. ....New Hope, PA
Cosel, Peter M. ....Newport, RI
Cosel, Robert V., Jr. ....New York, NY
Pelham, NY
Cosel, R. V. ....Pelham, NY
Cosel, Stephen R. ....Los Angeles, CA
Coselli, Lazor & Durham ....Houston, TX
Coselli, Paul J. ....Houston, TX
Coselli, Peter C. ....Houston, TX
Coselli, Ralph J. ....Houston, TX
Coselli, Richard ....Houston, TX
Cosens, Barbara A. ....Helena, MT
Cosentino, Andrew J. ....New York, NY
Cosentino & Christofeno ....Elkhart, IN
Cosentino, John ....Malibu, CA
Cosentino, John L. ....Gunnison, CO
Cosentino, John P. ....Las Cruces, NM
Cosentino, John R. ....Providence, RI
Cosentino, Joseph L. ....New Bedford, MA
Cosentino, Julia Satti ....Boston, MA
Cosentino, Julian D. ....St. Louis, MO
Cosentino, Lisa K. ....Yukon, OK
Cosentino, Michael A. ....Elkhart, IN
Cosentino, Michael B. ....Wellesley, MA
Cosentino, Patricia L. ....Chicago, IL
Cosentino, Philip S. ....Chambersburg, PA
Cosentino, Richard J. ....Chicago, IL
Cosentino, Richard N. ....Weedsport, NY
Cosentino, Richard V. ....Haddonfield, NJ
Cosentino, Robert E. ....White Plains, NY
Cosentino, Robert J. ....Providence, RI
Cosentino, Snyder & Snyder
New Hartford, NY
West Winfield, NY
Cosentino, Stephen J. ....Phoenix, AZ
Cosentino, Thomas ....San Francisco, CA
Cosentino, Victor J. ....North Hollywood, CA
Cosenza, Albert C. ....Brooklyn, NY
Cosenza, Diane Ried ....New Orleans, LA
Cosenza, George J. ....Parkersburg, WV
Ripley, WV
Cosenza, Louis J. ....New Orleans, LA
Cosenza, Matthew A. ....Cherry Hill, NJ
Blue Bell, PA
Cosenza, Thomas M. ....New York, NY
Cosenza, Todd G. ....New York, NY
Cosenza, Underwood & Merriman
Parkersburg, WV
Ripley, WV
Cosenzo, Joseph Carl ....Neptune, NJ
Coseo, John P. ....Saratoga Springs, NY
Coseo, Peter L. ....Saratoga Springs, NY
Cosetti, Joseph L. ....Pittsburgh, PA
Cosey, Gwendolyn D. ....Key West, FL
Cosey, Henri M. ....Houston, TX
Cosgrave, Carmel M. ....Chicago, IL
Cosgrave, John J. ....Portland, OR
Cosgrave, Vergeer & Kester, L.L.P.
Hillsboro, OR
Oregon City, OR
Portland, OR
Vancouver, WA
Cosgrave, Walter J. ....Portland, OR
Cosgriff, Bradley Thomas ....Hopkins, MN
Cosgriff, Elizabeth Frazer ....Portland, OR
Cosgriff, James H., III ....Buffalo, NY
Cosgriff, Peter ....Leadville, CO
Cosgriff, Roderick C. ....St. Paul, MN
Cosgriff, William J. ....St. Paul, MN
Cosgrove, Carol Atha ....Atlanta, GA
Cosgrove, Cathy Marie ....Livingston, NJ
Cosgrove, Charles A.
Department of the Army,
Office of the Judge Advocate General, GV
Cosgrove, Charles H.
Rancho Palos Verdes, CA
Cosgrove, Christopher M. ....Litchfield, CT
Cosgrove & Cosgrove ....Palm Desert, CA
Cosgrove, Daniel J. ....Des Moines, IA
Omaha, NE
Cosgrove, David B. ....Costa Mesa, CA
Cosgrove, David B. ....Newark, NJ
Cosgrove, David J. ....New Britain, CT
Cosgrove, David R. ....Short Hills, NJ
Cosgrove, Edward C. ....Buffalo, NY
Cosgrove, Eisenberg and Kiley, P.C.
Boston, MA
Quincy, MA
Cosgrove, Ellen M. ....Chicago, IL
Cosgrove, Emmet L. ....New London, CT
Cosgrove, Flynn & Gaskins, L.L.P.
Minneapolis, MN
Cosgrove, Francis P. ....Philadelphia, PA
Cosgrove, Frank ....Sioux City, IA
Cosgrove, Gail Y. ....Honolulu, HI
Cosgrove, Hugh J. ....Minneapolis, MN
Cosgrove, James F. ....Lewiston, ME
Old Bethpage, NY
Cosgrove, James F. ....Worcester, MA
Cosgrove, James F. X. ....Baltimore, MD
Cosgrove, James Leo ....Atlanta, GA
Cosgrove, Jeanne Schofield ....New York, NY
Cosgrove, Jeremiah P. ....Saratoga Springs, NY
Cosgrove, Jody L. ....Riverside, CT
Cosgrove, Joe ....Sioux City, IA
Cosgrove, John B. ....Clinton, NY
Cosgrove, John F. ....Miami, FL
Cosgrove, John L. ....Auburn, CA
Cosgrove, John R. ....Menlo Park, CA
Cosgrove, Joseph D. ....New York, NY
Cosgrove, Joseph Matthias ....Forty Fort, PA
Cosgrove, Joseph P. ....Great Falls, MT
Cosgrove, Kevin J. ....Norfolk, VA
Cosgrove, Leonard A. ....Lancaster, CA
Cosgrove, Leonard W., Jr. ....Concord, NH
Cosgrove, Martha A. Shaw ....Simsbury, CT
Cosgrove, Martin S. ....Boston, MA
Quincy, MA
Cosgrove, Michael F. ....Blakely, PA
Cosgrove, Michael J. ....Palm Desert, CA
Cosgrove, Michael S.
Federal Deposit Insurance Corporation,
Corporate Affairs Section, GV
Cosgrove, Nelson H. ....Buffalo, NY
Cosgrove, O'Connell & Blatt
Worcester, MA
Cosgrove, Patricia M. ....Chicago, IL
Cosgrove, Paul S. ....Portland, OR
Cosgrove, Paula M. ....Boston, MA
Cosgrove, Philip R. ....Los Angeles, CA
Cosgrove, Richard A. ....Chicago, IL
Cosgrove, Richd. M. ....Hartford, CT
Cosgrove, Robert A., The Law Offices of
San Diego, CA
Cosgrove, Robert C. ....Boston, MA
Cosgrove, Robert S. ....West Caldwell, NJ
Cosgrove, Robert T. ....Denver, CO
Cosgrove, Russel J. A. ....Oakland, CA
Cosgrove, Scott ....Miami, FL
Cosgrove, Sharon J. ....Joshua Tree, CA
Cosgrove, Shawn P. ....Billings, MT
Cosgrove, Stephen ....Rutland, VT
Cosgrove, Stephen, P.C. ....Rutland, VT
Cosgrove, Terrence R. ....Cincinnati, OH
Cosgrove, Terry B. ....Helena, MT
Cosgrove, Terry M. ....Chicago, IL
Cosgrove, Thaddeus E. ....Holstein, IA
Cosgrove, Thaddeus E. ....Ida Grove, IA
Cosgrove, Timothy R. ....Hendersonville, NC
Cosgrove, Timothy J. ....Cleveland, OH
Columbus, OH
Cosgrove, Webb & Oman ....Topeka, KS
Cosgrove, William N. ....Palm Desert, CA
Cosham, David E. ....Middletown, CT
Coshnear, Lawrence B. ....Baltimore, MD
Cosho, Ann L. ....Boise, ID
Cosho, Humphrey, Greener & Welsh, P.A.
Boise, ID
Nampa, ID
Cosiano, Ralph V. ....Cleveland, OH
Cosimi, Gregg B. ....Boston, MA
Cosimini, Mark D. ....Minneapolis, MN
Cosimini, R. Mark ....Urbana, IL
Cosio, Eduardo ....Miami, FL
Cosio, J. Raul ....Miami, FL
Cosio, Javier ....San Jose, CA
Cositore, Frank R., Jr. ....Freeport, NY
Coskey, Douglas R. ....Ann Arbor, MI
Coskey, Hal L. ....Los Angeles, CA
Coskey, Hal L., A Prof. Corp., Law Offices of
Los Angeles, CA
Coskey, Julia Bohlmann ....Titusville, FL
Coskey Law Offices ....Titusville, FL
Coskey, Susan L. ....Seattle, WA
Coskran, William G. ....Los Angeles, CA
Coskrey, Blaney A., III ....Columbia, SC
Cosky, Francis A. ....Moorestown, NJ
Coslett, Charles R. ....Kingston, PA
Coslett & Coslett ....Kingston, PA
Coslick, Ronald ....Washington, DC
Coslit, Michael E. ....Newark, NJ
Cosma, Thomas S. ....Roseland, NJ
Cosman, Marin ....San Diego, CA
Cosman, Shawn D. ....Louisville, KY
Cosmano, James Anthony ....Schaumburg, IL
Cosme, Keila D. ....Toledo, OH
Cosme Almeztica, Armando ....San Juan, PR
Cosmen, Franklin G., Jr. ....Miami, FL
Cosmi, John R. ....Paterson, NJ
Cosmic, John ....Amarillo, TX
Cosmich, John D. ....Jackson, MS
Cosmos, Jeanne K. ....Natick, MA
Cosner, Alan G. ....East Brunswick, NJ
Cosner, C. Kinian, Jr. ....Nashville, TN
Cosner & Cosner ....East Brunswick, NJ
Cosner, Dail W. ....Houston, TX
Cosner, Krista L. ....Chicago, IL
Cosner, Staci A. ....East Brunswick, NJ
Cosnowski, William, Jr.
Bloomfield Hills, MI
Cosper, Harvey L., Jr. ....Charlotte, NC
Cosper, Harvey L., Sr. ....Charlotte, NC
Coss, Anthony S. ....Phoenix, AZ
Coss, Christopher C. ....Paoli, PA
Coss, David P. ....Charlotte, NC
Coss, Edward G. ....Newport Beach, CA
Coss, Elizabeth C. ....Charlotte, NC
Coss, Jennifer Corcoran ....Charlotte, NC
Coss, Michele S. ....Phoenix, AZ
Coss, Raymond L. ....Nashville, TN
Coss, Richard E. ....Treasury Department,
Internal Revenue Service, GV
Coss, Rocky A. ....Hillsboro, OH
Coss, Stephen K. ....Charlotte, NC
Cossa, Kathleen R. ....Fairfax, VA
Cossaboom, David A. ....Santa Ana, CA
Cossaboom, Ewing O. ....Mt. Healthy, OH
Cossaboom, Richard B. ....Littleton, CO
Cossack, Roger L. ....Washington, DC
Cossairt, Kathleen J. ....Olathe, KS
Cossar & Cossar ....Charleston, MS
Cossar, George P., Jr. ....Charleston, MS
Cossar, L. Pepper ....Jackson, MS
Cosse, Clark R., III ....Baton Rouge, LA
Cossé, Irvy E., Jr. ....New Orleans, LA
Cossé, Steven A. ....El Dorado, AR
Cossel, John O. ....Kellogg, ID
Cossell, Marcia J. ....Indianapolis, IN
Cossette, W. J. ....Stockton, CA
Cossi, A. Dennis ....Ironwood, MI
Cossi, David A. ....Minneapolis, MN
Cossi, Lidia A. ....El Segundo, CA
Cossich & Associates, A Prof. Corp.
Belle Chasse, LA
Cossich, Philip F., Jr. ....Belle Chasse, LA
Cossidente, John G., Jr. ....Oak Forest, IL
Cossident-Italia, Cathleen ....Melrose Park, IL

Cossin, Alexander J. ....Pomona, NY
Cossingham, Kenneth A. North Andover, MA
Cossingham Law Office, P.C. North Andover, MA
Cossio, Raul A. ....Key Largo, FL
Cossitt, Erika L. ....Tucson, AZ
Cossitt, James H. ....Missoula, MT
Cossitt, James H., P.C. ....Missoula, MT
Cossitt, William B. ....Reno, NV
Cossman, Harry ....Newport Beach, CA
Cossman, Jill A. ....Los Angeles, CA
Cossman, Paul ....Anchorage, AK
Cossman, Paul, P.C., Law Offices of Anchorage, AK
Cossman, Peter J. ....Princeton, NJ
Cossman, Todd L. ....Anchorage, AK
Cosso, Dennis G. ....Arcadia, CA
Cossolini, Robert F. ....Short Hills, NJ
Cosson, David ....Washington, DC
Cosson, George ....Corpus Christi, TX
Cossu, Denise M. ....White Plains, NY
Cossum, John S. ....Houston, TX
Cost, Bradley P. ....New York, NY
Cost, Charles D. ....Yorba Linda, CA
Cost, Jeffrey S. ....San Carlos, CA
Cost, Jennifer Burns ....Falmouth, ME
Cost, John A. ....San Carlos, CA
Cost, John A., & Jeffrey S. Cost, A Professional Corporation ....San Carlos, CA
Cost, John J., (P.C.) ....Los Angeles, CA
Costa, Anthony M. ....Newark, NJ
Costa, Anthony P. ....Stratford, NJ
Costa, Carol A. ....Canton, OH
Costa, Catherine M. ....Morris Plains, NJ
Costa, Christine ....Rosemead, CA
Costa, Christopher K. ....Princeton, NJ
Costa, Christopher R. ....Washington, DC
Silver Spring, MD
Costa & Clark ....Norwich, CT
Costa, Claudia A. ....Newark, NJ
New York, NY
Costa & Costa ....Teaneck, NJ
Costa, Daniel P. ....Sacramento, CA
Costa, David E. ....Detroit, MI
Costa, David V. ....Oakland, CA
Costa, Dominic P. ....Oreland, PA
Costa, Donna ....White Plains, NY
Costa, Doreen Leavens ....Melville, NY
New York, NY
Costa, Edward Q. ....Decatur, IL
Costa, Giacinto G. ....New Haven, CT
Costa, Henry J., Jr. ....Blue Bell, PA
Costa, Jay, Jr. ....Pittsburgh, PA
Costa, Jennifer E. ....Sacramento, CA
Costa, Jennifer F. Paine ....Washington, DC
Costa, Jess Dale ....Bentleyville, PA
Costa, Jesse D. ....Bentleyville, PA
Costa, John ....Roanoke, VA
Costa, John A. ....Nyack, NY
Costa, John F. ....Stamford, CT
New York, NY
Costa, John R. ....Taunton, MA
Costa, Joseph P. ....Pacific Palisades, CA
Costa, Joseph S. ....Brooklyn, NY
Costa, Kristin N. ....Kansas City, MO
Costa, Leanne M. ....Providence, RI
Costa, Leilani Medina ....Pittsburgh, PA
Costa, Leonard A., Jr. ....Pittsburgh, PA
Wheeling, WV
Costa, Leonard F. ....Stratford, NJ
Costa, Loretta M. ....Sacramento, CA
Costa, Margaret L. ....Boston, MA
Costa, Mark A. ....Chicago, IL
Costa, Mary C. ....Los Angeles, CA
Costa, Mary Ellen ....Pittsburgh, PA
Costa, Matthew R. ....Tampa, FL
Costa, McKay & Donnelly ....Nyack, NY
Costa, Michael A. ....New York, NY
Costa, Nelson J. ....Newton, MA
Costa, Paul T. ....Norwich, CT
Costa, Penny M. ....Los Angeles, CA
Costa, Peter L. ....Buffalo, NY
Costa, Philip A. ....New Orleans, LA
Costa, Richard J. ....New York, NY
Costa, Richard M. ....Boston, MA
Costa, Salvatore R. ....Clarksville, MD
Costa, Sam, Jr. ....Boca Raton, FL
Costa, Samuel J. ....Syracuse, NY
Costa, Samuel J., P.C. ....Syracuse, NY
Costa, Santo J. ....Morrisville, NC
Costa, Sharon S. ....Mount Vernon, IL
Costa, Terri Salt ....Sarasota, FL
Costa, Theodore M. ....Mount Holly, NJ
Costa, Thomas ....Wexford, PA
Costa, Thomas E. ....Plainsboro, NJ
Costa, Thomas J., Jr. ....Teaneck, NJ
Costa, Thomas L. ....Melville, NY
Costa, Thomas L., LLP, Law Offices of Melville, NY
Costa, Thos. J. ....Teaneck, NJ
Costa, Wayne E., Jr. ....Honolulu, HI
Costa, William A. ....Boston, MA
Costabel, Attilio M. ....Miami, FL
Costabile, Gregory S. ....Cleveland, OH
Costa-Clarke, Rosalia J. ....Philadelphia, PA
Costagliola, Robert J. ....Philadelphia, PA
Costain, Bonnie J. ....Pierre, SD
Costakis, Arthur J. ....Manchester, NH
Costakis, Thomas J. ....Indianapolis, IN
Costakos, Jeffrey N. ....Denver, CO
Costalas, John K. ....Broomall, PA
Costalas, Stephen C. ....Philadelphia, PA
Costales, Dianne M. ....Los Angeles, CA
Costales, Elaine Rose ....Worcester, MA
Costales, Gary A. ....Miami, FL
Costales, Lynn B.K. ....Honolulu, HI
Costales, Marco D. ....Los Angeles, CA

Costamagna, David J. ....San Rafael, CA
Costan, Charlotte E. ....Burbank, CA
Costan, James M. ....Washington, DC
Costantakos, Christine P. ....Omaha, NE
Costantian, Gerard ....Las Vegas, NV
Costantin, Carrie A. ....Clayton, MO
Costantini, Anthony J. ....New York, NY
Costantini, Chris J. ....Harrisburg, PA
Costantini, Joseph J. ....Mays Landing, NJ
Costantini, Lawrence J. ....Milford, CT
Costantini, William P. ....Melville, NY
Costantino, Andrew A. ....New York, NY
Costantino, Cathy A. Federal Deposit Insurance Corporation, Liquidation Branch, GV
Costantino, David M. ....Indianapolis, IN
Costantino, John, Jr. ....Miami Beach, FL
Costantino, Karen Kaechele Washington, DC
Costantino, Mario A. ....Alexandria, VA
Costantino, Mark T. ....Mineola, NY
New York, NY
Costantino, Nicholas C. ....Buffalo, NY
Costantino, R. Scott ....Jacksonville, FL
Costantino, Ralph S. ....El Cajon, CA
Costantino, Robert A. ....Boston, MA
Costantino, Tracy L. ....Rochester, NY
Costantino, Tracy Wei ....Los Angeles, CA
Costantino, Vincent C. ....Department of Labor, Office of the Solicitor, GV
Costanza, Andrew A. ....Rochester, NY
Costanza, Angelo A. ....Rochester, NY
Costanza, Angelo J. ....Martinez, CA
Costanza, Jean M. ....Los Angeles, CA
Costanza, Jennifer M. ....Burbank, CA
Costanza, Joseph E. ....East Chicago, IN
Merrillville, IN
Costanza, Kevin S. ....Seattle, WA
Costanza, L. Damien ....Rochester, NY
Costanza, Marion G ....New Brunswick, NJ
Costanza, Nicholas J. ....Raleigh, NC
Costanza, Peter J. ....Boston, MA
Costanza, Ralph P., Jr. ....Norfolk, MA
Costanza, Richard John ....Southern Pines, NC
Costanzi, Charles J. ....Blue Bell, PA
Costanzo, Alfred J., Jr. ....Albany, NY
Costanzo, Anthony G. ....Alma, MI
Costanzo, Anthony J. ....Cleveland, OH
Costanzo, Catherine M. ....Dover, NH
Costanzo, Cathy E. ....Northampton, MA
Costanzo, Charles A. ....Union Beach, NJ
Costanzo, Charles P. ....Guilford, CT
Costanzo, David P. ....Chicago, IL
Costanzo, E. Marc ....Philadelphia, PA
Costanzo, Frank M. ....Orlando, FL
Costanzo, James V. ....Convent Station, NJ
Costanzo & Lazzaro ....Lakewood, OH
Costanzo, Lorin A. ....Vinton, VA
Costanzo, Margaret Ann North Kansas City, MO
Costanzo, Maridee L. ....Warren, OH
Costanzo, Neal E. ....Fresno, CA
Costanzo, R. Joseph, Jr. ....Aventura, FL
Costanzo, Raymond J. ....Lakewood, OH
Costanzo, Richard L. ....Toms River, NJ
Costanzo, Robert V. ....Lexington, KY
Middlesboro, KY
Costanzo, Rody J. ....Jersey City, NJ
Costanzo, Sally S. ....Costa Mesa, CA
Costanzo, Samuel L. ....Phoenix, AZ
Costanzo, Sarino R. ....Miami, FL
Costanzo, Vito A. ....Los Angeles, CA
Costar, Charles B., III ....Orlando, FL
Costas, Christophil B. ....New York, NY
Costas, Elliott H. ....Victoria, TX
Costas, H. Jonathon ....Valparaiso, IN
Costas, John M. ....Adrian, MI
Costas, Julia Cobb ....Tallahassee, FL
Costas, Norman & Clement ....Valparaiso, IN
Costas, Pamela G. ....Chicago, IL
Costas, Peter L. ....Hartford, CT
Costas, Stephen J. ....Irving, TX
Costas, Toby Wosk ....Dallas, TX
Costa-Sakelaris, Kris ....Hammond, IN
Costa-Sheedy, Valerie ....Phoenix, AZ
Costa-Traman, Cynthia A. White Plains, NY
Coste, Jeffrey A. ....Irvine, CA
Coste, John C. ....Philadelphia, PA
Costea, Natalia ....Los Angeles, CA
Costell, Alan Todd ....Smithtown, NY
Costell & Associates, PC ....Los Angeles, CA
Costell, Jeffrey Lee ....Los Angeles, CA
Costella, Andrew J., Jr. ....Garden City, NY
Costella, Joseph C. ....San Ramon, CA
Costella, Margaret Frances Marriottsville, MD
Costellia, Jeffrey L. ....McLean, VA
Costello, Alan R. ....Phoenix, AZ
Costello, Alexander S. ....Lowell, MA
Costello, Anita Coles ....Buffalo, NY
Costello, Ann S. ....Washington, DC
Costello, B. Patrick ....Greensburg, PA
Costello, Bartley A., Jr. ....Boulder, CO
Costello, Bartley A., Jr., P.C., Law Offices of Boulder, CO
Costello, Bartley J. ....Rutland, VT
Costello, Bartley J., III ....Albany, NY
Costello, Benjamin L. ....Washington, PA
Costello, Bradley H. ....Lombard, IL
Costello, Carrie Yang ....Berkeley, CA
Costello, Charles E. Agency for International Development, Other Offices of A.I.D., GV
Costello, Charles F., Jr. ....Wayne, NJ
Costello, Chris W. ....Deerfield Beach, FL
Costello, Christopher G. ....Tampa, KS
Costello, Christopher J. ....Washington, DC

Costello, Christopher M. Winter Park, FL
Costello, Christopher W. ....Westbury, NY
Costello, Claire M. ....New York, NY
Costello Cooney & Fearon, LLP Syracuse, NY
Costello & Costello, P.C. ....Carpentersville, IL
Costello, D. Brian ....Alexandria, VA
Costello, Daniel C. ....Annapolis, MD
Baltimore, MD
Costello, Daniel J. ....Baldwin, NY
Costello, Daniel W. ....Columbus, OH
Costello, David J ....Flossmoor, IL
Costello, David W. ....Washington, PA
Costello, Deborah Marie ....Richmond, VA
Costello, Dedee S. ....Panama City, FL
Costello, Dennis D. ....Sturgeon Bay, WI
Costello, Donald F., Law Offices of Santa Cruz, CA
Costello, Donald O. ....Bend, OR
Costello, Dorothy Stassun ....Berwyn, PA
Costello, Edward J. ....Tampa, KS
Costello, Edward J., Jr. Santa Monica, CA
Costello, Elizabeth ....Muncie, IN
Costello, Ellen M. ....New Haven, CT
Costello, Eric Owen ....Newark, NJ
Costello, Francis W. ....Los Angeles, CA
Costello, Frank J. ....Washington, DC
Costello, Frank R., Jr. ....Philadelphia, PA
Costello, Frederick A. ....Warwick, RI
Costello, Gail T. ....Stoneham, MA
Costello, George A. ....Library of Congress, Congressional Research Service, GV
Costello, George B. ....Upper Saddle River, NJ
Costello, Gerald T. ....Tacoma, WA
Costello, Gillian ....New York, NY
Costello, Gregory T. ....Seattle, WA
Costello, Harry G. ....St. Paul, MN
Costello & Hubacher ....Alexandria, VA
Costello, J Mcgarry ....New York, NY
Costello, James A. ....New York, NY
Costello, James A. ....Fairview, NC
Costello, James C. ....New York, NY
Costello, James J. ....Chicago, IL
Costello, James J., Jr. ....Springfield, IL
Costello, James L. ....Portland, ME
Costello, James M. ....Fort Myers, FL
Costello, James M., Jr. ....Bolingbrook, IL
Costello, James Paul ....Chicago, IL
Costello, James Paul, Ltd. ....Chicago, IL
Costello, Jan A. ....Darien, CT
Costello, Jan Clifford ....Los Angeles, CA
Costello, Jeanmarie P. ....Riverhead, NY
Costello, Jeannie ....New York, NY
Costello, John F. ....Irving, TX
Costello, John F. X. ....Lanham, MD
Costello, John J. ....New York, NY
Costello, John J. ....Rochester, NY
Costello, John J. ....Syracuse, NY
Costello, John J. ....Seattle, WA
Costello, John K. ....New Haven, CT
Costello, John L., Jr. ....Arlington, VA
Costello, John M. ....Rochester, NY
Costello, John M. ....Rapid City, SD
Costello, John M., Jr. ....New York, NY
Costello, John P. ....Buffalo, NY
Costello, John R. ....Baltimore, MD
Costello, John W. ....Chicago, IL
Costello, Joseph A., Jr. ....Monroe, MI
Costello, Joseph E. ....New York, NY
Costello, Joseph G. ....Brooklyn, NY
Costello, Joseph J. ....Philadelphia, PA
Costello, Joseph L. ....Sonoma, CA
Costello, Joseph M. ....Carmel, NY
Costello, Joseph M. ....New York, NY
Costello, Joseph O. ....Los Angeles, CA
Costello, Joseph Richard ....Brooklyn, NY
Costello, Karen M. ....Los Angeles, CA
Costello, Kathleen F. Federal Communications Commission, Cable Services Bureau, GV
Costello, Kelly A. ....Wilmington, DE
Costello, Kelly L. ....Chicago, IL
Costello, Kenneth R. ....Los Angeles, CA
Costello, Kevin G. ....Chicago, IL
Costello, Kevin M. ....Cherry Hill, NJ
Costello, Kevin M. ....Milwaukee, WI
Costello, Kevin R. ....Los Angeles, CA
Costello, Kevin S. ....Phoenix, AZ
Costello, Kim S. ....Peoria, AZ
Costello & Landrigan ....Somerville, MA
Costello Law Office ....Milwaukee, WI
Costello, Leo E. ....Birmingham, AL
Costello, Leo F. ....San Luis Obispo, CA
Costello, Leonard W. ....Port Orchard, WA
Costello, M. Patricia ....Monroe, MI
Costello & Mabie, A Professional Corporation ....Brattleboro, VT
Costello, Marcus Lee ....Tillamook, OR
Costello, Margaret A. ....Detroit, MI
Costello, Mark ....Rochester, NY
Costello, Mark A. ....New York, NY
Costello, Mark A. ....Rochester, NY
Costello, Mark E. ....Garden City, NY
Costello, Marsh, Ward & Christner Greensburg, PA
Costello, Martin J. ....St. Paul, MN
Costello, Mary Alice ....Houston, TX
Costello, Mary K. Downey Springfield, MA
Costello, Michael C. ....Cambridge, MA
Costello, Michael G. ....Southfield, MI
Costello, Michael J. ....Springfield, IL
Costello, Michael J. ....St. Louis, MO
Costello, Michael J. ....Ithaca, NY
Costello, Michael J. ....Seattle, WA
Costello, Michael L. ....Albany, NY

Costello, Nathan M. ....Las Vegas, NV
Costello, P. Keely ....Rochester, NY
Costello, Patrick D. ....Orofino, ID
Costello, Patrick J. Department Of Veterans Affairs, Board of Veterans Appeals, GV
Costello, Patrick J. ....Boston, MA
Costello, Patrick K. ....Heron Lake, MN
Lakefield, MN
Costello, Patrick M. ....Palo Alto, CA
Costello, Paul G. ....Smithtown, NY
Costello, Peter ....Redding, CA
Costello, Philip A. ....Monroe, MI
Costello, Philip N., Jr. ....Madison, CT
Costello, Porter, Hill, Heisterkamp, Bushnell & Carpenter, LLP ....Rapid City, SD
Costello, R. Richard ....Las Vegas, NV
Costello, Ralph F. ....West Babylon, NY
Costello, Richard G. ....Boston, MA
Costello, Robert C. ....Exeter, NH
Costello, Robert E. ....Somers Point, NJ
Costello, Robert E. ....Rockville Centre, NY
Costello, Robert H., Jr. ....Somerville, MA
Costello, Robert J. ....New York, NY
Costello, Robert J., Jr. ....Gainesville, FL
Costello, Robert K. ....Detroit, MI
Costello, Robert L. ....Chicago, IL
Costello, Robert M. ....Natick, MA
Costello, Robert P. ....Oklahoma City, OK
Costello, Robert T. ....Morristown, NJ
Costello, Robert V. ....Boston, MA
Costello, Sean M. ....Baltimore, MD
Costello, Sean P. ....Cleveland, OH
Costello, Selene H. ....New York, NY
Costello, Shannon L. ....Dayton, OH
Costello, Shea & Gaffney North Brunswick, NJ
New York, NY
Riverhead, NY
Rockville Centre, NY
Costello, Sims & Royston ....Fort Myers, FL
Costello, Stacy E. ....Washington, DC
Costello, Stephen J. ....Carpentersville, IL
Costello, Steven D. ....Lancaster, PA
Costello, Steven J. ....Chicago, IL
Costello, Stott and Grayson Birmingham, AL
Costello, Susan J. ....Philadelphia, PA
Costello, T. Brent ....Los Angeles, CA
Costello, Terrance A. ....Minneapolis, MN
Costello, Terrence W., IV ....Yorktown, VA
Costello, Thomas ....Massapequa, NY
Costello, Thomas ....Riverhead, NY
Costello, Thomas Christopher Baltimore, MD
Costello, Thomas G. ....Chicopee, MA
Costello, Thomas G. ....Troy, MI
Costello, Thomas J. ....Carmel, NY
Costello, Thomas M., Jr. Farmington Hills, MI
Costello, Thomas P. ....New York, NY
Costello, Thomas W. ....Brattleboro, VT
Costello, Timothy C. ....Philadelphia, PA
Costello, Timothy G. ....Milwaukee, WI
Costello, Timothy J. ....Rochester, NY
Costello, Timothy M. ....New York, NY
Costello, Truman J., (P.A.) Fort Myers, FL
Costello, Walter A., Jr. ....Salem, MA
Costello, William J., II ....Grand Island, NY
Costello, William L. ....Beachwood, OH
Costello, William L. Co., L.P.A. Beachwood, OH
Costello, Xiomara ....Redondo Beach, CA
Costelloe, John F. ....Boston, MA
Costelloe, Michael D. ....Pittsburgh, PA
Costelnock, Paul J. ....Washington, PA
Costen, John ....Memphis, TN
Costenbader, Charles M. ....Newark, NJ
Costenbader, Francis J. ....Nutley, NJ
Coster, Barbara J. ....Seattle, WA
Coster, Edgar M. ....Parsippany, NJ
Coster, James J. ....New York, NY
Coster, John G. H. ....Boston, MA
Coster, Kimberly A. ....Boise, ID
Coster, Michael J. ....Department of Justice, Immigration and Naturalization Service, GV
Costich, Emmett R. ....Postal Rate Commission, Office of the Consumer Advocate, GV
Costigan, Angela Maione ....Moorestown, NJ
Costigan & Company, P.C. ....New York, NY
Costigan, Dennis P. ....Bronx, NY
Costigan, J. Casey ....Bloomington, IL
Costigan, James V. ....New York, NY
Costigan, John M. ....Deerfield, IL
Costigan, John W. ....Tallahassee, FL
Costigan, Kathleen A. ....New York, NY
Costigan, Matthew D. ....Chicago, IL
Costigan, Maureen ....Arnold, MD
Costigan, Patricia A. ....Boston, MA
Costigan, Peter J. ....Port Jefferson Station, NY
Costigan, Philip P. ....Central Islip, NY
Costigan, Richard ....Philadelphia, PA
Costigan, Richard S., III ....Norcross, GA
Costigan, Thomas ....Boston, MA
Costigan, William F. ....Bloomington, IL
Costigan, William F. ....New York, NY
Costigan, William J. ....Akron, OH
Costigan & Wollrab, P.C. Bloomington, IL
Costiglio, Lawrence U. ....Uniondale, NY
Costikyan, Edward N. ....New York, NY
Costikyan, Haig ....New York, NY
Costilla, Frank, Jr. ....Brownsville, TX
Costilla, Frank, Jr., P.L.L.C. Brownsville, TX
McAllen, TX

Costilo, L. Barry
Federal Trade Commission, Bureau of Competition, GV
Costin, Charles A. ....Port St. Joe, FL
Costin, Christopher G. ....Santa Rosa, CA
Costin & Costin ....Port St. Joe, FL
Costin, Delida A. ....Palo Alto, CA
Costin, Rosemary ....Chicago, IL
Costin, Sandra Ward ....New York, NY
Costin, Sheila M. ....Alexandria, VA
Costin, Suzanne Hale ....Tulsa, OK
Costin, W. Dirk ....Denver, CO
Costine, Eric ....St. Clairsville, OH
Costine, J. Mark ....St. Clairsville, OH
Costine, John O. ....St. Clairsville, OH
Costine Law Firm The ....St. Clairsville, OH
Costis, Athena R. ....Oakland, CA
Costle, Caroline E. ....Alexandria, VA
Costle, Douglas M. ....Hartford, CT
Costle, Elizabeth R. ....Washington, DC
Costley, Cassandra LaVerne ....Baltimore, MD
Costley, J. Kevin ....Minneapolis, MN
Costley, John V., Jr. ....Covington, GA
Costley, Lloyd M. ....Washington, DC
Costley, Margaret V. ....Greensboro, NC
Costley, Mark F. ....Washington, DC
Costley, Mark O. ....Greensboro, NC
Costley, Mitchel H. ....Two Harbors, MN
Costley, Stephen L. ....Endicott, NY
Costley, Timothy A. ....Duluth, MN
Costley, William M. ....Ventura, CA
Costlow, Deborah C. ....Washington, DC
Costlow, Frederick F. ....Bangor, ME
Costlow, Gary Lee ....Johnstown, PA
Costo, John T. ....Seattle, WA
Costolo, William T. ....Orlando, FL
Coston, James E. ....Miami, FL
Chicago, IL
Coston & Lichtman ....Chicago, IL
Coston, P. Casey ....Detroit, MI
Coston, R. Richard ....Houston, TX
Coston, Ronald D. ....Boise, ID
Coston, William D. ....Washington, DC
Costonis, Theresa M. ....Nashville, TN
Costopoulos, Eve ....Kenilworth, NJ
Costopoulos, Foster and Fields
Lemoyne, PA
Costopoulos, George ....Philadelphia, PA
Costopoulos, William C. ....Lemoyne, PA
Costrini, Dorothea Summerell
Savannah, GA
Cot, José R. ....New Orleans, LA
Cota, Dennis M. ....Ontario, CA
Cotant, James C. ....Gaylord, MI
Cotant, Margaret ....Detroit, MI
Cotchett, Joseph W. ....Burlingame, CA
Los Angeles, CA
Cotchett, Pitre & Simon ....Burlingame, CA
Los Angeles, CA
San Mateo, CA
Cote, Alan Nelson ....North Andover, MA
Coté, Andrew C. ....Sharon, CT
Cote, Anne McPhilliamy ....Teterboro, NJ
Cote, Boyd C ....Glen Rock, NJ
Coté, C. Boyd ....Glen Rock, NJ
Cote & Casey ....Salem, MA
Cote, Cote & Hamann, P.A. ....Lewiston, ME
Cote, Craig G. ....Rancho Cucamonga, CA
Côté, Deborah L. ....San Francisco, CA
Cote, Denise ....New York, NY
Cote, Diane E. ....Lafayette, LA
Coté, Donna M. ....Chicago, IL
Cote, Earleen H. ....Fort Lauderdale, FL
Coté, Emily J. ....San Jose, CA
Cote, Eric B. ....Saco, ME
Cote, George J. B. ....Costa Mesa, CA
Cote & Guillory ....Saco, ME
Cote, James M. ....Salem, MA
Cote, James R. ....Bloomfield Hills, MI
Coté, Jennifer Wanty ....Brighton, MI
Cote, Johanna Gibbs ....Baltimore, MD
Coté, John L. ....East Lansing, MI
Cote, Joseph S., III ....Syracuse, NY
Cote, Karen R. ....St. Paul, MN
Cote, Kenneth J., Jr. ....Boston, MA
Coté, Lance R. ....Newport Beach, CA
Cote, Larry P. ....Falls Church, VA
Cote, Laurence ....Boston, MA
Cote & Limpert ....Syracuse, NY
Cote, Meredith A. ....Atlantic City, NJ
Cote, Michael A. ....Mineola, NY
Cote, Norma A. ....New York, NY
Cote, Paul A. ....Lewiston, ME
Cote, Paul A., Jr. ....Portland, ME
Cote, Raymond A. ....Elm Grove, WI
Cote, Richard P. ....Fullerton, CA
Cote, Robert A. ....New York, NY
Cote, Robert M. ....Syracuse, NY
Cote, Roger H. ....Kihei, HI
Cote, S. Raenele ....Villa Park, CA
Cote, Scott D. ....San Francisco, CA
Côté, Sean Andrew ....New York, NY
Coté, Steven J. ....Los Angeles, CA
Cote, Thomas J. ....Gorham, NH
Coté, Thomas J. ....Huntington, NY
Cote, Thomas J., P.C. ....Gorham, NH
Cote, Tracey Goyette ....Charlottesville, VA
Cote, William B. ....Lewiston, ME
Cotecchia, Alan B. ....Saugus, MA
Coteé,C. Boyd, P.C. ....Glen Rock, NJ
Cotelidis, Peter C. ....Mineola, NY
Cotellessa, Susan D. ....Williamsville, NY
Cotellesse, David P. ....Houston, TX
Cotera, Carol A. ....Phoenix, AZ
Cote-Sanders, Patricia J. ....Bakersfield, CA
Cotey, David E. ....Kingsport, TN
Cotgageorge, James ....Peabody, MA
Cotham, E. Ralph, IV ....Little Rock, AR
Cotham, Edward T., Jr. ....Houston, TX
Cotham, Harwell & Evans, P.C.
Houston, TX
Cotham, W. Mark ....Houston, TX
Cothern, Donald W. ....Tyler, TX
Cothern, Jas. H. ....Darby, MT
Cothern, John W. ....Memphis, TN
Cothorn, John A. ....Detroit, MI
Cothorn & Stanczyk, P.C. ....Detroit, MI
Cothran, C. Don, Jr. ....Atlanta, GA
Cothran, Darra Williamson
Columbia, SC
Cothran, Jack T. ....Flowery Branch, GA
Cothran, James C., Jr. ....Spartanburg, SC
Cothran, Joy D. ....Newport Beach, CA
Cothran, Monica L. ....Panama City, FL
Cothran, R. Ferrell, Jr. ....Manning, SC
Cothran, Ralph F. ....Manning, SC
Cothran & Robinson Law Firm
Manning, SC
Cothran, Samuel B., Jr. ....Charleston, SC
Cothran, Thomas P. ....Mount Pleasant, SC
Cothren, James P. ....Jackson, MS
Cothren Law Firm ....Jackson, MS
Coti, Ralph ....New York, NY
Coti & Sugrue ....New York, NY
Coticchia, Lori A. ....Rocky River, OH
Coticchia, Michael L. ....Cleveland, OH
Coticchio & Associates, P.C.
Grosse Pointe Woods, MI
Coticchio, Stephen A.
Grosse Pointe Woods, MI
Coticchio, Zotter, Sullivan, Molter, Skupin & Turner, Professional Corporation
Detroit, MI
Cotignola, Felice ....Millburn, NJ
Cotignola, Michael N. ....New York, NY
Cotiguala, Jac A. ....Chicago, IL
Cotillas, Eduardo M. ....Chicago, IL
Cotins, A. James ....New York, NY
Cotkin, Collins & Ginsburg, A Professional Corporation ....Los Angeles, CA
Santa Ana, CA
Cotkin, Raphael ....Los Angeles, CA
Cotlar, Ann LaPlace Paris ....Langhorne, PA
Cotlar, Sidney A., (A Professional Law Corporation) ....New Orleans, LA
Cotlar, Steven A. ....Doylestown, PA
Kintnersville, PA
Cotler, Alan K. ....Philadelphia, PA
Cotler, Craig B. ....Coconut Creek, FL
Cotler, Gregg N. ....San Juan, PR
Cotler, Lisa R. ....Chicago, IL
Cotler, Marcia G. ....Northbrook, IL
Cotler, Richard S. ....Hollywood, FL
Palm Beach, FL
Cotler, Richard S., P.A. ....Hollywood, FL
Palm Beach, FL
Cotler, Robin ....Hartsdale, NY
Cotleur, Michael D.
Federal Energy Regulatory Commission, Office of the General Counsel, GV
Cotner, David B. ....Missoula, MT
Cotner, James R. ....Bloomington, IN
Cotner, Jeffry J. ....Houston, TX
Cotner, John M. ....Troy, OH
Cotner, John W. ....Grand Rapids, MI
Cotner, K. Lee ....New Albany, IN
Cotner, Paul Stephen ....Moore, OK
Cotner, Roger G. ....Grand Haven, MI
Cotner, Roger G., P.C. ....Grand Haven, MI
Cotney, Hugh ....Jacksonville, FL
Cotney, Hugh, P.A.
Fernandina Beach, FL
Jacksonville, FL
St. Augustine, FL
Cotney, Joe W. ....Montgomery, AL
Cotney, N. Jackson, Jr. ....Marietta, GA
Cotney, Trent H. ....Tampa, FL
Cotnoir, Christopher J. ....Waterville, ME
Cotnoir, Ernest J. ....Putnam, CT
Cotnoir, Nelson H. ....Pompano Beach, FL
Coto, Malley & Tamargo ....San Juan, PR
Coto, Virginia P. ....Miami, FL
Coto, Yolanda R. ....Miami, FL
Cotogno, Gary A. ....New Orleans, LA
Cotoia, Margaret Ann ....Trenton, NJ
Coton, Daniel M. ....Plant City, FL
Coton, Luis D. ....Tampa, FL
Coton, Luis D., P.A. ....Tampa, FL
Coto-Ojeda, Ramón ....San Juan, PR
Cotora, Craig, Inc., A Professional Law Corporation ....Newport Beach, CA
Cotora, Craig, (P.C.) ....Newport Beach, CA
Cotov, Thomas Joseph ....Newark, NJ
Cotrel, Sally A. ....Los Angeles, CA
Cotrel, Thomas P. ....Burbank, CA
Cotro-Manes, Paul N. ....Salt Lake City, UT
Cotrona, M. Robyn ....Sarasota, FL
Cotronakis, Emanuel J. ....Cleveland, OH
Cotronei, P. Christopher ....Tuckahoe, NY
Cotroneo, Anthony ....Rochester, NY
Cotroneo, Paul ....Deerfield Beach, FL
Cotroneo, S. Thomas ....Johnston, RI
Cotroneo, Thomas F. ....Johnston, RI
Cotropia, Carla ....Houston, TX
Cotropia, Charles S. ....Dallas, TX
Cotruvo & Cusack ....Columbus, OH
Cotsirilos & Campisano
San Francisco, CA
Cotsirilos, George J. ....Chicago, IL
Cotsirilos, George J., Jr.
San Francisco, CA
Cotsirilos, John G. ....San Diego, CA
Cotsirilos, Stephenson, Tighe & Streicker, Ltd. ....Chicago, IL
Cotsonas, Carolyn E. ....Worcester, MA
Cott, Douglas M. ....Westport, CT
Cott, James L. ....New York, NY
Cott, Phillip M. ....Los Angeles, CA
Cott, Sharon H. ....New York, NY
Cotta, David ....New York, NY
Cottam, Charles C. ....Memphis, TN
Cottam, Dale W. ....Cheyenne, WY
Cottam, M. Catherine
Securities and Exchange Commission, Division of Enforcement, GV
Cotteleer, Michael A. ....Wheaton, IL
Cottell, Jennifer A. ....Philadelphia, PA
Cottemond, Mtesa Patrice ....Aiken, SC
Cotten, Alan ....St. Louis, MO
Cotten, Armeta D ....St. Louis, MO
Cotten, Cary L. ....Vista, CA
Cotten, Christopher E. ....Memphis, TN
Cotten, David P. ....Texarkana, TX
Cotten, Ernest W. ....Sparta, TN
Cotten, Jas. M. ....Weatherford, TX
Cotten, J. B., Jr., (P.C.) ....Lubbock, TX
Cotten, Larry E. ....Fort Worth, TX
Cotten, Marya N. ....Seattle, WA
Cotten, Mike ....Austin, TX
Cotten, Patti T. ....Knoxville, TN
Cotten, Robin O. ....Oxford, MS
Cotten & Selfon, P.L.L.C.
Washington, DC
Cotten, Vernon R. ....Carthage, MS
Cotten, Weston G. ....Baytown, TX
Cotter, Anne B. ....Chicago, IL
Cotter, Anthony J. ....Palatka, FL
Cotter, Arthur James ....St. Joseph, MI
Cotter, Barbara A. ....Sacramento, CA
San Francisco, CA
Cotter, Bernard T. ....San Mateo, CA
Cotter, Brenda M. ....Boston, MA
Cotter, Brian E. ....Danbury, CT
Cotter, Carrie W. ....Chicago, IL
Cotter & Cotter ....Rockland, MA
Cotter & Cotter, P.C. ....Great Falls, MT
Cotter & Cotter, P.C. ....Williamsville, NY
Cotter, Cotter and Sohon, P.C.
Bridgeport, CT
Milford, CT
New Haven, CT
Cotter, Daniel A. ....Chicago, IL
Cotter, Daniel W. ....Atlanta, GA
Cotter, David Alan ....Broken Arrow, OK
Cotter, David Andrew ....San Diego, CA
Cotter, David B. ....Williamsville, NY
Cotter, David G. ....Lansing, MI
Cotter, Dennis B. ....Detroit, MI
Cotter, Dennis J. ....Chicago, IL
Cotter, Edward F., Jr. ....Oakland, CA
Cotter, Edward J. ....Cambridge, MA
Cotter, Francis A. ....Bethesda, MD
Cotter, Francis P. ....Washington, DC
Cotter, Frank J. ....Arlington, VA
Cotter, Greenfield, Manfredi & Lenes, P.C.
Norwich, CT
Cotter, Gregory A. ....Washington, DC
Cotter, James J. ....Los Angeles, CA
Cotter, James J. ....New York, NY
Cotter, James J., III ....Milton, MA
Cotter, James M. ....New York, NY
Cotter, Jeffrey L. ....Minneapolis, MN
Cotter, Jerry ....Tawas City, MI
Cotter, John A. ....Norwich, CT
Cotter, John A. ....Minneapolis, MN
Cotter, John J. ....San Francisco, CA
Cotter, John J. ....Bridgeport, CT
Milford, CT
Cotter, John J. ....Boston, MA
Cotter, John J. ....Boston, MA
Cotter, John J., Jr. ....Buffalo, NY
Cotter, John K. ....Sacramento, CA
Cotter, John P. ....Sacramento, CA
Cotter, John P. ....Philadelphia, PA
Cotter, Joseph G. ....National City, MI
Cotter, Kay Kline ....San Antonio, TX
Cotter, Kenneth J. ....Winter Park, FL
Cotter, Kenneth P. ....South Bend, IN
Cotter, Kevin S. ....Providence, RI
Cotter, Leslie A., Jr. ....Columbia, SC
Cotter, Mark A. ....Salt Lake City, UT
Cotter, Mary Carole ....Battle Creek, MI
Cotter, Mary Jane ....New York, NY
Cotter, Michael F. ....Philadelphia, PA
Cotter, Michael L. ....Los Angeles, CA
Cotter, Michael P. ....Norfolk, VA
Cotter, Michael Patrick ....Elkhorn, WI
Cotter, Michael W. ....Department of State, Foreign Service Officers (Overseas), GV
Cotter, Michael W. ....Great Falls, MT
Cotter & Miller ....Philadelphia, PA
Cotter, Patricia M. ....New York, NY
Cotter, Patricia O'Brien ....Great Falls, MT
Cotter, Patrick J. ....Chicago, IL
Cotter, Patrick W. ....Milwaukee, WI
Cotter, Paul R. ....Sacramento, CA
Cotter, R. Hugo C. ....Albuquerque, NM
Cotter, R. Rainer, III ....Enterprise, AL
Cotter, Richard A. ....Austin, MN
Cotter, Richard J., Jr. ....Duxbury, MA
Cotter, Richard M. ....Acton, MA
Cotter, Richard T., (P.A.)
Fort Myers Beach, FL
Cotter, Robert W. ....Kansas City, MO
Cotter, Rochelle S. ....South Bend, IN
Cotter, Sandra M. ....Lansing, MI
Cotter, Shawn P. ....Rockland, MA
Cotter, Stephen L. ....Atlanta, GA
Cotter, Theodore J. G. ....Staten Island, NY
Cotter, Thomas A. ....Tampa, FL
Cotter, Thomas G. ....Tucson, AZ
Cotter, Thomas Galvin ....Bridgeport, CT
Cotter, Thomas J. ....St. Louis, MO
St. Louis, MO
Cotter, Thomas Michael ....Battle Creek, MI
Cotter, Thomas X. ....Westborough, MA
Cotter, Timothy J. ....Naples, FL
Cotter, Timothy J. ....Milwaukee, WI
Cotter, Timothy M. ....Buffalo, NY
Cotter, William A., Jr., (P.C.) ....Boston, MA
Cotter, William D. ....Greenwich, CT
Cotter, William J. ....Chicago, IL
Cotter, William J. ....Williamsville, NY
Cotter, William J. ....Durham, NC
Cotter, William R. ....Waterville, ME
Cotterell, Gregory F. ....Minneapolis, MN
Cotterell, Lindsey D. ....Longview, WA
Cotterman, Joseph E. ....Phoenix, AZ
Cottey, Frank ....Springfield, MO
Cottey, Tia L. ....Charlotte, NC
Cotthoff, David L. ....Hopkinsville, KY
Cottier, Derek L. ....Chicago, IL
Cottier, Geoffrey A. ....Toledo, OH
Cotting, Jeanette L. ....Portland, OR
Cotting, William W., Jr. ....Northborough, MA
Cottingham, Anne W. ....Washington, DC
Cottingham, Cynthia B. ....San Francisco, CA
Cottingham, Dale E. ....Oklahoma City, OK
Cottingham, David C. ....Bellingham, WA
Cottingham, Edward B., Jr.
Charleston, SC
Cottingham, Geo. L., Jr. ....Greenville, MS
Cottingham, J. Scott ....Salt Lake City, UT
Cottingham, John A. ....Rockville, MD
Cottingham, Patricia H. ....Jackson, MS
Cottingham & Porter, P.C. ....Douglas, GA
Cottingham, Rebecca D. ....Atlanta, GA
Cottingham, Sidney L. ....Douglas, GA
Cottingham, T. Thomas, III
Charlotte, NC
Cottington, Lisanne E.S. ....Washington, DC
Cottington, Robert B. ....Pittsburgh, PA
Cottle, Amber L. ....Washington, DC
Cottle, Bertrand E. ....Orange, CA
Cottle, Eric R.I. ....Pittsburgh, PA
Cottle, Jeffrey W. ....Baltimore, MD
Cottle, John I., III ....Tallassee, AL
Cottle, Karen O. ....Menlo Park, CA
Cottle, Lisa A. ....Los Angeles, CA
Cottle, Lisa Sullivan
Equal Employment Opportunity Commission, Office of the Commissioners, GV
Cottle, Richard C. ....Ashland, OR
Cottle, Robert W. ....Las Vegas, NV
Cottle, Sean A. ....Concord, CA
Cottle, T. Jeffery ....Orem, UT
Cottle, William R. ....Chicago, IL
Cottler, Steven Bruce ....Bronx, NY
Cottnair, David S. ....Seattle, WA
Cotto, Katayoon M. ....San Francisco, CA
Cottom, Roderick B., (P.C.) ....Muskegon, MI
Cotton, Alan C. ....Kansas City, MO
Cotton, Andrew M. ....College Point, NY
Cotton, Anthony J. ....Shaker Heights, OH
Cotton, Bledsoe, Tighe & Dawson, A Professional Corporation ....Houston, TX
Midland, TX
Cotton, Bolton, Hoychick & Doughty, L.L.P.
Monroe, LA
Rayville, LA
Cotton, C. John ....Gillette, WY
Cotton, Casey J. ....Wichita, KS
Cotton, Charles E. ....Wichita, KS
Cotton, Charles L. ....Houston, TX
Cotton, Christina A. ....New York, NY
Cotton, Clencie L. ....Holly Springs, MS
Cotton & Cooper ....Oneida, TN
Cotton & Cotton ....El Dorado, KS
Wichita, KS
Cotton & Cotton ....Snyder, TX
Cotton, Curtis ....San Diego, CA
Cotton, D. Douglas ....Dallas, TX
Cotton, Dan C. ....Snyder, TX
Cotton, Daniel I. ....Worcester, MA
Cotton, David G. ....College Point, NY
Cotton, David W. ....Snyder, TX
Cotton, Deborah L. ....Chicago, IL
Cotton, Don R. ....Austin, TX
Cotton, Earl Lee, Sr. ....Atlanta, GA
Cotton, Edwin T. ....Cordele, GA
Cotton, Eric C. ....Cleveland, OH
Cotton, Ernest L. (Buddy)
Fort Walton Beach, FL
Cotton, Eugene ....Chicago, IL
Cotton & Gates ....Fort Walton Beach, FL
Shalimar, FL
Cotton, George M. ....Baton Rouge, LA
Cotton, Gregory A. ....Bellaire, TX
Cotton, Gregory D. ....Memphis, TN
Cotton, H. Dean ....McPherson, KS
Cotton, Harold R. ....Jupiter, FL
Cotton, Harris Y. ....Woodbury, NJ
Cotton, Harvey D. ....Brookline, MA
Cotton, Horace D. ....Detroit, MI
Cotton, Howard E. ....New York, NY
Cotton, Huey P. ....Los Angeles, CA
Cotton, J. Kingsley, III
Bloomfield Hills, MI
Cotton, J. Robert ....Concord, NH
Cotton, Jack M. ....Bethesda, MD
Cotton, James Alexandre ....Houston, TX
Cotton, James L., Jr. ....Oneida, TN
Cotton, Janet F. ....New York, NY
Cotton, Jason M. ....Boston, MA
Cotton, Jeffrey D. ....Champlin, MN
Cotton, Jennifer A. ....New York, NY
Cotton, John H. ....Scottsdale, AZ
Las Vegas, NV

Cotton, John H., & Associates, Ltd.
Phoenix, AZ
Scottsdale, AZ
Las Vegas, NV
Cotton, John W. ... **Los Angeles, CA**
Cotton, Joseph G. ... **New Carrollton, MD**
Cotton, Julie A. ... Houston, TX
Cotton, Kathryn ... San Francisco, CA
Cotton, Kelly C. ... **Fort Lauderdale, FL**
Cotton, Kenneth W. ... **Wagner, SD**
Cotton, Knight & Baker ... Wichita Falls, TX
Cotton Law Office ... **Gillette, WY**
Cotton, Michael D. ... **Chicago, IL**
Cotton, Mitzi I. ... Austin, TX
Cotton, Patricia L. ... **Palo Alto, CA**
Cotton, Quincy ... **New York, NY**
Cotton, Raymond D. ... **Washington, DC**
Cotton, Richard ... **New York, NY**
Cotton, Richard B. ... New York, NY
Cotton, Robert J. ... Newton, MA
Cotton, Robert K. ... Southbridge, MA
Cotton, Robert L. ... Warren, NJ
Cotton, Ruffen H., Jr. ... Bonita Springs, FL
Cotton, Stacey W. ... Atlanta, GA
Cotton, Steve A. ... Wausau, WI
Cotton, Steven R. ... Salem, OR
Cotton, Steven S. ... Roanoke, VA
Cotton, Stuart ... **New York, NY**
Cotton, Tamara Todd ... Louisville, KY
Cotton, Thomas Clay ... Wichita Falls, TX
Cotton, Traci Lee ... Austin, TX
Cotton, Vincent J., Jr. ... Lexington, KY
Cotton, Ward A. ... Norristown, PA
Cotton, Wm. M. ... Austin, TX
Cottone, Anthony F. ... Providence, RI
Cottone, Kevin C. ... **Philadelphia, PA**
Cottone, S. John ... Scranton, PA
Cottongame, W. Brice ... **Fort Worth, TX**
Cottongame, W. Brice, A Prof. Corp., Law Office of ... **Fort Worth, TX**
Cottrell, Amelia A. ... **Chicago, IL**
Cottrell, Anne L. ... Salem, OR
Cottrell, Arthur J. ... **Edison, NJ**
Cottrell, Barbara D. ... Albany, NY
Cottrell, Bruce H. ... Los Alamos, NM
Cottrell, Debra Fischman
New Orleans, LA
Cottrell, Donald W. ... Leitchfield, KY
Cottrell, Edward Keenan ... **Jacksonville, FL**
Cottrell, Ernest E. ... Curtice, OH
Cottrell, Ernest E., Jr. ... Elmore, OH
Cottrell, Floyd G. ... **Newark, NJ**
Cottrell, Frank S. ... **Moline, IL**
Cottrell, Frederick L., III
Wilmington, DE
Cottrell, Gary R. ... Van Buren, AR
Cottrell, George A. ... Indianapolis, IN
Cottrell, James D. ... **Champaign, IL**
Cottrell, James L. ... **Cape Coral, FL**
Cottrell, James Ray ... **Alexandria, VA**
Fairfax, VA
Cottrell, Jane R. ... **Stamford, CT**
Cottrell, John H., Jr. ... Little Rock, AR
Cottrell, Jonathan W. ... Sandpoint, ID
Cottrell, Kristin A. ... Muscatine, IA
Cottrell, Matthew A. ... **Seattle, WA**
Cottrell, Patricia J. ... Nashville, TN
Cottrell, Paul ... **Philadelphia, PA**
Cottrell, Robert C., Jr. ... Dillon, CO
Cottrell, Sheryl A. ... **Seattle, WA**
Cottrell, Stephen E. ... Genoa, OH
Cottrell, Steven J. ... Lodi, CA
Cottrell, Tiffany M. ... Greenville, NC
Cottrell, Warchol, Merchant & Rollings
Cape Coral, FL
Fort Myers, FL
Cottrell, Wesley A. ... **Rogers, AR**
Joplin, MO
Cottrell, William G. ... **Minneapolis, MN**
Cottrell, William V. ... Omak, WA
Cottriel, Darren K. ... **Costa Mesa, CA**
Cottrill, G. Todd ... **Jacksonville, FL**
Cottrill, Kelly J. ... Zanesville, OH
Cottrill-Bell, Marlene (Neema) M.
Toledo, OH
Cotts, Eric M. ... **Norfolk, VA**
Cotty, William F. ... Columbia, SC
Cotugno, Lee W. ... **Beverly Hills, CA**
Cotugno, Michael C. ... El Centro, CA
Coty, Laura Ellen ... Louisville, KY
Cotz, George J. ... Ramsey, NJ
Cotzen, Michael L ... **Miami, FL**
Cotzin, Andrew, (P.A.)
Fort Lauderdale, FL
Couch, Alan J. ... Norman, OK
Couch, Allen B. ... **Southaven, MS**
Couch, Allen B., Jr. ... **Southaven, MS**
Couch, Andrew W. ... Newport Beach, CA
Couch, Betsy Ault ... Lansdale, PA
Couch, C. Deryl ... Fort Lauderdale, FL
Couch, Clinton A. ... **Pensacola, FL**
Couch, Clinton A., P.A. ... **Pensacola, FL**
Couch, David A. ... **Little Rock, AR**
Couch, David Allan ... **Detroit, MI**
Couch, David Harvey ... White City, OR
Couch, Dean A. ... Oklahoma City, OK
Couch and Deily ... **Hudson, NY**
Couch, Georgia Kaye Wisner ... Martinez, CA
Couch, H. Cleve, Jr., J.D. ... Easley, SC
Couch and Howard, P.C. ... **Albany, NY**
Couch, J. Christopher ... Houston, TX
Couch, James E. ... Columbus, OH
Couch, James G. ... Wakefield, RI
Warwick, RI
Couch, James R. ... **Elyria, OH**
Couch, James R., Jr. ... Chicago, IL
Couch, Jamir R. ... **Washington, DC**
Couch, Jill J. Jay ... Grove City, OH
Couch, J. O. Terrell ... Houston, TX
Couch, John C. ... **Hudson, NY**
Couch, John R., Jr. ... Stillwater, OK
Couch, Keith K. ... Overland Park, KS
Couch, Kevin A. ... Whippany, NJ
Couch, Kimberly S. ... **Portland, ME**
Couch, Laura P. ... **Irvine, CA**
Couch Law Firm ... **Southaven, MS**
Couch, Leslie F. ... **Albany, NY**
Couch, Mark W. ... Albany, NY
Saratoga Springs, NY
Couch, Mary Jane Bendon ... **Albany, NY**
Couch, Paul W. ... Brentwood, TN
Couch, Pierce, King & Hoffmeister, Chartered ... **Overland Park, KS**
Kansas City, MO
Couch, Richard ... Manchester, KY
Couch, Richard J. ... Grand Island, NY
Couch, Richard W. ... Tulsa, OK
Couch, Robert M. ... Birmingham, AL
Couch, Robert M. ... Lawrenceville, GA
Couch, Roger L. ... Spartanburg, SC
Couch, Steven E. ... **Houston, TX**
Couch, Steven William ... **Birmingham, AL**
Couch, Timothy R. ... Huntington, NY
Couch, V. Stuart ... **Greenville, NC**
New Bern, NC
Couch, Valerie K. ... Oklahoma City, OK
Couch, White, Brenner, Howard & Feigenbaum, LLP ... **Albany, NY**
Couch White, LLP ... **Washington, DC**
Albany, NY
Couch, William Clifford ... **Denton, TX**
Couchara, Vincent A. ... Norristown, PA
Couchman, Diane P. ... **Dallas, TX**
Couchman, Henry E., Jr. ... Kansas City, KS
Couchot, Paul J. ... **Newport Beach, CA**
Coudert Brothers ... **Los Angeles, CA**
Palo Alto, CA
San Francisco, CA
San Jose, CA
Denver, CO
Washington, DC
New York, NY
Coudert, Frederic R., III ... New York, NY
Coudrain, Andre G. ... **Hammond, LA**
Coudures, John M. ... Corona, CA
Coudurier, Diane L. ... Bloomfield Hills, MI
Couenhoven, Paul ... Berkeley, CA
Coufal, Rebecca M. ... **Spokane, WA**
Cougar, Michael ... Santa Cruz, CA
Couger, Warren D. ... Detroit, MI
Coughenour, Brian ... Port Angeles, WA
Coughenour, John C. ... Seattle, WA
Coughenour, Paul W. ... **Detroit, MI**
Coughenour, William C. ... Salisbury, NC
Coughlan, Barbara ... **Norwalk, CT**
Coughlan, Cheryl P. ... St. Paul, MN
Coughlan, Cornelius P. ... Larchmont, NY
Coughlan & Coughlan ... Boise, ID
Coughlan, Daniel M. ... Minneapolis, MN
Coughlan, Devon G. ... **Boca Raton, FL**
Coughlan, Glenn A. ... Boise, ID
Coughlan, James B. ... Washington, DC
Coughlan, Jonathan E. ... Buffalo, NY
Coughlan, Joseph D., Jr. ... Hartford, CT
Coughlan, Joseph M. ... Boise, ID
Coughlan, Kenneth L. ... **Chicago, IL**
Coughlan, Margaret E. ... Chicago, IL
Coughlan, Michael D. ... Stockton, CA
Coughlan, Peter B. ... Newport, KY
Coughlan, R. J. (Jerry), Jr.
San Diego, CA
Coughlan, Semmer & Lipman, LLP
San Diego, CA
Coughlan, Traci E. ... Philadelphia, PA
Coughlin, Anne M. ... **New York, NY**
Coughlin and Appleton, P.A.
North Miami, FL
Coughlin, Barbara B. ... High Point, NC
Coughlin, Barring ... Cleveland, OH
Coughlin, Brendan J. ... Santa Ana, CA
Coughlin, Carolyn Anne ... Brighton, CO
Coughlin, Casey William
Coral Springs, FL
Coughlin, Casey William, P.A.
Coral Springs, FL
Coughlin, Christine Nero ... **Greensboro, NC**
Coughlin, Christine P. ... **Boston, MA**
Coughlin, Cindy A. ... Sacramento, CA
Coughlin, Colleen ... Indianapolis, IN
Coughlin, Colleen D. ... Wheaton, IL
Coughlin & Coughlin ... Stratford, CT
Coughlin & Coughlin, S.C. ... Appleton, WI
Winneconne, WI
Coughlin, Craig J. ... South Amboy, NJ
Coughlin, Cregg W. ... Helena, MT
Coughlin, Cynthia Ann ... Sacramento, CA
Coughlin, Daniel D. ... **Greeneville, TN**
Coughlin, Daniel F. ... Boston, MA
Coughlin, Daniel F. ... **New York, NY**
Coughlin, Daniel J. ... Garden City, NY
Coughlin, Deborah L ... Arlington, MA
Coughlin, Dennis M. ... Wildwood, NJ
Coughlin, Donald J. ... Winchester, MA
Coughlin, Edith ... New York, NY
Coughlin, Edw. H. ... Buffalo, NY
Coughlin, Ellen Frances ... **Nashville, TN**
Coughlin, Emily G. ... **Boston, MA**
Coughlin, Eugene C., III ... Bangor, ME
Coughlin, Francis A. ... Arlington, MA
Coughlin, Francis J. ... New York, NY
Coughlin, Francis J., Jr. ... New York, NY
Coughlin, Francis R. ... New Canaan, CT
Coughlin, Francis X. J. ... New York, NY
Coughlin, Frank James ... Santa Ana, CA
Coughlin & Gargano ... Jersey City, NJ
Coughlin, George Gordon, Jr.
Binghamton, NY
Coughlin, George P. ... **Kansas City, MO**
Coughlin, Gerard J. ... Howell, MI
Coughlin & Gerhart, L.L.P. ... Afton, NY
Binghamton, NY
Deposit, NY
Owego, NY
Unadilla, NY
Coughlin, J. David ... **Baker City, OR**
Ontario, OR
Coughlin, J. Jeffrey ... **Prescott, AZ**
Coughlin, James J. ... Arcadia, CA
Coughlin, Jennifer Mary ... **Anchorage, AK**
Coughlin, John J. ... Milford, CT
Coughlin, John J. ... Mont Vernon, NH
Coughlin, John J. ... **Cherry Hill, NJ**
Coughlin, John P. ... **Beardstown, IL**
Coughlin, John R. ... Hollister, CA
Coughlin, John R. ... Malone, NY
Coughlin, John S. ... Providence, RI
Coughlin, John T. ... **Washington, DC**
Coughlin, John W. ... Denver, CO
Coughlin, Joseph E. ... **Chicago, IL**
Coughlin, Kathleen A. ... Jersey City, NJ
Coughlin, Kenneth F., Jr. ... Park Ridge, NJ
Coughlin, Kevin T. ... **Morristown, NJ**
Coughlin, Laurence L. ... Chicago, IL
Coughlin, Lawrence M. ... Galveston, TX
Coughlin, Leo J. ... Washington, DC
Coughlin, Leuenberger & Moon, P.C.
Baker City, OR
Ontario, OR
Coughlin, Lisa A. ... Denver, CO
Coughlin, Lynne ... **Paoli, PA**
Coughlin & Malone ... Milford, CT
Coughlin, Margaret A. ... **Detroit, MI**
Coughlin, Mary F. ... Appleton, WI
Coughlin, Melissa A. ... **Chicago, IL**
Coughlin, Michael D., Jr. ... New York, NY
Coughlin, Michael J.
Department of the Army,
Office of the Judge Advocate General, GV
Coughlin, Michael J., Jr. ... Sturbridge, MA
Coughlin, Michael P. ... **Cherry Hill, NJ**
Blue Bell, PA
Coughlin, Patrick ... **San Francisco, CA**
Coughlin, Patrick F. ... Appleton, WI
Winneconne, WI
Coughlin, Patrick J. ... Anchorage, AK
Coughlin, Patrick J., Jr. ... Baltimore, MD
Coughlin, Paul F. ... Flint, MI
Coughlin, Paul J., Jr. ... Washington, DC
Coughlin, Paula Jane ... **St. Louis, MO**
Coughlin, Paxton & Pipal, A Law Corporation
Hollister, CA
Coughlin, Peter J. ... Passaic, NJ
Coughlin, R. Lawrence ... **Washington, DC**
Coughlin, Rainboth & Murphy, P.A.
Portsmouth, NH
Coughlin, Raymond T. ... Jersey City, NJ
Coughlin, Richard A. ... **Greensboro, NC**
Coughlin, Richard E. ... St. Louis, MO
Coughlin, Richard H. ... Albany, NY
Coughlin, Robert B. ... **Dayton, OH**
Coughlin, Robert H., Jr. ... **Schenectady, NY**
Coughlin, Robert J. ... **Boston, MA**
Coughlin, Roberta J. ... Santa Ana, CA
Coughlin, Sean C. ... **San Diego, CA**
Coughlin, Sean J. ... **New York, NY**
Coughlin, Sharon A. ... Bedford, NH
Coughlin, Terrance J. ... Chicago, IL
Coughlin, Thomas A. ... **Washington, DC**
Coughlin, Thomas A. ... **McLean, VA**
Coughlin, Thomas B. ... Stratford, CT
Coughlin, Thomas C. ... Stratford, CT
Coughlin, Thomas Diffley ... Stanwood, WA
Coughlin, Thomas E. ... **Detroit, MI**
Coughlin, Thomas M. ... Irwindale, CA
Coughlin, Thomas M., Jr. ... **Cleveland, OH**
Coughlin, Timothy C. ... **Portsmouth, NH**
Coughlin, Timothy J. ... **Cleveland, OH**
Coughlin, Timothy L. ... Las Vegas, NV
Coughlin, Vincent E. ... Pawtucket, RI
Coughlin, William C. ... Worth, IL
Coughlin, William E. ... **Cleveland, OH**
Coughlin, William J. ... Auburn Hills, MI
Coughran, L. Craig ... Chatsworth, CA
Coughran, Wayne H. ... Livingston, TX
Coughter, Elizabeth P. ... **Charlottesville, VA**
Cougill, Patrick K. ... Portland, OR
Cougill, R. C. ... Lilburn, GA
Cougill, Thomas L. ... **Center, TX**
Houston, TX
Nacogdoches, TX
Couhig, Robert E., Jr. ... **New Orleans, LA**
Houston, TX
Couick, Michael N. ... Columbia, SC
Couick, Shirley B. ... Walnut Creek, CA
Couillard, Ronald M. ... Visalia, CA
Couillou, Chris M. ... Atlanta, GA
Coukos, Carolyn S. C. ... Bonita Springs, FL
Coukos, Marie J. ... Boston, MA
Coukos, Pamela ... **Washington, DC**
Coukos, Stephen J. ... **Boston, MA**
Coulahan, Kathleen A. ... **Timonium, MD**
Coulam, Dale T. ... Gardnerville, NV
Coulbourn, Edwin T. ... Suffolk, VA
Coulby, John N., III ... **Washington, DC**
Coules, Peter, Jr. ... Hinsdale, IL
Couleur, Douglas E. ... Santa Fe, NM
Couleur, Douglas E., P.A. ... Santa Fe, NM
Couling, Denise D. (Sheehan)
Grand Blanc, MI
Coulis, Karen M. ... Merrillville, IN
Coull, Shara Fosnight ... Concord, NH
Coulman, Lee John ... Forest Hills, NY
Coulom, Frank F., Jr. ... **Hartford, CT**
Coulombe Law Firm, The, A Professional Corporation ... **Costa Mesa, CA**
Coulombe, Maribeth A. ... **East Lansing, MI**
Coulombe, Ronald B. ... **Costa Mesa, CA**
Coulon, Jos. R. ... Southbury, CT
Coulson, Beth Gladden
North Little Rock, AR
Coulson, Charles E. ... Painesville, OH
Coulson, Charles G., Jr. ... **Cincinnati, OH**
Coulson, David A. ... **Miami, FL**
Chicago, IL
Coulson, Dawn M. ... **Los Angeles, CA**
Coulson, Debra McC. ... Pittsburgh, PA
Coulson, Edward A. ... Kansas City, MO
Coulson, Edward R. ... **Seattle, WA**
Coulson, George T. ... Wilmington, DE
Coulson, J. Mark ... **Baltimore, MD**
Coulson, Leslie A. ... Flint, MI
Coulson, Marilyn Olivo ... Oklahoma City, OK
Coulson, Mark C. ... **Pittsburgh, PA**
Coulson, Mary C. ... **Tulsa, OK**
Coulson, Michael I. ... **Jacksonville, FL**
Coulson, Michael R. ... **Oklahoma City, OK**
Coulson, Rebecca Stewart ... Houston, TX
Coulson, Richard E. ... **Oklahoma City, OK**
Coulson, Robert Edwards ... Waukegan, IL
Coulson, Scott E. ... **Tulsa, OK**
Coulson, Thomas P. ... Binghamton, NY
Coulson, W. Michael ... Houston, TX
Coulson, Wesley J. ... Edwardsville, IL
Coulston, Caroline E.
Cardiff-By-The-Sea, CA
Coulston, Clifford G. ... Mill Valley, CA
Coulston, Gerald F. ... Bronx, NY
Coulston, Judith ... **New York, NY**
Coulston, Michael S. ... **New York, NY**
Coulston, Wendy E. ... Santa Ana, CA
Coult, John H. ... Chicago, IL
Coult, Joseph ... Fair Lawn, NJ
Coultas, Edward O. ... Austin, TX
Coultas, Faye M. ... Osage Beach, MO
Coultas, Faye M., P.C. ... Osage Beach, MO
Coultas, Jennifer A. ... El Segundo, CA
Coultas, Robert ... **Miami, FL**
Coulter, Amber L. ... Lincoln, NE
Coulter, Ann Hart ... Washington, DC
Coulter, Arthur C. ... Seal Beach, CA
Coulter, Bruce R. ... Garden City, MI
Coulter, Calvin L. ... Bridgeport, NE
Coulter, Chad W. ... New York, NY
Coulter, Charles D. ... Boise, ID
Coulter, Charles E. ... Oregon City, OR
Coulter, Charles L. ... St. Louis, MO
Coulter, Charles R. ... **Davenport, IA**
Muscatine, IA
Coulter, Christopher R. ... Peoria, IL
Coulter, Clinton H., Jr. ... Tallahassee, FL
Coulter & Coulter ... **Roanoke, VA**
Coulter, Diane Ahearn ... Brockton, MA
Coulter, Dolores M. ... Flint, MI
Coulter, Donald B. ... Wausau, WI
Coulter, Donald E. ... Manassas, VA
Coulter, Donald E., P.C. ... Manassas, VA
Coulter, Donald H. ... **Grants Pass, OR**
Coulter, Douglas Glen ... Chicago, IL
Coulter, Everett B., Jr. ... **Spokane, WA**
Coulter, Fayedine ... Oakland, CA
Coulter, Fraser, Bolton, Bird & Ventre
Phoenix, NY
Syracuse, NY
Coulter, Gary L. ... Columbus, GA
Coulter, George P. ... Altadena, CA
Coulter, J. Greg ... **Phoenix, AZ**
Coulter, Jack B. ... **Roanoke, VA**
Coulter, James P. ... **Butler, PA**
Coulter, Janet M. ... Anaheim, CA
Coulter, Jay D. ... San Diego, CA
Coulter, Jean Walpole ... Tulsa, OK
Coulter, Jean Walpole, & Associates, Inc.
Tulsa, OK
Coulter, Johanna S. ... **Washington, DC**
Coulter, John D. ... **Little Rock, AR**
Coulter, John M. ... Poughkeepsie, NY
Coulter, John M., Jr. ... Treasury Department,
Internal Revenue Service, GV
Coulter, John S. ... Baton Rouge, LA
Coulter, Joseph C., Jr. ... Overland Park, KS
Coulter, Keith E. ... **Houston, TX**
Coulter, Lisa M. ... **Phoenix, AZ**
Coulter, Lisa Weekley ... **Columbus, OH**
Coulter, Livingston T. ... Schuylerville, NY
Coulter, Mark T. ... **Pittsburgh, PA**
Coulter, Nate ... **Little Rock, AR**
Coulter, Paul E. ... Culver City, CA
Coulter, Peter I. ... Flanders, NJ
Coulter, Philip C. ... **Roanoke, VA**
Coulter, Ray K. ... Palm Springs, CA
Coulter, Raymond C. ... Atlanta, GA
Coulter, Richard A. ... Spring, TX
Coulter, Robert F. ... Phoenix, NY
Syracuse, NY
Coulter, Robert K.
Department of Justice, GV
Coulter, Ronald G. ... **Durham, NC**
Coulter, Ted I. ... Marion, OH
Coulter, Terri Anne ... Oklahoma City, OK
Coulter, Thomas A. ... Department of Justice,
Civil Division, GV
Coulter, Vernoff & Pearson, A Professional Corporation ... Pasadena, CA
Coulter, Wayne R. ... **Port Richey, FL**
Spring Hill, FL
Coulter, William K. ... **Washington, DC**
Coulthard, William L. ... **Las Vegas, NV**
Coultoff, Daniel H. ... **Miami, FL**
Coulton, John S., II ... Springfield, MA
Coultrap, Boltz & Norman
Lancaster, OH

Coultrap, Martha F. ....New York, NY
Coumanis, Christ N. ....Mobile, AL
Coumaris, George Tom
Treasury Department, Internal Revenue Service, GV
Coumas, Angela ....Chicago, IL
Coumont, Donald A. ....Severna Park, MD
Coumont, Frank J. ....Gearhart, OR
Counard, Allen J. ....Trenton, MI
Counce, Amy E. ....Baton Rouge, LA
Counce, Carolyn Virginia ....Memphis, TN
Counce, David W. ....Phoenix, AZ
Council, Baradel, Kosmerl & Nolan, P.A.
Annapolis, MD
Baltimore, MD
Council, Brenda J. ....Omaha, NE
Council, Claude C., Jr. ....Pittsburgh, PA
Council, James F., Jr. ....Valdosta, GA
Council, James Godwin ....Glen Allen, VA
Council, John R. ....Dade City, FL
Council, Pauline Carter ....Valdosta, GA
Council, Ronald E. ....Annapolis, MD
Council, Ronald E., Jr ....Baltimore, MD
Council, William T. ....Juneau, AK
Council, William T., LLC ....Juneau, AK
Councill, Joseph G., Jr. ....Omaha, NE
Councill, W. Parker ....Smithfield, VA
Councilor, Terrence A. ....St. Louis, MO
Cound, Bronwen L. ....Minneapolis, MN
Cound, John J. ....Minneapolis, MN
Coundouris, Philip J. ....Port Washington, NY
Counelis, Steven G. ....Martinez, CA
Counihan, Edward A., IV ....Boston, MA
Counihan, Genevra Reed ....Concord, MA
Counihan, James A. ....Cambridge, MA
Counihan, Paul G. ....Cambridge, MA
Counihan, Victoria Watson ....Wilmington, DE
Counihan, Wm. J., Jr. ....Pawtucket, RI
Counos, William T., II ....St. Albans, VT
Counsell, Charles K. ....Tacoma, WA
Counsell, Jon M. ....Green Bay, WI
Counsell, Murphy & Bottiger, P.S.
Tacoma, WA
Counsman, Richard T. ....Detroit, MI
Countegan, Rita V. ....Southfield, MI
Counter, J. Nicholas, III ....Encino, CA
Counters, Lisa J. ....Scottsdale, AZ
Counters, Todd R. ....Apple Valley, MN
Countess, Frank Henisse ....York, PA
Countess • Gilbert • Andrews
East Berlin, PA
York, PA
Countess, Jeremy D. ....Moorestown, NJ
Countess, Jon C. ....York, PA
Countiss, James T. ....Honolulu, HI
Countiss, John R., III ....Jackson, MS
Countiss, Richard N. ....Houston, TX
Countiss, William F. ....Amarillo, TX
Country, Maria T. ....King Of Prussia, PA
Countryman, Byron E. ....Los Angeles, CA
Countryman, Clay J. ....Baton Rouge, LA
Countryman, Dayton W. ....Nevada, IA
Countryman, Joan
Administrative Office Of The United States Courts, GV
Countryman, John E. ....Fort Lauderdale, FL
Countryman, John W. ....Sycamore, IL
Countryman & McDaniel ....Los Angeles, CA
Countryman, Patricia L. McCurn
Schenectady, NY
Countryman, Perry K.
San Bernardino, CA
Countryman, Ralph P. ....Oakland, CA
Countryman, Sherry L. ....Boston, MA
Countryman, Thomas A.
San Antonio, TX
Countryman, Thomas M. ....St. Paul, MN
Countryman, Vance ....Riverton, WY
Counts, Anne Bradley ....Baltimore, MD
Counts, Braxton C., III ....Mobile, AL
Counts, Cynthia L. ....Atlanta, GA
Counts, George E. ....Charleston, SC
Counts, Henry, Jr. ....Alexandria, VA
Counts, James H., (P.C.) ....St. Joseph, MO
Counts, James Waylon ....Alamogordo, NM
Counts, Jay C. ....Dallas, TX
Counts, John E. ....Fenton, MO
Counts, John P. ....Washington, DC
Counts & Kanne, Chartered
Washington, DC
Counts, Lawrence C. ....Sacramento, CA
Counts, Leonard S., Jr. ....Marietta, GA
Counts, Marc D. ....Johnson City, TN
Counts, Richard A. ....Hindman, KY
Counts, Richard L., III ....Easton, MD
Counts, Stephen ....Austin, TX
Counts, Thomas A. ....San Francisco, CA
Counts, Thomas A., II ....Alexandria, VA
Counts, Thomas S. ....Columbus, OH
Counts, Tia A. ....New York, NY
Counts, W. David, III ....San Antonio, TX
Coup, Allen J. ....Church Hill, TN
Coupal, Jonathan M. ....Sacramento, CA
Coupe, Anita W. ....New York, NY
Coupe, James W. ....Universal City, CA
Coupe & Van Allsburg, P.C. ....Holland, MI
Coupe, William W. ....Holland, MI
Couper, Frank E. ....Rockville, MD
Couper, George E. ....Sacramento, CA
Coupey, Marc M., Law Offices of
Millwood, NY
Coupland Law Office ....Valentine, NE
Coupland, Robert D. ....Valentine, NE
Coupounas, George D. ....Brookline, MA
Courage, Thomas Roberts ....Providence, RI
Courageous, Sarah ....Honolulu, HI
Courard, Helene J. ....Arlington, VA
Courbois, Francis ....Oklahoma City, OK
Courchaine, Christine M. ....Eugene, OR
Courchesne, Nyles L. ....Palmer, MA
Courchesne, Richard P. ....Holyoke, MA
Coureas, Donald J. ....Norfolk, VA
Courey, Bruce Michael ....Cleveland, OH
Courey, Camille Marie ....San Jose, CA
Courey, Kosanda & Zimmer, P.A.
Minneapolis, MN
Courey, Marc Bennett ....Treasury Department, U.S. Customs Service, GV
Courey, Marc W. ....Minneapolis, MN
Courey, Richard N. ....Farmington Hills, MI
Courey, Sam T. ....Minneapolis, MN
Couri, Charles ....Peoria, IL
Couri & Couri ....Winnetka, IL
Couri, David M. ....Peoria, IL
Couri, Phillip A. ....Winnetka, IL
Couri, Phillip E. ....Winnetka, IL
Courie, David T. ....Fayetteville, NC
Courie, James R. ....Columbia, SC
Courie, John ....Detroit, MI
Courie, Yolanda C. ....Columbia, SC
Courington, Dorothy W., II
Savannah, GA
Courington, Kaye N. ....New Orleans, LA
Courington, Lea F. ....Dallas, TX
Cournane, Brendan M. ....Chicago, IL
Courney, Raymond J. ....Naperville, IL
Cournot, Pierre ....New York, NY
Cournoyer & Associates, P.C.
Framingham, MA
Hudson, MA
Marlborough, MA
Sudbury, MA
Cournoyer & Cournoyer, P.C.
Southbridge, MA
Cournoyer, Donald C. ....Southbridge, MA
Cournoyer, Donald C., Jr. ....Southbridge, MA
Cournoyer, Gerald S., Jr. ....Sudbury, MA
Cournoyer, Madonna E. ....Boston, MA
Courrier, James W., Jr. ....Keyser, WV
Cours, Claire ....Coral Springs, FL
Cours, Richard E., (P.A.) ....Tampa, FL
Course, Karen A. ....Irvine, CA
Courselle, Diane E. ....New York, NY
Coursen, Christopher D. ....Washington, DC
Coursen, David F.
Environmental Protection Agency, Office of the General Counsel, GV
Coursen-Neff, Zama ....Brooklyn, NY
Courser, D. Jeffrey ....Portland, OR
Vancouver, WA
Coursey, Daniel M., Jr. ....Decatur, GA
Coursey, James L., Jr. ....Savannah, GA
Coursey, Michael J. ....Washington, DC
Coursey, R Stevan ....Atlanta, GA
Coursey, Robert J., III ....Atlanta, GA
Coursey, Sheri R. ....Atlanta, GA
Courshon, Arthur H. ....Miami, FL
Courshon, Deanne Hope ....Aventura, FL
Courshon, Jack R. ....Miami Beach, FL
Courshon, James Robert ....San Mateo, CA
Coursol, Walter S. ....Englewood, CO
Coursolle, Victor A. ....Bloomington, MN
Courson, Donald C. ....Peoria, IL
Courson, Gardner G. ....Atlanta, GA
Courson, Marty Kevin ....San Francisco, CA
Courson, Richard J. ....Pendleton, OR
Courson, Timothy H. ....St. Louis, MO
Court, Leonard ....Oklahoma City, OK
Court, Richard F. ....Vandalia, OH
Court, Susan Brimley ....Mesa, AZ
Court, Susan J.
Federal Energy Regulatory Commission, Office of the General Counsel, GV
Courtade, A. David ....Fort Worth, TX
Courtade, A. David, Atty. and Coun. at Law, A P.C. ....Fort Worth, TX
Courtade, Bruce A. ....Grand Rapids, MI
Courtade, Colleen Ruth ....Rochester, NY
Courtade, John ....Fairfield, IA
Courtade, Ronald L., Jr. ....Metairie, LA
Courteau, Devin C. ....San Francisco, CA
Courteau, Diana L. ....El Segundo, CA
Courteau, Girard R. ....San Rafael, CA
Courteau, Michael A. ....Monroe, LA
Courtemanche, Patrick F.
Minneapolis, MN
Courtemanche, Richard Donald, Jr.
Tallahassee, FL
Courten, Dorothy A. ....Smithtown, NY
Courtenay, Adrian H. ....New York, NY
Courtenay, Forstall, Hunter & Fontana, L.L.P. ....New Orleans, LA
Courtenay, Francis A., Jr.
New Orleans, LA
Courtenay, Mary James
Colorado Springs, CO
Courter, Ann C. ....Chicago, IL
Courter, Craig E. ....San Diego, CA
Courter, James A. ....Orchard Lake, MI
Courter, James A. ....Hackettstown, NJ
Morristown, NJ
Trenton, NJ
Courter, Jeffrey William ....Des Moines, IA
Courter, Kobert, Laufer & Cohen, P.C.
Hackettstown, NJ
Morristown, NJ
Trenton, NJ
Courter, Quinn, Doran & Anderson
Boone, IA
Courtian, Jennifer B. ....New York, NY
Courtin, John C. ....Buffalo, NY
Courtin, Scott ....Aurora, IL
Courtis, Kathleen M. ....Washington, DC
Courtland, Elmer W. ....Tucson, AZ
Courtland, Robert D. ....Bethesda, MD
Courtland, Robert D., Chartered
Washington, DC
Bethesda, MD
Courtnage, Michael S. ....Seattle, WA
Courtnell, Paul W. A., Jr.
West Palm Beach, FL
Courtney, Aaron C. ....Portland, OR
Courtney, Alan W. ....Santa Ynez, CA
Courtney, Alan W., A Professional Corporation
Santa Ynez, CA
Courtney, Ann M. ....Portland, ME
Courtney, Anne B. ....Louisville, KY
Courtney, Barbara B. ....Palo Alto, CA
Courtney, Brian C. ....Hartford, CT
Courtney, Caren C. ....Canton, TX
Courtney, Catherine J. ....Minneapolis, MN
Courtney, Charles M. ....Harrisburg, PA
Courtney, Charles W., Jr. ....Belleville, IL
Courtney, Clifford R. ....Indianapolis, IN
Courtney, Cornelius M. ....New York, NY
Courtney & Courtney ....Somerset, PA
Courtney, Cynthia K. ....West Hartford, CT
Courtney, Darren L. ....Lebanon, OH
Courtney, David M., Jr. ....Tucker, GA
Courtney, Dawn R. ....Wilmington, DE
Westmont, NJ
Norristown, PA
Philadelphia, PA
Courtney, Dennis J. ....Murray, KY
Courtney, Don E. ....Algona, IA
Courtney, Donna S. ....Lander, WY
Courtney, Erik ....Miami, FL
Courtney, Eugene P ....Worcester, MA
Courtney, Grant E. ....Seattle, WA
Courtney, Haven P. ....Merced, CA
Courtney, Henry T., Law Offices of
Miami, FL
Courtney, Jack ....Belvedere-Tiburon, CA
Courtney, James B ....Somerset, PA
Courtney, James J. ....Los Angeles, CA
Courtney, James O., Jr. ....Somerset, PA
Courtney, Janet M. ....Orlando, FL
Courtney, Jeanne E. ....El Cajon, CA
Courtney, Jeffrey J. ....Wetumpka, AL
Courtney, Jerome H. ....Tucson, AZ
Courtney, Jerry D. ....Clarendon, TX
Courtney, John J. ....Malden, MA
Courtney, John J. ....Flushing, NY
Courtney, John K. ....Los Angeles, CA
Courtney, John P. ....Boston, MA
Courtney, John P. ....Amagansett, NY
Courtney, John P. ....Houston, TX
Courtney, John Patrick, III ....Mobile, AL
Courtney, John R. ....Springfield, MO
Courtney, John R., P.C. ....Springfield, MO
Courtney, John Richard, Jr. ....Springfield, MO
Courtney, John W. ....Klamath Falls, OR
Courtney, Joseph D. ....Vernon, CT
Courtney, Karen Anne ....Fort Wayne, IN
Courtney, Kathleen H.
Equal Employment Opportunity Commission, Office of Legal Counsel, GV
Courtney, Kathryn L. ....Redwood City, CA
Courtney, Keith A. ....Austin, TX
Courtney, Kevin L. ....Boston, MA
Courtney, Kevin Patrick ....Morgan Hill, CA
Courtney, Lawrence J. ....Medina, OH
Courtney, Lyle Y. ....Galveston, TX
Courtney, M. Jule ....Baconton, GA
Courtney, Maggie Murray
San Francisco, CA
Courtney, Marshall A. ....Albany, NY
Courtney, Mary G. ....Princeton, NJ
Courtney, Mary Llamas ....Cleveland, OH
Courtney, Maryanne ....Washington, DC
Courtney, Maston C. ....Amarillo, TX
Courtney, Michael A. ....Westland, MI
Courtney, Michael K. ....Danbury, CT
Courtney, Michael M. ....Cleveland, OH
Courtney, Norman P. ....Corona, CA
Courtney, Patrick C. ....Stillwater, MN
Courtney, Patrick M. ....Cedar Rapids, IA
Courtney, Paul E. ....Beaver, PA
Courtney, Paul M. ....Vandalia, OH
Courtney, Pledl & Molter, S.C.
Milwaukee, WI
Courtney, Rachel E. ....San Francisco, CA
Courtney, Ralph A., III ....Los Angeles, CA
Courtney, Ralston L. ....Fresno, CA
Courtney, Raymond S.
Santa Barbara, CA
Courtney, Richard A. ....Jackson, MS
Courtney, Robert E. ....Redondo Beach, CA
Courtney, Robert M. ....Milwaukee, WI
Courtney, Robin S. ....Columbia, TN
Courtney, Roger C. ....Burke, VA
Courtney, Ruth A. ....Harrisburg, PA
Courtney, Stephen J. ....New Haven, CT
Courtney, Steven C. ....Harrisburg, PA
Courtney, Thomas E., Jr. ....Memphis, TN
Courtney, Thomas F. ....Palos Heights, IL
Courtney, Thomas J. ....Milwaukee, WI
Courtney, Vincent J. ....St. Paul, MN
Courtney, Wendell V. ....State College, PA
Courtney, William D. ....Willowbrook, IL
Courtney, William F. ....Dallas, TX
Courtney, William H. ....Charleston, WV
Courtney, William J. ....Woodbury, NY
Courtney, William J., Law Offices of
Flemington, NJ
Morristown, NJ
Courtney, William V. ....Covington, LA
Courtney-Baigorri, Sara ....Miami, FL
Courtois, Kevin N. ....Colorado Springs, CO
Courtois, Maria J. ....Houston, TX
Courtois, Mark J. ....Houston, TX
Courtright & Courtright ....Allen Park, MI
Courtright, Elliott G. ....Houston, TX
Courtright, Felicia M. ....Allen Park, MI
Courtright, Gregory M. ....Charleston, WV
Courtright, John T. ....Allen Park, MI
Courtright, K. P. ....San Antonio, TX
Courtright, Margaret C. ....Decatur, GA
Courtright, Richard W. ....Medford, OR
Courtright, Thurman T. ....Lancaster, OH
Courtright, William R. ....Chicago, IL
Courts, Kathleen ....Oakland, CA
Courture, Peter J. ....Los Altos, CA
Courtway, John F. ....Little Rock, AR
Courtway, Thomas C. ....Conway, AR
Courtwright, Alison A. ....Dallas, TX
Courtwright, M. Ernest ....Warrensburg, MO
Courville, Carolyn P. ....Houston, TX
Courville, Craig Alan ....Atlanta, GA
Courville, Craig Anthony ....Austin, TX
Courville, Donna L. ....Lubbock, TX
Courville, Timothy J. ....Boston, MA
Courville, Traci Green ....Atlanta, GA
Coury, Anthony Joseph ....Phoenix, AZ
Coury, Brian A. ....Lake Mary, FL
Coury, Brian A. ....Orlando, FL
Coury, Christopher A. ....Phoenix, AZ
Coury, Elias J. ....Westlake, OH
Coury, Elie S. ....Danbury, CT
Coury, George A. ....New Haven, CT
Coury, John A. ....Port Huron, MI
Coury, John Douglas ....Oklahoma City, OK
Coury, John J. ....Scranton, PA
Coury, John M. ....Berea, OH
Coury, John S. ....Canton, OH
Coury, Malleck G. ....Tulsa, OK
Coury, Michael P. ....Memphis, TN
Coury, Rebecca L. ....Miami, FL
Coury, Renee M. ....Phoenix, AZ
Coury, Robert G. ....Woodsfield, OH
Coury, Robert P., Jr. ....Pittsburgh, PA
Coury & Walsh ....Scranton, PA
Coury, William J. ....Brooklyn, NY
Cousar, James E. ....Austin, TX
Couse, Conway M. ....Bainbridge, NY
Cousens, Mark H. ....Detroit, MI
Cousens, Mark H. ....Southfield, MI
Couser, R. Lamar ....Tucson, AZ
Couser, Richard B. ....Concord, NH
Cousin, Brian S. ....Livingston, NJ
New York, NY
Cousineau, Carol S. ....Lansing, MI
Cousineau, Helen M. ....Washington, DC
Cousineau, Henry A., Jr.
Minneapolis, MN
Cousineau, Maria Louise
Los Angeles, CA
Cousineau, McGuire & Anderson, Chartered
Ironwood, MI
Minneapolis, MN
Cousineau, Richard L. ....Dayton, OH
Cousineau, Sue A. ....Killingworth, CT
Cousino, Darrah Desmond ....Chicago, IL
Cousins & Associates
West Palm Beach, FL
Cousins, Avery B. ....Annandale, VA
Cousins, Avery B., III ....Dallas, TX
Cousins, Barry Wayne ....Lawton, OK
Cousins, Craig M. ....New Orleans, LA
Cousins, Deborah S. ....Cleveland, OH
Cousins, Donald C. ....Stratford, CT
Cousins, Ertharin ....Chicago, IL
Cousins, Harold P., Jr. ....Oak Ridge, TN
Cousins, Howard L., Jr. ....Bangor, ME
Cousins, James A. ....Niles, MI
Cousins, Jeffrey L. ....Kingwood, TX
Cousins and Johnson, P.C.
Bridgeport, CT
Fairfield, CT
New Haven, CT
Stratford, CT
Cousins, Kevin C. ....Richmond, VA
Cousins, Kevin M. ....Golden, CO
Cousins, Nathanael M. ....Chicago, IL
Cousins, Norman Leonard ....New York, NY
Cousins, Oswald B. ....San Francisco, CA
Cousins, Patricia Gillis ....Rockville, MD
Cousins, Patricia Melugin ....Modesto, CA
Cousins, Patrick St. George
West Palm Beach, FL
Cousins, Peter ....New York, NY
Cousins, R. B. ....Dallas, TX
Cousins, Robert B., Jr. ....Dallas, TX
Cousins, Robert B., Jr. ....Richmond, VA
Cousins, Robert J. ....Fort Lauderdale, FL
Cousins, Scott D. ....Wilmington, DE
Cousins, Sidney C., Jr. ....Rockville, MD
Cousins, Steven H. ....Stratford, CT
Cousins, Steven N. ....St. Louis, MO
Cousins, W. James, Jr. ....Stamford, CT
Wilton, CT
White Plains, NY
Cousins, William, Jr. ....Chicago, IL
Cousins, William R., III ....Dallas, TX
Cousins-Savage, Wendy ....Tampa, FL
Cousland, Charles W. ....Waukesha, WI
Couso Puccio, Linda ....Wayne, NJ
Coussan, Luke J. ....Carencro, LA
Coussons, Charles ....Houston, TX
Coussons, Irene ....Houston, TX
Coustan, Lily R. ....New York, NY
Coutant, Helen S. ....Binghamton, NY
Coutant, Kevin C. ....Tulsa, OK
Coutant, Richard H. ....Bellows Falls, VT
Coutant, Richard Norman ....Albany, NY
Coutant, Robert W. ....Binghamton, NY
Couter, John W. ....Decatur, IL
Coutilish, John G. ....Bloomfield Hills, MI
Coutilish, John G., P.C.
Bloomfield Hills, MI

Couto, Drew J. ... Lexington, KY
Couto, Tracey Pascale ... East Haven, CT
Coutrakon, Basil H. ... Springfield, IL
Coutras, A. A. ... Jacksonville, FL
Coutros, Lana H. ... Newark, NJ
Coutroulis, Chris S. ... Tampa, FL
Couts, Constance L. ... San Francisco, CA
Coutts, James V. ... Russellville, AR
Coutts, James V., Law Firm of
Russellville, AR
Coutts, Robert Patrick ... Ann Arbor, MI
Coutu, Roger L. ... Warwick, RI
Coutu, Ronald C. ... Wilmington, MA
Coutu, Stephanie Wexler ... Boston, MA
Couture, Alan J. ... Traverse City, MI
Couture, David J. ... Riverview, MI
Couture, Faye L. ... St. Louis, MO
Couture, George Allen ... Sacramento, CA
Couture, James A. ... Belchertown, MA
Couture, Jennifer L. ... Boston, MA
Couture, Jerold L. ... New York, NY
Couture, Jorene Michele ... Norwich, CT
Couture, Keith M. ... Chalmette, LA
Couture, Larry J. ... Tacoma, WA
Couture, Richard T. ... Hartford, CT
Couture, Thomas J.
Department of the Air Force, Office of the Judge Advocate General, GV
Couture, Timothy R. ... Chicago, IL
Couturier, Robert L. ... Lewiston, ME
Couvillion, D. Irvin
United States Tax Court, Special Trial Judges, GV
Couvillion, Dennis P. ... New Orleans, LA
Couvillon, Donald A.
Department of Justice, Civil Division, GV
Couvillon, Susan Teale ... Atlanta, GA
Couvillon, Tucker H., III
New Orleans, LA
Couvreur, Joseph G. ... Taylor, MI
Couzens, J. Richard ... Auburn, CA
Couzens, Jack S., II
Farmington Hills, MI
Couzens, John C., Jr. ... White Plains, NY
Couzens, Lansky, Fealk, Ellis, Roeder & Lazar, P.C. ... Detroit, MI
Farmington Hills, MI
Couzens, Richard M. ... Yardley, PA
Covacevich, Anthony J. ... Baltimore, MD
Covahey & Boozer, P.A. ... Baltimore, MD
Towson, MD
Covahey, Edward C., Jr. ... Towson, MD
Coval, Daniel S., Jr. ... Ardmore, PA
Coval, Michael A. ... Atlanta, GA
Coval, Paul J. ... Columbus, OH
Covalt, Victor E., III ... Lincoln, NE
Covarrubias, Marita T.
Santa Barbara, CA
Covas-Mendoza, Jorge L. ... San Juan, PR
Covatta, Anthony G., Jr. ... Cincinnati, OH
Covault, Carolyn ... Houston, TX
Covault, Ronald E. ... Pontiac, MI
Cove, Andrew N. ... Hollywood, FL
Cove & Associates, P.A. ... Hollywood, FL
Cove, John F., Jr. ... San Francisco, CA
Cove, Joseph C. ... Uxbridge, MA
Cove, Ruth L. ... New York, NY
Covel, Richard A. ... Waltham, MA
Coveler, Frederick E. ... Houston, TX
Coveler, Ira Alexander ... Houston, TX
Coveler & Katz, P.C. ... Houston, TX
Coveler, Matthew E. ... Houston, TX
Coveleski, James M. ... New York, NY
Covell, Andrea M. Gentile
Chevy Chase, MD
Covell, Calvin G. ... Cleveland, OH
Covell & Covell ... Baton Rouge, LA
Covell, Cynthia F. ... Denver, CO
Covell, Henry E., Jr. ... Richmond, CA
Covell, Jennifer A. ... New York, NY
Covell, John S. ... San Francisco, CA
Covell, Julie A. ... Los Angeles, CA
Covell, Kenneth L. ... Fairbanks, AK
Covell, Lauren Killebrew ... Baton Rouge, LA
Covell, Paul A. ... Christiansted, St. Croix, VI
Covell, Rebecca S. ... Dallas, TX
Covell, Robert M. ... Huntingdon, PA
Covell, Robert N. ... Rockville Centre, NY
Covell, Scott M. ... Pensacola, FL
Covell, Stephen E. ... Baton Rouge, LA
Covelli, Claude J. ... Madison, WI
Covelli, Gary L. ... Madison, WI
Covelli, Joseph P. ... Tampa, FL
Covelli, Victor M. ... Belmar, NJ
Covello, Alfred V. ... Hartford, CT
Covello, Cheryl R. ... New York, NY
Covello, Frank ... Wayne, NJ
Covello, Kim Marie ... Pottstown, PA
Covello, Timothy J. ... Simsbury, CT
Covello, Timothy S. ... San Luis Obispo, CA
Covelman, Joel David ... Irvine, CA
Coven, Brian S. ... Newark, NJ
Coven, Christine L. ... Akron, OH
Coven, David A. ... Fort Lauderdale, FL
Coven, David A., P.A. ... Fort Lauderdale, FL
Coven, Glenn E., Jr. ... Williamsburg, VA
Coven, Harry M. ... Chicago, IL
Coven, Janet ... Green Brook, NJ
Coven, Jules E. ... New York, NY
Coven, Lawrence S., Law Offices of, The
New York, NY
Coven, Lawrence S., The Law Offices of
Green Brook, NJ
Coven, Mark S. ... Somerville, MA
Coven, Michele R. ... New York, NY
Coven, Mitchell S. ... Staten Island, NY
Coven, Phyllis A.
Department of Justice, GV
Coven, Richard E. ... New York, NY
Coven, Roger B. ... Los Angeles, CA
Coveney, Kenneth G. ... San Diego, CA
Covensky, Harvey ... Southfield, MI
Coventon, Kevin E. ... Los Angeles, CA
Coventry, Dale E. ... Arlington Heights, IL
Coveny, Michael R. ... Chicago, IL
Cover, Charlotte A. ... Seminole, FL
Cover, David L. ... Peoria, IL
Cover, David M. ... San Francisco, CA
Cover, E. McIntosh ... Savannah, GA
Cover, Gary V. ... Clinton, MO
Cover, James N. ... Mission Viejo, CA
Cover, Kathi A. ... Dallas, TX
Cover, Krista M. ... San Antonio, TX
Cover, Marian L. ... Memphis, TN
Cover, Mark A. ... Dallas, TX
Cover, Richard L. ... Columbia, MD
Cover, Robert W., II
House of Representatives, Office of Legislative Counsel, GV
Cover, Thomas A. ... Detroit, MI
Cover, W. Curtis, Jr. ... Costa Mesa, CA
Coverdale, John F. ... Newark, NJ
Coverdale, William, (Inc.) ... San Rafael, CA
Coverdell, Jeffrey W. ... St. Louis, MO
Cover-Huntley, Dawn L. ... Providence, RI
Coverston, Harry S. ... Orlando, FL
Coverston, Janna M. ... Lafayette, CA
Coverstone, Thomas E.
Redwood City, CA
Covert, Barry Nelson ... Buffalo, NY
Covert, Carl W., Jr. ... San Antonio, TX
Covert, Charles W. ... St. Albans, WV
Covert, Cory John ... Farmingdale, NY
Covert, Derek F. ... San Francisco, CA
Covert, G. Stephen ... Baton Rouge, LA
Covert, George R. ... Baton Rouge, LA
Covert, John M. ... Washington, DC
Covert, Kasey A. ... San Diego, CA
Covert, Kevin M. ... Morristown, NJ
Covert, Mary Beth ... Buffalo, NY
Covert, Neil R. ... Clearwater, FL
Covert, P. Addison ... Sacramento, CA
San Francisco, CA
Covert, Rebecca L. ... Honolulu, HI
Covert, Richard W. ... San Francisco, CA
Covert, Robert E. ... Naples, FL
Covert, Spencer E., (P.C.) ... Tustin, CA
Covert, Stephen ... Palm Beach Gardens, FL
Covert, Wayne R., Jr. ... Columbia, SC
Covert, William H. ... Newark, NJ
Covey, Andrew W. ... Peoria, IL
Covey, Angeline A. ... Larkspur, CA
Covey, Anne ... Manasquan, NJ
Covey, Bonnie ... New York, NY
Covey, Bradley S. ... Batavia, IL
Covey, Brent R. ... Houston, TX
Covey, Charles A. ... Peoria, IL
Covey, Christine C. ... Cleveland, OH
Covey, David M. ... New York, NY
Covey, Donald E. ... Winner, SD
Covey, Frank M., Jr. ... Chicago, IL
Covey, J. Dow, IV ... Palm Coast, FL
Covey, J. Tyson ... Chicago, IL
Covey, Janet L. ... Forest Park, GA
Covey, Joseph M. R. ... Salt Lake City, UT
Covey, Julia Fayngold ... Washington, DC
Covey, Keith H. ... Oklahoma City, OK
Covey Law Office ... Winner, SD
Covey, Margaret Lee ... Los Angeles, CA
Covey, Maude ... Downers Grove, IL
Covey, Rebecca J., (P.A.)
Fort Lauderdale, FL
Covey, Richard B. ... New York, NY
Covey, Richard D. ... Los Angeles, CA
Covey, Robert O. ... Crystal Lake, IL
Covey, Roberts, Buchanan & McGroddy
North Palm Beach, FL
Katonah, NY
Covey, Russell D. ... Washington, DC
Covey, Steven K. ... Chicago, IL
Covey, William I. ... Peoria, IL
Covey, William R. ... Department of the Army, Office of the Judge Advocate General, GV
Covi, Kristopher J. ... Omaha, NE
Covich, Daniel G. ... Austin, TX
Coviello, Anthony L. ... Bloomfield, NJ
Coviello, Frank J. ... Gaithersburg, MD
Coviello, James A. ... Ridgefield, NJ
Coviello, Jane M. ... Boonton, NJ
Coviello, Joseph A. ... Cleveland, OH
Coviello, Joseph P. ... Clarks Summit, PA
Coviello, Joseph R. ... Summit, NJ
Coviello, Leonard P., Jr. ... Waterbury, CT
Coviello, Ninucio A. ... Roseland, NJ
Coviello, Philip E. ... New York, NY
Coviello, Rita A. ... Parsippany, NJ
Coviello, Robert A. ... Boston, MA
Coviello, Robert D. ... Santa Ana, CA
Coviello, Robert D., A Professional Law Corporation ... Santa Ana, CA
Coviello, Vincent F., Jr. ... Kirkland, WA
Coviello, Yvonne M. ... Washington, DC
Covill, Kitley S. ... Katonah, NY
Coville, John D. ... Woodhaven, NY
Coville, Robert A. ... Skaneateles, NY
Coville, Robert A., P.C. ... Skaneateles, NY
Covin, J. Robert ... Memphis, TN
Covin, Mark D. ... St. Paul, MN
Covine, Daniel G. ... Westfield, NJ
Covington, Alice L.
United States Postal Service, Law Department, GV
Covington, Ann K. ... Jefferson City, MO
Covington, Anthony B. ... Baltimore, MD
Covington, Barry T. ... Silver Spring, MD
Covington, Bobby L. ... Jackson, MS
Covington & Burling ... San Francisco, CA
Washington, DC
New York, NY
Covington & Crowe LLP
Los Angeles, CA
Ontario, CA
Pomona, CA
Rancho Cucamonga, CA
San Bernardino, CA
Covington, David L. ... San Francisco, CA
Covington, Deborah L. ... Saipan, TT
Covington, Douglas L. ... Tampa, FL
Covington, Earl G. ... Houston, TX
Covington, Eugene C., Jr. ... Greenville, SC
Covington, Forrest K. ... Birmingham, AL
Covington, George C. ... Charlotte, NC
Covington, George D. ... Bronx, NY
Covington, George M. ... Chicago, IL
Covington, George M. ... Lake Forest, IL
Covington, George W., Jr. ... Tomball, TX
Covington, George W., P.C. ... Tomball, TX
Covington, I. Boyce, III ... Winston-Salem, NC
Covington, J. Lee, II ... Little Rock, AR
Covington, J. Scott ... Harrison, AR
Covington, J. Wesley ... Durham, NC
Covington, James E., Jr. ... Richmond, VA
Covington, James R., III ... Springfield, IL
Covington, James S. ... Houston, TX
Covington, Jill M. ... Phoenix, AZ
Covington, JoAnn Corti ... Redwood City, CA
Covington, John P. ... Dallas, TX
Covington, John R. ... Lake Forest, IL
Covington, Joseph P. ... Washington, DC
Covington, Karen K. ... Atlanta, GA
Covington, Kelly Lee ... Atlanta, GA
Covington, Kenneth M. ... Martinsville, VA
Covington, Kevin B. ... Tallahassee, FL
Covington, L. Philip ... Garner, NC
Covington Law Office ... Harrison, AR
Covington, Linda W. ... Lexington, KY
Covington, M. Stanley ... Greenbelt, MD
Covington, Matthew Stone
San Francisco, CA
Covington, Pamela S. ... New York, NY
Covington, Patricia E.M. ... Glen Allen, VA
Covington, Patrick, Hagins, Stern & Lewis, P.A. ... Anderson, SC
Greenville, SC
Spartanburg, SC
Covington, Payton R. ... Lake Charles, LA
Covington, Peter J. ... Charlotte, NC
Covington & Poe ... Tulsa, OK
Covington, Polly J. ... Quitman, MS
Covington, Robert E., III ... Hayden Lake, ID
Covington, Robert E., Jr. ... Quitman, MS
Covington, Robert N. ... Nashville, TN
Covington, Sandra N. S. ... New York, NY
Covington, Susan B. ... Greenville, SC
Covington, Susan B., P.A. ... Greenville, SC
Covington, Suzanne ... Austin, TX
Covington, Timothy A. ... Palo Alto, CA
Covington, Timothy L. ... Atlanta, GA
Covington, Virginia M. ... Tampa, FL
Covington, Warren A. ... Portland, OR
Covington, William D. ... Carrollton, GA
Covington, William M. ... Oklahoma City, OK
Covington, William T., Jr. ... Charlotte, NC
Covino, A. Michael ... New York, NY
Covino, David W. ... Hamburg, NY
Covino, John A. ... Trenton, NJ
Covino, John D. ... East Syracuse, NY
Covinsky, Bryan O. ... Harrisonville, MO
Covit, Barrie B. ... New York, NY
Covitt, Regina ... Los Angeles, CA
Covitz, Morton R., Law Offices of
Englewood Cliffs, NJ
Covitz, Robert S. ... Aventura, FL
Covner, Andrew H. ... Ventura, CA
Covner, Ellen B. ... Philadelphia, PA
Covner, George S. ... Flushing, NY
Covolo, John J. ... Tarboro, NC
Covone, Mary Ann ... Chicago, IL
Covone, Neil A. ... Miami, FL
Covotta, Brian E. ... Palo Alto, CA
Covrett, C. Craig ... Toledo, OH
Covucci, George E. ... Washington, DC
Covy, Karen A. ... Chicago, IL
Cowal, Catherine Elaine ... Tallahassee, FL
Cowan, A. Halsey ... San Diego, CA
Cowan, Adam ... Cedar Grove, NJ
Cowan, Alfred W. ... Rockford, IL
Cowan, Amanda Aubry ... Orlando, FL
Cowan, Andrew S. ... Department of Justice, Antitrust Division, GV
Cowan, Antonia Z. ... Las Vegas, NV
Cowan, Arnold M. ... Long Beach, CA
Cowan & Associates, Chartered
Chicago, IL
Cowan, Barrie ... Menlo Park, CA
San Jose, CA
Cowan, Barry W. ... Dallas, TX
Cowan, Barton Z. ... Pittsburgh, PA
Cowan, Bruce M., (A Professional Corporation) ... San Francisco, CA
Cowan, Cameron L. ... Washington, DC
Cowan, Candace L. ... Houston, TX
Cowan, Caspar F. ... Portland, ME
Cowan, Charilyn W. ... Washington, DC
Cowan, Charles A. ... Washington, DC
Cowan, Charles D. ... Tyler, TX
Cowan, Charles D., P.C. ... Tyler, TX
Cowan, Christopher F. ... Dayton, OH
Cowan, Claiborne L. ... Austin, TX
Cowan, Claudia L. ... Irvine, CA
Cowan, Coleman M. ... Raleigh, NC
Cowan, Constance S. ... Chicago, IL
Cowan, Curtis R. ... Fort Lauderdale, FL
Cowan, Dale H. ... Cleveland, OH
Cowan, Dana T. ... Kennesaw, GA
Cowan, Daniel M. ... Boca Raton, FL
Cowan, David Clay ... Del Rio, TX
Cowan, David J. ... Los Angeles, CA
Cowan, David M. ... Birmingham, AL
Cowan, DeBaets, Abrahams & Sheppard LLP ... New York, NY
Cowan, Dennis G. ... Bloomfield Hills, MI
Cowan, Dennis K. ... Red Bluff, CA
Cowan, Dennis K. ... Redding, CA
Cowan, Douglas G. ... Walnut Creek, CA
Cowan, Douglas L. ... Bellevue, WA
Cowan, Elliott ... Baltimore, MD
Cowan, Elmer G. ... Cleveland, OH
Cowan, Eric W. ... Tysons Corner, VA
Cowan, Eugene G. ... Los Angeles, CA
Cowan, F. Neil, Jr. ... Richmond, VA
Cowan, Finis E. ... Houston, TX
Cowan, Finis E., III ... Galveston, TX
Cowan, Frank N. ... Richmond, VA
Cowan, Frederic J. ... Louisville, KY
Cowan, Gary ... Cleveland, OH
Cowan, Gary L. ... Houston, TX
Cowan, Gary R. ... Colorado Springs, CO
Cowan, George T. ... Seattle, WA
Cowan, Gordon M., Law Offices of
Reno, NV
Cowan, Grant S. ... Cincinnati, OH
Cowan, H. Mitchell ... Jackson, MS
Cowan, Hayne & Fox ... Bellevue, WA
Cowan & Hilgeman ... Dayton, OH
Cowan, Homer, Jr. ... Fort Scott, KS
Cowan & Hoover, P.C. ... Houston, TX
Cowan, Ivy A. ... Plantation, FL
Cowan, J. Donald, Jr. ... Greensboro, NC
Cowan, J. Stephen ... Daingerfield, TX
Cowan, Jacques T. ... Minneapolis, MN
Cowan, James K., Jr. ... Roanoke, VA
Cowan, James R. ... New York, NY
Cowan, James S.E. ... Houston, TX
Cowan, Jeffrey W. ... Los Angeles, CA
Cowan, Jennifer R. ... New York, NY
Cowan, Jerry L. ... Cincinnati, OH
Cowan, John ... El Paso, TX
Cowan, John A. ... Beaumont, TX
Cowan, John C. ... Fredericksburg, VA
Cowan, John J. ... South Charleston, WV
Cowan, John Robert ... Lexington, KY
Cowan, John S. ... Arvada, CO
Cowan, Josef M. ... Anaheim, CA
Cowan, Joseph L., II ... Birmingham, AL
Cowan, Joyce A. ... Washington, DC
Cowan, Judith N. ... Salem, MA
Cowan, Julie M. ... Pembroke Pines, FL
Cowan, Katherine H. ... Lake Oswego, OR
Cowan & Kelly, P.C. ... Langhorne, PA
Cowan, Kenneth W. ... Fort Smith, AR
Waldron, AR
Cowan, Kevin D. ... Miami, FL
Cowan, Kevin M. ... Wichita, KS
Cowan, Kristen Tosh ... Washington, DC
Cowan, Larry M. ... Lafayette, CA
Cowan, Lee W. ... Washington, DC
Cowan, Lewis R. ... New York, NY
Cowan, Liebowitz & Latman, P.C.
New York, NY
Cowan, Linda Scholle ... Louisville, KY
Cowan, Lisa ... Nashville, TN
Cowan, Luther F. ... Cordell, OK
Cowan, M. Benjamin ... Houston, TX
Cowan & MacDonald, P.C. ... Springfield, NJ
Cowan, Marcia K. ... Roswell, GA
Cowan, Mark A. ... Morristown, TN
Cowan, Mark E. ... Hagåtña, GU
Cowan, Martin B. ... New Rochelle, NY
Cowan, Martin D. ... Tarrytown, NY
Cowan, Marvin S. ... New York, NY
Cowan, Mary Margaret ... Tucson, AZ
Cowan, Melissa M. ... Los Angeles, CA
Cowan, Michael I. ... Santa Monica, CA
Cowan, Michael I., Professional Law Corporation ... Santa Monica, CA
Cowan, Nancy ... Harrisburg, PA
Cowan, Otis H. ... Kansas City, MO
Cowan & Owen, P.C. ... Chesterfield, VA
Richmond, VA
Cowan, Pamela S. ... Seattle, WA
Cowan, Paul I. ... Carson, CA
Cowan, Paul M. ... Miami, FL
Cowan, Peter S. ... Concord, NH
Manchester, NH
Cowan, Peter W. ... New York, NY
Cowan, Philip ... Chicago, IL
Cowan, Philip M. ... New York, NY
Cowan, R. Christopher ... Dallas, TX
Cowan, Rachel ... Cleveland, OH
Cowan, Rebecca Barge ... Canton, MS
Jackson, MS
Cowan, Rex P., Law Offices of
Winter Haven, FL
Cowan, Richard E. ... San Francisco, CA
Cowan, Richard E. ... Roselle, NJ
Cowan, Richard L. ... Salem, OR
Cowan, Robert Adam ... Dalton, GA
Cowan, Robert C., Jr. ... San Antonio, TX
Cowan, Robert C., Jr., Inc. ... San Antonio, TX
Cowan, Robert C., Sr. ... San Antonio, TX
Cowan, Robert J. ... Midland, TX
Cowan, Roger Brian ... New York, NY
Cowan, Ronald M. ... Murphy, NC
Cowan, Ruth E. ... Springfield, NJ
Cowan, Sally ... New York, NY
Cowan, Sandra Schilling ... Redmond, WA
Cowan, Scott W. ... Houston, TX
Cowan, Sid ... Del Rio, TX
Cowan, Spencer M. ... Chapel Hill, NC
Cowan, Stephen A. ... San Francisco, CA

Cowan, Steven J.
Overseas Private Investment Corporation, Investment Funds Department, GV
Cowan, Stewart M. ....San Diego, CA
Cowan, Stuart M., Law Offices of
Honolulu, HI
Cowan, Thomas A. ....Richland, WA
Cowan, Thomas C. ....New Orleans, LA
Houston, TX
Cowan, Thomas E., Jr. ....Elizabethton, TN
Cowan, Thomas W. ....Salem, OR
Cowan, Tracy J. ....St. Louis, MO
Cowan, Wade B. ....Nashville, TN
Cowan Walker, P.S. ....Kennewick, WA
Pasco, WA
Richland, WA
Cowan, Wallace E. ....New York, NY
Cowan, Walter G., Jr. ....Plano, TX
Cowan, Wendell F. ....Overland Park, KS
Cowan, William H. ....Chicago, IL
Cowan, William J.
Federal Energy Regulatory Commission, Office of the Administrative Law Judges, GV
Cowan, William M., Jr. ....Langhorne, PA
Cowan, William M. ("Mo") ....Boston, MA
Cowan, William Ray ....Raytown, MO
Cowan, William S. ....Georgetown, SC
Cowan, Wm. H. ....Austin, TX
Cowans, Daniel R. ....Los Altos, CA
Cowans, Timothy E. ....Columbus, OH
Coward, Carolyn Lloyd ....Asheville, NC
Coward, Clay H. ....Orlando, FL
Coward, Curtis M. ....McLean, VA
Coward, David Scott ....Raleigh, NC
Coward, George T. ....Lakeland, FL
Coward, Hicks & Siler, P.A. .....Cashiers, NC
Franklin, NC
Sylva, NC
Coward, J. K., Jr. ....Sylva, NC
Coward, John H. ....Cupertino, CA
Coward, Kimberly R. ....Cashiers, NC
Coward, Lloyd W. ....Rockville, MD
Coward, Mortimer F.
Department of Housing and Urban Development, Office of General Counsel, GV
Coward, Nicholas F. ....Washington, DC
Coward, Orville D. ....Sylva, NC
Coward, Orville D., Jr. ....Franklin, NC
Coward, P. Robert ....Moraga, CA
Coward, Thomas S. ....Portland, ME
Coward, William H. ....Franklin, NC
Cowardin, William C., Jr.
Newport News, VA
Cowart, Annette M. ....Decatur, GA
Cowart, B. Scott ....Baton Rouge, LA
Cowart, Carroll L. ....Savannah, GA
Cowart, Craig A. ....Memphis, TN
Cowart, Craig N. ....Macon, GA
Cowart, Dan S. ....Glennville, GA
Cowart, Dax S. ....Corpus Christi, TX
Cowart, Gary R. ....Fort Lauderdale, FL
Cowart, Greta E. (Gerberding)
Dallas, TX
Cowart, J. Douglas ....Macon, GA
Cowart, J. Walter ....Savannah, GA
Cowart, James D. ....Sugar Land, TX
Cowart, James M. ....Stockbridge, GA
Cowart, Joe A., Jr. ....Cocoa, FL
Cowart, John ....Llano, TX
Cowart, John D. ....La Jolla, CA
Cowart, John P., Jr. ....Atlanta, GA
Cowart, John T. ....Llano, TX
Cowart, Joseph H. (Joey) ....Statesboro, GA
Cowart, Kathy Lynn ....Snellville, GA
Cowart, Lawr. ....Oakhurst, TX
Cowart, Matthew M. ....San Antonio, TX
Cowart, Melanie Goins ....San Antonio, TX
Cowart, Melvin E. ....Pasadena, TX
Cowart, Patricia E. ....Miami, FL
Cowart, Richard G. ....Jackson, MS
Nashville, TN
Cowart, Richard M. ....Valdosta, GA
Cowart, Roy N. ....Warner Robins, GA
Cowart, Roy N., P.C. ....Warner Robins, GA
Cowart, T. David ....Dallas, TX
Cowart, Thomas B. ....Jackson, MS
Waco, TX
Cowart, Zollie S., III ....Bradenton, FL
Cowden & Cockrell ....Mount Sterling, KY
Cowden, David C. ....Grand Prairie, TX
Cowden, Fred E., Jr. ....Nashville, TN
Cowden, George, III ....San Antonio, TX
Cowden, George M. ....Austin, TX
Cowden, Gerald W. ....Akron, OH
Cleveland, OH
Cowden, Humphrey & Sarlson
Akron, OH
Cleveland, OH
Cowden, Jacqueline E.
Newport Beach, CA
Cowden, James L. ....Harrisburg, PA
Cowden, James N. ....Austin, TX
Cowden, Jax ....Houston, TX
Cowden, Jax, P.C. ....Houston, TX
Cowden, John M. ....Portland, OR
Cowden, John W. ....Kansas City, MO
Cowden, Karen G. ....Dallas, TX
Cowden, Marc G. ....San Jose, CA
Cowden, Paul David ....Mount Sterling, KY
Cowden, Pfarrer, Crew & Becker
Dayton, OH
Cowden, Robert E., III ....Boston, MA
Cowden, Roger R. ....Lexington, KY
Cowden, Tami D. ....Denver, CO
Cowden, Vance L. ....Columbia, SC
Cowden, William R. ....Washington, DC
Cowdery, Allen C. ....Tulsa, OK
Cowdery, Ecker & Murphy, L.L.C.
Hartford, CT
Cowdery, James T. ....Hartford, CT
Cowdery, Jane R. ....Tulsa, OK
Cowdery, Kathryn G. W. ....Tallahassee, FL
Cowdrey, Ann Marie ....Dallas, TX
Cowdrey, Elliott T. ....Lowell, MA
Cowdrey, Michael L. ....Orange, CA
Cowdrey, Robert F. ....Dayton, OH
Cowdrey, Robert L. ....Boston, MA
Cowdrey, Roy B., Jr. ....Easton, MD
Cowdrey, Sean D., Law Offices of
Ventura, CA
Cowdrey, Thompson & Karsten, P.A.
Annapolis, MD
Easton, MD
Cowdrick, Bruce A. ....Laurel, MD
Cowdrick, Bruce Alan, L.C. ....Laurel, MD
Cowdry, William R. ....Saginaw, MI
Cowee, John W. ....Aurora, CO
Cowel, Debbe Kay ....Boston, MA
Cowel, Steven N. ....Shreveport, LA
Cowell, Aaron D., Jr. ....Charlotte, NC
Cowell, Anthony ....Woodbridge, NJ
Cowell, Christina A. ....Red Bank, NJ
Cowell, Eugene F., III ....Houston, TX
Cowell, George I. ....Chicago, IL
Cowell, Heather Brantley ....Larned, KS
Cowell, Lloyd D., Jr. ....Columbus, OH
Cowell, Marion A., Jr. ....Charlotte, NC
Cowell, Marvin J., Jr. ....Staunton, VA
Cowell, Maryjane D. ....Roseland, NJ
Cowell, Michael A. ....Los Angeles, CA
Cowell, Robert R. ....Schaumburg, IL
Cowell, W. Richard ....Erie, PA
Cowell, Wes ....Chicago, IL
Cowell, William ....Gaylord, MN
Cowell Ross, Mary Riepma, (Mrs.)
New York, NY
Cowen, Adriene D. ....Highland Beach, FL
Cowen & Associates ....Washington, DC
McLean, VA
Cowen, Barbara E. ....Hackensack, NJ
Cowen, Bruce S. ....Fort Wayne, IN
Cowen, Cheryl C. ....Waynesburg, PA
Cowen, Crowley, Nord & Staub, P.C.
Chicago, IL
Cowen, David E. ....Galveston, TX
Cowen, Dorothy R. ....New Orleans, LA
Cowen, E. James ....Houston, TX
Cowen, Edward S. ....New York, NY
Cowen, Elizabeth B. ....New Orleans, LA
Cowen, George S. ....Hackensack, NJ
Cowen, Gerald ....Hollywood, FL
Cowen, Gerald G. ....Elmsford, NY
Cowen, Gretchen ....La Jolla, CA
Cowen & Grinch ....Hackensack, NJ
Cowen, Jacobs & Rothman
Hackensack, NJ
Cowen, James S. ....United States Senate, Committee Legal Personnel, GV
Cowen, John C. L. ....Green Valley, AZ
Cowen, Jon C. ....Boston, MA
Cowen, Jonathan M.
Federal Trade Commission, Bureau of Consumer Protection, GV
Cowen, Keitha Kay ....Southfield, MI
Cowen, Lawrence ....New York, NY
Cowen, Linda Friedner ....New York, NY
Cowen, Linda Sharpe ....Jonesboro, GA
Cowen, Louise ....South Gate, CA
Cowen, Martin H. ....Newark, NJ
Cowen, Maurice L. ....Louisville, KY
Cowen, Michael R. ....Brownsville, TX
Cowen, Michael R., P.C. ....Brownsville, TX
Cowen, Nancy S. ....Los Angeles, CA
Cowen, Rachel B. ....Chicago, IL
Cowen, Richard A. ....Chicago, IL
Cowen, Richard M. ....Melbourne, FL
Cowen, Robert E. ....Trenton, NJ
Cowen, Robert H. ....Williamston, NC
Cowen, Robert N. ....New York, NY
Cowen, Sandra E. ....Oak Brook, IL
Cowen, Sarah Pierce ....Houston, TX
Cowen, Sheldon ....Brooklyn, NY
Cowen, Stephen S. ....Atlanta, GA
Cowen, Steven E. ....Lakeside, CA
Cowen, Theodore E. ....Lexington, KY
Cowen, Thomas A. ....San Antonio, TX
Cowen, William B. ....McLean, VA
Cowen, Wilson
United States Court Of Appeals For The Federal Circuit, GV
Cowett, Alexei J. ....New York, NY
Cowett, Anne ....Phoenix, AZ
Cowett, C. Michael ....San Diego, CA
Cowett, Daniel J. ....San Bernardino, CA
Cowett, Patricia A. ....San Diego, CA
Cowger, Alfred R., Jr. ....New York, NY
Cowger, Christopher N. ....Topeka, KS
Cowger, Graciela G. ....Portland, OR
Cowger, Jeffrey L. ....Lansing, KS
Cowger, Walter S. ....Dallas, TX
Cowgill, Bradford L. ....Lexington, KY
Cowgill, Carol A.
Environmental Protection Agency, Office of the General Counsel, GV
Cowgill, Kenneth W. ....Washington, DC
Cowgill, Michael G. ....Albany, OR
Cowgill, Nancy L. ....Portland, OR
Cowgill, Sandra Cirricione ....Plainfield, IL
Cowgill, Thomas E. ....Joliet, IL
Cowherd, Charles B. ....Springfield, MO
Cowherd, John ....Mount Vernon, MO
Cowherd, Mary J. ....Austin, TX
Cowherd, Randy R. ....Springfield, MO
Cowherd, Robert E. ....Brookfield, MO
Chillicothe, MO
Cowherd, Stephen M. ....Westport, CT
Cowhey, Carol M. ....Philadelphia, PA
Cowhey, David J. ....Atlantic City, NJ
Cowhey, James R. ....White Plains, NY
Cowhig, Francis John ....Alhambra, CA
Cowhig, Hugh C. ....Lee, MA
Cowhig, John S. ....Orange, CA
Cowhig, Michael T., Jr. ....Boston, MA
Cowie, Evelyn D. ....Washington, DC
Cowie, Irvin S. ....Lakeland, FL
Cowie, James J. ....Atlanta, GA
Cowie, John R., Jr. ....Adams, MA
Cowie, Michael G. ....Washington, DC
Cowie & Mott, P.A. ....Baltimore, MD
Cowie, Nicholas D. ....Baltimore, MD
Cowie, Robert H. ....Houston, TX
Cowie, Robert J., Jr. ....Decorah, IA
Cowie, Roger B. ....Dallas, TX
Cowie, Thomas W. ....Plymouth, NH
Cowin, Jeffrey A. ....Danbury, CT
Cowin, Joseph P. ....Overland Park, KS
Cowin, Judith A. ....Boston, MA
Cowin, Merle Teitelbaum ....Chicago, IL
Cowin, William I. ....Boston, MA
Cowin, William L. ....Fresno, CA
Cowing, Mark W. ....Kansas City, MO
Cowing, Paul D. ....Kansas City, MO
Cowit, Elizabeth ....New York, NY
Cowitt, Stuart S. ....New York, NY
Cowle, Bradley L. ....Burnsville, MN
Cowles, C. Deming, IV
United States Senate, Senatorial Assistants, GV
Cowles, Colleen A. ....Eau Claire, WI
Cowles, D. Brooks, Jr. ....Atlanta, GA
Cowles, David R. ....Bristol, VT
Cowles, David W. ....Las Vegas, NV
Cowles, Donald T. ....Richmond, VA
Cowles, Douglas M. ....Gallipolis, OH
Cowles, Elizabeth ....Santa Ana, CA
Cowles, Frank L., Jr. ....Fairfax, VA
Cowles, Frederick O. ....New York, NY
Cowles, Jim E. ....Dallas, TX
Cowles, John Bertram, Jr. ....Toano, VA
Cowles, John E. ....Olathe, KS
Cowles, Julia K. ....New York, NY
Cowles, M. Christine ....Milwaukee, WI
Cowles, Macon, & Associates, P.C.
Boulder, CO
Cowles, Michael ....Duluth, MN
Cowles, Rinaldi, Judkins & Korjus, Ltd.
Fairfax, VA
Cowles, Robert L. ....Jacksonville, FL
Cowles, S. Macon, III ....Boulder, CO
Cowles & Shaughnessy, P.A.
Jacksonville, FL
Cowles, Shawn E. ....Newport Beach, CA
Cowles & Thompson, A Professional Corporation ....Dallas, TX
McKinney, TX
Tyler, TX
Cowley, Benjamin D. ....Elkton, MD
Cowley, Charles F., III ....Los Angeles, CA
Cowley, Charles H. ....Salt Lake City, UT
Cowley & Chidester, LLP
Rancho Santa Fe, CA
San Diego, CA
Cowley, Clark R. ....Fort Worth, TX
Cowley, Constance ....Plummer, ID
Cowley, Deborah A. ....Long Beach, CA
Cowley, Elmer ....Berkeley, CA
Cowley, James M. ....Rancho Santa Fe, CA
Cowley, John H., Jr. ....Southfield, MI
Cowley, Kevin S. ....Austin, TX
Cowley, Marcie K. ....Lansing, MI
Cowley, Michael C. ....Scranton, PA
Cowley, Raymond A. ....McAllen, TX
Cowley, Samuel C. ....Phoenix, AZ
Cowley, Stacey D. ....Tallahassee, FL
Cowley, Steven M. ....Boston, MA
Cowlin & Cowlin ....McHenry, IL
Cowlin, Curran & Coppedge, A Professional Corporation ....Crystal Lake, IL
Cowlin, Henry L. ....Woodstock, IL
Cowlin, James S. ....McHenry, IL
Cowlin, John L. ....Crystal Lake, IL
Cowlin, Thomas L. ....McHenry, IL
Cowlin, William J. ....Crystal Lake, IL
Cowlin, William J., Jr. ....Crystal Lake, IL
Cowlin, William J., Ltd. ....Crystal Lake, IL
Cowling, David E. ....Dallas, TX
Cowling, Dennis O'Neil ....New York, NY
Cowling, John F. ....St. Louis, MO
Cowling, John W. ....Mobile, AL
Cowling, Ken D., Jr. ....Lubbock, TX
Cowling, Robert L. ....Medford, OR
Cowling, Roger H. ....Redding, CA
Cowlishaw, Patrick R. ....Dallas, TX
Cowman, Jeffrey J. ....Denver, CO
Cowman, Jordan W. ....Dallas, TX
Cowne, John B., Jr. ....Falls Church, VA
Cownie, George L. ....Buffalo, NY
Cownie, William G. ....Lee's Summit, MO
Cowper, Albert W. ....Kinston, NC
Cowper, Gail Millar ....United States Senate, Committee Legal Personnel, GV
Cowper, Peter M. ....Dinuba, CA
Visalia, CA
Cowperthwait, Lindley M., Jr.
Norristown, PA
Cowperthwaite, John G. ....Oakland, CA
Cowsar, Christina Carolyn ......Birmingham, AL
Cowser, Danny L. ....Flagstaff, AZ
Cowser, D.L., M.S., J.D. Chartered
Flagstaff, AZ
Cowsert, Gregory Lejeune ....Miami, FL
Cowsert, William S. ....Athens, GA
Cowsert, William S., P.C. ....Athens, GA
Cox, A. Clay ....Bloomington, IL
Cox, A. Courtney ....Benton, IL
Cox, Adrian D., Jr. ....De Quincy, LA
Cox, Adrienne D. ....Jackson, MS
Cox, Aileen F. ....Ashland, MA
Cox, Alene ....Fayetteville, AR
Cox, Alfred Johnston ....Columbia, SC
Cox, Allan Meyers ....Pittsburgh, PA
Cox, Allen Howard ....San Francisco, CA
Cox, Alton B. ....Oklahoma City, OK
Cox, Amy L. ....Morganton, NC
Cox, Amy M. ....Oklahoma City, OK
Cox, Ancil L., Jr. ....Cleveland, MS
Cox, Andrea Marie ....Hollywood, FL
Cox, Andrew B. ....Louisville, KY
Cox, Andrew H. ....Boston, MA
Cox, Andrew M. ....Las Vegas, NV
Cox, Angela B. ....Houston, TX
Cox, Angela M. ....Newton, MA
Cox, Ann M. ....Olympia, WA
Cox, Anne ....New York, NY
Cox, Anne Randolph ....Englewood, CO
Cox, Anthony A. ....Hudson, OH
Cox, Archibald ....Cambridge, MA
Cox, Arthur ....New York, NY
New York, NY
Cox, Arthur R. ....Rochester, MI
Cox & Associates ....Wilmington, NC
Cox & Associates, P.C. ....Myrtle Beach, SC
Cox, B. Blake ....Fort Worth, TX
Cox, B. Kenneth, Jr. ....Tulsa, OK
Cox, Barbara F. ....Indianapolis, IN
Cox, Barbara L. ....New Haven, CT
Cox, Barry H. ....Guilford, CT
Cox, Barry J. ....St. Helena, CA
Cox, Bart A. ....Atlanta, GA
Cox, Barton J. ....Fremont, CA
Cox, Benjamin A. ....Dunwoody, GA
Cox, Benjamin G., Jr. ....Terre Haute, IN
Cox, Benjamin J. ....Leesburg, FL
Cox, Bennett L. ....Knoxville, TN
Cox, Berkeley C. ....Charlotte, NC
Cox, Beth L. ....Oregon, WI
Cox, Bobby Joe ....Dayton, OH
Cox, Bobby L. ....Natchez, MS
Cox, Boyd David ....Fayetteville, AR
Cox, Brenda G. ....Novato, CA
Cox, Brenda Jo ....Austin, TX
Cox, Brian ....Topeka, KS
Cox, Brian C. ....Charlotte, NC
Cox, Brian D. ....Eugene, OR
Cox, Brian D. ....Pittsburgh, PA
Cox, Bruce E. ....Spokane, WA
Cox, Bruce H. ....East Providence, RI
Cox, Bryan A. ....Las Vegas, NV
Cox, Buel L. ....Pensacola, FL
Cox & Burns, P.A. ....Tallahassee, FL
Cox, C. David, Jr. ....Toledo, OH
Cox, C. Lee ....Dallas, TX
Cox, C. Robert ....Reno, NV
Cox, Campbell ....Houston, TX
Nacogdoches, TX
Cox, Carla J. ....Austin, TX
Cox, Carol L. ....Miami, FL
Cox, Carol L. ....Atlantic City, NJ
Cox, Carolyn ....Washington, DC
Cox, Carolyn ....Salt Lake City, UT
Cox, Carrie ....Milwaukee, WI
Cox, Carrollyn C. ....Virginia Beach, VA
Cox, Castle & Nicholson LLP ....Irvine, CA
Los Angeles, CA
San Francisco, CA
Cox and Causey ....Shallotte, NC
Cox, Chad A. ....Dallas, TX
Cox & Chadwick ....St. Petersburg, FL
Cox, Chadwyn D. ....Dubuque, IA
Cox, Charles A. ....Minneapolis, MN
Cox, Charles A., III ....Minneapolis, MN
Cox, Charles E., Jr. ....Macon, GA
Cox, Charles L. A. ....Kellogg, ID
Cox, Charles M. ....Houston, TX
Cox, Charles M. ....Falls Church, VA
Cox, Charles Shepherd, Jr. ....Alexandria, VA
Cox, Charles W. ....Newport, ME
Cox, Charles W., II ....Los Angeles, CA
Cox, Cherry ....Indianapolis, IN
Cox, Cheryl M. ....New York, NY
Cox, Chip ....Mountain View, CA
Cox, Christa E. ....Columbia, SC
Cox, Christine C. ....West Covina, CA
Cox, Christopher D. ....New York, NY
Cox, Christopher H. ....Oklahoma City, OK
Cox, Christopher J. ....Menlo Park, CA
Cox, Christopher P. ....Clayton, MO
Cox, Christopher T. ....New York, NY
Cox, Christopher T. ....El Paso, TX
Cox, Clare Feler ....Louisville, KY
Cox, Clay ....Fort Myers, FL
Cox, Colleen M. ....Los Angeles, CA
Cox, Condé Thompson ....Austin, TX
Cox, Conrad L. ....Ukiah, CA
Cox, Constance E. ....Birmingham, AL
Cox & Cox ....Ashland, MA
Cox & Cox ....Dallas, TX
Cox and Cox ....Norfolk, VA
Virginia Beach, VA
Cox, Cox & Cox, Inc. ....Virginia Beach, VA
Cox, Cox & Filo ....Lake Charles, LA
Cox and Cox, L.L.P. ....Raleigh, NC
Cox, Cox & Stokes, P.C. ....Wellsboro, PA
Cox, Craig ....Campbellsville, KY
Cox, Craig D. ....Halstead, KS
Cox, Curtis N. ....San Antonio, TX
Cox, Cynthia L. ....Oakland, CA
Cox, Cynthia L. ....Vero Beach, FL
Cox, D. Sherman ....St. Louis, MO
Cox, Dale ....Glendive, MT
Cox, Dale G., Jr. ....Shreveport, LA

Cox, Dale O. ... **Orofino, ID**
Cox, Dallas W., Jr. ... St. Louis, MO
Cox, Dallas W., Jr., P.C. ... St. Louis, MO
Cox, Dana L. ... **Albuquerque, NM**
Cox, Daniel C. ... **St. Louis, MO**
Cox, Daniel H. ... **Naples, FL**
Cox, Daniel R., Jr. ... Marlborough, MA
Cox, Darrell F. ... Santa Rosa, CA
Cox, David B. ... **Atlanta, GA**
Cox, David G. ... Columbus, OH
Cox, David H. ... **Washington, DC**
Baltimore, MD
Rockville, MD
Vienna, VA
Cox, David M. ... **Atlanta, GA**
Cox, David M. ... Charlotte, NC
Cox, David M. ... **Houston, TX**
Cox, David N. ... Bloomington, MN
Cox, David R. ... Needham, MA
Cox, David S. ... **Los Angeles, CA**
Cox, David S. ... **Charleston, SC**
Cox, David T. ... **Phoenix, AZ**
Cox, David W. ... Xenia, OH
Cox, Deborah ... **Dallas, TX**
Cox, Deborah S. ... Boulder, CO
Cox, Debra D. ... Missoula, MT
Cox, Deirdre J. ... **San Francisco, CA**
Cox, Delbert M. ... Refugio, TX
Cox, Dempsey A., Jr. ... South Bend, IN
Cox, Derrick E. ... **Orlando, FL**
Cox, Desiree O. ... Santa Rosa, CA
Cox, DeWitt C. ... Sarasota, FL
Cox, Diana M. ... Rochester, NY
Cox, Donald A. ... Columbus, OH
Cox, Donald A., Jr. ... Mandeville, LA
Cox, Donald F., Jr. ... Department of Defense, Defense Legal Services Agency, GV
Cox, Donald F., Jr. ... Ledgewood, NJ
Cox, Donald J., Jr. ... **Hackensack, NJ**
Cox, Donald L. ... **Louisville, KY**
Cox, Donald L., Law Office of ... Antioch, CA
Cox, Don-Paul J. ... St. Petersburg, FL
Cox, Dorothy G. ... New Castle, KY
Cox, Douglas A. ... Logansport, IN
Cox, Douglas B.
Department of the Air Force, Office of the Judge Advocate General, GV
Cox, Douglas J. ... Denver, CO
Cox, Douglas M. ... **Chattanooga, TN**
Cox, Douglas R. ... **Washington, DC**
Cox, Duane E. ... Cleveland, OH
Cox, Dyson W. ... Upland, CA
Cox, E. Christopher ... **Raleigh, NC**
Cox, E. Thomas ... **Yorktown, VA**
Cox, Earl ... Palmetto, FL
Cox, Edw. J., Sr. ... Columbus, OH
Cox, Edward A. ... Youngstown, OH
Cox, Edward A., Jr. ... **Knoxville, TN**
Cox, Edward F. ... **New York, NY**
Cox, Edward J., Jr. ... Columbus, OH
Cox, Edward Leslie ... **Virginia Beach, VA**
Cox, Edward T., Jr. ... Winter Springs, FL
Cox, Edwin Carr ... **Richmond, VA**
Cox, Elizabeth Anne ... Atlanta, GA
Cox, Elizabeth Sherman ... Baton Rouge, LA
Cox, Ellen Gillerman ... **Albany, NY**
Cox, Elton E. ... Canyon, TX
Cox, Emmett Ripley ... Mobile, AL
Cox, Eric J. ... Plymouth Meeting, PA
Cox, Erin Nealy ... Dallas, TX
Cox, Ernest A., III ... **West Palm Beach, FL**
Cox, Evan R. ... **San Francisco, CA**
Cox, F. Kim ... Portland, OR
Cox & Ferguson ... **Laurens, SC**
Cox & Fields ... Memphis, TN
Cox, Frank G. ... Houston, TX
Cox, Frank J. ... San Rafael, CA
Cox, Frank R. ... Marietta, GA
Cox, Fred D., Jr. ... **Greenville, SC**
Cox, Frederic L. ... Ossipee, NH
Cox, Frederick E., Jr. ... Atlanta, GA
Cox, Gage and Sasser ... **Charlotte, NC**
Morganton, NC
Cox, Garen L. ... Coffeyville, KS
Cox, Garrison R. ... Louisville, KY
Cox, Garry M. ... West Des Moines, IA
Cox, Garth G. ... **Columbus, OH**
Cox, Gary ... Tulsa, OK
Cox, George B. ... Lexington, KY
Cox, George E., III ... Washington, DC
Cox, George M. ... **Los Angeles, CA**
Cox, George W. ... City of Industry, CA
Cox, George W., III ... Jefferson City, MO
Cox, George W., Jr. ... **Myrtle Beach, SC**
Cox, Gilbert C., Jr. ... **Detroit, MI**
Troy, MI
Cox, Gilbert W., Jr. ... Needham, MA
Cox, Ginamarie Bozkurt ... Birmingham, AL
Cox, Ginger & Leland ... Dayton, OH
Cox, Glenn L. ... Columbia, TN
Cox, Gordon E. ... **Chillicothe, MO**
Cox, Goudy, McNulty & Wallace, P.L.L.P.
Minneapolis, MN
St. Paul, MN
Cox, Gregory ... Stafford, TX
Cox, Gregory E. ... **Rockford, IL**
Cox, Gregory F. ... **Beaumont, TX**
Cox, Grover C., Jr. ... Owensboro, KY
Cox, Grover S. ... Louisville, KY
Cox, H. Clay, Jr. ... Hiwasse, AR
Cox, H. Morris, Jr. ... **Clemson, SC**
Cox, Harvey B., Jr. ... Glendale, AZ
Cox, Harvey L. ... Mexia, TX
Cox, Heather M. ... **Palo Alto, CA**
Cox, Heidi Bruegel ... Fort Worth, TX
Cox, Helen H. ... Department of Labor, Office of the Solicitor, GV
Cox, Henry Bartholomew
Fort Washington, MD
Cox, Henry R. ... **Overland Park, KS**
Kansas City, MO
Cox, Herman E. ... **Greenville, SC**
Spartanburg, SC
Cox, Herman F. ... Gulfport, MS
Cox, Hodgman & Giarmarco, P.C.
Detroit, MI
Troy, MI
Cox, Hugh D. ... Greenville, NC
Cox, J. Alan ... Tallahassee, FL
Cox, J. Alece ... Tacoma, WA
Cox, J. Clifton, (P.A.) ... Fort Lauderdale, FL
Cox, J. Craig ... New Castle, PA
Cox, J. Randall ... **Springfield, IL**
Cox, J. Stephen ... **Cincinnati, OH**
Cox, J. Thomas, Jr. ... **Wilmington, NC**
Cox, Jack S. ... Palm Beach Gardens, FL
Cox, Jack S., P.A. ... Palm Beach Gardens, FL
Cox, Jackson E., II ... **McDonough, GA**
Cox, Jacqueline P. ... Markham, IL
Cox, James ... **New Orleans, LA**
Cox, James A. ... Hemet, CA
Cox, James A. ... Lake Oswego, OR
Cox, James A. ... **Dallas, TX**
Cox, James B. ... **Boston, MA**
Cox, James C. ... **Oklahoma City, OK**
Cox, James C., Jr. ... Florence, SC
Hartsville, SC
Cox, James D. ... Durham, NC
Cox, James D., Jr. ... Phoenix, AZ
Cox, James E. ... Auburn, AL
Cox, James E. ... **Encino, CA**
Cox, James E. ... Pittsburg, CA
Cox, James F. ... Scotts Valley, CA
Cox, James F. ... Bangor, ME
Cox, James F. ... Dexter, ME
Cox, James F. ... Xenia, OH
Cox, James H. ... **Atlanta, GA**
Cox, James J. ... **Lake Charles, LA**
Cox, James L., Jr. ... **Aurora, CO**
Lincoln, NE
Cox, James M. ... **Long Beach, CA**
Cox, James M. ... **St. Louis, MO**
Cox, James M., Jr. ... Williamston, SC
Cox, James O. ... **Fort Smith, AR**
Cox, James P., III ... **Charlottesville, VA**
Cox, James R. ... Chicago, IL
Cox, James R. ... Louisville, KY
Cox, James R. ... **Springfield, MO**
Cox, James R. ... **Enid, OK**
Cox, James R., P.C. ... **Enid, OK**
Cox, James S. ... **Saratoga Springs, NY**
Cox, James S., & Associates ... Memphis, TN
Cox, James T. ... Jackson, MS
Cox, James T. ... Houston, TX
Cox, James T., P.C. ... Houston, TX
Cox, James W. ... Springfield, IL
Cox, James W. ... **Houston, TX**
Cox, James W., P.C., Law Offices of
Houston, TX
Cox, Janice L. ... Woodridge, IL
Cox, Janine ... Lawrence, KS
Cox, Jannet D. ... Jackson, MS
Cox, Jean M. ... Albany, NY
Cox, Jeffrey ... Port Orchard, WA
Cox, Jeffrey J. ... **Dallas, TX**
Cox, Jeffrey M. ... Chicago, IL
Cox, Jeffrey M. ... **Ann Arbor, MI**
Cox, Jeffrey M. ... Holdrege, NE
Cox, Jeffrey R. ... **Waco, TX**
Cox, Jeffrey S. ... **Shreveport, LA**
Cox, Jeffrey T. ... **Dayton, OH**
Cox, Jeffry M. ... Tupelo, MS
Cox, Jenelle C. L. ... **Palo Alto, CA**
Cox, Jennifer Dehner ... Dayton, OH
Cox, Jennifer J. ... Denver, CO
Cox, Jennifer L. ... **New Haven, CT**
Cox, Jeralynn (Jackee) ... Austin, TX
Cox, Jerry C. ... Memphis, TN
Cox, Jerry J. ... **Mount Vernon, KY**
Cox, Jerry W. ... **Washington, DC**
Cox, Jesse E. ... Lutherville, MD
Cox, Jesse E., P.A. ... Lutherville, MD
Cox, Jill S. ... **Winston-Salem, NC**
Cox, Jim W. ... Dublin, CA
Cox, Joachim P. ... Boulder, CO
Cox, Joe B. ... **Naples, FL**
Cox, Joe E. ... **Madison, IN**
Cox, Joe M. ... Mullins, SC
Cox, Joe Michael ... Juneau, AK
Cox, John C. ... **Dallas, TX**
Cox, John Coates ... Evansville, IN
Cox, John E. ... **Baton Rouge, LA**
Cox, John G. ... **Eugene, OR**
Cox, John H., III ... Greenville, MS
Cox, John H., (LTD.) ... Northbrook, IL
Cox, John L., Jr. ... Stanton, KY
Cox, John M. ... Mission, KS
Cox, John M. ... Columbia, SC
Cox, John M. ... **Dallas, TX**
Cox, John M., & Associates, P.C.
Dallas, TX
Cox, John M., Jr. (Co., L.P.A.)
Columbus, OH
Cox, John N. ... **Pittsburgh, PA**
Cox, John Philip ... Towson, MD
Cox, John R. ... Louisville, KY
Cox, John R. ... Morehead, KY
Cox, John R. ... Lansdale, PA
Cox, John Roger ... **The Woodlands, TX**
Cox, John S. ... Jacksonville, FL
Cox, John T., III ... **Dallas, TX**
Cox, John T., Jr. ... **Shreveport, LA**
Cox, John W. ... **New Orleans, LA**
Cox, John W., Jr. ... Galena, IL
Cox, Jon R. ... **Boise, ID**
Cox, Jonathan C. S. ... **Palo Alto, CA**
Cox, Jonathan R. ... Costa Mesa, CA
Cox, Joseph B., Jr. ... Raleigh, NC
Cox, Joseph C. ... Fowlerville, MI
Cox, Joseph K. ... Webberville, MI
Cox, Joseph L. ... Topeka, KS
Cox, Joseph M. ... Buffalo, NY
Cox, Joseph M. ... **Dallas, TX**
Cox, Joseph P. ... **Los Angeles, CA**
San Diego, CA
Washington, DC
Cox, Judith S. ... New York, NY
Cox, Julia Diamond ... **Chicago, IL**
Cox, Julie B. ... **Springfield, IL**
Cox, Juliet Ann ... **Kansas City, MO**
Cox, Justin Lamar ... **Jackson, MS**
Cox, Kaila A. ... Covington, KY
Cox, Karen A. ... **Dallas, TX**
Cox, Karen D. ... **Los Angeles, CA**
Cox, Kathleen Gallogly ... Towson, MD
Cox, Kathryn D. ... Oakland, CA
Cox, Kathy L. ... **Fort Worth, TX**
Cox & Keller ... Xenia, OH
Cox, Kenneth A. ... San Francisco, CA
Cox, Kenneth W., Jr. ... Troy, AL
Cox, Kent Eugene
Federal Trade Commission, Bureau of Competition, GV
Cox, Kerri L. ... Phoenix, AZ
Cox, Kevin C. ... **Memphis, TN**
Cox, Kevin C. ... St. Clair Shores, MI
Cox, Kevin D. ... **Buffalo, NY**
Cox, Kevin E. ... Dallas, TX
Cox, Kevin J. ... Southfield, MI
Cox, Kim A. ... Corpus Christi, TX
Cox, Kim C. ... San Diego, CA
Cox, Kimela Wright ... Memphis, TN
Cox, L. Catharine ... Atlanta, GA
Cox, L. DeLane
Securities and Exchange Commission, Division of Enforcement, GV
Cox, Lamb & Seeley ... Spartanburg, SC
Cox, Lance S. ... **Cincinnati, OH**
Cox, Lance S., Co., L.P.A. ... **Cincinnati, OH**
Cox, Larry J. ... Sacramento, CA
Cox, Larry R. ... **Bakersfield, CA**
Cox, Laura McAllister ... **Atlantic City, NJ**
Cox, Laura Picchietti ... Lake Forest, IL
Cox Law Firm, The, P.C. ... **St. Louis, MO**
Cox, Lawrence A. ... **Los Angeles, CA**
Cox, Lawrence A. ... Bloomfield, CT
Cox, Lawrence E. ... Portland, OR
Cox, Lawrence J. ... Torrance, CA
Cox, Lawson A., II ... Lithonia, GA
Cox, LeeAnne M. ... **Memphis, TN**
Cox, Leland E. ... Topeka, KS
Cox, Leo P. ... Red Bank, NJ
Cox, Lester B. ... Springfield, MO
Cox, LeVan, Sprader & Patton, P.L.L.C.
Nashville, TN
Cox, Lewis C., III ... **Lovington, NM**
Cox, Lila L. ... South Pasadena, CA
Cox, Linda C. ... **Tallahassee, FL**
Cox, Linda D. ... Seminole, FL
Cox, Lisa Renee ... Nashville, TN
Cox, L. J., Jr. ... Phoenix, AZ
Cox, Lois K. ... Iowa City, IA
Cox, Lucian B., III ... Virginia Beach, VA
Cox, Lynn M. ... Sacramento, CA
Cox, M. David ... **Nashville, TN**
Cox, Madeline E. ... **Newark, NJ**
Cox, Marcy Halterman ... **Houston, TX**
Cox, Margaret P.
Architect of the Capitol, GV
Cox, Marianne E. ... Philadelphia, PA
Cox, Marie K. ... Los Angeles, CA
Cox, Marjorie E. ... Oakland, CA
Cox, Mark A. ... **Oklahoma City, OK**
Cox, Marsha A. ... Danville, KY
Cox, Martha ... Oklahoma City, OK
Cox, Mary A. ... Honolulu, HI
Cox, Mary Carolyn ... **Washington, DC**
Cox, Mary E. ... Oklahoma City, OK
Cox, Mary Jane Truesdell ... **Littleton, CO**
Cox, Mary L. ... Minneapolis, MN
Cox, Mary T. ... **Chicago, IL**
Cox, Maryalyce W. ... **Beaumont, TX**
Cox, Matthew B. ... **Dover, NH**
Cox, Matthew J. ... Eugene, OR
Cox, Maureen Danehy ... **Waterbury, CT**
Cox, Maurice R. ... Montgomery, AL
Cox, Melvin M. ... Fort Lee, NJ
Cox, Michael A. ... Portland, OR
Cox, Michael C. ... **Omaha, NE**
Cox, Michael D. ... **Washington, DC**
Cox, Michael E. ... Key Largo, FL
Cox, Michael E. ... **Biloxi, MS**
Cox, Michael J. ... Evansville, IN
Cox, Michael J. ... **Lexington, KY**
Cox, Michael J. ... Columbia, SC
Cox, Michael K. ... **Lake Charles, LA**
Cox, Michael P. ... Lansing, MI
Cox, Michael T. ... Shallotte, NC
Cox, Michelle Agostino ... Evansville, IN
Cox, Millard, III ... Absarokee, MT
Cox, Milton R. ... Kelso, WA
Cox, Mitchell H. ... **Minneapolis, MN**
Cox, Mitchell M. ... New York, NY
Cox & Moore ... **Cleveland, MS**
Cox & Moyer, A Professional Corporation
San Francisco, CA
Cox, Mustain-Wood, Walker & Schumacher, LLC ... **Denver, CO**
Littleton, CO
Cox, Nicholas B. ... Tampa, FL
Cox, Niki D. ... Palo Alto, CA
Cox, Nona F. ... Bethesda, MD
Cox, Norman G. ... Wickes, AR
Cox, Ohman & Brandstetter, Chartered
Idaho Falls, ID
Cox, Oliver Seto ... Sacramento, CA
Cox Padmore Skolnik & Shakarchy
Palo Alto, CA
Cox Padmore Skolnik & Shakarchy
Denver, CO
Cox Padmore Skolnik & Shakarchy
New York, NY
Cox, Patricia ... Dayton, MD
Cox, Patrick E. ... **New York, NY**
Cox, Patrick F. ... Atlantic City, NJ
Cox, Patrick M. ... **New York, NY**
Cox, Paul J. ... **Lexington, KY**
Louisville, KY
Cox, Paul J. ... **Lake Charles, LA**
Cox, Paul L. ... Columbus, OH
Cox, Paul N. ... Indianapolis, IN
Cox, Paul Richard ... **Dover, NH**
Cox & Peterson ... Lake Oswego, OR
Cox, Phillips, Weber, Tedford & Heap, P.C.
Newton, IL
Oblong, IL
Robinson, IL
Cox, Phriness E. ... Irmo, SC
Cox, Phyllis ... Denver, CO
Cox, Phyllis, P.C., Law Offices of
Denver, CO
Cox, Ralph Frederick, Jr.
Hermosa Beach, CA
Cox, Ralph J. ... Severna Park, MD
Cox, Ralph W., II ... Rochester, NY
Cox, Randall Lee ... Oklahoma City, OK
Cox, Randall T. ... **Fort Worth, TX**
Cox, Randall T. ... **Gillette, WY**
Cox, Randall T., P.C. ... **Gillette, WY**
Cox, Randy J. ... **Missoula, MT**
Cox, Ray A. ... Dayton, OH
Cox, Ray F., Jr. ... **Little Rock, AR**
Cox, Ray L., Jr. ... **Houston, TX**
Cox, Ray N. ... Fresno, CA
Cox, Ray P. ... **Seattle, WA**
Cox, Raymon H. ... **Rome, GA**
Cox, Rebecca A. ... Miami, FL
Cox, Reed E. ... Marietta, GA
Cox & Reynolds ... Fort Lauderdale, FL
Cox, Richard A. ... Los Angeles, CA
Cox, Richard D. ... **Dallas, TX**
Cox, Richard H. ... Treasury Department, Internal Revenue Service, GV
Cox, Richard L.
Hot Springs National Park, AR
Cox, Richard L. ... **Asheboro, NC**
Cox, Richard L., Jr. ... Tampa, FL
Cox, Richard L., P.A.
Hot Springs National Park, AR
Cox, Richard P. ... Littleton, CO
Cox, Richard P. ... **Fairfax, VA**
Cox, Ricky J. ... **Gulfport, MS**
Cox, Rita Holbert ... Salemburg, NC
Cox, Robert A. ... Wheaton, IL
Cox, Robert A. ... **St. Louis, MO**
Cox, Robert A. ... **Memphis, TN**
Cox, Robert A., Jr. ... **Richmond, VA**
Cox, Robert Aubrey, Jr. ... **Charlotte, NC**
Cox, Robert B. ... **Hartford, CT**
Cox, Robert B. ... **Syracuse, NY**
Cox, Robert C. ... Dallas, TX
Cox, Robert D. ... **Temple, TX**
Cox, Robert D., Jr. ... **Worcester, MA**
Cox, Robert E. ... **Palo Alto, CA**
San Francisco, CA
Cox, Robert E. ... Newport, ME
Cox, Robert F. ... **Cranford, NJ**
Cox, Robert F., Jr. ... **Wellsboro, PA**
Cox, Robert H. ... **Washington, DC**
Cox, Robert J. ... **Birmingham, AL**
Mobile, AL
Cox, Robert J. ... **Cherry Hill, NJ**
Cox, Robert K. ... **Washington, DC**
McLean, VA
Cox, Robert L. ... **Clinton, MO**
Cox, Robert L. ... Oklahoma City, OK
Cox, Robert L. ... **Memphis, TN**
Cox, Robert L., III ... New York, NY
Cox, Robert L., Jr. ... Richmond, VA
Cox, Robert O. ... **Florence, AL**
Cox, Robert Scott ... Tallahassee, FL
Cox, Robert T. ... Columbia, MO
Cox, Robert W. ... Chicago, IL
Cox, Robert W. ... Tulsa, OK
Cox & Robinson ... Corpus Christi, TX
Cox, Rob't. D. ... Memphis, TN
Cox, Robt. J. ... Arcanum, OH
Cox, Rodger G. ... Campbellsville, KY
Cox & Rodnick ... **Austin, TX**
Cox, Roger A. ... **Ashland, MA**
Cox, Roger D. ... **Idaho Falls, ID**
Cox, Roger F. ... **Philadelphia, PA**
Cox, Roger P. ... **Lincoln, NE**
Cox, Roger S. ... **Amarillo, TX**
Cox, Ronald B. ... **Columbia, SC**
Cox, Ronald Carmen ... **Harlan, KY**
Cox, Ronald D. ... Lafayette, LA
Cox, Ronald H. ... Monroe, NC
Cox, Ronald W., Jr. ... Bethesda, MD
Cox, S. Barton ... **Honolulu, HI**
Cox, S. David ... Gainesville, FL
Cox, S. David, Chartered ... Gainesville, FL
Cox, S. Lance ... **Fayetteville, AR**
Cox, Samm T. ... Butte, MT
Cox, Samuel M. ... Tulsa, OK
Cox, Sandra H. ... Pasadena, CA
Cox, Sanford C., Jr. ... **El Paso, TX**
Cox, Sanford C., Jr., P.C. ... **El Paso, TX**
Cox, Sanford Curtis, III ... Tacoma, WA
Cox, Sarah A. ... Rochester, MI
Cox, Sarah D. Keller ... **Los Angeles, CA**

Cox, Scott A. .... Glendale, CA
Cox, Scott C. .... Louisville, KY
Cox, Scott L. .... Menomonie, WI
Cox, Scott R. .... Louisville, KY
Cox, Sean F. .... Detroit, MI
Cox, Sean P. .... Rochester, MI
Cox, Shannon F. .... Atlanta, GA
Cox, Shawn D. .... Hammond, IN
Cox, Shawn M. .... McLean, VA
Cox, Shelia June .... Charlotte, NC
Cox, Shirley A. .... Oklahoma City, OK
Cox, Sidney C. .... Covington, LA
Cox, Sinclair & Sheridans .... Rusk, TX
Cox & Smith Incorporated
San Antonio, TX
Cox, Stanley Brian .... Sedalia, MO
Cox and Stein, Co., L.P.A. .... Columbus, OH
Cox, Stephanie L. .... Burlington, IA
Cox, Stephen B. .... Frankfort, KY
Cox, Stephen E. .... Nashville, TN
Cox, Stephen G. .... Boston, MA
Cox, Stephen J. .... Knoxville, TN
Cox, Stephen L. .... Gilbert, AZ
Cox, Stephen M. .... Rock Hill, SC
Cox, Stephen T. .... San Francisco, CA
Cox, Steve R. .... Lewiston, ID
Cox, Steven A. .... Freeport, IL
Lena, IL
Cox, Steven A. .... Chesterfield, MO
Cox, Steven Carlos .... Minneapolis, MN
Cox, Steven J. .... El Segundo, CA
Cox, Steven M. .... Tucson, AZ
Cox, Steven M. .... Dayton, OH
Cox, Steven St. Leger .... Akron, OH
Cox, Stewart M. .... Birmingham, AL
Cox, Stuart T., Jr. .... Woodbridge, NJ
Cox, Stuart W. .... Baltimore, MD
Cox, Susan C. .... Dallas, TX
Cox, Susan D. .... Juneau, AK
Cox, Susan E. .... Chicago, IL
Cox, Susan G. .... Murfreesboro, TN
Cox, Susan W. .... Statesboro, GA
Cox, Susan Zimmer .... Amarillo, TX
Cox, Sylvester B., Jr. .... Baltimore, MD
Cox, T. Louis .... Spartanburg, SC
Cox, T. Randolph, Jr. .... Charleston, WV
Cox, Ted A., (P.C.) .... Houston, TX
Cox, Terence S. .... San Francisco, CA
Cox, Teresa Harkleroad .... Chevy Chase, MD
Cox, Terrill F. .... Lompoc, CA
Cox, Terry C. .... Collierville, TN
Cox, Terry L. .... Marshall, TX
Cox, Thaddeus R. .... New Castle, VA
Salem, VA
Cox, Theodore M. .... Sherman Oaks, CA
Cox, Theodore N., Law Office of
New York, NY
Cox, Thomas A. .... Atlanta, GA
Cox, Thomas A. .... Portland, ME
Cox, Thomas A. .... Ravenna, OH
Cox, Thomas F. .... St. Petersburg, FL
Cox, Thomas J. .... Kansas City, MO
Cox, Thomas J., Jr. .... Pittsburgh, PA
Cox, Thomas L., Jr. .... Dallas, TX
Cox, Thomas M. .... Hemet, CA
Cox, Thomas R. .... Hartford, CT
Cox, Thomas R. .... Detroit, MI
Cox, Thomas R., III .... Dallas, TX
Cox, Timothy W. .... Palm Beach, FL
Cox, Tracy B. .... Overland Park, KS
Cox, Trevor A. .... San Francisco, CA
Cox, Vicki Allane .... Tulsa, OK
Cox, Victor M. .... Kailua-Kona, HI
Cox, Vincent .... Los Angeles, CA
Cox, Virgil Q. .... Greer, SC
Cox, W. Donald .... Tampa, FL
Cox, W. Eugene .... Overland Park, KS
Cox, W. Jamison .... Charleston, SC
Cox, W. Reid, Jr. .... Laurens, SC
Cox, W. Robbins .... Raleigh, NC
Cox, Walter B. .... Fayetteville, AR
Cox, Walter C., Jr. .... Lexington, KY
Cox, Walter E. .... Bedford, VA
Cox, Walter Stephens .... Clarksdale, MS
Cox, Walter T., III
United States Court Of Appeals For the Armed Forces, GV
Cox, Wanda L. .... Inglewood, CA
Cox, Warren E. .... Jackson, MS
Cox, Wendell Scott .... Austin, TX
Cox, Wendy J. .... Minnetonka, MN
Cox, Wendy L. .... Washington, DC
Cox, William .... Long Beach, CA
Cox, William A., III .... Virginia Beach, VA
Cox, William B., Jr. .... Camden, SC
Cox, William C. .... Portland, OR
Cox, William D, Jr. .... Haverhill, MA
Cox, William D., Jr. .... Dallas, TX
Cox, William D., Jr., P.C. .... Dallas, TX
Cox, William E. .... Philadelphia, PA
Cox, William H. .... New York, NY
Cox, William H., Jr. .... Jackson, MS
Cox, William H., Jr. .... Chattanooga, TN
Cox, William J. .... Fredericksburg, VA
Cox, William K. .... Jeannette, PA
Cox, William M. .... East Alton, IL
Cox, William M. .... Newton, NJ
Cox, William M., Jr., Law Offices of
Williamsburg, KY
Cox, William N. .... Littleton, CO
Cox, William N. .... Lake Charles, LA
Cox, William O. .... Savannah, GA
Cox, William Painter .... Tallahassee, FL
Cox, William S. .... Houston, TX
Cox, William S., III .... Birmingham, AL
Cox, William T., Jr. .... Powder Springs, GA
Cox, William T., Jr., P.C.
Powder Springs, GA

Cox, William V. .... Denver, CO
Cox, Willoughby T., Jr. .... Orlando, FL
Cox, Wootton, Griffin & Hansen, LLP
San Francisco, CA
Cox, Young & Griffin .... Florence, AL
Cox, Yvette A. .... Columbus, OH
Cox, Z. Simpson .... Phoenix, AZ
Cox, Zwerner, Gambill & Sullivan
Terre Haute, IN
Cox-Brakefield, Cathy A. .... Atlanta, GA
Coxe, Bradley A. .... Wrightsville Beach, NC
Coxe & Coxe .... Baton Rouge, LA
Coxe, Henry M., III .... Jacksonville, FL
Coxe, Hugh M. .... Falmouth, ME
Coxe, James R., III .... Baton Rouge, LA
Coxe, Jas. R., Jr. .... Baton Rouge, LA
Coxe, Kent A. .... Kansas City, MO
Coxe, L. Robert, III .... Jacksonville, NC
Coxe, Mary C. .... Jacksonville, FL
Coxe, Tench C. .... Atlanta, GA
Coxe, Theodore S. .... Haverford, PA
Coxe, Theodore S., Jr. .... Haverford, PA
Coxe, William N., Jr. .... Baton Rouge, LA
Coxe, Wm. F. P., Jr. .... Asheville, NC
Coxhead, Amy Freivogel .... Key Largo, FL
Coxhead, Stephen F. .... Miami, FL
Coxhead, Wendy .... Tampa, FL
Cox-Korn, Carole .... Atlanta, GA
Coxon, Christopher .... Hartford, CT
Coxon, Franklin D. .... Florence, AZ
Coxon, Gary L. .... Conneaut, OH
Coxon, Jeffrey L. .... Ashtabula, OH
Cox-Ritter, Vicky .... Austin, TX
Coxsey & Coxsey .... Berryville, AR
Coxsey, J. Kent .... Berryville, AR
Coxsey, Ted P. .... Berryville, AR
Coxson, Harold P., Jr. .... Washington, DC
Cox-Warren, Robin L. .... San Antonio, TX
Coxwell and Coxwell .... Monroeville, AL
Coxwell, Franklin H., III .... Jackson, MS
Coxwell, J. Milton, Jr. .... Monroeville, AL
Coxwell, Katharine W. .... Monroeville, AL
Coxwell, Merrida P. .... Jackson, MS
Coy, C. Stephen .... Atlanta, GA
Coy, Cameron D. .... Orange, CA
Coy, Charles R. .... Richmond, KY
Coy, Edwin A. .... Toledo, OH
Coy, Gabriel Kristopher .... Los Angeles, CA
Coy, Gilbert & Gilbert .... Richmond, KY
Coy, Gregory B. .... Indianapolis, IN
Coy, John M. .... Richmond, KY
Coy, Julie .... Ballston Spa, NY
Coy, Kevin L. .... Washington, DC
Coy, Mark Stephen .... Jefferson City, MO
Coy, Mark W. .... Fountaintown, IN
Coy, Mary Frederick McCloy .... Toledo, OH
Coy, Robert W. .... Chicago, IL
Coy, Roderick S. .... Okemos, MI
Coy, Russell R., II .... Frankfort, KY
Coy, Silverio .... Washington, DC
Falls Church, VA
Coy, Thomas J. .... Lynnwood, WA
Coy, Tony D. .... Athens, GA
Coy, W. Gregory .... Vevay, IN
Coy, Wayne, Jr. .... Washington, DC
Coy, Wendy L. .... Phoenix, AZ
Coye & Copeland, P.A. .... Orlando, FL
Coye, Stephen E. .... Washington, DC
Coye, Wade B. .... Orlando, FL
Coyer, Bruce L. .... Scranton, PA
Coyer, Ronald W. .... Slippery Rock, PA
Coykendall, Robert W. .... Wichita, KS
Coyle, Adam P. .... Englewood, CO
Coyle & Alexander .... Pickens, SC
Coyle, Anna Margaret .... Laurel, MD
Coyle, Arlen B. .... Richmond, VA
Coyle, Brian J. .... Newark, NJ
Coyle, Carole J. .... Carol Stream, IL
Coyle, Charlotte M. .... Glenview, IL
Coyle, Christopher J. .... Detroit, MI
Coyle, Christopher J. .... Lebanon, PA
Coyle, Christopher L.
Glenwood Springs, CO
Coyle, Colleen .... Helena, MT
Coyle, Colleen M. .... Washington, DC
Coyle, Daniel J. .... Sacramento, CA
Coyle, David J. .... Toledo, OH
Coyle, David T. .... Coldwater, MI
Coyle, Denise Malley
Branchburg Township, NJ
Coyle, Dennis P. .... Juno Beach, FL
Coyle, Dorothy J. .... New York, NY
Coyle, Dunbar, Geoffrion & Rideout, P.A.
Springfield, MA
Coyle, Edward J. .... Lebanon, PA
Coyle, Francis J., Jr. .... Rock Island, IL
Coyle, Frank .... Newport Beach, CA
Coyle, Frank J. .... Greenwich, CT
Coyle, Frank J., Jr. .... Cedar Knolls, NJ
Coyle, Gilman & Stengel, Including a Prof. Corp. .... Rock Island, IL
Coyle, J. Redmond .... Pickens, SC
Coyle, Jack T. .... Winter Haven, FL
Coyle, James G. .... Alpharetta, GA
Coyle, James J. .... Palos Verdes Estates, CA
Coyle, James P. .... Kalamazoo, MI
Coyle, Jason R. .... Chicago, IL
Coyle, Jerry L. .... Dallas, TX
Coyle, Jill E. .... Minneapolis, MN
Coyle, John Anthony .... San Diego, CA
Coyle, John J., IV .... Wilmington, DE
Wildwood, NJ
Media, PA
Coyle, John J., Jr. .... Cumberland, MD
Coyle, John J., Jr. .... Phillipsburg, NJ
Coyle, John M., Law Offices of
Fairfield, CA
Coyle, John P. .... Washington, DC

Coyle, John R. .... McLean, VA
Coyle, John Stanley .... Fort Lauderdale, FL
Coyle, John T. .... Jersey City, NJ
Coyle, John W., III .... Oklahoma City, OK
Coyle, Katherine Gallagher .... Tulsa, OK
Coyle, Kellie A. .... Decatur, GA
Coyle, Kevin A. .... Sacramento, CA
Coyle, Kevin B. .... Springfield, MA
Coyle, Kevin J. .... Washington, DC
Coyle, Kevin J. .... Burlington, VT
Coyle, Leonard A. .... Osprey, FL
Coyle, Linda S. .... Brookfield, WI
Coyle, Lori A. .... Toledo, OH
Coyle, Lorraine V. K. .... Bronx, NY
Coyle, Lynn .... Chicago, IL
Coyle, M. Duane .... Wichita, KS
Coyle, Marshall A. .... Orange, CA
Coyle, Martin A. .... Cleveland, OH
Coyle & Martyak P.C. .... Belvidere, NJ
Hackettstown, NJ
Phillipsburg, NJ
Coyle, Matthew .... Bethesda, MD
Coyle, Matthew J. .... Olympia, WA
Coyle & McCoy, A Professional Corporation
Oklahoma City, OK
Coyle, Michael F. .... Omaha, NE
Coyle, Michael J. .... Dubuque, IA
Coyle, Michael J. .... New York, NY
Coyle, Michael L. .... Hartford, CT
Coyle, Michael P. .... Washington, DC
Coyle, Michele C. .... Los Angeles, CA
Coyle, N. Paul .... Chicago, IL
Coyle, Patrick M. .... Omaha, NE
Coyle, Patrick W. .... Santa Rosa, CA
Coyle, Peter J. .... Minneapolis, MN
Coyle, Philip W. .... Truckee, CA
Coyle, Richard C. .... Seattle, WA
Coyle, Rita R. .... St. Petersburg, FL
Coyle, Robert .... Fresno, CA
Coyle, Robert E. .... Fresno, CA
Coyle, Robert O. .... New York, NY
Coyle, Steven M. .... Springfield, MA
Coyle, Sylvia Halkousis .... Fresno, CA
Coyle, Thomas J., Jr. .... Elko, NV
Coyle, Timothy A. .... Norfolk, VA
Coyle, Timothy L. .... Fort Mitchell, KY
Cincinnati, OH
Coyle, Timothy O. .... Lakeland, FL
Coyle, Victoria A. .... Bethlehem, PA
Coyle, Vincent J., Jr. .... Mineola, NY
Coyle, Virginia A. .... Temple, TX
Coyle, William C. .... Indianapolis, IN
Coyle, William E. .... Bethel Park, PA
Coyle, William F. .... Flourtown, PA
Coyle, William J. .... Grosse Pointe Farms, MI
Coyle, William K., Jr. .... Chicago, IL
Coyle, William P. .... Huntington, NY
Coyle-Martyak, Maureen A.
Phillipsburg, NJ
Coyles, Donald B. .... Horseheads, NY
Coyne, Anthony J. .... Cleveland, OH
Coyne, Arthur S. .... Colonia, NJ
Coyne, Barry J. .... Pittsburgh, PA
Coyne, Barry L. .... St. Paul, MN
Coyne, Beth M. .... Winchester, VA
Coyne, Brian J. .... Olympia, WA
Coyne, Carol Elizabeth .... Albany, NY
Coyne, Carol J. .... Lowell, MA
Coyne, Charles B. .... Sacramento, CA
Coyne, Charles C. .... Philadelphia, PA
Coyne, Coleman G., Jr. .... Lewiston, ME
Coyne, Curtis J. .... Seattle, WA
Coyne, Daniel W. .... Chicago, IL
Coyne, Dennis M. .... Minneapolis, MN
Coyne, Dennis M. .... Cleveland, OH
Coyne, Donna Lynn .... Media, PA
Coyne, Ellen J. .... Rochester, NY
Coyne, Francis R. .... Drexel Hill, PA
Coyne, Frank J. .... Philadelphia, PA
Coyne, Frank M. .... Madison, WI
Coyne, Gerald J. .... Providence, RI
Coyne, H. Buckmaster, Jr. .... Ada, OK
Coyne, Henry F. .... Camp Hill, PA
Coyne, James E. .... Bridgeport, CT
Coyne, James E. .... Pittsburgh, PA
Coyne, James M. .... Caribou, ME
Coyne, Jeffrey B. .... Newport Beach, CA
Coyne, Jeffrey C. .... Altadena, CA
Coyne, Jennifer A. .... Chicago, IL
Coyne, Jennifer J. .... Towson, MD
Coyne, John E. .... Boston, MA
Coyne, John M., III .... Akron, OH
Coyne, John P. .... Cleveland, OH
Coyne, John T. .... Alexandria, VA
Coyne, John Thomas .... Morristown, NJ
Coyne, Joseph F. .... Chicago, IL
Coyne, Joseph F., Jr. .... Los Angeles, CA
Coyne, Julia A. .... Boston, MA
Coyne, Kathleen A. .... San Diego, CA
Coyne, Kenneth L. .... St. Louis, MO
Coyne, Kenneth P. .... Cincinnati, OH
Coyne, Kevin S. .... Bridgeport, CT
Coyne, Kieran J. .... St. Louis, MO
Coyne, Laura Ann .... Boston, MA
Coyne, Laureen M. .... New York, NY
Coyne, Loretta A. .... Cleveland, OH
Coyne, Lorraine .... Cleveland, OH
Coyne, Lynn H. .... Bloomington, IN
Coyne, M. Jeanne .... St. Paul, MN
Coyne, Madlyn Briody .... Boston, MA
Coyne, Mark E. .... New York, NY
Coyne, Marlene M. .... San Diego, CA
Coyne, Mary J. .... St. Paul, MN
Coyne, Mary L. .... Arlington, VA
Coyne, Michael F. .... New York, NY
Coyne, Michael F. .... Cleveland, OH
Coyne, Michael J. .... Treasury Department, Internal Revenue Service, GV

Coyne, Michael J. .... Springfield, MA
Coyne, Michael P. .... Cleveland, OH
Coyne, Michele A. .... New York, NY
Coyne, Niess, Schultz, Becker & Bauer, S.C.
Madison, WI
Coyne, Patricia A. .... San Diego, CA
Coyne, Patrick J. .... Washington, DC
Coyne, Pier-Alysia M. .... Washington, DC
Coyne, Randall T. E. .... Norman, OK
Coyne, Raymond M. .... Hoffman Estates, IL
Coyne, Richard F. .... Cleveland, OH
Coyne, Richard T. .... Cleveland, OH
Coyne, Robert F. .... Newark, NJ
Coyne, Robert J. .... Silver Spring, MD
Coyne, Robert P. .... Denver, CO
Coyne, Robert P. .... Mechanicsburg, PA
Coyne, Roderick J. .... New York, NY
Coyne, Russell J. .... Mineola, NY
Coyne, Sarah Edelman .... Madison, WI
Coyne, Terence J. .... St. Paul, MN
Coyne, Terrence H. .... Seattle, WA
Coyne, Thomas J. .... Cleveland, OH
Coyne, Timothy R. .... Philadelphia, PA
Coyne, Timothy S. .... Winchester, VA
Coyne, W. Carroll .... Syracuse, NY
Coyne, William F., Jr. .... Boston, MA
Coyne, William J. .... West Sacramento, CA
Coyne, William J. .... Cleveland, OH
Coyne, Wm. F. .... Boston, MA
Coyne, Wm. H. .... Willoughby, OH
Coyne-Hoerle, Helen .... Gig Harbor, WA
Coyner, Craig C. .... Bend, OR
Coyner, Craig C., III .... Bend, OR
Coyner, Douglas C. .... Farmington, NM
Coyner, Kelley S. .... Washington, DC
Coyoca, Lucia E., (A Professional Corporation) .... Los Angeles, CA
Coyr, Bruce L. .... Stroudsburg, PA
Coyte, Joseph R. .... Fort Collins, CO
Coyte, Ralph H. .... Fort Collins, CO
Coz, Steven P. .... Duluth, MN
Coz, Thomas A. .... Cincinnati, OH
Cozad, David C. .... Kansas City, KS
Cozad, Fredric R. .... Martin, SD
Cozad, Gregory D. .... Champaign, IL
Cozad, Jane Maxwell .... New York, NY
Cozad, John C. .... Kansas City, MO
Cozad, Karl V. .... Topeka, KS
Cozad & Krutcik .... Mission Viejo, CA
Cozad, Liza Marie E. .... Los Angeles, CA
Cozad, Peggy Duvieilh .... Miami, FL
Cozad, Richard A. .... New Orleans, LA
Cozad, Ronald J. .... Mission Viejo, CA
Cozad, Stacy Lancaster .... Dallas, TX
Cozakos, Shelly H. .... Boise, ID
Cozamanis, Steve C. .... Wilmington, DE
Cozart, Andrew C .... Fayetteville, AR
Cozart, Bert C. .... Los Angeles, CA
Cozart, Bruce W. .... La Mesa, CA
Cozart, John, Jr. .... Detroit, MI
Cozart, Richard M. .... Stamford, CT
Cozart, Stephen M. .... Gulfport, MS
Gulfport, MS
Cozart, Toby .... Piedmont, CA
Cozart, William T. .... Wilson, NC
Coze, Carissa Carol Wong
San Francisco, CA
Cozean, Ronald J., Jr. .... Cleveland, OH
Cozen and O'Connor, A Professional Corporation .... Los Angeles, CA
San Diego, CA
Wilmington, DE
Atlanta, GA
Newark, NJ
Westmont, NJ
New York, NY
Charlotte, NC
Philadelphia, PA
West Conshohocken, PA
Dallas, TX
Seattle, WA
Cozen, Stephen A. .... Philadelphia, PA
Cozens, Philip .... Sacramento, CA
Coziahr, Scott J. .... Omaha, NE
Cozier, Clifford G. .... Denver, CO
Cozier, J. Russell .... Mount Arlington, NJ
Cozier, Sophie S. .... Boca Raton, FL
Cozine, Madeleine H. .... Trenton, NJ
Cozine, Mark Reed .... Cherokee, IA
Cozine, Michael E. .... Nutley, NJ
Cozine, Michael E., P.A. .... Nutley, NJ
Cozine, Richard K. .... Minneapolis, MN
Cozort, Jack L. .... Raleigh, NC
Cozort, William J., Jr. .... Houston, TX
Cozy, Jack A. .... Palos Verdes Estates, CA
Cozza, Michael E. .... Cleveland, OH
Cozza, Michael J. .... White Plains, NY
Cozza, Sam F. .... Spokane, WA
Cozzarelli, Frank J. .... Belleville, NJ
Cozzarelli, Frank, Jr. .... Verona, NJ
Cozzens, Lawrence B. .... Billings, MT
Cozzens, R. Bruce, Jr. .... Mineola, NY
Cozzens, Tyler R. .... Palo Alto, CA
Cozzi, Annmarie .... Trenton, NJ
Cozzi, Matthew J. .... Chicago, IL
Cozzi, Michael J. .... Arlington Heights, IL
Cozzi, Paul C. .... Schaumburg, IL
Cozzi, Robert J. .... Chicago, IL
Cozzi, Vincent P. .... Lyndhurst, NJ
Cozzie, Robert M. .... McLean, VA
Cozzillio, Michael J. .... Wilmington, DE
Cozzini, Maria R. .... Mountainside, NJ
Cozzo, Kathryn E. .... Marietta, GA
Cozzola, Richard T. .... Chicago, IL
Cozzolino, Beth Gabel .... Hudson, NY
Cozzolino, Jeffrey Andrew .... Worcester, MA
Cozzolino, Joseph P. .... Mount Clemens, MI
Cozzolino, Marc C. .... Newark, NJ

Cozzolino, Michael ... Westerly, RI
Cozzolino, Michael Anthony ... Hudson, NY
Cprek, Kent ... Philadelphia, PA
Craane, Paul C. ... Chicago, IL
Craanen, Robert J. ... Appleton, WI
Crabb, Barbara B. ... Madison, WI
Crabb, David L. ... Chicago, IL
Crabb, Elizabeth A. ... Weslaco, TX
Crabb, Ferguson & Riesen
Oklahoma City, OK
Crabb, James Dennis ... South Lake Tahoe, CA
Crabb, Jefferson A., Jr. ... McAllen, TX
Crabb, Jennifer H. ... West Sacramento, CA
Crabb, Jerry J. ... Oklahoma City, OK
Crabb, Joe F. ... Houston, TX
Crabb, John
Department of Justice, GV
Crabb, Joseph M. ... Phoenix, AZ
Crabb, Kelli Hanley ... St. Petersburg, FL
Crabb, Kelly Charles ... Los Angeles, CA
Crabb, Michael R. ... Des Moines, IA
Omaha, NE
Crabb, Rocky Lee ... Covina, CA
Crabb, Roger A. ... Irving, TX
Crabb, Thomas S. ... Boulder, CO
Crabbe, Brown, Jones, Potts & Schmidt
Cincinnati, OH
Columbus, OH
Lancaster, OH
Crabbe, Cheryl C. ... Houston, TX
Crabbe, Danny W. ... Silver Creek, GA
Crabbe, Deborah A. ... Seattle, WA
Crabbe, Fred L. ... Tenafly, NJ
Crabbs & Crabbs ... Hanover, PA
Crabbs, John M. ... Hanover, PA
Crabbs, Karen Yvonne
Department of Justice,
Executive Office for Immigration Review, GV
Crabbs, Muriel Anne ... Hanover, PA
Crabill & Crabill, Ltd. ... Naperville, IL
Crabill, Elizabeth Faecher ... Raleigh, NC
Crabill, Frank W. ... New York, NY
Crabill, John C. ... Rye, NY
Crabill, Mary Jane ... Naperville, IL
Crabill, Robert A. ... Tampa, FL
Crabill, Warren E. ... Naperville, IL
Crabill, William E. ... Miami, FL
Crable, Francis R. ... Kennewick, WA
Crable, John A. ... Detroit, MI
Crable, John A. ... Troy, MI
Crable, Stephen E. ... Washington, DC
Crabtree, Andrew L. ... Uniondale, NY
Crabtree, Arthur George ... Santa Clarita, CA
Crabtree, Brooks ... San Diego, CA
Crabtree, Bruce I., III ... Atlanta, GA
Crabtree, C. Scott ... Denver, CO
Crabtree, C. D. ... San Antonio, TX
Crabtree, Charles W., Jr ... Tampa, FL
Crabtree, Christopher W. ... Lakewood, CO
Crabtree & Crabtree ... San Diego, CA
Crabtree, Dale T. ... Eugene, OR
Crabtree, Daniel B. ... San Diego, CA
Crabtree, Daniel D. ... Leawood, KS
Crabtree, David F. ... Salt Lake City, UT
Crabtree, Dean A. ... Bedford, PA
Crabtree, E. Hodge ... El Cajon, CA
Crabtree, Edwin H. ... Denver, CO
Crabtree, Ellen ... St. Louis, MO
Crabtree & Fallar ... Jacksonville, FL
Crabtree & Goforth ... London, KY
Crabtree, Graham K. ... Lansing, MI
Crabtree, Guy W. ... Durham, NC
Crabtree & Hoshibata ... Honolulu, HI
Crabtree, James L. ... Mission, KS
Crabtree, James W. ... Charlotte, NC
Crabtree, Jeffrey W. ... Daphne, AL
Robertsdale, AL
Crabtree, John E., III ... Minneapolis, MN
Crabtree, John G. ... Key Biscayne, FL
Crabtree, John G., P.A. ... Key Biscayne, FL
Miami, FL
Crabtree, Joseph H., Jr. ... Memphis, TN
Crabtree, Juli K. ... Chicago, IL
Crabtree, Karen M. ... Annapolis, MD
Crabtree, Kevin J. ... Los Angeles, CA
Crabtree, Larry D. ... Nashville, TN
Crabtree Law Offices ... Charleston, WV
Crabtree, Maril M. ... Mission, KS
Crabtree, Matthew W. ... Charleston, WV
Crabtree, Michael A. ... Washington, DC
Crabtree, Michael R. ... Twin Falls, ID
Crabtree, Michelle S. ... Charlotte, NC
Crabtree, Ralph R. ... Jacksonville, FL
Crabtree, Richard L. ... Anchorage, AK
Crabtree, Richard L. ... Chico, CA
Crabtree, Robert C. ... Tallahassee, FL
Crabtree, Robert K. ... Boston, MA
Crabtree, Robert W. ... Modesto, CA
Crabtree, Schmidt, Zeff, Jacobs & Farrar
Modesto, CA
Crabtree, Steven D. ... Stockton, CA
Crabtree, Susan A. ... Cary, NC
Crabtree, Sweet & Williams, P.C.
Daphne, AL
Robertsdale, AL
Crabtree, Thomas J. ... Bend, OR
Crabtree, Tony ... Dallas, TX
Crabtree, Valleri J. ... Columbus, OH
Crabtree, William G., II ... Hammond, IN
Crabtree, William G., II, P.C.
Hammond, IN
Crabtree, William H. ... Bloomfield Hills, MI
Crabtree, William Scott ... Franklin, KY
Crabtree, Wm. Gary ... London, KY
Cracas, Dorothea Garber ... Morristown, NJ
Cracas, Ronald J. ... Newark, NJ
Cracas, Teresa C. ... Fairfield, OH
Cracchiolo, Daniel ... Phoenix, AZ
Crace, Joseph B. ... Brentwood, TN
Crachiola, Gail Phillips ... Detroit, MI
Craciun, Joseph J. ... Garden Grove, CA
Crackel, Jeffrey A. ... Clifton Forge, VA
Cracken, Harkey & Payne, LLP
Dallas, TX
Cracken, John R. W. ... Dallas, TX
Cracker, Francine M. ... Marlton, NJ
Craco, Louis A. ... New York, NY
Craco, Louis A., Jr. ... New York, NY
Craco, Paul V. ... Uniondale, NY
Cracraft, Cristin M. ... Houston, TX
Cracraft, George K., Jr. ... Little Rock, AR
Cracraft, Michael B. ... Indianapolis, IN
Cracraft, Steven G. ... Indianapolis, IN
Craddick, Candland & Conti, Professional Corporation ... Danville, CA
Walnut Creek, CA
Craddick, Donald L. ... Sitka, AK
Craddick, Judy S. ... Martinez, CA
Craddick, Robert J. ... St. Louis, MO
Craddock, Allen T. ... San Antonio, TX
Craddock, Amy Elizabeth ... Houston, TX
Craddock, Christina A. ... Atlanta, GA
Craddock, Daniel K. ... Houston, TX
Craddock, Howard B. ... Charlottesville, VA
Craddock, J. Patrick ... Chicago, IL
Craddock, Jason R. ... Decatur, IL
Craddock, J. D., III ... Munfordville, KY
Craddock, Jean Marie ... Kernersville, NC
Craddock, John R. ... Houston, TX
Craddock, Kim A. ... Birmingham, AL
Craddock, Larry J., Jr. ... Austin, TX
Craddock, Michael J. ... Chicago, IL
Craddock, Michael J. ... Dallas, TX
Craddock, Nancy Anne ... Fresno, CA
Craddock, Reginald V. ... Ronkonkoma, NY
Craddock, Robert E., Jr. ... Memphis, TN
Craddock, Robin S. ... Louisville, KY
Craddock & Rosier, PLLC ... San Antonio, TX
Craddock, Scott London ... Nashville, TN
Craddock, Theodore J. ... Lynchburg, VA
Craddock, Thomas W. ... Dallas, TX
Craddock-Lee, Vera M. ... Stamford, CT
Craddock-Posey, Crystal Len
New Orleans, LA
Crader Crader & Dolan, LLP ... Sikeston, MO
Crader, D. David ... Sikeston, MO
Crader, Dwight ... Sikeston, MO
Crady, George E. ... Houston, TX
Crady, Jewett & McCulley, L.L.P.
Houston, TX
Crady, Thurston M. J. ... Louisville, KY
Crafa, Joseph R. ... Mineola, NY
New York, NY
Craff, Robert C. ... Tucson, AZ
Craffey, Kelly M. ... Mineola, NY
Craford, John K. ... Boston, MA
Craft, Allison Taylor ... Birmingham, AL
Craft, Barbara A. ... Grand Rapids, MI
Craft, Brenemen and Associates
Brandon, MS
Craft, Bruce A. ... Baton Rouge, LA
Craft, Carla Draluck ... Washington, DC
Craft, Carolyn D. ... Phoenix, AZ
Craft, Charles R. ... Lakewood, CO
Craft & Craft ... West Palm Beach, FL
Craft & Craft, A Professional Law Corporation
Baton Rouge, LA
Craft, D. Kay ... Bowling Green, KY
Craft, David L. ... Dallas, TX
Craft, David W. ... West Palm Beach, FL
Craft, David Ward ... Jackson, MI
Craft, Edward O. ... Bloomington, IN
Craft Fridkin & Rhyne, L.L.C.
Jefferson City, MO
Kansas City, MO
Craft, George S. ... Houston, TX
Craft, Hunter ... Houston, TX
Craft, James A. ... Phoenix, AZ
Craft, James M. ... Telluride, CO
Craft, James Wiley, II ... Whitesburg, KY
Craft, Jeffrey F. ... Los Angeles, CA
Craft, Jill L. ... Baton Rouge, LA
Craft, Jim B. ... Englewood, CO
Craft, John A. ... Sanford, FL
Craft, John C. ... Kansas City, MO
Craft, Joseph W., III ... Tulsa, OK
Craft, Judith J. ... Danville, CA
Craft, Karen J. ... Detroit, MI
Craft, Laura R. ... Emeryville, CA
Craft, Leslie Locke ... Rocky Mount, NC
Craft, Lewis John ... Villa Park, IL
Craft, Lewis John, & Associates
Villa Park, IL
Craft & McGhee, P.C. ... Christiansburg, VA
Craft, Orbie S. ... Brandon, MS
Craft, Patricia J. ... Decatur, GA
Craft, Patricia J., P.C. ... Atlanta, GA
Decatur, GA
Craft, Perry A. ... Nashville, TN
Craft, Peter L. ... Westport, CT
Craft, R. Brian ... Tyler, TX
Craft, Rance L. ... Atlanta, GA
Craft, Randal R., Jr. ... New York, NY
Craft, Rebecca A. ... Newark, NJ
Craft, Robert H., Jr. ... Washington, DC
Craft, Robert M. ... Jackson, MI
Craft, Robert M. ... Houston, TX
Craft, Robert W. ... Beaumont, TX
Craft, Ronald R. ... Fairfield, OH
Craft, S. Allen ... Moorestown, NJ
Craft, Susan Swilling ... Memphis, TN
Craft, Theodore, Law Offices ... Melrose, MA
Craft, Thomas J., Jr. ... Boca Raton, FL
Craft, Vicki O'Kelley ... Houston, TX
Craft, William C. ... Washington, DC
Craft, William R. L., Jr. ... Christiansburg, VA
Craft, Winfred O., Jr. ... Arlington, VA
Craft, Wm. E. ... Kenansville, NC
Crafton, B. Casey ... Baltimore, MD
Crafton, Constance J.D. ... Miamisburg, OH
Crafton, L. Joseph ... Ann Arbor, MI
Crafton, Martin, Ogburn & Zipperle, P.L.L.C. ... Louisville, KY
Crafton, Thomas E. ... Louisville, KY
Craft-Rochat, Julia A. ... Wichita, KS
Crafts, Alan L. ... Rancho Cucamonga, CA
Crafts, Edson S., III ... Huntingdon, PA
Crafts, James F., Jr. ... San Francisco, CA
Crafts, Jeffrey L. ... Orange, CA
Cragan, Paul H. ... Surprise, AZ
Crag-Chaderton, Rachael McMorris
Orlando, FL
Crager, Lynda M. ... Sanford, FL
Crager, Minor B. ... Houston, TX
Cragg, Brian T. ... San Francisco, CA
Cragg, Robert S. ... Hopkins, MN
Cragg, Walter Thorpe, Jr. ... Red Bluff, CA
Craggs, Ann Melinda ... Ocala, FL
Craggs, Dennis W. ... Houston, TX
Craghead, Laurie E. ... Gresham, OR
Cragin, Richard W. ... San Leandro, CA
Cragin, Timothy S. ... New Orleans, LA
Cragle, David R. ... Houston, TX
Crago, Dave H. ... Corpus Christi, TX
Crago, David C. ... Ada, OH
Crago, Jere L. ... Metairie, LA
Cragwall, J. A., Jr. ... Grand Rapids, MI
Crahan, Dyana J. ... Bedford, NH
Crahan, Lawrence G. ... St. Louis, MO
Crahan, Marcus E., Jr. ... Santa Barbara, CA
Crahan, Patrick J. ... San Diego, CA
Crahay, Francis X. ... Asbury Park, NJ
Craig, A. Douglas P. ... New York, NY
Craig, Alexander Joseph, III ... Fremont, CA
Craig, Allen B., III ... Houston, TX
Craig, Amziah W. ... Boston, MA
Craig, André A. ... Mayfield Village, OH
Craig, Andrew D. ... Durango, CO
Craig, Andrew F. ... Wayne, NJ
Craig, Andrew K. ... Parsippany, NJ
Craig, Andrew S. ... Portland, OR
Craig, Anne I. ... Lexington, MA
Craig, Barbara D. ... Portland, OR
Craig, Barbara Koerner ... Union City, NJ
Craig, Barbara Laughlin ... Mc Keesport, PA
Craig, Barbara S. ... Springfield, VA
Craig, Barry G. ... Miami, FL
Craig & Bartelsmeyer, P.C. ... Herrin, IL
Craig, Benjamin L. ... Lakewood, CO
Craig, Bernard D. ... Kansas City, MO
Craig, Brand, Lake & Hart
McMinnville, OR
Craig, Brent M. ... Decatur, AL
Craig, Brian D. ... Baltimore, MD
Craig, Brian D. ... Maumee, OH
Craig, Brian J. ... Reston, VA
Craig, Brian P. ... Locust Valley, NY
Craig & Brisson, P.A. ... Fayetteville, NC
Craig, Bruce A. ... Madison, WI
Craig, Bruce L. ... Colorado Springs, CO
Craig, Bruce W. ... Downers Grove, IL
Craig, C. York, III ... Jackson, MS
Craig, C. York, Jr. ... Jackson, MS
Craig, Carla E. ... New York, NY
Craig, Carmel A. ... Boston, MA
Craig, Carol Huston ... Augusta, GA
Craig, Carol S. ... Annapolis, MD
Craig, Carolyn J. ... Miami, FL
Craig, Carolyn L. ... Palo Alto, CA
Craig, Carrick D. ... Ann Arbor, MI
Craig, Caryn Leigh ... San Diego, CA
Craig, Cassin W. ... Blue Bell, PA
Craig, Charles D. ... Austin, TX
Craig, Charles D., Jr. ... Morristown, NJ
Craig, Christine L. ... Fairfield, CA
Napa, CA
Craig, Christine M. ... Concord, NH
Craig, Christopher B. ... Harrisburg, PA
Craig, Christopher H. ... Stamford, CT
Craig, Christopher L. ... Nashville, TN
Craig, Christopher Thomas ... McLean, VA
Craig, Clay ... Miami, FL
Craig, Colleen K. ... Morris Plains, NJ
Craig & Craig ... Benton, IL
Charleston, IL
Effingham, IL
Fairfield, IL
Marshall, IL
Mattoon, IL
McLeansboro, IL
Mount Vernon, IL
Nashville, IL
Paris, IL
Pinckneyville, IL
Salem, IL
Shelbyville, IL
Springfield, IL
Sullivan, IL
Toledo, IL
Tuscola, IL
Vandalia, IL
Craig, Cristy J. ... Seattle, WA
Craig, Curtis L. ... Tulsa, OK
Craig, Cynthia M. ... West Orange, NJ
Craig, D. Broward ... New York, NY
Craig, Dana M. ... Rock Island, IL
Davenport, IA
Craig, Daniel J. ... Augusta, GA
Craig, Daniel W. ... Kansas City, MO
Craig, Daniel Wayne ... Merriam, KS
Craig, David A. ... Cordova, TN
Craig, David B. ... Fayetteville, NC
Craig, David C. ... Des Moines, IA
Craig, David R. ... Herrin, IL
Craig, David Scott ... Jacksonville, FL
Craig, David W. ... Batesville, IN
Craig, David W. ... Allison Park, PA
Craig, Dawn M. ... Los Angeles, CA
Craig, Debbie F. ... Lake Oswego, OR
Craig, Dennis D. ... Jackson, MS
Craig, Dennis Patrick ... Daytona Beach, FL
Craig, D. F. Moore ... West Caldwell, NJ
Craig, Donald P. ... Voorhees, NJ
Craig, Donna, & Associates, PLC
Birmingham, MI
Craig, Donna J. ... Birmingham, MI
Craig, Douglas S., Jr. ... Houston, TX
Craig, Douglas W. ... Garden City, MI
Craig & Drake ... Nashville, TN
Craig, Edward A. ... Auburn Hills, MI
Craig, Edward B., IV ... Newnan, GA
Craig, Edward L., Jr. ... New Carlisle, OH
Craig, Elaine Hartung ... McMinnville, OR
Craig, Elisabeth Fandetti ... Baltimore, MD
Craig, Ellen C. ... Chicago, IL
Craig & Ells ... Old Greenwich, CT
New York, NY
White Plains, NY
Craig & Elrod ... Lawrenceville, GA
Craig, Eugene F. ... Staten Island, NY
Craig, Eugene J. ... Bellevue, WA
Craig, Eugene J., P.S. ... Bellevue, WA
Craig, Francis P. ... Boston, MA
Craig, Frank S., III ... Baton Rouge, LA
Craig, Frank S., Jr. ... Baton Rouge, LA
Craig, Garrett K. ... Los Angeles, CA
Craig, Geoffrey L. ... New York, NY
Craig, Geoffrey M. ... Durango, CO
Craig, George H., Jr. ... Pittsburgh, PA
Craig, George L. ... Oak Ridge, TN
Craig, George T. ... Athens, AL
Craig, Glen E. ... Columbia, SC
Craig, Glenn A. ... Melbourne, FL
Craig, Gordon A. ... Beaumont, TX
Craig, Gregory B. ... Washington, DC
Craig, H. Theodore, III ... Orinda, CA
Craig, H. Theodore, III, Inc., A P.C.
Orinda, CA
Craig, Harald F. ... Toledo, OH
Craig, Harold A., Jr. ... New York, NY
Craig, Harry E. ... Wickenburg, AZ
Craig, Harry E. ... Detroit, MI
Craig, Harry W., Jr. ... Topeka, KS
Craig, Henderson & Johnson, LLC
Landover, MD
Craig & Hirsch, P.C. ... Reston, VA
Craig, Hunter B. ... Pompano Beach, FL
Craig, Ian W. ... Sacramento, CA
Craig, Ian W., A Prof. Corp., Law Offices of Sacramento, CA
Craig, J. ... Charleston, WV
Craig, J. Blair, II ... Atlanta, GA
Craig, James A. ... Sioux Falls, SD
Craig, James E. ... McMinnville, OR
Craig, James L. ... Department of Labor,
Office of the Solicitor, GV
Craig, James M. ... Tampa, FL
Craig, James M., II ... Lakeland, FL
Craig, James P. ... Cedar Rapids, IA
Craig, James P. ... Ballston Spa, NY
Craig, James R. ... Dallas, TX
Craig, James W. ... Jackson, MS
Craig, James W. ... Manchester, NH
Craig, Jane Ellen ... Dripping Springs, TX
Craig, Janet ... Houston, TX
Craig, Janet A. ... Lexington, KY
Craig, Janice C. ... Ripley, TN
Craig, J. B. ... Wichita, KS
Craig, Jeanean W. ... Salem, OR
Craig, Jeffrey S. ... Haddonfield, NJ
Craig, Jennifer P. ... Knoxville, TN
Craig, Jeri B. ... Oklahoma City, OK
Craig, Jerome H. ... Los Angeles, CA
Craig, Jerry D. ... Arlington, VA
Craig, Jerry W. ... Mount Pleasant, SC
Craig, Jessup & Stratton ... Ellensburg, WA
Seattle, WA
Craig, Joan L. ... Brooklyn, NY
Craig, Joanne ... Boston, MA
Craig, Joel M. ... Durham, NC
Craig, John A. ... Hawthorne, NY
Craig, John C. ... Belleville, IL
Craig, John C. ... Boston, MA
Craig, John M. ... Washington, DC
Craig, John O., III ... High Point, NC
Craig, John W., III ... Los Angeles, CA
Craig, John W. L., II ... Roanoke, VA
Craig, Jon L. ... Charlottesville, VA
Craig, Jon R. ... Garden City, KS
Craig, Joyce I. ... Los Angeles, CA
Craig, Julia A. ... Kirkland, WA
Craig, Julia M. ... Mankato, MN
Craig, Karen A. ... Pittsburgh, PA
Craig, Karen D. ... Torrance, CA
Craig, Kenneth P. ... Incline Village, NV
Craig, Kenneth P. ... Moore, OK
Craig, Kevin James ... Minneapolis, MN
Craig, Kimberly M. ... Dearborn, MI
Craig, L. Clifford ... Cincinnati, OH
Craig & Laboe ... St. Louis, MO
Craig, Larry A. ... Riverside, CA
Craig, Larry D. ... Nashville, TN
Craig, Laura A. ... Larchmont, NY
Craig, Lauren L. ... Placerville, CA
Craig, Laurie B. ... Phoenix, AZ
Craig, Laurie J. ... Cedar Rapids, IA
Craig, Lawrance B., III ... Miami, FL
Craig, Lee ... Tampa, FL
Craig, Lee ... Richardson, TX
Craig, Lesley S. ... Denver, CO
Craig, Lisa Ritchey ... Atlanta, GA

Craig and Macauley, Professional Corporation ... Boston, MA
Craig, Margaret B. ... Fairfax, VA
Craig, Marion J., III, P.C. ... Roswell, NM
Craig, Marion J. (Jimmy), III ... Roswell, NM
Craig, Mark B. ... Decatur, AL
Craig, Mark J. ... Vicksburg, MI
Craig, Martha C.
Department Of Health And Human Services, Office of the General Counsel, GV
Craig, Martin Z. ... Evanston, IL
Craig, Mary Ellen ... Reston, VA
Craig, Mary R. ... Towson, MD
Craig, Mary Robin ... Cleveland, OH
Craig, Mary W. ... El Paso, TX
Craig, Michael A. ... Houston, TX
Craig, Michael D. ... Osprey, FL
Craig, Michael D. ... Buffalo Grove, IL
Bala Cynwyd, PA
Craig, Michael O. ... Benton, LA
Craig, Michael S. ... Lakeland, FL
Craig, Milton C. ... Chandler, OK
Craig, Nancy G. ... Luther, OK
Craig, Omar D., (P.A.) ... Oxford, MS
Craig, Oral C. ... Okemah, OK
Craig, Pamela ... Orlando, FL
Craig, Pamela Barnes ... Library of Congress, Law Library, GV
Craig, Patrick J. ... Eldora, IA
Hubbard, IA
Craig, Paul A. ... Chicago, IL
Craig, Paul Anthony ... St. Louis, MO
Craig, Paul G. ... Memphis, TN
Craig, Paul M., Jr. ... Washington, DC
Craig, Paula L. ... Washington, DC
Craig, Peter S. ... Washington, DC
Craig, Philip A. ... Vernon Hills, IL
Craig, Philippe B. ... San Luis Obispo, CA
Craig, Rachel M. ... Jefferson City, MO
Craig, Randall J., Jr. ... Landover, MD
Craig, Randall K., Law Offices of
Evansville, IN
Craig, Rebecca D. ... Ellensburg, WA
Seattle, WA
Craig, Rhonda P. ... Detroit, MI
Craig, Richard A. ... Chatham, NJ
Craig, Richard D. ... Norman, OK
Craig, Richard E. ... Vienna, VA
Craig, Richard F. ... Austin, TX
Craig, Richard M. ... Lawrenceville, GA
Craig, Richard M. ... Chicago, IL
Craig, Robert B. ... Covington, KY
Craig, Robert D. ... Burlington, NC
Craig, Robert E. ... Miami, FL
Craig, Robert F. ... Omaha, NE
Craig, Robert G. ... Marshfield, WI
Craig, Robert J. ... Vienna, VA
Craig, Robert L. (Bob), Jr., P.C.
Lubbock, TX
Craig, Robert M. ... Southfield, MI
Craig, Robert M., III ... Houston, TX
Craig, Robert T., III ... Prescott, AZ
Craig, Robin ... Evansville, IN
Craig, Roger E. ... Naples, FL
Craig, Roger P. ... Washington, DC
Craig, Ronnie F. ... Charlotte, NC
Charleston, SC
Craig, Roy A., Jr. ... Lakeland, FL
Lake Wales, FL
Winter Haven, FL
Craig, Royal W. ... Baltimore, MD
Craig, Royal W., P.C., Law Office of
Baltimore, MD
Craig, Rufus H. ... Montgomery, AL
Craig, Rufus H., Jr. ... Baton Rouge, LA
Craig, Russell Wells
Department of Commerce, Office of the General Counsel, GV
Craig, Sabra K. ... Sioux City, IA
Craig, Sandra L. ... St. Louis, MO
Craig, Sandra R. ... Philadelphia, PA
Craig, Sara M. ... Department of State, Director General—Foreign Service, GV
Craig, Scott ... Terre Haute, IN
Craig, Scott R., Law Offices of ... El Paso, TX
Craig, Sean M. ... Dallas, TX
Craig, Sindy Lee ... Burlington, VT
Craig, Stephen J. ... Phoenix, AZ
Craig, Stephen J. ... Lawrence, KS
Craig, Stephen Lance ... Louisville, KY
Craig, Stephen T. ... Boulder, CO
Craig, Stephen W. ... Phoenix, AZ
Craig, Steve A. ... Hilliard, OH
Craig, Steven E. ... Charleston, SC
Craig, Steven L. ... West Palm Beach, FL
Craig, Steven L. ... Canton, OH
Craig, Stuart L. ... Danville, VA
Craig, Susan ... Melrose, MA
Craig, Susan E. ... Department of Education, Office of the General Counsel, GV
Craig, Susan Eilers ... Brooklyn, NY
Craig, Ted C. ... Miami, FL
Craig, Terence G. ... Alexandria, VA
Craig, Terri Raye ... Wagoner, OK
Craig, Terrill & Hale, L.L.P.
Lubbock, TX
Craig, Theodore J. ... Aurora, IL
Craig, Theresa M. ... Phoenix, AZ
Craig, Thomas ... Manchester, NH
Craig, Thomas F., II ... Morristown, NJ
Craig, Thomas L. ... Huntington, WV
Craig, Thomas M. ... Chicago, IL
Craig, Thomas, P.A. ... Manchester, NH
Craig, Tim O. ... Greenville, AL
Craig, Timothy R. ... San Francisco, CA
Craig, Toni L. ... Destin, FL
Craig, Tracy A. ... Boston, MA
Craig, Vicki ... Washington, DC

Craig, W. Hal ... McDonough, GA
Craig, W. Walter ... Wichita, KS
Craig, Wallace S. ... Hurst, TX
Craig, Wendy A. ... Frankfort, KY
Craig, Wenners, Craig & Casinghino, P.A.
Manchester, NH
Craig, William A., Jr. ... New York, NY
Craig, William B. ... Costa Mesa, CA
Craig, William E. ... New Haven, CT
Craig, William E. ... Portland, OR
Craig, William G., Jr. ... Owensboro, KY
Craig, William H. ... Little Rock, AR
Craig, William H. ... Manchester, NH
Craig, William R. ... Charlotte, NC
Craig, William S. ... Verona, WI
Craig, William Tucker
Fort Lauderdale, FL
Tampa, FL
West Palm Beach, FL
Craig, Wilson & Flickinger
Independence, IA
Craig, Wm. Thomas ... Covington, GA
Craige, Archibald ... Keswick, VA
Craige, Brawley, Liipfert & Walker, L.L.P.
Winston-Salem, NC
Craige, Burton ... Raleigh, NC
Craige, Fitzgerald F. ... Egg Harbor City, NJ
Craige, Lawrence S. ... Wilmington, NC
Craige, Mark A. ... Tulsa, OK
Craighead Glick, LLP ... Boston, MA
Craighead, J. E., Jr. ... Dalhart, TX
Craighead, Jennifer L. ... Lancaster, PA
Craighead, M. Shane ... Monroe, LA
Craighead, Rodkey, Jr. ... Manchester, NH
Craighead, Susan S. ... Boston, MA
Craighead, Susan T. ... Atlanta, GA
Craighill, G. Bowdoin, Jr.
Washington, DC
Craighill, James B. ... Charlotte, NC
Craighill, Mayfield, Fenwick, Cromelin & Cobb, L.L.P. ... Washington, DC
Craighill, Polly W. ... United States Senate, Office of the Legislative Counsel, GV
Craighill & Smith ... Charlotte, NC
Craigie, Alex W. ... Los Angeles, CA
Craigie, McCarthy & Clow
San Francisco, CA
Craigie, Patricia T. ... Los Angeles, CA
Craigie, Peter W. ... San Francisco, CA
Craigie-Johnson, Cynthia ... Jacksonville, FL
Craigmile, Christine Anne ... Denver, CO
Craigmile, Jeffrey S.
Lake Buena Vista, FL
Craigmile, Kathleen E. ... Denver, CO
Craigmyle, Beach A. ... Louisville, KY
Craigo, Richard W. ... Los Angeles, CA
Craig-Olson, Robin D. ... San Francisco, CA
Craik, Charlotte J. ... Houston, TX
Crail, Elizabeth F. ... Des Moines, IA
Crail, H. Whitfield, Jr. ... Phoenix, AZ
Crain, Andrew D. ... Denver, CO
Crain, Andrew O. ... Natick, MA
Crain, Annette Brashier ... Tuscaloosa, AL
Crain, Bennett, Jr. ... Annapolis, MD
Crain, Billie W., P.C. ... McAlester, OK
Crain, Caton & James, A Professional Corporation ... Houston, TX
Crain, Charles H. ... Tulsa, OK
Crain, Charles H., P.C. ... Tulsa, OK
Crain, Christina Melton ... Dallas, TX
Crain, Christina Melton, P.C., Law Offices of
Dallas, TX
Crain, Christopher M. ... Cuero, TX
Crain, David F. ... Austin, TX
Crain, Donald L. ... Middletown, OH
Crain, E. Gene ... Newport Beach, CA
Crain, Edward B., Jr. ... Houston, TX
Crain, F. Carter, Jr. ... Houston, TX
Crain, Frank H. ... Victoria, TX
Crain, Frankie Adams ... Seattle, WA
Crain, Gayla Campbell ... Dallas, TX
Crain, Hillary J. ... Bogalusa, LA
Crain, J. Kevin ... Charleston, SC
Crain, James K. ... Cuero, TX
Crain, James T., III ... Louisville, KY
Crain, James T., Jr. ... Louisville, KY
Crain, John A. ... Mountain Home, AR
Crain, Julie J. ... Washington, DC
Crain, Katharine G. ... Houston, TX
Crain, Kathleen M. ... Los Angeles, CA
Crain, Kelly M. ... Dallas, TX
Crain, Ken ... Georgetown, TX
Crain, Larry L. ... Brentwood, TN
Crain, Laura Lee ... Portland, OR
Crain, Lawrence J. ... Chicago, IL
Crain, Leah Piersol ... Deadwood, SD
Crain, Leo L. ... Mobile, AL
Crain, Mac ... Dallas, TX
Crain, Matthew S. ... Centralia, IL
Crain, Michael I. ... Los Angeles, CA
Crain, Michael M. ... Los Angeles, CA
Crain, Michael O. ... Athens, GA
Atlanta, GA
Crain, Michele Romance ... Pittsford, NY
Crain, Molly Glover ... Memphis, TN
Crain, Nalda D. ... Oakland, CA
Crain, Patricia ... Medford, OR
Crain, Robert D. ... Dallas, TX
Crain, Robert M. ... Houston, TX
Crain, Rogers L. ... Houston, TX
Crain, Sam L., Jr. ... Memphis, TN
Crain, Shawn R. ... Milwaukee, WI
Crain & Sheppard ... Cuero, TX
Crain, Stephanie ... Houston, TX
Crain, Stephen B. ... Houston, TX
Crain, Stephen L. ... McAllen, TX
Crain, Stephen V. ... Gladstone, MO
Crain, Steven A. ... New York, NY

Crain, Steven B. ... Memphis, TN
Crain & Sullivan, L.L.C. ... Athens, GA
Atlanta, GA
Crain, Terry D. ... Media, PA
Crain, Veltman, Miller & Milner, Ltd.
Centralia, IL
Salem, IL
Crain, Wilbert O., Jr. ... Shreveport, LA
Crain, William J. ... Covington, LA
Crain, William P. ... Centralia, IL
Craine, Arnold H. ... Chicago, IL
Craine Associates, Inc. ... Bellevue, WA
Craine, Dean A. ... Bellevue, WA
Craine, Diana ... Lake Oswego, OR
Craine, Karl ... Vashon, WA
Craine, Kevin A. ... Columbus, OH
Craine & Love ... Lake Oswego, OR
Craine, Patrick K. ... Dallas, TX
Craine, Robert E., Jr. ... Tulsa, OK
Craine, Seth T. ... Tampa, FL
Craine, Teri ... Charlevoix, MI
Craine, William J., Jr. ... Laurens, SC
Crainer, Steven M. ... New York, NY
Crain-Rigg, Laurie S. ... El Segundo, CA
Crais, Arthur A., Jr. ... New Orleans, LA
Crake, Nancy A. ... Stuart, FL
Craley, D. Michael ... York, PA
Crall, David B. ... Orlando, FL
Crall, Debra L. ... Marysville, CA
Crall, Hugh C. ... Bradenton, FL
Cralle, Catherine W. ... Greenville, NC
Cralle, George L. ... Houston, TX
Cram, Donald H., III
Woodland Hills, CA
Cram, Douglas M. ... Purchase, NY
Cram, Eva J. ... Cedar Rapids, IA
Cram, Franklin W. ... Arlington, TX
Cram, Franklin W. ... Mansfield, TX
Cram, Richard L. ... Topeka, KS
Cram, Stanley ... Eugene, OR
Cram, William D., Jr. ... Fairfax, VA
Cramarosso, Michael A. ... Chicago, IL
Cramb, G. Stanley ... Hurst, TX
Cramb & Marling ... Fort Worth, TX
Hurst, TX
Cramblit, Miggie E. ... Minneapolis, MN
Cramer, A. Bradley, Jr. ... Pittsburgh, PA
Cramer, Adam B. ... Washington, DC
Cramer & Ahern ... Westport, CT
Cramer, Alan Barry ... Richmond Heights, MO
Cramer, Alfred F. ... Houston, TX
Cramer, Allan P. ... Westport, CT
Cramer, Amelia Craig ... Tucson, AZ
Cramer, Amelia Craig ... Tucson, AZ
Cramer & Anderson LLP ... Danbury, CT
Hartford, CT
Kent, CT
Litchfield, CT
New Milford, CT
Washington Depot, CT
Cramer, Andrew I. ... New York, NY
Cramer, Anne E. ... Burlington, VT
Cramer, Aric ... Salt Lake City, UT
Cramer, Arthur R. ... Fort Lauderdale, FL
Cramer, Bruce A. ... Findlay, OH
Toledo, OH
Cramer, C. Johnston, III ... Lexington, KY
Cramer, Carl A. ... Dayton, OH
Cramer, Carla DiPasquale
Palm Beach Gardens, FL
Cramer, Carol P. ... Hilton Head Island, SC
Cramer, Cathy Ann ... New York, NY
Cramer, Charles L. ... St. Louis, MO
Cramer, Charles W. ... Orlando, FL
Cramer and Cramer ... Chambersburg, PA
Cramer, Daniel J. ... Ann Arbor, MI
Cramer, Daniel M. ... Minneapolis, MN
Cramer, Daniel McN. ... Pittsburgh, PA
Cramer, Daryl, & Associates, P.A.
West Palm Beach, FL
Cramer, Daryl B. ... Miami, FL
West Palm Beach, FL
West Palm Beach, FL
Cramer, Daryl B., P.A. ... Miami, FL
Cramer & Davis, LLC
Salt Lake City, UT
Cramer, Dayton M. ... Department of the Army, Office of the General Counsel, GV
Cramer, Donald C. ... Edmonds, WA
Cramer, Dorcas ... Toledo, OH
Cramer, Dorothy J. ... Lakewood, CO
Cramer, Douglas I. ... Seal Beach, CA
Cramer, Edward M. ... New York, NY
Cramer & Egan, A Professional Corporation
San Diego, CA
Cramer, Eli L. ... Norwich, CT
Cramer, Elizabeth R ... Santa Barbara, CA
Cramer, Eric L. ... Philadelphia, PA
Cramer, Francis L., III ... Nashua, NH
Cramer, Gayle H. ... Pensacola, FL
Cramer, Geoffrey S. ... Neptune, NJ
Cramer, George F., Jr. ... Amherst, MA
Cramer, G. H. "Buddy", Jr. ... Dallas, TX
Cramer, Haber & McDonald, P.A.
Tampa, FL
Cramer, Harold ... Philadelphia, PA
Cramer, Herman Antony ... Silver Spring, MD
Cramer, James J. ... Overland Park, KS
Cramer, James S. ... Woodbridge, NJ
Cramer, Jeffrey A. ... Jacksonville, FL
Cramer, Jeffrey D. ... Moundsville, WV
Cramer, Jeffrey H. ... Boston, MA
Cramer, Jeffrey L. ... St. Louis, MO
Cramer, Jennifer G. ... Boston, MA
Cramer, John ... Lawton, OK
Cramer, John F. ... New York, NY
Cramer, John McN. ... Harrisburg, PA
Cramer, Jonathan P. ... New York, NY

Cramer, Jordan M. ... Chicago, IL
Cramer, Joseph B. ... Gainesville, FL
Cramer, Kathleen M. ... Redlands, CA
Cramer, Kathleen Walsh ... Chambersburg, PA
Cramer, Kay S. ... New Buffalo, PA
Cramer & Keib Smith, LLP
Syracuse, NY
Cramer, Keith C. ... Las Vegas, NV
Cramer, Keith C. ... Las Vegas, NV
Cramer, Keith H. ... Bakersfield, CA
Cramer, Kenneth ... Santa Monica, CA
Cramer, Kenneth D. ... Menlo Park, CA
Cramer & Klopman, Chartered
Rockville, MD
Cramer, Lauren B. ... New York, NY
Cramer, Laurence M. ... Philadelphia, PA
Cramer Law Firm, The ... Jacksonville, FL
Cramer, Lew W.
Department of Commerce, GV
Cramer, Lowell ... Miami, FL
Cramer, M. Michael ... Rockville, MD
Cramer, Mallon & Lamborn ... Burns, OR
Cramer, Mark C. ... Charlotte, NC
Cramer, Mark K. ... Buffalo, NY
Cramer, Mark R. ... Hartford, CT
Cramer, Mark T. ... Los Angeles, CA
Cramer, Martin R. ... New York, NY
Cramer, Megan Jennifer ... Kansas City, MO
Cramer, Michael ... West Covina, CA
Cramer, Michael H. ... Chicago, IL
Cramer, Michael J. ... Port Washington, WI
Cramer, Michael W. ... Houston, TX
Cramer, Milton L. ... Torrington, CT
Cramer, Minock & Gallagher, PLC
Ann Arbor, MI
Detroit, MI
Cramer, Multhauf & Hammes, LLP
Waukesha, WI
Cramer, Neal R. ... Pittsburgh, PA
Cramer, Patricia G. ... Philadelphia, PA
Cramer, Paul Andrew ... Cambridge, MA
Cramer, Paul M. ... Newington, CT
Cramer & Peavy ... Griffin, GA
Cramer, R. Norman, Jr. ... Golden, CO
Cramer, R. Scott ... Duncannon, PA
Cramer, Richard A. ... Menlo Park, CA
Cramer, Richard B. ... New Haven, CT
Cramer, Richard L. ... Syracuse, NY
Cramer, Richard R. ... Sheboygan, WI
Cramer, Richard S. ... Wethersfield, CT
Cramer, Richard W. ... Pittsburgh, PA
Cramer, Robert ... Los Angeles, CA
Cramer, Robert J. ... New York, NY
Cramer, Robert W. ... Malibu, CA
Cramer, Robert W. ... Charlotte, NC
Cramer, Roger A. ... Cleveland, OH
Cramer, Roger L. ... New York, NY
Cramer, Ronald D. ... Marion, OH
Cramer, Roy A. ... Wellesley, MA
Cramer, Scott S. ... Milwaukee, WI
Cramer, Stephen D. ... Federal Way, WA
Cramer, Stephen D., P.L.L.C.
Federal Way, WA
Cramer, Stephen M. ... Omaha, NE
Cramer, Steven ... New York, NY
Cramer, Steven J. ... Oakland, CA
Cramer, Steven J. ... North Palm Beach, FL
Cramer, Susan P. ... Des Moines, IA
Cramer, Swetz, McManus & Roach, P.C.
Stroudsburg, PA
Cramer, Thomas Dale ... Ithaca, NY
Cramer, Tim C. ... Griffin, GA
Cramer, Timothy M.
Department of Agriculture, Office of the General Counsel, GV
Cramer, Tyler W. ... San Diego, CA
Cramer, W. Mitchell ... Knoxville, TN
Cramer, W. D., Jr. ... Burns, OR
Cramer, Wesley A. ... Washington, PA
Cramer, William B. ... Stroudsburg, PA
Cramer, William C. ... Tampa, FL
Cramer, William C. ... Chambersburg, PA
Cramer, William C., Jr. ... Panama City, FL
Cramer, William D. ... Burns, OR
Cramer, William D. ... Grapevine, TX
Cramer, William T. ... Akron, OH
Crames, Charles F. ... New York, NY
Crames, Michael J. ... New York, NY
Cramin, Chet A. ... Santa Monica, CA
Cramin, Corey S. ... Santa Ana, CA
Cramme, C. William, III ... Richmond, VA
Crammer, Timothy M. ... Atlantic City, NJ
Crammond, John H. ... Bloomingdale, NJ
Cramp, Barry S. ... Pomfret, MD
Cramp, David S. ... Morristown, NJ
Cramp, John F. ... Media, PA
Crampe, Michiko Ito ... New York, NY
Crampton, Ann C. ... Kansas City, MO
Crampton, Barbara C. ... Wichita Falls, TX
Crampton & Crampton ... Wichita Falls, TX
Crampton, Don P. ... Phoenix, AZ
Crampton, Elizabeth Dianne
Oklahoma City, OK
Crampton, George W. ... Bath, NC
Crampton, Gregory B. ... Raleigh, NC
Crampton, Holly G. ... Wichita Falls, TX
Crampton, James Walter ... Omaha, NE
Crampton, Jeffery S. ... Grand Rapids, MI
Crampton, John Philip ... Philadelphia, PA
Crampton, Rebekah J. ... Springfield, MA
Crampton, Roger W. ... Wichita Falls, TX
Crampton, Scott P. ... Washington, DC
Crampton, Stephen R. ... Burlington, VT
Crampton, William D. ... St. Louis, MO
Crampton, William J. ... Kansas City, MO
Cramton, Charles D. ... Ithaca, NY
Cramton, Roger C. ... Ithaca, NY
Cran, Jonathan D. ... Minneapolis, MN

Cranberg, Marcia Ann ... Washington, DC
Crance, Frank M. ... Newport Beach, CA
Cranch, Constance W. ... New York, NY
Cranch, Laurence E. ... New York, NY
Crandall, Angela M. ... Minneapolis, MN
Crandall, Catherine B. ... Corning, NY
Crandall, Charles E., III ... Herkimer, NY
Crandall, Charles E., Jr. ... Herkimer, NY
Crandall, Charles E., Jr., Charles E. Crandall, III and John H. Crandall ... Herkimer, NY
Crandall, Clayton H. ... Oconomowoc, WI
Crandall, Colleen ... Boca Raton, FL
Crandall, Colleen Mary, P.A.
Boca Raton, FL
Crandall, Craig ... Thousand Oaks, CA
Crandall, Dale C. ... Burwell, NE
Crandall, Dale L. ... Salem, OR
Crandall, Dale R. ... Perrysburg, OH
Crandall, Daniel L. ... Roanoke, VA
Crandall, David E. ... Denver, CO
Crandall, David J. ... Cleveland, OH
Crandall, David J. ... Martinsville, VA
Crandall, David P. ... Irvine, CA
Crandall, Donna L. ... Santa Ana, CA
Crandall, Douglas K. ... Carthage, MO
Crandall, Douglas W. ... Boise, ID
Crandall, Duane C. ... Longview, WA
Crandall, Duane J. ... Burnsville, MN
Crandall, Elizabeth C. ... San Francisco, CA
Crandall, Emily S. ... New York, NY
Crandall, Eric L. ... Stillwater, MN
Crandall, Erika J. ... Weston, OH
Crandall, Frank R. ... Santa Barbara, CA
Crandall, Frith C. ... Hoffman Estates, IL
Crandall Gilman, L.L.P. ... Boise, ID
Crandall, Grant F. ... Charleston, WV
Crandall, Hanscom, Pease and Collins, P.A.
Rockland, ME
Crandall, James L. ... Irvine, CA
Crandall, Jas. J. ... Lake Station, IN
Crandall, Jeanne ... Dallas, TX
Crandall, Jeffery J. ... Coeur d'Alene, ID
Crandall, Jeffrey P. ... New York, NY
Crandall, John H. ... Herkimer, NY
Crandall, Karl N. ... Bowling Green, KY
Crandall, Krissell ... Anchorage, AK
Crandall, Laurie A. ... Salt Lake City, UT
Crandall, Martin E.
Dearborn Heights, MI
Crandall, Martin E., & Associates, P.C.
Dearborn Heights, MI
Detroit, MI
Crandall, Nancy ... Fairfield, CT
Crandall, Nelson D. ... Menlo Park, CA
Crandall, Nora L. ... Springfield, IL
Crandall, Penelope ... Charleston, WV
Crandall & Podleski ... Carthage, MO
Crandall Pyles Haviland & Turner, LLP
Charleston, WV
Crandall, Richard H. ... Manning, IA
Crandall, Ruth Ann ... Seal Beach, CA
Crandall, Stephen A. ... Sunnyvale, CA
Crandall, Stephen A. ... Burlington, WA
Crandall, Stephen A., Inc., P.S.
Burlington, WA
Crandall, Stephen S. ... Cleveland, OH
Crandall, Stephen T. ... San Diego, CA
Crandall, Susan Emlet, (Mrs.) ... San Jose, CA
Crandall, Terry Lynn
Research Triangle Park, NC
Crandall, Virginia Lea ... Honolulu, HI
Crandall, Vivian Lea ... Knoxville, TN
Crandall, Wayne R. ... Rockland, ME
Crandall, William A., III
Minneapolis, MN
Crandall, William H., Jr. ... St. Louis, MO
Crandell, Gary L. ... Denver, CO
Crandell, George M., Jr. ... Sacramento, CA
Crandell, Jennifer T. ... Las Vegas, NV
Crandell, Kevin S. ... Denver, CO
Crandell, Norman A. ... Kansas City, MO
Crandell, R. Timothy ... Tacoma, WA
Crandell, Ralph F. ... Denver, CO
Crandell, Rosaland M. ... Rolling Meadows, IL
Crandlemire, Donald C. ... Manchester, NH
Crandley, John G. ... Virginia Beach, VA
Crane, Adam M. ... Overland Park, KS
Crane, Alan R. ... West Palm Beach, FL
Crane, Allan C. ... New Orleans, LA
Crane, Andrew B. ... Jamaica Plain, MA
Crane, Angus E. ... Alexandria, VA
Crane, Ann L. ... Chicago, IL
Crane, Anne D. ... St. Louis, MO
Crane, Anne E. ... Wilton, CT
Crane, Anne J. ... Chicago, IL
Crane, B. Jean ... Cedartown, GA
Crane, Benjamin ... Boca Raton, FL
Crane, Benjamin F. ... New York, NY
Crane, Bernard F. ... Washington, DC
Crane, Bethiah Beale ... Durango, CO
Crane, Bruce A. ... Sacramento, CA
Crane, Catharine W. ... New York, NY
Crane, Catherine C. ... Denver, CO
Crane, Charles Bretton ... Tulsa, OK
Crane, Charles E. ... Petaluma, CA
Crane, Charlotte ... Chicago, IL
Crane, Clayton J. ... Streamwood, IL
Crane, Daniel A. ... New York, NY
Crane, David D. ... St. Louis, MO
Crane, David G. ... Bloomington, IN
Crane, David J. ... Eureka, CA
Crane, David M. ... Mott, ND
Crane, David W. ... Fort Lauderdale, FL
Crane, David W. ... Gulfport, MS
Crane, David W., P.A. ... Fort Lauderdale, FL
Crane, Debra D. ... Petoskey, MI
Crane, Debra K. ... Hamilton, OH
Crane, Donald B. ... Maryville, TN
Crane, Donald F., Jr. ... Princeton, NJ
Crane, Donald H. ... Pasadena, CA
Crane, Donald R. ... Klamath Falls, OR
Crane, Dorothy M. ... Pittsfield, MA
Crane, Duffy Doyle ... Austin, TX
Crane, Dunham & Drury ... Seattle, WA
Crane, Edward J., Jr. ... Boston, MA
Crane, Edward M. ... Chicago, IL
Crane, Elizabeth Loring ... Denver, CO
Crane, Ellen E. ... Boston, MA
Crane, Ellen E. ... Saginaw, MI
Crane, Eric J. ... Cotuit, MA
Crane, Eric R. ... Charlestown, MA
Crane, Erin ... San Francisco, CA
Crane, Ernest F. ... Auburn, WA
Crane, Eugene ... Chicago, IL
Crane, Franci Neely ... Houston, TX
Crane, Gayle L. ... Joplin, MO
Crane, George B. ... Pittsfield, MA
Crane, Gordon J. ... Roslyn, NY
Crane, Greene & Parente ... Albany, NY
Crane, Hal R. ... Carteret, NJ
Crane, Howard C. ... Marina Del Rey, CA
Crane, Howard D. ... Belle Mead, NJ
Crane, Howard R. ... Rochester, NY
Crane, Hyla Flaks ... Woodbridge, CT
Crane, J. Douglas ... Morgantown, WV
Crane, J. Randall ... Mobile, AL
Crane, James B., II ... Albany, NY
Crane, James Franklin ... Tucson, AZ
Crane, James L., Jr. ... Tucson, AZ
Crane, James M. ... Providence, RI
Crane, James Nelson ... Macon, GA
Crane, James S. ... Naples, FL
Crane, James S. ... Portland, OR
Crane, Jeff ... Houston, TX
Crane, Jeffrey E. ... Chicago, IL
Crane, Jennifer M. ... Atlanta, GA
Crane, Joanna P. ... Federal Trade Commission, Bureau of Consumer Protection, GV
Crane, John A. ... Austin, TX
Crane, John D. ... Richardson, TX
Crane, John F. ... Roseland, NJ
Crane, John Murdoch ... Hopkins, MN
Crane, Jonathan B. ... Los Angeles, CA
Crane, Jonathan O. ... Cleveland, OH
Crane, Jonathan R., (P.C.) ... Rochester, MI
Crane, Joseph Patrick ... Philadelphia, PA
Crane, J. T. Stephen ... Detroit, MI
Crane, Karen S. ... Chicago, IL
Crane, Kathianne Knaup ... St. Louis, MO
Crane, Kathleen D. ... Torrance, CA
Crane, Kenneth M. ... Chicago, IL
Crane, Kit C. Dean ... New Castle, IN
Crane, Kyle L. ... Cleveland, OH
Crane, L. Farrell, Jr. ... Houston, TX
Crane, Larry E., Jr. ... Little Rock, AR
Crane Law Firm ... Phoenix, AZ
Crane Law Office ... Mott, ND
Crane, Leake, Casey, Ehlers & Eggleston, A Professional Corporation ... Durango, CO
Crane, Leslie E. ... Boston, MA
Crane, Leslie P., Jr. ... Minneapolis, MN
Crane, Lili Best ... Madison, WI
Crane, Linda R. ... Chicago, IL
Crane, Louis A., P.C. ... Troy, MI
Crane, Manley C. ... Liverpool, NY
Crane, Mark ... Farmington Hills, MI
Crane, Mark, (P.C.) ... Chicago, IL
Crane, Martin J. ... Washington, DC
Crane, Maureen M. ... Detroit, MI
Crane, Melanie S. ... Lake Charles, LA
Crane, Melissa A. ... New York, NY
Crane, Michael A. ... Quincy, CA
Crane, Michael A. ... Wheeling, IL
Crane, Michael C. ... Los Angeles, CA
Crane, Michael E. ... Naples, FL
Milwaukee, WI
Crane, Michael E. ... Chicago, IL
Crane, Michael J. ... New York, NY
Crane, Michael L. ... Victoria, TX
Crane, Michael R. ... Charleston, WV
Crane, Michael S. ... Columbus, OH
Crane, Mitchell G. ... West Chester, PA
Crane, Monte E. ... Arlington, VA
Crane, Nancy J. ... Minneapolis, MN
Crane, Neil R. ... Hamden, CT
Crane, Newton D. ... Bloomfield, CT
Crane, Nicholas A. ... Miami, FL
Crane and Norcross ... Chicago, IL
Crane, Pamela J. ... Phoenix, AZ
Crane, Paul M. ... Phoenix, AZ
Crane, Paul N. ... Los Angeles, CA
Crane, Paula L. ... Montclair, NJ
Crane, Paula T. ... Silverdale, WA
Crane, Peter G.
Nuclear Regulatory Commission, Office of the General Counsel, GV
Crane, Peter R. ... San Francisco, CA
Crane, Philip A., Jr. ... San Diego, CA
Crane, Phillip Mark ... Chicago, IL
Crane, Phyllis A. ... East Rockaway, NY
Crane, R. A. ... Columbus, OH
Crane, Randall, Law Offices of
Oakland, CA
Crane, Randall, Law Offices of
San Francisco, CA
Crane, Randall P. ... San Benito, TX
Crane, Randy ... McAllen, TX
Crane, Richard A. ... Northbrook, IL
Crane, Richard G. ... Nashville, TN
Crane, Richard M. ... Denver, CO
Crane, Richard P., Jr. ... Los Angeles, CA
Crane & Richards ... Santa Barbara, CA
Crane, Robert C. ... Oakland, CA
Crane, Robert E. ... Durango, CO
Crane, Robert G. ... Knoxville, TN
Crane, Robert J. ... Wausau, WI
Crane, Robert L. ... West Palm Beach, FL
Crane, Robert L., Jr. ... Hudson, OH
Crane, Robert M. ... Anderson, IN
Crane, Robert Max ... Newark, NJ
New York, NY
Crane, Robert P. ... Cleveland, OH
Crane, Robert R. ... Rochester, NY
Crane, Robyn L. ... Akron, OH
Crane, Roderick B. ... Englewood, CO
Crane, Roderick J. ... Mayfield, OH
Crane, Ronald L. ... New York, NY
Crane, Sanford L. ... Burlington, MA
Crane, Sara W. ... Department of Commerce, Patent and Trademark Office, GV
Crane, Shannon Marie ... Santa Barbara, CA
Crane, Sharon E. ... Washington, DC
Crane, Shelly D. ... Clarksburg, WV
Crane, Stephen A. ... Tampa, FL
Crane, Stephen A. ... West Bloomfield, MI
Crane, Stephen C. ... Garland, TX
Crane, Stephen G. ... New York, NY
Crane, Stephen J. ... Seattle, WA
Crane, Stephen M. ... Bakersfield, CA
Crane, Stephen T., II ... Marietta, GA
Crane, Steve R. ... Magnolia, AR
Crane, Steven L. ... Lancaster, CA
Crane, Steven M. ... Los Angeles, CA
Crane, Sue M. ... Fulton, MO
Crane, Susan J. ... Sudbury, MA
Crane, Susan L. Loring ... New York, NY
Crane, Thomas C. ... Buffalo, NY
Crane, Thomas F. ... Rock Island, IL
Crane, Thomas J. ... Costa Mesa, CA
Crane, Thomas J. ... Naples, FL
Crane, Thomas J. ... Alexandria, LA
San Antonio, TX
Crane, Thomas S. ... Boston, MA
Crane, Warren H. ... Lawton, OK
Crane, William A. ... Saginaw, MI
Crane, William E. ... Oshkosh, WI
Crane, William G. ... Boston, MA
Crane, William Grace ... Poughkeepsie, NY
Crane-Oliver, Evelyn T. ... Menlo Park, CA
Craner, A. James ... Orlando, FL
Craner, Andrew ... Reno, NV
Craner, John A. ... Scotch Plains, NJ
Craner, Matthew L. ... New York, NY
Craner, Mitchel B. ... New York, NY
Craner, Nelson, Satkin & Scheer, P.A.
Scotch Plains, NJ
Cranert, Terrence L. ... Pasadena, CA
Craney, Jane S. ... Martinsville, IN
Cranfill, Paul L. ... Raleigh, NC
Cranfill, Steven R. ... Cody, WY
Cranfill, Sumner & Hartzog, L.L.P.
Charlotte, NC
Raleigh, NC
Cranfill, W. T., Jr. ... Charlotte, NC
Cranford, Bryant K. ... Little Rock, AR
Cranford, Charles H. ... Charlotte, NC
Cranford, Charles L. ... Jacksonville, FL
Cranford, Dwight L. ... Halifax, NC
Cranford, Elizabeth R. ... Salem, MA
Cranford, Evelyn L. ... Orlando, FL
Cranford, J. Mark ... Stoneham, MA
Cranford, James B., Jr. ... Texarkana, TX
Cranford, James M. ... Macon, GA
Cranford, John Herbert ... Newnan, GA
Cranford, Lee Evans ... Nashville, TN
Cranford, Page D. ... Norfolk, VA
Cranford, Randy L. ... Thomasville, NC
Cranford, Schultze and Tomchin, P.A.
Charlotte, NC
Cranford, Scott M. ... Littleton, NC
Cranford, Steven L. ... St. Louis, MO
Cranford, Todd L.
Securities and Exchange Commission, Division of Enforcement, GV
Cranford, Victoria M. ... Shreveport, LA
Crangle, John Vernon ... Columbia, SC
Crangle, Joseph F. ... Buffalo, NY
Crangle, Mary L. ... Cherry Hill, NJ
Northfield, NJ
Crangle, Robert D. ... Lincoln, KS
Crangle, William J., Jr. ... Fonda, NY
Cranham, Bruce ... Sault Ste. Marie, MI
Crank, Christopher M. ... Kansas City, MO
Crank, Robert H. ... Walnut Ridge, AR
Cranley, Grace Winkler ... Chicago, IL
Cranley, John P. ... Irving, TX
Cranley, Paul D. ... Chicago, IL
Cranman, Kevin A. ... Atlanta, GA
Cranmer, Douglas C. ... Wichita, KS
Cranmer, John D. ... Haddonfield, NJ
Cranmer, Kathy Eaton ... Denver, CO
Cranmer, Mary L. ... Grand Rapids, MI
Cranmer, Michael R. ... Denver, CO
Cranmer, R. Bruce ... Coral Springs, FL
Cranmer, R. Bruce, P.A. ... Coral Springs, FL
Cranmer, Rex W. ... Redlands, CA
Cranmer, Sheridan M. ... Woodland Hills, CA
Cranmer, Thomas W.
Bloomfield Hills, MI
Cranmer, Wesley E.
Saint Simons Island, GA
Cranmore, FitzGerald & Meaney
Hartford, CT
Cranmore, Floyd W. ... Beverly Hills, CA
Cranmore, J. J. ... Hartford, CT
Cranna, Kenneth G. ... Philmont, NY
Cranna, William F. ... Hudson, NY
Crannage, Sonia B. ... Carmel, NY
Cranner, Bruce Arne ... New Orleans, LA
Cranney, Marilyn Kanrek ... New York, NY
Cranny, Scott P. ... San Diego, CA
Crano, Marie A. ... Lake Wales, FL
Cranor, Nancy C. ... Lake Charles, LA
Cranshaw, Bradford William ... Columbia, SC
Cranshaw, David W. ... Atlanta, GA
Cranshaw & Lunsford
Daytona Beach, FL
Ormond Beach, FL
Cranshaw, T. Jay ... Tucson, AZ
Cranshaw, Todd M. ... Ormond Beach, FL
Cranston, Beth K. ... Santa Monica, CA
Cranston, Charles K. ... Kenai, AK
Cranston & Cranston, P.C. ... Barre, MA
Cranston, David E. ... Los Angeles, CA
Cranston, Earl M. ... Billings, MT
Cranston, Francis J. ... Barre, MA
Cranston, H. Stephen ... San Marino, CA
Cranston, Mary B. ... San Francisco, CA
Cranston, Michael C. ... Baltimore, MD
Cranston, Paul M. ... Barre, MA
Cranston, Paul R. ... Morgantown, WV
Cranston, Sylvia M. ... Santa Ana, CA
Cranston, Theodore J. ... San Diego, CA
Cranston, Thomas K. ... Canton, OH
Cranton, Timothy W. ... Redmond, WA
Cranwell, C. Richard ... Vinton, VA
Cranwell, George E. ... Arlington, VA
Cranwell, Moore & Bullington
Roanoke, VA
Vinton, VA
Cranwell & O'Connell ... Arlington, VA
Cranwell, Thomas G. ... Alexandria, VA
Crapenhoft, Michael L. ... Los Angeles, CA
Crapis, Jerry G. ... Bloomfield, NJ
Crapo, David J. ... Salt Lake City, UT
Crapo, David N. ... Newark, NJ
Crapo, Michael D. ... Idaho Falls, ID
Crapple, George E. ... New York, NY
Crapps, Thomas ... Tallahassee, FL
Crapse, Kathleen M. ... Reidsville, NC
Crapsi, Paul ... Buffalo, NY
Crapster, Gary C., (P.C.) ... Dallas, TX
Crary, Bruce A. ... Sioux City, IA
Crary, Bruce P. ... Ventura, CA
Crary, Buchanan, Bowdish, Bovie, Roby, Beres, Negron & Thomas, Chartered
Fort Pierce, FL
Port St. Lucie, FL
Stuart, FL
Crary, Byron R. ... Clarklake, MI
Crary, Calvert D. ... Waccabuc, NY
Crary Clark Domanico, P.S. ... Spokane, WA
Crary, David R. ... Sioux City, IA
Crary, Donna L. ... Laurel, MD
Crary, Donna L., P.A. ... Laurel, MD
Takoma Park, MD
Crary, E. Avery ... Irvine, CA
Crary, Evans, Jr. ... Stuart, FL
Crary, Gordon B. ... Irvine, CA
Crary, Huff, Inkster, Hecht & Sheehan
South Sioux City, NE
Sioux City, IA
Dakota Dunes, SD
Crary, Lawrence Evans, III ... Stuart, FL
Crary, Lowell J. ... Gilbert, AZ
Crary, Miner D., Jr. ... New York, NY
Crary, Paul T. ... Fargo, ND
Crary, Peter B. ... Fargo, ND
Crary, Peter G. ... Albany, NY
Crary, R. "Mike" ... Port St. Lucie, FL
Stuart, FL
Crary, Robert B. ... Spokane, WA
Crary, Robert J. ... Sioux City, IA
Crary, Roger V. ... Minneapolis, MN
Crary, Stephen A. ... Seattle, WA
Crary, Thomas S. ... Auburn, CA
Crary, William F. ... Stuart, FL
Crary, William F., II ... Stuart, FL
Crase, Christine M. ... Dallas, TX
Craske, Duane ... Wedderburn, OR
Crass, Charles J. ... Kingston, TN
Crass, Cynthia Johnston ... Salt Lake City, UT
Crass, David A. ... Madison, WI
Crass, Harold L. ... Woodbury, NJ
Crass, Kevin A., (P.A.) ... Little Rock, AR
Crass, Timothy A. ... Miami, FL
Crassweller, James R. ... St. Paul, MN
Crasto, Anthony C ... Kew Gardens, NY
Crastz, Jennifer Witherell ... Encino, CA
Crateau, Margaret Daly ... Salem, MA
Crater, Anne ... Northfield, NJ
Crater, Nancy B. ... Topanga, CA
Crates, James L. ... Kenton, OH
Crates, Randy L. ... Kenton, OH
Cratis, Samuel R. ... Miami Beach, FL
Craton, Curt R. ... Long Beach, CA
Craton, John F. ... Crowley, LA
Cratsenberg, Andrew C., Jr. ... Seattle, WA
Cratsley, John C. ... Boston, MA
Craun, Christopher L. ... Lake City, FL
Craun, Galen G., III ... Winston-Salem, NC
Craun, J. Mark ... San Antonio, TX
Craun, Ned L. ... Canton, MA
Craun, Rhonda ... Indianapolis, IN
Crause, Kenneth W. ... Tecumseh, MI
Crauwels, Patricia D. ... Sarasota, FL
Cravath, B. Jeffrey ... Washington, DC
Cravath, Bernard J. ... Potomac, MD
Cravath, Steven G. ... Washington, DC
Cravath, Swaine & Moore ... New York, NY
Craven, Anthony B. ... Honolulu, HI
Craven, Charles L. ... Yancey, TX
Craven, Charles W. ... Philadelphia, PA
Craven & Craven ... Chicago, IL
Craven, Daniel H. ... Gulf Shores, AL
Craven, Daniel H., P.C., Law Firm of
Bay Minette, AL
Foley, AL
Gulf Shores, AL
Craven, David J. ... Chicago, IL
Craven, David Leigh ... Winston-Salem, NC
Craven, Donald B. ... Washington, DC

Craven, Donald M. .... **Springfield, IL**
Craven, Eric F. .... Austin, TX
Craven, Erica L. .... Washington, DC
Craven, George W. .... **Chicago, IL**
Craven, Harold L. .... Chicago, IL
Craven, J. Jeffrey .... **Washington, DC**
Craven, Jack S. .... Chicago, IL
Craven, James B., III .... **Durham, NC**
Craven, James C. .... **Springfield, IL**
Craven, James O. .... **New Haven, CT**
Craven, James S. .... **Spokane, WA**
Craven, John D. .... Boston, MA
Craven, John J., Jr. .... Boston, MA
Craven, John P. .... **Chicago, IL**
Craven, John P., Jr. .... Portland, OR
Craven, John W. .... Austin, TX
Craven, Joseph Harris .... **Durham, NC**
Craven, Joseph P., III .... Boston, MA
Craven, Judith .... Boston, MA
Craven, Kathryn A. .... Alexandria, VA
Craven, Kett R. .... Columbia, MO
Craven, Lexie L. .... **Atlanta, GA**
Craven, Mary Nell .... **Winston-Salem, NC**
Craven, Michael C. .... Chicago, IL
Craven, Nancy .... **Bend, OR**
Portland, OR
Craven, Pamela F. .... **Murray Hill, NJ**
Craven, R. Daniel .... **Indianapolis, IN**
Craven, Rebecca .... Lewiston, ID
Craven, Rex P. .... Pierre, SD
Craven, Richard C. .... **Aberdeen, NC**
Craven, Richard E. .... Midland, MI
Craven, Richard T. .... **Fayetteville, NC**
Craven, Robert A. .... **Tampa, FL**
Craven, Robert E. .... Providence, RI
Craven, Robert F. .... Indianapolis, IN
Craven, Samuel H. .... Alexandria, LA
Craven, Scott & Randow .... Alexandria, LA
Craven, Stanley E. .... **Kansas City, MO**
Craven, Susan J. .... Des Plaines, IL
Craven, Susan S. .... Saluda, NC
Craven, T. Peter .... Glenwood Springs, CO
Craven, Terry M. .... Boston, MA
Craven, Thomas A. "Tac"
Sacramento, CA
Craven, Thoms .... Winston-Salem, NC
Craven & Thornton, P.C. .... **Springfield, IL**
Craven Vieira & DiGianfilippo
Providence, RI
Craven, William G. .... **Jamestown, TN**
Craven, William J. .... Westerly, RI
Craven-Guischard, Pamela A.
New York, NY
Cravens, Christopher D. .... **Nashville, TN**
Cravens, Claude S. .... Slaton, TX
Cravens & Cravens .... Paris, AR
Cravens, David R. .... Paris, AR
Cravens, Garland W., Jr. .... **Evansville, IN**
Cravens, J. Thompson .... Richmond, VA
Cravens, J. Thompson, & Associates, P.C.
Richmond, VA
Cravens, Jack D. .... West Covina, CA
Cravens, James R., Jr. .... Schaumburg, IL
Cravens, John A. .... **Wausau, WI**
Cravens, Louise Dickson .... Tulsa, OK
Cravens, Richard J. .... Evanston, IL
Cravens, Sheri M. .... **Wichita Falls, TX**
Cravens, William S. D. .... **Boston, MA**
Cravens, Yvonne .... Arcadia, OK
Craver, Adelaide A. .... Shelby, NC
Craver, Barbara R. .... Juneau, AK
Craver, Brian W. .... Washington, DC
Craver, C. Penn, Jr. .... **Winston-Salem, NC**
Craver, Charles B. .... Washington, DC
Craver, Elizabeth Nowlin .... Plainview, TX
Craver, G. Rhodes .... **Durham, NC**
Craver, James B. .... **Columbus, OH**
Craver, James S. .... Centerville, IA
Craver, John P. .... **Denver, CO**
Craver, Michael .... **Lewisville, TX**
Craver, Nolan C., Jr. .... Urbana, IL
Craver, Perry C. .... Fort Lauderdale, FL
Craver, Ty Michael .... **Indianapolis, IN**
Craver, William E., III .... **Charleston, SC**
Cravero, Joseph P. .... Moline, IL
Cravey, Dale W. .... **Tampa, FL**
Cravey, Lynn V. .... **St. Petersburg, FL**
Cravey, Robin Theobald .... Austin, TX
Cravey, Zack D., Jr. .... **Atlanta, GA**
Cravez, Glenn E. .... **Anchorage, AK**
Cravinho, Lynn T. .... **Groton, CT**
Cravins, Donald Ray, Jr.
Baton Rouge, LA
Craw, Frederick G. .... San Francisco, CA
Craw, Marc D. .... Newtonville, NY
Craw, Michael J. .... Greenville, SC
Crawfis, Robert P. .... Huntington Beach, CA
Crawford, A. Kevin .... Albany, NY
Crawford, A. Lindsey
Agency for International Development, Office of the General Counsel, GV
Crawford, Andrea L. .... **New York, NY**
Crawford, Anita C. .... Champaign, IL
Crawford, Anna V. .... Windsor, CT
Crawford, Anne W. .... New York, NY
Crawford, Anthony E. .... Rapid City, SD
Crawford, Anthony J. .... Thousand Oaks, CA
Crawford & Anzelmo .... **Monroe, LA**
Crawford, Arthur R. .... **Arlington, VA**
Crawford, B. Hayden .... **Tulsa, OK**
Crawford, B. Lee, Jr. .... **Diboll, TX**
Crawford, B. Lindsay, III .... **Columbia, SC**
Crawford & Bangs, LLP
City of Industry, CA
Covina, CA
Los Angeles, CA
San Diego, CA
Crawford, Barbara L. .... **Denver, CO**

Crawford, Barrett L. .... Hickory, NC
Crawford, Baxter & James, P.S.C.
Carrollton, KY
Crawford, Benjamin F., III .... Larkspur, CA
Crawford, Beth A. .... Hartford, CT
Crawford, Beth A. .... Northampton, MA
Crawford, Beverly Diane .... Richmond, VA
Crawford, Beverly J. .... Spring Park, MN
Crawford, Billy-Joe Hoot .... Panama City, FL
Crawford, Bonnie Brade .... High Point, NC
Crawford, Brad, Jr. .... Lubbock, TX
Crawford, Bradley C. .... **San Francisco, CA**
Crawford, Brian Douglas .... Volcano, HI
Crawford, Brian E. .... **Monroe, LA**
Crawford, Bridget .... **New York, NY**
Crawford, Bruce C. .... St. Petersburg, FL
Crawford, Bruce D. .... **Tempe, AZ**
Crawford, Bruce N. .... **Chicago, IL**
Crawford, Bruce Nelson
Minneapolis, MN
Crawford, Bryce, III .... Omaha, NE
Crawford, C. Robert .... Midland, TX
Crawford, Callestyne Hall .... Greenwood, MS
Crawford, Carl M., Jr. .... Pittsburgh, PA
Crawford, Carol A. .... Orlando, FL
Crawford, Carol T.
United States International Trade Commission, Office of the Commissioners, GV
Crawford, Cassie N. .... **Vancouver, WA**
Crawford, Charles .... Melbourne, FL
Crawford, Charles .... **Cartersville, GA**
Crawford, Charles D. .... Newport Beach, CA
Crawford, Charles F., Jr. .... Fayetteville, TN
Crawford, Charles Gilbert, IV .... Decatur, AL
Crawford, Charles J. .... **McKinney, TX**
Crawford, Charles J. .... Stevenson, WA
Crawford, Charles R. .... **Memphis, TN**
Crawford, Charles T. .... New York, NY
Crawford, Cheryl Ann .... Department of Justice, Office of Justice Programs, GV
Crawford, Christa Foster
Los Angeles, CA
Crawford, Christine Ann .... Blue Bell, PA
Crawford, Christopher J. .... **New York, NY**
Crawford, Christopher S. .... **Chicago, IL**
Crawford, Clan, Jr. .... **Ann Arbor, MI**
Crawford, Claudia .... **Seattle, WA**
Crawford, Claudia Gayheart
Albuquerque, NM
Crawford, Clay E. .... **Houston, TX**
Crawford, Clay E., P.C. .... **Houston, TX**
Crawford, Colin .... Brooklyn, NY
Crawford, Craig L. .... Gainesville, FL
Crawford & Crawford .... Chattanooga, TN
Crawford, Crawford & Newton
Maryville, TN
Crawford, Crystal D. .... Los Angeles, CA
Crawford, Cynthia .... **Houston, TX**
Crawford, D. Sims .... Birmingham, AL
Crawford, Dale A. .... Columbus, OH
Crawford, Dale L. .... Arcadia, CA
Crawford, Dan J. .... Kennett, MO
Crawford, Daniel A. .... **Burlingame, CA**
Crawford, Daniel J. .... **San Francisco, CA**
Crawford, Daniel L. .... Tulsa, OK
Crawford, Daniel M. .... **San Francisco, CA**
Crawford, David B. .... **Palo Alto, CA**
Crawford, David E. .... **St. Paul, MN**
Crawford, David E., Jr. .... **St. Louis, MO**
Crawford, David H. .... Chicago, IL
Crawford, David H. .... **Charleston, SC**
Crawford, David, III .... **Los Angeles, CA**
Crawford, David L. .... Omaha, NE
Crawford, David L., Jr.
Treasury Department, Internal Revenue Service, GV
Crawford, David Lee .... **Houston, TX**
Crawford, David P. .... San Diego, CA
Crawford, David R. .... Winston-Salem, NC
Crawford, Dawson G. .... **Los Gatos, CA**
Crawford, Debra Kay Smith .... Topeka, KS
Crawford, Debra Vaniman
Beverly Hills, CA
Crawford, Denise Voigt .... Austin, TX
Crawford, Dennis J. .... Haddonfield, NJ
Crawford, Dennis M. .... Neptune, NJ
Crawford, Dennis P. .... Lincoln, NE
Crawford, Derek G. .... Hamlet, NC
Crawford, Dewey B. .... **Chicago, IL**
Crawford & Diamond .... Radnor, PA
Crawford, Don D. .... Victoria, TX
Crawford, Donald J. .... **Rockville, MD**
Crawford, Donald M. .... Tampa, FL
Crawford, Donald M.
Bloomfield Hills, MI
Crawford, Donna Negus .... **Carrollton, GA**
Crawford, Douglas C. .... Las Vegas, NV
Crawford, Duncan V. .... **Maryville, TN**
Crawford, Durwood D. .... **Dallas, TX**
Crawford, Edward H. .... West Branch, MI
Crawford, Edward J. .... Uniondale, NY
Crawford, Edwin L. .... Albany, NY
Crawford, Francis N. .... Morgan Hill, CA
Crawford, Frank P. .... Terre Haute, IN
Crawford, Franklin J. .... United States Senate, Senatorial Assistants, GV
Crawford, Fred D., IV .... Montebello, CA
Crawford, Frederick A. .... **Columbia, SC**
Crawford, Fronefield, Jr.
West Chester, PA
Crawford, G. Ian .... Canton, OH
Crawford, G. Irene .... Flagstaff, AZ
Crawford, Gary B. .... Minneapolis, MN
Crawford, Gary L. .... **Gaithersburg, MD**
Crawford, Geoffrey W. .... **Burlington, VT**
Crawford, George F. .... **Overland Park, KS**
Crawford, George H. .... Medford, MA

Crawford, George V., III .... **Nashville, TN**
Crawford, George V., Jr. .... **Nashville, TN**
Crawford, George W., II .... Philadelphia, PA
Crawford, Gerald M. .... Racine, WI
Crawford, Gerald W. .... Des Moines, IA
Crawford, Gloria J.
Federal Labor Relations Authority, Authority Member Staff, GV
Crawford, Gordon R. .... Baton Rouge, LA
Gonzales, LA
Crawford, Gregory J.
Oklahoma City, OK
Crawford, Gregory N. .... **Savannah, GA**
Crawford, H. Frank .... **Tacoma, WA**
Crawford and Halligan .... Tenafly, NJ
Crawford, Harvey J. .... Floydada, TX
Crawford, Hilary H., Jr. .... San Francisco, CA
Crawford, Hinesley & Jennings
Savannah, GA
Crawford, Howard A. .... **Kansas City, MO**
Crawford, Ian .... **Boston, MA**
Crawford, Ian R. .... **Darien, CT**
New York, NY
Crawford, Ivan W. .... Flint, MI
Crawford, J. Andrew .... **Newark, OH**
Crawford, J. Craig .... Washington, DC
Crawford, J. Hamilton, Jr. .... New York, NY
Crawford, J. Nick .... **Boise, ID**
Crawford, J. Richard .... Shawnee, KS
Kansas City, MO
Crawford, J. Stephen .... **Bonita Springs, FL**
Crawford, J. Stephen, Chartered
Bonita Springs, FL
Crawford, Jac A. .... San Luis Obispo, CA
Crawford & Jackson .... Martinsburg, WV
Charles Town, WV
Crawford, James A. .... Tenafly, NJ
Crawford, James Alvin, II .... Wichita, KS
Crawford, James B. .... Department of Labor, Office of the Solicitor, GV
Crawford, James B., III
Charles Town, WV
Martinsburg, WV
Crawford, James C. (Clay) .... **Houston, TX**
Crawford, James D. .... **Philadelphia, PA**
Crawford, James E. .... **Elkhart, IN**
Crawford, James E., Jr. .... Catonsville, MD
Crawford, James E., Jr., P.A.
Catonsville, MD
Crawford, James F. .... Collingswood, NJ
Crawford, James H. .... Cleveland, OH
Crawford, James L. .... Terre Haute, IN
Crawford, James L. .... Harrisburg, PA
Crawford, James M. .... De Funiak Springs, FL
Crawford, James M. .... Atlanta, GA
Crawford, James M. .... Carrollton, KY
Crawford, James M., Jr. .... **Davis, CA**
Crawford, James P. .... Juneau, AK
Crawford, James R. .... **New York, NY**
Crawford, James S. .... Sacramento, CA
Crawford, James T., Jr. .... **Indianapolis, IN**
Crawford, James W. .... Mars, PA
Crawford, Jane A. .... Painted Post, NY
Crawford, Janice K. .... **Phoenix, AZ**
Crawford, Jason C. .... Durango, CO
Crawford, Jason L. .... **Atlanta, GA**
Columbus, GA
Crawford, Jeffrey A. .... Minneapolis, MN
Crawford, Jeffrey C. .... **New York, NY**
Crawford, Jennifer M.
Bloomfield Hills, MI
Crawford, John A. .... **Jackson, MS**
Crawford, John A., Jr. .... **San Diego, CA**
Crawford, John A., Jr. .... **Jackson, MS**
Crawford, John Allen .... Olympia, WA
Crawford, John D. .... Chicago, IL
Crawford, John D. .... Dallas, TX
Crawford, John D., A Professional Corporation
Dallas, TX
Crawford, John E. .... Inglewood, CA
Crawford, John G., Jr. .... **Portland, OR**
Crawford, John H., Jr. .... Southampton, MA
Crawford, John L. .... Houston, TX
Crawford, John M. .... Tacoma, WA
Crawford, John R. .... **Jacksonville, FL**
Crawford, John R. .... **Minneapolis, MN**
Crawford, John W. .... Fallbrook, CA
Crawford, Jonathan H. .... Braintree, MA
Crawford, Jonathan K.M.
Philadelphia, PA
Crawford, Joseph C. .... **Philadelphia, PA**
Crawford, Joseph L. .... Emeryville, CA
Crawford, Joseph P. .... **San Mateo, CA**
Crawford, Joseph V. .... **Austin, TX**
Crawford, Julé A. .... Middletown, CT
Crawford, Karen Aldridge .... **Columbia, SC**
Crawford, Karen J. .... Cambridge, MA
Crawford, Karen Shichman
Pittsburgh, PA
Crawford, Katherine B. .... Boise, ID
Crawford and Keith .... Newport Beach, CA
Crawford, Kelly M. .... **Dallas, TX**
Crawford, Kelly Strange .... **Morristown, NJ**
Crawford, Kenneth B. .... **Carrollton, GA**
Crawford, Kenneth E., Jr. .... Mount Olive, MS
Crawford, Kenneth L. .... Columbia, MD
Crawford, Kevin .... Salem, OR
Crawford, Kevin B. .... **Houston, TX**
Crawford, Kim .... **Nashville, TN**
Crawford & Kline, P.L.C. .... **Phoenix, AZ**
Tempe, AZ
Crawford, Lance D. .... Jacksonville, FL
Crawford, Laura L. .... Everett, WA
Crawford Law Firm .... Des Moines, IA
Crawford Law Offices .... **Corbin, KY**
Crawford, Leland .... Santa Barbara, CA

Crawford, Leslie R.
Federal Deposit Insurance Corporation, Resolutions Section, GV
Crawford & Lewis, A Professional Law Corporation .... **Baton Rouge, LA**
Lafayette, LA
New Orleans, LA
Austin, TX
Crawford, Lewis Charles .... Louisville, KY
Crawford, Linda, & Associates
Hallowell, ME
New York, NY
Crawford, Linda S. .... Columbus, OH
Crawford, Linda Sibery .... Hallowell, ME
New York, NY
Crawford, Linton K. .... Cornelia, GA
Crawford, Lisa L. .... **Dallas, TX**
Crawford, Lloyd V. .... Memphis, TN
Crawford, Lonnie E. .... Huntsville, TX
Crawford, Lonnie L., Jr. .... Philadelphia, PA
Crawford, Malcolm D., (P.C.) .... Denver, CO
Crawford, Malcolm G. .... Lexington, VA
Crawford, Marie M. .... Eagan, MN
Crawford, Mark A. .... **Atlanta, GA**
Crawford, Mark D. .... **Washington, DC**
Crawford, Mark G. .... **Newport Beach, CA**
San Francisco, CA
Crawford, Marshall R. .... Lafayette, IN
Crawford, Martelia T. .... Cookeville, TN
Crawford, Martha .... Washington, DC
Crawford, Mary Hazel .... Oak Park, IL
Crawford, Mary R. .... Phoenix, AZ
Crawford, McGilliard, Peterson, Yelish and Dixon .... Port Orchard, WA
Crawford & McKinney .... **Houston, TX**
Crawford, Melissa .... Chicago, IL
Crawford, Melton L. .... **Seattle, WA**
Crawford, Michael A. .... **Baton Rouge, LA**
Crawford, Michael E. .... **Arlington, VA**
Crawford, Michael H.
Hot Springs National Park, AR
Crawford, Michael H. .... Clarkesville, GA
Crawford, Michael J. .... Tucson, AZ
Crawford, Michael K. .... Houston, TX
Crawford, Michael S. .... New York, NY
Crawford, Michael T. .... **Tyler, TX**
Crawford, Michon L. .... **Philadelphia, PA**
Crawford, Mitchell .... Nashville, TN
Crawford, Muriel E.
Department of Commerce, Patent and Trademark Office, GV
Crawford, Nancy King .... Nashville, TN
Crawford, Nancy L. .... **Omaha, NE**
Crawford, Nanette J. .... Denver, CO
Crawford, Nick .... Greenville, MS
Crawford & Olesen, L.L.P.
Beaumont, TX
Crawford, Pamela D. .... Milwaukee, WI
Crawford, Pamela Denise
Department Of Health And Human Services, Social Security Administration, GV
Crawford, Patricia A. .... Naples, FL
Crawford, Paul E. .... **Wilmington, DE**
Crawford, Paul G. .... Marshalltown, IA
Crawford, Paul S. .... Montgomery, AL
Crawford, Paul V. .... Greenbelt, MD
Crawford, Peter D., Jr. .... **Blue Bell, PA**
Crawford, Phil N. .... Lakeport, CA
Crawford, Philip John .... Los Gatos, CA
Crawford, Philip W. .... **Newark, NJ**
Crawford, Phillip W., Jr. .... New York, NY
Crawford, PLLC .... Minneapolis, MN
Crawford, Quincy M., III .... **Baltimore, MD**
Crawford, Randall D. .... Kansas City, MO
Crawford, Rebecca Bellows
Baton Rouge, LA
Crawford, Reid W. .... Ames, IA
Crawford & Reimann LLP
Los Angeles, CA
Crawford, Renee Billings .... **Raleigh, NC**
Crawford, Richard Barry .... Horsham, PA
Crawford, Richard H. .... Memphis, TN
Crawford, Richard L. .... **Baton Rouge, LA**
Crawford, Robert A. .... Waterford, MI
Crawford, Robert A. .... Jackson, MS
Crawford, Robert A. .... **Knoxville, TN**
Crawford, Robert C. .... Whitefish Bay, WI
Crawford, Robert E., Jr. .... **Dallas, TX**
Crawford, Robert F. .... **Phoenix, AZ**
Crawford, Robert F. .... **Scottsdale, AZ**
Crawford, Robert H. .... Chattanooga, TN
Crawford, Robert H., Jr. .... Chattanooga, TN
Crawford, Robert J. .... **Portland, ME**
Crawford, Robert J. .... Minneapolis, MN
Crawford, Robert K. .... San Mateo, CA
Crawford, Robert L. .... Danbury, CT
Crawford, Robert L. .... **Memphis, TN**
Crawford, Robert Lee .... Memphis, TN
Crawford, Robert Mallery .... Zebulon, GA
Crawford, Robert Michael .... Springfield, TN
Crawford, Robert S., Jr. .... Uvalde, TX
Crawford, Robert W.
Fort Lauderdale, FL
Crawford, Robert W. .... Cincinnati, OH
Crawford, Robert W., P.A.
Fort Lauderdale, FL
Crawford, Robin V. .... Fairfax, VA
Crawford, Roger Clint .... White Plains, NY
Crawford, Roger K. .... **Riverside, CA**
Crawford, Rollin H. .... **South St. Paul, MN**
Crawford, Ronald C. .... Savannah, GA
Crawford, Ronald K. .... San Luis Obispo, CA
Crawford, Rosemary C. .... **Pittsburgh, PA**
Crawford, Roxane .... Milwaukee, WI
Crawford, Roy D. .... Maryville, TN
Crawford, Roy E., III .... **San Francisco, CA**
Crawford, Roy J. .... **Birmingham, AL**
Crawford, Ruby M. .... Atlanta, GA

Crego, John W. .... Utica, NY
Crego, Phillip W. .... Jonesboro, AR
Crego, Robert O. .... Belleville, IL
Crego, Sue Anne .... Fairfield, CT
Cregor, Douglas E. .... Indianapolis, IN
Cregor, John M., Jr. .... Honolulu, HI
Crehan, Joseph E., P.C. .... Naples, FL
Crehan, Joseph E., P.C. .... Naples, FL
Crehan, Matthew J. .... Hamilton, OH
Crehan, Patrick J. .... Ridgefield, CT
Crehan, Thomas M. .... Santa Maria, CA
Crehore, Charles A. .... Wickliffe, OH
Crehore, Charles M. H. .... Paradise Valley, AZ
Creidy, Henry .... New York, NY
Creigh, David Edward .... Avalon, CA
Creigh, James C. .... Palo Alto, CA
Creighton, Allen F. .... Columbia, SC
Creighton, Andrew J. .... Denver, CO
Creighton, Andrew J. .... Indian Head Park, IL
Creighton, Ann K. .... Dallas, TX
Creighton, Brent B. .... Lakeland, FL
Creighton, C. Brandon .... Conroe, TX
Creighton, Carl V. .... Livonia, MI
Creighton, Catherine .... Buffalo, NY
Creighton, Chas. W., Jr. .... Salem, OR
Creighton, Darryl B. .... Tampa, FL
Creighton, G. Mark .... Conroe, TX
Creighton, Geoffrey M. .... Foster City, CA
Creighton, Gerald J., Jr. .... Conroe, TX
Creighton, J. Kenneth .... Reno, NV
Creighton, James B., Law Offices of
San Mateo, CA
Creighton, James F. .... White Plains, NY
Creighton, John, III .... Austin, TX
Beaumont, TX
Creighton, John N. .... Oakland, CA
Creighton, John R. .... Arlington, TX
Creighton, Joseph R. .... Melbourne, FL
Creighton, Lisa C. .... Kansas City, MO
Creighton & Lott, P.A. .... Lakeland, FL
Creighton, Mark G. .... Fort Worth, TX
Mineral Wells, TX
Creighton, Michael J. .... Pittsburgh, PA
Creighton, Michael T. .... Claremont, CA
Creighton, Myra K. .... Atlanta, GA
Creighton, Oris .... Covington, LA
Creighton, Patricia A. .... San Jose, CA
Creighton & Pullis, LLP .... Conroe, TX
Creighton, Richard L., Jr. .... Cincinnati, OH
Creighton, Robert A. .... Atwood, KS
Creighton, Robert C. .... Uniondale, NY
Creighton, Roberta J. .... Lakeland, FL
Creighton, Sandra A. .... Fairfield, NJ
Creighton, Sandy .... Mountain View, CA
Creighton, Susan A. .... Palo Alto, CA
Creighton, Thomas D. .... Minneapolis, MN
Creighton, Thomas E. .... Denver, CO
Flagler, CO
Creighton, Tom .... Mineral Wells, TX
Creighton, Virginia Morton .... Denver, CO
Creighton, William S. .... Youngstown, OH
Creim, Jerry A. .... Seattle, WA
Creim, Macias & Koenig LLP
Los Angeles, CA
Creim, Marjorie R. .... Pasadena, CA
Creim, William B. .... Los Angeles, CA
Creitz, Daniel D. .... Erie, KS
Creitz, Joseph Andrew .... San Francisco, CA
Crelin, Barry W. .... Edison, NJ
Crelin, R. Bruce .... Newark, NJ
Crell, Marvin S. .... Fort Wayne, IN
Crell, Steven M. .... Indianapolis, IN
Crellin, Jack L. .... Salt Lake City, UT
Crellin, Rose M.
Federal Communications Commission,
Wireless Telecommunications Bureau, GV
Crellin, Terry M. .... LaVerkin, UT
Cremaldi, Russel J. .... Franklin, LA
Creme, Matthew J., Jr. .... Lancaster, PA
Creme, Paul D. .... Nashua, NH
Cremeans, Kay E. .... Columbus, OH
Cremeens, Charlene A., P.C. .... Belleville, IL
St. Louis, MO
Cremeens-Strong, Sally L. .... Cincinnati, OH
Cremen, Frank J. .... Las Vegas, NV
Cremens, J. Elizabeth .... Boston, MA
Cremens, John F. .... Cambridge, MA
Crement, Anthony J. .... Chicago, IL
Cremer, Allen .... New York, NY
Cremer, Charles F., Jr. .... Indianapolis, IN
Cremer, Frank N., Jr. .... Midland, TX
Cremer, James M. .... Aberdeen, SD
Cremer, John A. .... Indianapolis, IN
Cremer, Karen E. .... Pierre, SD
Cremer, Kathy L. .... Miami, FL
Cremer, Kopon, Shaughnessy & Spina
Chicago, IL
Wheaton, IL
Cremer Miller & Burroughs
Indianapolis, IN
Cremer, Paul L. .... Pierre, SD
Cremer, Richard A. .... Roseburg, OR
Cremer, Susan M. .... Atlanta, GA
Cremer, William J. .... Chicago, IL
Cremerius, Edward P. .... Palatine, IL
Cremerius, Kathryn M. .... Palatine, IL
Cremieux, Richard J. .... Chicago, IL
Cremin, J. Patrick .... Tulsa, OK
Cremin, Richard T. .... Stuart, FL
Cremin, Susan E. .... Chicago, IL
Cremin, Timothy D. .... San Francisco, CA
Cremins & Associates, P.C.
Alexandria, VA
Arlington, VA
Fairfax, VA
Cremins, James S. .... Richmond, VA
Cremins, Jennifer Eileen .... Fairfax, VA
Cremins, William C. .... Knoxville, TN
Cremins, William D. .... Fairfax, VA
Cremins, William T. .... Naugatuck, CT
Cremo, Roger .... Anchorage, AK
Cremons, David M. .... Minneapolis, MN
Creney, John C. .... Yarmouth Port, MA
Creney, John C., P.C.
Yarmouth Port, MA
Crenna, Lloyd R. .... San Francisco, CA
Crennen, Christopher L. .... Denver, CO
Crenney, Lynne Nordenberg .... Pittsburgh, PA
Crenney O'Keefe P.C. .... Pittsburgh, PA
Crenney, Thomas E. .... Pittsburgh, PA
Crenshaw, Ander .... Jacksonville, FL
Crenshaw, André G. .... Miami, FL
Crenshaw, Ann Kiley .... Front Royal, VA
Winchester, VA
Crenshaw, Augustus P., III
Chevy Chase, MD
Crenshaw, Braxton .... Lexington, KY
Crenshaw, Charles E. .... Austin, TX
Crenshaw, Craig M., Jr. .... Arlington, VA
Crenshaw, D. Kerry .... Detroit, MI
Crenshaw, Dal M. .... Meridian, MS
Crenshaw, David A. .... Kenilworth, NJ
Crenshaw, Dupree & Milam, L.L.P.
Brownfield, TX
Crosbyton, TX
Floydada, TX
Levelland, TX
Littlefield, TX
Lubbock, TX
Plainview, TX
Post, TX
Tahoka, TX
Crenshaw, Francis N. .... Norfolk, VA
Crenshaw, Hal D. .... Memphis, TN
Crenshaw, Henry T., Jr. .... Dallas, TX
Crenshaw, J. Timothy .... Brentwood, TN
Crenshaw, James B. .... Jefferson City, MO
Crenshaw, Jeanne Dawes .... Gainesville, FL
Crenshaw, John L. .... North Chicago, IL
Crenshaw, John R. .... Atlanta, GA
Crenshaw, Julia T. .... Hopkinsville, KY
Crenshaw, K. Suzanne .... Nashville, TN
Crenshaw, Kenneth B. .... Palm Springs, FL
Crenshaw, Kenneth B., P.A.
Palm Springs, FL
Crenshaw, Kyle L. .... Newport Beach, CA
Crenshaw, Louis U. G. .... Okemos, MI
Crenshaw, Margaret P.
Postal Rate Commission,
Office of the Secretary, GV
Crenshaw, Marva L. .... Tampa, FL
Crenshaw, Mayron R. .... Chicago, IL
Crenshaw, McCarthy .... Orange Park, FL
Crenshaw, McCarthy, Jr.
Green Cove Springs, FL
Crenshaw, Paul M. .... Fayetteville, NC
Crenshaw, Phillip T. .... Lake Worth, FL
Crenshaw, Richard N. .... Phoenix, AZ
Crenshaw, Todd Lyndell .... Eudora, KS
Crenshaw, Ware and Martin, P.L.C.
Norfolk, VA
Portsmouth, VA
Virginia Beach, VA
Crenshaw, Waverly D., Jr. .... Nashville, TN
Crenshaw, William C. .... Washington, DC
Crenshaw, Zena D. .... Gary, IN
Crepeau, Dewey L. .... Columbia, MO
Crepeau, Victor F. .... Kremmling, CO
Crepps, Janet L. .... New York, NY
Creppy, Michael J. .... Department of Justice,
Executive Office for Immigration Review,
GV
Creps, Clay D. .... Portland, OR
Creque, Arthur J. .... Perry, GA
Crerend, William C. .... New York, NY
Cresap, Joan Marshall .... Rye, NY
Cresap, Paul H. .... Sidney, MT
Cresap, Todd L. .... Minot, ND
Cresap, Wayne G. .... Chalmette, LA
Crescenzo, Alphonse T. .... Glen Rock, NJ
Crescenzo, Ronald E.
West Palm Beach, FL
Cresci, Carl .... New York, NY
Cresci, Peter J. .... Scotch Plains, NJ
New York, NY
Cresenzo, J. Randolph .... Eden, NC
Cresham, John C. .... McLean, VA
Cresitello, Mark C. .... New York, NY
Cresitello, Michael V., Jr.
Saddle Brook, NJ
Creskoff & Doram LLP .... Pasadena, CA
Washington, DC
Creskoff, Howard J. .... Philadelphia, PA
Creskoff, Stephen M. .... Washington, DC
Creson, John L. .... Atlanta, GA
Creson, John L. .... Augusta, GA
Creson, John L. .... Aiken, SC
Creson, Larry B., Jr. .... Memphis, TN
Creson, Marie G. .... Seattle, WA
Crespi, Michael .... Dothan, AL
Crespi, Racquel .... New York, NY
Crespi, Robert H. .... Westfield, NJ
Crespi, Ted .... Fort Lauderdale, FL
Crespi, Ted, P.A. .... Fort Lauderdale, FL
Crespin, Alan J. .... Denver, CO
Crespin, Kerns and Furman, L.L.C.
Fort Morgan, CO
Crespin, Margo .... New York, NY
Crespin, Stuart P. .... Fort Morgan, CO
Crespo, Diana .... New York, NY
Crespo, Elvin J. .... Hackensack, NJ
Crespo, Emmanuel .... Wayland, MA
Crespo, John C. .... Washington, DC
Crespo, John P. .... Houston, TX
Crespo, Manuel A. .... Nashville, TN
Crespo, Manuel L. .... Miami, FL
Crespo, Rafael .... San Mateo, CA
Crespo-Kortright, Nicolas .... San Juan, PR
Crespy, Gregory Paul .... Cleveland, OH
Cress, Daniel P. .... Soquel, CA
Cress, James F. .... Denver, CO
Cress, Joseph Michael .... Sacramento, CA
Cress, Kathleen O. .... Sarasota, FL
Cress, Lloyd R. .... Covington, KY
Lexington, KY
Louisville, KY
Cress, Lloyd R., Jr. .... Frankfort, KY
Lexington, KY
Cress, Mark D. .... Springfield, MA
Cress, Sheila .... San Jose, CA
Cress, Walter L. .... El Centro, CA
Cressend, Joy G. .... Harvey, LA
Cressey, Albert E., III
Rancho Santa Fe, CA
Cressey, Anne H. .... Portland, ME
Cressey, Bryan C. .... Chicago, IL
Cressey, Michael F. .... San Diego, CA
Cressey-Yates, Amy K. .... San Diego, CA
Cressler, Douglas E. .... Indianapolis, IN
Cressler, Michael A. .... Moscow, ID
Cressler, William J. .... Harrisburg, PA
Cressman, Mark P. .... West Palm Beach, FL
Cressman, Paul R., Jr. .... Seattle, WA
Cressman, Paul R., Sr. (P.S.) .... Seattle, WA
Cresson, Catharine B. .... Washington, DC
Cresson, Jeanne T. .... Metairie, LA
Cresson, Kathleen C. .... New Orleans, LA
Cresson, Louisa K. .... Philadelphia, PA
Cresson, Melissa M. .... Baton Rouge, LA
Cresswell, Cake & Echeguren, A Professional Corporation .... Oakland, CA
Cresswell, Charles W. .... Las Cruces, NM
Cresswell and Froberger, P.C. .... Utica, MI
Cresswell, Jana L. .... Philadelphia, PA
Cresswell, John H. .... Utica, MI
Cresswell, Ronald R. .... Dallas, TX
Cresswell, Thomas B., Jr. .... Nashville, TN
Cresswell, Thomas J. .... Midland, MI
Cresswell, William E. .... United States Senate,
Senatorial Assistants, GV
Cressy, Joseph C. .... Edgartown, MA
Cresta-Savage, Patricia A. .... Washington, DC
Cresto, Dominic F. .... Providence, RI
Cresto, John J. .... Chicago, IL
Crestol, Jack .... Massapequa Park, NY
Creston, Donald P. .... Washington, DC
Creswell, C. Celeste .... Atlanta, GA
Creswell, C. Edward .... Amarillo, TX
Creswell, Clayton Michael .... Washington, DC
Creswell, Jennifer L. .... Annapolis, MD
Creswell, Kathryn E. .... Wheaton, IL
Creswell, Lori L. .... Treasury Department,
Internal Revenue Service, GV
Creswell, Nancy J. .... Burlington, VT
Creswell, Richard W. .... Macon, GA
Creta, Vincent M. .... Phoenix, AZ
Cretan, Clifford V. .... San Mateo, CA
Cretella, Albert W., Jr. .... New Haven, CT
Cretella, Andrew D. .... Trumbull, CT
Cretella, Henry A. .... Lincoln, MA
Cretella, Lauren J. .... Basking Ridge, NJ
Cretella, Ralph George .... New Brunswick, NJ
Cretella, Victor E. .... Frederick, MD
Creutz and Creutz .... Los Angeles, CA
Creutz, Mary G. .... Los Angeles, CA
Creutzmann, Harry F. .... Stamford, CT
Creuzot, John C. .... Dallas, TX
Crevasse, Christopher A.
Chattanooga, TN
Crevasse, Clayton W. .... Fort Myers, FL
Creveling, Curtis C. .... Allentown, PA
Creveling, Kelley Bertoux
Indianapolis, IN
Creveling, Lesa A., (P.C.) .... Tulsa, OK
Creveling, Michael A. .... Akron, OH
Creveling, Wendy S. .... Akron, OH
Creveling, Wilbur C., Jr. .... Allentown, PA
Crevi, Peter M. .... New York, NY
Crevier, David B. .... Springfield, MA
Crevier & Ryan, L.L.P. .... Springfield, MA
Crevina, Martin N. .... Glen Rock, NJ
Crevis, John M., Jr. .... Snellville, GA
Crew, Brent M. .... Vancouver, WA
Crew & Buchanan .... Dayton, OH
Crew & Crew .... Sioux Falls, SD
Crew & Crew, P.A. .... Fort Walton Beach, FL
Crew, D. Bruce, III .... Elmira, NY
Crew, Darren R. .... Washington, DC
Crew, Eugene .... San Francisco, CA
Crew, James B., Jr. .... Atlanta, GA
Jasper, GA
Crew, James Leonard .... San Ramon, CA
Crew, Jill W. .... Fort Walton Beach, FL
Crew, John Michael .... San Francisco, CA
Crew, Karen L. .... Sioux Falls, SD
Crew, Margaret .... Vermillion, SD
Crew, Michael B. .... Sioux Falls, SD
Crew, Michael D. .... Portland, OR
Crew, Michael H. .... Fort Walton Beach, FL
Crew, Michelle A. .... Buffalo, NY
Crew, Mitchell .... Portland, OR
Crew, Phillips B. .... Vermillion, SD
Crew, Robert B. .... Dayton, OH
Crew, Robert B., Jr. .... Denver, CO
Crew, Shannon L. .... Pittsburgh, PA
Crew, Stephen F. .... Portland, OR
Crew, W. Lunsford .... Roanoke Rapids, NC
Crew, Wendy Brooks .... Birmingham, AL
Crewdson, Jas. H. .... Charleston, WV
Crewdson, Robert L. .... Atlanta, GA
Crewe, Trenton G., Jr. .... Wytheville, VA
Crewe, Trenton G., Jr., P.C.
Wytheville, VA
Crewe-Allen, Pamela L. .... Fairfax, VA
Crews, Bryan W. .... Orlando, FL
Crews, Chantel .... El Paso, TX
Crews, Claibourne Curran .... Little Rock, AR
Crews, Connie Pecori .... Weston, FL
Crews, David W. .... Conroe, TX
Crews, Donald R. .... San Antonio, TX
Crews, Evangeline Levison .... Chicago, IL
Crews, Frank T., Jr. (P.C.) .... Galveston, TX
Crews, Franklin K. .... Hutchinson, KS
Crews, Gary J. .... Caro, MI
Crews, Gary W. .... Tulsa, OK
Crews, Gary W. .... Tulsa, OK
Crews, George P., Jr. .... Chattanooga, TN
Crews, Glenna England .... Houston, TX
Crews, Grasty, II .... Falls Church, VA
Crews, Grasty, II, P.C. .... Falls Church, VA
Crews, Gregory K., (P.A.) .... Jacksonville, FL
Crews, Gretchen E. .... San Francisco, CA
Crews, Halbert O. .... Chicago, IL
Crews & Hancock, P.L.C. .... Fairfax, VA
Richmond, VA
Roanoke, VA
Virginia Beach, VA
Crews, Howard Ross, Jr. .... Huntington, WV
Crews, J. Arthur, II .... Jackson, TN
Crews, Jack D. .... Tulsa, OK
Crews, Jack R. .... Temple, TX
Crews, James M., III .... Canton, MS
Crews, James P. .... Charlotte, NC
Crews, Joe K. .... Austin, TX
Crews, John .... Lubbock, TX
Crews, John R. .... Dallas, TX
Crews, John William .... Richmond, VA
Crews, Kenneth D. .... Chicago, IL
Crews, Kenneth D. .... Indianapolis, IN
Crews, Kenneth D. .... McAllen, TX
Crews, Kevin W. .... Miami, FL
Crews & Klein, P.C. .... Charlotte, NC
Crews, Kyle J. .... Tacoma, WA
Crews, Nanette W. .... Mercer, PA
Crews, R. Brent .... Newport, AR
Crews, Raymond E., Jr. .... Lawrence, KS
Crews, Richard A. .... Portland, OR
Crews, Richard W. .... Beaver, WV
Crews, Richard W., Jr.
Corpus Christi, TX
Crews, Roy M. A. .... Centerville, TN
Crews, Samuel F., III .... Columbia, SC
Crews, Steven D. .... Natchitoches, LA
Crews, Steven L. .... Huntsville, TX
Crews, Ted J. .... Phoenix, AZ
Crews, Thomas M. .... San Diego, CA
Crews, Thomas R. .... Jackson, MS
Crews, Waits, Brownlee, Berger & Hoop
Kansas City, MO
Crews, Wendell W. .... Athens, TN
Crews, William B., Jr. .... Southern Pines, NC
Crews, William E. .... Atlanta, GA
Crews, William P., Jr. .... Natchitoches, LA
Crews, William P., Jr., L.L.C., The Law Offices of .... Natchitoches, LA
Crewson, Thomas S. .... Tulsa, OK
Creyaufmiller, Timothy P. .... Los Angeles, CA
Creyke, Geoffrey, Jr. .... Alexandria, VA
Creyke, Stephen R. .... Bethesda, MD
Criaco, Adam P. .... Houston, TX
Criado, Antonio .... Houston, TX
Criado, Carrie Anna .... Murfreesboro, TN
Criazzo, Jas. J. .... Auburn, NY
Cribari, Arnold D., Jr. .... White Plains, NY
Cribari, James M. .... Denver, CO
Cribari, Kathleen Colette .... Boulder, CO
Cribari, Stephen J. .... Baltimore, MD
Cribb, Jos. W. .... Canandaigua, NY
Cribbet, John E. .... Urbana, IL
Cribbin, Robert D. .... Department of the Army,
Office, Chief of Engineers/Headquarters,
U.S. Army Corps of Engineers, GV
Cribbin, Theresa M. .... White Plains, NY
Cribbs, C. Haden, Jr. .... Beaumont, TX
Cribbs, Daniel A. .... Los Angeles, CA
Cribbs, Debra L. .... Greensburg, PA
Cribbs, Ferdinand P., Jr. .... Houston, TX
Cribbs, Graham Anderson .... Indio, CA
Cribbs, Gregory D. .... Pittsburgh, PA
Cribbs, Gregory M. .... Newport Beach, CA
Cribbs, Ian M. .... Palo Alto, CA
Cribbs, James A. .... Arlington, TX
Cribbs & McFarland, A Professional Corporation .... Arlington, TX
Fort Worth, TX
Cribbs, Sandra R. .... Seattle, WA
Cribley, James M. .... Honolulu, HI
Crice, Thomas E. .... Bronx, NY
Crichlow, Claudia A. .... Washington, DC
Crichlow, David A. .... New York, NY
Crichton, Anne .... Department Of The Interior,
Office of the Solicitor, GV
Crichton, Carolyn S. .... Winter Park, FL
Crichton, David H. .... Bolivar, TN
Crichton, David R. .... Tarrytown, NY
Crichton, James W. .... Danville, CA
Crichton, Kimberly .... New York, NY
Crichton, Rob J. .... Seattle, WA
Crichton, Roni Michele .... El Segundo, CA
Crichton, Scott J. .... Shreveport, LA
Crichton, Thomas, IV .... Dallas, TX
Crichton, William .... Parkersburg, WV
Crick, Derek D. .... Seattle, WA
Crick, Gene E., Jr. .... Orlando, FL
Crick, Glen D. .... Chicago, IL
Crick, Glen D., Ltd. .... Chicago, IL
Crick, Robert H. .... Spokane, WA
Crick, Steven E. .... Independence, MO
Crickard, Jack A. .... Los Angeles, CA
Crickenberger & Associates, P.C.
Fairfax, VA
Crickenberger, I. J. .... Fairfax, VA

Crittenden, J. Alan ... Pittsburgh, PA
Crittenden, John M. ... Oklahoma City, OK
Crittenden, John W. ... San Francisco, CA
Crittenden, Judith S. ... Birmingham, AL
Crittenden, Laurie ... Chatham, NJ
New York, NY
Crittenden, Leianne S. ... Redwood City, CA
Crittenden, Lisa R. ... Texarkana, TX
Crittenden • Martin ... Birmingham, AL
Crittenden, Max D. ... Abilene, TX
Crittenden, Robert R. ... Winter Haven, FL
Crittenden, Roger L. ... Frankfort, KY
Crittenden, Ronald L. ... Dexter, MI
Crittenden, Thomas D. ... Virginia Beach, VA
Crittenden, Tracy Lee
Kennedy Space Center, FL
Crittenden, Vanessa G. ... Columbia, SC
Crittendon, Christophe L. ... Atlanta, GA
Crittendon, Krystal Alisa ... Detroit, MI
Crittendon, Renée ... Washington, DC
Crittendon, Shari Fawn ... Baltimore, MD
Critton, Beth Bryan ... Waterbury, CT
Critton, Robert D., Jr. (P.A.)
North Palm Beach, FL
Critz, Boyd R., III ... Peoria, IL
Critz, Robert M. ... Concord, NC
Critz, Robert M., P.A., Law Offices of
Concord, NC
Critzer & McDade, LLP ... Modesto, CA
Critzer, S. Scott ... Atlanta, GA
Critzer, Stephen A. ... Modesto, CA
Critzman, Francina ... Baltimore, MD
Critzos, John, II ... Oxon Hill, MD
Crivaro, Alan J. ... Santa Ana, CA
Crivella, Vincent L.
General Services Administration, Office of the General Counsel, GV
Crivelli, Eileen M. ... Boonton, NJ
Crivelli, Frank M. ... Trenton, NJ
Crivelli, John G. ... Tampa, FL
Crivelli, Robert A. ... New York, NY
Crivelli, Rosanna J. ... New York, NY
Crivello, Carlson, Mentkowski & Steeves, S.C. ... Milwaukee, WI
Crivello, Frank T. ... Milwaukee, WI
Crivello, Frank T., II ... Milwaukee, WI
Crivlare, Laura A. ... Chicago, IL
Criz, Jesse A. ... Chicago, IL
Crlenjak, Jack ... Fortuna, CA
Crnich, Joseph E. ... Tigard, OR
Croak, Carolyn A.
Department of Commerce, Office of the Inspector General, GV
Croak, Francis R. ... Milwaukee, WI
Croak, Gonzalez & Croak ... Madison, WI
Croak, Martin F. ... Madison, WI
Croak, Michael A., (P.A.) ... Tavares, FL
Croak, Philip J. ... Madison, WI
Croak, Richard ... Albany, NY
Croak, Thomas E. ... Longmont, CO
Croak, Thomas E., Jr. ... Fort Bragg, CA
Croak, Thomas E., Sr. ... Covina, CA
Croak, Thomas M. ... Chicago, IL
Croake, Paul A. ... Madison, WI
Croall, David T. ... Cincinnati, OH
Croas, M. Lynn ... Midland, TX
Croasdell, Jeffrey M. ... Albuquerque, NM
Crocamo, Romilda P. ... Scranton, PA
Crocco, Charles A., Jr. ... New York, NY
Crocco, Kathleen A. ... Newark, NJ
Crocco, Louis Patrick ... Johnstown, PA
Croce, Arthur C. ... Wellfleet, MA
Croce, Carl R. ... Newton, MA
Croce, Carl R., P.C. ... Newton, MA
Croce, Christine Loretta ... Akron, OH
Croce, Edward J. ... Brooklyn, NY
Croce, Joseph A. ... Taunton, MA
Croce, Lenny L. ... Oak Ridge, TN
Croce, Louis S. ... Philadelphia, PA
Croce, Paul W. ... Louisville, KY
Croce, R. Richard ... Glastonbury, CT
Croce, Stephen P. ... San Diego, CA
Crocenzi, Michael J. ... Harrisburg, PA
Crochet, Anne J. ... Baton Rouge, LA
Crochet, Carla Lynn ... Tustin, CA
Crochet, Diane L. ... Baton Rouge, LA
Crochet, Gerald J., Jr. ... Little Rock, AR
Crochet, Gerald, PLLC, & Associates
Little Rock, AR
Crochet, Gregory R. ... Atlanta, GA
Crochet, John M. ... Lake Charles, LA
Crochet, Vicki M. ... Baton Rouge, LA
Crochet, Wayne T. ... Harahan, LA
Crochetiere, David P. ... Los Angeles, CA
Crochiere, Paul G. ... Wakefield, MA
Crociata, Joseph S. ... Washington, DC
Baltimore, MD
Rockville, MD
Crock, James Dickson
Daytona Beach, FL
Crock, James Dickson, P.A.
Daytona Beach, FL
Crock, Jane E. ... Des Moines, IA
Crock, Jane E. ... Charlotte, NC
Crockard, James E., III ... Pittsburgh, PA
Crockatt, Dale M. ... Hopewell Junction, NY
Crockatt, Joann Kealy ... Somers, NY
Crockenberg, Christine S. ... Brooklyn, NY
Crockenberg, David W. ... Pueblo, CO
Crocker, Andrew Wycoff
Silver Spring, MD
Crocker, Bathsheba Nell
Department of State, Office of the Legal Adviser, GV
Crocker, Benjamin D.
Bowling Green, KY
Crocker, Berthenia S. ... Lander, WY
Crocker, Blake D. ... Kalamazoo, MI

Crocker, Boyce Andrew ... Winchester, KY
Crocker, Bruce I. ... Pittsburgh, PA
Crocker, C. Timothy ... Milan, TN
Crocker, Charles A. ... Houston, TX
Crocker, Claudia L. ... Austin, TX
Crocker, Colleen M. ... Princeton, NJ
Crocker & Crocker, P.C. ... Pottstown, PA
Crocker, Cynthia R. ... Pittsburgh, PA
Crocker, Daniel S. ... Everett, WA
Crocker, David G. ... Kalamazoo, MI
Crocker, David P. ... Portland, ME
Crocker, Duane G. ... Victoria, TX
Crocker, Gary B. ... Charlotte, NC
Crocker, Glen M. ... Lumberton, TX
Crocker, H. Christopher ... Pottstown, PA
Crocker, Henry T. ... Pottstown, PA
Crocker, James A., III ... Lafayette, LA
Crocker, James W., (P.C.) ... Atlanta, GA
Crocker, Janet Jobe ... Franklin, KY
Crocker, Jeffrey R. ... Jaffrey, NH
Crocker, John D. ... Delhi, NY
Crocker, John Lawrence ... New York, NY
Crocker, Julian ... Boston, MA
Crocker, Kevin T. ... Dallas, TX
Crocker, Kit ... Novato, CA
Crocker Kuno, LLC ... Seattle, WA
Crocker Law Firm ... Milan, TN
Crocker, Linda Darnell ... Santa Rosa, CA
Crocker, Martha R. ... Jaffrey, NH
Crocker, Mason L. ... New York, NY
Crocker, M. D. ... Fresno, CA
Crocker, Michael ... Wakefield, RI
Crocker, Michael Pue ... Bel Air, MD
Crocker, Ottis B., III ... Gulfport, MS
Crocker, Ottis B., Jr. ... Bruce, MS
Crocker, Pamela R. ... Rochester, NY
Crocker, Patrick D. ... Kalamazoo, MI
Crocker, Randall D. ... Milwaukee, WI
Crocker, Samuel K. ... Nashville, TN
Crocker, Samuel S. ... Houston, TX
Crocker, Saône Baron ... Washington, DC
Crocker, Scott K. ... Bowling Green, KY
Crocker, Scott S. ... Dallas, TX
Crocker, Shelly ... Seattle, WA
Crocker, Susan M. ... Ketchikan, AK
Crocker, Thomas E., Jr. ... Washington, DC
Crocker, Timothy J. ... Franklin, KY
Crocker, Walter C., III ... Dallas, TX
Crocker & Wilkey ... Franklin, KY
Crocker, Wm. R. ... Austin, TX
Crocket, Mary Beth ... York Harbor, ME
Crocket, Will G. ... Reno, NV
Crockett, Alexander G.
San Francisco, CA
Crockett, Allen Bruce ... Golden, CO
Crockett, Bonnie J. ... Baltimore, MD
Crockett & Brown PLLC ... Little Rock, AR
Crockett, C. Richard ... Little Rock, AR
Crockett, C. Taylor ... Birmingham, AL
Crockett, C. Webb ... Phoenix, AZ
Crockett, Carrie H. ... San Francisco, CA
Crockett, Catherine Grayson ... Rockville, MD
Crockett, Charles A. ... Smethport, PA
Crockett, Clyde C. ... La Jolla, CA
Crockett, Clyde H. ... Indianapolis, IN
Crockett, Craig M. ... Fort Worth, TX
Crockett, Cynthia ... Phoenix, AZ
Crockett, David E. ... Elizabethton, TN
Crockett, David E., Jr.
Treasury Department, GV
Crockett, David G. ... Atlanta, GA
Crockett, David G. ... Southern Pines, NC
Crockett, David G., Law Office
Southern Pines, NC
Crockett, David G., (P.A.) ... Wichita, KS
Crockett, David G., P.C. ... Atlanta, GA
Crockett, David L. ... Newport Beach, CA
Crockett, Denise Brody, (P.A.) ... Miami, FL
Crockett, Don W. ... Department of Energy, Office of the General Counsel, GV
Crockett, Douglas M. ... Willimantic, CT
Crockett, Ed R. ... Tulsa, OK
Crockett, Elizabeth S. ... Washington, DC
Crockett & Fish ... Fullerton, CA
Crockett, Florine G. ... Oklahoma City, OK
Crockett Franklin & Chasen
Miami Beach, FL
Crockett, George W., III ... Detroit, MI
Crockett & Gilhousen ... Wichita, KS
Crockett, Gregory L. ... Idaho Falls, ID
Crockett, Gwendolyn B. ... Forestville, MD
Crockett, Harold L. ... Atlanta, GA
Crockett, J. Richard ... Seattle, WA
Crockett, James S., Jr. ... Richmond, VA
Crockett, Janet S. ... Fort Lauderdale, FL
Crockett, Jeffrey B. ... Miami, FL
Crockett, Jeffrey Webb ... Phoenix, AZ
Crockett, Jerry B. ... Miami, FL
Crockett, Joe Vaulx, III ... Nashville, TN
Crockett, John C. ... Auburn, ME
Crockett, John M. ... Pryor, OK
Crockett, John R., III ... Louisville, KY
Crockett, J. R., Jr. ... Las Vegas, NV
Crockett, Julie B. ... New York, NY
Crockett, K. David ... Fullerton, CA
Crockett, Karen B. ... San Francisco, CA
Crockett, Karen G. ... New York, NY
Crockett, Kim L. ... Boston, MA
Crockett, Leon W. ... Salt Lake City, UT
Crockett, Lisa King ... Bristol, TN
Crockett, Margaret B. ... Boston, MA
Crockett, Mark P. ... Knoxville, TN
Crockett, Michael A. ... Little Rock, AR
Crockett & Myers, Ltd., A Professional Corporation ... Las Vegas, NV
Crockett Nakamura & Schmidt
Wailuku, HI
Crockett, Patricia Alice ... Belchertown, MA

Crockett, Paul Hampton ... Miami Beach, FL
Crockett, Paula M. ... Fort Worth, TX
Crockett, Philbrook & Crouch, P.A.
Auburn, ME
Crockett, Phyllis N. ... Boston, MA
Crockett, Robert D. ... Los Angeles, CA
Crockett, Robert J. ... San Francisco, CA
Crockett, Robert W. ... San Francisco, CA
Crockett, Scott M. ... Overland Park, KS
Crockett, Sonia R. ... Tampa, FL
Crockett, Stephen G. ... Salt Lake City, UT
Crockett, Steven F.
Nuclear Regulatory Commission, Commission, GV
Crockett, Tabania L. ... San Francisco, CA
Crockett, Tamara R. ... Arlington, VA
Crockett, Theophilus C. ... Milwaukee, WI
Crockett, Thomas W. ... Jackson, MS
Crockett, William E. ... Encino, CA
Crockett, William F. ... Wailuku, HI
Crockett Graham, Julie ... Weslaco, TX
Crockin, Susan L. ... Newton, MA
Crockwell, Craig D. ... Los Angeles, CA
Crocoll, Kathleen J.
Department of Labor, GV
Croegaert, Clark & Hough, Ltd. ... Olney, IL
Croegaert, Paul A., Sr. ... Olney, IL
Croen & Barr LLP ... Milwaukee, WI
Croen, Frederick R. ... Milwaukee, WI
Croen, Philip W. ... Milwaukee, WI
Croes, Jane E. ... New York, NY
Croessmann, J. David ... Springfield, MO
Croessmann, Philip R. ... Washington, DC
Croessmann, Robert W. ... Rochester, NY
Croffoot-Suede, Lance ... New York, NY
Crofford, Greta Rapstine ... Amarillo, TX
Crofford, Laurence R. ... Martinsburg, WV
Crofford, Stephen ... Nashville, TN
Crofoot, Betty I. ... Portland, OR
Crofoot, Clyde H. ... Toms River, NJ
Crofoot, Emory J. ... Portland, OR
Crofoot, Ernest A. ... Bel Air, MD
Crofoot, Thomas H. ... Santa Ana, CA
Croft, Alan B. ... Washington, DC
Croft, Arnold T. ... Lynn, MA
Croft, Bradley L. ... Boston, MA
Croft, Bryant H. ... Salt Lake City, UT
Croft, Catherine S. ... Manassas, VA
Croft, Chancy ... Anchorage, AK
Croft, Christopher D. ... Palo Alto, CA
Croft, Colin ... Omaha, NE
Croft, David J. ... Philadelphia, PA
Croft, David R. ... Wheeling, WV
Croft, Gregory E. ... Neenah, WI
Croft, James B. ... Minneapolis, MN
Croft, Janice Claire ... Glendale, CA
Croft, John W. ... Dallas, TX
Croft, Julia E. ... Department of Justice, Drug Enforcement Administration, GV
Croft, Kenneth J., III ... Waltham, MA
Croft, M. Kathryn ... Akron, OH
Croft, Manly R. ... Glenview, IL
Croft, Mark S. ... Houston, TX
Croft, Richard E. ... Minneapolis, MN
Croft, Richard S. ... Breckenridge, CO
Croft, Ronald ... St. Petersburg, FL
Croft, Sidney F. ... Torrance, CA
Croft, Terrence Lee ... Atlanta, GA
Croft, Thomas A. ... Atlanta, GA
Croft, Thomas C. ... St. Louis, MO
Croft, Thomas R. ... Richardson, TX
Croft, William Hodge ... Sumter, SC
Croft, William L., & Associates
Las Vegas, NV
Crofton, Miriam K. ... Huntington, WV
Crofton, Peter M. ... Atlanta, GA
Crofton, Ralph L. ... Oakland, CA
Crofton, Stephen E. ... Phoenix, AZ
Crofts, Callaway & Jefferson, A Professional Corporation ... San Antonio, TX
Crofts, Christopher A. ... Cheyenne, WY
Crofts, George D., Jr. ... Buffalo, NY
Crofts, J. Michael ... San Diego, CA
Crofts, Michael L. ... Liberty Lake, WA
Crofts, Robert D. ... Salt Lake City, UT
Crofts, Thomas H., Jr. ... San Antonio, TX
Crofts, Thos. H. ... Terrell, TX
Croft-Walsh, Kathleen A.
San Antonio, TX
Crogan, James X., Jr. ... Baltimore, MD
Croghan, Michael J., Jr.
Webster Groves, MO
Croghan, Richard ... Chicago, IL
Crognale, Corey V. ... Columbus, OH
Crohan, Richard Bryan ... Atlanta, GA
Crohan, Robert J., Jr. ... Melbourne, FL
Crohn, Linda R. ... Chicago, IL
Crohn, Mark I. ... Seattle, WA
Crohn, Max H., Jr. ... New York, NY
Croisant, Catherine S. ... Boston, MA
Croissant, Robert P. ... Tustin, CA
Croiter, Richard L. ... Florence, KY
Croke, Claire ... New York, NY
Croke, Jerome P. ... Chicago, IL
Croke, Kevin G. ... San Francisco, CA
Croke, Pamela A. ... Glenside, PA
Croke, William F. ... Denver, CO
Croke, William P. ... Milwaukee, WI
Croker, C. Joseph ... Grand Junction, CO
Moab, UT
Croker, C. Joseph, P.C.
Grand Junction, CO
Moab, UT
Croker, Huck, Kasher, DeWitt, Anderson & Gonderinger, P.C. ... Omaha, NE
Croker, James E., Jr. ... Washington, DC
Croker, Joan M. ... Los Angeles, CA
Croker, Richard E. ... Omaha, NE

Croker, Richard J. ... Kansas City, MO
Crokin, Richard H. ... Englewood, FL
Crolan, Karen Routt ... Columbia, MD
Croland, Barry I., P.C. ... Hackensack, NJ
Croland, James E. ... Little River, SC
Croland, Leslie J. ... Miami, FL
Croley, Daniel A. ... San Francisco, CA
Croley, Davidson & Huie ... Knoxville, TN
Croley, Jeanette L. ... Tampa, FL
Croley, Moore & Snell ... La Grange, KY
Croley, Paul K., II ... Williamsburg, KY
Croley, Robert R. ... Knoxville, TN
Croley, Russell L. ... Central City, KY
Croley, Steven P. ... Ann Arbor, MI
Croley, William P. ... La Grange, KY
Crolius, Clinton T. ... Boston, MA
Croll, Alan D. ... Los Angeles, CA
Croll, Andrew M. ... Baltimore, MD
Croll, Billy M. ... Oklahoma City, OK
Croll, Howard R. ... Woonsocket, RI
Croll, Mark W. ... Glenview, IL
Croll, Samuel W., III ... Westfield, NJ
Croll, Stephanie Ellen ... Seattle, WA
Croll, Timothy Rex ... Palo Alto, CA
Crollard, Homer A. ... Yakima, WA
Crolle, James A., III ... Washington, DC
Crollett, Richard J. ... Albuquerque, NM
Crollett, Robert ... Taos, NM
Crollett & Sanchez, P.A. ... Taos, NM
Croly, Mary Sembrot ... White Plains, NY
Croly, Peter B. ... Larchmont, NY
Crom, Timothy S. ... St. Paul, MN
Croman, Charlotte ... Old Saybrook, CT
Croman, Dennis R. ... Irving, TX
Croman, Dennis R., Inc., A Professional Corporation ... Fort Worth, TX
Irving, TX
Croman, Earl L. ... San Antonio, TX
Croman, Earl L., P.C. ... San Antonio, TX
Croman, Kelly S. ... Olympia, WA
Cromartie, Eric R. ... Dallas, TX
Cromartie, Ernest W., II ... Columbia, SC
Cromartie, Hendrick L., III ... Rome, GA
Cromartie, John L., Jr. ... Atlanta, GA
Cromartie, Martha A. ... Charlotte, NC
Cromartie, Martin L., Jr. ... Washington, DC
Cromartie, Martin L., Jr. ... Tarboro, NC
Cromartie, Nancy Lee ... New Orleans, LA
Cromartie & Williams ... Columbia, SC
Cromarty, Arthur M. ... Bay Shore, NY
Crombie, Timothy J. ... New York, NY
Crome, Jennifer M. ... Los Angeles, CA
Cromelin, Paul B., III ... Washington, DC
Cromer, Anderson D. ... King, NC
Cromer, Andrew M., Jr. ... Camden, AL
Cromer, Brian A. ... Louisville, KY
Cromer, Brian E. ... San Diego, CA
Cromer, Charles L. ... Raleigh, NC
Cromer & Faber ... Dayton, OH
Cromer, Gail K. ... Brooklyn, NY
Cromer, George A. ... Las Vegas, NV
Cromer, George A., Professional Corporation of
Las Vegas, NV
Cromer, George E. ... Las Vegas, NV
Cromer, J. Lewis ... Columbia, SC
Cromer, John B. ... Pittsburgh, PA
Cromer, John R. ... Indianapolis, IN
Cromer, Julie D. ... Chicago, IL
Cromer, Kamela A. ... Dallas, TX
Cromer & Mabry ... Columbia, SC
Cromer, Michele McPeak ... Pittsburgh, PA
Cromer, Raymond W. ... Pittsburgh, PA
Cromer Reinbold ... Pittsburgh, PA
Cromer, Richard J. ... Pittsburgh, PA
Cromer, Robert J. ... Pittsburgh, PA
Cromer, Robin Sloan ... Anderson, SC
Cromer, S. Kelly ... Wrightwood, CA
Cromer, Terry M. ... Birmingham, AL
Cromer, William M. ... Dayton, OH
Cromes, Bernard A.
Federal Energy Regulatory Commission, Office of the General Counsel, GV
Cromett, Michael F. ... St. Paul, MN
Cromheecke, Jennifer B. ... Chicago, IL
Cromidas, Stacy ... Bronx, NY
Cromie, John D. ... Roseland, NJ
Cromie, John J. ... Ballston Spa, NY
Cromie, Wayne R. ... Willow Grove, PA
Cromley, Brent R. ... Billings, MT
Cromley, David W. ... Philadelphia, PA
Cromley, J. Timothy ... Chicago, IL
Cromley, Robert E., Jr. ... Columbus, OH
Cromley, Terri Fay ... Bradenton, FL
Cromley, William R. ... Columbus, OH
Crommett, Herbert A. ... Portland, ME
Crompton, Charles S., III
Menlo Park, CA
Crompton, Charles S., Jr.
Wilmington, DE
Crompton, David M. ... Minneapolis, MN
Crompton, George H. ... Pittsburgh, PA
Crompton, John Stone ... Tampa, FL
Crompton Law Group ... Tampa, FL
Crompton, R. Michael ... Washington, DC
Crompton, Richard M. ... San Mateo, CA
Crompton, Robert ... Braintree, MA
Crompton, Robert A. ... Braintree, MA
Crompton, Seager & Tufte, LLC
Minneapolis, MN
Cromwell, Brian S. ... Charlotte, NC
Cromwell, Charles W. ... Corpus Christi, TX
Cromwell, Cynthia ... Glastonbury, CT
Cromwell, Gregory F. ... Kent, WA
Cromwell, James H. ... Rusk, TX
Cromwell, James J. ... Rockville, MD
Cromwell, James R. ... Roanoke, VA
Cromwell, James T. ... Virginia Beach, VA
Cromwell, Jan R. ... Fort Smith, AR

Cromwell, John M. .... Mineola, NY
Cromwell, Judith A. .... St. Louis, MO
Cromwell, L. David .... Shreveport, LA
Cromwell, Louise M. .... Washington, DC
Cromwell, M. Jenkins, Jr. .... Baltimore, MD
Cromwell, Margrit E., Law Office of
Tucson, AZ
Cromwell, Marion M.
North Palm Beach, FL
Cromwell, Michael A .... Baton Rouge, LA
Cromwell, P. McEvoy .... Baltimore, MD
Cromwell, Payton Dickinson
Virginia Beach, VA
Cromwell, Pfaffenberger, Dahlmeier, Barner, Griffin & Colton .... North Palm Beach, FL
Cromwell, Ralph E., Jr. .... Seattle, WA
Cromwell, Richard Joshua .... Norfolk, VA
Cromwell, Robert B., Jr. .... Virginia Beach, VA
Cromwell, Robert D. .... New York, NY
Cromwell, Robert F. .... North Palm Beach, FL
Cromwell, William G. .... Atlanta, GA
Cromwell, William M. .... Fort Smith, AR
Cromwell, William T. .... Portland, OR
Cromwell & Yerman .... Mineola, NY
Cron, Dan .... Santa Fe, NM
Cron, Dan, Law Firm, P.C. .... Santa Fe, NM
Cron & Israels .... Los Angeles, CA
Santa Monica, CA
Sherman Oaks, CA
Van Nuys, CA
Cron, James J. .... Ocala, FL
Cron, Lawrence M. .... Irvine, CA
Cron, Nicholas J. .... Toledo, OH
Cron, Richard B. .... Houston, TX
Cron, Richard J. .... Cutchogue, NY
Cron, Steven M. .... Santa Monica, CA
Crona, Spencer J. .... Denver, CO
Cronan, Charles J., IV .... Louisville, KY
Cronan, J. Michael .... Kansas City, MO
Cronan, James P. .... Portland, OR
Cronan and Messick .... Kansas City, MO
Cronan, Patrick C. .... Minneapolis, MN
Cronan Pearson Quinlivan, P.A.
Minneapolis, MN
Cronan, R. Todd .... Boston, MA
Cronan, Sarah G. .... Chicago, IL
Cronan, Sheila K. .... Department of Labor, Office of the Solicitor, GV
Cronan, Thomas E. .... Madison, CT
Cronan, Timothy M. .... Sacramento, CA
Cronan, Virginia J. .... Department of Justice, Tax Division, GV
Cronan-Yorick, Anne .... Morgantown, WV
Cronauer, Adrian .... Washington, DC
Cronauer, Charles E. .... Sycamore, IL
Cronauer & Kruizenga .... De Kalb, IL
Sycamore, IL
Crone, Alan G. .... Memphis, TN
Somerville, TN
Crone, Andrea Lee .... Pittsburgh, PA
Crone, Brian .... Sacramento, CA
Crone, Chester F. .... Cleveland, OH
Crone, Douglas C. .... Chicago, IL
Crone, Gary L. .... South Bend, IN
Crone, John W., III .... Hickory, NC
Crone, Marcia Cain .... Houston, TX
Crone, Mark E. .... Hartford, CT
Crone & Mason, P.L.C. .... Memphis, TN
Somerville, TN
Crone, Maya R. .... McLean, VA
Crone, Paul A., Jr. .... St. Louis, MO
Crone, Prudence Wilson .... Charleston, SC
Crone, Richard H. .... Department of Labor, Office of the Solicitor, GV
Crone, Richard S. .... Pittsburgh, PA
Crone, Robert L., Jr. .... Lakeport, CA
Crone, Steven S. .... Owensboro, KY
Crone, Terry A. .... South Bend, IN
Crone, Thomas R. .... Madison, WI
Crone, Thor L. .... Stamford, CT
Croneberger, Rebecca C. .... New York, NY
Cronen, Michael J. .... Oakland, CA
Cronenwalt, Nancy .... Encino, CA
Cronenwett, Debra A. .... Lebanon, NH
Cronenwett, Mark D. .... Dallas, TX
Croner, Charles R. .... Chatsworth, CA
Croner & Croner .... Chatsworth, CA
Croner, Fred B., Jr. .... Indianapolis, IN
Croner, George W. .... Philadelphia, PA
Croner, John F. .... Boise, ID
Croner, Melissa A. .... Chatsworth, CA
Croney, J. Kenneth .... Norristown, PA
Croney, Vance M. .... Salem, OR
Cronfel, Ada .... Laredo, TX
Crongeyer, James J., Jr. .... Jackson, MS
Crongeyer, Robert L. .... Pensacola, FL
Cronheim, Alan J. .... Portsmouth, NH
Cronheim, Daniel D. .... Chatham, NJ
Cronheim, George K. .... Columbus, OH
Cronic, Horace F. .... Houston, TX
Cronic, Jason P. .... Washington, DC
Cronig, Steven Carlyle .... Miami, FL
Cronig, Steven Carlyle, P.A., & Associates
Miami, FL
Cronin, Ailen M. .... Seattle, WA
Cronin, Albert E., Jr. .... Stockton, CA
Cronin, Ann Reid .... Los Angeles, CA
Cronin, Barbara A. .... Chicago, IL
Cronin, Beth Anne .... Tampa, FL
Cronin, Brad W. .... Mineola, NY
Cronin, Caren J. .... Central Islip, NY
Cronin, Catherine A. .... Annapolis, MD
Cronin, Charles F. .... Worcester, MA
Cronin, Charles J. .... Syracuse, NY
Cronin, Cheryl M. .... Boston, MA
Cronin, Colleen M. .... Garden City, NY
Cronin & Cronin .... Escondido, CA
Cronin, Cronin & Harris, P.C.
Mineola, NY
Cronin, Daniel I., Jr. .... Braintree, MA
Cronin, Daniel J. .... Escondido, CA
Cronin, Daniel J. .... Oakbrook Terrace, IL
Cronin, Daniel L., (P.C.) .... John Day, OR
Cronin, Daniel P. .... New York, NY
Cronin, Daniel Ward .... Worcester, MA
Cronin, David L. .... Stoneham, MA
Cronin, Denis F. .... New York, NY
Cronin, Dennis C. .... New York, NY
Cronin, Dennis C. .... Spokane, WA
Cronin, Dennis J. .... Boston, MA
Cronin, Dennis M., Jr. .... Westwood, MA
Cronin, Dennis P. .... Bonita Springs, FL
Naples, FL
Cronin, Donald A., Jr. .... McDonough, GA
Cronin, Donald J. .... Bethesda, MD
Cronin, Doreen A. .... New York, NY
Cronin, Edward F. .... Department of Justice, Tax Division, GV
Cronin, Eileen M. .... Bronx, NY
Cronin, Elizabeth A. .... Tulsa, OK
Cronin, Eugene M. .... New York, NY
Cronin, Frank .... Irvine, CA
Cronin, Franklin J. .... Boston, MA
Cronin, Frederick R. .... Lynn, MA
Cronin, Fried, Sekiya, Kekina & Fairbanks, Attorneys at Law, A Law Corporation
Honolulu, HI
Cronin, George F., Jr. .... Boston, MA
Cronin, George T. .... San Francisco, CA
Cronin, Harry R. .... Fairmont, WV
Cronin, James J. .... Denver, CO
Cronin, James J. .... Minneapolis, MN
Cronin, Jeremiah A. .... Wallingford, CT
Cronin, Jill M. .... Austin, TX
Cronin, Joel S., (P.A.) .... Lake Worth, FL
West Palm Beach, FL
Cronin, John A. .... Valley Center, CA
Cronin, John G. .... Manchester, NH
Cronin, John J. .... Chicago, IL
Cronin, John J., III .... Bennington, NH
Cronin, John J., III, P.C. .... Bennington, NH
Cronin, John M. .... Indianapolis, IN
Cronin, John O'Shea .... Escondido, CA
Cronin, John P. .... North Billerica, MA
Cronin, John P. .... Forest Hills, NY
Cronin, John W. .... San Diego, CA
Cronin, Joseph D. .... Philadelphia, PA
Cronin, Joseph I. .... Minden, NV
Cronin, Joseph P. .... Woodlyn, PA
Cronin, Joseph V. .... Needham, MA
Cronin, Julia R. .... Altoona, PA
Cronin, Julie Thomas .... Mayfield Heights, OH
Cronin, K. Elizabeth .... Los Angeles, CA
Cronin, Kathleen M. .... Chicago, IL
Cronin, Kevin B. .... Madison, WI
Cronin, Kevin G. .... Albany, CA
Cronin, Kevin P. .... Philadelphia, PA
Cronin, Kimberley P. .... Boston, MA
Cronin, Larry V. .... Goodyear, AZ
Cronin, Laurence V. .... Wilmington, DE
Cronin, Lillian M. .... Lake Grove, NY
Cronin, Linda M. .... Lake Success, NY
Cronin, Lisa Conly .... Newport News, VA
Cronin, Margaret D. .... Quincy, MA
Cronin, Margaret Mary .... Braintree, MA
Cronin, Margaret Mary .... Shirley, MA
Cronin, Mark A. .... Fort Washington, PA
Cronin, Martin G. .... Newark, NJ
Cronin, Mary C. .... Phoenix, AZ
Cronin, Mary Ellen .... Braintree, MA
Cronin, Mary K. .... Wheaton, IL
Cronin, Matthew J. .... Mineola, NY
Cronin, Maureen R. .... New York, NY
Cronin, Michael A. .... Phoenix, AZ
Cronin, Michael E., Jr. .... Old Saybrook, CT
Cronin, Michael F. .... Armonk, NY
Cronin, Michael J. .... Chicago, IL
Cronin, Michael J. .... Hightstown, NJ
Cronin, Michael J. .... Spokane, WA
Cronin, Michael K. .... Chicago, IL
Cronin, Michael T. .... Clearwater, FL
Cronin, Michael T. .... Cleveland, OH
Cronin, Monica .... Miami, FL
Cronin, Nancy Anne .... Albuquerque, NM
Cronin, Neil P. .... Spokane, WA
Cronin, Nelda Davis .... Manchester, NH
Cronin, Patricia L. F. .... Elizabeth, NJ
Cronin, Patrick J. .... Cincinnati, OH
Cronin, Patrick J. .... Spokane, WA
Cronin, Patrick T. .... Haddonfield, NJ
Cronin, Patti Wright .... Madison, WI
Cronin, Paul F. .... Honolulu, HI
Cronin, Paul J. .... Chicago, IL
Cronin, Paul J. .... Boston, MA
Cronin, Paul S. .... Albuquerque, NM
Cronin, Paul T. .... Newton, MA
Cronin and Peters, P.C. .... Chicago, IL
Cronin, Philip F., Jr. .... Rochester, NY
Cronin, Philip M. .... Boston, MA
Cronin, Phillip S. .... Fresno, CA
Cronin, Richard A., Jr.
Department of Energy, Office of Hearings and Appeals, GV
Cronin, Robert A. .... Rincon, GA
Cronin, Robert E. .... Chicago, IL
Cronin, Robert S., Jr. .... Phoenix, AZ
Cronin & Scardino .... Fort Washington, PA
Cronin, Scott A. .... Philadelphia, PA
Cronin, Skilton & Skilton .... Nashua, IA
Cronin & Stanewich .... Phoenix, AZ
Tucson, AZ
Cronin, Steven M. .... Spokane, WA
Cronin, T. Michael .... Jackson, MS
Cronin, Thomas C. .... Chicago, IL
Dallas, TX
Cronin, Thomas E. .... St. Paul, MN
Cronin, Thomas G. .... Chicago, IL
Cronin, Thos. R. .... North Hollywood, CA
Cronin, Timothy E. .... Bloomingdale, IL
Cronin, Timothy G. .... Sacramento, CA
Cronin, Timothy L. .... Plymouth, MI
Cronin, Timothy P. .... Spokane, WA
Cronin, Val C. .... Dallas, TX
Cronin, William F. .... Seattle, WA
Cronin, William J. .... New York, NY
Croninger, Marsha S. .... Los Angeles, CA
Cronis, Charles .... Lynn, MA
Cronise, Elizabeth Haines
Washington, DC
Croniser, Gretchen E. .... Toledo, OH
Cronk, C. Tabor .... Richmond, VA
Cronk, Crystal S. .... Keosauqua, IA
Cronk, Gary E. .... Port Orchard, WA
Cronk, George .... North Haledon, NJ
Cronk, Harold J. .... Savannah, GA
Cronk, Harold J., P.C. .... Savannah, GA
Cronk, Jerome R. .... Seattle, WA
Cronk, Jerome R., P.S. .... Seattle, WA
Cronk, Kay-Margaret .... West Sand Lake, NY
Cronk, Peter J. .... Cherry Hill, NJ
Philadelphia, PA
Cronk, Robert M. .... New York, NY
Cronk, Shanler D. .... Bogart, GA
Cronk, Stacey M. .... Issaquah, WA
Cronkhite, James V. .... Houston, TX
Cronkhite, Willis D., (III) .... Little Rock, AR
Cronkite, Maber W., Jr. .... Edgewater, MD
Cronkright, Douglas L. .... Alpharetta, GA
Cronlund, Jayne Renee .... Lake Oswego, OR
Cronmiller, Rae E. .... Arlington, VA
Cronmiller, Thomas B. .... Rochester, NY
Cronn, Jeffrey S. .... Portland, OR
Cronon, James A. .... Tucker, GA
Cronovich, Lenore A. .... Detroit, MI
Cronrath, Carl D., Jr. .... Reading, PA
Cronson, Robert G. .... Chicago, IL
Cronthall, André J. .... Los Angeles, CA
Cronvich, Alwynn J. .... Metairie, LA
Cronvich, James T. .... Harahan, LA
Cronvich, Wambsgans & Michalczyk
Metairie, LA
Cronyn, Robert L. .... Buffalo, NY
Croog, Elizabeth A. .... Washington, DC
Croog, Martha E. .... West Hartford, CT
Croog, Robert D. .... Rochester, NY
Croog, Robert L. .... New York, NY
Crook, Alice M. .... Owego, NY
Crook, Anne Michele .... Pylesville, MD
Crook, Betty R. .... Waco, TX
Crook, Charles M. .... Montgomery, AL
Crook, Christopher S .... San Francisco, CA
Crook, Clyde Tyree .... Houston, TX
Crook, Courtney A. .... Columbia, SC
Crook, D. Clifford, III
Department of Energy, Office of the General Counsel, GV
Crook, D. Scott .... Salt Lake City, UT
Crook, David .... Augusta, ME
Crook, David .... McAllen, TX
Crook, David W. .... Rutherford, NJ
Crook, Debra Hawes .... Birmingham, AL
Crook, Donald L. .... San Antonio, TX
Crook, Donald M. .... Dallas, TX
Crook and Edwards, A Professional Corporation
Smithfield, VA
Crook, George D. .... Sherman Oaks, CA
Crook, H. Woodrow, Jr. .... Smithfield, VA
Crook, Heather Buyrn .... Chesapeake, VA
Crook, James J. .... El Paso, TX
Crook, James L., Jr. .... New Bedford, MA
Crook, James R., Jr. .... Baltimore, MD
Crook, Jeffrey A. .... Sandy, OR
Crook, Jennifer M. .... New York, NY
Crook, John A. .... Edwardsville, IL
Crook, John R. .... Department of State, Office of the Legal Adviser, GV
Crook, John R. .... Barrington, RI
Crook, Kendall C. .... Indianapolis, IN
Crook, Lee W., III
General Services Administration, Office of Regional Counsel, GV
Crook, Lowry A. .... Washington, DC
Crook, Patricia Lee .... Pasadena, CA
Crook, Penny Lozon .... Tampa, FL
Crook, Robert L. .... Ruleville, MS
Crook, Robert L., Jr. .... Birmingham, AL
Crook, Ronald R. .... Birmingham, AL
Crook, Wannell M. .... Denver, CO
Crook, William M. .... Houston, TX
Crook, William W. .... Belmont, MA
Crooke, Elizabeth Lane .... Los Angeles, CA
Crooke, Richard R. .... Ocala, FL
Crooke, Steven C. .... Irvine, CA
Santa Ana, CA
Crooke, Steven F. .... Mission Woods, KS
Crooker, Constance H. .... Portland, OR
Crooker, John H., Jr. .... Houston, TX
Crooker, Richard A. .... Parsippany, NJ
Crookes, Harold R. .... Irvine, CA
Crookes, Thomas R. .... Akron, OH
Crookham, Charles S. .... Portland, OR
Crookham, Joe P. .... Oskaloosa, IA
Crooks, Bridget King .... Philadelphia, PA
Crooks, Charles J. .... Morgantown, WV
Crooks, David W. .... Grand Rapids, MI
Crooks, Deborah L. .... Mayfield, KY
Crooks, Donna C. .... Daleville, AL
Crooks, Gary V. .... Goleta, CA
Crooks, Geoffrey .... Olympia, WA
Crooks, James H. .... Tacoma, WA
Crooks, Kendal A. .... Chicago, IL
Crooks, Kenneth C. .... Melbourne, FL
Crooks, Kenneth E. .... Indialantic, FL
Crooks, Kevin P. .... Louisville, KY
Crooks, Kevin P. .... Wausau, WI
Crooks, Kim D. .... Kalamazoo, MI
Crooks, Leonard William .... New Orleans, LA
Crooks, Leonard William, P.L.C.
New Orleans, LA
Crooks, Low, Connell & Rottier, S.C.
Marathon, WI
Wausau, WI
Crooks, Lynn E. .... Fargo, ND
Crooks, Lynn Lawandales
Mount Pleasant, SC
Crooks, Michael P. .... Madison, WI
Crooks, N. Patrick .... Madison, WI
Crooks, Patrick L. .... Wausau, WI
Crooks, Robert G. .... Durham, NH
Crooks, Robert M. .... Greenwich, CT
Crooks, Roy G. .... Kansas City, MO
Crooks, Scott B. .... Cincinnati, OH
Crooks, Steven R. .... Sacramento, CA
Crooks, Susan Davis .... Raleigh, NC
Crooks, Thomas C. .... Chicago, IL
Crooks, Wilbur E. .... Chicago, IL
Crooks, William E. .... Baton Rouge, LA
Crookshank, Dorothy V. .... Grand Rapids, MI
Crookston, J. A. .... Atlanta, GA
Crookston, Wayne G., Jr. (P.A.)
Meridian, ID
Croom, Claudia C. .... Raleigh, NC
Croom, Craig .... Raleigh, NC
Croom, Jacques H. .... Bethesda, MD
Croom, James B. .... Lansing, MI
Croom, John H., IV .... Philadelphia, PA
Croom, Michael F. .... Albuquerque, NM
Croom, Sam G., Jr. .... Houston, TX
Croomes, E. Steven .... Athens, AL
Crooms, Lisa A. .... Washington, DC
Croot, John E., Jr. .... Morristown, NJ
Cropp, J. Wayne .... Chattanooga, TN
Cropp, Jeffrey Mark .... Clarksburg, WV
Cropper, Gregory L. .... Salt Lake City, UT
Cropper, Hugh, IV .... Ocean City, MD
Cropper, James R. .... Phoenix, AZ
Cropper, Jeffrey B. .... Snow Hill, MD
Cropper, Mariann C. .... Palm Desert, CA
Cropper, Mark Spencer .... Ocean City, MD
Cropper, Michael D. .... Midland, TX
Cropper, Michael Edward .... Houston, TX
Cropper, Stephen W. .... New York, NY
Cropper, Walter H. .... Omaha, NE
Cropsey, Alan L. .... Lansing, MI
Cropsey, Conrad F. .... Albion, NY
Cropsey & Cropsey .... Albion, NY
Cropsey, Douglas John .... Dearborn, MI
Cropsey, Henry C. .... Springfield, MA
Crosbie, Connie W. .... Buzzards Bay, MA
Crosbie, Michael D. .... Orlando, FL
Crosbie, Scott A. .... Lexington, KY
Crosbie, Thomas B. .... San Diego, CA
Crosby, Abe .... Macon, GA
Crosby, Alexander C. .... Carmel, CA
Crosby, Allen B., (P.C.) .... Houston, TX
Crosby, Anthony .... West Hartford, CT
Crosby & Associates, P.C., A Law Office of,
Rockford, IL
Crosby, Belock & O'Brien, Co., L.P.A.
Cleveland, OH
Crosby, Brian P. .... Buffalo, NY
Crosby, Carole .... Troy, MI
Crosby, Charles Patrick, Jr. .... Raleigh, NC
Crosby, Christina Nelson
San Francisco, CA
Crosby, Craig W., Sr. .... Portland, TX
Crosby, Cynthia L. .... Van Nuys, CA
Crosby, Dana L. .... Tampa, FL
Crosby, Danya .... Anchorage, AK
Crosby, David C. .... Juneau, AK
Crosby, David F. .... Boston, MA
Crosby, David M. .... Las Vegas, NV
Crosby, David R. .... Minneapolis, MN
Crosby, David U. .... Atlanta, GA
Crosby, Donald L. .... Ponte Vedra Beach, FL
Crosby, Donna R. .... Cambridge, MA
Crosby, Douglas A. .... Oakland, CA
Crosby, Douglas G. .... Las Vegas, NV
Crosby, E. Howell .... New Orleans, LA
Crosby, Elizabeth A. .... Cleveland, OH
Crosby, Eugene J. .... Faribault, MN
Crosby, Eva Mae .... Columbus, OH
Crosby, Evan .... Wellesley, MA
Crosby, F. Pen .... Indianapolis, IN
Crosby, G. Lee, Jr. .... Phoenix, AZ
Crosby, Gary L. .... Schaumburg, IL
Fort Worth, TX
Crosby & Gladner, P.C. .... Phoenix, AZ
Crosby, Grace M. .... Detroit, MI
Crosby, Grady L. .... Winston-Salem, NC
Crosby, Guenzel, Davis, Kessner & Kuester
Lincoln, NE
Crosby, Hans J. .... Philadelphia, PA
Crosby, Heafey, Roach & May, Professional Corporation .... Los Angeles, CA
Oakland, CA
San Francisco, CA
Santa Rosa, CA
Crosby, Horace E. .... Silver Spring, MD
Crosby, J. Ellis, Jr. .... Jacksonville, FL
Crosby, J. Wayne .... Orlando, FL
Crosby, J. Wayne, P.A. .... Orlando, FL
Crosby, James D. .... San Diego, CA
Crosby, James H. .... Mobile, AL
Crosby, James P. .... Dallas, TX
Crosby, Jane E. .... Springfield, MA
Crosby, Jefferson C. .... Lancaster, PA
Crosby, Joanna L. .... West Orange, NJ
Crosby, Joe M. .... Georgetown, SC
Crosby, Joel S. .... Santa Barbara, CA
Crosby, John B. .... Chicago, IL

Crosby, John D. ... Tifton, GA
Crosby, John R. ... Houston, TX
Crosby, Joseph H. ... Tulsa, OK
Crosby, Joseph Raymond, III
Montgomery, AL
Crosby, Judd F. ... Pittsburgh, PA
Crosby, Judith K. ... Boston, MA
Crosby, Karen Matcke ... Walnut Creek, CA
Crosby, Kenneth Lee ... Warren, PA
Crosby, Kevin M. ... Reno, NV
Crosby, Kevin P. ... Fort Lauderdale, FL
Crosby, Kristen W. ... Chicago, IL
Crosby, L. Clint ... Atlanta, GA
Crosby, Laura S. ... Palo Alto, CA
Crosby, Lawrence H. ... St. Paul, MN
Crosby, Lisa Ann ... Washington, DC
Crosby, M. Elizabeth ... Boston, MA
Crosby, Magara Lee ... Los Angeles, CA
Crosby, Margaret C. ... San Francisco, CA
Crosby, Margaret M. ... Chicago, IL
Crosby, Mark R. ... New York, NY
Crosby, Mary Anne ... San Antonio, TX
Crosby, Matthew A. ... Saratoga, CA
Crosby, Matthew S. ... Harrisburg, PA
Lancaster, PA
Crosby, Michael H. ... San Diego, CA
Crosby, Michael J. ... Rochester, NY
Crosby, Michael S. ... Rockford, IL
Crosby, Michael W. ... Gulfport, MS
Crosby, Michele Whitesell
Baton Rouge, LA
Crosby, Mike W. ... Niskayuna, NY
Crosby, Peter J. ... Anchorage, AK
Crosby, Peter J., IV ... San Francisco, CA
Crosby, Philip C. ... San Francisco, CA
Crosby, Robert A. ... Atlanta, GA
Crosby, Robert B. ... Lincoln, NE
Crosby, Robert D. ... Warren, MI
Crosby, Robert L. ... Minneapolis, MN
Crosby, Roger J. ... Deer Harbor, WA
Crosby, Ronnie L. ... Hampton, SC
Crosby, Samuel G. ... Lakeland, FL
Crosby, Samuel N. ... Bay Minette, AL
Daphne, AL
Foley, AL
Crosby, Scott J. ... Memphis, TN
Crosby, Sean L. ... Orlando, FL
Crosby, Thomas C. ... San Francisco, CA
Crosby, Thomas E. ... Guilford, CT
Crosby, Thomas F., III ... Marion, IL
Crosby, Thomas F., Jr. ... Santa Ana, CA
Crosby, Thomas M., Jr. ... Minneapolis, MN
Crosby, Tommy J. ... Tampa, FL
Crosby, William E. ... New York, NY
Crosby, William H., Jr. ... New York, NY
Crosby, William I. ... Roswell, GA
Crosby, William K. ... Springfield, MO
Crosby, William M. ... Irvine, CA
Crosby, William M. ... Cleveland, OH
Crosby Halstead, Kara ... Tucson, AZ
Crosco, Leslie ... Wheeling, WV
Crose, Gayle L. ... Minneapolis, MN
Crose, John A., Jr. ... Santa Monica, CA
Crose, Joy Murakami ... Torrance, CA
Croshal, James M. ... Pueblo, CO
Croshaw, Cathy L. ... San Francisco, CA
Croshaw, Fred E. ... St. Helena, CA
Croshaw, Glenn R. ... Norfolk, VA
Virginia Beach, VA
Crosier, Byron ... Cleburne, TX
Crosier, Diane M. ... San Diego, CA
Crosier, Don Alan ... Houston, TX
Crosier, Douglas A. ... Honolulu, HI
Crosier, William L. ... Greeley, CO
Croskell, Henry ... Dallas, TX
Croskery, Robert Forsythe
West Chester, OH
Croskey, H. Walter ... Los Angeles, CA
Croskey, Thomas P. ... Miamisburg, OH
Crosky, Morris ... Hartford, CT
Crosland, David W. ... Washington, DC
Crosland, Edward B. ... Washington, DC
Crosland, Edward B., Jr. ... Washington, DC
Crosland, James C. ... Miami, FL
Orlando, FL
Crosland, J. W. ... Dallas, TX
Crosland, Lee K. ... Columbia, SC
Crosland, Malcolm M., Jr.
Charleston, SC
Crosland, Martha S.
Department of Energy, GV
Crosland, Royda ... Mill Valley, CA
Crosland, Sandra L. ... Ogden, UT
Salt Lake City, UT
Crosland, Strand, Freeman & Mayock
Washington, DC
Crosley, John C. ... Cleveland, OH
Crosley, Marianne ... Chagrin Falls, OH
Crosley, Roy H. ... Dulles, VA
Crosley, Stanley W. ... Indianapolis, IN
Crosley, Thomas A. ... San Antonio, TX
Crosman, Christopher A.
Los Angeles, CA
Crosmer, Andrew A. ... Munster, IN
Crosmun, Jean R. ... Cincinnati, OH
Crosner, Albert L. ... Manhattan Beach, CA
Crosnoe, Michael P. ... Farwell, TX
Crosnoe, R. Caven ... Wichita Falls, TX
Crosnoe, Wade C. ... Dallas, TX
Cross, Alix Coulter ... Nashville, TN
Cross, Andrew J. ... St. Louis, MO
Cross, Andrew P. ... Pittsburgh, PA
Cross, Audrey Tittle ... New York, NY
Cross, Bernard H. ... Mechanicsville, VA
Cross, Bruce Michael ... Seattle, WA
Cross, Bryan D. ... Denver, CO
Cross, C. Felix, III ... Richmond, VA
Cross, C. Thomas ... Cincinnati, OH

Cross, Carl D. ... Dallas, TX
Cross, Carole ... Arlington, TX
Cross, Caroline Lee ... Wilmington, DE
Cross, Carolyn C. ... Cleveland, OH
Cross, Cary Jay ... Irving, TX
Cross, Charles A. ... Columbia, MD
Cross, Charles A. ... Columbia, MD
Cross, Charles W. ... Chicago, IL
Cross, Charmel L. ... Columbus, OH
Cross, Chester J. ... Chicago, IL
Cross, Christopher G. ... New York, NY
Cross, Christopher H. ... Indianapolis, IN
Cross, Clinton F. ... El Paso, TX
Cross, Colleen R. (IBA) ... Washington, DC
Cross & Cross ... Mechanicsville, VA
Cross, Cynthia Rebecca ... Washington, DC
Cross, Dan S. ... Denver, CO
Cross, Daniel ... Portland, OR
Cross, Daniel R. ... Appleton, WI
Cross, David B. ... Wellsburg, WV
Cross, David D. ... Sacramento, CA
San Diego, CA
Cross, David L. ... Weaverville, CA
Cross, David M. ... Albany, KY
Cross, David M. ... Jamestown, KY
Cross, David R. ... Bowie, MD
Cross, David R. ... Milwaukee, WI
Cross, Dean B. ... Las Cruces, NM
Cross, Donald L. ... Phoenix, AZ
Cross, Dustan J. ... New Ulm, MN
Cross, Earl W. ... Dallas, TX
Cross, Edward L., Jr. ... Manchester, NH
Cross, Ellen Christina ... Englewood, CO
Cross, Elmo G., Jr. ... Mechanicsville, VA
Cross, Eugene A. ... Wall Township, NJ
Cross, Francois R. ... Beacon, NY
Cross, Freda J. ... Oklahoma City, OK
Cross, Frederick K. ... Overland Park, KS
Cross, Frederick M. ... Sterling Heights, MI
Cross, Gary E. ... Washington, DC
Cross, Geoffrey C. ... Tacoma, WA
Cross, Gregory A. ... Baltimore, MD
Cross, Gunter, Witherspoon & Galchus, P.C.
Little Rock, AR
Cross, H. Kay ... Washington, DC
Cross, Harry M., Jr. ... Kalispell, MT
Cross, Iris J. ... Brooklyn, NY
Cross, J. Bruce ... Little Rock, AR
Cross, J. Emory ... Charlotte, NC
Cross, J. Harry ... Baltimore, MD
Cross, J. Stanton, Jr. ... Conway, SC
Cross, James D. ... New York, NY
Cross, James E. ... Phoenix, AZ
Cross, James E. ... Los Angeles, CA
Cross, James E. ... Dayton, OH
Cross, James E., Jr. ... Oxford, NC
Cross, James O. ... Canton, OH
Cross, Janis Alexander ... Amarillo, TX
Cross, Jeannette Bickner ... Phoenix, AZ
Cross, Jeffery M. ... Chicago, IL
Cross, Jeffrey ... Louisville, KY
Cross, Jeffrey D. ... Columbus, OH
Cross, Jeffrey G. ... New York, NY
Cross, Jenks, Mercer and Maffei
Baraboo, WI
Lake Delton, WI
Cross, Jennefer J. ... Charlotte, NC
Cross, Jerome R., II ... Longmont, CO
Cross, Jesse R. ... San Antonio, TX
Cross, John C. ... Boston, MA
Cross, John F.
Environmental Protection Agency,
Program Office Attorneys, GV
Cross, John J., III ... Washington, DC
Cross, John M., Jr. ... Greensboro, NC
Cross, John Milton, Jr. ... Caldwell, ID
Cross, John T. ... Louisville, KY
Cross, Jonathan ... Tuscaloosa, AL
Cross, Jonathan A. ... Denver, CO
Cross, Jonathan E. ... Philadelphia, PA
Cross, Jonathan W.
Department of Transportation,
Federal Aviation Administration, GV
Cross, Joseph Matthew ... Fort Worth, TX
Cross, Joseph R., Jr. ... Columbia, SC
Cross, Judith A. ... Springfield, MA
Cross, Judith A. ... Medina, OH
Cross, Junius Bracy, Jr. ... Little Rock, AR
Cross, Kathleen E. ... Boston, MA
Cross, Keith F. ... Colorado Springs, CO
Cross, Kenneth C. ... Austin, TX
Cross, Kenneth C., Jr. ... Chiefland, FL
Cross, Kim R. ... Department of Justice,
Office of Justice Programs, GV
Cross & Kimenker ... Needham, MA
Cross, L. Warren, II ... Stafford, TX
Cross, Laura L. ... Oklahoma City, OK
Cross, LeAnn Wainscott ... Dallas, TX
Cross, Lee ... Brooklyn, NY
Cross, Leland B., Jr. ... Indianapolis, IN
Cross & Lieberman, P.A. ... Phoenix, AZ
Cross, Lisa A. ... Anaheim, CA
Cross, Lisa C. ... Birmingham, AL
Cross, Lisa M. ... San Diego, CA
Cross, Mark Austin ... Oregon City, OR
Cross, Mark Austin, P.C. ... Oregon City, OR
Cross, Marshall, Schuck, DeWeese, Cross & Feick, Professional Corporation
Muncie, IN
Cross, Martin L. ... Manassas, VA
Cross, Mary Alice ... Minneapolis, MN
Cross, Melanie B. ... Tifton, GA
Cross, Meredith B. ... Washington, DC
Cross, Merrill N. ... Norton, MA
Cross, Michael A. ... Los Angeles, CA
Cross, Michael E. ... Baltimore, MD
Cross, Michael E. ... Bartlett, TN
Cross, Michael J. ... Hampton, IA

Cross, Michael R. ... Visalia, CA
Cross, Milton H. ... Philadelphia, PA
Cross, Murphy, Smuck & Houston
Washington, DC
Cross, Nancy L. ... Indianapolis, IN
Cross, Neil S. ... Chicago, IL
Cross, Noble C. ... Dallas, TX
Cross, Nola J. Hitchcock ... Milwaukee, WI
Cross, Nori J. McCann ... Salem, OR
Cross, Othello ... Pine Bluff, AR
Cross, P. Gregory ... Muncie, IN
Cross, Pamela F. ... Harrisburg, PA
Cross, Patricia Foy ... Barrington, IL
Cross, Patrick S. ... Indianapolis, IN
Cross, Pearcy & Burgess ... Nashville, IL
Cross, Peter A., (P.C.) ... New York, NY
Cross, Philip D. ... Portsmouth, NH
Cross, Phillip Samuel ... Washington, DC
Cross, R. Graham ... Longview, WA
Cross, R. Scott ... Ocala, FL
Cross, Raymond R. ... New Smyrna Beach, FL
Cross, Richard A. ... Berkeley, CA
Cross, Richard A. ... Los Angeles, CA
Cross, Richard G. ... Livingston, AL
Cross, Richard H., Jr. ... Wilmington, DE
Cross, Richard R. ... Woodstock, IL
Cross, Richard W. ... Baraboo, WI
Lake Delton, WI
Cross & Robbins, P.A. ... Ocala, FL
Cross, Robert C. ... Sacramento, CA
Cross, Robert C. ... Blue Island, IL
Cross, Robert Curtis ... Cleveland, OH
Cross, Robert L. ... Santa Clara, CA
Cross, Robert L. ... Nashville, IL
Cross, Robert P., IV ... Chicago, IL
Cross, Robert R. ... San Francisco, CA
Cross, Robert W. ... New York, NY
Cross, Robert W. M. ... Selma, CA
Cross, Roberta Buchman ... El Paso, TX
Cross, Rona West ... Boston, MA
Cross, Ronald D. ... Austin, TX
Cross, Ronald L. ... Richmond, IN
Cross & Rose Co., L.P.A. ... Canton, OH
Cross, Ryan N. ... Bartlesville, OK
Cross, Sandra L. ... San Francisco, CA
Cross, Scott G. ... Fresno, CA
Cross, Shaun M. ... Spokane, WA
Cross, Silas G., Jr. ... Tuscaloosa, AL
Cross, Spencer C. ... Ocoee, FL
Cross, Stanley A. ... Sacramento, CA
Cross, Stephen F. ... Borger, TX
Cross, Steven C. ... St. Paul, MN
Cross, Susan Anne ... Rock Hill, SC
Cross, Susan Lynn ... La Crescenta, CA
Cross, Terence H. ... Palo Alto, CA
Cross, Terry I. ... Dallas, TX
Cross, Theodore L. ... New York, NY
Cross, Thomas F., Jr. ... Minnetonka, MN
Cross, Thomas H., III ... Joliet, IL
Cross, Thomas R. ... Colorado Springs, CO
Cross, Thomas R., P.C.
Colorado Springs, CO
Cross, T.J. ... Nashville, TN
Cross, Tracy J. ... Durango, CO
Cross, Valerie L. ... Ithaca, NY
Cross, W. Dennis ... Kansas City, MO
Cross, Wanda W. ... Memphis, TN
Cross, Wayne A. ... New York, NY
Cross, William A., Jr. ... Needham, MA
Cross, William S., (P.C.)
Fort Lauderdale, FL
Cross Wrock, A Professional Corporation
Washington, DC
Detroit, MI
Harbor Springs, MI
Livonia, MI
Petoskey, MI
Crossan, Amy Christine ... Huntington, WV
Crossan, James E. ... Towson, MD
Crossan, John R. ... Chicago, IL
Crossdale, Carol F. ... Purchase, NY
Crosse, Charles G., IV ... Denver, CO
Crosse, Kester I. H. ... Newark, DE
Wilmington, DE
Crosse Law Office, P.C. ... Denver, CO
Crossen, Edward T. ... Boston, MA
Crossen, Gary C. ... Boston, MA
Crossen, James E. ... Pottsville, PA
Crossen, James R. ... Morgan Hill, CA
Crossen, Janet S.
Board of Governors Of The Federal Reserve System,
Office of the General Counsel, GV
Crossen, Kevin J. ... Danbury, CT
Crossen, Martha J. ... Terre Haute, IN
Crossen, Michael K. ... Boston, MA
Crossen, Sarah (IBA) ... New York, NY
Crossen, Trevor J. ... Indianapolis, IN
Crosser, Robert M. ... Lansing, MI
Crossett, David S. ... Chicago, IL
Crossett, Edgar L., III ... Atlanta, GA
Crossett, Edgar L., III, P.C. ... Atlanta, GA
Crossett, Jennifer A. ... New York, NY
Crossett, John M. ... Liberty, MO
Crossett, Kevin Stephen ... Plainsboro, NJ
Crossett, Lynn ... Austin, TX
Crossett & Mevec ... Syracuse, NY
Crossett, Peter J. ... Syracuse, NY
Crossett, Robert P. ... Marietta, GA
Crossett, William W., IV ... Syracuse, NY
Crossetta, William J., Jr. ... Buffalo, NY
Crossette, Sheldon M. ... Overland Park, KS
Crossfield, Charles D. ... Round Rock, TX
Crossin, Agnes A. ... Larchmont, NY
Crossin, Richard P. ... South Orange, NJ
Crossin, William J. ... Larchmont, NY
Crossing, Randall F. ... Memphis, TN

Crossland, Daniel T., Law Offices of
Wilmington, DE
Crossland, Donna L. ... Brunswick, GA
Crossland, Edward C. ... Cumberland, MD
Crossland, Hugh J. ... Newton, MA
Crossland, Jeffrey J. ... Lewisburg, PA
Crossland, Jennifer E. ... Chesterfield, VA
Crossland, Julia A. ... Boise, ID
Crossland, Lisa K. W. ... Wilmington, DE
Crossland, Margaret J. ... San Francisco, CA
Crossland, Mark T. ... Woodbridge, VA
Crossland, Robert D., Law Offices of
Fresno, CA
San Mateo, CA
Crossland, Robert S. ... Fresno, CA
Crossland, Ross S., Law Office of
Austin, TX
Crossland, Stephen R. ... Cashmere, WA
Wenatchee, WA
Crossland, Wendy Davis ... Seattle, WA
Crossland, William L. ... Fresno, CA
Crossley, Benjamin L. ... Lansing, MI
Crossley, Conly K. ... Monroe, MI
Crossley, Dennis J. ... Garden City, NY
Crossley, Elizabeth Wood
Greensboro, NC
Crossley, John F. ... Wilmington, NC
Crossley Law Firm, The, A Professional Corporation ... Knoxville, TN
Crossley McIntosh Prior & Collier
Wilmington, NC
Crossley, R. Louis, Jr. ... Knoxville, TN
Crossley, Robert L. ... Knoxville, TN
Crossley, Troy L. ... Provo, UT
Crosslin, Gregory Dale ... Montgomery, AL
Crosslin, Slaten & O'Connor, P.C.
Birmingham, AL
Huntsville, AL
Mobile, AL
Montgomery, AL
Crossman, Avery Naomi ... Phoenix, AZ
Crossman, Darryl H. ... Cleveland, OH
Crossman, David A. ... Chicago, IL
Crossman, F. Ann ... Dayton, OH
Crossman, Fred L., Jr. ... Chicago, IL
Crossman, Harlan J. ... Phoenix, AZ
Crossman, Harlan J., P.C. ... Phoenix, AZ
Crossman & Hosford ... Omaha, NE
Crossman, John K. ... Denver, CO
Chicago, IL
Boston, MA
New York, NY
Philadelphia, PA
Crossman, Laurel M. ... Provo, UT
Crossman, Raymond M., Jr. ... Omaha, NE
Crossman, Richard C. ... Fresno, CA
Crossman, Robert M. ... Arthur, IL
Crossman, Scott B. ... Minneapolis, MN
Crossman, Stephanie A ... Tallahassee, FL
Crossman, William Vaughton
Canon City, CO
Crossmore, Edward Y. ... Ithaca, NY
Crossmore Law Office ... Ithaca, NY
Crosson, Cathy E. ... Bloomington, IN
Crosson, Elaine M. ... Central Islip, NY
Crosson, Kenneth L. ... Fairfax, VA
Crosson, Lynn A. ... Birmingham, AL
Crosson, Matthew T. ... New York, NY
Crosson, Michael W. ... Sacramento, CA
Crossot, Eugene A. ... Mequon, WI
Crossroads Law Center, P.C. ... Chicago, IL
Crossroads Law Offices ... Oklahoma City, OK
Crosswell, Harry B. ... Pottsville, PA
Crosswell, William C. ... Lancaster, PA
Crosswhite, Christopher L.
Washington, DC
Crosswhite, Craig S. ... Jetmore, KS
Crosswhite, Donna Richards
St. Louis, MO
Crosswhite, Ilona T. ... Hartford, CT
Crosswhite, Joseph N. ... Statesville, NC
Crosswhite, Kristine A. ... Baltimore, MD
Crosswhite, Lloyd R. ... Fort Worth, TX
Crosswhite, Mark A. ... Birmingham, AL
Crosswhite, McKenna & Limbrick, LLP
Baltimore, MD
Crosswhite, Robert N. ... Lakeside, MT
Crosswhite, William E. ... Statesville, NC
Crost, Hillard ... Buffalo Grove, IL
Crost, Katharine I. ... New York, NY
Crost, Paul E. ... Los Angeles, CA
Los Angeles, CA
Crost, Paul E. ... Orange, CA
Riverside, CA
Crost, Paul E. ... San Bernardino, CA
Crost, Paul E. ... San Bernardino, CA
Crosthwait, Frank O., Jr. ... Indianola, MS
Jackson, MS
Crosthwait, Joe ... Joplin, MO
Crosthwait, M. Joe, Jr. ... Midwest City, OK
Crosthwait & Reneau ... Midwest City, OK
Oklahoma City, OK
Crosthwait Terney & Noble, PLLC
Indianola, MS
Crosthwait Terney, PLLC ... Jackson, MS
Crosthwaite, Daryl A. ... Cincinnati, OH
Croston, Alyssa Silver ... Hauppauge, NY
Croston, Jerome L. ... Garland, TX
Croston, Michael John ... West Babylon, NY
Croswell & Adams Co., L.P.A.
Cincinnati, OH
Croswell, Brewington W. ... Philadelphia, PA
Croswell, David Lee ... Reedville, VA
Croswell, Jeffrey N. ... Riverside, CA
Croswell, R. Scott, III ... Cincinnati, OH
Croswell, William V. ... Tucson, AZ
Croteau, Francis L. ... Fountain Valley, CA
Croteau, Norman R. ... Auburn, ME

Croteau, Raymond, Jr. ....Manassas, VA
Croteau, Roger P. ....Las Vegas, NV
Croteau, Roger P. & Associates, Ltd. Las Vegas, NV
Crothamel, Donna M. ....Philadelphia, PA
Crothers, Cathy L. ....Sacramento, CA
Crothers, Daniel J. ....Fargo, ND
Crothers, Diane ....Department of Labor, Employment Standards Administration, GV
Crothers & Hansen, P.C. ....Salem, OR
Crothers, Joanne M., Chrtd. ....Alexandria, VA
Crothers, Leah W. S. ....Boston, MA
Crothers, Robert T. ....Washington, PA
Crothers, William C. ....Salem, OR
Crotser, Larry A. ....Highland Park, IL; Westwood, NJ
Crotser, Michele L. ....Willoughby, OH
Crotta, Carol A. ....Los Angeles, CA
Crotta, Daniel W. ....San Diego, CA
Crotta, David J., Jr. ....New Haven, CT
Crotte, Alberto D. ....Toledo, OH
Crotteau, Craig A. ....Washington, DC
Crotteau, James ....Lamoine, ME
Crotteau, Richard D. ....Chattanooga, TN
Crotteau, Richard D., Jr. ....Reston, VA
Crotts, Amy K. ....Department of Commerce, Office of the General Counsel, GV
Crotts, Milton B. ....Clemmons, NC
Crotts, Troy J. ....St. Petersburg, FL
Crotts, William P. ....Phoenix, AZ
Crotty, Anne L. ....San Marino, CA
Crotty, Anne L. ....Kittanning, PA
Crotty, Anne M. ....Danvers, MA
Crotty & Bartlett, P.A. Daytona Beach, FL
Crotty, Bernard W. ....Los Angeles, CA
Crotty, Carole ....Sherman Oaks, CA
Crotty, Cassandra A. ....Chicago, IL
Crotty, Donald S. ....Bridgewater, MA
Crotty, Douglas M., III ....Garden City, KS
Crotty, Edward R., Jr. ....Kansas City, MO
Crotty & Fitzgerald ....Pocahontas, IA
Crotty, Francis P. ....Morristown, NJ
Crotty, J. Desmond ....Pocahontas, IA
Crotty, James T. ....Chicago, IL
Crotty, Jason A. ....San Francisco, CA
Crotty, Jerome F. ....Chicago, IL
Crotty & Johansen, L.L.P. ....Dallas, TX
Crotty, John F. ....Red Bank, NJ
Crotty, John M. ....Orlando, FL
Crotty, John M. ....Albany, NY
Crotty, John T. ....Phoenix, AZ
Crotty, Jonathan M. ....Charlotte, NC
Crotty, Kathleen L. ....Daytona Beach, FL
Crotty Law Office, P.A. ....Garden City, KS
Crotty, Lisa M. ....Charlotte, NC
Crotty, Mary C. ....New York, NY
Crotty, Michael D. ....Daytona Beach, FL
Crotty, Michael F. ....Washington, DC
Crotty & Mindlin ....Sherman Oaks, CA
Crotty, Paul A. ....New York, NY
Crotty, Peter ....Albany, NY
Crotty, Philip A. ....New Windsor, NY
Crotty, Rebecca ....Garden City, KS
Crotty, Richard D. ....Council Bluffs, IA
Crotty, Richard G. ....Northbrook, IL
Crotty, Richard G. ....Worcester, MA
Crotty, Robert B. ....Dallas, TX
Crotty, Robert E. ....New York, NY
Crotty, Robert J. ....Spokane, WA
Crotty, Sean B. ....Chicago, IL
Crotty, Sheila ....Newark, NJ
Crotty, Thomas L., Jr. ....Boston, MA
Crotty, Thomas P. ....New Bedford, MA
Crotty, W. Garrett (Gary) Daytona Beach, FL
Crotty, William R. ....Albany, NY
Crotty-Steinmetz, Karen A. ....Albany, NY
Crotwell, Amelia G. ....Knoxville, TN
Crotzer, Darold E., Jr. ....St. Louis, MO
Crotzer and Ford ....St. Louis, MO
Crouch, A. G., III ....Alvin, TX
Crouch, Allen L. ....Philadelphia, PA
Crouch, Auley M., III ....Wilmington, NC
Crouch & Bannasch, P.C. ....San Diego, CA
Crouch, Bob W. ....Springfield, MO
Crouch, Bonnie S. ....Miami, FL
Crouch, Carolyn ....Hickory, NC
Crouch, Charles L., III Santa Monica, CA
Crouch & Crouch ....Arlington, VA
Crouch, Davis & Rykowski ....Springfield, MO
Crouch, Delia T. ....Newnan, GA
Crouch, Donald A., Jr. ....New York, NY
Crouch, Ford W. ....Minneapolis, MN
Crouch, Franklin M. ....Chicago, IL
Crouch, Fred W. ....Kansas City, MO
Crouch, Garrett R. ....Warrensburg, MO
Crouch, Garrett R., II ....Warrensburg, MO
Crouch, Howard E. ....Pawcatuck, CT
Crouch, Hubert A., III ....Dallas, TX
Crouch & Inabnett ....Dallas, TX
Crouch, J. Michael ....Birmingham, AL
Crouch, James A. ....Raleigh, NC
Crouch, James A ....Houston, TX
Crouch, James C. ....Forsyth, MO
Crouch, James E. ....Springdale, AR
Crouch, James E. ....Hamilton, TX
Crouch, James R. ....Las Cruces, NM
Crouch, Jeffrey L. ....Dallas, TX
Crouch, Jewell C. ....Des Moines, IA
Crouch, Jimmy E. ....Denton, TX
Crouch, Joel N. ....Dallas, TX
Crouch, John E. ....Auburn, ME
Crouch, John H. ....Long Beach, MS
Crouch, John H., IV ....Dallas, TX
Crouch, John Howard ....Arlington, VA
Crouch, John P. ....Indianola, IA
Crouch, John W. ....Victorville, CA
Crouch, Julie McIntyre ....Pasadena, CA
Crouch, Karen A. ....San Antonio, TX
Crouch, Keith M. ....Boulder, CO
Crouch, Keith N. ....South Pasadena, CA
Crouch, Kimberley R. ....Detroit, MI
Crouch, Larry J. ....Hanford, CA
Crouch, Laurence E. ....Menlo Park, CA; San Francisco, CA
Crouch Law Office ....Alvin, TX; Missouri City, TX
Crouch, Leslie M. ....San Diego, CA
Crouch, Linda M. ....Johnson City, TN
Crouch, Melinda Haynie ....Wilmington, NC
Crouch & Miner, P.A. Hallandale Beach, FL
Crouch, Moira A. ....New York, NY
Crouch, R. Milton ....Atlanta, GA
Crouch, Richard E. ....Arlington, VA
Crouch, Robert C. ....Greenville, TX
Crouch, Robert C., P.C. ....Greenville, TX
Crouch, Robert G. ....Boulder, CO
Crouch, Robert P., Jr. ....Roanoke, VA
Crouch, Ronald W. ....Pittsburgh, PA
Crouch, S. Lee ....Hallandale Beach, FL
Crouch, Spangler & Douglas ....Belton, MO; Harrisonville, MO
Crouch, Spencer K. ....Wichita Falls, TX
Crouch, Steven L. ....Kansas City, MO
Crouch, Suzanne S. ....Indianapolis, IN
Crouch, T. Allen ....Gainesville, FL
Crouch, Thomas G. ....Dallas, TX
Crouch, Thomas G., Inc. ....Dallas, TX
Crouch, Thomas H. ....Minneapolis, MN
Crouch, Thomas T., Jr. ....Seattle, WA
Crouch, Thos. C., Jr. ....Richmond, VA
Crouch, Victor R. ....Toledo, OH
Crouch, Walter H. ....Nashville, TN
Crouch and White ....Hamilton, TX
Crouch, Wm. E. ....Houston, TX
Croucher and Jones ....Canandaigua, NY
Crouchet, Jack H. ....Denver, CO
Crouchley, Daniel G. ....Omaha, NE
Crouchley, John S. ....Los Angeles, CA
Crouchley, Robert G. ....Warwick, RI
Crouchman, William A. ....St. Clair Shores, MI
Croudace & Dietrich ....Irvine, CA
Croudace, Virginia P. ....Irvine, CA
Crough, Maureen M. ....New York, NY
Crouppen, Terry B. ....St. Louis, MO
Crouse, Charles M., Jr. ....Frankfort, IN
Crouse Cobb & Bays ....Charleston, IL; Edwardsville, IL
Crouse, Daniel D. ....Redmond, WA
Crouse, Dee Ann Wunschel ....Carroll, IA
Crouse, Gerald L., Jr. ....Waukesha, WI
Crouse, Gordon J. ....Denver, CO
Crouse, Gregory A. ....Painesville, OH
Crouse, Jacqueline S. ....Los Angeles, CA
Crouse, James Teague ....Arlington, VA
Crouse, Jeanne M. ....Department of Justice, Executive Office for United States Trustees, GV
Crouse, John O. ....Hillsboro, OH
Crouse, Joseph R. ....Baltimore, MD
Crouse, Kevin D. ....Jasper, IN
Crouse, Lawrence W. ....Denver, CO
Crouse, Lewis R., II ....Santa Ana, CA
Crouse, Lynda M. ....Atlanta, GA
Crouse, M. Therese ....Scottsdale, AZ
Crouse, Margaret A. ....Boston, MA
Crouse, Peter J. ....Broomfield, CO
Crouse, R. Daniel ....Southfield, MI
Crouse, Robert N. ....Raleigh, NC
Crouser, Bradley A. ....Charleston, WV
Crouse-Smith, Elizabeth ....Hillsboro, OH
Croushore, Bruce J. ....Mobile, AL
Croushore, Paul ....Cincinnati, OH
Crousore, Andrew P. ....Palo Alto, CA
Croussouloudis, Artemis ....New York, NY
Crout, Charles M. ....Washington, DC
Crout, Daniel W. ....Covington, KY
Crout, John K. ....Mount Pleasant, SC
Crout, Joseph M. ....Memphis, TN
Crout, William B. ....El Paso, TX
Croutch, Barbara L. ....Los Angeles, CA
Croutch, Todd E. ....Woodland Hills, CA
Croutch, William H. ....Overland Park, KS
Crouter, Jerrol A. ....Portland, ME
Crouter, Mary Jean ....Augusta, ME
Crouter, Mary M. Department of Transportation, Office of the General Counsel, GV
Crouter, Mary R. ....Austin, TX
Crouter, Richard Van ....Yucca Valley, CA
Crouthamel, Roger P. ....Hagåtña, GU
Crouther, LeRoy, Jr. ....St. Louis, MO
Croutier, William J. ....Rockville Centre, NY
Croutier, William J., Jr. ....Mineola, NY
Crovella, Dennis C. ....San Diego, CA
Crovella, Linda S. Harris ....Buffalo, NY
Crovo, Marie D. ....Cambridge, MA
Crow, Alexander J. ....Rockville, MD
Crow, Carl A., Jr., & Associates Hot Springs National Park, AR
Crow, Carl A., Jr., & Associates Hot Springs Village, AR
Crow, Carl T. ....Seattle, WA
Crow, Carl V. ....Houston, TX
Crow, Carl V., PLLC ....Houston, TX
Crow, Carol A. ....Covina, CA
Crow, Charles S., III ....Princeton, NJ
Crow, Cheri L. ....Reading, MA
Crow, Cherie N. ....Olathe, KS
Crow, Christina D. ....Union Springs, AL
Crow, Clothier & Bates ....Leavenworth, KS
Crow and Crow ....Pomeroy, OH
Crow, Dan C. ....San Antonio, TX
Crow, Daniel W. ....Topeka, KS
Crow, David E., Jr. ....East Haven, CT
Crow, David F. ....West Palm Beach, FL
Crow, Debra ....Santa Rosa, CA
Crow, Donna L. ....St. Clairsville, OH
Crow, Douglas G. ....Clearwater, FL
Crow, Douglas M. ....New York, NY
Crow, Duncan R. ....Mobile, AL
Crow, Fred W., III ....Pomeroy, OH
Crow, Frederick W. ....Indianapolis, IN
Crow, Glenn L. ....Westminster, CO
Crow, Gregory L. ....Paragould, AR
Crow, Harvey M., Jr. ....Rapid City, SD
Crow, I. Carson ....Pomeroy, OH
Crow, James H., III ....Birmingham, AL
Crow, James M. ....Hastings, MN
Crow, Jeff A., Jr. ....Memphis, TN
Crow, Jeff A., Jr., P.C. ....Memphis, TN
Crow, Jerald D. ....Conroe, TX
Crow, Jerry O. ....Fort Jones, CA; Ventura, CA
Crow, Jim ....Waco, TX
Crow, John ....Tucson, AZ
Crow, John C. ....Springfield, MO
Crow, John Emmett ....Pasadena, TX
Crow, John J., Jr. ....Water Valley, MS
Crow, John L. ....St. Joseph, MI
Crow, Jonathan D ....Albany, OR
Crow & Joseph ....Tarpon Springs, FL
Crow, Keith S. ....Chicago, IL
Crow, Kenneth H. ....Waco, TX
Crow, Kenneth V. ....Little Rock, AR
Crow, Lauren Meyer ....Detroit, MI
Crow Law Firm, The, A Professional Corporation ....Phoenix, AZ; Tempe, AZ; Tucson, AZ; Sacramento, CA; San Dimas, CA; Amarillo, TX
Crow, Lawrence D. ....Tarpon Springs, FL
Crow, Liza M. ....San Antonio, TX
Crow, Lon Worth, IV ....Avon Park, FL
Crow, M. Carter ....Houston, TX
Crow, Margaret B. ....Oakland, CA
Crow, Mark A. ....Burlington, VT
Crow, Martha Burnett ....Leavenworth, KS
Crow, Melissa E. ....Washington, DC
Crow, Michael ....Leavenworth, KS
Crow, Michael D. ....Farmington Hills, MI
Crow, Michael G. ....New Orleans, LA
Crow, Michael J. ....Montgomery, AL
Crow, Michael L. ....Sacramento, CA
Crow, Nancy R. ....Denver, CO
Crow, Nelson T. ....Muskogee, OK
Crow, Patricia Renner ....Indianapolis, IN
Crow, Patrick F. ....Newcastle, WY
Crow, Patrick F., Law Offices of Newcastle, WY
Crow, Patrick Q. ....Dallas, TX
Crow, Paula Elliott ....Conroe, TX
Crow, R. Allen ....Anniston, AL
Crow, Reynolds, Shetley & McVey, LLP Caruthersville, MO; Kennett, MO
Crow, Richard Anthony ....Houston, TX
Crow, Richard E. ....Sacramento, CA
Crow, Richard E., II ....Sacramento, CA
Crow, Robert G. ....Oakland, CA
Crow, Robin C. ....McAllen, TX
Crow, Robroy Lee ....Findlay, OH
Crow, Sam A. ....Topeka, KS
Crow, Samuel J. ....Asheville, NC
Crow, Scot C. ....Columbus, OH
Crow, Sonia F. ....Washington, DC
Crow, Stanley D. ....Boise, ID
Crow, Steven L. ....Smyrna, GA
Crow & Tartanella ....Princeton, NJ
Crow, Vincent E. ....Rock Springs, WY
Crow, Wade R. ....Bennettsville, SC
Crow, Wade R. ....Florence, SC
Crow, Wendell W. ....Kennett, MO
Crow, William B., P.C. ....Portland, OR
Crow, William L. ....Vallejo, CA
Crowden, Beverly Ashley ....Waco, TX
Crowder, A. Courtney ....Tuscaloosa, AL
Crowder, Albert M., Jr. Colorado Springs, CO
Crowder, Angela J. ....New York, NY
Crowder, Barbara L. ....Edwardsville, IL
Crowder, Charles B. ....Long Beach, CA
Crowder, Charles H., III ....South Hill, VA
Crowder, Charles R. ....Birmingham, AL
Crowder, Cheryl D. ....Everett, MA
Crowder, Dale F. ....Irving, TX
Crowder, Daniel F. ....Houston, TX
Crowder, Debra A. ....Rochester, NY
Crowder, Douglas A. ....Van Nuys, CA
Crowder, Douglas A., Law Offices of, A Professional Corporation ....Van Nuys, CA
Crowder, Douglas S. ....Eufaula, OK
Crowder, Edwin A. ....Boydton, VA
Crowder, Elizabeth ....Chicago, IL
Crowder, Elizabeth H. ....Dallas, TX
Crowder, Floyd E. ....Columbia, IL
Crowder, J. Lane ....Seattle, WA
Crowder, Jack A., Jr. ....Falls Church, VA
Crowder, James F., Jr. ....Miami, FL
Crowder, James L. ....Santa Barbara, CA
Crowder, James L. ....Chattanooga, TN
Crowder, James M. ....Land O'Lakes, FL
Crowder, Jason M. ....Mattoon, IL
Crowder, Jerry, Jr. ....St. Louis, MO
Crowder, John T., Jr. ....Mobile, AL
Crowder, Jonathan M. ....Lakeland, FL
Crowder, Kimberly A. ....Washington, DC
Crowder, Kirk R. ....St. Louis, MO
Crowder, Mark S. ....Goshen, IN
Crowder, Martin T. ....Seattle, WA
Crowder, Mary Kay ....Marion, OH
Crowder, Mildred S. ....Coral Gables, FL
Crowder, Nathion F. ....Houston, TX
Crowder, Paul J., Jr. ....Scottsdale, AZ
Crowder, Richard D. ....Wichita, KS
Crowder, Richard R. ....Lynchburg, VA
Crowder, Richard W. ....Goshen, IN
Crowder, Robert B. ....Houston, TX
Crowder, Robert S. ....Los Angeles, CA
Crowder, Ronald G. ....Colorado Springs, CO
Crowder, Ronald G., P.C. Colorado Springs, CO
Crowder, Russell H. ....Minneapolis, MN
Crowder, Sarah A. ....Raleigh, NC
Crowder & Scoggins, Ltd. ....Columbia, IL; Waterloo, IL
Crowder & Seltzer, P.C. ....Houston, TX
Crowder & Taliana ....Edwardsville, IL
Crowder, Thomas E. ....Jacksonville, FL
Crowder, Travis C. ....Houston, TX
Crowder, Wayner P. ....Atlanta, GA
Crowder, William Craig ....Tampa, FL
Crowder, Winston P. ....Houston, TX
Crowder-Dorsey, Kathy ....Circleville, OH
Crowdis, David G. ....Sacramento, CA
Crowdus, W. Warren, III Washington, DC
Crowe, A. Evans ....Mobile, AL
Crowe, Alice M. ....Washington, DC
Crowe, Ann C. ....St. Paul, MN
Crowe, Anne Smith ....Dallas, TX
Crowe, Ara M., Jr. ....Baltimore, MD
Crowe, Austin W., Jr. ....Portland, OR
Crowe, Bernard F. ....Ridgefield, CT
Crowe, Betsy L. ....Houston, TX
Crowe, Billie L. ....Treasury Department, Internal Revenue Service, GV
Crowe, Brian L. ....Chicago, IL
Crowe, Bruce F. ....St. Louis, MO
Crowe, Christine M. ....Washington, DC
Crowe, Christopher N. ....Richmond, VA
Crowe & Crowe, Inc. ....Oklahoma City, OK
Crowe, Cynthia M. ....Houston, TX
Crowe, Daniel A. ....St. Louis, MO
Crowe, Daniel F. ....Westfield, NJ
Crowe, Daniel T. ....Chicago, IL
Crowe, Daniel W. ....Visalia, CA
Crowe, Danny C. ....Columbia, SC
Crowe, David ....Athens, GA
Crowe, David L. ....San Francisco, CA
Crowe, David M. ....New York, NY
Crowe, David W. ....Dallas, TX
Crowe & Day LLP ....Los Angeles, CA; Santa Monica, CA
Crowe, Deegan & Dickson Glen Cove, NY; Mattituck, NY; **Mineola, NY**
Crowe, Donald R. ....Chicago, IL
Crowe, Donna M. ....Birmingham, AL
Crowe & Dunlevy ....Norman, OK; Oklahoma City, OK; Tulsa, OK
Crowe & Dunn ....Boston, MA
Crowe, Eric M. ....Los Angeles, CA
Crowe, Eugene F. ....Ridgewood, NY
Crowe, Gary A. ....Kalispell, MT
Crowe, Guthrie F. ....Fort Lauderdale, FL
Crowe, H. Kent ....Newton, NC
Crowe, Harry M., Jr. ....Tulsa, OK
Crowe, J. Michael, (A Professional Corporation) ....Santa Monica, CA
Crowe, Jack ....Chicago, IL
Crowe, Jaime M. ....Washington, DC
Crowe, James A. ....New York, NY
Crowe, James B. ....Coeur d'Alene, ID
Crowe, James E., Jr. ....St. Louis, MO
Crowe, James J. ....Cincinnati, OH
Crowe, James R. ....Springfield, MA
Crowe, Jean N. ....Nashville, TN
Crowe, Joel P. ....Portsmouth, VA
Crowe, John J. ....New York, NY
Crowe, John L. ....Chesterfield, MO
Crowe, John T. ....Visalia, CA
Crowe, John W. ....Rochester, NY
Crowe, John W., Jr. ....Buffalo, NY
Crowe, Katherine M. ....Phoenix, AZ
Crowe, Kay Gaffney ....Columbia, SC
Crowe, Kevin F. ....Jersey City, NJ
Crowe Law Offices, The ....Visalia, CA
Crowe, Lawrence E. ....Rockford, IL
Crowe, Lorenzo W., Jr. ....Easton, PA
Crowe, Marcia A. ....Flemington, NJ
Crowe, Mark A. ....Lancaster, PA
Crowe, Martin A. ....Darien, CT
Crowe, Martin J. ....Belfast, ME
Crowe, Michael A. ....Newton, MA
Crowe, Michael C. ....Canton, NY
Crowe, Michael R. ....Austin, TX
Crowe, Michael S. ....Kansas City, MO
Crowe, Norman J., Jr. ....Sylvester, GA
Crowe, Patricia ....Madison, WI
Crowe, Patricia J. ....Boston, MA
Crowe, Patrick J. ....Mineola, NY
Crowe, Philip J., Jr. ....Boston, MA
Crowe, R. Denning ....Oklahoma City, OK
Crowe, R. William ....Jacksonville, FL
Crowe, Rae M. ....Mobile, AL
Crowe, Richard M. ....Austin, TX
Crowe, Robert B., (P.C.) ....Washington, DC; Boston, MA
Crowe, Robert J. ....Department of Commerce, Patent and Trademark Office, GV
Crowe, Robert K., Law Office of San Francisco, CA
Crowe, Robert L. ....Brunswick, GA

Crowe, Robert W. .... **Newark, DE**
Wilmington, DE
Crowe, Robert W. .... Winnetka, IL
Crowe, Roger L., Jr. .... Beaufort, NC
Crowe, Roger L., Jr., P.A. .... Beaufort, NC
Crowe, Samuel J. .... **Conyers, GA**
Crowe, Samuel P. .... **Ontario, CA**
Crowe & Scott, P.A. .... **Phoenix, AZ**
Crowe, Stephen C. .... Milford, OH
Crowe, Susan L. .... Kingston, NY
Crowe, Suzanne S. .... Edina, MN
Crowe, Thomas E. .... **Las Vegas, NV**
Crowe, Thomas E., Professional Law Corporation .... **Las Vegas, NV**
Crowe, Thomas K. .... **Washington, DC**
Crowe, Thomas K., P.C., Law Offices of .... **Washington, DC**
Crowe, Thomas L. .... Columbia, MD
Crowe, Tom .... **Phoenix, AZ**
Crowe, Vincent W. .... **White Plains, NY**
Crowe, Walter M., Jr. .... Brooklyn, NY
Crowe & Welch .... Milford, OH
Crowe, William D. .... **Boston, MA**
Crowe, William J. .... **Louisville, KY**
Crowe, William J., Jr. .... Syosset, NY
Crowe, William L., Sr. .... New Orleans, LA
Crowe, William R. .... **Wethersfield, CT**
Crowe, William R. .... Buffalo, NY
Crowe, Williams G. .... Springfield, MO
Crowe & Zimmer .... Kingston, NY
Crowell, Amanda G. .... **Lebanon, TN**
Crowell, Ann C. .... Saratoga Springs, NY
Crowell, Anthony O. .... Bluffton, IN
Crowell, Anthony William .... New York, NY
Crowell, Barbara D. .... Wilmington, DE
Crowell, Barry E.
Department Of The Interior, Office of Legislation, GV
Crowell, C. Wesley .... **Kennebunk, ME**
Crowell, Carl D. .... Salem, OR
Crowell, Caron D. .... New Orleans, LA
Crowell, Chancey C. .... Wenatchee, WA
Crowell and Chapin, P.C. .... **Casper, WY**
Crowell, Charles F. .... Dennis, MA
Crowell, Constance J. .... Apple Valley, MN
Crowell, David A. .... Seattle, WA
Crowell, David J. .... **New York, NY**
Crowell, Dean W. .... **Washington, DC**
Crowell, Donald N. .... **Winter Park, FL**
Crowell, Donald R. .... Phoenix, AZ
Crowell, Donald R., II .... Danbury, CT
Crowell, Douglas G. .... **Los Angeles, CA**
Crowell, Dwight L., III .... **Salisbury, NC**
Crowell, Eldon H. .... **Washington, DC**
Crowell, Frederick P. .... **San Diego, CA**
Crowell, Gail A. .... **Biloxi, MS**
Crowell, George Bradford .... Rolla, MO
Crowell, Gustav H. .... Tavernier, FL
Crowell, Hendrick S. .... Suisun City, CA
Crowell, James Douglas .... **Irving, TX**
Crowell, James N. .... Redondo Beach, CA
Crowell, Jane Orci .... Department of Justice, Bureau of Prisons, GV
Crowell, Jason Glennon
Cape Girardeau, MO
Crowell, John B., Jr. .... **Portland, OR**
Crowell, John P. .... **Portland, OR**
Crowell, John W. .... **Columbus, MS**
Crowell, Joseph M. .... Gulf Breeze, FL
Crowell, Judith .... Providence, RI
Crowell, Kenneth E. .... **New York, NY**
Crowell, Larry G. .... Englewood, OH
Crowell, Lawrence .... Canton, OH
Crowell, M. Catherine .... **Durham, NC**
Crowell, Melissa Garland
San Francisco, CA
Crowell, Merrie-Roxie, (P.A.)
Clearwater, FL
Crowell, Michael .... **Raleigh, NC**
Crowell & Moring LLP .... **Irvine, CA**
Los Angeles, CA
Washington, DC
Crowell, Nicholas P. .... **New York, NY**
Crowell, Nuckols, Layman & Aust
Pulaski, VA
Crowell & Otten .... Red Bank, NJ
Crowell and Owens, L.L.C.
Alexandria, LA
Crowell, Patrick C. .... **Orlando, FL**
Crowell, Patrick C., P.A. .... **Orlando, FL**
Crowell & Porter, P.A. .... **Salisbury, NC**
Crowell, Raymond L. .... **Gainesville, GA**
Crowell, Richard B. .... **Alexandria, LA**
Crowell, Richard E., Jr. .... Warwick, RI
Crowell, Robert L. .... **Carson City, NV**
Crowell Ruff, LLP .... Salem, OR
Crowell, Scott D. .... Kirkland, WA
Crowell, Steven J. .... Pfafftown, NC
Crowell, Susich, Owen & Tackes, Ltd., A Prof. Law Corp. .... **Carson City, NV**
Crowell, Theodore .... Houston, TX
Crowell, Thomas G. .... **Seattle, WA**
Crowell, Thomas Martin
San Francisco, CA
Crowell, Thomas N. .... Houston, TX
Crowell, Victor L. .... **Baton Rouge, LA**
Crowell, Whitney .... Red Bank, NJ
Crowell, William D. .... **Harwich Port, MA**
Crowell, William E., Jr. .... Hyannis, MA
Crowell, William F. .... Diamond Springs, CA
Crowell, William J., Jr. .... **Carson City, NV**
Crowell, William Y., III .... **Albany, NY**
Crowfoot, William A. .... **Los Angeles, CA**
Crowgey, Guy C. .... Richmond, VA
Crowgey, Rodney G. .... **Christiansburg, VA**
Crowgey, Rodney G., P.C.
Christiansburg, VA
Crow-Johnson, June Richelle .... Topeka, KS
Crowl, James M. .... Topeka, KS
Crowl, Katherine S. .... Richmond, VA
Crowl, Matthew C. .... Chicago, IL
Crowl, Richard D., Jr. .... **Council Bluffs, IA**
Crowl, Ronald D. .... Omaha, NE
Crowl, Thomas L., Jr. .... Huber Heights, OH
Crowle, Henry W. .... **Sacramento, CA**
Crowle, Jacqueline C. .... San Diego, CA
Crowley, Andrea L. .... **Boston, MA**
Crowley, Angeline M. .... Minneapolis, MN
Crowley, Ann V. .... Department of Justice, Civil Division, GV
Crowley, Ann V. .... Marblehead, MA
Crowley, Appel, Starkey & Holbrook, LLC
Atlanta, GA
Crowley, Arthur E., Jr. .... Rutland, VT
Crowley & Associates .... Madison, WI
Crowley, Barbara W. G. .... **Los Angeles, CA**
Crowley Barrett & Karaba, Ltd.
Chicago, IL
Crowley, Beryl Ponton .... Austin, TX
Crowley, Bonnie J. .... **Boston, MA**
Crowley, Brian S. .... Arlington Heights, IL
Crowley & Bunger .... Burlington, IA
Crowley, Carl A., III, P.C. .... **Atlanta, GA**
Crowley, Carol B. .... Milwaukee, WI
Crowley, Carolyn Wagner .... Los Angeles, CA
Crowley, Catherine J. .... New York, NY
Crowley, Catherine M. .... **New York, NY**
Crowley, Catherine T. .... Skokie, IL
Crowley, Christine Runte
Department Of Veterans Affairs, Board of Veterans Appeals, GV
Crowley, Christopher .... **New York, NY**
Crowley, Christopher M.
Kansas City, MO
Crowley, Christopher W. .... Naples, FL
Crowley, Clayton Ewing
Albuquerque, NM
Crowley, Colleen M. .... **Charlotte, NC**
Crowley, Considine & Dray .... Boston, MA
Crowley, Dale A. .... Hastings, MI
Crowley, Daniel F. .... **Sacramento, CA**
Santa Rosa, CA
Crowley, Daniel H. .... **Washington, DC**
Crowley, Daniel M. .... **Costa Mesa, CA**
Los Angeles, CA
Crowley, Danna M. .... Boston, MA
Crowley, David A. .... Tallahassee, FL
Crowley, David F. .... Binghamton, NY
Crowley, David J. .... Houston, TX
Crowley, David M. .... Boston, MA
Crowley, David R. .... Mercer, PA
Crowley, Deborah L. .... **Minneapolis, MN**
Crowley, Diane R. .... **San Francisco, CA**
Crowley, Donald F. .... Hartford, CT
Crowley, Donald L. .... Rahway, NJ
Crowley, Donald L. .... Newark, NY
Crowley, Douglas J. .... Niagara Falls, NY
Crowley & Douglas, L.L.P. .... **Houston, TX**
Crowley, Douglas M. .... Santa Monica, CA
Crowley, Duane E., Jr. .... Austin, TX
Crowley, E. Todd .... Salt Lake City, UT
Crowley, Eileen .... **Atlanta, GA**
Crowley, Eileen V. .... Port Washington, NY
Crowley, Ellen M. .... Phoenix, AZ
Crowley, Eugene F. .... Binghamton, NY
Crowley, Francis L., Jr. .... Beverly Hills, CA
Crowley, Francis X. .... **Media, PA**
Crowley, Frank & Ahlers, Co., LPA
Cincinnati, OH
Crowley, Frank C. .... **Helena, MT**
Crowley, Frederic C. .... Pawtucket, RI
Crowley, Garrett F.X. .... Brookline, MA
Crowley, George A. .... **Fort Worth, TX**
Crowley, George D., Jr. .... Chevy Chase, MD
Crowley, George W. .... Boston, MA
Marblehead, MA
Crowley, Gerald E. .... Ellwood City, PA
Crowley, Gerald L. .... Helena, MT
Crowley, Gerald S. .... **New York, NY**
Crowley, Gregory G. .... **Hopkinton, MA**
Crowley, Haughey, Hanson, Toole & Dietrich, P.L.L.P. .... **Billings, MT**
Helena, MT
Kalispell, MT
Williston, ND
Crowley, Henry D. .... Madison, ME
Crowley, Henry P. .... Brookline, MA
Crowley & Hiemer .... Anchorage, AK
Crowley, Hoge & Fein, P.C.
Washington, DC
Crowley, J. Brian .... Denver, CO
Crowley, J. Wayne .... Macon, GA
Crowley, James C. .... **Chicago, IL**
Crowley, James C., IV .... Cincinnati, OH
Crowley, James C., Jr. .... **Worcester, MA**
Crowley, James E. .... Riverside, CA
Crowley, James I. .... Washington, DC
Crowley, James J. .... Quincy, MA
Crowley, James J., Jr. .... **Newark, NJ**
Crowley, James M. .... Chicago, IL
Crowley, James M. .... **Bloomfield Hills, MI**
Crowley, James M. .... **Philadelphia, PA**
Crowley, James Sidney .... Sugar Land, TX
Crowley, James W. .... Hilliard, OH
Crowley, James W. .... Dallas, TX
Crowley, Jerome P. .... Stoneham, MA
Crowley, Joan .... Toms River, NJ
Crowley, John A. .... Federal Trade Commission, Bureau of Consumer Protection, GV
Crowley, John A., Jr. .... New York, NY
Crowley, John F. .... Bloomfield, NJ
Crowley, John G. .... Ayer, MA
Crowley, John G. .... **New York, NY**
Crowley, John J.
Department Of Veterans Affairs, Board of Veterans Appeals, GV
Crowley, John J., Jr. .... **Mobile, AL**
Crowley, John J., Jr. .... Boston, MA
Crowley, John K. .... San Jose, CA
Crowley, John L. .... Stuart, FL
Crowley, John P. .... **Rutland, VT**
Crowley, John P., III .... Saco, ME
Crowley, John R. .... Walled Lake, MI
Crowley, John W. .... **San Francisco, CA**
Crowley, Jonathan .... **Boston, MA**
Crowley, Juanita A. .... **Washington, DC**
Crowley, Karen M. .... **Portsmouth, VA**
Crowley, Kathleen A. .... Orchard Park, NY
Crowley, Kenneth C. .... Wilsonville, OR
Crowley, Kenneth G. .... **New York, NY**
Crowley, Kevin E. .... **New York, NY**
Crowley, Kevin T. .... Lexington, MA
Crowley, Kevin X. .... **Tallahassee, FL**
Crowley Law Offices, P.S. .... **Seattle, WA**
Crowley, Lawrence J., Jr. .... **Boston, MA**
Crowley, Leo .... Flagstaff, AZ
Crowley, Leo T. .... **New York, NY**
Crowley, Lionel L. .... Madison, WI
Crowley, M. Lisanne .... **Washington, DC**
Crowley, Marc D. .... **Morristown, NJ**
Crowley, Margaret A. .... Washington, DC
Crowley, Margaret M. .... Reno, NV
Crowley, Marilyn L. .... Madison, WI
Crowley, Mark Brian .... Santa Monica, CA
Crowley, Mark V. .... Bluemont, VA
Crowley, Martin J. .... Smithtown, NY
Crowley, Mary L. .... Syracuse, NY
Crowley, Matthew S. .... **San Francisco, CA**
Crowley, Matthew S. .... **Topeka, KS**
Crowley, Maureen A. .... **Chicago, IL**
Crowley, Michael C. .... El Paso, TX
Crowley, Michael E. .... **New York, NY**
Crowley, Michael J. .... **Eureka, CA**
Crowley, Michael J. .... Chicago, IL
Crowley, Michael J. .... **Boston, MA**
Crowley, Michael J. .... **Garden City, NY**
Crowley, Michael J. .... **Austin, TX**
Crowley, Michael L. .... San Diego, CA
Crowley, Michael T. .... **Indianapolis, IN**
Crowley, Michael T., III .... Milwaukee, WI
Crowley, Neal A. .... Omaha, NE
Crowley, Neil R.
Federal Housing Finance Board, Office of General Counsel, GV
Crowley, Noel C. .... **Morristown, NJ**
Crowley, Patricia A. .... Bowling Green, OH
Crowley, Patricia C. .... **Washington, DC**
Crowley, Patricia M. .... **New Orleans, LA**
Crowley, Patrick .... Bowling Green, OH
Crowley, Patrick W. .... **Seattle, WA**
Crowley, Paul C. .... Anchorage, AK
Crowley, Paul G. .... Hood River, OR
Crowley, Peter J. .... Chicago, IL
Crowley, Philip J. .... **Traverse City, MI**
Crowley, Philip O. .... **Houston, TX**
Crowley, Philip P. .... New Brunswick, NJ
Crowley, Pickens & Martin .... **Enid, OK**
Crowley, Rebecca R. .... **Waycross, GA**
Crowley, Richard A. .... **New York, NY**
Crowley, Richard P. .... **Boston, MA**
Osterville, MA
Crowley, Richard P., Attorney at Law, P.C.
Osterville, MA
Crowley, Robert E. .... Biddeford, ME
Crowley, Robert L., Jr. .... Rigby, ID
Crowley, Robert L., Jr., Chartered .... Rigby, ID
Crowley, Robert W. .... Boston, MA
Crowley, Ronda Lynn .... Los Angeles, CA
Crowley, Rosemary .... Boston, MA
Crowley, Ruth .... Salem, OR
Crowley, Sarah G. .... **Princeton, NJ**
Crowley, Scott C. .... **Waycross, GA**
Crowley, Scott Gregory .... Morristown, NJ
Crowley, Shawn .... Seattle, WA
Crowley, Steven J. .... Burlington, IA
Crowley, Susan Garrett .... Hood River, OR
Crowley, Suzanne Marie .... **Chicago, IL**
Crowley, Theresa E. .... **Douglaston, NY**
Crowley, Thomas Earl .... Butler, PA
Crowley, Thomas J. .... Boston, MA
Crowley, Thomas M. .... Worcester, MA
Crowley, Tim J. .... **Enid, OK**
Crowley, Timothy G. .... **Columbus, OH**
Crowley, Timothy J. .... Santa Rosa, CA
Crowley, Timothy J. .... Lisle, IL
Crowley, Timothy J. .... **Houston, TX**
Crowley, Timothy W. .... **Stamford, CT**
Crowley, W. Timothy .... Vincennes, IN
Crowley, Walter L. .... Chicago, IL
Crowley, Wilbert F., Jr. .... **Chicago, IL**
Crowley, William F. .... Reading, MA
Crowley, William J. .... **Washington, DC**
Baltimore, MD
Crowley, William J. .... **Boston, MA**
Crowley, William J. .... **Seattle, WA**
Crowley, William L. .... **Missoula, MT**
Crown, Allen R. .... Watsonville, CA
Crown, Barry G. .... East Lansing, MI
Crown, Barry G., P.C. .... East Lansing, MI
Crown, Bradley D. .... Colorado Springs, CO
Crown, Daryl B. .... Houston, TX
Crown, Howard L. .... **Naples, FL**
Crown, James S. .... Chicago, IL
Crown, Jeffrey L. .... Berlin, CT
Crown, Joseph T., Jr. .... Capitol Heights, MD
Crown, Larry J. .... **Phoenix, AZ**
Crown, Marla R. .... Scottsdale, AZ
Crown, Michele F. .... **Washington, DC**
Crown, Nancy E. .... Boca Raton, FL
Crown, Patricia .... **New York, NY**
Crown, Robert L .... **Naples, FL**
Crown, Ross L. .... **Albuquerque, NM**
Crown, Steven A. .... **Redmond, WA**
Crown, Thaine M., Jr. .... Phoenix, AZ
Crown, Valerie J. .... **New City, NY**
Crowne, James D. .... Washington, DC
Crowne, Stephen G. .... Lexington, MA
Crowner, Brian P. .... **Philadelphia, PA**
Crownhart, George W. .... Madison, WI
Crownover, Blair .... Washington, DC
Crownover, Coleman, Standridge & Mitchell
Tuscaloosa, AL
Crownover, Derek C., Law Offices of
Nashville, TN
Crownover, Dick R. .... Abilene, TX
Crownover Law Firm .... Abilene, TX
Crownover, Walter P. .... Tuscaloosa, AL
Crowns, Arthur J., Jr. .... Wichita, KS
Crowns, Byron C. .... Wisconsin Rapids, WI
Crowns, Midthun, Metcalf & Quinn, S.C.
Wisconsin Rapids, WI
Crowson, Cecil V., Jr. .... Nashville, TN
Crowson, Celine Jimenez
Washington, DC
Crowson, Christopher R. .... San Diego, CA
Crowson, Daniel A. .... Columbiana, AL
Crowson, David L. .... **Longview, TX**
Crowson, Harold E., Jr. .... **El Paso, TX**
Crowson & Ingram .... **El Paso, TX**
Crowson, Jane A. .... **Longview, TX**
Crowson, Jason P. .... Houston, TX
Crowson, Jennifer M. .... **El Paso, TX**
Crowson, Jennifer R. .... **Jackson, MS**
Crowson, Timothy B. .... Madison, AL
Crowson, Walker F. .... **El Paso, TX**
Crowson, William S. .... **Birmingham, AL**
Crowther, Curtis J. .... **Wilmington, DE**
Crowther, F. Bosley, 3rd .... **Palmyra, VA**
Crowther & Gardner, P.C.
Salt Lake City, UT
Crowther, Geoffrey D. .... Newport Beach, CA
Crowther, Harold F. .... Santa Monica, CA
Crowther, J. Wesley .... Malad City, ID
Crowther, Joanne .... San Francisco, CA
Crowther, John .... Tampa, FL
Crowther, John B. .... **DeLand, FL**
Deltona, FL
Crowther, John B. .... **Orange City, FL**
Crowther, Lawrence S. .... **Cleveland, OH**
Crowther, Mark O. .... **Charlotte, NC**
Crowther, Marshall L. .... Lawrence, KS
Crowther, Pamela A. .... **Philadelphia, PA**
Crowther, Philip E. .... Wichita, KS
Crowther, Richard S. .... **Galveston, TX**
Crowther, Robert P. .... **Anchorage, AK**
Crowther, Robyn Carrico
Los Angeles, CA
Crowther, Steven P. .... **Burlington, VT**
Crowther, Thomas N. .... **Salt Lake City, UT**
Crowther, Wayne R. .... Bala Cynwyd, PA
Crow-Willard, Dorothy C. .... Denver, CO
Croxen, Edith A. .... Tucson, AZ
Croxton, Cheryl H. .... **Philadelphia, PA**
Croxton, Gayle T. .... New Orleans, LA
Croxton, Hardy W. .... **Rogers, AR**
Croxton, Hardy W., Jr. .... Rogers, AR
Croxton, J. Huff .... **Atlanta, GA**
Croxton, Jessica .... Santa Monica, CA
Croy, James B. .... Oklahoma City, OK
Croy, Judy Greenbaum .... Atlanta, GA
Croy, Kenneth R. .... Marietta, GA
Croy, Kevin J. .... **Dallas, TX**
Croy, Lorrain Rae .... Lindsey, OH
Croy, Louis L. .... Manitowoc, WI
Croy, Paul E. .... Perrysburg, OH
Croydon, Stanley O., Jr.
Department of Labor, Office of the Solicitor, GV
Croyle, Kimberly S. .... **Morgantown, WV**
Croyle, Lizabeth B. .... Altoona, PA
Croyle, Robert G. .... Houston, TX
Croyle, Robert J. .... Buffalo, NY
Croyle, Ronald P. .... Suffern, NY
Croyle, Sherry A. .... **Cleveland, OH**
Croyle & Williams .... Suffern, NY
Croysdale, David W. .... **Milwaukee, WI**
Crozier, Barbara J. .... Muskegon, MI
Crozier, Brian W. .... **Austin, TX**
Crozier, Carol .... Delray Beach, FL
Palm Beach Gardens, FL
Crozier, Christopher .... New York, NY
Crozier, John B. .... Grand Rapids, MI
Crozier, John H. .... Trumbull, CT
Crozier, Kevin D. .... Yonkers, NY
Crozier, Lyn S. .... Baltimore, MD
Crozier, Ralph C. .... Waterbury, CT
Crozier, Richard L. .... **Austin, TX**
Crozier, Scott A. .... Phoenix, AZ
Cruanes, Carlos .... **Miami, FL**
Cruce, Jane Ann .... Mesquite, TX
Cruciani, Gary .... **Dallas, TX**
Cruciani, John Joseph .... Overland Park, KS
Cruciani, Joseph A. .... Detroit, MI
Cruciani, Joseph R. .... Charlotte, NC
Cruciani Professional Association
Charlotte, NC
Crucillo, Joycelyn .... **Denver, CO**
Crucs, John .... Boston, MA
Crudale, Jean N. .... North Attleboro, MA
Crudden, Kevin L. .... **Minneapolis, MN**
Crudder, Henry A., III .... Adrian, MI
Crudele, De Lima & Shiroma .... Hilo, HI
Crudele, Robert J. .... Hilo, HI
Cruden, Irene Kopelman .... **Houston, TX**
Cruden, John C. .... Department of Justice, Environment and Natural Resources Division, GV
Cruden, Tabatha L. .... **Raleigh, NC**
Crudo, Alexander J. .... Brooklyn, NY
Crudo, Anthony F. .... Salem, OR
Crudo, Crudo & Russo, P.C. .... Brooklyn, NY
Crudo, Peter L. .... **Honolulu, HI**

Cuadra, D. Elizabeth .... Juneau, AK
Cuadra, Veronica .... Dallas, TX
Cuadrado, Manuel A. .... Miami, FL
Cuadros, Joe F. .... Encino, CA
Cuan, Manuel Chong, Jr. .... Miami, FL
Cuatrecasas .... New York, NY
New York, NY
Cuatto, Jan Robert .... Phoenix, AZ
Cuatto, Raymond R., Jr. .... Hartford, CT
Cuba, Benjamin J. .... Temple, TX
Cuba, Brenda A. Coppola .... West Orange, NJ
Cuba, Court .... Temple, TX
Cuba & Cuba, Professional Legal Corporation .... Temple, TX
Cuba, Donald L. .... San Antonio, TX
Cuba, Jill A. .... Chicago, IL
Cubar, John C. .... Cleveland, OH
Cubas, Alexander G. .... Miami, FL
Cubas, Alexander G., P.A. .... Miami, FL
Cubbage, Amy D. .... Louisville, KY
Cubbage, Benjamin C. .... Henderson, KY
Cubbage, Brenda Turner .... Dallas, TX
Cubbage, Brian .... Alexandria, VA
Cubbage & Cubbage .... Cushing, OK
Cubbage, Jerome K. .... Des Moines, IA
Cubbage, Richard T. .... Evanston, IL
Cubbage, S. Todd .... Chicago, IL
Cubbage, Stephen B. .... Cushing, OK
Cubbage, Thomas L., III .... Washington, DC
Cubbage, T. L., II .... Bartlesville, OK
Cubbage, William R. .... Cushing, OK
Cubberley, Douglas B. .... Norman, OK
Cubberley, Mark D. .... Hamilton, NJ
Cubberley, William C. .... New York, NY
Cubberly, Howard B. .... Jersey City, NJ
Cubbie & Pepper, Ltd. .... Milwaukee, WI
Cubbie, Rodney L. .... Milwaukee, WI
Cubbin, Claire .... Fort Lauderdale, FL
Cubbin, Robert S. .... Detroit, MI
Cubbison, Theo. R. .... Youngstown, OH
Cubbon Assoc. Co., L.P.A. .... Toledo, OH
Cubbon, Denise Navarre .... Toledo, OH
Cubbon, Frank W., Jr. .... Toledo, OH
Cubbon, Kyle Alison .... Toledo, OH
Cubbon, Stuart F. .... Toledo, OH
Cubell, Howard A. .... Boston, MA
Cubello, Kristofer P. .... Baltimore, MD
Cuber, Baird .... New York, NY
Cubert, Burleigh M. .... Olympia, WA
Cubert, Jack S. .... Washington, DC
Cubert, Jeremy A. .... Washington, DC
Cubeta, David B. .... Washington, DC
Cubete, Samuel .... Huntington Beach, CA
Cubia, Gil R. .... Chicago, IL
Cubie, James M. .... United States Senate, Committee Legal Personnel, GV
Cubine, Irvin .... Virginia Beach, VA
Cubit, Thomas Mark .... Fort Lauderdale, FL
Cubit, William A. .... Sharon Hill, PA
Cubita, Peter N. .... New York, NY
Cubitt, Cubitt & Trowhill .... Bad Axe, MI
Cubitt, E. Duane .... Bad Axe, MI
Cubitt, H. Dale .... Bad Axe, MI
Cubitto, Robert J. .... New York, NY
Cubley & Cubley, P.C. .... Potsdam, NY
Cubley, David N. .... Potsdam, NY
Cuca, Ralph P., Jr. .... Lincoln, NE
Cuca, Roberto E. .... Washington, DC
Cuccaro, Julia E. Trimarchi .... Indiana, PA
Cucchiara, Anne .... St. Clair Shores, MI
Cucchiara, Gary J. .... Rutherford, NJ
Cucchissi, Michael S. .... Newport Beach, CA
Cucci, Gardenia P. .... New York, NY
Cucci, John, Jr. .... Deer Park, NY
Cucci, Stephen N. .... Brick, NJ
Cucci, Vincent E. .... Brooklyn, NY
Cuccia, Christine .... New York, NY
Cuccia, Edward J. .... New York, NY
Cuccia, Frederick J. .... New York, NY
Cuccia, Jos. F. .... New York, NY
Cuccia, Oster & Hansburg .... New York, NY
Cuccia, Robert P. .... Houma, LA
Cuccia, Robert P., PLC .... Houma, LA
Cuccia, Royal R. .... East Hampton, NY
Cuccias, Edward P. .... Fairfax, VA
Cuccias Law Office .... Arlington, VA
Fairfax, VA
Vienna, VA
Cuccias, Matthew J. .... Washington, DC
Cuccinello, Glen R. .... New York, NY
Cuccio and Cuccio .... Hackensack, NJ
Cuccio, Emil S. .... Hackensack, NJ
Cuccio, Frank J. .... Hackensack, NJ
Cucco, Michael J. .... Chicago, IL
Cucco, Robert J. .... Bloomfield Hills, MI
Pontiac, MI
Cucco, Robert J., P.C. .... Pontiac, MI
Cucco, William P., Jr. .... Newark, NJ
Cuccurullo, Jodie D. .... Phoenix, AZ
Cuchiara, Charles R., Jr. .... Lakewood, CO
Pueblo, CO
Cuchiara, Charles R., Jr., P.C.
Lakewood, CO
Pueblo, CO
Cuchna, Ronald J. .... Chicago, IL
Cuchna, Wayne M. .... Wheaton, IL
Cucin, Robert Louis .... New York, NY
Cucinell, Robert G. .... White Plains, NY
Cucinotta, Ann Marie .... Reading, PA
Cucinotta, Salvatore J. .... Philadelphia, PA
Cucinotta, Salvatore J., P.C.
Philadelphia, PA
Cuclis, James L. .... Houston, TX
Cuco, Victor A. .... Arlington, VA
Cucolo, K. Jody .... Pearl River, NY
Cucolo, Richard J. .... Albany, NY
Cucovatz, Larry R. .... Santa Ana, CA
Cuculic, Lawrence M. .... Lafayette, IN

Cucullu, Karen M. .... New Orleans, LA
Cucullu, Michael D. .... Monument, CO
Cuculo, Paula M. .... Providence, RI
Cuculo, Ralph D. .... Providence, RI
Cucurullo, Stephanie E.S. .... Stoughton, MA
Cucuzza, Michelle .... New York, NY
Cucuzzella, Lucinda C. .... Wilmington, DE
Cuda, Anthony .... Chicago, IL
Cuda, Charles Nicholas .... Walnut Creek, CA
Cuda, Francis T. .... St. Johnsville, NY
Cuda, Michael D. .... Dallas, TX
Cuda, Steven J. .... Woodstock, IL
Cudahy, Michael C. .... Phoenix, AZ
Cudahy, Richard D. .... Chicago, IL
Cudahy, Richard D., Jr. .... Milwaukee, WI
Cudahy, W. B. .... Palm Beach, FL
Cudak, Gail L. .... Brecksville, OH
Cudd & Associates .... Denver, CO
Cudd, Howard V. .... Sterling City, TX
Cudd, J. Earl .... Minneapolis, MN
Cudd, Patricia .... Denver, CO
Cudd, Robert A. N. .... New York, NY
Cudd, Robert C., III .... Monroe, LA
Cudd, Stacy Elizabeth .... St. Paul, MN
Cuddahy, John P. .... New Hyde Park, NY
Cuddeback & Onofry .... Port Jervis, NY
Cuddeback, William L. .... Binghamton, NY
Cuddigan, Timothy J., (P.C.) .... Omaha, NE
Cuddihy, Peter S. .... Westmont, NJ
Cuddire, Michael L. .... Boston, MA
Cuddy, Andrew K. .... Lockport, NY
Cuddy, C. Emery, Jr. .... Santa Fe, NM
Cuddy, Charles R. .... Riverhead, NY
Cuddy, Christine S. .... Los Angeles, CA
Cuddy, Danl. H. .... Anchorage, AK
Cuddy, Edward M., III .... New York, NY
Cuddy & Feder & Worby LLP
Norwalk, CT
Stamford, CT
New York, NY
White Plains, NY
Cuddy, Francis X. .... Boston, MA
Cuddy, James G. .... Auburn, NY
Cuddy, Jineen T. .... Modesto, CA
Cuddy, John Cooper .... New York, NY
Cuddy, Kevin M. .... Bangor, ME
Cuddy & Lanham .... Bangor, ME
Cuddy, Laura Kristine .... Torrance, CA
Cuddy, Michael J. .... New York, NY
Cuddy, Michael J., Jr. .... Medina, NY
Cuddy, Sharon A. .... Rochester, NH
Cuddy, Stephen R. .... Seattle, WA
Cuddy, William H. .... Hartford, CT
Cuddy, William V. .... White Plains, NY
Cude, Donna Smith .... Houston, TX
Cude, Jerry C. .... Lawton, OK
Cude, Martin C., Jr. .... Dallas, TX
Cude, Melton D. .... Decatur, TX
Cude, Susan Bird .... Portland, OR
Cudkowicz, Ariel D. .... Boston, MA
Cudlip, Robert E. .... Sacramento, CA
Cudlipp, Katherine Y. .... United States Senate, Committee Legal Personnel, GV
Cudlipp, William S., Jr. .... Richmond, VA
Cudney, Kevin A. .... Denver, CO
Cudney, Kim W. .... Washington, KS
Cudney, Mark D. .... Cameron Park, CA
Cudney, Tyren .... Portage, MI
Cudnowski, David P. .... Chicago, IL
Cudnowski, David P., Ltd. .... Chicago, IL
Cudrin, Richard N. .... Carteret, NJ
Cudworth, Jon A. .... Aiken, SC
Cudzik, Walter J. .... New Orleans, LA
Cue, Brandon .... Wheaton, IL
Cue, Molly J. .... Lexington, KY
Cuebas Tañon, Hector .... San Juan, PR
Cuellar, Armando G., Jr. .... Oakland, CA
Cuellar, David D. .... Valrico, FL
Cuellar, Enrique R. .... Laredo, TX
Cuellar, James E. .... Houston, TX
Cuellar, Jesse .... Dallas, TX
Cuellar, Jesse, P.C., Law Offices of
Dallas, TX
Cuellar, John A. .... Dallas, TX
Cuellar, Mary Lou .... Tampa, FL
Cuellar, Michael M. .... Melbourne, FL
Cuellar, Norbert .... Minneapolis, MN
Cueller, Albert, III .... Chicago, IL
Cueller, Daniel .... Indianapolis, IN
Cueller, Gerry .... Chicago, IL
Cuello, Rosary A. .... Corpus Christi, TX
Cuen, Elise Jacobs .... Santa Ana, CA
Cuen, Robert M. .... Los Angeles, CA
Cuerdon-Kahn, Kathleen .... Chicago, IL
Cuervo, Asela M. .... Vienna, VA
Cuervo, Jose R. .... Miami, FL
Cuervo, Manuel H. .... Miami, FL
Cuervo, Raul A. .... Washington, DC
Miami, FL
Cuesta-Aragon, Angeli .... Los Angeles, CA
Cueto, Anthony R. .... New York, NY
Cueto, Christopher F. .... Belleville, IL
Cueto, Santiago A. .... Miami, FL
Cueto, Victor M. .... Santa Ana, CA
Cueto, William F. .... Miami, FL
Cueva, Maria Elizabeth Joaquino
Brooklyn, NY
Cuevas, Andrew .... Miami, FL
Cuevas, Carlos J. .... Chicago, IL
Cuevas, Carlos J. .... New York, NY
Cuevas, George S. .... Santa Ana, CA
Cuevas, Hector B. .... Montebello, CA
Cuevas, Joseph K. .... Hattiesburg, MS
Cuevas Kuinlam & Bermúdez
San Juan, PR
Cuevas, Leslie J. .... Phoenix, AZ
Cuevas, Michael R. .... Schenectady, NY
Cuevas, Robert A., Jr. .... Miami, FL

Cuevas & Rubin, P.A., Law Offices of
Miami, FL
Cuevas, Shelby L. .... Phoenix, AZ
Cuevas, Steven J. .... Seattle, WA
Cuevas Kuinlam, Rafael .... San Juan, PR
Cuevas Segarra, Jose .... San Juan, PR
Cuevas-Silva, Javier .... San Juan, PR
Cuff, Adam G. .... Seattle, WA
Cuff, Brian C. .... Tustin, CA
Cuff, Mary Catherine .... Freehold, NJ
Cuff, Robert G., Jr. .... Palm Coast, FL
Cuff, Terence F. .... Los Angeles, CA
Cuff, Walter G. .... Brooklyn, NY
Cuffe, Brian T. .... Newburyport, MA
Cuffe, Elizabeth C. K.
United States Court Of Veterans Appeals, GV
Cuffe, Kathryn LoPresti .... Boston, MA
Cuffe, Matthew J. .... Missoula, MT
Cuffe, Ronald F. .... Washington, DC
Cuffe, T. Richard, Jr. .... Lynn, MA
Cuffie & Associates, P.C. .... Atlanta, GA
Cuffie, Frances H. .... Oxon Hill, MD
Cuffie, Thomas F. .... Atlanta, GA
Cuffman, Phillip P. .... Little Rock, AR
Cuffman & Phillips .... Little Rock, AR
Cuffman, Stephen K. .... Little Rock, AR
Cufley, James E., Jr. .... Seattle, WA
Cugini, Crissa .... Bellevue, WA
Cugini, Frank A. .... Fryeburg, ME
Cugno, Jeffrey P. .... Berlin, CT
Cui, Steven X. .... Palo Alto, CA
Cuiffo, Frank W. .... New York, NY
Cuillerier, Ian .... New York, NY
Cuillier, Gary M. .... Yakima, WA
Cuilwik, Alysia A. .... Department of Justice, Drug Enforcement Administration, GV
Cuisinier, Francis P. .... Chicago, IL
Cuisinier, Lori G. .... New York, NY
Cuizon, Roy D. .... Honolulu, HI
Cujé, Maury L. .... Englewood, CO
Cuker, Mark R. .... Philadelphia, PA
Cukerbaum, Neal .... Plano, TX
Cukier, Carol J. .... Lansing, MI
Cukier, Dorothy Erstling .... Keedysville, MD
Cukier, Eduardo A. .... New York, NY
Cukier, Linda .... Los Angeles, CA
Cukier, Linda .... Los Angeles, CA
Cukier, Lisa M. .... Brookline, MA
Cukjati, Curtis L. .... San Antonio, TX
Cukor, Martha S. .... Baltimore, MD
Cukras, Roger .... New York, NY
Culas, Roberto G. .... Provo, UT
Culberson, David A. .... Lexington, SC
Culberson, Eugene B. .... East Peoria, IL
Culberson, John A. .... Houston, TX
Culberson, Mary Elizabeth .... Wetumpka, AL
Culberson-Smith, Louise .... Boulder, CO
Culbert, A. .... Scottsdale, AZ
Culbert & Adkins .... Toledo, OH
Culbert, Amy E. .... Minneapolis, MN
Culbert, Andrew C. .... Boston, MA
Culbert & Culbert .... Fremont, OH
Culbert, David C. .... Leesburg, VA
Culbert, David C., P.L.C. .... Leesburg, VA
Culbert, David E. .... Minneapolis, MN
Culbert, David E. & Associates, P.A.
Minneapolis, MN
Culbert, Mary B. .... Los Angeles, CA
Culbert, Noel D. .... Owosso, MI
Culbert, Peter V. .... Santa Fe, NM
Culbert, R. Bradford .... Fremont, OH
Culbert, Roger A. .... Fremont, OH
Culbert, Steven E. .... Minneapolis, MN
Culbert, T. Andrew .... Redmond, WA
Culbert, William M. .... Toledo, OH
Culberth, Celeste E. .... Minneapolis, MN
Culbertson, Andrew
Equal Employment Opportunity Commission, Office of Federal Operations, GV
Culbertson, Benjamin H. .... Georgetown, SC
Culbertson, Benjamin H., Professional Association .... Georgetown, SC
Culbertson & Christophillis, P.A.
Greenville, SC
Culbertson, Craig R. .... Chicago, IL
Culbertson, Culbertson & Allen .... Delavan, IL
Culbertson, David E. .... Akron, OH
Culbertson, Davisson D. .... Nogales, AZ
Culbertson, Edward S. .... Reston, VA
Culbertson, Edward T. .... St. Petersburg, FL
Culbertson, Edwin M. .... Cynthiana, KY
Culbertson, Hal R. .... South Bend, IN
Culbertson, John D. .... Charles City, IA
Culbertson, Katheryn C. .... Nashville, TN
Culbertson, Kaydee M. .... Albuquerque, NM
Culbertson, M. Andriette .... Aliso Viejo, CA
Culbertson, Manning Y. .... Greenville, SC
Culbertson, Mary M. .... Cleveland, OH
Culbertson, R. Wayne .... Kingsport, TN
Culbertson, R. Wayne, P.C.
Kingsport, TN
Culbertson, Richard A. .... Orlando, FL
Culbertson, Richard D. .... Fort Worth, TX
Culbertson, Robert E. .... Washington, DC
Culbertson, Robert M., Jr. .... Delavan, IL
Culbertson, Robin Duncan
Washington, DC
Culbertson, Rodney A. .... Greenville, SC
Culbertson, Russell D. .... Austin, TX
Culbertson, Teri A. .... Treasury Department, Internal Revenue Service, GV
Culbertson, Theodore R. .... Clearwater, FL
Culbertson, Thomas A. .... Santa Ana, CA
Culbertson, Thomas M. .... Spokane, WA
Culbertson, W. Paul .... Laurens, SC

Culbertson, Weiss, Schetroma and Schug, P.C. .... Meadville, PA
Culbertson, William J. .... Cleveland, OH
Culbertson, Wm. S. .... Cincinnati, OH
Culbreath, Andrew Scott .... Orangeburg, SC
Culbreath, Anne Ross .... Orangeburg, SC
Culbreath, Gray Thomas .... Columbia, SC
Culbreath, Stanlee E. .... Columbus, OH
Culbreth, Archie B. .... Alpharetta, GA
Culbreth, Hallet M. .... Richmond, VA
Culbreth, Jackson L. .... Atlanta, GA
Culbreth, James H., Jr. .... Charlotte, NC
Culbreth, James P. .... Wheat Ridge, CO
Culbreth, James W. .... Atlanta, GA
Culbreth, Kenneth M., Jr.
Corpus Christi, TX
Culbreth & Sharony .... Atlanta, GA
Culbreth, Stephen E. .... Burgaw, NC
Culbreth, Stephen E. .... Wilmington, NC
Culbreth, William R. .... Richmond, VA
Culcasi, Rosemary .... Woodbridge, NJ
Culclasure, Margaret G. .... Savannah, GA
Culclasure, Thomas P. .... St. Matthews, SC
Culet, Gregory M. .... Weiser, ID
Culgin, Donald M. .... Bedford, MA
Culham, Dorothy Abzanka .... Dallas, TX
Culham, Dorothy Abzanka, Law Offices, P.C.
Dallas, TX
Culhan, Edward J. (Ted) .... Orlando, FL
Culhane, Daniel J. .... Denver, CO
Culhane, Edward J. .... Boston, MA
Culhane, Eileen A. .... Mineola, NY
Culhane, Floyd C., Jr. .... Boston, MA
Culhane, Frank J. .... Bay Shore, NY
Culhane, James E. .... Denver, CO
Culhane, James E. .... Milwaukee, WI
Culhane, John G. .... Wilmington, DE
Culhane, John L., Jr. .... Philadelphia, PA
Culhane, Kevin R., (Inc.)
Sacramento, CA
Culhane, Marianne Baldrige .... Omaha, NE
Culhane, Martin A., III .... Minneapolis, MN
Culhane, Michael Langdon
Bloomington, MN
Culhane, Shelley R. .... Bethesda, MD
Culhane, Stephen .... New York, NY
Culhane, Thomas A. .... New York, NY
Culhane, Thomas J. .... Omaha, NE
Culic, Maria L. .... Seattle, WA
Culichia, James W. .... Colorado Springs, CO
Culin, Cassandra A. .... Louisville, KY
Culin, Robert G., Jr. .... Fairfax, VA
Culin, Sharp & Autry, P.L.C. .... Fairfax, VA
Culiner, Helen B. .... San Francisco, CA
Culkar, D. J. .... Lansing, MI
Culkin, Donald S. .... Leesburg, VA
Winchester, VA
Culkin, F. Hosmer .... Oswego, NY
Culkin, Francis K. .... Denver, CO
Culkin, Jeffrey T. .... Latham, NY
Culkins, L. William .... Alhambra, CA
Culkowski, Kathleen M.
Bowling Green, OH
Cull, Frederick B. .... Houston, TX
Cull & Hayden, A Prof. Serv. Corp., Law Offices .... Frankfort, KY
Cull, James M. .... Southfield, MI
Cull, Laramie & Lubbers, P.C.
Southfield, MI
Cull, Marie Alagia .... Frankfort, KY
Cull, William J. .... Cleveland Heights, OH
Cull, William J., Sr. .... Highland Heights, OH
Cullan, Daniel B. .... Omaha, NE
Cullan, Daniel M. .... Chicago, IL
Cullan, David J. .... Omaha, NE
Cullan, Samuel K. .... Kansas City, MO
Cullar, R. John .... Waco, TX
Cullari, Samuel F. .... Washington, DC
Cullaro, Erin Collins .... Tampa, FL
Cullaro, John J. .... Tampa, FL
Culleen, Lawrence E. .... Washington, DC
Culleen, Lawrence E.
Environmental Protection Agency, Program Office Attorneys, GV
Culleiton, Joseph E. .... Pittsburgh, PA
Cullem, John P. .... St. Petersburg, FL
Cullen, Albert F., Jr. .... Boston, MA
Cullen, Barbara L. .... Newton, MA
Cullen, Bernard D. .... Yardley, PA
Cullen & Bernstein .... Seattle, WA
Cullen, Brendan P. .... Los Angeles, CA
Cullen, Brian J. .... Atlantic City, NJ
Cullen, Brian J. S. .... Boston, MA
Cullen, Brian M. .... Boston, MA
Cullen & Butters .... Boston, MA
Cullen, Carsner, Seerden & Cullen, L.L.P.
Bay City, TX
Victoria, TX
Cullen, Catherine .... Boston, MA
Cullen, Catherine J. .... King Of Prussia, PA
Cullen, Charlene P. .... Birmingham, AL
Cullen, Charles E., Jr. .... Shrewsbury, MA
Cullen, Christian Robert .... Poughkeepsie, NY
Cullen, Christopher .... Santa Fe, NM
Cullen, Christopher J. .... Kansas City, MO
Cullen, Cornelius W. .... San Jose, CA
Cullen, Dale .... Auburn, NE
Cullen, Daniel F. .... Chicago, IL
Cullen, Daniel F. .... King Of Prussia, PA
Cullen, David D. .... Olympia, WA
Cullen, David P. .... Cherokee, OK
Cullen, Dennis P., Jr. .... Pittsburgh, PA
Cullen, Diane Ault .... Toms River, NJ
Cullen, Diane Ault, P.C. .... Toms River, NJ
Cullen and Dykman .... Washington, DC
Newark, NJ
Brooklyn, NY
Garden City, NY

Cullen, Edward F., Jr. ....San Jose, CA
Cullen, Edward J., Jr. ....Philadelphia, PA
Cullen, Elizabeth A. ....Washington, DC
Cullen, Eugene Kelly ....Southfield, MI
Cullen, Eugene T. ....Great Neck, NY
Cullen, Eugene W. ....Short Hills, NJ
Cullen, Francis P. ....Woburn, MA
Cullen, Frank ....Yorktown Heights, NY
Cullen, Garrett J., Jr. ....Needham, MA
Cullen, Gary P. ....Chicago, IL
Cullen, Gary S. ....Palo Alto, CA
Cullen, George J. ....Chicago, IL
Cullen, H. Regina ....Seattle, WA
Cullen, Insley, Hanson & Benson, LLP
Salisbury, MD
Cullen, J. Joseph ....Washington, DC
Philadelphia, PA
Cullen, Jack J. ....Seattle, WA
Cullen & Jacobson ....Norwalk, CT
Cullen, James D. ....Erie, PA
Cullen, James D., Jr. ....Naples, FL
Cullen, James D., P.A. ....Naples, FL
Cullen, James G. ....Groton, MA
Cullen, James J., Jr. ....Chicago, IL
Cullen, James P. ....Minneapolis, MN
Cullen, James P. ....New York, NY
Cullen, James P. ....Fairview Park, OH
Cullen, James P. ....Lancaster, PA
Cullen, James P., Jr. ....Philadelphia, PA
Cullen, Jean M. ....Cleveland, OH
Cullen, Jean Smetana ....Victoria, TX
Cullen, Jeanne M. ....Chicago, IL
Cullen, Jennifer J. ....Minneapolis, MN
Cullen, Jerry Bob ....Jackson, TN
Cullen, Joan ....Quincy, MA
Cullen, John E. ....New Rochelle, NY
Cullen, John J. ....San Francisco, CA
Cullen, John J. ....New York, NY
Cullen, John L. ....Cleveland, OH
Cullen, John M. ....Philadelphia, PA
Cullen, John R. ....Louisa, VA
Cullen, John S. ....Seattle, WA
Cullen, Joseph A., Jr. ....Doylestown, PA
Cullen, Joseph J. ....Irvine, CA
Cullen, Karen J. ....Orlando, FL
Cullen, Kathleen J. ....Delmar, NY
Cullen, Kenneth A., Jr. ....Albuquerque, NM
Cullen, Kevin D. ....Victoria, TX
Cullen, Kevin J. ....Weston, CT
Cullen, Kim Michael ....Orlando, FL
Cullen, Laura Waller ....Atlanta, GA
Cullen Law Firm, Ltd. ....Minneapolis, MN
Cullen Law Firm, The, PLLC
Washington, DC
Cullen Law Office ....Olympia, WA
Cullen, Lawrence V. ....Forest Hills, NY
Cullen, Lawrence W. ....St. Louis, MO
Cullen, Lee ....Madison, WI
Cullen, Mark J. ....Des Moines, IA
Cullen, Mark K. ....Springfield, IL
Cullen, Mary Clare ....Cuyahoga Falls, OH
Cullen, Mary R. ....Lakewood, CO
Cullen, MaryAnne Motter ....Lancaster, PA
Cullen, Michael C. ....Boston, MA
Cullen, Michael G. ....Media, PA
Cullen, Michael G., P.C. ....Media, PA
Cullen, Michael J. ....Palo Alto, CA
Cullen, Michael S. ....Washington, DC
Cullen, Nancy M. ....Boston, MA
Cullen, Patricia A. ....Princeton, NJ
Cullen, Patrick G. ....Baltimore, MD
Cullen, Patrick J. ....Omaha, NE
Cullen, Paul ....Seattle, WA
Cullen, Paul D., Jr. ....Washington, DC
Cullen, Paul D., Sr. ....Washington, DC
Cullen, Paul Michael ....Houston, TX
Cullen, Pauline M. ....Armonk, NY
Cullen, Peter S. ....Stamford, CT
Cullen, Philip J. ....Newport Beach, CA
Cullen, Philip M., Jr. ....Lancaster, PA
Cullen, Philip Michael, III
Fort Lauderdale, FL
Cullen, Philip Michael, III, Chartered
Fort Lauderdale, FL
Cullen, R. Laurence ....Hampton, NH
Cullen, Raymond T. ....Philadelphia, PA
Cullen, Richard ....Richmond, VA
Cullen, Richard D. ....Victoria, TX
Cullen, Rick S. ....Boca Raton, FL
Cullen, Robert L. ....Philadelphia, PA
Cullen, Robert W. ....San Jose, CA
Cullen, Robert W. ....Atlanta, GA
Cullen, Roger E. ....Newtown, PA
Cullen, Russell H., Jr. ....Key Largo, FL
Cullen, Russell H., P.A. ....Key Largo, FL
Cullen, Scott M. ....New Orleans, LA
Cullen, Shannon ....Fullerton, CA
Cullen, Sharon Elliott ....Houston, TX
Cullen, Siobhan A. ....San Diego, CA
Cullen, Stephen J. ....Baltimore, MD
Cullen, Steven P. ....West Palm Beach, FL
Cullen, Terrance M. ....St. Paul, MN
Cullen, Terrence J. ....Seattle, WA
Cullen, Thomas A. ....New York, NY
Cullen, Thomas F., Jr. ....Washington, DC
Cullen, Thomas J. ....Norwalk, CT
Cullen, Thomas J. ....Lilburn, GA
Cullen, Thomas J., Jr. ....Baltimore, MD
Cullen, Thomas Sean ....Savannah, GA
Cullen, Thomas V. ....Plainsboro, NJ
Cullen, Thomas W. ....New York, NY
Cullen, Timothy James ....Little Rock, AR
Cullen, Tonia K. ....Framingham, MA
Cullen, Veronica A. ....Cambridge, MA
Cullen Weston Pines & Bach ....Madison, WI
Cullen, William C. ....Los Angeles, CA
Cullen, William E., Jr. ....Olympia, WA
Cullen, William J. ....New York, NY
Cullen, William M. ....Melville, NY
Cullen, William T. ....Pittsburgh, PA
Cullen, William Z. ....Birmingham, AL
Cullenberg, David P. ....Orford, NH
Cullenberg, Ronald J. ....Farmington, ME
Cullens, Andree Matherne
New Orleans, LA
Cullens & Cullens, LLP ....Cartersville, GA
Cullens, Heather A. ....New York, NY
Cullens, J.E., Jr. ....New Orleans, LA
Cullens, Joseph R. ....Cartersville, GA
Cullens, J. R. ....Cartersville, GA
Culler, E. Olen ....Richmond, VA
Culler, J. Burke, Jr. ....West Palm Beach, FL
Culler, J. Burke, Jr., P.A.
West Palm Beach, FL
Culler, Jena Page ....Charlotte, NC
Culler, M. Patricia ....Cleveland, OH
Culler, Mark S. ....Mocksville, NC
Culler, Richard A. ....Charlotte, NC
Cullers, James J. ....Mt. Vernon, OH
Cullers, Mark E. ....Fresno, CA
Cullers, Michael A. ....Chicago, IL
Cullers, Randy D. ....Ord, NE
Cullers, Romney B. ....Cleveland, OH
Cullerton, John J. ....Chicago, IL
Cullerton, Patrick J. ....Chicago, IL
Culleton, Christopher J. ....Philadelphia, PA
Culleton, James J. ....Englewood, NJ
Bronx, NY
White Plains, NY
Culleton, Marinaccio & Foglia
Englewood, NJ
Bronx, NY
White Plains, NY
Culley, Christopher M. ....Columbus, OH
Culley, David G. ....Wilmington, DE
Culley, Harold ....Raleigh, IL
Culley, J. Kent ....Harrisburg, PA
Pittsburgh, PA
Culley, John H. ....Aurora, CO
Culley, Marcia L. ....Metairie, LA
Culley, Marks, Tanenbaum & Pezzulo
Rochester, NY
Culley, Mary M. ....Wilmington, DE
Culley, Patricia ....Livermore, CA
Culley, Peter W. ....Portland, ME
Culley, Scott H. ....Boulder, CO
Culligan, Colleen ....Littleton, CO
Culligan, Kevin J. ....New York, NY
Culligan, Lawrence J. ....St. Paul, MN
Culligan, Michelle T. ....Minneapolis, MN
Cullimore, Howard Michael
Indian Harbour Beach, FL
Cullimore, Kirk A. ....Sandy, UT
Cullin, Brian K. ....Detroit, MI
Cullina, John S. ....Arlington, VA
Cullina, Karen M. ....Farmington, CT
Cullina, William M. ....Hartford, CT
Cullinan, Marybeth ....Buffalo, NY
Cullinan, Michael N. ....Tremont, IL
Cullinan, Patrick J. ....Chicago, IL
Cullinan, Paul H. ....Washington, DC
Cullinan, R. Keith ....Louisville, KY
Cullinan, Ronald P. ....Lakeland, FL
Cullinan, Sean P. ....Chicago, IL
Cullinan, William G. ....Springfield, MA
Cullinane, Catriona M. ....New York, NY
Cullinane, John S. ....St. Louis, MO
Cullinane, Lara G. ....Atlanta, GA
Cullinane, Paul B. ....Boston, MA
Cullinane, Robert L. ....Dover, NH
Culling, Michael A. ....Deer Park, TX
Manvel, TX
Cullins, Douglas D. ....Laguna Hills, CA
Cullins, F. William ....Coffeyville, KS
Cullins & Grandy ....Laguna Hills, CA
Cullins, Jeanna ....Washington, DC
Cullins, Michael D. ....Southfield, MI
Cullis, David H. ....Greensburg, PA
Cullison, Alan D. ....Hartford, CT
Cullison, Bennett, Jr. ....Harlan, IA
Cullison, Claudia ....Portland, OR
Cullison and Cullison, P.C. ....Harlan, IA
Cullison, Patricia H. ....San Francisco, CA
Cullison, Richard A. ....Covington, KY
Cullison, Stephen R. ....Hillsboro, IL
Cullitan, Reginald K. ....Spokane, WA
Culliton, Daniel J. ....Los Angeles, CA
Culliton, David A. ....Dorchester, MA
Culliton, Ellen Champagne ....Geneva, IL
Culliton, James M. ....Sacramento, CA
Culliton, Katherine ....Washington, DC
Culliton, Stephen J. ....Chicago, IL
Cullity, John F. ....Manchester, NH
Cullity, John F., P.A. ....Manchester, NH
Cullman, Lori M. ....Bakersfield, CA
Cullman, Louis C. ....Newport Beach, CA
Cullman, Virginia A. ....Naples, FL
Boyne City, MI
Cullo, Leonard A., Jr. ....Pittsburgh, PA
Cullom Burland Bacon Overpeck & Nelder, A Professional Corporation
San Francisco, CA
Cullom, Charles J. ....Orlando, FL
Cullom, Freeman D. ....San Francisco, CA
Cullom, Jewell A. ....Juno Beach, FL
Cullom, June E. ....Houston, TX
Cullom, Paul C., Jr. ....Seattle, WA
Cullotion, Dennis P. ....Chicago, IL
Cullotta, Peter ....Chicago, IL
Cullum, Carole S. ....San Francisco, CA
Cullum, Daniel ....San Francisco, CA
Cullum, Edward L., Jr. ....Little Rock, AR
Cullum, Frank R. ....Savannah, GA
Cullum, James E. ....Glens Falls, NY
Cullum, Janet L. ....Palo Alto, CA
Cullum Law Firm, P.C. ....Dallas, TX
Cullum, Paul F., III ....Newark, NJ
Cullum, Rita Bragg ....Columbia, SC
Cullum & Sena ....San Francisco, CA
Cullum, Tony S. ....Flagstaff, AZ
Cullum, Tony S., P.C., Law Office of
Flagstaff, AZ
Sedona, AZ
Cullum, William Bennett ....Dallas, TX
Cully, Herbert J. ....Utica, NY
Cully, John ....Bronx, NY
Cully, Michael K. ....Springfield, MO
Cully, Michael R. ....Huntington Beach, CA
Cully & Ryan, A Professional Corporation
Huntington Beach, CA
Cully, Sandra J. ....San Jose, CA
Culmer, Charles W. ....Treasury Department, Internal Revenue Service, GV
Culmer, Marjorie M. ....Waukegan, IL
Culmo, Thomas A. ....Miami, FL
Culmo, Thomas A., P.A. ....Miami, FL
Culnan, Brian M. ....Albany, NY
Culnan, David E. ....Kahului, HI
Culnane, Janice ....Minneapolis, MN
Culotta, Charles C., Jr. ....Patterson, LA
Culotta, Janice M. ....New Orleans, LA
Culotta, John T., (P.L.C.) ....Metairie, LA
Culotta, Kenneth S. ....Houston, TX
Culotta, Rodi W. ....New Orleans, LA
Culotta, Samuel A. ....Baltimore, MD
Culotta, Vincent A. ....Painesville, OH
Culow, Fernando ....Houston, TX
Culp, Allan R. ....Kansas City, MO
Culp, Benjamin B., Jr. ....Atlanta, GA
Culp, Bethany K. ....St. Paul, MN
Culp, Charles A., Jr. ....Nashville, TN
Culp, Charles W. ....Indianapolis, IN
Culp, Charles W., A Professional Corporation ....Indianapolis, IN
Culp, Chesley K., III (P.C.) ....Denver, CO
Culp, Christopher E. ....Okanogan, WA
Culp, Christopher J. ....Charlotte, NC
Culp, Donald A. ....Kansas City, MO
Culp, Douglass ....Birmingham, AL
Culp, Dudley H. ....Oklahoma City, OK
Culp Elliott & Carpenter, P.L.L.C.
Charlotte, NC
Culp, Ellisa Huguley ....Greenville, SC
Culp, Florence E. ....San Francisco, CA
Culp, Glenn W. ....Metairie, LA
Culp, Gordon C. ....Seattle, WA
Culp, Henry P. C. ....Santa Rosa, CA
Culp, J. Clayton ....Alpharetta, GA
Culp, James D. ....Johnson City, TN
Culp, King R. ....Fort Wayne, IN
Culp, Lloyd J. ....Houston, TX
Culp, Marc S. ....Dallas, TX
Culp, Margaret H. ....Minneapolis, MN
Culp, Marylin E. ....Tampa, FL
Culp, Michael ....Medina, NY
Culp, Michael Joseph ....Des Moines, IA
Culp, Nathan C. ....Little Rock, AR
Culp and Parsons ....West Jefferson, OH
Culp, Patricia E. ....Russell, KY
Culp, Paul ....Boynton Beach, FL
Culp, Phyllis J. ....San Francisco, CA
Culp, Rex E. ....Kansas City, KS
Culp, Robert Alan ....New York, NY
Culp, Robert H. ....Binghamton, NY
Culp, Vann ....Midland, TX
Culp, W. Wallace, III ....Greenville, SC
Culp, W. Wallace, III ....Seneca, SC
Culp & Wade, P.C. ....Kansas City, MO
Culp, William P. ....Havertown, PA
Culp, William R., Jr., (P.A.)
Charlotte, NC
Culpepper, A. Hope ....Winterville, NC
Culpepper, Bobby L., (P.C.) ....Jonesboro, LA
Culpepper, Bruce ....Tallahassee, FL
Culpepper & Culpepper ....Yakima, WA
Culpepper, David A. ....Chicago, IL
Culpepper, David C., P.C. ....Portland, OR
Culpepper, David M. ....New Orleans, LA
Culpepper, Deborah A. ....Yakima, WA
Culpepper, Donna J. ....Macon, GA
Culpepper, Duncan McRae ....Prescott, AR
Culpepper, G. Bryant ....Macon, GA
Culpepper, George B., III ....Fort Valley, GA
Culpepper, George R. ....Meridian, MS
Culpepper, Gina K. ....Dallas, TX
Culpepper, Glenn E. ....Silver Spring, MD
Culpepper, Howard O. ....Santa Monica, CA
Culpepper, J. Scott ....Atlanta, GA
Culpepper, James A. ....Palo Alto, CA
Culpepper, James Bruce ....Tallahassee, FL
Culpepper, Jim L. ....Houston, TX
Culpepper, Jim L., & Associates, Inc.
Houston, TX
Culpepper, John C., Jr. ....College Station, TX
Culpepper, John K. ....Chattanooga, TN
Culpepper, Kimber M. ....Lawrenceville, GA
Culpepper, L. Polk ....Cashiers, NC
Culpepper & Liipfert ....Fort Valley, GA
Culpepper, Luther B., IV ....Rich Square, NC
Culpepper, Malcolm ....Jonesboro, AR
Culpepper, Michael L. ....Chapel Hill, NC
Culpepper, Milton I., Jr. ....Cropwell, AL
Culpepper, P. Melton, Jr. ....Cordele, GA
Culpepper, Paul E. ....Hickory, NC
Culpepper & Pfeiffer ....Cordele, GA
Culpepper, Philip Bruce ....Tallahassee, FL
Culpepper, Rebecca A. ....Atlanta, GA
Culpepper, Robert A. ....Atlanta, GA
Culpepper, Robert S. ....Lexington, VA
Culpepper, Ronald E. ....Tacoma, WA
Culpepper, S. Gardner, III ....Atlanta, GA
Culpepper, Sterling G., Jr.
Montgomery, AL
Culpepper, Thomas A. ....Dallas, TX
Culpepper, VanNoy ....Yakima, WA
Culpepper, Vernon M. ....Geneva, FL
Culpepper, Virginia Blair ....Tampa, FL
Culpepper, William T., III ....Edenton, NC
Culpepper, Wm. A. ....Alexandria, LA
Culter, Brandon S ....Denver, CO
Cultice & Brown ....Zanesville, OH
Cultice, Peter N. ....Zanesville, OH
Cultice, Robert D. ....Boston, MA
Culton, Robert H., II
Altamonte Springs, FL
Culton, William E., Jr ....Boston, MA
Culvahouse, Arthur B., Jr.
Washington, DC
Culver, Allan J., Jr. ....Bel Air, MD
Culver, Allison ....Dallas, TX
Culver, Carter C. ....Chicago, IL
Culver, Chandler F. ....Hudson, MI
Culver, Charlene Rudio ....Los Angeles, CA
Culver, Curtis L. ....Tulsa, OK
Culver, Curtis N. ....Sugar Land, TX
Culver, C. W. ....Houston, TX
Culver, Dan S. ....Dallas, TX
Culver, David C. ....Santa Rosa, CA
Culver, David H. ....Huntsville, AL
Culver, David, Law Office of
Santa Rosa, CA
Culver, Deborah S. ....Houston, TX
Culver, Donna L. ....Wilmington, DE
Culver, Edwin S. ....Denver, CO
Culver, Everett L. ....Tyler, TX
Culver, Fred C., Jr. ....Muskegon, MI
Culver, Howard L. ....Long Beach, CA
Culver, Jarel G. ....Santa Rosa, CA
Culver, Jill A. ....Ellsworth, ME
Culver, John A. ....Lakewood, CO
Culver, John A. ....Chicago, IL
Culver, John C. ....Washington, DC
Culver, John Dodd ....San Diego, CA
Culver, John H., III ....Charlotte, NC
Culver, Karig P. ....Enid, OK
Culver, Kathryn Frazzini ....Akron, OH
Culver, Lillard W., Jr. ....Cedarburg, WI
Culver, Marianne W. ....Chicago, IL
Culver, Mariclare Thinnes
Des Moines, IA
Culver, Marilyn Martin ....Irvine, CA
Culver, Marjorie R. ....Seattle, WA
Culver, Michael S. ....Alexandria, VA
Culver, Nada Leslie Wolff ....Lakewood, CO
Culver, Nancy P. ....Santa Monica, CA
Culver, Ralph K. ....San Antonio, TX
Culver, Ray C., III ....United States Senate, Committee Legal Personnel, GV
Culver, Richard D. ....Greenfield, IN
Culver, Richard W. ....Schaumburg, IL
Culver, Robert E. ....Columbia, SC
Culver, Robert W., (A P.C.) ....Wilson, WY
Culver, Russell L. ....Baker, MT
Culver, Sheridan, Knowlton, Even & Franks, P.C. ....Muskegon, MI
Culver, Taylor R. ....Oakland, CA
Culver, Thomas R., III ....Richmond, TX
Culver, Timothy J. ....Boston, MA
Culver, Tracy M. ....Atlanta, GA
Culver, Triel Dustin ....Billings, MT
Culver, Willis L. ....Rio Nido, CA
Culver, Wm. Eric ....Tulsa, OK
Culverhouse, Brad ....Fort Pierce, FL
Culverhouse, C. Gregory ....Cartersville, GA
Culverhouse, C. Gregory, & Associates, P.C.
Cartersville, GA
Culverhouse, Hugh F., Jr. ....Miami, FL
Culverhouse, Hugh F., Jr., P.A. ....Miami, FL
Culverwell, Kathleen E. ....Pasadena, CA
Culviner, William H. ....Poway, CA
Culwell, J. Todd ....Houston, TX
Culwell, Pamela ....Phoenix, AZ
Culy, Michael D. ....Fresno, CA
Culyba, Basil C. ....Washington, DC
Cumalander, Tonya C. ....Fuquay-Varina, NC
Cumalander, W. Mark ....Fuquay-Varina, NC
Cumare, Rosa M. C. ....Pasadena, CA
Cumba Torres, Jose L. ....Catano, PR
Cumberbatch, Ashton G., Jr. ....Austin, TX
Cumberland & Coates
San Luis Obispo, CA
Cumberland, David M.
San Luis Obispo, CA
Cumberland, Elizabeth G. ....Martindale, TX
Cumberland & Erly, LLC
Prince Frederick, MD
Cumberland, Frank J., Jr. ....Cleveland, OH
Cumberland, J. Michael ....New Orleans, LA
Cumberland, Laurence W. B.
Prince Frederick, MD
Cumberland, Patrick J. ....Philadelphia, PA
Cumberland, William E. ....Washington, DC
Cumberledge, George B. ....Glencoe, MO
Cumbest, A. Scott ....Pascagoula, MS
Cumbest, Arvis V. "Sid" ....Pascagoula, MS
Cumbest, Cumbest, Hunter & McCormick, P.A. ....Bay St. Louis, MS
Biloxi, MS
Gulfport, MS
Hattiesburg, MS
Jackson, MS
Pascagoula, MS
Cumbest, Halsey ....Pascagoula, MS
Cumbey, Constance E. ....Lake Orion, MI
Cumbie, B. Allen ....Bay City, TX
Cumbie, Fred H., II ....Kissimmee, FL
Cumbie, James C. ....Jacksonville, FL
Cumbie, James E. ....Baltimore, MD
Cumbie, Lee D. ....Dunn, NC
Cumbie, William C. ....Eastpoint, FL
Cumbo, James A. ....Rochester, NY
Cumbow, Robert C. ....Seattle, WA

Cumby, Dorothy E. ....New York, NY
Cumfer, Eric M. ....Salem, OR
Cuminale, James W. ....Greenwich, CT
Cuming, Samuel J., Jr. ....Spring, TX
Cumings, Anne Flower ....Oakland, CA
Cumings, Charles B. ....Flint, MI
Cumings, Col. Charles S. ....Fort Pierce, FL
Cumings & Johnston ....Flint, MI
Cumings, Michael W. ....Des Moines, IA
Cumins, Gail T. ....Washington, DC
New York, NY
Cumler, Robert B. ....Waldoboro, ME
Cummer, Andrew W. ....Bradenton, FL
Cummer, Catharine Wildenthal
Washington, DC
Cummer, Jas. W. ....Indianapolis, IN
Cummerford, Edward F. ....Sun City, AZ
Cummerford, John E. ....Phoenix, AZ
Cumming, Charles S. ....Oyster Bay, NY
Cumming, Cumming & Esary
Griffin, GA
Cumming, David Robert, Jr. ....Atlanta, GA
Cumming, Deborah K. ....Grants Pass, OR
Cumming, Douglas S. ....Sacramento, CA
Cumming, Elizabeth A. ....Minneapolis, MN
Cumming, George A., Jr.
San Francisco, CA
Cumming, Hatchett & Jordan, A Professional Corporation ....Hampton, VA
Newport News, VA
Cumming, Isabel Mercedes ....Towson, MD
Cumming, James C. ....Helena, MT
Cumming, James H. ....San Francisco, CA
Cumming, Jennifer L. ....Minneapolis, MN
Cumming, John A. ....Dayton, OH
Cumming, John E. ....Dayton, OH
Cumming, John W. ....Eureka, CA
Cumming, Justin D. ....Denver, CO
Cumming, Kathleen Smyth ....Orlando, FL
Cumming, Lawrence G. ....Hampton, VA
Cumming, Margaret ....Dearborn, MI
Cumming, Mark S. ....Flagstaff, AZ
Cumming, Michael G.
Bloomfield Hills, MI
Cumming, Newell E. ....San Diego, CA
Cumming, R. Malcolm ....Grand Rapids, MI
Cumming, Richard C. ....Folsom, CA
Cumming, Richard E. ....Dallas, TX
Cumming, W. Barron ....Griffin, GA
Cumming, Wayne K. ....Sidney, MT
Cumming, William A. ....Minneapolis, MN
Cumming, William R.
Federal Emergency Management Agency, Office of the General Counsel, GV
Cummings, Alan G. ....Woodstock, VT
Cummings, Alexander L. ....Annapolis, MD
Cummings, Allen D. ....Houston, TX
Cummings, Alyson B. ....Augusta, ME
Cummings, Amory ....Chicago, IL
Cummings, Ana Guerrero ....Houston, TX
Cummings, Andrea J. ....Palo Alto, CA
Dallas, TX
Cummings, Andrea T. ....Washington, DC
Cummings, Andrew D. ....Boston, MA
Providence, RI
Cummings, Andrew M. ....Park Ridge, NJ
Cummings, Anthony W. ....Atlanta, GA
Cummings, Anthony W. ....Charlotte, NC
Cummings, Ashley ....Atlanta, GA
Cummings, Asunción
Department of Justice, Antitrust Division, GV
Cummings, Barbara ....Department of State, Foreign Service Officers (Overseas), GV
Cummings, Barbara W. ....Rye, NY
Cummings, Bobby L. ....Waco, TX
Cummings, Brian D. ....Nashville, TN
Cummings, C. DeForest, Jr. ....Buffalo, NY
Cummings, Candace S. ....Greensboro, NC
Cummings, Charles B. ....New York, NY
Cummings, Charles D. ....Los Angeles, CA
Cummings, Charles J. ....Milwaukee, WI
Cummings, Charles R. ....Brattleboro, VT
Cummings, Christopher E. ....Malvern, PA
Cummings, Christopher J. ....Homewood, IL
Cummings, Christopher Ward
Commodity Futures Trading Commission, Division of Trading and Markets, GV
Cummings, Corlis P ....Atlanta, GA
Cummings, Courtney H., Jr.
Wilmington, DE
Cummings, Cummings & Dudenhefer, A Professional Law Corporation
New Orleans, LA
Cummings, Cynthia C. ....Dublin, OH
Cummings, Dana Emerson
Cleveland, OH
Cummings, Daniel ....Chicago, IL
Cummings, Daniel L. ....Portland, ME
Cummings, Daniel M. ....Seattle, WA
Cummings and Dashiell ....Baltimore, MD
Cummings, David A. ....Rocky River, OH
Cummings, David B. ....Richmond, VA
Cummings, David S. ....Ponca City, OK
Cummings, Dennis P. ....Anchorage, AK
Cummings, Donald E. ....Lubbock, TX
Cummings, Donna J. ....Grand Blanc, MI
Cummings, Donna J. ....Olympia, WA
Cummings, Donna S. ....New Orleans, LA
Cummings, Douglas K.
Salt Lake City, UT
Cummings, Douglas P., Jr. ....Sioux Falls, SD
Cummings & Duda, Ltd. ....Homewood, IL
Cummings, Dunckel & Campany, LLP
Lowville, NY
Cummings, Edward A. ....Stevensville, MT
Cummings, Edward H.
Newport Beach, CA
Santa Ana, CA
Cummings, Edward J., III ....Boston, MA
Cummings, Edward R. ....Department of State, Office of the Legal Adviser, GV
Cummings, Elijah E. ....Baltimore, MD
Cummings, Ellen M. ....Maynard, MA
Cummings, Emma M. ....Los Angeles, CA
Cummings, Eugene M. ....Chicago, IL
Cummings, F. Alan ....Fort Lauderdale, FL
Tallahassee, FL
Cummings, F. Marion ....Cedartown, GA
Cummings, Frank, (P.C.)
Washington, DC
New York, NY
Cummings, Fred L. ....Fort Worth, TX
Cummings, Fred V. ....Oakland, CA
Cummings, Frederick M. ....Phoenix, AZ
Cummings, Frederick R., Jr.
New York, NY
Cummings, Geoffrey K. ....Portland, ME
Cummings, George F D. ....Bullhead City, AZ
Cummings, George T., Law Office of
Park Ridge, IL
Cummings, Glenn P. ....Pittsburgh, PA
Cummings, Gordon L. ....Keizer, OR
Cummings, Gregory J. ....Tallahassee, FL
Cummings, H. Don ....Washington, DC
Cummings, H. Preston ....Chicago, IL
Cummings, Harold R. ....South Windsor, CT
Cummings, Harriet E. ....Carson City, NV
Cummings, Helen ....Newark, NJ
Cummings, Henry W. ....St. Charles, MO
Cummings, Howard J. ....Raleigh, NC
Cummings, Humphrey S. ....Charlotte, NC
Cummings, J. Greer, Jr. ....Nashville, TN
Cummings, James A. ....Peoria, IL
Cummings, James B. ....Pittsburgh, PA
Cummings, James J., III ....Rochester, NY
Cummings, James L. ....Neenah, WI
Cummings, James W. ....Ridgefield, CT
Cummings, Jane Anne ....Hillsborough, NH
Cummings, Jasper L., Jr. ....Raleigh, NC
Cummings, Jay P. ....Springfield, MO
Cummings, Jean Kelly ....West Hartford, CT
Cummings, Jeffrey I. ....Chicago, IL
Cummings, Jill ....Washington, DC
Cummings, John C. ....Cincinnati, OH
Cummings, John E., Jr ....Grove City, OH
Cummings, John F. ....Northbrook, IL
Cummings, John G. ....Port Huron, MI
Cummings, John H., Jr.
San Francisco, CA
Cummings, John J. ....Parsippany, NJ
Cummings, John J., III ....New Orleans, LA
Cummings, John L. ....Huntington, WV
Cummings, John M. ....Fort Worth, TX
Cummings, John M., Jr.
Department of Justice, Drug Enforcement Administration, GV
Cummings, John R. ....Hinsdale, IL
Cummings, John R., III ....Tampa, FL
Cummings, Judith ....Omaha, NE
Cummings, Kelly L. ....Naperville, IL
Cummings & Kemp, A Professional Corporation ....Los Angeles, CA
Riverside, CA
Santa Ana, CA
Cummings, Kenneth ....Kingwood, TX
Cummings, Kenneth J. ....Canton, OH
Cummings, Kent J. ....Chicago, IL
Cummings, Kerry D. ....Glenview, IL
Cummings, Kevin M. ....Seattle, WA
Cummings, King & MacDonald
Boston, MA
Newton, MA
Cummings, L. Edward ....Vincennes, IN
Cummings & Lanza, L.L.C.
South Windsor, CT
Cummings Legal Services ....Canton, OH
Cummings, Linda E. ....Newport Beach, CA
Cummings, Lindsey Clay ....Dallas, TX
Cummings, Lisa A. ....Round Rock, TX
Cummings & Lockwood ....Greenwich, CT
Hartford, CT
New Haven, CT
Stamford, CT
Bonita Springs, FL
Naples, FL
Palm Beach, FL
Vero Beach, FL
Cummings, M. Neil, & Associates
Los Angeles, CA
Cummings, M. Wayne ....Amarillo, TX
Cummings, Mark D. ....Arlington, VA
Cummings, Mary Griffin ....Wilkes-Barre, PA
Cummings, Matthew L. P.
Greensboro, NC
Cummings, Maupin ....Keizer, OR
Cummings, McClorey, Davis, Acho & DaCorsi ....Woodland Hills, CA
Cummings, McClorey, Davis, Acho & Day, P.L.C. ....Phoenix, AZ
Cummings, McClorey, Davis & Acho, P.C.
Battle Creek, MI
Farmington Hills, MI
Livonia, MI
Cummings, McClorey, Davis, Acho & Tremp, P.C. ....Traverse City, MI
Cummings, Michael ....New York, NY
Cummings, Michael ....Reston, VA
Cummings, Michael J. ....New York, NY
Cummings, Michael J. ....Virginia Beach, VA
Cummings, Michael O. ....New York, NY
Cummings, Michele Kane
Fort Lauderdale, FL
Cummings, Nancy J. ....Scottsdale, AZ
Cummings, Nathan K. ....Washington, DC
Cummings, Neil ....Los Angeles, CA
Cummings, Newsom C. ....Gainesville, GA
Cummings, Nika A. J. ....Wichita, KS
Cummings, Norbert E., Jr. ....Summerville, SC
Cummings, Owen J. ....Livonia, MI
Cummings, Patricia A. ....Binghamton, NY
Cummings, Patrick C. ....Red Bank, NJ
Cummings, Patrick M. ....Chicago, IL
Cummings, Paul D. ....Sherman Oaks, CA
Cummings, Paul L. ....Pensacola, FL
Cummings, Paul L. ....Newton, MA
Cummings, Paul M. ....Miami, FL
Cummings, Peter E. ....San Luis Obispo, CA
Cummings, Philip R. ....Cincinnati, OH
Cummings, Philip T. ....Washington, DC
Cummings, R. Scott ....Tampa, FL
Cummings, Rachel R. ....Charlotte, NC
Cummings, Ralph E., Jr. ....Charlotte, VT
Cummings, Randall S. ....Honolulu, HI
Cummings, Richard A. ....Boise, ID
Cummings, Richard C. ....Lowville, NY
Cummings, Richard C., Jr. ....Chicago, IL
Cummings, Richard L. ....Nashville, TN
Cummings, Richard M. ....New York, NY
Cummings, Richard T. ....Wheaton, IL
Cummings, Richard T. ....Houston, TX
Cummings, Robert C. ....Salt Lake City, UT
Cummings, Robert E. ....Belleville, IL
Cummings, Robert E., Jr. ....Bennington, VT
Cummings, Robert, Jr. ....Baltimore, MD
Cummings, Robert L. ....Tallahassee, FL
Cummings, Robert L. ....Morehead City, NC
Cummings, Robert S., (P.C.) ....Boston, MA
Cummings, Rochelle S. ....Hartford, CT
Cummings, Roger H.
Bloomfield Hills, MI
Cummings, Ronald E. ....Anchorage, AK
Cummings, Ronald G. ....Hartford, CT
Cummings, Russell W. ....Jacksonville, FL
Cummings, S. Lynn ....Altamonte Springs, FL
Cummings, Samuel R. ....Lubbock, TX
Cummings, Sasha M. ....San Francisco, CA
Cummings, Scott A. ....West Palm Beach, FL
Cummings, Scott Alexander ....Fort Worth, TX
Cummings, Scott W. ....Alexandria, VA
Cummings & Snyder, P.A.
Fort Lauderdale, FL
Tallahassee, FL
Cummings, Stacey L. ....Wilmington, DE
Cummings, Stan ....Pine Bluff, AR
Cummings, Stephen P., II ....Atlanta, GA
Cummings, Stephen T. ....San Diego, CA
Cummings, Steven E. ....Kalispell, MT
Cummings, Tamara Lynn ....St. Louis, MO
Cummings, Terence P. ....New York, NY
Cummings, Theodore F., III ....Hickory, NC
Cummings, Thomas B. ....Santa Ana, CA
Cummings, Thomas E. ....Los Angeles, CA
Cummings, Thomas E. ....Charlotte, NC
Cummings, Thomas J. ....Wellesley Hills, MA
Cummings, Thomas L. ....St. Paul, MN
Cummings, Thomas P. ....Scranton, PA
Cummings, Thomas, (P.C.) ....St. Louis, MO
Cummings, Timothy J. ....Watertown, SD
Cummings, Timothy R. ....Norwich, CT
Cummings, Tom M. ....Oklahoma City, OK
Cummings, Tom M., P.C.
Oklahoma City, OK
Cummings, Walter D. ....Homewood, IL
Cummings, Wayne L. ....Belleville, IL
Cummings, William B. ....Alexandria, VA
Cummings, William B., P.C.
Alexandria, VA
Cummings, William C. ....Jacksonville, AR
Cummings, William F. ....Juneau, AK
Cummings, William F. ....Hartford, CT
Cummings, William F. ....Wichita, KS
Cummings, William H., Jr. ....Wilson, NY
Cummings, William Leamon
Gardena, CA
Cummings, William M., II ....Atlanta, GA
Cummings, William Paul ....Boston, MA
Cummings, William R. ....Milwaukee, WI
Cummings, William S. ....Anchorage, AK
Cummings, William V. ....Spartanburg, SC
Cummings & Wilson, Law Offices of
Spartanburg, SC
Cummings-Spickler, Maureen
Department of Transportation, Federal Aviation Administration, GV
Cummins, Alisa Gross ....Baltimore, MD
Cummins, Andrew W. ....Canonsburg, PA
Cummins, Arthur B., Jr. ....Salem, OR
Cummins, Arthur B., Jr., P.C. ....Salem, OR
Cummins, Barbara M. ....New York, NY
Cummins, Barney J. ....Fort Lauderdale, FL
Cummins, Bernard F. ....Martinez, CA
Cummins, Brad, (P.C.) ....Austin, TX
Cummins, Brendan D. ....Minneapolis, MN
Cummins, Carl W., III ....St. Paul, MN
Cummins, Carolyn C. ....Oklahoma City, OK
Cummins, Charles F., Jr. ....San Jose, CA
Cummins, Clark H. ....Leavenworth, KS
Cummins, D. Scott ....Newnan, GA
Cummins, Daniel E. ....Scranton, PA
Cummins, David C. ....Lubbock, TX
Cummins, David L. ....Holdenville, OK
Cummins, David R. ....Franklin, KY
Cummins, Dennis J., Jr. ....Fair Lawn, NJ
Cummins, Don M., III ....Katonah, NY
Cummins, Donal D. ....San Ramon, CA
Cummins, Dwight P. ....Bayport, MN
Hastings, MN
Cummins, Elliott C. ....McMinnville, OR
Cummins, George S. ....Blackstone, VA
Cummins, Gervais & Blocher, Ltd.
Bayport, MN
Hastings, MN
Stillwater, MN
Cummins, Goodman, Fish & Platt, P.C.
McMinnville, OR
Cummins, Guylyn R. ....San Diego, CA
Cummins, Harry A. ....New York, NY
Cummins, H. E. ....Little Rock, AR
Cummins, Herbert A. ....Woodcliff Lake, NJ
Cummins, J. Gerard ....New York, NY
Cummins, J. Scott ....Santa Barbara, CA
Cummins, James E. ....Corsicana, TX
Cummins, James R. ....Cincinnati, OH
Cummins, Jerold D. ....Arlington, VA
Cummins, Jill Reid ....Greenbelt, MD
Cummins, John D. ....Washington, DC
Cummins, John D., Jr. ....Chicago, IL
Cummins, John F. ....Carefree, AZ
Cummins, John J. ....Naples, FL
Cummins, John J. ....Chicago, IL
Cummins, John P. J., III ....Fairfax, VA
Cummins, John R. ....Louisville, KY
Cummins, John R. ....Cincinnati, OH
Cummins, Judith M. ....Buffalo, NY
Cummins, Justin David ....Minneapolis, MN
Cummins, Kara Pitchford ....Conroe, TX
Cummins & Kneidel, P.C. ....Franklin, GA
Greenville, GA
Newnan, GA
Cummins, Manley L., III ....Daphne, AL
Cummins, Mark E. ....Lansing, MI
Cummins, Michael J. ....San Francisco, CA
Cummins, Michael J. ....Chicago, IL
Lake Forest, IL
Cummins, Michael J. ....Columbia, MO
Cummins, Michael R. ....San Francisco, CA
Cummins, Michael Timothy ....Cleveland, OH
Cummins, Michael W. ....Jacksonville, TX
Cummins, Norman C. ....Clermont, FL
Leesburg, FL
Cummins, Norman C., P.A. ....Clermont, FL
Leesburg, FL
Cummins, Richard ....Aspen, CO
Cummins, Richard E., (P.C.)
Grand Rapids, MI
Cummins, Richd. E. ....San Jose, CA
Cummins, Robert P. ....Chicago, IL
Cummins, Robert T. ....Helena, MT
Cummins, Ruth Wagonheim ....Hanover, MD
Cummins, Sally J. ....Department of State, Office of the Legal Adviser, GV
Cummins, Scott C. ....San Diego, CA
Cummins, Seth J. ....New York, NY
Cummins, Susan E. ....Alexandria, VA
Cummins, Suzanne C. ....Tucson, AZ
Cummins, Theresa E. ....Fairfax, VA
Cummins, Walter M., Jr. ....Orlando, FL
Cummins & White, LLP
Newport Beach, CA
Cummins, Woods & Panek
East Lansing, MI
Lansing, MI
Cummis, Clive S. ....Atlantic City, NJ
Newark, NJ
New York, NY
Cummis, Deborah G. ....Los Angeles, CA
Roseland, NJ
Cummis, Philip B. ....Newark, NJ
Cummiskey, David R. ....Waterville, MN
Cummiskey, John W. ....Grand Rapids, MI
Cummiskey, Keith B. ....Dallas, TX
Cummiskey, Paul J. ....Stamford, CT
Cummiskey, Timothy B. ....New York, NY
Cummo, Aimée M. ....Newark, NJ
Cump, Charles E. ....Denver, CO
Cumpian, Joe G. ....San Antonio, TX
Cumpiano, Flavio ....Washington, DC
Cumpiano, Lady E. ....Pittsburgh, PA
Cumpston, H. Max ....Enid, OK
Cumpston & Shaw ....Rochester, NY
Cumpston, Thomas D. ....Placerville, CA
Cumpton, Michael L. ....Mobile, AL
Cunabaugh, Linda A. ....McHenry, IL
Cunahan, Wm. E. ....Youngstown, OH
Cunan, Richard C. ....Clayton, CA
Cunard, Janet E. ....Pawling, NY
Cunard, Jeffrey P. ....Washington, DC
Cunard, Paul F. ....Deptford, NJ
Cunat, Marc N. ....Cumming, GA
Cuncannan, J. William ....Chicago, IL
Cuncannan, Jacqueline K.
Washington, DC
Cunconan-Lahr, Robin L. ....Des Moines, IA
Cundall, Cheryl L. ....Syracuse, NY
Cundari, Frank J. ....Las Vegas, NV
Cundiff, Barry V. ....Kirksville, MO
Cundiff, Candace M. ....Charleston, WV
Cundiff, Don R. ....Shepherdsville, KY
Cundiff, Elizabeth A. ....Chicago, IL
Cundiff, Ellsworth, Jr. ....St. Charles, MO
Cundiff, James H. ....Chicago, IL
Cundiff, James N. ....Tulsa, OK
Cundiff, Melvin ....Louisville, KY
Cundiff, Shelley A. ....Poteau, OK
Cundiff, Susan K. ....Benton Harbor, MI
Cundiff, Terry ....St. Charles, MO
Cundiff, Turken & Londoff ....St. Charles, MO
Cundiff, Victoria A. ....New York, NY
Cundra, Steven D. ....Washington, DC
Cundy, Cecil A. ....Sundance, WY
Cundy, Joyce L. ....Minneapolis, MN
Cuneo, Black, Ward & Missler
Sacramento, CA
Cuneo, David K. ....Collingswood, NJ
Cuneo, Donald L. ....New York, NY
Cuneo, Eileen ....LaGrangeville, NY
Cuneo, Frank P. ....Miami, FL

Cuneo & Hensler ... Collingswood, NJ
Cuneo & Hoover, Professional Corporation ... Los Angeles, CA
Cuneo, J. Christopher ... Minneapolis, MN
Cuneo, J. Nicholas ... Los Angeles, CA
Cuneo, J. Vince ... Connellsville, PA
Cuneo, James B. ... Sacramento, CA
Cuneo, James C. ... Sacramento, CA
Cuneo, Jonathan W. ... Washington, DC
Cuneo Law Group, The, P.C. ... Washington, DC
Cuneo, Richard P. ... Toledo, OH
Cuneo, Sandra W. ... Washington, DC
Cuneo, Steven R., Jr. ... Los Angeles, CA
Cung, Niki Trang ... Fort Smith, AR
Cung, Raphael Dang-Quang ... Los Angeles, CA
Cung, Thao H. ... San Francisco, CA
Cunha, Fernando S. ... Providence, RI
Cunha, Gary William ... Waco, TX
Cunha & Holcomb, P.C. ... Boston, MA
Cunha, James R. ... Palo Alto, CA
Cunha, John H., Jr. ... Boston, MA
Cunha, Mark G. ... New York, NY
Cunha, McKiernan & Wheeler ... Providence, RI
Cunha, Richard M. ... Sacramento, CA
Cunha, Robert E. ... El Segundo, CA
Cunha, Roberto ... Benton Harbor, MI
Cuni, Ferguson, Wolfgang & LeVay Co., L.P.A. ... Cincinnati, OH
Cuni, Thomas L. ... Cincinnati, OH
Cunial, Gary Donald, Law Offices of ... Encino, CA
Cunico, Gerald J. ... Lockport, IL
Cuniff, Clifford W. ... Baltimore, MD
Cunilio, James ... Bryn Mawr, PA
Cunill-Fals, Monica ... Miami, FL
Cuningham, John R. ... Edmonds, WA
Cunio, Christopher J. ... Boston, MA
Cunis, David W. ... Cambridge, MA
Cunliffe & Cook, A Professional Corporation ... Hagåtña, GU
Cunliffe, Erika B. ... Chicago, IL
Cunliffe, F. Randall ... Hagåtña, GU
Cunliffe, Robert W. ... Washington, DC
Cunnagin, Carl ... McKee, KY
Cunnagin and Cunnagin ... London, KY
Cunnagin, Elmer, Jr. ... London, KY
Cunnagin, Willis C. ... London, KY
Cunnane, Deirdre A. ... Boston, MA
Cunnane, Mary C. ... Philadelphia, PA
Cunnane, Thomas F. ... Philadelphia, PA
Cunnane, W. Dennis ... Walnut Creek, CA
Cunnane, William J. ... Jersey City, NJ
Cunneen, Jennifer M. ... San Jose, CA
Cunneen, John M. ... New York, NY
Cunneen, O'Gorman & Rotella ... South Orange, NJ
Cunneen, Raymond L. ... South Orange, NJ
Cunney, Paul ... Honolulu, HI
Cunniff, James A. ... Dedham, MA
Cunniff, John A. ... Wellesley, MA
Cunniff, Kenneth L., (Ltd.) ... Chicago, IL
Cunniff, Martin F. ... Washington, DC
Cunniff, Michael J. ... Wayne, NJ
Cunniff, Sarah A. ... San Francisco, CA
Cunniff, Thomas A. ... Cleveland, OH
Cunniffe, Christopher T. ... Charleston, SC
Cunnigham, Patrick J. ... San Francisco, CA
Cunning, Andrea M. ... St. Louis, MO
Cunning, James S. ... Indianapolis, IN
Cunning, Patrick Paul ... Youngstown, OH
Cunning, Stacy Lynn ... Wichita, KS
Cunningham, Alan T. ... Los Angeles, CA
Cunningham, Albert F. ... Redding, CA
Cunningham, Alice Welt ... New York, NY
Cunningham, Allyson ... Charlotte, NC
Cunningham, Amy ... Pocatello, ID
Cunningham, Amy S. ... Greensburg, PA
Cunningham, Andra E. ... Federal Communications Commission, GV
Cunningham, Andrea P. ... Albany, NY
Cunningham, Ann Recker ... Ottawa, OH
Cunningham, Anne M. ... New York, NY
Cunningham, Anthony W. ... Tampa, FL
Cunningham, Arthur B. ... New Philadelphia, OH
Cunningham, Arthur K. ... San Bernardino, CA
Cunningham & Associates ... Baton Rouge, LA
Cunningham & Associates, A Professional Corporation ... Lansing, MI
Cunningham & Associates, P.C. ... Chicago, IL
Cunningham, Audrey Davidson ... Piscataway, NJ
Cunningham, Barbara A. ... Worcester, MA
Cunningham, Barbara Lewis ... Foster City, CA
Cunningham, Ben J. ... Austin, TX
Cunningham, Bill ... Eddyville, KY
Cunningham, B. J., Jr. ... Grand Island, NE
Cunningham, Blackburn, Francis, Brock & Cunningham ... Grand Island, NE
Cunningham, Bounds, Yance, Crowder & Brown, L.L.C. ... Mobile, AL
Cunningham, Brian C. ... Palo Alto, CA
Cunningham, Brian D. ... Gilroy, CA
Cunningham, Brian D. ... Salt Lake City, UT
Cunningham, Brian G. ... Chicago, IL
Cunningham, Bruce E. ... Denver, CO
Cunningham, Bruce E. ... Worcester, MA
Cunningham, Bruce T., Jr. ... Southern Pines, NC
Cunningham, Burke & Brooks, L.L.P. ... Houston, TX
Cunningham & Byck ... Marlton, NJ
Cunningham, Cameron M. ... Santa Rosa, CA
Cunningham, Candace M. ... Hartford, CT
Cunningham, Carl E. ... Franklin, TN
Cunningham, Carol Lynette ... New York, NY
Cunningham, Carolyn ... Rye, NY
Cunningham, Catherine A. ... Columbus, OH
Cunningham, Cathy ... Irving, TX
Cunningham, Charles ... Scarsdale, NY
Cunningham, Charles D. ... New York, NY
Cunningham, Charles D., Jr. ... Omaha, NE
Cunningham, Charles J., III ... Havertown, PA
Philadelphia, PA
Cunningham, Charles L., Jr. ... Louisville, KY
Cunningham, Charles R., (P.C.) ... Corpus Christi, TX
Cunningham, Charles T. ... Winston-Salem, NC
Cunningham, Charles W. ... Dallas, TX
Cunningham & Chernicoff, P.C. ... Carlisle, PA
Harrisburg, PA
York, PA
Cunningham, Christine ... New York, NY
Cunningham, Christopher H. ... Seattle, WA
Cunningham, CiCi ... Las Vegas, NV
Cunningham, Claire E. ... McLean, VA
Cunningham, Clarence E., Jr. ... Morristown, TN
Cunningham, Clark D. ... St. Louis, MO
Cunningham, Clark & Greiwe, P.A. ... Tampa, FL
Cunningham, Clay H. ... Pittsburgh, PA
Cunningham, Clell I., III ... Oklahoma City, OK
Cunningham, Craig Carnell ... Chicago, IL
Cunningham & Cunningham ... Gloucester, MA
Cunningham & Cunningham ... Worcester, MA
Cunningham & Cunningham ... Ottawa, OH
West Palm Beach, FL
Cunningham, Cynthia E. ... New York, NY
Cunningham, D. John ... Seattle, WA
Cunningham, Dale V. ... Sherman Oaks, CA
Cunningham Dalman, P.C. ... Allegan, MI
Grand Haven, MI
Holland, MI
Saugatuck, MI
Cunningham, Daniel ... Eden Prairie, MN
Cunningham, Daniel A. ... Administrative Office Of The United States Courts, GV
Cunningham, Daniel D. ... Albany, NY
Cunningham, Daniel J. ... Chicago, IL
Cunningham, Daniel M. ... Natick, MA
Cunningham, Daniel P. ... New York, NY
Cunningham, Daniel P. ... Akron, OH
Cunningham, Daniel R. ... Niantic, CT
Cunningham, Darla K. ... Woodland Hills, CA
Cunningham, Darlow, Zook & Chapoton, LLP ... Houston, TX
Cunningham, Darryl W. ... York, PA
Cunningham, David B. ... Beaverton, OR
Cunningham, David C. ... Topeka, KS
Cunningham, David E. ... Quincy, MA
Cunningham, David F. ... Santa Fe, NM
Cunningham, David L. ... Ventura, CA
Cunningham, David L. ... Rock Island, IL
Cunningham, David M. ... Bonaire, GA
Cunningham, David P. ... Houston, TX
Cunningham, David S., III ... Los Angeles, CA
Cunningham, Deborah D. ... Omaha, NE
Cunningham, Dedmond, Petersen & Smith ... Southern Pines, NC
Cunningham, Denise R. ... Washington, DC
Cunningham, Diana G. ... Syracuse, NY
Cunningham, D. J. ... Centralia, WA
Cunningham, Don ... Sallisaw, OK
Cunningham, Donald J. ... Avon-By-The-Sea, NJ
Cunningham, Donald L., Jr. ... Baton Rouge, LA
Cunningham, Donna Grandy ... Los Angeles, CA
Cunningham, Donna J. ... Barrington, IL
Cunningham, Douglas C. ... Lansing, MI
Cunningham, Douglas R. ... Sacramento, CA
Cunningham, Drury B. ... Lake Charles, LA
Cunningham, E. Brice ... Dallas, TX
Cunningham, Ed ... Austin, TX
Cunningham, Edselle K. ... Baton Rouge, LA
Cunningham, Edward ... Gadsden, AL
Cunningham, Edward ... Dallas, TX
Cunningham, Edward C. ... El Reno, OK
Cunningham, Edward F. ... Rego Park, NY
Cunningham, Edward I. ... Washington, DC
Cunningham, Edward J. ... Springfield, IL
Cunningham, Edward VK., Jr. ... Poughkeepsie, NY
Cunningham, Elizabeth A. McGee ... Dayton, OH
Cunningham, Elizabeth C. ... Clearfield, PA
Cunningham, Elizabeth G. ... Roswell, NM
Cunningham, Ernest D. ... Irvine, CA
Cunningham, Eugene W., Jr. ... Towson, MD
Cunningham, F. Malcolm, Jr., (P.A.) ... West Palm Beach, FL
Cunningham, Francis J., III (A.P.C.) ... Woodland Hills, CA
Cunningham, Francis X. ... Revere, MA
Cunningham, Frank C. ... San Jose, CA
Cunningham, Fred A., (P.A.) ... Palm Beach Gardens, FL
Cunningham, Frederick M. ... Alameda, CA
Cunningham, G. Alan ... Minneapolis, MN
Cunningham, G. Bruce ... Atlanta, GA
Cunningham, G. Kevin ... Houston, TX
Cunningham, Galloway & Marett ... Scarsdale, NY
Cunningham, Gary A. ... Bremerton, WA
Cunningham, Gary H. ... Bloomfield Hills, MI
Cunningham, Gary M. ... Fenton, MO
Cunningham, Gary R. ... Springfield, MO
Cunningham, George D. ... Milwaukee, WI
Cunningham, George G. ... Hooksett, NH
Cunningham, George G. ... Wilkesboro, NC
Cunningham, George H. ... Stockton, CA
Cunningham, George V. ... Watertown, SD
Cunningham, Gerald ... Atlanta, GA
Cunningham, Gerald Michael ... Fort Lauderdale, FL
Cunningham, Gerald P. ... Los Angeles, CA
Cunningham, Gerard W. ... New York, NY
Cunningham, Glen ... Superior, WI
Cunningham, Glenn M. ... Hartford, CT
Cunningham, Glenn W. ... Houston, TX
Cunningham, Gordon H. ... Holland, MI
Cunningham & Gray, P.A. ... Wilkesboro, NC
Cunningham, Greg ... Oklahoma City, OK
Cunningham, Gregory M. ... Portland, ME
Cunningham, Grover B., Jr. ... Austin, TX
Cunningham, Guy H. ... Columbus, OH
Cunningham, Harold D., Jr. ... Dover, NH
Cunningham, Heather Anne ... Boise, ID
Cunningham, H. N., III ... Dallas, TX
Cunningham, Howard L. ... Reno, NV
Cunningham, Hugh J. ... Kinder, LA
Cunningham, J. Calvin, Law Offices of ... Lexington, NC
Cunningham, J. Russell ... Sacramento, CA
Cunningham, Jack M. ... Centralia, WA
Cunningham, Jack R. ... Phoenix, AZ
Cunningham, Jack R. ... Lexington, KY
Cunningham, James ... Orlando, FL
Cunningham, James A. ... San Diego, CA
Cunningham, James A. ... Gilbertsville, PA
Cunningham, James C., Jr. ... Fort Lauderdale, FL
Cunningham, James F. ... Pittsburgh, PA
Cunningham, James L. ... Simi Valley, CA
Cunningham, James L. ... Denver, CO
Cunningham, James M., III ... Rayne, LA
Cunningham, James P. ... Phoenix, AZ
Cunningham, James P. ... San Francisco, CA
Cunningham, James P. ... Birmingham, MI
Cunningham, James R. ... Orlando, FL
Cunningham, James R. ... Cincinnati, OH
Cunningham, James R. ... Olympia, WA
Cunningham, James T. ... New York, NY
Cunningham, James V. ... Peoria, IL
Cunningham, James V. ... Baltimore, MD
Cunningham, James W. ... Syracuse, NY
Cunningham, Jan Marie ... Muskogee, OK
Cunningham, Janice G. ... Plymouth Meeting, PA
Cunningham, Janice K. ... Lansing, MI
Cunningham, Janine P. ... New York, NY
Cunningham, Janis A. ... Seattle, WA
Cunningham, Jean M. ... Washington, DC
Cunningham, Jean R. ... New Albany, IN
Cunningham, Jean W. ... Richmond, VA
Cunningham, Jeanne M. ... Chicago, IL
Cunningham, Jeffrey L. ... Athens, TN
Cunningham, Jeffrey P. ... Seal Beach, CA
Cunningham, Jerry G. ... Maryville, TN
Cunningham, Jesse P. ... Beaumont, TX
Cunningham, Jesse P., P.C. ... Beaumont, TX
Cunningham, Joe Bruce ... Fort Worth, TX
Cunningham, Joel C. ... Halifax, VA
Cunningham, Joel C., P.C. ... Halifax, VA
Cunningham, Joel D. ... Seattle, WA
Cunningham, John ... Rock Island, IL
Cunningham, John A. ... Brunswick, ME
Cunningham, John C. ... Department of Justice, Civil Division, GV
Cunningham, John C. ... Fort Lauderdale, FL
Cunningham, John C. ... Houston, TX
Cunningham, John C., P.A. ... Fort Lauderdale, FL
Cunningham, John D., III ... Gloucester, MA
Cunningham, John F. ... Wailuku, HI
Cunningham, John J. ... Albany, NY
Cunningham, John J., III ... Philadelphia, PA
Cunningham, John J., IV ... West Chester, PA
Cunningham, John K. ... Miami, FL
Cunningham, John M. ... Silver Spring, MD
Cunningham, John M. ... Grand Island, NE
Cunningham, John Oliver ... Natick, MA
Cunningham, John P. ... St. Petersburg, FL
Cunningham, John P. ... Belleville, IL
St. Louis, MO
Cunningham, John P., Jr. ... Temple, TX
Cunningham, John R., III ... Davidson, NC
Cunningham, John R., III, P.A. ... Davidson, NC
Cunningham, John Roy ... Symsonia, KY
Cunningham, Joi M. ... Detroit, MI
Cunningham, Jon A. ... St. Charles, MO
Cunningham, Jonathan J. ... Dallas, TX
Cunningham, Jordan D. ... Harrisburg, PA
Cunningham, Joseph Cotten ... Annapolis, MD
Cunningham, Joseph F., Jr. ... Fairview Heights, IL
Cunningham, Joseph Francis ... Alexandria, VA
Cunningham, Joseph Francis, & Associates ... Alexandria, VA
Cunningham, Joseph P., III ... Crystal City, MO
Cunningham, Joseph W. ... Southfield, MI
Cunningham, Joseph W. ... Philadelphia, PA
Cunningham, Judith K. ... Pontiac, MI
Cunningham, Judson T. ... Thousand Palms, CA
Cunningham, Julie Beth ... Houston, TX
Cunningham, Kara L. ... Washington, DC
Cunningham, Kate ... Louisville, KY
Cunningham, Kathleen B. ... Minot, ND
Cunningham, Kathryn, A. ... Mineola, NY
Cunningham, Kathryn M. ... Hartford, CT
Cunningham, Keith E. ... Tampa, FL
Cunningham, Keith J. ... Portland, ME
Cunningham, Kelley J. ... Buckhannon, WV
Cunningham, Kelly W. ... Santa Monica, CA
Cunningham, Ken ... Chicago, IL
Cunningham, Kendall R. ... Wichita, KS
Cunningham, Kenneth C. ... Fort Worth, TX
Cunningham, Kevan J. ... Taunton, MA
Cunningham, Kevin F. ... Princeton, NJ
Cunningham, Kevin M. ... Washington, DC
Cunningham, Kevin R. ... Philadelphia, PA
Cunningham, Kieran F. ... Bloomfield Hills, MI
Cunningham, Kirk B. ... Des Moines, IA
Cunningham, Kyle D. ... Missoula, MT
Cunningham & Lansden ... Lancaster, CA
Modesto, CA
Oxnard, CA
Simi Valley, CA
Ventura, CA
Cunningham Law Firm ... Phoenix, AZ
Cunningham Law Firm, The ... West Palm Beach, FL
Cunningham, Lawrence A. ... New York, NY
Cunningham, LeeAnn ... Long Valley, NJ
Cunningham, Leo P. ... Palo Alto, CA
Cunningham, Leslie Blanco ... Chicago, IL
Cunningham, Linda N. ... Los Angeles, CA
Cunningham, Lisa ... Tacoma, WA
Cunningham, Lisa L. ... New York, NY
Cunningham, Lloyd R., Jr. ... Houston, TX
Cunningham, Lorinne J ... Milwaukee, WI
Cunningham, Lynn E. ... Washington, DC
Cunningham & Lyons, S.C. ... Milwaukee, WI
Cunningham, M. Edward, II ... Huntington, WV
Cunningham, Margaret S. ... Atlanta, GA
Cunningham, Marina F. ... Hartford, CT
Cunningham, Marjorie F. ... Tucson, AZ
Cunningham, Mark A. ... Westminster, CO
Cunningham, Mark A. ... Washington, DC
Cunningham, Mark A. ... New Orleans, LA
Cunningham, Mark A. ... Marlton, NJ
Cunningham, Mark A. ... Chattanooga, TN
Cunningham, Mark G. ... Los Angeles, CA
Cunningham, Mark M. ... Detroit, MI
Cunningham, Martin B. ... Douglaston, NY
Cunningham, Martin C. ... Harrisburg, PA
Cunningham, Martin J., III ... Lexington, KY
Cunningham, Mary I. ... Natick, MA
Cunningham, Mary Kathryn ... Charleston, SC
Cunningham, Mary Lee ... New York, NY
Cunningham, Mary M. ... Chicago, IL
Cunningham, Maryanne ... New York, NY
Cunningham, Matthew A. ... Ottawa, OH
Cunningham, Matthew B. ... Phoenix, AZ
Cunningham, Maureen J. ... Pelham, NY
Cunningham, Maurice F. ... Lynnfield, MA
Cunningham, M. C., II ... Bartlesville, OK
Cunningham, Melisse S. ... Portland, OR
Cunningham Meyer & Vedrine, P.C. ... Wheaton, IL
Cunningham, Michael E. ... Trenton, NJ
Cunningham, Michael J. ... Chicago, IL
Cunningham, Michael J. ... Chicago, IL
Cunningham, Michael J. ... Des Moines, IA
Cunningham, Michael J. ... Southfield, MI
Cunningham, Michael J. ... Albany, NY
Cunningham, Michael R. ... Minneapolis, MN
Cunningham, Michael R. ... Austin, TX
Cunningham, Michael T. ... Houston, TX
Cunningham, Michael W. ... Watonga, OK
Cunningham, Miller, Heffernan, Hamilton & Wolfe, LLP ... Marathon, FL
Cunningham, Mitchell, Hicks & Rocconi, P.L.L.C. ... Clarksville, TN
Cunningham & Mullinax ... La Fayette, GA
Cunningham, Myles C. ... Rockville Centre, NY
Cunningham, Myron K. ... Oklahoma City, OK
Cunningham, Nancy J. ... Santa Monica, CA
Cunningham, Neal J. ... Lafayette, NY
Cunningham, Nelson W. ... Washington, DC
Cunningham, Noel B. ... New York, NY
Cunningham, Norris ... Indianapolis, IN
Cunningham, P. Michael ... Baltimore, MD
Cunningham, Patricia ... Nashville, TN
Cunningham, Patricia Bayer ... Atlanta, GA
Cunningham, Patrick J. ... San Francisco, CA
Cunningham, Patrick J. ... Anderson, IN
Cunningham, Patrick J. ... Syracuse, NY
Cunningham, Patrick J., Jr. ... Anderson, IN
Cunningham, Patrick K. ... Fall River, MA
Cunningham, Patrick R. ... Bradenton, FL
Cunningham, Paul A. ... Washington, DC
Cunningham, Paul H. ... Ottawa, OH
Cunningham, Paul Y., Jr. ... South Padre Island, TX
Cunningham, Paul Y., Jr., P.C. ... South Padre Island, TX

Cunningham, Paula M. ....Gassaway, WV
Cunningham, Peggy Bevard ....Yukon, OK
Cunningham, Penelope R. ....Cincinnati, OH
Cunningham, Peter C. ....Tallahassee, FL
Cunningham, Phillip M. ....Sacramento, CA
Cunningham, Phillip M., A Law Corporation Sacramento, CA
Cunningham, Pierce E. ....Cincinnati, OH
Cunningham, R. Gregory Cathedral City, CA
Cunningham, R. Scott ....Dalton, GA
Cunningham, R. Scott, P.C. ....Dalton, GA
Cunningham, Ralph E., Jr. ....Marathon, FL
Cunningham, Richard B. ....San Francisco, CA
Cunningham, Richard D. ....Houston, TX
Cunningham, Richard H. ....Smithtown, NY
Cunningham, Richard H. G. ....Stamford, CT
Cunningham, Richard J. ....New York, NY
Cunningham, Richard J., Jr. New York, NY
Cunningham, Richard O. Washington, DC
Cunningham, Richard P. ....Lynchburg, VA
Cunningham, Richard P., & Associates, P.C. Lynchburg, VA
Cunningham, Richard T. ....Akron, OH
Cunningham, Rick ....Alva, OK
Cunningham, Rita Baldwin ....Little Rock, AR
Cunningham, Robert B. ....Atlanta, GA
Cunningham, Robert D. ....Burbank, CA
Cunningham, Robert E. ....Pontiac, MI
Cunningham, Robert F. ....St. Paul, MN
Cunningham, Robert H. ....Quincy, MA
Cunningham, Robert J. ....Englewood, CO
Cunningham, Robert J. ....Chicago, IL
Cunningham, Robert J. ....Houston, TX
Cunningham, Robert J., Jr. ....Fairfax, VA
Cunningham, Robert L., Jr. New York, NY
Cunningham, Robert M. ....Brunswick, GA
Cunningham, Robert M., P.C. Brunswick, GA
Cunningham, Robert Michael, II Pascagoula, MS
Cunningham, Robert P. ....Springfield, MA
Cunningham, Robert P. ....St. Cloud, MN
Cunningham, Robert T. ....Mobile, AL
Cunningham, Robert T., Jr. ....Mobile, AL
Cunningham, Robert T., Jr. ....Akron, OH
Cunningham, Robert W. ....Gloucester, MA
Cunningham, Rodney ....Philadelphia, PA
Cunningham, Roger A. ....Ann Arbor, MI
Cunningham, Roger S. ....Pittsburgh, PA
Cunningham, Ronald E. ....Knoxville, TN
Cunningham, Roscoe D., (Ltd.) Lawrenceville, IL
Cunningham, Roy H ....Buffalo, NY
Cunningham, R. P. ....Columbus, OH
Cunningham, Russell B., III Philadelphia, PA
Cunningham, Russell N. ....Dublin, OH
Cunningham, Samuel S. ....Englewood, CO
Cunningham, Scott D. ....Houston, TX
Cunningham, Scott & Denius, L.L.P. Austin, TX
Cunningham, Sean B. ....Washington, DC
Cunningham, Sean C. ....San Diego, CA
Cunningham, Shawn M. ....Phoenix, AZ
Cunningham, Sheila Jordan ....Memphis, TN
Cunningham, Shirley Allen, Jr. Georgetown, KY
Lexington, KY
Cunningham, Stanley L. Oklahoma City, OK
Cunningham, Stephanie Corning Tacoma, WA
Cunningham, Stephen C. ....New York, NY
Cunningham, Steven A. ....Atlanta, GA
Cunningham, Stewart A. ....Morristown, NJ
Cunningham, Susan O. ....Washington, DC
Cunningham, Teresa A. ....Fairfield, CA
Napa, CA
Cunningham, Theodore S. ....New York, NY
Cunningham, Theresa L. ....Santa Rosa, CA
Cunningham, Thomas A. ....St. Louis, MO
Cunningham, Thomas A. ....St. Helens, OR
Cunningham, Thomas D. ....Chicago, IL
Cunningham, Thomas E. ....Indianapolis, IN
Cunningham, Thomas E., Jr. ....Tampa, FL
Cunningham, Thomas F. ....Washington, DC
Cunningham, Thomas J. West Palm Beach, FL
Cunningham, Thomas J. ....Chicago, IL
Cunningham, Thomas M. ....Des Moines, IA
Cunningham, Thomas M. ....Arlington, VA
Cunningham, Thomas M. ....Wheeling, WV
Cunningham, Thomas P. ....Albany, NY
Buffalo, NY
Cunningham, Thomas P., Jr. ....Chicago, IL
Cunningham, Thomas R. Philadelphia, PA
Cunningham, Thomas W. ....Milwaukee, WI
Cunningham, Tom Alan ....Houston, TX
Cunningham & Treadwell Woodland Hills, CA
Cunningham, Vickers L., Sr. ....Dallas, TX
Cunningham, Vincent A. ....Nashville, TN
Cunningham, W. Eric ....Cape Girardeau, MO
Cunningham, W. Peyton, Jr. Natchitoches, LA
Cunningham, Walker C., Jr. Louisville, KY
Cunningham, Whitney ....Flagstaff, AZ
Cunningham, William A. ....Dalhart, TX
Cunningham, William B., Jr. St. Louis, MO
Cunningham, William Briggs New York, NY
Cunningham, William D. ....Cincinnati, OH
Cunningham, William David La Fayette, GA
Cunningham, William F. ....Wheaton, IL
Cunningham, William J. ....Highland, IN
Cunningham, William J., III ....Mineola, NY
Cunningham, William J., Jr. ....Buffalo, NY
Cunningham, William M., Jr. ....Mobile, AL
Cunningham, William M., Jr. ....Beloit, WI
Cunningham, William P. ....Toms River, NJ
Cunningham, William Paul Florham Park, NJ
Cunningham, William R. ....Erie, PA
Cunningham III, Eric A. ....Chicago, IL
Cunnington and Burnett ....Kankakee, IL
Cunnington, Thomas W. ....Kankakee, IL
Cunnison, Stephen D. ....Riverside, CA
Cunnyngham, Maxine Brown Oklahoma City, OK
Cuntz, Warren A., Jr. ....New Orleans, LA
Cuny, Linda M. ....Palo Alto, CA
Cunyus, George ....Dallas, TX
Cuoco, Deborah A. ....Wilmington, DE
Cuoco, Lillian M. ....Berlin, CT
Cuomo, Andrew M. ....New York, NY
Cuomo, Anthony A. ....Palm Bay, FL
Cuomo & Cuomo ....Wellsburg, WV
Cuomo, Dennis E. ....Baltimore, MD
Cuomo, Diana L. ....Sacramento, CA
Cuomo, Frank ....Wellsburg, WV
Cuomo, Frank N. ....Amherst, NY
Cuomo, Jason Adam ....Wellsburg, WV
Cuomo, Jerry A. ....Newark, NJ
Cuomo, John A. ....Miami, FL
Cuomo, John N. ....Glen Oaks, NY
Cuomo, Joseph V. ....New York, NY
Cuomo, Lori F. ....Fairfax, VA
Cuomo, Madeline C. ....New York, NY
Cuomo, Mario M. ....New York, NY
Cuomo, Matthew A. ....New York, NY
Cuomo, Neil N. ....Amherst, NY
Cuomo, Paul C. ....Washington, DC
Cuono, Marco D. ....Miami, FL
Cuonzo, Angelo A. ....Newark, NJ
Cuozzi, William F., III ....New York, NY
Cuozzi, William F., Jr. ....West Orange, NJ
Cuozzo, Donald H. ....Pittsburgh, PA
Cupelli, Redino J. ....New York, NY
Cupelo, William ....Boston, MA
Cupero, Hamil M., Jr. ....Beaumont, TX
Cupero, James J. ....Goshen, NY
Cupero, Kelly McFarland ....Beaumont, TX
Cupery, Joanne G. Bagin ....Beaver Dam, WI
Cupick, Linda S. ....Daytona Beach, FL
Cupit, Danny E., Law Offices of Jackson, MS
Cupit Law Office ....Norfolk, VA
Cupit, Linda Lee ....Norfolk, VA
Cupit, Michael B. ....Brookhaven, MS
Cupita, Jos. F. ....Omaha, NE
Cupka, Brian J. ....Wayne, NJ
Cupka, Ellen M. ....Somerville, NJ
Cupkovic, Walter D. ....Chicago, IL
Cupo, Leonard V. ....Jersey City, NJ
Cupo-Cruz, Mary L. ....Trenton, NJ
Cupp, Ann Agnew ....Lexington, SC
Cupp, Cathy L. ....Englewood, CO
Cupp & Cupp ....Bedford, PA
Uniontown, PA
Cupp and Cupp, P.C. ....Harrisonburg, VA
Cupp, Emilie J. ....Bedford, PA
Uniontown, PA
Cupp, Jenifer D. ....Harrisonburg, VA
Cupp, John S., Jr. ....Bedford, PA
Uniontown, PA
Cupp, Melissa N. ....Culpeper, VA
Cupp, Richard L., Jr. ....Malibu, CA
Cupp, Robert R. ....Lima, OH
Cupp, Ruth Williams ....Charleston, SC
Cupp, Scott H. ....Fort Myers, FL
Cupp, Steven R., (P.C.) ....New Orleans, LA
Cupp, Timothy E. ....Harrisonburg, VA
Cuppage, David M. ....Cleveland, OH
Cupples, Gary M. ....Kansas City, MO
Cupples, Ronald L. ....St. Louis, MO
Cupples, Stephen E. ....St. Louis, MO
Cupp-Moreno, Kimberley Fay New York, NY
Cupps, David S. ....Columbus, OH
Cupps, Donald L. ....Cassville, MO
Cupps, Terry C. ....Wichita, KS
Cuppy, Frederick M. ....Merrillville, IN
Cuprill, Hector R. ....Ponce, PR
Cuprill & Pedrosa ....Ponce, PR
Cuprill, Raymond W. Department of Transportation, Federal Highway Administration, GV
Cuprill-Comas, Alice M. ....Austin, TX
Cura, Danicet Mairim ....Tampa, FL
Cura, Juan Carlos ....Coral Gables, FL
Cura, Peter J. ....Boston, MA
Curan, Michael B. ....Garden City, NY
Curan, Michael E. ....New York, NY
Curan, Michael E., P.C., The Law Offices of New York, NY
Curato, Randy J. ....Chicago, IL
Curatola, Neal T. ....Anaheim, CA
Curatolo, Joseph G. ....Westlake, OH
Curbelo, Pamela J. ....Windsor, CT
Curbo, Charles R. ....Memphis, TN
Curbow, William E. ....New York, NY
Curchack, Walter H. ....New York, NY
Curchin, Alexander B., III ....Joplin, MO
Curci, Angela Surace ....Brooklyn, NY
Curci, Frank X. ....Seattle, WA
Curci, Nicholas R. ....Lorain, OH
Curciarello, Gerry V. ....Chicago, IL
Curcillo, Jody T. ....Marlton, NJ
Media, PA
Philadelphia, PA
Curcillo, Joseph A., III ....Harrisburg, PA
Huntingdon Valley, PA
Curcillo & Langton, P.C. ....Marlton, NJ
Media, PA
Philadelphia, PA
Curcillo, Tara K. ....New York, NY
Curcio, Andrea L. (Lori) ....Southfield, MI
Curcio, Barry M. ....Groton, MA
Curcio, Benjamin C. ....Parsippany, NJ
Curcio, Craig P., Law Offices of Middletown, NY
Curcio, David S. ....Houston, TX
Curcio, Dominic S. ....New York, NY
Curcio, Gregory J. ....New York, NY
Curcio, James ....Hammonton, NJ
Curcio, Jeffrey W. ....Sacramento, CA
Curcio, John B. ....Lansing, MI
Curcio, Joseph R. ....Chicago, IL
Curcio, Joseph R., Ltd. ....Chicago, IL
Curcio, Mary G. ....General Accounting Office, Office of the General Counsel, GV
Curcio, Paul V. ....Boston, MA
Providence, RI
Curcio, Peter ....Bristol, VA
Curcio, Rick V. ....Los Angeles, CA
Curcio, Robert ....New Haven, CT
Curcio, Samuel A. ....Hammonton, NJ
Curcio, Samuel A., Jr. ....Hammonton, NJ
Curcio, Susan H. ....Mays Landing, NJ
Curcio, Thomas J. ....Alexandria, VA
Curcio, Walter W. ....Boston, MA
Curcione, Paul L. ....Lawrenceville, GA
Curd, Ann Marie ....New York, NY
Valley Stream, NY
Curd, David Wilson ....Chandler, AZ
Curd, Joseph D. ....Long Beach, CA
Curd, Philip L. ....Cleveland, OH
Curd, Sarah Coursey ....Murray, KY
Curd, Stephanie Staples Fort Lauderdale, FL
Curda, Dale O. ....Bethel, AK
Curdie, Don N. ....Little Rock, AR
Curdts, William R. ....White Stone, VA
Cure, Candy ....Barrington, NJ
Cure, Carol ....Scottsdale, AZ
Cure & Francis, A Professional Association Killeen, TX
Temple, TX
Cure, Harding B. ....Phoenix, AZ
Cure, Harry L., Jr. ....Fort Worth, TX
Cure, Harry L., Jr., P.C. ....Fort Worth, TX
Cure, Ira ....New York, NY
Cure, James O. ....Killeen, TX
Temple, TX
Cure, Kevin T. ....Galena, KS
Cure Law Firm, The ....Scottsdale, AZ
Curelop, Jean-Cristophe ....Los Angeles, CA
Curenton, James G., Jr. ....Fairhope, AL
Curenton, James G., Jr., P.C. Bay Minette, AL
Fairhope, AL
Gulf Shores, AL
Curet, Adolph B., III ....Franklin, LA
Curet & Barron ....Hammond, LA
Curet, Blaise S. ....San Francisco, CA
Curet, Douglas T. ....Hammond, LA
Curet, Louis D. ....Baton Rouge, LA
Curet, Ronald A. ....Hammond, LA
Cureton, Caplan & Clark, P.C. Mount Laurel, NJ
Cureton, Cheryl ....Owensboro, KY
Cureton, Debbie Russell ....Clearwater, FL
Cureton, Frank W. ....Columbia, SC
Cureton, H. J., Jr. ....Meridian, TX
Cureton, Jasper M. ....Columbia, SC
Cureton, Jeffrey L. ....Fort Worth, TX
Cureton, Jerald R. ....Mount Laurel, NJ
Cureton, Kenneth A. ....Treasury Department, Office of Thrift Supervision, GV
Cureton, Robert H. ....Walhalla, SC
Cureton, Steven R. ....Clemson, SC
Curfiss, Robert C. ....Houston, TX
Curfman, Charles A. ....Wichita, KS
Curfman, Lawrence E., III Belvedere-Tiburon, CA
Curfman, Shirley E. ....Los Angeles, CA
Curhan, Allan R. ....Boston, MA
Curhan, Jenifer J. ....Washington, DC
Curhan, Michael C. ....Troy, MI
Curi, Eli, Jr. ....New York, NY
Curi, Marcelo ....Miami Beach, FL
Curi, Marcelo ....Miami Beach, FL
Curi, Sarah Elisabeth ....Boston, MA
Curia, Frank S. ....Charleston, WV
Curia, Joseph A. ....Clarksburg, WV
Curiale Dellaverson Hirschfeld Kelly & Kraemer, LLP ....Los Angeles, CA
San Francisco, CA
Curiale, Matthew A. ....Greensburg, PA
Curiale, Richard J. ....San Francisco, CA
Curiale, Salvatore R. ....New York, NY
Curiel, Antonio J. ....Chicago, IL
Curiel, Gloria M. ....Santa Monica, CA
Curiel, Gonzalo P. ....San Diego, CA
Curiel & Parker, Law Offices of Santa Monica, CA
Curielli, John Peter ....Barrington, IL
Curington, Gerald B. ....Tallahassee, FL
Curington, John Wesley ....Dallas, TX
Curington, Tim W. ....Houston, TX
Curko, Sandy A. ....Boston, MA
Curl, Ann H. ....Los Angeles, CA
Curl, Cathleen M. ....Millbrae, CA
Curl, Dean E. ....Mt. Gilead, OH
Curl, Jeffrey R. ....Hannibal, MO
Curl, Paul T. ....San Antonio, TX
Curl, Paul T., A Professional Corporation San Antonio, TX
Curl, Wesley L. ....Department of Labor, Office of the Solicitor, GV
Curland, Dennis J. ....Chesterfield, MO
Curland, Hillard ....Randallstown, MD
Curle, David H. ....Minneapolis, MN
Curle, Wilson ....Redding, CA
Curlee, Allan E. ....Fairbanks, AK
Curlee, Allan, P.C. ....Fairbanks, AK
Juneau, AK
Curlee, Brett B. ....Los Angeles, CA
Curlee, C. Durbrow ....St. Louis, MO
Curlee, Emery D. ....Alexandria, LA
Curlee, Glen ....Wetumpka, AL
Curlee, Steven A. ....Atlanta, GA
Curless, Charles D. ....Lamar, MO
Curless, Douglas W. ....Department of Justice, Bureau of Prisons, GV
Curley, Alan F. ....Chicago, IL
Curley, Anne D. ....Washington, DC
Curley, Arthur W. ....San Francisco, CA
San Rafael, CA
Curley, Brian F. ....Warren, NJ
Curley, C. Philip ....Chicago, IL
Curley, Charles R., Jr ....Jacksonville, FL
Curley, Charles V. ....Cherry Hill, NJ
Harrisburg, PA
King Of Prussia, PA
Curley, Christine M. ....North Kingstown, RI
Curley & Curley, P.C. ....Boston, MA
Curley, Denise ....Boston, MA
Curley, Edward ....Dover, DE
Curley, Edward K. ....San Diego, CA
Curley, Frank E. ....Scottsdale, AZ
Curley, Frederick N. ....Spokane, WA
Curley, G. Joseph ....West Palm Beach, FL
Curley, Gregory M. ....New York, NY
Curley, Jay J. ....Wakefield, MA
Curley, Jennifer M. ....Washington, DC
Curley, John E. ....Southfield, MI
Curley, John E. ....Montvale, NJ
Curley, John E. ....Pittsburgh, PA
Curley, John F. ....Chicago, IL
Curley, John H. ....Morristown, NJ
Curley, John J. ....Hoboken, NJ
Jersey City, NJ
Curley, John J. ....Chappaqua, NY
Curley, John J., III ....Leominster, MA
Curley, John O. ....Oxon Hill, MD
Curley, John P. ....New York, NY
Curley, John P., Jr. ....Barnstable, MA
Curley, John T. ....Trumbull, CT
Curley, Karen Khan ....Somerset, NJ
Curley, Kathleen L. ....Westborough, MA
Curley, Kathleen M. ....Englewood, CO
Curley, Kathleen O. ....Hackensack, NJ
Curley, Kevin J. ....New York, NY
Curley, Mark M. ....Wakefield, MA
Curley, Michael A. ....New York, NY
Curley, Michael J. ....Phoenix, AZ
Curley, Patricia S. ....Milwaukee, WI
Curley, Patrick G. ....Los Angeles, CA
Curley, Paul J. ....New York, NY
Curley, Paul McCourt ....Richmond, VA
Curley, Richard L. ....Hyannis, MA
Curley, Richard O., Jr. ....Denver, CO
Curley, Richard T. ....Lancaster, PA
Curley, Robert A. ....Boston, MA
Curley, Robert A., Jr. ....Boston, MA
Curley, Robert Charles ....Providence, RI
Curley, Robert E. ....Chicago, IL
Curley, Robert J. ....Red Bank, NJ
Curley, Robert M. ....Cudahy, WI
Curley, Robert P. ....Washington, DC
Curley, Roger D. ....Phoenix, AZ
Curley, Sarah Sharer ....Phoenix, AZ
Curley & Sciarra ....Hoboken, NJ
Jersey City, NJ
Curley, Sean B. ....Greensboro, NC
Curley, Stephen C. ....New York, NY
Curley, Stephen J. ....Stamford, CT
Curley, W. Charles ....Columbus, OH
Curley, Wilfred F. ....Livonia, MI
Curley, William P., III ....Brea, CA
Curliano, Jason J. ....Oakland, CA
Curlin, David P. ....New Orleans, LA
Curlin, Lyn M. ....New Orleans, LA
Curlin, William P., Jr. ....Frankfort, KY
Curling, Julius O. ....Southfield, MI
Curls, G. Michael ....Los Angeles, CA
Curme, Ann M. ....Minneapolis, MN
Curnan, Robert J. ....Dubuque, IA
Curney, John, Jr. ....San Antonio, TX
Curnick, B. Dwight ....Temecula, CA
Curnin, Kevin J. ....New York, NY
Curnin, Paul C. ....New York, NY
Curnin, Rebecca T. ....New York, NY
Curnin, Thomas F. ....New York, NY
Curnow, David P. ....San Diego, CA
Curnow, Rodger P. ....Oakland, CA
Curnow, Roy D. ....Red Bank, NJ
Curnutt, Kelly J. ....Dallas, TX
Curnutt, Richard A. ....Costa Mesa, CA
Curnutte, Mark W. ....Grove, OK
Vinita, OK
Curnyn, John ....Chicago, IL
Curoe, Andrew H. ....Detroit, MI
Curoe, Michael R. ....Overland Park, KS
Curosh, Christine Hajduch ....Hammond, IN
Curosh, Joseph L. ....Griffith, IN
Curosh, William J. ....Phoenix, AZ
Curott, Phyllis Winifred ....New York, NY
Curott, Richard W. ....Milaca, MN
Curotto, Alexis Joseph ....Mountain View, CA
Curotto, David ....Overland Park, KS
Curotto, Donald J. ....Orlando, FL

Curotto, John F. ... Santa Cruz, CA
Curp, John H. ... Dayton, OH
Curp, John P. ... Columbus, OH
Curp, W. Anthony ... Kansas City, MO
Curphey, James D. ... Columbus, OH
Curphey, John M. ... Toledo, OH
Curphey, William E. ... Tampa, FL
Curphy, R. James ... San Antonio, TX
Currais, Maria Victoria ... Miami, FL
Currall, Geoffrey G. ... Ketchikan, AK
Currall, William G. ... Westfield, NJ
Curran, Albert F. ... Boston, MA
Curran, Alice T. Valder ... Washington, DC
Curran, Alicia Hayes ... Dallas, TX
Curran, Alicia S. ... Los Angeles, CA
Curran, Ann ... North Syracuse, NY
Curran, Arthur B. ... Rochester, NY
Curran, Barbara A. ... Chicago, IL
Curran, Barbara Sanson ... Wilmington, DE
Curran & Benedict ... Indianapolis, IN
Curran & Byrne, P.C. ... Media, PA
Philadelphia, PA
Curran, Caitlin T. ... Pottsville, PA
Curran, Carol A. ... Montrose, CO
Curran, Catherine A. ... Scarsdale, NY
Curran, Catherine M. ... Charlotte, NC
Curran, Charles A. ... Miami, FL
Curran, Charles D. ... Dulles, VA
Curran, Charles E. ... Chevy Chase, MD
Curran, Charles E., III ... Cincinnati, OH
Curran, Charles P. ... Kent, WA
Curran, Chas. ... McArthur, OH
Curran, Christopher J. ... Davenport, IA
Curran, Christopher J., Jr. ... Rockwall, TX
Curran, Christopher M. ... Washington, DC
Curran & Clifford ... Osage Beach, MO
Curran, Coffey & Moran, LLP
Boston, MA
Salem, MA
Curran, Colleen ... Minneapolis, MN
Curran & Curran ... Fort Lauderdale, FL
Curran & Curran ... Paramus, NJ
Curran, Daniel A. ... Adamsville, RI
Curran, Daniel F. ... Crystal Lake, IL
Curran, Daniel F. ... Bloomfield Hills, MI
Curran, Daniel J. ... San Diego, CA
Curran, Daniel J. ... Cincinnati, OH
Curran, Daniel S. ... Glenview, IL
Curran, David G. ... Lawrenceville, NJ
Curran, Deborah J. ... Escanaba, MI
Curran, Deborah K. ... Laurel, MD
Curran, Denis A. ... Palo Alto, CA
Curran, Dennis J. ... Phoenix, AZ
Curran, Dennis J. ... Boston, MA
Curran, Dennis L. ... New York, NY
Curran, Desmond P. ... Chicago, IL
Curran, Diane ... Washington, DC
Curran, Dianne ... Providence, RI
Curran, Donald W. ... Oakland, CA
Curran, Douglas A. ... Worthington, OH
Curran, Douglas Y. ... Kansas City, MO
Curran, Edmund T. ... Hartford, CT
Curran, Edwin J., Jr. ... Mobile, AL
Curran, Eileen D. ... Las Cruces, NM
Curran, Elizabeth ... New York, NY
Curran, Francis J. ... Detroit, MI
Curran, Francis J., Jr. ... Media, PA
Curran, Francis M. ... Tampa, FL
Curran, G. Michael ... Dallas, TX
Curran, George F., III ... Southfield, MI
Curran, Gerald R. ... Fairfax, VA
Curran, Gregory S. ... Birmingham, AL
Curran, Gruner & O'Connor
Kingston, NY
Curran, Harold J. ... Anchorage, AK
Curran, Hollenbeck & Orton, S.C.
Mauston, WI
Curran, Hugh C. ... Bridgeport, CT
Curran, Hugh R. ... Hartford, CT
Boston, MA
Curran, J. Charles ... Fairfax, VA
Curran, J. Donald ... Spokane, WA
Curran, J. Joseph, III ... Baltimore, MD
Curran, J. Joseph, Jr. ... Baltimore, MD
Curran, James ... Fort Lauderdale, FL
Curran, James D. ... San Francisco, CA
Curran, James E. ... Phoenix, AZ
Curran, James F. ... Sacramento, CA
Curran, James J., Jr. ... Pottsville, PA
Curran, James M. ... East Brunswick, NJ
Curran, James P. ... Phoenix, AZ
Curran, James P. ... New York, NY
Curran, James P. ... Kent, WA
Curran, James, P.A. ... Fort Lauderdale, FL
Curran, Jeffrey A. ... Oklahoma City, OK
Curran, John A. ... Bedford, NH
Curran, John B. ... Osterville, MA
Curran, John D. ... Quincy, MA
Curran, John E. ... Fairfield, CT
Curran, John E. ... Osage Beach, MO
Curran, John F., Jr. ... New York, NY
Curran, John G. ... Rochester, NY
Curran, John J. ... Indianapolis, IN
Curran, John J. ... Syracuse, NY
Curran, John J. ... Cleveland, OH
Curran, John M. ... Boston, MA
Curran, John M. ... Buffalo, NY
Curran, John P. ... New York, NY
Curran, John P. ... New York, NY
Curran, John Paul ... Media, PA
Philadelphia, PA
Curran, John R. ... Fairfield, CT
Curran, John R. ... Providence, RI
Curran, John S. ... Framingham, MA
Curran, John T. ... New York, NY
Curran, John W. ... St. Paul, MN
Curran, John-Patrick ... New York, NY
Curran, Joseph B. ... Hartford, CT
Curran, Joseph F. ... Woodbridge, VA
Curran, Joseph P. ... Boston, MA
Providence, RI
Curran, Joseph P. ... Springfield, MA
Curran, Judy L. ... Kansas City, MO
Curran, Karen A. ... Coral Gables, FL
Curran, Karin Ranta ... Longmont, CO
Curran, Kathleen M. ... Chicago, IL
Curran, Keelin A. ... Seattle, WA
Curran, Kenneth G. ... New York, NY
Curran, Kevin C. ... St. Louis, MO
Curran, Kevin J. ... Santa Fe, NM
Curran, Kevin M. ... New York, NY
Curran, Kevin M. ... New York, NY
Curran, Kimberly A. ... Los Angeles, CA
Curran, Kris E. ... Chicago, IL
Curran Law Offices ... Pottsville, PA
Curran, Lowell F., Jr. ... Princeton, NJ
Curran, M. Glenn, III
Fort Lauderdale, FL
Curran, M. Kate ... Stamford, CT
Curran, M. Prial ... Chicago, IL
Curran, M. Scot ... Washington, PA
Curran, Margaret M. ... Orchard Park, NY
Curran, Margaret S. ... Blue Bell, PA
Curran, Margaret Sleater ... Kirkwood, MO
Curran, Mark C. ... Chicago, IL
Curran, Marshall G., Jr.
Fort Lauderdale, FL
Curran, Martha A. ... Boston, MA
Curran, Martha Hawkins ... Charlotte, NC
Curran, Mary ... San Francisco, CA
Curran, Mary Jane ... Fairmont, WV
Curran, Maureen E. ... Boston, MA
Curran, Maurice F. ... Mount Kisco, NY
Curran Mendoza, P.S. ... Kent, WA
Curran, Michael A. ... Lakewood, CO
Curran, Michael D. ... Phoenix, AZ
Curran, Michael F. ... East Islip, NY
Curran, Michael P. ... Canton, MA
Curran, Michael V. ... New York, NY
Curran, Michaela C. ... San Diego, CA
Curran, Michele W. ... Department of Labor, Office of the Solicitor, GV
Curran, Pamela A. ... Minneapolis, MN
Curran, Pamela J. ... Lawrence, KS
Curran & Parry ... Las Vegas, NV
Curran, Patricia Ann ... Southport, CT
Curran, Patrick B. ... Buffalo, NY
Curran, Patrick F. ... Ottumwa, IA
Curran, Patrick H. ... Stockton, CA
Curran, Patrick Louis ... Crestwood, KY
Curran, Patrick M. ... Mill Creek, WA
Curran, Patrick Timothy ... Bedford, TX
Curran, Paul J. ... New York, NY
Curran, Paul M. ... Treasury Department, Financial Management Service, GV
Curran, Paul S. ... Mauston, WI
Curran, Peter K. ... Lawrence, KS
Curran, Peter V. ... Houston, TX
Curran, R. Timothy ... Marietta, GA
Curran, Raymond L. ... Los Angeles, CA
Curran, Richard F. ... New York, NY
Curran, Richard J. ... Fullerton, CA
Curran, Richard J., Jr. ... Crystal Lake, IL
Curran, Richard Woodruff ... Boulder, CO
Curran, Richd. J. ... San Diego, CA
Curran, Robert B. ... Baltimore, MD
Curran, Robert D., Jr. ... Paramus, NJ
Curran, Robert D., Sr. ... Paramus, NJ
Curran, Robert E. ... Chevy Chase, MD
Curran, Robert E. J. ... Media, PA
Philadelphia, PA
Curran, Robert F. ... San Francisco, CA
Curran, Robert F. ... Plantation, FL
Curran, Robert J. ... Hillsboro, MO
Curran, Robert J. ... Bay Shore, NY
Curran, Robert J. ... Seattle, WA
Curran, Robert T. ... Yonkers, NY
Curran, Robert W. ... Newport News, VA
Curran, Roger ... Pittsburgh, PA
Curran, Roger ... Wexford, PA
Curran, Rosemary ... Hasbrouck Heights, NJ
Curran, Sean D. ... Pottsville, PA
Curran, Sheila T. ... Brockton, MA
Curran, Stephen J. ... Seal Beach, CA
Curran, Stuart R. ... San Francisco, CA
Curran, Susan O. ... Pittsburgh, PA
Curran, Thomas A. ... Phoenix, AZ
Curran, Thomas C. ... Queensbury, NY
Curran, Thomas E., III ... San Francisco, CA
Curran, Thomas H. ... Boston, MA
Curran, Thomas P. ... Waltham, MA
Curran, Thomas P. ... New York, NY
Curran, Thomas P. ... Cleveland, OH
Curran, Thomas R., Jr. ... Ada, MI
Bloomfield Hills, MI
Curran, Thos. J. ... Milwaukee, WI
Curran, Timothy J. ... Crystal Lake, IL
Curran, Timothy L. ... Overland Park, KS
Curran, Va Lena, (Mrs.) ... Spokane, WA
Curran, Virginia A.
Hilton Head Island, SC
Curran, Vivian ... Pittsburgh, PA
Curran and Watson ... Fullerton, CA
Curran & Whittington, P.C. ... Woodbridge, VA
Curran, William A. ... Providence, RI
Curran, William P. ... Las Vegas, NV
Curran, William T. ... Hackensack, NJ
Curran, William T. ... Mauston, WI
Currans, Brenda A. ... West Des Moines, IA
Currans, Michael E. ... Omaha, NE
Currault, Donna Phillips
New Orleans, LA
Currault, Douglas N., II
New Orleans, LA
Currault, Nestor L., Jr. ... Gretna, LA
Curray, Emily J. ... Denver, CO
Currea, Michael A. ... Miami, FL
Currell, Daniel G. ... Minneapolis, MN
St. Paul, MN
Curren, Conrad A. ... Greenfield, OH
Curren, Denise Anne ... Orange, CA
Curren, J. Edward ... Okeechobee, FL
Currence, Benjamin A.
Charlotte Amalie, St. Thomas, VI
Currence, Peter G. ... Columbia, SC
Sumter, SC
Currens, Timothy C. ... Mooresville, IN
Current, Dana B. ... Warrenton, VA
Current, Diane C. ... Charleston, SC
Current, H. C., and Associates, P.C.
Longmont, CO
Current, Howard C. ... Longmont, CO
Current, Richard A. ... Decatur, IL
Current, Sara M. ... Charlotte, NC
Current, T. Randy ... Clinton, IA
Current, Thomas W. ... Lynchburg, VA
Currer, Christopher J. ... Pasadena, CA
Currer, Nicole L. ... Beverly Hills, CA
Currer, Paul M. ... Alexandria, VA
Curreri, Anthony ... Ridge, NY
Curreri, Geoffrey C. ... Fort Lauderdale, FL
Curreri, Michael P. ... Richmond, VA
Curreri, Richard A. ... Albany, NY
Currey, Billie Keith ... Abilene, TX
Currey, Brian S. ... Los Angeles, CA
Currey, Charles R. ... Santa Ana, CA
Currey, Charles T. ... Ithaca, NY
Currey & Currey ... Mishawaka, IN
Currey, Jack K. ... Abilene, TX
Currey, Kathleen O. ... Atlanta, GA
Currey, R. Scott ... Flagstaff, AZ
Currey, Ralph B., III ... New York, NY
Currey, Rebecca Smith ... Flagstaff, AZ
Currey, Richard C. ... Mishawaka, IN
Currey, Richard F. ... Colorado Springs, CO
Currey, Robt. S. ... Mishawaka, IN
Currey-Wilson, Robert T. ... Portland, OR
Curriden, Dale A. ... Asheville, NC
Curriden, Daniel E. ... Las Vegas, NV
Currie, Allan B. ... Belvedere-Tiburon, CA
Currie, Allyson B. ... St. Augustine, FL
Currie, Andrew J. ... Detroit, MI
Currie, Arthur D. ... Jackson, MS
Currie, Brenda ... Jackson, MS
Currie, Brian E. ... Jacksonville, FL
Currie, Cameron McGowan ... Florence, SC
Currie, Colleen C. ... Northampton, MA
Currie, Craig A. ... Minneapolis, MN
Currie, David B. ... Needham, MA
Currie, David P. ... Chicago, IL
Currie, David S. ... Atlanta, GA
Currie, Donald E. ... Delphi, IN
Currie, Donald J. ... West Palm Beach, FL
New York, NY
Currie, Donald M. ... Seattle, WA
Currie, Douglas I. ... Somerville, MA
Currie, Duncan S. ... Rockwall, TX
Currie, Edward J., Jr. ... Jackson, MS
Currie, Francis S. ... New York, NY
Currie, Frank J. ... Venice, FL
Currie, Gaye Nell Lott ... Jackson, MS
Currie, Geo. G. ... Hattiesburg, MS
Currie, Geo. W. & Geo. G. ... Hattiesburg, MS
Currie, J. Craig ... Cherry Hill, NJ
Philadelphia, PA
Currie, Jennifer A. ... Boston, MA
Currie, John A. ... Richmond, VA
Currie, John K. ... West Hartford, CT
Currie, John P. ... Havertown, PA
Currie, John W. ... Columbia, SC
Currie Johnson Griffin Gaines & Myers, PLLC ... Jackson, MS
Currie, Julie ... Philadelphia, PA
Currie Kendall Polasky Meisel, PLC
Bay City, MI
Midland, MI
Saginaw, MI
Currie, Kenneth A. ... Stoneham, MA
Currie, L. Rodger ... Washington, DC
Currie, M. Cecelia ... Lake Forest, IL
Currie, Matthew I. ... Irvine, CA
Currie, Matthew T. ... Los Angeles, CA
Currie, Michael R. ... Portland, ME
Currie, Michael W. ... Columbus, OH
Currie, Nathaniel ... Raleigh, NC
Currie, Overton A. ... Atlanta, GA
Currie, Patrick Wade ... Albemarle, NC
Currie, Peter George ... Waltham, MA
Currie, Richard D. ... Pleasant Hill, CA
Currie, Richard M., Jr. ... Kingsport, TN
Currie, Robert A. ... Atlanta, GA
Currie, Robert B. ... Saginaw, MI
Currie, Robert E. ... Costa Mesa, CA
Currie, Robert J. ... Houston, TX
Currie, Robert M. ... Southfield, MI
Currie, Stephen L. ... Park River, ND
Currie & Strawley ... Cherry Hill, NJ
Philadelphia, PA
Currie, Susan ... Santa Ana, CA
Currie, Thomas F. ... Syracuse, NY
Currie, Thomas J. ... Cedar Rapids, IA
Currie, W. Keith ... Hayti, MO
Currie, Walter L. ... Asheville, NC
Currie, Warner S. ... Atlanta, GA
Currie, William E. ... Cleveland, OH
Currie-Johnson, Clara E. ... Sonora, TX
Currie Pittard, Kathrine E. ... Sacramento, CA
Currier, Allen A. ... Danbury, CT
Currier, Amy L. ... Philadelphia, PA
Currier, Barry A. ... Birmingham, AL
Currier, C. Wesley G. ... Glynco, GA
Currier, Charles G. ... Knoxville, TN
Currier, Charles L. ... Costa Mesa, CA
San Diego, CA
Currier, Christopher J. ... Boston, MA
Currier, David E. ... Portland, ME
Currier, Diane L., (P.C.) ... Boston, MA
Currier, Douglas P. ... Portland, ME
Currier, Everett W., Jr. ... Beattyville, KY
Currier, Gary L. ... College Station, TX
Currier, Gene M. ... Dearborn Heights, MI
Currier, Gene M., P.C., Law Office of
Dearborn Heights, MI
Currier, Gilda W. ... Noblesville, IN
Currier, Gregory O. ... Metairie, LA
Currier, Heidi Willis ... Roseland, NJ
Currier, Henrietta S. (Rhett)
San Francisco, CA
Currier, James A. ... Providence, RI
Currier, James R. ... Port Huron, MI
Currier, Jane Ellen ... Westwood, MA
Currier, John Alton ... Wayne, NJ
Currier, John M. ... New Orleans, LA
Currier, Keith J. ... Windsor Locks, CT
Currier, Lawrence E. ... Philadelphia, PA
Currier, Lori Jeanne ... Goshen, NY
Currier, Marjorie Hamano ... Los Angeles, CA
Currier, Michael F. ... Garden Grove, CA
Currier, Michelle P. ... Nashua, NH
Currier, Philip R. ... Nashua, NH
Currier, Philip R., P.C. ... Nashua, NH
Currier, Randall L. ... Trenton, NJ
Currier, Richard L. ... Presque Isle, ME
Currier, Teresa K. D. ... Wilmington, DE
Currier, Thomas E. ... Rockford, IL
Currier, Timothy J. ... Bloomfield Hills, MI
Currier & Trask, P.A. ... Presque Isle, ME
Currin, Cynthia M. ... Raleigh, NC
Currin, Deborah Hogan ... Kingwood, TX
Currin, George B. ... Raleigh, NC
Currin, Hugh M. ... Oxford, NC
Currin, Hugh M., Jr. ... Oxford, NC
Currin, Julie Amarie ... Glen Allen, VA
Currin Law Firm, PLLC ... Raleigh, NC
Wilmington, NC
Currin, Margaret E. ... Chicago, IL
Currin, Margaret Person ... Raleigh, NC
Currin, Michael D. ... Spokane, WA
Currin, Patrick William ... Pleasanton, CA
Currin, Richard A. ... Anchorage, AK
Currin, Richard N. ... Wills Point, TX
Currin, Robert G., Jr. ... Columbia, SC
Currin, Rodney A. ... New Bern, NC
Raleigh, NC
Currin, Sam B., III ... Oxford, NC
Currin, Samuel T. ... Raleigh, NC
Currin, Thomas L. ... Oxford, NC
Currin, Thomas L., P.A. ... Oxford, NC
Currivan, John D. ... Cleveland, OH
Currivan, Robt. C. ... Mansfield, MA
Curro, Kelly M. ... Troy, NY
Curry, Al ... Fort Worth, TX
Curry, Alan K. ... Houston, TX
Curry, Alicia L. ... Houston, TX
Curry, Alton F. ... Houston, TX
Curry, Antje Flegel ... Salt Lake City, UT
Curry, Arden J. ... Charleston, WV
Curry, Arden J., II ... Charleston, WV
Curry, Arlene T. ... Sioux City, IA
Curry & Associates ... Hyannis, MA
Curry & Associates, P.A., Law Offices
Brandon, FL
Plant City, FL
Sun City Center, FL
Tampa, FL
Curry & Associates, P.C.
San Antonio, TX
Curry, Barbara A. ... Los Angeles, CA
Curry, Barbara L. ... Salisbury, NC
Curry, Ben ... Merced, CA
Curry, Bernadette S. ... San Leandro, CA
Curry, Bruce A. ... Columbus, OH
Curry, Bryan E. ... Chicago, IL
Curry, B. W., III ... Hattiesburg, MS
Curry, Caran ... Little Rock, AR
Curry, Cassandra L. ... Chicago, IL
Curry, Charles B. ... Bartow, FL
Curry, Charles C. ... Grandview, MO
Curry, Charles E. ... Dillon, SC
Curry, Charles E., P.C. ... Dillon, SC
Curry, Charles E., Sr. ... Youngstown, OH
Curry, Charles N. ... Euless, TX
Fort Worth, TX
Curry, Charles W. ... Lexington, KY
Curry, Christian A.M. ... San Diego, CA
Curry, Christina E. ... Staten Island, NY
Curry, Christopher C. ... Orlando, FL
Curry, Clayton S., Jr. ... Charlotte, NC
Curry, Clifford M. ... Seattle, WA
Curry, Clifton C., Jr. ... Brandon, FL
Curry and Curry ... Merced, CA
Curry & Curry ... Phillipsburg, NJ
Curry, Curry & Counts, P.A. ... Charleston, SC
Curry, D. Scott ... Irving, TX
Curry, Daniel A. ... Los Angeles, CA
Curry, Daniel J. ... New York, NY
Curry, Daniel L. ... La Porte, IN
Curry, Daniel R. ... Thousand Oaks, CA
Curry, David A. ... Hartford, CT
Curry, David G. ... Washington, DC
Curry, David M. ... Pittsburgh, PA
Curry, David S. ... Chicago, IL
Curry, Dennis J. ... Ebensburg, PA
Curry, Diane M. ... Cleveland, OH
Curry, Donald J. ... New York, NY
Curry, Donald L. ... Lubbock, TX
Curry, Donald R. ... Fort Worth, TX
Curry, Douglas L. ... Lincoln, NE
Curry, Doyle W. ... Marshall, TX
Curry, E. Bruce ... Kerrville, TX
Curry, Earl M., Jr. ... Cleveland, OH
Curry, Eduardo K. ... Charleston, SC

Curry, Elizabeth A. .... West Hartford, CT
Curry, Ellen Jenkins .... Mount Vernon, IL
Curry, Ellen K. .... Davenport, IA
Curry, Ellen K., P.C. .... Davenport, IA
Curry, Ellis Rexwood .... Tampa, FL
Curry, Eugene R. .... Barnstable, MA
Curry, F. Thomas .... Arkadelphia, AR
Curry & Friend, A Professional Law Corporation .... New Orleans, LA
Curry, Geo. C. .... Hattiesburg, MS
Curry, George S. .... Lancaster, WI
Curry, Gerald E. .... Canoga Park, CA
Curry, Glenna Jo .... Frankfort, KY
Curry, Greg W. .... Dallas, TX
Curry, Guy Christopher
New Orleans, LA
Curry, H. Bruce .... Beaver, PA
Curry, H. Matthew .... Phillipsburg, NJ
Curry, Hannah Bishop .... Charleston, WV
Curry, Harold J. .... Phillipsburg, NJ
Curry, Henry .... Covington, KY
Curry, Holly B. .... Lexington, NC
Curry, I. Gregg, IV .... Kaukauna, WI
Curry, Irving G., III .... Kaukauna, WI
Curry, J. Stanton .... Phoenix, AZ
Curry, James .... Atlanta, GA
Curry, James E. .... Los Angeles, CA
Curry, James E. .... Woodland Hills, CA
Curry, James E. .... Ava, MO
Curry, James J. .... Cranbury, NJ
Curry, James J., Jr. .... Toms River, NJ
Curry, James L. .... Marysville, CA
Curry, James T. .... Lake Pleasant, NY
Curry, James W. .... Richmond, VA
Curry, James W., Jr. .... Memphis, TN
Curry, Jeffery V. .... Chattanooga, TN
Curry, J. L. (Buddy), Jr. .... Lubbock, TX
Curry, John B., II .... Waynesboro, VA
Curry, John C. .... Seattle, WA
Curry, John E. .... East Meadow, NY
Curry, John J., Jr. .... Chicago, IL
Curry, John Paul .... Cincinnati, OH
Curry, John S. .... Edina, MN
Curry, John Shaw .... Quincy, FL
Curry, John T., III .... New York, NY
Curry, Jon D. .... Tyler, TX
Curry, Judi Abbott .... New York, NY
Curry, K. Todd .... San Diego, CA
Curry, Kathleen .... Washington, DC
Curry, Kathleen .... San Antonio, TX
Curry, Kathleen M. .... Boston, MA
Curry, Kathryn C. .... Redwood City, CA
Curry, Kay O. .... Strafford, NH
Curry, Kenneth C. .... Fort Worth, TX
Curry, Kevin C. .... Baton Rouge, LA
Curry, Kevin P. .... Boston, MA
Curry, Kristen Mckenzie .... Mesa, AZ
Curry, Landis V., Jr. .... Ocala, FL
Curry, Lauren P. .... Cambridge, MA
Curry, Leonard C. .... Santa Rosa, CA
Curry, Leslie Cameron .... Grand Rapids, MI
Curry, Linda Bryant .... Atlanta, GA
Curry, Margaret A. .... Detroit, MI
Curry, Marilyn A. .... Portland, OR
Curry, Marilyn P. .... Alturas, CA
Curry, Mark S. .... Sacramento, CA
Curry, Mark T. .... Houston, TX
Curry, Marlo L. .... Houston, TX
Curry, Mary G. .... Stamford, CT
Curry, Mary Judith .... Los Angeles, CA
Curry, Mary K. .... Tallahassee, FL
Curry, Maynard T.
Department of Housing and Urban Development, GV
Curry, Michael .... Austin, TX
Curry, Michael J. .... Indianapolis, IN
Curry, Michael J.
West Conshohocken, PA
Curry, Michael L. .... Omaha, NE
Curry, Michael, P.C. .... Austin, TX
Curry, Michel E. .... Midland, TX
Curry, Monte D. .... Nashville, TN
Curry, Morin and Goudarzi, P.C.
Marshall, TX
Curry, Nancy L. .... Baton Rouge, LA
Curry, Niamh A. .... New York, NY
Curry, Norman D. .... Columbus, IN
Curry, Othello Herbert, III .... Sacramento, CA
Curry & Pasqualone .... Geneva, OH
Curry, Patrick .... Stockton, CA
Curry, Patrick W. .... East Meadow, NY
Curry, Paul F. .... Westfield, NY
Curry, Paula G. .... Waltham, MA
Curry, Peter H. .... Nashville, TN
Curry, Peter J. .... Bethlehem, PA
Harrisburg, PA
Curry, Peter L. .... Boston, MA
Curry, Peter L. .... Uniondale, NY
Curry, Peter Michael .... San Antonio, TX
Curry, Philip W. .... Azle, TX
Curry, R. Raye .... Jacksonville, FL
Curry, Ralph F. .... St. Louis, MO
Curry, Randy K. .... Hyannis, MA
Curry, René A., Jr. .... New Orleans, LA
Curry, Richard A. .... Baton Rouge, LA
Curry, Richard C. .... Palmyra, PA
Curry, Richard L. .... Chicago, IL
Curry, Richard R. .... Sacramento, CA
Curry, Robert A. .... Tulsa, OK
Curry, Robert E., III .... Palo Alto, CA
Curry, Robert E., Jr. .... New York, NY
Curry, Robert F. .... Geneva, OH
Curry, Robert L. .... Westlake, OH
Curry, Robert L. .... Madison, WI
Curry, Robert Lee, III .... Monroe, LA
Curry, Robert M. .... Dayton, OH
Curry, Robert W. .... Boston, MA
Curry, Roger D. .... Fairmont, WV

Curry, Ronald E. .... Austin, TX
Curry, Sarah .... Las Cruces, NM
Curry, Scott .... Wichita, KS
Curry, Sean Patrick .... Knoxville, TN
Curry & Shamas .... Coral Gables, FL
Curry, Stanley W., Jr. .... San Antonio, TX
Curry, Stephen E. .... Augusta, GA
Curry, Stephen L. .... Little Rock, AR
Curry, Steven M. .... Central City, NE
Curry, Susan J. .... St. Paul, MN
Curry, Suzanne L. .... Marquette, MI
Curry, Tamara C. .... Charleston, SC
Curry, Terry R. .... Indianapolis, IN
Curry, Thomas J. .... Castle Rock, CO
Curry, Thomas J. .... Boston, MA
Curry, Thomas M. .... Merced, CA
Curry, Thomas M. .... West Trenton, NJ
Curry, Thomas R. .... Livermore, CA
Curry, Tim .... Fort Worth, TX
Curry, Timothy J. .... Simsbury, CT
Curry, Timothy R. .... Palo Alto, CA
Curry, Tonda L. .... Tyler, TX
Curry, Tyronda Michelle .... Southfield, MI
Curry, Vincent A. .... Seattle, WA
Curry, Vincent E. .... Mineola, NY
Curry & Westgate .... Stockton, CA
Curry, William E. .... Washington, DC
Curry, William J. .... Boston, MA
Curry, William J., Jr. .... Metairie, LA
Curry, William P., Jr. .... New Orleans, LA
Curry, William T. .... Seminole, TX
Curry-Johnson, Leslie .... Pulaski, TN
Curseaden, Kevin J. .... Bridgeport, CT
Cursinella, Joanne M. .... New York, NY
Cursio, Ralph M. .... Mineola, NY
Cursio, Valerie F. .... New York, NY
Curson, C. Randolph .... Houston, TX
Curt, Suzanne G.
Department of Justice, GV
Curtas, John A. .... Las Vegas, NV
Curtas, Mary Ellen .... Kirkland, WA
Curtes, Cynthia A. .... Mount Horeb, WI
Curth, Daniel C. .... Chicago, IL
Curthoys, Brian A. .... Tulsa, OK
Curthoys, Karen McGivern .... Tulsa, OK
Curti, Thomas A. .... Tucson, AZ
Curtice, Lawrence L. .... San Francisco, CA
Curtice, Wm. L., Jr. .... Seminole, FL
Curtin, Anne F. .... Albany, NY
Curtin, Christopher J. .... Wilmington, DE
Curtin, Colleen Erin .... Irvine, CA
Curtin, Cynthia K. .... Hudson, OH
Curtin, Daniel D. .... New Haven, CT
Curtin, Daniel F. .... Poughkeepsie, NY
Curtin, Daniel J., Jr. .... Walnut Creek, CA
Curtin, Daniel M. .... Pittsburgh, PA
Curtin, David J. .... Washington, DC
Curtin, David M. .... Vienna, VA
Curtin, Dennis D. .... Plattsburgh, NY
Curtin, Edward R. .... New York, NY
Curtin, Edward R., P.C. .... New York, NY
Curtin, G. Michael .... Cleveland, OH
Curtin, Geo. M. .... Wilmington, DE
Curtin, Gerard V., Jr. .... Cambridge, MA
Curtin & Heefner, LLP .... Trenton, NJ
Doylestown, PA
Morrisville, PA
Curtin, J. Barry .... West Palm Beach, FL
Curtin, Jack L. .... Juliaetta, ID
Curtin, James B. .... New Haven, CT
Curtin, James B. .... Columbus, OH
Curtin, James H. .... Phoenix, AZ
Curtin, James H.
Environmental Protection Agency, Office of the General Counsel, GV
Curtin, James K. .... Chicago, IL
Curtin, James S. .... Chicago, IL
Curtin, John E. .... McLean, VA
Curtin, John I. .... Adams, MA
Curtin, John J., Jr. .... Boston, MA
Curtin, John M. .... Scottsdale, AZ
Curtin, John M., P.C., Law Offices of
Scottsdale, AZ
Curtin, John T. .... Buffalo, NY
Curtin, John T. .... Philadelphia, PA
Curtin, John V. .... Boston, MA
Curtin, Joseph P. .... Washington, DC
Curtin, Joseph P. .... Boston, MA
Curtin, Judi A. .... Costa Mesa, CA
Curtin, Judi A., A P.C .... Costa Mesa, CA
Curtin, Katherine G. .... New York, NY
Curtin, Kathleen K. .... Prospect Heights, IL
Curtin, Kenneth C. .... Columbus, OH
Curtin, Kenneth M.
West Palm Beach, FL
Curtin, Kevin G. .... Washington, DC
Curtin, Kevin J. .... Cambridge, MA
Curtin, Lawrence N. .... Tallahassee, FL
Curtin, Mary Anne .... Treasury Department, Internal Revenue Service, GV
Curtin, Mary E. .... Hopkins, MN
Curtin, Michael F. .... Washington, DC
Curtin, Murphy & O'Reilly, P.C.
Boston, MA
Curtin, Nancy Clark .... Boston, MA
Curtin, Neal J. .... Boston, MA
Curtin, Nolan, Gallagher & Mroz, Ltd.
Vienna, VA
Curtin, Patricia E. .... Danville, CA
Curtin, Patricia M. .... Binghamton, NY
Curtin, Patrick E., Jr. .... New York, NY
Curtin, Paul J., Jr. .... Syracuse, NY
Curtin, Paul Sean .... Stamford, CT
New York, NY
Curtin, Peter J. .... Washington, DC
Baltimore, MD
Curtin, Philip F. .... Manchester, NH

Curtin, Philip G. .... Cherry Hill, NJ
Philadelphia, PA
Curtin, Philip J. .... New York, NY
Curtin, Richard A. .... Anchorage, AK
Curtin, Richard N. .... Boston, MA
Curtin, Richard P. .... Lancaster, CA
Curtin, Richard T. .... Minneapolis, MN
Curtin, Robert F. .... Sauk City, WI
Curtin, Sandra K. .... Malvern, PA
Curtin, Sean H. .... McLean, VA
Curtin, Shawn J. .... San Rafael, CA
Curtin & Steingart, P.A.
Minneapolis, MN
Curtin, T. Shane .... Oklahoma City, OK
Curtin, Theodore Charles .... Washington, DC
Fairfax, VA
Curtin, Thomas F. .... Walnut Creek, CA
Curtin, Thomas H. .... New York, NY
Curtin, Thomas M. .... White Plains, NY
Curtin, Thomas R. .... Morristown, NJ
Curtin, Timothy F. .... Chicago, IL
Curtin, Timothy J. .... Grand Rapids, MI
Curtin, Timothy Murray .... Atlanta, GA
Curtin, Timothy R. .... Rochester, NY
Curtin, William A., Jr. .... Boston, MA
Curtin, William J. .... Washington, DC
Curtin, William J., III .... Washington, DC
Curtis, Adam B. .... New York, NY
Curtis, Alexander, McCampbell & Morris
Greenville, TX
Curtis, Amber Dahlgreen
Westminster, MD
Curtis, Amy M. .... Richmond, VA
Curtis, Amy Ray .... Dallas, TX
Curtis, Andrew, Jr. .... Seattle, WA
Curtis & Arata, A Professional Corporation
Modesto, CA
Curtis, Arthur D. .... Vancouver, WA
Curtis, Arthur E. .... Springfield, MO
Curtis, Arthur R. .... Traverse City, MI
Curtis, Augustus T. .... Athens, GA
Curtis, Barbara A. .... Fort Lauderdale, FL
Curtis, Benjamin J. .... Poteau, OK
Curtis, Brian W., II .... Sugar Land, TX
Curtis, Brinckerhoff & Barrett, P.C.
Darien, CT
Greenwich, CT
New Canaan, CT
Stamford, CT
Curtis, C. Kerry .... Phenix City, AL
Curtis, C. William, III .... Jacksonville, FL
Curtis, Calvin C. .... Salt Lake City, UT
Curtis, Cari L. .... Houston, TX
Curtis, Carol L. .... Vail, CO
Curtis, Carolyn .... Rye, NY
Curtis, Cecil M. .... Charlotte, NC
Curtis, Cecil M., P.A. .... Charlotte, NC
Curtis, Charles B. .... Washington, DC
Curtis, Charles Emeride .... Los Angeles, CA
Curtis, Charles G., Jr. .... Madison, WI
Curtis, Charles L. (Jack) .... Hays, KS
Curtis, Charles L., (P.C.)
Fort Lauderdale, FL
Curtis, Charles R. .... Chicago, IL
Curtis, Charles T., Jr. .... New Orleans, LA
Curtis, Chester H. .... Clarksdale, MS
Oxford, MS
Southaven, MS
Curtis, Christian A. .... McLean, VA
Curtis, Christopher C. .... Boston, MA
Curtis, Christopher J. .... Las Vegas, NV
Curtis, Christopher J. .... Dallas, TX
Curtis, Christopher T. .... Falls Church, VA
Curtis, Clifford F. .... Bellevue, WA
Curtis, Clinton A. .... Lakeland, FL
Lake Wales, FL
Winter Haven, FL
Curtis, Clinton J. .... Morristown, NJ
Curtis & Cunningham .... Tucson, AZ
Curtis & Curtis .... Plymouth, MA
Curtis & Curtis .... Imperial, NE
Curtis & Curtis, P.A.
Fort Lauderdale, FL
Curtis, Curtis & Thomson, P.C.
Jackson, MI
Curtis, Cynthia Ley .... Clark, NJ
Curtis, D. Jay .... Salt Lake City, UT
Curtis, Dan G. .... Scottsdale, AZ
Curtis, Dana .... Sausalito, CA
Curtis, Dana, Mediation
San Francisco, CA
Sausalito, CA
Curtis, Danny L. .... Kansas City, MO
Curtis, David M. .... Dallas, TX
Curtis, David S. .... Dallas, TX
Curtis & Dean .... Farmington, NM
Curtis, Debra Moss .... Brandon, FL
Curtis, Deirdre F. .... New York, NY
Curtis, Diane B. .... Waukegan, IL
Curtis, Diane M. .... Chicago, IL
Curtis, Donna M. .... Los Angeles, CA
Curtis, Dorene M. .... San Francisco, CA
Curtis, Douglas E. .... Columbus, OH
Curtis, Douglas E., & Co., L.P.A.
Columbus, OH
Curtis, Douglas F. .... Washington, DC
New York, NY
Curtis, E. Alton, Jr. .... Smyrna, GA
Curtis, E. Glion .... Overland Park, KS
Curtis, Edward R. .... Fort Lauderdale, FL
Curtis, Edwin C. .... Seattle, WA
Curtis, Eric J. .... Milwaukee, WI
Curtis, Francine S. .... Novato, CA
Curtis, Frank Bradford .... St. Louis, MO
Curtis, Frank J. .... Wayne, NJ
Curtis, Frank R. .... New York, NY
Curtis, Gaylen .... Birmingham, MI
Curtis, Gaylen, P.C. .... Birmingham, MI

Curtis, Geoffrey A. .... Woburn, MA
Curtis, George B. .... Denver, CO
Curtis, George E. .... Quincy, MA
Curtis, George E. .... Utica, NY
Curtis, George G. .... Portland, OR
Curtis, George H. .... Tucson, AZ
Curtis, George N. .... Albany, NY
Curtis, George W. .... Oshkosh, WI
Curtis, Gerald .... Bingham Farms, MI
Curtis, Greg P. .... Appleton, WI
Curtis, Gregory T. .... Lowell, MA
Curtis, Greth S. .... Los Angeles, CA
Curtis & Griffin .... Orono, ME
Curtis, Guy G. .... Imperial, NE
Curtis, Harold F. .... Greenville, TX
Curtis, Harry A. .... Reynoldsburg, OH
Curtis, Harvey W. .... Denver, CO
Curtis, Henry J., Jr. .... Woburn, MA
Curtis, Herbert, III .... Ventura, CA
Curtis, Hope .... Montgomery, AL
Curtis, Howard G., II .... Oakland, CA
Curtis, J. Vaughan .... Atlanta, GA
Curtis, Jack .... Cleveland, OH
Curtis, Jack S. .... Springfield, MO
Curtis, James A. .... Grass Valley, CA
Curtis, James B. .... Los Angeles, CA
Curtis, James G., Jr. .... La Crosse, WI
Curtis, James H. .... Portland, OR
Curtis, James L. .... Chicago, IL
Curtis, James M.
Securities and Exchange Commission, Division of Investment Management, GV
Curtis, James P. .... Minneapolis, MN
Curtis, James T. .... Lowell, MA
Curtis, James T. .... Fort Worth, TX
Curtis, James T., Jr. .... Lowell, MA
Curtis, James W. .... Athens, GA
Curtis, James W., Jr. .... Indianapolis, IN
Curtis, Jared C. .... Bellevue, WA
Curtis, Jean M. .... Walnut Creek, CA
Curtis, Jeanette A. .... Plymouth, MA
Curtis, Jeanne C. .... New York, NY
Curtis, Jeffrey L. .... Dallas, TX
Curtis, Jennifer Tolson .... Richland, WA
Curtis, Jim .... El Paso, TX
Curtis, Jodi A. .... Salem, MA
Curtis, Joel R. .... Washington, DC
Curtis, John A. .... Dallas, TX
Curtis, John B., Jr. .... Chattanooga, TN
Curtis, John C. .... Chattanooga, TN
Curtis, John D. .... Dallas, TX
Curtis, John J. .... San Antonio, TX
Curtis, John Jay
Rancho Santa Margarita, CA
Curtis, John S. .... Los Angeles, CA
Curtis, Jonathan C. .... Los Angeles, CA
Curtis, Joseph K. .... Mineola, NY
Curtis, Jude A. .... Boston, MA
Curtis, Judith A. .... Detroit, MI
Curtis, Judith A. .... Grosse Pointe Park, MI
Curtis, Justin B. .... Glendale, CA
Curtis, K. William .... Sacramento, CA
Curtis, Karen Haynes .... Miami, FL
Curtis, Katherine R. .... Kalispell, MT
Curtis, Kenneth M. .... Portland, ME
Curtis, Kenneth W. .... Costa Mesa, CA
Curtis, Kenneth W. .... Fairfax, VA
Curtis, Keri R. .... Los Angeles, CA
Curtis, Kevin J. .... Spokane, WA
Curtis, Kevin M. .... Houston, TX
Curtis, Kristi F. .... Sumter, SC
Curtis, Kristi L. .... Redwood City, CA
Curtis & Lambert .... New Iberia, LA
Lafayette, LA
Curtis, Lance J .... Sacramento, CA
Curtis, Larry Mauthner .... New York, NY
Curtis, Larry R. .... Ames, IA
Curtis, Lauren S. .... Tampa, FL
Curtis Law Firm, The, P.C.
Kansas City, MO
Curtis Law Office .... Woburn, MA
Curtis Law Office .... Milwaukee, WI
Curtis Law Office .... Oshkosh, WI
Curtis, Lawrence H. .... Rockville, MD
Curtis, Lawrence N. .... Lafayette, LA
Curtis, Lawrence T. .... Toledo, OH
Curtis, Lee P. .... Washington, DC
Curtis, LeGrand R., Jr.
Salt Lake City, UT
Curtis, Leland B. .... St. Louis, MO
Curtis, Lesley Beth .... Sacramento, CA
Curtis, Linda Duggan .... Hampton, VA
Curtis, Linda L. .... Los Angeles, CA
Curtis, Luther C. .... Atlanta, GA
Curtis, Lynn M. .... Kansas City, MO
Curtis, Mallet-Prevost, Colt & Mosle LLP
Stamford, CT
Washington, DC
Newark, NJ
New York, NY
Houston, TX
Curtis, Mark .... Long Beach, CA
Curtis, Mark C. .... Chatham, NJ
Curtis, Marshall M. .... Reston, VA
Curtis, Martha A. .... Tampa, FL
Curtis, Martha Y. .... New Orleans, LA
Curtis, Mary R. .... Oshkosh, WI
Curtis, Matthew G. .... Southfield, MI
Curtis, Michael .... Palo Alto, CA
Curtis, Michael A. .... Phoenix, AZ
Curtis, Michael A. .... Houston, TX
Curtis, Michael G. .... Plymouth, MA
Curtis, Michael J. .... Ashland, KY
Curtis, Michael J. .... Buffalo, NY
Curtis, Michael K. .... Winston-Salem, NC
Curtis, Michael S. .... Seattle, WA
Curtis, Michelle R. .... Rockville, MD
Curtis, Mildred Adams .... Cincinnati, OH

Curtis, Myron K. ....Overland Park, KS
Curtis, Nancy M. ....Lexington, KY
Curtis, Nancy Vaughan ....Summit, NJ
Curtis, Oetting, Heinz, Garrett & Soule, P.C.
St. Louis, MO
Curtis, Orlie L. ....Stockton, CA
Curtis, Pamela L. ....Big Rapids, MI
Curtis, Patricia J. ....Las Vegas, NV
Curtis, Paul C. ....Duluth, GA
Curtis, Paul D. ....Madison, WI
Curtis, Paul T. ....Sacramento, CA
Curtis, Penny J. ....Lee's Summit, MO
Curtis, Peter L. ....Williamsville, NY
Curtis, Philip H. ....New York, NY
Curtis, Philip J. ....Park Ridge, IL
Curtis, Philip J. ....Jackson, MI
Curtis, R. Wade ....Boise, ID
Curtis, Ralph S. ....Modesto, CA
Curtis, Ralph W. ....Salt Lake City, UT
Curtis, Richard A. ....Pomona, CA
Curtis, Richard A. ....Philadelphia, PA
Curtis, Richard B. ....San Francisco, CA
Curtis, Richard D. ....Eugene, OR
Curtis, Richard G. ....Rochester, NY
Curtis, Richard M. ....Salinas, CA
Curtis & Riess-Curtis, P.C.
New York, NY
Curtis, Robert A. ....San Juan Capistrano, CA
Curtis, Robert Elliot, Jr. ....Andover, MA
Curtis, Robert J. ....Irvine, CA
Curtis, Robert J. ....Albuquerque, NM
Curtis, Robert Kern ....Hackensack, NJ
Curtis, Robert M. ....Fort Lauderdale, FL
Curtis, Robert M. ....Novelty, OH
Curtis, Robert N. ....Jackson, MI
Curtis, Robert R. ....Mill Valley, CA
Curtis, Robin Elizabeth ....Houston, TX
Curtis, Robt. E., Jr. ....Boston, MA
Curtis, Ronald C. ....Milwaukee, WI
Curtis, Ronald E. ....Bridgeport, CT
Curtis, Russell E. ....Cedar Falls, IA
Curtis, Ryan C. ....Jacksonville, FL
Curtis, Santhia L. ....Atlanta, GA
Curtis, Sarah ....Boston, MA
Curtis, Scott M. ....Farmington, NM
Curtis, Scott P. ....Brookline, MA
Curtis, Shelley S. ....Redwood City, CA
Curtis & Sides ....Poteau, OK
Curtis & Sindeband, LLP ....Andover, MA
Curtis, Stephanie D. ....Dallas, TX
Curtis, Stephen P. ....Albuquerque, NM
Curtis, Stephen P., Attorney At Law, P.C.
Albuquerque, NM
Curtis, Steve ....Chicago, IL
Curtis & Strickland ....Eugene, OR
Curtis, Stuart A. ....Ahoskie, NC
Curtis, Susan G. ....New York, NY
Curtis, Susan M. ....New York, NY
Curtis, T. Lon ....Belton, TX
Curtis, Tanya L. ....Chicago, IL
Curtis, Ted C. ....Gainesville, FL
Curtis Thaxter Stevens Broder & Micoleau LLC ....Augusta, ME
Portland, ME
Curtis, Theodore S., Jr. ....Orono, ME
Curtis, Thomas A. ....New York, NY
Curtis, Thomas D. ....Lafayette, LA
Curtis, Thomas Michael ....Alexandria, VA
Curtis, Thomas Percy ....Harlingen, TX
Curtis, Tom ....Austin, TX
Curtis, Tom ....Austin, TX
Curtis, Tracy P. ....Lafayette, LA
Curtis, V. Cecil ....Phenix City, AL
Curtis, V. Kay ....Overland Park, KS
Curtis, Vance W. ....Tipton, IN
Curtis, Vincent J., Jr. ....Washington, DC
Arlington, VA
Curtis, Vorbeck and Associates, LLC
Lee's Summit, MO
Curtis, W. Robert ....New York, NY
Curtis, Warren & Fori ....Coxsackie, NY
Curtis, Warren S. ....Sumter, SC
Curtis, Wendy Butler ....Austin, TX
Curtis, Wesley W. ....Champaign, IL
Curtis, William B. ....Dallas, TX
Curtis, William D. ....Monterey, CA
Curtis, William H. ....Lafayette, CA
Curtis, William H. ....Smyrna, GA
Curtis, William M. ....Laguna Hills, CA
Curtis, William Patrick, Jr. ....Media, PA
Curtis, William R. ....Wilton, CT
Curtis, William T. ....Springfield, IL
Curtis, Yvonne ....Seattle, WA
Curtis, Zaklukiewicz, Vasile, Devine & McElhenny ....Merrick, NY
Riverhead, NY
Curtis Morris, Leah ....Greenville, TX
Curtiss, Alan ....Alliance, NE
Curtiss, Alan H. ....Emerson, NE
Curtiss, Alice A. ....Buffalo, NY
Curtiss, Ann Eleanor ....Chicago, IL
Curtiss, Bruce D. ....Plainview, NE
Curtiss, Catherine ....Washington, DC
Curtiss, Catherine L. ....Palo Alto, CA
Curtiss, Christine L. ....Derby, CT
Curtiss, David W. ....Laurel, NE
Curtiss, Davin C. ....Dubuque, IA
Curtiss, Gary L. ....Canandaigua, NY
Curtiss, Gayle Libby ....Rockville, MD
Curtiss, Gregory ....Littleton, CO
Curtiss, Harold T. ....Emerson, NE
Curtiss, J. Arthur ....Lincoln, NE
Curtiss, Jack D. ....Greenfield, MA
Curtiss, James C. ....Livonia, MI
Curtiss, James R. ....Washington, DC
Curtiss, Jeffrey E. ....Skokie, IL
Curtiss, John A. ....Tampa, FL
Curtiss, Kenneth E. ....Dallas, TX
Curtiss Law Office ....Emerson, NE
Curtiss, Leibell & Shilling, P.C. ....Carmel, NY
Curtiss, Moravek, Curtiss & Margheim
Alliance, NE
Curtiss, Nicholas E. ....Fairfield, NJ
Curtiss, Robin C. ....Orford, NH
Curtiss, Terry J. ....Alliance, NE
Curtiss, Thomas, Jr. ....Los Angeles, CA
Curtiss, Timothy J. ....Carmel, NY
Curtiss, Timothy L ....Mount Pleasant, MI
Saginaw, MI
Curtiss, W. David ....Ithaca, NY
Curtiss, William H., Law Offices of
Ross, CA
Curtiss, William H., Law Offices of
San Francisco, CA
Curtiss, William S. ....Menlo Park, CA
Curtiss, Wynn ....Hopkins, MN
Curtiss, Zelda G. ....Pittsburgh, PA
Curtiss-Lusher, Barry ....Denver, CO
Curtner, Gregory L. ....Ann Arbor, MI
New York, NY
Curtner, Patricia M. ....Chicago, IL
Curtner, Tracy Chappell ....Raleigh, NC
Curto, Alan P. ....Hartford, CT
Curto, Andrew E. ....Melville, NY
Mineola, NY
Curto, Anthony V., Jr. ....Melville, NY
Mineola, NY
Curto, Daniel A. ....Boston, MA
Curto, Joseph R. ....Yonkers, NY
Curto, Michael A. ....Washington, DC
Curto, Michael J. ....Yonkers, NY
Curto, Michael W. ....Maitland, FL
Curtright, Norman G. ....Denver, CO
Curts, T. Jay ....Carmel, IN
Curtz, Chauncey S.R. ....Lexington, KY
Curuby, Nicholas G. ....Lynn, MA
Curvin, Steven P. ....Buffalo, NY
Curvin, Thomas W. ....Atlanta, GA
Curving, Glenn D. ....Morristown, NJ
Curwen, Gregory B. ....Seattle, WA
Tacoma, WA
Curwen, Mary Jo
Palos Verdes Peninsula, CA
Curwin, Gary P. ....New York, NY
Curwin, Michael S. ....Woodbury, NJ
Curwin, S Mark ....Minneapolis, MN
Curwin, Steven M. ....Rockville, MD
Curwood, James M. ....New York, NY
Cury, Alexandra ....Hot Springs, NC
Cury, Bruce P. ....Bartow, FL
Curylo, Christopher J. ....New York, NY
Curylo, Patricia A. ....Flint, MI
Curzan, Myron P. ....Washington, DC
Curzan, Robert L. ....Middletown, CT
Curzi and Artigliere ....Phillipsburg, NJ
Curzi, D. Scott, P.A. ....Phillipsburg, NJ
Curzi, Jeffrey D. ....Clinton, NJ
Curzio, Daniel M. ....Chicago, IL
Curzon, Christopher D. ....Omaha, NE
Curzon, Elliott R. ....Washington, DC
Curzon, Thomas H. ....Phoenix, AZ
Cusa, Thomas C. ....Westport, CT
New York, NY
Cusack, Beth Anne ....Philadelphia, PA
Cusack, Charles R., Jr. ....Vancouver, WA
Cusack, Daniel P., (P.C.) ....Peoria, IL
Cusack, David J. ....Dayton, OH
Cusack, Dennis C. ....Chicago, IL
Cusack, Dennis M. ....San Francisco, CA
Cusack, Fleming, Gilfillan & O'Day
Peoria, IL
Cusack, Francis William ....Nahant, MA
Cusack, James J. ....Tampa, FL
Cusack, Jaramillo, Romero & Associates, P.C. ....Roswell, NM
Cusack, Jennifer A. ....Troy, NY
Cusack, John F., Jr. ....Tucson, AZ
Cusack, John T. ....Chicago, IL
Cusack, John T. J. ....Chicago, IL
Cusack, Kenneth J. ....Seattle, WA
Cusack & Knowles ....Washington, DC
Seattle, WA
Cusack, Laurence R. ....Philadelphia, PA
Cusack, Lauric J. ....Houston, TX
Cusack, Mark E. ....San Marcos, TX
Cusack, Mary Jo ....Columbus, OH
Cusack, Michael E. ....Albany, NY
Cusack, Nancy S. ....Roswell, NM
Cusack, Patrick M. ....Hialeah, FL
Cusack, Raymond R. ....Tucson, AZ
Cusack, Richard W. ....Hinsdale, IL
Cusack, Robert E. ....Chicago, IL
Cusack & Stiles LLP ....New York, NY
Cusack, Thomas F. ....New York, NY
Cusack, Thomas M., III ....Philadelphia, PA
Cusack, Timothy J. ....Peoria, IL
Cusack, Timothy J. ....Roswell, NM
Cusack, William W. ....Columbus, OH
Cusack-Lehmann, Lynmarie
Manchester, NH
Cusanelli, Gabriel H. ....New Haven, CT
Cusano, John N. ....Lebanon, CT
Cusano, Louis J. C. ....New York, NY
Cusano, Ronald S. ....Pittsburgh, PA
Cusato, Elisa Ann ....San Diego, CA
Cusato, Patrick L. ....Rochester, NY
Cuscaden, Douglas R. ....St. Charles, IL
Cusce, Brian J. ....Chesterfield, VA
Cusenbary, C. Lee, Jr. ....San Antonio, TX
Cushing, Ann Bryce ....Canyon Country, CA
Cushing, Ann M. ....Boston, MA
Cushing, Charles M., Jr. ....Atlanta, GA
Cushing, Christine M. ....Dover, NH
Cushing, Daniel S. ....Mobile, AL
Cushing, David J. ....Washington, DC
Cushing & Dolan, P.C. ....Boston, MA
Norwood, MA
Westborough, MA
Wilmington, MA
Woburn, MA
Cushing, Donald W. ....Scarborough, ME
Cushing, Douglas P. ....Portland, OR
Cushing, George A. ....Albany, NY
Cushing, George L. ....Boston, MA
Cushing, Gerard J. ....Riverhead, NY
Cushing, Glenn L. ....Madison, WI
Cushing, James E., Jr. ....Bothell, WA
Cushing, James R. ....Tacoma, WA
Cushing, Keric J. ....Santa Maria, CA
Cushing, Kevin M. ....St. Louis, MO
Cushing, Kym S. ....Las Vegas, NV
Cushing, Laur. A. ....Grants Pass, OR
Cushing, Leo J. ....Boston, MA
Norwood, MA
Westborough, MA
Wilmington, MA
Woburn, MA
Cushing, Mary T. ....Cleveland, OH
Cushing, Matthew J. ....Boston, MA
Cushing, Michael
Office of Personnel Management, GV
Cushing, Morris, Armbruster & Jones, LLP
Atlanta, GA
Cushing, Paul G. ....Boston, MA
Cushing, Paul M. ....Atlanta, GA
Cushing, Peter ....Orlando, FL
Cushing, Richard G. ....New York, NY
Cushing, Richard P. ....Clinton, NJ
Cushing, Robert W. ....Chicago, IL
Cushing, Terry M. ....Louisville, KY
Cushing, Thomas F. ....San Francisco, CA
Cushing, Willard L. ....McMinnville, OR
Cushingberry, Sharon K. ....Houston, TX
Cushion, R. Paul, II ....Cleveland, OH
Cushman, Anne F. ....Columbia, SC
Cushman, Benjamin D. ....Olympia, WA
Cushman, Bernard ....Silver Spring, MD
Cushman, Charles A. ....Alexandria, VA
Cushman, Charles V. B., III ....Camden, SC
Cushman, Christopher A. ....Kansas City, MO
Cushman, Constance ....New York, NY
Cushman, Daniel C. ....San Diego, CA
Cushman, Dawn ....Sherman Oaks, CA
Cushman, Edward C., Jr. ....Aiken, SC
Cushman, Eugene C. ....New London, CT
Cushman, Francis N. ....Issaquah, WA
Cushman, James G. ....Norwich, NY
Cushman, John P. ....Grosse Pointe Farms, MI
Cushman, Jon E. ....Olympia, WA
Cushman, Kenneth C. ....Santa Ana, CA
Cushman, Kenneth M. ....Philadelphia, PA
Cushman Law Offices, P.S. ....Olympia, WA
Cushman, Linda Joanne ....Springfield, OH
Cushman, Patrice Marie ....Ivy, VA
Cushman, Paul A. ....Richmond, VA
Cushman, Paull M. ....Raynham, MA
Cushman, Ralph B. ....Anchorage, AK
Cushman, Ralph B., P.C., Law Offices of
Anchorage, AK
Cushman, Robert F. ....Philadelphia, PA
Cushman, Robert S. ....Chicago, IL
Cushman, Stan ....Gainesville, FL
Cushman, Susan ....Vail, CO
Cushman, Thomas E. ....St. Augustine, FL
Cushman, Thomas R. ....St. Petersburg, FL
Cushman, Thomas R. ....Gooding, ID
Cushmore, Stephen M. ....Philadelphia, PA
Cushner, Alan J. ....Boston, MA
Cushner & Bloom, P.C. ....Boston, MA
Cushner, Lawrence S. ....Brooklyn, NY
Cushner, Stacey L. ....Boston, MA
Cushner, Stephen S. ....West Hartford, CT
Cushnie, Colin Christopher ....Stuart, FL
Cushnie, Douglas F. ....Saipan, TT
Cushnir, Andrew ....Los Angeles, CA
Cushwa, David J. ....Barrington, IL
Cushwa, Mara E. ....Cleveland, OH
Cusic, Daniel W. ....Pensacola, FL
Cusic, Jeffery ....Chicago, IL
Cusic, Sharon L. ....Newport Beach, CA
Cusick, Alan P., Jr. ....Denver, CO
Cusick, Charles S., Jr. ....New Castle, PA
Cusick, Colleen Healy ....Oak Brook, IL
Cusick, Daniel F. ....Pittsburgh, PA
Cusick, David M. ....Winsted, CT
Cusick, David P. ....Spooner, WI
Cusick, Derek R. ....Gulfport, MS
Cusick, Ernest G. ....Schenectady, NY
Cusick, Hacker & Murphy, LLP
Albany, NY
Latham, NY
Schenectady, NY
Troy, NY
Cusick, James P. ....Chicago, IL
Cusick, Kenneth Albert ....Corpus Christi, TX
Cusick, Mark A. ....Cleveland, OH
Cusick, Maurice J.
Christiansted, St. Croix, VI
Cusick, Michael F. ....New York, NY
Cusick, Michael J. L. ....Bozeman, MT
Cusick, Michael P. ....Fort Lauderdale, FL
Cusick, Patrick T. ....Lancaster, PA
Reading, PA
Cusick, Paul L., Jr. ....Rockland, MA
Cusick, Paulette J. ....Chicago, IL
Cusick, Peter ....Staten Island, NY
Cusick, Peter P. ....Staten Island, NY
Cusick, Richard ....Cleveland, OH
Cusick, Richard A. ....Birmingham, AL
Cusick, Robert E. ....Pittsburgh, PA
Cusick, Robert I. ....Louisville, KY
Cusick, Robert W. ....Mount Laurel, NJ
Cusick, Roger J. ....Latham, NY
Cusick, Stephen K. ....Melbourne, FL
Cusick, Stephen W. ....San Francisco, CA
Cusick, Thomas E., (Ltd.) ....Barrington, IL
Cusick, William H. ....New York, NY
Cusimano & Aswell ....Farmerville, LA
Cusimano, Charles V., II ....Gretna, LA
Cusimano, Frank N., III ....Midland, TX
Cusimano, Gregory S. ....Gadsden, AL
Cusimano, Jennifer B. ....Cleveland, OH
Cusimano, John M. ....New York, NY
Cusimano, Joseph A., Jr. ....Farmerville, LA
Cusimano, Joseph J. ....Cleveland, OH
Cusimano, Keener, Roberts & Kimberley, P.C. ....Gadsden, AL
Cusimano, Salvador M. ....Metairie, LA
Cusimano, Thomas W., Jr.
Binghamton, NY
Cusimano, V. Charles ....Baton Rouge, LA
Cuskaden, Everett L. ....Honolulu, HI
Cusker & Cusker ....Rochester, NY
Cusker, Dorothy Hickey ....Rochester, NY
Cusker, Eugene R. ....Rochester, NY
Cusker, John C. ....Pasadena, CA
Cusker, Richard E. ....Rochester, NY
Cusker, Thomas J. ....Rochester, NY
Cusma, Stephen J. ....Princeton, NJ
Cusmano, Joseph ....Romeo, MI
Cusmano, Virginia ....Detroit, MI
Cusmano, William M. ....Arlington, VA
Cussen, Deborah A. ....San Francisco, CA
Cussen, John ....Virginia Beach, VA
Cussen, Michael P. ....Cincinnati, OH
Cussen, William M. ....Cincinnati, OH
Cusson, David M. ....Macon, GA
Cusson, Jennifer Lynn ....Tampa, FL
Cusson, Molly S. ....New York, NY
Cusson-Cobb, Jody Marie ....Indianapolis, IN
Custar, David B. ....Oklahoma City, OK
Custard, Robert F. ....State College, PA
Custen, Martin W. ....Ogden, UT
Custer, Andy M. ....Hollywood, FL
Custer, B. Scott, Jr. (IBA) ....Washington, DC
Custer, Barbara Ann ....Los Angeles, CA
Custer, B. H. ....Washington, DC
Custer, Brian Benham ....Honolulu, HI
Custer, C. Gay ....Syracuse, NY
Custer, Cawthon Hester ....Albany, GA
Custer, Charles S. ....San Francisco, CA
Custer, Clayton M. ....Winston-Salem, NC
Custer & Custer ....Albany, GA
Custer, Daniel J. ....San Francisco, CA
Custer, Eric J. ....Los Angeles, CA
Custer, Fred A. ....Madison Heights, MI
Custer, Henry Clayton ....Albany, GA
Custer & Hill, P.C. ....Atlanta, GA
Marietta, GA
Custer, John S., Jr. ....Newtown Square, PA
Custer, Karen J. ....Grand Rapids, MI
Custer, Kelly J. ....Boulder, CO
Custer, Lawrence B. ....Marietta, GA
Custer, Max W., Jr. ....Patterson, NY
Custer, Oliver C. ....Reno, NV
Custer, Patricia Jo ....San Diego, CA
Custer, Robert Duff ....Albuquerque, NM
Custer, Russell R., Jr. ....Oak Brook, IL
Custer, Susan Warriner ....Richmond, VA
Custer, William J., III ....Crofton, MD
Custer, William V., IV ....Atlanta, GA
Custin, Richard E. ....Lake Villa, IL
Custis, A. Taylor ....New York, NY
Custis, Dion J. ....Cheyenne, WY
Custis, Dion J., P.C. ....Denver, CO
Fort Collins, CO
Cheyenne, WY
Custis, Douglass L. ....Cincinnati, OH
Custis, Henry P., Jr. ....Accomac, VA
Custis, Keith A. ....Boston, MA
Custis, Lewis & Dix, L.L.P. ....Accomac, VA
Custis, Robert J. ....Salem, OR
Custis, Stilley & Bischoff ....Salem, OR
Custodio, Laura Lee ....Newbury Park, CA
Custody Center, The, P.C.
Virginia Beach, VA
Cusumano, Barbara A. ....Gainesville, FL
Cusumano, Barbara A., P.A., Bankruptcy Law Firm of ....Gainesville, FL
Cusumano, Jerry J. ....Monroe, NY
Cusumano, Leanne ....Rockville, MD
Cusumano, Robert F. ....New York, NY
Cusumano, Robert P. ....Poughkeepsie, NY
Cutaia, Rory J. ....Mineola, NY
Cutajar, Frank H. ....Philadelphia, PA
Cutaia-Watchilla, Dawn M. ....York, PA
Cutajar, Valerie Hope ....Garden City, NY
Cutbirth, Joyce G. ....Houston, TX
Cutchen, D. Michael ....Mesa, AZ
Cutchen & Setlow, P.L.C. ....Mesa, AZ
Phoenix, AZ
Cutcher, Timothy R. ....Cincinnati, OH
Cutchin, John F. ....Newton, NC
Cutchin, John F., P.A. ....Newton, NC
Cutchin, John W. ....San Diego, CA
Cutchins, Clifford A., IV ....Deerfield, IL
Cutcliff, Lee S. ....Murray Hill, NJ
Cutcliffe, Conrad M. ....Providence, RI
Cute, Brian A. ....McLean, VA
Cutelis, Susan J. ....Chelmsford, MA
Cuthbert, Charles H., Jr. ....Petersburg, VA
Cuthbert, Henry L. ....Madison, WI
Cuthbert Law Offices, A Professional Corporation ....Petersburg, VA
Cuthbert, Maryellen ....Chelmsford, MA
Cuthbert, Rolfe ....San Mateo, CA
Cuthbert, Sheila Mary ....San Francisco, CA
Cuthbert, Thos. C. ....Salt Lake City, UT
Cuthbert, Vicki Trammell ....Marietta, GA
Cuthbertson, Frank E. ....Tacoma, WA
Cuthbertson, Hugh W. ....New Haven, CT

Cuthbertson, J. Douglas ....Richmond, VA
Cuthbertson, Mark A. ....Melville, NY
Cuthbertson, Patricia Casey — Cleveland, OH
Cutherell, Robt. S. ....Houston, TX
Cuthill, David M. ....Mercer Island, WA
Cuthrell & Cuthrell ....Corpus Christi, TX
Cuthrell, Keith C., Jr. ....Norfolk, VA
Cuthrell, Tamara Tejml ....Corpus Christi, TX
Cuthrell, V. Camp, III ....Corpus Christi, TX
Cuti, John R. ....New York, NY
Cuticello, Vincent J. ....New York, NY
Cutillo, Kenneth J. ....Chicago, IL
Cutini, Drake ....Department of Justice, Civil Division, GV
Cutino, Annette M. ....Salinas, CA
Cutler, Adam Harris ....Philadelphia, PA
Cutler, Alfred H. ....Boston, MA
Cutler, Alisande ....Ann Arbor, MI
Cutler, Alison B. ....Fort Lauderdale, FL
Cutler, Allan H. ....Pacific Palisades, CA
Cutler, Andrew N. ....New York, NY
Cutler, Arnold R. ....Boston, MA
Cutler, Audrey S. ....Boston, MA
Cutler, Barbara W. ....New York, NY
Cutler, Barry J. ....Washington, DC
Cutler, Beverly W. ....Palmer, AK
Cutler, Bruce ....New York, NY
Cutler, Bruce ....Aberdeen, SD
Cutler, Catherine E. ....San Francisco, CA
Cutler, Charles E. ....Des Moines, IA
Cutler, Clinton E. ....Minneapolis, MN
Cutler, Cynthia J. ....Lexington, KY
Cutler, Dal H. ....Salt Lake City, UT
Cutler, Daniel David ....Rockville, MD
Cutler, Daryl S. ....Ballston Spa, NY
Cutler, David A. ....San Francisco, CA
Cutler, David M. ....Nashville, TN
Cutler, Donahoe & Mickelson, LLP — Sioux Falls, SD
Cutler, Donald M. ....Southfield, MI
Cutler, Edward I. ....Tampa, FL
Cutler, Eliot R. ....Denver, CO; Washington, DC
Cutler, Felice R. ....Beverly Hills, CA
Cutler & Fish ....New York, NY
Cutler, Gary B. ....Philadelphia, PA
Cutler, Gary L. ....New York, NY
Cutler, George C. ....South Hamilton, MA
Cutler, Gordon B. ....Los Angeles, CA
Cutler, H. Jeffrey ....Miami, FL
Cutler, Helen Elmquist — Pacific Palisades, CA
Cutler, Henry M., III ....Fort Collins, CO
Cutler, Hollie S. ....Annapolis, MD
Cutler, Irwin H., Jr. ....Louisville, KY
Cutler, James M. ....Livingston, NJ
Cutler, Jay B. ....Washington, DC
Cutler, Jay L. ....Canton, OH
Cutler, Jay M. ....San Francisco, CA
Cutler, Jeffrey L. ....Encino, CA
Cutler, Jeffrey M. ....Wendell, NC
Cutler, Jeffrey N. ....Knoxville, TN
Cutler, Jennifer L. ....Sacramento, CA
Cutler, Jerry M. ....Baltimore, MD
Cutler, Joel B. ....Garden City, NY
Cutler, John A. ....Washington, DC
Cutler, John C. ....Chicago, IL
Cutler, John E. ....Idaho Falls, ID
Cutler, John H. ....San Francisco, CA
Cutler, John M., Jr. ....Washington, DC
Cutler, J. T. ....Virginia Beach, VA
Cutler, Judith Chanoux ....Boston, MA
Cutler, Karen McDade ....Atlanta, GA
Cutler, Kate ....San Francisco, CA
Cutler, Kathryne ....Omaha, NE
Cutler, Kenneth A. ....Boca Raton, FL
Cutler, Kenneth B. ....New York, NY
Cutler, Kenneth L. ....Minneapolis, MN
Cutler, Kent R. ....Sioux Falls, SD
Cutler, Laurence J. ....Morristown, NJ
Cutler, Lawrence M. ....Phoenix, AZ
Cutler, Linda L. ....Minneapolis, MN
Cutler, Lloyd N. ....Washington, DC
Cutler, Louisiana W. ....Anchorage, AK
Cutler, Lynn S. ....Santa Maria, CA
Cutler, M. Richard ....Irvine, CA
Cutler, Mark E. ....Sacramento, CA
Cutler, Mark I. ....Washington, DC
Cutler, Martin I. ....Los Angeles, CA
Cutler, Mary Coppinger ....San Ramon, CA
Cutler, Matthew Lawrence ....St. Louis, MO
Cutler, Maury K. ....Blackwood, NJ
Cutler, Michael D. ....Brookline, MA
Cutler, Michael E. ....Washington, DC
Cutler, Michael H. ....Southfield, MI
Cutler, Miriam ....Arlington, VA
Cutler, Murray ....Brooklyn, NY
Cutler, Norton ....Denver, CO
Cutler & Nylander, A Professional Service Corporation ....Seattle, WA
Cutler, Paul S. ....Marietta, GA
Cutler, Paul W. ....Northbrook, IL
Cutler, Peter P. ....Olympia, WA
Cutler, Philip E. ....Redmond, WA; Seattle, WA
Cutler, Priscilla R. Dorn ....Osceola, WI
Cutler, Richard A. ....Sioux Falls, SD
Cutler, Richard B. ....Beverly Hills, CA
Cutler, Richard J. ....Fresno, CA
Cutler, Richard J. ....New York, NY
Cutler, Richard W. ....New York, NY
Cutler, Richard W. ....Milwaukee, WI
Cutler, Robert E., Jr. ....Foxboro, MA
Cutler, Robert H. ....San Diego, CA
Cutler, Roger F. ....Salt Lake City, UT
Cutler, Ronald ....Daytona Beach, FL
Cutler & Schulman, P.C. ....Marietta, GA
Cutler, Scott R. ....San Diego, CA
Cutler, Sewall C., Jr. ....Dallas, TX
Cutler, Sheldon ....Poughkeepsie, NY
Cutler • Smith, P.C. ....Dallas, TX
Cutler & Stanfield, L.L.P. ....Denver, CO; Washington, DC
Cutler, Stanley ....Somerset, NJ
Cutler, Stephan L. ....Philadelphia, PA
Cutler, Stephanie ....Washington, DC
Cutler, Stephen M. — Securities and Exchange Commission, Executive Staff, GV
Cutler, Steven W., (P.A.) — Fort Lauderdale, FL
Cutler, Stuart J. ....Portland, OR
Cutler, Thomas H. ....Portland, OR
Cutler, Thomas P. ....Washington, DC
Cutler, Timothy K. ....Boston, MA
Cutler, Todd D. ....Philadelphia, PA
Cutler, William D. ....Santa Rosa, CA
Cutler-Jones, Michelle C. ....Boston, MA
Cutler-Levine, Robin ....Pittsburgh, PA
Cutlip, Edward C., Jr. ....Detroit, MI
Cutlip, Justin Bradley — Federal Labor Relations Authority, Washington Regional Office, GV
Cutlip, Meikka A. ....Alexandria, VA
Cutlip, Quinton B. ....Redwood City, CA
Cutner & Associates, P.C. ....New York, NY
Cutner, David A. ....New York, NY
Cutner, Helen H. ....Philadelphia, PA
Cutner, Rolande Regat ....Brooklyn, NY
Cutone, Angela A. ....Hauppauge, NY
Cutone, Kathaleen K. ....Boston, MA
Cutrell, Charles C., III ....Boston, MA
Cutrell, Jay D. ....Georgetown, OH
Cutrer, Anita K. ....Fort Worth, TX
Cutrer, Dan K. ....Dallas, TX
Cutrer, Emilia ....Sacramento, CA
Cutrer, G. Winston ....Tylertown, MS
Cutrer & Jefferson ....Houston, TX
Cutrer, Kenneth N. ....Fort Worth, TX
Cutrer, L. Michelle ....Palo Alto, CA
Cutrer, Lilynn A. ....Lake Charles, LA
Cutrera, Terri A. ....Trenton, NJ
Cutrera, William J. ....Lake Charles, LA
Cutri, Susan L. ....Boca Raton, FL
Cutri, Susan L. ....Fort Lauderdale, FL
Cutright, Carol Tuggle ....Signal Mountain, TN
Cutright & Cutright ....Toledo, IL
Cutright & Cutright ....Chillicothe, OH
Cutright, David A. ....Chillicothe, OH
Cutright, Ervin J. ....Seattle, WA
Cutright, James K. ....Chillicothe, OH
Cutright, James M. ....Chillicothe, OH
Cutright, John ....Austin, TX
Cutright, John O. ....Toledo, IL
Cutright, Roger L. ....Morgantown, WV
Cutright, Stephen Ray ....Glen Allen, VA
Cutro, James J. ....New York, NY
Cutro, Joseph E. ....Fort Lauderdale, FL
Cutrona, Angelina C. ....Binghamton, NY
Cutrona, Anthony J. ....Brooklyn, NY
Cutrone, Camille A. ....New Orleans, LA
Cutrone, Francesca L. ....Brooklyn, NY
Cutrone, Jerrard B. ....Miami, FL
Cutrone, John M. ....Chicago, IL
Cutrone, Louis J. ....Woodland Hills, CA
Cutrone, Paul W. ....Glendale, NY
Cutrone, Roseann M. ....Washington, DC
Cutrone, Verlander & Meyer — New Orleans, LA
Cutroni, Paul C. ....Belmont, MA
Cutrow, Allan B., (A Professional Corporation) ....Los Angeles, CA
Cutruzzula, Arthur, & Associates — Pittsburgh, PA
Cutsforth, Thomas William ....Fossil, OR
Cutshall, Bruce A. ....Lincoln, NE
Cutshall, Ronny L. ....Salt Lake City, UT
Cutshall, Thomas C. ....Minneapolis, MN
Cutshaw, David J. ....Indianapolis, IN
Cutshaw, J. Michael ....Baton Rouge, LA
Cutshaw, Jimmy Gray ....Greeneville, TN
Cutshaw, John W., Jr. ....Cambridge City, IN
Cutshaw, Kenneth A. ....Atlanta, GA
Cutsinger and Schafstall ....Franklin, IN
Cutson, Amy ....Altamonte Springs, FL
Cutt, David A. ....Salt Lake City, UT
Cutter, C. Brooks ....Sacramento, CA
Cutter, Corey N. ....Chicago, IL
Cutter, David F. ....Washington, DC
Cutter, Edward A. ....Oakland, CA
Cutter, Edward J. ....Dexter, ME
Cutter, G. Terry ....Carmel, IN
Cutter, Gail E. ....New York, NY
Cutter, James M. ....Columbus, OH
Cutter, Jeff ....Yakima, WA
Cutter, John H., III ....Charlotte, NC
Cutter, John H., III, P.A. ....Charlotte, NC
Cutter, Kerry E. ....Sacramento, CA
Cutter, Lawrence D. ....Poughkeepsie, NY
Cutter, Mary E. ....Lexington, KY
Cutter, Nick S. ....Honolulu, HI
Cutter, Patrick S. ....Philadelphia, PA
Cutter, Richard A. ....Wilmington, MA
Cutter, Richard G., III ....Waterford, NY
Cutter, Robert C. ....Glenwood Springs, CO
Cutter, Stephanie A. — Executive Office Of The President, GV
Cutting, Curt ....Los Angeles, CA
Cutting, Ernest E. ....Minneapolis, MN
Cutting, Ernest E., P.A. ....Minneapolis, MN
Cutting, H. Rebecca ....Worcester, MA
Cutting, JoAnn Cooper ....Memphis, TN
Cutting, Robert H., Jr. ....Santa Barbara, CA
Cuttino, John E. ....Columbia, SC
Cuttino, Kathy Ward ....Sumter, SC
Cuttita & Cuttita ....New York, NY
Cuttita, Francis V. ....New York, NY
Cuttita, Victoria ....New York, NY
Cuttita, Vincent J. ....New York, NY
Cuttitta, Peter H. ....Truckee, CA; Reno, NV
Cuttle, Allan E. J. ....Brooklyn, NY
Cuttle, Marcie M. ....Chicago, IL
Cuttler, Michele K. ....Los Angeles, CA
Cuttler, Sandra H. ....Atlanta, GA
Cuttner, David A. ....Farmington Hills, MI
Cuttner, David A., P.C ....Farmington Hills, MI
Cuttone, Brian K. ....Fresno, CA
Cutts, Anita S. ....Mount Prospect, IL
Cutts, H. Buck ....Surfside Beach, SC
Cutts, John A., III — United States Court Of Appeals For The Armed Forces, GV
Cutts, John G., Jr. ....Des Plaines, IL
Cutts, Karen D. ....Pasadena, CA
Cutts, Matthew D. ....Washington, DC
Cutts, William J. ....Moorestown, NJ
Cuva, Anthony John ....Tampa, FL
Cuva, Robert F. ....Woodbury, NJ
Cuvelier, Steven D. ....Terre Haute, IN
Cuviello, Anthony B. ....Atlanta, GA
Cuykendall, Clydia J. ....Houston, TX
Cuykendall, Frank Paul — Santa Barbara, CA
Cuyler, Aviva ....Emeryville, CA
Cuyler Burk ....Florham Park, NJ; Morristown, NJ; Newark, NJ; Parsippany, NJ; New York, NY
Cuyler, Devin Rainey ....Chicago, IL
Cuyler, Kenneth B. ....Naples, FL
Cuyler, Renaye B. ....Brooklyn, NY
Cuyler, Stephen D. ....Parsippany, NJ
Cuypers, Charles J. ....Grand Island, NE
Cuza, Jesús E. ....San Juan, PR
Cuzdey, Stephen ....Atlanta, GA
Cuzmanes, Paul T. ....Baltimore, MD
Cuzzo, Maria W. ....Duluth, MN
Cuzzo, Michael J. ....Duluth, MN
Cuzzolino, Gregory J. ....Newark, NJ
Cuzzucoli, Christopher W. ....Hauppauge, NY
Cvach, Paul R. ....Baltimore, MD
Cvarch, John A. ....Hartford, CT
Cvejanovich, John Adam ....Springfield, MA
Cvengros, David A. ....Traverse City, MI
Cvengros, James M. ....Burlingame, CA
Cvengros, Steve A. ....Rockville, IN
Cvetanovich, Danny L. ....Columbus, OH
Cvetetic, Elizabeth T. ....Huntsville, AL
Cvetich, Ilija ....Sacramento, CA
Cvitan, Alexander B. ....Los Angeles, CA
Cvitanovic, Steven M. ....Pleasanton, CA
Cwagenberg, Philip ....Birmingham, MI
Cwalina, Christopher G. ....Baltimore, MD
Cwalina, Jon A. ....Pittsburgh, PA
Cwalinski, Alexander A. ....Adams, MA
Cwayna, James R. ....Bloomington, MN
Cweiber, Elaine Harris ....Owings Mills, MD
Cweren, Brian P. ....Houston, TX
Cweren, Michelle ....Houston, TX
Cwern, Mark L. ....Pasadena, CA
Cwiek, Mark A. ....Taylorville, IL
Cwik, David L. ....Chicago, IL
Cwik, Joseph E. ....Chicago, IL
Cwiklo, David P. ....Woodland Hills, CA
Cwik-Martin, Cynthia H. ....San Diego, CA
Cwirka, Karen J. ....Springfield, MA
Cwirko, Claris K. ....Southfield, MI
Cybak, Robert ....Chicago, IL
Cyboron, John L. ....Colorado Springs, CO
Cybriwsky, Wolodymyr ....Prestonsburg, KY
Cybul, Bruce S. ....New York, NY
Cybulski, Alec E. ....Springfield, MA
Cybulski, David P. — United States Postal Service, GV
Cybulski, Donald ....Cleveland, OH
Cybulski, Joan W. — Department Of Veterans Affairs, Office of the General Counsel, GV
Cybulski, Lisa Ann ....Mountainside, NJ
Cybulsky, Joseph ....Tucson, AZ
Cycmanick, Michael F. ....Orlando, FL
Cyester, Tod A. ....Piqua, OH
Cygal, Everett J. ....Chicago, IL
Cygan, Jeanne A. ....New York, NY
Cygan, Stanley J., Jr. ....Chicago, IL
Cyganiewicz, Edmund K. ....Brownsville, TX
Cyganowski, Melanie L. ....Hauppauge, NY
Cygelman, Stanley ....Wellesley, MA
Cyko, Geo. L. ....Arlington, TN
Cykon, Phillip J. ....Montpelier, VT
Cylar, Lisa A. ....Birmingham, MI
Cylkowski, Clare M. ....Detroit, MI
Cylkowski, Jeffrey ....New York, NY
Cylkowski, Laurie A. ....St. Paul, MN
Cymbal, Kenneth M. ....Boston, MA
Cymbler, Jeffrey K. ....New York, NY
Cymerman, Barbara G. ....Pittsburgh, PA
Cymerman, Barry M. ....Milwaukee, WI
Cymerman, Patricia ....Los Angeles, CA
Cymrot, Lloyd ....Novato, CA
Cymrot, Mark A. ....Washington, DC
Cymrot, Steven L. ....Washington, DC
Cynamon, David J., (P.C.) — Washington, DC
Cynamon, Jeff P. ....Fort Lauderdale, FL
Cynamon, Jeffrey P. ....Fort Lauderdale, FL
Cynar, Walter P. ....Warren, MI
Cyncynatus, Jerry M. ....Moreland Hills, OH
Cynkar, Robert J. ....Washington, DC
Cynn, Jin-Ho ....Annandale, VA
Cynor, Thomas J. ....Belleville, IL
Cypel, Kirk ....San Diego, CA
Cypen & Cypen ....Miami Beach, FL
Cypen, Irving ....Miami Beach, FL
Cypen, Marcia K. ....Miami, FL
Cypen, Myles G. ....Miami Beach, FL
Cypen, Stephen H. ....Miami Beach, FL
Cypen, Wayne A. ....Miami Beach, FL
Cypers, Michael L. ....Los Angeles, CA
Cyperski, Nancy L. ....Canton, OH
Cyperski, Robert H. ....Canton, OH
Cypert, Crouch, Clark & Harwell — Bentonville, AR; Fayetteville, AR; Rogers, AR; Springdale, AR
Cypert, James D. ....Springdale, AR
Cypert, Mark G. ....Houston, TX
Cypert, Wayne A. ....Nogales, AZ
Cypher, James R. ....Oakland, CA
Cypher, Thomas H. ....Grand Rapids, MI
Cyphers, Carol Poli ....Coquille, OR
Cyphers, Christopher D. ....Anchorage, AK
Cyphers, Harlan L. ....Denver, CO
Cyphers, Jeannette A. ....Seattle, WA
Cyphers, Jeannette A., P.S. ....Seattle, WA
Cyphers, Joseph A., Jr. ....Harrisburg, PA
Cyphers, Kenneth Richard ....New York, NY
Cyphers, R. Wayne ....Seattle, WA
Cyphert, Michael A. ....Cleveland, OH
Cypser, Darlene A. ....Boulder, CO
Cyr, Anne C. ....Los Osos, CA; San Luis Obispo, CA
Cyr, Conrad K. ....Bangor, ME
Cyr, Danielle D. ....New York, NY
Cyr, Douglas D. ....Lincoln, NE
Cyr, Henry Bruce ....Montgomery, AL
Cyr, Howard M., III ....Cherry Hill, NJ; Philadelphia, PA
Cyr, John ....Houston, TX
Cyr, Joseph P. ....New York, NY
Cyr, Karen D. — Nuclear Regulatory Commission, Office of the General Counsel, GV
Cyr, Kenneth J. ....Methuen, MA
Cyr, Kevin W. ....Minneapolis, MN
Cyr, Leslie Martinelli ....Philadelphia, PA
Cyr, Mark F., (P.C.) ....Moline, IL; Ottawa, IL
Cyr, Paula ....Beaumont, TX
Cyr, Robert N. ....Biddeford, ME
Cyr, Robertson & Associates ....Moline, IL; Ottawa, IL
Cyr, Steven M. ....Portland, OR
Cyr, Susan E. ....Greenville, SC
Cyr, Susan T. J. ....Springvale, ME
Cyra, Nancy A. ....Reno, NV
Cyranoski, Debra M. ....Chicago, IL
Cyranoski, Steven E. ....Chicago, IL
Cyrelson, Florane ....West Collingswood, NJ
Cyriax, Conrad G. ....South Amboy, NJ
Cyril & Crowley LLP ....San Francisco, CA
Cyril, Paul H., (A Professional Corporation) — San Francisco, CA
Cyril, William ....Corona Del Mar, CA
Cyrlin, Alan I. ....Los Angeles, CA
Cyrluk, Jonathan M. ....Chicago, IL
Cyron, Wayne F. ....Alexandria, VA
Cyron, Wayne F. ....Arlington, VA; Fairfax, VA
Cyrs, Michael T. ....Rockford, IL
Cyrul, Richard E. ....New Baltimore, MI
Cyruli, Robert J. ....New York, NY
Cyrus, Dwayne E. ....Charleston, WV
Cyrus, Eugene B. ....Eagle River, AK
Cyrus, John F. ....Huntington, WV
Cyrus, Phyllis H. ....Huntington, WV
Cyrus, Robert R. ....Leesburg, FL
Cyrus, Rose A. ....Ashland, KY
Cys, Richard L. ....Washington, DC
Cytron, Benson ....House Springs, MO
Cytron, Bradford J. ....St. Louis, MO
Cytron, John M. ....Chicago, IL
Cytryn, Dan ....Tamarac, FL
Cyze, Mary Beth ....Chicago, IL
Cyzen, Keith M. ....Chicago, IL
Cyzio, Chester T. ....Philadelphia, PA
Czaban, James Nicholas ....Washington, DC
Czachor, Curtis R. ....Green Bay, WI
Czack, Michael W. ....Cleveland, OH
Czaczkes & Czaczkes ....Norwich, CT
Czaczkes, Edward ....Norwich, CT
Czaczkes, Morris ....Norwich, CT
Czadowski, Edward W. ....Chicago, IL
Czaiko, Michael F. ....Oregon City, OR
Czaja, Claude P. ....Smyrna, GA
Czaja, Edward D. ....Naples, NY
Czaja, Richard F. ....New York, NY
Czaja, Stanley C. ....Chicago, IL
Czaja, Timothy A. ....Minneapolis, MN
Czajka, Paul ....Hudson, NY
Czajka, Terri Ann ....Indianapolis, IN
Czajkowski, Frank H. ....Greenwich, CT
Czajkowski, James P. ....Prairie du Chien, WI
Czajkowski, Joseph J. ....Florham Park, NJ
Czajkowski, Mark E. ....Rochester, NY
Czajkowski, Ned J. ....Milwaukee, WI
Czajkowski & Rider, S.C. — Prairie du Chien, WI
Czajkowsky (Shy-kow-ski), Stanley T. — Wilmington, DE
Czajkowskyj, Cyril ....Glendale, CA
Czamanske, Daniel M. ....Platte City, MO
Czamanske, Daniel M., Jr. — Clarksdale, MS
Czamanske, David ....South Pasadena, CA
Czap, David P. ....Newtown Square, PA
Czapanskiy, Karen ....Baltimore, MD
Czapiga, James M. ....Hartford, CT

Daghe, Laura B. ... Indianapolis, IN
Dagher, Renee ... Farmington Hills, MI
Dagher-Margosian, Jeanice A.
Ann Arbor, MI
Daghir, Christian S. ... Elizabethville, PA
Harrisburg, PA
Millersburg, PA
Daghir & Daghir ... St. Marys, PA
Daghir, George L. ... St. Marys, PA
Daghir, George N. ... St. Marys, PA
Daghir, Gordon J. ... St. Marys, PA
Daghir, Roberta Kienast ... Baltimore, MD
Daghlian, Peter ... Hoboken, NJ
Dagilis, Steven C. ... Prescott, AZ
d'Agincourt, Carolyn G. ... Boston, MA
Dagle, C. Paul ... Portland, OR
Dagley, John L. ... Houston, TX
Dagley, Michael L. ... Nashville, TN
Dagli, Riza I. ... Lawrenceville, NJ
Daglian, Charles P. ... Jersey City, NJ
Daglio, Michael R. ... Richmond, VA
Dagner, Deana R. ... Englewood, CO
Dagon, George A., Jr. ... Hartford, CT
Dagon, John N. ... Hornell, NY
Dagonese, Gerard R. ... San Bernardino, CA
Dagonese, Joseph C. ... Buffalo, NY
Dagosta, Alicia M. ... Phoenix, AZ
D'Agostine, Julian J. ... Boston, MA
D'Agostini, Altero ... San Francisco, CA
D'Agostini, Eugene A. ... Sterling Heights, MI
D'Agostini, Lorenzo A. ... Southfield, MI
D'Agostini, Mary Lou Flagg ... Plymouth, CA
D'Agostini and Ruggeri, Professional Corporation ... Sterling Heights, MI
D'Agostino, Albert A. ... Valley Stream, NY
D'Agostino, Alfred A., Jr. ... New York, NY
D'Agostino, Andrea ... Riviera Beach, FL
D'Agostino, Angelo Chas. ... White Plains, NY
D'Agostino & Budz ... Fort Myers, FL
D'Agostino, Cindy E.
Palm Beach Gardens, FL
D'Agostino, Clare ... Philadelphia, PA
D'Agostino, Daniel D. ... York, SC
D'Agostino, Diane M. ... Hillsboro, OR
D'Agostino, Edward E. V. ... Providence, RI
D'Agostino, Harry J. ... Albany, NY
D'Agostino, Hoblock & Greisler P.C.
Albany, NY
D'Agostino, James S., Jr. ... Nashville, TN
D'Agostino, Joe ... Santa Ana, CA
D'Agostino, John ... New York, NY
D'Agostino, John B. ... Hartford, CT
D'Agostino, Karen J. ... Rochester, NY
D'Agostino, Krackeler, Baynes & Maguire, P.C. ... Albany, NY
D'Agostino, L. James ... McLean, VA
D'Agostino, Lani M. ... Springfield, NJ
D'Agostino, Lea Purwin ... Van Nuys, CA
D'Agostino Levine & Landesman, L.L.P.
New York, NY
D'Agostino, Louis D. ... Naples, FL
D'Agostino, Mae A. ... Albany, NY
D'Agostino, Mary R. ... Roseland, NJ
D'Agostino, Michael ... New York, NY
D'Agostino, Michael C. ... New Haven, CT
D'Agostino, Michael J. ... Fort Myers, FL
D'Agostino, Michael S. ... Saddle Brook, NJ
D'Agostino & O'Donnell ... Providence, RI
D'Agostino, Raymond R. ... Syracuse, NY
D'Agostino, Reneé C. ... Novato, CA
D'Agostino, Richard J. ... Lawrence, MA
D'Agostino, Rita M. ... Kansas City, MO
D'Agostino, Rocco F. ... White Plains, NY
D'Agostino, Sam J. ... Eden, NY
D'Agostino, Thomas C. ... Buffalo, NY
D'Agostino, Vincent ... Roseland, NJ
D'Agresta, Suzanne ... Orlando, FL
DaGrosa, Jessica E. ... Miami, FL
D'Agrosa, Paul J. ... Clayton, MO
Daguanno, James E. ... Carle Place, NY
Daguanno, Richard ... Farmington Hills, MI
D'Aguanno, Vincent A. ... Plymouth, MI
Dague, Laurence W. ... Harrisburg, PA
Dague, Linda Clark ... Muncie, IN
Dague, Raymond J. ... Syracuse, NY
Dagurt, Sheldon G. ... Baltimore, MD
D'Agustino, Elena M. ... Vallejo, CA
Dahan, David ... New York, NY
Dahan, David M. ... New York, NY
Dahan, David R. ... Voorhees, NJ
Philadelphia, PA
Dahan, Israel ... New York, NY
Dahan, Leslie Abella ... Washington, DC
Dahan, M. Marc ... New York, NY
Dahan, Nancy W. ... Beverly Hills, CA
Dahan & Nowick ... New York, NY
Dahar, Eleanor Wm. ... Manchester, NH
Dahar, S. William, II ... Manchester, NH
Dahar, Victor W. ... Manchester, NH
Dahar, Victor W., Jr. ... Manchester, NH
Dahar, Victor W., Professional Association
Manchester, NH
Dahdah de Surillo, Laura A.
Mayaguez, PR
Dahdouh, Thomas N. ... San Francisco, CA
Daheim, Warren J. ... Tacoma, WA
Daher, Georganne V. ... Philadelphia, PA
Daher, Rosemary L. ... Detroit, MI
Dahill, Daniel D. ... Logan, WV
Dahill, John B. ... Austin, TX
Dahill, William F. ... New York, NY
Dahl, Alrich W. ... Belvedere-Tiburon, CA
Dahl, Annabelle H. ... San Marino, CA
Dahl, Barry J. ... Longview, WA
Dahl, Brian A. ... Indianapolis, IN
Dahl, Bruce E. ... Denver, CO
Dahl, Christine Stebbins ... Portland, OR
Dahl, Christopher L. ... Seattle, WA
Dahl, Christopher T. ... Boston, MA
Dahl, Collin J. ... Sturgeon Bay, WI
Dahl, David D. ... Newport Beach, CA
Dahl, David D. ... Raleigh, NC
Dahl, David H. ... Omaha, NE
Dahl, David L. ... Wichita, KS
Dahl, Erik ... Chicago, IL
Dahl, Everett E. ... Midvale, UT
Dahl, Garyt W. ... Okemos, MI
Dahl, Gerald E. ... Denver, CO
Dahl, Gloria C. ... Jamestown, RI
Dahl, Gregory G. ... Lafayette, CA
Dahl, Harry W., III ... Des Moines, IA
Dahl, Harry W., P.C. ... Des Moines, IA
Dahl, Henry ... Charlottesville, VA
Dahl, James A. ... New Brighton, MN
Dahl, James E., & Associates ... Chicago, IL
Dahl, James G. ... Plano, TX
Dahl, Jay L. ... Geneva, IL
Dahl, Jay L., Ltd. ... Geneva, IL
Dahl, Jeffrey A. ... Albuquerque, NM
Dahl, Jeffrey E. ... San Antonio, TX
Dahl, John E. ... Springfield, MA
Dahl, John M. ... Minneapolis, MN
Dahl, John P. ... Seattle, WA
Dahl, Joyle C. ... Portland, OR
Dahl, Kathryn J. ... Annapolis, MD
Dahl, Kelly R. ... Omaha, NE
Dahl, Kirby ... Cold Spring, MN
Dahl, Kristian M. ... Springfield, VA
Dahl, Lance Christopher ... Seattle, WA
Dahl, Larry J. ... Phoenix, AZ
Dahl, Loren S. ... Sacramento, CA
Dahl, Merlin W. ... Edina, MN
Dahl, Michael B. ... Trenton, NJ
Dahl, Milford W., Jr. ... Costa Mesa, CA
Dahl, Nancy K. ... San Diego, CA
Dahl & Osterloth, LLP ... Boulder, CO
Colorado Springs, CO
Denver, CO
Fort Collins, CO
Dahl, Pamela Greenman ... Des Moines, IA
Dahl, Philip Y. ... St. Paul, MN
Dahl, Richard A. ... Newport Beach, CA
Dahl, Richard M. ... Minneapolis, MN
Dahl, Robert A. ... Washington, DC
Dahl, Robert E. ... Orlando, FL
Dahl, Robert H. ... Los Angeles, CA
Dahl, Ronald W. ... Sacramento, CA
Dahl, Sarah A. ... New York, NY
Dahl, Scott S. ... Department of Justice, Criminal Division, GV
Dahl, Sonja M. ... Walnut Creek, CA
Dahl, Stephen J. ... North Las Vegas, NV
Dahl, Stephen M. ... Edison, NJ
Dahl, Torger N. ... Rochester, NY
Dahl, Tyrus V., Jr. ... Winston-Salem, NC
Dahl, Walter P. ... Chicago, IL
Dahl, Walter R. ... Sacramento, CA
Dahl, William A. ... Fresno, CA
Dahlberg, Edwin C. ... Beloit, WI
Dahlberg, James L. ... Washington, DC
Dahlberg, James P. ... Morehead, KY
Dahlberg, Jeffry A. ... Loves Park, IL
Dahlberg, John N. ... San Francisco, CA
Dahlberg, Julia A. ... Washington, DC
Dahlberg, Lyle F. ... Bloomfield Hills, MI
Dahlberg, Melanie J. ... Minneapolis, MN
Dahlberg, Paul ... Rochester, MN
Dahlberg, Robin ... New York, NY
Dahlberg, Troy A. ... Los Angeles, CA
Dahlbo, Robert M. ... Del Mar, CA
Dahlborg, Lynne D. ... Boston, MA
Dahlby, Gary L. ... Palo Alto, CA
Dahle, Bridget K. ... White Plains, NY
Dahle, Christopher T. ... Alamosa, CO
Dahle, David S. ... Los Angeles, CA
Dahle, Dennis V. ... Salt Lake City, UT
Dahle, Gary C. ... Mounds View, MN
Dahle, Gary C. ... Shoreview, MN
Dahle, John N. ... Denver, CO
Dahle, Mark F. ... Lakeland, FL
Dahle, Mark F., P.A., Law Offices of
Lakeland, FL
Orlando, FL
Dahle, Regan S. ... Detroit, MI
Dahle, Robert D. ... Sandy, UT
Dahle, Scott L. ... Los Angeles, CA
Dahle, Sheila R. ... Fullerton, CA
Dahle, Thomas A. ... Sioux Falls, SD
Dahle, Thomas A. ... Hudson, WI
Dahle, Vincent S. ... New Brighton, MN
Dahlem, John F. ... Virginia, IL
Dahlem, Steven W. ... Mariposa, CA
Dahlen, Jane H. ... Deerfield, IL
Dahlen, Karl A. ... Fitchburg, WI
Dahlen, Michael F. ... Carbondale, IL
Dahlen, Peter ... Northfield, MN
Dahlen, Peter Rolf ... United States Senate, Committee Legal Personnel, GV
Dahlen, Richard G. ... Wilmington, DE
Dahlen, Richard L. ... Hershey, PA
Dahler, Erik T. ... Lytle, TX
Dahler, Fred W. ... Canton, OH
Dahlgaard, Erik A. ... Sarasota, FL
Dahlgaard, Patricia L. ... Carlsbad, CA
Dahlgren, Becky L. ... Oak Brook, IL
Dahlgren, Becky Lynn, Ltd. ... Oak Brook, IL
Dahlgren and Close ... Washington, DC
Dahlgren & Dauenhauer, P.C. ... Seattle, WA
Dahlgren, Donald C. ... Seattle, WA
Dahlgren, Gregory R. A. ... Chicago, IL
Dahlgren, Jeffery C. ... Wichita, KS
Dahlgren, Joel J. ... New Ulm, MN
Dahlgren, Kathleen R. ... Milwaukee, WI
Dahlgren, Lawrence F. ... Pontiac, MI
Dahlgren, Lisa D. Fox ... Wichita, KS
Dahlgren, Norman H., Jr. ... San Diego, CA
Dahlgren, Ward E. ... Sarasota, FL
Dahlgren, Wilbur D. ... Binghamton, NY
Dahlin, C. William ... Santa Ana, CA
Dahlin, Dale D. ... Lincoln, NE
Dahlin, Eric L. ... Portland, OR
Dahlin, Eric T. ... North Bend, OR
Dahlin, Lewis W. ... Medford, OR
Dahlin, Peter D. ... Spokane, WA
Dahlin, Roland E., II ... Houston, TX
Dahlin, Ronald A. ... San Diego, CA
Dahling, Alfred E. ... Warren, OH
Dahling, William D., Jr. ... Riverside, CA
Dahlinquist, Anna Newman ... Reno, NV
Dahlk, Thomas H. ... Omaha, NE
Dahlke, Donn H. ... Montello, WI
Dahlke, Gary A. ... Spokane, WA
Dahlke, Kirk L. ... Aventura, FL
Dahlke, Lawrence T. ... Schenectady, NY
Dahlman, Andrea J. ... Phoenix, AZ
Dahlman, Dennis S. ... Hopkins, MN
Dahlman, Jeffrey Stuart ... Short Hills, NJ
Dahlman, Nora Jean ... New York, NY
Dahlman, Paul E. ... New York, NY
Dahlman, Terrell W. ... Corpus Christi, TX
Dahlmann, Donald J. ... Belleville, IL
Dahlmeier, David M. ... Minneapolis, MN
Dahlmeier, Frederick M.
North Palm Beach, FL
Dahlmeyer, Fred D. ... Durham, CT
Dahlquist, Charles W., II
Salt Lake City, UT
Dahlquist, James S. ... Minneapolis, MN
Dahlquist, John W ... Lombard, IL
Dahlquist, Karl S. ... Phoenix, AZ
Memphis, TN
Dahlquist, Pamela J. ... Omaha, NE
Dahlquist, Robert P. ... San Diego, CA
Dahlson, Richard F. ... Dallas, TX
Dahlsten, Andrea ... San Diego, CA
Dahlstrom, A. Winton ... Montague, MI
Dahlstrom, Carrie Ellen ... New Bedford, MA
Dahlstrom, Christopher M. ... Harvard, MA
Dahlstrom, Eric N. ... Phoenix, AZ
Dahlstrom, John A. ... Salt Lake City, UT
Dahlstrom, Patrick V. ... New York, NY
Dahlstrom, William S. ... Dallas, TX
Dahlstrom Jr., John A.
Salt Lake City, UT
Dahlstrum, Jack A. ... Cathedral City, CA
Dahm, Albert J. ... Fort Wayne, IN
Dahm, Martha M. ... Chicago, IL
Dahm, Peter F. ... Essexville, MI
Dahm, Robert W. ... Bloomfield Hills, MI
Dahm, Stephen L. ... San Francisco, CA
Dahm, Susan ... Boulder, CO
Dahman, Marc ... Jacksonville, IL
Dahman, Victor C. ... Madera, CA
Dahman, William H. ... St. Louis, MO
Dahmani, Pierre A. ... Chicago, IL
Dahmen, Gene D. ... Boston, MA
Dahmer, Douglas M. ... Columbus, OH
Dahmer, Woody ... Atlanta, GA
Dahmes, Dwight A. ... New Orleans, LA
Dahms, Christopher Hayes
San Francisco, CA
Dahms, Kenneth C. ... Dayton, OH
Dahn, Douglas C. ... Detroit, MI
Dahn, Mark D. ... Franklin, NJ
Dahnk, Jeannie P. ... Fredericksburg, VA
Dahnke, Duane A. ... Albuquerque, NM
Dahnke, George W. ... Oklahoma City, OK
Dahnke, Jeffery T. ... Denver, CO
Dahnke, Joel L. ... Alexandria, VA
Arlington, VA
Dahodwala, Fatema ... North Reading, MA
Dahood, Wade J. ... Anaconda, MT
Dahowski, Michael T. ... Poughkeepsie, NY
Dahut, Henry ... Sherman Oaks, CA
Dahut, John M. ... Kensington, MD
Dai, Alexander M. ... Glendale, CA
Dai, Benjamin Menzel ... Kensington, CA
Dai, Christopher John ... Staten Island, NY
Dai, Michael Minxiang ... St. Paul, MN
Dai, Miwako ... Washington, DC
Daiber, Kent E. ... Harrison, NY
Daiber, Theodore E. ... Boston, MA
Daichman, Jeffrey H. ... New York, NY
Daicoff Baskin, Susan D. ... Columbus, OH
Daidone, Benj. ... Niles, IL
Daidone, Sal B., (P.A.) ... Voorhees, NJ
Daiek, Joseph R. ... Birmingham, MI
Daiek, Joseph R. ... Rochester Hills, MI
Daiell, Michael S. ... Brooklyn, NY
Daiell, Michael S., P.C. ... Brooklyn, NY
Daiello, Thomas D. ... Wildwood, FL
Daigel, Grace C. ... Chicago, IL
Daiger, Gordon W. ... Department of Justice, Civil Division, GV
Daigh, Gary E. ... Los Angeles, CA
Daigle, Daniel J. ... New Orleans, LA
Daigle, Daryl J. ... New Orleans, LA
Daigle, Dominigue T. ... New Orleans, LA
Daigle, Edward S. ... Portland, ME
Daigle, Ellen M. ... Shreveport, LA
Daigle, Ellis J. ... Eunice, LA
Daigle, Eric M. ... New Orleans, LA
Daigle, Howard, Jr. ... Covington, LA
Daigle, James H., (A Professional Law Corporation) ... New Orleans, LA
Daigle, James H., Jr. ... New Orleans, LA
Daigle, Janie L. ... Sacramento, CA
Daigle, Joseph R. ... Norwood, MA
Daigle, Lesley E. ... Atlanta, GA
Daigle, Michael R. ... Golden, CO
Daigle, Mimi ... Tallahassee, FL
Daigle, P. Keith ... Metairie, LA
Daigle, Paul N. ... Seattle, WA
Daigle, Peter M. ... Centerville, MA
Daigle, Raymond A., Jr. ... Metairie, LA
New Orleans, LA
Daigle, Robert W. ... Lafayette, LA
D'Aigle, Rod F. ... Rogers, MN
Daigle, Ronald A. ... Caribou, ME
Daigle, Sullivan, Dupré & Aldous, A Professional Law Corporation ... Metairie, LA
Provo, UT
Daigle, Susan A. ... Lafayette, LA
Daigle, Tommy M. ... Lafayette, LA
Daignault, Marilyn C. ... New York, NY
Daignault, Ronald A. ... Minneapolis, MN
Daignault, Ronald M. ... New York, NY
Daigneault, Abel & Daigneault
Torrance, CA
Daigneault, Alessandra F. Via ... Vienna, VA
Daigneault, Kathleen Reynolds
Fitchburg, MA
Daigneault, Michelle M. ... Palo Alto, CA
Daigneault, Philip ... Torrance, CA
Daigneault, Philip M. ... Torrance, CA
Daigneault, Taylor J. ... Torrance, CA
Daigre, Robert J. ... New Orleans, LA
Daijogo, Maki ... Larkspur, CA
Daiker, Bertram B. ... Port Washington, NY
Daiker, Bertram B., & Reed P. Whittemore
Port Washington, NY
Daiker, Duane A. ... Tampa, FL
Daiker, Paul B. ... Cleveland, OH
Daiker, Stephen B. ... St. Louis, MO
Daiker, Victoria ... Hamilton, OH
Daiker-Middaugh, Pamela Ann
Cleveland, OH
Dail, Francis E. ... Raleigh, NC
Dail, Halbert T. ... Chesapeake, VA
Dailard, Cynthia B. ... Washington, DC
Dailard, Scott D. ... Washington, DC
Daileader, Dale Lucas ... Fairfield, NJ
Daileader, Robert L., Jr. ... Washington, DC
Dailey, Anna Marie ... Charleston, WV
Dailey & Associates ... West Bridgewater, MA
Dailey & Associates, Chtd.
Washington, DC
Dailey, Bonnie C. ... Hartford, CT
Dailey, Brian Thomas
Farmington Hills, MI
Dailey, Carol Anne ... Bryn Mawr, PA
Dailey, Coleen Hall ... East Liverpool, OH
Dailey & Dailey, P.C. ... Manchester, VT
Dailey, David N. ... Moline, IL
Dailey, Dianne K. ... Portland, OR
Dailey, Donald B., Jr. ... Portland, TX
Dailey, Douglas M. ... Yankton, SD
Dailey, Edward J. ... Boston, MA
Dailey, Edward W. ... Burlington, IA
Dailey, Edward W., Law Office, P.C.
Burlington, IA
Dailey, Elaine R. ... Albuquerque, NM
Dailey, Elizabeth W. ... Salem, MA
Dailey, Erin Lee ... Sarasota, FL
Dailey, Frank M. ... Springfield, KY
Dailey, Frank W. ... Indianapolis, IN
Dailey, Garrett C. ... Oakland, CA
Dailey, Gary F. ... Colorado Springs, CO
Dailey, George E. ... Ponte Vedra Beach, FL
Dailey, Gerald E. ... Columbus, OH
Dailey, Gina B. ... Boston, MA
Dailey & Grisham, P.C. ... Birmingham, AL
Dailey, H. Kay ... Carlisle, PA
Dailey, Henry ... Birmingham, AL
Dailey, J. Robert ... New York, NY
Dailey, Jacob E. ... Pottstown, PA
Dailey, James H. ... Renton, WA
Dailey, James J. ... Mobile, AL
Dailey, James J. ... Mankato, MN
Dailey, James R. ... Erie, PA
Dailey, James T., Jr. ... Kingwood, WV
Dailey, Jeanne L. ... Marysville, OH
Dailey, Joan P. ... Washington, DC
Dailey, Joanna ... Department of Education, Office of the General Counsel, GV
Dailey, John J. ... Erie, PA
Dailey, John L. ... Denver, CO
Dailey, John M. ... Albion, NY
Dailey, John T. ... San Antonio, TX
Dailey, John W., Jr. ... Marysville, OH
Dailey, Jonathan Christian
Washington, DC
Dailey, Joseph P. ... New York, NY
Dailey, Joyce Cullinan ... Pittsburgh, PA
Dailey, Kara D. ... Elizabethtown, KY
Dailey, Kathleen M. ... Portland, OR
Dailey, Kevin M. ... Clifton Park, NY
Dailey, L. Scot ... Dallas, TX
Dailey Law Office ... Mankato, MN
Dailey, Lawrence ... Glendale, CA
Dailey, Lisa M. ... Colorado Springs, CO
Dailey, Lisa M., P.C.
Colorado Springs, CO
Dailey, Margaret E. ... Newport, OR
Dailey, Margaret S. ... Washington, DC
Dailey, Marilyn Adams ... Pleasant Ridge, MI
Dailey, Mark L. ... Huntington Woods, MI
Dailey, Marlee Hendrix ... Birmingham, AL
Dailey, Mary Reagan ... Marcellus, NY
Dailey, Maurice ... Granite City, IL
Dailey, Michael Alan ... Atlanta, GA
Dailey, Michael L. ... Greenbelt, MD
Dailey, Michael T. ... Matawan, NJ
Dailey, P. Jill ... Cincinnati, OH
Dailey, Patricia A. ... Cincinnati, OH
Dailey, Peter H. ... Hackensack, NJ
Dailey, Peter J. ... Greensburg, PA
Dailey, R. Thomas ... Farmington, NM
Dailey, R. Thomas, P.C. ... Farmington, NM
Dailey, Restifo & Dailey ... Erie, PA
Dailey, Richard A. ... Muncie, IN
Dailey, Richard C. ... West Bridgewater, MA

Dailey, Richard M., Jr. .... Greensboro, NC
Dailey, Richard R. .... New York, NY
Dailey, Robert G. .... Omaha, NE
Dailey, Rosemary E. .... Washington, DC
Dailey, Shannon M. .... San Diego, CA
Dailey, Stephen Paul .... Millersburg, OH
Dailey, Steven M. .... Santa Ana, CA
Dailey, Susan Burley .... Manchester, VT
Dailey, Terry J. .... Atlantic City, NJ
Dailey, Thomas A. .... Alamo, CA
Dailey, Thomas Arthur
Agency for International Development, Other Offices of A.I.D., GV
Dailey, Thomas F. .... Princeton, NJ
Dailey, Thomas M. .... King Of Prussia, PA
Dailey, Thomas M. .... Reston, VA
Dailey, Timothy P. .... Sacramento, CA
Dailey and Walker, P.C. .... Granite City, IL
Dailey, William B. .... Boston, MA
Dailey, William F.
Department of Agriculture, Food Safety and Inspection Service, GV
Dailey, William H. .... Moline, IL
Dailey, William H., Ltd. .... Moline, IL
Dailey, William J., III .... Boston, MA
Dailey, William J., Jr. .... Boston, MA
Dailey, William M. .... Stamford, CT
Dailey McManus, Elizabeth T.
New York, NY
Dailing, Joseph A. .... Rockford, IL
Dailly, Eleonore .... New York, NY
Dailor, Joseph F. .... Albany, NY
Daily, Arthur C. .... Aspen, CO
Daily, Brian L. .... St. Louis, MO
Daily, Charles F., Jr. .... Buda, TX
Daily, Cheryl K. .... San Diego, CA
Daily, F. Michael, Jr. .... Merchantville, NJ
Daily, F. W., Tax Law Offices of
San Francisco, CA
Daily, Frank F. .... Baltimore, MD
Daily, Frank J. .... Milwaukee, WI
Daily, Frederick W., III
San Francisco, CA
Daily, James D. .... Irvine, CA
Daily, John A. .... Uniontown, OH
Daily, John D. .... McLeansboro, IL
Daily, Joseph A. .... Indio, CA
Daily, Kirk A. .... Ottumwa, IA
Daily, LaVone A. .... Kansas City, KS
Daily Law Office, P.C. .... Glasgow, MO
Daily, Leo F. .... Spokane, WA
Daily, N. Alexandra .... New York, NY
Daily, Nicholas S. .... Wichita, KS
Daily, Richard M. .... Ilion, NY
Daily, Richard W. .... Denver, CO
Daily, Robert F. .... Sun Valley, ID
Daily, Robert Lee .... Torrance, CA
Daily, Robert Lee, A Professional Corporation .... Torrance, CA
Daily, Sharon F. .... St. Louis, MO
Daily, Steven C. .... Riverwoods, IL
Daily, Steven R. .... San Diego, CA
Daily, Terrence J. .... San Jose, CA
Daily, Thomas A. .... Fort Smith, AR
Daily, William E. .... Indianapolis, IN
Daily, William J. .... Glasgow, MO
Daily, Wm H. .... Pinetop, AZ
Daily & Woods, P.L.L.C. .... Booneville, AR
Charleston, AR
Fort Smith, AR
Greenwood, AR
Ozark, AR
Paris, AR
Van Buren, AR
Dain, Anthony J. .... Phoenix, AZ
San Diego, CA
Dain, Daniel P. .... Boston, MA
Dain, David L. .... Department of Justice, Environment and Natural Resources Division, GV
Dain & Li .... Phoenix, AZ
San Diego, CA
Dain, Robert D. .... Reston, VA
Daine, Kimberly A. .... New Haven, CT
Daines, Kendall Welch .... Washington, DC
Daines, Luther I. .... Kalamazoo, MI
Daines, N. George, III .... Logan, UT
Daines, Robert W. .... Brigham City, UT
Daingerfield, Richard P. .... New York, NY
Dainow, J. David .... New York, NY
Dains, Jeffrey A. .... San Bernardino, CA
Dains, Michelle .... Austin, TX
Daire, Virginia .... Tallahassee, FL
Dairman, Dennis W. .... Mesa, AZ
Daisak, Daniel N. .... Linthicum, MD
Daise, Michelle Denise .... Wichita, KS
Daise, R. Bruce .... Wichita, KS
Daisey, Robert J. .... Philadelphia, PA
Daisley, Michel C. .... Charlotte, NC
Daisley, Robert M. .... Tampa, FL
Daisley, William P. .... Bethesda, MD
Daisy, William L. .... Greensboro, NC
Daitch, Jeffrey A. .... Burbank, CA
Daitch, Marvin C. .... Southfield, MI
Daitch, Michael E. .... Las Vegas, NV
Daitch, Michael E., P.C. .... Las Vegas, NV
Daitz, Jeffrey M. .... River Edge, NJ
Daitz, Michele A. .... Princeton, NJ
Daitz, Ronald F. .... New York, NY
Daitzman, Lynn .... Denver, CO
Daitzman, Myles .... New Milford, NJ
D'Aiuto, Leonard N., (Professional Association)
Altoona, FL
Daiuto, Ralph A. .... Stamford, CT
D'Aiuto, Ronald J. .... Stockton, CA
D'Aiutolo, Diane V. .... Baltimore, MD
Daiy, Michael G. .... Lafayette, LA

Daiy, Michael G., (A Professional Law Corporation) .... Lafayette, LA
Dajani, F. Martin
Federal Trade Commission, Bureau of Competition, GV
Dajani, Mollie T. .... Chicago, IL
Dajani, Mona E. .... Chicago, IL
Dajnowicz, Robert G. .... Bingham Farms, MI
Dajos, Benjamin W., Jr. .... Coldwater, MI
Dakan, Stephen L. .... Sarasota, FL
Dakan, William E. .... Wichita, KS
Dake, Amanda Christine .... Dallas, TX
Dake, James M. .... Fremont, NE
Dake, Jon C., (P.C.) .... Phoenix, AZ
Dake, Kenneth M. .... Sedalia, MO
Dake, Norman W. .... Santa Barbara, CA
Dake, Stephen M. .... Bakersfield, CA
Dake, T. Gale .... Phoenix, AZ
Dake, Terry A. .... Phoenix, AZ
Dakich, Roy .... Merrillville, IN
Dakich, Thomas P. .... Indianapolis, IN
Dakin, Andy .... Jackson, MS
Dakin & Benelli, P.C. .... Chester, VT
Dakin, Carol F. .... Cleveland, OH
Dakin, Christopher M. .... Salisbury, CT
Dakin, Deborah .... Treasury Department, Office of Thrift Supervision, GV
Dakin, Dorothy .... Boone, IA
Dakin, Herbert W. .... Woodstock, IL
Dakin, Karl J. .... Englewood, CO
Dakin, L. Jorn
Federal Energy Regulatory Commission, Office of the General Counsel, GV
Dakin LawTech, LLC .... Englewood, CO
Dakin, Lloyd E., Jr. .... Livermore, CA
Dakin, Melvin G. .... Baton Rouge, LA
Dakin, Michael Norman .... New York, NY
Dakin, Paul A. .... Lafayette, LA
Dakin, Robert F. .... Cleveland, OH
Dakin, William E., Jr. .... Chester, VT
Dakin, William G. .... Fairfax, VA
Dakin, William J. .... Vernon, CT
Dakin-Grimm, Linda .... Los Angeles, CA
Dakin-Mitchell, Barbara A. .... Frisco, TX
Dakis, John .... New York, NY
Dakis, Linda .... Miami, FL
Dakmak, George P. .... Detroit, MI
Dakoff, Alan .... New Port Richey, FL
Dakoff, Howard S. .... Chicago, IL
Dakolias, Maria M. .... Washington, DC
Dakopolos, Paul A. .... Salem, OR
Dakoyannis, Louis J. .... Norwood, MA
Daks, Jonathan B. .... Sherman Oaks, CA
Dalack, Basil E. .... Tequesta, FL
Dalager, Joe C. .... South St. Paul, MN
Dalager, Jon K. .... Georgetown, KY
Dalager, Robert .... Phoenix, AZ
Dalager, Robert V. .... Morris, MN
Dalaker, Lawrence .... Monroe, CT
Dalal, Ankur P. .... Baltimore, MD
Dalal, Kosha K. .... Baltimore, MD
Dalal, Mirut P. .... Dallas, TX
Dalal, Nitin .... Boston, MA
Dalal, Suresh H. .... Iselin, NJ
Dalan & Katz, P.L. .... Brooksville, FL
Clearwater, FL
New Port Richey, FL
St. Petersburg, FL
Tampa, FL
Dalan, Rick .... Clearwater, FL
Dalayanis, Antoni .... Akron, OH
D'Alba, Joel A. .... Chicago, IL
D'Albani, Thomas L. .... Bemidji, MN
Dalberg, Jon L. R. .... Los Angeles, CA
Dalberth, Elizabeth A. .... Haddonfield, NJ
Philadelphia, PA
Dalbey, Betty England .... Roswell, GA
Dalbey, Garry D. .... Mansfield, OH
Dalbey, John D. .... Atlanta, GA
Dalbey, William Blair .... La Quinta, CA
Dalby, Carol Canneddy .... Texarkana, TX
Dalby, Cheryl J. .... Minneapolis, MN
Dalby, David I. .... San Francisco, CA
Dalby, Docia L. .... Baton Rouge, LA
Dalby, Lena L. .... Sacramento, CA
Dalby, Linda S. .... Boston, MA
Dalby, Robert A. .... Hayward, CA
Dalby, Ronald E. .... Salt Lake City, UT
Dalby, Ronald K. .... Detroit, MI
Dalby, Stephen H. .... Libby, MT
Dalby, Virgil R. .... Sacramento, CA
Dalcanton, Carol L. .... Pittsburgh, PA
Dalcher, Bruce P.
Department of Transportation, U. S. Coast Guard, GV
Dal Cielo, Douglas W. .... San Jose, CA
D'Alcomo, Joanne .... Boston, MA
DalCortivo, Kathleen Meehan
Trenton, NJ
Dale, A. Ennis .... Phoenix, AZ
Dale, Alan S. .... Houston, TX
Dale, Alice L. .... Salem, OR
Dale, Angelyn L. .... Tulsa, OK
Dale, Anthony J.
Federal Communications Commission, Common Carrier Bureau, GV
Dale, Bald, Showalter & Mercier, P.A.
Jacksonville, FL
Dale, Barry J. .... Phoenix, AZ
Dale, Ben E. .... Sacramento, CA
Dale, Braden & Hinchcliffe, A Professional Law Corporation .... Los Angeles, CA
San Diego, CA
Ventura, CA
Walnut Creek, CA
Dale, Brian C. .... Everett, WA
Dale, Candace L. .... Minneapolis, MN
Dale, Candy Wagahoff .... Boise, ID

Dale, Charles A., III .... Boston, MA
Dale, Charles E. .... Levelland, TX
Dale, Charles S., Jr. .... Fort Lauderdale, FL
Dale, Charles S., P.A. .... Fort Lauderdale, FL
Dale, Charles V. .... Library of Congress, Congressional Research Service, GV
Dale, Colleen M. .... Jefferson City, MO
Dale, David C. .... Lakeland, FL
Dale, David C. .... Bluffton, IN
Dale, David S. .... Denver, CO
Dale, Dick B. .... Richmond, MO
Dale, Dinah M. .... Benton, AR
Dale, Don .... Guymon, OK
Dale, Douglas Don .... Guymon, OK
Dale, E. Lee .... Denver, CO
Dale, E. Randolph .... Westport, CT
Dale, Eben .... Honolulu, HI
Dale, Edward M. .... Willimantic, CT
Dale & Eke, Professional Corporation
Indianapolis, IN
Dale, Elizabeth .... Clemson, SC
Dale, Ellen Horowitz .... Fort Lee, NJ
Dale, Eric J. .... Norwalk, CT
New York, NY
Dale, Flynn & McBride .... St. Joseph, MO
Dale, Frank K. .... Columbia, TN
Dale, Frank M., Jr. .... Washington, DC
Dale, Frank Rodolf .... Ardmore, OK
Dale, G. Allen .... Washington, DC
Dale, George D. .... Los Angeles, CA
Las Vegas, NV
Dale, George F. .... Philadelphia, PA
Dale, Gillian .... Denver, CO
Dale, Gloria Ralph .... Nashville, TN
Dale, Gordon G. .... Santa Ana, CA
Dale & Gordon LLP .... Fort Lee, NJ
Dale, Gregory N. .... Indianapolis, IN
Dale, Harvey P. .... New York, NY
Dale, Howard L. .... Jacksonville, FL
Dale, Jacobs & Gensburg, P.C. .... Chicago, IL
Dale, Jacqueline .... San Francisco, CA
Dale, James C. .... Boise, ID
Dale, James C., III .... Nashville, TN
Dale, James Cary .... Houston, TX
Dale, James M. .... Rancho Santa Fe, CA
Dale, James Y. .... Greenwood, MS
Dale, Janice .... Albuquerque, NM
Dale, Jeffrey B. .... Ballwin, MO
Dale, Jerry M. .... Miami, FL
Dale, Jo Ann .... Louisville, KY
Dale, John B., Jr.
Department of the Navy, GV
Dale, John D., Jr. .... Taylorsville, KY
Dale, John J. .... Fort Worth, TX
Dale, John S. .... Hyannis, MA
Dale, John T., Jr. .... New Orleans, LA
Dale, Jordan .... New York, NY
Dale, Joseph G. .... Wenonah, NJ
Dale, Julie A. .... Burlington, VT
Dale, Kenneth P. .... Cincinnati, OH
Dale, Kenton L. .... Oak Harbor, WA
Dale, Kevin F. .... Nantucket, MA
Dale, Kimberlee J. .... Albany, NY
Dale & Klein, L.L.P. .... Brownsville, TX
McAllen, TX
Dale & Korolishin, P.C. .... Philadelphia, PA
Dale, Kristin W. .... Denver, CO
Dale, Lance C. .... Chicago, IL
Dale, Lawrence B. .... Dallas, TX
Dale, Lisa M. .... Irvine, CA
Dale, Lon J. .... Missoula, MT
Dale, Lorna Gene .... Bend, OR
Dale, Louise D. .... Sherman Oaks, CA
Dale, Margaret Antinori .... New York, NY
Dale, Mary M. .... Moline, IL
Dale, Mary Margaret .... Washington, DC
Dale, Michael J. .... Fort Lauderdale, FL
Dale & Mitchell .... Washington, DC
Dale, Mitchell W. .... Arlington, VA
Dale, Myron L. .... Cincinnati, OH
Dale, Nicholas D. .... Bethesda, MD
Dale, Peter J. .... Boston, MA
Dale, Randy E. .... Georgetown, TX
Dale, Rex A. .... Lenoir City, TN
Dale, Richard .... Sioux Falls, SD
Dale, Richard M. .... Chicago, IL
Dale, Richard R., Law Offices of
Mill Valley, CA
Dale, Robert J. .... Salt Lake City, UT
Dale, Robert M. .... Sacramento, CA
Dale, Rosenberg & Kleinfelter
Nashville, TN
Dale, Roy S., (P.C.) .... Brownsville, TX
McAllen, TX
Dale, Scott Douglas .... Poplar Bluff, MO
Dale, Sebe, Jr. .... Columbia, MS
Dale, Shana .... House of Representatives, Committee on Science, GV
Dale, Stanley I. .... St. Joseph, MO
Dale, Stephen A. .... Northglenn, CO
Dale, Suzanne .... Winston-Salem, NC
Dale, T. Gregory .... Medina, NY
Dale, Tara L .... Austin, TX
Dale, Ted J. .... Kansas City, MO
Dale, Thomas E. .... Dallas, TX
Dale, Thomas H. .... Orlando, FL
Dale, Thomas P. .... Reston, VA
Dale, Thomas W. .... Milwaukee, WI
Dale, Tobin E. .... Seattle, WA
Dale, Virginia R., (Mrs.) .... Columbus, NC
Dale, Wheeler .... Morganton, NC
Dale, William H. .... Portland, ME
Dale, William H., Jr. .... Columbia, TN
Dale, William J. .... Vista, CA
Dale, William J. .... Henryetta, OK
Dale, William J., Jr. .... Indianapolis, IN

Dale, William P. .... Washington, DC
Bowie, MD
Alexandria, VA
Dale, Woodard, Montgomery, Greenfield & Pemrick, A Professional Corporation
Franklin, PA
Dalebout, Richard S. .... Provo, UT
Dalebroux, Gary J. .... Casco, WI
Dalebroux, Jeffrey M. .... Chicago, IL
Dalebroux Law Office, S.C. .... Casco, WI
Dalehite, Henry G., Jr. .... Galveston, TX
Dalehite, William M., Jr. .... Jackson, MS
Daleiden, Christine M. .... Koror, TT
Daleiden, Norbert A.
Arlington Heights, IL
Daleiden & Tremaine, Ltd.
Arlington Heights, IL
Chicago, IL
d'Alelio, Ellen .... Washington, DC
D'Alemberte, Talbot "Sandy", (P.A.)
Tallahassee, FL
Dalen, Dennis E. .... Minneapolis, MN
Dalen, DuWayne J. .... Newton, IA
Dalen, Keith B. .... New York, NY
Dalena, Albert F. .... Madison, NJ
Dalena, Anne M. .... Newark, NJ
Dalena, Christine M. .... Hackettstown, NJ
Morristown, NJ
Trenton, NJ
Dalena, Dalena & DeStefano .... Madison, NJ
Dalena, Daniel T. .... Morristown, NJ
Dalena, Elizabeth A. .... Madison, NJ
Dalen-Bard, Kristin S. .... Milwaukee, WI
Dalenberg, David .... Warren, MI
Dalenberg, Heidi .... Chicago, IL
Dalenberg, Jack .... South Holland, IL
Dalenberg, Robert V. R. .... San Francisco, CA
Daleo, Robert C. .... Morristown, NJ
D'Aleo, Robert I. .... Garden City, NY
Daleo, Vito .... Melrose Park, IL
Dales, David G. .... Columbus, NE
Dales, Douglas S., Jr. .... Albany, NY
Dales, E. Scott .... Riverside, CA
Dales, Kathy .... Philadelphia, PA
Dales, Philip A., III .... Annapolis, MD
Dales, Ronald P. .... Sheboygan, WI
Dales, Scott W. .... New York, NY
Dalesandro, Anne V. .... Camden, NJ
Dalesandro, Jil .... San Jose, CA
D'Alesandro & Miliman, P.A.
Baltimore, MD
D'Alesandro, Nicholas M., Jr.
Salt Lake City, UT
D'Alesandro, Thomas J., III .... Baltimore, MD
D'Alesio, Joseph D. .... Bridgeport, CT
Dalesio, Stephen J. .... Pittsburgh, PA
Wheeling, WV
D'Alessandri, Richard J. .... New York, NY
D'Alessandro, A. Gregory
Basking Ridge, NJ
D'Alessandro, Alessandra M.
Philadelphia, PA
D'Alessandro, Anna M. .... Irvine, CA
D'Alessandro, Arthur G. .... Basking Ridge, NJ
D'Alessandro, Beth Anne .... Jersey City, NJ
D'Alessandro, Carmine G. .... Towson, MD
D'Alessandro, Carol G. .... Newark, NJ
D'Alessandro, Carolyn P. .... Bartow, FL
D'Alessandro, Christine C.
Washington, DC
D'Alessandro, Christopher Frank
Southfield, MI
D'Alessandro & D'Alessandro
Basking Ridge, NJ
D'Alessandro, Daniel A. .... Jersey City, NJ
D'Alessandro, Daniel A., P.C.
Jersey City, NJ
D'Alessandro, David .... Washington, DC
D'Alessandro, David C. .... Dallas, TX
D'Alessandro, Dianne .... Hackensack, NJ
D'Alessandro, Douglas M.
Basking Ridge, NJ
D'Alessandro, Edward G.
Florham Park, NJ
New York, NY
D'Alessandro, Edward G., Jr.
Florham Park, NJ
New York, NY
D'Alessandro, Frank D. .... Presque Isle, ME
D'Alessandro, Guido B. .... Marlborough, MA
D'Alessandro, Jacovino & Gerson
Florham Park, NJ
Morristown, NJ
New York, NY
D'Alessandro, James J. .... Boston, MA
D'Alessandro, James P. .... Fair Lawn, NJ
D'Alessandro, Jas. G. .... Detroit, MI
D'Alessandro, Jennifer A. .... Denver, CO
D'Alessandro, John J. .... Woburn, MA
D'Alessandro, John P. .... Bronx, NY
D'Alessandro, Joseph P. .... Fort Myers, FL
D'Alessandro, Kenneth .... San Jose, CA
D'Alessandro, Leonardo .... New York, NY
D'Alessandro, Mark T. .... Columbus, OH
Dalessandro, Marye Ann .... Vestavia Hills, AL
D'Alessandro, Michael .... Rahway, NJ
D'Alessandro, Michael A. .... Philadelphia, PA
D'Alessandro, Nicholas M. .... Philadelphia, PA
D'Alessandro, Nicholas M., Jr.
Philadelphia, PA
D'Alessandro, Paul David
Huntington Beach, CA
D'Alessandro, Peter A. .... Tulsa, OK
D'Alessandro, Ralph .... Valencia, CA
Wilsonville, OR
D'Alessandro, Richard V. .... Albany, NY
D'Alessandro, Richard V., Professional Corporation .... Albany, NY

D'Alessandro & Ritchie, A Professional Corporation .... San Jose, CA
D'Alessandro, Ronald, Jr. .... Albany, NY
Dalessandro, Sherry A. .... Wilkes-Barre, PA
D'Alessandro, William .... Amherst, NH
Dalessandro, William .... Garden City, NY
Dalessi, William T. .... Long Beach, CA
D'Alessio, Anthony P. .... Springfield, NJ
D'Alessio, C. Salvatore, Jr.
Department of Justice, Civil Division, GV
D'Alessio, Edward P. .... Fairfield, NJ
D'Alessio, Gary A. .... Chicago, IL
D'Alessio, Gerard V., Jr. .... Corpus Christi, TX
D'Alessio, James A. .... Columbia, SC
Dalessio, James J. .... San Diego, CA
d'Alessio, Jon W. .... Ross, CA
D'Alessio, Lauran S.
Whitehouse Station, NJ
D'Alessio, Lori S. .... Augusta, GA
D'Alessio, Michael, Jr. .... West Orange, NJ
Dalessio, Ralph J. .... Naples, FL
D'Alessio, Thomas .... Atlanta, GA
Daleure, Gus G., Jr. .... Louisville, KY
Daley, Annamarie A. .... Minneapolis, MN
Daley & Baldwin .... Hillsdale, NY
Daley, Balyeat, Balyeat & Leahy
Lima, OH
Daley, Bernard C. .... Cleveland, OH
Daley, Bernard F., Jr. .... Tallahassee, FL
Daley, Bryan Begley .... Lexington, KY
London, KY
Daley, Charles C., Jr. .... Haddonfield, NJ
Daley, Charles W. .... Lima, OH
Daley, Darrell M. .... Boulder, CO
Daley, Darren E. .... St. Louis, MO
Daley, David B. .... East Peoria, IL
Daley, Deborah D. .... Milwaukee, WI
Daley, Dennis R. .... Minneapolis, MN
Daley, Dennis W. .... Solana Beach, CA
Daley, Donald F. .... Syracuse, NY
Daley, Donald J. .... Falls Church, VA
Daley, Dorian E. .... Redwood City, CA
Daley, Douglas A. .... Lima, OH
Daley, E. Neal .... Norwalk, CA
Daley, Edmund P. .... Boston, MA
Daley, Elene M. .... Long Beach, CA
Daley, Erin M. .... Wichita, KS
Daley, Erisman & van Ogtrop
Newark, DE
Wilmington, DE
Daley, Frank J., Jr. .... Lincoln, NE
Daley, Frederick J. .... Chicago, IL
Daley, Frederick J., Ltd. .... Chicago, IL
Daley and George, Ltd. .... Chicago, IL
Daley, Gerard F. .... Los Angeles, CA
Daley, Gordon R. .... Medford, OR
Daley & Heft .... Solana Beach, CA
Daley, Henry J. .... Washington, DC
Daley, James Allen .... Alexandria, KY
Daley, James J. .... New York, NY
Daley, James P. .... Chicago, IL
Daley, James P. .... Chicago, IL
Daley, James P. .... Janesville, WI
Daley, James R. .... Inglewood, CA
Daley, James W. .... Orange, CA
Daley, Jennifer .... Miami, FL
Daley, Jennifer E. .... Fort Lauderdale, FL
Daley, John .... Pittsburgh, PA
Daley, John J. .... Boston, MA
Daley, John J., III .... Chicago, IL
Daley, John M. .... San Francisco, CA
Daley, John M. .... Pittsburgh, PA
Daley, John P. .... La Porte, IN
Daley, John T. .... Boston, MA
Daley, Joseph Charles .... New York, NY
Daley, Joseph D. .... San Diego, CA
Daley, Joseph F. .... Kalispell, MT
Daley, Judith Walsh .... Kingston, PA
Daley, Kathleen Alice .... Washington, DC
Daley, Kevin G. .... San Jose, CA
Daley, Kevin M. .... Warwick, RI
Daley, Kevin V. .... Boston, MA
Daley, Kevin W. .... Boulder, CO
Daley, Linda .... Denver, CO
Daley, Linda B. .... Menlo Park, CA
Daley, M. James .... Kansas City, MO
Daley, M. Teresa .... New York, NY
Daley, Marcia L. .... Universal City, CA
Daley, Margaret A. .... Chicago, IL
Daley, Marleigh White .... Menlo Park, CA
Daley, Maureen E. .... Philadelphia, PA
Daley, Michael .... Chicago, IL
Daley, Michael D. .... Omaha, NE
Daley, Michael E. .... Herkimer, NY
Daley, Michael F. .... Grand Forks, ND
Daley, Michael J. .... Oakland, CA
Daley, Michael J. .... Chicago, IL
Daley, Michael J., The Law Office of
McAllen, TX
Daley, Michelle L. .... New Haven, CT
Daley & Mohan, P.C. .... Chicago, IL
Daley, Pamela .... Fairfield, CT
Daley, Paul P. .... Boston, MA
Daley, Peter J., & Associates, P.C.
California, PA
Daley, Peter John, II .... California, PA
Daley, Richard C. .... Columbus, OH
Daley, Richard E., II
Christiansted, St. Croix, VI
Daley, Richard J. .... Chicago, IL
Daley, Richard M. .... Chicago, IL
Daley, Robert E. .... Newark, DE
Wilmington, DE
Daley, Robert E. .... New York, NY
Daley, Robert F. .... Pittsburgh, PA
Daley, Robert H. .... Westfield, NY
Daley, Rodger C. .... Denver, CO

Daley, Roger W. .... New Brunswick, NJ
Daley, Stephen C. .... Syracuse, NY
Daley, Stephen D. .... Glen Ellyn, IL
Daley, Susan J. .... Chicago, IL
Daley, Terrence J. .... Manchester, NH
Daley, Thomas A. .... Pittsburgh, PA
Daley, Thomas F. .... Gretna, LA
Daley, Thomas G. .... Albany, NY
Daley, Timothy A. .... Suffield, CT
Daley, Timothy B. .... Burlington, WI
Daley, Timothy J. .... San Diego, CA
Daley, Todd A. .... Los Angeles, CA
Daley, William D. .... Chula Vista, CA
Daley, William E. .... Fort Wayne, IN
Daley, William J., Jr. .... Boston, MA
Daley, William P. .... Oakland, CA
Daley, William P. .... San Diego, CA
Daley-Duncan, Yasmin M. .... Brooklyn, NY
Daley-Watson, Christopher J. .... Seattle, WA
Dalfen, Sahra .... New York, NY
Dalferes, William V., Jr., (P.C.)
New Orleans, LA
D'Alfonso, Gina M. .... Harrisburg, PA
Dalfonso, Lisa M. .... Hartford, CT
D'Alfonso, Margaret M.S.
North Kingstown, RI
D'Alfonso, Mario J. .... Haddon Heights, NJ
D'Alfonso, Mario J., A Professional Corporation .... Haddon Heights, NJ
D'Alfonso, Wendy .... Rochester, NY
Dal Gallo, Lisa J. .... San Francisco, CA
Dalgetty, J. William .... Fairfax, VA
Dalgleish, Douglas R. .... Kansas City, MO
Dalglish, Leslie E. B. .... Minneapolis, MN
Dalglish, Lucy A. .... Minneapolis, MN
Dalglish, Thomas K. .... Seattle, WA
Dalgoutté, Christopher N.
New Windsor, NY
Dalheim, Karen L.
Office Of Special Counsel, GV
Dalheim, Theodore J. .... Concord, OH
Dalheim, Theodore J., Jr. .... Concord, OH
Dalhuisen, Albert J. .... Sunnyvale, CA
Daliana, Michela .... New York, NY
Dalianis, Linda Stewart .... Nashua, NH
Dalickas, Gail A. .... Philadelphia, PA
Dalier, John D. .... Department of Commerce, Patent and Trademark Office, GV
Daliere, Mark W. .... Phoenix, AZ
Dalimonte, Alphonse B. .... Moran, MI
Dalimonte, Anthony W. .... Dearborn, MI
D'Alimonte, Christa A. .... New York, NY
Dalimonte, John A. .... Boston, MA
D'Alimonte, John S. .... New York, NY
Dalin, Andrew .... New York, NY
Dalinka, Alan S. .... Chicago, IL
Dalins, Andrew .... Huntsville, AL
Dalious, Jack A. .... Midland, TX
Dalis, John S. .... Augusta, GA
Dalke, David P. .... Costa Mesa, CA
Dalke, Dean .... Beatrice, NE
Dalke, Jeffrey A. .... Philadelphia, PA
Dalke, Smith, Harris & Nelson
Beatrice, NE
Dalke, Terry J. .... Tucson, AZ
Dalki, Christopher J. .... Chicago, IL
Dall, Anne .... Portland, OR
Dall, Benjamin V. .... Syracuse, NY
Dall, James Monte .... Houston, TX
Dall, Mark E. .... Indianapolis, IN
Dall, Terrance S. .... Orange, CA
DallaGrana, Walter .... Florence, WI
Dallaire, Chloe E. .... Atlanta, GA
Dallaire, Gregory R. .... Seattle, WA
Dallam, Roger I. .... Gretna, LA
Dallara, Mark J. .... New York, NY
Dallarda, Carl .... Princeton, NJ
Philadelphia, PA
Dallarda, Pedro C. .... Riverside, CA
Dallas, Albert H. (Buddy) .... Thomson, GA
Dallas, Bert .... Houston, TX
Dallas, Bobby L. .... Jackson, MS
Dallas, Bruce K. .... New York, NY
Dallas, Carla Foreman .... Louisville, KY
Dallas, Christopher S. .... Irvine, CA
Dallas, Dana E. .... Richmond, VA
Dallas, David L., Jr. .... Richmond, VA
Dallas, Evridiki (Vicki) .... Costa Mesa, CA
Dallas, George M. .... Boston, MA
Dallas, H. Richard .... New York, NY
Dallas, James R. .... El Paso, TX
Dallas, Lynne L. .... San Diego, CA
Dallas, Michael C. .... Grand Rapids, MI
Dallas, Nickolas .... Skokie, IL
Dallas, Nickolas, P.C. .... Skokie, IL
Dallas, Robert F. .... Atlanta, GA
Dallas, Ronald K. .... Fort Lauderdale, FL
Dallas, Stephen K., (P.S.C.) .... Florence, KY
Dallas, Steven .... Roselle, IL
Dallas, T. Walton .... Jackson, MS
Dallas, Traci A. .... Beverly Hills, CA
Dallas, Wanda .... Atlanta, GA
Dallas, William D. .... Chicago, IL
Dallas, William M., III .... Griffin, GA
Dallas, William M., Jr. .... New York, NY
Dallas, William R., Jr. .... Louisville, KY
Dalla Santa, Cassie .... Chicago, IL
Dalla Valle, Mark A. .... San Francisco, CA
Dalldorf, Cathleen A. .... Walnut Creek, CA
Dalle Mura, Steven L. .... Richmond, VA
Dallenbach, Anich & Haukaas, S.C.
Ashland, WI
Dallenbach, Keith W. .... Ashland, WI
Dalle Pazze, James P. .... Wilmington, DE
Daller Greenberg & Dietrich, LLP
Haddon Heights, NJ
Fort Washington, PA
Philadelphia, PA

Daller, Morton F. .... Fort Washington, PA
Dallet, Bradley I. .... Milwaukee, WI
Dallett, Estelina L. .... Washington, DC
Dallett, Matthew C. .... Boston, MA
D'Alleva, Dominick .... Astoria, NY
D'Alleva, Jacqueline Ermalinda
Boston, MA
D'Alleva, Karla J. .... Marlborough, MA
Dalley, George A. .... Washington, DC
Dalley, Jason Steven .... West Palm Beach, FL
Dalley, John A. .... New York, NY
Dalley, Karla A. .... Hartford, CT
Dalley, Paula J. .... Oklahoma City, OK
Dallimore, Suzanne M. .... Phoenix, AZ
Dalling & Dalling .... Idaho Falls, ID
Dalling, Dean, (Chartered) .... Idaho Falls, ID
Dalling, William R., (Chartered)
Idaho Falls, ID
Dallinger, Timothy G. .... Sherman Oaks, CA
Dallis, Barbara D. .... Newton, MA
Dallis Law Firm, P.A. .... Charleston, SC
Columbia, SC
Mount Pleasant, SC
Dallis, W. Alex, Jr. .... Charleston, SC
Columbia, SC
Dallison, Julie McDaniel .... Houston, TX
Dallman, Robert E. .... Milwaukee, WI
Dallmann, Peggy D. .... Indianapolis, IN
Dallmeyer, Ford R. .... Stamford, CT
Dallmeyer, Michael A. .... Jefferson City, MO
Dallmeyer, Suzanne Beman .... Northfield, IL
Dallner, Daniel K. .... Joliet, IL
Dallob, Naomi C. .... Cincinnati, OH
Dallosto, Philip S. .... Glenview, IL
Dall'Osto, Raymond M. .... Milwaukee, WI
Dallow, Howard S. .... Middletown, NY
Dalluge, Bruce .... Tecumseh, NE
D'Allura, Noelle D. .... Columbus, OH
Dall Vechia, John T. .... Kingston, NY
Dally, Carl E. F. .... Austin, TX
Dally, Craig A. .... Nazareth, PA
Dally, Dally & Wilson LLP .... Redlands, CA
Dally, Henry E. .... Palm Springs, CA
Dally, Michael Jay .... Appleton, WI
Dally, Rebecca Polston .... Social Circle, GA
Dally, Rebecca Polston, P.C.
Social Circle, GA
Dally, Richard L. .... Denver, CO
Dally, Richard L., P.C. .... Denver, CO
Dally, Robert L. .... Redlands, CA
Dally, Robert L., Jr. .... Redlands, CA
Dallyn, Selwyn L. .... Tempe, AZ
Dalm & Dalm, P.L.C. .... Kalamazoo, MI
Dalm, Jacob A., Jr. .... Kalamazoo, MI
Dalm, William W. .... Kalamazoo, MI
Dalman, Holly L. .... Chicago, IL
Dalman, Ronald L. .... Holland, MI
Dalmas, Victoria A. .... Syracuse, NY
Dalmaso, Nicholas .... Oakbrook Terrace, IL
Dalmaso, Roseann .... Oak Brook, IL
Dalmass, Kelly R. .... Westmont, NJ
Dalmau, Frank .... San Juan, PR
Dalmau, Gayl C. .... Freedom, CA
Dalmazio, Christine R .... Brooklyn, NY
Dalmbert, Robert L. .... Columbus, IN
D'Almeida, Arthur B. .... Boca Raton, FL
D'Almeida, Arthur B., P.A.
Boca Raton, FL
Dalmore, Jean A. .... Los Angeles, CA
Dalmut, Pete M. .... Department of Commerce, Office of the General Counsel, GV
Dalmy, Adam M. .... Denver, CO
Dalmy, Diane D. .... Denver, CO
Dalnekoff, Barry J. .... Annapolis, MD
Dalnekoff & Mason, P.A. .... Annapolis, MD
Glen Burnie, MD
D'Aloia, David J. .... Newark, NJ
D'Aloise, Lawrence T., Jr.
White Plains, NY
D'Aloise, Scott Lawrence .... New York, NY
Daloisio, James J. .... Camden, NJ
D'Alonzo, Jane R. .... Philadelphia, PA
Dalonzo, Joseph Raymond
Port Washington, NY
D'Alonzo, Thomas W.
Research Triangle Park, NC
Dalonzo-Baker, Sarah .... Raleigh, NC
Dal Piaz, Christopher C. .... New York, NY
Dalpiaz, Leslae Jane .... Missoula, MT
Dal Poggetto, Newton .... Sonoma, CA
Dal Ponte, Don A. .... Zanesville, OH
Dal Porto, Steven David .... Oakland, CA
Dal Pos, Leila .... Concord, NH
Dal Pra, Merrilee A. Parr .... Coeur d'Alene, ID
Dalrymple, Brian C. .... San Francisco, CA
Dalrymple, Bruce L. .... Saginaw, MI
Dalrymple, C. Robert .... Frederick, MD
Silver Spring, MD
Dalrymple, Charles G. .... Silver Spring, MD
Dalrymple, Christopher K. .... New York, NY
Dalrymple, Clovia Jennalyn
West Columbia, SC
Dalrymple, Dwight A. .... Tulsa, OK
Dalrymple, Elizabeth H. .... Bartlesville, OK
Dalrymple, Gail .... San Antonio, TX
Dalrymple, J. Jeffrey .... Fort Myers, FL
Dalrymple & Jacobs, P.A. .... Fort Myers, FL
Dalrymple, James D. .... Gaithersburg, MD
Dalrymple, James D., P.C.
Gaithersburg, MD
Dalrymple, James F. .... Traverse City, MI
Dalrymple, Jeffrey G. .... Matthews, NC
Dalrymple, JoAnn .... Austin, TX
Dalrymple, John E. .... White Plains, NY
Dalrymple, Joseph T. .... Alexandria, LA
Dalrymple, Kenda B. .... Austin, TX
Dalrymple, Noelle M. .... Laredo, TX
Dalrymple, Rich .... Redding, CA

Dalrymple, Robert K. .... Indianapolis, IN
Dalrymple, Ronald D. .... Los Angeles, CA
Dalrymple, Shelly L. .... Tulsa, OK
Dalrymple, Stevan B. .... Pine Bluff, AR
Dalrymple, Thomas L. .... Toledo, OH
Dal Santo, Diane .... Albuquerque, NM
Dal Santo, James S. .... Highland, IN
Dalsemer, Lawrence H. .... Philadelphia, PA
Dalsey, Ferrara, Townsend & Albano
Springfield, MA
Dalsey, John F. .... Springfield, MA
Dalsimer, Dennis V. .... Crestline, CA
Dalsimer, Vincent S. .... Long Beach, CA
Dalsimer, William R. .... New York, NY
Dal Soglio, Robin D. .... Los Angeles, CA
Dalsted, G. Leonard .... Bismarck, ND
Dalsted, Kenneth L. .... Jamestown, ND
Daltan, Gerald F. .... Fredericksburg, VA
Daltan, Joseph E. .... Lincoln, NE
Dalthorp, David C. .... Helena, MT
Dalthorp, George C. .... Billings, MT
Daltner, Diane .... New York, NY
Dalto, Angelo H. .... Edison, NJ
Dalto, Livio C. .... Palisades, NY
Dalton, A. Todd .... Biloxi, MS
Dalton, Albert B. .... Boston, MA
Dalton, Amy Gottlieb .... Fall River, MA
Dalton, Andrew J. .... Albany, NY
Dalton, Andrew T., Jr. .... Tulsa, OK
Dalton, Barbara A. .... Mineola, NY
New York, NY
White Plains, NY
Dalton, Barbara E. .... Los Angeles, CA
Dalton & Baron .... Andover, MA
Dalton, Bartholomew J. .... Wilmington, DE
Dalton, Bartholomew P. .... Los Angeles, CA
Dalton & Bicknell .... Eureka, CA
Dalton, Carol Ann, Law Office
Washington, DC
Dalton, Charlene Wilkinson .... Glen Ridge, NJ
Dalton, Charles D. .... Bridgewater, NJ
Dalton, Charles F., Jr. .... Andover, MA
Dalton, Charles R., Jr. .... Norfolk, VA
Dalton, Christopher S. .... Boston, MA
Dalton, Clare .... Boston, MA
Dalton, Craig G., Jr. .... Raleigh, NC
Dalton, Cynthia L. .... Agoura Hills, CA
Dalton, D. Michael .... Houston, TX
Dalton, D. Patrick .... Ocala, FL
Dalton, Daniel E. .... Tewksbury, MA
Dalton, Daniel J. .... Whitehouse Station, NJ
Dalton, Daniel P. .... Farmington Hills, MI
Dalton, Daniel T. .... St. Louis, MO
Dalton, David A. .... St. Charles, MO
Dalton, David L. .... Bowling Green, KY
Dalton, David M. .... Miamisburg, OH
Dalton, Debra L. .... Atlanta, GA
Dalton, Debra L. .... Des Moines, IA
Dalton, Debra Lee .... Norcross, GA
Dalton, Dewey M., (P.C.) .... Dallas, TX
Dalton, Donald E. .... St. Charles, MO
Dalton, Donald L. .... San Diego, CA
Salt Lake City, UT
Dalton, Douglas .... Los Angeles, CA
Dalton, Edward C., Jr. .... Cape Elizabeth, ME
Dalton, Elizabeth A. .... Provo, UT
Dalton, Ellen Douglass .... Alexandria, VA
Dalton, Frances Estabrook
Philadelphia, PA
Dalton, G. Bradley .... Seattle, WA
Dalton, Gary F. .... Dover, DE
Dalton, George E. .... San Diego, CA
Salt Lake City, UT
Dalton, George E. .... Charlotte, NC
Dalton, Gerald B. .... Monterey, CA
Dalton, Glenn L. .... St. Louis, MO
Dalton Gotto Samson & Kilgard, P.L.C.
Phoenix, AZ
Dalton, Gregory J. .... Houston, TX
Dalton, Gregory L. .... Buffalo, NY
Dalton, Harlon L. .... New Haven, CT
Dalton, Harriett Brown .... Philadelphia, PA
Dalton, Henry .... Oklahoma City, OK
Dalton, J. Michael .... Louisville, KY
Dalton, Jack E. .... Dodge City, KS
Dalton, James C. .... Doylestown, PA
Dalton, James F. .... Wilsonville, OR
D'Alton, James F., Jr. .... Petersburg, VA
Dalton, James L. .... East Lansing, MI
Dalton, James P. .... Jefferson City, MO
Dalton, James P., P.C. .... Jefferson City, MO
Dalton, Jane Leslie .... Philadelphia, PA
Dalton, Jennifer Rose .... Florham Park, NJ
Dalton, John D. .... Chicago, IL
Dalton, John Hall .... Kennett, MO
Dalton, John Hall, Jr. .... Kennett, MO
Dalton, John J. .... New York, NY
Dalton, John J. .... Rhinebeck, NY
Dalton, John J., Jr. .... Cedar Grove, NJ
Dalton, John J., P.C. .... Atlanta, GA
Dalton, John M. .... Eureka, CA
Dalton, John N., Jr. .... Radford, VA
Dalton, John R., Jr. .... Washington, DC
Dalton, John T. .... Seattle, WA
Dalton, Jonathan F. .... Jefferson City, MO
St. Louis, MO
Dalton, Joseph F. .... Lynnfield, MA
Dalton, Joseph M. .... Nashville, TN
Dalton, Joshua M. .... Boston, MA
Dalton, Karen L. .... Houston, TX
Dalton & Kelley, PPLC .... San Diego, CA
Salt Lake City, UT
Dalton, Kenneth M. .... New York, NY
Dalton, Kevin Joseph .... Glen Burnie, MD
Dalton, Kevin M. .... Beverly, MA
Dalton, Larry R. .... Milwaukee, WI
Dalton, Lawrence X. .... Morristown, NY
Dalton, Lawrence X., Jr. .... Rochester, NY

Dalton, LeRoy L. ..... Madison, WI
Dalton, Lori L. ..... Dallas, TX
Dalton, M. Anne ..... Fort Myers, FL
Dalton, Margaret A. ..... San Diego, CA
Dalton, Mark J. ..... Dover, MA
Dalton, Marsha ..... Huntington, WV
Dalton, Mary Colleen ..... McLean, VA
Dalton, Mary Lynne ..... Mandeville, LA
Dalton, Maryanne G. ..... Oxnard, CA
Dalton, Mary-Margaret ..... Cheshire, CT
Dalton, Matthew J. ..... Long Beach, CA
Dalton, Matthew R. ..... Denver, CO
Dalton, Michael A. ..... Atlanta, GA
Dalton, Michael J. ..... Oakland, CA
Dalton, Michael J. ..... Dallas, TX
Dalton, Moira M. ..... Billings, MT
Dalton & Moore, P.C. ..... Radford, VA
Dalton, Neil C. ..... Winston-Salem, NC
Dalton, Patrick J. ..... Rochester, NY
Dalton, Patrick J. ..... Spokane, WA
Dalton, Phillip S. ..... Los Angeles, CA
Dalton, R. Douglas ..... Phoenix, AZ
Dalton, R. Toms, Jr. ..... Waynesboro, VA
Dalton, Randall S. ..... Phoenix, AZ
Dalton, Raymond F., Jr. ..... Elgin, IL
Dalton, Richard A. ..... Mashpee, MA
Dalton, Richard C. ..... Broussard, LA
Dalton, Richard J. ..... Gridley, IL
Dalton, Robert B. ..... Hartford, CT
Dalton, Robert C. ..... Stockton, CA
Dalton, Robert E. ..... Department of State,
Office of the Legal Adviser, GV
Dalton, Robert J. ..... Department of Labor,
Office of Secretary, GV
Dalton, Roger ..... Blacksburg, VA
Dalton, Roy B., Jr. ..... Orlando, FL
Dalton, Samuel Poage ..... Dallas, TX
Dalton, Scott M. ..... Department of the Army,
Office, Chief of Engineers/Headquarters,
U.S. Army Corps of Engineers, GV
Dalton, Sean F. ..... Glassboro, NJ
Dalton, Shannah Smoller ..... Ardsley, NY
Dalton, Stephen E. ..... Fort Myers, FL
Dalton, Stephen L., & Associates
Richmond, VA
Dalton, Steven M. ..... Middletown, NJ
Dalton, Susan T. ..... Andover, MA
Dalton, Terry J., Jr. ..... Beaumont, TX
D'Alton, Theresa Benedict ..... Kent, CT
Dalton, Thomas P. ..... Beaumont, TX
Dalton, T. M., Jr. ..... Dallas, TX
Dalton, Tony C. ..... Brevard, NC
Dalton, Tony R. ..... Knoxville, TN
Dalton, Tracy J. ..... Los Angeles, CA
Dalton, Treasure & Mowrer
Caruthersville, MO
Kennett, MO
Dalton, Virginia Moses ..... Denver, CO
Dalton, Walter B. ..... Norfolk, VA
Dalton, Walter H. ..... Rutherfordton, NC
Dalton, Warren K. ..... Lincoln, NE
D'Alton, William A. ..... Billings, MT
Dalton, William Andrew ..... Atlanta, GA
Dalton, William A. R. ..... Springfield, MO
Dalton, William H. ..... Department of Defense,
Office of the General Counsel, GV
Dalton, William J. ..... Boston, MA
Dalton, William M., II ..... Warsaw, IN
Dalton, Wm. L. ..... Moline, IL
Daluga, William G., Jr. ..... Chicago, IL
Daluvoy, Sunil
Federal Communications Commission,
Cable Services Bureau, GV
da Luz, Therese I. ..... San Francisco, CA
Daluz, Tobey M. ..... Philadelphia, PA
Dalva, Morris ..... Pacific Palisades, CA
Dalvano, Barbara Ann
Colorado Springs, CO
D'Alvia, Patricia ..... New York, NY
Daly, Adam K. ..... Exeter, NH
Daly, Adam K. ..... Exeter, NH
Daly, Ann Marie ..... Doylestown, PA
Daly, Anna ..... Charlotte, NC
Daly, Anne M. ..... Seattle, WA
Daly, Astrid M. Stevens ..... Manchester, NH
Daly, Barbara H. ..... New York, NY
Daly, Barbara M. ..... Philadelphia, PA
Daly, Barrett B. ..... New Orleans, LA
Biloxi, MS
Daly, Beatrice S. ..... Timonium, MD
Daly, Bernard J. ..... Commack, NY
Daly, Bohling & O'Connor ..... Eagan, MN
Daly, Brenda J. ..... San Diego, CA
Daly, Brian ..... Montvale, NJ
Daly, Bryan D. ..... Los Angeles, CA
Daly, C. Brian ..... Union, NJ
Daly, C D, Law Corporation ..... Irvine, CA
Daly, Carol M. ..... Yonkers, NY
Daly, Catherine S. ..... San Francisco, CA
Daly, Charles Dion ..... Irvine, CA
Daly, Charles J. ..... Philadelphia, PA
Daly, Charles W. ..... Schenectady, NY
Daly, Christine C. ..... Lake Wales, FL
Daly, Christine McCue ..... New Orleans, LA
Daly, Christopher J. ..... Missoula, MT
Daly, Christopher Kevin
Glenwood Springs, CO
Daly, Christopher P. ..... Uniondale, NY
Daly, Christopher W. T. ..... Covington, GA
Norcross, GA
Daly, Colin Michael ..... Nashville, TN
Daly, Colleen M. ..... Boston, MA
Daly, Cornelius ..... Harrisburg, PA
Daly, Cornelius F., Jr. ..... Boston, MA
Daly, Craig A. ..... Detroit, MI
Daly & Daly ..... Salem, MA
Daly & Daly, P.A. ..... Charlotte, NC
Daly, Daniel Emerson ..... Fairfax, VA
Daly, Daniel F. ..... Tampa, FL
Daly, Daniel W., III ..... Houston, TX
Daly, David J. ..... Boston, MA
Daly, David J. ..... Newport News, VA
Daly, David M. ..... Winchester, IN
Daly, David M. ..... New York, NY
Daly, David S. ..... New Orleans, LA
Daly, David T. ..... Auburn Hills, MI
Daly, Deborah Anne ..... Raleigh, NC
Daly, Deirdre M. ..... Southport, CT
New York, NY
Daly, Denis G. ..... Dayton, OH
Daly, Dennis ..... Atlantic City, NJ
Daly, Dennis P. ..... Gurnee, IL
Daly, Diane M. ..... Santa Monica, CA
Daly, Donald J. ..... Port Jefferson, NY
Daly, Donald W. ..... Council Bluffs, IA
Daly, Dorothy T. ..... Philadelphia, PA
Daly, Edward J., Jr. ..... Hartford, CT
Daly, Elena L. ..... New York, NY
Daly, Elizabeth ..... Oak Brook, IL
Daly, Elizabeth A. ..... Boston, MA
Daly, Elizabeth A. ..... Livingston, NJ
Daly, Ellen ..... Treasury Department,
U.S. Customs Service, GV
Daly, Eric A. ..... Las Vegas, NV
Daly, Erin ..... Wilmington, DE
Daly, Eugene C. ..... Milwaukee, WI
Daly, Eugene J. ..... New York, NY
Daly, Eugene M. ..... Chicago, IL
Daly, Frank P., Jr. ..... New York, NY
Daly, Frank W. ..... Media, PA
Daly, Gene B. ..... Helena, MT
Daly, George ..... Charlotte, NC
Daly, George F. ..... Winchester, IN
Daly, George R. ..... New York, NY
Daly, Gerald J. ..... Danbury, CT
Daly, Hugh F. "Trey" ..... Cincinnati, OH
Daly, J. Frank ..... Westmont, IL
Daly, J. Joseph ..... St. Joseph, MI
Daly, J. Kevin ..... Albany, NY
Daly, J. Michael, Jr. ..... Metairie, LA
Daly, J. Spencer ..... Vero Beach, FL
Daly, Jack F. ..... Minneapolis, MN
Daly, James C. ..... Freeport, NY
Daly, James F. ..... Chicago, IL
Daly, James F. ..... Milwaukee, WI
Daly, James J. ..... Northfield, IL
Daly, James J., Jr. ..... Warner Robins, GA
Daly, James J., Jr. ..... Southampton, PA
Daly, James L. ..... Hopewell Junction, NY
Daly, James R. ..... Chicago, IL
Daly, James S. ..... Schenectady, NY
Daly, James T. ..... Baton Rouge, LA
Daly, James W. ..... Adrian, MI
Daly, James W., IV ..... Philadelphia, PA
Daly, Jeffrey N. ..... Novato, CA
Daly, Jeffrey W. ..... Seattle, WA
Daly, Joan Devlin ..... Media, PA
Daly, John ..... Marion, IL
Daly, John A. ..... Los Angeles, CA
Daly, John A. ..... Washington, DC
Daly, John A. ..... Bradford, MA
Daly, John E. ..... New York, NY
Daly, John F. ..... Federal Trade Commission,
Office of the General Counsel, GV
Daly, John G. ..... Medfield, MA
Daly, John J. ..... Hartford, CT
Daly, John J.
Department of Housing and Urban
Development,
Office of General Counsel, GV
Daly, John J. ..... Philadelphia, PA
Daly, John J. ..... Vienna, VA
Daly, John K. ..... Chicago, IL
Daly, John Kieran ..... New York, NY
Daly, John L. ..... Boston, MA
Daly, John L., Jr. ..... Framingham, MA
Daly, John Louis ..... Taylor, MI
Daly, John M. ..... Gillette, WY
Daly, John P. ..... Orlando, FL
Daly, John P. ..... Louisville, KY
Daly, John P., Jr. ..... Indianapolis, IN
Daly, John Paul ..... San Luis Obispo, CA
Daly, John R. ..... Staten Island, NY
Daly, John V. ..... Hampton, NH
Daly, Jordan Z. ..... Newport News, VA
Daly, Joseph A. ..... Collingswood, NJ
Philadelphia, PA
Daly, Joseph C., Jr. ..... Imperial, CA
Daly, Joseph F. ..... Lauderdale-By-The-Sea, FL
Daly, Joseph G. ..... Austin, TX
Daly, Joseph K. ..... Albuquerque, NM
Daly, Joseph P. ..... Washington, DC
Daly, Joseph P. ..... Chicago, IL
Daly, Joseph S. ..... Omaha, NE
Daly, Joseph T. ..... Secaucus, NJ
Daly, Julian ..... Weston, MA
Daly, Karen Siobhan ..... San Francisco, CA
Daly, Katharine A. ..... Concord, NH
Daly, Kathleen O. ..... Costa Mesa, CA
Daly, Kehoe & Crosson, L.L.P. ..... Boston, MA
Daly, Kelly A. ..... Washington, DC
Daly, Kenna Irene ..... Hartford, CT
Daly, Kenneth ..... Traverse City, MI
Daly, Kenneth Collins ..... Brewster, NY
Daly, Kenneth E. ..... Delray Beach, FL
Daly, Kenneth J., P.C. ..... Traverse City, MI
Daly, Kevin ..... Gainesville, FL
Daly, Kevin J. ..... Jackson, MI
Daly, Kevin J. ..... Cranford, NJ
Daly, Kevin J., Jr. ..... Waterbury, CT
Daly, Kevin J., P.C. ..... Cranford, NJ
Daly, Kevin Laurence ..... Denver, CO
Daly, Kevin R. ..... Cheshire, CT
Daly, Kevin T. ..... Salem, MA
Daly, Laura L. ..... Minneapolis, MN
Daly Lavery & Hall ..... Ossining, NY
White Plains, NY
Daly Law Associates, P.C. ..... Gillette, WY
Daly Law Offices, The, LLC
Manchester, NH
Daly, Lawrence F. ..... Missoula, MT
Daly, Leo Gerard ..... Pittsburgh, PA
Daly, Leo M. ..... Minneapolis, MN
Daly, Linda R. ..... New York, NY
Daly, Lisa Colleen ..... Sacramento, CA
Daly, Lisa M. ..... House of Representatives,
Office of Legislative Counsel, GV
Daly, Lisa S. ..... Newark, NJ
Daly, M. Cecilia ..... Burlington, VT
Daly and MacFie ..... Tacoma, WA
Daly, Margaret Anne ..... Minneapolis, MN
Daly, Mark F. ..... Boston, MA
Daly, Mark J. ..... Omaha, NE
Daly, Martha A. ..... Santa Fe, NM
Daly, Martin J. ..... Utica, NY
Daly, Mary C. ..... New York, NY
Daly, Mary C. ..... New York, NY
Daly, Mary M. ..... Baton Rouge, LA
Daly, Matthew T. ..... Burlington, VT
Daly, Micaela M. ..... Chicago, IL
Daly, Michael C. ..... Bristol, CT
Daly, Michael J. ..... Gardiner, ME
Daly, Michael M. ..... San Diego, CA
Daly, Michael P. ..... Syracuse, NY
Daly, M. J., III ..... Waterbury, CT
Daly, Noreen M. ..... Markham, IL
Daly, O'Brien & Bongaardt, P.C. ..... Media, PA
Daly, Patricia A. ..... Fort Wayne, IN
Daly, Patrick E. ..... Wayne, NJ
Daly, Patrick F. ..... Palos Heights, IL
Daly, Patrick J. ..... Cambridge, MA
Daly, Patrick K. ..... Tacoma, WA
Daly, Paul ..... Springfield, NJ
Daly, Paul N. ..... Princeton, NJ
Daly & Pitts ..... Syracuse, NY
Daly, R. Lawrence ..... Evansville, IN
Daly, Reona J. ..... Carbondale, IL
Daly, Richard D. ..... Houston, TX
Daly, Richard E. ..... Salem, MA
Daly, Richard F. ..... Amherst, NY
Daly, Richard G. ..... Eureka, CA
Daly, Richard, Inc. ..... Eureka, CA
Daly, Richard J. ..... Detroit, MI
Daly, Richard L. ..... St. Louis, MO
Daly, Richard M. ..... Treasury Department,
Internal Revenue Service, GV
Daly, Richard P. ..... Denver, CO
Daly, Richard P., P.C. ..... Denver, CO
Daly, Robert C. ..... Torrance, CA
Daly, Robert C., Jr. ..... Oconomowoc, WI
Daly, Robert E. ..... Eagan, MN
Daly, Robert J. ..... Philadelphia, PA
Daly, Robert John ..... Ann Arbor, MI
Daly, Robert P. ..... Darien, CT
Daly, Robert P. ..... Long Island City, NY
Daly, Robert V., Jr. ..... Minneapolis, MN
Daly, Roger A. ..... Hackensack, NJ
Daly, Roswald B., Jr. ..... Ahoskie, NC
Rocky Mount, NC
Daly, Russell F. ..... Media, PA
Daly, Sean ..... Daytona Beach, FL
Daly, Seaton M. ..... Spokane, WA
Daly, Stephen C. ..... Manhattan Beach, CA
Daly, Stephen R. ..... St. Paul, MN
Daly, Susan Lee ..... San Diego, CA
Daly, Susan M. ..... Boca Raton, FL
Daly, Sybil J. ..... Santa Barbara, CA
Daly, Tad T. ..... Gillette, WY
Daly, Taylor Tapley ..... Atlanta, GA
Daly, Thomas ..... Mineola, NY
Daly, Thomas D. ..... Redwood City, CA
Daly, Thomas F. ..... Newark, NJ
Daly, Thomas Francis ..... Hawthorne, CA
Daly, Thomas J. ..... Pasadena, CA
Daly, Thomas J. ..... North Haven, CT
Daly, Thomas J. ..... Kansas City, MO
Daly, Thomas P., Jr. ..... Bakersfield, CA
Daly, Thomas R. ..... Washington, DC
Daly, Timothy J. ..... Boston, MA
Daly, Timothy Joseph ..... Huntington, NY
Daly, Vincent ..... Treasury Department,
Internal Revenue Service, GV
Daly, W. Edward, Jr. ..... Houston, TX
Daly, Warren B., Jr.
Steamboat Springs, CO
Daly, Weihing & Bochanis
Bridgeport, CT
Daly, William J. ..... Ossining, NY
Daly, William L., III ..... New York, NY
Daly, William L., Sr. ..... Phoenix, MD
Daly, William P., Jr. ..... Vienna, VA
Daly, William T. ..... Dayton, OH
Daly-Rivera, Victor G. ..... Bronx, NY
Dalzell, Earl W. ..... Kalamazoo, MI
Dalzell, Elizabeth M. ..... Washington, DC
Dalzell, Sally Mozley
Environmental Protection Agency,
Office of Enforcement and Compliance
Assurance, GV
Dalzell, Stewart ..... Philadelphia, PA
Dalzell, William A. ..... West Trenton, NJ
Dalzell-Finger, Heidi ..... Department of Labor,
Office of the Solicitor, GV
Dalziel, Charles M., Jr. ..... Atlanta, GA
Dalziel, Charles M., Sr. ..... Savannah, GA
Dam, Kenneth W. ..... Chicago, IL
Dam, Lawrence W. ..... Los Angeles, CA
Dama, Marty J. ..... Dallas, TX
Damadeo, Maria ..... Lynbrook, NY
Damalouji, Robert I. ..... Washington, DC
Daman, Douglas F. ..... Irving, TX
Daman, Willem A. ..... Treasury Department,
U.S. Customs Service, GV
D'Amanda, Christopher H. ..... Rochester, NY
D'Amanda, John F. ..... Rochester, NY
D'Amanda, Louis ..... Rochester, NY
D'Amanda, Richard ..... Rochester, NY
Damani, Rashmi M. ..... Washington, DC
D'Amante, Richard A. ..... Boston, MA
Damanti, Patrick J. ..... Darien, CT
New York, NY
Damaré, Mary L. ..... Mendenhall, MS
Damari, Tamir D. ..... Washington, DC
D'Amaro, Katherine J. ..... Chicago, IL
D'Amaro, Louis ..... North Babylon, NY
D'Amaro, Paul T. ..... Deer Park, NY
Damas, Patrick ..... Ozone Park, NY
Damas, Raymond J. ..... Lansing, MI
Damas, Stanislaw S. ..... Denver, CO
Damasco, E. John ..... San Diego, CA
Damasco, Gino P. ..... New York, NY
Damasco, Julia Mandeville
San Francisco, CA
Damascus, Dennis A. ..... New York, NY
Damaser, Hilary R. ..... Columbus, OH
Damashek, George ..... Scarsdale, NY
Damashek, Godosky & Gentile
New York, NY
Damashek, Jay B. ..... New York, NY
Damashek, Jonathan S. ..... New York, NY
Damashek, Philip ..... New York, NY
Damashek, Philip M. ..... New York, NY
Damashek, Ronald A. ..... Chicago, IL
Damasiewicz, Jeffrey A. ..... Honolulu, HI
Damas-Rodriquez, Ofelia ..... Miami, FL
Damast, Craig A. ..... New York, NY
Damast, Irving ..... New York, NY
Damast, Michael J. ..... New York, NY
Damast, Robert ..... White Plains, NY
D'Amato, Anthony ..... Chicago, IL
D'Amato, Anthony D. ..... Chicago, IL
D'Amato, Armand P. ..... Lloyd Harbor, NY
Damato, Charles A. ..... New York, NY
D'Amato, Charles R., Jr.
United States Senate,
Committee Legal Personnel, GV
D'Amato, D. Donald ..... Bayside, NY
D'Amato & D'Amato ..... Floral Park, NY
D'Amato, Ellen A. ..... Kansas City, MO
D'Amato, Fred Gerard ..... Chicago, IL
D'Amato, George G. ..... Los Angeles, CA
New York, NY
D'Amato, Janice M. ..... Bellevue, WA
D'Amato, Jennifer R. ..... Milwaukee, WI
D'Amato, John J. ..... Honolulu, HI
D'Amato, John James ..... Albuquerque, NM
D'Amato, John M. ..... Staten Island, NY
D'Amato, John P. ..... Los Angeles, CA
Damato, Joseph R. ..... Washington, DC
D'Amato, Julius J. ..... Floral Park, NY
D'Amato, Kenneth F. ..... Morristown, NJ
Damato, Kenneth J. ..... Fairfield, CT
D'Amato, Laura E. ..... Boston, MA
D'Amato, Lawrence L. ..... Bayside, NY
D'Amato, Louis M. ..... Rochester, NY
D'Amato & Lynch ..... New York, NY
D'Amato & Maloney ..... Honolulu, HI
D'Amato, Mary Ann ..... New York, NY
Damato, Paul ..... East Norwich, NY
D'Amato, Paul R. ..... Linwood, NJ
D'Amato, Paul R., P.C. ..... Linwood, NJ
D'Amato, Rudolph R. ..... Floral Park, NY
D'Amato, Tara P. ..... Jersey City, NJ
Damazo, Herbert Lane ..... Treasury Department,
Internal Revenue Service, GV
Dambach, Bernard W. ..... North Scituate, RI
Dambach & Dambach ..... Northridge, CA
Dambach, James J. ..... Northridge, CA
Dambacher, Gary P. ..... Sonora, CA
Dambly, Dennis C.
Nuclear Regulatory Commission,
Office of the General Counsel, GV
Dambold, Richard P. ..... Amarillo, TX
D'Ambra, Cindy Ellen ..... East Hills, NY
Dambra, Georgiana ..... West Palm Beach, FL
D'Ambra, James S. ..... Providence, RI
Dambrink, Lauralee F. ..... Pottstown, PA
Dambrino, Robert J., III ..... Grenada, MS
Jackson, MS
New Albany, MS
Oxford, MS
Dambroff, David ..... White Plains, NY
D'Ambrose, James J. ..... Brockton, MA
D'Ambrosi, Fred L. ..... Burlington, WA
D'Ambrosia, Lisa A. ..... Denver, CO
D'Ambrosio, A. Daniel ..... Newark, NJ
D'Ambrosio, Alan A. ..... New York, NY
D'Ambrosio, Cynthia L. ..... San Diego, CA
D'Ambrosio, Denise J. ..... New York, NY
D'Ambrosio, Doris B. ..... Farmington, CT
D'Ambrosio, Felix J. ..... Arlington, VA
D'Ambrosio, George J. ..... West Chester, PA
D'Ambrosio, Jack R., Jr. ..... Hackensack, NJ
D'Ambrosio, James J. ..... Irvington, NY
D'Ambrosio, Jo Katherine, (P.C.)
Houston, TX
D'Ambrosio, Joan N. ..... San Francisco, CA
D'Ambrosio, John P. ..... Irvington, NY
D'Ambrosio, Joseph ..... New York, NY
D'Ambrosio, Lawrence A. ..... Erie, PA
D'Ambrosio, Lillian M. ..... Boston, MA
D'Ambrosio, Mary A.
Fort Lauderdale, FL
D'Ambrosio, Michael T. ..... Bronx, NY
D'Ambrosio, Nicholas J. ..... Elmira, NY
D'Ambrosio, Nicholas J., Jr. ..... Albany, NY
D'Ambrosio, Nicholas, Jr. ..... Houston, TX
D'Ambrosio, Peter M. ..... Vienna, VA
D'Ambrosio, Sheila ..... San Francisco, CA
d'Ambrosio, Thomas A. ..... Chicago, IL
Hoffman Estates, IL

D'Ambrosio, Thomas V. …. New York, NY
D'Ambrosio, Vincent T. …. Brooklyn, NY
Dambrot, Donna Lise …. Long Island City, NY
Dambrov, Alan S. …. Springfield, MA
Dambrov, Matthew …. Oakland, CA
Dambrov, Robert L. …. Springfield, MA
D'Ambrozio, Dominick N. …. Hawthorne, NY
Dambruch, Stephen G. …. Providence, RI
D'Ambruoso, Dom S. …. Concord, NH
D'Ambruoso, Joseph A. …. Dix Hills, NY
Dame, Jill Langford …. Jacksonville, FL
Dame, Lisa D. …. Washington, DC
Dame, Norman J. …. Plattsburgh, NY
Dame, Peter L. …. Jacksonville, FL
Dame, Robert F. …. Charlottesville, VA
Dame, Thomas C. …. Baltimore, MD
D'Amelia, Gerald D., Jr. …. Albany, NY
Damelin, Fara
Department Of Health And Human Services, Office of the General Counsel, GV
Damelin, Harold …. Washington, DC
Damelin, Rachel B. …. Washington, DC
Damelio, Anthony J., Jr. …. Cleveland, OH
D'Amelio, Lawrence J., III …. Greensboro, NC
Damelio, Marillyn Fagan …. Cleveland, OH
D'Amelio, Michael C. …. San Francisco, CA
D'Amelio, Michael J. …. Cincinnati, OH
D'Amelio, Salvatore E. …. Chatham, NJ
Damer, Nicholas R. …. El Granada, CA
Dameris & Kuniansky …. Houston, TX
Dameris, Peter T. …. Houston, TX
Dameris, Thad T. …. Houston, TX
Dameris, Thano …. Houston, TX
Dameron, Burgin & Parker, P.A. …. Marion, NC
Dameron, Del Stiltner …. Washington, DC
Dameron, E. Penn, Jr. …. Marion, NC
Dameron, Elizabeth Brown …. Greenville, SC
Dameron, Emerson P. …. Marion, NC
Dameron, E. S. W., Jr. …. Burlington, NC
Dameron, James L., III …. Gaithersburg, MD
Dameron, Jonathan P. …. Cincinnati, OH
Dameron, Nancy Jane …. Cincinnati, OH
Dameron, Robert L. …. Kansas City, KS
Dameron, Russell S. …. Kansas City, MO
Dameron, Sharon L.
Federal Energy Regulatory Commission, Office of the General Counsel, GV
Dameron, Zechariah Clifton …. New York, NY
Damerville, Deborah K. …. Hilo, HI
Damerville, Ricky R. …. Hilo, HI
Dames, John …. Chicago, IL
Dames, John William …. Los Angeles, CA
Dames, Kristan M. …. St. Louis, MO
Dames, Mark A. …. San Jose, CA
Dames, Robert D. …. Medford, OR
Dames, Robert D., Jr. …. Portland, OR
Dames, William S. …. Medford, OR
Damesyn, Jan K. …. Sacramento, CA
Damesyn, Richard F. …. Edgewood, MD
Damewood, Thomas C. …. Charleston, WV
Dameyer, Richard W. …. Yakima, WA
Damgaard, Jens H. …. Harrisburg, PA
Damgaard, Roger W. …. Sioux Falls, SD
Damgard, Michael T. …. Richmond, VA
Damgen, Jeanne M. …. Hackensack, NJ
New York, NY
Dami, Paul A. …. Chicago, IL
Damia, A. Peter …. Danbury, CT
Damia, Michael A. …. Rochester, NY
Damian & Amato, P.C. …. Pittsburgh, PA
Damian, Anita Sani …. Houston, TX
Damian, August C. …. Pittsburgh, PA
Damian, August M. …. Pittsburgh, PA
Damian, Charles M. …. Passaic, NJ
Damian, Kathleen H. …. Dearborn, MI
Damian, Michelle N. …. Miami, FL
Damian, Vincent E., Jr. …. Miami, FL
Damiani, Amelia T. …. Poughkeepsie, NY
Damiani, Byron D., Jr. …. Sacramento, CA
Damiani, Gerard M. …. New City, NY
Damiani, John F. …. Irvine, CA
Damiani, Lisa J. …. San Diego, CA
Damiani, Lora R. …. Miami, FL
Damiani, Louis C. …. Cleveland, OH
Damiani, Patrick J. …. Phoenix, AZ
Damiano, Anthony D. …. Paoli, PA
Damiano, Anthony J. …. Philadelphia, PA
Damiano, Anthony M. …. Cheboygan, MI
Damiano, Dennis A. …. Encino, CA
Damiano, Frank A., Jr. …. Troy, MI
Damiano, Linda A. …. Syracuse, NY
Damiano, Michael …. Portland, OR
Damiano, Robert S. …. West Paterson, NJ
Damianos, John E. …. Smithtown, NY
Damich, Edward J. …. Washington, DC
Damicis, Daniel …. West Haven, CT
Damick, David N. …. St. Louis, MO
Damico, Alfonse J. …. Syracuse, NY
D'Amico, Andrew J. …. Media, PA
D'Amico, Andrew T., Jr. …. New York, NY
D'amico, Andrew T., Jr. …. New York, NY
D'Amico, Ann M. …. Lyndhurst, OH
D'Amico, Anthony J. …. Pittsburgh, PA
D'Amico, Antonio …. Los Angeles, CA
Damico & Associates …. Washington, DC
D'Amico, Barbara S. …. New York, NY
D'Amico, Cheryl A. …. Cleveland, OH
Damico, Chester, Jr. …. Cupertino, CA
D'amico, D. Joseph …. Providence, RI
Damico, David A. …. Pittsburgh, PA
Damico, David J. …. Roanoke, VA
D'Amico, Dominic J. …. Bloomfield, NJ
Damico, Donald A. …. Syracuse, NY
D'Amico, Frank J., (A Prof. Law Corp.)
New Orleans, LA
D'Amico, Frank J., Jr. …. New Orleans, LA

D'Amico, George P. …. Bridgeport, CT
D'Amico, Griffin & Pettinicchi, L.L.C.
Waterbury, CT
D'Amico, Howard B. …. Westminster, MA
Damico, J. David …. Syracuse, NY
D'Amico, James M.P. …. Milwaukee, WI
D'Amico, Jason A. …. Pittsburgh, PA
D'Amico, Jeffrey Robert …. Garden City, NY
Damico, Jennifer G. …. Bingham Farms, MI
D'Amico, Jodelle M. …. Reynoldsburg, OH
Damico, John A. …. Rochester, NY
Damico, John A., Jr. …. Rochester, NY
D'Amico, John E. …. Hartford, CT
D'Amico, John, Jr. …. Freehold, NJ
D'Amico, John M. …. Boston, MA
D'Amico, John R. …. Fort Worth, TX
D'Amico, Joseph A. …. Staten Island, NY
D'Amico, Joseph A. (IBA) …. **Charlotte, NC**
Damico, Joseph A., Jr. …. Media, PA
D'Amico, Joseph B. …. Harrisburg, PA
D'Amico, Joseph S., Jr. …. Allentown, PA
D'Amico, Kirk M. …. New York, NY
D'Amico, Linda …. Park Ridge, NJ
D'Amico, Louis Anthony
Mayfield Village, OH
Damico, Maria E. …. Boston, MA
D'Amico, Marie A. …. Seattle, WA
D'Amico, Marisa …. San Francisco, CA
Damico, Mark D. …. Media, PA
D'Amico, Mark V. …. Burlington, VT
D'Amico, Matthew P. …. New York, NY
D'Amico, Michael A. …. Waterbury, CT
D'Amico, Michael J. …. Franklin, OH
Springboro, OH
D'Amico, Michael L. …. Buffalo, NY
D'Amico, Mitchell …. Mentor, OH
Damico & Moore …. Baton Rouge, LA
Damico, Nicholas P. …. Washington, DC
Damico, Paul A. …. West Palm Beach, FL
D'Amico, Peter P. …. Providence, RI
d'Amico, Raymond A. …. Albany, NY
D'Amico, Richard J. …. Daytona Beach, FL
D'Amico, Richard J. …. Atlanta, GA
D'Amico, Robert A., II …. Providence, RI
D'Amico, Sam J. …. Baton Rouge, LA
D'Amico, Sam J., A P.L.C.
Baton Rouge, LA
D'Amico, Scott S. …. Fort Worth, TX
D'Amico, Sebastian …. San Diego, CA
Damico, Thomas C. …. Baton Rouge, LA
D'Amico, Thomas J. …. Washington, DC
D'Amico & White, P.L.L.C.
Garden City, NY
D'Amico, William S. …. Washington, DC
Damicone, Mary T. …. Munroe Falls, OH
Damien, Javier …. New York, NY
Damir, James C. …. Sacramento, CA
Damir, Robert M. …. San Francisco, CA
Damir, Robert M., A Prof. Corp.
San Francisco, CA
Damirgian, Jeanne K.
Fort Lauderdale, FL
Damis, James J. …. Portland, OR
Damis, Spirro …. Tacoma, WA
Damisch, John W. …. Chicago, IL
Wheaton, IL
Damitz, Barbara J. …. Harrisburg, PA
Damkroger, Rick A. …. Lincoln, NE
Damlos, Barbara J. …. San Francisco, CA
Damm, Camille Wintch …. Las Vegas, NV
Damm, Frederick R. …. Detroit, MI
Damm, Harold F. …. Mineola, NY
Damm, J. Gregory …. Las Vegas, NV
Damm, Jacqueline M. …. Chicago, IL
Damm, John S. …. Logansport, IN
Damm, Lawrence H. …. Pacific Palisades, CA
Damm, Michael C. …. Mount Laurel, NJ
Damm, Paul …. Chicago, IL
Damm, Robert C. …. Fort Lee, NJ
Damm, Robert C., P.C. …. Fort Lee, NJ
Damman, Gregory C. …. Seward, NE
Damman Law Office …. Seward, NE
Dammann, Peter A. …. Friday Harbor, WA
Dammann, Polly A. …. Department of Justice, Civil Division, GV
Damme, Lora L. …. Talmage, NE
Dammeier, Dieter C.
Rancho Cucamonga, CA
Dammeyer, Eric C. …. Minneapolis, MN
Dammeyer, Robt. E. …. Annapolis, MD
D'Ammora, Victor J. …. White Plains, NY
Damon, C. F., Jr. …. Honolulu, HI
Damon, Charles E. …. Grand Rapids, MI
Damon, Claudia Cords …. Concord, NH
Manchester, NH
Damon, Conrad …. West Palm Beach, FL
Damon, Doneene Keemer
Wilmington, DE
Damon, Eric P. …. Boston, MA
Damon, Gary G. …. Sacramento, CA
Damon, James G., III
Newport Beach, CA
Damon, Jennifer M. …. Orange, CA
Damon, John A. …. Whitehall, WI
Damon, John E. …. Grand Rapids, MI
Damon, Jonathan A. …. New York, NY
Damon, Jonathan S. …. Grand Rapids, MI
Damon, Kathryn Fife …. Brigham City, UT
Damon Key Leong Kupchak Hastert, Attorneys at Law, A Law Corporation
Honolulu, HI
Damon, Lisa J. …. Boston, MA
Damon, Martha J. …. Dallas, TX
Damon, Matthew E. …. Minneapolis, MN
Damon, Max …. Pacific Palisades, CA
Damon & Morey LLP …. Buffalo, NY
Rochester, NY

Damon, Oosterhouse & Witte, L.L.P.
Grand Rapids, MI
Damon, Richard E. …. Santa Cruz, CA
Damon, Richard E., A P.C. …. Santa Cruz, CA
Damon, Robert J. C. …. Northfield, IL
Damon, Scott E. …. Orlando, FL
Damon, Susan Straight …. Boulder, CO
Damone, Robert P. …. Long Beach, CA
Damonte, Audrey P. …. Carson City, NV
Damonte, Jonathan James …. Largo, FL
Damoorgian, Dorian K. …. Fort Lauderdale, FL
Damoose, George L. …. San Diego, CA
D'Amore, Alfred A. …. Bridgeport, CT
D'Amore, Anthony A. …. New York, NY
D'Amore & Associates, P.C. …. Portland, OR
Vancouver, WA
Damore, David A. …. Phoenix, AZ
Damore, David R. …. Daytona Beach, FL
Damore, Dennis M. …. Portland, OR
D' Amore, Frank Michael …. St. Louis, MO
Damore, Janet L. …. Olathe, KS
D'Amore, Jeffrey S. …. Lake Park, FL
D'Amore, John Domenico …. McLean, VA
D'Amore, Joseph R. …. Phoenix, AZ
Damore, Lawrence J. …. Youngstown, OH
D'Amore, Mark S. …. Berlin, NJ
D'Amore, Matthew M. …. New York, NY
Damore, Michael A. …. Sacramento, CA
D'Amore, Robert A. …. West Palm Beach, FL
D'Amore & Shamiss …. Bridgeport, CT
D'Amore, Stephen V. …. Chicago, IL
D'Amore, Thomas D. …. Portland, OR
D'Amore Donnelly, Mary Katherine
South Barrington, IL
Damoudt, Axel J. …. New York, NY
D'Amour, Annmarie …. New York, NY
D'Amour, Charles L. …. Springfield, MA
D'Amour, Denise M.
National Labor Relations Board, Office of Board Members, GV
Damour, Frederick W. …. Denver, CO
D'Amour, Kevin F. …. Princeton, NJ
D'Amour, Richard G. …. Evansville, IN
D'Amours, Norman E. …. Manchester, NH
D'Amours, Richard J. …. Ossipee, NH
Damp, Ronald W. …. Plymouth, WI
Dampeer, John L. …. Cleveland, OH
Dampf, Edwards, Thibaut, Melanson, Delatte & Marcantel …. Baton Rouge, LA
Dampf, Jack M. …. Baton Rouge, LA
Dampf, Robert S. …. Lake Charles, LA
Dampier, Harold D., Jr. …. Houston, TX
Dampier, M. Stephen …. Mobile, AL
Damrath, Joseph E. …. Hornell, NY
Damrau, Mason …. Fairbanks, AK
Damrauer, Carol L. …. Toledo, OH
Damrell, Frank C., Jr. …. Sacramento, CA
Damrell, Nelson, Schrimp, Pallios & Ladine, A Professional Corporation …. Modesto, CA
Oakdale, CA
Damren, Samuel C. …. Bloomfield Hills, MI
Damron, David J. …. Phoenix, AZ
Damron, James S. …. Austin, TX
Damron, Jeffrey D. …. Prestonsburg, KY
Damron, John T. …. Frankfort, KY
Damron, Loretta A. …. Philadelphia, PA
Damron, Phillip D. …. Prestonsburg, KY
Damron, Robert H. …. Yuba City, CA
Damron, Scott A. …. Huntington, WV
Damron & Taylor, PLLC
Huntington, WV
Damron, Whitney B., P.A. …. Topeka, KS
Damron, Whitney Blair …. Topeka, KS
Damrosch, Lori Fisler …. New York, NY
Damschen, Darrell D. …. Evergreen, CO
Damschroder, Timothy R. …. Ann Arbor, MI
Damsel, Charles H., Jr.
West Palm Beach, FL
Damsel, Charles H., Jr., P.A.
West Palm Beach, FL
Damsgaard, Dennis D. …. Waterloo, IA
Damsgaard, Kell M. …. Philadelphia, PA
Damsker, Lee S. …. Tampa, FL
Damski, Frederick J. …. Fort Lauderdale, FL
Damsky, Edward J. …. Rockville Centre, NY
Damsky, Gerald D. …. Boca Raton, FL
Damsky, Gerald, P.A …. Boca Raton, FL
Damsky, Mitchell H. …. Birmingham, AL
Damsky, Sheldon W. …. Saranac Lake, NY
Damslet, Otis Reidar …. New York, NY
Damstra, Daniel L. …. Berwyn, PA
Damtoft, Russell W. …. Chicago, IL
Damudar, Amitesh …. Studio City, CA
Damus, Charles M. …. Las Vegas, NV
Damus, Charles M., A Professional Law Corporation …. Las Vegas, NV
Damus, David P. …. Los Angeles, CA
Damus, Robert G.
Executive Office Of The President, Office of Management and Budget, GV
Damuth, Brenda Jeffers …. Dallas, TX
Damuth, G. Scott …. Dallas, TX
Dan, Brian D. …. Delray Beach, FL
Dan, Hideo …. Teaneck, NJ
Dan, Jeffrey C. …. Chicago, IL
Dan, Michael A.K., A Professional Corporation …. Los Angeles, CA
Dan, Michael A. K. …. Los Angeles, CA
Dana, A. Fairfield …. New York, NY
Dana, Andrew C. …. Bozeman, MT
Dana & Associates …. Mesa, AZ
Dana, Christopher S. …. Media, PA
Dana, Craig U. …. Newton, NJ
Dana, Donald E. …. San Francisco, CA
Dana, Frank J., III …. Greenville, SC
Dana, Frederick J. …. St. Louis, MO
Dana, George W. …. Houston, TX
Dana, Howard H., Jr. …. Portland, ME

Dana, Jane T. …. Washington, DC
Dana, John A. …. Sandersville, GA
Dana, John F. …. South Portland, ME
Dana, John R. …. New York, NY
Dana, Jonathan M. …. Washington, DC
Dana, Lauren Elizabeth …. Los Angeles, CA
Dana Law Firm …. Greenville, SC
Dana, Mark Lawrence …. Long Beach, CA
Dana, Mark W. …. Providence, RI
Dana, Matthew S. …. Mesa, AZ
Dana, Michel …. Long Island City, NY
Dana & Pariser, Co., L.P.A. …. Columbus, OH
Dana, Patrick R. …. San Francisco, CA
Dana, Randall M. …. Columbus, OH
Dana, Raymond E. …. Minneapolis, MN
Dana, Richard A. …. Burlingame, CA
Dana, Richard G. …. New York, NY
Dana,, Richard L., Jr. …. Warren, OH
Dana, Saml. M. …. Los Angeles, CA
Dana, Stacey J. …. San Francisco, CA
Dana, Thomas V. …. New York, NY
Dana, Valerie …. Englewood, CO
Dana, William H. …. Fremont, CA
Dana-Bashian, Pauline …. New York, NY
Danaceau, Alison …. Orlando, FL
Danaher, Brian E. …. Washington, DC
Danaher, Charles A. …. San Diego, CA
Danaher, Christian J. …. Syracuse, NY
Danaher, Daniel …. Hillsdale, NJ
Danaher, James R. …. West Bend, WI
Danaher, James T. …. Palo Alto, CA
Danaher, James T., Jr. …. Santa Cruz, CA
Danaher, John E. …. Grosse Pointe, MI
Danaher, M. Joseph …. Elmira, NY
Danaher, Maria Greco …. Pittsburgh, PA
Danaher, Maureen C. …. Canton, NY
Danaher, Michael J. …. Palo Alto, CA
Danaher, Michael J. …. Milwaukee, WI
Danaher, Michael J., Jr. …. Endicott, NY
Danaher, Philip J. …. East Greenbush, NY
Danaher, R. Cornelius, Jr. …. Hartford, CT
Danaher, Richard G. …. Chicago, IL
Danaher, Robert C. …. Hartford, CT
Danaher, Robert L. …. Southport, CT
Danaher, Tedford, Lagnese & Neal, P.C.
Hartford, CT
Baltimore, MD
New York, NY
Danaher, Thomas W. …. Tampa, FL
Danaher, William A., Jr. …. Elmira, NY
Danaher, William K., Jr. …. Springfield, MA
Danahy, Mary J. …. Chicago, IL
Danahy, Matthew R. …. Tampa, FL
Danahy, Paul S. …. Boston, MA
Danahy, Paul W., Jr. …. Tampa, FL
Danahy, Scott D. …. Orlando, FL
Danais, Conrad …. Manchester, NH
Danais & Danais …. Manchester, NH
Danamraj, Shreen K. …. Dallas, TX
Danas, Andrew M. …. Washington, DC
Danas, Joseph P., Jr. …. Milwaukee, WI
Danberg, Carl Christian …. Wilmington, DE
Danberg, M. Edward …. Wilmington, DE
Danberg, Neil B., Jr. …. Omaha, NE
Danberry, Cheryl A. …. Greencastle, IN
Danborn, Paul R. …. Arvada, CO
Danburg, Debra …. Houston, TX
Danbury, Michael J. …. Treasury Department, Internal Revenue Service, GV
Dance, D. Craig …. Lexington, KY
Dance, Dance & Lane …. Nashville, TN
Dance, Fred C. …. Nashville, TN
Dance, Gary T. …. Idaho Falls, ID
Pocatello, ID
Dance, James B. …. Carthage, TN
Dance, Richard …. Nashville, TN
Dance, Simon E. …. Washington, DC
Dance, William H. …. Troy, MI
Dancer, Andrena G. …. Upland, CA
Dancer, Donald R. …. Duluth, GA
Dancer, Mark R. …. Traverse City, MI
Dancer, Neal …. Corpus Christi, TX
Dancey, Burt L. …. Pekin, IL
Dancey, David L. …. Waukesha, WI
Dancey, Elizabeth E. …. Mount Clemens, MI
Danch, Christopher …. Ojai, CA
Danch & Danch …. Ojai, CA
Danch, John R. …. Ojai, CA
Danchak, Michael G. …. Columbus, OH
Danchi, Theodore S. …. Apex, NC
Danchuk, Kathleen M. …. Atherton, CA
Danchuk, William A. …. Pittsburgh, PA
Dancigers, George J. …. Norfolk, VA
Dancis, Mordecai …. Palm Beach, FL
Danciu, Charlotte H. …. Boca Raton, FL
Danciu, Charlotte H., P.A. …. Boca Raton, FL
Dancks, Thérèse Wiley …. Fayetteville, NY
Danco, Ernest J. …. Reynoldsburg, OH
Danco, Sharon Docherty …. Tampa, FL
D'Ancona & Pflaum LLC …. Chicago, IL
Dancsecs, Mark S. …. Los Angeles, CA
Dancu, David A. …. Naples, FL
Dancy, Blair …. Austin, TX
Dancy, Robert L. …. Reading, MA
Dancy, Shenia Marie …. Dorchester, MA
Dancy, Victoria A. …. Dallas, TX
Danda, David E. …. Atlanta, GA
Danda, David E., P.C. …. Atlanta, GA
Dandar & Dandar, P.A. …. Tampa, FL
Dandar, Debra L. …. St. Petersburg, FL
Dandar, James P. …. Honolulu, HI
Dandar, Kennan G. …. Tampa, FL
Dandar, Thomas J. …. Tampa, FL
Dandeker, Rebecca L. …. Washington, DC
Dandelles, Stefan Roane …. Chicago, IL
Dandenault, Bryan C. …. Battle Creek, MI
Dandeneau, Debra A. …. Miami, FL
Dandes, Benjamin I. …. Peabody, MA

Dandino, Patrick E. ... Cleveland, OH
Dando, Brian R. ... Phoenix, AZ
Dandola, John A. ... Flushing, NY
Dandona, Jean M. ... Santa Barbara, CA
Dandora, Reetu ... Philadelphia, PA
Dandos, Phillip S. ... Sioux City, IA
D'Andrade, Hugh A. ... Madison, NJ
D'Andrea, Alfred A., Jr. ... New York, NY
D'Andrea, Dennis ... Mineola, NY
D'Andrea, Donato A. ... Newport, RI
D'Andrea, Elisa A. ... Washington, DC
D'Andrea, Erich J. ... Detroit, MI
D'Andrea, Frank H., Jr. ... Stamford, CT
D'Andrea & Goldstein ... Scarsdale, NY
D'Andrea, James L. ... Jacksonville, FL
D'Andrea, James Milo ... Hicksville, NY
D'Andrea, John J. ... Washington, DC
Albany, NY
D'Andrea, Norman E. ... Providence, RI
D'Andrea, Patrick J. ... Akron, OH
Dandrea, Richard K. ... Pittsburgh, PA
D'Andrea, Vincent P. ... Scarsdale, NY
Dandridge, Albert S., III ... Philadelphia, PA
Dandridge, James H. ... Charlottesville, VA
Dandridge, Lori S. ... Charleston, SC
Dandridge, Paul A. ... Philadelphia, PA
Dandridge, Sherilyn R. ... New York, NY
Dandridge, Tasha T. ... Buffalo, NY
Syracuse, NY
Dandurand, Andre ... Louisville, CO
Dandurand, Craig R. ... Sacramento, CA
Dandurand, Joseph P. ... Warrensburg, MO
Dandurand, Thomas J. ... San Francisco, CA
Dane, Alan J. ... Birmingham, AL
Dane, Beth-Ann ... Forest Hills, NY
Dane, Brady & Haydon, LLP
Concord, MA
Dane & Dane ... Forest Hills, NY
Dane, Edmund M. ... Forest Hills, NY
Dane, Edward G. ... Los Angeles, CA
Dane, Frank ... Portland, OR
Dane, Harold John, III ... Davenport, IA
Dane, Henry J. ... Concord, MA
Dane & Howe, LLP ... Boston, MA
Dane, John K. ... Hamilton, MA
Dane, Michael ... Cleveland, OH
Dane, Nathan, III ... Bangor, ME
Dane, Paul N. ... Martinez, CA
Dane, Philomena M. ... Columbus, OH
Dane, Ronnie ... New York, NY
Dane, Stephen M. ... Findlay, OH
Toledo, OH
Dane, Tara Miller ... Naples, FL
Dane, Ted G. ... Los Angeles, CA
Dane, William H., Jr. ... Orlando, FL
Danecki, Robert R. ... Little Rock, AR
Danehey, John F. ... Boston, MA
Danehower, Robert G. ... Lansdale, PA
Danehy, Jack D. ... Fort Wayne, IN
Danehy, James S. ... Cincinnati, OH
Danek, Gregory C. ... Chicago, IL
Danek, Jeffrey C. ... Itasca, IL
Danek, Marie F. ... Albany, NY
Danek, Stanley M. ... Tallahassee, FL
Danekas, Steven E. ... Chicago, IL
Daneker, David C. ... Baltimore, MD
Daneker, Eva L. ... Jacksonville, FL
Ponte Vedra Beach, FL
Daneker, Mark J. ... Baltimore, MD
Daneker, McIntire, Davis, Schumm, Prince & Goldstein, P.C. ... Baltimore, MD
Daneker, Michael D. ... Washington, DC
Danell, Albin E. ... San Jose, CA
Danella, Brian D. ... Palo Alto, CA
Danella, Joseph R. ... Philadelphia, PA
Danello, Daniel F. ... Washington, DC
Danello, John Joseph ... Cambridge, MA
Danello, Paul F. ... Washington, DC
Columbus, OH
Danello, Timothy F. ... Charlotte, NC
Danelo, Peter A. ... Seattle, WA
Danelski, David J. ... Seattle, WA
Daneman, Cara R. ... Los Angeles, CA
Daneman, David ... Baltimore, MD
Daneman, Donald ... Baltimore, MD
Daneman, Donald, P.A. ... Baltimore, MD
Daneman, Erika F ... Baltimore, MD
Daneman, Sara Jane ... Gahanna, OH
Danen, Philip J. ... Green Bay, WI
Danen, Richard A. ... Waterbury, CT
Danenbarger, W. Wright ... Manchester, NH
Danenberg, Gregory E. ... New York, NY
Danenhauer, George P. ... New York, NY
Daner, Adam M. ... San Diego, CA
Daner, William E., Jr. ... Richmond, VA
Daneri, Eugene L. ... Hicksville, NY
Daneri, Robert W. ... San Francisco, CA
Daneri, Roxanne T. ... Sacramento, CA
Daneri, Roxanne T., P.C. ... Sacramento, CA
Danese, Gregory ... Stockton, NJ
Danese, Richard, Jr. ... Newtown, PA
Danesh, Young Lee ... Boston, MA
Daneshrad, Joseph, Law Offices of
Los Angeles, CA
Daneshrad, Shari S. ... Encino, CA
Danet, Gloria J. ... Brooklyn, NY
Danett, Paula R. ... New York, NY
Danetz, Stephen S. ... Great Neck, NY
Daney, Michael H. ... Baltimore, MD
Daney, Tamara K. ... San Francisco, CA
Danfelser, John W. ... Caballo, NM
Danford, Caroline S. ... New York, NY
Danford, Caroline Swan ... New York, NY
Danford, Daniel E. ... Lexington, KY
Danford, Darl R. ... La Jolla, CA
Danford, Mary Thurston ... Portland, OR
Danford, Ormond S. ... Williamsburg, MI
Danforth, Ann R. ... San Jose, CA
Danforth, Brian D. ... Hartford, CT
Danforth, Cleary & Grenier
North Haven, CT
Danforth, Daniel M. ... Spokane, WA
Danforth, Dorothy Duncan ... St. Louis, MO
Danforth, Frederick W., Jr.
North Haven, CT
Danforth, George H. ... Huron, SD
Danforth, Henry D. ... McLean, VA
Danforth, John B. ... Jefferson, WI
Danforth, John C. ... Washington, DC
St. Louis, MO
Danforth, John D. ... Milpitas, CA
Danforth, Kimberly H. ... Indianapolis, IN
Danforth, Lee J. ... Redwood City, CA
Danforth, Meierhenry & Meierhenry, LLP
Sioux Falls, SD
Danforth, Richard R. ... Troy, MI
Danforth, Robert B. ... Elk River, MN
Danforth, Robert T. ... Lexington, VA
Danforth, Timothy J. ... Seattle, WA
Dang, Bradford Jen-Wei ... Honolulu, HI
Dang, Charles H.Y. ... Honolulu, HI
Dang, Douglas Y. ... Oakland, CA
Dang, Hieu T. ... Houston, TX
Dang, Kenneth H. Q. ... Woodcliff Lake, NJ
Dublin, OH
Dang, Kha Q. ... Seattle, WA
Dang, Le T. ... San Jose, CA
Dang, Marvin S. C. ... Honolulu, HI
Dang, Robert M. ... San Francisco, CA
Dang, Sakang Chong
South San Francisco, CA
Dang, Thu A. ... Alexandria, VA
Dang & Trachuk ... Oakland, CA
Dang, Trina L. ... Treasury Department, Internal Revenue Service, GV
Dang, Van T. ... San Jose, CA
Dangeau, Jeffrey L. ... Fayetteville, AR
Dangel, Edward T., III ... Boston, MA
Dangel and Fine, LLP ... Boston, MA
D'Angel, Robert M. ... Mount Holly, NJ
Dangel, Ruth Bope ... Columbus, OH
Dangel, Stephanie A. J. ... Pittsburgh, PA
Dangelica, Domenick Leonard
New York, NY
D'Angelillo, Robert M. ... Bay Shore, NY
D'Angelo, Alfred J., Jr. ... Wilmington, DE
Philadelphia, PA
D'Angelo, Andrew M. ... Boston, MA
D'Angelo, Carl A. ... White Plains, NY
D'Angelo, Carlo ... Fort Lauderdale, FL
D'Angelo, Charles N. ... Santa Fe, NM
D'Angelo, Christine ... Los Angeles, CA
D'Angelo, Christopher A. ... New York, NY
D'Angelo, Christopher Scott
Philadelphia, PA
D'Angelo, Dana ... Butler, NJ
D'Angelo & D'Angelo ... Butler, NJ
D'Angelo, Daniel ... Boston, MA
D'Angelo, David S. ... Philadelphia, PA
D'Angelo, Drew P. ... Jenkintown, PA
D'Angelo, Elisa M. ... San Diego, CA
D'Angelo and Eurell ... Philadelphia, PA
D'Angelo, Francesca ... Spokane, WA
D'Angelo, Frank G., Jr. ... Garden City, NY
D'Angelo, Frank J. ... Nutley, NJ
D'Angelo, George A. ... Philadelphia, PA
d'Angelo, George V. ... Washington, DC
D'Angelo, Gregory G. ... Metairie, LA
D'Angelo, Ida ... Melville, NY
D'Angelo, Jack M. ... New York, NY
Dangelo, James ... Huntington, NY
D'Angelo, James L. ... Myrtle Beach, SC
D'Angelo, James P. ... Wilmington, DE
D'Angelo, James S. ... Los Angeles, CA
D'Angelo, Janeen L. ... San Diego, CA
D'Angelo, Jason A. ... New York, NY
D'Angelo, Joanne Milazzo ... Woodbridge, CT
D'Angelo, John G. ... Butler, NJ
D'Angelo, Joseph Bryan ... Bay Minette, AL
D'Angelo, Joseph D. ... New York, NY
D'Angelo, Joseph M. ... Toledo, OH
D'Angelo, Julie A. ... Madison, WI
Dangelo, Kathleen Birkel ... Chagrin Falls, OH
D'Angelo, Laura A. ... Lexington, KY
D'Angelo, Leonard M. ... Metairie, LA
D'Angelo, Lorraine ... New York, NY
D'Angelo, Louis J. ... Allison Park, PA
D'Angelo, Madelyne L. ... Pittsburgh, PA
D'Angelo, Mario ... Shreveport, LA
D'Angelo, Mario D. ... Bay Shore, NY
D'Angelo, Michael D. ... Morristown, NJ
Dangelo, Michael D. ... New York, NY
D'Angelo, Michael L. ... Irvine, CA
D'Angelo, N. Michael ... Oakland, IA
D'Angelo, Nicholas A. ... Painesville, OH
D'Angelo, Patricia J. ... Waukesha, WI
D'Angelo, Patrick A. ... Cleveland, OH
D'Angelo, Peter T. ... Phoenix, AZ
D'Angelo, Robert V., Jr. ... Naugatuck, CT
D'Angelo, Robert W., (P.C.)
Pasadena, CA
D'Angelo, Ronald James ... Brooklyn, NY
D'Angelo, Scott L. ... Chicago, IL
D'Angelo, Susan W. ... Long Valley, NJ
D'Angelo, Victoria L. ... Williamsville, NY
D'Angelo, Vincent P. ... Los Angeles, CA
D'Angelo, William, III ... Costa Mesa, CA
Danger, Marlene B. ... Miami, FL
Dangerfield, Cari M. ... Tucson, AZ
Dangerfield, Joel R. ... Salt Lake City, UT
Dangerfield, Lloyd ... Lafayette, LA
Dangerfield, Mark C. ... Phoenix, AZ
Dangerfield, Richard S. ... San Francisco, CA
D'Angio, Carl E., Jr. ... Waltham, MA
D'Angio, Louis A. ... Waltham, MA
D'Angio, Robert A., Jr.
West Palm Beach, FL
D'Angiolillo, Marc ... Morristown, NJ
Dangl, John R., Jr. ... Los Angeles, CA
Dangle, Robert F. ... Carrollton, GA
Dangler, Richard Hale ... Sacramento, CA
Dangoia, W. James
Department Of Veterans Affairs, Office of the General Counsel, GV
Dangora, James T. ... Billerica, MA
Dangott, Morris A. ... Oakland, CA
Danhausen, Martha J. ... Kankakee, IL
Danhof, Calvin R. ... Grand Rapids, MI
Danhof, Robert J. ... Holland, MI
Danhof, William J. ... Lansing, MI
Dani, William P. ... Grand Rapids, MI
Danian, Michael S. ... Waukegan, IL
Danian, Michael S., Professional Corporation
Waukegan, IL
Danias, Anastasia T. ... New York, NY
Danias, Peter G. ... New York, NY
Danie, Robert J. ... Agawam, MA
Daniel, A. E., III ... La Grange, GA
Daniel, A. L. Butler
Wrightsville Beach, NC
Daniel, Al J., Jr. ... New York, NY
Daniel, Allen J. ... Orlando, FL
Daniel, Anne D. ... Albuquerque, NM
Daniel, Arthur B., Jr. ... Richmond, VA
Daniel, Aubrey M., III ... Washington, DC
Daniel, Baker & Howard ... Tulsa, OK
Daniel, Barton N. ... Virginia Beach, VA
Daniel, Ben, Jr. ... Ocala, FL
Daniel, Ben, Jr., P.A. ... Ocala, FL
Daniel, Ben L. ... Memphis, TN
Daniel, Benjamin ... Miami, FL
Daniel, Bruce B. ... Boston, MA
Daniel, Bruce M. ... Houston, TX
Daniel, Burton & Associates
Murfreesboro, TN
Daniel, C. Edward ... Knoxville, TN
Daniel, C. Welborn ... Daytona Beach, FL
Maitland, FL
Daniel, Carol H. ... Anchorage, AK
Daniel, Carol V. ... Dallas, TX
Daniel, Carrie Anderson
San Francisco, CA
Daniel, Charles D. ... Melville, NY
Daniel, Charles E. ... Drumright, OK
Daniel, Charles Lee, III ... Dalton, GA
Daniel, Charles R., II ... New Orleans, LA
Daniel, Christina Lidot ... Houston, TX
Daniel, Christine S. ... Berkeley, CA
Daniel, Christopher G.
Winston-Salem, NC
Daniel, Clampett, Powell & Cunningham, L.L.C. ... Springfield, MO
Daniel, Clarence H. ... Chagrin Falls, OH
Daniel, Clyde P. ... Garden City, KS
Daniel Coker Horton & Bell, P.A.
Gulfport, MS
Jackson, MS
Oxford, MS
Daniel, Cornelius W., III ... Point Pleasant, NJ
Daniel, Creed A. ... Rutledge, TN
Daniel, D. Mark ... Fort Worth, TX
Daniel & Daniel ... Pawleys Island, SC
Daniel & Daniel ... Houston, TX
Daniel & Daniel ... Houston, TX
Daniel, Darden E. ... Irving, TX
Daniel, David E. ... Pittsburgh, PA
Daniel, David M. ... Boise, ID
Daniel, David O., III ... Chicago, IL
Daniel, David P. ... Rossville, GA
Daniel, David S. ... Merion, PA
Daniel, David W. ... Raleigh, NC
Daniel, D. C., Jr., P.C. ... Murfreesboro, TN
Daniel, Deborah A.
Rancho Cucamonga, CA
Daniel, Denise A. ... Concord, NH
Daniel, Donald G. ... Olympia, WA
Daniel, Donald L. ... Lafayette, IN
Daniel, Dorris Caldwell, Jr.
Murfreesboro, TN
Daniel, Doug ... Harrison, AR
Daniel, E. Anderson ... West Linn, OR
Daniel, E. Bart ... Charleston, SC
Daniel, Ed ... Little Rock, AR
Daniel, Ed, IV ... Little Rock, AR
Daniel, Eleanor ... Los Angeles, CA
Daniel, Elizabeth Kehoe ... Memphis, TN
Daniel, Emily ... New York, NY
Daniel, Eric L. ... Detroit, MI
Daniel, Eva S. ... Chicago, IL
Daniel, Frederick R. ... Tiffin, OH
Daniel, Frederick T. ... Pickerington, OH
Daniel, George B. ... Yanceyville, NC
Daniel, Hadden, Alford& Graham, P.C.
La Grange, GA
Daniel, Harold T., Jr. ... Atlanta, GA
Daniel, Hartman C. ... Metairie, LA
Daniel, H. D. ... Los Angeles, CA
Daniel, Helene L. ... Tampa, FL
Daniel, Herman C., III ... Richmond, VA
Daniel, Houston L. ... Liberty, TX
Daniel, Isaak ... Wauwatosa, WI
Daniel, J. Henry ... Falls Church, VA
Daniel, J. Howard ... Greenville, SC
Daniel, J. Mark ... Atlanta, GA
Daniel, J. Murrell ... Lynchburg, VA
Daniel, J. Neil ... Abilene, TX
Daniel, J. Nixon, III ... Pensacola, FL
Daniel, J. Reese ... Pawleys Island, SC
Daniel, J. Robert ... Macon, GA
Daniel, Jack ... Huntsville, AL
Daniel, Jack ... Fresno, CA
Daniel, Jack C. ... Macon, GA
Daniel, James A. L. ... Danville, VA
Daniel, James A.L., Jr. ... Charlotte, NC
Daniel, James C. "Chris" ... Tulsa, OK
Daniel, James E. ... Charlotte, NC
Daniel, James Edwards ... Memphis, TN
Daniel, James H. ... Jacksonville, FL
Daniel, James L., Jr. ... Houston, TX
Daniel, James M., Jr. ... Richmond, VA
Daniel, Jeffrey Stuart ... Gardendale, AL
Daniel, Jeffrey Zane ... Knoxville, TN
Daniel, Jerry M. ... Waynesboro, GA
Daniel, Joe H. ... Jackson, MS
Daniel, Joel A. ... Washington, DC
Greenville, SC
Daniel, John A. ... Dallas, TX
Daniel, John B., Jr. ... Temple, TX
Daniel, John C., III ... Macon, GA
Daniel, John E. ... Washington, DC
Daniel, John E. ... New York, NY
Daniel, John F. ... Panama City, FL
Daniel, John Furman, Jr. ... Greenville, SC
Daniel, John P. ... Pensacola, FL
Daniel, John R. ... Rockingham, NC
Daniel, John T. ... Charlotte, NC
Daniel, John W., II ... Richmond, VA
Daniel, Jonathan L. ... Los Angeles, CA
Daniel, Joseph S. ... Murfreesboro, TN
Daniel, Joseph T. ... La Quinta, CA
Daniel, Josiah M., III ... Dallas, TX
Daniel, Judith Palotay ... Palm Springs, CA
Daniel, Judy J. ... High Point, NC
Daniel, Julianne T. ... Olympia, WA
Daniel, Julie ... Philadelphia, PA
Daniel, June E. ... Boston, MA
Providence, RI
Daniel, Kara L. ... Paducah, KY
Daniel, Karen N. ... Montgomery, AL
Daniel and Kasbee ... Pittsburgh, PA
Daniel, Kimberly W. ... Richmond, VA
Daniel & Komarek ... Bonifay, FL
Chipley, FL
De Funiak Springs, FL
Marianna, FL
Port St. Joe, FL
Panama City, FL
Daniel, Kris ... Chicago, IL
Daniel, Lance ... Sacramento, CA
Daniel, Larry O., Jr. ... Huntsville, AL
Daniel, Laurie Webb ... Atlanta, GA
Daniel Law Firm ... Memphis, TN
Daniel Law Firm, The, L.L.C.
Breckenridge, CO
Daniel Law Offices, P.C. ... Belleville, IL
Lake Ozark, MO
St. Louis, MO
Daniel, Lawson, Tuggle & Jerles, L.L.P.
Perry, GA
Warner Robins, GA
Daniel, LeAnne ... Arkadelphia, AR
Daniel, Lee Dawn ... Greenfield, MA
Northampton, MA
Springfield, MA
Daniel, Lisa H. ... New York, NY
Daniel, Lisa K. ... Phoenix, AZ
Daniel, Lori Vanhoose ... Paintsville, KY
Daniel & Lowe ... Augusta, GA
Martinez, GA
Daniel, Luke L. ... Houston, TX
Daniel, Lundy W. ... Memphis, TN
Daniel, M. David ... Salem, OR
Daniel, M. Irene ... Los Angeles, CA
Daniel, Marc A. ... Chicago, IL
Daniel, Marc R. ... New York, NY
Daniel, María A. ... Cherry Hill, NJ
Daniel, Marilyn S. ... Lexington, KY
Daniel, Mark G. ... Fort Worth, TX
Daniel, Mark R. ... Rahway, NJ
Daniel, Mark Stephen ... Hinesville, GA
Daniel, Mark W. ... Wheaton, IL
Daniel, Martin B. ... Memphis, TN
Daniel, Martin N. ... Los Angeles, CA
Daniel, Marvin V. ... Burlington, WI
Daniel, Mary L. C. ... Winchester, VA
Daniel, Matthew L. ... New York, NY
Daniel, Maurice ... San Diego, CA
Daniel, Mayer A. ... San Mateo, CA
Daniel, Melvin R. ... Indianapolis, IN
Daniel, Michael C. ... Athens, GA
Daniel, Michael G. ... Tulsa, OK
Daniel, Michael R. ... Columbia, SC
Daniel, Michael R. ... Pawleys Island, SC
Daniel, Miriam W. ... Rockville, MD
Daniel, N. Kenneth, (P.C.) ... Augusta, GA
Daniel, Nicole Chrisman ... Roanoke, VA
Daniel, Noble D. ... Pawhuska, OK
Daniel & Oberman ... Knoxville, TN
Daniel, Orrel A. ... Brighton, CO
Daniel and Otey, L.L.P. ... Tulsa, OK
Daniel, Paul ... Bethesda, MD
Daniel, Paul G. ... Washington, DC
Daniel, Peter F. ... Kansas City, MO
Daniel, Peter K. ... Atlanta, GA
Daniel, R. Dolores ... Peachtree City, GA
Daniel, R. Michael ... Pittsburgh, PA
Daniel, Ralph S. ... Lubbock, TX
Daniel, Ray W. ... Omaha, NE
Daniel, Remer C. ... Macon, GA
Daniel, Remer Craig ... Atlanta, GA
Daniel, Rhetta Moore ... Hanover, VA
Mechanicsville, VA
Daniel, Rhetta Moore ... Richmond, VA
Daniel, Robert C. ... Chicago, IL
Daniel, Rodney A. ... Chicago, IL
Daniel, Roxann Gray ... Columbus, GA
Daniel, Royal, III ... Breckenridge, CO
Daniel, Royal T., III ... Raleigh, NC
Daniel, Royal T., III, P.A., The Law Office of
Raleigh, NC
Daniel, Samuel P. ... Tulsa, OK

Daniel, Samuel P., III ..... Tulsa, OK
Daniel, Sandra K. ..... Houston, TX
Daniel, Scott ..... Murfreesboro, TN
Daniel, Scott D. ..... Galveston, TX
Daniel, Scott E. ..... Garden City, KS
Daniel, Scott E. ..... Omaha, NE
Daniel, Seymour & Grossman, P.C.
Flint, MI
Daniel, Sharon C. ..... Greensboro, NC
Daniel, Shonnie L. ..... Houston, TX
Daniel & Shoultz, L.L.P. ..... Dallas, TX
Daniel, Stephanie A. ..... Tallahassee, FL
Daniel, Stephen C. ..... Fort Wayne, IN
Daniel, Stephen T. ..... Morganton, NC
Daniel, Susan ..... Port Orchard, WA
Daniel, Susan K. ..... Binghamton, NY
Daniel, T. Christopher ..... Atlanta, GA
Daniel, Ted Cameron ..... Houston, TX
Daniel, Teresa ..... Fayetteville, WV
Daniel, Teresa A. ..... Huntington, WV
Daniel, Teresa D. ..... Fairmont, WV
Daniel, Theodore D. ..... New Carlisle, OH
Daniel, Theodore W. ..... Dallas, TX
Daniel, Theresa Jenkins ..... Union Springs, AL
Daniel & Thom, P.C. ..... Colorado Springs, CO
Daniel, Thomas Alan, (P.A.) ..... Gainesville, FL
Daniel, Thomas C. ..... Richmond, VA
Daniel, Thomas H. ..... Austin, TX
Daniel, Thomas J., IV
Oklahoma City, OK
Daniel, Thomas M. ..... Anchorage, AK
Daniel, Thomas R. ..... Honolulu, HI
Daniel, Tia L. ..... Houston, TX
Daniel, Timothy ..... Cleveland, OH
Daniel, Timothy W. ..... Drumright, OK
Daniel, Tod O. ..... Janesville, WI
Daniel, Tom W. ..... Perry, GA
Daniel, Troy B. ..... Roscommon, MI
Daniel, Vaughan, Medley & Smitherman, P.C. ..... Danville, VA
Martinsville, VA
South Boston, VA
Daniel, W. Jonathan ..... Birmingham, AL
Daniel, W. Zane, (P.C.) ..... Knoxville, TN
Daniel, Walter E., IV ..... Houston, TX
Daniel, Wiley Y. ..... Denver, CO
Daniel, William A., Jr. ..... Miami, FL
Daniel, William A., Jr., P.A., Law Offices of ..... Miami, FL
Daniel, William B. ..... Detroit, MI
Daniel, William (Bill) Partlow
Houston, TX
Liberty, TX
Daniel, William H. ..... Yanceyville, NC
Daniel, William H. ..... Austin, TX
Daniel, William J. ..... Philadelphia, PA
Daniel, William J. ..... Arlington, VA
Daniel, William L., II ..... Frankfort, KY
Daniel, William P. ..... Flint, MI
Daniel, William R. ..... Tampa, FL
Daniel, William S. ..... Belleville, IL
Lake Ozark, MO
St. Louis, MO
Daniel, William T., Jr. ..... Savannah, GA
Daniel, William Todd ..... Knoxville, TN
Daniel, William W. ..... Atlanta, GA
Daniele, Anthony ..... Rochester, NY
Daniele, Anthony R. ..... New York, NY
Daniele, Barbara E. ..... Stamford, CT
Daniele, Frank A. ..... New York, NY
Daniele, Jennie R. ..... Bronx, NY
Daniele, Julie E. ..... Boston, MA
Daniele, Mark A. ..... Newark, NJ
Daniele, Michele ..... Cherry Hill, NJ
Philadelphia, PA
Daniele, Paul R. ..... Newark, NJ
Daniele, Rhonda Lee ..... Norristown, PA
Daniele, Theresa M. ..... White Plains, NY
Daniele, Vanessa M. ..... Wilkes-Barre, PA
Williamsport, PA
Daniele, Vanessa M., P.C. ..... Williamsport, PA
Danieleski, John J., Jr. ..... Saginaw, MI
Danielewicz, Michael J. ..... Chicago, IL
Danielewicz, Raymond F. ..... Berlin, NJ
Daniel-Grobler, Anne M. ..... Washington, DC
Danieli, Ann Elizabeth ..... Seattle, WA
Danieli, Hadar R. ..... Chicago, IL
Danielian, Arsen ..... Glendale, CA
Danielian, Jason Frank ..... Markham, IL
Daniell, David F. ..... Mobile, AL
Daniell, Grace Elaine ..... Chattanooga, TN
Daniell, John R. ..... Newport Beach, CA
Daniell, Roy B., III ..... Decatur, GA
Daniell, William P. ..... Durham, NC
Danielle, Suzanne W. ..... Federal Way, WA
D'Aniello, Jerry S. ..... Somerville, NJ
Daniello, John P. ..... Wilmington, DE
D'Aniello, Michael J. ..... Norristown, PA
D'Aniello, Phil A. ..... Miami, FL
Daniells, Thomas M. ..... Hartford, CT
Danielpour, Michael ..... Los Angeles, CA
Daniels, Alan H. ..... Orlando, FL
Daniels, Albert L. ..... Elmhurst, IL
Daniels, Alfred J. ..... Guttenberg, NJ
Daniels, Allen B. ..... Houston, TX
Daniels, Allison D. ..... Oakland, CA
Daniels, Alys Nagler
North Palm Beach, FL
Daniels, Ann G. ..... San Francisco, CA
Daniels, Anthea R. ..... Cleveland, OH
Daniels, Arthur H. ..... Corpus Christi, TX
Daniels Associates, PLC ..... Louisville, KY
Daniels, Barbara Ann ..... Newark, NJ
Daniels, Bethany C. ..... Pittsburg, KS
Daniels, B. J. ..... Miami Beach, FL
Daniels, Bonnie L. ..... Miami, FL
Daniels, Branch H., Jr. ..... Portsmouth, VA
Daniels, Brian P. ..... New Haven, CT
Daniels, Bruce F. ..... New Hartford, NY
Daniels, Bruce F., P.C. ..... New Hartford, NY
Daniels, Bruce J. ..... North Palm Beach, FL
Daniels, Bryant J. ..... Redondo Beach, CA
Daniels, C. Fred ..... Birmingham, AL
Daniels, C. William, Jr. ..... Mobile, AL
Daniels, Carl A. ..... Tantallon, MD
Daniels, Carney D. ..... Wakefield, MA
Daniels, Carol Tipton ..... Sudbury, MA
Daniels, Carolyn E. ..... Denver, CO
Daniels, Charic M. ..... Houston, TX
Daniels, Charlene G. ..... New York, NY
Daniels, Charles E. ..... Bartlesville, OK
Daniels, Charles M. ..... Pensacola, FL
Daniels, Charles M. ..... Greenup, KY
Daniels, Charles W. ..... Albuquerque, NM
Daniels, Cheryl Furstace ..... Madison, WI
Daniels, Christine Carey ..... Schenectady, NY
Daniels, Christopher B. ..... Houston, TX
Daniels, Christopher D. ..... Madison, WI
Daniels, Christopher J. ..... Columbia, SC
Daniels, Christopher M. ..... Minneapolis, MN
Daniels, Constance ..... Tampa, FL
Daniels, D. Scott ..... Vallejo, CA
Daniels, Daniel L. ..... Stamford, CT
Daniels & Daniels ..... San Antonio, TX
Daniels & Daniels, P.A.
Research Triangle Park, NC
Daniels, David A. ..... Pawling, NY
Daniels, David E. ..... Pawling, NY
Daniels, David M. ..... Sacramento, CA
Daniels, David R. ..... Los Angeles, CA
Daniels, David R. ..... Biloxi, MS
Daniels, David W.T. ..... Washington, DC
Daniels, Deana M. ..... Miamisburg, OH
Daniels, Deborah ..... Columbia, MO
Daniels, Deborah D. ..... New York, NY
Daniels, Deborah J. ..... Indianapolis, IN
Daniels, Diana M. ..... Washington, DC
Daniels, Donald L. ..... Orange, CA
Daniels, Donna Ross ..... New York, NY
Daniels, Douglas A. ..... Daytona Beach, FL
Daniels, Douglas A. ..... Houston, TX
Daniels, Douglas H. ..... New York, NY
Daniels, Douglas R. ..... New Haven, CT
Daniels, E. Kent, Jr. ..... Cleveland, OH
Daniels, Earl F. (Sam), III ..... Tucson, AZ
Daniels, Edmund D. ..... Houston, TX
Daniels, Edward C., Jr. ..... Cape Coral, FL
Daniels, Edward L. ..... Albany, OR
Daniels, Edwin H. ..... New Bern, NC
Daniels, Elaine C. ..... Mount Pleasant, MI
Daniels, Elizabeth J. ..... Clearwater, FL
Daniels, Eric D. ..... Hartford, CT
Daniels, Eric S. ..... Department of Justice,
Justice Management Division, GV
Daniels, Erin Leigh ..... Palm Springs, CA
Daniels, Eugene O. ..... Denver, CO
Daniels, Fine, Israel & Schonbuch, LLP
Los Angeles, CA
Daniels, Franklin G. ..... Myrtle Beach, SC
Daniels, Fred G. ..... Lake Success, NY
Daniels, Frederick J. ..... Orlando, FL
Daniels, Gary L. ..... Mount Holly, NJ
Daniels, Gena H. ..... Mobile, AL
Daniels, George B. ..... New York, NY
Daniels, George F. ..... Pittsburgh, PA
Daniels, George G. ..... Orlando, FL
Daniels, George P. ..... Casselberry, FL
Daniels, Georgia Lynn ..... Medford, OR
Daniels, Gordie O. ..... Miami, FL
Daniels, Graham C. ..... Chester, VA
Daniels, Harold F. ..... Pickens, SC
Daniels, Harry T. ..... Boston, MA
Daniels, Howard F. ..... Los Angeles, CA
Daniels, Isiah, III ..... Columbus, OH
Daniels, J. Christopher
Oklahoma City, OK
Daniels, J. Martelle ..... Grand Junction, CO
Daniels, J. Steve ..... Livingston, TN
Daniels, James B. ..... Roseland, NJ
Daniels, James D. ..... Short Hills, NJ
Daniels, James E. ..... New York, NY
Daniels, James F. B. ..... Kansas City, MO
Daniels, James L. ..... Jennings, LA
Lafayette, LA
Daniels, James L. ..... Golden Valley, MN
Daniels, James P. ..... Albany, NY
Daniels, James W. ..... Costa Mesa, CA
Daniels, Janean Acevedo ..... Santa Barbara, CA
Daniels, Jeffrey C. ..... Garden City, NY
Daniels, Jennifer L. ..... Dakota Dunes, SD
Daniels, Jennifer M. ..... Armonk, NY
Daniels, Jere F. ..... Winter Park, FL
Daniels, Jere F., Jr. ..... Norcross, GA
Daniels, Jere Franklin, Jr.
Winter Park, FL
Daniels, Jerry ..... Lawrenceville, GA
Daniels, Joan C. ..... Anaheim, CA
Daniels, Joan T. ..... Los Angeles, CA
Daniels, Joel B. ..... Houston, TX
Daniels, Joel L. ..... Buffalo, NY
Daniels, John A. ..... San Antonio, TX
Daniels, John B. ..... New York, NY
Daniels, John D. ..... Chicago, IL
Daniels, John D. ..... Sioux City, IA
Daniels, John F., III ..... Phoenix, AZ
Daniels, John F. "Jack" ..... Wilmington, DE
Daniels, John H. ..... Phoenix, AZ
Daniels, John H. ..... Mineola, NY
Daniels, John H., III ..... Greenville, MS
Daniels, John H., Jr. ..... Minneapolis, MN
Daniels, John P., (Inc.) ..... Los Angeles, CA
Daniels, John S. ..... Dallas, TX
Daniels, John W., Jr. ..... Milwaukee, WI
Daniels, Joseph F. ..... Palo Alto, CA
Daniels, Juliette E. ..... Dallas, TX
Daniels, Justin J. ..... New York, NY
Daniels, Justin S. ..... Atlanta, GA
Daniels & Kaplan, P.C. ..... Birmingham, MI
Kansas City, MO
Daniels, Kara L. ..... Washington, DC
Daniels, Karen Kelly ..... Macon, GA
Daniels, Kashtan & Fornaris, P.A.
Coral Gables, FL
Fort Lauderdale, FL
Miami, FL
Palm Beach, FL
Daniels, Katherine E. ..... Blythewood, SC
Daniels, Katherine J. ..... New York, NY
Daniels, Keith Allan ..... Albany, NY
Daniels, Keith B., Jr. ..... Chicago, IL
Daniels, Keith E. ..... Fort Worth, TX
Daniels, Kelli R. ..... Austin, TX
Daniels, Kelly L. ..... Norfolk, VA
Daniels, Kenneth F. ..... Minneapolis, MN
Daniels, Kenneth G. ..... Alexandria, LA
Daniels, Kenneth R. ..... Denver, CO
Daniels, Kerrie A. ..... Southfield, MI
Daniels, Kimberly R. ..... San Francisco, CA
Daniels, L. Mickele, & Associates
Houston, TX
Daniels Law Firm ..... Pickens, SC
Daniels Law Firm, P.L.L.C.
Charleston, WV
Daniels Law Offices, P.C. ..... Boston, MA
Daniels, Lawrence R. ..... Towson, MD
Daniels, Lee A. ..... Chicago, IL
Daniels, Leslie J. ..... San Jose, CA
Daniels, Linda L. ..... San Antonio, TX
Daniels, Linda Markus
Research Triangle Park, NC
Daniels, Lisa ..... Lynbrook, NY
Daniels, Lisa Leonard ..... Fort Lauderdale, FL
Daniels, Louis D. ..... Memphis, TN
Daniels, Lucy A. ..... Overland Park, KS
Daniels, Lynne Caryl ..... Irvine, CA
Daniels, M. Lee, Jr. ..... Greenville, SC
Daniels, Mack T. ..... Chester, VA
Daniels, Marci S. ..... Rancho Santa Fe, CA
Daniels, Mark ..... Thousand Oaks, CA
Daniels, Martin P. ..... New Canaan, CT
New York, NY
Daniels, Mauro & Pinsel ..... Waukegan, IL
Daniels, Michael D. ..... Beverly Hills, CA
Daniels, Michael D., A Professional
Corporation ..... Beverly Hills, CA
Daniels, Michael J. ..... New Orleans, LA
Daniels, Michael J. ..... Ocean City, NJ
Daniels, Michael Joseph ..... Los Angeles, CA
Daniels, Michael K. ..... Albuquerque, NM
Daniels, Michael O. ..... Bakersfield, CA
Daniels, Michael P. ..... Washington, DC
Daniels, Michael Paul ..... Southfield, MI
Daniels, Michael R. ..... Honolulu, HI
Daniels, M. K. ..... Deer Lodge, MT
Daniels, Nancy A. ..... Tallahassee, FL
Daniels, Nicholas ..... Petersburg, VA
Daniels, Nicholas M. ..... Miami, FL
Daniels, Nora M. ..... Needham, MA
Daniels, Norman T., Jr. ..... Charleston, WV
Daniels, Patricia C. ..... San Francisco, CA
Daniels, Patricia M. ..... Houston, TX
Daniels, Patrick W. ..... San Diego, CA
Daniels, Paul A. ..... Washington, DC
Alexandria, VA
Daniels, Paula A. ..... Los Angeles, CA
Daniels, Peter A. ..... Binghamton, NY
Daniels, Peter Gary ..... Wheaton, IL
Daniels, Quentin A. ..... Jackson, MS
Daniels, Raymond ..... Cranston, RI
Daniels, Reuben, Jr. ..... Milwaukee, WI
Daniels, Rhoda T. ..... Louisville, KY
Daniels, Rhonda L. ..... Washington, DC
Daniels, Richard C. ..... Waukegan, IL
Daniels, Richard C. ..... College Park, MD
Daniels, Richard G. ..... Miami, FL
Daniels, Richard H. ..... Millville, NJ
Daniels, Richard J. ..... San Jose, CA
Daniels, Richard L. ..... Los Angeles, CA
Daniels, Richard S. ..... Asheville, NC
Daniels, Richard S., Jr. ..... Boston, MA
Daniels, Rita Everding ..... St. Louis, MO
Daniels, Robert C. ..... Philadelphia, PA
Daniels, Robert C., Ltd. ..... Philadelphia, PA
Daniels, Robert D. ..... Los Angeles, CA
Daniels, Robert G. ..... Nashua, NH
Daniels, Robert H. ..... San Francisco, CA
Daniels, Robert L., Jr. ..... Orlando, FL
Daniels, Robin Patrick ..... Boston, MA
Daniels, Rochelle Jadek
Fort Lauderdale, FL
Daniels, Rona ..... New York, NY
Daniels, Ronald L., (P.C.) ..... Tulsa, OK
Daniels, Roosevelt, Jr. ..... Jackson, MS
Daniels, Ruth Ann Norton ..... Dallas, TX
Daniels, Samantha S. ..... New York, NY
Daniels, Sanders, Pianowski, Todd & Thomas ..... Elkhart, IN
Goshen, IN
South Bend, IN
Daniels, Scott ..... Salt Lake City, UT
Daniels, Scott A. ..... Manchester, NH
Daniels, Scott M. ..... Washington, DC
Daniels, Sean J. ..... New York, NY
Daniels, Shawn B. ..... Fayetteville, AR
Daniels, Shepperd ..... Westbury, NY
Daniels, Sherri Giffin ..... Naperville, IL
Daniels & Sooter, L.L.C. ..... Alexandria, LA
Daniels, Spencer W. ..... Olympia, WA
Daniels, Stephen H. ..... Cleveland, OH
Daniels, Stephen M.
General Services Administration,
Board of Contract Appeals, GV
Daniels, Steven H. ..... Springfield, NJ
Daniels, Steven J. ..... Wilmington, DE
Daniels, Steven K. ..... Waterloo, IA
Daniels, Steven L. ..... Boca Raton, FL
West Palm Beach, FL
Daniels, Steven R. ..... Austin, TX
Daniels, Steven W. ..... Oklahoma City, OK
Daniels, Tammy ..... Detroit, MI
Daniels & Taylor, P.C. ..... Lawrenceville, GA
Daniels, Theodore ..... Garden City, NY
Daniels, Thomas C. ..... Cleveland, OH
Daniels, Thomas E. ..... Ann Arbor, MI
Ypsilanti, MI
Daniels, Thomas J. ..... St. Paul, MN
Daniels, Thomas R. ..... Scranton, PA
Daniels, Timothy A. ..... Dallas, TX
Daniels, Timothy F. ..... New Orleans, LA
Daniels, Timothy J. ..... San Antonio, TX
Daniels, Timothy P. ..... St. Paul, MN
Daniels, Valerie L. ..... San Antonio, TX
Daniels, Vernon R. ..... Omaha, NE
Daniels, Walter E.
Research Triangle Park, NC
Daniels, Walter E., Jr. ..... Birmingham, AL
Daniels, Wendel E. ..... Lakewood, NJ
Daniels, Wesley A., III ..... Watertown, NY
Daniels, Westwell R. ..... Coral Gables, FL
Daniels, W. F. ..... Fayette, MO
Daniels, Wilbur ..... New York, NY
Daniels, William A. ..... Los Angeles, CA
Daniels, William B. ..... Monterey, CA
Daniels, William Boone, II ..... Sebastopol, CA
Daniels, William Boone, II, P.C.
Sebastopol, CA
Daniels, William F., Jr. ..... Carmel, IN
Daniels, William L. ..... Chicago, IL
Daniels, William R., Jr., (P.A.)
Monticello, AR
Daniels, William Stanbert ..... Carlisle, PA
Daniels, William Thomas ..... Houston, TX
Danielsen, Dan ..... Boston, MA
Danielsen, David J. ..... San Diego, CA
Danielsen, Robert G. ..... Plymouth, MN
Danielson, Allen H., Jr. ..... New Orleans, LA
Danielson, Andrew W. ..... Minneapolis, MN
Danielson, April B. ..... Bessemer, AL
Danielson, Barry K. ..... Elgin, IL
Danielson, Brent ..... Manistee, MI
Danielson, Brian L. ..... Marshalltown, IA
Danielson, Carmen S. ..... Boulder, CO
Danielson, Clarke, Charbonneau & Platt, P.A. ..... West Palm Beach, FL
Danielson, Cynthia H. ..... Mt. Pleasant, IA
Danielson, David A.
West Palm Beach, FL
Danielson, David, (P.S.) ..... Seattle, WA
Danielson, Edward J.
Department of the Navy,
Office of the Judge Advocate General, GV
Danielson, Elizabeth W. ..... Waldron, AR
Danielson, Erin R. ..... New Orleans, LA
Danielson, Gary R. ..... St. Clair Shores, MI
Danielson, George E. ..... Los Angeles, CA
Danielson, Gregory R. ..... Denver, CO
Danielson Group, The, P.C.
St. Clair Shores, MI
Danielson, Guettinger, Richie & Manydeeds, S.C. ..... Eau Claire, WI
Danielson, Gustav A.
Charlotte Amalie, St. Thomas, VI
Danielson Harrigan & Tollefson, LLP
Seattle, WA
Danielson, James M. ..... Moses Lake, WA
Wenatchee, WA
Danielson, Joan Lewis ..... Los Angeles, CA
Danielson, John C. ..... Punta Gorda, FL
Danielson, Kevin ..... Tulsa, OK
Danielson, Larry Robert ..... Los Angeles, CA
Danielson, Laura J. ..... Minneapolis, MN
Danielson, Lauren G. ..... Atlanta, GA
Danielson Law Office, P.C. ..... Mt. Pleasant, IA
Danielson, Linda M. ..... Eau Claire, WI
Danielson, Lisa A. ..... Milwaukee, WI
Danielson, Mark C. ..... Iowa City, IA
Danielson, Mark J. ..... Palo Alto, CA
Danielson, Mark R. ..... Richardson, TX
Danielson, Michele M. ..... St. Paul, MN
Danielson, Michelle L. ..... Milwaukee, WI
Danielson, Paul E. ..... Booneville, AR
Danielson, Paul V. ..... Columbus, OH
Danielson, Philip R. ..... Burlington, VT
Danielson, Richard ..... United States Senate,
Office of Senate Legal Counsel, GV
Danielson, Robert E. ..... Portland, ME
Danielson, Robert G. ..... Sweet Home, OR
Danielson, Silas L. ..... Mankato, MN
Danielson, Steven G. ..... Eau Claire, WI
Danielson-Kube, Kari ..... Wenatchee, WA
Daniels-Stock, Howard R. ..... Agoura Hills, CA
Daniel-Weeks, Bernell ..... Durham, NC
Danieri, T. W. Ronald ..... Corona, CA
Danieu, John P. ..... Buffalo, NY
Danieu, Kimberlee Lupton ..... Buffalo, NY
Danikolas, Chris T. ..... Bloomfield Hills, MI
Danikolas, James ..... Gary, IN
Danilack, Michael ..... Washington, DC
Danilek, Donald J. ..... New York, NY
Daniloff, Deborah A. ..... San Francisco, CA
Danilov, Dan P. ..... Seattle, WA
Danilow, Greg A. ..... New York, NY
Danilowicz, L. Paul ..... Quincy, MA
Danilson, David R. ..... Boone, IA
Daniluck, John V. ..... Indianapolis, IN
Daniluk, Suzanne M. ..... Houston, TX
Danin, Gerald G. ..... Harbor Springs, MI
Daninhirsch, Hilary Sue ..... Pittsburgh, PA
Danio, Leslie A. ..... Springfield, MA
Danis, David O. ..... St. Louis, MO
Danis, Gary F. ..... Summit, NJ
Danis, Jeffrey N. ..... Manchester, NH

Dapper, David P. ....Los Angeles, CA
Dapper, John ....Austin, TX
Dapper, Robert E., Jr. ....Pittsburgh, PA
D'Appolito, Alan E. ....Upper Marlboro, MD
DaPrile, Denise A. ....Neptune, NJ
D'Aprile, Denise B. ....Port Charlotte, FL
D'Aprile, Denise B., P.A., Law Office of
Port Charlotte, FL
D'Aprile, Gina M. ....New York, NY
Daprile, Joseph R. ....Cleveland, OH
D'Aprile, Rocco ....Glen Mills, PA
DaProcida, Joseph ....New York, NY
Dapron, Charles E. ....St. Louis, MO
Dapser, Wayne R. ....Huntington Beach, CA
D'Apuzzo, Alfonso M. ....Medford, MA
D'Aquila, Barbara Jean ....Minneapolis, MN
D'Aquila, C. Jerome ....New Roads, LA
D'Aquila, Jean M. ....Hartford, CT
D'Aquila, Roy M. ....Kenner, LA
D'Aquilla, SamuelC. ....Jackson, LA
d'Aquin, Joseph F., III ....Metairie, LA
D'Aquin, Leila A. ....Dallas, TX
D'Aquino, Albert J. ....Buffalo, NY
Dara, Joseph Martin ....Baldwin, NY
Daraban, Louis M. ....San Pedro, CA
Darabaris, Elizabeth B. ....San Ramon, CA
Daraee, Hafez ....Portland, OR
Daragan, Joseph J. ....Arlington, VA
Darakjy, Jack C. ....Oradell, NJ
Daray, Michael J. ....Traverse City, MI
Darbee, Bosco & Hammond, P.C.
Bay City, MI
Darbee, Donald H. ....Oakdale, NY
Darbee, William H. ....Bay City, MI
Darbinian, Azniv ....Walnut Creek, CA
Darbinian, Silva ....Santa Rosa, CA
Darbo, Howard H. ....Carol Stream, IL
Darbut, Douglas F. ....Miami, FL
Darby, Alvin L. ....Philadelphia, PA
Darby, Amanda M. ....Newport Beach, CA
Darby, Ben H., Jr. ....Lakeland, FL
Darby & Darby, Professional Corporation
Los Angeles, CA
New York, NY
Darby, David Alan, Law Office of
Tucson, AZ
Darby, Delano & Price ....Winona, MN
Darby, G. Harrison ....Los Angeles, CA
Darby, George E. ....Greenville, SC
Darby, Gregory J. ....Keystone Heights, FL
Darby, Harwell M., Jr. ....Roanoke, VA
Darby, Herbert F., (P.A.) ....Lake City, FL
Darby, J. Patrick ....Birmingham, AL
Darby, James L., Jr. ....Savannah, GA
Darby, Jeffery S. ....San Antonio, TX
Darby, Joan M. ....Washington, DC
Darby, John M. ....Diboll, TX
Darby, Joseph B., III ....Boston, MA
Darby, Joseph J. ....San Diego, CA
Darby, Joseph M. ....Ossining, NY
Darby, Karen S. ....Columbus, OH
Darby, Ken M. ....Altus, OK
Darby, Kenneth V. ....Morton Grove, IL
Darby Laundon Stearns Thorndike & Kolter
Stowe, VT
Waterbury, VT
Darby, Lawrence A., III ....New York, NY
Darby, Leslie F. ....Portland, OR
Darby, Michael A. ....Flint, MI
Darby, Michael M. ....Manchester, CT
Darby, P. Matthew ....Baltimore, MD
Darby, Peele, Bowdoin, Payne & Kennon
Lake City, FL
Darby, Perry E. ....Baltimore, MD
Darby, Regina L. ....New York, NY
Darby, Richard B. ....Altus, OK
Darby, Richard H. ....Winona, MN
Darby, Richard W. ....Waterbury, VT
Darby, Robert E. ....Los Angeles, CA
Darby, Roland B. ....Houston, TX
Darby, Ronald E. ....Camden, TN
Darby, Sandra L. ....Southport, NC
Darby, Shelly J. ....Costa Mesa, CA
Darby, Shirley D. ....Atmore, AL
Darby, Shirley D., P.C. ....Atmore, AL
Darby, Timothy J. ....Washington, DC
Darby, W. Drew ....San Angelo, TX
Darby, William L. ....Oakland, CA
Darby, Willis C., Jr. ....Mobile, AL
Darby, Willis C., Jr., Professional Corporation ....Mobile, AL
Darby-Reid, Michele ....Marietta, GA
Darbyshire, Glen M. ....Atlanta, GA
Savannah, GA
Darbyshire, J. Hobart ....Davenport, IA
d'Arcambal, Michelle J. ....New York, NY
d'Arcambal, Nicole ....Chicago, IL
D'Arcangelo, Frederick A. ....Summit, NJ
D'Arcangelo, Joseph M. ....Toledo, OH
D'Arcangelo, Julie M. ....Toledo, OH
D'Arcangelo, Michael J. ....Toledo, OH
Darce, Noel J. ....New Orleans, LA
Darcey, Jeanne P. ....Boston, MA
Darch, Douglas A. ....Chicago, IL
D'Arche, Douglas D. ....Houston, TX
Darche, Gary M. ....Kew Gardens, NY
Darche, Gary M. ....New York, NY
Darche, John P. ....Whippany, NJ
Darche, Michael ....Brockton, MA
Darchuk, Walter ....North Little Rock, AR
D'Arco, Thomas R. ....Riverside, CA
D'Arcy, Andrew J. ....Morristown, NJ
D'Arcy, Anita M. ....Lincolnshire, IL
D'Arcy, Charles E., III ....Sacramento, CA
D'Arcy, Charles J. ....Akron, OH
Darcy, D. Alexander ....Chicago, IL
Darcy, Daniel Philip ....Chicago, IL
Darcy, Denise A. ....Chicago, IL
Darcy, Dwight D. ....New York, NY
D'Arcy, Edward D., Jr. ....Chicago, IL
Darcy, Francis J., Jr. ....Dearborn, MI
Darcy, James M. ....Woodside, NY
Darcy, John F. ....Ridgewood, NJ
Darcy, John J. ....Fairfield, CT
Darcy, John J. ....Pittsford, NY
Rochester, NY
Darcy, Jonathan M. ....Princeton, NJ
Darcy, Lynne ....New York, NY
Darcy, Mary Ellen ....Cleveland, OH
Darcy, Paul T. ....New York, NY
Darcy, Sally M. ....Tucson, AZ
D'Arcy, Sean G. ....Washington, DC
Darcy, Stathy ....Chicago, IL
D'Arcy, Theodore B. ....Colorado Springs, CO
Darcy, Thomas J. ....Middletown, NY
Dardaganis, Eftihia ....Rochester, NY
Dardani, Thomas E. ....Southport, CT
Dardano, David W. ....Lake Oswego, OR
Dardarian, Linda M. ....Oakland, CA
Dardashti, Sean S. ....Beverly Hills, CA
Dardeck, Stephen Alan ....Rutland, VT
Darden, Allen D. ....Baton Rouge, LA
Darden, Christopher Allen ....Los Angeles, CA
Darden, David P. ....Marietta, GA
Darden, Edwin C. ....Springfield, VA
Darden, Elise Bryant ....Richmond, VA
Darden, Eric J. ....Washington, DC
Darden, Fowler and Creighton, L.L.P.
Conroe, TX
Darden, George (Buddy) ....Atlanta, GA
Darden, J. Christopher ....Tulsa, OK
Darden, Joe W. ....Memphis, TN
Darden, John A., III ....Las Cruces, NM
Darden, Josephine R. ....Raleigh, NC
Darden, Kelly M., Jr.
North Miami Beach, FL
Darden, Larry W. ....Pasadena, CA
Darden, Linnie L., III ....Hinesville, GA
Darden, M. Taylor ....New Orleans, LA
Darden, Millard P., Jr. ....Atlanta, GA
Darden, Rita Henderson ....Madisonville, TX
Darden, Robert D., Jr.
Morehead City, NC
Darden, Stephen M. ....Johnson City, TN
Kingsport, TN
Darden, Thomas F., II ....Raleigh, NC
Darden, Thomas M. ....Minneapolis, MN
Darden, William C. ....Chino, CA
Darden, William H.
United States Court Of Appeals For The Armed Forces, GV
Darden, William H. ....Raton, NM
Darden, William T. ....Sacramento, CA
Dardenne, Desha D. ....Atlanta, GA
Dardenne, John L., Jr. ....Baton Rouge, LA
Dardeno, Frank N. ....Somerville, MA
Dardeno, Frank N., Jr. ....Somerville, MA
Dardeno, Ronald A. ....Somerville, MA
Dardes, Susan E. ....Newtown, PA
Dardess, James A. ....Sheffield, AL
Dardi, Peter S. ....Minneapolis, MN
Dardick, Christina M. ....Chicago, IL
Dardick, Lewis A. ....Owings Mills, MD
Dardick, Nathan H. ....Chicago, IL
Dardinski, Gerald J. ....Annapolis, MD
Dardis, Edward G. ....Damariscotta, ME
Dardis, Erin E. ....Miami, FL
Dardis, Frederic J. ....Tucson, AZ
Dardis & Hippert, P.C. ....Tucson, AZ
Dardy, William A. ....Mount Clemens, MI
Dardzinski, Michael H. ....Washington, DC
Dare, Byron L. ....Honolulu, HI
Dare, David M. ....St. Louis, MO
Dare, David T. ....Omaha, NE
Dare, Joseph C. ....Coral Gables, FL
Dare, Marilyn Tiki ....Palo Alto, CA
Dare, Paul W. ....Stone Harbor, NJ
Dare, Paul W., P.A. ....Avalon, NJ
Cape May Court House, NJ
Stone Harbor, NJ
Dare, R. Mark ....Falls Church, VA
Dare, Robyn ....Loudonville, NY
Dare, Virginia C. ....Harper Woods, MI
D'Arelli, Paul David ....Los Angeles, CA
Darensburg, Darlene ....Mesquite, TX
Darensburg, June B. ....Metairie, LA
Darer, Brian D. ....Raleigh, NC
Darflinger, Joseph J. ....Decatur, IL
Dargan, Catherine Janine
Washington, DC
Dargan, Daniel M. ....Mill Valley, CA
Dargan, Howard ....West Palm Beach, FL
Dargan, Perrin Q., III ....Charleston, SC
Dargan, Richard L.
Federal Judicial Center, GV
Dargan, Thomas J. ....Melville, NY
Dargatis, David G. ....Washington, DC
Dargay, Susan R. ....Mount Holly, NJ
Dargel, Michael E. ....Chandler, OK
Dargene, Dan C. ....Dallas, TX
D'Argenio, Rinaldo M.
Englewood Cliffs, NJ
Darger, Daniel ....Salt Lake City, UT
Darger, Jennifer W. ....New York, NY
Darger, Richard J. ....Midland, MI
Dargin, John F., Jr. ....Milton, MA
Dargis, Robert J. ....Chicago, IL
Dargitz, Stephen D. ....Wilmington, DE
Dargo, George ....Boston, MA
D'Ari, Paul
Federal Communications Commission, Wireless Telecommunications Bureau, GV
Daria, Jason A. ....Philadelphia, PA
Darian, Charles ....Glendale, CA
Darias, Alicia ....Las Vegas, NV
Darienzo, Anthony C.
Huntington Station, NY
Darienzo, Eleanor J. ....Woodbury, NY
D'Arienzo, Felix L., Jr. ....New York, NY
Darienzo, John A., Jr. ....Brooklyn, NY
Darienzo, Marie B. ....New York, NY
Darigan, Melissa E. ....Providence, RI
Darin, Bruce G. ....Joliet, IL
Darin, Darin & McMillan
Bloomfield Hills, MI
DaRin, Edward J. ....Pasadena, CA
DaRin, Edward J., Inc., A Law Corporation
Pasadena, CA
Darin & Gerjel, P.A. ....Daytona Beach, FL
Maitland, FL
Ocala, FL
Darin, Holly Quackenbush ....Killingworth, CT
Darin, John R., II ....Daytona Beach, FL
Maitland, FL
Ocala, FL
Darin, Thomas F. ....Rockford, IL
Daringer, Carolyn P. Lanzillo ....Reading, PA
Daringer, James Allen ....Reading, PA
Dario, Ronald A. ....Hackensack, NJ
Dariotis, Terrence T. ....Tallahassee, FL
Darius, Jean-Jacques Antoine ....Tampa, FL
Darji, Sachin Jay ....Minneapolis, MN
Dark, Charles K. ....Cleveland, TX
Dark, Clayton E., Jr. ....Lufkin, TX
Dark, David M. ....Kalamazoo, MI
Dark, Edward Allen ....Wooster, OH
Dark, L. Talton, III ....Morganton, NC
Dark, L. T., Jr. ....Siler City, NC
Dark, Okianer Christian ....Portland, OR
Darke, Ann L. ....Kansas City, MO
Darke, Kristen L. ....Red Bank, NJ
Darke, Richard F., (P.C.)
Grosse Pointe Woods, MI
Darke, Richard P. ....Chicago, IL
Darke, Roy R. ....Kansas City, MO
Darke & Wilson ....Grosse Pointe Woods, MI
Darken, Kevin J. ....Tampa, FL
Darkes, Barbara ....Harrisburg, PA
Darkey, Joanne M. ....New York, NY
Darkey, Kermit L. ....Denver, CO
Darknall, Judith C. ....Tempe, AZ
Darko, Richard J. ....Indianapolis, IN
Darks, H. Maxwell ....Oklahoma City, OK
Darlak, Lawrence C. ....Reston, VA
Darland, David S. ....Crofton, MD
Darland, Jack D. ....Davenport, IA
Eldridge, IA
Darland, S. Thomas ....Plentywood, MT
Darland, Tye G. ....Wichita, KS
Darley, Lon Jackson, III ....Tulsa, OK
Darley, Roger G. ....Austin, TX
Darling, Brian H. ....Boston, MA
Darling, Brian K. ....Louisville, KY
Darling, Carol A. ....Dallas, TX
Darling, Charles M., IV ....Washington, DC
Darling, Chester ....Boston, MA
Darling, Curtis ....Bakersfield, CA
Darling & Darling ....Winterset, IA
Darling, David J. ....Chicago, IL
Darling, Donnalynn N. ....Mineola, NY
Darling, Douglas K. ....San Francisco, CA
Darling, E. Suzanne ....Richmond, VA
Darling, Elizabeth C. ....Denver, CO
Darling, Ellen L. ....Irvine, CA
Darling, Eric S. ....Wauwatosa, WI
Darling, Gerald E. ....Haddonfield, NJ
Darling, Gordon K. ....Winterset, IA
Darling, Gordon K., Jr. ....Winterset, IA
Darling, Hall & Rae, LLP
Los Angeles, CA
Darling, Harris I. ....Worthington, MN
Darling, Hyman G. ....Springfield, MA
Darling, James C. ....New Ulm, MN
Darling, James E. ....McAllen, TX
Darling, Jeffrey A. ....Lexington, KY
Darling, John D. ....Pasadena, CA
Darling, John E. ....Salem, MA
Darling, John E. ....Troy, NY
Darling, John H. ....Bloomington, MN
Darling, John P. ....Alexandria, VA
Darling, Joseph W. ....Norton, VA
Darling, Kathryn Midboe ....Austin, TX
Darling & Keister ....Columbus, OH
Darling, Marc C. ....Denver, CO
Darling, Margery Lee J. ....Denver, CO
Darling, Mark A. ....Boston, MA
Darling, Mark C. ....Worcester, MA
Darling, Melanie M. ....Oakland, CA
Darling, Milton A. ....Bloomfield Hills, MI
Darling, Peter R. ....Nashville, AR
Darling, Peter S. ....Newtown, CT
Darling, Phillip H. ....Woodland Hills, CA
Darling, Ray H., Jr.
Occupational Safety and Health Review Commission, Office of the Executive Secretary, GV
Darling & Reynolds, P.S.C.
Lexington, KY
Darling, Robert A. ....Worthington, MN
Darling, Robert H. ....Southfield, MI
Darling, Ronald Everett ....Costa Mesa, CA
Darling, Scott E., (A Professional Corporation)
Riverside, CA
Darling, Stanton G. ....Columbus, OH
Darling, Stanton G., II ....Columbus, OH
Darling, Stephen E. ....Charleston, SC
Darling, Stephen R. ....Corpus Christi, TX
Darling, Thomas A. ....Sacramento, CA
Darling, Thomas S. ....Minneapolis, MN
Darling, Thomas W. ....Gretna, LA
Darling, William D., (P.C.) ....Austin, TX
Darling, William J. ....Albuquerque, NM
Darling, William J., & Associates, P.A., A Prof. Assn. ....Albuquerque, NM
Darling, Wm. Webster, II ....Rogers, AR
Darlington, Amy Elliott ....Radnor, PA
Darlington, Ann Gaines ....Chattanooga, TN
Darlington, Chester F., Jr.
Philadelphia, PA
Darlington, E. Dillwyn ....Feasterville, PA
Darlington, Fred. L. ....Cincinnati, OH
Darlington, G. Ronald ....Harrisburg, PA
Darlington, John ....Nevada City, CA
Darlington, Joyce A. ....New Orleans, LA
Darlington, Michael
Rancho Cucamonga, CA
Darlington, Stephen M. ....Cleveland, OH
Darlington, Susan W. ....Hempstead, NY
Darlow, David ....Miami, FL
Darlow, Debbie Crupain ....Houston, TX
Darlow, Julia Donovan ....Detroit, MI
Darlson, John A. ....Palm City, FL
Darmafol, Claudia ....Needham, MA
D'Armagnac, Kathleen L.
San Francisco, CA
Darman, Leslie J.
Environmental Protection Agency, Office of the General Counsel, GV
Darman, Lisa B. ....Boston, MA
Darman, Sumner ....Boston, MA
Darmanian, Denise G. ....Flemington, NJ
New York, NY
Darmanin, Maureen A. ....Newark, NJ
Darmer, Karenina M. ....Boston, MA
Darmer, Roman E., II ....Costa Mesa, CA
D'Arminio, Louis L. ....Woodcliff Lake, NJ
Darmody, Stephen J. ....Washington, DC
Darmody, Thomas G. ....New York, NY
Darmofal, Claudia Maria ....Bryan, TX
Darmon, Elaine P. ....Franklin, MI
D'Armond, William R. ....Baton Rouge, LA
Darmstadter, Henry C., III
Department of Justice, Tax Division, GV
Darmstadter, Howard M. ....New York, NY
Darmstadter Elliott, Celeste
New Orleans, LA
Darnall, C. Jackson ....Addison, IL
Darnall, Carl M. ....Rochester, NY
Darnall, Danny E. ....Elizabethtown, KY
Darnall, Darleen R. ....Portland, OR
Darnall, Eleanor B. ....Austin, TX
Darnall, Elizabeth A. ....Dallas, TX
Darnall, Karen ....Camarillo, CA
Darnall, Marcy Bradshaw, III ....Nashville, TN
Darnall, Polachek & Krantz ....Addison, IL
Darnall, Richard M. ....Cherry Hill, NJ
Darnbrough, Douglas J. ....Fall River, MA
Darneal, Thomas L., II
Colorado Springs, CO
Darneille, Alan R. ....Sacramento, CA
Darneille, Diane Davenny ....Washington, DC
Darneille, Hopewell H., III
Washington, DC
Darnel, David H. ....Setauket, NY
Darnel, James ....Denver, CO
Darnell, Alan M. ....Woodbridge, NJ
Darnell, Alex W. ....Clarksville, TN
Darnell, Anne ....Tulsa, OK
Darnell, Charles E. ....Lebanon, MO
Darnell, Chester E. ....Houston, TX
Darnell, Clifton E. ....Memphis, TN
Darnell, Dan A. ....Farmington Hills, MI
Darnell, David L. ....Georgetown, TX
Darnell, David N. ....Kingsport, TN
Darnell, Donald C. ....Ann Arbor, MI
Darnell, Eric B. ....El Paso, TX
Darnell, Eric B., P.C. ....El Paso, TX
Darnell & Flynn ....Frankfort, KY
Darnell, Jim ....Dallas, TX
El Paso, TX
Darnell, Jim, P.C. ....El Paso, TX
Darnell, Jonathan N. ....San Antonio, TX
Darnell, Joseph D. ....Anchorage, AK
Darnell, Michael C. ....New Orleans, LA
Darnell, Michael J. ....Louisville, KY
Darnell, Philip B. ....Naples, FL
Darnell, R. William ....Lincoln, NE
Darnell, Robert W.
Environmental Protection Agency, Program Office Attorneys, GV
Darnell, Robert W. ....Sarasota, FL
Darnell, Roger D. ....Newport Beach, CA
Darnell, Stephen E. ....New York, NY
Darnell, Steve R. ....Clarksville, TN
Darnell, William David ....Memphis, TN
Darnell-Anderson, Lois Marie
Richmond, UT
Darner, Robert G. ....Bloomington, IL
Darner, Thomas A.
Environmental Protection Agency, Office of the General Counsel, GV
Darnieder, Julie J. ....Milwaukee, WI
Darnieder, Mark C. ....Milwaukee, WI
Darnieder, West, Davis & Geraghty
Milwaukee, WI
Darnielle, Gary L. ....Eugene, OR
Darnley, James D., Jr. ....Indianapolis, IN
Kalamazoo, MI
Darnold, David ....Nevada, MO
Darnold, Douglas D. ....Dallas, TX
Darnton, James E. ....Benton Harbor, MI
Darnton, Rutzky & Dodge, P.C.
Ann Arbor, MI
Darnton, Thomas B. ....Ann Arbor, MI
Daro, Gina ....St. Petersburg, FL
Daroca, Sylvan P., III ....Pasadena, CA
Daroci, Robert G. ....Freehold, NJ
Daroff, Charles, II ....Cleveland, OH
Daroff, Herbert K. ....Quincy, MA
Daroff, William C. ....Cleveland, OH

Daroga, N. (Norrie) ... Brown Deer, WI
Darold, Jane Marie ... Pound Ridge, NY
Daron, Harold M. ... Salem, OR
Daronco, Peter J.
Federal Communications Commission, Wireless Telecommunications Bureau, GV
Da Rosa, Carlos D.
Environmental Protection Agency, Environmental Appeals Board, GV
Da Rosa and Miller ... Wheaton, IL
Da Rosa, Ronald A. ... Wheaton, IL
Daross, James A. ... El Paso, TX
Darpel, Paul J. ... Crestview Hills, KY
D'Arpino, Ann M. ... Boston, MA
D'Arpino, John J. ... Rochester, NY
D'Arpino, Vincent A. ... New York, NY
Darque, Michelle ... Hicksville, NY
Darques-Lane, Florence ... New York, NY
Darr, James E., Jr. ... Little Rock, AR
Darr, J. W. ... Hillsboro, OR
Darr, Kelly L. ... Philadelphia, PA
Darr, Kenneth E., Jr. ... Spartanburg, SC
Darr, Kurt J. ... Washington, DC
Darr, Lanny H., II ... Alton, IL
Darr, Leslie M. ... Covington, TN
Darr, Stephanie R ... Tulsa, OK
Darr, William M. ... Indiana, PA
Darrach, Donald M. ... Miami, FL
Darragh, Daniel M. ... Buffalo, NY
Pittsburgh, PA
Darragh, Edward ... Fort Lauderdale, FL
Darragh, George F., Jr. ... Great Falls, MT
Darragh, Neil C. ... Northampton, MA
Darragh, Thomas C. ... Bridgeview, IL
Darrah, C. Rex ... Des Moines, IA
Darrah, Charles B., & Associates
Denver, CO
Darrah, Diane C. ... Baltimore, MD
Darrah, Dorothy A. ... Washington, DC
Darrah, George R. ... Flint, MI
Darrah, James L. ... Chapman, KS
Darrah, James P. ... Stockton, CA
Darrah, John W. ... Wheaton, IL
Darrah, Joseph E. ... Powell, WY
Darrah, Mark S. ... Tulsa, OK
Darrah, Micheal L. ... Oklahoma City, OK
Darrah, Paula J. ... Severna Park, MD
Darrah, Ryan D. ... Boston, MA
Darrah, W. Timothy ... East Meadow, NY
Darrah, William C. ... Honolulu, HI
Darras, Frank N. ... Claremont, CA
Darreff, Brian C. ... Cherry Hill, NJ
Darrell, Barton D. ... Bowling Green, KY
Darrell, David J. ... Des Moines, IA
Darrell, John G. ... Brockton, MA
Darrell, Joseph A. ... San Francisco, CA
Darrell, Keith B., (P.A.) ... Boca Raton, FL
Darrell, Mark C. ... Richmond, VA
Darrell, Norris, Jr. ... New York, NY
Darrell-Kemp, Judith ... Boston, MA
Darricades, Jeanne (Gigi) ... Gillette, WY
Darrigo, Angelo ... Newburgh, NY
D'Arrigo, Charles J. ... Staten Island, NY
D'Arrigo, Cristen P. ... Bridgeton, NJ
D'Arrigo & D'Arrigo ... Bridgeton, NJ
D'Arrigo, JoAnn C. ... Bridgeton, NJ
D'Arrigo, Joseph C. ... Salem, MA
D'Arrigo, Mario ... Liverpool, NY
Darrigo, Patricia M. ... Boston, MA
Darrigo, Richard A. ... Fresh Meadows, NY
Darrigo, Ronald D. ... Tampa, FL
Darrin, David ... Palm Springs, CA
Darrin, William A., Jr. ... Milford, CT
Darringer, Bruce S. ... New York, NY
Darroch, David ... San Francisco, CA
Darroch, Elaine M.
Securities and Exchange Commission, Division of Market Regulation, GV
Darroch, Robert M. ... Atlanta, GA
Darroch, Teresa D. ... Atlanta, GA
Darron, Leah A. ... Richmond, VA
Darrough, J. William ... Fort Collins, CO
Darrough, Matthew S. ... St. Louis, MO
Darrough, Paul G., Jr.
Snowmass Village, CO
Darrouzet, Deirdre ... Austin, TX
Darrouzet, J. P. ... Austin, TX
Darrow, Andrew T. ... Mound, MN
Darrow, Bert N. ... Cabot, AR
Darrow, Carolyn Schnack ... Honolulu, HI
Darrow, Carroll L. ... San Ramon, CA
Darrow, Christopher ... Los Angeles, CA
Darrow, Clarence A. ... Rock Island, IL
Darrow, David J. ... West Orange, NJ
Darrow, Dietrich & Hawley, S.C.
Random Lake, WI
Darrow, Dietrich & Hawley, S.C.
Sheboygan, WI
Darrow, Douglas H. ... Houston, TX
Darrow, Duncan ... New York, NY
Darrow, Dwight D. ... Sheboygan, WI
Darrow, Earl N. ... San Bernardino, CA
Darrow, George E. ... Oklahoma City, OK
Darrow, Geraldine ... Long Beach, CA
Darrow & Helmsing ... Delta, CO
Darrow, Irving ... Baltimore, MD
Darrow, James D. ... Washington, DC
Darrow, James L. ... El Centro, CA
Darrow, Jessica Lynne ... New York, NY
Darrow, Jill E. ... New York, NY
Darrow, John A. ... Chicago, IL
Darrow, Kenneth F. ... Miami, FL
Darrow, Kim L. ... West Brentwood, NY
Darrow, Laurel Susan
Oklahoma City, OK
Darrow, Marc ... Santa Monica, CA
Darrow, Mary Jude ... New Orleans, LA
Darrow & Merrill ... Long Beach, CA
Darrow, Michael P. ... Annapolis, MD
Darrow, Nicholas E. ... Delta, CO
Darrow, P. Clarence ... Naples, FL
Darrow, Peter H. ... New York, NY
Darrow, Peter P., Law Offices of
Ann Arbor, MI
Darrow, Peter V. ... New York, NY
Darrow, Philip H. ... Phoenix, AZ
Darrow, Robert H. ... Santa Cruz, CA
Darrow, Russell M. ... West Bend, WI
Darrow, Sarah T. ... Trenton, NJ
Darrow, Stephen Hal ... Long Beach, CA
Darrow, Tanja L. ... Los Angeles, CA
Darrow, V. Alexandra ... Schaumburg, IL
Darrow, Warren R. ... Prescott, AZ
Darrow, William B. ... Burlington, VT
Darrow, William J. ... Evergreen, CO
Darsa, George J. ... White Plains, NY
Darsey, Alison Ann ... Lafayette, LA
New Orleans, LA
Darsey, Elton A. ... Houma, LA
Darsey, Julius H. ... Albuquerque, NM
Darsie, Charles ... Durham, NC
Darsie & Elste ... Lexington, KY
Darsky, Richard H. ... New York, NY
Darsow, Jill C. ... Walnut Creek, CA
Darsow, Paul E. D. ... Minneapolis, MN
Darst, Brian A. ... Washington, DC
Darst, Donald W. ... Walnut Creek, CA
Darst, Evelyn M. ... Kaufman, TX
Darst, John L., (Mrs.) ... Williamsburg, VA
Darst, Nancy Lee ... Wareham, MA
Darst, Richard L. ... Indianapolis, IN
Darst, Sandy ... Indianapolis, IN
Darst, Tamara J. ... Aberdeen, WA
Dart Adamson Donovan & Hanson
Salt Lake City, UT
Dart, B. L., (P.C.) ... Salt Lake City, UT
Dart, Gary W. ... Tulsa, OK
Dart, Geraldine Mele, Law Offices of
Beverly Hills, CA
Dart, Henry Attorneys at Law, A Professional Corporation ... Metairie, LA
Dart, Henry P., III ... Tucson, AZ
Dart, Henry Tutt ... Metairie, LA
Dart, John M. ... Sarasota, FL
Dart, Judith C. ... Detroit, MI
Dart, Laurie A. ... Bangor, ME
Dart, Patricia A. ... Palmyra, VA
Dart, Penelope S., Law Office of
Gambrills, MD
Dart, Stephen H. ... Harbor Springs, MI
Dart, Stephen P. ... St. Francisville, LA
Dart, Thomas H. ... Sarasota, FL
Dart, Timothy J. ... Chicago, IL
Dart, Walter A., Jr. ... Erie, PA
Darter, Charles W. ... Wellington, TX
Darter, Lewie J., III ... Atlanta, GA
Darter, O. Lloyd, Jr. ... Chapel Hill, NC
Dartez, Scott A. ... Lafayette, LA
Dartigue, Natasha Marie ... Baltimore, MD
Dartland, Walter T. ... Tallahassee, FL
Dartley, Edward T. ... Roseland, NJ
Darton, Thomas R. ... San Diego, CA
Dartt, Donald D. ... Portland, OR
Dartt, Jon A. ... Columbus, IN
Darty & Ball ... Winston-Salem, NC
Darty, Kenneth Bernard ... Winston-Salem, NC
Darugh, David G. ... Aiken, SC
Daruty, Diane Smith ... Irvine, CA
Daruty, Scott J. ... Newport Beach, CA
Darval, M. Barry ... Willmar, MN
Darvanan, Avetis G. ... Youngstown, OH
Darvas, Andrea A. ... Seattle, WA
Darvey, Diane L. ... Los Angeles, CA
Darvey, Frederick Lee ... Encino, CA
Darvick, Martin I. ... Detroit, MI
Darville, Brian B. ... Washington, DC
Darville, Lionel C. ... Belle Glade, FL
Darville, Wyndel G. ... Sarasota, FL
Darvin, Michelle G. ... Newark, NJ
Darvin, Peter L. ... Portland, ME
Darwak, John J. ... Kingston, NY
Shokan, NY
Darweesh, Callen, Lewis & Von Dohlen
Rochester, NY
Darweesh, Joseph N. ... Rochester, NY
Darwell, Robert A. ... Los Angeles, CA
Darwin, Amanda D. ... Boston, MA
Darwin, Andrew Todd ... Columbia, SC
Darwin, Anna Maria ... Greenville, SC
Darwin, David L. ... Manhasset, NY
Darwin, Florrie ... Cambridge, MA
Darwin, Lesli Brown ... Columbia, SC
Darwin, Richard C. ... San Francisco, CA
Darwin, William B., Jr. ... Spartanburg, SC
Darwish, Sayed M. ... Oakland, CA
Darwish-Esposit, Amel B. ... San Diego, CA
Daryanani, Protima ... New York, NY
Daryanani, Raj ... Chicago, IL
Das, Anjali C. ... Rolling Meadows, IL
Das, Arun ... Denver, CO
Das, Bal G. ... New York, NY
Das, Kalyan ... New York, NY
Das, Micky ... Houston, TX
Dasaro, Rose M. ... Livonia, MI
Dascanio, Dennis A. ... Santa Ana, CA
Dascenzo, Daniel P. ... Youngstown, OH
D'Ascenzo, David S. ... Portland, OR
Dascenzo, Don E. ... Bellevue, WA
Dascenzo, Janine M. ... Cincinnati, OH
D'Ascenzo, Ronald A. ... Pittsburgh, PA
Dasch, Darrell D. ... Plano, TX
Dasch, Ramon E. ... Austin, TX
Dasch, Susan M ... Trenton, NJ
Daschbach, Cooper, Hotchkiss & Csatari, Professional Association ... Hanover, NH
Lebanon, NH
Daschbach, Cory Owen ... Pittsburgh, PA
Daschbach, Joseph F. ... Lebanon, NH
Daschbach, Richard J. ... Washington, DC
Dascher, Laura L. ... Covington, VA
Dascoli, Carl John, Jr. ... Charleston, WV
Dascoli, Julie A. ... Manchester, NH
Dase, Wolfgang Arthur ... New York, NY
Dasef, David ... Bethesda, MD
Dasent, Andre C. ... Philadelphia, PA
Dasent, Carlton J. ... New Bedford, MA
D'Asero, Marcelo A. ... Norwalk, CA
Dash, A. Penny ... Department of Labor, Office of the Solicitor, GV
Dash, Abraham ... Baltimore, MD
Dash, Adam ... Somerville, MA
Dash, Andrew S. ... New York, NY
Dash, B. Alan ... Cherry Hill, NJ
Philadelphia, PA
Dash, Glen R. ... Boxborough, MA
Dash, James M. ... Chicago, IL
Dash, Jeffrey L. ... Chicago, IL
Dash, Larry M. ... Newport News, VA
Dash, Lawrence J. ... Bala Cynwyd, PA
Dash, Michael ... Cherry Hill, NJ
Philadelphia, PA
Dash, Michael L. ... Boston, MA
Dash, Ralph B. ... Los Angeles, CA
Dash, Robert Edward ... Mineola, NY
Dash, Samuel ... Washington, DC
Dashe, Joseph ... New York, NY
Dashef, Alysia A. ... New York, NY
Dashefsky, Lowell ... New York, NY
Dashefsky, Michael
Federal Trade Commission, Bureau of Competition, GV
Dashefsky, Richard L. ... Washington, DC
Dasher, Gregg ... Houston, TX
Dasher, K. Alan ... Albany, GA
Dasher, Susan J. ... Austin, TX
Dashevsky, Edwin ... Philadelphia, PA
Dashevsky, Horwitz, DiSandro, Kuhn, Dempsey and Novello, P.C.
Haddonfield, NJ
Philadelphia, PA
Dashevsky, Jeffrey L. ... Philadelphia, PA
Dashiell, Charles R., Jr. ... Salisbury, MD
Dashiell, David A., Jr. ... Norfolk, VA
Dashiell, Douglas J. ... Austin, TX
Dashiell, E. Katherine ... Sacramento, CA
Dashiell, Frederick E. ... Boston, MA
Dashiell, James R. ... Chicago, IL
Dashiell, Laurence B. ... Sacramento, CA
Dashiell, Pamela M. ... Maynard, MA
Dashiell, Robert Fulton ... Baltimore, MD
Dashiell, Russell C., Jr. ... Salisbury, MD
Dashiell, Thomas C. ... Berkeley, CA
Dashjian & Dashjian
San Luis Obispo, CA
Dashjian, Michael B.
San Luis Obispo, CA
Dashjian, Sylvia M. (Beth)
San Luis Obispo, CA
Dashman, Daniel David
Croton-On-Hudson, NY
Dashner, Geoffrey Brian ... Bedford, TX
Dashner, Jerome A. ... Street, MD
Dashoff, Arnold D. ... Baltimore, MD
Dashoff, Stephen L. ... Martinsville, VA
Dashosh, Jack ... Randolph, NJ
Dashow, Jules ... Chicago, IL
Dashow, Robert A. ... New York, NY
Dashow, Sharon Weintraub ... Brooklyn, NY
Da Silva, Albert I. ... New York, NY
DaSilva, Andrew L. ... New York, NY
DaSilva, Anthony P., Jr. ... Albany, NY
Dasilva, Eric S. ... Westport, CT
Da Silva, Eugene H. ... Wilmington, NC
DaSilva, Hilowitz & McEvily LLP
Garden City, NY
Mineola, NY
New City, NY
DaSilva, Jennifer Bancroft ... New York, NY
DaSilva, Kimberly E. ... San Francisco, CA
DaSilva, Rosemarie ... Morristown, NJ
DaSilva, Russell J. ... New York, NY
DaSilva, Willard H. ... Garden City, NY
DaSilva, Willard H. ... New City, NY
da Silva Cornell, David S. ... Miami, FL
DaSilva-Kilgore, Honoria ... Taunton, MA
Da Silveira Neves, Yolanda M.
San Juan, PR
Dasinger, Michael A., III ... Robertsdale, AL
Dasinger, Thomas Edgar ... Foley, AL
Daskais, Georgiana ... Ventura, CA
Daskal, Bernard ... Jersey City, NJ
New York, NY
Daskal, David C. ... Chicago, IL
Daskal, Dean S. ... Atlanta, GA
Daskal, Frona C. ... Chicago, IL
Daskal, Robert H. ... Chicago, IL
Daskalakis, Antonios G. ... White Plains, NY
Daskalakis, Olympia ... New York, NY
Daskam, William S., IV ... Tampa, FL
Dasnanjali, Nina ... West Hills, CA
Dasovich, Caroline L. ... Irvine, CA
Dasovich, W. Jeffrey ... Oklahoma City, OK
Daspin, D. Albert ... Chicago, IL
Daspin, Michael J. ... Orlando, FL
Daspit, Charles E. ... Baton Rouge, LA
Daspit, Jacqueline M. ... New Orleans, LA
Daspit, Laurence F. ... Harahan, LA
Daspit, Nancy R. ... Atlanta, GA
Daspit, Paul S., Jr. ... St. Martinville, LA
Dassance, David ... Los Angeles, CA
D'Assaro and Hall, P.A. ... Orlando, FL
D'Assaro, Vincent M. ... Orlando, FL
Dassau, Jennifer A. ... Califon, NJ
Dasse, Kimberly Ann ... New York, NY
Dasse, Thomas F. ... Phoenix, AZ
Dasse & Vakula, P.C. ... Phoenix, AZ
Scottsdale, AZ
Dassel, Jeanne Ellefson ... Dallas, TX
Dassel, Kathleen A.T. ... Seattle, WA
Dassenko, Paul ... Los Angeles, CA
Dassin, Lev L. ... New York, NY
Dasso, James D. ... Chicago, IL
Dasso, William J. ... Chicago, IL
Dassoff, Glenn D. ... Costa Mesa, CA
Dassoff, Nancy L. ... Los Angeles, CA
Dassori, F. Davis, (P.C.) ... Boston, MA
Dassow, Robert T. ... Indianapolis, IN
Dasta, Joseph R. ... Spartanburg, SC
Dasteel, Jeffrey H. ... Los Angeles, CA
Dasti, Jerry J. ... Forked River, NJ
Dasti, Murphy & Wellerson, P.C.
Forked River, NJ
Dastin, Barry L. ... Los Angeles, CA
Dastin, Robert E. ... Concord, NH
Manchester, NH
D'Astous, Paul ... Meriden, CT
Daswick, Michael ... Los Angeles, CA
Daszkiewicz, Rosemary ... Seattle, WA
Data, Sharon P. ... Sparta, TN
Datan, Merav R. ... Cambridge, MA
Date, Rajeev V. ... Washington, DC
Date, Sanjeev ... San Diego, CA
Date, Vandana ... Menlo Park, CA
Date, Winifred H. ... Chicago, IL
D'Ateno, Lisa ... New York, NY
Dates, John A. ... Denver, CO
Datesh, J. Nicholas, Jr. ... Pittsburgh, PA
Datesh, LuAnn R. ... Pittsburgh, PA
Datesman, Susan K. ... Baltimore, MD
Dati, James D. ... Syracuse, NY
Datig, Cregor G. ... Riverside, CA
Datillio, Ralph C. ... Tallahassee, FL
Datlow, Philip Israel ... Washington, DC
Datner and Murphy, P.C. ... Woodbury, NJ
Philadelphia, PA
Datner, Robert ... Woodbury, NJ
Philadelphia, PA
Datnow, Paul R. ... San Diego, CA
Dato, Joseph, Jr. ... Tampa, FL
Dato, Margaret M. ... Floral Park, NY
Dato, Robert M. ... Costa Mesa, CA
Dato, William S. ... San Diego, CA
Datomi, Christopher A.
Sherman Oaks, CA
Datomi, Jan M. ... Los Angeles, CA
Datri, Alan M. ... Department of Commerce, Patent and Trademark Office, GV
D'Atri, E. Lang ... Canton, OH
D'Atri, Justin W. ... New York, NY
Datsko, James R. ... Manchester, MI
Datsko, Patricia L. ... Everett, PA
Datson, Brian L. ... East Wakefield, NH
Datsopoulos, MacDonald & Lind, P.C.
Hamilton, MT
Missoula, MT
Polson, MT
Datsopoulos, Melina ... Boise, ID
Datsopoulos, Milton ... Missoula, MT
Datt, Douglas A. ... Rockville, MD
Alexandria, VA
Datta, Jivan Borja ... Miami, FL
Datta, Manjari M. ... New York, NY
Datta, Neal Richardson ... New York, NY
Datta, Ruchi B. ... Mount Laurel, NJ
Datta, Saheli ... Los Angeles, CA
Dattan, Dattan Scott, Law Offices of
Anchorage, AK
Dattani, Sheela P. ... Wilmington, DE
Dattaro, James G. ... Bethesda, MD
Datte, Deborah A. ... Hanover, PA
Lancaster, PA
Reading, PA
York, PA
Datte, Paul J. ... Pottsville, PA
Dattel, Saml. M. ... Memphis, TN
D'Attelo, Anne Marie ... Farmington, CT
Dattilo, David L. ... Louisville, KY
Dattilo, James A. ... Pittsburgh, PA
Dattilo, Joseph T. ... Cleveland, OH
Dattilo, Philip B. ... Rochester, NY
Dattilo, Philip B., Jr. ... Honeoye Falls, NY
Dattilo, Samuel B. ... Penfield, NY
Dattilo, Thomas M. ... Madison, IN
Datto, Brett A. ... Philadelphia, PA
Dattola, Rita C. ... New York, NY
Dattolo, Alphonse R.
General Services Administration, Office of Regional Counsel, GV
Dattolo, Angelo ... West Orange, NJ
D'Attomo, Daniel F. ... Joliet, IL
D'Attomo, John J. ... Chicago, IL
Dattore, Eugene F. ... Lake Mary, FL
Las Vegas, NV
Datz, A. Harold ... Philadelphia, PA
Datz, Albert J. ... Jacksonville, FL
Datz and Goldberg ... Philadelphia, PA
Datz, Harold J.
National Labor Relations Board, Office of Board Members, GV
Datz, Jacobson, Lembcke & Wright, P.A.
Jacksonville, FL
Datz, Lawrence C. ... Jacksonville, FL
Datzker, Leigh A. ... Calabasas, CA
Dau, Paolo M. (Paul) ... Palo Alto, CA
Dau, Ralph W. ... Los Angeles, CA
Daub, Harold J., Jr. ... Washington, DC
Daub, Janilyn Brouwer ... South Bend, IN
Daub, Michael H. ... Minneapolis, MN
Daub & Nelson ... Omaha, NE
Daub, Peter M. ... Washington, DC
Daub, Robert L. ... Hutchinson, KS
Daub, Russell S. ... Omaha, NE

Daub, Wayne C. .... Louisville, KY
Daubach, James L. .... Chicago, IL
Daubaras, Jeanette B. .... Des Plaines, IL
Daube, Linda L. .... Los Angeles, CA
Daubenberger, Richard C. .... Media, PA
Daubenfeld, Alfred F. .... Pacifica, CA
Dauber, Edward J. .... Newark, NJ
Dauber, Eric L. .... Plantation, FL
Dauber, Harriet S. .... Pasadena, CA
Dauber, Shannon Harrington .... Seattle, WA
Dauber, Susan G. .... Princeton, NJ
New York, NY
Dauber, William R. .... New York, NY
Daubert, Amy Griffith .... Harrisburg, PA
Daubert, Daniel D. .... Wausau, WI
Daubert, Eugene D. .... Oklahoma City, OK
Daubert, Jon K. .... San Antonio, TX
Daubert Law Firm .... Stratford, WI
Wausau, WI
Daubert, Todd D. .... Washington, DC
D'Aubin, Leo J. .... Baton Rouge, LA
Daubman, Allen E. .... Omaha, NE
Daubner, Susan Moore .... Elmira, NY
Daubney, James S. .... Boise, ID
Daubney, John E. .... St. Paul, MN
Daucher, Brian M. .... Costa Mesa, CA
Daucher, Donald A. .... Los Angeles, CA
Dauchez, Christine H. .... Kenilworth, NJ
Madison, NJ
Dauchot, Luke L. .... Cleveland, OH
Dauchy, Craig E. .... Menlo Park, CA
Dauchy, Lee Beauchamp .... Albany, GA
Daudet, Robert M. .... Phoenix, AZ
Daudish, Joseph E. .... Oak Forest, IL
Daudt, Michael D. .... Seattle, WA
Daue, E. Craig .... Missoula, MT
Dauenhauer, Mark W. .... Madison, GA
Dauenhauer, Paul J. .... Seattle, WA
Dauer, Charles W. .... Needles, CA
Dauer, Edward A. .... Denver, CO
Dauer, Gene A. .... Lexington, KY
Dauer, Jennifer L. .... Sacramento, CA
Dauer, John L., Jr. .... New York, NY
Dauer, Lisa D. .... Pittsburgh, PA
Dauer, Mark P., (P.C.) .... New Orleans, LA
Dauer, Paul F. .... Sacramento, CA
Dauer, Rachel P. .... Denver, CO
Dauer, Risa C. .... Los Angeles, CA
Dauer, Robert E. .... Pittsburgh, PA
Dauer, Robert E., Jr. .... Pittsburgh, PA
Dauer & Thompson .... Sacramento, CA
Dauerer, Louis M. .... Poughkeepsie, NY
Dauerty, Guy P. .... New York, NY
Daugaard, Lisa .... New York, NY
Daugerdas, Paul M. .... Chicago, IL
Daugert, Larry .... Bellingham, WA
Daughaday, John T. .... Mayfield, KY
Daughan, Francis P. .... York, ME
Daughan & Geyer .... York, ME
Daughdrill, John Wesley, Jr. .... Jackson, MS
Daughdrill, Stephanie M. .... Dallas, TX
Daugherity, Eugene P. .... Ottawa, IL
Streator, IL
Daugherty & Addison .... Itasca, IL
Daugherty, Alan L. .... St. Paul, MN
Daugherty, Alison W. .... Portland, OR
Daugherty and Associates, A Professional Corporation .... Amarillo, TX
Daugherty, C. Hunter .... Nicholasville, KY
Daugherty, Charles C. .... Indianapolis, IN
Daugherty, Charles V. .... Canyon Country, CA
Daugherty, Craig M. .... Tyler, TX
Daugherty, David D. .... Warren, OH
Daugherty, David D., Jr. .... Cincinnati, OH
Daugherty, David H. .... Huntington, WV
Daugherty, David W. .... Los Angeles, CA
Daugherty, Dennis A. .... San Francisco, CA
Daugherty, Donald A., Jr. .... Milwaukee, WI
Daugherty, Donald F. .... Atlanta, GA
Daugherty, Duncan W. .... Huntington, WV
Daugherty, E. Bloxom, III .... Moneta, VA
Daugherty, E. Duane .... Rensselaer, IN
Daugherty, Edw. L., Jr. .... Itasca, IL
Daugherty, Elizabeth G., (P.A.)
Fort Lauderdale, FL
Daugherty, Fowler, Peregrin & Haught, A Professional Corporation
Oklahoma City, OK
Daugherty, Fred H. .... Barrington, IL
Daugherty, Frederick A. .... Oklahoma City, OK
Daugherty, G. Thomas .... California, MD
Daugherty, George A. .... Elkview, WV
Daugherty, Guy E. .... Norfolk, VA
Daugherty, Harry K., Jr. .... Charlotte, NC
Daugherty, Hilary D. .... Raleigh, NC
Daugherty, Holly A. .... Covington, KY
Daugherty, Jack .... Granite City, IL
Daugherty, James E. .... Merrillville, IN
Daugherty, James Lee .... Euclid, OH
Daugherty, James R. .... Little Rock, AR
Daugherty, Jay A. .... Kansas City, MO
Daugherty, J. C. .... Holdenville, OK
Daugherty, John B. .... Beulah, MI
Daugherty, John B., P.L.C. .... Beulah, MI
Daugherty, John Burton .... Beulah, MI
Daugherty, John F. .... Atlanta, GA
Daugherty, John L. .... Department of Justice, Executive Office for United States Trustees, GV
Daugherty, Kathleen H. .... Orinda, CA
Daugherty, Kendra L. .... Batavia, OH
Daugherty, L. Valson .... Inglewood, CA
Daugherty, Laurie Curry .... McLean, VA
Daugherty Law Offices, L.C. .... Elkview, WV
Daugherty, Lawrence M. .... Hemet, CA
Daugherty, Leslee K. .... Charlotte, NC
Daugherty, M. Dennis
Department Of The Interior, Office of the Solicitor, GV
Daugherty, Maria St. John
Fort Lauderdale, FL
Daugherty, Marie St. John .... Miami, FL
Daugherty, Marie B. .... Leonardtown, MD
Daugherty, Mark Alan .... Graham, WA
Daugherty, Mary K. .... Frankfort, KY
Daugherty & Maupin, P.C.
Leonardtown, MD
Daugherty, Michael J. .... Denver, CO
Daugherty, Michael T. .... Xenia, OH
Daugherty & Parker
Fort Lauderdale, FL
Daugherty, Patricia L. .... Orlando, FL
Daugherty, Patrick D. .... Charlotte, NC
Daugherty, Patrick J. .... Mentor, OH
Daugherty, Phil E. .... Oklahoma City, OK
Daugherty, Ralph H. .... Austin, TX
Daugherty, Richard B. .... San Francisco, CA
Daugherty, Ron D., Law Office of
Houston, TX
Daugherty, Ronald L. .... Philadelphia, PA
Daugherty, Sally J. .... Philadelphia, PA
Daugherty, Sam .... Dallas, TX
Daugherty, Scott R. .... Raleigh, NC
Daugherty, Silas Clark, V .... Norfolk, VA
Daugherty, Suzanne Westerman
Elkview, WV
Daugherty, Teresa Rice .... Hubbard, OH
Daugherty, Tracy C. .... Stamford, CT
Daugherty, Troy L. .... Kansas City, MO
Daugherty, Veva .... Watonga, OK
Daugherty, Virginia Ellen .... Amarillo, TX
Daugherty, W. Emory .... Deerfield Beach, FL
Daugherty, William .... Auburn, CA
Daughney, Brian C. .... New York, NY
Daughrity, C. Lynn .... Port Arthur, TX
Daughters, Carrie L. .... San Francisco, CA
Daughters, Turpen A. .... Pinole, CA
Daughtery, Nancy M. Rundin .... Chicago, IL
Daughtery, Peter J. .... Atlanta, GA
Columbus, GA
Daughton, Donald .... Phoenix, AZ
Daughton, James R., Jr. .... Tallahassee, FL
Daughtrey, Lawrence A. .... McLean, VA
Daughtrey, Martha Craig .... Nashville, TN
Daughtrey, Sarah Carran .... Nashville, TN
Daughtrey, William H., Jr. .... Richmond, VA
Daughtrey-Kramer, Tana .... San Ramon, CA
Daughtridge, John A. .... Windermere, FL
Daughtry, Alan B. .... Houston, TX
Daughtry, Billy I., Jr .... Elberton, GA
Daughtry, Bruce L. .... Ahoskie, NC
Daughtry, Charles A. .... Houston, TX
Daughtry, Douglas W. .... Salem, OR
Daughtry, John R. .... Raleigh, NC
Daughtry, Kelly K. .... Smithfield, NC
Daughtry, Lloyd D. .... Stamford, CT
Daughtry, N. Leo .... Smithfield, NC
Daughtry, Woodard, Lawrence & Starling
Smithfield, NC
Daugirda, John P. .... Eugene, OR
Daugs, E. John .... Beaufort, SC
Daugs, Tedder, Newman & McDougall
Jonesboro, GA
Beaufort, SC
Hilton Head Island, SC
Dauguste, James Edward .... Long Beach, NY
Dauhajre, Ivonne .... North Bergen, NJ
Daukas, John B. .... Boston, MA
Dauksch, James C., Jr. .... Daytona Beach, FL
Dauksewicz, Peter .... Boston, MA
Daul, James A. .... Vallejo, CA
Dault, Richard Douglas .... Phoenix, AZ
Daulton, Jack .... Chicago, IL
Daulton, Julie R. .... Minneapolis, MN
Daulton, Quinten A. .... Chattanooga, TN
Daulton, Stephen W. .... Columbus, OH
Daum, Angela M. .... Fremont, CA
Daum, Carter A. .... Eugene, OR
Daum, Elliot L. .... Santa Rosa, CA
Daum, John A. .... Omaha, NE
Daum, John F. .... Los Angeles, CA
Daum, Kurt G. .... Houston, TX
Daum, Rachel Ariadne .... Doraville, GA
Daum, Roslyn G., (P.C.) .... Boston, MA
Daume, David O.
Treasury Department, GV
Daume, William H. .... Terrytown, LA
Daumen, Michael P. .... East Aurora, NY
Daumit, Debra M. .... Washington, DC
Daun, Fara .... Olympia, WA
Daunhauer, Jenifer Tarter .... Louisville, KY
Daunis, Diana L. .... Providence, RI
D'Aunno, Lisa E. .... Chicago, IL
Daunno, Theodore W. .... Clifton, NJ
D'Aunoy, Yvette A. .... New Orleans, LA
Daunt, Jacqueline A. .... Palo Alto, CA
Daunt, Philip J. .... Monterey, CA
Daunt, Robert T. .... Monterey, CA
Dauphin, Brian .... Manchester, NH
Dauphin, Charles A. .... Birmingham, AL
Dauphin Law Center, P.C. .... Mobile, AL
Dauphin, Richard B. .... Houston, TX
Dauphin, Robert J. .... San Rafael, CA
Dauphin, William M., Jr. .... Lafayette, LA
Dauphinais, Raymond J. .... Detroit, MI
Dauphinais, Richard .... Washington, DC
Dauphine, Dawn L. .... Phoenix, AZ
Dauphiné, Susan M. .... Salinas, CA
Dauphinee, Paul F. .... Fitchburg, MA
Dauphinot, Lee Ann .... Fort Worth, TX
Dauphinot, Wes .... Fort Worth, TX
D'Aurelio, Michael J. .... Atlanta, GA
D'Auria, Alfred J. .... Avon-By-The-Sea, NJ
D'Auria, Anthony J. .... New York, NY
D'Auria, Frank A. .... New York, NY
D'Auria, Gregory Thomas .... Hartford, CT
D'Auria, Robert H. .... Bedford, MA
D'Auria, Robert H., P.C., Law Offices of
Bedford, MA
D'Aurio, Anthony .... Atlanta, GA
D'Aurizio, Franklin .... Rochester, NY
D'Aurizio, John F. .... Rochester, NY
D'Aurora, Jack .... Columbus, OH
Daus, Christopher J. .... St. Louis, MO
Daus, Thomas E. .... Grass Valley, CA
Dausch, Michael J., III .... Baltimore, MD
Dausch, Thomas J. .... Pittsburgh, PA
Dausch, Thomas J., P.C. .... Pittsburgh, PA
Dauscher, Raymond G. .... Cleveland, OH
Dauscher, Scott K. .... Cerritos, CA
Dau-Schmidt, Kenneth .... Bloomington, IN
Dauster, Marjorie Allen .... North Haven, CT
Dauster, William G. .... United States Senate, Committee Legal Personnel, GV
Daut, Alan M. .... Altoona, IA
Daut, Robert F. .... Boston, MA
Dautch, Harold A. .... Amherst, NY
Dautel, Susan Styer .... Albany, NY
Dautel, Timothy P. .... Charlotte, NC
Dauterive, Ronald E. .... Lafayette, LA
Dauterman, Steven L. .... Cincinnati, OH
Dauterman, William D. .... Fostoria, OH
D'Auteuil, Daniel A., Jr. .... Lewiston, ME
D'Auteuil, Mark D. .... Little Rock, AR
Dautremont, James H. .... Media, PA
Dautrich, David R. .... Reading, PA
Dautrich, Kathleen D. .... Reading, PA
Dauzat, Falgoust, Caviness & Bienvenu, L.L.P. .... Opelousas, LA
Dauzat, Jimmy L. .... Opelousas, LA
Davagian, John S., II .... Boston, MA
Davan, Karissa J. .... Carlsbad, CA
Davant, Fred C. .... Miami, FL
Davant & Morris .... Houston, TX
Davant, Robert M. .... Houston, TX
D'Avanzo, Barbara Toop
Englewood Cliffs, NJ
DaVanzo, Frank J. .... Los Angeles, CA
D'Avanzo, Jerry .... Detroit, MI
D'Avanzo, Jerry P. .... Southgate, MI
D'Avanzo, Joseph A. .... New York, NY
D'Avanzo, Robert Lewis
Cape May Court House, NJ
Davczyk, Terrance E. .... Milwaukee, WI
Wausau, WI
Dave, Andrew .... Scarsdale, NY
Davé, Aparna .... North Potomac, MD
Silver Spring, MD
Dave, Danelle K. .... Los Angeles, CA
Dave, Jamiel G. .... Los Angeles, CA
Dave, Mahesh M. .... New York, NY
Dave, Michael G. .... Los Angeles, CA
Davé, Raj S. .... Washington, DC
Dave, Rita .... Mineola, NY
Davee, Gerald S. .... San Diego, CA
Davee, Robert A. .... Galveston, TX
Davee, Robert C. .... Houston, TX
Davell, William C. .... Fort Lauderdale, FL
D'Avella, Bernard J., Jr. .... Roseland, NJ
D'Avella, Denise M.
National Transportation Safety Board, Office of the General Counsel, GV
D'Avella, Victor J. .... Bel Air, MD
Davenport, Alice C. .... New York, NY
Davenport, Alicia B. .... Berlin, CT
Davenport, Andrew A. .... Atlanta, GA
Davenport, April L. .... Louisville, KY
Davenport, Barbara B. .... Austin, TX
Davenport, Bert A., (P.A.) .... Panama City, FL
Davenport, Beth R. .... Santa Fe, NM
Davenport, Bettite Jean .... Norman, OK
Davenport, Billie J. .... Lexington, KY
Davenport, Bradfute W., Jr.
Richmond, VA
Davenport, Brian L. .... Reno, NV
Davenport, Brian L., Ltd. .... Reno, NV
Davenport, Bryan B. .... Franklin, IN
Davenport, Bryan B., P.C. .... Franklin, IN
Davenport, C. Thomas, Jr. .... Bristol, TN
Davenport, Candace C. .... San Rafael, CA
Davenport, Carolyn W. .... New York, NY
Davenport, Charles .... McLean, VA
Davenport, Charles A., III
Costa Mesa, CA
Davenport, Clifford M. .... Indianapolis, IN
Davenport, Clydia A. .... New Orleans, LA
Davenport, Colleen M. .... Minneapolis, MN
Davenport, Craig J. .... Yakima, WA
Davenport, Cynthia M. .... St. Louis, MO
Davenport, D. Denby, Jr. .... Greenville, SC
Davenport, Dale A. .... Harrisonburg, VA
Davenport, Damian E. .... Salt Lake City, UT
Davenport, Darius LeMoyne .... Austin, TX
Davenport, David A. .... Waseca, MN
Davenport, David C., Jr. .... Santa Fe, NM
Davenport, David J. .... Minneapolis, MN
Davenport, David M. .... Oklahoma City, OK
Davenport, David M. .... Richmond, VA
Davenport, David S. .... Boston, MA
Davenport, David W. .... Atlanta, GA
Davenport, Dawn .... Dallas, TX
Davenport, Deborah L. .... Newport Beach, CA
Davenport, Dennis A. .... Fayetteville, GA
Davenport & Dodds, LLP .... Santa Fe, NM
Davenport, Eric K. .... Salt Lake City, UT
Davenport, Erwin .... Wichita Falls, TX
Davenport, Evans, Hurwitz & Smith, L.L.P.
Sioux Falls, SD
Davenport, Files & Kelly, L.L.P.
Monroe, LA
Davenport, Frank T. .... Chicago, IL
Davenport, Fred B., Jr. .... Wilmington, NC
Davenport, G. William .... Birmingham, AL
Davenport, Gary B. .... Jacksonville, FL
Davenport, Gary C. .... Denver, CO
Davenport, George B. .... Soldotna, AK
Davenport, Gerald B. .... Tulsa, OK
Davenport & Gerstner .... Walnut Creek, CA
Davenport, Gordon E., Jr. .... Alvin, TX
Davenport, Gordon, III .... Madison, WI
Davenport, Gregory R. .... Stockton, CA
Davenport, Horace A. .... Norristown, PA
Davenport, Howard C.
Federal Communications Commission, Wireless Telecommunications Bureau, GV
Davenport, Hugh M. .... Jacksonville, FL
Davenport, Hugh M. .... Atlanta, GA
Davenport, Iris S. .... Decatur, GA
Davenport, J. Kent .... Dallas, TX
Davenport, Jack B. .... Hickory Hills, IL
Davenport, James & Cothran
Panama City, FL
Davenport, James P. .... Washington, DC
Davenport, James P. .... Manassas, VA
Davenport, James R. .... Dallas, TX
Davenport, Jane Detra .... Allentown, PA
Davenport, Jill B. .... Dallas, TX
Davenport, Joan .... Baltimore, MD
Davenport, John E. .... Nashville, NC
Davenport, John E., P.A. .... Nashville, NC
Rocky Mount, NC
Davenport, John L. .... Boston, MA
Davenport, John P. .... Portland, OR
Davenport, Jos., Jr. .... Port Gibson, MS
Davenport, Julie A. .... Findlay, OH
Davenport, Katherine Elizabeth .... Raleigh, NC
Davenport, Kay .... Tyler, TX
Davenport, Kimberly S. .... San Francisco, CA
Davenport, Kirk A. .... New York, NY
Davenport, Kristen L. .... Daytona Beach, FL
Davenport, Laura C. .... Jackson, MI
Davenport Law Firm .... Alvin, TX
Davenport, Leslie L. .... Hartford, CT
Davenport, Linda E. .... Westmont, IL
Davenport, Lisa M. .... Washington, DC
Davenport, Lonie .... Sacramento, CA
Davenport, Loretta Hopkins .... Chicago, IL
Davenport, Lynn E. .... New York, NY
Davenport, Marcia J. .... Helena, MT
Davenport, Margaret Andrews
New York, NY
Davenport, Marian D. .... Houston, TX
Davenport, Mark T. .... Dallas, TX
Davenport, Maurice D. .... Atlanta, GA
Davenport, Melanie D. .... Richmond, VA
Davenport, Michael A. .... Houston, TX
Davenport, Michael J. .... Kingsport, TN
Davenport, Michael Joseph
Council Bluffs, IA
Red Oak, IA
Davenport, Michael T. .... Minneapolis, MN
Davenport, Michelle S. .... Marietta, GA
Davenport, Mitchell G. .... Jacksboro, TX
Davenport, Nan A. .... Harrisburg, PA
Davenport, Nancy Stover .... Kingston, NY
Davenport, Nikole M. .... Atlanta, GA
Davenport, Norma G. .... Houston, TX
Davenport, Patricia A. .... Los Angeles, CA
Davenport, Patricia E. .... Tampa, FL
Davenport, Patrick H. .... Birmingham, AL
Davenport, Paul E. .... Albany, NY
Davenport, Paul H. .... Richmond, VA
Davenport, Paul J. .... Belmont, MA
Davenport, Paul M., Jr. .... New Orleans, LA
Davenport, Peter A. .... Troy, MI
Davenport, Priscilla K. .... Dallas, TX
Davenport, Randy P. .... Elizabeth, NJ
Davenport, Raven .... Austin, TX
Davenport, Rebecca H. .... Blountville, TN
Davenport, Richard L. .... Sparks, NV
Davenport, Richard M. .... Brentwood, TN
Davenport, Robert H. .... Denver, CO
Davenport, Robert L., Jr.
Department of the Army, Office of the General Counsel, GV
Davenport, Robert N. .... Allentown, PA
Davenport, Ronald G. .... Montgomery, AL
Davenport, Rustin T. .... Mason City, IA
Davenport, Samuel F. .... Boston, MA
Davenport, Scott J. .... Houston, TX
Davenport, Scott Wm. .... San Diego, CA
Davenport, Seth I. .... Montclair, NJ
Davenport, Sheree A. .... Belton, SC
Davenport, Stephanie N. .... Everett, WA
Davenport, Stephen C. .... Boston, MA
Davenport, Stephen T., Jr.
Walnut Creek, CA
Davenport, Taylor M. .... Cary, NC
Davenport, Teresa D. .... Birmingham, AL
Davenport, Teresa J. .... Miami, FL
Davenport, Thomas, III .... Santa Rosa, CA
Davenport, Thomas W., Jr. .... Monroe, LA
Davenport, Toni M. .... Opelousas, LA
Davenport, Tracy L. .... Huntsville, TX
Davenport, Valorie W. .... Houston, TX
Davenport, Vanessa Aching .... Oakland, CA
Davenport, W. Kirk .... Birmingham, AL
Davenport, William A. .... Spokane, WA
Davenport, William B. .... Chicago, IL
Davenport, William F., Jr.
St. Petersburg, FL
Davenport, William H.
Federal Communications Commission, Common Carrier Bureau, GV
Davenport, William J. .... Boston, MA
Davenport, William R. .... Pensacola, FL
Davenport, William W. .... Chesterfield, VA
Davenport, Wortham D. .... Laurel, MD
Davenport & Yacobi, P.A. .... Greenville, SC

Davidson, J. Scott .... Batesville, AR
Davidson, J. Scott .... Arlington, VA
Davidson, J. Valerie .... Monterey Park, CA
Davidson, Jack H. .... Anaheim, CA
Davidson, Jack S. .... Jefferson, GA
Davidson, James .... Rockland, ME
Davidson, James A. .... Glens Falls, NY
Davidson, James A. .... Midland, TX
Davidson, James B. .... Chicago, IL
Davidson, James E. .... Santa Barbara, CA
Davidson, James E. .... Morristown, NJ
Davidson, James E. .... Columbus, OH
Davidson, James G. .... Washington, DC
Davidson, James G. .... Tulsa, OK
Davidson, James H. .... United States Senate, Committee Legal Personnel, GV
Davidson, James J., III .... Lafayette, LA
Davidson, James P. .... Salina, KS
Davidson, James P. .... Dayton, OH
Davidson, James Vance .... Birmingham, AL
Davidson, Jan Meadows .... Atlanta, GA
Davidson, Jan P. .... Red Wing, MN
Davidson, Janet Toll .... Costa Mesa, CA
Davidson, Janice Burnett .... Denver, CO
Davidson, Janice Watson .... Tarboro, NC
Davidson, Jeanne E. .... Department of Justice, Civil Division, GV
Davidson, Jeffery S. .... Philadelphia, PA
Davidson, Jeffrey H. .... Los Angeles, CA
Davidson, Jeffrey J. .... Washington, DC
Davidson, Jeffrey L. .... Beverly Hills, CA
Davidson, Jeffrey O. .... Fort Wayne, IN
Davidson, Jeffrey S. .... Los Angeles, CA
Davidson, Jennifer A. .... Washington, DC
Davidson, Jerrold R. .... Brownsville, TX
Davidson, Joanne T. .... Phoenix, AZ
Davidson, Joe M. .... San Diego, CA
Davidson, Joe R. .... Houston, TX
Davidson, Joe R., P.C. .... Houston, TX
Davidson, Joel E. .... New York, NY
Davidson, Joel R. .... Washington, DC
Davidson, Joel R. .... Quincy, MA
Davidson, John .... San Francisco, CA
Davidson, John .... Flint, MI
Saginaw, MI
Davidson, John A. E., (A Prof. Law Corp.) Metairie, LA
Davidson, John B. .... Chicago, IL
Davidson, John C. .... Alexandria, LA
Davidson, John E. .... Charlottesville, VA
Davidson, John Edward .... Eugene, OR
Davidson, John H. .... Vermillion, SD
Davidson, John H. .... Terrell, TX
Davidson, John H., Jr. .... Youngstown, OH
Davidson, John J. .... Treasury Department, Office of Thrift Supervision, GV
Davidson, John L. .... Baton Rouge, LA
Davidson, John L. .... St. Louis, MO
Davidson, John L., P.C. .... St. Louis, MO
Davidson, John M. .... Houston, TX
Davidson, John P. .... Troy, MI
Davidson, John P., Law Offices of Raton, NM
Davidson, John R. .... Billings, MT
Davidson, John R. .... Brattleboro, VT
Davidson, John S. .... Hershey, PA
Davidson, John W. .... Columbia, SC
Davidson, John W. .... San Antonio, TX
Davidson, Jon Warren .... Los Angeles, CA
Davidson, Jonathan Marc .... Tallahassee, FL
Davidson, Joseph B. .... Houston, TX
Davidson, Joseph R. .... Granite City, IL
Davidson, Joshua .... Houston, TX
Davidson, Jossi KvZ. .... Silverton, OR
Davidson, Julia Loewy .... Palo Alto, CA
Davidson, Julie .... New Brunswick, NJ
Davidson, Julius M. .... Minneapolis, MN
Davidson, Justin H. .... Los Angeles, CA
Davidson, Karen L. .... Providence, RI
Davidson, Karen P. .... Chapel Hill, NC
Davidson, Karen R. .... San Bernardino, CA
Davidson, Karla .... Beverly Hills, CA
Davidson, Kathleen Fuller .... Glen Ellyn, IL
Davidson, Keith L., & Associates Chicago, IL
Davidson, Keith S. .... Rockville Centre, NY
Davidson & Kelly .... Houston, TX
Davidson, Kelly Gallops .... Auburn, AL
Davidson, Kelly J. .... Baltimore, MD
Davidson, Kenneth E. Colorado Springs, CO
Davidson, Kenneth H. .... Kirkland, WA
Davidson, Kenneth L. .... De Kalb, IL
Davidson, Kenneth M. Federal Trade Commission, Bureau of Competition, GV
Davidson, Kevin J. .... Baltimore, MD
Davidson, Kevin J. .... St. Louis, MO
Davidson, Kim .... Birmingham, AL
Davidson, Kimberly Geller Sherman Oaks, CA
Davidson, Kimberly K .... Torrance, CA
Davidson, Kristi L. .... Cincinnati, OH
Davidson, L. Edward, Jr. .... Houston, TX
Davidson, Lance S. .... Scottsdale, AZ
Davidson, Larry M. .... Spokane, WA
Davidson, Larry W. .... Troy, MI
Davidson, Laura .... New York, NY
Davidson, Laurie Pineau .... Columbia, SC
Davidson Law Firm, Ltd. .... Little Rock, AR
Davidson Law Offices, L.P.A. Hamilton, OH
Davidson, Lawrence .... Las Vegas, NV
Davidson, Lawrence H. Newport Beach, CA
Davidson, Lawrence I. .... Chicago, IL
Davidson, Lawrence R. .... Portland, OR
Davidson, Lawrence U., III .... Charlotte, NC

Davidson, Lee J. .... Olathe, KS
Davidson, Leonard H. .... North Miami, FL
Davidson, Leonard M. .... Newton, MA
Davidson, Leslye B. .... New York, NY
Davidson, Lester C. .... Phoenix, AZ
Davidson, Linda E. .... Sun City Center, FL
Highland Park, IL
Davidson, Lisa J. .... Hopkins, MN
Davidson, Lisanne P. .... Dallas, TX
Davidson, Lloyd T. .... Largo, FL
Davidson, Lori E. .... Dallas, TX
Davidson, Louren G. .... Springfield, MO
Albuquerque, NM
Davidson, Lydia Pruitt .... Charleston, SC
Davidson, M. Katharine .... Los Angeles, CA
Davidson, M. McCoy .... Tuscaloosa, AL
Davidson, M. Wayne .... Kansas City, MO
Davidson, Malcolm L. .... Boston, MA
Davidson Mandell & Menkes .... Chicago, IL
Davidson, Marc L. .... Radnor, PA
Davidson, Margaret A. .... Charleston, SC
Davidson, Margaret E. .... Albuquerque, NM
Davidson, Marie .... Seattle, WA
Davidson, Marie A. .... Coral Gables, FL
Davidson, Mark .... Greensboro, NC
Raleigh, NC
Davidson, Mark A. .... Denver, CO
Davidson, Mark D. .... Houston, TX
Davidson, Mark E. .... New York, NY
Davidson, Mark F. .... Detroit, MI
Davidson, Mark H. .... Port Huron, MI
Davidson, Mark S. .... Chicago, IL
Davidson, Mark S. .... Seattle, WA
Davidson, Marshall .... Prestonsburg, KY
Davidson, Marvin S. .... Orange, NJ
Davidson, Matthew S. .... Three Rivers, MI
Davidson, Meaux, Sonnier, McElligott & Swift .... Lafayette, LA
Davidson, Melissa E. .... San Francisco, CA
Davidson, Michael D. .... Las Vegas, NV
Davidson, Michael H. .... Tallahassee, FL
Davidson, Michael I. .... Philadelphia, PA
Davidson, Michael J. .... Richland, WA
Davidson, Michael M. .... Washington, DC
Davidson, Michael S. .... Irvine, CA
Davidson, Michele S. .... Philadelphia, PA
Davidson, Miles E. .... Tulsa, OK
Davidson, Milton Jay .... Woodland Hills, CA
Davidson, Milton Jay, A Professional Corporation .... Woodland Hills, CA
Davidson, Mindy G. .... Houston, TX
Davidson, Mitchell .... Chicago, IL
Davidson, Mitchell A. .... New York, NY
Davidson, Monica B. .... Louisville, KY
Davidson Morrison & Lindemann, P.A. Columbia, SC
Davidson & Naylor .... Norwalk, CT
Davidson, Neil .... Irving, TX
Davidson, Nelson M. (Mike), Jr. Dripping Springs, TX
Davidson, Nix & Jones, A Professional Law Corporation .... Shreveport, LA
Davidson, Norman .... Arcadia, CA
Davidson & O'Mara, P.C. .... Elmira, NY
Davidson, Orlando R. .... Honolulu, HI
Davidson, Pamela A. .... Chicago, IL
Davidson, Pamela J. .... Bloomington, IN
Davidson, Patricia L. .... Worcester, MA
Davidson, Patrick C. .... Montgomery, AL
Davidson, Patrick G. .... Gillette, WY
Davidson, Paul G. .... Arlington, TX
Davidson, Paul L. .... Bentonville, AR
Davidson, Paul S. .... Nashville, TN
Davidson, Peter A. .... Los Angeles, CA
Davidson, Peter B. House of Representatives, Committee Legal Personnel, GV
Davidson, Peter F. .... Chappaqua, NY
Davidson, Phillip L. .... Nashville, TN
Davidson, R. Eddie .... Nashville, TN
Davidson, Rachel N. .... Newark, NJ
Davidson, Randall S. .... Shreveport, LA
Davidson, Rebecca J. .... Lillington, NC
Davidson, Richard A. Rancho Cucamonga, CA
Davidson, Richard A. .... Rock Island, IL
Davenport, IA
Davidson, Richard A., Jr. .... Boston, MA
Davidson, Richard C. .... Auburn Hills, MI
Davidson, Richard D. .... Orlando, FL
Davidson, Richard E. .... Oxford, NY
Davidson, Richard G. .... Clarinda, IA
Davidson, Richard H. .... Clarinda, IA
Davidson, Richard L. .... Southfield, MI
Davidson, Robert .... Dallas, TX
Davidson, Robert A. .... Ventura, CA
Davidson, Robert B. .... New York, NY
Davidson, Robert D. .... Jackson, MS
Davidson, Robert E. .... Stamford, CT
Davidson, Robert G. .... Chicago, IL
Davidson, Robert J. .... Los Angeles, CA
Davidson, Robert L. .... Minneapolis, MN
Davidson, Robert L. .... New York, NY
Davidson, Robert M. .... Norwalk, CT
Davidson, Robert P. .... Medford, OR
Davidson, Robert S. .... Marion, OH
Davidson, Robert T. H. .... Killingworth, CT
Davidson, Robin C. .... New York, NY
Davidson, Roger K. .... Akron, OH
Davidson, Roger V. .... Denver, CO
Davidson, Ronald H. .... Hudson, OH
Davidson, Russ & Harris .... Gardena, CA
Davidson, Ruth M. .... St. Petersburg, FL
Davidson, Ruth M., P.A. .... St. Petersburg, FL
Davidson, S. Gerald .... Rochester, NY
Davidson, S. Thomas .... Wilmington, DE
Davidson, Sakolosky, Moseley & Tiller, P.C. Lynchburg, VA

Davidson, Samuel .... Palm Beach, FL
Davidson, Samuel L. .... Monroe, LA
Davidson, Sander M. .... Rockville, MD
Davidson, Scott .... Jonesboro, AR
Davidson & Scott .... Chicago, IL
Davidson, Scott A. .... Louisville, KY
Davidson, Scott I. .... New York, NY
Davidson, Scott K. .... Newport Beach, CA
Davidson, Scott M. .... Albuquerque, NM
Davidson, Scott W. .... Portland, OR
Davidson, Selmer A. .... Lacey, WA
Davidson, Seth A. .... Washington, DC
Davidson, Sheila Kearney .... New York, NY
Davidson, Sheldon .... Chicago, IL
Davidson, Shelley .... Macon, GA
Davidson, Shepard .... Boston, MA
Davidson, Sherrill I. .... Baton Rouge, LA
Davidson, Shirley .... Beverly Hills, CA
Davidson, Sidney D. .... Peoria, IL
Davidson, Stacey L. .... New York, NY
Davidson, Staiger and Hill, P.C. Port Huron, MI
Davidson, Stanley J. .... Chicago, IL
Davidson, Stephen J. .... Minneapolis, MN
Davidson, Stephen P. .... New York, NY
Davidson, Steven D. .... Omaha, NE
Davidson, Steven D. .... Dallas, TX
Davidson, Steven K. .... Washington, DC
Davidson, Steven R. .... Chicago, IL
Davidson & Strain .... Rome, GA
Davidson, Stuart W. .... Harrisburg, PA
Philadelphia, PA
Davidson, Sue .... Cheyenne, WY
Davidson, Susan B. .... Chicago, IL
Davidson, Susan Joan .... Palo Alto, CA
Davidson, Susan M. .... Naperville, IL
Davidson, Susan W. .... Houston, TX
Davidson, Suzanne Mouron .... Glendale, CA
Davidson, Teresa D. .... Greensboro, NC
Davidson, Tessa T. .... Albuquerque, NM
Davidson, Thomas B., Jr. .... Richmond, VA
Davidson, Thomas E. .... Jackson, MS
Davidson, Thomas M. .... Washington, DC
Davidson, Thomas M. .... McLean, VA
Davidson, Timothy A., II .... Houston, TX
Davidson, Timothy S. .... Overland Park, KS
Kansas City, MO
Davidson, Timothy T. .... Monterey Park, CA
Davidson, Tina B. .... Far Rockaway, NY
Davidson, Todd S. Rancho Palos Verdes, CA
Davidson, Todd W. .... Salina, KS
Davidson, Tom .... Mertzon, TX
Davidson, Tom W. .... Washington, DC
Davidson, Tonya J. .... Terre Haute, IN
Davidson & Troilo, A Professional Corporation .... Austin, TX
San Antonio, TX
Davidson, Van M., Jr. .... Dickinson, TX
Davidson, Vern G. .... Spokane, WA
Davidson, W. Keith .... Lawrenceville, GA
Davidson, W. Keith .... Snellville, GA
Davidson, Wayne D. .... Houston, TX
Davidson, Wendell R. .... Hallowell, ME
Davidson, Wiggins, Jones & Coleman, P.C. Birmingham, AL
Tuscaloosa, AL
Davidson, Wilbur L., Jr. United States Postal Service, GV
Davidson, Wilbur S. .... Port Huron, MI
Davidson, William C. .... Davenport, IA
Davidson, William C. .... Port Chester, NY
Davidson, William C. .... Austin, TX
Davidson, William E. .... Houston, TX
Davidson, William E., Jr. .... Rome, GA
Davidson, William F. .... San Antonio, TX
Davidson, William G., III .... Rockville, MD
Fairfax, VA
Davidson, William H., II .... Columbia, SC
Davidson, William L. .... Minneapolis, MN
Davidson, William M. .... Duluth, GA
Davidson, William M. .... Northville, MI
Davidson, William S. .... Richmond, VA
Davidson, William T. .... Pikeville, KY
Davidson, William W. .... Houston, TX
Davidson, Winn C. .... Palatine, IL
Davie, Alan W. .... Wichita, KS
Davie, Carole S. .... New York, NY
Davie, J. Clayton, Jr. .... New Orleans, LA
Davie, James H., II Green Cove Springs, FL
Davie, John W. .... New York, NY
Davie, Kenneth P. .... Harrison, NJ
Davie, Michael J. .... Jacksonville, FL
Davie, Mose J. .... Nashville, TN
Davie, Robert S. .... Fort Worth, TX
Davie, Roger C. .... El Paso, TX
Davie, Stephen S. .... Syracuse, NY
Davie, Thomas P., Jr. .... Richmond, VA
Davies, Albert E., III .... Bridgeport, OH
Davies, Amy G. .... Washington, DC
Davies, Anne C. .... Eugene, OR
Davies, Arthur B., III .... Lynchburg, VA
Davies, Arthur L. .... Olympia, WA
Davies, Bankhead T. .... Arlington, VA
Davies, Bankhead Thornton .... Arlington, VA
Davies, Barbara J. .... Buffalo, NY
Davies, Barrell, Will, Lewellyn & Edwards, P.C. .... Charlottesville, VA
Culpeper, VA
Fredericksburg, VA
Davies, Bruce O. .... Olympia, WA
Davies, Caleb, IV .... Alpharetta, GA
Davies, Carol G. .... Houston, TX
Davies, Catherine L. .... Milwaukee, WI
Davies, Charles M. .... Waukesha, WI
Davies, Charles P. .... Tucson, AZ
Davies, Charles R. .... Washington, DC

Davies, Christopher A. .... Janesville, WI
Davies, Christopher K. .... Chicago, IL
Davies, Christopher N. .... Fort Myers, FL
Davies, Christopher N., P.A. .... Fort Myers, FL
Davies, Christopher R.L. .... Washington, DC
Davies, Colette Baumgardner Billings, MT
Davies, Colleen T. .... Oakland, CA
Davies, D. Douglas .... Walnut Creek, CA
Davies, D. Schuyler .... Delavan, WI
Davies, Daniel R. .... North Olmsted, OH
Davies, Danielle Wrobel .... New York, NY
Davies, Darlene Thomas .... Baltimore, MD
Davies, David C. .... Lake Oswego, OR
Davies, David G. .... Phoenix, AZ
Davies, David G. .... Cleveland, OH
Davies, David G., Ltd., Law Offices of Phoenix, AZ
Davies, David H. .... Willoughby, OH
Davies, David N. .... San Jose, CA
Davies & Davies .... Centereach, NY
Davies & Davies .... Arlington, VA
Davies & Davies .... Lynchburg, VA
Davies, Davies & Sandberg, P.A. Paterson, NJ
Totowa, NJ
Davies, Diane B. .... Denver, CO
Davies, Diane E. .... Morro Bay, CA
Davies, Donald A. .... Columbus, OH
Davies, Douglas R. .... Fairfax, VA
Davies, Doyle J. .... Lusk, WY
Davies, E. Reynolds, Jr. .... Nashville, TN
Davies, Ed Reynolds .... Nashville, TN
Davies, Edward E. .... Tulsa, OK
Davies, Elizabeth E. .... Philadelphia, PA
Davies, Ellen White .... Hattiesburg, MS
Davies, Frank J., Jr. .... Totowa, NJ
Davies, Frederick P. .... Syracuse, NY
Davies, George .... Aurora, CO
Davies, George H. .... Seattle, WA
Davies, George N. .... Birmingham, AL
Davies, Glen E. .... Salt Lake City, UT
Davies, Gregory L. .... Everett, WA
Davies, Harry F., Jr. Department of Housing and Urban Development, Office of General Counsel, GV
Davies, Holly P. .... Chandler, AZ
Davies & Humphreys .... Nashville, TN
Davies, Ian T. .... Staten Island, NY
Davies, Jack .... St. Paul, MN
Davies, Jacqueline E. Maitland Washington, DC
Davies, James A. .... Seattle, WA
Davies, James E. .... New York, NY
Davies, James H. .... Monroe, MI
Davies, James R. .... Glens Falls, NY
Davies, Jennifer Margiotta Philadelphia, PA
Davies, John .... Downey, CA
Davies, John G. .... Wasilla, AK
Davies, John G. .... Los Angeles, CA
Davies, John G. .... San Diego, CA
Davies, John H. .... Haddonfield, NJ
Davies, John J., III .... Culpeper, VA
Davies, John L. .... Columbus, OH
Davies, John W. .... Sacramento, CA
Davies, Jonathan E. .... Lynchburg, VA
Davies, Joseph A. .... Denver, CO
Davies, Joseph A., P.C. .... Denver, CO
Davies, Julie .... Sacramento, CA
Davies, Julie Lynn .... Austin, TX
Davies, Katherine Department of Housing and Urban Development, Office of General Counsel, GV
Davies, Kathleen J. .... Pittsburgh, PA
Davies, Kenneth E. .... Peoria, IL
Davies, Kenneth F. .... Baltimore, MD
Davies, Kenneth M. .... Detroit, MI
Davies, Kenneth T. .... Charlotte, NC
Davies, Kimberly A. .... Encinitas, CA
Davies, Kristie Porter .... Columbia, SC
Davies Law Firm, A Professional Corporation Syracuse, NY
Davies, Lee Clarke .... Akron, OH
Davies, Lesley Akers .... Lake Mary, FL
Davies, Leslie .... Boston, MA
Davies, Lori K. .... Irvine, CA
Davies, Louis M. .... Youngstown, OH
Davies, Lynn S. .... Salt Lake City, UT
Davies, M. Randel .... Los Angeles, CA
Davies, Marc .... Philadelphia, PA
Davies, Mariann Sarah .... Orlando, FL
Davies, Mark I. .... Boston, MA
Davies, Mark L. .... Tarrytown, NY
Davies, Mark R. .... Houston, TX
Davies, Mary M. .... Winnetka, IL
Davies McFarland & Carroll, P.C. Pittsburgh, PA
Davies, Michael G. .... New York, NY
Davies, Norleen O. .... Plymouth Meeting, PA
Davies, Olivia C. .... Los Gatos, CA
Davies, Patrick S. .... Washington, DC
Davies, Paul J. .... Palatine, IL
Davies, Paul L., Jr. .... San Francisco, CA
Davies, Paul R. .... Chicago, IL
Davies Pearson, P.C. .... Tacoma, WA
Davies, Philip T. .... New York, NY
Davies, R. Nigel .... Bowling Green, OH
Pemberville, OH
Davies, R. Scott .... Minneapolis, MN
Davies, Ralph A. .... Pittsburgh, PA
Davies, Rebecca S. .... Farmington Hills, MI
Davies, Richard .... Medina, OH
Davies, Richard B. .... Houston, TX

Davies, Richard J. ....Cherry Hill, NJ
Harrisburg, PA
King Of Prussia, PA
Davies, Richard J. ....Seattle, WA
Davies, Richard L. ....Window Rock, AZ
Davies, Richard N. ....Albert Lea, MN
Davies, Richard P. ....New York, NY
Davies, Richard W. ....Orange, CT
Davies, Robert E. ....Fairfield, CA
Sacramento, CA
Davies, Robert E. Lee ....Franklin, TN
Davies, Robert F. ....Totowa, NJ
Davies, Robert K. ....Albany, NY
Davies, Robert N. ....Indianapolis, IN
Davies, Robert Ogsbury ....Atlanta, GA
Davies, Robert R. ....Knoxville, TN
Davies, Robert R. ....Nashville, TN
Davies, Robert S. ....Villa Park, CA
Davies, Roberts & Reid LLP ....Seattle, WA
Davies, Ronald C. ....Centereach, NY
Davies, Rosalie G. ....Narberth, PA
Davies, Ross E. ....Washington, DC
Davies, Roy H. ....Pacifica, CA
Davies & Ruck ....Bowling Green, OH
Pemberville, OH
Davies, Samuel E. ....Barbourville, KY
Corbin, KY
Davies, Samuel E., P.S.C.
Barbourville, KY
Davies, Sarah A. ....Madison, WI
Davies, Sarah E. ....Philadelphia, PA
Davies, Scott M. ....Denver, CO
Davies, Shannon F. ....Edmond, OK
Davies, Sharon L. ....New York, NY
Davies, Stanton W., II ....Newport Beach, CA
Davies, Sterling G. ....Columbia, SC
Davies, Steven W. ....Tacoma, WA
Davies, Susan M. ....Chicago, IL
Davies, Susan M. ....New York, NY
Davies, Thomas A. ....Fargo, ND
Davies, Thomas A., Ltd. ....Fargo, ND
Davies, Thomas E. ....Morton, IL
Davies, Thomas E., P.C. ....Morton, IL
Davies, Thomas I. ....Austin, TX
Davies, Thomas M. ....Hickman, NE
Lincoln, NE
Davies, Thomas R. ....Lancaster, PA
Davies, Thomas W. ....Saratoga, CA
Davies, Thomas Y. ....Knoxville, TN
Davies, Timothy Q. ....Fargo, ND
Davies, Timothy R. ....Centereach, NY
Davies, Todd E. ....Moline, IL
Davies, Tracey B. ....Austin, TX
Davies, Veronica P. ....Los Angeles, CA
Davies, Victoria Lynn ....Centereach, NY
Davies, Wade V. ....Knoxville, TN
Davies, Wallace M. ....Signal Mountain, TN
Davies, Wayne A. ....St. Paul, MN
Davies, Wayne R. ....Milford, MA
Davies, Wendell L. ....Amarillo, TX
Davies, Wendy J. ....Hartford, CT
Davies, William A. ....Sacramento, CA
Davies, William Boyd ....Barton, VT
Davies, William F. ....La Mesa, CA
Davies, William L. ....Billings, MT
Davies, William S., Jr. ....Columbia, SC
Davies, William T. ....Streamwood, IL
Davies-Sekle, Michael P. ....Reston, VA
Daviess-White, Laurie A. ....Wenatchee, WA
Davies-Watson, Melissa J. ....Lakewood, OH
Daviet, Mary Patricia ....Greeley, CO
D'Avignon, David Allan ....Cincinnati, OH
D'Avignon, R. Joseph ....Lexington, MA
Davignon, Robert E. ....Providence, RI
Da Vigo, Anthony S. ....Sacramento, CA
Davik-Galbraith, Christine S. ....Chicago, IL
Dávila, Carlos V. J. ....San Juan, PR
Davila, Edward J. ....San Jose, CA
Davila, Emilio Chito ....Laredo, TX
Davila, Emilio, Jr. ....Laredo, TX
Davila, Frank, II ....San Antonio, TX
Davila, Gilbert D. ....Austin, TX
Davila, Gregory D. ....Key West, FL
Dávila, Jaime ....Miami, FL
Davila, Jose R., Jr. ....Richmond, VA
Davila, Linda E. ....San Francisco, CA
Davila, Michelle B. ....New York, NY
Davila, Nino R. ....Chicago, IL
Davila, Patricia A. ....San Antonio, TX
Davila & Polverino ....San Jose, CA
Davila, Rivas & Goyco ....Ponce, PR
Davila, Robert ....Houston, TX
Davila, Roberto E. ....Ponce, PR
Davila, Teresita B. ....Miami, FL
Davila-Bloise, Edwin G. ....Washington, DC
Dávila-Carlos, Ramón E. ....San Juan, PR
Davila-Garcia, Migdalia ....San Juan, PR
Davila Lanausse, Jose N. ....San Juan, PR
Davila Lopez, Roberto E. ....Ponce, PR
Dávila-Rivera, Raúl ....San Juan, PR
Dávila-Thomas, Rafael E. ....San Juan, PR
Davilla, Raymond J., Jr. ....San Jose, CA
Davillier, Daniel E. ....New Orleans, LA
Davimos, Robert S. ....Boca Raton, FL
Davin, Denise M. ....New York, NY
Davin, Elizabeth A. ....Columbus, OH
Davin, James M. ....Houston, TX
Davine, Amy C. ....Washington, DC
Davine, Howard M. ....Burbank, CA
Davine, Jeffrey D. ....Los Angeles, CA
Davine, Jeffrey R. ....Denver, CO
D'Avino, Carey R. ....New York, NY
D'Avino, Richard ....Stamford, CT
Davis, A. Arthur, 3rd ....Somerville, NJ
Davis, A. David ....Boston, MA
Davis, A. John, III ....Salt Lake City, UT
Davis, A. Kimbrough ....Atlanta, GA
Davis, A. Thomas ....Tompkinsville, KY
Davis, Adam C. E. ....Mesa, AZ
Phoenix, AZ
Scottsdale, AZ
Sun City, AZ
Davis, Adam S. ....Ashland, KY
Davis, Adelaide E. ....Oviedo, FL
Davis, Aileen S. ....Tampa, FL
Davis, Aimee B. ....New York, NY
Davis, Aimee R. ....Greenville, SC
Davis, Al ....Marshall, TX
Davis, Alan C. ....San Francisco, CA
Davis, Alan C. ....Ridgefield, CT
Davis, Alan D. ....San Gabriel, CA
Davis, Alan E. ....Woodbridge, NJ
Davis, Alan H. ....Melrose, MA
Davis, Alan J. ....Philadelphia, PA
Davis, Alan K. ....Dallas, TX
Davis, Alan R. ....Phoenix, AZ
Davis, Alan R. ....Sherman Oaks, CA
Davis, Alan S. ....Marietta, GA
Davis, Alan T. ....Chicago, IL
Davis, Albert F. ....Los Angeles, CA
Davis, Albert P. ....Marble Falls, TX
Davis, Aldrich B. ....Baltimore, MD
Davis, Alfred P. ....Loveland, CO
Davis, Alfred W. (Fred), III ....Bryan, TX
Davis, Alice J.B.
Department of Justice, GV
Davis, Alison Nadine ....Baltimore, MD
Davis, Allan B. ....St. Petersburg, FL
Davis, Allan F. ....Newport Beach, CA
San Diego, CA
Davis, Allan H. ....Findlay, OH
Davis, Allan W. ....Southfield, MI
Davis, Allen A., Jr. ....Baltimore, MD
Davis, Allene D. ....Oklahoma City, OK
Davis, Allison ....Brooklyn, NY
Davis, Allison A. ....San Francisco, CA
Davis, Allyn W. ....Florence, CO
Davis, Althea W. ....Department of Justice,
Civil Division, GV
Davis, Alton T. ....Grayling, MI
Davis, Alvin A. ....Lawrenceville, GA
Davis, Alvin Bruce ....Miami, FL
Davis, Ames ....Nashville, TN
Davis, Amy Alandt ....New York, NY
Davis, Amy E. ....New York, NY
Davis, Amy Elaine ....Dallas, TX
Davis, Amy Fogel ....Philadelphia, PA
Davis, Amy Hope ....Sacramento, CA
Davis, Amy S. ....Detroit, MI
Davis, Amy Sweeny ....Kansas City, MO
Davis, Ana C. ....Atlanta, GA
Davis, André M. ....Baltimore, MD
Davis, Andrea Shapiro ....Flushing, NY
Davis, Andrea Y. ....Cleveland, OH
Davis, Andrew G. ....San Francisco, CA
Davis, Andrew H., Jr. ....Providence, RI
Davis, Andrew I. ....Portland, OR
Davis, Andrew J. ....San Francisco, CA
Davis, Andrew N. ....Hartford, CT
Davis, Andrew P. ....New York, NY
Davis, Andrew W. ....Providence, RI
Davis, Angela D. ....Houston, TX
Davis, Angela Edwards ....Atlanta, GA
Davis, Angela Jordan ....Washington, DC
Davis, Angela W. ....Tallahassee, FL
Davis, Ann E. ....Orlando, FL
McLean, VA
Davis, Ann G. ....Lafayette, IN
Davis, Ann H. ....Santa Rosa, CA
Davis, Ann Hines ....Waynesville, NC
Davis, Anna Holmquist ....Arlington, VA
Davis, Anna L. ....Towson, MD
Davis, Anne Megan ....Chicago, IL
Davis, Ansel L. ....Atlanta, GA
Davis, Anthony Craig ....Prestonsburg, KY
Davis, Anthony E. ....San Francisco, CA
Davis, Anthony E. ....Denver, CO
New York, NY
Davis, Anthony G. M. ....Manchester, NH
Davis, Anthony J. ....Parsippany, NJ
Davis, April McCurdy ....Enid, OK
Davis, Aretha Delight ....Philadelphia, PA
Davis, Arneil Law Firm, LLP
Wenatchee, WA
Davis, Arnold ....New York, NY
Davis, Arnold, Haynes & Sanders, P.L.L.C.
Knoxville, TN
Davis, Arnold L., Jr. ....Beaumont, TX
Davis, Arrie W. ....Baltimore, MD
Davis, Arthur A., Jr. ....Kingston, NY
Davis, Arthur H. K. ....Berlin, NH
Davis, Arthur S. ....Boca Raton, FL
Davis, Artie Fultz, (Mrs.) ....Navasota, TX
Davis, Aryeh ....New York, NY
Davis, Ashby W. ....Greenville, SC
Davis & Associates ....Rockville, MD
Davis, Audrey H. ....Cleveland, OH
Davis Augello Matteliano & Gersten, LLP
Buffalo, NY
Williamsville, NY
Davis, A. W. ....Bryan, TX
Davis, A. W., Jr. ....Newton, TX
Davis, B Ford ....Baltimore, MD
Davis, B. Joan ....Raleigh, NC
Davis, B. Mark ....Tiffin, OH
Davis, B. Martin, III
Manhattan Beach, CA
Davis & Baldwin ....Seattle, WA
Davis & Balmuth ....Irvine, CA
Davis, Barbara Ann ....Asheville, NC
Davis, Barbara B.
Agency for International Development,
Other Offices of A.I.D., GV
Davis, Barbara C. ....Daytona Beach, FL
Davis, Barbara H. ....Buffalo, NY
Davis, Barbara J. ....Chicago, IL
Davis, Barbara J. ....Cherry Hill, NJ
Davis, Barbara Willman ....Lakeland, FL
Davis, Barbra L. ....Los Angeles, CA
Davis, Barnett, II ....Redwood City, CA
Davis, Barry ....Houston, TX
Davis, Barry L. ....Miami, FL
Davis, Barry M. ....Tucson, AZ
Davis, Barry R. ....Oklahoma City, OK
Davis, Bart M. ....Idaho Falls, ID
Davis, Barton B. ....Manassas, VA
Davis, Baxter L. ....Atlanta, GA
Davis, Beall, McGuire & Thompson, Chartered
Leavenworth, KS
Davis, Benjamin F. ....San Francisco, CA
Davis, Benjamin F., Jr. ....Greensboro, NC
Davis, Benjamin Franklin, Jr.
Metairie, LA
Davis, Benjamin K. ....Corbin, KY
Davis Bennett Barr & Spiess ....Wayne, PA
Davis & Bentzen, PLLC ....Washington, DC
Davis, Bernard ....Chicago, IL
Davis, Bernard ....Southfield, MI
Davis, Bernard E. ....Chester, NY
Davis, Bernard R. ....Mansfield, OH
Davis, Bernard S. ....Newark, NJ
Davis, Berthlynn J. ....Albany, NY
Davis, Bertrand A. ....Fort Wayne, IN
Davis, Beryl Ray ....Henryetta, OK
Davis, Beth Boosalis ....Evanston, IL
Davis, Beth H. ....Nashua, NH
Davis, Beth Margolis ....New York, NY
Davis, Betty M. ....London, KY
Davis, Beverly A., III ....Rocky Mount, VA
Davis, Beverly J. ....Fort Worth, TX
Davis, Beverly McDonald ....Radford, VA
Davis, B. G. (Ben) ....Carlsbad, NM
Davis, Bill J. ....El Dorado, AR
Davis, Billy A. ....Lubbock, TX
Davis, Billy H., Jr. ....Jackson, MS
Waco, TX
Davis, Birnbaum, Marcou, Seymour & Colgan
La Crosse, WI
Davis, Blair ....San Antonio, TX
Davis, Blake S. ....Secaucus, NJ
Davis, Bobbi J.W. ....Department of the Army,
U.S. Army Legal Services Agency, GV
Davis, Bobby, Jr. ....Cleveland, OH
Davis, Bobby Wayne ....Virginia Beach, VA
Davis & Boghigian, P.C. ....Nashua, NH
Davis, Bond ....San Antonio, TX
Davis, Bonni G. ....New York, NY
Davis, Bonnie C. ....Chesterfield, VA
Davis, Bonnie J. ....Baton Rouge, LA
Davis & Bostwick ....Portland, OR
Davis, Boyce R. ....Lincoln, AR
Davis, Boyce R., Associates ....Lincoln, AR
Davis, Bradford L. ....Council Bluffs, IA
Davis, Bradley B. ....New York, NY
Davis, Bradley G. ....Seattle, WA
Tacoma, WA
Davis, Bradley J. ....Orlando, FL
Davis, Bradley S. ....Kansas City, MO
Davis, Brandon T. ....New York, NY
Davis, Brandt W. ....Knoxville, TN
Davis, Brant ....Atlanta, GA
Davis, Brent ....Jonesboro, AR
Davis, Brent A. ....Peru, IN
Davis, Brent L. ....Minnetonka, MN
Davis, Brent W. ....Birmingham, AL
Davis, Bret D. ....Oklahoma City, OK
Davis, Bret H. ....Myrtle Beach, SC
Davis, Bret J. ....Los Angeles, CA
Davis, Brett ....Kansas City, MO
Davis, Brett D. ....Fairfield, CA
Davis, Brett D. ....Prestonsburg, KY
Davis and Brewer ....Clemmons, NC
Davis, Brian A. ....Department of Justice,
Federal Bureau of Investigation, GV
Davis, Brian A. ....Fort Lauderdale, FL
Davis, Brian A., (P.C.) ....Boston, MA
Davis, Brian C. ....Modesto, CA
Davis, Brian E. ....Pittsburgh, PA
Davis, Brian E. ....Houston, TX
Davis, Brian F. ....Wendell, NC
Davis, Brian H. ....St. Paul, MN
Davis, Brian J. ....Jacksonville, FL
Davis, Brian J. ....East Meadow, NY
Davis, Brian J. ....San Antonio, TX
Davis, Brian J. ....San Antonio, TX
Davis, Brian M. ....Charlotte, NC
Davis, Brian R. ....Redwood City, CA
Davis, Brian R. ....Austin, TX
Davis, Brian T. ....Southampton, NY
Davis, Bridget J. ....San Francisco, CA
Davis, Britt K. ....Houston, TX
Davis, Britton A. ....Winnetka, IL
Davis & Brown ....Walnut Creek, CA
Davis, Brown, Koehn, Shors & Roberts, P.C.
Des Moines, IA
Davis, Browning & Schnitker
Madison, FL
Davis, Bruce C. ....Santa Ana, CA
Davis, Bruce D., Jr. ....Baltimore, MD
Davis, Bruce E. ....Bethlehem, PA
Davis, Bruce E. ....Charleston, SC
Davis, Bruce G. ....Lansing, MI
Davis, Bruce G. ....Franklin, NC
Davis, Bruce H. ....Crescent City, FL
Davis, Bruce K. ....Frankfort, KY
Davis, Bruce N. ....Washington, DC
Davis, Bryan E. ....Atlanta, GA
Davis, Bryan H., Jr. ....Nacogdoches, TX
Davis & Brynteson, P.C. ....Chesapeake, VA
Davis & Bucco, P.C. ....Spring House, PA
Davis and Bujold ....Concord, NH
Manchester, NH
Davis, Byron, Jr. ....Nashville, TN
Davis, Byron P. ....Houston, TX
Davis, C. A., & Son ....Memphis, TN
Davis, C. Andrea ....New York, NY
Davis, C. Clay ....Savannah, GA
Davis, C. Clinton, Jr. ....Dallas, TX
Davis, C. Dean ....Austin, TX
Davis, C. Larry ....San Diego, CA
Davis, C. Lee ....Marietta, GA
Davis, C. Melvin ....Oxford, MS
Davis, C. Michael ....Alvin, TX
Davis, C. Morris ....Austin, TX
Davis, C. Nathan ....Albany, GA
Davis, C. Paul ....Huntsville, AL
Davis, C. Richard ....Richmond, VA
Davis, C. Stephen ....Los Angeles, CA
Davis, C. Thomas ....Atlanta, GA
Davis, C. Thomas ....Beaverton, OR
Davis, C. VanLeer, III ....Philadelphia, PA
Davis, C. Wayne ....Baltimore, MD
Davis, C. Wayne ....St. Louis, MO
Davis, C. William ....Bluefield, WV
Davis, Calvin E. ....Los Angeles, CA
Davis & Campbell L.L.C.
Washington, DC
Chicago, IL
Peoria, IL
Davis, Candace P. ....Chicago, IL
Davis & Cannon ....Cheyenne, WY
Sheridan, WY
Davis, Cara H. ....Lexington, KY
Davis, Carey Scott ....Houston, TX
Davis & Carico LLP ....Los Angeles, CA
Manhattan Beach, CA
Davis, Carl B. ....Wichita, KS
Davis, Carl E. ....San Bernardino, CA
Davis, Carl K. ....Beaverton, OR
Davis, Carl M. ....Dillon, MT
Davis, Carl M., II ....Atlanta, GA
Davis, Carl R. ....Daphne, AL
Davis, Carla D. ....Chicago, IL
Davis, Carle E. ....Richmond, VA
Davis, Carleton A. (Joe) ....Austin, TX
Davis, Carol E. ....Vail, CO
Davis, Carol Elaine ....Houston, TX
Davis, Carol N. ....Leesburg, FL
Davis, Carol O. ....Spokane, WA
Davis, Carole E. L. ....Georgetown, DE
Davis, Caroline D. ....Seattle, WA
Davis, Carolyn Curie (Peck) ....Naples, FL
Davis, Carolyn J. ....Los Angeles, CA
Davis, Carolyn Kimbrough ....Midland, MI
Davis, Carolyn L. ....Department of Justice,
Antitrust Division, GV
Davis, Carolyne K., P.C. ....Dallas, TX
Davis, Carolyne Koval ....Dallas, TX
Davis, Carroll P. ....Miami, FL
Davis, Cary E. ....Greenville, KY
Davis, Catherine ....Bronx, NY
Davis, Catherine A. ....Cleveland, OH
Davis, Catherine E. ....Midland, MI
Davis, Catherine F. ....Albuquerque, NM
Davis, Catherine M. ....Lansing, MI
Davis, Cecelia Oneathia-Lucenda
Arlington, VA
Davis, Cecil L., Jr. ....Tallahassee, FL
Davis, Cedillo & Mendoza, Incorporated
San Antonio, TX
Davis, Celeste Harriet ....Chicago, IL
Davis & Ceriani, P.C. ....Denver, CO
Davis, Champ W., Jr. ....Chicago, IL
Davis, Charlene D. ....Wilmington, DE
Davis, Charles A., Jr. ....Bartow, FL
Davis, Charles A., Jr. ....Chicago, IL
Davis, Charles A., Jr. ....Nappanee, IN
Davis, Charles A., (P.C.) ....Novato, CA
Davis, Charles Alexander ....Tucson, AZ
Davis, Charles B. ....Oklahoma City, OK
Davis, Charles C., Jr.
Securities and Exchange Commission,
Office of the General Counsel, GV
Davis, Charles D. ....Gallatin, MO
Davis, Charles E. ....Mesa, AZ
Davis, Charles E. ....Springdale, AR
Davis, Charles E. ....Mebane, NC
Davis, Charles Evans ....Orlando, FL
Davis, Charles G. ....New City, NY
Davis, Charles H. ....Liberty Corner, NJ
Davis, Charles H., Jr. ....Atlanta, GA
Davis, Charles L. ....Fairbanks, AK
Davis, Charles L. ....Buffalo, NY
Davis, Charles M. ....Baltimore, MD
Davis, Charles M. ....Louisburg, NC
Davis, Charles M. ....Seattle, WA
Davis, Charles S. ....Huntsville, TX
Davis, Charles W. ....Seattle, WA
Davis, Charlotte L. Poole
Christiansted, St. Croix, VI
Davis, Cherie Thompson ....Livermore, CA
Davis, Cheryl ....New York, NY
Davis, Cheryl L. ....New York, NY
Davis, Cheryl L. ....Knoxville, TN
Davis, Cheryl L. ....Charleston, WV
Davis, Cheryl-Ann ....Boston, MA
Davis, Chester George, Jr. ....Lanham, MD
Davis, Chester L., Jr. ....Indianapolis, IN
Davis, Chester R., Jr. ....Chicago, IL
Davis, Chris P. ....Portland, OR
Davis, Christi L. ....Pittsburgh, PA
Davis, Christina Robinson ....Boston, MA
Davis, Christine F.
General Accounting Office,
Office of the General Counsel, GV
Davis, Christine L. ....Moorestown, NJ
Philadelphia, PA
Davis, Christopher A. ....Gulfport, MS
Davis, Christopher A. ....Romney, WV
Davis, Christopher F. ....Salisbury, MD
Davis, Christopher L. ....Los Angeles, CA
Davis, Christopher L. ....Burlington, VT

Davis, Christopher M. ....Washington, DC
Davis, Christopher O. ....New Orleans, LA
Davis, Christopher P. ....Boston, MA
Davis, Christopher P. ....New York, NY
Davis & Cichorski ....Chicago, IL
Davis, Cindy Dobler ....San Diego, CA
Davis, Cindy J.K. ....Atlanta, GA
Davis, Clarence ....Columbia, SC
Davis, Clarence, Jr. ....Washington, DC
Davis, Clarice M., (P.C.) ....Dallas, TX
Davis, Clark H. ....Olathe, KS
Davis, Clark S. ....Pontiac, MI
Davis, Claude D. ....Austin, TX
Davis, Claude J. ....Jerseyville, IL
Davis, Claude-Leonard ....Athens, GA
Davis, Claudia L. ....Riverside, CA
Davis, Clay H. ....Springdale, AR
Davis, Clay S., Jr. ....Knoxville, TN
Davis, Clayton A. ....McLean, VA
Davis, Clayton A. L. ....Lake Charles, LA
Houston, TX
Davis, Clayton L., Jr. ....Detroit, MI
Davis, Cletus A. ....Houston, TX
Davis, Cletus, P.C. ....Houston, TX
Davis, Cliff ....Houston, TX
Davis, Clifford ....West Hartford, CT
Davis, Clifford L. ....Monticello, FL
Davis, Clifford L. ....White Plains, NY
Davis, Clifford L. ....Akron, OH
Davis, Clint B. ....Los Angeles, CA
Boston, MA
Davis, Clive ....New York, NY
Davis, Clyde L., Jr. ....Tyler, TX
Davis, Clyde N., Jr. ....Columbia, SC
Davis, Cody Fowler ....Tampa, FL
Davis, Coleen R. ....Odessa, TX
Davis, Colette T. ....Los Angeles, CA
Davis & Company, P.C. ....Irvine, CA
Davis, Connie Burk ....Westminster, MD
Davis, Constance Collins ....Washington, DC
Davis, Corbin R. ....Lansing, MI
Davis & Cox ....Fort Smith, AR
Van Buren, AR
Davis, Cox & Wright, PLC
Bentonville, AR
Fayetteville, AR
Rogers, AR
Springdale, AR
Davis, Craig A. ....Fresno, CA
Davis, Craig A. ....Washington, IA
Davis, Craig A. ....Lafayette, LA
Davis, Craig A., PLC ....Lafayette, LA
Davis, Craig C. ....Los Angeles, CA
Davis, Craig D. ....Grand Prairie, TX
Davis, Craig E. ....Austin, TX
Davis, Craig K. ....Columbia, SC
Davis, Craig K., P.C. ....Columbia, SC
Davis & Crain ....Tuscaloosa, AL
Davis, Craver, Hagood & Kerr, P.A.
Charleston, SC
Davis, Crowley A., Jr. ....Memphis, TN
Davis, Crystal A. ....Newton, NC
Davis, Curtis Wilburn ....Bonita, CA
Davis, Cynthia D. ....Gloster, MS
Davis, Cynthia D. ....Columbus, OH
Davis, Cynthia Fields ....Crossville, TN
Davis, D. Brent ....Miami, FL
Davis, D. Derrell ....Benton, AR
Davis, D. Edward ....Amarillo, TX
Davis, D. Frank ....Birmingham, AL
Davis, D. Jason ....Los Angeles, CA
Davis, D. Mark ....Dallas, TX
Davis, D. Nathan ....Charleston, SC
Davis, D. Paul ....Miami, FL
Davis, D. Scott ....Fairbanks, AK
Davis, D. William ....Bellaire, OH
Davis, Dale G. ....Piqua, OH
Davis, Dale L. ....Springfield, MO
Davis, Dan J. ....Tupelo, MS
Davis, Dana D. ....Charleston, WV
Davis, Dana H. ....Raleigh, NC
Davis, Dana R. ....Mustang, OK
Davis, Daniel ....Miami, FL
Davis, Daniel ....St. Louis, MO
Davis, Daniel E. ....Santa Rosa, CA
Davis, Daniel J. ....New York, NY
Davis, Daniel J. ....Dallas, TX
Davis, Daniel John ....Corpus Christi, TX
Davis, Daniel M. ....Sacramento, CA
Davis, Daniel S. ....Brookfield, WI
Davis, Daniel W. ....Mercer, PA
Davis, Danielle T., (Mrs.) ....Sebastopol, CA
Davis, Danny E. ....Waynesville, NC
Davis, Darlene R. ....Baltimore, MD
Davis, Darragh J. ....Herndon, VA
Vienna, VA
Davis, Darrell ....Mission, TX
Davis, Darrell E. ....Phoenix, AZ
Davis, Darrell J. ....Minneapolis, MN
Davis, Daryl E. ....New York, NY
Davis, David A. ....Oklahoma City, OK
Davis, David B. ....Huntington Beach, CA
Davis, David B. ....Clifton Forge, VA
Davis, David C. ....Vernon, CT
Davis, David C. ....Belleville, IL
Davis, David C. ....St. Louis, MO
Davis, David D. ....Osprey, FL
Davis, David E. ....Tampa, FL
Davis, David E. ....Bristol, PA
Davis, David E. ....Wichita Falls, TX
Davis, David E., P.A. ....Tampa, FL
Davis, David F. ....Buffalo, NY
Davis, David I. ....Spring House, PA
Davis, David J. ....Santa Barbara, CA
Davis, David J. ....Chicago, IL
Davis, David, Jr. ....Bloomington, IL
Davis, David L. ....Woodbridge, NJ
Davis, David M. ....Birmingham, MI
Davis, David M. ....Preston, MS
Davis, David M. ....Austin, TX
Davis, David M. ....Sandy, UT
Davis, David M., Jr. ....Milwaukee, WI
Davis, David P. ....Cincinnati, OH
Davis, David S. ....Louisville, KY
Davis, David S. ....St. Louis, MO
Davis, David W. ....Phoenix, AZ
Davis, David W. ....Tulsa, OK
Davis, Davidson & McLaughlin
Auburn, AL
Davis & Davis ....Daphne, AL
Davis & Davis ....Beverly Hills, CA
Davis & Davis ....Washington, DC
Davis & Davis ....Decatur, GA
Davis & Davis ....Greenfield, IN
Davis & Davis ....Council Bluffs, IA
Lexington, KY
Davis & Davis ....Columbia, MS
Davis and Davis ....New City, NY
Davis & Davis ....New York, NY
White Plains, NY
Davis & Davis ....Swanquarter, NC
Davis & Davis ....Youngstown, OH
Davis and Davis ....Ebensburg, PA
Davis & Davis ....Uniontown, PA
Davis & Davis ....Memphis, TN
Davis & Davis, A Professional Corporation
Anchorage, AK
Davis & Davis, A Professional Corporation
Bryan, TX
Davis, Davis & Davis ....Radford, VA
Davis, Davis, Davis & Rice
Rocky Mount, VA
Davis, Davis & Kaar ....Milton, PA
Davis Davis & Langan ....Indianapolis, IN
Davis, Davis & Layson ....Corydon, IN
Davis & Davis LLP ....Los Angeles, CA
Davis & Davis, P.A. ....Leesburg, FL
Davis & Davis, P.C. ....New York, NY
Davis & Davis, P.C. ....Austin, TX
Davis & Davis, Prof. Corp. ....Elkhart, IN
Davis, Dawn R. ....Atlanta, GA
Davis, Dean M. ....Bloomington, IL
Davis, Dean R. ....Wilmington, NC
Davis, Deanna L. ....Raleigh, NC
Davis, Deborah A. ....San Francisco, CA
Davis, Deborah D. ....Albany, NY
Davis, Deborah D. ....New York, NY
Davis, Deborah Lynn ....New York, NY
Davis, Deborah Neufeld ....Los Angeles, CA
Davis, Deborah Selph ....Tupelo, MS
Davis, Deborah Sullivan ....Tampa, FL
Davis, Dee Jon ....Houston, TX
Davis, DeForest P. ....Chicago, IL
Davis, Delaina J. ....Kinston, NC
Davis & Delanois, P.C. ....Danville, IL
Davis, Delta Anne ....Nashville, TN
Davis, DeMar W. ....Lake San Marcos, CA
Davis, Denise C. ....Goshen, IN
Davis, Dennis D. ....San Francisco, CA
Davis, Dennis D. ....Greenville, TX
Davis, Dennis J. ....Bryant, AR
Davis, Dennis L. ....Kansas City, MO
Davis, Dennis M. ....Coeur d'Alene, ID
Davis, Denny R. ....Cameron Park, CA
Davis, Derek ....Boston, MA
Davis, Derek L. ....Austin, TX
Davis, Derek S. ....Dallas, TX
Davis Devine Goodman & Wells
Miami, FL
Davis, D. G. Jason ....Oakland, CA
Davis, Diana L. ....Juno Beach, FL
Davis, Diana L. ....Houston, TX
Davis, Diane ....Albany, NY
Davis, Diane Corey ....Seattle, WA
Davis, Diane Vulich ....Toledo, OH
Davis, Dianna ....Mayfield, KY
Davis, Dianna M. ....San Diego, CA
Davis, Dianne James ....Alexander City, AL
Davis, Dick ....Tyler, TX
Davis, D. J. ....Greenfield, IN
Davis, D'Lesli M. ....San Diego, CA
Nashville, TN
Davis, Dolores M. ....Yucca Valley, CA
Davis, Don ....Charlotte, NC
Davis, Don A. ....Phoenix, AZ
Davis, Don C. ....Lawton, OK
Davis, Don G. ....East Lansing, MI
Davis, Don L. ....Austin, TX
Davis, Don, P.A. ....Charlotte, NC
Davis, Don W. ....Tallahassee, FL
Davis, Don W. ....Dallas, TX
Davis, Donald A. ....Grand Rapids, MI
Davis, Donald B., Jr. ....Baltimore, MD
Davis, Donald D. ....Indianapolis, IN
Davis, Donald E. ....Marina Del Rey, CA
Davis, Donald E. ....Cumberland, MD
Davis, Donald F. ....Ankeny, IA
Davis, Donald G. ....Los Angeles, CA
Davis, Donald G. ....New York, NY
Davis, Donald G. ....Dallas, TX
Davis, Donald Jay, Jr. ....Charleston, SC
Davis, Donald K. ....Fairfax, VA
Davis, Donald K. ....Seattle, WA
Davis, Donald L. ....Vega, TX
Davis, Donald Lee ....Kansas City, MO
Davis, Donald M. ....Los Angeles, CA
Davis, Donald M. ....Philadelphia, PA
Davis, Donald R. ....Gold River, CA
Davis, Donald R. ....Kentfield, CA
Davis, Donald R. ....Palo Alto, CA
Davis, Donald W. ....Oklahoma City, OK
Davis, Donald W., Jr. ....Akron, OH
Davis, Donen ....Columbia, SC
Davis, Donn E. ....Lincoln, NE
Davis, Donn M. ....Chicago, IL
Davis, Donna Ambler, P.C. ....Chapel Hill, NC
Davis, Donna D. ....Bend, OR
Davis, Donna EM ....Dunmore, PA
Davis, Donna Jo ....Clearwater, FL
Davis, Donna R. ....Knoxville, TN
Davis, Donna S. ....Long Beach, CA
Davis, Donnell P. ....Norfolk, VA
Davis, Doreen S. ....Philadelphia, PA
Davis, Dorin, Curtis & Neil, P.C.
Birmingham, AL
Davis, Dorothy A. ....Pittsburgh, PA
Davis, Dorothy K. ....Mission Viejo, CA
Davis & Dorward ....Hayward, CA
Davis, Douglas E. ....Phoenix, AZ
Davis, Douglas E., P.C. ....Phoenix, AZ
Davis, Douglas J., (P.C.) ....Atlanta, GA
Davis, Douglas L. ....Charleston, WV
Davis, Douglas R. ....Anchorage, AK
Davis, Douglas R. ....Austell, GA
Davis, Douglas R. ....New York, NY
Davis, Douglas R. ....Salt Lake City, UT
Davis, Douglas R. ....Seattle, WA
Davis, Douglas W. ....Malibu, CA
Davis, Douglas W. ....Chesapeake, VA
Davis, Douglas W. ....Richmond, VA
Davis, Drew Anna ....Shawnee, KS
Davis, Drew F. ....Kansas City, MO
Davis, Drew M. ....Washington, DC
Davis & Durham ....Huntsville, TX
Davis, Dwight E. ....Cleveland, OH
Davis, Dwight J. ....Atlanta, GA
Davis, E. Brian ....New Albany, IN
Davis, E. Brian ....Louisville, KY
Davis, E. Darrell, Jr. ....St. Charles, MO
Davis, E. Lawrence, III ....Raleigh, NC
Davis, E. Lee ....Statesboro, GA
Davis, E. Marcus, (P.C.) ....Atlanta, GA
Davis, E. Purnell ....Warrenton, GA
Davis, E. Wright, Jr. ....Pensacola, FL
Davis, Earl P. (Pat) ....Memphis, TN
Davis, Earon S. ....Wilmette, IL
Davis, Eden R. ....Fort Worth, TX
Davis, Edmond R. ....Los Angeles, CA
Davis, Edmund M. ....Monticello, NY
Davis, Edmund R. ....New York, NY
Davis, Edward A. ....Butler, GA
Davis, Edward A. ....New York, NY
Davis, Edward A. ....Dallas, TX
Davis, Edward A., III ....Houston, TX
Davis, Edward A., P.C. ....Butler, GA
Davis, Edward B. ....Miami, FL
Davis, Edward E. ....Phoenix, AZ
Davis, Edward H. ....San Francisco, CA
Davis, Edward H., Jr. ....Miami, FL
Davis, Edward I. ....Morganville, NJ
Davis, Edward J. ....New York, NY
Davis, Edward, Jr. ....Baton Rouge, LA
Davis, Edward N. ....Butler, GA
Davis, Edward P., Jr. ....Palo Alto, CA
Davis, Edward S. ....New York, NY
Davis, Edwin D., II ....South Daytona, FL
Davis, Edwin L. ....Tuskegee, AL
Davis, Edwin Theodore ....Houston, TX
Davis, Edwin W. ....Dallas, TX
Davis, Egbert L., IV ....Charlotte, NC
Davis, Eileen J. ....St. Cloud, MN
Davis & Eisenberg ....New York, NY
Davis, Elaine C. ....Baltimore, MD
Davis, Elbridge B. ....Calais, ME
Davis, Elisa L. ....Chicago, IL
Davis, Elise ....Easton, MD
Davis, Elizabeth ....Joplin, MO
Davis, Elizabeth A. ....Flint, MI
Davis, Elizabeth Bolton ....Atlanta, GA
Davis, Elizabeth K. ....Tampa, FL
Davis, Elizabeth M. ....Birmingham, AL
Atlanta, GA
Davis, Elizabeth M. ....St. Louis, MO
Davis, Elizabeth N. ....Akron, OH
Cleveland, OH
Davis, Elizabeth Wilson ....Austin, TX
Davis, Ella Jane P. ....Tallahassee, FL
Davis, Ellen ....Sorrento, ME
Davis, Ellen Estes ....Shreveport, LA
Davis, Ellen T. ....Washington, DC
Davis, Elliot S. ....Pittsburgh, PA
Davis, Emerson S.
Securities and Exchange Commission,
Division of Investment Management, GV
Davis, Emily ....Minneapolis, MN
Davis, Emily S. ....White River Junction, VT
Davis, Eppstein & Terry, L.L.C.
Tucson, AZ
Davis, Eric ....North Wilkesboro, NC
Davis, Eric B. ....New York, NY
Davis, Eric J. ....Annapolis, MD
Davis, Eric K. ....Los Angeles, CA
Davis, Eric L. ....Franklin, TN
Davis, Eric M. ....Wilmington, DE
Davis, Eric M. ....New York, NY
Davis, Eric S. ....Department of Transportation,
Surface Transportation Board, GV
Davis, Erik G. ....Salt Lake City, UT
Davis, Ervin D. ....St. Charles, MO
Davis, Erwin L. ....Fayetteville, AR
Davis, Ethan I. ....Boston, MA
Davis, Eugene J. ....Marysville, CA
Davis, Eugene L. ....San Diego, CA
Davis, Eugene S. ....St. Louis, MO
Davis, Eva Herbst ....Los Angeles, CA
Davis, Evaleen M. ....Addison, TX
Davis, Evan A. ....New York, NY
Davis, Evan J. ....Department of Justice,
Tax Division, GV
Davis, Everett Conley ....San Diego, CA
Davis, E'Vinski L. ....Baton Rouge, LA
Davis, F. Barrett ....Dallas, TX
Davis, F. Curtis, Jr. ....Trevose, PA
Davis, F. Elwood ....Washington, DC
Davis, F. Eugene, IV ....Stamford, CT
Davis, F. Eugene, IV ....Stamford, CT
Davis, F. Gary
Office of Government Ethics,
Office of the Director, GV
Davis, F. Kelly ....Wilkes-Barre, PA
Davis, F. Leary, Jr. ....Buies Creek, NC
Davis, F. Patrick ....St. Louis, MO
Davis, F.C. (Rick), II ....Wichita, KS
Davis & Feder ....Mobile, AL
Gulfport, MS
Davis & Fernandes, Sr., P.A.
Gainesville, FL
Davis & Fields, P.C. ....Daphne, AL
Davis & Finucane ....Elizabethtown, NY
Davis Firm, The ....Bremerton, WA
Everett, WA
Seattle, WA
Davis and Flanagan ....Shreveport, LA
Davis, Florence A. ....New York, NY
Davis, Florence K. S. ....Hartford, CT
Davis, Floyd D. ....Winchester, TN
Davis & Forehand ....Cordele, GA
Vienna, GA
Davis & Fox ....Los Angeles, CA
Davis, Frances E. ....Emmetsburg, IA
Davis, Frances K. ....Berwyn, PA
Davis, Frances M. ....Oakland, CA
Davis, Francis J. ....Urbana, IL
Davis, Francis M. ....Boston, MA
Davis, Frank ....Melville, NY
Davis, Frank B. ....Houston, TX
Davis, Frank C. ....Live Oak, FL
Davis, Frank C., III ....Dallas, TX
Davis, Frank G. ....Cincinnati, OH
Davis, Frank M. ....Dillon, MT
Davis, Frank R. ....Dedham, MA
Davis, Frank T., III ....Greenville, SC
Davis, Frank W. ....Guthrie, OK
Davis, Frank W., Jr. ....Colorado Springs, CO
Davis, Franklin G.
Office of Personnel Management, GV
Davis, Fred ....New York, NY
Davis, Fred Bunker ....Omaha, NE
Davis, Fred D., III ....Pine Bluff, AR
Davis, Fred E. ....Austin, TX
Davis, Fred, The Law Firm of
New York, NY
Davis, Fred W. ....Lafayette, LA
Davis, Frederic H. ....Louisville, KY
Davis, Frederick ....Memphis, TN
Davis, Frederick T. ....New York, NY
Davis, French C. ....Daytona Beach, FL
Davis, Friedman, Zavett, Kane & MacRae
Chicago, IL
Davis, F. T., Jr., (P.C.) ....Atlanta, GA
Davis, Furby & Rogers, P.L.L.C.
Jackson, MS
Davis, G. Eric ....Santa Rosa, CA
Davis, G. Gervaise, III ....Monterey, CA
Davis, G. Gordon ....Elizabethtown, NY
Davis, G. Jack, Jr. ....Dayton, OH
Davis, G. Kay ....Newport Beach, CA
Davis, G. Phillip ....Buckhannon, WV
Davis, G. Sander ....Northfield, NJ
Philadelphia, PA
Davis, G. Terrell ....Atlanta, GA
Davis, G. Thomas ....Atlanta, GA
Davis, Gabrielle B. ....New York, NY
Davis, Gabrielle V. ....New York, NY
Davis & Gaffney ....Baltimore, MD
Davis, Gail Reiner ....New York, NY
Davis, Gardiner B. ....Kansas City, MO
Davis, Gardner F. ....Jacksonville, FL
Davis, Garnett S. ....Kingsville, TX
Davis, Garrett V. ....Washington, DC
Davis, Garry E. ....Decatur, IL
Davis, Gary A. ....St. Paul, MN
Davis, Gary B. ....Greenville, NC
Davis, Gary D. ....Grass Valley, CA
Davis, Gary D. ....La Porte, IN
Davis, Gary E. ....Santa Ana, CA
Davis, Gary E. ....Denver, CO
Davis, Gary E. ....Bowie, MD
Davis, Gary E. ....New York, NY
Davis, Gary E. ....Columbus, OH
Davis, Gary F.
General Services Administration,
Office of Regional Counsel, GV
Davis, Gary J. ....Cincinnati, OH
Davis, Gary L. ....Miami, FL
New Port Richey, FL
Davis, Gary L. ....Boise, ID
Davis, Gary L. ....St. Paul, MN
Davis, Gary L. ....Helena, MT
Davis, Gary M. ....Pittsburgh, PA
Davis, Gary S. ....Modesto, CA
Davis, Gary Scott ....Miami, FL
Davis, Gary V., Law Offices of
McLean, VA
Davis, Gary W. ....Cheyenne Wells, CO
Eads, CO
Davis, Gary W. ....Oklahoma City, OK
Davis, Gary W. ....Wakefield, RI
Davis, Gary Ward, Jr. ....Austin, TX
Davis, Gayle ....Newport Beach, CA
Davis, Gaylon Keith ....Wellington, TX
Davis, Gene C. ....Lake Forest, IL
Davis, Gene S. ....Troy, MI
Davis, Geo. Thomas, Jr. ....Swanquarter, NC
Davis, Geoffrey B. ....Providence, RI
Davis, Geoffrey G. ....Washington, DC
Davis, Geoffrey H. ....Bingham Farms, MI
Davis, Geoffrey H. ....Toledo, OH
Davis, Geoffrey M. ....Boise, ID
Davis, Geoffrey M. ....Chicago, IL
Davis, Geoffrey Scott ....Alamo, CA
Davis, George A. ....Dubuque, IA

Davis, George B. ....Greenfield, IN
Davis, George B. ....Grand Rapids, MI
Davis, George C.
United States Postal Service, Law Department, GV
Davis, George C. ....Baltimore, MD
Davis, George D. ....Oklahoma City, OK
Davis, George H., III ....Bowling Green, VA
Davis, George H., Jr. ....Columbia, SC
Davis, George L., III ....Portsmouth, OH
Davis, George M. ....Los Angeles, CA
Davis, George P., Jr. ....Murphy, NC
Davis, George R. ....Lowville, NY
Davis, George T. ....Kamuela, HI
Davis, Gerald ....Seattle, WA
Davis, Gerald C. ....Farmington Hills, MI
Davis, Gerald D. ....St. Petersburg, FL
Davis, Gerald J. ....Phoenix, AZ
Davis, Gerald K. ....Bakersfield, CA
Davis, Gerald K., Jr. ....Juneau, AK
Davis, Gerald L. ....Akron, OH
Davis, Gerald W. ....Pine River, MN
Davis, Gerard H. ....New York, NY
Davis, Gilbert H. ....Atlanta, GA
Davis, Gilbert K. ....Fairfax, VA
Davis & Gilbert LLP ....New York, NY
Davis, Gilbert T., Jr. ....Clemmons, NC
Davis Gillette & Clark, P.C. ....Mesa, AZ
Davis, Gilstrap, Hearn, Shaw, Saladoff & Smith, A Professional Corporation
Yreka, CA
Ashland, OR
Grants Pass, OR
Klamath Falls, OR
Medford, OR
Davis, Gleam O. ....Los Angeles, CA
Davis, Glenn B. ....Los Angeles, CA
Davis, Glenn E. ....San Francisco, CA
Washington, DC
Davis, Glenn E. ....Belleville, IL
St. Louis, MO
Davis, Glenn E. ....Woodbridge, NJ
Davis, Glenn E. ....Bartlesville, OK
Davis, Glenn E. ....Philadelphia, PA
Davis, Glenn E., Jr. ....Indianapolis, IN
Davis, Glenn E., Sr. ....Indianapolis, IN
Davis, Glenn M. ....Phoenix, AZ
Davis, Glenn R. ....Harrisburg, PA
Davis, Glenn T. ....Somers, CT
Davis, Glenn V. ....Trinidad, CO
Davis and Goldie ....Harrison, AR
Yellville, AR
Davis & Gooch ....Washington, DC
Davis, Gordon & Doner, P.A.
West Palm Beach, FL
Davis, Gordon J. ....New York, NY
Davis, Gordon P. ....San Diego, CA
Davis, Gowin ....Wichita Falls, TX
Davis, Gractia S. ....Centerville, OH
Davis, Grady M. ....Chico, CA
Davis, Graham & Stubbs LLP
Boulder, CO
Denver, CO
Davis, Grant L. ....Kansas City, MO
Davis, Grass, Goldstein & Housouer
Upland, CA
Davis, Grayson L. ....Houston, TX
Davis, Greg ....West Hills, CA
Davis, Greg L. ....Montgomery, AL
Davis, Greg R. ....Phoenix, AZ
Davis, Gregg C. ....Dallas, TX
Davis, Gregory C. ....Boston, MA
Davis, Gregory J. ....Wayne, PA
Davis, Gregory L. ....Louisville, KY
Davis, Gregory L. ....Buffalo, NY
Davis, Gregory M. ....Chicago, IL
Davis, Gregory R. ....Williamsburg, VA
Davis, Gregory S. ....Chicago, IL
Davis, Gregory V. ....Department of Justice, Tax Division, GV
Davis, Greta L. ....Romney, WV
Davis, Grimm & Payne ....Seattle, WA
Davis, Grover B. ....Indianapolis, IN
Davis & Gugerty ....Forest Hills, NY
Davis, Gus L., Jr. ....Morehead City, NC
Davis, Guy E., Jr. ....Atlanta, GA
Davis, Guy Stephen ....Dyersburg, TN
Davis, Guy-Michael B. ....Toledo, OH
Davis, H. Brian ....Camas, WA
Davis, H. Glenn ....Shelbyville, IL
Davis, H. Glenn ....Winston-Salem, NC
Davis, H. Lee, Jr. ....Winston-Salem, NC
Davis, H. Russell ....Arcadia, LA
Davis, H. Sam ....Dallas, TX
Davis, H. Scott, Jr. ....Louisville, KY
Davis, H. Thomas, Jr. ....New York, NY
Davis, H. A. ....Lombard, IL
Davis, Hal A. ....Carrabelle, FL
Davis, Hal S. ....New York, NY
Davis, Hal S., III ....Plano, TX
Davis, Hal W. ....Fort Smith, AR
Davis, Hamilton C. ....Shippensburg, PA
Davis, Hamilton G. ....Lake Bluff, IL
Davis & Hamrick, L.L.P.
Winston-Salem, NC
Davis, Hardge, Jr. ....Newark, NJ
Davis, Harland W. ....Apollo Beach, FL
Davis & Harman ....Washington, DC
Davis, Harold ....New York, NY
Davis, Harold C., Jr.
Department of Transportation, Federal Aviation Administration, GV
Davis, Harold T. ....Hingham, MA
Davis, Harold V. ....Albany, MO
Davis, Harrel L., III ....El Paso, TX
Davis, Harry L. ....Fairbanks, AK
Davis, Harry P., Jr. ....Marietta, GA
Davis, Harry S. ....New York, NY
Davis, Harry W. ....New York, NY
Davis, Harry W., Jr. ....Columbia, SC
Davis, Harvey L. ....Dallas, TX
Davis & Harwell, P.A.
Winston-Salem, NC
Davis, Hatley, Haffeman & Tighe, P.C.
Great Falls, MT
Davis, Hay, Wittenburg, Davis & Caldwell, L.L.P. ....San Angelo, TX
Davis, Hayden D., Jr. ....Terrace Park, OH
Davis, Hayden E. ....Jericho, NY
Davis, Hayward H. ....Lake Placid, FL
Davis, H. C. Tanner ....Memphis, TN
Davis, Heather Elayne ....Los Angeles, CA
Davis, Heather L. ....Lincoln, NE
Frisco, TX
Davis, Heather M. ....Golden, CO
Davis, Helen R. ....Phoenix, AZ
Davis and Hengelbrok ....Cincinnati, OH
Davis, Henry A., Jr. ....Chatham, VA
Davis, Henry B., Jr. ....Grand Rapids, MI
Davis, Henry Clay, III ....Georgetown, DE
Davis, Henry Clay, III, P.A.
Georgetown, DE
Davis, Henry E. ....Jacksonville, FL
Davis, Henry E. ....Lexington, KY
Davis, Henry P. ....New York, NY
Davis, Henry S., Jr. ....Laurel, MS
Davis, Henry W. ....Youngstown, OH
Davis, Herbert ....Naples, FL
Davis, Herbert C. ....St. Louis Park, MN
Davis, Herbert Gordon ....San Antonio, TX
Davis, Herbert H. ....Prosser, WA
Davis, Herbert H., III ....Denver, CO
Davis, Herbert H., Jr. ....Jacksonville, FL
Davis, Herbert J. ....Chicago, IL
Davis, Herbert O. ....Greensboro, NC
Davis, Herbert, (P.C.) ....Los Angeles, CA
Davis, Heywood H. ....Kansas City, MO
Davis, Hillary Galloway ....Towson, MD
Davis Hoffman Crumpton & Roth, LLP
New York, NY
Davis & Holiman ....Little Rock, AR
Davis, Holly A. ....Ocala, FL
Davis, Homer A. ....Dalhart, TX
Davis, Horace H. ....Seattle, WA
Davis, Howard A. ....Chicago, IL
Davis, Howard E. "Ben" ....San Antonio, TX
Davis, Howard J. ....Philadelphia, PA
Davis, Howard M. ....West Orange, NJ
Davis, Howard M., P.C. ....Newark, NJ
West Orange, NJ
Davis, Howard P. ....Tenafly, NJ
Davis, Howard P., P.C. ....Tenafly, NJ
Davis, Howard Q., Jr. ....Indianola, MS
Davis, Howard S. ....New York, NY
Davis, Howard W. ....Boston, MA
Davis, Hugh A., II ....Leesburg, FL
Davis, Hugh J. ....Seattle, WA
Davis, Hugh M., Jr. ....Detroit, MI
Davis, Hugh W., II ....Raleigh, NC
Davis & Humbert, P.A. ....Mebane, NC
Davis, Hutchinson & Wilkerson, L.L.P.
Corpus Christi, TX
Davis, Hutson S., Jr. ....Beaufort, SC
Davis, I. Kenneth ....Portland, OR
Davis, Ian E. ....Fort Worth, TX
Davis, Ira L. ....Austin, TX
Davis, Irwin N., (P.C.) ....Buffalo, NY
Davis, J. Alan ....Los Angeles, CA
Davis, J. Alan, P.C. ....Los Angeles, CA
Davis, J. Anderson ....Rome, GA
Davis, J. Bratton ....Columbia, SC
Davis, J. Christopher ....Tulsa, OK
Davis, J. Daniel ....San Francisco, CA
Davis, J. Glenn ....Buffalo, NY
Davis, J. Harvey ....Ocilla, GA
Davis, J. Herbert ....Evansville, IN
Davis, J. Jefferson ....Nashua, NH
Davis, J. Kennerly, Jr. ....Richmond, VA
Davis, J. Layne ....Boise, ID
Davis, J. Mac ....Waukesha, WI
Davis, J. Mark ....Little Rock, AR
Davis, J. Mark ....Houston, TX
Davis, J. Mason, Jr. ....Birmingham, AL
Davis, J. Maston ....Warsaw, VA
Davis, J. Max ....Decatur, GA
Davis, J. Michael ....St. Augustine, FL
Davis, J. Michael ....Atlanta, GA
Davis, J. Michael ....Portland, ME
Davis, J. Richard, Jr. ....Columbia, MS
Davis, J. Riley ....Tallahassee, FL
Davis, J. Robert, Jr. ....Houston, TX
Davis, J. Roger ....Columbus, OH
Davis, J. Ross ....Winter Park, FL
Davis, J. Russell ....San Antonio, TX
Davis, J. Stark ....Woodward, OK
Davis, J. Thomas ....Forest City, NC
Davis, J. Todd ....Columbus, OH
Davis, J. Toliver ....Asheville, NC
Davis, J. Tucker ....Westlake Village, CA
Davis, Jack ....Mesa, AZ
Davis, Jack ....Evansville, IN
Davis, Jack ....Ashland, OR
Davis, Jack C., (P.C.) ....Lansing, MI
Davis, Jack H. ....Dallas, TX
Davis & Jack, L.L.C. ....Wichita, KS
Davis, Jack R. ....Chicago, IL
Davis, Jack R. ....Seattle, WA
Davis, Jackson B. ....Shreveport, LA
Davis, Jacob B. ....Glen Burnie, MD
Davis, Jacob E. ....Cincinnati, OH
Davis, Jacob E., II ....Columbus, OH
Davis, Jacqulin F. ....Columbus, OH
Davis, Jacqueline E. ....Washington, DC
Davis, Jacqueline E. ....New York, NY
Davis, James ....Oxon Hill, MD
Davis, James A. ....Fremont, NE
Davis, James A. ....Salisbury, NC
Davis, James A. ....Winston-Salem, NC
Davis, James A. ....Memphis, TN
Davis, James Allen, & Associates, P.C.
Fremont, NE
Davis, James B. ....Fort Lauderdale, FL
Davis, James B. ....Chagrin Falls, OH
Davis, James B. ....Carrizo Springs, TX
Davis, James B. ....Vienna, VA
Davis, James B., (P.C.) ....Alameda, CA
Davis, James Benjamin
Department of the Army, Office of the General Counsel, GV
Davis, James Bruce ....Arlington, VA
Davis, James C. ....Des Moines, IA
Davis, James C. ....Concord, NC
Davis, James C., II ....Plant City, FL
Davis, James C., Jr. ....Niskayuna, NY
Davis, James C., Jr. ....Charlotte, NC
Davis, James D. ....Richmond, VA
Davis, James E. ....Texarkana, AR
Davis, James E. ....Thornton, CO
Davis, James E. ....Greenfield, IN
Davis, James E. ....Albany, NY
Davis, James E. ....Akron, OH
Davis, James E. ....Tunkhannock, PA
Davis, James E. ....Dallas, TX
Davis, James E. ....Yakima, WA
Davis, James E., Jr. ....Huntsville, AL
Davis, James E., Jr. ....Montgomery, AL
Davis, James F. ....Wilmington, DE
Davis, James F. ....Washington, DC
Davis, James F. ....Oklahoma City, OK
Davis, James Fred ....Worland, WY
Davis, James G. ....Upland, CA
Davis, James G. ....Baltimore, MD
Davis, James G. ....Nashville, TN
Davis, James H. ....Birmingham, AL
Davis, James H. ....Rockville, MD
Davis, James H. ....Boston, MA
Davis, James H. ....Shrub Oak, NY
Davis, James H. ....Youngstown, OH
Davis, James H., III ....Quincy, MA
Davis, James H., Jr. ....Kansas City, MO
Davis, James Hornor, III ....Charleston, WV
Davis, James Hornor, IV ....Charleston, WV
Davis, James J. ....Boise, ID
Davis, James J., III ....San Francisco, CA
Davis, James J., Jr. ....Juneau, AK
Davis, James K. ....Hamilton, AL
Davis, James K., Jr. ....Sacramento, CA
Davis, James L. ....Reading, PA
Davis, James L. (Jim), III ....Gulfport, MS
Davis, James L., Jr. ....Atlanta, GA
Davis, James L. (Jim), III ....Biloxi, MS
Davis, James Lee ....New Bern, NC
Davis, James Lynn, A Prof. Law Corp.
Many, LA
Davis, James M. ....Chicago, IL
Davis, James M. ....New York, NY
Davis, James M. ....Morristown, TN
Davis, James M., Jr. ....Midland, TX
Davis, James Martin ....Omaha, NE
Davis, James Miller, Jr. ....Columbia, SC
Davis, James O., III ....Tampa, FL
Davis, James P., II ....Bellevue, WA
Davis, James R. ....Sacramento, CA
Davis, James R. ....Lansing, MI
Davis, James R. ....Houston, TX
Davis, James R., II ....Washington, DC
Davis, James Randall ....Lexington, SC
Davis, James Romeyn ....Keene, NH
Davis, James S. ....Rancho Cucamonga, CA
Davis, James S. ....Boston, MA
Davis, James S. ....Portland, OR
Davis, James T. ....Little Rock, AR
Davis, James T. ....Uniontown, PA
Davis, James V. ....Albany, GA
Davis, James W. ....Birmingham, AL
Davis, James W. ....Shreveport, LA
Davis, James W. ....St. Charles, MO
Davis, James W. (Jim) ....Douglasville, GA
Davis, James W., Jr. ....New Cumberland, WV
Davis, James Willard ....Westminster, MD
Davis, JaNan Arnold, (P.A.)
Little Rock, AR
Davis, Jane A. ....Birmingham, AL
Davis, Jane Clay ....El Cerrito, CA
Davis, Jane E. ....San Antonio, TX
Davis, Jane F. ....Hyannis, MA
Davis, Jane G. ....York, PA
Davis, Jane Thompson ....Charleston, SC
Davis, Janet E. ....Mason, OH
Davis, Janet R. ....Chicago, IL
Davis, Janice ....Washington, DC
Davis, Janice Z. ....Dallas, TX
Davis, Jaret L. ....Miami, FL
Davis, Jarrod G. ....Boise, ID
Davis, Jas. E. ....Birmingham, AL
Davis, Jason Robert ....Norfolk, VA
Davis, Jay ....Garden City, NY
Davis, Jay G. ....Atlanta, GA
Davis, Jay L. ....Phoenix, AZ
Davis, Jay M. ....Los Angeles, CA
Davis, Jay R. ....Los Angeles, CA
Davis, Jay R. ....Chicago, IL
Fort Worth, TX
Davis, Jayne Tracy ....Boise, ID
Davis, J. D. ....New York, NY
Davis, Jean Carey ....Danvers, MA
Davis, Jean J. ....Brooklyn, NY
Davis, Jean M. ....Minneapolis, MN
Davis, Jeannine M. ....Elkhart, IN
Davis, Jed ....Augusta, ME
Davis, Jeff Jr. ....Little Rock, AR
Davis, Jeff W. ....Rapid City, SD
Davis, Jefferson B. ....Houston, TX
Nacogdoches, TX
Davis, Jefferson James ....Decatur, GA
Davis, Jefferson, Jr. ....Atlanta, GA
Davis, Jefferson L., Jr. ....Cartersville, GA
Davis, Jeffery W. ....Chicago, IL
Davis, Jeffrey ....Camden, NJ
Davis, Jeffrey ....Syracuse, NY
Davis, Jeffrey A. ....Houston, TX
Davis, Jeffrey C. ....Chicago, IL
Davis, Jeffrey G. ....Washington, DC
Davis, Jeffrey J. ....Charlotte, NC
Davis, Jeffrey L. ....Chicago, IL
Davis, Jeffrey M. ....Champaign, IL
Davis, Jeffrey M. ....Roseland, NJ
Davis, Jeffrey N. ....St. Louis, MO
Davis, Jeffrey O. ....Milwaukee, WI
Davis, Jeffrey P. ....Fresno, CA
Davis, Jeffrey P. ....Marietta, GA
Davis, Jeffrey R. ....Miami, FL
Davis, Jeffrey R. ....Atlanta, GA
Davis, Jeffrey R. ....Columbus, OH
Davis, Jeffrey R. ....San Antonio, TX
Davis, Jeffrey S. ....Washington, DC
Davis, Jeffrey S.
Department Of Health And Human Services, Office of the General Counsel, GV
Davis, Jeffrey S. ....Portland, OR
Davis, Jeffrey S. ....Houston, TX
Davis, Jeffrey T. ....Springfield, MO
Davis, Jeffrey W. ....Lawrence, KS
Davis, Jeffrey W. ....New York, NY
Davis, Jeffrey W. ....Harrisburg, PA
Davis, Jeffrey W. ....Seattle, WA
Davis, Jeffry A. ....San Diego, CA
Davis, Jeffry R. ....Fort Worth, TX
Davis, Jenifer Melander ....Gainesville, FL
Davis, Jennifer A. ....Denver, CO
Davis, Jennifer B. ....Washington, DC
Davis, Jennifer Elizabeth ....Fort Wayne, IN
Davis, Jennifer L. ....Boston, MA
Davis, Jennifer Leigh ....Birmingham, AL
Davis, Jennifer Lynn ....Wilmington, NC
Davis, Jennifer Lynn ....Houston, TX
Davis, Jennifer Smith ....Sacramento, CA
Davis, Jennifer Wilson ....Dallas, TX
Davis, Jeraldine B. ....Philadelphia, PA
Davis, Jerome L. ....West Palm Beach, FL
Davis, Jerrod ....Gilmer, TX
Davis, Jerry ....Houston, TX
Davis, Jerry A. ....Danville, IL
Davis, Jerry A. ....Aberdeen, MS
Davis, Jerry F. ....Baton Rouge, LA
Davis, Jerry L. ....New Boston, TX
Davis, Jess W. ....Walnut Creek, CA
Davis, Jessica L. ....Chicago, IL
Davis, Jill Wachtel ....Lake Havasu City, AZ
Davis, Jillian S. ....Cleveland, OH
Davis, Jimmy F. ....Dimmitt, TX
Davis, Jimmy Kyle ....Knoxville, TN
Davis, Jo Ann ....Prospect Heights, IL
Davis, Jo Ann M. ....Baltimore, MD
Davis, Jo Robin ....Farmington Hills, MI
Davis, Jo-Ann W. ....Springfield, MA
Worcester, MA
Davis, Joanne Fatse ....Middlebury, CT
Davis, Joe A. ....Dallas, TX
Davis, Joe L., Jr. ....Wauchula, FL
Davis, Joe M. ....New Albany, MS
Davis, Joe R. ....Kingsville, TX
Davis, Joe W., Jr. ....Collegedale, TN
Davis, Joel C. ....Boulder, CO
Davis, Joel G. ....Oakdale, LA
Davis, Joel Richard ....Chicago, IL
Davis, Joel Scott ....Louisville, KY
Davis, John A. ....Dallas, TX
Davis, John A., III ....Bentonville, AR
Fort Smith, AR
Little Rock, AR
Davis, John A., Jr. ....Houston, TX
Davis, John A. (Zan), IV ....Little Rock, AR
Davis, John Allen "Jad", Jr. ....Midland, TX
Davis, John B. ....Oklahoma City, OK
Davis, John B., II ....Baton Rouge, LA
Davis, John C. ....Eureka, CA
Davis, John C. ....Kansas City, MO
Davis, John C., Jr. ....Tuscaloosa, AL
Davis, John D. ....Little Rock, AR
Davis, John E. ....Manhattan Beach, CA
Davis, John E. ....Washington, DC
Davis, John E. ....Lexington, KY
Davis, John E. ....New York, NY
Davis, John E. ....Grants Pass, OR
Davis, John E., III ....Tucson, AZ
Davis, John F. ....Sacramento, CA
Davis, John F. ....Des Moines, IA
Davis, John F. ....Silver Spring, MD
Davis, John F. ....Boston, MA
Davis, John F. ....Manchester, NH
Davis, John F. ....Rio Rancho, NM
Davis, John F., Jr. ....Decatur, GA
Davis, John F., Jr. ....Greenville, MS
Davis, John F., Jr., Law Firm of
Decatur, GA
Davis, John F., P.C., Law Office of
Rio Rancho, NM
Davis, John G. ....Clayton, GA
Davis, John Gary ....Little Rock, AR
Davis, John H. ....San Antonio, TX
Davis, John H., Jr. ....Denver, CO
Davis, John I., Jr. ....Chicago, IL
Davis, John J. ....Pikeville, KY
Davis, John J. ....Boston, MA
Davis, John J. ....Angleton, TX
Davis, John J., III ....Louisville, KY
Davis, John J., Jr. ....San Francisco, CA
Davis, John K. ....Seattle, WA
Davis, John L. ....Department of Justice, Civil Division, GV
Davis, John L. ....Decatur, IL

Davis, John L. .... Greenfield, IN
Davis, John L., Jr. .... Houston, TX
Davis, John M. .... Indianapolis, IN
Davis, John M. .... Raleigh, NC
Davis, John M. .... Seattle, WA
Davis, John M., Jr. .... Dallas, TX
Davis, John N. .... Cordele, GA
Vienna, GA
Davis, John P. .... Butte, MT
Davis, John P. .... Tonopah, NV
Davis, John P. .... New York, NY
Davis, John P., III .... Pittsburgh, PA
Davis, John P., Jr. .... Pittsburgh, PA
Davis, John R. .... Los Angeles, CA
Davis, John R. .... Chicago, IL
Waukegan, IL
Davis, John Randolph .... Lawton, OK
Davis, John S. .... Atlanta, GA
Davis, John S. .... Dallas, TX
Davis, John W. .... Whittier, CA
Davis, John W. .... Brunswick, GA
Davis, John W. .... Springfield, MA
Davis, John W. .... Worland, WY
Davis, John W., Jr. .... Rossville, GA
Davis, John W., P.C. .... Worland, WY
Davis, John Wm., Jr. .... Goshen, IN
Davis, John Wyatt .... Louisburg, NC
Davis, Johnnie F. .... Austin, TX
Davis & Johnson, LLP
Dripping Springs, TX
Davis, Jon S. .... Marshfield, MA
Davis, Jon T. .... Columbus, OH
Davis, Jonathan .... Wellesley, MA
Davis, Jonathan D. .... New York, NY
Davis, Jonathan D., A Professional Corporation .... New York, NY
Davis, Jonathan E. .... San Francisco, CA
Davis, Jonathan E. .... Brooklyn, NY
Davis, Jonathan F. .... Glendale, CA
Davis, Jonathan G. .... Washington, DC
Davis, Jonathan J. .... Fort Lauderdale, FL
Davis, Jonathan M. .... Wilton, ME
Davis, Jonathan R. .... San Angelo, TX
Davis, Jonathan S. .... Hackensack, NJ
Davis, Jones E. .... Jacksonville, FL
Davis & Jones, P.A. .... Coral Gables, FL
Miami, FL
Davis & Jordan, P.C. .... Brentwood, TN
Davis, Jos. B. .... Muncie, IN
Davis, Joseph .... Louisville, KY
Davis, Joseph A. .... Los Angeles, CA
Davis, Joseph A. .... Meridian, MS
Davis, Joseph A., Sr. .... Louisville, KY
Davis, Joseph E. .... Chicago, IL
Davis, Joseph F. .... Sumter, SC
Davis, Joseph G. .... Santa Ana, CA
Davis, Joseph G. .... Washington, DC
Davis, Joseph G. (Gray) .... Sacramento, CA
Davis, Joseph G., III .... Rockingham, NC
Davis, Joseph G., Jr. .... Atlanta, GA
Davis, Joseph G., Jr. .... Rockingham, NC
Davis, Joseph H. .... Dunwoody, GA
Davis, Joseph H. .... Goldsboro, NC
Davis, Joseph H., III .... Kingsport, TN
Davis, Joseph H., Jr. .... Kokomo, IN
Davis, Joseph I. .... Miami, FL
Davis, Joseph I., Jr. .... Miami, FL
Davis, Joseph L. .... Seattle, WA
Davis, Joseph M. .... Department of Defense, Defense Legal Services Agency, GV
Davis, Joseph M. .... Tampa, FL
Davis, Joseph M. .... Roseland, NJ
Davis, Joseph P., III .... Boston, MA
Davis, Joseph R. .... Costa Mesa, CA
Davis, Joseph R. .... House of Representatives, Committee Legal Personnel, GV
Davis, Joseph Ross .... Portland, OR
Davis, Joseph S., Jr. .... Olathe, KS
Davis, Joseph W., Jr. .... Orford, NH
Davis, Joshua .... Boston, MA
Davis, Joshua M. .... Boston, MA
Davis, Joshua P. .... San Francisco, CA
Davis, Joshua S. .... Los Angeles, CA
Davis, Joslin .... Winston-Salem, NC
Davis, Joyce A. .... New York, NY
Davis, Joyce E. .... Boston, MA
Davis, Joyce L., & Associates .... Raleigh, NC
Davis, J. P. .... Waco, TX
Davis, Judith M. .... Columbia, SC
Davis, Judith Sproul .... Placerville, CA
Davis, Julia A. .... Columbus, OH
Davis, Julia Brooke .... Jacksonville, FL
Davis, Julia M. .... Los Angeles, CA
Davis, Julia Paschal .... Baltimore, MD
Davis, Julia Ruth .... Bronx, NY
Davis, Julianne R. .... Portland, OR
Davis, Julie A. .... Greensboro, NC
Davis, Julie B. .... Palo Alto, CA
Davis, Julie J. .... Chicago, IL
Davis, Julie W. .... Washington, DC
Davis, Justin M. .... Pontiac, MI
Davis, Justin R. .... Columbia, MO
Davis, K. Elizabeth .... Greenwood, MS
Davis, K. Neal .... Charlotte, NC
Davis, K. Paul .... Charleston, WV
Davis, K. Robert .... Elizabethtown, NC
Davis, Kaplan, Dystrup and Hoster, P.C.
Joliet, IL
Davis, Kara Albert .... Atlanta, GA
Davis, Karen .... St. Louis, MO
Davis, Karen Alicia .... Oakland, CA
Davis, Karen C. .... Alexandria, VA
Davis, Karen E. .... Tigard, OR
Davis, Karen F. .... St. Louis, MO
Davis, Karen Heaphy .... Philadelphia, PA
Davis, Karen J. .... Detroit, MI
Davis, Karen J. Mellencamp .... Seymour, IN
Davis, Karen L.
Treasury Department, GV
Davis, Karen M. .... Morehead, KY
Davis, Karen S. .... Glendale, CA
Davis, Karen T. .... Indianapolis, IN
Davis, Karen Wetherell .... Seattle, WA
Davis, Karin Engstrom .... Philadelphia, PA
Davis, Karl E. .... Washington, DC
Rockville, MD
Davis, Karl L., Jr. .... Pacific Palisades, CA
Davis, Karla M. .... Madison, WI
Davis, Katessa Charles .... Los Angeles, CA
Davis, Katharyn B. .... St. Louis, MO
Davis, Kathe Kates .... Bakersfield, CA
Davis, Katherine H. .... Lumberton, NC
Davis, Kathleen H. .... Burlington, VT
Davis, Kathleen M. .... Minneapolis, MN
Davis, Kathleen M.P. .... Sarasota, FL
Davis, Kathleen O. .... Green Cove Springs, FL
Davis, Kathy A. .... Covington, GA
Davis, Kathy Michelle .... Topeka, KS
Davis, Kathy R. .... Birmingham, AL
Davis, Kay Marcus .... Pittsburgh, PA
Davis, Kearns .... Greensboro, NC
Davis, Keith Christophe .... Los Angeles, CA
Davis, Keith D. .... San Bernardino, CA
Davis, Keith E. .... Los Angeles, CA
Davis, Keith E. .... Dallas, TX
Davis, Keith Eugene .... Chicago, IL
Davis, Keith Warren .... Fort Pierce, FL
Davis, Kelley R. .... Los Angeles, CA
Davis, Kelly S. .... Cheyenne, WY
Davis, Ken W. .... Tallahassee, FL
Davis, Kenneth .... Riverside, CA
Davis, Kenneth A. .... Oakland, CA
Davis, Kenneth A. .... San Francisco, CA
Davis, Kenneth B., Jr. .... Madison, WI
Davis, Kenneth D. .... Tuscaloosa, AL
Davis, Kenneth E. .... Phenix City, AL
Davis, Kenneth E. .... Moody, OK
Davis, Kenneth Geoffrey .... San Diego, CA
Davis, Kenneth J. .... Boston, MA
Davis, Kenneth R. .... New York, NY
Davis, Kenneth R. .... Oklahoma City, OK
Davis, Kenneth Ray, II .... Portland, OR
Davis, Kenneth S. .... Lake City, FL
Davis, Kent W. .... Seminole, FL
Davis, Keven J. .... Seattle, WA
Davis, Kevin G. .... Akron, OH
Davis, Kevin M. .... Los Angeles, CA
Davis, Kevin M. .... Boston, MA
Davis, Kevin R. .... Chicago, IL
Davis, Kevin R. .... Topeka, KS
Davis, Kevin R. .... Nashville, TN
Davis, Kilmarx, Swan & Bowling, LLP
Providence, RI
Davis, Kimberly .... Hartford, CT
Davis, Kimberly Ann .... Des Plaines, IL
Davis, Kimberly S. .... Boston, MA
Davis, Kimberly S. .... Columbus, OH
Davis, Kip A. .... Stuart, FL
Davis & Kirby .... Richmond, VA
Davis, Kirk .... Boise, ID
Davis, Kirk S. .... Tampa, FL
Davis, Kirsten L. .... New York, NY
Davis & Kreitzer .... Rossville, GA
Davis, Kristopher S. .... Los Angeles, CA
Davis & Kuelthau, S.C. .... Green Bay, WI
Madison, WI
Milwaukee, WI
Sheboygan, WI
Davis & Kuhnke, P.C. .... Ann Arbor, MI
Davis, Kyle A. .... Bryan, TX
Davis, L. Burton .... Washington, DC
Davis, L. Clifford .... Fort Worth, TX
Davis, L. Dow, IV .... Department of Energy, Office of the General Counsel, GV
Davis, L. Franklin .... Accomac, VA
Davis, L. Joe, Jr. .... Tampa, FL
Davis, L. Kelly .... Hinesville, GA
Davis, L. Kym .... Washington, DC
Davis, L. Park .... Joliet, IL
Davis, L. Tiffany Hawkins
New Orleans, LA
Davis, Lamar W. .... Roanoke, VA
Davis, Lamar W., Jr. .... Savannah, GA
Davis, Lana Parks .... Little Rock, AR
Davis, Lance B. .... St. Joseph, MO
Davis, Langston C. .... Department of Defense, Defense Legal Services Agency, GV
Davis, Lanny J. .... Washington, DC
Davis, Lant B. .... Birmingham, AL
Davis, Lara Gersholowitz
Charlottesville, VA
Davis, Larry .... Hollywood, FL
Davis, Larry A. .... Des Plaines, IL
Davis, Larry Ray .... Patchogue, NY
Davis, Larry W. .... Charlottesville, VA
Davis, Laura .... Danville, PA
Davis, Laura A. .... Monterey, CA
Salinas, CA
Davis, Laura C. .... Martinsburg, WV
Davis, Laura D. .... New York, NY
Davis, Laura L. .... Fort Collins, CO
Davis, Laura L. .... Barrington, IL
Davis, Laura Prosser .... Baton Rouge, LA
Davis, Laurel Elizabeth .... Las Vegas, NV
Davis, Laurel J. .... Tempe, AZ
Davis, Lauren J. .... Baton Rouge, LA
Davis, Laurie C. .... Marietta, GA
Davis, Laurie C., P.C. .... Marietta, GA
Davis, Laurie E. .... Sacramento, CA
Davis, Laurie K. .... Lake City, CO
Davis Law Firm .... Gainesville, FL
Ocala, FL
Davis Law Firm .... Indianola, MS
Davis Law Office .... Columbus, OH
Davis Law Office, L.L.C. .... Shreveport, LA
Davis, Lawrence E. (Larry)
Oklahoma City, OK
Davis, Lawrence H. .... Northridge, CA
Davis, Lawrence L. .... Fort Lauderdale, FL
Davis, Lawrence L. .... Ebensburg, PA
Davis, Lawrence L., P.A.
Fort Lauderdale, FL
Davis, Leah D. .... Los Angeles, CA
Davis, Leah J. .... Greensburg, PA
Davis, LeAnne L. .... Oxford, MS
Davis, Lee .... Chattanooga, TN
Davis, Lee C. .... Atlanta, GA
Davis, Lee S. .... Smyrna, GA
Davis, Lee W. .... Pittsburgh, PA
Davis & Leiman, P.C. .... Washington, DC
Davis, Lennie F. .... Columbus, GA
Davis, Lenore S. .... Woodmere, NY
Davis, Leonard .... Cleveland, OH
Davis, Leonard A. .... New York, NY
Davis, Leonard A., (A Professional Law Corporation) .... New Orleans, LA
Davis, Leonard E. .... San Antonio, TX
Davis, Leonard E. .... Tyler, TX
Davis, Leonard E., P.C. .... San Antonio, TX
Davis, LeRoy R. .... Los Angeles, CA
Davis, Lesley C. .... Phoenix, AZ
Davis, Lesley C., P.C. .... Phoenix, AZ
Davis, Leslie A. .... Belleville, IL
St. Louis, MO
Davis, Leslie A. .... Philadelphia, PA
Davis, Leslie E. .... Boston, MA
Davis, Leslie Hollowell .... Raleigh, NC
Davis, Leslie J. .... Stamford, CT
Davis Levin Livingston Grande
Honolulu, HI
Davis, Lewis U., Jr. .... Pittsburgh, PA
Davis, Linda .... Mount Clemens, MI
Davis, Linda K. .... Newport Beach, CA
Davis, Linda Kay .... Washington, DC
Davis, Linda M. .... Pittsburgh, PA
Davis, Linda S. .... Baltimore, MD
Davis, Lindsay Reeves, Jr.
Greensboro, NC
Davis, Lindsey Mussleman .... Florence, AL
Davis, Linn .... Norco, CA
Davis, Linn .... New York, NY
Davis, Linwood L. .... Winston-Salem, NC
Davis, Lisa A. .... Palo Alto, CA
Davis, Lisa A. .... King Of Prussia, PA
Philadelphia, PA
Davis, Lisa E. .... New York, NY
Davis, Lisa Kimberly .... Owings Mills, MD
Davis, Lisa L. .... Dallas, TX
Davis, Lisa N. .... Los Angeles, CA
Davis, Lisa N. .... New Haven, CT
Davis, Lisa Poe .... Surfside Beach, SC
Davis, Lisa Tipping .... Oklahoma City, OK
Davis, Lisa Waxman .... Carle Place, NY
Davis, Lloyd S. .... South Pasadena, CA
Davis, Lois C. .... New Orleans, LA
Davis, Lois W. .... Wynnewood, PA
Davis, Lon F. .... Boise, ID
Davis, Lonnie G. .... Bellevue, WA
Davis, Lora G. .... Dallas, TX
Davis, Lori .... Frankfort, KY
Davis, Lori Ann .... Topeka, KS
Davis, Lorraine C.
Equal Employment Opportunity Commission, Office of the General Counsel, GV
Davis, Louis J. .... Englewood, CO
Davis, Louis J. .... Houston, TX
Davis, Louis James .... Morehead City, NC
Davis, Louis P., Jr. .... Sarasota, FL
Davis, Louis R. .... Lafayette, LA
Davis & Lowe, P.C. .... Phoenix, AZ
Davis, Lowell B. .... Carle Place, NY
Davis, L.P. Lonny .... Tulsa, OK
Davis, Lucille G. .... Orange, CA
Davis, Lucy M. .... St. Louis, MO
Davis & Luttrell, L.L.P. .... San Antonio, TX
Davis, Lynn A., (Mr.) .... Little Rock, AR
Davis, Lynn W. .... Provo, UT
Davis, Lynne M. .... New York, NY
Davis, Lynnette M. .... Boise, ID
Davis, Lyonnette M. .... Atlanta, GA
Davis, M. Alicia .... Malvern, PA
Davis, M. Betts .... Dover, NH
Davis, M. Catharine .... Detroit, MI
Davis, M. Donald, Jr. .... Mobile, AL
Davis, M. Ellen .... Andrews, NC
Davis, M. Jefferson .... Crownsville, MD
Davis, M. Shane .... Atlanta, GA
Davis, M. Stephen .... Beverly Hills, CA
Davis, M. Windle, Jr. .... Atlanta, GA
Davis, Mack A. .... Atlanta, GA
Davis, Maclin P., Jr. .... Nashville, TN
Davis, Maer I. .... Waukegan, IL
Davis, Magda Montiel, (P.A.) .... Miami, FL
Davis & Maginot, P.C. .... St. Louis, MO
Davis, Malcolm H. .... New York, NY
Davis, Malm & D'Agostine, P.C.
Boston, MA
Davis & Manley .... El Dorado, KS
Davis, Mannix & McGrath .... Chicago, IL
Davis, Mansfield .... San Francisco, CA
Davis, Marc B. .... Lansdale, PA
Davis, Marcia .... Gainesville, FL
Davis, Marcus J. .... Alexandria, VA
Davis, Margaret L. .... Los Angeles, CA
Davis, Marguerite H. "Ditti" .... Tallahassee, FL
Davis, Marianne B. .... Plymouth, MN
Davis, Marilyn Pearl .... New City, NY
Davis, Marjorie Beth .... Jackson, MS
Davis, Mark .... Little Rock, AR
Davis, Mark .... San Francisco, CA
Davis, Mark .... Lafayette, IN
Davis, Mark A. .... Bloomfield Hills, MI
Davis, Mark A. .... Grand Rapids, MI
Davis, Mark A. .... Raleigh, NC
Davis, Mark A. .... Providence, RI
Davis, Mark B. .... San Rafael, CA
Davis, Mark B. .... Louisville, KY
Davis, Mark C. .... Austin, TX
Davis, Mark D. .... Denver, CO
Davis, Mark D. .... De Funiak Springs, FL
Davis, Mark David .... Washington, DC
Davis, Mark E. .... San Jose, CA
Davis, Mark E. .... Washington, DC
Davis, Mark E. .... Christiansted, St. Croix, VI
Davis, Mark E., P.C., Law Offices of
Christiansted, St. Croix, VI
Davis, Mark F. .... Fairfax, VA
Davis, Mark G. .... Washington, DC
Davis, Mark H. .... San Francisco, CA
Davis, Mark J. .... House of Representatives, Committee Legal Personnel, GV
Davis, Mark J. .... New Orleans, LA
Davis, Mark J. .... Baltimore, MD
Davis, Mark J. .... Prince Frederick, MD
Davis, Mark J. .... Lincoln, NE
Davis, Mark J. .... Portland, OR
Davis, Mark J. .... Spokane, WA
Davis, Mark L. .... Johnson City, TN
Davis, Mark M. .... Grand Rapids, MI
Davis, Mark R. .... Anchorage, AK
Davis, Mark R. .... Denver, CO
Davis, Mark R. .... Chicago, IL
Davis, Mark R. .... Freeport, TX
Lake Jackson, TX
Davis, Mark R. .... Richmond, VA
Davis, Mark S. .... Chicago, IL
Davis, Mark S., (A Law Corporation)
Honolulu, HI
Davis, Mark T. .... Montgomery, AL
Davis, Mark T. .... Sacramento, CA
Davis, Mark T. .... Jackson, MS
Davis, Mark T. .... Taylorsville, NC
Davis, Mark W. .... Gulfport, MS
Davis, Mark W. .... Princeton, NJ
Davis, Mark W. .... Kent, WA
Davis, Marlin R. .... Tulsa, OK
Davis, Marshall D. .... Jacksonville, FL
Davis, Marshall S. .... Newton, MA
Davis, Martha .... Vermillion, SD
Davis, Martha F. .... New York, NY
Davis, Martha L. .... Department of Justice, Executive Office for United States Trustees, GV
Davis, Martha M. .... Windsor, VT
Davis, Martha S. .... Houston, TX
Davis, Martin C. .... Corpus Christi, TX
Davis, Martin D. .... Nashville, TN
Davis, Martin Jefferson
Treasury Department, Office of Thrift Supervision, GV
Davis, Marty E., (P.A.) .... Miami, FL
West Palm Beach, FL
Davis, Marvin .... Phoenix, AZ
Davis, Marvin H .... La Crosse, WI
Davis, Mary .... Portland, ME
Davis, Mary .... Cleveland, OH
Davis, Mary B. .... Canton, MS
Davis, Mary Christina .... Cleburne, TX
Davis, Mary E. .... Washington, DC
Davis, Mary E. .... Elkhart, IN
Davis, Mary E. .... Waltham, MA
Davis, Mary Elizabeth .... Asheville, NC
Davis, Mary J. .... Winston-Salem, NC
Davis, Mary J. .... Berwyn, PA
Davis, Mary Lee .... Atlanta, GA
Davis, Mary McLaughlin .... Paoli, PA
Philadelphia, PA
Davis, Mary P.
Federal Deposit Insurance Corporation, Professional Liability Section, GV
Davis, Marydene .... Brooklyn, NY
Davis, Matthew D. .... San Francisco, CA
Davis, Matthew E. .... Columbia, SC
Davis, Matthew J. .... Charlotte, NC
Davis, Matthew Neill .... Enid, OK
Davis, Matthew S. .... Los Angeles, CA
Davis, Matthews & Quigley, P.C.
Atlanta, GA
Davis, Mattie Belle .... Coral Gables, FL
Davis, Maxon R. .... Great Falls, MT
Davis, Maxwell S., Jr. .... Evanston, IL
Davis, Maynard D. .... Los Angeles, CA
Davis, M.C. .... Chicago, IL
Davis, Megan P. .... New York, NY
Davis, Melanie E. .... Maryville, TN
Davis, Melinda A. .... Bloomfield Hills, MI
Davis, Melissa A. .... Dallas, TX
Davis, Melissa Atkinson .... Tampa, FL
Davis, Melissa M. .... Syracuse, NY
Davis, Melissa Robin .... Greensboro, NC
Davis, Mendel J. .... Mount Pleasant, SC
Davis, Merle E. .... White Plains, NY
Davis, M.G. .... Dallas, TX
Davis, Michael .... Chicago, IL
Davis, Michael .... Minneapolis, MN
Davis, Michael .... North Brunswick, NJ
Davis, Michael .... Houston, TX
Davis, Michael .... San Antonio, TX
Davis, Michael A. .... Denver, CO
Davis, Michael A. .... Des Moines, IA
Davis, Michael A. .... Knoxville, TN
Davis, Michael Arlen, Jr. .... Austin, TX
Dallas, TX
Davis, Michael B. .... West Palm Beach, FL
Davis, Michael C. .... St. Paul, MN
Davis, Michael C. .... Norfolk, VA
Davis, Michael "Cael" S.
San Francisco, CA
Davis, Michael D. .... Hackensack, NJ
Davis, Michael D. .... Tulsa, OK

Davis, Michael Duane ... Riverside, CA
San Bernardino, CA
Davis, Michael E. ... Pomona, CA
Davis, Michael E. ... Goshen, NY
Davis, Michael E. ... Pittsburgh, PA
Davis, Michael Geo. F. ... Safety Harbor, FL
Davis, Michael H. ... Orlando, FL
Davis, Michael H. ... Cleveland, OH
Davis, Michael Hart ... Baltimore, MD
Davis, Michael Hart ... Towson, MD
Davis, Michael I. ... New York, NY
Davis, Michael J. ... Oak Brook, IL
Davis, Michael J. ... Minneapolis, MN
Davis, Michael J. ... Kansas City, MO
Davis, Michael J. ... Cincinnati, OH
Lebanon, OH
Davis, Michael J. ... Mason, OH
Davis, Michael J. ... Pearisburg, VA
Davis, Michael K. ... Fort Lauderdale, FL
Davis, Michael K. ... Indianapolis, IN
Davis, Michael K. ... Providence, RI
Davis, Michael K. ... Sheridan, WY
Davis, Michael Keith ... Dunlap, TN
Davis, Michael L. ... Orlando, FL
Davis, Michael L. ... Houston, TX
Davis, Michael L. ... Falls Church, VA
Davis, Michael M. ... Mobile, AL
Davis, Michael M. ... Boston, MA
Davis, Michael P. ... Atlanta, GA
Davis, Michael P. ... Round Rock, TX
Davis, Michael R. ... Washington, DC
Davis, Michael R. ... Atlanta, GA
Davis, Michael R. ... Dallas, TX
Davis, Michael R. ... Virginia Beach, VA
Davis, Michael R. ... Madison, WI
Davis, Michael S. ... Fort Lauderdale, FL
Davis, Michael S. ... St. Petersburg, FL
Davis, Michael S. ... Tampa, FL
Davis, Michael S. ... Paramus, NJ
Davis, Michael S. ... New York, NY
Davis, Michael Scott ... New Bern, NC
Davis, Michael V. ... Leonardtown, MD
Davis, Michael V. ... Albuquerque, NM
Davis, Michael W. ... Department of Justice,
Tax Division, GV
Davis, Michael W. ... Chicago, IL
Davis, Michael W. ... Columbia, MD
Davis, Michael W. ... Chambersburg, PA
Hanover, PA
Harrisburg, PA
Lancaster, PA
Reading, PA
York, PA
Davis, Michael William ... Cincinnati, OH
Davis, Michele L. ... Atlanta, GA
Davis, Michele R. ... St. Louis, MO
Davis, Michelle Ann ... Lawrence, KS
Davis, Michelle D. ... Winston-Salem, NC
Davis, Michelle E. ... Los Angeles, CA
Davis, Michelle L. ... Paoli, PA
Davis, Michelle M. ... Boston, MA
Davis, Mickey R. ... Houston, TX
Davis, Mike ... Austin, TX
Davis, Miles ... Pensacola, FL
Davis and Miles, P.A. ... Orlando, FL
Winter Park, FL
Davis, Mindy G. ... Washington, DC
Davis, M. L. Jack ... Flat River, MO
Davis, Molly M. ... Tacoma, WA
Davis, Monroe R., (P.C.) ... Monticello, NY
Davis, Montague E. ... Tucson, AZ
Davis, Monte K. ... Atlanta, GA
Davis, Monty ... New York, NY
Davis, Morgan Drew ... Las Vegas, NV
Davis, Morris E. ... Oakland, CA
Davis, Muller, (P.C.) ... Chicago, IL
Davis, Murphy & Stone, LLP
Westminster, MD
Davis, Murray I. ... Swampscott, MA
Davis, Murrell & Tate Law Firm, A
Professional Corporation ... Kokomo, IN
Davis, Murrelle & Lumsden, P.A.
Beaufort, NC
Davis & Myers, A Professional Corporation
Northfield, NJ
Philadelphia, PA
Davis, Myron Y., Jr. ... Cincinnati, OH
Davis, Nadia M. ... Santa Ana, CA
Davis & Nance, P.S.C. ... Glasgow, KY
Davis, Nancy E. ... Dallas, TX
Davis, Nancy J. ... Auburn, AL
Davis, Nancy J. ... Tucson, AZ
Davis, Nancy J. ... Philadelphia, PA
Davis, Nancy Lynn ... Tulsa, OK
Davis, Nancy M. ... Cranston, RI
Davis, Nancy Worth ... Charleston, SC
Davis, Nanette L. ... Department of Justice,
Tax Division, GV
Davis, Natalie Naftzger ... San Marino, CA
Davis, Nathaniel M. ... Florham Park, NJ
Davis, Neal ... Houston, TX
Davis, Neil ... Troy, MI
Davis, Neil A. ... Indianapolis, IN
Davis, Neil S. ... Framingham, MA
Davis, Neil S. ... Worcester, MA
Davis, Neil S. ... Newburgh, NY
Davis, Neil V. ... Fayetteville, NC
Davis, Newton ... New York, NY
Davis, Newton & Davis, P.C. ... Freeport, TX
Lake Jackson, TX
Davis, Nicholas E., Jr. ... Dayton, OH
Davis, Noel C. ... Aurora, IL
Davis, Nondas M. ... Jacksonville, FL
Davis, Noran L., Sr. ... Council Bluffs, IA
Davis, Noreen Bermel ... Walpole, MA
Davis, Noreen S. ... Tallahassee, FL
Davis, Norma L. ... Bronx, NY
Davis, Norman ... Miami, FL
Davis, Norman ... Detroit, MI
Davis, Norman C. ... Marfa, TX
Davis, Norman H., Jr. ... Mobile, AL
Davis, Norman J. ... Phoenix, AZ
Davis, Norman S. ... San Antonio, TX
Davis, Norvell & Norvell ... Decatur, GA
Davis, O. Curt ... Somerset, KY
Davis, O. Luke, III ... Dallas, TX
Davis, O. Wayne ... Indianapolis, IN
Davis, Oliver E. ... Anadarko, OK
Davis, Oneil ... Wichita, KS
Davis & Opper, P.C. ... Austin, TX
Houston, TX
Davis, Oretsky & Guilfoyle, P.C.
Houston, TX
Davis, Osby ... Vallejo, CA
Davis, Oscar E., Jr. (P.A.) ... Little Rock, AR
Davis, Paige Maddox ... Birmingham, AL
Davis, Palmer C. ... Bartow, FL
Davis, Pamela Ann ... Gretna, LA
Davis, Pamela G. ... Orlando, FL
Davis, Pamela Hammond
San Francisco, CA
Davis, Pamela R. ... Palo Alto, CA
Davis, Patrice M. ... New York, NY
Davis, Patricia A. ... Mobile, AL
Davis, Patricia K. ... Charlotte, NC
Davis, Patricia Kunze ... Decatur, GA
Davis, Patricia L. ... Washington, DC
Topeka, KS
Davis, Patricia M. ... Phoenix, AZ
Davis, Patricia M. ... Houston, TX
Davis, Patricia P. ... Cinnaminson, NJ
Davis, Patricia R. ... Department of Justice,
Civil Division, GV
Davis, Patricia S. ... Chicago, IL
Davis, Patrick A. ... Clearwater, FL
Davis, Patrick B. ... Chicago, IL
Davis, Patrick C. ... Carrollton, IL
Davis, Patrick J. ... Phoenix, AZ
Davis, Paul ... Palo Alto, CA
Davis, Paul ... Austin, TX
Davis, Paul A. ... Los Angeles, CA
Davis, Paul Brantley ... Atlanta, GA
Davis, Paul C. ... Tampa, FL
Davis, Paul D. ... Bloomfield Hills, MI
Davis, Paul D. ... Raleigh, NC
Davis, Paul E. ... Raleigh, NC
Davis, Paul H., Jr. ... Syracuse, NY
Davis, Paul K. ... Atlanta, GA
Davis, Paul K. ... Bend, OR
Davis, Paul L., and Associates, Law Offices
of ... Anchorage, AK
Davis, Paul M. ... Los Angeles, CA
Davis, Paul M. ... San Mateo, CA
Davis, Paul M. ... Buffalo Grove, IL
Davis, Paul M. ... Spokane, WA
Davis, Paul Michael ... Baltimore, MD
Davis, Paul M., Law Offices Of
San Mateo, CA
Davis, Paul N. ... Jackson, MS
Davis, Paul R. ... Independence, MO
Davis, Paul S. ... Boston, MA
Davis, Paul Treanor ... Lawrence, KS
Davis, Paul W. ... Scottsdale, AZ
Davis, Paul W. ... Laguna Beach, CA
Davis, Paul W. ... Baltimore, MD
Davis, Peggy A. ... Chicago, IL
Davis, Peggy C. ... New York, NY
Davis, Penny ... University, AL
Davis, Penny L. ... Portland, OR
Davis, Perry, Jr. ... Cincinnati, OH
Davis, Perry, Jr. ... Odessa, TX
Davis, Peter A. ... Ann Arbor, MI
Davis, Peter Eric ... San Ramon, CA
Davis, Peter F. ... Boston, MA
Davis, Peter F. ... Kalamazoo, MI
Davis, Peter G. ... Madison, WI
Davis, Peter I. J. ... Rockville, MD
Davis, Peter James ... Washington, DC
Davis, Peter Justis ... Pittsburgh, PA
Davis, Peter L. ... New York, NY
Davis, Peter M. ... Chicago, IL
Davis, Peter N. ... Columbia, MO
Davis, Peter W. ... San Francisco, CA
Davis, Peter W. ... Dayton, OH
Davis, Pfahl & Fix, P.C. ... New York, NY
Davis, Philip ... Flushing, NY
Davis, Philip, (A Professional Corporation)
Los Angeles, CA
Davis, Philip B. ... Albuquerque, NM
Davis, Philip C. ... Toledo, OH
Davis, Philip G. ... Woodland Hills, CA
Davis, Philip J. ... Washington, DC
Davis, Philippe G. ... Menlo Park, CA
Davis, Phillip A. ... Los Angeles, CA
Davis, Phillip M. ... Boston, MA
Davis, Phillips S. ... Worcester, MA
Davis, Platt W., III ... Houston, TX
Davis Polk & Wardwell ... Menlo Park, CA
Washington, DC
New York, NY
Davis & Poovey, Inc. ... Eureka, CA
Davis & Prager, P.C. ... Patchogue, NY
Davis, Preston L. ... Milton, PA
Davis, Price & Young ... Atlanta, GA
Davis, Priscilla Irene ... Sonora, CA
Davis, Punelli & Keathley LLP
Newport Beach, CA
Davis & Quat ... New York, NY
Davis, R. Alon ... Piedmont, MO
Davis, R. Andrew ... Bedford, VA
Davis, R.B., & Associates, P.A.
Gainesville, FL
Davis, R. Brooks ... Pensacola, FL
Davis, R. Christian ... Madison, WI
Davis, R. Cresap ... Smithsburg, MD
Davis, R. Gene, Jr. ... Raleigh, NC
Davis, R. Hamilton ... Lafayette, LA
Davis, R. Heath ... Barrington, IL
Chicago, IL
Davis, R. Horton ... Americus, GA
Davis, R. Jefferson, Jr. ... Atlanta, GA
Davis, R. Keenan ... Davis, CA
Davis, R. Leonard, III ... Allentown, PA
Doylestown, PA
Stroudsburg, PA
Davis, R. Mark ... Columbia, SC
Davis, R. Scott ... Salisbury, MD
Davis, R. Scott ... Spartanburg, SC
Davis, R. Scott, P.C. ... Spartanburg, SC
Davis, R. Stephen ... Beckley, WV
Davis, R. Theodore, Jr. ... Wilmington, NC
Davis, R. Townsend, Jr. ... New York, NY
Davis, R. Walton, III ... Asheville, NC
Davis, Rachel ... Chicago, IL
Davis, Rachel A. ... Atlanta, GA
Davis, Rachel O. ... Hartford, CT
Davis, Ralph G.
Department Of Veterans Affairs,
Office of the General Counsel, GV
Davis, Ralph M. ... Bellevue, WA
Davis, Ralph W. ... Nashville, TN
Davis, Randal Kevin ... Tuscaloosa, AL
Davis, Randall H ... Eureka, CA
Davis, Randall H. ... Cartersville, GA
Davis, Randall J. ... Brighton, CO
Davis, Randall S. ... Walnut Creek, CA
Davis, Randle S. ... Nashville, TN
Davis, Ransom E. ... Baltimore, MD
Davis, Ransom J. ... Baltimore, MD
Davis, Rantson E. ... Leesburg, FL
Davis, Ray Jay ... Provo, UT
Davis, Raymond C. ... Montrose, PA
Susquehanna, PA
Davis, Raymond D. ... Houston, TX
Davis, Raymond E. ... Richmond, VA
Davis, Raymond L. ... Seattle, WA
Davis, Raymond M. ... Lansing, MI
Davis, R. B. ... Gainesville, FL
Davis, Rebecca ... Stockton, CA
Davis, Rebecca ... Statesboro, GA
Davis, Rebecca Carroll ... Batavia, OH
Davis, Rebecca J. ... Houston, TX
Davis, Rebecca R. ... Hamilton Square, NJ
Davis, Reberkenny & Abramowitz, A
Professional Corporation ... Camden, NJ
Cherry Hill, NJ
Davis, Reed J. ... Pittsburgh, PA
Davis, Reed James ... Pittsburgh, PA
Davis, Reese A. ... Wayne, PA
Davis, Reginald D. ... San Francisco, CA
Davis, Reginald R. ... Klamath Falls, OR
Davis Reilly, P.C. ... Pittsburgh, PA
Davis, Reinena L. ... New York, NY
Davis, Rendall A., Jr.
Federal Trade Commission,
Bureau of Competition, GV
Davis, Rene Domingue ... Houston, TX
Davis & Reno ... San Francisco, CA
Davis, Reuben ... Tulsa, OK
Davis, Reuben K. ... Rochester, NY
Davis, Rex D. ... Waco, TX
Davis, Rex L. ... Houston, TX
Davis, Rhonda G. ... Beverly Hills, CA
Davis, Rhonda Gail ... Akron, OH
Davis, Rhonda L. ... Williamsport, PA
Davis, Rhonda L. ... Houston, TX
Davis, Richard ... Tucson, AZ
Davis, Richard A. ... South Portland, ME
Davis, Richard A. ... Charlottesville, VA
Davis, Richard A., III ... Bellingham, WA
Davis, Richard A., IV ... Austin, TX
Davis, Richard B. ... Northbrook, IL
Davis, Richard B. ... Milwaukee, WI
Davis, Richard C. ... Arlington, VA
Davis, Richard D. ... Los Angeles, CA
Davis, Richard D. ... Austin, TX
Davis, Richard D. ... Canton, TX
Davis, Richard D. ... Midland, TX
Davis, Richard D., Jr. ... Midland, TX
Davis, Richard E. ... Daphne, AL
Davis, Richard E. ... Seal Beach, CA
Davis, Richard E. ... Tampa, FL
Davis, Richard E. ... Springfield, MO
Davis, Richard E. ... Canton, OH
Salem, OH
Davis, Richard E., Jr. ... Barre, VT
Davis, Richard E., P.A. ... Tampa, FL
Davis, Richard Eldon ... Birmingham, AL
Davis, Richard F. ... Los Angeles, CA
Davis, Richard G. ... Tampa, FL
Davis, Richard Glenn ... El Paso, TX
Davis, Richard H., Jr. ... Tulsa, OK
Davis, Richard J. ... Grosse Pointe Park, MI
Davis, Richard J. ... St. Paul, MN
Davis, Richard J. ... New York, NY
Davis, Richard J. ... New York, NY
Davis, Richard J. ... McLean, VA
Davis, Richard J., Jr. ... Houston, TX
Davis, Richard K. ... Princeton, NJ
New York, NY
Davis, Richard L. ... Denver, CO
Davis, Richard L. ... Washington, DC
Davis, Richard L. ... Hillsboro, OH
Davis, Richard Lorne ... Sherman Oaks, CA
Davis, Richard M. ... Scottsdale, AZ
Davis, Richard M. ... Jacksonville, FL
Davis, Richard M. ... Miami, FL
Davis, Richard M. ... Merrillville, IN
Davis, Richard M., Jr. ... Cheyenne, WY
Sheridan, WY
Davis, Richard O. ... Selinsgrove, PA
Davis, Richard R. ... New York, NY
Davis, Richard Russell ... Shallotte, NC
Davis, Richard S. ... Los Angeles, CA
Davis, Richard S. ... Washington, DC
Davis, Richard S. ... West Palm Beach, FL
Davis, Richard S. ... New York, NY
Davis, Richard S. ... Tipp City, OH
Davis, Richard S., L.P.A. ... Tipp City, OH
Davis, Richard T. ... West Palm Beach, FL
Davis, Richard T., Jr. ... Los Angeles, CA
Davis, Richard V. ... Greenville, SC
Davis, Richard W. ... Los Angeles, CA
Davis, Richard W. ... San Diego, CA
Davis, Richard W. ... Radford, VA
Davis, Richard W., Jr. ... Elkhart, IN
Davis, Richard W., Jr. ... Radford, VA
Davis, Richard W. B. ... Bryan, TX
Davis, Richard Wm. ... Portland, OR
Davis, Richmond, Law Offices of
Silver Spring, MD
Davis, Richmond T. P. ... Silver Spring, MD
Davis, Rick G. ... Denver, CO
Davis, Ricky B. W. ... Stamford, CT
Davis, Ridout, Jones & Gerstner, L.L.P.
Houston, TX
Davis & Riebman ... Des Plaines, IL
Davis, Rikke K. ... Washington, DC
Davis, Riter, Parry & Tyler, A Professional
Corporation ... Philadelphia, PA
Davis, Robert A., Jr. ... Hemet, CA
Davis, Robert A., Jr. ... Washington, DC
Davis, Robert B. ... Long Beach, CA
Davis, Robert B. ... New York, NY
Davis, Robert B. ... Austin, TX
Davis, Robert C. ... Gadsden, AL
Davis, Robert C. ... Boston, MA
Davis, Robert C., Jr. ... Washington, DC
Davis, Robert D. ... Macon, GA
Davis, Robert E. ... Topeka, KS
Davis, Robert E. ... Cleveland, OH
Davis, Robert E. ... Spartanburg, SC
Davis, Robert E. ... Dallas, TX
Davis, Robert Edwin ... Dallas, TX
Davis, Robert F. ... Mount Kisco, NY
Davis, Robert G. ... Auburn, CA
Davis, Robert G. ... Boston, MA
Davis, Robert G. ... Battle Creek, MI
Davis, Robert G. ... Hancock, NY
Davis, Robert Guy ... Dallas, TX
Davis, Robert J. ... Calabasas, CA
Davis, Robert J. ... Bay City, MI
Davis, Robert Jacob ... Dallas, TX
Davis, Robert L. ... Chico, CA
Davis, Robert L. ... Newport Beach, CA
Davis, Robert L. ... Wichita, KS
Davis, Robert L. ... Baltimore, MD
Davis, Robert L. ... Minneapolis, MN
Davis, Robert L. ... Union, MO
Davis, Robert L. ... Cincinnati, OH
Davis, Robert L. ... Austin, TX
Davis, Robert L., (P.C.) ... San Francisco, CA
Davis, Robert M. ... New York, NY
Davis, Robert M., III ... Shreveport, LA
Davis, Robert N. ... Oakland, CA
Davis, Robert N. ... Hagåtña, GU
Davis, Robert N. ... University, MS
Davis, Robert N., Jr. ... Bethesda, MD
Davis, Robert P. ... Washington, DC
Davis, Robert P. ... Chicago, IL
Davis, Robert P. ... New York, NY
Davis, Robert R., Jr. ... Seattle, WA
Davis, Robert S. ... Santa Ana, CA
Davis, Robert S. ... St. Louis, MO
Davis, Robert S. ... New York, NY
Davis, Robert S. ... Philadelphia, PA
Davis, Robert S. ... Philadelphia, PA
Davis, Robert S. ... Tyler, TX
Davis, Robert S., II ... Basking Ridge, NJ
Davis, Robert Spink ... Providence, RI
Davis, Robert T. ... Chattanooga, TN
Davis, Robert T. ... Austin, TX
Davis, Robert W. ... Kershaw, SC
Davis, Robert W. ... Derby Line, VT
Davis & Roberts, P.C. ... Arlington, TX
Grand Prairie, TX
Irving, TX
Davis, Robin Jean ... Charleston, WV
Davis, Robin Kuttner ... Gainesville, FL
Davis, Robin M. ... Lancaster, PA
Davis, Robyn N. ... Omaha, NE
Davis, Rodney B. ... Fayetteville, NC
Davis, Rodney Stephen
Santa Monica, CA
Davis, Roger Barry ... Miami, FL
Davis, Roger D. ... Corydon, IN
Davis, Roger E. ... Troy, MI
Davis, Roger H. ... Los Angeles, CA
Davis, Roger K.
Nuclear Regulatory Commission,
Commission, GV
Davis, Roger L. ... San Francisco, CA
Davis, Roger S. ... Boston, MA
Davis, Roland C. ... San Francisco, CA
Davis, Rollin D., Jr. ... Pensacola, FL
d'Avis, Ronald ... Indianapolis, IN
Davis, Ronald E. ... Columbus, OH
Davis, Ronald H. ... Charlotte, NC
Davis, Ronald J. ... Palos Verdes Estates, CA
Davis, Ronald J. ... Atlanta, GA
Davis, Ronald J. ... Silver Spring, MD
Davis, Ronald Joseph, II ... Miami, FL
Davis, Ronald L. ... Tuscaloosa, AL
Davis, Ronald L. ... North Miami Beach, FL
Davis, Ronald L. ... Cartersville, GA
Davis, Ronald L. ... Silver Spring, MD
Davis, Ronald L. ... Franklin, TN
Davis, Ronald L., P.A.
North Miami Beach, FL
Davis, Ronald P. ... Mobile, AL
Davis, Ronald R. ... San Diego, CA
Davis, Ronald R. ... Winston-Salem, NC

Davis, Ronald W. ....**New York, NY**
Davis & Roose ....Goshen, IN
Davis, Rosa Gunter Hamlett
Montgomery, AL
Davis, Rosalee H. ....Columbia, SC
Davis, Rosalie V. ....San Francisco, CA
Davis, Rosemary V. ....**Sterling Heights, MI**
Davis, Rosetta N. ....Nashville, TN
Davis, Ross G. ....Medford, OR
Davis, Ross, Jr. ....Vail, CO
Davis, Roxanne A., Law Offices of
Los Angeles, CA
Davis, Roy ....Mentor, OH
Davis, Roy A. ....Keller, TX
Davis, Roy G. ....**Peoria, IL**
Davis, Roy H. ....St. Petersburg, FL
Davis, Roy J. ....Edmond, OK
Davis, Roy W., Jr. ....**Asheville, NC**
Davis & Rubin ....Boston, MA
Davis and Ruffner, P.C. ....Alexandria, VA
Davis, Russell A. ....Solana Beach, CA
Davis, Russell B. ....**Marietta, GA**
Davis, Russell D. ....Santa Ana, CA
Davis, Russell H., Jr. ....**Pikeville, KY**
Davis, Russell L. ....**Indian Wells, CA**
Davis, Russell L. ....**Palm Springs, CA**
Davis, Ruth B. ....Tucson, AZ
Davis, Ruth D. ....**Hagåtña, GU**
Davis, Ryan E. ....**Orlando, FL**
Davis, Ryan P. ....South Lake Tahoe, CA
Davis, S. Brett ....Daphne, AL
Davis, S. Eric ....**Newport Beach, CA**
Davis, S. Grace ....**Grand Rapids, MI**
Davis, S. Joseph, Jr. ....Sanford, FL
Davis, S. Nyles ....Wichita, KS
Davis, S. Scott ....Albuquerque, NM
Davis, S. Scott, P.C. ....Albuquerque, NM
Davis, Sadie L. ....Trenton, NJ
Davis & Sallinger, L.L.P ....Dallas, TX
Davis, Sally L. ....New York, NY
Davis, Sally S. ....Fallon, NV
Davis, Sam B. ....Ashland, OR
Davis, Sam W., Jr. ....Houston, TX
Davis, Samuel B., Jr. ....Newport News, VA
Davis, Samuel F., Jr. ....**Concord, NC**
Davis, Samuel H. ....East Brunswick, NJ
Davis, Samuel J. ....Uniontown, PA
Davis, Samuel L. ....Teaneck, NJ
Davis, Samuel M. ....Athens, GA
Davis, Samuel R. ....**New York, NY**
Davis, Samuel S. ....Philadelphia, PA
Davis, Sandra E. ....**Greensburg, PA**
Davis, Sandra K. ....**Waterbury, CT**
Davis, Sandra L. ....Rockford, MI
Davis, Sandra Lea ....Edmonds, WA
Davis, Sandra W. ....**Lancaster, OH**
Davis, Sanford J. ....**Greenwich, CT**
Davis Saperstein, P.C. ....Teaneck, NJ
Davis, Sara B. ....**New York, NY**
Davis, Sara H. ....Asheville, NC
Davis, Sarah B. ....San Francisco, CA
Davis, Sarah E. ....**Washington, DC**
Davis & Sauer ....San Francisco, CA
Davis, Saul ....Department of Justice, Civil Division, GV
Davis, Saul ....Pittsburgh, PA
Davis, Saunders, Arata & Rome, A Professional Law Corporation ....Metairie, LA
Davis, Saundra, & Associates, P.A.
Lawrenceville, GA
Davis & Scarritt, P.A. ....**Tampa, FL**
Davis & Schroeder, P.C. ....**Monterey, CA**
Davis, Scott ....Tupelo, MS
Davis, Scott ....**New York, NY**
Davis, Scott C. ....**Tampa, FL**
Davis, Scott J. ....**Chicago, IL**
Davis, Scott L. ....**Dallas, TX**
Davis, Scott M. ....Wellesley Hills, MA
Davis, Scott M. ....**Forest Hills, NY**
Davis, Scott Paul ....Live Oak, FL
Davis, Scott R. ....Westborough, MA
Davis, Scott S. ....**Denver, CO**
Davis, Sean M. ....Thousand Oaks, CA
Davis & Selwyn ....**Houston, TX**
Davis, Seth A. ....**New York, NY**
Davis, Shanna R. ....**Santa Monica, CA**
Davis, Sharon B. ....**Chicago, IL**
Davis, Sharon Kennedy ....Chicago, IL
Davis, Sharon L. ....**Washington, DC**
Davis, Sharon L. ....Bethpage, NY
Davis, Sharon L. ....Cottage Grove, OR
Davis, Sharon Lock ....Dallas, TX
Davis, Shedrick O., III ....**Los Angeles, CA**
Davis, Sheldon P. ....Ventnor City, NJ
Davis, Shelia Cochran ....Chicago, IL
Davis, Shelley ....San Francisco, CA
Davis, Shelley F. ....Washington, DC
Davis, Shelley T. ....Phoenix, AZ
Davis, Shelly M. ....St. Cloud, MN
Davis, Shepard Andrew ....Milwaukee, WI
Davis, Sherri E. ....East Amherst, NY
Davis, Sherri L. ....Buffalo, NY
Pittsburgh, PA
Davis, Sherry D. ....**Portsmouth, OH**
Davis, Shessy Thomas ....**Houston, TX**
Davis, Shirleymae ....La Jolla, CA
Davis, Sidney D., Jr. ....Mendenhall, MS
Davis, Sidney F. ....Atlanta, GA
Davis, Sidney H., Jr. ....**Dallas, TX**
Davis, Sidney P., Jr. ....**Fayetteville, AR**
Davis, Silver & Levy ....Miami, FL
West Palm Beach, FL
Davis & Singer, P.C. ....**White Plains, NY**
Davis & Singleton, A Professional Law Corporation ....Shreveport, LA
Davis, Smith W., (P.C.) ....**Washington, DC**
Davis, Sonya Meyers ....**St. Louis, MO**
Davis, S. P. ....Shreveport, LA

Davis, Spencer E., Jr. ....Foley, AL
Davis, St. Clair O. ....New York, NY
Davis, Stacey Campbell ....**Spartanburg, SC**
Davis, Stan ....Madison, WI
Davis, Stanley A. ....Nashville, TN
Davis, Stanley D. ....Sebastopol, CA
Davis, Stanley D. ....**Kansas City, MO**
Davis & Stanley, LLC ....**Fairfax, VA**
Davis, Stephanie ....**New York, NY**
Davis, Stephanie C. ....Atlanta, GA
Davis, Stephanie M. ....Los Angeles, CA
Davis, Stephanie N. ....Oswego, NY
Davis, Stephen ....New York, NY
Davis, Stephen ....**White Plains, NY**
Davis, Stephen A. ....Omaha, NE
Davis, Stephen A. ....Summersville, WV
Davis, Stephen B. ....**Princeton, NJ**
Davis, Stephen B. ....Bellevue, WA
Davis, Stephen D. ....**Chicago, IL**
Davis, Stephen E. ....Cincinnati, OH
Davis, Stephen E. ....Bristol, RI
Davis, Stephen H. ....Jacksonville, FL
Davis, Stephen J. ....**Minneapolis, MN**
Davis, Stephen J. ....Austin, TX
Davis, Stephen L. ....Sacramento, CA
Davis, Stephen M. ....**New York, NY**
Davis, Stephen O. ....**Warren, NJ**
Davis, Stephen R. ....**Norfolk, VA**
Davis, Stephen T. ....Escanaba, MI
Davis, Stephen V. ....San Antonio, TX
Davis, Stephen W. "Steve"
Oklahoma City, OK
Davis, Steve Chang ....Orlando, FL
Davis, Steve J. ....Atlanta, GA
Davis, Steven A. ....**Lancaster, OH**
Davis, Steven B ....Daphne, AL
Davis, Steven B. ....**Harrison, AR**
Davis, Steven B. ....San Diego, CA
Davis, Steven B. ....**Philadelphia, PA**
Davis, Steven Brian ....San Diego, CA
Davis, Steven C. ....**Cincinnati, OH**
Davis, Steven C. ....**Oklahoma City, OK**
Davis, Steven Clark ....**Seattle, WA**
Davis, Steven D. ....**Santa Monica, CA**
Davis, Steven E. ....Galesburg, IL
Davis, Steven G. ....**Indianapolis, IN**
Davis, Steven G. ....**New York, NY**
Davis, Steven H. ....**New York, NY**
Davis, Steven J. ....**San Diego, CA**
Davis, Steven J. ....**Dayton, OH**
Davis, Steven L. ....**Emporia, KS**
Davis, Steven L. ....**St. Louis, MO**
Davis, Steven L. ....**Englewood, NJ**
Davis, Steven M. ....**Miami, FL**
Davis, Steven P. ....**Chicago, IL**
Davis, Steven R. ....Brunswick, ME
Davis, Steven R. ....**Oklahoma City, OK**
Davis, Steven S. ....**Los Angeles, CA**
Davis, Steven S. ....Cleveland, OH
Davis, Steven T. ....**Philadelphia, PA**
Davis, Steven W. ....**Miami, FL**
Davis, Stewart D. ....**Rochester, NY**
Davis, Stuart E. ....North Massapequa, NY
Davis, Stuart E., P.C.
North Massapequa, NY
Davis, Sturges & Tomlinson
Henderson, NC
Louisburg, NC
Warrenton, NC
Davis, Sumpter B., III ....**Baton Rouge, LA**
Davis, Susan ....**New York, NY**
Davis, Susan A. ....Ann Arbor, MI
Davis, Susan Frederick ....Columbia, SC
Davis, Susan L. ....Hillsboro, OH
Davis, Susan M. ....Richmond, VA
Davis, Susan McMillan ....Columbia, MD
Davis, Susan R. ....**Seattle, WA**
Davis, Susan S. ....**Los Angeles, CA**
Davis, Susan Walsh ....**Boston, MA**
Davis, Suzanne Quinlan ....**Houston, TX**
Davis, Sybil Anne ....Sierra Madre, CA
Davis, Sydney M. ....Newton, MA
Davis, Sylvia D. ....**Washington, DC**
Davis, Syndy Arnold ....Houston, TX
Davis, Syrie R. ....Cambridge, MA
Davis, T. Hoyt, Jr. ....Cordele, GA
Vienna, GA
Davis, T. Martin ....**Little Rock, AR**
Davis, T. Richard ....**Salt Lake City, UT**
Davis, T. Wayne, Jr. ....Jacksonville, FL
Davis, Tamara L. ....**Dodge City, KS**
Davis, Tammy A. ....New York, NY
Davis, Tania L. ....**Los Angeles, CA**
San Francisco, CA
Davis, Tanya S. ....Sherman, TX
Davis, Tawana E. ....Department of Justice, Civil Rights Division, GV
Davis, Taylor S. ....Davenport, IA
Davis, Teresa B. ....**Oklahoma City, OK**
Davis, Terrance K. ....**Toledo, OH**
Davis, Terrel E. ....**Englewood, CO**
Davis, Terrence O. ....**Washington, DC**
Davis, Terrie A. ....Winston-Salem, NC
Davis, Terry ....Leander, TX
Davis, Terry A. ....Omaha, NE
Davis, Terry A. ....**La Crosse, WI**
Davis, Terry G. ....**Montgomery, AL**
Davis, Terry G., P.C. ....**Montgomery, AL**
Davis, Terry Hunter, Jr. ....**Norfolk, VA**
Davis, Terry K. ....Santa Ana, CA
Davis, Texanna ....Austin, TX
Davis, T. G. ....**Carthage, TX**
Davis, Thad A. ....**New York, NY**
Davis, Theodore E. ....**San Diego, CA**
Davis, Theodore H., Jr. ....**Atlanta, GA**
Davis, Theodore M. ....New York, NY
Davis, Theodore T. ....Pueblo, CO
Davis, Theodore Z. ....Camden, NJ

Davis, Theresa C. ....**Cedar Rapids, IA**
Davis, Theresa L. ....**Chicago, IL**
Davis, Thomas ....Norwalk, CA
Davis, Thomas ....Zion, IL
Davis, Thomas A. ....**Birmingham, AL**
Davis, Thomas A. ....**Washington, DC**
Davis, Thomas A. ....**Portland, OR**
Davis, Thomas C. ....**Beaufort, SC**
Davis, Thomas E. ....Gadsden, AL
Davis, Thomas E. ....Springfield, IL
Davis, Thomas E. ....Albuquerque, NM
Davis, Thomas E. ....Akron, OH
Davis, Thomas E. ....Bethune, SC
Davis, Thomas E. ....**Dallas, TX**
Davis, Thomas F. ....**Dublin, OH**
Davis, Thomas G. ....Austin, TX
Davis, Thomas H. ....**Kansas City, MO**
Davis, Thomas H., III ....Sumter, SC
Davis, Thomas H., Jr. ....**Raleigh, NC**
Davis, Thomas J. ....**Tucson, AZ**
Davis, Thomas J. ....Oakdale, LA
Davis, Thomas J. ....Rockville, MD
Davis, Thomas J., Jr. ....**Fort Myers, FL**
Davis, Thomas J., Jr. ....New York, NY
Davis, Thomas Kelly ....Grand Rapids, MI
Davis, Thomas Kelly, P.C.
Grand Rapids, MI
Davis, Thomas L. ....**Indianapolis, IN**
Davis, Thomas L. ....Indianapolis, IN
Davis, Thomas L. ....**Columbus, OH**
Davis, Thomas L. ....**Dallas, TX**
Davis & Thomas L.L.P. ....**Houston, TX**
Davis, Thomas M. ....**San Bernardino, CA**
Davis, Thomas M., III ....McLean, VA
Davis, Thomas N., Jr. ....Lawrenceville, GA
Davis, Thomas O. ....Decatur, GA
Davis, Thomas P. ....**Laguna Beach, CA**
Davis, Thomas R. ....Los Angeles, CA
Davis, Thomas R. ....**Peoria, IL**
Davis, Thomas R. ....Kansas City, MO
Davis, Thomas R. ....Poughkeepsie, NY
Wappingers Falls, NY
Davis, Thomas S. ....Columbia, MO
Davis, Thomas Todd ....**Shelbyville, KY**
Davis, Thomas W. ....Gainesville, FL
Davis, Thomas W. ....Glasgow, KY
Davis, Thomas W., II ....**Las Vegas, NV**
Davis & Thompson ....**Grove, OK**
Jay, OK
Davis, Thos. M. ....West Liberty, KY
Davis, Tiffany E. ....**Charleston, WV**
Davis, Timothy ....Dallas, TX
Davis, Timothy A. ....**Kansas City, MO**
Davis, Timothy C. ....**Birmingham, AL**
Davis, Timothy C. ....**Menlo Park, CA**
Davis, Timothy D. ....**Birmingham, AL**
Davis, Timothy E. ....**Philadelphia, PA**
Davis, Timothy J. ....Riverside, CA
Davis, Timothy J. ....**St. Joseph, MO**
Davis, Timothy L. ....**Los Angeles, CA**
Davis, Timothy Lee ....San Diego, CA
Davis, Timothy O. ....**Albany, GA**
Davis, Timothy O. ....**Edina, MN**
Davis, Timothy O., & Associates, Ltd.
Edina, MN
Davis, Timothy S. ....Washington, DC
Davis, Timothy Scott ....Rochester, NY
Davis, Tina A. ....Stamford, CT
Davis & Tobin, P.C. ....**Barre, VT**
Davis, Todd ....**Murphy, NC**
Davis, Todd P. ....**Atlanta, GA**
Davis, Todd S. ....**Cleveland, OH**
Davis, Tom H., P.C. ....**Austin, TX**
Davis, Tom L. ....Springfield, VA
Davis, Tom M., Jr. ....**Houston, TX**
Davis, Tommy K. ....**Dallas, TX**
Davis and Tompkins, P.A.
Lake Placid, FL
Davis, Tony M. ....**Houston, TX**
Davis, Tonya DeAnne ....Pensacola, FL
Davis, T. R. "Rick" ....Columbus, OH
Davis, Tracee E. ....New York, NY
Davis, Tracey L. ....**Boston, MA**
Davis, Tracy Hamrick ....**Raleigh, NC**
Davis, Tracy Hope ....New York, NY
Davis, Tracy K. ....**Marietta, GA**
Davis, Tracy L. ....**San Francisco, CA**
Davis, Tracy T. ....**Santa Monica, CA**
Davis, Tracy Y. ....Montclair, NJ
Davis, Trayton M. ....**New York, NY**
Davis, Trigg T. ....**Anchorage, AK**
Davis & Trotta ....Millerton, NY
Davis, Tupper & Grimsley, L.L.P.
Beaufort, SC
Hilton Head Island, SC
Davis, Turner S. ....Griffin, GA
Davis, Tyrone ....Argonne, IL
Davis, Unrein, Hummer, McCallister, Biggs & Head, L.L.P. ....**Topeka, KS**
Davis & Upton ....**Prince Frederick, MD**
Davis, Valerie A. ....**Lake Buena Vista, FL**
Davis, Valerie J. ....Sarasota, FL
Davis, Valerie J., P.A. ....Sarasota, FL
Davis, Vaughn, Jr. ....**Jackson, MS**
Davis, Vernon A. ....Fort Worth, TX
Davis, Veronica L. ....West Columbia, TX
Davis, Veronica M. ....**Freehold, NJ**
Davis, Vicki M. ....Mobile, AL
Davis, Vickie Kaye ....Columbia, MO
Davis, Victor A., Jr. ....**Junction City, KS**
Manhattan, KS
Davis, Victoria ....Cuero, TX
Davis, Victoria ....**Salt Lake City, UT**
Davis, Victoria E. ....Woodland, CA
Davis, Victoria M. ....**Atlanta, GA**
Davis, Vincent W. ....Monterey Park, CA
Davis, Virginia A. ....**Washington, DC**
Davis, Virginia E. ....**Augusta, ME**

Davis, Vivian ....Floral Park, NY
Davis, W. Brett ....Weston, MA
Davis, W. Eugene ....Lafayette, LA
Davis, W. Jeremy ....Grand Forks, ND
Davis, W. Keith ....**Bloomington, IL**
Davis, W. Kenneth, Jr. ....**Chicago, IL**
Davis, W. Leon ....Charlotte, NC
Davis, W. Leon, P.C. ....Charlotte, NC
Davis, W. Randolph ....San Antonio, TX
Davis, W. Richard, (P.C.) ....**Dallas, TX**
Davis, W. Russell ....**Palo Alto, CA**
Davis, W. Sidney, Jr. ....**Miami, FL**
New York, NY
Davis, W. Van ....Pell City, AL
Davis, Wagner & Ehler ....Dayton, OH
Davis, Walker & Associates, P.C.
Douglasville, GA
Davis, Wallace F. (Rusty) ....**El Dorado, KS**
Davis & Wallace, PLC ....Chattanooga, TN
Davis, Walter Alan ....**Oxford, MS**
Davis, Walter Allen ....Huntsville, AL
Davis, Walter L. ....**Hayward, CA**
Davis, Walter L. ....Bow, WA
Davis, Walter Lee, Jr. ....**Johnson City, TN**
Davis, Walter Lee, Jr., A Professional Corporation ....**Johnson City, TN**
Davis, Walter P., Jr. ....Atlanta, GA
Davis, Walter R., Jr. ....Bernardsville, NJ
Davis, Walter S. ....**Milwaukee, WI**
Davis, Walter W. ....Millerton, NY
Davis, Walter William ....**Brentwood, TN**
Davis, Walter Winn ....Glasgow, KY
Davis, Walton, Jr. ....Chicago, IL
Davis, Walton V. ....Gettysburg, PA
Davis, Wanda J. ....St. Petersburg, FL
Davis, Warren & Hritsco ....**Dillon, MT**
Davis, Warren J. ....**Beaufort, NC**
Davis, Warren N. ....**Washington, DC**
Davis, Warren W. ....**Belleville, IL**
St. Louis, MO
Davis, Watts E. ....Birmingham, AL
Davis, Wayne B. ....Goliad, TX
Davis, Wayne H. ....Cambridge, MA
Davis, Wayne H. ....**New York, NY**
Davis, Wayne M. ....Albany, NY
Davis, Wayne M., P.C. ....Albany, NY
Davis, W. B. Rodman ....**Greensboro, NC**
Davis, W. C. ....Austin, TX
Davis Weber & Edwards ....**Miami, FL**
Davis Weber & Edwards P.C.
New York, NY
Davis & Weisman, P.C. ....**Clayton, MO**
St. Louis, MO
Davis, Wendell G., Jr. ....**Hartford, CT**
Davis, Wendell, Jr. ....New York, NY
Davis, Wendell N., Jr. ....Detroit, MI
Davis, Wendy ....**Rosemead, CA**
Davis, Wendy B. ....Boston, MA
Davis, Wendy W. ....Denver, CO
Davis, Wendy W. ....**Fort Wayne, IN**
Davis, Wesley L. ....Irvine, CA
Davis White & Pettingell, P.C.
Boston, MA
Davis, Whitney A. ....**Sacramento, CA**
Davis, Wiley H. ....Atlanta, GA
Davis, Wilfred L. ....New York, NY
Davis, Wilfred L., & Stephen Davis, P.C.
New York, NY
Davis & Wilkerson, P.C. ....**Alpine, TX**
Austin, TX
Davis, Will D. ....**Austin, TX**
Davis, Willard J. ....Edina, MN
Davis, William ....**Bowie, MD**
Davis, William ....**Winston-Salem, NC**
Davis, William A. ....Washington, DC
Davis, William A. ....**Washington, DC**
Davis, William A. ....Ghent, KY
Davis, William A. ....Columbus, OH
Davis, William A., II ....Chicago, IL
Davis, William A., II ....**Winston-Salem, NC**
Davis, William A., Jr. ....**Winter Park, FL**
Davis, William A., Jr. ....Valdosta, GA
Davis, William Alan ....**Portland, OR**
Davis, William Anthony, III
Birmingham, AL
Davis, William B ....Fort Myers, FL
Davis, William B. ....**Merrillville, IN**
Davis, William C. ....**Cherry Hill, NJ**
Davis, William C., III ....Coral Gables, FL
Davis, William C., III ....**Rockville, MD**
Davis, William C., Jr. ....Lewistown, IL
Davis, William C., Jr. ....**Carson City, NV**
Las Vegas, NV
Reno, NV
Davis, William D. ....Dripping Springs, TX
Davis, William E. ....Berkeley, CA
Davis, William E. ....Ceres, CA
Davis, William E. ....Washington, DC
Davis, William E. ....**Miami, FL**
Davis, William E. ....Gary, IN
Davis, William E. ....Davenport, IA
Davis, William E. ....Columbus, OH
Davis, William E. ....**Kennewick, WA**
Davis, William E., Jr. ....Houston, TX
Davis, William F. ....**Los Angeles, CA**
Davis, William F. ....**Nebraska City, NE**
Davis, William F. ....Albuquerque, NM
Davis, William F. ....Suffolk, VA
Davis, William F., & Associates, P.C.
Albuquerque, NM
Davis, William G. ....Baton Rouge, LA
Davis, William G. ....**Rocky Mount, VA**
Davis, William Guy, Jr. ....**Pensacola, FL**
Davis, William H. ....**Sacramento, CA**
Davis, William H. ....**Orlando, FL**
Davis, William H. ....**Tallahassee, FL**
Davis, William H. ....**Corydon, IN**

Dawson, John E. .... Las Vegas, NV
Dawson, John J. .... Phoenix, AZ
Dawson, John M. .... Meadville, PA
Dawson, John R. .... Portland, OR
Dawson, John R. .... Milwaukee, WI
Dawson, John T. .... San Jose, CA
Dawson, Jon S. .... Anchorage, AK
Dawson, Jonathan T. .... Southport, CT
Dawson, Joseph, III .... Charleston, SC
Dawson, Joseph J. .... New York, NY
Dawson, Joseph P. .... Toledo, OH
Dawson, Joseph R. .... Fort Lauderdale, FL
Dawson, Joseph R., P.A.
Fort Lauderdale, FL
Dawson, Julia .... North Miami, FL
Dawson, Keith A. .... Corona Del Mar, CA
Dawson, Kenneth R. .... Hollywood, FL
Dawson, Kent J. .... Henderson, NV
Dawson, Larry .... El Centro, CA
Dawson, Laura E. B. .... Stamford, CT
Dawson, Laura J. .... San Francisco, CA
Dawson, Lauri Brown .... Ventura, CA
Dawson, Leighton B. .... Corsicana, TX
Dawson, Linda .... Madison, WI
Dawson, Linda C. .... Paris, KY
Dawson, Linda L. .... Lynnwood, WA
Dawson, Lois J. .... Wilmington, DE
Dawson, M. Perry
Christiansted, St. Croix, VI
Dawson, Mark L. .... Pleasanton, CA
Dawson, Martha J. .... Seattle, WA
Dawson, McGinty & Parker .... Scottsboro, AL
Dawson & Meade .... Spokane, WA
Dawson, Michael C. .... Gunnison, CO
Dawson, Michael G. .... Claremont, CA
Dawson, Michael J. .... Las Vegas, NV
Dawson, Michael S. .... Washington, DC
Dawson, Michele S. .... Canonsburg, PA
Dawson, Michelle L. .... Martinez, CA
Dawson, Milton C. .... Murrieta, CA
Dawson, Mitchell J. .... Beverly Hills, CA
Dawson, Mitchell J., A Professional Law Corporation .... Beverly Hills, CA
Dawson, Moira L. .... San Francisco, CA
Dawson, Monette P. .... Washington, DC
Dawson, Mylan W. .... Baton Rouge, LA
Dawson, Nina Smeltzer .... Bel Air, MD
Dawson, Norma Ann .... Los Angeles, CA
Dawson, Passafuime & Bowden, A Professional Corporation .... Scotts Valley, CA
Dawson, Patrick A. .... Marietta, GA
Dawson, Paul R. (Dick) .... Baytown, TX
Dawson, Peter J. .... Worcester, MA
Dawson, Peter L. .... Alexandria, VA
Dawson, Peter P., III .... Dallas, TX
Dawson, Peter T., Law Office of
Augusta, ME
Dawson, Peter W. .... St. Clair Shores, MI
Dawson, Petrina R. .... New York, NY
Dawson, Philip H. .... St. Clair Shores, MI
Dawson, Philip M. .... Cleveland, OH
Dawson, Phyllis I. .... Cincinnati, OH
Dawson, R. Matt .... Corsicana, TX
Dallas, TX
Dawson, R. Wayne .... Richmond, VA
Dawson, Rachel Miller
Federal Trade Commission,
Office of the General Counsel, GV
Dawson, Ralph C. .... New York, NY
Dawson, Ray C. .... Baton Rouge, LA
Dawson, Rena C. .... New York, NY
Dawson, Rhett B. .... Washington, DC
Dawson, Richard T. .... Tampa, FL
Dawson, Richard W. .... New York, NY
Dawson, Richd. M. .... Louisville, KY
Dawson, Rick .... Salem, OR
Dawson, Robbin R. .... Panhandle, TX
Dawson, Robert A.
Department of Commerce,
Patent and Trademark Office, GV
Dawson, Robert Alec .... New York, NY
Dawson, Robert C. .... Midlothian, VA
Dawson, Robert E. .... Palo Alto, CA
Dawson, Robert H. .... Midland, TX
Dawson, Robert H., Jr. .... Dallas, TX
Dawson, Robert K. .... Washington, DC
Dawson, Robert K. .... Seattle, WA
Dawson, Robert M. .... Los Angeles, CA
Dawson, Robert O. .... Austin, TX
Dawson, Robert R. .... Richmond, VA
Dawson, Robert T. .... Fort Smith, AR
Dawson, Robert W. .... Los Angeles, CA
Dawson, Ronald G. .... Annapolis, MD
Dawson & Rosenthal, P.C. .... Phoenix, AZ
Dawson, Rudolph V. .... East Chicago, IN
Dawson, Russell H. .... Seattle, WA
Dawson, Seth R. .... Everett, WA
Dawson, Shane M. .... Columbus, OH
Dawson, Sherry R. .... Winston-Salem, NC
Dawson, Sheryl Westfall .... Portland, OR
Dawson, Sodd & Beard, P.C.
Corsicana, TX
Dawson, Stephen D. .... Englewood, CO
Dawson, Stephen E. .... Bloomfield Hills, MI
Dawson, Stephen R. .... Fargo, ND
Dawson, Steven C. .... Phoenix, AZ
Dawson, Steven J. .... Los Angeles, CA
Dawson, Susan C. .... Boston, MA
Dawson, Susan H. .... Alexandria, VA
Dawson, Suzanne S. .... Deerfield, IL
Dawson, Tammy D. .... Jacksonville, FL
Dawson, Teresa E. .... Washington, DC
Dawson, Terry W. .... Indianapolis, IN
Dawson, Thomas B. .... Lincoln, NE
Dawson, Thomas C. .... Bardstown, KY
Dawson, Thomas C., Jr. .... Norfolk, VA
Dawson, Thomas D. .... East Liverpool, OH
Dawson, Thomas J. .... Walnut Creek, CA
Dawson, Thomas J. .... Madison, WI
Dawson, Thomas L. .... Detroit, MI
Dawson, Thomas M. .... Leavenworth, KS
Dawson, Thomas M. .... New York, NY
Dawson, Thomas W. .... Oxford, MS
Dawson, Timothy J. .... Bismarck, ND
Dawson, Timothy S. .... San Francisco, CA
Dawson, Todd A. .... Warsaw, IN
Dawson, Todd K. .... Lander, WY
Dawson, Townes L. .... Temple Hills, MD
Dawson, Toya T. L. .... Denver, CO
Dawson, Tracey .... Englewood, CO
Dawson, Tracey B. .... Martinsburg, WV
Dawson, Valerie M. .... Palo Alto, CA
Dawson, Vance R. .... Orlando, FL
Dawson, W. Penn, III .... Tampa, FL
Dawson, Walter F. .... Lowell, MA
Dawson, Warren H. .... Tampa, FL
Dawson, Warren J. .... White Plains, NY
Dawson, Wayne G. .... Anchorage, AK
Dawson, Wayne H. .... Dayton, OH
Dawson, Wendell C. .... Nashville, TN
Dawson, Wendell T. .... Watkinsville, GA
Dawson, William B. .... Dallas, TX
Dawson, William L., Jr. .... Belfast, ME
Dawson, William M. .... Birmingham, AL
Dawson, William R. .... Palo Alto, CA
Dawson, William S., III .... Chantilly, VA
Dawson, Willie C. .... Winston-Salem, NC
Dawson Berry, Judy .... Camden, NJ
Dawson-Brown, Claire S. .... Austin, TX
Dawson-Tibbits, Susan .... Peoria, IL
Dax, John C. .... Vernon Hills, IL
Dax, John W. .... Albany, NY
Daxe, Jeffrey A. .... Marietta, GA
Day, Alison M. .... Columbus, OH
Day, Allen T. .... Lanham, MD
Day, Allison R. .... Miami, FL
Day, Americo P., Jr. .... Mansfield, MA
Day, Amy Carron .... New York, NY
Day, Amy L. Y. .... Westport, CT
Day, Arnold R., Jr. .... Kansas City, MO
Day, Barbara Breier .... Austin, TX
Day, Barbara P. .... Bel Air, MD
Day, Bartley F. .... Portland, OR
Day, Bartley F., A Prof. Corp., Law Offices of .... Portland, OR
Day, Barton D. .... Washington, DC
Day, Ben F. .... Baton Rouge, LA
Day, Ben Louis .... Baton Rouge, LA
Day, Berry & Howard LLP
Greenwich, CT
Hartford, CT
Stamford, CT
Boston, MA
Day, Beth Jackson .... Ellicott City, MD
Day & Birdwell, P.C. .... Cookeville, TN
Day, Bradford R. .... Belvidere, NJ
Day, Brett A. .... Neosho, MO
Day, Brian L. .... Irvine, CA
Day, Brian M. .... Boston, MA
Day, Bruce W. .... Oklahoma City, OK
Day, Bryan K. .... Las Vegas, NV
Day & Brzustowicz, A Professional Corporation .... McMurray, PA
Day, C. Lynne .... Chardon, OH
Day & Campbell, LLP .... Costa Mesa, CA
Day Casebeer Madrid & Batchelder, L.L.P.
Cupertino, CA
Day, Charles B. .... Greenbelt, MD
Day, Charles E. .... Monroe, GA
Day, Charles E., Jr. .... Grand Rapids, MI
Day, Charles F. .... Laguna Niguel, CA
Day, Charles M. .... Galax, VA
Day, Charles T., III .... Atlanta, GA
Day, Charles Williamson, Jr.
Washington, DC
Day, Christian C. .... Syracuse, NY
Day, Christian V. .... Portland, OR
Day, Christopher J. .... Tustin, CA
Day, Christopher J. .... Cherry Hill, NJ
Philadelphia, PA
Day, Christopher M. .... Northfield, NJ
Day, Christopher M. .... Arlington, VA
Day, Christopher R. .... Washington, DC
Day, Clarence A. .... Toledo, OH
Day, Claude M. .... Jefferson City, MO
Day, Claudia S. .... Grand Rapids, MI
Day, Conrad .... Bellville, TX
Day & Cook, A Legal Professional Association .... Columbus, OH
Day, Craig R. .... Lancaster, WI
Day, Cynthia Page .... Columbus, OH
Day, Daniel S. .... Salt Lake City, UT
Day, Daryl K. .... Stanford, KY
Day, David .... Cookeville, TN
Day, David B. .... Visalia, CA
Day, David C. .... Ottawa, IL
Day, David F. .... Honolulu, HI
Day, David H. .... Murray, UT
Day, David J. .... Inverness, FL
Day, David L. .... Columbus, OH
Day, David L. .... Mount Vernon, WA
Day, David R. .... Indianapolis, IN
Day and Day .... Tustin, CA
Day & Day, P.C. .... Fort Worth, TX
Day, Deanna Elaine .... Phoenix, AZ
Day, Denise M. .... Philadelphia, PA
Day, Dennis G. .... Grinnell, IA
Day, Dennis G. .... Columbus, OH
Day, Dennis M. .... Detroit, MI
Day, Diana L. .... San Diego, CA
Day, Don C. .... Bloomington, MN
Day, Donald P. .... Naples, FL
Day, Donald R. .... Phoenix, AZ
Day, Donald S. .... Buffalo, NY
Day, Douglas L., (A Professional Corporation) .... Santa Monica, CA
Day, Dwayne .... Houston, TX
Day, Edward F., Jr. .... Newark, NJ
Day, Edwards, Federman, Propester & Christensen, P.C. .... Oklahoma City, OK
Day, Elizabeth .... Boston, MA
Day, Elizabeth C. .... Tacoma, WA
Day, Ernest B., Jr. .... Tulsa, OK
Day, Esther Sanders .... Tulsa, OK
Day, Fadra LeBlanc .... Waco, TX
Day, F. B. Webster .... Roanoke, VA
Day, Frank D. .... Whiteford, MD
Day, Frederick J., Jr. .... Falls Church, VA
Day, Gary .... New York, NY
Day, Gary E. .... Carlsbad, CA
Day, Gary L. .... Miles City, MT
Day, George C. .... San Francisco, CA
Day, George C., Jr. .... Gadsden, AL
Day, George C., Jr., P.C. .... Gadsden, AL
Day, George E., (P.A.)
Fort Walton Beach, FL
Day, George W. .... Bloomfield Hills, MI
Day, Gloria E. .... McLean, VA
Day, Grace S. .... St. Joseph, MO
Day, Graham L. W. .... Los Angeles, CA
Day, Gregg A. .... West Palm Beach, FL
Day, Gregory Paul .... Morristown, NJ
Day, Gregory S. .... Encinitas, CA
Day, Gregory T. .... Grants Pass, OR
Day, H. Talmage, Jr.
Department of Agriculture,
Farm Service Agency, GV
Day, Hayward F., Jr. .... Far Hills, NJ
Day, H. E., Jr. .... Sun City West, AZ
Day, Heather N.
Department of Labor, GV
Day, Henry Cleaves .... Warrenton, VA
Day, Isabel Scott .... Charlotte, NC
Day, J. Edward .... Chevy Chase, MD
Day, J. Marcus .... San Diego, CA
Day, J. Philip .... Columbus, GA
Day, J. Rick .... San Antonio, TX
Day, Jack G. .... Cleveland, OH
Day, James B. .... Colorado Springs, CO
Day, James B. .... O'Fallon, MO
Day, James E. .... Washington, DC
Day, James E., Jr. .... Dallas, TX
Day, James F. .... Bath, ME
Day, James L. .... Seattle, WA
Day, James M. .... Washington, DC
Day, James M. .... Raleigh, NC
Day, James M., Jr. .... Sacramento, CA
Day, James W. .... Carrollton, IL
Day, Janna B. .... Phoenix, AZ
Day, Jean A. .... Jackson, WY
Day, Jeanette L. .... San Diego, CA
Day, Jeffrey M. .... Bay City, MI
Day, Jennifer E. .... Cincinnati, OH
Day, Jerry .... Oklahoma City, OK
Day, J. K. MacKendree .... Chicago, IL
Day, Joanne Reed .... Orlando, FL
Day, Joe, Jr. .... Fort Worth, TX
Day, John A. .... New York, NY
Day, John A. .... Nashville, TN
Day, John B. .... Danbury, CT
Day, John F. .... Scottsdale, AZ
Day, John F. .... Cleveland, OH
Day, John F., P.C. .... Scottsdale, AZ
Day, John G. .... Bloomfield, CT
Day, John L., Jr. .... Cincinnati, OH
Day, John R. .... Belleville, MI
Farmington Hills, MI
Day, John R., (P.A.) .... Miami, FL
West Palm Beach, FL
Day, John S. .... Boston, MA
Day, John T. .... Stevenson, WA
Day, John W. .... St. Petersburg, FL
Day, Jonathan S. .... Houston, TX
Day, Joseph E. .... Cedar Rapids, IA
Day, Joseph Martin .... Louisville, KY
Day, Julia F. .... San Jose, CA
Day, Julie Hottle .... Fairfax, VA
Day, Kahlil A. .... Oviedo, FL
Day, Karen L. .... Alexandria, VA
McLean, VA
Day, Karin S. .... New York, NY
Day, Katherine A. .... Department of Justice,
Bureau of Prisons, GV
Day, Kavanaugh & Blommel, A Professional Corporation .... Mesa, AZ
Day, Kelley R. .... Shreveport, LA
Day, Kendall Paul .... Kansas City, MO
Day, Kenneth C. .... Raleigh, NC
Day, Ketterer, Raley, Wright & Rybolt, Ltd.
Canton, OH
Day, Kevin L. .... San Diego, CA
Day, Kirsten J. .... San Francisco, CA
Day, Larry R. .... Rancho Cucamonga, CA
Day, Lauren LeBlanc .... Oklahoma City, OK
Day Law Offices .... Alameda, CA
Oakland, CA
Day, Leroy S. .... Fairfield, ME
Day, Lesa Fugate .... Knoxville, TN
Day, Lisa A. .... Rockford, IL
Day, Lisa K. .... Portland, OR
Day, Lisa M. .... Ewing, NJ
Day, Lloyd R., Jr. .... Cupertino, CA
Day, Lois Ann .... Eugene, OR
Day, M. Elizabeth .... Palo Alto, CA
Day, M. Henry, Jr. .... Atlanta, GA
Day, M. Michelle .... Oak Brook, IL
Day, Marcel P. .... Houston, TX
Day, Margaret Ranft .... New Fairfield, CT
Day, Maribeth D. .... Indianapolis, IN
Day, Marilyn J. .... Lansing, MI
Day, Marjorie W. .... Tustin, CA
Day, Marshall J. .... Fort Worth, TX
Day, Martha .... Wakefield, RI
Day, Martha L. .... Westbrook, ME
Day, Mary Kathleen .... Tulsa, OK
Day, Matthew Jacob .... New York, NY
Day and Meade, P.A.
Fort Walton Beach, FL
Day Meeker Lamping & Schlegel
Washington, IA
Day, Meigs M. .... Grand Rapids, MI
Day, Melissa A. .... Buffalo, NY
Day, Michael A. .... St. George, UT
Day, Michael B. .... San Francisco, CA
Day, Michael G. .... Hagerstown, MD
Day, Michael J. .... Apollo Beach, FL
Day, Michael J. .... St. Francis, KS
Day, Michael W. .... Belle Fourche, SD
Rapid City, SD
Day, Michelle R. Loy .... Oklahoma City, OK
Day, Montie S. .... Alameda, CA
Day, Nancy Thygesen .... Seattle, WA
Day, Neil M. .... Trenton, NJ
Day, Nere E., Jr. .... Norfolk, VA
Day, Nicholas .... Philadelphia, PA
Day, Pamela Triplett .... Irving, TX
Day, Patricia A. .... Baltimore, MD
Day, Patricia A. .... Boston, MA
Day, Patricia Ann .... Madisonville, KY
Day, Patricia L. .... Houston, TX
Day, Patrick J. .... Philadelphia, PA
Day, Patrick R., (P.C.) .... Cheyenne, WY
Day, Paul J. .... Baltimore, MD
Day, Paul W. .... St. Paul, MN
Day, Paula A. .... Anson, ME
Day, Paulee Coughlin .... Clearwater, FL
Day, Peter R. .... Seattle, WA
Day, Philip S. .... Chevy Chase, MD
Day, Phillip G. .... Tampa, FL
Day, Phillip J. .... Abilene, TX
Day, R. Christopher .... Jacksonville, TX
Day, R. Daniel, Jr. .... Seneca, SC
Day, R. Wilson .... Raleigh, NC
Day, Randall E., III .... Hollandale, MS
Day, Randy G. .... Garland, ME
Day, Reed B. .... McMurray, PA
Day, Richard A. .... Chicago, IL
Day, Richard A., III .... La Plata, MD
Day, Richard E. .... Columbia, SC
Day, Richard E. .... Casper, WY
Day, Richard G. .... Edina, MN
Day, Richard J. .... St. Elmo, IL
Day, Richard J. .... Buffalo, NY
Day, Richard R. .... Santa Rosa, CA
Day, Richard V. .... Napa, CA
Day, Robert .... Washington, IA
Day, Robert A. .... Santa Ana, CA
Day, Robert D., Jr. .... Bethesda, MD
Day, Robert E. .... Detroit, MI
Day, Robert G. .... Palo Alto, CA
Day, Robert G., Jr. .... Peoria, IL
Day, Robert L. .... Woodland, CA
Day, Robert L., Jr. .... Dubuque, IA
Day, Robert R. .... Saginaw, MI
Day, Robert S., Jr. .... Nashville, TN
Day, Robin L. .... Alamo, CA
Day, Robt. G., Sr. .... Peoria, IL
Day, Roger F. .... Columbus, OH
Day, Roland B., (P.C.) .... San Diego, CA
Day, Ronald L. .... Cookson, OK
Day, Rowland W., II .... Costa Mesa, CA
Day, Rutherford .... Oakland Park, FL
Day & Sackheim .... Boulder, CO
Day, Sam J., III .... Fort Worth, TX
Day, Samuel A. .... New Albany, IN
Day, Sandra A. .... Mesa, AZ
Day, Sarah E. .... Greenville, SC
Day & Sawdey, A Professional Corporation
Grand Rapids, MI
Day and Schneider, P.A. .... Hagerstown, MD
Day, Scott M. .... Naperville, IL
Day, Scott M., P.C. .... Naperville, IL
Day, Sean R. .... College Park, MD
Day, Selim B. .... Palo Alto, CA
Day, Shannon L. .... Madison, WI
Day, Sharon S. .... Decatur, AL
Huntsville, AL
Day Shell & Liljenquist, L.C. .... Murray, UT
Day, Stephen E. .... Jacksonville, FL
Day, Stephen J. .... Seattle, WA
Day, Stephen L. .... Seattle, WA
Day, Steve Woodward, Jr. .... Scranton, PA
Day, Steven C. .... Wichita, KS
Day, Steven L. .... Las Vegas, NV
Day, Steven M. .... Kansas City, MO
Day, Steven M. .... Salt Lake City, UT
Day, Stuart R. .... Casper, WY
Day, Suzanne F. .... Wickliffe, OH
Day, Thomas D. .... Boulder, CO
Day, Thomas L. .... San Francisco, CA
Day, Timothy .... Osgood, IN
Day, Timothy C. .... Haverhill, MA
Day, Timothy C. .... Jackson, WY
Day, Timothy Quinn .... Santa Ana, CA
Day, Ursula B. .... New York, NY
New York, NY
Day, Vallerina F. .... McDonough, GA
Day, Victor R. .... Tulsa, OK
Day, Virgil B., (P.C.) .... New York, NY
Day, W. Gregory .... Sacramento, CA
Day & White, P.A. .... Raleigh, NC
Day, William A. .... Birmingham, MI
Day, William A., Jr. .... Omaha, NE
Day, William F., Jr. .... Sioux Falls, SD
Day, William J. .... Brecksville, OH
Day, William K. .... Oakland, CA
Day, William S. .... Canton, MA
Day, Willis F., IV .... Toledo, OH
Day, Winston R. .... Baton Rouge, LA
Day, Wm. Bruce .... Overland Park, KS
Kansas City, MO
Dayal, Anjali .... Chicago, IL

Dayal, Ashima A. .... **New York, NY**
Dayal, Sujata T. .... **North Chicago, IL**
Dayan, Allen N., & Associates .... **Anchorage, AK**
Dayan, David .... **Palo Alto, CA**
Dayan, Jeannette .... **New York, NY**
Dayan, Leon .... **Washington, DC**
Dayan, Lisa E. .... **Parsippany, NJ**
New York, NY
Dayan, Marshall .... **Raleigh, NC**
Dayan, Michael D. .... **New York, NY**
Dayan, Rodney S. .... Newport Beach, CA
Dayan, Scott M. .... **Atlanta, GA**
Dayan & Wensel, P.C. .... Anchorage, AK
Dayani, Hamid .... Davis, CA
Dayani, Hooman .... **Los Angeles, CA**
Dayanim, Behnam .... **Washington, DC**
Dayanim, Pooya .... Beverly Hills, CA
Daye, Bowie & Beresko, A Professional Law Corporation .... **Shreveport, LA**
Daye, Charles E. .... Chapel Hill, NC
Daye, David P. .... **Shreveport, LA**
Daye, Emilie Melancon .... **Houma, LA**
Daye, Joseph L., (P.A.) .... Fort Lauderdale, FL
Daye, Robert E. .... Menlo Park, CA
Dayen, Michael .... **Los Angeles, CA**
Dayes, A.R. "Trey", III .... Pleasant Grove, UT
Dayhoff, Charles S., III .... Palm Harbor, FL
Dayhuff, Travis .... **Columbia, SC**
Dayian, Daryl E. .... **Providence, RI**
Dayich, Louis M. .... Waynesburg, PA
Daykin, Frank W. .... Carson City, NV
Daykin, Linda Nagy .... Reno, NV
Dayley, Kristen J. .... **Los Angeles, CA**
Daylor, Lane H. .... Pottstown, PA
Daymon, Matt S. .... Grand Junction, CO
Daymude, Janet .... New Brunswick, NJ
Daymude, Michael R. .... Encino, CA
Daynard, Matthew
Federal Trade Commission, Bureau of Consumer Protection, GV
Daynard, Richard A. .... Boston, MA
Dayne, Stanley J. .... Sacramento, CA
Dayner, Judith C. .... Bloomfield, CT
Daynes, Wendy Waller .... Beverly Farms, MA
Dayno, Karen Shecter .... **Blue Bell, PA**
Days, Drew S., III .... **Washington, DC**
Days, Virginia M. .... San Jose, CA
Dayter, F. Charles .... Albany, NY
Dayton, A. Kimberley .... Lawrence, KS
Dayton, Carrie I. .... **Newark, DE**
Baltimore, MD
Dayton, Charles K. .... **Minneapolis, MN**
Dayton, Christopher A. .... San Diego, CA
Dayton Countryman Law Offices, P.C.
Nevada, IA
Dayton & D'Amato, P.C. .... Bayside, NY
Dayton, David-Eric A. .... Atlanta, GA
Dayton, Douglas E. .... East Hampton, NY
Dayton, Edgar M. .... New Orleans, LA
Dayton, Gwen M. .... Gresham, OR
Dayton, Joel K. .... **Canton, OH**
Dayton, John W., III .... Department of State, Foreign Service Officers (Overseas), GV
Dayton, Keith David .... Cortland, NY
Dayton, Kenneth A. .... Tampa, FL
Dayton, Lee H. .... Westerville, OH
Dayton, Lee W. .... **Los Angeles, CA**
Dayton, Marie E. .... Richmond, VA
Dayton, Michael R. .... Medford, OK
Dayton, Pamela A. .... Denver, CO
Dayton, Paul J. .... **Seattle, WA**
Dayton, Peter S. .... **Missoula, MT**
Dayton, Ralph L. .... East Hampton, NY
Dayton, Ray J. .... Anaconda, MT
Dayton, Robert D. .... **Portland, OR**
Dayton, Sheila C. .... **Grand Rapids, MI**
Dayton, Steven A. .... Long Beach, CA
Dayton & Voorhees .... East Hampton, NY
Dayton, William H., Jr. .... **Lehigh Valley, PA**
Dayvault, David M. .... Wichita, KS
Dayvault, Jay J. .... Los Angeles, CA
Daza, Raul .... Beverly Hills, CA
Dazé, D. Timothy .... Studio City, CA
Daze, Douglas E. .... **Jacksonville, FL**
Dazé, Michel A. .... **Washington, DC**
Dazey, William B. .... San Antonio, TX
Dazey, William H., Jr. .... Indianapolis, IN
Dazzio, P. Thomas, Jr. .... **Birmingham, AL**
Dazzio, Peter T. .... **Baton Rouge, LA**
Dazzo, George E. .... Commack, NY
D'Costa, Ophelino .... Denver, CO
D'Cruz, R. Jason .... **Atlanta, GA**
D'Cruz, Sheila .... **Chicago, IL**
De, Sona .... **New York, NY**
Dea, Hong S. .... Los Angeles, CA
Dea, Mark T. .... **Rancho Santa Fe, CA**
Dea, Michael S. .... **Rancho Santa Fe, CA**
De Abreu, David O. .... Taunton, MA
de Abreu, Orlando F. .... Fall River, MA
Taunton, MA
Deachman & Cowie, P.A. .... Plymouth, NH
Deachman, Ross V. .... Plymouth, NH
Deacon, Bruce E. .... **Denver, CO**
Deacon, Carrell Van, Jr. .... Cleveland, TN
Deacon, Charles A. .... **San Antonio, TX**
Deacon, Edward S. .... **Sacramento, CA**
Deacon, J. Barry .... **Jonesboro, AR**
Deacon, James W., II .... **Washington, DC**
Deacon, John C. .... **Jonesboro, AR**
Deacon, John D., Jr. .... **Providence, RI**
Deacon, Kenneth C., Jr.
St. Petersburg, FL
Deacon, Linda Van Winkle
Los Angeles, CA
Deacon & Moulds, P.A.
St. Petersburg, FL
Deacon, Robert F. .... **Cleveland, OH**
Deacon, Rush B. .... Little Rock, AR
Deacon, Walter E., III .... **Erie, PA**
Deacons Graham & James .... **New York, NY**
Deaconson, David N. .... **Waco, TX**
Deacy and Deacy, LLP
Prairie Village, KS
Kansas City, MO
Deacy, Thomas E., Jr. .... **Kansas City, MO**
Deacy, Thomas M. .... **Kansas City, MO**
Deaderick, Robert H., Jr.
Fredericksburg, VA
Deaderick, Wm. David .... **Austin, TX**
Deadman, Bruce B. .... Green Bay, WI
Deadman, Glenn J. .... San Antonio, TX
Deadman, Glenn J., P.C. .... San Antonio, TX
Deadman, Robert M. .... New York, NY
Deadman, William G. .... **Coshocton, OH**
Deadrich, Charles H. .... San Leandro, CA
Deadrich, Paul E. .... Duarte, CA
Deady, Conan R. .... Waltham, MA
Deady, Douglas L. .... **Kansas City, MO**
Deady, H. Brian .... Baltimore, MD
Deady, John B. .... Brockton, MA
Deady, Patrick E. .... **Chicago, IL**
de Aenlle, Theia C. .... Anaheim, CA
Deagazio, Christopher R. .... **Boston, MA**
DeAgazio, Richard M. .... **Short Hills, NJ**
Deagen, Kimberli J. .... Houston, TX
Deagle, Brian J. .... **Seattle, WA**
Deagle, Donald C. .... Denver, CO
Deagle, Marianne .... Topeka, KS
DeAgostino, L. Gene .... **Troy, MI**
De Agostino, Paul V.
Department of the Army, U.S. Army Legal Services Agency, GV
DeAgostino, Thomas M.
Auburn Hills, MI
DeAguero, Andres D. .... Santa Fe, NM
Deaguero, Richard J. .... **Dallas, TX**
Deahl, Michael A. .... **Dallas, TX**
Deahl, Richard J. .... **South Bend, IN**
Deahl, Warren A. .... **South Bend, IN**
Deak, Richard A. .... Langhorne, PA
Deak, Tom .... **Carlsbad, CA**
Deake, Edward D. .... Ann Arbor, MI
Deakin, Barbara J. .... Washington, DC
Deakin, David A. .... Boston, MA
Deakin, Jennifer Dowd .... **New Haven, CT**
Deakin, Michael Cuff .... Shelton, CT
Deakins, Homer L., Jr. .... **Washington, DC**
Atlanta, GA
Greenville, SC
Nashville, TN
Deakins, Misty A. .... Stuart, FL
Deakle, John Mark .... **Mobile, AL**
Deakle, Margaret Molette .... **Mobile, AL**
Deakle, Sherry S. .... Hattiesburg, MS
Deaktor, Michael W. .... **Glendale, CA**
Deakyne & James .... **St. Petersburg, FL**
Deakyne, James E., Jr., (P.A.)
St. Petersburg, FL
Deal, Betty Barry .... Alameda, CA
Deal, Blake F., III .... **Jacksonville, FL**
Deal, Cathryn V. .... St. Paul, MN
Deal, Charles M. .... **Tampa, FL**
Deal, Charles T. .... Clemson, SC
Deal, Christopher E. .... **Los Angeles, CA**
Deal, David R. .... Department of Commerce, Patent and Trademark Office, GV
Deal, David T. .... Washington, DC
Deal & Deal, P.A. .... Clemson, SC
Deal, Dianne C. DiGiamber .... Salem, NJ
Deal, Donna Marlea .... Boston, MA
Deal, Edwin M. .... Cotuit, MA
Deal, Eugene A. .... Atlanta, GA
Deal, Gary F. .... Eugene, OR
Deal, Geo. L. .... Canton, OH
Deal, Gregory R. .... **Lakeland, FL**
Deal, J. Ray .... Graham, NC
Deal, J. Thomas .... **San Ramon, CA**
Deal, James B. .... **Norcross, GA**
Deal, James E. .... Brazil, IN
Deal, James M., Jr. .... **Boone, NC**
Deal, Jason J. .... Gainesville, GA
Deal, Jill B. .... **Washington, DC**
Deal, John C. .... **Columbus, OH**
Deal, John F. .... Richmond, VA
Deal, John L. .... **Norfolk, VA**
Deal, Joseph D. .... **Cherry Hill, NJ**
Deal, Keith M. .... Jacksonville, FL
Deal, L. Anthony .... Memphis, TN
Deal, L. Anthony, P.C. .... Memphis, TN
Deal, Leonard E. .... Fresno, CA
Deal, Mary E. .... Basking Ridge, NJ
Deal, Michael .... Seattle, WA
Deal, Michael S. .... Lima, OH
Deal & Moseley .... **Boone, NC**
Deal & Norris .... Monroe, LA
Deal, Pamela A. E. .... Clemson, SC
Deal, Paul B. .... **New Orleans, LA**
Deal, Philip T. .... Monroe, LA
Deal & Pineo, P.A. .... Virginia, MN
Deal, R. Brandt .... **Winston-Salem, NC**
Deal, Reha Kamâa .... **Salt Lake City, UT**
Deal, Ricky Joe .... Houston, TX
Deal, Roger F. .... Columbus, OH
Deal, Ronald B. .... Chipley, FL
Deal, Sharon S. .... Seattle, WA
Deal, Stepen Joseph .... Bethesda, MD
Deal, Thomas A., (P.C.) .... Speedway, IN
Deal, Todd E. .... Virginia, MN
de Alcuaz, Anthony .... **Palo Alto, CA**
Deale, Frank E. .... New York, NY
Dealey, Sam J. .... **Dallas, TX**
De Almeida, Dolores M. .... **Livingston, NJ**
de Almeida, Douglas .... **Fort Lauderdale, FL**
DeAlmeida, Patrick .... Trenton, NJ
Dealy, John F. .... McLean, VA
Dealy, Peter S. .... Santa Monica, CA
Dealy, William J. .... New York, NY
Dealy-Browning, Deborah .... Monmouth, OR
Deam, Ann W. .... Miami, FL
Deam, Michael T. .... **Fort Wayne, IN**
Deamer, Bartley C. .... **Palo Alto, CA**
San Francisco, CA
Deamer, Michael L. .... Salt Lake City, UT
Deamicis, Amy M. .... Los Angeles, CA
DeAmicis, Brian .... **Sacramento, CA**
DeAmicis, Don S. .... **Boston, MA**
De Amicis, Marilyn A. .... Worcester, MA
DeAmorin, Joseph S. .... Newark, NJ
Deamud & Bennett, PLC, Law Offices of
Prudenville, MI
Deamud, James R. .... **Prudenville, MI**
Dean, Aaron .... **Seattle, WA**
Dean, Aaron A. .... **Minneapolis, MN**
Dean, Aaron A. .... Sidney, NY
Dean, Alan .... **New York, NY**
Dean, Amy N. .... Miami, FL
Dean, Anthony A. .... **New Brunswick, NJ**
New York, NY
Dean, Arnold Y. .... Arlington, VA
Dean, Barbara J. .... **Charlotte, NC**
Dean & Barrett .... **Auburn, AL**
Opelika, AL
Dean, Barry R. .... Randolph, NJ
Dean, Beale .... **Fort Worth, TX**
Dean, Beni T. .... San Antonio, TX
Dean, Benj. E. .... Owego, NY
Dean, Benjamin .... **New York, NY**
Dean, Benjamin E. .... Owego, NY
Dean, Benjamin Masur .... **Washington, DC**
Dean, Benjamin P. .... Raleigh, NC
Dean, Beryl R. .... Bryn Mawr, PA
Dean, Bill V., Jr. .... Jones, OK
Dean, Billie K. .... Chattanooga, TN
Dean Blakey & Moskowitz .... Washington, DC
Dean, Brian J. .... **St. Louis, MO**
Dean, Brian L. .... Venice, FL
Dean, Bruce A. .... **Marietta, GA**
Dean, Bruce Adams .... Cambridge, MA
Dean, Bruce Alan .... Atlanta, GA
Dean, Bruce C. .... **Metairie, LA**
Dean, Bruce L. .... **Dallas, TX**
Dean, C. Rees .... **Flint, MI**
Dean, Cameron .... Flint, MI
Dean, Camille E. .... Louisville, KY
Middletown, KY
Dean & Casella .... Venice, FL
Dean, Catherine Palmer .... **Osceola, AR**
Dean, Cathy J. .... **Kansas City, MO**
Dean, Chad W. .... Henderson, TX
Dean, Charles A. .... **Troy, MI**
Dean, Charles F., Jr. .... Cleveland, OH
Dean, Christine P. .... Jones, OK
Dean, Christine Witcover .... Raleigh, NC
Dean, Clarence J., Jr. .... Springfield, OH
Dean, Clifford A. .... North Chicago, IL
Dean, D. William .... **Manitowoc, WI**
Dean, Danette C. .... Philadelphia, PA
Dean, Daniel A., Jr. .... **New York, NY**
Dean, Daniel B. .... **Laurinburg, NC**
Dean, Daniel F. .... Palestine, TX
Dean, Daniel Lee .... Atlanta, GA
Dean, Daniel P. .... **San Francisco, CA**
Dean, Daniel W. .... Fort Collins, CO
Dean, David A. .... Dallas, TX
Dean, David A. & Associates, P.C.
Dallas, TX
Dean, David B. .... **Minneapolis, MN**
Dean, David J. .... Deer Park, NY
Dean, David J. .... **Mineola, NY**
New York, NY
Dean, David Johnson .... Montgomery, AL
Dean, David Lawrence .... **Birmingham, AL**
Dean, David M. .... Renton, WA
Dean, David P. .... **Washington, DC**
Dean and Dean, L.L.P. .... Ocala, FL
Dean, Dean, Segar & Hart, P.C. .... Flint, MI
Dean, Delany .... Kansas City, MO
Dean, Denis .... Tallahassee, FL
Dean, Denise Best .... Falmouth, KY
Dean, Dennis P.
Department Of Veterans Affairs, Board of Veterans Appeals, GV
Dean, Derek F. .... Charleston, SC
Dean, Diana L. .... Department of Energy, Office of the General Counsel, GV
Dean, Don M. .... **Amarillo, TX**
Dean, Donald M., Jr. .... Novato, CA
Dean, Donna M. .... **Beverly Hills, CA**
Dean, E. Joseph .... **Portland, OR**
Dean, Edward A. .... **Mobile, AL**
Dean, Edward F. .... Crystal Lake, IL
Dean, Edward R., Jr. .... Lowell, MA
Dean, Elizabeth M.
Farm Credit Administration, GV
Dean, Eric D. .... **Los Angeles, CA**
Dean, Eric T., Jr. .... **New Haven, CT**
Dean, Erin D. .... **Beaufort, SC**
Dean, Eugene J., Jr. .... Waquoit, MA
Dean, Eula M. .... Sacramento, CA
Dean, Florence .... Brooklyn, NY
Dean, Frank D. .... Stockton, CA
Dean, Frederick S. .... Tucson, AZ
Dean, Fredk. J., III .... Chesapeake, VA
Dean & Fulkerson, P.C. .... **Detroit, MI**
Troy, MI
Dean, G. Douglas .... Opelousas, LA
Dean, Gale A. .... Tucson, AZ
Dean, Gale A., P.C. .... Tucson, AZ
Dean, Gary Daniel .... **Los Angeles, CA**
Dean, Gary J. .... Pryor, OK
Dean, George A. .... **Nashville, TN**
Dean, George B. .... Boston, MA
Dean, George B., Jr., (P.C.) .... **Monroe, LA**
Dean, George R. .... Atlanta, GA
Dean, Gibson, II .... Buford, GA
Dean, Gibson, II, P.C. .... Buford, GA
Dean & Gibson, L.L.P. .... **Charlotte, NC**
Dean, Goble D. .... **Orlando, FL**
Dean, Gregory A. .... Overland Park, KS
Dean, Gregory B. .... Opelousas, LA
Dean, Gregory J. .... King Of Prussia, PA
Dean, H. Edward .... Ocala, FL
Dean, Harlin R., Jr. .... **Dallas, TX**
Dean, Harold .... Southfield, MI
Dean, Harold B. .... New London, CT
Dean, Harvey R. .... Warren, MI
Dean, Heather M. .... Charlottesville, VA
Dean, Henry .... Tallahassee, FL
Dean, Herbert W., Jr. .... Richmond, CA
Dean, Homer E., Jr. .... Alice, TX
Dean, Howard .... Washington, DC
Dean, Howard .... Tarrytown, NY
Dean, Howard, P.C. .... Tarrytown, NY
Dean, Hugh E., Jr. .... Bloomfield Hills, MI
Dean, Iris Susan .... **New York, NY**
Dean, Irwin J., Jr. .... Pittsburgh, PA
Dean, J. Christopher .... **Houston, TX**
Dean, J. Thomas .... Madison, OH
Dean, James B. .... **Denver, CO**
Dean, James B., P.C. .... **Denver, CO**
Dean, James Hadden .... **Danville, KY**
Dean, James J. .... **Tallahassee, FL**
Dean, James J. .... **Iselin, NJ**
Dean, James P. .... **Troy, MI**
Dean, James P. .... Corinth, MS
Dean, James Webb .... Denver, CO
Dean, January E. .... Columbus, OH
Dean, Jay Douglas .... New York, NY
Dean, Jeffery B. .... Falmouth, KY
Dean, Jeffrey H. .... **Chicago, IL**
Dean, Jeffrey J. .... **Dalton, GA**
Dean, Jeffrey L. .... **Solon, OH**
Dean, Jeffrey M. .... Zephyrhills, FL
Dean, Jennifer L. .... **Baltimore, MD**
Dean, Jill D. .... West Bloomfield, MI
Dean, Jill Weber .... **Madison, WI**
Dean, Joe N. .... Groveton, TX
Dean, John A., Jr. .... **Farmington, NM**
Dean, John B. .... **Minneapolis, MN**
Dean, John C. .... Glenwood, IA
Dean, John C. .... **Providence, RI**
Dean, John E. .... Washington, DC
Dean, John G. .... **Scranton, PA**
Dean, John J. .... Baltimore, MD
Dean, John O. .... Tulsa, OK
Dean, John P. .... **Washington, DC**
Dean, John R. .... Batavia, OH
Dean, John R. .... Montrose, PA
Dean, John R. .... **Rutland, VT**
Dean, John W. .... **White Plains, NY**
Dean, John W., III .... Philadelphia, PA
Dean, Jonathan .... Akron, OH
Dean, Jonathan S. .... Ocala, FL
Dean, Joseph L., Jr. .... **Opelika, AL**
Dean, Joseph W. .... Raleigh, NC
Dean, Judith N. .... Haverford, PA
Dean, Juliene Lee .... Chico, CA
Dean, Kala R. .... **Little Rock, AR**
Dean, Karen .... Charlotte, NC
Dean, Karl F. .... Nashville, TN
Dean, Ken S. .... Madisonville, KY
Dean, Kenneth D. .... Columbia, MO
Dean, Kenneth L. .... Stone Mountain, GA
Dean, Kevin Paul .... **New Haven, CT**
Dean, Kevin R. .... Blakely, GA
Dean, Kimberly J. .... Nashville, TN
Dean, Kristen D. .... **Norton, VA**
Dean, Kristi Weiler, Law Offices of
Encino, CA
Dean, Kristi Weiler, Law Offices of
Los Angeles, CA
Dean, Laura Hansen .... Indianapolis, IN
Dean, Lauren A. .... **Los Angeles, CA**
Dean Law Firm, The, P.C. .... **Buffalo, NY**
Grand Island, NY
Niagara Falls, NY
Dean, Lawrence K.
Colorado Springs, CO
Dean, Lee M. .... Harrodsburg, KY
Dean, Lee W. .... San Bernardino, CA
Dean, Leslie A. .... Tucson, AZ
Dean, Lisa Harris .... **McLean, VA**
Dean, Lisa L. .... **Cincinnati, OH**
Dean & Lomenick .... Opelousas, LA
Dean, Luana M. .... Department of Labor, Office of Secretary, GV
Dean, L. W. "Rusty" .... Tyler, TX
Dean, Lyn E. .... **Austin, TX**
Dean, Lynn A. .... Roseville, CA
Dean, M. Victoria .... Gaithersburg, MD
Dean, Margaret E. .... Kansas City, MO
Dean, Margaret G. .... New Haven, CT
Dean, Margaret G. .... Indianapolis, IN
Dean, Mark H. .... **Hartford, CT**
Dean, Mark H., P.C. .... **Hartford, CT**
Dean, Mark J. .... **St. Louis, MO**
Dean, Mark W. .... **Concord, NH**
Manchester, NH
Dean, Martha A., Law Offices of
Hartford, CT
Dean, Martha F. .... Canal Winchester, OH
Dean, Martin L. .... San Francisco, CA
Dean, Mary .... Newark, NJ
Dean, Mary E. .... Treasury Department, Internal Revenue Service, GV
St. Paul, MN
Dean, Mary Frances .... **Pittsburgh, PA**
Dean, MaryAnn E. .... Miamisburg, OH
Dean, Max .... Flint, MI
Dean, Mead, Egerton, Bloodworth, Capouano & Bozarth, P.A. .... **Orlando, FL**

Dean, Mead, Minton & Klein
Fort Pierce, FL
Dean, Mead, Spielvogel, Goldman & Boyd
Melbourne, FL
Merritt Island, FL
Dean, Merrianne E. ....San Diego, CA
Dean, Michael ....London, KY
Dean, Michael A. ....Oakland, CA
Dean, Michael D. ....Waukesha, WI
Dean, Michael E. ....Ocala, FL
Dean, Michael F. ....Sacramento, CA
San Francisco, CA
Dean, Michael K. ....El Paso, TX
Dean, Michael M. ....Philadelphia, PA
Dean, Michael P. ....North Canton, OH
Dean, Mickey ....Kansas City, MO
Dean, Mitchell D. ....Solana Beach, CA
Dean, Morris J. ....Philadelphia, PA
Dean, Nannette B. ....Columbus, OH
Dean, Norman C. ....New Braunfels, TX
Dean, Norman C., P.C. ....New Braunfels, TX
Dean & O'Dea, P.C. ....Bessemer, MI
Crystal Falls, MI
Iron Mountain, MI
Ironwood, MI
Ontonagon, MI
Ashland, WI
Florence, WI
Hurley, WI
Washburn, WI
Dean & Ongert, P.C. ....Galveston, TX
Houston, TX
Dean, Otis Auburn ....Salem, NH
Dean, Pamela Prator ....New Orleans, LA
Dean, Patricia ....Denver, CO
Dean, Patricia A. ....Metairie, LA
Dean, Patricia Ann ....Washington, DC
Dean, Paul E. ....Emporia, KS
Dean, Paul R. ....Falls Church, VA
Dean, Paul R., Jr. ....Falls Church, VA
Dean, Paula D. ....Charleston, WV
Dean, Penny S. ....Concord, NH
Dean, Peter H. ....Atlanta, GA
Dean, Peter L. ....Escondido, CA
Dean, Preston ....Kansas City, MO
Dean, Ralph H., Jr. ....Washington, DC
Dean, Ralph M., III ....Oxford, MS
Dean, Randal L. ....Fort Worth, TX
Dean, Randall J. ....Los Angeles, CA
Dean, Randy L. ....Jackson, MS
Dean, Reagan W. ....Marietta, GA
Dean, Rebecca ....Seattle, WA
Dean, Rebecca Orin ....New Orleans, LA
Dean & Reid, L.L.C. ....Fort Collins, CO
Dean, R. G. ....Montrose, PA
Dean, Rice & Kane, P.A. ....Concord, NH
Manchester, NH
Dean, Richard A. ....Washington, DC
Dean, Richard C., Jr. ....Montgomery, AL
Dean, Richard H., Jr. ....Ann Arbor, MI
Dean, Richard N. ....Washington, DC
Dean, Richard W. ....Boca Raton, FL
Dean, Ringers, Morgan and Lawton, P.A.
Orlando, FL
Dean, Robert ....New York, NY
Dean, Robert A. ....Grand Island, NY
Dean, Robert C. ....Tallahassee, FL
Dean, Robert C. ....Greenville, MS
Dean, Robert Everett ....Irvine, CA
Dean, Robert L. ....Rockville, MD
Dean, Robert M. ....Tustin, CA
Dean, Rodney A. ....Charlotte, NC
Dean, Ronald ....Pacific Palisades, CA
Dean, Ronald Craig ....Wheeling, WV
Dean, Ronald J. ....Torrance, CA
Dean, Ronald W. ....Provo, UT
Dean, Roy E. ....Sarasota, FL
Dean, Russell B. ....Santa Monica, CA
Dean, Russell J. ....Indianapolis, IN
Dean, S. Bobo ....Washington, DC
Dean, Samuel L., Jr. ....Rockford, IL
Dean, Sandra W. ....Camden-Wyoming, DE
Dean & Schnaufer ....New York, NY
White Plains, NY
Dean, Scott J. ....Cleveland, OH
Dean, Shari L. ....Blythe, CA
Dean, Shelly A. ....Richmond, VA
Dean, Sheri Y. ....Houston, TX
Dean, Shirley D. ....Durham, NC
Dean, Smith & Therrell, P.A. ....Atlanta, GA
Dean, Stanley P. ....Winston-Salem, NC
Dean, Stephanie J. ....San Mateo, CA
Dean, Stephen G. ....Rayville, LA
Dean, Stephen M. ....Redding, CA
Dean, Stephen T. ....Orlando, FL
Dean, Steven O. ....Dayton, OH
Dean, Stuart ....New York, NY
Dean, Susan E. ....Ocala, FL
Dean, Susan M. ....Haddonfield, NJ
Philadelphia, PA
Dean, Sydney G. ....Harker Heights, TX
Dean, Theresa Smith ....Opelika, AL
Dean, Thomas B. ....Gallatin, TN
Dean, Thomas F. ....Richmond, VA
Dean, Thomas M. ....Buffalo, NY
Dean, Thomas R. ....Newark, NJ
Dean, Thomas S. ....Boston, MA
Dean, Timothy M. ....Ironwood, MI
Dean, Timothy S. ....Ocala, FL
Dean, V. Gerald ....Monroe, LA
Dean, Verdell ....Pittsburgh, PA
Dean, Verdell, and Associates, P.C.
Pittsburgh, PA
Dean, W. Earl ....Harrodsburg, KY
Dean, W. Edward ....San Francisco, CA
Dean, Walter Scott ....Austin, TX
Dean, Walter W. ....Tuscaloosa, AL
Dean, Warren C., Jr. (Professional Corporation)
Newport Beach, CA
Dean, Warren L., Jr. ....Washington, DC
Dean & Wheeler ....Indianapolis, IN
Dean, Wilbur R. ....Moore, OK
Dean, William A. ....Miami, FL
Dean, William C. ....Coral Springs, FL
Dean, William E. ....Boise, ID
Dean, William J. ....New York, NY
Dean, William S. ....Washington, DC
Dean, William S. ....Somerset, KY
Dean, William T., Jr. ....Atlanta, GA
Dean Yuen Allison, LLP ....Sacramento, CA
San Francisco, CA
De Anda, James ....Houston, TX
De Anda Law Firm ....Laredo, TX
De Anda, Ricardo ....Laredo, TX
DeAndrea, Vincent P., Jr. ....Metuchen, NJ
DeAndreis, Annette ....West Sacramento, CA
DeAndreis, Peter ....McMinnville, OR
Deane, Charles B., Jr. ....Rockingham, NC
Deane, Dana D. ....North Chicago, IL
Deane, Eileen ....Chicago, IL
Deane, Elaine ....San Francisco, CA
Deane, George I., III (Professional Corporation)
Sonora, CA
Deane, Irvin B. ....Baltimore, MD
Deane, James R. ....New York, NY
Deane, Jeffrey W. ....Beverly Hills, CA
Deane, Jeffrey W. ....Overland Park, KS
Deane, Jesse ....Cape May, NJ
Deane, John Russell, III ....Washington, DC
Deane, Kathleen M. ....Chicago, IL
Deane, Kenneth B. ....New York, NY
Deane, M. Elizabeth ....San Francisco, CA
Deane, Marvin T. ....San Antonio, TX
Deane, Richard E. ....Jacksonville, FL
Deane, Richard H. ....Atlanta, GA
Deane, Robert B. ....New Orleans, LA
Deane, Robert B. ....Westbury, NY
Deane, Ruth M. ....Lincoln Park, NJ
Deane, Sherry C. ....Washington, DC
Deane, William J., Jr. ....Philadelphia, PA
Deanehan, Alan F. ....Baltimore, MD
Deaner, Charles W. ....Las Vegas, NV
Deaner, Deaner, Scann, Malan & Larsen
Las Vegas, NV
Deaner, Stephanie E. ....Los Angeles, CA
Deaner, Ted E. ....Rochester, MN
DeAngeli, Darin A. ....Boise, ID
de Angeli, John A. ....Yonkers, NY
de Angeli, Michael M. ....Rockville, MD
de Angeli, Michael M., P.C.
Washington, DC
Rockville, MD
De Angeli, Phil E. ....Boise, ID
DeAngelis, Diana F. ....Pittsburgh, PA
DeAngelis, Donald D. ....Delmar, NY
DeAngelis, Frank J. ....New York, NY
DeAngelis, Ildiko P. ....Washington, DC
DeAngelis, Jennifer L. ....Tulsa, OK
DeAngelis, John A. ....Chicago, IL
DeAngelis, John L., Jr. ....Melbourne, FL
DeAngelis, John M. ....Greensboro, NC
DeAngelis, Joseph ....Providence, RI
De Angelis, Joseph G. ....Sacramento, CA
DeAngelis, Joseph J. ....Warwick, RI
DeAngelis, Kaplowitz, Murphy, Runion, Fritts & Whiting ....Delmar, NY
DeAngelis, L. Mark ....Los Angeles, CA
DeAngelis Law Firm, The ....Pittsburgh, PA
DeAngelis, Mark E. ....New York, NY
DeAngelis, Mark J. ....Willimantic, CT
De Angelis, Michael A. ....Palo Alto, CA
DeAngelis, Michael A. ....New York, NY
DeAngelis, Michael Gordon
San Francisco, CA
DeAngelis, Patricia A. ....Delmar, NY
DeAngelis, Paul P. ....San Francisco, CA
De Angelis, R. Quinn, Jr. ....Phoenix, AZ
DeAngelis, Regina M. ....San Francisco, CA
De Angelis, Regina M. ....Media, PA
De'Angelis, Richard J. ....Framingham, MA
De Angelis, Richard P., Jr. ....Morristown, NJ
Trenton, NJ
DeAngelis, Robert J. ....New York, NY
DeAngelis, Robert J., Jr. ....Louisville, KY
DeAngelis, Roberta ....Trenton, NJ
DeAngelis, Samuel F. ....Madison, NJ
De Angelo, Charles S. ....Fredonia, NY
Jamestown, NY
DeAngelo, Edward J. ....Boston, MA
DeAngelo, Edward M. ....Cleveland, OH
DeAngelo, Edward S. ....Boardman, OH
DeAngelo, James P. ....Harrisburg, PA
DeAngelo, Kathryn Cook
Surfside Beach, SC
DeAngelo, Kristen M. ....Boston, MA
DeAngelo, Michael ....Boise, ID
DeAngelo, P. Michael ....Columbus, OH
DeAngelo, Paula K. ....Chicago, IL
DeAngelo, Vincent M. ....Bristol, CT
DeAngelo, Walter A. ....New Brunswick, NJ
DeAngelus & DeAngelus ....Clifton Park, NY
De Angelus, Donald J. ....Clifton Park, NY
De Angelus, Ronald P. ....Clifton Park, NY
Deanhardt, W. Clay ....Palo Alto, CA
Deano and Deano ....Mandeville, LA
Deano, Edward J., Jr. ....Mandeville, LA
Deano, Guy L., Jr. ....Mandeville, LA
DeAno, James L. ....Chicago, IL
Wheaton, IL
Dean-Richardson, Laura L. ....Anaheim, CA
Deans & Collins ....Glastonbury, CT
Deans, Dorcas H. ....North Conway, NH
Deans, Errol C., Jr. ....New York, NY
Deans, Gregory L. ....Houston, TX
Deans, James H. ....Salt Lake City, UT
Deans, John B. ....West Hartford, CT
Deans, John E. ....Glastonbury, CT
Deans, Jolyn M. ....Santa Ana, CA
Deans, Kimberly N. ....Elizabethtown, NC
Fayetteville, NC
Jacksonville, NC
New Bern, NC
Shallotte, NC
Wilmington, NC
Deans, Marcia M. ....Raleigh, NC
Deans, Stuart R. ....Stamford, CT
Deans, Thomas S. ....Mendota Heights, MN
Deans, Thomas W. ....Melbourne, FL
Deans, William C. ....Newport Beach, CA
Deans, William C., A Professional Corporation
Newport Beach, CA
DeAntonio Law Firm, L.L.C.
Charleston, SC
DeAntonio, Stephen F. ....Charleston, SC
Dean-Webster, Deanna A.
Indianapolis, IN
Dear, Alan E. ....Alameda, CA
Dear, Diane M. ....Phoenix, AZ
Dear, Jake ....San Francisco, CA
Dear, James F. (Jim) ....Dripping Springs, TX
Dear, John K. ....Kansas City, KS
Dear & Kelley LLP ....Pasadena, CA
Dear, Maureen B. ....Mill Valley, CA
Dear, Richard D. ....Pasadena, CA
Dear, Ronald B. ....Houston, TX
de Arango, Fernando F. ....Greenwich, CT
de Araujo, Roberta L. ....Hallowell, ME
de Araya, Cathleen Colvin ....New York, NY
Dearbaugh, William C. ....Dayton, OH
Dearborn, Amanda P. ....Atlanta, GA
Dearborn, Charles H., III
Mountain View, CA
Dearborn, David ....Cambridge, MA
Dearborn, Henry C. ....White Plains, NY
Dearborn, Joel A. ....Brewer, ME
Dearborn, Luther H. ....Bloomington, IL
Dearborn, Nancy Lawver ....Menlo Park, CA
Dearborn, Philip M., III ....Washington, DC
Dearborn, Richard W. ....Worcester, MA
Dearborn, William H. ....Naples, FL
Dearden, Albert B. ....Arlington, VT
Dearden, Charles C. ....Columbia Falls, MT
Dearden, Ralph D. ....Santa Maria, CA
Deardorff & Associates ....Cincinnati, OH
Deardorff, Craig S. ....Baltimore, MD
Deardorff, Daniel K. ....Carlisle, PA
Deardorff, Dionna D. ....Oklahoma City, OK
Deardorff, Elizabeth K. ....Dallas, TX
Deardorff, Julie A. ....Cincinnati, OH
Deardorff, Michelle H. ....Los Angeles, CA
Deardorff, Robert C. ....Indianapolis, IN
Deardorff, Timothy J. ....Cincinnati, OH
Deardorff, Virginia ....Towson, MD
Deardorff, Yvonne Y. ....Baltimore, MD
Deardurff, Dayle D. ....Cincinnati, OH
De Are, Donald H. ....Greeley, CO
Deare, James D. ....Springdale, AR
Dearie, Christopher F. ....Old Westbury, NY
Dearie, Harold E., II ....Metairie, LA
Dearie, James A. ....Dayton, OH
Dearie, John P., Jr. ....New York, NY
Dearie & Killian ....Metairie, LA
Dearie, Raymond J. ....Brooklyn, NY
Dearien, James N. ....Dallas, TX
Dearing, David Earl ....Indianapolis, IN
Dearing, David P. ....Jacksonville, FL
Dearing, Deborah Carter ....Clayton, MO
Dearing, Dennis A. ....Towson, MD
Dearing and Hartzog, L.C. ....Clayton, MO
Dearing, Henry H. ....Los Angeles, CA
Dearing, James E. ....Clayton, MO
Dearing, James E., Jr. ....Atlanta, GA
Dearing, James M. ....Lexington, KY
Dearing, Jo C. ....Chattanooga, TN
Dearing & Klauber, P.C. ....Atlanta, GA
Dearing, Mark C. ....Jacksonville, FL
Dearing, Melissa A. ....Jacksonville, FL
Dearing, Peter L. ....Jacksonville, FL
Dearing, Robin ....Roanoke, VA
Dearing, Teresa E. ....Indianapolis, IN
Dearing, Theodore D. ....Clayton, MO
Dearing, Thomas C., (P.C.)
Jacksonville, FL
Dearing, Vicki M. ....Jacksonville, FL
Dearing, William R. ....Chattanooga, TN
Dearinger, Jerry W. ....Salt Lake City, UT
Dearington, Michael ....New Haven, CT
Dearlove, Catherine G. ....Wilmington, DE
Dearman, C. Dudley ....Kingwood, TX
Dearman, John E. ....San Francisco, CA
Dearman, William T. ....Houston, TX
De Armas, J. Alfredo ....Coral Gables, FL
de Armas, Luis A. ....Miami, FL
deArmas, Orbein A. ....New York, NY
de Armas, R. David ....Orlando, FL
de Armas, Rafael G. ....Punta Gorda, FL
DeArmas-Ricci, Brenda J. ....New Orleans, LA
DeArment, Claudia ....York, PA
DeArment, Lisa M. ....Lewistown, PA
DeArment, Roderick Allen
Washington, DC
DeArmey, Milo F. ....Santa Ana, CA
Dearmin, Diana M. ....Seattle, WA
Dearmon, A. Delys ....Destin, FL
DeArmon, Edd W., Jr. ....Davidson, NC
DeArmon, Michael J. ....Springfield, MO
DeArmon, Shari Groce ....Springfield, MO
Dearmond, Ann Larsen ....Wasilla, AK
DeArmond, Craig H. ....Danville, IL
De Armond, Forest N., Sr. ....Indio, CA
De Arnavat, Ghislaine Chávez
New York, NY
Dearr, Craig R. ....Miami, FL
Dearr, Craig R., P.A. ....Miami, FL
de Arrigoitia, C. Teresa ....Winter Park, FL
Dears, Elizabeth C. ....Albany, NY
Dearstyne, Donovan D. ....Park Rapids, MN
Dearth, Mark C. ....Upland, CA
Dearth, Markham & Jack, Chartered
Independence, KS
Parsons, KS
Pittsburg, KS
Dearth, Miles B. ....Charlotte, NC
Dearth, Richard C. ....Parsons, KS
Deary, David R. ....Dallas, TX
Houston, TX
Dearybury, Sheila A.
House of Representatives,
Committee on Armed Services, GV
Deas, Brian Timothy ....Columbus, OH
Deas, Charles D. ....Maryville, TN
Deas, John F. ....New Orleans, LA
Deas & Olivier ....Metairie, LA
Deas, Richard A. ....Metairie, LA
Deas, Thomas Allen ....Mobile, AL
Deas, Thomas J. ....Mineola, NY
Deas, Vergil Ard ....Summerville, SC
Deas, William G. ....Dayton, OH
Deas, William J. ....Jacksonville, FL
Deas, William J., P.A. ....Jacksonville, FL
DeAscentis, Arthur M. ....Fall River, MA
Mattapoisett, MA
de Ases, Eduardo E. ....Corpus Christi, TX
Deasey, Francis J. ....Philadelphia, PA
Deasey, Mahoney & Bender, Ltd.
Haddonfield, NJ
Philadelphia, PA
Deason, Chance H. ....Nashville, TN
Deason, Charles A., Jr. ....Las Cruces, NM
Deason, Charles A., Jr. ....El Paso, TX
Deason, Donald L. ....Oklahoma City, OK
Deason, Edward J. ....Los Angeles, CA
Deason, Edward J. ....Torrance, CA
Deason, George T. ....New York, NY
Deason, Herold McC. ....Detroit, MI
Deason, James R. ....Portland, OR
Deason, Lawrence L. ....Yuma, AZ
Deason, Lawrence L., Ltd. ....Yuma, AZ
Deason, Marshall C., Jr. ....Tampa, FL
Deason, Susan Bryant ....Los Angeles, CA
Deason, Tina Taylor ....Oklahoma City, OK
Deasy & Dwyer, P.A. ....Nashua, NH
Deasy, J. Michael ....Manchester, NH
Deasy, James D. ....Philadelphia, PA
Deasy, John F. ....Pittsburgh, PA
Deasy, Michael J. ....Wausau, WI
Deasy, Michael P. ....Mystic, CT
Deasy, Oonagh L. ....Washington, DC
Deatherage, H. Kenneth ....Kingston, TN
Deatherage, James W. ....Irving, TX
Deatherage, Loral ....Phoenix, AZ
Deatherage, Loral, P.C. ....Phoenix, AZ
Deatherage, Marion ....Lakewood, CA
Deatherage, Mark ....Phoenix, AZ
Deatherage, Myers, Self & Lackey
Cadiz, KY
Hopkinsville, KY
Deatherage, Scott D. ....Dallas, TX
Deatherage, Stephen Forrest
Portland, OR
Deatherage, Susan N. ....Collinsville, VA
Deatherage, Todd W. ....Dallas, TX
Deatherage, William G., Jr.
Hopkinsville, KY
Deatherage, William V. ....Medford, OR
DeAtley, James H. ....San Antonio, TX
Deaton, Alfred L. ....Houston, TX
Deaton, Alfred L., III ....Houston, TX
Deaton and Allen ....Tarpon Springs, FL
Deaton, Austin R., Jr. ....Ada, OK
Deaton & Biggers, P.L.L.C. ....Shelby, NC
Deaton, Cary J. ....New Orleans, LA
Deaton, Charles M. ....Greenwood, MS
Deaton, Chris H. ....Tupelo, MS
Deaton, Christine A. ....Atherton, CA
Deaton, Dana G. ....Tupelo, MS
Deaton, Daniel M. ....Houston, TX
Deaton, David B. ....Houston, TX
Deaton, Davison & Kessinger, A Professional Corporation ....Ada, OK
Deaton & Deaton, P.A. ....Tupelo, MS
Deaton, Douglas R. ....Greensboro, NC
Deaton, Evelyn L. ....San Francisco, CA
Deaton, J. Reno ....Cincinnati, OH
Deaton, James F. ....Okemah, OK
Deaton, Janice M. ....San Diego, CA
Deaton, Jo Anne ....Tulsa, OK
Deaton, Joe S., III ....Jackson, MS
Deaton, Kenneth D. ....Columbus, GA
Deaton, Margaret E. ....Tarpon Springs, FL
Deaton, Maria F. ....Yuma, AZ
Deaton, Mark D. ....Naperville, IL
Deaton, Michael F. ....Lexington, KY
Deaton, Nathan Brian ....Hazlehurst, GA
Deaton, Paul ....Paintsville, KY
Deaton, Robert E. ....Suffolk, VA
Deaton, Stephen B. ....Charlottesville, VA
Deaton, Steven A. ....Tulsa, OK
Deaton, Theodore E. ....Bellevue, WA
Deaton, Thomas Patrick, Jr.
St. Louis, MO
Deaton, Thomas W. ....Lufkin, TX
Deaton, W. Edward ....Reidsville, NC
Deaton, W. Robinson, Jr. ....Shelby, NC
Deaton, Wesley L. ....Lincolnton, NC
Deaton, William W., Jr. ....Albuquerque, NM
Deatrick, David R., Jr. ....Louisville, KY
Deatrick, Sherry R. ....Louisville, KY
Deatrick & Spies, P.S.C. ....Louisville, KY
Deats, B. Craig ....Austin, TX
Fort Worth, TX

deCamara, Donald M. ... El Cajon, CA
De Camara, Jennifer M. ... New York, NY
De Camillis, John A. ... Louisville, KY
DeCamp, Allen, Jr. ... Kansas City, MO
DeCamp, Antoinette ... Los Angeles, CA
DeCamp, Clifford L. ... Akron, OH
de Camp, Donald T. ... Bakersfield, CA
DeCamp, Michael L. ... St. Louis, MO
DeCamp, Patterson A. ... Lexington, KY
DeCamp, Paul ... Los Angeles, CA
DeCamp, Richard R. ... Fort Wayne, IN
DeCamp, Roth & Michael ... Akron, OH
DeCampo, Diamond & Ash
New York, NY
DeCampo, Joseph A. ... New York, NY
DeCamps, C. Michael ... Richmond, VA
DeCandia, Anthony ... Hackensack, NJ
DeCandia, Donald A. ... Albuquerque, NM
DeCandia, Robert F. ... Union, NJ
Decandia, Stephanie Maria ... Boston, MA
DeCandido, William V. ... Forest Hills, NY
DeCandio, Michael J. ... Jacksonville, FL
DeCann, Andrew P. ... Tulsa, OK
DeCant, Cher ... Santa Ana, CA
Decapio, Thomas J. ... Weirton, WV
De Capito, Alberta ... Warren, OH
De Capo, Thomas A. ... Boston, MA
DeCaporale, Joseph L., Jr. ... Providence, RI
DeCaprio, Dolores D. ... Vero Beach, FL
DeCaprio, M. Fred ... Hartford, CT
Decapua, Gerard A. ... Rockville Centre, NY
DeCapua, Michael F. ... Newark, NJ
De Capua, Pacifico M. ... Milford, MA
De Carbonnières, Tanguy
Washington, DC
de Cardenas, Alberto I. ... Miami, FL
De Cardenas, Mario E. ... Miami, FL
de Cardona, Lisa Ann ... Department of Justice, Executive Office for Immigration Review, GV
DeCardy, William D. ... Bloomington, IL
Decaria, Mark R. ... Ogden, UT
Decaria, Mary Anne ... Reno, NV
de Carion, David P. ... San Jose, CA
DeCarion, George H. ... Coral Gables, FL
DeCarion, George H., P.A. ... Coral Gables, FL
deCaris, Mario ... Cleveland, OH
DeCarli & Irwin ... Austin, TX
DeCarli, Robert C. ... Austin, TX
De Carli, Silvio J. ... Wilmington, DE
DeCarlis, William N. ... Gainesville, FL
Ocala, FL
DeCarlis, William N., P.A. ... Gainesville, FL
Ocala, FL
DeCarlo, Connor & Selvo, A Professional Corporation ... Los Angeles, CA
De Carlo, Connor & Selvo, A Professional Corporation ... Washington, DC
DeCarlo, Daniel C. ... Los Angeles, CA
De Carlo, Donald T. ... New York, NY
DeCarlo, Frank ... Pittsburgh, PA
DeCarlo, Gioia ... Framingham, MA
DeCarlo, Jacqueline ... Middletown, NJ
DeCarlo, James J. ... New York, NY
DeCarlo, Jeffrey D. ... Miami, FL
DeCarlo, Jeffrey D. ... Miami, FL
DeCarlo, John H. ... Rochester, MI
De Carlo, John Paul ... Birmingham, AL
DeCarlo, John T. ... Los Angeles, CA
DeCarlo, Joseph, Jr. ... New York, NY
DeCarlo, Kari Dawn ... Akron, OH
DeCarlo, Kean J. ... Atlanta, GA
De Carlo, Luciana M. ... Long Island City, NY
DeCarlo, Michael ... Akron, OH
DeCarlo, Michael ... Tulsa, OK
DeCarlo, Michael J. ... Washington, DC
Decarlo, Nicholas ... Washington, DC
De Carlo, Patricia L. ... San Juan, PR
De Carlo, Paul M. ... Staten Island, NY
DeCarlo, Paul R. ... Garden City, NY
DeCarlo, Thomas D. ... West Palm Beach, FL
DeCarlo, Thomas D., P.A.
West Palm Beach, FL
DeCarlo, Vito D. ... Chicago, IL
DeCarlo, Vito D., P.C. ... Chicago, IL
DeCarlo, William S. ... Chicago, IL
De Carmine, India ... New York, NY
DeCaro, A. Roy ... Philadelphia, PA
DeCaro, Barbara Morlan ... Los Gatos, CA
DeCaro, Dennis J. ... Chicago, IL
DeCaro, Doran, Siciliano, Gallagher & DeBlasis, LLP ... Washington, DC
Lanham, MD
Upper Marlboro, MD
Alexandria, VA
De Caro, Francis M. ... Bronx, NY
DeCaro, Jeffrey R. ... Lanham, MD
DeCaro, John J., Jr. ... New Castle, PA
De Caro, Philip A. ... Purchase, NY
DeCaro, Phillip S. ... Colorado Springs, CO
DeCaro, Phillip S., A Prof. Corp., Law Offices of ... Colorado Springs, CO
De Caro, Shana ... New York, NY
De Caro, Thomas G. ... Purchase, NY
DeCarolis, Mary Ann ... New York, NY
DeCarolis, Patrick, Jr. ... Los Angeles, CA
De Carolis, Paul M. ... Nashua, NH
DeCarolis, Saenz & Trope, LLP
Los Angeles, CA
de Carvalho, Eunice P. ... Minneapolis, MN
Decas, George C. ... Middleboro, MA
Wareham, MA
Decas, Murray & Decas ... Middleboro, MA
Wareham, MA
Decas, William C. ... Middleboro, MA
De Castro, Alfredo F. ... Miami, FL
de Castro, Ana M. ... Burbank, CA
DeCastro, Bernadette ... Newark, NJ
de Castro, Hugo D. ... Los Angeles, CA
de Castro, J. Edmund, Jr. ... Buffalo, NY
De Castro, Luis C. ... Santa Monica, CA
DeCastro, Mark J. ... San Jose, CA
DeCastro, Michelle ... Chico, CA
de Castro, Teresa C. ... Seattle, WA
de Castro, Thomas Rui ... New York, NY
de Castro, Vicki Fern ... Modesto, CA
De Castro, West, Chodorow, Glickfeld & Nass, Inc. ... Los Angeles, CA
Decataldo and Decataldo ... Schenectady, NY
Decataldo, Kathleen R. ... Schenectady, NY
Decataldo, Robert T. ... Schenectady, NY
de Catalogne, Bettina ... New York, NY
Decato Law Offices ... West Lebanon, NH
Decato, R. Peter ... Lebanon, NH
West Lebanon, NH
Decator, Eric R. ... Chicago, IL
Decator, Jay A., III ... Viera, FL
DeCaulp, Bobara E. ... Oklahoma City, OK
Decea, Nanette E. ... Elmsford, NY
Decea, Thomas B. ... White Plains, NY
DeCecco, Joseph R. ... Sheboygan, WI
Dececco, Lisa L. ... Pittsburgh, PA
DeCell, Jane B.
Department of Transportation, Office of the General Counsel, GV
DeCelle, Malcolm E., Jr. ... West Monroe, LA
DeCelles, David ... Arlington, MA
DeCelles, Gerard M. ... Smithfield, RI
Decello, Anthony D. ... Cleveland, OH
Decena, M. Virginia ... New York, NY
Decensi, Patricia Marie Bunn
Cleveland, OH
DeCenso, Weber & Knapp ... Cincinnati, OH
De Censo, William A. ... Cincinnati, OH
DeCenzo, Paul D. ... Framingham, MA
DeCerbo, David ... Garden City, NY
de Cervens, Jeanne ... Baltimore, MD
Decesare, Dale Marino ... Denver, CO
DeCesare, Jim L. ... Midland, MI
De Cesare, Nicholas, Jr. ... Flushing, NY
DeCesare, Vincent A. ... Providence, RI
DeCesare-Treitler, Diana ... Jersey City, NJ
New York, NY
DeCesaris, Annette ... Bowie, MD
DeCessna, Donald A. ... Bowling Green, OH
DeCew, Annine M. ... Santa Monica, CA
De Cew, Sperry A. ... New Canaan, CT
Dech, Janet E. ... Oklahoma City, OK
Dech, Merle R., Jr. ... Toledo, OH
Dech, Robert W. ... Annandale, VA
Dech and Welther ... Annandale, VA
de Chabert, Gisele F. ... New York, NY
DeChaine, Dean D., P.C. ... Portland, OR
DeChaine, John R. ... Santa Rosa, CA
De Chambeau, Robert A. ... Madison, WI
DeChance, Paul Michael ... Woodbury, NY
Dechant, Donald ... San Diego, CA
Dechant, Donald J. ... La Jolla, CA
Dechant, Edmund B. ... Santa Rosa, CA
Dechant, Maurice L. ... Grand Junction, CO
De Chant, Thomas H. ... Cleveland, OH
De Charles, Patrick Michael, II
New York, NY
de Chateauvieux, Charles M. ... Dallas, TX
DeChazal, Claire D. ... Chicago, IL
De Chellis, Robert ... Clinton, NJ
DeChello, Anthony R. ... New Haven, CT
Dechene, James C. ... Chicago, IL
De Cherrie, Robert T. ... Chicago, IL
Dechert Price & Rhoads ... Hartford, CT
Washington, DC
Boston, MA
Princeton, NJ
New York, NY
Harrisburg, PA
Philadelphia, PA
Dechery, Laurie J. ... Minneapolis, MN
De Chiara, Adam C. ... New York, NY
DeChiara, Dominick P. ... New York, NY
De Chiara, Michael K. ... New York, NY
DeChiara, Peter D. ... New York, NY
DeChicco, Mari ... New Albany, OH
Dechman, Lynne Le Vee ... Chattanooga, TN
Dechovitz, Susan L. ... Miami, FL
Dechow, Gerald A. ... Roanoke, VA
Dechter, Eugene E. ... Chicago, IL
Dechter, Hyman ... Brooklyn, NY
Dechter, Mitchell ... Waterford, MI
Dechter, Nathan ... Long Beach, NY
DeChurch, James Douglas ... Miami, FL
DeCiantis, Joseph R. ... Venice, FL
DeCiantis, Joseph R., P.C. ... Venice, FL
DeCiccio, Daniel ... Winter Park, FL
DeCiccio, Johnson, Herzfeld & Rubin
Winter Park, FL
DeCiccio, Sheila Gupta ... Winter Park, FL
De Cicco, Andrew ... Santa Ana, CA
DeCicco, Anthony J. ... Long Beach, NY
DeCicco, Fred A. ... New York, NY
De Cicco, Gibbons & McNamara, P.C.
New York, NY
deCicco, Jack M. ... Albertson, NY
De Cicco, John J. ... Newark, NJ
DeCicco, John R., Jr. ... Bound Brook, NJ
Decicco, Mark J. ... Garden City, NY
DeCicco, Michelle Anne ... Overland Park, KS
Decicco, Philip A. ... Hicksville, NY
De Cicco, Philip A. ... New York, NY
DeCicco, Philip M. ... Bronx, NY
De Cicco, Roy C. ... New York, NY
DeCicco, William A.
Department of the Navy, Office of the Judge Advocate General, GV
Decie, Kevin C. ... Teaneck, NJ
Decile, Jeffrey Mark ... Columbus, OH
Decillis, Leslie R. ... Fort Worth, TX
DeCillis, Steven B. ... Durham, NC
DeCinti, James ... Harrisburg, PA
De Cintio, Anthony J. ... Ozone Park, NY
Decio, Jamee ... Los Angeles, CA
Decius, Scott A. ... Farmington Hills, MI
DeCiutiis, Joseph C. ... New York, NY
Deck, Alice A. ... Wayne, PA
Deck & Baron ... Kankakee, IL
Deck, Carol A. ... Denver, CO
Deck, Dayna F. ... St. Louis, MO
Deck & Deck ... Sioux City, IA
Deck, Gary L. ... Abington, PA
Deck, Gregory A. ... Kankakee, IL
Deck, Louis J. ... Martinsville, NJ
Deck, Lucky G. ... Indianapolis, IN
Deck, Michael S. (Steve) ... McAllen, TX
Deck, Paul W., Jr. ... Sioux City, IA
Deck, Paul W., Sr. ... Sioux City, IA
Deck, Robert B. ... Sioux City, IA
Deck, Susan Marie ... New Hyde Park, NY
Deck, William G. ... Sioux City, IA
Deckard, Diane C. ... Alameda, CA
San Jose, CA
Deckard, Harry W. ... Austin, TX
Deckard, John G. ... Indianapolis, IN
Deckard Law Firm, The ... Alameda, CA
San Jose, CA
Deckard & O'Brien ... Danville, IN
Deckbar, Daniel C. ... Atlanta, GA
Deckelbaum, Ariel J. ... New York, NY
Deckelbaum, David A. ... Washington, DC
Deckelbaum, Gerald E. ... Portland, OR
Deckelbaum, Nelson ... Bethesda, MD
Deckelbaum Ogens Reiser Shedlock & Raftery, Chartered ... Bethesda, MD
Deckelman, Arthur D. ... Palm Harbor, FL
Deckelman, Arthur D., & Associates, P.A.
Palm Harbor, FL
Deckelman, William L., Jr. ... Austin, TX
Decker, Adam D. ... Crown Point, IN
Decker, Alan B. ... New York, NY
Decker, Amy Michelle ... Wichita, KS
Decker, Amy VanVarick ... Parsippany, NJ
Decker, Andrew J. ... Arlington, VA
Decker, Andrew J., III ... Live Oak, FL
Decker, Andrew J., III, P.A. ... Live Oak, FL
Decker, Ann E. ... Rochester, MN
Decker, Antoinette ... Los Angeles, CA
Decker, Arnold ... Marlboro, NJ
Decker, Arthur W., Jr. ... Staten Island, NY
Decker & Associates ... Houston, TX
Decker, Bruce L., Jr. ... Erie, PA
Decker, Bryan C. ... Boston, MA
Decker, Byrne J. ... Portland, ME
Decker, Cardon, Thomas, Weintraub & Neskis ... Norfolk, VA
Decker, Carey D. ... Chicago, IL
Decker, Carmel Joy ... Livingston, NJ
Decker, Catherine E. ... Portland, ME
Decker, Charles D. ... Dothan, AL
Decker, Charles F. ... Treasure Island, FL
Decker, Charles W. ... Gualala, CA
Decker, Christopher Randolph
Colorado Springs, CO
Decker, Christopher Shawn ... Chesapeake, VA
Decker, Clarence A. ... Englewood, CO
Decker, Constance Gorman
Huntsville, TX
Decker, D. Lee ... Phoenix, AZ
Decker & Darcy ... Middletown, NY
Decker, David A. ... Waukegan, IL
Decker, David J. ... Hollywood, CA
Decker, David R. ... Los Angeles, CA
Decker, Deborah E. ... Chicago, IL
Decker, Devon H. ... Houston, TX
Decker, Donald L. ... Terre Haute, IN
Decker, Doug ... Albuquerque, NM
Decker, Doug ... Pierre, SD
Decker, Elizabeth Bernstein ... Hazleton, PA
Decker, Francis K., Jr. ... New York, NY
Decker, Frank A. ... Cobleskill, NY
Decker, Frank C., (P.A.) ... Jacksonville, FL
Decker, Frank N., Jr. ... Fayetteville, NY
Decker, Fred D. ... Filer City, ID
Decker, Gary Scott ... Sacramento, CA
Decker, George A. ... Detroit, MI
Decker, George K. ... Westbury, NY
Decker, George T. ... Endwell, NY
Decker, Gregory L. ... Spokane, WA
Decker & Hallman ... Atlanta, GA
Decker, Harold J. ... Bridgewater, NJ
Decker, Heather Wright ... Portland, OR
Decker, Heidi T. ... Portland, OR
Decker Hubbard Welden & Sweeney
New York, NY
Decker, Ira J. ... Parsippany, NJ
Decker, Jack W. ... Columbus, OH
Decker, James D. ... Anchorage, AK
Decker, James G. ... Fort Myers, FL
Decker, James H., Jr. ... Trevose, PA
Decker, Jannell L. ... Wilkes-Barre, PA
Decker, Jarett B. ... Minneapolis, MN
Decker, Jason A. ... Fresno, CA
Decker, Jeffrey E. ... Orlando, FL
Decker, Jennifer Henson ... Louisville, KY
Decker, Jennifer L. ... Buffalo, NY
Decker, Jerry M. ... Jamaica, NY
Decker, John A. ... Saginaw, MI
Decker, John A. ... Milwaukee, WI
Decker, John C., II ... Burke, VA
Decker, John E. ... Melbourne, FL
Decker, John F. ... Chicago, IL
Decker, John L. ... Lincoln, NE
Decker, John R. ... Tulsa, OK
Decker, John S. ... Washington, DC
Decker, Jones, McMackin, McClane, Hall & Bates, A Professional Corporation
Dallas, TX
Fort Worth, TX
Decker, Joseph ... Pittsburgh, PA
Decker, Joseph P. ... Pittsburgh, PA
Decker, Julia J. ... Houston, TX
Decker, Karl R. ... Idaho Falls, ID
Decker, Kathryn M. ... Morristown, NJ
Decker, Katrina C. ... Oakland, CA
Decker, Ken C. ... South Bend, IN
Decker, Kimberly J. ... Hanover, PA
York, PA
Decker, Kristin D. ... Charlotte, NC
Decker, Kurt E. ... Tallahassee, FL
Decker, Kurt H. ... Reading, PA
Decker, Laura L. ... Princeton, NJ
Decker & Lawyer ... Anderson, IN
Decker, Lee A. ... East Lansing, MI
Flint, MI
Decker & Linn, Ltd. ... Waukegan, IL
Decker, Lisa Kay ... Indianapolis, IN
Decker, Lisa M. ... Baltimore, MD
Decker, L. J. "Jim" ... Houston, TX
Decker, L. J. "Mike", III ... Houston, TX
Decker, Lori W. ... Toledo, OH
Decker, M. Lee ... Chesterfield, VA
Decker, Marcia J.
Research Triangle Park, NC
Decker, Mariam W. ... Columbia, MO
Decker, Mark ... Groveport, OH
Decker, Mark Gordon ... Brooklyn, NY
Decker, Mark R. ... Westfield, NJ
Decker, Marla Graff ... Richmond, VA
Decker, Martin E. ... St. Paul, MN
Decker, Mary Clare ... Providence, RI
Decker, Mary J. ... Los Angeles, CA
Decker, Melinda M. ... Hartford, CT
Decker, Melissa M. ... Los Angeles, CA
Decker, Michael E. ... Toledo, OH
Decker, Michael J. ... Denver, CO
Decker, Michael J. ... Omaha, NE
Decker, Michael Kenneth
Coral Gables, FL
Decker, Michael L. ... Oklahoma City, OK
Decker, Norman E. ... Los Angeles, CA
Decker, Peter G., III ... Norfolk, VA
Decker, Peter G., Jr. ... Norfolk, VA
Decker, Philip E. ... San Jose, CA
Decker, Philip E., P.C. ... San Jose, CA
Decker, Philip G., II ... Anderson, IN
Decker, Phillip ... New Durham, NH
Decker & Quattlebaum, L.L.P.
Houston, TX
Decker, R. Grant ... McLean, VA
Decker, R. Joseph ... Long Beach, CA
Decker, Rachel Scott ... Greensboro, NC
Decker, Ralph G., (P.A.) ... Orlando, FL
Decker, Randall K. ... Tucson, AZ
Decker, Randy L. ... Minneapolis, MN
Decker, Raymond Henry, Jr.
Covington, KY
Decker, Rex H. ... Chandler, AZ
Decker, Richard J. ... Los Angeles, CA
Decker, Richard P. ... Atlanta, GA
Decker, Robert C. ... St. Petersburg, FL
Tampa, FL
Decker, Robert E. ... San Francisco, CA
Decker, Robert G. ... Omaha, NE
Decker, Robert J. ... Cambridge, MA
Decker, Robert S. ... Chicago, IL
Decker, Robert W. ... Fort Worth, TX
Decker, Roger C. ... Mesa, AZ
Decker, Ronald A. ... Baltimore, MD
Decker, Ronald O. ... Oak Park, IL
Decker, Ryan W. ... Philadelphia, PA
Decker, Scott A. ... New Orleans, LA
Decker, Scott A. ... Everett, WA
Decker, Scott T. ... Daytona Beach, FL
Decker, Stephen O. ... Tampa, FL
Decker, Steven R. ... Chicago, IL
Decker, Susan E. ... Binghamton, NY
Decker, Suzzanne W. ... Baltimore, MD
Decker, Tarrell S. ... Bainbridge Island, WA
Decker, Teresa S. ... Grand Rapids, MI
Decker, Theodore ... Copiague, NY
Decker, Thomas A. ... Berwyn, PA
Decker, Thomas D. ... Chicago, IL
Decker, Thomas D., and Associates, Ltd.
Chicago, IL
Decker, Thomas J. ... Millburn, NJ
Decker, Vernon L. ... El Paso, TX
Decker, Victor A., III ... Hawley, PA
Decker, Vonau, Sybert, Lackey & Viets Co., L.P.A. ... Groveport, OH
Decker, Wendy R. ... Baton Rouge, LA
Decker, William S., II ... Jersey City, NJ
Decker, William W., Jr.
Farmington Hills, MI
Grand Rapids, MI
Decker, William W., Jr., P.C.
Grand Rapids, MI
Decker, Wilmot ... Middletown, NY
Decker, Wm. D. ... Galveston, TX
Decker and Woods ... Chandler, AZ
Deckert, Gregory W. ... Minneapolis, MN
Deckert, James R. ... Kansas City, MO
Deckert, Raymond R. ... Valrico, FL
Deckert, Timothy R. ... Harrisburg, PA
Deckhut, Joseph A. ... Spring Lake, NJ
Deckinger, Harold ... Pompano Beach, FL
Deckinger, Nancy J. ... New York, NY
Deckman, Adrienne L. ... Cleveland, OH
Deckman, Lawrence G. ... Eugene, OR
Deckman, Michael R. ... Mount Wolf, PA
Deckman, William L. ... Mayfield Heights, OH
Decko, Kenneth O. ... Hartford, CT
Deckoff, Marvin J. ... New York, NY

Deckro, Stephen A. ... Morrison, IL
Deckter, Louis L. ... Tucson, AZ
Deckter, Louis L., P.C. ... Tucson, AZ
deClaire, George F. ... Boca Raton, FL
DeClaire, Lawrence A. ... Denver, CO
DeClark, Candice R. ... Middletown, OH
Declark, Peter O. ... Toledo, OH
de Clef Piñeiro, John ... New York, NY
DeClement, David M. ... Pitman, NJ
DeClerck, Edward A. ... Enid, OK
DeClerck, Richard A. ... Portland, OR
DeClerck, Russell ... New York, NY
Tarrytown, NY
DeClerck, Tim E. ... Enid, OK
Declet, Carlos M. ... San Juan, PR
Declet, Rafael A., Jr. ... New York, NY
DeCleva, Paul, Jr. ... Dallas, TX
De Clue, Albert S. ... Bainbridge, NY
DeClue, Curtis L. ... Indianapolis, IN
De Clue, David A. ... Bainbridge, NY
de Clue, David Marshall ... St. Louis, MO
Declues, J. Michael ... Santa Ana, CA
DeCluitt, Kristi D. ... College Station, TX
Decocq, Paul L. ... Howell, MI
Decof & Grimm, A Professional Corporation
Newport, RI
Providence, RI
Decof, Leonard ... Newport, RI
Providence, RI
Decof, Mark B. ... Providence, RI
Decolator, John V. ... Lake Success, NY
Decolator, Joseph L. ... Lake Success, NY
DeColibus, Amy M. ... Cleveland, OH
Decolvenaere, Frank D. ... New York, NY
DeConca, Richard A. ... Red Bank, NJ
DeConcilis, Patricia A. ... Monessen, PA
DeConcini, Christina ... Washington, DC
DeConcini, Dennis ... Washington, DC
Deconcini, Matthew D ... Washington, DC
DeConcini McDonald Yetwin & Lacy, P.C.
Phoenix, AZ
Tucson, AZ
Washington, DC
DeConti, Elizabeth A. ... Tampa, FL
DeConti, Giulio A., Jr. ... Boston, MA
DeConti, Merlin A. ... Cranston, RI
DeCook, Brian F. ... Lombard, IL
Matteson, IL
DeCook, Rebecca B. ... Denver, CO
Decora, Andrew W. ... Laramie, WY
DeCorato, Linda J. ... New York, NY
DeCordova, Donald L. ... Beaumont, TX
de Cordova, Donald W. ... Hackensack, NJ
deCordova, Noel, Jr. ... Poughkeepsie, NY
DeCore, Julianne K. ... Trenton, NJ
Decorie, Clyde W. ... Springfield, MA
De Corso, Anthony A. ... Los Angeles, CA
De Corso, Nicholas ... Anaheim, CA
DeCort, Donald P. ... Tampa, FL
DeCosky, Richard L., Jr. ... Lakewood, OH
DeCosse, Stephen J. ... San Francisco, CA
DeCosta, Frank A., III ... Washington, DC
DeCosta, Janet K. ... Washington, DC
DeCosta, Janet K., P.C. ... Washington, DC
de Costa, Karl ... Los Angeles, CA
Decosta, Steven C. ... New York, NY
De Costa, Virginia L. ... Tacoma, WA
DeCoster, Barbara M. ... Chicago, IL
DeCoster, Jules V. ... Monticello, MO
de Coster, Lawrence O.
Rolling Hills Estates, CA
DeCoster, Paul H. ... New York, NY
De Coster, Richard J. ... Canton, MO
DeCoteau, Jerilyn A. ... Denver, CO
De Coteau, Pamela L. ... Glen Burnie, MD
DeCotiis, Alfred C. ... Teaneck, NJ
De Cotiis, Daniel C. ... West Trenton, NJ
DeCotiis, Fitzpatrick & Gluck, LLP
Ramsey, NJ
Sayreville, NJ
Teaneck, NJ
Trenton, NJ
DeCotiis, Joseph M. ... Teaneck, NJ
DeCotiis, M. Robert ... Teaneck, NJ
Trenton, NJ
DeCotiis, Michael R. ... Teaneck, NJ
DeCotis, Henry A. ... Albany, NY
DeCou, Richard T. ... Mount Laurel, NJ
DeCoudres, Don G. ... Birmingham, AL
Decoulos & Decoulos ... Peabody, MA
Decoulos, James N. ... Peabody, MA
Decoulos, Nicholas J. ... Peabody, MA
DeCourcey, James M. ... Grants Pass, OR
Decourcey, Stephen W. ... Boston, MA
DeCourcy, Dara A. ... Pittsburgh, PA
de Courcy, Felicia H. ... Tazewell, VA
De Courcy, Michael ... Franklin, IN
DeCourcy, Michael T. ... St. Paul, MN
DeCoursey, Eleanor M. ... Glenville, NY
De Coursey, James H., Jr. ... Topeka, KS
DeCoursey, John Paul ... Wichita, KS
DeCoursey, Kevin J. ... Whippany, NJ
De Coursey, Robert A. ... Kansas City, KS
DeCoursey, Susan Perry ... Kansas City, MO
DeCoursey, Thomas ... Kansas City, KS
DeCourt, Jill M. ... New Iberia, LA
DeCourval-Freedman, Mary ... Flint, MI
DeCoux & DeCoux ... Houston, TX
DeCoux, Elizabeth L. ... Indianapolis, IN
DeCoux, Jacque ... Houston, TX
DeCoux, Jeanne C. ... Houston, TX
DeCrane, Alfred C., Jr. ... White Plains, NY
DeCresce, Joseph P. ... Springfield, MA
DeCrescenzo, Robert M. ... Hartford, CT
Decreus, Walda M. ... New York, NY
DeCristo, Lorraine S. ... Sherman Oaks, CA
Decristofaro, Daniel ... Medford, MA
De Cristofaro, Elizabeth M.
New York, NY
DeCristoforo, Anthony J.
Sacramento, CA
DeCristoforo, Anthony, Jr. ... Sacramento, CA
DeCristoforo, Cheryl A. ... Hopedale, MA
DeCristoforo, Michele M. ... Sacramento, CA
DeCristopher, Joseph R. ... Sunbury, PA
De Croce, Alexander M., Jr.
Syracuse, NY
Decroo, Audrey A. ... Carlsbad, CA
DeCross, Karen Kinberg ... Rochester, NY
Decrosta, Anthony E. ... Hartford, CT
DeCrow, Karen ... Jamesville, NY
de Cruz, Sonia, (P.A.) ... Miami, FL
Dector, Andrew M. ... Boca Raton, FL
DeCubellis, Daniel L. ... Orlando, FL
DeCubellis, Frederick A. ... New Bedford, MA
DeCubellis & Meeks, P.A. ... Orlando, FL
DeCuir, Charles Arthur ... Folsom, CA
De Cuir, Dennis W. ... Sacramento, CA
Decuir, Donna T. Budwin
Citrus Heights, CA
Decuir, Jon S. ... New Iberia, LA
Decuir, Oswald A. ... New Iberia, LA
DeCuir, Robert D. ... Treasury Department, Office of Thrift Supervision, GV
De Cuir & Somach, A Professional Corporation ... Sacramento, CA
DeCuir, Winston G. ... Baton Rouge, LA
DeCuir, Winston G., & Associates
Baton Rouge, LA
DeCuir, Winston G., Jr. ... New Orleans, LA
DeCusati, Albert J. ... Atlanta, GA
DeCusatis, Anthony C. ... Philadelphia, PA
Decusatis, Gerard C. ... Amsterdam, NY
Decuyper, Joseph Y., Jr. ... Kansas City, MO
DeCuyper, Joseph Y., Sr. ... Kansas City, MO
DeCuzzi, James ... New York, NY
Decyk, Julian B. ... Los Angeles, CA
Decyk, Roxanne J. ... Chicago, IL
Deda, David ... Phillips, WI
De Dakis, N. George ... Marietta, GA
Deddens, Darcy L. ... Toledo, OH
Deddens, Randy L. ... Louisville, KY
Deddens, Robert L. ... Dayton, OH
Dedekam, Robert C. ... Eureka, CA
Dedenbach, Marc T. ... Haslett, MI
DeDent, Pamela A. ... Columbus, OH
De Deo, Carol A. ... Department of Labor, Office of the Solicitor, GV
De Deo, James F. ... Fairfax, VA
Dederer, Anne C. ... Seattle, WA
Dederer, James W. ... Los Angeles, CA
Dederick, Gerald G. ... Minneapolis, MN
Dederick, Mary J. ... Pasadena, CA
Dederick, Ronald Osburn ... Greenwich, CT
Stamford, CT
Dedes, William C. ... Rochester, NY
DeDeyn, Carey P. ... Atlanta, GA
DeDiana, L. Christian ... Greensburg, PA
De Die, Ann Marie ... Walnut Creek, CA
De Diego, Armando ... Dallas, TX
De Diego, Armando, P.C., The Law Offices of
Dallas, TX
De Diego-Collar, Alberto ... San Juan, PR
Dedina, Josephine A. ... Imperial Beach, CA
Dedina, Steven J. ... Palm Desert, CA
Dedinas, Vilia M. ... Chicago, IL
Dedinsky, Scott C. ... Omaha, NE
de Dios, Gonzalo ... Washington, DC
Deditch, Aaron C. ... Iselin, NJ
New York, NY
Dedman, David A. ... Bethesda, MD
Dedman, F. William, Jr. ... Sacramento, CA
Dedman, James C. ... Urbana, IL
Dedman, James M., III ... Houston, TX
Dedman, Linda T. ... Dallas, TX
Dedman, Marc O. ... Nashville, TN
Dedman, Robt. H. ... Dallas, TX
Dedmon, Charles D. ... Topeka, KS
Dedmon, Dean P. ... Dyersburg, TN
Dedmon, Judith ... Dallas, TX
Dedmon, Shelly G. ... Cleveland, OH
Dedmond, Richard E.
Southern Pines, NC
Dedmond, Sybil J. ... Pensacola, FL
Dedo, Drew J. ... Philadelphia, PA
DeDobbelaere, Lori K. ... Portland, OR
Dedola, Anthony S., Jr. ... Uniontown, PA
De Dolph, Scott ... Fort Collins, CO
DeDomenico, Dennis T. ... Pleasanton, CA
de Domínguez, Carmen Irizarry
San Juan, PR
de Dominici, Paula G. ... Hackensack, NJ
New York, NY
DeDominicis, Felicia ... Hartford, CT
Dedon, John P. ... Fairfax, VA
DeDonato, Joseph ... Livingston, NJ
DeDoncker, David ... Moline, IL
DeDoncker, John D. ... Davenport, IA
Dedopoulos, Stuart ... Durham, NH
Dedrick, D. Fred ... Fort Lauderdale, FL
Dedrick, Katherine Smith ... Chicago, IL
Dedvukaj, Joseph ... Southfield, MI
Dedvukaj, Joseph, P.C. ... Southfield, MI
Dedyo, David F. ... San Francisco, CA
Dedyo, John J. ... New York, NY
Dee, Christopher ... New York, NY
Dee, David A. ... Hartford, CT
Dee, David A. ... Tampa, FL
Dee, David B. ... Salt Lake City, UT
Dee, David S. ... Tallahassee, FL
Dee, Debra S. ... Hebron, CT
Dee, Dennis J. ... Buffalo, NY
Dee, Dennis J., Jr. ... New York, NY
Dee, Elizabeth Anne ... New York, NY
Dee, Emanuel P. ... Houston, TX
Dee, Francis X. ... Newark, NJ
Dee, Harold ... Mount Kisco, NY
New York, NY
Dee, Harold, P.C. ... Mount Kisco, NY
New York, NY
Nyack, NY
Poughkeepsie, NY
White Plains, NY
Dee, James D. ... Jenkintown, PA
Dee, John ... Plattsburgh, NY
Dee, John F., Jr. ... Denver, CO
Dee, John J. ... Los Angeles, CA
Dee, John J. ... Syracuse, NY
Dee, John P. ... Tucson, AZ
Dee, John P. ... Buffalo, NY
Dee, Kenneth J. ... Milaca, MN
Dee, Lynda M. ... Baltimore, MD
Dee, M. Joseph ... St. Louis, MO
Dee, MacGregor, Fales & MacGregor, L.L.P.
Grangeville, ID
Dee, MaryJeanette ... New York, NY
Dee, Michael A. ... Des Moines, IA
Dee, Patricia L. ... Mount Laurel, NJ
Dee, Paul J., Jr. ... Boston, MA
Dee, Paul T. ... Coral Gables, FL
Dee, Robert Henry ... Wray, CO
Dee, Stacy Leshock ... Pittsburgh, PA
Dee, Susan Giroux ... Wellesley, MA
Dee, T. Christopher ... Kenosha, WI
Dee, Terrence J. ... Chicago, IL
Dee, Thomas F. ... Chicago, IL
Dee, Thomas F., Ltd. ... Chicago, IL
Dee, Thomas J. ... New York, NY
Dee, Thomas M. ... St. Louis, MO
Dee, Thomas R. ... Chicago, IL
Dee, William F. ... Manchester, NH
Deeb, Brian P. ... Clearwater, FL
Deeb, Charles G. ... Willoughby, OH
Deeb, Daniel J. ... Fort Wayne, IN
Deeb & Deeb ... Grand Rapids, MI
Deeb and Deeb, P.S.C. ... Louisville, KY
Deeb, Edna L. ... Encino, CA
Deeb, G. Phillip, Jr. ... Louisville, KY
Deeb, G. Phillip, Jr., P.S.C. ... Louisville, KY
Deeb, G. Phillip, Sr. ... Louisville, KY
Deeb, Gary P. ... Palm Desert, CA
Deeb, John D. ... Grand Rapids, MI
Deeb, John Geary ... Bowling Green, KY
Deeb, Joseph F., Jr. ... Grand Rapids, MI
Deeb & Lamont, P.A. ... Clearwater, FL
Deeb, Peter J. ... Cherry Hill, NJ
Philadelphia, PA
Deeb, Phyllis ... Louisville, KY
Deeb, Renda ... Homestead, FL
Deeb, Renda Frank ... Miami, FL
Deeb, Richard A. ... Los Angeles, CA
Deeb, Robert M., Jr.
Hilton Head Island, SC
Deeb, Ronald George ... Aurora, CO
Deeb, Sam ... Louisville, KY
Deeb, Terry J. ... Clearwater, FL
St. Petersburg, FL
Deeb, Theresa A. ... Clearwater, FL
Deeba Sauter Herd ... St. Louis, MO
Dee-Bilka, Patricia ... New York, NY
Deede, Randy A. ... Devils Lake, ND
Deeds, C. Jason ... Dover, OH
Deeds, G. Robt. ... Wichita, KS
Deeds, Gary W. ... Columbus, OH
Deeds, Jean A. ... San Francisco, CA
Deeds, Michael W. ... Houston, TX
Deeds, R. Creigh ... Monterey, VA
Warm Springs, VA
Deedy, Judith G. ... Cleveland, OH
Deedy-Sincali, Elaine ... Quaker Hill, CT
Deef, Francis H. ... Piscataway, NJ
Deegan & Dadey ... Syracuse, NY
Deegan, Daniel P. ... Glen Cove, NY
Mattituck, NY
Deegan, David J. ... New York, NY
Deegan & Deegan, L.L.P. ... Hempstead, NY
Mineola, NY
New York, NY
Riverhead, NY
Deegan, Donald E. ... Hempstead, NY
Deegan, F. Timothy ... Cleveland, OH
Deegan, Francis W. ... Glen Cove, NY
Mattituck, NY
Deegan, Glenn E. ... Boston, MA
Deegan, James V. ... Hempstead, NY
Deegan, John J. ... New York, NY
Deegan, John P. (Jack) ... Petoskey, MI
Deegan, Joseph E. ... Leland, MI
Deegan, Joseph Edward ... Cleveland, OH
Deegan, Joseph F., Jr. ... Edison, NJ
Deegan, Kathleen M. ... Sioux City, IA
Deegan, Kenneth A. ... Huntington, NY
Deegan, Marian F. ... Milwaukee, WI
Deegan, Marie J. ... Helena, MT
Deegan, Martha E.H., LLC
Greenwich, CT
Deegan, Martha E.H. ... Greenwich, CT
Deegan, Maura O'Halloran ... Newark, NJ
Deegan & McGarry ... Cleveland, OH
Deegan, Michael D. ... Fort Worth, TX
Deegan, Michael J.
Fort George G. Meade, MD
Baldwin, NY
Deegan, Michael N. ... Gillette, WY
Deegan, Nan Marie ... Jonesboro, GA
Deegan, Peter E. ... Port Huron, MI
Deegan, Richard J. ... Sarasota, FL
Deegan & Strong, LLC
Rockville Centre, NY
Deegan, Susanne H. ... Cleveland, OH
Deegan, Teryl A. ... Agawam, MA
Deege, J. Michael ... West Des Moines, IA
Deege, John P. ... Quincy, IL
Deegear, James O., III ... Boerne, TX
Deehan, Paul G. ... Summit, NJ
Deehl, David L. ... Miami, FL
Deehl, David L., P.A. ... Miami, FL
Deehl, Robert M. ... Miami, FL
Deehr, Manya S. ... Philadelphia, PA
Deeken, James A. ... Dallas, TX
Deel, Bradford Wayne
South Charleston, WV
Deel, Dineen T. ... Denver, CO
Deeley, C. Carey, Jr. ... Baltimore, MD
Towson, MD
Deeley, Elizabeth Lee ... Washington, DC
Deeley, Harold P., Jr. ... Annandale, VA
Deeley, James P. ... Harrisburg, PA
Deeley, Karen A. ... Boston, MA
Deeley, King & Pang ... Honolulu, HI
Deeley, William J., (Atty. at Law, A Law Corp.) ... Honolulu, HI
Deely, Ann Doyle ... Lee, MA
Deely, J. Patrick ... San Antonio, TX
Deely, Jessie Doyle ... Lee, MA
Deely, Lynn Fusco ... Chicago, IL
Deely, Martin J. ... Schaumburg, IL
Deely, Richard J. ... New York, NY
Deely, Sheila H. ... Chicago, IL
Deely, Stephen G. ... Chicago, IL
Deem, Charles L. ... San Diego, CA
Deem, David A. ... Vincennes, IN
Deem, J. Christopher ... Tampa, FL
Deem, James L., (P.C.) ... Dallas, TX
Deem, Joseph M. ... Vancouver, WA
Deem, Lori L. ... Chicago, IL
Deem, Patricia A. ... Washington, DC
Deem, Patrick D. ... Clarksburg, WV
Deem, Tonya R. ... Winston-Salem, NC
Deem, William W. ... Jacksonville, FL
Deemer, Elizabeth E. ... Pittsburgh, PA
Deemer, Patricia L. ... Naperville, IL
Deems, Daniel R. ... Cartersville, GA
Deems, Douglas H. ... Santa Monica, CA
Deems, Harry B. ... Panorama City, CA
Deems, Joseph E. ... Los Angeles, CA
Deems Law Offices ... Los Angeles, CA
Deems, Mark F. ... Central Point, OR
Deems, Michael R. ... Chico, CA
Deems, Nyal D. ... Grand Rapids, MI
Deems, William W. ... Evansville, IN
Deen & Cameron ... Meridian, MS
Deen, Inmond L. ... Bay St. Louis, MS
Deen, James R. ... Houston, TX
Deen, Jana B. ... Cincinnati, OH
Deen, Jeffrey D. ... Altamonte Springs, FL
Deen, M. Elizabeth ... San Francisco, CA
Deen, Michael S. ... Englewood, CO
Deen, Robert B., Jr. ... Meridian, MS
Deen, Sanders B. ... Marietta, GA
Deen, Shella ... San Jose, CA
Deen, T. Jefferson, III ... Mobile, AL
Deen, Thomas D. ... Dermott, AR
Deen, Thomas O. ... Houston, TX
Deener, Feingold & Stern, A Professional Corporation ... Hackensack, NJ
Deener, Jerome A. ... Hackensack, NJ
Deener, Larry C. ... Lexington, KY
Deener-Agus, Elisa T. ... Boston, MA
Deeney, Raymond M. ... Trenton, NJ
Deenis, Nicholas ... Philadelphia, PA
Deeny, Raymond M.
Colorado Springs, CO
Deeny, Robert J. ... Phoenix, AZ
Deep, Charles David ... Henderson, KY
Louisville, KY
Deep, Colleen A. ... Columbus, OH
Deep, David Gregory ... Pittsburgh, PA
Deep, Michael ... Frankfort, KY
Deep, Michael A. ... Macon, GA
Deep, Norman Paul ... Clinton, NY
Deep, W. Mitchell, Jr. ... Henderson, KY
Deep & Womack ... Evansville, IN
Henderson, KY
Louisville, KY
Deer, A. Ross ... Overland Park, KS
Deer, Dwayne G. ... Mc Comb, MS
Deer, Jeffrey Wade ... Chicago, IL
Deer, Jill Verdeyen ... Birmingham, AL
Deer, Montie R. ... Wichita, KS
Deer, R. Alan ... Birmingham, AL
Deer, Richard E. ... Indianapolis, IN
Deer & Stone, P.C. ... Chicago, IL
Deer, Thomas E. ... Indianapolis, IN
Deer, William K. ... Indianapolis, IN
Deere, Beth M. ... Little Rock, AR
Deere, Elizabeth A. ... Los Angeles, CA
Deere, Heather L. ... Longmont, CO
Deere, Monte M., Jr. ... Dallas, TX
Deere, Timothy A. ... Chattanooga, TN
Deering, Charles V. ... El Dorado Hills, CA
Deering, Christopher W. ... Birmingham, AL
Deering, Claudia L. ... San Rafael, CA
Deering, Dana Edwin ... Covington, KY
Deering, Daniel 'La P. ... Minneapolis, MN
Deering, Fred A., Jr. ... Denver, CO
Deering, Harold H., Jr. ... Sioux Falls, SD
Deering, Jennifer K. ... Cincinnati, OH
Deering, Joseph E., Jr. ... Santa Monica, CA
Deering, Matt C. ... Champaign, IL
Deering, Paegan L. ... Westford, MA
Deering, Patrick D. ... Atlanta, GA
Deering, Patrick D., & Associates P.C.
Atlanta, GA
Deering, Perry A., II ... Houston, TX
Deering, Randy D. ... Waverly, OH
Deering, Thomas P. ... Portland, OR
Deering, Walther & Sands
Santa Monica, CA
Deeringer, James L. ... Sacramento, CA
Deerson, Adele S. ... Lake Success, NY

Deerson, Bruce A. ......Raleigh, NC
Deerwester, Steven J. ......Columbus, OH
Deery, Carol Moravec ......White Plains, NY
Deery, G. Edward ......Houston, TX
Deery, J. Jeffrey ......Orlando, FL
Deery, James A. ......Elyria, OH
Deery, Joseph S., Jr. ......Utica, NY
Deery-Schmitt, John P. ......Seattle, WA
Dees, A. Jerome ......Mobile, AL
Dees, Anse ......Greenville, MS
Dees, Anselm (Buddy) J., Jr.
Vicksburg, MS
Dees, C. Stanley ......Washington, DC
Dees, Daniel L. ......San Jose, CA
Dees, David L. ......Oakland, CA
Dees, Deborah Shelby ......Jackson, MS
Dees, Don A. ......Clarksdale, MS
Dees, Don L. ......Tulsa, OK
Dees, Elizabeth A. ......Washington, DC
Dees, Giles, Tedder, Tate & Gaylord
Greensboro, NC
Dees, Harry C., Jr. ......South Bend, IN
Dees, Harry P. ......Evansville, IN
Dees, J. Gordon ......Houston, TX
Dees, J. Gordon, A Professional Corporation
Houston, TX
Dees, Jeffrey L. ......Daytona Beach, FL
Dees, Jodie D. ......Mansfield, OH
Dees, Joe ......Vandalia, IL
Dees, John E., Jr. ......Dallas, TX
Dees, John W. ......Goldsboro, NC
Dees, John W. (Jay), II ......Goldsboro, NC
Dees, Julius, Jr. ......Greensboro, NC
Dees, Linda P. ......Kansas City, MO
Dees, Margaret Widman ......Jacksonville, FL
Dees, Michael K. ......Lake Charles, LA
Dees, Morris S., Jr. ......Montgomery, AL
Dees, Patricia Brown ......Mishawaka, IN
Dees, Richard L. ......Chicago, IL
Dees, Robert G. ......Houston, TX
Dees, Robert M. ......Jacksonville, FL
Dees, Smith, Powell, Jarrett, Dees & Jones
Goldsboro, NC
Dees, Stacy R. ......Washington, DC
Dees, Stephen P. ......Kansas City, MO
Dees, William A., Jr. ......Goldsboro, NC
DeEsch, Dennis A. ......Easton, PA
Deese, C. Michael ......Washington, DC
Deese, Crystal S. ......Washington, DC
Deese, James W. ......Frankfort, KY
Deese, Pamela M. ......Washington, DC
Deese, Patrick J. ......Melbourne, FL
Deese, Patrick J., P.A. ......Melbourne, FL
Deese, Renny W. ......Fayetteville, NC
de Espinosa, Raymond J. ......Montebello, CA
De Esso, Frank E. ......Scarsdale, NY
Deeter, Ellen M. ......Indianapolis, IN
Deeter, Leann R. ......Columbus, OH
Deetjen, Jose M. ......San Marino, CA
Deetman, Bernard Richard ......San Diego, CA
Deetman, Gregory E. ......Arcadia, CA
Deets, Charles R., III ......Lafayette, IN
Deets, Darryl W. ......Manitowoc, WI
Deets, Edward H., Jr. ......Charlottesville, VA
Deets, James A. ......Dallas, TX
Deets, Nicholas C. ......Lafayette, IN
Deets, Susan ......Miami, FL
Deetsch, D. L. ......Louisville, KY
Deetz, Richard E. ......Stroudsburg, PA
Deetz, Tonya S. ......Los Angeles, CA
Deeves, Christopher J. ......San Antonio, TX
DeFabio and Fenn, P.A. ......Coral Gables, FL
Miami, FL
DeFabio, George J. ......Miami, FL
DeFabis, Mark V. ......Indianapolis, IN
DeFabrizio, Nicholas J. ......Newark, NJ
DeFalaise, Louis ......Department of Justice, Executive Office for United States Attorneys, GV
DeFalco, Edward P. ......Providence, RI
De Falco, John A. ......Haddonfield, NJ
Defalco, Marcelline ......Wheaton, IL
Defalco, Marie T. ......Roseland, NJ
DeFalice & Douglas, P.C. ......Pittsburgh, PA
DeFalice, Vincent A. ......Pittsburgh, PA
De Falla, Emily M. ......San Francisco, CA
DeFanti, Michael P. ......Boston, MA
Providence, RI
DeFao, Michael E. ......Boston, MA
DeFazio, David G. ......Richmond, VA
DeFazio, Gary M. ......Newark, NJ
DeFazio, Hugh E., Jr. ......Dover, NJ
DeFazio, J. Diane ......Salem, OH
DeFazio, John T. ......Canfield, OH
DeFazio, Joseph ......Staten Island, NY
DeFazio, Joseph C. ......Woodbridge, NJ
DeFazio, M. Edward ......Surf City, NJ
DeFazio, Tamara J. ......Fairmont, WV
De Fea, Robt. J. ......San Francisco, CA
Defebaugh, James E., IV ......Troy, MI
Defehr, James M. ......Cornelius, NC
DeFehr, Lawrence R. ......Sacramento, CA
Defeis, Elizabeth Frances ......Newark, NJ
De Feis, Nicholas M. ......New York, NY
De Feis O'Connell & Rose, P.C.
New York, NY
DeFelice, Anthony C. ......Teaneck, NJ
De Felice, Benedetto ......Arlington, VA
DeFelice, Dale A. ......Spokane, WA
DeFelice, Diane C. ......Los Angeles, CA
DeFelice, Eugene V. ......Redmond, WA
DeFelice, Joseph F. ......Kew Gardens, NY
DeFelice, Laura A. ......New York, NY
DeFelice, Ronald J. ......Irvine, CA
DeFelice, Rudolph ......Los Angeles, CA
Defenbach, Will S. ......Boise, ID
Defenbaugh, George ......Shawnee, OK
DeFendis, Matthew D. ......Fresno, CA

DeFeo, Charles A. ......Havertown, PA
DeFeo, Daniel T. ......Kansas City, MO
DeFeo, Jennifer R. ......Boston, MA
DeFeo, Jennifer R., P.C., Law Offices of
Boston, MA
DeFeo, John E. ......Dallas, TX
DeFeo, John M. ......Philadelphia, PA
DeFeo, Louis C., Jr. ......Jefferson City, MO
DeFeo, Morris F., Jr. ......Washington, DC
DeFeo, Nancy A. ......Morgantown, WV
DeFeo, Peter R. ......Hingham, MA
DeFeo, Ralph R. ......Malvern, PA
De Feo, Robert M. ......Los Angeles, CA
DeFeo, Stephen J. ......Camden, NJ
Westmont, NJ
Defeo, William Paul ......Brewster, NY
De Fernandez, Lilian Castellani
St. Louis, MO
de Fernandez, Teresa Isabel Leger
Santa Fe, NM
de Ferranti, Margot E. ......Department of Justice, GV
Defevers, Jack J. ......Cincinnati, OH
Deffebach, Harry L. ......Palm Bay, FL
Deffenbaugh, Robert W. ......Springfield, IL
Deffense, Clare ......Los Angeles, CA
Defferding, Wayne C. ......Appleton, WI
Deffet, James P. ......Wichita, KS
Deffet, Michael E. ......Hauppauge, NY
Deffina, Thomas V. ......New York, NY
Deffner, J. Stephen ......Encinitas, CA
Deffner Law Firm, S.C. ......Wausau, WI
Deffner, Roger L. ......Wausau, WI
Defiesta, Lenore C. ......San Francisco, CA
DeFilippi, Peter R. ......Mineola, NY
DeFilippis, John P. ......New York, NY
deFilippis, Lisa M. ......Cleveland, OH
de Filippis, Louis R. ......Maplewood, NJ
De Filippis, Peter A. ......New York, NY
Defilippis, Steve M. ......San Jose, CA
DeFilippo, Angel M. ......Edison, NJ
DeFilippo, Diane ......Oklahoma City, OK
DeFilippo, Frederick J. ......Elmira, NY
DeFilippo, Gerald E. ......Elmira, NY
DeFilippo, Joseph N. ......Stamford, CT
DeFilippo, Lisa A. ......Columbus, OH
DeFilippo, Paul R. ......Newark, NJ
DeFilippo, Richard M., Jr ......Columbus, OH
Defilippo, Rosemary K. ......Woodbridge, CT
DeFilipps, Thomas C. ......Palo Alto, CA
DeFillippo, David J. ......Red Bank, NJ
Defillo-Rosas, Luis A. ......San Juan, PR
De Fina, Vincent R. ......Stamford, CT
Define, William T. ......Baltimore, MD
DeFino, Anthony J. ......Philadelphia, PA
DeFino, Anthony M. ......West New York, NJ
Defino, Joseph F. ......Oakhurst, NJ
De Fino, Michael Anthony ......Philadelphia, PA
DeFino, Michael G. ......Media, PA
Defio, Daniel N. ......Syracuse, NY
Defiore, Paul Phillip ......Long Island City, NY
De Fiori, Victor A. ......Columbia, SC
Defley, Joseph E., Jr. ......Port Sulphur, LA
DeFloria, Gregory James ......Greensburg, PA
DeFoe, Daniel R. ......Blue Springs, MO
DeFoor, Don F. ......Douglasville, GA
DeForce, Mark H., III ......Oakland, CA
DeFord, Don K. ......Glenwood Springs, CO
DeFord, Julie Adams ......Idaho Falls, ID
DeFord, Paul S. ......Kansas City, MO
de Forest, Alicia ......Department of Energy, Office of the General Counsel, GV
de Forest, Benjamin B. ......Akron, OH
De Forest & Duer ......Greenwich, CT
Hackensack, NJ
New York, NY
DeForest, Ginger K. ......Metairie, LA
DeForest & Koscelnik ......Pittsburgh, PA
DeForest, Laura I. ......New York, NY
De Forest, Russell W. ......Medford, OR
DeForest, Stephen E. ......Seattle, WA
DeForest, Walter P., III ......Pittsburgh, PA
DeForge, Dale R. ......Irvine, CA
DeFors, Michael J. ......Lansing, MI
Defosse, Thomas L., III ......Broomall, PA
Defossez, Mark E. ......Columbus, OH
De Four, Jan Gilbert
Grosse Pointe Woods, MI
DeFour, Wayne L.
Grosse Pointe Woods, MI
DeFoy, Ernest D. ......Cleveland, OH
DeFoyd, Jim L. ......Houston, TX
DeFoyd, Jim L., and Associates, P.C.
Houston, TX
DeFraga, Allan ......Martinez, CA
DeFrain, Andrea M., (P.C.)
Southfield, MI
DeFraites, Judith A. ......New Orleans, LA
DeFrances, Guy R. ......Meriden, CT
DeFrances, Ronald F. ......Baton Rouge, LA
DeFrancesch, Fred ......Baton Rouge, LA
DeFranceschi, Daniel J. ......Wilmington, DE
DeFranceschi, Edward ......Boston, MA
DeFranceschi, Edward, P.C. ......Boston, MA
Defranceschi, Gary M. ......Bridgewater, NJ
De Francesco & De Francesco
Bridgman, MI
De Francesco, Frank J. ......Bridgman, MI
DeFrancesco, Joseph G. ......Saginaw, MI
DeFrancesco, Joseph J. ......Sierra Vista, AZ
De Francesco, Roccy M. ......Bridgman, MI
De Francesco, Roccy Michael
Bridgman, MI
Defrancis, Alexander A. ......Commack, NY
DeFrancis, Victor F. ......New York, NY
De Francis, William F. ......Nyack, NY
DeFrancisco, John A. ......Syracuse, NY
DeFrancisco, Mark J. ......Boston, MA

DeFrancisco, Mary T. ......Salem, MA
DeFranco, Carl M., Jr. ......Boston, MA
DeFranco, Denise W. ......Boston, MA
DeFranco, Edward J. ......New York, NY
DeFranco, Eva M. ......Danbury, CT
DeFranco, James E. ......Belleville, IL
DeFranco, James P., Jr. ......New York, NY
DeFranco, Jennifer M. ......Grayslake, IL
De Franco, Joseph ......Washington, DC
DeFranco, Judith A. ......San Carlos, CA
DeFranco, Leonard S. ......Oakbrook Terrace, IL
DeFranco, Marisa A. ......Peabody, MA
DeFranco, Michael A. ......Durham, NC
DeFranco, Michael J. ......Seattle, WA
De Franco, Ralph T. ......Cleveland, OH
DeFrancq, Donald J. ......Portland, OR
DeFrang, Gary R. ......Portland, OR
DeFrank, Maureen A. ......Eugene, OR
DeFrank, Michael E. ......Fort Mitchell, KY
Defrank, Michael L. ......San Diego, CA
De Frank, Sam ......Northbrook, IL
DeFrank, Steven J. ......New Haven, CT
DeFranks, John J. ......Buffalo, NY
DeFrantz, Anita L. ......Los Angeles, CA
De Franzo, Dennis P. ......Burbank, CA
DeFreece, Darek A. ......San Francisco, CA
DeFreece, LaRee M. ......St. Louis, MO
Defrees, Allison Leigh ......Austin, TX
Defrees & Fiske ......Chicago, IL
DeFreest, Eric S. ......Eugene, OR
DeFreitas, B. Eugene ......Saugus, MA
DeFreitas, Blaine J. ......Maynard, MA
DeFreitas, Louis Allen, Jr.
Crystal River, FL
Melbourne, FL
Orlando, FL
DeFreitas, Maury L. ......Gaithersburg, MD
de Freitas, Michael A.O.
Williamsville, NY
de Freitas, Paul C. ......New York, NY
deFreitas, Rhonda E. ......Wilmette, IL
De Frenza, Marcello F. ......Costa Mesa, CA
DeFreytas, C. Douglas ......Riverside, CA
De Fries, Anthony Wayne ......Chicago, IL
deFries, Hiriam A. ......Costa Mesa, CA
DeFries, S. Lucky ......Topeka, KS
DeFrino, Robert A. ......Hartford, CT
de Fritsch, Carol R. ......New York, NY
De Fuccio, Charles M. ......Hackensack, NJ
DeFuccio, DeAnne C. ......Hackensack, NJ
De Funis & Balint, P.S. ......Seattle, WA
De Funis, Marco ......Seattle, WA
DeFur, Voran, Hanley, Radcliff & Reed, LLP
Muncie, IN
de Furia, Guy G. ......Media, PA
DeFuria, Joseph A. ......Springfield, NJ
DeFurio, Amy P. ......Indiana, PA
DeFurio, Frank A. ......Los Angeles, CA
DeFurio, James R. ......Clearwater, FL
DeFusco, Arthur J. ......Lawrence, MA
Defusco, Arthur J., II ......Lawrence, MA
DeFusco & DeFusco ......Lawrence, MA
DeFusco, Leopold P. ......Bridgeport, CT
DeFusco & Lyman-Askew ......Bridgeport, CT
DeFusco, Robert G. ......Cincinnati, OH
DeFusco, Salvatore P. ......Providence, RI
Dega, Anne-Marie ......Chicago, IL
DeGabrielle, Don J. ......Houston, TX
DeGaetani, Frank J., Jr. ......Richmond, VA
De Gaetano, Anthony J. ......Albany, NY
DeGaetano, George A. ......New York, NY
De Gaetano, Marco Hall ......Denver, CO
De Gaetano, Peter F. ......New York, NY
DeGailler, Brian D. ......Orlando, FL
De Galan, J. B. ......Belleair Beach, FL
DeGallery, Lisa M. ......Hillsboro, OH
Degan, Blanchard & Nash, A Professional Law Corporation ......New Orleans, LA
Degan, Michael S. ......Omaha, NE
Degan, Nancy Scott ......New Orleans, LA
Degan, Sidney W., III ......New Orleans, LA
DeGance, Joseph ......Fort Lauderdale, FL
DeGance, Joseph, P.A. ......Fort Lauderdale, FL
Degand, Mark A. ......Secaucus, NJ
Degani, Orly ......Los Angeles, CA
Deganis, Sergio C. ......Glastonbury, CT
DeGaris, Annesley H. ......Birmingham, AL
DeGarlais, Vincent C. ......Denver, CO
Degarmo, Alana J. ......Simi Valley, CA
DeGarmo, Dale A. ......Flint, MI
De GarmoVon Allman, Nanette
New Philadelphia, OH
DeGasparis, Ernest W. ......Santa Maria, CA
De Gasper, Kenneth A. ......Buffalo, NY
DeGasperin, Toni L. ......Laguna Hills, CA
DeGaudenzi, Bianca M. ......New York, NY
Dege, Susan M. ......Litchfield, MN
DeGeer, Kirsten ......Detroit, MI
DeGeest, Randy S. ......Oskaloosa, IA
DeGeeter, John P. ......Houston, TX
Degel, James A. ......Seattle, WA
Degele-Mathews, Danielle Noel
Honolulu, HI
DeGelleke, Peter G. ......Concord, MA
DeGeller, Donald J. ......Novato, CA
Degen, A. Robert ......Philadelphia, PA
Degen, Charlene ......Chicago, IL
Degen, Frederick C. ......Utica, NY
Degen, Lynn S. ......Livingston, NJ
Degen, Margaret J. ......Marion, IL
Degen, Richard A. ......Mascoutah, IL
Degen, Ronald D. ......New York, NY
Degen, William E. ......Santa Barbara, CA
De Genaro, George ......Boca Grande, FL
DeGenaro, Mary ......Youngstown, OH
De Genaro, Paul A. ......Southport, CT
Degener, Carol M. ......New York, NY
deGeneres, John L. ......Baton Rouge, LA

de Generes, Tasker O. ......Northbrook, IL
Degenfelder, Jeffrey G. ......Dallas, TX
Degenhardt, Walter P. ......Waynesboro, GA
Degenhart, Lara A. ......Washington, DC
Degenhart Law Firm ......Columbia, SC
Degenhart, Paul V. ......Columbia, SC
DeGenna, Dirk M. ......Santa Ana, CA
DeGennaro, Albert A. ......Harleysville, PA
DeGennaro, Alfred ......Asbury Park, NJ
De Gennaro, Barbara L. ......Derby, CT
De Gennaro, Gina ......San Antonio, TX
DeGennaro, Mark J. ......West Haven, CT
DeGennaro, Mark L. ......La Grange, GA
DeGenova, Damian P. ......Struthers, OH
DeGenova, Jacqueline F. ......Columbus, OH
DeGenova, Lisa M. ......Cherry Hill, NJ
DeGenova-Carter, Catherine A.
Springfield, IL
Degenshein, Dale J. ......New York, NY
Degenshein, I Braun ......San Francisco, CA
DeGeorge, R. Steven ......Charlotte, NC
DeGeorge, Robert ......Trenton, NJ
DeGeorge, Rudolph V. ......Jenkintown, PA
DeGeorge, Steven R. ......New York, NY
DeGeorge, Steven W. ......Washington, DC
DeGeorge, Susan G. ......Dobbs Ferry, NY
DeGeorgio, Barbara A. ......Houston, TX
DeGeorgio, Barbara A., P.C. ......Houston, TX
Degerman, David C. ......Los Angeles, CA
DeGette, Diana L. ......Washington, DC
DeGeurin, Mike ......Houston, TX
Deggendorf, Rose M. ......Hillsboro, OR
Degginger, Grant S. ......Seattle, WA
deGhetaldi, Dario B. ......Millbrae, CA
DeGiacomo, Diane M. ......Pittsfield, MA
DeGiacomo, James R. ......Boston, MA
DeGiacomo, Lynne Callahan ......Boston, MA
DeGiacomo, Mark G. ......Boston, MA
DeGiacomo, Rosamond J. ......Seattle, WA
Degidio, Anthony J., Jr. ......Toledo, OH
Degiorgio, Joan ......Salt Lake City, UT
DeGiorgio, Kenneth D. ......Santa Ana, CA
De Giorgis, Alessandro C. ......New York, NY
DeGiovanni, Jack R. ......East Providence, RI
Degiovanni, James ......St. Cloud, MN
DeGirolamo, Anthony J. ......Akron, OH
DeGirolamo, Joseph A. ......Orinda, CA
DeGirolamo, Joseph A. ......New York, NY
De Giulio, Frank P. ......Camden, NJ
New York, NY
Philadelphia, PA
DeGiulio, Paul S. ......Newark, NJ
De Giuseppe, Joseph, Jr.
White Plains, NY
DeGiusti, Anthony D.
Oklahoma City, OK
DeGiusti, Elaine Thompson
Oklahoma City, OK
DeGiusti, Stephen L. ......Oklahoma City, OK
DeGiusti, Timothy D.
Oklahoma City, OK
deGlee, James C. ......Boise, ID
Degler, Mark W. ......Chattanooga, TN
Degling, Donald E. ......New York, NY
Deglomine, Anthony, III ......Orlando, FL
DeGlopper, Douglas J. ......Indianapolis, IN
Deglow, Terry L. ......Spokane, WA
Degnan, Charles A. ......Lewiston, MN
Degnan, Daniel ......Carmel, NY
Degnan, Daniel R. ......Oak Brook, IL
Degnan, Donald A. ......Boulder, CO
Degnan, Edward J. ......Canisteo, NY
Degnan, Frederick H. ......Washington, DC
Degnan, James G. ......Los Angeles, CA
Degnan, John J. ......Warren, NJ
Degnan, John M. ......Minneapolis, MN
Degnan, L. John ......Guttenberg, IA
Degnan, Lauren A.
United States Court Of Appeals For The Federal Circuit, GV
Degnan, Martin J. ......Wooster, OH
Degnan, Mary F. ......Pleasantville, NY
Degnan, Michael J. ......Boston, MA
Degnan, Michael J. ......Newark, NJ
Degnan, Michael J.C.
Fort Lauderdale, FL
Degnan, Peter J. ......Mendon, NY
Degnan, Peter M. ......Atlanta, GA
Degnan, Philip James ......Newark, NJ
Degnan, Ruth M. ......Chicago, IL
Degnan, Terrance J. ......Pittsburgh, PA
Degner, Lorelei J. ......Madison, WI
Degnon, Thomas P. ......Boston, MA
deGoede, Arthur C. ......Los Angeles, CA
De Goede, Dale A. ......Fresno, CA
de Goede, Mary Beth ......Fresno, CA
De Golia, James B. ......San Francisco, CA
De Golia, Peter C. ......Santa Rosa, CA
deGolian, Robert R. ......Louisville, KY
deGolian, William D. ......Atlanta, GA
DeGomez, John P. ......Pasadena, CA
DeGonge, Samuel A., Law Offices of
Belleville, NJ
Degonia, John B., Jr. ......Covington, GA
Degonia, Thomas M., II ......Department of State, GV
DeGood, Ball, Easley, Wabeke & Brummet
Loveland, CO
DeGood, F. Ray ......Loveland, CO
De Gooyer, Harlan W. ......Arvada, CO
DeGooyer, John G. ......Washington, DC
DeGory, Stanley P. ......Indiana, PA
de Gotay, Ramonita Pérez ......San Juan, PR
De Goytisolo, Agustin ......Miami, FL
DeGraaf, Lawrence G. ......Greensboro, NC
de Graauw, John S. ......Baton Rouge, LA
DeGraff, Enoh T. ......Boston, MA

DeGraff, Foy, Holt-Harris and Kunz, LLP
Albany, NY
Saratoga, NY
Schenectady, NY
Troy, NY
DeGraff, Garrett E. ... Albany, NY
Degraff, Gregory P. ... Troy, MI
DeGraff, Harold R. ... Menlo Park, CA
DeGraff, John C. ... Carson City, NV
DeGraff, John T., Jr. ... Albany, NY
DeGraff, Martha H.
General Services Administration, Board of Contract Appeals, GV
De Graff, Randy W. ... South Holland, IL
DeGraff, Shawn E. ... Shawnee, KS
DeGraff, Shawn E., P.A. ... Shawnee, KS
DeGraff, Steven ... Chicago, IL
DeGraffenreid, Jeff P. ... Wichita, KS
DeGraffenreid, Paul E. ... Oklahoma City, OK
DeGraffenreid, Ann-Marie ... Hartford, CT
DeGraffenreidt, James H., Jr.
Washington, DC
de Graffenried, Adrian T. L.
Agency for International Development, Other Offices of A.I.D., GV
deGraffenried, Ryan, Jr. ... Tuscaloosa, AL
Degraffgnreidt, Carol Elizabeth
Fort Lauderdale, FL
Degraft, J. Cobbie ... Alexandria, VA
de Gramont, Alexandre ... Washington, DC
de Gramont, Jacqueline ... Washington, DC
DeGrand, Daniel R. ... Escanaba, MI
DeGrand, Karen Kies ... Chicago, IL
DeGrand, Luke ... Chicago, IL
DeGrand, Robert J. ... Escanaba, MI
DeGrandi, Donna M. ... New York, NY
DeGrandis, Fred M. ... Westlake, OH
DeGrandis, Paula A. ... Portland, OR
DeGrandis, Ronald L. ... Cleveland, OH
DeGrandis, William D. ... Washington, DC
DeGrandpre, Charles A. ... Portsmouth, NH
De Grandpre, Jocelyn T.
Environmental Protection Agency, Office of the General Counsel, GV
deGrandpre, John B., Jr. ... Washington, DC
De Grandy, Miguel ... Miami, FL
DeGrange, Dianne D. ... Chicago, IL
DeGrasse, Frank ... White Plains, NY
deGrasse, Kathleen M. ... Norridge, IL
de Grasse, Michael E. ... Walla Walla, WA
deGrasse, Rocco J. ... Chicago, IL
De Grave, Douglas M. ... Santa Ana, CA
DeGrave, Susan V. ... Springfield, MA
deGravelles, John W. ... Baton Rouge, LA
deGravelles, Palmintier & Holthaus
Baton Rouge, LA
de Gravelles, Patrick P. ... Washington, DC
DeGraw, Alan L. ... Ecorse, MI
DeGraw & Assocs., P.A. ... Winter Park, FL
DeGraw, D. Kevin ... St. George, UT
DeGraw, David J. ... Grand Rapids, MI
DeGraw, David J. ... Marshall, MI
DeGraw, Frances D. ... Winter Park, FL
De Graw, Harold E. ... Nevada City, CA
DeGraw, James S. ... Boston, MA
DeGraw, Ronald J. ... Marshall, MI
DeGraw, Sheley L. ... Detroit, MI
DeGraw, William R., Jr. ... Winston-Salem, NC
DeGrazia, Basil M., Jr. ... Pittsburgh, PA
DeGrazia, Edward ... New York, NY
DeGrazia, James I. ... Bloomfield Hills, MI
DeGrazia, Joel J. ... Elmhurst, IL
DeGrazia, Lee A. ... Anchorage, AK
Degree, Michael Keith ... Staten Island, NY
DeGreen, Keith P. ... Phoenix, AZ
DeGregori, Alice E. ... Houston, TX
DeGregorie, Robert P. ... New York, NY
DeGregorio, Anthony, Jr. ... Boston, MA
De Gregorio, David ... New York, NY
DeGregorio, Edmonde P. ... Cincinnati, OH
DeGregorio, Jacqueline A.
Parsippany, NJ
De Gregorio, John R. ... Roswell, GA
DeGregorio, Michael J. ... Pittsfield, MA
Degregoris, Albert ... Mineola, NY
DeGregoris, Gerard, Jr. ... Mineola, NY
Degrendel, Grant B. ... Rochester, MI
DeGrezia, Christopher H. ... Princeton, NJ
DeGrezia, Donna Markey ... Trenton, NJ
De Grim, Frank E. ... New York, NY
De Groat, Charles W. ... West Haverstraw, NY
DeGroat, Eric J. ... Lansing, MI
DeGroat, Michael P. ... Walton, NY
DeGroff, Christopher J. ... Chicago, IL
DeGroff, Eric A. ... Virginia Beach, VA
Degroff, Forrest Alan ... Hoboken, NJ
DeGroff, Ginger ... Tampa, FL
DeGroff, Joseph E. ... Indianapolis, IN
DeGrood, George M., III ... Southfield, MI
DeGroot, Bruce W. ... St. Louis, MO
De Groot, Case ... Coloma, MI
DeGroot, David A. ... San Francisco, CA
de Groot, John A. ... San Diego, CA
DeGroot, John F. ... Garden City, NY
DeGroot, John W., Jr. ... Madera, CA
De Groot, Keller, Vincent & Almassian, P.L.C. ... Grand Rapids, MI
De Groot, Murray B. ... Grand Rapids, MI
de Groot, Robert J. ... Deltona, FL
DeGroot, Robert J. ... Newark, NJ
de Groot, Steven J. ... Atlanta, GA
De Groot, Susan M. ... Madison, WI
DeGroot, Thomas J. ... St. Louis, MO
DeGroote, Jennifer L. ... Fort Wayne, IN
DeGroote, Jessica B. ... Jackson, MS
DeGroote, John Sabine ... Dallas, TX
DeGroote, Timothy W. ... Fort Wayne, IN
DeGroote-Striano, Maryanne ... New York, NY

DeGross, Charles M.
Warrensville Heights, OH
DeGrow, Dan L. ... Port Huron, MI
DeGruttola, Carmela ... New York, NY
DeGruy, Lisa ... Ponchatoula, LA
Deguardia, Joseph M. ... Bronx, NY
de Guardiola, Eduard J. ... Atlanta, GA
Deguc, Vincent A. ... Beaverton, OR
DeGuerin, Dick ... Houston, TX
DeGuerin & Dickson ... Houston, TX
De Guia, Julius A. ... San Diego, CA
DeGuilio, Jon E. ... South Bend, IN
DeGuire, Frank C. ... Milwaukee, WI
DeGuire, Frank C., Jr. ... Milwaukee, WI
DeGulis, Gregory J. ... Cleveland, OH
Degulis, Joseph M. ... Boynton Beach, FL
Manchester, NH
DeGunther, Richard N. ... Rockford, IL
DeGuzman, Arnold M. ... Palo Alto, CA
de Guzman, Dennis M. ... Seattle, WA
De Guzman, Emiliano T. ... New York, NY
De Guzman, Iona ... San Francisco, CA
Chicago, IL
de Guzmán-Vendrell, Guillermo
San Juan, PR
de Haaff, Stuart M. ... Calabasas, CA
DeHaan & Bach, Co., L.P.A.
Cincinnati, OH
DeHaan, Elizabeth Slone ... Cincinnati, OH
DeHaan, Ellen Hirsch ... Clearwater, FL
St. Petersburg, FL
DeHaan, Harry C. ... Twin Falls, ID
De Haan, Karen L. ... Louisville, KY
Dehaan, May Lin ... Monterey, CA
DeHaan, Peter R. ... Cincinnati, OH
DeHaan, Richard L. ... Department of Justice, Executive Office for United States Attorneys, GV
De Haan & Richter, P.C. ... Chicago, IL
DeHaan, Robert A. ... Washington, DC
De Haan, Ronald M. ... Chicago, IL
Dehaan, Scott R. ... San Diego, CA
DeHaan, Stephen J. ... Grandville, MI
DeHaan, Tamara D. ... San Diego, CA
DeHaan, William R. ... Phoenix, AZ
DeHaas, Ernest P., III ... Uniontown, PA
De Haas, Louis H. ... Los Angeles, CA
de Haas, Philip R. ... Emporia, VA
Dehan, Hani E. ... Shreveport, LA
DeHarde, Anita F. ... Royal Oak, MI
De Hardit, John E. ... Gloucester, VA
DeHardt, Jay D. ... Kansas City, MO
DeHart, A. Jeffrey ... Placerville, CA
DeHart, Barbara B. ... Rochester, NH
DeHart, Barbara B., Law Offices, P.A.
Rochester, NH
DeHart, Charles J., III ... Harrisburg, PA
DeHart, Gloria F. ... San Francisco, CA
De Hart, Gordon F. ... Aurora, IL
DeHart, J. Cort ... Fort Worth, TX
DeHart, James L. ... Concord, NH
De Hart, James M. ... Fort Lauderdale, FL
DeHart, June Langston (Walton)
Washington, DC
DeHart, Kenneth D. ... Alpine, TX
DeHart, V. L., Jr. ... Danbury, NC
DeHaven, Catherine I. ... Harahan, LA
DeHaven, Dara L. ... Atlanta, GA
DeHaven, George K. ... Uniondale, NY
DeHaven, J. Lynn ... Washington, PA
DeHaven, M. Travis ... Atlanta, GA
De Haven, Mark ... Spokane, WA
Dehaven, Michael G. ... Towson, MD
DeHay & Elliston, L.L.P. ... Beaumont, TX
Dallas, TX
DeHayes, Karina H. ... Chicago, IL
De Heer, Gerda C. ... New York, NY
Dehel, Francis E. ... Philadelphia, PA
Dehen, Robert E. ... Springfield, IL
DeHenzel, Robert J., Jr.
Federal Deposit Insurance Corporation, Professional Liability Section, GV
de Herdt, Erik ... Plano, TX
DeHerdt, R. Dave ... Chelmsford, MA
DeHerrera & DeHerrera ... Aurora, CO
DeHerrera, Guillermo A. ... Aurora, CO
DeHerrera, Juan "Leo" ... Rawlins, WY
DeHerrera, Rosemary Y. ... Aurora, CO
Dehgan, Alex ... Chicago, IL
Dehghan, Koorosh ... Alexandria, VA
DeHihns, Lee A., III ... Atlanta, GA
De Hill, Kelly ... Salt Lake City, UT
Dehler, Carol Muratore ... Milwaukee, WI
Dehler, Douglas P. ... Milwaukee, WI
Dehler, Leo H. ... St. Paul, MN
Dehler, Mark F. ... Decatur, GA
Dehler, Mark F., LLC ... Atlanta, GA
Decatur, GA
Dehler, Martin D. ... Garden City, NY
Dehlinger, Charles A.
Altamonte Springs, FL
Dehlinger, Peter J. ... Palo Alto, CA
Dehm, Curtis R. ... Rochester, NY
Dehm & Dehm ... Fallbrook, CA
Dehm, Greg ... Fallbrook, CA
Dehm, Marisa ... Fallbrook, CA
Dehmand, Sharon ... Falmouth, MA
Dehmel, Paul R. ... New York, NY
Dehmler, Bridget M. ... Rochester, NY
Dehmler, Michael F. ... Rochester, NY
Dehn, Douglas J. ... Anoka, MN
Dehn, Elizabeth ... Novato, CA
Dehn, Francis X. ... New York, NY
Dehn, James E. ... Cambridge, MN
Dehn, Kenneth W. ... Bothell, WA
Dehncke, Richard J. ... Denver, CO
Dehner, Christopher C.
Walnut Creek, CA

Dehner & Ellis, P.S.C. ... Morehead, KY
Dehner, Gerald G. ... Lincoln, IL
Dehner, H. Lee ... Sarasota, FL
Dehner, Jeff S. ... Atlanta, GA
Dehner, Joseph J. ... Cincinnati, OH
Dehner, Michael Raymond ... Portland, OR
Dehner, Truman L. ... Morehead, KY
Dehney, Robert F. ... Garden City, NY
Dehney, Robert J. ... Wilmington, DE
Dehnke, William T. ... Treasury Department, Office of the Comptroller of the Currency, GV
DeHoek, William R. ... Grand Rapids, MI
DeHoff, Harold E. ... Canton, OH
DeHoff, Paul T. ... Murfreesboro, TN
de Holczer, Paul D. ... Columbia, SC
deHoll, Paul B. ... Arlington, VA
deHoll, Robert A. ... Greenville, SC
DeHon, Frederic T., Jr.
Palm Beach Gardens, FL
Dehon, Jeffrey A. ... Kansas City, KS
Dehon, Jeffrey A., P.A. ... Kansas City, KS
De Hond, Wayne F. ... East Rochester, NY
De Hoogh, John F. ... Sheldon, IA
DeHope, Edward K. ... Morristown, NJ
De Hope, Joseph J., Jr. ... Davis, CA
De Horn, Jon M. ... Detroit, MI
de Hoyos, Debora ... Chicago, IL
De Hoyos, Rick ... San Angelo, TX
Deiana, Robert V. ... Worcester, MA
Deibel, Gilbert A. ... Saginaw, MI
Deibel, John W. ... Barberton, OH
Deibel, Thos. E. ... Saginaw, MI
Deibert, Anne M. ... San Francisco, CA
Deibert, Donald G. ... Midland, MI
Deibert, Douglas M. ... Sioux Falls, SD
Deibert, Edward A. ... San Francisco, CA
Deibert, Karen S. ... New York, NY
Deibert, Kathleen D. ... San Francisco, CA
Deibert, Raymond H. ... Winnetka, IL
Deibert, Thomas ... Princeton, NJ
Deible, Charles R. ... Hammond, IN
Deich and Meece ... Portland, OR
Deich, Richard F. ... Portland, OR
Deichert, James M. ... Atlanta, GA
Deiches & Ferschmann, A Professional Corporation ... Haddonfield, NJ
Deiches, Ira R. ... Haddonfield, NJ
Deichler, Anthony C. ... Lafayette, CA
Deichler, Clark L. V. ... Piedmont, CA
Deichmeister, Robert L. ... Fairfax, VA
Deicken, Jennifer L. ... Santa Cruz, CA
Deickler, Beverly L. ... Woodbury, CT
New York, NY
Deiermann, Mark S. ... St. Louis, MO
Deife, Mark D. ... Seattle, WA
Deifik, Celia Ellen ... Naples, FL
Deifik, Joel A. ... Naples, FL
Deifik, Mark G. ... Albertson, NY
Deig, Glenn A. ... Evansville, IN
Deig, Mary R. ... Evansville, IN
Deig, Steven K. ... Evansville, IN
Deigaer, Nicole C. ... Menlo Park, CA
Deighan, Jean M. ... Portland, ME
Deighan, Michael P. ... Southfield, MI
Deighan, Neil F., Jr. ... Westmont, NJ
Deighan, Thomas M. ... Bloomington, IL
Deight, Blanche ... Huntington Beach, CA
Deignan, Paul T. ... Indianapolis, IN
Deignan, Robert E. ... Chicago, IL
Deignan, Robert L. ... Lowell, MA
Deihl, Colin C. ... Denver, CO
Deihl, Kenneth R. ... Girard, IL
Deihl, Richard T. ... Santa Ana, CA
Deike, Keith L. ... Waseca, MN
Deike, Robert J. ... Edina, MN
Deikman, Eugene L., (P.C.) ... Denver, CO
Deily, Dautel & Mooney, LLP
Brookline, MA
Albany, NY
Deily, Elspeth K. ... San Francisco, CA
Deily, John P., Law Offices of
Laguna Hills, CA
Deily, Johnna J. ... Carlisle, PA
Deily, Jonathan D. ... Albany, NY
Deily, Robert J. ... Catskill, NY
Deily and Schaefer ... Catskill, NY
Deily, Testa & Dautel, LLP ... Albany, NY
Deily, William E. ... Hudson, NY
Deimen, James M. ... Ann Arbor, MI
Deimer, Mary S. ... Washington, DC
Deimling, Margaret Ware, (Mrs.)
Atlanta, GA
Deimund, Michael ... Cape Girardeau, MO
de Imus, Carlos C. ... Seattle, WA
Dein, Henry Y. ... Indianapolis, IN
Dein, Judith G. ... Boston, MA
Deinard, Lile H. ... New York, NY
Deiner, Howard D. ... Washington, DC
Deiner, John B. ... Ormond Beach, FL
Deines & Deines ... Wa Keeney, KS
Deines, E. Jay ... Wa Keeney, KS
Deinhardt, Barbara C. ... Brooklyn, NY
Deinhart, Martin F. ... Hagåtña, GU
Deininger, Christopher L. ... Jersey City, NJ
New York, NY
Deininger, David G. ... Madison, WI
Deininger, Mark A. ... Atlanta, GA
Deininger, Neil D. ... North Little Rock, AR
Deinken, John J. ... Thousand Oaks, CA
Deinlein, James Nichol ... Charlottesville, VA
Deinoff, Pelle ... Washington, DC
Deioma, David B. ... Cleveland, OH
de Iongh, Bailey R. ... Seattle, WA
DeIorio, Patrick V. ... New York, NY
Purchase, NY
DeIorio, Vincent A. ... New York, NY
Purchase, NY

DeIorio, Vincent A., The, Law Firm
New York, NY
Purchase, NY
White Plains, NY
Deiotte, James T. ... Des Moines, IA
Deisch and Marion, P.C. ... Denver, CO
Deisch, Phillip S. ... Houston, TX
Deise, Jerome E., Jr. ... Baltimore, MD
Deisenroth, Craig ... Tulsa, OK
Deisher, Jonathan C. ... Philadelphia, PA
Deisinger, Francis W. ... Milwaukee, WI
Deisinger, William R. ... Red Bank, NJ
Deisler, Sandra W. ... Orlando, FL
Deisley, David L. ... Salt Lake City, UT
Deisley, Susan Gorey ... Salt Lake City, UT
Deisner, Vicki L. ... Columbus, OH
Deison, R. A. "Mickey" ... Conroe, TX
Deiss, Andrew G. ... Salt Lake City, UT
Deiss, William D. ... North Pomfret, VT
Deissler, Ronald T. ... Riverside, CA
Deist, John H. ... San Francisco, CA
Deister, Thomas M. ... Grand Junction, CO
De Ita & Lowe, LLP ... San Mateo, CA
De Ita, Nancy Ligon ... San Mateo, CA
Deitch, Alex ... Philadelphia, PA
Deitch, Daniel C. ... Philadelphia, PA
Deitch, David ... Bethpage, NY
Deitch, David B. ... Washington, DC
Deitch, Gerald E. ... Wilmington, DE
Deitch, Gilbert H. ... Atlanta, GA
Deitch, I. Walter ... Chicago, IL
Deitch, Jack ... Staten Island, NY
Deitch, Jason A. ... Hallandale Beach, FL
Deitch, Jason A., P.A. ... Hallandale Beach, FL
Deitch, Jeffrey ... Durango, CO
Deitch, John M. ... Cranford, NJ
Deitch, Laurence B. ... Southfield, MI
Deitch, Lisa ... Los Angeles, CA
Deitch, Lynne E. ... Detroit, MI
Deitch, Michael, Law Offices of
Austin, TX
Deitch, Michele Yve ... Toledo, OH
Deitch, Penny L. ... Farmington Hills, MI
Deitch, Philip ... Beverly Hills, CA
Deitch, Robert C. ... Gettysburg, PA
Deitch, Russell ... Los Angeles, CA
Deitch, William H. ... Oakmont, PA
Deitchler, Dale L. ... Minneapolis, MN
Deitchler, M. Douglas ... Lincoln, NE
Deitchman, B. Buzz ... Dallas, TX
Deitchman, David ... Dallas, TX
Deitchman, Roy ... Mount Kisco, NY
Deitel, Arthur ... Princeton, NJ
Deitelbaum, John E. ... Springfield, MA
Deitelzweig, Craig M. ... New York, NY
Deitemeyer, Ailsa DePrada, (P.C.)
Boston, MA
Deiter, Charles J. ... Indianapolis, IN
Deiter, Daniel W. ... Montgomery City, MO
Deiter, Jennifer A. ... Cherry Hill, NJ
Deiter, Paul D. ... Pasadena, CA
Deitering, Sandra K. ... Topeka, KS
Deiters, Cynthia A. ... Clayton, MO
Deiters, Kelly Ann ... Smithtown, NY
Deitle, Chas. M. ... Akron, OH
Deitrich, David K. ... Bradenton, FL
Deitrich & St. Paul, P.A. ... Bradenton, FL
Deitrick, Robert J., Jr. ... Charlotte, MI
Deitrick, William E. ... Chicago, IL
Deits, David H. ... Seattle, WA
Deitsch, David H. ... New York, NY
Deitsch, Goldberg & Marin
New York, NY
Deitsch, Greggory M. ... Birmingham, AL
Deitsch, Ira J. ... Boston, MA
Deitsch, Stephen M. ... Wheaton, IL
Deitsch, Stephen P. ... Riverside, CA
Deitschel, J. Thomas ... Dallas, TX
Deitsch-Perez, Deborah ... New York, NY
Deitz, Adrian J.S. ... New York, NY
Deitz, Anne E. ... Seattle, WA
Deitz & Aronson ... Pennington, NJ
Deitz, David L. ... New York, NY
Deitz & Freeburger, P.S.C.
Henderson, KY
Deitz, Kenneth J. ... Doylestown, PA
Deitz, Merritt S., Jr. ... Henderson, KY
Deitz, Morton ... Pennington, NJ
Deitz, Randolph W. ... Columbia, MD
Deitz, Robert L. ... Department of Defense, Defense Legal Services Agency, GV
Deitz, Robert N. ... Detroit, MI
Deitz, Roger M. (IBA) **... New York, NY**
Deitzer, Lynn ... Boston, MA
Provincetown, MA
Deitzer, Moran, Abraham & Hallett, LLP
Boston, MA
Provincetown, MA
Deitzler, Harry G. ... Charleston, WV
DeIulio, Regina Leigh ... Tampa, FL
DeIulis, Patrick Joseph ... Salem, MA
Deivanayagam, Virkram S. ... Waco, TX
Deixel, Vardon E. ... Woodmere, NY
Deixler, Bert H. ... Los Angeles, CA
Deixler, Janet Hand ... Albany, NY
Deiz, Mercedes F. ... Portland, OR
Deja, Daniel R. ... Stevensville, MI
Deja, Sharon K. ... Benton Harbor, MI
DeJaco, Frani B. ... Deerfield Beach, FL
DeJager, Pamela ... Bronxville, NY
De Jana, Richard ... Kalispell, MT
de Janes, J. Michael ... Atlanta, GA
DeJanes, Sherry D. ... Kansas City, MO
DeJarnatt, James W. ... Manhattan, KS
DeJarnatt, Susan L. ... Philadelphia, PA
DeJarnett, David A. ... Martinsburg, WV
De Jarnett, Shawn Robert ... Wellington, KS

DeJarnette, Edmund T., Jr. ... **Richmond, VA**
DeJarnette, Elliott H. ... Culpeper, VA
De Jarnette, Jeannette M. ... Metairie, LA
DeJarnette, Kenneth G. ... **San Francisco, CA**
DeJean, Bradley S. ... **Oakland, CA**
DeJean, Broderick C. ... Opelousas, LA
DeJean, DeJean & DeJean ... Opelousas, LA
De Jean, Felix A., III ... Opelousas, LA
DeJean, Howard C. ... Opelousas, LA
DeJean, Kenneth Clay ... Baton Rouge, LA
DeJean, Kenneth W. ... **Lafayette, LA**
DeJean, Kent S. ... Eunice, LA
DeJean, Marcie Swayze ... Baton Rouge, LA
De Jean, Richard F. ... Sumner, WA
De Jean, Robert F., Jr. ... Opelousas, LA
DeJean, Samantha Bley ... **San Francisco, CA**
DeJean, Thomas J. ... Opelousas, LA
De Jesus, Alma ... Brooklyn, NY
De Jesus, Ana Elba ... San Juan, PR
de Jesus, David J. ... **Oakland, CA**
deJesus, Joel ... **Washington, DC**
De Jesus, Milton A. ... Little Rock, AR
DeJesus, Mireya ... Hollywood, FL
De Jesus, Riza E. ... **Seattle, WA**
De Jesus, Susan ... Staten Island, NY
de Jesus, Vivian ... San Juan, PR
De Jesús-Annoni, Gerardo ... **San Juan, PR**
DeJesus-Bonney, Petra M. ... San Francisco, CA
de Jesús Kellogg, Sara E. ... San Juan, PR
de Jesús Navarro-García, Teresita ... San Juan, PR
de Jesús-Schuck, Francisco ... **San Juan, PR**
Dejnozka, Jan ... Detroit, MI
De John, Robt. N. ... San Francisco, CA
DeJohn, Stephen E. ... Lakewood, OH
DeJohn, Timothy W. ... Rochester, NY
Dejoie, Jessy ... **New York, NY**
Dejoie, Louis A. ... **Harrisburg, PA**
De Joie, Mark P. ... Lynn, MA
DeJong, Alex C. ... Chicago, IL
DeJong, Alvin W. ... Chicago, IL
De Jong, Barbara DePaola ... Long Beach, CA
De Jong, Bradley K. ... **Orange City, IA**
De Jong, Brent A. ... Ritzville, WA
DeJong, Danielle ... Muskegon, MI
DeJong, David J. ... Chicago, IL
De Jong, David J. ... **Red Wing, MN**
De Jong, David S. ... **Rockville, MD**
DeJong, Eric A. ... **Seattle, WA**
de Jong, Hendrik ... **New York, NY**
DeJong, James G. ... **Milwaukee, WI**
DeJong, Jane Ann ... Kansas City, MO
De Jong, Jeffrey P. ... **Chicago, IL**
De Jong, Johannes M. ... Philadelphia, PA
de Jong, Jonathan James ... **Wichita, KS**
DeJong, Lauren Evans ... **Chicago, IL**
DeJong, Philip ... Ukiah, CA
De Jong, Ralph E. ... **Chicago, IL**
De Jong, Remko B. ... New York, NY
de Jong, Renee ... Santa Barbara, CA
DeJong, Robert L. ... **Grand Rapids, MI**
Dejong, Timothy ... **Portland, OR**
deJong, Tina E. ... **New York, NY**
DeJong, Tracy Barger ... Vienna, VA
de Jonge, Kathleen R. ... Department of Commerce, Patent and Trademark Office, GV
de Jonge, Kathleen Russell ... Richmond, VA
deJonge, Peter M. ... **Sandy, UT**
De Jongh, J. Paul ... **Research Triangle Park, NC**
de Jongh, John P. ... **Charlotte Amalie, St. Thomas, VI**
De Jonghe, Thomas G. ... **San Francisco, CA**
DeJoode, Jeffrey W. ... Macomb, IL
DeJoode, Troy M. ... Cedar Falls, IA
Dejoras, Lisa D. ... **Minneapolis, MN**
DeJordin, Bradford J. ... **Los Angeles, CA**
DeJordy, Eugene A. ... Washington, DC
DeJoseph, Brian F. ... Syracuse, NY
DeJoseph, Paula C. ... Hazleton, PA
de Journette, Jo A. ... **North Wilkesboro, NC**
Dejowski, Edmund F. ... New York, NY
DeJoy, Robert W., Jr. ... **New York, NY**
DeJulia, Alicia ... Altoona, PA
DeJulio, Douglas P. ... Las Vegas, NV
DeJulio, Leonard A. ... Bellevue, PA
De Julio, Lois A. ... Jersey City, NJ
DeJuneas, Patricia A. ... Hartford, CT
DeJung, Theodore J. ... Santa Rosa, CA
De Jute, David A. ... Culver City, CA
Deka, David J. ... San Diego, CA
Dekajlo & Associates ... East Meadow, NY
Dekajlo, Oleh N. ... East Meadow, NY
Dekajlo, Orest T. ... East Meadow, NY
De Kalb, Rebecca ... Orinda, CA
DeKalb, Stacey A. ... **Minneapolis, MN**
Dekan, Marsha L. ... **Dallas, TX**
De Kany, Mark T. ... Memphis, TN
DeKavis, Donna L. ... Hampton Falls, NH
DeKay, Harold G. ... Atlantic, IA
deKelaita, Robert T. ... Sacramento, CA
DeKelaita, Robert W. ... Glenview, IL
Dekelebaum, Ron H. ... Addison, TX
Deken, Christine E. ... Columbus, OH
deKieffer, Donald E. ... **Washington, DC**
deKieffer & Horgan ... **Washington, DC**
Dekker, Christina M. ... **Chicago, IL**
Dekker, Christopher F. ... **Chicago, IL**
Dekker, David T. ... **Washington, DC**
Dekker, Deon H. ... Dallas, TX
Dekker, John ... Wichita, KS
Dekker, Kathleen F. ... Tallahassee, FL
Dekker, Laura A. ... Fairfield, CA
Dekker, Peter H. ... **Walnut Creek, CA**
Dekker, Randall M. ... Zeeland, MI
Dekker, Susan A. ... Santa Clarita, CA
Dekle, David P., (P.C.) ... **Augusta, GA**
Dekle, Donne R. ... Charlotte, NC
Dekle, George R. ... Live Oak, FL
Dekle, Hal P. ... Tampa, FL
Dekle, Martha F. ... Brunswick, GA
Dekle, Martha F., P.C. ... Brunswick, GA
Dekle, Patrick H. ... **Tampa, FL**
Dekle, Patrick H., P.A. ... **Clearwater, FL**
St. Petersburg, FL
Tampa, FL
Dekle, W. Richard ... **Savannah, GA**
de Klerk, Andrew S. ... **New Orleans, LA**
De Klerk, Stephen M. ... **Sunnyvale, CA**
De Kleva, James J. ... Sanford, FL
Dekleva, Michael Joseph ... **Albuquerque, NM**
DeKline, Cheryl M. ... **New Providence, NJ**
DeKlotz, Fred W., Jr. ... San Jose, CA
de Kluiver, Julia Symon ... **Washington, DC**
DeKoatz, Matthew R. ... El Paso, TX
DeKoch, Mark ... **Corpus Christi, TX**
DeKock, Bruce W. ... **Portland, OR**
De Kock, Paola M.G. ... New York, NY
DeKock, Robert H. ... Muscatine, IA
Dekom, Peter J. ... Beverly Hills, CA
de Koninck, Jessica G. ... Upper Montclair, NJ
DeKoster & DeKoster ... **Hull, IA**
Sioux Falls, SD
DeKoster, Jim D. ... **Waterloo, IA**
DeKoster, John G. ... **Hull, IA**
DeKoster, Lucas J. ... **Hull, IA**
Sioux Falls, SD
DeKoster, Paul Ronald ... **San Francisco, CA**
DeKoter, Daniel E. ... **Sibley, IA**
DeKoter, Thole & Dawson, P.L.C. ... **Sibley, IA**
De Koven, Herman J. ... **Chicago, IL**
De Koven, Kenneth A. ... Paramus, NJ
DeKoven, Ronald ... New York, NY
Dekoven, Seymour Samuel ... Winnetka, IL
de Kowzan, John E. ... New Carrollton, MD
Dekraai, Stephanie R. ... **Baltimore, MD**
Dekreon, Gail ... San Francisco, CA
DeKruif, Rodney D. ... **Milwaukee, WI**
DeKuiper, Kristin A. ... **Boston, MA**
DeKuyper, Frederick T. ... Baltimore, MD
Del, Ernest ... **Los Angeles, CA**
DeLaat, Mary H. ... Phoenix, AZ
DeLaat-Maher, Kelly ... **Tacoma, WA**
de La Barre, Francois D. V. ... New Orleans, LA
Delabarre, Mitchell P. ... **Moses Lake, WA**
Wenatchee, WA
de la Bastide, Thomas V., III ... **New York, NY**
DeLabio, Erin P. ... **Buffalo, NY**
de Labry, Colette O. ... Palm Beach, FL
de la Camara, Rosa M. ... **Miami, FL**
de la Carrera, Antonio M. ... Paterson, NJ
de la Carrera, Miguel ... Paterson, NJ
Delacato, Carl H., Jr. ... **Philadelphia, PA**
Delacenserie, Nancy J. ... **Madison, WI**
Delacenserie, Richard J. ... **Madison, WI**
DeLacerda, Melissa ... **Ponca City, OK**
DeLacerda, Melissa ... **Stillwater, OK**
de la Cerna, Patricia M. ... Chicago, IL
de la Cerna, Manuel Federico ... **La Jolla, CA**
De La Cerra, Rebeca D. ... Los Angeles, CA
DeLacey, Charles H. ... **San Francisco, CA**
De La Chapelle, D.F.X. ... **New York, NY**
de la Chapelle, Philippe ... New York, NY
Delacourt, John T. ... **Washington, DC**
Delacourt, Scott D. ... **Washington, DC**
Delacroix, Scott E. ... **New Orleans, LA**
de la Cruz, Alfred M. ... **San Diego, CA**
De la Cruz, Andrés ... **New York, NY**
DeLaCruz, Cedric G. ... Boston, MA
Delacruz, Charles M. ... Baltimore, MD
DeLaCruz, Christopher P. ... Canton, OH
De La Cruz & Cutler, P.A. ... Miami, FL
Dela Cruz, Jose ... Saipan, TT
de la Cruz, La Dessa M. ... Wichita, KS
De La Cruz, Luis F., Jr. ... Miami, FL
de la Cruz, Peter L. ... **Washington, DC**
de la Cruz, Ramon ... Ridgefield, NJ
de la Cruz, Vito ... Yakima, WA
de la Cruz-Figueroa, Jorge ... San Juan, PR
de la Cruz-Muñoz, Jorge ... **Miami, FL**
Dela Cruz Sierra, Bautista ... Vega Baja, PR
De la Cruz-Torres, Lillian T. ... **San Juan, PR**
De Lacy, David G., Jr. ... Sacramento, CA
de la Fé, Ernesto J. ... Miami, FL
de la Fé, Ernesto J., P.A. ... Miami, FL
Delafield, Caroline M. ... New York, NY
Delafield, Darren T. ... Roanoke, VA
Delafield, Gary A. ... **State College, PA**
Delafield, George S. ... San Diego, CA
Delafield, Hope & Linker ... New York, NY
Delafield, Joseph A. ... Lake Charles, LA
Delafield, Joseph L., III ... **Portland, ME**
Delafield, McGee, Jones & Kauffman ... **Bellefonte, PA**
State College, PA
de la Flor, George L. ... **La Mesa, CA**
de la Forest, Charles P. ... Santa Rosa, CA
de la Forest, John M. ... Beaverton, OR
de la Fuente, Andrew Joseph ... Miami Beach, FL
DeLaFuente, Charles ... Latham, NY
de la Fuente, D.G. (Bob), Jr ... **Miami, FL**
De La Fuente, Estela S. ... Dallas, TX
Delafuente, Frances Sosa ... Miami, FL
Delafuente, Jacqueline ... Flushing, NY
de la Fuente, Jose E. ... **Austin, TX**
De La Fuente-Cowan, Maria Elena ... Miami, FL
Delagardelle, Elizabeth A. ... **Kansas City, MO**
de la Garza & Associates, P.C. ... Dallas, TX
De La Garza, Beatriz E. ... Austin, TX
De La Garza, Bill ... **Houston, TX**
De La Garza, Bill, & Associates, P.C. ... **Houston, TX**
De La Garza, Charles H. ... **Minneapolis, MN**
de la Garza, Edward ... Houston, TX
de la Garza, Henry E. ... Albuquerque, NM
De La Garza, Kimberly ... Houston, TX
de la Garza, Leland C. ... Dallas, TX
de la Garza, Luis A. ... San Antonio, TX
De La Garza, Pete ... Kingsville, TX
de La Garza, Randy Waldman ... Houston, TX
de la Garza, Richard ... San Diego, CA
De La Garza, Robert E. ... Edinburg, TX
de la Garza, Rudy ... Brownsville, TX
De La Garza De Garcia, Cecilia ... **Brownsville, TX**
de la Guardia, Oscar G. ... Sunrise, FL
de la Guardia, Ramon M. ... Sacramento, CA
Delahanty, John D. ... **Portland, ME**
Delahanty, Kathryn A. ... **Baltimore, MD**
Delahanty, Mary Lou ... **Lawrenceville, NJ**
Delahanty, Raymond A., Jr. ... Philadelphia, PA
Delahanty, Sean R. ... Louisville, KY
Delahanty, Thomas E., II ... Auburn, ME
Delahay, Benjamin T., Jr. ... Los Alamos, NM
Delahaye, John L. ... **Plaquemine, LA**
Delahaye, Louis W. ... Plaquemine, LA
Delahaye, Thomas C. ... Plaquemine, LA
Delahoussaye, Chanelle T. ... **Lafayette, LA**
De La Houssaye, Edw. A., III ... Franklin, LA
Delahoussaye, Gary J. ... **Lafayette, LA**
Delahoussaye-Turner, Audre ... Los Angeles, CA
de la Hoz, Fernando J. ... **Miami, FL**
De La Hoz, Lillian Arango ... **Miami, FL**
Delahunt, Donald A. ... **Providence, RI**
De La Hunt, Jill A. ... Anchorage, AK
Delahunt, Thos. E. ... Cheektowaga, NY
Delahunt, Timothy E. ... **Washington, DC**
Delahunt, William D. ... Dedham, MA
Delahunty, Peter J. ... **Miami, FL**
Delahunty, Robert C. ... **Salt Lake City, UT**
Delahunty, Robert J. ... Department of Justice, Office of Legal Counsel, GV
Delahunty, Terence J., Jr. ... **Orlando, FL**
De Laine, Allan C. ... Clayton, NC
DeLair, Sidney C. ... Naperville, IL
Delaitsch, Paul G. ... Montgomery, AL
DeLaittre, Carter ... **Minneapolis, MN**
De Lallo, Brett ... Stamford, CT
Delaloza, Arthur, Jr. ... Huntington Beach, CA
de la Loza, Edward T. ... Arcadia, CA
Delamadrid-Gautier, Eugenio G. ... San Juan, PR
De La Mar, John R. ... Urbana, IL
DeLaMar, Shannon M. ... **Champaign, IL**
de la Mata-Melendez, Arlene ... **San Juan, PR**
Delamater, David J. ... **Syracuse, NY**
De La Mater & Hagg Law Office ... Weirton, WV
Delamater, John O. ... New York, NY
De La Mater, W. Dean ... Weirton, WV
DeLamatre & DeLamatre ... Huron, OH
DeLamatre, Richard D. ... Huron, OH
Delamatre, Robert Charles ... Huron, OH
de Lambert, Guy M., III ... St. Paul, MN
de Lambert, John R. ... **Minneapolis, MN**
Delamere, Stephen J. ... **Stoughton, MA**
De Lamielleure, Richard J. ... Canton, MI
DeLamielleure, Ronald A. ... Canton, MI
del Amo, Carlos C. ... Coral Gables, FL
de la Mora & de la Mora ... Elm Grove, WI
de la Mora, Hector ... Elm Grove, WI
de la Mora, Linda C. ... Elm Grove, WI
De La Mora, Richard G. ... **Los Angeles, CA**
de la Motte, Melvin A., Jr. ... San Luis Obispo, CA
de la Motte, Melvin A., Jr., A Law Corporation ... San Luis Obispo, CA
Delan, Daniel ... New York, NY
Delana, Sumner ... Boise, ID
DeLancett, John G. ... **Orlando, FL**
Delancey, Leah E. ... **Long Beach, CA**
DeLancey, Merle Miller, Jr. ... **Washington, DC**
De Lancie, Nicolas ... **San Francisco, CA**
Delancy, Adrian C. ... **Miami, FL**
Delancy, Benjamin I. ... **Washington, DC**
DeLancy, David P., Jr. ... Palm Desert, CA
Delancy, Michelle Ashby ... **Miami, FL**
Deland, Alexander T. ... **New York, NY**
DeLand, Jeffrey A. ... Sacramento, CA
DeLand, Loni F. ... Salt Lake City, UT
De Landri, Adria ... **New York, NY**
DeLaneuville, Laura B. ... Norco, LA
Delaney, Amy Jeanne ... Houston, TX
DeLaney, Amy Parise ... Portland, OR
Delaney & Associates ... West Chester, PA
Delaney, Barbara G. ... Florham Park, NJ
DeLaney, Barbara H. ... Charlotte, NC
Delaney, Bernard A., Jr. ... Oceanside, CA
Delaney, Brian L. ... Missoula, MT
Delaney, Bruce ... New York, NY
DeLaney, Chris C. ... Mobile, AL
DeLaney, Cormac B. ... **Toledo, OH**
Delaney, Cynthia P. ... **Denver, CO**
Delaney, Dale W. ... Largo, FL
Delaney, Dale W., P.A. ... Largo, FL
Delaney, Daniel J. ... **Chicago, IL**
Delaney, Daniel P. ... **Los Angeles, CA**
Delaney, Daniel P. ... **Harrisburg, PA**
Delaney, Daniel R. ... **Pittsburgh, PA**
Delaney, Daniel V. ... Indiana, PA
Delaney, David Brooke ... Fairfax, VA
Delaney, David L. ... **Plymouth, MA**
Delaney, David M. ... **Gainesville, FL**
Delaney, David M. ... Caro, MI
Delaney, David R. ... Hanover, MA
DeLaney & DeLaney ... Mobile, AL
Delaney & Delaney ... Indiana, PA
Delaney, Dennis J. ... Monroe, CT
Delaney, Dennis R. ... **Boston, MA**
Delaney, Dexter L., (P.C.) ... Missoula, MT
Delaney, Duane B. ... Washington, DC
Delaney, Edgar M. ... Phoenix, AZ
Delaney, Edmund T. ... Chester, CT
DeLaney, Edward O. ... **Indianapolis, IN**
Delaney, Elizabeth A. ... **Washington, DC**
DeLaney, Ernest S., Jr. ... Charlotte, NC
DeLaney, Ernest S. (Mike), III ... **Charlotte, NC**
Delaney, Frank G. ... **Corpus Christi, TX**
Delaney, George ... San Jose, CA
Delaney, George T. ... Bronx, NY
Delaney, H. Jean ... Savannah, GA
Delaney, Helen L. ... Los Angeles, CA
DeLaney, Herbert W., Jr. ... **Denver, CO**
DeLaney, Herbert W., Jr., Professional Corporation ... **Denver, CO**
Delaney, James F. ... **New York, NY**
Delaney, James J. ... **Anchorage, AK**
Delaney, James J. ... **New York, NY**
Delaney, James L. ... Grand Blanc, MI
Delaney, James M. ... **Seattle, WA**
Delaney, James R. ... Webster, SD
Delaney, Jeffrey J. ... **New York, NY**
Delaney, Jennifer K. ... **San Antonio, TX**
Delaney, Jerome P. ... West Seneca, NY
Delaney, Jill M. Davis ... Portland, ME
Delaney, Joan Colette ... New York, NY
Delaney, John B ... New York, NY
Delaney, John B. ... **Alexandria, VA**
Delaney, John E., Jr. ... **Salt Lake City, UT**
Delaney, John F. ... Hartford, CT
Delaney, John F. ... **New York, NY**
Delaney, John J. ... **Washington, DC**
Delaney, John J. ... **Columbia, MD**
Silver Spring, MD
Delaney, John J. ... **Rapid City, SD**
DeLaney, John J., Jr. ... **Summit, NJ**
DeLaney, John M. ... **Syracuse, NY**
Delaney, John M. ... Bryan, TX
Delaney, John M., Jr. ... East Alton, IL
DeLaney, John V. ... Pelham, NY
Delaney, John W. ... **Boston, MA**
Delaney, Joseph A. ... **San Diego, CA**
Delaney, Joseph E. ... **Seattle, WA**
Delaney, Joseph H. ... Flint, MI
Delaney, Joseph M. ... **Wallingford, CT**
Delaney, Joseph P. ... Las Vegas, NV
Delaney, Joshua C. ... Silver Spring, MD
Delaney, Karoline A. ... **Newport Beach, CA**
DeLaney, Kathleen A. ... **Indianapolis, IN**
Delaney, Kathleen M. ... **Washington, DC**
Delaney, Kathleen M. ... Lake Charles, LA
Delaney, Kent J. ... Webster, SD
Delaney, Kevin C. ... **Redwood City, CA**
Delaney, Kevin P. ... **Tyler, TX**
Delaney, Kimberly Y. ... **Houston, TX**
Delaney, Lawrence S. ... **Worcester, MA**
Delaney, Leo F. ... Falmouth, MA
Delaney, Lisa J. ... Braintree, MA
Delaney, Lisa L. ... Milford, MA
Delaney, Martin A., III ... Chicago, IL
Delaney, Martin J. ... Mineola, NY
Delaney, Mary Ann ... Lexington, KY
Delaney, Mary C. ... Santa Monica, CA
Delaney, Mary Jane ... San Francisco, CA
Delaney, Maureen A. ... **Washington, DC**
Delaney, McCarthy, Colton & Botzin, P.C. ... **Alexandria, VA**
Delaney & Melkonoff ... Phoenix, AZ
Delaney, Michael Arthur ... Manchester, NH
Delaney, Michael B. ... Cincinnati, OH
DeLaney, Michael C. ... Mobile, AL
Delaney, Michael F. ... **Kansas City, MO**
Delaney, Michael J. ... Los Angeles, CA
Delaney, Michael J. ... Nanticoke, PA
Delaney, Michael James ... **Atlanta, GA**
Delaney, Michael P. ... Houston, TX
Delaney, Michael S. ... Indiana, PA
Delaney & Muncey, P.C. ... **Plymouth, MA**
Weymouth, MA
Delaney, Nancy E. ... **New York, NY**
Delaney, Nancy J. ... Dedham, MA
Delaney, Nancy K. ... **Eureka, CA**
DeLaney and O'Connor LLP ... **Syracuse, NY**
Delaney, Pamela Michele ... Chicago, IL
DeLaney, Patricia A. ... **Houston, TX**
Delaney, Patricia C. ... Commack, NY
Delaney, Patrick ... **Minneapolis, MN**
Delaney, Patrick J. ... Hermiston, OR
Delaney, Patrick M. ... Lancaster, CA
Delaney, Patrick R. ... **Cherry Hill, NJ**
Delaney, Paul F. ... New York, NY
DeLaney, Paul H., Jr. ... Washington, DC
DeLaney, Philip A. ... **Gainesville, FL**
Delaney, Raighne C. ... Alexandria, VA
Delaney, Raymond T. ... **Somerville, MA**
DeLaney, Richard ... **Huntington, IN**
Warren, IN
Delaney, Richard P. ... Houston, TX
Delaney, Robert ... Carbondale, CO

Delaney, Robert Emmett ......West Chester, PA
Delaney, Robert J. ......Richmond, IN
Delaney, Robert J. ......New Orleans, LA
Delaney, Robert L. ......Nashville, TN
Delaney, Robert R., Jr. ......Deerfield, IL
Delaney, Robert S. ......Spokane, WA
Delaney, Rose H. ......New Orleans, LA
Delaney, Sean ......Flemington, NJ
Delaney, Sean C. ......Boston, MA
Delaney, Sean T. ......Boston, MA
Delaney, Sheila K. ......Department of Justice, Civil Rights Division, GV
Delaney, Stacia Bank ......Denver, CO
Delaney, Stephen ......Redwood City, CA
Delaney, Stephen B. ......New Britain, CT
Delaney, Steven D. ......Richmond, VA
Delaney, Steven J. ......Plantation, FL
Delaney, Steven M. ......Bellevue, NE
Delaney & Sumner ......Rapid City, SD
Delaney, Thomas A. ......Irvine, CA
Delaney, Thomas Edward ......Charleston, WV
Delaney, Thomas F. ......West Chester, PA
Delaney, Thomas J. ......Washington, DC
Delaney, Tim ......Phoenix, AZ
Delaney, Timothy J. ......Cleveland, OH
Delaney, Timothy Q. ......Chicago, IL
Delaney, Trisha W. ......Uniondale, NY
Delaney, Vander Linden & Delaney
Webster, SD
Delaney, Warren R., Jr. ......Boston, MA
Delaney, Wiles, Hayes, Gerety, Ellis & Young, Inc. ......Anchorage, AK
Delaney, William F., Jr. ......Rochester, NY
Delaney, William J. ......Providence, RI
Delaney, William R. ......Mobile, AL
Delaney, William R. ......San Francisco, CA
De Laney, William R. ......Elmira, NY
Delaney, Wm. Patrick ......Erie, PA
Delaney, Zemetis, Donahue, Durham & Noonan, P.C. ......Guilford, CT
New Haven, CT
Wallingford, CT
DeLange, Brett T. ......Boise, ID
DeLange, Darrin J. ......Phoenix, AZ
De Lange, Hudspeth, McConnell & Tibbets, L.L.P. ......Houston, TX
De Lange, J. F. Henry ......Lockport, NY
DeLange, Robert S. ......Houston, TX
DeLange, Timothy A. ......San Diego, CA
De Lange, Tracey Lynn Kovall
San Diego, CA
de Langis, Mark K. ......San Francisco, CA
deLanglade-Spriggs, Elise M.
Columbus, OH
DeLanis, James A. ......Nashville, TN
Delanney, Bertrand J. ......New York, NY
Delanney, Susana D. ......New York, NY
De Lannoy, Amy B. ......Bridgeport, CT
DeLano, Arthur A., Jr. ......Baltimore, MD
Delano, Caryl E. ......Tampa, FL
Delano, Dare F. ......Newport Beach, CA
San Diego, CA
Delano, G. Kristin ......St. Petersburg, FL
Delano, Jonathan W. ......Pittsburgh, PA
Delano, M. Dare Fuller ......San Diego, CA
Delano, Mario J. ......Asbury Park, NJ
DeLano, Mary ......Portland, ME
Delano, Robert B., Jr. ......Richmond, VA
Delano, Stephen J. ......Winona, MN
Delano, Stuart P. ......Brockton, MA
Delano, William A. ......New York, NY
Delano, William G., Jr. ......San Antonio, TX
Delanois, Barbara L. ......Danville, IL
Delanoit, Heidi L. ......West Des Moines, IA
DeLanoit, Peter S. ......Des Moines, IA
Delanoy, Cathleen Russo ......Trenton, NJ
DeLanoy, Drake ......Las Vegas, NV
DeLanoy, Drake, A Prof. Corp., Law Offices of
Las Vegas, NV
Delanoy, Edward James, Jr. ......Toms River, NJ
DeLanoy, English, Schuetze & McGaha, A Professional Corporation ......Las Vegas, NV
Delanoy, Jesse D. ......Owings Mills, MD
De Lanoy, John Scott ......Minneapolis, MN
Seattle, WA
Delany, B. Cort ......Greenwich, CT
Delany, Francis E., Jr. ......Newark, NJ
Delany, Frank J. ......Riverside, CA
DeLany, Jack V. ......Memphis, TN
Delany, Logan D., Jr. ......Irvington, NY
Delany, Teresa Ann ......New York, NY
Delany, William J. ......Washington, DC
Delany, William J. ......Philadelphia, PA
Delao, Alice E. ......Milwaukee, WI
de la O, Jose M. ......Coral Gables, FL
de la O, Miguel M. ......Miami, FL
de la O & Marko ......Miami, FL
de la Osa, Jorge ......Orlando, FL
Delap, Herbert A. ......Denver, CO
Delap, Herbert A., & Associates, P.C.
Denver, CO
de la Parte, Edward P., Jr. ......Tampa, FL
de la Parte, Gilbert & Bales, Professional Association ......Tampa, FL
de la Parte, L. David ......Tampa, FL
de la Parte, Louis A. ......Tampa, FL
de la Paz, Andrew G. ......Landover, MD
De La Paz, David M. ......Tallahassee, FL
de la Pena, Federico A. ......Pomona, CA
de la Peña, Gregory R. ......Emeryville, CA
San Francisco, CA
De La Peña, Leoncio E. ......Miami, FL
de la Pena, Nancy A. ......Santa Cruz, CA
de la Peña, Nuria ......Washington, DC
de la Peña, Patricia M. ......Austin, TX
de la Peña, Richard ......Stockton, CA
De La Peña, Villanueva & Bajandas, L.L.P.
Miami, FL

DeLapenha, Monique Y. ......Philadelphia, PA
Delaplain, James Wesley
Minneapolis, MN
Delapoer, James V. B. ......Albany, OR
Delaporta, Gregg A. ......Washington, DC
de la Portilla, Maria R. ......Coral Gables, FL
De La Portilla, Miguel Diaz ......Miami, FL
de la Poterie, Marceline A.
Los Angeles, CA
Delapp, Curtis ......Bartlesville, OK
DeLapp, Mark L. ......Portland, OR
DeLapp, Mark L., P.C. ......Portland, OR
De Lara, Nannette ......San Francisco, CA
DeLara Luck, Leslie ......Atlanta, GA
de la Rama, Christopher ......New York, NY
de la Reza, Mercedes E. ......Hackensack, NJ
DeLargy, Elisabeth ......Austin, TX
DeLargy, Krista ......Washington, DC
de Larios, F. Jose ......South San Francisco, CA
deLarios, Patricia B. ......Dallas, TX
De La Riva, Jesús ......Los Angeles, CA
de la Rocha, Raquelle ......Universal City, CA
DeLaroche, Steven N.J.
Daytona Beach, FL
De La Rosa, Andrew ......Chicago, IL
de la Rosa, Dan M. ......New York, NY
de la Rosa, Dora M. ......Torrance, CA
De la Rosa, Jennifer J. ......Houston, TX
De la Rosa, John G. ......New York, NY
Delarosa, Kathleen ......Phoenix, AZ
De La Rosa, Luis Antonio ......Los Angeles, CA
de la Rosa, Melandro T. ......Woodland, CA
De La Rosa, Michael A. ......Round Rock, TX
Dela Rosa, Noelle E. ......San Diego, CA
De la Rosa, Oscar L. ......Houston, TX
DelaRosa, Regina M. ......Columbus, OH
De La Rosa-Tolgyesi, Haydee ......Miami, FL
De La Rosa-Tolgyesi, Haydee, P.A.
Miami, FL
Delarose, Ronald ......Houston, TX
Delarue, Earl G. ......Timonium, MD
DeLarue, Marcia B. ......Orange, TX
de Lasa, Jose M. ......North Chicago, IL
DeLascio, John E. ......Chicago, IL
Delashaw, Kenneth L., Jr. ......Marietta, OK
DeLashmet, W. Pemble ......Mobile, AL
Delashmit, Preston C. ......Atlanta, GA
De Lasho, S. Jas. ......Yonkers, NY
de la Sota, Richard ......Los Angeles, CA
Delate, Thomas E. ......Yardley, PA
de la Teja, Magdalena H. ......Austin, TX
Delaterre, Norman F. ......Long Beach, CA
DeLateur, Steven W. ......Los Angeles, CA
Delatore, John A. ......Victorville, CA
De La Torre, Cris ......Fort Collins, CO
de la Torre, Dale R. ......Beverly Hills, CA
de la Torre, Frank J. ......Fort Lauderdale, FL
De La Torre, Helio ......Miami, FL
De La Torre, Jasmine ......Chicago, IL
de la Torre, Martin John ......Houston, TX
de la Torre, Pedro ......Philadelphia, PA
DeLaTorre, Phillip E. ......Lawrence, KS
Delatorre, Richard P.
Rancho Cucamonga, CA
De La Torre, Ruben A. ......Ventura, CA
de la Torriente, Cosme J., (P.A.) ......Miami, FL
Delatour, Marjorie C. ......Dallas, TX
Delatte, Glynn J., Jr. ......Baton Rouge, LA
DeLaughter, Bobby B. ......Jackson, MS
de Launay, Gerald C. ......Erath, LA
Lafayette, LA
deLaunay, William H., Jr. ......Alexandria, LA
Delaune, Harvey P. ......Bossier City, LA
DeLaune, Jeffrey S. ......Bossier City, LA
DeLaune, Patrick L. ......Austin, TX
Delaune, Timothy A. ......Concord, NH
Delaune, Warner J., Jr. ......Baton Rouge, LA
deLaup, Mickey S. ......Metairie, LA
New Orleans, LA
de Laup, René ......New Orleans, LA
deLaup, S. Guy ......Metairie, LA
DeLaura, Michael V. ......Norfolk, VA
Delaurenti, Charles J., II ......Renton, WA
DeLaurenti, John L. ......Greenville, IL
de Laurentiis, Jennifer ......Washington, DC
Delaurentiis, Joseph H. ......Lincoln Park, MI
DeLaurentis, Anthony J. ......Kensington, MD
DeLaurentis, Brian M. ......New York, NY
De Laurentis, Dina M. ......Venice, CA
DeLaurentis, Dominic A., Jr.
Mount Laurel, NJ
DeLaurentis, Dominic J., Jr. ......Boardman, OH
de Laurentis, John M. ......Cherry Hill, NJ
Delaus, Daniel M., Jr. ......Rochester, NY
Delauter, Michael H. ......Frederick, MD
Delavan, Charles F. ......Annapolis, MD
de LaVan, Joseph M. ......Chicago, IL
DeLave, Joseph W. ......Bloomfield Hills, MI
de la Vega, Constance M. V.
San Francisco, CA
de la Vega, Frederick ......New York, NY
De la Vergne, Hugues J., II
New Orleans, LA
de la Vergne, James V. ......Sacramento, CA
de la Vergne, Louis V. ......New Orleans, LA
de la Vergne & McMurtry, A Professional Corporation ......Sacramento, CA
DeLaVergne, Ralph J. ......Vienna, VA
De La Vergne, Warren T. ......Drain, OR
Delavigne, John A. ......Los Angeles, CA
De La Villa, Marcos L. ......San Juan, PR
Delay, Brendan E. ......Cleveland, OH
De Lay, Clara Black ......Stone Mountain, GA
Delay, Curran, Thompson, Pontarolo & Walker, P.S. ......Spokane, WA
DeLay, John K., Jr. ......Dallas, TX
Delay, Joseph P. ......Spokane, WA
Delay, Lawrence C. ......Friday Harbor, WA

Delay, Michael J. ......Spokane, WA
Delay, Paul J. ......Seattle, WA
DeLay, Paul R. ......Monterey, CA
DeLay, Roy E., III ......Dallas, TX
DeLay, Thomas H. ......Norfolk, NE
DeLay, Thomas S. ......Jackson, OH
DeLayo, Dianne ......Santa Fe, NM
DeLayo, Leonard J., Jr. ......Albuquerque, NM
DeLayo, Leonard J., Jr., P.C.
Albuquerque, NM
Del Baglivo, Emil A. ......Jersey City, NJ
Delbaum, Charles M. ......New Orleans, LA
Delbaum, David S. ......New York, NY
Del Beccaro, Thomas G. F.
Walnut Creek, CA
Del Beccaro, Thomas M. ......Chicago, IL
Delbecq, Bruce R. ......Southfield, MI
DelBello, Alfred B. ......White Plains, NY
DelBello Donnellan Weingarten & Tartaglia, LLP ......New York, NY
White Plains, NY
DelBello, James E. ......Media, PA
DelBello, James E. ......Philadelphia, PA
Del Bello, Robert A. ......Atlanta, GA
Del Ben, Reno A. ......Tenafly, NJ
Del Bene, Frank J. ......North Merrick, NY
Del Bene, LaPolla & Thomas ......Warren, OH
Delbert, Susan M. ......Washington, DC
Del Bianco, H. Peter, Jr. ......Portland, ME
Del Bianco, Jane R. ......Bronx, NY
Del Bianco, Mark C. ......Washington, DC
Delbick, Judi A. ......Glendale, CA
Del Bino, Jon J. ......Auburn, CA
Del Bino, Jon J. ......Roseville, CA
Delbon, David A. ......Burlingame, CA
Del Bonis, Anthony F. ......Providence, RI
DelBove, Peter P. ......Roswell, GA
Delbridge, Jane Becker-Smith ......Fairfax, VA
Delbridge, William L. ......Vashon, WA
Delbruck, Jonathan ......Del Mar, CA
Del Buono, Carl ......New Hartford, NY
Del Buono & Diodati, LLP
New Hartford, NY
Del Buono, John A. ......Watertown, CT
del Calvo, Jorge A. ......Palo Alto, CA
Delcambre, Paul J., Jr. ......Gulfport, MS
Delcamp, Rex E. ......St. Petersburg, FL
Delcamp & Siegel ......St. Petersburg, FL
DelCampo, J. Antonio ......Greenville, SC
Del Campo, John F. ......Herndon, VA
Del Campo, Joseph A. ......Chicago, IL
Delcampo, Lil G. ......Santa Ana, CA
Del Campo, Rafael A. ......Chicago, IL
del Campo, Robert A. ......Arroyo Grande, CA
Del Carlo, Edw. R. ......San Francisco, CA
Del Carlo, Shari ......Los Angeles, CA
Del Caro, Lyn ......Louisville, CO
Del Carpio, Carlos ......Manchester, NH
Del Casale, John J. ......Philadelphia, PA
Del Casino, Anne J. ......Mineola, NY
Del Casino, F. Casey, P.C. ......Nashville, TN
Del Casino, Francis (Casey) ......Nashville, TN
del Castillo, Albert A. ......Miami, FL
del Castillo, Barbara Carey
Fort Lauderdale, FL
del Castillo, Diamela ......Miami, FL
del Castillo, Rafael G. ......Honolulu, HI
DelCastillo, Rey ......Miami, FL
Delchamps, Alfred F., III ......Birmingham, AL
Delcher, Mark J. ......Linwood, NJ
Delchin, Steven A. ......Cleveland, OH
Delchop, Patrick J. ......Los Angeles, CA
Del Col, John V. ......Stamford, CT
Del Colliano, Arthur G. ......Hackensack, NJ
Del Collo, John N. ......Ridley Park, PA
Del Collo & Mazzanti ......Paoli, PA
Del Collo, Michael J. ......Merion, PA
Del Collo, Peter R. ......Paoli, PA
Del Compare, Lisa
Department Of The Interior, GV
DelConte, Scott J. ......Syracuse, NY
Delcore, Colleen E. ......Indian Lake, NY
Del Core, Jeanmarie ......Great Neck, NY
Delcore, Joseph C. ......Everett, MA
Del Cotto, Dennis D. ......Monroeville, PA
DelCotto, Laura Day ......Lexington, KY
Del Cotto, Louis A. ......Buffalo, NY
Del Cotto, Ronald D. ......Monroeville, PA
Del Cotto, Steven J. ......Pittsburgh, PA
Delcour, David W. ......Denver, CO
Del Deo, Ralph N. ......Newark, NJ
Deldin, Lisa ......Bronx, NY
Del Duca, Andrea ......Charlotte, NC
Del Duca, Damien O. ......Haddonfield, NJ
Del Duca, Frances H. ......Carlisle, PA
Del Duca, Joseph A. ......Haddonfield, NJ
Del Duca, Louis F. ......Carlisle, PA
Del Duca, Mark Thomas ......Milwaukee, WI
DelDuca, Matthew V. ......Princeton, NJ
Del Duca, Maureen F. ......Washington, DC
Del Duca, Patrick ......Los Angeles, CA
Del Duca, Ronald M., Jr.
Virginia Beach, VA
Del Duca, Tiffany N. ......Naples, FL
DelDuchetto, Ernest A. ......Syracuse, NY
DelDuchetto & Potter ......Syracuse, NY
Delduco, A. Alfred ......West Chester, PA
Delea, Martha A. ......Baltimore, MD
Delea, Michael F., Jr. ......Towson, MD
DeLear, Vera Ann ......Hackensack, NJ
Deleault, Robert R. ......Manchester, NH
Delecke, Janet H. ......Troy, MI
DeLee, Brent K. ......Baton Rouge, LA
DeLee, Garrison G. ......Los Angeles, CA
DeLee, James A. ......Port Arthur, TX
Deleery, Elizabeth Gibson ......Austin, TX
de Leeuw, Emily ......Saratoga, CA
De Leeuw, Marc ......New York, NY

de Leeuw, Michael Birney ......New York, NY
deLeeuw, Michael J. ......Norfolk, VA
DeLeeuw, Murray ......Pittsford, NY
Delegal Law Offices, P.A. ......Jacksonville, FL
Delegal, Mark K. ......Tallahassee, FL
Delegal, Susan F. ......Fort Lauderdale, FL
Delegal, Thomas A. "Tad", III
Jacksonville, FL
Delehant, David M. ......Sacramento, CA
Delehant, David M., A Professional Law Corporation ......Sacramento, CA
Delehant, Jean E. ......Omaha, NE
Delehant, John W. ......Sacramento, CA
Delehant, Joseph H. ......Danvers, MA
Delehanty, Andrew J. J. ......Washington, DC
Delehanty, Garrett J., Jr. ......Hartford, CT
Delehanty, Gary W. ......Rochester, NY
Delehanty, Jeanne Mazur ......Simsbury, CT
Delehanty, John D. ......Tupper Lake, NY
Delehanty, Kevin ......Boston, MA
Delehanty, Mark W. ......Rochester, MN
Delehanty, Terrence D. ......Boca Raton, FL
Delehaunty, James F. ......Worcester, MA
Delehey, C. Mark ......Philadelphia, PA
Delehey, Charles A. ......Trenton, NJ
Delehey, Lauren Graham ......Princeton, NJ
Delehunt, Michael E. ......San Francisco, CA
de Leiris, Betsy G. ......Newport, RI
Deleissegues, Richard L. ......San Diego, CA
Delekta, Diane Hubel ......Memphis, MI
Delekta, Diane Hubel, P.C. ......Memphis, MI
Delelio, James D. ......Chicago, IL
DeLellis, Anthony J. ......San Diego, CA
San Diego, CA
Delello, Richard J. ......Los Angeles, CA
Roseland, NJ
New York, NY
Delello, Robert ......Boston, MA
Delemar, Isaiah David ......Miami, FL
Delemarre, Michelle T.
Department of Justice, GV
deLemos, Donald R. ......Palo Alto, CA
deLemos, Pedro R. ......Department of Justice, Civil Rights Division, GV
DeLena, Robert C. ......Boston, MA
DeLeo, Alfred F. ......Los Angeles, CA
DeLeo, Angell, Palmer & Zenkert
Westfield, MA
DeLeo, Charles G. ......Miami, FL
De Leo, Donald W. ......Hackensack, NJ
De Leo, Frank L. ......Lincolnwood, IL
De Leo, Joseph B. ......Westfield, MA
DeLeo, Joseph E. ......Cocoa, FL
De Leo, Joseph M. ......New York, NY
DeLeo, Laura D. ......Englewood, CO
DeLeo, Michael S. ......Seattle, WA
DeLeo, Patricia A. ......Tampa, FL
DeLeo, Robert A. ......Revere, MA
De Leo, Robin Ronquillo ......Mandeville, LA
De Leo, Shelley R. (Barber)
San Francisco, CA
DeLeo, Stephen A. ......Bristol, RI
DeLeo, Vincenzo A. ......New York, NY
De Leon, Albert V. ......New York, NY
DeLeon, Anna Maria ......McAllen, TX
de Leon, Armando ......Phoenix, AZ
DeLeon, Boggins & Icenogle, A Professional Corporation ......Austin, TX
Deleon, Charles ......Herndon, VA
deLeon, Dennis ......New York, NY
DeLeon, Edgar ......New York, NY
De Leon, Fernando ......Sacramento, CA
Deleon, Florecita Vivas ......San Francisco, CA
DeLeon, Hector ......Austin, TX
DeLeon, J. Russell ......San Francisco, CA
De Leon, Jacqueline M. ......Miami Beach, FL
DeLeon, Joan D. ......Orange, CA
DeLeon, John Louis ......Miami, FL
DeLeon, John R. ......Chicago, IL
de Leon, Josie E. ......Department of Justice, Tax Division, GV
de Leon, Josefino P. ......Arlington, VA
DeLeon, Keith B. ......Charlotte, NC
Deleon, Kenneth J. ......Palo Alto, CA
De Leon, Kirk Dennison ......Miami, FL
DeLeon, Lara Cardin ......Houston, TX
de Leon, Leon M. ......Washington, DC
DeLeon, Louis A. ......St. Louis, MO
De Leon, Maria Guadalupe ......Houston, TX
de Leon, Melina ......Honolulu, HI
DeLeon, Nancy L. ......Dallas, TX
De Leon, Pablo, Jr. ......Los Angeles, CA
De Leon, Patrick ......Watertown, CT
DeLeon, Patrick H. ......United States Senate, Senatorial Assistants, GV
Deleon, Primitivo R. ......New York, NY
De Leon, Rafael
Environmental Protection Agency, Office of the General Counsel, GV
DeLeon, Ruben C. ......Dallas, TX
De León, Ruth N. ......San Juan, PR
de Leon, Sylvia A. ......Washington, DC
De Leonardis & Dermody ......Jersey City, NJ
De Leonardis, Francis ......Jersey City, NJ
DeLeonardis, Louis ......Bloomingdale, IL
DeLeonardo, Prisca M. ......Birmingham, AL
DeLeone, James F. ......Columbus, OH
de Leon Vergel de Dios, Richard
Anaheim, CA
Deleranko, Florence K. ......Seattle, WA
Delerme, Augusto N. ......Altoona, PA
Pittsburgh, PA
Delerme & Gallimore ......Altoona, PA
Pittsburgh, PA
Delery, Carolyn H. ......Milwaukee, WI
Delery, Oliver S. ......New Orleans, LA
Delery, Stuart F. ......Washington, DC
Delery, Winifred M. ......New Orleans, LA

Delesdernier, Michael R. ....Metairie, LA
Delesdernier, Michael R.
New Orleans, LA
Delesie, J. Craig, Jr. ....Tampa, FL
Delesie, James Craig, Sr. ....Tampa, FL
Delesk, Suzanne M. ....Laguna Niguel, CA
Delesky, Edward ....Roseland, NJ
DeLessio, Kathleen ....Freeport, NY
DeLett, Robert ....Reno, NV
Deleuran, Mette ....Philadelphia, PA
Delev, Gregory D. ....Cincinnati, OH
Delev, Gregory D., Co., L.P.A.
Cincinnati, OH
DeLeve, Gene A. ....Kansas City, MO
deLevie, Alvin F. ....Philadelphia, PA
Delevie, Harold J. ....Los Angeles, CA
Delevie, Harold J., Incorporated
Los Angeles, CA
Delevie, Hugo A. ....Southfield, MI
deLevie, Raymond M. ....Columbus, OH
Delevie, Thomas L. ....Philadelphia, PA
Deley, Lisa ....Anderson, IN
Deley-Shimer, Julie A. ....Columbus, OH
DelFavero, Jane L. ....New York, NY
Delfeld, David W. ....Azle, TX
Delfine, Michael P. ....Portage, IN
Delfino, Alan P. ....Watsonville, CA
Delfino, Brett D. ....New York, NY
Delfino, Chrisopher A.
Department of Commerce,
Office of the General Counsel, GV
Delfino Green & Green ....Oakland, CA
San Francisco, CA
San Rafael, CA
Delfino, Patrick F. ....Coeur d'Alene, ID
Spokane, WA
Delfino, Rebecca ....Los Angeles, CA
Delfino Green, Sharon ....San Francisco, CA
Delflache, Marc L. ....Houston, TX
DelForge, Clarence Joe, III ....Raleigh, NC
Delforge, Dean P. ....Waukesha, WI
Delforge, Ralph H. ....Milwaukee, WI
Delforge, Richard D. ....Oconto, WI
DelFranco, Randolph A. ....New York, NY
Delfs, Elizabeth ....New York, NY
Del Fuoco, Jeffrey John ....Tampa, FL
Delgadillo, Albert G. ....Corinth, MS
Tupelo, MS
Delgadillo, Bryant S. ....Philadelphia, PA
Delgadillo, Hortencia ....Tucson, AZ
Delgadillo, Maria Elena ....Brownsville, TX
Del Gadio, Robert G., Law Offices of
Uniondale, NY
Delgado, Acosta, Braden & Jones, P.C.
El Paso, TX
Delgado, Andree D. ....Atlanta, GA
Delgado, Ann-Marie C. ....Washington, DC
Delgado, Antonio Cuevas ....San Juan, PR
Delgado & Bickett ....Bakersfield, CA
Delgado, Blas H., Jr. ....San Antonio, TX
Delgado, Carlos ....Chicago, IL
Delgado, Charles X. ....Irvine, CA
Delgado, David ....Chicago, IL
Delgado, Deborah Harvey
Treasury Department,
Internal Revenue Service, GV
Delgado, Denise ....New York, NY
Delgado, Donna M. ....Miami Beach, FL
Delgado, Evan L. ....Redding, CA
Delgado, Fernández & Rodriguez, LLP
San Juan, PR
Delgado, Hector ....El Paso, TX
Delgado, John D. ....Columbia, SC
Delgado, Juan C. ....Costa Mesa, CA
Delgado, Juan P. ....Miami, FL
Delgado, Lee ....White Plains, NY
Delgado, Lou Ann ....San Juan, PR
Delgado, Luis E. ....Miami, FL
Delgado, Marco ....El Paso, TX
Delgado, Marcus ....Atlanta, GA
Delgado, Mario R. ....Coral Gables, FL
Delgado, Michael P. ....Arlington, TX
Delgado, Michelle M. ....New York, NY
Delgado, Michelle M., Law Offices of, P.C.
New York, NY
Delgado, Natalia ....Chicago, IL
Delgado, Oscar J. ....Miami Lakes, FL
Delgado, Raul G. ....Miami, FL
Delgado, Robert W. ....Washington, DC
Delgado, Rodolfo ....Edinburg, TX
Delgado, Rolando ....Miami, FL
Delgado, Ronaldo P. ....Moses Lake, WA
Delgado, Thomas M. ....Tempe, AZ
Delgado, Tracy M. ....Atlanta, GA
Delgado, Vincent E. ....Indian Orchard, MA
Delgado-Cadilla, José L. ....San Juan, PR
Delgado-Hernández, Pedro A.
San Juan, PR
Delgado Kuinlam, Fernando
San Juan, PR
Delgado-Munoz, Billy E. ....Perth Amboy, NJ
Delgado-Sosa, Maria de los Angeles
San Juan, PR
Del Gallo, Rinaldo ....Washington, DC
Delgass, Michael N. ....Chicago, IL
New York, NY
Del Gatto, Brian T. ....New York, NY
Del Gaudio, Victor H. ....Trenton, NJ
Del Genio, Edward D. ....Chicago, IL
DelGeorge, Louis O. ....Naperville, IL
Delger, Edw. F. ....San Rafael, CA
DelGiorno, Matthew ....Washington, DC
Del Giudice, Michael J. ....Charleston, WV
Del Giudice, Peter M. ....Dearborn, MI
Del Giudice, Richard A. ....Chicago, IL
Del Gizzi, Ronald E.
Department of Commerce,
Patent and Trademark Office, GV

Del Grande, Donald ....Burlingame, CA
Del Grande, Lee F. ....San Jose, CA
Del Greco, Peter F. ....Los Angeles, CA
DelGreco, Phylliss A. ....Melville, NY
Del Greco, Robert G., Jr. ....Pittsburgh, PA
DelGreco, Terri ....Saddle Brook, NJ
DelGross, Claudia A. ....Wilmington, DE
Delgrosso, Lisa S. ....Akron, OH
DelGrosso, Peter ....Montgomery, AL
Del Grosso, William K. ....Hoover, AL
Del Guercio, James P. ....Los Angeles, CA
Del Guercio, Nicholas P. ....Stony Brook, NY
Del Guercio, Richard A. ....Los Angeles, CA
Del Guercio, Ronald J. ....Los Angeles, CA
Del Guercio, Stephen A. ....Los Angeles, CA
Del Guercio, Victor R. ....Port Chester, NY
DelGuzzi, Bernard D. ....Ravenna, OH
Delhagen, Michael R. ....New York, NY
DelHagen, William T. ....Los Angeles, CA
Delhey, Duncan C. ....Milwaukee, WI
Delhey, William F. ....Saline, MI
del Hierro, Edwin S. ....Chicago, IL
DelHomme, Beverly A. ....Dallas, TX
Delhomme, Monique S. ....Washington, DC
Delhommer, Harold J. ....Houston, TX
Delhotal Law Offices, P.A. ....Wichita, KS
Delhotal, Van R. ....Wichita, KS
D'Elia, Anthony J. ....Binghamton, NY
D'Elia, Anthony V. ....Hackensack, NJ
Delia, Bernard J. ....Department of Justice,
Office of the Deputy Attorney General, GV
D'Elia & Cavanaugh ....Orleans, MA
D'Elia, Edmund P. ....New York, NY
DeLia, Elis J. ....Utica, NY
D'Elia, Filomena ....Washington, DC
D'Elia, Frank A. ....Port Washington, NY
D'Elia, Frank R. ....Lynbrook, NY
D'Elia, Gerry ....Park City, UT
Delia, James J. ....Paramus, NJ
D'Elia, Jason ....San Diego, CA
D'Elia, John J. ....New Haven, CT
D'Elia, Joseph ....Huntington, NY
D'Elia, Joseph H. ....Orleans, MA
Delia, Lesley Magaril ....Mineola, NY
D'Elia, Susan F. ....Stamford, CT
D'Elia, Vincent ....Mount Laurel, NJ
D'Elia, Vincent J. ....Englewood, NJ
Delianites, Dean G. ....Flushing, NY
D'Elia-Wilson, Robin ....New York, NY
De Libera, John S. ....Columbus, OH
De Libera, Lyons and Bibbo ....Columbus, OH
DeLiberato, Vincent C., Jr. ....Harrisburg, PA
Delibert, Arthur C. ....Washington, DC
Delibert, Steven A. ....New York, NY
Deliberto, Thomas A., (P.C.)
Washington, DC
Baltimore, MD
De Liberty, Peter A. ....Broomall, PA
De Liberty, Richard A.
San Francisco, CA
Chicago, IL
Delicari, Alexia ....New York, NY
Delich, Sam D. ....San Francisco, CA
D'Elicio, Christine Pillsbury
Baltimore, MD
Delie, David L., Jr. ....Troy, MI
De Liee, Charles T. ....Treasury Department,
Internal Revenue Service, GV
De Liema, Max B. ....Laguna Hills, CA
Deligan, Todd D. ....Everett, WA
Deliganis, Chryssa V. ....Seattle, WA
Deligiorgis, Maria ....Washington, DC
Delikanakis, John S. ....Las Vegas, NV
Delikat, Michael ....New York, NY
Delile, Tammy A. ....Goshen, NY
De Lillo, Albert P. ....Staten Island, NY
De Lima, Brian J. ....Hilo, HI
delima, Richard F. ....Cambridge, MA
Delin, Richard C., Jr.
North Brunswick, NJ
Delin, Sylvia K. ....Birmingham, MI
DeLince, J. Patrick ....New York, NY
Deline, Douglas N. ....Midland, MI
DeLine, James E. ....Detroit, MI
Deline, Thomas C. ....Denver, CO
de Liniere, Victor H. ....Kirkwood, MO
Delinko, Steven C. ....Paramus, NJ
Delinsky, Eric R. ....Washington, DC
Delinsky, Stephen R. ....Boston, MA
DeLio, Anthony P. ....New Haven, CT
Delio, Jaime Vincent ....New York, NY
Delio, Melissa T. ....Durango, CO
Delio, Peter M. ....Erie, PA
DeLio & Peterson, LLC ....New Haven, CT
de Lipkau, Ross E. ....Reno, NV
Delis, Alexander E. ....Peabody, MA
Delis, John A. ....Santa Ana, CA
DeLisa, Lynn Haeberle ....Woodbury, NY
Delise, Amedee & Hall ....Metairie, LA
Delise, Bobby J. ....Metairie, LA
DeLise, Christopher J. ....Chicago, IL
Delisi & Associates ....Clarkston, MI
De Lisi, Lynne Marie ....Ridgewood, NJ
DeLisi, Paul M. ....Morristown, NJ
Delisi, Robert D. ....Clarkston, MI
Delisi, Samuel P. ....Greensburg, PA
DeLisio Moran Geraghty & Zobel, P.C.
Anchorage, AK
Fairbanks, AK
DeLisio, Stephen S. ....Anchorage, AK
DeLisio, Therese B. ....Rockville Centre, NY
Delisle, Allison Marie ....Charlottesville, VA
DeLisle, Edward L. ....Philadelphia, PA
Delisle, Gary P. ....Schenectady, NY
DeLisle, Jennifer N. ....Chicago, IL
deLisle, Melinda L. ....Philadelphia, PA
DeLisle, Sandra J. ....Milwaukee, WI
de Lisle, Victoria M. ....New Orleans, LA

Deliso, John C. ....Boston, MA
Deliso, Joseph A. ....New York, NY
DeLissa, Janna ....Leoti, KS
de Lisser, Margaret A. ....Washington, DC
de Lissovoy Mayrer, Jane Goodhue
Baltimore, MD
Delius, Bryan E. ....Sevierville, TN
Delius, Scott D. ....Atlanta, GA
Delivorias, Linda ....Washington, DC
Deliyannis, Theodore ....Hackensack, NJ
Delizonna, Harry ....San Jose, CA
Delk, Craig R. ....Las Vegas, NV
Delk, David L., Jr. ....Wheeling, WV
Delk, Edward C. ....New York, NY
Delk, Elizabeth Abraham ....Wheeling, WV
Delk, Glenn A. ....Atlanta, GA
Delk, Joseph C., III ....Lenoir, NC
Delk, Paulette J. ....Memphis, TN
Delk, Philip D. ....Chicago, IL
Delk, Rodham T., Jr. ....Suffolk, VA
Delk, Russell ....Dallas, TX
Delker, Wilja ....Downers Grove, IL
Dell, Adrienne S. ....San Jose, CA
Dell, Alex C. ....Binghamton, NY
Dell & Anspach ....Tiffin, OH
Dell'Ario, A. Charles, P.C. ....Oakland, CA
Dell, Becky E. ....Farmington, NM
Dell, Brian M. ....Oklahoma City, OK
Dell, Brian M., A Professional Corporation
Oklahoma City, OK
Dell, David H. ....Rosemont, IL
Dell & Dell, P.C. ....Indianapolis, IN
Dell, Denise D. ....Orlando, FL
Dell, Donna M. ....San Francisco, CA
Dell, Elizabeth Connolly ....Woodbridge, NJ
Dell, Ernest R. ....Pittsburgh, PA
Dell, George M. ....Los Angeles, CA
Dell Graham, P.A. ....Gainesville, FL
Dell, Harry N. ....Royal Oak, MI
Dell'Italia, Affinito, Jerejian & Santola
Orange, NJ
New York, NY
Dell, James P. ....Indianapolis, IN
Dell, Jane C. ....Tiffin, OH
Toledo, OH
Dell, John Donald ....Dallas, TX
Dell, John W. ....West Palm Beach, FL
Dell, J.V., Jr. ....Macon, GA
Dell, Kevin J. ....Oceanport, NJ
Dell, Kristin L. ....Newton, MA
Dell, Louis P. ....Los Angeles, CA
Dell, Martitia M. ....Portland, OR
Dell, Michael E. ....Milwaukee, WI
Dell, Michael J. ....New York, NY
Dell, Ralph C. ....Tampa, FL
Dell, Richard W. ....Pittsburgh, PA
Dell, Robert M. ....San Francisco, CA
Dell & Schaefer, P.A. ....Hollywood, FL
Dell, Steven G. ....West Palm Beach, FL
Dell, Steven J. ....Hollywood, FL
Dell, Suanne M. ....Denver, CO
Dell, Sue ....Tujunga, CA
Dell, Thomas D. ....Lancaster, PA
Dell, Wayne Eric ....West Columbia, SC
Dell & Winkle, LLP ....Lancaster, PA
Della Cioppa & Bogosian ....Carmel, NY
Della-Badia, David ....Denville, NJ
Della Badia, Joseph ....Cranford, NJ
Dellaccio, Douglas A., Jr.
Birmingham, AL
Della Cioppa, Alfred ....Carmel, NY
Dellacona, Tracey L. ....Macon, GA
Dell'Acqua, Dawn M. ....San Diego, CA
Della Croce, Thomas A. ....Newark, NJ
Della-Donna, Alphonse ....Fort Lauderdale, FL
Della Donna, Annee M. ....Laguna Beach, CA
Della Fera, Richard F. ....Fort Lauderdale, FL
Dellafiora, Mary Jane ....Torrance, CA
Dellagloria, John C. ....North Miami, FL
Della Grotta, John F. ....Costa Mesa, CA
Della Grotte, Ronald L. ....Somerville, MA
Della Guardia, Joseph L. ....Philadelphia, PA
Della-Gustina, Jo-Ann Subotin
New York, NY
Dell'Alba, Jennette ....York, PA
Dellamano, Paul M. ....Torrance, CA
Dellamarggio, Jean F. ....Hartford, CT
Della Maria, Joseph P., Jr. ....Chicago, IL
Dellamonaca, Michael D. ....Fitchburg, MA
Della Monica, Armand A. ....New York, NY
Dell'Angelo, Michael C., IV
Philadelphia, PA
DellAngelo, Robert L. ....Los Angeles, CA
Dell'Anno, Marlea F. ....Visalia, CA
de Llanos, Estela ....Los Angeles, CA
Dellapa, Fred M. ....Coral Gables, FL
Dellapa, George C. ....New York, NY
Dell'Apa, James M. ....Sarasota, FL
Dellapa, John A. ....Hampton, NH
Dellapa Lewis & Perseo ....New York, NY
Della Pelle, Anthony F. ....Morristown, NJ
Della Pia, Max H. ....Wausau, WI
Della Pietra, Anthony P., Jr.
New York, NY
Dellapina, Peter W. ....Fort Lauderdale, FL
Della Porta, Armand J., Jr.
Wilmington, DE
Philadelphia, PA
Della Porta, Edmond A. ....Glendale, NY
Della Porta, James J. ....Albany, NY
Della Porta, Mark P. ....Groton, CT
Dellaportas, John ....New York, NY
Della Posta, Frank P. ....Gowanda, NY
Della Posta, Mark P. ....Buffalo, NY
Dell'Aquila, Louis J. ....Sewickley, PA
Dellaquila, Thomas ....North Massapequa, NY
Dellaquila, Thomas, Jr.
North Massapequa, NY

Dell'Aquilo, John J., Jr. ....Marlton, NJ
Dellar, Neil A. ....Washington, DC
Della Ratta, Andrew F.J. ....Jericho, NY
Della Ratta, John P. ....Greenvale, NY
Della Ratta, John P., Jr. ....Manhasset, NY
Della Ratta, Richard G. ....Schenectady, NY
Dell'Ario, A. Charles ....Oakland, CA
Della Rocca, David Thomas
Palo Alto, CA
Della Rocca, John S. ....Albany, NY
Della Rocca, Steven ....New York, NY
DellaRocco, Kenneth A. ....Stamford, CT
Della Rosa, Ralph T. ....Rumford, RI
Della-Rose, Thomas F. ....Klamath Falls, OR
Dellas, Hercules Alexander ....Phoenix, AZ
Dellasala, Eleanor ....New York, NY
Dellasala, Eleanor R. ....Staten Island, NY
Dellasala, Gerald L. ....New York, NY
Della Santa, Bernard J. ....Walnut Creek, CA
Della Santina, Philip S. ....Flint, MI
Saginaw, MI
Dellasega, Paul J. ....Bethlehem, PA
Harrisburg, PA
Della Torre, Cynthia L. ....Troy, MI
Della Torre, Gerald R. ....Morristown, NJ
Della Torre, Louis E., Jr. ....Jersey City, NJ
Della Valle, Patrick J. ....Scranton, PA
Della Valle, Robert M. ....San Francisco, CA
Dellavecchia, Gina A. ....Washington, DC
Della Vecchia, Michael A. ....Pittsburgh, PA
Della Vecchia, Samuel G. ....Columbia, MD
Dellavella, Robert N. ....Philadelphia, PA
Dellaverson, JoAnne ....San Francisco, CA
Dellaverson, John J., (A P.C.)
Los Angeles, CA
della Volpe, Dean A. ....Cleveland, OH
Della Volpe, Nicholas A. ....Knoxville, TN
Dellay, Patrick J. ....New York, NY
Dellea, William J. ....Boston, MA
Dellechiaie, Donna M. ....New York, NY
Dellecker, Robert H. "Bob" ....Orlando, FL
Dellecker, Wilson & King, P.A.
Orlando, FL
Delle Donne, Frank A. ....New York, NY
Delle Donne, Victor R. ....Pittsburgh, PA
Dellehunt, David A. ....Hudson, NY
D'Ellena, Carmine J. ....East Greenwich, RI
Dellenbach, David B. ....Salt Lake City, UT
Dellenbach, Robert B. ....San Francisco, CA
Dellenbach, Winter S. ....Palo Alto, CA
Dellenbaugh, Elizabeth Gordon
Alexandria, VA
Dellenbaugh, Geoffrey G. ....Morris Plains, NJ
Dellenbusch, Caroline M. Davis
Grand Rapids, MI
Delleney, Francis G. (Greg), Jr.
Chester, SC
Great Falls, SC
Deller, Eric Paul ....San Diego, CA
Deller, Gerald ....Fort Wayne, IN
Deller, Jeffery A. ....Pittsburgh, PA
Deller, Jill Theresa ....Honolulu, HI
Deller, Nicole S. ....New York, NY
Deller, Scott G. ....Toledo, OH
Dellera, John P. ....New York, NY
Dellera, Peter A., Jr. ....Kailua, HI
Dellerman, Karen M. ....Enka, NC
Dellett, John P. ....Portland, OR
Dellett, Stephen D. ....Austin, TX
Dellett and Walters ....Portland, OR
Dellheim, Helen Lee ....Baltimore, MD
Dellheim, Richard A. ....Towson, MD
Delli Bovi, Carolyn W. ....Sandusky, OH
DelliCarpini, Christopher J.
Washington, DC
Dellicarpini, John M., (P.C.) ....Deer Park, NY
Dellicarri, Anthony R. ....Suffern, NY
Dellick, F. Theresa ....Youngstown, OH
Dellick, John T. ....Youngstown, OH
Delligatti, Angelo A. ....Glen Cove, NY
Delligatti, Anthony, Jr. ....Columbus, OH
Delligatti, Michael J. ....Columbus, OH
Delligatti, Stephen ....White Plains, NY
Delling, Anthony R. ....Los Angeles, CA
Delling, Michael Carl ....Lapeer, MI
Dellinger, Dellinger & Smith
Monticello, IN
Dellinger, Elizabeth A. ....Cleveland, OH
Dellinger, Eydie Jae ....Westminster, SC
Dellinger, Hampton Y. ....Raleigh, NC
Dellinger, Jacqueline C. ....Fairfax, VA
Dellinger, L. Dowal ....Monticello, IN
Dellinger, L. Gray ....Melbourne, AR
Dellinger, Lewis D., Jr. ....Monticello, IN
Dellinger, Mark ....Roanoke, VA
Dellinger, Mark H. ....Wheeling, WV
Dellinger, Peter ....Rochester, NY
Dellinger, Richard ....Orlando, FL
Dellinger, Stephen D. ....Charlotte, NC
Dellinger, Walter E. ....Washington, DC
Delli Paoli, Edward ....Staten Island, NY
Dell'Isola, Mark A. ....Stamford, CT
Dell'Italia, John P. ....Orange, NJ
DelliVeneri, Richard ....Denver, CO
Delli Venneri, John ....New York, NY
Dellner, Thomas A. ....Columbus, OH
Delloff, Robert J. ....Brooklyn, NY
Delloff, Stefan T. ....Fair Lawn, NJ
Dello Iacono, Paul M. ....Charlotte, NC
Dell'Olio, Donna ....Colorado Springs, CO
Dellon, Leslie K. ....Washington, DC
Dell'Orfano, Shannon ....Council Bluffs, IA
DelloRusso, Paul E. ....Newark, NJ
Dell'Osa, Daniel A. ....San Dimas, CA
Dell'Osa, Robert V. ....Philadelphia, PA
Dell'Osso, Mario L. ....Houston, TX
Dell'Osso, Monica ....Oakland, CA

DeLuca-Katchmeric, Karen ....Annandale, VA
DeLucca, Anthony J.
North Miami Beach, FL
DeLucca, Joseph R. ....Boca Raton, FL
Delucca, Leopoldo C. ....San Juan, PR
Delucchi, Alfred A. ....Oakland, CA
De Lucchi, Steven M. ....Union City, CA
Delucchi, William F. ....Redwood City, CA
De Luccia, Joseph J. ....North Haledon, NJ
De Luccia, Ralph L., Jr. ....Paterson, NJ
DeLuccie, Karen M. ....Independence, MO
DeLuce, David W. ....Lemoyne, PA
De Luce, Richard D. ....Los Angeles, CA
Deluce-Taylor, Penny ....Roseville, MN
De Lucia, Concetta R. ....Hackensack, NJ
DeLucia, Frank A., Jr. ....New York, NY
DeLucia, George David ....Rochester, NY
De Lucia, Joseph J. ....Bridgeport, CT
DeLucia, Louis T. ....Woodbridge, NJ
DeLucia, Richard L. ....New York, NY
DeLucia, Robert J. ....Washington, DC
De Lucia, S. Victor ....Rutherford, NJ
DeLucia, Treacy & Ader-Duncan, P.A.
Rutherford, NJ
DeLucio, Marco L. ....Evansville, IN
DeLucry, Richard F. ....Atlantic City, NJ
Delude, Sandra J.
Federal Energy Regulatory Commission, Office of the General Counsel, GV
DeLue, Amy R. ....Henderson, NV
Delukey, John C. ....Brooklyn, NY
de Luna, Benjamin A. ....Jacksonville, FL
Deluna, Daniel A ....Troy, NY
DeLuna, Luis Reynaldo ....Garland, TX
De Luna, Maria ....Newport Beach, CA
de Luna, Renato M. ....Cambridge, MA
De Luna-Colon, Yvette ....San Juan, PR
DeLung, Gerald L. ....Fort Smith, AR
DeLung, Harry L., Jr. ....Chicago, IL
DeLury, Bernard E., Jr. ......Atlantic City, NJ
DeLuzio, Maria E. ....Boston, MA
Deluzio, Vincent C. ....Pittsburgh, PA
Delva, Paul D. ....Philadelphia, PA
Delvac, William F. ....Los Angeles, CA
Del Vacchio, Richard ....Flemington, NJ
Del Valle, Augustine A. ....San Francisco, CA
del Valle, Bernard J. ....Pasadena, CA
Del Valle, Cristina ....New York, NY
del Valle, Ignacio G. ....Miami, FL
Del Valle, Jesus M. ....San Juan, PR
Del Valle, Jorge I.G. ....Miami, FL
Del Valle, Joseph K. ....Middleton, MA
Del-Valle, M. Christina, (P.A.) ....Miami, FL
Del Valle, Marguerite ....New York, NY
Del Valle, Sandra ....New York, NY
Del Valle, Sonia H. ....Los Angeles, CA
Del Valle, Telesforo, Jr. ....New York, NY
DelValle, W. Bruce ....Orlando, FL
DelValle, W. Bruce, P.A., Law Offices of
Orlando, FL
Del Valle-Aguilera, Ana M. ....Miami, FL
Del Valle-Armstrong, Maria M.
Ponce, PR
Del Valle-Armstrong, Waldemar
Ponce, PR
Del Valle Cruz, Carlos A. ....San Juan, PR
Del Valle-Emmanuelli, Luis F.
San Juan, PR
Del Valle Lecároz, Suzette M.
San Juan, PR
Del Vecchio, Amelia T. ....White Plains, NY
Del Vecchio, Anthony ....New York, NY
Del Vecchio, Antimo A. ....Montvale, NJ
Del Vecchio, Daniel ....North Attleboro, MA
Del Vecchio, David Leonardo
St. Petersburg, FL
Del Vecchio, Debra A. ....Salem, MA
DelVecchio, Dyann ....Boston, MA
Del Vecchio, Frank V. ....Belmont, MA
Del Vecchio & Houseman ....Salem, MA
Del Vecchio, John F. ....Syracuse, NY
Del Vecchio, John M. ....Buffalo, NY
Del Vecchio, Joseph N. ....Buffalo, NY
Delvecchio, Laurence M. ....Lancaster, PA
Del Vecchio, Nicholas A. ....Las Vegas, NV
delVecchio, Paul E. ....Pittsburgh, PA
del Vecchio, Peter ....Houston, TX
DelVecchio, Peter M. ....Los Angeles, CA
Del Vecchio, Regina Ann ....Buffalo, NY
Del Vecchio, Robert A. ....Florham Park, NJ
Del Vecchio, Steven M. ....Garden City, NY
Del Vecchio, Suzanne Vitagliano
Boston, MA
Del Vecchio, Victor D. ....Boston, MA
Delvecchio, Wendy A.
Fort Lauderdale, FL
Delventhal, Harry A., Jr. ....Ocean City, NJ
Delventhal, Robert W. ....Morristown, NJ
Delventhal, Thomas M. ....Columbus, OH
Del Vento, Benjamin M. ....West Orange, NJ
Del Vento, Ronald R. ....Austin, TX
Delves, Daniel P., P.A. ....Orange Park, FL
Del Vescovo, Anthony C.
Ocean Springs, MS
del Villar, Ramoán M. ....Houston, TX
Del Virginia, Gabriel ....New York, NY
Delwiche & Von Dollen ....Santa Barbara, CA
Delworth, James C ....St. Louis, MO
Delworth, John J., Jr. ....Rochester, IN
Dely, Robert E. ....Richmond, VA
Delyani, Anthony ....Portsmouth, NH
Dely-Lazard, Regine ....New York, NY
DeLynne, Brandyn ....San Diego, CA
Delzell, Lynn E. ....Chicago, IL
Delzer, Carol ....Gold River, CA
Delzer, Carol, A Professional Corporation
Gold River, CA
Roseville, CA
Sacramento, CA
Delzer & Coulter ....Port Richey, FL
Spring Hill, FL
Delzer, Harvey V. ....Port Richey, FL
Spring Hill, FL
Delzer, Michael Armand ....Brookfield, WI
Delzer, Stacy Alvarez ....Milwaukee, WI
Delzotti, Lisa A. ....Tampa, FL
Delzotti, Patricia H. ....Newark, NJ
Dem, Stephen P. ....Encino, CA
Dema, John K.
Christiansted, St. Croix, VI
Dema, John K., P.C., Law Offices of
Christiansted, St. Croix, VI
Charlotte Amalie, St. Thomas, VI
DeMaere, Guido ....Chapel Hill, NC
DeMaertelaere, Philip P. ....Chicago, IL
DeMaertelaere, Ray J.
Elk Grove Village, IL
DeMaggio, David ....New York, NY
DeMaggio, Steven ....New York, NY
deMahy, Paul J. ....St. Martinville, LA
DeMahy, Pete L. ....Miami, FL
de Maigret, Clarke J. ....Palo Alto, CA
Demain, Jeffrey B. ....San Francisco, CA
Demain, Sanford R. ....Chatsworth, CA
De Maine, Philip M. ....Tacoma, WA
De Maio, Alexandra Marie ....Tampa, FL
DeMaio, Andrew J. ....Matawan, NJ
DeMaio, Daniel F. ....Hudson, WI
DeMaio, David M. ....Miami, FL
DeMaio & DeMaio ....Matawan, NJ
De Maio, John Henry ....New York, NY
DeMaio, John P. ....New York, NY
De Maio, Louis J. ....Baltimore, MD
De Maio, Luigi P. ....New York, NY
DeMaio, Maureen ....Santa Barbara, CA
DeMaio, Pat, Jr. ....New Haven, CT
DeMaio, Stephen J. ....Philadelphia, PA
DeMaio, Tanya M. ....Northport, NY
DeMaio, Vincent C. ....Matawan, NJ
Demakis, Charles ....Lynn, MA
Demakis, Gregory C. ....Lynn, MA
Demakis Law Offices, P.C. ....Lynn, MA
Demakis, Lisa J. ....New Bedford, MA
Demakis, Spyro J. ....Wheaton, IL
Demakis, Thomas C. ....Lynn, MA
Demakis, Timothy W. ....Salem, MA
Demakopoulos, Christina M. ....Boston, MA
DeMallie, Campbell ....Dedham, MA
DeMallie, Gardener G., Jr.
Charlottesville, VA
DeManche, Gregory F. ....Wethersfield, CT
Demanelis, Ernie K. ....Cleveland, OH
Demanes, Floyd A. ....Burlingame, CA
Demange, Julie Ann ....Hammond, IN
DeMangin, Tiffany ....Houston, TX
de Manio, Peter M. ....Sarasota, FL
Demanski, David A. ....San Diego, CA
D'Emanuele, Ross ....Minneapolis, MN
DeMar, Eric S. ....Warren, IL
De Mar, Gretchen E. ....Alexandria, VA
Demaras, Matthew P. ....Lowell, MA
Demaras, Patricia L. ....New York, NY
Demaray, C. Drew ....Birmingham, AL
Demaray, Mark M. ....Seattle, WA
DeMarb, Rebecca R. ....Madison, WI
DeMarcay, Lawrence R., III
New Orleans, LA
DeMarce, James L. ....Department of Labor, Employment Standards Administration, GV
DeMarché, Douglas M., Jr. ....Utica, NY
Demarchena, Debra A. ....Mineola, NY
DeMarchi, Darvin, Jr. ....Cleveland, OH
DeMarchi, Virginia K. ....Palo Alto, CA
Demarco, A. John ....Washington, DC
De Marco, A. F. ....San Jose, CA
De Marco, Alex V., (Co., L.P.A.)
Vandalia, OH
Demarco, Anne Marie ....Northport, NY
DeMarco, Anthony F. ....Providence, RI
DeMarco, Anthony J.
Department of Housing and Urban Development, Office of General Counsel, GV
DeMarco, Anthony J. ....Lynn, MA
DeMarco, Anthony J., Jr. ....Brooklyn, NY
DeMarco, Anthony J., Jr., P.C.
Brooklyn, NY
DeMarco, Carl T.
Department Of Health And Human Services, Food & Drug Administration, GV
DeMarco, Carmine A. ....Hackensack, NJ
De Marco, Cathleen M. ....Morristown, NJ
DeMarco, Celeste K. ....Boston, MA
DeMarco, Christopher M. ....Lancaster, PA
DeMarco, Christopher P. ....Hamden, CT
DeMarco, Cindy R. ....Cranston, RI
DeMarco, Daniel A. ....Cleveland, OH
DeMarco, Daniel J. ....Chicago, IL
DeMarco, Daniel L. ....Pittsburgh, PA
DeMarco, Daniel R. ....Braintree, MA
DeMarco & DeMarco ....Malden, MA
DeMarco & DeMarco ....Philadelphia, PA
DeMarco, Donna L. ....Irvine, CA
DeMarco, Edward J., Jr. ....Philadelphia, PA
De Marco, Frank, Jr. ....Arcadia, CA
DeMarco, G. Lawrence ....Philadelphia, PA
DeMarco, J. Christopher
Cuyahoga Falls, OH
De Marco, J. Garfield ....Hammonton, NJ
DeMarco, James J. ....Philadelphia, PA
DeMarco, James J., Jr. ....Philadelphia, PA
DeMarco, James R. ....Irvine, CA
DeMarco, James V. ....White Plains, NY
DeMarco, Jefferson M. ....Monterey, CA
San Bernardino, CA
DeMarco, Jennifer C. ....New York, NY
DeMarco, John A. ....Lake Orion, MI
DeMarco, John L. ....Rochester, NY
DeMarco, John M. ....Los Angeles, CA
DeMarco, John M. ....Morristown, NJ
DeMarco, John V. ....Pittsburgh, PA
DeMarco, John W. ....White Plains, NY
DeMarco, Joseph ....Secaucus, NJ
De Marco, Joseph M. ....Beverly Hills, CA
DeMarco, Joseph M. ....Media, PA
De Marco, Joseph V. ....New York, NY
DeMarco, Julianne M. ....Los Angeles, CA
DeMarco, Kara M. ....Pittston, PA
DeMarco, Kenneth F. ....Philadelphia, PA
DeMarco, Leo, II ....Malden, MA
DeMarco, Leo P. ....Malden, MA
DeMarco, Lisa A. ....Philadelphia, PA
DeMarco & Lore ....Dunellen, NJ
De Marco, Louis M. ....Akron, OH
DeMarco, L. R. ....Nashville, TN
DeMarco, Margaret M. ....Valley Forge, PA
DeMarco, Marianne M. ....Newark, NJ
Demarco, Mario L. ....Port Chester, NY
DeMarco, Mark S. ....Bronx, NY
DeMarco, Matthew J. ....Garden City, NY
DeMarco, Michael ....Boston, MA
De Marco, Michael D. ....Pittsburgh, PA
DeMarco, Michael F. ....Philadelphia, PA
DeMarco, Michelle Lee ....St. Clair Shores, MI
DeMarco, Patrick C. ....North Haledon, NJ
De Marco, Paul ....Providence, RI
DeMarco, Paul J. ....Birmingham, AL
De Marco, Paul M. ....Cincinnati, OH
DeMarco, Peri ....Concord, CA
deMarco, Perry P. ....Philadelphia, PA
DeMarco, Peter D. ....Andover, MA
DeMarco, Ralph C. ....New York, NY
DeMarco, Raymond ....New York, NY
De Marco, Raymond P. ....Dunellen, NJ
DeMarco, Robert A. ....West Hartford, CT
DeMarco, Robert J. ....Alhambra, CA
DeMarco, Robert P. ....Cleveland, OH
DeMarco, Robert T. ....Gold River, CA
DeMarco, Robert V., (P.A.) ....Charleston, SC
DeMarco, Rocco C. ....Burke, VA
DeMarco and Sage, P.C. ....Lake Orion, MI
De Marco, Thomas ....Media, PA
DeMarco, Thomas J. ....Camden, NJ
DeMarco, Vincent ....Baltimore, MD
De Marco, William J. ....Wayne, NJ
DeMarcus, M. Rachel
General Accounting Office, Office of the General Counsel, GV
de Mare, Barbara L. ....Hackensack, NJ
Fort Plain, NY
DeMarea, Andrew M. ....Overland Park, KS
Kansas City, MO
DeMarea, Christine H. ....Kansas City, MO
Demaree, Bruce F. ....Phoenix, AZ
Demaree, D. Derk ....Mt. Vernon, OH
Demaree, Dartt J.
Department of the Air Force, Office of the General Counsel, GV
Demaree, David R. ....Trenton, NJ
Demaree, Jennifer Andrews ....Boston, MA
Demaree, L. Steven ....Las Vegas, NV
Demareski, Craig ....Morristown, NJ
Demarest, Andrew E. ....Bensalem, PA
Demarest, Barbara Geisz ....Harleysville, PA
Demarest, Daniel A. ....New York, NY
Demarest, David C. ....Los Angeles, CA
Demarest, Francis J., Jr. ....New Orleans, LA
Demarest, J. Paul ....New Orleans, LA
Demarest, Jacqueline M. ....New York, NY
Demarest, James T. ....Naples, FL
Demarest, John A. ....Woodland Hills, CA
Demarest, Michelle R. ....Mandeville, LA
Demarest, Smith, Jones, Giunta & Moore, P.L.L.C. ....Dallas, TX
Demarest, Stephen H. ....Friday Harbor, WA
Demarest, Sylvia M. ....Dallas, TX
Demarest, Thomas J. ....Chatham, NJ
Demarest, William F., Jr. ....Washington, DC
Demaret, Douglas A. ....Simi Valley, CA
Demaret, John O. ....Glenview, IL
DeMaret, Victoria C. ....Boston, MA
DeMaria, Alfred T. ....New York, NY
DeMaria, Anthony J. ....Concord, CA
DeMaria, Anthony N. ....Fresno, CA
DeMaria & Associates, P.C. ....Boston, MA
DeMaria, Christine ....La Jolla, CA
DeMaria Ellis & Bauch L.L.C.
Newark, NJ
De Maria & Gallina ....Rochester, NY
DeMaria, Gerald C. ....Providence, RI
DeMaria, James P. ....Boston, MA
De Maria, Jos. R. ....Chicago, IL
DeMaria, Joseph A. ....Miami, FL
West Palm Beach, FL
De Maria, Joseph C. ....King Of Prussia, PA
De Maria, Joseph G. ....Rochester, NY
DeMaria, Kathleen K. ....Pensacola, FL
DeMaria, Matthew P. ....Elmwood Park, NJ
DeMaria, Robert J. ....Jamesburg, NJ
DeMaria, Ronald H. ....Newark, NJ
DeMaria, Roseanna ....New York, NY
Demaria, Susan ....Northampton, MA
Demaria, William D. ....Hempstead, NY
DeMarie, Anthony J. ....Buffalo, NY
DeMarie, Joseph ....Buffalo, NY
DeMarie, Lawrence ....Ardmore, PA
DeMarie & Schoenborn, P.C. ....Buffalo, NY
de Marigny, Barbara Spudis
San Antonio, TX
DeMarini, William S. ....Sacramento, CA
de Marino, Thomas J. ....Denver, CO
DeMario, Gordon L. ....Morristown, NJ
New York, NY
Demario, Kenneth E. ....New York, NY
DeMaris, Susan F. ....Detroit, MI
DeMark, Kolbe & Brodek, S.C.
Racine, WI
Demarko, Ken ....Jesup, GA
DeMarko, Michael J. ....Pensacola, FL
DeMarlo, Anthony ....Decatur, GA
DeMaro, John A. ....Mineola, NY
DeMaro, Kimberly A. ....New York, NY
DeMarr, Edward M. ....Cleveland, OH
Demarr, Jean A. ....Cleveland, OH
DeMarrais, Jennifer A. ....New York, NY
DeMars, Allan J. ....Chicago, IL
de Mars, Andrew Lane ....Scottsdale, AZ
Demars, David J. ....Corpus Christi, TX
DeMars, David T. ....Fargo, ND
DeMars, Gordon, Olson & Shively
Lincoln, NE
DeMars, Gregory J. ....Detroit, MI
DeMars, James J. ....Lincoln, NE
de Mars, Susan Strawn ....Scottsdale, AZ
DeMars & Turman, Ltd. ....Moorhead, MN
Fargo, ND
DeMars, William B., Jr. ....Phoenix, AZ
DeMarsh, Stephen E. ....Sarasota, FL
DeMarte, Vincent ....White Plains, NY
de Marteleire, Margaret M. ....Philadelphia, PA
DeMartin, Charles P. ....Huntington, NY
DeMartin, Joan ....Columbus, OH
DeMartin, Michael D. ....Baltimore, MD
DeMartin, Thomas ....Trenton, NJ
de Martínez, Dianna Soler ....San Juan, PR
DeMartini, Alfred F. ....Camden, NJ
DeMartini, Alfred J., Jr. ....Daly City, CA
Demartini, Arthur Joseph ....Huntington, NY
DeMartini, D'Aquila & Volk, A Professional Law Corporation ....Kenner, LA
New Orleans, LA
DeMartini, Edward J. ....Kenner, LA
De Martini, Frank T. ....Los Angeles, CA
DeMartini, James F. ....Cloverdale, CA
DeMartini, Lori ....San Francisco, CA
Demartini, Paul ....Brooklyn, NY
DeMartini, Raymond D. ....Antioch, IL
Demartini, Sally H. ....Augusta, ME
DeMartini, Vincent J. ....San Rafael, CA
DeMartini & Walker ....San Rafael, CA
Demartinis, Adolfo S. ....Englewood, NJ
DeMartino, Christopher W.
San Antonio, TX
DeMartino, David J. ....Salem, OR
De Martino Finkelstein Rosen & Virga
Washington, DC
New York, NY
DeMartino, Gaelynn T. ....Washington, DC
De Martino, James E. ....Belle Mead, NJ
DeMartino, Karen ....Hamden, CT
Demartino, Laura Jean
Federal Trade Commission, Bureau of Consumer Protection, GV
DeMartino, Nicholas J. ....Syracuse, NY
DeMartino, Nick F. ....Coral Gables, FL
DeMartino, Scott P. ....Greenwich, CT
deMartino, Valerie K. ....Long Beach, CA
Demary, Robert F. ....Portland, OR
DeMarzo, James M. ....Morristown, NJ
DeMarzo, Joseph L. ....New York, NY
DeMarzo, Lisa Ann ....Florham Park, NJ
DeMarzo, Maria C. ....Madison, NJ
De Marzo, Vincent F. ....Pasadena, CA
Demas, Elizabeth M. ....Burlington, VT
Demas, George N. ....Colchester, VT
Demas, John N. ....Sacramento, CA
Demas, Leonidas G. ....Short Hills, NJ
Demas, Louis ....Sacramento, CA
Demas, Peter J. ....Monessen, PA
Demas, Redmond & Rosenthal
Sacramento, CA
Demas, Thomas L. ....Chicago, IL
Demas, Thomas T. ....Lake City, FL
Demas, Thomas T., P.A. ....Lake City, FL
Demas, Vivian ....Chatham, NJ
Demas, William Chris ....St. Petersburg, FL
De Mase, Lauren J. ....White Plains, NY
Demase, Lawrence A. ....Pittsburgh, PA
Demase, Patricia ....Pittsburgh, PA
De Masi, Blaise J. ....Mountain Lakes, NJ
DeMasi, Deborah A. ....Washington, DC
DeMasi & DeMasi ....Phillipsburg, NJ
DeMasi, J. Scott ....Phillipsburg, NJ
DeMasi, Joseph V. ....Phillipsburg, NJ
DeMasi, Juliet M. ....New York, NY
Demasi, Michelle L. ....Morgantown, WV
DeMasi, Timothy E. ....New York, NY
Demaske, Susan J. ....Cleveland, OH
DeMaso, Jeffrey A. ....Middletown, CT
De Massa, Philip A. ....San Diego, CA
DeMasse, Elaine ....Philadelphia, PA
DeMassi, John ....Scotch Plains, NJ
DeMasters, Peter T. ....Fairmont, WV
Morgantown, WV
Demastus, Julie A. ....Oklahoma City, OK
de Mateis, Candace Somers ....Raleigh, NC
Dematteis, Claire Marie ....Wilmington, DE
Dematteis, L. B. ....Redwood City, CA
De Matteis, Martin D. ....Niles, OH
De Matteo De Matteo & De Matteo
Schenectady, NY
Dematteo, Donna M. ....San Francisco, CA
DeMatteo, John, III ....New York, NY
DeMatteo, Joseph R. ....New York, NY
DeMatteo, Madelyn M. ....New Haven, CT
De Matteo, Raymond E. ....Schenectady, NY
De Matteo, Raymond E., Jr.
Schenectady, NY
DeMatteo, Ronald F. ....Fairfield, CT

De Matteo, Salvatore T. ... Brooklyn, NY
DeMatteo, Stephen P. ... St. Petersburg, FL
De Matteo, Susan M. Trusselle ... Boston, MA
Dematteis, Nicholas C., Jr.
Florham Park, NJ
New York, NY
DeMatthew, Jeffrey A. ... Racine, WI
DeMattia, Gregory ... Newark, NJ
DeMauro, Joseph A. ... Bronx, NY
DeMauro, Peter G. ... Sacramento, CA
DeMay, Daniel J. ... Sarasota, FL
DeMay, DeMay, Donnelly & Todd, P.C.
Bethel Park, PA
Demay, Douglas M. ... Boston, MA
DeMay, John A. ... Bethel Park, PA
DeMay, Joseph F., Jr. ... New York, NY
DeMay, Kristine ... Brainerd, MN
DeMay, Marsha J. ... Chicago, IL
DeMay, Patrick J. ... Bethel Park, PA
DeMay, Robert L. ... Minneapolis, MN
DeMay, Thomas J. ... Oak Brook, IL
De Mayo, Anthony V. ... East Haven, CT
de Mayo, Benjamin P. ... Santa Ana, CA
DeMayo, Michael A. ... Charlotte, NC
DeMayo, Michael A., L.L.P., Law Offices of
Charlotte, NC
De Mayo, Richard T. ... Norcross, GA
DeMayo, Thomas J. ... Hampton Bays, NY
Dembe, David ... Trenton, NJ
Dembe, Harold N. ... University Heights, OH
Dembeck, John ... New York, NY
Dembeck, Louise E. ... New York, NY
Dember, John V. ... Princeton, NJ
New York, NY
Dember, Stuart B. ... Princeton, NJ
Demberg, Jennifer Gayle ... Miami, FL
Dembert, David C. ... Baltimore, MD
Dembia, Andrew K. ... Newark, NJ
Dembia, Robert ... New York, NY
Dembicer, Edwin H. ... Brooklyn, NY
Dembicer & Lederer ... Brooklyn, NY
Dembicer, Melissa E. ... Encino, CA
Dembicer, Michael A.
Woodland Hills, CA
Dembicer, Tracy S. ... New York, NY
Dembiec, Walter F., Jr. ... Parsippany, NJ
Dembin, Nathan L. ... New York, NY
Dembin, Nathan L., & Associates, P.C.
New York, NY
Dembinsky, Joel H. ... Glenwood Springs, CO
Dembitz, Marla Bark ... Northbrook, IL
Dembitzer, David H. ... New York, NY
Dembitzer & Dembitzer LLP
New York, NY
Dembitzer, Herbert M. ... Wilton, CT
Dembitzer, Lester ... New York, NY
Dembitzer, Naftali Z. ... New York, NY
Dembitzer, Stephen A. ... New York, NY
Dembling, Marc L. ... Morristown, NJ
Neptune, NJ
Dembling, Paul G. ... Washington, DC
Dembling, Ross W. ... Falls Church, VA
Demblowski, Denis A. ... Pittsburgh, PA
Dembo, Barry S. ... Asheville, NC
Dembo, Harold S. ... Chicago, IL
Dembo, Leon D. ... Cherry Hill, NJ
Dembo, Mitchell S. ... Flint, MI
Dembo, Murray ... Lake Worth, FL
Dembo, Steven R. ... West Hartford, CT
Dembosky, Luke E. ... Philadelphia, PA
Dembowski, Christopher J. ... Lansing, MI
Dembowski, Edward H. ... Marquette, MI
Dembrosky, Katherine C. ... Brooklyn, NY
Dembrow, Dana Lee ... Silver Spring, MD
Dembrow, Ira J. ... New York, NY
Dembrowsky, John F. ... Stoughton, MA
Dembs, Marcy Robinson ... Syracuse, NY
Dembski, Sandra A. ... Department of State, Foreign Service Officers (Overseas), GV
Demby, Michael H. ... Sherman Oaks, CA
Demby, Steven C. ... Denver, CO
Demchak, Michael D. ... Canton, OH
Demchak, Robert P. ... Brooklyn, NY
Demchak, Teresa ... Oakland, CA
Demcisak, John M. ... Willow Grove, PA
Demco, John W. ... Seattle, WA
Demczuk, Peter Arthur, Jr.
Grosse Pointe, MI
Demczyk, Michael V. ... Uniontown, OH
de'Medici, Bruce E. ... Chicago, IL
Demedis, Emanuel ... Prince Frederick, MD
DeMeester, Mark A. ... Boise, ID
DeMeester, Thomas A. ... Grand Rapids, MI
DeMeire, Jana L. ... Los Angeles, CA
Demel, Ana ... New York, NY
DeMelia, Robert W. ... Little Silver, NJ
DeMelis, Linda ... Menlo Park, CA
De Mell, Harry A. ... New York, NY
DeMello, Jill A. ... Manchester, NH
de Mello, Joseph F. ... Taunton, MA
DeMent, Angela L. ... Raleigh, NC
DeMent, Askew, Gammon, DeMent & Overby ... Raleigh, NC
Dement, Christopher T.
Grand Rapids, MI
DeMent, Daniel L. ... Kalamazoo, MI
De Ment, Ira ... Montgomery, AL
DeMent, James A., Jr. ... Houston, TX
Dement, Kenneth L. ... Sikeston, MO
Dement, Kenneth L., Jr. ... Sikeston, MO
DeMent and Marquardt, P.L.C.
Kalamazoo, MI
Dement, Randolph S. ... Englewood, CO
DeMent, Russell W., Jr. ... Raleigh, NC
DeMent, Sandra H. ... Lanham, MD
Dement, Thomas J., II ... Nashville, TN
Dement, Vandivort and Dement
Benton, MO
Cape Girardeau, MO
Sikeston, MO
De Meo, Albert V ... Brooklyn, NY
DeMeo, Alfonse A. ... Belleville, NJ
DeMeo, Anthony J. ... Lima, OH
Demeo & Associates, P.C. ... Boston, MA
DeMeo, Bradford J. ... Santa Rosa, CA
DeMeo, Christopher D. ... Houston, TX
DeMeo & DeMeo ... Santa Rosa, CA
De Meo, Emilia M. ... Newark, NJ
DeMeo, John F. ... Santa Rosa, CA
Demeo, Joseph L. ... Boston, MA
DeMeo, Karen L. ... New York, NY
DeMeo & LaVista, P.C. ... Belleville, NJ
DeMeo, Ralph A. ... Tallahassee, FL
DeMeo, Raymond T. ... Hartford, CT
DeMeo, Regina A. ... Washington, DC
De Meo, Rhonda S. ... Jericho, NY
DeMeo, Rocco J. ... Chicago, IL
DeMeo, Rudolph E. ... Towson, MD
Demer, Adrian J. ... Cleveland, OH
Demer, Gregory W. ... Cleveland, OH
Demer, John A. ... Cleveland, OH
DeMera, James V., III ... Lodi, CA
Demerath, Jeffrey T. ... St. Louis, MO
Demerath, Larry R. ... Valley, NE
DeMerchant, Daniel C. ... Hartford, CT
Demerdjian, Elise ... Los Angeles, CA
DeMere, McCarthy ... Memphis, TN
Demeree, Wendy Allen ... Sapulpa, OK
Demergasso, John ... San Francisco, CA
Demergian, David K. ... San Diego, CA
Demerjian, David E. ... Los Angeles, CA
Demerle, Angela M. ... Buffalo, NY
Demeroto, Cathy A. ... Tucson, AZ
Demers, Amanda ... New York, NY
deMers & Benson, Inc., P.S.
Federal Way, WA
Demers, David A. ... St. Petersburg, FL
Demers, David E. ... Santa Fe, NM
Demers, David J. ... Dublin, OH
DeMers & Donovan, A Professional Corporation ... Sacramento, CA
Demers, Gregory T. ... Bay City, MI
deMers, Harrison H. ... Federal Way, WA
Demers, Henri A. ... Albertson, NY
DeMers, Jay ... Seattle, WA
Demers, Jeanne E. ... Boston, MA
Demers, Kristin Alexandra
St. Petersburg, FL
DeMers, Louis A. ... Sacramento, CA
Demers, Margaret S. ... Washington, DC
Demers, Mike J. ... Pelham, NH
Demers, Roger R. ... Providence, RI
Demers, Ronald F. ... Enfield, CT
Demers, Susan S. ... St. Petersburg, FL
Demers, Timothy F. ... Reading, PA
DeMersseman, Clyde ... Durango, CO
Albuquerque, NM
DeMersseman Jensen, L.L.P.
Rapid City, SD
DeMersseman, Michael B. ... Rapid City, SD
DeMersseman, William P. ... Dexter, GA
Demert, Jennifer M. ... Buffalo, NY
Demet & Demet, S.C. ... Milwaukee, WI
Demet, Donal Moffatt ... Milwaukee, WI
Demet, James D. ... Los Angeles, CA
Demet, Kevin J. ... Milwaukee, WI
Demet, Margadette Moffatt
Milwaukee, WI
Demeter, Bruce R. ... Trenton, NJ
Demeter, David J. ... Albany, NY
Demeter, John C. ... Indianapolis, IN
DeMeter, Kathleen C. ... Department of Transportation, GV
Demeter, Patricia Briggs ... Woodbridge, NJ
Demeter, Richard V. ... Painesville, OH
DeMeter, Robert F. ... Los Angeles, CA
Demeter, Thomas P. ... Cleveland, OH
Demeter-Doughty, Diane ... New Castle, PA
Demetracopoulos, Anthony ... Dover, NH
Demetras, J. Craig, Law Offices of
Reno, NV
Demetras, Stephen G. ... Stockton, CA
Demetre, Dean A. ... Costa Mesa, CA
Demetri, Adam C. ... Garden City, NY
Demetriades, Christopher Paul
Orlando, FL
Demetriades, Todd ... Fort Lauderdale, FL
Demetriades, W. Todd ... Orlando, FL
DeMetrick, Linda Lee ... San Francisco, CA
Demetrio, Michael K. ... Chicago, IL
Demetrio, Thomas A. ... Chicago, IL
Demetriou, Andrew J. ... Los Angeles, CA
Demetriou, Del Guercio, Springer & Moyer, LLP ... Los Angeles, CA
Demetriou and Demetriou ... Garden City, NY
Demetriou, Eleni M. ... New York, NY
Demetriou, Harriet A. ... Tucson, AZ
Demetriou & Howell, P.C. ... Saginaw, MI
Demetriou, James P. ... Mineola, NY
Doylestown, PA
Demetriou, Michael ... Garden City, NY
Demetriou, Thomas J. ... Saginaw, MI
De Metro & Congett LLC ... Kearny, NJ
De Metro, Nicholas M. ... Kearny, NJ
DeMetros, Christopher R.
Jacksonville, FL
Demetros, Spencer Christie ... Boston, MA
Demetroulakos, Beatrice N.
Chelmsford, MA
Demetroulakos, Lewis G. ... Lowell, MA
Demetry, James A. ... Atlanta, GA
DeMetz, Kathleen S. ... Cleveland, OH
DeMetz, Robert A. ... Atlanta, GA
De Metz, Robert A., Jr. ... Marietta, GA
De Meules, James H. ... Los Angeles, CA
DeMeules, Rita Coyle ... Minneapolis, MN
Demeur, Basil E. ... Miami, FL
Demeure, Joseph A. ... Pittsburgh, PA
Demeure, Joseph A., P.C. ... Pittsburgh, PA
DeMeuse, Jeffrey T. ... Green Bay, WI
DeMeyer, Gary D. ... Middleton, ID
De Meyere, Patricia A. ... New York, NY
deMeza, William B., Jr. ... Tampa, FL
Demgen, Katharine ... San Francisco, CA
Demian, Mark J.A. ... Cleveland, OH
Demian, Simon P. ... Cleveland, OH
Demianczuk, Yolanda Marie
Washington, DC
DeMicco, Michael A. ... New York, NY
DeMichael, Joseph J. ... Oak Forest, IL
De Michaelis, Dante J. ... Boston, MA
De Michele, Peter H. ... Houston, TX
DeMichele, Richard A., Jr. ... Atlantic City, NJ
DeMichelis, Clement J. ... Cincinnati, OH
D'Emidio, Michael A. ... Oakland, CA
Demiduke, Robert D. ... Tampa, FL
DeMier, Fred Will ... Tulsa, OK
De Mier, María I. ... San Juan, PR
deMier-LeBlanc, Louis A. ... Rio Piedras, PR
De Miguel, Norma ... Miami, FL
DeMik, Roger L. ... Kingsport, TN
DeMik, William J. ... Boynton Beach, FL
Demilio, Carole S. ... Baltimore, MD
Demilio, Carole S., P.A. ... Baltimore, MD
D'Emilio, Deanne H. ... Pittsburgh, PA
Demilio, Gerard ... Riverhead, NY
Demille, Jason C. ... Whittier, CA
DeMille, John F. ... Houston, TX
De Mille, Louis J., Jr. ... Trenton, NJ
DeMille & Moore, P.C. ... Houston, TX
DeMille, Thomas W. ... Hartford, CT
DeMille-Wagman, Lawrence
Federal Trade Commission, Office of the General Counsel, GV
de Milliano, Maryanne ... Hillsboro, OH
DeMilly, Preston ... Tallahassee, FL
De Milt, Marc S. ... New York, NY
Deming, Bruce R. ... Walnut Creek, CA
Deming, David J. ... Nashville, TN
Deming, Donald L. ... New York, NY
Deming, Donna Claxton ... Tacoma, WA
Deming, E. Huntington ... New Haven, CT
Deming, Frank S. ... Philadelphia, PA
Deming, Hudson E. ... Grand Ledge, MI
Deming, Hughey, Chapman, Richardson & Bosch, P.C. ... Kalamazoo, MI
Deming, Joseph C. ... Houston, TX
Deming, Joseph E. ... Fairfield, NJ
Deming, Judith E. ... Orange, CA
Deming, Kristin A. ... Washington, DC
Deming Law Associates, LLC
Lawrenceville, GA
Norcross, GA
Deming, Leighton B., Jr. ... Norcross, GA
Deming, Leslie H. ... Watertown, NY
Deming, Michael D. ... Covington, GA
Norcross, GA
Deming, Michael R. ... Atlanta, GA
Deming, N. Karen ... Atlanta, GA
Deming, Nancy K. ... Delhi, NY
Deming, Parker, Hoffman, Green & Campbell, P.C. ... Atlanta, GA
Covington, GA
Cumming, GA
Lawrenceville, GA
Norcross, GA
Deming, Peter A. ... Bellevue, WA
Deming, Rachel E. ... Tarrytown, NY
Deming, Renée Raimondi
Menlo Park, CA
Deming, Sheila Robertson ... Lansing, MI
Deming, Stuart H. ... Washington, DC
Kalamazoo, MI
Deming, Thomas A. ... Annapolis, MD
Deming, Vernon K. ... Sacramento, CA
Demirali, Agim M. ... Denver, CO
DeMiranda, Adelio ... Boston, MA
Demiris, Harry C., Jr. ... New York, NY
Demirjian, Charles A. ... Chicago, IL
DeMiro, Michael A. ... Verona, NJ
Demis, George J. ... New Philadelphia, OH
DeMis, Nancy ... Media, PA
Demis, Spero Peter ... Denver, CO
Demissie, Derege ... Roxbury, MA
DeMita, Michael A. ... Washington, DC
Demitrack, Thomas ... Cleveland, OH
Demitz, Carol K. ... New York, NY
Demko, Andrew ... Mount Holly, NJ
Demko, Edward Lee ... Columbia, SC
Demko, Joseph N. ... San Francisco, CA
Demkovich, Allen ... Connersville, IN
Demkovitz, Peter H. ... Philadelphia, PA
Deml, Gail M. ... San Antonio, TX
Demleitner, Nora Verena ... San Antonio, TX
Demler, Armstrong & Rowland
Long Beach, CA
San Diego, CA
Demler, Edison J. ... Long Beach, CA
Demler, Eric C. ... Long Beach, CA
Demler, Everett E. ... Long Beach, CA
Demling, John W. ... Chicago, IL
Demling, Thomas G. ... Grand Rapids, MI
Demlong, William M. ... Phoenix, AZ
Demlow, Amy L. ... Wooster, OH
Demlow, Daniel J. ... Lansing, MI
Demlow, James C. ... Golden, CO
Demm, Stephen P. ... Atlanta, GA
Demma, Anthony D., Jr. ... Tallahassee, FL
Demma, James J. ... Rockville, MD
Demma, Michael B. ... Oak Brook, IL
Demma, Nicholas G. ... Thousand Oaks, CA
Demman, Kristen L. ... Las Vegas, NV
Demman, Michael D. ... Las Vegas, NV
Demme, Elizabeth G. ... Tallahassee, FL
Demmel, Jill A. ... Sacramento, CA
Demmer, Alan B. ... Minneapolis, MN
Demmer, David M. ... Phoenix, AZ
Demmerle, Daniel H., II ... Cincinnati, OH
Demmerle, Kenneth T. ... Orange, CA
Demmerle, Peter K. ... New York, NY
Demmerly, Frank R., Jr. ... Haddonfield, NJ
Demmi, John D. ... Miami, FL
Demmings, Eddie M., Jr. ... New York, NY
Demmler, John H. ... Pittsburgh, PA
Demmo, Nicholas G. ... New York, NY
Demmon, William M. ... Laguna Vista, TX
Demmon, William M., Jr. ... Monterey, CA
Demmons, Larry E. ... New Orleans, LA
Demmy, John D. ... Wilmington, DE
Demo, Bernelle, (Mr.) ... Spartanburg, SC
Demo, David B. A. ... San Francisco, CA
Demo & Rainey ... Geneva, IL
Demoff, Allison L. ... Los Angeles, CA
Demoff, Marvin A., (A Professional Corporation) ... Los Angeles, CA
Demoga, Paul J. ... Worcester, MA
DeMoisey, J. Fox ... Louisville, KY
DeMoisey & Smither ... Louisville, KY
deMoll, Harry T. ... Frederick, MD
DeMonaco, Charles A. ... Pittsburgh, PA
DeMonaco, Marykim ... Staten Island, NY
DeMonaco & Sabian ... Staten Island, NY
Demonbreun, Richard A., Law Offices of
Nashville, TN
DeMond, Gorton M., Jr. ... Washington, DC
Demond, Walter ... Austin, TX
DeMonsi, Frank A. ... Cherry Hill, NJ
De Mont, Jason P. ... Whippany, NJ
DeMont, Kathleen K. ... Reading, MA
Demont, Michael E. ... Jacksonville, FL
Demont, Valerie ... New York, NY
De Mont, William E. ... La Palma, CA
De Monte, Leonard F. ... Woodland Hills, CA
DeMonte, Robert J. ... Piedmont, CA
deMontesquiou, Paul A. ... Calabasas, CA
deMontluzin, Brooke E. ... New Orleans, LA
deMontmollin, Stephen J. ... Gainesville, FL
De Montrond, George A., III ... Houston, TX
DeMoor, Laura J. ... Chicago, IL
De Moore, Christina L. ... Petoskey, MI
Demopoulos, Gregory D. ... Livonia, MI
Demopoulos, Amelia H. ... Department of Labor, Office of Secretary, GV
Demopoulos, Harold W. ... Providence, RI
DeMordaunt, Lorin J. ... Charlotte, NC
DeMore, George E. ... Syracuse, NY
DeMore, Paula M. ... Phoenix, AZ
DeMore, Robert S. ... Fabius, NY
Lafayette, NY
DeMore, William G. ... Hartford, CT
Demorest, Jon D. ... San Diego, CA
Demorest, Lawrie E. ... Atlanta, GA
Demorest, Mark S., Law Offices of
Dearborn, MI
Troy, MI
De Morgan, Dennise Noemi Longo
Baltimore, MD
Demoruelle & Cunningham ... Kinder, LA
Demoruelle, John E. ... Kinder, LA
Demory, Betty J., (P.A.) ... Little Rock, AR
DeMory, Denise M. ... San Francisco, CA
Demory, M. Yvonne ... Alexandria, VA
Demos, Angelo P. ... Miami, FL
Demos, Angelo P., P.A. ... Miami, FL
Demos, Barbara M. ... Chicago, IL
Demos, Bessie S. ... Baltimore, MD
Demos & Brake ... Chicago, IL
Demos, Charles Mark
North Miami Beach, FL
Demos, George C. ... Los Angeles, CA
Newport Beach, CA
Demos, Gregory John ... Lebanon, OH
Demos, James ... Chicago, IL
Demos, James Thomas, (Ltd.) ... Chicago, IL
Demos, John ... Kettering, OH
Demos, John C., Jr.
Department of Commerce, Patent and Trademark Office, GV
Demos & Madden ... Tempe, AZ
Demos, Margaret A. ... Laconia, NH
Demos, Martin C. ... Tempe, AZ
Demos, Peter J. ... New York, NY
Demos, Stephanie E. ... Miami, FL
Demos, Theodore P. ... Denver, CO
Yuma, CO
Demosky, Lee R. ... Greensburg, PA
DeMoss, Carey R. ... Dallas, TX
DeMoss, Charles C. ... Minneapolis, MN
DeMoss, Christine C. ... Edina, MN
DeMoss, Clarence W. ... Nashville, IL
DeMoss, Darrell L. ... Philadelphia, PA
DeMoss, David A., & Associates
Indianapolis, IN
DeMoss, David Brian ... Columbus, OH
DeMoss, David J. ... Sharon, MA
DeMoss, Diane M. ... Edina, MN
DeMoss, Douglas P. ... Newport News, VA
DeMoss, Harold R., Jr. ... Houston, TX
deMoss, Jacques E. ... Lafayette, LA
DeMoss, Joanne ... Edina, MN
DeMoss, John A. ... Mount Clemens, MI
DeMoss, John B. ... Mount Clemens, MI
De Moss, John C. ... Minneapolis, MN
DeMoss, John C., Ltd. ... Minneapolis, MN
DeMoss, Jon W. ... Chicago, IL
DeMoss, Lisa Sewell ... Detroit, MI
De Moss, Michael C. ... Edina, MN
DeMoss, Philip F. ... Sheffield, IA
DeMoss, Renee ... Tulsa, OK
DeMoss, Richard E. ... Mount Carroll, IL

DeMoss, Robert C. .... Denver, CO
DeMoss, Robert Lee, II .... Montgomery, AL
DeMoss & Thompson .... Mount Clemens, MI
DeMoss, William C. .... Nashville, IL
Demotses, James A. .... Peabody, MA
DeMott, Deborah A. .... Durham, NC
DeMott, Howard L. .... Garden City, NY
DeMott, John J., P.C. .... Portland, OR
DeMott, Joseph B. .... San Antonio, TX
DeMott, Russell A. .... Allegan, MI
DeMott, Russell A., P.C. .... Allegan, MI
DeMotte, James R. .... Jasper, IN
DeMoulin, William P. .... Golden, CO
De Moully, James L. .... St. Petersburg, FL
DeMoura, Kenneth J. .... Boston, MA
DeMouy, Marshall J. .... Mobile, AL
DeMouy, Maura L. .... Baltimore, MD
de Moya, Desirée V. .... Nanuet, NY
Dempcy, Birney N. .... Bellevue, WA
Dempf, Louis, Jr. .... Albany, NY
Dempf, R. Christopher .... Albany, NY
Dempler, JoAnn F. .... Pittsburgh, PA
Demps, Anita C. .... Stockton, CA
Demps, Jesse Edgar .... Portsmouth, VA
Demps, Katherine Hicks .... Hopkinsville, KY
Demps, Patricia Redd
Oklahoma City, OK
Dempsey, Aime G. .... New York, NY
Dempsey, Alford J., Jr. .... Atlanta, GA
Dempsey, Andrew F., Jr., (P.C.)
Washington, DC
Baltimore, MD
Dempsey, Andrew J. .... Fort Wayne, IN
Dempsey, Angela C. .... Tallahassee, FL
Dempsey, Ann T. .... Rockford, IL
Dempsey, Anna Marie .... Dallas, TX
Dempsey, Ashley E. .... Los Angeles, CA
Dempsey, Bernard H., Jr. .... Orlando, FL
Dempsey, Bernard S. .... Wilmington, DE
Dempsey, Beverly D. .... Wichita, KS
Dempsey, Bourne P. .... Cleveland, OH
Dempsey, Brian K. .... Garden City, KS
Dempsey, Brian P. .... Castleton, VT
Dempsey, C. Bert .... Louisville, CO
Dempsey, D. Terrell .... Hannibal, MO
Dempsey, David B. .... Washington, DC
Dempsey, David C. .... Peekskill, NY
Dempsey, David J. .... Atlanta, GA
Dempsey & Deliberto .... Washington, DC
Baltimore, MD
Dempsey & Dempsey .... Buffalo, NY
Dempsey, Dempsey & Riggs, P.C.
Hannibal, MO
Dempsey, Dempsey & Sheehan
Elizabeth, NJ
Summit, NJ
Dempsey, Dennis J. .... New York, NY
Dempsey, Don J. .... Englewood, CO
Dempsey, Donald B. .... DeLand, FL
Dempsey, Douglas .... Clinton Township, MI
Dempsey, Edward A., Jr. .... Jacksonville, FL
Dempsey, Edward J. .... Hartford, CT
Dempsey, Francis P. .... Livonia, MI
Dempsey, Frederick R. .... Chicago, IL
Dempsey, Gerard E. .... Chicago, IL
Dempsey, Gordon .... Indianapolis, IN
Dempsey, Guy C., Jr. .... New York, NY
Dempsey, Hayden R. .... Tallahassee, FL
Dempsey, Helen Kaney .... Buffalo, NY
Dempsey, James A. .... Princeton, NJ
Dempsey, James C. .... Darien, CT
Dempsey, James H., Jr. .... Cleveland, OH
Dempsey, James W. .... Jackson, MI
Dempsey, Jeffrey J. .... Albuquerque, NM
Dempsey, Jennifer L. .... Waltham, MA
Dempsey, Jerry R. .... Summit, NJ
Dempsey, John C. .... Washington, DC
Dempsey, John D. .... Chicago, IL
Dempsey, John E. .... Oshkosh, WI
Dempsey, John J. .... Flagstaff, AZ
Dempsey, John J. .... Hartford, CT
Springfield, MA
Dempsey, John M. .... Lansing, MI
Dempsey, John M. .... Buffalo, NY
Dempsey & Johnson, P.C.
Los Angeles, CA
Dempsey, Joseph F. .... Las Vegas, NV
Dempsey, Justin M. .... Department of Justice,
Antitrust Division, GV
Dempsey, Karen A. .... San Francisco, CA
Dempsey, Karen M. .... Brighton, MI
Dempsey, Kathryn Powell .... Portland, OR
Dempsey, Kevin .... Washington, DC
Dempsey, Kevin P. .... Indianapolis, IN
Dempsey, Kimberly J. .... Atlanta, GA
Dempsey & Kingsland, P.C.
Kansas City, MO
Dempsey & Langan .... Peekskill, NY
Dempsey Law Firm .... Clayton, MO
Washington, MO
Dempsey, Leland F. .... Kansas City, MO
Dempsey, Louise Pomeroy .... Cleveland, OH
Dempsey, Lynn Althaus .... Camarillo, CA
Dempsey, Magnusen, Williamson & Lampe, LLP .... Oshkosh, WI
Dempsey, Margaret M. .... Scranton, PA
Dempsey, Mark F. .... Charlottesville, VA
Dempsey, Mary T. .... New York, NY
Dempsey, Matthew D. .... Scranton, PA
Dempsey, Maureen M.
West Springfield, MA
Dempsey, Melissa A. .... Washington, DC
Dempsey, Michael C. .... Union, MO
Dempsey, Michael D. .... Los Angeles, CA
Dempsey, Michael Gerard .... New York, NY
Dempsey, Michael J. .... Philadelphia, PA
Dempsey, Nancy L. .... Denver, CO
Dempsey, Nancy Phinney .... East Dennis, MA

Dempsey, Owen E. .... Oakland Park, FL
Dempsey, Pamela A. .... Irvine, CA
Dempsey, Pamela L. .... New York, NY
Dempsey, Patricia A. .... Miami, FL
Dempsey, Patricia A. .... Melville, NY
Riverhead, NY
Dempsey, Paul F. .... Quincy, MA
Dempsey, Paul S. .... Denver, CO
Dempsey, Pearson & Cummins .... Daphne, AL
Dempsey, Randy A. .... Birmingham, AL
Dempsey, Rebecca A. .... Santa Fe, NM
Dempsey, Rhona Spitz .... Detroit, MI
Dempsey, Richard B. .... Washington, MO
Dempsey, Richard B., Jr. .... Clayton, MO
Dempsey, Robert N. .... Department of Justice,
Civil Rights Division, GV
Dempsey, Robert R. .... Greensboro, FL
Dempsey, Robert W. .... Cliffside Park, NJ
Dempsey, Robert W. .... Summit, NJ
Dempsey, Roberts & Smith, Ltd.
Las Vegas, NV
Dempsey & Sasso .... Orlando, FL
Dempsey, Scott M. .... Urbana, IL
Dempsey, Sean E. .... Saddle Brook, NJ
Dempsey, Stanley .... Denver, CO
Dempsey, Steed, Stewart & Keever, P.C.
Birmingham, AL
Dempsey, Susan H. .... Garden City, NY
Dempsey, Susan J. .... Chesterfield, VA
Dempsey, Terence M. .... St. James, MN
Dempsey, Terrence E. .... Scranton, PA
Dempsey, Terry L. .... Russellville, AL
Dempsey, Thomas C. .... Atlanta, GA
Dempsey, Thomas J. .... Comstock Park, MI
Dempsey, Thomas J. .... Pittsburgh, PA
Dempsey, Thomas J., Jr. .... Pittsburgh, PA
Dempsey, Thomas L. .... Tacoma, WA
Dempsey, Thomas M. .... Los Angeles, CA
Dempsey, Timothy M. .... Oshkosh, WI
Dempsey, Vicki A. .... Hannibal, MO
Dempsey, W. Glenn ..... West Palm Beach, FL
Dempsey, Wade T. .... Mineola, NY
Dempsey, Wallace G. .... Tuckahoe, NY
Dempsey, William Edward
Overland Park, KS
Dempsey, William H. .... Washington, DC
Dempsey, William J. .... Mineola, NY
Dempsey, William J. .... Scranton, PA
Dempsey, William J., Jr. .... Mineola, NY
Dempsey, Wm. F. .... Cleveland, OH
Dempsey-Swopes, Danielle D.
Lawrence, KS
Dempski, Katherine M. .... Groton, CT
Dempster, Allen .... San Francisco, CA
Dempster & Edwards, L.L.C.
Sikeston, MO
Dempster, George M. .... Trevose, PA
Dempster, Georgia .... Houston, TX
Dempster, Hazen H. .... Atlanta, GA
Dempster, J. Robert .... Los Gatos, CA
Dempster, James W. .... McMinnville, TN
Dempster, Joseph B., Jr. .... Raleigh, NC
Dempster, Katie A. .... South Pasadena, CA
Dempster, Michael J. .... Pittsburgh, PA
Dempster, Richd. A. .... Atchison, KS
Dempster, Roberta Nicol
San Francisco, CA
Dempster, Seligmann & Raineri
Los Gatos, CA
Dempster, Theodore R. .... Hollywood, FL
Dempster, Thomas, III ...... Mount Laurel, NJ
Dempster, Thomas, III, Law Offices of
Mount Laurel, NJ
Dempster, William J. .... Washington, DC
Dempze, Nancy E. .... Boston, MA
Demro, James M. .... Nashua, IA
Demro, Paul W. .... Cedar Falls, IA
Demsey, Christine K. .... Wilmington, DE
Demsey, James O. .... Fresno, CA
Demsey, Richard L. .... Cleveland, OH
Demsey, Seubert & Sale .... Wilmington, DE
Demsher, Ronald R. .... Boston, MA
Demski, Raymond B. .... Lawrenceville, NJ
Demski, Thomas J. .... Newark, NJ
New York, NY
Demsky, Leon S. .... Arlington, VA
Demsky, Lisa J. .... Los Angeles, CA
Demsky, Melinda J. .... San Francisco, CA
Demsky, William E. .... Massillon, OH
Demund, Dann S. .... Sacramento, CA
DeMuniz, Paul J. .... Salem, OR
DeMunno, James F. .... Chicago, IL
DeMuro, David A. .... New York, NY
DeMuro, David R. .... Denver, CO
DeMuro, Francis D. .... Towson, MD
DeMuro, Paul .... Tulsa, OK
DeMuro, Paul R. .... Los Angeles, CA
San Francisco, CA
DeMuth, Alan C. .... Denver, CO
Demuth, C. Jeanne .... Kingwood, TX
DeMuth, Christopher C. .... Washington, DC
DeMuth & DeMuth .... Denver, CO
DeMuth, Howard E., Jr. .... Baltimore, MD
DeMuth, John A. .... Paulding, OH
DeMuth, Lael S. .... Denver, CO
DeMuth, Laurence W., III .... Boulder, CO
DeMuth, Laurence W., Jr. .... Englewood, CO
Demuth, Peter F. .... Wellesley Hills, MA
DeMuth, Thomas P. .... Milwaukee, WI
Demuth, Troy .... Louisville, KY
Demy, Dale Stull .... New York, NY
Demyan, Susan .... Glen Burnie, MD
Demyanek, Walter .... Rancho Mirage, CA
Den, Emily .... Boston, MA
Dena, Stephen P. .... Montebello, CA
Denaburg, Charles L. .... Birmingham, AL
Denaco, Parker A. .... Concord, NH
DeNapoli, Albert A. .... Boston, MA

DeNapoli, James J. .... Bethesda, MD
Denard, Dennis P. .... Richboro, PA
DeNardis, Ann M. Ponichtera
New Bedford, MA
DeNardis, Antonio Daniel
New Bedford, MA
DeNardis, McCandless & Muller, P.C.
Detroit, MI
DeNardis, Richard R. .... Detroit, MI
DeNardis, Ronald F. .... Detroit, MI
DeNardo, Christopher A. .... Malvern, PA
DeNardo, James P. .... Chicago, IL
DeNardo, R. Douglas .... Pittsburgh, PA
Denardo, Scott E. .... Easton, PA
Denaro, Anthony D. .... Hempstead, NY
Denaro, Charles T. .... Philadelphia, PA
Denaro, Gerald A. .... Staten Island, NY
Denaro, Gregory C. .... Miami, FL
Denaro, Gregory C., P.A. .... Miami, FL
DeNaro, Stephen .... Florham Park, NJ
Denaro, Susan N. .... Reading, PA
Denaro, Victor A. .... Boston, MA
DeNatale, Andrew P. .... New York, NY
DeNatale, Carole Egan .... Parsippany, NJ
DeNatale, Leonard P. .... Yonkers, NY
DeNatale, Peter J. .... Wellesley, MA
DeNatale, Richard .... San Francisco, CA
DeNatale, Thomas V., Jr. .... Bakersfield, CA
Denault, Adrianne S. .... San Diego, CA
DeNault, Donald P., Jr
Sterling Heights, MI
Denault, Laura P. .... Orlando, FL
Denbaum, Lewis H. .... Fairfield, IA
D'Enbeau, Madelyn Starrett .... Haiku, HI
Denbeaux, Marcia W. .... Westwood, NJ
Denbeaux, Mark P. .... Newark, NJ
Denberg, Kenneth H. .... Chicago, IL
Denberg, Michael B. .... Miami, FL
Denberg, Paul S. .... Newark, NJ
DenBeste, Daniel .... Cedar Rapids, IA
Denbin, Howard D. .... Philadelphia, PA
Denbo, Alexander .... Burlington, NJ
Denbo, James R. .... Washington, DC
Denbo, Mark B. .... Washington, DC
Denbo, Susan M. .... Burlington, NJ
den Boer, David H. .... Houston, TX
Denbow, Don .... Weatherford, TX
Denbow, Thomas M. .... Shively, KY
Denbow-Hubbard, Stefania A.
Columbus, OH
Den Brok-Perez, Carolina .... Atlanta, GA
Denburg, Dorian S. .... Atlanta, GA
Denburg, Howard S. .... New York, NY
Denburg, Ruth .... Los Angeles, CA
Denburg, Samuel A. .... Hoboken, NJ
Denby, David E. .... Garden City, NY
Denby, John M. .... Melville, NY
Denby, Meno, Bloomer & Denby
Carlinville, IL
Jerseyville, IL
Denby, Michael L. .... Phoenix, AZ
Denby, Peter .... Pittsburgh, PA
Denby, Robert L. .... Chicago, IL
Denby, Stephanie H. .... Chicago, IL
Denby, Thomas D. .... Carlinville, IL
Denby, Walter A. .... New York, NY
Denby, W. W. .... Benld, IL
Carlinville, IL
Denby, Wynn, Meno & Bloomer .... Benld, IL
Dence, Edward W., Jr. .... Providence, RI
Dench, Bryan M. .... Auburn, ME
Dench, Donald S.
Rancho Cucamonga, CA
Dench, Donald S. .... Seal Beach, CA
Dencker, Joseph M. .... Denver, CO
Dencker, Lester J. .... Milwaukee, WI
Dender, Annie E. .... Canoga Park, CA
Dender, David S. .... New York, NY
Dender, Robert E. .... Miami Lakes, FL
Dender, Wm. M. .... Etowah, TN
Dendinger, Eugene A. .... Sewickley, PA
Dendinger, James D. .... Dallas, TX
Dendinger, Lowell E. .... Tipton, IA
Dendinger, Michael .... Atlanta, GA
Den-Dulk, John D. .... Orinda, CA
Dendy, Carl V. .... Conyers, GA
Dendy, Charles R. .... Lufkin, TX
Dendy, Cheryl G. .... Gretna, LA
Dendy, D. Michael .... Gretna, LA
Dendy, Geoffrey B. .... Atlanta, GA
Dendy, James L. .... Baton Rouge, LA
Dendy, James, P.A. .... Little Rock, AR
Dene, Joseph F. .... Abingdon, VA
Dené, Kathleen Anne .... San Diego, CA
Dene, Louis .... Abingdon, VA
Denea, Michael P. .... Phoenix, AZ
Deneau, Irene W.
Department of Housing and Urban
Development, GV
Denebeim, Bruce K. .... San Francisco, CA
Denebeim, James E. ...... Belvedere-Tiburon, CA
Denebeim, Robert L. .... Los Altos, CA
Denebeim, Steven K. .... Sausalito, CA
Denechaud, Charles I., III
New Orleans, LA
Denechaud, Charles I., Jr.
New Orleans, LA
Denechaud, Deirdre T. .... Atlanta, GA
Denechaud and Denechaud
New Orleans, LA
Denechaud, Edward B. .... New Orleans, LA
Denecke, Anne E. .... Portland, OR
Denecke, David R. .... Portland, OR
DeNee, Alan G. .... Elmwood Park, NJ
Deneen, Daniel G. .... Bloomington, IL
Deneen & Deneen .... Bloomington, IL
Deneen, Donald J. .... Windsor, CT
Deneen, Henry L. .... West Columbia, SC

DeNeen, James F. .... Joplin, MO
Deneen, Kevin M. .... Windsor, CT
Deneen, Michael F. .... Montrose, CO
Deneen, Michael P. .... Windsor, CT
Deneen, Robert G. .... Bloomington, IL
Deneen, Terrence M.
Pension Benefit Guaranty Corporation,
Office of the General Counsel, GV
Denefe, J. Terrence .... Ottumwa, IA
Denefe, Mary Elizabeth .... Chicago, IL
Denègre, George .... New Orleans, LA
Denegre, George, Jr. .... New Orleans, LA
Denegre, John G. .... Topeka, KS
Denegre, Julia Baird .... New Orleans, LA
Denegre, Louise .... Livingston, NJ
Denègre, Stanhope B. .... New Orleans, LA
Denegre-Tosun, Louise .... New York, NY
Denehan, Stephen P. .... Smithtown, NY
Denehy, Mark O. .... Boston, MA
Providence, RI
Deneka, H. Michael .... Roanoke, VA
Denekas, Craig N. .... Portland, ME
Denekas, Marvin E. .... Santa Rosa, CA
Deneke, Albert J., Jr. .... Dayton, OH
Denelle, Marilee .... Narragansett, RI
Denemark, Howard A. .... Akron, OH
Denempont, Geoffrey L. .... Tucson, AZ
Denena, Andrea K. .... Houston, TX
Denena, Anthony M. .... Houston, TX
Denenberg, Alice E. .... Philadelphia, PA
Denenberg, Alan F. .... Menlo Park, CA
San Francisco, CA
Denenberg, Barry A. .... Oakland, CA
Denenberg, Brian S. .... Northfield, IL
Denenberg, Daniel K. .... San Francisco, CA
Denenberg, David H. .... Philadelphia, PA
Denenberg, David S. .... Secaucus, NJ
Denenberg, David W. .... New York, NY
Denenberg, Herbert S. .... Philadelphia, PA
Denenberg, Howard M. .... Chicago, IL
Denenberg, Jay D. .... Highland Park, IL
Denenberg, Julian .... East Meadow, NY
Denenberg, Julius .... Bingham Farms, MI
Denenberg, Norman .... Omaha, NE
Denenberg, Seth .... New York, NY
Denenberg, Simon J. .... Philadelphia, PA
Denenberg, Stevan L. .... San Diego, CA
Denenberg, Susan V. .... Portsmouth, NH
Denenberg, Todd B. .... Bingham Farms, MI
Denenea, John H., Jr. .... New Orleans, LA
Denenfeld, Stephen M. .... Kalamazoo, MI
Denenholz, Cynthia A. .... Santa Rosa, CA
Denenholz, Judy Rimelspach
Burbank, CA
Denenholz, Susan Joyce .... New York, NY
Denero, Carolyn A. .... Austin, TX
Denery, Juli Gaylia .... Costa Mesa, CA
Denes, Gregory L. .... Miami, FL
Denes, Jane N. .... Springfield, IL
Denes, Richard F. .... Fairfield, NJ
Denesha, Tammy A. .... Norwalk, CT
Denetsosie, Warren M. .... Phoenix, AZ
Deneufbourg, Daniel J. .... Chicago, IL
de Neuville, Helene .... Washington, DC
DeNeve, Alexandra Nicole .... Chicago, IL
DeNevi, Mary .... Boston, MA
Deneweth, Ronald A. .... Troy, MI
de Newton, Lourdes Monserrat
Santa Fe, NM
Denfield, George H. .... Lansing, MI
Deng, Joseph W. .... Los Angeles, CA
Dengel, Carl W. .... Lafayette, NY
Dengel, Paul E. .... Chicago, IL
Denger, Michael L. .... Washington, DC
Denger, Peter .... Rock Island, IL
Dengler, Arnold B. .... Columbus, OH
Dengler, Cynthia Love .... Norristown, PA
Dengler, Dengler & Dengler
New York, NY
Dengler, Laurence G. .... New York, NY
Dengler, Mary McWilliams
Columbus, OH
Dengler, Norbert .... New York, NY
Dengler, Patricia M. .... Wichita, KS
Dengler, Ralph Albert .... Bronx, NY
Dengler, Theobald J. .... New York, NY
Dengler, Timothy J. .... Woodbridge, NJ
Dengler, William E. .... Media, PA
Dengler, William H., Jr. .... Cherry Hill, NJ
Denha, Randall A. .... Detroit, MI
Denham, Alfred T., Law Office of
McAllen, TX
Denham, Alison A. .... Portland, ME
Denham, Earl Lamar ...... Ocean Springs, MS
Denham & Ford, P.C. .... Moulton, AL
Denham, Glenn W. .... Middlesboro, KY
Denham, Golden and Nagle
Middlesboro, KY
Pineville, KY
Tazewell, TN
Denham, James H. .... Albany, OR
Denham & King, PLLC .... Biloxi, MS
Gulfport, MS
Jackson, MS
Ocean Springs, MS
Pascagoula, MS
Denham, Matthew B. .... Riverside, CA
San Diego, CA
Denham, Monica L. .... Little Rock, AR
Denham, Reid L. .... Los Angeles, CA
Denham, Robert E. .... Los Angeles, CA
Denham, Robert E. .... Cincinnati, OH
Denham, S. Mark .... Los Angeles, CA
Denham, Thomas B. .... Moulton, AL
Denham, V. Robert, Jr. .... Atlanta, GA
Denhardt, James W. .... St. Petersburg, FL
Denhardt, Robert B. .... Lander, WY
DenHartigh, David L. .... Salem, OR

Dennis, Paul M., Jr. ... Greensboro, NC
Dennis, Peter R. ... Frankfort, IL
Dennis, R. Markley ... Moncks Corner, SC
Dennis, R. Markley, Jr. ... Moncks Corner, SC
Dennis, R. Ray ... Spartanburg, SC
Dennis, Ralph E., Jr. ... Muncie, IN
Dennis, Richard A. ... Louisville, KY
Dennis, Richard G. ... Houston, TX
Dennis, Robert D. ... Carlsbad, CA
Dennis, Robert D. ... Oklahoma City, OK
Dennis, Robert F. ... Palo Alto, CA
Dennis, Robert L. ... Okeechobee, FL
Dennis, Robert L., Jr. ... San Jose, CA
Dennis, Roger J. ... Camden, NJ
Dennis, Ronald Ned ... Marshall, TX
Dennis, Sam D. ... Valdosta, GA
Dennis, Samuel E. ... Philadelphia, PA
Dennis, Samuel S., 3rd, (P.C.) Boston, MA
Dennis, Sandra J.P. ... Washington, DC
Dennis, Sarah H. ... Tampa, FL
Dennis, Schottky, Swanberg & Braunstein, A Professional Corporation Sacramento, CA
Dennis, Shaw & Ford, LLC Spartanburg, SC
Dennis, Sheryl J. ... Boston, MA
Dennis, Stephen A. ... Palo Alto, CA
Dennis, Steven D. ... Columbia, SC
Dennis, Syna N. ... Los Angeles, CA
Dennis, Ted W. ... Belleville, IL
Dennis, Terry ... Bakersfield, CA
Dennis, Theo ... Waltham, MA
Dennis, Thomas John ... Phoenix, AZ
Dennis, Tracy J. ... White Plains, NY
Dennis, Vereen A. ... Greenville, SC
Dennis & Vertesch ... Richmond, IN
Dennis, Victoria E. ... Hermosa Beach, CA
Dennis, Walter M. ... Raleigh, NC
Dennis, Walter M. ... Knoxville, TN
Dennis, Warren L. ... Washington, DC
Dennis, Wenger & Abrell, Prof. Corp., Law Offices of ... Muncie, IN
Dennis, William C. ... New York, NY
Dennis, William E. ... Claremont, CA
Dennis, William F. ... Detroit, MI
Dennis, William L. ... Riverside, CA
Dennis, William L. ... Greenville, SC
Dennis and Williams Co., L.P.A. Wilmington, OH
Dennis, Willie E. ... New York, NY
Dennis, Zane ... Macon, GA
Dennison, Bennett & Press, LLP Los Angeles, CA
Dennison, Bruce B. ... Los Angeles, CA
Dennison, Caroline D. ... Alexandria, VA
Dennison, Charles E., Law Office of Swarthmore, PA
Dennison, Dennison & Harper Brookville, PA
Dennison, Donald J. ... Brookville, PA
Dennison, Donald L. ... Arlington, VA
Dennison, Gary F. ... Liberty, TX
Dennison, Gregory T. ... New York, NY
Dennison, Heidi Ulrich ... Brookville, PA
Dennison, James D. ... Brookville, PA
Dennison, John B. ... Minneapolis, MN
Dennison, John C., II ... Brookville, PA
Dennison, Judith L. ... Marysville, OH
Dennison, Karen D. ... Reno, NV
Dennison Law Offices, P.C. ... Brookville, PA
Dennison, Lee S. ... Mount Holly, NJ
Dennison, Lia Pappas ... Boise, ID
Dennison, Meserole, Scheiner & Schultz Arlington, VA
Dennison, Michelle R. ... Rochester, NY
Dennison, Randall G. ... New Castle, IN
Dennison, Robert A., III ... Pago Pago, TT
Dennison, Robert D. ... El Segundo, CA
Dennison, Robert R., II ... Atlanta, GA
Dennison, W. Eric ... Houston, TX
Dennison, Wayne F. ... Boston, MA
Dennison, William J. ... Department of Energy, Office of the General Counsel, GV
Dennison-Leonard, Sarah E. ... Seattle, WA
Dennis-Strathmeyer, Jeffrey A. Berkeley, CA
Denniston, Brackett B., III ... Fairfield, CT
Denniston, Debra Keyes ... Tarzana, CA
Denniston, James R. ... Chicago, IL
Denniston, Jeannie L. ... Morrilton, AR
Denniston, John A. ... San Diego, CA
Denniston, John B. ... Washington, DC
Denniston, John L. ... Chicago, IL
Denniston, Lavinia H. ... New York, NY
Denniston, Michael S. ... Birmingham, AL
Denniston, Robert P. ... Mobile, AL
Denniston, Sean Curtin ... Dorchester, MA
Dennis-White, Beatrice ... Columbia, SC
Denno, Dale J. ... Portland, ME
Denno, Deborah W. ... New York, NY
Denny, Bobbie J. ... Fairfax, VA
Denny, Bryce J. ... Shreveport, LA
Denny, Charles W. (IBA) **... Oakland, CA**
Denny, Collins, III ... Richmond, VA
Denny, David ... Dallas, TX
Denny, David R. ... Johnson City, TN
Denny, Douglas R. ... Cleveland, OH
Denny, F. Otway, III ... New Orleans, LA
Denny, George V., III ... Los Angeles, CA
Denny, Gregory B. ... Toledo, OH
Denny, Gregory T. ... Birmingham, AL
Denny, James E. ... Gaithersburg, MD
Denny, James M. ... Skokie, IL
Denny, Jeffrey S. ... Cedartown, GA
Denny, John R. ... Los Angeles, CA
Denny, Joyce ... Fontana, CA
Denny, Karen M. ... Petaluma, CA
Denny, Larry J ... Dayton, OH
Denny, Larry O. ... Kansas City, MO
Denny, Leslie Anne ... Los Angeles, CA
Denny, Marcia J. ... Midland, TX
Denny, Michael C. ... Department of the Army, Office of the Judge Advocate General, GV
Denny and Milliken ... Johnson City, TN
Denny, Otway B., Jr. ... Houston, TX
Denny, P. Thomas ... Charleston, WV
Denny, Ralph K. ... Des Moines, IA
Denny, Richard G. ... Miamisburg, OH
Denny, Richard S. ... New York, NY
Denny, Ronald W. ... Waynesboro, VA
Denny, Steven A. ... Chicago, IL
Denny, Steven A., P.C., Law Office of Chicago, IL
Denny, William A. ... Elm Grove, WI
Denny, William R. ... Wilmington, DE
Denny & Yanisch ... Elm Grove, WI
Deno, Darcy Niles ... Southlake, TX
Deno, James E. ... Everett, WA
Deno, Millikan, Dale & Decker Everett, WA
De Noble, Brad D. ... Anchorage, AK
Denoce, Kevin Glenn ... Ventura, CA
DeNoewer, Frank E. ... San Diego, CA
Denoi, Kacey ... Albuquerque, NM
DeNoia, Americo J., Jr. ... Red Bank, NJ
DeNoia, John ... Woodbridge, NJ
DeNoia, Thomas ... Red Bank, NJ
Toms River, NJ
Denomme, Linda D. ... Flint, MI
Denomy, Robert W., Jr. ... Tacoma, WA
DeNooyer, LeRoy L. ... Carrollton, TX
Denooyer, Lynn C., Law Office of Dallas, TX
DeNora, John ... San Diego, CA
Denorfia, Anthony A. ... Southington, CT
DeNorscia, James C. ... Hackensack, NJ
Denosky, Michael E. ... Austin, TX
DeNoto, Michael P. ... Bay Shore, NY
DeNoto, Peter ... New York, NY
DeNotto, Gerald F. ... Buffalo Grove, IL
Den Ouden, Matthew W. ... Hartford, CT
Denove, John F. ... Los Angeles, CA
DeNovio, Nicholas J. ... Miami, FL
Denowitz, Alfred P. ... Plantation, FL
Denowitz, David C. ... New York, NY
Denowitz, Francine M. ... Plantation, FL
Densberger, Joan Cole ... Concord, MA
Densborn, Donald K. ... Indianapolis, IN
Densen, Beatrice ... New York, NY
Densen, Gregory T. ... Denver, CO
Densen-Gerber, Judianne ... New York, NY
Densford, Daniel D. ... Houston, TX
Densford, David W. ... Leonardtown, MD
Densford, David W., P.A. Leonardtown, MD
Densford, James H. ... Andrews, TX
Densford, Joseph R. ... Lexington Park, MD
Densford, Thomas E. ... Bloomington, IN
Denslaw, Larry W. ... Tempe, AZ
Densley, James A. ... Tacoma, WA
Densley, Steven T. ... Salt Lake City, UT
Denslow, L. Alton ... Occoquan, VA
Densmore, Douglas W. ... Roanoke, VA
Densmore, F. Trent ... Bethany, OK
Densmore, Gerald P. ... Randolph, MA
Densmore, Harold R. ... Newman, CA
Densmore, James H. ... Corinth, NY
Densmore, Leroy E., Jr. ... Kalamazoo, MI
Densmore, Lin B. ... San Francisco, CA
Densmore, Mark Alan ... Detroit, MI
Densmore, Stephen J. ... Los Angeles, CA
Denson, Alexander B. ... Raleigh, NC
Denson, Bradley Jay ... Atlanta, GA
Denson, Bruce H. ... St. Petersburg, FL
Denson, Carl T., Jr. ... Houston, TX
Denson, David L. ... Nashville, TN
Denson, Donald N., P.A. ... Ocala, FL
Denson, Fred L. ... Webster, NY
Denson, John V. ... Opelika, AL
Denson, K. Terrence ... New York, NY
Denson, Lucy Hojo Greenwood Village, CO
Denson, William D. ... Mineola, NY
Denson, William F., III ... Birmingham, AL
Denson-Low, Wanda K. ... El Segundo, CA
Dent, Arthur L. ... Wilmington, DE
Dent, Arthur L., III ... Houston, TX
Dent, Barbara A. ... Chicago, IL
Dent, Charles W. ... Puyallup, WA
Dent & Cook, P.A. ... Sarasota, FL
Dent, Dan V. ... Hillsboro, TX
Dent, DeWitt R. ... Appling, GA
Dent, DeWitt R. ... Augusta, GA
Dent, Don D. ... Dallas, TX
Dent, Douglas F. ... Greenville, SC
Dent, Dwain ... Fort Worth, TX
Dent, G. Richard ... Washington, DC
Dent, George E. ... Tupelo, MS
Dent, George M., III ... Mobile, AL
Dent, George W., Jr. ... Cleveland, OH
Dent, Gregory R. ... Baltimore, MD
Dent, Harold J., Jr. ... St. George, UT
Dent, Harry S. ... Columbia, SC
Dent, Hayden Segrest ... Pascagoula, MS
Dent, Janeece Lichte ... Lee's Summit, MO
Dent, Jennifer P. ... Birmingham, AL
Dent, John A. ... Waterford, MI
Dent, John C., Jr. ... Sarasota, FL
Dent, John F. ... Greensburg, PA
Dent, John R. ... Los Angeles, CA
Dent, John R. ... Fort Lupton, CO
Dent, Joseph F ... Cocoa Beach, FL
Dent, Joseph W. ... Albany, GA
Dent, Kathleen ... Portland, OR
Dent, Kevin B. ... Washington, DC
Dent, Larry B. ... Anacortes, WA
Dent Law Firm, The ... Fort Worth, TX
Dent, Leslie A. ... Atlanta, GA
Dent, Leslie Dawn ... Chicago, IL
Dent, Lloyd A. ... Valley Village, CA
Dent, Lynne A. ... Sterling, VA
Dent, Mary J. ... Washington, DC
Dent, Miriam J. ... Atlanta, GA
Dent, Mollie J. ... San Jose, CA
Dent, Paul M. ... Kansas City, KS
Dent, Rawley J. "Judd" ... Independence, KS
Dent, Rebecca Holloway ... Cleveland, OH
Dent, Richard B. ... Marietta, GA
Dent, Robyn L. ... Chicago, IL
Dent, Sara Boswell ... Frankfort, KY
Dent, Sharon E. ... Charlotte, NC
Dent, Thomas A. ... Garden City, NY
Dent, Thomas G. ... Chicago, IL
Dent, Valerie P. ... New York, NY
Dent, Walter J. ... Department of Agriculture, Farm Service Agency, GV
Dent & Witschieben ... Garden City, NY
Dente, Christina Fichera ... Springfield, NJ
Dente, James M. ... Phoenix, AZ
Dente, Joseph A. ... Kingston, PA
Dente, Ronald A., Jr. ... West Palm Beach, FL
Dentel, Christopher W. ... Fair Haven, MI
Dentel, Eric A. ... Orlando, FL
Denten, Christophe Peter ... Santa Clara, CA
Denten, Raymond T. ... Oakbrook Terrace, IL
Dentes, George M. ... Ithaca, NY
Denti, Kenneth M. ... Cherry Hill, NJ
Denti, Kevin A. ... Naples, FL
Dentice, Jeanne L. ... Pittsburgh, PA
Dentice, M. Angela ... Brookfield, WI
Dentinger, Tammy M. ... Salem, OR
Dentino, Anthony A. ... Rochester, NY
Dentino, Cammarata & Byrnes Rochester, NY
Dentino, Michael P., III ... Chicago, IL
Dentino, William ... Sacramento, CA
Dentler, Deborah ... Glendale, CA
Dentler, John L. ... Olympia, WA
Denton, Adam Scott ... Tulsa, OK
Denton, Allen D. ... Quitman, GA
Denton & Associates, A Professional Corporation ... Dallas, TX
Denton, Aubrey E. ... Lafayette, LA
Denton, Barbara Besore ... Indianapolis, IN
Denton, Betty F. ... Waco, TX
Denton, Brad A. ... Mesa, AZ
Denton, Brad A., Ltd. ... Mesa, AZ
Denton, Brett J. ... Charlotte, NC
Denton, Brian B. ... San Francisco, CA
Denton, Callie Jill ... Topeka, KS
Denton & Cary ... Bolivar, TN
Denton, Charles M. ... Oakland, CA
Denton, Charles M., II ... Grand Rapids, MI
Denton, Christopher ... Elmira, NY
Denton, Clark W. ... Green Valley, AZ
Denton, Dan R. ... Beaufort, SC
Denton, Daniel G. ... Seattle, WA
Denton, David B. ... Bradenton, FL
Denton, David O. ... Blackwell, OK
Denton, David W. ... New York, NY
Denton, Deborah J. ... Chicago, IL
Denton, Deborah S. ... Little Rock, AR
Denton, Debra L. ... Los Angeles, CA
Denton, Desiree P. ... Chapel Hill, NC
Denton, Donald A. ... Syracuse, NY
Denton, Donald D. ... Yardley, PA
Denton, Donna L. ... New Hyde Park, NY
Denton, Duane R. ... Indianapolis, IN
Denton, E. Brady ... Saginaw, MI
Denton, G. Hallett ... New York, NY
Denton, Gary L. ... Richmond, VA
Denton, Geo. N. ... Austin, TX
Denton, Glenn D. ... Paducah, KY
Denton, Gregory J. ... Los Angeles, CA
Denton, H. Morris ... Bolivar, TN
Denton, Harold L. ... Cedar Rapids, IA
Denton, Janet Miller ... Bedford, TX
Denton, Joe D. ... Dallas, TX
Denton, John H. ... Roseland, NJ
Denton, Joy D. ... Bowling Green, KY
Denton, Julie Anne Grow ... Syracuse, NY
Denton, Justin B. ... Portland, OR
Denton, Kenneth G. ... Laguna Beach, CA
Denton & Keuler ... Paducah, KY
Denton, Kevin A. ... Pawling, NY
Denton, Keyser, LaBrecque & Moore Elmira, NY
Denton & Lopez ... Las Vegas, NV
Denton, Lowell Frank ... San Antonio, TX
Denton, Mark R. ... Las Vegas, NV
Denton, Mary K. ... Meridian, ID
Denton, McKamie & Navarro, A Professional Corporation ... San Antonio, TX
Denton & McLaughlin, P.C. ... Pawling, NY
Denton, Melissa ... Tumwater, WA
Denton, Michael D., Jr. ... Mustang, OK
Denton, Michael E. ... Austin, TX
Denton, Michael G. ... Dallas, TX
Denton, Michael J. ... Olathe, KS
Denton, N. Edward ... Bridgeport, CA
Denton, Natalie R. ... Charlotte, NC
Denton, Nita G. ... Stuart, FL
Denton, Philip C. ... St. Louis, MO
Denton, R. Michelle ... Boulder, CO
Denton, Ralph L. ... Las Vegas, NV
Denton, Rhonda L. ... Houston, TX
Denton, Richard ... Elmira, NY
Denton, Robert W. ... Beverly Hills, CA
Denton, Roger C. ... St. Louis, MO
Denton, Russell A. ... San Antonio, TX
Denton, Sarah P. ... Austin, TX
Denton, Sheila Anne ... Bridgeport, CT
Denton, Shelby T. ... Owensboro, KY
Denton, Stephania Camp ... Seattle, WA
Denton, Steven R. ... San Diego, CA
Denton, Tammy Besaw ... Rutland, VT
Denton, W. David ... Paducah, KY
Denton, Wayne E. ... Austin, TX
Denton, William Boyette ... Bolivar, TN
Denton, William J. ... St. Louis, MO
Denton, William L. ... Biloxi, MS
Denton, William L., Law Office of Biloxi, MS
Gulfport, MS
Jackson, MS
Pascagoula, MS
Denton, William M. ... Victoria, TX
Denton, William T. ... Maryville, TN
Denton, Wm. J. ... Baltimore, MD
D'Entremont, Charles D. ... Bedford, MA
d'Entremont, James ... Metairie, LA
Dentz, Edward J. ... Naperville, IL
Dentz, Edwin J. ... Burke, VA
Dentzer, James H. ... Alexandria, VA
Dentzer, John L. ... Buffalo Grove, IL
Denue, Gregory L. ... Las Vegas, NV
Denum, Barrett A. ... Georgetown, TX
Denum, Bart D. ... Austin, TX
Denum, Craig R. ... Houston, TX
Denum, Gretchen H. ... Houston, TX
DeNune, Ralph, III ... Toledo, OH
Den Uyl, James ... North Brunswick, NJ
Denuzze, Andrew P. ... Kensington, CT
DeNuzzo, Noreen ... Cleveland, OH
Denver, Paul F. ... Boston, MA
Denver, Thomas H. R. ... San Jose, CA
Denvir, James P., III ... Washington, DC
Denvir, Jim ... Pagosa Springs, CO
Denvir, John R. ... Bakersfield, CA
Denvir, Quin ... Sacramento, CA
Denvir, Robert F. ... Chicago, IL
Denvir, Sean J. ... Kingston, NY
Denwalt, Lisa K. Hammond Oklahoma City, OK
Denwicz, Chester M. ... Palm Desert, CA
Denwood, Peter R. ... San Francisco, CA
Denworth, Joanne R. ... Philadelphia, PA
Denyes, Nancy E. ... San Diego, CA
Denys, Barbara Brigham Philadelphia, PA
Denys, Karen A. ... Newark, NJ
Denys, Sylvia ... Pittsburgh, PA
Denys, Todd A. ... Princeton, NJ
Denz, Michael D. ... Buffalo, NY
Denzel, Kent ... Columbia, MO
Denzer, James ... St. Paul, MN
Denzer, Paul P. ... Overland Park, KS
Denzler, Julius J. ... Morristown, NJ
Deobler, Eric B. ... Earlville, IL
Ottawa, IL
de Oddone, Barbara S. ... Santa Rosa, CA
Deol, Neil S. ... Livonia, MI
Deola, Linda M. ... Helena, MT
De Oliveira, Cristina, (P.A.) Coral Gables, FL
DeOliveira, Lidia Outor Berkeley Heights, NJ
Deon, Grace M. ... Doylestown, PA
de Ona, Laura Cristina ... Boca Raton, FL
Deonarine, Barry ... New York, NY
Deones, Jack E. ... Mountain Lakes, NJ
Deoras, Monica B. ... Pittsburgh, PA
De Orchis, Corsa & Hillenbrand, LLP Miami, FL
De Orchis, M. E. ... New York, NY
De Orchis, Vincent M. ... New York, NY
De Orchis, Walker & Corsa, LLP Stamford, CT
Boston, MA
Union, NJ
New York, NY
DeOreo, Linda H. ... Cleveland, OH
DeOreo, Matthew ... New York, NY
Deorocki, Christopher D. Newburyport, MA
DeOrsey and Thompson ... Rockville, MD
Deosdade, Anthony L. ... San Antonio, TX
Deoudes, Katherine Kimi Department of Justice, GV
Deoul, Gerard ... New York, NY
De Pace, Gerald ... Woodbury, NY
DePaco, Mark A. ... Santa Barbara, CA
DePaepe, Davison & Paisley, P.C. Taylorville, IL
DePaepe, Louis A. ... Taylorville, IL
DePalma, Jerome A. ... Las Vegas, NV
De Palma, Joseph J. ... Newark, NJ
De Palma, Karen R. ... Provincetown, MA
de Palma, Leonard S. ... Elmwood Park, NJ
DePalma, Michael G. ... Bridgeport, CT
DePalma, Nicholas V. ... North Arlington, NJ
Depalma, Ralph, III ... New York, NY
DePalma, Rebecca G. ... Birmingham, AL
Washington, DC
De Palma, Richard A. ... New York, NY
DePalma, Russell J. ... Dallas, TX
DePalma, Stephen ... Bronx, NY
DePalma, Timothy E. ... Orlando, FL
DePalo, Anna M. ... New York, NY
DePalo, Anne-Louise ... Staten Island, NY
DePalo, Christopher F. ... East Providence, RI
DePanfilis, Anthony J. ... Norwalk, CT
DePanfilis & Vallerie, LLC ... Norwalk, CT
DePaola, Antoinette T. ... Clark, NJ
De Paola, Antonia Ann ... West Trenton, NJ
De Paola, Bruce S. ... New York, NY
DePaola, Donna M. ... Ventura, CA
DePaola, Felicia Goldstein ... Levittown, NY
DePaola, Jeanmarie M. ... New York, NY
DePaola, John J. ... Montclair, NJ
De Paola, Karen M. ... Morristown, NJ

DePaola, Leonard F. ... Boston, MA
DePaola, Rinaldo A. ... Towanda, PA
DePaola, Susan Shirock ... Montgomery, AL
DePaoli, David A. ... Sherman Oaks, CA
Depaoli & Frenkel, P.C. ... Arlington, VA
Depaoli, George A. ... Arlington, VA
DePaoli, Gordon H. ... Reno, NV
Depaoli, L. Robert ... Walnut Creek, CA
DePaoli, Michael T. ... Scottsdale, AZ
DePaolis, Diane Mary ... Eugene, OR
DePaolis, Peter C. ... Falls Church, VA
DePaolis & Shepard ... Eugene, OR
DePaolo, Anthony R. ... Cheshire, CT
DePaolo, Audra ... Saddle Brook, NJ
De Paolo, David J. ... Thousand Oaks, CA
De Paolo, John P. ... Worcester, MA
DePaolo, Joseph F., Jr. ... Plantsville, CT
de Para, Manuel J. ... Chicago, IL
DePardo, Gerald L. ... Wallingford, CT
de Parry, Astrid ... DeLand, FL
DePascale, Diane K. ... Columbus, OH
De Pascale, Edward J. ... Jersey City, NJ
DePascale, Ernest ... Athens, GA
DePascale, Paul A. ... Columbus, OH
De Pascale, Paul M. ... Jersey City, NJ
De Pascale, Vincent ... Columbus, OH
De Paso, Thomas J. ... Washington, DC
DePasquale, Constance Catherine
Scranton, PA
Depasquale, David F. ... Canton, OH
DePasquale, David L. ... Pasadena, CA
DePasquale, Frank C., Jr.
Haddon Heights, NJ
Philadelphia, PA
DePasquale, James E. ... Pittsburgh, PA
DePasquale, Jeanine M. ... New York, NY
De Pasquale, John A. ... Oakland, CA
De Pasquale, Leonard ... Albany, NY
DePasquale, Mark J. ... Phoenix, AZ
DePasquale, Paul R., Law Offices of
Los Angeles, CA
DePasquale-Erker, Nancy ... Tustin, CA
de Pass, Vincent Earl ... Huntington, NY
DePass, W. Keith, IV ... New Orleans, LA
De Passalacqua, John L. A. ... San Juan, PR
Depastina, Anthony Carmen ... Baltimore, MD
De Paul, Andrew V. ... Chicago, IL
De Paul, Anthony K. ... Wallingford, PA
De Paul, Edmund E. ... Philadelphia, PA
DePaul, Guy L. ... Danbury, CT
De Paul, Joseph A. ... Greenbelt, MD
DePaul, Louis A. ... Pittsburgh, PA
DePaul, Ross ... Houston, TX
De Paula, Robert A. ... Schenectady, NY
DePauli, Frank E. ... Fairview Heights, IL
De Pauli, Louis E. ... Gallup, NM
De Pauli, Louis Edward, Jr. ... Gallup, NM
DePazzo, Louis L. ... Baltimore, MD
Depcik, Alan M. ... Chicago, IL
DePeel, Scott W. ... Sacramento, CA
DePekary, Denise Marra ... Manasquan, NJ
DePena & DePena, P.A. ... Fort Myers, FL
DePena, Frank E. ... Fort Myers, FL
De Pena, Hector ... Corpus Christi, TX
DePena, Olimpia B. ... Fort Myers, FL
Depenbrock, John F., Jr.
Department of Labor,
Office of the Solicitor, GV
de Pender, Norman ... Colbert, WA
De Pento, Nicholas ... San Diego, CA
De Peppe, Douglas M. ... Neptune, NJ
De Peralta, Vernon S ... San Diego, CA
DePerine, Gary A. ... Anaheim, CA
DePerno, Matthew S. ... Kalamazoo, MI
De Persia, Robert E., II ... Haddonfield, NJ
DePersia, Rocco A. ... Haddonfield, NJ
DePersis, Dominic S. ... Binghamton, NY
DePeter, Edward A. ... Mineola, NY
DePeter, Thomas G. ... Newberry, FL
DePeter, Thomas G., P.A. ... Newberry, FL
DePeters, Marcella ... Milwaukee, WI
de Petra, Laura Miller ... San Francisco, CA
DePetrillo, Mary Anne ... Orlando, FL
DePetris & Bachrach ... New York, NY
De Petris, Celeste V. ... Long Beach, CA
de Petris, Cynthia Ann ... Los Angeles, CA
DePetris, David A. ... Merrick, NY
De Petris, Emil F. ... Riverhead, NY
DePetris, Paul ... Mount Laurel, NJ
De Petris, Richard E. ... Riverhead, NY
DePetris, Ronald E. ... New York, NY
DePetro, J. Matthew ... Englewood, CO
Depew, Anne G. ... Boston, MA
DePew, Brian D. ... Los Angeles, CA
Depew, Calvin R., Jr. ... Norfolk, VA
DePew, Chauncey M. ... Kansas City, MO
Depew, Craig V. ... Houston, TX
Depew, David A. ... Burbank, CA
Depew, Dennis D. ... Neodesha, KS
Depew, Douglas D. ... Neodesha, KS
Depew and Gillen, L.L.C. ... Wichita, KS
De Pew, Grimes & De Pew
Bloomington, IL
Heyworth, IL
Depew, Harry L. ... Neodesha, KS
Depew, Jacqueline R. ... Washington, DC
De Pew, James R. ... Bloomington, IL
Heyworth, IL
Depew, Kenneth C.
Department of Education,
Office of the General Counsel, GV
Depew Law Firm ... Neodesha, KS
DePew, Lloyd G., Jr. ... Columbus, OH
De Pew, Russell E. ... Bloomington, IL
Depew, Spencer L. ... Wichita, KS
de Peyster, James A., Jr.
Hastings-On-Hudson, NY
Depfer, Joan P. ... Collingswood, NJ
Philadelphia, PA
DePhillips, Christopher P.
Morristown, NJ
De Phillips, Guy P. ... Jamaica, NY
DePhillips, Russell M.
Cardiff-By-The-Sea, CA
Dephoure, Emily A. ... Los Angeles, CA
Dephtereos, David L. ... Westport, CT
De Piano, Salvatore C. ... Bridgeport, CT
de Picciotto, Maurice M. ... Liberty Corner, NJ
de Picciotto, Philip ... McLean, VA
DePiero, Daniel R. ... Cleveland, OH
de Pierro, Ann ... Boston, MA
De Pietro, Albert ... Garden City, NY
DePietro, Deborah ... Covina, CA
DePietro, Gina K. ... Doylestown, PA
DePillis, Kathleen Quinn ... Allentown, PA
DePillis, Mark S. ... Philadelphia, PA
dePillis, Suzanne Hasson ... Cherry Hill, NJ
DePillis, Vincent B. ... Seattle, WA
dePillis, V.P. ... Philadelphia, PA
DePinto, Jessica T. ... Chicago, IL
De Pippo, Frank A. ... Boston, MA
DePippo, Henry J. ... New York, NY
Rochester, NY
Depka, Richard ... Milwaukee, WI
Depke, John E. ... New York, NY
Depke, Robert J. ... Chicago, IL
Depke, S. Robert ... Chicago, IL
Des Plaines, IL
DePlaza, Laurence A. ... Dallas, TX
Depler, Thomas A. ... Shelby, OH
De Plois, Jacques P. ... Coos Bay, OR
DePlonty, Scott W. ... Saginaw, MI
DePodesta, John F. ... Washington, DC
DePodwin, Andrew H. ... Nanuet, NY
DePodwin & Murphy ... Ridgewood, NJ
Nanuet, NY
New City, NY
Depoian, Donna L. ... Danvers, MA
DePoint, James ... Palmyra, NY
DePol, Bruce F. ... Santa Ana, CA
Depolo, David A. ... Walnut Creek, CA
DePolo, George M., P.C. ... Manassas, VA
Depolo, John L. ... Clarksburg, WV
DePolo, Michael J. ... Detroit, MI
DePolo & Morissette, Law Offices
Manassas, VA
Deponai, Pierre L. ("Pete") ... Broomfield, CO
DePont, Maurice J.
Federal Communications Commission,
Wireless Telecommunications Bureau, GV
DePont, Robert A. ... Annapolis, MD
Deporter, Kent J. ... Dayton, OH
DePorre, Paul A. ... Birmingham, MI
De Porter, Dennis A. ... Rock Island, IL
De Porter, Gregory L. ... Colona, IL
de Poto, Robert M. ... Syosset, NY
DePould, Diane Elizabeth ... Los Angeles, CA
DePoy, Diane A. ... Boca Raton, FL
DePoy, Jack F. ... Harrisonburg, VA
DePoy, Scott ... Charlotte, NC
dePozsgay, George ... Miami, FL
Deppa, Jennifer L. ... Creedmoor, NC
Durham, NC
Greensboro, NC
Raleigh, NC
Deppe, Betsy L. ... Silver Spring, MD
Deppe, Brian J. ... Franklin, IN
Deppe, Charles D. ... Jewell, IA
Story City, IA
Deppe Fredbeck & Boll ... Columbus, IN
Franklin, IN
Deppe, John W., Jr. ... Hinsdale, IL
Deppe, Robyn A. ... Azusa, CA
Deppenbrock, Bonnie L. ... Danbury, CT
Depper, Estelle M. ... San Francisco, CA
Depper Law Firm ... El Dorado, AR
Depper, Robert L., Jr. ... El Dorado, AR
Deppert, Gael S. ... Indianapolis, IN
Deppman, Benjamin Hollingsworth
Middlebury, VT
Deppman & Foley, P.C. ... Middlebury, VT
Deppman, John C. ... Middlebury, VT
dePrado, Alfred F. M.
Yorktown Heights, NY
De Pree, Howard J. ... Phoenix, AZ
DePree, Kathryn J. ... Ossipee, NH
DePree, Michael ... Davenport, IA
DePrekel, Thomas W. ... Saginaw, MI
De Prenger, Claudia S. ... Denver, CO
De Prest, Geert ... Washington, DC
DePrez, Anne N. ... Indianapolis, IN
DePrez, Arthur W. ... Indianapolis, IN
Deprez, Deborah A. ... Lansing, MI
DePrez, John C., IV ... Shelbyville, IN
Deprez, Michel Gerard
Benton Harbor, MI
DePrez, Peter G. ... Shelbyville, IN
DePrez, Susan M. ... Highlands Ranch, CO
DePriest, Darryl L. ... Chicago, IL
DePriest, Elizabeth D.
Department of Justice, Tax Division, GV
DePriest, Jonathan W. ... Houston, TX
DePriest, Roy H. ... Piqua, OH
DePriest, Thomas B. ... Department of Energy,
Office of the General Counsel, GV
DePrima, Anthony E. ... Phoenix, AZ
De Prisco, Nicholas, Jr. ... Riverside, CA
Deprospero, Richard L. ... Overland Park, KS
DeProspo, John M. ... Brooklyn, NY
DeProspo, William L. ... Newburgh, NY
DeProw, Grant Christopher
Blytheville, AR
Depta, Scott J. ... San Diego, CA
Depta, Sylvia L. ... San Diego, CA
Deptula, David M. ... Dayton, OH
Deptula, George C. ... Boston, MA
Deptula, George C., P.C. ... Boston, MA
Deptula, George S. ... Syracuse, NY
Deptula, Walter J., III ... Long Beach, CA
Depué, Ronald S. ... Grand Island, NE
DePumpo, Daniel G
Department of Commerce,
Patent and Trademark Office, GV
DePumpo, Joseph F. ... Dallas, TX
Deputy, Darrell, Jr. ... Lebanon, MO
DePuy, David W. ... Livingston, MT
DePuy, Jacques B. ... Washington, DC
DePuy, R. David ... Manchester, NH
De Puy, Walter A., Jr. ... Springfield, OR
Depuy, Warner K. ... Stamford, CT
DePuy, William D. ... Denver, CO
Depuydt, Daniel G. ... Denver, CO
Dequaine, Rodney W. ... Green Bay, WI
De Quesada, Jorge C. ... San Francisco, CA
de Quevedo, Deborah A. ... Honolulu, HI
Dequick, Clara G. ... Detroit, MI
Dequinze, Robert M. ... Medina, OH
Der, Jackie L. ... Seattle, WA
Der, James J., Jr. ... Milpitas, CA
DeRaedt, Kathleen M. ... Cleveland, OH
de Raismes, Joseph N., III ... Boulder, CO
Deramee, Edmond L., Jr. ... Cut Off, LA
Thibodaux, LA
Deramee & Pitre, L.L.P. ... Cut Off, LA
Thibodaux, LA
D'Eramo, Francis J.
Christiansted, St. Croix, VI
D'Eramo, Loretta Lynn ... Bridgeport, CT
de Ramon, Roderick E. ... Newburgh, NY
DeRamus, Judson D., Jr.
Winston-Salem, NC
DeRamus, Lesley S. ... Birmingham, AL
Deramus, Osly F. ... Dallas, TX
DeRan, Craig H. ... Bel Air, MD
Havre de Grace, MD
Der Ananian, Souran M. ... Andover, MA
Deranger, Andrew H.
Department of Defense,
Defense Legal Services Agency, GV
DeRango, Christopher A. ... Rockford, IL
Derango, Ralph J. ... Belleville, IL
Derania, Paul J. ... San Jose, CA
Deras, Warren C. ... Portland, OR
Deraska, Tricia F. ... Boston, MA
D'Erasmo, Joseph J., Law Offices of
Rockville, MD
D'Erasmo, Raymond M. ... New York, NY
Deratany, David C. ... West Harwich, MA
Deratzian, David L. ... Philadelphia, PA
DeRaymond, Raymond J. ... Easton, PA
Derba, John A., Jr. ... Peabody, MA
Derber, David P. ... Fort Worth, TX
Derbes, Albert J., III ... Metairie, LA
Derbes, Albert J., IV ... Metairie, LA
Derbes, Eric J. ... Metairie, LA
Derbes, James G. ... New Orleans, LA
Derbes Law Firm, The, L.L.C.
Metairie, LA
New Orleans, LA
Derbes, Lorraine G. ... Denver, CO
Derbes, Peter D. ... New Orleans, LA
Derbes, Richard S. ... Baton Rouge, LA
Derbes, Richard S., A P.L.C.
Baton Rouge, LA
Derbes & Waldrup ... New Orleans, LA
Derbidge, Warren S. ... Boise, ID
Derbigny, Darryl Anthony ... New Orleans, LA
Derbin, Robert C., Jr. ... Berkeley, CA
Der Boghosian, April L. ... Haverhill, MA
Derby, Charles P. ... Norwalk, OH
Derby, Cook, Quinby & Tweedt LLP
San Francisco, CA
Derby, Daniel H. ... Huntington, NY
Derby, Deborah M. ... Benton Harbor, MI
Derby, E. Stephen ... Baltimore, MD
Derby, Frank E. ... Newark, NJ
Derby, Jonathan J. ... Newton, MA
Derby, Loyd P. ... Los Angeles, CA
Derby, Mark S. ... Wolfeboro, NH
Derby, Marri ... Santa Ana, CA
Derby, Matthew S. ... Troy, MI
Derby, Matthew W. ... Roseburg, OR
Derby, Michael D. ... Washington, DC
Derby, Robert J. ... San Antonio, TX
Derby, Stephanie R. ... Phoenix, AZ
Derby, Steven Leo ... Walnut Creek, CA
Derbyshire, George W. ... Trumbull, CT
Derbyshire, Kevin M. ... Memphis, TN
Derbyshire, Ralph C. ... Boston, MA
Derchin, Woodrow J. ... Brooklyn, NY
Dercks, Lisa Hurwitz ... Minneapolis, MN
D'Ercole, John Dominick ... New York, NY
D'Ercole, S. Frank ... Hartford, CT
Boston, MA
Manchester, NH
Derdarian, Christine A. ... Lansing, MI
Derden, A. Christopher ... Houston, TX
Derden, Terry L. ... Little Rock, AR
Derdenger, Patrick ... Phoenix, AZ
Derderian, Setrak K. ... Beverly, MA
Derderian, Stephen H.
Greenwood Lake, NY
Derderian, Thomas H. ... Okemos, MI
Derdeyn, Michael E. ... Charlottesville, VA
Derdiger & Cohen ... Los Angeles, CA
Derdiger, Ira G. ... Los Angeles, CA
Derdiger, Jan Alan ... Deerfield, IL
Dere, Abraham J. ... Richmond, VA
de Recat, Craig J. ... Los Angeles, CA
Derecho, Augusto T. ... Arcadia, CA
D'Eredita, Anthony M. ... North Syracuse, NY
D'Eredita, Ruth Moors ... Syracuse, NY
DeRee, Debra P. ... Colorado Springs, CO
de Regt, Mark A. ... Seattle, WA
De Reign & De Reign ... Caruthersville, MO
De Reign, James A. ... Caruthersville, MO
De Reitzes, E. Foster ... Washington, DC
Deremer, Francis H. ... Corriganville, MD
DeRemer, Janis M. ... Grand Forks, ND
de Remer, Nicole A. ... Palo Alto, CA
DeRemer, Richard L. ... Rolling Meadows, IL
Deremigio, Thomas E. ... Redwood City, CA
Deremo, Donald C. ... Anderson, SC
Deren, Edward G. ... Katonah, NY
Deren, Genett & Macreery, P.C.
Katonah, NY
Deren, Joseph V., Jr. ... Buffalo, NY
Deren, Patrick T. ... Earling, IA
Harlan, IA
DeRenard, Lisa A. ... Paducah, KY
Derenberger, Edward A. ... Glen Burnie, MD
Derengoski, Robt. A. ... East Lansing, MI
Derengoski, William W. ... Lansing, MI
DeRensis, Paul R. ... Boston, MA
Nantucket, MA
Derenthal & Dannhauser
San Francisco, CA
Derenthal, Paul J. ... San Francisco, CA
Derenze, James V. ... Mineola, NY
DeRenzi, Bruce D. ... New York, NY
DeRenzo and Karraker, P.A.
Altamonte Springs, FL
DeRenzo, Linda ... Boston, MA
Derenzo, Ronald T. ... Pottsville, PA
Derer, Gary J. ... Garland, TX
de Resendiz, Susan Barnes ... Houston, TX
Dereshinsky, Ralph M. ... New York, NY
DeRespino, Joseph G. ... Philadelphia, PA
De Respino, Laurence J. ... Phoenix, AZ
Deretich, George ... St. Paul, MN
Deretich & Sarazin, P.A. ... St. Paul, MN
DeReuil, Louis J. ... Pompano Beach, FL
de Reus, Elizabeth A. ... Berkeley, CA
Derevan, Richard A. ... Irvine, CA
Derevlany, Louise A. ... New York, NY
Derevlany, Michael J.
Yorktown Heights, NY
Derewetzky, Marc J. ... Walnut Creek, CA
Derewicz, Kristine Grady
Philadelphia, PA
de Reyna, David R. ... Detroit, MI
Derezinski, Anthony A. ... Ann Arbor, MI
Toledo, OH
Derfel, Blumie R. ... Daytona Beach, FL
Derfelt, JoAnna Lynn ... Hutchinson, KS
Derfler, James T. ... San Diego, CA
Derfner, Armand G. ... Charleston, SC
Derfner, Armand, P.A. ... Charleston, SC
Derfner, Donald A. ... New York, NY
Derfner & Mahler, LLP ... New York, NY
DerGarabedian, Michael
Rockville Centre, NY
Dergosits, Michael E. ... San Francisco, CA
Dergosits & Noah LLP
San Francisco, CA
de Rham, Casimir, Jr. ... Boston, MA
Derham, Donald A. ... Bellerose, NY
Derham, Robert J. ... Fort Lauderdale, FL
DeRhodes, Jon M. ... Kent, OH
Deri, Lynne M. ... Ozone Park, NY
Derian, Cathryn Blue ... Chapel Hill, NC
Derian, James G. ... Southfield, MI
Derian, Robert A. ... Canton, MA
Derian, Steven K. ... Los Angeles, CA
Derian, Susan M. ... Torrance, CA
Deric, Arthur J. ... Lansdale, PA
DeRicco, Steven Paul ... White Plains, NY
Derichsweiler, Teresa M. ... Sacramento, CA
Derickson, David G. ... Phoenix, AZ
Derickson, David G., P.C. ... Phoenix, AZ
Derico & Associates, P.C. ... Chicago, IL
Derico, James T., Jr. ... Chicago, IL
de Ridder, Craig A. ... Washington, DC
de Ridder, Karen J. ... Boston, MA
De Ridder, Patrick A. ... Richmond, VA
De Ridder, Raymond B.
Saratoga Springs, NY
DeRienzis, Joshua H. ... Islandia, NY
DeRienzo, Daniel J. ... Saipan, TT
Derifield, J. Bradford ... Frankfort, KY
De Riggi, Anthony P. ... Massapequa, NY
DeRiggi, Brendan J. ... East Meadow, NY
De Riggi, De Riggi & De Riggi
Massapequa, NY
Deright, Alan H. ... Seattle, WA
DeRight, Robert E., Jr. ... New York, NY
Derigo, Timothy N. ... Midland, TX
Deriman, Nicholas ... Alamo, CA
Derin, Greg David ... Los Angeles, CA
Dering, David J. ... Cedar Knolls, NJ
Dering, James E. ... Albany, NY
De Rise, Raymond J. ... Pittsburgh, PA
DeRiso, Jerome ... Pittsburgh, PA
Deriso, Walter M., Jr. ... Albany, GA
De Ritter, Elmer, Jr. ... Newark, NJ
Derivan, Sharon Katherine ... Akron, OH
Derivaux, J. Allen, Jr. ... Vicksburg, MS
Der, James J., Jr. ... San Jose, CA
Derkach, Mary M. ... Pittsburgh, PA
Derkacz, Patrick J. ... Southfield, MI
Derke, Shirley A. ... Las Vegas, NV
Derkin, William Scott ... Cleveland, OH
Derkovitz, Mark P. ... Lake Orion, MI
Derkum, Sharon F. ... Los Angeles, CA
Derkum, Stephen A. ... Twentynine Palms, CA
Derleth, Dean ... Riverside, CA
Derleth, Thomas J. ... Rochester, NY
Derman, Adam K. ... Roseland, NJ
Derman, Andrew B. ... Dallas, TX
Derman, Barbara S. ... New York, NY
Derman, Bret S. ... New York, NY

Derman, Harriet ..... Trenton, NJ
Derman, Herbert B. ..... New York, NY
Derman, Lisa S. ..... New York, NY
Derman & Turkelson ..... Bellaire, MI
Derman, William F., Jr. ..... Bellaire, MI
Der Manuelian, Christopher, Jr.
San Mateo, CA
DerManuelian, Mark J. ..... Ann Arbor, MI
DerMarderosian, Armen ..... Needham, MA
Der Marderosian, Lia ..... Boston, MA
Dermer, Martin D. ..... Los Gatos, CA
Dermer, Stephen F. ..... Atlanta, GA
Dermer, Stephen N. ..... Roseland, NJ
Dermody, Debra H. ..... Pittsburgh, PA
Dermody, Edward S. ..... Binghamton, NY
Dermody, Francis J. ..... Pittsburgh, PA
Dermody, Gerard F. ..... San Diego, CA
Dermody, Kelly M. ..... San Francisco, CA
Dermody, Larry James ..... Coronado, CA
Dermody, Michael ..... New Brunswick, NJ
Dermody, Michael J. ..... Oklahoma City, OK
Dermody, Michael L. ..... Jersey City, NJ
Dermody, Terrence R. ..... Stockton, CA
Dermott, Cutler & McLaughlin
Santa Rosa, CA
Dermott, Edw. ..... Santa Rosa, CA
Dermott, Jon ..... Joplin, MO
Dermott, Jon Sharrock ..... Little Rock, AR
Dermott, Sharrock
Hot Springs Village, AR
Little Rock, AR
DerMovsesian, Albert ..... Willow Grove, PA
Dern, Dixon Q. ..... Los Angeles, CA
Dern, Dixon Q., P.C. ..... Los Angeles, CA
Dern, Karen Podhurst ..... Miami, FL
Dern, Mark R. ..... Boca Raton, FL
Dern, Warren D. ..... Los Angeles, CA
Dernago, Theodore P., Jr. ..... Southwick, MA
Dernbach, John C. ..... Harrisburg, PA
Dernberger, Rebecca A. ..... Louisville, KY
Dernelle, Gary J.
Commodity Futures Trading Commission, Division of Enforcement, GV
Derner, Mary P. ..... Santa Rosa, CA
Dernier, Matthew Brooke ..... New York, NY
Dernis, Craig ..... Coral Gables, FL
Dernis & Dernis ..... Coral Gables, FL
Dernis, Martin M. ..... Coral Gables, FL
Dernis, Melanie Anne ..... Miami, FL
Dernis, Sanford F. ..... Miami, FL
Dernoga, Thomas E. ..... Highland, MD
De Robbio, Albert E. ..... Providence, RI
DeRobertis, L. Richard ..... Honolulu, HI
Deroberts, Jeffrey ..... Syracuse, NY
DeRocco, Gary D. ..... University Heights, OH
De Roche, Chas. P. ..... Washington, DC
DeRoche, Debra L. ..... Cleveland, OH
DeRoche, James A. ..... Cleveland, OH
DeRoche, James D. ..... Los Angeles, CA
DeRoche, Jo A. ..... Washington, DC
DeRoche, Kenneth H. ..... Oviedo, FL
deRochemont, Sarah ..... Redwood City, CA
de Roetth, Peter ..... Boston, MA
DeRogatis, Dante J. ..... Brick, NJ
DeRogatis, Rosemarie Ann
Staten Island, NY
DerOhannesian & DerOhannesian
Albany, NY
DerOhannesian, Paul ..... Albany, NY
DerOhannesian, Paul, II ..... Albany, NY
DeRoin, Jan E. ..... Boise, ID
DeRojas, Gina Butera ..... Gretna, LA
DeRojas, Isidro René ..... Metairie, LA
DeRoma, Silas R. ..... Department of the Army, U.S. Army Legal Services Agency, GV
Deromedi, David R. ..... Detroit, MI
Deron, Edward M. ..... Detroit, MI
DeRonde & DeRonde, Law Offices of
Fairfield, CA
DeRonde, Glen A. ..... Fairfield, CA
DeRonde, John A. ..... Vacaville, CA
DeRonde, John A., Jr. ..... Fairfield, CA
DeRoo, Curtis J. ..... Detroit, MI
DeRoon, Louis, III ..... Phoenix, AZ
DeRoon & Seyffer ..... Phoenix, AZ
deRoos, Carolyn ..... Friday Harbor, WA
De Roos, Dirk W. ..... Denver, CO
DeRoos, George E. ..... Denver, CO
de Roos, Juanita G. ..... Morristown, NJ
de Roos, Shelli N. W. ..... Atlanta, GA
Deros, John S. ..... Baltimore, MD
Deros, John S., P.A. ..... Baltimore, MD
de Rosa, Barth X. ..... Washington, DC
DeRosa, Christine Lynn ..... Boston, MA
DeRosa, Christine M. ..... Boston, MA
DeRosa, Franca L. ..... Hartford, CT
DeRosa, Francis J. ..... Princeton, NJ
De Rosa, Frank J. ..... New York, NY
DeRosa, Frank V. ..... East Meadow, NY
De Rosa, Frederick J. ..... Philadelphia, PA
DeRosa, John B. ..... North Adams, MA
De Rosa, John-Paul ..... Portland, ME
DeRosa, Joseph C. ..... Cleveland, OH
De Rosa, Judith ..... Fairfield, NJ
De Rosa, Kenneth R. ..... Philadelphia, PA
De Rosa, Marianne ..... Mineola, NY
DeRosa, Matina Marguerite ..... Lynchburg, VA
DeRosa, Michelle M.
Fort Lauderdale, FL
DeRosa, Paul J. ..... Pittsburgh, PA
De Rosa, Ralph A. ..... Tarrytown, NY
DeRosa, Suzanne J. ..... Los Angeles, CA
deRosa, Thomas R. ..... Orlando, FL
DeRosa, Vincent J. ..... Elmont, NY
Derosby, Anthony R. ..... Portland, ME
Newburyport, MA
DeRose, Aladean M. ..... South Bend, IN
De Rose, Albert G. ..... Denver, CO
De Rose, Anthony J. ..... Olean, NY
De Rose, Barry ..... Globe, AZ
Chicago, IL
DeRose, Daniel A. ..... Olean, NY
De Rose, David A. ..... Waukegan, IL
DeRose, David S. ..... Greensburg, PA
DeRose, Dominic A. ..... Denver, CO
DeRose, James D. ..... Westfield, NJ
DeRose, John P. ..... Burr Ridge, IL
DeRose, Julie M. ..... Los Angeles, CA
DeRose, Lisa M. ..... Newark, NJ
DeRose, Louis E., Jr. ..... Chicago, IL
DeRose, Nancy A. ..... New Haven, CT
DeRose, P. Louis ..... Greensburg, PA
De Rose, Peter L. ..... Austin, TX
De Rose, Ralph C. ..... Nutley, NJ
De Rose, Richard ..... New York, NY
DeRose, Victor A. ..... Indianapolis, IN
De Rosier & Barrett ..... Lake Charles, LA
DeRosier, John F. ..... Lake Charles, LA
Derosier, Margaret F. ..... Salem, MA
DeRosier, Phillip J. ..... Detroit, MI
Derosier, Robert M. ..... Exeter, NH
DeRoss, Joseph J., Jr. ..... Fort Pierce, FL
deRosset, Elizabeth M. ..... Atlanta, GA
deRosset, James B. ..... Miami, FL
Derossi, Gina L. ..... Boston, MA
DeRouen, Lynn A. ..... New Iberia, LA
DeRouen, Patrick D. ..... New Orleans, LA
DeRouen & Wattigny ..... New Iberia, LA
Derouin, James G. ..... Phoenix, AZ
Derouin, Laura A. ..... Chicago, IL
Derounian, Paul D. ..... New York, NY
Derounian, Paul D., P.C. ..... New York, NY
Derounian, Steven B. ..... Austin, TX
DeRousie, Charles S. ..... Columbus, OH
DerOvanesian, Martin ..... Fort Myers, FL
DerOvanesian, Todd, Jr. ..... San Diego, CA
DeRoy, Cathy ..... Burbank, CA
DeRoy, George ..... Beverly Hills, CA
Derque, Joseph A., III ..... Jefferson City, MO
Derr, Allen ..... Boise, ID
Derr, Antoinette ..... Spokane, WA
Derr, Dailey J. ..... Durham, NC
Derr, Dailey J., P.A. ..... Durham, NC
Raleigh, NC
Derr, Dale A. ..... Bloomsburg, PA
Derr, Dennis Lee ..... Pittsburgh, PA
Derr, J Russell ..... Omaha, NE
Derr, Jacque D. ..... Winnfield, LA
Derr, James M.
Charlotte Amalie, St. Thomas, VI
Derr, Jay P. ..... Seattle, WA
Derr, Kathryn J. ..... Omaha, NE
Derr, Kevin R. ..... Williamsport, PA
Derr, Lawrence R. ..... Portland, OR
Derr, Lisa L. ..... Beaver Dam, WI
Derr, Maria St. Ann ..... New York, NY
Derr, Pursel, Luschas & Norton
Bloomsburg, PA
Derr, Richard L. ..... Allentown, PA
Derr, Sara B. ..... Spokane, WA
Derr, Vicki B. ..... Somerset, OH
Derrenbacher, Christopher J.
Raleigh, NC
Derrendinger, Regine ..... Los Angeles, CA
Derrevere, Jon D. ..... West Palm Beach, FL
Derrevere, Suzette W. ..... Washington, DC
Derrick, A. Scott ..... Nashville, TN
Derrick, Beth Roberts ..... Nashville, TN
Derrick & Briggs ..... Oklahoma City, OK
Derrick, Butler C., Jr. ..... Washington, DC
Derrick, Christopher W. ..... Lake Junaluska, NC
Derrick, Clark L. ..... Phoenix, AZ
Derrick, Dennis P. ..... Essex, MA
Derrick, Dirk J. ..... Conway, SC
Derrick, Elizabeth O. ..... Atlanta, GA
Derrick, Eugene J. ..... Melville, NY
Derrick, G. Conrad ..... Florence, SC
Derrick, Gary W. ..... Oklahoma City, OK
Derrick, Jack H. ..... Wake Forest, NC
Derrick, James V., Jr. ..... Houston, TX
Derrick, Jean Perrin ..... Lexington, SC
Derrick, Jerry ..... Tuba City, AZ
Derrick Law Firm ..... Conway, SC
Derrick, Mark M. ..... Searcy, AR
Derrick, Michael E. ..... Tampa, FL
Derrick, Michael G. ..... Memphis, TN
Derrick, Paul H. ..... Greenville, SC
Derrick, Raymond Todd ..... Dothan, AL
Derrick, Ritter & Williams, P.A. ..... Seneca, SC
Derrick, Robert S. ..... Redmond, WA
Derrick, Tyree C., Jr. ..... St. Louis, MO
Derrick, William A., Jr. ..... Cleveland, OH
Derrick, William F. ..... Seneca, SC
Derrick, William J. ..... El Paso, TX
Derrick, William J., P.C. ..... El Paso, TX
Derrick, William S. ..... Marion, SC
Derrick-Hamon, Annick
South Pasadena, CA
Derrickson, Dorothy ..... New York, NY
D'Errico, Anne M. ..... East Greenwich, RI
Derrico, Donald G. ..... New York, NY
Derrico, Jeffrey P. ..... Washington, PA
Derrico, Joseph A., Jr. ..... Charlottesville, VA
D'errico, Larraine D. ..... Mineola, NY
D'Errico, Lisa Van Gordon
Northampton, MA
D'Errico, Maria ..... Langhorne, PA
Derrico, Michelle C. Feinberg
Roanoke, VA
Derrico, Patrick C. ..... Washington, PA
d'Errico, Peter ..... Amherst, MA
Derrico, Richard L. ..... Roanoke, VA
Derrig, Ellen N. ..... Hartford, CT
Derrig, James T. ..... Seattle, WA
Derrig, Joanne M. ..... Northbrook, IL
Derrin, Stacie E. ..... Westport, CT
Derringer, Steven ..... Denver, CO
Derrington, Keith R. ..... Houston, TX
Derrin-Lieberson, Rhona ..... Westport, CT
Derrota, Luis H. ..... Houston, TX
Derry, Carol D. ..... Los Angeles, CA
Derry, Douglass L. ..... Trenton, NJ
Derry, Peter E. ..... Chevy Chase, MD
Derry, Richard W. ..... Mineola, NY
New York, NY
White Plains, NY
Derry, William R., Jr. ..... Richmond, VA
Derryberry, Barry Lindsey ..... Tulsa, OK
Derryberry, Daryl L. ..... Tyler, TX
Derryberry, Eugene E. ..... Roanoke, VA
Derryberry, George M. ..... Chattanooga, TN
Derryberry, Glenn H. ..... Lima, OH
Derryberry, Jack W., Jr. ..... Nashville, TN
Derryberry, Kenneth B. ..... Bloomington, IN
Derryberry, Larry ..... Oklahoma City, OK
Derryberry, Quentin M., II ..... Wapakoneta, OH
Derryberry, Quigley, Solomon & Naifeh
Oklahoma City, OK
Derryberry, Reggie ..... Fresno, CA
Dersch, Julie R. ..... Indianapolis, IN
Dersch, Wilbur D. ..... Peoria, IL
Derschowitz, Harold J. ..... New York, NY
Derse, Arthur R. ..... Milwaukee, WI
Dersh, Irving ..... Northridge, CA
Dershaw, Terry P. ..... Philadelphia, PA
Dershem, Larry D. ..... San Diego, CA
Dershowitz, Alan M. ..... Cambridge, MA
Dershowitz & Eiger, P.C. ..... New York, NY
Dershowitz, Jamin S. ..... New York, NY
Dershowitz, Marilyn Barlach ..... New York, NY
Dershowitz, Michael
Federal Trade Commission, Bureau of Consumer Protection, GV
Dershowitz, Morris ..... New York, NY
Dershowitz, Nathan Z. ..... New York, NY
Dershowitz, Rana ..... New York, NY
Dersom, Charles R. ..... Columbus, OH
Derstine, J. Matthew ..... Tucson, AZ
Derstine, Lauren L. ..... San Diego, CA
Derstine, Roger B. ..... Chicago, IL
Dertke, Daniel R. ..... Department of Justice, Environment and Natural Resources Division, GV
Derucki, Michael A. ..... Merrillville, IN
DeRue, Patricia L. ..... Syracuse, NY
deRuntz, K. Alison ..... San Francisco, CA
Derus, Margaret M. ..... Milwaukee, WI
DeRusha, Pamela J. ..... Spokane, WA
Derusseau, Ginnie Chase
Overland Park, KS
DeRussy, John G. ..... New Orleans, LA
DeRuyter, Daniel B. ..... Spokane, WA
De Ruyter, Rebecca L. ..... Department of Labor, Office of the Solicitor, GV
DeRuyter, Steven D. ..... Minneapolis, MN
Dervaes, R. Scott, II, Law Offices of
San Diego, CA
Derveloy, Thomas S., Jr. ..... Mandeville, LA
Dervishi, Brian S. ..... Fort Lauderdale, FL
Miami, FL
Dervishian, Robert W. ..... Richmond, VA
Dervishian, William A. ..... Richmond, VA
Derwart, Alfred Rees ..... Indiana, PA
Derwent, Mark E. ..... Grand Rapids, MI
Derwin, Douglas K. ..... Menlo Park, CA
Derwin, John M. ..... Boston, MA
Derwin, Jordan ..... New York, NY
Derwin, Nancy ..... Los Angeles, CA
Dery, Jennifer Slack ..... Garden City, NY
Dery, Kenneth A. ..... New York, NY
Derycz, Diana ..... Santa Monica, CA
de Ryss, Diane Giselle ..... Seattle, WA
Derzaw, Richard L. ..... New York, NY
Derzis, Ann ..... Birmingham, AL
Derzko, Natalie M. ..... Washington, DC
Derzon, Alan L. ..... Milwaukee, WI
Derzon, Mark A. ..... Bakersfield, CA
Derzon, Menard & Noonan, S.C.
Milwaukee, WI
De Sa, Emily ..... Brooklyn, NY
DeSabato, Anthony A. ..... Bensalem, PA
de Sa e Silva, Marco ..... Seattle, WA
Desai, Aashish Y. ..... Irvine, CA
Desai, Anuj Chang ..... Seattle, WA
Desai, Apurva Drupad
Pension Benefit Guaranty Corporation, Office of the General Counsel, GV
Desai, Asim K. ..... Los Angeles, CA
Desai, Bina ..... Silver Spring, MD
Desai, Dimple H. ..... Austin, TX
Desai, Mitul I. ..... New York, NY
Desai, Prasant ..... Boston, MA
Desai, Riddhi P. ..... Houston, TX
Desai, Sahil W. ..... San Francisco, CA
Desai, Sajeet T. ..... Palo Alto, CA
Desai, Samir S. ..... Washington, DC
Desai, Sonia A. ..... Chicago, IL
Desai, Sophia ..... Weymouth, MA
Desai, Spencer P. ..... St. Louis, MO
Desai, Umesh M. ..... Houston, TX
Desai, Urvi Patel ..... Rockville, MD
de Saillan, Charles ..... Santa Fe, NM
de St. Aubin, Mark C. ..... Atlanta, GA
De Saint Phalle, Alexandra
Springfield, IL
de Saint Phalle, Eustace
San Francisco, CA
de Saint Phalle, Pierre ..... New York, NY
de Saint Phalle, Richard ..... San Francisco, CA
DeSaix, James K. ..... Beresford, SD
DeSales, Stephan A. ..... Fullerton, CA
DeSales, Stephan A., A Professional Law Corporation ..... Fullerton, CA
DeSalle, David M. ..... Harrisburg, PA
DeSalle-Pittman, Robin M.
New Orleans, LA
DeSalles, Albert R. ..... Kailua-Kona, HI
DeSalvo, Anthony J. ..... Jersey City, NJ
De Salvo, C. John ..... Ocala, FL
De Salvo, C. John, P.A. ..... Ocala, FL
DeSalvo, E. Alexander, Jr. ..... Denver, CO
DeSalvo, Frank G. ..... New Orleans, LA
DeSalvo, Frank J. ..... Wheaton, IL
DeSalvo, Frank J., Jr. ..... White Plains, NY
DeSalvo & Harris ..... Baton Rouge, LA
DeSalvo, Jack J. ..... Wayne, NJ
DeSalvo, Joseph D. ..... White Plains, NY
DeSalvo, Karen J. ..... Mineola, NY
DeSalvo, Peter, Jr. ..... Roseland, NJ
DeSalvo, Ramona P. ..... Nashville, TN
DeSalvo, Russell E. ..... Pueblo, CO
De Salvo, Steven ..... Los Angeles, CA
DeSalvo, Vincent J. ..... Baton Rouge, LA
DeSanctis, Christine A. ..... Lafayette, IN
DeSanctis, Christy Hallam
Washington, DC
DeSanctis, Joseph J. ..... New Haven, CT
DeSanctis, Julio ..... Orrington, ME
De Sanctis, Michael A. ..... Denver, CO
DeSanctis, Michael B. ..... Washington, DC
De Sanctis, Richard C. ..... New York, NY
DeSandro, Bradley K. ..... Salt Lake City, UT
DeSano, John A. ..... Providence, RI
DeSano, John A., Jr. ..... Warren, RI
DeSano, John A., Jr., P.C., Inc. ..... Warren, RI
DeSano, John A., Law Office, Inc.
Providence, RI
DeSano, Philip R. ..... Providence, RI
DeSanti, Richard J. ..... Fairfax, VA
DeSanti, Susan S.
Federal Trade Commission, Policy Planning, GV
DeSantis, Angela C. ..... Syracuse, NY
DeSantis, Blaine J. ..... Reading, PA
DeSantis, Carl ..... New York, NY
DeSantis, Conrad J.
North Palm Beach, FL
DeSantis, Conrad J., III ..... New York, NY
DeSantis, Debra Morena ..... Philadelphia, PA
DeSantis, Dennis M. ..... Trenton, NJ
De Santis & De Santis ..... Utica, NY
DeSantis, DeSantis & Essig ..... Reading, PA
DeSantis, Emily ..... Fort Lauderdale, FL
DeSantis, Frank, Law Office of
San Diego, CA
DeSantis, Frank R. ..... Cleveland, OH
DeSantis, Frank V. ..... Queensbury, NY
DeSantis, Gabrielle ..... San Diego, CA
DeSantis, Gaskill, Smith & Shenkman, P.A.
North Palm Beach, FL
DeSantis, Gennaro M. ..... Denver, CO
De Santis, Gerard D. ..... Carle Place, NY
De Santis, Gerard D. ..... Mineola, NY
Riverhead, NY
DeSantis, John P., Jr. ..... Millburn, NJ
New York, NY
DeSantis, Joseph E. ..... Reading, PA
DeSantis, Karen McCartan
Washington, DC
DeSantis, Kathleen K. ..... Fresno, CA
DeSantis, Kevin V. ..... San Diego, CA
DeSantis, Lourdes Mendoza ..... Atlanta, GA
De Santis, Lynette S. ..... Cleveland, OH
DeSantis, M. David ..... Oakland, CA
DeSantis, Michael A. ..... Lanham, MD
DeSantis, Michael J. ..... Silver Spring, MD
De Santis, Michael P. ..... Utica, NY
DeSantis, Michael V. ..... Uniondale, NY
De Santis, Michael V. ..... Utica, NY
De Santis, Michele M. ..... Hackensack, NJ
DeSantis, Nicole M. ..... Sacramento, CA
DeSantis, Pasquale ..... Boston, MA
DeSantis, Richard A. ..... Los Angeles, CA
DeSantis, Robert J. ..... Wilton, CT
DeSantis, Salvatore J. ..... New York, NY
DeSantis, Shauna M. ..... Clifton Park, NY
DeSantis, Sheryl A. ..... Bridgewater, NJ
DeSantis, Victor J. ..... Washington, DC
DeSantis, Vincent ..... Gloversville, NY
DeSantis, William J. ..... Cherry Hill, NJ
DeSanto & Barlow ..... Scranton, PA
Desanto, Catherine Carol ..... Riverhead, NY
DeSanto, Debra J. ..... Columbus, OH
DeSanto & DeSanto ..... Poland, OH
DeSanto, Donald J. ..... Poland, OH
DeSanto, Frank J. ..... Scranton, PA
DeSanto, James J. ..... Libertyville, IL
DeSanto, James J., A Professioanl Corporation ..... Chicago, IL
Libertyville, IL
Waukegan, IL
DeSanto, Jason C. ..... Chicago, IL
DeSanto, Jeanne Bitonte ..... Poland, OH
DeSanto, John E. ..... Duluth, MN
DeSanto, Joseph D. ..... Poland, OH
DeSanto, Joseph R. ..... Fairfax, VA
DeSanto, Ralph P. ..... New York, NY
DeSanto, Richard J. ..... Fort Lauderdale, FL
DeSanto, Robert A. ..... Vineland, NJ
DeSanto, Robert P. ..... Ashland, OH
DeSanto, Sara J. ..... Department of Justice, Antitrust Division, GV
De Santos, Diana ..... Dallas, TX
DeSantos, Laura E. ..... Houston, TX
DeSantos, Thomas ..... Hanford, CA
Visalia, CA
Desany, Jessica A. ..... Albany, NY
DeSanze, Christine M. ..... New York, NY
De Sapio, Gaetano M. ..... Frenchtown, NJ
de Saram, Jetsun Auer ..... New York, NY
DeSarbo, D. Richard ..... North Haven, CT

DeSarbo, Reichert & Gradoville, P.C. North Haven, CT
Desaretz, Sheri ..... Collingswood, NJ
DeSario, Daniel J. ..... Los Angeles, CA
DeSario, Jack P. ..... Cleveland, OH
Desarlo, Joanne ..... New York, NY
Des Armo, Candace J. ..... Milwaukee, WI
De Sarno, Paul A. ..... Sayreville, NJ
DeSarno, Peter A. ..... Edison, NJ
De Saro, Jolie Ann ..... New York, NY
Desatnik, Colyn B. ..... Irvine, CA
DeSaulnier, Paula M. ..... Portsmouth, NH
DeSaulnier & Siegal, P.A. ..... Portsmouth, NH
Desaulniers, Eugene R., II ..... Hampton, VA
Desaulniers, Helen T. General Accounting Office, Office of the General Counsel, GV
de Saussure, Ariane L. Department of the Air Force, Office of the General Counsel, GV
deSaussure, Charlton, Jr. ..... Charleston, SC
DeSaussure, Hamilton ..... Akron, OH
DeSaussure, Hamilton, Jr. ..... Akron, OH
DeSaussure, Richard L., III ..... Memphis, TN
Desautels, Clement T. ..... Southbridge, MA
Desautels, Diane C. ..... Springfield, MA
Desautels, Gerald W. ..... Burlington, VT
Desautels, Jeffrey H. ..... Denver, CO
Desautels, Michael L. ..... Albany, NY
Desautels, Raymond A., III ..... Oxford, MA
Des Barres, John Brian ..... Tulsa, OK
Desberg, Gary S. ..... Cleveland, OH
Desbois, Annie J. ..... Scarsdale, NY
des Bordes, Lee H. (Hank), Jr. Baton Rouge, LA
DeScala, Joseph, Jr. ..... San Anselmo, CA
Descalso, Judith A. ..... Escondido, CA
Descalso, Michael G. ..... San Mateo, CA
DesCamp, Robin C. ..... Portland, OR
Descarage, Susan Marie ..... Springfield, MA
Desch, Theodore E. ..... Chicago, IL
Deschaine, Micheline A. ..... Stratham, NH
Deschambault, Danielle ..... Philadelphia, PA
Deschamps, Deborah A. ..... Willimantic, CT
Deschamps, Robert L., III ..... Missoula, MT
DesChamps, William W., Jr. Myrtle Beach, SC
DesChamps, William W., Jr., P.A. Myrtle Beach, SC
Deschamps-Braly, Dania ..... Ada, OK
Deschauer, John J., Jr. ..... Washington, DC
Des Chenes, Alexander M., Jr. ..... Adrian, MI
Deschenes, Denise J. ..... Montpelier, VT
St. Johnsbury, VT
Deschênes, Diane Lyne ..... Calabasas, CA
Deschenes, Douglas C. ..... Boston, MA
Deschenes, Gary S. ..... Great Falls, MT
Deschenes, Gregory P. ..... Boston, MA
Deschenes, John E. ..... Wareham, MA
Deschenes, John J. ..... Sarasota, FL
Deschenes Law Office ..... Great Falls, MT
Deschenes, Richard ..... Swansea, MA
Descher, Joanne Martin ..... St. Louis, MO
Descher & Schultz ..... St. Louis, MO
Deschere, Linda M. ..... Troy, MI
DeScherer, Christopher K. ..... Raleigh, NC
Descherer, Dorinda D. ..... Tenafly, NJ
DeScherer, Nilufer O. ..... Roseland, NJ
DeScherer, Richard K. ..... New York, NY
Deschler, Michael C. ..... Bethlehem, PA
Deschler, Peter W. ..... Manitowoc, WI
deSchweinitz, Allan B. ..... Medford, OR
deSchweinitz & Hamilton Klamath Falls, OR
Medford, OR
d'Esclapon, Pierre F. de Ravel New York, NY
Descoteaux, Gemma L. ..... Dallas, TX
Descoteaux, Joan M. ..... Walpole, MA
DeSear, Edward M. ..... New York, NY
De Seguin-Hons, Suzan ..... Denver, CO
de Seife, Rodolphe J. A. ..... De Kalb, IL
Desel, Paula M. ..... New York, NY
Desell, Linda J. ..... Springfield, VA
DeSelm & Baker ..... Cambridge, OH
DeSelm, David H. ..... Cambridge, OH
DeSelms, L. Kaye ..... Olney, IL
Deselms, Margaret A. ..... Holdrege, NE
De Sena, Benjamin P. ..... Wayne, NJ
DeSena, Jennifer Rice ..... Cape Elizabeth, ME
Desena, Jennifer Susan ..... New York, NY
Desena, Louis John ..... Uniondale, NY
DeSena, Nicolette C. ..... Newark, NJ
DeSena, Ralph A. ..... New York, NY
DeSena, Ralph E., Jr. ..... New York, NY
Desenberg, B. R. ..... Buchanan, MI
Desenberg, Carl R. ..... St. Louis, MO
Desenberg & Colip, P.C., A Professional Corporation ..... Buchanan, MI
Desenberg, Dana ..... Houston, TX
Desenberg, Jon P. ..... Detroit, MI
Desenberg, Louis A. ..... Buchanan, MI
De Seno, Thomas ..... Shrewsbury, NJ
Deser, Michael Dean ..... Madison, WI
Deseran, Sophia M. ..... Cleveland, OH
DeSerio, Alan E. ..... Tampa, FL
DeSerio, Gary W. ..... Houston, TX
Deserio, Kim M. ..... Bethesda, MD
De Serna, Alexander C. ..... Miamisburg, OH
DeSeve, Karren A. ..... Washington, DC
de Séve, Richard J. ..... Concord, NH
DeSevo, Alex R. ..... Secaucus, NJ
De Sevo Cerutti & Lombardi, P.A. Jersey City, NJ
De Sevo, Ralph A. ..... Jersey City, NJ
De Sevo, Richard A. ..... New York, NY
Desfor, Bruce D. ..... Harrisburg, PA
Desgalier, Kari Mason ..... San Diego, CA
des Groseilliers, Jennifer ..... Brentwood, NH
Kingston, NH
Desha, John R., II ..... Honolulu, HI
DeSha, Roy C., Jr. ..... Nashville, TN
DeSha, Wallace E. ..... San Francisco, CA
Deshaies, Marc R. ..... New Bedford, MA
Deshaies, Robert J. ..... Amesbury, MA
Desharnais, Kevin G. ..... Chicago, IL
Desharnais, Richard R. ..... Albany, NY
De Shazer, Randal A. ..... Las Vegas, NV
DeShazer, Samuel H. ..... Louisville, KY
Deshazo, Andrea P. ..... San Francisco, CA
DeShazo, Diane Lea ..... Atlanta, GA
DeShazo, Gary F., & Associates Austin, TX
DeShazo, Nikki T. ..... Dallas, TX
DeShazo, Preston ..... Dallas, TX
De Shazo, Sharon T. ..... Orlando, FL
Deshensky, George O. ..... New York, NY
DeSheplo, John R. ..... Fort Lee, NJ
De Shetler, Kenneth E. ..... Columbus, OH
de Shetler, Michael M. ..... Corpus Christi, TX
DeShields-Minnis, Tarra R. ..... Baltimore, MD
Deshler, Christine P. ..... Boston, MA
Deshler, Dana A. ..... Columbus, OH
Deshmukh, Jay R. ..... Cincinnati, OH
DeShon, A. Michelle ..... Cleveland, OH
De Shong, Amy P. ..... Blue Bell, PA
Deshong, John K. ..... Fairfax, VA
Deshong, Leanne ..... Kansas City, MO
Deshong, Tery D. ..... Tulsa, OK
Deshotel, C. Kenneth ..... Opelousas, LA
Deshotel, Joseph D. ..... Beaumont, TX
Deshotels & Deshotels ..... Kaplan, LA
Deshotels, Errol D. ..... Oberlin, LA
Deshotels, John B. ..... Ville Platte, LA
Deshotels, O. H., III ..... Kaplan, LA
DesHotels, Paul J. ..... Minneapolis, MN
DesHotels, Paul J., Ltd., Law Offices of Minneapolis, MN
Deshur, James E. ..... Milwaukee, WI
DeSibio, Nicholas ..... Hewlett, NY
DeSibio, Nicholas, P.C. ..... Hewlett, NY
Desideri, Lawrence R. ..... Chicago, IL
Desiderio, David Ernest ..... Philadelphia, PA
Desiderio, Frank J. ..... New York, NY
Desiderio, Gina K. ..... Twinsburg, OH
Desiderio, John M. ..... New York, NY
Desiderio, John M., P.C. and Associates New York, NY
Desiderio, Marc F. ..... Englewood Cliffs, NJ
Desiderio, Peter L. ..... Fort Lauderdale, FL
Desiderio, Robert J. ..... Albuquerque, NM
Desiderio, Roger J. ..... West Orange, NJ
Desiderio, Virginia L. ..... Monongahela, PA
De Siena, Charles L. ..... Bridgeport, CT
DeSiena & Gallucci ..... Bridgeport, CT
DeSieno, Diane E. ..... Princeton, NJ
DeSieno, Timothy B. ..... Hartford, CT
Desierto, Julie Sparling ..... Chicago, IL
Desilets, Gerard E. ..... Boston, MA
Desilets, Lawrence E. ..... Framingham, MA
Desilets, Robert A., Jr. ..... Treasury Department, Internal Revenue Service, GV
Desilets, Roland B., Jr. ..... Mount Laurel, NJ
De Silva, Angelita V. ..... New York, NY
De Silva, Archangela M. ..... Houston, TX
de Silva, Edward B., Jr. ..... Davenport, IA
DeSilva, Edward T. ..... New York, NY
DeSilva, Eric W. ..... Washington, DC
De Silva, James T. ..... New York, NY
De Silva, Joseph R. ..... Stockton, CA
DeSilva, Kathleen ..... Houston, TX
DeSilva, Lionel A. ..... Bridgeport, CT
DeSilva, Michael G. ..... Wilmington, NC
De Silva, Michael R. ..... Irvine, CA
de Silva, Raymond J., Jr. ..... Syracuse, NY
de Silva & Rhinehart ..... Syracuse, NY
DeSilva, Robert J. ..... Holtsville, NY
De Silva, Rohini P. ..... North Hollywood, CA
Desilva, Susan R. ..... New York, NY
DeSilva, Tim E. ..... Hilo, HI
DeSilva, Tim E., Attorney at Law, A Law Corporation ..... Hilo, HI
DeSimon, Thomas A. ..... Rochester, NY
DeSimone, Alyssa ..... New York, NY
DeSimone, Anne K. ..... New York, NY
De Simone & Associates Agoura Hills, CA
Los Angeles, CA
DeSimone, Beth S. ..... Washington, DC
Desimone, Bruce N. ..... Camp Springs, MD
Desimone, D. Mark ..... Minneapolis, MN
DeSimone, D. Peter ..... Mineola, NY
DeSimone, David J. ..... Kansas City, MO
De Simone, Dominic J. ..... Camden, NJ
Philadelphia, PA
DeSimone, Douglas R. ..... Providence, RI
DeSimone, Ernest P. ..... Boston, MA
DeSimone, Frank ..... Philadelphia, PA
De Simone, Frank L. ..... Medford, OR
De Simone, Gerald ..... Agoura Hills, CA
DeSimone, Herbert F. ..... Providence, RI
DeSimone, Herbert F., Jr. ..... Providence, RI
DeSimone, James M. ..... Orlando, FL
DeSimone, James W. ..... Pasadena, CA
DeSimone, Jean M. ..... New York, NY
DeSimone, John C. ..... Boston, MA
Worcester, MA
Desimone, John P. ..... Westlake, OH
DeSimone, Joseph ..... New York, NY
DeSimone & Leach, A Professional Corporation ..... Providence, RI
DeSimone, Louis A., Jr. ..... Warwick, RI
DeSimone, Margaret A. ..... Philadelphia, PA
DeSimone, Michael ..... Fair Lawn, NJ
DeSimone, Michael M. ..... Philadelphia, PA
De Simone, Michael P. ..... New York, NY
DeSimone, Nancy E. Charlotte Amalie, St. Thomas, VI
De Simone, Patricia M. ..... Chicago, IL
DeSimone Pearson, L.C. Kansas City, MO
de Simone, Richard ..... Albany, NY
DeSimone, Ronald ..... Mount Laurel, NJ
Desimone, Ronald Joseph ..... Houston, TX
Desimone, Salvatore ..... Northridge, CA
DeSimone, Samuel G. ..... Woodbury, NJ
DeSimone, Samuel R. ..... Worcester, MA
DeSimone, Samuel R., Jr. ..... Portland, OR
Desimone, Thomas M. ..... White Plains, NY
De Simone, Thomas R. ..... Providence, RI
DeSimone, Toby Susan ..... Garden City, NY
DeSimone, Vincent James ..... Venice, CA
Desimone, Wayne Lawrence New York, NY
Desind, Laurence ..... River Edge, NJ
De Sio, Isabel R. ..... Oak Brook, IL
Desio, Paula J. ..... Washington, DC
Desio, Roberta ..... New Orleans, LA
De Sio, Thomas A. ..... Des Moines, IA
DeSipio, Adam A. ..... Norristown, PA
Philadelphia, PA
DeSipio, George ..... New York, NY
DeSipio, Richard L. ..... Norristown, PA
DeSisco, Nicholas J., Jr. ..... Bel Air, MD
DeSisti & Keeffe ..... Sayre, PA
DeSisti, Michael J. ..... Sayre, PA
DeSisto, Anthony ..... Providence, RI
DeSisto, Donald J. ..... Fairfax, VA
DeSisto, Jamie L. ..... Greenbelt, MD
DeSisto, John A. ..... Denver, CO
DeSisto Law Offices ..... Providence, RI
DeSisto, Marc ..... Providence, RI
DeSisto, Michael A. ..... Providence, RI
Des Jardins & Berens ..... Chicago, IL
Des Jardins and Brown, P.C. ..... Owosso, MI
Desjardins, Cathleen ..... San Francisco, CA
Desjardins, Douglas ..... Washington, DC
Cleveland, OH
DesJardins, Fernandez & Smith, LLP Riverside, CA
San Bernardino, CA
Desjardins, Garry ..... Hartford, CT
DesJardins, Hal E. ..... Topeka, KS
Desjardins, Jay A. ..... Collegeville, PA
Des Jardins, Jerry L. ..... Owosso, MI
Des Jardins, Leonard A. ..... Chicago, IL
DesJardins, Lucille A. ..... Santa Cruz, CA
DesJardins, Michael A. ..... Riverside, CA
DesJardins, Michelle A. ..... San Diego, CA
Desjardins, Mimi ..... Olympia, WA
Desjardins, Paul D. ..... Lancaster, NH
Desjardins, Richard P. ..... Westport, MA
Des Jardins, Robert P. ..... Santa Ana, CA
Desjarlais, Mary Lynn ..... Sarasota, FL
Desjarlais, Mary Lynn, P.A. ..... Sarasota, FL
Desjourdy, Kathleen Pierce ..... Newark, NJ
Deskevich, Duane A. ..... Richmond, VA
Deskins, Heather L. ..... Beckley, WV
Deskins, Herbert, Jr. ..... Pikeville, KY
Deskins, Kathleen Campbell Lexington, KY
Deskins, Larry L. ..... St. Louis, MO
Deskins, Maureen Madigan ..... Tampa, FL
Deskins, Sharlene A. Department of Agriculture, Office of the General Counsel, GV
Desky, Robert M. ..... San Mateo, CA
Deslaurier, Toni ..... Bethel, VT
Des Laurier, Victor A. ..... Chicago, IL
Deslauriers, Frank ..... Covington, TN
Des Lauriers, Stephane P. Washington, DC
Desler, Peter ..... Boise, ID
Desloge, Angela B. ..... St. Louis, MO
Desloge, Taylor S. ..... St. Louis, MO
Desloovere, Muriel ..... Tampa, FL
Desmarais, Charles R. ..... New Bedford, MA
Desmarais, Dennis F. ..... Springfield, MA
Desmarais, Douglas W. ..... Baltimore, MD
Desmarais, Edward S., Jr. Washington, DC
Desmarais, Harrington & FitzGerald, P.C. New Bedford, MA
DesMarais, James F. ..... Boston, MA
Desmarais, John M. ..... New York, NY
Desmarais, Josee ..... Mill Valley, CA
Desmarais, Mark B. ..... Honolulu, HI
Desmarais, Michael G. ..... Campbell, CA
Desmarais, Roland G. ..... Fall River, MA
Desmarais, Stanley F. ..... Olympia, WA
Desmarais, Tracy S. ..... Louisville, KY
Desmarais, Victoria M. ..... Bay City, MI
Desmarais, Wilfred J. ..... Manchester, NH
Desmarais-Gordon, Christine Manchester, NH
Des Marteau, George J. ..... Rochester, NY
Desmery, Martin P. ..... Boston, MA
DeSmet, Ervin A., Jr. ..... Seattle, WA
De Smet, Robert F. ..... Point Richmond, CA
Desmet, Thierry Olivier ..... Miami, FL
DesMeules, Olmstead & Ostler Norwich, VT
DesMeules, Peter J. ..... Norwich, VT
DeSmidt, Jody Ollyver ..... Minneapolis, MN
De Smith, Steven R. ..... San Francisco, CA
Desmond, Allen R. ..... Fridley, MN
Desmond, Angela M. Board of Governors Of The Federal Reserve System, Division of Banking Supervision and Regulation, GV
Desmond, Brenda C. ..... Missoula, MT
Desmond, Cecilia M. Federal Energy Regulatory Commission, Office of the General Counsel, GV
Desmond, Charles S., II ..... Buffalo, NY
Desmond & Cooper, P.A. ..... Westbrook, ME
Desmond, Daniel J. ..... Westbrook, ME
Desmond, Daniel P. ..... Dallas, TX
Desmond, David S. ..... Amityville, NY
Desmond, Deirdre C. ..... Eagle Butte, SD
Desmond & Desmond ..... Sacramento, CA
Desmond, Elizabeth L. ..... Boston, MA
Desmond, George R. ..... Framingham, MA
Desmond, Gerald J. ..... Sacramento, CA
Desmond, Gerald J., Jr. ..... Sacramento, CA
Desmond, Gerald, Law Offices of Santa Rosa, CA
Desmond, James D. ..... Louisville, KY
Desmond, James L. ..... Portland, OR
Desmond, James M. ..... Duxbury, MA
Desmond, James M. ..... Sugar Land, TX
Desmond, Jennifer M.Dillion ..... Hamburg, NY
Desmond, John F. ..... Centerville, MA
Desmond, John M. ..... Ridgeland, MS
Desmond, John O. ..... Framingham, MA
Desmond, John P. ..... Las Vegas, NV
Reno, NV
Desmond, John P. ..... Madison, WI
Desmond, Joseph ..... Boston, MA
Desmond, Joseph A. ..... San Francisco, CA
Desmond, Leo T. ..... Benton, IL
Desmond, Leo W. ..... West Palm Beach, FL
Desmond, Louis N., (A Law Corporation) Sacramento, CA
Desmond, Marie Barraza ..... Eugene, OR
Desmond, Marjorie Turk ..... Long Beach, CA
Desmond, Maura Campbell ..... Hamburg, NY
Desmond, Michael J. ..... Department of Justice, Tax Division, GV
Desmond, Michael K. ..... Chicago, IL
Desmond, Miller & Desmond Sacramento, CA
Desmond, Nicholas J. ..... Miami, FL
Desmond, Patrick J. ..... Toledo, OH
Desmond, Richard F. ..... Sacramento, CA
Desmond, Richard K. ..... Cleveland, OH
Desmond, Robert G. ..... New York, NY
Desmond, Robin J. ..... Denver, CO
Desmond, Scott M. ..... New York, NY
Desmond, Sean J. ..... San Francisco, CA
Desmond, Susan Fahey ..... New Orleans, LA
Desmond, Thomas P. ..... Chicago, IL
Desmond, Timothy P. ..... Brevard, NC
Desmond, Walter J. ..... Long Beach, CA
Desmond & Webster, LLP ..... Ridgeland, MS
Desmond, William J. ..... Cincinnati, OH
Desmond, Wm. T. ..... Billerica, MA
Desmonde, Corinne ..... Cold Spring, NY
Desmuke Hawkins, Odele S. ..... Chicago, IL
Desnet, Holly E. ..... Skokie, IL
Desnick, Lori C. ..... West Palm Beach, FL
Desnoyers, Dale A. ..... Hudson, NY
Deso, Robert E. ..... Washington, DC
Deso, Thomas, Spevack, Weitzman & Rost, P.C. ..... Washington, DC
de Socarraz, Elena ..... Miami, FL
de Socarraz, Elena, P.A. ..... Miami, FL
Desoer, Michele M. ..... Los Angeles, CA
De Sola, Isabella M. ..... New York, NY
de Solenni, Mario E. ..... Crescent City, CA
Deson-Fried, Sarah G. ..... Birmingham, MI
DeSonier, Louis G., Jr. ..... Metairie, LA
Desormier-Cartwright, Anné West Palm Beach, FL
Desotelle, Charles R. ..... Flint, MI
De Soto, Ernesto ..... Tucson, AZ
De Soto, Hector E. ..... Newark, NJ
DeSoto, Karen F. ..... Somerville, NJ
DeSoto, Kurt E. ..... Washington, DC
de Soto Cicchetti, Tammy ..... Tallahassee, FL
De Sousa, Frank A. ..... Farmingdale, NY
de Sousa, Gregory ..... Scarsdale, NY
de Sousa, Paula C. P. ..... San Diego, CA
De Sousa, Robert J. ..... Harrisburg, PA
DeSouza, Anne M. ..... Boston, MA
De Souza, Barbara Dillon ..... Las Vegas, NV
De Souza, Donnise A. ..... Miami, FL
Desouza, Jacqueline ..... Berkeley, CA
DeSouza, Jas. L. ..... Phoenix, AZ
Desouza Law Offices, P.C. ..... Berkeley, CA
San Francisco, CA
de Souza, Lawrence E. ..... Fairfield, CA
De Souza, Marcele Tavares New York, NY
Des Pain, David L. ..... Collinsville, IL
DeSpain, Donald E. ..... Oklahoma City, OK
Despard, Mary Allison ..... Chicago, IL
Despas, Katina ..... New York, NY
Despeaux, L. Sandra ..... Baltimore, MD
de Spelder, Robert ..... Pasadena, CA
Desper, Oscar E., III ..... Seattle, WA
D'Espies, Kevin J. ..... Fort Lauderdale, FL
D'Espies, Kevin J., P.A. Fort Lauderdale, FL
Despina, Eleanore ..... San Francisco, CA
Despins, Luc A. ..... New York, NY
Despins, Martin P. ..... Kent, OH
DeSpirito, Carolyn ..... Melrose, MA
Desplaines, Danielle M. ..... Salem, MA
Despo, William A. ..... Newark, NJ
Desport, Cheree D. ..... Covina, CA
DesPortes, Betty Layne ..... Richmond, VA
Desposito, Angelo J., III ..... Louisville, KY
D'Esposito, Frank G. ..... Bardonia, NY
D'Esposito, James J. ..... New York, NY
D'Esposito, Jeanne ..... White Plains, NY
D'Esposito, John V. ..... Tampa, FL
D'Esposito, Julian C., Jr. ..... Chicago, IL

Despotakis, Constantine A.
White Plains, NY
Despotopulos, David P. ... Worcester, MA
Despotovich, Dean ... Clifton, NJ
Despotovich, Steven ... West Des Moines, IA
Despoy and Nelson ... Altoona, PA
Ebensburg, PA
Hollidaysburg, PA
Despoy, Terry W. ... Altoona, PA
Despres, Leon M. ... Chicago, IL
Despres, Schwartz & Geoghegan
Chicago, IL
Despriet, John G. ... Atlanta, GA
Desrochers, Christopher ... Winter Haven, FL
Desrochers, Gerard A. ... Houston, TX
Des Rochers, Mark S. ... Chilton, WI
Desrochers, Michael J. ... Boston, MA
Desrochers, Paul A. ... Portland, OR
Des Roches, Cary A. ... New Orleans, LA
Des Roches, Stuart E. ... New Orleans, LA
DesRosier, Thomas J. ... Cambridge, MA
Desrosiers, Albert E. ... Stratford, CT
DesRosiers, Denise L. ... Tampa, FL
des Rosiers, Jared S. ... Portland, ME
Desrosiers, Ronald L. ... Chelmsford, MA
DesRuisseaux, Ann ... Houston, TX
Desruisseaux, Richard E. ... Las Vegas, NV
Dessaint, Marigene Abbott ... Phoenix, AZ
Dessaint, Noel K. ... Phoenix, AZ
Dessau, Peter V. ... San Jose, CA
Dessauer, Mark S. ... Johnson City, TN
Kingsport, TN
Dessaules, Jonathan A. ... Phoenix, AZ
Dessausure, Ernest Latony ... Columbia, SC
Dessberg, Claudio J. ... New York, NY
Dessecker, James W., Jr. ... Boca Raton, FL
Dessel, William ... Providence, RI
Desselle, H. Kent ... Independence, MO
Desselle Law Offices ... Independence, MO
Dessem, R. Lawrence ... Knoxville, TN
Dessen, David S. ... Jenkintown, PA
Media, PA
Philadelphia, PA
Dessen, Eric M. ... New York, NY
Dessen, Moses & Sheinoff ... Cherry Hill, NJ
Jenkintown, PA
Media, PA
Philadelphia, PA
Dessen, Stanley B. ... New York, NY
Dessent, Michael H. ... San Diego, CA
Desser, Christina L. ... San Francisco, CA
Desser, David B. ... Chicago, IL
Desser, Franklin M. ... Los Angeles, CA
Desser, Irwin H. ... Baltimore, MD
Desser, Jennifer ... Chicago, IL
Desser, Leonard I. ... Towson, MD
Desser, Richard B. ... Towson, MD
Dessert, Edward E. ... Park Rapids, MN
Desseyn, Donald M. ... Cleveland, OH
Dessler, Marvin J. ... Bowie, MD
Dessner, Angela M. ... Monroe, WI
Dessoffy, Rebecca J. ... Cleveland, OH
Dessommes, Genevieve M.
New Orleans, LA
Dessonville, Loren E. ... Omaha, NE
Dessy, Fawn Kennedy ... Bakersfield, CA
Dessy, Ronald Daniel ... Bakersfield, CA
Dest, Michael M. ... Twin Peaks, CA
De Staffan, Anthony J. ... Newark, NY
Destaffan, Peter A. ... Syracuse, NY
DeStaffan & Saracino, P.C. ... Newark, NY
DeSt.Croix, Maureen ... Carlsbad, CA
de Stefan, Dwight Deane ... Hackensack, NJ
DeStefanis, John L. ... Milwaukee, WI
de Stefanis, Lena ... Pound Ridge, NY
DeStefano, Albert A. ... New York, NY
DeStefano, Alfred D. ... Saugus, MA
Destefano, Anthony R. ... Americus, GA
DeStefano, Corinne M. ... Madison, NJ
DeStefano, Darren K.
Securities and Exchange Commission,
Division of Corporation Finance, GV
DeStefano, David P. ... Warwick, RI
DeStefano, Emanuele J. ... Mount Pocono, PA
De Stefano, Ernest ... Hammonton, NJ
Philadelphia, PA
De Stefano, Francis ... Jersey City, NJ
DeStefano & Gabor ... Mount Pocono, PA
DeStefano, Gina M. ... Baltimore, MD
DeStefano, Jill L. ... Pittsburgh, PA
DeStefano, John J. ... Boston, MA
De Stefano, John V. ... Chicago, IL
De Stefano, L. Robert ... Los Angeles, CA
DeStefano, Louis M. ... Newark, NJ
De Stefano, Nicholas E. E. ... Greenwich, CT
De Stefano, Paul R. ... Palo Alto, CA
DeStefano, Peter ... Harrison, AR
DeStefano, Philip F., Jr. ... Greenwich, CT
DeStefano, Ralph J. ... Montville, NJ
DeStefano, Ralph T. ... Pittsburgh, PA
De Stefano, Rhonda ... Mount Olive, NJ
DeStefano, Richard ... El Prado, NM
Destefano, Robert J. ... New York, NY
DeStefano, Rocco W. ... Hollywood, FL
DeStefano, Rudolph W. ... Norristown, PA
DeStefano, Salvatore A. ... Succasunna, NJ
DeStefano, William A. ... Philadelphia, PA
deSteiguer, Darla R. ... Tahlequah, OK
DeSteno, Richard L. ... New York, NY
De Stephanis, Alfred ... Palmyra, NJ
De Stephens, William P. ... Lima, OH
Dester, James M. ... Salt Lake City, UT
de Steuben, Karla J. ... Worcester, MA
D'Esti, Joellen M. ... Boston, MA
DeStigter, Melanie S. ... Grand Rapids, MI
Destino, David A. ... Los Angeles, CA
Destito, Samuel G. ... Morristown, NJ
Princeton, NJ
Destocki, Paul E. ... Ironton, OH
Destouet, Maurice P. ... Los Angeles, CA
D'Estrada, Richard D. ... Denver, CO
Destribats, Campbell, DeSantis, Magee & O'Donnell ... Freehold, NJ
New Brunswick, NJ
Princeton, NJ
Somerville, NJ
Trenton, NJ
Destribats, Jay G. ... Trenton, NJ
Destro, Robert A. ... Washington, DC
Destry, Matthew I. ... Fort Lauderdale, FL
DeSue, Christine L. ... New Orleans, LA
DesVeaux, James J. ... Chicago, IL
Desvernine, Eugene M. ... Richmond, VA
DeSylvia, Terry ... Portland, OR
DeTamble, Jacqueline E. ... Honolulu, HI
Detamore, James R. ... Lebanon, IN
Detamore, James Scott ... Lakewood, CO
Detamore, William T., Jr. ... Tulsa, OK
DeTar, Richard A. ... Easton, MD
DeTar, Richard F. ... Melbourne, FL
Detar, Suzanne ... Charleston, SC
DeTardo & DeTardo ... Hollywood, FL
DeTardo, Douglas M. ... Hollywood, FL
DeTardo, Nicholas J. ... Hollywood, FL
De Tasnady, Stephen Nicholas ... Seattle, WA
Detch, Andrew ... Highland Beach, FL
Detch, John L. ... Lewisburg, WV
Detchemendy, Deanna Wollam
Burbank, CA
Detec, David A. ... Warren, OH
DeTella, Joel R. ... Chicago, IL
DeTemple, Matthew J. ... Columbus, OH
Detenbeck, Lee C. ... Horseshoe Bay, TX
Deter, Chet D. ... San Francisco, CA
Deter, Kurt A. ... St. Cloud, MN
Deter, Linc S. ... St. Paul, MN
Deterding, F. Marshall ... Tallahassee, FL
Deterling, Sheri L. ... Dallas, TX
Determan, Dann J. ... Vienna, VA
Determan, Dean W. ... New Orleans, LA
Determan, Donald P. ... San Diego, CA
Determan, John D. ... Chino, CA
Determan, Katherine Miller
New Orleans, LA
Determan, Margaret S. ... Irvington, NY
Determan, Mark S. ... Department of Justice,
Tax Division, GV
Determan, Sara-Ann ... Washington, DC
Deters, Benzinger & LaVelle, P.S.C.
Covington, KY
Independence, KY
Cincinnati, OH
Hamilton, OH
Deters, Charles H. ... Covington, KY
Deters, Duane A. ... Mattoon, IL
Deters, Eric C., & Associates
Covington, KY
Deters, Eric C., & Associates
Cincinnati, OH
Deters, Jed K. ... Covington, KY
Deters, Jeremy J. ... Cincinnati, OH
Deters, Joseph T. ... Cincinnati, OH
Deters, Loren A. ... Irvine, CA
Detert, Eugene E. ... Hales Corners, WI
Detgen, Gretchen A. ... St. Joseph, MI
Detherage, Andrew J. ... Indianapolis, IN
Detherow, Dori B. ... St. Louis, MO
Dethlefs, Darrell C., Law Office of
Camp Hill, PA
Dethlefs, Thomas M. ... Denver, CO
Dethlefsen, Carolyn B. ... San Rafael, CA
Dethlefsen, Shawn M. ... Allentown, PA
Dethman, John P. H. ... Denver, CO
Dethmers, Rebecca Ann
Inver Grove Heights, MN
DeThomasis & Buchanan, P.A.
Gainesville, FL
DeThomasis, Craig C. ... Gainesville, FL
Dethrow, Brian L. ... Dallas, TX
Detiberiis, Marina Cora ... New York, NY
Detiere, Ann L. ... New York, NY
De Tine, Linda J. ... Buffalo, NY
Detisch & Christensen ... San Diego, CA
Detisch, Donald W. ... San Diego, CA
Detisch, John ... Omaha, NE
Detjen, David W. ... New York, NY
Detjen, Mary L. ... Chicago, IL
Detjens, John, III ... Portland, OR
Detkin, Barbara J. ... New York, NY
Detkin, Peter N. ... Santa Clara, CA
Detlefs, Dale R. ... Louisville, KY
Detlefs, Jeff., P.C. ... Denver, CO
Detlefs, Jeffrey S. ... Denver, CO
Detlefsen, Guy Robert, Jr.
Wisconsin Rapids, WI
Detlefsen, Jeffrey E. ... Portland, OR
Detlefsen Law Office, P.C. ... Portland, OR
Detlie, H. Edwin ... Ottumwa, IA
Detling, James S. ... Greenville, OH
Detling, Karen ... Baltimore, MD
Detloff, Janis H. ... Houston, TX
Detloff, Martin P. ... Houston, TX
Detloff, Tamara L. ... Bethesda, MD
Detlor, John S. ... Kirkland, WA
Detmer, Rosalie Beck ... Madison, WI
Detmer, Thomas R. ... Madison, WI
DeToffol, David J. ... Mineola, NY
New York, NY
de Toledo, Victoria ... Stamford, CT
DeTommasi, Anthony J. ... Albany, NY
White Plains, NY
DeTommaso, Michael A. ... Philadelphia, PA
DeTora, Alice E. ... Hartford, CT
Detora, Leighton C. ... Barre, VT
DeTore, John A. ... Boston, MA
DeTore, Stephen M.
Securities and Exchange Commission,
Office of Compliance Inspections and
Examinations, GV
de Torres, Eduardo X. ... Newton, NC
DeTour, Michele E. ... Houston, TX
DeTraglia, Gustave J., Jr. ... Utica, NY
DeTraglia, Salvatore, III ... Lisle, IL
DeTrano, Denise Wilber ... Modesto, CA
Detre, Peter A. ... San Francisco, CA
Detrich, Donald L. ... Tulsa, OK
Detrick, Brian S. ... Wilmington, CA
Detrick, Herbert H., II ... New York, NY
Detrick, J. Paul ... Hampton, SC
Detrick, Joanne F. Weber ... Columbus, OH
Detrick, Judson W. ... Denver, CO
Detrick, Lisa Ann ... Los Angeles, CA
Detrick, Paul C. ... Browns Mills, NJ
Detrick, Robert P. ... Denver, CO
Detring, Cara L. ... Farmington, MO
Detrio, Joseph M. ... Winter Park, FL
Detrixhe, Edward B. ... Ames, KS
Detrizio, Charles S. ... New York, NY
De Trizio, Raffaella ... Princeton, NJ
DeTro, W. Scott ... Omak, WA
DeTroy, Benjamin E. ... Auburn, ME
DeTroy, Peter J., III ... Portland, ME
DeTrude, Howard J. ... Indianapolis, IN
Dettelbach, Brian Andrew
United States Senate,
Committee Legal Personnel, GV
Dettelbach, Sam G. ... Atlanta, GA
Dettelbach, Sicherman & Baumgart, A Legal Professional Association ... Cleveland, OH
Dettelbach, Steven M. ... Department of Justice,
Executive Office for United States Attorneys,
GV
Dettelbach, Thomas L.
Mayfield Heights, OH
Dettery, Linda R. ... New York, NY
Dettinger, James F. ... Toledo, OH
Dettinger, Warren W. ... North Canton, OH
Dettling, Aaron ... Mobile, AL
Dettling, Edwin J. ... Pompano Beach, FL
Dettling, Ethan R. ... Birmingham, AL
Dettling, Fannie M. ... Hudson, MA
Dettling, Faye Duckett ... Sugar Land, TX
Dettling, Rosemary ... Department of Justice,
Civil Rights Division, GV
Dettling, Theresa A. ... Glendale, CO
Dettloff, Richard W. ... Ferndale, MI
Dettman, Donald D. ... Benton Harbor, MI
Dettman, Edwin, Jr. ... Golden, CO
Dettman, Kurt L. ... Boston, MA
Dettman, Robert M. ... Dallas, TX
Dettmann, Darrell R. ... Marquette, MI
Dettmann, David A. ... Davenport, IA
Dettmann, Jonathan W. ... Minneapolis, MN
Dettmann, Marc J. ... Madison, WI
Dettmann, Steven J. ... Los Angeles, CA
Dettmar, Joseph H.
Department of Transportation,
Surface Transportation Board, GV
Dettmer, Anne R. ... Dayton, OH
Dettmer, Dale A., (P.A.) ... Melbourne, FL
Dettmer, Dennis A. ... Detroit, MI
Dettmer, Ethan D. ... San Francisco, CA
Dettmer, Frederick R., Law Office of
New York, NY
Dettmer, Marilyn J. ... Charles City, IA
Dettmer, Michael H. ... Grand Rapids, MI
Dettmer, Robert G. ... Harrison, NY
Dettmer, Robin O'Day ... Fort Worth, TX
Dettmer, Scott C. ... Menlo Park, CA
Dettmer, Teri M. ... Seattle, WA
Dettmer, Thomas H. ... San Jose, CA
Dettmering, P.C. ... Douglasville, GA
Dettmering, W. O'Neal, Jr.
Douglasville, GA
Dettner, John R. ... San Francisco, CA
Detton, David K. ... Salt Lake City, UT
Dettor, Arnold A. ... Syracuse, NY
Dettor, Christine Woodcock ... Syracuse, NY
Dettor, Douglas P. ... Greensboro, NC
Dettor, Robert W. ... Fayetteville, NY
Dettore, Raymond, Jr. ... Providence, RI
Dettra, Norman E., Jr. ... Reading, PA
Detty, John L. ... Jackson, OH
DeTulleo, Charles T. ... West Chester, PA
Detuno, Joseph E. ... Chicago, IL
De Turris, Teresa A. ... New York, NY
Detweiler, Donald J. ... Wilmington, DE
Detweiler, Frank H. ... New York, NY
Detweiler, George C. ... Twin Falls, ID
Detweiler, Keith M. ... New Orleans, LA
Detweiler, Robert A. ... Philadelphia, PA
Detweiler, Robert A. ... Swarthmore, PA
Detweiler, Robert T. ... Brighton, MI
Detweiler, Sean Douglas ... Foxboro, MA
Detweiler, William J. ... Akron, OH
Detweiler, William M. ... New Orleans, LA
Detwiler, Alice W. ... Washington, DC
Detwiler, Harold W. ... Summerton, SC
Detwiler, Harry R., Jr. ... Tallahassee, FL
Detwiler, Jeffrey B. ... San Francisco, CA
Detwiler, Kathy E. ... Rochester, NY
Detwiler, Leslie C. ... San Diego, CA
Detwiler, Lisa C. ... Harrisburg, PA
Philadelphia, PA
Detwiler, Philip R. ... Blue Bell, PA
Detwiler, Philip R., & Associates, P.C.
Blue Bell, PA
Detwiler, Richard C. ... Columbia, SC
Detwiler, Robert W. ... Jacksonville, NC
Detwiler, Robert W., P.A. ... Jacksonville, NC
Detwiler, R.P. ... Department of Energy,
Office of the General Counsel, GV
Detwiler, William F. ... New York, NY
Detzel, Christopher A. ... Santa Monica, CA
Detzel, Lauren Y. ... Orlando, FL
Detzer, Ronald J. ... La Mesa, CA
Detzky, Michael L. ... Freehold, NJ
Detzner, John A. ... Washington, DC
Deubel, Charles C., III ... South Orange, NJ
Deubel & Deubel ... South Orange, NJ
Deuben, David C. ... Wheat Ridge, CO
Deuber, Fred J. ... Barberton, OH
Deubner, K. Mark ... Dallas, TX
Deuel, Patti Olson ... Chicago, IL
Deuel, Peter L. ... Medford, OR
Deuel, Peter M. ... Chicago, IL
Deuhs, Joseph J., Jr. ... Minneapolis, MN
Deukmejian, George ... Los Angeles, CA
Deull, Ellis M. ... Merrick, NY
De Ulloa, Joseph R. ... San Francisco, CA
Deuman, Leanne Barnes
Sault Ste. Marie, MI
Deupi, Carlos J. ... Miami, FL
Deupree, Darcie A. ... Atlanta, GA
Deupree, William J., III ... Covington, KY
Deupree, William J., Jr. ... Covington, KY
Deuprey, Dan H. ... San Diego, CA
Deuprey, Solveig Store ... San Diego, CA
Deuring, Stuart R. ... Minneapolis, MN
Deurso, Darren ... Harrison, NY
Deus, Roderick S. ... New Orleans, LA
Deuschle, Brian C. ... Fort Lauderdale, FL
Deuschle, Brian C., Chartered
Fort Lauderdale, FL
Deuschle, James K. ... Tulsa, OK
Deuschle, James K., P.C. ... Tulsa, OK
Deuschle, Kurt J. ... Boston, MA
Deuschle, Thomas A. ... Buffalo, NY
Deuser, Charles W., II ... Dayton, OH
Deuser, Richard F. ... Wasilla, AK
Deusner, E. Earl, II ... Selmer, TN
Deusner & Kennedy, A Professional Association ... Selmer, TN
Deuster, Donald E. ... Libertyville, IL
Deutch, Alan H. ... Milwaukee, WI
Deutch & Falk, A Professional Corporation
Flemington, NJ
Linden, NJ
New Brunswick, NJ
Princeton, NJ
Somerville, NJ
Woodbridge, NJ
New York, NY
Deutch, Howard E. ... Rockville, MD
Deutch, Jeffrey A., (P.A.) ... Boca Raton, FL
Deutch, Joann R. ... Studio City, CA
Deutch, Paul H. ... New York, NY
Deutch, Philip J. ... Washington, DC
Deutch, Richard E., Jr. ... Miami, FL
Deutch, Roni Lynn ... Sacramento, CA
Deutch, Samayla D. ... New York, NY
Deutch, Theodore Eliot ... Boca Raton, FL
Deutch, Victor A. ... Woodbridge, NJ
Deutchman, Leonard ... Philadelphia, PA
Deutchman, Murray L. ... Rockville, MD
Deutchman, Richard ... Edison, NJ
Deutchman, Scott M. ... Washington, DC
Deutcsh, Elsie M. ... Birmingham, AL
Deuterman, Daniel L. ... Raleigh, NC
Deutinger, Mark W. ... Fresno, CA
Deutsch, Adam ... Chicago, IL
Deutsch, Adam B. ... Chicago, IL
Deutsch, Alex ... New York, NY
Deutsch, Alfred L. ... West Bloomfield, MI
Deutsch, Alvin ... New York, NY
Deutsch, Amy E. ... Los Angeles, CA
Deutsch, Andrea M. ... Philadelphia, PA
Deutsch, Andrew L. ... New York, NY
Deutsch, Anthony S. ... San Diego, CA
Deutsch, Ayala ... New York, NY
Deutsch, Barbara W. ... New Haven, CT
Deutsch, Barry E. ... Shelton, CT
Deutsch, Barry J. ... Brooklyn, NY
Deutsch, Benjamin P. ... New York, NY
Deutsch, Bennett I. ... New York, NY
Deutsch & Blumberg, P.A. ... Miami, FL
Deutsch, Brad
Federal Communications Commission,
Mass Media Bureau, GV
Deutsch, Brett S. ... New York, NY
Deutsch, Brunswick G., (P.L.C.)
New Orleans, LA
Deutsch, Cathleen M. ... Mineola, NY
Deutsch, Christine R. ... Philadelphia, PA
Deutsch, Coffey & Metz, LLP
Mamaroneck, NY
New York, NY
Deutsch, Daniel R. ... Boston, MA
Deutsch, Daryl A. ... Bellevue, WA
Deutsch, David ... Department of Justice,
Civil Rights Division, GV
Deutsch, David ... Miami, FL
Deutsch, David ... New York, NY
Deutsch, David B. ... Farmington Hills, MI
Deutsch, David E. ... Merced, CA
Deutsch, David M. ... Dayton, OH
Deutsch, David M., Co., L.P.A.
Dayton, OH
Deutsch, David R. ... Los Angeles, CA
Deutsch, Debbie ... Culver City, CA
Deutsch, Dennis S. ... Hackensack, NJ
New York, NY
Deutsch & Deutsch ... Rock Island, IL
Deutsch, Douglas E. ... Dallas, TX
Deutsch, Earl A. ... Chicago, IL
Deutsch, Edward B. ... Boca Raton, FL
Deutsch, Edward B. ... Morristown, NJ
Deutsch, Eliot J. ... Mineola, NY
Deutsch, Ellen S. ... Washington, DC
Deutsch, Elliot A. ... Cedarhurst, NY
Deutsch, Eric A. ... Boston, MA

Deutsch, Gary A. ... Cherry Hill, NJ
Deutsch, Gary B. ... Akron, OH
Deutsch, Gerald S. ... Port Washington, NY
Deutsch, Gregory G. ... Treasury Department, Office of Regulations and Rulings, GV
Deutsch, Harvey E. ... Denver, CO
Deutsch, Herbert I. ... Mamaroneck, NY
New York, NY
Deutsch, Herbert M. ... Garden City, NY
Deutsch, Howard D. ... New York, NY
Deutsch, Ilene Siegel ... Brooklyn, NY
Deutsch, Ira T. ... Agoura Hills, CA
Deutsch, Irwin F. ... Palm Beach, FL
Deutsch, Ivan D. ... New York, NY
Deutsch, James B. ... Jefferson City, MO
Deutsch, James H. ... New York, NY
Deutsch, Jamie Alter ... New York, NY
Deutsch, Jan G. ... New Haven, CT
Deutsch, Jeffrey R. ... Miami, FL
Deutsch, Jeremy E. ... New York, NY
Deutsch, Jeremy J. ... New York, NY
Deutsch, Jerry ... Brooklyn, NY
Deutsch, Joel A. ... Rock Island, IL
Deutsch, Joel David, (P.C.)
Los Angeles, CA
Deutsch, Joseph ... New City, NY
Deutsch, Joshua ... Glendale, NY
Deutsch, Kathleen L., (P.A.) ... Miami, FL
Deutsch, Kathryn A. ... Newport Beach, CA
Deutsch, Kerrigan & Stiles, L.L.P.
Lafayette, LA
New Orleans, LA
Gulfport, MS
Deutsch Klagsbrun & Blasband
New York, NY
Deutsch, Larrimore, Farnish & Andersson, L.L.P. ... Philadelphia, PA
Deutsch, Laurence E. ... New York, NY
Deutsch, Laurence M., Law Firm
New York, NY
Deutsch, Lawrence ... Philadelphia, PA
Deutsch, Lee K. ... Jericho, NY
Deutsch, Leslie S. ... Brooklyn, NY
Deutsch, Levy & Engel, Chartered
Chicago, IL
Wheaton, IL
Deutsch & Lipner ... Garden City, NY
Deutsch, M. Robert ... Bethesda, MD
Deutsch, Marshall A. ... Department of Labor, Office of the Solicitor, GV
Deutsch, Marshall J. ... Clearwater, FL
Deutsch, Martin R. ... San Jose, CA
Deutsch, Mc Cormick & D'Amato
Oyster Bay Cove, NY
Deutsch, Melvin P. ... Oyster Bay Cove, NY
Deutsch, Meredith L. ... New York, NY
Deutsch, Michael C. ... Elgin, IL
Deutsch, Michael E. ... New York, NY
Deutsch, Morris H. ... Washington, DC
Deutsch, Morris L. ... Boston, MA
Deutsch, Nancy Packer
Department of Education, Office of the General Counsel, GV
Deutsch, Nathaniel M.
Department of Agriculture, GV
Deutsch, Neil H. ... Hackensack, NJ
Deutsch, Norman T. ... Albany, NY
Deutsch, Paul ... Everett, WA
Deutsch, Paul A. ... New York, NY
Deutsch, Peter R. ... Hollywood, FL
Deutsch, Phyllis Z. ... Los Angeles, CA
Deutsch, Randolph W. ... San Francisco, CA
Deutsch, Resnick, Green & Gramigna
Hackensack, NJ
Springfield, NJ
Deutsch, Robert ... Los Angeles, CA
Deutsch, Robert J. ... Asheville, NC
Deutsch, Robert S. ... New York, NY
Deutsch, Ronald S. ... Towson, MD
Deutsch, Rory M. ... New York, NY
Deutsch & Salberg ... New York, NY
Deutsch, Sarah B. ... Arlington, VA
Deutsch & Schneider ... Glendale, NY
Deutsch, Sheldon ... San Diego, CA
Deutsch, Shirley D. ... Los Angeles, CA
Deutsch, Spillane & Reutzel, P.C.
Denver, CO
Deutsch, Stanley I. ... New York, NY
Deutsch, Stephanie ... Fort Lauderdale, FL
Deutsch, Stephen B. ... Boston, MA
Deutsch, Stephen H. ... New York, NY
Deutsch, Steven K. ... Miami, FL
Deutsch, Steven W. ... Fort Lauderdale, FL
Deutsch, Stewart ... Arlington, VA
Deutsch, Stuart L. ... Chicago, IL
Deutsch Tane Waterman & Wurtzel, P.C.
New York, NY
Deutsch, Theodore Z. ... Hialeah, FL
Deutsch, Theodore Z., P.A. ... Hialeah, FL
Deutsch Williams Brooks DeRensis Holland & Drachman, P.C. ... Boston, MA
Nantucket, MA
Deutscher, Ann R. ... Tacoma, WA
Deutscher, Layne A. ... Dallas, TX
Deutscher, Robert I., Law Offices of
Tacoma, WA
Deutschman, Alfred L. ... Inverness, FL
Deutschman, Jeffrey Scott ... Chicago, IL
Deutschman, Jolie S. ... Rockville, MD
Deutschman, Michael R. ... Timonium, MD
Deutschmeister, Jason S. ... New York, NY
DeVaan, Kevin R. ... Minneapolis, MN
Devack, Mitchell J. ... East Meadow, NY
Devadason, Sneha ... New York, NY
DeVagno, Angelo A. ... Whitestone, NY
Devagno, Borchert, Levine & LaSpina, P.C.
Whitestone, NY
DeValerio, Glen ... Boston, MA
DeValk, Carrie L. ... Chicago, IL
DeValk, Richard L. ... Lyons, NY
Sodus, NY
Devall, Carrie J. ... Tucson, AZ
DeVall, David F. ... Saratoga Springs, NY
DeVall & DeVall ... Saratoga Springs, NY
Devall, James L. (IBA) ... **Washington, DC**
DeVall, Richard F. ... Saratoga Springs, NY
de Valpine, Jean E. ... Cambridge, MA
Devamithran, Joseph A. ... Fairfax, VA
Devan, Deborah Hunt ... Baltimore, MD
DeVan, Jon W. ... Burbank, CA
Devan, Joseph F. ... Manchester, NH
DeVan, Mark R. ... Cleveland, OH
Devan, Mark S. ... Towson, MD
DeVan, William A. ... Richmond, VA
DeVance, Curtis
Department Of Health And Human Services, Social Security Administration, GV
Devane, Brian W. ... Albany, NY
Devane, Christopher ... Mineola, NY
Devane, David L. ... Charleston, SC
DeVane, Eleanor Stuart ... New Haven, CT
Devane, Fogarty & Ribezzo
West Warwick, RI
Devane, Joseph F. ... Dublin, CA
Devane, Mark F. ... Chicago, IL
Devane, Michael A. ... West Warwick, RI
DeVane, Milton P. ... New Haven, CT
Devane, Paul T. ... Albany, NY
DeVane, Robert S. ... Johnson City, TN
DeVane, Susan C. ... Columbus, GA
DeVane, William N., Jr. ... Marathon, FL
Devaney, Amy J. ... Newton, MA
Devaney, Brian A. ... San Antonio, TX
DeVaney, Charles A. ... Augusta, GA
Devaney, Daniel H., IV ... Honolulu, HI
Devaney, Deborah A. ... Chicago, IL
Devaney, Deirdre A. ... Hartford, CT
Devaney, Dennis M. ... Detroit, MI
DeVaney, Donna Brookes ... Tampa, FL
DeVaney, Edward D., Jr. ... Norcross, GA
Devaney, Francis M. ... San Diego, CA
Devaney, Hubert J. ... Greenlawn, NY
Devaney, James T. ... Plant City, FL
Devaney, John M. ... Washington, DC
Devaney, John M. ... Overland Park, KS
De Vaney, Kathleen D. ... Los Angeles, CA
Devaney, Kevin D. ... Toledo, OH
Devaney, Leslie E. ... San Diego, CA
DeVaney, M. Jay ... Greensboro, NC
Devaney, Nicole ... Middletown, NJ
Devaney, Stephen A. ... New York, NY
Devaney, Thomas M. ... New York, NY
Devaney, Thomas R. ... Atlanta, GA
Devaney, William B.
Federal Labor Relations Authority, Office of the Administrative Law Judges, GV
Devaney, William H. ... New York, NY
Devanie, Michael J. ... La Crosse, WI
Devanna, Sharon M. ... Chicago, IL
Devanney, Diane Summers ... Southeastern, PA
Devanney, Joseph J. ... Philadelphia, PA
Devanney, Kevin A. ... Blue Bell, PA
Devanney, Patrick A. ... New York, NY
Devany, David M. ... Akron, OH
Devany, Eugene Patrick ... New York, NY
DeVany and Gors ... Vermillion, SD
DeVany, John S. ... Vermillion, SD
De Varso, James F. ... New York, NY
DeVasher, William A., Jr. ... Wellesley, MA
Devashrayee, Jeffery J. ... Salt Lake City, UT
DeVasto, Diane Vinson ... Tyler, TX
DeVaughn, C. Elizabeth ... Valdosta, GA
DeVaughn, Donald L. ... Plainview, MN
DeVaughn, Dustin L. ... Wichita, KS
DeVaughn Law Office ... Plainview, MN
DeVaughn, Marynell
Department of Commerce, Office of the General Counsel, GV
Devaul, William D. ... New York, NY
DeVault, Charlton R., Jr. ... Kingsport, TN
DeVault, Jerry A. ... Houston, TX
DeVault, John A., III ... Jacksonville, FL
DeVault, Sara Meredith ... Nashville, TN
De Vault, Sharon L. ... Chicago, IL
deVaux, Arthur F. ... Detroit, MI
Devay, Daniel Alan ... Raleigh, NC
Devé, Philippe W. ... Coral Gables, FL
Deveau, Colton & Marquis ... Atlanta, GA
De Veau, David R. ... Manchester, NH
Deveau, Frank J. ... Indianapolis, IN
Deveau, Kimberly M. Urban ... Brockton, MA
De Veau, Robert C. ... St. Paul, MN
Deveau, Robert W. ... Salem, NH
DeVeau, Ronald E. ... Kill Devil Hills, NC
DeVeau, Ronald E., P.C. ... Corolla, NC
Kill Devil Hills, NC
Manteo, NC
Nags Head, NC
Deveau, Todd ... Atlanta, GA
DeVeaux & Associates, Inc. ... Anchorage, AK
Deveaux, Clinton E. ... Atlanta, GA
De Veaux, Gerard P. ... Rutherford, NJ
DeVeaux, LeRoy E. ... Anchorage, AK
DeVecchio, Warren J. ... Washington, DC
Devecka, Joseph M. ... State College, PA
Devecka & Rayman ... State College, PA
d'Evegnee, Charles P. ... Ashland, VA
De Vellis, Claudio A. ... New York, NY
DeVellis, Patricia Burke ... Arlington, MA
DeVellis, Raymond J. ... Boston, MA
Devellis, Robert A. ... Stamford, CT
DeVencentes, Philip A. ... Hackensack, NJ
Devendorf, Alfred E. ... Mineola, NY
Devendorf, David C. ... Port Huron, MI
Devendorf, Joan A. ... Loveland, CO
Devendorf, Jon P. ... Syracuse, NY
Devendorf, Lee Earl ... Norfolk, VA
Deveney, Brian T. ... Garden City, NY
Deveney, Dennis R. ... New York, NY
Deveney & Hagopian ... Cranston, RI
Deveney, James E. ... Fall River, MA
Deveney, James R., II ... Baltimore, MD
DeVeney, Jeannie M. ... Overland Park, KS
Deveney, John Patrick ... New York, NY
Deveney, Marie R. ... Ann Arbor, MI
Deveney, Susan Elaine ... Cranston, RI
Deveney, William Drummond
Atlanta, GA
Devenney, Sean T. ... Wilmington, DE
DeVennish, Joseph Briggs ... Columbus, OH
DeVenny, T. Alston, Jr. ... Lancaster, SC
Devenport, Lezley Kuntz ... New Orleans, LA
Devenport, Marc E. ... Metairie, LA
New Orleans, LA
Devenport, Russell Alan ... Amarillo, TX
Devens, Charles J. ... Danville, IL
Devens, Gordon E. ... Fort Lauderdale, FL
Devens, Henry F., III ... Pittsburgh, PA
Devens, Lawrence P. ... Chicago, IL
Devens, Mignon ... Jersey City, NJ
Devens, Nakano, Saito, Lee, Wong & Ching
Honolulu, HI
Devens, Paul, (A Law Corporation)
Honolulu, HI
Devens, Paula ... Honolulu, HI
Devens, Robert S., Jr. ... Palo Alto, CA
Devens, Vladimir Paul ... Kailua, HI
De Venuto, Richard ... Astoria, NY
DeVeny, Dain N. ... Dayton, OH
Deveny, Lori E. ... Portland, OR
Deveny, Robert G. ... Portland, OR
Deveny, Thomas A., III ... Akron, OH
Deveny, Thomas J. ... Edina, MO
Devenyi, Susan ... New York, NY
Devenyns, Michael L. ... Denver, CO
DeVenzio, Trent ... Beaumont, TX
Dever, A. Steven ... Lakewood, OH
Dever, C. Nicholas ... Ann Arbor, MI
Dever, Dana A. ... Ann Arbor, MI
Dever, Donna M. ... Harleysville, PA
Dever, Edward J., Jr. ... Boston, MA
Dever, Francis J. ... Quincy, MA
Dever, H. Michael ... Atlanta, GA
Dever, James C., III ... Raleigh, NC
Dever, James R. ... Rockville, MD
Dever, James R., P.A. ... Rockville, MD
Dever, Joseph E. ... Towson, MD
Dever, Joseph P. ... Lynnfield, MA
Dever, Joseph P., Jr. ... New York, NY
Dever, Karen P. ... Boston, MA
Dever, Leon A. ... Salt Lake City, UT
Dever, Mark F. ... Washington, DC
Dever, Martin J. ... Wyckoff, NJ
Dever, Martin J., Jr. ... Hackensack, NJ
Dever, Michael L. ... Pittsburgh, PA
Dever, Mitch ... Panama City Beach, FL
Dever, Mitch, P.A. ... Panama City Beach, FL
Dever, Professional Corporation
Ann Arbor, MI
Dever, Richard W. ... Rochester, NY
Dever, Robert E. ... Portsmouth, OH
Dever, Robert R. ... Portsmouth, OH
Dever, Stephen E. ... Fort Wayne, IN
Dever, Theresa Finn ... Boston, MA
Dever, Timothy J. ... Toledo, OH
Dever, Veronica M. ... Fairview Park, OH
Dever, William A., Jr.
Federal Communications Commission, Common Carrier Bureau, GV
Dever, William C. ... Dallas, TX
Deveraux, Valerie J. ... San Francisco, CA
DeVere, Brent A. ... Austin, TX
DeVere, Clark ... Harrisburg, PA
Devereaux, Daniel R. ... St. Louis, MO
Devereaux, Dennis M. ... Lillydale, MN
Devereaux & Hamlett, L.L.C.
Greenville, AL
Montgomery, AL
Prattville, AL
Troy, AL
Tuskegee, AL
Wetumpka, AL
Devereaux, James O. ... San Francisco, CA
Devereaux, John R. ... Boston, MA
Devereaux, Meghan R. ... St. Louis, MO
Devereaux, Michael ... Sacramento, CA
Devereaux, Michael J. ... New York, NY
Devereaux, N. Paul ... Glendale, CA
Devereaux, Paula M. ... Boston, MA
Devereaux, Peter W. ... Los Angeles, CA
Devereaux, Scott D. ... Palo Alto, CA
Devereaux, Stefanie ... Rochester, NY
Devereaux, Stephen B. ... Atlanta, GA
Devereaux, Stokes & Nolan, P.C.
St. Louis, MO
Devereaux, Wanda D. ... Montgomery, AL
Devereaux, William P. ... Providence, RI
Devereux, Aimee M. ... San Francisco, CA
Devereux, Anthony Q. ... Pawleys Island, SC
Devereux, Benjamin F., III ... Knoxville, TN
Devereux, Clarke P. ... San Francisco, CA
Devereux, Joseph F., Jr. ... St. Louis, MO
Devereux, Madeline Henricks ... Chicago, IL
Devereux, Mary ... Covington, LA
Devereux, Mary Ellen ... Irvine, CA
Devereux, Mary Patricia ... Maywood, IL
Devereux, Matthew J. ... Chicago, IL
Devereux, Murphy, Striler, Brickey & Sher, L.L.C. ... St. Louis, MO
Devereux, Robert L. ... St. Louis, MO
Devereux, Robin J. ... Los Angeles, CA
Devereux, Sean Patrick ... Asheville, NC
Devereux, Timothy F. ... Decatur, IL
San Antonio, TX
Devereux, Timothy F. ... St. Louis, MO
de Verges & de Verges, Ltd.
New Orleans, LA
de Verges, Edw. J., Jr. ... New Orleans, LA
de Verges, Eugene P. ... Tulsa, OK
de Verges, George L. ... Worcester, MA
de Verges & Katsonis ... Worcester, MA
Deverich, Jay W. ... Irvine, CA
Deverin, Sean ... Morristown, NJ
Deverman, Beth A. ... Chicago, IL
Devermont, Dennis H. ... Santa Monica, CA
Devermont & Devermont ... Santa Monica, CA
DeVerna, Edward W., Jr. ... East Moriches, NY
DeVerna, Robert W. ... Hauppauge, NY
Devers, Daniel J. ... Philadelphia, PA
Devers, Daniel P. ... Kansas City, MO
Devers, Douglas P. ... Portland, OR
Devers, John P. ... Washington, DC
Devers, Peter D. ... Southampton, NY
Devers, Robert L., Jr. ... Phoenix, AZ
Devers, William E. ... Louisville, KY
Devers, William J., Jr. ... Orchard Lake, MI
DeVerter, Paul L., II ... Houston, TX
Devery, Elizabeth ... Austin, TX
Devery, Gerald P. ... Glen Ellyn, IL
Devery, Jennifer Ruth ... Baltimore, MD
Devery, Kelly Ann ... Mount Laurel, NJ
Devery, Loree A. ... Portland, OR
DeVesa, Frederick P. ... Trenton, NJ
de Vesty, Malcolm W. ... Albuquerque, NM
Devetski, Robert G. ... South Bend, IN
Devetski, Timothy J. ... Houston, TX
Devey, Mark R. ... Rancho Cucamonga, CA
de Veyra Gonzalez, Ferdinand
Laguna Hills, CA
Devgun, Dharminder S. ... Minneapolis, MN
Devich, Robert R. ... Los Angeles, CA
Devience, Alexander, Jr., (Ltd.) ... Chicago, IL
DeVierno, John A. ... Washington, DC
DeVigne, Renee ... Washington, DC
Devik, Timothy R. ... Plymouth, MA
Devil's Advocate, The ... Alexandria, VA
DeVilbiss, Gail Cook ... Radford, VA
DeVilbiss, J. E. ... Aspen, CO
DeVilbiss, Preston, Jr. ... Sarasota, FL
DeVille, Roman A. ... Marietta, GA
de Villefranche, Maxine ... Los Angeles, CA
de Villefranche, Maxine ... Northridge, CA
De Villegas, Elena Diaz ... Miami, FL
de Villeneuve, David Andrew ... Eugene, OR
DeVillers, Lea ... St. Paul, MN
De Villier, Emma Jean ... Morgan City, LA
Devillier, Stacey Caillet ... New Roads, LA
DeVillier, Veil David ... Baton Rouge, LA
de Villiers, P. Francois ... Palo Alto, CA
DeVilliers, W. Rodney, Jr.
Oklahoma City, OK
Devin, Abigail A. ... Omaha, NE
Devin, Clayton E. ... Dallas, TX
Devin, Donald B. ... Mount Freedom, NJ
Devin & Drohan, P.C. ... Hingham, MA
Devin, Francine Romano ... Springfield, MA
Devin, Julia A. ... Seattle, WA
Devin, Marilyn ... Los Angeles, CA
Devin, Michael D. ... Oakland, CA
Devin, Paul R. ... Boston, MA
Devin, Robert L. ... Hingham, MA
DeVincens, John J. ... Toms River, NJ
DeVincent, Frank A. ... Atlanta, GA
DeVincenzi, Jeanne Meyer
San Francisco, CA
Devincenzi, Joseph L. ... San Francisco, CA
Devincenzi, Kathryn R. ... San Francisco, CA
DeVincke, Thomas F. ... Providence, RI
Devine, Alicia S. ... Norfolk, VA
Devine, Andy ... Toledo, OH
Devine, Anthony W. ... Traverse City, MI
Devine, Antoine M. ... San Francisco, CA
Devine, Ariel Sarah ... New York, NY
Devine, Barrows & Devine ... Boston, MA
DeVine, Barry F. ... Lansing, MI
Devine, Bernard M. ... Portland, ME
Devine, Bernard M., Jr. ... Boston, MA
Devine, Brian P. ... New York, NY
Devine, Carl D. ... Lexington, KY
Devine, Charles G., Jr. ... Boston, MA
Devine, Christine E. ... Worcester, MA
De Vine, Clifford J. ... Southfield, MI
Devine, Daniel C. ... Bloomfield Hills, MI
Devine, Daniel C., Jr. ... Bloomfield Hills, MI
Devine, Daniel E. ... Philadelphia, PA
Devine, David A., (P.C.) ... Anchorage, AK
Devine, David C. ... Philadelphia, PA
Devine, Deborah Anne ... Lansing, MI
DeVine, Derek Wade ... Tiffin, OH
DeVine, DeVine, Kantor and Serr
Ann Arbor, MI
Devine, Don R. ... Denver, CO
Devine, Donald F. ... New York, NY
Devine, Donn ... Wilmington, DE
Devine, Earl L. ... Des Moines, IA
Devine, Edgar F., Jr. ... Clark, NJ
DeVine, Edmond F. ... Ann Arbor, MI
Devine, Edward T. ... South Portland, ME
Devine, Erin R. ... Arlington, VA
Devine, Eugene P., Jr. ... Albany, NY
Devine, Evelyn R. ... Philadelphia, PA
Devine, F. Patrick ... Bloomfield Hills, MI
Devine, Faith A. ... Los Angeles, CA
Devine, Foy R. ... Atlanta, GA
Devine, Francis P., III ... Philadelphia, PA
Devine, Frank ... Yakima, WA
Devine, Gary G. ... Santa Rosa, CA
Devine, George J. ... La Crosse, WI
Devine, Georgia Patriakeas ... Boston, MA
Devine, Ginger R. ... Mexico, MO
Devine, Gregory M. ... Pittsburgh, PA
Devine, Harry T. ... Philadelphia, PA

Devine, Helen C. ....New York, NY
Devine, J. Dennis ....Little Rock, AR
Devine, J. Martin ....Boston, MA
Devine, J. Neil ....Parishville, NY
Devine, James A. ....Kankakee, IL
Watseka, IL
Devine, James D. ....Northbrook, IL
Devine, James D., Law Offices of
Bainbridge Island, WA
Devine, James Dennis ....Heber Springs, AR
Devine, James E. ....Melville, NY
Devine, James F. ....Schenectady, NY
Devine, James F. ....Philadelphia, PA
Devine, James F., III ....Lancaster, PA
Devine, James G. ....Newton, NJ
Devine, James I. ....Philadelphia, PA
Devine, James J. ....Norwich, CT
Devine, James J., Jr. ....Oneida, NY
Devine, James P. ....Rockford, IL
Devine, James R. ....Columbia, MO
Devine, Jeanne N. ....Treasury Department,
Office of the Comptroller of the Currency, GV
Devine, Jennifer C.
Federal Maritime Commission,
Office of the General Counsel, GV
Devine, Jill A. ....Harrisburg, PA
DeVine, John B. ....Ann Arbor, MI
Devine, John C. ....Harrisburg, PA
Devine, John D. ....Portland, ME
Devine, John J. ....Swampscott, MA
Devine, John J., Jr. ....Mount Pleasant, MI
DeVine, John K. ....Chicago, IL
Devine, John M. ....Santa Ana, CA
Devine, John M. ....Albany, NY
Devine, John P. ....Cambridge, MA
Devine, John Preston ....San Francisco, CA
Devine, John R. ....Baltimore, MD
Devine, John W. ....Miami, FL
Devine, Jon P., Jr.
Environmental Protection Agency,
Office of the General Counsel, GV
Devine, Joseph C. ....Columbus, OH
Devine, Joseph J. ....Cherry Hill, NJ
Philadelphia, PA
Devine, Joseph M. ....San Francisco, CA
Devine, Kevin Cutler ....Manchester, NH
De Vine & Kohn, PLLC ....Detroit, MI
Southfield, MI
Devine, Kristin C. ....St. Paul, MN
Devine, Luann ....Covington, KY
Devine, Lynne L. ....Philadelphia, PA
Devine, M. Colette ....Washington, DC
DeVine & Mallory ....Lansing, MI
Devine, Marie C. ....Clearwater, FL
Devine, Marilyn J. ....Nashville, TN
Devine, Mary B. ....Gray, ME
Devine, Michael C. ....New York, NY
Devine, Michael J.
Department of Transportation,
U. S. Coast Guard, GV
Devine, Michael J. ....Chicago, IL
Wheaton, IL
Devine, Michael J. ....Bloomfield Hills, MI
Devine, Michael V. ....Port Jefferson, NY
Devine, Michael V., P.C. ....Port Jefferson, NY
Devine, Michael W. ....Salt Lake City, UT
Devine, Millimet & Branch, Professional
Association ....Andover, MA
Manchester, NH
North Hampton, NH
Devine & Mulhern, P.C. ....Newton, NJ
DeVine, Myles J. ....Britton, SD
Devine & Nyquist ....Concord, NH
Manchester, NH
Devine, Pamela J. ....Philadelphia, PA
Devine, Patrick ....Houston, TX
Devine, Patrick A. ....Columbus, OH
Devine, Patrick C., Jr. ....Norfolk, VA
Devine, Patrick J. ....San Francisco, CA
Devine, Patrick J. ....Plaistow, NH
Devine, Patrick J. ....Seattle, WA
Devine, Patrick P. ....Merrillville, IN
Devine, Patrick Thomas ....Norwood, MA
Devine, Paul F. ....St. Louis, MO
Devine, Paul J. ....San Diego, CA
Devine, Paul S. ....Merrick, NY
Devine, Philip J. ....Oneonta, NY
Devine, Rhial N. ....Las Vegas, NV
Devine, Richard A. ....Chicago, IL
Devine, Richard Q. ....Norwich, NY
Devine, Robert ....Lake Success, NY
Devine, Robert A. ....Hermosa Beach, CA
Devine, Robert G. ....Westmont, NJ
Devine, Robert T. ....Jacksonville, FL
Devine, Shane ....Concord, NH
Devine, Sharon J. ....Denver, CO
DeVine, Suzanne L. ....Ann Arbor, MI
Devine, Terence J. ....Albany, NY
Devine, Terence P. ....Lakota, ND
Devine, Therese M. ....Des Plaines, IL
Devine, Thomas E., III ....Little Rock, AR
Devine, Thomas G. ....Austin, TX
Devine, Thomas J. ....Waterbury, VT
Devine, Thomas M. ....Racine, WI
Devine, Thomas R. ....Washington, DC
Devine, Timothy A. ....Dearborn, MI
Devine, Tod A. ....Burbank, CA
Devine, Vicki H. ....Norfolk, VA
Devine, W. Thomas ....Chippewa Falls, WI
Devine, Walter J. ....Massapequa, NY
Devine, William F. ....Norfolk, VA
Devine, William F., Jr. ....Menlo Park, CA
Devine, William M. ....Atlanta, GA
Devinger, David W. ....Schaumburg, IL
Devinney, Daniel P. ....Pittsburgh, PA
Devinney, James G. ....Ponca City, OK
DeVinny, Robert F. ....Anoka, MN

Devins, Alicia B. ....Carle Place, NY
Devins, Arthur S. ....West Palm Beach, FL
Devins, Edward J. ....Brooklyn, NY
Devins, Jeffrey L. ....Evansville, IN
Devins, Michael B. ....Morristown, NJ
Devins, Neal E. ....Williamsburg, VA
Devins, Sharon E. ....Norristown, PA
Devins, Thomas A., Jr. ....San Jose, CA
Devins, Thomas V. ....New York, NY
Devinsky, Paul ....Washington, DC
DeVirgilio, Charles J. ....Latrobe, PA
DeVirgilis, John ....Philadelphia, PA
Devirian, Donald B. ....Los Angeles, CA
Devirian, Richard C. ....Wilmington, CA
Devirian & Shinmoto, A Professional
Corporation ....Los Angeles, CA
Devirian, Utley & Detrick ....Wilmington, CA
Devison, Roderick A. ....Fairmont, WV
DeVita, Daniel F. ....Garden City, NY
De Vita, Danielle ....Woodcliff Lake, NJ
DeVita, David ....Cincinnati, OH
DeVita, Donna M. ....Scranton, PA
De Vita, E. Michele ....Los Angeles, CA
Devita, Gerard A. ....Commack, NY
DeVita & Howe ....Cincinnati, OH
DeVita, James A. ....Department of Justice,
Environment and Natural Resources
Division, GV
DeVita, James R. ....New York, NY
Devita, John Anthony, II ....Golden, CO
De Vita, Lenore ....Glendale, CA
DeVita, Melissa R. ....Los Angeles, CA
DeVita, Richard D. ....Hoboken, NJ
DeVita, Stephen Lawrence ....Dayton, OH
DeVita, Thomas P. ....Clifton, NJ
De Vita, Vincent S. ....Brooklyn, NY
DeVito, Albert S. ....Chicago, IL
DeVito, Andrew F.
Department Of The Interior, GV
De Vito, Anthony J. ....New York, NY
DeVito, Anthony M., III ....Darien, CT
DeVito, Cara ....Woodland Hills, CA
DeVito, Christopher Michael
Cleveland, OH
Devito and Colen, P.A. ....Largo, FL
DeVito, Curtis J. ....New York, NY
DeVito, Daniel A. ....New York, NY
DeVito, Danielle ....Fort Lauderdale, FL
DeVito, Edward R. ....Coldwater, MI
Devito, Eric M. ....Washington, DC
DeVito, Felix R. ....White Plains, NY
De Vito, Francesco A. ....Boston, MA
DeVito, Francis D. ....Newton, MA
De Vito, Francis J. ....Hackensack, NJ
Devito, Francis M. ....Danville, CA
DeVito, Frank D. ....Rahway, NJ
DeVito, Gary A. ....Cherry Hill, NJ
Jersey City, NJ
Philadelphia, PA
DeVito, Gina Marie ....San Francisco, CA
Devito, James A. ....Largo, FL
Devito, James A. ....Forest Hills, NY
DeVito, Janet F. ....Concord, NH
DeVito, Janet F., P.C. ....Concord, NH
Devito, Joseph ....New York, NY
Devito, Joseph J. ....Detroit, MI
DeVito, Lawrence J. ....Roseville, MI
DeVito, Leo V., Jr. ....Bethlehem, PA
DeVito, Mathias J. ....Columbia, MD
DeVito, Michael ....Cedarhurst, NY
DeVito, Michael A., Jr. ....Dedham, MA
DeVito, Robin A. ....Carlsbad, CA
Devito, Roger R. ....Santa Monica, CA
DeVito, Ronald A. ....Warren, OH
DeVito, Ronald J. ....Garden City, NY
DeVito, Steven Henry ....Denver, CO
DeVito, Victor ....New York, NY
De Vito, Victor F. ....Jersey City, NJ
De Vito, Vincent ....Boston, MA
DeVito, William P. ....New York, NY
De Vitre, Mark ....Los Angeles, CA
Devitt, Aoifinn ....New York, NY
Devitt, Christene M. ....Cheboygan, MI
Devitt, Dennis M. ....Los Angeles, CA
Devitt, Donald W. ....Chicago, IL
Devitt, Fred B., III ....Delray Beach, FL
Devitt, Fred B., Jr. ....Delray Beach, FL
Devitt, James I. ....Malibu, CA
Santa Monica, CA
Devitt, James J. ....Baton Rouge, LA
Devitt, Jerald J. ....Golden, CO
Devitt, John R. ....Milwaukee, WI
Devitt, Laura K. ....Houston, TX
Devitt, Michael R. ....Phoenix, AZ
Devitt, Patrick A. ....La Jolla, CA
Devitt, Patrick J. ....Wauwatosa, WI
Devitt & Porada, Ltd. ....Chicago, IL
Devitt, R. Michael ....San Luis Obispo, CA
Devitt, Russell W. ....Whitewater, WI
Devitt, Sonja M. ....Norwalk, CT
Devitt & Spellman ....Smithtown, NY
Devitt, Thistle & Devitt, P.A.
Delray Beach, FL
Devitt, Veronica Colby ....San Francisco, CA
Devitt, William E. ....Chicago, IL
Devitt, Wm. L. ....St. Paul, MN
DeVittorio, James H. ....Ridgway, PA
DeVivo, Donald A. ....New Britain, CT
DeVivo, Edward C. ....New York, NY
DeVivo, Margaret ....Deer Park, NY
DeVivo, Thomas G., Jr. ....Mineola, NY
De Vizcarrondo, Heberto J. ....San Juan, PR
Devlaeminck, Vic. J. ....Vancouver, WA
de Vlaming, Denis M. ....Clearwater, FL
de Vlaming, Denis M., P.A.
Clearwater, FL
de Vlaming, Douglas M. ....Clearwater, FL
DeVleming, John F. ....Seattle, WA

De Vlieger, Paul T. ....Philadelphia, PA
DeVlieger, Tracy Blake ....West Chester, PA
Devlin, Andrew L. ....Jacksonville, FL
Devlin, Arthur V. ....Pebble Beach, CA
Devlin, Austa S. ....New York, NY
Devlin, Brian D. ....Lansing, MI
Devlin, Cathleen M. ....Philadelphia, PA
Devlin, Christopher J. ....Portland, ME
Devlin, Cittadino & Shaw, P.C.
Trenton, NJ
Devlin, Darren John ....San Diego, CA
Devlin, Donald M. ....Chicago, IL
Devlin, Elizabeth M. ....Villanova, PA
Devlin, Faune ....New York, NY
Devlin, Francis J. ....Houston, TX
Devlin, Frank C., Jr. ....Washington, DC
Devlin, Frith & Phillips ....Houston, TX
Devlin, Geo. J. ....Boston, MA
Devlin, Gerard F. ....Upper Marlboro, MD
Devlin, Gerard M., Jr. ....Houston, TX
Devlin, Glenn H. ....Houston, TX
Devlin, Greg M. ....Spokane, WA
Devlin, James J. ....Braintree, MA
Devlin, James P. ....Taunton, MA
Devlin, James Richard ....Westwood, KS
Devlin, Jane P. ....Cambridge, MA
Devlin, John F. ....Kew Gardens, NY
Devlin, John G. ....Trenton, NJ
Devlin, John Gerard ....East Brunswick, NJ
Westmont, NJ
Allentown, PA
Philadelphia, PA
Wilkes-Barre, PA
Devlin, John Gerard, & Associates, P.C.
East Brunswick, NJ
Westmont, NJ
Allentown, PA
Philadelphia, PA
Wilkes-Barre, PA
Devlin, John M. ....Baton Rouge, LA
Devlin, John M. ....Houston, TX
Devlin, John M., Attorney at Law, P.C.
Houston, TX
Devlin, John Michael ....Marlton, NJ
Devlin, John R., Jr., P.A. ....Greenville, SC
Devlin, John Robert, Jr. ....Greenville, SC
Devlin, John S., III ....Seattle, WA
Devlin, John W. ....Trenton, NJ
Devlin, Joseph E. ....Harvard, MA
Devlin, Joseph F. ....Glen Burnie, MD
Devlin, Judson F. ....Louisville, KY
Devlin, Kathleen J. ....Bedminster, NJ
Devlin, Kauffman & Shilling ....Harrisburg, PA
Devlin, Kelly A. ....Plymouth, MA
Devlin, Lisa M. Sommer ....Phoenix, AZ
Devlin, Marvin A. ....Atlanta, GA
Devlin, Mary ....Los Angeles, CA
Devlin, Mary Beth ....Houston, TX
Devlin, Mary Elizabeth
Environmental Protection Agency,
Office of Enforcement and Compliance
Assurance, GV
Devlin, Mary M. ....Chicago, IL
Devlin, Mary-Ellen M. ....Ridgefield, CT
Devlin, Michael J. ....Somers, CT
Devlin, Michael P. ....Milford, CT
Devlin, Naylor & Turbyfill, P.L.L.C.
Houston, TX
Devlin, Patricia ....Honolulu, HI
Devlin, Patrick J. ....Grand Rapids, MI
Devlin, Paul A. ....Trenton, NJ
Devlin, Peter J. ....Treasury Department,
Internal Revenue Service, GV
Devlin, Peter J. ....Boston, MA
Devlin and Peters ....Somers, CT
Devlin & Pignuolo, P.C. ....Houston, TX
Devlin, Rene M. ....Chicago, IL
Devlin, Richard G., III ....Philadelphia, PA
Devlin, Robert G. ....Pittsburgh, PA
Devlin, Robert G., P.C. ....Houston, TX
Devlin, Robert J. ....Metuchen, NJ
Devlin, Robert J., Jr. ....New Haven, CT
Devlin, Robert P. ....New York, NY
Devlin, Rosemary Ann ....Chicago, IL
Devlin, Sean ....Warren, NJ
Devlin, Terry E. ....Apopka, FL
Devlin, Thomas C. ....Washington, DC
Devlin, Thomas M. ....Philadelphia, PA
Devlin, Timothy G. ....Philadelphia, PA
Devlin, Timothy M. ....Washington, DC
Devlin, Timothy N. ....Denver, CO
Devlin, Tracy L. ....Boston, MA
Devlin, William B. ....San Diego, CA
Devlin, William J., Jr. ....Harrisburg, PA
Devlin, William R. ....Las Vegas, NV
Devling, Madonna L. ....Costa Mesa, CA
Devney, Denise L. ....Cincinnati, OH
Devney, John L. ....St. Paul, MN
De Voe, Alice A. ....New Brunswick, NJ
DeVoe, Anne ....Columbus, OH
DeVoe, Charles H. ....Portland, OR
Devoe, Dana C. ....Bangor, ME
De Voe, George W. ....New Brunswick, NJ
Devoe, Harry L., Jr. ....Cherry Hill, NJ
DeVoe, Jeffrey A. ....Boise, ID
DeVoe, John C. ....Portland, OR
Devoe, Melanie T. ....Treasury Department,
Bureau of Alcohol, Tobacco and Firearms, GV
Devoe, Michael P. ....Orlando, FL
DeVoe, Robert C. ....Sacramento, CA
DeVoe, Russell G., Jr. ....Severna Park, MD
DeVoe, S. Curtis ....Indianapolis, IN
DeVoe, Stephen E. ....Indianapolis, IN
DeVoe, Steve A. ....Greensboro, NC
DeVoe, Thomas R. ....Indianapolis, IN
Devoe, William B. ....Bangor, ME
De Voe, William D. ....Seattle, WA

DeVoesick, Jeffrey F. ....Columbus, OH
Devoid, Katharine B. ....Montgomery, AL
Devokaitis, Gerald F. ....Hartford, CT
DeVol, Anthony R. ....Bethesda, MD
DeVolder, Steven P. ....Des Moines, IA
Devoll, Glenn A. ....Enid, OK
DeVoll, Tracy ....Waterville, ME
DeVoll, Willys D. ....New York, NY
Devolve, Robert F. ....Minneapolis, MN
Devon, Donald F., Jr. ....Baltimore, MD
Devon, Marcia A. ....Long Beach, CA
Devon, Richard R. ....San Antonio, TX
Devone, Lokelani ....San Francisco, CA
Devonish, Mayleen E. ....New York, NY
Devonshire, Linda B. ....Hartford, CT
DeVooght, Carlton A. ....Brunswick, GA
Devor, James W. ....New York, NY
Devor, Morton C. ....Los Angeles, CA
Devor, Richard C., Jr. ....McLean, VA
DeVore Acton & Stafford, P.A.
Charlotte, NC
De Vore, Allan ....Oklahoma City, OK
DeVore, Andrew C. ....New York, NY
DeVore, Bradford A. ....Charlotte, NC
DeVore, Cheryl H. ....Dublin, OH
De Vore, Daun Aline ....Palm Springs, CA
Devore, David L. ....South Lake Tahoe, CA
Devore & Devore, P.A.
West Palm Beach, FL
Devore, Dianna L. ....Palo Alto, CA
DeVore, Fred W., III ....Charlotte, NC
Devore, Gene S. ....West Palm Beach, FL
DeVore, J. Russ, Jr. ....Amarillo, TX
DeVore, Jason E. ....Chicago, IL
Devore, Jeffrey A. ....West Palm Beach, FL
DeVore, Joel S. ....Eugene, OR
DeVore, Jon M. ....Anchorage, AK
Devore, Joseph A. ....Atlanta, GA
DeVore, Kevin W. ....Eden Prairie, MN
Devore, Laurie B. ....East Setauket, NY
De Vore Law Firm, The, A Professional
Corporation ....Oklahoma City, OK
De Vore, Lawrence M. ....Washington, DC
DeVore, Linda J. ....Tacoma, WA
Devore, Linda S. ....Fayetteville, NC
Devore, Mark S. ....Santa Ana, CA
DeVore, P. Cameron ....Seattle, WA
DeVore, Robert H. ....Bradenton, FL
Devore, Scott D. ....West Palm Beach, FL
DeVore, Stewart W., Jr. ....Arlington, TX
DeVore, Thomas J. ....Las Vegas, NV
DeVoren, Ivan S. ....Philadelphia, PA
Devorkin, Gregory I. ....Milwaukee, WI
Devorkin, Michael S. ....New York, NY
Devorkin, Rhonda ....Milwaukee, WI
Devorris, Guy E. ....Los Angeles, CA
Devorsetz, Sidney ....Syracuse, NY
Devorsetz Stinziano Gilberti Heintz & Smith,
P.C. ....Albany, NY
Syracuse, NY
Harrisburg, PA
De Vos & Co., PLLC ....New York, NY
De Vos, Daniel M. ....Sunnyvale, CA
Austin, TX
DeVos, Joseph E. ....Stamford, CT
DeVos, Lawrence S. ....Atlanta, GA
DeVos, Leanne B. ....Denver, CO
De Vos, Lloyd ....New York, NY
DeVos, Robert ....Alexandria, VA
DeVos, Susan Belle ....St. Paul, MN
DeVoss, Hugh A. ....Dallas, TX
De Voss, Jay M. ....Decatur, IN
DeVoss, Jeffrey Scott ....Denver, CO
De Voss, Johnson, Baker & Ainsworth,
Professional Corporation ....Decatur, IN
DeVoss, Patricia A. ....Alexandria, MN
Devoti, Matthew Joseph ....St. Louis, MO
Devoto, Cesar A. ....New York, NY
DeVoto, Louis J. ....Cherry Hill, NJ
DeVoto & Paperner ....Alton, IL
St. Louis, MO
DeVoto, Robert L., (L.C.) ....Alton, IL
St. Louis, MO
DeVoto, Thomas C., (P.C.) ....St. Louis, MO
Devoy, James C. ....San Francisco, CA
DeVoy, James M. ....Buffalo, NY
Devoy, Kimball J. ....Minneapolis, MN
DeVoy, Mary E. ....San Diego, CA
Devoy, Robert F. ....Brookfield, MO
Devoy, William P. ....Brookfield, MO
DeVoy Clutter, Anna ....Evansville, IN
DeVree, Jeffrey A. ....Grand Rapids, MI
DeVriendt, Charles J. ....Chicago, IL
DeVries, Andrea L. ....Boston, MA
deVries & Associates, P.C. ....Kansas City, MO
deVries, B. Janeen ....Kansas City, MO
DeVries, Benjamin H. ....Houston, TX
DeVries, Brian ....Tampa, FL
DeVries, Christopher ....Ann Arbor, MI
Troy, MI
DeVries, Daniel J. ....Monterey, CA
DeVries, David J. ....Harrisburg, PA
DeVries, Donald J. ....San Jose, CA
DeVries, Donald L., Jr. ....Baltimore, MD
DeVries, Douglas D. ....Enosburg Falls, VT
deVries, Douglas K. ....Sacramento, CA
deVries, Frank Coulter ....Kansas City, MO
Devries, Garrett A. ....Dallas, TX
DeVries, James C. ....Jenison, MI
De Vries, James H. ....Chicago, IL
DeVries, John M. ....Grand Rapids, MI
DeVries, John R. ....Manistee, MI
DeVries, Jolene L. ....Canon City, CO
DeVries, Keith ....New York, NY
DeVries, Kenneth J. ....Kalamazoo, MI
DeVries, Laurence J. ....Chicago, IL
DeVries, Margaret B. ....Charlotte, NC
DeVries, Mark W. ....Bellevue, IA

De Vries, Martin J. ... Fond du Lac, WI
DeVries, Matthew J. ... Fairfax, VA
De Vries, Melissa Hoogendoorn
Chicago, IL
DeVries, Michael D. ... Grand Rapids, MI
DeVries, Mildred E. ... Austin, TX
De Vries, Price & Davenport, A Professional Corporation ... Mason City, IA
De Vries, Robert ... San Francisco, CA
DeVries, Robert K. ... Parsippany, NJ
De Vries, Rosalee J. ... Washington, DC
DeVries, Scott P. ... San Francisco, CA
DeVries, Sharon F. ... Rye, NH
DeVries & Solmonson ... San Jose, CA
DeVries, Steven ... Anchorage, AK
DeVries, Tania A. Hricik
Rochester Hills, MI
De Vries, Warren L. ... Mason City, IA
DeVries, William R. ... Homer, AK
DeVuono, Richard R. ... Addison, TX
DeVylder, Edgar P. ... Stamford, CT
Dew & Blaney ... Madison, WI
Dew, Bruce ... Columbia, SC
Dew, Carlos, Jr. ... West Newbury, MA
Dew, Carol ... Monroe, GA
Dew, Duncan M., III ... Florence, SC
Dew, Edgar Jerome ... Detroit, MI
Dew, Elizabeth J. Gaut ... Newburyport, MA
Dew, Jennifer ... Palo Alto, CA
Dew, John A. ... New Century, KS
Dew, John C. ... St. Petersburg, FL
Dew, Kevin W. ... New York, NY
Dew, Mathew J. ... Madison, WI
Dew, Michael J. ... Phoenix, AZ
Dew, Paul E. ... Ripley, TN
Dew, Scott C. ... Los Angeles, CA
Dew and Smith, L.L.C. ... Monroe, GA
Dew, Stephen D. ... Fairfax, VA
Dew, Thomas E. ... Ann Arbor, MI
Dewa, Roger Y. ... Honolulu, HI
Wahiawa, HI
De Waal, Gary Alan ... New York, NY
DeWaele, Richard C. ... Honolulu, HI
DeWaele, Richard M. ... Lowell, MA
DeWaele, Sharon A. ... Detroit, MI
DeWahl, David A. ... Ho-Ho-Kus, NJ
Dewald, Bruce W. ... Colorado Springs, CO
DeWald, Carole K. ... Kansas City, MO
Dewald, Jay ... Fort Worth, TX
De Wald, Jean ... Dallas, TX
DeWald, Jennifer K. ... Portland, OR
De Wald, John E. ... Newark, NJ
DeWald, John W. ... Brockton, MA
Hyannis, MA
Dewald, Kevin J. ... Burlingame, CA
DeWald, Lee F. ... Arlington Heights, IL
Dewald, Linus J., Jr. ... Roseville, CA
DeWald, Ronald G. ... Washington, DC
Silver Spring, MD
DeWald, Scott ... Phoenix, AZ
DeWald, Terrance (Tracy) S. ... Omaha, NE
DeWall, David ... San Antonio, TX
Dewalt, Deborah N. ... Burnsville, MN
DeWalt, Eric R. ... San Francisco, CA
DeWalt, Harold J. J., Jr. ... Easton, PA
DeWalt, Suzanne L. ... Pittsburgh, PA
DeWalt, Timothy A. ... Riverside, CA
Dewan, Bradford N. ... Oakland, CA
DeWan, Daniel P. ... North Branch, MN
Dewan, Debra Siedman ... Brooklyn, NY
Dewan & Lally, L.L.P. ... Austin, TX
Dewan, Margaret Wood ... Cincinnati, OH
Dewan, Maureen ... Fairfield, CT
Dewan, Raman N. ... Austin, TX
Dewane, Dewane, Kummer, Lambert & Fox
Manitowoc, WI
Dewane, John E. ... St. Joseph, MI
Dewane, John J. ... St. Joseph, MI
Dewane, John P. ... Manitowoc, WI
Dewane, Patrick A., Jr. ... Manitowoc, WI
Dewar, Benjamin M. ... New York, NY
Dewar, Debra ... Atlanta, GA
Dewar, Frank G. ... Waltham, MA
Dewar, Glen Hudson ... Dayton, OH
Dewar & Johnson ... Seattle, WA
Dewar, Marvin A. ... Gainesville, FL
Dewar, Peter B. ... Dallas, TX
Dewar, Robert C. ... Richmond, VA
Dewar and Rockwood, A Professional Corporation ... Monterey, CA
Dewar, Roderick L. ... Monterey, CA
Dewar, Stephen M. ... Los Angeles, CA
Dewar, Warren L. ... Seattle, WA
DeWar, William D. ... Pasadena, MD
DeWare, Jesse M., IV ... Jefferson, TX
Dewart, John W. ... Willows, CA
Dewart, William F., Jr. ... Rochester, NY
DeWaters, Edward A., Jr. ... Towson, MD
DewBerry, Carla M. ... Seattle, WA
Dewberry, Charlon K. ... Defiance, OH
Dewberry, E. Dale ... Alpharetta, GA
Dewberry, Elister H. ... Lee's Summit, MO
Dewberry, Frederick L. ... Baltimore, MD
Dewberry, George M. ... Greenville, MI
Dewberry, Michael J. ... Jacksonville, FL
Dewberry, Michael K. ... Los Angeles, CA
Dewberry, Richard L. ... Whittier, CA
Dewberry, Robert H. ... Whittier, CA
Dewberry, Steven, A Prof. Corp., Law Offices of ... Pasadena, CA
Dewberry, Steven E. ... Pasadena, CA
Dewberry, Susan A. ... Atlanta, GA
Dewberry, Thomas E. ... Baltimore, MD
Dewbre & Dewbre, P.C.
Oklahoma City, OK
Dewbre, James K. ... Oklahoma City, OK
Dewbre, J. W. ... Dallas, TX
Dewbre, Kenneth ... Oklahoma City, OK
Dewbre, Ross J. ... Oklahoma City, OK
DeWease, Wanda A. ... Roanoke, VA
DeWeerdt, John L.
United States Postal Service, Law Department, GV
Dewees, Cheryl P. ... Sherborn, MA
Dewees, Christopher S. ... Palo Alto, CA
DeWees, Edward E., Jr. ... San Antonio, TX
Dewees, Jennifer T. ... Tupelo, MS
Dewees, Paul J. ... Kansas City, MO
Dewees, Robert L., Jr. ... Boston, MA
Dewees, Wayne T. ... Memphis, TN
DeWeese, Allen J. ... West Palm Beach, FL
DeWeese, Chloethiel (Cokey) W.
Seattle, WA
DeWeese, David S. ... Wildwood, NJ
DeWeese, James ... Mansfield, OH
DeWeese, J. H. ... Piqua, OH
DeWeese, Mary Jane ... Washington, DC
Chicago, IL
DeWeese, Michael B. ... Sacramento, CA
DeWeese, Robert C. ... Mill Creek, WA
Deweese, Stephen S. ... Worthington, OH
DeWeese, Thomas L. ... Muncie, IN
DeWeese, Wendy M. ... Covina, CA
DeWeil, Dawn S. ... New York, NY
Dewell, John C. ... Los Angeles, CA
Dewell, John H. ... Haines City, FL
Dewell, John P. ... Pierre, SD
Dewell, Julian C. ... Everett, WA
Dewell, Kenneth R. ... Rapid City, SD
Dewell, Louise ... Los Angeles, CA
DeWenter, John C. ... Springfield, OR
DeWenter, John C., P.C. ... Springfield, OR
Dewerff, Edward E. ... Clarksville, TN
De Werff, J. Kenneth ... Minneapolis, MN
DeWerth-Jaffe, Henry J. ... Philadelphia, PA
DeWester, Gerald M. ... Noblesville, IN
Dewey, Addison E. ... Columbus, OH
Dewey, Alicia M. ... Corsicana, TX
Dallas, TX
Dewey, Allen C., Jr. ... Albuquerque, NM
Dewey, Andrew M. ... Glastonbury, CT
Dewey Ballantine LLP ... Los Angeles, CA
Washington, DC
New York, NY
Dewey, Blair H. ... Urbandale, IA
Dewey, Charles N., Jr. ... Grand Rapids, MI
Dewey, David K. ... Pittsburgh, PA
Dewey, David W. ... Wichita, KS
Dewey, Dennis J. ... Newburgh, IN
Dewey & Dewey ... Clyde, OH
Dewey, Earl F., II ... New London, CT
Dewey, Elizabeth R. ... Washington, DC
Dewey, Eric S. ... Portland, OR
Dewey, Ericka ... New York, NY
Dewey, George D., Jr ... Jacksonville, FL
Dewey, H. Stanley ... Richmond, CA
Dewey, H. Tucker ... Memphis, TN
Dewey, Henry B. ... Worcester, MA
Dewey, James C. ... New Roads, LA
Dewey, Jane M. ... Boston, MA
Dewey, Jeff ... Wichita, KS
Dewey, Joel A. ... Baltimore, MD
Dewey, John D. ... Chicago, IL
Dewey, John E. ... Lake Jackson, TX
Dewey, John M. ... New York, NY
Dewey, John P. ... Clyde, OH
Dewey, Josias N. ... Miami, FL
Dewey, Julia M. ... Seattle, WA
Dewey, Kathryn C. ... San Diego, CA
Dewey, Laura G. ... Santa Barbara, CA
Dewey, Lee S.
Nuclear Regulatory Commission, Atomic Safety and Licensing Board Panel, GV
Dewey, Lisa C. ... Chesterfield, VA
Dewey and Lund, L.L.P. ... Wichita, KS
Dewey, Michael J. ... Riverside, CA
Dewey, Paul ... Bend, OR
Dewey, Paul Carpenter
Newtown Square, PA
Dewey Pegno & Kramarsky LLP
New York, NY
Dewey, Richard B. ... Houston, TX
Dewey, Robert J. ... Davidson, NC
Dewey, Robert J., P.C. ... Davidson, NC
Dewey, Robert L. ... Norfolk, VA
Dewey, Robert M. ... Minneapolis, MN
Dewey, Robert V., Jr. ... Peoria, IL
Dewey, Sandra A. ... Los Angeles, CA
Dewey, Thomas E. L. ... New York, NY
Dewey, Thomas F. ... Clyde, OH
Dewey, Thomas F., Jr. ... Clyde, OH
Dewey, Walter R., Esq. ... Hawthorne, NJ
Dewey, William F. ... Anchorage, AK
Dewez, Brigitte M. ... El Segundo, CA
Dewhirst, Linda N. ... Sandy Hook, CT
Dewhirst, Peter A. ... Toledo, OH
Dewhirst, Robert C. ... Manchester, NH
Dewhirst, Scot E. ... Columbus, OH
Dewhurst, Stephen B.
Department of Agriculture, Office of Budget and Program Analysis, GV
Dewick, David P. ... Wisconsin Dells, WI
de Wied, Warren S. ... New York, NY
De Wild, Tamara ... Springfield, MO
De Wilde, Margret ... Manassas, VA
DeWind, Adrian W. ... New York, NY
DeWind, Margaret S. ... Madison, WI
DeWind, Wendy K. ... Binghamton, NY
De Wine, R. Michael ... Xenia, OH
DeWine, R. Patrick ... Cincinnati, OH
Dewing, Douglass W. ... Norfolk, VA
DeWinne, Werner K. ... Los Angeles, CA
DeWinter, Laurent ... Washington, DC
de Winter, Rudolph ... New York, NY
deWinter, William J., III
Glenwood Springs, CO
Dewire, Mark A. ... Washington, DC
Baltimore, MD
Dewire, Mary H. ... Long Beach, CA
Dewis, Karen A. ... Washington, DC
DeWitt, A. Gardner, Jr. ... Louisville, KY
de Witt, Alexander S. ... Charlottesville, VA
DeWitt Algorri & Algorri
Los Angeles, CA
Pasadena, CA
DeWitt, Anne A. ... Denver, CO
DeWitt, Balke & Vincent, P.L.C.
Detroit, MI
DeWitt, Beverly J. ... Boston, MA
DeWitt, Brian L. ... Los Angeles, CA
DeWitt, Brian W. ... San Diego, CA
DeWitt, Brydon Mark ... Richmond, VA
DeWitt, Carey A. ... Detroit, MI
DeWitt, Caroline L. ... Beverly Hills, CA
DeWitt, Charles C., Jr. ... Detroit, MI
DeWitt, Charles E., Jr. ... Boston, MA
DeWitt, Christiane ... Austin, TX
DeWitt, Christine E. ... Silver Spring, MD
deWitt, Clinton J. ... Sacramento, CA
DeWitt, Clyde F. ... Los Angeles, CA
DeWitt, Daniel K. ... Grand Rapids, MI
DeWitt, David S. ... Midland, MI
Dewitt, Derrick T. ... Oklahoma City, OK
DeWitt, Donald C. ... Troy, NY
DeWitt, Donald D. ... Wichita, KS
DeWitt, Dorothy D. ... New York, NY
DeWitt, Edward, III ... Falmouth, MA
DeWitt, Edward J. ... Falmouth, MA
De Witt, Franklin R. ... Conway, SC
De Witt and Higgins ... Elmhurst, NY
Port Washington, NY
DeWitt, Jack R. ... Madison, WI
DeWitt, James D. ... Fairbanks, AK
DeWitt, John R. ... Madison, WI
De Witt, John W. ... Idabel, OK
DeWitt, Jon F. ... Grand Rapids, MI
DeWitt, Julia A. ... Portland, OR
DeWitt, Kim Marie ... Elgin, IL
DeWitt, LaVonda R. ... Atlanta, GA
DeWitt Law Firm ... Alvin, TX
DeWitt Law Firm, P.A. ... Orlando, FL
DeWitt, Linda E. ... Indio, CA
DeWitt Lockman & DeWitt
New York, NY
DeWitt, Louis E. ... Pasadena, CA
DeWitt, Marcia P. ... Baltimore, MD
DeWitt, Mark E. ... Washington, DC
DeWitt, Mark Edward ... Washington, DC
DeWitt, Michael W. ... Columbus, OH
Dewitt, Myron B. ... Susquehanna, PA
DeWitt, Nancy Dirkse ... Cincinnati, OH
DeWitt, Neisa King ... Miami, FL
DeWitt, Nicholas ... Los Angeles, CA
DeWitt, Patricia A. ... Norwalk, CT
White Plains, NY
Dewitt, Phyllis A., (Mrs.) ... Tulsa, OK
DeWitt, Richard A. ... Omaha, NE
DeWitt, Rick ... Englewood, CO
DeWitt, Robert A. ... Houston, TX
DeWitt, Robert A., (P.C.)
Los Angeles, CA
DeWitt, Robert D. ... Kansas City, MO
DeWitt, Robert E. ... Atlanta, GA
Dewitt, Robert P., Jr. ... Troy, MI
DeWitt & Roberts LLP ... Los Angeles, CA
DeWitt & Rogers, S.C. ... Madison, WI
DeWitt Ross & Stevens S.C. ... Madison, WI
DeWitt, Sherri K. ... Orlando, FL
DeWitt, Sonja L. ... Cambridge, MA
De Witt, Susan J. ... Los Angeles, CA
DeWitt, Theresa G. ... New York, NY
DeWitt, Theresa R. ... Toledo, OH
DeWitt, Thomas H. ... Salem, NH
DeWitt, Thomas M. ... Alvin, TX
DeWitt, Thomas W. ... Grand Rapids, MI
DeWitt, Timothy A. ... Oakland, CA
Dewitt, Timothy R. ... Washington, DC
De Witt, Victor ... Fullerton, CA
DeWitt, W. Donald ... Elmhurst, NY
Port Washington, NY
DeWitt, Ward, Jr. ... Nashville, TN
De Witt, Wayne K., Jr. ... Alpharetta, GA
DeWitt, Wendy G. ... San Diego, CA
DeWitt, William W. ... Grand Rapids, MI
DeWitt & Zeldin, P.C. ... Kansas City, MO
DeWitte, Vincent L.
Department of Agriculture, Office of the General Counsel, GV
De Wolf, Buckmaster ... Menlo Park, CA
Dewolf, Daniel I. ... New York, NY
De Wolf, David K. ... Spokane, WA
DeWolf, Gerard J. ... Albany, NY
DeWolf, Gregory William
Fountain Valley, CA
DeWolf, Steven K. ... Dallas, TX
DeWolf, Thomas B. ... Orlando, FL
DeWolf, Thomas B., P.A. ... Orlando, FL
DeWolfe, Elena M. ... Chicago, IL
deWolfe, Geoffrey H. ... Colorado Springs, CO
De Wolfe, Gregory S. ... Dayton, OH
DeWolfe, John C., Jr. ... Chicago, IL
DeWolfe, Kerry B. ... Barre, VT
DeWolfe, L. James ... Woburn, MA
DeWolfe, Paul B. ... Rockville, MD
DeWolfe, Poynton & Stevens ... Chicago, IL
DeWolfe, Ruthanne K. ... Chicago, IL
DeWolfe, William R., (P.C.) ... Riverside, CA
Dewoody, Jeanette Alice ... Caldwell, ID
DeWoskin, A. Thomas ... St. Louis, MO
DeWoskin, Alan E. ... St. Louis, MO
DeWoskin, Alan E., P.C. ... St. Louis, MO
DeWoskin, Henry M. ... St. Louis, MO
DeWoskin, Kathleen H. ... Creve Coeur, MO
DeWoskin, Linda J. ... Evanston, IL
Dewrell, George I. ... Shalimar, FL
Dewrell, J. LaDon, (P.A.)
Fort Walton Beach, FL
Dewrell & Shaw ... Fort Walton Beach, FL
Dewrell, Tracey K. ... Miami, FL
Dews, Georgina R. ... Santa Cruz, CA
Dews, Julie ... Marion, NC
Dewsnup, King & Olsen
Salt Lake City, UT
Dewsnup, Ralph L. ... Salt Lake City, UT
DeWulf, James N. ... Moline, IL
DeWulf, John E. ... Phoenix, AZ
DeWulf, Mark W. ... Odessa, WA
DeWulf, Martin G. ... Kewanee, IL
Dewyer, William P. ... Bridgeview, IL
Dex, Daniel D. ... New York, NY
Dexheimer, James P. ... Beverly Hills, CA
Dexheimer, Karl D. ... Belleville, IL
Dexheimer, Robt. S. ... New Orleans, LA
Dexter, Alan G. ... Charlotte, NC
Dexter, Angelike I. ... Los Angeles, CA
Dexter, Bobby L. ... Washington, DC
Dexter, Bruce H. ... Hackensack, NJ
Dexter, Calvin R. ... Wausau, WI
Dexter, Catherine M. ... Portland, OR
Dexter, Cecily ... New York, NY
Dexter, Daniel Alan ... Santa Rosa, CA
Dexter, Deirdre O'Neil E. ... Tulsa, OK
Dexter, Douglas D. ... Lincoln, NE
Dexter, Douglas E. ... San Francisco, CA
Dexter, Edwin T. ... Kansas City, MO
Dexter, Forrest L. ... Spokane, WA
Dexter, Forrest L., P.S., Law Office of
Spokane, WA
Dexter, Judith A. ... Bethlehem, PA
Dexter, Nathaniel T. ... Boston, MA
Dexter, Paul B. ... Boston, MA
Dexter, Philip ... St. Louis, MO
Dexter, Robert F. ... Malibu, CA
Dexter, Roland A. ... Melbourne, FL
Dexter, Scott J., Law Office of
Upland, CA
Dexter, Vicki L. ... Baltimore, MD
Dexter, William R. ... Owensboro, KY
Dey, Dorothy H. ... Milwaukee, WI
Dey, Jeffrey R. ... Newport Beach, CA
Dey, Joseph S. ... Milford, CT
Dey, Sally C. ... Culver City, CA
Dey, Smith & Associates ... Milford, CT
Dey, Stephen G. ... Los Angeles, CA
Deye & Browning ... Morgantown, KY
Deye, Richard J. ... Morgantown, KY
Deye, Thomas E. ... Cincinnati, OH
Deyerle, Henry Price, Jr. ... Gilford, NH
Deyerle, Kristie A. ... Wilmington, DE
Deyeso, Frederick J., Jr. ... San Antonio, TX
Deyle, David A. ... Omaha, NE
Deyling, Robert P.
Administrative Office Of The United States Courts, GV
Deyne, Herbert G. ... Chicago, IL
Deyo, Kenneth D. ... Euclid, OH
Deyo, Richard N. ... Norwalk, CA
Deyo, Russell C. ... New Brunswick, NJ
Deyo, Tanya V. ... Philadelphia, PA
Deyo, William B., Jr. ... New York, NY
De Yoe, David P. ... Chicago, IL
DeYoe Heissenbuttel, L.L.C.
Hackensack, NJ
Morristown, NJ
Newark, NJ
Paterson, NJ
Wayne, NJ
DeYoe, John M. ... Asheville, NC
De Yoe, Mark R. ... San Diego, CA
DeYoe, Wood M. ... Wayne, NJ
DeYong, Dirk ... St. Louis, MO
DeYong, J. Michael ... Edmond, OK
DeYong, Ryan & Rischard, P.A.
Edmond, OK
Oklahoma City, OK
DeYonker, Alex J. ... Grand Rapids, MI
DeYoung, Bruce R. ... Akron, OH
De Young, Cathryn Brogan ... Santa Ana, CA
Deyoung, Constance ... Evanston, IL
DeYoung, D. Tobyn ... Tampa, FL
De Young, David A. ... Chicago, IL
DeYoung, Donald J. ... Grand Rapids, MI
DeYoung, Edwin R. ... Dallas, TX
De Young, Erin Lee ... Orlando, FL
DeYoung, Gordon P. ... Sparta, MI
De Young, Howard F. ... Grand Rapids, MI
DeYoung, J. Worthen ... Kansas City, MO
DeYoung, Jacqueline S. ... Detroit, MI
DeYoung, Jan Hart ... Anchorage, AK
DeYoung, Joel J. ... San Francisco, CA
DeYoung, Laurie ... Los Angeles, CA
Deyoung, M. Alisandra ... Tampa, FL
DeYoung, Margaret Evatt ... Boston, MA
DeYoung, Mark E. ... Lafayette, IN
DeYoung, Mary R. ... Seattle, WA
DeYoung, Neal A. ... New York, NY
DeYoung, Patricia Lynn ... Houston, TX
De Young, Richard C., III ... New Bern, NC
De Young, R. R. ... Anchorage, AK
DeYoung, Steven S. ... Hyannis, MA
DeYoung, Susan C. ... Wheaton, IL
De Young, Timothy J. ... Albuquerque, NM
De Young, Vincent G. ... Las Vegas, NV
DeYoung, William F. ... Chicago, IL
DeYulia, Kathryn E. ... Milledgeville, GA
De Yurre, Victor H. ... Miami, FL
Deza, Paula ... Washington, DC
DeZago, Ralph J. ... Herington, KS
de Zayas, Carlos L. ... Miami, FL
de Zayas, Martha ... Miami, FL

de Zayas-Green, Eileen S. ....Barranquitas, PR
DeZee, John V. ....Los Angeles, CA
Dezelan, Deborah E. ....Chicago, IL
De Zelar, James M. ....Chicago, IL
Dezen, David A. ....Denver, CO
Dezen, Phillip M. ....North Hollywood, CA
Dezen & Pollin ....Denver, CO
Dezendorf, Burton E., Jr. ....Reno, NV
DeZengremel, Richard A. ....Englewood, CO
Dezern, Ray W., Jr. ....Norfolk, VA
Dezern, Roy E. ....Jacksonville, FL
DeZern, Thomas J. ....Spartanburg, SC
Dezes, Basil G. ....Los Angeles, CA
Deziel, Colleen A. ....Long Beach, CA
Deziel, Ronald F. ....Dearborn, MI
Dezii, Dawn ....Westmont, NJ
Dezio, John A. ....Charlottesville, VA
Dezio, Richard Allen ....Alexandria, VA
DeZorett, Michael J. ....New York, NY
De Zorett, Wm. J. ....New York, NY
Dezort, Robert E. ....Cleveland, OH
DeZotti, Flavia N. ....New York, NY
DeZube, Douglas Keith ....Overland Park, KS
Dezube, Esther C. S. ....Boston, MA
DeZure, Thomas J. ....Dearborn, MI
Dezurick, Bradford Lawrence
Oakland, CA
Dezurick, Paul A. ....Oakland, CA
Dezzani, David J. ....Honolulu, HI
Dezzani & Petersen ....Placerville, CA
Dezzani, Wendy S. ....Sacramento, CA
Dhaliwal, Kai ....Los Angeles, CA
Dhaliwal, Mahindar K. ....San Francisco, CA
Dhall & Douglas, P.C. ....Dallas, TX
Dhall, Kamla M. ....Dallas, TX
Dhanraj, Edward ....Richmond Hill, NY
Dhawan, Sanjiv S. ....Palo Alto, CA
d'Hemecourt, Jules A., IV .....Baton Rouge, LA
Dhillon, Janet L. ....Los Angeles, CA
Dhillon, Jennifer K. W. ....San Francisco, CA
Dhillon, Sabina ....Staten Island, NY
Dhillon, Uttam ....Los Angeles, CA
Dhima, Artan ....Washington, DC
Dhindsa, Ranjit S. ....Washington, DC
Dhir, Rashi ....New York, NY
Dholakia, Ullasini ....Anaheim, CA
Dhong, Edward Young Chul
San Francisco, CA
Dhooge, Lucien J. ....Stockton, CA
Dhuey, Andrew J. ....Berkeley, CA
Dhuey, John A. ....Palo Alto, CA
Diab, F. Joseph ....Raleigh, NC
Diab, G. Stephen ....Wilmington, NC
Diab, George Stephen ....Rocky Mount, NC
Diab, Malik R. ....Chicago, IL
Diabo, Tina M. ....Pompano Beach, FL
Diachenko, Thomas M. ....San Diego, CA
Diachishin, Christine M. ....Rochester, NY
Diaco, Joseph F., Jr. ....Tampa, FL
Diaco, Stephen C. ....Tampa, FL
Diaconis, John S. ....New York, NY
Diacou, Nicholas H. ....Chicago, IL
Diacovo, Nannette M. ....Burbank, CA
Di Adamo, Carmine W. ....Lawrence, MA
DiAdamo, Robert A. ....Boston, MA
DiAdamo, William H. ....Boston, MA
Di Addezzio, Fred J. ....Bryn Mawr, PA
Diaddigo, John E. ....Pittsburgh, PA
Diadul, Daniel ....Philadelphia, PA
Diagonale, Dina F. ....Westport, CT
Diak, Patricia ....Birmingham, AL
Diakos, Maria L. ....Buffalo, NY
Diakow, Nicholas T. ....New York, NY
Diakun, Andrew ....Williamsville, NY
Dial, Alan R. ....Washington, DC
Dial, Ardie Jean ....Talladega, AL
Dial & Associates ....Anaheim, CA
Dial, Audra A. ....Atlanta, GA
Dial, Curtis ....Keokuk, IA
Dial, David A. ....Atlanta, GA
Dial, Edward C., Jr. ....Manchester, NH
Dial, Ellen Conedera ....Seattle, WA
Dial, Gary ....Memphis, MO
Dial, George L., Jr. ....Columbia, SC
Dial, J. Donald ....Columbia, SC
Dial, J. Donald, Jr. ....Columbia, SC
Dial, James F. ....Princeton, NJ
Dial, Justine R. ....Evanston, IL
Dial, Karl G. ....Dallas, TX
Dial, Kelley A. ....Cartersville, GA
Dial, Looze & May, Chartered
Pocatello, ID
Dial, Stephen F. ....Anaheim, CA
Dial, Terri Fay ....Roanoke, VA
Dial, Thomas F. ....Pocatello, ID
Dial, William H. ....Orlando, FL
Dial, William K. ....Los Angeles, CA
DiAlbert, John E. ....Westerville, OH
DiAlberto, Robert V. .....Fort Lauderdale, FL
Dialessi, Julie A. ....Chicopee, MA
Dials, John J., Jr. ....Warrendale, PA
Diamandis, Elizabeth C. ....Tampa, FL
Diamandis, John T. ....Tampa, FL
Diamant, Aviva F. ....New York, NY
Diamant, Irene R. ....Santa Monica, CA
Diamant, Jeffrey Nolan ....Houston, TX
Diamant, Laura Jo ....Chicago, IL
Diamant, Lawrence A. ....Los Angeles, CA
Diamant, Marc C. ....Denver, CO
Diamant, Michael H. ....Cleveland, OH
Diamant, Tal ....Denver, CO
Diamant, Violet ....New York, NY
Diamant, William ....Hinsdale, IL
Diamante, Joseph ....New York, NY
Diamantopulos, George C. ....Pittsburgh, PA
Diambri, Paul P. ....Highwood, IL

Diambri & Vicari, P.C. ....Gurnee, IL
Highland Park, IL
Lake Forest, IL
Diambri, Walter ....Gurnee, IL
Diament, Nathan J. ....New York, NY
Diament, Sahra H. ....New York, NY
Diamomd, Regina ....Philadelphia, PA
Diamond, Afflitto & Raimondi ....Wayne, NJ
Diamond, Alan J. ....Beverly Hills, CA
Diamond, Albert D. ....Miami, FL
Diamond, Alison D. K. ....Sterling, VA
Diamond, Alison S. ....New York, NY
Diamond, Allan B. ....Dallas, TX
Houston, TX
Diamond, Andrew R. ....Atlanta, GA
Diamond, Andrew R. ....New York, NY
Diamond, Ann ....Fort Worth, TX
Diamond, Ann Cynthia ....New York, NY
Diamond, Ann L. ....Ross, CA
Diamond, Anthony J. ....Fort Myers, FL
Diamond, Anthony P. ....Hamburg, NY
Diamond, Arthur M. ....South Bend, IN
Diamond, Arthur M. ....Garden City, NY
Diamond, Arthur M. ....Mineola, NY
Diamond & Baker ....Cedar Ridge, CA
Diamond, Barbara J. ....Portland, OR
Diamond, Barbara M. ....Boston, MA
Diamond, Barbara S. ....Miami, FL
Diamond, Barry ....Miami, FL
Diamond, Barry A. ....Coral Springs, FL
Diamond, Barry A., P.A. ....Coral Springs, FL
Diamond, Barry R. ....Alexandria, VA
Diamond, Basil S. ....Lantana, FL
Diamond, Benjamin D. ....Washington, DC
Diamond, Bernard R. ....New York, NY
Diamond, Beth D. ....New York, NY
Diamond, Brian ....New York, NY
Diamond, Brian J. ....Wheaton, IL
Diamond, Bruce M. ....Washington, DC
Diamond, Bruce W. ....Waterbury, CT
Diamond, Charles M. ....Ashtabula, OH
Diamond, Charles P. ....Los Angeles, CA
Diamond, Christine C. ....New York, NY
Diamond, Cindy A. ....San Jose, CA
Diamond, Cindy R. ....Baltimore, MD
Diamond, Claudia A ....Baltimore, MD
Diamond, Clifford A. ....New York, NY
Diamond, Craig A. ....Cedar Ridge, CA
Diamond, Cyrus M. ....Mineola, NY
New York, NY
Diamond, Dale A. ....Chicago, IL
Diamond, Dale A. ....New York, NY
Diamond, Dan D. ....Denver, CO
Diamond, David A. ....Napa, CA
Diamond, David A. ....Sonoma, CA
Diamond, David A. ....Albany, NY
Diamond, David A. ....Hempstead, NY
Diamond, David Arthur ....Palm Beach, FL
Diamond, David H. ....New York, NY
Diamond, David J. ....Sierra Vista, AZ
Tucson, AZ
Diamond, David J. ....Katonah, NY
Diamond, David M. ....Chicago, IL
Diamond, David N. ....Chicago, IL
Diamond, Dennis
Agency for International Development,
Office of the General Counsel, GV
Diamond and Diamond ....South Bend, IN
Diamond and Diamond, P.A.
Fort Myers, FL
Diamond and Diamond, P.A.
Flemington, NJ
Millburn, NJ
Morristown, NJ
Somerville, NJ
Warren, NJ
Watchung, NJ
Diamond, Donald ....Napa, CA
Diamond, Donna G. ....Seal Beach, CA
Diamond, Dubsky & Ford Co., L.P.A.
Ashtabula, OH
Diamond, Emily ....New York, NY
Diamond, Eric J. ....Beverly Hills, CA
Diamond, Eric L. ....South Bend, IN
Diamond, Eugene C. ....Chicago, IL
Diamond, Fischer & Wurman
Elkins Park, PA
Diamond, G. Kimberley ....St. Louis, MO
Diamond, Gary M. ....Rocklin, CA
Diamond, Gary W. ....Atlanta, GA
Diamond, Gary Wayne ....Kensington, MD
Diamond, George L. ....Dallas, TX
Diamond, George P. ....Glen Ridge, NJ
Diamond, Gregory T. ....Seattle, WA
Diamond, Gustave ....Pittsburgh, PA
Diamond, H. Jeffrey ....Shawnee, OK
Diamond, H. Joshua ....Miami, FL
Diamond, Harley David ....New York, NY
Diamond, Harold ....Philadelphia, PA
Diamond, Harris ....New York, NY
Diamond, Harry B. ....Louisville, KY
Diamond, Harvey S. ....Cincinnati, OH
Diamond, Hasser & Frost ....Mobile, AL
Diamond, Helen ....Santa Ana, CA
Diamond, Henry L. ....Washington, DC
Diamond, Howard M.
Colorado Springs, CO
Diamond, Howard S. ....Morristown, NJ
Diamond, Ilene ....San Francisco, CA
Diamond, Ivan M. ....Louisville, KY
Diamond, J. Christopher ....Houston, TX
Diamond, J. Leonard ....Miami Beach, FL
Diamond, Jack ....Sherman Oaks, CA
Diamond, Jack ....Totowa, NJ
Diamond, Jack T. ....Akron, OH
Diamond, James A. ....Gardena, CA
Diamond, James A. ....Harrisburg, PA

Diamond, James D. ....New Canaan, CT
Ridgefield, CT
Diamond, James L. ....Belmont, MA
Diamond, James T., Jr. ....Oakland, CA
Diamond, Janet W. ....New York, NY
Diamond, Jay H. ....Islandia, NY
Diamond, Jeff, Law Firm ....Carlsbad, NM
Diamond, Jeffrey A. ....West Sacramento, CA
Diamond, Jeffrey B. ....Carlsbad, NM
Diamond, Jeffrey D. ....Encino, CA
Diamond, Jeffrey D., A Professional
Corporation ....Encino, CA
Diamond, Jeffrey L. ....Houston, TX
Diamond, Jeffrey M. ....New York, NY
Diamond, Jeffry B. ....Sacramento, CA
Diamond, Jerome ....Miami, FL
Diamond, John D. ....Ojai, CA
Diamond, Jonathan R. ....Sacramento, CA
Diamond, Josef ....Seattle, WA
Diamond, Joseph ....New York, NY
Diamond, Joseph B. ....Bronx, NY
Diamond, Joseph I. ....Radnor, PA
Diamond, Joshua R. ....Montpelier, VT
Diamond, Judith E. ....Brookline, MA
Diamond, Julieann ....Albany, NY
Diamond, Keith D. ....Miami, FL
Diamond, Kenneth A. ....Tampa, FL
Diamond, Kenneth B. ....Phoenix, AZ
Diamond, Kenneth J. ....Seattle, WA
Diamond, Kenneth S. ....Westbury, NY
Diamond, Kevin R. ....Las Vegas, NV
Diamond, Kimberly E. ....New York, NY
Diamond, Konstantine J. ....Southfield, MI
Diamond, Kristin M. ....San Jose, CA
Diamond, Larry ....Los Angeles, CA
Diamond, Larry A. ....Memphis, TN
Diamond, Lauren H. ....Great Neck, NY
Diamond, Laurence A. ....St. Paul, MN
Diamond, Lawrence J.
West Palm Beach, FL
Diamond, Lawrence P. ....Flushing, NY
Diamond, Lawrence W. ....Newark, NJ
Diamond, Leonard W. ....New York, NY
Diamond, Leslie K. ....Norfolk, VA
Diamond, LeSueur, Roth & Feetterer, P.C.
McHenry, IL
Diamond, Liszt & Grady, P.A.
Minneapolis, MN
Diamond, Louis E. ....Staten Island, NY
Diamond, Louis H. ....Washington, DC
Diamond, Lucia Marie
Belvedere-Tiburon, CA
Diamond, M. Gregg ....Bethesda, MD
Diamond, M. Jerome ....Montpelier, VT
Diamond, Margaret G. ....New Orleans, LA
Diamond, Margaret-joyce ....Boston, MA
Diamond, Maria S. ....Seattle, WA
Diamond, Mark ....Stamford, CT
Diamond, Mark R. ....New York, NY
Diamond, Marla E.
Environmental Protection Agency,
Office of the General Counsel, GV
Diamond, Martin ....Albuquerque, NM
Diamond, Marvin J. ....Washington, DC
Diamond, Marylin G. ....New York, NY
Diamond, Michael ....Union, NJ
Diamond, Michael A. ....Tansboro, NJ
Diamond, Michael H. ....Los Angeles, CA
Diamond, Michael J. ....Philadelphia, PA
Diamond, Michael K. ....Wayne, NJ
Diamond, Michael R. ....Washington, DC
Diamond, Mitchell L. ....Roslyn, NY
Diamond, Murray J. ....Brooklyn, NY
Diamond, Nancy B. ....San Rafael, CA
Diamond, Nancy H. ....Portland, OR
Diamond, Nathan ....Rego Park, NY
Diamond, Nathan P. ....Miami, FL
Diamond, Norman ....Washington, DC
Diamond & Ostrow LLP .....Los Angeles, CA
Diamond, P. Andrew ....Pittsburgh, PA
Diamond, Patricia D.
Rancho Cucamonga, CA
Diamond, Paul R. ....Chicago, IL
Diamond, Paul S. ....Philadelphia, PA
Diamond, Peter K. ....Glendale, CA
Diamond, Philip A. ....Orlando, FL
Diamond, Philip E. ....San Francisco, CA
Diamond, Philip R. ....San Francisco, CA
Diamond, Polsky & Bauer
Deerfield Beach, FL
Media, PA
Philadelphia, PA
Diamond, Priscilla M. ....Cambridge, MA
Diamond, Priscilla Seiderman
Louisville, KY
Diamond, Ralph ....Garden City, NY
Diamond, Rand J. ....Cleveland, OH
Diamond Rash Gordon & Jackson, P.C.
El Paso, TX
Diamond, Raymond T. ....New Orleans, LA
Diamond, Richard ....Washington, DC
Diamond, Richard Harris ....New York, NY
Diamond, Richard I. ....Minneapolis, MN
Diamond, Richard K., (A Professional
Corporation) ....Los Angeles, CA
Diamond, Richard L. ....Rockville Centre, NY
Diamond, Richard L., P.C.
Rockville Centre, NY
Diamond, Richard S. ....Santa Monica, CA
Diamond, Richard S. ....Millburn, NJ
Diamond, Rick N. ....Minneapolis, MN
Diamond, Robert ....Millburn, NJ
Diamond, Robert A. ....Washington, DC
Diamond, Robert L. ....Woodland Hills, CA
Diamond, Robert L. ....Grand Rapids, MI
Diamond, Robert M. ....Washington, DC
Diamond, Robert M. ....Falls Church, VA
Diamond, Roberta W. ....Chicago, IL

Diamond, Robin S. ....Sacramento, CA
Diamond & Robinson, P.C.
Montpelier, VT
Diamond, Roger Jon ....Santa Monica, CA
Diamond, Ronald N. ....Elkins Park, PA
Diamond, Ross M., III ....Mobile, AL
Diamond, Rutman, Costello & Silberglitt
New York, NY
Diamond, Samuel ....Philadelphia, PA
Diamond, Samuel J. ....McHenry, IL
Diamond, Sandra Fascell
St. Petersburg, FL
Seminole, FL
Diamond & Scharnberger ....Encino, CA
Ventura, CA
Woodland Hills, CA
Diamond, Scott R. ....Los Angeles, CA
San Diego, CA
Diamond, Seth ....New York, NY
Diamond, Shari S. ....Chicago, IL
Diamond, Sidney J. ....El Paso, TX
Diamond, Stanley ....New York, NY
Diamond, Stanley A. ....Brooklyn, NY
Diamond, Stanley J. ....Los Angeles, CA
Diamond, Stella ....Fort Myers, FL
Diamond, Stephen ....Los Angeles, CA
Diamond, Stephen B. ....Chicago, IL
Diamond, Stephen C.F. ....White Plains, NY
Diamond, Stephen E. ....Poughkeepsie, NY
Diamond, Stephen P., Jr. ....New York, NY
Diamond, Steven M. ....San Jose, CA
Diamond, Steven M. ....Houston, TX
Diamond, Steven S. ....Washington, DC
Diamond, Stewart H. ....Chicago, IL
Diamond, Stuart ....New York, NY
Diamond, Susan C. ....Los Angeles, CA
Diamond, Susan R. ....San Francisco, CA
Diamond, Tami J. ....Chicago, IL
Diamond, Terrance Lee ....Chicago, IL
Diamond, Thomas A. ....Costa Mesa, CA
Diamond, Timothy J. ....Wheaton, IL
Diamond, Tom ....El Paso, TX
Diamond, Tracey E. ....Philadelphia, PA
Diamond, Valerie ....San Francisco, CA
Diamond, Virginia R. ....Richmond, VA
Diamond, William A. ....Richmond, VA
Diamond, William H. ....Reading, MA
Diamond, William H. ....New York, NY
Diamond, William J. ....New York, NY
Diamond & Wilson ....Los Angeles, CA
Diamondstein, Lee M. ....Philadelphia, PA
Diamondstone, Fred ....Seattle, WA
Diamondstone, Jessica S. ....Bedford, PA
Diamonstein, Alan A. ....Newport News, VA
Diamonstein, Kevin M. ....Newport News, VA
Diamonstein, Richard G. ....Norfolk, VA
DiAmore-Siah, Carmen, Law Office of
Honolulu, HI
Diana, Anthony J. ....New York, NY
Diana, Brenda Sweeny ....Boston, MA
Diana, Carl ....Spokane, WA
Diana, Conti, Tunila & Comollo
Manchester, CT
Diana, Corinne ....Woburn, MA
Diana, George I. ....Spokane, WA
Diana, James C. ....Washington, DC
Diana Law Office, P.S. ....Spokane, WA
Diana, Leo V. ....Manchester, CT
Diana, Leonard P. ....New York, NY
Diana, Mark ....Morristown, NJ
Diana, Natalie H. ....Treasury Department,
Financial Management Service, GV
Diana, Ronald S. ....New York, NY
Diana, Stewart K. ....Baltimore, MD
Diana, Vincent L. ....Manchester, CT
Diana, Wilfred P. ....Somerville, IL
DiAndrea-Iversen, Laura ....Chicago, IL
DiAngelo, Christopher J. ....New York, NY
Dianiska, Mary M. ....New York, NY
Diankov, Nikolay P. ....Pittsburgh, PA
Dianno, Mark J. ....Philadelphia, PA
DiAntonio, Janet V. ....Baltimore, MD
DiAntonio, Mark A. ....Baltimore, MD
DiAntonio, Vincent G., Jr.
Philadelphia, PA
Diarmit, Frank O. ....Portland, OR
Dias, Amy E. ....Pittsburgh, PA
Dias, Antonio F. ....Pittsburgh, PA
Dias, Becky J.W. ....Fremont, NE
Wahoo, NE
Dias, Blake Edward ....Seattle, WA
Dias, Christopher A. ....Honolulu, HI
Dias, Claudia A. ....Citrus Heights, CA
Dias, Frederick J. ....Phoenix, AZ
Dias, Gregory S. ....East Providence, RI
Dias, Julianne B. ....Gloucester, VA
Dias, Kathleen M.
Federal Energy Regulatory Commission,
Office of the Commissioners, GV
Dias, Kathleen O'Loughlin ....Boston, MA
Dias, Kathy Smith ....Albany, NY
Dias, Ligia M. ....Medford, MA
Dias, Mark S. ....Boston, MA
Dias, Michael A. ....Hanford, CA
Dias, Sean D. ....Secaucus, NJ
Dias, Thomas E. ....Santa Ana, CA
Dias, Virginia M. ....Philadelphia, PA
Diase, Soraya
Charlotte Amalie, St. Thomas, VI
Diaso, Janet L. ....New York, NY
Diasparra, Diana J. ....New York, NY
Diaz, Adrian ....San Diego, CA
Diaz, Albert ....Raleigh, NC
Diaz, Alejandro J. ....Atlanta, GA
Diaz, Alina C. ....Miami, FL
Diaz, Alyce M. ....Yardley, PA
Diaz, Andrew Gerald ....Tampa, FL
Diaz, Aristides J. ....Orlando, FL

Diaz, Arturo ..... New York, NY
Diaz, Beatriz Beato ..... San Juan, PR
Diaz, Benito H. ..... Miami, FL
Diaz, Benjamin A. ..... Sacramento, CA
Diaz, Bert ..... Miami, FL
Diaz, Carlos M. ..... San Juan, PR
Diaz, Charles C. ..... Reno, NV
Diaz, Charles R. ..... Los Angeles, CA
Diaz, Cheryl E. ..... Dallas, TX
Diaz, Christina L. ..... Philadelphia, PA
Diaz, Claire ..... Denver, CO
Diaz, Daniel, Jr. ..... San Antonio, TX
Diaz, David ..... Woodbury, NY
Diaz, David ..... Corpus Christi, TX
Diaz, David M. ..... Dallas, TX
Diaz, Debora Ann ..... New Port Richey, FL
Diaz, Denise L. ..... Washington, DC
Diaz, Dennis S. ..... Los Angeles, CA
Diáz, Edith ..... New York, NY
Diaz, Edw. T. ..... Golden Meadow, LA
Diaz, Edward ..... West Palm Beach, FL
Diaz, Elena ..... Austin, TX
Diaz, Ena Teresa ..... Miami, FL
Diaz, Eric ..... Philadelphia, PA
Diaz, Felix, Jr. ..... Miami, FL
Diaz, Frances L. ..... Beverly Hills, CA
Diaz, Glenn E. ..... Chalmette, LA
Diaz, Gregory G. ..... Irvine, CA
Diaz, Gregory T.
Office of Personnel Management, GV
Diaz, Gus F. ..... Hagåtña, GU
Diaz, Henry N. ..... New York, NY
Diaz, Humberto ..... Los Angeles, CA
Diaz, Idris M. ..... Washington, DC
Diaz, Inez M. ..... New Haven, CT
Diaz, Isauro ..... West Covina, CA
Diaz, James E. ..... Lafayette, LA
Diaz, James E., Jr. ..... Lafayette, LA
Diaz, Jessica A. ..... Philadelphia, PA
Diaz, Joe ..... Buford, GA
Diaz, Joe C. ..... Albuquerque, NM
Diaz, John A. ..... New York, NY
Diaz, John E. ..... Salt Lake City, UT
Diaz, Jorge ..... Miami, FL
Diaz, Jose A. "Cheo" ..... Flushing, NY
Diaz, Jose O. ..... Miami, FL
Diaz, Joseph ..... Tampa, FL
Diaz, Joseph M. ..... Tacoma, WA
Diaz, Joseph T. ..... New York, NY
Diaz, Karen Ann ..... Doylestown, PA
Diaz, Kathryn E. ..... New York, NY
Diaz, Liza G. ..... Chicago, IL
Diaz, Luis E. ..... Miami, FL
Diaz, Luis E. ..... Union City, NJ
Diaz, Luis J. ..... Phoenix, AZ
Diaz, Luis O. ..... New York, NY
Diaz, M. Pilar ..... Atlanta, GA
Diaz, Manuel A. ..... Miami, FL
Diaz, Manuel J. ..... Beverly Hills, CA
Diaz, Margarita ..... New York, NY
Diaz, Maria B. ..... New York, NY
Diaz, Marilyn
Department of Housing and Urban Development,
Office of General Counsel, GV
Diaz, Mario E., (A Professional Corporation)
Los Angeles, CA
Diaz, Mark A. ..... Houston, TX
Diaz, Martin A. ..... Iowa City, IA
Diaz, Martin, Law Firm ..... Iowa City, IA
Diaz, Mary Jo ..... Olympia, WA
Diaz, Michael, Jr., Law Offices of
Miami, FL
Diaz, Modesto ..... Santa Ana, CA
Diaz & Morel-Saruski ..... Coral Gables, FL
Fort Lauderdale, FL
Miami, FL
Diaz, Nelson A. ..... Philadelphia, PA
Diaz, O. Rene ..... San Antonio, TX
Diaz, Oliver E., Jr. ..... Jackson, MS
Diaz, Patricia J. ..... New York, NY
Diaz, Patricia L. ..... Miami, FL
Diaz, Patrick ..... Boston, MA
Diaz, Paul J. ..... Beltsville, MD
Diaz, R. Scott ..... San Francisco, CA
Diaz, Ramon V. ..... Hagåtña, GU
Diaz, Raymond Alexis ..... Kentfield, CA
Diaz, Raymond J. ..... Vienna, VA
Diaz, Reynaldo L., Jr. ..... San Antonio, TX
Diaz, Reynaldo L., Jr., P.C.
San Antonio, TX
Diaz, Ricardo J. ..... Pensacola, FL
Diaz, Ricardo M. ..... Los Angeles, CA
Diaz, Richard H. ..... Covina, CA
Diaz, Richard S. ..... Newport, OR
Diaz, Robert E. ..... New York, NY
Diaz, Robert E. ..... Arlington, TX
Diaz, Robert H., Jr. ..... Milwaukee, WI
Diaz, Robert L. ..... Albuquerque, NM
Diaz, Roberto J. ..... Miami, FL
Diaz, Rodolfo R. ..... San Diego, CA
Diaz, Rodrigo J. ..... Harrisburg, PA
Diaz, Rolando A. ..... Miami, FL
Diaz, Roxanne M. ..... Los Angeles, CA
Diaz, Roy A. ..... Fort Lauderdale, FL
Diaz, Rudolph A. ..... El Monte, CA
Diaz, Samuel, Jr. ..... Riverside, CA
Diaz, Soren E. ..... Sacramento, CA
Diaz, Steven A. ..... Washington, DC
Diaz, Susan M. ..... Chicago, IL
Diaz, Suzanne M. ..... Fort Lauderdale, FL
Diaz, Temys M. ..... Miami, FL
Diaz, Teresa L. ..... Gaithersburg, MD
Diaz, Theodore E. ..... Alton, IL
Diaz, Theodore R. ..... Wood River, IL
Diaz, Thomas ..... La Puente, CA
Diaz, Thomas J. ..... Little Rock, AR
Diaz, Thomas P. ..... New Orleans, LA
Diaz, Tina ..... Denver, CO
Diaz, Victor A. ..... Maitland, FL
Diaz, Victor M., Jr. ..... Miami, FL
Diaz, Victoria S. ..... Cardiff-By-The-Sea, CA
Díaz-Angueira, Arturo ..... San Juan, PR
Diaz-Arrastia, George R. ..... Houston, TX
Diaz Asencio, Jose B. ..... San Juan, PR
Diaz-Asper, Jose A. ..... Washington, DC
Diaz-Balart, Lincoln ..... Miami, FL
Diaz-Bergnes, Gabriel T., (P.A.) ..... Miami, FL
Diaz-Buxo, Nydia Maria ..... Caguas, PR
Diaz-Cruz, Mario, III ..... New York, NY
Díaz de Aldrey, Iván ..... San Juan, PR
Díaz-Díaz, Ruy V. ..... San Juan, PR
Diaz-Fontana, Guillermo R. ..... Baltimore, MD
Diaz-Francisco, Angel L. ..... Miami, FL
Diaz-Garcia, Agustin ..... Ponce, PR
Diaz-Granados, Rafael ..... New York, NY
Diaz-Laureano, Benito ..... Aguadilla, PR
Díaz-López, Iván ..... San Juan, PR
Diaz-Matos, Andrew B. ..... New York, NY
Diaz-Miranda, Melissa ..... New York, NY
Díaz-Olmo, Eldia M. ..... Guaynabo, PR
Diaz-Padron, Carlos ..... Coral Gables, FL
Diaz Palenque, Angel L. ..... Caguas, PR
Diaz Rivera, Miguel A. ..... San Juan, PR
Diaz-Rodriguez, José R. ..... Mayaguez, PR
Diaz-Santiago, Peter ..... San Juan, PR
Diaz-Silveira, Albert ..... Miami, FL
Diaz-Silveira, Jorge, (P.A.) ..... Miami, FL
Diaz-Tejera, Jose G. ..... San Juan, PR
Díaz-Toro, Karín G. ..... San Juan, PR
Diaz Valdes, Julio A. ..... San Juan, PR
Diaz-Vega, Jose Carlos ..... San Juan, PR
Díaz-Velasco, Ana Cristina ..... San Juan, PR
Diaz Vivo, Carlos ..... San Juan, PR
Diaz-Yaeger, Elia ..... Metairie, LA
Dib, Albert ..... Madison, CT
Dib, Albert J. ..... Detroit, MI
DiBacco, Alicia R. ..... New York, NY
DiBari, David D. ..... Washington, DC
Di Bari, Mary Ann C. ..... Pound Ridge, NY
Di Bart, Joseph R. ..... Hartsdale, NY
DiBartolo, Annamarie ..... Simsbury, CT
Di Bartolo, CharCretia V. ..... Boston, MA
Providence, RI
Di Bartolo, Ferdinand F., Jr.
Clarence Center, NY
Dibartolo, John P. ..... Northampton, MA
Di Bartolomeo, Anthony L. ..... Foster City, CA
DiBartolomeo, Dean F. ..... Miami, FL
DiBartolomeo & DiBartolomeo ..... Miami, FL
DiBartolomeo, Joseph ..... Miami, FL
DiBartolomeo, Lisa ..... Boston, MA
DiBasio, Lawrence B. ..... Livonia, MI
DiBattista, Jason C. ..... Newark, NJ
DiBattiste, Carol ..... Department of Justice,
Executive Office for United States Attorneys,
GV
Dibb, Alfred W. ..... Medford, OR
Dibb, Bruce L. ..... Salt Lake City, UT
Dibb Lupton Alsop ..... New York, NY
Dibble, Ann E. ..... Santa Clara, CA
Dibble, Barbara A. ..... Findlay, OH
Dibble, Barbara J. ..... Garden Grove, CA
Dibble, Charles E. ..... Contoocook, NH
Dibble, Charles L. ..... Columbia, SC
Dibble, Christine L.
Environmental Protection Agency,
Program Office Attorneys, GV
Dibble, Daniel M. ..... Kansas City, MO
Dibble, David ..... Oakland, CA
Dibble, David P. ..... Eureka, CA
Dibble, Francis D., Jr. ..... Springfield, MA
Dibble, Gerald W. ..... Rochester, NY
Dibble, John C. ..... Washington, DC
Dibble, Jonathan A. ..... Salt Lake City, UT
Dibble, Kevin Michael ..... New York, NY
Dibble Law Offices ..... Columbia, SC
Dibble, Leland H., Jr. ..... Santa Rosa, CA
Dibble & Miller, P.C. ..... Rochester, NY
Dibble, Oliver O. ..... Orlando, FL
Dibble, Robert W., Jr. ..... Columbia, SC
Dibble, Samuel C. ..... Los Angeles, CA
Dibble, Stephen J. ..... Dover, NH
Dibblee, Jack H. H. ..... Spokane, WA
Dibblee, Richard C. ..... Salt Lake City, UT
Dibbs, Jean-Charles ..... Miami, FL
Dibbs, Scott W. ..... Tampa, FL
DiBella, D. Randall ..... New Milford, CT
DiBella & Geer, P.C. ..... Pittsburgh, PA
Di Bella, John B. ..... New York, NY
Di Bella, John E. ..... Brooklyn, NY
Di Bella, Joseph ..... Arlington, VA
DiBella, Nicolas M. W. ..... Redding, CA
DiBella, Richard W. ..... Pittsburgh, PA
DiBella, Robert M. ..... White Plains, NY
DiBello, Darin A. ..... Miami, FL
DiBello, Lucille ..... New York, NY
DiBenedetto, Anthony R. ..... Chicago, IL
DiBenedetto, Daniel J. ..... Roseland, NJ
Di Benedetto, Dennis V. ..... Petersburg, WV
DiBenedetto, Donald S. ..... Syracuse, NY
Di Benedetto, Florence L.
Sacramento, CA
DiBenedetto, James L. ..... Lisle, IL
Di Benedetto, Joseph ..... San Pedro, CA
DiBenedetto, Joseph A. ..... New York, NY
DiBenedetto, Joseph C. ..... Pleasantville, NY
DiBenedetto, Joseph J.
Long Island City, NY
Di Benedetto, Joseph J.
Rockville Centre, NY
Di Benedetto, Richard K. ..... Whitestone, NY
DiBerardini-Albrecht, Danielle
Stamford, CT
DiBerardino, Philip J., Jr. ..... New York, NY
DiBernardi, John J., Jr. ..... Brooklyn, NY
DiBernardino, John ..... Lehighton, PA
DiBernardo, Fred J. ..... San Pedro, CA
DiBernardo, Ian G. ..... New York, NY
DiBernardo, Lisa M. ..... York, PA
DiBernardo, S. James ..... Palo Alto, CA
Dibert, Nickolas J. ..... Portland, OR
Dibert, Robert W. ..... Louisville, KY
Dibia, Ike Paul ..... Burtonsville, MD
Brooklyn, NY
Dibiaggio, Deirdre J. ..... Miami, FL
DiBiagio, Gladstone & Wilsman, LLC
Annapolis, MD
DiBiagio, Raymond E., Jr. ..... Annapolis, MD
DiBiagio-Wood, Elyse M.
Environmental Protection Agency,
Office of Enforcement and Compliance
Assurance, GV
DiBianco, Gary ..... Washington, DC
DiBianco, Gustave J. ..... Syracuse, NY
DiBiase, A. Joseph ..... Newburyport, MA
DiBiase, Bruna, Ms. ..... Bayside, NY
DiBiase, David T. ..... Los Angeles, CA
DiBiase, Michael ..... Providence, RI
DiBiase, Michael J., (P.C.)
Los Angeles, CA
Di Biase, Peter A. ..... Providence, RI
DiBiase, Peter A., Inc. ..... Providence, RI
Di Biase, Roberta ..... Brick, NJ
DiBiase, Thomas J. ..... Boston, MA
DiBiasi, Thomas S. ..... Nutley, NJ
Dibiaso, Nickolas J. ..... Fresno, CA
DiBiccaro, Robert A. ..... Boston, MA
Diblasi, Frank A ..... Buffalo, NY
DiBlasi, Gandolfo V. ..... New York, NY
DiBlasi, Jill Lynch ..... Buffalo, NY
Di Blasi, John, Jr. ..... Short Hills, NJ
Di Blasi, John P. ..... White Plains, NY
DiBlasi, Joseph P. ..... North Reading, MA
Di Blasi, Vincent A. ..... Brooklyn, NY
DiBlasio, Henry A. ..... Youngstown, OH
DiBlasio, William J. ..... Browns Mills, NJ
Dible, Jeffrey S. ..... Indianapolis, IN
Dibler, Dennis E., (P.C.) ..... Grandview, MO
Dibler, Lindsay A. ..... St. Louis, MO
Dibley, Allison M. ..... Minneapolis, MN
Dibling, Wilburn C., Jr. ..... Roanoke, VA
DiBoise, James A. ..... Palo Alto, CA
DiBoise, Sarah J. ..... Burlingame, CA
DiBona, Caroline A.
Environmental Protection Agency,
Office of Enforcement and Compliance
Assurance, GV
DiBona, Peter D. ..... Brooklyn, NY
DiBonaventura, Stephen ..... Philadelphia, PA
DiBonaventura, Victoria L. ..... Paris, TN
Dibrell, Chas G., Jr. ..... Galveston, TX
Dibrell, Cooper G. ..... San Antonio, TX
Dibrell, Dotson, Dibrell & Dibrell
San Antonio, TX
Dibrell, E. Walter ..... San Antonio, TX
Dibrell, George E. ..... Port Arthur, TX
Dibrell, Joe B., Jr. ..... Austin, TX
Dibrell, Joseph B., Jr. ..... Seguin, TX
Dibrell, Samuel D. ..... San Antonio, TX
Dibrell, Will W. ..... Austin, TX
DiBrigida, Joseph A., Jr. ..... Manchester, NH
Dibsie, Gregory C. ..... Cherry Hill, NJ
DiBuono, Anthony J. ..... Marlborough, MA
Di Buono, V. William ..... Bridgewater, NJ
DiCalvo, Al A. ..... Miami, FL
DiCamillo, Angelo J. ..... Camden, NJ
Di Camillo, Joseph G. ..... Chicago, IL
DiCamillo, Margrit Mary ..... Niagara Falls, NY
DiCamillo, Raymond J. ..... Wilmington, DE
Dicanio, Jack P. ..... Los Angeles, CA
Di Canio, Michael J. ..... Glendale Heights, IL
Di Capo, Baldassaro (Bill)
Sacramento, CA
Di Caprio, Anthony J., Jr. ..... Syracuse, NY
DiCaprio, Anthony P. ..... Syracuse, NY
Di Caprio & Di Caprio ..... Syracuse, NY
Dicaprio, Joseph A. ..... Rockford, IL
DiCaprio, Patrick T. ..... Merrick, NY
DiCaprio-Lee, Lori A. ..... Westlake Village, CA
DiCara, Lawrence S., (P.C.) ..... Boston, MA
DiCara, Mark Michael ..... Barrington, IL
DiCara, Phyllis M. ..... Rocky Hill, CT
DiCarlantonio, Pamela S. ..... Chicago, IL
DiCarlo, Dana M. ..... Washington, DC
DiCarlo, David Jon ..... Washington, PA
DiCarlo, Denise ..... Revere, MA
DiCarlo, Donald P. ..... Philadelphia, PA
DiCarlo, Gregory C. ..... Moorestown, NJ
Philadelphia, PA
DiCarlo, Gregory G. ..... Old Greenwich, CT
White Plains, NY
DiCarlo, Joseph W. ..... Revere, MA
DiCarlo, Louis D. ..... White Plains, NY
Di Carlo, Mark A. ..... Corpus Christi, TX
DiCarlo, Mary C. ..... Boston, MA
DiCarlo, Nicholas J. ..... Phoenix, AZ
DiCarlo, Patrick C. ..... Atlanta, GA
DiCarlo, Vincent, Law Office of
Sacramento, CA
DiCarlo, Wayne R. ..... Boston, MA
DiCaro, John M. ..... Phoenix, AZ
DiCaro, John R. ..... San Diego, CA
Santa Ana, CA
DiCaro Nield & Coppo ..... San Diego, CA
Santa Ana, CA
Di Castri, Andrea ..... Benton Harbor, MI
DiCastri, Damon ..... Chicago, IL
DiCastri, Frank W. ..... Chicago, IL
Di Cato, Edward M. ..... Akron, OH
Dicce, Marie F. ..... Margate, FL
Dicce, Peter W. ..... Media, PA
Dicdican, Leonor Y. ..... Atlanta, GA
Dice, Bruce E. ..... Pittsburgh, PA
Dice, Denis C. ..... Philadelphia, PA
Dice, Eugene E. ..... Harrisburg, PA
Dice, Frank W. ..... Salinas, CA
Dice, Joseph S. ..... Tuscaloosa, AL
Dice, Karen N. ..... Tuscaloosa, AL
Dice, Michael R., and Company, L.L.C.
Denver, CO
Dice, Richard A. ..... Cheshire, CT
DiCecco, Fant & Burman, L.L.P.
Houston, TX
DiCecco, Joseph W. ..... Houston, TX
Dicecco, Peter M. ..... Burbank, CA
DiCeglio, Gary M. ..... Akron, OH
Dice-Goldberg, Bert ..... Newark, NJ
Dicello, Francis P. ..... Washington, DC
DiCello, Robert J. ..... Mentor, OH
DiCello, Robert J., Co., L.P.A. ..... Mentor, OH
Dicembre, Michael D. ..... Orlando, FL
DiCenso, David J. ..... Lincoln, ME
San Antonio, TX
Di Censo, Gregory V. ..... Troy, MI
Dicenzo, Frank D., Jr. ..... Pittsburgh, PA
DiCenzo, Nancy P. ..... Sacramento, CA
DiCerbo, Nicholas A. ..... Olean, NY
DiCerbo & Palumbo ..... Olean, NY
Di Cesare & Behle, LLP ..... Costa Mesa, CA
Di Cesare, Davidson & Barker, P.A.
Lakeland, FL
DiCesare, Francis J. ..... Cincinnati, OH
Di Cesare, James J. ..... Costa Mesa, CA
Di Cesare, Joseph ..... New York, NY
DiCesare, Pat T., II ..... Lakeland, FL
Di Cesare, Thor D. ..... Reading, PA
DiCesare, Thor Dominic ..... Canonsburg, PA
Dicey, James E., Jr. ..... Portland, OR
Dicharry, Christopher J.
Baton Rouge, LA
Dicharry, Gregory ..... New Orleans, LA
Dicharry, Guy ..... Albuquerque, NM
Dicharry, Paul O. ..... New Orleans, LA
Dicharry, Richard N. ..... New Orleans, LA
Dichele, Ernest Michael ..... Orange, CT
DiChiara, Anthony P. ..... Palo Alto, CA
DiChiara, Donna M.
West Palm Beach, FL
Di Chiara, Douglas M. ..... Essex Fells, NJ
Di Chiara, Gerald J. ..... New York, NY
DiChiara, John B. ..... Fort Lauderdale, FL
Di Chiara, Laura ..... New York, NY
DiChiara, Michael ..... Cambridge, MA
DiChiara, Peter ..... New York, NY
Dichiara, Peter M. ..... Boston, MA
DiChiara, Richard, Jr. ..... Bethlehem, PA
DiChiara, Thomas J. ..... Red Bank, NJ
DiChiaro, Joseph, Jr. ..... Derry, NH
DiChiaro, Michael ..... Chestnut Ridge, NY
DiChiro, Patrick ..... Cleveland, OH
Dichner, Ellen ..... New York, NY
Dicht, Stephen P. ..... Gibbsboro, NJ
Philadelphia, PA
Dichter, Arthur J. ..... Miami, FL
Dichter, Barry J. ..... New York, NY
Dichter, Eric ..... Valley Forge, PA
Dichter, Fredric R. ..... Milwaukee, WI
Dichter, Harold B. ..... New York, NY
Dichter, Joel R. ..... New York, NY
Dichter, Mark S. ..... Philadelphia, PA
Dichter, Philip J. ..... Beverly Hills, CA
Dichter, Spector & Karpel
Beverly Hills, CA
Dichter, Stephen M. ..... Phoenix, AZ
Dichtl, Ralph L. ..... Wheaton, IL
Diciaccio, Angela Monica ..... Boston, MA
DiCianni, Thomas G. ..... Chicago, IL
DiCianni, Vincent L. ..... Boston, MA
DiCianno, Adrian C. ..... Washington, DC
DiCicco, Bruce M. ..... New York, NY
DiCicco, David R. ..... Boston, MA
DiCicco, Debra A. ..... Brooklyn, NY
DiCicco, Diane Marie ..... Boston, MA
Di Cicco, Jessica R. ..... Baltimore, MD
DiCicco, John A. ..... Department of Justice,
Tax Division, GV
DiCicco, Joseph M. ..... Newark, NJ
Di Cicco, Leslie B. ..... Worcester, MA
DiCicco, Margaret C. ..... Stratford, CT
DiCicco, Michael M. ..... Lakewood, NJ
DiCicco, Richard D. ..... Wickliffe, OH
DiCicco, Robert A. ..... Towson, MD
DiCicco, Robin A. ..... Southfield, MI
DiCicco, Susan Felice ..... New York, NY
Dicig, Mary E. ..... Chicago, IL
DiCindio, William J. ..... South Plainfield, NJ
DiCintio, Timothy J. ..... Washington, DC
Di Cioccio, Stephen J. ..... New York, NY
DiCioccio, Vincent S. ..... Philadelphia, PA
DiCiurcio, William T. ..... Cherry Hill, NJ
Dick, Adam ..... New York, NY
Dick, Allen C. ..... Northbrook, IL
Dick, Anthony S., (A Law Corporation)
Sacramento, CA
Dick, Arlene R. ..... Washington, DC
Dick, Bernard E. ..... Medina, OH
Dick, Brett R. ..... San Francisco, CA
Dick, Bruce E. ..... Bellevue, WA
Dick, Carol J. ..... St. Louis, MO
Dick, Carolyn ..... Albany, NY
Dick, Cathleen H. ..... New York, NY
Dick, Charles ..... Boston, MA
Dick, Charles H., Jr. ..... San Diego, CA
Dick, Daniel R. ..... Rochester, NY
Dick, David ..... Oklahoma City, OK
Dick, David A. ..... St. Louis, MO
Dick, David E. ..... Morgantown, WV
Dick & Dick ..... The Dalles, OR
Dick, Donald J. ..... Berrien Springs, MI
Dick, Douglas P. ..... Washington, DC
Dick, Edison Warner ..... Washington, DC

Dick, Eric S. ... Augusta, ME
Dick, Geo. F., III ... Bloomington, IL
Dick, Geoffrey C. ... Gastonia, NC
Dick & Hague, Ltd. ... Johnston, RI
Dick and Harris ... Chicago, IL
Dick, Hemmer & Wagner
Sacramento, CA
Dick, Henry N., III ... Biloxi, MS
Dick, Ilene ... San Francisco, CA
Dick, James V. ... Washington, DC
Dick, Jerome J. ... Washington, DC
Dick, Jerry, (A Professional Corporation)
Oklahoma City, OK
Dick, Jerry W. ... Woodward, OK
Dick, Joel S. ... Winter Park, FL
Dick, John C. ... Evanston, IL
Dick, John H. ... Chandler, AZ
Dick, John M. ... San Francisco, CA
Dick, John R. ... Longview, WA
Dick, Karen J. ... Tyler, TX
Dick, Kathleen R. ... Albany, NY
Dick, Kenneth E. ... St. Louis, MO
Dick, L. Mitchell ... McLean, VA
Dick, Lawrence ... New York, NY
Dick, Lenore D. ... Herndon, VA
Dick, Lynne Bice ... Monroe, LA
Dick, Michael J. ... Ithaca, NY
Dick, Norman C. ... Longview, WA
Dick, Patricia Alyn Macke ... Hutchinson, KS
Dick, Paul Anthony, Jr. ... Canton, OH
Dick, Paul C. ... Bedford, MA
Dick, Paul C., Prof. Corp., Law Offices of
Bedford, MA
Dick, Paul K. ... Jacksonville, FL
Dick, Randall G. ... San Francisco, CA
Dick, Rebecca P. ... Department of Justice, Antitrust Division, GV
Dick, Richard E. ... Huntsville, AL
Dick, Richard Eugene ... Chicago, IL
Dick, Richard J. ... Indianapolis, IN
Dick, Robert N. ... Tulsa, OK
Dick, Robert P. ... Tacoma, WA
Dick, Roger L. ... The Dalles, OR
Dick, Ronald L. ... Sacramento, CA
Dick, Sam W. ... Sugar Land, TX
Dick, Sandra Y. ... Newark, NJ
Dick, Shelly D. ... Baton Rouge, LA
Dick, Sheryl L. ... Prairie Village, KS
Dick, Steven I. ... Santa Cruz, CA
Dick, Steven K. ... Indianapolis, IN
Dick, Terese M. ... Milwaukee, WI
Dick, Terry S. ... St. Paul, MN
Dick, Thomas E. ... Anniston, AL
Dick, Thomas S. ... Washington, DC
Dick, Trafford ... Zanesville, OH
Dick, William C. ... Orlando, FL
Dick, William G., II ... The Dalles, OR
Dick, William J. ... West Palm Beach, FL
Dick, William J. ... Emporia, KS
Dick, William M. ... Northfield, OH
Dick, William S. ... Greencastle, PA
Waynesboro, PA
Dickard, P. David ... Denver, CO
Dickas, William D. ... Portland, OR
Dickason, Oren E. ... Lima, OH
Dicke, Billig & Czaja, P.A.
Minneapolis, MN
Dicke, Diane D. ... Slidell, LA
Dicke, John A. ... Golden, CO
Dicke, Karen M. ... New Orleans, LA
Dicke, Kristine L. ... Rochester, MN
Dicke, Lowell M. ... Palo Alto, CA
Dicke, Michael S. ... San Francisco, CA
Dicke, Patricia A. ... Vienna, VA
Dicke, Richard M. ... New York, NY
Dicke, Stephen P. ... Washington, DC
Dicke, Steven E. ... Minneapolis, MN
Dickel, Marion Stanwood ... Chicago, IL
Dickel, Morris ... Crookston, MN
Dickel, Ronald D. ... Chicago, IL
Dickel, William M. ... Wayzata, MN
Dickelman, Robert E. ... Scottsdale, AZ
Dicken, Buddy M. ... Sherman, TX
Dickens, Albert, Jr. ... Jackson, MS
Dickens, Angelia M. ... New York, NY
Dickens, Benjamin H., Jr.
Washington, DC
Dickens, David ... Eugene, OR
Dickens, Dorrance D. ... Washington, DC
Dickens, G. Lee, Jr. ... Milledgeville, GA
Dickens, Gordon S. ... Rochester, NY
Dickens, Grady P. ... Dallas, TX
Dickens, J. Pink ... Mason, TX
Dickens, James A. ... Greensboro, NC
Dickens, James R., P.C. ... Seattle, WA
Dickens, Jennifer Ransbottom
Huntington, WV
Dickens, Jeremy W. ... New York, NY
Dallas, TX
Dickens, John A. ... Milwaukee, WI
Dickens, John F. ... Melrose Park, IL
Dickens, Julie E. ... Seattle, WA
Dickens, Lynette C. ... Cheverly, MD
Dickens, Marie T. ... Costa Mesa, CA
Dickens, Mary C. ... New York, NY
Dickens, Peter B. ... Austin, TX
Dickens, Raymond A., Jr. ... Houston, TX
Dickens, Royce L.
Federal Communications Commission, Cable Services Bureau, GV
Dickens, Scott T. ... Louisville, KY
Dickens, Theresa McCarthy ... Durham, NC
Dickens, William F., Jr.
Roanoke Rapids, NC
Dickens Dean, Donna Lisa ... Louisville, KY
Dickensheid, Diane M. ... New York, NY
Dickenson, Bob ... Eastland, TX
Dickenson, Charles H. ... Napa, CA
Dickenson, Daniel D., III ... Norfolk, VA
Dickenson, David B. ... Boca Raton, FL
Dickenson, Gregory B., (P.A.) ... Jupiter, FL
Dickenson, Howard G. ... Napa, CA
Dickenson, Jennifer L. ... Atlanta, GA
Dickenson, Murdoch, Rex and Sloan, Chartered ... Boca Raton, FL
Dickenson, Nancy C. ... Lebanon, VA
Dickenson, Peatman & Fogarty, A Professional Law Corporation ... Napa, CA
Dickenson, Scott J. ... St. Louis, MO
Dickenson, Thomas B. ... Roanoke, VA
Dickenson, Thomas H. ... Knoxville, TN
Dicker, Brian S. ... Culver City, CA
Dicker, Clifford S. ... Culver City, CA
Dicker, David H. ... Encino, CA
Dicker, David J. ... Chicago, IL
Dicker & Dicker ... Encino, CA
Dicker & Dicker ... Chicago, IL
Dicker, E. Carolyn Hochstadter
Philadelphia, PA
Dicker, Edward A. ... West Palm Beach, FL
Dicker, Eli Jay ... Miami, FL
Dicker, Eric S. ... Kenilworth, NJ
Dicker, Gary H. ... Columbus, OH
Dicker, Gerald R. ... Wayland, MA
Dicker, Herbert ... New York, NY
Dicker, Howard B. ... New York, NY
Dicker, Howard W. ... Encino, CA
Dicker, Joanne Pyes ... Chicago, IL
Dicker, Joshua ... New York, NY
Dicker, Kevin S. ... Beverly Hills, CA
Dicker, Lawrence D. ... Bronx, NY
Dicker, Lee T., (A Professional Corporation)
Beverly Hills, CA
Dicker, Marvin ... New York, NY
Dicker, Morton B. ... New York, NY
Dicker, Ross T. ... Washington, DC
Dicker, Ruth ... Jacksonville, FL
Dicker, Stephen W. ... New York, NY
Dicker, Steven Michael ... Chicago, IL
Dickerman & Bayne ... Los Angeles, CA
Dickerman, Donald E. ... Tucson, AZ
Dickerman, Dorothea W. ... Washington, DC
Dickerman, George F. ... Riverside, CA
Dickerman, James E. ... Baltimore, MD
Dickerman, John M. ... Washington, DC
Dickerman, Lola ... Boston, MA
Dickerman, Stephen G. ... New York, NY
Dickerman, William ... Los Angeles, CA
Dickerson, Anne E. ... Chicago, IL
Dickerson, Barbara J. ... Lubbock, TX
Dickerson, Barry C. ... Mesa, AZ
Dickerson, Billy R. ... Houston, TX
Dickerson, Bradley H. ... Breckenridge, CO
Dickerson, Brett L. ... Modesto, CA
Dickerson, Brian C. ... Vincennes, IN
Dickerson, Brian E. ... Columbus, OH
Dickerson, Butler, Rabb & Rodriquez, P.C.
Tucson, AZ
Dickerson, C. David ... Sacramento, CA
Dickerson, Catherine A. ... Houston, TX
Dickerson, Charles C. ... Carthage, TX
Dickerson, Charles E., III ... Arcadia, CA
Dickerson, Chris L. ... Chicago, IL
Dickerson, Claire Taylor ... Jackson, MS
Dickerson, Claudia W. ... Nashville, TN
Dickerson, Colleen Treacy
Virginia Beach, VA
Dickerson, Daniel L. ... Florence, KY
Dickerson, David D. ... Virginia Beach, VA
Dickerson, David M. ... Whittier, CA
Dickerson, David W. ... Scottsdale, AZ
Dickerson, Debra Jean ... Cambridge, MA
Dickerson, Denise A. ... Cleveland, OH
Dickerson, Dickerson, Consul & Pocker
Las Vegas, NV
Dickerson, Donald D. ... Irvine, CA
Dickerson, Donald G. ... Cookeville, TN
Dickerson, Donald H. ... Marshall, MI
Dickerson, Donald L.
Cape Girardeau, MO
Dickerson, Donald R. ... Hillsborough, NC
Dickerson, Donald R., P.A. ... Durham, NC
Graham, NC
Hillsborough, NC
Raleigh, NC
Dickerson, Dwight E. ... Oakland, CA
Dickerson, Elizabeth Brinkley
Washington, DC
Dickerson, Francis L. ... Bardstown, KY
Dickerson, Frank S., III ... Tulsa, OK
Dickerson, George M. ... Las Vegas, NV
Dickerson, George T. ... Waynesboro, MS
Dickerson, Glen M. ... San Jose, CA
Dickerson, Harry Ashby ... Abingdon, VA
Dickerson, Henry P., III ... Staunton, VA
Dickerson, Henry R., Jr. ... Corvallis, OR
Dickerson, Jack W.
Hot Springs National Park, AR
Dickerson, Jaffe D. ... Los Angeles, CA
Dickerson, James H., Jr. ... Freeport, TX
Dickerson, Jeffrey A. ... Atlanta, GA
Dickerson, Jeffrey A. ... Las Vegas, NV
Dickerson, Jeffrey A. ... Reno, NV
Dickerson, Jeffrey S. ... Corpus Christi, TX
Dickerson, Jill Conley ... Farmville, VA
Dickerson, John A. ... Toccoa, GA
Dickerson, John C., III ... Bay City, TX
Dickerson, John G. ... Houston, TX
Dickerson, John J. ... Lutherville, MD
Dickerson, John K. ... Dearborn, MI
Dickerson, Joseph B., Jr. ... St. Louis, MO
Dickerson, Joseph Michael ... Laredo, TX
Dickerson, Joy Edna Margaret
Laguna Beach, CA
Dickerson, K. Alex ... New York, NY
Dickerson, Kenneth M. ... San Carlos, CA
Dickerson, Kenneth R. ... Los Angeles, CA
Dickerson, Kenneth W. ... El Reno, OK
Dickerson, L. Clifton, III ... Lockport, LA
Dickerson, M. Ashley, (Mrs.)
Anchorage, AK
Dickerson, M. Joseph ... Brandon, FL
Dickerson, Mark S. ... Phoenix, AZ
Dickerson, Mary A. ... Camdenton, MO
Dickerson, Mary Irene ... Macon, GA
Dickerson, Norvin K., III ... Charlotte, NC
Dickerson, Onnie D., III ... Birmingham, AL
Dickerson, Paul ... Houston, TX
Dickerson, Paul L. ... Texarkana, TX
Dickerson & Reilly ... New York, NY
Dickerson, Rice, Spaeth, Heisserer, Summers & Remley, L.C. ... Cape Girardeau, MO
Dickerson, Richard W. ... Pueblo, CO
Dickerson, Robert C., II ... Seattle, WA
Dickerson, Robert P. ... Las Vegas, NV
Dickerson, Robert W. ... Los Angeles, CA
Dickerson, Robert W. ... Winston-Salem, NC
Dickerson, Robert W. B., A Professional Corporation ... Houston, TX
Dickerson, Robert W.B. ... Houston, TX
Dickerson, Roger K. ... Prairie Village, KS
Dickerson, Ruth L. ... Moraga, CA
Dickerson, Stefnee Ashlock ... Houston, TX
Dickerson, Stephen G. ... Kansas City, KS
Dickerson, Steven L. ... Addison, TX
Dickerson, Steven L. ... Dallas, TX
Dickerson, Susanne E. ... Akron, OH
Dickerson, Thomas A. ... Yonkers, NY
Dickerson, Thomas P.
Environmental Protection Agency, Office of Congressional and Legislative Affairs, GV
Dickerson, Thomas P. ... New York, NY
Dickerson, Timothy B. ... Sierra Vista, AZ
Dickerson, Vernon F. ... Tucson, AZ
Dickerson, W. Brinkley, Jr. ... Atlanta, GA
Dickerson, William M. ... Coatesville, PA
Dickerson, William M. ... Philadelphia, PA
Dickert, C. Stewart ... South Salem, NY
Dickert, Don C. ... Brundidge, AL
Dickert, Linda K. ... Nashville, TN
Dickert, Neal W. ... Augusta, GA
Dickert, Robert B. ... Bristol, VA
Dickert, Sheila E. ... Philadelphia, PA
Dickes, Don D. ... Canton, OH
Dickett, Diane M. ... Chicago, IL
Dickett, Gust W. ... Chicago, IL
Dickett, James E. ... Chicago, IL
Dickett, William G. ... Chicago, IL
Dickey, Alan A. ... Sanford, FL
Dickey, Alan T. ... Dallas, TX
Dickey, Andrew C. ... Springfield, MA
Dickey, Audrey F. ... Milpitas, CA
Dickey, Barbara B. ... Berkeley, CA
Dickey, Bill ... Tampa, FL
Dickey, Carol D. ... Fayetteville, NC
Dickey, Charles R. ... New York, NY
Dickey, Clayton E. ... Kansas City, MO
Dickey, D. Pittman ... Fayetteville, NC
Dickey, Darryl O. ... Los Angeles, CA
Dickey, David C. ... Stanardsville, VA
Dickey, David Dallas ... Tampa, FL
Dickey, David H. ... Savannah, GA
Dickey, David R.
Federal Energy Regulatory Commission, Office of the General Counsel, GV
Dickey, David R. ... Oklahoma City, OK
Dickey, David S. ... Berlin, PA
Dickey, Denise A. ... Santa Barbara, CA
Dickey & Dickey ... Oklahoma City, OK
Dickey, Don A. ... Salem, OR
Dickey, Edward A. ... Little Rock, AR
Dickey, Everett W. ... Newport Beach, CA
Dickey, Frank C., Jr. ... San Angelo, TX
Dickey, Frank E., Jr. ... Kingman, AZ
Dickey, Frank G., Jr. ... Lexington, KY
Dickey, Gene A. ... Brea, CA
Dickey, Gordon J.
United States Information Agency, Office of the General Counsel, GV
Dickey, H. Eldridge, Jr. ... Fort Worth, TX
Dickey, Harrison G. ... Tucson, AZ
Dickey, J. Charles ... Sunnyvale, CA
Dickey, Jack W. ... Thomas, OK
Dickey, James R. C. ... Miami, FL
Dickey, Jay W., Jr. ... Pine Bluff, AR
Dickey, Jeanne Henderson ... Anchorage, AK
Dickey, Jeffrey S. ... Westfield, NJ
Dickey, John C. ... Dallas, TX
Dickey, John F. ... Wilmington, DE
Dickey, John M. ... El Paso, TX
Dickey, John P. ... Jackson, MI
Dickey, John W. ... New York, NY
Dickey, Jonathan C. ... Palo Alto, CA
Dickey, Joshua M. ... Las Vegas, NV
Dickey, Kathryn ... Montgomery, AL
Dickey, M. Jane ... Little Rock, AR
Dickey, Mark D. ... San Diego, CA
Dickey, Martha L. ... Washington, DC
Dickey, Michael P. ... Panama City, FL
Dickey, Patricia B. ... Norfolk, VA
Dickey, Patricia L. ... Toledo, OH
Dickey, Perry J. ... Bartlesville, OK
Dickey, Phillip A. ... Oklahoma City, OK
Dickey, Richard D. ... Wadsworth, OH
Dickey, Robert B. ... Keokuk, IA
Dickey, Robert E., Jr. ... Reno, NV
Dickey, Robert R. ... Medford, OR
Dickey, Robert R., Jr. ... Medford, OR
Dickey, Robert W. ... Louisville, KY
Dickey, Robert W. ... New York, NY
Dickey, Roger V. ... McKinney, TX
Dickey, Sam ... Springfield, MO
Dickey, Smith, Kultala and Boddicker
Keokuk, IA
Dickey, Steven M. ... Oklahoma City, OK
Dickey, Steven T. ... Newark, NJ
Dickey, Sue A. ... Olathe, KS
Dickey, Thomas A. ... Indianapolis, IN
Dickey, Thomas J. ... Saint Simons Island, GA
Dickey, Thomas M. ... Altoona, PA
Hollidaysburg, PA
Dickey, Todd R. ... Los Angeles, CA
Dickey, Trent S. ... Newark, NJ
New York, NY
Dickey, Valerie L. ... Houston, TX
Dickey, Victoria B. ... Sebastopol, CA
Dickey, Walter J. ... Madison, WI
Dickey, Walter M. ... Kansas City, MO
Dickey, Wayne ... Waco, TX
Dickey, Will G. ... Houston, TX
Dickey, William H., Jr. ... Charlottesville, VA
Dickey, William K. ... Collingswood, NJ
Dickey, William R. ... Largo, FL
Dickey, Wm. Robert ... Seminole, FL
Dickey-Tomlinson, Margaret L.
Washington, DC
Dickgrafe, Sharon L. ... Wichita, KS
Dick-Greenstein, Michelle ... Miami, FL
Dickhaner, Ray ... Hillsboro, MO
Dickhaus, Beth A. ... Denver, CO
Dickhaus, Karl W. ... St. Louis, MO
Dick-Hurwitz, Rebecca J. ... Pittsburgh, PA
Dickhute, Mark S. ... Omaha, NE
Dickie, Dean A. ... Chicago, IL
Dickie, Jess C. ... Amarillo, TX
Dickie, Lawrence F. ... Purchase, NY
Dickie, Martha S. ... Austin, TX
Dickie, McCamey & Chilcote
Wheeling, WV
Pittsburgh, PA
Dickie, Robert B. ... Weston, MA
Dickie, Robert Q. ... St. Paul, MN
Dickie, Walter M., Jr. ... Oakland, CA
Dickie, William A. ... Seekonk, MA
Providence, RI
Dickieson, David H. ... Washington, DC
Dickinson & Abel, A Professional Corporation
Indianapolis, IN
Dickinson, Albert W. ... Scituate, MA
Dickinson, Amy B. ... Kansas City, MO
Dickinson, Andrew D. ... Boulder, CO
Denver, CO
Chicago, IL
Dickinson, Anne W. ... Conway, NH
Dickinson, Arthur W. ... Minnetonka, MN
Dickinson & Associates
Rancho Santa Margarita, CA
Dickinson, Benjamin L. ... Glasgow, KY
Dickinson, Breese M. ... Hagerstown, MD
Dickinson, Bruce Scott ... Las Vegas, NV
Dickinson, Calhoun ... Seattle, WA
Dickinson, Charles B., Jr. ... Laredo, TX
Dickinson, Chris J. ... Everett, WA
Dickinson, Christopher C. ... Chicago, IL
Dickinson, Clair E. ... Akron, OH
Dickinson, Clayton R. ... Tacoma, WA
Dickinson, Curtis J. ... Indianapolis, IN
Dickinson, D. Bradley, (P.C.) ... Dallas, TX
Dickinson, Dan ... Kansas City, MO
Dickinson, Daniel S., III ... Watertown, NY
Dickinson, Daniel W., Jr. ... Wheeling, WV
Dickinson, Danl. S., Jr. ... Binghamton, NY
Dickinson, David B. ... Houston, TX
Dickinson, David F. ... Monroe, GA
Dickinson, David J. ... Millburn, NJ
Dickinson, David L. ... Durango, CO
Dickinson, Debbie A. ... Atlanta, GA
Dickinson, Deborah Kane ... Concord, NH
Dickinson, Dena C. ... Siloam Springs, AR
Dickinson, Derek ... Washington, DC
Dickinson, Donald R. ... Aurora, IL
Dickinson, Douglas ... Burbank, CA
Dickinson, Dwight ... Washington, DC
Dickinson, Elizabeth C. ... Memphis, TN
Dickinson, Elizabeth H. ... Rockville, MD
Dickinson, Elizabeth Morison ... Madison, CT
Dickinson, Emily D. ... Scarborough, ME
Dickinson, Eugene B. ... Burbank, CA
Dickinson, Eugene B., Inc. ... Burbank, CA
Dickinson, Everstine & Prud'Homme
Denver, CO
Dickinson, Floyd M. ... Richmond, VA
Dickinson, Frank H., III ... Baton Rouge, LA
Dickinson, Frank P. ... Gunnison, CO
Dickinson, Fred A. ... Carmel, NY
Dickinson, Georgett B. ... Atlanta, GA
Dickinson, Gerald, Jr. ... West Memphis, AR
Dickinson & Gibbons, P.A. ... Sarasota, FL
Dickinson, Gilbert A. ... Denver, CO
Dickinson, Glenn J. ... Oxnard, CA
Dickinson, Greg A. ... Des Moines, IA
Dickinson, Henry H. ... Louisville, KY
Dickinson, H. T. ... Sweet Home, AR
Dickinson, James B. ... Mound, MN
Dickinson, James G. ... Cleveland, OH
Dickinson, James L. ... Frankfort, KY
Dickinson, Jane T. ... Jacksonville, FL
Dickinson, Jess H. ... Gulfport, MS
Dickinson, Jo Ann A. ... Yankton, SD
Dickinson, JoAnne Walton
Wichita Falls, TX
Dickinson, John C. ... Birmingham, MI
Dickinson, John E. ... Buffalo, NY
Dickinson, John E. ... Houston, TX
Dickinson, John F. ... Jacksonville, FL
Tampa, FL
Dickinson, John F., Jr. ... Trenton, NJ
Dickinson, John J. ... New York, NY
Dickinson, Jon M. ... Palo Alto, CA
Portland, OR

Dickinson, Joseph A. ... Concord, NH
Dickinson, Judith A. ... Norcross, GA
Dickinson, Judith R. ... Milwaukee, WI
Dickinson, Katherine J. ... Berwyn, PA
Dickinson, Kelly Leigh ... Jacksonville, FL
Dickinson, Kenneth L., (P.C.) Richmond, VA
Dickinson, Kimberly J. ... West Chester, PA
Dickinson, L. Eugene ... Charleston, WV
Dickinson Landmeier LLP Washington, DC
Dickinson, Laurence Mason Fredericksburg, VA
Dickinson, Lisa M. ... Department of Justice, United States Marshals Service, GV
Dickinson, Lloyd J. ... Milwaukee, WI
Dickinson, Lynn T. Commission on Civil Rights, Office of the General Counsel, GV
Dickinson, Mackaman, Tyler & Hagen, P.C. Des Moines, IA
Dickinson, Mark C. ... Des Moines, IA
Dickinson, Martin B., Jr. ... Lawrence, KS
Dickinson, Marty Joe ... Newton, KS
Dickinson & Mixson ... Monroe, GA
Dickinson, Nancy ... Boulder, CO
Dickinson, Patrick H. ... Sarasota, FL
Dickinson, Paul R., Jr. ... Charlotte, NC
Dickinson, Paula ... Andover, MA
Dickinson, Peter S. ... Burbank, CA
Dickinson, Philip C. ... Grosse Pointe Park, MI
Dickinson, Philip D. ... St. Petersburg, FL
Dickinson, Q. Todd Department of Commerce, Patent and Trademark Office, GV
Dickinson, Richard H., Jr. ... Cleveland, OH
Dickinson, Richard J. ... Columbus, OH
Dickinson, Robert A. ... Englewood, FL
Dickinson, Robert C., III ... Palm Harbor, FL
Dickinson, Robert C., III, P.A. Palm Harbor, FL
Dickinson, Robert E. ... East Falmouth, MA
Dickinson, Robert G. ... Eugene, OR
Dickinson, Roger ... Sacramento, CA
Dickinson, Roy L. ... Franklin, IN
Dickinson, Roy L. ... Indianapolis, IN
Dickinson, Sarah R. ... Ridgway, PA
Dickinson, Scott D. ... Atlanta, GA
Dickinson, Scott J. ... Laguna Hills, CA
Dickinson, Sheryl L. ... Tampa, FL
Dickinson, Steven J. ... Des Moines, IA
Dickinson, Steven L. Rancho Santa Margarita, CA
Dickinson, Steven M. ... Seattle, WA
Dickinson, Suetta W. ... Frankfort, KY
Dickinson, Susan Brooks Rocky River, OH
Dickinson, Susan H. ... Richmond, VA
Dickinson, Susan S. ... Grand Rapids, MI
Dickinson, Temple ... Glasgow, KY
Dickinson, Thomas A. ... Houston, TX
Dickinson, Thomas M., Jr. ... Winchester, VA
Dickinson, Thomas More ... Providence, RI
Dickinson, Thomas W. ... Charlotte, NC
Dickinson, Timothy L. ... Washington, DC
Dickinson, Todd R. ... Grand Rapids, MI
Dickinson, W. Gordon ... Roswell, NM
Dickinson, W. A. ... Roanoke, VA
Dickinson, Walter M. ... Little Rock, AR
Dickinson, Wheelock, Smith & Cerasuolo, P.C. ... Houston, TX
Dickinson, William B. ... Norwalk, CT
Dickinson, William C. ... Washington, DC
Dickinson, William W., Jr. ... Wallingford, CT
Dickinson Wright PLLC ... Washington, DC
Ann Arbor, MI
Bloomfield Hills, MI
Detroit, MI
Flint, MI
Grand Rapids, MI
Lansing, MI
Pontiac, MI
Dickison, Gregory C. ... Moscow, ID
Dickison, J. Mark ... Boston, MA
Dickler, Gerald ... New York, NY
Dickler, Marshall N. ... Arlington Heights, IL
Dickler, Marshall N., Ltd. Arlington Heights, IL
Dickler, Richard ... New York, NY
Dickman, Barry ... Hackensack, NJ
New York, NY
Dickman, Bruce A. ... Chicago, IL
Dickman, Charles H. ... Helena, MT
Dickman, Claudia ... San Francisco, CA
Dickman, David G. ... Washington, DC
Dickman, Don B. ... Corvallis, OR
Dickman, G. Emerson, III ... Maywood, NJ
Dickman, H. Brunner ... Cincinnati, OH
Dickman & Holt ... Riverside, CA
Dickman, Irwin L. ... New York, NY
Dickman, J. Jerry ... Tulsa, OK
Dickman, Jacquelyn S. ... Columbia, SC
Dickman, James L. ... Zanesville, OH
Dickman, Janis Y. ... Atlanta, GA
Dickman, John G. ... Riverside, CA
Dickman, John M. ... Chicago, IL
Dickman, Judith A. ... Oakland, CA
Dickman, K. Eric ... Seattle, WA
Dickman, Marjorie J. ... Washington, DC
Dickman, Martin J. ... Chicago, IL
Dickman, Mary M. ... New York, NY
Dickman, Michael ... Santa Fe, NM
Dickman, Michael B. ... Rockville, MD
Dickman, Michael J. ... Chicago, IL
Dickman, Norbert J. ... Larkspur, CA
Dickman, Robert H. ... Philadelphia, PA
Dickman, Robert J. ... Miami, FL
Dickman, Robert J., P.A. ... Miami, FL
Dickman, Sherry C. ... Miami, FL
Miami, FL
Dickman, Sherry C., P.A., Law Offices of Miami, FL
Dickman, Stephen C. ... Austin, TX
Dickman, Steven M. ... Los Angeles, CA
Dickman, Toby Lynn ... Lansdale, PA
Dickmann, Charles H. ... Anderson, IN
Dickmann, David R. ... Stevens Point, WI
Dickmann, John P. ... Anderson, IN
Dickmann, Reason and Bogigian Greenfield, IN
Dickon-Matney, Rachel E. Federal Maritime Commission, Other Offices of the Commission, GV
Dickos, George D. ... Pittsburgh, PA
Dickos, Harry F. ... Akron, OH
Dickover, Donnelly, Donovan & Biagi, LLP Goshen, NY
Middletown, NY
Newburgh, NY
Warwick, NY
Dickover, Robert J. ... Goshen, NY
Dickover, Stanley R., Jr. ... San Francisco, CA
Dickow & Associates Farmington Hills, MI
Dickow, Diane L. ... Pontiac, MI
Dickow, Mark B. ... Farmington Hills, MI
Dickrell, Peter A. ... Fresno, CA
Dickrell, Robert A. ... Sherman Oaks, CA
Dicks & Coglianese ... Scottsdale, AZ
Aliso Viejo, CA
San Diego, CA
Westlake Village, CA
Dicks, Dennis D. ... Chicago, IL
Dicks, Jack W. ... Longwood, FL
Dicks, John L. ... Plant City, FL
Dicks, Joseph G. ... San Diego, CA
Dicks, Joseph G., A.P.C., The Law Offices of San Diego, CA
Dicks, Mark Jeffry ... Los Angeles, CA
Dicks, Michael Drew ... Scottsdale, AZ
Aliso Viejo, CA
San Diego, CA
Westlake Village, CA
Dicks, Norman D. ... United States Senate, Senatorial Assistants, GV
Dicks, Vivian I. ... Detroit, MI
Dicks, Xavier C. ... Stone Mountain, GA
Dicksion, Archie M. ... Santa Ana, CA
Dickson, Andrea Roumell ... Detroit, MI
Dickson, Anthony G. ... West Trenton, NJ
Dickson, Archie L. ... Gulfport, MS
Dickson, Ashenfelter, Slous, Tanner & Trevenen LLP ... Upper Montclair, NJ
Dickson, B. Alan ... Los Angeles, CA
Dickson, Barbara Beck ... Lisle, IL
Dickson, Blake A. ... Cleveland, OH
Dickson, Brent E. ... Indianapolis, IN
Dickson, Carolyn F. ... Dover, NH
Dickson, Charles B. ... Greeley, CO
Dickson, Christina E. ... Pasadena, CA
Dickson, Claire ... Chinle, AZ
Dickson, Clarence H., III ... Waynesville, NC
Dickson, Craig P. ... Austin, TX
Fort Worth, TX
Houston, TX
Dickson, David B. ... Petersburg, OH
Dickson, David C., Jr. ... Berwick, PA
Dickson, David F. ... Tallahassee, FL
Dickson, David K. ... Ames, IA
Dickson, David M. ... St. Louis, MO
Dickson, Delavan Jon ... Cedar Glen, CA
Dickson & Dickson ... Greeley, CO
Dickson, Don L. ... Bellville, TX
Dickson, Donald W., II ... Port Arthur, TX
Dickson, Douglas G. ... Santa Ana, CA
Dickson, Edgar W. ... Orangeburg, SC
Dickson, Elizabeth B. ... Denver, CO
Dickson, Eric J. ... Schenectady, NY
Dickson, Frank P., Jr. ... Los Alamos, NM
Dickson, Frederick H. ... Aurora, IL
Dickson, G. Wells, Jr. ... Charleston, SC
Kingstree, SC
Dickson, G. Wells, Jr. ... Florence, SC
Dickson, Gary L. ... Los Angeles, CA
Dickson, George A. ... Anchorage, AK
Dickson, George, Jr. ... Sarasota, FL
Dickson and Gordner ... Berwick, PA
Dickson, Graham J. ... New York, NY
Dickson, J. Craig, III Upper Montclair, NJ
Dickson, J. David ... Waco, TX
Dickson, James E. ... Jonesboro, AR
Dickson, James M. ... Clover, SC
Dickson, James N., III ... Harrisonburg, VA
Dickson, Jane J. ... New York, NY
Dickson, Janet H. ... Valencia, CA
Dickson, Janet M. ... Greeley, CO
Dickson, John B. ... Alameda, CA
Dickson, John L. ... Whitesboro, TX
Dickson, Joseph A. ... Morristown, NJ
Dickson, Joseph C., Jr. Upper Montclair, NJ
Dickson, Judge A. ... Stamford, CT
Dickson, Julie D. ... St. Helena, CA
Dickson, Karen S. ... Cassopolis, MI
Dickson, Karen V.E. ... Fullerton, CA
Dickson, Kathleen Deegan ... Glen Cove, NY
Mattituck, NY
Dickson, Kathryn Burkett ... Oakland, CA
Dickson, Kenneth C. ... Murrieta, CA
Dickson, Kimberly Roy ... Milford, CT
Dickson, Kyle L. ... League City, TX
Dickson, L. Bruce ... Birmingham, AL
Dickson, L. James ... Clearwater, FL
Dickson, Lawrence H. ... New Britain, CT
Dickson, Leslie N. ... Fairbanks, AK
Dickson, Lewis ... Houston, TX
Dickson, Mark F. ... Garden City, NY
Dickson, Mark K. ... Menlo Park, CA
Dickson, Mary J. ... Trenton, NJ
Dickson, Mary LePique ... Los Angeles, CA
Dickson, Neil H. ... Atlanta, GA
Dickson, Pamela L. ... San Francisco, CA
Dickson, Patricia L. K. ... Chickasha, OK
Dickson, Peter D. ... Princeton, NJ
Dickson & Pope, P.A. ... Topeka, KS
Dickson, R. Bruce ... Washington, DC
Dickson, R. Temple ... Sweetwater, TX
Dickson, Richard K., II ... Newport Beach, CA
Dickson, Richard L. ... Palo Alto, CA
Dickson, Richard L. ... Wichita, KS
Dickson, Richard L. ... Oklahoma City, OK
Dickson, Richard Lee ... Athens, GA
Dickson, Robert B. ... Concord, NH
Dickson, Robert F. ... Pittsburgh, PA
Dickson, Robert J. ... Anchorage, AK
Dickson, Robert L. ... Los Angeles, CA
Dickson, Robert M. ... New York, NY
Dickson, Robert MacGregor ... Fullerton, CA
Dickson, Roger W. ... Chattanooga, TN
Dickson, Russell K., Jr. ... Orlando, FL
Dickson, Russell M. ... Portland, OR
Dickson, Sam G. ... Atlanta, GA
Dickson, Sarah S. ... League City, TX
Dickson, Stacy E. ... Houston, TX
Dickson, Stanley B., Jr. ... Detroit, MI
Dickson, T. Dean ... Orlando, FL
Dickson, Theodore F. ... New York, NY
Dickson, Thomas A. ... Bismarck, ND
Dickson, Thomas C. ... Everett, WA
Dickson, Thomas G. ... Minneapolis, MN
Dickson, Thomas L. ... Kent, WA
Dickson, Thomas L. ... Tacoma, WA
Dickson, Thomas W. ... Tampa, FL
Dickson, Timothy David ... Richmond, VA
Dickson, V. James ... St. Petersburg, FL
Tampa, FL
Dickson, V. Paul ... Fort Worth, TX
Dickson, Walter D. ... Birmingham, AL
Dickson, William H. ... Canton, OH
Dickson, William M. ... Chicago, IL
Fort Worth, TX
Dickson, William T. ... Tulsa, OK
Dickson Fontaine, Kathryn Redwood City, CA
Dickstein, Adam J. ... Philadelphia, PA
Dickstein, Beth J. ... Chicago, IL
Dickstein, Diane R. ... Oakland, CA
Dickstein, Gary Stuart West Palm Beach, FL
Dickstein, Harold D. ... San Diego, CA
Dickstein, Howard L. ... Sacramento, CA
Dickstein, Ira L. ... Yorba Linda, CA
Dickstein, Jeffrey A. ... Condon, MT
Dickstein, Jeffrey W. ... Miami, FL
Dickstein, Jerry I. ... New York, NY
Dickstein, Jonathan S. ... San Francisco, CA
Dickstein, Joy ... Levittown, PA
Dickstein, Lisa ... Boston, MA
Dickstein, Matthew ... San Francisco, CA
Dickstein, Mel I. ... Minneapolis, MN
Dickstein & Merin ... Sacramento, CA
Dickstein, Phyllis Claire ... Yorba Linda, CA
Dickstein, Reynolds & Woods, P.A. West Palm Beach, FL
Dickstein, Robert S. ... Hackensack, NJ
Dickstein, Sallie L. ... Pasadena, CA
Dickstein & Scutti ... Somerdale, NJ
Philadelphia, PA
Dickstein Shapiro Morin & Oshinsky LLP Washington, DC
New York, NY
Dickstein, Sidney ... Washington, DC
New York, NY
Dickstein, Steven ... Somerdale, NJ
Philadelphia, PA
Dickstein, Zena Manes, (P.A.) ... Miami, FL
DiClemente, John ... Deerfield, IL
DiClemente, Lisa M. ... Perrysburg, OH
Di Clerico, Joseph A., Jr. ... Concord, NH
DiCola, Annemarie Germano New York, NY
DiCola, Anthony J. Hot Sulphur Springs, CO
Di Cola, Joan B. ... Boston, MA
DiConsiglio, Keith ... Parsippany, NJ
DiConza, Gerard ... New York, NY
DiConza, Peter J., Jr. ... Manhasset, NY
DiConza, William A. ... Melville, NY
Mineola, NY
Di Corcia, Joseph G. ... Rochelle Park, NJ
DiCorleto, Dominic A. ... Bloomfield, CT
DiCorrado, Richard A. ... Glendale, CA
Dicosola, Gyda M. ... Concord, NH
Di Costanzo & Cutrona, P.C. ... Brooklyn, NY
DiCostanzo, Linda F. ... Chicago, IL
DiCostanzo, Mary Ann ... Haddon Heights, NJ
Di Costanzo, Nicholas M. ... Bronxville, NY
Di Costanzo, Philip F. ... Brooklyn, NY
DiCrescenzo, Mary V. ... Washington, DC
DiCrescenzo, Nick ... Chicago, IL
DiCristofaro, Maureen S. ... Providence, RI
DiCristofaro, Paul T. ... Providence, RI
Di Croce, Camille Holton Manchester, NH
DiCroce, Joseph A. ... Wall Township, NJ
DiCroce & Maggs ... Wall Township, NJ
Dicterow, Steven M. ... Irvine, CA
Dictor, Cary L., Law Offices of Alameda, CA
Oakland, CA
Dictrow, Joel P. ... New York, NY
DiCuccio, N. Gerald ... Columbus, OH
Dicum, Henry D. ... San Francisco, CA
DiCunto, J. Donald ... Brooklyn, NY
DiCuollo, Lino ... Newark, NJ
Dicus, Aubrey O., Jr. ... St. Petersburg, FL
Dicus, Brian G. ... Dallas, TX
Dicus, Carroll C., Jr. ... Department of Defense, Armed Services Board of Contract Appeals, GV
Dicus, Clarence H. ... Kansas City, MO
Dicus, Davis, Sands & Collins, P.C. Kansas City, MO
Dicus, Henry L. ... Dunedin, FL
Dicus, Joanne M. ... Baltimore, MD
Dicus, Martha ... Columbus, GA
Dicus, Stephen H. ... Kansas City, MO
Dicus, Todd C. ... Kansas City, MO
Dicus, William A. ... Dunedin, FL
Dicus, William A., P.A. ... Dunedin, FL
Diczok, Paul D. ... Basking Ridge, NJ
Didak & Jack ... Los Angeles, CA
Didak, Mark F. ... Los Angeles, CA
Didaleusky, C. Matthew ... Palo Alto, CA
Washington, DC
Didamo, Valerie T. ... Stamford, CT
Didat, Louisa Jackson ... New Albany, IN
Didat, Rebecca L. ... Louisville, KY
Diddel, A. Glenn, III ... Houston, TX
Diddel, Heather D. ... Albany, NY
Didden, George A., III ... Washington, DC
Diddle, Samuel A. ... Boise, ID
Didelius, William E. ... Sandusky, OH
Didesch, Bruce E. ... Nespelem, WA
Didget, Carol E. ... Boston, MA
Didia, Victor E. ... New York, NY
Didier, Alain C. ... Atlanta, GA
Didier, Alfred L. ... Oakbrook Terrace, IL
Didier, Daniel J. ... Santa Ana, CA
Didier, Dawn C. ... Wheaton, IL
Didier, Deborah Dupuy ... Marksville, LA
Didier, Gordon W. ... Birmingham, MI
Didier, Henry N., Jr. ... Orlando, FL
Didier, Jacqueline M. ... New York, NY
Didier, Jean M. ... St. Cloud, MN
Didier, Terrie Springer ... Tallahassee, FL
DiDio, Arthur S. ... Washington, DC
Di Dio, Johanna F. ... Philadelphia, PA
DiDio, Kevin M. ... Bloomfield Hills, MI
Didio, Mildred C. ... New York, NY
Didlake, William M. ... Dallas, TX
Di Domenicis, Robert P. ... Philadelphia, PA
Di Domenico, Andrea J. ... Mechanicville, NY
Di Domenico, Donald M., II ... Livingston, NJ
DiDomenico, Frank ... Vineland, NJ
DiDomenico, Patrick V. ... New York, NY
di Domenico, Philip ... New York, NY
DiDomenico, Richard E. ... Chicago, IL
Di Domenico, Timothy E. ... New York, NY
DiDomenico, Vincent B. ... Paramus, NJ
DiDonato, Ann ... Des Moines, IA
Di Donato, Donna M. ... Providence, RI
DiDonato, Edward J. ... Philadelphia, PA
DiDonato, Eugene J. ... Billerica, MA
DiDonato, Harry J. ... West Chester, PA
DiDonato, J. Brooks ... Marlton, NJ
DiDonato, John M. ... Voorhees, NJ
Philadelphia, PA
DiDonato, Joseph A. ... Hackensack, NJ
Didonato, Michelle ... Catonsville, MD
Didonato, Susan Mcgettrick ... Albany, NY
DiDonato & Winterhalter, P.C. Marlton, NJ
Blue Bell, PA
Philadelphia, PA
DiDonna, Karen Rasmusson ... La Jolla, CA
Di Donna, Louis A. ... Kingston, NY
Didorosi, Michelle C. ... Birmingham, MI
Didrick, Robert M. ... Chicago, IL
Didrickson, Mark Evan ... Vancouver, WA
Didriksen, Michael W. E. ... New York, NY
Didszun, Michael D. ... Pasadena, CA
Didway, J.A. (Trey), III ... Lubbock, TX
Didway, Kevin D. ... Houston, TX
Didzerekis, Paul P. ... Wheaton, IL
Dieball, Scott Alan ... Houston, TX
Diebel, Jeffrey P. ... St. Paul, MN
Diebenow, Steven ... Jacksonville, FL
Diebling, Christopher A. ... Honolulu, HI
Diebner, Gerard F. ... New York, NY
Diebold, Charles R. ... Buffalo, NY
Diebold, David K. ... Washington, DC
Diebold, Donald A. ... Santa Ana, CA
Diebold & Farmelo, P.C. ... Buffalo, NY
Diebold, Francis X. ... Philadelphia, PA
Diebold, Gregory G. ... Jersey City, NJ
Diebold, Lynn B. ... Memphis, TN
Diebold, Mary Ann T. ... Charlestown, MA
Diebold, Richard J. ... Buffalo, NY
Diebold, Thomas G. ... Portland, ME
Diebolt, Karen ... Waterbury, CT
Diecidue, Anthony F. ... Tampa, FL
Diecidue, Dennis G. ... Tampa, FL
Diecidue, Dennis G., P.A. ... Tampa, FL
Diecidue, Jeffrey J. ... New York, NY
Dieckhoff, William S. ... Yuma, AZ
Dieckman, Lloyd F. ... Raymore, MO
Dieckmann, Anjum Sahai ... Milwaukee, WI
Diederich, Bernard F. Department of Transportation, Office of the General Counsel, GV
Diederich, Daniel B., A Professional Corporation ... Torrance, CA
Diederich, Daniel K. ... Salina, KS
Diederich, Mathias J. ... Woodland Hills, CA
Diederich, Michael D., Jr. ... Stony Point, NY
Diederich, Theresa L. ... Glendale, CA
Diederichs, Brenda L. ... Los Angeles, CA
Diedolf, Robert H. ... Patchogue, NY
Diedrich, Alexandra L.W. ... Easton, MA
Diedrich, Curtis R. ... Boston, MA

Diedrich, Dawn M. ....**Decatur, GA**
Diedrich, Edward F. ....De Kalb, IL
Diedrich, Michael C. ....**Chicago, IL**
Diedrich, Michael G. ....**Rapid City, SD**
Diedrich, Peter J. ....**Los Angeles, CA**
Diedrich, Robert S. ....Bloomfield Hills, MI
Diedrich, S. Elaine ....**Pittsburgh, PA**
Diedrich, William A. ....Stevens Point, WI
Diedrich, William L., Jr. ....San Francisco, CA
Diedrichs, Clayton R.
Department of the Army,
U.S. Army Legal Services Agency, GV
Diedrichs, Frank M. ....**Cincinnati, OH**
Diedrick, L. G. ....Rocky Mount, NC
DiEdwards, Gerald D. ....New York, NY
Diefenbach, Joan M. ....Pennington, NJ
Diefenderfer & Hoover ....Pittsburgh, PA
Diefenderfer, James N. ....Allentown, PA
Diefenderfer, John Philip
Quakertown, PA
Diefenderfer, William M., III ......Pittsburgh, PA
Diefendorf, Richard R. ....**Washington, DC**
Dieffenbach, Albert W., Jr. ....**Hillsboro, MO**
Dieffenbach, Richard P. ....**Long Beach, CA**
Dieffenbach, Roxann H. ....**Cincinnati, OH**
Dieffenbach, Witt & Birchby ....Paramus, NJ
Diegel, Glenn A. ....**Southfield, MI**
Diegel, Mary Jo ....Shelby Township, MI
Diegel, Ronald B. ....**Columbia, SC**
Diegleman, Joel ....Sparta, WI
Diegnan, Patrick J., Jr. ....South Plainfield, NJ
Diego, Beverly L. ....Brooklyn, NY
Diego, Jonathan E. ....Newark, NJ
Dieguez, Anthony ....Hialeah, FL
Dieguez, Paul A. ....Indialantic, FL
Dieguez, Paul A. & Barker, Sabrina L., P.A.,
Law Office of ....Indialantic, FL
Dieguez, Richard P. ....Roslyn Heights, NY
Diehl, Barbara R. ....Yorktown Heights, NY
Diehl, Benjamin G. ....Los Angeles, CA
Diehl, Carl ....New York, NY
Diehl, Charles Frederick ....Raleigh, NC
Diehl Clayton & Jacobsen ....Newton, IA
Diehl, Deborah H. ....**Baltimore, MD**
Diehl, Donald L. ....Coralville, IA
Diehl, Duke B. ....Eureka, CA
Diehl, Eileen M. ....Allentown, PA
Diehl, Erich Mark ....Mechanicsburg, PA
Diehl & Fosnocht ....West Chester, PA
Diehl, Frank D. ....Lawrence, KS
Diehl & Gibson ....**Raeford, NC**
Diehl, Glen M. ....Secaucus, NJ
Diehl, Glenn R. ....West Chester, PA
Diehl, Gregg A. ....Traverse City, MI
Diehl, Gregg A., P.C. ....Traverse City, MI
Diehl, Henry C. ....Tucson, AZ
Diehl, James E. ....Bangor, ME
Diehl, James J. ....**San Francisco, CA**
Diehl, James P. ....**Pottsville, PA**
Diehl, John C. ....Lakeland, FL
Diehl, John E. ....**Minneapolis, MN**
Diehl, John J. ....Rochester, NY
Diehl, John J., Jr. ....**St. Charles, MO**
Diehl, Joseph W. ....Stockton, CA
Diehl, Joseph W., Jr.
San Luis Obispo, CA
Diehl, Katia T. ....**Palo Alto, CA**
Diehl, Kevin L. ....**Topeka, KS**
Diehl, Lauren T. ....**Los Angeles, CA**
Diehl Law Offices, P.C. ....Allentown, PA
Diehl, Lawrence D. ....**Hopewell, VA**
Diehl, Lawrence D. ....**Richmond, VA**
Diehl, Lawrence S. ....Harrisburg, PA
Diehl, Les E. ....**Topeka, KS**
Diehl, Marc M. ....Omaha, NE
Diehl, Mary Ann ....Albert City, IA
Storm Lake, IA
Diehl, Mary Grace ....**Atlanta, GA**
Diehl, Michael
United States International Trade
Commission,
Office of the General Counsel, GV
Diehl, Michael ....**Austin, TX**
Diehl, Michael R. ....New York, NY
Diehl, Millicent G. ....Raeford, NC
Diehl, Nancy J. ....Detroit, MI
Diehl, Paul A. ....Cleveland, OH
Diehl, Paul W. ....Shelton, CT
Diehl, Philip A. ....**Raeford, NC**
Diehl, R. Anthony ....**Philadelphia, PA**
Diehl, Rachel L. ....**Newark, NJ**
Diehl, Richard J. ....Honolulu, HI
Diehl, Richard P. ....Rochester Hills, MI
Diehl, Rita J.
Charlotte Amalie, St. Thomas, VI
Diehl, Robert A. ....**Lake Oswego, OR**
Diehl, Robert E. ....**Hays, KS**
Diehl, Robert E. ....**Minneapolis, MN**
Diehl, Robert E., Jr. ....**Sunbury, PA**
Diehl, Robert J. ....Grosse Pointe Park, MI
Diehl, Robert J., Jr. ....**Detroit, MI**
Diehl, Robert S., Jr. ....Chicago, IL
Diehl, Robert W. ....**Chicago, IL**
Diehl & Rodewald, A Professional
Corporation ....**San Luis Obispo, CA**
Diehl, Rosanne K. ....Pittsburgh, PA
Diehl, Sarah J. ....Pacific Grove, CA
Diehl, Shane F. ....Grosse Pointe Woods, MI
Diehl & Sobczak, P.C. ....Rochester Hills, MI
Diehl, Susan A. ....Cedar Rapids, IA
Diehl, Susan Mashour ....**Dundee, MI**
Diehl, Thomas ....Iowa City, IA
Diehl, Thomas J. ....Lebanon, OH
Diehl & Weger ....Honolulu, HI
Diehl, William D. ....Columbus, OH
Diehl, William F. ....**Indianapolis, IN**
Diehl, William K., Jr. ....**Charlotte, NC**
Diehlmann, Elten ....New Hyde Park, NY

Diehm, James W. ....Wilmington, DE
Diehm, Paul C. ....Columbus, OH
Diehn, Daniel S. ....Black River Falls, WI
Diehr, Beverly Hunt ....Tampa, FL
Diekema, Connie L. ....**Des Moines, IA**
Diekemper, Hammond, Shinners, Turcotte &
Larrew, P.C. ....St. Louis, MO
Diekemper, Herbert T., Jr. ....St. Louis, MO
Diekemper, Jerome A. ....St. Louis, MO
Diekemper, Tracy A. ....**St. Louis, MO**
Dieker & Dieker ....Columbus, OH
Dieker, James W. ....Champaign, IL
Dieker, Jeannie K. ....Columbus, OH
Dieker, Lawrence L. ....Columbus, OH
Dieker, Lawrence L., Jr. ....Columbus, OH
Diekhoff, Mary Ellen Stanzione
Bloomington, IN
Diekmann, Gilmore F., Jr.
San Francisco, CA
Diekmann-Dicicco, Madeline L.
Las Vegas, NV
Diel, Diane S. ....Hales Corners, WI
Diel, Diane S., S.C. ....Hales Corners, WI
Diel, Isaac L. ....Grandview, MO
Diel, Tracy T. ....Lawrence, KS
Dielman, Kirk A. ....Chicago, IL
Dielmann, Heinz J. ....**Washington, DC**
Dielschneider, Janmarie ....Bend, OR
Diem, Amy L. ....West Palm Beach, FL
Diem, Ann G. ....Oakland, CA
Diem, Lisa M. ....**Cleveland, OH**
Diemand, Timothy A. ....**New Haven, CT**
Diemer, Charles ....Hastings, MN
Diemer, Clare M. ....**Philadelphia, PA**
Diemer, Daniel E. ....Clayton, MO
Diemer, Daniel E., LLC ....Clayton, MO
Diemer, Dennis J. ....Cleveland, OH
Diemer, Harvey H. ....Los Gatos, CA
Diemer, John D. ....**Beverly Hills, CA**
Diemer, Kathryn J. ....**San Jose, CA**
Diemer, Robert A. ....Beltsville, MD
Diemer, Robert C. ....**San Francisco, CA**
Diemert, Jacob C. ....**Acton, MA**
Diemert, Joseph W., Jr. ....Cleveland, OH
Diemert, Joseph W., Jr. & Associates, Co.,
L.P.A. ....Cleveland, OH
Diemoz, Dennis K. ....Houston, TX
Dienelt, John F. ....**Washington, DC**
Diener, Ann G. ....Carpinteria, CA
Diener, Ashley L. ....Miami, FL
Diener, David ....Baltimore, MD
Diener, Erwin ....Monroe, MI
Diener, G. Edward ....San Jose, CA
Diener, Jerre S. ....Baltimore, MD
Diener, Lawrence B. ....**Hackensack, NJ**
Diener, Michael A. ....**Boston, MA**
Diener, S. Robert ....Berkeley, CA
Diener, Scott ....**Hackensack, NJ**
Diener, Sol ....Westfield, NJ
Diener, Walter M., Jr. ....**Reading, PA**
Diener, William P. ....**Indianapolis, IN**
Dienes, C. Thomas ....Washington, DC
Dienes, Lauren A. ....**New York, NY**
Dienes, Louis R. ....**New York, NY**
Dienes, Mary Ellen ....Northfield, IL
Dienes, Scott A. ....**Grand Rapids, MI**
Dienna, William D. ....**Norristown, PA**
Dienner, John A., III ....**Chicago, IL**
Dienner, John A., Jr. ....Highland Park, IL
Diennor, Martin ....**New York, NY**
Dienst, Gary John ....Morristown, NJ
Dienst, Gerald A. ....Toms River, NJ
Dienst, Richard A. ....**New York, NY**
Dienst & Serrins, LLP ....**New York, NY**
Dienst, Victoria Winter ....**New York, NY**
Dienstag, Abbe L. ....**New York, NY**
Dienstag, Cynthia J. ....Miami, FL
Dienstag, Cynthia J., P.A. ....Miami, FL
Dienstag, Gary E. ....**Barrington, IL**
Chicago, IL
Dienstag, Glenn ....New York, NY
Dienstag, Jerome ....Rochester, NY
Dienstag, Mark A. ....Miami, FL
Dienstag, Matthew E. ....New York, NY
Dienstag, Robert V. ....Great Neck, NY
Diepenbrock, Anthony B.
San Francisco, CA
Diepenbrock, Anthony B., III
Palo Alto, CA
Diepenbrock, Anthony C.
Sacramento, CA
Diepenbrock & Costa ....**Sacramento, CA**
Diepenbrock, Daniel H. ....**Liberal, KS**
Diepenbrock, Eileen M. ....**Sacramento, CA**
Diepenbrock, J. Thomas, Law Offices of
San Jose, CA
Diepenbrock, John V. ....**Sacramento, CA**
Diepenbrock, Karen L. ....**Sacramento, CA**
Diepenbrock Law Firm, The, A Professional
Corporation ....**Sacramento, CA**
Diepenbrock, Mary L. ....Sacramento, CA
Diepenbrock, R. James ....**Sacramento, CA**
Dieperink, Ann L. ....Stillwater, MN
Dier, Hilton H., Jr. ....Middlebury, VT
Dier, Jeffrey M. ....Baltimore, MD
Dier, Jerry L. ....Clarksville, MD
Dier, John E. ....Holdrege, NE
Dier, John G. ....Lake George, NY
Dier, Wendy J. ....Alturas, CA
Dierauf, Elizabeth M. Fay
Hendersonville, NC
Dierberg, James F. ....St. Louis, MO
Dierberg, Michael J. ....Treasury Department,
Office of the Comptroller of the Currency,
GV
Dierberger, Wesley A. ....Los Angeles, CA
Diercks, David G. ....**Madison, WI**
Diercks, Robert J. ....**Seattle, WA**

Diercks, Walter E. ....**Washington, DC**
Dierdorf, Elizabeth T. ....Fort Worth, TX
Dierdorf, Paul J., Jr. ....Watertown, NY
Dierdorff, David R. ....Juneau, AK
Dierenfeld, Paula S. ....**Des Moines, IA**
Dierenfield, David R. ....Minneapolis, MN
Dieringer, Beatriz ....Los Angeles, CA
Dieringer, Cheryl A. ....Brookfield, WI
Dieringer, Christine M.
Colorado Springs, CO
Dieringer, Jon A. ....**Tustin, CA**
Dieringer, Lana R. ....Houston, TX
Dierker, Ernest W. ....Sweet Springs, MO
Dierker, James A. ....**Denver, CO**
Dierker, John W. ....Dallas, TX
Dierker, Julia Church ....**Troy, MI**
Dierker, Ray F., Jr. ....St. Louis, MO
Dierker, Robert H., Jr. ....St. Louis, MO
Dierker, Roland F. ....Watertown, WI
Dierkes, Robert J., (P.C.) ....Columbia, MO
Dierking, Anne V. ....Far Rockaway, NY
Dierking, Bruce D. ....**Boulder, CO**
Dierking, Carmen Chittick ....St. Paul, MN
Dierking, James K. ....**Irvine, CA**
Dierking, James W. ....**Minneapolis, MN**
St. Paul, MN
Dierking, John C., Jr. ....Hagåtña, GU
Dierking, John R. ....**Orlando, FL**
Dierking, Lavinia Keefer ....**Heathrow, FL**
Dierking, Lowell ....Caldwell, KS
Dierking, Roger F. ....Portland, OR
Dierking & Schuster ....Portland, OR
Dierks, Jennifer T. ....Kansas City, MO
Dierks, Marieluise H. ....Chicago, IL
Dierks, Mark N. ....Cincinnati, OH
Dierksen, John T. ....**New Braunfels, TX**
Diers, Ann D. ....**Lincoln, NE**
Diers, Robert ....Davie, FL
Diersen, Daniel A. ....Oak Brook, IL
Diersen, Ronald L. ....Kenosha, WI
Diersing, Charles M. ....Delaware, OH
Diersing, George A., Jr. ....Cincinnati, OH
Dierssen-Morice, Rikke A.
Minneapolis, MN
Dierstein, M. Lois ....Chicago, IL
Dies, David ....Orange, TX
Dies, George A., Jr. ....Garden City, NY
Dies, Henderson & Carona ....**Orange, TX**
Dies, Jack ....Austin, TX
Dies, Kenneth P. ....Houston, TX
Dies, Martin, Jr. ....Beaumont, TX
Dies, Martin W. ....**Orange, TX**
Diesa, Arthur L. ....Stamford, CT
Diesel, Louis M. ....**Flagstaff, AZ**
Diesel, Peter L. ....**Grand Blanc, MI**
Diesen, Charles F. ....**Redmond, WA**
Diesen, Wittman & Graves
Redmond, WA
Diesenhof, Kenneth Marc ....Boston, MA
Diesenhouse, Margo ....New York, NY
Dieseth, Paul R. ....**Minneapolis, MN**
Diesi, Salvador L. ....Opelousas, LA
Diesing, Daryl L. ....**Milwaukee, WI**
Diesing, Gary R. ....**Toledo, OH**
Diesman, Kathleen O. ....Torrance, CA
Dieso, Joseph ....Hartford, CT
Diess, Louis W., III ....**Washington, DC**
Diessner, Charles F. ....**Minneapolis, MN**
Diessner, Karl F. ....Minneapolis, MN
Diessner, Michael F. ....Phoenix, AZ
Diestel, Richard S. ....**San Francisco, CA**
Diestelmeier, Mark S. ....**Milwaukee, WI**
Dietch, Henry X. ....Homewood, IL
Dietchman, Alan M. ....Liberty, MO
Dietchweiler, Daniel O. ....**New York, NY**
Dietchweiler, Michael L. ....Kankakee, IL
Dietderich, Andrew G. ....**New York, NY**
Dietel, John E. ....Seekonk, MA
Dieter, David L. ....**Chicago, IL**
Dieter, Denise Lynn ....Jersey Shore, PA
Dieter, James G. ....**Houston, TX**
Dieter, Rebecca L. ....Golden, CO
Dieter, Richard C. ....Washington, DC
Dieter, Robert J. ....Boulder, CO
Dieter, Robert J. ....**Cedar Falls, IA**
Dieterich, Christopher H. ....Los Angeles, CA
Dieterich, Eric R. ....Columbus, OH
Dieterich, James M. ....**Denver, CO**
Dieterich, Kristen Lynn ....**Edwardsville, IL**
Dieterich, L. Elise ....Seattle, WA
Dieterich, Linda M. ....**Riverhead, NY**
Dieterich, Linda M., P.C. ....**Riverhead, NY**
Dieterich, Michael G. ....Burlington, IA
Dieterich, Neil B. ....**St. Paul, MN**
Dieterich, Neil B., P.A. ....**St. Paul, MN**
Dieterich, Thomas A. ....**New York, NY**
Dieterich, William H. ....Menomonee Falls, WI
Dieterich, Wm. J. ....Quincy, IL
Dieterle, Donnah J. ....**Dayton, OH**
Dieterle, Gordon A. ....**Boca Raton, FL**
Dieterle Judge, Dianne ....Dayton, OH
Dieterly, Douglas K. ....**South Bend, IN**
Dieterly, Richard ....**Clinton, NJ**
Dietert, Hank Lee ....San Antonio, TX
Dieth, Ford J. ....**New Orleans, LA**
Dieth and Martin ....**New Orleans, LA**
Dietlein, Lawrence Frederick, Jr.
Georgetown, TX
Dietlein & Smoot, PLLC ....Georgetown, TX
Dietrich, Alan D. ....Huron, SD
Dietrich, Brian S. ....East Norriton, PA
Dietrich & Cassavaugh, A Professional
Corporation ....Detroit, MI
Dietrich, Charles C. ....Sausalito, CA
Dietrich, Christopher M. ....Bakersfield, CA
Dietrich, Clayton A. ....Baltimore, MD
Dietrich & Cline ....Springfield, IL
Dietrich, D. David ....Escondido, CA

Dietrich, David J. ....**Billings, MT**
Dietrich, Dean M. ....Sheboygan, WI
Dietrich, Dean R. ....**Wausau, WI**
Dietrich, Debra M. ....**Irvine, CA**
Dietrich, Diana L. ....**Washington, DC**
Dietrich & Dietrich ....**Cleveland, TN**
Dietrich, Dietrich & Mikulski, P.A.
Hamilton, NJ
Trenton, NJ
Dietrich, Donald Paul ....Orlando, FL
Dietrich, Donald Paul, II ....**Orlando, FL**
Dietrich, Donna K. ....Yankton, SD
Dietrich, Edgar J. ....Detroit, MI
Dietrich, Edward H. ....**New Canaan, CT**
Westport, CT
New York, NY
Dietrich, Edward P. ....Minneapolis, MN
Dietrich, Elaine D. ....Trenton, NJ
Dietrich, Elena Bocca ....San Ramon, CA
Dietrich, Elizabeth Anne ......San Francisco, CA
Dietrich, Erin ....Bakersfield, CA
Dietrich, Frederick T. ....San Francisco, CA
Dietrich, G. Philip ....**Kalamazoo, MI**
Dietrich, George A. ....**Akron, OH**
Dietrich, Gerhard P.
Fort Washington, PA
Dietrich, Glasrud, Mallek & Aune
Fresno, CA
Dietrich, Glen A. ....Maryville, MO
Dietrich, Howard N. ....Portland, OR
Dietrich, Ivan ....Falls Church, VA
Dietrich, J. Raymond ....Trenton, NJ
Dietrich, Joanne M. ....Hamilton, NJ
Trenton, NJ
Dietrich, John F. ....Scottsburg, IN
Dietrich, John M. ....**Billings, MT**
Dietrich, John W. ....**Cerritos, CA**
Dietrich, John W. ....Elk Grove Village, IL
Dietrich, Julie S. ....Washington, DC
Dietrich, Karen B. ....**Boston, MA**
Dietrich, L. Elise ....**Washington, DC**
Dietrich, Laura Giannone ....Springfield, IL
Dietrich Law Offices ....**Billings, MT**
Dietrich, Lisa Luschen
Oklahoma City, OK
Dietrich, Marian Faye ....Pittsburgh, PA
Dietrich, Mark K. ....New York, NY
Dietrich, Merwyn J. ....Baton Rouge, LA
Dietrich, Paul George ....Washington, DC
Dietrich, Paul H. ....**Cleveland, TN**
Dietrich, Philip W. ....**Kalamazoo, MI**
Dietrich, Richard C. ....Pelham, NH
Dietrich, Ronald R. ....**Chicago, IL**
Dietrich, Samia Haddad ....Minneapolis, MN
Dietrich, Sarah Sharlot ....**Houston, TX**
Dietrich, Sharon M. ....Philadelphia, PA
Dietrich, Smith, Howard & VanderRoest,
P.C. ....**Kalamazoo, MI**
Dietrich, Stephen J. ....**Denver, CO**
Dietrich, Susan Ellen ....Brooksville, FL
Dietrich, Thomas W. ....**Phoenix, AZ**
Dietrich, Thomas W. ....Columbus, OH
Dietrich, Timothy G. ....Kutztown, PA
Reading, PA
Dietrich, Val G. ....Palos Verdes Estates, CA
Dietrich, Virginia M. ....Trenton, NJ
Dietrich, William A. ....West Trenton, NJ
Dietrich, William F. ....**San Francisco, CA**
Dietrich, William G. ....**Kansas City, MO**
Dietrich, William H. ....**Madison, SD**
Dietrich, William J., III ....Atlantic City, NJ
Dietrich, Wolf C. ....Woodridge, IL
Dietrich & Young, P.C. ....East Norriton, PA
Dietrichs, Mark T. ....**Atlanta, GA**
Dietrick, Daniel W. ....Carnegie, PA
Dietrick, Evans, Scholz & Williams, L.L.C.
Atlanta, GA
Dietrick, John D. ....**St. Louis, MO**
Dietrick, John R. ....Topeka, KS
Dietrick, Joseph F. ....Camp Hill, PA
Dietrick, Kenneth L. ....Chesapeake, VA
Dietrick, Michael E. ....San Rafael, CA
Dietrick, Paul A. ....**Atlanta, GA**
Dietsch, Alfred J. ....Aspen, CO
Dietsch, Gary J. ....**Cleveland, OH**
Dietsch, Paul R. ....**Omaha, NE**
Dietsch, Terry D. ....Evansville, IN
Dietterick, Scott A. ....**Hershey, PA**
Diettrich, Robert J. ....**Boston, MA**
Dietz, Angela Elbert ....**Chicago, IL**
Dietz and Associates, P.C. ....Round Rock, TX
Dietz, Bernard C. ....Washington, DC
Dietz, Brian M. ....Bloomfield Hills, MI
Dietz, Carol K. ....Boston, MA
Dietz, Charlton ....North Oaks, MN
Dietz, Christopher P. ....Cincinnati, OH
Dietz, Cynthia M. ....**Baltimore, MD**
Dietz, Daniel G. ....Bloomfield Hills, MI
Dietz, Darrin M. ....Schoharie, NY
Dietz, David F., (P.C.) ....**Boston, MA**
Dietz, David H. ....Salem, OR
Dietz, David J. ....New York, NY
Dietz, Dennis A. ....Ames, IA
Dietz & Dietz ....Poughkeepsie, NY
Dietz, Ethelinda ....Albuquerque, NM
Dietz, George A. ....**Sarasota, FL**
Dietz & Hardman ....Osborne, KS
Dietz, Jacqueline F. ....Golden Valley, MN
Dietz, James ....Ashland, OR
Dietz, James A. ....**Covington, KY**
Dietz, James B. ....**Youngstown, OH**
Dietz, James M. ....**Columbus, OH**
Delaware, OH
Dietz, Jennifer A. ....Tampa, FL
Dietz, Jennifer M. ....Lake Elmo, MN
Dietz, John A. ....Rochester, NY
Dietz, John A. ....Fargo, ND
Dietz, John F. ....Santa Fe, NM

Dietz, John H. ... Cincinnati, OH
Dietz, John K. ... Austin, TX
Dietz, John P. ... New York, NY
Dietz, John W. ... Westport, CT
Dietz, Joseph M. ... Indianapolis, IN
Dietz, Julia A. ... New Orleans, LA
Dietz, Kathryn L. ... Bismarck, ND
Dietz, Kenneth J. ... Covington, KY
Dietz, Lawrence D. ... Sunnyvale, CA
Dietz, Little & Haas ... Bismarck, ND
Dietz, Marc D. ... Covington, KY
Dietz, Margaret M. ... San Francisco, CA
Dietz, Mark W. ... Vernon, CT
Dietz, Martha Bakos ... Brooklyn, NY
Dietz, Mary C. ... Dearborn, MI
Dietz, Mary Schaerdel ... Austin, TX
Dietz, Matthew W. ... Miami, FL
Dietz, Melissa Grant ... Round Rock, TX
Dietz, Melvin E. ... Auburn, WA
Dietz, Michael S. ... Rochester, MN
Dietz, Paul T. ... Minneapolis, MN
Dietz, Philip E. L., Jr. ... Easton, MD
Dietz, Phyllis P. ... Washington, DC
Dietz, R. Mark ... Round Rock, TX
Dietz, Rebecca L. ... Baltimore, MD
Dietz, Richard A. ... Detroit, MI
Dietz, Richard E. ... Osborne, KS
Dietz, Richard J. ... Green Bay, WI
Dietz, Robert A. ... Annapolis, MD
Dietz, Robert A. ... Laconia, NH
Dietz, Robert B. ... Poughkeepsie, NY
Dietz, Robert D. ... La Crosse, WI
Dietz, Robert E., Jr. ... Fort Myers, FL
Dietz, Robert L. ... Orlando, FL
Dietz, Robert M. ... Hartsdale, NY
Dietz, Roderic A. ... Upland, CA
Dietz, Stephanie A. ... Elsmere, KY
Dietz, Stephen E. ... New York, NY
Dietz, Stephen P. ... McAllen, TX
Dietz, Steven B. ... Buffalo, NY
Dietz, Thomas E. ... Poughkeepsie, NY
Dietz, Thorsten H. ... New York, NY
Dietz, Timothy C. ... Phoenix, AZ
Dietz, Victor H. ... Overland Park, KS
Dietz, Wallace W. ... Nashville, TN
Dietz, William F. ... Phoenix, AZ
Dietze and Davis, P.C. ... Boulder, CO
Dietze, Errol John ... Cuero, TX
Dietze, Jennifer Rolf ... Dallas, TX
Dietze, John F. (Jeff) ... Rockport, TX
Dietze, Paul E. ... Washington, DC
Dietze, Peter C. ... Boulder, CO
Dietze & Reese ... Cuero, TX
Dietzen & Atchley ... Chattanooga, TN
Dietzen, Carolyn I. ... Lafayette, LA
Dietzen, Charles Richard ... Chattanooga, TN
Dietzen, Christopher J. ... Minneapolis, MN
Dietzen, Gregory A. ... Anderson, IN
Dietzen, John W. ... Chattanooga, TN
Dietzen, Leonard J. ... Tallahassee, FL
Dietzgen, Charles A. ... New York, NY
Dietzler, Dennis J. ... Richfield, MN
Dietzmann, Elizabeth Moore ... Rolla, MO
Dietzmann, F. Blake ... San Antonio, TX
Dieu, Loren E. ... Sacramento, CA
Diez, Charles, Jr. ... Englewood, FL
Diez and Floyd ... Englewood, FL
Diez, Gabriel ... New York, NY
Diez, Santiago ... Miami, FL
Diez, Santiago, P.A. ... Miami, FL
Diez-Arguelles, Carlos R. ... Kissimmee, FL
Orlando, FL
Diez-Arguelles, Jose A. ... Tallahassee, FL
Diez Hidalgo, Ricardo J. ... Houston, TX
DiFabio, Andrea M. ... Boston, MA
DiFabio, E. Michael ... Albany, NY
DiFabio, Louis A. ... Geneva, OH
Di Fabio, Michael D. ... Albany, NY
DiFabio, Tommaney and Legnard, Professional Corporation ... Albany, NY
DiFabio, Vincent P. ... Marlton, NJ
Paoli, PA
DiFalco, John P. ... Fort Collins, CO
DiFalco, John P., & Associates, P.C.
Denver, CO
Fort Collins, CO
DiFazio, Charles A. ... Philadelphia, PA
DiFazio, John E., Jr. ... Alexandria, VA
DiFazio, Lucien P., Jr. ... Chester, CT
Di Fazio, Radom, Wetter & Bennett
Somerville, NJ
DiFazio, S. Russ ... Huntington, NY
Di Fazio, Salvatore P. ... Somerville, NJ
DiFebbo, Michael E., Jr. ... Philadelphia, PA
Difede, James R. ... Washington, DC
Di Fede, Jos. ... Bronx, NY
Di Fede, M. Victor ... Yonkers, NY
DiFelice, Daniel C. ... Braintree, MA
Difenderfer, William H. ... Pittsburgh, PA
DiFeo, Joseph C. ... Jersey City, NJ
DiFerrante, Barbara M. ... Seattle, WA
Di Ferrante, Chris ... Houston, TX
Diffenbach, David B. ... Lancaster, PA
Diffendal, Harry A. ... Arlington, VA
Diffenderfer, Robert P.
West Palm Beach, FL
Diffenderfer, William J. ... Fairfield, CA
Differderffer, Charles R. ... Towson, MD
Differ, Anthony L. ... Norristown, PA
Differding, Gayle Y. ... Sonoma, CA
Differt, Thomas D. ... Tempe, AZ
Diffin, Edward Wilson, Jr. ... Philadelphia, PA
DiFiglia, Catherine ... New York, NY
Di Figlia, Vincent Paul ... San Diego, CA
DiFilippi, Anthony J. ... New York, NY
DiFilippo, Anthony, III ... East Aurora, NY
DiFilippo, Anthony, IV ... East Aurora, NY
DiFilippo, Anthony J., Jr. ... Jacksonville, FL
DiFilippo, Bennett & Daumen
East Aurora, NY
DiFilippo & Clark, P.A. ... Jacksonville, FL
Di Filippo, Deborah D. ... San Antonio, TX
DiFilippo, LeeAnne ... McLean, VA
DiFilippo, Robert A. ... Bala Cynwyd, PA
DiFilippo, Tanya E. ... Tampa, FL
DiFiore, Albert A. ... Providence, RI
Di Fiore, Andrew D. ... Houston, TX
DiFiore, Andrew D., Law Office
Houston, TX
Difiore, Barbara A. ... Yonkers, NY
DiFiore, David V. ... Akron, OH
DiFiore, Gerard S. ... Newark, NJ
DiFiore, Janet M. ... White Plains, NY
DiFiore, Julius C. ... Yonkers, NY
DiFiore & Retta ... Yonkers, NY
DiFlorio, Aldo L. ... Lockport, NY
DiFlorio, Marco P. ... Marlton, NJ
DiFonzo, J. Herbie ... Hempstead, NY
DiFrancesca, Donald J. ... Norwich, CT
DiFrancesca & Steele, P.C. ... Norwich, CT
DiFrancesco, Donald T. ... Warren, NJ
Di Francesco, James R. ... Johnstown, PA
DiFrancesco, Marci ... Roseland, NJ
Di Francesco, Samuel R., Jr. ... Johnstown, PA
DiFranco, Diane ... New York, NY
Di Franco, Thomas M., Law Offices of
San Francisco, CA
Di Franco, Thomas, The Law Offices
San Francisco, CA
Di Franco, Tina ... Baltimore, MD
DiFranza, Barbara A. ... Salinas, CA
DiFronzo, Louis J., Jr. ... Boston, MA
DiFronzo, Michael A. ... Washington, DC
Di Fronzo, Pascal W. ... Irvine, CA
DiFruscia, Anthony R. ... Lawrence, MA
DiFruscia, Anthony R., and Kathleen Sullivan DiFruscia, Law Offices of ... Lawrence, MA
Di Fruscia, Celeste McDonald
Lawrence, MA
DiFruscia, Kathleen Sullivan ... Lawrence, MA
DiGaetano, Michele ... Rochester, NY
Digaetano, Scott Mathew ... Salem, NH
Digan, Thomas E. ... Washington, DC
DiGangi & Legasey, Law Offices of
Salem, MA
DiGangi, Peter C. ... Salem, MA
DiGangi, Roberta L. ... Brooklyn, NY
Digardi & Campbell ... Oakland, CA
Digardi, Edward M. ... Oakland, CA
Digati, Philip A. ... Fort Lauderdale, FL
Digati, Philip A., P.A. ... Fort Lauderdale, FL
Digby, Darin N. ... San Antonio, TX
Digby, Matthew E. ... Los Angeles, CA
Digby, Patrick R. ... Atlanta, GA
Digel, Gregory J. ... Atlanta, GA
DiGenio, Anna M. ... Boston, MA
Digenis, Emily M. ... Louisville, KY
Di Gennaro, Anthony R. ... Massapequa, NY
DiGennaro, Iris Beth ... Boca Raton, FL
DiGennaro, Janice J. ... Uniondale, NY
DiGennaro, Judith ... San Diego, CA
DiGennaro, Philip R., Jr.
Philadelphia, PA
DiGennaro, Robert C. ... Suffield, CT
diGenova, Joseph E. ... Washington, DC
DiGenova, Michael Hansen
Philadelphia, PA
diGenova & Toensing ... Washington, DC
DiGeronimo, Michael E. ... Sacramento, CA
Walnut Creek, CA
Digesti, Ronald D. ... San Jose, CA
Digges, Dudley H. ... Clifton, VA
Digges, Randolph E., III ... Cleveland, OH
Digges, Robert S., Jr. ... Alexandria, VA
Digges, Thomas F. ... Fairfax, VA
Diggins, Abigail King ... Portland, ME
Diggins, Bernard J. ... Philadelphia, PA
Diggins, Daniel F. ... Kendallville, IN
Diggins, John J. ... Dallas, TX
Diggins, John J., P.C. ... Dallas, TX
Diggins, Mary M. ... Boston, MA
Diggins, Merritt W. ... Kendallville, IN
Diggins, S. Sheldon ... Baltimore, MD
Diggins, Timothy W. ... Boston, MA
Diggins, William J. ... Buffalo, NY
Diggs, Ariyike Oshunkoya ... New York, NY
Diggs, Barbara D. ... New York, NY
Diggs, Bradley C. ... Seattle, WA
Diggs, Cheryl Harris ... Houston, TX
Diggs, Cynthia Thomson ... Dallas, TX
Houston, TX
Diggs, D. Lester ... Aiken, SC
Diggs, David V. ... Baltimore, MD
Diggs, Edward W. ... Pittsburgh, PA
Diggs, James B. ... Oklahoma City, OK
Diggs, James C. ... Pittsburgh, PA
Diggs, Janet E. ... San Diego, CA
Diggs, Marshall R., Jr. ... Denver, CO
Diggs, Melvin M. ... Fort Worth, TX
Diggs, Robert M. ... Olean, NY
Diggs, Robert W. ... Atlanta, GA
Diggs, Shelia D. ... Newark, NJ
Diggs, Terry P.
Hot Springs National Park, AR
Diggs, Walter E., Jr. ... St. Louis, MO
Diggs, Weldon ... Rancho Mirage, CA
Diggs, Weldon, A Prof. Law Corp.
Rancho Mirage, CA
Diggs, William Isaac ... Myrtle Beach, SC
Diggs-Miller, Sandra ... New Orleans, LA
Dighe, Kris S. ... Detroit, MI
Dighe, Kristin W. ... Detroit, MI
Dighello, Richard M., Jr. ... Hartford, CT
Dighero, James E. ... Fair Oaks, CA
Dightman, Maureen J. ... Seattle, WA
DiGia, Kenneth W. ... New York, NY
DiGiacinto, Christopher E. ... New York, NY
DiGiacinto, Joseph W. ... White Plains, NY
DiGiacobbe, Kimberley L. ... Dallas, TX
DiGiacobbe, Toni L. ... Wexford, PA
Digiacomo, Albert D. ... Mattydale, NY
Di Giacomo, Anthony M. ... Stamford, CT
DiGiacomo & Baffa ... Philadelphia, PA
DiGiacomo, Bernard V. ... Conshohocken, PA
DiGiacomo, Brian D.
Department of Commerce, Office of the General Counsel, GV
DiGiacomo, Carol A. ... Chicago, IL
DiGiacomo, Daniel J. ... Philadelphia, PA
DiGiacomo, David R. ... Arvada, CO
DiGiacomo & DeTommasi, L.L.P.
Madison, NJ
Albany, NY
White Plains, NY
DiGiacomo, Frank ... Stuart, FL
DiGiacomo, Frank A. ... Cherry Hill, NJ
DiGiacomo, Frank A. ... Buffalo, NY
DiGiacomo & Jaggers ... Arvada, CO
DiGiacomo, John L. ... Paoli, PA
DiGiacomo, Kunkle and Levin ... Paoli, PA
Di Giacomo, Louis J. ... Philadelphia, PA
DiGiacomo, Michael ... Buffalo, NY
DiGiacomo, Paul D. ... Madison, NJ
Albany, NY
White Plains, NY
DiGiacomo, Paula Cosenza ... Meadville, PA
DiGiacomo, Richard F. ... Buffalo, NY
DiGiacomo, Ron ... Evansville, IN
DiGiacomo, Ruth & Stern
Conshohocken, PA
DiGiacomo, Tina Maria ... Philadelphia, PA
DiGiaimo, Louis P. ... Morristown, NJ
DiGiamberardino, John A. ... Temple, PA
Wyomissing, PA
DiGiandomenico, Judith Nallin ... Newark, NJ
DiGiandomenico, Linda M. ...
Small Business Administration, GV
DiGianfilippo, Joseph M. ... Providence, RI
DiGianfilippo, Stephen J. ... Providence, RI
Di Giantonio, Laura ... Chicago, IL
DiGidio, Mark D. ... Roseland, NJ
DiGiglia, J. Mike ... Baton Rouge, LA
DiGiglio, Frank S. ... Garden City, NY
Digilio, Craig T. ... Poughkeepsie, NY
Digilio, Susan E. ... New York, NY
Di Gioia, Anthony J., Jr. ... West Chester, PA
DiGioia, Donald A. ... Mountainside, NJ
DiGioia, Gina R. ... New York, NY
DiGioia, Victor J. ... New York, NY
Digiorgio, Christopher ... Birmingham, AL
Di Giorgio, Davis, Klein, Wegis, Duggan & Friedman ... Bakersfield, CA
Di Giorgio, Frank C., Sr. ... Baltimore, MD
DiGiorgio, G. Richard (Rick)
Birmingham, AL
DiGiorgio, Jeanne M. ... Boston, MA
DiGiorgio, Joseph M. ... Pittsburgh, PA
Di Giorgio, Joseph P. ... Paoli, PA
Di Giorgio, Philip A. ... Albany, NY
Di Giorgio, V.P., Inc. ... Bakersfield, CA
DiGiorgio, Valentino F. ... Malvern, PA
Di Giorgio, Vincent P. ... Bakersfield, CA
DiGiosia, Lori Beth ... Fairfax, VA
DiGiovanna, Lawrence F. ... Brooklyn, NY
DiGiovanna, Michael D. ... New York, NY
Di Giovanna, Richard ... Albany, NY
DiGiovanni, Carolyn B. ... Philadelphia, PA
DiGiovanni, Cynthia M. ... Palo Alto, CA
Digiovanni, Donna ... Saugus, MA
DiGiovanni, Francis ... Wilmington, DE
DiGiovanni, Frank ... Westfield, NJ
DiGiovanni, Frank R. ... Chicago, IL
DiGiovanni, Joseph ... Reading, MA
DiGiovanni, Joseph A., Jr. ... Washington, DC
DiGiovanni, Kim M. ... Clinton, MD
DiGiovanni, Nicholas, Jr. ... Boston, MA
DiGiovanni, Nick J. ... Chicago, IL
DiGiovanni, Patricia J. ... Cambridge, MA
DiGiovanni, Peter M. ... Leawood, KS
Kansas City, MO
Digiovanni, Peter W. ... Gradyville, PA
DiGiovanni, Philip E. ... Elizabeth, NJ
Di Giovanni, Robert M. ... Washington, DC
DiGiovanni, Thomas G. ... New York, NY
DiGiovanni, Tracy E. ... Port Orchard, WA
DiGirolamo, Alan P. ... Akron, OH
DiGirolamo, Richard G. ... Somerville, MA
Digirolamo, Samuel ... St. Louis, MO
DiGirolamo, Thomas M.
Hagerstown, MD
DiGirolamo, V. Anthony ... Englewood, NJ
Di Girolomo, Alfred C., Jr.
Garden City, NY
DiGirolomo, Lucille S. ... Forest Hills, NY
Digital Law P.A. ... St. Paul, MN
Di Giulian, Bruno L.
Fort Lauderdale, FL
Di Giulian, Teri L. ... Aventura, FL
Di Giulian, Thomas M. ... Decatur, AL
Di Giulio, Barbara ... Chicago, IL
Di Giulio, Christopher P. ... New York, NY
DiGiulio, James M. ... Wakefield, MA
Di Giulio, John E. ... Baton Rouge, LA
New Orleans, LA
Di Giulio, Joseph ... Marina Del Rey, CA
DiGiulio, Lawrence C. ... Buffalo, NY
Di Giulio, Paul J. ... Fort Lauderdale, FL
Di Giulio, Robert T. ... Rochester, NY
Di Giuseppe, James ... Los Angeles, CA
DiGiuseppe, Joseph ... Philadelphia, PA
DiGiuseppe, Stephen A.
Westlake Village, CA
Di Giusto, John E. ... Sacramento, CA
DiGivlian, Maria T. ... Washington, DC
Diglio, Salvatore L. ... Hamden, CT
Dignam, Brett ... New Haven, CT
Dignam, Michael F. ... Fort Myers, FL
Dignam, Michael F., P.A. ... Fort Myers, FL
Dignam, Rhea Kemble ... New York, NY
Dignam, Robert J. ... Merrillville, IN
Dignan, Brian D. ... Brewster, NY
Dignan, Jos. J. ... San Francisco, CA
Dignan, Mary ... Sacramento, CA
Dignan, Robert A., Jr. ... Milford, MA
Dignan, Serena C. ... New York, NY
Dignan, Terrance P. ... Owosso, MI
Dignan, Thomas G. ... Garden City, NY
Dignan, Thomas G., Jr. ... Boston, MA
Dignan, Thomas J. ... Owosso, MI
Dignan, William J. ... Quincy, MA
Dignazio, Michael P. ... Media, PA
Di Grappa, Frank S. ... Denver, CO
DiGrazia, Anthony A. ... Hinsdale, IL
Di Grazia, Anthony R. ... Chicago, IL
Di Grazia, Gary E. ... Elko, NV
di Grazia, Robert P. ... Salem, MA
DiGrazia, Thomas A. ... Kailua, HI
DiGregorio, Andrea M. ... Bronx, NY
Di Gregorio, Anthony J. ... Mineola, NY
DiGregorio, Jennifer J. ... Plymouth, MA
Di Gregorio, Michael A. ... Wilmington, DE
DiGregory, James E. ... Pittsburgh, PA
DiGrigoli, Tomasina ... New York, NY
DiGrigolis, Julie Alyssa ... Baltimore, MD
Towson, MD
Digrugilliers, Renee A. ... Forest Hills, NY
Dihle, Gordon D. ... Evergreen, CO
DiIaconi, Barbara M. ... Klamath Falls, OR
Diianni, Maryann ... Pittsburgh, PA
Di Ianni, Pat ... Hawthorne, NJ
DiIlio, Saundra L. ... Philadelphia, PA
DiIorio, Elena-Faye ... Houston, TX
Di Iorio, John P. ... Hackensack, NJ
DiIorio, Lisa ... Dallas, TX
Di Iorio, Peter ... New York, NY
Dijkman, Christiana ... Houston, TX
Di Joseph, Arnold E., III ... New York, NY
Di Joseph, Portegello & Schuster
New York, NY
Di Julio, Joseph A. ... Virginia Beach, VA
DiJulio, P. Stephen ... Seattle, WA
DiJulio, R. David ... Glendale, CA
DiJulio, Robert L. ... Seattle, WA
Dik, Daniel K. ... Anaheim, CA
Dike, Alexander T. ... Worcester, MA
Dike, Bronstein, Roberts & Cushman
Marlborough, MA
Boston, MA
Dike, Jack A. ... Lincoln, NE
Dike, Jennifer ... Seattle, WA
Dike, Karen D. ... Lincoln, NE
Dike, Tom ... Owensville, IN
Dikeakos, Stephanie P. ... Renton, WA
Dikeman, Mark P. ... Miami, FL
Dikeman, Marvin D. ... Atlanta, GA
Dikeou, Deno P. ... Fern Park, FL
Diker, Ronald M. ... Minneapolis, MN
Dikes, Patti L. ... San Diego, CA
Dikitanan, Rosalinda C. ... New York, NY
Dikman, David S. ... Lake Success, NY
Dikman and Dikman ... Jamaica, NY
Lake Success, NY
Dikman, Jeffrey M. ... Tallahassee, FL
Dikman, Leo ... Lake Success, NY
Dikman, Michael ... Jamaica, NY
Lake Success, NY
Dikmen, Theodore ... San Diego, CA
Dikranis, Frank D. ... Long Beach, NY
Diktas, Christos J. ... Cliffside Park, NJ
Diktas Gillen ... Cliffside Park, NJ
Dikter, Harvey B. ... Philadelphia, PA
DiLabbio, Larry V. ... Sylvania, OH
Dilalla, Salvatore ... Rochester, NY
DiLallo, Kevin S. ... Washington, DC
Di Lando, Michael A. ... Los Angeles, CA
San Francisco, CA
DiLapi, Ellen A. ... New York, NY
DiLascio, Rudolph M., Jr. ... Hollywood, FL
DiLauro, John P. ... Syracuse, NY
DiLauro, Michael A. ... Reston, VA
DiLazzero, Jeffrey A. ... Vineland, NJ
DiLazzero & Minato, P.C. ... Bridgeton, NJ
Vineland, NJ
Dilbeck, Delbert N. ... Chicago, IL
Dilbeck, J. Kevan ... Dallas, TX
Dilbeck, James P., Jr. ... Louisville, KY
Dilbeck, Mark R. ... Woodland Hills, CA
Dilday, Clarence E. ... Roxbury, MA
Dilday, James S. ... Boston, MA
Dilday, Judith Nelson ... Boston, MA
Dildine, Dan B. ... Troy, MO
Dildine, Diane K. ... Washington, DC
Dile, Madelyn M. ... Columbus, OH
DiLella, Anthony C. ... Cedar Grove, NJ
DiLella, Nancy S. ... Nutley, NJ
DiLello, Anthony C. ... Graham, NC
Dilello, Dario ... White Plains, NY
Di Lello, Edward V. ... New York, NY
Dileno, Jon M. ... Cleveland, OH
Dilenschneider, David V. ... Denver, CO
Dilenschneider, John J. ... Columbus, OH
DiLeo, Anthony M., (P.C.)
New Orleans, LA
Dileo, Diana M. D'Alessio ... Mineola, NY
Di Leo, Gregory P. ... New Orleans, LA
Di Leo, Gregory P., A Professional Law Corporation ... New Orleans, LA
Di Leo, Louis M. J. ... Linden, NJ
DiLeo, Lucille A. ... Worcester, MA
Dileo, Matthias D. ... Woodbridge, NJ
DiLeo, Michael J. ... New York, NY
Dileonard, Gary C. ... Forest Hills, NY

DiLeonardo, Joseph W. ....Santa Rosa, CA
DiLeonardo, Thomas S.
Department of Justice, Tax Division, GV
DiLeone, Ralph J. ....Raleigh, NC
DiLettuso, David N. ....Pittsburgh, PA
Di Leva, Charles E. ....Washington, DC
Dilg, G. Robertson ....Orlando, FL
Dilg, Joseph C. ....Houston, TX
Dilgart, Sally L. ....Chicago, IL
Dilger, Craig Christman ....Louisville, KY
Dilger, Kathleen M. ....Rochester Hills, MI
Dilger, Kathleen M., P.C.
Rochester Hills, MI
Dilger, Nathaniel L. ....Irvine, CA
Dilger, Sarah Hulette ....Louisville, KY
DiLibero, Robert J. ....Boston, MA
Dilibero, William A. ....North Kingstown, RI
Dilibert, Karen J. ....Itasca, IL
Diliberti, Mark J. ....Milwaukee, WI
DiLiberti-Goldsmith, Cher
Laguna Beach, CA
DiLiberto, Grace ....Chesterfield, VA
Diliberto, Michael R. ....Los Angeles, CA
DiLiberto, Richard A., Jr.
Wilmington, DE
Diliberto, Robert J. ....New Orleans, LA
Diliberto, Salvatore A. ....New York, NY
Diliberto, Salvatore A.
Queens Village, NY
Dilimetin, Anthony K. ....New York, NY
Dilimetin and Dilimetin ....New York, NY
Dilimetin, Laura M. ....New York, NY
diLiscia, Elenora R. ....Chicago, IL
diLiscia & Keenan ....Chicago, IL
diLiscia-Everett, Rose C. ....Ann Arbor, MI
DiLisi, Richard A. ....Cleveland, OH
DiLisio, Carl A. ....St. Louis, MO
DiLisio, Kelli Ryan ....Springfield, MA
Dilk, Andrew J., Jr.
Department of Transportation,
Federal Aviation Administration, GV
Dilk, Gary L. ....Fishers, IN
Indianapolis, IN
Dilkes, C. Edward ....Los Angeles, CA
Dilkes, Eleanor M. ....Iowa City, IA
Dilks, Joseph G. ....Haddonfield, NJ
Dilks, Park B., Jr. ....Philadelphia, PA
Dilks, Rodeen & Gibson & Smith, Ltd.
Paxton, IL
Dilks, Russell C. ....Madison, NJ
Dilks, Sidney H. ....Paxton, IL
Dilks, William D. ....Gloucester City, NJ
Dill, Alexander C. ....New York, NY
Dill, Alonzo T., III
Federal Deposit Insurance Corporation,
Professional Liability Section, GV
Dill, Barbara J. ....New York, NY
Dill, Craig H. ....Saginaw, MI
Dill, Cynthia A. ....Portland, ME
Dill, Daniel F. ....Orlando, FL
Dill, David G. ....Newport Beach, CA
Dill, Dill, Carr, Stonbraker & Hutchings, P.C. ....Denver, CO
Dill, Donald L. ....Denver, CO
Dill, Everett C. ....Portage, MI
Dill, Fountain, Hoyle, Pridgen, Stroud & Naylor, L.L.P. ....Rocky Mount, NC
Dill, Franklin A. ....Orinda, CA
Dill, Fred H. ....Redlands, CA
Dill, G. Redmond, Jr. ....Valdese, NC
Dill, Glenn ....Kenmare, ND
Dill, Gordon J., Jr. ....Ashland, KY
Dill, Gordon J., P.S.C. ....Ashland, KY
Dill, H. Alan ....Denver, CO
Dill, J. Anthony ....St. Louis, MO
Dill, James M. ....Lafayette, LA
Dill, James R. ....Northbrook, IL
Dill, Jeffrey ....Costa Mesa, CA
Dill, Jimmy D. ....Pine Bluff, AR
Dill, John L. ....St. Louis, MO
Dill, John W. ....Winter Park, FL
Dill, Jon W. ....Rapid City, SD
Dill, Karen A. ....St. Louis, MO
Dill, Larry L. ....Wolcott, IN
Dill, Matthew T. ....Wilmington, NC
Dill, Michael W. ....Dallas, TX
Dill, Pamela W. ....Jackson, MS
Dill, Peter F. ....Seattle, WA
Dill, Peter J. ....Westborough, MA
Dill, R. Joseph ....Jacksonville, FL
Dill, Ralph E. ....Columbus, OH
Dill, Randy ....Huntsville, AL
Dill, Richard E. ....Lancaster, NH
Dill, Richard J. ....Marlton, NJ
Dill, Robert A. ....Denver, CO
Dill & Showler ....Redlands, CA
Dill, Terrance D., Jr. ....Houston, TX
Dill, Terry ....Long Beach, MS
Dill, Thomas A. ....Tampa, FL
Pioche, NV
Dill, Thomas A. ....Sharon, PA
Dill, Thomas C. ....Waukesha, WI
Dill, Thomas G. ....Rocky Mount, NC
Dill, Trudi ....Temple, TX
Dill, W. Allen ....Sharon, PA
Dill, Wamser Bamvakais & Newsham, P.C.
St. Louis, MO
Dill, Warren W. ....Sebastian, FL
Dill, William Glenn, Jr. ....Miami, FL
Dill, William R. ....Norman, OK
Dill, William S. ....Valentine, NE
Dill, Winston E. ....Baltimore, MD
Dillabough, Elizabeth S. Gioiosa
New York, NY
Dillaha, Theo. A., Jr. ....Little Rock, AR
Dillahey, Wayne R. ....Philadelphia, PA
Dillahunty, Benjamin P. ....La Jolla, CA
Dillahunty, Larry L. ....St. Petersburg, FL
Dillahunty, Larry L., P.A. ....St. Petersburg, FL
Dillahunty, Mary Ann ....Redwood City, CA
Dillahunty, T. Gene ....Redwood City, CA
Dillahunty, W. H. ....Little Rock, AR
Dillane, John W. ....St. Louis, MO
Dillaplain, Courtney A. ....Los Angeles, CA
Dillard, A. Fleet, III ....Tappahannock, VA
Dillard, A. Wayne ....Kansas City, MO
Dillard, Alexander F., Jr.
Tappahannock, VA
Dillard, Arthur L. ....Paoli, IN
Dillard & Bower ....Douglas, GA
Waycross, GA
Woodbine, GA
Dillard, Brian L. ....Silver Spring, MD
Dillard, C. Denise ....Houston, TX
Dillard, Carol C. ....Chicago, IL
Dillard, Craig S. ....Montgomery, AL
Dillard, Cynthia L. ....Kansas City, MO
Dillard, David A. ....Pasadena, CA
Dillard, Dennis A. ....Little Rock, AR
Dillard, Denver D. ....Cedar Rapids, IA
Dillard, G. Douglas ....Atlanta, GA
Dillard & Galloway, LLC ....Atlanta, GA
Dillard, Godfrey J. ....Detroit, MI
Dillard, J. Amy Gretchen ....Alexandria, VA
Dillard, J. Tilden ....Decatur, AL
Dillard, Jack W. ....Bryan, TX
Dillard, James C. ....Flint, MI
Dillard, Jeffery D. ....Chicago, IL
Dillard, Joel E. ....Birmingham, AL
Dillard, Joelle Jackson ....Jacksonville, FL
Dillard, John M. ....Greenville, SC
Dillard, John M., Law Offices of
Santa Ana, CA
Dillard, John R. ....Asheville, NC
Dillard, Joseph F. ....Detroit, MI
Dillard, Judith Loucks ....Tallahassee, FL
Dillard and Katona ....Tappahannock, VA
Warsaw, VA
Dillard, Kirk W. ....Chicago, IL
Dillard, L. Bradley ....Tupelo, MS
Memphis, TN
Dillard, Lester L. ....South Boston, VA
Dillard, Luecretia D. ....Houston, TX
Dillard, McElvaney & Kovach, L.L.P.
Houston, TX
Dillard, Michael E., (P.C.) ....Dallas, TX
Dillard, Michael L. ....Sacramento, CA
Dillard, Michelle Hargis ....Denver, CO
Dillard & Noel ....Chicago, IL
Dillard, Pamela H. ....Athens, GA
Dillard, R. Geoffrey ....Toccoa, GA
Dillard, R. Howard ....Cape Girardeau, MO
Dillard, Richard T. ....Dover, DE
Dillard, R. L., Jr. ....Dallas, TX
Dillard, Robert L., III ....Dallas, TX
Dillard, Roger Lee, Jr. ....Winston-Salem, NC
Dillard, Stephen C. ....Houston, TX
Dillard, Stephen Louis A. ....Macon, GA
Dillard, Terry A. ....Waycross, GA
Dillard, Thomas D., Jr. ....Las Vegas, NV
Dillard, Thomas S. ....San Clemente, CA
Dillard, Timothy L. ....Birmingham, AL
Dillard, Truett O. ....Livingston, TX
Dillard, William E., III ....Savannah, GA
Dillard, William Thomas, III
Knoxville, TN
Dillard, William V. ....Birmingham, AL
Dillard, W. O. ....Jackson, MS
Dillaway, Steven B. ....San Diego, CA
Dillawn, J. Stephen ....Austin, TX
Dille, Benjamin B. ....Shakopee, MN
Dille, Brent F. ....Seattle, WA
Dille, Bryce H., (P.S.) ....Puyallup, WA
Dille, David H. ....Pittsburgh, PA
Dille, Deborah L. ....Birmingham, AL
Dille, Robert E. ....Baton Rouge, LA
Dille, Timothy W. ....Fairfield, IA
Dillehay, Kristin A. ....Palo Alto, CA
Dillemuth, Walter F. ....La Jolla, CA
Dillen, Jeffrey S. ....Minneapolis, MN
Dillenbeck, Richard R. ....New York, NY
Dillender, David C. ....Nashville, TN
Dillender, Melanie Valunas ....Nashville, TN
Dillenseger, Dominique
Federal Election Commission,
Office of the General Counsel, GV
Diller, Edward D. ....Cincinnati, OH
Diller, Jon N. ....Pandora, OH
Diller, Kathleen L. ....Findlay, OH
Diller, Mark N. ....New York, NY
Diller, Matthew ....New York, NY
Diller, Michael L. ....Trenton, NJ
Diller, Nicole A. ....San Francisco, CA
Diller, Ralph L. ....Worcester, MA
Diller, Samuel W. ....Bluffton, OH
Diller, Steven L. ....Toledo, OH
Van Wert, OH
Diller, Tom D. ....Portland, IN
Dilley, A. Newton ....Grand Rapids, MI
Dilley, Albert R. ....Grand Rapids, MI
Dilley and Associates, Ltd. ....Appleton, WI
Dilley, David D. ....Cranbury, NJ
Dilley, David E., Jr. ....San Antonio, TX
Dilley, Dean M. ....Washington, DC
Dilley & Dewey, P.C. ....Grand Rapids, MI
Dilley, Dilley, Murkowski & Goller
Grand Rapids, MI
Dilley, Donald C. ....Grand Rapids, MI
Dilley, Douglas E. ....San Antonio, TX
Dilley, Frederick D. ....Grand Rapids, MI
Dilley, Jan L. ....Peoria, AZ
Dilley, Jan L., P.L.C. ....Peoria, AZ
Dilley, Jeffrey S. ....Clarksdale, MS
Dilley, Lorn M. ....Appleton, WI
Dilley, Nancy J. ....St. Louis, MO
Dilley, Nancy L. ....Grand Rapids, MI
Dilley, Patricia E. ....Tacoma, WA
Dilley, Ralph J. ....Traverse City, MI
Dilley, Robert W. ....Grand Rapids, MI
Dilley & Rominger ....Grand Rapids, MI
Dilley, Steven C. ....East Lansing, MI
Dilley, Thomas R. ....Grand Rapids, MI
Dilli, John J., Jr. ....Baltimore, MD
Dillian, James A., (P.A.) ....Miami, FL
Dillick, Steven A. ....San Francisco, CA
Dilligan, Michael A. ....San Diego, CA
Dilliha, Gary L. ....Springfield, TN
Dillin, Hiram S. ....Roseville, CA
Dillin, Hiram S., Inc. ....Roseville, CA
Sacramento, CA
Dillin, S. Hugh ....Indianapolis, IN
Dilling & Deutinger ....Fresno, CA
Dilling, Diana J. ....Northbrook, IL
Dilling & Dilling ....Chicago, IL
Dilling, James A. ....Fresno, CA
Dilling, Kirkpatrick W. ....Chicago, IL
Dilling, Robert M. ....Falls Church, VA
Dilling, Thomas A. ....Columbus, OH
Dillinger, Jane E. ....Dallas, TX
Dillinger, Jason Patrick ....Washington, DC
Dillinger, Robert H. ....Clearwater, FL
Dillingham, Blase P. ....Los Angeles, CA
Dillingham, Bruce E. ....Southport, CT
Dillingham, Charles ....Brenham, TX
Dillingham, Charles, P.C. ....Brenham, TX
Dillingham Cross, P.L.L.C. ....Phoenix, AZ
Dillingham, James W. ....Bend, OR
Dillingham, John L. ....Phoenix, AZ
Dillingham, Kenneth E. ....Elkton, KY
Dillingham & Murphy, LLP
San Francisco, CA
Dillingham, Nancy K. ....Flint, MI
Dillingham, Nicole A. ....San Francisco, CA
Dillingham, Paul W. ....Rock Hill, SC
Dillingham, Ruth A. ....Quincy, MA
Dillingham, Wayne E. ....Kingwood, TX
Dillingham, William O.
San Francisco, CA
Dillion, Bosch, Daw & Bock, Chartered
Boise, ID
Dillion, Charles B. ....Denver, CO
Dillion, Clarissa Friend ....Pikeville, KY
Dillion, Cynthia Shimon
Newport Beach, CA
Dillion, Gregory L. ....Newport Beach, CA
Dillion, Lee B. ....Boise, ID
Dillman, Alvin E., Jr. ....Pittsburgh, PA
Dillman, Andrea R. ....Houston, TX
Dillman, Harold E. ....Corydon, IN
Dillman, Holbrook, Wurtz, Roth & Rostollan
Sheboygan, WI
Dillman, Howard ....Homestead, FL
Dillman, James S.
Department of Transportation,
Federal Aviation Administration, GV
Dillman, Jeffrey D. ....Ann Arbor, MI
Dillman, John M. ....Danbury, CT
Dillman, John P. ....Houston, TX
Dillman, Kirk D. ....Los Angeles, CA
Dillman, Linda Watson ....Orlando, FL
Dillman, Lisa M. ....Indianapolis, IN
Dillman, Lori Huff ....Los Angeles, CA
Dillman, Louis W. ....Brunswick, ME
Dillman, Noreen A. ....Wethersfield, CT
Dillman, Rodney J. ....Hartford, CT
Dillmann, Brendan J. ....Milwaukee, WI
Dillmann, Delores M. ....Treasury Department,
Internal Revenue Service, GV
Dillmann, Todd A. ....Fond du Lac, WI
Dillmeier, William E. ....Garden City, NY
Dillner, J. David ....South Holland, IL
Dillner, Scott ....South Holland, IL
Dillof, Anthony Morris ....Fort Worth, TX
Dillof, Henry H. ....New York, NY
Dillof, Robert ....New York, NY
Dillof, William R. ....New York, NY
Dilloff, Neil J. ....Baltimore, MD
Dillon, Andrew D. ....St. Louis, MO
Dillon, Andrew J. ....Austin, TX
Dillon, Ann G. ....Austin, TX
Dillon, Anthony ....Greensboro, NC
Dillon, Arthur A. ....Blauvelt, NY
Dillon, Barbara Reist ....Ephrata, PA
Lancaster, PA
Lititz, PA
Dillon, Bitar & Luther ....Morristown, NJ
Dillon, Bradley D. ....Hutchinson, KS
Dillon, Bradley E. ....Louisville, KY
Dillon, Bryan J. ....New Albany, IN
Louisville, KY
Dillon, C. Brien ....Houston, TX
Dillon, Carol K. ....Palo Alto, CA
Dillon, Carol M. ....Amsterdam, NY
Dillon, Caroline M.W. ....Charleston, SC
Dillon, Carrol F. ....Sarasota, FL
Dillon, Charles E. ....Butler, PA
Dillon, Charles T. ....St. Petersburg, FL
Dillon, Christopher D. ....Menlo Park, CA
San Francisco, CA
Dillon, Christopher H. ....New York, NY
Dillon, Christopher S., & Associates, P.L.C.
Richmond, VA
Dillon, Christopher S. ....Richmond, VA
Dillon, Constance M. ....Olympia, WA
Dillon, Daniel H. ....Buffalo, NY
Dillon, Daniel J. ....Rockville Centre, NY
Dillon, Daniel T. ....Janesville, WI
Dillon, David B. ....Hutchinson, KS
Dillon, David C. ....Chicago, IL
Dillon, David M. ....Rapid City, SD
Dillon, David M. ....Austin, TX
Dillon, David Reid ....Ironton, OH
Dillon, David S. ....Salt Lake City, UT
Dillon, Dawn M. ....Raleigh, NC
Dillon, Debora J. ....White Plains, NY
Dillon, Deirdre A. ....New York, NY
Dillon, Denis ....Boston, MA
Dillon, Denis E. ....Mineola, NY
Dillon, Dennis M. ....Tallman, NY
Dillon, Diane L. ....Napa, CA
St. Helena, CA
Dillon, Dianne M. ....Springfield, MA
Dillon & Dillon, P.C. ....Plymouth, MI
Dillon, Donald E. ....Bryan, TX
Dillon, Donald R., Jr. ....Birmingham, MI
Columbus, OH
Dillon, Dorothy P. ....Rocky Mount, VA
Dillon, Dorothy S. ....Little Rock, AR
Dillon, Douglas J. ....Houston, TX
Dillon, Edward B., Jr. ....Little Rock, AR
Dillon, Edward E., Jr. ....Slatersville, RI
Dillon, Elizabeth J. ....Washington, DC
Dillon, Elizabeth M. ....San Francisco, CA
Chicago, IL
Dillon, Erica E. ....New York, NY
Dillon, Erika ....Chicago, IL
Dillon, Field, Monk & Stedham, P.A.
Anniston, AL
Dillon & Findley, P.C. ....Anchorage, AK
Juneau, AK
Dillon, Forrest O. ....Detroit, MI
Dillon, Francis B. ....Sacramento, CA
Dillon, Francis X. ....Newtown, PA
Dillon, Frank P. ....Merrick, NY
Dillon, Geary P. ....Whitwell, TN
Dillon, Gerard M. ....Mandeville, LA
Dillon, G. L. ....Utica, NY
Dillon, Gregory R. ....Beverly Hills, CA
Dillon, Haber & Dillon ....Roslyn Heights, NY
Dillon, Haradon M. ....Pleasant Hill, CA
Dillon, Heath ....Baton Rouge, LA
Dillon, Helen C. ....Portland, OR
Dillon, Herbert J. ....Roslyn Heights, NY
Dillon, J. Alexander ....Farmington Hills, MI
Dillon, J. Matthew ....Charleston, SC
Dillon, J. Russell ....Olathe, KS
Dillon, J. Scott ....Greensboro, NC
Dillon, J. Terrance ....Grand Rapids, MI
Dillon, James E. ....Charlotte, NC
Dillon, James J., (P.C.) ....Boston, MA
Dillon, James L. ....San Francisco, CA
Dillon, Janet J. ....Oxnard, CA
Pasadena, CA
Dillon, Jannell C. ....Fort Smith, AR
Dillon, Jean H. ....Monmouth Beach, NJ
Dillon, Jennifer L. ....Chicago, IL
Dillon, Jesse A. ....Allentown, PA
Dillon, Jessica L. ....Denver, CO
Dillon, Joan L. ....Atlanta, GA
Dillon, John A. ....Buffalo, NY
Dillon, John B. ....Chicago, IL
Dillon, John David ....Franklin, NC
Dillon, John J. ....Chevy Chase, MD
Dillon, John J. ....Garden City, NY
Dillon, John, Jr. ....New City, NY
Dillon, John M. ....Bridgeport, CT
Dillon, John M. ....Detroit, MI
Dillon, John Ryder
Grosse Pointe Farms, MI
Dillon, John T. ....Guilford, CT
Dillon, John W. ....Utica, NY
Dillon, Joseph F. ....Detroit, MI
Dillon, Judith L. ....Burlington, VT
Dillon, Karen L. ....Los Angeles, CA
Dillon, Kathryn A. ....Cranston, RI
Dillon, Kelly A. ....Minot, ND
Dillon, Kevin M. ....Buffalo, NY
Dillon, Larry B. ....Florence, KY
Dillon, Lauren K. Heggestad
Wellesley, MA
Dillon Law Office ....Rapid City, SD
Dillon, Lewis & Young, A Professional
Corporation ....Bryan, TX
Dillon, Linda M. H. ....Utica, NY
Dillon, Lura L. ....Mather, CA
Dillon, M. Raymond ....Kansas City, KS
Dillon, Marian J. ....Somers, NY
Dillon, Mark C. ....White Plains, NY
Dillon, Mark D. ....Scottsdale, AZ
Dillon, Mark J. ....Carlsbad, CA
Dillon, Mary Jo ....Butler, PA
Cranberry Township, PA
Saxonburg, PA
Dillon, Mary Margaret ....Raleigh, NC
Dillon McCandless King Coulter & Graham L.L.P. ....Butler, PA
Cranberry Township, PA
Saxonburg, PA
Dillon, Melissa S. ....Atlanta, GA
Dillon, Michael A. ....Forsyth, GA
Dillon, Michael A. ....Harrisburg, PA
Dillon, Michael David ....Nashville, TN
Dillon, Michael J. ....Jersey City, NJ
Dillon, Michael R. ....Philadelphia, PA
Dillon, Molly L. ....Los Angeles, CA
Dillon & Nash, Ltd. ....Chicago, IL
Dillon, Neal ....Logan, OH
Dillon, Neal, Co., L.P.A. ....Logan, OH
Dillon, Otis J. ....Houston, TX
Dillon, Patricia M. ....New York, NY
Dillon, Paul J. ....Plymouth, MI
Dillon, Paul J. ....Livingston, NJ
Dillon, Paul L. ....Juneau, AK
Dillon, Paul L. ....New York, NY
Dillon, Paul O. ....Exeter, ME
Dillon, Peter Gardner ....Oklahoma City, OK
Dillon, Raymond L. ....Mansfield, OH
Dillon, Rebecca L. ....Lancaster, PA
Dillon, Richard T. ....St. Petersburg, FL
Dillon, Richd. E. ....Columbus, OH
Dillon, Robert C. ....Anniston, AL
Dillon, Robert E. ....Coral Springs, FL

Dillon, Robert E. .... Rye, NY
Dillon, Robert E. .... Philadelphia, PA
Dillon, Robert W. .... Sacramento, CA
Dillon, Robert W. .... Miami, FL
Dillon, Roberta S. .... Sterling, IL
Dillon, Robin L. .... Jackson, MS
Dillon & Rodgers .... Sacramento, CA
Dillon, Rodney L. .... Sarasota, FL
Dillon, Ronald C. .... Coral Springs, FL
Dillon, Rosemary .... Albuquerque, NM
Dillon, Sean M. .... Orlando, FL
Dillon, Shawna Dawn .... Vincennes, IN
Dillon, Sidney G. .... Morristown, NJ
Dillon, Stephen P. .... Houston, TX
Dillon, Theresa Ann .... Brockton, MA
Dillon, Thomas .... New York, NY
Dillon, Thomas A. .... Columbus, OH
Dillon, Thomas A., Jr. .... Chicago, IL
Dillon, Thomas J. .... Chicago, IL
Dillon, Thomas J., III .... Richmond, VA
Dillon, Thomas J., Jr. .... Tustin, MI
Dillon, Thomas M. .... Anchorage, AK
Dillon, Thomas M., P.C. .... Anchorage, AK
Dillon, Thomas P. .... Toledo, OH
Dillon, Thomas W. .... Geneva, IL
Dillon, Thos J. .... Savannah, GA
Dillon, Timothy C. .... Aurora, IL
Dillon, Timothy K. .... Cannon Falls, MN
Dillon, Timothy P. .... Claremont, CA
Dillon, Timothy P. .... La Jolla, CA
Dillon, Timothy P. .... Ansonia, CT
Dillon, Tom .... Atlanta, GA
Dillon, Trace .... Atlanta, GA
Dillon, Veronica .... Washington, DC
Dillon, W. Lyman .... Atlanta, GA
Dillon, Wells H. .... St. Marys, WV
Dillon, Wendy A. .... Cleveland, OH
Dillon, Wilburn, Jr. .... Topeka, KS
Dillon, William A. .... Chicago, IL
Dillon, William B., III .... Payette, ID
Dillon, William Daniel .... Atlanta, GA
Dillon, William E. .... Oakbrook Terrace, IL
Dillon, William H. .... Boston, MA
Dillon, William M. .... Santa Barbara, CA
Dillon, William S. .... Chicago Ridge, IL
Dillon, William S., Jr. .... Wheaton, IL
Dillon, Wm. J. .... St. Paul, MN
Dillon-D'Orsi, Tara .... Newark, NJ
Dillow, John D. .... Seattle, WA
Dillow, Larry R. .... Kingsport, TN
Dillow, Ralph M., Jr. .... Bristol, VA
Dillow, Robert Eugene, Jr. .... Wilmington, NC
Dillow, Willard A., III .... Branson, MO
Dillport, Donald B. .... New York, NY
Dillport, Sue Ann G. .... New York, NY
Dills, Alan B. .... Toledo, OH
Dills, Jonathan S. .... Winston-Salem, NC
Dills, Jonathan S. The Law Offices of, P.A.
Winston-Salem, NC
Dills, Leighton Ralph .... Sacramento, CA
Dills, Patrice Raye .... Oklahoma City, OK
Dillsaver, Joe D. .... Tulsa, OK
Dillworth & Dillworth, P.C. .... Hollis, NY
Dillworth, Drew M. .... Miami, FL
Dillworth, Richard Scott .... Hollis, NY
Dillworth, Robt. S. .... Hollis, NY
DiLonardo, Anna M. .... Garden City, NY
Dilorati, Daniel E .... Boston, MA
DiLorenzo, Chris M. .... Hackensack, NJ
DiLorenzo & Hamel, P.A. .... Ocala, FL
DiLorenzo, Jack T. .... Washington, DC
DiLorenzo, James D. .... Ocala, FL
DiLorenzo, John A., Jr. .... Portland, OR
Di Lorenzo, John F., Jr. .... Columbus, OH
DiLorenzo, Kirby W. .... Troy, NY
DiLorenzo, Louis P. .... Syracuse, NY
Di Lorenzo, Maria F. .... Hoffman Estates, IL
DiLorenzo, P. Charles .... Bloomfield, NJ
Di Lorenzo, Robert J. .... Nevada City, CA
DiLorenzo & Rush .... Hackensack, NJ
DiLorenzo, Sarah .... Chicago, IL
DiLorenzo, Stephen L. .... New York, NY
DiLorenzo, Theodore J. .... Hartford, CT
DiLorenzo, Vincent .... Jamaica, NY
DiLoreto, Cosentino & Bolinger
Chambersburg, PA
Harrisburg, PA
DiLoreto, Denis M. .... Chambersburg, PA
Di Loreto & Di Loreto .... Winchester, MA
Di Loreto, Elizabeth A. .... Winchester, MA
Di Loreto, Emidio .... Winchester, MA
DiLoreto, Frank L. .... Chicago, IL
Di Loreto, Joseph E. .... Downey, CA
Di Loreto, Mario .... Manchester, CT
DiLoretto, Daniel V. .... Philadelphia, PA
Dils, Arthur K. .... Harrisburg, PA
Dils & Bergdoll .... New Whiteland, IN
Dils, Jan .... Parkersburg, WV
Dils, Jimmy B. .... New Whiteland, IN
Dilsaver, Nelson & Schnibben
Charleston, IL
Mattoon, IL
Dilschneider, Henry Adolphus .... Tulsa, OK
Dilsheimer, James B. .... Philadelphia, PA
Dilthey, Ronald C. .... Raleigh, NC
Dilts, Dee W. .... Dallas, TX
Dilts, Fred W., III .... Douglas, WY
Dilts, George M. .... Flemington, NJ
Dilts, Gregory A. .... Torrance, CA
Dilts, Jon Paul .... Bloomington, IN
Dilts, Joseph L. .... Cincinnati, OH
Dilts, Macary and Calvin
Fort Washington, PA
Dilts, Mark N. .... Fort Washington, PA
Dilts, Robert D. .... Covington, KY
Dilts, Robt. .... Ridgewood, NJ
Dilts, Thomas H. .... Somerville, NJ
Diltz, Peter C. .... Sturgeon Bay, WI

DiLucci, Raymond J. .... Concord, NH
DiLucci, Raymond J., P.A. .... Concord, NH
Di Luccio, Jeffrey M. .... Mineola, NY
Diluccio, Patrick M. .... Valley Stream, NY
Di Lucia, Gilbert A. .... Cooperstown, NY
DiLuglio, Charles H. .... East Greenwich, RI
DiLuglio, Raymond A. .... Boise, ID
DiLuglio, Thomas R. .... Johnston, RI
DiLuia, Edward A. .... Flossmoor, IL
DiLullo, Thomas F. .... Hackensack, NJ
DiLuna, Francis A. .... Woburn, MA
Di Luna, R. Lisa .... Boston, MA
DiLuzio, Adrian L. .... Mineola, NY
DiLuzio, C. Bruce .... Spokane, WA
DiLuzio, Louis Michael .... New York, NY
Dilweg, Vivi L. .... Green Bay, WI
Dilworth, Amy K. .... Richmond, VA
Dilworth, Andrew I. .... San Francisco, CA
Dilworth & Barrese .... Mineola, NY
New York, NY
Riverhead, NY
Uniondale, NY
Dilworth, Christopher W. .... Falmouth, ME
Dilworth, Edmond J., Jr.
Birmingham, MI
Dilworth, Edward L., III .... Norway, ME
Dilworth, George T. .... Portland, ME
Dilworth, Hal C., Jr. .... Huntsville, AL
Dilworth, Harrison P. .... St. Paul, MN
Dilworth, James W. .... Riverside, CA
Dilworth, Keith .... Richmond, IN
Dilworth, Lee C. .... Nashville, TN
Dilworth, Lucienne F. .... San Francisco, CA
Dilworth, Michael P. .... Uniondale, NY
Dilworth, Norman E. .... Bloomfield Hills, MI
Dilworth, Pamela S. .... Houston, TX
Dilworth Paxson LLP .... Wilmington, DE
Cherry Hill, NJ
Turnersville, NJ
Harrisburg, PA
Media, PA
Philadelphia, PA
Dilworth, Peter G. .... Uniondale, NY
Dilworth, Robert H. .... Washington, DC
Dilworth, Robert J., Jr. (IBA)
New York, NY
Dilzer, Daniel .... New Britain, CT
Dim, Martin L. .... Deerfield, IL
DiMaggio, Anthony .... Newark, NJ
DiMaggio, Dale Paul
Fort Lauderdale, FL
Miami, FL
West Palm Beach, FL
DiMaggio, Debra .... Chicago, IL
DiMaggio, Diana .... Lemon Grove, CA
DiMaggio, Frank V. .... Perryville, MO
Ste. Genevieve, MO
Dimaggio, Kathleen A. .... Perryville, MO
Di Maggio, Richard L., Jr. .... Clifton Park, NY
DiMaggio, Samuel A. .... Grand Ledge, MI
DiMaggio, Susan L. .... New London, CT
Di Maio, Dominick A. .... New York, NY
DiMaio & George, Inc. .... Pawtucket, RI
DiMaio, Joseph-Anthony .... Pawtucket, RI
Di Maio, Mary Ann .... Philadelphia, PA
Dimaio, Mary Malloy .... Towson, MD
Di Maio, Paul J. .... Warren, NJ
DiMaio, Samantha Ann .... Houston, TX
Di Maio, Thomas J. .... New York, NY
DiMaiolo, Mindy .... New York, NY
DiMaiolo, Vincent, Jr. .... Parsippany, NJ
DiMaiti, Mary C. .... Boston, MA
Dimalanta, John Erick .... Walnut Creek, CA
Dimaline, A.J., IV .... San Antonio, TX
DiMango, Patricia M. .... Brooklyn, NY
DiManna & Jackson .... Denver, CO
DiManna, Michael F., (P.C.) .... Denver, CO
DiManni, Margherita L. .... New York, NY
DiManno, Gerald T. .... New York, NY
Di Marco, Andrew J. .... Santa Ana, CA
Di Marco, Araujo & Montevideo, A Prof. Law Corp. .... Santa Ana, CA
DiMarco, Bret M. .... Palo Alto, CA
DiMarco, Carla V. .... Rome, NY
DiMarco, Cerio A. .... New Orleans, LA
DiMarco, Cynthia A. .... Staten Island, NY
Di Marco, David C. .... Rochester, NY
DiMarco, Deborah A. .... Dallas, TX
Di Marco, Felicia M.
Securities and Exchange Commission, Office of Compliance Inspections and Examinations, GV
Di Marco, Frank P. .... New Rochelle, NY
DiMarco, Gerard D. .... Rochester, NY
Di Marco, Richard J. .... Bridgeport, CT
Westport, CT
DiMarco, Richard P. .... Mayfield Heights, OH
Di Marco, Steven J. .... Santa Ana, CA
DiMare, Charles A. .... Medford, MA
DiMare, Charles J. .... Amherst, MA
Di Mare, Frank S. .... Staten Island, NY
Dimare, Leonard E. .... Philadelphia, PA
Di Mare, Louis A., Jr. .... Westfield, NJ
DiMari, John M. .... Omaha, NE
Di Maria, Carmen J. .... Morristown, NJ
Di Maria & Cone .... Palo Alto, CA
Di Maria & Di Maria .... Lodi, NJ
Di Maria, Frederick M. .... Lodi, NJ
DiMaria, Joseph F. .... Mandeville, LA
Di Maria, Joseph S. .... Paramus, NJ
DiMaria, Mark E. .... Los Angeles, CA
Di Maria, Philip A. .... Palo Alto, CA
DiMaria, Susan M. .... Philadelphia, PA
DiMariano, Eugene A., Jr. .... Concord, NH
Di Marino, Anthony J., III
Cherry Hill, NJ
Philadelphia, PA
Di Marino, Frank J. .... Savannah, GA

Di Marino, Louis P. .... Olean, NY
DiMario, Michael F.
Government Printing Office, GV
DiMario, Salvatore D. .... East Moline, IL
DiMarsico, Andrew J.
New Brunswick, NJ
DiMartini, Nancy McRandal .... Monaca, PA
Di Martini, Patrick W. .... Jersey City, NJ
DiMartini, Stuart .... New York, NY
DiMartino, Anthony J., Jr. .... Oswego, NY
DiMartino, Horace R. .... Washington, DC
DiMartino, I. V. .... Pennsauken, NJ
DiMartino, Lisa T. .... Los Angeles, CA
DiMartino, Michele A. .... Media, PA
DiMartino, Rose F. .... New York, NY
DiMartino, Theresa M. .... New York, NY
DiMarzio, David A. .... Providence, RI
DiMarzio, Dennis D. .... Bowling Green, OH
Di Marzio, Philip L. .... St. Charles, IL
DiMarzo, Audrey Price .... Boston, MA
DiMarzo, Mario D. .... Brockton, MA
Dimas, Anthony .... Pleasant Hill, CA
Dimas, James J. G. .... Louisville, KY
Dimas, Marilyn D. .... Rockville, MD
Dimas, Simos C. .... New York, NY
Di Mascio, Denise M. .... Fresno, CA
Dimascio, Dianne .... Santa Monica, CA
DiMascio, John P., Jr. .... Garden City, NY
DiMascio, John P., The Law Offices of
Garden City, NY
DiMasi, Brian M. .... Erie, PA
DiMasi, Heather J. .... Erie, PA
Di Masi, John L. .... Winter Park, FL
Di Masi, Rebecca S. C. .... Austin, TX
Dimasi, Vincent A. .... Cincinnati, OH
Di Massa, Anthony M. .... Philadelphia, PA
Di Massa Associates, Ltd. .... Philadelphia, PA
Di Massa, Rudolph J. .... Philadelphia, PA
DiMassa, Rudolph J., Jr. .... Philadelphia, PA
Dimassimo, James D. .... Rochester, NY
Di Matteo, Anthony
West Palm Beach, FL
DiMatteo, David M. .... Warsaw, NY
DiMatteo, John M. .... New York, NY
DiMatteo, Philip S. .... Sun City West, AZ
DiMatteo, Philip S., P.C.
Sun City West, AZ
DiMatteo, Vincent J. .... Middletown, NJ
DiMattia, A.J. .... Ridgefield, CT
Di Mattia, Michael J. .... New York, NY
Dimauro, Andrew T. .... Springfield, MA
di Mauro, Geoffrey B. .... Orlando, FL
Di Mauro, Joseph F. .... Bolton Landing, NY
DiMauro, Joseph F., P.A.
Bolton Landing, NY
Dimauro, Michael A. .... Staten Island, NY
Di Mauro, Nicholas J. .... Boston, MA
DiMauro, Robert J. .... Hollywood, FL
DiMauro, Thomas M. .... Worcester, MA
Dimeff, Carl L. .... Encinitas, CA
Dimeff, Stephen J. .... San Diego, CA
DiMeglio, James .... Pontiac, MI
DiMeglio, David J. .... Los Angeles, CA
DiMeglio, Gregory .... McLean, VA
DiMeglio, John F. .... North Providence, RI
Di Meglio, Marisa .... New York, NY
DiMeglio, Ruth .... Providence, RI
DiMeglio, Samuel J., Jr. .... Deer Park, NY
Dimeling, William R. .... Philadelphia, PA
Dimengo, Steven A. .... Akron, OH
DiMenno, Joseph A. .... Pittsburgh, PA
Dimenstein & Celentano .... Milford, CT
Dimenstein, Morton J. .... Milford, CT
Diment, Barbara J. .... West Des Moines, IA
Diment, Dana Garrett .... Carrollton, GA
Diment, Donald D., Jr. .... Eugene, OR
Diment, J. Kester, II .... San Francisco, CA
Diment, Richard A. .... Carrollton, GA
Diment & Walker .... Eugene, OR
DiMento, Anthony F. .... Cherry Hill, NJ
DiMento, Carol A. G. .... Swampscott, MA
DiMento & DiMento .... Swampscott, MA
DiMento, Francis J. .... Boston, MA
DiMento, Francis J., Jr. .... Boston, MA
DiMento & Sullivan .... Boston, MA
DiMento, Vincent J. .... Boston, MA
DiMento, William R. .... Swampscott, MA
DiMeo, Arthur T. .... Denver, CO
Di Meo, Frank N., Jr. .... Philadelphia, PA
DiMeo, Roman .... Niagara Falls, NY
DiMeo, Rose Marie .... Marlton, NJ
DiMeolo, Amelia A. .... Boca Raton, FL
Dimerling, Marguerite E. .... Beaumont, TX
Dimery, Velmer J. .... Norman, OK
Dimes, Edwin K. .... Westport, CT
Di Mezza, Deborah Ferro .... Ballston Spa, NY
DiMiceli, Joseph A. .... New York, NY
Dimich, John .... Grand Rapids, MN
DiMichael, Nicholas J. .... Washington, DC
Dimichele, Donn A. .... San Bernardino, CA
DiMichele, Elizabeth E. .... New York, NY
Dimichele, James .... Forest Hills, NY
Dimick, Joseph I. .... Orem, UT
Dimick, Julia E. .... Indianapolis, IN
Dimick, Martha A. Holton
Minneapolis, MN
Dimick, Paul M. .... Cedarburg, WI
Dimick, Richard A. .... Oklahoma City, OK
Dimick, Sara K. .... Tavares, FL
DiMickele, Susan M. .... Columbus, OH
Dimieri, Robin J. .... Boston, MA
Dimiero, Alfred D. .... Short Hills, NJ
DiMillo, A. Angelo .... Lockport, NY
Dimin, William N. .... Englewood, NJ
Dimino, Alfred M. .... Garden City, NY
Dimino, Franklin J. .... Lake Forest, CA
Dimino, Joseph C. .... Norfolk, VA
Dimino, Mark .... Newport Beach, CA

Dimino & Nigro .... Lake Forest, CA
Dimino, Robert A. .... Fremont, CA
DiMino, Robert L. .... New York, NY
Dimino, Robyn .... Santa Ana, CA
DiMino, S. Tina .... Garden City, NY
Dimitri, Dean .... North Riverside, IL
DiMitri, Lea A. .... Fort Lauderdale, FL
Dimitri, Martha J. .... North Riverside, IL
Dimitrief, Alex .... Chicago, IL
Dimitrijevich, Robert .... San Luis Obispo, CA
Dimitrijevs, James A. .... Cleveland, OH
Dimitriou, Andrew .... San Francisco, CA
Dimitriou, Demetrios .... San Francisco, CA
Dimitriou, Emmanuel H. .... Reading, PA
Dimitriou, Emmanuel H., P.C.
Lancaster, PA
Pottsville, PA
Reading, PA
Dimitris, Jason E. .... Miami, FL
Dimitroff, Anton .... San Diego, CA
Dimitroff, Douglas W. .... Buffalo, NY
Dimitroff, Sashe D. .... Houston, TX
Dimitrouleas, William P.
Fort Lauderdale, FL
Dimitrova, Kristine L. .... Boston, MA
Dimitruk, David B. .... Irvine, CA
Dimitry, Douglas B. .... Inkster, MI
Dimitry, Edward S. .... Enon, OH
Dimitry, Richard K. .... New Orleans, LA
Dimkoff, Graydon W. .... Fremont, MI
Dimler, Robert D. .... Plymouth, MA
Dimlich, Stephen H., Jr. .... Houston, TX
Dimling, Robert A. .... Cincinnati, OH
Dimmers, Alan M. .... Hillsdale, MI
Dimmers & Boyd .... Hillsdale, MI
Dimmers, David A. .... Hastings, MI
Dimmers & McPhillips .... Hastings, MI
Dimmich, Guldin, Dinkelacker & Brienza, P.C. .... Allentown, PA
Orefield, PA
Dimmich, Jeffrey R. .... Orefield, PA
Dimmick, Carolyn R. .... Seattle, WA
Dimmick, Lucille Goins .... Fresno, CA
Dimmick, Martha "Mimi" .... Baton Rouge, LA
Dimmick, Patricia L. .... San Francisco, CA
Dimmick, Radford Harlan .... Nashville, TN
Dimmick, Steven W. .... Treasury Department, Office of Thrift Supervision, GV
Dimmick, Teri A. .... Peoria, IL
Dimmig, Howard L., II .... Bartow, FL
Dimmig, William J. .... Miami, FL
Dimmitt, David A. .... St. Louis, MO
Dimmitt, Donald L. .... Wenatchee, WA
Dimmitt, Jacqueline A. .... St. Louis, MO
Dimmitt, Lawrence A. .... Topeka, KS
Dimmitt, William W., Jr. .... Sapulpa, OK
Dimmock, Avary, Jr. .... Ellijay, GA
Dimmock, Clarence O. .... New York, NY
Dimmock & Dodd .... Raleigh, NC
Dimmock & Hill .... Ellijay, GA
Dimmock, Katherine H. .... Indianapolis, IN
Dimmock, Thomas J. .... Raleigh, NC
Dimock, Dalia M. .... Southfield, MI
Dimock, Stanley W. .... West Hartford, CT
Dimock, Whiting G. .... Washington, DC
Dimoff, Roderick .... Seattle, WA
Dimoh, Irene Bookhard .... Brooklyn, NY
DiMola, Sandi .... New York, NY
Dimon, Edward J. .... Toms River, NJ
Dimon, Helenkay .... Rockville, MD
Dimon, Samuel .... New York, NY
DiMona, Joseph J. .... New York, NY
Dimond, Alan J. .... Newton, MA
Dimond, Alan T. .... Miami, FL
Dimond, Cynthia E. .... Kew Gardens, NY
Dimond, Diane .... Durham, NC
Dimond, Douglas A. .... Mayfield Heights, OH
Dimond, Karen J. .... Chicago, IL
Dimond, Kendra L. .... Washington, DC
Dimond, Marc J .... Chicago, IL
Dimond, Paul R. .... Ann Arbor, MI
Dimond, Richard L. .... Columbus, OH
Dimond, Scott Michael .... Miami, FL
Dimond, Thomas W. .... Chicago, IL
DiMondi, Joseph A. .... New York, NY
DiMondi, William J. .... Wyoming, DE
Di Monte, Eugene A. .... Park Ridge, IL
DiMonte, Karen Fisher .... Chicago, IL
Di Monte & Lizak .... Chicago, IL
Park Ridge, IL
Di Monte, Riccardo A. .... Park Ridge, IL
DiMonte, Vincent A. .... Providence, RI
Dimopoulos, Arthur .... Washington, DC
Dimos, Brown, Erskine & Burkett
Monroe, LA
Dimos, C. L. .... Washington, DC
Dimos, C. L. .... Middleburg, VA
Dimos, James .... Indianapolis, IN
Dimos, Jimmy N. .... Monroe, LA
DiMotto, Jean W. .... Milwaukee, WI
DiMotto, John J. .... Milwaukee, WI
Dimovski, Lolita .... Detroit, MI
D'Imperio, Anthony M. .... Boston, MA
Dimperio, Joseph C. .... Pittsburgh, PA
Dimsey, Dennis J. .... Department of Justice, Civil Rights Division, GV
Di Mucci, Salvatore, Jr. .... Palatine, IL
DiMugno, John .... Belmont, CA
DiMura, Halina C. .... Albany, NY
DiMuro, Bernard J. .... Alexandria, VA
DiMuro, Christopher M. .... Newark, NJ
DiMuro, George N. .... Providence, RI
DiMuro, Ginsberg & Mook, P.C.
Alexandria, VA
Di Muro, Joseph V. .... Universal City, CA
DiMuro, Kathleen G. .... Cranston, RI
DiMuro, Sharon A. .... Tallahassee, FL
DiMuzio, David A. .... Rochester, NY

DiMuzio, David C. ... Cincinnati, OH
DiMuzio, Gary M. ... Houston, TX
DiMuzio, Kenneth A., (P.C.) ... Woodbury, NJ
DiMuzio, Theodore P. ... Philadelphia, PA
Dimyan, Joseph ... Danbury, CT
Dinaburg, Barry A. ... New York, NY
Dinackus, Thomas D.
Department of Justice, Civil Division, GV
Dinallo, Gerald A., Jr. ... Hawthorne, NY
Dinallo, Richard N. ... San Francisco, CA
Dinan, Althea, II ... Bridgeport, CT
Dinan, Althea S. ... Bridgeport, CT
Dinan, Christopher C. ... Portland, ME
Dinan, Daniel J. ... United States Tax Court, Special Trial Judges, GV
Dinan & Dinan, P.C. ... Bridgeport, CT
Dinan, Donald R. ... Washington, DC
Dinan, James Charles ... New York, NY
Dinan, James H. ... Washington, DC
Dinan, Jay P. ... Tampa, FL
Dinan, Joseph H., Jr. ... Jacksonville, FL
Dinan, Kevin M. ... Washington, DC
Dinan, Ronald, & Associates
Santa Rosa, CA
Dinan, Ronald M. ... Santa Rosa, CA
Dinan, Terence D. ... West Chester, OH
Dinan, William P. ... Duluth, MN
DiNapoli, Daniel P. ... New York, NY
DiNapoli, Leonard F., Jr. ... New York, NY
DiNapoli, Paula Ann ... Woodcliff Lake, NJ
DiNapoli, Uzzi & Sibley ... San Jose, CA
Di Nardi, David W. ... Boston, MA
Dinardi, Peter D. ... Morgantown, WV
Di Nardo, Bruno ... New York, NY
DiNardo, Charles A. ... Irvine, CA
Di Nardo & Co., P.C., Law Office
New York, NY
Dinardo, Daniel ... Coraopolis, PA
DiNardo, Deborah ... Providence, RI
Di Nardo, Elise ... Jersey City, NJ
DiNardo, John A. ... Washington, DC
DiNardo, Joseph ... Buffalo, NY
DiNardo, Karen A. ... Rochester, NY
DiNardo, Lawrence A. ... Quincy, MA
DiNardo, Lawrence C. ... Chicago, IL
Dinardo, Nicholas J. ... Cincinnati, OH
Dinardo, Patrick P. ... Boston, MA
DiNardo, Richard L. ... Chicago, IL
DiNardo, Robert E. ... Walden, NY
DiNardo, Sheila Smith ... Pittsburgh, PA
Di Nardo, Thomas ... New York, NY
Dinari, Ray ... Garden Grove, CA
DiNatale, Joseph N. ... Chicago, IL
DiNatale, Mario ... Stamford, CT
Di Natale, Natale V. ... Bridgeport, CT
Dinberg, Douglas I. ... Oil City, PA
Dince, David M. ... New York, NY
Dincel, Kim O. ... San Francisco, CA
Dinces, Franklin G. ... Seattle, WA
Dinces, Jerard M. ... Ontario, CA
Dinces Law Firm ... Bellevue, WA
Gig Harbor, WA
Seattle, WA
Dinces, Stephen L. ... McLean, VA
Dincman, Holly Ashby ... Tallahassee, FL
D'Incognito, Myrna L. ... Los Angeles, CA
Dinday, Brian R. ... San Francisco, CA
Dinday, Mary Krauklis ... San Rafael, CA
Dindinger, Frederick J. ... Denver, CO
Dindoffer, Fredrick J. ... Detroit, MI
Dindoffer, Joan R. ... Detroit, MI
Dine, Christopher J. ... Detroit, MI
Dine, Jennifer B ... Washington, DC
Dine, Karen B. ... New York, NY
Dineen, Carolyn B., (Mrs.) ... Houston, TX
Dineen, Claire E. ... Denver, CO
Dineen, Daniel B. ... New York, NY
Dineen, Daniel R. ... Slinger, WI
Dineen, Daniel T. ... Carlisle, PA
Dineen, Denis F. ... Albany, NY
Dineen, Francis X. ... New Haven, CT
Dineen, Jeremiah R., III
Yorktown Heights, NY
Dineen, John K. ... Portland, ME
Boston, MA
Dineen, John R. ... Closter, NJ
Dineen, John W. ... Providence, RI
Dineen, Joseph P. ... New York, NY
Dineen Law Offices, S.C. ... Milwaukee, WI
Dineen, Matthew G. ... New York, NY
Dineen, Michael Francis
Fresh Meadows, NY
Dineen, Michelle L. ... Boston, MA
Dineen, Patricia C. ... Yorktown Heights, NY
Dineen, Patricia M. ... New York, NY
Dineen & Pratt, P.C. ... Yorktown Heights, NY
Dineen, Robert E., Jr. ... New York, NY
Dineen, Robert N. ... Youngstown, OH
Dineen, William P. ... Milwaukee, WI
Dineff, Beverly E. ... Summit, IL
Dineff, Laurel V. ... Chicago, IL
Dinegar, Wilbur Ward ... Bridgeport, CT
Dinell, Mark ... Tucson, AZ
Dinella, Roger W. ... New York, NY
Dinelli, Peter L. ... Albuquerque, NM
Dinenberg, Gary, (P.C.) ... Northfield, NJ
DiNenna, S. Eric ... Baltimore, MD
Diner, David N. ... Englishtown, NJ
Diner, Helena G. ... Irvine, CA
Diner, Jesse H. ... Hollywood, FL
Diner, Manuel ... Miami, FL
Diner, Manuel, P.A. ... Miami, FL
Dinerman, David ... San Francisco, CA
Dinerman, Irving P. ... New York, NY
Dinerman, Kristina H. ... Los Angeles, CA
Dinerman, Lisa ... Providence, RI
Dinerman, Marshall B. ... Atlanta, GA
Dinerstein & Lesser, P.C. ... Commack, NY
Dinerstein, Paula N. ... Washington, DC
Dinerstein, Robert ... Treasury Department, Office of Regulations and Rulings, GV
Dinerstein, Robert C. ... Stamford, CT
New York, NY
Dinerstein, Robert D. ... Washington, DC
Dinerstein, Robert Jay ... Commack, NY
Dines, Aaron ... Clifton, NJ
Dines & English ... Clifton, NJ
Dines, Gross & Esquivel, P.C.
Albuquerque, NM
Dines, James M. ... Albuquerque, NM
Dines, Odalys Perez ... New York, NY
Dines, Tyson, III ... Denver, CO
Dine Wagner, Jennifer ... Washington, DC
Arlington, VA
Di Nezza, Todd R. ... Providence, RI
Ding, Boise A. ... Los Angeles, CA
Ding, George M. ... New York, NY
Ding, Walter ... Champaign, IL
Ding, William K. ... New York, NY
Dingée, John L. ... New Bedford, MA
Dingel, James D. ... Minnetonka, MN
Dingel, Lori A. ... Boise, ID
Dingel, M. Allyn, Jr. ... Boise, ID
Dingel, Michael M. ... Boise, ID
Dingeldine, David G. ... Tucson, AZ
Dingeman, Dancer & Christopherson, P.L.C.
Cadillac, MI
Charlevoix, MI
Kalkaska, MI
Petoskey, MI
Traverse City, MI
Dingeman, Daniel J. ... Traverse City, MI
Dingeman, David ... Cedar Hill, TX
Dinger, Angela B. ... New York, NY
Dinger, Henry C., (P.C.) ... Boston, MA
Dinger, Judith Ransom ... La Habra, CA
Dinger, Larry M. ... Department of State, Foreign Service Institute, GV
Dinger, Paul L. ... Minneapolis, MN
Dinger, Rita Marilyn ... Lincoln, NE
Dinges, Christina L. ... Williamsport, PA
Dinges, Lorelei A.
Department of Transportation, Federal Aviation Administration, GV
Dingess, John R. ... Pittsburgh, PA
Dingfelder, Jessica ... Charlotte, NC
Dingfelder, John J. ... Tampa, FL
Dingilian, Edward G. ... San Francisco, CA
Dingilian, Timothy R. ... Washington, DC
Baltimore, MD
Rockville, MD
Dingle, Carrie D. ... Willingboro, NJ
Dingle, Erik N. ... Wilkes-Barre, PA
Dingle, Julie Ann ... Albany, NY
Dingle, Karen L. ... St. Paul, MN
Dingle, Larry M. ... Atlanta, GA
Dingle, Michael W. ... Boston, MA
Dingle, Phillip S. ... Tampa, FL
Dingledine, L. Brooke ... Barre, VT
Dingledy, Jay R. ... Columbus, OH
Dingler, Crystal L. ... Edmonds, WA
Dingler, Donna G. ... St. Augustine, FL
Dingler, William M., IV ... Midland, TX
Dingley, James M. ... Burlington, VT
Dingley, Mark A. ... Providence, RI
Dingman, Brian M. ... Westborough, MA
Dingman, Charles F. ... Augusta, ME
Dingman, E. Wallace ... Riverside, CA
Dingman, Harry D. ... St. Petersburg, FL
Dingman, Harry D. ... Lee's Summit, MO
Dingman, Jeffrey Wade ... Dallas, TX
Dingman Labowitz, P.C. ... Alexandria, VA
Dingman, Michael S. ... Falls Church, VA
Dingman, Peter Allan ... Alexandria, VA
Dingmann, Lawrence C., Jr.
Minneapolis, MN
Dingott, Marvin M. ... White Plains, NY
Dingus, Jonathan W. ... Panama City, FL
Dingus, M. Shawn ... Mt. Gilead, OH
Dingus, Titee M. ... Cleveland, OH
Dingwall, Craig D. ... Washington, DC
Dingwall, Thos. M. ... Jacksonville, FL
Dingwall, Walter M. ... Fort Lauderdale, FL
Dingwall-Williams, Suzanne ... San Mateo, CA
Dingwell, David L. ... Canton, OH
Dingwell, Maurice D. ... Omaha, NE
Dingwerth, James A. ... Kansas City, MO
Dinh, Phong T. ... Boston, MA
Dinh, Thuy Tu Bich
Commodity Futures Trading Commission, Office of the General Counsel, GV
Dinh, Toni N. ... Dallas, TX
Dinh, Truong T. ... Palo Alto, CA
Dinh-Cohen, Michael ... Uniondale, NY
Dinhofer, Michael S. ... New York, NY
Dinhofer, Philip J. ... New York, NY
Dini, Cynthia ... Mount Prospect, IL
Dini, Marina Rose ... Los Angeles, CA
Dini, Michael G. ... Oakland, CA
Dini, Robert U. ... Winnetka, IL
Dinice, Louis J. ... Hackensack, NJ
Dinicola, Brian K. ... Eatontown, NJ
DiNicola & DiNicola ... Carneys Point, NJ
Di Nicola, Gino O. ... Pottsville, PA
DiNicola, John W. ... Providence, RI
DiNicola, John W., II ... Morristown, NJ
DiNicola, Joseph M. ... Carneys Point, NJ
Di Nicola, Patricia A. ... Carneys Point, NJ
DiNicola, Ronald A., (A Professional Corporation) ... Los Angeles, CA
Dinielli, David C. ... Los Angeles, CA
Dinielli, Jacquelyn ... New York, NY
DiNieri, Robert A. ... Clyde, NY
Dinin, John R. ... White Plains, NY
Dinino, Karen R. ... Los Angeles, CA
Dinis, Edmund ... New Bedford, MA
Di Nitto, Anthony A. ... Rochester, NY
Dinius, Anne-Marie ... San Diego, CA
Diniz, Roland A. ... New York, NY
Dinizulu, Yao O. ... Chicago, IL
Dinkel, Deborah J. ... Laguna Beach, CA
Dinkel, E. John, III ... Tampa, FL
Dinkel, Mark J. ... Salina, KS
Dinkel, Mary A. ... Grand Rapids, MI
Dinkel, Mary A., P.L.L.C.
Grand Rapids, MI
Dinkel, Norman J., Jr. ... Chicago, IL
Dinkel, Polly A. ... Palo Alto, CA
Dinkel, R. Dean ... Sharon Springs, KS
Dinkel, William H. ... Lancaster, PA
Dinkelacker, Patrick T. ... Cincinnati, OH
Dinkelacker, Thomas H. ... Orefield, PA
Dinkelman, Jennifer L. ... Los Angeles, CA
Dinkelmeyer, Kurt ... New York, NY
Dinkelmeyer, Paul D. ... East Meadow, NY
Dinkelspiel, Richard C., Jr.
San Geronimo, CA
Dinkelspiel, Robert L. ... Memphis, TN
Dinkelspiel, Steven E. ... Redwood City, CA
Dinkes, Michael ... Baldwin, NY
Dinkes, William ... New York, NY
Dinki, Edward J. ... Clarence, NY
Dinkin, Jeffrey A. ... Santa Barbara, CA
Dinkin, Mitchell A.
Palm Beach Gardens, FL
Dinkins, Benjamin A. ... Fairfax, VA
Dinkins, Carol E. ... Houston, TX
Dinkins, Jennifer M. ... Houston, TX
Dinkins Kelly Lenox & Lamb, L.L.P.
Houston, TX
Dinkins, Lewis E. ... Ocala, FL
Dinkins, Lewis E., P.A. ... Ocala, FL
Dinkins, O. Theodore, Jr. ... Houston, TX
Dinkins, Richard H. ... Nashville, TN
Dinklage, Ingolf R. ... San Diego, CA
Dayton, OH
Dinkler, Sara Church ... San Francisco, CA
Dinkoff, Allan ... New York, NY
Dinlenc, Ata ... New York, NY
Dinman, Bruce C. ... Kailua, HI
Dinn, Hochman and Potter, LLC
Cleveland, OH
Mayfield Heights, OH
Dinn, Irwin J. ... Cleveland, OH
Dinna, Edward T. ... Fort Lauderdale, FL
Dinnan, Maureen Sullivan ... Cheshire, CT
Dinndorf, Beth ... Minneapolis, MN
Dinnebier, King & Werts, P.C. ... Tustin, CA
Dinnebier, Richard A. ... Tustin, CA
Dinneen, Edith N. ... Tampa, FL
Dinneen, James F. X. ... Boston, MA
Dinneen, James T. ... Cheyenne, WY
Dinneen, Kevin G. ... Winter Park, FL
Dinneen, Michael D. ... Cleveland, OH
Dinneen, Vicky L. ... Warrenton, VA
Dinneen-Long, Christian B.
Kansas City, MO
Dinner, Dara L. ... King Of Prussia, PA
Dinner, Dean M. ... Phoenix, AZ
Dinner, Gary L. ... Cleveland, OH
Dinner, Janice M. ... Phoenix, AZ
Dinner, Melvin ... Greeley, CO
Dinner, Melvin, P.C. ... Greeley, CO
Dinner, Scott M. ... Harrisburg, PA
Dinnerstein, Julie E. ... New York, NY
Dinnerstein, Michael ... New York, NY
Dinney, Michael S. ... Bryn Mawr, PA
Dinnin & Dunn, P.C. ... Troy, MI
Dinnin, Michael L. ... Dallas, TX
Dinnin, Michael R. ... Troy, MI
Dinning, Brian R. ... Norfolk, VA
Dinning & Dinning ... Helena, AR
Dinning, Douglas L. ... Roseville, MI
Dinning & Greve, P.L.C. ... Roseville, MI
Dinning, Michael B. ... Alameda, CA
Dinning, Ronald S. ... Seattle, WA
Dinning, Wm. G., Jr. ... Helena, AR
Dinning, Woodford W., Jr. ... Demopolis, AL
Linden, AL
Dinolfo, Elise ... Livingston, NJ
Dinolfo, Joseph F. ... Rochester, NY
Dinolfo, Pat V. ... Rochester, NY
Dinolfo, Pat V., P.C. ... Rochester, NY
DiNolfo, Stephen H. ... Wheaton, IL
Dinolfo, Vincent M. ... Rochester, NY
DiNome, Anthony J. ... New York, NY
Di Nome, John A. ... Philadelphia, PA
Dinon, Laura M. ... Petoskey, MI
Dinon, Richard A. ... Petoskey, MI
Dinopoulos, Thomas J. ... Boston, MA
Dinos, Mark ... Chicago, IL
DiNota, Anthony S. ... New York, NY
Di Noto, Frank J. ... Newport Beach, CA
DiNoto, John ... Mineola, NY
DiNoto, John C. ... Buffalo, NY
Dinoto, Joseph D. ... Cherry Hill, NJ
DiNovi, Mark ... Bridgewater, NJ
DiNovis, Stephen E. ... Lititz, PA
DiNovo, Andrew ... Austin, TX
DiNovo, Thomas J. ... Albany, NY
Dinow, Adam M. ... New York, NY
Dinowitz, Jay ... New York, NY
Dinowitz, Michael A. ... New York, NY
Dinsdale, Christine E. ... Seattle, WA
Dinsdale, Denise M. ... Modesto, CA
Dinse, Jill Goldsmith ... Portland, OR
Dinse, John M. ... Burlington, VT
Dinse, Knapp & McAndrew, P.C.
Burlington, VT
Dinse, Ralph H. ... West Branch, MI
Dinse, Ralph H., P.C. ... West Branch, MI
Dinsmoor, R. Keith ... Kihei, HI
Dinsmoor, Robert ... El Paso, TX
Dinsmoor, Theodore E. ... Boston, MA
Dinsmore, Barbara Flynn ... Sioux Falls, SD
Dinsmore, Courtney A. ... New York, NY
Dinsmore, Danielle S. ... Lancaster, PA
Dinsmore, Donald L. ... Casselberry, FL
Dinsmore, Evans & Bryant
Virginia Beach, VA
Dinsmore, F. Clement ... United States Senate, Committee Legal Personnel, GV
Dinsmore, J. Tyler ... Charleston, WV
Dinsmore, James P. ... Columbus, OH
Dinsmore, John B. ... Virginia Beach, VA
Dinsmore, John W. ... Birmingham, AL
Dinsmore, Mark J. ... Indianapolis, IN
Dinsmore, Richard J. ... Omaha, NE
Dinsmore, Robert E. ... Boston, MA
Dinsmore, Robert W. ... Morgantown, WV
Dinsmore, Scott D. ... Manhattan Beach, CA
Dinsmore & Shohl LLP ... Lexington, KY
Louisville, KY
Cincinnati, OH
Columbus, OH
Dayton, OH
Dinsmore, Stephen R. ... Boston, MA
Dinsmore, Wiley ... Cincinnati, OH
Dinstein, Orrie ... New York, NY
Dintaman, Robert E., Jr. ... Cleveland, OH
D'Intino, John, Jr. ... Marlton, NJ
Dintino, Robert P. ... Haddon Heights, NJ
Dintzer, Daniel L. ... Beverly Hills, CA
Dintzer, Jeffrey D. ... Los Angeles, CA
Dintzer, Kenneth M. ... Department of Justice, Civil Division, GV
DiNubile, Suzanne D. ... San Francisco, CA
DiNucci, Jennifer Fonner ... Palo Alto, CA
DiNucci, John A. ... Falls Church, VA
DiNunzio, Edward J. ... Port Jefferson, NY
Di Nunzio, James C. ... Belmont, MA
DiNunzio, Nicholas Paul ... Washington, DC
Dinur & Associates, P.C. ... Atlanta, GA
Dinur, Daniel D. ... Atlanta, GA
DiNuzzo, Joseph A.
Federal Deposit Insurance Corporation, Regulation and Legislation Section, GV
Dinverno, Armond A. ... Oak Brook, IL
Dinverno, Diana U. ... Detroit, MI
Dinverno & Foltz ... Oak Brook, IL
Dinwiddie, Bruce W. ... Metairie, LA
Dinwiddie, Candy F. ... Calumet City, IL
Dinwiddie, Harry E., Jr. ... Edina, MN
Dinwiddie, J. William ... Lynchburg, VA
Dinwiddie, James F. ... Leitchfield, KY
Dinwiddie, Sharon ... Destin, FL
Panama City, FL
Dinwiddie, Thomas W. ... Indianapolis, IN
Dinwoodey, David T. ... Boston, MA
Dio, Lawrence A. ... Port Lavaca, TX
Diodati, David R. ... New Hartford, NY
Diodati, Marijane ... Boston, MA
DioGuardi, Anthony M., II ... Canton, OH
Dioguardi, Mark D. ... Phoenix, AZ
Dioguardi, Michael J. ... Minneapolis, MN
Diokno, Jose Miguel ... Itasca, IL
Dioli, Martin D. ... Palo Alto, CA
Dion, Alan E. ... Atlanta, GA
Dion, Alan J. ... Philadelphia, PA
Dion, Edward A. ... Tallahassee, FL
Dion, Faye A. ... Hartford, CT
Dion, Gary S. ... Philadelphia, PA
Dion, Gregory T. ... Los Angeles, CA
Dion, John J. ... Department of Justice, Criminal Division, GV
Dion, Jonathan W. ... Charlotte, NC
Dion, Marc R., Sr. ... Akron, OH
Dion, Melvin, (A Professional Corporation)
Philadelphia, PA
Dion, Norman M. ... New York, NY
Dion, Pamela J. ... Phoenix, AZ
Dion, Paul J. ... San Francisco, CA
Dion, Philip J., Jr. ... Phoenix, AZ
Dion, Raymond C. ... Los Angeles, CA
Dion, Ronald A. ... Plantation, FL
Dion, Rosenau & Smith ... Norristown, PA
Philadelphia, PA
Dion, Sarah ... New York, NY
Dion, Valerie J. ... Princeton, NJ
Dion, William T. ... Cherry Hill, NJ
Blue Bell, PA
Dioneda, Gregory L. ... Granite City, IL
Dioneda, Steven M. ... St. Louis, MO
Dionise, Michael C. ... Lapeer, MI
Dionisi & Andersen, A Professional Corporation ... Marlborough, MA
Dionisi, Robert F., Jr. ... Marlborough, MA
Dionisio, Gaudencio D. ... Sacramento, CA
Dionisio, Regina Reyes ... Beverly Hills, CA
Dionisopoulos, George A. ... Milwaukee, WI
Dion-Kindem, Peter R. ... Los Angeles, CA
Dion-Kindem, Peter R., P.C.
Los Angeles, CA
Dionne, Arthur F. ... Springfield, MA
Dionne & Dionne ... Tuscaloosa, AL
Dionne, Donald L. ... Tuscaloosa, AL
Dionne & Gass ... Boston, MA
Dionne, James J. ... Seattle, WA
Dionne, Melinda Murphy ... Tuscaloosa, AL
Dionne, Paul H. ... Fort Stockton, TX
Dionne, Paula L. ... Los Angeles, CA
Dionne, Richard A. ... Perris, CA
Dionne, Richard D. ... Boston, MA
Dionne & Rorick ... Seattle, WA
DiOrio, Anthony J. ... White Plains, NY
D'Iorio, Anthony M. ... Hawthorne, NY
Diorio, Charles J. ... Malvern, PA
Diorio, Edmond Michael ... Watertown, CT
Di Orio, Joseph M. ... Providence, RI
Diorio, Leonard P. ... Chicago, IL
D'Iorio, Megan Kochell ... Wilmington, DE
DiOrio, P. Christopher ... North Attleboro, MA

D'Iorio, Ralph B. ... Media, PA
DiOrio, Rana B. ... San Francisco, CA
DiOrio, Robert M. ... Media, PA
DiOrio & Sereni, LLP ... Media, PA
Philadelphia, PA
Diorio, Thomas F. ... Orlando, FL
DiOrio, Veronica M. ... Wilmington, MA
Diorio-Dwyer, Maria ... Boston, MA
Dios, Anthony M. ... New York, NY
Dios, John J. ... Newark, NJ
Diosegy, Arlene J. ... Raleigh, NC
Dioszeghy, Joseph L. ... Overland Park, KS
DiPace, Steven B. ... Fitchburg, MA
DiPadova, Anthony F., Jr. ... Newport, NH
DiPadova, Arthur A. ... Haddonfield, NJ
Di Paglia, Raymond ... Des Moines, IA
DiPalma, Douglas A. ... Cleveland, OH
DiPalma, John T. ... Bay Shore, NY
Di Palma, Joseph A. ... New York, NY
DiPalma, Joseph W. ... Syracuse, NY
DiPalma, Robert S. ... Burlington, VT
DiPalma, William J. ... Mentor, OH
DiPanfilo, Chas. J. ... Woburn, MA
Di Paola, Andrew J. ... Mineola, NY
DiPaola, Mary T. ... Ridgewood, NJ
Di Paola, Robert B. ... New York, NY
Di Paola, Suzanne M. ... Sacramento, CA
Di Paola, Thomas S. ... New York, NY
Di Paoli, Raymond P. ... Floral Park, NY
DiPaolo, Anthony ... Uniondale, NY
DiPaolo, Barrett S. ... New York, NY
Di Paolo, Mark ... New York, NY
DiPaolo, Paul A. ... Sebastopol, CA
DiPaolo, R. Eugene ... New York, NY
Di Paolo, Roger F. ... Ravenna, OH
DiPaolo, Sharon F. ... Pittsburgh, PA
Di Paolo, Thomas F. ... San Diego, CA
DiPaolo, William J. ... Pittsburgh, PA
DiPasqua, Angelo A. ... Media, PA
DiPasquale, Anita A. ... Bronx, NY
Di Pasquale, Anne L. ... New York, NY
DiPasquale, Benn S. ... Milwaukee, WI
DiPasquale, Charles G. ... Buffalo, NY
DiPasquale, Christopher A.
Rochester, NY
DiPasquale, Joseph J. ... West Orange, NJ
DiPasquale, Linda M. ... Amherst, NY
Buffalo, NY
Di Pasquale, Maria Teresa ... Palm Beach, FL
Di Pasquale, Meghan Mc Manus
Rochester, NY
Di Pasquale, Richard J. ... Baltimore, MD
DiPasquale, Thomas J. ... St. Paul, MN
Di Pasquantonio, Francis J. ... Raleigh, NC
DiPaul, John J., II ... Philadelphia, PA
DiPaula, Anthony J. ... Towson, MD
DiPentima, Alexandra Davis ... Kent, CT
DiPentima, Anthony F. ... Wethersfield, CT
DiPentima, Anthony F., LLC
Wethersfield, CT
DiPerna, Raymond A. ... New York, NY
DiPerrio, Anthony J., II ... Danbury, CT
DiPersia, John G. ... New Haven, CT
DiPersio, Denise T. ... Wilmington, DE
Di Petrillo, Anthony ... Providence, RI
Di Petrillo, Carmine R. ... Providence, RI
DiPetrillo, William J. ... Coral Springs, FL
Di Petta, Deanna Lynn ... Cleveland, OH
DiPiazza, Barbara ... Syracuse, NY
DiPiazza, Carl J. ... Hackensack, NJ
DiPiazza, Nicholas C. ... Mount Sinai, NY
DiPiazza, Paul J. ... Bethesda, MD
DiPiazza, Thomas M., Jr. ... Rochester, NY
DiPiero, Andrew E., Jr. ... Philadelphia, PA
DiPiero, Deborah S. ... Laguna Niguel, CA
Di Piero, Frank A. ... Cleveland, OH
DiPiero, J. Timothy ... Charleston, WV
DiPiero, Vincent F. ... Chicago, IL
Dipierro, Gaetano ... New York, NY
Dipierro, Joseph V. ... Raleigh, NC
Di Pierro, Robert ... New York, NY
DiPietrantonio, John ... Cambridge, MA
DiPietro, Andrew M., Jr. ... New Haven, CT
DiPietro, Andrew M., Jr., P.C.
New Haven, CT
DiPietro, Anthony ... New York, NY
DiPietro, Anthony ... Sandy, UT
DiPietro, Anthony R. ... Saugus, MA
DiPietro, Arthur ... Westhampton Beach, NY
Di Pietro, Brian G. ... Avondale, AZ
Di Pietro, Dario E. ... Columbus, OH
DiPietro & Day, P.C. ... Belleville, MI
Di Pietro, Elaine P. ... Sacramento, CA
Di Pietro, Francesco A. ... New York, NY
Dipietro, Joanne M. ... Norwood, MA
DiPietro, John A. ... Conshohocken, PA
DiPietro, Joseph Anthony
North Little Rock, AR
DiPietro, Joseph L., Jr. ... Philadelphia, PA
DiPietro, Lisa G. ... Philadelphia, PA
DiPietro, Louis ... San Francisco, CA
DiPietro, Louis ... Boston, MA
DiPietro, Mark J. (IBA) ... Minneapolis, MN
DiPietro, Mary-Lynne ... Roseland, NJ
DiPietro, Melanie, S.C. ... Pittsburgh, PA
Di Pietro, Michael A. ... Towson, MD
Di Pietro, Patrick Thomas
Fort Lauderdale, FL
Miami, FL
DiPietro, Ralph J. ... Washington, DC
DiPietro, Rosann ... Boston, MA
Di Pietro, Susanne D. ... Anchorage, AK
DiPietro, Thomas K. ... Belleville, MI
di Pietro, Vincent J. ... Baltimore, MD
DiPietro, Vito J. ... Department of Justice,
Civil Division, GV
DiPietro-Gerace, Donna ... Philadelphia, PA
DiPilato, George D., III ... Philadelphia, PA
DiPilla, Thomas J., Jr. ... Moorestown, NJ
DiPinto, Ilse Harle ... Newport Beach, CA
DiPinto, Lawrence J. ... Irvine, CA
DiPinto & Shimokaji, P.C.
Newport Beach, CA
DiPippa, John M. A. ... Little Rock, AR
DiPippa, Kathy O'Brien
Treasury Department,
United States Secret Service, GV
Di Pippo & Associates, Law Offices of
Mineola, NY
Di Pippo, Maria A. ... Mineola, NY
DiPippo, Philip A. ... New York, NY
DiPirro, Elizabeth M. ... Akron, NY
Di Placido, Carmen A. ... Department of State,
Bureau of Consular Affairs, GV
Dipolito, Frank X. ... Long Beach, CA
DiPompo, Charles R. ... Foxboro, MA
DiPonio, Lisa R. ... Englewood, CO
Di Ponio, Tony F. ... Southfield, MI
DiPonzio, Jason S. ... Rochester, NY
Dippel, C. Charles ... Houston, TX
Dippel, Eric ... San Jose, CA
Dippel, Kenneth C. ... Dallas, TX
Dippel & McCann, P.C.
Council Bluffs, IA
Dippel, Richard J. ... St. Louis, MO
Dippel, Tieman H., Jr. ... Austin, TX
Dippel, William Kenneth C. ... Dallas, TX
Dippell, Steven B. ... San Jose, CA
Dippert, William H. ... New York, NY
Dippery, James H., Jr. ... Weaverville, CA
Dippo, Robert E., (P.C.) ... Boulder, CO
Dippold, John C. ... Seattle, WA
Dippold, Karen L. ... New York, NY
Dippold, Kristine A. ... Seattle, WA
Dippold, Lynn W. ... Somerset, NJ
D'Ippolito, Alex H. ... Pittsburgh, PA
Dippolito, Michaelangelo L. ... Exton, PA
D'Ippolito & Paladin ... Pittsburgh, PA
Dippolito, William F. ... Tacoma, WA
Dippolito, William F., P.S., Inc.
Tacoma, WA
Di Preta, Manlio ... New York, NY
DiPreta, Richard S. ... Norwalk, CT
DiPrete, James, Jr. ... Cranston, RI
DiPrete, Roberta Ann ... San Francisco, CA
DiPrete, Thomas H. ... Cranston, RI
DiPrima, Frank P. ... Madison, NJ
Di Prima, John A. ... Naperville, IL
DiPrima, Joseph F. ... Rahway, NJ
DiPrima, Stephen Richard ... New York, NY
DiPrimo, Marie ... Syosset, NY
DiPrinzio, Eugene A. ... Wilmington, DE
DiPrisco, Dominic ... Lake Success, NY
DiPrisco, Frank C. ... New York, NY
DiPuccio, Dominic A. ... Cleveland, OH
DiPuccio, John M. ... Cincinnati, OH
DiQuinzio, Diane ... Denver, CO
Di Quinzio, P.J. ... West Chester, PA
Dir, David J. ... Phoenix, AZ
Diracles, James C. ... Minneapolis, MN
DiRaddo, Raymond S. ... Rochester, NY
Di Raimo & D'Agostino ... Rochester, NY
Di Raimo, Vincent J. ... Rochester, NY
Dircks, Durwood W. ... Clarence, IA
Dircks, Richard J. ... New York, NY
Dircks, Ridenour & Macek ... Clarence, IA
Davenport, IA
Dircks, Russell A. ... Clarence, IA
DiRe, Daniel M. ... Encinitas, CA
DiRe, Douglas J. ... Anaconda, MT
Di Re, Mario J. ... Staten Island, NY
Dire, Robert Oz ... Lynnwood, WA
Director, Alan L. ... Jenkintown, PA
Director, Brett S. ... New York, NY
Director, Gerald ... New York, NY
Director, Jerald J. ... House of Representatives,
Office of Law Revision Counsel, GV
Director, Jonathan ... New York, NY
Director, Mark D. ... Washington, DC
Director, Michael C. ... Garden City, NY
Director, Richard D. ... Allentown, PA
Director, Steven R. ... Wilmington, DE
Direktor, Kenneth S.
West Palm Beach, FL
Direnfeld, Barry B. ... Washington, DC
Di Renzo and Bomier, LLC ... Neenah, WI
Di Renzo, Robert C. ... Neenah, WI
DiResta, Anthony E. ... Washington, DC
Di Resta, Thomas J. ... New York, NY
DiResta, Timothy D. ... Stamford, CT
Dirga, Eric J. ... Orlando, FL
Dirga, Eric J., P.A., Law Office of, The
Orlando, FL
Dirgo, David ... Lincoln, NE
Diri, Phyl A. ... Ukiah, CA
Dirickson, Donna Lynn ... Weatherford, OK
DiRienzo, Carmen M. ... New York, NY
Dirienzo, John J., Jr. ... Somerset, PA
DiRienzo, Joseph ... Fanwood, NJ
Dirienzo, Mario E. ... Iselin, NJ
Dirinna, John G. ... Columbus, OH
DiRita, David M. ... Plymouth, MI
DiRito, Vincent J. ... Ponte Vedra Beach, FL
Dirker & Hawk ... Akron, OH
Dirker, Louis A. ... Akron, OH
Dirkes, Daniel F. ... Bloomington, IL
Dirkes, George R. ... San Francisco, CA
Dirkes, Mary A. ... Southfield, MI
Dirkes, Mary C. ... Detroit, MI
Dirkin, Jennifer M. ... Chicago, IL
Dirks, Alfred E. ... St. Paul, MN
Dirks, Darrell D. ... Tampa, FL
Dirks, Denise L. ... Roseville, CA
Dirks, Donald N. ... New York, NY
Dirks, Jerry A. ... Arnold, MO
Dirks, John A. ... Bloomington, IL
Dirks, Marilyn K. ... Hartford, CT
Dirks, Scott M. ... Pelican Rapids, MN
Dirks, Stanley J. ... San Francisco, CA
Dirks, Susan K. ... Pittsburgh, PA
Dirkse, Paul ... Mosinee, WI
Dirksen, Charles Andrew
San Francisco, CA
Dirksen, Lawrence G. ... Olympia Fields, IL
Dirksen, Linda K. ... Orlando, FL
Dirksen, Peter T. ... Nashville, TN
Dirksen, Thomas A. ... Bellevue, WA
Dirks-Linhorst, P. Ann ... Jefferson City, MO
Dirksmeyer, Anton C. ... Dallas, TX
Dirlam, Charles F.
Department Of Health And Human Services,
Social Security Administration, GV
Dirlam, Gary L. ... Orlando, FL
Dirmann, James R. ... Sarasota, FL
Dirmann, James R., P.A. ... Bradenton, FL
Sarasota, FL
DiRoberto, Joseph P. ... Sierra Vista, AZ
DiRocco, Albert P., Jr. ... Orange, CA
DiRocco, John J., Jr. ... Philadelphia, PA
Diroll, David J. ... Columbus, OH
Di Rosa, Jos. V. ... New Orleans, LA
Di Rosa, Joseph V., Jr. ... New Orleans, LA
Di Rosa, Louis A. ... New Orleans, LA
Di Rosa, Paolo ... Department of State,
Office of the Legal Adviser, GV
DiRosario, Daniel ... Pasadena, CA
DiRosario, Lewis J. ... Columbus, OH
DiRosario, Robert P. ... Columbus, OH
DiRose, Dean R. ... Fort Lauderdale, FL
Dirr, Angela H. ... Atlanta, GA
Dirr, James P. P. ... Atlanta, GA
Dirrim, Craig C. ... Lincoln, NE
Dirrim, Delbert E. ... Omaha, NE
Dirrim, Lysle R. ... Brighton, CO
Dirsa, Ann Marie ... Manchester, NH
Dirsa, Barbara Ann ... Boston, MA
Dirscherl, Joseph D. ... Colorado Springs, CO
Dirska, Alfred J. ... Columbia, MD
Dirska & Levin ... Columbia, MD
DiRuggiero, Patricia H. ... Alexandria, VA
DiRusso, Elizabeth A. ... Cambridge, MA
DiRusso, F. Christian ... Mount Airy, NC
DiRusso, Michael J. ... Keene, NH
Dirvonas, Thomas F. ... Stroudsburg, PA
Di Sabatino, Arthur F. ... Wilmington, DE
DiSabatino, David W. ... Philadelphia, PA
DiSabatino, Frank ... Van Nuys, CA
DiSabato, Daniel A. ... Bolingbrook, IL
DiSabato, David J. ... Newark, NJ
Di Sabato, Jos. P. ... Harrison, NJ
Di Saia, Steven D. ... Los Angeles, CA
DiSalle, Anthony B. ... Toledo, OH
Di Salle & Arcuri, P.C. ... Washington, PA
DiSalle, Francis J. ... Pittsburgh, PA
DiSalle, John D. ... Maumee, OH
Di Salle, John F. ... Washington, PA
DiSalle, Lisa N. ... Cleveland, OH
DiSalle, Richard ... Pittsburgh, PA
Washington, PA
DiSalvo, Allan A. ... Woodbury, NY
DiSalvo, Charles R. ... Morgantown, WV
DiSalvo, Joseph A. ... Bronxville, NY
DiSalvo, Joseph R. ... Newark, NJ
DiSalvo, Loraine M. ... Atlanta, GA
Di Salvo, Richard J. ... Boulder, CO
DiSalvo, Richard S. ... Manassas, VA
Disalvo, Rosemary ... White Plains, NY
DiSalvo, Samuel C. ... Washington, DC
DiSalvo, Scott A. ... Fort Lauderdale, FL
DiSalvo, Theodore L. ... Boca Raton, FL
DiSalvo, Thomas J. ... Webster, NY
DiSalvo, Thomas J., P.C. ... Webster, NY
DiSandro, E. Douglas ... Haddonfield, NJ
Philadelphia, PA
DiSandro, Edmond A. ... Providence, RI
DiSano, Dane E. ... St. Petersburg, FL
DiSano, Dane E., P.A. ... St. Petersburg, FL
Di Sano, Samuel L. ... Providence, RI
DiSante, Frank L. ... Littleton, CO
DiSante, Marie D. ... Irvine, CA
DiSanti, Alexander A. ... Media, PA
DiSanti, Alexander D. ... Media, PA
DiSanti, Anthony ... Central Islip, NY
Di Santi, Anthony S. ... Boone, NC
Di Santi, Francis M. ... West Springfield, MA
DiSanti, Gerard J. ... West Springfield, MA
Di Santi Watson & Capua ... Boone, NC
Di Santis, Ernest J., Jr. ... Erie, PA
DiSantis, John A. ... West Chester, PA
Disantis, John P. ... Aurora, OH
DiSantis, Linda K. ... Atlanta, GA
Disantis, Richard J. ... Cleveland, OH
DiSanto, Carrie J. ... Chicago, IL
DiSanto, Edmund ... Syracuse, NY
DiSanto, Thomas J. ... Providence, RI
Disare, Melinda G. ... Buffalo, NY
Disare, Thomas F. ... Buffalo, NY
Disario, Sandra L. ... Sacramento, CA
DiSarro, Anthony ... New York, NY
DiSarro, Frances J. ... New York, NY
DiSarro, Stephanie D. ... Warwick, RI
DiSavino, Frances L. ... San Francisco, CA
DiSavino, Rosemary ... Nutley, NJ
Disbrow, D. Jeffrey ... Washington, DC
Disbrow, Jason C. ... Southport, NC
Disburg, Leo ... Pierre, SD
Discafani, Michael ... New York, NY
DiScala, Francis J., Jr. ... Norwalk, CT
DiScala, Francis J., Law Offices of
Norwalk, CT
Discenza, Francis A. ... Cortland, NY
Discenza, John Michael ... Springfield, MA
Discenza, John Michael, & Associates, P.C.
Springfield, MA
Discenza, Joseph J. ... West Orange, NJ
Discepolo, John T. ... Mount Holly, NJ
Discepolo, Sara, The Law Office of
Boston, MA
Disch, K. Annette ... Houston, TX
Disch, Robert M. ... Washington, DC
Dischell, Bartle, Yanoff and Dooley, A Professional Corporation ... Lansdale, PA
Dischell, Mark B. ... Lansdale, PA
Discher, David P. ... San Francisco, CA
Discher, Gregory Scott ... Reston, VA
Dischinger, Joseph B. ... Denver, CO
Dischinger, Joseph B., P.C. ... Denver, CO
Disciascio, Laura C. ... Irvine, CA
Discipio, Francis J. ... Oak Brook, IL
Di Scipio, Joseph M. ... Washington, DC
Di Scipio, Robert M. ... New Canaan, CT
DiSciullo, Alan M. ... New York, NY
DiSciullo, Alfred J., Jr. ... Waltham, MA
DiSciullo, Guido B. ... Boston, MA
DiSciullo, Jeffrey G. ... Washington, DC
DiSciullo, John B. ... Boston, MA
DiSciullo, Robert J. ... Purchase, NY
Di Sciullo, Tylene Kay ... Arlington, TX
Disco, Matthew D. ... San Francisco, CA
Discoe, Tony A. ... Santa Ana, CA
Discon, John G. ... Metairie, LA
Discon, Thomas M. ... Mandeville, LA
Dise & Associates, P.C. ... Southfield, MI
Dise, John H., Jr. ... Southfield, MI
DiSegna, Thomas B. ... Cranston, RI
Diseker, Roger C. ... Fort Worth, TX
Disend, Bruce L. ... Puyallup, WA
Disenhaus, Helen E. ... Washington, DC
Disenhouse, Bruce E. ... Riverside, CA
Diserio, Eugene A. ... Stamford, CT
Diserio Martin O'Connor & Castiglioni, LLP ... Stamford, CT
D'Isernia, Alfred L. ... Panama City, FL
Disert, Patricia Leigh ... Santa Fe, NM
Di Sesa, Christopher F. ... Leominster, MA
DiSesa & DiSesa ... New Haven, CT
DiSesa, Victoria M. ... New Haven, CT
Disharoon, Robert ... Santa Rosa, CA
Dishell, Amy B. ... Salt Lake City, UT
Disher, David Alan ... Houston, TX
Disher, Michael J. ... Danville, CA
Disheroon, Fred R. ... Department of Justice,
Environment and Natural Resources
Division, GV
Disheroon, Gary M. ... Chattanooga, TN
Dishler, Hal S. ... Aspen, CO
Dishman, Amy P. ... Crestwood, KY
Dishman, Mike L. ... Anchorage, AK
Dishman, William M., Jr. ... Danville, KY
Dishner, Jerry E. ... Gate City, VA
Dishon, Aaron ... Irvine, CA
Dishon, Aaron ... Newport Beach, CA
Dishong, George W. ... Jaffrey, NH
Dishongh, Randy ... Houston, TX
Dishongh, Randy, P.C. ... Houston, TX
Dishowitz, Martin R. ... Fort Lauderdale, FL
Dishuck, Jane K. ... Tuscaloosa, AL
Dishuck & LaCoste, P.C.
Birmingham, AL
Tuscaloosa, AL
DiSibio, Carol K. ... Richland, WA
D'Isidoro, Robert A. ... Carmel, CA
DiSilvestri, Jay Francis ... Petaluma, CA
DiSilvestro, Michael J. ... Wichita, KS
Di Silvestro, Robert F. ... Chicago, IL
DiSilvestro, Robert J. ... Chicago, IL
DiSilvestro, Stephen P. ... Chicago, IL
Di Silvio, Marilena ... Cleveland, OH
DiSipio, Basil A. ... Philadelphia, PA
Diskant, George E., III ... Santa Barbara, CA
Diskant, Gregory L. ... New York, NY
Diskey, Daniel D. ... New Port Richey, FL
Diskin, Francis J. ... Seattle, WA
Diskin, John A. ... Southgate, KY
Diskin, Laurence ... Ocean Ridge, FL
Diskin, Mark J. ... Washington, DC
Kansas City, MO
Diskin, Peter J. ... Atlanta, GA
Diskin, Sharon R.
Federal Communications Commission,
Office of the General Counsel, GV
Diskin, Thomas A. ... Westhampton Beach, NY
Diskint, Peter G. ... New York, NY
Diskint, Robert ... Greenbrae, CA
Disler, Donald ... San Francisco, CA
Disler, Joan A. ... Los Angeles, CA
Roseland, NJ
New York, NY
Disler, Mark R. ... United States Senate,
Committee Legal Personnel, GV
Disler, Michael M. ... Sebring, FL
Dismer, William E.
Saint Simons Island, GA
Dismond, Timothy A. ... Kansas City, MO
Dismuke, David A. ... Atlanta, GA
Dismuke, William L. ... Arlington, TX
Dallas, TX
Dismukes, Dee E. ... Tulsa, OK
Dismukes, Edward P. ... Chicago, IL
Dismukes, Glenn P., Jr. ... Pascagoula, MS
Dismukes, Jim B. ... Fair Oaks, CA
Dismukes, K. Terrell, Jr. ... Dallas, TX
Dismukes, Scott R. ... Pittsburgh, PA
Disner, Eliot G., (P.C.) ... Beverly Hills, CA
Disner, Marshall C. ... West Bloomfield, MI
Disner, Marshall C., P.C.
West Bloomfield, MI
Disney, David B. ... Harrisburg, PA
Disney, David E. ... DeLand, FL
Disney, David E., P.A. ... DeLand, FL
Disney, James H. ... Concord, CA
Disney, John G. ... Baltimore, MD

Disney, Mitchell F. ...Ventura, CA
Disney, Neil K. ...Bloomfield Hills, MI
Disney, Rick K. ...Fort Worth, TX
Disney, William J. ...Douglas, WY
D'Isola, Michael M. ...Boston, MA
DiSomma, Jennine ...Newark, NJ
DiSomma, Ralph F. ...New York, NY
Dison, Carol A. ...Urbana, IL
Dispensa, Paul C. ...Schaumburg, IL
Dispenza, Samuel A., Jr.
East Rochester, NY
DiSpigna, Frederic J. ...Boca Raton, FL
DiSpigna, Frederic J., P.A., Law Offices of
Boca Raton, FL
Dispoto, Mark ...Hackensack, NJ
Dispute Resolvers ...Lafayette, CA
Disque, Carl W. ...Hagerstown, MD
Disque, Carl W., P.C. ...Hagerstown, MD
Disque, Charles R. ...Indianapolis, IN
Disque, Donald J. ...Redmond, WA
Disque, Philip A. ...Fort Lauderdale, FL
Diss, Fred J. ...Denver, CO
Diss, William T. ...Denver, CO
Disselhorst, Earl J. ...San Francisco, CA
Disselhorst, John R. ...Burlington, IA
Disselhorst, Thomas M. ...Bismarck, ND
Disselkamp, Linda B. ...Washington, DC
Disselkoen, Fred S., Jr. ...Ormond Beach, FL
Dissen, James H. ...Charleston, WV
Dissen, Richard W. ...Pittsburgh, PA
Dissen, Walter C. ...Norfolk, VA
Dissette, Michael J. ...Boston, MA
Dissinger, Deanne L. ...Philadelphia, PA
Dissinger & Dissinger ...Camp Hill, PA
Marysville, PA
Dissinger, Mary A. Etter ...Camp Hill, PA
Marysville, PA
Dissinger, Sharon Rau ...Baltimore, MD
Dissinger, William C. ...Camp Hill, PA
Marysville, PA
Dissly, Jayme Smith ...Fayetteville, AR
Disspayne, Laurenn Sharp ...Nashville, TN
Distad, Eric A. ...Casper, WY
Distad, Robert ...Minneapolis, MN
DiStasi, Daniel J. ...Cherry Hill, NJ
Di Stasi, Lewis C., Jr. ...Highland, NY
Di Stasi and Moriello, P.C. ...Highland, NY
Distasio, Anthony R. ...Reading, PA
Distasio, Daniel J., Jr. ...Wilkes-Barre, PA
Distasio, Frank A., Jr. ...Bethesda, MD
DiStasio, Lynne E. ...New York, NY
Distasio, Scott P. ...Tampa, FL
Di Stefano, Arcangelo ...Putnam Valley, NY
DiStefano, Biagio J. ...Wampsville, NY
DiStefano, Charles E. ...Phoenix, AZ
DiStefano, David J. ...Bangor, MI
DiStefano & Erca ...Durham, NC
Di Stefano, Frank J. ...Chicago, IL
Distefano, Gregory V. ...New York, NY
Distefano, Henry Peter ...Bay Shore, NY
Di Stefano, James G. ...Syracuse, NY
di Stefano, James Michael ...Washington, DC
DiStefano, Joann ...Chicago, IL
DiStefano, Joseph ...Washington, DC
Di Stefano, Joseph A. ...Brooklyn, NY
DiStefano, Joseph R. ...Providence, RI
DiStefano, Lamberto ...Clawson, MI
Plymouth, MI
Di Stefano, Laurence Joseph, Jr.
Millville, NJ
Di Stefano, Matthew E.
Jackson Heights, NY
DiStefano, Nancy B. ...Wilmington, DE
DiStefano, Pamela R. ...Durham, NC
DiStefano, Rebecca Gibson
Fort Lauderdale, FL
DiStefano, Regina G. ...Cherry Hill, NJ
DiStefano, Richard ...New York, NY
Di Stefano, Richard R. ...Philadelphia, PA
Di Stefano, Richard T. ...Albany, NY
DiStefano, Robert F. ...Atlantic City, NJ
DiStefano, Robert P. ...Washington, DC
Distel, John F. ...San Diego, CA
Distel, Michael J. ...Grand Rapids, MI
Distel, Richard H. ...Warren, MI
Distelhorst, Michael ...Columbus, OH
Distell, Gary N. ...New York, NY
Distelman, Jacqueline W. ...Floral Park, NY
Distenfeld, Jeffrey S. ...Bethesda, MD
Distenfeld, Yvonne ...Rockville, MD
Di Stephan, Vincent P. ...Lake Success, NY
Disterheft, Arthur H. ...San Rafael, CA
Distler, Bernard E. ...Pasadena, CA
Distler, M. David ...New York, NY
Distler, Thomas R. ...New York, NY
Distler, Vivian B. ...Palo Alto, CA
Dita, Joseph, III ...Reno, NV
D'Italia, Alexandra ...San Francisco, CA
D'Italia, Arthur N. ...Jersey City, NJ
Di Talia, Carmela M. ...Riverhead, NY
D'Italia, Russell V. ...Morristown, NJ
DiTanna, Kevin A. ...Tampa, FL
Di Taranto, Frank M. ...New York, NY
DiTaranto, Joann M. ...East Meadow, NY
DiTaranto, Joseph J. ...Woodbury, NJ
DiTaranto, Mark A. ...New York, NY
DiTata, Barbara ...White Plains, NY
Di Tata, Jerry A. ...Staten Island, NY
DiTata, Maureen Rothschild
New York, NY
Ditch, Luther B. ...Towson, MD
Ditchek, Neil I. ...Washington, DC
Ditchen, Meredith W. ...Woodstock, GA
Ditchik, Alan ...New York, NY
Ditchik, Joel ...New York, NY
Ditchik, Michael ...Tukwila, WA
Dite, Barbara M. ...St. Louis, MO
Ditelberg, Dennis L. ...Boston, MA
Ditelberg, Jane Gorham ...Chicago, IL
Ditelberg, Joshua L. ...Chicago, IL
Ditges, Laura A. ...Denver, CO
Dithmar, John U. ...Baraboo, WI
Dithrich, Charles W. ...Sewickley, PA
Ditka, Anthony Ashton ...Pittsburgh, PA
Ditka, Laura Ann ...Pittsburgh, PA
Ditkof, Martin L. ...Milwaukee, WI
Ditkoff, James H. ...Washington, DC
Ditkowich, Robin Ann ...New York, NY
Ditkowsky & Contorer ...Chicago, IL
Ditkowsky, Kenneth K. ...Chicago, IL
Ditlevson, Richard L. ...Olympia, WA
Ditlevson, Rodgers & Hanbey, P.S.
Olympia, WA
Ditman, Melvin ...New Haven, CT
Ditmars, Kathryn T. ...Chicago, IL
Ditmars, Linda J. ...Trenton, NJ
Ditmars, Lyle W. ...Council Bluffs, IA
Dito, Frank Joseph, Jr. ...New York, NY
Dito, Jeffrey A. ...San Francisco, CA
Dito, John A. ...Los Angeles, CA
Ditocco, Anthony ...Fort Lauderdale, FL
DiTocco, Robyn ...Fort Lauderdale, FL
Di Tolve, Anthony W. ...Charlottesville, VA
DiTomaso, Richard D. ...Moorestown, NJ
Ditomassi, Elisabeth A. ...Boston, MA
DiTomasso, Edward A. ...New York, NY
Di Tomasso, Edward T. ...New York, NY
Di Tomasso, Michael R.
Yorktown Heights, NY
Di Tomasso, Michael R., P.C.
Yorktown Heights, NY
Di Tomasso, Susan A.
Yorktown Heights, NY
DiTommaso, Anthony L. ...Pittsburgh, PA
DiTommaso & Berman, P.C.
Oakbrook Terrace, IL
DiTommaso, Joseph F. ...Marlborough, MA
DiTommaso, Vincent L.
Oakbrook Terrace, IL
DiTomo, Joseph L., Jr. ...Philadelphia, PA
Ditonto, Douglas P. ...Rosemead, CA
Ditora, David L. ...Sacramento, CA
Ditora, Lisa Lauritzen ...Sacramento, CA
Ditore, Deborah D. ...Sacramento, CA
Ditore, Jerome C. ...Brooklyn, NY
DiTrani & Butler ...Camp Springs, MD
DiTrani, Leslie Tuttle ...Boston, MA
DiTrani, Louis J. ...Camp Springs, MD
DiTrapano, Barrett & DiPiero, P.L.L.C.
Charleston, WV
DiTrapano, L. Dante ...Charleston, WV
DiTrapano, Lia M. ...Charleston, WV
DiTrapano, Rudolph L. ...Charleston, WV
Ditsch, Brian E. ...Scottsdale, AZ
Ditsch, Charles A. ...Phoenix, AZ
Ditslear, Christopher R. ...DeLand, FL
Ditsler, John W. ...Linden, NJ
Ditsworth, John R. ...Tempe, AZ
Ditta, George Joseph, II ...New Orleans, LA
Ditta, Louis M. ...Houston, TX
Ditta, Roland A. ...Gretna, LA
Dittberner, Janet L. ...Woodland Hills, CA
Dittberner, Michael D. ...Edina, MN
Dittelman, Lawrence R. ...White Plains, NY
Dittemore, Richard D. ...Englewood, CO
Dittenhoefer, Marc M. ...New York, NY
Ditter, George B. ...Ambler, PA
Ditter, J. William, III ...Norristown, PA
Ditter, J. William, Jr. ...Philadelphia, PA
Ditter, Mark M. ...Milwaukee, WI
Ditter, Michael ...San Diego, CA
Dittert, J. Lee, Jr. ...Sealy, TX
Ditfurth, David A. ...San Antonio, TX
Ditthardt, Brian J., (P.A.) ...Hollywood, FL
Ditthavong, Keth ...Washington, DC
Dittlinger, Stephen L. ...San Antonio, TX
Dittman, Derryck H. ...Tigard, OR
Dittman, John C. ...Anchorage, AK
Dittman, John C., P.C., Law Offices of
Anchorage, AK
Dittman, Mitchell R. ...Troy, MI
Dittman, Robert A. ...Delray Beach, FL
Dittman, Stevan C. ...New Orleans, LA
Dittman, Wilber & Associates, PLC
Troy, MI
Dittmann, Albert S., Jr. ...New Orleans, LA
Dittmann, Jo Ann Smith ...Chambersburg, PA
Dittmann, Lisa A. ...Minneapolis, MN
Dittmann, M. Carton, Jr. ...Gladwyne, PA
Dittmann, Scott S. ...Metairie, LA
Dittmar, Ann Marie ...Rockford, IL
Dittmar, C. Harris ...Jacksonville, FL
Dittmar, Carol M. ...Tampa, FL
Dittmar, Carol S. ...Eau Claire, WI
Dittmar, Charles H., Jr. ...Tampa, FL
Dittmar, David N. ...Steubenville, OH
Weirton, WV
Dittmar, David P. ...Miami, FL
Dittmar, Dawn M. ...Norwalk, CT
Dittmar, Harold A. ...White Plains, NY
Dittmar & Hauser, P.A. ...Miami, FL
Dittmar, James S. ...Boston, MA
Dittmar, Kevin S. ...Milwaukee, WI
Dittmar, Maria J. ...Newark, NJ
Dittmeier, Anthony T. ...Cincinnati, OH
Dittmeier, Thomas E. ...St. Louis, MO
Dittmer, C. Suzanne ...New Orleans, LA
Dittmer, Charles W., Jr. ...Metairie, LA
Dittmer, E. B., II ...Bogalusa, LA
Mandeville, LA
Dittmer & Hartman ...Metairie, LA
Dittmer, Jeffrey A. ...Columbus, OH
Dittmer, Kaija Kristine ...White Plains, NY
Dittmer, Robert F. ...Howell, NJ
Dittmer, Terrance H. ...Maitland, FL
Dittmer, Wohlust & Wilkins, P.A.
Maitland, FL
Orlando, FL
Dittmeyer, Edward B. ...Quincy, IL
Dittner, Derek E. ...Charlotte, NC
Ditto, Dale S., & Associates, P.S.C.
Lexington, KY
Ditto, Dale Stewart ...Lexington, KY
Ditto, David G. ...Cheyenne, WY
Ditto, J. Kane ...Jackson, MS
Ditto, Michael E. ...Dallas, TX
Ditto, Richard L. ...St. Paul, MN
Ditto, Steven M. ...Yukon, OK
Ditto, Steven M., P.C. ...Yukon, OK
Ditto, W. Paul, Jr. ...Dallas, TX
Dittoe, John E. ...Oakland, CA
Dittrich, Brian E. ...Tulsa, OK
Dittrich, Gregory D. ...St. Paul, MN
Dittrich, H. M. ...Detroit, MI
Dittrich, Mark A. ...Minneapolis, MN
Dittrich, Raymond J. ...Minneapolis, MN
Dittrich, Robert ...Stuttgart, AR
Dittrich, William E. ...Hammond, IN
Dittrick, William G. ...Omaha, NE
Dittus, Sandra B. ...Grand Forks, ND
Dittus, Timothy R. ...Grand Forks, ND
Ditty, Anthony T. ...San Diego, CA
Ditty, Bradley Nelson ...Wilmington, DE
Ditty, Christine M ...Edina, MN
Ditty, John Paul ...San Francisco, CA
DiTucci, Cosmo J. ...Kew Gardens, NY
Ditullio, Dino A. ...Fort Collins, CO
Di Tullio, Donna M.
Federal Labor Relations Authority,
Federal Service Impasses Panel, GV
Ditullio, Jessica K. ...Columbus, OH
DiTullio, John D. ...Phoenix, AZ
Ditullio, Mark ...Columbus, OH
DiTullio, Sheila A. ...Buffalo, NY
DiTullio, Stephen A. ...Madison, WI
Ditunno, Christopher A. ...Boston, MA
Ditus, R. Stanley ...Anchorage, AK
Ditusa, Robert Anthony ...Buffalo, NY
Ditz, Paul J. ...Shelby, NC
Ditzhazy, Shelly L. ...Palmdale, CA
Ditzhazy, William Matthew ...Palmdale, CA
Ditzian, Michael D. ...New York, NY
Ditzler, Austin D. ...Minneapolis, MN
Ditzler, J.C. ...Seattle, WA
DiUbaldo, Robert F. ...Warren, NJ
Diuguid, John M. ...Wurtsboro, NY
Diulio, Jeanne M. ...Brooklyn, NY
Diulus, Gregory P. ...Pittsburgh, PA
Diulus-Myers, A. Patricia ...Pittsburgh, PA
Diumenti, George S., II ...Bountiful, UT
Divack, Joshua I. ...New York, NY
Divak, Jodi L. ...New York, NY
Divak, Russell A. ...New York, NY
Divalentino, Karen Michele
Newburgh, NY
DiValerio, Richard M. ...Orchard Park, NY
Divaris, Angela ...Hempstead, NY
Diveglia, Archie V. ...Harrisburg, PA
Diveglia, Archie V., P.C. ...Harrisburg, PA
Divelbiss, Bruce A. ...Bakersfield, CA
Divelbiss, Carl W. ...Phoenix, AZ
Divelbiss, Divelbiss & Bonzell, LLP
San Francisco, CA
Divelbiss, Mark J. ...San Francisco, CA
Divelbiss, Robert O. (Rod)
San Francisco, CA
Divelbliss, Elaine M. ...New York, NY
Diveley, E. Marie Tucker ...Richmond, VA
Diveley, Terry A. ...Richardson, TX
Dively and Dively ...Vienna, VA
Dively, Lane D. ...Pittsburgh, PA
Dively, Mary Jo Howard ...Pittsburgh, PA
Dively, Michael A. ...Key West, FL
Dively, Robert R. ...Vienna, VA
Dively, Robert Ray, Jr. ...Vienna, VA
Diven, Warren B. ...Solana Beach, CA
DiVenere, Anthony J. ...Cleveland, OH
DiVenere, Thomas M. ...Chicago, IL
Divens, Jon A. ...Los Angeles, CA
DiVenuta, Dennis M. ...Mendham, NJ
Diver, David M. ...Riverside, CA
Diver, Grach, Quade & Masini
Waukegan, IL
Diver, Jeffrey R. ...Wheaton, IL
Diver, Joseph W. ...Colorado Springs, CO
Diver, Thomas W. ...Waukegan, IL
DiVergilis, James J. ...Pennsauken, NJ
Philadelphia, PA
DiVernieri, DiVernieri & Cotter
Staten Island, NY
DiVernieri, Rose M. ...Staten Island, NY
DiVernieri, Roseann F. ...Staten Island, NY
DiVerniero, Kristyn ...Daytona Beach, FL
Divers, Brett D. ...Tampa, FL
Diviacchi Law Office ...Boston, MA
Diviacchi, Valeriano ...Boston, MA
Diviak, Paul J. ...Buffalo, NY
Divin, Rory ...Fort Worth, TX
DiVincenti, Roy J., III ...Baton Rouge, LA
DiVincenzo, Anthony S. ...Chicago, IL
DiVincenzo, Joseph P.
Newport Beach, CA
DiVincenzo, Joseph P. ...Buffalo, NY
Di Vincenzo, Louis H. ...Buffalo, NY
DiVincenzo, Mark C. ...Boston, MA
Divine, Carol L. ...New York, NY
Divine, Cheryl ...Bloomington, MN
Divine, Dorough & Sizemore ...Albany, GA
Divine & Estes, P.A. ...Orlando, FL
Divine, Hugh W. ...Winston-Salem, NC
Divine, Jennifer S. ...Seattle, WA
Divine, Richard H. ...Burlingame, CA
Divine, Richard W. ...Dayton, OH
Divine, Robert C. ...Chattanooga, TN
Johnson City, TN
Divine, Russell W. ...Orlando, FL
Divine, Scott E. ...Sacramento, CA
Divine, Thomas M. ...Hartford, CT
Divine, W. Douglas ...Albany, GA
Divine, William G. ...Indianapolis, IN
Divine, William T., Jr. ...Albany, GA
Diviney, Catherine A. ...Syracuse, NY
Diviney, Craig D. ...Minneapolis, MN
Diviney, Richard J. ...Westport, CT
Divino, Amy F. ...New York, NY
Divino, Jong Sook ...Chicago, IL
Diviny, Christopher ...Philadelphia, PA
DiVirgilio, James M. ...Hartford, CT
Divis, Daniel J. ...Moorestown, NJ
Philadelphia, PA
Divis, Deborah B. ...Downers Grove, IL
Divita, DesireéHalkias ...Charleston, WV
Divita, Fred A. A., (Professional Corporation)
Eugene, OR
Divita, Fred A. A. ...Eugene, OR
DiVita, Nicholas L. ...Kansas City, MO
DiVita, Robert G. ...Williamsville, NY
DiVita, Robert R. ...Newark, NJ
Di Vita, Stephanie A. ...New York, NY
Di Vito, Gary F. ...Philadelphia, PA
DiVito, Gino L. ...Chicago, IL
Di Vito & Higham, P.A.
St. Petersburg, FL
Divito, Joann Rowe ...Clearwater, FL
Di Vito, John J. ...St. Petersburg, FL
Di Vito, Joseph A. ...St. Petersburg, FL
Di Vito, Julie B. ...Melbourne, FL
Divney, Jeffrey A. ...Denver, CO
Divola, Julie A. ...San Francisco, CA
Divoll, Marcia K. ...Boston, MA
Divoll, Natt L., Jr. ...Bellows Falls, VT
Divoll, Vicki J. ...Washington, DC
Divone, Charles D. ...McLean, VA
Di Voni, Donnino ...Fanwood, NJ
Divozzo, Wendy A. ...Bloomfield Hills, MI
Diwik, James P. ...San Francisco, CA
Dix, Barry D. ...Belleville, IL
Dix, C. Raymond ...Tallahassee, FL
Dix, Diane Stehle ...Cincinnati, OH
Dix, Forman & Kern, P.C. ...Tucson, AZ
Dix, Genevieve M. ...Memphis, TN
Dix, Genevieve M., P.C. ...Memphis, TN
Dix, George E. ...Austin, TX
Dix, Harold G. ...Pittsburgh, PA
Dix, J. Stephen ...Tucson, AZ
Dix, James G.
Securities and Exchange Commission,
Division of Enforcement, GV
Dix, Jeffrey P. ...Jackson, MO
Dix, Julius A. ...Van Nuys, CA
Dix, Julius A., A P.C. ...Van Nuys, CA
Dix, Karl, Jr. ...Atlanta, GA
Dix, Kathleen ...Albany, NY
Dix, Kenneth M. ...Boca Raton, FL
Dix, Laurie ...New York, NY
Dix, Leonard J. ...Stockton, KS
Dix, Lloyd D. ...Van Nuys, CA
Dix, Lois F. ...New York, NY
Dix, Martin R. ...Tallahassee, FL
Dix, Mary Ann ...Columbus, OH
Dix, Mitchell A. ...New York, NY
Dix, Nancy O. ...San Diego, CA
Dix, R. Victor ...Wooster, OH
Dix, Randy K. ...Butte, MT
Helena, MT
Dix, Robert M. ...Princeton, NJ
Dix, Scott L. ...Norcross, GA
Dix, Simon ...Los Angeles, CA
Dix, Stephen David ...Sunnyvale, CA
Dix, Steven A. ...Murfreesboro, TN
Dix, Thomas B., Jr. ...Accomac, VA
Dix, Timothy V. ...Colorado Springs, CO
Dix, William K. ...La Jolla, CA
Dixie, Chris J. ...Houston, TX
Dixie, George C. ...Dallas, TX
Grand Prairie, TX
Dixie & Mauzy, L.L.P. ...Dallas, TX
Grand Prairie, TX
Dixit, Mayankkumar M. ...San Jose, CA
Dixit, Parmesh ...Atlanta, GA
Dixit, Raj K. ...Orange, CA
Las Vegas, NV
Dixler, Alan O. ...Whitehouse Station, NJ
Dixler, Kevin Lawrence ...Chicago, IL
Dixon, A. Bryce ...Las Vegas, NV
Dixon, Alan J. ...Washington, DC
St. Louis, MO
Dixon, Alex L. ...La Grange, GA
Dixon, Alicia M. ...Washington, DC
Dixon, Allan ...Troy, NY
Dixon, Amanda M. ...Philadelphia, PA
Dixon, Amy L. ...Los Angeles, CA
Dixon, Amy T. ...Washington, DC
Dixon, Angela ...Atlanta, GA
Dixon, Anne M. ...Philadelphia, PA
Dixon, Anthony J. ...Hazleton, PA
Dixon Attorneys PLLC ...Omaha, NE
Dixon, Augustus M. ...Columbia, SC
Dixon, Barbara T. ...Bronx, NY
Dixon, Ben F. ...Washington, DC
Dixon, Billy Don ...Houston, TX
Dixon, B. J. ...Jonesboro, GA
Dixon, Bonnie Lynn ...New York, NY
Dixon, Brenda A. ...Tuscaloosa, AL
Dixon, Brendan M. ...Brea, CA
Dixon, Brett W. ...Stamford, CT
Dixon, Brian A. ...Sacramento, CA
Dixon & Brooks, P.C. ...Winsted, CT
Dixon, Bryan A. ...Minneapolis, MN
Dixon, Bryan C. ...Oklahoma City, OK
Dixon, Byron H. ...Tampa, FL

Dixon, C. Douglas ... New York, NY
Dixon, C. Warren, III ... Department of Transportation, U. S. Coast Guard, GV
Dixon, Carl F. ... Kenilworth, IL
Dixon, Carmen E., (Ms) ... San Jose, CA
Dixon, Carol ... New York, NY
Dixon, Cazeline Hebert ... Baton Rouge, LA
Dixon, Chappell E. ... Houston, TX
Dixon, Charles D. ... Hickory, NC
Dixon, Charles R. ... Federal Mine Safety and Health Review Commission, Office of the General Counsel, GV
Dixon, Charles W. ... Worcester, MA
Dixon, Charley Greene, Jr. ... Barbourville, KY
Dixon, Cressida A. ... Rochester, NY
Dixon, Cynthia Pyle ... King Of Prussia, PA
Dixon, Dan D. ... Seattle, WA
Dixon, Daniel B. ... Pittsburgh, PA
Dixon, Daniel R. ... Raleigh, NC
Dixon, Danielle K. ... Des Moines, IA
Dixon, David ... Pompton Plains, NJ
Dixon, David A. ... Milwaukee, WI
Dixon, David C. ... Southfield, MI
Dixon, David D. ... Oskaloosa, IA
Dixon, David M. ... Department of Justice, Immigration and Naturalization Service, GV
Dixon, David R. ... Avon, NC
Dixon, David S. ... Traverse City, MI
Dixon, David W. ... Irving, TX
Dixon, Deanna L. ... Detroit, MI
Dixon, Debra J. ... Cleveland, OH
Dixon, Diana L. ... Fort Walton Beach, FL
Dixon, Diana M. ... Doylestown, PA
Dixon & Dixon ... Avon, NC; Nags Head, NC; Raleigh, NC
Dixon & Dixon ... Toledo, OH
Dixon, Donald D. ... Overland Park, KS
Dixon, Donna B. ... Minneapolis, MN
Dixon, Donna K. ... Warroad, MN
Dixon, Donna L. ... Paducah, KY
Dixon, Doub & Conner ... Greenville, NC
Dixon, Douglas J. ... Houston, TX
Dixon, Douglas M. ... Overland Park, KS
Dixon, Douglas P. ... Environmental Protection Agency, Office of Enforcement and Compliance Assurance, GV
Dixon, E. Scot ... Houston, TX
Dixon, E. A., Jr. ... Wayne, PA
Dixon, Edward H. ... Washington, DC
Dixon, Edward K. ... Pittsburgh, PA
Dixon, Elise ... Chicago, IL
Dixon, Elliott J. ... Long Beach, CA
Dixon, Eric D. ... Portales, NM
Dixon, Eric D., Attorney and Counselor at Law, P.A. ... Clovis, NM; Portales, NM
Dixon, Erin K. ... Houston, TX
Dixon, Eugene B. ... Maryville, TN
Dixon, Evan ... Houghton, MI
Dixon, Frank J. ... Portland, OR
Dixon, Fred W. ... Bloomfield Township, MI
Dixon, G. Dallas, (P.C.) ... Trenton, NJ
Dixon, G. Grant, III ... Chicago, IL
Dixon, Gary V. ... Washington, DC
Dixon, Gerald E. ... Wilmington, DE
Dixon, Gerald G. ... Albuquerque, NM
Dixon & Giesen ... Dixon, IL
Dixon, H. Dale, III ... Omaha, NE
Dixon, H. Diane W. ... Hixson, TN
Dixon, Hallie S. ... Mobile, AL
Dixon & Hamilton, LLP ... Getzville, NY
Dixon, Harold M. ... Aiken, SC
Dixon, Harry D., Jr. ... Omaha, NE
Dixon, Harry T., Jr. ... Getzville, NY
Dixon, Henry S. ... Amboy, IL; Dixon, IL
Dixon, Henry Sherwood ... Dixon, IL
Dixon, Herbert B., Jr. ... Washington, DC
Dixon, Howard W. ... Miami, FL
Dixon, Howell, Westmoreland & Newman ... Los Angeles, CA
Dixon, Isabella Darlynn ... Columbus, OH
Dixon, Isaiah, III ... Towson, MD
Dixon, J. Michael ... Columbus, OH
Dixon, J. Mikel ... Knoxville, TN
Dixon, J. Reed ... Sweetwater, TN
Dixon, J. Tobias ... Chicago, IL
Dixon, Jack Charles ... Montgomery, AL
Dixon, Jacqueline B. ... Nashville, TN
Dixon, James ... Schenectady, NY
Dixon, James A., Jr. ... Tallahassee, FL
Dixon, James B. ... Edmond, OK
Dixon, James C. ... Baton Rouge, LA
Dixon, James E. ... Dixon, IL
Dixon, James J. ... New York, NY
Dixon, James J. ... Olympia, WA
Dixon, James M. ... Bloomington, IN
Dixon, James O. ... Dallas, TX
Dixon, Janet L. ... Houston, TX
Dixon, Janet Sue ... Sterling Heights, MI
Dixon, Jas. S. ... Peoria, IL
Dixon, Jean Louise C. ... Avon, NC; Nags Head, NC
Dixon, Jeffery M. ... Dallas, TX
Dixon, Jeffrey H. ... Pine Bluff, AR
Dixon, Jennifer L. ... Hartford, CT
Dixon, Jennifer S. ... Des Moines, IA
Dixon, Jenny L. ... San Francisco, CA
Dixon, Jerome F. ... Bartlett, IL
Dixon, Jerre W. ... Denver, CO
Dixon, Jesse C. ... La Grange, KY
Dixon, Jessica R., Law Offices of ... Dallas, TX
Dixon, Jimmie C. ... Granbury, TX
Dixon, Joe H., Jr. ... Monroe, LA
Dixon, John D. ... Atlanta, GA
Dixon, John E. ... Los Alamitos, CA
Dixon, John Fletcher ... Western Springs, IL
Dixon, John J. ... Warminster, PA
Dixon, John M. ... Chicago, IL
Dixon, John M., Jr. ... Hopkinsville, KY
Dixon, John R. ... Tampa, FL
Dixon, John W. ... Lake Bluff, IL
Dixon & Johnston ... Belleville, IL
Dixon, Joseph A. ... Cincinnati, OH
Dixon, Joseph L. ... Department of Commerce, Patent and Trademark Office, GV
Dixon, Joseph T., III ... New York, NY
Dixon, Joseph T., Jr. ... Minneapolis, MN
Dixon, Joyce A. ... Omaha, NE
Dixon, Judith A. ... Winsted, CT
Dixon, Judith B. ... DeWitt, MI
Dixon, Julie C. ... Indianapolis, IN
Dixon, June Marie ... Streator, IL
Dixon, Karen K. ... Chicago, IL
Dixon, Karen L. ... Oklahoma City, OK
Dixon, Karen M. ... Chicago, IL
Dixon, Katherine D. ... Atlanta, GA
Dixon, Kathleen B. ... Casper, WY
Dixon, Kelly K. ... San Francisco, CA
Dixon, Kevin K. ... Inverness, FL
Dixon, Kimberly ... Okemos, MI
Dixon, Kurt L. ... Raleigh, NC
Dixon, Kyle D. ... Federal Communications Commission, Office of the Commissioners, GV
Dixon, L. Allyn, Jr. ... Irving, TX
Dixon, Lance R. ... Los Angeles, CA
Dixon, Larry L. ... Jackson, CA
Dixon, LaVerne A. ... Lake Forest, IL
Dixon Law Firm ... Dardanelle, AR
Dixon Law Offices, A Professional Corporation ... Philadelphia, PA
Dixon, Lee J., II ... Washington, DC
Dixon, Lefler, Lorenzen & Myers ... Tampa, FL
Dixon, Lisa James ... Raleigh, NC
Dixon, Lori A. ... Denver, CO
Dixon, Lorraine Kay Tunley ... Dallas, TX
Dixon, LuAnn C. ... Topeka, KS
Dixon, M. Brad ... Arlington, TX
Dixon, M. Ellen ... Blue Bell, PA
Dixon & MacDonald, P.C. ... Southfield, MI
Dixon, Marian A. ... Chicago, IL
Dixon, Marjorie M. ... Ann Arbor, MI
Dixon, Mark W. ... Tulsa, OK
Dixon, Mary Alice ... Charlotte, NC
Dixon, Matthew ... Culver City, CA
Dixon, Matthew John ... Cary, NC
Dixon, Maynard H., Jr. ... Department of Transportation, Surface Transportation Board, GV
Dixon, Megan ... Washington, DC
Dixon, Michael B. ... Getzville, NY
Dixon, Michael C. ... Manassas, VA
Dixon, Michael J. ... Washington, DC
Dixon, Michael P. ... Juneau, AK
Dixon, Michael W. ... Waco, TX
Dixon, Miriam Ann ... Charlotte, NC
Dixon, Monroe ... Miami, FL
Dixon, Nancy ... Kansas City, MO
Dixon, Nancy M. ... Wichita, KS
Dixon, Pamela B. ... Little Rock, AR
Dixon, Pat D., Jr. ... Atlanta, GA; Atlanta, GA
Dixon, Patrick ... Casper, WY
Dixon, Patrick J. ... Geneva, IL
Dixon, Paul E. ... Rye, NY
Dixon, Paul L. ... Las Vegas, NV
Dixon, Paul R. ... Norwalk, CA
Dixon, Paul V. ... Summit, MS
Dixon, Peter ... San Francisco, CA
Dixon, Philip D., III ... Fort Worth, TX
Dixon, Philip E. ... Little Rock, AR
Dixon, Philip H. ... Albany, NY
Dixon, Philip R. ... Searcy, AR
Dixon, Phillip R., Sr. ... Greenville, NC
Dixon, Phineas S. ... Catonsville, MD
Dixon, Phinorice Boldin ... Philadelphia, PA
Dixon, R. Brian ... San Francisco, CA
Dixon, R. Eddie, Jr. ... Round Rock, TX
Dixon, R. Glenn, Jr. ... Salisbury, NC
Dixon, Ralph F. ... Newport Beach, CA
Dixon, Randall C. ... Toledo, OH
Dixon, Randall W. ... Dardanelle, AR
Dixon, Randy Kevin ... Lufkin, TX
Dixon, Raymond H. ... Alexandria, VA
Dixon, R. C. ... Anderson, IN
Dixon, Richard D. ... New London, CT
Dixon, Richard D. ... Dearborn, MI
Dixon, Richard D.S., III ... United States Court Of Appeals For The Armed Forces, GV
Dixon, Richard E. ... Duncan, OK
Dixon, Richard E. ... Fairfax, VA
Dixon, Richard L. ... Glens Falls, NY
Dixon, Robert ... Miami, FL
Dixon, Robert A. ... Cleveland, OH
Dixon, Robert B. ... Toledo, OH
Dixon, Rodger L. ... Warren, OH
Dixon, Ronald ... Washington, DC
Dixon, Ronald R. ... Clinton Township, MI
Dixon, Ronda R. ... Beverly Hills, CA
Dixon, Ronnie E. ... Atlanta, GA
Dixon, Sallie Donarovich ... Little Falls, NJ
Dixon, Samuel Bobbitt ... Edenton, NC
Dixon, Scott ... Belleville, IL
Dixon, Scott E. ... Pensacola, FL
Dixon, Scott M. ... Atlanta, GA
Dixon, Sean G. ... Baltimore, MD
Dixon, Sharon Quinn ... Miami, FL
Dixon, Sherrie Rosen ... Chicago, IL
Dixon, Simon ... Lawrence, MA
Dixon and Snow, P.C. ... Denver, CO
Dixon, Spencer H. ... Butler, NJ
Dixon, Stephen D. ... Bend, OR
Dixon, Steven ... New York, NY
Dixon, Steven B. ... Waikoloa, HI
Dixon, Steven B. ... Port Orchard, WA
Dixon, Steven J. ... Salt Lake City, UT
Dixon, Stewart S. ... Chicago, IL
Dixon & Stutts ... Sweetwater, TN
Dixon, Susan E. ... Winsted, CT
Dixon, Susani N.H. ... Denver, CO
Dixon, Terence A. ... Philadelphia, PA
Dixon, Terry D. ... North Miami, FL
Dixon, Terry E. ... Irvine, CA
Dixon, Thomas A. ... Columbus, OH; Toledo, OH
Dixon, Thomas B. ... Phoenix, AZ
Dixon, Thomas E. ... Chattanooga, TN
Dixon, Thomas E. ... Seattle, WA
Dixon, Thomas E., III ... Atlanta, GA
Dixon, Thomas H. ... Dallas, TX
Dixon, Thomas J. ... Fort Wayne, IN
Dixon, Thomas M. ... Detroit, MI
Dixon, Thomas R., Jr. ... Amarillo, TX
Dixon, Thomas W., Jr. ... Staunton, VA
Dixon, Timothy A. ... Baltimore, MD
Dixon, Timothy E. ... Baltimore, MD
Dixon, Truman & Kelleher ... Las Vegas, NV; St. George, UT
Dixon, Tyler Charles, (P.C.) ... Atlanta, GA
Dixon, Victor A. ... Washington, DC
Dixon, Virgil F. ... Des Moines, IA
Dixon, W. McGregor, Jr. ... Troy, OH
Dixon, Wade M. ... Tribune, KS
Dixon, Wallace W. ... Raleigh, NC
Dixon, Wanda J ... Upper Marlboro, MD
Dixon, Willard ... Memphis, TN
Dixon, William B. ... Columbus, OH
Dixon, William B., (P.C.) ... Pittsburgh, PA
Dixon, William C., III ... Rochester, NY
Dixon, William Charles ... Philadelphia, PA
Dixon, William D. ... Vienna, VA
Dixon, William H., (P.A.) ... Palm Bay, FL
Dixon, William J. ... Lake Odessa, MI
Dixon, William L., V ... Tacoma, WA
Dixon, William M. ... Troy, OH
Dixon, William P. ... Phoenix, AZ
Dixon, William P. ... Madison, WI
Dixon, William S. ... Atlanta, GA
Dixon, William S. ... Albuquerque, NM
Dixon, Willie O., IV ... Charlotte, NC
Dixon, Wright T., Jr. ... Raleigh, NC
Dixon, Yolanda Johnson ... Baton Rouge, LA
Dixon, Yoniece Mitchell ... Tampa, FL
Dixon, Yvonne Teresa ... National Labor Relations Board, Office of the General Counsel, GV
Dixon-Moses, Clarke M. ... Aptos, CA
Dixon-Thayer, Denelle M. ... Los Angeles, CA; San Francisco, CA
Dixson, K. DeAnne ... Los Angeles, CA
Dixson, Mark A. ... Owego, NY
Diz, Carlos E. ... General Accounting Office, Office of the General Counsel, GV
Dizard, Seth E. ... Waukesha, WI
Dize, James K. ... Vienna, VA
Dizenfeld, Bruce E. ... Los Angeles, CA
Dizenfeld, David G. ... Beverly Hills, CA
Dizengoff, Bruce Brian ... Department of Justice, Washington, D.C. District Office, GV
Dizengoff, Ira S. ... New York, NY
Dizenhuz, Robert S. ... Cincinnati, OH
di Zerega, James G. ... Englewood, CO
Diznoff, Laurel B. ... Pittsburgh, PA
Dizon, Carolyn A. ... New York, NY
Dizon, Eileen S. ... Mountain View, CA
Dizon, Kirk ... San Francisco, CA
Dizozza, Nicholas F. ... Forest Hills, NY
Dizozza, Peter W. ... Long Island City, NY
Dizzia, John Paul ... Upper Montclair, NJ
Djaha, David C. ... New York, NY
Djang, Edward B. ... Costa Mesa, CA
Djavaherian, Michael M. ... Del Mar, CA
Djerassi, Ramy I. ... Philadelphia, PA
Djernaes, Christina ... San Francisco, CA
Djeu, Deborah Daphne ... Los Angeles, CA
Djinis, Anthony W. ... Washington, DC
Djokic, Richard ... Denver, CO
Djokic, Walter H. ... West Palm Beach, FL
Djordjevic, Diane Eshleman ... Chicago, IL
Djordjevic, Michael M. ... Akron, OH
Djordjevic, Michael M., Co. LPA ... Akron, OH
Djordjevich, Alexander ... Washington, DC
Djordjic, Mira ... Chicago, IL
Djou, Charles K. ... Honolulu, HI
Djurasovic, George ... New York, NY
Djuric, Nikola Richard ... Atlanta, GA
Djurisic, Paul I. ... Chicago, IL
Dladla, Paula Jones ... New York, NY
D'Lauro & Dickerson, P.C. ... Philadelphia, PA
D'Lauro, John J., III ... Philadelphia, PA
Dlin, Ella ... New York, NY
Dlin, Geoffrey William ... Allentown, PA
D'Lizarraga, Stacey Coe ... Fort Worth, TX
Dloski, Lawrence W. ... Mount Clemens, MI
Dlott, George E. ... Sharon, MA
Dlott, Steven P. ... Columbus, OH
Dlott, Susan J. ... Cincinnati, OH
Dlouhy, Francina A. ... Indianapolis, IN
Dlug, Sam ... Los Angeles, CA
Dlugach, Michael S. ... Memphis, TN
Dlugajczyk, Robert R. ... Chicago, IL
Dlugatch, Harvey E. ... Reseda, CA
D'Luge, Christine ... Southfield, MI
D'Luge, Miles & Miles, P.L.C. ... Mount Clemens, MI
Dluge, Robert L., Jr. ... Elysburg, PA
D'Luge, Thomas G. ... Mount Clemens, MI
Dlugie, David R. ... Chicago, IL
D'Lugin, Jeri Kay ... Greensboro, NC
D'Lugo, Michael R. ... Orlando, FL
Dlugoff, Marc A. ... New York, NY
Dlugokecki, Frederick ... Naugatuck, CT
Dlugokinski, Dennis J. ... Farmington Hills, MI
Dlugosz, Robert W. ... Lorain, OH
Dlutman, Roselyn C. ... New York, NY
Dlutowski, Christopher J. ... New York, NY
Dluz, Peter M. ... Stamford, CT
Dmitrovich, Veda ... Chicago, IL
Dmoch, Gary John ... Flushing, NY
Dmochowski, Charles P. ... Lansing, MI
Dmyterko, Michael Philip ... Chicago, IL
Dmytryk, Peter ... San Francisco, CA
Do, Andrew H. ... Santa Ana, CA
Do, Anne H. ... Encino, CA
Do, Caroline T. ... Costa Mesa, CA
Do, Hieu D. ... San Jose, CA
Do, Kim Huong ... Securities and Exchange Commission, Division of Corporation Finance, GV
Do, Liem H. ... Westminster, CA
Do, Quoc-Huy D. ... San Francisco, CA
Do, Thao H. V. ... New York, NY
Do, Thi Bao ... San Francisco, CA
Doak & Associates, P.C. ... Billings, MT
Doak, Barbara ... Nashville, TN
Doak, D. Fred ... Oklahoma City, OK
Doak, David M. ... Stover, MO
Doak, Jerome R. ... Dallas, TX
Doak, John F. ... Rock Island, IL
Doak, John G., Sr. ... Nashville, TN
Doak, Jon E. ... Billings, MT
Doak, Samuel C. ... Knoxville, TN
do Amaral, Paulina ... San Francisco, CA
Doan, Burgess L. ... Newport, KY; Fairfax, OH
Doan, Charles H. ... Cincinnati, OH
Doan, Darby Vincent ... Texarkana, TX
Doan, Dinh Q. ... New York, NY
Doan, D T ... Des Moines, IA
Doan, Glenda K. ... Hanford, CA
Doan, James N. ... Cleveland, OH
Doan, Jennifer Haltom ... Texarkana, TX
Doan, Kathryn M. ... Washington, DC
Doan, Kirk H. ... Kansas City, MO
Doan, Otis, Jr. ... Harlan, KY
Doan, R. Stephen ... Los Angeles, CA
Doan, Robert L. ... New York, NY
Doan, Rupert A. ... Cincinnati, OH
Doan, Tien V. ... Westminster, CA
Doan, Xuyen V. ... San Jose, CA
Doane, David ... Centerville, VA
Doane, Douglas D. ... Denver, CO
Doane, Gary E. ... Orlando, FL
Doane, James K. ... Seattle, WA
Doane, Kenneth G., Jr. ... New Albany, IN
Doane, M. Lee ... Department of Justice, Antitrust Division, GV
Doane, Marcia E. ... Bedford Park, IL
Doane, Margaret M. ... Nuclear Regulatory Commission, Office of Commission Appellate Adjudication, GV
Doane, Mark A. ... Buffalo, NY
Doane, Michael L. ... Washington, DC
Doane, Randell C. ... West Palm Beach, FL
Doane, Rebecca G. ... West Palm Beach, FL
Doane, Robt. E. ... Boston, MA
Doane, Ronald J. ... Fort Salonga, NY
Doane, Wayne P. ... Bangor, ME
Doar Devorkin & Rieck ... New York, NY
Doar, Drill & Skow, S.C. ... Baldwin, WI; New Richmond, WI
Doar, John ... New York, NY
Doar, Kathleen ... Minneapolis, MN
Doar, Michael ... Boca Raton, FL
Doar, Michael ... Rockford, IL
Doar, William W., Jr. ... Georgetown, SC
Doar, W. T., Jr. ... New Richmond, WI
Dobal, Carlos H. ... Fort Lauderdale, FL
Dobal, Malena ... Santa Monica, CA
Dobash, Tanya J. ... Stamford, CT; Minneapolis, MN
Dobashi, Sunny D. ... Gold River, CA
Dobb, Richard P. ... Norcross, GA
Dobbels, Dennis J. ... Kansas City, MO
Dobben, Brian L. ... Chicago, IL
Dobberfuhl, Mark O. ... Barron, WI
Dobberpuhl, Eugene E. ... Aberdeen, SD
Dobberpuhl, William E. ... Long Beach, CA
Dobberstein & Dobberstein ... St. Louis, MO
Dobberstein, Eric, & Associates ... Henderson, NV
Dobberstein, Patricia ... New York, NY
Dobberstein, Paul L., Jr. ... St. Louis, MO
Dobberstein, Ralph A. ... St. Louis, MO
Dobberteen, Eric L. ... Los Angeles, CA
Dobberteen, Kenyon F. ... Los Angeles, CA
Dobberteen & Luna ... Los Angeles, CA
Dobbin, Deborah L. ... Brooklyn, NY
Dobbin, James J. ... La Mesa, CA
Dobbin, Robert F. ... Bronxville, NY
Dobbins, A. Marvin ... Anderson, SC
Dobbins, Alexander W. ... Washington, DC
Dobbins & Associates ... Akron, OH
Dobbins & Aveis ... Woodland Hills, CA
Dobbins, B. Alan, III ... Fort Lauderdale, FL

Dobbins, B. Knox ..... Atlanta, GA
New York, NY
Dobbins & Barre, L.L.P. ..... Corpus Christi, TX
Dobbins Beardslee & Grinage, P.C.
Marshall, MI
Dobbins, Burford C. ..... Corpus Christi, TX
Dobbins, C. Dean ..... Greenfield, IN
Dobbins, Carolyn B. ..... Atlanta, GA
Dobbins, Charles W., Jr. ..... Louisville, KY
Dobbins, D. Cameron ..... Champaign, IL
Dobbins, Daniel P. ..... Taylor, MI
Dobbins, Daniel W. ..... Tallahassee, FL
Dobbins, Daniel W., P.A. ..... Tallahassee, FL
Dobbins, David F. ..... New York, NY
Dobbins, Dean ..... Greenfield, IN
Dobbins, Deborah Wood ..... Blacksburg, VA
Pulaski, VA
Dobbins, Donald W. ..... Willows, CA
Dobbins, Dot ..... Nashville, TN
Dobbins, E. Fred ..... Leakesville, MS
Dobbins, Edward F., Jr. ..... Chicago, IL
Dobbins, Fraker, Tennant, Joy & Perlstein, A Professional Corporation ... Champaign, IL
Danville, IL
Urbana, IL
Dobbins, Howard W. ..... Richmond, VA
Dobbins, James Matthew ..... Glendale, CA
Dobbins, Jeff ..... Mountain View, AR
Dobbins, Jeffrey C. ..... Department of Justice, Environment and Natural Resources Division, GV
Dobbins, Julia ..... Fort Worth, TX
Dobbins, Keith E. ..... Washington, DC
Dobbins, Keith S. ..... Woodland Hills, CA
Dobbins, L. Guerry, Jr. ..... Lakeland, FL
Dobbins, Linda ..... Newark, NJ
Dobbins, Lloyd R. ..... North Olmsted, OH
Dobbins, M. David ..... Washington, DC
Dobbins, Madeliene H. ..... Washington, DC
Dobbins, Mark L. ..... Tahlequah, OK
Dobbins, Mark Wesley ..... Louisville, KY
Dobbins, Mary G. ..... Minneapolis, MN
Dobbins, McCurdy & Yu ..... Portland, OR
Dobbins, Michelle A. ..... Golden, CO
Dobbins, Raymond E. ..... Fort Lauderdale, FL
Dobbins, Richard E. ..... Akron, OH
Dobbins, Richard G. ..... Portland, OR
Dobbins, Richard L. ..... Marshall, MI
Dobbins, Robert N. ..... Laguna Hills, CA
Dobbins, Sharon M. ..... Sacramento, CA
Dobbins, Sherry Weldon ..... Fort Payne, AL
Dobbins, Susan Diane ..... Galveston, TX
Dobbins, Teri J. ..... Houston, TX
Dobbins, Thorne ..... Pasadena, TX
Dobbins & Venick ..... Nashville, TN
Dobbins, W. Lee ..... Fort Pierce, FL
Dobbins, William G. ..... Greenville, SC
Dobbins-Bucklad, Mary ..... Marietta, OH
Dobbins-Mccary, Renee ..... Cleveland, OH
Dobbrow, Allison Lindley
Redwood City, CA
Dobbs, Ann ..... Los Angeles, CA
Dobbs, Brent ..... Sugar Land, TX
Dobbs & Bunting, P.C. ..... Corpus Christi, TX
Dobbs, C. Edward ..... Atlanta, GA
Dobbs, Carney H. ..... Birmingham, AL
Dobbs, Carter, Jr. ..... Aberdeen, MS
Amory, MS
Dobbs, David A. ..... San Francisco, CA
Dobbs, David M. ..... Scottsdale, AZ
Dobbs, Diane M. ..... Trenton, NJ
Dobbs, Donovan D. ..... Wagoner, OK
Dobbs, Gary A. ..... Morris, IL
Dobbs, Gary C. ..... Irving, TX
Dobbs, Guy Peter ..... Livonia, MI
Dobbs, Hubert Lee, Jr. ..... Phoenix, AZ
Dobbs, J. Robert, Jr. ..... Tyler, TX
Dobbs, James B. ..... Columbus, OH
Dobbs, James C. ..... Springfield, VA
Dobbs, James D. ..... Ackerman, MS
Dobbs, James M. ..... Eufaula, OK
Dobbs, James W. ..... Oklahoma City, OK
Dobbs, John C. ..... Montgomery, AL
Dobbs, Jonathan ..... Commack, NY
Dobbs, Judith ..... Foster City, CA
Dobbs, Kathryn A.
Department of Commerce, Patent and Trademark Office, GV
Dobbs, Keely D. ..... Shawneetown, IL
Dobbs, Lauren W. ..... Yakima, WA
Dobbs, Marcus L. ..... Houston, TX
Dobbs, Marian F. ..... New York, NY
Dobbs, Mary Jane ..... Roseland, NJ
Dobbs, Michael D. ..... Gaithersburg, MD
Dobbs, Michael W. ..... Dallas, TX
Dobbs & Neidle ..... Detroit, MI
Livonia, MI
Dobbs, Pamela Beckman
Ruidoso Downs, NM
Dobbs, Preston ..... Dallas, TX
Dobbs, Robert A. ..... Dothan, AL
Dobbs, S. Jay ..... St. Louis, MO
Dobbs, Schroeder & Middleton
Oklahoma City, OK
Dobbs, Steven ..... Oklahoma City, OK
Dobbs, Stuart ..... Carlinville, IL
Dobbs, Tammy L. ..... Birmingham, AL
Dobbs, Thomas H. ..... Tulsa, OK
Dobbs, William F., Jr. ..... Charleston, WV
Dobbs-Ramey, Kimberly ..... Decatur, AL
Dobby, Stanley M. ..... Plymouth, MI
Dobbyn, Colm James ..... Purchase, NY
Dobbyn, John F. ..... Villanova, PA
Dobe, Carl F. ..... Syracuse, NY
Dobeck, Robert B. ..... Washington, DC
Dobeck, Timothy G. ..... Parma Heights, OH
Dobek, Robert F. ..... Washington, DC
Dobek, Sheryl L. ..... Fort Lauderdale, FL
Dobel, Kathryn E. ..... Berkeley, CA
Dobel, Maureen E. ..... Denver, CO
Dobelbower, Peter M. ..... Oklahoma City, OK
Dobell, Elizabeth ..... New York, NY
Dobelstein, Ronald E. ..... Roswell, GA
Dobelstein, Ronald E., P.A. ..... Roswell, GA
Doberman, Amy R. ..... Hartford, CT
Doberman, Jeffrey J. ..... Encino, CA
Doberneck, Charles N. ..... Fishers, IN
Indianapolis, IN
Doberneck, K. Megan ..... Denver, CO
Dobes, Alison ..... Atlanta, GA
Dobes, Heidi K. ..... Walhalla, SC
Dobes, Margaret Alison ..... Atlanta, GA
Dobias, Gary F. ..... Jim Thorpe, PA
Dobias, Mark L. ..... Sault Ste. Marie, MI
Dobias, Mark L., P.C.
Sault Ste. Marie, MI
Dobie, Brian J. ..... Boston, MA
Dobie, Dudley R., Jr. ..... Austin, TX
Dobie, Linda M. ..... Torrance, CA
Dobie, W. Gordon ..... Chicago, IL
Dobiel, Maryrita ..... Albany, NY
Dobies, Mark M. ..... New York, NY
Dobiesz, Mark R. ..... Louisville, KY
Dobin, Andrea ..... Trenton, NJ
Dobin, David M. ..... Miami Beach, FL
Dobin, Edward I. ..... Morrisville, PA
Dobin, Elliott ..... Boston, MA
Dobin & Jenks, LLP ..... Jupiter, FL
Dobin, Joshua ..... Miami, FL
Dobin, Marc S. ..... Jupiter, FL
Dobin, Phyllis J. ..... Washington, DC
Silver Spring, MD
Dobinski, Karla ..... Washington, DC
Dobis, Beth A. ..... Easton, PA
Dobis, James S. ..... Livingston, NJ
Dobis & Reilly, P.A. ..... Livingston, NJ
Dobise, John J., Jr. ..... Williston Park, NY
Dobkin, Charles H. ..... Brooklyn, NY
Dobkin, Donald S. ..... Farmington, MI
Dobkin, Joseph Martin ..... Miami, FL
Dobkin, Judith F. ..... Chicago, IL
Dobkin, Kenneth L. ..... Miami, FL
West Palm Beach, FL
Dobkin, Kenneth S. ..... Fort Lauderdale, FL
Dobkin, Laurence B. ..... Chicago, IL
Dobkin, Richard B. ..... Tucker, GA
Doble, Arthur V. ..... Huntington Beach, CA
Dobler, Clifford I. ..... Moscow, ID
Dobler, Craig O. ..... Riverside, CA
Dobler, James B. ..... Lincoln, NE
Dobler, John J. ..... Bellaire, TX
Doble-Ruiz, Mayra Del C. ..... San Juan, PR
Doblick, Donna M. ..... Pittsburgh, PA
Doblie & Associates, P.C. ..... Portland, OR
Doblie, Gerald C. ..... Portland, OR
Doblin, Debra L. ..... Bayside, NY
Doblin, Marvin H. ..... Bayside, NY
Dobmeier, Eric L. ..... Kirkland, WA
Dobner, Ari ..... Philadelphia, PA
Dobnicker, Allan D. ..... Lima, OH
Dobosh, Laurence D. ..... New York, NY
Dobosiewicz, Elizabeth J. ..... Buffalo, NY
Dobosiewicz, Raymond A. ..... Brooklyn, NY
Dobosz, Glen T. ..... Elgin, IL
Dobosz, Michael D. ..... Highland, IN
Dobosz, Philip F. ..... San Diego, CA
Dobozin, Carl H. ..... Buffalo, NY
Dobra, Charles W., Ltd. ..... Roselle, IL
Dobra, Michael L. ..... Warren, MI
Dobran, James M. ..... Youngstown, OH
Dobranski, Bernard ..... Washington, DC
Dobranski, Edward J. ..... San Francisco, CA
Dobransky, Joann K. ..... Newark, NJ
Dobratz, Steve ..... Great Bend, KS
Dobreff, David Albert ..... Warren, MI
Dobreff, Edward ..... Warren, MI
Dobreff, Steven F. ..... Farmington Hills, MI
Dobreff, Wendy E. Hige
Bingham Farms, MI
Dobrer, Jean ..... Chicago, IL
Dobres, Sheldon N. ..... Baltimore, MD
Dobrescu, Steven L. ..... Ely, NV
Dobrescu, Steven L., A Professional Corporation ..... Ely, NV
Dobriansky, Larisa E. ..... Washington, DC
Dobrin, Clifford P. ..... San Diego, CA
Dobrin, Daniel A. ..... Rancho Cucamonga, CA
Dobrin, Jon-Marc ..... San Francisco, CA
Dobrin, Jon-Marc, A Prof. Corp., Law Offices of ..... Fairfield, CA
San Francisco, CA
Walnut Creek, CA
Dobrin, Michael K. ..... Sacramento, CA
Dobrinic, Kathryn Slepicka ..... Hillsboro, IL
Dobrinsky, Manuel L. ..... Miami, FL
Dobris, Joel C. ..... Davis, CA
Dobris, Roger S. ..... New Haven, CT
Dobrish, Robert Z., (P.C.) ..... New York, NY
Dobro, Maxine I. ..... San Diego, CA
Dobro & Schwartz ..... San Diego, CA
Dobrofsky, Steven R. ..... Chicago, IL
Dobronos, Michael G. ..... Cleveland, OH
Dobroski, John D. ..... Milwaukee, WI
Dobroth, John E. ..... Ventura, CA
Dobrott, James E., Jr. ..... Irvine, CA
Dobrov, Michael L. ..... Redwood City, CA
Dobrovic, Claudia Marie ..... McLean, VA
Dobrovir, William A., Chartered
Warrenton, VA
Dobrovits, Paul
Department of the Navy, GV
Dobrovolny, Collin P. ..... Minot, ND
Dobrovolny, James L. ..... Urbana, IL
Dobrovolny, Janet Lee ..... Emeryville, CA
Dobrovolny, Leo P., Jr. ..... Alliance, NE
Dobrovolski, Edward C. ..... Woodbridge, NJ
Dobrovsky, Janet E. ..... Auburn, NY
Dobrow, Richard ..... Boca Raton, FL
Dobrowalski, Lauren E. ..... Kingston, PA
Dobrowitsky, Margaret A. ..... Auburn Hills, MI
Dobrowolski, Jos. S. ..... New Haven, CT
Dobrowski, Francis R. ..... Quincy, MA
Dobrowski, Paul J. ..... Houston, TX
Dobrowski, Stanley J. ..... Columbus, OH
Dobrusin, Charles E. ..... Chicago, IL
Dobrusin, Eric M. ..... Bloomfield Hills, MI
Dobrutsky, Jay S. ..... Chicago, IL
Dobry, Stanley T. ..... Warren, MI
Dobscha, Stephen F. ..... Mayfield Village, OH
Dobshinsky, Neal S. ..... Morganville, NJ
Dobson, Allen C. ..... Little Rock, AR
Dobson, Anne M. ..... Richmond, VA
Dobson, Arthur F., Jr. ..... Buffalo, NY
Dobson, Beth ..... Portland, ME
Dobson & Brown, P.A. ..... St. Augustine, FL
Dobson, Carol W. ..... Red Bank, NJ
Dobson, Casey L. ..... Austin, TX
Dobson, David H. ..... Oklahoma City, OK
Dobson, Earl C. ..... Denton, TX
Dobson, Edward M. ..... Bozeman, MT
Dobson, Eleanor Spence ..... Arlington, VA
Dobson, Frederick Page ..... Oklahoma City, OK
Dobson, Geoffrey B. ..... St. Augustine, FL
Dobson, Houser & Dobson ..... Renton, WA
Dobson, James H. ..... Indianapolis, IN
Dobson, Jane ..... New York, NY
Dobson, Janet K. ..... Overland Park, KS
Dobson, Jennifer Lynn ..... Columbia, SC
Dobson, Jerome J. ..... St. Louis, MO
Dobson, John D. ..... Portland, OR
Dobson, John J. ..... Oneonta, AL
Dobson, John S. ..... Ann Arbor, MI
Dobson, John W. ..... Renton, WA
Dobson, Jon A. ..... Richfield, MN
Dobson Jones & Ball, P.A. ..... Greenville, SC
Dobson, Kevin S. ..... Wilmington, DE
Dobson, Lisa S. ..... Lakeland, FL
Dobson, Lynn M. ..... San Jose, CA
Dobson, Lynne F. ..... Columbia, SC
Dobson, Mark ..... Fort Lauderdale, FL
Dobson, Mary Virginia ..... Atlanta, GA
Dobson, Matthew G. ..... Baltimore, MD
Dobson, Michael B. ..... Detroit, MI
Dobson, Mitzie L. ..... Los Angeles, CA
Dobson, Nathaniel, Jr. ..... Atlanta, GA
Dobson, Page ..... Oklahoma City, OK
Dobson, Paul A. ..... Toledo, OH
Dobson & Pinci ..... New York, NY
New York, NY
Dobson, R. Grant ..... Chattanooga, TN
Dobson, Richard E. ..... Westport, CT
Dobson, Robert J. ..... New York, NY
Dobson, Stephen S., III ..... Tallahassee, FL
Dobson, Stephen S., III, P.A.
Tallahassee, FL
Dobson, Steven F. ..... Chattanooga, TN
Dobson, Thomas R. ..... Mercer, PA
Dobson, Thomas W. ..... Los Angeles, CA
Dobson, Tommy R. ..... Sylacauga, AL
Dobson, Tyson Y., Jr. ..... Smithfield, NC
Dobson, W. J., & Assoc., P.C. ..... McLean, VA
Dobson, William D. ..... Galt, CA
Dobson, William J., Jr. ..... McLean, VA
Dobson, Wm. Greg ..... Macon, GA
Dobson, Wyman K. ..... Renton, WA
Dobush, Stephen E. ..... Bedford, OH
Doby & Beaver ..... Albemarle, NC
Doby, Henry C., Jr. ..... Albemarle, NC
Doby, Julian M. ..... Graham, NC
Doby, Robert M., III ..... Fort Worth, TX
Doby, Robert M., Jr. ..... Fort Worth, TX
Doby, S. Bryan ..... Bishopville, SC
Dobyns, J. Michael ..... Blanchester, OH
Wilmington, OH
Dobyns, Richard E. ..... Houston, TX
Dobyns, Thomas ..... Tustin, CA
Dobyns, Thomas, Inc., A Professional Corporation ..... Tustin, CA
Dobyns, Timothy J. ..... Columbus, OH
Do Campo, James A. ..... Hackensack, NJ
do Campo, Orlando ..... Miami, FL
Docan, Carol A. ..... Northridge, CA
Docherty, James M. ..... Roseland, NJ
Docherty, Jennifer Ann ..... New York, NY
Docherty, John F. ..... United States Senate, Committee Legal Personnel, GV
Docherty, Michael R. ..... St. Paul, MN
Docherty, Pamela A. ..... Cleveland, OH
Docherty, Robert A. ..... New Ulm, MN
Docherty, Robert F., Jr. ..... White Plains, NY
Dochney, Francis X. ..... Philadelphia, PA
Dochney, Joseph J. ..... Toms River, NJ
Dochter, Ivan M. ..... Manhasset, NY
Docimo, Gregory A. ..... Montebello, CA
Docken, John D. ..... Marshall, MN
Dockendorf, Margo ..... San Diego, CA
Dockens, Elaine B. ..... Chicago, IL
Docker, W. F. ..... Fresno, CA
Docker, William F. ..... Fresno, CA
Dockerty, Suzanne A. ..... Miami, FL
Dockery, Daniel P. ..... Milwaukee, WI
Dockery, David F. ..... Englewood, CO
Dockery, Elfreda ..... Chicago, IL
Dockery, Harva Ruth ..... Dallas, TX
Houston, TX
Dockery, John P. ..... New York, NY
Dockery, Judith ..... Virginia Beach, VA
Dockery, Kirk Wayne ..... Floresville, TX
Dockery, Martin J. ..... New York, NY
Dockery, Michael S. ..... Billings, MT
Dockery, Patricia J. ..... Detroit, MI
Dockery, Raymond E., Jr. ..... Dallas, TX
Dockery, Robert J. ..... Tarpon Springs, FL
Dockery, Robert W. ..... Dallas, TX
Dockery, Virginia G. ..... Charlotte, NC
Raleigh, NC
Dockery, William J. ..... New York, NY
Dockett, Sonya D. ..... Blue Bell, PA
Docking, George R. ..... Kansas City, KS
Docking, Kent ..... Kansas City, KS
Docking, Thomas R. ..... Wichita, KS
Dockins, Dennis S. ..... Springfield, MO
Dockins, Halbert E., Jr. ..... Jackson, MS
Dockins, John D. ..... Nashville, TN
Dockins, William S. ..... Bozeman, MT
Dockrey, Jasper W. ..... Chicago, IL
Dockry, John J., (P.C.) ..... New York, NY
Dockry, Kathleen A. ..... Wayne, NJ
Dockry, Michael B. ..... Youngstown, OH
Dockser, Ronald D. ..... Natick, MA
Dockser, Sidney J. ..... Needham Heights, MA
Dockser, William B. ..... Rockville, MD
Docksey, J. Ross ..... Chicago, IL
Dockstader, Kim J. ..... Boise, ID
Dockstader, Robert A. ..... Tacoma, WA
Dockter, Dennis D. ..... Bismarck, ND
Dockter, Heather ..... Atlanta, GA
Dockter, Thomas A. ..... Louisville, KY
Dockterman, Alan S. ..... Alexandria, VA
Dockterman, Michael ..... Chicago, IL
Docktor, Susan A. ..... York, PA
Dockum, Bobbye J. ..... Bethany, OK
Dockweiler & Dockweiler ..... Los Angeles, CA
Dockweiler, Frederick C. ..... Los Angeles, CA
Docobo, Richard ..... Miami, FL
Docs, Deborah A. ..... New York, NY
Docter, Charles A. ..... Washington, DC
Docter, Docter & Lynn, P.C.
Washington, DC
Docter, Henry David Will
Washington, DC
Docter, James N. ..... Port Orchard, WA
Docter, Karen J. ..... De Witt, NY
Docter, Marcia K. ..... Washington, DC
Docter, Stephen H. ..... Chicago, IL
Docter, Thomas J. ..... Cross Plains, WI
Doctor, Gregory L. ..... Short Hills, NJ
Doctor, Marsh D. ..... Wellington, KS
Doctor, Nancy M. ..... Oakland, CA
Doctor, Randall A. ..... San Francisco, CA
Doctorian, Sherry L. ..... Jefferson City, MO
Doctorman, Gary E. ..... Salt Lake City, UT
Doctoroff, Andrew S. ..... Detroit, MI
Doctoroff, Isadore ..... Belmont, MA
Doctoroff, Jeffrey A. ..... Boston, MA
Doctoroff, Martin M. ..... Southfield, MI
Doctoroff, Richard M. ..... San Francisco, CA
Doctors, Jerome P. ..... Los Angeles, CA
Doctors, Rachel ..... Springfield, IL
Doctors, Samuel I. ..... Hayward, CA
Doctrow, Michael A. ..... Harrisburg, PA
Doctrow, Robert M. ..... Frankfort, KY
Doctrow, Sherman ..... Encino, CA
Dod, Barry W. ..... Portland, OR
Doda, Kyle ..... Houston, TX
Doda, Paul F. ..... Newark, NJ
New York, NY
Dodaro, James J. ..... Pittsburgh, PA
Dodaro, Kennedy & Cambest ..... Pittsburgh, PA
Dodart, Mark C. ..... New Orleans, LA
Dodd, Alan F. ..... Westborough, MA
Dodd, Allen P., III ..... Louisville, KY
Dodd, Andrew W. ..... Torrance, CA
Dodd, Andrew W., A Professional Corporation
Torrance, CA
Dodd, Angela D. ..... Oak Park, IL
Dodd, B. Joan ..... Green River, WY
Dodd & Batla, P.C. ..... Austin, TX
Dodd, Bette J. ..... Indianapolis, IN
Dodd, Burton F. ..... Atlanta, GA
Dodd, Catherine M. ..... Phoenix, AZ
Dodd, Christopher J. ..... Wethersfield, CT
Dodd, D. Michael ..... Austin, TX
Dodd, David A. ..... Marietta, GA
Dodd, David W. ..... Schaumburg, IL
Dodd, Debra Westhoff ..... Brighton, CO
Dodd and Dennis, P.C. ..... Valdosta, GA
Dodd & Dodd ..... Louisville, KY
Dodd, Donald H. ..... Oswego, NY
Dodd, Donald L. ..... Urbana, OH
Dodd, Douglas D. ..... New Orleans, LA
Dodd, E. Allen, Jr. ..... Fort Payne, AL
Dodd, Edward T., Jr. ..... Cheshire, CT
Dodd, Elizabeth M. ..... Louisville, KY
Dodd, Futterman & Dupree LLP
San Francisco, CA
Dodd, Gary A. ..... Asheville, NC
Dodd, George T. ..... Elkhart, IN
Fort Wayne, IN
Dodd, Gerald M. ..... Los Angeles, CA
Dodd, Glenn T. ..... San Jose, CA
Dodd & Godwin ..... Wichita, KS
Dodd, Gregory L. ..... Ypsilanti, MI
Dodd, Herbert K. ..... Wichita, KS
Dodd, Hiram, Jr. ..... Birmingham, AL
Dodd, J. David ..... Fort Payne, AL
Dodd, James A. ..... Lakewood, CO
Dodd, James B. ..... Jacksonville, FL
Dodd, Jan E. ..... Belleville, IL
St. Louis, MO
Dodd, Jason Evans ..... Norfolk, VA
Dodd, Jeanne D. ..... Midland, MI
Dodd, Jeff C. ..... Houston, TX
Dodd, Jerry L. ..... Grove City, OH
Dodd, Jill S. ..... San Francisco, CA
Dodd, John David, III ..... Dallas, TX
Dodd, John F. ..... Kansas City, MO
Dodd, John H. ..... San Francisco, CA
Dodd, Julia J. ..... Dallas, TX
Dodd, Karetha A. ..... Chicago, IL
Dodd, Kiann Caprice ..... Kansas City, KS
Dodd, L. Michael ..... Raleigh, NC

Dodd, Lawrence Roe ....Baton Rouge, LA
Dodd, Lesa M. ....Fresno, CA
Dodd, Lessack, Ranando & Dalton, L.L.C.
Cheshire, CT
Waterbury, CT
Dodd, Martin H. ....San Francisco, CA
Dodd, Martin H. ....New Haven, CT
Dodd, Maureen Moore ....Annapolis, MD
Baltimore, MD
Dodd & McClellan, P.C. ....Champaign, IL
Dodd, Michael Brady ....Pittsburgh, PA
Dodd, Michael C. ....Birmingham, AL
Dodd, Michael L. ....Syracuse, NY
Dodd, O. Kenneth, Jr. ....Beaumont, TX
Dodd, P. Douglas ....Syracuse, NY
Dodd, Peter J. ....Hornbrook, CA
Dodd, Philip K. ....Montpelier, VT
Dodd, Quin D. ....Washington, DC
Dodd, Richard A. ....Cameron, TX
Dodd, Richard B. ....Seattle, WA
Dodd, Richard S., II ....Washington, DC
Dodd, Robert H., Jr. ....Denver, CO
Dodd, Robert J., Jr. ....New Lexington, OH
Dodd, Robert W. ....Champaign, IL
Dodd, Robert W. ....Virden, IL
Dodd, Roger J. ....Valdosta, GA
Dodd, S. Douglas ....Tulsa, OK
Dodd, Shirley D. ....Chicago, IL
Dodd, Stephen H. ....Columbus, OH
Dodd, Stephen M. ....Norwell, MA
Dodd, Stephen M. ....Philadelphia, PA
Wayne, PA
Dodd, Susan Bowers ....Atlanta, GA
Dodd, Susan Young ....Wheeling, WV
Dodd, Thomas C. ....Harlan, KY
Dodd, Thomas J. ....San Antonio, TX
Dodd, Timothy H. ....Minneapolis, MN
Dodd, Timothy J. ....Boston, MA
Dodd, Timothy J. ....New York, NY
Dodd, Timothy R. ....Evansville, IN
Dodd, Travis L. ....San Diego, CA
Dodd, Travis M. ....Tulsa, OK
Dodd, Vickie R. ....Charleston, WV
Dodd, Victoria Jeannette ....Boston, MA
Dodd, William C. ....Morristown, NJ
Dodd, William F. ....Houma, LA
Dodd, William H. ....Honolulu, HI
Dodd, Wm. H. ....Carlisle, PA
Doddato, Frank A. ....Williston Park, NY
Dodderidge, Dana B. ....Manhattan, KS
Dodderidge, Nancy Meredith
New York, NY
Doddington, Donald G. ....Tampa, FL
Doddo, James E. ....Miami, FL
Dodd-o, James J. ....Bethlehem, PA
Harrisburg, PA
Doddo, Michael ....Fort Lauderdale, FL
Doddo, Michael, P.A. ....Fort Lauderdale, FL
Dodds, Amy Lauren
National Labor Relations Board, Office of the General Counsel, GV
Dodds, Bradford C. ....Columbus, GA
Dodds, Bruce W. ....Santa Barbara, CA
Dodds, Christina Carlson ....Austin, TX
Dodds, David A. ....Dallas, TX
Dodds, Deborah D. ....Pittsburgh, PA
Dodds, Debra A. ....Newport Beach, CA
Dodds, Donald J. ....Boston, MA
Dodds, Douglas D. ....Austin, TX
Dodds, F. Alison ....Chicago, IL
Dodds, Frederick J., III ....Wichita, KS
Dodds, Gary D. ....Detroit, MI
Dodds & Hennessy ....Charleston, SC
Mount Pleasant, SC
Dodds, James M. ....Nevada City, CA
Dodds, James R. ....Stockton, CA
Dodds, Jenelle Celine ....Boston, MA
Dodds, John A. ....Department of the Air Force, Office of the General Counsel, GV
Dodds, John C. ....Philadelphia, PA
Dodds, John H. ....Sacramento, CA
Dodds, John J. ....Seattle, WA
Dodds, John J., III ....Mount Pleasant, SC
Dodds, Katherine L. ....Houston, TX
Dodds, Kathleen A. ....Portland, OR
Dodds, Kenneth W.
Small Business Administration, Office of the General Counsel, GV
Dodds, Kidd, Ryan & Moore
Little Rock, AR
Dodds, Lawrence A., Jr. ....Charleston, SC
Mount Pleasant, SC
Dodds, Lawrence D. ....Philadelphia, PA
Dodds, Marcy L. ....Memphis, TN
Dodds, Mark Lee ....Las Vegas, NV
Dodds, Pamela B. ....Minneapolis, MN
Dodds, Paul G. ....Portland, OR
Dodds, R. Harcourt ....Elmsford, NY
New York, NY
Dodds, Ralph P. ....Troy, NY
Dodds, Robert F. ....Fairfax, VA
Dodds, Robert J., III ....Santa Fe, NM
Dodds, Robert J., Jr. ....Pittsburgh, PA
Dodds, Robert S. ....Mount Pleasant, SC
Dodds, Sarah C. ....New York, NY
Dodds, Tony C., Law Office of
Lakeland, FL
Dodds, William K. ....New York, NY
Dodds-Eastman, Leanne ....Phoenix, AZ
Eden Prairie, MN
Dodds-Marshall, Belinda Dawn
Mineola, NY
Doddy, Robert V. ....Los Angeles, CA
Dodek, Oscar I., Jr. ....Washington, DC
Dodek, Rosemary Chun ....Boston, MA
Dodelin & Kelly ....Columbus, GA
Dodelin, Richard F. ....Columbus, GA
Dodell, Herbert ....Los Angeles, CA
Dodell, Herbert, A Law Corporation
Los Angeles, CA
Dodell, Leib ....Simsbury, CT
Dodell, Nathan ....Rockville, MD
Dodell, Neal D. ....Alpharetta, GA
Dodell, Roslyn I. ....Atlanta, GA
Dodell, Sue Ellen ....New York, NY
Doden, Maci M. ....Fort Wayne, IN
Dodero, William B. ....San Francisco, CA
Dodes, Ivy B. ....New York, NY
Dodez, Richard D. ....Canton, OH
Dodge, Andrea Tyler ....Rome, NY
Dodge & Associate ....Knox, IN
Dodge, Austin P. ....Minden, NE
Dodge, Beverly K. ....Minneapolis, MN
Dodge, Carl F., Jr. ....Fallon, NV
Dodge, Chester J., Jr. ....Huntington, NY
Dodge, Christopher J. ....Madison, WI
Dodge, Conway, Jr. ....Boston, MA
Dodge, Courtney L. ....Charlotte, NC
Dodge, Cynthia E. ....Pulaski, VA
Dodge, Cynthia M. ....Kansas City, MO
Dodge, David A. ....Grand Rapids, MI
Dodge, David A., P.C. ....Grand Rapids, MI
Dodge, David D. ....Phoenix, AZ
Dodge, David Orin ....Atlanta, GA
Dodge, David Wilson ....Dallas, TX
Dodge, Deborah K. ....Springfield, MO
Dodge, Diana B. ....Duluth, MN
Dodge, Diane E. ....Evergreen, CO
Dodge, Don F. ....Scottsdale, AZ
Trenton, MI
Dodge, Don F., P.C. ....Scottsdale, AZ
Trenton, MI
Dodge, Don W. ....Cedar Rapids, IA
Dodge, Douglas C. ....Department of Justice, Office of Justice Programs, GV
Dodge, Douglas C. ....New York, NY
Dodge, Elizabeth L. ....Houston, TX
Dodge, Ethel L. Wiley ....Houston, TX
Dodge, Fazio, Anderson & Jones, P.C.
Dallas, TX
Dodge, Frank S. ....Colorado Springs, CO
Dodge, Franklin D. ....Phoenix, AZ
Dodge, Fred C. ....Lafayette, CA
Dodge, Frederick M., II ....Rome, NY
Dodge, Garen E. ....Washington, DC
Dodge, Gary A. ....Salt Lake City, UT
Dodge, Gary R. ....Dover, DE
Dodge, Gary R., P.A. ....Dover, DE
Dodge, George W. ....Arlington, VA
Dodge, Harold T., Jr. ....Tacoma, WA
Dodge, James ....Portland, OR
Dodge, James C. ....Sublette, KS
Dodge, James C. ....West Liberty, OH
Dodge, Jason M. ....Glastonbury, CT
Dodge, Jennifer Lynn ....Los Angeles, CA
Dodge, John ....Washington, DC
Dodge, John A. ....Federal Way, WA
Dodge, John C. ....Bentonville, AR
Dodge, John D. ....Washington, DC
Dodge, John F., Jr. ....Grosse Pointe Farms, MI
Dodge, Jonathan K. ....Cheshire, CT
Dodge, Joseph Francis ....Coopersville, MI
Dodge, Katharine S. ....Brattleboro, VT
Dodge, Kenneth W. ....West Palm Beach, FL
Dodge, Kenneth W. ....Minneapolis, MN
Dodge, Kirstin S. ....Bellevue, WA
Dodge, Linda I. ....Warrenton, VA
Dodge, Lisa B. ....St. Petersburg, FL
Dodge, Lynn ....Department of Justice, Environment and Natural Resources Division, GV
Dodge, Mark S. ....Irvine, CA
Dodge, Mary Elizabeth ....Edwardsburg, MI
Dodge, Michael C. ....Dallas, TX
Dodge, Michael E. ....Cassopolis, MI
Dodge, Michael John ....Southfield, MI
Dodge & Minikes ....New York, NY
Dodge, Patricia L. ....Pittsburgh, PA
Dodge, Peter J. ....Ann Arbor, MI
Dodge, Peter X. ....Mineola, NY
Dodge, R. Stanton ....Littleton, CO
Dodge, Ralph E. ....Syracuse, NY
Dodge, Raymond G., Jr. ....Spokane, WA
Dodge, Richard E. ....Walnut Creek, CA
Dodge, Richard J. ....St. Louis, MO
Dodge, Richard S. ....Dayton, OH
Dodge, Robert C. ....Beaufort, NC
Dodge, Robert G. ....Leavenworth, WA
Wenatchee, WA
Dodge, Robert I. ....Department of Justice, Environment and Natural Resources Division, GV
Dodge, Robert L., III ....Fredericksburg, VA
Dodge, Ryan E., Jr. ....Seattle, WA
Dodge, S. Regina ....New York, NY
Dodge, Scott H. ....La Jolla, CA
Dodge, Shari A. ....Caldwell, ID
Dodge, Shelley Phelps ....Denver, CO
Dodge, Stanford ....Moose Lake, MN
Dodge, Stephanie Lee ....Chicago, IL
Dodge, Steven A. ....Knox, IN
Dodge, Steven M. ....Brighton, MI
Dodge, Virginia N. H. ....Marblehead, MA
Dodge & Warp ....Moose Lake, MN
Dodge, Wesley Scott ....Omaha, NE
Dodge, William E. ....New York, NY
Dodge, William S. ....San Francisco, CA
Dodgen, Andrew C. ....Columbus, GA
Dodgen, Walter A. ....Huntsville, AL
Dodi, Kwesi Addo ....Austin, TX
Dodick, Dorothy M. ....Arvada, CO
Dodick, John O. ....Erie, PA
Dodier, Emilie ....Los Angeles, CA
Dodier, Grace M ....Chicago, IL
Dodig, Chris S. ....Adams, MA
Dodig, John M. ....Haddonfield, NJ
Dodig, Michael S. ....Kansas City, MO
Dodman, Donald P. ....Buffalo, NY
Dodorico, Paul A. ....Miller Place, NY
Dodrill, James G., II ....New York, NY
Dodrill, Louis A. ....Little Rock, AR
Dods, John C. ....Kansas City, MO
Dods, Sandra J. ....Edwardsville, IL
Dods, Sarah C. ....Seattle, WA
Dods, Walter K., Law Offices of
San Rafael, CA
Dodson, Alison T. ....Denver, CO
Dodson, Ann S. ....Norfolk, VA
Dodson, Anthony J. ....Houston, TX
Dodson and Associates, P.C. ....Denver, CO
Dodson Breeze Kister & Roberts
Festus, MO
Hillsboro, MO
Dodson, C. Richard ....Long Beach, CA
Dodson, Carlton B. ....Amarillo, TX
Dodson, Carr G. ....Macon, GA
Dodson, Catherine S., (Mrs.)
Oklahoma City, OK
Dodson, Charles F. ....East Falmouth, MA
Dodson, Charles H., Jr. ....Mobile, AL
Dodson, Charles M. ....Coeur d'Alene, ID
Dodson, Charles W. ....Tallahassee, FL
Dodson, Charles W., P.A. ....Tallahassee, FL
Dodson, Christophe Thomas ....Bismarck, ND
Dodson, Christopher William ....Rockford, IL
Dodson, Claiborne B. ....Amarillo, TX
Dodson, Daniel J. ....Columbia, MO
Jefferson City, MO
Dodson, David W. ....Fort Lauderdale, FL
Dodson, Davida J. ....Ravenna, OH
Dodson, Denise Avery ....Birmingham, AL
Dodson, Don B. ....El Dorado, AR
Dodson, Doreen D. ....St. Louis, MO
Dodson, Edwin ....Phoenix, AZ
Dodson, Ella W. ....New York, NY
Dodson, Erik H. ....Akron, OH
Dodson, F. Brian ....Pittsburgh, PA
Dodson & Feldman, L.L.P. ....Atlanta, GA
Dodson, Frank B. ....Kingsport, TN
Dodson, Frank M. ....Shreveport, LA
Dodson, G. Diane ....Washington, DC
Dodson, Gary W. ....Sparta, TN
Dodson, Geoffrey C. ....Falls Church, VA
Dodson, Gerald P. ....Palo Alto, CA
Dodson, Hannah Metcalf ....Columbia, SC
Dodson, Harlan, III ....Nashville, TN
Dodson, J. Daryl
Charlotte Amalie, St. Thomas, VI
Dodson, J. Lucian, III ....Walnut Creek, CA
Dodson, Jack R., III ....Jackson, MS
Dodson, Jack R., Jr. ....Clarksdale, MS
Dodson, James H. ....Beaver City, NE
Dodson, James O. ....Fort Worth, TX
Dodson, James R. ....San Diego, CA
Dodson, James W. ....Clearwater, FL
Dodson, Jason D. ....St. Louis, MO
Dodson, Jeffrey C. ....New York, NY
Dodson, Joe Michael ....Beaumont, TX
Dodson, Joel E. ....Douglasville, GA
Dodson, John C. ....Louisville, KY
Dodson, John C. ....Nashville, TN
Dodson, John D. ....Champaign, IL
Dodson, John E. ....Chesterfield, VA
Dodson, John W. ....Birmingham, AL
Dodson, Karen C. ....New York, NY
Dodson Law Office, The ....Beaver City, NE
Dodson, Lisa P. ....Gulfport, MS
Dodson & Lowe ....Uvalde, TX
Dodson, Mark S. ....Portland, OR
Dodson, Mary Jane ....Washington, DC
Dodson, Maxwell G. ....New Orleans, LA
Dodson, Melene Rowe ....Corpus Christi, TX
Dodson, Michael J. ....San Jose, CA
Dodson, Michael Pearce ....Tallahassee, FL
Dodson, Michael R. ....Delta, CO
Dodson, Parker, Dinkins & Behm, P.C.
Nashville, TN
Dodson, Patricia M. ....Jacksonville, FL
Dodson, Patricia McGee ....Birmingham, AL
Dodson, Patrick Doyle ....Chattanooga, TN
Dodson, Paul ....Corpus Christi, TX
Dodson, Paulette Rennalls ....Chicago, IL
Dodson, Pence & Viar ....Roanoke, VA
Dodson, Peter H. ....Boston, MA
Dodson, Peter M. ....Washington, DC
Dodson Piraino & Associates
Champaign, IL
Dodson, Preston L. ....Tomball, TX
Dodson, Raymond G. ....Charleston, WV
Dodson, Richard J. ....Baton Rouge, LA
Dodson, Richard N. ....Texarkana, TX
Dodson, Richard S., Jr. ....Canton, OH
Dodson, Robert C. ....Festus, MO
Dodson, Robert D. ....Columbia, SC
Dodson, Robert E. ....Texarkana, TX
Dodson, Robert M. ....San Diego, CA
Dodson, Rocco A. ....Denver, CO
Dodson, Roland W. ....Portsmouth, VA
Dodson, Roland W., Ltd. ....Portsmouth, VA
Dodson, Ronald C. ....Columbia, SC
Dodson, S. Catherine ....Norfolk, VA
Dodson, Stanley K. ....Pittsburg, CA
Dodson, Sue ....San Antonio, TX
Dodson, T. Ryland ....Danville, VA
Dodson, Tammy R. ....Kansas City, MO
Dodson, Timothy R. ....Atlanta, GA
Dodson & Vidrine, A Professional Law Corporation ....Baton Rouge, LA
Dodson, W. Patrick ....Uvalde, TX
Dodson, Walter S., Jr. ....Paterson, NJ
Dodson, William C. ....St. Louis, MO
Dodson, William D. ....Pasadena, CA
Dodson, William H., II ....Atlanta, GA
Dodson, William H., Sr. ....Sallisaw, OK
Dodson, William L., Jr. ....Greenville, SC
Dodson, William P. ....Oxford, MS
Dodson, William S., Jr. ....Birmingham, AL
Dodson, Wilson B., III ....Norfolk, VA
Dodson, Wm. W., Jr. ....Harrisburg, PA
Dodulik, Louis ....Elm Grove, WI
Dody, Barbara Wade ....Austin, TX
Dodyk, Paul M. ....New York, NY
Dodys, Nick A. ....Atlanta, GA
Doe, Doreen Ellen Chiodo
St. Petersburg, FL
Doe, Robert B. ....Golden Valley, MN
Doebbert, Belvin L. ....Glenwood, MN
Doebele, Daniel J. ....New York, NY
Doeg, Bruce C. ....Knoxville, TN
Doeg, Donald W. ....Hartford, CT
Doehl, Robert A. K. ....Department of Justice, Civil Division, GV
Doehle, Christine A. ....Crescent City, CA
Doehling & Associates, P.C.
Grand Junction, CO
Doehling, Gary L. ....Grand Junction, CO
Doehrel, Andrew E. ....Columbus, OH
Doehring & Doehring ....Houston, TX
Doehring, Richard L. ....Houston, TX
Doehring, Sweeney J., Jr. ....Houston, TX
Doehrman, John W. ....Jeffersonville, IN
Doehrman, Thomas C. ....Indianapolis, IN
Doele, Joseph H. ....Grand Rapids, MI
Doell, Thomas J. ....Chicago, IL
Doelling, Robert E., Jr. ....Fort Wayne, IN
Doellman, Norbert M., Jr. ....Hamilton, OH
Doelze, Kurt J. ....Wilmington, DE
Doelze, Kurt J., P.A. ....Wilmington, DE
D'Oench, Russell G., III ....New York, NY
Doenges, William S. ....Tulsa, OK
Doepfner, Phillip R. ....Dallas, TX
Doepke, Ervin L. ....Beaver Dam, WI
Doepke & Hannan, Chartered
Beaver Dam, WI
Doepke, Hannan, Elbert & Pfitzinger, Chartered
Juneau, WI
Doepke, Nancy Louise ....Rockford, IL
Doepken Keevican & Weiss, Professional Corporation ....Washington, DC
Bloomfield Hills, MI
Cleveland, OH
Harrisburg, PA
Pittsburgh, PA
Doepken, William L. ....Washington, DC
Bloomfield Hills, MI
Harrisburg, PA
Pittsburgh, PA
Doepker, James A. ....Fort Thomas, KY
Doerfel, Ken Sue ....Lawton, OK
Doerfer, Gordon L. ....Needham, MA
Doerfler, Christopher A. ....Phoenix, AZ
Doerfler, James M. ....Pittsburgh, PA
Doerfler, Karyn L. ....Chicago, IL
Doerflinger, W. Charles ....Lawrenceburg, TN
Doerge, Michal ....Harrisburg, IL
Doerhoff, Dale C. ....Jefferson City, MO
Doering, Albert L., III ....Philadelphia, PA
Doering & Associates, P.C.
Kansas City, MO
Doering, Christopher A.
Greenwood Village, CO
Doering, David M. ....Denver, CO
Doering, David W. ....Alpharetta, GA
Doering Diversified, Ltd. ....Escondido, CA
Doering, Donald K. ....Torrance, CA
Doering, Edw. A. ....Cincinnati, OH
Doering, Grisell & McFarland, P.A.
Garden City, KS
Doering, Henry H., III ....San Francisco, CA
Doering, John P., III ....Modesto, CA
Doering, Karen M. ....Tampa, FL
Doering, Kevin P. ....Augusta, ME
Doering, Lee E. ....Marshall, MN
Doering, Michael C. ....Garden City, KS
Doering, Michael D. ....Kansas City, MO
Doering, R. Earl ....Dassel, MN
Doering, Steven B. ....Garnett, KS
Doering, Vivian Velichkoff ....Escondido, CA
Doeringer, Jeffrey W. ....Costa Mesa, CA
Doeringer, John H. ....Matteson, IL
Doerksen, Charles L. ....Fresno, CA
Doermer, Richard D. ....Chicago, IL
Doernberg, Alan M. ....Pittsburgh, PA
Doernberg, Donald L. ....White Plains, NY
Doernberg, Richard L. ....Atlanta, GA
Doernberger, Edwin L. ....New Haven, CT
Doernberger, Edwin L., P.C.
New Haven, CT
Doerner, Brian D. ....Philadelphia, PA
Doerner, David W. ....Toledo, OH
Doerner, Maureen A. ....Cleveland, OH
Doerner, Sally R. ....Miami, FL
Doerner, Saunders, Daniel & Anderson, L.L.P. ....Oklahoma City, OK
Tulsa, OK
Doerpinghaus, Charles J., Jr. ....Benton, AR
Doerr, Brian D. ....Kansas City, MO
Doerr, Donald C. ....Syracuse, NY
Doerr, Donald D., Jr. ....Bay Minette, AL
Doerr, Jean ....Buffalo, NY
Doerr, Jeffrey M. ....Neligh, NE
Doerr, Jeffrey S. ....Clifton Park, NY
Doerr, John A. ....Twin Falls, ID
Doerr, John H. ....Buffalo, NY
Doerr, John M. ....Malvern, PA
Doerr, Judith ....Tacoma, WA
Doerr, Kenneth D. ....Sarasota, FL
Doerr & Knudson, P.A. ....Clovis, NM
Portales, NM
Doerr Law Firm ....Bay Minette, AL
Doerr, Peter M. ....Mount Morris, MI
Doerr, Peter M., P.C. ....Mount Morris, MI

Doerr, Richard F. .... St. Charles, IL
Doerr, Stephen .... Clovis, NM
Portales, NM
Doerr, Thomas M. .... Rosemont, IL
Doerr, Thomas S. .... Westfield, NJ
Doerr, William R. .... Eagle River, WI
Doerr, William R .... St. Germain, WI
Doerre, Laura W. .... Houston, TX
Doerrer, Amanda F. .... San Diego, CA
Doerrer, John A., II .... Chicago, IL
Doerries, Eric W. .... Houston, TX
Doerries, Michael F. .... Chicago, IL
Doerring, Erik P. .... Columbia, SC
Doerring, Lora Lee Flowers
San Francisco, CA
Doersch, Patricia H.
Department of Transportation, Federal Highway Administration, GV
Doersch, Richard C. .... Cleveland, WI
Doerstling, Karl W. .... Santa Monica, CA
Doerty, James A. .... Saipan, TT
Doery, Richard .... Treasury Department, Office of the Inspector General, GV
Doescher, Louis R. .... Carson City, NV
Doesken, Don .... Topeka, KS
Doesschate, Judy L. .... Albany, NY
Doetsch, Douglas A. .... Chicago, IL
Doetsch, Frederick R., Jr. .... Detroit, MI
Doetzel, Daniel J. .... St. Louis, MO
Doetzer, Amie M. .... San Francisco, CA
Doezema, James B. .... Grand Rapids, MI
Doezie, Janice J. .... Orange, CA
Doezie, Michael .... Bellevue, WA
Doffermyre, Everette L. .... Atlanta, GA
Doffermyre, L. Randolph, III .... Dunn, NC
Doffermyre, Shields, Canfield, Knowles & Devine .... Atlanta, GA
Doffing, Michelle R. .... Minneapolis, MN
Doffing, Sylvester F. .... St. Paul, MN
Dofflemyre, Michael L. .... San Diego, CA
Doft, Alan .... New York, NY
Doft, Jonathan .... New York, NY
Doft, Peter S. .... San Diego, CA
Doft, Peter S., A PC .... San Diego, CA
Doga, Burleigh G. .... Crowley, LA
Dogali, Anthony Anderson Benton
St. Petersburg, FL
Tampa, FL
Dogan & Associates .... New York, NY
Dogan, David W., III .... Jackson, MS
Dogan, Kevin W. .... Indianapolis, IN
Indianapolis, IN
Dogan, Mel .... New York, NY
Dogan, Stacey L. .... Washington, DC
Dogan, Thomas M. .... Merrillville, IN
Dogan, Vivian B. .... Providence, RI
Dogan & Wilkinson, PLLC .... Jackson, MS
Pascagoula, MS
Austin, TX
Doganiero, Antonio F. .... Berlin, NJ
Doganiero, John A., III .... Willoughby, OH
Doganiero, Lori A. .... Tampa, FL
Doganiero, Mara Grame .... Cleveland, OH
Dogger, David G. .... Saginaw, MI
Doggett, Andrew T. .... Boston, MA
Doggett, David L. .... San Antonio, TX
Doggett, Dianne Elizabeth .... Austin, TX
Doggett, Donald Lee .... St. Louis, MO
Doggett, Edward W. .... Florence, AL
Doggett, Edward W., P.C. .... Florence, AL
Doggett, Janice Frankino .... Helena, MT
Doggett, Jeffery L. .... Houston, TX
Doggett, Jeffrey S. .... San Diego, CA
Doggett, John J., III .... Glynco, GA
Doggett, John P. .... Alexandria, LA
Doggett, Kenneth A. .... Alexandria, LA
Doggett, Knight E. .... Alexandria, LA
Doggett, Mary Belan .... San Antonio, TX
Doggett & McEvilley .... Cincinnati, OH
Doggett, Monty L. .... Natchitoches, LA
Doggett, Pamela .... Lexington, KY
Doggett, Robert I. .... Cincinnati, OH
Doggett, Robert W. .... Dallas, TX
Doggett, Scott T. .... Dallas, TX
Doggett, Stephen A. .... Richmond, TX
Doggett, Suzanne W. .... McLean, VA
Doggette, Billy C. .... Laurel, MS
Doggrell, Henry P. .... Memphis, TN
Dogmetchi, Laya .... Irvine, CA
Dognazzi, Heather A. .... Newnan, GA
Dogostino, Leanne A. .... Haddon Heights, NJ
Dogum, John P. .... Philadelphia, PA
Dogwill, Nicole P. .... Detroit, MI
Dohan, Andrew H. .... Kennett Square, PA
Malvern, PA
Dohan, John W.
Grosse Pointe Woods, MI
Dohan, John W., P.C. .... Detroit, MI
Grosse Pointe Woods, MI
Dohan, Marc .... Boston, MA
Dohanich, John P. .... Ambridge, PA
Dohanick, Rhonda K. .... Marlton, NJ
Dohar, Julie A. .... Austintown, OH
Doheney, Clyde T. .... Agoura Hills, CA
Doheney, William C. .... San Pedro, CA
Doheny, Edward L. .... Los Angeles, CA
Doheny, Frank P., Jr. .... Louisville, KY
Doheny, James J., Jr. .... Chicago, IL
Doheny, John T. .... Cleveland, OH
Doheny, John V. .... St. Louis, MO
Doheny, Matthew A. .... New York, NY
Doheny, Michael W.
Federal Labor Relations Authority, Washington Regional Office, GV
Doheny, Peggy Ann .... Oak Park, IL
Doheny, William H., Jr. .... Los Angeles, CA
Doherty, Aileen M. .... New York, NY
Doherty, Alex & Tadano .... Phoenix, AZ

Doherty, Amy Lynn .... Newport Beach, CA
Doherty, Amy R. .... Boston, MA
Doherty, Ashley
Federal Deposit Insurance Corporation, Professional Liability Section, GV
Doherty, Barbara Vogler .... Murphysboro, IL
Doherty, Brendan P. .... Boston, MA
Doherty, Brian .... Boston, MA
Doherty, Brian B., P.C. .... Portland, OR
Doherty, Brian C. .... Jersey City, NJ
Doherty, Brian J. .... Overland Park, KS
Kansas City, MO
Doherty, Brian M. .... Anchorage, AK
Doherty, Casey W. .... Houston, TX
Doherty, Catherine M. .... Brockton, MA
Doherty & Catlow, A Law Corporation
Los Angeles, CA
Doherty, Charles J. .... Newton, MA
Doherty, Charlotte L. .... Darlington, WI
Doherty, Christopher J. .... Glenview, IL
Doherty, Christopher J. .... Bethesda, MD
Doherty, Colleen .... San Francisco, CA
Doherty, Colleen M. .... Orange, CA
Doherty, Cornelius H., Jr.
Washington, DC
Vero Beach, FL
Fairfax, VA
Doherty, Daniel B. .... Houston, TX
Doherty, Daniel C. .... Boulder, CO
Doherty, Daniel E. .... Westwood, KS
Doherty, Daniel E. .... Braintree, MA
Doherty, Daniel J., III .... Crofton, MD
Doherty, Daniel L. .... Albany, NY
Doherty, Daniel T., Jr. .... Frederick, MD
Doherty, Daniel W. .... Danvers, MA
Doherty, David P. .... New York, NY
Doherty, David P. .... Syracuse, NY
Doherty, David Scott .... Thomasville, NC
Doherty, Dawn Kahle .... Dallas, TX
Doherty, Deidre A. .... Boston, MA
Doherty, Dennis D. .... Hermiston, OR
Doherty, Dennis M. .... Chicago, IL
Doherty, Dennis M. .... Detroit, MI
Doherty, Dennis O. .... Atlanta, GA
Doherty, Diane .... San Diego, CA
Philadelphia, PA
Doherty & Doherty .... Cohoes, NY
Doherty, Doherty & Adams, L.L.P.
Houston, TX
Doherty, Donald P. .... St. Louis, MO
Doherty, Edward L. .... New York, NY
Doherty, Eileen P. .... Garden City, NY
Doherty, Eric P. .... Lakeview, NY
Doherty, Eugene G. .... Rockford, IL
Doherty, Francis J. .... Hamden, CT
Doherty, Francis X., (P.C.)
San Francisco, CA
Doherty, George M. .... Chatham, NJ
Doherty, Gerald F. .... Mount Clemens, MI
Doherty, Gerald T. .... Boston, MA
Doherty, Gerard F. .... Boston, MA
Doherty, Glen P. .... Albany, NY
Doherty, Hamilton, Jr. .... Springfield, MA
Doherty, Heather Ann .... Baltimore, MD
Doherty, H. V. .... Port Angeles, WA
Doherty, J. Mark .... Rockford, IL
Doherty, J. Michael .... Pittsburgh, PA
Doherty, J. Patrick .... Chicago, IL
Doherty, J. Patrick .... Houston, TX
Doherty, J. Peter .... Sharon Springs, NY
Doherty, James A. .... Bellingham, WA
Doherty, James A., Jr. .... Scranton, PA
Doherty, James D. .... Boston, MA
Doherty, James E. .... New York, NY
Doherty, James F., Jr. .... Severna Park, MD
Doherty, James J. .... Camarillo, CA
Doherty, James J. .... Denver, CO
Doherty, James J. .... Chicago, IL
Doherty, James M. .... Austin, TX
Doherty, James N. .... Cambridge, MA
Doherty, James P., III .... Lafayette, LA
Doherty, James P., Jr. .... Opelousas, LA
Doherty, James T. .... Hamden, CT
Doherty, Jane M. .... Wellesley, MA
Doherty, Jeffrey C. .... Boston, MA
Doherty, Jennifer K. .... Stockton, CA
Doherty, Joanne J. .... Houston, TX
Doherty, John C. .... Andover, MA
Doherty, John C. .... Boston, MA
Doherty, John C. .... New York, NY
Doherty, John E. .... Tracy, CA
Doherty, John F. .... Newark, NJ
Doherty, John F. .... Philadelphia, PA
Doherty, John F. .... Pittsburgh, PA
Doherty, John H. .... Port Angeles, WA
Doherty, John J. .... Phoenix, AZ
Doherty, John J. .... Los Angeles, CA
Doherty, John J. .... San Francisco, CA
Doherty, John J. .... Minneapolis, MN
Doherty, John J., Jr. .... Cohoes, NY
Doherty, John L. .... Pittsburgh, PA
Doherty, John M. .... Carpentersville, IL
Doherty, John Patrick .... New York, NY
Doherty, John R. .... Bridgeport, CT
New Haven, CT
Doherty, John R. .... Rutland, VT
Doherty, Joseph G. .... West Bend, WI
Doherty, Joseph J. .... Knoxville, TN
Morristown, TN
Doherty, Joseph L., Jr. .... Boston, MA
Doherty, Judith E. .... Wynnewood, PA
Doherty, Julie A. .... Phoenix, AZ
Doherty, Julie A. .... Minneapolis, MN
Doherty, Karen M. .... Washington, DC
Doherty, Kelly L. .... Simsbury, CT
Doherty, Kerry A. .... Boston, MA
Doherty, Kevin M. .... Atlanta, GA
Doherty, Kevin M. .... New City, NY

Doherty, Larry J. .... Houston, TX
Doherty, Laurie A.
Securities and Exchange Commission, Division of Enforcement, GV
Doherty, Lawrence .... Philadelphia, PA
Doherty, Lewis S., III .... Baton Rouge, LA
Doherty, Louis W. .... Winston-Salem, NC
Doherty, Mark J. .... New Orleans, LA
Doherty, Martin J. .... Mission Viejo, CA
Doherty, Mary C. .... Woburn, MA
Doherty, Mary Catherine .... Santa Rosa, CA
Doherty, Mary Cushing .... Norristown, PA
Doherty, Mary E. .... Chicago, IL
Doherty, Mary Katherine .... Seattle, WA
Doherty, Mary T. .... Indianapolis, IN
Doherty, Maura C. .... Boston, MA
Doherty, Maureen L. .... Milton, MA
Doherty, Michael A. .... New York, NY
Doherty, Michael G. .... Boston, MA
Doherty, Michael H. .... Arlington, VA
Doherty, Michael J. .... Westfield, NJ
Doherty, Michael James .... Alexandria, VA
Doherty, Michael P. .... Franklin, MA
Doherty, Michelle A. .... Tampa, FL
Doherty, Michelle J. .... Waterford, MI
Doherty, Mimi E. .... Prairie Village, KS
Kansas City, MO
Doherty, Moira .... Los Angeles, CA
Doherty, Moira A. .... New York, NY
Doherty, Neil F. .... Jamaica, NY
Doherty, Nicklas & Prete, P.A.
Annapolis, MD
Frederick, MD
Doherty, Oonagh C. .... Holyoke, MA
Doherty, Patk. H. .... Mendota Heights, MN
Doherty, Patricia A. .... Orlando, FL
Doherty, Patricia Brody .... Boston, MA
Doherty, Patrick D. .... Sylva, NC
Doherty, Patrick D., P.A. .... Sylva, NC
Doherty, Paul E. .... New York, NY
Doherty, Paul F. .... Birmingham, MI
Doherty, Paul S. .... Springfield, MA
Doherty, Pearl B. .... Raleigh, NC
Doherty, Penelope D. .... Los Angeles, CA
Doherty, Penelope D. .... Los Angeles, CA
Doherty, Peter H. .... Denver, CO
Doherty, Philip M. .... Boston, MA
Doherty, Rebecca F. .... Lafayette, LA
Doherty, Richard C. .... Youngstown, NY
Doherty, Richard E. .... Miami, FL
Doherty, Richard J. .... Chicago, IL
Doherty, Risa C. .... Roslyn Heights, NY
Doherty, Robert J. .... Barrington, RI
Doherty, Robert J., Jr. .... Chicago, IL
Doherty, Robert Leo .... Tallahassee, FL
Doherty, Robert P. .... Medford, MA
Doherty, Robert P., Jr. .... Salem, VA
Doherty, Ronan P. .... Washington, DC
Doherty, Rumble & Butler, A Professional Corporation .... Denver, CO
Doherty, Ryan P. .... Edison, NJ
Doherty, Sean .... Department of Agriculture, Board of Contract Appeals, GV
Doherty, Sean .... Boston, MA
Doherty, Sean M. .... Coral Springs, FL
Doherty, Sharon A. .... Chicago, IL
Doherty, Sharon T. .... Chicago, IL
Doherty, Sheridan & Grimaldi, L.L.P.
Bethesda, MD
Doherty & Sheridan, L.L.P.
Washington, DC
Vero Beach, FL
Fairfax, VA
Doherty, Stephen A. .... Great Falls, MT
Doherty, Stephen G. .... Livingston, NJ
Doylestown, PA
Doherty, Stephen P. .... Kansas City, KS
Doherty, Susan M. .... Bronx, NY
Doherty, Suzanne E. .... Kansas City, MO
Doherty, Therese M. .... New York, NY
Doherty, Thomas F. .... Newark, NJ
Doherty, Thomas G. .... Chicago, IL
Doherty, Thomas J. .... Washington, DC
Doherty, Thomas J.
Environmental Protection Agency, Office of the General Counsel, GV
Doherty, Thomas L. .... De Kalb, IL
Doherty, Thomas P. .... Milwaukee, WI
Doherty & Venezia, A Professional Corporation .... Phoenix, AZ
Doherty & Wagner .... Houston, TX
Doherty, Wallace, Pillsbury and Murphy, P.C. .... Northampton, MA
Springfield, MA
Doherty, William A., Jr.
South Harwich, MA
Doherty, William P., Jr. .... Bridgeton, NJ
Doherty-Minicozzi, Colleen
Washington, DC
Dohi, Gregory A. .... Los Angeles, CA
Dohl, Bert R. .... Salamanca, NY
Dohlman, Marlin .... Washington, DC
Dohm, Dennis M. .... Markham, IL
Dohm, Dolores H. .... Chicago, IL
Dohm, Jerome E. .... Rockford, IL
Dohm, Kelly C. .... Waconia, MN
Dohm, Mark D. .... Palos Park, IL
Dohmann, George R. .... Summit, NJ
Dohmen, Luke R. .... Maple Grove, MN
Dohms, David B. .... Honolulu, HI
Dohn, John C., II .... Troy, MI
Dohn, Robert P. .... Scarsdale, NY
Dohnal, David E. .... Akron, OH
Dohnal, Dennis W. .... Richmond, VA
Dohnalek, Charles W. .... Tulsa, OK
Dohnalek, Marilyn Ann .... Tulsa, OK
Dohner, John M. .... Akron, OH
Dohoney, Betty R. .... Hillsboro, TX

Dohoney, James P. .... Pittsfield, MA
Dohoney, Patrick S. .... Fort Worth, TX
Dohoney, Tanya S. .... Fort Worth, TX
Dohr, Heidi L. .... Los Angeles, CA
Dohr, Michael J. .... Aurora, CO
Dohr, Peter R. .... Madison, WI
Dohra, Michelle V. .... Chicago, IL
Dohrer, Suzanne M. .... Phoenix, AZ
Dohrer, Thomas A. .... Chicago, IL
Dohrer & Watts, P.L.C. .... Phoenix, AZ
Dohring, Paul J. .... Stockton, CA
Dohrman, Greg H. .... Williamsburg, VA
Dohrman, Malvin D. .... Kilauea, HI
Dohrmann, Dawn M. .... Falls Church, VA
Dohrmann, Henry C. .... Lititz, PA
Dohrmann, Jeffrey C. .... Williamsport, PA
Dohrmann, Rebekah Ann Solberg
Bismarck, ND
Dohrmann, Robert M. .... Los Angeles, CA
Dohse, Roberta S. .... Corpus Christi, TX
Doi, Gavin Kazuo .... Honolulu, HI
Doi, Kathryn .... San Francisco, CA
Doi, Keith C. .... South Bend, IN
Doi, Mary M. .... Bryn Mawr, PA
Doi, Masato .... Honolulu, HI
Doi, Philip M. .... Honolulu, HI
Doi, Steven J. .... San Francisco, CA
Doidge, J. Richard .... Department of Justice, Antitrust Division, GV
Doig, Cornell & Mandel .... Goshen, NY
New City, NY
Doig, Douglas N. .... Englewood, CO
Doig, Gordon A. .... Austin, TX
Doig, Jacqueline .... Midland, MI
Doig, Jo .... Lawrenceville, NJ
Doig, John C. .... Alma, MI
Doig, Julia K. .... Department of Justice, Immigration and Naturalization Service, GV
Doig, Marilyn Brock
Colorado Springs, CO
Doig, Robert J. .... Colorado Springs, CO
Doigan, Lloyd .... Dearborn, MI
Doino, William D. .... New York, NY
Doiron, David J. .... Baton Rouge, LA
Doiron, James V. .... Rancho Cucamonga, CA
Doischen, William .... Jericho, NY
Doise, Dennis L. .... Lafayette, LA
Dojlidko, Michael .... New York, NY
Dok, Douglas J., Jr. .... Grand Rapids, MI
Dok, Levy & Perrin .... San Jose, CA
Dok, William L., (Inc.) .... San Jose, CA
Doke, Marshall J., Jr. .... Dallas, TX
Doke, Susan A. .... Oklahoma City, OK
Do-Khanh, Daniel D. .... Garden Grove, CA
Dokken, Craig T. .... Minneapolis, MN
Dokken, David E. .... Lewiston, ID
Dokken, Sheila K. .... Minneapolis, MN
Dokla, Luke T. .... Hopewell Junction, NY
Dokos, Daniel S. .... New York, NY
Dokovna, Aran H. .... Santa Monica, CA
Dokson, Robert N. .... Atlanta, GA
Doktor, Joseph R. .... Randolph, MA
Doktor, Joseph R., P.C. .... Randolph, MA
Dokurno, Anthony D. .... Alexandria, VA
Dola, Mark S. .... Washington, DC
Dolack, Hansler, Loran, Rowan & Ritchie, P.S.
Tacoma, WA
Dolack, Jennifer A. .... Indianapolis, IN
Dolack, Richard J. .... Tacoma, WA
Dolack, Robert F. .... Indianapolis, IN
Dolak, Andrew .... Newport Beach, CA
Dolak, Yolanda T. .... Beverly Hills, CA
Dolan, Alice E. .... Chicago, IL
Dolan, Amy M. .... Pittsburgh, PA
Dolan, Andrew K. .... Seattle, WA
Dolan & Associates .... Brighton, CO
Dolan, Bernadette .... Garden City, NY
Dolan, Brendan G. .... San Francisco, CA
Dolan, Brian F. .... Georgetown, DE
Dolan, Brian M. .... Monmouth Junction, NJ
Dolan, Brian O. .... Norfolk, VA
Dolan, Brian T. .... Denver, CO
Dolan, Caroline McS. .... New Orleans, LA
Dolan, Carrie A. .... Chicago, IL
Dolan, Charles E. .... Springfield, MA
Dolan, Christine .... Mineola, NY
Dolan, Christopher B. .... San Francisco, CA
Dolan, Christopher J. .... Minneapolis, MN
Dolan, Christopher Kent .... Cedar Rapids, IA
Dolan, Christopher M. .... San Francisco, CA
Dolan, Colleen .... St. Louis, MO
Dolan, Colleen A. .... Reno, NV
Dolan, Cynthia .... White Plains, NY
Dolan, D. Kevin .... Washington, DC
Dolan, Daniel A. .... New York, NY
Dolan, Daniel A., (P.A.) .... Las Cruces, NM
Dolan, Daniel D., II .... Miami, FL
Dolan, Daniel G. .... Chicago, IL
Dolan, Daniel G. .... Omaha, NE
Dolan, Daniel G., P.C. .... Omaha, NE
Dolan, Daniel M. .... Ketchum, ID
Dolan, Daniel R., II .... Albuquerque, NM
Dolan, David A. .... Sikeston, MO
Dolan, David M. .... St. Louis, MO
Dolan, David M. .... Dallas, TX
Dolan, David T. .... St. Louis, MO
Dolan & Dolan .... Turners Falls, MA
Dolan and Dolan, P.A. A Professional Corporation .... Blairstown, NJ
Newton, NJ
Dolan and Domenici, P.C.
Albuquerque, NM
Dolan, Donald P., II .... Scranton, PA
Dolan, Edward C. .... Washington, DC
Dolan, Edward J. .... New Haven, CT
Dolan, Erin A. .... Skillman, NJ
Dolan & Escalona, P.A. .... Miami, FL
Dolan, Eugene P. .... Denville, NJ

Dolan, Eva Haas ....Chagrin Falls, OH
Dolan, Francis E., Jr. ....Turners Falls, MA
Dolan, Frank A. ....Newton, NJ
Dolan, Frank J. ....Chicago, IL
Dolan, Frederick M., Jr.
Federal Maritime Commission,
Office of Administrative Law Judges, GV
Dolan, Glenn P. ....New York, NY
Dolan, Harry A. ....Houston, TX
Dolan, Hugh J. ....
Department of Commerce, GV
Dolan, J. Benjamin ....Detroit, MI
Dolan, J. Lawrence ....Albany, NY
Dolan, James ....Garden City, NY
Dolan, James B. ....New York, NY
Dolan, James B., Jr. ....Boston, MA
Dolan, James C. ....New York, NY
Dolan, James F. ....New York, NY
Dolan, James Michael ....Media, PA
Dolan, James Reilly
Federal Trade Commission,
Bureau of Consumer Protection, GV
Dolan, James V. ....Fort Lauderdale, FL
Dolan, James V. ....Omaha, NE
Dolan, James V., Chartered Law Offices of,
Chartered Law Offices of
Fort Lauderdale, FL
Dolan, Janice Forrester ....Gladstone, NJ
Dolan, Joan G. ....Boston, MA
Dolan, JoAnn ....Department of State,
Office of the Legal Adviser, GV
Dolan, John A. ....Clinton, MI
Dolan, John Barr ....Boston, MA
Dolan, John F. ....Detroit, MI
Dolan, John F. ....Lyndhurst, OH
Dolan, John F. ....Providence, RI
Dolan, John F., Jr. ....Barrington, NH
Dolan, John Fitzgerald
Department of Commerce,
Patent and Trademark Office, GV
Dolan, John J. ....New Orleans, LA
Dolan, John J. ....Attleboro, MA
Dolan, John L., Jr. ....Memphis, TN
Dolan, John Patrick ....Brea, CA
Dolan, John R. ....Turners Falls, MA
Dolan, John T. ....Newark, NJ
Dolan, Joseph A. ....Pomona, CA
Dolan, Joseph C. ....Phoenix, AZ
Dolan, Joseph F. ....Englewood, CO
Dolan, Joseph G. ....Florham Park, NJ
Dolan, Judith A. ....Hollywood, FL
Dolan, Judith E. ....Birmingham, AL
Dolan, Julie C. ....Sikeston, MO
Dolan, Kate ....Houston, TX
Dolan, Kathleen S. ....Washington, DC
Dolan, Kent Bradley ....New York, NY
Dolan, Kerry A. ....Pasadena, CA
Dolan, Kevin D. .... Elizabethtown, PA
Lancaster, PA
Dolan, Kevin M. ....Boston, MA
Norwood, MA
Westborough, MA
Wilmington, MA
Woburn, MA
Dolan, Kimberly M. ....Philadelphia, PA
Dolan Law Firm, The ....Los Angeles, CA
Dolan Law Firm, The ....San Francisco, CA
Dolan Law Offices, The ....Brea, CA
Dolan, Lawrence ....Chicago, IL
Dolan, Lawrence E., (P.A.) ....Orlando, FL
Dolan, Lawrence J. ....Chardon, OH
Dolan, Lawrence P. ....Lynnwood, WA
Dolan, Leigh Ann ....Atlanta, GA
Dolan, Leslie C. ....Denver, CO
Dolan, Lisa R. ....Philadelphia, PA
Dolan, Louis E., Jr. ....Washington, DC
Dolan, Lynne B. ....Providence, RI
Dolan, Maria Hidalgo ....Allenwood, NJ
Dolan, Mark J. ....Albany, NY
Dolan, Mark P. ....Providence, RI
Dolan, Mark V. ....Wichita, KS
Dolan, Mark V. ....Binghamton, NY
Dolan, Martin ....Portland, OR
Dolan, Martin A. ....Chicago, IL
Naperville, IL
Dolan, Mary S. ....Chicago, IL
Dolan, Matthew J. ....Washington, DC
Dolan, Matthew J. ....Chardon, OH
Dolan, Michael ....New Haven, CT
Dolan, Michael A. ....Brighton, CO
Dolan, Michael C. ....Oakland, CA
Dolan, Michael F. ....Chicago, IL
Dolan, Michael F. ....New Brunswick, NJ
Dolan, Michael F.X., Jr. ....Quincy, MA
Dolan, Michael G. ....New York, NY
Dolan, Michael J. ....Alexandria, MN
Dolan, Michael J. ....Newark, NJ
Dolan, Michael Patrick ....Nashville, TN
Dolan, Michael R. ....Providence, RI
Dolan, Michael T. ....Philadelphia, PA
Dolan, Michael W. ....
Administrative Office Of The United States
Courts, GV
Dolan, Patricia Ann ....St. Paul, MN
Dolan, Patricia K. ....Boston, MA
Dolan, Patrick D. ....Chicago, IL
Dolan, Patrick D. ....Reno, NV
Dolan, Patrick D. ....New York, NY
Dolan, Patrick J. ....Boston, MA
Dolan, Paul J. ....Syracuse, NY
Dolan, Paul J. ....Chardon, OH
Dolan, Peggy A. ....Miami Beach, FL
Dolan, Peter B. ....Department of Labor,
Office of the Solicitor, GV
Dolan, Peter Brown ....Los Angeles, CA
Dolan, Peter M., Jr. ....Denver, CO
Dolan, Philip E. ....Coeur d'Alene, ID
Dolan, Philip G., II ....Bethlehem, PA

Dolan, Rachel E. ....Austin, TX
Dolan & Regan ....Lynn, MA
Dolan, Richard E. ....St. Clairsville, OH
Dolan, Richard H. ....New York, NY
Dolan, Richard J. ....Bozeman, MT
Dolan, Robert E. ....Houston, TX
Dolan, Robert E., Jr. ....St. Louis, MO
Dolan, Robert P., III ....Greenfield, MA
Dolan, Robert T. ....Los Angeles, CA
Dolan, Robert T. ....Minneapolis, MN
Dolan, Robert T. ....Price, UT
Dolan, Robt. J. ....San Francisco, CA
Dolan, Ronald J. ....St. Louis, MO
Dolan, Sabrina A. ....Edina, MN
Dolan, Sean A. ....Wilmington, DE
Dolan, Sean P. ....Athens, GA
Dolan & Shannon, A Professional Corporation
Chicago, IL
Naperville, IL
Dolan, Sheila A. ....San Francisco, CA
Dolan, Stephen Michael ....Kinderhook, NY
Dolan, Stephen R. ....Raleigh, NC
Dolan, Susan S. ....Miami, FL
Dolan, Thomas D. ....Lynn, MA
Dolan, Thomas E. ....Brown Deer, WI
Dolan, Thomas H. ....Boston, MA
Dolan, Thomas J. ....Washington, DC
Dolan, Thomas J. ....Poughkeepsie, NY
Dolan, Thomas M. ....Worcester, MA
Dolan, Timothy J. ....Richmond, VA
Dolan, Timothy M. ....Garibaldi, OR
Dolan, Valerie J. ....El Cajon, CA
Dolan, William A. ....Fullerton, CA
Dolan, William A., II ....Newton, NJ
Dolan, William A., Law Offices of, Inc.
Fullerton, CA
Dolan, William D., III (P.C.) ....McLean, VA
Dolan, William F. ....Chicago, IL
Dolan, William H. ....Minnetonka, MN
Dolan, William J. ....Hartford, CT
Dolan, William M., III ....Providence, RI
Dolan, William T. ....Minneapolis, MN
Dolan, William T. K. ....
Architect of the Capitol, GV
Dolan, William W. ....Sarasota, FL
Doland Gould & Fingerman LLP
Los Angeles, CA
Doland, Marie N. ....Washington, DC
Doland, Michael C. ....Los Angeles, CA
Doland, Nelson C., Jr. ....Boonton, NJ
Dolas, Mary D. ....Fresno, CA
Dolasinski, Brian P. ....Phoenix, AZ
Dolata, Leo ....Angola, NY
Dolatly, George C. ....New York, NY
Dolatly, Marguerita B. ....Newark, NJ
Dolatowski, John J. ....Brunswick, OH
Dolatowski, Thomas E. ....Burlington, WI
Dolbashian, Kenneth R. ....Portsmouth, RI
Dolbear, Bernard S. ....New Orleans, LA
Dolbeare, Kenneth ....Falls Church, VA
Dolbeare, Robert L. ....Richmond, VA
Dolbeare, Robert L., P.C. ....Richmond, VA
Dolbec, McGrath, Crowley & White
Boston, MA
Dolbec, Robert P. ....Boston, MA
Dolbec, Robert P., Jr. ....Boston, MA
Dolber, Frederick A. ....Bronx, NY
Dolberg, Allen ....New York, NY
Dolberg, David S. ....Point Richmond, CA
Dolberg, Nancy A. ....Boston, MA
Dolberg, Steven P. ....Missoula, MT
Dolbey, Holly E. ....Detroit, MI
Dolbin, Cyrus Palmer ....Pottsville, PA
Dolbin, Donald D. ....Pottsville, PA
Dolce, Amy Allred ....Salt Lake City, UT
Dolce, Anthony J. ....Hartford, CT
Dolce, Carla J. ....Dallas, TX
Dolce, Cyrus G. ....New York, NY
Dolce, Joan Dell ....Kerrville, TX
Dolce, Julia Wagner ....Lake Worth, FL
Dolce, Marcus P. ....Department of Commerce,
Patent and Trademark Office, GV
Dolce, Michael Thomas
West Palm Beach, FL
Dolce, Richard James ....West Columbia, SC
Dolce, Rosa Maria ....Ridgewood, NY
Dolce & Thomas, L.L.P. ....Dallas, TX
Dolcetti, Daniel J., Jr. ....New York, NY
Dolchin, Jerry H. ....Philadelphia, PA
Falls Church, VA
Dolchin, Marla R. ....Columbus, OH
Dolchin, Slotkin & Todd, P.C.
Cherry Hill, NJ
Philadelphia, PA
Falls Church, VA
Dolchin, Steven B., (P.A.) ....Hollywood, FL
Dolci, Charles F., Jr. ....Palo Alto, CA
Dolci, Dominick P. ....Oakbrook Terrace, IL
Dolci, Lawrence H., III ....Kansas City, MO
Dolcimascolo, Samuel B. ....Tampa, FL
Dolcino, Chiara G. ....Concord, NH
Dold, Douglas H. ....Grosse Pointe, MI
Troy, MI
Dold, Elizabeth Thomas ....Washington, DC
Dold, Jennifer A. ....Seattle, WA
Dold, Paul M. ....Honolulu, HI
Dold, Ronald J. ....Houston, TX
Dold, Scott A. ....Lawrence, KS
Dold, Spath & McKelvie, P.C.
Grosse Pointe, MI
Troy, MI
Dolde, William G. ....North Miami Beach, FL
Dolder, Nancy S. ....Department of Labor,
Office of Secretary, GV
Dolder, Richard E., Jr. ....Atlanta, GA
Doldo, Todd J. ....Watertown, NY
Dole, Christopher J. ....Boston, MA

Dole, Coalwell, Clark, Mountainspring & Mornarich, P.C. ....Roseburg, OR
Dole, Donald A. ....Roseburg, OR
Dole, George V. ....Paris, IL
Dole, James K. ....Falmouth, MA
Dole, James R. ....Grants Pass, OR
Dole, Joseph C. ....Syracuse, NY
Dole, Kathleen D. ....Syracuse, NY
Dole, Kathryn Riley
Federal Communications Commission,
Common Carrier Bureau, GV
Dole, Linda Ingols ....Houston, TX
Dole, Peter T. ....Paris, IL
Dole, Richard F. ....San Francisco, CA
Dole, Richard F., Jr. ....Houston, TX
Dole, Robert J. ....Washington, DC
Dole, Stuart R. ....San Francisco, CA
Dole, Susan M. ....Montpelier, VT
Dole, Timothy Karam ....Seattle, WA
Dole, W. Melville ....Aurora, CO
Dole, William R. ....San Bernardino, CA
Doleac, Charles B. ....Portsmouth, NH
Doleac, M. Ronald ....Hattiesburg, MS
Dolecki, Kenneth C. ....Hackensack, NJ
Dolecki, Lawrence L. ....Houston, TX
Dolega, John H. ....Dearborn, MI
Dolega, Thomas E. ....Troy, MI
Dolegowski, Wence W. ....Pittsburgh, PA
Dolehanty, Darrin ....Richmond, IN
Dolehide, Beth S. ....Chicago, IL
Dolejs, Richard F. ....Cleveland, OH
Dolen, Raymond F. ....San Bernardino, CA
Dolence, John S. ....Joplin, MO
Dolenga, Michael D. ....Dearborn, MI
Dolente, Michael J. ....Philadelphia, PA
Dolentz, Patricia W. ....St. Cloud, MN
Doles, Edward A. ....Chesterland, OH
Doles, Gilbert C. ....Honolulu, HI
Doles, James Edward ....Ventura, CA
Doles, Paul W, II ....Miamisburg, OH
Doles, Troy Andrew ....St. Louis, MO
Dolesh, Michael J., (P.C.) ....Chicago, IL
Dolewski, Daniel A.
Port Jefferson Station, NY
Dolezal, Dave P. "Duke" ....El Paso, TX
Dolezal, David G. ....Austin, TX
Dolezal, John R. ....Beaumont, TX
Dolezal, Kenneth F. ....Cedar Rapids, IA
Dolezal, Trey L. ....Austin, TX
Dolezal, Wayne Elliott ....Lincoln, NE
Dolezalek, J. Stephan ....Palo Alto, CA
Dolfi, Christine M. ....Pittsburgh, PA
Dolfi, Glenn D. ....Pittsburgh, PA
Dolfman, Bruce M. ....Philadelphia, PA
Dolfman, Douglas L. ....Philadelphia, PA
Dolfman, Murray B. ....Philadelphia, PA
Dolge, Creig A. ....Santa Barbara, CA
Dolgen, Jonathan L. ....Los Angeles, CA
Dolgenas, Ilyse S. ....New York, NY
Dolgenos Newman & Cronin LLP
New York, NY
Dolgin, Aaron ....Tarzana, CA
Dolgin, Barbara L. ....New York, NY
Dolgin, Cassandra K. ....Jefferson City, MO
Dolgin, Daniel L. ....New York, NY
Dolgin, David A. ....Martinez, CA
Dolgin, Gary S. ....Tampa, FL
Dolgin, Harlan G. ....St. Louis, MO
Dolgin, Janet L. ....Hempstead, NY
Dolgin, Jay L. ....Chicago, IL
Dolgin, Joseph J. ....St. Louis, MO
Dolgin, Kalmon ....New York, NY
Dolgin, Robert M. ....St. Louis, MO
Dolgin & Watts, P.C. ....St. Louis, MO
Dolginer, Charles I. ....Los Angeles, CA
Dolgin-Kmetz, Stacey L. ....White Plains, NY
Dolginoff, Stanford M. ....Arlington, TX
Dolginoff, Todd A. ....Dallas, TX
Fort Worth, TX
Dolginoff, Todd A. ....Plano, TX
Dolgoff, Barry ....Williamsville, NY
Dolgorukov, D. Edward ....Toledo, OH
Dolian, Robert P. ....Stamford, CT
Dolida, Michael D. ....San Diego, CA
Dolido, Edward ....New York, NY
Dolifka, Dale L. ....Soldotna, AK
Dolin, Albert H. ....Highland Park, IL
Dolin & Associates, P.C. ....Rochester, NY
Dolin, Eliza A. ....New York, NY
Dolin, Jason M. ....Canal Winchester, OH
Dolin, Kenneth R. ....Chicago, IL
Dolin, Laura D. ....Plantation, FL
Dolin, Lawrence S. ....Cleveland, OH
Dolin, Lester ....New York, NY
Dolin, Lisa L. ....Plantation, FL
Dolin, Lonny H. ....Rochester, NY
Dolin, Mark L. ....Farmington Hills, MI
Dolin, Mitchell F. ....Washington, DC
Dolin, Norman M., Law Offices of
Beverly Hills, CA
Dolin, Richard A. ....Louisville, KY
Dolin, Stewart ....Chicago, IL
Dolin, Susan L. ....Hollywood, FL
Dolin, Thomas E. ....Albany, NY
Dolina, Thomas J. ....Towson, MD
Dolinar, Sarah J. ....New York, NY
Doliner, Anne E. ....Lancaster, PA
Doliner, Deborah S. ....Miami, FL
Doliner, Elliot A. ....Midland Park, NJ
Doliner, Harlan M. ....Boston, MA
Doliner, Nathaniel L. ....Tampa, FL
Doling, Stuart P. ....Albany, NY
Dolinger, Craig M. ....Woodbury, NY
Dolinger, Michael H. ....New York, NY
Dolinger, Miles J. ....San Francisco, CA
Dolinger, Peter M. ....Cherry Hill, NJ
Philadelphia, PA
Dolinick, Karen J. ....Oak Brook, IL

Dolinko, Adam R. ....Palo Alto, CA
Dolinko, Alan R. ....Chicago, IL
Dolinko, Robert A. ....San Francisco, CA
Dolins, Mark R. ....Boston, MA
Dolinsky, Joan M. ....Los Angeles, CA
Dolinsky, Nancy E. ....Stamford, CT
Dolinsky, William S. ....Santa Monica, CA
D'Olio, Anthony J. ....Las Vegas, NV
Dolkas, David Henry ....Palo Alto, CA
Doll, A. Robert ....Louisville, KY
Doll, Amy J. ....Morris, MN
Doll, Bruce E. ....Burton, MI
Doll, Craig A. ....Harrisburg, PA
Doll, Cynthia Blevins ....Louisville, KY
Doll, David A. ....Kenmore, NY
Doll, Donald K. ....Oak Park, IL
Doll, Earl R. ....York, PA
Doll, Gregory L. ....Los Angeles, CA
Doll, John H. ....Chicago, IL
Doll, John K. ....Louisville, KY
Doll, John R. ....Dayton, OH
Doll, Linda L. ....West Barnstable, MA
Doll, Mary T. ....Southfield, MI
Doll, Maurice E. ....Vincennes, IN
Doll, Michael A. ....Dodge City, KS
Doll, Michael S. ....Long Beach, CA
Doll, Troy W. ....New York, NY
Doll and Webb ....Vincennes, IN
Doll, William E., Jr. .... Frankfort, KY
Lexington, KY
Dollahite, M. Keith ....Tyler, TX
Dollahite, Sam ....Marlin, TX
Dollahon, Willard E. ....Houston, TX
Dollar, Beverly M. ....Bartlesville, OK
Dollar, Dawn De Keyser ....Chicago, IL
Dollar, Edward E. ....Santa Ana, CA
Dollar, Gerald G. ....Tuscaloosa, AL
Dollar, John P. ....West Des Moines, IA
Dollar, Johnny E., (P.L.C.) ....Monroe, LA
Dollar Laird, L.L.P. ....Monroe, LA
Dollar, Lorrie L. ....Raleigh, NC
Dollar, Rachel M. ....Santa Rosa, CA
Dollar, Steve W. ....San Jose, CA
Dollar, Tim E. ....Kansas City, MO
Dollar, W. Mason ....Auburn, AL
Dollard, Adrian Emmett
San Francisco, CA
Dollard, Anne ....Emeryville, CA
Dollard, Elizabeth K. ....New York, NY
Dollard, J. Donald ....Florissant, MO
Dollard, James A. ....Staten Island, NY
Dollard, James P., Jr. ....Kew Gardens, NY
Dollard, Leo D. ....St. Louis, MO
Dollarhide, Barbara Miller ....Oxford, MS
Dollarhide, Charles L., II
Oklahoma City, OK
Dollarhide, Mary C. ....Stamford, CT
Dollars, Robert A. ....Austin, TX
Dollase, Christopher R. ....Baltimore, MD
Columbia, MD
Dollbaum, Margaret R. ....Los Angeles, CA
San Francisco, CA
Dolle, Carol L. ....Los Angeles, CA
Dolle and Dolle, A Professional Corporation
Los Angeles, CA
Dolle, Hodge L., Jr. ....Los Angeles, CA
Dolle, Robert E. ....Cincinnati, OH
Dolle, Robert H. ....Cincinnati, OH
Dolle, Rueger & Mathews Co., L.P.A.
Cincinnati, OH
Dollens, John R. ....Scottsburg, IN
Dollet, Loren M. ....New York, NY
Dolley, Leland C. ....Los Angeles, CA
Dolley, Michelle A. ....Winslow, ME
Dollin, Elizabeth Wizeman ....Newark, NJ
Dollin, James A. ....New York, NY
Dollinger, David M. ....Rochester, NY
Dollinger & Dollinger, A Professional Corporation ....Paramus, NJ
Dollinger, Douglas R. ....Garden City, NY
Dollinger, Edmund ....Hackensack, NJ
Tarrytown, NY
Dollinger, Gonski & Grossman
Fairfield, NJ
Carle Place, NY
Mineola, NY
Dollinger, Harold J., Jr. ....Dallas, TX
Dollinger, Jay L. ....Melville, NY
Dollinger, Jeffrey D. ....Livingston, NJ
Dollinger, Jeffrey R. ....Gainesville, FL
Dollinger, Martin E. ....Paramus, NJ
Dollinger, Matthew ....Carle Place, NY
Dollinger & Ostrowsky ....Livingston, NJ
Dollinger, Richard A. ....Webster, NY
Dollinger, Scot G. ....Baytown, TX
Dollinger, Stephan G. ....Laurel, MD
Dollinger, Stephen H. ....Reno, NV
Dollinger, Steve C. ....Houston, TX
Dollinger, Steven D. ....Melville, NY
Dollinger, Susan B. ....Carlisle, MA
Dollinger, Thomas W. ....Los Angeles, CA
Dollison, Allan L. ....Los Angeles, CA
Dollison, Allan, Law Offices of
Los Angeles, CA
Dollison, Charles B. ....Charleston, WV
Dollison, Fred R. ....Sheridan, WY
Dollison, Richard H.
Charlotte Amalie, St. Thomas, VI
Dolliver, James M. ....Olympia, WA
Dolliver, Keith R. ....Redmond, WA
Dolliver, Leslie Henges ....Austin, TX
Dollmann, Kenneth C. ....Holbrook, NY
Dolloff, Arthur Dean ....Topsham, ME
Dolloff, David J. ....San Jose, CA
Dolloff, Paul W. ....Buffalo, NY
Dolman, Carl L. ....Walters, OK
Dolman, Charles M. ....Cincinnati, OH
Dolman, Gerald ....New York, NY

Dolman, James B. ......Ardmore, OK
Dolman, James L. ......Ardmore, OK
Dolman Law Offices ......Ardmore, OK
Dolman, Maurice H., (P.C.)
Los Angeles, CA
Dolman & Samuels ......Los Angeles, CA
Dolmanisth, Steven J. ......Washington, DC
Dolmatch, Minda Solomon ......New York, NY
Dolmatch, Stephen J. ......Ridgefield Park, NJ
Dolmat-Connell, Carrie ......Boston, MA
Dolney, Theo. J. ......Vermillion, SD
Dolnick, Jeremy D. ......Fullerton, CA
Dolnick, L. Rachel ......Boca Raton, FL
Dolny, Carmen R. ......Tucson, AZ
Doloboff, Joseph M. ......Los Angeles, CA
Dolotta, Peter E. ......New York, NY
Dolowich, Ivan J. ......New York, NY
Dolowitz, David S. ......Salt Lake City, UT
Dolph, Becky Ingrum ......Kansas City, MO
Dolph, Bob ......Jonesboro, GA
Dolph, Cyrus A., IV ......Norfolk, VA
Dolph, David A. ......Overland Park, KS
Dolphin, John L. ......Philadelphia, PA
Dolphin, Verginald L. ......Washington, DC
Dolqueist, Lori Anne ......Washington, DC
Dols, Richard J. ......Alexandria, VA
Dolsky, Robin R. ......New York, NY
Dolson, Edward M. ......Overland Park, KS
Kansas City, MO
Dolson, Laurie L. ......Fairfax, VA
Dolson, Laurie L., P.C. ......Fairfax, VA
Dolson, Scott W. ......Louisville, KY
Dolson, William F. ......Louisville, KY
Dolt, Frederick C. ......Louisville, KY
Dolt, Furkin & Thompson, P.S.C.
Louisville, KY
Dolter, Elizabeth L. ......San Francisco, CA
Dolton, Gregory N. ......Menlo Park, CA
Dolton, Robert G. ......Clackamas, OR
Doluisio, Michael S. ......Philadelphia, PA
Dolve, Elmer J. ......Billings, MT
Dolven, Earl P. ......Berkeley, CA
Dolven, Frank J. ......San Francisco, CA
Dolven, Lynn Bolinske ......Denver, CO
Dolven, Thomas R. ......Denver, CO
Dolwig, Richard J., Jr. ......Montecito, CA
Dolyk, W. Zack ......Sandusky, OH
Vermilion, OH
Domagala, Donna ......Newton, MA
Domagalski, J. Andrew ......Richland, MI
Domagalski, James P. ......Buffalo, NY
Domagalski, Philip W. ......Chicago, IL
Domagas, Benjamin J. ......Keller, TX
Domalakes, John E. ......Pottsville, PA
Domalakes, Paul G. ......Frackville, PA
Domalewski, Craig A. ......Cranford, NJ
Domalik, Anita J. ......Pittsburgh, PA
Doman, Andrew P. ......St. Maries, ID
Doman, Bruce K. ......Upper Black Eddy, PA
Doman, Daniel F. ......Mineola, NY
Doman, Daniel J. ......Dearborn, MI
Doman, Laurence B. ......Dearborn, MI
Doman Law Offices, P.C. ......St. Maries, ID
Doman, Michael P. ......Chicago, IL
Doman, Nicholas R. ......New York, NY
Doman, Nicholas R., The Law Firm of
New York, NY
Doman, Paul M. ......Cleveland, OH
Domangue, Julie Sullivan ......Houma, LA
Domanico, Gene T. ......New York, NY
Domanico, James A. ......Spokane, WA
Domanish, Michael J. ......Philadelphia, PA
Scranton, PA
Domann, Craig E. ......Bolingbrook, IL
Domann, G. Kyle ......Springfield, MO
Domanovic, Dieter ......Cleveland, OH
Domanski, Paula R. ......Waltham, MA
Domanskis, Alexander R. ......Chicago, IL
Domansky, Edward C. ......Bloomington, IL
Domansky, Elissa Deborah ......New York, NY
Domaratius, Stephen W. ......Chicago, IL
Domas, George A. ......Chicago, IL
Domaz, James H. ......Tempe, AZ
Domb, Alexander L. ......Pembroke Pines, FL
Domb, Martin ......New York, NY
Dombai, Les ......Chicago, IL
Dombai, Thomas J. ......Chicago, IL
Dombal, Sheila J. ......Washington, DC
Dombalagian, Onnig H. ......Washington, DC
Dombalis, Nicholas J., II ......Raleigh, NC
Dombchik, Adam D. ......Los Angeles, CA
Dombeck, James E. ......Rochester, NY
Dombek, Arthur E. ......Cleveland, OH
Dombek, Curt M. ......Santa Monica, CA
Domber, Harlan R. ......Sarasota, FL
Domber, Harlan R., Law Office of, P.A.
Sarasota, FL
Domber, Jeffrey H.
General Services Administration,
Office of the General Counsel, GV
Domber, Matthew J. ......New York, NY
Dombey, Philip L. ......Perrysburg, OH
Dombkowski, Dale Edward
San Francisco, CA
Dombo, Frederick T. ......Washington, DC
Dombo, Frederick T., III ......Washington, DC
Dombosch, Gina A. ......Miami, FL
Dombourian, Joyce M., (P.C.)
New Orleans, LA
Dombrink, Stephen ......Oakland, CA
Dombro, Sandra B. ......Burlington, VT
Dombroff & Gilmore ......Washington, DC
Miami, FL
New York, NY
Dombroff, Mark A. ......Washington, DC
Dombroff, Robert M. ......Hartford, CT
New York, NY
Dombroski, James M. ......Petaluma, CA
Dombroski, Knapsack & Hillis, LLC
New Haven, CT
Dombroski, Stan R. ......New Haven, CT
Dombrosky, Joseph P. ......Hartford, CT
Dombrow, Anthony E. ......Chicago, IL
Dombrow, Richard L. ......Santa Ana, CA
Dombrowski, Anna H. ......Princeton, NJ
Dombrowski, Bonnie S. ......Tucson, AZ
Dombrowski, Cass E. ......Frisco, CO
Dombrowski, Chris J. ......Dearborn, MI
Dombrowski, Donald J. ......Houston, TX
Dombrowski, Garrett J. ......New York, NY
Dombrowski, Gerald M. ......Chicago, IL
Dombrowski, John M. ......Leominster, MA
Dombrowski, John W., Jr. ......Hartford, CT
Dombrowski, Kenneth S.
Bloomfield Hills, MI
Dombrowski, Leo P. ......Chicago, IL
Dombrowski, Michael G. ......Brown Deer, WI
Dombrowski, Nadia A. ......Stamford, CT
Dombrowski, Neil T. ......Philadelphia, PA
Dombrowski, Paul J. ......Madison, WI
Dombrowski, Stefan S. ......New York, NY
Dombrowski, Thaddeus M.
Mount Clemens, MI
Dombrowski, Valerie Mattson
Los Angeles, CA
Dombrowsky, Alan H. ......Miami, FL
Domby, Arthur H. ......Atlanta, GA
Dome, Lauren G. ......New York, NY
Dome, Leonard S. ......New York, NY
Domeck, Corneal L., III ......Louisville, KY
Domeck, John W. ......Mayfield Village, OH
Domecus, Kevin L. ......San Francisco, CA
Domeika, Hilary Buckley ......Seattle, WA
Domeika, John P. ......Seattle, WA
Domel, Lori Jane ......Austin, TX
Domel, Mark ......Austin, TX
Domen, Victor J., Jr. ......Nashville, TN
Domen-Broshears, Carolyn M.
Los Angeles, CA
Domene, David ......Louisville, KY
Domengeaux, James H. ......Lafayette, LA
Domengeaux, Jerome E. ......Lafayette, LA
Domengeaux Wright & Roy, A Professional Law Corporation ......Lafayette, LA
Domenichini, Frank ......Orange, CA
Domenici, David ......Washington, DC
Domenici, Peter V., Jr. ......Albuquerque, NM
Domenick, Heide E. ......Santa Monica, CA
Domenick, Robert P. ......Greensburg, PA
Domenico, Calvin J., Jr. ......Rome, NY
Domenico, Geoffrey A. ......Brockton, MA
Domenico, Kathleen Franco ......Denver, CO
Domenico Law Offices ......Rome, NY
Domenico, Lawrence B. ......Atlanta, GA
Domeny, Paul Z. ......Kalamazoo, MI
Domer, Cindy Kendrick ......Washington, DC
Domer, Michelle Berry ......Bloomington, IN
Domer, Thomas M. ......Milwaukee, WI
Domers, Alan ......Marlton, NJ
Domers & Bonamassa ......Marlton, NJ
Domescik, G. Kirk ......Atlanta, GA
Domesick, Michael H. ......Palo Alto, CA
Domesick, Stephen R. ......Boston, MA
Domestico & Barry ......Boston, MA
Framingham, MA
Worcester, MA
Domestico, Charles J. ......Framingham, MA
Domeyer, Mark T. ......Woodland Hills, CA
Domeyer, Tamra S. ......Chicago, IL
Domholt, Richard ......Burlingame, CA
Domiano, Johnny L., Jr.
New Orleans, LA
Domiano, Joseph C. ......Marco Island, FL
Cleveland, OH
Domicello, Marc Jeffrey ......White Plains, NY
Domich, Brooke Bowden ......Sacramento, CA
Domico, William D. ......Memphis, TN
Domike, Joan R. ......Treasury Department,
Internal Revenue Service, GV
Domike, Julie Ronder ......Washington, DC
Domin, Ann C. ......Tulsa, OK
Domin, Timothy A. ......Charleston, SC
Domina, Daren R. ......New York, NY
Domina, David A. ......Omaha, NE
Domina Law pc ......Omaha, NE
Dominczyk, Thomas R. ......Bridgewater, NJ
Domine, Jeffrey B. ......Sherman Oaks, CA
Domingo, Richard B. ......Palo Alto, CA
Domingue, Barry L. ......Lafayette, LA
Domingue, Billy J. ......Lafayette, LA
Domingue, C. Dean ......Lafayette, LA
Domingue, Curtis, Jr. ......Houston, TX
Domingue, Goldie C. ......Chicago, IL
Domingue, Harold L., Jr. ......Lafayette, LA
Domingue, John Forsyth ......San Jose, CA
Domingue, Lamont P. ......Lafayette, LA
Domingue, Michael J. ......Baton Rouge, LA
Domingue & Smith, P.C. ......Houston, TX
Domingue & Waddell, PLC ......Lafayette, LA
Domingues, E. John ......Rockville, MD
Domingues, E. John, P.A. ......Rockville, MD
Dominguez, Abel A. ......San Antonio, TX
Dominguez, Adrienne ......Bethesda, MD
Dominguez, Adrienne E. ......Dallas, TX
Dominguez, Alberto Luis ......Monticello, FL
Dominguez, Alfonso, Jr. ......El Paso, TX
Dominguez, A. M., Jr. ......Greeley, CO
Dominguez, Carmen J. ......San Francisco, CA
Dominguez, Carol Lee ......Albuquerque, NM
Dominguez, Christopher E.
Washington, DC
Dominguez, Daniel L. ......Chicago, IL
Dominguez, Darin R. ......Newport Beach, CA
Dominguez, David ......Provo, UT
Dominguez, Ernesto J. ......McAllen, TX
Dominguez, Errol M. ......Boston, MA
Dominguez, Esther B. ......Boston, MA
Dominguez, Francisco X. ......El Paso, TX
Dominguez, G. Luis ......Miami, FL
Dominguez, Humberto R. ......Miami, FL
Dominguez, Humberto S. ......New York, NY
Dominguez, Iris Aguilar ......Edinburg, TX
Dominguez, James V. ......Tampa, FL
Dominguez, Jesse V., (P.A.) ......Tampa, FL
Dominguez, John P. ......Washington, DC
Dominguez, Joseph ......Philadelphia, PA
Dominguez, Juan Carlos ......Los Angeles, CA
Dominguez, Juan J. ......Los Angeles, CA
Dominguez, Lu-ann Mancini
Fort Lauderdale, FL
Dominguez, M. Carmen ......Miami, FL
Dominguez, Manuel ......Long Beach, CA
Dominguez, Maria Del Rosario
Opa Locka, FL
Dominguez, Marialina H. ......Brooklyn, NY
Dominguez, Marina R. ......McAllen, TX
Dominguez, Maureen F. ......Chicago, IL
Dominguez, Mauricio ......Charlotte, NC
Dominguez, Richard E., II ......Washington, DC
Dominguez, Winifred H. ......San Antonio, TX
Dominguez-Urban, Ileana ......Carbondale, IL
DoMinh, Bernard T.
Department Of Veterans Affairs,
Board of Veterans Appeals, GV
Domini, James A. ......New York, NY
Dominianni, Emilio A. ......New York, NY
Dominianni, Paul A. ......Bloomfield, CT
Dominic, Donald Louis ......Covina, CA
Dominic, John A. ......Southfield, MI
Dominici, Letitia ......Chicago, IL
Dominick, Alan R. ......Lansing, MI
Dominick, Bobbi Killian ......Boise, ID
Dominick, Charles A. ......Wilkes-Barre, PA
Dominick, Christopher B. ......Denver, CO
Dominick, D. Clinton, III ......Newburgh, NY
Dominick, David D. ......Cody, WY
Dominick, Dean V. ......York, PA
Dominick, Fletcher, Yeilding, Wood & Lloyd, P.A. ......Birmingham, AL
Dominick, Frank ......Birmingham, AL
Dominick, Gayer G. ......Olympia, WA
Dominick & Handley ......Olympia, WA
Dominick, Julian K. ......Orlando, FL
Dominick, Julian K., Jr. ......Orlando, FL
Dominick, L. Allison ......Minneapolis, MN
Dominick Law Offices ......Boise, ID
Dominick, Paul A. ......Charleston, SC
Dominick, Sherry L. ......New Haven, CT
Dominick, Thomas B. ......Boise, ID
Dominick, Thomas W.
San Bernardino, CA
Dominiecki, Thomas F. ......South River, NJ
Dominik, Cynthia A.
Department of Transportation,
Federal Aviation Administration, GV
Dominik, Jack E. ......Miami, FL
Dominik, Knechtel, Demeur & Samlan
Miami, FL
Chicago, IL
Dominik, Paula S. ......Shalimar, FL
Dominique, Eugene M. ......San Francisco, CA
Dominique, P. Pierre ......Jefferson City, MO
Dominis, Dori ......Palo Alto, CA
Dominitz, Erica J. ......Washington, DC
Dominitz, Jennifer S. ......Universal City, CA
Dominsky, John ......Stamford, CT
Dominy, Mary Ann ......Washington, DC
Dominy, Michael A. ......Atlanta, GA
Dominy, Shawn R. ......Columbus, OH
Delaware, OH
Dominy, William S. ......Decatur, GA
Domiquez-calbi, Bertica ......Kansas City, MO
Domitrovic, Gerald J. ......Wichita, KS
Domitrovic, Leah J. ......Chicago, IL
Domitrovich, Stephanie ......Erie, PA
Domke, Howard J. ......Van Nuys, CA
Domke, Jenel M. ......Sumter, SC
Domm, Alice ......New Brunswick, NJ
Domm, Gavin J. ......Chicago, IL
Domm, William A. ......Northbrook, IL
Domm, William A., P.C. ......Northbrook, IL
Domme, Thomas M. ......Albuquerque, NM
Dommel, Julia M. ......La Jolla, CA
Dommerich, John William ......Fort Myers, FL
Dommermuth, Brestal, Cobine and West, Ltd. ......Aurora, IL
Chicago, IL
Naperville, IL
Wheaton, IL
Dommermuth, Michael J. ......Denver, CO
Dommers, Christa L. ......New Haven, CT
Domnarski, Edward S. ......Old Saybrook, CT
Domnick, Sean C. ......West Palm Beach, FL
Domning, Bryan A. ......Houston, TX
Domnitz, Avin M. ......Milwaukee, WI
Domnitz, H. Ronald ......San Diego, CA
Domnitz, Mawicke, Goisman & Rosenberg, S.C. ......Kenosha, WI
Milwaukee, WI
Domnitz, Merrick R. ......Milwaukee, WI
Domnitz, Robert H. ......Lexington, MA
Domolky, Serena ......Weston, MA
Domon, Margo P.
Federal Communications Commission,
Cable Services Bureau, GV
Domoney, J. Darcy ......Paola, KS
Domonkos, Julie A. ......New York, NY
Domonkos, Michael ......Brevard, NC
Domoracki, Gary S. ......Wenham, MA
Domow, Penny P. ......New York, NY
Domozick, Daniel D. ......Cleveland, OH
Dompier, Robert N. ......Spokane, WA
Dompieri, Arnold B. ......Westfield, NJ
Dompkowski, Joseph Paul ......Mineola, NY
Domsky, Ronald Z. ......Chicago, IL
Domstein, David J. ......Bingham Farms, MI
Domurad, John Matthew ......Albany, NY
Domzal, David A. ......Farmington Hills, MI
Domzalski, David J. ......Philadelphia, PA
Domzalski, Kenneth S. ......Burlington, NJ
Domzalski, Kurts and Gunn ......Burlington, NJ
Don, Amy I. ......New York, NY
Don, Arthur ......Chicago, IL
Don, Berek P. ......Fort Lauderdale, FL
Don, Beth L. ......General Accounting Office,
Personnel Appeals Board, GV
Don Carlos, Shapiro & Hahn, L.L.P.
Phoenix, AZ
Sun City, AZ
Sun City West, AZ
Don, David ......South Burlington, VT
Don, David J. ......Scottsdale, AZ
Don, David M. ......Washington, DC
Don, Harold K., Jr. ......Mechanicsburg, PA
Don, Hiller & Galleher, A Professional Corporation ......Denver, CO
Don, James E. ......Florence, AZ
Don, Jeffrey J. ......Torrance, CA
Don, John A. ......San Diego, CA
Don, Michael E. ......Washington, DC
Don, Robert E. ......North Riverside, IL
Don, Roselynn G. ......Chicago, IL
Don, Shelley B. ......Denver, CO
Don, Susan M. Salt ......Melrose, MA
Donabed, Ralph A. ......Boston, MA
Donabedian, Diana L. ......Palo Alto, CA
Donabedian, Kristine L. ......Boston, MA
Providence, RI
Donaca, Thomas C. ......Portland, OR
Donadee, Michael A. ......Pittsburgh, PA
Donadio, Babette L. ......New York, NY
Donadio, Catherine ......Montclair, NJ
Donadio, David R. ......Novato, CA
Donadio, Donald A. ......Raleigh, NC
Donadio Law Office ......Greenville, OH
Donadio, Mark C. ......Buffalo, NY
Donadio, R. Richard ......Towson, MD
Donadio, Raymond M., Jr.
Greenville, OH
Donadio, Robert E. ......Timonium, MD
Donaghe, E. Bruce ......Dallas, TX
Donaghue & Bradley ......Media, PA
West Chester, PA
Donaghue, Ethel F., (Miss) ......Hartford, CT
Donaghue, Hugh A. ......Media, PA
Donaghue, James F. ......Atlanta, GA
Donaghue, Paul R., Jr. ......Chelmsford, MA
Donaghy, Andrew J. ......Media, PA
Donaghy, Donna K. ......Boston, MA
Donaghy, James F.
General Accounting Office,
Resources Community and Economic
Development Division, GV
Donaghy, John K. ......Brandywine, MD
Donaghy, John W. ......Morrisville, PA
Donaghy, Kevin P. ......Orlando, FL
Donaghy, Linda A. ......Department of Justice,
Justice Management Division, GV
Donaghy, Maryanne T. ......Philadelphia, PA
Donaghy, Michael R. S. ......Hampton, NH
Donaghy, Peardon ......Montpelier, VT
Donaghy, Robert J. ......Newtown, PA
Donaghy, Sandra N. Craig ......Cleveland, TN
Donaghy, Susan Winslow ......Media, PA
Donahe, Heidi Pederson ......Portland, OR
Donaher, Donna M. ......Pittsburgh, PA
Donaher, Matthew M. ......New York, NY
Donaher, Paul J. ......Boston, MA
Donahey, Joseph G., Jr. ......Clearwater, FL
Donahey, M. Scott ......Palo Alto, CA
Donahey, Michael M. ......Phoenix, AZ
Donahey, Richard S. ......Columbus, OH
Donahey, Teague I. ......San Jose, CA
Donahey, William F. ......Cleveland, OH
Donaho and Dockery, P.C. ......Floresville, TX
Donaho, Maureen Ann ......Edwardsville, IL
Donaho, Scott R. ......Floresville, TX
Donaho, Stephanie E. ......Houston, TX
Donahoe, Brian J. ......Sioux Falls, SD
Donahoe, C. Mark ......Jackson, TN
Donahoe, Daniel B. ......Pittsburgh, PA
Donahoe, Daniel J. ......Elmira, NY
Donahoe, Edward A. ......Omaha, NE
Donahoe, Gary E. ......Phoenix, AZ
Donahoe, Henry M. ......Lee, MA
Donahoe, James F. ......New York, NY
Donahoe, John E. ......Fort Lauderdale, FL
Donahoe, Karen Phillips, Law Offices of
Los Angeles, CA
Donahoe, Keith W. ......Greenbelt, MD
Donahoe, Laurence K. ......Oklahoma City, OK
Donahoe, Laurence K., P.C.
Oklahoma City, OK
Donahoe, Mara Jill ......Chesterland, OH
Donahoe, Michael J. ......Indianapolis, IN
Donahoe, Nancy A. ......Chicago, IL
Donahoe, Pecaro & Vollender, P.A.
Fort Lauderdale, FL
Donahoe, Peter H. ......Indianapolis, IN
Donahoe, Robert J. ......Pittsburgh, PA
Donahoe, Roger F. ......Seattle, WA
Donahoe, Terry Trexler ......Pittsburgh, PA
Donahoe, Thomas Christopher
Convent Station, NJ
Donahoe, Thomas L., Jr. ......Pittsburgh, PA
Donahoe, Thomas P. ......San Diego, CA
Donahoe, Timothy C. ......Encino, CA
Donahoo, Ball & McMenamy, P.A.
Jacksonville, FL
Donahoo, Eugenia H. ......Jacksonville, FL
Donahoo, John W., Jr. ......Jacksonville, FL
Donahoo, Richard ......Tustin, CA

Donahoo, Richard E. .... Tustin, CA
Donahoo, Thomas M. .... Jacksonville, FL
Donahoo, Thomas M., Jr. Jacksonville, FL
Donahower, Frederick L. Fort Lauderdale, FL; Biloxi, MS
Donahue, A. C. .... Somerset, KY
Donahue, Alicia A. .... Lowell, MA
Donahue, Alicia J. .... San Francisco, CA
Donahue, Allan J. .... Winter Park, FL
Donahue & Allen .... Derby, CT
Donahue, Anne de la Blanchetai New York, NY
Donahue, Arthur M., Jr. .... Kingston, MA
Donahue, Battle and Donahue Philadelphia, PA
Donahue, Bernard E., Jr. .... Riverside, CA
Donahue, Beth E. .... Hammond, IN
Donahue, Bonnie Kay Winston-Salem, NC
Donahue, Braun, Hagan, Klein & Newsome, P.C. .... Hackensack, NJ; Morristown, NJ; Short Hills, NJ
Donahue, Brendan M. .... Little Rock, AR
Donahue, Brendan P. .... Fairfield, CT
Donahue, Brian Charles North Little Rock, AR
Donahue, Carol E., Law Offices of Orlando, FL
Donahue, Carol E., Law Offices of Winter Park, FL
Donahue, Charles A. .... Keene, NH
Donahue, Charles B., II .... Cleveland, OH
Donahue, Charles, Jr. .... Cambridge, MA
Donahue, Craig .... Dallas, TX
Donahue, Craig R. .... Glendale, CA
Donahue & Cross, P.C. Northampton, MA; Springfield, MA
Donahue, Daniel G. .... St. Louis, MO
Donahue, Daniel J. .... North Hollywood, CA
Donahue, Daniel J. .... Santa Ana, CA
Donahue, Daniel K. .... Newport Beach, CA
Donahue, Daniel M. .... Washington, DC
Donahue, Daniel M. .... Rockford, IL
Donahue, Daniel W. .... Winston-Salem, NC
Donahue, David C. .... Boston, MA
Donahue, David P. .... Birmingham, AL
Donahue, Deirdre E. .... McLean, VA
Donahue, Dennis J., Jr. .... Clinton, CT; West Haven, CT
Donahue, Dennis J. M., III .... St. Louis, MO
Donahue, Diana D. .... Waldorf, MD
Donahue & Donahue, Attorneys, P.C. Boston, MA; Lowell, MA
Donahue, Duane .... Cary, IL; Crystal Lake, IL
Donahue, E. Victor .... Washington, DC
Donahue, Edward J., Jr. .... Boston, MA
Donahue, Eileen A. .... Derby, CT
Donahue, Elizabeth A. .... Glens Falls, NY
Donahue, Emily Stacy .... Dallas, TX
Donahue & Faesser, P.C. .... Pawnee City, NE
Donahue, Francis W. .... Short Hills, NJ
Donahue, Frank Rogers, Jr. Philadelphia, PA
Donahue, Frank Scott .... Philadelphia, PA
Donahue, Gallagher, Woods & Wood, LLP Mill Valley, CA; Oakland, CA; Walnut Creek, CA
Donahue, George M. .... New York, NY
Donahue, Gerald T. Cornwall-On-Hudson, NY
Donahue, Gregory J. .... Traverse City, MI
Donahue, Gregory J. .... Troy, MI
Donahue, Hoey, Rawls & Skedsvold, LLC Atlanta, GA
Donahue, J. Christopher .... Pittsburgh, PA
Donahue, James A. .... Great Falls, MT
Donahue, James E. .... Sacramento, CA
Donahue, James F., III .... Columbus, OH
Donahue, James M. .... McLean, VA
Donahue, James P. .... San Francisco, CA
Donahue, James P., Jr. .... Cumberland, MD
Donahue, James R. .... Fairfield, CA; Sacramento, CA
Donahue, James R. .... Cleveland, OH
Donahue, James T. .... West Springfield, MA
Donahue, Jay .... Herndon, VA
Donahue, Jeffrey O. .... Hartford, CT
Donahue, Joan W.D. .... Middlebury, VT
Donahue, John A. .... Chicago, IL
Donahue, John A. .... Salt Lake City, UT
Donahue, John E. .... Milwaukee, WI
Donahue, John F. .... Chicago, IL
Donahue, John F. .... Geneva, IL; Lisle, IL
Donahue, John F. .... Springfield, MA
Donahue, John James .... Lakewood, NJ; Morrisville, PA
Donahue, John L. .... Palo Alto, CA
Donahue, John L., Jr. .... Tucson, AZ
Donahue, John M. .... Hartford, CT
Donahue, John M. .... St. Joseph, MI
Donahue, John M. .... Philadelphia, PA
Donahue, John P. .... Arlington, MA
Donahue, John P. .... Cranbury, NJ
Donahue, John P. .... Perrysburg, OH
Donahue, John R., Jr. .... Sarasota, FL
Donahue, John T. .... Boston, MA
Donahue, John W. .... Joliet, IL
Donahue, John W. .... Dayton, OH
Donahue, Joseph F. .... Rocky River, OH
Donahue, Joseph G. .... Augusta, ME
Donahue, Joseph P. .... Washington, DC
Donahue, Joseph P., Jr. .... Lowell, MA
Donahue, Joseph R. .... Newark, NJ
Donahue, Kara S. .... Riverside, CT
Donahue, Kathleen M. .... Chicago, IL
Donahue, Kathleen M. .... Baltimore, MD
Donahue, Kenneth B. .... Atlanta, GA
Donahue, Kevin D. .... Torrance, CA
Donahue, Laura J. .... Derby, CT
Donahue, Laura Marie .... Peoria, IL
Donahue, Lauri .... Valley Village, CA
Donahue Law Group, P.S.C. Somerset, KY
Donahue, Leo F. .... Gold River, CA
Donahue, Leslie D. .... Kansas City, MO
Donahue, Linda .... New York, NY
Donahue, Lisa Kaye .... City of Industry, CA
Donahue, Lisa R. .... Boston, MA
Donahue, Malcolm M. .... Boston, MA
Donahue, Mark D. .... Corvallis, OR
Donahue, Mark F. .... Laguna Hills, CA
Donahue, Mark H. .... Somerville, MA
Donahue, Mark L. .... Worcester, MA
Donahue, Mary Jo .... Department of Justice, Civil Division, GV
Donahue, Mary Johnson .... Norfolk, VA
Donahue, Matthew C. .... Lowell, MA
Donahue, Matthew Paul .... Sacramento, CA
Donahue, Maureen E. .... Cornwall, CT
Donahue, Maureen E. .... Washington, DC
Donahue Mesereau & Leids L.L.P. Los Angeles, CA
Donahue, Michael B. .... Boston, MA
Donahue, Michael C. .... Dedham, MA; South Easton, MA
Donahue, Michael C., P.C. South Easton, MA
Donahue, Michael D., (A Professional Corporation) .... Los Angeles, CA
Donahue, Michael G. .... Princeton, NJ
Donahue, Michael J. .... Pawnee City, NE
Donahue, Michael J. .... Exeter, NH
Donahue, Michael J., III .... Pawnee City, NE
Donahue, Michael K. .... Annapolis, MD
Donahue, Michael P. .... Washington, DC
Donahue, Michael Wayne .... Modesto, CA
Donahue, Nancy A. .... Washington, DC
Donahue, Norbert F. .... Kalispell, MT
Donahue & Nunnari .... Perrysburg, OH
Donahue, Patricia .... Chicago, IL
Donahue, Patricia A. .... New York, NY
Donahue, Patricia J. .... Denver, CO
Donahue, Patrick .... Santa Ana, CA
Donahue, Patrick B. .... Omaha, NE
Donahue, Patrick H. .... Topeka, KS; Kansas City, MO
Donahue, Patrick J. .... Moosic, PA
Donahue, Patrick Michael .... Annapolis, MD; Baltimore, MD
Donahue, Patrick S. General Accounting Office, Resources Community and Economic Development Division, GV
Donahue, Paul F. .... Chicago, IL
Donahue, Paul T. .... Ottawa, IL
Donahue, Paul V. .... Pittsfield, MA
Donahue, Peter A. .... Chicago, IL
Donahue, Peter J. .... Dayton, OH
Donahue, Pierre M. .... Washington, DC
Donahue, Richard K. .... Lowell, MA
Donahue, Richard K., Jr. .... Lowell, MA
Donahue, Richard M. .... Covington, LA
Donahue, Riker J. .... Stamford, CT
Donahue & Riley .... La Plata, MD
Donahue, Robert A. .... Vero Beach, FL
Donahue, Robert J. .... Hyannis, MA
Donahue, Robert J. .... Norwood, MA
Donahue, Robert J. .... Yarmouth Port, MA
Donahue, Robert M. .... Birmingham, MI
Donahue, Robert M. .... Staten Island, NY
Donahue, Roger J. .... Boston, MA
Donahue, Roger J., Jr. .... Boston, MA
Donahue, Sally M. .... Uniondale, NY
Donahue, Sean .... Portland, OR
Donahue, Sean H. .... Department of Justice, Environment and Natural Resources Division, GV
Donahue & Seidman, LLC .... Waldorf, MD
Donahue, Shannon L. .... Albuquerque, NM
Donahue, Sharon M. .... Washington, DC
Donahue, Shawn L. .... McHenry, IL
Donahue, Shawn R. .... Providence, RI
Donahue, Sheila M. .... Portland, ME
Donahue, Sowa & Bugos .... Geneva, IL; Lisle, IL
Donahue, Stephanie F. .... Washington, DC; Annapolis, MD; Baltimore, MD
Donahue, Stephen F. .... Southport, CT
Donahue, Stephen J. .... Springfield, NJ
Donahue, Susan F. .... Boston, MA; Providence, RI
Donahue, Terrence J. .... Tacoma, WA
Donahue, Theodore A., Jr. .... Hartford, CT
Donahue, Theodore R. .... Miami Shores, FL
Donahue, Thomas E. .... Los Angeles, CA
Donahue, Thomas F. .... Carlsbad, CA
Donahue, Thomas J., Jr. .... Worcester, MA
Donahue, Thomas M. .... Des Moines, IA
Donahue, Thomas M., Jr. .... Seattle, WA
Donahue, Thomas P. .... Dallas, TX
Donahue, Timothy B. .... New York, NY
Donahue, Timothy J. .... Santa Ana, CA
Donahue, Timothy P. .... Birmingham, AL
Donahue, Timothy W. .... Wallingford, CT
Donahue, Tucker & Ciandella .... Dover, NH; Exeter, NH; Portsmouth, NH
Donahue, Vicki S. .... Pittsfield, MA
Donahue, Votto & DeGennaro, P.C. Clinton, CT; West Haven, CT
Donahue & Warenda .... Lakewood, NJ; Morrisville, PA
Donahue, William C. .... Columbus, OH
Donahue, William F. .... Worcester, MA
Donahue, William H., Jr. .... Westmont, NJ
Donahue, William J. White River Junction, VT
Donahue, William T. .... Danville, IL
Donahue, Wood, Loving, Myers & Vogel Fairfield, CA
Donahue, Wood, Loving & Vogel Sacramento, CA; Stockton, CA
Donais, Craig S. .... Chelmsford, MA
Donais, William L. .... Auburn, WA
Donald, Andrew L. .... Livingston, NJ
Donald, Bernice B. .... Memphis, TN
Donald, Brenda Stone .... Irondale, AL
Donald, Dan L., Jr. .... Jennings, LA
Donald, Henry F. .... Woodbury, NY
Donald, J. Scott .... Sacramento, CA
Donald, J. Wylie .... Newark, NJ
Donald, James P. .... Morton, MS
Donald, John R. .... Palo Alto, CA
Donald, John W., Jr. .... Mobile, AL
Donald, Karen L. .... Los Angeles, CA
Donald, Laura A. .... Menlo Park, CA
Donald L. Mackie & Associates, Inc. Canton, CT
Donald, M. Randall .... Monroe, LA
Donald, Marcie L. .... Pasadena, CA
Donald, Mark A. .... Denver, CO
Donald, Michael B. .... Shreveport, LA
Donald, Milton L. .... Madison, WI
Donald, Norman H., III .... New York, NY
Donald, Randall, Donald & Tipton Demopolis, AL; Fayette, AL; Tuscaloosa, AL
Donald, Robert A., III .... Louisville, KY
Donald, Robert L. .... Fort Myers, FL
Donald, William J. .... Tuscaloosa, AL
Donald, William J., III .... Tuscaloosa, AL
Donald, Williamson P. .... Wilmington, DE
Donaldes, Leslie G., (A Professional Corporation) .... Beverly Hills, CA
Donaldson, Alan P. .... New Canaan, CT
Donaldson, Alan S. .... Bellevue, WA
Donaldson, Amy L. .... Dallas, TX
Donaldson, Andreoli & Truitt .... Lebanon, IN
Donaldson, Andreoli and Truitt Zionsville, IN
Donaldson, Arthur J. .... Greensboro, NC
Donaldson Associates, P.C. Traverse City, MI
Donaldson, Bell & Pickett, P.C. Albany, GA
Donaldson & Black, P.A. .... Greensboro, NC
Donaldson, Bruce D. .... Indianapolis, IN
Donaldson, Bryan D. .... Jonesboro, AR
Donaldson, Carol Stephens .... Polson, MT
Donaldson, Caroline Wight Washington, DC
Donaldson, Clyde E. .... Elizabethtown, PA
Donaldson, Craig J. .... Morristown, NJ
Donaldson, Craig O. .... Chicago, IL
Donaldson, David H., Jr. .... Austin, TX
Donaldson, David M. .... Philadelphia, PA
Donaldson, David R. .... Birmingham, AL
Donaldson, Diana S. .... Philadelphia, PA
Donaldson, D. L. .... Longview, WA
Donaldson & Donaldson, P.C. Savannah, GA
Donaldson, Dorothea E. .... Winter Park, FL
Donaldson, Dorothy L. .... Raleigh, NC
Donaldson, Douglas C. .... Albany, CA
Donaldson, Douglas J. .... Traverse City, MI
Donaldson, Dwight .... Houston, TX
Donaldson, Earl R. .... Oklahoma City, OK
Donaldson, Frank W. .... Birmingham, AL
Donaldson, Gail .... Emeryville, CA
Donaldson, Gene S. .... Richmond, CA
Donaldson, Geo. R., Jr. .... Baltimore, MD
Donaldson, George, Law Offices of San Francisco, CA
Donaldson, George P., III .... Albany, GA
Donaldson, Grady W., Jr. .... Lynchburg, VA
Donaldson, Gretchen G. .... Pittsburgh, PA
Donaldson, Guin & Slate, LLC Birmingham, AL
Donaldson, Harry W. .... Pittsburgh, PA
Donaldson, J. Bruce .... Traverse City, MI
Donaldson, Jack B. .... Memphis, TN
Donaldson, James F. .... Denver, CO
Donaldson, Jeff .... Jasper, AL
Donaldson, Jeffrey C. .... Savannah, GA
Donaldson, Jeffrey L. .... Worcester, MA
Donaldson, Jennifer A. .... Washington, DC
Donaldson, Jerry B. .... Austin, TX
Donaldson, John B. .... Somers, NY
Donaldson, John D. .... Mansfield, OH
Donaldson, John E., Jr. .... Falls Church, VA
Donaldson, John I. .... Yazoo City, MS
Donaldson, John M. .... Mount Clemens, MI
Donaldson, John P. .... Atlanta, GA
Donaldson, John W. .... Lebanon, IN
Donaldson, K. John Department of Transportation, National Highway Traffic Safety Administration, GV
Donaldson, Kathleen A. Department of Agriculture, Farm Service Agency, GV
Donaldson, Kiel & McKenzie, P.S. Seattle, WA
Donaldson & Knigge .... Seattle, WA
Donaldson, Larry A. .... Fresno, CA
Donaldson, Laura Beth .... St. Joseph, MO
Donaldson, Lawrence R. .... Detroit, MI
Donaldson, L. Clark .... Salt Lake City, UT
Donaldson, LeAnn Bradley .... Edmond, OK
Donaldson, Linda F. .... Washington, DC
Donaldson, Lisa .... Seattle, WA
Donaldson, Lorraine M. .... Del Mar, CA
Donaldson, Lynn .... Claremont, CA
Donaldson, Lynn Clark Salt Lake City, UT
Donaldson, M. Andrew .... Montgomery, AL
Donaldson, Marc H., Jr. .... Crown Point, IN
Donaldson, Mark A. .... Edmond, OK
Donaldson, Mark S. .... Harrisburg, PA
Donaldson, Matthew S., Jr. .... Media, PA
Donaldson, Michael C. .... Beverly Hills, CA
Donaldson, Michael L. .... Livonia, MI
Donaldson, Michael P. .... Houston, TX
Donaldson, Michael Patrick Tallahassee, FL
Donaldson, Michael W. .... Columbus, OH
Donaldson, Monica H., P.C. .... Mesa, AZ
Donaldson, Monica Hope .... Mesa, AZ
Donaldson, Monte S. .... Houston, TX
Donaldson, Paige .... Chicago, IL
Donaldson, Patricia F. .... Bloomfield Hills, MI
Donaldson, Paul A. .... Rutland, VT
Donaldson, R. Kelly, & Associates Beaumont, TX
Donaldson, Ray S. .... Tierra Verde, FL
Donaldson, R. B., Jr. .... Savannah, GA
Donaldson, Rebecca .... Colton, CA
Donaldson, Richard B., Jr. Newport News, VA
Donaldson, Richard C. .... McLean, VA
Donaldson, Richard E. .... Las Vegas, NV
Donaldson, Richard E., Chtd. Las Vegas, NV
Donaldson, Richard L. .... Dallas, TX
Donaldson, Richard M. .... Cherry Hill, NJ; Philadelphia, PA
Donaldson, Richard P. .... Seattle, WA
Donaldson, Robert D. .... Los Angeles, CA
Donaldson, Robert M. .... Lake Forest, CA
Donaldson, Robert W. .... Detroit, MI
Donaldson, Robert W. .... Portland, OR
Donaldson, Russell G. .... Rochester, NY
Donaldson, Samuel A. .... Bellevue, WA
Donaldson - Schwebs .... Claremont, CA; Ontario, CA; Pasadena, CA; Pomona, CA; San Bernardino, CA; Santa Ana, CA
Donaldson, Scott M. .... Seattle, WA
Donaldson, Stacey J. .... Houston, TX
Donaldson, Susan C. .... Chattanooga, TN
Donaldson, Susan Marie .... Chestnut Hill, MA
Donaldson, Thomas F., Jr. .... Memphis, TN
Donaldson, Thomas J. .... Carson City, NV
Donaldson, Timothy J. .... Walla Walla, WA
Donaldson, W. Scott .... Tuscaloosa, AL
Donaldson, W. Scott .... Phoenix, AZ
Donaldson, Warren A. .... Lake Ozark, MO
Donaldson, William A. .... Mobile, AL
Donaldson, William E. .... Beverly, MA
Donaldson-Adams, Phyllis .... Ann Arbor, MI
Donaldson-Swift, Julie .... Washington, DC
Donalson, George E., III .... Houston, TX
Donalty, Barry M. .... Utica, NY
Donan, Patrick M. .... Philadelphia, PA
Donan, Thomas A. .... Bardstown, KY
Donan & Vick .... Greenville, KY
Donan, William D. .... Madisonville, KY
Donarski, Michelle M. .... Moorhead, MN; Fargo, ND
Donarski, William J. .... Elkhorn, WI
Donart, James G. .... Fallbrook, CA
Donat, Anthony F. .... Batavia, IL
Donat & Donat .... Batavia, IL
Donat, Greg S. .... New York, NY
Donat, Gregory J. .... Lafayette, IN
Donat, Joseph E. .... New York, NY
Donat, Marshall J. .... White Plains, NY
Donat, Peter M. .... Batavia, IL
Donat, Walter J. .... Batavia, IL
Donatelle, Michael J. .... Boston, MA
Donatelle, Sharon E. .... Brockton, MA
Donatelli, Alan .... Buffalo, NY
Donatelli & Coules, Ltd. .... Hinsdale, IL
Donatelli, Dean J. .... Florham Park, NJ
Donatelli, Frank J. .... Washington, DC
Donatelli, Guy A. .... West Chester, PA
Donatelli, Jos. N. .... Clifton, NJ
Donatelli, Lori Novak .... West Chester, PA
Donatelli, Mark H. .... Santa Fe, NM
Donatelli, Mark R. .... Hinsdale, IL
Donatelli, Mike M. .... New York, NY
Donatelli, Randolph H. .... New York, NY
Donatelli, Robert A. .... Syosset, NY
Donatelli, Robert E. .... Allentown, PA
Donatelli, Robert E. .... Easton, PA
Donatelli, William F. .... Bradenton, FL
Donath, Glen .... Washington, DC
Donath, Nicole B. .... Washington, DC
Donath, Patricia L. Bates .... Holt, MI
Donathen, James D. .... Buffalo, NY
Donati and Associates, P.C. .... Memphis, TN
Donati, Donald A. .... Memphis, TN
Donati, Donna J. .... Detroit, MI
Donati, Gianni .... Princeton, NJ
Donati, Peter F. .... Chicago, IL
Donati, Victoria L. .... Chicago, IL
Donatiello, Guy T. .... Philadelphia, PA

Donato, Anthony J. ... Brighton, MA
Donato, Arthur T., Jr. ... Media, PA
Donato, Brian J. ... Irvine, CA
Donato, Cecelia A. ... Newark, NJ
Donato, Charles J. ... New Haven, CT
Donato, Christopher R. ... Dedham, MA
Donato, Elaine ... New York, NY
Donato & Fairbairn ... Charleston, SC
Donato, Frank M. ... Paterson, NJ
Donato, James ... San Francisco, CA
Donato, Jodi Ann ... Holtsville, NY
Donato, Jodi Ann, P.C. ... Holtsville, NY
Donato, Mario J., Jr. ... Fort Worth, TX
Donato, Michele R. ... Lavallette, NJ
Donato, Michele R., P.A. ... Lavallette, NJ
Donato, Minx & Brown, PLLC
Houston, TX
Donato, Paula M. ... Chicago, IL
Donato, Randy ... Houston, TX
Donato, Richard T. ... Hollywood, FL
Donato, Richard W. ... Yuma, AZ
Donato, Robert R. ... Charleston, SC
Donato, Robin A. ... Morristown, NJ
Donato, Stephen A. ... Syracuse, NY
Donato, Trini L. ... West Palm Beach, FL
Donatoni, Robert J. ... West Chester, PA
Donatoni, Robert J., & Associates, P.C.
West Chester, PA
Donatucci, Joseph N. ... Philadelphia, PA
Donatucci, Robert J. ... New York, NY
Donatucci, Ronald R. ... Philadelphia, PA
Donaty, Marc R. ... Baltimore, MD
Donau, Alfred S., III ... Tucson, AZ
Donau & Bolt ... Tucson, AZ
Donaubauer, Michael W. ... Chicago, IL
Donavan, Mary Sue ... Washington, DC
Donavon, Michelle L. ... Troy, IL
Donawick, Peter M.
Department Of Veterans Affairs, Office of the General Counsel, GV
DonCarlos, Stephen H. ... Baytown, TX
Don Carlos, Waldo E. ... Sun City West, AZ
Don Carlos, William W. ... Sun City, AZ
Sun City West, AZ
Doncaster, Steve ... Tempe, AZ
Donch, Sarah A. ... Dallas, TX
Donchess, James M. ... Youngstown, OH
Donchess, James W. ... Nashua, NH
Donchess, Joseph S. ... Youngstown, OH
Donchess & Notinger, P.C. ... Nashua, NH
Donchin, David B. ... Oklahoma City, OK
Dondanville, Jeffrey W. ... Irvine, CA
Dondanville, John W. ... Chicago, IL
Dondanville, Joyce R. ... La Jolla, CA
Dondanville, Patricia ... Chicago, IL
Dondero, Doreen L. ... Parsippany, NJ
Dondero, John ... Silver Spring, MD
Dondero, Valerie A. ... Miami, FL
Dondershine, Scott Allan ... Vienna, VA
Dondis, Harold B. ... Boston, MA
Dondis, Lynn ... Portland, ME
Dondrea, John A. ... Dallas, TX
Dondzila, Bruce E. ... Wintersville, OH
Doneff, Andrea ... Atlanta, GA
Donegan, A.J., Jr. ... Brockton, MA
Donegan, Charles E. ... Washington, DC
Donegan, Chas. H., Jr. (P.C.) ... Seguin, TX
Donegan, Evelyn A. ... Newark, NJ
Donegan, George J. ... Springfield, MO
Donegan, Harold C. ... New Haven, CT
Donegan, James G. ... Chicago, IL
Donegan, James Michael ... Summit, NJ
Donegan, James S., Sr. ... Fresno, CA
Donegan, James W. ... Ann Arbor, MI
Donegan, Jayne M. ... Providence, RI
Donegan, John C. ... Los Angeles, CA
Donegan, John E. ... Branford, CT
Donegan, John H. ... Honolulu, HI
Donegan, John M. ... Palo Alto, CA
Donegan, John O. ... Jamesville, NY
Donegan, Joseph M. ... Bedminster, NJ
Donegan, Judy J. ... Plymouth, MI
Donegan, Michael P. ... Hartford, CT
Donegan, Michael P. ... Providence, RI
Donegan, Patrick J., Jr. ... New York, NY
Donegan, Patrick M. ... Alexandria Bay, NY
Donegan, Susan L. ... Provincetown, MA
Donegan, Thomas M., Jr. ... Atlanta, GA
Donegan, Thomas P. ... Milwaukee, WI
Doneghey, Allison B. ... Sarasota, FL
Doneghy, Charles J. ... Toledo, OH
Doneghy, Joseph E.
Department Of Health And Human Services, Social Security Administration, GV
Donehoo, Dean B. ... Chatsworth, GA
Donehower, James ... Detroit Lakes, MN
Donehue, David C. ... Pittsburgh, PA
Doneker, Beverly J. ... Allentown, PA
Donelan, Charles ... Boston, MA
Donelan, Clare R.
Department of Transportation, Federal Aviation Administration, GV
Donelan, Cleary, Wood & Maser, P.C.
Washington, DC
Donelan, Edward D., Jr. ... New York, NY
Donelan, James M. ... Warwick, RI
Donelan, John F. ... Washington, DC
Donelan, John T. ... Alexandria, VA
Donelan, Stephen M. ... Tallahassee, FL
Donelan, William P., Jr. ... Columbia, SC
Donell, Donald R. ... Weirton, WV
Donellan, Betty ... Newport Beach, CA
Donelli, Kathleen ... White Plains, NY
Donelon, Brendan J. ... Kansas City, MO
Donelon, James J. ... Metairie, LA
Donelon, Thomas G. ... Metairie, LA
Donelson, J. Morgan ... Princeton, MO
Donelson, James H., (P.C.) ... Des Moines, IA
Donelson, Jeffrey Howard
Highlands Ranch, CO
Donelson, Kenneth W. ... Sacramento, CA
Donelson, Kevin R. ... Oklahoma City, OK
Donelson, Larry D. ... Kansas City, MO
Donelson, Lewis R., III ... Washington, DC
Chattanooga, TN
Huntsville, TN
Knoxville, TN
Memphis, TN
Nashville, TN
Donelson, Linda L. ... Tahlequah, OK
Donelson, Martin, III ... Danville, VA
Donelson, Sheldon ... Round Rock, TX
Donelson, Stephen W. ... Denver, CO
Donelson, Thomas P. ... Burke, VA
Donelson, Vivian Ray ... Memphis, TN
Donen, Steven R. ... Cromwell, CT
Donenberg, Barbara A. ... Chicago, IL
Donenfeld, Alice G. ... Los Angeles, CA
Donenfeld, Glenn L. ... Fort Lauderdale, FL
Donenfeld, J. Douglas ... Chicago, IL
Donenfeld, Jack A. ... Chicago, IL
Cincinnati, OH
Donenfeld, Jack A., A Legal Prof. Assn., Law Offices of ... Cincinnati, OH
Doner, Adam S. ... West Palm Beach, FL
Doner & Castro ... Berlin, NJ
Doner, Ezra J. ... New York, NY
Doner, Gary W. ... Perrysburg, OH
Doner, Henry L. ... Berlin, NJ
Doner, Joel M. ... Berlin, NJ
Doner, Karen A. ... Washington, DC
Doner, Paul N. ... Bay City, MI
Donerly, Brian J. ... Tampa, FL
Dones, Susan ... Southfield, MI
Donesa, Christopher A.
House of Representatives, Congressional Assistants, GV
Doneski, David J. ... Boston, MA
Donesky, R. Douglas ... Ontario, CA
Donesley, Brian N. ... Boise, ID
Donet, David A. ... Miami, FL
Donet, Dennis A. ... Miami, FL
Doneth, Dan ... Okemos, MI
Donewald, Kent J. ... Northbrook, IL
Doney, Crowley, Bloomquist & Uda, P.C.
Helena, MT
Doney, David M. ... Tampa, FL
Doney, Edward ... Tempe, AZ
Doney, Eric W. ... Mill Valley, CA
Oakland, CA
Doney, Jack C. ... Severna Park, MD
Doney, John C. ... Phoenix, AZ
Doney, Timothy J. ... Columbus, OH
Doney, William P. ... West Palm Beach, FL
Donfeld, Jeffrey E., (A Professional Corporation) ... Los Angeles, CA
Donfeld, Kelley & Rollman
Los Angeles, CA
Donfeld, Robert B. ... Tucson, AZ
D'Onfro, Paul J. ... Worcester, MA
Dong, B. Randall ... Columbia, SC
Dong, Daniel Louis ... Ontario, CA
Dong, David ... Flushing, NY
Dong, Deborah B. ... Boston, MA
Dong, Donald D. ... Oakland, CA
Dong, Edward K.H. ... Department of State, Foreign Service Officers (Overseas), GV
Dong, Jing ... Atlanta, GA
Dong, Nelson G. ... Minneapolis, MN
Dongell, Richard A. ... Los Angeles, CA
Dongoske, Scott J. ... Minneapolis, MN
St. Paul, MN
Dongvillo, Henry J. ... Scottville, MI
Donham, Cary E. ... Chicago, IL
Donham, John C. ... Overland Park, KS
Donhauser, Linda V. ... Baltimore, MD
Donheiser, Mark M. ... Dallas, TX
Donica, Herbert R. ... Tampa, FL
Donica, Herbert R., P.A. ... Tampa, FL
Donica, Janice Norman ... Tampa, FL
Donica, Kimberly Ann ... Miami, FL
Donica, Marion Sidney ... Woodbridge, NJ
Donich, Alfred J., Jr. ... Deer Lodge, MT
Donig, Reuben J. ... Redwood City, CA
Doniger, Alan F. ... New York, NY
Doniger, Anthony M. ... Boston, MA
Doniger, David D. ... Washington, DC
Doniger & Engstrand ... New York, NY
Doniger & Fetter ... Los Angeles, CA
Doniger, Jeffrey David ... Denver, CO
Doniger, Stephen M. ... Marina Del Rey, CA
Doniger, Thomas ... Los Angeles, CA
Doniger, Wende A. ... New York, NY
Donilon, Thomas E. ... Washington, DC
Donin, Dean M. ... Los Angeles, CA
Donin, Jeffrey S. ... New York, NY
Donin, Rena G. ... New York, NY
Donin, Robert B. ... Cambridge, MA
Donine, Barbara ... West Covina, CA
Donine & Donine ... West Covina, CA
Donine, Marvin D. ... West Covina, CA
Doninger, Chris ... Summit, NJ
Doninger, Clarence H. ... Indianapolis, IN
Doninger, John A. ... Orlando, FL
Donington, John Scott ... Clinton, NJ
Donini, Edward S. ... New Smyrna Beach, FL
Donini, Michael L. ... Wall Township, NJ
Donio, Ann Marie ... Hammonton, NJ
Donio, Bertman & Donio ... Hammonton, NJ
Donio, Samuel A. ... Hammonton, NJ
Donio, William S. ... Hammonton, NJ
Donis, Lisa B. ... Department of Justice, Civil Division, GV
Donisi, John Philip ... Austin, TX
Donisi, Philip A. ... Houston, TX
Donisthorpe, Oscar L. ... Bloomfield, NM
Donius, Kathleen S. ... Milwaukee, WI
Donjacour, Micheline M. ... Santa Monica, CA
Donk, Terry K. ... Odessa, TX
Donkel, Kenneth J. ... Olympia Fields, IL
Donker, Norman W. ... Midland, MI
Donkersley, Jason A. ... Phoenix, AZ
Donkersloot, James A. ... Zeeland, MI
Donlan, Dan J. ... Seattle, WA
Donlan, James F. ... Los Angeles, CA
Donlan, John F. ... Park Ridge, IL
Donlan, John M. ... New York, NY
Donlan, Martin A., Jr. ... Richmond, VA
Donlan, Michael F. ... Boston, MA
Donlan, Michael J. ... Kennebunk, ME
Donlan, Robert R. ... Luray, VA
Donleavy, Pamela L. ... Philadelphia, PA
Donlevie, John C. ... Malvern, PA
Donlevy, John D. ... Chicago, IL
Donlevy, Mary P. ... Newport Beach, CA
Donlevy-Rosen, Patricia ... Miami, FL
Donlevy-Rosen & Rosen, Professional Association ... Coral Gables, FL
Fort Lauderdale, FL
Miami, FL
Palm Beach, FL
Donley, Billy M. ... Houston, TX
Donley, Charles F., II ... Washington, DC
Donley, Craig A. ... Montgomery, AL
Donley, David Arthur "Dave"
Anchorage, AK
Donley, Dennis W., Jr. ... Austin, TX
Donley, Donald E. ... Homewood, IL
Donley, Elizabeth L.R. ... Madison, WI
Donley, Garrett C. ... Troy, MI
Donley, Jack E. ... Colorado Springs, CO
Donley, James A. ... Kansas City, MO
Donley, Jerry A. ... Colorado Springs, CO
Donley, John ... Chicago, IL
Donley, John P., II ... Greeley, CO
Donley, John W. ... Weatherford, OK
Donley, Joseph F. ... New York, NY
Donley, Joseph M. ... Philadelphia, PA
Donley, Latricia C. ... Hialeah, FL
Donley, Mark W. ... Wichita, KS
Donley and Murphy ... Elk Point, SD
Donley, Orlan L. ... San Luis Obispo, CA
Donley, Owen J. ... United States Senate, Senatorial Assistants, GV
Donley, P. Kelly ... Wichita, KS
Donley, Ray N. ... Austin, TX
Donley, Roger S. ... Houston, TX
Donley, Sarah ... Kansas City, MO
Donley-Hoopes, Maureen A.
Washington, DC
Donlin, Charles L. ... Bismarck, ND
Donlin, David L. ... Minneapolis, MN
Donlin, J. Gregory ... Baltimore, MD
Donlin, John F. J. ... Baltimore, MD
Donlin, Patrick J., Sr. ... Warren, OH
Donlin, Paul G. ... St. Paul, MN
Donlin, R. David ... Balsam, NC
Donlon, Anne M. ... Scarborough, ME
Donlon, Donna M. ... Washington, DC
Donlon, Edward ... Garden City, NY
Donlon, Elizabeth Pollina
Garden City, NY
Donlon, James F. ... Staten Island, NY
Donlon, Jane P. ... New York, NY
Donlon, John J. ... Jacksonville, FL
Donlon, Kimberly A. ... Los Angeles, CA
Donlon, Robert M.
Palm Beach Gardens, FL
Donlon, Robert M. ... Charlotte, NC
Donlon, Rosalie L. ... Bridgeport, CT
Donlon, Roy A. ... Boston, MA
Donlon, Thomas J. ... New York, NY
Donlon, William J. ... Bokeelia, FL
Donlon, William J., Jr. ... Denver, CO
Donn, Allan G. ... Norfolk, VA
Donn, Ronald P. ... Norfolk, VA
Donna, David A. ... Minneapolis, MN
Donna, John C. ... Pittsfield, MA
Donna, John C., Law Firm of ... Pittsfield, MA
Donna, Robert W. ... Pittsfield, MA
Donnahoe, Alan S. ... Richmond, VA
Donnahoe, George D. ... West Union, WV
Donnahoe, Prince A., IV ... Plantation, FL
Donnally, Robert A. ... Palo Alto, CA
Donnan, John M. ... Pleasanton, CA
Donnan, Morton, Davis & Snyder, P.A.
Greenville, SC
Donnan, Phillip D. ... Greenville, SC
Donnan, Susan L. ... Baton Rouge, LA
Donnantuoni, Peter M. ... St. Petersburg, FL
Donnard, Brian ... New York, NY
Donnaruma, Walter ... Albany, NY
Donnarumma, Francis M. ... New Haven, CT
Donnay, Michelle ... New York, NY
Donnell, Ben A. ... Corpus Christi, TX
Houston, TX
Donnell, Bradley K. ... Oklahoma City, OK
Donnell, Brian J. ... Hartford, CT
Donnell, Cathlin ... Denver, CO
Donnell, Comer L. ... Lebanon, TN
Donnell, Douglas A. ... Grand Rapids, MI
Donnell, Gregory L. ... Angleton, TX
Donnell, Jack L. ... Greensboro, NC
Donnell, James ... Houston, TX
Donnell, James C. ... The Dalles, OR
Donnell, Jeffrey A. ... Laramie, WY
Donnell, Kerry M. ... Alpine, CA
Donnell, Milton L., Jr. ... Metairie, LA
Ponchatoula, LA
Donnell, Richard H. ... Jackson, TN
Donnell, Thomas M., Jr. ... Nashville, TN
Donnell, William S. ... San Diego, CA
Donnell, William T. ... Louisville, KY
Donnella, Amy Gershenfeld ... St. Davids, PA
Donnella, Michael Andre ... Basking Ridge, NJ
Donnellan, Alfred E. ... White Plains, NY
Donnellan, Andrew B., Jr. ... New York, NY
Donnellan, Christopher P. ... New York, NY
Donnellan, Deanne Zindell ... San Rafael, CA
Donnellan, Deidre A. ... Joliet, IL
Donnellan, Edward J. ... Chicago, IL
Donnellan, Edward L. ... Springfield, MA
Donnellan, Gerard J. ... San Francisco, CA
Donnellan, J. James, III ... Miami, FL
Donnellan, Joan C. ... Los Angeles, CA
Donnellan, Jonathan R. ... New York, NY
Donnellan, Michael T. ... Department of Justice, Environment and Natural Resources Division, GV
Donnellan, Nancy K. ... Bradenton, FL
Donnellan, Philip J. ... Kansas City, MO
Donnellan, Rebecca A. ... Washington, DC
Donnellan, Robert I. ... Kansas City, MO
Donnellan, Robert J. ... Dearborn, MI
Donnellan, Teresa G. ... Saratoga Springs, NY
Donnellan, Thomas M. ... Flint, MI
Donnellan, Thomas P. ... Derby, VT
Donnelley, Elise Montgomery
Anchorage, AK
Donnelley, Katharine S. ... Helena, MT
Donnelley, Lisa H. ... Anchorage, AK
Donnelley, Robert G. ... Chicago, IL
Donnelli, Jennifer A. ... Kansas City, MO
Donnellon, Daniel J. ... Cincinnati, OH
Donnellon, Donnellon and Miller, A Legal Professional Association ... Cincinnati, OH
Donnellon, Edward J. ... Cincinnati, OH
Donnellon, Terrence M. ... Cincinnati, OH
Donnellon, Thomas E. ... Cincinnati, OH
Donnelly, Andrew P. ... Stamford, CT
Donnelly, Arthur E., III ... Cherry Hill, NJ
Donnelly & Associates ... Dallas, TX
Donnelly, Baldwin and Wilhite, P.C.
Lebanon, MO
Donnelly, Barbara H. ... Paw Paw, MI
Donnelly, Basil S. ... Philadelphia, PA
Donnelly, Brian J. ... New York, NY
Donnelly, Brian M. ... Wantagh, NY
Donnelly, Brian Philip ... San Francisco, CA
Donnelly, Brian R. ... Pompton Plains, NJ
Donnelly, Brian V. ... Palo Alto, CA
Donnelly, Celia Moffie ... West Hartford, CT
Donnelly, Charles F. ... Scottsdale, AZ
Donnelly, Charles P.
National Labor Relations Board, Office of the General Counsel, GV
Donnelly, Christine Walsh ... Chicago, IL
Rockford, IL
Donnelly, Christopher J.
San Francisco, CA
Donnelly, Christopher J. ... New York, NY
Donnelly, Clark, Chase & Smiland
Los Angeles, CA
Donnelly, Conroy & Gelhaar, LLP
Boston, MA
Donnelly, Daniel ... Garrison, NY
Donnelly, Daniel ... New York, NY
Donnelly, Daniel J. ... Chicago, IL
Donnelly, Daniel J. ... Chicago, IL
Donnelly, Daniel Thomas ... Hemet, CA
Donnelly, Darren ... Palo Alto, CA
Donnelly, David ... Lebanon, MO
Donnelly, David C. ... West St. Paul, MN
Donnelly, David P. ... Eatontown, NJ
Donnelly, David T. ... Boston, MA
Donnelly, David T. ... Bethel Park, PA
Donnelly, Deirdre ... Department of Justice, Tax Division, GV
Donnelly, Dennis C. ... St. Louis, MO
Donnelly, Dennis M. ... Chatham, NJ
Donnelly, Dennis M. ... Troy, OH
Donnelly, Diane ... New York, NY
Donnelly & DiRusso ... Mount Airy, NC
Donnelly, Donal B. ... El Centro, CA
Donnelly, Dorothy J. ... Trenton, NJ
Donnelly, Douglas R. ... Santa Barbara, CA
Donnelly, E. Gerald, Jr. ... Philadelphia, PA
Donnelly, Edward C.
Port Jefferson Station, NY
Donnelly, Edward F., Jr. ... Cambridge, MA
Donnelly, Edward W ... Nyack, NY
Donnelly, Eleanore B. ... Houston, TX
Donnelly, F. James ... Denver, CO
Donnelly, Francis J. ... Shawnee, KS
Donnelly, Francis J., P.A. ... Shawnee, KS
Donnelly, Francis X. ... Cherry Hill, NJ
Donnelly, Frank P. ... Mitchellville, MD
Donnelly, George ... Wheaton, IL
Donnelly, Gerard T. ... Worcester, MA
Donnelly, Gina-Maria ... Belleville, MI
Donnelly & Gross, P.A. ... Gainesville, FL
Donnelly, Gus L. ... Mount Airy, NC
Donnelly, Hugh J. ... New York, NY
Donnelly, J. Brian ... Norfolk, VA
Donnelly, J. Brian ... Virginia Beach, VA
Donnelly, J. Kirk ... Irvine, CA
Donnelly, James ... Sycamore, IL
Donnelly, James A. ... Jamestown, RI
Donnelly, James A., Jr. ... Fall River, MA
Donnelly, James C., Jr. ... Worcester, MA
Donnelly, James D. ... Cherry Hill, NJ
Donnelly, James F. ... Holyoke, MA
Donnelly, James L. ... Chicago, IL
Donnelly, James P. ... Clarence, NY
Donnelly, James S. ... San Francisco, CA
Donnelly, James T. ... Glens Falls, NY
Donnelly, James W. ... Sea Girt, NJ
Donnelly, Jean K. ... Boston, MA
Donnelly, Jean M. ... Costa Mesa, CA
Donnelly, Jerry L. ... Lawrence, KS
Donnelly, Joan Hockert ... Sarasota, FL
Donnelly, Joan M. ... Freehold, NJ

Donohue, Thomas J. ....Long Grove, IL
Donohue, Thomas J. ....Hudson, NY
Donohue, Thomas J., Jr. ....Hartford, CT
Simsbury, CT
Donohue, Thomas J., Jr. ....Pittsfield, MA
Donohue, Thomas P. ....Warren, MI
Donohue, Thomas P. ....Monroe, WI
Donohue, Thomas W. ....Scottsdale, AZ
Donohue, Timothy M. ....Chatham, NJ
Donohue & Van Scoy, P.C. ......Rockville, MD
Donohue, Vincent T. ....West Chester, PA
Donohue, William J. ....Girdwood, AK
Donohue, William J. ....Philadelphia, PA
Donohue, William J., P.C. ....Girdwood, AK
Donohue-Babiak, Amy L.
Philadelphia, PA
Donoian, James H. ....New York, NY
Donoughue, Timothy M. ....Houston, TX
Donovan, Aileen W. ....Red Bank, NJ
Donovan, Amy Huestis ....Dedham, MA
Donovan, Andrew H. ....New York, NY
Donovan, Andrew P. ....Rochester, NY
Donovan, Ann C. ....Fayetteville, AR
Donovan, Ann M. ....Newton, MA
Donovan, Arrie Jan ....El Paso, TX
Donovan, Arthur R. ....Evansville, IN
Donovan, Arthur S. ....Hartford, CT
Donovan, Audrey M. ....Boston, MA
Donovan, Brendan ....Riverside, IL
Donovan, Brian C. ....Aurora, CO
Donovan, Brian E. ....Englewood, CO
Donovan, Brian F. ....Fitchburg, MA
Donovan, Brian J. ....Newport Beach, CA
Donovan, Brian K. ....Brooklyn, NY
Donovan, Brian L. ....Ada, MI
Donovan, Brian P. ....Stamford, CT
Donovan & Broderick, P.C.
Silver Spring, MD
Donovan, C. Richard ....Pueblo, CO
Donovan, C. Steven ....Newark, NJ
New York, NY
Donovan, Carey A. ....Elmwood Park, NJ
Donovan, Carol A. ....Boston, MA
Donovan, Carol Crabtree ....Dallas, TX
Donovan, Caroline ....Goldens Bridge, NY
Donovan, Catherine M. ....New York, NY
Donovan, Charles J., Sr. ....Austin, TX
Donovan, Charles S. ....San Francisco, CA
Donovan, Christina C. ....Detroit, MI
Donovan, Christine Lynn ....Irvine, CA
Donovan, Christopher J. ....Boston, MA
Donovan, Christopher R.
Department of Justice,
Federal Bureau of Investigation, GV
Donovan, Colleen R. ....Morristown, NJ
New York, NY
Donovan, Constance A. ....Rockville, MD
Donovan, D. Brendan ....Atlanta, GA
Donovan, Daniel J. ....Baltimore, MD
Donovan, Daniel J. ....Yonkers, NY
Donovan, Daniel M., Jr. ....New York, NY
Donovan, Daniel P. .....Point Reyes Station, CA
Donovan, Daniel P. ....Dallas, TX
Donovan, Daniel R. ....Bath, ME
Donovan, Daniel T. ....Washington, DC
Donovan, Daniel V. ....Great Falls, MT
Donovan, Darin H. ....Palo Alto, CA
Donovan, David A. ....Goshen, NY
Donovan, David D. ....Peabody, MA
Donovan, David M. ....Little Rock, AR
Donovan, David P. ....Washington, DC
Donovan, Deborah Curtis ....Portland, ME
Donovan, Deborah Swindells
Richmond, VA
Donovan, Denis M. ....Sacramento, CA
Donovan, Dennis F. ....Fallbrook, CA
Donovan, Donald Francis ....New York, NY
Donovan, Donald R. ....Douglasville, GA
Donovan & Donovan, P.C. ....Hicksville, NY
Donovan & Draheim, A Professional
Corporation ....Fullerton, CA
Riverside, CA
Donovan, Dwight C. ....San Francisco, CA
Donovan & Eastham ....Capistrano Beach, CA
Donovan, Edmund T. ....New York, NY
Donovan, Edward C. ....Washington, DC
Donovan, Edward F. ....Biloxi, MS
Donovan, Edward G. ....Denver, CO
Donovan, Edward J. ....Brooklyn, NY
Donovan, Edward T. ....New York, NY
Donovan, Edward V., Jr. ....Chicago, IL
Donovan, Eileen ....New York, NY
Donovan, Eileen A.
Commodity Futures Trading Commission,
GV
Donovan, Elisa Macia ....Houston, TX
Donovan, Elizabeth M. ....Detroit, MI
Donovan, Emery & Hewetson ....Bedford, IN
Donovan, Emily R. ....Boston, MA
Donovan, Eric T. ....Boston, MA
Donovan, Erin ....Tulsa, OK
Donovan, Frances M. ....Boston, MA
Donovan, Francis J. ....Hicksville, NY
Donovan, Francis T. ....Conway, AR
Donovan, Gail K. ....Baltimore, MD
Donovan, Gary N. ....Fullerton, CA
Riverside, CA
Donovan, George E. ....Boston, MA
Donovan, Geraldine ....St. Davids, PA
Donovan, Gerard K. ....Tulsa, OK
Donovan & Giannuzzi ....New York, NY
Donovan, Herbert C. ....Detroit, MI
Donovan, Hugh E. ....Silver Spring, MD
Donovan, J. Kevin ....San Francisco, CA
Donovan, J. Patrick ....Chicago, IL
Donovan, J. Patrick, P.C., Law Office of
Chicago, IL
Donovan, J. Rickard ....Fort Wayne, IN

Donovan, J. Stephen ....Sacramento, CA
Donovan, J. Ted ....New Hyde Park, NY
Donovan, James ....Napoleon, OH
Donovan, James D. ....Bristol, CT
Donovan, James D. ....Erie, PA
Donovan, James F. ....Chicago, IL
Donovan, James H. ....Melrose, MA
Donovan, James H., II ....Cape Coral, FL
Donovan, James L. ....Fresno, CA
Donovan, James L. ....Metairie, LA
Donovan, James L., Jr. ....Metairie, LA
Donovan, James M. ....Bedford, MA
Donovan, James M. ....Springfield, MA
Donovan, James M., Law Offices of
Los Angeles, CA
Santa Ana, CA
Donovan, James Neil ....Woodbury, NY
Donovan, James P. ....New York, NY
Donovan, Jane F. ....Stamford, CT
Donovan, Janet ....Wellesley, MA
Donovan, Jeffery L. ....Sunnyvale, CA
Donovan, Jeremiah ....Old Saybrook, CT
Donovan, John ....Napoleon, OH
Donovan, John A. ....Los Angeles, CA
Donovan, John A., III ....Boston, MA
Donovan, John A., Jr. ....Boston, MA
Donovan, John D., Jr. ....Boston, MA
Donovan, John E. ....Atlanta, GA
Donovan, John F. ....San Francisco, CA
Donovan, John F. ....Department of Justice,
Executive Office for Immigration Review,
GV
Donovan, John F. ....Buffalo, NY
Donovan, John F., III ....St. Louis, MO
Donovan, John J. ....Milton, MA
Donovan, John J. ....South Salem, NY
Donovan, John M. ....Duluth, MN
Donovan, John M. ....New York, NY
Donovan, John M. ....New York, NY
Donovan, John M., Jr. ....Philadelphia, PA
Donovan, John P. ....Scottsdale, AZ
Donovan, John P. ....Santa Ana, CA
Donovan, John P. ....Weymouth, MA
Donovan, John P. ....Weymouth, MA
Donovan, John R. ....Cromwell, CT
Meriden, CT
Donovan, John S. ....Roswell, GA
Donovan, John T. ....Philadelphia, PA
Donovan, John W. ....Houston, TX
Donovan, John W., Atty. at Law, P.C., Law
Office of ....Houston, TX
Donovan, Jos. R., Jr. ....Albany, NY
Donovan, Joseph B. ....Red Bank, NJ
Donovan, Joseph E. ....Chicago, IL
Donovan, Karen ....San Francisco, CA
Donovan, Karla M. ....Princeton, NJ
Donovan, Katherine E. ....Fresno, CA
Donovan, Kathleen A. ....Lyndhurst, NJ
Donovan, Kathleen A. ....New York, NY
Donovan, Kathryn E. ....Sacramento, CA
Donovan & Kayser ....Colorado Springs, CO
Donovan, Keith E. ....Wilmington, DE
Donovan, Kelly Riley ....Washington, DC
Donovan, Kevin C. ....Newark, NJ
Donovan, Kevin F. ....Colorado Springs, CO
Donovan, Kevin M. ....Philadelphia, PA
Donovan, Kevin P. ....Albany, NY
Donovan, Kevin R. ....Morristown, NJ
Donovan, Kevin Wm. ....Elyria, OH
Donovan, Kimberly A. ....Redwood City, CA
Donovan, Kreag ....Rochester, NY
Donovan, Larry M. ....Cheyenne, WY
Donovan & Lawler, A Professional Law
Corporation ....Metairie, LA
New Orleans, LA
Donovan, Lawrence ....Bronxville, NY
Donovan, Lawrence J., Jr. ....Denver, CO
Donovan, Lawrence Michael, Jr.
Savannah, GA
Donovan, Lawrence P., III ....El Monte, CA
Donovan, Linda L. ....Clifton Park, NY
Donovan, Lori A. ....Boston, MA
Donovan, Love & Twinney
Grand Rapids, MI
Donovan, M. Shaun ....Superior, MT
Donovan, Martha M. ....Atlantic City, NJ
Donovan, Martha N. ....Somerville, NJ
Donovan, Martin K. ....Providence, RI
Donovan, Mary A. ....Irvine, CA
Donovan, Mary A. ....Omaha, NE
Donovan, Mary A. ....New York, NY
Donovan, Mary Elizabeth ....Dayton, OH
Donovan, Mary S. ....Macon, GA
Donovan, Matthew Thomas ....Hicksville, NY
Donovan, Maureen D. ....New York, NY
Donovan, Maurice J. ....West Orange, NJ
Donovan, Michael ....Concord, NH
Donovan, Michael D. ....Philadelphia, PA
Donovan, Michael F. ....Ketchum, ID
Donovan, Michael G. ....Modesto, CA
Donovan, Michael G. ....Boston, MA
Donovan, Michael J. ....Yuma, AZ
Donovan, Michael J. ....Boise, ID
Donovan, Michael J. ....Austin, TX
Donovan, Michael J. ....Milwaukee, WI
Donovan, Michael K. ....Duluth, MN
Donovan, Michael L. ....San Francisco, CA
Donovan, Michael P. ....Southfield, MI
Donovan, Michael R. ....Palm Desert, CA
Donovan, Michael T. ....Chicago, IL
Donovan, Michael T. ....Chicago, IL
Donovan, Michael W. ....Grand Rapids, MI
Donovan, Michelle ....Stoneham, MA
Donovan Miller, LLC ....Philadelphia, PA
Donovan, Monique D. ....Wilmington, MA
Donovan & Morello, LLP ....Cromwell, CT
Meriden, CT
Donovan, Nathan F. ....Lincoln, NE

Donovan, Nicholas T. ....New York, NY
Donovan, Noreen A. ....Jericho, NY
Donovan & O'Connor, LLP ....Adams, MA
Pittsfield, MA
Bennington, VT
Donovan Parry Carbin McDermott &
Radzik ....Brooklyn, NY
New York, NY
Donovan, Patricia A. ....Philadelphia, PA
Donovan, Patrick A. ....Hazen, ND
Donovan, Patrick J. ....Washington, DC
Donovan, Patrick J. ....New York, NY
Donovan, Patrick W. ....Mission, SD
Donovan, Paul F. ....Boston, MA
Donovan, Paul F. ....Lancaster, NH
Donovan, Paul F. ....Madison, WI
Donovan, Paul F., Professional Corporation
Lancaster, NH
Donovan, Paul J. ....Baltimore, MD
Donovan, Paul M. ....Washington, DC
Donovan, Paul M. ....Elmira, NY
Donovan, Peter L. ....Austin, TX
Donovan, Peter M. ....Metairie, LA
Donovan, Philip J. ....Los Angeles, CA
Donovan, Priscilla A. ....Ellicott City, MD
Donovan, R. Stephen ....Martinsville, IN
Donovan, Richard E. ....Parsippany, NJ
New York, NY
Donovan, Richard J. ....Columbus, OH
Donovan, Richard J., & Associates Co.,
L.P.A. ....Columbus, OH
Donovan, Richard P. ....New York, NY
Donovan, Richard T. ....Little Rock, AR
Donovan, Robert B. ....Exeter, NH
Donovan, Robert F., Jr. ....Chicago, IL
Donovan, Robert I. ....Marietta, GA
Donovan, Robert I., P.C. ....Marietta, GA
Donovan, Robert J. ....Marianna, AR
Donovan, Robert J. ....San Francisco, CA
Donovan, Robert M. ....Doylestown, PA
Donovan, Robert P. ....Roseland, NJ
Donovan, Robert W. ....Naples, ME
Donovan, Robert W. ....Wenham, MA
Donovan and Roberts, P.C. ....Wheaton, IL
Donovan, Rose, Nester, Szewczyk & Joley,
P.C. ....Belleville, IL
Benton, IL
Edwardsville, IL
Donovan, Russell B. ....Birmingham, AL
Donovan & Sapienza, A Prof. Corp., Law
Offices of ....Santa Monica, CA
Donovan, SaraBeth ....Omaha, NE
Donovan, Scott H. ....Manassas, VA
Donovan, Sean P. ....Dayton, OH
Donovan, Sharon A., (P.C.)
Salt Lake City, UT
Donovan, Sharon E. ....Norwalk, CT
Donovan, Sheila M. ....Lexington, KY
Donovan, Sherri ....New York, NY
Donovan, Stacey L. ....Topeka, KS
Donovan, Stephen ....Capistrano Beach, CA
Donovan, Stephen ....Washington, DC
Donovan, Stephen H. ....Concord, CA
Donovan, Teresa DeNafio ....Laconia, NH
Donovan, Teresa L. ....Alexandria, VA
Donovan, Teresa L., P.C. ....Alexandria, VA
Donovan, Terry S. ....Old Saybrook, CT
Donovan, Theodore M. ....Bristol, CT
Donovan, Thomas A. ....Pittsburgh, PA
Donovan, Thomas B. ....Los Angeles, CA
Donovan, Thomas B. ....Frankfort, IL
Donovan, Thomas C., Jr.
Colorado Springs, CO
Donovan, Thomas J. ....Chicago, IL
Donovan, Thomas J. ....Manchester, NH
Donovan, Thomas J. ....Mineola, NY
Rye, NY
Donovan, Thomas J. ....Burlington, VT
Donovan, Thomas M. ....Santa Monica, CA
Donovan, Thomas M. ....Peabody, MA
Donovan, Thomas M. ....Williamsville, NY
Donovan, Timothy J. ....San Jose, CA
Donovan, Timothy J. ....Lansing, MI
Donovan, Timothy M. ....Fresno, CA
Donovan, Timothy M. ....Melville, NY
Donovan, Timothy R. ....Chicago, IL
Donovan, Valerie B. ....Albany, NY
Donovan, W. Denis ....White Plains, NY
Donovan, W. Howard, III
Birmingham, AL
Donovan, W. Robert, Jr. ....Baltimore, MD
Donovan, Walter J. ....Bay Shore, NY
Donovan, William A. ....Naples, FL
Donovan, William A. ....White Plains, NY
Donovan, William A., P.A. ....Naples, FL
Donovan, William E. ....Sacramento, CA
Donovan, William E. ....New York, NY
Donovan, William E. ....San Antonio, TX
Donovan, William F. ....State College, PA
Donovan, William J. ....Manchester, NH
Donovan, William J. ....Pittsburgh, PA
Donovan, William J., Jr. ....Washington, DC
Donovan, William M. ....Bloomfield Hills, MI
Donovan, William M. ....Marinette, WI
Donovan, William M., P.C.
Bloomfield Hills, MI
Donovan, William P. ....Brooklyn, NY
Donovan, William P., Jr. ....Washington, DC
Donovan & Yee LLP ....New York, NY
Donovan-DiRocco, Anita ....Montclair, NJ
Donovan-Maher, Kathleen M.
Boston, MA
Donowitz, Michael ....Boston, MA
Donoyan, Maral ....Los Angeles, CA
Donsanto, Craig C. ....Department of Justice,
Criminal Division, GV
Donsavage, Paulette ....San Francisco, CA
Donsbach, Jan S. J. ....Long Beach, CA

Donsky, Calman L. ....Dallas, TX
Donsky, Eli N. ....Philadelphia, PA
Donsky, Marvin H. ....Philadelphia, PA
Donsky, Maurice E. ....Miami, FL
Donsky, Soffian, Allen & Bor, A Professional
Corporation ....Philadelphia, PA
Donsky, Steven M. ....Rochester, NY
Donsky, Tracy ....Palo Alto, CA
Donson, G. Jack, Jr. ....Cincinnati, OH
Donson, Kristen Goddard ....Carlisle, PA
Dontzin Law Firm, The ....New York, NY
Dontzin, Mary Hillyer ....New York, NY
Dontzin, Matthew S. ....New York, NY
Dontzin, Michael J., Hon. ....New York, NY
Donweber, Stephen M. ....Philadelphia, PA
Donworth, Robert B., Jr. ....Birmingham, AL
Donza, Donna Maria ....Hollywood, FL
Donze, George S. ....Media, PA
Donzella, Niccolò N. ....Baltimore, MD
Donzella, Niccolò N., P.A. ....Baltimore, MD
Donziger, Steven R. ....New York, NY
Doo, Cheryl M. L. ....San Francisco, CA
Doo, Helen ....New York, NY
Doobay, Sedesh ....Philadelphia, PA
Doocey, Edward C. ....Quincy, MA
Dood, John J. ....Okemos, MI
Dood, John Lindsey ....Grand Rapids, MI
Dood and Wilson ....Okemos, MI
Doodan, Michael M. ....Beverly Hills, CA
Doody, Dennis J. ....New York, NY
Doody, Donald J. ....Fort Lauderdale, FL
Doody, James J., III ....Glastonbury, CT
Doody, James P. ....Scarsdale, NY
Doody, James P., Jr. ....Boston, MA
Doody, John R. "Jack" ....Phoenix, AZ
Doody, John T., Jr. ....Homewood, IL
Doody, Patrick A. ....Danbury, CT
Doody, Patrick C. ....Chicago, IL
Doody, Peter S. ....San Diego, CA
Doody, Richard L. ....Fort Lauderdale, FL
Doody, Stephen ....New York, NY
Doogal, Daljit S. ....Troy, MI
Doogan, James P., Jr. ....Fairbanks, AK
Dooge, Daniel L. ....Madison, WI
Dooge, Gregg H. ....Milwaukee, WI
Doohan, Mary Elizabeth ....Chicago, IL
Doohan, Pauline E. ....Detroit, MI
Doohen, Stephen E. ....Des Moines, IA
Dooher, Daniel W. ....Department of Justice,
Environment and Natural Resources
Division, GV
Dooher, Patrick G. ....Washington, DC
Dool, Carl D. ....Barberton, OH
Dool, Scott D. ....Los Angeles, CA
Dool, Scott F. ....Thousand Oaks, CA
Dool, Scott F., Inc. ....Thousand Oaks, CA
Doolan, Devin John ....Chevy Chase, MD
Doolan, Roy F. ....San Francisco, CA
Doolan, Sean M. ....Washington, DC
Albany, NY
Doolan, Thomas C. ....Knoxville, TN
Doolen, Lawrence ....Denver, CO
Dooley, Albert J. ....Lexington, SC
Dooley, Albert J., Jr. ....Lexington, SC
Dooley, Andrew J. ....Taunton, MA
Dooley, Ann ....Tulsa, OK
Dooley, Athena M. ....Philadelphia, PA
Dooley, Brendan J. ....San Francisco, CA
Dooley, C. Douglas ....Chattanooga, TN
Dooley, Cary D. ....Oklahoma City, OK
Dooley, Charles W. ....Chattanooga, TN
Dooley, Christopher R.
Department of the Air Force,
Office of the Judge Advocate General, GV
Dooley, Colleen M. ....Toledo, OH
Dooley, Cynthia C. ....Columbia, SC
Dooley, Cynthia G. ....Dallas, TX
Dooley, Daniel M. ....Visalia, CA
Dooley, David W. ....Hagåtña, GU
Dooley, Dooley, Spence & Parker, P.A.
Lexington, SC
Dooley, Edward M. ....Orange Beach, AL
Dooley, Edward W. ......Huntington Station, NY
Dooley, Edwin G. ....Fort Smith, AR
Dooley, Eileen V. ....Philadelphia, PA
Dooley, Estella W. ....San Francisco, CA
Dooley, Fintan L. ....Bismarck, ND
Dooley, Francis E., Jr. ....Boston, MA
Dooley, Francis M. ....Lakeville, CT
Dooley, Frederick E., Jr. ......Washington, DC
Dooley, H. Kathleen ....McLean, VA
Dooley, Helen I. ....Washington, DC
Dooley, Herr & Williams, LLP ....Visalia, CA
Dooley & Hoerster, L.L.P.
Fredericksburg, TX
Dooley, Howard B. ....Omaha, NE
Dooley, James H. ....Salisbury, NC
Dooley, James H., Jr. ....Salisbury, NC
Dooley, James J. ....Paramus, NJ
Dooley, James L. ....Charlottesville, VA
Dooley, James T., III ....Redding, CA
Dooley, Jas. R. ....Los Angeles, CA
Dooley, John J. ....Jersey City, NJ
Dooley, John T. ....Lansdale, PA
Dooley, John T. ....Philadelphia, PA
Dooley & Johnston L.L.P. ....Dallas, TX
Dooley, Joseph G. ....Boca Raton, FL
Dooley, Joseph M., III ....Chicago, IL
Dooley, Karen Ervin ....Memphis, TN
Dooley, Kathleen H. ....Florham Park, NJ
Dooley, Kevin C. ....Minneapolis, MN
Dooley, Kevin P. ....Binghamton, NY
Dooley Lannen Roberts & Fowler LLP
Hagåtña, GU
Dooley & Leibovitz ....Orinda, CA
Dooley, Lisa M. ....Philadelphia, PA
Dooley, Mark P. ....Milwaukee, WI
Dooley, Marlene ....Trenton, NJ

Dorfzaun, Richard S. .... Pittsburgh, PA
Dorgan, Dana L. .... New York, NY
Dorgan, Donna J. .... Rutherford, NJ
Dorgan, Glen F. .... San Diego, CA
Dorgan, James Richard .... Fairhope, AL
Gulf Shores, AL
Dorgan, Joan G. .... Pittsburgh, PA
Dorgan, John R. .... Minneapolis, MN
Dorgan, Walter J., Jr. (P.A.) .... Paramus, NJ
Dorgan, Wanda R. .... Los Angeles, CA
Dorgan, William J. .... Wilmington, DE
Dorger, Paul D. .... Cincinnati, OH
Dorhout, Kevin L. .... Oxnard, CA
Dori, Yaron .... Washington, DC
Doria, Cynthia Ann .... St. Louis, MO
Doria, Joseph M. .... Harrisburg, PA
Doria, Marilyn L. .... Washington, DC
Doria, Nicholas R. .... Hackensack, NJ
Doria, Stephanie A. .... San Francisco, CA
Dorian, Barbara Bucci .... Chicago, IL
Dorian, Brett .... Fresno, CA
Dorian, Charissa .... Los Angeles, CA
Dorian, Christopher B. .... Fresno, CA
Dorian, Harry A. .... Philadelphia, PA
Dorian, Harry A., Jr. .... Bensalem, PA
Philadelphia, PA
Dorian, Howard M. .... Cliffside Park, NJ
Dorian, Ira D. .... Cranford, NJ
Dorian, Max C. .... Annandale, VA
Dorian, Raymond W. .... Camp Hill, PA
Dorigan, John P. .... Palm Springs, CA
Dorigan, William E. .... Denver, CO
Dorin, Bradley H. .... Roslyn, NY
Dorin, Paul E. .... St. Louis, MO
Doring, Matthew P. .... Newburyport, MA
Dorini, Brian J. .... Washington, DC
Dorini, Helen H. .... Boston, MA
Doris, Alan .... Cleveland, OH
Doris, Carole R. .... Chicago, IL
Doris, Daniel .... Tulsa, OK
Doris, Ian C. .... Hackensack, NJ
Doris, Robert L. .... South Orange, NJ
Dorisio, Andrew D. .... Lexington, KY
Dorit, J Niley .... San Francisco, CA
Dority, Avery E. .... Sacramento, CA
Dority, John P. .... Sarasota, FL
Dority, Julian W. .... Greenville, SC
Dority, Larry W. .... Kansas City, MO
Dority & Manning, P.A. .... Columbia, SC
Greenville, SC
Spartanburg, SC
Dorius, Dale M. .... Brigham City, UT
Dorius, Ralph W. .... Coral Gables, FL
Dorius, Steven M. .... Memphis, TN
Dorizas, Angelo J. .... Jackson, MS
Dorka, Lilian L. Sotolongo
Department of Education,
Office for Civil Rights, GV
Dorkey, Charles E., III .... New York, NY
Dorkin, Eric .... Chicago, IL
Dorkin, Frederic E. .... Kirkland, WA
Dorkin, Robert S. .... Springfield, NJ
Dorl, James J. .... Marathon, FL
Dorl, Richard E. .... Somerset, NJ
Dorlack, Joseph J. .... Milwaukee, WI
Dorland, Dana I., (Ms.) .... Chehalis, WA
Dorland, Deborah S. .... Detroit, MI
Farmington Hills, MI
Dorliae, Cecile Mathis .... Buffalo, NY
Dorlon, John H., Jr. .... San Antonio, TX
Dormady, Patricia C. .... Brockton, MA
Dormady, Valerie A. .... Nashville, TN
Dorman, Andrew J. .... Cleveland, OH
Dorman, Benjamin N. .... Baltimore, MD
Dorman, Bradley P. .... Providence, RI
Dorman, Cary .... Fort Worth, TX
Dorman, Charles W.
Department of the Navy,
Office of the Judge Advocate General, GV
Dorman, Christopher G. .... New York, NY
Dorman, Dennis Paul, & Associates
San Diego, CA
Dorman, Don D. .... Tulare, CA
Dorman, Donald D. .... Chicago, IL
Dorman and Dorman .... Lemon Grove, CA
Dorman, Elizabeth D. .... Oakland, CA
Dorman, Erin A. .... East Hartford, CT
Dorman & Fredrick .... Santa Ana, CA
Dorman & Gilbert, P.A. .... Tulsa, OK
Dorman, Gregg M. .... Schaumburg, IL
Dorman, Ira S. .... East Hartford, CT
Dorman, J. Michael .... Houston, TX
Dorman, J. Wesley, Jr. .... Houston, TX
Dorman, James V. .... Lemon Grove, CA
Dorman, Jay M. .... New York, NY
Dorman, Jeffrey Howard .... Santa Ana, CA
Dorman, Jeffrey L. .... Chicago, IL
Dorman, Joel H. .... Pella, IA
Dorman, John D. .... Houston, TX
Dorman, Keith A. .... Chicago, IL
Dorman, Kenneth J. .... Oakland, CA
Dorman, Kerri J. .... Houston, TX
Dorman, Larry .... Kew Gardens, NY
Dorman, Laura J. .... San Francisco, CA
Dorman, Lori M. .... Bradenton, FL
Dorman, Malcolm E. .... Orange, TX
Dorman, Mary J. .... Tallahassee, FL
Dorman, Melissa A. .... El Paso, TX
Dorman, Monique .... Bloomfield, NJ
Dorman, Neal T. .... New York, NY
Dorman, Nicole D. .... West Hartford, CT
Dorman, "R" "H" .... San Diego, CA
Dorman, Richard H. .... St. Clair Shores, MI
Dorman, Richard T. .... Mobile, AL
Dorman, Roderick G. .... Los Angeles, CA
Dorman, Shawn D. .... Las Vegas, NV
Dorman, Stanley J. .... New York, NY
Dorman, Wallace D. .... Lemon Grove, CA
Dorman, Wendy S.
Department Of The Interior,
Office of the Solicitor, GV
Dorman, William S. .... Tulsa, OK
Dorman, Wm. T. .... Bellaire, TX
Dorman-Davis, Jessica S. .... Costa Mesa, CA
Dorman-Rodriguez, Deborah
Santa Fe, NM
Dorment, James, Jr. .... Jersey City, NJ
Dormer, Robert A. .... Washington, DC
Dormer, Robert R. .... Denver, CO
Dormer, Scott Bradley .... Marina Del Rey, CA
Dormer, Stephen G. .... Washington, DC
Dormeyer, David C. .... Carmichael, CA
Dormin, John W. .... Putnam Valley, NY
Dorminey, A. Blair, III .... Fayetteville, GA
Dorminey, Elizabeth K. .... Atlanta, GA
Dormitzer, Deborah .... Maynard, MA
Dormont, April Denise .... Sapulpa, OK
Dormont, Daniel .... Department of Justice,
Drug Enforcement Administration, GV
Dormont, David .... Philadelphia, PA
Dormsjo, Ture O., Jr. .... Hackensack, NJ
Dorn, Alan S. .... Chicago, IL
Dorn, Albert A. .... Los Angeles, CA
Dorn & Associates, P.C. .... Brooklyn, NY
Dorn, Bruce Farrel .... Chicago, IL
Dorn, Bruce Farrel, & Associates
Chicago, IL
Dorn, Carl H. .... Beverly Hills, CA
Dorn, David P. .... Birmingham, AL
Dorn, Elbert S. .... Columbia, SC
Dorn, Ellen Eisenlohr .... Dallas, TX
Dorn, Franz E. .... Deltona, FL
Dorn, Gail Danette Couse
Corpus Christi, TX
Dorn, Gerald M. .... Reno, NV
Dorn, Heather M. .... Southfield, MI
Dorn, James Michael .... Chino, CA
Dorn, Jerrold S. .... Chicago, IL
Dorn, Joseph W. .... Washington, DC
Dorn, Kenneth J. .... Pittsburgh, PA
Dorn & Klamp, P.C. .... Washington, DC
Dorn, Kristine A. .... Omaha, NE
Dorn, Marguerite M. .... Belmont, MA
Dorn, Marybeth .... Minneapolis, MN
Dorn, McEachran, Jambor & Keating
Chicago, IL
Dorn, Melissa R. .... Little Rock, AR
Dorn, Paul C. .... St. Paul, MN
Dorn, Peter E. .... Portland, OR
Dorn, Philip G. .... Santa Ana, CA
Dorn, Richard L. .... New York, NY
Dorn, Sally A. .... Atlanta, GA
Dorn, Steven J. .... Brooklyn, NY
Dorn, Susan E. .... Washington, DC
Dorn, Trilby C.E. .... Seattle, WA
Dorn, Watson L. .... Greenwood, SC
Dornagon, Mandares Melad .... Bellerose, NY
Dornak, David .... Las Vegas, NV
Dorna-Llompart, Mariemma
San Juan, PR
Dornan, Donald C., Jr. .... Biloxi, MS
Dornan, Donald C., Jr. .... Gulfport, MS
Hattiesburg, MS
Jackson, MS
Pascagoula, MS
Dornan, Dorothy R. (Dari) .... Houston, TX
Dornan, Earle M. .... Phoenix, AZ
Dornan, Kevin W. .... Jacksonville, FL
Dornan, Stuart J. .... Omaha, NE
Dornay, Chris B. .... Clovis, CA
Dornay, Val J. .... Clovis, CA
Dornbaum, Michael L. .... Garden City, NY
Dornbaum, Neil S. .... Newark, NJ
Dornberger, John W. .... Harrisburg, PA
Dornberger, Kevin D. .... Sioux Falls, SD
Dornblaser, David .... Glen Ellyn, IL
Dornblaser, Kenneth E. .... Tulsa, OK
Dornbos, William A. .... Kalamazoo, MI
Dornbrand, Faith D. .... Washington, DC
Dornbusch, Arthur A., II .... Iselin, NJ
Dornbush, Darwin C. .... New York, NY
Dornbush, Jerold P. .... New York, NY
Dornbush Mensch Mandelstam & Schaeffer, LLP .... New York, NY
Dorne, Craig M. .... Miami, FL
Dorne, David J. .... San Diego, CA
Dorne, Michael W. .... Rogers, AR
Dorne, Robert .... Los Angeles, CA
Dorne, Steven H. .... Rockville, MD
Dorner, Bruce L. .... Londonderry, NH
Dorner, Dale, (Ms.) .... Greenville, NY
Dorner, Hillery .... Belmont, MA
Dorner, Renisa A. .... Toledo, OH
Dorner, T. Michael .... Mansfield, OH
Dornette, John J. .... Lawrenceburg, IN
Dornette, William H. L. .... Kensington, MD
Dornette, William Stuart .... Cincinnati, OH
Dorney, Colleen T. .... Costa Mesa, CA
Dorney, Edward R. .... Bayside, NY
Brooklyn, NY
New York, NY
Dorney, Linda M. .... Rockville, MD
Dorney, Maureen S. .... Palo Alto, CA
Dorney, Michael J. .... New Haven, CT
Dorney, Sheryl Ann .... York, PA
Dornfeld, Daniel S. .... Jericho, NY
Dornfeld, Kivie .... Teaneck, NJ
Dornfeld, Sharon Wicks .... Danbury, CT
Dornfried, Joseph E. .... Waterbury, CT
Dornhaffer, Robert B. .... Meadville, PA
Dornic, Myron Dusan .... Dallas, TX
Dornier, Russell L. .... Baton Rouge, LA
Dornig, Joseph A., Jr. .... Los Altos, CA
Dornik, John M. .... Minneapolis, MN
Dornish, Bradley S.
Cranberry Township, PA
Pittsburgh, PA
Dornish, Cynthia M. .... Pittsburgh, PA
Dornish & Scolieri, P.C. .... Beaver, PA
Butler, PA
Cranberry Township, PA
Greensburg, PA
Pittsburgh, PA
Washington, PA
Dornon, Sherrie J. .... Peoria, IL
Dornshuld, Carl L. .... Medina, OH
Dornstein, Judith C. .... Los Angeles, CA
Dornstein, Judith C., Inc., The Law Office of
Los Angeles, CA
Dornstein, Laurence A. .... Los Angeles, CA
Dorny, Brett N. .... Boston, MA
Dorny, D. Matthew .... Salt Lake City, UT
D'Oro, Frank J. .... Pasadena, CA
Doro, Holly Geyer .... Parkland, FL
Doro, Holly Geyer, P.A. .... Parkland, FL
Dorobek, David A. .... Fremont, OH
Dorocak, John R. .... Parma, OH
Dorocak, Michael K. .... Bloomfield Hills, MI
Dorocke, Lawrence F. .... Indianapolis, IN
Doros, Jerrold T. .... New York, NY
Doroshow, Eric M. .... Wilmington, DE
Doroshow, James E. .... Pasadena, CA
Doroshow, Kenneth L.
Department of Justice, GV
Doroshow, Pasquale, Krawitz, Siegel & Bhaya .... Wilmington, DE
Doroshow, Robin J. .... Minneapolis, MN
Dorosin, Daniel A. .... Morgan Hill, CA
Dorosin, Joshua L. .... Department of State,
Office of the Legal Adviser, GV
Dorosin, Mark Edward .... Carrboro, NC
Dorosin, Norman .... Aptos, CA
Dorosin, Robert N. .... Department of Justice,
Tax Division, GV
Dorotheo, Lakandula Duke .... Washington, DC
Dorothy, Bill B., II .... St. Louis, MO
Dorothy, Catherine S. .... Kansas City, MO
Dorothy, Charles .... Sioux Falls, SD
Dorothy & Henoch, LLC .... Lenexa, KS
Dorothy, James A. .... Keosauqua, IA
Dorothy Law Firm, P.C. .... Sioux Falls, SD
Dorothy & Lytle .... Keosauqua, IA
Dorothy, Wade A. .... Lenexa, KS
Dorough, David N., Jr. .... Decatur, GA
Dorough & Dorough, LLC .... Atlanta, GA
Decatur, GA
Dorough, John R. .... Ocala, FL
Dorough, Kathy Kraft .... Decatur, GA
Dorough, Keith T. .... Albany, GA
Dorough, Kermit S., Jr. .... Albany, GA
Dorough, Lisa Hudson .... Birmingham, AL
Dorough, R. Lee .... Orlando, FL
Dorow, Monica Lindstrom, (Ltd.)
Minneapolis, MN
Dorph, Martin S. .... Philadelphia, PA
Dorr, Carson, Sloan & Birney, P.C.
Denver, CO
Dorr, David H. .... Grand Rapids, MI
Dorr, David T. .... Houston, TX
Dorr, Donald W. .... Hanover, PA
Dorr, Fred L. .... Des Moines, IA
Dorr, Gregory .... Omaha, NE
Dorr, Gregory P. .... Bangor, ME
Dorr, James M. .... Barstow, CA
Dorr, James P. .... Chicago, IL
Dorr, Jas. W. .... Cincinnati, OH
Dorr, John Van N., III .... Durham, NH
Dorr, Karl .... Evergreen, CO
Dorr, Kathleen M. .... Rochester, NY
Dorr, Lisa C. .... Washington, DC
Dorr, Luther M., Jr. .... Birmingham, AL
Dorr, Patrick Charles .... Philadelphia, PA
Dorr, Rachael Macindoe .... Boston, MA
Dorr, Richard E. .... Springfield, MO
Dorr, Robert C. .... Denver, CO
Dorr, Roderick A. .... Albuquerque, NM
Dorr, Stephen M. .... Philadelphia, PA
Dorr, William Lent .... Rochester, NY
Dorr, Williams P. .... Chicago, IL
Dorrance, Arthur C., Jr. .... Philadelphia, PA
Dorrance, Bradford .... Harrisburg, PA
Dorrance, Christopher W. .... Odessa, MO
Dorrance, Jerry M. .... Santa Barbara, CA
Dorrance, Meredith Winters .... Seattle, WA
Dorrell, Jeffrey L. .... Houston, TX
Dorrell, John S. .... Cleveland, OH
Dorrell, Robert B. .... Corpus Christi, TX
Dorrestein, Ronald .... Graham, NC
Dorrian, Julia L. .... Columbus, OH
Dorrian, Krista Bean .... Washington, DC
Dorrier, Lindsay G., Jr. .... Richmond, VA
Dorrier, Thomas B. .... Washington, DC
Dorrill, George L. .... Kosciusko, MS
Dorrill, Jeff W. .... Dallas, TX
Dorrington, Michael A. .... Boston, MA
Dorris, Beth S. .... Los Angeles, CA
Dorris, David V. .... Bloomington, IL
Chicago, IL
Dorris, Douglas N. .... Marion, IL
Dorris, Evanjerl .... Department of Justice,
Civil Rights Division, GV
Dorris, Gregory C. .... Washington, DC
Dorris, Howard S. .... Jericho, NY
Dorris, Jennifer S. E. .... New York, NY
Dorris, John E. .... Victoria, TX
Dorris, John Hamilton .... Hattiesburg, MS
Dorris, Kevin M. .... Knoxville, TN
Dorris, Malcolm S. .... New York, NY
Dorris, Michael P. .... Department of Justice,
Federal Bureau of Investigation, GV
Dorris, Michael S. .... Tampa, FL
Dorris, Paul A. .... Sacramento, CA
Dorris, Richard A. .... McMinnville, TN
Dorris, Terry W. .... Fort Worth, TX
Dorris, Thomas B. .... Chicago, IL
Dorris, Tomi L. .... Columbus, OH
Dorris, William E. .... Atlanta, GA
Dorrity, Francis X., & Associates
Jersey City, NJ
Dorrity, Kristen .... Seattle, WA
Dorrity, Tracey A. .... Jersey City, NJ
Dorroh, Charles R. .... Memphis, TN
Dorroh, Joel F. .... Tuscaloosa, AL
Dorroh, Joel F., P.C. .... Tuscaloosa, AL
Dorroh, Lawrence G. .... Caruthersville, MO
Dorroh, Paul E. .... West Des Moines, IA
Dorroh, Walter E., Jr. .... Jena, LA
Dorros, Kenneth M. .... Wethersfield, CT
Dorrough, Carl L. .... Tyler, TX
Dorrough, Richard H. .... Montgomery, AL
Dorrough, Shirley C. .... Montgomery, AL
Dorry, Steven F. .... Morristown, NJ
Dorsa, John .... Houston, TX
Dorsa, Joseph P. .... Corona, NY
Dorsa, Vincent W. .... Mahwah, NJ
Dorsaneo, William V., III
Corpus Christi, TX
Dorsay, Craig J. .... Portland, OR
Dorsch, Daniel B. .... Kansas City, MO
Dorsch, Eric M .... Manchester, NH
Dorsch, James A. .... Alexandria, VA
Dorsch, Jay A. .... New York, NY
Dorsch, William M. .... Burlington, VT
Dorschel, Griffin G. .... Madison, WI
Dorse, Kevin A. .... Los Angeles, CA
Dorsen, David M. .... Washington, DC
Dorsen, Harriette K. .... New York, NY
Dorsen, Norman .... New York, NY
Dorset, Katherine J. .... Monterey, CA
Dorsett, Ann Terrell .... Charlotte, NC
Dorsett, C. Powers, Jr. .... Fort Mill, SC
Dorsett, Charles B., Jr. .... Santa Rosa, CA
Dorsett, Charles H. .... Troy, NC
Dorsett, Charles H., Jr. .... Doylestown, PA
Dorsett, D. Keith .... Waco, TX
Dorsett, James K., III .... Raleigh, NC
Dorsett, James K., Jr. .... Raleigh, NC
Dorsett, Stuart B. .... New Bern, NC
Dorsett, Suzanne C. .... Huntsville, AL
Dorsett, Wm. N. .... Marshall, TX
Dorsey, Ansley Head .... Magnolia Springs, AL
Dorsey, Arthur M. .... Gatesville, TX
Dorsey & Aulbert .... Florissant, MO
Dorsey & Bell .... Boonton, NJ
Dorsey, Benjamin H. .... Potomac, MD
Dorsey, Benjamin R., IV .... Richmond, VA
Dorsey, Bernard William .... Kansas City, MO
Dorsey, Brian J. .... Wenatchee, WA
Dorsey, Bryan F. .... Atlanta, GA
Dorsey, C. Michele .... Scituate, MA
Dorsey, Cam D., Jr. .... Atlanta, GA
Dorsey, Carmen M. .... Augusta, ME
Dorsey, Cecil D. .... Atlanta, GA
Dorsey, Charles N. .... Roanoke, VA
Dorsey, Christine Schunmann
Middletown, CT
Dorsey, Christopher J. .... New Britain, CT
Dorsey, Dan R., (A Prof. Law Corp.)
River Ridge, LA
Dorsey, Dan Richard .... Covington, LA
Dorsey, Daniel K. .... Washington, DC
Dorsey, David A. .... Coos Bay, OR
Dorsey, David A., P.C. .... Coos Bay, OR
Dorsey, David H. .... Rockville, MD
Dorsey, David J. .... Wenatchee, WA
Dorsey, Dee Ann .... Atlanta, GA
Dorsey, Donald P. .... Kerrville, TX
Dorsey, Donald T. .... Meriden, CT
Dorsey, Douglas C. .... Pittsburgh, PA
Dorsey, Edward .... Carbondale, IL
Dorsey, Edward S. .... Cincinnati, OH
Dorsey, Elbert .... St. Louis, MO
Dorsey, Elizabeth L. .... Boston, MA
Dorsey, Emerson L., Jr. .... Baltimore, MD
Dorsey & Foley, P.C. .... Annapolis, MD
Leonardtown, MD
Dorsey, Forrest J. .... Corpus Christi, TX
Dorsey, Francis E. .... Saratoga Springs, NY
Dorsey, Francis P. .... West Des Moines, IA
Dorsey, Frederick L. .... New Haven, CT
Dorsey, Gray L. .... St. Louis, MO
Dorsey, Gregory Alan .... Westminster, MD
Dorsey, H. Bruce .... Baltimore, MD
Dorsey, Harriet D. .... Blacksburg, VA
Dorsey, Hugh M., III .... Savannah, GA
Dorsey, J. Bonner .... Corpus Christi, TX
Dorsey, Jack V. .... Decatur, GA
Dorsey, James B. .... Saratoga Springs, NY
Dorsey, James B., Jr. .... Saratoga Springs, NY
Dorsey, James E. .... Minneapolis, MN
Dorsey, James E., (P.C.) .... Atlanta, GA
Dorsey, James J. .... University City, MO
Dorsey, James R. .... Minneapolis, MN
Dorsey, Jeffrey C. .... Washington, DC
Dorsey, John C. .... Raleigh, NC
Dorsey, John E. .... Charleston, WV
Dorsey, John G. .... Kansas City, MO
Dorsey, John H. .... Boonton, NJ
Dorsey, John K. .... Charles Town, WV
Dorsey, John L. .... New Orleans, LA
Dorsey, John M., III
Federal Deposit Insurance Corporation,
Professional Liability Section, GV
Dorsey, John Stanton .... Rapid City, SD
Dorsey, John T. .... Wilmington, DE
Dorsey, Jonathan R. .... Walnut Creek, CA
Dorsey, Karen O. .... Treasury Department,
Office of the General Counsel, GV
Dorsey, Kathleen A. .... Watertown, MA

Doucette, Robert O. ....Leominster, MA
Doucette, Ronald G. ....Vienna, VA
Doucette, Sharon S. ....Upper Marlboro, MD
Doucette, Stephen G. ....Boston, MA
Doucette-Ashman, Linda J.
West Paterson, NJ
Doucher, Kimberley A. ....Columbus, OH
Doucher, Paul M. ....Columbus, OH
Douchkess, Donald N. ....Philadelphia, PA
Doud, Alden L. ....Washington, DC
Doud, David H. ....Sunriver, OR
Doud, Deborah Sue ....Kansas City, MO
Doud, John H., III ....Baltimore, MD
Doud, Mary Teresa Anastasia
Washington, DC
Doud, Michael Patrick ....Saginaw, MI
Doud, Randall H. ....New York, NY
Doud, Richard J. ....Flint, MI
Saginaw, MI
Doud, Robert H. ....Hempstead, NY
Doud, Thomas J., Jr. ....Baltimore, MD
Doud, William E. ....Centreville, VA
Doudera, A. Edward, Jr. ....Camden, ME
Doudna, Heather L. ....Clearwater, FL
Doudnikoff, Catherine E. ....Seattle, WA
Douds, Anne S. ....Beaufort, SC
Douds, Gregory T. ....La Plata, MD
Douds, H. James ....Washington, DC
Douek, Andre M.
Federal Deposit Insurance Corporation,
Professional Liability Section, GV
Dougal, Elizabeth M. ....Chicago, IL
Dougal, Leonard H. ....Austin, TX
Dougal, Stephen A. ....Florence, MA
Dougall, Cristian ....Houston, TX
Dougall, Thomas F. ....Columbia, SC
Dougan, Arthur L. ....Wickliffe, OH
Dougan, Charles R. ....Rogers, AR
Dougan, Hugh M. ....New York, NY
Dougan, Patricia ....Struthers, OH
Dougan, Stacey Pastel ....Miami, FL
Dougan, Stephen J. ....Sacramento, CA
Dougan, Thomas J. ....Oberlin, OH
Dougher, Constance M. ....Limerick, PA
Dougher, Joseph P. ....Philadelphia, PA
Dougher, Robert J. ....Philadelphia, PA
Dougherty, Alan A. ....San Carlos, CA
Dougherty, Amy E. ....Frankfort, KY
Dougherty, Andrew A. ....Holyoke, MA
Dougherty, Ann M. ....Toms River, NJ
Dougherty, Ann R. ....King Of Prussia, PA
Dougherty, Annamary Catherine
Little Rock, AR
Dougherty, Anne H. ....Nashville, TN
Dougherty, Anne Vachon ....Thornwood, NY
Dougherty, Anthony W. ....Mercer Island, WA
Dougherty & Associates ....Charlotte, NC
Dougherty, Barbara K.
Equal Employment Opportunity
Commission,
Office of the General Counsel, GV
Dougherty, Bernard J. ....Phoenix, AZ
Dougherty, Bernard J. ....Tucson, AZ
Dougherty, Bethenia J. ....Albuquerque, NM
Dougherty, Bradley J. ....Indianapolis, IN
Dougherty, Brian J. ....Pueblo, CO
Dougherty, Brian J. ....Philadelphia, PA
Dougherty & Brogan ....Toms River, NJ
Dougherty, Burtis M., Jr.
Department of Justice,
Civil Rights Division, GV
Dougherty, C. Clark, Jr.
Oklahoma City, OK
Dougherty, C. Gordon ....Rosemont, IL
Dougherty, C. Michael ....Newark, NJ
New York, NY
Dougherty, Carolann Jackson
Philadelphia, PA
Dougherty, Charles H. ....Buffalo, NY
Dougherty, Charles R. ....Boston, MA
Dougherty, Christopher ....Chicago, IL
Dougherty, Christopher E.
Newtown Square, PA
Dougherty, Clement J., Jr.
Sacramento, CA
Dougherty, Clifford Clark, III
Oklahoma City, OK
Dougherty, Colleen B. ....Orange, CA
Dougherty, Daniel G. ....Whitehall, PA
Dougherty, David E. ....Falls Church, VA
Dougherty, David L. ....Treasury Department,
Office of the General Counsel, GV
Dougherty, Dennis ....Charlottesville, VA
Dougherty, Donald G. ....San Jose, CA
Dougherty, Donna ....Philadelphia, PA
Dougherty & Dougherty ....Sioux Falls, SD
Dougherty & Dougherty ....Houston, TX
Dougherty, Dougherty & Vecchiolla
Greenwich, CT
Norwalk, CT
Stamford, CT
Dougherty, Douglas B. ....Columbus, OH
Dougherty, Douglas B. ....Houston, TX
Dougherty, Duane C. ....Omaha, NE
Dougherty, E. Lynn ....Bristol, TN
Dougherty, E. Paul, Jr. ....Los Angeles, CA
Dougherty, Ed ....Kansas City, MO
Dougherty, Edward W., Jr.
Tallahassee, FL
Dougherty, Elizabeth Cary ....Metairie, LA
Dougherty, Erin L. ....Bloomfield Hills, MI
Dougherty, Erin P. ....Annapolis, MD
Dougherty, Eugene R. ....Irvington, NY
Dougherty, Euguene E. ....Chicago, IL
Dougherty, Frank ....Merced, CA
Dougherty, Frank ....Mission Viejo, CA
Dougherty, Frank J., Jr. ....Louisville, KY
Dougherty, Frank M. ....Homer, LA
Dougherty, Frank M. ....Albuquerque, NM
Dougherty, George R. ....Chicago, IL
Dougherty, George T. ....Lawrenceville, NJ
Dougherty, Gerard M. ....Westlake Village, CA
Dougherty, Gina M. ....Columbus, OH
Dougherty, H. Morgan, III ....Indio, CA
Dougherty & Hessin ....Oklahoma City, OK
Dougherty, Hildre, Dudek & Haklar
San Diego, CA
Dougherty, Hofmann & Goodwin, P.C.
Danville, IL
Dougherty, Hugh ....Mill Valley, CA
Dougherty, Hugh Bruce ....Greenwich, CT
Dougherty, J. Allen ....Atlanta, GA
Philadelphia, PA
Dougherty, J. Charles ....Little Rock, AR
Dougherty, J. Chrys ....Austin, TX
Dougherty, J. Michael, Jr.
Upper Marlboro, MD
Dougherty, Jack P. ....Oakland, CA
Dougherty, James Bruce ....Greenwich, CT
Dougherty, James C. ....Washington, DC
Dougherty, James C. ....Lake Toxaway, NC
Dougherty, James D. ....New York, NY
Dougherty, James E. ....Orange, CA
Dougherty, James F. ....Palo Alto, CA
Dougherty, James Kevin ....New York, NY
Dougherty, James L., Jr. ....Houston, TX
Dougherty, James P. ....New York, NY
Dougherty, James P. ....Harrisburg, PA
Dougherty, James S. ....Indianola, IA
Dougherty, James S. ....Houston, TX
Dougherty, James T. ....Springfield, IL
Dougherty, James W. ....Jersey City, NJ
Dougherty, Janeen Olsen ....Radnor, PA
Dougherty, Janet Jule ....Syracuse, NY
Dougherty, Jennifer J. ....Omaha, NE
Dougherty, Jerome C. ....St. Helena, CA
Dougherty, Jill Edwards ....Charlottesville, VA
Dougherty, Joann H. ....St. Paul, MN
Dougherty, John ....McLean, VA
Dougherty, John A. ....New York, NY
Dougherty, John B. ....Harrisburg, PA
Dougherty, John Caleb ....Baltimore, MD
Dougherty, John D., Jr. ....Cohasset, MA
Dougherty, John E. ....Atlanta, GA
Dougherty, John E. ....Chicago, IL
Dougherty, John F. ....Baltimore, MD
Dougherty, John F., Jr. ....Philadelphia, PA
Dougherty, John H. ....Newtown, CT
Dougherty, John J. ....Decatur, AL
Dougherty, John P. ....West Des Moines, IA
Dougherty, John P. ....Boston, MA
Dougherty, John P. ....Malvern, PA
Dougherty, Joseph A. ....Paoli, PA
Dougherty, Joseph D. ....Charlottesville, VA
Dougherty, Joseph J. ....Berkley, MA
Dougherty, Joseph J. ....West Chester, PA
Dougherty, Joseph M., II ....Springfield, PA
Dougherty, Joseph R. ....Atlantic City, NJ
Dougherty, Judith A. ....Bethlehem, PA
Dougherty, Judith J. ....Tallahassee, FL
Dougherty, Judy K. ....Houston, TX
Dougherty, Kara A. ....Philadelphia, PA
Dougherty, Katharine E. ....Newtown, CT
Dougherty, Katherine ....Austin, TX
Dougherty, Kathleen M. ....Syracuse, NY
Dougherty, Kathy A. ....Columbus, OH
Dougherty, Kenneth P. ....Tyler, TX
Dougherty, Kenwyn M. ....Philadelphia, PA
Dougherty, Kevin G. ....Grand Rapids, MI
Dougherty, Kirkman T. ....Fort Smith, AR
Dougherty & Landon ....Westlake Village, CA
Dougherty Law Firm, P.C. ....Tyler, TX
Dougherty, Lawrence T. ....San Diego, CA
Dougherty, Leventhal & Price, LLP
Kingston, PA
Dougherty, Linda Fairbanks ....Ross, CA
Dougherty, Linda M. ....Lyndhurst, NJ
Dougherty, Lucia A. ....Miami, FL
Dougherty, Marc C. ....Harvey, LA
Dougherty, Maren J. ....Chicago, IL
Dougherty, Margaret M. ....Elizabeth, NJ
Dougherty, Marlene A. ....Winsted, CT
Dougherty, Marybeth ....Chicago, IL
Dougherty, Maureen ....Malverne, NY
Dougherty, Michael ....East Hanover, NJ
Dougherty, Michael G. ....Apple Valley, MN
Dougherty, Michael H. ....Los Angeles, CA
Dougherty, Michael J.
Equal Employment Opportunity
Commission,
Office of Federal Operations, GV
Dougherty, Michael J. ....New York, NY
Dougherty, Michael Joseph ....Naples, FL
Dougherty, Michael P. ....New York, NY
Dougherty, Michael R. ....Oakland, CA
Dougherty, Michael R. ....Ventura, CA
Dougherty, Michael T. ....Dallas, TX
Dougherty, Michele J. ....Los Angeles, CA
Dougherty, Modin & Holloway
Kansas City, MO
Dougherty, Nancy C. ....Baton Rouge, LA
Dougherty, Pamela A. ....Morristown, NJ
Dougherty, Patricia A. ....Columbus, OH
Dougherty, Patrick A. ....Baldwin, MI
Beulah, MI
Dougherty, Patrick A. ....Manistee, MI
Dougherty, Patrick D. ....Missoula, MT
Dougherty, Patrick E. ....Kingston, PA
Dougherty, Patrick J. ....Valparaiso, IN
Dougherty, Patrick T. ....Sioux Falls, SD
Dougherty, Paul C. ....Collingswood, NJ
Dougherty, Paul M. ....Ojai, CA
Dougherty, Paul V. ....Cleveland, OH
Dougherty, Philip R. ....Sacramento, CA
Dougherty, R. Wade ....New York, NY
Dougherty, Ralph H. ....Charlotte, NC
Dougherty, Robert A. ....Tampa, FL
Dougherty, Robert C. ....Portland, OR
Dougherty, Robert E. ....Ontario, CA
Dougherty, Robert F. ....Tulsa, OK
Dougherty, Robert J. ....Baltimore, MD
Dougherty, Robert K. ....Syracuse, NY
Dougherty, Robert Louis ....Garden City, NY
Dougherty, Robert P. ....Fort Smith, AR
Dougherty, Robert P. ....Newnan, GA
Dougherty, Robert P., Jr. ....Tyler, TX
Dougherty, Ronald W. ....Canton, OH
Salem, OH
Dougherty, Russell D. ....Louisville, KY
Dougherty, Russell E. ....McLean, VA
Dougherty, Ryan, Giuffra, Zambito & Hession
New York, NY
Dougherty, Salliann S.M.
Department of Justice,
Civil Rights Division, GV
Dougherty & Schneider ....Baldwin, NY
Dougherty and Scott ....Fairmont, MN
Dougherty, Sean O. ....New York, NY
Dougherty, Sharon ....Philadelphia, PA
Dougherty, Sharon E. ....Dunwoody, GA
Dougherty, Shawn ....Wilmington, DE
Dougherty, Sherry D. ....Kingsport, TN
Dougherty, Stephen J. ....Syracuse, NY
Dougherty, Steven W. ....Salt Lake City, UT
Dougherty, Terence A. ....Glen Mills, PA
Dougherty, Terrence ....New York, NY
Dougherty, Terry C. ....Lincoln, NE
Dougherty, Thomas A. ....Minneapolis, MN
Dougherty, Thomas A. ....Bridgeville, PA
Dougherty, Thomas E. ....Treasury Department,
United States Secret Service, GV
Dougherty, Thomas E. ....Roseville, MN
Dougherty, Thomas F. ....Minneapolis, MN
Dougherty, Thomas H.
Palm Beach Gardens, FL
Dougherty, Thomas H., P.A.
Palm Beach Gardens, FL
Dougherty, Thomas J. ....Boston, MA
Dougherty, Thomas J., Jr.
Washington, DC
Dougherty, Thomas K. ....Tyler, TX
Dougherty, Thomas M. ....Fort Myers, FL
Dougherty, Thomas P. ....Baldwin, NY
Dougherty, Thomas P., Jr. ....Houston, TX
Dougherty, Thos. E. ....Fairmont, MN
Dougherty, Timothy J. ....Merrillville, IN
Dougherty, Timothy J. ....Sioux Falls, SD
Dougherty, Timothy M. ....Baldwin, NY
Dougherty, Tom K. ....Clermont, FL
Dougherty, Veronica M. ....Cleveland, OH
Dougherty, William A. ....Villa Park, CA
Dougherty, William D. ....Florham Park, NJ
Dougherty, William F. ....New York, NY
Dougherty, William J., Jr.
Newport News, VA
Dougherty, William O. ....San Diego, CA
Dougherty, William P. ....Memphis, TN
Dougherty-Hogg, Anne ....Tampa, FL
Doughten, David L. ....Cleveland, OH
Doughten, Nancy M. N. ....Wilmington, DE
Doughten, Robert E. ....Johnstown, OH
Doughtery, Robert S. ....Indiana, PA
Doughtie, JoAnn ....Dahlonega, GA
Doughtie, Nath C. ....Gainesville, FL
Doughtie, Richard T., III ....Memphis, TN
Doughton, Richard L. ....Sparta, NC
Doughton, Susan Dominick
Birmingham, AL
Doughton, Thomas J. ....Winston-Salem, NC
Doughty, Bruce W. ....Chicago, IL
Doughty, Carol A. ....Sheridan, WY
Doughty, Clark G. ....Southfield, MI
Doughty, David A. ....Charlotte, NC
Doughty, David P. ....Rayville, LA
Doughty, Dennis G. ....Oklahoma City, OK
Doughty & Doughty ....Springfield, OH
Doughty, Edward R. ....Atlantic City, NJ
Linwood, NJ
Doughty, Francis E. ....Beacon, NY
Doughty, H. Cort, Jr. ....Columbus, OH
Doughty, James A. ....Springfield, OH
Doughty, Jason E. ....Houston, TX
Doughty, Jon A. ....Springfield, OH
Doughty, Kristi J. ....Mount Laurel, NJ
Doughty, Maria S. ....Northbrook, IL
Doughty, Mark A., Law Offices Of
Yuba City, CA
Doughty, R. Stephen ....Nashville, TN
Doughty, Robert M., II ....Alamogordo, NM
Doughty, Robert M., III
Albuquerque, NM
Doughty, Ross E., Jr. ....Uvalde, TX
Doughty, Stefan K. ....Oklahoma City, OK
Doughty, Stephen P. ....Wilmington, DE
Mount Laurel, NJ
Philadelphia, PA
Doughty, Tatyana ....New York, NY
Doughty, Terry A. ....Rayville, LA
Douglas, Alan C. ....San Diego, CA
Douglas, Alexa, Koeppen & Hurley
Valparaiso, IN
Douglas, Alexander S., II
Winter Park, FL
Douglas, Alfred J. ....Palm Desert, CA
Douglas, Alison C. ....Naples, FL
Douglas, Alroy L. ....Omaha, NE
Douglas, Amy B. ....Shoreham, VT
Douglas, Andrew G. ....Columbus, OH
Douglas, Anthony P. ....Oakland, CA
Douglas & Barnhill, P.C.
San Antonio, TX
Douglas, Benjamin A. ....Fort Worth, TX
Douglas, Benjamin L. ....San Francisco, CA
Douglas, Beverly, Jr. ....Columbia, TN
Douglas, Bradley D ....Washington, DC
Douglas, Bradley K. ....Austin, TX
Douglas, Brandon J. ....Boca Raton, FL
Douglas & Brown, P.A. ....Phoenix, AZ
Douglas, Bruce A. ....Bloomfield, CT
Douglas, Bruce E. ....Salem, OR
Douglas, Bruce J. ....Minneapolis, MN
Douglas, Bruce M. ....Denver, CO
Douglas, Bruce R. ....Buffalo, MN
Douglas, Carl E., Law Offices of
Beverly Hills, CA
Douglas, Carol M. ....Chicago, IL
Douglas, Caroline G. ....Concord, NH
Douglas, Catherine M. ....Raynham, MA
Douglas, Charles C. ....Indianapolis, IN
Douglas, Charles E. ....Norman, OK
Douglas, Charles G., III ....Concord, NH
Douglas, Charles L., Jr. ....Greenup, KY
Douglas, Charles T. ....Winston-Salem, NC
Douglas, Charles V., III ....San Diego, CA
Douglas, Charles W. ....Chicago, IL
Douglas, Christian D. ....Brookline, MA
Douglas, Christina U. ....Winston-Salem, NC
Douglas, Claybourne M. ....Longmont, CO
Douglas, Clifford, (A Prof. Law Corp.)
Rancho Santa Fe, CA
Douglas, Clifford E. ....Evanston, IL
Douglas & Conroyd, P.C. ....Salem, OR
Douglas, Craig McKinney ....Austin, TX
Douglas, D. Scott ....Belleair Beach, FL
Douglas, Dale S. ....Pittsburgh, PA
Douglas, Damon ....Athens, TX
Douglas, Darren V. ....Annapolis, MD
Douglas, Daryl J. ....Kansas City, MO
Douglas, David C. ....Treasury Department,
Office of the Comptroller of the Currency,
GV
Douglas, David C. ....Lockport, NY
Douglas, David E. ....Socorro, NM
Douglas, David Gray ....San Rafael, CA
Douglas, David Lloyd ....Tustin, CA
Douglas, David M. ....Austin, TX
Douglas, David S. ....New York, NY
Douglas, David W. ....Columbus, OH
Douglas, David W. ....Austin, TX
Douglas, Davison M. ....Williamsburg, VA
Douglas, Denham, Rogers & Hood
Portland, ME
Douglas, Dennis L. ....Spokane, WA
Douglas, Dennis O. ....Fairview Heights, IL
Douglas, Donald A. ....Helena, MT
Douglas, Donald C., Jr. ....Monroe, LA
Douglas, Donald D. ....Glendale, CA
Douglas, Donald W. ....Portland, OR
Douglas, Douglas & Douglas ....Carlisle, PA
Douglas & Douglas, L.L.C. ....Neosho, MO
Douglas, Dubignion ....Dublin, GA
Douglas, E. Scott ....Hermosa Beach, CA
Douglas, E. Sid, III ....Kansas City, MO
Douglas, E. Vernon ....Lake City, FL
Douglas, Earl M. ....Memphis, TN
Douglas, Eden, Phillips & Deruyter
Spokane, WA
Douglas, Edward L. ....Titusville, FL
Douglas, Edward L., Jr. ....Seattle, WA
Douglas, Edward M. ....Albany, NY
Douglas, Edward W. ....San Diego, CA
Douglas, Edwin L. ....Warrenville, IL
Douglas, Elvin S., Jr. ....Belton, MO
Harrisonville, MO
Douglas, Flach ....Cincinnati, OH
Milford, OH
Douglas, Flach, & Co., LPA ....Milford, OH
Douglas, Franklin ....New York, NY
Douglas, Frederick A. ....Washington, DC
Douglas, Frederick L. ....Atlanta, GA
Douglas, G. Kay ....Huntsville, TX
Douglas, Garey, Hammill & Robinson
Los Angeles, CA
Douglas, Gary D. ....Midland, TX
Douglas, Gary J. ....Jericho, NY
Douglas, Gene ....Wilton Manors, FL
Douglas, George C., Jr. ....Birmingham, AL
Douglas, George F., III ....Carlisle, PA
Douglas, George R., Jr. ....Arlington, VA
Douglas, George Walker
Winston-Salem, NC
Douglas, Gerald P. ....Garden City, NY
Douglas, Glenn M. ....Houston, TX
Douglas, Gregory A. ....Long Beach, CA
Douglas, H. Dwight ....Neosho, MO
Douglas, Harry E., IV ....Los Angeles, CA
Douglas, Herbert ....Neosho, MO
Douglas, Herbert K. ....Valparaiso, IN
Douglas, J. Andrew ....Los Angeles, CA
Douglas, J. Paul ....Gastonia, NC
Douglas, Jack W. ....Houston, TX
Douglas, James A. ....Department of Defense,
Defense Legal Services Agency, GV
Douglas, James A. ....Seattle, WA
Douglas, James Boyd, Jr. ....Auburn, AL
Douglas, James D. ....Washington, DC
Douglas, James D. ....Washington, DC
Douglas, James E. ....Hermitage, PA
Douglas, James E., Jr. ....Juneau, AK
Douglas, James H. ....Valparaiso, IN
Douglas, James J. ....Westbury, NY
Douglas, James M. ....New York, NY
Douglas, James Matthew ....Houston, TX
Douglas, James W. ....Sutton, WV
Douglas, Jane Nussbaum ....Charleston, SC
Douglas, Jeffrey J. ....Los Angeles, CA
Douglas, Jeffrey J. ....Santa Monica, CA
Douglas & Jenkinson ....Martinsburg, WV
Douglas, Jerry Mack, Jr. ....Virginia Beach, VA
Douglas, Jo Ann Neuhoff ....New York, NY
Douglas, Joan Capps ....Houston, TX
Douglas, Jodi K. ....Parsons, WV

Douglas, Joel Bruce ....Los Angeles, CA
Douglas, John E. ....Los Angeles, CA
Douglas, John E. ....Oklahoma City, OK
Douglas, John H. ....San Francisco, CA
Douglas, John H. ....Charleston, SC
Douglas, John Hilton ....Indianapolis, IN
Douglas, John L. ....Washington, DC
Atlanta, GA
Douglas, John P. ....Dallas, TX
Douglas, John R. ....Omaha, NE
Douglas, John R. ....Dallas, TX
Douglas, John T. ....Aynor, SC
Douglas, John W. ....Washington, DC
Douglas & Joseph ....Hermitage, PA
Sharon, PA
Douglas, Joseph H. ....Bettendorf, IA
Douglas, Karen L. ....Matthews, NC
Douglas, Karen Y. ....Department of Justice, Antitrust Division, GV
Douglas, Katherine Cole ....Philadelphia, PA
Douglas, Kathleen L. ....Garden City, NY
Douglas, Kathleen M. ....Honolulu, HI
Douglas, Keith W., Law Offices of
Northridge, CA
Douglas, Kelly Capen ....San Diego, CA
Douglas, Kelly M. ....Billerica, MA
Douglas, Kenneth A. ....Corsicana, TX
Douglas, Kenneth J. ....Franklin Park, IL
Douglas, Kerry D. ....Bolivar, MO
Douglas, Kevin H. ....Nashville, TN
Douglas, Larry B. ....Houston, TX
Douglas, Larry D., (P.A.) ....Springdale, AR
Douglas, Laura ....Fort Lauderdale, FL
Douglas, Laura G. ....Bronx, NY
Douglas, Laura L. ....Southfield, MI
Douglas Law Firm, P.C. ....Libby, MT
Douglas, Linda Trombly ....Essex, CT
Douglas, Lisa R. ....Santa Monica, CA
Douglas, Loretta C. ....Chicago, IL
Douglas, Louis ....New Orleans, LA
Douglas, Lynch, Haun & Kirksey, P.C.
Bolivar, MO
Douglas, Lynne M. ....Overland Park, KS
Douglas, M. Joy ....Salt Lake City, UT
Douglas, Malcolm C. ....Cleveland, OH
Douglas, Marilyn P. ....Wallingford, CT
Douglas, Marion Elizabeth ....Los Angeles, CA
Douglas, Martica S. ....Portland, ME
Douglas, Matthew J. ....Denver, CO
Douglas, Melanie P. ....Colorado Springs, CO
Douglas, Melvyn L. ....Dallas, TX
Douglas, Merrilynn R. ....Grafton, MA
Douglas, Michael E. ....Frankfort, IN
Douglas, Michael I. ....Los Angeles, CA
Douglas, Michael R. ....Tampa, FL
Douglas, Michelle M. ....Kentfield, CA
Douglas, Morris T. ....Richmond, VA
Douglas, Nancy L. ....San Francisco, CA
Douglas, Nathaniel ....Department of Justice, Environment and Natural Resources Division, GV
Douglas, Nils R. ....New Orleans, LA
Douglas, Ollis, Jr. ....Newark, NJ
Douglas, P. Lanier ....Jackson, MS
Douglas, Pamela L. ....Duarte, CA
Douglas, Patrice Raye Dills
Oklahoma City, OK
Douglas, Patricia Byrne ....Baltimore, MD
Douglas, Patricia H. ....Baton Rouge, LA
Douglas, Patricia Labarta ....Tampa, FL
Douglas, Patricia S. ....Washington, DC
Douglas, Patricia W. S. ....Washington, DC
Douglas, Paul A. ....New York, NY
Douglas, Paul F., Jr. ....San Bernardino, CA
Douglas, Paul I. ....Boston, MA
Douglas, Paul I. ....Norfolk, MA
Douglas, Paul P. ....New York, NY
Douglas, Paul T. ....West Palm Beach, FL
Douglas, Peter R. ....New York, NY
Douglas, Philip ....Port Chester, NY
Douglas, Philip Le B. ....New York, NY
Douglas, Phyllis O. ....Miami, FL
Douglas, Preston J. ....New York, NY
Douglas, Priscilla H. ....Santa Ana, CA
Douglas, Ralph P., Jr. ....Tallahassee, FL
Douglas, Ralph Paul ....DeLand, FL
Douglas, Randall R., (P.C.) ....Phoenix, AZ
Douglas, Ravenel, Hardy & Crihfield, L.L.P.
Greensboro, NC
High Point, NC
Douglas, Raymond G. ....Metuchen, NJ
Douglas, R. D., Jr. ....Greensboro, NC
Douglas, Rebecca Lyn ....New York, NY
Douglas, Renee Riley ....Midland, TX
Douglas, Richard A. ....Scottsbluff, NE
Douglas, Richard E. ....Miami, FL
Douglas, Richard J. ....Department of Justice, Criminal Division, GV
Douglas, Richard L. ....Martinsburg, WV
Douglas, Richard W. ....Hagerstown, MD
Douglas, Robert C. ....Baltimore, MD
Douglas, Robert C., Jr. ....Denver, CO
Douglas, Robert D., III ....Greensboro, NC
Douglas, Robert E. ....Downers Grove, IL
Douglas, Robert E. ....St. Joseph, MO
Douglas, Robert E. ....Charleston, WV
Charleston, WV
Douglas, Robert J. ....San Francisco, CA
Douglas, Robert J., Jr. ....Des Moines, IA
Douglas, Robert L., (Ltd.) ....Robinson, IL
Douglas, Robert M. ....Greenwich, NY
Douglas, Robert S. ....Topeka, KS
Douglas, Robinson, Leonard & Garvey, P.C.
Concord, NH
Douglas, Rodney Scott ....Washington, DC
Douglas, Roger E. ....Valdosta, GA
Douglas, Ronald G. ....Mount Pleasant, MI
Douglas, Ronald P. ....Spokane, WA

Douglas, Roxanne ....Atlanta, GA
Douglas, Scott S. ....Carthage, MO
Douglas, Sharon ....Tucson, AZ
Douglas, Stacy L. ....Los Angeles, CA
Douglas, Stephen Allen ....Valhalla, NY
Douglas, Stephen J. ....Jacksonville, FL
Douglas, Steven C. ....Crossville, TN
Douglas, Steven R. ....West Frankfort, IL
Douglas, Sue Marie ....Cleveland, OH
Douglas, Ted S. ....Lenoir, NC
Douglas, Terry A. ....Dallas, TX
Douglas, Thomas C. ....Millersburg, OH
Douglas, Thomas J., Jr. ....Garden City, NY
Douglas, Thomas L., Jr.
Department Of Veterans Affairs, Board of Veterans Appeals, GV
Douglas, Thomas M. ....Southfield, MI
Douglas, Thomas S. ....Sylvania, OH
Douglas, Troy R. ....Fort Smith, AR
Douglas, Walter M. ....Glendora, CA
Douglas, Warren C. ....Cherry Hill, NJ
Douglas, Wayne R. ....Portland, ME
Douglas, Wayne W. ....Gleneden Beach, OR
Douglas, Wilhelmina G. ....Philadelphia, PA
Douglas, Willard H., Jr. ....Richmond, VA
Douglas, William A. ....Libby, MT
Douglas, William D. ....Tampa, FL
Douglas, William Dan, Jr. ....Ripley, TN
Douglas, William H. ....Phoenix, AZ
Douglas, William James ....Gold River, CA
Douglas, William P. ....Carlisle, PA
Douglas, Winston H. ....Treasury Department, Internal Revenue Service, GV
Douglas, Wuester & Disney, P.C.
Fort Worth, TX
Douglas-Gershowitz, Melissa Ann
Charlotte, NC
Douglas-Hamilton, Margaret H.
New York, NY
Douglas-Ntagha, Pamela ....Richmond, TX
Douglass, Andrew Ian ....Boston, MA
Providence, RI
Douglass, Anne Sheffler ....Bradenton, FL
Douglass, B. Scott ....San Francisco, CA
Douglass, Bedford, Jr. ....Mesa, AZ
Douglass, Charles R. ....Dunwoody, GA
Douglass, Charlotte N. B.
Library of Congress, Copyright Office, GV
Douglass & Chew ....El Paso, TX
Douglass, Clifton F., III ....San Antonio, TX
Douglass, Craig S. ....Dallas, TX
Douglass, Cynthia B. ....Upland, CA
Douglass, Daniel B. ....Spencer, WV
Douglass, Daniel B., II ....Spencer, WV
Douglass, Daniel W. ....Los Angeles, CA
Douglass, David L. ....Washington, DC
Douglass, David M., & Associates
Cleveland, OH
Douglass & DeFoy ....Cleveland, OH
Douglass, Donald G. ....Scranton, PA
Douglass & Douglass ....Raleigh, NC
Douglass & Douglass ....Spencer, WV
Douglass, Ellen E. ....Chicago, IL
Douglass, Ernest M. ....Spencer, WV
Douglass, Eugene G., Jr. ....Bartlett, TN
Douglass & Ferrarino ....Mesa, AZ
Douglass, Frank ....Austin, TX
Dallas, TX
Douglass, Fredk. C. ....Chokoloskee, FL
Douglass, Gene ....Wichita Falls, TX
Douglass, Georgette Sosa
Fort Lauderdale, FL
Douglass, Gregory K. ....Beaver, PA
Douglass, Heather Kirk ....Drexel Hill, PA
Douglass, Howard F. ....Lexington, TN
Douglass, J. Stuart ....Metairie, LA
Douglass, J. Stuart, A.P.L.C. ....Metairie, LA
Douglass, James D. ....Broomfield, CO
Douglass, James H. ....Portland, ME
Douglass, James M., (P.A.) ....Venice, FL
Douglass, James R. ....Cleveland, OH
Douglass, John E. ....Apple Valley, CA
Douglass, John G. ....Richmond, VA
Douglass, John Jay ....Houston, TX
Douglass, John P. ....North Oaks, MN
Douglass, John R. ....Amarillo, TX
Douglass, John W. ....Fort Lauderdale, FL
Douglass, Joseph D. ....Washington, DC
Douglass, Judith N. ....San Jose, CA
Douglass, Julianne G. ....Atlanta, GA
Douglass, Kent R. ....Livingston, MT
Douglass, Kevin K. ....Pittsburgh, PA
Douglass Law Firm, P.A. ....Tallahassee, FL
Douglass, Malcolm C. ....Abilene, TX
Douglass, Maria T.
Export-Import Bank of The United States, Office of the General Counsel, GV
Douglass, Mary McCafferty ....Lansing, MI
Douglass, Michael A. ....Liberty, IN
Douglass, Michael C. ....Phoenix, AZ
Tucson, AZ
Douglass, Michele A. ....Long Beach, CA
Douglass, Michelle J. ....Vineland, NJ
Douglass, Neria R. ....Auburn, ME
Douglass, Orion L., (P.C.) ....Brunswick, GA
Douglass, Paul M. ....El Paso, TX
Douglass, Paul S. ....Lewiston, ME
Douglass, R. Daniel, (P.C.) ....Atlanta, GA
Douglass, Richard L. ....Columbia, MS
Douglass, Robert A., P.A.
St. Petersburg Beach, FL
Douglass, Robert E. ....St. Joseph, MO
Douglass, Robert P. ....Bullhead City, AZ
Douglass, Robert R. ....New York, NY
Douglass, S. Preston, Jr. ....Kerrville, TX
Douglass, Sam P. ....Houston, TX
Douglass, Samuel L. ....Pittsburgh, PA

Douglass, Sharon L. ....Los Angeles, CA
Douglass, Steven N. ....Memphis, TN
Douglass, Susan G. ....Houston, TX
Douglass, Susan Upton ....New York, NY
Douglass, Teresa K. ....Mexico, MO
Douglass, Thomas E. ....St. Louis, MO
Douglass, Thomas E. ....North Olmsted, OH
Douglass, Thomas G. ....Raleigh, NC
Douglass, Thomas G., Jr. ....Atlanta, GA
Douglass, Thomas N., Jr. ....Indio, CA
Douglass, W. Birch, III ....Richmond, VA
Douglass, W. Bruce, Jr. ....Houston, TX
Douglass, W. Dexter ....Tallahassee, FL
Douglass, Wallace P. ....San Francisco, CA
Douglass, West & Associates
Drexel Hill, PA
Douglass, William B. ....Naples, FL
Douglass, William D. ....Orinda, CA
Douglass, William D.
Department of State, GV
Douglass, William F. ....Eureka Springs, AR
Douglass, William T., Jr. ....Charleston, WV
Douglass, William V.
San Luis Obispo, CA
Douglass, Willis B. ....Mission Viejo, CA
Douglass, Wylie B. ....Chicago, IL
Douglass-Talley, Rita ....Oklahoma City, OK
Doukas, Andrew J. ....Portland, ME
Doukas & Hewell ....San Diego, CA
Doukas, John M. ....Boston, MA
Doukas, Karla J. ....Boston, MA
Doukas, Kenneth J., Jr.
New Brunswick, NJ
Doukas, Michael E. ....San Diego, CA
Doukas, Patricia A. ....Darien, CT
Douma, Alyson C. ....Clark, NJ
Douma, Carl T. ....Pasadena, CA
Douma, Edward L. ....Richmond, VA
Douma, Philip K. ....Lansing, MI
Doumani, Edward M. ....Los Angeles, CA
Doumani, Peter J. ....Los Angeles, CA
Doumani, Roy ....Venice, CA
Doumar, Allsworth, Curtis, Cross, Laystrom, Perloff, Voigt, Wachs & Mac Iver
Fort Lauderdale, FL
Miami, FL
Tallahassee, FL
West Palm Beach, FL
Doumar, Charles C. ....New York, NY
Doumar, George R. A. ....Washington, DC
Doumar, Raymond A., (P.C.)
Fort Lauderdale, FL
Doumar, Raymond J. ....Augusta, GA
Doumar, Robert G. ....Norfolk, VA
Doumar, Roger Alfred ....Baltimore, MD
Doumas, Alexandra ....Roseland, NJ
Doumas, Leonidas P. ....Bayonne, NJ
Doumazios, Ted ....Mineola, NY
Doummar, Richard H. ....Virginia Beach, VA
Dounias, Peter ....Central Islip, NY
Dounson, Pepos S. ....San Antonio, TX
Douoguih, Augustin ....Reston, VA
Doupé, G. E. Craig ....Richland, WA
Douple, Daryl R. ....Dayton, OH
Dourbetas, Nico A. ....Santa Ana, CA
Dourian, Robert, Law Offices of
Pasadena, CA
Douros, George, Jr. ....St. Louis, MO
Douros, Irene V. ....Manchester, MO
Douros, Timothy J. ....Boston, MA
Dourson, Martha Culler ....Cincinnati, OH
Douse, David B. ....Salisbury, MD
Douse, Steven C. ....Nashville, TN
Doussard Hodel & Markman, Professional Corporation ....Lakewood, CO
Doussard, Joseph E. ....Lakewood, CO
Douthat, Charles R. ....New Haven, CT
Douthat, James F. ....Roanoke, VA
Douthat, Kenneth E. ....Nashville, TN
Douthett, Breaden M. ....Cleveland, OH
Douthett, Jill A. ....Philadelphia, PA
Douthett, Marshall B. ....Jackson, OH
Douthit, Claire E. ....Denver, CO
Douthit, Dawn M. ....Dallas, TX
Douthit, Durell ....Honolulu, HI
Douthit, Eric M. ....Indianapolis, IN
Douthit, Evan A. ....Kansas City, MO
Douthit Frets Rouse & Gentile, L.L.C.
Kansas City, MO
Douthit, Marc Anthony ....Miami, FL
Douthit, Zona C. ....Walnut Creek, CA
Douthitt, Troy, Jr. ....Wichita Falls, TX
Douthitt, Troy, Jr. & Associates, Inc.
Wichita Falls, TX
Douthwaite, Charles K. ....Tacoma, WA
Douthwaite, David T. ....Portland, OR
Douvan, Eugene V. ....Ann Arbor, MI
Douvan, Thomas A. ....San Francisco, CA
Douvas, Augustus G. ....Darien, IL
Douveas, Julie A. ....Irvine, CA
Douville, Leo E. ....Baltimore, MD
Douville, Louise M. ....Santa Ana, CA
Douville, Susanni ....Damariscotta, ME
Doval, Juan F. ....San Juan, PR
Dovalina, Jesus M. ....Eagle Pass, TX
Dovbish, Alfred ....Corte Madera, CA
Dove & Chill ....Greenwood, MS
Jackson, MS
Dove, David J. ....Seattle, WA
Dove, Douglas S. ....St. Louis, MO
Dove & Dove ....Shelbyville, IL
Dove, Ellen C. ....Sacramento, CA
Dove, Frank P. ....Kerrville, TX
Dove, Franklin E. ....Shelbyville, IL
Dove, Haven Lee ....Mesa, AZ
Dove, Henry P. ....Easton, MD
Dove, Ira L. ....Morristown, TN

Dove, J. Matthew ....Lake City, SC
Surfside Beach, SC
Dove, Jay R. ....Santa Rosa, CA
Dove, Jeffrey A. ....Syracuse, NY
Dove, John W. ....San Antonio, TX
Dove, Joyce S. ....Tallahassee, FL
Dove, L. Dale ....Rock Hill, SC
Dove, Luke ....Greenwood, MS
Jackson, MS
Dove, Mark J. ....North Vernon, IN
Dove, Mathew ....Jackson, MS
Waco, TX
Dove, Maureen Mullen ....Baltimore, MD
Dove, Michael S. ....New Ulm, MN
Dove, Paul D. ....Minneapolis, MN
Dove, Paulette Fiorentino ....Springfield, IL
Dove, Rhett P., III ....Miami, FL
Dove, Richard Allan ....Columbus, OH
Dove, Ronald G. ....Washington, DC
Dove, Sharon Schwartz ....New York, NY
Dove, Stephen A. ....Department of Energy, Office of the General Counsel, GV
Dove, T. Clark ....Phoenix, AZ
Dove, Thomas P. ....San Francisco, CA
Dove, Tonetta Tollefson
South St. Paul, MN
Dove, Valerie Denise ....Cleveland, OH
Dove, W. Scott ....New York, NY
Dove-Coleman, Evelyn ....Kinston, NC
Dovel, Gregory S. ....Los Angeles, CA
Dovel, J. Newton ....Luray, VA
Dovenbarger, Daniel B. ....Indianapolis, IN
Dover, Agnes Pek ....Washington, DC
Dover, Albert P. ....Nevada City, CA
Dover, Brian Douglas ....Philadelphia, MS
Dover, Dale Warren ....Alexandria, VA
Dover, Darrell D. ....Little Rock, AR
Dover & Dixon, P.A. ....Little Rock, AR
Dover, J. Michael ....Valdosta, GA
Dover, James R. ....Dillon, CO
Dover, James R., P.C., Law Office of
Dillon, CO
Dover, Jeffrey ....Atlanta, GA
Dover, Jeffrey H., P.C. ....Atlanta, GA
Dover, Jennifer ....Chicago, IL
Dover, Mark A. ....Kansas City, MO
Dover, Marleigh Diane
Department of Justice, Civil Division, GV
Dover, Michael A. ....Dallas, TX
Dover, P. B., Jr. ....Deer Park, TX
Dover, Sleeter C. ....Cheyenne, WY
Dover, Thomas E. ....Cleveland, OH
Dover, Thomas J. ....Bakersfield, CA
Dover, Willard D. ....Fort Lauderdale, FL
Doverman, Elizabeth J. ....Philadelphia, PA
Doverspike, John David ....Atlanta, GA
Doverspike, Terry R. ....Tulsa, OK
Dove-Taylor, Jeanne, Law Office of
Dahlgren, VA
Dovey, Clayton C., III ....Johnstown, PA
Dovi, Susan A. ....San Francisco, CA
Doviak, Alison R. ....New York, NY
Dovidio, Joseph A. ....Philadelphia, PA
Dovidio, Kathleen Ann ....Oakland, CA
Dovidio, Thomas P. ....Diamond Bar, CA
Dovin, Edward J. ....Atlanta, GA
Dovith, Melvin W. ....Mobile, AL
Dovitz, Clifford J. ....Bloomfield Hills, MI
Dovitz, Susan B. ....Farmington Hills, MI
Dovletian, Garineh S. ....Morristown, NJ
New York, NY
Dovnik, Karl, Jr. ....Wales, WI
Dovre, Gary L. ....Farmington Hills, MI
Dow, Alan E. ....St. Louis, MO
Dow, Alex A. ....Fort Lauderdale, FL
Dow, Andrea C. ....Boston, MA
Dow, Bernard O. ....Houston, TX
Dow, Charles A. ....Augusta, ME
Dow, Chas E. ....Boston, MA
Dow, Cheryl A. ....Newport Beach, CA
Dow, Christopher J. ....Buffalo, NY
Dow, Cogburn & Friedman, P.C.
Houston, TX
Dow, David A. ....New York, NY
Dow, David C. ....Norway, ME
Dow, David J. ....San Diego, CA
Dow, David P. ....Amesbury, MA
Dow, David R. ....Houston, TX
Dow, David W. ....Phoenix, AZ
Dow, De'Ana H.
Commodity Futures Trading Commission, Division of Trading and Markets, GV
Dow, Denise Jarrett ....Chicago, IL
Dow, Dennis R. ....Kansas City, MO
Dow, Diane L. ....Dearborn Heights, MI
Dow, Edson H. ....Tacoma, WA
Dow, Einhaus & Mattison, P.A.
Owatonna, MN
Dow, Elizabeth Hoskins ....Joliet, IL
Dow, Francis V. ....Albany, NY
Dow, George E., Jr. ....Owatonna, MN
Dow, Gregory C. ....Kennewick, WA
Dow, H. Cushman ....San Diego, CA
Dow, Harmon B. ....Chicago, IL
Dow, Howell & McClinton, L.L.P.
Waco, TX
Dow, J. Greg ....Houston, TX
Dow, J. Luke ....Austin, TX
Dow, J. Matthew ....Austin, TX
Dow, Jeffrey L. ....Lexington, MA
Dow, John Ferris ....Somerville, MA
Dow, John Mack ....Tooele, UT
Dow, Joseph Sheffield ....Brookline, MA
Dow, Juliane M. ....Boston, MA
Dow, Karen B. ....Palo Alto, CA
Dow, Karen R. ....Houston, TX
Dow, Kenneth J. ....Wayne, NJ

Dow Law Firm, The, LLC
Fort Collins, CO
Dow & Lewis, P.C. ... Boston, MA
Dow, Linda A. ... West Hartford, CT
Dow, Lohnes & Albertson, PLLC
Washington, DC
Atlanta, GA
Dow, Margaret Joanne ... Bemidji, MN
Dow, Mark C. ... Albuquerque, NM
Dow, Martin P. ... Toledo, OH
Dow, Melvin A. ... Houston, TX
Dow, Michael H. ... Sioux Falls, SD
Dow, Patricia T. ... Fort Collins, CO
Dow, Paul A. ... Tujunga, CA
Dow, Paula T. ... Newark, NJ
Dow, Peter F. ... Boston, MA
Dow, Randolph C. ... Southern Pines, NC
Dow, Randy R. ... West Palm Beach, FL
Dow, Rebecca Wilcox ... Denver, CO
Dow, Reema ... Detroit, MI
Dow, Robert ... Huntington Beach, CA
Dow, Robert F. ... Atlanta, GA
Dow, Robert L. ... Lake Charles, LA
Dow, Robert M., Jr. ... Chicago, IL
Dow, Rodney H. ... Milwaukee, WI
Dow, Russell B. ... Portland, ME
Dow's Law Office, P.A. ... Norway, ME
Dow, Sanford L. ... Houston, TX
Dow, Scott A. ... Suffern, NY
Dow, Sharon Kale ... Cary, NC
Dow, Steven H. ... Tulsa, OK
Dow, Steven J. ... San Francisco, CA
Dow, Steven M. ... Waco, TX
Dow, Stuart J. ... Houston, TX
Dow, T. Andrew ... Dallas, TX
Dow, Timothy J. ... Fort Collins, CO
Dow, Wallace M. ... Baltimore, MD
Dow, William F., III ... New Haven, CT
Dow, William W. ... Bradford, MA
Dowben, Carla ... Dallas, TX
Dowcett, Daniel F. X. ... Boston, MA
Dowcett, John P. ... Boston, MA
Dowd, A. Joseph ... New York, NY
Dowd, Adam J. ... Northfield, MN
Dowd, Anne P. ... Boston, MA
Dowd, Barbara C. ... Brooklyn, NY
Dowd, Barry W. ... Monroe, LA
Dowd, Bloch & Bennett ... Chicago, IL
Dowd & Blount ... Dallas, TX
Dowd, Bonnie Lee ... Seattle, WA
Dowd, Bradley Michael ... Leawood, KS
Kansas City, MO
Dowd, C. Wayne ... Texarkana, AR
Dowd, Cathy A. ... East Hartford, CT
Dowd, Cindra M. ... Norfolk, VA
Richmond, VA
Dowd, Daniel G. ... Phoenix, AZ
Dowd, Daniel J. ... Des Plaines, IL
Dowd, David D. ... Boston, MA
Dowd, David D., III ... Birmingham, AL
Dowd, David D., Jr. ... Akron, OH
Dowd, David F. ... Washington, DC
Dowd, Deborah ... Seattle, WA
Dowd, Debra J.C. ... Richmond, VA
Dowd, Donald W. ... Villanova, PA
Dowd, Donald W. ... Linden, TX
Dowd, Douglas P. ... St. Louis, MO
Dowd & Dowd ... Omaha, NE
Dowd & Dowd, Ltd. ... Chicago, IL
Des Plaines, IL
Lake Geneva, WI
Dowd, Dowd & Mertes, Ltd.
Des Plaines, IL
Dowd & Dowd, P.C. ... St. Louis, MO
Dowd, Duane J. ... Omaha, NE
Dowd, Earl M. ... Rockville, IN
Dowd, Edward C. ... Escondido, CA
Dowd, Edward C., A Prof. Corp.
Escondido, CA
Dowd, Edward H. ... McLean, VA
Dowd, Edward J. ... Dayton, OH
Dowd, Edward L. ... St. Louis, MO
Dowd, Edward L., Jr. ... St. Louis, MO
Dowd, Ellen J. ... La Jolla, CA
Dowd, Garrett J. ... New York, NY
Dowd, Glenn W. ... Hartford, CT
Dowd, Harrelson, Moore & Giles
Texarkana, AR
Texarkana, TX
Dowd, Haseltine, Poertner & Redmond
St. Louis, MO
Dowd, Hector G. ... New York, NY
Dowd, J. Peter ... Chicago, IL
Dowd, Jacqueline H. ... Orlando, FL
Dowd, James A. ... Mountainside, NJ
Dowd, James E. ... Concord, MA
Dowd, James E. ... Springfield, MA
Dowd, James F. ... New York, NY
Dowd, James F., III ... St. Louis, MO
Dowd, James L. ... Syosset, NY
Dowd, James M. ... Washington, DC
Boston, MA
Dowd, James M. ... St. Louis, MO
Dowd, James P. ... New York, NY
Dowd, Joanne ... Forest Hills, NY
Dowd, Joanne Jordan ... Roseland, NJ
Dowd, John A. ... Garden City, NY
Dowd, John C. ... Cleveland, OH
Dowd, John C. ... Milwaukee, WI
Dowd, John C., S.C. ... Milwaukee, WI
Dowd, John F. ... Mahopac, NY
Dowd, John G. ... Binghamton, NY
Lewiston, NY
Dowd, John M. ... Washington, DC
Dowd, John P. ... Omaha, NE
Dowd, John R. ... Shalimar, FL
Dowd, Joseph P. ... Des Plaines, IL
Dowd, Joseph V. ... Chicago, IL
Des Plaines, IL
Dowd, Judith A.
Federal Energy Regulatory Commission,
Office of the Administrative Law Judges, GV
Dowd, Karen L. ... Phoenix, AZ
Dowd, Karen M. ... Westbury, NY
Dowd, Kellian Hall ... San Francisco, CA
Dowd, Kelvin J. ... Washington, DC
Dowd, Kennedy & Dowd ... Oak Lawn, IL
Dowd, Kevin M. ... Hartford, CT
Dowd, Kevin M. ... Norwich, NY
Dowd, Kevin T. ... Newburgh, NY
Dowd, Lucy F. ... Morristown, NJ
Dowd, Lynn D. ... Chicago, IL
Dowd, Mark K. ... New York, NY
Dowd & Marotta, P.C. ... New York, NY
Dowd, Martin F. ... Newark, NJ
Dowd, Mary Joanne ... Washington, DC
Dowd, Matthew J. ... Topeka, KS
Dowd, Matthew J. ... New York, NY
Dowd, Maureen O. ... South Bend, IN
Dowd, Melissa Ann ... Monterey, VA
Dowd, Michael F. ... Princeton, MA
Dowd, Michael G. ... New York, NY
Dowd, Michael G. ... Richmond, VA
Dowd, Michael J. ... San Diego, CA
Dowd, Michael J. ... Lewiston, NY
Dowd, Michael J. ... Sayre, PA
Dowd, Michael P. ... Omaha, NE
Dowd, Michael V. ... Boston, MA
Dowd, Nancy E. ... Gainesville, FL
Dowd, Patrick C. ... Chicago, IL
Des Plaines, IL
Lake Geneva, WI
Dowd, Patrick C. ... Chesterfield, MO
Dowd, Patrick K. ... Seattle, WA
Dowd, Paul A. ... Manchester, NH
Dowd, Raymond J. ... New York, NY
Dowd & Reilly ... Red Bank, NJ
Dowd, Richard K. ... St. Louis, MO
Dowd, Robert E. ... Bakersfield, CA
Dowd, Robert E. ... Beachwood, OH
Dowd, Robert G., Jr. ... St. Louis, MO
Dowd, Robert K. ... Dallas, TX
Dowd, Robert M. ... Hanford, CA
Dowd, Robert S., Jr. ... Hackensack, NJ
Dowd, Rodney B. ... Longview, TX
Dowd, Ronald B. ... Hutchinson, KS
Dowd, Rosalie ... Hyannis, MA
Dowd, Sean ... Palo Alto, CA
Dowd, Steven M. ... Diboll, TX
Dowd, Susan Heckard ... Indianapolis, IN
Dowd, Terry Bancroft ... Washington, DC
Dowd, Thomas A. ... Chicago, IL
Dowd, Thomas F. ... Clayton, MO
Dowd, Thomas F. ... Omaha, NE
Dowd, Thomas P. ... Fairfield, CT
Dowd, Thomas P. ... Baltimore, MD
Dowd, Thomas R. ... St. Louis, MO
Dowd, Thomas S. ... Charlottesville, VA
Dowd, Thos. M. ... Kenton, OH
Dowd, Timothy C. ... Oklahoma City, OK
Dowd, Timothy K. ... San Diego, CA
Dowd, W. Timothy ... Oklahoma City, OK
Dowd, William C. ... Oak Lawn, IL
Dowd, William F. ... Red Bank, NJ
Dowd, William T. ... St. Louis, MO
Dowd, Willis F., IV ... Charlotte, NC
Dowda, D. Lamar ... Greensboro, NC
Dowda and Fields, Chartered ... Palatka, FL
Dowdal, Bridgid E. ... Department of Justice,
Civil Division, GV
Dowdal, Emmett ... White Bear Lake, MN
Dowdal, Mullen J. ... Minneapolis, MN
Dowdall & Associates, P.C. ... Boston, MA
Dowdall, Colleen M. ... Missoula, MT
Dowdall, J. Patrick ... Boston, MA
Dowdall, Janice L. ... St. Paul, MN
Dowdalls, Thomas J. ... Walnut Creek, CA
Dowdell, Donald A. ... Tallahassee, FL
Dowdell, John E. ... Tulsa, OK
Dowdell, Patricia Alicia
Department of Labor, GV
Dowdell, Paul F. ... Phoenix, AZ
Dowdell, Stacey A. ... Phoenix, AZ
Dowdell, Thomas E. ... Washington, DC
Dowdell, Thomas J., III ... Marathon, FL
Dowden, Albert R. ... New York, NY
Dowden, Alvin C., Jr. ... Leesville, LA
Dowden, Anne Marie ... Los Angeles, CA
Dowden, Cindy M. ... New York, NY
Dowden, Daniel Drew ... Laguna Niguel, CA
Dowden, Don L. ... Memphis, TN
Dowden, Donald S. ... New York, NY
Dowden, Hicks & Lambright
Leesville, LA
Dowden, James F. ... Little Rock, AR
Dowden, James H. ... Jersey City, NJ
Dowden, Leigh A. ... Atlanta, GA
Dowden, Lisa G. ... Washington, DC
Dowden, Susan ... Baton Rouge, LA
Dowden, Zdancewicz & Camp
Jackson, TN
Memphis, TN
Dowdey, Landon Gerald ... Washington, DC
Dowdie, Cathleen M. ... Washington, DC
Dowding, Dowding & Dowding
Grand Island, NE
Lincoln, NE
Dowding, Joseph C. ... Lincoln, NE
Dowding, Phillips M. ... Newport News, VA
Dowding, Steven W. ... Grand Island, NE
Dowding, Vince ... Grand Island, NE
Dowdle, Brenda M. ... Nashville, TN
Dowdle, Michael D. ... Morgan Hill, CA
Dowdle, Michael L. ... Salt Lake City, UT
Dowdle, Patrick D. ... Westminster, CO
Dowdle, Richd. E. ... Chicago, IL
Dowds, John Stevens ... Louisville, KY
Dowds, Norman R. ... Los Angeles, CA
Dowds, Patricia E. ... Charlotte, NC
Dowdy, Alicia K. ... Houston, TX
Dowdy, David H. ... Northport, AL
Dowdy, Geo. W. ... Humble, TX
Dowdy, Irene ... Trenton, NJ
Dowdy, James Jeffery ... Sanford, FL
Dowdy, Jeff ... Winter Springs, FL
Dowdy, John M., Jr. ... Jackson, MS
Dowdy, John V., Jr. ... Arlington, TX
Dowdy, John V., Jr. ... Fort Worth, TX
Dowdy, Kenneth A. ... Birmingham, AL
Dowdy, L. Craig ... Atlanta, GA
Dowdy, Lemuel W.
Federal Trade Commission,
Bureau of Consumer Protection, GV
Dowdy & Nielsen, P.A. ... Winter Springs, FL
Dowdy, Robert A. ... Tacoma, WA
Dowdy, T. William ... Dillwyn, VA
Springfield, VA
Dowdy, T. William ... Fairfax, VA
Dowdy, Theresa M. ... Boston, MA
Dowdy, Timothy W. ... Dallas, TX
Dowdy, Wayne ... Magnolia, MS
Dowdy, William C., Jr. ... McKinney, TX
Dowdy, William C. (Trey), III, (P.C.)
Dallas, TX
Dowe, Capetanakis & Preite
New York, NY
Dowe, Daniel W. ... New York, NY
Dowe, Everett B., III ... Windsor, CT
Dowe, Janet L. ... New York, NY
New York, NY
Dowell, A. Yates, III ... Arlington, VA
Dowell, A. Yates, Jr. ... Arlington, VA
Dowell, Anthony E. ... Chicago, IL
Dowell, Arthur E., III ... Arlington, VA
Dowell & Bromley ... Houston, TX
Dowell, Dale ... Beaumont, TX
Dowell, David Bradley ... Fort Worth, TX
Dowell, David C. ... Orlando, FL
Dowell, David J., Jr. ... Gretna, LA
Dowell, David L. ... Towson, MD
Dowell, David R. ... Lacey's Spring, AL
Dowell, Donald C. ... San Bernardino, CA
Dowell, Douglas M. ... Frankfort, KY
Dowell & Dowell, P.C. ... Washington, DC
Arlington, VA
Dowell, Earl Simeon ... Falls Church, VA
Dowell, Edwina E. ... Los Angeles, CA
Dowell, Gavin C. ... Boston, MA
Dowell, J. Daniel ... Miami, FL
Dowell, Jairl P. ... Amarillo, TX
Dowell, Jeremy D. ... Tampa, FL
Dowell, John H. ... St. Louis, MO
Dowell, John R. ... Topeka, KS
Dowell, Jonathan R. ... San Francisco, CA
Dowell, Kelli M. ... Jackson, MS
Dowell, L. Eric ... Phoenix, AZ
Dowell, Laurie B. ... Newport, KY
Dowell Law Offices ... Bellevue, WA
Dowell, Mary L. ... Los Angeles, CA
Dowell, Michael A. ... Los Angeles, CA
Dowell, Neva Jane Burns ... Houston, TX
Dowell, Nobel Y., Jr. ... Mount Vernon, IL
Dowell, Ralph A. ... Arlington, VA
Dowell, Robert L. ... Greensburg, KY
Dowell, Rodney S. ... Boston, MA
Dowell, Steven R. ... Covington, KY
Dowell, Theresa E. ... Bellevue, WA
Dowell, W. Curtis ... Beach Haven, NJ
Dowell, William A. ... Savannah, GA
Dowell, William L. ... Burlington, IA
Dowell, William L. ... Longview, WA
Dower, Jennifer C. ... Washington, DC
Dower, Robert K. ... Winter Park, FL
Dower, Thomas A. ... Hutchinson, KS
Dower-LaBastille, Naomi R. ... Trenton, NJ
Dowers, Camille D. ... Enid, OK
Dowery, Brenda L. ... Bronx, NY
Dowgialo, James J. ... San Francisco, CA
Dowgiello, Bernard A.
Department Of Health And Human Services,
Social Security Administration, GV
Dowgin, Michael V. ... Dayton, NJ
Dowhan, Christine M. ... Detroit, MI
Dowhan, William R. ... Aurora, CO
Dowhower, Brian S. ... Atlanta, GA
Dowie, Donald N., Jr.
Department of Justice, Tax Division, GV
Dowis, Joan R. ... Auburn, CA
Dowis, Lenore ... Smithtown, NY
Dowlen, George E. ... Amarillo, TX
Dowler, April L. ... Shepherdstown, WV
Dowler, Harry L., Jr. ... Marion, OH
Dowler & Hill ... Shepherdstown, WV
Dowler, Julie E. ... Huntington, WV
Dowler, Michael H. ... Lafayette, IN
Dowler, Michael S. ... Houston, TX
Dowler, Moulton S., Jr. ... San Antonio, TX
Dowler, Peter C. ... Ventura, CA
Dowler, Robert D. ... Lakewood, CO
Dowler, Robert W. ... Fairfax, VA
Dowless, Ann-Charlotte ... Greensboro, NC
Dowley, Joel E. ... Spring Arbor, MI
Dowley, Joseph K. ... Washington, DC
Dowley, Michael F. ... Middletown, CT
Dowlin, Winn E., Jr. ... Billings, MT
Dowling, Aaron & Keeler, Incorporated
Bakersfield, CA
Fresno, CA
Madera, CA
Dowling, Alan G. ... Los Angeles, CA
Dowling, Andrew H. ... Harrisburg, PA
Dowling, Ann C. ... New Orleans, LA
Dowling, Anthony H. ... Boston, MA
Dowling, B. Jay ... Belleville, IL
Dowling, Barron W. ... San Antonio, TX
Dowling, Brian W. ... Dothan, AL
Dowling, Carl P. ... Augusta, GA
Dowling, Charles T. ... New York, NY
Dowling, Christie L. ... Arlington, VA
Dowling, Curtis F. ... San Francisco, CA
Dowling, Curtis W. ... Columbia, SC
Dowling, Daniel J. ... Arlington, VA
Dowling, David B. ... Harrisburg, PA
Dowling, David K. ... Montgomery City, MO
Dowling, Dawn M. ... Cleveland, OH
Dowling, Diana S. ... Helena, MT
Dowling, Donald C. ... Delray Beach, FL
Dowling, Donald C., Jr. ... Lincolnshire, IL
Dowling, Donald J. ... San Bruno, CA
Dowling, Donald J., Jr. ... Alpena, MI
Dowling and Dowling ... Hartford, CT
Simsbury, CT
Dowling, Duncan B., III, (P.A.)
Orlando, FL
Dowling, Edith L. ... Mansfield, PA
Dowling, Edward D., IV ... Port Jefferson, NY
Dowling, Elaine M. ... Oklahoma City, OK
Dowling, Elizabeth B. ... New Orleans, LA
Dowling, Elizabeth E. ... Little Rock, AR
Dowling, G. G. ... Beaufort, SC
Dowling, Gregory P. ... Bloomer, WI
Dowling, J. Michael ... Denver, CO
Dowling, J. Michael, & Associates, P.C.
Denver, CO
Dowling, James C. ... Fulton, MO
Dowling, James E. ... Indianapolis, IN
Dowling, James G., Jr. ... Hartford, CT
Dowling, James J. ... Palm Harbor, FL
Dowling, James W. ... Encinitas, CA
Dowling, Joab M., Jr. ... Beaufort, SC
Dowling, Joan E. ... Plainfield, NJ
Dowling, John C. ... Enterprise, AL
Dowling, John C. ... Harrisburg, PA
Dowling, John C. ... Madison, WI
Dowling, John J. ... Annapolis, MD
Dowling, John James, III ... New York, NY
Dowling, John L. ... Lakewood, OH
Dowling, Jon C. ... Dayton, OH
Dowling, Joseph P. ... Cleveland, OH
Dowling, July L. ... Dothan, AL
Dowling, Keri L. ... Cleveland, OH
Dowling, Kerry B. ... Cincinnati, OH
Dowling, Kevin B. ... Woodbury, NJ
Dowling, Kevin P. ... New York, NY
Dowling, Kimberly ... Fair Oaks, CA
Dowling, Kimberly S. ... Muncie, IN
Dowling, Lara ... Washington, DC
Dowling Law Firm, P.A. ... Beaufort, SC
Dowling, Lexa E. ... Dothan, AL
Dowling, M. Catherine ... Baltimore, MD
Dowling, Madeleine J. ... New York, NY
Dowling, Margaret A. ... Juneau, AK
Dowling, Maria-Kate
National Labor Relations Board,
Office of Board Members, GV
Dowling, Marianne M. ... New York, NY
Dowling, Mark B.
General Accounting Office,
Office of the General Counsel, GV
Dowling, Martin P. ... San Diego, CA
Dowling, Mathew M. ... Oklahoma City, OK
Dowling, Michael A. ... Fairfield, CT
Dowling, Michael D. ... Fresno, CA
Dowling, Michael P. ... Fresno, CA
Dowling, Michael R. ... Ashland, KY
Dowling, Myers and Helm, LLP
Las Vegas, NV
Dowling, Nancy Kabara ... Baltimore, MD
Dowling, Pamela Jane ... West Hartford, CT
Dowling, Patrick J. ... Treasury Department,
Internal Revenue Service, GV
Dowling, R. Oak ... San Rafael, CA
Dowling, R. Oak, Inc. ... San Rafael, CA
Dowling, Ralph E. ... Indianapolis, IN
Muncie, IN
Dowling, Renee D.
Christiansted, St. Croix, VI
Dowling, Richard J. ... Annapolis, MD
Dowling, Robert G. ... Milwaukee, WI
Dowling, Ruth T. ... Boston, MA
Dowling, Sarah T. ... Providence, RI
Dowling, Sean P. ... Nevada City, CA
Dowling, Stacy Ann
Securities and Exchange Commission,
Division of Enforcement, GV
Dowling, Theresa M. ... Las Vegas, NV
Dowling, Thomas F. ... Helena, MT
Dowling, Thomas J. ... Santa Barbara, CA
Dowling, Thomas M. ... Rutland, VT
Dowling, Thomas P. ... New York, NY
Dowling, Timothy J. ... Washington, DC
Dowling, Timothy M. ... Boulder, CO
Longmont, CO
Dowling, Timothy P. ... Corpus Christi, TX
Dowling, Victor J. ... Simsbury, CT
Dowling, Victor J., Jr. ... Simsbury, CT
Dowling, Vincent J. ... Hartford, CT
Dowling, Virginia M. ... Chicago, IL
Dowling, William D., Jr. ... Akron, OH
Dowling, William F. ... Annapolis, MD
Dowling, William F. ... New York, NY
Dowling, William F. ... Syracuse, NY
Dowling, William G. ... Chicago, IL
Dowling, William J. ... Bronxville, NY
Dowling, William L. ... Milwaukee, WI
Dowling-DiBella, Lori ... Hartford, CT
Dowling-Fitzpatrick, Carla R.
Columbus, OH
Dowlut, Robert ... Fairfax, VA
Down, Carl V. ... San Ramon, CA
Downard, Jonathan L. ... Union, MO

Downard, William S. ... Walnut Creek, CA
Downen, Alan C. ... McLeansboro, IL
Downen, Allan T. ... Augusta, GA
Downen, Donald E. ... Caldwell, ID
Downer, Carol A. ... Los Angeles, CA
Downer, Daniel G., Jr. ... Annapolis, MD
Downer, Daniel G., Jr., P.A.
Annapolis, MD
Downer, Elizabeth A. ... Bloomington, IL
Downer, Hugh C., Jr. ... Gold Beach, OR
Downer, Huntington B., Jr., (P.C.)
Houma, LA
Downer, Jeffrey P. ... Seattle, WA
Downer, John D. ... Indianapolis, IN
Downer, John M. ... Costa Mesa, CA
Downer, Kyle & Wilhite, L.L.C.
Shreveport, LA
Downer, Michael J. ... Los Angeles, CA
Downer, Philip E., III ... Shreveport, LA
Downer, Richard R. ... Alva, OK
Downer, Robert H., Jr. ... Charlottesville, VA
Downer, Robert N. ... Iowa City, IA
Downer, Steven D. ... Pasadena, CA
Downer, Susan Q. ... Signal Mountain, TN
Downer, Thomas T. ... Charlotte, NC
Downes, Bradley G. Bledsoe
Costa Mesa, CA
Downes, Christopher ... New York, NY
Downes, Daniel J. ... Chicago, IL
Downes, Daniel J., P.C., Law Offices of
Chicago, IL
Downes, David A. ... Front Royal, VA
Downes, David D. ... Towson, MD
Downes, David W. ... Watertown, MA
Downes, Dennis E. ... Marco Island, FL
Downes, Dennis E. ... Southampton, NY
Downes, Elizabeth ... Bethesda, MD
Downes, Gile R. ... Portland, OR
Downes and Gregory ... Centreville, MD
Downes & Hurst ... Columbus, OH
Downes, J. Kevin ... Tustin, CA
Downes, James J. ... White Plains, NY
Downes, James S. ... Chicago, IL
Downes, James T., Jr. ... Waltham, MA
Downes, John J. ... Larkspur, CA
Downes, Jonathan J. ... Columbus, OH
Downes, Kenneth C. ... Albuquerque, NM
Downes, Kenneth C., & Associates, P.C.
Albuquerque, NM
Los Lunas, NM
Rio Rancho, NM
Downes, Kevin P. ... New York, NY
Downes, Larry ... Chicago, IL
Downes, Lawrence ... New York, NY
Downes, MacDonald & Levengood, P.C.
Fairbanks, AK
Downes, Michael T. ... Everett, WA
Downes, Patrick N. ... Los Angeles, CA
Downes, Paul K. ... Minneapolis, MN
Downes, Richard H. ... Sparta, NJ
Downes, Robert B. ... Fairbanks, AK
Downes, Robert W., Jr. ... Miami Beach, FL
Downes, Robert Wilson ... New York, NY
Downes, Roger P. ... San Bernardino, CA
Downes, Ruth B. ... Houston, TX
Downes, Sean P. ... Tulsa, OK
Downes, Stephen A. ... New York, NY
Downes, Terence B. ... Lowell, MA
Downes, W. Patrick ... Hammond, IN
Downes, Walter J. ... Ionia, MI
Downes, William F. ... Casper, WY
Downes, William W., Jr.
Salt Lake City, UT
Downey, Alicia L. ... Boston, MA
Downey, Ann M. ... Lafox, IL
Downey, Anne Fox ... Buffalo, NY
Downey, Arthur H. ... Denver, CO
Downey, Arthur T. ... Washington, DC
Downey, Athena M. ... Peoria, IL
Downey, Barbara P. ... Park City, UT
Downey, Barry K. ... Baltimore, MD
Downey, Brand, Seymour & Rohwer LLP
Sacramento, CA
Downey, Brandt C., III ... Clearwater, FL
Downey, Brian J. ... Longmeadow, MA
Downey, Brian James ... Columbus, OH
Downey, Brian P. ... Cleveland, OH
Downey, Brian P. ... Harrisburg, PA
Downey, Brian W. ... Buffalo, NY
Downey, Bruce J., III ... Montgomery, AL
Downey, Caroline J. ... New York, NY
Downey, Carolyn M.
Cleveland Heights, OH
Downey, Charles J., III ... Stamford, CT
Downey, Christine D. ... Apple Valley, MN
Downey, Christopher J. ... New York, NY
Downey & Cleveland, LLP ... Marietta, GA
Downey, Daniel ... Palm Beach, FL
Downey, Daniel M. ... Houston, TX
Downey, Daniel T. ... Columbus, OH
Downey, Denis A. ... Brownsville, TX
Downey & Downey, P.A. ... Palm Beach, FL
West Palm Beach, FL
Downey & Downey, P.C. ... New Bedford, MA
Downey, Edw. J. ... Boston, MA
Downey, Edward ... Palm Beach, FL
Downey, Edward B. ... Albany, NY
Downey, Edward E. ... Millerton, NY
Downey, Edward F. ... Chicago, IL
Downey, Edward F. ... Jefferson City, MO
Downey, Edward K. ... Quincy, IL
Downey, Eileen ... Hazel Park, MI
Downey, Elizabeth A. ... Southfield, MI
Downey, Erin ... San Diego, CA
Downey, Gerald B. ... Green Bay, WI
Downey, Gerard P. ... Philadelphia, PA
Downey, Gregory M. ... New Bedford, MA
Downey Haab & Murphy, PLLC
Millerton, NY
Downey, Heather Carnes
Birmingham, AL
Downey, Henry M. ... Springfield, MA
Downey, Howard Yeilding
Birmingham, AL
Downey, J. Michael ... Waukee, IA
Downey, J. Patrick ... Phoenix, AZ
Downey, J. Patrick ... Youngstown, OH
Downey, J. Richard ... Franklin, KY
Downey, James A., III ... Bristol, PA
Langhorne, PA
Downey, James C. ... West Palm Beach, FL
Downey, James E. ... Norwich, NY
Downey, James F. ... New York, NY
Downey, James H. ... Englewood, CO
Downey, James M. ... Boulder, CO
Downey, James P. ... Fairfax, VA
Downey, James S. ... New York, NY
Downey, Jane Harris ... Columbia, SC
Downey, Jeffrey J. ... Washington, DC
Downey, Jeremiah J. ... Coronado, CA
Downey, Jody L. ... Placentia, CA
Downey, John B., Jr. ... Nashville, TN
Downey, John D. ... Dallas, TX
Downey, John H. ... Jackson, MS
Downey, John H. ... Warren, OH
Downey, John J. ... Chicago, IL
Downey, John M. ... New York, NY
Downey, John R. ... Hartford, CT
Downey, John T. ... New Haven, CT
Downey, Joseph W. ... Columbia, MO
Downey, Julia Noelle ... Killeen, TX
Downey, Julie P. ... Los Angeles, CA
Downey, Kathleen A. ... Topeka, KS
Downey, Keary Acca ... White Plains, NY
Downey, Kevin M. ... Washington, DC
Downey, Kevin M. ... Washington, DC
Downey, Kirk C. ... Hagerstown, MD
Downey & Knickrehm, A Professional Corporation ... Denver, CO
Downey Law Firm, P.C. ... Denver, CO
Downey, L. E. ... Ashtabula, OH
Downey, Lynn A. ... Marietta, GA
Downey, Mark D. ... Dallas, TX
Downey, Mary Alice ... San Marino, CA
Downey, Mary C. ... Coronado, CA
Downey, Mary F. Kelley
Department of Commerce,
Patent and Trademark Office, GV
Downey, Mary M. ... Charleston, WV
Downey, Matthew J. ... New Bedford, MA
Downey, Maurice F. ... New Bedford, MA
Downey, Michael C. ... Dixon, IL
Downey, Michael Patrick ... Kansas City, MO
Downey, N. Ronald, III ... Birmingham, AL
Downey, Noel Christopher ... Brooklyn, NY
Downey, Patrick J. ... Ann Arbor, MI
Findlay, OH
Toledo, OH
Downey, Patrick J. ... Spokane, WA
Downey, Paul J. ... Philadelphia, PA
Downey, Paul V. ... Dallas, TX
Downey, Paula S. ... Pebble Beach, CA
Downey, Pauline C. ... Ashtabula, OH
Downey, Philip A. ... Norristown, PA
Downey, Philip F. ... Columbus, OH
Downey, Richard L., & Associates, Law Offices of ... Fairfax, VA
Downey, Richard Morgan ... Washington, DC
Downey, Richard R ... Cambridge, MA
Downey, Robert F. ... West Hartford, CT
Downey, Robert L. ... Pittsburgh, PA
Downey, Robert M. ... Boca Raton, FL
Miami, FL
Downey, Robert M., P.A. ... Boca Raton, FL
Miami, FL
Downey, Roy J. ... Pikeville, KY
Downey, Shawn M. ... Big Rapids, MI
Downey, Sheridan, III ... Oakland, CA
Downey & Sosin, P.C. ... Southfield, MI
Downey, Steven D., Law Offices of
Bowling Green, KY
Downey, Steven M. ... Plymouth, MA
Downey, Storrs W. ... Chicago, IL
Downey, Sullivan & FitzGerald
Kansas City, MO
Downey, Thomas A. ... San Francisco, CA
Downey, Thomas E., Jr. ... Denver, CO
Downey, Thomas H. ... Pasadena, CA
Downey, Thomas J. ... Jefferson City, MO
Downey, Thomas M. ... Oakland, CA
Downey, William F. ... New York, NY
Downey, William G. ... Philadelphia, PA
Downey, William J. ... Phoenix, AZ
Downey, William J., III ... Atlantic City, NJ
Downey, William J., P.C. ... Phoenix, AZ
Downie, Brian T. ... Washington, DC
Downie, Jason W. ... Colorado Springs, CO
Downie, Margaret H. ... Phoenix, AZ
Downie, Nancy A. ... Bloomfield Hills, MI
Downie, R. Hayden ... Tulsa, OK
Downie, R. Hayden, P.C. ... Tulsa, OK
Downie, R. Rex ... Beaver Falls, PA
Downie, Robert C., II ... Tallahassee, FL
Downie, Robert K. ... Houston, TX
Downie, Thomas A. ... Lorain, OH
Downing, Abbie Joe, Jr. ... Denver, CO
Downing, Alexander, Wood and Ilg
Kearney, NE
Omaha, NE
Superior, NE
Downing, Allison L. ... New York, NY
Downing, Andrew D. ... Tulsa, OK
Downing, B. Patricia ... Atlanta, GA
Downing, Betty Ann ... Los Angeles, CA
Downing, Bruce E. ... Winchester, VA
Downing, Carl B. ... Southfield, MI
Downing, Carl S. ... New Orleans, LA
Downing, Catherine ... Santa Fe, NM
Downing, Catherine F. ... Boston, MA
Downing, Catherine Stewart ... New York, NY
Downing, Charles ... San Pedro, CA
Downing, Conway A., Jr. ... Washington, DC
Downing, David B. ... Indio, CA
Downing, David B. ... Superior, NE
Downing, David, Cockman & Downing
Fayetteville, NC
Downing, Denise M. ... Safety Harbor, FL
Downing, Dennis J.
Great Barrington, MA
Downing, Dickerson M. ... New York, NY
Downing, Don M. ... St. Louis, MO
Downing, Dwain ... Arlington, TX
Downing, Edward F., III ... Metairie, LA
Downing, Edward K., Jr. ... Odessa, TX
Downing, Emily Leach ... Buffalo, NY
Downing, Eugene W., Jr. ... Lexington, MA
Downing & Flynn ... Boston, MA
Downing, Frank O. ... Savannah, GA
Downing, George ... Cleveland, OH
Downing, George A. ... Palm City, FL
Downing, George L. ... Detroit, MI
Downing, Gerard D. ... Pittsfield, MA
Downing, Gordon R. ... Berwyn, PA
Downing, Grant T. ... Winter Park, FL
Downing, Harold D. ... Fayetteville, NC
Downing, Harold L. ... Orlando, FL
Downing, Herbert J. ... Essex Junction, VT
Downing, Howard N. ... Nicholasville, KY
Downing, J. Calvin, III ... Kansas City, MO
Downing, James C. ... Middletown, CA
Downing, James S. ... Rolling Meadows, IL
Downing, Jefferson ... Lincoln, NE
Downing, Jeffrey S. ... Tampa, FL
Downing, John G. ... San Francisco, CA
Downing, John L. ... Lower Burrell, PA
Downing, John M. ... New York, NY
Downing, John M., Jr. ... New York, NY
Downing, John T.
Federal Deposit Insurance Corporation,
Trial Litigation Section, GV
Downing, John W., Jr. ... Arlington, MA
Downing, Joseph A. ... Tipp City, OH
Downing, Kathleen R. ... Boston, MA
Downing, Kimberly ... Atlanta, GA
Downing, Lawrence, & Associates
Rochester, MN
Downing, Lawrence D. ... Rochester, MN
Downing & Liu, LLP ... San Francisco, CA
Downing, Margaret Ryan ... Portland, ME
Downing, Marjorie Mosburg
Oklahoma City, OK
Downing & Mehrtens, P.C.
New York, NY
Downing, Michael D. ... Glenview, IL
Downing, Michael J. ... Cleveland, OH
Downing, Michael P. ... Tucson, AZ
Downing, Michael W. ... Kansas City, MO
Downing, Paul A. ... North Chicago, IL
Downing, Peter W. ... Denver, CO
Downing, Randall Scott ... Dallas, TX
Downing, Richard C. ... Little Rock, AR
Downing, Richard C., P.A.
Little Rock, AR
Downing, Richard G., II ... Newark, NJ
Downing, Richard, Jr. ... Denver, CO
Downing, Robert A. ... Chicago, IL
Downing, Robert B. ... Findlay, OH
Downing, Robert D. ... Baton Rouge, LA
Downing, Robert F. ... Teaneck, NJ
Downing, Robert J. ... Glenview, IL
Downing, Scott P. ... Chicago, IL
Downing, Scott T. ... Gresham, OR
Downing, Sean P. ... Quincy, MA
Downing, Thaddeus P. ... Fayetteville, NC
Downing, Thomas N. ... Newport News, VA
Downing, Thomas R. ... Lewiston, ME
Downing, Timothy J. ... Cleveland, OH
Downing, Trudy A. ... Wayne, NJ
Downing & Uhl ... Decatur, IL
Downing, Valerie ... Faribault, MN
Downing, Vincent ... New York, NY
Downing, Walter J. ... Denver, CO
Downing, Warwick, II ... Denver, CO
Downing, William A. ... Sioux Falls, SD
Downing, William L. ... Baton Rouge, LA
Downing, William L. ... Seattle, WA
Downing, William T. ... Decatur, IL
Downing & Willmott ... Lexington, KY
Downs, Alan J. ... St. Louis, MO
Downs, Andrew B. ... San Francisco, CA
Downs, Anthony S. ... Duluth, MN
Downs & Associates ... Coral Gables, FL
Pembroke Pines, FL
Downs, B. Boozer, Jr. ... Woodstock, AL
Downs, Barbara A. ... Chicago, IL
Oak Park, IL
Downs & Berg ... Woodstock, AL
Downs, Bertis E., IV ... Athens, GA
Downs, Bryan A. ... Decatur, GA
Downs, Charity A. ... Wells, VT
Downs, Christine R. ... Chicago, IL
Downs, Christopher Donald ... Columbia, SC
Downs, Christopher F. ... Denver, CO
Downs, Clark Evans ... Washington, DC
Downs, Craig T. ... Coral Gables, FL
Downs, Darrell W. ... Claremore, OK
Downs, David L. ... San Antonio, TX
Downs, Donald R. ... Corinth, MS
Downs, Donald Ray, P.A. ... Corinth, MS
Downs, Doris L. ... Atlanta, GA
Downs, E. Ross, Jr. ... Bastrop, LA
Downs, Edward F. ... Las Vegas, NV
Downs, Edward J. ... Mount Prospect, IL
Downs, Erin Sheehey ... Bristol, VA
Downs, E. T. ... Southfield, MI
Downs, G. Warthen ... Richmond, VA
Downs, Gary P. ... San Francisco, CA
Downs, H. Elizabeth ... Houston, TX
Downs, Harold A. ... Naples, FL
Downs, Harry ... Atlanta, GA
Downs, Helen Kathryn ... Birmingham, AL
Downs, J. Anthony ... Boston, MA
Downs, James F. ... Albany, NY
Downs, James P. ... San Francisco, CA
Downs, James U. ... Franklin, NC
Downs, Jay R. ... Dallas, TX
Downs, Jerome F. ... San Francisco, CA
Downs, John E. ... St. Joseph, MO
Downs, John H. ... St. Johnsbury, VT
Downs, Joseph Edward ... King, NC
Downs, Joseph P. ... Laguna Hills, CA
Downs, Joseph W., III ... Miami, FL
Downs, Joseph W., IV ... New York, NY
Downs, Judin & Stanford, A Professional Corporation ... Dallas, TX
Downs, Karen D. ... Baton Rouge, LA
Downs, Kenneth G. ... San Francisco, CA
Downs, Kenneth R. ... Pineville, NC
Downs, Kermit M. (Mac) ... Gadsden, AL
Downs, Kevin Chad Bourne
Marblehead, MA
Downs, Kirsten Gettys
Department of Justice,
Office of Attorney Personnel Management,
GV
Downs, Larry R. ... Evansville, IN
Downs Law Offices, P.C. ... Chicago, IL
Oak Park, IL
Downs, Leslie Scott ... Montrose, CO
Downs, Mary Alane ... Baltimore, MD
Hunt Valley, MD
Downs, Mary E. ... Washington, DC
Downs, Maureen Creighton ... Chicago, IL
Downs, Mayanne ... Orlando, FL
Downs, Michael A. ... Chicago, IL
Downs, Pamela S. ... Marietta, GA
Downs, Patrick ... Everett, WA
Downs, Paul B. ... Cleveland, OH
Downs, Paul D. ... New York, NY
Downs Rachlin & Martin PLLC
Littleton, NH
Brattleboro, VT
Burlington, VT
Montpelier, VT
St. Johnsbury, VT
Downs, Richard ... Kirkland, WA
Downs, Robert A. ... Luray, VA
Downs, Robert A., P.L.C. ... Luray, VA
Downs, Robert C. ... Kansas City, MO
Downs, Robert J., Jr. ... Philadelphia, PA
Downs, Robert K. ... Chicago, IL
Oak Park, IL
Downs, Robert S. ... Baltimore, MD
Downs, Ryan D. ... Denver, CO
Chicago, IL
Downs, Sandra E. ... Georgetown, KY
Downs, Sean ... New York, NY
Downs, Stephen F. ... Albany, NY
Downs, Stephen H. ... North Manchester, IN
Wabash, IN
Downs, Terence J. ... Delavan, WI
Downs, Thomas C. ... Washington, DC
Downs, Thomas D. ... Marietta, GA
Downs, Thomas E., IV ... Old Bridge, NJ
Downs, Thomas K. ... Indianapolis, IN
Downs, Thomas M. ... Washington, DC
Downs, Timothy ... Southfield, MI
Downs, Timothy N. ... Duluth, MN
Downs, Tom ... Lansing, MI
Downs, Tom, P.C. ... Lansing, MI
Downs, Travis E., III ... San Diego, CA
Downs, Willis A. ... Brockton, MA
Downs, Woodrow F. ... Bardstown, KY
Downton, Carol Ann Beem ... Nashville, TN
Dowrey, Carl G. ... Snohomish, WA
Dowse, Geoffrey J. ... Kenosha, WI
Dowsley, Felix R., III ... Nashville, TN
Dowton, Polly Rutherford ... St. Louis, MO
Dowton, Tamara Y. ... Owings Mills, MD
Dox, Jonathan W. ... Alexandria, VA
Doxey, Deborah A. ... Buffalo, NY
Doxey, Diane ... New York, NY
Doxey, Evelyn N. ... Nashville, TN
Doxey, James R. ... Houston, TX
Doxey, Janice McPherson ... Norfolk, VA
Doxey, Stephen B. ... Salt Lake City, UT
Doxsee, Donald D. ... Fort Wayne, IN
Doxzen, Michael J. ... Baltimore, MD
Doy, Samuel J. ... Chicago, IL
Doyaga, David J. ... Brooklyn, NY
Doyal, Bret C. ... Houston, TX
Doyal, Larry Little ... Montgomery, AL
Doyal, Scot M. ... Austin, TX
Doyal, Tom R. ... Austin, TX
Doyel, Michael E. ... St. Louis, MO
Doyel, Robert L. ... Bartow, FL
Doyen, John G. ... St. Louis, MO
Doyen, Michael R. ... Los Angeles, CA
Doying, William A.E.
Federal Trade Commission,
Bureau of Competition, GV
Doyle, A. Patrick ... Washington, DC
Doyle, Alexander L. ... Houma, LA
Doyle, Alison L. ... Washington, DC
Doyle, Amy J. ... Milwaukee, WI
Doyle, Andrew J. ... Department of Justice,
Environment and Natural Resources
Division, GV
Doyle, Ann Elizabeth Bands ... Baltimore, MD
Doyle, Anne Marie ... Chester, NJ

Doyle, Anthony D. M. ....Anchorage, AK
Doyle, Anthony P. ....Pittsfield, MA
Doyle, Appel & Davis, A P.C.
Phoenix, AZ
Doyle, Arthur J. ....Kansas City, MO
Doyle, Arthur T. ....New York, NY
Doyle & Associates ....Danville, IL
Hoopeston, IL
Urbana, IL
Doyle & Associates, LLC ....Greeley, CO
Doyle, Austin J., Jr. ....Washington, DC
Doyle, Austin J., Jr., P.C. ....Washington, DC
Doyle & Bachman ....Arlington, VA
Doyle, Bernard E. ....Washington, DC
Doyle, Bernard F., Jr. ....Chicago, IL
Doyle & Bolotin, Ltd., A Professional Corporation ....Chicago, IL
Doyle and Brady ....Kearny, NJ
Doyle, Brenda A. ....Providence, RI
Doyle, Brian ....San Jose, CA
Doyle, Brian A. ....Rocky Hill, CT
Doyle, Brian K. ....Chicago, IL
Doyle, Brooks S., Jr. ....El Segundo, CA
Doyle, C. Bronson ....New Orleans, LA
Doyle, Carol A. ....Chicago, IL
Doyle, Cary C. ....Anderson, SC
Doyle, Catherine M. ....Milwaukee, WI
Doyle, Catherine T. ....Lafayette, CA
Doyle, Cathryn M. ....Albany, NY
Doyle, Charles ....Library of Congress, Congressional Research Service, GV
Doyle, Charles A. ....Oradell, NJ
Doyle, Charles B., II ....Fort Worth, TX
Doyle, Charles E., Jr. ....Peekskill, NY
Doyle, Charles M. ....White Plains, NY
Doyle, Chas. R. ....Boston, MA
Doyle, Cheryl Secrest ....South Pasadena, CA
Doyle, Christine ....Silver Spring, MD
Doyle, Christine ....New York, NY
Doyle, Christine A. ....Burlingame, CA
Doyle, Christopher E. ....New York, NY
Doyle, Christopher Hart ....Sacramento, CA
Doyle, Christopher J. ....New York, NY
Doyle, Christopher J. ....Arlington, TX
Doyle, Christopher L. ....Buffalo, NY
Doyle, Christopher R. ....Los Angeles, CA
Doyle, Clare H. ....Houston, TX
Doyle, Colleen P. ....Los Angeles, CA
Doyle, Colleen P. ....Buffalo, NY
Doyle, Conal ....Tampa, FL
Doyle, Connie P. ....Greensboro, NC
Doyle, Craig D. ....Fort Wayne, IN
Indianapolis, IN
Doyle, Daniel D. ....Rockford, IL
Doyle, Daniel D. ....St. Louis, MO
Doyle, Daniel J. ....Rochester, NY
Doyle, Daniel J. ....Joliet, IL
Doyle, Daniel L. ....Kansas City, MO
Doyle, Daniel S. ....Media, PA
Doyle, Daniel T. ....Fort Lauderdale, FL
Doyle, Daniel T. ....Blackstone, MA
Doyle, Daniel W. ....Irvine, CA
Doyle, David ....Dallas, OR
Doyle, David A. ....Gallatin, TN
Doyle, David C. ....San Diego, CA
Doyle, David Douglas ....Fresno, CA
Doyle, David E. ....Chicago, IL
Doyle, David J. ....Chicago, IL
Doyle, David L. ....Chicago, IL
Doyle, David L. ....Boston, MA
Doyle, David O, Jr ....Orlando, FL
Doyle, David P. ....Morristown, NJ
Doyle, David S. ....New Haven, CT
Doyle, David T. ....Salem, MA
Doyle, David T. ....Detroit, MI
Doyle, David Wilson ....Grand Rapids, MI
Doyle, Deborah A. ....West Chester, PA
Doyle, Delia ....Ormond Beach, FL
Doyle, Dennis T. ....White Plains, NY
Doyle, Dermot J. ....Hackensack, NJ
Doyle, Diana Slyfield ....Chicago, IL
Doyle, Dirk Edward ....Hood River, OR
Doyle, Donald H., Jr. ....Waterbury, CT
Doyle, Donald V. ....Sioux City, IA
Doyle, Donald W. ....New Orleans, LA
Doyle, Donald W., Jr. ....New Orleans, LA
Doyle, Donna Canina ....Orlando, FL
Doyle, Douglas F. ....Hawthorne, NJ
New York, NY
Doyle & Doyle ....Newark, NJ
Short Hills, NJ
Doyle & Doyle ....Troy, NY
Doyle & Doyle ....Rapid City, SD
Doyle, Doyle & Doyle ....New Orleans, LA
Doyle, Duane L. ....Twinsburg, OH
Doyle, Edward M. ....Houston, TX
Doyle, Edward R. ....Wethersfield, CT
Doyle, Edward W. ....Peekskill, NY
Doyle, Eleanor Janosek ....Short Hills, NJ
Doyle, Elizabeth A. ....San Francisco, CA
Doyle, Elizabeth A. ....Hollidaysburg, PA
Doyle, Ellen M. ....Pittsburgh, PA
Doyle, Ellie A. ....Atlanta, GA
Doyle, Eric L. ....Troy, MI
Doyle, Eugene E. ....Lady Lake, FL
Doyle, Eugene F. ....Morristown, NJ
Doyle & Fraley ....Taylorville, IL
Doyle, Francis Burton ....Campbell, CA
Doyle, Francis J. ....Dorchester, MA
Doyle, Francis X., Jr. ....Washington, DC
Doyle, Frank A. ....Houston, TX
Doyle, Fred P. ....Secaucus, NJ
Doyle, Fredk. T. ....Boston, MA
Doyle, Gartland, Nelson, McCleery & Wade, P.C. ....Eugene, OR
Doyle, George M. ....Chicago, IL
Doyle, George P. ....Chapel Hill, NC
Doyle, Gerard F. ....Arlington, VA
Doyle, Gerard S., Jr. ....Short Hills, NJ
Doyle, Glenn F. ....Bay City, MI
Doyle, Gloria L. ....La Crosse, WI
Doyle, Gordon P. ....Muncie, IN
Doyle, Gregory M. ....Braintree, MA
Doyle, Gregory Michael ....Oakland, CA
Santa Rosa, CA
Doyle Group Attorneys ....Sarasota, FL
Lansing, MI
Macatawa, MI
Doyle, Guinn P. ....Indianapolis, IN
Doyle, H. Eugene ....Dothan, AL
Doyle, Harold C. ....Sioux Falls, SD
Doyle & Harris, A Professional Corporation
Tulsa, OK
Doyle, Henry M. ....Zebulon, NC
Doyle, Hugh J. ....Chicago, IL
Doyle, Hugh J. ....Newburyport, MA
Doyle, J. Bradford ....Corte Madera, CA
Doyle, J. Michael ....Bozeman, MT
Doyle, J. Michael ....Helena, MT
Doyle, J. Michael ....Philadelphia, PA
Doyle, J. Richard ....San Jose, CA
Doyle, J. Stuart ....Chicago, IL
Doyle, James ....Geneva, IL
Doyle, James A. ....Washington, DC
Doyle, James B. ....Lake Charles, LA
Doyle, James B. ....Rochester, NY
Doyle, James B., III ....Rochester, NY
Doyle, James C., Jr. ....Arlington, MA
Doyle, James D. ....Rochester, NY
Doyle, James D., III ....Austin, TX
Doyle, James E., IV ....Lexington, NE
Doyle, James Eloi ....Houston, TX
Doyle, James F. ....New York, NY
Doyle, James F. X. ....Bohemia, NY
Doyle, James G. ....Milwaukee, WI
Doyle, James J. ....Rapid City, SD
Doyle, James J., III ....Annapolis, MD
Doyle, James J., Jr. ....Towson, MD
Doyle, James J., Jr. ....Houston, TX
Doyle, James M. ....Boston, MA
Doyle, James M., Jr. ....San Antonio, TX
Doyle, James P. ....Springfield, VA
Doyle, James P., Jr. ....New York, NY
Doyle, James R., II ....Atlanta, GA
Doyle, James R., Jr. ....Cincinnati, OH
Doyle, James W. ....Houston, TX
Doyle, Jane Loveland ....Rapid City, SD
Doyle, Janet Heck ....Evergreen, CO
Doyle, Janet R. ....Department Of The Interior, Office of Hearings & Appeals, GV
Doyle, Jeffrey A. ....Raleigh, NC
Doyle, Jeremiah W., IV ....Newburyport, MA
Doyle, Jeremiah W., 3rd ....Newburyport, MA
Doyle, Jeremy L. ....Houston, TX
Doyle, Jerome P. ....Atlanta, GA
Doyle, Jim ....Houston, TX
Doyle, John A. ....Chicago, IL
Doyle, John C. ....Phoenix, AZ
Doyle, John C. ....Pasadena, CA
Doyle, John C. ....Chicago, IL
Doyle, John D. ....Rochester, NY
Doyle, John F. ....Pleasanton, CA
Doyle, John F. ....Washington, DC
Doyle, John H., III ....New York, NY
Doyle, John J. ....San Francisco, CA
Doyle, John J. ....Sarasota, FL
Lansing, MI
Macatawa, MI
Doyle, John J., III ....Philadelphia, PA
Doyle, John J., Jr. ....Winston-Salem, NC
Doyle, John L. ....Richmond, VA
Doyle, John M. ....Naperville, IL
Doyle, John M. ....Winnemucca, NV
Doyle, John M. ....San Antonio, TX
Doyle, John P. ....Van Nuys, CA
Doyle, John P., Jr. ....Portland, ME
Doyle, John P., Jr. ....Auburn, NY
Doyle, John Paul ....Toms River, NJ
Doyle, John R. ....Chicago, IL
Doyle, John R. ....Lincoln, NE
Doyle, John R., III ....Norfolk, VA
Doyle, John R., Jr. ....San Francisco, CA
Doyle, John T. ....Chicago, IL
Doyle, John T. ....Verona, NJ
Doyle, John T. ....Pine Bush, NY
Doyle, John V. ....DeLand, FL
Doyle, Jon F. ....San Francisco, CA
Atlanta, GA
Doyle, Jon R. ....Augusta, ME
Doyle, Jonathan J. ....Atlanta, GA
Doyle, Joseph A. ....New York, NY
Doyle, Joseph E. ....Chicago, IL
Doyle, Joseph E. ....Marlton, NJ
Doyle, Joseph L. ....Waynesboro, PA
Doyle, Joseph P. ....Plainview, NY
Doyle, Joseph T. ....Quincy, MA
Doyle, Joseph T. ....Media, PA
Doyle, Joseph T., Jr. ....Boston, MA
Quincy, MA
Doyle, Joyce A. ....New York, NY
Doyle, Julie A. ....Chicago, IL
Doyle, Justin E.
Agency for International Development, Legal Advisers-Overseas, GV
Doyle, Justin P. ....Rochester, NY
Doyle, Karen Leslie ....New York, NY
Doyle, Kathleen ....New York, NY
Doyle, Kathleen J. ....Casper, WY
Doyle, Kathryn R. ....Philadelphia, PA
Doyle, Kelly Michael ....Portland, OR
Doyle & Kennedy ....Yankton, SD
Doyle, Kenneth J. ....Albany, NY
Doyle, Kerry Elizabeth ....Boston, MA
Doyle, Kevin A. ....Atlanta, GA
Doyle, Kevin J. ....Audubon, NJ
Doyle, Kevin J. ....New York, NY
Doyle, Kevin M. ....East Hartford, CT
Doyle, Kevin Pierce ....Tulsa, OK
Doyle, Kevin R. ....Wellesley, MA
Doyle, Kieran ....New York, NY
Doyle, Kimberly Hall ....Hollywood, FL
Doyle, L. Owen ....Lexington, KY
Doyle, Laura E. ....Boston, MA
Doyle, Laura O. ....Los Angeles, CA
Doyle Law ....Lafayette, CA
Doyle Law Office, S.C. ....La Crosse, WI
Doyle, Lawrence M. ....Royal Oak, MI
Doyle, Leo W. ....Annapolis, MD
Doyle, Lewis & Warner ....Toledo, OH
Doyle, Linda M. ....Chicago, IL
Doyle, Louis F. ....San Martin, CA
Doyle & Mansfield ....Northampton, MA
Doyle, Marcia E. Green ....Paxton, MA
Doyle, Marcia Jean ....Troy, NY
Doyle, Maria C. ....Louisville, KY
Doyle, Marjorie W. ....Wilmington, DE
Doyle, Mark A. ....Dallas, TX
Doyle, Mark C. ....Irvine, CA
Doyle, Martin ....Chicago, IL
Doyle, Martin E. ....Miami, FL
Doyle, Martin E., P.A. ....Miami, FL
Doyle, Martin J. ....Philadelphia, PA
Doyle, Mary ....Coral Gables, FL
Doyle, Mary E. ....Sunnyvale, CA
Doyle, Mary Ellen ....Rumson, NJ
Doyle, Mary L. ....Lincoln, NE
Doyle, Maura Sweeney ....Boston, MA
Doyle, Maureen A. McLinden
Abington, MA
Doyle, Maurice C. ....Buffalo, NY
Doyle, Maurice E. ....Cambridge, MA
Doyle, Michael A. ....Atlanta, GA
Doyle, Michael C. ....Pasadena, CA
Doyle, Michael D. ....Elyria, OH
Doyle, Michael J. ....Mesa, AZ
Doyle, Michael J. ....New York, NY
Doyle, Michael J. ....Tuxedo Park, NY
Doyle, Michael P. ....Houston, TX
Doyle, Michael W. ....Titusville, FL
Doyle, Michael W. ....Eugene, OR
Doyle & Mone ....Wellesley, MA
Doyle, Nancy J. ....Chicago, IL
Doyle & Nelson ....Augusta, ME
Doyle, Nora L. ....Harrisburg, PA
Doyle, Norman A., Jr. ....Kearny, NJ
Doyle & O'Rourke, P.A. ....Anderson, SC
Doyle, Pamela S. ....Elmira, NY
Doyle, Patricia ....New York, NY
Doyle, Patricia E. ....East Meadow, NY
Doyle, Patricia K. ....Los Angeles, CA
Doyle, Patricia M. ....Belvedere-Tiburon, CA
Doyle, Patrick E. ....Silverton, OR
Doyle, Patrick F. ....Galveston, TX
Doyle, Patrick O. ....Chicago, IL
Doyle, Patrick W. ....Winter Park, FL
Doyle, Paul A., Jr. ....Calabasas, CA
Doyle, Paul F. ....New York, NY
Doyle, Paul M. ....Needham, MA
Doyle, Paul R. ....Wethersfield, CT
Doyle, Paul R. ....Chicago, IL
Doyle, Paula K. ....Madison, WI
Doyle, Peggy S. ....San Francisco, CA
Doyle, Penner, Bradley & Seymour
Fresno, CA
Sacramento, CA
Doyle, Peter C. ....Rock Island, IL
Doyle, Peter C. ....Dearborn, MI
Doyle, Peter C., P.C. ....Dearborn, MI
Doyle, Peter D. ....New York, NY
Doyle, Peter F., Jr. ....Salem, MA
Doyle, Peter H.
Federal Communications Commission, Mass Media Bureau, GV
Doyle, Peter M. ....El Dorado Hills, CA
Doyle, Peter V. ....Portsmouth, NH
Doyle, Philip ....Department of Justice, Tax Division, GV
Doyle, Philip J. ....Moraga, CA
Doyle, Philip J. ....North Andover, MA
Doyle, R. Christopher ....Columbus, OH
Doyle, Rachel J. ....Dallas, TX
Doyle, Rani Elizabeth
Securities and Exchange Commission, Division of Corporation Finance, GV
Doyle, Richard B. ....Miami, FL
Doyle, Richard B., Jr.
Fort Lauderdale, FL
Doyle, Richard D. ....South Bend, IN
Doyle, Richard H. ....Des Moines, IA
Doyle, Richard J. ....Danville, IL
Hoopeston, IL
Urbana, IL
Doyle, Richard M. ....Boston, MA
Doyle, Richard M. ....Rochester, NY
Doyle, Richard N. ....Greeley, CO
Doyle, Richard P., Jr. ....Lafayette, CA
Doyle, Richard T., Jr. ....Philadelphia, PA
Doyle, Rider, Restrepo, Harvin & Robbins, L.L.P. ....Houston, TX
Doyle, Robert C. ....Omaha, NE
Doyle, Robert E., Jr. ....Naples, FL
Doyle, Robert F. ....Nashville, TN
Doyle, Robert H. ....Potomac, MD
Doyle, Robert H. ....Valley, NE
Doyle, Robert J. ....Indianapolis, IN
Doyle, Robert J. ....Boston, MA
Doyle, Robert M.
Environmental Protection Agency, Program Office Attorneys, GV
Doyle, Robert S. ....Brighton, CO
Doyle, Robert T., Jr. ....Northampton, MA
Doyle, Robert W. ....Riverhead, NY
Doyle, Robert W., Jr. ....Washington, DC
Doyle, Robert W., Jr. ....Melville, NY
Doyle, Rodger P., Jr. ....Buffalo, NY
Doyle, Ronald E. ....Tulsa, OK
Doyle, RoxAnne ....Kansas City, MO
Doyle, Ruth M. ....Buzzards Bay, MA
Doyle & Salisbury ....Tulsa, OK
Doyle, Sallie ....Yorba Linda, CA
Doyle, Sara L. ....Atlanta, GA
Doyle, Scott W. ....Denver, CO
Doyle, Scott W. ....Carson City, NV
Doyle, Sean C. ....New York, NY
Doyle, Sharon Steele ....Houston, TX
Doyle, Shea ....Rock Island, IL
Doyle, Sheri A. ....Seattle, WA
Doyle, Shirley A. ....Worcester, MA
Doyle, Stan P. ....Tulsa, OK
Doyle, Stanley B., Jr. ....Massapequa, NY
Doyle, Stephanie E. ....Richmond Heights, OH
Doyle, Stephen J. ....Cambridge, MA
Doyle, Stephen J. ....Portland, OR
Doyle, Stephen M. ....Department of Justice, Civil Division, GV
Doyle, Stephen P. ....San Diego, CA
Doyle, Stephen P. ....Washington, DC
Doyle, Stephen P. ....Wayzata, MN
Doyle, Steven P. ....La Crosse, WI
Doyle, Susan E. ....New Bedford, MA
Doyle, Susan M. ....Walnut Creek, CA
Doyle, Suzan Gail ....Costa Mesa, CA
Doyle, T. Michael ....Lansing, MI
Doyle, Terence N. ....St. Paul, MN
Doyle, Terry ....Port Arthur, TX
Doyle, Theresa B. ....Seattle, WA
Doyle, Thomas A. ....Chicago, IL
Doyle, Thomas A. ....Chicago, IL
Doyle, Thomas B. ....Chelmsford, MA
Doyle, Thomas C. ....Pittsfield, MA
Doyle, Thomas E. ....Taylorville, IL
Doyle, Thomas E. ....Rockville, MD
Doyle, Thomas F. ....San Francisco, CA
Doyle, Thomas H. ....Newington, CT
Doyle, Thomas J. ....Sacramento, CA
Doyle, Thomas J. ....Flint, MI
Saginaw, MI
Doyle, Thomas J. ....St. Paul, MN
Doyle, Thomas K. ....Portland, OR
Doyle, Thomas M. ....Chicago, IL
Doyle, Thomas M., II ....Washington, DC
Doyle, Thomas P. ....Rockville, MD
Doyle, Thomas R. ....Portland, ME
Doyle, Timothy J. ....Farmington, MI
Doyle, Timothy M. ....Rice Lake, WI
Doyle, Todd E. ....Irvine, CA
Doyle, Trek C. ....Austin, TX
Doyle, Valerie M. ....White Plains, NY
Doyle, Victoria J.B. ....New York, NY
Doyle, Vincent E., III ....Buffalo, NY
Doyle, Vincent E., Jr. ....Buffalo, NY
Doyle, Wendie J. ....Sacramento, CA
Doyle, William E. ....Frankfort, KY
Doyle, William E. ....Allentown, PA
Doyle, William E., Jr. ....Harrisburg, PA
Doyle, William H. ....Phoenix, AZ
Doyle, William J. ....New Haven, CT
Doyle, William J. ....Boston, MA
Doyle, William J. ....Tulsa, OK
Doyle, William J., III ....Troy, NY
Doyle, William J., Jr. ....Boston, MA
Doyle, William J., Jr. ....Troy, NY
Doyle, William L. ....Avenel, NJ
Doyle, William M. ....Mobile, AL
Doyle, William M., Jr. ....Chicago, IL
Doyle, William T. ....Cleveland, OH
Doyle & Winthrop, P.C. ....Phoenix, AZ
Doyle-Kossick, Patricia ....Tempe, AZ
D'Oyley, Hope R. ....Princeton, NJ
Doyno, Barry L. ....New York, NY
Doyno, Brian M. ....Hackensack, NJ
Doyon, Keith W. ....Colorado Springs, CO
Doyscher, David E. ....Stillwater, MN
Dozark, Patrick F. ....Houston, TX
Dozeman, Douglas A. ....Grand Rapids, MI
Dozer, Daniel W. ....Pawnee, OK
Dozer, Hilary M. ....Santa Barbara, CA
Dozer, Jodi L. ....Columbus, OH
Dozer, Stephen C. ....Kaukauna, WI
Dozier, A. Bradley, Jr. ....Atlanta, GA
Dozier and Associates, P.C. ....Richmond, VA
Dozier, Bill ....Stockton, CA
Dozier, Bradford J. ....Stockton, CA
Dozier, Bruce E. ....Wilmington, DE
Dozier, Cary L. ....Troy, AL
Dozier, Darlene M. ....Tiburon, CA
Dozier, D. C. Jim ....Conroe, TX
Dozier, Dennis G., Sr. ....Rincon, GA
Dozier, Dennis G., Sr., P.C., Law Office of
Rincon, GA
Dozier & Dozier ....Los Altos, CA
Dozier & Dozier ....Sarasota, FL
Dozier, Erin ....Washington, DC
Dozier, Eugene J. ....Fort Worth, TX
Dozier, G. Sheppard W. ....Ocala, FL
Dozier, George L., Jr. ....Marietta, GA
Dozier, Gilbert Hennigan ....Lafayette, LA
Dozier, Heather A. ....Irvine, CA
Dozier, Henry C., III ....Ocala, FL
Dozier, Jack C. ....Stockton, CA
Dozier, James H. ....Los Altos, CA
Dozier, Jas. M., Jr. ....Farmerville, LA
Dozier, Jerry B. ....Alvin, TX
Dozier, John W., Jr. ....Richmond, VA
Dozier, Joseph W. ....Los Altos, CA
Dozier, L. Zack, Jr. ....Macon, GA
Dozier, Lamar B. ....Sarasota, FL
Dozier, Lee, Graham & Sikes ....Macon, GA
Dozier, Linda Beliveau ....Sacramento, CA
Dozier, Marguerite Ann ....Cincinnati, OH
Dozier, Michael D. ....Folsom, CA

Dozier, Miller, Pollard & Murphy
Charlotte, NC
Dozier & Moore ... San Clemente, CA
Dozier, Phillip C. ... Orlando, FL
Dozier, Reginald G. ... Detroit, MI
Dozier, Robert E. ... Department of Justice, Tax Division, GV
Dozier, Robert L. ... Nashville, TN
Dozier, Ronald C. ... Bloomington, IL
Dozier, Russell W., Jr. ... Oklahoma City, OK
Dozier, Steve R. ... Nashville, TN
Dozier, Susan K. ... Los Angeles, CA
Dozier, Thomas A. ... Sarasota, FL
Dozier, Turner & Braceful, A Professional Corporation ... Detroit, MI
Dozier, W. Joseph, Jr. ... Charlotte, NC
Dozier, Walter B. ... San Clemente, CA
Dozier, Wilene D., Law Office of
Jacksonville, FL
Dozier, William M. ... Norfolk, VA
Dozois, Laura K. ... Chicago, IL
Dozois, Timothy ... Portland, OR
Dozor Auslander & Stein ... Collingdale, PA
Dozor, Barry C. ... Collingdale, PA
Dozoretz, Bernice R. ... Binghamton, NY
Draa, Charles M. ... Youngstown, OH
Draa, Tyler G. ... Saratoga, CA
Drabant, Robert J. ... Sacramento, CA
Drabble, Nancy S. ... Sacramento, CA
Drabek & Associates, P.C. ... Harlingen, TX
Drabek, Cynthia ... Great Falls, VA
Drabek, Jaime A. ... Harlingen, TX
Drabenstadt, Scott ... Louisville, KY
Drabicki, Judy ... New Hartford, NY
Drabick, Jr., Thomas C. ... Columbus, OH
Drabik, Lisa M. ... Winston-Salem, NC
Drabin, Lee S. ... Van Nuys, CA
Drabkin, Eva Garfinkel ... East Hills, NY
Drabkin, Harry P. ... Modesto, CA
Drabkin, Jess H. ... New York, NY
Drabkin, Jules ... McMinnville, OR
Drabkin, Murray ... Washington, DC
Drabkin, Nathaniel ... New York, NY
Drabkin, Ralph J. ... New York, NY
Drabkin & Tankersley ... McMinnville, OR
Drablos, Scott C. ... Dallas, TX
Drabot, Lawrence J. ... Chicago, IL
Wheaton, IL
Drace, Denise L. ... Chicago, IL
Drach, Jeffery J. ... Wausau, WI
Drach, John E. ... Plymouth Meeting, PA
Drach Law Firm ... Wausau, WI
Drach, Sally A. ... San Francisco, CA
Drachler, Dan ... Seattle, WA
Drachler, Paul ... Seattle, WA
Drachlis, Bernard P. ... Los Angeles, CA
Drachman, Allan W. ... Boston, MA
Drachman, Annette Roney ... Charleston, SC
West Columbia, SC
Drachman, Frank E., Jr. ... San Diego, CA
Drachman, Steven S. ... New York, NY
Drachsler, David A. ... Department of Labor, Office of Secretary, GV
Drack, Marshall N. ... Sacramento, CA
Dracup, Jeffrey A. ... Santa Ana, CA
Dracup & Patterson, A Law Corporation
Santa Ana, CA
Draddy, Elizabeth ... New York, NY
Draddy, James J., Jr.
Securities and Exchange Commission, Office of Compliance Inspections and Examinations, GV
Draeb, August C. ... Hebron, ND
Richardton, ND
Draeger, Dina M. ... High Point, NC
Draeger, James M. ... Menlo Park, CA
Draeger, Terry P. ... Anchorage, AK
Draesel, Herbert G. ... River Edge, NJ
Draesel, Sunshine, Atkins, Minassian & Tafuri, P.A. ... River Edge, NJ
Draffen, Jennifer Adams ... New York, NY
Draffin, Jill M. ... Irvine, CA
Draffin, Michael C. ... Long Beach, CA
Draffin, Stephen T. ... Columbia, SC
Draftz, Susan M. Youngers ... Sheldon, IA
Drag, Michael J. ... Murrysville, PA
Drag, Walter F. ... Dunkirk, NY
Dragan, Dennis T. ... Monrovia, CA
Dragan, Sharon A. ... Flemington, NJ
Dragan, William P. ... Shelton, CT
Draganchuk, Joyce Ann ... Lansing, MI
Draganosky, David J. ... Lansdale, PA
Draganov, Bronislav M. ... Beverly Hills, CA
Dragas, M. Linda ... New York, NY
Drage, Christine E. ... Pasadena, CA
Drage, de Beaubien, Knight, Simmons, Mantzaris & Neal ... Orlando, FL
Drage, Jonathan S. ... Chicago, IL
Drage, Thomas B., Jr. ... Orlando, FL
Dragelevich & Blair ... Niles, OH
Dragelevich, J. Walter ... Niles, OH
Drager, Arthur L., The Law Offices of
Baltimore, MD
Drager, Christine
National Labor Relations Board, Office of the General Counsel, GV
Drager, Natalie Weidener ... Washington, DC
Drager, Paul ... Peekskill, NY
Dragg, Joe L.
Federal Energy Regulatory Commission, Office of Administrative Litigation, GV
Dragga, Callahan, Hannon & Hessler, L.L.P.
Rockville, MD
Dragga, Patrick W. ... Rockville, MD
Draghi, Brenda A. ... Ellington, CT
Draghi, John D. ... New York, NY
Draghi, John M. ... Concord, NH
Draghi, Thomas A. ... Garden City, NY
Dragich, Stephen J. ... Chicago, IL
Dragna, Gerard Joseph ... New Orleans, LA
Dragna, James J. ... Los Angeles, CA
Dragna, Steve ... Anaheim, CA
Drago, Alexander J. ... New York, NY
Drago, Anthony, Jr. ... Boston, MA
Drago, Domenic C. ... San Diego, CA
Drago, Donald J. ... Austin, TX
Drago, Frank J. ... Napa, CA
Drago, Joseph A. ... Fort Worth, TX
Drago, Linda S. ... Pittsburgh, PA
Drago, Mary C. ... Universal City, CA
Drago, Nicholas V. ... Somerville, MA
Drago, Scott M. ... New York, NY
Drago, Thomas J. ... New York, NY
Dragojevic, Julia ... Westlake Village, CA
Dragon, Albert ... Philadelphia, PA
Dragon, Edward A. ... Washington, DC
Dragon, James C. ... Lowell, MA
Nahant, MA
Dragon, James C., P.C., Law Offices of
Lowell, MA
Nahant, MA
Dragon, Jean E. ... Chicago, IL
Dragon, Jeffrey F., (P.A.) ... Cherry Hill, NJ
Dragone, Roy ... Baltimore, MD
Dragone, Victor G., Jr. ... Everett, MA
Dragonette, John A. ... Los Angeles, CA
Dragoo, Denise A. ... Salt Lake City, UT
Dragotta, Roy S. ... Hauppauge, NY
Dragseth, Jason A. ... New York, NY
Dragseth, John A. ... Minneapolis, MN
Dragseth-Kleinschmidt, Carolyn ... Boutte, LA
Dragun, Anthony J. ... Irvine, CA
Dragunas, Ruta M. ... New York, NY
Dragus, George H. ... Hammond, IN
Dragutinovich, Zoran ... Chicago, IL
Draheim, David B. ... Oakland, CA
Draheim, Jennifer E. ... Fullerton, CA
Riverside, CA
Draheim, Philip Earl ... St. Louis, MO
Draher, Allen B. ... Seattle, WA
Drahos, Carl C. ... Bemidji, MN
Drahos, Leslie Acerra ... Fremont, CA
Drahos & Young ... Bemidji, MN
Drahozal, Christopher R. ... Washington, DC
Draigh, David P. ... New York, NY
Draikiwicz, Ellyn A. ... Summit, NJ
Draikiwicz, John D. ... Newark, NJ
Draim, Ida Wurczinger ... Washington, DC
Draim, Robert E. ... McLean, VA
Drain, Aluanda R. ... Greenbelt, MD
Drain, Diane L. ... Phoenix, AZ
Drain, J. Michael ... Chagrin Falls, OH
Drain, John M. ... Cleveland, OH
Drain, Joseph A. ... Rocky River, OH
Drain, Kurt B. ... Los Angeles, CA
Drain, Lewis D. ... White Bear Lake, MN
Drain, Loyd G. ... Bellaire, TX
Drain, Patricia W. ... Falls Church, VA
Drain, Randall G. ... New York, NY
Drain, Robert D. ... New York, NY
Draine, Francis T. ... Columbia, SC
Draine, Kathleen A. ... Upper Nyack, NY
Drais, Daniel G. ... Seattle, WA
Draisen, Daniel L. ... Anderson, SC
Draisin, Stephen J. ... Hackensack, NJ
Drakas, Gary A. ... Philadelphia, PA
Drake, Adrienne C.M. ... Sioux Falls, SD
Drake, Alicia R. ... Minneapolis, MN
Drake, Andrew R. ... Indianapolis, IN
Drake, Anna W. ... Salt Lake City, UT
Drake, Anna W., P.C. ... Salt Lake City, UT
Drake & Associates ... Birmingham, AL
Drake, Barbara S. ... Arlington, VA
Drake, Beckler & Drake ... Metairie, LA
Ponchatoula, LA
Drake, Brenda Jackson ... San Francisco, CA
Drake & Burrell ... Port Gibson, MS
Drake, Carol Sparks ... Indianapolis, IN
Drake, Charles A. ... Inlet, NY
Utica, NY
Drake, Charles E. ... Inlet, NY
Utica, NY
Drake, Charles E. ... Stillwater, OK
Drake, Charlotte J. ... Metairie, LA
Ponchatoula, LA
Drake, Chester W., Jr. ... Detroit, MI
Drake, Christine McKoy ... Cullman, AL
Drake, Christopher D. ... Albany, NY
Drake, Christopher S. ... Bronx, NY
Drake, Claire Fried ... Raleigh, NC
Drake, Claire Kathryn ... Chicago, IL
Drake, Criston L. ... Brainerd, MN
Drake, Criston L., P.A. ... Brainerd, MN
Drake, Curtis J. ... Salt Lake City, UT
Drake, Curtis L. ... Metairie, LA
Drake, D. Flint ... Dubuque, IA
Drake, Dale ... McKinney, TX
Drake, Dana L. ... Huntington Beach, CA
Drake, Daniel A. ... Rochester, NY
Drake, Daniel G. ... Brandon, FL
Drake, Daniel W. ... New York, NY
Drake, Daniel W. ... Columbus, OH
Drake, Danny A. ... Jackson, MS
Drake, David A. ... Atlanta, GA
Drake, David A. ... Chapel Hill, NC
Drake, David D. ... West Des Moines, IA
Drake, David L. ... Springfield, IL
Drake, David Randall
Mountain Home, AR
Drake, David W. ... Atlanta, GA
Drake, Denise K. ... Kansas City, MO
Drake, Dennis K. ... San Antonio, TX
Drake, Denny ... Des Moines, IA
Drake, Diane J. ... Philadelphia, PA
Drake, Donald M. ... Columbus, OH
Drake, Donald W. ... Niagara Falls, NY
Drake, Donna ... Washington, DC
Drake, Dorothy R. ... Birmingham, AL
Drake, Douglas H. ... Reno, NV
Drake & Drake ... Cullman, AL
Drake and Drake ... Inlet, NY
Utica, NY
Drake, Dwight F. ... Columbia, SC
Drake, Dwight J. ... Seattle, WA
Drake, E. Thayer ... Avon, CT
Drake, E. Whitney
Federal Deposit Insurance Corporation, Appellate Litigation Section, GV
Drake, Eduardo E. ... Minneapolis, MN
Drake, Edward J. ... Dallas, TX
Drake, Edward J., III ... Dallas, TX
Drake, Edward J., III, P.C. ... Dallas, TX
Drake, Edwin G. ... Singer Island, FL
Drake, Edwin P. ... Pittsburgh, PA
Drake, Eileen ... Portland, OR
Drake, Elizabeth ... Minneapolis, MN
Drake, Elizabeth Mullikin ... Colchester, VT
Drake, Ernest G., Jr. ... Metairie, LA
Ponchatoula, LA
Drake, Eugene E. ... Englewood, CO
Drake & Franco, PLC ... Southfield, MI
Drake, Franklin ... Raleigh, NC
Drake, G. Curt ... Helena, MT
Drake, G. Whit ... Birmingham, AL
Cullman, AL
Drake, George H., Jr. ... Denver, CO
Drake, George T. ... Lake Forest, IL
Drake, Georgette ... Little Falls, NY
Drake, Glen L. ... Helena, MT
Drake, Gregory S. ... Stamford, CT
Drake, Gurden E. ... Department of Defense, Office of the General Counsel, GV
Drake, H. Michael ... Salt Lake City, UT
Drake, Harold M., Jr. ... Canton, MA
Drake, Heather L. ... Tulsa, OK
Drake, Henry T. ... Marshville, NC
Wadesboro, NC
Drake, Hileman & Davis, P.C.
Allentown, PA
Doylestown, PA
Stroudsburg, PA
Drake, Ian J. ... Greensboro, NC
Drake, Irving R. ... Houston, TX
Drake, J. Kevin ... Sarasota, FL
Drake, J. Kevin, P.A. ... Sarasota, FL
Drake, James H. ... St. Louis, MO
Drake, James J. ... Wyandotte, MI
Drake, James L., Jr. ... Savannah, GA
Drake, James M. ... Chicago, IL
Drake, James M. ... Springfield, IL
Drake, Janet L. ... Atlanta, GA
Drake, Janet Stansberry ... Aurora, CO
Drake, Jeanne S. ... Loveland, CO
Drake, Jeffrey A. ... Allentown, PA
Doylestown, PA
Stroudsburg, PA
Drake, Jeffrey T. ... Boise, ID
Drake, Jennifer Bales
Fort Lauderdale, FL
Drake, Jody Haller ... Arlington, VA
Drake, John C. ... Cincinnati, OH
Drake, John E. ... Corpus Christi, TX
Drake, John J. ... Fort Worth, TX
Drake, John W. ... Northampton, MA
Drake, John Walter ... Decatur, GA
Drake, Jonathan L. ... Philadelphia, PA
Drake, J. T., Jr. ... Port Gibson, MS
Drake, Juliet A. ... New York, NY
Drake, Karen L. ... Cambridge, MA
Drake, Kathleen ... Edina, MN
Drake, Kathryn S. ... Louisville, KY
Drake, Kelly L. ... Lawrence, KS
Drake, Kenneth ... New York, NY
Drake, Kenneth R. ... Miami, FL
Drake, Kenneth W. ... Sherman Oaks, CA
Drake, Kevin R. ... Boston, MA
Drake, Kimberly A. ... Lewisville, TX
Drake, Laura Lynn ... Cincinnati, OH
Drake, Leslie A. ... Kirkland, WA
Drake, Linda A. ... Tucson, AZ
Drake, Linda Copeland ... Gary, IN
Drake, Lyle R. ... St. George, UT
Drake, Margaret Cronan ... Elmira, NY
Drake, Mark D. ... McGehee, AR
Drake, Mark J. ... Kansas City, MO
Drake, Mary ... Oak Park, IL
Drake, Mason H. ... New York, NY
Drake, Matthew R. ... San Francisco, CA
Drake, Matthew T. ... Union, MO
Drake, Melvin L., Jr. ... Atlanta, GA
Drake, Michael ... Tucson, AZ
Drake, Michael J. ... Springfield, IL
Drake, Monique Michal ... Denver, CO
Drake, Nancy E. Caldwell ... Columbia, SC
Drake, Naomi G. ... Daphne, AL
Drake, Narup & Mead, P.C.
Springfield, IL
Drake, Patrick J. ... Southfield, MI
Drake, Paul ... Chicago, IL
Drake, Paul S. ... Austin, TX
Drake, Paula ... Boston, MA
Drake, Paula B. ... Santa Ana, CA
Drake, Philip M. ... Greenwich, CT
Drake, Phillips, Kuenzli & Clark
Findlay, OH
Drake & Pleasant ... Marshville, NC
Wadesboro, NC
Drake, R. Larry ... Crossville, TN
Drake, Randy A. ... Reno, NV
Drake, Raymond B. ... Clinton, NJ
Drake, Richard J. ... Newburgh, NY
Drake, Richard N. ... Winston-Salem, NC
Drake, Robert C. ... Philadelphia, PA
Drake, Robert M. ... Albany, GA
Drake, Robert N. ... Newark, OH
Drake, Robert P. ... Big Flats, NY
Drake, Robert S. ... Big Bear Lake, CA
Drake, Robert S., Jr. ... Warsaw, MO
Drake, Robert W. ... Alameda, CA
Drake, Robert W. ... Findlay, OH
Drake, Robin J. ... El Paso, TX
Drake, Russell Jackson ... Birmingham, AL
Drake, Russell L. ... Trinity, TX
Drake, Rusty W. ... Pasadena, TX
Drake, Sara J. ... Sacramento, CA
Drake, Sidney E. ... Centerville, IA
Drake, Sommers, Loeb, Tarshis & Catania, PLLC ... Goshen, NY
Kingston, NY
Monroe, NY
Newburgh, NY
White Plains, NY
Drake, Stephen N. ... Bronx, NY
Drake, Stephen R. ... Boise, ID
Drake, Steve ... Absecon, NJ
Drake, Stuart A. C. ... Washington, DC
Drake, Stuart B. ... Farmer City, IL
Drake, Susan D. ... Washington, DC
Drake, Susie Stuart ... Lynchburg, VA
Drake, Ted N. ... Pine Bluff, AR
Drake, Thomas D. ... Findlay, OH
Drake, Thomas E., II ... Cullman, AL
Drake, Thomas J., Jr. ... Nashville, TN
Drake, Thos. G. ... Minneapolis, MN
Drake, Tim E. ... Dallas, TX
Drake, Tom ... Cullman, AL
Drake, Tracy V. ... Baltimore, MD
Drake, W. Homer, Jr. ... Newnan, GA
Drake, Walker H., Jr. ... Chalmette, LA
Drake, Walter P. ... Berlin, MD
Drake, Wilfred F. ... Durham, NC
Drake, William A. ... Los Angeles, CA
Drake, William D. ... San Diego, CA
Drake, William E. ... Minneapolis, MN
Drake, William F., Jr. ... Philadelphia, PA
Drake, William H. ... Colon, MI
Drake, William N., Jr. ... St. Petersburg, FL
Drakeford, Garrett L. ... La Grange, KY
Drakeford, Rosalind T. ... Atlanta, GA
Drakeley, James T. ... Addison, TX
Draker, Courtneay B. ... Houston, TX
Drakesmith, Burke, Linson & Briscoe, LLP
St. Charles, MO
Drakesmith, Frederick W.
St. Charles, MO
Drakos, Peter G. ... New York, NY
Drakos, Steven A. ... Oxford, MI
Drakotos, Penelope A. ... New York, NY
Drakulich & Carlson, P.C. ... Portland, OR
Drakulich, Gene S. ... Reno, NV
Drakulich, Kathleen Morello ... Reno, NV
Drakulich, Nicholas J. ... San Diego, CA
Drakulich, Nick A. ... Portland, OR
Drakulich, Victor G. ... Reno, NV
Dralla, Gloria G. ... Santa Clara, CA
Draluck, Jonathan D. ... Washington, DC
Dramer, Daniel L. ... Oceanside, CA
Dramis, George J., III ... Sarasota, FL
Drana, John E. ... Milwaukee, WI
Drandell, Harry M. ... Fresno, CA
Drane, J. Frank ... Louisville, KY
Drane, Robert E. ... Louisville, KY
Drane, Scott A. ... Chicago, IL
Drane, W. Harding, Jr. ... Wilmington, DE
Draneas, John H. ... Portland, OR
Draneas, Streicher & Huglin, P.C.
Portland, OR
Dranetz, Charles S. ... Pompano Beach, FL
Dranetz, Marshall M. ... Hyannis, MA
Draney, Michael ... Lee's Summit, MO
Draney, Shawn E. ... Salt Lake City, UT
Drange, Harold R. ... Denver, CO
Drange, Steven E. ... Benson, MN
Drangel, Alfred ... Great Neck, NY
Drangel, Jason M. ... New York, NY
Dranginis, Anne C. ... Litchfield, CT
Dranginis, Peter J., Jr.
Briarcliff Manor, NY
Drangula, Carey B. ... New Brunswick, NJ
Dranias, Nicholas C. ... Chicago, IL
Dranit, Warren L. ... Santa Rosa, CA
Dranitzke, Alan ... Washington, DC
Dranitzke, Anna-Sigga ... Brooklyn, NY
Dranitzke, Lechtrecker & Trabold
Center Moriches, NY
Patchogue, NY
Dranitzke, William ... Center Moriches, NY
Patchogue, NY
Drankoski, Bernadette M. ... Atlanta, GA
Dranoff, Albert S. ... Long Beach, NY
Dranoff, Arnold ... Philadelphia, PA
Dranoff, David L. ... Chicago, IL
Dranoff, Eric ... New York, NY
Dranoff & Goldschmidt, L.L.P.
Elmsford, NY
New York, NY
Pearl River, NY
Dranoff & Patrizio ... Philadelphia, PA
Dranoff, Peter D. ... New York, NY
Dranoff, Sanford S. ... Elmsford, NY
New York, NY
Pearl River, NY
Dranoff, Sarah E. ... Brooklyn, NY
Dranoff, Steven M. ... Exton, PA
Hamlin, PA
Philadelphia, PA
Scranton, PA
Dranoff-Perlstein Associates ... Exton, PA
Hamlin, PA
Philadelphia, PA
Scranton, PA
Dransfield, Robert D. ... Dallas, TX

Dransite, Geraldine Helen ... **Elmsford, NY**
Pearl River, NY
Drantch, Mitchel S. ... Denver, CO
Dranttel, Elizabeth M. ... **Albuquerque, NM**
Dranttel, Jack G. ... Churchton, MD
Drapalski, Henry J., Jr. ... Holyoke, MA
Drapanas, Mark T. ... Harahan, LA
Drapatsky, Alexander ... Chicago, IL
Drape, Dana L. ... Des Moines, IA
Drapeau, David R. ... Ventura, CA
Drapeau, Diane M. ... Boston, MA
Drapeau, Francis X. ... Rockville, CT
Drapeau, John W. ... San Diego, CA
Drapeau, Kathleen A. ... **New York, NY**
Drapekin, Steven C. ... **St. Louis, MO**
Draper, Ann M. ... San Francisco, CA
Draper, Brian C. ... Rogers City, MI
Draper, Brian C., P.C. ... Rogers City, MI
Draper, Carl R. ... **Springfield, IL**
Draper, Carol ... Kissimmee, FL
Draper, Charles B. ... **Kissimmee, FL**
Draper, Chris Alan ... **Maitland, FL**
Draper, Clare H., IV ... **Atlanta, GA**
Draper, Daniel C. ... New York, NY
Draper, Daniel D., Jr. ... Stillwater, OK
Draper, Daniel, Jr. ... **Miami, FL**
Draper, Daniel S. ... **Lake Geneva, WI**
Draper, David ... **Knoxville, TN**
Draper, David B. ... **San Jose, CA**
Draper, David R. ... Grosse Pointe Park, MI
Draper, David R. ... Chehalis, WA
Draper, David W., Jr. ... Leesburg, VA
Draper, Deborah ... Lacey, WA
Draper, Delbert M., III ... Salt Lake City, UT
Draper, Douglas S. ... Woodland Hills, CA
Draper, Douglas S. ... **New Orleans, LA**
Draper, Douglas S., A Law Corporation
Woodland Hills, CA
Draper, Duane D. ... **Tampa, FL**
Draper, Elsie C. ... **Tulsa, OK**
Draper, Franklin Warner, IV ... Baltimore, MD
Draper, Gary M. ... **Crossett, AR**
Draper, Gerald L. ... **Columbus, OH**
Draper, Glenn S. ... **Seattle, WA**
Draper & Goldberg, P.L.L.C. ... Leesburg, VA
Draper, Harold A., Jr. ... Flint, MI
Draper, Hayward L. ... **Des Moines, IA**
Draper, J. William ... Philadelphia, PA
Draper, Jack A., Inc., Law Offices of
Bakersfield, CA
Los Angeles, CA
Draper, Jack Alden, II (IBA)
Bakersfield, CA
Los Angeles, CA
Draper, Jack B. ... **Knoxville, TN**
Draper, Jacqueline M. ... Trenton, NJ
Draper, James W. ... **Detroit, MI**
Draper, James W. ... Bellevue, WA
Draper, John B. ... **Santa Fe, NM**
Draper, John H., IV ... **Burlington, VT**
Draper, John M. ... Englewood, CO
Draper, Kenneth J. ... Washington, DC
Draper Law Office ... **Kissimmee, FL**
Draper, Lindsey D. ... Wauwatosa, WI
Draper, Louise P. ... Covington, LA
Draper, Margaret H. ... Chicago, IL
Draper, Mark A. ... **Punta Gorda, FL**
Draper, Mark E. ... **Springfield, MA**
Draper, Marti Ann ... Pasadena, CA
Draper, Monette E. ... Carmel, IN
Draper, Patricia Ann ... Tallahassee, FL
Draper, Paul D. ... Costa Mesa, CA
Draper, Paul E. ... **Baltimore, MD**
Draper, Paul E., P.A. ... **Baltimore, MD**
Draper, Robert Linn ... **Washington, DC**
Draper, Robert S. ... **Los Angeles, CA**
Draper, Ronald G. ... Chicago, IL
Draper, Shelley McIntyre ... Boston, MA
Draper, Thomas B. ... **Boston, MA**
Draper, Thomas G., Jr. ... **New York, NY**
Draper, Thomas N. ... Mission Hills, CA
Draper, Virginia L. ... Denver, CO
Draper & Walsh ... Costa Mesa, CA
Drapiewski, Daniel ... San Francisco, CA
Drapkin, Andrew L. ... Houston, TX
Drapkin, Dennis B. ... **Dallas, TX**
Drapkin, Donald G. ... New York, NY
Drapkin, Larry C., (A Professional Corporation) ... **Los Angeles, CA**
Drapkin, Michael L. ... Boulder, CO
Drapkin, Steven, Law Offices of
Los Angeles, CA
Drapola, Steven M. ... Mineola, NY
Drapos, Alexander E. ... **Worcester, MA**
Drasco, Dennis J. ... **Roseland, NJ**
Drasco, Mitchell I. ... Laguna Beach, CA
Drash, David W. ... Richmond, VA
Drasheff, Barbara ... **Roseland, NJ**
Drasheff, Gerald R. ... **New York, NY**
Drasin, John S. ... Eagan, MN
Drasin, Judith ... Philadelphia, PA
Drasin, Lawrence ... Los Angeles, CA
Drasin, Resa T. ... Roseland, NJ
Drasites, Thomas E. ... **Cape Coral, FL**
Draskovic, John W. ... **Erie, PA**
Draskovich, Robert M., Jr. ... **Las Vegas, NV**
Drasner, Fred ... Washington, DC
Drasnin, David B. ... Farmington Hills, MI
Drasnin, Mark W. ... **Philadelphia, PA**
Drasser, Charles G. ... Aberdeen, MD
Dratch, Barbara McMahon
New Milford, CT
Dratch, John E. ... Abington, PA
Dratch, Stephen N. ... **Livingston, NJ**
New York, NY
Dratch, Todd Anthony ... Abington, PA
Dratel, Joshua L. ... New York, NY
Dratel, William M. ... New York, NY
Dratfield, Paul ... **Glastonbury, CT**
Dratfield, Sherri F. ... Secaucus, NJ
Drath, Clifford, Murphy, Wennerholm & Hagen, A Professional Corporation
San Diego, CA
San Francisco, CA
Drath, Constance M. ... Washington, DC
Drath & Dwyer ... Washington, DC
Drath, John M. ... **San Francisco, CA**
Drath, Lawrence I. ... New York, NY
Drathman, Ronald Wm. ... Homer, AK
Draths, Thomas G. ... **Chicago, IL**
Dratler, Eric N. ... **Albany, NY**
Dratler, Jay, Jr. ... Honolulu, HI
Dratler, Sylvia Lederman ... Meadville, PA
Dratt, Arnold H. ... Chicago, IL
Drattell, Eric M. ... Washington, DC
Dratz, John Paul, Jr. ... San Francisco, CA
Dratz, Mary C. ... Oklahoma City, OK
Draucker, Carl A. ... **Cleveland, OH**
Draude, James T. ... **Washington, DC**
Draudt, James P. ... Portland, OR
Draugelis & Ashton, L.L.P. ... **Clawson, MI**
Detroit, MI
Plymouth, MI
Draugelis, Edward F. ... **Clawson, MI**
Plymouth, MI
Draughn, Charles M., III ... Franklinton, NC
Draughn, James Worth, Jr.
Washington, DC
Draughn, Joe L. ... **Houston, TX**
Draughon, Ashley H. ... **Atlanta, GA**
Draughon, Donald S. ... Santa Rosa, CA
Draughon, John A. ... **Macon, GA**
Draughon, Professional Association
Jacksonville, FL
Draughon, Richard Scott ... **Jacksonville, FL**
Draughon, Scott W. ... Tulsa, OK
Draughton, Nancy Akel ... Jacksonville, FL
Draus, Andrew J. ... **Chicago, IL**
Draut, A. Andrew ... **Louisville, KY**
Draut, James W. ... Cincinnati, OH
Draut, Terrence G. ... **Torrance, CA**
Draves, Allan C. ... Orlando, FL
Draves, Brian ... **Palo Alto, CA**
Draves, Daren Kimberly ... Burlingame, CA
Draves, Donna L. ... Orlando, FL
Dravid, Aditi ... **Dallas, TX**
Dravillas, Kathleen ... Chicago, IL
Dravis, Bruce ... **Sacramento, CA**
Dravis, Ted E. ... **Houston, TX**
Drawbert, David A. ... Breckenridge, CO
Drawdy, Mary Lynne Witt ... Tecumseh, OK
Drawdy, Vance E. ... **Greenville, SC**
Drawe, Patricia S. ... Salt Lake City, UT
Drawe, Scott P. ... **Minneapolis, MN**
Drawec, John W. ... Belchertown, MA
Drawz, John E. ... **Minneapolis, MN**
Draxl, Gregory L. ... Little Rock, AR
Dray, Andrea F. ... **Asheville, NC**
Dray, Barbara Glidden ... Bayside, CA
Dray, David L. ... Hull, MA
Dray, Elaine R. ... Boston, MA
Dray, Judith M. ... **Atlanta, GA**
Dray, Mark S. ... **Richmond, VA**
Dray, Powers & Sasse Co., L.P.A.
Painesville, OH
Dray, Sandra A. ... Painesville, OH
Dray, Thomson & Dyekman, P.C.
Cheyenne, WY
Dray, W. Perry ... **Cheyenne, WY**
Draycott, Mark Justin
Department of Justice, Civil Division, GV
Drayden, Charles L. ... Bellaire, TX
Drayer, Anna Lee ... Austin, TX
Drayer, Calvin S., Jr. ... Norristown, PA
Drayer, H. John ... **Clarion, PA**
Drayer, Lonnie R. ... Columbus, OH
Drayer, Michael ... Tampa, FL
Drayer, Robin ... Chicago, IL
Draymore, Mark R. ... Springfield, MA
Draymore, Mastin & Goldberg, P.A.
Springfield, MA
Drayo, Samuel L., Jr. ... Fredonia, NY
Drayovitch, Debra Adami
Fort Worth, TX
Drayton, Douglas L. ... **Glastonbury, CT**
Drayton, Douglas P. ... **San Francisco, CA**
Drayton, Gloria Frances ... Torrance, CA
Walnut Creek, CA
Drayton, Joseph M. ... **New York, NY**
Drayton, Melvin ... Kingwood, TX
Drayton, Michael R. ... **Sacramento, CA**
Drayton, V. Michael ... La Porte, IN
Drazan, Daniel ... New York, NY
Drazan, Daniel J. ... **Eugene, OR**
Drazdys, Vilia M. ... **Chicago, IL**
Drazek, Joseph A. ... **Phoenix, AZ**
Drazen, Franklin A. ... Milford, CT
Drazen, James A. ... Branford, CT
Drazen, James M. ... Troy, IL
Drazen, Martin ... **White Plains, NY**
Drazen, Stanton M. ... Binghamton, NY
Drazen-Smith, Melissa M. ... Denver, CO
Drazewski, Scott D. ... Bloomington, IL
Drazic, Blair K. ... Chesterfield, MO
Drazich, Brian F. ... **Los Angeles, CA**
Drazin, Brian D. ... **Red Bank, NJ**
Drazin, Dennis A. ... **Brick, NJ**
Red Bank, NJ
Drazin & Drazin, P.A. ... Columbia, MD
Drazin, Israel ... Columbia, MD
Drazin, Robert S. ... Detroit, MI
Drazin, Ronald S. ... **Red Bank, NJ**
Drazin, Stephen A. ... Columbia, MD
Drazin and Warshaw ... **Brick, NJ**
Hazlet, NJ
Red Bank, NJ
Drazkowski, John E. ... **Phoenix, AZ**
Drazkowski, Kenneth D. ... Seattle, WA
Drazner, Richard J. ... Chicago, IL
Draznin, Anne L. ... Springfield, IL
Draznin, Neal A. ... Chicago, IL
Drcar, Theodore S. ... **San Diego, CA**
Drea, Arthur S., Jr. ... Annapolis, MD
Dreaden, James S. ... **Chattanooga, TN**
Drean, Robert E. ... **Orlando, FL**
Dreben, Raya S. ... Boston, MA
Dreben, Ron N. ... **Washington, DC**
Drebes, Dana ... **Livonia, MI**
Drebsky, Dennis J. ... **New York, NY**
Drechen, Martin J. ... Cicero, IL
Drechsel, Katy Anne ... **Houston, TX**
Drechsel, Lea-Marise ... **Los Angeles, CA**
Drechsler, Bea Krain ... **New York, NY**
Drechsler, David L. ... **Akron, OH**
Drechsler, Larkin & Walters, P.C.
Baltimore, MD
Drechsler, R. Roger ... **Baltimore, MD**
Drechsler, Robert H. ... New York, NY
Drechsler, Thomas ... **Boston, MA**
Dreckman, Patrick M. ... Katy, TX
Dreckmel, Paul C. ... **Salt Lake City, UT**
Drecktrah, Louis I. ... Black River Falls, WI
Dredge, David ... Westerly, RI
Dredge & Lallatin, L.C. ... Provo, UT
Dredge, Richard Kim ... Boise, ID
Dredge, Sandra ... Provo, UT
Dredger, Thomas A. ... Glen Cove, NY
Dredze, Mitchell G. ... Chicago, IL
Dreeben, Helen L. ... Mission Viejo, CA
Dreeben, Linda J.
National Labor Relations Board, Office of the General Counsel, GV
Dreeben, Michael R. ... Department of Justice, Office of the Solicitor General, GV
Dreeland, Allan E. ... Bridgeville, PA
Dreeman, Cynthia J. ... **Morristown, NJ**
New York, NY
Drees, Barry D. ... **Dallas, TX**
Drees, Catherine A. ... Daytona Beach, FL
Drees, Catherine A., P.A.
Daytona Beach, FL
Drees, Michelle J. ... **Sacramento, CA**
Drees, Nicholas T. ... Des Moines, IA
Dreesen, Duane M. ... **Omaha, NE**
Dreesen, Joseph ... **Omaha, NE**
Dreeszen, Steven K. ... Boston, MA
Drefke, Kyle W. ... **Washington, DC**
Dreger, Jonathan M. ... Golden, CO
Dreger, Marilyn A. ... Verona, WI
Dreger & McClelland ... **Cumming, GA**
Roswell, GA
Dreger, Richard J. ... **Roswell, GA**
Dreger, Robert M. ... Chicago, IL
Dregier, Daniel J., Jr. ... **Towson, MD**
Dregne, Matthew P. ... **Madison, WI**
Dregne, Nancy M. ... Phoenix, AZ
Dreher, Darrell L. ... **Mandeville, LA**
Columbus, OH
Dreher, Frederick W. ... **Philadelphia, PA**
Dreher, Garfinkle & Watson
San Francisco, CA
San Mateo, CA
Dreher, Joseph D. ... **Cleveland, OH**
Dreher, Kenneth R. ... Jackson, MS
Dreher Langer & Tomkies L.L.P.
Mandeville, LA
Columbus, OH
Dreher, Leanna Denise ... Santa Maria, CA
Dreher, Marie-Anne deRosier
New York, NY
Dreher, Nancy C. ... Minneapolis, MN
Dreher, Nancy L. ... Tampa, FL
Dreher, Nicholas C. ... **Honolulu, HI**
Dreher, Robert E. ... **Des Moines, IA**
Dreher, Robert G.
Environmental Protection Agency, Office of the General Counsel, GV
Dreher, Robert Scott ... **San Diego, CA**
Dreher, Simpson & Jensen, P.C.
Des Moines, IA
Dreher, Stephen C. ... **San Francisco, CA**
Dreher, Timothy J. ... Colorado Springs, CO
Dreher, Yolanda L. ... **Bryant, AR**
Memphis, TN
Drehkoff, W. Dennis ... **Chicago, IL**
Dreibelbis, Bessie P. ... Richmond, CA
Dreibelbis, Jon ... Des Moines, IA
Dreier, Alexander E. ... **Washington, DC**
Dreier & Baritz, LLP ... Boca Raton, FL
Dreier & Baritz LLP ... **New York, NY**
Dreier, David H. ... **New York, NY**
Dreier, Elizabeth A. ... Palm Springs, CA
Dreier, Gary L. ... **Stevens Point, WI**
Dreier Law Office ... **Norfolk, NE**
Dreier, Marc S. ... **New York, NY**
Dreier, Max G. ... **Norfolk, NE**
Dreier, Patricia ... **Norwalk, CT**
Dreier, Shari E.B. ... **New York, NY**
Dreier, William A. ... **Somerville, NJ**
Dreifach, Kenneth M. ... New York, NY
Dreifke, Stuart L. ... Columbus, OH
Dreifke, Stuart L. Co., L.P.A.
Columbus, OH
Dreifort, Ronald W. ... Corning, CA
Dreifus, Amy A. ... Las Vegas, NV
Dreifus, David ... **Raleigh, NC**
Dreifus, Suzanne Elaine
West Bloomfield, MI
Dreifuss, David A. ... Merrick, NY
Dreifuss, David C. ... **Livingston, NJ**
New York, NY
Dreifuss, Jeffrey M. ... Columbia, MD
Dreifuss, Shelley S.
Postal Rate Commission, Office of the Consumer Advocate, GV
Dreiling & Associates, P.C. ... St. Louis, MO
Dreiling, Bieker & Hoffman, LLP
Hays, KS
Dreiling, Fred D. ... Corpus Christi, TX
Dreiling, Geri L. ... St. Louis, MO
Dreiling, Janice P. ... Bartlesville, OK
Dreiling, Michael P. ... **Liberal, KS**
Dreiling, Norbert R. ... **Hays, KS**
Dreiling, Robert K. ... **Kansas City, MO**
Dreiling, Theresa G. ... Tulsa, OK
Dreiling, Thomas R. ... Seattle, WA
Dreilinger, Evan M. ... **New York, NY**
Dreilinger, Gwen B. ... Farmington, CT
Dreilinger, Lloyd A. ... **Hartford, CT**
Dreis, David G. ... Milwaukee, WI
Dreisbach, Daniel A. ... **Wilmington, DE**
Dreisbach, Leroy E. ... Olympia, WA
Dreiser, Daniel L. ... Chicago, IL
Dreises, Howard Ira ... Brooklyn, NY
Dreisewerd, Sherry K. ... **St. Louis, MO**
Dreishmire, Lisa A. ... **Dallas, TX**
Dreishpoon, Michael ... Richmond Hill, NY
Dreisig, W. Patrick ... **Southfield, MI**
Dreismeier, Craig M. ... **Council Bluffs, IA**
Dreispuc, Tracy ... **New York, NY**
Dreitler, Beth L. ... **Dublin, OH**
Dreitler, Joseph R. ... **Columbus, OH**
Dreitzer, Richard Ian ... **Las Vegas, NV**
Dreizen, Alison M. ... **New York, NY**
Dreizen, Harry R. ... New York, NY
Dreizen, Pamela L. ... Cupertino, CA
Dreizen, Samuel ... Santa Ana, CA
Dreizler, Dina B. ... San Pedro, CA
Drelich, David
Environmental Protection Agency, Office of Enforcement and Compliance Assurance, GV
Drelich, Norma ... **Washington, DC**
Drell, Bradley L. ... Alexandria, LA
Drell, David A. ... **Casper, WY**
Drell, Dee D. ... **Alexandria, LA**
Drell, Jill Leslie ... Deerfield, IL
Drell, Lea Armstrong ... Joliet, IL
Drell, Michael, (A Prof. Corp.)
Los Angeles, CA
Drella, Ann Marie ... White Plains, NY
Drella, Michael S. ... **Crystal Lake, IL**
Drelling, Francis M. ... Tustin, CA
Dremann, Andrew E. ... Media, PA
Dremann, Christopher C. ... **Charlotte, NC**
Dremann, Christopher C., P.C.
Charlotte, NC
Dremann, James E. ... Nevada City, CA
Dremluk, Robert W. ... **New York, NY**
Dremluk, Robert W., The Law Firm of
New York, NY
Dremousis, Anna M. ... Seattle, WA
Drenan, Teresa R. ... **San Diego, CA**
Drench, Zachary D. ... **Boston, MA**
Drenckhahn, Arthur A. ... Oslo, MN
Stephen, MN
Warren, MN
Drenckhahn & Williams, P.A.
Crookston, MN
Oslo, MN
Stephen, MN
Warren, MN
Drenckpohl, Rachael M. ... Kenyon, MN
Drendall, Stephen G. ... South Bend, IN
Drendel, Gerald A. ... Streator, IL
Drendel, Gilbert X., Jr. ... **Batavia, IL**
Drendel, John Squire ... **Reno, NV**
Drendel, Kevin G. ... **Batavia, IL**
Drendel Tatnall, A Professional Corporation
Batavia, IL
Geneva, IL
Drendel, Thomas E. ... **Reno, NV**
Drenk, Douglas ... Addison, IL
Drenkow, Rodney D. ... Waverly, IA
Drennan & Associates ... **Washington, DC**
Drennan, D. Jane ... **Washington, DC**
Drennan, D'Ann Nichols ... **Fort Worth, TX**
Drennan, Douglas J. ... **Menlo Park, CA**
Denver, CO
Drennan, F. Richard ... Pittsfield, MA
Drennan, James B., III ... **Spartanburg, SC**
Drennan, James C. ... Raleigh, NC
Drennan, James Derek ... **Birmingham, AL**
Drennan, James H. ... **Bakersfield, CA**
Drennan, James S. ... **Oklahoma City, OK**
Drennan, J. C. ... Medford, OK
Drennan, Jocelyn C. ... **Albuquerque, NM**
Drennan, John L. ... North Charleston, SC
Drennan, Joseph Peter ... Alexandria, VA
Drennan, Richard X. ... Pittsfield, MA
Drennan, William A., II ... **St. Louis, MO**
Drennen, Daniel E., II ... Chester, PA
Drennen, Edward G., II ... Florence, KY
Drennen, Jas. M. ... Waverly, OH
Drenner, Stephen O. ... **Austin, TX**
Drenner & Stuart, L.L.P. ... **Austin, TX**
Drenning, John B. ... **Buffalo, NY**
Drenning, Laura G. ... **San Francisco, CA**
Drennon, Charles C., III ... **Memphis, TN**
Drenth, Thomas L. ... Grand Rapids, MI
Drentlaw, Stacey L. ... **Minneapolis, MN**
Drenttel, Edward J. ... **Minneapolis, MN**
St. Paul, MN
Dreos, George C. ... Upper Marlboro, MD
Dreps, Robert J. ... **Madison, WI**
Dresbach, Mary L. ... Detroit, MI
Dresben, Fred C. ... Los Angeles, CA
Dresbold, Joel M. ... Pittsburgh, PA
Drescher, Allen G. ... Ashland, OR
Drescher, Ann Marie ... **Atlanta, GA**

Drescher & Associates, P.A. **Baltimore, MD**
Drescher, Cathy S. .... North Royalton, OH
Drescher & Cheslow, P.A. .... Manalapan, NJ
Drescher, D. Scott .... Charleston, SC
Drescher, Deborah L. .... Lansing, MI
Drescher, Debra Pulenskey .... Delmar, NY
Drescher & Drescher, S.C. .... Appleton, WI
Drescher, Gordon A. .... Wasco, CA
Drescher, Gregory P. .... Chicago, IL
Drescher, Howard L. .... Manalapan, NJ
Drescher, James H. .... Nashville, TN
Drescher, John M., Jr. .... St. Louis, MO
Drescher, John W. .... Norfolk, VA
Drescher, Kathleen Ebben .... Appleton, WI
Drescher, Kevin .... Ventura, CA
Drescher, Lisa Anne .... Oklahoma City, OK
Drescher, M. Donald .... Miami, FL
Drescher, McConica, Onstot & Schuck **Santa Paula, CA** **Ventura, CA**
Drescher, Michael P. .... Burlington, VT
Drescher, Park M. .... Appleton, WI
Drescher, Philip C. .... Santa Paula, CA
Drescher, Robert E. .... Valencia, CA
Drescher, Ronald J. .... Baltimore, MD
Drescher, Stephen W. .... Caldwell, ID
Drescher, Susan L. .... Scottsdale, AZ
Drescher, Tammy Cohen .... Baltimore, MD
Drescher, Thomas D. .... Palo Alto, CA **Chicago, IL**
Drescher, Udo M. .... New York, NY
Drescher, William B. .... Nashville, TN
Drescher, William R. .... Milford, NH
Drescher, Wolfgang .... Sylvania, OH
Dresden, Dennis S. .... Houston, TX
Dresdner, Katherine V., Law Office of **Pennington, NJ**
Dresdner, Robert P. Environmental Protection Agency, Office of Enforcement and Compliance Assurance, GV
Dresher, J. David .... Birmingham, AL
Dresher, Judith Illene .... San Francisco, CA
Dresie, Grey .... Wichita, KS
Dresie, Lee A. .... Los Angeles, CA
Dreskin, Edward A., (P.C.) .... Newark, NJ
Dreskin, Laura .... Monterey Park, CA
Dreslin, Courtney J. .... Dallas, TX
Dresner, Arthur .... New York, NY
Dresner, Byron .... New York, NY
Dresner, Cheryl Faye .... New York, NY
Dresner & Henle .... New York, NY
Dresner, Jeri D. .... Miami, FL
Dresner, Jerry .... Baltimore, MD
Dresner, Kenneth .... Colorado Springs, CO
Dresner, Maryann .... San Francisco, CA
Dresner, Zita Zatkin .... Rockville, MD
Dresnick & Ellsworth, P.A. **Coral Gables, FL** **Miami, FL**
Dresnick, Mark A. .... Miami, FL
Dresnick, Paul, A Professional Corporation Hayward, CA
Dresnick, Ronald C. .... Miami, FL
Dresnin, Benjamin .... Boca Raton, FL
Dresnin, Michael .... Philadelphia, PA
Dresow, Charles M. .... Belvedere-Tiburon, CA
Dress, Roger E. .... Hartford, CT
Dressel, Abigail O'Brien .... Tampa, FL
Dressel, David L. .... Olympia, WA
Dressel, Delverne A. .... Towson, MD
Dressel, E. Richard .... Cherry Hill, NJ Philadelphia, PA
Dressel, Elizabeth .... Menlo Park, CA
Dressel, Frederick W. .... Dayton, OH
Dressel & Hatab, P.C. .... New York, NY
Dressel, Henry F. .... New York, NY
Dressel, Hugh A. .... Spokane, WA
Dressel, Laura M. .... San Francisco, CA
Dressel, Mark L. .... Chicago, IL
Dressel, Quinton R. .... Springfield, OH
Dressel, Scott M. .... Morgantown, WV
Dressel, William F. .... Fort Collins, CO
Dresselhaus, Carl D. .... Los Angeles, CA
Dresselhuis, Ellen .... New Hope, MN
Dresselhuis, George W. .... Odebolt, IA
Dresselhuis and Heidenreich .... Odebolt, IA
Dresselhuis Law Office, P.A. New Hope, MN
Dresselhuys, Camilla Ann .... San Diego, CA
Dresser, Brayton .... New York, NY
Dresser, Dresser, Gilbert & Haas, P.C. **LaGrange, IN** **Coldwater, MI** **Sturgis, MI** **Three Rivers, MI**
Dresser, Duane W. .... San Francisco, CA
Dresser, George L. .... Worcester, MA
Dresser, Glen .... North Hollywood, CA
Dresser, Gregory P. .... San Francisco, CA
Dresser, James N. .... Arlington, VA
Dresser, John Clark, Jr. .... Aspen, CO
Dresser, John R. .... Sturgis, MI
Dresser, Raymond H., Jr. .... Sturgis, MI
Dresser, Rebecca Susan .... Cleveland, OH
Dresser, Richard I. .... St. Johns, MI
Dresser, Robert S. .... Sacramento, CA
Dresser, Scott Geoffrey .... New York, NY
Dresser, W. Donald .... Bells, TN
Dresser, William C. .... San Jose, CA
Dressing, John W. .... Cincinnati, OH
Dressing, Julie Stumpe .... Washington, DC
Dressing, Patrick X. .... Cincinnati, OH
Dresslar, John H. .... San Francisco, CA
Dressler, Alan A. .... San Francisco, CA
Dressler, Bennett .... New York, NY
Dressler, Brett E. .... Houston, TX
Dressler, Christopher K.H. .... Albany, NY
Dressler, Dennis A. .... Springfield, MO
Dressler, Dennis J. .... Spokane, WA
Dressler, Donald G. .... Irvine, CA
Dressler, Donald J. .... Canton, OH
Dressler, Donna M. .... Cocoa Beach, FL
Dressler, E. Michael .... Belmont, MA
Dressler, Francis A. .... Lake Charles, LA
Dressler, James R., Sr. .... Cocoa Beach, FL
Dressler, Jeffrey P. .... Hartford, CT
Dressler, Jennifer L. .... Madison, WI
Dressler, Joshua .... Sacramento, CA
Dressler, Lawrence S. .... New Haven, CT
Dressler, Michael R. .... East Rutherford, NJ
Dressler, Paul M. .... Waseca, MN
Dressler, Peter .... Oak Brook, IL
Dressler Rein Evans & Sestanovich LLP **Los Angeles, CA**
Dressler, Robert A. .... Fort Lauderdale, FL
Dressler, Robert L. .... Portland, OR
Dressler, Roy D. .... Kent, OH
Dressler, Steven C. .... Wilkes-Barre, PA
Dressler, Thomas W. .... Los Angeles, CA
Dressler-Fiks, Sara .... Philadelphia, PA
Dressman, James A., III .... Covington, KY
Dressman, James A., Jr. .... Covington, KY
Dressner, Howard R. .... New York, NY
Dressner, Joseph S. .... Springfield, MO
Dressner, Robert G. .... New York, NY
Dressner, Tracy J. .... Los Angeles, CA
Dreste, John W. .... New York, NY **Rochester, NY**
Dretke, Brian Craig .... Pendleton, OR
Dretler, David D. .... Marblehead, MA
Dretler, Jeffrey A. .... Boston, MA
Dretzin, David .... New York, NY
Dreufus, Bethany .... North Hollywood, CA
Dreuil, Emile J., Jr. .... New Orleans, LA
Dreuth, Sybille .... Los Angeles, CA
Dreux, Anthony .... Washington, DC
Dreux, Mark S., Sr. .... Washington, DC
Drever, Mark J. .... Salinas, CA
Dreves, Thomas J. .... New York, NY
Drevlow, Robert R. .... San Francisco, CA
Drevo, David A. .... Elmwood, NE Lincoln, NE
Drew, Alexander .... Washington, DC
Drew, Bernard E., Jr. .... Waukegan, IL
Drew & Carlson, LLC .... Gillette, WY
Drew, Carolyn Marie .... Vancouver, WA
Drew, Charles L. .... Atlanta, GA
Drew, Christopher S. .... Avon, CT
Drew, Cooper & Anding **Grand Rapids, MI**
Drew, Cynthia A. .... Department of Justice, Environment and Natural Resources Division, GV
Drew, Daniel D. .... Chicago, IL
Drew, David C. .... Lyndonville, VT
Drew, David Marc .... Chicago, IL
Drew, David P. .... Stow, OH
Drew, Davidoff & Edwards **Monticello, NY**
Drew, Dean A. .... Buffalo, NY
Drew, Dean M. .... Buffalo, NY
Drew, Dean M. .... Rochester, NY
Drew, Donald J. .... Arcadia, CA
Drew, E. Lanier .... Jacksonville, FL
Drew Eckl & Farnham, LLP .... Atlanta, GA Brunswick, GA
Drew, Elizabeth M. .... Milwaukee, WI
Drew, Ellis B., III .... Winston-Salem, NC
Drew, Ellis B., Jr. .... Anderson, SC
Drew, Gayden, IV .... Jackson, TN
Drew, George Raymond .... Cincinnati, OH
Drew, Glen D. .... Rockville, MD
Drew, Glenn A. .... Burlington, NC
Drew, Gregory P. .... Blair, NE
Drew, Helen A. .... Buffalo, NY
Drew, Horace R., Jr. .... Jacksonville, FL
Drew, J. Imani .... Chicago, IL
Drew, Jacqueline A. Charlotte Amalie, St. Thomas, VI
Drew, James B., Jr. (P.C.) .... Atlanta, GA
Drew, James J. .... Toms River, NJ
Drew, James M. .... Hampton, IA
Drew, Jay L. .... Atlanta, GA
Drew, Jean T. .... Shreveport, LA
Drew, Jerry I. .... Philadelphia, PA
Drew, John E. .... Avon, CT
Drew, John F. .... Boston, MA
Drew, Julie L. .... Costa Mesa, CA
Drew, Katherine A. .... Dallas, TX
Drew, Kathleen F. .... New Orleans, LA
Drew, Kathy A. Department of Labor, GV
Drew, Kenneth W. .... Apopka, FL
Drew, Kiply Suzanne .... Bloomington, IN
Drew Law Firm, P.C. .... Des Moines, IA **Hampton, IA**
Drew Law Offices Charlotte Amalie, St. Thomas, VI
Drew, Lionel E., Jr. .... Savannah, GA
Drew, M. Sherman, Jr. .... Niles, MI
Drew, Margaret B. .... Norwood, MA
Drew, Mark K. .... Los Angeles, CA
Drew, Mark L. .... Birmingham, AL
Drew, Melinda F. .... Boston, MA
Drew & Mersereau, P.C. .... Avon, CT
Drew, Michael A. .... Columbus, OH
Drew, Michael G. .... Boston, MA
Drew, Michael L. .... Bloomfield Hills, MI
Drew, Michael Shaefer .... Denver, CO
Drew, Michael V. .... Stone Mountain, GA
Drew, Mowitt S. .... Niles, MI
Drew, Natasha L. .... San Diego, CA
Drew, Paul J. .... Gillette, WY
Drew, R. Harmon .... Minden, LA
Drew, R. Harmon, Jr. .... Minden, LA
Drew, Raymond P. .... Hampton, IA
Drew, Richard M. .... Durham, NC
Drew, Robert A. .... Marion, IL
Drew, Roger J. .... Huntington, NY
Drew, Rollin E. .... Oklahoma City, OK
Drew, Sean W. .... Niles, MI
Drew, Shakun M. .... Washington, DC
Drew, Sharon A. .... Greenfield, WI
Drew, Stephen .... Dinuba, CA
Drew, Stephen R. .... Grand Rapids, MI
Drew, Steven J. .... Boston, MA
Drew, Steven J., P.C., Law Offices of Boston, MA
Drew, Terese A. .... St. Louis, MO
Drew, Theodore .... Monticello, NY
Drew, Theresa A. .... Buffalo, NY
Drew, Thomas J. .... Westport, CT
Drew, Tom L. .... Des Moines, IA
Drew, Viola Sellers .... Atlanta, GA
Drew & Ward, A Legal Professional Association .... Cincinnati, OH
Drew, William A. .... Portland, OR
Drew, William F., Jr. .... Charlotte, NC
Drew, William J. .... Kohler, WI
Drew, William K. Department of Justice, GV
Drew, William Ryan .... Milwaukee, WI
Drewek, Katherine M. .... Waukesha, WI
Drewelow, James B. .... Wenatchee, WA
Drewes, Donna N. .... Framingham, MA
Drewes, W. Christian .... New York, NY
Drewes, William H. .... New York, NY
Drewes-Silton, Heidi M. .... Minneapolis, MN
Drewett, Craig J. .... Flint, MI
Drewett, Randy E. .... Beaumont, TX
Drewitz, Mary Lyn Badiali **Washington, PA**
Drewitz, Paul W. .... San Francisco, CA
Drewke, Susan W. .... Chicago, IL
Drewko, Margaret M. .... Chicago, IL
Drewniak, Christopher J. .... Annapolis, MD
Drewniak, Erik W. .... Hawthorne, NY
Drewniak, Inga Oesterle .... Annapolis, MD
Drewniany, Jeffrey J. .... Middletown, CT
Drewry, Anthony B. .... Los Angeles, CA
Drewry, B. Leigh, Jr. .... Lynchburg, VA
Drewry, Diane M. .... Minneapolis, MN
Drewry, Eric B. .... Newark, DE
Drewry, James S. W. .... Washington, DC
Drewry, Janet M. .... San Antonio, TX
Drewry, Jimmie D. .... Memphis, TN
Drewry, John F. .... Boston, MA
Drewry, Michael F. .... Indianapolis, IN
Drewry, Michael K. .... Carrollton, TX
Drewry, Philip M. .... Los Angeles, CA
Drewry, Robert G. .... Memphis, TN
Drewry, Timothy W. .... Courtland, VA
Drewry, W. Shepherd, Jr. Virginia Beach, VA
Drews, Barbara A. .... Cedar Falls, IA
Drews, Christopher R. .... Burbank, CA
Drews, Elizabeth Hagan .... Austin, TX
Drews, Fred .... Fort Washington, PA
Drews, Gregory A. .... Whitehouse, NJ
Drews, Karl D. .... Houston, TX
Drews, Michael S. .... Sarasota, FL
Drews, Richard A. .... Omaha, NE
Drewsen, Jeanne K. .... New York, NY
Drewski & Lindberg, P.A. .... Sauk Rapids, MN
Drewski, Ronald .... Sauk Rapids, MN
Drewyer, Michelle L. .... Wailuku, HI
Drexel, Baron J. .... Oakland, CA
Drexel, Ray P. .... Columbus, OH
Drexel, Robert A. .... Hackensack, NJ
Drexel, Scott J. .... San Francisco, CA
Drexel, Victor L. .... Northeast Harbor, ME
Drexelius, John Roger, Jr. .... Kenmore, NY
Drexler, Caryl L. .... New York, NY
Drexler, Charles .... Oakland, CA
Drexler, David .... Sherman Oaks, CA
Drexler, David A. .... Wilmington, DE
Drexler, David E. .... Memphis, TN
Drexler, David J. .... Mesa, AZ
Drexler, Deborah L. .... Lima, OH
Drexler, Douglas J. .... Florence, WI
Drexler, Elias J. .... New York, NY
Drexler, Elliot M. .... Warminster, PA
Drexler, Eugene .... Rockville Centre, NY
Drexler, Fred .... San Francisco, CA
Drexler, Gale A. .... Littleton, CO
Drexler, Harry J., Jr .... Surf City, NJ
Drexler, Henry J. .... Norwich, NY
Drexler, Jessica N. .... Silver Spring, MD
Drexler, Kenneth .... San Rafael, CA
Drexler, Kenneth J. .... Washington, DC
Drexler, Kimberley S. .... New York, NY
Drexler, Lawrence S. .... Wilmington, DE
Drexler & Leach .... San Rafael, CA
Drexler, Lyons & McGuffin .... Warminster, PA
Drexler, Mark A. .... Rochester, NY
Drexler, Ray F. .... Chicago, IL
Drexler, Regina T. .... Denver, CO
Drexler, Robert J. .... Akron, OH
Drexler, Robert J., Jr. .... Los Angeles, CA
Drexler, Ruth .... Encino, CA
Drexler, Stanley L., (P.C.) .... Denver, CO
Drexler, Stephen .... Pittsburgh, PA
Drexler, Thomas W. .... Chicago, IL
Drexler, Wald & Moats .... Denver, CO
Drexler, William F. .... Camillus, NY
Drey, Elizabeth A. .... Allentown, PA
Drey, Norman W., Jr. .... St. Louis, MO
Drey, Paul A. .... Des Moines, IA
Drey, Stephanie L. Brick .... Des Moines, IA
Dreyer, Anthony J. .... New York, NY
Dreyer, Babich, Buccola & Callaham, LLP **Sacramento, CA**
Dreyer, Barbara J. .... Anchorage, AK
Dreyer Boyajian LLP .... Albany, NY
Dreyer, Dain A. .... San Antonio, TX
Dreyer, Darryl Joseph .... Goshen, NY
Dreyer, David E. .... West Palm Beach, FL
Dreyer, David J. .... Indianapolis, IN
Dreyer, David J. .... Harrison, MI
Dreyer, Dorothy E. .... Gainesville, FL
Dreyer, Douglas L. .... Newnan, GA
Dreyer, Douglas P. .... Jenkintown, PA
Dreyer, Foote, Streit, Furgason and Slocum, A Professional Association .... Aurora, IL
Dreyer, George J. .... New York, NY
Dreyer, Gerald T. .... Houston, TX
Dreyer, Harold E. .... Belmont, MA
Dreyer, Helene P. .... Palm Springs, CA
Dreyer & Hovey .... Harrison, MI
Dreyer, Ivan W. .... New York, NY
Dreyer, James A. .... Medford, OR
Dreyer, James D. .... Sarasota, FL
Dreyer, James Daniel, Jr. .... Sarasota, FL
Dreyer, John E. .... Aurora, IL
Dreyer, John J. .... Cincinnati, OH
Dreyer, Kevin T. .... Cincinnati, OH
Dreyer, Kirk D. .... Houston, TX
Dreyer, Kyle H. .... Dallas, TX
Dreyer, Laurence M. .... Boston, MA
Dreyer, Leo P. .... Kansas City, MO
Dreyer, Mark E. .... Tulsa, OK
Dreyer, Mary E. .... Saratoga Springs, NY
Dreyer, Mary F. .... Indianapolis, IN
Dreyer, Nancy R. .... Watertown, MA
Dreyer, Noreen S. .... Port St. Lucie, FL
Dreyer, Norman L. .... Lynbrook, NY
Dreyer, Raymond F. .... Belvedere-Tiburon, CA
Dreyer, Roger A. .... Sacramento, CA
Dreyer, Roger M. .... Gonzales, TX
Dreyer, Scott Monro .... Los Angeles, CA
Dreyer, Stanley B. .... New York, NY
Dreyer, Steven D. .... New York, NY
Dreyer, Theodore D. .... St. Cloud, MN
Dreyer, Thomas A. .... Media, PA
Dreyer, William J. .... Albany, NY
Dreyer, William M. .... Atlanta, GA
Dreyfus, Andra Todd .... Clearwater, FL
Dreyfus, Andra Todd, P.A. **Clearwater, FL**
Dreyfus, David B. .... Los Angeles, CA
Dreyfus, Donald .... Chicago, IL
Dreyfus, Donald J. .... Merrillville, IN
Dreyfus, Edward D. .... Mountainside, NJ
Dreyfus, Eric M. .... New York, NY White Plains, NY
Dreyfus & Evans .... Meridian, MS
Dreyfus, James K. .... New York, NY
Dreyfus, Jared .... Sebastopol, CA
Dreyfus, Karen .... Newport Beach, CA
Dreyfus, Katherine A. .... Portland, OR
Dreyfus, Larry M. .... Placitas, NM
Dreyfus, Lee S., Jr. .... Waukesha, WI
Dreyfus, Mary Kay Gara .... Chicago, IL
Dreyfus, Richard B. .... Houston, TX
Dreyfus, Robert M., Jr. .... Meridian, MS
Dreyfus, Ruth .... Stamford, CT
Dreyfuss, Daniel W. .... Cleveland, OH
Dreyfuss, David .... New York, NY
Dreyfuss, Dorian Leopold .... Los Altos, CA
Dreyfuss, Gilbert .... Los Angeles, CA
Dreyfuss, Karen E. .... Los Angeles, CA
Dreyfuss, Kenneth A. .... Oakland, CA
Dreyfuss, Kenneth R. .... Miami, FL
Dreyfuss, Lawrence J. .... Santa Ana, CA
Dreyfuss, Lawrence J. .... Houston, TX
Dreyfuss, Rochelle C. .... New York, NY
Dreyfuss, Stephen L. .... Newark, NJ
Dreyspool, Anthony A. .... New York, NY
Dreyspool, Phyllis C. .... New York, NY
Drez, David J., III .... Fort Worth, TX
Drezin, Alan .... Brooklyn, NY
Drezin, Norman A. Department Of Health And Human Services, Food & Drug Administration, GV
Dreznick-Waller, Lisa Jane .... Bronx, NY
Drian, Allan H. Y. .... Goshen, NY
Driano, Dominick V. .... Seattle, WA
Driano, Dominick V., Jr. .... Bellevue, WA
Driano, Nancy A. .... Seattle, WA
Driansky, Richard .... Durham, NC
Dribin, Eileen Wilansky .... Los Angeles, CA
Dribin, Leland G. .... Los Angeles, CA
Dribin, Michael A., (P.A.) .... Miami, FL
Dribinsky, Leonard M. Office Of Special Counsel, GV
Dribusch, Christian H. .... Albany, NY
Dribusch, Elizabeth C. .... Glenmont, NY
Drichta, Jeffrey H. .... New York, NY
Drick, Jay R. .... Howell, MI
Drickey, Steven L. .... Chicago, IL
Drickey-Prohow, Judy .... Tucson, AZ
Drickman, Miriam R. .... Denver, CO
Drickman, Phyllis H. .... Tampa, FL
Drics, John Thomas .... Indianapolis, IN
Driebe, Charles J. .... Atlanta, GA **Jonesboro, GA**
Driebe, Charles J., Jr. .... Atlanta, GA **Jonesboro, GA**
Driebe & Driebe, P.C. .... Atlanta, GA **Jonesboro, GA**
Driegert, Robert S. .... Dallas, TX
Driemeyer, Jeffrey A. .... Cedar Glen, CA
Drier, John C. .... Valparaiso, IN
Drier, Marc S. .... Jersey Shore, PA
Dries, James J. .... Brookfield, WI
Dries, John D. .... Milwaukee, WI
Driesel, Willard L., Jr. .... Idabel, OK
Driesen, George B. .... Washington, DC
Driesman, Daniel L. .... Brooklyn, NY

Driessen, Anthony H. .... **Madison, WI**
Milwaukee, WI
Driessen, Karyn J. .... Santa Ana, CA
Driggars, Charles R. .... **Birmingham, AL**
Driggers, Dennis J. .... Noblesville, IN
Spring, TX
Driggers, Donald S. .... **Hightstown, NJ**
Driggers, Douglas R. .... Las Cruces, NM
Driggers, Johnny F. .... North Charleston, SC
Driggers, Marcia B. .... Las Cruces, NM
Driggers, Martin S. .... Hartsville, SC
Driggers, Robert O. .... Birmingham, AL
Driggers, Schultz & Herbst, A Professional Corporation .... **Troy, MI**
Driggers, Stephen G. .... **Raleigh, NC**
Driggers, Thomas V. .... Dallas, GA
Driggers, Timothy G. .... Lexington, SC
Driggers, William Gerald
Washington, DC
Driggins, Twila Charlyse .... Baltimore, MD
Driggs, Adrian P. .... Naples, FL
Driggs, Adrian P., III .... **New York, NY**
Driggs, Charles M. .... **Mentor, OH**
Driggs, J. Douglas, Jr. .... **Las Vegas, NV**
Driggs, Kenneth D. .... Austin, TX
Driggs, Lucas, Brubaker & Hogg Co., L.P.A.
Chardon, OH
Cleveland, OH
Mentor, OH
Driggs, Mario F. .... **Philadelphia, PA**
Driggs, Matthew W. .... Salt Lake City, UT
Driggs, Nancy L. .... Brockton, MA
Driggs, Rebecca R. .... **Phoenix, AZ**
Driggs, Warren W. .... Murray, UT
Drigotas, Elizabeth E. .... **Dallas, TX**
Driker, Eugene .... **Detroit, MI**
Driks, Jordan J. .... Merion, PA
Drill, Irina J. .... **Los Angeles, CA**
Drill, James A. .... New Richmond, WI
Drill, Jonathan E. .... Cedar Grove, NJ
Drill, Keith E. .... **Kansas City, MO**
Drill, Lisa M. .... New Richmond, WI
Drilling, Martin J. .... Plymouth, MA
Drillings, Jay M. .... Monticello, NY
Drillock Law Firm .... Marlette, MI
Drillock, Linda R. .... Marlette, MI
Drillock, William J. .... Marlette, MI
Drimer, Jeffrey Lee .... Syracuse, NY
Drimmer, James B. .... **San Diego, CA**
Drimmer, Jonathan C.
Department of Justice, Criminal Division, GV
Drimmer, Saul E. .... Coconut Creek, FL
Drinan, Francis B. .... **Bay City, MI**
Drinan, James M. .... St. Louis, MO
Drinan, Mary M. .... **San Francisco, CA**
Drinan, Robert F. .... Washington, DC
Drinan, Ronald J. .... Bloomington, IL
Drinane, Monica .... New York, NY
Drinane, William M. .... **Minneapolis, MN**
Dring, Catherine A. .... **Menlo Park, CA**
Dring, John P., Jr. .... Alexandria, VA
Dringman, Page C. .... **Big Timber, MT**
Dringman, Patrick N. .... **Big Timber, MT**
Drinka, Judith A. .... **Milwaukee, WI**
Drinka, Levine & Masson, S.C.
Milwaukee, WI
Drinkard, C. Daryl .... **Grove Hill, AL**
Drinkard, Edward W. .... Prattville, AL
Drinkard, Maria P. .... Atlanta, GA
Drinkard, Natalie Paige .... **Towson, MD**
Drinkard, Newton & Cumpton
Bay Minette, AL
Mobile, AL
Drinkard, Stephen W. .... **Montgomery, AL**
Drinkard, Vaughan, Jr. .... **Mobile, AL**
Drinkard, Wade .... Linden, AL
Drinker Biddle & Reath LLP
Washington, DC
Princeton, NJ
New York, NY
Berwyn, PA
Philadelphia, PA
Drinker Biddle & Shanley LLP
Florham Park, NJ
Drinko, John D. .... **Cleveland, OH**
Drinkwater, Arthur S. .... North Reading, MA
Drinkwater, Clover M. .... **Elmira, NY**
Drinkwater, Darrell A. .... Virginia Beach, VA
Drinkwater, Darrell A., P.C.
Virginia Beach, VA
Drinkwater, Robert D. .... **Jackson, MS**
Drinkwater, Stanley N., III .... Berlin, NJ
Drinkwater, W. Wayne, Jr. .... **Jackson, MS**
Drinkwater, William .... **Virginia Beach, VA**
Drinkwater, William, P.C.
Virginia Beach, VA
Drinkwine & McBride, P.C. .... Englewood, CO
Drinnon, James E., Jr. .... Knoxville, TN
Drinnon, Rodney L. .... **Cincinnati, OH**
Drinnon, Stephen W. .... **Dallas, TX**
Dripchak, Michael P. .... Montvale, NJ
Dripps, Roy C. .... **Wood River, IL**
Dris & Kouskoutis, Law Offices of
Tarpon Springs, FL
Dris, Michael E. .... Tarpon Springs, FL
Driscol, Alfred W., III .... Chico, CA
Driscoll, Adrian G. .... **San Francisco, CA**
Driscoll, Arlen M. .... **Houston, TX**
Driscoll & Associates .... Lodi, CA
Driscoll, Brian D. .... Cranford, NJ
Driscoll, Brian G. .... **Washington, DC**
Driscoll, Brian M. .... San Francisco, CA
Driscoll, Christopher L. .... Los Angeles, CA
Driscoll, Clara Maehara .... Pasadena, CA
Driscoll, Cynthia D. .... **Pittsburgh, PA**
Driscoll, Daniel F. .... **Saco, ME**
Driscoll, Daniel H., III .... El Paso, TX
Driscoll, Daniel J. .... Boston, MA
Driscoll, Daniel L. .... Jackson Heights, NY
Driscoll, Daryl A. .... Darien, CT
Driscoll, David C., Jr. .... **Rockville, MD**
Driscoll, David E. .... Riverside, CA
Driscoll, David F. .... Salem, MA
Driscoll, David J. .... Fairfield, CA
Driscoll, David J., (P.C.) .... **Boulder, CO**
Driscoll, David M. .... Taunton, MA
Driscoll, David M. .... **El Paso, TX**
Driscoll, David R. .... **Minneapolis, MN**
Driscoll, David R., Jr. .... Louisville, KY
Driscoll & Delaney .... **New York, NY**
Driscoll, Denis Francis .... **Hackensack, NJ**
Driscoll, Denise .... Sherman Oaks, CA
Driscoll, Dennis G. .... Detroit, MI
Driscoll, Dennis W. .... **Glastonbury, CT**
Driscoll, Donald F. .... Pittsburgh, PA
Driscoll, Donald J. .... Hartford, CT
Driscoll & Draude .... **Washington, DC**
Driscoll and Driscoll .... Russell, KS
Driscoll, Edw. R. .... Torrington, CT
Driscoll, Edward J. .... **Minneapolis, MN**
Driscoll, Ellen F. .... Pasadena, CA
Driscoll, Erin M. .... **St. Louis, MO**
Driscoll & Fox .... **Los Angeles, CA**
Driscoll, Frank .... **Rapid City, SD**
Driscoll, Frank B. .... Arnold, CA
Driscoll, Freeman & Associates
Lynnfield, MA
Driscoll, Gary G. .... Costa Mesa, CA
Driscoll, Gerald J. .... Dumont, NJ
Driscoll & Gibson .... **Duxbury, MA**
Marshfield, MA
Plymouth, MA
Driscoll, Gilberte N. .... New York, NY
Driscoll, J. Ward .... St. Louis, MO
Driscoll, Jacques D. .... St. Paul, MN
Driscoll, James .... Woodbury, NJ
Driscoll, James C., III .... **Bethel, CT**
Driscoll, James C., Jr. .... **Southbury, CT**
Driscoll, James Coy, Law Offices of
San Francisco, CA
Driscoll, James D. .... Fresno, CA
Driscoll, James G. .... **San Francisco, CA**
Driscoll, James L. .... **Pittsburgh, PA**
Driscoll, James O. .... Windermere, FL
Driscoll, James O., P.A. .... Windermere, FL
Driscoll, James P. .... Weston, CT
Driscoll, Jan Shirley .... **Chula Vista, CA**
Driscoll, Jean Strauten .... Boston, MA
Driscoll, Jeanine C. .... **New York, NY**
Driscoll, Jeffrey L. .... Grand Junction, CO
Driscoll, Jeffry .... Fort Lauderdale, FL
Driscoll, Jerry E. .... Russell, KS
Driscoll, John C. .... Norwich, CT
Driscoll, John C. .... Portsmouth, NH
Driscoll, John C. .... East Hills, NY
Driscoll, John F. .... Birmingham, AL
Driscoll, John F. .... Fall River, MA
Driscoll, John H. .... **St. Louis, MO**
Driscoll, John J. .... **Chicago, IL**
Driscoll, John J. .... Chelmsford, MA
Driscoll, John J. .... **Holyoke, MA**
Driscoll, John J. .... **New York, NY**
Driscoll, John J. .... Greensburg, PA
Driscoll, John M. .... Bloomingdale, IL
Driscoll, John M., III .... **New York, NY**
Driscoll, John M., P.C. .... Bloomingdale, IL
Driscoll, John P. .... **Richmond, VA**
Driscoll, John P., Jr. .... **Boston, MA**
Driscoll, John Q. .... Troy, NY
Driscoll, John R. .... Hauppauge, NY
Driscoll, John T. .... **New York, NY**
Driscoll, John W. .... **Placerville, CA**
Driscoll, Joseph Edward .... San Diego, CA
Driscoll, Joseph P. .... Garland, TX
Driscoll, Joseph R. .... Quincy, MA
Driscoll, J. P. .... Chicago, IL
Driscoll, Justin E., III .... **New York, NY**
Driscoll, Keith J. .... Beverly, MA
Driscoll, Kenneth J. .... Silver Spring, MD
Driscoll, Kevin F. .... **Boston, MA**
Driscoll, Kevin J. .... Washington, DC
Driscoll, Kevin J. .... **Des Moines, IA**
Driscoll, Kimberlee M. .... Bedford, MA
Driscoll & Kober, P.C. .... **Boston, MA**
Driscoll, Lane, Mannion & Driscoll
Bethel, CT
Driscoll Law Firm, The .... **Houston, TX**
Driscoll, Leo J. .... Spokane, WA
Driscoll, Lisa Caron .... Boston, MA
Driscoll, Lois R. .... Cos Cob, CT
Driscoll, M. Cathlene .... **Norristown, PA**
Philadelphia, PA
Driscoll, Margaret Connors .... Bridgeport, CT
Driscoll, Marie V. .... **New York, NY**
Driscoll, Martin K. .... Fort Lauderdale, FL
Driscoll, Mary Ann .... Boston, MA
Driscoll, Mary E. .... Norwich, CT
Driscoll, Mary K. .... **Sacramento, CA**
Driscoll & Mattingly, P.C. .... Brockton, MA
Driscoll, Maureen E. .... **Fairfield, CT**
Driscoll, Maureen M. .... Northampton, MA
Driscoll, Michael D. .... **New York, NY**
Driscoll, Michael E. .... **Norwich, CT**
Driscoll, Michael F. .... St. Paul, MN
Driscoll, Michael H. .... Houston, TX
Driscoll, Michael John .... New York, NY
Driscoll, Michael N. .... Manassas, VA
Driscoll, Michele R. .... Auburn, NY
Driscoll, Neil J., P.C. .... Portland, OR
Driscoll, Neil Joseph, III .... Portland, OR
Driscoll, Neil R. .... Lynnfield, MA
Driscoll, Nora T. .... Worcester, MA
Driscoll, Patricia A. .... Syracuse, NY
Driscoll, Patricia T. .... Dallas, TX
Driscoll, Patrick T., Jr. .... **Chicago, IL**
Driscoll, Patrick W. .... **Davenport, IA**
Driscoll, Paul Arthur .... **Virginia Beach, VA**
Driscoll, Paul F. .... **Portland, ME**
Driscoll, Paul J. .... **Marshfield, MA**
Driscoll, Perry F. .... Toledo, OH
Driscoll, Peter .... Columbia, MD
Driscoll, Peter E. .... **Haddonfield, NJ**
Driscoll, Peter J. .... **New York, NY**
Driscoll & Prats, P.A. .... St. Petersburg, FL
Driscoll & Redlich .... **New York, NY**
Driscoll, Richard C., Jr. .... Brockton, MA
Driscoll, Richard E. .... Auburn, CA
Driscoll, Richard E. .... Groveland, MA
Driscoll, Richard J. ....
Department of State, GV
Driscoll, Richard W. .... **Washington, DC**
Fairfax, VA
Driscoll, Richard W. .... **Tampa, FL**
Driscoll, Richard W., P.A. .... **Tampa, FL**
Driscoll, Robert E. .... New York, NY
Driscoll, Robert E., III .... Vermillion, SD
Driscoll, Robert J. .... **San Diego, CA**
Driscoll, Robert J. .... **New York, NY**
Driscoll, Robert L. .... **Kansas City, MO**
Driscoll, Robert N. .... **Boston, MA**
Driscoll, Robert O., Jr. .... Columbus, OH
Driscoll, Robert P. .... Columbus, OH
Driscoll, Robert W. .... San Marino, CA
Driscoll & Rozanski .... Woodbury, NJ
Driscoll, Stephen J. .... **Philadelphia, PA**
Driscoll, Steven M. .... Costa Mesa, CA
Driscoll, Susan Bernstein
Kennebunk, ME
Driscoll, Suzanne M.
Fort Lauderdale, FL
Driscoll, Talarico, Frizzell, Olivo & Driscoll
Bethel, CT
Bridgeport, CT
Danbury, CT
Newtown, CT
Southbury, CT
Stamford, CT
Driscoll, Tamara J. .... Helena, MT
Seattle, WA
Driscoll, Thomas D. .... Minneapolis, MN
Driscoll, Thomas H., Jr. .... Lynn, MA
Driscoll, Thomas J., Jr. .... Lodi, CA
Driscoll, Thomas L. .... **San Francisco, CA**
Driscoll, Timothy J. .... **Greenbelt, MD**
Driscoll, Timothy P. .... St. Petersburg, FL
Driscoll, Timothy S. .... Washington, DC
Driscoll, Virginia M. .... Houston, TX
Driscoll, Wilfred C., Jr. .... Fall River, MA
Driscoll, William J. .... Washington, DC
Driscoll, William J. .... Louisville, KY
Driscoll, William P. .... **Los Angeles, CA**
Driscoll, William P. .... **Helena, MT**
Driscoll, William T. .... Forest Hills, NY
Drisdale, John K., Jr. .... **Austin, TX**
Drisgula, A. Randall .... Hillsdale, NJ
Drish, Mark J. .... Cedar Rapids, IA
Driskell, Cynthia Frierson .... Houston, TX
Driskell, Robert L. .... Glendora, CA
Driskill, Jack P. .... **Lubbock, TX**
Driskill, John M. .... **Dallas, TX**
Houston, TX
Driskill, Linda R. .... Oklahoma City, OK
Driskill, Mitchell A. .... **El Centro, CA**
Palm Springs, CA
San Diego, CA
Driskill, Roger M. .... Liberty, MO
Driskill, Tameria S. .... Gadsden, AL
Driskill, Timothy W. .... Tulsa, OK
Driskill, Tsinena Bruno
Oklahoma City, OK
Drisko, Diana M. .... **St. Louis, MO**
Drisko, William M. .... **Lexington, KY**
Drislane, William E. .... Burlington, VT
Dritsas, Catherine .... **Royal Oak, MI**
Dritsas, James B. .... **Bloomfield Hills, MI**
Dritsas, Paul C. .... **Newark, NJ**
Dritsas, William J. .... **San Francisco, CA**
Dritz, Stanley B. .... **Columbus, OH**
Drivas, Dimitrios T. .... **New York, NY**
Drivdahl, Heidi M. .... **Seattle, WA**
Driveness, Glen A. .... Wilsonville, OR
Driver, Albert G. .... Haddon Heights, NJ
Driver, B. J. .... Palm Harbor, FL
Driver, Bridgette N. .... Memphis, TN
Driver, Cecil .... North Adams, MA
Driver, Dante J. .... **Seattle, WA**
Driver, David R. .... Sacramento, CA
Driver, Douglas G. .... Broadway, VA
Driver, Driver & Hunt, A Professional Association .... Sacramento, CA
Driver, Gary Ray, Jr. .... Tallahassee, FL
Driver, Gayle Marie Brown .... Rockville, MD
Driver, Guy F., Jr. .... **Raleigh, NC**
Winston-Salem, NC
Driver, Janet Carol .... Ann Arbor, MI
Driver, Joan L. .... Portland, OR
Driver, John P. .... Murfreesboro, TN
Driver, Joseph H. .... **Birmingham, AL**
Driver, Judy Lynn .... San Bernardino, CA
Driver, Kenneth B. .... **Washington, DC**
Driver, Mark L. .... **Denver, CO**
Driver, Mark L., P.C. .... **Denver, CO**
Driver, Michael J. .... **Denver, CO**
Driver, N. LaDonna .... **Springfield, IL**
Driver & Pagnotta .... North Adams, MA
Driver, Philip F. .... Gold River, CA
Driver, R. Temple .... Wichita Falls, TX
Driver, Richard J. .... **Roseland, NJ**
Driver, Ronald S. .... Austin, TX
Driver, Samuel .... Haddon Heights, NJ
Driver, Susan K. .... Portland, OR
Driver, Toni D. .... **Fort Worth, TX**
Driver, Walter W., Jr. .... **Atlanta, GA**
Drivon, David E. .... Stockton, CA
Drivon, James A. .... Sacramento, CA
Drivon, Laurence .... Stockton, CA
Drivon, Laurence E. .... Stockton, CA
Drivon & Tabak, A Professional Law Corporation .... Stockton, CA
Drizin, Lee A. .... **Las Vegas, NV**
Drizin, Robert C. .... Chicago, IL
Drizin, Steven A. .... Chicago, IL
Drizner, Paul S. .... **Chicago, IL**
Drlicka, Erick M. .... **Pensacola, FL**
Drmacich, Mary P. .... Niagara Falls, NY
Drnec, James E. .... **Wilmington, DE**
Drobac & Drobac .... Santa Cruz, CA
Drobac, Martin .... Santa Cruz, CA
Drobac, Nick J. .... Santa Cruz, CA
Drobac, Peter Jacob .... **San Francisco, CA**
Drobak, John N. .... St. Louis, MO
Drobbin, Paul D. .... **Newark, NJ**
Drobenko & Piddoubny .... **Astoria, NY**
Drobenko, Walter .... **Astoria, NY**
Drobile, James A. .... **Philadelphia, PA**
Drobka, Mary Elizabeth .... **Seattle, WA**
Drobner, David S. .... **Miami, FL**
Drobnich, Dawn M. .... **Birmingham, MI**
Birmingham, MI
Drobny, Dane .... **Chicago, IL**
Drobny, Irving, (P.C.) .... Chicago, IL
Drobny Law Offices .... **Sacramento, CA**
Stockton, CA
Drobny, Mark S. .... **Sacramento, CA**
Stockton, CA
Drobny, Pablo J. .... Los Angeles, CA
Drobot, Ann E. .... **Boston, MA**
Droby, Costine A. .... Dallas, TX
Drociak, Joseph L. .... Los Angeles, CA
Drockton, Leslie A. .... **Cleveland, OH**
Droder & Miller Co., L.P.A. .... Cincinnati, OH
Droege, Calvin L. .... Huntington Beach, CA
Droege, Calvin L., (A Prof. Corp.)
Huntington Beach, CA
Droege, Daniel I., Jr. .... Madison, WI
Droege, Esther K. .... Doraville, GA
Droege, J. Charles, Law Offices of
Overland Park, KS
Droege, J. Robert .... Potomac, MD
Droege, James N. .... Chicago, IL
Droege, John F. .... La Porte, IN
Droegemueller, Glen .... Greeley, CO
Droegemueller, Glen, P.C. .... Greeley, CO
Droeger, Gregory L., Law Offices of
Nogales, AZ
Droeger, Michelle J. .... Calabasas, CA
Droegkamp, Donald H. .... Brookfield, WI
Droesch, Dana Cuoco .... Larchmont, NY
Droese, Karl E., Jr. .... Oakland, CA
Droessler, Julie A. .... **Dayton, OH**
Drogalis, Mark A. .... Harrisburg, PA
Droge, Robert J. .... Brooklyn, NY
Drogen, Andrew M. .... **New York, NY**
Drogin, Carol A. .... New York, NY
Drogin, Ira .... New York, NY
Drogin, Jack
Securities and Exchange Commission, Division of Market Regulation, GV
Drogin, Karen L. .... New Rochelle, NY
Drogin, Laurent S. .... New York, NY
Drogin, Morris .... Fort Lee, NJ
Drogin, Susan F. .... **Boston, MA**
Drogin, Victoria Roberts .... **New York, NY**
Drogula, Jennifer M. .... **Washington, DC**
Drogus, Valerie M. .... **San Jose, CA**
Drohan, David H. .... Hingham, MA
Drohan & Drohan .... Ghent, NY
Drohan & Drohan LLP .... New York, NY
Drohan, James P. .... **Fishkill, NY**
Scarsdale, NY
Drohan, John P., III .... Ghent, NY
New York, NY
Drohan, Thomas B. .... **Boston, MA**
Drohan, Thomas H. .... Boston, MA
Drohan, Toni Mileo .... Manhasset, NY
Drohan, Tracey .... **Washington, DC**
Drohan, Vivian R. .... Ghent, NY
New York, NY
Drohosky, Stephen J. .... Woburn, MA
Droke, Michael W. .... **Seattle, WA**
Droker, Herbert J. .... Bellevue, WA
Droker, Howard A. .... Seattle, WA
Drolet, E. Peter .... **Detroit, MI**
Drolet, Freeman, Cotton & Norris, P.C.
Bloomfield Hills, MI
Detroit, MI
Drolet, Joseph J. .... Atlanta, GA
Droll, Robert W. .... Rock Island, IL
Drolla, F. Joseph, Jr. .... **Metairie, LA**
Drolla, John C. D., Jr. .... Austin, TX
Drollas, Anthony T. .... Nutley, NJ
Drollas, Anthony T., Jr. .... **Trenton, NJ**
Droller, Deborah S. .... Oakton, VA
Droller, Lester W. .... **Washington, DC**
Drollinger, William C. .... Orchard Lake, MI
Drollman, Donald W. .... Livermore, CA
Drolshagen, John A. .... **Fresno, CA**
Dromgoole, Armond J., Jr. .... Berkeley, CA
Dromsky, B. Joseph, Jr. .... Augusta, GA
Dromsky-Reed, Susan K. .... **Roseland, NJ**
Dron, Diana M. .... **Santa Ana, CA**
Drone, James L. .... Houston, TX
Drone, Robert Michael .... **Carmi, IL**
Dronen, Keith G. .... Chicago, IL
Dronet, Gina .... La Jolla, CA
Droney, Christopher F. .... Hartford, CT
Droney, John F., Jr. .... **Farmington, CT**
Droney, Patricia M. .... West Hartford, CT
Dronson, Kevin G. .... **Cherry Hill, NJ**
Philadelphia, PA
Dronzek, James F. .... **Jersey City, NJ**

Dronzek, Marvin ... Providence, RI
Drooff, Michael Jeffrey ... Manchester, NH
Droogan, Cornelius J. ... Garden City, NY
Droogan, Michael T., Jr.
Mount Laurel, NJ
Philadelphia, PA
Droogmans, Johan ... Atlanta, GA
Drook, Helen ... New York, NY
Drook, Jerry T. ... Marion, IN
Drooks, Bruce J. ... Franklin Square, NY
Drooks, Mark T. ... Los Angeles, CA
Droomers, Warren C. ... St. Clair Shores, MI
Droomers, Warren C., P.C.
St. Clair Shores, MI
Droop, Christian ... New York, NY
Drooyan, Richard E. ... Los Angeles, CA
Drooz, David T. ... Raleigh, NC
Drooz, Deborah ... Los Angeles, CA
Drooz, Harold ... Los Angeles, CA
Dropick, Dorothy K. ... Simsbury, CT
Dropick, John J. ... Hartford, CT
Dropiewski, Larry ... Bloomfield Hills, MI
Dropkin, Allen H. ... Chicago, IL
Dropkin, Charles E. ... New York, NY
Dropkin, Keith ... San Francisco, CA
Dropkin, Martin B. ... Lexington, MA
Dropkin, Philip ... Monticello, NY
Dropkin, Robert F. ... New Hartford, NY
Dropkin, Shelley J. ... New York, NY
Droppert, V. Marc ... Redmond, WA
Droppleman, John J. ... Clarksburg, WV
Dror, Asaf ... Garden City, NY
Drory, Daniel M. ... Dallas, TX
Drosdick, Claire K. ... Bellevue, WA
Drosdick, John R. ... Newark, NJ
Drosdick, Scott E. ... Langhorne, PA
Drosdik, Vincent A., Jr. ... Farmington, ME
Drose, R. Michael ... Charleston, SC
Drosen, Alfred A., Jr. ... West Allis, WI
Drosen, Christopher M. ... West Allis, WI
Drosen, Wandt & Rustad ... West Allis, WI
Drosky, Todd C. ... Boca Raton, FL
Drosman, Anapoell & Salis, LLP
Costa Mesa, CA
Drosman, C. Thomas ... Costa Mesa, CA
Drosman, Daniel Steven ... San Diego, CA
Drosnes, Andrea J. ... Cherry Hill, NJ
Drosnes, Larry A. ... Galveston, TX
Drosnes, Morton M. ... New York, NY
Drosnin, Deborah ... Boston, MA
Drosnin, Roberta Gale ... New York, NY
Dross, Irving ... Waldorf, MD
Dross, Justin Steven ... Greenbelt, MD
Dross, Levenstein, Perilman & Kopstein
Greenbelt, MD
Waldorf, MD
Drossel, Norlen E. ... Berkeley, CA
Drossel, Robert J. ... Oroville, CA
Drossman, Leslie J. ... Brooklyn, NY
Drossman, Mitchell A. ... New York, NY
Drost, Albin F. ... Department of Commerce, Patent and Trademark Office, GV
Drost, Bryan C. ... Blue Ridge, GA
Drost, Catherine S. ... Department of Defense, Defense Legal Services Agency, GV
Drost, George T. ... Arlington Heights, IL
Drost, John A. ... Arlington Heights, IL
Drost, John E., Jr. ... Springfield, MA
Drost, Kenneth B. ... Chicago, IL
Drost & Kivlahan, Ltd.
Arlington Heights, IL
Drost, Marianne ... Irving, TX
Drost, Skipper Maurice ... Sulphur, LA
Droste, Alan J. ... Costa Mesa, CA
Droste, Donald C. ... Wayne, NJ
Droste, Norman K. ... Traverse City, MI
Droster, Jill M. ... Highland, IN
Drott, Earl A. ... Tyler, TX
Drott, Earl, P.C. ... Tyler, TX
Drotz, John E. ... Honolulu, HI
Drotzer, Arthur S. ... Croton-On-Hudson, NY
Drotzer, Karen S. ... New York, NY
Drotzmann, Christopher J. ... Portland, OR
Drouant, Robert W. ... New Orleans, LA
Drouet, Brett C. ... Santa Monica, CA
Drouet, Martha L. ... Arlington, MA
Drought, Drought & Bobbitt, L.L.P.
San Antonio, TX
Drought, Ellen ... Milwaukee, WI
Drought, Gerald T. ... San Antonio, TX
Drought, James L. ... San Antonio, TX
Drought, Thomas ... San Antonio, TX
Drought, Thomas J. ... Milwaukee, WI
Droughton, Aileen F. ... Newark, NJ
Drouilhet, Patrick W. ... Houston, TX
Drouillard, Jerome R. ... Dearborn, MI
Drouin, Donald G. ... Bedford, MA
Droumbanis, Nadia K. ... Philadelphia, PA
Droutman, Erik L. ... McLean, VA
Drover, W. Gary ... Camdenton, MO
Drowatzky, John N. ... Toledo, OH
Drown, Daniel D. ... Los Angeles, CA
Drown, Jack ... Westminster, CA
Drown, James A. ... Winchester, VA
Drown, Steven A. ... Davis, CA
Drown, William T. ... Johnstown, OH
Drowos, Stuart B. ... Wilmington, DE
Drowota, Frank F., III ... Nashville, TN
Droz, Danna E. ... Frankfort, KY
Droz, Marvin I. ... Pittsburgh, PA
Droz, Paul C. ... Salt Lake City, UT
Drozd, Dale A. ... Sacramento, CA
Drozd, Donald L. ... Santa Ana, CA
Drozd, Leon F., Jr. ... San Francisco, CA
Drozd, Linda M. ... San Antonio, TX
Drozda, Robert L. ... Boise, ID
Drozdoff, Vladimir V. ... New York, NY
Drozdoski, Joanne C. ... Kensington, MD
Drozdowski, Gerardyne M.
Grand Rapids, MI
Drozdowski, James M. ... Cleveland, OH
Drozdowski, Raymond F. ... Camden, NJ
Drozdzik, Ronald L. ... Chicago, IL
Droze, William M. ... Atlanta, GA
Drozen, Melvin S. ... Washington, DC
Drozenski, Diane C. ... Lexington, MA
Drozin, Garth Matthew ... Los Angeles, CA
Drozt, Robert Allen ... Chicago, IL
Druar, Robert B. ... Buffalo, NY
Druary, J. William, Jr. ... Waterville, ME
Drubach, Leonardo D. ... San Bruno, CA
Drubel, Richard B. ... Hanover, NH
Armonk, NY
Drubner, Hartley, O'Connor & Mengacci
Waterbury, CT
Drubner, Norman S. ... Waterbury, CT
Druby, Kendall W. ... Anchorage, AK
Druby, Richard B. ... Harrisburg, PA
Drucas, Chris ... Salem, MA
Druce, Michelle S. ... Portland, OR
Druce, Tracy W. ... San Antonio, TX
Druch, Andrew W. ... New York, NY
Druck, Edward N. ... Chicago, IL
Druck, Thomas W. ... New Berlin, WI
Drucker, A. Norman
North Miami Beach, FL
Drucker, Alison R. ... Department of Justice, Civil Division, GV
Drucker, Andrea Holtzman
Philadelphia, PA
Drucker, Andrew H. ... Coral Gables, FL
Drucker, Andrew H., P.A. ... Coral Gables, FL
Drucker, Arnold W. ... Flushing, NY
Drucker Associates ... San Francisco, CA
Drucker, Barry A. ... Los Angeles, CA
Drucker, Bruce D., (P.C.) ... Chicago, IL
Uniondale, NY
Drucker, Cecily A. ... San Francisco, CA
Drucker, Christine M. ... Minneapolis, MN
Drucker, David G. ... New York, NY
Drucker, Deborah J. ... Rockville, MD
Drucker, Dennis ... New York, NY
Drucker, Douglas R. ... Houston, TX
Drucker, Douglas R., Jr. ... New York, NY
Drucker & Drucker ... Bohemia, NY
Drucker, Ellen R. ...
Department Of Health And Human Services, GV
Drucker, Emily J. ... New York, NY
Drucker, Fred L. ... Chicago, IL
Drucker, Gary J. ... Coral Springs, FL
Drucker, Geoffrey A.
United States Postal Service, Law Department, GV
Drucker, George W., Jr. ... Monterey, CA
Drucker, Howard A. ... New York, NY
Drucker, I. Morley, (A Professional Corporation) ... Los Angeles, CA
Drucker, Jacquelin F. ... New York, NY
Drucker, James D. ... Fort Lauderdale, FL
Drucker, Jesse S. ... Bohemia, NY
Drucker, Joel A. ... New York, NY
Drucker, Joelle M. ... Beverly Hills, CA
Drucker, John H. ... New York, NY
Drucker, Jon E. ... Los Angeles, CA
Drucker, Jonathan D. ... New York, NY
Drucker, Jonathan M. ... Coral Gables, FL
Drucker, Joseph ... Red Bank, NJ
Drucker, Julie F. ... Coral Gables, FL
Drucker, Kenneth Bruce ... Miami, FL
Drucker, Lawrence C. ... New York, NY
Drucker, Linda Price ... San Francisco, CA
Drucker, Lisa B. ... Guaynabo, PR
Drucker, Mark S. ... Jackson Heights, NY
Drucker, Marvin ... Cleveland, OH
Drucker, Michael S. ... Los Angeles, CA
Oak Park, CA
Drucker, Michael Stuart ... Atlanta, GA
Drucker, Mitchell S. ... New York, NY
Drucker, Paul J. ... Philadelphia, PA
Drucker, Peri J. ... Los Angeles, CA
Drucker, Peter A. ... New York, NY
Drucker, Richard A. ... New York, NY
Drucker, Richard H. ... Brooklyn, NY
Drucker, Richard H. ... Cleveland, OH
Drucker, Robert A. ... River Edge, NJ
New York, NY
Drucker, Ronald H. ... Philadelphia, PA
Drucker, Scott Michael ... Atlanta, GA
Drucker, Sheldon M. ... Boston, MA
Drucker, Stanley W. ... Newport News, VA
Drucker, Steven B. ... Atlanta, GA
Drucker, Vanessa ... New York, NY
Drucker, William B. ... Needham, MA
Drucker, Wm. A. ... New York, NY
Druckman & Breslow, Professional Association ... Fort Lauderdale, FL
Miami, FL
Druckman, Hernandez and Sennello, P.C.
Elizabeth, NJ
Druckman, Howard E. ... New York, NY
Druckman, Ira J. ... Miami, FL
Druckman, Jack P. ... North Miami Beach, FL
Druckman, James P. ... New York, NY
Druckman, Jeffrey J. ... Portland, OR
Druckman, Jeffrey J., P.C., Law Office of
Portland, OR
Druckman, Jonathan S. ... Elizabeth, NJ
Druckman, Kenneth ... Key Largo, FL
Druckman, Marc L. ... Miami, FL
Druckman, Michael N. ... Washington, DC
Druckman Raphan & Sinel ... New York, NY
Druckman, Rebecca Carol ... Lakeport, CA
Druckman, Stuart L. ... New York, NY
Druckman, William S. ... Charleston, WV
Drucks, Howard E. ... Atlantic City, NJ
Drudi, John J. ... Los Angeles, CA
Druding, Michael J. ... Orange, CA
Druehl, Craig P. ... New York, NY
Drueke, Patrick ... Grand Rapids, MI
Druen, W. Sidney ... Columbus, OH
Druet, Kathryn F. ... Weymouth, MA
Druffner, David C. ... Dallas, TX
Drugach, Claire ... Newark, NJ
Drugan, George S., III ... San Antonio, TX
Drugan, Margaret M. ... Irvine, CA
Drugan, Mary ... New York, NY
Drugas, Constantine G. ... Evergreen Park, IL
Drugas, Peter T. ... Orland Park, IL
Druggs, Merrill J. ... Gibsonia, PA
Druhan, J. Michael, Jr. ... Mobile, AL
Druhet, Rogers J., III ... Lincoln, NE
Druhot, Denise M. ... Springfield, IL
Druhot, Raymond M. ... Olmsted Falls, OH
Druin, Wade D. ... Watertown, SD
Druitt, Beverly F.
National Labor Relations Board, Office of the General Counsel, GV
Druker, David W. ... New York, NY
Druker, Harry ... Marshalltown, IA
Druker, Isaac E. ... New York, NY
Druker, James O. ... Garden City, NY
Mamaroneck, NY
Druker, Michele A. ... Des Moines, IA
Drukker, William R. ... Los Alamitos, CA
Drukman, Melvin ... Atlanta, GA
Drukman, Melvin, P.C. ... Atlanta, GA
Druks, Richard L., (P.A.) ... Miami Beach, FL
Druley, Ray M. ... Fort Branch, IN
Druliner, Kathryn M. ... Sacramento, CA
Druliner, Ross D., Jr. ... Aurora, NE
Drum, Jack D. ... Gastonia, NC
Drum, John F. ... Dennis, MA
Drum, Joseph F. ... Stratford, CT
Drum, Keith, (P.C.) ... Beaver, OK
Drum, LeAndrea E. ... Tampa, FL
Drum, Sydney Maria ... New York, NY
Drum & Venable ... Beaver, OK
Drumheller, Anthony D. ... Houston, TX
Drumheller, Barbara A. ... Houston, TX
Drumheller, Betty L. ... Bellevue, WA
Drumheller, Holly Lynn ... Baltimore, MD
Drumheller, Scott ... Chicago, IL
Drumheller, Woodson T. ... Richmond, VA
Drumke, Michael W. ... Chicago, IL
Drumke, Ronald A. ... Evanston, IL
Drumm, Alfred Wendall ... San Jose, CA
Drumm, Bernhardt C., Jr. ... Clayton, MO
Drumm, Cynthia J. ... Worthington, OH
Drumm, David G. ... Dallas, TX
Drumm, Francis J., Jr. ... Hartford, CT
Drumm, Gerard T. ... New York, NY
Drumm, Janet ... Royal Oak, MI
Drumm, John G. ... Phoenix, AZ
Drumm, Larry L. ... San Francisco, CA
Drumm, Lawrence E. ... Los Angeles, CA
Drumm, Lawrence R. ... Chicago, IL
Drumm, Manuel ... Sikeston, MO
Drumm, Maria Lapi ... Fort Myers, FL
Drumm, Michael R. ... Buffalo, NY
Drumm & Thornton ... Sikeston, MO
Drumm, William H. ... Rochester, NY
Drummer, Charlene M. (Walker)
San Francisco, CA
Drummer, Dorothy J. ... Austin, TX
Drummer, Mary ... Golden Valley, MN
Drummer, Robert G. ... Alexandria, VA
Drummer, Robert H. ... Laurel, MD
Drummey, Charles E. ... Hartford, CT
Drummey, George F., Jr.
St. Clair Shores, MI
Drumming, George, Jr. ... Tallahassee, FL
Drummond, Alison M. ... Atlanta, GA
Drummond & Ashenbrener, P.S.
Spokane, WA
Drummond, Brian C. ... Fairfax, VA
Drummond, Bryan K. ... Tulsa, OK
Drummond, Cecil G. ... Tulsa, OK
Drummond, Christopher F.
Centreville, MD
Drummond, Donald F. ... San Francisco, CA
Drummond, Donald G. ... Pueblo, CO
Drummond, Dougherty and Schwartz, P.C.
Pueblo, CO
Drummond & Drummond, LLP
Portland, ME
Drummond & Duckworth
Newport Beach, CA
Drummond, Edward P., Jr.
Livingston, NJ
Drummond, Elaine G. ... Stamford, CT
Drummond, Elaine R. ... San Pedro, CA
Drummond, Eric H. ... Austin, TX
Drummond, F. Ford ... Bartlesville, OK
Drummond, Forrest S. ... Pasadena, CA
Drummond, Gary A. ... Phoenix, AZ
Drummond, Gary T. ... Walnut Creek, CA
Drummond, Gentner F. ... Tulsa, OK
Drummond, Gerard K. ... Portland, OR
Drummond, Gregory ... Summit, NJ
Drummond, I. Michele ... Tulsa, OK
Drummond, J. Alan ... Summit, NJ
Drummond, J. Gregory ... White Plains, NY
Drummond, James Alexander ... Norman, OK
Drummond, James E. ... San Diego, CA
Drummond, James F., Jr.
Environmental Protection Agency, Office of the General Counsel, GV
Drummond, Jan T. ... Edmonds, WA
Drummond, Jeffery P. ... Dallas, TX
Drummond, John A. ... Lakeport, CA
Drummond, Kevin A. ... Summit, NJ
Drummond, Kimberly Ann ... Philadelphia, PA
Drummond, Larry A. ... Houston, TX
Drummond Law Group, The, P.C.
Atlanta, GA
Drummond, Mark A. ... Quincy, IL
Drummond, Mark A. ... Indianapolis, IN
Drummond, Nancy C. ... Birmingham, AL
Drummond & O'Brien
Upper Marlboro, MD
Drummond & Owren ... Summit, NJ
Drummond, P. Wayne, Jr. ... Charlotte, NC
Drummond, Patricia Nimmerrichter
Upper Marlboro, MD
Drummond, Paul A. ... San Antonio, TX
Drummond, Paula G. ... Pensacola, FL
Drummond, Peter C. ... Staunton, IL
Drummond, Raymond & Drummond
Tulsa, OK
Drummond, Robert G. ... Great Falls, MT
Drummond, Robert J. ... Chicago, IL
Drummond, Robert K. ... Milwaukee, WI
Drummond, Robert Keith, (P.C.)
Dallas, TX
Drummond, Stephen ... Spokane, WA
Drummond, Steven J. ... Alexandria, MN
Drummond, Temple H. ... Tampa, FL
Drummond, Thaddeus E. ... Mount Holly, NJ
Drummond, Thomas E. ... Tulsa, OK
Drummond, Tucker ... Boston, MA
Drummond, William H.
Newport Beach, CA
Drummond, William H. ... Scarsdale, NY
Drummond, Winslow ... Little Rock, AR
Drummond Woodsum & MacMahon
Portland, ME
Drummonds, Henry H. ... Portland, OR
Drummy, James P. ... Los Angeles, CA
Drummy, John B. ... Indianapolis, IN
Drummy, Kathleen L. Houston
Los Angeles, CA
Drummy King White & Gire, A Professional Corporation ... Costa Mesa, CA
Newport Beach, CA
Drummy, Stephen C. ... Costa Mesa, CA
Drummy, William W. ... Terre Haute, IN
Drumright, Donald A. ... Palo Alto, CA
Drumwright, James R. ... Haverford, PA
Drungole, Paula E. ... Starkville, MS
Drunken Driving Defense Lawyers of Illinois, Ltd. ... Chicago, IL
Drury, Cathleen J. ... Westlake Village, CA
Drury, Charles J. ... Portage, WI
Drury, David C.
Bellefontaine Neighbors, MO
Drury, David C., P.C.
Bellefontaine Neighbors, MO
Drury, Dennis C. ... Troy, MI
Drury, Douglas V. ... Scottsdale, AZ
Drury, Elizabeth H. ... Charlotte, NC
Drury, Geoffrey ... Canaan, CT
Drury, Glenn R. ... Minneapolis, MN
Drury, James Creighton ... Roseland, NJ
Drury, James J. ... Staten Island, NY
Drury, John B. ... Reston, VA
Drury, John L. ... North Attleboro, MA
Drury, Larry D. ... Chicago, IL
Drury, Laura ... Baltimore, MD
Drury, Lloyd L., III ... New Orleans, LA
Drury, Mark E. ... Casper, WY
Drury, Mary E. ... Portage, WI
Drury, Mary J. ... Las Vegas, NV
Drury & Matisoff ... Westlake Village, CA
Drury, Michael ... Los Angeles, CA
Drury, Michael B. ... Denver, CO
Drury, Richard Toshiyuki
San Francisco, CA
Drury, Ronald E. ... Greenwood, IN
Drury, Scott R. ... Chicago, IL
Drury, Sidney H. ... Chicago, IL
Drury, Thomas J. ... Buffalo, NY
Drury, Timothy J. ... Buffalo, NY
Drury, W. A. ... Jasper, FL
Drury, William W., Jr. ... Phoenix, AZ
Drusch, Walter S., Jr.
Cape Girardeau, MO
Druse, Harold ... Warren, NJ
Drushal, Bonnie C. ... Wooster, OH
Drushal, J. Douglas ... Wooster, OH
Drushall, Stephen D. ... Los Angeles, CA
Drushel, Kelly E. ... Cleveland, OH
Drushel, Kelly E. ... Cleveland, OH
Drushel, William H., Jr. ... Houston, TX
Druskin, Victor ... Henderson, NV
Druss, Lewis R. ... Plantation, FL
Druss, Lewis R., P.A. ... Plantation, FL
Drust, Joann L. ... Philadelphia, PA
Drutchas, Grantland G. ... Chicago, IL
Drutchas, Gregory G. ... Detroit, MI
Druten, Charles A. ... Palm Desert, CA
Druten, Kelly ... Phoenix, AZ
Drutman, Evan Michael ... New York, NY
Drutman, Robin I. ... Clearwater, FL
Drutz, Mark W. ... Prescott, AZ
Drutz, Natalie M. ... New York, NY
Druxman, Louis M. ... Albuquerque, NM
Druyan, B. Martin ... New York, NY
Druyan, Kira E. ... Chicago, IL
Druz, Dan A. ... Manasquan, NJ
Druzbick, Carol L. ... Alexandria, VA
Druziako, Victor ... Philadelphia, PA
Druzinski, Diane Marie ... St. Clair Shores, MI
Dry, Fred Mark ... Chicago, IL
Dry & Higgins ... Plano, TX
Dry, Laurence R., & Associates
Atlanta, GA
Oak Ridge, TN
Dry, Laurence R., & Associates
Knoxville, TN
Dry, Maureen R. ... Baltimore, MD
Dry, N. Elton ... Houston, TX

Dry, P. Ray .... Baton Rouge, LA
Dry, Robert T., Jr. .... Plano, TX
Dry & Tassin, L.L.P. .... Houston, TX
Dryburgh, Bruce S. .... Farmers Branch, TX
Dryburgh, Erik D. .... San Francisco, CA
Dryburgh and Moraine, L.L.P.
Farmers Branch, TX
Dryden, Cathy A. .... Baltimore, MD
Dryden, Daryl A. .... Pascagoula, MS
Dryden, Dianna Timm .... Belfair, WA
Dryden, Grossheim & Sutton
Beaumont, TX
Dryden, Jacqueline Renee .... Miami, FL
Dryden, James W. .... Annapolis, MD
Dryden, Margoles, Schimaneck, Kelly & Wait, A Law Corporation
Claremont, CA
Los Angeles, CA
Riverside, CA
San Bernardino, CA
San Francisco, CA
Santa Ana, CA
Dryden, Michael G. .... Philadelphia, PA
Dryden, Robert E. .... San Francisco, CA
Dryden, Robert E. .... Dallas, TX
Dryden, Robert R. .... Aliso Viejo, CA
Dryden, Stephen F. .... Wilmington, DE
Dryden, Thomas M. .... Fort Myers, FL
Dryden, Wayne S. .... Pasadena, CA
Dryden, William G. .... Boise, ID
Dryden, Woodson E. .... Beaumont, TX
Drye, Janice A. .... Spokane, WA
Drye, John Monroe .... Atlanta, GA
Drye, Michael L. .... Winston-Salem, NC
Drye, Michael W. .... Asheville, NC
Drye, Michael W., P.C. .... Asheville, NC
Dryer, Aaron A. .... Columbus, OH
Dryer, Andrea Jordan .... Independence, IA
Dryer, C. Shawn .... Columbia, SC
Dryer, David E. .... Boston, MA
Dryer, David M. .... Indianola, IA
Dryer, Dryer & Weinstock
New Rochelle, NY
Dryer, Edwin Jason .... Washington, DC
Dryer, Gary Hugh .... Charlotte, MI
Dryer, Howard L. .... New Rochelle, NY
Dryer, Joel L. .... Oelwein, IA
Dryer, Jonathan .... Philadelphia, PA
Dryer, Kathy Davis .... Salt Lake City, UT
Dryer, Lee E. .... Tampa, FL
Dryer, Leo A., Jr. .... Columbia, SC
Greenville, SC
Dryer, Mark .... New York, NY
Dryer, Paul A. .... Waynesboro, VA
Dryer, R. Craft .... Duluth, MN
Dryer, Randy L. .... Salt Lake City, UT
Dryer, Rhoda K. .... New Rochelle, NY
Dryfoos, Glenn A. .... Los Angeles, CA
Dryfoos, Robert J. .... New York, NY
Dryfuss, Claire D. .... Tallahassee, FL
Dryja, Michael A. .... Minneapolis, MN
Dryjanski, Andrew L. .... Chicago, IL
Drylie, Deborah Carolyn .... Gainesville, FL
Drymalski, Peter G. .... Rockville, MD
Drymalski, Raymond H. .... Chicago, IL
Drymon, Clinton H. .... Dover, NJ
Drymon, James J. .... Sarasota, FL
Drymonis, Kyriakos .... Daytona Beach, FL
Dryovage, Mary M., Law Offices of
San Francisco, CA
Drysdale, Don M. .... Newport Beach, CA
Newport Beach, CA
Drysdale, Douglas B. .... Chicago, IL
Drysdale, Douglas D. .... Washington, DC
Drysdale, Douglas R. .... Bozeman, MT
Drysdale, Leon P.J. .... Boston, MA
Drysdale, McLean & Nellen, P.C.
Bozeman, MT
Drysdale, Michael R. .... Minneapolis, MN
Drysdale, Philip E. .... Oakland, CA
Dryvynsyde, Geoffrey B. .... San Francisco, CA
Drzal, Michael P. .... Richmond, VA
Drzewiecki, Claire M. .... Warren, NJ
DSC Communications Corp. .... Plano, TX
D'Souza, Gerard I. .... Cleveland, OH
D'Souza, Lisa J. .... Weslaco, TX
D'Souza, Maureen Devine
Gaithersburg, MD
Du, Miranda M. .... Reno, NV
Du, Miriam M. .... Philadelphia, PA
Duan & Duan Law Firm .... Seattle, WA
Duan, Q. H. Charles .... Seattle, WA
Duane, Elizabeth Stevens .... Allentown, PA
Duane, Harley W., III .... Richmond, VA
Duane, James J., III .... Boston, MA
Duane, Jennifer A. .... Washington, DC
Duane, John F. .... New York, NY
Duane, Kenneth J., P.C. .... East Brunswick, NJ
Duane, Lyman, Seltzer & Gorelick
Berkeley, CA
Duane, Michael J. .... Morristown, NJ
Duane, Morris & Heckscher LLP
San Francisco, CA
Dover, DE
Wilmington, DE
Washington, DC
Miami, FL
Palm Beach, FL
Chicago, IL
Boston, MA
Cherry Hill, NJ
Newark, NJ
Princeton, NJ
New York, NY
Allentown, PA
Harrisburg, PA
Philadelphia, PA
Wayne, PA
Houston, TX
Duane, Richard P. .... Berkeley, CA
Duane, Rosanne M. .... Palm Beach, FL
Duane and Shannon, P.C. .... Richmond, VA
Duane, W. Ford .... Orlando, FL
Duane, William F., P.A. .... Winter Park, FL
Duane, William Francis .... Winter Park, FL
Duany, Michael G. .... Vergennes, VT
Duany, Tracy .... Fort Lauderdale, FL
Duara, Juliette Gregory .... Chicago, IL
Duarte, Albert A. .... Visalia, CA
Duarte, Alex M. .... Denver, CO
Duarte, Antonio, III .... Tampa, FL
Duarte, Benjamin .... San Jose, CA
Duarte, Charlotte J. .... Honolulu, HI
Duarte, Demetrio, Jr. .... San Antonio, TX
Duarte, Demetrio, Jr., and Associates, P.C.
San Antonio, TX
Duarte, Dennis D. .... Tustin, CA
Duarte, Dennis D., A Professional Law Corporation .... Tustin, CA
Duarte, Elena J. .... Sacramento, CA
Duarte, Elena M. .... Chicago, IL
Duarte, Eugenio .... Miami, FL
Duarte, Frances E. .... Greenville, SC
Duarte, Garrett B.M. .... Washington, DC
Duarte, James J., Jr .... Salinas, CA
Duarte, James M. .... Foothill Ranch, CA
Duarte, Jorge A. .... South Miami, FL
Duarte, Leroy W. .... Albuquerque, NM
Duarte, Lisa .... San Francisco, CA
Duarte, Maria Cristina .... Washington, DC
Duarte, Michael J. .... Los Angeles, CA
Duarte, Patricia A. .... Walnut Creek, CA
Duarte, Richard .... Miami, FL
Duarte, Richard, P.A. .... Miami, FL
Duarte, Ruben Gabriel .... El Paso, TX
Duarte, Stephen E. .... Department of Energy, Office of the General Counsel, GV
Duarte, Susan J. .... San Jose, CA
Duarte, Thomas C. .... Marietta, GA
Duax, John T. .... Chicago, IL
Dub, Allen W. .... Chicago, IL
Highland Park, IL
Northbrook, IL
Dub & Grande, Ltd., Law Offices of
Pawtucket, RI
Dub, Larry .... Pawtucket, RI
Dub, Stanley M. .... Cleveland, OH
Duba, Christopher J. .... Chicago, IL
Duba, Donald E. .... Grand Rapids, MI
Duback, Steven R. .... Milwaukee, WI
Dubail Judge, A Professional Corporation
St. Louis, MO
Dubail, W. Donald .... St. Louis, MO
Duban, Janice L. .... Chicago, IL
Duban, Jeffrey M., Law Offices of
New York, NY
Duban, Michael C. .... White Plains, NY
Duban, Michael C., P.C. .... White Plains, NY
Dubanevich, Keith S. .... Portland, OR
DuBarry, Deonne .... Metairie, LA
DuBarry, Deonne .... New Orleans, LA
Dubas, Marlene C. .... Skokie, IL
Dubault, Robert A. .... Muskegon, MI
Dubay & Andreini .... Hartford, CT
Dubay, Christopher F. .... Detroit, MI
DuBay, Dennis B. .... Detroit, MI
Dubay, James V. .... Richmond, MI
Dubay, Jennifer M. .... Phoenix, AZ
DuBay, John L. .... Portland, OR
DuBay, Keith Edward, Jr. .... Hartford, CT
Dubay, Kevin G. .... Hartford, CT
DuBay, Mark D. .... Paw Paw, MI
DuBay, Michael Dennis .... Chicago, IL
DuBay, Roger L. .... Cleveland, OH
Dubbeld, Kaelber & Sage, P.A.
St. Petersburg, FL
Dubbeld, Paul J. .... Daytona Beach, FL
Dubbeld, Peter H. .... St. Petersburg, FL
Dubbelde, Robert J. .... Austin, TX
Dubberly, B. Danial, Jr. .... Glennville, GA
Dubberly, B. Daniel, III .... Glennville, GA
Dubberly, David E. .... Columbia, SC
Dubberly & McGovern .... Glennville, GA
Dubberly, Paula
Securities and Exchange Commission, Division of Corporation Finance, GV
Dubberstein & Lilly .... Oklahoma City, OK
Dubberstein, Mark J.
Oklahoma City, OK
Dubbin, Murray H. .... Miami Beach, FL
Dubbin, Samuel J. .... Miami, FL
Dubbin, William M. .... San Jose, CA
Dubbin, William M., Inc. .... San Jose, CA
Dubbs, Elizabeth .... New York, NY
Dubbs, John W. .... Northfield, IL
Dubbs, John W., III .... Chicago, IL
Dubbs, Judith Lockman
Redondo Beach, CA
Dubbs, Maryanne .... Baltimore, MD
Dubbs, Melissa A. .... Mountain View, CA
Dubbs, Rita K. .... Northfield, IL
Dubbs, Robert Morton .... Philadelphia, PA
Dubbs, Seymour .... Nanuet, NY
Dub Carlson, Daria A. .... Santa Monica, CA
Dubcoff, Gary K. .... San Francisco, CA
Dube, Bertram J. .... Glens Falls, NY
Dube, Cheryl Scott .... Southfield, MI
Dube, Christopher M. .... Manchester, NH
Dube, Christopher N. .... Wrens, GA
Dubé, Dale R. .... Wilmington, DE
Dube, Daniel A. .... New Bedford, MA
Dube, Diane M. .... Minneapolis, MN
Dube, Douglas A. .... San Diego, CA
Dubé & Goodgal, P.C. .... Washington, DC
Baltimore, MD
Dube, James F. .... Pawtucket, RI
Dubé, Lawrence E., Jr. .... Washington, DC
Baltimore, MD
Dube, Mark S. .... Houston, TX
Dube, Monte .... Chicago, IL
Dube, Patricia Kay .... Houston, TX
Dube, Patricia Kay, P.C. .... Houston, TX
Dube, Philip C. .... Los Angeles, CA
Dube, Phillip E. .... Washington, DC
Dubé, Priscilla Bondy .... Burlington, VT
Dubé, Robert L. .... Miami, FL
Dube, Steven Louis .... Boston, MA
Dubé and Wright, P.A., Law Offices of
Miami, FL
DuBeau, Guy J. .... Madison, WI
DuBeau, Robert C. .... Vernon, CT
DuBeau, Ryan & Boyan, P.C. .... Vernon, CT
Dubeck, John B. .... Washington, DC
Dubecq, Cheryl A. .... Wilmington, DE
Dubel, Thomas S. .... Elmira, NY
Dubelier, Eric A. .... Washington, DC
Dubelier, Kristin L. .... Treasury Department, U.S. Customs Service, GV
Dubelko, James M. .... North Olmsted, OH
Duben, Ernest C. .... Kew Gardens, NY
Dubendorf, Donald R. .... Pittsfield, MA
Williamstown, MA
Dubensky, Abraham .... Westbury, NY
Dubensky & Dubensky .... Westbury, NY
Dubensky, Joyce S. .... Brooklyn, NY
Dubensky, Peter A. .... Bradenton, FL
Dubensky, Seymour .... Westbury, NY
Duber, Michael J. .... Cleveland, OH
Duber, Robert, II .... Globe, AZ
Du Berchin, Marjorie S. .... San Diego, CA
Duberchin, Michael S. .... Calabasas, CA
Duberg, James S. .... Chula Vista, CA
Duberman, James R. .... New York, NY
Duberstein, Conrad B. .... Brooklyn, NY
Duberstein, Donald J. .... White Plains, NY
Duberstein, Douglas R. .... Bethesda, MD
Duberstein, Maxine K. .... Brooklyn, NY
Duberstein, Norman .... Columbia, MD
Duberstein, Ronnie .... Los Angeles, CA
Duberstein, Wilbur .... San Ramon, CA
Dubert, Carl A. .... Washington, DC
DuBester, Ernest W.
National Mediation Board, GV
Dubetz, Michael, Jr. .... Denver, CO
Dubey, James M. .... Santa Clara, CA
Du Bey, Lynn Edelstein .... Seattle, WA
Dubey, Paul William .... Midland, TX
Du Bey, Richard A. .... Seattle, WA
Dubey, Susmita
Environmental Protection Agency, Office of the General Counsel, GV
Dubia, Christian F., Jr. .... Irvine, CA
Dubiac, Diane L. .... New York, NY
Dubiac & Perlmutter .... New York, NY
Dubiansky, Joseph M. .... Deerfield, NH
Dubick, Julie P. .... San Diego, CA
Dubick, Mitchell B. .... San Diego, CA
Dubicki, David J. .... Peoria, IL
Dubicki, Henry J. .... Alexandria, VA
Dubicki, Nancy Z. .... New London, CT
Dubie, Carol .... Philadelphia, PA
Dubiel, Edwin J. .... Woodland Hills, CA
Dubiel, Joseph A. .... Haleiwa, HI
Dubik, Deborah A. .... Davenport, IA
Dubill, Robert A. .... Alexandria, VA
Dubin, Aaron S. .... St. Louis, MO
Dubin, Alan S. .... Washington, DC
Dubin, Arlene G. .... New York, NY
Dubin, Balistreri & Schelble, Ltd.
Milwaukee, WI
Dubin, Barry A. .... San Francisco, CA
Dubin, Brock T. .... Stamford, CT
Dubin, Carl L. .... Milwaukee, WI
Dubin, Chas. T. .... Baltimore, MD
Dubin, Cindy Zimmerman
Los Angeles, CA
Dubin, Daphne S.W. .... New York, NY
Dubin, David I. .... Narberth, PA
Dubin, David M. .... Riverhead, NY
Southampton, NY
Dubin, Deborah F. .... San Francisco, CA
Dubin, Eric J. .... Costa Mesa, CA
Dubin, Franklin R. .... Milwaukee, WI
Dubin, Gary Victor .... Honolulu, HI
Dubin, Gary W. .... Cleveland, OH
Dubin, Harry .... Brooklyn, NY
Dubin, Herbert Alan .... Rockville, MD
Dubin, Israel D. .... Hackensack, NJ
Dubin, James M. .... New York, NY
Dubin, Jeffrey E. .... Cleveland, OH
Dubin, Jeffrey S. .... Huntington, NY
Dubin, Jon C .... San Antonio, TX
Dubin, Joseph & Shagrin .... Cleveland, OH
Dubin, Joshua L. .... Aventura, FL
Miami, FL
Dubin, Laurie Phillips .... Larkspur, CA
Dubin, Lawrence .... New York, NY
Dubin, Lawrence A. .... Northford, CT
Dubin, Lawrence A. .... Birmingham, MI
Dubin, Lawrence M., (P.C.) .... Chicago, IL
Dubin, Leonard .... Philadelphia, PA
Dubin, Leonard R. .... Los Angeles, CA
Dubin, Leonard R., A Professional Corporation
Los Angeles, CA
Dubin, Lorne B. .... San Francisco, CA
Dubin, Marla .... Chestnut Hill, MA
Dubin, Marvin T. .... Buffalo, NY
Dubin, Michael A. .... St. Louis, MO
Dubin, Michael B. .... Jenkintown, PA
Dubin, Morton .... New York, NY
Dubin, M. R. .... Salisbury, CT
Dubin, Nellie J. .... Milford, CT
Dubin, Richard M. .... Chicago, IL
Dubin, Robert A. .... Detroit, MI
Dubin, Robert J. .... Buffalo, NY
Dubin, Roger E. M. .... New York, NY
Dubin, Scott B. .... Trenton, NJ
Dubin, Seth H. .... New York, NY
Dubin, Sommerstein & Hunter .... Buffalo, NY
Dubin, Stanford .... Camp Springs, MD
Dubin, Stanton .... Philadelphia, PA
Dubin, Stephen L. .... Los Angeles, CA
Dubin, Stephen V. .... Philadelphia, PA
Dubin, Steven G. .... Southampton, PA
Dubin, Stuart B. .... Chicago, IL
Dubin, Stuart B., Ltd. & Associates
Chicago, IL
Dubin, Susan B. .... Lutherville, MD
Dubin, Thomas I. H. .... Morris Plains, NJ
Dubin, Vivian L. .... New York, NY
Dubina, Joel F. .... Montgomery, AL
Dubiner, Jay L. .... New York, NY
Dubiner, Michael .... West Palm Beach, FL
Dubiner & Wilensky, PA
West Palm Beach, FL
Dubini, G. Beatriz .... Los Angeles, CA
Dubinski, Joseph P. .... Kansas City, MO
Dubinski, Leon E. .... Prospect Heights, IL
Dubinsky, David J. .... Boston, MA
Dubinsky, Donna Dikman
Lake Success, NY
Dubinsky, Duggan & Horwitz
St. Louis, MO
Dubinsky, Irvin .... St. Louis, MO
Dubinsky, Jack .... New York, NY
Dubinsky, Jamie L. .... Los Angeles, CA
Dubinsky, Joan Elise .... Kensington, MD
Dubinsky, Joseph .... New York, NY
Dubinsky, Kerre R. .... Palo Alto, CA
Dubinsky, Melvin .... New York, NY
Dubinsky, Paul R. .... Washington, DC
Dubinsky, William J. .... Chicago, IL
Dubis, Christina E. .... St. Louis, MO
Dubis, Edward S. .... Tucson, AZ
Dubis, Melanie L. Black .... Raleigh, NC
Dubis, Michael F., (S.C.) .... Waterford, WI
Dubishar, Wm. Craig .... McLean, VA
Dubitsky, Alexander A. .... Washington, DC
Dubitsky, Ira L. .... Miami, FL
Dubitsky, Ira L., P.A. .... Miami, FL
Dubitsky, Randolph J. .... Detroit, MI
Dubitzky, Anne J. .... Boston, MA
Dubitzky, Dan R. .... Seattle, WA
Dubitzky, Jonathan B. .... Boston, MA
Dubitzky & Zarky, P.S. .... Seattle, WA
Duble, Steven M. .... Houston, TX
Dubler, Leo B., III .... Atlantic City, NJ
Dubler, Leo B., (P.C.) .... Woodbury, NJ
Dubler, Nancy N. .... New York, NY
Dublikar, Ralph F. .... Canton, OH
Dublin, Allen I. .... Gilford, NH
Dublin, Kirk A. .... San Francisco, CA
Seattle, WA
Dublin, Peter B. .... Great Barrington, MA
Dublin, Philip C. .... New York, NY
Dublin, Robert A.
Department Of Health And Human Services, Office of the General Counsel, GV
Dublinske, Bret A. .... Des Moines, IA
Dublinsky, Neal A. .... Beverly Hills, CA
Dublirer, Harold .... New York, NY
Dubner, Barry H. .... Lansing, MI
Dubner, Robin A. .... Oakland, CA
Dubner, Steven .... Atlanta, GA
Dubnick, Harry L. .... Chicago, IL
Dubno, Abraham M. .... Brooklyn, NY
Dubno, Erica T. .... New York, NY
Dubno, Herbert .... Bronx, NY
Dubno, Robert C. .... Brooklyn, NY
Dubnoff, Ira S. .... Syracuse, NY
Dubnow, Linda B. .... Chicago, IL
Dubnow, Stacie F. .... Baltimore, MD
Duboc, Robert M. .... Kansas City, MO
DuBoe, Burton V. .... Skokie, IL
Duboff, Allan B. .... Beverly Hills, CA
DuBoff & Associates, Chartered
Silver Spring, MD
DuBoff, Dorband, Cushing & King, PLLC
Portland, OR
Du Boff, Joel .... Silver Spring, MD
DuBoff, Keith B. .... Enfield, CT
Duboff, Kenneth R. .... North Miami, FL
DuBoff, Leonard D. .... Portland, OR
Du Boff, Michael H. .... New York, NY
DuBoff, Robert S. .... Lexington, MA
DuBoff, Samuel J. .... Wallingford, CT
Du Boff, Sandra J. .... New York, NY
DuBoff, Scott M. .... Washington, DC
Dubofsky, Frank N. .... Boulder, CO
Dubofsky, Jean E. .... Boulder, CO
Dubofsky, Jean E., P.C. .... Boulder, CO
Dubograev, Dmitri I. .... Washington, DC
Du Bois, A. Harold .... Baltimore, MD
Dubois, Alan F. .... Morehead City, NC
DuBois, Allan K. .... San Antonio, TX
DuBois, Amanda .... Seattle, WA
DuBois Billig Loughlin Conaty & Weisman
Mineola, NY
Rock Hill, NY
White Plains, NY
DuBois, Charles H. .... Dallas, TX
DuBois, Cheryl A. .... Milford, CT
Dubois, Christine .... Santa Rosa, CA
DuBois, Christopher John
Tallahassee, FL
Dubois, Cooksey, Bischoff and Ferreri, P.A.
Albuquerque, NM
DuBois & Cruickshank, P.A.
Tallahassee, FL
DuBois, D. Christopher .... Rock Hill, NY
DuBois, David R. .... Portage, IN
DuBois, Duane R. .... Brookfield, WI

DuBois and DuBois, P.C. ....Columbia, TN
Dubois, George A. ....Albuquerque, NM
DuBois, H. Keith ....Grayling, MI
DuBois, H. Keith, P.C. ....Grayling, MI
Du Bois, Herbert G. ....Camden, NJ
DuBois, Iris M. ....Sarasota, FL
DuBois, J. Thomas ....Columbia, TN
DuBois, James J. ....Mobile, AL
DuBois, James J. ....Denver, CO
DuBois, James T. ....Columbia, TN
DuBois, Jan E. ....Philadelphia, PA
DuBois, Jann P. ....Colorado Springs, CO
Dubois, Jeffrey S. ....Du Bois, PA
DuBois, Jonathan D. ....New York, NY
DuBois, Joseph E. ....Irvine, CA
Du Bois, Kathleen Collins ....St. Louis, MO
Dubois, Kristina ....Cleveland, OH
DuBois, Lawrence D. ....Cavalier, ND
Du Bois, Madison S. ....Camden, NJ
Dubois, Marc N. ....New Orleans, LA
Dubois, Mark A. ....New London, CT
Dubois, Michael L. ....Lewiston, ME
DuBois, Nicholas J. ....Roseland, NJ
New York, NY
Dubois, Pascale Hélène ....Washington, DC
Dubois, Philip L. ....Boulder, CO
Dubois, Philip L., P.C. ....Boulder, CO
DuBois, Richard H. ....Redwood City, CA
DuBois, Robert F., III ....Austin, TX
Dubois, Roland
Environmental Protection Agency, Office of the General Counsel, GV
DuBois, Sam ....Bloomfield Hills, MI
DuBois, Sheehan, Hamilton & Levin
Camden, NJ
Cherry Hill, NJ
DuBois, Steve R. ....Gaylord, MI
DuBois, Steven M. ....Alexandria, VA
Du Bois, William H. ....Oakland, CA
DuBoise, Hengst & Henderson ....Houston, TX
DuBoise, Robert S. ....Houston, TX
Dubón & Dubón ....San Juan, PR
Dubon, Jose R. ....San Juan, PR
Dubón, Luis E., III ....San Juan, PR
Dubón, Luis E., Jr. ....San Juan, PR
Dubón, Luis E., Sr. ....San Juan, PR
Dubón, Manuel H. ....San Juan, PR
Dubord, Daniel J. ....Waterville, ME
Dubord, David R. ....Lewiston, ME
Dubord, Stephen F. ....Waterville, ME
Dubord, William P. ....Waterville, ME
Dubord & Deganis ....Glastonbury, CT
DuBorg, George J. ....Glastonbury, CT
DuBorg, George J., Law Offices of
Glastonbury, CT
Dubos, Michael L. ....Monroe, LA
DuBosar, Howard D. ....Boca Raton, FL
DuBose, Ben K. ....Dallas, TX
DuBose, C. Jones, Jr. ....Columbia, SC
DuBose, C. Wilson ....Atlanta, GA
DuBose, Charles O. ....Charlotte, NC
DuBose, Clarke W. ....Columbia, SC
DuBose and Cushman ....Camden, SC
DuBose, David C., (P.C.) ....Austin, TX
DuBose, E. Keith ....Sarasota, FL
DuBose, Eugene Zemp ....Dallas, TX
DuBose, Eugene Zemp, P.C. ....Dallas, TX
DuBose, Gale R. ....Columbia, SC
Du Bose, Guy ....Irvine, CA
DuBose, J. Kennedy, Jr. ....Camden, SC
Dubose, J. Mark, Jr. ....San Antonio, TX
DuBose, Jesse ....Lumpkin, GA
DuBose, John E., Jr. ....Frostproof, FL
Orlando, FL
DuBose, John P. ....Pensacola, FL
Dubose, Kevin H. ....Houston, TX
DuBose, Lenora ....Austin, TX
DuBose, Margaret Anne Bumgardner
Columbia, SC
DuBose, Mark Kevin ....Winston-Salem, NC
DuBose, Michael Mann
Treasury Department, Office of the General Counsel, GV
Dubose, Robert B. ....Houston, TX
DuBose & Short ....Montgomery, TX
DuBose, Stuart C., Law Offices of
Jackson, AL
Thomasville, AL
DuBose, Susan Drake ....Columbia, SC
DuBose, Theodore B. ....Columbia, SC
DuBose, Tracy N. ....Montgomery, TX
DuBose, Victor A. ....Hattiesburg, MS
DuBose, Waymon G., Jr. ....Dallas, TX
DuBose, Willie B. ....Midland, TX
DuBose-Schmitt, M. Gwyn ....Lexington, SC
Dubosh, Anthony P. ....Virden, IL
Dubosky, Daniel D. ....Venice, FL
Dubosky, David ....Pawtucket, RI
DuBosque, Geoffrey ....Newburyport, MA
Dubovich, Debra Lynch ....Highland, IN
DuBovy, N Jane ....Pacific Palisades, CA
Dubow, Adam R. ....New York, NY
Dubow, Alan ....Alexandria, VA
Dubow, Alan M. ....White Plains, NY
Dubow, Aneta B. ....Los Angeles, CA
Dubow, David A. ....Ithaca, NY
Dubow & Dubow ....Dania, FL
Dubow, Jason B. ....Dania, FL
Dubow, Jay A. ....Philadelphia, PA
Dubow, Les W. ....San Diego, CA
Dubow, Michael B. ....Bronx, NY
Dubow, Mitchell A. ....Virginia, MN
Dubow, Nancy R. ....Philadelphia, PA
Dubow, Paul J. ....San Francisco, CA
Dubow, Rachel L. ....New York, NY
Dubow, Robert E. ....Dania, FL
Dubow, Robert M. ....New York, NY
Dubow & Smith ....Bronx, NY
Dubow, Steven ....Philadelphia, PA
Dubow, Tod R. ....Los Angeles, CA
Dubowski, Joseph ....Douglaston, NY
Dubowsky, Bari Michelle ....Parsippany, NJ
Dubowsky, Fred S. ....Edison, NJ
Dubowsky, Martin J. ....Chicago, IL
Dubowsky, Peter ....Las Vegas, NV
Dubowsky, Scott M. ....New York, NY
Dubrasich, Paul N. ....San Francisco, CA
Dubrawski, Peter A. ....Santa Monica, CA
Dubreuil, Francis W. ....Palo Alto, CA
Dubreuil, John M. ....Covington, LA
Dubridge, Jo Ann ....Lowell, MI
Dubriel, M. Ricardo ....New York, NY
DuBrin, Harry L., Jr. ....Troy, NY
Dubrinsky and Dubrinsky ....Birmingham, MI
Dubrinsky, Marvin ....Birmingham, MI
Dubrinsky, Seymour N. ....Birmingham, MI
DuBrock, Daniel J. ....Chicago, IL
DuBrock, Roger W. ....Anchorage, AK
DuBroff, Allen B. ....Philadelphia, PA
Dubroff, Andrew J. ....Washington, DC
Dubroff, Charles M. ....New York, NY
DuBroff, Diana D. ....New York, NY
Dubroff, Harold ....Albany, NY
DuBroff, Kenneth ....White Plains, NY
Du Broff, Roger ....New York, NY
Dubroof, Linda B.
Federal Communications Commission, International Bureau, GV
Dubrovsky, Anna ....Menlo Park, CA
Dubrow, Barbara Tobin ....Cherry Hill, NJ
Philadelphia, PA
Dubrow, David L. ....Concord, NH
Dubrow, David L. ....New York, NY
Dubrow, David Noah ....Maplewood, NJ
Dubrow, Dennis R. ....Los Angeles, CA
Dubrow, Eli B. ....Los Angeles, CA
Dubrow, Eve L. ....Washington, DC
Dubrow, Herbert B. ....Skokie, IL
Dubrow, Jon B. ....Washington, DC
Dubrow, Kenneth M. ....Philadelphia, PA
Dubrow, Lisa B. ....New York, NY
Dubrow, Lowell H. ....Bala Cynwyd, PA
Dubrow, Michelle R. ....Columbus, OH
DuBrow, Phyllis E. ....New York, NY
Dubrow, Robert G. ....New Hyde Park, NY
Dubrow, Robert R. ....Beverly Hills, CA
Dubrowski, William A. ....Lakewood, NJ
Du Brul, Karen ....Philadelphia, PA
Dubsky, Duane J. ....Ashtabula, OH
Dubuar, James D. ....Seattle, WA
Dubuar, Lirhus & Engel, LLP
Seattle, WA
Dubuc, Brian M. ....Atlanta, GA
Dubuc, Carroll E. ....Alexandria, VA
Arlington, VA
Dubuc, Steven C. ....Washington, DC
Dubuclet, Victor A., III ....Metairie, LA
Du Buisson, Charles D. ....Winston-Salem, NC
Dubuisson and Dubuisson ....Opelousas, LA
Dubuisson, Edward B. ....Opelousas, LA
Dubuisson, James G. ....Opelousas, LA
Dubuisson, Susan A. ....Olympia, WA
DuBuque, Joan E. ....Seattle, WA
Dubuque, Louis T. ....Dumas, TX
Dubuque, Louis T., P.C. ....Dumas, TX
Dubuque, Marianne Barbino
Waterbury, CT
Dubus, Michael W. ....Atlanta, GA
Duby, James R., Jr. ....Lansing, MI
Duby, Ronald S. ....Boston, MA
Dubyak & Goldense Co., L.P.A
Cleveland, OH
Dubyak, Joseph A. ....Cleveland, OH
Dubyak, Robert J. ....Cleveland, OH
Dubyn, Jerome M. ....Philadelphia, PA
Duca, James F., II ....Milwaukee, WI
Duca, James N. ....Honolulu, HI
Duca, Lauren E. ....Boston, MA
Duca, Paul J. ....Philadelphia, PA
Duca and Prim ....Philadelphia, PA
Ducanis, Joseph T., Jr.
Fort Lauderdale, FL
Du Canto, Joseph N. ....Chicago, IL
Ducar, Timothy D. ....Phoenix, AZ
Ducas, William J. ....Boston, MA
Ducassou, Kathy Lynn ....Baltimore, MD
Ducatman, Robert P. ....Cleveland, OH
Ducayet, James W. ....Chicago, IL
Duce, Bastian & Peterson ....Everett, WA
Duce, David W., (P.S.) ....Everett, WA
Duce, Wesley K. ....Everett, WA
Ducey & Associates, P.C. ....Belleville, IL
Ducey, C. Patout ....Belleville, IL
Ducey, Cornelius T., Jr. ....Belleville, IL
St. Louis, MO
Ducey, Cornelius T., Sr. ....Belleville, IL
St. Louis, MO
Ducey, Cynthia L. ....Anchorage, AK
Ducey, Donald G. ....Detroit, MI
Ducey, Ernest D. ....Toledo, OH
Ducey, Feder & Ducey, Ltd. ....St. Louis, MO
Ducey, Marylou ....Woodbridge, NJ
Ducey, Mitchell F. ....Santa Monica, CA
Ducey, Richard V. ....Wellesley Hills, MA
Duch, John G. ....Clifton, NJ
Duch, Thomas J. ....Elmwood Park, NJ
Duchak, Joseph T. ....Brick, NJ
Duchak, Kathleen E. ....Columbus, OH
Duchardt, Frederick A., Jr. ....Kearney, MO
DuCharme & Cohen ....San Francisco, CA
Ducharme, David R. ....Coeur d'Alene, ID
Ducharme, Dennis T. ....Manchester, NH
DuCharme, Elaine G. ....Seattle, WA
Ducharme, Gerald D. ....Dearborn, MI
Ducharme, Gerald J. ....Canton, NY
DuCharme, James A. ....San Francisco, CA
DuCharme, John B. ....Clifton Park, NY
DuCharme, Kathryn L. ....Carlisle, PA
Ducharme, Kimberly O'Leary ....Anderson, IN
Ducharme, Moriarty & Turcott
Holyoke, MA
DuCharme, Nancy K. ....Chicago, IL
Ducharme, Ronald A. ....Waterville, ME
Ducharme, Sean Paul ....Richmond, VA
Ducharme, Wayne B. ....Los Angeles, CA
Ducharme, Willard C. ....Southfield, MI
DuChateau, Judith Emick ....St. Louis, MO
Duchateau, Laurie S. ....Pittsburgh, PA
Du Chateau, Richard ....Los Angeles, CA
Duchek & Buckley ....Omaha, NE
Duchek, Douglas F. ....Omaha, NE
Duchek, Susan M.
United States Postal Service, Law Department, GV
Duchelle, John W. ....Washington, DC
DuChemin & Associates ....Orlando, FL
DuChemin, Claire A. ....Tallahassee, FL
DuChemin, Claire A., P.A. ....Tallahassee, FL
Duchemin, James R. ....Eau Claire, WI
Duchemin, Matthew J. ....Milwaukee, WI
Duchemin, Michael A. ....Seattle, WA
DuChemin, Robert A. ....Orlando, FL
Duchen, Robert M. ....Englewood, CO
Duchene, Dennis A. ....Costa Mesa, CA
DuChene, Jennifer Belt ....Cleveland, OH
Duchene, Kate W. ....Los Angeles, CA
DuChene, Todd M. ....Hampton, NH
Duchene, Wade D. ....San Diego, CA
Duchenes, Terri Groen ....Minneapolis, MN
Ducheny, Denise Moreno ....San Diego, CA
Duchesne, June ....Boston, MA
Duchesneau, Peter R. ....Los Angeles, CA
DuChez, Neil A. ....Cleveland, OH
Duchin, Morris G. ....New York, NY
Duchnick, James L. ....San Diego, CA
Duchon, Darryn L. ....Indianapolis, IN
Duchovny, Daniel F. ....Washington, DC
Duchrow & Barker LLP ....Los Angeles, CA
Santa Monica, CA
Duchrow, David J. ....Santa Monica, CA
Duck, Aaron ....Sulphur, OK
Duck, Berkley W. ....Indianapolis, IN
Duck, Calhoun & Taylor ....Fairhope, AL
Duck, Emily F. ....Indianapolis, IN
Duck, John M. ....New Orleans, LA
Duck, John V. ....Fairhope, AL
Duck, John W. ....Memphis, TN
Duck, Kevin R. ....Lafayette, LA
Duck, Robert J. ....North Palm Beach, FL
Duck, Thomas S. ....Birmingham, AL
Duck, William G. ....San Francisco, CA
Duckenfield, Thomas A., III
Washington, DC
Ducker, Aubrey Harry, Jr.
Winter Park, FL
Ducker, Brian L. ....Santa Ana, CA
Ducker, Bruce ....Denver, CO
Ducker, Charles R., Jr.
Department of Commerce, Patent and Trademark Office, GV
Ducker, John L. ....Altamonte Springs, FL
Ducker, John T. ....Dayton, OH
Ducker, Montgomery & Lewis, P.C.
Denver, CO
Ducker, Richard D. ....Chapel Hill, NC
Ducker, William L. ....Purvis, MS
Duckers, David K. ....Kansas City, KS
Duckers, Edward C. ....Washington, DC
Duckers, Sarah A. ....Houston, TX
Duckett, Daniel ....Manchester, NH
Duckett, Douglas E. ....Hamilton, OH
Duckett, Gregory M. ....Memphis, TN
Duckett, James A. ....Greenville, SC
Duckett, James M. ....Little Rock, AR
Duckett, Jerome P. ....Reno, NV
Duckett, Joan ....Cambridge, MA
Duckett, L. L. ....El Campo, TX
Duckett, Michael H. ....Lafayette, IN
Duckett, Nicole M. ....Los Angeles, CA
Duckett, Tracey Lenhardt ....Washington, DC
Duckett, Virginia Lynn ....Washington, DC
Duckett, Warren B., III ....Baltimore, MD
Duckett, Warren B., Jr. ....Baltimore, MD
Duckler, Geordie ....Lake Oswego, OR
Ducklo, Robert L., III ....Memphis, TN
Duckman, Lorin M., (Mr.) ....New York, NY
Duckor, Ildiko ....New York, NY
Duckor, Michael J. ....San Diego, CA
Duckor, S. Gerald ....Loudonville, NY
Duckor Spradling & Metzger, A Law Corporation ....San Diego, CA
Duckson & Carlson, LLC
Minneapolis, MN
Duckson, Todd A. ....Minneapolis, MN
Duckstad, Jon R. ....St. Paul, MN
Duckstad, Robert J. ....Minneapolis, MN
Duckstein, Mark E. ....Newark, NJ
Duckstein, Norbert ....Chicago, IL
Duckstein, Sonja S. ....Phoenix, AZ
Duckwall, Robert H. ....Fort Myers, FL
Duckwall, Robert H., P.A.
Fort Myers, FL
Duckworth, B. Christine
Running Springs, CA
Duckworth, Brian F. ....Orlando, FL
Duckworth, Brian J. ....San Jose, CA
Duckworth, Bryce C. ....Las Vegas, NV
Duckworth, David G. ....Newport Beach, CA
Duckworth, David R. ....Dallas, TX
Duckworth, Edward G. ....Denver, CO
Duckworth, Edward Kent ....Ronan, MT
Duckworth, Edward K. Law Office, P.C
Ronan, MT
Duckworth, Frank A. ....Washington, DC
Duckworth, Gary F. ....Oklahoma City, OK
Duckworth, James T., III ....Oxford, NC
Duckworth, Kevin, & Associates
Chicago, IL
Duckworth, Kevin B. ....Chicago, IL
Duckworth, Liza B. ....Pasadena, CA
Duckworth, Marvin E. ....Des Moines, IA
Duckworth, Michael E. ....Phoenix, AZ
Duckworth, Pamela A. ....Boston, MA
Duckworth, R. Demarest, III
New York, NY
Duckworth, Robert W. ....Orlando, FL
Duckworth, Russel B. ....Charlotte, NC
Duckworth, Thomas E.
San Francisco, CA
Duckworth, Timothy J. ....Bethlehem, PA
Duckworth, V. Denise ....Dallas, TX
Duckworth, Vincent L. ....Lima, OH
Duckworth, William F. ....Columbus, OH
Duckworth, William H., Jr.
Jonesboro, GA
Ducley, Richard E. ....San Rafael, CA
Duclos, Catherine F. ....Atlanta, GA
Duclos, Suzanne L. ....Rockville, MD
Duclos, Todd A. ....Evanston, IL
Ducloux, Claude E. ....Austin, TX
Ducloux, Philip R. ....Bastrop, TX
Ducmanis, Ruth Ann ....Bay City, MI
Duco, Bernard A., Jr. ....St. Louis, MO
Ducoff & Chanon ....Houston, TX
Ducoff, Ronni Elise ....Cleveland, OH
Ducoff, Russell C. ....Bellaire, TX
DuComb, Anthony W. ....Burlingame, CA
Ducomb, Darby N. ....Seattle, WA
DuComb, Robert J., Jr. ....Phoenix, AZ
Ducommun, Steven E. ....Chicago, IL
Ducore, Daniel P.
Federal Trade Commission, Bureau of Competition, GV
Ducote, Andre F. ....Jackson, MS
Ducote, Daniel C. ....Beaumont, TX
DuCote, Harold A., Jr. ....Costa Mesa, CA
Ducote, Keith A. ....San Jose, CA
Ducote, Monte J. ....New Orleans, LA
Ducote, Wayne C. ....New Orleans, LA
Ducre, Julian I. ....San Dimas, CA
DuCroz, Charles L. ....Houston, TX
Ducworth, George M. ....Anderson, SC
Duczer, Stephen A. ....Slidell, LA
Duczkowski, Donald E. ....Cheboygan, MI
Duczynski, John M. ....Chicago, IL
Duczynski, Margaret S. ....Chicago, IL
Duda, Anthony G. ....Oak Brook, IL
Duda, Donald A., Jr. ....Hubbard, OH
Duda, Francis X. ....St. Louis, MO
Duda, Frederick R. ....Moraga, CA
Duda, Frederick R., P.C. ....Moraga, CA
Duda, Fritz L. ....Dallas, TX
Duda, James C. ....Springfield, MA
Duda, James T. ....Homewood, IL
Duda, John E., (Co., L.P.A.) ....Cleveland, OH
Duda, John P. ....Hollywood, FL
Duda, Lisa A. ....Philadelphia, PA
Duda, Mary Beth ....Jewett City, CT
Duda, Nicholas, Jr. ....Clearwater, FL
Duda, Paul E. ....Syracuse, NY
Duda, Philip M. ....Wilbraham, MA
Duda, Richard J. ....Jewett City, CT
Duda, Richard J., P.C. ....Jewett City, CT
Duda, Terrie-Anne ....Voorhees, NJ
Duda, Thomas A. ....St. Louis, MO
Duda, Thomas W. ....Arlington Heights, IL
Chicago, IL
Duda-Chapman, Tracy ....Oviedo, FL
Dudas, David G. ....Appleton, WI
Dudas, Jonathan W.
House of Representatives, Committee Legal Personnel, GV
Dudash, Mark J. ....Pittsburgh, PA
Dudda, Barbara S. ....Toledo, OH
Dudden, Michelle Leigh ....Palmyra, VA
Dudden, Richard A. ....Ogallala, NE
Dudderar, Frederick A., Jr. ....Duluth, MN
Dudderer, John R., Jr. ....Westminster, MD
Duddlesten, Kevin M. ....Phoenix, AZ
Duddleston, David J. ....Minneapolis, MN
Duddy, Christina C. ....Boston, MA
Duddy, Helene ....Beach Haven, NJ
Duddy, Martin J. ....Syosset, NY
Duddy, Michael A. ....Augusta, ME
Bangor, ME
Duddy, R. Terrance ....Portland, ME
Duddy, Roy A. ....Bedford, NH
Dude, Cornelia ....New York, NY
Dude, Cynthia Mace ....Colorado Springs, CO
Dude, William Kelly
Colorado Springs, CO
Dudeck, Arlene Ann ....Johnstown, PA
Dudeck, John A., Jr. ....Department of Justice, Tax Division, GV
Dudeck, Ronald D. ....Johnstown, PA
Dudek, Andrea M. ....Chicago, IL
Dudek, Brian P. ....Braintree, MA
Dudek, Charles J. ....Windsor, CT
Dudek, Frederick M. ....San Diego, CA
Dudek, Gregory J. ....Buffalo, NY
Dudek, Jean K. ....Washington, DC
Dudek, Lawrence M. ....Detroit, MI
Dudek, Michael J., (P.C.) ....Chicago, IL
Dudek, Nancy Kay ....Los Angeles, CA
Dudek, Patricia E. Kefalas ....Troy, MI
Dudek, Paul M.
Securities and Exchange Commission, Division of Corporation Finance, GV
Dudek, Richard T. ....Sacramento, CA
Dudek, Robert A. ....Milwaukee, WI
Duden, Christine E. ....Edwardsville, IL
Duden, H. Richard, III ....Lanham, MD

Duden, Nancy McCutchan ... Annapolis, MD
Duden, Paul R. ... Portland, OR
Dudenbostel, Rayburn K. ... Elma, WA
Dudenhefer, Frank C., Jr. ... New Orleans, LA
Dudensing, Carl ... Houston, TX
Dudensing, Edward P. ... Sacramento, CA
Dudensing and Webb ... Houston, TX
Duderstadt, Janet F. ... Pittsburgh, PA
Dudgeon, David M. ... Boca Raton, FL
Dudgeon, John M. ... Lakewood, CO
Dudgeon, Laurie K. ... Lexington, KY
Dudgeon, Thomas C. ... Oak Brook, IL
Dudick, Chester F., Jr. ... Wilkes-Barre, PA
Dudick, Decker & Shovlin, P.C.
Wilkes-Barre, PA
Dudik, Betty E. ... Silver Spring, MD
Dudik, Duane A. ... Pittsburgh, PA
Dudine, William F., III ... New York, NY
Dudine, William F., Jr. ... New York, NY
Dudinyak, Richard G. ... Freeland, PA
Dudis, John B., Jr. ... Kalispell, MT
Dudkowski, Alyssa A. ... Chicago, IL
Dudley, Adriane J.
Charlotte Amalie, St. Thomas, VI
Dudley, Arthur, II ... Detroit, MI
Dudley, B. Dane ... Hartford, CT
Dudley, Bruce K. ... Louisville, KY
Dudley, Carter G. ... Oklahoma City, OK
Dudley, Charles F. ... Provincetown, MA
Dudley, Charles Frederick
Tallahassee, FL
Dudley, Chas. D. ... Oklahoma City, OK
Dudley, Christina G. ... Richmond, VA
Dudley, Clarence R. ... Birmingham, AL
Dudley Clark & Chan
Christiansted, St. Croix, VI
Charlotte Amalie, St. Thomas, VI
Dudley, D. Dennis ... Lansing, MI
Dudley, D. Michael ... East Lansing, MI
Dudley, Danny L. ... Des Moines, IA
Dudley, David A. ... Lincoln, NE
Dudley, David L. ... Reston, VA
Dudley, David R. ... Albany, NY
Dudley, D. Michael ... Lansing, MI
Dudley, Dudley & Windle ... El Paso, TX
Dudley, Dwight R. ... St. Petersburg, FL
Dudley, Earl C., Jr. ... Charlottesville, VA
Dudley, Edward R. ... New York, NY
Dudley, Everett H., Jr., (P.A.)
Boca Raton, FL
Dudley, Frank S., Jr. ... Queenstown, MD
Dudley, Fred B. ... Englewood, CO
Dudley, Frederick R. ... Bonita Springs, FL
Dudley, Galumbeck & Necessary
Bland, VA
Bluefield, VA
Tazewell, VA
Wytheville, VA
Dudley, George E. ... Louisville, KY
Dudley, George H. T.
Charlotte Amalie, St. Thomas, VI
Dudley, Godfrey D.
Equal Employment Opportunity
Commission,
Office of Federal Operations, GV
Dudley, Gordon E. ... Phoenix, AZ
Dudley, J. Jeffrey ... Portland, OR
Dudley, J. Matthew ... Waukegan, IL
Dudley, Jacqueline Marie ... Riverhead, NY
Dudley, James B. ... Ellicott City, MD
Dudley, James B. ... Metuchen, NJ
Dudley, James C. ... Silverdale, WA
Dudley, James H. ... Comanche, TX
Dudley, James W. ... Bluefield, VA
Dudley, Jane Saindon ... Washington, DC
Dudley, Janet ... Redwood City, CA
Dudley, Joan D. ... Farmington Hills, MI
Dudley, John A. ... Washington, DC
Dudley, John Henry, Jr. ... Ann Arbor, MI
Detroit, MI
Dudley, Jonathan H. ... Milwaukee, WI
Dudley, Joseph J., Jr. ... St. Paul, MN
Dudley, Joseph J., Sr. ... St. Paul, MN
Dudley, Joseph P. ... New Smyrna Beach, FL
Dudley, Joyce E. ... Santa Barbara, CA
Dudley, Julia C. ... Roanoke, VA
Dudley, Karen A. ... St. Paul, MN
Dudley, Kathie Blackman ... Bloomington, IL
Dudley, Kathryn L. ... St. Louis, MO
Dudley, L. Ragan ... Statesville, NC
Dudley, Leslie S. ... Bridgton, ME
Dudley, Mark K. ... Indianapolis, IN
Dudley, Mark Z. ... Palo Alto, CA
Wilmington, DE
Dudley, Marshall N. ... Guilford, CT
Dudley, Mary K. McMahon
Downers Grove, IL
Dudley, Matthew G. ... San Francisco, CA
Dudley, Nathaniel J. ... Boston, MA
Dudley, Patrick A. ... Buffalo, NY
Dudley, Paul W. ... Portland, OR
Dudley, Paul W. ... El Paso, TX
Dudley, Penni A. ... Atlanta, GA
Dudley, Remmel H. ... Falls Church, VA
Dudley, Richard O. ... Indianapolis, IN
Dudley, Robert J. ... Miami, FL
Dudley, Robert W. ... Park Ridge, IL
Dudley, Ronald T., Jr. ... Birmingham, AL
Dudley, Sharon King ... Baltimore, MD
Dudley, Sharon King, P.A. ... Baltimore, MD
Dudley and Smith, A Professional Association ... St. Paul, MN
Dudley, Stewart R. ... Birmingham, AL
Dudley, Susan A. ... Wethersfield, CT
Dudley, Thomas D., Jr. ... East Lansing, MI
Dudley, Thomas E., III ... Greenville, SC
Dudley, Thomas M., Jr. ... Portsmouth, NH
Dudley, Timothy O. ... Little Rock, AR

Dudley, Topper and Feuerzeig
Christiansted, St. Croix, VI
Charlotte Amalie, St. Thomas, VI
Dudley, Vincent B. ... Cleveland, OH
Dudley, Waller T. ... McLean, VA
Dudley, William A. ... Raleigh, NC
Dudley, William A. ... Corpus Christi, TX
Dudley, William C. ... Vancouver, WA
Dudley, William C. (Pat) ... El Paso, TX
Dudley, William H. ... Americus, GA
Dudley, William M. ... Denver, CO
Dudley, William R. ... Toms River, NJ
Dudley, Yvette V. ... South Ozone Park, NY
Dudman, Jan M. ... Santa Ana, CA
Dudman, Matthew P. ... Sacramento, CA
Dudman, Paul W. ... Oklahoma City, OK
Dudney, Doris A. ... Tampa, FL
Dudney, Margaret H. ... Chattanooga, TN
Dudnick, Andrew L. ... San Francisco, CA
Dudnick, Carol Lee ... Danbury, CT
Dudnick Detwiler Rivin & Stikker LLP
San Francisco, CA
Dudnik, Robert M. ... Los Angeles, CA
Dudor, Walter J. ... Northridge, CA
Dudrey, John ... Portland, OR
Dudugjian & Maxey, A Law Corporation
Roseville, CA
Dudugjian, Robert P. ... Roseville, CA
Dudukovich, James A. ... Atlanta, GA
Dudula-Salkowski, Patrice
Charlton City, MA
Dudum, Richard M. ... San Francisco, CA
Dudyshyn, Denise M. ... New York, NY
Dudziak, Emile ... Wakefield, MA
Dudziak, Ralph P. ... Chicago, IL
Dudzic, Paul F. ... Chicago, IL
Dudzik, Carol J. ... Western Springs, IL
Dudzik, Carolyn M. ... Raleigh, NC
Dudzik, Christine A. ... Chicago, IL
Dudzik, Darrell S. ... Chicago, IL
Dudzik, Joseph A., Jr. ... Adelphi, MD
Dudzinski, Chester A. ... Pittsburgh, PA
Dudzinsky, William S., Jr.
Washington, DC
Due, Barbara K. ... Milwaukee, WI
Due, Brian G. ... Norridge, IL
Dué, Caballero, Price & Guidry, (A Professional Association)
Baton Rouge, LA
Due, Danford R. ... Indianapolis, IN
Due, Lydia Charlotte ... Dallas, TX
Due, Mary Jane C. ... United States Senate,
Senatorial Assistants, GV
Dué, Paul H. ... Baton Rouge, LA
Due, Robert W. ... Minneapolis, MN
Duea, Bradford David ... Los Angeles, CA
Duebbert, Ronald R. ... Belleville, IL
Duebbert, Victoria M. ... Cedarburg, WI
Dueber, Thomas L. ... Greeley, CO
Duechle, Gary P. ... Fort Wayne, IN
Duecker, Stephanie Michelle ... McKinney, TX
Duecy, Charles M. ... Tempe, AZ
Duedall, Mark I. ... Atlanta, GA
Dueffert, Paul K. ... Washington, DC
Dueholm, James A. ... Minneapolis, MN
Duehr, Victoria M. ... Brookings, SD
Dueker, Alice K. ... Camden, NJ
Dueker, Jane E. ... St. Louis, MO
Dueker, John J. ... St. Louis, MO
Duel, Arthur B., III ... Greenwich, CT
Duell, Andrew J. ... New York, NY
Duell, Charles M. ... Fayetteville, AR
Duell, Delmar A. ... San Jose, CA
Duell, Diana Blackman ... Fayetteville, AR
Duell, Diane L. ... Richmond, VA
Duell, Emery C. ... Montvale, NJ
Duell, Joan K. Harty ... Syracuse, NY
Duell, Kim L. ... Hartford, CT
Duell, Mark E. ... Columbus, OH
Duell, Richard C., III ... Birmingham, AL
Duell, Robert L. ... Syracuse, NY
Duell, Teresa K. ... Fountain Valley, CA
Duell, Yearout & Spina, P.C.
Birmingham, AL
Duell-Cazes, Tracy L. ... San Jose, CA
Duellman, Clark J. ... Irvine, CA
Duelly, Elizabeth Anne ... Newark, NJ
Duemler, R. Leigh ... Bonita Springs, FL
New York, NY
Duemling, Arnold H. ... Fort Wayne, IN
Duemmler, Frank L. ... Stamford, CT
Duenas, Andrea Hall ... Charleston, SC
Duenas, Cristobal C. ... Hagåtña, GU
Dueno, David D. ... New York, NY
Duenow, Christopher J.
San Luis Obispo, CA
Duenow, James M. ... San Luis Obispo, CA
Duenow, James M., A Law Corporation
San Luis Obispo, CA
Duenser, Mark W. ... Houston, TX
Duenser, Ruth E. ... Houston, TX
Duensing, Emily Y. ... Tulsa, OK
Duensing, Margaret A., (P.C.)
Charlotte Amalie, St. Thomas, VI
Duensing, Matthew J., (P.C.)
Charlotte Amalie, St. Thomas, VI
Duepner, John J., Jr. ... Clayton, MO
Duer, A. Adgate ... Baltimore, MD
Duer, D. Holbrook ... Lancaster, PA
Duer, Donna D. ... Department of Justice,
Environment and Natural Resources
Division, GV
Duer, E. McMaster ... Princess Anne, MD
Duer, Philip W. ... Nashville, TN
Duerbeck, Charles A. ... San Bernardino, CA
Duerbeck, Heidi B. ... New York, NY
Duerden, Suzanne K. ... San Rafael, CA
Duerinck, Kevin F. ... Deerfield, IL

Dueringer, Christopher L.
Santa Monica, CA
Dueringer, William J. ... Gibson City, IL
Duerksen, Darla K. ... Fresno, CA
Duerksen, William ... San Diego, CA
Duerr, Charles A., Jr. ... Ann Arbor, MI
Duerr, Douglas H. ... Atlanta, GA
Duerr, Finn F. ... Decatur, GA
Duerr, Keith D. ... Louisville, KY
Duerr, Patrick T. ... Detroit, MI
Duerr, Rhonda Denise ... Barbourville, KY
Duerr, Richard E., Jr. ... Memphis, TN
Duerr, Robert K. ... North Tonawanda, NY
Duerr, Stephen R. ... Jackson, WY
Duerr, William Christopher
King Of Prussia, PA
Duerre, Blake W. ... Minneapolis, MN
Duerre, Ralph E. ... Anchorage, AK
Duerring, Burton C. ... Pittsburgh, PA
Duerson and Duerson ... Berea, KY
Duerson, Guy K., Jr. ... Berea, KY
Duerson, Kendall L. ... Berea, KY
Duerst, Jonathan R. ... Bend, OR
Dues, Theodore R., Jr. ... Charleston, WV
Dues, Wilfrid G. ... Eaton, OH
Duesberry, Philip T. ... Norman, OK
Duescher, Gary ... Newark, NJ
Duesdieker, George S. ... San Mateo, CA
Duesenberg, John R. ... Englewood, CO
Duesenberg, Mark H. ... Washington, DC
Duesenberg, Robert H. ... Falls Church, VA
Duesing, Christopher A. ... Milwaukee, WI
Duesing, Jerome A. ... Cincinnati, OH
Duesing, Steven J. ... Las Vegas, NV
Duesler, Donald W., & Associates
Beaumont, TX
Duesler, Thomas W. ... Beaumont, TX
Duessel, Nancy Figg ... Dallas, TX
Duesterdick, Paul S. ... Albany, NY
Duesterhaus, Joseph A. ... Quincy, IL
Duet, Keith P. ... Mandeville, LA
Duett, Blanche A. ... Houston, TX
Duettra, Andrew W. ... Dallas, TX
Duey, Joseph G. ... Baltimore, MD
Duez, David J. ... Chicago, IL
Dufallo, Paul J. ... Pottsville, PA
DuFauchard, Preston P.
San Francisco, CA
DuFault, David T. ... Charlotte, NC
Dufault, Douglas C., Jr. ... Providence, RI
Dufault & Dufault ... New London, NH
Dufault, Larry Bernard ... New London, NH
Dufault, Mary Louise ... New London, NH
Dufault, Michael S. ... Department of Justice,
Civil Division, GV
Dufault, Paul E. ... Royal Oak, MI
Dufek, Penny J. ... Anchorage, AK
Dufek, Robert A. ... Washington, DC
Dufendach, Carl W. ... Grand Rapids, MI
Duff, Alec ... Seattle, WA
Duff, Alicia M. ... Boston, MA
Duff, Amy H. ... Costa Mesa, CA
Los Angeles, CA
Duff, Andrea Eva ... Framingham, MA
Duff, Andrew R. ... Akron, OH
Duff, Barbara A. ... Denver, CO
Duff, Brian ... Jersey City, NJ
Duff, Brian Barnett ... Chicago, IL
Duff & Brown ... Miami, FL
Duff, Bruce F. ... Bellevue, WA
Duff, Candace R. ... Miami, FL
Duff, Charles H. ... Great Falls, VA
Duff, Clair V. ... Pittsburgh, PA
Duff, Daniel ... Washington, DC
Duff, Daniel V., III ... New York, NY
Duff, Daniel V., Jr. ... New York, NY
Duff, David A. ... New York, NY
Duff, David H., (P.C.) ... Palo Alto, CA
Duff, David L. ... Fairfax, VA
Duff, David L., P.C. ... Fairfax, VA
Duff, David T. ... Columbia, SC
Duff, David W. ... Warren, OH
Duff, Donald ... Frankfort, KY
Duff, Dubberly, Turner, White & Boykin, L.L.C. ... Columbia, SC
Duff, Edwin H., III ... Daytona Beach, FL
Duff, Ellar ... Edwardsville, IL
Duff, Ernest Ray ... Columbia, MS
Duff, F. Ellen ... Chicago, IL
Duff, Frank X. ... Wheeling, WV
Duff, George M., III ... San Francisco, CA
Duff, George M., Jr. ... Fishkill, NY
Duff, Gerald P. ... St. Clairsville, OH
Duff, Gordon J. ... Sacramento, CA
Duff, Gregory J. ... Seattle, WA
Duff, H. Thompson ... Bluffton, OH
Duff, Howard ... Woodbridge, NJ
Duff, James C. ...
Supreme Court Of The United States, GV
Duff, James C. ... Pittsburgh, PA
Duff, James H. ... Detroit, MI
Duff, James, P.C. ... Washington, DC
Duff, James T. ... Los Angeles, CA
Duff, Jane L. ... Fort Lauderdale, FL
Duff, Jerome J. ... St. Louis, MO
Duff, Jerome J., & Associates, P.C.
St. Louis, MO
Duff, John F. ... San Francisco, CA
Duff, John F. ... Boston, MA
Duff, John M., Jr. ... San Francisco, CA
Duff, Johnette S. ... Houston, TX
Duff, Karl J. ... Kennesaw, GA
Duff, Kevin B. ... Chicago, IL
Duff, Larry R. ... Rupert, ID
Duff, Leo W. ... Cortland, OH
Duff, Lydia Belknap ... Baltimore, MD
Duff, Mary Elizabeth ... Richmond, TX
Duff, Michael A. ... Reading, PA

Duff, Michael C. ... Philadelphia, PA
Duff, Michael J. ... Lorain, OH
Duff, Michael J. ... Alexandria, VA
Duff, Michael O. ... Los Angeles, CA
Duff, Nancy H. ... Boston, MA
Duff, Patrick M. ... Portland, MI
Duff, Renée L. ... Scarsdale, NY
Duff, Robert H. ... Melbourne, FL
Duff, Robert P. ... Detroit, MI
Duff, Ronald B. ... Grand Junction, CO
Duff, Susan Droppleman ... Tampa, FL
Duff, Thomas J. ... Des Moines, IA
Duff, Timothy J. ... Denver, CO
Duff, Timothy J. ... Cleveland, OH
Duff, Virginia E. ... Ferris, TX
Duff, William B. ... New York, NY
Duff & Zinser, L.L.C. ... Denver, CO
Duffack, William C., Jr. ... Tallahassee, FL
Duffala, Donald P. ... San Francisco, CA
Duffalo, Deidra L. ... Fort Washington, PA
Duffalo, Jan H. ... New York, NY
Duffee, Cecil G. ... Birmingham, AL
Duffee, David K. ... New York, NY
Duffee, Lisa Greenwood ... Dallas, TX
Duffee, Michael W. ... Chicago, IL
Duffee, Robert T. ... West Palm Beach, FL
Duffell, David K. ... Providence, RI
Duffett, Benton S., III ... Alexandria, VA
Duffett, Benton S., Jr. ... Alexandria, VA
Duffett, David J. ... Alexandria, VA
Duffett, Henry P. ... Ormond Beach, FL
Duffett, Kathleen ... New York, NY
Duffett, Neale A. ... Portland, ME
Duffett, Paul A. ... Ormond Beach, FL
Duffett, Robert J. ... Falls Church, VA
Duffey, Aubrey G. ... Carrollton, GA
Duffey, Brian C. ... Boston, MA
New York, NY
Duffey, Claudia ... Boca Raton, FL
Duffey & Dolan, P.A. ... Sarasota, FL
Duffey & Duffey ... Rome, GA
Boca Raton, FL
Duffey, Gregg A. ... Houston, TX
Duffey, Harl C., III ... Rome, GA
Duffey, Harl C., Jr. ... Rome, GA
Duffey, Jeffery C. ... Montgomery, AL
Duffey, John C. ... Lafayette, IN
Duffey, John J. ... Worthington, OH
Duffey, Joseph P. ... Milwaukee, WI
Duffey Law Office, S.C. ... Milwaukee, WI
Duffey, Lynne Plum ... Chicago, IL
Duffey, Martin P. ... Philadelphia, PA
Duffey, Mary S. ... Columbus, OH
Duffey, Melissa C. ... Atlanta, GA
Duffey, Michael M. ... Van Nuys, CA
Duffey, Richard J., Jr. ... Muskegon, MI
Duffey, Robert Michael ... Washington, DC
Duffey, Samuel S. ... Sarasota, FL
Duffey, Sean N. ... Milwaukee, WI
Duffey, Thomas E. ... Concord, MA
Duffey, Thomas J. ... Milwaukee, WI
Duffey, Thomas J., Jr. ... Milwaukee, WI
Duffey, Walter E. ... Huntsville, AL
Duffey, William E., Jr. ... Brownsville, TN
Duffey, William S., Jr. ... Atlanta, GA
Dufficy, Ann B. ... Richmond Hill, NY
Dufficy, James J. ... Santa Ana, CA
Dufficy, Michael B. ... San Rafael, CA
Dufficy, Thomas J. ... Harrison, NY
Dufficy, Timothy J. ... Jamaica, NY
Duffie, Elbert O., III ... Walterboro, SC
Duffie, Jerry R. ... Lemoyne, PA
Duffie, L. Traywick ... Atlanta, GA
Duffie, Mark C. ... Lemoyne, PA
Duffie, Rebecca ... Colonial Heights, VA
Duffie, Virgil W., III ... Columbia, SC
Duffie, Virgil W., Jr. ... Columbia, SC
Duffield, Anne E. ... Dallas, TX
Duffield, Brigid A. ... Glen Ellyn, IL
Duffield, Edward H.
Research Triangle Park, NC
Duffield, George C. ... Venice, FL
Duffield, Kathleen V. ... Atlanta, GA
Duffield, L. David ... Huntington, WV
Duffield Law Firm ... Huntington, WV
Duffield, Lisa G. ... Dallas, TX
Duffield, R. Bruce ... Chicago, IL
Duffield, Richard ... Green Valley, AZ
Tucson, AZ
Duffield, Theodore T. ... Des Moines, IA
Duffield, Thomas A. ... Decatur, IL
Duffield, Young, Adamson & Alfred, P.C.
Green Valley, AZ
Tucson, AZ
Duffin, David D. ... Cherry Hill, NJ
Philadelphia, PA
Duffin, Francis J. ... New Haven, CT
Duffin, Gene R. ... Goshen, IN
Duffin, John P. ... Toledo, OH
Duffin, M. Patrick ... Idaho Falls, ID
Duffin, Ryan G. ... Indianapolis, IN
Duffin, Thomas A. ... Salt Lake City, UT
Duffin, William E. ... Milwaukee, WI
Duffis, Kevin A. ... Los Angeles, CA
Duffley, Peter J. ... Raleigh, NC
Duffly, Fernande R. V. ... Boston, MA
Duffner, John T. ... Marco, FL
Duffney, Charles L., Jr. ... Rockville, MD
Dufford & Brown, P.C.
Colorado Springs, CO
Denver, CO
Dufford, Philip G. ... Denver, CO
Dufford, Waldeck, Milburn & Krohn, L.L.P.
Grand Junction, CO
Duffus & Associates, P.A. ... Fayetteville, NC
Greenville, NC
Raleigh, NC
Duffus, J. David, Jr. ... Greenville, NC

Dugard, Gregory G. ... **Chicago, IL**
Dugard, Thomas M. ... **Chicago, IL**
Dugas, Clay, Law Offices of ... Orange, TX
Dugas, Clifton M., III ... **Dallas, TX**
Dugas, David R. ... **Lafayette, LA**
New Iberia, LA
Dugas, Evin G. ... **Houston, TX**
Dugas, Floyd J. ... **Milford, CT**
Dugas, Francis F. ... Thibodaux, LA
Dugas & Inselmann, P.C. ... **Houston, TX**
Dugas, John L. ... **Baton Rouge, LA**
Dugas, Joseph E., Jr. ... New Orleans, LA
Dugas, Julian R. ... Washington, DC
Dugas, Karen Eddlemon ... Plaquemine, LA
Dugas, Malcolm J., Jr. ... Donaldsonville, LA
Dugas, Michael C. ... Treasury Department, Office of the Comptroller of the Currency, GV
Dugas, Stephen L. ... Hollidaysburg, PA
Dugas, Steven J. ... Marblehead, MA
Dugas, Thomas F. ... **Greenville, SC**
Dugas, Troy M. ... Baton Rouge, LA
Dugat, William D., III ... **Austin, TX**
Dugaw, Paul J. ... Centralia, WA
Dugdale, Bradley E., Sr. ... **Havre, MT**
Dugdale, James R ... San Francisco, CA
Dugdale, Jeff S. ... **Denver, CO**
Dugdale, John ... **Dallas, TX**
Dugdale, Robert B. ... Eugene, OR
Duggan, Andrew Thomas ... Purchase, NY
Duggan, Anne F. ... Pittsburgh, PA
Duggan, Barbara J. ... **San Jose, CA**
Duggan, Ben O., Jr. ... Chattanooga, TN
Duggan, Caccavaro & Ciapciak
East Hartford, CT
Boston, MA
Norwood, MA
Providence, RI
Duggan, Catherine ... San Francisco, CA
Duggan, Catherine F. ... **New York, NY**
Duggan, Charles S. ... **New York, NY**
Duggan, Christopher A. ... **Boston, MA**
Duggan, Clifford E. ... Merrillville, IN
Duggan, Crotty & Dunn, P.C.
New Windsor, NY
Duggan, Dan W., Jr. ... Brandon, MS
Duggan, Daniel S. ... **Denver, CO**
Duggan, David G. ... **Chicago, IL**
Duggan, David R. ... **Maryville, TN**
Duggan, Deborah A. ... Oakland, CA
Duggan, Dennis M., Jr. (P.C.) ... **Boston, MA**
Duggan, Dennis R. ... **Vancouver, WA**
Duggan, Edmund A. ... San Rafael, CA
Duggan, Edward J. ... **Boston, MA**
Duggan, Eileen C. ... **New London, CT**
Duggan, Francis A. ... Atlanta, GA
Duggan, Francis J. ... **Washington, DC**
Duggan, Francis J. ... **Worcester, MA**
Duggan, George ... Newark, NJ
Duggan, I. Stewart ... **Rome, GA**
Duggan, J. James ... **Charleston, SC**
Duggan, J. Robert, (P.A.) ... **Leesburg, FL**
Duggan, James E. ... Carbondale, IL
Duggan, James E. ... Concord, NH
Duggan, James F. ... Toledo, OH
Duggan, James G. ... Lake Forest, IL
Duggan, James J. ... **Buffalo, NY**
Duggan, James T. ... **Buffalo, NY**
Duggan, James Thomas ... Carmel, NY
Duggan, Jennifer E. ... **Sacramento, CA**
Duggan, Jeremiah J. ... Roswell, GA
Duggan, John B. ... **Greer, SC**
Duggan, John C. ... Boca Raton, FL
Duggan, John E. ... Anchorage, AK
Duggan, John F. ... **Norwich, CT**
Duggan, John F. ... Harrisburg, PA
Duggan, John J. ... Woodbridge, NJ
Duggan, John M. ... Kansas City, MO
Duggan, John P. ... **Aurora, IL**
Duggan, John P. ... Seattle, WA
Duggan, John Peter ... Red Bank, NJ
Duggan, John R. ... Dedham, MA
Duggan, Karen L. ... **Leawood, KS**
Duggan, Kathleen G. ... New York, NY
Duggan, Kathleen M. ... Redwood City, CA
Duggan, Kevin G. ... Sarasota, FL
Duggan, Kristen K. ... **Atlanta, GA**
Duggan, Lee, Jr. ... Houston, TX
Duggan, Lisa M. ... **Washington, DC**
Duggan, Lynch & Fons, S.C. ... Greenfield, WI
Duggan, Mark J. ... **Boston, MA**
Duggan, Marsha M. ... Chula Vista, CA
Duggan, Mary Ann ... West Palm Beach, FL
Duggan, Michael C. ... Los Angeles, CA
Duggan, Michael C. ... Seattle, WA
Duggan, Michael E. ... Caldwell, ID
Duggan, Michael F., The Law Office of
Christiana, DE
Duggan, Michael J. ... Chicago, IL
Duggan, Michael J. ... Hinsdale, IL
Duggan, Michael J. ... North Attleboro, MA
Duggan, Moira Clare ... **Philadelphia, PA**
Duggan, Patrick J. ... Detroit, MI
Duggan, Patrick M. ... **St. Louis, MO**
Duggan, Patrick O. ... Saginaw, MI
Duggan, Paul Hanley ... Bryan, OH
Duggan, Powell Lawson ... **Warrenton, VA**
Duggan, Richard E. ... Cotuit, MA
Duggan, Richard E. ... Horseshoe Bay, TX
Duggan, Robert ... **Boston, MA**
Duggan, Robert B., Jr. ... Catlettsburg, KY
Duggan, Robert D. ... **Seattle, WA**
Duggan, Robert J. ... St. Helena, CA
Duggan, Robert N. ... Miami, FL
Duggan, Rose L. ... Portland, ME
Duggan Schlotfeldt & Welch PLLC
Vancouver, WA
Duggan, Scott F. ... **Boston, MA**

Duggan, Shadwick & Doerr, P.C.
Kansas City, MO
Duggan, Sharon E. ... San Francisco, CA
Duggan, Sheila ... **New York, NY**
Duggan, Stacy L. ... Pittsburgh, PA
Duggan, Stephen A. ... **Manchester, NH**
Duggan, Stephen J. ... Santa Rosa, CA
Duggan, Stephen P. ... New York, NY
Duggan, Stephen P., III ... New Windsor, NY
Duggan, Tara A. ... **Englewood Cliffs, NJ**
Duggan, Thomas E. ... New York, NY
Duggan, Thomas G. ... Milwaukee, WI
Duggan, Thomas M.
San Luis Obispo, CA
Duggan, Timothy E. ... Springfield, IL
Duggan, Timothy J. ... **Norwood, MA**
Duggan, Timothy P. ... Jefferson City, MO
Duggan, Timothy P. ... **Princeton, NJ**
Duggan, Virginia S. ... Daly City, CA
Duggan, W. Dennis ... Albany, NY
Duggan, Wendy M. ... **Casa Grande, AZ**
Duggan, William H., Jr.
East Hampton, NY
Duggan, William, Jr. ... Stamford, CT
Duggan, William, Jr. ... Detroit, MI
Duggan, Wyman R. ... **Jacksonville, FL**
Duggar, Bruce R. ... Jacksonville, FL
Duggar, Elaine N. ... **Tallahassee, FL**
Duggar, Rolfe D. ... St. Petersburg, FL
Duggar, Rolfe D., P.A. ... St. Petersburg, FL
Dugger, Ashley P. ... Kansas City, MO
Dugger & Associates ... **Houston, TX**
Dugger & Cole ... **Elizabethton, TN**
Dugger, Cynthia Shdeed
Oklahoma City, OK
Dugger, Darin D. ... **Kansas City, MO**
Dugger, Donna Marie ... Tallahassee, FL
Dugger, Gary W. ... **Houston, TX**
Dugger, George F., Jr. ... **Elizabethton, TN**
Dugger, Glen A. ... **Columbus, OH**
Dugger, Jas. W. ... Wichita Falls, TX
Dugger, Jay E. ... **Hampton, VA**
Dugger, Jessica Dawn ... **Lebanon, TN**
Dugger, Jill Barron ... **Orlando, FL**
Dugger, John F., Jr. ... Morristown, TN
Dugger, John L. ... Nashville, TN
Dugger, Kathryn J. ... **Elizabethton, TN**
Dugger, Llezelle Agustin ... Charlottesville, VA
Dugger, Mark S. ... **Elizabethton, TN**
Dugger, Richard L. ... Lawton, OK
Dugger, Robert Keith ... **Kansas City, MO**
Dugger, Terry D. ... **Little Rock, AR**
Dugger, Virgil E. ... Portland, OR
Dugger, William D. ... Chickasha, OK
Duggin, Marshall E. ... Woodbury, TN
Duggin, Sarah H. ... Washington, DC
Duggins, David C. ... **Austin, TX**
Duggins, David D. ... **New Orleans, LA**
Duggins, J. Nathan, III ... **Greensboro, NC**
Duggins, James N., Jr. ... **Greensboro, NC**
Duggins, Ralph ... Jefferson City, MO
Duggins, Ralph H. ... **Fort Worth, TX**
Duggins, Robert E. ... **Raleigh, NC**
Duggins, Stephen S. ... Chattanooga, TN
Dughi and Hewit, A Professional Corporation ... **Cranford, NJ**
Marlton, NJ
Dughi, Louis John, Jr. ... **Cranford, NJ**
Marlton, NJ
Dughi, Robert L. ... Parsippany, NJ
Dughie, John V. ... Kalamazoo, MI
Dugi, Aimee ... **Dallas, TX**
Dugic, Melody Gazda ... Youngstown, OH
Duginger, Robert E. ... **Irvine, CA**
Duginski, Michael J. ... Milwaukee, WI
Dugo, Dominic I. ... San Diego, CA
Dugoni, Cristina Kapela ... **Seattle, WA**
Dugoni, Laurence P. ... **Redwood City, CA**
Dugoni, Lisa M. ... **San Mateo, CA**
Dugoni, Lisa M., P.C., Law Offices of
San Jose, CA
San Mateo, CA
Dugovics, Jill T. ... Cleveland, OH
Duguay, Paul Allan ... Caledonia, MI
Duh, Ernest F. ... Phillipsburg, NJ
Duh, Ernest F., A Professional Corporation
Phillipsburg, NJ
Duh, William A. ... Hellertown, PA
Duhaime, Amanda Conti ... **Troy, MI**
Duhaime, Diane ... **Hartford, CT**
Duhaime, Paul J. ... Troy, MI
Duhaime, William E. ... Medford, OR
Duhamel, D. Ty ... Wenatchee, WA
Duhamel, Diane D. ... **Glastonbury, CT**
Duhamel, Marcel C. ... **Cleveland, OH**
Duhamel, Nadine M. ... **New York, NY**
Duhamel & Schoolcraft LLC
Glastonbury, CT
Hartford, CT
Duhan, Bernard ... New York, NY
Duhart, Jake Jerome ... Chicago, IL
Duhart, Myron C. ... Toledo, OH
Duhe, Charles J., Jr. ... **Baton Rouge, LA**
Duhe, John M., Jr. ... Lafayette, LA
Duhig, John H. ... Miami, FL
Duhig, Michael J. ... Oak Brook, IL
Duhigg, Cronin and Spring, P.A.
Albuquerque, NM
Duhigg, David L. ... Albuquerque, NM
Duhigg, Doris ... Albuquerque, NM
Duhigg, John J. ... Albuquerque, NM
Duhl, Emilie A. ... **Chicago, IL**
Duhl, Glenn A. ... **New Haven, CT**
Duhl, Gregory M. ... **Chicago, IL**
Duhl, Lisa D. ... Milford, CT
Duhl, Steven R. ... West Palm Beach, FL
Duhl, Stuart ... **Chicago, IL**
Duhon, Bernard F. ... Abbeville, LA

Duhon, Carl M. ... **Lafayette, LA**
Duhon, Daniel L. ... Baton Rouge, LA
Duhon, Gary Wayne ... **Reno, NV**
Duhon, John F. ... Austin, TX
Duhon Law Firm ... **Lafayette, LA**
Duhy, Gregory S. ... Chalmette, LA
Duignan & Cella ... New York, NY
Duignan, Christine M.
Fort Lauderdale, FL
Duignan, David K. ... Denver, CO
Duignan, Gerard P. ... St. Petersburg, FL
Duignan, Kathleen A. ... United States Court Of Appeals For The Armed Forces, GV
Duignan, Lawrence D., (A P.C.)
San Diego, CA
Duignan, Maureen
Federal Communications Commission, Office of the General Counsel, GV
Duignan, Maureen ... **Pensacola, FL**
Duignan, Richard M. ... New York, NY
Duignan, Thomas P. ... Bridgewater, NJ
Duimstra, Larry E. ... Santa Cruz, CA
Duimstra, Robert N. ... **Appleton, WI**
Duitch, Robert M. ... Colorado Springs, CO
Duitch, Robert M., P.C.
Colorado Springs, CO
Duitsman, Robert L. ... Culver City, CA
Duitsman, Roger G. ... Culver City, CA
Duiven, Linda L. ... **San Francisco, CA**
Duiven, Stephanie L. ... Ventura, CA
Dujack, Susan M. ... **McLean, VA**
Dujmich, Louis C. ... **New York, NY**
Dujovne, Miguel (Mike) Esteban
Melbourne, FL
Dukakis, Michael S. ... Boston, MA
Dukarich, Gary ... **Irvine, CA**
Dukatz, Victoria A. ... **Milwaukee, WI**
Duke, A. Frank ... **Southfield, MI**
Duke, Alan ... **Burbank, CA**
Duke, Branch & Box ... San Antonio, TX
Duke and Brown ... Goldsboro, NC
Duke, Bryan W. ... Fort Lauderdale, FL
Duke, Byrd V., Jr. ... Plantation, FL
Duke, Carol Burns ... Gaithersburg, MD
Duke, Charles E. ... Washington, DC
Duke, Charles J. ... **Bradford, PA**
Duke, Charles T., Jr. ... San Diego, CA
Duke, Christopher S.
West Palm Beach, FL
Duke, Claude W. ... Pass Christian, MS
Duke, Daniel ... Tyrone, GA
Duke, Daniel J. ... Midland, MI
Duke, Daniel J. ... **Green Bay, WI**
Duke, David ... Arlington, TX
Duke, David E. ... Griffin, GA
Duke, David J. ... **Austin, TX**
Duke, David M. ... Washington, DC
Duke, David M. ... **Raleigh, NC**
Duke, Davis W., Jr. ... **Fort Lauderdale, FL**
Duke, Debora ... Peabody, MA
Duke, Deirdre J. ... Garden City, NY
Duke, Douglas A. ... Washington, DC
Duke, Douglas R. ... **Jackson, MS**
Duke, Dwight ... Scottsboro, AL
Duke, Edward C. ... Memphis, TN
Duke, Edward E., II ... Bloomfield Hills, MI
Duke, Elizabeth A. ... **Los Angeles, CA**
Duke, Emily E. ... **Minneapolis, MN**
Duke, Gary W. ... Sacramento, CA
Duke, George F. ... Mill Valley, CA
Duke Gerstel Shearer, LLP ... Phoenix, AZ
Tucson, AZ
Costa Mesa, CA
Los Angeles, CA
Palm Springs, CA
San Diego, CA
San Francisco, CA
Duke, Harold W. ... Greenville, MS
Duke, Hilary ... **Washington, DC**
Duke, Holzman, Yaeger & Photiadis LLP
Buffalo, NY
Duke, Ivy Wafford ... Bethesda, MD
Duke, J. Richard ... **Birmingham, AL**
Duke, Jack E. ... Lake Charles, LA
Duke, James L. ... Buffalo, NY
Duke, Jennie R. ... Arlington, TX
Duke, Joey D. ... **Birmingham, AL**
Duke, John E. ... Goldsboro, NC
Duke, Jonathan M. ... Salt Lake City, UT
Duke, Kenneth A. ... Buffalo, NY
Duke, Kenneth J. ... **Durham, NC**
Duke, Kevin E. ... **Dulles, VA**
Duke, Lance G. ... Corpus Christi, TX
Duke Law Firm, P.C. ... **Birmingham, AL**
Jasper, AL
Duke Law Firm, P.C. ... Arlington, TX
Duke, Leon G. ... **Mobile, AL**
Duke, Lonnie W. ... Austin, TX
Duke, Mary K. ... New York, NY
Duke, Melissa Jaron ... Bingham Farms, MI
Duke, Melvin K. ... Hardinsburg, KY
Duke, Michael C. ... West Chester, PA
Duke, Michelle L. ... Reno, NV
Duke, Miriam D. Wansley ... Macon, GA
Duke, Mullin & Galloway, P.A.
Fort Lauderdale, FL
Duke, Neil E ... **Baltimore, MD**
Duke, Nicole Chapin ... **Washington, DC**
Duke, Norman E. ... Winter Park, FL
Duke, P. Benjamin ... **New York, NY**
Duke, Patrick L. ... Louisville, IL
Duke, Paul R. ... Washington, DC
Duke, R. Stephen ... Beverly Hills, CA
Duke, Randall W. M. ... Dallas, TX
Duke, Rebecca F. ... West Palm Beach, FL
Duke, Richd. H. ... Denver, CO
Duke, Robert C. ... Austin, TX

Duke, Robert D. ... Glen Allen, VA
Duke, Robert N. ... Fort Lauderdale, FL
Duke, Samuel E. ... Lake Wales, FL
Duke, Stephen B., (P.A.) ... St. Petersburg, FL
Duke, Steven B. ... **San Diego, CA**
Duke, Steven B. ... New Haven, CT
Duke, Susan N. ... Harrisburg, PA
Duke, Susanna N. ... Seattle, WA
Duke, T. Harrison ... Pensacola, FL
Duke, Thomas A. ... Lexington, KY
Duke, Thomas H. ... Dallas, TX
Duke, Thomas Howard ... Fort Lauderdale, FL
Duke, Thomas W., Jr. ... Atlanta, GA
Duke, Tommy B. ... **Denver, CO**
Duke, Tommy B., P.C. ... **Denver, CO**
Duke, Vera ... Richmond, VA
Duke, W. Gregory ... **Greenville, NC**
Duke, W. Russell, Jr. ... Greenville, NC
Duke, William K. ... **Oxford, MS**
Duke, William R., Jr. ... Birmingham, AL
Duke, William S. ... Montgomery, AL
Duke, Winston L. ... Barrington, IL
Duke, Wm. David ... **Little Rock, AR**
Dukehart, Deborah Glenn ... Flagler Beach, FL
Dukellis, Gregory John ... **Irvine, CA**
Dukelow, Gayle L., (Mr.) ... Los Angeles, CA
Dukelow, Lisa M. ... Durham, NC
Dukelow, Owen W. ... **Palo Alto, CA**
Portland, OR
Dukelow, Ruth H. ... Lansing, MI
Duke-Mims, Sheila Renee ... Columbia, SC
Dukeminier, Jesse ... Los Angeles, CA
Duker, Denis C. ... Florissant, MO
Duker, Judith ... Boston, MA
Duker, Kenneth A. ... **Ottumwa, IA**
Dukes, Amy M. ... **North Palm Beach, FL**
Dukes, Carroll W. ... **Danville, IL**
Dukes, Carter H. ... **Birmingham, AL**
Dukes, Charlene D. ... Baltimore, MD
Dukes, Charles A., Jr. ... Laurel, MD
Dukes, David E. ... **Columbia, SC**
Dukes, Dukes, Keating and Faneca, P.A.
Biloxi, MS
Gulfport, MS
Jackson, MS
Dukes, Gene W. ... St. George, SC
Dukes, Gilbert F., III ... **Mobile, AL**
Dukes, Grady K. ... McDonough, GA
Dukes, Harold E., Jr. ... Rehoboth Beach, DE
Dukes, James K. ... **Hattiesburg, MS**
Dukes, James K., Jr. ... **Hattiesburg, MS**
Dukes, James O. ... **Gulfport, MS**
Hattiesburg, MS
Dukes, John P. ... Anchorage, AK
Dukes, John Townsend ... **Mobile, AL**
Dukes, Katharine L. ... Austin, TX
Dallas, TX
Dukes, Linda Creek ... Montgomery, AL
Dukes, Marie D. ... **Louisville, KY**
Dukes, Mark C. ... **Columbia, SC**
Dukes, Marshall Burke ... **Atlanta, GA**
Dukes, Martin, Ryan, Meyer & Johnson, Ltd. ... **Champaign, IL**
Danville, IL
Urbana, IL
Dukes, Marvin H. ... **Beaufort, SC**
Dukes, Marvin H., III ... **Beaufort, SC**
Dukes, M. W. ... Sandersville, GA
Dukes, Patrick M. ... Cleveland, OH
Dukes, Robert A. ... Pomona, CA
Dukes, Rory C. ... **Tyler, TX**
Dukes, Thomas A., Jr. ... Farmville, VA
Dukes, Thomas E., III ... **Orlando, FL**
Dukes, Walter W. ... **Gulfport, MS**
Dukes, William F. ... **Gulfport, MS**
Dukes, Williams, Infinger & Ruff, P.A.
Beaufort, SC
Dukess, A. Carleton ... **New York, NY**
Dukess, Jeffrey W. ... Brockton, MA
Duket, David G. ... Bakersfield, CA
Duket, Tim A. ... Marinette, WI
Dukowski, Darryl J. ... Painesville, OH
Dul, John A. ... Skokie, IL
Dula, Arthur M. ... **Houston, TX**
Dula, Tamea A. ... **Houston, TX**
Dulac, Donald T., Jr. ... **Pittsburgh, PA**
DuLac, Douglas D. ... Edina, MN
Dulacki, Mary J. ... Aurora, CO
Dulak, Norman C. ... Madison, NJ
Dulan, Julia A. ... Atlanta, GA
Dulan, Steven ... East Lansing, MI
Dulaney, Andrew G. ... San Francisco, CA
Dulaney, Andrew T. ... **Tunica, MS**
Dulaney, April D. ... **New Orleans, LA**
Dulaney, Carol J. ... **Nashville, TN**
Dulaney Engel & Phillips ... Dayton, OH
Dulaney, Gene L. ... Snyder, TX
Dulaney, Geo. D. ... Alexandria, VA
Dulaney, H. Scott ... **Orlando, FL**
Dulaney, John W., Jr. ... **Tunica, MS**
Dulaney, Joseph R. ... **Tunica, MS**
Dulaney Law Firm, L.L.P. ... **Tunica, MS**
Dulaney, Lincoln G. ... Charlottesville, VA
Dulaney, Marian F. ... Tunica, MS
Dulaney, Richard A. ... Culpeper, VA
Dulaney, Robert B., III ... **Atlanta, GA**
Dulaney, Samantha ... **New York, NY**
Dulaney, Sim C., Jr. ... Port Gibson, MS
Dulaney, Stephen R. ... San Jose, CA
du Laney, Valerie ... **Seattle, WA**
Dulaney, William H., III ... Dayton, OH
Dulaney, William P. ... **Tunica, MS**
Dulansey, David G. ... Pittsburgh, PA
Dulany, Benjamin W. ... **Washington, DC**
Vienna, VA
Dulany, George B. ... Belton, TX
Dulany, James P. ... Exeter, NH
Dulany, Jeffrey A., P.C. ... **Monroe, MI**

Dulany & Leahy, LLP ....**Baltimore, MD**
Westminster, MD
Dulany, Richard B. ....El Paso, TX
Dulany, T. Patrick ....**McLean, VA**
Dulany, William B. ....**Westminster, MD**
Dulas, DeAnne L. ....Inver Grove Heights, MN
DuLaurence, Henry J., III ....Boston, MA
Dulay, Gail A. ....San Diego, CA
Dulberg, Andrea L. ....New York, NY
Dulberg, Gary S. ....Oakland, CA
Dulberg, Jay M. ....Norwalk, CT
Dulberg, Jeffrey W. ....**Los Angeles, CA**
Dulberg, Joel K. ....New City, NY
Dulberg, Matthew S.
Jackson Heights, NY
Dulberg, Michael S. ....**Phoenix, AZ**
Dulberg, Robert A. ....Miami, FL
Dulberg, Samuel E. ....Jamaica, NY
Dulberg, Sharon Margaret
San Francisco, CA
Dulcan, James N. ....Bethesda, MD
Dulchinos, Carolyn F. ....Boulder, CO
Dulchinos, Dean A. ....**Springfield, MA**
Dulcich, James F., P.C. ....**Portland, OR**
Dulcich, Thomas V. ....**Portland, OR**
Dulde, T. A. ....Milwaukee, WI
Duleba, Alicia R. ....**Austin, TX**
Dulebohn, Diana G. ....Waynesfield, OH
Dulen, Maureen T. ....Department of Justice,
Civil Rights Division, GV
Duley, Lisa Kent ....Richmond, VA
Duley, Patrick R. ....Upper Marlboro, MD
Duley, Thomas E. ....**Menlo Park, CA**
Duley, Thomas F. ....Upper Marlboro, MD
Dulgarian, George H. ....Los Angeles, CA
Dulich, Kendall ....**San Diego, CA**
Dulick, Harry L. ....Cleburne, TX
Dulik, Gregg N. ....**San Francisco, CA**
Dulik, Richard ....**Washington, DC**
Dulin, Amy G. ....**Miami, FL**
Dulin, Betsy Ennis ....South Charleston, WV
Dulin, Carol J. ....Wilmington, DE
Dulin & Dulin, Ltd. ....Gulfport, MS
Dulin, Edwin R., Jr. ....Uvalde, TX
Dulin, George H. ....Greenwood, MS
Dulin, Irene L. ....**St. Louis, MO**
Dulin, Jacques M. ....**Palo Alto, CA**
Dulin, John P., Jr. ....**Birmingham, AL**
Dulin, Joseph P., Jr. ....Syracuse, NY
Dulin, Kimberly A. ....Boston, MA
Dulin, King, Parres, McDowell & McDowell, LLP ....**St. Louis, MO**
Dulin, Sue Esther ....Gulfport, MS
Dulin & Tarski ....Uvalde, TX
Dulin, Thomas N. ....Albany, NY
Dulin, Tommy ....Gulfport, MS
Duling, Matthew ....Santa Rosa, CA
Duling, Robert Webster ....Richmond, VA
Duling, Thomas D. ....**Woodbridge, VA**
Dulisse, Carole L. ....**Oklahoma City, OK**
Dulit, Kathryn L. ....Boston, MA
Dulitz, Elchanan I. ....Teaneck, NJ
Dulitz, Harris M. ....New Orleans, LA
Dulka, Mary K. ....**New York, NY**
Dulka, Matthew J. ....Castro Valley, CA
Dulksnys, Audra L. ....**Chicago, IL**
Dull, Christopher J. ....Antioch, TN
Dull, David A. ....Irvine, CA
Dull, David A., Sr. ....Warren, OH
Dull, David Austin, Jr. ....Warren, OH
Dull, David L.
Environmental Protection Agency,
Program Office Attorneys, GV
Dull, J. Terrence ....Niles, OH
Dull, James A. ....Cleveland, OH
Dull, James E. ....Mount Vernon, IL
Dull, Jeffrey L. ....Osceola, MO
Dull, John E. ....**Wilmington, DE**
Dull, Kay Ellen ....**Sioux City, IA**
Dull, Patrick M. ....Columbus, OH
Dull, Robert J. ....Le Mars, IA
Dull, Stacy L. ....**Los Angeles, CA**
D'Ull, Walter ....New York, NY
Dullaghan, Matthew P. ....Waynesboro, VA
Dullaghan, Victoria White ....Staunton, VA
Dullahan, Thomas J. ....Palermo, ME
Dullanty, F. J., Jr. ....**Spokane, WA**
Dullanty, Margaret O. ....**Charleston, SC**
Dullanty, Richard C., Jr. ....Spokane, WA
Dullanty, Richard E. ....Rockford, WA
Spokane, WA
Dulle, Joseph R. ....**St. Louis, MO**
Dullea, Michael E. ....San Diego, CA
Dullea, Paul D. ....Boston, MA
Dullea, Peter A. ....Los Olivos, CA
Dullea, William J. ....Braintree, MA
Dullinger, Dennis R. ....St. Cloud, MN
Dullnig, Arnold J. ....Kerrville, TX
Dullnig, Darrell Scott ....San Antonio, TX
Dullum, Dana Andrew ....Edina, MN
Dully, Bertram J. ....Hartford, CT
Dulmage, Claudia H. ....Department of Justice,
Antitrust Division, GV
Dulmage, Philip L., (P.C.) ....Flint, MI
Dulman, Wendy Friedman ......**New York, NY**
Dulmer, John J. ....Venice, FL
Dulmer & Tracy, Chartered ....Venice, FL
Dulock, David F. ....**Houston, TX**
Dulong, Harold C. ....**Burlington, MA**
Dulong, Kristin A. ....**Boston, MA**
Duls, Thomas G. ....Sylva, NC
Dulske, John C. ....**San Antonio, TX**
Dulski, Laura ....Madison, WI
Dulsky, Beryl I., (Mr.) ....Phoenix, AZ
Dulsky, Michele G. ....Burlingame, CA
Dultz, Alisa ....**Stamford, CT**
Hackensack, NJ
New York, NY

Dulweber, Vincent L. ....Longview, TX
Dulweber, Vincent L., P.C. ....Longview, TX
Dulworth, Daniel J. ....**Detroit, MI**
Dulworth, Georgette Borrego ....Detroit, MI
Dulworth, James M. ....Dallas, TX
Dulzaides, Raquel M. ....**San Juan, PR**
Duma, John M. ....Kansas City, KS
Dumain, Rita D. ....New York, NY
Dumain, Sanford P. ....**New York, NY**
Dumais, Kathleen M. ....**Bethesda, MD**
Dumais, Richard J. ....Baltimore, MD
Duman, Fred M. ....Castro Valley, CA
Duman, Jon ....Castro Valley, CA
Duman, Suzanne ....Chicago, IL
Duman, Thomas J. ....**Pittsburgh, PA**
Dumanis, Bonnie M. ....San Diego, CA
Dumaresq, John E. ....New York, NY
Dumark, Frank J. ....Branford, CT
Dumark, Gregory James ....Washington, DC
Dumark & Lindsay ....Branford, CT
DuMars, Charles T. ....**Albuquerque, NM**
Torreon, NM
DuMars, Christina Bruff
Albuquerque, NM
Torreon, NM
DuMars, Karen A. ....Trenton, NJ
Dumas, Arthur H. ....Sanford, ME
Dumas & Associates ....Los Angeles, CA
Dumas & Associates, Law Coporation
Baton Rouge, LA
Dumas, Barre C. ....Mobile, AL
Dumas, Beth F. ....Santa Barbara, CA
Dumas, Cecily A. ....**San Francisco, CA**
Dumas, Charles B. ....**Albany, NY**
Saratoga Springs, NY
Dumas, Claudia J. ....
Agency for International Development, GV
Dumas, David M. ....**Akron, OH**
Dumas, David W. ....**Waco, TX**
Dumas, Dennis R. ....**New York, NY**
Dumas, Donald L. ....Austin, TX
Dumas, Edward P. ....**Rensselaer, IN**
Dumas, Elizabeth M. ....**Albany, NY**
Dumas, Eugene R. ....Janesville, WI
Dumas, Gloria A. ....Nashville, TN
Dumas, James A., Jr. ....Los Angeles, CA
Dumas, James F., Jr. ....Aurora, CO
Dumas, James L. ....**Portland, OR**
Dumas, Jennifer L. ....**New York, NY**
Dumas, John W. ....Waldport, OR
Dumas, Lawrence, III ....**Birmingham, AL**
Dumas, Lorena ....Lake Charles, LA
Dumas, Lori A. ....North Wales, PA
Dumas and McPhail, L.L.C. ....Mobile, AL
Dumas & Moriarty ....**Rensselaer, IN**
Dumas, Nanette ....San Jose, CA
Dumas, Paul F. ....**Morrilton, AR**
Dumas, Paul R., Jr. ....Mexico, ME
Dumas, Richard A. ....Grand Blanc, MI
Dumas, Robin A. ....**Boston, MA**
Dumas, Veronica Gabrielli ....Albany, NY
Dumas, Walter C. ....**Baton Rouge, LA**
Dumasius, John G. ....**Dearborn, MI**
Dumaw, Kurtis R. ....**Ann Arbor, MI**
Dumaw, Lisa S. ....**Boulder, CO**
Denver, CO
Dumbacher, David ....Cincinnati, OH
Dumbacher & Dumbacher ....Cincinnati, OH
Dumbacher, John P. ....Cincinnati, OH
Dumbaugh, Daniel F. ....Tucson, AZ
Dumbaugh, John D. ....**Sarasota, FL**
Dumbrill, R. Douglas ....**Gillette, WY**
Dumbrill, Richard S. ....Newcastle, WY
Dumbroff, David H. ....Ledgewood, NJ
Dumeer, Melinda S. ....**Raleigh, NC**
Dumenil, Ann M. ....**Phoenix, AZ**
Dumeny, Marcel J. ....Little Rock, AR
Orlando, FL
Dumer, Gary E., Jr. ....**Baltimore, MD**
Dumerer, James E. ....Dallas, TX
Dumes, Robert M. ....Middletown, OH
Dumesnil, Bryan S. ....**Houston, TX**
Dumestre, Mary L., (P.C.)
New Orleans, LA
DuMez, Robert I. ....**Kenosha, WI**
Dumezich, Daniel ....**Chicago, IL**
Dumford, Donald Jacob ....Marietta, GA
Dumich, Nicholas G. ....**Atlanta, GA**
Dumire, Howard ....Washington, PA
Dumit, Thomas A. ....Oak Harbor, WA
Dumitrescu, Gabriel ....**Atlanta, GA**
Dumke, Michael E. ....**St. Joseph, MI**
Dumke, Richard A. ....Lafayette, CA
Dumke, William E. ....**White Plains, NY**
Dumler, Douglas M. ....**Fort Collins, CO**
Dumler, Egon ....**Los Angeles, CA**
Dumler & Giroux ....New York, NY
Dumler, John H. ....Baltimore, MD
Dumler, Mark M. ....**Baltimore, MD**
Dumm, Angela L. ....**Harrisburg, PA**
Dumm, Christopher Jesse ....Vancouver, WA
Dumm, Christopher W. ....Joplin, MO
Dumm, Mark H. ....**Denver, CO**
Dumm, Markelle Medlock
Virginia Beach, VA
Dummer, Christine Lynne ....Knoxville, TN
Dummer, Donald W. ....Santa Rosa, CA
Dummer, Melissa K. Sviggum
Owatonna, MN
Dummer, Rosanne M. ....Dallas, TX
Dummer, William L. ....Pleasanton, CA
Dummigan, R Brendan ....Portland, OR
Dummit and Associates
Winston-Salem, NC
Dummit, Craig S. ....**Los Angeles, CA**
Dummit, E. Clarke ....**Winston-Salem, NC**

Dummit, Faber, Briegleb & Diamond
Los Angeles, CA
Sacramento, CA
San Diego, CA
Las Vegas, NV
Dumoff, Alan ....Washington, DC
Dumon, Denise ....**Dallas, TX**
DuMond, Amy L. ....**Minneapolis, MN**
Dumond, Carol ....San Francisco, CA
DuMond, J. William ....**Plainfield, IN**
Dumont, Dan ....Montgomery, AL
Dumont, Earle J., Jr. ....Chandler, AZ
DuMont, Edward C. ....Department of Justice,
Office of the Solicitor General, GV
Dumont, Gabriel O., Jr. ....Boston, MA
DuMont, Glen J. ....Woodbridge, NJ
DuMont, Gregory T. ....**Washington, DC**
DuMont, Harry ....Asheville, NC
Dumont, James A. ....Middlebury, VT
Dumont, Janet S. ....**Tulsa, OK**
Dumont, Jeanine M. ....**Hartford, CT**
Dumont, John H. ....**Princeton, NJ**
Dumont, Jon Michael ....**Philadelphia, PA**
Dumont, Judith Owen ....**New York, NY**
Dumont, Kala Scott ....**San Antonio, TX**
Dumont, Kathleen ....**Garden City, NY**
Dumont, Kristen Garcia ....Palo Alto, CA
Dumont, Martin G. ....Colorado Springs, CO
Dumont, Marybeth ....Plattsburgh, NY
Dumont, Richard D. ....**San Francisco, CA**
Dumont, W. Hunt ....Paterson, NJ
Dumontet, Gilbert M. ....Beverly Hills, CA
DuMontier, Clarissa W. ....Boonville, MO
Dumornay, Denise ....**Boca Raton, FL**
DuMouchel, David F. ....**Detroit, MI**
DuMouchel, David F., P.C. ....**Detroit, MI**
Dumouchel, Robert J. ....**Providence, RI**
DuMouchelle, Elizabeth A. ....**Detroit, MI**
Dumoulin, Frederick E. ....Dallas, TX
Dumpis, Juris ....Redwood City, CA
Dumser, Karen ....Newton, MA
Dumser, Stephen R. ....Cherry Hill, NJ
Dumville, S. Lawrence, Independence Law Center ....**Norfolk, VA**
Dumville, S. Lawrence, Independence Law Center ....**Virginia Beach, VA**
Dumville, S. Miles ....**Richmond, VA**
Dun, David H. ....**Eureka, CA**
Dun & Martinek, LLP ....**Eureka, CA**
Dunaetz, Nancy L. ....Los Angeles, CA
Dunagan, Christopher H. ....**Alpharetta, GA**
Dunagan, Craig A. ....Austin, TX
Dunagan, Danny A. ....Morrison, IL
Dunagan, David N. ....Martin, TN
Dunagan, Georgia Crossley ....Marietta, GA
Dunagan, Kevin Scott ....**Houston, TX**
Dunagan, Michael W. ....**Dallas, TX**
Dunagan, O. Paul ....**Dallas, TX**
Dunagan, Patrick E. ....Bloomington, IL
Dunagan, Sidney G. ....**Oklahoma City, OK**
Dunagan, Walter B. ....Daytona Beach, FL
Dunagan - Weichert - Houston ....Austin, TX
Dunagin, David L. ....Fort Smith, AR
Dunah, Patrick E ....San Diego, CA
Dunahoe, Edwin ....**Natchitoches, LA**
Dunahoo, Kermit L. ....Des Moines, IA
Dunai, Rebecca Voth ....Pensacola, FL
Dunaj, Michelle ....Miami, FL
Dunaj, Sherryll Martens ....**Miami, FL**
Dunaj, William J. ....**Fort Lauderdale, FL**
Dunajeski, Melanie Morgan
Hammond, IN
Dunakey, David D. ....Waterloo, IA
Dunakey & Klatt, P.C. ....Waterloo, IA
Dunalewicz, Micheal B. ....Overland Park, KS
Dunavan, Dylan M. ....**Itasca, IL**
Dunavant, D. Michael ....Ripley, TN
Dunavant, Leonard C., Jr. ....**Memphis, TN**
Dunavant, Marilyn Kay ....Memphis, TN
Dunavant, Richard H. ....Pulaski, TN
Dunaway & Associates ....**Anderson, SC**
Dunaway, Baxter ....Malibu, CA
Dunaway, Bridget L. ....**London, KY**
Dunaway, C. Glenn ....**Atlanta, GA**
Dunaway, Carlyle M., Jr. ....**New York, NY**
Dunaway & Cross, A Professional Corporation ....**Washington, DC**
Dunaway, David B. ....**Thomaston, GA**
Dunaway, David H., & Associates, Law Offices of ....**La Follette, TN**
Dunaway, G. Baxter ....Malibu, CA
Dunaway & Greenway, L.L.P.
Anniston, AL
Auburn, AL
Birmingham, AL
Florence, AL
Gadsden, AL
Huntsville, AL
Montgomery, AL
Tuscaloosa, AL
Dunaway, Harold Edward ....Glendale, KY
Dunaway, Jack ....Los Angeles, CA
Dunaway, James R. ....Orange, TX
Dunaway, James R., P.C. ....Orange, TX
Dunaway, Johnny V. ....La Follette, TN
Dunaway, Kathryn ....Paso Robles, CA
Dunaway, Kevin Hays ....**Springfield, MO**
Dunaway, Mac S. ....**Washington, DC**
Dunaway, Matthew A. ....Anniston, AL
Birmingham, AL
Florence, AL
Gadsden, AL
Huntsville, AL
Dunaway, Rhett Conlon ....Charleston, SC
Dunaway, Rhonda J. ....Council Bluffs, IA
Dunaway, Rhonda J. ....Omaha, NE
Dunaway, Roger W., Jr. ....Thomson, GA
Dunaway, Sally Putnam ....Washington, DC

Dunaway, Thiele R. ....**Oakland, CA**
Dunaway, Thomas W., III ....**Anderson, SC**
Dunaway, Vicki W. ....**Billings, MT**
Dunaway, Wayland F. ....State College, PA
Dunaway, Weyandt, McCormick, Gerace & McGlaughlin ....**Bellefonte, PA**
State College, PA
Dunay, Gary S. ....**Boca Raton, FL**
Dunay, Myron S. ....**Delray Beach, FL**
Dunay, Myron S., P.A. ....**Delray Beach, FL**
Dunay, Ricard John ....Charlottesville, VA
Dunbar, Amy Kimball ....Washington, DC
Dunbar, Anthony P., & Associates
New Orleans, LA
Dunbar & Associates ....**La Jolla, CA**
San Diego, CA
Dunbar & Associates, P.A. ....Charleston, SC
Columbia, SC
Spartanburg, SC
Dunbar, Barbara B. ....New Orleans, LA
Dunbar, Blake E., Jr. ....Blue Bell, PA
Dunbar, Byron H. ....Billings, MT
Dunbar, Carol F. ....Waterloo, IA
Dunbar & Casey ....Brownsburg, IN
Dunbar, Charles D. ....**Charleston, WV**
Dunbar, Charles Edward, III
New Orleans, LA
Dunbar, Claude R. ....Spartanburg, SC
Dunbar, Colleen A. ....**Dallas, TX**
Dunbar, Craig B. ....Washington, DC
Dunbar, Crowley & Hegeman, L.L.P.
El Paso, TX
Dunbar, D. Joseph ....Brownsburg, IN
Dunbar, Daniel Alan ....Lawrence, KS
Dunbar, Daniel H. ....Columbus, OH
Dunbar, Daniel W., Law Office of
Los Angeles, CA
Dunbar, Daniel W., Law Office of
Torrance, CA
Dunbar, David C. ....**Jackson, MS**
Dunbar, David F. ....San Diego, CA
Dunbar, David M. ....**Chicago, IL**
Dunbar, Donald E., Jr. ....San Diego, CA
Dunbar, Douglas Scott ....West Linn, OR
Dunbar & Dunbar ....Waterloo, IA
Dunbar & Dunbar, Professional Law Corp.
San Diego, CA
Dunbar, Edward A. ....Boynton Beach, FL
Dunbar, Edward W. ....El Paso, TX
Dunbar, Gary D. ....**Coraopolis, PA**
Dunbar, Grace Gilchrist ....Spartanburg, SC
Dunbar, Grace Gilchrist, P.A.
Spartanburg, SC
Dunbar, Harder & Benson, LLP
Houston, TX
Dunbar, Harold E. ....Silver Spring, MD
Dunbar, Henry O., Jr. ....Buies Creek, NC
Dunbar, Howard R. ....**Johnson City, TN**
Dunbar, J. Mark ....**La Jolla, CA**
Dunbar, Jack F. ....**Oxford, MS**
Dunbar, Jacqueline ....Albany, NY
Dunbar, James A. ....**Towson, MD**
Dunbar, James V., Jr. ....Charleston, SC
Columbia, SC
Spartanburg, SC
Dunbar, Jeffrey D. ....**Seattle, WA**
Dunbar, Jesse R. ....**New York, NY**
Dunbar, John D. ....**Kansas City, MO**
Dunbar, John H. ....**Oxford, MS**
Dunbar, John Joseph ....**Portland, OR**
Dunbar, John P. ....Honolulu, HI
Dunbar, Joseph W. ....**Buffalo, NY**
Dunbar, Julie L. ....**Ann Arbor, MI**
Dunbar, Kevin T. ....Rolling Hills Estates, CA
Dunbar, Lawrence G. ....**Houston, TX**
Dunbar, Lynn B. ....West Branch, MI
Dunbar, Marc W. ....**Tallahassee, FL**
Dunbar, Margaret M. ....**St. Louis, MO**
Dunbar, Mary M. ....Washington, DC
Dunbar, Michael C. ....Waterloo, IA
Dunbar, Patricia M. ....Springfield, MA
Dunbar, Paul H., III ....**Augusta, GA**
Dunbar, Peggy Elizabeth ....**Kerrville, TX**
Dunbar, Peter M. ....**Tallahassee, FL**
Dunbar, Richard D. ....**Parkersburg, WV**
Dunbar, Ronald W., Jr. ....**Boston, MA**
Dunbar, Rosemary J. ....Minneapolis, MN
Dunbar, Sandra ....Cleveland, OH
Dunbar, Stanley K. ....Limestone, TN
Dunbar, Stephen H. ....Moorestown, NJ
Dunbar, Steven F. ....Phillipsburg, NJ
Dunbar, Susan ....**Costa Mesa, CA**
Dunbar, Thomas T. ....Oxford, MS
Dunbar, Thomas W. ....**Chesapeake, VA**
Dunbar, Timothy C. ....Waterloo, IA
Dunbar, Vernon F. ....**Columbia, SC**
Dunbar & Vodonick, A Law Corporation
Roseville, CA
Dunbar, Wiiliam ....Baton Rouge, LA
Dunbar, William F. ....Sun Valley, ID
Dunbar, William L. ....Roseville, CA
Dunbar, Wylene W. ....Oxford, MS
Dunbaugh, Frank M., III ....Annapolis, MD
Dunbeck, Joseph T., Jr. ....Heber City, UT
Dunberg, Richard G. ....Miami, FL
Dunbrack, Timothy ....Orlando, FL
Duncan, Adam D., Jr. ....Los Angeles, CA
Duncan, Adam M. ....Salt Lake City, UT
Duncan, Alan C. ....**Dallas, TX**
Duncan, Alan W. ....**Greensboro, NC**
Duncan, Albert Ray, Jr. ....Vicksburg, MS
Duncan, Alex G., III ....**Tucson, AZ**
Duncan, Alison MacDonald
Washington, DC
Duncan & Allen ....**Washington, DC**
Duncan, Allyson K. ....**Raleigh, NC**
Duncan, Alva ....Lake City, FL
Duncan, Angela Denise ....Doraville, GA

Duncan, Anne H. .... **Irvine, CA**
Duncan, Anne Marie V. .... San Bernardino, CA
Duncan, Anthony L. .... **Atlanta, GA**
Duncan, Arthur, Jr. .... **Kansas City, MO**
Duncan, Ball, Evans & Ubaldi, A Professional Corporation
Sacramento, CA
Duncan, Basil R. .... **Guilford, CT**
Duncan, Benjamin R. .... Los Angeles, CA
Duncan, Bernadette A., P.C. .... Cherry Hill, NJ
Duncan, Bernadette A. .... Cherry Hill, NJ
Duncan, Beth M. .... **Brunswick, GA**
Duncan, Bette Wolf .... Des Moines, IA
Duncan & Blaich .... Poplar Bluff, MO
Duncan, Blair M. .... New York, NY
Duncan, Bradley R. .... **McLean, VA**
Duncan & Brandt, P.C. .... Peru, IL
Duncan, Brian L. .... **Fresno, CA**
Duncan, Brooke H., II .... New Orleans, LA
Duncan, Brooke, III .... **New Orleans, LA**
Duncan, Bruce .... Excelsior, MN
Duncan, Bruce D. .... Doraville, GA
Duncan, Bruce G. .... Mount Dora, FL
Duncan, C. Emerson, II .... **Washington, DC**
Duncan, Carol M. .... Jonesboro, AR
Duncan, Carolyn L. .... **Birmingham, AL**
Duncan, Charles G. .... Eugene, OR
Duncan, Charles G., P.C. .... Eugene, OR
Duncan, Charles L., Jr. .... Philadelphia, PA
Duncan, Cheri .... Houston, TX
Duncan, Christina Henley
Manchester, TN
Duncan, Christopher E. .... **Angleton, TX**
Duncan, Clarence J. .... Phoenix, AZ
Duncan, Clifford F., Jr. .... Louisville, KY
Duncan & Courington, L.L.C.
New Orleans, LA
Duncan, Dale E. .... **Silver Spring, MD**
Falls Church, VA
Duncan, Dan R. .... Cincinnati, OH
Duncan, Dan R., P.C. .... Cincinnati, OH
Duncan, Dana L. .... Alameda, CA
Duncan, Dana W. .... **Wisconsin Rapids, WI**
Duncan, Daniel A. .... Kansas City, KS
Duncan, Daniel B. .... Mobile, AL
Duncan, Daniel E. .... Albuquerque, NM
Duncan, Dann L. .... West Covina, CA
Duncan, David .... **Boston, MA**
Duncan, David C. .... West Des Moines, IA
Duncan, David C. .... Dearborn, MI
Duncan, David K. .... Phoenix, AZ
Duncan, David N. .... Amarillo, TX
Duncan, David R. .... Columbia, SC
Duncan, David R. .... San Angelo, TX
Duncan, David R. .... Bothell, WA
Duncan, David T., & Associates
Brownsville, TX
Duncan, David W. .... Cortez, CO
Duncan, David W., P.C. .... Cortez, CO
Durango, CO
Duncan, Debra J. .... **Washington, DC**
Duncan, Debra S. .... Topeka, KS
Duncan, Debra S. .... West Bend, WI
Duncan, Deidre G. .... Department of the Army, Office of the General Counsel, GV
Duncan, Dennis H. .... Chesterfield, VA
Duncan, Dennis J. .... **Stockton, CA**
Duncan, Dennis L. .... **Macon, GA**
Duncan, Dennis L. .... **Parker, SD**
Duncan, Donald C. .... Houston, TX
Duncan, Donald R. .... **Springfield, MO**
Duncan, Donald R. .... Athena, OR
Duncan, Donald W. .... Palm Coast, FL
Duncan, Donald W., P.A. .... Palm Coast, FL
Duncan, Douglas .... **West Palm Beach, FL**
Duncan, Douglas M. .... Redmond, WA
Duncan, Douglas W. .... **Atlanta, GA**
Duncan, Duncan, Jelkin & Walker
Alma, NE
Franklin, NE
Hildreth, NE
Duncan, Dwight G. .... North Dartmouth, MA
Duncan, E. David, Law Offices of
Albany, NY
Duncan, E. Kenneth .... Bowling Green, KY
Duncan, E. Townes .... Nashville, TN
Duncan, Earl R. .... Panama City, FL
Duncan, Ed E. .... **Cleveland, OH**
Duncan, Eddirland .... **Boston, MA**
Duncan, Edgar M. .... **San Antonio, TX**
Duncan, Edward C., III .... Maitland, FL
Duncan, Edward R., Jr. .... Wheaton, IL
Duncan, Edwin W. .... **Los Angeles, CA**
Duncan, Elaine C. .... Louisville, KY
Duncan, Elizabeth Anne .... Durham, NC
Duncan, Elizabeth Q. .... New York, NY
Duncan, Elton F., III .... **New Orleans, LA**
Duncan, Eric C. .... Green Bay, WI
Duncan, Ernest L., Jr.
Corpus Christi, TX
Duncan, Farris A. .... Goldsboro, NC
Duncan, Farris A., P.A. .... Goldsboro, NC
Duncan, Frank P. .... Los Angeles, CA
Duncan, Freeman B. .... Post Falls, ID
Duncan, Geo. R., Jr. .... Stayton, OR
Duncan, George E., Jr. .... **Atlanta, GA**
Duncan, George Gary .... **Santa Fe, NM**
Duncan, Glen E. .... Seattle, WA
Duncan, Glenn A. .... Laramie, WY
Duncan, Glenn L. .... **Elkhart, IN**
Mishawaka, IN
Duncan, Gordon A., Jr. .... Jacksonville, FL
Duncan, Gordon R. .... **Fort Myers, FL**
Duncan, Green, Brown, Langeness & Eckley, A Professional Corporation
Des Moines, IA
Duncan, Gregory S. .... Charlottesville, VA
Duncan, Gregory W. .... **Helena, MT**

Duncan & Grogan .... Bowling Green, KY
Duncan, Harold .... El Paso, TX
Duncan, Harold F., Jr. .... San Antonio, TX
Duncan, Harold S. .... Chattanooga, TN
Duncan, Hearst R. (Randy), Jr.
Des Moines, IA
Duncan, Heather .... **San Diego, CA**
Duncan, Heidi .... **Washington, DC**
Duncan, Helen L. .... **Los Angeles, CA**
Duncan, Herbert H., Jr. .... Baton Rouge, LA
Duncan • Honn, P.C. .... **Portland, OR**
Duncan & Hopkins, P.C. .... Alexandria, VA
Duncan, Howard T. .... Omaha, NE
Duncan, Howard T., P.C. .... Omaha, NE
Duncan, H. R. .... Des Moines, IA
Duncan, Hugh M. .... Casper, WY
Duncan, J. Eileen .... **St. Louis, MO**
Duncan, J. Kelly .... **New Orleans, LA**
Duncan, J. Michael .... Raleigh, NC
Duncan, J. Stuart .... Irvine, CA
Duncan, Jack G. .... Washington, DC
Duncan, Jack G. .... Washington, DC
Duncan, Jack L. .... Flat River, MO
Duncan, Jackson E., III .... **Huntsville, AL**
Tuscaloosa, AL
Duncan, Jacqueline Phelps .... Arapaho, OK
Duncan, Jacqueline Syers .... **Frankfort, KY**
Lexington, KY
Duncan, James B. .... San Francisco, CA
Duncan, James B., III .... Augusta, GA
Duncan, James F. .... **Kansas City, MO**
Duncan, James G. .... Department of Justice, Office of Professional Responsibility, GV
Duncan, James H., Jr. .... San Francisco, CA
Duncan, James M. .... **Bakersfield, CA**
Duncan, James M. .... Dallas, TX
Duncan, James M., P.C. .... Dallas, TX
Duncan, James R. .... **Irvine, CA**
Los Angeles, CA
Duncan, James R. .... **Pasadena, CA**
Duncan, James T. .... Portland, OR
Duncan, James T., Jr. .... New York, NY
Duncan, James V. .... **Broken Bow, NE**
Duncan, James W., Jr. .... Baltimore, MD
Duncan, Janell Mayo .... **Washington, DC**
Rockville, MD
Duncan, Jayne F. .... Elizabethtown, PA
Duncan, Jeffery M. .... **Chicago, IL**
Duncan, Jerry M. .... **Sacramento, CA**
Duncan, Jerry S., Law Office
Oklahoma City, OK
Duncan, Jimmie .... Cypress, TX
Duncan, Jimmie K. .... Murfreesboro, TN
Duncan, Jimmy A. .... Nashville, TN
Duncan, Joan B. .... Collegeville, PA
Duncan, Joanne K. .... Inez, KY
Duncan, Joe D. .... Knoxville, TN
Duncan, Joe M. .... **Memphis, TN**
Duncan, John A. .... **Orange, CA**
Duncan, John A., A Professional Corporation
Irvine, CA
Newport Beach, CA
Orange, CA
Duncan, John B. .... **Menlo Park, CA**
Duncan, John Bruce .... **Greenwich, CT**
New Canaan, CT
Duncan, John C., III .... Alexandria, VA
Duncan, John Clifton, Jr. .... Fort Worth, TX
Duncan, John D. .... **El Cajon, CA**
Duncan, John D. .... **Portland, ME**
Duncan, John D., Jr. ....
Department of State, GV
Duncan, John Earl .... Lexington, SC
Duncan, John G. .... Syracuse, NY
Duncan, John K. .... Long Beach, CA
Duncan, John M. .... French Lick, IN
Duncan, John P.C. .... **Chicago, IL**
Duncan, John R., Jr. .... San Diego, CA
Duncan, John S., III .... **La Salle, IL**
Duncan, Jon A. .... **Oak Park, IL**
Duncan, Jonathan F. .... **Kansas City, MO**
Duncan, Julie A. .... Costa Mesa, CA
Duncan, Julie Lippert .... Cincinnati, OH
Duncan, Julienne S. .... **Morristown, NJ**
Duncan, Kalliope B. .... **Bloomfield Hills, MI**
Minneapolis, MN
Duncan, Karen .... Vinton, IA
Duncan, Karen C. .... New Orleans, LA
Duncan, Karen Lee .... **Norfolk, VA**
Duncan, Kathleen M. .... Edmond, OK
Duncan & Kazragis, P.A. .... **Sedona, AZ**
Duncan, Kelly K. .... Lincoln, NE
Duncan, Kenneth Addison .... Baton Rouge, LA
Duncan, Kent E. .... St. Louis, MO
Duncan, Kevin T. .... **Washington, DC**
Duncan, Kimi Lyn .... St. Louis, MO
Duncan, Krista L. .... Mesa, AZ
Duncan, Kristi A. .... **Jackson, MS**
Duncan, Laney .... **Oklahoma City, OK**
Duncan, Laura M. .... **St. Louis, MO**
Duncan, Laura T. .... Westbury, NY
Duncan Law Firm .... **Hattiesburg, MS**
Jackson, MS
Duncan, Lawrence, III .... **Washington, DC**
Duncan, LeRoy E. .... Williamsville, IL
Duncan, M. Elizabeth .... **Portland, OR**
Duncan, M. Kathleen .... Trenton, NJ
Duncan, M. Troy .... New York, NY
Duncan, Madeline L. .... Wheat Ridge, CO
Duncan, Mal Stanley .... **Atlanta, GA**
Duncan, Malcolm J. .... **Chicago, IL**
Duncan, Mallory B. .... Washington, DC
Duncan & Mangiafico, P.C. .... **Atlanta, GA**
Duncan, Margaret M. .... **San Diego, CA**
Duncan, Margaret M. .... **Chicago, IL**
Duncan, Mark Gregory .... **New York, NY**
Duncan, Mary Carter .... **St. Louis, MO**
Duncan, Mary E. .... **Billings, MT**

Duncan, Mary M. .... Jamesville, NY
Duncan, Matthew J. .... Alameda, CA
Duncan, Matthew S. .... Costa Mesa, CA
Duncan, Maureen .... **San Francisco, CA**
Duncan, Mel F. .... Sonoma, CA
Duncan, Michael A. .... **Covington, KY**
Duncan, Michael B. .... **Panama City, FL**
Duncan, Michael D. .... **Wilkesboro, NC**
Duncan, Michael D. .... **Oklahoma City, OK**
Duncan, Michael J. .... San Diego, CA
Duncan, Michael J.
Colorado Springs, CO
Duncan, Michael L. .... **Jacksonville, FL**
Duncan, Michael Louis .... Somerset, KY
Duncan, Michael N. .... Spartanburg, SC
Duncan, Michael P. .... **Des Plaines, IL**
Duncan, Michael T. .... **Houston, TX**
Duncan, Michael W. H. .... Malvern, PA
Duncan, Michele R. .... **Charleston, WV**
Duncan & Mosley .... **Chattanooga, TN**
Duncan, Myrl L. .... Topeka, KS
Duncan, Natalie F. .... Austin, TX
Duncan, Nicholas Dale .... Austin, TX
Duncan, Nicole .... **New York, NY**
Duncan, Nora Kathryn .... Oakdale, LA
Duncan, Ostrander & Dingess, P.C.
Denver, CO
Duncan, P.B., & Associates, L.L.C.
Montgomery, AL
Duncan, P. Michelle D. .... Baker, LA
Duncan, Parker W., Jr. .... **Louisville, KY**
Nashville, TN
Duncan, Patricia .... **Burbank, CA**
Duncan, Patricia A. .... Santa Ana, CA
Duncan, Patrick A. .... Franklin, NE
Duncan, Patrick Casey
Merit Systems Protection Board, Office of Appeals Counsel, GV
Duncan, Patti L. .... Dallas, TX
Duncan, Paul C., Jr. .... Oklahoma City, OK
Duncan, Peter L. .... **San Diego, CA**
Duncan, Phillip J., (P.A.) .... **Little Rock, AR**
Duncan & Phillips .... Greenfield, OH
Duncan, Priscilla Black .... Montgomery, AL
Duncan, R. Andrew .... Tampa, FL
Duncan & Rainwater, Trial Lawyers, A Prof. Assn. .... **Forrest City, AR**
Fort Smith, AR
Jonesboro, AR
Little Rock, AR
Russellville, AR
Duncan, Randa L. .... **Houston, TX**
Duncan, Randal J .... Radford, VA
Duncan, Randall L. .... **Portland, OR**
Duncan, Randall T. .... **Claremore, OK**
Tulsa, OK
Duncan, Randolph Mathieson (Matt)
Des Moines, IA
Duncan, Richard A. .... **Minneapolis, MN**
Duncan, Richard A. .... Pierre, SD
Duncan, Richard D. .... St. Louis, MO
Duncan, Richard F. .... Lincoln, NE
Duncan, Richard G., Jr. .... **Irvine, CA**
Orange, CA
Duncan, Richard L. .... Dayton, OH
Duncan, Richard L. .... **Knoxville, TN**
Duncan, Richard W. .... **San Antonio, TX**
Duncan, Robert A. .... Indianapolis, IN
Duncan, Robert B. .... **Washington, DC**
McLean, VA
Duncan, Robert E., II .... Topeka, KS
Duncan, Robert F. .... **Lexington, KY**
Duncan, Robert F., Jr. .... Oak Brook, IL
Duncan, Robert K. .... Dayton, OH
Duncan, Robert L. .... **Lubbock, TX**
Duncan, Robert L. .... Cheyenne, WY
Duncan, Robert L., Jr. .... New York, NY
Duncan, Robert M. .... Inez, KY
Duncan, Robert M. .... Columbus, OH
Duncan, Robert R. .... Denver, CO
Duncan, Roger L. .... Tucson, AZ
Duncan, Ronda Mae .... Fresno, CA
Duncan, Rosario Portuondo
Coral Gables, FL
Duncan, Russell .... Gainesville, TX
Duncan, Russell D. .... **Washington, DC**
Duncan, Russell P. .... **New York, NY**
Duncan, Sally Schneider .... **Phoenix, AZ**
Duncan, Samuel J. .... **Hattiesburg, MS**
Duncan, Sara .... Denver, CO
Duncan, Sarah C. .... Greenfield, OH
Duncan, Scott J. .... **Corpus Christi, TX**
Duncan, Scott P. .... **Des Moines, IA**
Duncan - Senecal, Chartered .... Atchison, KS
Leavenworth, KS
Duncan, Sharon J. .... **Orlando, FL**
Duncan, Stephen M. .... McLean, VA
Duncan, Stephen S. .... Kansas City, MO
Duncan, Steven P. .... Laguna Beach, CA
Duncan, Stuart E. .... **Chattanooga, TN**
Duncan, Stuart Kyle .... Houston, TX
Duncan, Susan R. .... Canton, CT
Duncan, T. Scott .... Lawrenceville, GA
Duncan, Tamara .... **Palo Alto, CA**
Duncan, Tanis A. .... Tucson, AZ
Duncan & Tardif, P.A., A Professional Association .... **Cape Coral, FL**
Fort Myers, FL
Duncan, Terrance .... Salinas, CA
Duncan, Thomas A. .... **Kansas City, MO**
Duncan, Thomas C. .... **Greensboro, NC**
Duncan, Thomas G.
House of Representatives, Office of Parliamentarian, GV
Duncan, Thomas H. .... **Denver, CO**
Duncan, Thomas J. .... Setauket, NY
Duncan, Thomasenia P.
Corporation for National and Community Service, Office of the General Counsel, GV
Duncan, Thomasson, Leonard & Shattuck
Franklin, GA
La Grange, GA
Duncan, Thurman E. .... **La Grange, GA**
Duncan, Timothy .... Cambridge, MA
Duncan, Timothy R. .... **Minneapolis, MN**
Duncan, Tristan Layle .... **Kansas City, MO**
Duncan, Ulman, Weakley & Bressler, Inc.
San Antonio, TX
Duncan, Vernon F. .... Franklin, NE
Duncan, Virginia I. .... **Sedona, AZ**
Duncan, Wallace L. .... **Washington, DC**
Duncan, Wallace L. .... Poplar Bluff, MO
Duncan, Weinberg, Genzer & Pembroke, P.C. .... **San Jose, CA**
Washington, DC
Portland, OR
Duncan, William .... El Paso, TX
Duncan, William A. .... **Cleveland, OH**
Duncan, William L. .... **Spartanburg, SC**
Duncan, William M. .... Hornbrook, CA
Duncan, William M. .... Hartford, CT
Duncan, William Michael .... Columbia, SC
Duncan, William S. .... **Georgetown, SC**
Surfside Beach, SC
Duncan, William Stuart, Law Firm of
Georgetown, SC
Duncan, Xollie .... Bentonville, AR
Duncan-Brice, Jennifer .... Chicago, IL
Duncan-Harrison, Lucia .... **Atlanta, GA**
Duncan-Peters, Stephanie .... Washington, DC
Duncanson, Ella J. .... **Palo Alto, CA**
Duncanson, Mark J. .... Jamestown, NY
Duncanson, Robert J. .... Murrieta, CA
Duncanson, William F. .... Jamestown, NY
Duncanson, William F. .... Jamestown, NY
Duncheon, Michael A. .... **San Francisco, CA**
Dunchock, Arnold .... Corunna, MI
Dunck, H. Thomas, Jr. .... Richmond, VA
Dunck, Shelley L. .... Chicago, IL
Dunckel, Donald H., II .... Kalamazoo, MI
Dunckel, Earl B. .... **Lowville, NY**
Dunckel, Priscilla Lynn .... **Dallas, TX**
Dunckel, Robert B. .... Fort Lauderdale, FL
Dunckelman, William H. .... Houma, LA
Duncker, Conrad O. .... Chicago, IL
Duncliffe, Neil E. .... Georgetown, KY
Duncombe, Barbara A. .... **Dayton, OH**
Duncombe, Raynor B. .... Schoharie, NY
Dundas, David G. .... **Irvine, CA**
Dundas, Derek D. .... **Costa Mesa, CA**
Dundas, Garrison M. .... **Fort Pierce, FL**
Dundas, Gerald P. .... Farmington Hills, MI
Dundas, Jana L. .... Houston, TX
Dundas, John A., II .... Pasadena, CA
Dundas, Mary Jane .... Tempe, AZ
Dundas, Natalie Sibbald .... **Costa Mesa, CA**
Dundas, Philip B., III .... New York, NY
Dundas, Philip B., Jr. .... **New York, NY**
Dundee, Mark W. .... **Los Angeles, CA**
Dunder, Keith A. .... Minneapolis, MN
Dundes, Raymond J. .... Dayton, OH
Dundis, Stephen P. .... Chicago, IL
Dundon, Jeffrey R. .... **Centerville, OH**
Dundon, Matthew J. .... **New York, NY**
Dundon, Thomas H. .... **Nashville, TN**
Dundon, Thomas R. .... Traverse City, MI
Dundy, Michael W. .... Houston, TX
Dune, Steve C. .... New York, NY
Dunec, JoAnne L. .... **San Francisco, CA**
Dunefsky, Allyse B. .... **White Plains, NY**
Dunefsky, Brian .... **New York, NY**
Dunegan, L. Jean .... Hudson, MI
Dunegan, Richard E. .... **Orlando, FL**
Dunegan, Stephen D. .... **Orlando, FL**
Dunesky, Allyse B. .... **New York, NY**
Dunetz, Charles S. .... **Livingston, NJ**
Dunetz, Jeffrey L. .... **New York, NY**
Dunetz, Marcus, Brody & Weinstein, L.L.C.
Livingston, NJ
Dunetz, Roger M. .... Miami, FL
Dunevant, Thomas, III .... Phoenix, AZ
Dunfee, Jack C., Jr. .... Johns Island, SC
Dunfee, John W. .... **Washington, DC**
Dunfee, Thomas W. .... Philadelphia, PA
Dunfield, Chris W. .... Corvallis, OR
Dunford, George M., III .... Salem, OR
Dunford, James B. .... Shreveport, LA
Dunford, Robin Commons .... Tampa, FL
Dunford, Thomas M. .... **Seattle, WA**
Dungan, Charles B., Jr. .... Maryville, TN
Dungan, Christopher .... Sarasota, FL
Dungan, Darryl C. .... Fort Lauderdale, FL
Dungan & LeFevre, A Legal Professional Association .... Covington, OH
Dayton, OH
Piqua, OH
Troy, OH
Dungan, Mark C. .... **Sarasota, FL**
Dungan and Meares .... Maryville, TN
Dungan, Nelson V. N. .... Somerville, NJ
Dungan, Robert E. .... Asheville, NC
Dungan, Robert E., P.A. .... Asheville, NC
D'Unger, Gerald F. .... **Dallas, TX**
Dunger, James E. .... Santa Ana, CA
Dungey, Richard J. .... **Stuart, FL**
Dunham, Barbara M. .... **Wallingford, CT**
Dunham, Boman & Leskera .... **Belleville, IL**
Collinsville, IL
Dunham, Bradley W. .... **Peoria, IL**
Dunham, Buel W. .... Tustin, CA
Dunham, Carl M., Jr. .... New Milford, CT
Dunham, Catherine Ross .... **Fayetteville, NC**
Dunham, Christopher C. .... **New York, NY**
Dunham, Corydon B. .... **Washington, DC**
New York, NY

Dunham, Cynthia C. .... Olathe, KS
Dunham, D. Scott .... Minneapolis, MN
Dunham, Dan S. .... Morris Plains, NJ
Dunham, Daniel R. .... Columbia, MO
Dunham, Darrell W. .... Carbondale, IL
Dunham, David C. .... West Palm Beach, FL
Dunham, David E. .... Austin, TX
Dunham, Douglas K. .... Dallas, TX
Dunham, Douglas S. .... Seattle, WA
Dunham, Douglas W. .... New York, NY
Dunham, Edgar Alden, IV .... Trenton, NJ
Dunham, Edward M., Jr.
Philadelphia, PA
Dunham, Edward Wood .... New Haven, CT
Dunham, Ellen M. .... Boston, MA
Dunham, Frank W., III .... New York, NY
Dunham, Frank W., Jr. .... Alexandria, VA
Arlington, VA
Dunham, Geoffrey .... New York, NY
Dunham, Gilbert H. .... New York, NY
Dunham, Giuliana H.
Department of Justice, Criminal Division, GV
Dunham & Grassi, P.C. .... Hillsdale, MI
Dunham, Harvey A. .... Spokane, WA
Dunham, James David .... Griffin, GA
Dunham, James S. .... Russellville, AR
Dunham, James W., Jr. .... Tulsa, OK
Dunham, Jeff .... Fayetteville, NC
Dunham, John J. .... Southington, CT
Dunham, John M. .... Hartford, CT
Dunham, John N. .... Sparks, MD
Dunham, John Raymond, III
Sarasota, FL
Dunham, Kathleen L. .... Santa Ana, CA
Dunham, Kenneth F. .... Marietta, GA
Dunham, Kimberly F. .... Greenville, SC
Dunham, Lawrence P.
Department of State, GV
Dunham, Lester R., Jr. .... Clifton, NJ
Dunham, Mary Ann .... Pittsburgh, PA
Dunham, Milton G. .... Minneapolis, MN
Dunham, Patrick .... Seattle, WA
Dunham, Paul J. .... Austin, TX
Dunham, Ralph Wesley .... Andover, MA
Dunham & Ramey, P.A. .... Russellville, AR
Dunham, Robert B. .... Beaumont, TX
Dunham, Robert Brett .... Philadelphia, PA
Dunham, Roderick R. .... Hillsdale, MI
Dunham, Roger E. .... Seattle, WA
Dunham, Ronald L. .... Tempe, AZ
Dunham, Scott H. .... Los Angeles, CA
Dunham, Stephen S. .... Denver, CO
Dunham, Thomas M. .... Washington, DC
Dunham, W. Lee H. .... Boston, MA
Dunham, Walter, Jr. .... Corpus Christi, TX
Dunham, William F. .... Hagerstown, MD
Dunham, Wm. H. .... Manchester, ME
Dunham, Wolcott B., Jr. .... New York, NY
Dunham, Yuko Uezumi .... New York, NY
Duni, Rollin F. .... Fallbrook, CA
Dunican, Patrick C., Jr. .... New York, NY
Dunick, Duane .... Dearborn Heights, MI
Dunie, Maurice R. .... Bethesda, MD
Dunietz, Jerry S. .... Rockville, MD
Dunigan, E. Bryan, III .... Chicago, IL
Dunigan, Elizabeth A. .... Cambridge, MA
Dunigan, Terrence J. .... Austin, TX
Dunigan, Thomas E. .... Washington, DC
Dunigan, Thomas L. .... Santa Fe, NM
Duning, J. William .... Lebanon, OH
Duning, T. P. .... Lewisburg, TN
Dunipace, H. Richard .... Bowling Green, OH
Dunipace, I. Douglas .... Phoenix, AZ
Dunipace, John M. .... Bowling Green, OH
Dunipace, Thomas M. .... Colfax, CA
Dunitz, Jonathan M. .... Portland, ME
Dunitz, Nelson I. .... Chicago, IL
Dunivan, Karen E. .... Richmond, VA
Dunivan, Lindell P. .... Farmington, MO
Dunivan, Lori L. .... San Diego, CA
Duniway, Sarah .... Minneapolis, MN
Dunk, Andrew P. P., III .... San Diego, CA
Dunk, John C. S. .... San Diego, CA
Dunkel, Charles A. .... San Francisco, CA
Dunkel, Gary M. .... West Palm Beach, FL
Dunkel, John A. .... Columbus, OH
Dunkelberg, A. G. .... Osage, IA
Dunkelberg, McKinley, Folkers & Walk
Osage, IA
Dunkelberg, Ryk A. .... Tulsa, OK
Dunkelberger, Christy A. .... Atlanta, GA
Dunkelberger, H. Edward, Jr.
Washington, DC
Dunkel-Bradley, Dorothy A.
Los Angeles, CA
Dunkelman, Brett L. .... Phoenix, AZ
Dunkelman, Paul R. .... Frisco, CO
Dunkelman, Robert A. .... Shreveport, LA
Dunker, Dawn M. .... Columbus, OH
Dunker, Deborah M.
Greenwood Village, CO
Dunker, Henry T. .... Weymouth, MA
Dunker, Leonard R. .... Lincoln, NE
Dunker, Steven A. .... Grand Rapids, MI
Dunker, Steven J. .... Casper, WY
Dunker, William L. .... Cranford, NJ
Dunkerley, Debra L. .... Columbus, OH
Dunkerley, Michele A. .... Round Rock, TX
Dunkerly, Edward L. .... Vancouver, WA
Dunkin, Craig L. .... Los Angeles, CA
Dunkin, David A. .... Englewood, FL
Dunkin, David A., P.A. .... Englewood, FL
Dunkin, David C. .... Chicago, IL
Dunkin, Ellen R. .... New York, NY
Dunkin, Sol R. .... Jamaica, NY
Dunkin, Warren C. .... Lakewood, CO
Dunkirk, David R. .... Oak Ridge, TN
Dunkirk, Jean H. .... Oak Ridge, TN
Dunkle & Bunecky, P.A. .... Sarasota, FL
Dunkle, David S. .... Birmingham, AL
Dunkle, Kurt H. .... Jacksonville, FL
Dunkle, Mark F. .... Dover, DE
Dunkle, Randal C. .... Sarasota, FL
Dunklee, David V. .... Denver, CO
Dunkless, Robert C. .... Boston, MA
Dunkley, Bennett & Christensen, P.A.
Minneapolis, MN
Dunkley, Chad .... Plymouth, MN
Dunkley, Denzil R. .... Newark, NJ
Dunkley, J. Reed .... Spokane, WA
Dunkley, Patrick H. .... Palo Alto, CA
Dunkley, William M. .... Minneapolis, MN
Dunklin, Garth K. .... Charlotte, NC
Dunklin, Larry G. .... Little Rock, AR
Dunks-Iley, Mary K. .... Denver, CO
Dunkum, B. Craig .... Richmond, VA
Dunkum, Bennie L. .... Richmond, VA
Dunkum, Betty L. .... Washington, DC
Dunkum, Marvin H., Jr. .... Buckingham, VA
Dunlap, Aklilu D .... Minneapolis, MN
Dunlap, Andrew A. .... Dallas, TX
Dunlap, Angela F. .... Indianapolis, IN
Dunlap, Anna B. .... Jacksonville, OR
Dunlap, Anne A. .... Dallas, TX
Dunlap, Arthur M. .... Boston, MA
Dunlap, Benjamin Charles, Jr.
Harrisburg, PA
Dunlap, Brenda N. .... Blanchester, OH
Lebanon, OH
Dunlap & Brown, Ltd. .... Libertyville, IL
Dunlap, Bryan R. .... New York, NY
Dunlap & Burdick, A Professional Law Corporation .... Santa Cruz, CA
Dunlap, Calvin R. X. .... Reno, NV
Dunlap, Carolyn N. .... Dearborn, MI
Dunlap, Caswell .... Dallas, TX
Dunlap, Caswell L. .... Dallas, TX
Dunlap, Celia Muller .... Frankfort, KY
Dunlap, Charles E. .... St. Louis, MO
Dunlap, Charles E. .... Canfield, OH
Dunlap, Charles L. .... Orlando, FL
Dunlap, Charles L. .... Honolulu, HI
Dunlap, Charles R. .... Muncie, IN
Dunlap, Charles T. (Tom) .... Roswell, NM
Dunlap, Chet D. .... Trumann, AR
Dunlap, Codding & Rogers, P.C.
Oklahoma City, OK
Dunlap, Craig .... Salt Lake City, UT
Dunlap, David G. .... Houston, TX
Dunlap, David H. .... West Plains, MO
Dunlap, David J. .... Topeka, KS
Dunlap, David L. .... Indianapolis, IN
Dunlap, David Lewis .... Hermitage, TN
Dunlap, David M. .... Jacksonville, FL
Dunlap, David M. .... Memphis, TN
Dunlap, David W.
Federal Energy Regulatory Commission, Office of the General Counsel, GV
Dunlap, Davisson F., Jr. .... Tallahassee, FL
Dunlap, Edgar B., II .... Gainesville, GA
Dunlap, Elizabeth Bower .... Richardson, TX
Dunlap, Eric Dwayne .... Orlando, FL
Dunlap, F. Thomas, Jr. .... Santa Clara, CA
Dunlap, Gary J. .... Lompoc, CA
Dunlap, Gary, P.C. .... Lompoc, CA
Dunlap, George C. .... Dallas, TX
Dunlap, George C., Jr. .... Dallas, TX
Dunlap, George T., III .... Bartow, FL
Dunlap, Gerry A. .... Milford, NE
Dunlap, Grace E. .... Tampa, FL
Dunlap, Gregory E. .... Harrisburg, PA
Dunlap, Hanna-Aurelia .... Lancaster, PA
Dunlap Herzig .... San Francisco, CA
Dunlap, Holly Green .... Jacksonville, FL
Dunlap, J. Daniel .... Walnut Creek, CA
Dunlap, Jack .... Berlin, MD
Dunlap, Jackson R., Jr. .... Georgetown, DE
Dunlap, James A. .... Gainesville, GA
Dunlap, James B. .... Lakewood, CO
Dunlap, James E. .... Pasadena, CA
Dunlap, James L. .... Waukesha, WI
Dunlap, Janet M. .... Boston, MA
Dunlap, Jay L. .... Milford, NE
Dunlap, Jeffrey D. .... Akron, OH
Dunlap, Jeffrey S. .... Cleveland, OH
Dunlap, Jerry J. .... Oklahoma City, OK
Dunlap, Jerry J., II .... Oklahoma City, OK
Dunlap, Jim .... Austin, TX
Dunlap, Jimmie G. .... Marked Tree, AR
Dunlap, John Anthony .... New Orleans, LA
Dunlap, John B., III .... Baton Rouge, LA
Dunlap, John C. .... Minneapolis, MN
Dunlap, John F. .... Napa, CA
Dunlap, John F. .... Arlington, VA
Dunlap, John K. .... Library of Congress, Copyright Office, GV
Dunlap, John K. .... Atlanta, GA
Dunlap, John K. .... Dallas, TX
Dunlap, John P. .... Redding, CA
Dunlap, John R. .... Memphis, TN
Dunlap, John T. .... New York, NY
Dunlap, Julia M. .... Escondido, CA
Dunlap, Karin R. .... Rockville, MD
Dunlap, Kenneth J. .... Milwaukee, WI
Dunlap, Kevin A. .... Spartanburg, SC
Dunlap, Larry .... Riverside, CA
Dunlap, Laura Lee .... Butte, MT
Dunlap, Laurence M. .... Libertyville, IL
Dunlap, Laurie A. .... Sacramento, CA
Dunlap, Lora A. .... Orlando, FL
Dunlap, M. Lynn .... Twin Falls, ID
Dunlap, M. Richard .... Pittsburgh, PA
Wheeling, WV
Dunlap, Mark E. .... Portland, ME
Dunlap, Marvin J., Jr. .... Katy, TX
Dunlap, Mary C. .... San Francisco, CA
Dunlap, Mary H. .... Rochester, MN
Dunlap, Michael E. .... Santa Cruz, CA
Dunlap, Mollie Busterud .... Long Beach, CA
Dunlap & Moran, P.A. .... Fort Myers, FL
Sarasota, FL
Dunlap, Nancy K. .... Dallas, TX
Dunlap, Paul D. .... Des Moines, IA
Dunlap, Peter L. .... Lansing, MI
Dunlap, Phil .... Beaumont, TX
Dunlap, Philip A. .... Renton, WA
Dunlap, R. Terren .... Scottsdale, AZ
Dunlap, Ray M. .... Kirkland, WA
Dunlap, Richard J. .... Seattle, WA
Dunlap, Richard L., III .... Paris, TN
Dunlap, Richd. H. .... Los Angeles, CA
Dunlap, Robert B., II .... Saipan, TT
Dunlap, Robert E. .... Bellefontaine, OH
Dunlap, Robert H. .... Wilmington, DE
Dunlap, Robert Hunt, Jr. .... Atlanta, GA
Dunlap, Robert, P.C. .... Colorado Springs, CO
Dunlap, Robert William .... San Francisco, CA
Dunlap & Russell, P.A. .... Jacksonville, FL
Dunlap, Scott W. .... Sarasota, FL
Dunlap & Seeger, P.A. .... Austin, MN
Rochester, MN
Winona, MN
Dunlap & Soderland, P.S. .... Seattle, WA
Dunlap, Stephen J. .... Hudson, WI
Dunlap, Tavner B. .... Versailles, KY
Dunlap, Thomas M. .... Fulton, MO
Dunlap, Thomas Mansfield .... Leesburg, VA
Dunlap, Thomas Paine .... Los Angeles, CA
Dunlap, Thos. D. .... Humboldt, TN
Dunlap, Tom .... Santa Clara, CA
Dunlap, Tracy .... Hailey, ID
Dunlap, Trudy I. .... Laguna Hills, CA
Dunlap, Virginia Jo .... Sacramento, CA
Reno, NV
Dunlap, W. Gray .... St. Petersburg, FL
Dunlap, W. Gray, Jr. (P.A.) .... Tampa, FL
Dunlap, Walter H., Jr. .... Dallas, TX
Dunlap, Whitney, III .... Richmond, KY
Dunlap, William E., Jr. .... Columbus, OH
Dunlap, William P., (P.A.) .... Seminole, FL
Dunlap, William V. .... Hamden, CT
Dunlap, William W., Jr. .... Memphis, TN
Dunlavey, Colin Patrick .... Wilmington, DE
Dunlavey, David A. .... Presque Isle, ME
Dunlavey, Dean C. .... Los Angeles, CA
Dunlavey, Dean G. .... Costa Mesa, CA
Dunlavey, James .... Oakland, CA
Dunlavey, Walter F .... Seattle, WA
Dunlay, Catherine T. .... Columbus, OH
Dunlay, Edward L. .... El Paso, TX
Dunlay, F. Charles, IV .... Kansas City, KS
Dunlay, Jonathan W. .... Dallas, TX
Dunleavy, April Z. .... New York, NY
Dunleavy, Denise M. .... New York, NY
Dunleavy, Edward T. .... Rockaway Point, NY
Dunleavy, James A. .... Philadelphia, PA
Dunleavy, James M. .... Presque Isle, ME
Dunleavy, James P. .... Presque Isle, ME
Dunleavy, John K. .... Montpelier, VT
Dunleavy, Jonathan H. .... Chicago, IL
Dunleavy, Kevin J. .... Washington, DC
Dunleavy Law Offices, P.A.
Presque Isle, ME
Dunleavy, Patricia Godwin .... Ila, GA
Dunleavy, Robert E., Jr. .... Collingswood, NJ
Dunleavy, Terence M. .... Chicago, IL
Dunleavy, William J. .... Dallas, TX
Dunlevey, Karen T. .... Dayton, OH
Dunlevey, Mahan & Furry, A Legal Professional Association .... Dayton, OH
Dunlevey, Robert T., Jr. .... Dayton, OH
Dunlevie, Michael R. .... Avon, CO
Dunlevie, Steven S. .... Atlanta, GA
Dunlevy, Cynthia M. .... La Jolla, CA
Dunlevy, Diann L. .... Minneapolis, MN
Dunlevy, F.W., Jr., A Professional Corporation
Oklahoma City, OK
Dunlevy, F. W. "Rick", Jr.
Oklahoma City, OK
Dunlevy, Kevin J. .... Minneapolis, MN
Dunlevy, Patrick Mark .... Los Angeles, CA
Dunlevy, Shawn M. .... Duluth, MN
Dunlevy, Susan D. .... Tampa, FL
Dunlevy, Terry T. .... Baton Rouge, LA
Dunlevy, William S. .... Camarillo, CA
Dunley, Candace M. .... Denver, CO
Dunlop, Brian D. .... St. Louis, MO
Dunlop, Charles A. .... Crystal Lake, IL
Dunlop, Diana Knowles .... Winter Park, FL
Dunlop, Dudley C. .... St. Louis, MO
Dunlop, Dunlop & Dunlop, P.A.
Orlando, FL
Winter Park, FL
Dunlop, Fred H. .... Houston, TX
Dunlop, J. Erwin .... Winter Park, FL
Dunlop, James C. .... Chicago, IL
Dunlop, Janet R. .... Department of Labor, Office of the Solicitor, GV
Dunlop, John E. .... Washington, DC
Dunlop, Karen O. .... Chicago, IL
Dunlop, Karlin Rene .... Las Vegas, NV
Dunlop, Lisl J. .... New York, NY
Dunlop & McCarter .... St. Louis, MO
Dunlop, Pamela R. .... Dallas, TX
Dunlop, Philip T. .... Winter Park, FL
Dunlop, Richard E.
Equal Employment Opportunity Commission, Office of Legal Counsel, GV
Dunlop, Roberta L. .... Kew Gardens, NY
Dunlop, Robin E. .... Treasury Department, Bureau of the Public Debt, GV
Dunlop, Scott G. .... Pittsburgh, PA
Dunlop, Thomas G. .... Brookfield, WI
Dunlop, William N. .... Boise, ID
Dunlop, William R. .... New York, NY
Dunlow, John Marshall .... Oxford, NC
Dunmire, Fisher & Hastings .... Hastings, NE
Dunmire, John D. .... Norristown, PA
Dunmire, Lawrence .... Hastings, NE
Dunmire, Terrance D. .... Phoenix, AZ
Dunmire, Thea D. .... Clearwater, FL
Dunmire, Virginia J. .... Kansas City, MO
Dunn, A. Kelley .... Washington, PA
Dunn, Abe .... Houston, TX
Dunn, Abplanalp & Mauriello, P.C.
Eagle, CO
Vail, CO
Dunn, Alan Gary .... Denver, CO
Dunn, Alan M. .... Washington, DC
Dunn, Albert C., Jr .... Charleston, WV
Dunn, Alton G., Jr. .... Cooperstown, NY
Dunn, Alvin .... Washington, DC
Dunn, Andrew D. .... Manchester, NH
Dunn, Andrew Donelson .... Nashville, TN
Dunn, Andrew J. .... Des Moines, IA
Dunn, Andrew M. .... Oneida, NY
Dunn, Andrew S. .... Hamlin, NY
Dunn, Angela .... Columbiana, AL
Dunn, Arin M. .... Seattle, WA
Dunn, Arin M., P.S. .... Seattle, WA
Dunn & Associates .... Newfane, NY
Dunn, B. Michael .... Mason City, IA
Dunn, Barbara .... Chicago, IL
Dunn, Barbara E. .... Pasadena, CA
Dunn, Barbara Fox .... Minneapolis, MN
Dunn, Barry E. .... Tallahassee, FL
Dunn, Benjamin A., II .... Columbia, SC
Dunn, Bernard J. .... Topeka, KS
Dunn, Bernard L. .... Loudonville, NY
Dunn, Bertram F. .... Department of State, Foreign Service Officers (Overseas), GV
Dunn, Boyd W., (P.C.) .... Tempe, AZ
Dunn, Brendan C. .... Salem, OR
Dunn, Brett E. .... San Antonio, TX
Dunn, Brian H. .... Kansas City, MO
Dunn, Brian J. .... La Jolla, CA
Dunn, Brian J., A Professional Law Corporation .... La Jolla, CA
San Diego, CA
Dunn, Brian T. .... Los Angeles, CA
Dunn & Browne, L.L.C. .... Closter, NJ
Dunn, Bruce C., Sr. .... New Windsor, NY
Dunn, Bruce H. .... Malibu, CA
Dunn, Bryna Stokes .... Greenville, SC
Dunn, C. Burnett .... Tulsa, OK
Dunn, C. Burton .... Birmingham, AL
Dunn, Carney, Allen, Higgins & Tongue
Portland, OR
Dunn, Carol Rose .... Nashville, TN
Dunn, Cassandra .... Fresno, CA
Dunn, Catherine M.
Environmental Protection Agency, Program Office Attorneys, GV
Silver Spring, MD
Dunn, Cathy H. .... Spartanburg, SC
Dunn, Cecil F. .... Lexington, KY
Dunn, Charles .... Lubbock, TX
Dunn, Charles A., Jr. .... DeLand, FL
Dunn, Charles C. .... Fairfax, VA
Dunn, Charles E. .... Bloomfield Hills, MI
Dunn, Charles H. .... Birmingham, AL
Dunn, Charles J. .... Manchester, NH
Dunn, Charles J., Jr. .... Boston, MA
Dunn, Charles J., Jr. .... Manhasset, NY
Dunn, Charles J., Jr., A Prof. Corp., Law Offices of .... Boston, MA
Dunn, Charles L. .... Madison, MS
Dunn, Charles O. .... Yazoo City, MS
Dunn, Charles R. .... Houston, TX
Dunn, Charles S. .... Charleston, WV
Dunn, Cheryl J. .... Springfield, MA
Dunn, Christopher A. .... Washington, DC
Dunn, Christopher J. .... United States Senate, Committee Legal Personnel, GV
Dunn, Christopher R. .... Lanham, MD
Dunn, Christopher S. .... Nashville, TN
Dunn & Clark, P.A. .... Rigby, ID
Dunn, Claudia Sue .... New Orleans, LA
Dunn, Clement .... Longview, TX
Dunn, Clifford V. .... St. George, UT
Dunn, Clyde A. .... Newport, TN
Dunn, Clyde A., And Associates
Newport, TN
Dunn, Cynthia Bullock .... Irving, TX
Dunn & Daffern, P.A. .... Tulsa, OK
Dunn, Damon E. .... Chicago, IL
Dunn, Daniel Andrew, Jr .... Rockford, IL
Dunn, Daniel E., S.C. .... La Crosse, WI
Dunn, Daniel J. .... Denver, CO
Dunn, Daniel J. .... Fargo, ND
Dunn, Daniel M. .... New York, NY
Dunn, Daniel S. .... Machiasport, ME
Dunn, Danni Sternfeld .... San Francisco, CA
Dunn, Darlene E. .... Ocala, FL
Dunn, Darlene E., P.A. .... Ocala, FL
Dunn, Darlene Jeanne .... Toledo, OH
Dunn, Darlene S. .... San Diego, CA
Dunn, David .... New York, NY
Dunn, David .... Pierre, SD
Dunn, David A. .... Orange, TX
Dunn, David C. .... Manchester, NH
Dunn, David E., III .... Washington, DC
Dunn, David F., Law Offices .... Allentown, PA
Dunn, David J. .... La Fayette, GA
Dunn, David J. .... Ringgold, GA
Dunn, David J. .... Trenton, GA
Dunn, David J. .... Corpus Christi, TX
Dunn, David N. .... Brattleboro, VT
Dunn, David S. .... Bloomington, IL

Dunn, David W. ... **Des Moines, IA**
Eldora, IA
Dunn, David W., Law Firm, PLC
Eldora, IA
Dunn, Deborah ... **Chicago, IL**
Dunn, Denis M. ... **Media, PA**
Dunn, Denise A. ... Newport News, VA
Dunn, Dennis C. ... **Houston, TX**
Dunn, Dennis R. ... Atlanta, GA
Dunn, Diedre S. ... **Chicago, IL**
Dunn, Dolores A. ... Cincinnati, OH
Dunn, Donald F. ... **The Dalles, OR**
Dunn, Donald J. ... New Bern, NC
Dunn, Donald J., P.A. ... New Bern, NC
Dunn, Donald L. ... Lincoln, NE
Dunn, Donya Hicks ... Oklahoma City, OK
Dunn, Douglas L. ... Knoxville, TN
Dunn, Douglas R. ... Dallas, TX
Dunn, Drew A. ... Department of Commerce, Patent and Trademark Office, GV
Dunn, Duane D. ... Marrero, LA
Dunn & Dunn ... **Salt Lake City, UT**
Dunn & Dunn, Attorneys, P.A.
St. Petersburg, FL
Dunn, Dunn & Mitchell, L.L.P.
Columbia, SC
Dunn & Dunn, P.C. ... Eldora, IA
Dunn, Dunn, Stoller & Pittman, L.L.P.
New Bern, NC
Dunn, E. Thomas, Jr. ... Santa Ana, CA
Dunn, Edgar H., Jr. ... Otto, NC
Dunn, Edgar M., Jr. ... **Daytona Beach, FL**
Dunn, Edgar M., Jr., P.A.
Daytona Beach, FL
Dunn, Edward K. ... **Sacramento, CA**
Dunn, Edward P. ... Fulton, NY
Dunn, Edward S. ... Holton, KS
Dunn, Edward W. ... **Springfield, OH**
Dunn, Edwin R. ... **Chicago, IL**
Dunn, Eileen K. ... Springfield, MA
Dunn, Eleanor A. Putnam ... Lynchburg, VA
Dunn, Elizabeth A.
Department of Commerce, Patent and Trademark Office, GV
Dunn, Elizabeth B. ... **Boston, MA**
Dunn, Elizabeth Eleanor ... Brainerd, MN
Dunn, Elizabeth Jucius ... **Springfield, OH**
Dunn, Ellen M. ... **New York, NY**
Dunn, Eric L. ... **Costa Mesa, CA**
Dunn & Ferrari ... San Jose, CA
Dunn, Francis Joseph ... **Marlton, NJ**
Philadelphia, PA
Dunn, Francis M. ... Springfield, MA
Dunn, Frank J. ... Morris Plains, NJ
Dunn, Franklin & Murphy
Lexington, KY
Dunn, Franklin T. ... **Los Angeles, CA**
Dunn, G. William ... Long Beach, CA
Dunn, Gary S. ... Levittown, NY
Dunn, Gary W. ... **New York, NY**
Dunn, Geoffrey R. ... Corte Madera, CA
Dunn, George Harvey, III ... **Dallas, TX**
Dunn, George J. ... **Cleveland, OH**
Dunn, George R. ... St. Paul, MN
Dunn, George S. ... South Haven, MI
Dunn, George T. ... Rye, NY
Dunn, George T. ... Lockhart, TX
Dunn, Gerard W. ... Media, PA
Dunn, Gilbert T. ... Carle Place, NY
Dunn, Gloria Y. ... Monterey Park, CA
Dunn, Gregory J. ... **Columbus, OH**
Dunn, Gregory Scott ... Indianapolis, IN
Dunn, Gregory T. ... Honolulu, HI
Dunn, Gregory T. ... **Albuquerque, NM**
Dunn, Gregory Y. ... Horse Cave, KY
Dunn, H. Glenn ... **Raleigh, NC**
Dunn, H. Stewart, Jr. ... **Washington, DC**
Dunn, Harry F., Jr. ... Media, PA
Dunn, Harry H. ... Hutchinson, KS
Dunn, Harvey ... **Columbus, OH**
Dunn, Henry M., Jr. ... **Savannah, GA**
Dunn, Henry R. ... Longview, WA
Dunn, Herbert I. ... General Accounting Office, Office of the General Counsel, GV
Dunn, Howard A. ... Cleveland, OH
Dunn, I. John ... **Erie, PA**
Dunn, Irving E. ... Miami, FL
Dunn, J. Morris, III ... Metairie, LA
Dunn, J. Morton ... West Hartford, CT
Dunn, J. Thomas, Jr. ... Charlotte, NC
Dunn, Jack H. ... Tigard, OR
Dunn, James ... Sherman, TX
Dunn, James A. ... Cincinnati, OH
Dunn, James A. ... **Houston, TX**
Dunn, James Bruce ... Nashville, TN
Dunn, James E. ... Greenwood, IN
Dunn, James E., Jr. ... Atlanta, GA
Dunn, James F. ... **Los Angeles, CA**
Dunn, James F. ... **St. Paul, MN**
Dunn, James F. ... New York, NY
Dunn, James F. ... Marietta, OH
Dunn, James F., & Associates, P.A.
St. Paul, MN
Dunn, James G. ... Pittsburgh, PA
Dunn, James J. ... Cleveland, OH
Dunn, James J. ... Burlington, VT
Dunn, James M. ... **Philadelphia, PA**
Dunn, James M. ... Salt Lake City, UT
Dunn, James Melvin ... **Fort Smith, AR**
Dunn, James, P.C. ... Sherman, TX
Dunn, James R. ... **San Bernardino, CA**
Dunn, James S. ... Springfield, IL
Dunn, James T. ... Bloomfield Hills, MI
Dunn, James T. ... **Portland, OR**
Dunn, James T. ... Midvale, UT
Dunn, Jan Karen Greenspan ... Southfield, MI
Dunn, Jane Sylvia ... Clearwater, FL
Dunn, Janice Belucci ... Santa Maria, CA
Dunn, Janine W. ... Sneads Ferry, NC
Dunn, Jason A. ... **Washington, DC**
Dunn, Jason E. ... **Boston, MA**
Dunn, Jason M. ... Waltham, MA
Dunn, Jean McNeil ... **Eldora, IA**
Dunn, Jeanne M. ... Glen Mills, PA
Dunn, Jeff M. ... West Bloomfield, MI
Dunn, Jeffrey A. ... **Washington, DC**
Baltimore, MD
Dunn, Jeffrey D. ... Jacksonville, FL
Dunn, Jeffrey D., (P.C.) ... **Dallas, TX**
Dunn, Jeffrey H.
General Services Administration, Office of Regional Counsel, GV
Dunn, Jeffrey T. ... **Tulsa, OK**
Dunn, Jeffrey V. ... **Riverside, CA**
Dunn, Jerry R. ... Englewood, CO
Dunn, Jill A. ... Albany, NY
Dunn, Jim ... Conway, SC
Dunn, John B. ... Takoma Park, MD
Dunn, John B. ... Stroudsburg, PA
Dunn, John B., Jr. ... **Greenville, NC**
Dunn, John C. ... San Francisco, CA
Dunn, John D. ... **Grand Rapids, MI**
Dunn, John D. ... Brownwood, TX
Dunn, John E. ... **Milwaukee, WI**
Dunn, John F. ... Chicago, IL
Dunn, John F. ... Decatur, IL
Dunn, John F. ... **Boston, MA**
Boston, MA
Dunn, John J. ... El Cerrito, CA
Dunn, John J. ... Denver, CO
Dunn, John J. ... Central Islip, NY
Dunn, John J., Sr. ... Scranton, PA
Dunn, John K. ... Providence, RI
Dunn, John L. ... Roslyn, NY
Dunn, John M. ... **Modesto, CA**
Dunn, John M. ... **San Diego, CA**
Dunn, John P. ... **Worcester, MA**
Dunn, John P. ... **Cleveland, OH**
Dunn, John T. ... San Francisco, CA
Dunn, John W. ... **Vail, CO**
Dunn, John W., Jr. ... Oklahoma City, OK
Dunn & Johnson, P.A. ... Miami, FL
Dunn, Jonathan J. ... **Los Angeles, CA**
Dunn, Joseph ... Swampscott, MA
Dunn, Joseph ... Somerville, NJ
Dunn, Joseph A. ... **Springfield, OH**
Dunn, Joseph E. ... Chicago, IL
Dunn, Joseph L. ... **Newport Beach, CA**
San Diego, CA
Dunn, Joseph P., Jr. ... Falmouth, MA
Dunn, Joseph W. ... **Bloomington, IL**
Dunn, Judith C. ... Treasury Department, Internal Revenue Service, GV
Dunn, K. Elizabeth ... **San Diego, CA**
Dunn, K. Kristine ... **Los Angeles, CA**
Dunn, Kacal, Adams, Pappas & Law, A Professional Corporation ... **Houston, TX**
Dunn, Karen L. ... Bellevue, WA
Dunn, Kathleen ... Bala Cynwyd, PA
Dunn, Kathleen Erin ... Newport, OR
Dunn, Keller, Gillespie, Johnston & Latz, L.C. ... **Kansas City, MO**
Dunn, Kelly ... Richmond, CA
Dunn, Kenneth A. ... Lowell, MA
Dunn, Kenneth C. ... Chicago, IL
Dunn, Kevin W. ... Medina, OH
Dunn, Kim ... **Anchorage, AK**
Dunn, Kristin E.D. ... **Long Beach, CA**
Dunn, Landon A. ... **Charlotte, NC**
Dunn, Landon A., P.A. ... **Charlotte, NC**
Dunn, Larry K. ... Reno, NV
Dunn, Larry K., & Associates, Chartered
Reno, NV
Dunn, Lawrence A. ... **Norfolk, VA**
Dunn, Lawrence A., Jr. ... **New York, NY**
Dunn, Lawrence D., II ... Lynn, MA
Dunn, Lawrence M. ... Englewood, CO
Dunn Leader & Allen ... **Worcester, MA**
Dunn, Leanne Rosle ... **New York, NY**
Dunn, Lee J., Jr. ... **Boston, MA**
Dunn, Lee & Keary ... **Irvine, CA**
Dunn, Leo J., III ... **Boston, MA**
Dunn, Leo Wm., Jr. ... **Chester, MD**
Dunn, Leo Wm., Jr., P.A. ... **Chester, MD**
Dunn, Leslie ... South Burlington, VT
Dunn, Leslie D. ... **Cleveland, OH**
Dunn, Lew ... Longview, TX
Dunn, Linda J. ... Seattle, WA
Dunn, Linda L. ... **New York, NY**
Dunn, Lisa Anne ... Gretna, LA
Dunn, Lisa Bondy ... **Los Angeles, CA**
Dunn, Lloyd A. ... Houston, TX
Dunn, Lonnie R. ... Quincy, IL
Dunn, Loren R. ... **Seattle, WA**
Dunn, Loretta L. ... United States Senate, Committee Legal Personnel, GV
Dunn, Louise E. ... Albany, NY
Dunn, Lynne A. ... **Toms River, NJ**
Dunn, M. Douglas ... **New York, NY**
Dunn, MacDonald & Coleman, P.C.
Knoxville, TN
Dunn, Malcolm G. ... Kingsport, TN
Dunn, Malson & Kozera, P.C.
Grand Rapids, MI
Dunn, Marcia T. ... Miami, FL
Dunn, Marcus D. ... **Columbus, OH**
Dunn, Margaret E. ... Tulsa, OK
Dunn, Maria C. ... **Bartlesville, OK**
Dunn, Marilyn P. ... Chicago, IL
Dunn, Mark E. ... St. Louis, MO
Dunn, Mark L. ... Syracuse, NY
Dunn, Mark P. ... **Troy, MI**
Dunn, Mark R. ... **St. Louis, MO**
Dunn, Mark S. ... Tallahassee, FL
Dunn, Mark T. ... **Bloomington, IL**
Dunn, Marla Becker ... **New York, NY**
Dunn, Martin J. ... South Hadley, MA
Dunn, Martin & Miller, Ltd. ... **Joliet, IL**
Dunn, Martiné R. ... **Cincinnati, OH**
Dunn, Mary E. ... Morris Plains, NJ
Dunn, Matthew J. ... Chicago, IL
Dunn, Matthew S. ... **New York, NY**
Dunn, Maureen ... Knoxville, TN
Dunn, Maureen S. ... Sacramento, CA
Dunn, Maureen S. ... Atlanta, GA
Dunn, Maureen Z. ... **Columbia, SC**
Dunn, McCormack & MacPherson
Fairfax, VA
Dunn & McMenamin ... Springfield, IL
Dunn, Mel ... Casper, WY
Dunn, Melanie ... Chicago, IL
Dunn, Melissa J. ... Miami Beach, FL
Dunn, Melvin E. ... Geneva, IL
Dunn, Michael A. ... Schaumburg, IL
Dunn, Michael A. ... Port Orchard, WA
Dunn, Michael B. ... **New York, NY**
Dunn, Michael E. ... **Oklahoma City, OK**
Dunn, Michael F. ... Glenside, PA
Dunn, Michael J. ... **Grand Rapids, MI**
Dunn, Michael J. ... **Haddonfield, NJ**
Philadelphia, PA
Dunn, Michael L. ... Newfane, NY
Dunn, Michael L. ... **Longview, TX**
Dunn, Michael M. ... Fort Worth, TX
Dunn, Michael O. ... **Lincoln, NE**
Dunn, Michael P. ... San Jose, CA
Dunn, Michael P. ... **Milwaukee, WI**
Dunn, Michael R. ... Detroit, MI
Mount Clemens, MI
Dunn, Michael R. ... Falls City, NE
Dunn, Michael T. ... Costa Mesa, CA
Dunn, Mike ... Sherman, TX
Dunn and Miller ... Media, PA
Dunn & Miller, P.C. ... St. Louis, MO
Dunn, Milton, (Co., L.P.A.) ... Cleveland, OH
Dunn, Nancy G. ...
United States Court Of Appeals District Of Columbia Circuit, GV
Dunn, Neal J. ... Melbourne, FL
Dunn, Nina Laserson ... **Parsippany, NJ**
Dunn, Nutter, Morgan & Shaw
Texarkana, AR
Texarkana, TX
Dunn, Pamela E. ... **Los Angeles, CA**
Dunn, Patricia ... Flushing, NY
Dunn, Patricia A. ... Department of Justice, Executive Office for Immigration Review, GV
Dunn, Patricia C. ... Houston, TX
Dunn, Patricia Colleen ... Tallahassee, FL
Dunn, Patricia McDonough ... **Portland, ME**
Dunn, Patrick L. ... **Kansas City, MO**
Dunn, Patrick T. ... **Auburn Hills, MI**
Dunn, Paul E. ... **Knoxville, TN**
Dunn, Paul J. ... Prescott, AZ
Dunn, Paul J., P.C. ... Prescott, AZ
Dunn, Peter A. ... **Philadelphia, PA**
Dunn, Peter G. ... **Phoenix, AZ**
Dunn, Peter I. ... **Boston, MA**
Dunn, Peter J. ... Babylon, NY
Dunn, Peter M. ... **Oneida, NY**
Dunn, Philip E., Jr. ... Bakersfield, CA
Dunn, Philip H. ... Santa Monica, CA
Dunn, Philip J. ... Boston, MA
Dunn, Philip M. ... **Closter, NJ**
Dunn, Philip R. ... **Westlake Village, CA**
Dunn, Philip R. ... New Britain, CT
Dunn, Philip R., Jr. ... **Hartford, CT**
Dunn & Phillips, P.C. ... Springfield, MA
Dunn, Pierce B. ... Lawrenceville, NJ
Dunn, R. Elliott, Jr. ... Wesley Chapel, FL
Dunn, R. Rogge ... **Dallas, TX**
Dunn, Ralph ... Richwood, WV
Dunn, Ralph B. ... Malden, MA
Dunn, Randall L. ... Portland, OR
Dunn, Randy E. ... **Denver, CO**
Dunn, Raney & Schmidt ... **Dallas, TX**
Dunn & Rasch, Ltd. ... Metairie, LA
Dunn, Ray A. ... Houston, TX
Dunn, Raymond E. ... **New Bern, NC**
Dunn, Raymond E., Jr. ... **New Bern, NC**
Dunn, Raymond V. M. ... Palo Alto, CA
Dunn, Reagan B. ... **Bellevue, WA**
Dunn, Reginald A. ... **Sacramento, CA**
Dunn, Richard E. ... **Wheaton, MD**
Dunn, Richard E., Jr. ... Honolulu, HI
Dunn, Richard N. ... Eldora, IA
Dunn, Richard, (P.A.) ... **Miami, FL**
Dunn, Richard S. ... **Baton Rouge, LA**
Dunn, Richard T. ... **Bloomington, IL**
Dunn, Richard W. ... Cleveland, OH
Dunn, Robert A. ... **Troy, MI**
Dunn, Robert A. ... Spokane, WA
Dunn, Robert C. ... **Vallejo, CA**
Dunn, Robert C. ... Corsicana, TX
Dunn, Robert C. ... **Alexandria, VA**
Dunn, Robert D. ... **Miami, FL**
Dunn, Robert E. ... **Morristown, NJ**
Dunn, Robert E., Jr. ... **Manchester, NH**
Dunn, Robert G., Jr. ... Cambridge, MA
Dunn, Robert J. ... Bay City, MI
Dunn, Robert J., III ... **Lake Wales, FL**
Dunn, Robert J., P.C. ... Bay City, MI
Dunn, Robert L. ... San Francisco, CA
Dunn, Robert N. ... Indio, CA
Dunn, Robert Nicholas ... **Millburn, NJ**
New York, NY
Dunn, Robert R. ... **Columbus, OH**
Dunn, Robert R. ... Houston, TX
Dunn, Robert S. ... San Diego, CA
Dunn, Robert Steven ... New York, NY
Dunn, Robert T. ... San Diego, CA
Dunn, Robert T. ... Bedford, MA
Dunn, Robin D. ... Rigby, ID
Dunn, Robt. B. ... Seattle, WA
Dunn, Robt. H. ... Marietta, GA
Dunn, Rod ... Albuquerque, NM
Dunn, Rogaski, Preovolos & Weber
Vallejo, CA
Dunn, Ronald G. ... **Albany, NY**
Dunn, S. Michael ... **Austin, TX**
Dunn, Samuel E. ... Houston, TX
Dunn and Sanderson ... **Thousand Oaks, CA**
Westlake Village, CA
Dunn, Sandra K. ... **Sacramento, CA**
Dunn, Schouten and Snoap, A Professional Corporation ... **Grand Rapids, MI**
Wyoming, MI
Dunn, Scott ... Brooklyn, NY
Dunn, Scott W. ... **Longmont, CO**
Dunn, Sean P. ... **Columbus, OH**
Dunn, Shari L. ... Milwaukee, WI
Dunn, Stanczak & Willard
Bloomington, IL
Dunn, Stanley L. ... Gardena, CA
Dunn, Stephanie Erin ... **Denver, CO**
Dunn, Stephen A. ... **Raleigh, NC**
Dunn, Stephen E. ... Lynchburg, VA
Dunn, Stephen J. ... **Baltimore, MD**
Bel Air, MD
Dunn, Stephen J. ... **Troy, MI**
Dunn, Stephen J. ... **Charlotte, NC**
Dunn, Stephen J., P.C. ... **Troy, MI**
Dunn, Stephen R. ... Providence, KY
Dunn, Stephen S. ... **Pocatello, ID**
Dunn, Stephen W. ... **Irvine, CA**
Dunn, Steven J. ... Gates Mills, OH
Dunn, Steven R. ... **Dallas, TX**
Dunn, Stuart H. ... **Richmond, VA**
Dunn, Susan A. ... **Palo Alto, CA**
Dunn, Susan Black ... **Salt Lake City, UT**
Dunn, Susan King ... Charleston, SC
Dunn, Susan M. ... Bronx, NY
Dunn, Susan Stevens
Research Triangle Park, NC
Dunn, Susan Zeller ... **Cincinnati, OH**
Dunn, Swan & Cunningham, P.C.
Oklahoma City, OK
Dunn, Teena P. ... **Oklahoma City, OK**
Dunn, Terence H. ... Portland, OR
Dunn, Terrance J. ... **Lynchburg, VA**
Dunn, Terrence M. ... **New York, NY**
Dunn, Theodore E. ... **Wyoming, MI**
Dunn, Theodore M., Jr. ... **Cleveland, OH**
Dunn, Theodore R. ... **Bozeman, MT**
Dunn, Theresa ... Brooklyn, NY
Dunn, Thomas A. ... Joliet, IL
Dunn, Thomas A. ... Tyler, TX
Dunn, Thomas Churchill
St. Petersburg, FL
Dunn, Thomas E. ... **New York, NY**
Dunn, Thomas F. ... **Washington, DC**
Dunn, Thomas F. ... **Boston, MA**
Dunn, Thomas F. ... Arlington, TX
Dunn, Thomas F. X. ... New York, NY
Dunn, Thomas G. ... **San Mateo, CA**
Dunn, Thomas H. ... Chicago, IL
Dunn, Thomas Jack ... **Albuquerque, NM**
Dunn, Thomas M. ... **Denver, CO**
Dunn, Thomas W. ... **Montvale, NJ**
Dunn, Tim Dalton ... **Salt Lake City, UT**
Dunn, Timothy J., II ... **Closter, NJ**
Dunn, Timothy J., III ... **Baldwin, NY**
Dunn, Timothy M ... **Fayetteville, NC**
Dunn, Timothy M., P.A., Law Offices of
Fayetteville, NC
Dunn, Timothy P. ... Aloha, OR
Dunn, Timothy W. J. ... Golden Valley, MN
St. Paul, MN
Dunn, Toole, Coats, Carter & Sosnkowski, LLP ... **The Dalles, OR**
Dunn, Tracy J. ... Palo Alto, CA
Dunn, Travis ... **Oklahoma City, OK**
Dunn, Troy D. ... Houston, TX
Dunn, Vincent ... **New York, NY**
Dunn, Vincent dePaul ... Concord, NH
Dunn, Vincent P. ... **Boston, MA**
Dunn, Vindigni & Bruno ... **Oneida, NY**
Dunn, W. David ... **Columbus, MS**
Dunn, W. Elliott ... Waukegan, IL
Dunn, W. Mark ... Richmond, VA
Dunn, W. Michael ... **Concord, NH**
Manchester, NH
Dunn & Walker ... **Lubbock, TX**
Dunn, Wallace B. ... Waukegan, IL
Dunn, Walter C. ... **Monroe, LA**
Dunn, Warren E. ... Denville, NJ
Dunn & Weathered, P.C.
Corpus Christi, TX
Dunn, Webb, McEwen & Studdard, P.A.
Columbus, MS
Dunn, Wendell B. ... Whitefish, MT
Dunn, Wesley B. ... Sharpsburg, GA
Dunn, Will T., Jr. ... Greenville, SC
Dunn, Will T., Jr., P.A. ... Greenville, SC
Dunn, William ... LaGrangeville, NY
Dunn, William B. ... Wetumpka, AL
Dunn, William B. ... **Detroit, MI**
Dunn, William Beal ... San Francisco, CA
Dunn, William C. ... Dayton, TN
Dunn, William D. ... New York, NY
Dunn, William David ... **Dallas, TX**
Dunn, William F. ... Del Norte, CO
Dunn, William F. ... Edwardsville, KS
Dunn, William Gerald ... Caledonia, IL
Dunn, William H. ... San Jose, CA
Dunn, William H. ... Vancouver, WA
Dunn, William H., Law Offices of
Claremont, NH
Dunn, William Howard ... Claremont, NH
Dunn, William J. ... **Omaha, NE**
Dunn, William M. ... **Chicago, IL**

Dunn, William Michael ..... Baltimore, MD
Dunn, William M. S. ..... Columbus, OH
Dunn, William N. ..... Birmingham, AL
Dunn, William R. ..... Oak Lawn, IL
Dunn, William R. ..... Berwick, ME
Dunn, William R. ..... Greenwood, SC
Dunn, William W. ..... Charlottesville, VA
Dunn, Winford L., Jr. ..... Texarkana, AR
Dunn & Zuckerman, P.C. ..... New York, NY
Dunnagan, Charles A. ..... Anchorage, AK
Dunnagan, Marciann ..... Boston, MA
Dunnahoo, Michael G.
Corpus Christi, TX
Dunnahoo, William M. ..... Atlanta, GA
Dunnam & Dunnam, L.L.P. ..... Waco, TX
Dunnam, Gregory J. ..... Utica, MI
Dunnam, James R. ..... Waco, TX
Dunnam, Michael P. ..... Philadelphia, PA
Dunnam, Myrna J. ..... Baytown, TX
Dunnam, Vance ..... Waco, TX
Dunnam, Vance, Jr. ..... Waco, TX
Dunnam, W. V., Jr. ..... Waco, TX
Dunnan, Douglas M. ..... New York, NY
Dunnan, Weaver W. ..... Bethesda, MD
Dunnavant, Barbara Ann
Department of Labor, Office of Secretary, GV
Dunnavant, Edward F. ..... Wilmington, NC
Dunnaville, Clarence M., Jr. ..... Richmond, VA
Dunnaway, S. Kelly ..... Walnut Creek, CA
Dunne, Anthony J. ..... Santa Ana, CA
Dunne, Arthur L. ..... Chicago, IL
Dunne, Brian ..... St. Louis, MO
Dunne, Bruce W. ..... Washington, DC
Dunne, Carey R. ..... New York, NY
Dunne, Carleen A. ..... Buffalo, NY
Dunne, Christopher ..... Springfield, VA
Dunne, Christopher E. ..... Wilmington, DE
Dunne, Cynthia S. ..... Wichita, KS
Dunne, Daniel J. ..... Seattle, WA
Dunne, Debra S. ..... Philadelphia, PA
Dunne, Dennis F. ..... New York, NY
Dunne, Edward Fitzsimmons ..... Chicago, IL
Dunne, Edward J. ..... Downers Grove, IL
Dunne, Edward M. ..... Succasunna, NJ
Dunne, Francis H. ..... Detroit, MI
Dunne, Frank C. ..... Chesterfield, MO
Dunne, Frederick R., Jr. ..... Kearny, NJ
Dunne, Gerald M. ..... St. Louis, MO
Dunne, Gerald T. ..... St. Louis, MO
Dunne, Gerard F. ..... New York, NY
Dunne, Gerard F., P.C. ..... New York, NY
Dunne & Healy ..... Sea Cliff, NY
Dunne, James L. ..... Sea Cliff, NY
Dunne, John C. ..... Houston, TX
Dunne, John P. ..... Seminole, FL
Dunne, John P. ..... Mineola, NY
Dunne, John R. ..... Albany, NY
Dunne, John W. ..... Mineola, NY
Dunne, Joseph E., III ..... Durango, CO
Dunne, Joseph P. ..... Salem, OR
Dunne, Julie A. ..... San Diego, CA
Dunne, Kevin A. ..... Baltimore, MD
Dunne, Kevin J. ..... San Francisco, CA
Dunne, Lawrence R. ..... Merchantville, NJ
Dunne, Linda ..... Hackensack, NJ
Dunne, Lisa J. ..... Los Angeles, CA
Dunne, Marci Gardner ..... San Francisco, CA
Dunne, Margaret Ann ..... Diamond Bar, CA
Dunne, Martin F.
Department Of Veterans Affairs, Board of Veterans Appeals, GV
Dunne, Mary Elizabeth T. ..... Albany, NY
Dunne, Mary Maguire ..... Department of Justice, Executive Office for Immigration Review, GV
Dunne, Michael J. ..... Morristown, NJ
Dunne, Nancy E. ..... Los Angeles, CA
Dunne, Paul J. ..... Indianapolis, IN
Dunne, Peter J. ..... St. Louis, MO
Dunne, Philip T. ..... Albany, NY
Dunne, Raymond W. ..... Fresno, CA
Dunne, Richard A. ..... Springfield, NJ
Dunne, Robert E. ..... San Jose, CA
Dunne, Robert E., A Prof. Law Corp., The Law Offices of ..... San Jose, CA
Dunne, Roderick T. ..... Chicago, IL
Dunne, Steven M. ..... Washington, DC
Dunne, Susan S. ..... Washington, DC
Dunne, Thomas A. ..... New York, NY
Dunne & Thompson, P.C. ..... Kearny, NJ
Dunne, Timothy R. ..... Houston, TX
Dunne, William J. ..... Dover, DE
Dunneback, James F. ..... Palos Heights, IL
Dunnegan, William ..... New York, NY
Dunnell, Adey May ..... Fairfield, CA
Dunnell, Christina G. ..... Hartford, CT
Dunnell, John R. ..... Wakefield, MA
Dunnells, G. Richard ..... Washington, DC
Dunnells, Shirley A. ..... Woodland, CA
Dunnem, Alvin E. ..... Cambridge, NY
Dunnem & Imhof ..... Cambridge, NY
Dunner, Donald R. ..... Washington, DC
Dunner, Lisa Ann ..... Washington, DC
Dunnet, Wallace J. ..... Southborough, MA
Dunnett, Carolyn M. S. ..... Long Beach, CA
Dunnett, Cynthia M. ..... Los Angeles, CA
Dunnewold, Ruth D. ..... Harrisburg, PA
Dunnigan, Brady W. ..... Lexington, KY
Dunnigan, E. Vaughn ..... Atlanta, GA
Dunnigan, Janette ..... Bradenton, FL
Dunnigan, Keith D. ..... Westport, CT
Dunnigan, Ronnie G. ..... Lexington, KY
Dunnigan, Stephen A. ..... Newport News, VA
Dunnill, William C. ..... Dallas, TX
Dunning, Abigail F., (Mrs.) ..... Anchorage, AK
Dunning, Aldorah F. ..... Naperville, IL
Dunning, Beth A. ..... Nashville, TN
Dunning, Brian C. ..... New York, NY
Dunning, Carol A. ..... New York, NY
Dunning, David P. ..... Fort Worth, TX
Dunning, Donald T. ..... San Diego, CA
Dunning, Donald T., P.C. ..... San Diego, CA
Dunning, Douglas K. ..... Mobile, AL
Dunning, Douglas K., P.C. ..... Mobile, AL
Dunning, Edward ..... Dublin, OH
Dunning, Elizabeth T. ..... Salt Lake City, UT
Dunning, Forman, Kirrane & Terry, L.L.P. ..... Mashpee, MA
Dunning, Gina D. ..... Paducah, KY
Dunning, Joyce Ann ..... Colorado Springs, CO
Dunning, Kenneth S. ..... Lawrenceville, GA
Dunning, Kim G. ..... Orange, CA
Dunning, Mary Louise ..... Parma, OH
Dunning, Matthew G. ..... Omaha, NE
Dunning, Michael A. ..... Mashpee, MA
Dunning, Neal K. ..... Denver, CO
Dunning, Richard A., Jr. ..... Menlo Park, CA
Dunning, Richard L. ..... Omaha, NE
Dunning, Robert E., Jr. ..... Concord, NH
Dunning, Russell K. ..... Boston, MA
Dunning, Ruth M. ..... Chicago, IL
Dunning, Scott T. ..... San Francisco, CA
Dunning, Steven J. ..... Laguna Niguel, CA
Dunning, Sue Hynds ..... Gallatin, TN
Dunning, Timothy ..... Omaha, NE
Dunninger, Bonnie H. ..... Washington, DC
Dunnings & Frawley, P.C. ..... Charlotte, MI
Corunna, MI
Ionia, MI
Jackson, MI
Lansing, MI
Mason, MI
St. Johns, MI
Dunnings, Shauna L. ..... Lansing, MI
Dunnings, Steven D. ..... Lansing, MI
Dunnings, Stuart J., III ..... Lansing, MI
Dunnings, Stuart J., Jr. ..... Lansing, MI
Dunnings, Susan E. ..... Washington, DC
Dunnington, Bartholow & Miller, LLP
Westlake Village, CA
Dunnington, Bartholow & Miller LLP
New York, NY
Dunnington, Eugene E. ..... Garden Grove, CA
Dunnington, Eugene E., Law Offices of, A Professional Corp. ..... Garden Grove, CA
Dunnington, Thomas C., Jr. ..... Dover, NH
Dunnion Law Firm, The ..... Monterey, CA
Dunnion, Thomas J. ..... Monterey, CA
Dunn-Kraus, John ..... San Clemente, CA
Dunn-Rankin, Dean ..... Irvine, CA
Dunnum, Carroll M. ..... Long Beach, CA
Dunnum, Priscilla McKinney ..... Downey, CA
Dunnwald, Thomas G., Law Offices of ..... Minneapolis, MN
Dunn-Walters, Kellee P. ..... Overland Park, KS
Dunoff, Jeffrey Lawrence ..... Philadelphia, PA
Dunovan, Kimberly A. ..... Omaha, NE
Dunphy, Deirdre A. ..... New York, NY
Dunphy, Dennis J. ..... Seattle, WA
Dunphy, Edward J., Jr. ..... Syracuse, NY
Dunphy, Elizabeth R. ..... Springfield, MA
Dunphy, James J.
Department Of Veterans Affairs, Board of Veterans Appeals, GV
Dunphy, James M. ..... Westerville, OH
Dunphy, James Michael, Jr.
Washington, DC
Boston, MA
Dunphy, John Robert ..... Tallahassee, FL
Dunphy, Kevin V. ..... Chicago, IL
Dunphy, Megan L.
Securities and Exchange Commission, Division of Investment Management, GV
Dunphy, Ned E. ..... Bakersfield, CA
Dunphy, Patrick K. ..... Dayton, OH
Dunphy, Patrick O. ..... Brookfield, WI
Dunphy, Richard T. ..... Rutherford, NJ
Dunphy, Sean M. ..... Northampton, MA
Dunsay, Richard C. ..... Los Angeles, CA
Dunscomb, George A. ..... Tucson, AZ
Dunscomb & Shepherd, P.C. ..... Tucson, AZ
Dunseath, Frances N. ..... Akron, OH
Dunseath, William N. ..... Reno, NV
Dunsford, John E. ..... St. Louis, MO
Dunsford, Kelly D. ..... Clayton, MO
Dunsford, Robert ..... Kansas City, MO
Dunshee, Mark B. ..... New York, NY
Dunshee, Stephen M. ..... Norwich, NY
Sherburne, NY
South Edmeston, NY
Dunsizer, Jennifer B. ..... Dublin, OH
Dunsky, Christopher J. ..... Detroit, MI
Dunsky, Frederic S. ..... San Antonio, TX
Dunsky, Gregory P. ..... Dayton, OH
Dunsky, Lisa A. ..... Chicago, IL
Dunsmoor, John S. ..... Lakewood, CO
Dunsmore, Billy D. ..... Irvine, CA
Dunsmore, Dean K. ..... Anchorage, AK
Dunsmore, E. Edward ..... Knightstown, IN
Dunsmore, John W., Jr. ..... Lincolnton, GA
Dunsmore, Keith A. ..... Washington, DC
Dunsmore, Lorri A. ..... Seattle, WA
Dunsmore, Robert B. ..... Rocky River, OH
Dunsmore, Walter B. ..... Norristown, PA
Dunson, Daniel ..... New York, NY
Dunson & Dunson ..... Cleveland, OH
Dunson, Gwendolyn Kaye ..... Stephenville, TX
Dunson, James A., Jr. ..... Cleveland, OH
Dunson, Jas. A. ..... Cleveland, OH
Dunson, Kendall C. ..... Montgomery, AL
Dunson, Philip M. ..... Columbus, OH
Dunson, Robin D. ..... Atlanta, GA
Dunson, Stephen D. ..... Columbus, OH
Dunst, Alan I. ..... New Brunswick, NJ
Dunst, Isabel P. ..... Washington, DC
Dunst, Kathleen A. ..... Harrisburg, PA
Dunst, Lee G. ..... Brooklyn, NY
Dunst, Robert Alan ..... Mattoon, IL
Dunstan, Allen C. ..... Memphis, TN
Dunstan, Bernard S., Jr. ..... Augusta, GA
Dunstan, Dunstan & Cleary ..... Augusta, GA
Dunstan, J. Richard ..... Augusta, GA
Dunstan, James E. ..... Arlington, VA
Dunstan, Kerrie L. ..... Menlo Park, CA
Dunston, George A., Jr.
Whitehouse Station, NJ
Dunston, Jerri U. ..... Arlington, VA
Dunston, Leigh E. ..... Miami, FL
Dunston, Michael C.
Charlotte Amalie, St. Thomas, VI
Dunstone, William F. ..... Scranton, PA
Dunten, Frank G., P.C.
Grand Rapids, MI
Dunten, Jack P. ..... LaGrange, IN
Dunten, Wilbur H. (Pete) ..... Dickinson, TX
Dunton, Ammon G. ..... White Stone, VA
Dunton, Ammon G., Jr. ..... White Stone, VA
Dunton, Fred W. ..... Pittsburgh, PA
Dunton, Gary E. ..... Paw Paw, MI
Dunton, Simmons & Dunton, L.L.P.
Heathsville, VA
Lancaster, VA
Saluda, VA
White Stone, VA
Dunton-Ilievski, Gloria R. ..... Jersey City, NJ
Dunty, R. P., Jr. ..... Lake Placid, FL
Dunwody, W. E., III, P.A. ..... Highlands, NC
Dunwody, W. E., III ..... Highlands, NC
Dunwody White & Landon, P.A.
Fort Lauderdale, FL
Miami, FL
Naples, FL
Palm Beach, FL
West Palm Beach, FL
Dunwoodie, Judith I. ..... East Lansing, MI
Dunwoody, Dana J. ..... San Diego, CA
Dunwoody, Grant ..... Houston, TX
Dunwoody, Stuart R. ..... Seattle, WA
Dunworth, Gerald J. ..... New York, NY
Dunworth, Michael P. ..... New York, NY
Dunworth, Moira ..... Philadelphia, PA
Dunyon-Hansen, Jill L. ..... Stanbury Park, UT
Duong, David L ..... Houston, TX
Duong, Peter ..... San Francisco, CA
Duong, Tan N. ..... Milpitas, CA
Duong, Wendy Nichole ..... Houston, TX
Duong-Tran, Hien C. ..... Santa Clara, CA
Duoos, Deborah L. ..... Edina, MN
Dupaix, Laura B ..... Salt Lake City, UT
DuPar, Richard C. ..... Pasadena, CA
Dupart, Louis H. ..... Washington, DC
Dupart, Theresa M. ..... Chevy Chase, MD
Dupee, David Douglas ..... Atlanta, GA
Dupee & Dupee, P.C. ..... Goshen, NY
Dupee, Jon C., Jr. ..... Goshen, NY
Dupee, Jon Charles ..... Goshen, NY
Dupée, Michael G. ..... Cleveland, OH
Dupere, Richard A. ..... Carmel, CA
Duperier, Laurie Plessala ..... New York, NY
Duperrault, David V. ..... San Jose, CA
Duphorne, Darin H. ..... Houston, TX
Dupignac, Frank J., Jr. ..... Toms River, NJ
Duplack, Ronald P. ..... Chicago, IL
Duplaga, Edward K. ..... Chicago, IL
Duplantier, Adrian G. ..... New Orleans, LA
Du Plantier, Angelo A., III ..... Orange, CA
Duplantier, David L. ..... New Orleans, LA
Duplantier, John C. (Sandy) ..... New Orleans, LA
Duplantier, Jon-al ..... Houston, TX
Duplantier, Margaret ..... Houston, TX
Duplantier, Michael A. ..... New Orleans, LA
Duplantier, Richard G., Jr.
New Orleans, LA
Duplantier, Thomas R. ..... Lafayette, LA
Duplantis, B. J., (A P.L.C.) ..... Lafayette, LA
Duplantis, Gregory G. ..... Lafayette, LA
Duplass, Lawrence J. ..... Metairie, LA
Duplass, Zwain & Bourgeois
New Orleans, LA
Metairie, LA
Duplechain, G. Steven ..... Baton Rouge, LA
Duplechain, G. Steven, A Professional Law Corporation ..... Baton Rouge, LA
Duplechain, Garett ..... Opelousas, LA
Duplechain, Gary P. ..... Slidell, LA
Duplechian, Donna J. ..... Alexandria, LA
Duplechin and Associates, Law Corporation ..... Gretna, LA
Duplechin, D. James ..... Crestview, FL
Duplechin, Giles J. ..... Gretna, LA
Dupler, Bryan L. ..... Tulsa, OK
Dupler, Gary T ..... Knoxville, TN
Dupler, Jeffrey E. ..... New York, NY
Dupler, Mitchell S. ..... Washington, DC
Dupler, Paul A. ..... Boulder, CO
Duplessie, Richard D. ..... Eau Claire, WI
DuPlessis, James A., Jr. ..... Brielle, NJ
Duplinsky, Warren ..... Gaithersburg, MD
DuPlissey, Donnie R. ..... Houston, TX
Duplissey, Rick W. ..... Monroe, LA
Duplissis, Diane M. ..... Colorado Springs, CO
Dupnik, Christine A. ..... Phoenix, AZ
Dupon, John Patrick ..... Timonium, MD
Dupont, A. Jerome ..... Kaneohe, HI
DuPont, Amanda Cramer
Minneapolis, MN
duPont, Ann S. ..... Klamath Falls, OR
DuPont, Annemarie ..... Plainsboro, NJ
Dupont, Antoinette L. ..... Hartford, CT
DuPont, Augustus I. ..... Stamford, CT
duPont, Chae A. ..... Miami, FL
duPont, Charles E., Jr. ..... Encinitas, CA
Dupont, Deborah A.
Federal Communications Commission, Mass Media Bureau, GV
Dupont, Debra Yaniko ..... Fort Worth, TX
DuPont, Douglas N. ..... Summit, IL
Dupont & Dupont ..... Plaquemine, LA
DuPont, Eric C. ..... Boston, MA
Dupont, Gerald H. ..... West Springfield, MA
Dupont, Gerard J. ..... Attleboro, MA
Du Pont, Gregory S. ..... Columbus, OH
Dupont, James H. ..... Plaquemine, LA
Dupont, Joseph B. ..... Plaquemine, LA
Dupont, Lorraine Adrienne ..... Baton Rouge, LA
Dupont, Mark A. ..... Chicago, IL
Dupont, Mark P. ..... St. Louis, MO
Dupont, Mary Nan ..... Overland Park, KS
DuPont, Michael J. ..... Minneapolis, MN
DuPont, Michael R. ..... Red Bank, NJ
du Pont, Nancy C. ..... Santa Ana, CA
Dupont, Natasha ..... New York, NY
Dupont, Norman A. ..... Santa Monica, CA
Dupont, Philip R. ..... Kansas City, MO
du Pont, Pierre S. ..... Wilmington, DE
Dupont and Radlauer, L.L.P.
New London, CT
Dupont, Ralph P. ..... New London, CT
DuPont, Robert John ..... Pasadena, CA
Dupont, Robyn Meyer
Equal Employment Opportunity Commission, Office of Federal Operations, GV
Dupont, Stephane R.
Hallandale Beach, FL
Dupont, Steven ..... Boulder, CO
Denver, CO
Dupont, Thomas E. ..... Danielson, CT
Dupont, Wesley D. ..... Stamford, CT
du Pont, William B., Jr. ..... Wilmington, DE
Dupont, William C. ..... Plaquemine, LA
Dupont, William E. "Bill" ..... Houston, TX
Dupper, Ervin E. ..... Mobridge, SD
Duppler, Alan ..... Stanton, ND
Dupps, David Scott ..... Louisville, KY
Dupras, Fred J. ..... Reedley, CA
Dupray, William M. ..... Falls Church, VA
Dupre, Alvin J., Jr. ..... Metairie, LA
Dupre, Anthony C. ..... Ville Platte, LA
Dupré, Arthur D., Jr. ..... Metairie, LA
Dupre, Barbara H. ..... Northfield, NJ
Dupre, Charles C. ..... Coventry, RI
Dupre, Cornelius, II ..... Lafayette, LA
DuPre, Daniel A. ..... Chicago, IL
DuPré, Daniel F. ..... Charlotte, NC
Dupré, Deborah A. ..... Nashville, TN
Dupre, Donald R. ..... Hartford, CT
Dupre, Durward D. ..... Dallas, TX
Dupré, Eric L. ..... San Francisco, CA
Dupré, Forrest Henri ..... Milwaukee, WI
Dupre, Frederic L. ..... Worcester, MA
Dupre, Helen P. ..... Plano, TX
Dupre, James T. ..... Oklahoma City, OK
Dupre, Jennifer L. ..... Boston, MA
Dupré, Jennifer R. ..... Cupertino, CA
DuPré, John L. ..... Lexington, MA
Dupre, Lynda M. ..... Ligonier, PA
Dupré, Marc F. ..... Boston, MA
DuPre, Martha A. ..... Toledo, OH
DuPre, Patricia Ariana ..... Glendale, CA
Dupre, Simone Chachere ..... Lafayette, LA
DuPré and Small, P.C. ..... Ogdensburg, NY
Dupré, Steven C. ..... St. Petersburg, FL
Dupré, Suzanne
Corporation for National and Community Service, Office of the General Counsel, GV
DuPré, Thomas E. ..... Ogdensburg, NY
DuPré, William A., IV ..... Atlanta, GA
Dupree, Anita J. ..... Red Bank, NJ
DuPree, Beth H. ..... Jackson, TN
DuPree, Billy Glenn, Jr. ..... Rexburg, ID
Dupree, Charles P. ..... Chattanooga, TN
DuPree, Clifford H. R. ..... Pleasantville, NY
Dupree, David H. ..... Washington, DC
DuPree, David J. ..... Fort Myers, FL
DuPree, David J., P.A. ..... Fort Myers, FL
Dupree, E. Scott ..... San Diego, CA
Dupree, Eric A. ..... San Diego, CA
Dupree, Hylton B., Jr. (P.C.)
Marietta, GA
Dupree, James M. ..... Chicago, IL
Dupree, Jamie L. ..... San Francisco, CA
Dupree, John Benton ..... Knoxville, TN
Dupree, Johnson, Poole & King
Marietta, GA
Dupree, Joseph B., II ..... Greenville, NC
Dupree, Scott E. ..... Kansas City, MO
Dupree, Stanley M. ..... San Francisco, CA
Dupree, Thomas H., Jr. ..... Washington, DC
Duprey, Allan W. ..... Tucson, AZ
Duprey, Anthony R. ..... Vergennes, VT
Duprey, Mary Ellen ..... Columbus, OH
Duprey, Michelle M. ..... Farmington, CT
Duprey, Susan V. ..... Manchester, NH
DuPriest, Douglas M. ..... Eugene, OR
DuPriest, Joanna Garbush ..... Philadelphia, PA
DuPriest, Robert ..... Sapulpa, OK
DuPris, Cheryl Schrempp ..... Pierre, SD
Dupuis, C. Thomas ..... Cincinnati, OH
Dupuis, Daniel G. ..... Fontana, CA
DuPuis, Elizabeth A. ..... Bellefonte, PA
State College, PA
Dupuis, Fay Danner ..... Cincinnati, OH
Dupuis, Gerard A. ..... New York, NY
Dupuis & Harson ..... Lafayette, LA
Dupuis, Jean-Baptiste ..... New York, NY
DuPuis, Linda H. ..... Jacksonville, FL
Dupuis, Renee P. ..... New Bedford, MA

DuPuis, Sharon B. ....Rancho Cucamonga, CA
Dupuis, Steven J. ....Lafayette, LA
Dupuis, Thomas I. ....Los Angeles, CA
Dupuy, Brett M. ....Metairie, LA
DuPuy, Carolyn M. ....Washington, DC
Dupuy, Clarence O., Jr. ....Metairie, LA
Dupuy, Cullen J. ....Baton Rouge, LA
Dupuy & Didier ....Marksville, LA
Dupuy, Gregory A. ....Metairie, LA
Dupuy, Howard M., Jr. ....Portland, OR
Dupuy, John E. Department of Housing and Urban Development, Office of the Inspector General, GV
DuPuy, John S. ....Charlotte, NC
Dupuy, Juliet M. Securities and Exchange Commission, Division of Enforcement, GV
Dupuy, Marc, Jr. ....Marksville, LA
Dupuy, Matthew J. ....West Yarmouth, MA
Dupuy, R. René ....Washington, DC
DuPuy, Robert A. ....Milwaukee, WI
DuPuy, Robert K. ....Des Moines, IA
Dupuy, Robert W. ....Dallas, TX
Dupuy, Sandra L. ....Boston, MA
Dupwe, Warren ....Jonesboro, AR
Duque, Thomas E. ....Los Angeles, CA
Duquella, Michel J. ....San Diego, CA
duQuesnay, Michael S. ....Los Angeles, CA
Duquet, Robert W. ....Braintree, MA
Duquette, David J., Jr. ....Princeton, NJ
Duquette, Dennis W. ....Greensboro, NC
Duquette, Donald N. ....Ann Arbor, MI
Duquette, Lois B. ....Hershey, PA
Duquette, Richard ....Carlsbad, CA
Duquette & Tipton LLP ....Princeton, NJ
Dura, Maribeth Egert ....Peoria, IL
Duraiswamy, Vijayalakshmi D., (Ms.) El Segundo, CA
Durako, JoAnne ....Villanova, PA
Durall, Richard M. ....Redding, CA
Duran, Adriana ....Chicago, IL
Duran, Alfredo G. ....Miami, FL
Duran, David ....El Paso, TX
Duran, David A. ....Freeport, TX
Duran, Don W. ....Lufkin, TX
Duran, Edward N. ....Santa Ana, CA
Duran, Eugene A. ....Denver, CO
Duran, George C. ....New York, NY
Duran, Grace B. ....Las Cruces, NM
Duran, Joe A. ....Albuquerque, NM
Duran, John J. ....Los Angeles, CA
Duran, Juan C. ....Austin, TX
Duran, Lawrence J. ....Sacramento, CA
Duran, Leandro H. ....Berkeley, CA
Duran, Lisa Dibbern ....Phoenix, AZ
Duran, Lois J. ....Dallas, TX
Duran, Loquvam & Robertson Los Angeles, CA
Duran, Michael M., (P.C.) New Orleans, LA
Durán & Pandos, P.C. ....Mountainside, NJ
Durán, Paulino G. ....Sacramento, CA
Duran, Percy ....Pasadena, CA
Duran, Robert A. ....El Paso, TX
Duran, Robert N. ....Los Angeles, CA
Duran, Rowena M. ....Mountainside, NJ
Duran, Samuel M. ....Cincinnati, OH
Duran, Stanley J. ....Minneapolis, MN
Duran, Ysidro E. ....Defiance, OH
Durana, Aurelio ....Coral Gables, FL
Durance, Stephen E. ....Midland, MI
Duranczyk, Richard P. ....Lansing, MI
Durand, Allan L. ....Erath, LA
Lafayette, LA
Durand, Anna L. Department Of Health And Human Services, GV
Durand & Assocs., P.C. ....Lewisville, TX
Durand, Cherie K. Dibbell Charleston, SC
Durand, Daniel C., III ....Lewisville, TX
Durand, Edward N. ....Pittsburgh, PA
Durand, Harry W., Jr. ....Nashville, TN
Durand, Janine ....Washington, DC
Durand, Jean-Paul ....Tampa, FL
Durand, John Donald ....Riverside, CA
Durand, Kemper B. ....Memphis, TN
Durand, Kent D. ....Juneau, AK
Durand, Marty A. ....Idaho Falls, ID
Durand, Michael G. ....Lafayette, LA
Durand, Paulette J. ....Albuquerque, NM
Durand, Peter J. ....Southfield, MI
Durand, Philip P. ....Knoxville, TN
Durand, Robert A. ....Camden, NJ
Durand, Robert J. ....Allentown, PA
Durand, Sherri M. ....Durham, NC
Durand, Steven D. ....Little Rock, AR
Durand, Whitney ....Chattanooga, TN
Durand, William D. ....Braintree, MA
Durando, Antonio R. ....Tucson, AZ
Portland, OR
Durando, Birdwell & Janke, LLP Tucson, AZ
Durando, Nann Novinski ....Tucson, AZ
Durán-González, Néstor ....San Juan, PR
Duran Guzmán, Nerisvel C. ....San Juan, PR
Duranleau, Karen L. ....Wichita, KS
Duran Reed, Clara I. ....Los Angeles, CA
Duranske, George L., III ....Bemidji, MN
Duranske Law Offices ....Bemidji, MN
Durant, Amy J. ....Cheboygan, MI
Durant, Charles A. ....North St. Paul, MN
Durant, Charles W. ....McLean, VA
Durant, David E. ....Oakland, CA
Durant & Durant ....Philadelphia, PA
Durant, E. Terry ....Bridgeport, CT
DuRant, Frank H. ....Myrtle Beach, SC
Durant, Harry L. (IBA) ....Houston, TX
Durant, James A. ....Los Angeles, CA
Durant, James B. ....Tulsa, OK
Durant, James M., III Department of the Air Force, Office of the Judge Advocate General, GV
Durant, James R. ....Kalamazoo, MI
Durant, Joretta ....Kinston, NC
DuRant, Joseph M. ....Hampton, VA
Durant, Katherine ....Forest Park, GA
Durant, Kevin M. ....New York, NY
Durant, Lawrence A. ....Baton Rouge, LA
Durant, Lisa Parks ....Lafayette, CA
Walnut Creek, CA
Durant, Marc ....Philadelphia, PA
Durant, Maria R. ....Boston, MA
DuRant & Martin ....Myrtle Beach, SC
Durant, Michael A. ....Jacksonville, FL
DuRant, N. David ....Surfside Beach, SC
DuRant, N. David, and Associates, P.A., Law Offices of ....Surfside Beach, SC
Durant, N. Joseph, Jr. ....Miami, FL
Durant, Nancy K. ....New Orleans, LA
Durant, Nichols, Houston, Mitchell & Sheahan, P.C. ....Bridgeport, CT
Durant, Peter H. ....Rochester, NY
Durant, Piper & Sorci ....Kalamazoo, MI
Durant, Richard ....Detroit, MI
Durant, Richard K. ....Rosemead, CA
Durant, Rita M. ....Philadelphia, PA
Durant, Sandra B. ....New York, NY
Durant, Stephen C. ....San Francisco, CA
Durant, Stephen H. ....Jacksonville, FL
Durant, Susan Gibson ....Cherry Hill, NJ
Philadelphia, PA
Durant, Timothy E. ....Clearfield, PA
Durant, W. Clark, III ....Detroit, MI
DuRant, William E., Jr. ....Sumter, SC
Durant, Yvette ....Truckee, CA
Durante, Charles J. ....Wilmington, DE
Durante, Charles T. ....Reno, NV
Durante, Felix L. ....Los Angeles, CA
Durante, James P. ....New York, NY
Durante, Joseph ....Campbell, CA
Durante, Joseph C., Jr. ....Visalia, CA
Durante, Michael N. ....Great Neck, NY
Durante, Philip ....Jersey City, NJ
Durard, Forest A., Jr. ....Shelbyville, TN
DuRard, Gangemi, McKenna & Borg, A Professional Corporation ....San Mateo, CA
DuRard, Suzanne ....Kent, WA
Duraski, Russell T. ....Montgomery, AL
Durava, Richard J. ....Chicago, IL
Duray, Michael P. ....Dallas, TX
Durback, Nick V. ....Walton Hills, OH
Durbak, Tatiana B. ....Albany, NY
Durban, Lee E. ....Columbus, OH
Durbano, Douglas M. ....Ogden, UT
Durbano & Merrill ....Ogden, UT
Durben, Irwin ....Garden City, NY
Durben, Richard H. ....Boston, MA
Durben & Tosti ....Garden City, NY
Durbin, Alan C. ....Oklahoma City, OK
Durbin, Anna M. ....Ardmore, PA
Durbin, Anna M. ....Philadelphia, PA
Durbin, D. Greg ....Fresno, CA
Durbin, David P. ....Washington, DC
Durbin, Diana C. ....San Antonio, TX
Durbin, Diane Davidson Kansas City, MO
Durbin, Durbin & Borde Denham Springs, LA
Durbin, Elizabeth E. ....Lisle, IL
Durbin, Erlo J. ....Denham Springs, LA
Durbin, Fithian L. ....Kettering, OH
Durbin, Fletcher M. ....Chicago, IL
Durbin, Gerald E., II Oklahoma City, OK
Durbin, Iveth P. ....Seattle, WA
Durbin, James A. ....Overland Park, KS
Kansas City, MO
Durbin, James E. ....Los Angeles, CA
Durbin, James E. ....Denham Springs, LA
Durbin, Jennifer G. ....San Antonio, TX
Durbin, John F. ....Hilton Head Island, SC
Durbin, Larimore & Bialick, P.C. Oklahoma City, OK
Durbin, Lynne M. ....Columbia, MD
Durbin, Marie A. ....St. Louis, MO
Durbin, Mark L. ....Chicago, IL
Durbin, Paul J. ....Honolulu, HI
Durbin, Paul J. ....Columbia, MD
Durbin, Peter ....San Diego, CA
Durbin, Richard J. ....Springfield, IL
Durbin, Valerie Anne ....Santa Monica, CA
Durbin, William Blaine ....St. Petersburg, FL
Durbin, William P., Jr. ....Dallas, TX
Durbin Willman & Associates, P.C. Columbia, MD
McLean, VA
Durbin, Winfield T. ....La Jolla, CA
Durby, Ronald W. ....Chattanooga, TN
Durcan, Martha L. ....Waltham, MA
Durchanek, Julia H, Esq. ....Holyoke, MA
Durchfort, David E. ....Beverly Hills, CA
Durchslag & Durchslag ....Chicago, IL
Durchslag, Melvyn R. ....Cleveland, OH
Durchslag, M. L. ....Chicago, IL
Durchslag, Stephen P. ....Chicago, IL
Durchslag, Tracy M. ....Phoenix, AZ
Durdaller, Paul G. ....Atlanta, GA
Durden, Adie N., Jr. ....Albany, GA
Durden, Anne Latta ....Swainsboro, GA
Durden, Brenna M. ....Jacksonville, FL
Durden, Bruce V. ....Dublin, GA
Vidalia, GA
Durden, Chauncey W., III Department Of Veterans Affairs, Office of Employment Discrimination Complaints Adjudication, GV
Durden, Daniel E. ....Washington, DC
Durden, Deborah Brooks ....Columbia, SC
Durden, Gregory ....Fort Lauderdale, FL
Durden, J. Thomas, Jr. ....Hinesville, GA
Durden, Nelson T. ....Hampton, VA
Durden, R. Dale ....Birmingham, AL
Durden, Richard J. ....Grand Rapids, MI
Durden, Robert R. ....Fort Worth, TX
Durden, Stan ....Athens, GA
Durden, Stan, P.C. ....Athens, GA
Durden, Stephen M. ....Jacksonville, FL
Durden, Wayne M. ....Bartow, FL
Durden, William L. ....Jacksonville, FL
Durdik, Paul A. ....Palo Alto, CA
Durea, Ann M. ....Columbus, OH
Duree, David M. ....O'Fallon, IL
St. Louis, MO
Duree, David M., and Associates, P.C.
O'Fallon, IL
St. Louis, MO
Duree, Edward G. ....Fairfield, CA
Duree, John R., Jr. ....Sacramento, CA
Duree, John Rex, Jr., Inc. ....Sacramento, CA
Duree, Terry Alan ....Fairfield, CA
Durek & Harth ....Woodbridge, NJ
Durek, James P. ....Woodbridge, NJ
Durell, Jay ....Odessa, TX
Durell, Richard A. ....Grand Rapids, MI
Duren, B. Kwaku ....Los Angeles, CA
Duren, David L. ....Dublin, OH
Duren, Glen E. ....Oakland, CA
Duren, Katherine M. ....Green Bay, WI
Duren, Mark W. ....Dayton, OH
Duren, Orlesia A. ....Austin, TX
Duren, Tom F. ....Goldthwaite, TX
Dureska, David Patrick ....Canton, OH
Durette, Philippe L. ....Rahway, NJ
Durfee, Amy L. ....Denver, CO
Durfee, Benjamin B. ....Toledo, OH
Durfee, David A. ....Phoenix, AZ
Durfee, David R., Jr. ....Baltimore, MD
Durfee, Douglas I. ....Dearborn, MI
Durfee, John T. ....Bethesda, MD
Durfee, Karen M. ....Los Angeles, CA
Durfee, Louise ....Providence, RI
Durfee, Peter A. ....Albany, NY
Durfee, Randall G. ....Boise, ID
Durfee, Richard E., Jr. ....Phoenix, AZ
Durfee, Sally E. ....Orchard Lake, MI
Durfee, Scott A. ....Houston, TX
Durfey, Miles C. ....Columbus, OH
Durfey, Rosemary G. ....Canton, MS
Durgala, Milan M. ....Auburn, NY
Durgin, Eugene J. ....Boise, ID
Durgin, Eugene A. ....Boston, MA
Durgin, John C., Jr. ....Stoneham, MA
Durgin, Robert Ellsworth ....Warsaw, IN
Durgom-Powers, Jane E. ....Rockford, IL
Durham, Albert F. ....Charlotte, NC
Durham, Barbara ....Olympia, WA
Durham, Bart, Law Office of ....Nashville, TN
Durham, Betty Ann ....Scotts Valley, CA
Durham, Brenda ....Washington, DC
Durham, Burney Thomas ....Gallatin, TN
Durham, Carl M., Jr. ....San Jose, CA
Durham, Charles W. ....Radcliff, KY
Durham, Chas. J. ....Chicago, IL
Durham, Christine M. ....Salt Lake City, UT
Durham, Corbett Q., Jr. ....Cincinnati, OH
Durham, Dane J. ....San Francisco, CA
Durham, Danny L. ....Augusta, GA
Durham, Darryl W. ....Louisville, KY
Durham, David F. ....San Francisco, CA
Durham, David S. ....San Francisco, CA
Durham, Donna Baysinger ....Richmond, VA
Durham, Douglas M. ....Houston, TX
Durham, Drew T. ....Georgetown, TX
Durham, Edward D. ....Montrose, CO
Durham, Edwin L. ....Chicago, IL
Durham, Eleanor ....Seattle, WA
Durham, Elsa R. ....Seattle, WA
Durham, F. Colin, Jr. ....Dallas, TX
Durham, G. Vincent, Jr. Rocky Mount, NC
Durham, Gena L. ....Los Angeles, CA
Durham, Gregory P. ....Cape Canaveral, FL
Durham, H. Hunter ....Columbia, KY
Durham, Harold E. United States Postal Service, Law Department, GV
Durham, Harry B., III ....Casper, WY
Durham, Hugh M. ....Arlington, VA
Durham, J. Bryant, Jr. ....Rome, GA
Durham, J. Douglas ....Mather, CA
Santa Monica, CA
Durham, J. Frank ....Greencastle, IN
Durham, J. Porter, Jr. ....Chattanooga, TN
Nashville, TN
Durham, James B. ....Brunswick, GA
Durham, James D. ....Atlanta, GA
Durham, James D., Jr. ....Amarillo, TX
Durham, James F., II ....Miami, FL
Durham, James Geoffrey ....Dayton, OH
Durham, James W. ....Philadelphia, PA
Durham, Joan Drake ....Dayton, OH
Durham, Joe B. ....Cleburne, TX
Durham, John C. ....Windermere, FL
Durham, Jones & Pinegar ....Telluride, CO
Durham Jones & Pinegar, A Professional Corporation ....Ogden, UT
Salt Lake City, UT
Durham, Joshua Blake ....Charlotte, NC
Durham, Lee B., Jr. ....Birmingham, MI
Durham, Leona L. ....Cincinnati, OH
Durham, Lisa K. ....Dallas, TX
Durham, Lyn Head ....Bessemer, AL
Durham, Lynn D., Jr. ....Midland, TX
Durham, M. Freeman ....Cincinnati, OH
Durham, Mary Frances ....Dallas, TX
Durham, Mary Lynn ....Cleveland, OH
Durham, Matthew M. ....Salt Lake City, UT
Durham, Michael E. ....Little Rock, AR
Durham, Michael G. ....Guilford, CT
Durham, Michael L. ....Houston, TX
Durham, Michael V. ....Huntsville, TX
Durham, Patricia A. ....Fremont, CA
Durham, Patricia L. ....Louisville, KY
Durham, Paul H. ....Bartlesville, OK
Durham, Paul J. ....Miami, FL
Durham, Paul M. ....Salt Lake City, UT
Durham, Paul W. ....Colorado Springs, CO
Durham, Peter A. ....Newnan, GA
Durham, R. Gregory ....Evanston, IL
Durham, Randy L. ....Tacoma, WA
Durham, Ricardo M. Federal Communications Commission, Compliance and Information Bureau, GV
Durham, Richard M. ....Winston-Salem, NC
Durham, Robert ....Cookeville, TN
Knoxville, TN
Durham, Robert A. ....Indianapolis, IN
Durham, Robert B., Jr. ....Norristown, PA
Durham, Robert D. ....Salem, OR
Durham, Robert H., Jr., ...Denver, CO
Durham, Robert J. ....La Jolla, CA
Durham, Robert J., Jr. ....La Jolla, CA
San Diego, CA
Durham, Rodney F. ....Victoria, TX
Durham, Sharon ....Boise, ID
Durham, Sheldon D. ....Los Altos, CA
Durham, Shirley W. ....Jacksonville, FL
Durham, Sidney D. ....Kalamazoo, MI
Durham, Stephen A. ....Media, PA
Durham, Susan Carole ....Columbus, OH
Durham, Susan H. ....Dallas, TX
Durham, Suzanne Chauvin ....Hammond, LA
Durham, Sylvie A. ....New York, NY
Durham, Terri P. ....Greensboro, NC
Durham, Thomas A. ....Alexandria, LA
Durham, Thomas C. ....Chicago, IL
Durham, Thomas H., Jr. ....Memphis, TN
Durham, W. Cole, Jr. ....Provo, UT
Durham, William A. ....Houston, TX
Durham, William L. ....Huntsville, TX
Durham, William L., II ....Atlanta, GA
Durham, William Werner ....Huntsville, TX
Durham, Wm. F. ....Gallatin, TN
Durham & Zornes ....Columbia, KY
Duric, Nicholas M. ....Chicago, IL
Durick, B. Timothy ....Bismarck, ND
Durick, Patrick W. ....Bismarck, ND
Durick, Steven T. ....Des Moines, IA
Duricko, Michael K. ....Wilkes-Barre, PA
Durie, Daralyn Jeannine San Francisco, CA
Durigon, Albert Peter ....Cambridge, MA
Durigon, Dru A. ....Pittsburgh, PA
Duringer, David R. ....Coronado, CA
Duringer, Elizabeth A. ....Chicago, IL
Durio, James J. ....New Orleans, LA
Durio, Joseph F. ....Baton Rouge, LA
Durio, McGoffin & Stagg, Professional Corporation ....Lafayette, LA
Durio, Steven G. ....Lafayette, LA
Durio, William H. ....Lafayette, LA
Duris, Colleen M. ....Ocala, FL
Duris, Maureen J. ....Santa Barbara, CA
Duris, Pamela L. ....Princeton, NJ
Durity, Harry L. ....Upper Marlboro, MD
Durkalec, Carol Ann ....Norristown, PA
Durkan, Frank ....New York, NY
Durkan, Jenny A. ....Seattle, WA
Durkan, John O. ....Curlew, WA
Durkan, Martin J. ....Seattle, WA
Durkan, T. Ryan ....Seattle, WA
Durkay, John J. ....Beaumont, TX
Durkee, Alice W. ....Birmingham, AL
Durkee, Bill ....Houston, TX
Durkee, C. David ....Miami, FL
Durkee, Donald R. Department of Transportation, Federal Transit Administration, GV
Durkee, Ellen J. ....Department of Justice, Environment and Natural Resources Division, GV
Durkee, Emily ....San Diego, CA
Durkee & Hennessey ....Bellevue, WA
Seattle, WA
Durkee, Joe W. ....Houston, TX
Durkee, Marie T. ....Sacramento, CA
Durkee, Michael P. ....San Francisco, CA
Durkee, Paul ....Worcester, MA
Durkee, Paul D. ....Boston, MA
Durkee, Stephen R. ....Bellevue, WA
Durkee, Tanya Anne ....Bend, OR
Durkee & Uhle ....Batavia, OH
Milford, OH
Durket, Matthew J. ....San Jose, CA
Durket, Steven Lorne ....Longwood, FL
Durkheimer, John H. ....Portland, OR
Durkin, Albert E., Jr. ....Chicago, IL
Durkin & Boggia ....Ridgefield Park, NJ
Durkin, Brian J. ....Philadelphia, PA
Durkin, Carrie A. ....Chicago, IL
Durkin, Catherine E. ....Woburn, MA
Durkin, Catherine M. ....Wilmington, NC
Durkin, Daniel A. ....Wilmington, DE
Durkin, David L. ....Washington, DC
Durkin, Dawn M. ....Youngstown, OH
Durkin, Denis L. ....Orlando, FL
Durkin, Dennis A. ....West Caldwell, NJ
Durkin, Dennis J. ....Redwood City, CA
Durkin, Douglas S. ....Leonardtown, MD
Durkin & Durkin ....West Caldwell, NJ
Durkin, Elizabeth M. ....West Caldwell, NJ

Dutton, C. Gilmore, III ....Louisville, KY
Shelbyville, KY
Dutton, Carey J. ....Beverly Hills, CA
Dutton, C. B. ....Indianapolis, IN
Dutton, Channing L.
West Des Moines, IA
Dutton, Christine S. ....Harrisburg, PA
Dutton, Christopher L. ....Colchester, VT
Dutton, David C., Jr. ....Hayward, CA
Dutton, David J. ....Waterloo, IA
Dutton, Diana C., (P.C.) ....Dallas, TX
Dutton, Don E. ....Ruidoso, NM
Dutton, Donald D. ....San Diego, CA
Dutton, Donn S. ....Miami, FL
Dutton, Douglas L. ....Knoxville, TN
Dutton & Dutton, P.C. ....Washington, DC
Dutton, Edward Drew ....New York, NY
Dutton, Edward F. ....Park Ridge, IL
Dutton, F. Mitchell ....Columbus, OH
Dutton Firm, The, Ltd. ....Ruidoso, NM
Dutton, Frederick G. ....Washington, DC
Dutton, Gillian ....Yakima, WA
Dutton, Granville ....Dallas, TX
Dutton, Harold H., Jr. ....Manassas, VA
Dutton, Harold V., Jr. ....Houston, TX
Dutton, James D. ....San Diego, CA
Dutton, James J., Jr. ....Norwich, CT
Dutton, James Kevin ....Jasper, TX
Dutton, Janet B. ....Raleigh, NC
Dutton, Janna, & Associates, P.C.
Chicago, IL
Dutton, Janna S. ....Chicago, IL
Dutton, Jeanne M. ....Somerset, NJ
Dutton, Jefferson A. ....Houston, TX
Dutton, John C., Jr. ....Phoenix, AZ
Dutton, John D., Jr. ....Richmond, VA
Dutton, John J. ....Auburn, CA
Dutton, Karen T. ....San Francisco, CA
Dutton, L. Garrett, Jr. ....Philadelphia, PA
Dutton, Lynn B. ....Portsmouth, VA
Dutton, Mark A. ....Moulton, AL
Dutton, Michael J. ....Overland Park, KS
Dutton, Michael M. ....Hyannis, MA
Dutton, Nancy Hogan ....Washington, DC
Dutton & Overman, A Professional Corporation
Indianapolis, IN
Dutton, Patrick F. ....Alta Loma, CA
Dutton, Paul M. ....Youngstown, OH
Dutton, Philip M. ....Groton, CT
Norwich, CT
Dutton, Richard L. ....New York, NY
Dutton, Robert A. ....Richland, WA
Dutton, Rosanne B. ....Los Angeles, CA
Dutton, Scott W. ....Tampa, FL
Dutton, Sharon C. ....Oakland, CA
Dutton, Stephen J. ....Indianapolis, IN
Dutton, Terence G. ....San Diego, CA
Dutton, Thomas C. ....Quitman, GA
Dutton, Thomas E. ....Chicago, IL
Dutton, Thomas E. ....Columbus, OH
Dutton, Tom ....Birmingham, AL
Dutton, Uriel E. ....Houston, TX
Dutton, Vernon L. ....Little Rock, AR
Dutton, Yvonne M. ....San Diego, CA
Dutton-Johnson, Myra ....Muskegon, MI
Dutton-Mitchell, Kathryn R. ....Frankfort, KY
Duty, Daniel Morgan, III
Minneapolis, MN
Duty, Davis ....Fort Smith, AR
Duty, Gerald S. ....Hollywood, FL
Duty, Jeff ....Rogers, AR
Duty, Jennifer E. ....Greenville, SC
Duty, John C. ....Oklahoma City, OK
Duty, Mary-Leslie ....Chesterfield, VA
Duty, Michael Shannon ....Cincinnati, OH
Duty, Robert L. ....Bloomfield Hills, MI
Duty, William R. ....Owensboro, KY
Duglas, Darlene ....Los Angeles, CA
Duus, F. Martin ....Media, PA
Duus, Gordon C. ....Hackensack, NJ
Duva, Giacomo ....Colts Neck, NJ
Duva, Jason A. ....Boston, MA
Duva, Joseph A. ....Youngwood, PA
D'Uva, Raymond P. ....Newark, NJ
Duva & Skatell, P.C. ....Youngwood, PA
Duval, Anne-Gwin ....Lafayette, LA
DuVal, Benjamin S., Jr. ....Michigan City, IN
Duval, Bernard A. ....Alexandria, VA
Duval, C. Berwick, II ....Houma, LA
DuVal, Clive L., II ....McLean, VA
DuVal, Daniel H. ....McLean, VA
DuVal, David V. ....Richmond, VA
Duval, Frank J. ....Port Washington, NY
Duval, Funderburk, Sundbery, Lovell & Watkins, A Professional Law Corporation
Houma, LA
Duval, Gordon W. ....Pleasant Grove, UT
Duval, Hansen, Witt & Morley
Pleasant Grove, UT
DuVal, Harvie S. ....North Miami, FL
DuVal, J. Todd ....Richmond, VA
Duval, John R. ....Fort Collins, CO
DuVal, Kathleen ....Richmond, VA
Duval, Leo V., III ....Staten Island, NY
Duval, Leslie E. ....Basking Ridge, NJ
Duval, Louis J. ....Boston, MA
DuVal, Mark E. ....St. Paul, MN
Duval, Michael J. ....Springfield, MA
Duval, Nancy O. ....West Sacramento, CA
Duval, Nicole R. ....Sacramento, CA
Duval, Patrick W. ....New York, NY
DuVal, Philip L. ....Chattanooga, TN
DuVal, Richard S. ....Honolulu, HI
Duval, Robert M. ....Dallas, TX
DuVal, Robert T. ....Jersey City, NJ
Duval & Stachenfeld LLP ....New York, NY
Duval, Stanwood R., Jr. ....New Orleans, LA
DuVal, Thomas B. ....Chicago, IL

Duval, William L., Jr. ....Santa Barbara, CA
Duvall, Adrienne ....Norristown, PA
Duvall, Alan ....Dayton, OH
Duvall, Charles T. ....Department of Defense, Armed Services Board of Contract Appeals, GV
Duvall, Clifford R. ....Greenup, KY
Duvall, Cornelius H. ....Falcon Heights, TX
Duvall, Diane Pedicini
Overland Park, KS
Duvall, Donald Knox ....Washington, DC
Duvall & Duvall, L.L.P. ....Ocean City, MD
Salisbury, MD
Duvall, Gardner M. ....Baltimore, MD
Duvall, Gary C. ....Towson, MD
Duvall, Gary R. ....Seattle, WA
Duvall, H. Daniel ....Charleston, WV
Duvall, Harrigan, Hale & Hassan, P.L.C.
Fairfax, VA
Duvall, Homer, III ....St. Petersburg, FL
Duvall, Hubert G., Jr. ....Eugene, OR
DuVall, J. Kyle ....Dallas, TX
Duvall, James ....Columbus, OH
Duvall, James J. ....Alma, WI
Duvall, Jeffries H., (P.A.) ....Tallahassee, FL
Duvall, Jim, Law Offices of
San Marcos, TX
Duvall, John A. ....Coudersport, PA
Duvall, John E. ....Jacksonville, FL
Duvall, John H. ....Alexandria, VA
Duvall, John H., P.C. ....Alexandria, VA
Duvall, Joseph L. ....Fairfax, VA
Duvall, Leslie ....Indianapolis, IN
Duvall, Lindsey W. ....Millersville, MD
DuVall, Louise M. ....Long Beach, CA
Duvall, Marc J. ....Seattle, WA
Duvall, Mareen L., Jr. ....Annapolis, MD
Duvall, Mark E. ....Oklahoma City, OK
Duvall, Mark N. ....Danbury, CT
Duvall, Martha J. ....Lumberton, NC
Duvall, Mary Louise ....Plainfield, NJ
Duvall, Michael Alan ....Rocky River, OH
Duvall, Nancy L. ....Dayton, OH
Duvall, Paul H. ....San Diego, CA
DuVall, Randolph C. ....Virginia Beach, VA
Duvall, Reuter, Pruyne & Ondrey
Dushore, PA
Le Raysville, PA
Towanda, PA
Duvall, Richard M. ....Salisbury, MD
Duvall, Richard O. ....Washington, DC
Falls Church, VA
DuVall, Richard R. ....Poughkeepsie, NY
Duvall, Robert A. ....Bella Vista, AR
Duvall, Robert E. ....Springfield, VA
Duvall, Roger L. ....Scottsburg, IN
Duvall, Ruud L. ....Fayetteville, AR
Duvall, Scot A. ....Louisville, KY
Duvall, Sharon C. ....Atlanta, GA
Duvall, Susan E. ....Washington, DC
Duvall, Suzanne M., (Ms.) ....Dallas, TX
Duvall, Thomas O., Jr. ....Atlanta, GA
Duvall, Tyler D. ....McLean, VA
Duvall, Weems W., Jr. ....Pasadena, MD
Duvall, Weems W., Jr., P.A.
Pasadena, MD
Duvall, William G. ....Salisbury, MD
Duvall, Willis A. ....Edison, GA
DuVall, Willis A., Jr. ....Albany, GA
Duvanel, Fonda ....New York, NY
DuVarney, Andrée A., (Ms.)
Department of Agriculture, Farm Service Agency, GV
Duvauchelle & Kakinami ....Kalaheo, HI
Duve, Cherie ....Chicago, IL
Duve, James C., (P.C.)
Colorado Springs, CO
Duvel, Perla J. ....Santa Ana, CA
Duvelius, Carolyn A. ....Lebanon, OH
Duven, Dawn R. ....Waterloo, IA
Duven, William Charles
Colorado Springs, CO
Duver, Theodore F. ....New York, NY
Duvernay, Marc S. ....Los Angeles, CA
Duverney, Daphne ....Brooklyn, NY
Duverney, Ulric N. ....Huntington Beach, CA
Duvernoy, Austin A. ....Ithaca, NY
Duvick, David F. ....St. Paul, MN
Duvieilh, John L. ....New Orleans, LA
Duvieilh, Milton L., Jr. ....New Orleans, LA
DuVilla, Philipp ....Woodbury, NJ
Duvin, Cahn & Hutton, A Legal Professional Association ....Southfield, MI
Cleveland, OH
Duvin, Marc A. ....Cleveland, OH
Duvin, Robert P. ....Cleveland, OH
DuVivier, Katharine K. ....Boulder, CO
du Von, Jay ....Arlington, VA
Woodbridge, VA
DuWaldt, Karen ....Denver, CO
DuWaldt, Michael J. ....Marengo, IL
Duwe, Barry K. ....Overland Park, KS
Duwe, Brian W. ....Chicago, IL
Duwel, Todd T. ....Dayton, OH
Duwell, John F. ....West Bend, WI
Duwve, Lori L. ....Denver, CO
Dux, Kathryn A. ....Philadelphia, PA
Duxbury, Lloyd L. ....Washington, DC
Duxbury, Richard M. ....Lincoln, NE
Duxstad, Robert S. ....Monroe, WI
Duxstad, Vale, Bestul & Gartzke, S.C.
Monroe, WI
Duxstad, Vale, Bestul & Gartzke, S.C.
Darlington, WI
New Glarus, WI
Duyck, Daniel L. ....Portland, OR
Duyer, Katherine S. ....Rockville, MD
Duyk, Martin L. ....Edison, NJ

Duzan, James R. ....Salt Lake City, UT
Duzane, George J. ....Nashville, TN
Duzane, Jerre G. ....Memphis, TN
Duzane, Kooperman & Mondelli
Nashville, TN
Duzey, Robert Lindsey ....Downey, CA
Duzinskas, Debra L. ....Peoria, IL
Duzyk, Darren J. ....Lexington, KY
Duzyk, David M. ....New York, NY
Dveirin, Brant H. ....Los Angeles, CA
Dveirin, Jack L. ....New Orleans, LA
D'Vileskis Morgan, Christine M.
Chelmsford, MA
Dvonch, Richard F. ....Honolulu, HI
Dvorachek, Ronald S. ....Georgetown, OH
Dvorak, Brian G. ....Las Vegas, NV
Dvorak, David A. ....East Peoria, IL
Dvorak, David C. ....Mentor, OH
Dvorak, David M. ....Omaha, NE
Dvorak, Diane L. ....St. James, NY
Dvorak, Edwin A. ....Countryside, IL
Dvorak, Frank A. ....Minneapolis, MN
Dvorak, George F., (P.C.) ....Chicago, IL
Dvorak, James P., Jr. ....McLean, VA
Dvorak, John E. ....Chicago, IL
Dvorak, John K. ....Boston, MA
Dvorak, Joseph J. ....Florham Park, NJ
Dvorak, Joseph M., III ....Riverside, IL
Dvorak, Joseph M., Jr. ....North Riverside, IL
Dvorak, Kathleen B. ....South Bend, IN
Dvorak, Liberty P. ....North Riverside, IL
Dvorak, Linda J. ....Redwood City, CA
Dvorak, Lori A. ....North Brunswick, NJ
Dvorak, Louis B. ....Bend, OR
Dvorak, Mark S. ....Ashland, KY
Dvorak, Michael A. ....South Bend, IN
Dvorak, Michael W. ....Minneapolis, MN
Dvorak and Orum ....Chicago, IL
Dvorak, Richard D. ....Leawood, KS
Dvorak, Robert J. ....Milwaukee, WI
Dvorak, Robyn ....Coeur d'Alene, ID
Dvorak, Shirley A. ....Grand Forks, ND
Dvorak, Suzanne H ....Chicago, IL
Dvorak, Thomas E. ....Boise, ID
Dvorak, Thomas P. ....Houston, TX
Dvorak, Wendy Cox ....Boise, ID
Dvorchak, Kimberly E.
Colorado Springs, CO
Dvores, Harris N. ....Orlando, FL
Dvores, Lawrence B. ....Livingston, NJ
Dvores, Marilyn D. ....Orlando, FL
Dvoretzky, Sharon L. ....Houston, TX
Dvorin, Donald I. ....Newark, NJ
Dvorin, Jeffrey M. ....Albany, NY
Dvorin, Joshua E. ....New Brunswick, NJ
Dvorin, Lawrence A. ....Hartford, CT
Dvorin, Shirley R. ....Des Plaines, IL
Dvorken, Rachel ....Chicago, IL
Dvorkin, Elizabeth ....New York, NY
Dvorkin, Sidney H. ....Roseland, NJ
Dvorkin, Stephen A. ....New York, NY
Dvornik & Associates, P.A. ....Clearwater, FL
Dvornik, D. A. Skip ....Clearwater, FL
Dvorocsik, Madeline V. ....Dallas, TX
Dvorscak, Mark P. ....Argonne, IL
Dvorsky, Kristin L. ....Chicago, IL
Dvoskin, Alicia L. ....Melville, NY
Mineola, NY
Dvoskin, Gary E. ....Mineola, NY
Riverhead, NY
Dwan, H. Michael ....Saginaw, MI
Dwan, Ralph H., Jr. ....Washington, DC
Dwan, Timothy J. ....Lancaster, NY
Dwares, David Mark ....Fort Lauderdale, FL
Dwares, David R. ....Washington, DC
Dwares, Peter L. ....San Francisco, CA
Dwares, Rachel A. ....Wilmington, DE
Dwarica, Leonard A. ....West Haven, CT
Dwars, Gail Beesen ....Chicago, IL
Dweck, H. P. Sean ....New York, NY
Dweck, Jack S. ....New Canaan, CT
New York, NY
White Plains, NY
Dweck, Jacob ....Washington, DC
Dweck Law Firm, The ....New Canaan, CT
New York, NY
White Plains, NY
Dweck, Milizio & Capell ....New York, NY
Dweck, Ralph S. ....Washington, DC
Dweck, Ronald A. ....Bethesda, MD
Dweck, Sari L. ....New York, NY
Dweck, Shoshana R. ....Armonk, NY
Dweck, Stuart M. ....New York, NY
Dwelle, Anne Zier ....Moscow, ID
Dwelle, Cynthia L. ....Stamford, CT
Dwelle, Dorsey K. ....Fresno, CA
Dwelle & Dwelle ....Fresno, CA
Dwigans, Dean L. ....Kansas City, MO
Dwiggins, George Albert ....Charlotte, NC
Dwiggins, Richard H. ....Palo Alto, CA
Dwight, Amanda V. ....Laguna Beach, CA
Dwight, Charles B., III ....Honolulu, HI
Dwight, Charles B., IV ....Kailua-Kona, HI
Dwight, David F. ....Lake Charles, LA
Dwight, Deborah J. ....Phoenix, AZ
Dwight, George H. P. ....New York, NY
Dwight, George, II ....Cincinnati, OH
Dwight, Joseph L., IV ....Kailua, HI
Dwight, Lita Mercedes ....New York, NY
Dwight, M. Diane ....Beaumont, TX
Dwight, Ronald A. ....Department of State, Foreign Service Officers (Overseas), GV
Dwight, Thomas T. ....St. Paul, MN
Dwin, Dasha Smith ....New York, NY
Dwin, Harold P. ....Baltimore, MD
Dwinn, Arnold H. ....Chicago, IL
Dwire, Edgar Wm. ....Wichita, KS
Dworak, Anton V. ....Longmont, CO

Dworak, Joseph E. ....San Jose, CA
Dworakowski, Daryl A. ....Santa Ana, CA
Dworakowski, David A. ....Santa Ana, CA
Dworek, Richard D. ....Pittsburgh, PA
Dworetsky, David H. ....Rockaway Park, NY
Dworetsky, Samuel H. ....Whippany, NJ
Dworetzky, Jeanne J. ....Camden, NJ
Philadelphia, PA
Dworetzky, Joseph A. ....Philadelphia, PA
Dworin, Christopher D. ....Berkeley, CA
Dworin, Jeffrey Z. ....Washington, MI
Dworjanyn, Peter H. ....Columbia, SC
Dwork, Bernard A. ....Boston, MA
Hyannis, MA
Dwork, David P. ....Boston, MA
Dwork, Joel ....Glendale, CA
Dwork, Stuart D. ....Dallas, TX
Dworken & Bernstein Co., L.P.A., A Professional Corporation
Painesville, OH
Dworken, David M. ....Painesville, OH
Dworken, Martin A. ....Bridgeport, CT
Dworken, Marvin P. ....Painesville, OH
Dworkin, Adam M. ....New York, NY
Dworkin, Alan T. ....Warwick, RI
Dworkin, Alan T., Ltd. ....Warwick, RI
Dworkin, Bernard ....New York, NY
Dworkin, Bradley S. ....Chicago, IL
Dworkin, Brian M. ....New York, NY
Dworkin, Carl G. ....Albany, NY
Dworkin, Chambers & Williams, P.C.
Denver, CO
Dworkin, David J. ....Denver, CO
Dworkin, David M. ....Shaker Heights, OH
Dworkin, Douglas A.
Department of Defense, Office of the General Counsel, GV
Dworkin, Howard S. ....Plainview, NY
Dworkin, Irving ....Farmington Hills, MI
Dworkin, Jeremy ....Londonderry, VT
Dworkin, Jerold H. ....Tustin, CA
Dworkin, John C. ....New York, NY
Dworkin, Jonathan S. ....Amherst, OH
Dworkin, Joseph E. ....Arvada, CO
Dworkin, Judith M. ....Scottsdale, AZ
Dworkin, Karen S. ....Department of Justice, Environment and Natural Resources Division, GV
Dworkin, Lawrence R. ....Chester, PA
Dworkin, Marcy G. ....New York, NY
Dworkin, Michael H. ....Montpelier, VT
Dworkin, Michael L., and Associates
San Francisco, CA
Dworkin, Michael L., and Associates
San Mateo, CA
Dworkin, Neil J. ....Irvington, NJ
Dworkin, Roger B. ....Bloomington, IN
Dworkin, Terry Morehead ....Bloomington, IN
Dworman, James M. ....Troy, MI
Dworman, Michael B. ....Worcester, MA
Dwornick, Robert F. ....St. Louis, MO
Dworniczek, Kelly A. ....Chicago, IL
Dwornik, Frances P. ....Fairfax, VA
Dwornik, Richard M. ....Omaha, NE
Dwornik & Sigerson ....Omaha, NE
Dworski, David H. ....Bridgeport, CT
Dworski, William V. ....New Britain, CT
Dworski, William V., P.C. ....New Britain, CT
Dworsky, Alan L. ....Minnetonka, MN
Dworsky, Clara W. ....Houston, TX
Dworsky, Donald L. ....Glen Echo, MD
Dworsky, Edgar ....Boston, MA
Dworsky, Marc T. G. ....Los Angeles, CA
Dworsky, Martin ....Sherman Oaks, CA
Dworsky, Roger L. ....Niskayuna, NY
Dworsky, Tamara L. ....Scottsdale, AZ
Dworsky, Tamara L. ....Sun City, AZ
Dworzanowski, Gregory W. ....Tampa, FL
Dwoskin, Howard P. ....Philadelphia, PA
Dwoskin, Joan Thomson ....Orlando, FL
Dwoskin, Judith ....New York, NY
Dwoskin, Linda S. ....Philadelphia, PA
Dwoskin, Peter M. ....New York, NY
Dwoskin, Robert P. ....Charlottesville, VA
Dwoskin-Smith, Kate M. ....Morganville, NJ
Dwyeer, John J., Jr. ....Chicago, IL
Dwyer, Adrienne K. ....Department of Labor, Office of the Solicitor, GV
Dwyer, Albert Hayden ....Tenafly, NJ
Dwyer, Alice Lorraine ....El Paso, TX
Dwyer, Ami C. ....Towson, MD
Dwyer, Amy S. ....Washington, DC
Dwyer, Anabel L. ....Lansing, MI
Dwyer, Andrew ....Newark, NJ
Dwyer, Andrew P., II ....Trumbull, CT
Dwyer, Anthony D. ....Rockville, MD
Dwyer, Benjamin R. ....Rochester, NY
Dwyer, Bernard J. ....Boston, MA
Dwyer & Black, P.C. ....Belmont, NY
Little Valley, NY
Olean, NY
Wellsville, NY
Dwyer & Brennan ....New York, NY
Dwyer & Cambre, A Professional Law Corporation ....Covington, LA
Metairie, LA
New Orleans, LA
Dwyer & Canellis, P.A. ....Westfield, NJ
Dwyer & Caramagno ....Portsmouth, NH
Dwyer, Carol Jones ....Hastings, MI
Dwyer, Catherine A. ....San Jose, CA
Dwyer, Christopher D. ....Chicago, IL
Dwyer, Christopher E. ....Glendale, CA
Dwyer & Collora, LLP ....Boston, MA
Dwyer, Connell & Lisbona ....Fairfield, NJ
Dwyer, Cornelius J., Jr. ....New York, NY
Dwyer, Craig E. ....San Diego, CA
Dwyer, D. Michael ....Overland Park, KS

Dwyer, Daisy Hilse ... New York, NY
Dwyer, Daly, Brotzen & Bruno, LLP
Los Angeles, CA
Dwyer, Damian P. ... Boykins, VA
Dwyer, Daniel J. ... Boston, MA
Dwyer, Daniel James ... New York, NY
Dwyer, Daniel L. ... Dade City, FL
Dwyer, Daniel M. ... Ridgewood, NJ
Dwyer, Daniel P. ... Philadelphia, PA
Dwyer, Daniel Patrick ... Hagerstown, MD
Dwyer, Daniel R. ... Washington, DC
Dwyer, Danl. D. ... Wichita, KS
Dwyer, David E. ... Fort Collins, CO
Dwyer, Dawn M. B. ... Maple Grove, MN
Dwyer, Deborah A. ... Seattle, WA
Dwyer, Deborah E. ... Columbia, MD
Dwyer, Debra L. ... Rockville, MD
Dwyer, Dennis M. ... Culver City, CA
Dwyer & Dwyer ... Boston, MA
Dwyer, Dwyer & Dwyer, P.C.
Ridgewood, NJ
Dwyer, Dykes & Thurston
Overland Park, KS
Dwyer, Edmond J., Jr. ... Fairfield, NJ
Dwyer, Edward P., Jr. ... Joplin, MO
Dwyer, Edward W. ... Springfield, IL
Dwyer, Ellen Moran ... Washington, DC
Dwyer & Ellis, L.L.C. ... Newark, NJ
Dwyer, Eugene F. ... Davenport, IA
Dwyer, Felicia M. ... Chicago, IL
Dwyer, Francis J. ... Pelham Manor, NY
Dwyer, Frank X. ... Denver, CO
Dwyer, Frederick H. N. ... Mandeville, LA
Dwyer, G. Edward, Jr. ... Frederick, MD
Dwyer, Gary J. ... New York, NY
Dwyer, Gerald A. ... Schenectady, NY
Dwyer, Gerald P. ... New Haven, CT
Dwyer, Gerald P. ... New York, NY
Dwyer, Glynn J., Jr. ... Kendall Park, NJ
Dwyer, Gregg A. ... Bethel, CT
Dwyer, Gregory W. ... Sacramento, CA
Dwyer, Huddleson & Ray, P.C.
Fort Collins, CO
Dwyer Imanaka Schraff Kudo Meyer & Fujimoto, Attorneys at Law, A Law Corporation ... Honolulu, HI
Dwyer, J. Matthew, Jr. (P.C.) ... Atlanta, GA
Dwyer, J. Michael ... Portland, OR
Dwyer, J. Patrick ... Glastonbury, CT
Dwyer, James B. ... Erie, PA
Dwyer, James C. ... New York, NY
Dwyer, James F. ... Syracuse, NY
Dwyer, James G. ... Chicago, IL
Dwyer, James J. ... New York, NY
Dwyer, James J. ... New York, NY
Dwyer, James P. ... Portland, OR
Dwyer, James R. ... Chicago, IL
Dwyer, James W. ... Wauwatosa, WI
Dwyer, Janet
Pension Benefit Guaranty Corporation, Other Lawyers in Staff or Executive Positions, GV
Dwyer, Janice M. ... Sacramento, CA
Dwyer, J. D. ... Washington, IN
Dwyer, Jeffry R. ... Washington, DC
Dwyer & Jenkins, Attorneys At Law, P.C.
Boston, MA
Dwyer, Joan S. ... St. Louis, MO
Dwyer, John ... Philadelphia, PA
Dwyer, John B. ... West Milford, NJ
Dwyer, John Charles ... Palo Alto, CA
Dwyer, John D. ... Los Angeles, CA
Dwyer, John D. ... Boston, MA
Dwyer, John D., Jr. ... Clayton, MO
Dwyer, John F. ... San Francisco, CA
Dwyer, John F. ... Des Moines, IA
Dwyer, John F. ... New York, NY
Dwyer, John H., Jr. ... Louisville, KY
Dwyer, John J. ... Washington, DC
Dwyer, John J. ... Lanham, MD
Dwyer, John J. ... Cleveland, OH
Dwyer, John, Jr. ... Boston, MA
Dwyer, John M. ... San Diego, CA
Dwyer, John P. ... Los Angeles, CA
Dwyer, John P. ... Newark, NJ
Dwyer, John R., Jr. ... Honolulu, HI
Dwyer, John V., Jr. ... Nashua, NH
Dwyer, John W. ... Bismarck, ND
Dwyer, Joseph C. ... Olean, NY
Dwyer, Joseph R. ... Vista, CA
Dwyer, Judith H. ... Washington, IN
Dwyer, Kathleen ... Salem, NH
Dwyer, Kathleen M. ... Portsmouth, NH
Dwyer, Kathleen M. ... Albany, NY
Dwyer, Kathleen P. ... Danvers, MA
Dwyer, Kathryn ... Blue Bell, PA
Dwyer, Kelly J. ... Austin, TX
Dwyer, Kerry E. ... Milwaukee, WI
Dwyer, Kevin C. ... Washington, DC
Dwyer, Kevin F. ... Newport, RI
Dwyer, Kevin J. ... McLean, VA
Dwyer, Kinburn & Hall, A Professional Corporation ... Paterson, NJ
Totowa, NJ
Dwyer, Lawrence A. ... Omaha, NE
Dwyer, Lawrence M. ... San Antonio, TX
Dwyer, Linda Marie ... Fairfax, VA
Dwyer, Lisa M. ... Washington, DC
Philadelphia, PA
Dwyer, Lorna M. ... West Hartford, CT
Dwyer, Louis C., Jr. ... Wildwood, NJ
Dwyer, M. Andrew, Jr. ... Troy, NY
Dwyer, Margaret M. ... Chicago, IL
Dwyer, Mark E. ... New York, NY
Dwyer, Mark R. ... New York, NY
Dwyer, Martha M., Law Offices of
New York, NY
Dwyer, Mary C. ... San Francisco, CA
Dwyer, Mary J. ... Lansing, MI
Dwyer, Mary Jane ... Marion, IL
Dwyer, Matthew E. ... Boston, MA
Dwyer, Matthew H. ... Lake Placid, NY
Dwyer, Matthew R., Jr. ... Hampton Bays, NY
Dwyer, Maureen C. ... Bedford, NH
Dwyer, Maureen Ellen ... Washington, DC
Dwyer, Maureen Galvin ... Northport, NY
Dwyer, Michael A. ... Bismarck, ND
Dwyer, Michael C. ... Rochester, NY
Dwyer, Michael D. ... Seattle, WA
Dwyer, Michael G. ... Chatsworth, CA
Dwyer, Michael G., Jr. ... Kenmore, NY
Dwyer, Michael J. ... Concord, CA
Dwyer, Michael J. ... Eagan, MN
Dwyer, Michael J. ... Ridgewood, NJ
Dwyer, Michael J. ... Milwaukee, WI
Dwyer, Michael J. ... Milwaukee, WI
Dwyer, Michael L. ... Utica, NY
Dwyer, Michael T. ... Winchester, MA
Dwyer, Michael W. ... Miami, FL
Dwyer & Miller ... Portland, OR
Dwyer, Nancy E. ... Baltimore, MD
Dwyer, Nora E. ... Sacramento, CA
Dwyer, Oswald S., Jr. ... Topeka, KS
Dwyer, Pat E., Sr. ... El Paso, TX
Dwyer, Patrick E. ... Chicago, IL
Dwyer, Patrick E., & Associates, Ltd.
Chicago, IL
Dwyer, Patrick J. ... Newark, NJ
New York, NY
Dwyer, Patrick M., PC ... Seattle, WA
Dwyer, Patrick Michael ... Seattle, WA
Dwyer, Patrick William ... Austin, TX
Dwyer, Paul E. ... Santa Monica, CA
Dwyer, Paul E., Jr. ... Providence, RI
Dwyer, Paul F., Jr. ... Albany, NY
Dwyer, Paul S., Jr. ... Washington, DC
Dwyer, Peter A. ... Santa Fe, NM
Dwyer, Peter C. ... Baltimore, MD
Dwyer, Philip J. ... East Lansing, MI
Dwyer, Philip J. ... New York, NY
Dwyer, Ralph D., Jr. ... New Orleans, LA
Dwyer, Reneé W. ... Hartford, CT
Dwyer, Rex W. ... Dallas, TX
Dwyer, Richard E. A. ... San Jose, CA
Dwyer, Richard J., III ... Alexandria, VA
Dwyer, Robert A., Jr. ... Chicago, IL
Dwyer, Robert E. ... Indianapolis, IN
Dwyer, Robert E. ... Buffalo, NY
Dwyer, Robert F. ... Norwell, MA
Dwyer, Robert F., III ... Beaverton, OR
Dwyer, Robert G. ... Erie, PA
Dwyer, Robert J. ... New York, NY
Dwyer, Robert J., Jr. ... New York, NY
Dwyer, Robert Martin ... Denver, CO
Dwyer, Robert P. ... Syracuse, NY
Dwyer, Robert V., Jr. ... Omaha, NE
Dwyer, Robin V. ... San Antonio, TX
Seguin, TX
Dwyer, Roderick T. ... Washington, DC
Dwyer, Ronald A. ... Los Angeles, CA
Dwyer, Rosetta ... Ridgefield, CT
Dwyer, Roy ... Eugene, OR
Dwyer & Ryan ... New York, NY
Dwyer & Sanderson ... Hadley, MA
Dwyer, Sandra Erica Ann ... New York, NY
Dwyer, Scott E. ... Grand Rapids, MI
Dwyer & Sheridan ... Glastonbury, CT
Dwyer, Shlesinger, deVilleneuve & Potter, P.C. ... Albany, OR
Bend, OR
Coos Bay, OR
Corvallis, OR
Eugene, OR
Medford, OR
Roseburg, OR
Salem, OR
Dwyer, Smith, Gardner, Lazer, Pohren, Rogers & Forrest ... Omaha, NE
Dwyer, Stephen C. ... Washington, DC
Dwyer, Stephen I. ... Covington, LA
Metairie, LA
Dwyer, Stephen J. ... Edmonds, WA
Dwyer, Stephen J., P.S. ... Edmonds, WA
Dwyer, Susan T. ... New York, NY
Dwyer, Suzanne R. ... Wichita, KS
Dwyer, Terrence ... Totowa, NJ
Dwyer, Terrence J. ... Bronxville, NY
Dwyer, Theresa ... Phoenix, AZ
Dwyer, Thomas C. ... Portsmouth, NH
Dwyer, Thomas D. ... Springfield, MO
Dwyer, Thomas E., Jr. ... Boston, MA
Dwyer, Thomas E., Sr. ... Boston, MA
Dwyer, Thomas F. ... Westfield, NJ
Dwyer, Thomas J. ... Chicago, IL
Dwyer, Thomas P. ... Santa Cruz, CA
Dwyer, Thomas P. ... Philadelphia, PA
Dwyer, Thomas W. ... East Williston, NY
Dwyer, Timothy J. ... St. Paul, MN
Dwyer, Timothy P. ... Crystal Lake, IL
Dwyer, Tom ... Brighton, CO
Dwyer, Virginia A. ... Eagan, MN
Dwyer, Warren R. ... Brunswick, ME
Dwyer & White ... Atlanta, GA
Dwyer, William E., Jr. ... Hadley, MA
Dwyer, William Emmett ... New York, NY
Dwyer, William F., II ... Washington, DC
Dwyer, William G. ... Houston, TX
Dwyer, William J. ... Albany, NY
Dwyer, William K., Jr. ... Chicago, IL
Dwyer, William L. ... Seattle, WA
Dwyer, William Newton
Mammoth Lakes, CA
Dwyer, William T., Jr. ... Chicago, IL
Dwyer & Wing, P.C. ... Davenport, IA
Dwyer, W. P., Jr. ... Loomis, CA
Dwyre, John S. ... San Antonio, TX
Dy, Cynthia A. ... Palo Alto, CA
Dyal, Gary E. ... Chicago, IL
Dyal, J. Patrick ... Fort Lauderdale, FL
Dyal, Jonathan Paul ... Biloxi, MS
Dyal, Lucius M., Jr. ... Tampa, FL
Dyal, Margaret ... Lavonia, GA
Dyal, Nola S. ... La Quinta, CA
Dyal, R. Carson ... Tallahassee, FL
Dyal, Sylvia Anne ... Los Angeles, CA
Dyar, Catherine E. ... Chicago, IL
Dyar, John W. ... Decatur, IL
Dyar, Paul J. ... Louisville, KY
Dyar, Richard W. ... Indianapolis, IN
Dyas, Charles R., Jr. ... Cincinnati, OH
Dyas, Eric J. ... Mobile, AL
Dyas, Mildred W. ... Alexandria, VA
Dyatt, Betty Marie ... San Marcos, CA
Dyba, Cecilia P. ... Los Angeles, CA
Dybala, Ray A. ... Schaumburg, IL
Dybeck, Alfred C. ... Pittsburgh, PA
Dybens, Bruce A. ... Long Beach, CA
Dybens, Mary T. ... Los Angeles, CA
Dybing, Genevieve K. ... Richmond, VA
Dybing, Robert A. ... Richmond, VA
Dybner, Ariel M. ... New York, NY
Dybner, Mariela Markelis ... New York, NY
Dybvig, David F. ... Tucson, AZ
Dybvig & Dybvig ... Dayton, OH
Dybvig, Roger S. ... Dayton, OH
Dycaico, Peter J. ... San Francisco, CA
Dych, Joseph A. ... Philadelphia, PA
Dyche, John David ... Louisville, KY
Dyche, Robert W., III ... London, KY
Dyche, Scott A. ... Dallas, TX
Dyches, A. Fletcher ... Tampa, FL
Dyches, A. Fletcher, A Prof. Assn.
Tampa, FL
Dyches, Donald E., Jr. ... Savannah, GA
Dyches, Ryan P. ... Mesa, AZ
Dyches, Steven T. ... Portland, OR
Dycio, Mark R. ... Washington, DC
Dycio & Shea ... Fairfax, VA
Dyck, John D. ... Parma, OH
Dyck, Wendell ... Tukwila, WA
Dyckman, Deborah A. ... Mineola, NY
New York, NY
White Plains, NY
Dyckman, Ezra ... New York, NY
Dyckman, Jacob M. ... New York, NY
Dyckman, Linda A. ... Cortland, NY
Dyckman, Matthew ... Washington, DC
Dyckman, Samuel A. ... New York, NY
Dycus, Joe A. ... Memphis, TN
Dycus, Linda F. ... Kansas City, MO
Dycus, Stephen ... South Royalton, VT
Dycus, Susan L. ... St. Petersburg, FL
Dyczek, Carl ... Cleveland, OH
Dydynsky, George T. ... Lehighton, PA
Dydzak, Daniel D., Law Offices of
Los Angeles, CA
Dye, A. Rowland ... Augusta, GA
Dye, Alan L. ... Washington, DC
Dye, Alan P. ... Washington, DC
Dye, Alexander M. ... New York, NY
Dye, Brad ... Jackson, MS
Dye, Bradford J., Jr. ... Jackson, MS
Dye, Carolyn A. ... Los Angeles, CA
Dye, Christopher deR. ... Bradford, VT
Dye, Clinton E., III ... Birmingham, AL
Dye, Dana Lloyd ... Centerville, TN
Dye, David A. ... Columbus, OH
Dye, Dewey A., Jr. ... Bradenton, FL
Dye, Don D. ... Tallahassee, FL
Dye, Donald H. ... Carlsbad, CA
Dye, Douglas G. ... Philadelphia, PA
Dye, Edward R. ... Fairlawn, OH
Dye Foley Krohn & Shannon, S.C.
Racine, WI
Dye, Garry L. ... Denver, CO
Dye, Gary G. ... Los Angeles, CA
Dye, Gregory R. ... Cleveland, OH
Dye, Harold V. ... Missoula, MT
Dye, Hugh B. ... Birmingham, AL
Dye, James D. ... Bradenton, FL
Dye, James D. ... Wichita, KS
Dye, James Javier ... Orlando, FL
Dye, Jeffrey L. ... Portland, OR
Dye, Jerry B. ... Augusta, GA
Dye, Jim L. ... Tallahassee, FL
Dye, Jimmy ... Tallahassee, FL
Dye, John V. ... Eaton, OH
Dye, Josephine V. ... Boston, MA
Dye, Karey Dubiel ... Houston, TX
Dye Law Firm The, P.A. ... Tallahassee, FL
Dye, Luther V. ... Jamaica, NY
Dye, Martha ... Washington, DC
Dye, Michael B. ... Salem, OR
Dye & Moe, P.L.L.P. ... Missoula, MT
Dye, Noelle C. ... Chicago, IL
Dye, Paul Scott ... Omaha, NE
Dye, Paul T. ... Los Angeles, CA
Dye, Pauline Peppercorn ... Wichita, KS
Dye, Peter W. ... Burbank, CA
Dye, Phillip B., Jr. ... Houston, TX
Dye, R. Harvey, Law Offices of
Phoenix, AZ
Dye, Ralph D., Jr. ... McConnelsville, OH
Dye, Richard M. ... Jackson, MS
Dye, Richard W. ... Houston, TX
Dye, Robert A. ... Los Angeles, CA
Dye, Robert C. ... Farmingville, NY
Dye, Robert E. ... Irvine, CA
Dye, Scott A. ... Dallas, TX
Dye & Scott, P.A. ... Bradenton, FL
Dye, Sherman ... Cleveland, OH
Dye, Sherrill L. ... Portland, OR
Dye, Stephen H. ... San Francisco, CA
Dye, Stephen R. ... Bradenton, FL
Dye, Steven Michael ... Longmont, CO
Dye, Stuart S. ... Washington, DC
Dye, Thomas A. ... Fort Lauderdale, FL
Dye, Thomas W. ... Macomb, IL
Dye, Tucker, Everitt, Long & Brewton
Appling, GA
Louisville, GA
Thomson, GA
Washington, GA
Waynesboro, GA
Augusta, GA
Dye & Vander Horst ... Centerville, TN
Dye, William E. ... Racine, WI
Dye, William H. ... Wichita, KS
Dye, William M., Jr. ... Oxford, MS
Dye-Chiew, KahBo ... Honolulu, HI
Dyekman, Curtis, Cohen & Karow, P.L.C.
Phoenix, AZ
Scottsdale, AZ
Dyekman, Donald E. ... Scottsdale, AZ
Dyekman, Gregory C. ... Cheyenne, WY
Dyen, Randall E. ... Philadelphia, PA
Dyer, A. Gill ... Covington, LA
Dyer, Adair ... Austin, TX
Dyer, Allen R. ... Baltimore, MD
Dyer & Associates ... McAllen, TX
Dyer, Benjamin L. ... Houston, TX
Dyer, Bill M. ... Somerset, KY
Dyer, Billy Coe ... Houston, TX
Dyer, Boyd K. ... Salt Lake City, UT
Dyer, Brent E. ... Overland Park, KS
Dyer, Cecilia Ridgway
Hot Springs National Park, AR
Pine Bluff, AR
Dyer, Charles A. ... Menlo Park, CA
Dyer, Charles H. ... Jacksonville, FL
Dyer, Charles J. ... Phoenix, AZ
Dyer, Charles J. ... Boston, MA
Dyer, Charles M. ... Phoenix, AZ
Dyer, Charles R. ... San Diego, CA
Dyer, Charles T. ... Dyersburg, TN
Dyer, Christina L. ... San Diego, CA
Dyer, Christopher S. ... Rancho Cordova, CA
Dyer, Chuck ... Van Buren, AR
Dyer, Colin R. C. ... Fort Mill, SC
Dyer, Constance E. ... Portland, OR
Dyer, Curtis B. ... Corpus Christi, TX
Dyer, Daniel E. ... Syracuse, NY
Dyer, Daniel J. ... Norfolk, VA
Dyer, Danny Paul ... Knoxville, TN
Dyer, David B. ... Dallas, TX
Dyer, David P. ... Kansas City, MO
Dyer, David R. ... New Orleans, LA
Dyer, David W. ... Indialantic, FL
Dyer, Deborah Lovett ... Haverhill, MA
Dyer, Dee R. ... Appleton, WI
Dyer & Dilts, P.C. ... Cortez, CO
Dyer, Dion G. ... San Diego, CA
Dyer, Don ... Long Beach, CA
Dyer Donnelly ... Denver, CO
Dyer, Dustin W. ... Washington, DC
Dyer, Dyer, Jones & Daniels, A Professional Association ... Greenville, MS
Dyer, Edwin W. F., III ... Bismarck, ND
Dyer Ellis & Joseph, A Professional Corporation ... Washington, DC
Dyer, Erin P. ... Pittsburgh, PA
Dyer, Gaines S. ... Greenville, MS
Dyer, Garofalo, Mann & Schultz, A Legal Professional Association ... Dayton, OH
Lima, OH
Middletown, OH
Piqua, OH
Springfield, OH
Dyer, George L., Jr. ... Port Ludlow, WA
Dyer, George N., Jr. ... Ventura, CA
Dyer, Gilford McKenna ... York, PA
Dyer, Glenn T. ... Roseland, NJ
Dyer & Goodall ... Augusta, ME
Dyer, Gregory C. ... Mill Valley, CA
Dyer, Gregory F. ... Sacramento, CA
Reno, NV
Dyer, Gregory M. ... Newark, NJ
Dyer & Gustafson ... Augusta, ME
Dyer, Guy B., Jr. ... Cortez, CO
Dyer, Hollis O. ... Woodland Hills, CA
Dyer, Holly A. ... Wichita, KS
Dyer, Howard, III ... Greenville, MS
Dyer, J. Scott ... New York, NY
Dyer, Jack N. ... Orange Beach, AL
Dyer, James A. ... Dayton, OH
Dyer, James David ... Kent, OH
Dyer, James H. ... Tucson, AZ
Dyer, James H. ... Houston, TX
Dyer, James K., Jr. ... Birmingham, AL
Dyer, James L. ... Battle Creek, MI
Dyer, James P. ... Austin, TX
Dyer, Jeffrey N. ... Midland, MI
Dyer, John G. ... Kansas City, MO
Dyer, John G., III ... Medford, NJ
Dyer, John H., Jr. ... Orlando, FL
Dyer, John M. ... Miami, FL
Dyer, John R., Jr. ... Truro, MA
Dyer, Jonathan P. ... Napa, CA
Dyer, Joseph J. ... Washington, DC
Dyer, Joseph P. ... Fairfax, VA
Dyer, Joseph R. ... Dallas, TX
Dyer, J. W. ... McAllen, TX
Dyer, Karen Caudill ... Orlando, FL
Armonk, NY
Dyer, Kate ... San Francisco, CA
Dyer, Kathleen M. ... Albuquerque, NM
Dyer, Kenneth J. ... Washington, DC
Dyer, Kenneth J. ... Baltimore, MD
Dyer, Kevin M. ... New York, NY
Dyer Law Offices ... Clarksburg, WV
Dyer, Lawrence, Cooney & Penrose
Carson City, NV

Dyer & Libby ... Houston, TX
Dyer, Linda Smith ... Augusta, ME
Dyer, Lloyd E., Jr. ... Wheaton, IL
Dyer, Lynn L. ... Boston, MA
Dyer, Mann & Berens, LLP ... Phoenix, AZ
Dyer, Marion M., (Mr.) ... Broken Arrow, OK
Dyer, Mark J. ... Dallas, TX
Dyer, Marshall K. ... Broken Arrow, OK
Dyer, Martin A. ... Baltimore, MD
Dyer, Martin E. ... Ardmore, OK
Dyer, Martin Patrick ... San Diego, CA
Dyer, Mary Lou ... Augusta, ME
Dyer, Matthew C. ... Lewiston, ME
Dyer, Matthew F. ... Augusta, ME
Dyer, Maureen C. ... East Lansing, MI
Dyer, Michael Dean ... Jefferson City, MO
Dyer, Michael E. ... Dayton, OH
Dyer, Michael E. ... Salt Lake City, UT
Dyer, Michael J. ... Stockton, CA
Dyer, Michael J. ... Laurel, MD
Dyer, Michael J. ... Omaha, NE
Dyer, Michael W. ... Carson City, NV
Dyer, Michele L. ... McLean, VA
Dyer & Nielsen ... San Diego, CA
Dyer, Noel J. ... San Francisco, CA
Dyer, Norman C. ... Columbia, MD
Dyer, Pat T. ... Houston, TX
Dyer, Patrick J. ... Houston, TX
Dyer, Paul E. ... Little Compton, RI
Dyer, Phillip W., Law Offices of
Salt Lake City, UT
Dyer, Preston L. ... Lewes, DE
Dyer, Ralph A. ... Portland, ME
Dyer, Ralph A., P.A., Law Offices of
Portland, ME
Dyer, Ralph R. ... Valrico, FL
Dyer, Richard P. ... New York, NY
Dyer, Richard W. ... Manchester, CT
Dyer, Robert ... Orlando, FL
Dyer, Robert E. ... Wheaton, IL
Dyer, Robert G., Law Offices of
Encinitas, CA
Dyer, Robert J., III ... Denver, CO
Dyer, Robert M. ... Canton, GA
Dyer, Robert M. ... Sandy, UT
Dyer, Robert O. ... Phoenix, AZ
Dyer, Rodney N. ... Laconia, NH
Dyer, Roger C. ... Yorba Linda, CA
Dyer, Savannah Lee ... Plano, TX
Dyer, Sharon L. ... Binghamton, NY
Dyer, Sherry R. ... Needham, MA
Dyer, Stephen E. ... Ardmore, OK
Dyer, Stephen G. ... Honolulu, HI
Dyer, Stephen T. ... Houston, TX
Dyer, Stephen W. ... Monterey, CA
Dyer, Steven D. ... Lancaster, PA
Dyer, Steven E. ... St. Louis, MO
Dyer, Sue M. ... Nashville, TN
Dyer & Summers, P.C. ... Bismarck, ND
Dyer, T. Stephen ... Chicago, IL
Dyer, Thomas G. ... Clarksburg, WV
Dyer, Thomas H. ... Manlius, NY
Dyer, Thomas M. ... Washington, DC
Dyer, Thomas R. ... Memphis, TN
Dyer, Tommy R., Jr. ... Jay, OK
Dyer, Tracy J. ... Bozeman, MT
Dyer, Treeca J., (Miss) ... Little Rock, AR
Dyer, Treeca J., P.A. ... Little Rock, AR
Dyer, Victoria J. ... Moline, IL
Dyer, Virginia L. ... New York, NY
Dyer, W. Robert, Jr. ... Dallas, TX
Dyer, W. Wallace, Jr. ... Jenkintown, PA
Dyer & White LLP ... Menlo Park, CA
Dyer, Wilfred M., Jr. ... Clinton, MD
Dyer, William ... Smithville, TN
Dyer, William B., III ... Atlanta, GA
Dyer, William J. ... Houston, TX
Dyerly, Rodney B. ... Chesterton, IN
Dyers, Sean Patrick ... Seattle, WA
Dyess, Arthur D., Jr. ... Houston, TX
Dyess, Arthur D., Jr., P.C. ... Houston, TX
Dyess, Bobby D. ... Dallas, TX
Dyess, Carl F. ... Portland, OR
Dyess, Jeffrey D. ... Birmingham, AL
Dyess, Robert W., Jr. ... Newport Beach, CA
Dyess, William A.
Federal Deposit Insurance Corporation, GV
Dyess, William D. ... New Orleans, LA
Dygert, Diane V. ... Chicago, IL
Dygert, Edward C. ... Irvine, CA
Dygert, George H., & Associates
Charlottesville, VA
Dygert, Harold P., III ... Olympia, WA
Dygert, Jeffrey H.
Federal Communications Commission,
Common Carrier Bureau, GV
Dygert, Jerry G. ... Minneapolis, MN
Dygert Law Office ... Minneapolis, MN
Dygert, Robert W. ... Minneapolis, MN
Dyhrberg, Thomas A. ... Scarborough, ME
Dyhrkopp, Anthony W. ... Shawneetown, IL
Dyhrkopp, Erik F. ... Chicago, IL
Dyk, Timothy B. ... Washington, DC
Dykas, Cecile L. ... Fort Lauderdale, FL
Dykas, David A. ... West Plains, MO
Dykas, Frank J. ... Boise, ID
Dykas, Frank J., P.A. ... Boise, ID
Dyke, Charles M. ... San Francisco, CA
Dyke, Donald J. ... Madison, WI
Dyke, Ellen F. ... McLean, VA
Dyke, Henry, Goldsholl & Winzerling, P.L.C.
Little Rock, AR
Dyke, J. Benton, Jr. ... Little Rock, AR
Dyke, James R. ... Stockton, CA
Dyke, James T. ... Little Rock, AR
Dyke, James Webster, Jr. ... McLean, VA
Dyke, Lori Anne E. ... Cleveland, OH
Dyke, Thomas A. ... Austin, TX
Dyke, Thomas W. ... Louisville, KY
Dyke, William D. ... Mineral Point, WI
Dyke, William H. ... Oklahoma City, OK
Dykehouse, James B. ... Chicago, IL
Dykema, Daniel D. ... Hollywood, FL
Dykema Gossett PLLC ... Washington, DC
Chicago, IL
Ann Arbor, MI
Bloomfield Hills, MI
Detroit, MI
Grand Rapids, MI
Lansing, MI
Dykema, Jayne A. ... Grand Rapids, MI
Dykema, John R. ... Detroit, MI
Dykema Law Offices, P.C.
Grand Rapids, MI
Dykema, Peter Kryn ... Washington, DC
Dykema, Steven L. ... Grand Rapids, MI
Dykeman, Christine M. ... Des Moines, IA
Dykeman, Daryl E. ... St. Louis, MO
Dykeman, David B. ... Oklahoma City, OK
Dykeman, David Jack ... Minneapolis, MN
Dykeman & Dykeman, Inc. A Professional Corporation ... Oklahoma City, OK
Dykeman, Greg M. ... Beaumont, TX
Dykeman & Rosenthal ... Winchester, KY
Dykeman, W. Samuel
Oklahoma City, OK
Dykeman, William A. ... Winchester, KY
Dykeman, William S. ... Oklahoma City, OK
Dykes, Barbara ... Everett, WA
Dykes, Gerald W. ... Overland Park, KS
Dykes, James D. ... Newark, DE
Dykes, Jeffrey L. ... Englewood, CO
Dykes, Joe G., Jr. ... DeLand, FL
Dykes, Lillian E. ... Memphis, TN
Dykes, Mark E. ... Houston, TX
Dykes, Mark W. ... Salt Lake City, UT
Dykes, Osborne J., III ... Houston, TX
Dykes, Robert G. ... Columbus, OH
Dykes, Robert M. ... Tustin, CA
Dykes, Roger F. ... Rockledge, FL
Dykes, Teresa E. ... Washington, DC
Dykes, Toby ... Birmingham, AL
Dykes, William T. F., A Law Corporation
Shreveport, LA
Dykes, William T. F. ... Shreveport, LA
Dykhouse, David J. ... Detroit, MI
Dykhouse, David W. ... New York, NY
Dykhouse, Richard R. ... Carmel, IN
Dykhuizen, Dennis F. ... Fort Wayne, IN
Dykhuizen, Joseph M. ... Indianapolis, IN
Dykman, Charles P. ... Madison, WI
Dykman, Craig, Law Offices of
Petaluma, CA
Dykman, Craig, Law Offices of
San Rafael, CA
Dykman, Peter J. ... Madison, WI
Dykstra, A. Richard ... Seattle, WA
Dykstra, Arlene V. ... Denver, CO
Dykstra, C. Kevin ... Phoenix, AZ
Dykstra, Daniel D. ... Sioux City, IA
Dykstra, Daniel J. ... Davis, CA
Dykstra, Daniel R. ... Kansas City, MO
Dykstra, Deborah A. ... Montclair, NJ
Dykstra & Grill ... Kansas City, MO
Dykstra, Hessel ... Sanborn, IA
Dykstra, Jason G. ... Great Falls, MT
Dykstra, Julie Ann ... Grand Rapids, MI
Dykstra, Kurt D. ... Milwaukee, WI
Dykstra, Mark T. ... Sarasota, FL
Dykstra, Michelle B. ... Los Angeles, CA
Dykstra, Orville L. ... Walnut Creek, CA
Dykstra, Paul A. ... Hasbrouck Heights, NJ
Dykstra, Paul D. ... Peoria, IL
Dykstra, Paul H. ... Chicago, IL
Dykstra, Peter H. ... Seattle, WA
Dykstra, Tamara S. ... Chicago, IL
Dykxhoorn, Jacob C. ... Lakeland, FL
Lake Wales, FL
Winter Haven, FL
Dyl, Antony B. ... Denver, CO
Dyl, Mark S. ... Glendora, CA
Dylan, Jones R. K. ... Honolulu, HI
Dylan, Tyler ... Palo Alto, CA
Dyler, Pattie ... Los Angeles, CA
Dyleski, Mary Grace ... Orlando, FL
Dylewski, Dennis M. ... Houston, TX
Dylewski & Douglass, A Professional Corporation ... Houston, TX
Dylis, David P. ... Ballston Spa, NY
Dylla, Edward V. ... San Antonio, TX
Dyller, Barry H. ... Wilkes-Barre, PA
Dylong, Frank E., Jr ... Washington, DC
Dym, Herbert ... Washington, DC
Dym, Kenneth I. ... New York, NY
Dym, Lori Joan
United States Postal Service,
Law Department, GV
Dym, Mark S. ... Chicago, IL
Dymally, Hazel M. ... Los Angeles, CA
Dymarkowski, Daniel W. ... Toledo, OH
Dymarkowski, Douglas A. ... Sylvania, OH
Dyme, Rochelle Secemsky ... Chicago, IL
Dymecki, Kimberly A. ... Atlanta, GA
Dyment, Jeffrey B. ... Houston, TX
Dyment, Jeffrey B., & Associates
Houston, TX
Dymersky, Michael A. ... Washington, DC
Dymkar & Brandt ... Rochester, NY
Dymkar, Irene K. ... Rochester, NY
Dymoke, Rachel Johnson ... Fergus Falls, MN
Dymoke, Scott E. ... Fergus Falls, MN
Dymond, Alan L. ... Studio City, CA
Dymond, F. Irvin ... New Orleans, LA
Dymond, Kenneth ... Albany, NY
Dymond, Lewis W., Jr. ... Englewood, CO
Dymond, Lynn A. ... Baltimore, MD
Dymond, Richard V. ... Gulfport, MS
Dymond, Steven H. ... Denver, CO
Dymond, Steven H., P.C. ... Denver, CO
Dymond, William T., Jr. ... Orlando, FL
Dymott, Thomas M. ... San Diego, CA
Dymowski, Julianne Erin
Washington, DC
Dynda, Frank J. ... Department of the Army,
U.S. Army Legal Services Agency, GV
Dynek, Sigrid E. ... Menomonee Falls, WI
Dyner, Mark A.
Environmental Protection Agency,
Office of the General Counsel, GV
Dyner, Morris G. ... Chicago, IL
Dynes, Andrea F. ... Washington, DC
Dynes, Brandon D. R. ... Cleveland, OH
Dynes, George T. ... Dickinson, ND
Dynes, Jane L. ... Fargo, ND
Dynice, Barry P. ... Leominster, MA
Dynkowski, Darius W. ... Troy, MI
Dynner, Alan R. ... Boston, MA
Dyre, Arnold D. ... Jackson, MS
Dyre, Jon T. ... Kalispell, MT
Dyre, Mary Scrim ... Kalispell, MT
Dyre & Smith ... Jackson, MS
Dyreson, Jerry T., P.S. ... Spokane, WA
Dyroff, David R., Jr. ... St. Louis, MO
Dyroff, Joann N. Lynch ... St. Louis, MO
Dyrseth, Mary M. ... St. Paul, MN
Dyrud, Harlan M. ... Grand Forks, ND
Dyrud, John Oliver ... Miami, FL
Dyrud, Jonathan A. ... St. Paul, MN
Dyrud, Kenneth R. ... Missoula, MT
Dysard, W. Henderson ... Ashland, KY
Dysart, Daniel L. ... Chalmette, LA
Dysart & Dubick, LLP ... San Diego, CA
Dysart, James H. ... Spring Hill, FL
Dysart, Lewis A. ... Kansas City, MO
Dysart, Nathan D. ... Olympia, WA
Dysart, Pandora ... Dallas, TX
Dysart, Patricia L. ... Richmond, VA
Dysart, Sanborn & Tabary
Chalmette, LA
New Orleans, LA
Dysart, Sara E. ... San Antonio, TX
Dysart, Sara E., P.C. ... San Antonio, TX
Dysart Taylor Lay Cotter & McMonigle, P.C. ... Kansas City, MO
Dysart, William E. ... San Diego, CA
Dysinger & Stewart, A Legal Professional Association ... Tipp City, OH
Dysinger, Thomas E. ... Tipp City, OH
Dysland, Robert C. ... Silver Spring, MD
Dyslin, Daniel R. ... Northbrook, IL
Dyson, Albert H., III
Department of Defense,
Office of the General Counsel, GV
Dyson, David P. ... Eagan, MN
Dyson, Edward E. ... Washington, DC
Dyson, Edward R., Jr. ... Kingsville, TX
Dyson, Elizabeth D. ... Washington, DC
Dyson, Frederic Eckhart, III ... Boulder, CO
Dyson, James D. ... Atlanta, GA
Dyson, James H. ... DeLand, FL
Dyson, Juliann R. ... Englewood, CO
Dyson, Marianna G. ... Washington, DC
Dyson, Michael Ryan ... Raleigh, NC
Dyson, Michael Thomas ... Washington, DC
Dyson, Sandra ... Treasury Department,
Bureau of the Public Debt, GV
Dyson, Schmidlin & Foulds, Co., L.P.A.
Mayfield Heights, OH
Dyson, Victoria L. ... South Lake Tahoe, CA
Dystrup, Alderman ... Lemont, IL
Dystrup, Andrew C. ... Joliet, IL
Dytrych, Terrence F.
West Palm Beach, FL
Dytrych, Terrence F., P.A., The Law Office of ... West Palm Beach, FL
Dyttmer, Dyan M. ... Augusta, ME
Dywan, Jeffrey J. ... Hammond, IN
Dyze, Thomas D. ... Detroit, MI
Dzakovich, Angela Allegra ... Northbrook, IL
Dzeguze, Andrew B. ... Indianapolis, IN
Dzenitis, Talis ... Department of Commerce,
Patent and Trademark Office, GV
Dziadulewicz, Lisa A. ... Sheboygan, WI
Dzialga, Daniel A. ... Pittsburgh, PA
Dzialo, Edward W., Jr. ... Lawton, OK
Dzialo, John T. ... Fullerton, CA
Dzialo, Michael G. ... New York, NY
Dzialo, Pickett & Allen, P.C.
Middletown, CT
Old Saybrook, CT
Dzialo, Robert L. ... Detroit, MI
Rochester Hills, MI
Dzialowski, Michael H. ... Kalamazoo, MI
Dziatkiewicz, Elizabeth A.
Department of State,
Foreign Service Officers (Overseas), GV
Dzida, Carey & Steinman ... Irvine, CA
Dzida, Joseph S., Jr. ... Los Angeles, CA
Dzida, Steven J. ... Irvine, CA
Dziedziak, John F. ... Chicago, IL
Dziedzic, Charles E.
Federal Communications Commission,
Mass Media Bureau, GV
Dziedzic, Jennifer L. ... Washington, DC
Dziedzic, Raymond J. ... Buffalo, NY
Dziedzina, Eugene J., Jr. ... Brewster, MA
Dziedziula, Richard F. ... Manhasset, NY
Dziegielewski, Greg ... Chicago, IL
Dziejma, Thomas P. ... Oxford, MA
Dziekan, Carl S. ... New Hartford, NY
Dziekonski, Thadeus J., Jr. ... Buffalo, NY
Dzieman, Thomas J. ... Medford, OR
Dzien, Kenneth E. ... Pasadena, CA
Dziennik, Francis F. ... Baltimore, MD
Dzienny & Associates, LPA ... Toledo, OH
Dzienny, Michael A. ... Toledo, OH
Dzierlenga, Gary W. ... Houston, TX
Dzierzanowski, Brigid F. ... Fort Myers, FL
Dziesinski, Kenneth L. ... San Francisco, CA
Dziewisz, John ... Barberton, OH
Dziewit, Halina S. ... Boulder, CO
Dziezak, Judie D. ... Chicago, IL
Dzija, John D. ... Cross Lanes, WV
Dzik, Robert B. ... Tinley Park, IL
Dziki, Steven M. ... Lake Villa, IL
Dzikiewicz, Agatha N. ... Iselin, NJ
Short Hills, NJ
Dzikowski, Patricia A., (P.A.)
Fort Lauderdale, FL
Dzikowski & Walsh ... Fort Lauderdale, FL
Dzilenski, William P. ... Providence, RI
Dziuba, Catherine ... Los Angeles, CA
Dziuba, Daniel C. ... Portland, OR
Dziuba, Helen Tompkins ... Portland, OR
Dziubek, Kerry A. ... New York, NY
Dziubla, Robert W. ... Los Angeles, CA
Dziurgot, Cynthia A. ... Clinton, MA
Dzivi, Bartly A. ... San Francisco, CA
Dzivi, Richard ... Great Falls, MT
Dzivi, Richard, P.C. ... Great Falls, MT
Dziwis, Gregory J. ... Utica, NY
Dzodin, Harvey C. ... New York, NY
Dzubur, Eric G., Law Offices of
Castro Valley, CA
Dzubur, Karen S. ... Castro Valley, CA
Dzul, George O. ... Grosse Pointe, MI
Dzuranin, Stephen J. ... Harrisburg, PA
Dzurik, John G. ... Bridgeport, CT
Westport, CT
D'Zurilla, David ... Arlington, VA
D'Zurilla, William T. ... New Orleans, LA
Dzwilewski, Allan P. ... Florham Park, NJ
Dzwilewski, Daniel R. ... La Jolla, CA
Dzwonczyk, Michael R. ... Washington, DC

E, Wei Qun ... San Jose, CA
Eaby, Bradley S. ... Dover, DE
Eaby, Christian Earl ... Leola, PA
Eaby, D. Scott ... Ephrata, PA
Eaby and Eaby ... Brownstown, PA
Denver, PA
Ephrata, PA
Lancaster, PA
Eaby, Mark R., Jr. ... Brownstown, PA
Denver, PA
Ephrata, PA
Lancaster, PA
Eaby, Thelia Jean ... Brownstown, PA
Denver, PA
Ephrata, PA
Lancaster, PA
Eacho, Harrison C., Jr. ... King William, VA
Eacret, Gene B. ... Roseville, CA
Eaddy, Carolene S. ... New York, NY
Eaddy, H. Blake ... Durham, NC
Eaddy, Michele R. ... Okemos, MI
Eaddy, W. Randy ... Atlanta, GA
Eade, Ellen R. ... Monroe, LA
Eade, Kenneth G. ... Oxnard, CA
Eade, Richard D. ... Fort Lauderdale, FL
Eade & Verlander, L.L.P. ... Monroe, LA
Eades, Brian C. ... Omaha, NE
Eades, Christopher C. ... Hammond, IN
Eades, Cynda L. ... Tucker, GA
Eades, David L. ... Charlotte, NC
Eades, Gregory A. ... Milwaukie, OR
Eades, Marilyn G. ... San Antonio, TX
Eades, Natalie A.
Department Of The Interior,
Office of the Solicitor, GV
Eades, R. Timothy ... Fredonia, NY
Eades, Robert Oren ... Hickory, NC
Eades, Ronald W. ... Louisville, KY
Eades, Tanya Andrews ... Lawrenceville, GA
Eades, Walter J. ... Gulfport, MS
Eades, William B., Jr. ... San Rafael, CA
Eadie, Richard D., P.S. ... Seattle, WA
Eadie, Scott James ... Newport Beach, CA
Eadie-Daniels, L., (Mrs.) ... Chicago, IL
Eadington, George ... Newport Beach, CA
Eadington, Merhab & Eadington, A Professional Corporation
Newport Beach, CA
Eadon, Sherod H., Jr. ... Columbia, SC
Eads, Arthur C. ... Belton, TX
Eads, Bruce S. ... Oakland, CA
Eads, Darcy L. ... Andover, KS
Eads, James R., Jr. ... Atlanta, GA
Eads, Joan L. ... Madison, WI
Eads, Joel M. ... Princeton, NJ
Philadelphia, PA
Eads, John T., III ... Bloomfield Hills, MI
Eads, John Trimble, III
Farmington Hills, MI
Eads, John W. ... Oxford, MS
Eads, Kevin M. ... Anderson, IN
Eads, Kristin R. ... Minneapolis, MN
Eads, Mary G. ... Fort Worth, TX
Eads & Murray, P.C. ... Indianapolis, IN
Eads, Parker W. ... Louisville, KY
Eads, Patricia C. ... Austin, TX
Eads, Ralph S. ... Chicago, IL
Eads, Roselee Adlin ... Marietta, GA
Eads, Scott A. ... Wichita, KS
Eads, Scott D. ... Houston, TX
Eads, Terence L. ... Indianapolis, IN
Eads, Wayne B. ... Raleigh, NC
Eads, William R. ... Cedar Rapids, IA
Eady, Edsell M., Jr. ... Los Angeles, CA
San Diego, CA
San Francisco, CA

Eady, Jonathan E. ... Atlanta, GA
Eady, Karen E. ... Charlotte, NC
Eady, Michael W. ... Austin, TX
Eady, Nancy L. ... Alexander City, AL
Eady, S. Keith ... Talladega, AL
Eady, Veronica S. ... Roxbury, MA
Eagal, Richard ... Trenton, MI
Eagal, Richard, P.C. ... Taylor, MI
Trenton, MI
Wyandotte, MI
Eagan, Alicia Kay ... Salem, OR
Eagan, Barbara Anne ... Orlando, FL
Eagan, Christopher M. ... Seattle, WA
Eagan, Claire V. ... Tulsa, OK
Eagan, David E. ... New York, NY
Eagan, Dina M. ... Willow Grove, PA
Eagan & Donohue ... West Hartford, CT
Eagan, Emmett E., Jr. ... Russells Point, OH
Eagan, Ewell E. (Tim), Jr., (A P.L.C.)
New Orleans, LA
Eagan, F. Owen ... Hartford, CT
Eagan, Gail ... Boston, MA
Eagan, Gayle L. Vaillancourt ... Buffalo, NY
Eagan, J. Christopher ... New York, NY
Eagan, Jaime B. ... St. Petersburg, FL
Eagan, James E. ... Milford, CT
Eagan, James J. ... Florissant, MO
Eagan, James K., III ... Columbia, MD
Eagan, John B. ... Boston, MA
Eagan, John J. ... Somerville, NJ
Eagan, Joseph A., Jr. ... Philadelphia, PA
Eagan, Kerry P. ... Lincoln, NE
Eagan, Marc T. ... Fullerton, CA
Eagan, Mark Christopher
Birmingham, AL
Eagan, Mark J. ... New York, NY
Eagan, Michael L. ... Dallas, TX
Eagan, Michael Q. ... San Francisco, CA
Eagan, Michele Stawinski ... Lancaster, PA
Eagan, Monica J. ... Buffalo, NY
Eagan, Owen P. ... West Hartford, CT
Eagan, Patrick J. ... East Lansing, MI
Eagan, Paul A. ... Detroit, MI
Eagan, Robert, Law Offices of
Orlando, FL
Eagan, Thomas M. ... New York, NY
Eagan, Thomas P. ... Louisville, KY
Eagan, Thomas V., (P.A.) ... Miami, FL
Eagan, William B. ... Willow Grove, PA
Eagan, William L. ... Orlando, FL
Eagans, Gerald W. ... Riverside, CA
Eagar, James ... Hillsboro, OR
Eagel, Lawrence P. ... New York, NY
Eagelston, Mary Ellen ... Wyoming, IL
Eagen, Eagen & Adkins ... Durham, NC
Eagen, Elizabeth S. ... Durham, NC
Eagen, Michael D. ... Cincinnati, OH
Eagen, Michael J., Jr. ... Stroudsburg, PA
Eagen, Richardson Todd ... Scranton, PA
Eagen, Thomas H. ... Durham, NC
Eagen, Thomas L., Jr. ... Cincinnati, OH
Eagen, William J. ... San Jose, CA
Eagen, Wykoff & Healy Co., L.P.A.
Cincinnati, OH
Eager, George H. ... Lancaster, PA
Eager, Henry G. ... Anaheim, CA
Eager, L. Prentice, III ... Atlanta, GA
Eager, Richard B. ... Evansville, WI
Eager, Robert C. ... Washington, DC
Eager, Rosalind
United States Court Of Veterans Appeals, GV
Eager, Samuel W., Jr. ... Middletown, NY
Eager-Vance, Holly A. ... Salem, OR
Eagle, Adam W. ... New York, NY
Eagle, Alan C. ... Uniondale, NY
Eagle, Alexander F., III ... Los Gatos, CA
Eagle, Alissa M. ... Davis, CA
Eagle, Bart J. ... New York, NY
Eagle, Brett R. ... New York, NY
Eagle, Brian A. ... Indianapolis, IN
Eagle & Crawford ... Los Gatos, CA
Eagle, David R. ... San Antonio, TX
Eagle, David S. ... Wilmington, DE
Eagle, David W. ... Phoenix, AZ
Eagle & Eagle ... St. Petersburg, FL
Eagle & Eagle ... Rock Island, IL
Eagle, Edw. L., Jr. ... Rock Island, IL
Eagle, Elizabeth ... Rock Island, IL
Eagle & Fein ... Indianapolis, IN
New York, NY
Eagle, James Brian ... Rock Island, IL
Eagle, Jerry L. ... Greensboro, NC
Eagle, Joan M. ... Chicago, IL
Eagle, Judith G. ... Bel Air, MD
Eagle, Kenneth H. ... Berlin, CT
Eagle, Kenneth L. ... Cary, NC
Eagle, Kristine ... Stockton, CA
Eagle, Marcia R. ... Hackensack, NJ
Eagle, Paul F. ... Seattle, WA
Eagle, Richard A. ... St. Petersburg, FL
Eagle, Robert A. ... Rock Island, IL
Eagle, Ross M. ... Rosemont, IL
Eagle, Russ F. ... Murfreesboro, TN
Eagle, Sara B.
Pension Benefit Guaranty Corporation, Office of the General Counsel, GV
Eagle, Saul L. ... Bronx, NY
Eagle, Sidney ... New York, NY
Eagle, Steven J. ... Arlington, VA
Eagle, Thomas G. ... Franklin, OH
Eagle, Thomas G., Co., L.P.A.
Franklin, OH
Lebanon, OH
Middletown, OH
Eagle, Timothy E. ... Grand Rapids, MI
Eagle, Warren E. ... Chicago, IL
Eagleburger, G. Gregory ... Phoenix, AZ

Eagleman, Patrick S. ... St. Louis, MO
Eagles, Catherine C. ... Greensboro, NC
Eagles, Michael J. ... Philadelphia, PA
Eagles, Sidney Smith, Jr. ... Raleigh, NC
Eagles, William A. ... Greensboro, NC
Eaglesfield, R. Davy, III ... Indianapolis, IN
Eagleson & Eagleson ... Columbus, OH
Eagleson, Elizabeth K. ... San Diego, CA
Eagleson, Freeman T. ... Columbus, OH
Eagleson, John M. ... Houston, TX
Eagleson, Judith Mentor ... Bremerton, WA
Eagleson, Stuart D. ... Columbus, OH
Eagleston, Ronald T. ... Upper Marlboro, MD
Eagleton, E. John ... Tulsa, OK
Eagleton, Eagleton and Harrison, Inc.
Tulsa, OK
Eagleton, James R. ... Tulsa, OK
Eagleton, John M. ... Tulsa, OK
Eagleton, Nicholson, Pordos & Pardue, P.C.
Chandler, OK
Oklahoma City, OK
Eagleton, Norma ... Tulsa, OK
Eagleton, Richard E. ... Peoria, IL
Eagleton, Richard J. ... Tulsa, OK
Eagleton, Thomas F. ... St. Louis, MO
Eagleton, William L., IV ... Tulsa, OK
Eaglin, James B.
Federal Judicial Center, GV
Eaglin, Patrick G. ... Canton, CT
Eaglin, Paul B. ... Fairbanks, AK
Eagloski, N. Edward, II ... Charleston, WV
Eagon, Diana S. ... Minneapolis, MN
Eak, Gerald J. ... Brick, NJ
Eakeley, Douglas S. ... Roseland, NJ
Eaken, Bruce W., Jr. ... New York, NY
Eaker, Jamie D. ... Titusville, FL
Eaker, John H. ... Houston, TX
Eaker, Lawrence H., Jr.
West Palm Beach, FL
Eaker, Lloyd E. ... Clayton, MO
Eakes, Charles F. ... Winston-Salem, NC
Eakes, James S. ... Anderson, SC
Eakes, M. Garey ... Arlington, VA
Eakes, Martin D. ... Durham, NC
Eakes & Thompson, PLLC ... Arlington, VA
Eakin, Alan Jay ... Marina Del Rey, CA
Eakin, Christi W. ... Knoxville, TN
Eakin, Donald W., (P.A.)
Fort Lauderdale, FL
Eakin, Edward M., Jr. ... Hopewell, VA
Eakin, Eva ... Austin, TX
Eakin, Heidi F. ... Lancaster, PA
Eakin, Ira D. ... Billings, MT
Eakin, James E. ... Menlo Park, CA
Eakin, Jane ... Laramie, WY
Eakin, John M. ... Mechanicsburg, PA
Eakin, Larkin C., Jr. ... Houston, TX
Eakin, Lenden A. ... Roanoke, VA
Eakin, Margo M. ... Palo Alto, CA
Eakin, Myndi M. ... Phoenix, AZ
Eakin, Paul M. ... Atlantic Beach, FL
Eakin, Ronald L. ... Manassas, VA
Eakin, Ronald L., P.C. ... Manassas, VA
Eakin, Sneed & Catalan ... Atlantic Beach, FL
Eakin, W. Craig ... Fort Lauderdale, FL
Eakins, Alan Dale ... Columbus, OH
Eakins, Brett W. ... Denver, CO
Eakins, Greg ... Gahanna, OH
Eakins, J. Richard ... Dallas, TX
Eakins, Jan Elizabeth ... Los Angeles, CA
Eakins, William S. ... New York, NY
Eakle, Joanne M. ... San Antonio, TX
Eakman, Glen E. ... Fort Worth, TX
Eakman, Steven P. ... Seattle, WA
Ealick, Mary Catherine ... Atlanta, GA
Ealick, Perry L. ... Ponca City, OK
Ealy, David H. ... Rochester, NY
Ealy, Jonathan B. ... Anchorage, AK
Ealy, Lawrence O. ... Ocean City, NJ
Ealy, Stephen T. ... Hudson, OH
Ealy, W. Curt ... Palm Springs, CA
Eaman, Frank D. ... Detroit, MI
Eamer, Richard K. ... Los Angeles, CA
Eames, Anthony L. ... Auburn, CA
Eames, David T. ... New York, NY
Eames, Donald E. ... Skowhegan, ME
Eames, Frederick R. ... Washington, DC
Eames, John B. ... Littleton, NH
Eames, Laura R. ... Los Angeles, CA
Eames, Leslie H. ... Morris Plains, NJ
Eames, Mark A. ... Seattle, WA
Eames, Patricia E. ... Detroit, MI
Eames, Rex ... Troy, MI
Eames, Robert N. ... Denton, TX
Eames, W. Brent ... Rexburg, ID
Eames Wilcox ... Detroit, MI
Eamick, Dennis L. ... Dillingham, AK
Eandi, David R. ... Beverly Hills, CA
Eandi, Joseph M. ... Palo Alto, CA
Eandi, Susan F. ... Palo Alto, CA
Eannace, John Jay ... Chicago, IL
Eannace Law Firm, The, LLP ... Utica, NY
Eannace, Ralph J., Jr. ... Utica, NY
Eanni, Carmen A. ... Fresno, CA
Eapen, Rajan Paul ... Washington, DC
Eardley, David J. ... Chardon, OH
Eardley, Elizabeth Anne ... Berea, KY
Eardley, Eugenie B. ... Cannonsburg, MI
Eardley, James M. ... Grand Rapids, MI
Eardley, John F. ... Cannonsburg, MI
Eardley Law Offices, P.C.
Cannonsburg, MI
Grand Haven, MI
Ionia, MI
Muskegon, MI
Eardley, Robert H. ... Lexington, KY
Eardley, Ross ... Elko, NV

Eardley, Zulandt & Smalheer
Chardon, OH
Eargle, Alton Haskell, Jr. ... Columbia, SC
Eargle, Steve ... Fort Worth, TX
Earhart, David R. ... Dallas, TX
Earhart, Farleigh H. ... Washington, DC
Earhart, James A. ... Louisville, KY
Earhart, Rhonda Lurene ... Richmond, VA
Earhart, Scott William ... Dayton, OH
Earhart, Thomas B. ... Pittsburgh, PA
Earhart, Thomas W. ... Warsaw, IN
Earhart, Victoria C. ... Lansing, MI
Earhart, Warren S. ... Sun City, AZ
Earisman, Peggy ... Paterson, NJ
Earl, Allan R. ... Las Vegas, NV
Earl, Anthony M. ... Las Vegas, NV
Earl, Anthony S. ... Madison, WI
Earl & Associates, A Professional Corporation ... San Antonio, TX
Earl, Blank, Kavanaugh & Stotts, Professional Association ... Miami, FL
Sarasota, FL
Earl, Boyd L. ... Buffalo, NY
Earl, Brent A. ... Battle Mountain, NV
Earl, Brian Edward ... Vancouver, WA
Earl, Curley & Lagarde, P.C.
Phoenix, AZ
Earl, Cynthia S. ... Mount Laurel, NJ
Earl, Daniel A. ... Charleston, WV
Huntington, WV
Earl, David B. ... Phoenix, AZ
Earl, David L. ... Schaumburg, IL
Earl, David Lawrence ... San Antonio, TX
Earl, David W. ... Phoenix, AZ
Earl, De Lange, May, Jones and Hogan
Lockport, NY
Earl, Douglas K. ... Moses Lake, WA
Earl & Earl ... Las Vegas, NV
Earl & Earl, Inc., P.S. ... Moses Lake, WA
Earl, Edward D. ... Clinton, NY
Earl, Jack J. ... Cincinnati, OH
Earl, Jeffrey A. ... Alexandria, VA
Earl, Jeffrey B. ... Moses Lake, WA
Earl, John C. ... Little Rock, AR
Earl, Kathleen Reardon ... St. Louis, MO
Earl, Kevin D. ... Batavia, NY
Earl, Lance C. ... Las Vegas, NV
Earl, Laurie M. ... Sacramento, CA
Earl, Leslie R., Jr. ... Tulsa, OK
Earl, Lewis H. ... Post, TX
Earl, Marshall H., Jr. ... Chicago, IL
Richmond, VA
Earl, Patrick O. ... Moses Lake, WA
Earl, Richard J. ... Aptos, CA
Earl, Richard V. ... Albuquerque, NM
Earl, Rulon A. ... Las Vegas, NV
Earl, Ryan J. ... Reno, NV
Earl, Sari K. ... Atlanta, GA
Earl, Stephen C. ... Phoenix, AZ
Earl, Ted ... Columbus, OH
Earl, Thomas J. ... Moses Lake, WA
Earl, Tiffany Ann ... Kansas City, MO
Earl, Timothy C. ... San Diego, CA
Earl, Trevor L. ... Louisville, KY
Earl, Warburton, Adams & Davis, A Legal Professional Association ... Columbus, OH
Earl, William H. ... Lockport, NY
Earl, William L. ... Miami, FL
Earle, Anthony F. ... San Francisco, CA
Earle & Baird ... Greenville, KY
Earle, Bartholomew V. ... Burlington, MA
Earle, Berry B., III ... Thomasville, GA
Earle, Beverley H. ... Boston, MA
Earle, C. Terry ... Greenville, KY
Earle, Christopher C. ... Indianapolis, IN
Earle, Dana E. ... West Palm Beach, FL
Earle, David B. ... Stuart, FL
Earle, David J. ... Glendale, CA
Earle, David J. ... Los Angeles, CA
Santa Ana, CA
Earle, Douglas R. ... Lansing, MI
Earle and Earle ... St. Petersburg, FL
Earle, Eleanor M. ... Hartford, CT
Earle, Frank Trumbull, III ... Boston, MA
Earle, George M. ... Savannah, GA
Earle, George Randle ... Dallas, TX
Earle, Henry, III ... Detroit, MI
Earle, Hubert P. ... Philadelphia, PA
Earle, J. William ... Houston, TX
Earle, Jacqueline L. S. ... Honolulu, HI
Earle, James C. ... Irvine, CA
Earle, James E. ... Charlotte, NC
Earle, James T., Jr. ... St. Petersburg, FL
Earle, Jane Stewart ... New York, NY
Earle, John Burns, III ... Harrisonburg, VA
Earle, John C. ... Bloomfield Hills, MI
Earle, John G. ... Warwick, RI
Earle, Linda A. ... St. Petersburg, FL
Earle, Linda H. ... Houston, TX
Earle, Luman C. ... Hazlehurst, GA
Earle, Mary Jo ... Dallas, TX
Earle, Michael J. ... Pittsburgh, PA
Earle & Patchen, Professional Association
Miami, FL
Earle, Patrick T. ... Milwaukee, WI
Earle, Peter ... Milwaukee, WI
Earle, Richard Alan ... Washington, DC
Earle, Richard T., III ... St. Petersburg, FL
Earle, Richard T., Jr. ... St. Petersburg, FL
Earle, Robert Dennis ... Baltimore, MD
Columbia, MD
Earle, Robert L., (P.C.) ... Sedona, AZ
Earle, Robert M. ... Columbia, SC
Earle, Robert R. ... Farmerville, LA
Earle & Romero, L.L.P. ... Dallas, TX
Earle, Ronald ... Austin, TX
Earle, Suzanne E. ... Westminster, SC
Earle, Thomas G. ... Columbia, SC

Earle, Thomas H. ... Philadelphia, PA
Earle, William G. ... Portland, OR
Earle, William George ... Miami, FL
Earl-Ennen & Ennen ... Newark, OH
Earl-Ennen, Kathleen Ann ... Newark, OH
Earles, Carl A. ... Los Angeles, CA
Earles, John A. ... Atlanta, GA
Earles, Kristian D. ... Crowley, LA
Earles, Richard L. ... Charleston, WV
Earley, Anthony F., Jr. ... Detroit, MI
Earley, Anthony L. ... New York, NY
Earley, Billy J. ... Nacogdoches, TX
Earley, E. Franklin, III ... Houston, TX
Earley, Francis J. ... New York, NY
Earley, George J. ... Eaton, OH
Earley, George Michael ... North Andover, MA
Earley, J. Fred ... Parkersburg, WV
Earley, J. Fred, II ... Parkersburg, WV
Earley, Jack M., Law Office of, The
Costa Mesa, CA
Earley, James M. ... West Des Moines, IA
Earley, James P. ... North Hollywood, CA
Earley, Jeanne E. ... Lowell, MA
Earley, Jerome A. ... Pittsburgh, PA
Earley, John F. A., III ... Valley Forge, PA
Earley, John F. A., Jr., (P.C.)
Valley Forge, PA
Earley, John J. ... Coaldale, PA
Earley, Joseph M., III ... Paradise, CA
Earley, Karen M. ... Columbus, GA
Earley, Keith H. ... McLean, VA
Earley, Kerry L. ... Las Vegas, NV
Earley, Loyd Ross ... Dallas, TX
Earley, M. Jay ... Indiana, PA
Earley, Mark L. ... Norfolk, VA
Earley, M. Jay, P.C. ... Indiana, PA
Earley, Phillip B. ... Chelmsford, MA
Earley, Richard P. ... Morristown, NJ
Earley, Robert C. ... Indiana, PA
Earley, Robert E. ... Nashua, NH
Earley, Roberta Jean ... Colorado Springs, CO
Earley Savage ... Las Vegas, NV
Earley, William P. ... Oklahoma City, OK
Earley, William T. ... San Diego, CA
Earl-Hubbard, Michele L. ... Seattle, WA
Earlin, Jeffrey L. ... Milford, PA
Earl-Ray, Neal ... Richmond, KY
Earls, Claudia ... Cloverdale, IN
Earls, Donald E. ... Norton, VA
Earls, Donna R. ... Gaffney, SC
Earls, Hugh C. ... Allentown, PA
Earls, James J. ... Westwood, MA
Earls, Karen Bernice ... Los Angeles, CA
Earls, Thomas A. ... Cary, NC
Earls, Thomas P. ... Dallas, TX
Earls, Trisha M. ... Atlanta, GA
Earls, William T., Jr. ... Cincinnati, OH
Earls, William W. ... Terre Haute, IN
Early, A. Doyle, Jr. ... High Point, NC
Early, Alexander R., III ... Glendale, CA
Early, Arnold & Ziemer, LLP
Evansville, IN
Early, Bert H. ... Chicago, IL
Early, C. Fielding, Jr. ... Austin, TX
Early & Chandler, P.A.
Rocky Mount, NC
Early Cochran & Olson, L.L.C.
Chicago, IL
Early, Collison, Tousey, Regan, Wlodek & Morrow ... Elgin, IL
Early, Darrell G. ... Boise, ID
Early, Dennis J. ... Alexandria, VA
Early, Doyet A., III ... Bamberg, SC
Early, E. Gary ... Tallahassee, FL
Early & Early
Charlotte Court House, VA
Early, Edward J., Jr. ... Lowell, MA
Early, Edward W.
Charlotte Court House, VA
Early, Eric P. ... Los Angeles, CA
Early, Francine Davis ... Newington, CT
Early, J. Michael ... New Orleans, LA
Early, James B. ... St. Paul, MN
Early, James F. ... New Haven, CT
Boston, MA
New York, NY
Early, James H., Jr. ... Greensboro, NC
Early, James H., Jr. ... Winston-Salem, NC
Early, James R. ... Lexington, KY
Early, Janet Fritz
Charlotte Court House, VA
Early, Jeffrey C. ... Madison, VA
Stanardsville, VA
Early, Joanne ... Dallas, TX
Early, John D. ... Irvine, CA
Early, John F. ... Elgin, IL
Early, John J. ... Battle Creek, MI
Early, John J. ... Arlington, VA
Early, John L. ... Sarasota, FL
Early, Joseph D., Jr. ... Worcester, MA
Early, Kathryn Morris ... Ipswich, MA
Early, Lawrence G. ... New York, NY
Early, Lennon, Peters & Crocker, P.C.
Kalamazoo, MI
Early, Leslie R. ... New Philadelphia, OH
Early, Linda Moore ... Houston, TX
Early, Ludwick & Sweeney, L.L.C.
New Haven, CT
Early, Mark ... Dallas, TX
Early, Maslach, Price & Baukol
Los Angeles, CA
Early, Matthew T.E. ... Sioux City, IA
Early, Maurice D. ... St. Louis, MO
Early, Mavis S. ... New Orleans, LA
Early, Melinda R. ... Findlay, OH
Early, Michael D. ... San Francisco, CA
Early, Michael J. ... Haverhill, MA
Early, Michael W. ... Chicago, IL

Early & Ness ...... Bamberg, SC
Early, Norman F. ...... Denver, CO
Early, Norman S., Jr. ...... Denver, CO
Early, Richard J. ...... Northridge, CA
Early, Richard M. ...... Berlin, CT
Early, Ronald L. ...... Bethesda, MD
Early, S. Allen ...... Detroit, MI
Early, S. Allen, & Associates ...... Detroit, MI
Early, Scott E. ...... Chicago, IL
Early, Sean P. ...... New Orleans, LA
Early, Stephen B. ...... Louisville, KY
Early, Steven G., (P.C.) ...... Atlanta, GA
Early & Strauss, LLC ...... New York, NY
Early, Susan J. ...... Overland Park, KS
Early, Tara C. ...... Orlando, FL
Early, Thomas W. ...... Detroit, MI
Early, Valrey W., III ...... Birmingham, AL
Early, Vincent T. ...... Kalamazoo, MI
Early, W. Alvin ...... Houston, TX
Early, W. Blaine, III ...... Lexington, KY
Early, Walter J. ...... Rocky Mount, NC
Early, William B. ...... Klamath Falls, OR
Early, William C. ...... Philadelphia, PA
Early, William N.
United States Court Of Appeals For The Armed Forces, GV
Early, William Peele ...... Bamberg, SC
Early, William T. ...... Harlan, IA
Missouri Valley, IA
Early-Hubelbank, David ...... New York, NY
Early-Hubelbank, Latonia ...... Westbury, NY
Earlywine, Gary J. ...... St. Peters, MO
Earman, David W. ...... Harrisonburg, VA
Earman, Susan Friedlander ...... McLean, VA
Earne, Richard M. ...... Bowmansville, NY
Earnest, Broughton M. ...... Easton, MD
Earnest, David W. ...... Chicago, IL
Earnest, Elizabeth ...... New Orleans, LA
Earnest, Foster, Eder & Levi
Rushville, IN
Earnest, G. Lane ...... Boulder, CO
Earnest, Jack E. ...... Houston, TX
Earnest, James H. ...... Miami, FL
Earnest, Jason Lane ...... Las Vegas, NV
Earnest, John A. ...... Fredericksburg, VA
Earnest, John C., Jr. ...... Birmingham, AL
Earnest, Joseph E. ...... Santa Fe, NM
Earnest, Joseph E., P.C. ...... Santa Fe, NM
Earnest, Lante K. ...... Indianapolis, IN
Earnest, Mary M. ...... Davie, FL
Earnest, Phillip R. ...... Pittsburgh, PA
Earnest, Ray L. ...... Easton, MD
Earnest, Rebecca C. ...... Seattle, WA
Earnest, Robert A. ...... Los Angeles, CA
Earnest, Robert L. ...... Atlanta, GA
Earnest, Robert L. ...... Russell, KS
Earnest, Stephen L. ...... Atlanta, GA
Earnest, Susan E. ...... New Orleans, LA
Earnest, T. Craig ...... Blakely, GA
Earnest, W. Merrill, Jr. ...... Atlanta, GA
Earnest, William M. ...... Atlanta, GA
Earnhardt, Cameron Turner
Birmingham, AL
Earnhardt, Charles E. ...... Jacksonville, FL
Earnhardt, John A. ...... Birmingham, AL
Earnhardt, Kent C. ...... Atlanta, GA
Earnhardt, Thomas Wright ...... Durham, NC
Earnhardt Breen, Melany ...... Hillsborough, NC
Earnhart, Mark ...... Sterling, CO
Earnhart, Steven C. ...... Indianapolis, IN
Earnhart, William Andrew
Anchorage, AK
Earnheart, Chas. E., Jr. ...... Oklahoma City, OK
Earnheart, Frank J. ...... Dresher, PA
Earnshaw, Donald E. ...... Bucks, AL
Earnshaw, George W. ...... Merriam, KS
Earnshaw, Kathleen M. ...... Amherst, NH
Earnshaw, Sylvia Jung ...... Fort Collins, CO
Earnshaw-Hobbs, Catherine
Lee's Summit, MO
Earnst, Kurt R. ...... Michigan City, IN
Earp, Anita C. ...... Ahoskie, NC
Earp, Bret Van ...... Austin, TX
Earp Cohn P.C. ...... Westmont, NJ
Philadelphia, PA
Earp, J. Michael ...... Westminster, MD
Earp, James H. ...... Melbourne, FL
Earp, Jonathan P. ...... Oakland, CA
Earp, Robert D. ...... El Paso, TX
Earp, Robert H., III ...... Dayton, OH
Earp, Stephen W. ...... Greensboro, NC
Earp, Thomas L. ...... Westmont, NJ
Earsley, Jacqueline M. ...... Long Beach, CA
Earsom, Deryl L. ...... St. Louis, MO
Earsy, Nancy Franklin ...... Boston, MA
Earthman, B. Douglas ...... Memphis, TN
Earthman, James B., III ...... Galveston, TX
Earthman, James B., III & Associates, P.C.
Galveston, TX
Earthman, William W., III ...... Nashville, TN
Earwicker, Harley ...... Vista, CA
Earwood, Carla W. ...... Dallas, TX
Earwood, Dale C. ...... Shreveport, LA
Earwood, John Thomas ...... Raleigh, NC
Earwood, Kristi D. ...... Franklin, TN
Earwood, Michael E. ...... Jackson, MS
Easa & Easa ...... Hempstead, NY
Easa, Easa ...... Hempstead, NY
Easa, Elizabeth A. ...... Hempstead, NY
Easa, Jack ...... Hempstead, NY
Easa, James ...... Cleveland, OH
Easey, Ken Ryan ...... Orange, CA
Eash, David E. ...... Coeur d'Alene, ID
Spokane, WA
Eash, Paul D. ...... Elkhart, IN
Easland, Bradley C. ...... Norfolk, NE
Easley, Aaron R. ...... Woodbridge, NJ
Easley, Allen K. ...... Topeka, KS
Easley, B. Michael ...... Forrest City, AR
Easley, Blair, Jr. ...... Oklahoma City, OK
Easley, Brian W. ...... Chicago, IL
Easley, Charles D., Jr. ...... Columbus, MS
Easley, Clifton (Cliff) R., Jr. ...... Bruce, MS
Easley & Cooper ...... Bruce, MS
Easley, Daniel G. ...... Dallas, TX
Easley, Dorothy F. ...... Coral Gables, FL
Easley, George G. ...... Morristown, NJ
Easley, Glenn E. ...... Columbia, MO
Easley, H. Michael ...... West Palm Beach, FL
Easley, Hicky, Cline & Hudson
Forrest City, AR
Easley, Jeffrey D., P.C. ...... Lakewood, CO
Easley, Jeffrey Dana ...... Lakewood, CO
Easley, Joe Tom ...... Hudson, NY
Easley, John W. ...... Loveland, CO
Easley, Joseph C. ...... Sacramento, CA
Easley, Kevin O. ...... Greenville, NC
Easley, L. Guen ...... Topeka, KS
Easley, Leesa M. ...... Cleveland, OH
Easley, Mark Doyle ...... Rogers, AR
Easley, Mark E. ...... Houston, TX
Easley & Marquis ...... Plano, TX
Easley, Mary Pipines ...... Durham, NC
Easley, Michael J. ...... Red Bluff, CA
Easley, Peter R. ...... Washington, DC
Easley, Preston ...... San Pedro, CA
Easley, R. Sidney ...... Murray, KY
Easley, Rex L., Jr. ...... Victoria, TX
Easley, Saville W. ...... Gresham, OR
Easley, Sharon M. ...... Plano, TX
Easley, Sue A. ...... Westerville, OH
Easlick, David K., Jr.
Grosse Pointe Farms, MI
Easom, Gary ...... Jacksonville, FL
Easom & Peirce ...... Jacksonville, FL
Eason, Alan D. ...... Baltimore, MD
Eason, Brooks ...... Jackson, MS
Eason, Carl A. ...... Virginia Beach, VA
Eason, Carl Edward, Jr. ...... Suffolk, VA
Eason, D. Russell ...... Haleyville, AL
Eason, David E. ...... Livonia, MI
Eason, David R. ...... Denver, CO
Eason, Douglas G. ...... Oklahoma City, OK
Eason, Elizabeth H. ...... Atlanta, GA
Eason, F. Jackson, Jr. ...... Wake Forest, NC
Eason, James Kerry ...... Houston, TX
Eason, Joseph W. ...... Raleigh, NC
Eason, Katherine W. ...... Virginia Beach, VA
Eason, Kendra J. ...... Cleveland, OH
Eason, Leroy ...... Bronxville, NY
Eason, Linton B. ...... Tallahassee, FL
Eason, Loutitia Denison ...... Oklahoma City, OK
Eason, Marcia J. Meredith
Chattanooga, TN
Eason, Matthew R. ...... Sacramento, CA
Eason, Melissa A. ...... Austin, TX
Eason, Michael J. ...... Des Moines, IA
Eason, Nathan W. ...... San Antonio, TX
Eason, Paul B. ...... Greenbelt, MD
Eason, Richard B., II ...... New Orleans, LA
Eason, Richard B., Jr. ...... Atlanta, GA
Eason, Richard L. ...... Denver, CO
Eason, Rosalyn Doyle ...... Kenner, LA
Eason, Shelley T. ...... Raleigh, NC
Eason, Thos. R. ...... Sylvester, GA
Eason, Wendy Kay ...... New York, NY
Eason, William E., Jr. ...... Atlanta, GA
Norcross, GA
Eassa, Robert D. ...... Oakland, CA
Easson, David A. ...... New Orleans, LA
East, C. Scott ...... Bellevue, WA
East, C. Scott, Law Offices of, Inc. P.S.
Bellevue, WA
East & East, P.C. ...... San Antonio, TX
East, Elmer V. ...... Lubbock, TX
East, Ernest E. ...... Barrington, IL
East, Gary W. ...... Seattle, WA
East, George Todd ...... Kingsport, TN
East, Gita E. ...... Boston, MA
East, Jack, III ...... Little Rock, AR
East, Jack, III, P.A. ...... Little Rock, AR
East, James L. ...... San Antonio, TX
East, James W., Jr. ...... Hinsdale, IL
East, Joseph E. ...... Waycross, GA
East, Joseph E., P.C. ...... Waycross, GA
East, Kenneth W. ...... Tulsa, OK
East, Lisa ...... Tallahassee, FL
East, Martin D. ...... Nicholasville, KY
East, Michael C. ...... Littleton, CO
East, Myron E., Jr. ...... San Antonio, TX
East, Nathan A. ...... Portland, TX
East & O'Connor ...... Lubbock, TX
East, Thomas ...... Purchase, NY
East, Van P., III ...... Nashville, TN
East, W. David ...... Houston, TX
East, William J. ...... Jackson, MS
East, William R., Jr. ...... Dallas, TX
Eastaugh, Robert L. ...... Anchorage, AK
Eastberg, Kathleen
Department Of Veterans Affairs, Office of Management, GV
Eastburn, Ann M. ...... Denver, CO
Eastburn, Arthur M., Jr. ...... Doylestown, PA
Eastburn, Benjamin S. ...... Aztec, NM
Eastburn, D. Rodman ...... Doylestown, PA
Eastburn & Gray, P.C. ...... Doylestown, PA
New Hope, PA
Newtown, PA
Eastburn, Lawrence S. ...... Woodstock, GA
Eastburn, Robert, Jr. ...... Fort Worth, TX
Eastburn, Thomas J. ...... Wilmington, DE
Eastburn, William H., III ...... Doylestown, PA
Eastepp, D. Dean ...... Colorado Springs, CO
Easter, Alvis P. ...... Mount Clemens, MI
Easter, Cavosie & Pastore
Indianapolis, IN
Easter, Dana Jene ...... Golden, CO
Easter, David Norman, II ...... Edmond, OK
Easter, Donald L. ...... Oklahoma City, OK
Easter, Faith V. ...... Framingham, MA
Easter, Gerald F. ...... Memphis, TN
Easter, J. Greg ...... Indianapolis, IN
Easter, John R. ...... Richmond, VA
Easter, Kent Wycliffe ...... Palo Alto, CA
Easter, Kim ...... Jackson, MI
Easter, Laurie B. ...... Houston, TX
Easter, Len D. ...... New York, NY
Easter, Mark A. ...... Riverside, CA
Easter, Sally Allen ...... Denver, CO
Easter, Scott B. ...... Seattle, WA
Easter, Stanley G. ...... Costa Mesa, CA
Easter, Stephen J. ...... Canton, NY
Easter, Suzanne M. ...... Miamisburg, OH
Easter, Terese M. ...... Dallas, TX
Easter, Timothy L. ...... Brentwood, TN
Easterberg, John C. ...... Richmond, IL
Easterbrook, Frank H. ...... Chicago, IL
Easterbrook, John W. ...... San Jose, CA
Easterbrook, Samuel G., III
Daytona Beach, FL
Easterby, B. Katherine ...... Houston, TX
Easterby, E. Armistead ...... Houston, TX
Easterday, Adam R. ...... Richmond, VA
Easterday, Debra S. ...... Indianapolis, IN
Easterday, James E. ...... Culver, IN
Plymouth, IN
Easterday, Jeffrey A. ...... Dublin, OH
Easterday, Jeffrey L. ...... Kansas City, MO
Easterday, Roger L. ...... Spring, TX
Easterday, Thomas V. ...... Lafayette, IN
Easterday & Ummel ...... Culver, IN
Plymouth, IN
Easterday, Victoria Lynne ...... Charlotte, MI
Easterlin, Benjamin F., IV ...... Americus, GA
Easterling, C. David ...... Houston, TX
Easterling, Charles A. ...... Houston, TX
Easterling, Danny K. ...... Houston, TX
Easterling, Donna M. ...... Grand Prairie, TX
Easterling & Easterling, P.C.
Houston, TX
Easterling, Elaine A. ...... Stow, OH
Easterling & Goodall ...... Stafford, VA
Easterling, Harry R. ...... Bennettsville, SC
Easterling, Harry R., Jr. ...... Bennettsville, SC
Easterling, James M., Jr. ...... Houston, TX
Easterling, James T. ...... Chicago, IL
Easterling, Kenneth L. ...... Newport, KY
Easterling, Lisa A. ...... New Orleans, LA
Easterling, Lynn M. ...... San Jose, CA
Easterling, Michelle D. ...... West Point, MS
Easterling, Orlando A., Jr. ...... Monroe, LA
Easterling, Richard B. ...... Baton Rouge, LA
Easterling, Robert B. ...... Stafford, VA
Easterling, S. Wayne ...... Hattiesburg, MS
Easterling, William K. ...... Myrtle Beach, SC
Easterly, A. Shelby, III
Denham Springs, LA
Easterly, Alan B. ...... Chattanooga, TN
Easterly & Armstrong, A Professional Corporation ...... Elko, NV
Easterly, Bill, & Associates ...... Nashville, TN
Easterly, C. Thomas ...... Miami, FL
Easterly, Eric G. ...... Elko, NV
Easterly, Ernest S., III ...... Watson, LA
Easterly, James C. ...... Scottsdale, AZ
Easterly Law Office ...... Baton Rouge, LA
Denham Springs, LA
Easterly, Robert W. ...... Troy, MI
Easterwood, Cynthia A. ...... Toledo, OH
Easterwood, Larry J. ...... Carson, CA
Easterwood, Oliver H.
General Accounting Office, Office of the General Counsel, GV
Easterwood, Paul ...... Houston, TX
Easterwood, Rex W. ...... Hereford, TX
Easterwood, Terry S. ...... St. Clairsville, OH
Eastham, Catherine Mode
Milwaukee, WI
Eastham, James Michael ...... Chicago, IL
Eastham, James S. ...... Milwaukee, WI
Eastham, John P. ...... Albuquerque, NM
Eastham Johnson Monnheimer & Jontz, P.C.
Albuquerque, NM
Eastham, Melissa D. ...... Clovis, NM
Eastham, Meyer & Vorpahl ...... Houston, TX
Eastham, R. Dabney ...... La Jolla, CA
Eastham, Ryan G. ...... Columbus, OH
Eastham, Stephen Carl ...... Potomac, MD
Eastham, Watson, Dale & Forney, L.L.P.
Houston, TX
Easthom, James R. ...... Durham, NC
Easthom-Rowsey, Sharon ...... Ashland, KY
Easthope, Christopher Sean ...... Ypsilanti, MI
Easthope, Joseph ...... Fort Lauderdale, FL
Eastin, Keith E. ...... Washington, DC
Eastlack, David P. ...... Cranbury, NJ
Fort Washington, PA
Eastlack, John C., Jr. ...... Blackwood, NJ
Eastlack, John C., (P.C.)
Colorado Springs, CO
Eastland, Henry B. ...... Colorado Springs, CO
Eastland, Henry B., P.C.
Colorado Springs, CO
Eastland, Hiram C., Jr. ...... Greenwood, MS
Eastland, John J. ...... Tyler, TX
Eastland, Oliver ...... Kensington, MD
Eastland, S. Stacy ...... Houston, TX
Eastling, John R. ...... Menlo Park, CA
Eastlund, Solstad, Cade & Hutchinson, Ltd.
Minneapolis, MN
Savage, MN
Eastlund, Warren E. ...... Minneapolis, MN
Eastman & Apolinsky, L.L.P. ...... Atlanta, GA
Decatur, GA
Eastman, Bruce ...... Florissant, MO
Eastman, C. Dana, Jr. ...... Alton, IL
Eastman, Charles D. ...... Kewanee, IL
Eastman, Daniel J. ...... Madison, WI
Eastman, David A. ...... Decatur, GA
Eastman, David D. ...... Tallahassee, FL
Eastman, David R. ...... Cuyahoga Falls, OH
Eastman, Diane Wilkens ...... Palm Desert, CA
Eastman, Donald N. ...... Los Angeles, CA
Eastman & Eastman ...... New York, NY
Eastman & Eastman ...... Cuyahoga Falls, OH
Eastman, Edward C., Jr. ...... Freehold, NJ
Eastman, Elrich A. ...... New York, NY
Eastman, F. David ...... Clear Lake, IA
Eastman, Forest E. ...... Waterloo, IA
Eastman, Frank E. ...... Waltham, MA
Eastman, Fred E. ...... Cuyahoga Falls, OH
Eastman, G. Perry, III ...... New Orleans, LA
Eastman, Gary T. ...... Kansas City, MO
Eastman, Gerald F. ...... Fort Worth, TX
Eastman, Gerald G. ...... Phoenix, AZ
Eastman, Harold A., Jr. ...... Gettysburg, PA
Eastman, Herbert A. ...... St. Louis, MO
Eastman, Hope ...... Bethesda, MD
Eastman, James F. ...... San Francisco, CA
Eastman, James L.
Securities and Exchange Commission, Office of the General Counsel, GV
Eastman, James M. ...... Omaha, NE
Eastman, Jan S. ...... Burlington, VT
Eastman, Jean Y. ...... Redwood City, CA
Eastman, Jeffrey M. ...... Ogallala, NE
Eastman, Jeffrey S. ...... Gladstone, MO
Eastman, John L. ...... New York, NY
Eastman, John W. ...... New York, NY
Eastman, Laura B. ...... Houston, TX
Eastman, Lynn R., (Mr.) ...... Canyon Lake, CA
Eastman, Margaret E. ...... Santa Ana, CA
Eastman, Mariah A ...... Lewistown, MT
Eastman, Mark H. ...... Studio City, CA
Eastman, Martha Marie
Winston-Salem, NC
Eastman, Michael J.
House of Representatives, Congressional Assistants, GV
Eastman, Pervil G. ...... New York, NY
Eastman, Richard A. ...... Los Angeles, CA
New York, NY
Eastman, Robert E. ...... Palm Springs, CA
Eastman, Robert G. ...... Hartwood, VA
Eastman, Robert L. ...... Coffeyville, KS
Eastman, Robert W. ...... Burlington, VT
Eastman, Robert W., P.C. ...... Burlington, VT
Eastman & Short, L.L.P. ...... Baltimore, MD
Eastman & Smith Ltd.
Bowling Green, OH
Columbus, OH
Perrysburg, OH
Toledo, OH
Eastman, Susan ...... Santa Ana, CA
Eastman, Tad J. ...... Midland, MI
Eastman, Thomas B. ...... Baltimore, MD
Eastman, Thomas G. ...... Aventura, FL
Eastman, Todd J. ...... San Diego, CA
Eastment, Thomas J. ...... Washington, DC
Eastmond, M. Dirk ...... Sandy, UT
Eastmond, Scott ...... Phoenix, AZ
Eastmond-Bright, Cheryl ...... Bronx, NY
Eastmoore, E. L. ...... Palatka, FL
Eastmoore, Theodore C. ...... Sarasota, FL
Easton, Bradd S. ...... Skokie, IL
Easton, Brian ...... Anchorage, AK
Easton, Brian W. ...... Costa Mesa, CA
Easton, Burton C. ...... Clearwater, FL
Easton & Clark ...... Levittown, NY
Easton, David ...... Madison, WI
Easton, Eric Bennett ...... Baltimore, MD
Easton, George H. ...... Kenosha, WI
Easton, Harold ...... Oakton, VA
Easton, Harold, (P.C.) ...... Los Angeles, CA
Easton, John F. ...... Houston, TX
Easton, John O. ...... Washington, DC
Fairfax, VA
Easton, Karren L. ...... Walnut Creek, CA
Easton, Kelly Mark ...... Elizabethtown, KY
Easton, Lory Barsdate ...... Chicago, IL
Easton, Margaret S. ...... Seattle, WA
Easton, Mark ...... Levittown, NY
Easton, Mark C. ...... Los Angeles, CA
Easton, Reed W. ...... Pompton Plains, NJ
Easton, Reed W., P.C. ...... Pompton Plains, NJ
Easton, Richard L. ...... Wilmington, DE
New York, NY
Easton, Robert G. ...... Princeton, NJ
Easton, Robert H. ...... New York, NY
Easton, Robert P. ...... San Diego, CA
Easton, Rosa Kwon ...... Los Angeles, CA
Easton & Schiff ...... Los Angeles, CA
Easton, Stephen D. ...... Columbia, MO
Easton, Stephen K. ...... Martinez, CA
Easton, Stephen W. ...... Albany, NY
Easton, Susan M. ...... Melrose Park, IL
Easton, Thomas ...... Crescent City, CA
Easton, W. Douglas, Law Offices of
Costa Mesa, CA
Easton, Wayne B. ...... Bloomington, MN
Easton, William E., Law Offices of
Rochester, NY
Easton, William S. ...... Port Huron, MI
Easton, William T. ...... Rochester, NY
Eastridge, Christopher J. ...... Elkton, MD
Eastridge, Kenneth E. ...... Houston, TX
Eastridge, Michael A. ...... Johnson City, TN
Eastridge, Ronald T. ...... Columbia, PA
Eastridge, Thomas ...... San Francisco, CA
Eastus, Matthew P. ...... Houston, TX
Eastus, Victoria L. ...... Arlington, VA
Eastwick, Carl E. ...... Baltimore, MD

Eastwick Rose & Wright, P.A.
Baltimore, MD
Eastwood, C. William ... Greeley, CO
Eastwood, Catherine V. ... Needham, MA
Eastwood, Charles R. ... National Aeronautics And Space Administration, GV
Eastwood, Edwin C., Jr. ... North Bergen, NJ
Eastwood, Elizabeth Ann
Washington, DC
Eastwood, J. Marquis ... Minneapolis, MN
Eastwood, James A. ... Washington, DC
Eastwood, James Thomas ... Garden City, NY
Eastwood, John A. ... Cleveland, OH
Eastwood, Lawrence S., Jr. ... Nashville, TN
Eastwood, Lisa K. ... New York, NY
Eastwood, Marla ... Atlanta, GA
Eastwood, Mary O. ... South Wayne, WI
Eastwood, Myles E. ... Atlanta, GA
Eastwood, Robert J. ... Chicopee, MA
Eastwood, Roland H. ... Fort Myers, FL
Eastwood, Sandra A. ... Corpus Christi, TX
Eastwood, Thomas I. ... Hudson Falls, NY
Eastwood, Valerie J. ... Washington, DC
Easum, Nancy G. ... Springfield, IL
Eates, Antoinette M.
Equal Employment Opportunity Commission, Office of Federal Operations, GV
Eatherly-Legate, Pamela ... Austin, TX
Eatherton, Lewis H., III ... Houston, TX
Eathington, Kenneth R. ... Peoria, IL
Eatinger, Robert J.
Department of Defense, GV
Eatman & Eatman ... Shreveport, LA
Eatman, Edward L., Jr. ... Charlotte, NC
Eatman, Jerome R., Jr. ... Raleigh, NC
Eatman, Louis P. ... Los Angeles, CA
Eatman, Robert E. ... Shreveport, LA
Eatman, Robert E., Jr. ... Shreveport, LA
Eatman, Thomas D., Jr. ... Charlotte, NC
Eatmon, Buford J. ... Dallas, TX
Eatmon, Nile W. ... Salt Lake City, UT
Eaton, Aaron P. ... Rutland, VT
Eaton, Adam R. ... Denver, CO
Eaton, Albert C. ... Orlando, FL
Eaton, Allen O. ... Boston, MA
Eaton, Allen T. ... Washington, DC
Philadelphia, PA
Eaton, Arthur G. ... Sun City Center, FL
Eaton, Barney E., III ... Jackson, MS
Eaton, Bart ... Baton Rouge, LA
Eaton, Barton Denis ... White Plains, NY
Eaton, Berrien C. ... Phoenix, AZ
Eaton, Carol L. ... Carbondale, IL
Eaton & Chandler, P.C. ... Andover, MA
Eaton, Christopher J. ... Kansas City, KS
Eaton, Claudia ... Burbank, CA
Eaton, Clyde L. ... Havana, IL
Eaton, Coleman C., Jr. ... Jonesboro, GA
Eaton and Cottrell, P.A.
Bay St. Louis, MS
Biloxi, MS
Gulfport, MS
Hattiesburg, MS
Jackson, MS
Pascagoula, MS
Eaton, Craig A. ... Brooklyn, NY
Eaton, Craig L. ... Boston, MA
Providence, RI
Eaton, Curtis H. ... Twin Falls, ID
Eaton, Dale M. ... Ladysmith, WI
Eaton, Daniel E. ... San Diego, CA
Eaton, Daniel V. ... Sacramento, CA
Eaton, David A. ... St. Petersburg, FL
Eaton, David A., P.A. ... St. Petersburg, FL
Eaton, David C. ... Harrisburg, PA
Eaton, David F. ... Omaha, NE
Eaton, David G. ... Tampa, FL
Eaton, David H. ... Phoenix, AZ
Eaton, David J. ... Ashland, WI
Eaton, David L. ... Chicago, IL
Eaton, David M. ... Atlanta, GA
Eaton, David R. ... Baltimore, MD
Eaton, Denise R. ... San Francisco, CA
Eaton, Donald E. ... Friday Harbor, WA
Eaton, Donald J. ... Boise, ID
Eaton, Douglas F. ... New York, NY
Eaton, Douglas Fredric ... Miami, FL
Eaton, E. Howard ... Taylorsville, MS
Eaton, Edward E. (Gene) ... Glenwood, IA
Shenandoah, IA
Eaton, Edward E. (Gene) ... Sidney, IA
Eaton, Edward F. ... Wilmington, DE
Eaton, Elizabeth W. ... Woodbridge, NJ
Eaton, Fernin F. ... Baton Rouge, LA
Eaton, Frank L. ... Miami, FL
Eaton, Gary A., Law Office ... Tulsa, OK
Eaton, Gary Bruce ... Placentia, CA
Eaton, Gary M. ... Bridgeport, CT
Eaton, George F., II ... Bangor, ME
Eaton, Gerald M. ... Manchester, NH
Eaton, Gordon & Sawyer ... West Hartford, CT
Tampa, FL
West Palm Beach, FL
Eaton, Gregory M. ... Baton Rouge, LA
Eaton, Gregory M. ... Littleton, NH
Eaton, Gregory N. ... Andover, MA
Eaton, Griffith & DeGroat ... Sidney, NY
Walton, NY
Eaton, Harold E., Jr. ... Woodstock, VT
Eaton & Hayes, A Professional Corporation
Woodstock, VT
Eaton, Holly R. ... Washington, DC
Silver Spring, MD
Eaton, Holly Taebel ... Austin, TX
Eaton, J. Jackson, III ... Allentown, PA
Eaton, J. Timothy ... Chicago, IL
Eaton, Jacqueline M. ... Daytona Beach, FL
Eaton, Jade Alice ... Department of Justice, Antitrust Division, GV
Eaton, James C. ... Barron, WI
Eaton, James H., III ... Andover, MA
Eaton, Jane M. ... Robbinston, ME
Eaton, Janet Lane ... Mukilteo, WA
Eaton, Jason Hale ... Portland, OR
Eaton, Jay ... Des Moines, IA
Eaton, Jay R. ... Prescott, AZ
Eaton, Jay R., P.C. ... Prescott, AZ
Eaton, Jeffery G. ... Chicago, IL
Eaton, Jimmy ... Little Rock, AR
Eaton, Joe ... Miami, FL
Eaton, Joel D. ... Miami, FL
Eaton, John Butler ... Fort Worth, TX
Eaton, John D. ... Miami, FL
Eaton, John E. ... Southfield, MI
Eaton, John H. ... McAllen, TX
Eaton, John M. ... Coos Bay, OR
Eaton, John M., Jr. ... Concord, MA
Eaton, John S. ... Snyder, NY
Eaton, John Wilson, III ... Memphis, TN
Eaton, Jonathan C., Jr. ... Minot, ND
Eaton and Jones ... Santa Barbara, CA
Eaton, Joseph G. ... Indianapolis, IN
Eaton, Joseph H. ... Los Angeles, CA
Eaton, Joshua P. ... New York, NY
Eaton, Judith Anne ... Denver, CO
Eaton, K. Wade ... Rochester, NY
Eaton, Kim D. ... Pittsburgh, PA
Eaton, Kingsley B. ... Daly City, CA
Eaton, Kristin Winnie ... West Linn, OR
Eaton, Larry James ... Fayetteville, GA
Eaton, Larry L. ... Versailles, IN
Eaton, Larry R. ... Chicago, IL
Eaton, Laurence D. ... Torrance, CA
Eaton, Leslie A. ... Denver, CO
Eaton, Lori A. ... Danbury, CT
Eaton, Louis F., Jr. ... Cohasset, MA
Eaton, Maja Campbell ... Chicago, IL
Eaton, Margaret L. ... Palo Alto, CA
Eaton, Marie L. ... Asheville, NC
Eaton, Marilynn M.
Department of Agriculture, Board of Contract Appeals, GV
Eaton, Mark L. ... Pleasanton, CA
Eaton, Mark R. ... Washington, DC
Eaton, Martinez & Hart, P.C.
Albuquerque, NM
Las Vegas, NM
Eaton & McClellan ... Washington, DC
Philadelphia, PA
Eaton & McIninch ... Manchester, NH
Eaton, Melissa L. ... Sandusky, OH
Eaton, Michael M. ... Washington, DC
Eaton, Michael W. ... New City, NY
Eaton, O. H., Jr. ... Sanford, FL
Eaton, P. Scott ... Albuquerque, NM
Eaton, Paul D. ... Little Rock, AR
Eaton, Paul F. ... Walton, NY
Eaton, Paul F., Jr. ... Sidney, NY
Eaton, Paul W. ... Amarillo, TX
Eaton, Paula R. ... Phoenix, AZ
Eaton, Peabody, Bradford & Veague, P.A.
Augusta, ME
Bangor, ME
Blue Hill, ME
Brunswick, ME
Dover-Foxcroft, ME
Eaton, Phillip D. ... Santa Ana, CA
Eaton, Phoebe M. ... Milwaukee, WI
Eaton & Powell ... Tampa, FL
Eaton, R. B. ... Redding, CA
Eaton, Reka R. ... Atlanta, GA
Eaton, Richard E. ... Mount Clemens, MI
Eaton, Richard K. ... Washington, DC
Eaton, Rita Bash ... Columbus, OH
Eaton, Robert A. ... Salisbury, MD
Eaton, Robert A., P.A. ... Ocean City, MD
Salisbury, MD
Eaton, Robert E. ... Ashland, WI
Eaton, Robert E. L., Jr. ... Washington, DC
Eaton, Robert F. ... Duluth, MN
Eaton, Robert I. ... Manchester, NH
Eaton, Robert I. ... Seattle, WA
Eaton, Robert J. ... Bangor, ME
Eaton, Roger V. ... Albuquerque, NM
Eaton & Romweber ... Batesville, IN
Versailles, IN
Eaton, Samuel K., Jr. ... Santa Barbara, CA
Eaton, Scott A. ... Las Vegas, NV
Eaton, Scott, P.C., Law Offices of
Albuquerque, NM
Eaton, Susan J. ... Lakewood, CO
Eaton, Thomas A. ... Athens, GA
Eaton, Tracy ... Dallas, TX
Eaton, Van de Streek & Ward ... Minot, ND
Eaton & Van Winkle ... New York, NY
Eaton, W. Kenneth, Jr. ... Florence, SC
Eaton, Wendy C. ... Brooklyn, NY
Eaton, William D. ... San Francisco, CA
Eaton, William E., Jr. ... Jupiter, FL
Eaton, William H. ... Jersey City, NJ
Eaton, William J. ... Royal Oak, MI
Eaton, William L. ... Concord, MA
Eatroff, Michael ... Westfield, NJ
Eavenson, Jesse W. ... Middletown, NJ
Eavenson, L. Chandler
Sautee-Nacoochee, GA
Eavenson, Stuart G. ... Farmington Hills, MI
Eaves, Angela M. ... Baltimore, MD
Eaves, Bardacke, Baugh Kierst & Kiernan, P.A. ... Albuquerque, NM
Eaves, G. Jyles ... Jackson, MS
Eaves, James C., Jr. ... Louisville, KY
Eaves, Jessica A. ... Seattle, WA
Eaves, John Arthur ... Jackson, MS
Eaves, John Arthur, Jr. ... Jackson, MS
Eaves, John Arthur, Law Firm
Jackson, MS
Eaves, John M. ... Albuquerque, NM
Eaves, Mary G. ... Louisville, KY
Cincinnati, OH
Eaves, Melissa K. ... Los Angeles, CA
Eaves, Michael K. ... Beaumont, TX
Eaves, Michael R. ... Richmond, KY
Eaves, Sylvia G. ... Marietta, GA
Eavey, Henry H. ... San Mateo, CA
Eayrs, Sonja Trom ... Boca Raton, FL
Plymouth, MN
Ebach, Hillary A. ... Chicago, IL
Ebacher, Cathleen A. ... Milwaukee, WI
Ebacher, Laurie A. ... Amesbury, MA
Ebacher, Timothy J. ... Lowell, MA
Ebanks, Alberto A. ... New York, NY
Ebanks, James D. ... Houston, TX
Ebanks, Jennifer S. ... Clearwater, FL
Ebanks, Kenneth D. ... San Francisco, CA
Ebanks & Sattler, LLP ... New York, NY
Ebaugh, Christian M. ... Fern Park, FL
Ebaugh, Dwight D. ... Lansing, MI
Ebaugh, Linda J. ... San Antonio, TX
Ebaugh, Nelson S. ... Addison, TX
Ebb, Carmel P. ... Washington, DC
Ebb, Lawrence F. ... Washington, DC
Ebb, Nancy Elizabeth ... Washington, DC
Ebb, Peter L. ... Boston, MA
Ebbe, Robert D. ... Appleton, WI
Ebben, David W. ... Rhinelander, WI
Ebben, William H. ... Cincinnati, OH
Ebbers, Carolyn Ann ... Dallas, TX
Ebberson, Linda Kelley ... Seattle, WA
Ebberson, Randal W. ... Seattle, WA
Ebbert, L. Eric ... Kingsport, TN
Ebbert, Richard P. ... Los Angeles, CA
Ebbert, Richard P. ... Pasadena, CA
Denver, CO
Ebbesen, Bob B. ... Lamberton, MN
Redwood Falls, MN
Ebbesen & Sarrazin ... Lamberton, MN
Redwood Falls, MN
Ebbesmier, Kristine A. ... St. Petersburg, FL
Ebbeson, James O. ... Sturgeon Bay, WI
Ebbets, Armstrong, Chamberlin & Traster
Daytona Beach, FL
Ebbets, Chobee, P.A. ... Daytona Beach, FL
Ebbin, Marc J. ... San Francisco, CA
Ebbinghouse, Richard J.
Birmingham, AL
Ebbott, Christopher J. ... Flint, MI
Ebbott, John F. ... Milwaukee, WI
Ebbott, Richard H. ... Flint, MI
Ebbs, Robert H., P.C., Law Office of
Indianapolis, IN
Ebbs, Robert Henry ... Indianapolis, IN
Ebby, David A. ... Philadelphia, PA
Ebby, Robert L. ... Philadelphia, PA
Ebby, Stuart F. ... Philadelphia, PA
Ebdon, Priscilla Ragle ... Charleston, IL
Ebe, Jason ... Phoenix, AZ
Ebe, Nancy ... Austin, TX
Ebe, Robert L. ... San Francisco, CA
Ebeid, Evon M. ... Detroit, MI
Ebel, C. Thomas ... Richmond, VA
Ebel, David M. ... Denver, CO
Ebel, David R. ... Seattle, WA
Ebel, Deanne M. ... Cedar Rapids, IA
Ebel, Deborah S. ... Atlanta, GA
Ebel, Eileen M. ... Nutley, NJ
Ebel, Jack E. ... Littleton, CO
Ebel, James H. ... Farmington, MI
Ebel, James V., II ... Warrenville, IL
Ebel, John S. ... Seattle, WA
Ebel, Karen Beth ... Sacramento, CA
Ebel, Karen E. ... New London, NH
Ebel, Mark D. ... Denver, CO
Ebel, Martin S. ... Boston, MA
Ebel, Pamela L. ... New Orleans, LA
Ebel, Walter M., III (P.A.)
Little Rock, AR
Ebelhar, Melinda W. ... Glendale, CA
Ebelhare, Mary A. ... Fort Collins, CO
Ebeling, Dellinda J. ... Lubbock, TX
Ebeling, Louise B. ... San Francisco, CA
Ebeling, Patricia L. ... Houston, TX
Ebeling, Richard C. ... White Plains, NY
Ebelini, Madeline ... Fort Myers, FL
Ebelini, Madeline, P.A. ... Fort Myers, FL
Ebelini, Mark A. ... Fort Myers, FL
Ebell, C. Walter ... Seattle, WA
Ebeltoft, Paul F., Jr. ... Dickinson, ND
Eben, James R. ... Milwaukee, WI
Ebenal, Shelley D. ... Anchorage, AK
Fairbanks, AK
Ebendorf, Thomas A. ... Louisville, KY
Ebener, Brian S. ... Waukegan, IL
Ebener, Kenneth W. ... West Columbia, SC
Ebenfeld, Cindy L. ... Miami, FL
Ebenfeld, Gregory A. ... Hollywood, FL
Ebenfeld, Gregory A., P.A.
Fort Lauderdale, FL
Hollywood, FL
Ebenger, David E. ... Winthrop, WA
Ebenger, Joseph R. ... Dayton, OH
Ebenholtz, Keith Herschel ... Tampa, FL
Ebenstein, Barbara J. ... New York, NY
Ebenstein, Daniel S. ... New York, NY
Ebenstein, Jerome S. ... New York, NY
Ebenstein, Robert A. ... Santa Barbara, CA
Eber, Alan R. ... Encino, CA
Eber, David ... Boston, MA
Eber, Jennifer A. ... Concord, NH
Eber, Loraine P. ... Irvine, CA
San Francisco, CA
Eber, Louis R. ... New York, NY
Eber, Martin H. ... Palo Alto, CA
San Francisco, CA
Eber, Michele ... Las Vegas, NV
Eber, Samuel ... New York, NY
Eber, Scott T. ... Bal Harbour, FL
Eberhard, Bill D., Jr. ... LaGrange, IN
Eberhard, Daniel T. ... Brookfield, CT
Eberhard, David C.C.
Sterling Heights, MI
Eberhard & Eberhard ... Brookfield, CT
Eberhard, Eric D. ... Seattle, WA
Eberhard, Jeffrey D. ... Portland, OR
Eberhard, Robert V. ... Brookfield, CT
Eberhard, Steven J. ... Houston, TX
Eberhardt, Charles N. ... Bellevue, WA
Eberhardt, Clyde W. ... Roswell, GA
Eberhardt, Daniel H. ... Elkhorn, WI
Eberhardt, David B. ... Columbia, MD
Eberhardt and Eberhardt ... Littleton, CO
Eberhardt, Eric ... Albany, GA
Eberhardt, Eric E. ... Port Washington, WI
Eberhardt, Gary A. ... St. Louis, MO
Eberhardt, Gretchen A. ... Littleton, CO
Eberhardt, Harold H. ... Jefferson, WI
Eberhardt, J. Warren ... Baltimore, MD
Eberhardt, Jan M. ... Huntsville, AL
Eberhardt, Leslie A. ... Monterey, CA
Eberhardt, Michael C. ... Lancaster, CA
Eberhardt, Michael C. ... Dallas, TX
Eberhardt, Michael D. ... Chesapeake, VA
Eberhardt, Nancy C. ... Morristown, NJ
Eberhardt, Paul E. ... Portland, OR
Eberhardt, Robert L. ... Pittsburgh, PA
Eberhardt, Robert S. ... Littleton, CO
Eberhardt, U. Richard ... Morristown, NJ
Eberhardy, Jane ... Las Vegas, NV
Eberhart & Buytendyk Co., L.P.A.
Wooster, OH
Eberhart, Caryn S. ... Northbrook, IL
Eberhart, David R. ... San Francisco, CA
Eberhart, Edward K. ... Wooster, OH
Eberhart, John M. ... Fairbanks, AK
Eberhart, Lance G. ... St. Louis, MO
Eberhart, Max E. ... Wichita, KS
Eberhart, Peter D. ... Pittsburgh, PA
Eberhart, Robert L. ... Columbus, OH
Eberharter, Frank J. ... Seattle, WA
Eberight, William J. ... New York, NY
Eberle, Ann E. ... Louisville, KY
Eberle, Berlin, Kading, Turnbow & McKlveen, Chartered ... Boise, ID
Eberle, Brian G. ... Denver, CO
Eberle, C. Raymond, (P.S.) ... Spokane, WA
Eberle, Donald C. ... Denver, CO
Eberle, Edmond R. ... New Orleans, LA
Eberle, Edward J. ... Oklahoma City, OK
Eberle, Ingrid A. ... New York, NY
Eberle, John T., Law Offices of
Oklahoma City, OK
Eberle, Karen E. ... Menlo Park, CA
Eberle, Kevin Roger ... Charleston, SC
Eberle, Louis J. ... Catonsville, MD
Eberle, Mary C. ... Doylestown, PA
Eberle, Mary E. ... Madison, WI
Eberle, Mary U. ... Bloomfield, CT
Eberle, Robert Alan ... Pittsburgh, PA
Eberle, Shelley Precivale ... Palo Alto, CA
Eberle, Stephan L. ... San Francisco, CA
Eberle, Susan A. ... Buffalo, NY
Eberle, Susan L. ... Orlando, FL
Eberle, Susan L., P.A. ... Orlando, FL
Eberle, Thomas F. ... Milford, OH
Eberle, Todd B. ... Lexington, KY
Eberle, William F. ... Salem, NY
Eberle, William S., (P.A.)
Washington, DC
Eberlein, Arthur L. ... Wausau, WI
Eberlein, Frederic ... Shawano, WI
Eberlein, Menard and Martell ... Shawano, WI
Eberlein, Michael G. ... Shawano, WI
Eberley, David B. ... Bakersfield, CA
Eberlin, James M. ... Chicago, IL
Eberling, Kathleen G. ... Canon City, CO
Eberly, David A. ... Cincinnati, OH
Eberly, Dennis J. ... Tiffin, OH
Eberly, Donald A. ... Canton, OH
Eberly & Eberly ... Tiffin, OH
Eberly, James C., Sr. ... Duncansville, PA
Eberly, John E. ... Chattanooga, TN
Eberly, John H., Jr. ... Eugene, OR
Eberly, Mary Rogan ... Chattanooga, TN
Eberly, Silver B. ... Louisville, KY
Eberly, Stephen S. ... Cincinnati, OH
Eberly, Thomas J. ... Tiffin, OH
Ebers, Earl S., Jr. ... Olympia Fields, IL
Ebersbach, Kurt D. ... Atlanta, GA
Ebersbach, Randy J. ... Newnan, GA
Ebersbacher, Susan M. ... Chesterland, OH
Ebersberger, John M., Jr. ... Annapolis, MD
Ebersberger, Rudolph P. ... Minneapolis, MN
Ebershoff, David A. ... Los Angeles, CA
Ebersohl, James L. ... Worth, IL
Ebersohl, Lori Vaughn ... Washington, DC
Ebersol, Charles R. ... Torrington, CT
Ebersol, Charles R., Jr. ... Torrington, CT
Ebersol, J. Michael ... South Bend, IN
Ebersol & McCormick, LLC
Torrington, CT
Ebersold, Louis A. ... Potomac, MD
Ebersole, C. R. ... Houston, TX
Ebersole, David A. ... San Diego, CA
Ebersole, Eugene F. ... Salem, OR
Ebersole, Gary R. ... Buffalo, NY
Ebersole, Jodi K. ... Baltimore, MD
Ebersole, John McCoy ... Atlanta, GA
Ebersole, Joseph L. ... Washington, DC
Ebersole, Mary Frances ... Baltimore, MD

Ebersole, Maureen Bevans
San Francisco, CA
Ebersole, Thomas E. ..... Fresno, CA
Ebersole, Todd M. ..... Glendale, CA
Eberspacher, David Y. ..... Mattoon, IL
Eberspacher, Edward C., III ..... Shelbyville, IL
Eberspecher, Kelly J. ..... Chicago, IL
Eberstein, Allison L. ..... Dallas, TX
Eberstein & Associates ..... Dallas, TX
Eberstein, Brian A. ..... Dallas, TX
Ebert, Alfred H., Jr. ..... Houston, TX
Ebert, Allan ..... Washington, DC
Ebert, Arthur L., Jr. ..... Milwaukee, WI
Ebert, Brian V. ..... McLean, VA
Ebert, C. Houston ..... Elsmere, KY
Ebert, Carey Dalton ..... Hurst, TX
Ebert, Carl H., & Assoc. ..... Chicago, IL
Ebert, Christine ..... Boston, MA
Ebert, D. Michael ..... San Diego, CA
Ebert, Darlene M. ..... Denver, CO
Ebert, David Bruce ..... Hurst, TX
Ebert, David G. ..... New York, NY
Ebert, Dobin and Green ..... Washington, DC
Silver Spring, MD
Alexandria, VA
Ebert, Douglas E. ..... Marion, OH
Ebert, Dyan J. ..... St. Cloud, MN
Ebert, E. Bruce ..... Hurst, TX
Ebert, Eugene ..... Washington, DC
Silver Spring, MD
Alexandria, VA
Ebert, Frederick C. ..... Fort Collins, CO
Ebert, Frederick C. ..... Utica, NY
Ebert, Gary A. ..... Cleveland, OH
Ebert, J. William ..... Las Vegas, NV
Ebert, J. William, Ltd., Law Office of
Las Vegas, NV
Ebert, James A. ..... East Alton, IL
Ebert, James R. ..... Irvine, CA
Ebert, Jessica ..... Burlington, VT
Ebert, John William ..... Reno, NV
Ebert, Julianna ..... Milwaukee, WI
Ebert, Juliette M. ..... San Francisco, CA
Ebert, Kathleen ..... San Antonio, TX
Ebert, Kim F. ..... Indianapolis, IN
Ebert Law Offices, P.C. ..... Hurst, TX
Ebert, Lawrence B. ..... New York, NY
Ebert, Lorraine R. ..... Lutherville, MD
Ebert, Louis J. ..... Baltimore, MD
Ebert, Mark C. ..... Springfield, VA
Ebert, Mark V. ..... Tucson, AZ
Ebert, Merle L., Jr. ..... Harrisburg, PA
Ebert, Paul B. ..... Manassas, VA
Ebert, Paul S. ..... Washington, DC
Ebert, Regan D. ..... Chicago, IL
Ebert, Robert T. ..... Washington, DC
Ebert, Robert T. ..... St. Louis, MO
Ebert, Robert T., Jr. ..... St. Louis, MO
Ebert, Robt. A. ..... St. Paul, MN
Ebert, Steven D. ..... Madison, WI
Ebert, Tina M. ..... Pittsburgh, PA
Ebert, William B. ..... Springfield, IL
Ebert, William F. ..... Topeka, KS
Ebert, William F., P.A. ..... Topeka, KS
Eberth, Michael D. ..... Dearborn, MI
Ebertowski, Rodney J. ..... Bismarck, ND
Eberts, F. Samuel, III ..... North Chicago, IL
Eberts, F. William ..... Delray Beach, FL
Eberwein, Thomas C. ..... Hamilton, OH
Eberwein, Tony L. ..... Clayton, MO
Eberz, James G. ..... White Plains, NY
Eberz, Robert J. ..... Owego, NY
Ebesugawa, Michael M. ..... Honolulu, HI
Ebetino, James M. ..... Somers, NY
Ebey, Amanda L. ..... San Francisco, CA
Ebey, Frederick H. ..... Watsonville, CA
Ebihara, Daniel D. ..... Las Vegas, NV
Ebin, Linda ..... Miami, FL
Ebin, Robert F. ..... New York, NY
Ebiner, Lawrence P. ..... Irvine, CA
Ebiner, Michael G. ..... West Covina, CA
Ebiner, Robert M. ..... West Covina, CA
Ebinger, Robert F. ..... Columbus, OH
Ebinger, Robert M. ..... Las Vegas, NV
Ebinger, Robert M., Chtd. ..... Las Vegas, NV
Ebisch, Jane G. ..... Denver, CO
Ebisu, Geneva Wong ..... San Jose, CA
Ebisui, Edwin A., Jr. ..... Wahiawa, HI
Ebitz, Elizabeth Kelly ..... Bangor, ME
Ebitz & Thornton, P.A. ..... Bangor, ME
Ebke, Stephen C. ..... Council Bluffs, IA
Eble, Louis B. ..... Houston, TX
Eble, Timothy E. ..... Charleston, SC
Eblen, Ann T. ..... Louisville, KY
Eblen, Carol Ann ..... Honolulu, HI
Eblen, David M. ..... Columbia, MO
Eblen, Elmer E. ..... Kingston, TN
Eblin, Robert L. ..... Columbus, OH
Ebling, George L. ..... Sacramento, CA
Ebling, Keith J. ..... Maryland Heights, MO
Ebling, Louis K. ..... Cincinnati, OH
Ebling, Philip H. ..... San Francisco, CA
Ebling, Samuel C. ..... St. Louis, MO
Ebling, Samuel C., A Prof. Corp., Law Offices of ..... St. Louis, MO
Ebling, Susan ..... Philadelphia, PA
Ebner, David A. ..... Pueblo, CO
Ebner, David G. ..... Denver, CO
Ebner, Drake W. ..... Cincinnati, OH
Ebner, Elizabeth
Federal Mine Safety and Health Review Commission, Office of the Commissioners, GV
Ebner, Frank G. ..... Farmington Hills, MI
Ebner, Henry F. ..... Oak Lawn, IL
Ebner, John F. ..... St. Paul, MN
Ebner, Kenneth R. ..... Philadelphia, PA
Ebner, Lawrence S. ..... Washington, DC
Ebner, Margaret E. ..... La Crosse, WI
Ebner, Randall Miles ..... Houston, TX
Ebner & Riker Co., L.P.A.
Cincinnati, OH
Ebner, Ruth ..... Los Angeles, CA
Ebner, Stephen A. ..... Calabasas, CA
Ebner, Susan Warshaw ..... Fairfax, VA
Eboch, Donald K. ..... Fairfax, VA
Eboli, Danilo M. ..... San Juan, PR
Ebrahimoff, Rosalyn Joan ..... Brooklyn, NY
Ebright, Albert H. ..... Los Angeles, CA
Ebright, Howard A. ..... Wayne, NJ
Ebright, James N. ..... Los Angeles, CA
Ebright, Jeffrey L. ..... San Diego, CA
Ebright, Mitchell A. ..... Los Angeles, CA
Ebright, Peter ..... Morristown, NJ
Ebrom, Charles E. ..... San Antonio, TX
Ebron-Fubara, Erania M. ..... New York, NY
Ebroon, David A. ..... Chicago, IL
Ebsary, W.F. "Casey", Jr. ..... Tampa, FL
Ebsen, Ann E. ..... Papillion, NE
Ebstein, Gregory E. ..... San Francisco, CA
Ebstein, Jeffrey D. ..... Sausalito, CA
Eburuche-Ekeanyanwu, Thecla
Washington, DC
Eby, C. Arthur, Jr. ..... Towson, MD
Eby, C. Richard ..... Cincinnati, OH
Eby, David P. ..... Manchester, NH
Eby, Dayle M. ..... Indianapolis, IN
Eby, Gary L. ..... Cleveland, OH
Eby, Gary Moore ..... Cincinnati, OH
Eby, Jaelle Paige ..... Farmington Hills, MI
Eby, James K. ..... Oswego, NY
Eby, Louis K.
Environmental Protection Agency, Program Office Attorneys, GV
Eby, Lynn C. ..... Albuquerque, NM
Eby, Mark J. ..... Ann Arbor, MI
Eby, Matthew Bryce ..... Chicago, IL
Oak Park, IL
Eby, Michael ..... Boston, MA
Eby, Raymond B. ..... Minneapolis, MN
Eby, Rickey L. ..... Laguna Niguel, CA
Eby, Robert J. ..... Lebanon, PA
Ebzery, Bertram T. ..... Chicago, IL
Ebzery, Thomas E. ..... Billings, MT
Ebzery, Thomas E., P.C. ..... Billings, MT
Ecabert, Peter L. ..... Lexington, KY
Ecal, Michael Joselito ..... Paramus, NJ
Ecanow, Elise A. ..... Suffern, NY
Ecanow, Karen Julie ..... Chicago, IL
Eccard, Walter T. ..... Treasury Department, Bureau of the Public Debt, GV
Eccher, James D. ..... Ferndale, PA
Eccher & Jungblut ..... Ferndale, PA
Eccles, Beth Ann ..... Austin, TX
Eccles, C. Hope ..... Park City, UT
Eccles, James "Beau" ..... Austin, TX
Eccles, Katie A. ..... Salt Lake City, UT
Eccles, Pamela J. ..... Cincinnati, OH
Eccles, Peter R. ..... New York, NY
Eccles, Robert N. ..... Washington, DC
Eccles, Robert W. ..... Springfield, MA
Eccleston, Archibald, III ..... Baltimore, MD
Eccleston, Brendan ..... Parsippany, NJ
Eccleston, James J. ..... Chicago, IL
Eccleston, Lynn E. ..... Washington, DC
Eccleston and Wolf, A Professional Corporation ..... Washington, DC
Baltimore, MD
Fairfax, VA
Ecclestone, Arthur G., Jr. ..... Plymouth, MA
Ecclestone, Frederick G. ..... Novi, MI
Ecclestone, Frederick G., P.C. ..... Novi, MI
Ecclestone, John S., II ..... Dearborn, MI
Ecclestone, John S., II, P.C. ..... Dearborn, MI
Ecenia, Stephen A. ..... Tallahassee, FL
Echan, Cheryl ..... Binghamton, NY
Echan, George W., Jr. ..... Zephyr Cove, NV
Echard, Robert A. ..... Ogden, UT
Echard, Roberta M.
Administrative Office Of The United States Courts, GV
Echavarren, Daniel ..... Department of Justice, Executive Office for Immigration Review, GV
Echavarria, Andrew ..... Manhattan Beach, CA
Echavarria, Camilo ..... Los Angeles, CA
Echavarria, Lorraine B. ..... Los Angeles, CA
Echavarria, Roland ..... San Antonio, TX
Echavarria & Rork, P.C. ..... San Antonio, TX
Echavarri-Junco, Christian M.
San Juan, PR
Echaveste, María
Executive Office Of The President, GV
Echeguren, Ronald D. ..... Oakland, CA
Echelbarger, Fred R. ..... Fostoria, OH
Echeles, Julius Lucius ..... Pompano Beach, FL
Echemendia, Rafael J. ..... Bartow, FL
Echemendia, Santiago D. ..... Miami, FL
Echer, Joy D. ..... Astoria, NY
Echerd, J. Hartly ..... Chattanooga, TN
Echerd, Mark R. ..... Irving, TX
Echeruo, Ike O. ..... New York, NY
Echevarria & Associates, P.A. ..... Tampa, FL
Echevarría, George W. ..... Mount Kisco, NY
Echevarria, J. Michael ..... Los Angeles, CA
Echevarria, Margaret D. ..... Los Angeles, CA
Echevarria, Michael ..... Angleton, TX
Echevarria, Michael J. ..... Tampa, FL
Echevarria, Suzanne Y. ..... Houston, TX
Echeverria, Ben ..... San Marcos, CA
Echeverria, John ..... San Francisco, CA
Echeverria, Luis F. ..... Flushing, NY
Echeverria, Peter ..... Reno, NV
Echeverria, Ricardo ..... Claremont, CA
Echeverria, Rodolfo, Law Office of
Vista, CA
Echeverria, Rodolfo R. ..... Vista, CA
Echeveste, Diana ..... Los Angeles, CA
Echeveste, Marc A. ..... Phoenix, AZ
Echikson, Thomas G. ..... Washington, DC
Echlin, Bernard J. ..... Chicago, IL
Echlin, Lewis H. ..... Grosse Pointe, MI
Echnoz, James ..... Boca Raton, FL
Echo, John F. ..... Boston, MA
Echohawk, John E. ..... Boulder, CO
Echohawk, Larry J. ..... Provo, UT
Echo Hawk, Walter R. ..... Boulder, CO
Echols, Bradley R. ..... Longview, TX
Echols, Charlene R. ..... Dallas, TX
Echols, Clinton J. ..... Houston, TX
Echols & Cotter ..... Fort Myers Beach, FL
Echols, D. Daryle, Jr. ..... Waco, TX
Echols, Danny D. ..... Lindale, TX
Echols, David W. ..... Oklahoma City, OK
Echols, Douglas A. ..... Farmington, NM
Echols, F. Stanley ..... Washington, DC
Echols & Hyman ..... Arlington, VA
Echols, Jim ..... Tyler, TX
Echols, John Bryan ..... Nashville, TN
Echols, John C., (P.A.) ..... Little Rock, AR
Echols, John D. ..... Tulsa, OK
Echols, Judy A. ..... Houston, TX
Echols, Julianne T. ..... New Orleans, LA
Echols, Larry A., (P.A.)
Fort Myers Beach, FL
Echols, M. Patton ..... Gresham, OR
Echols, M. Patton, Jr. ..... Arlington, VA
Echols, Margaret A. ..... Bloomington, IL
Echols, Marsha A. ..... Washington, DC
Echols, Michele M. ..... New Orleans, LA
Echols, Michelle Dauphinais
Washington, DC
Echols, P. Burks, III ..... Richmond, VA
Echols, Paul E. ..... Modesto, CA
Echols, Percy W. ..... Department of Commerce, Patent and Trademark Office, GV
Echols, Robert L. ..... Nashville, TN
Echols, Robert M., Jr. ..... Birmingham, AL
Echols, Robert M., Jr., P.C.
Birmingham, AL
Echols, Ruth M. ..... Decatur, GA
Echols, Stephen L. ..... Wilson, NC
Echols, Ted M. ..... Boise, ID
Echols, Ted N. ..... Forest Park, GA
Echols, William R. ..... Charlotte, NC
Echols-Pitts, Leslie ..... Dallas, TX
Echsner, Stephen H. ..... Pensacola, FL
Echt, Jeffrey D. ..... Chicago, IL
Echter, Martin S. ..... New Haven, CT
Echterling, Caleb M. ..... Harrisonburg, VA
Echternach, Kathy L. ..... Philadelphia, PA
Echternach, Steven G. ..... Bartlett, IL
Echtman, Elyse D. ..... New York, NY
Echtman, Irwin M. ..... New York, NY
Eck, Amber L. ..... San Diego, CA
Eck, Carl A. ..... Pittsburgh, PA
Eck, Christopher C. ..... Bend, OR
Eck, Collins & Marstiller ..... Richmond, VA
Eck, Daniel W. ..... Chicago, IL
Minneapolis, MN
Eck, E. Edwin ..... Bozeman, MT
Eck & Elliott, L.L.P. ..... Bend, OR
Eck, F. Thomas, III ..... Napa, CA
Reno, NV
Eck, F. Thomas, IV ..... Treasury Department, Office of the Comptroller of the Currency, GV
Eck, Francis T. ..... Richmond, VA
Eck, Franklin E., Jr. ..... Columbus, OH
Eck, Franklin, Jr. ..... Ellenville, NY
Eck, George G. ..... Minneapolis, MN
Eck, Jennifer M. ..... Washington, DC
Eck, John C. ..... Santa Barbara, CA
Eck, John T. ..... Fort Worth, TX
Eck, Kathleen S. ..... Vail, CO
Eck, Lonnie D. ..... Tulsa, OK
Eck, Margaret Kadel ..... Washington, DC
Eck, Mark A. ..... Pittsburgh, PA
Eck, Paul S. ..... Orange, CA
Eck, Peter K. ..... New York, NY
Eck, Phillip D. ..... Denver, CO
Eck, R. Paul ..... Westmont, IL
Eck, Robert J. ..... Rye Brook, NY
Eck, Steven R. ..... St. Davids, PA
Eck, William B. ..... Miami, FL
Eckard, Garry ..... Boston, MA
Eckard, Kenneth L. ..... York, PA
Eckard, Linda J. ..... Washington, DC
Eckard, Robert David ..... Clearwater, FL
Eckardt, David E. ..... St. Paul, MN
Eckardt & Khoury ..... Los Angeles, CA
Eckardt, Marc A. ..... San Francisco, CA
Eckardt, Peter J. ..... Milwaukee, WI
Eckardt, Richard W. ..... Los Angeles, CA
Eckart, Dennis E. ..... Washington, DC
Eckart, Harvey H. ..... St. Paul, MN
Eckart, Joan C. ..... San Francisco, CA
Eckart, Julia P. ..... Tampa, FL
Eckart, Susan E. ..... Fort Wayne, IN
Eckas, Scott E. ..... New York, NY
Eckber, Jeffrey ..... Berkeley, CA
Eckberg, David ..... Chicago, IL
Eckberg, David K. ..... Seattle, WA
Eckberg, Lammers, Briggs, Wolff & Vierling, P.L.L.P. ..... Stillwater, MN
Eckberg, Lyle J. ..... Stillwater, MN
Eckblad, James D. ..... Madison, WI
Eckdish, Stephen D. ..... San Francisco, CA
Eckel, Charles T. ..... Cardiff, NJ
Eckel, Frederick C., Jr. ..... Westerly, RI
Eckel, G. Mitchell, III ..... Boston, MA
Eckel, Gindi L. ..... Fort Worth, TX
Eckel, Grason John-Allen ..... Cambridge, MD
Eckel, Grason John-Allen ..... Cambridge, MD
Eckel, Hodgson G. ..... Austin, TX
Eckel, John ..... Galveston, TX
Eckel, John M. ..... Chicago, IL
Eckel, Kelly D. ..... Philadelphia, PA
Eckel, Lee N. ..... Los Angeles, CA
Eckel, Mark E. ..... San Diego, CA
Eckel, Matthew Edward ..... Rockville, MD
Eckel, Neal A. ..... Tucson, AZ
Eckel, P. Cory ..... Perrysburg, OH
Eckel, Robin D. ..... Doylestown, PA
Eckel, Timothy C. ..... Watkins Glen, NY
Eckel, William K. ..... Johnstown, PA
Eckelberger, Jerrie F. ..... Englewood, CO
Eckelberger, Robert M, Jr.
Johnson City, NY
Eckelberry, Kirk R. ..... Bismarck, ND
Eckelberry, Robert L. ..... Littleton, CO
Eckelkamp, Cynthia Marie ..... Union, MO
Eckelkamp, Eckelkamp, Wood & Kuenzel
Washington, MO
Eckelkamp, L. B., Jr. ..... Washington, MO
Eckelkamp, Louis B. "Buzz", III
Washington, MO
Eckelkamp, William W. ..... Washington, MO
Eckell, Murray S. ..... Media, PA
Eckell, Sparks, Levy, Auerbach, Monte, Rainer & Sloane, A Professional Corporation ..... Media, PA
Philadelphia, PA
West Chester, PA
Eckelman, Derek S. ..... Naples, FL
Eckelman, Eugene M. ..... Portland, OR
Eckels, Howard R. ..... Springfield, OH
Eckels, Jack P., (P.C.) ..... Houston, TX
Eckels, Jane ..... Seattle, WA
Eckels, John S. ..... Kansas City, MO
Eckels, Mark K. ..... Jacksonville, FL
Eckels, T. Lynne ..... Houston, TX
Eckenbrecht, Margaret M. ..... Atlanta, GA
Eckenrod, Beth S. ..... Redwood City, CA
Eckenrode, Howard C. ..... Milford, CT
Eckenrode, J. Thaddeus ..... St. Louis, MO
Eckenrode, Robert A. ..... Williamsport, PA
Eckensberger, William H., Jr.
Lehigh Valley, PA
Eckenstein, John T. ..... Chicago, IL
Eckenswalder, Joan ..... Carmel, NY
Eckenwiler, Mark ..... Department of Justice, Criminal Division, GV
Ecker, Arthur S. ..... Del Mar, CA
Ecker, Bart E. ..... Hazleton, PA
Ecker, Deborah I. ..... Boston, MA
Ecker, Deborah Pitluk ..... Columbus, OH
Ecker, Ecker & Ecker ..... Pittsburgh, PA
Ecker, Gene T. ..... St. Paul, MN
Ecker, Howard ..... Las Vegas, NV
Ecker, James M. ..... Pittsburgh, PA
Ecker, Janet E. B. ..... Washington, DC
Ecker, Jerome ..... Durham, NC
Ecker, Karen M. ..... Cincinnati, OH
Ecker, Lawrence H. ..... Yonkers, NY
Ecker, Loehr, Ecker & Ecker, L.L.P.
New York, NY
White Plains, NY
Yonkers, NY
Ecker, Lori D. ..... Chicago, IL
Ecker, Lori D., PC, Law Office of
Chicago, IL
Ecker, Louis A. ..... New York, NY
Yonkers, NY
Ecker, Michael D. ..... Philadelphia, PA
Ecker, N. Boyd ..... Washington, DC
Ecker, Peder K. ..... Sioux Falls, SD
Ecker, Robert L. ..... Yonkers, NY
Ecker, Rochelle B. ..... Kansas City, MO
Ecker, Roger J. ..... Washington, PA
Ecker, Rome, Simpson & DeAngelis, P.C.
Pittsburgh, PA
Ecker & Standish, Chartered
Las Vegas, NV
Ecker, Steven D. ..... Hartford, CT
Ecker, Tammi L. ..... North Salem, NY
Eckerle, Audra J. ..... Louisville, KY
Eckerle, Bettina R. ..... New York, NY
Eckerle, Donald J. ..... Louisville, KY
Eckerle, Glenn A. ..... Beverly Hills, CA
Eckerle, Jana L. ..... Madison, WI
Eckerle, Laura Ann ..... Hicksville, NY
Eckerle, Michael L. ..... Indianapolis, IN
Eckerle, Thomas C. ..... Madison, WI
Eckerle, Thomas N. ..... Indianapolis, IN
Eckerling, Herbert ..... Westlake Village, CA
Eckerman, H. Charles ..... San Francisco, CA
Eckerman, Theodore C. ..... Los Angeles, CA
Eckerman, Theodore C. ..... Pasadena, CA
Eckerman, Thomas Patrick ..... Gastonia, NC
Eckersen, Carol A. ..... Minneapolis, MN
Eckersley, M. David ..... Salt Lake City, UT
Eckerson, James B. ..... Mariposa, CA
Eckerson, Michael A. ..... Yorba Linda, CA
Eckerson, Rick A. ..... Houston, TX
Eckerson, Tracy C. ..... Houston, TX
Eckerstrom, Paul L. ..... Phoenix, AZ
Eckerstrom, Peter J. ..... Tucson, AZ
Eckert, Alan W.
Environmental Protection Agency, Office of the General Counsel, GV
Eckert, Alcorn & Goering ..... Madison, IN
Eckert, Amy ..... Denver, CO
Eckert, Ann Marie ..... Washington, DC
Eckert, Anna U. ..... Wellesley, MA
Eckert, Annette A. ..... Belleville, IL
Eckert, Anthony W., III ..... New York, NY
Eckert, Beverlyn Bowen ..... Little Rock, AR
Eckert, Brenda A. ..... Hartford, CT
Eckert, Bruce M. ..... Plymouth Meeting, PA
Eckert, C. Marie ..... Portland, OR
Eckert, Carl M. ..... Detroit, MI

Eckert, Charles A., II ... Cincinnati, OH
Eckert, Charles M. ... Houston, TX
Eckert, Charles V., III ... Goleta, CA
Eckert, Daniel D. ... DeLand, FL
Eckert, David J. ... Wausau, WI
Eckert, Denis R. ... Sioux City, IA
Elk Point, SD
Eckert, Douglas E. ... Birmingham, AL
Washington, DC
Eckert, Eckert & Craven
Indianapolis, IN
Eckert, Eckert & Eckert ... Cincinnati, OH
Eckert, James D. ... St. Petersburg, FL
Eckert, Jennifer K. ... Downers Grove, IL
Eckert, Jody ... Norwich, NY
Eckert, John B. ... Auburndale, FL
Eckert, John C. ... Cincinnati, OH
Eckert, John C. ... Cincinnati, OH
Eckert, Joseph E. ... Austin, TX
Eckert Kost & Vocke ... Rhinelander, WI
Eckert, Lawrence T. ... New York, NY
Eckert, Lorraine D. ... Norwich, CT
Eckert, Margaret E. ... Springfield, MA
Eckert, Michael L. ... Rhinelander, WI
Eckert, Milton K. ... Houston, TX
Eckert, Patricia ... San Francisco, CA
Eckert, Paul A. ... Harahan, LA
Eckert, Paul J. ... Tinley Park, IL
Eckert, Paul R. ... Washington, DC
Eckert, Pete ... Dallas, TX
Eckert, Philip C. ... Indianapolis, IN
Eckert, Philip F., Jr. ... Richmond, VA
Eckert, Philip J. ... West Bend, WI
Eckert, Phillip W. ... Akron, OH
Eckert, Richard A. ... Huntington Station, NY
Eckert, Richard F. ... Freeport, IL
Eckert, Richard L. ... Anchorage, AK
Eckert, Richard T. ... Detroit, MI
Eckert, Richard V. ... Topeka, KS
Eckert, Robert J. ... Laguna Niguel, CA
Eckert, Robert L. ... Wahpeton, ND
Eckert, Roger B. ... Department of Commerce, National Oceanic and Atmospheric Administration, GV
Eckert, Roger C. ... Cincinnati, OH
Eckert, Roland A ... Chicago, IL
Vernon Hills, IL
Eckert, Ruth A. ... Chicago, IL
Eckert Seamans Cherin & Mellott, LC
Fort Lauderdale, FL
Washington, DC
Boston, MA
Haddonfield, NJ
Harrisburg, PA
Philadelphia, PA
Pittsburgh, PA
Eckert & Smith, P.A. ... Jacksonville, FL
Orange Park, FL
Eckert, Stacy A. ... Orange City, FL
Eckert, Stacy A., P.A. ... Orange City, FL
Eckert, Stephen P. ... Indianapolis, IN
Eckert, Thomas I. ... Hazard, KY
Eckert, Thomas L. ... Roanoke, VA
Eckert, W. Kelsea ... Jacksonville, FL
Orange Park, FL
Eckert, William A. ... Magnolia, AR
Eckert, William H. ... Metairie, LA
Eckhard, Richard D. ... Tampa, FL
Eckhardt, Adolph J. ... Baldwin, NY
Eckhardt, Albert ... Aurora, CO
Eckhardt, Andrea M. ... Kew Gardens, NY
Eckhardt, August G. ... Tucson, AZ
Eckhardt, Carl W., Jr. ... Phoenix, AZ
Eckhardt, Cheryl E. ... Bridgeport, CT
Eckhardt, Elizabeth M. ... Baltimore, MD
Eckhardt, John H. ... Springfield, VA
Eckhardt, John Milton ... Denver, CO
Eckhardt, Lana ... Oak Brook, IL
Eckhardt & Lee ... Gibson City, IL
Eckhardt, Robert C. ... Austin, TX
Eckhardt, Rodney D. ... Denver, CO
Eckhardt, Sarah ... Austin, TX
Eckhardt & Stillman ... Indio, CA
Eckhardt, Terry E. ... Gibson City, IL
Eckhardt, Thomas A. ... Glen Ellyn, IL
Eckhardt, Thomas K. ... Indio, CA
Eckhardt, William ... Albany, GA
Eckhardt, William R., III ... Houston, TX
Eckhardt Reed, Sheridan, (Ms.)
San Diego, CA
Eckhart, Anne E. ... Columbus, OH
Eckhart, Daniel W. ... Kansas City, KS
Eckhart, Dennis P. ... Sacramento, CA
Eckhart, Edward L. ... Austin, TX
Eckhart, Elizabeth Wadley ... Kansas City, KS
Eckhart, Henry W. ... Columbus, OH
Eckhart, James F. ... Tallahassee, FL
Eckhart, James M. ... Miami, FL
Eckhart, Kimberly A. ... San Francisco, CA
Eckhart, McSwain, Silliman and Sears
Chicago, IL
Eckhart, Michael R. ... Dayton, OH
Eckhart, Morris L. ... Vinton, IA
Eckhaus, Fred Ira ... North Brunswick, NJ
Eckhaus, Jay E. ... Fort Lauderdale, FL
Eckhaus, Joseph
Federal Trade Commission, Bureau of Competition, GV
Eckhaus, Larry S. ... Derry, NH
Eckhaus & Olson ... New York, NY
Eckhaus, Steven G. ... New York, NY
Eckhause, Melissa M. ... Cleveland, OH
Eckhoff & Hoppe ... San Francisco, CA
Eckhoff, James D. ... St. Louis, MO
Eckhoff, P. Grant ... Wheaton, IL
Eckhoff, Robert G. ... Redding, CA
Eckhold, Scott R. ... Gaylord, MI
Eckhouse, Jacqueline ... New York, NY
Eckinger, Robert D. ... Birmingham, AL
Eckinger, Robert W. ... Canton, OH
Eckis, Stephen M. ... El Cajon, CA
Eckl, Andrea D. ... Glen Cove, NY
Eckl, Fred A. ... Brookfield, WI
Eckl, James H. ... Rochester, NY
Eckl, W. Wray ... Atlanta, GA
Eckland, Bliss ... Colorado Springs, CO
Eckland, Deborah Causey
Minneapolis, MN
Eckland, Jeff H. ... Minneapolis, MN
Eckland, Todd W. ... New York, NY
Eckland, William S. ... Washington, DC
Eckle, David J. ... Monroeville, PA
Eckles, David A. ... San Francisco, CA
Eckles, Kenneth C. ... Plainfield, NJ
Eckles, Linda M. ... Metairie, LA
Eckles, Paul M. ... Los Angeles, CA
Eckley & Associates, P.C. ... Phoenix, AZ
Eckley, Gerald B. ... Kingwood, TX
Eckley, James R. ... Phoenix, AZ
Eckley, Robert ... Phoenix, AZ
Eckley, Stephen R. ... Des Moines, IA
Eckley, Timothy S. ... Des Moines, IA
Eckloff, E. Keith ... Rockville, MD
Ecklund, Carl A. ... Rockford, IL
Ecklund & Frutkin, LLC
Indianapolis, IN
Ecklund, Gary L. ... Rockford, IL
Ecklund, Kareen R. ... St. Paul, MN
Ecklund, Peter S.
Grosse Pointe Farms, MI
Ecklund, Rodney H. ... Minneapolis, MN
Ecklund, William K. ... Minneapolis, MN
Eckmair, Kelley M. ... Oneonta, NY
Eckman, Alexander L. ... Pittsburgh, PA
Eckman, Benjamin D. ... Elizabeth, NJ
Eckman, D. Richard ... Lancaster, PA
Eckman, David W. ... Houston, TX
Eckman, Gordon P. ... Pyatt, AR
Eckman, Mark L. ... Vienna, VA
Eckman, Richard P. ... Wilmington, DE
Eckman, Stephen S. ... Minneapolis, MN
Eckman Strandness & Egan, P.A.
Minneapolis, MN
Eckman, Susan May ... Chadds Ford, PA
Eckman, W. Paul ... Fort Collins, CO
Eckmann, James K. ... San Diego, CA
Eckmann, Michael K. ... San Diego, CA
Eckold, Dennis C. ... Kansas City, MO
Eckold, Lisa D. ... Kansas City, MO
Eckrem, Joyce Oline ... Sacramento, CA
Eckrich, Paula L. ... St. Louis, MO
Ecksmith, Linda M. ... Atlanta, GA
Eckstein, Andrew B. ... New York, NY
Eckstein, Barbara Patricia ... Carle Place, NY
Eckstein, Barry S. ... Oberlin, OH
Eckstein, Deece ... San Antonio, TX
Eckstein, Donald A. ... Englewood, CO
Eckstein, Franklin D. ... St. Petersburg, FL
Eckstein, Gabriel E. (IBA) ... Washington, DC
Eckstein, Georgia L. ... Cleveland, OH
Eckstein, John A. ... Denver, CO
Eckstein, Joseph Michael ... New York, NY
Eckstein, Kenneth H. ... New York, NY
Eckstein, Maya M. ... Richmond, VA
Eckstein, Michael L. ... New Orleans, LA
Eckstein, Michael L., Attorney At Law, A Prof. Corp. ... New Orleans, LA
Eckstein, Neil J. ... Louisville, CO
Eckstein, Paul F. ... Phoenix, AZ
Eckstein, Ray A. ... Cassville, WI
Eckstein, Sarah Thomas ... New Orleans, LA
Eckstein, Sharon B. ... Philadelphia, PA
Eckstein, Steven D. ... Bucyrus, OH
Eckstein, Suzy ... Rockville, MD
Eckstein, Timothy J. ... Phoenix, AZ
Eckstein, William A. L. ... Old Bridge, NJ
Eckstine, Gary E. ... Jacksonville, FL
Eckstrand, Elton A. ... St. Clair Shores, MI
Eckstrom, David C. ... Columbia, SC
Eckweiler, Karl T. ... Stamford, CT
Eclov, Jon P. ... Walker, MN
Eclov, Timothy P. ... Minneapolis, MN
Ecoff, Lawrence C. ... Beverly Hills, CA
Econom, Kim ... Northridge, CA
Economides, Constantine Z. ... Media, PA
Economides & Economides ... Media, PA
Economides, James A. ... Albany, NY
Economides, Lambros ... Media, PA
Economidis, Peter ... Tucson, AZ
Economidy, John M. ... San Antonio, TX
Economon, Ariane C. ... New York, NY
Economon, Paul David ... Annandale, VA
Economopoulos, John B. ... Escanaba, MI
Economos, Gregory G. ... Los Angeles, CA
Economos, Larry C. ... Greenville, NC
Economos, Peter C. ... Chicago, IL
Economos-Jenkins, Betsy M. ... Radiant, VA
Economou, Andoni ... West New York, NJ
Economou, Chris ... Tulsa, OK
Economou, Chris A. ... Fort Lauderdale, FL
Economou, Dena ... Chicago, IL
Economou, Diane ... Palos Heights, IL
Economou, Donna W. ... Wellesley, MA
Economou, Forrester & Ray
Alexandria, VA
Economou, Jack ... Poughkeepsie, NY
Economou, John S. ... New York, NY
Economou, Nicole Vivian ... Hillsborough, CA
Economou, Stewart C. ... Alexandria, VA
Economou, Theodora D. ... Morris, MN
Economou, Vangelis ... Chicago, IL
Economus, Dale S. ... Northfield, OH
Economus and Economus ... Youngstown, OH
Economus, George C. ... Youngstown, OH
Economus, Peter C. ... Youngstown, OH
Economy, Andria Nicole ... Denver, CO
Economy, R. George ... Lansing, MI
Ecton, Douglas B. ... Spokane, WA
Ecton, Kraig S. ... Fort Collins, CO
Ecton, Walter G., Jr. ... Richmond, KY
Ector, Chiquita ... Torrance, CA
Ecube, Cynthia V. ... Hagåtña, GU
Ecuyer, Edward P. ... New Orleans, LA
Ecuyer, Michael J. ... New Orleans, LA
Edalgo, Catherine S. ... High View, WV
Edberg, Hugo C. ... Tampa, FL
Edbril, Donna E. ... New York, NY
Edde, Kristine M. ... Salt Lake City, UT
Eddens, Houston T. ... Birmingham, AL
Eddie, Kim W. ... Lansing, MI
Eddie, Relinda ... Washington, DC
Eddinger, Kevin G. ... Salisbury, NC
Eddingfield, Joseph W. ... Wabash, IN
Eddings, Charles ... Denver, CO
Eddings, Delisa Flowers ... Memphis, TN
Eddings, Michael C. ... Houston, TX
Eddings, Mike ... Calhoun, GA
Eddington, Brian A. ... Baton Rouge, LA
Eddington, Gregory Neil
Oklahoma City, OK
Eddington, James A. ... Torrington, WY
Eddington, Jeffrey S. ... San Diego, CA
Eddington, Keith E. ... West Jordan, UT
Eddington & McArthur ... West Jordan, UT
Eddington & Pryor, Law Offices
Norman, OK
Eddington, Richard L. ... Corpus Christi, TX
Eddington, Virginia K. ... Walnut Creek, CA
Eddington, Warren L. ... Brownsville, TX
Houston, TX
Eddins, Alta B. ... Potomac, MD
Eddins & Bennett Law Firm LLP
Beaumont, TX
Port Arthur, TX
Eddins, Gerald W. ... Port Arthur, TX
Eddins, H. Kevin ... Louisville, KY
Eddins, Katherine M. ... Columbus, GA
Eddins, Linda S. ... Atlanta, GA
Eddins, Phyllis ... Little Rock, AR
Eddins & Ridlehoover ... Milton, FL
Pensacola, FL
Eddins, Robert C. ... Bethel Park, PA
Eddins, Ronald C. H. ... Fort Worth, TX
Eddins, William E. ... Pensacola, FL
Eddison, Jonathan B. ... Irvine, CA
Eddleman, Clark & Rosen ... Dallas, TX
Eddleman, Claude S., Jr. ... Louisville, KY
Eddleman, James H. ... Anna, IL
Eddleman, Joseph K., Jr.
Mount Pleasant, SC
Eddleman, Robert L. ... Columbus, MT
Eddleman, William R. ... Dallas, TX
Eddowes, David J. ... Bridgeton, NJ
Eddows, William R. ... Boston, MA
Edds, Carole B. ... Jackson, MS
Edds, John R., Jr. ... New York, NY
Edds, Stephen C. ... Jackson, MS
Edds, William L. ... Topeka, KS
Eddy, Alfred B. ... Potomac, MD
Eddy, Bruce D. ... Little Rock, AR
Eddy, Charles H. ... Morrilton, AR
Eddy, Cheryl L. ... Chesapeake, VA
Eddy, Cynthia Reed ... Pittsburgh, PA
Eddy, Dana Franklin ... Charleston, WV
Eddy, David B., (P.A.) ... Ocala, FL
Eddy, David C. ... Washington, DC
Eddy, David L. ... Russellville, AR
Eddy, David Sherwood, III
Federal Labor Relations Authority, Authority Member Staff, GV
Eddy, Derek B. ... Philadelphia, PA
Eddy, Domenica A. ... Kissimmee, FL
Eddy, Domenica A., P.A., Law Office of
Kissimmee, FL
Eddy, Donald F. ... Chicago, IL
Eddy, Edward D., III ... Los Angeles, CA
Eddy, Harold N., Jr. ... Stamford, CT
Eddy, Harry L. (Les) ... Wichita, KS
Eddy, Helen B. ... Portland, ME
Eddy, James R., (P.A.) ... Pompano Beach, FL
Eddy, James S. ... San Rafael, CA
Eddy, Jeffrey C. ... Old Saybrook, CT
Eddy, Jeffrey T. ... Charleston, SC
Eddy, John C. ... Des Moines, IA
Eddy, Jonathan A. ... Seattle, WA
Eddy & Jones ... Oklahoma City, OK
Eddy, Kathleen ... Sacramento, CA
Eddy, Marshall H. ... Middlebury, VT
Eddy, Matthew J. ... St. Louis, MO
Eddy, Meryl L. K. ... Baltimore, MD
Eddy, Michael B. ... San Diego, CA
Eddy, Nicholas B. ... Pleasant Valley, CT
Eddy & Osterman ... Pittsburgh, PA
Eddy, Patrice ... Minneapolis, MN
Eddy, Paul H. ... Hartford, CT
Eddy, Peter B. ... Wayne, NJ
Eddy, Ralph G. ... Hartford, CT
Eddy, Rand C. ... Oklahoma City, OK
Eddy, Robert H. ... Cleveland, OH
Eddy, Robert K. ... Tampa, FL
Eddy, Robert L., III ... Metairie, LA
Eddy, Robert L., Jr. ... Hartford, CT
Eddy, Ronald M. ... Denver, CO
Eddy, Stetson Winslow ... Tiverton, RI
Eddy, Teresa A. ... Armonk, NY
Eddy, Theron F. ... North Olmsted, OH
Eddy, Thomas R. ... Pittsburgh, PA
Eddy, W. David, Jr. ... White Plains, NY
Eddy, William A. ... San Diego, CA
Eddy, William A. ... Osceola, IA
Eddy, William H., Jr. ... Eddyville, KY
Eddy, William J. ... Bristol, CT
Ede, Daniel R. ... Tulsa, OK
Ede, Douglas E. ... South Miami, FL
Edee, Allen B. ... Austin, TX
Edee, James P. ... Atlanta, GA
Edeen, Lars O. ... Hamden, CT
Edeiken, Yale F. ... Allentown, PA
Edel, Christopher C. ... New York, NY
Edel, Frederick C. ... Hempstead, NY
Edel, George A. ... Philadelphia, PA
Edel, Gillian H. ... Pacific Palisades, CA
Edel, Martin D. ... New York, NY
Edel, Robert P. ... New Orleans, LA
Edel, Roger J. ... Buffalo, NY
Edel, Scott ... Los Angeles, CA
Edel, Tod B. ... Dallas, TX
Edelbaum, Philip R. ... New York, NY
Edelberg, David ... Hackensack, NJ
Edelberg, Harry W. ... Madison, CT
Edelberg, Irving M. ... Monticello, GA
Edelberg, Paul B. ... Darien, CT
Edelberg, Sherwin C. ... Encino, CA
Edelblum, David M. ... Hackensack, NJ
Edelblute, William ... Spokane, WA
Edelbrock, Jack ... Chicago, IL
Edelbrock, Mark D.
Rancho Cucamonga, CA
Edelbrock & Martin
Rancho Cucamonga, CA
Edelen, Collings J., Jr. ... Surfside, FL
Edelen, Linda L. ... Syracuse, NY
Edelen, Timothy L. ... Bowling Green, KY
Edelfelt, Jonathan D. ... Houston, TX
Edelheit, Susan L. ... Department of Justice, Antitrust Division, GV
Edelhertz, Herbert ... Kirkland, WA
Edelin, Charlisa Holloway
Philadelphia, PA
Edell & Associates ... Morristown, NJ
New York, NY
Edell, Ira C. ... Rockville, MD
Edell, Linda F. ... Nashville, TN
Edell, Marc Z. ... Morristown, NJ
Edell, Miriam Fost ... Greenville, DE
Edell, Robert T. ... Minneapolis, MN
Edelman, A. Sheldon ... New York, NY
Edelman, Alan I. ... United States Senate, Committee Legal Personnel, GV
Edelman, Albert I. ... New York, NY
Edelman, Allan M. ... Clifton, NJ
Edelman, Alvin ... Chicago, IL
Edelman, Amos S. ... New York, NY
Edelman, Ann E. ... Denver, CO
Edelman, Anne P. ... Uniondale, NY
Edelman, Barbara B. ... Lexington, KY
Edelman, Barry H. ... San Antonio, TX
Edelman, Bernard ... Clayton, MO
Edelman, Bernard P. ... Chicago, IL
Edelman, Charles D. ... Burlington, NC
Edelman, Charlotte ... New York, NY
Edelman, Cheryl A. ... Boston, MA
Edelman, Combs & Latturner
Chicago, IL
Edelman, Daniel A. ... Chicago, IL
Edelman, Daniel B. ... Washington, DC
Edelman, Daniel D. ... New York, NY
Edelman, Daniel J. ... Arlington, VA
Edelman, David ... New York, NY
Edelman, Diane Penneys ... Philadelphia, PA
Edelman, Doreen M. ... Washington, DC
Edelman and Edelman, Chartered
Chicago, IL
Edelman & Edelman, P.C. ... New York, NY
Edelman, Elaine D. ... Carbondale, IL
Edelman, Elizabeth A. ... Atlanta, GA
Edelman, Emily Shappell ... Los Angeles, CA
Edelman, Frank A. ... Chicago, IL
Edelman, Frank A., Ltd. ... Chicago, IL
Edelman, Gilbert ... Fort Lauderdale, FL
Edelman, Glen S. ... Lake Success, NY
Edelman & Goldstein, P.C. ... New York, NY
Edelman, Hal M. ... New York, NY
Edelman, Henry D. ... Washington, DC
Edelman, Herbert M. ... Mineola, NY
Edelman, Herbert S. ... New York, NY
Edelman, Howard C. ... Rockville Centre, NY
Edelman, Janet ... Newark, NJ
Edelman, Jeffrey E. ... Livingston, NJ
Edelman, Jeffrey R. ... Denver, CO
Edelman, Jeffrey R., P.C. ... Denver, CO
Edelman, Jerome ... Tustin, CA
Edelman, Jerome ... New York, NY
Edelman, Joel ... Denver, CO
Edelman, Joel I. ... Santa Monica, CA
Edelman, Joseph ... Hicksville, NY
Edelman, Joyce D. ... Columbus, OH
Edelman, Kathryn J. ... Gillette, WY
Edelman, Kenneth, (P.A.) ... Boca Raton, FL
Edelman, Laurence ... New York, NY
Edelman, Laurence H. ... Portland, OR
Edelman, Lawrence C. ... Iselin, NJ
Edelman, Lawrence M. ... Hampton, NH
Edelman, Leon F. ... Chicago, IL
Edelman, Lester ... Department of the Army, Office, Chief of Engineers/Headquarters, U.S. Army Corps of Engineers, GV
Edelman, Marc R. ... Tampa, FL
Edelman, Mark S. ... Cleveland, OH
Edelman, Marsha ... Harrison, NY
Edelman and Martin ... Lakeside, AZ
Edelman, Martin L. ... New York, NY
Edelman, Martin W. ... New York, NY
Edelman, Michael J. ... New York, NY
Edelman, Michael N. ... Palo Alto, CA
Edelman, Michael R. ... White Plains, NY
Edelman, Milton ... New York, NY
Edelman, Minna J. ... Bronx, NY
Edelman, Mira Vayda ... Washington, DC
Edelman & Ness ... Hicksville, NY
Edelman, Paul B. ... Carle Place, NY
Edelman, Paul S. ... New York, NY

Edelman, Peri B. ... New York, NY
Edelman, Peter F. ... New York, NY
Edelman, Peter T. ... Reading, PA
Edelman, Philis H. ... Miami, FL
Edelman, Raymond M. ... Lawrenceburg, KY
Edelman, Richard H. ... Houston, TX
Edelman, Richard M. ... New York, NY
Edelman, Richard S. ... Washington, DC
Edelman, Robert J. ... Rochester, NY
Edelman, Rochelle M. ... East Hanover, NJ
Edelman, Ronnie L. ... Department of Justice, Criminal Division, GV
Edelman, Samuel I. ... Bronx, NY
Edelman, Sandra ... New York, NY
Edelman, Sanford J. ... Lakeside, AZ
Edelman, Sara Lynn ... New York, NY
Edelman, Scott A. ... Los Angeles, CA
Edelman, Scott A. ... New York, NY
Edelman, Scott R. ... New York, NY
Edelman, Stacey E. ... Bradenton, FL
Edelman, Stuart J. ... Miami, FL
Edelman, Theodore ... New York, NY
Edelman, Todd Eric ... Washington, DC
Edelman, Warren S. ... New Orleans, LA
Edelman, William J. ... Gillette, WY
Edelman, William W. ... Metairie, LA
Edelmann, Thomas K. ... St. Louis, MO
Edelmayer, Robert J. ... Norristown, PA
Edelmayer, Robert J., P.C. ... Norristown, PA
Edelschick, Douglas G. ... Washington, DC
Edelsohn, Joan Deborah B.
Walnut Creek, CA
Edelson, Bernard ... Bala Cynwyd, PA
Media, PA
Edelson, Bernard, P.C. ... Bala Cynwyd, PA
Media, PA
Philadelphia, PA
Edelson, Bernard S. ... Bloomfield Hills, MI
Edelson, Charles Z. ... Hillsboro, OR
Edelson, Christopher P. ... Washington, DC
Edelson, David B. ... San Francisco, CA
Edelson, Gary L. ... Toms River, NJ
Edelson, Gary M. ... Philadelphia, PA
Edelson, Gilbert S. ... New York, NY
Edelson, James I. ... New York, NY
Edelson, Jay ... Chicago, IL
Edelson, Jeffrey M. ... Portland, OR
Edelson, Leon I., Law Office of ... Chicago, IL
Edelson, Marc H. ... Doylestown, PA
Edelson, Maurice F. ... New York, NY
Edelson, Michael ... Newark, NJ
Edelson, Mitchell D. ... Chicago, IL
Edelson, Rebecca ... Los Angeles, CA
Edelson, Robert ... Baltimore, MD
Edelson, Ruth Cheris ... New Brunswick, NJ
Edelson, Stephanie D. ... Morristown, NJ
Edelstein, Aaron J. ... North Miami, FL
Edelstein, Alan M. ... Newton, MA
Edelstein, Barbara I. ... Chicago, IL
Edelstein, Bernard S. ... Miami Beach, FL
Edelstein & Brown ... Brooklyn, NY
Edelstein, Charles D. ... Miami, FL
Edelstein, David M. ... Miami, FL
Edelstein & Edelstein, P.C. ... Chicago, IL
Edelstein, Edward ... New York, NY
Edelstein, Edward L. ... Philadelphia, PA
Edelstein, George ... New York, NY
Edelstein, Gerald A. ... Glendale, CA
Edelstein, Gerald F. ... Los Angeles, CA
Edelstein, Harry ... Haverstraw, NY
Edelstein, Haskell ... New York, NY
Edelstein, Howard S. ... New York, NY
Edelstein, I. Scott ... Yonkers, NY
Edelstein, Jan M., (Ms.) ... Washington, DC
Edelstein, Janet C.
Department of Labor, GV
Edelstein, Jay L. ... Philadelphia, PA
Edelstein, Jeffrey S. ... New York, NY
Edelstein, Joanna ... San Francisco, CA
Edelstein, Laird & Sobel, LLP
Los Angeles, CA
Edelstein, Lara Judith ... Fort Lauderdale, FL
Edelstein, Leonard B. ... Philadelphia, PA
Edelstein & Lochner LLP
Mount Kisco, NY
Edelstein, Mady J. ... New York, NY
Edelstein, Mark ... Los Angeles, CA
Edelstein, Mark S. ... Chicago, IL
Edelstein, Mark S. ... New York, NY
Edelstein, Martin A. ... New York, NY
Edelstein, Marvin I. ... West Hempstead, NY
Edelstein, Mary Louise Eisnor ... Miami, FL
Edelstein, Michael Z. ... Northampton, MA
Edelstein, Michelle J. ... Greenbelt, MD
Edelstein, Morton ... Baltimore, MD
Edelstein, Nathan L. ... Philadelphia, PA
Edelstein, Nathan M. ... Lawrenceville, NJ
Edelstein, Norman ... Chicago, IL
Edelstein, Paul Jon ... Brooklyn, NY
Edelstein, Peter M. ... Mount Kisco, NY
Edelstein, Ralph J. ... Beverly, MA
Edelstein, Raymond L. ... Oshkosh, WI
Edelstein, Robert ... Beachwood, OH
Edelstein, Robin I. ... Chicago, IL
Edelstein, Roy D. ... Boston, MA
Edelstein, Saul ... Brooklyn, NY
Edelstein, Scott A. ... Los Angeles, CA
Edelstein, Sidney ... Chicago, IL
Edelstein, Stacy L. ... Atlanta, GA
Edelstein, Stanley B. ... Philadelphia, PA
Edelstein, Stephen J. ... Florham Park, NJ
Edelstein, Steven A. ... Coral Gables, FL
Edelstein, Steven A. ... Miami, FL
Edelstein, Steven J. ... Atlanta, GA
Edelstein, Stewart I. ... Bridgeport, CT
Westport, CT
Edelstein, Stuart T. ... Chicago, IL
Edelstein, Stuart T., Ltd. ... Chicago, IL

Edelstein, Walter ... New York, NY
Edelstien and Levine ... Haverstraw, NY
Edelston, Clarissa B. ... Bangor, ME
Edelston, Clifford D. ... Winter Park, FL
Edelston, Clifford D., P.A.
Winter Park, FL
Edelstone, Gary H. ... Los Angeles, CA
Edem, Emmanuel E. ... Oklahoma City, OK
Edemon, J. Mark ... San Antonio, TX
Eden, Avi D. ... Philadelphia, PA
Eden, Ben F. ... Gunnison, CO
Eden, C. J. ... Breckenridge, TX
Eden, Courtney ... Washington, DC
Eden, David ... New York, NY
Eden, Donna Z. ... Baltimore, MD
Eden, Fred J., Jr. ... Damascus, MD
Eden, Jane ... Worcester, MA
Eden, Jeffrey S. ... Portland, OR
Eden, Jennifer S. ... Orlando, FL
Eden, John H., IV ... Inverness, FL
Eden, John H., IV, P.A. ... Inverness, FL
Eden, Joy D. ... Los Angeles, CA
Eden, Lawrence E. ... Encinitas, CA
Eden, Morton A. ... Detroit, MI
Eden, Nathan E. ... Key West, FL
Eden, Robert E. ... Freeport, IL
Eden, Robert L. ... Dallas, TX
Eden, Steven M. ... Ventura, CA
Eden, Teddy J. ... Van Nuys, CA
Eden, Thomas M., III ... Birmingham, AL
Eden, Tolins & Rafferty ... Worcester, MA
Eden, Van N. ... Tulsa, OK
Eden, William D. ... Spokane, WA
Edenbaum, Andrew J. ... San Diego, CA
Edenbaum, Thomas A. ... Florham Park, NJ
Edenfield, B. Avant ... Savannah, GA
Edenfield, Bruce M. ... Atlanta, GA
Edenfield, Christine E.W. ... Columbia, SC
Edenfield, Cox, Bruce & Classens, P.C.
Pembroke, GA
Statesboro, GA
Edenfield, Edwin E., Jr. ... Atlanta, GA
Edenfield, Gerald M. ... Statesboro, GA
Edenfield, J. Franklin ... Swainsboro, GA
Edenfield, Martha J. ... Tallahassee, FL
Edenfield, Mary A. ... Orlando, FL
Edenfield, Michael S. ... Brandon, FL
Edenfield, Tom A. ... Savannah, GA
Edenfield, V. Anne ... Roanoke, VA
Edenharter, Fred K. ... Reading, PA
Edenhofer, Carl R., Jr. ... Salem, WI
Edenhofer Law Offices, S.C. ... Salem, WI
Edens, Ann M. ... Chester, NJ
Edens, Frank D., Sr. ... Brandon, MS
Edens, Geraldine E. ... Washington, DC
Edens, J. Jeffrey ... Lebanon, IN
Edens, J. Wesley ... Bristol, TN
Edens, Lloyd R. ... Pineville, KY
Edens, Michael O. W. ... Columbia, SC
Edens, Michelle O. W. ... Dallas, TX
Edens, Robert J. ... Lodi, CA
Edens, Rod T., Jr. ... Austin, TX
Edens, Stella J. ... Kennewick, WA
Edensword-Breck, George ... Seattle, WA
Edep, Monique M. ... La Jolla, CA
Eder, Elaine A.
Department of Transportation, U. S. Coast Guard, GV
Eder, Elliot D. ... Washington, DC
Eder, Eugene J. ... Oak Creek, WI
Eder, H. Philip ... Portland, OR
Eder, Harold N. ... Valley Cottage, NY
Eder, James A. ... West Hartford, CT
Eder, James J. ... Altamont, IL
Effingham, IL
Eder, James N. ... San Francisco, CA
Eder, James Robert ... Cleveland, OH
Eder, Jan B. ... Milwaukee, WI
Eder, Michele Longo ... Newport, OR
Eder, N. George ... Salem, OR
Eder, Robert J. ... Rushville, IN
Eder, Robert N. ... Whiteville, NC
Eder, William H., Jr. ... Cincinnati, OH
Ederer, Alan C. ... Mineola, NY
Ederer, C. Michael ... Tyler, TX
Ederer, John Edward ... Seattle, WA
Ederer, Louis S. ... New York, NY
Ederer & Price, L.L.C. ... San Antonio, TX
Ederer, Rodger T. ... Okemos, MI
Ederer, Ronald F. ... San Antonio, TX
Ederington, L. Benjamin ... Washington, DC
Eder-Kaufman, Terry ... New York, NY
Ederle, Douglas R. ... Boston, MA
Ederr, Suzanne J. ... Fort Myers, FL
Edersheim, Judith Gallen ... Chestnut Hill, MA
Edes, Brian E. ... Wilmington, NC
Edes & Edes, Inc., A Professional Corporation ... Concord, MA
Edes, F. Davie ... Concord, MA
Edes, Heather V. ... Boston, MA
Edes, Richmond T. ... Concord, MA
Edes & Rosen ... Chicago, IL
Edeus, Keith E., Jr. ... Rockford, IL
Edewaard, C. Robert ... Gainesville, FL
Edgar, Alexander L. ... South Bend, IN
Edgar, Carolyn A. ... New York, NY
Edgar, Cary B. ... Phoenix, AZ
Edgar, Charles Ernest, IV
Washington, DC
Edgar, Charles W., III
West Palm Beach, FL
Edgar, Christopher L. ... Grand Rapids, MI
Edgar, Dallas S. ... Hayward, CA
Edgar, David Alan ... Pittsburgh, PA
Edgar, David J. ... Houlton, ME
Edgar, David W. ... Kansas City, MO
Edgar & De Soto, P.C. ... Tucson, AZ
Edgar, Donald L. ... Walnut Creek, CA

Edgar, Donald S. ... Santa Rosa, CA
Edgar, Frank A., Jr. ... Norfolk, VA
Edgar, George L. ... Washington, DC
Edgar, Gerald L. ... Irving, TX
Edgar, Glynis C. ... Oklahoma City, OK
Edgar, Harold S. H. ... New York, NY
Edgar, J. Hadley, Jr. ... Dallas, TX
Lubbock, TX
Edgar, J. Roger ... St. Louis, MO
Edgar, James A. ... Evansville, IN
Edgar, James H. ... East Lansing, MI
Edgar, James L. ... Tulsa, OK
Edgar, James N. ... Cary, NC
Edgar, Jerry A. ... West Bend, WI
Edgar, John F. ... Independence, MO
Edgar, John M. ... Kansas City, MO
Edgar, John P. ... Baltimore, MD
Edgar, John P. ... Pittsburgh, PA
Edgar, Joseph L. ... Colorado Springs, CO
Edgar, Karl F. ... Burlington, NC
Edgar, Kasey J. ... Wenatchee, WA
Edgar, Kenneth C., Jr. ... New York, NY
Edgar, Kevin R. ... Washington, DC
Edgar, Leigh A. ... Lake Success, NY
Edgar, Mary Ann Dominy
Washington, DC
Edgar, Mary C. B. ... East Lansing, MI
Edgar, Mary F. ... Department of Justice, Environment and Natural Resources Division, GV
Edgar, Orna A. ... Seattle, WA
Edgar, Patricia A. ... Euless, TX
Edgar, Perigo & Hilsabeck, A Professional Corporation ... Broken Arrow, OK
Tulsa, OK
Edgar, Peter S. ... Cincinnati, OH
Edgar, R. Allan ... Chattanooga, TN
Edgar, Russell G., Jr. ... Tallahassee, FL
Edgar, Sheryl Lynn ... Orange, CA
Edgar, Steven E. ... Tulsa, OK
Edgar, Thomas E. ... Chico, CA
Edgar, Timothy H. ... Washington, DC
Edgar, William C. ... Washington, DC
Edgar, William J. (Sam) ... Alma, GA
Edgar, William Robledo ... Oakland, CA
Edgar, Wm. R., Jr. ... Ironton, MO
Edgar, Zada ... Tucson, AZ
Edgar-Sprinkle, Caroletta L. ... Detroit, MI
Edgarton, A. D. ... Fond du Lac, WI
Edgarton, Robert V. ... Fond du Lac, WI
Edgarton, St. Peter, Petak, Massey & Bullon
Fond du Lac, WI
Edgcomb & Blocker LLP
Portola Valley, CA
San Francisco, CA
Edgcomb, John D. ... Portola Valley, CA
San Francisco, CA
Edge, Amy R. ... Oxford, NC
Edge, Armond D. ... Spartanburg, SC
Edge, Arthur B., IV ... Newnan, GA
Edge, Beverly S. ... La Fayette, GA
Edge, Elizabeth T. ... Bellmawr, NJ
Edge, Eugene F. ... Calhoun, GA
Edge, J. Dexter, Jr., P.C. ... Atlanta, GA
Edge, J. Vincent ... Dothan, AL
Edge, Jay G. ... Kansas City, MO
Edge, Joe D. ... Washington, DC
Edge, John A. ... Houston, TX
Edge, Katheryn Reed ... Nashville, TN
Edge, Kathleen M. ... Virginia Beach, VA
Edge, Kathleen M., P.C. ... Virginia Beach, VA
Edge, Peter ... Chicago, IL
Edge, Robert ... Hollywood, FL
Edge, Robert G. ... Atlanta, GA
Edgecombe, Karen Hammack ... Dunkirk, MD
Edgecombe, Wallace E., Jr.
Pittsburgh, PA
Edgecumbe, Craig H. ... Torrance, CA
Edgehouse, Gregory J. ... Cleveland, OH
Edgell, Elise M. ... Orange, CA
Edgell, G. Paul ... Washington, DC
Edgell, Joseph W., Jr. ... Keizer, OR
Edgell, Katherine C. ... Brooklyn, NY
Edgeller, Charles A. ... Kansas City, MO
Edgemon, Charles F. ... Campbell, CA
Edgemon, Pauline D. ... Corte Madera, CA
Edgerly, James R. ... New Castle, PA
Edgerly, Keith N. ... Peoria, AZ
Edgerton, Dorothy H. ... Columbia, SC
Edgerton, Laura A. ... Raleigh, NC
Edgerton, Lynne Todd ... Los Angeles, CA
Edgerton, Malcolm J., Jr. ... New York, NY
Edgerton, Michael F. ... Boston, MA
Edgerton, Michael P. ... West Chicago, IL
Edgerton, Richard L. ... Omaha, NE
Edgerton, Samuel Y., III
Hermosa Beach, CA
Torrance, CA
Edgerton, Tracy J. ... Omaha, NE
Edgett, Eugene A., Jr. ... Baltimore, MD
Edgett, Michael ... Clinton, MO
Edgeworth, Arthur B., Jr. ... Washington, DC
Edgeworth, Dee R. ... San Bernardino, CA
Edgeworth, Myron H. ... Nashville, TN
Edgin, Gordon R. ... Valrico, FL
Edgington, Helen M. ... Baton Rouge, LA
Edgington, M. Shane ... Denver, CO
Edgington, Ray H. ... Sioux City, IA
Edgington, Richard P. ... Kennett, MO
Edgington, Thomas J. ... Pittsburgh, PA
Edgington, Todd Andrew ... New Haven, CT
Edginton, John A. ... San Francisco, CA
Edginton, Ruthanne ... Fresno, CA
Edgley, Ryan M. ... Yakima, WA
Edgmon, Allison ... Chattanooga, TN
Edgmon, Jerry R. ... Long Beach, CA
Edgren, Idalis O. ... Rockford, IL
Edhlund, Sandra A. ... Milwaukee, WI

Edic, William S. ... Los Angeles, CA
Edick, David G. ... Lansing, MI
Edick, Dawn A. ... Boston, MA
Edick, Robert E. ... Detroit, MI
Edick, Roxanne L. ... Braintree, MA
Edick, William D. ... Washington, DC
Edidin, Gary R. ... Highland Park, IL
Edidin and LaPlaca, P.C. ... Washington, DC
Edidin, Laura ... New York, NY
Edidin, Orrin J. ... Chicago, IL
Edie, John A. ... United States Senate, Committee Legal Personnel, GV
Edie, Mark ... Dearborn, MI
Edie, William Gordon
Colorado Springs, CO
Ediger, Catherine C. ... Fort Wayne, IN
Ediger, Gerald D. ... Fort Wayne, IN
Ediger, Rick L. ... Scottsbluff, NE
Ediger, Steven Alan ... Hutchinson, KS
Kansas City, MO
Edin, Charles T., P.C. ... Bismarck, ND
Edin, David L. ... St. Paul, MN
Edin, Jonathan Allen ... Staples, MN
Edinburg, Elaine G., (P.C.) ... Denver, CO
Edinburgh, Howard S. ... New York, NY
Edinburgh, Janis Roney ... Franklin, MA
Edinger & Blakley, P.C.
Oklahoma City, OK
Edinger, Brook A. ... Washington, DC
Edinger, Donald ... Kansas City, MO
Edinger, Gary S. ... Gainesville, FL
Edinger, John Sinclair, Jr. ... Wilmington, DE
Edinger, Pamela K. ... Corvallis, OR
Edinger, Paul R. ... West Long Branch, NJ
Edinger, Richard Edward ... Moorhead, MN
Edinger, Robert D. ... Oklahoma City, OK
Edinger, Roger J. ... Syracuse, NY
Edinger, Stephanie B. ... Denver, CO
Edingfield, Tracy L. ... Wichita, KS
Edington, Alice Smith ... Benton Harbor, MI
Edington, Bruce S. ... Newark, NJ
Edington, Judith G. ... Boston, MA
Edington, Mark M. ... Emerald Isle, NC
Edington, Robert L. ... Miamisburg, OH
Edington, Robert O. ... Cincinnati, OH
Edington, Robert S. ... Mobile, AL
Edip, Derin ... New York, NY
Edises, Bertram ... Prescott, AZ
Edises, Higgins and Learn ... Oakland, CA
Edises, Victoria ... Oakland, CA
Edison, Andrew M. ... Houston, TX
Edison, Brent J., P.C. ... Bismarck, ND
Edison, Chris A. ... Fargo, ND
Edison, Gail D. ... Topeka, KS
Edison, Glenn ... Redmond, WA
Edison, John E. ... Stanwood, WA
Edison, Lois Howcott ... Greenville, SC
Edison, Mark E. ... Louisville, KY
Edison, Mark E. ... Shepherdsville, KY
Edison, Philip M. J. ... Chicago, IL
Edison, Sally E. ... Pittsburgh, PA
Edison, Sheri H. ... Cleveland, OH
Edison, Thomas E. ... Astoria, OR
Edison-Smith, Lisa Kay ... Fargo, ND
Edlavitch, Ronald B. ... Camp Springs, MD
Edlavitch, Susan T. ... Washington, DC
Edlefsen, F. Leon ... San Diego, CA
Edlein, Susan Eichler ... Atlanta, GA
Edleman, Jeffrey G. ... Elyria, OH
Edler, Beth ... Houston, TX
Edler, Jacqueline M. ... Geneva, IL
Edler, Robert P. ... St. Louis, MO
Edler, Robert W. ... Chicago, IL
Cincinnati, OH
Edles, Gary J. ... Washington, DC
Edleson, L. B. Chip ... San Diego, CA
Edleston, William R. ... Phillipsburg, NJ
Edley, Christopher F., Jr. ... Cambridge, MA
Edley, Elliot B. ... Wilkes-Barre, PA
Edley & Reishtein ... Wilkes-Barre, PA
Edlich, Theodore J., IV ... Richmond, VA
Edlin, Aaron S. ... Berkeley, CA
Edlin, Dorothy M. ... Berkeley, CA
Edlin, Douglas E. ... Roseland, NJ
Edlin, Gene K. ... Chicago, IL
Edlin, Gene K., Ltd. ... Chicago, IL
Edlin, Kenneth M. ... San Francisco, CA
Edlin, Noel ... San Francisco, CA
Edlin, Richard A. ... New York, NY
Edlin, Shiel G. ... Atlanta, GA
Edlin, Theodore R. ... Berkeley, CA
Edling, C. Matthew ... Austin, TX
Edling, Shelley K. ... Hillsboro, OR
Edling, Susan K. ... Sacramento, CA
Edlow, David J. ... Susanville, CA
Edlund, Curtis E. ... Park Ridge, IL
Edlund, Lee A. ... San Francisco, CA
Edlund, Mitchell J. ... Chicago, IL
Edlund, Philip A. ... Scottsdale, AZ
Edlund, Ruth Laura ... Bellevue, WA
Edlund, William I. ... San Francisco, CA
Edman, Arnold ... Brooklyn, NY
Edman, John A. ... Fairmont, MN
Edman, John M. ... Clearwater, FL
Edman, Leland M. ... Fresno, CA
Edman, Paul C. ... Fairmont, MN
Edman, Sean ... Boston, MA
Edmands, Bruce W. ... Boston, MA
Edmands, Peter L. ... Biddeford, ME
Edminister, Joseph A. ... Ithaca, NY
Edminister, Michael Edward ... Akron, OH
Edmison, William R. ... Tulsa, OK
Edmisten, Rufus L. ... Raleigh, NC
Edmister, Richard R. ... Cleveland, OH
Edmiston, Charles N., II ... Bloomington, IL
Macomb, IL
Peoria, IL
Quincy, IL

Rushville, IL
Springfield, IL
Edmiston, Diana .....Wichita, KS
Edmiston, Donna M. .....Los Angeles, CA
Edmiston, James G., III .....Billings, MT
Edmiston, James P. .....Cincinnati, OH
Edmiston, John H. .....Warrensburg, MO
Edmiston, Keith L. .....Knoxville, TN
Edmiston, Mark A. .....Tulsa, OK
Edmiston, Michael P. .....Harrisburg, PA
Edmiston, Michael S. .....Los Angeles, CA
Edmiston, Paul D. .....Frankfort, IN
Edmiston, Robert Gray .....Cincinnati, OH
Edmiston, Robert Q. .....Huntsville, TX
Edmiston, Robert R. .....Tulsa, OK
Edmiston, Steven W. .....Seattle, WA
Edmon, Lee Smalley .....Los Angeles, CA
Edmond, Ellen Randi .....Department of Labor, Office of the Solicitor, GV
Edmond, John A. .....Washington, DC
Edmond, Julie M. .....Washington, DC
Edmond, Landon R. .....San Francisco, CA
Edmonds, Alan B. .....Charlotte, NC
Edmonds, Ann M. .....Chicago, IL
Edmonds & Assocs. .....Borger, TX
Edmonds, Bobbie .....Fort Worth, TX
Edmonds, Brian O. .....Houston, TX
Edmonds & Bruno, P.C. .....Branford, CT
Edmonds, Christian P. .....Branford, CT
Edmonds, Clyde E. .....Plainfield, NJ
Edmonds, Clydene J. .....McLean, VA
Edmonds & Co., P.C. .....New York, NY
Edmonds, Cole, Hargrave, Givens & Witzke, P.C. .....Oklahoma City, OK
Wewoka, OK
Edmonds, Cornell A., Jr. .....Princeton, NJ
Edmonds, David C. .....St. Louis, MO
Edmonds, David E. .....Boston, MA
Edmonds, David W. .....Oklahoma City, OK
Edmonds, Doris L. .....Virginia Beach, VA
Edmonds, Douglas J. .....Kansas City, MO
Edmonds, Edmund P. .....New Orleans, LA
Edmonds, Elizabeth A.
Department of Justice, Environment and Natural Resources Division, GV
Edmonds, Ellen M. .....Belleville, IL
Edmonds, Finley L. .....Corpus Christi, TX
Edmonds, Finley L., Inc., A Professional Corporation .....Corpus Christi, TX
Edmonds, Glenda Ellis .....Tucson, AZ
Edmonds, Helen L. .....Augusta, ME
Edmonds, Hollis E. .....Russell Springs, KY
Edmonds, J. Robert .....Edwardsville, IL
Edmonds, James C. .....Salem, OR
Edmonds, James M. .....Candler, NC
Edmonds, James N. .....Tulsa, OK
Edmonds, James Q., II .....Henderson, TN
Edmonds, Jay D. .....Salt Lake City, UT
Edmonds, Jerry B. .....Seattle, WA
Edmonds, John J. .....Houston, TX
Edmonds, John P. .....Chillicothe, IL
Edmonds, John T. .....Seattle, WA
Edmonds, John W., III .....Richmond, VA
Edmonds Law Center .....Edmonds, WA
Edmonds, Lisa Frances .....Barnstable, MA
Edmonds, Lisa I. .....Chicago, IL
Edmonds, Marie Mirro .....Medina, OH
Edmonds, Marie Mirro, Co., L.P.A.
Medina, OH
Edmonds, Mark D. .....Johnson City, TN
Edmonds, Mary Frances .....Tulsa, OK
Edmonds, Nathan J. .....Troy, MI
Edmonds, Norman Robb
Overland Park, KS
Edmonds, Robert C. .....New York, NY
Edmonds, Robert E. .....Topeka, KS
Edmonds, Robert Scott .....New York, NY
Edmonds, Rocklon L. .....Cheyenne, WY
Edmonds, Rodney S. .....Kansas City, MO
Edmonds, Scott Keith .....Tallahassee, FL
Edmonds, Sonnet C. .....Topeka, KS
Edmonds, Steven M. .....Richmond, VA
Edmonds, Thomas A. .....Richmond, VA
Edmonds, Thomas H. .....Portland, OR
Edmonds, Thomas L. .....Borger, TX
Edmonds, Thomas N. .....Kalamazoo, MI
Edmonds, Walter I., Jr. .....Salem, OR
Edmonds, Warner, Jr. .....Santa Barbara, CA
Edmonds, William G. .....Lady Lake, FL
Edmonds, William L. .....Sioux City, IA
Edmonds, William S. .....Kemmerer, WY
Edmondson, Barbara A. .....Washington, IA
Edmondson, Beth .....Atlanta, GA
Edmondson, Charles W. .....Montgomery, AL
Edmondson, Chas. E. .....Cambridge, MD
Edmondson, Dale M. .....Palo Alto, CA
Edmondson, Darryl W. .....Knoxville, TN
Edmondson, David J. .....Washington, DC
Edmondson, Eric D. .....Washington, DC
Edmondson, F. Ty .....Princeton, NJ
Edmondson, Faye Hutchinson .....Dadeville, AL
Edmondson, Frank K., Jr. .....Olympia, WA
Edmondson, Garry L. .....Covington, KY
Edmondson, Guenther & Rylee
Covington, KY
Edmondson, Horatio A. O. .....Atlanta, GA
Edmondson, J. Richard .....New York, NY
Edmondson, James E. .....Muskogee, OK
Edmondson, James Larry .....Atlanta, GA
Edmondson, James W. .....Washington, DC
Edmondson, Janalyn Sue .....Santa Fe, NM
Edmondson, Jennifer Lee .....Appleton, WI
Edmondson, John B. .....Appleton, WI
Edmondson, Joseph D., Jr.
Washington, DC
Edmondson, L. Steve .....Shelton, WA
Edmondson, Lucy E. .....Raleigh, NC
Edmondson, Mary Elizabeth
Washington, DC
Edmondson, Patricia B. .....Charlotte, NC
Edmondson, Paul D. .....Yakima, WA
Edmondson, Paul W. .....Washington, DC
Edmondson, Robert B. .....Long Beach, CA
Edmondson, Ron .....Dallas, TX
Edmondson, Stephanie James
Greenville, NC
Edmondson, Thomas E. .....Houston, TX
Edmondson, Thomas L. .....Nashville, TN
Edmondson, Timothy H. .....New York, NY
Edmondson, W. A. Drew
Oklahoma City, OK
Edmondson, Wiley W. .....Geneva, IL
Edmonson, A. Root .....Raleigh, NC
Edmonson, Barbara M. .....Huntington, NY
Edmonson, Biggs & Mozingo, P.A.
Columbus, MS
Jackson, MS
Starkville, MS
Edmonson, Jamie L. .....Los Angeles, CA
Edmonson, Milton B. .....Greenwood, MO
Edmonson, Randy D. .....Oklahoma City, OK
Edmonson, Richard L. .....Houston, TX
Edmonson, Richard M. .....Jackson, MS
Edmonson, Richard M., Jr. .....Jackson, MS
Edmonson, Steven A. .....Chicago, IL
Edmonson, Susan M. .....Seabrook, TX
Edmonson, Susan M., P.C. .....Seabrook, TX
Edmonson, Tammy J. .....Mill Valley, CA
Edmonson, Tracy K. .....San Francisco, CA
Edmonston, Craig A. .....Bakersfield, CA
Edmund, George A. .....Atlanta, GA
Edmund, Jack T. .....Fort Meade, FL
Edmund, John Adam .....Harrison, NE
Edmund, Robert W. .....Columbus, OH
Edmunds, Alan V. .....Encinitas, CA
Oceanside, CA
Edmunds, Alan V. .....San Diego, CA
Edmunds & Associates .....Bellevue, WA
Edmunds, C. Coleman G.
Fort Lauderdale, FL
Edmunds, Carmela N. .....Washington, DC
Edmunds, David L., Jr. .....Buffalo, NY
Edmunds, Douglas A. .....Vancouver, WA
Edmunds, Eric F., Jr. .....Los Angeles, CA
Edmunds, H. Noh .....Washington, DC
Edmunds, Howard W. .....Houston, TX
Edmunds, J. Timothy .....Brunswick, OH
Edmunds, James E. .....Halifax, VA
Edmunds, James R. .....Chicago, IL
Edmunds, Jeffrey G. .....Dublin, VA
Edmunds, Jeffrey P. .....Sunbury, PA
Edmunds, John M. .....Los Angeles, CA
Edmunds, John S. .....Honolulu, HI
Edmunds Maki Verga & Thorn
Honolulu, HI
Edmunds, Michael W. .....Flint, MI
Edmunds, Nancy Garlock .....Detroit, MI
Edmunds, Renne .....Omaha, NE
Edmunds, Robert K. .....San Diego, CA
Edmunds, Wayne L. .....Petersburg, VA
Edmunds, Wesley N., Jr. .....Bellevue, WA
Edmunds & Willetts, P.C. .....Waynesboro, VA
Edmunds, William C. .....Birmingham, MI
Edmunds, William F. .....Louisville, KY
Edmunds & Williams, P.C.
Lynchburg, VA
Edmundson & Burnette, L.L.P.
Oxford, NC
Edmundson, C. Scott, Jr. .....Meridian, MS
Edmundson, D. Barclay .....Los Angeles, CA
Edmundson, Daniel C. .....New York, NY
Edmundson, Dean P. .....Fort Collins, CO
Edmundson, Dean P., P.C.
Fort Collins, CO
Edmundson, Donna Lynn .....Houston, TX
Edmundson, Ellen Mandell
Washington, DC
Edmundson, James J. .....Rocky Mount, NC
Edmundson, James K. .....Washington, DC
Edmundson, James K. .....Washington, DC
Edmundson, Jasper N. .....Poplar Bluff, MO
Edmundson & Lincoln .....Emerald Isle, NC
Edmundson, Matthew S.
Poplar Bluff, MO
Edmundson, Misty Anne .....Seattle, WA
Edmundson, Paul B., Jr. .....Goldsboro, NC
Edmundson, R. Gene .....Emerald Isle, NC
Oxford, NC
Edmundson, Robert C. .....Pittsburgh, PA
Edmundson, Stephen B. .....Houston, TX
Edmundson, Terando, Hopkins and Henson
Cape Girardeau, MO
Poplar Bluff, MO
Edmundson, Vangi M. .....Los Angeles, CA
Edmunson, James L. .....Eugene, OR
Edney, Andrea La'Verne .....Jackson, MS
Edney, Deborah L. .....Charlotte, NC
Edney, Marsha S. .....Department of Justice, Civil Division, GV
Ednie, Regina M.
Department of Labor, GV
Edoga, Delia V. .....Morristown, NJ
Edouard, Marceau J., Jr. .....Bronx, NY
Edozie, John .....Bronx, NY
New York, NY
Edozien, Margaret E.O. .....Menlo Park, CA
Edquist, David J. .....Milwaukee, WI
Edquist, Matthew B. .....Angleton, TX
Edquist, Ronald K. .....Lakewood, CO
Edralin, Stella M. .....San Francisco, CA
Edraos, Patricia Tongue .....Boston, MA
Edrich, Marc S. .....Hartford, CT
Edridge, R. Michael .....Allentown, PA
Edrington, Frank R., II .....Warrenton, VA
Edrington, Jack B. .....Houston, TX
Edrington, Laura Giles .....Houston, TX
Edrington, Peter P. .....Walnut Creek, CA
Edrington, Richard L. .....La Place, LA
Edrington, Schirmer & Murphy
Walnut Creek, CA
Edrington, Teresa R. .....Santa Ana, CA
Edris, Brown, Johnson & Feeback
Bluffton, IN
Edris, John H., Jr. .....Bluffton, IN
Edsall, Alexandra T. Victor
Treasury Department, Office of the General Counsel, GV
Edsall, David Edward .....Camarillo, CA
Edsall, Michael T. .....Washington, DC
Edsall, Richard L. .....Dayton, OH
Edsall, Robert D. .....Greenville, MI
Edsey, David R. .....Chicago, IL
Edsill, Henry E. .....Waterloo, IA
Edson and Bruer .....Southold, NY
Edson, Cassandra .....Montpelier, VT
Edson, Charles L. .....Washington, DC
Edson, David W. .....San Francisco, CA
Edson, Eldon S. .....Los Angeles, CA
Edson, Elizabeth M. .....Department of Justice, Bureau of Prisons, GV
Edson, Gail D. .....Kansas City, MO
Edson, Gerald W. .....Port Huron, MI
Edson, Gery W. .....Boise, ID
Edson, Gery W., P.C. .....Boise, ID
Edson & Hastings, P.C. .....Port Huron, MI
Edson, Jack B. .....Commerce City, CO
Edson, James W. .....Norwalk, CA
Edson, John D. .....San Diego, CA
Edson, John J., V .....Pittsburgh, PA
Edson, Judith L. .....Eureka, CA
Edson, Kenneth T. .....Hempstead, NY
Edson, Laplante & Spinelli
Sacramento, CA
Edson, Lyle R. .....South San Francisco, CA
Edson, Michael A. .....Tucson, AZ
Edson, Michael M. .....Phoenix, AZ
Edson, Noel Marie .....Sacramento, CA
Edson, Richard J. .....Sacramento, CA
Edson, Thomas J. .....Woodland Hills, CA
Edstrom, Bromm, Lindahl & Sohl
Fremont, NE
Wahoo, NE
Edstrom, David A. .....Denver, CO
Edstrom, David J. .....Portland, OR
Edstrom, Dean R. .....Minneapolis, MN
Edstrom, Dean R., Professional Association
Minneapolis, MN
Edstrom, Jane E. .....Chicago, IL
Edstrom, John J. .....Wahoo, NE
Educato, John S. .....Grand Rapids, MI
Educato, Louis J. .....Grand Rapids, MI
Edvalson, Ian B. .....Palo Alto, CA
Edward, Carol L. .....Seattle, WA
Edwards, A. Clifford .....Billings, MT
Edwards, A. G., and Associates, P.C.
Birmingham, MI
Edwards, A. Michael .....Marion, NC
Edwards, Aaron M. .....Indianola, MS
Edwards, Alan G. .....Birmingham, MI
Edwards, Alex H. .....Tampa, FL
Edwards, Alice J. .....Shawnee, KS
Edwards, Alice Riedman .....Chicago, IL
Edwards, Alison H. .....Chicago, IL
Edwards, Allen M. .....Baton Rouge, LA
Edwards, Allison G. .....Fort Lauderdale, FL
Edwards, Allyson L. .....Pelham, AL
Edwards, A. M., Jr. .....West Point, MS
Edwards, Amelia E. .....Providence, RI
Edwards, Amy L. .....Washington, DC
Edwards, Amy L. .....Chicago, IL
Edwards, Amy M.E. .....Richmond, VA
Edwards, Andrea D. .....Statesville, NC
Edwards, Andrew R. .....Pasadena, CA
Edwards, Angela Logan .....Louisville, KY
Edwards & Angell, LLP .....Hartford, CT
Palm Beach, FL
Boston, MA
Short Hills, NJ
New York, NY
Newport, RI
Providence, RI
Edwards, Anne Duncan .....New Bern, NC
Edwards, Anne G. .....Houston, TX
Edwards, Anne K. .....Los Angeles, CA
Edwards, Anne Schultze .....Boston, MA
Edwards & Antholis, P.C.
Morristown, NJ
Edwards, Anthony C. .....Costa Mesa, CA
Edwards, Anthony C. .....Weaverville, CA
Edwards, Arlene C. .....Baton Rouge, LA
Edwards, Arthur A. .....Brooklyn, NY
Edwards, Arthur M., III .....Jackson, MS
Edwards, Ashley Ann .....Hammond, LA
Edwards, Ashley M. .....Wilmington, NC
Edwards, Ashton & Gin, LLP
Glendale, CA
Los Angeles, CA
Edwards, Atwater & Andrews
Siler City, NC
Edwards, Aubrey .....Big Lake, TX
Edwards, Aymara K. .....Spring, TX
Edwards, B. Richard .....Anchorage, AK
Edwards, Ballard, Bishop, Sturm, Clark & Keim, P.A. .....Spartanburg, SC
Edwards, Ballard, Clark, Barrett and Carlson, P.A. .....Winston-Salem, NC
Edwards, Barbara Anne .....Fair Lawn, NJ
Edwards, Barbara Jean .....Austin, TX
Edwards, Barbara Rockhill .....Tallahassee, FL
Edwards, Barry D. .....Honolulu, HI
Edwards, Barry G. .....Los Angeles, CA
Edwards, Barry R. .....Los Angeles, CA
Edwards, Bedford D. .....Waco, TX
Edwards, Belinda E. .....Atlanta, GA
Edwards, Belk, Hunter & Kerr
El Paso, TX
Edwards, Bernard E. .....South Bend, IN
Edwards, Bernard F., Jr. .....St. Louis, MO
Edwards, Berry H. .....El Paso, TX
Edwards, Bert M. .....Louisville, KY
Edwards, Beth J. .....Smithfield, VA
Edwards, Beverly L. .....Aurora, CO
Edwards, Beverly Z. .....Kansas City, MO
Edwards, Billie Ruth .....Cheyenne, WY
Edwards, Billy G. .....Jamestown, NC
Edwards, Billy John .....Abilene, TX
Edwards, Billy S. .....Houston, TX
Edwards, Bingham D. .....Decatur, AL
Edwards, Bingham D., Jr.
Birmingham, AL
Edwards, Blaine D. .....Houston, TX
Edwards, Bob L. .....Fremont, CA
Edwards, Bonnie .....New York, NY
Edwards, Boykin, Jr. .....Decatur, GA
Edwards, Boykin, Jr., P.C. .....Decatur, GA
Edwards, Brady .....Houston, TX
Edwards, Brian C. .....Louisville, KY
Edwards, Brian D. .....Atlanta, GA
Edwards, Brian S. .....Newport Beach, CA
Edwards, Brian T. .....Monticello, NY
Edwards, Bridnetta D. .....Washington, DC
Edwards, Bruce A. .....San Francisco, CA
Edwards, Bruce Neil .....Seattle, WA
Edwards, Bryant B. .....Los Angeles, CA
Edwards, Bryna L. .....New York, NY
Edwards, Byard, Jr. .....Ponchatoula, LA
Edwards, C. Luke .....Lafayette, LA
Edwards, C. Thomas .....Morganton, NC
Edwards & Caldwell .....Hawthorne, NJ
Trenton, NJ
New York, NY
Edwards, Calvert and Aruffo .....Houston, TX
Edwards and Campbell .....Nashville, TN
Edwards, Carl .....Topeka, KS
Edwards, Carl D., Jr. .....Ashland, KY
Ironton, OH
Edwards, Carl E. .....Amarillo, TX
Edwards, Carl E., Jr. .....Dallas, TX
Edwards, Carl N. .....Dover, MA
Edwards, Carl T. .....Seattle, WA
Edwards, Carlos D. .....Carrollton, MO
Edwards, Caroline Achey .....Newtown, PA
Edwards, Carolyn M. .....Milwaukee, WI
Edwards & Carstarphen .....Washington, DC
Miami, FL
Edwards, Catherine Bonczak .....Detroit, MI
Edwards, Catherine Duke .....Louisville, CO
Edwards, Catherine Sue .....Philadelphia, PA
Edwards, Cathleen C. .....Phoenix, AZ
Edwards, Cecil A., Jr. .....Phoenix, AZ
Edwards, Cecile C. .....Jackson, MS
Edwards, Charla .....San Angelo, TX
Edwards, Charlene .....Lillington, NC
Edwards, Charles A. .....Raleigh, NC
Edwards, Charles B., Sr. .....Fort Myers, FL
Edwards, Charles F. .....Orlando, FL
Edwards, Charles G. .....Port Richey, FL
Edwards, Charles G. .....Little Compton, RI
Edwards, Charles H. .....Atlanta, GA
Edwards, Charles L. .....Chicago, IL
Edwards, Charles M. .....Joplin, MO
Edwards, Charles P. .....Indianapolis, IN
Edwards, Charles P. .....Spartanburg, SC
Edwards, Charles R., Jr. .....Sevierville, TN
Edwards, Charles S. .....Syracuse, NY
Edwards, Charles W. .....Reedley, CA
Edwards, Charles W. .....Spencer, IN
Edwards, Charles W. .....Clark, NJ
Edwards, Charles W., II
San Bernardino, CA
Edwards, Chris D. .....Cody, WY
Edwards, Christine A. .....Riverwoods, IL
Edwards, Christine A. .....Houston, TX
Edwards, Christopher A. .....Lafayette, LA
Edwards, Christopher P. .....Farmville, NC
Edwards, Clark G. .....Boulder, CO
Edwards, Clay .....Louisville, KY
Edwards, Cleddie F. .....Lubbock, TX
Edwards, Cohen & Jacobs, P.A.
Jacksonville, FL
Edwards, Corie A. .....San Francisco, CA
Edwards, Corwin V. .....Fort Belvoir, VA
Edwards, Craig K. .....Bend, OR
Edwards, Craig R. .....Lincolnshire, IL
Edwards, Craig T. .....Quakertown, PA
Edwards, Crawford B., Jr. .....Macon, GA
Edwards, Cynthia G. .....Kansas City, MO
Edwards, D. Rix
Department of Defense, GV
Edwards, Dan .....New York, NY
Edwards, Dana .....New York, NY
Edwards, Dana Maxeen .....Olathe, KS
Edwards, Daniel A. .....San Angelo, TX
Edwards, Daniel F. .....Columbus, OH
Edwards, Daniel H. .....Amite, LA
Edwards, Daniel P. .....Colorado Springs, CO
Edwards, Danny R. .....Kerrville, TX
Edwards, Darrell C. .....Glenarm, MD
Edwards, Darren Keith .....Fort Lauderdale, FL
Edwards, Daryle A. .....Kansas City, MO
Edwards, David .....Wilmington, DE
Edwards, David B. .....Dallas, TX
Edwards, David B. .....Houston, TX
Edwards, David E. .....Philadelphia, PA
Edwards, David F. .....New Orleans, LA
Edwards, David G. .....Fresno, CA
Edwards, David G. .....Pittsburgh, PA
Edwards, David J. .....Jacksonville, FL
Edwards, David J. .....Rochester, NY
Edwards, David L. .....Redding, CA
Edwards, David L. .....Charlotte, NC

Edwards, David L. ... Aberdeen, WA
Edwards, David N., Jr. ... Chapel Hill, NC
Edwards, David O. ... Springfield, IL
Edwards, David R. ... Southlake, TX
Edwards, David R. ... Burlington, VT
Edwards, David S. ... Okanogan, WA
Edwards, David Timothy ... San Angelo, TX
Edwards, David W. ... Greenville, SC
Edwards, Davis E. ... Louisville, KY
Edwards, Debby B. ... Raleigh, NC
Edwards, Deborah A. ... Warner Robins, GA
Edwards, Deborah A. ... Addison, TX
Edwards, Deborah L. ... Charlotte, NC
Edwards, Deborah Mordecai ... Miami, FL
Edwards, Deborah Ruffin ... Trenton, NJ
Edwards, Debra Ann ... Albertson, NY
Edwards, Debra Cole ... Cary, NC
Edwards, Dell H. ... Pinellas Park, FL
Edwards, Dena R. ... Houston, TX
Edwards, Dennis, Jr. ... New York, NY
Edwards, Denver G. ... New York, NY
Edwards, Derek ... Olympia, WA
Edwards, Dirk L. ... Portland, OR
Edwards, Dona C. ... San Francisco, CA
Edwards, Donald A. ... Victoria, TX
Edwards, Donald E. ... Oklahoma City, OK
Edwards, Donald P. ... Atlanta, GA
Edwards, Donald P. ... Atlanta, GA
Edwards, Donald S. ... Columbus, IN
Edwards, Donald W. ... Anchorage, AK
Edwards, Donna M. ... Dallas, TX
Edwards, Douglas ... Spokane, WA
Edwards, Douglas A. ... Houston, TX
Edwards, Douglas H. ... New Orleans, LA
Edwards, Douglas M. ... Las Vegas, NV
Edwards, Douglas R. ... Charlotte, NC
Edwards, Douglas W. ... Los Angeles, CA
Edwards, D. R. ... Chicago, IL
Edwards, Drew E. ... Los Angeles, CA
Edwards & Duggan, P.C.
East Hampton, NY
Edwards, Duggan, Reese and McKinney, P.A.
Greer, SC
Edwards, Duncan L. ... Newark, DE
Edwards, Durwood ... Del Rio, TX
Edwards, Duval A. ... Tucson, AZ
Edwards, E. Byrne ... Lafayette, LA
Edwards, E. John, III ... Kansas City, MO
Edwards, E. Perry ... Greenville, SC
Edwards, E. Ray ... Houston, TX
Edwards, Earl Franklin, III ... Fort Collins, CO
Edwards, Edith M. ... Valdosta, GA
Edwards & Edwards ... Tallassee, AL
Wetumpka, AL
Edwards & Edwards ... Van Buren, AR
Valdosta, GA
Edwards & Edwards ... Freeport, NY
Edwards & Edwards ... Hertford, NC
Lancaster, OH
Edwards & Edwards, A Prof. Corp.
Anaheim, CA
Edwards Edwards & Bodin ... Duluth, MN
Edwards & Edwards, L.L.P.
Greenville, NC
Edwards, E. E., III ... Nashville, TN
Edwards, E. L., III ... Nashville, TN
Edwards, Eleanor H. ... Bellevue, WA
Edwards, Elgin C. ... Santa Ana, CA
Edwards, Elizabeth ... Treasury Department,
Internal Revenue Service, GV
Edwards, Elizabeth A. ... Wilton, CT
Edwards, Elizabeth Flannagan
Richmond, VA
Edwards, Elizabeth M. ... Baltimore, MD
Edwards, Ellen Caslavka ... Tulsa, OK
Edwards, Ellen E., Ms. ... Brooklyn, NY
Edwards, Elwood L. ... Memphis, TN
Edwards, Emma-Louise ... Austin, TX
Edwards, Eric ... Washington, DC
Edwards, Eric Nathan ... Enid, OK
Fairview, OK
Edwards, Ernest L., Jr. (A Professional Law Corp.) ... New Orleans, LA
Edwards, Ersel L. ... Nevada City, CA
Edwards, Eugene T., Jr. ... Stamford, CT
Edwards, Evans G. ... Atlanta, GA
Edwards, F. Anthony ... San Francisco, CA
Edwards, F. Anthony ... Walnut Creek, CA
Edwards, Frances E. ... Stamford, CT
Edwards, Frances Lea ... Houston, TX
Edwards, Frank D. ... Chicago, IL
Edwards, Frank R. ... Rock Island, IL
Edwards, Frederick A., Jr.
Rockville Centre, NY
Edwards, Frederick E. ... Conroe, TX
Edwards, Frederick L. ... Fairfax, VA
Edwards, G. Kent ... Anchorage, AK
Edwards, G. Kip ... Palo Alto, CA
Edwards, Galen B. ... Waco, TX
Edwards, Gary J. ... San Jose, CA
Edwards, Gary L. ... San Diego, CA
Edwards, Gary R. (IBA) **... Washington, DC**
Edwards, Gene H. ... Fort Worth, TX
Edwards, Geo. N. ... Houston, TX
Edwards, George E. ... Pompano Beach, FL
Edwards, George R. ... Edwardsville, IL
Edwards, George R. ... Houston, TX
Edwards, George W. ... Tacoma, WA
Edwards, Gordon W., Jr.
Oklahoma City, OK
Edwards, Gregory C. ... Roanoke, VA
Edwards, Gregory D. ... Jonesville, VA
Edwards, Gregory J. ... Jamestown, NY
Edwards, Gregory W. ... Albany, GA
Edwards, H. Jack ... Goldsboro, NC
Edwards, H. Lynn ... Annandale, VA
Edwards & Hagen ... Aberdeen, WA

Edwards, Hale, Sturman & Atkin, Ltd.
Las Vegas, NV
Edwards, Harold M. ... Charlotte, NC
Edwards, Harrison J., Jr. ... Freeport, NY
Edwards, Harry L. ... Greenville, SC
Edwards, Harry Philip ... Boston, MA
Edwards, Harry T.
United States Court Of Appeals District Of Columbia Circuit, GV
Edwards & Hayden, Law Offices of
San Diego, CA
Santa Ana, CA
Edwards, H. B., III ... Valdosta, GA
Edwards, Helen Odeal ... Baton Rouge, LA
Edwards, Herbert H. ... Harbor Springs, MI
Edwards, Herbert O. ... Stone Mountain, GA
Edwards, Herman ... Murphy, NC
Edwards, Hilda B. ... Comanche, TX
Edwards & Huffman, L.L.P. ... Tulsa, OK
Edwards, Ira L., Jr. ... Tulsa, OK
Edwards, J. Angus ... Salt Lake City, UT
Edwards, J. Blake ... Benkelman, NE
Ogallala, NE
Edwards, J. Bruce ... Anaheim, CA
Edwards, J. Bryan ... Morgantown, WV
Edwards, J. Dewey, Jr. ... Jacksonville, NC
Edwards, J. Duke ... Salt Lake City, UT
Edwards, J. Kenneth ... Raleigh, NC
Edwards, J. Max, Jr. ... Pontotoc, MS
Tupelo, MS
Edwards, J. Stanley ... Phoenix, AZ
Edwards, Jack ... Mobile, AL
Washington, DC
Edwards, Jack L. ... Dimmitt, TX
Edwards, James ... Comanche, TX
Edwards, James A. ... San Bernardino, CA
Edwards, James A. ... Maitland, FL
Edwards, James A. ... New York, NY
Edwards, James A. ... Lancaster, OH
Edwards, James A. ... Lufkin, TX
Edwards, James B. ... Houston, TX
Edwards, James C. ... Encino, CA
Edwards, James Charles ... Madison, TN
Edwards, James E. ... Charlottesville, VA
Edwards, James E., Jr. ... Baltimore, MD
Edwards, James F., Jr.
Winston-Salem, NC
Spartanburg, SC
Edwards, James G., II ... Decatur, GA
Edwards, James H. ... Wilmington, DE
Edwards, James K. ... Providence, RI
Edwards, James L. ... Las Vegas, NV
Edwards, James L. ... Gillette, WY
Edwards, James M. ... Montgomery, AL
Edwards, James M. ... Denver, CO
Edwards, James M. ... Monroe, LA
Edwards, James M. ... Detroit, MI
Edwards, James M. ... New York, NY
Edwards, James M., P.C. ... Denver, CO
Edwards, James O. ... Wichita, KS
Edwards, James R. ... San Diego, CA
Edwards, James R. ... Aurora, IL
Edwards, Jane ... Salem, OR
Edwards, Janet ... Knoxville, TN
Edwards, Janine ... Honesdale, PA
Edwards, Jean C. ... Washington, DC
Edwards, Jeanette G. ... Miami, FL
Edwards, Jeanette G., P.A., Law Office of
Miami, FL
Edwards, Jeffrey G. ... Benton, KY
Edwards, Jeffrey P. ... Louisville, KY
Edwards, Jeffrey Robert ... St. Louis, MO
Edwards, Jeffrey S. ... Philadelphia, PA
Edwards, Jeffrey T. ... Portland, ME
Edwards, Jeffry M. ... Phoenix, AZ
Edwards, Jehanne McIntyre ... Annapolis, MD
Edwards, Jennifer C. H. ... Biloxi, MS
Edwards, Jerome ... Los Angeles, CA
Edwards, Jerry L. ... Charleston, IL
Edwards, Jimmie M. ... St. Louis, MO
Edwards, Jimmy ... Houston, TX
Edwards, J. O., Jr. ... Oklahoma City, OK
Edwards, Joan C. ... Houston, TX
Edwards, Jodi L. ... North Miami Beach, FL
Edwards, Joe E. ... Oklahoma City, OK
Edwards, Joe S., Jr. ... Lima, OH
Edwards, John ... Chino, CA
Edwards, John B. ... Pascagoula, MS
Edwards, John C. ... La Jolla, CA
Edwards, John C. ... San Diego, CA
Edwards, John C. ... Macon, GA
Edwards, John C. ... Marietta, GA
Edwards, John Charles ... United States Senate,
Senatorial Assistants, GV
Edwards, John D. ... Des Moines, IA
Edwards, John D. ... Opelousas, LA
Edwards, John E. ... San Diego, CA
Edwards, John F.
United States Court of Federal Claims,
Office of Special Masters, GV
Edwards, John F. ... Amherst, MA
Edwards, John H. ... East Islip, NY
Edwards, John H, ("J"), IV ... Mansfield, TX
Edwards, John K. ... Houston, TX
Edwards, John Kent ... Valdosta, GA
Edwards, John L.T. ... Boise, ID
Edwards, John M. ... Boston, MA
Edwards, John M., Jr. ... Atlanta, GA
Edwards, John P., Jr. ... Mount Olive, NC
Edwards, John R. ... Flossmoor, IL
Edwards, John R. ... New York, NY
Edwards, John R. ... Milwaukee, WI
Edwards, John R., Jr. ... Woodcliff Lake, NJ
Edwards, John S. ... Lincoln, ME
Edwards, John S. ... New City, NY
Edwards, John S. ... Roanoke, VA
Edwards, John T. ... Oklahoma City, OK
Edwards, John U. ... Glendale, CA

Edwards, John V. ... Norfolk, VA
Edwards, John W. ... Columbus, OH
Edwards, John W., II ... Cleveland, OH
Edwards, Jon H. ... Augusta, ME
Edwards, Jon L. ... San Francisco, CA
Edwards, Jonathan E. ... Freeport, NY
Edwards, Jonathan P. ... Yarmouth Port, MA
Edwards, Jonathan Ralph ... Monticello, KY
Edwards, Jordan & O'Connor ... Aurora, IL
Edwards, Joseph B. ... Anaheim, CA
Edwards, Joseph C. ... Dallas, TX
Edwards, Joseph D. ... Tampa, FL
Edwards, Joseph E. ... Rochester, NY
Edwards, Joseph E., III ... Carbondale, CO
Edwards, Joseph E., Jr. ... Carbondale, CO
Edwards, Joseph F. ... Cookeville, TN
Edwards, Joseph H. B. ... Boston, MA
Edwards, Joseph L., Jr. ... Lawrence, MA
Edwards, Joseph T. ... Greenville, NC
Edwards, Judith L. ... Lancaster, OH
Edwards, Jules D., III ... Lafayette, LA
Edwards, June
National Aeronautics And Space Administration,
Office of the General Counsel, GV
Edwards, Karen Anne ... Stanton, NJ
Edwards, Karen M. ... Washington, DC
Edwards, Karen M. ... Atlanta, GA
Edwards, Kate ... New York, NY
Edwards, Katherine B. ... Washington, DC
Edwards, Katherine J. ... Santa Monica, CA
Edwards, Kathleen S. ... Boston, MA
Edwards, Kathleen V. ... Wilmington, DE
Edwards, Kathryn H. ... San Francisco, CA
Edwards, Kathy J. ... Nampa, ID
Edwards, Kaye Holland ... San Angelo, TX
Edwards, Keith ... Las Vegas, NV
Edwards, Kelly M. ... San Diego, CA
Edwards, Kenneth E. ... Boston, MA
Edwards, Kenneth Evan ... Chicago, IL
Edwards, Kenneth W. ... Palm Beach, FL
Edwards, Kerry Lynn ... Washington, DC
Edwards, Kevin L. ... Boca Raton, FL
Edwards, Kevin S. ... Southfield, MI
Edwards, Kimberly ... Danville, IL
Edwards, Kimberly T. ... Washington, NC
Edwards & Klein Co., L.P.A. ... Russell, KY
Ironton, OH
Edwards, Knight ... Providence, RI
Edwards, Krista L. ... Washington, DC
Edwards, Kristine A. ... Madison, WI
Edwards, Lance W. ... Washington, DC
Edwards Law Firm ... Lafayette, LA
Edwards, Lawrance A. ... Bothell, WA
Edwards, Lawrence J. ... Albany, NY
Edwards, Leland S., Jr. ... Anchorage, AK
Edwards, Lennon C. ... New York, NY
Edwards, Leonard P. ... San Jose, CA
Edwards, Lillian Brown ... Garland, TX
Edwards, Linda Gray ... Austin, TX
Edwards, Linda H. ... Macon, GA
Edwards, Linda Harrison
Los Angeles, CA
Edwards, Linda Lee ... Phoenix, AZ
Edwards, Linda M. ... Los Angeles, CA
Edwards, Linda Pearce ... Columbia, SC
Edwards, Lisa M. ... Macon, GA
Edwards, Lisa T. Levin ... Richardson, TX
Edwards, Lisa W. ... Department of Justice,
Civil Rights Division, GV
Edwards, Lonzy F. ... Macon, GA
Edwards, Lucius ... Hernando, MS
Edwards, LuEllen W. ... Pacific Palisades, CA
Edwards & Lupton ... San Angelo, TX
Edwards, Lynn Catherine ... Concord, NH
Edwards, Lynn K. ... Towson, MD
Edwards, M. Christopher
West Palm Beach, FL
Edwards, M. Ray ... Van Buren, AR
Edwards, Mahlon ... Las Vegas, NV
Edwards, Malcolm L. ... Seattle, WA
Edwards & Malzahn, Ltd. ... Anoka, MN
Edwards, Manuel F. ... Cookeville, TN
Edwards, Marc ... Oklahoma City, OK
Edwards, Marc L. ... San Francisco, CA
Edwards, Marcy L. ... Portland, OR
Edwards, Marcy S. ... Chicago, IL
Edwards, Margaret A. ... Lake Charles, LA
Edwards, Margaret Hart
San Francisco, CA
Edwards, Margaret LaHaye ... Opelousas, LA
Edwards, Margot Willis ... Portland, OR
Edwards, Maridee Farnquist
Los Angeles, CA
Edwards, Marilyn E. ... Clarksville, TN
Edwards, Marion F. ... Gretna, LA
Edwards, Mark B. ... Charlotte, NC
Edwards, Mark C. ... Redlands, CA
San Bernardino, CA
Edwards, Mark C. ... New Haven, CT
Edwards, Mark C. ... Sweetwater, TX
Edwards, Mark E. ... Santa Ana, CA
Edwards, Mark E. ... Nashville, NC
Edwards, Mark E. ... Nashville, TN
Edwards, Mark Everette ... Durham, NC
Edwards, Mark L. ... Beverly Hills, CA
Edwards, Mark L. ... McAlester, OK
Edwards, Mark P. ... Philadelphia, PA
Edwards, Mark S. ... Morgan Hill, CA
Edwards, Mark S. ... Hialeah, FL
Edwards, Mark U. ... Glendale, CA
Edwards, Marsha Epps ... Washington, DC
Edwards, Martin ... Chicago, IL
Edwards, Martin I. ... Jacksonville, FL
Edwards and Martinuzzi, P.C.
Southfield, MI
Edwards, Mary Alice C. ... Lafayette, LA
Edwards, Mary Baker ... Towson, MD

Edwards, Mary Ellen ... Red Bank, NJ
Edwards, Mary J. ... Buffalo, NY
Edwards, Matthew B. ... Olympia, WA
Edwards and McLeod, P.C.
Douglasville, GA
Edwards, Melvin ... Twin Falls, ID
Edwards, Mia Squeri ... New York, NY
Edwards, Michael A. ... Phoenix, AZ
Edwards, Michael B. ... Lincoln, NE
Edwards, Michael J. ... Tulsa, OK
Edwards, Michael L. ... Birmingham, AL
Edwards, Michael L. ... Jacksonville, FL
Edwards, Michael L. ... Savannah, GA
Edwards, Michael M. ... San Diego, CA
Las Vegas, NV
Edwards, Michael M., Jr. ... San Diego, CA
Las Vegas, NV
Edwards, Michael T. ... Gaylord, MI
Edwards, Michael W. ... Hendersonville, TN
Edwards, Micheal A. ... West Palm Beach, FL
Edwards, Micheal A., Law Office of, P.A.
West Palm Beach, FL
Edwards, Michelle E. ... Atlanta, GA
Edwards, Mitchell L. ... Park City, UT
Edwards, Mitchell & Reeves ... Decatur, AL
Edwards, Mona Gillis ... Greensboro, NC
Edwards, Monica D. ... Nashville, TN
Edwards, Monique C. Carkum
New York, NY
Edwards, Monique M. ... Orlando, FL
Edwards, Monte R. ... Washington, DC
Edwards, Moranda C. ... Chicago, IL
Edwards, Nada L. ... Santa Ana, CA
Edwards, N. D. ... Van Buren, AR
Edwards, Neill
Research Triangle Park, NC
Edwards, Nina G. ... Boston, MA
Edwards, Ninian M. ... St. Louis, MO
Edwards, Nolan G. ... Lafayette, LA
Edwards, Norman B. ... Stanton, NJ
Edwards, Norman L. ... Newton, MA
Edwards, Norman M. ... Memphis, TN
Edwards, Norman W. ... Miami, FL
Edwards, O. Brandt ... Houston, TX
Edwards, O. Carlisle, Jr. ... Columbia, SC
Edwards, Oliver ... New York, NY
Edwards, Orida Broussard ... Lafayette, LA
Edwards, Pamela Kaye ... Bloomington, IL
Edwards & Parsons ... Cookeville, TN
Edwards, Patrick J. ... Chicago, IL
Edwards, Paul B. ... Burlington, WI
Edwards, Paul F. T. ... Memphis, TN
Edwards, Paul N. ... Cleveland, OH
Edwards, Paul R. ... Santa Monica, CA
Edwards, Paul S. ... Colorado Springs, CO
Edwards, Paul T. ... Hartford, CT
Edwards, Peter G. ... Indianapolis, IN
Edwards, Peter H. ... Miami, FL
Edwards, Phil S. ... Siler City, NC
Edwards, Philip J. ... Reading, PA
Edwards, R. Deryl ... Joplin, MO
Edwards, R. Gregg ... Fayetteville, NC
Edwards, R.L. " ... Rocky Mount, NC
Edwards, R. Randle ... New York, NY
Edwards, R. Randy ... Atlanta, GA
Edwards, Ralph ... St. Louis, MO
Edwards, Randall K. ... Salt Lake City, UT
Edwards, Randall W. ... San Francisco, CA
Edwards, Randy L. ... Hanford, CA
Edwards, Ray H. ... Laguna Hills, CA
Edwards, Raymond W. ... Kilmarnock, VA
Edwards, Reed R. ... Little Rock, AR
Edwards, Regina B. ... Wetumpka, AL
Edwards, Regina S. ... Louisville, KY
Edwards, Rex L., Jr. ... Culpeper, VA
Edwards, Rexford P. ... San Diego, CA
Edwards, Richard ... West Liberty, WV
Edwards, Richard A. ... New York, NY
Edwards, Richard A. ... Slaton, TX
Edwards, Richard A. ... West Bend, WI
Edwards, Richard A., P.C. ... Portland, OR
Edwards, Richard C. ... Tampa, FL
Edwards, Richard C. ... Springfield, IL
Edwards, Richard D. ... Stamford, CT
Edwards, Richard D. ... Reno, NV
Edwards, Richard H. ... St. Louis, MO
Edwards, Richard H. ... Malone, NY
Edwards, Richard L. ... Boston, MA
Edwards, Richard Mark ... Paducah, KY
Edwards, Richard W. ... Louisville, KY
Edwards, Rick ... Los Angeles, CA
Edwards, Rick, Inc. ... Los Angeles, CA
Edwards, Rita M. ... Mount Vernon, OR
Edwards, R.L. ... Miami, FL
Edwards, Robert ... Searcy, AR
Edwards, Robert ... Anoka, MN
Edwards, Robert A. ... San Francisco, CA
Edwards, Robert A. ... Akron, OH
Edwards, Robert B. ... Douglasville, GA
Edwards, Robert B. ... Smithfield, VA
Edwards, Robert C. ... Knoxville, TN
Edwards, Robert E. ... Dallas, TX
Edwards, Robert F. ... St. Johns, AZ
Edwards, Robert H., Jr. ... Washington, DC
Edwards, Robert J. ... San Francisco, CA
Edwards, Robert J. ... Atlanta, GA
Edwards, Robert J.E. ... Kansas City, MO
Edwards, Robert L. ... Winston-Salem, NC
Edwards, Robert M. ... Worthington, OH
Edwards, Robert M., Jr. ... South Bend, IN
Edwards, Robert N. ... Liberty Corner, NJ
Edwards, Robert P., Jr. ... Atlanta, GA
Edwards, Robert R. ... Fort Lauderdale, FL
Edwards, Robert S. ... Plant City, FL
Edwards, Robert T. ... Denver, CO
Edwards, Robert W. ... Salt Lake City, UT
Edwards, Robert W., Jr. ... Providence, RI
Edwards, Roberta L. ... Rocky Mount, NC

Edwards, Roberta M. ... Oklahoma City, OK
Edwards, Robin M. ... San Francisco, CA
Edwards, Robyn Haring
Cape Girardeau, MO
Edwards, Rodney A. ... Tulsa, OK
Edwards, Rodney E. ... Duluth, MN
Edwards, Rodney J. ... Duluth, MN
Edwards, Roger C. ... Abbeville, LA
Edwards, Roger C., Jr., (P.C.) ... Abbeville, LA
Edwards, Roger D. ... Anchorage, AK
Edwards, Roger H. ... Miami, FL
Edwards, Roger J. ... Aransas Pass, TX
Edwards, Roger Lee ... Long Beach, NC
Edwards, Roger Lee, P.A.
Long Beach, NC
Edwards, Ronald K. ... Greer, SC
Edwards, Roy D. ... Lodi, CA
Edwards, Royce Deryl, Jr. ... Joplin, MO
Edwards, Rudolph L. ... Durham, NC
Edwards, R.W.L. ... New York, NY
Edwards, S. Dan, Jr. ... Dallas, TX
Edwards, S. Mahlon ... Las Vegas, NV
Edwards, S. Mark ... Junction City, KS
Edwards, Sally Ketchum
Oklahoma City, OK
Edwards, Sally M. ... Terrace Park, OH
Edwards, Sam ... Encinitas, CA
Edwards, Sam B., III ... Hagåtña, GU
Edwards, Sam H. ... Shallotte, NC
Edwards, Samantha G. ... Wilmington, NC
Edwards, Samuel H. ... Nashville, TN
Edwards, Sandra ... Glenview, IL
Edwards, Sandra B. ... Hamilton, MA
Edwards, Sandra L. ... Baton Rouge, LA
Edwards, Sarah E. ... Selma, NC
Edwards, Scott D. ... Bloomfield Hills, MI
Edwards, Scott G. ... Dallas, TX
Edwards, Scott M. ... Seattle, WA
Edwards, Scott Nesbitt ... Miami, OK
Edwards, Scott Wesley ... Reno, NV
Edwards, Sean G. ... San Diego, CA
San Francisco, CA
Edwards, Sean P. ... Annapolis, MD
Edwards, Seth H. ... Washington, NC
Edwards, Shannon L.
Oklahoma City, OK
Edwards, Sharon-Lee ... Detroit, MI
Edwards, Sharpe & Wickham, P.A.
Durham, NC
Edwards, Sharron R. ... Greenville, NC
Edwards, Sherilyn D. ... Houston, TX
Edwards, Sheryl A. ... Sarasota, FL
Edwards, Sheryl A., P.A. ... Sarasota, FL
Edwards, Sidney G. ... New York, NY
Edwards, Sieh, Smith & Goodfriend, P.S.
Seattle, WA
Edwards, Simmons & Oliver ... Nashville, TN
Edwards Singer Witte and Spoeneman, LLP
St. Louis, MO
Edwards, Sooy & Byron, A Professional Corporation ... San Diego, CA
Las Vegas, NV
Edwards, Spencer ... Houston, TX
Edwards, Spencer L. ... Sikeston, MO
Edwards, Stacy L. ... Escondido, CA
Edwards, Stefanski & Zaunbrecher
Crowley, LA
Lafayette, LA
Edwards, Stephanie ... Lilburn, GA
Edwards, Stephen A. ... Atlanta, GA
Edwards, Stephen B. ... Austin, TX
Edwards, Stephen D. ... Fort Myers, FL
Edwards, Stephen E. ... Houston, TX
Edwards, Stephen J. ... Chatham, NJ
Edwards, Stephen L. ... Nashville, TN
Edwards, Stephen M. ... Boston, MA
Edwards, Stephen W. ... La Jolla, CA
Edwards, Stephen W. ... New York, NY
Edwards, Steve J. ... Grove City, OH
Edwards, Steve W. ... Smithfield, VA
Edwards, Steven A. ... Louisville, KY
Edwards, Steven J. ... Decatur, GA
Edwards, Steven L. ... Newport Beach, CA
Edwards, Steven M. ... New York, NY
Edwards, Steven W. ... St. Louis, MO
Edwards, Storey, Marshall & Helveston, LLP ... West Point, MS
Edwards, Susan L. ... Socorro, NM
Edwards, Susan M. ... Houston, TX
Edwards, Susan V. ... Berwyn, PA
Edwards, Suzanne Dye ... Montgomery, AL
Edwards, T. Ashley ... Worcester, MA
Edwards, T. Mark ... Dallas, TX
Edwards, T. Michael ... Atlanta, GA
Edwards, Tamara G. ... Honolulu, HI
Edwards, Tawana Louise ... Louisville, KY
Edwards, Ted B. ... Orlando, FL
Edwards, Terence D. ... San Francisco, CA
Edwards, Teresa ... Boston, MA
Edwards, Terry A. ... Jamaica, NY
Edwards, Terry R. ... Florence, KY
Edwards, Theodore C., II ... Raleigh, NC
Edwards, Theodore G., IV ... Lafayette, LA
Edwards, Theresa Bland
Fort Lauderdale, FL
Edwards, Theresa Bland, P.A.
Fort Lauderdale, FL
Edwards, Thomas A. ... San Diego, CA
Edwards, Thomas A. ... Miami, FL
Edwards, Thomas A, P.A., Law Offices of
Miami, FL
Edwards, Thomas C. ... Fullerton, CA
Edwards, Thomas C. ... San Jose, CA
Edwards, Thomas F., Jr. ... Philadelphia, PA
Edwards, Thomas H. ... Los Angeles, CA
Edwards, Thomas H. ... Pasadena, CA
Edwards, Thomas R. ... Wetumpka, AL
Edwards, Thomas R. ... Lafayette, LA
Edwards, Thomas S., Jr. ... Jacksonville, FL
Edwards, Thomson F. ... Malvern, PA
Edwards, Tim ... Memphis, TN
Edwards, Tim, & Associates, P.S., Law Firm of
Auburn, WA
Edwards, Timothy D. ... Fayetteville, NC
Edwards, Timothy G. ... Auburn, WA
Edwards, Timothy H. ... Savannah, GA
Edwards, Todd Allan ... Houston, TX
Edwards, Tolstedt & Frickle ... Billings, MT
Edwards, Tom ... Houston, TX
Edwards, Tommy B. ... Anderson, SC
Edwards, Tony M. ... Washington, DC
Edwards, Tony W. ... McAlester, OK
Edwards, Tracey K. ... San Jose, CA
Edwards, Travis G. ... Victoria, TX
Edwards, Troy A. ... Costa Mesa, CA
Edwards, Trudy McKelvey
Winchester, TN
Edwards, Tynise Y. ... Rochester, NY
Edwards, Valerie Robinson ... Phoenix, AZ
Edwards, Van E., III ... Columbia, SC
Edwards, Vernelle S. ... Oxnard, CA
Edwards, Vicki Jo ... Simla, CO
Edwards, Virginia Adkins ... Richmond, VA
Edwards, Virginia C. ... San Francisco, CA
Edwards, Virginia M. ... Hackensack, NJ
Edwards, W. Cary ... Hawthorne, NJ
Trenton, NJ
Edwards, W. David ... Winston-Salem, NC
Edwards, W. Jeffery ... Richmond, VA
Edwards, W. Joseph ... Columbus, OH
Columbus, OH
Edwards, W. Mark ... Biloxi, MS
Pascagoula, MS
Edwards, Wallace A. ... Baton Rouge, LA
Edwards, Walter G., Jr. ... Hertford, NC
Edwards, Warren E. ... Hartford, CT
Edwards, Warren H. ... Bonifay, FL
Edwards, Wayne G. ... East Meadow, NY
Edwards, Wesley F. ... New Bremen, OH
Edwards & West ... Cedartown, GA
Edwards, Weston A. ... Los Angeles, CA
Edwards, Wilbur P., Jr. ... Boston, MA
Edwards, William A. ... Cleveland, OH
Edwards, William B. ... Detroit, MI
Edwards, William B. ... Amery, WI
Edwards, William Carl ... Birmingham, AL
Edwards, William D. ... Washington, DC
Edwards, William D. ... Valdosta, GA
Edwards, William D. ... Cleveland, OH
Edwards, William Evans, Jr. ... Bend, OR
Edwards, William F. ... Inverness, FL
Edwards, William F. ... Greenbelt, MD
Edwards, William G. ... Miami, FL
Edwards, William H. ... San Francisco, CA
Edwards, William H. ... Metairie, LA
Edwards, William H. ... St. Paul, MN
Edwards, William H., Jr. ... Little Rock, AR
Edwards, William J. ... Cleveland, OH
Edwards, William K.
Research Triangle Park, NC
Edwards, William R. ... Garden Grove, CA
Edwards, William T., Jr. ... Middleburg, FL
Edwards, William W. ... Tucson, AZ
Edwards, Winston W. ... Montgomery, AL
Edwards & Winterton, Chtd.
Las Vegas, NV
Edwards, W. L. ... Chattanooga, TN
Edwards-Chung, Penny ... Santa Ana, CA
Edwardsen, J. Chris ... Portland, OR
Edwards-Gordon, Claudia J. ... Atlanta, GA
Edwardsneumann, Christine Yvonne
Hempstead, NY
Edwardson, Eric John ... Washington, DC
Edwardson, Eric Paul ... Beaumont, TX
Edwardson, Ronald W. ... Seattle, WA
Edwards-Smith and Edwards ... Akron, OH
Edwards-Smith, Karen ... Akron, OH
Edwin, Gail I. ... New York, NY
Edy, William T. ... Cape Coral, FL
Edy, William T. ... Fort Myers, FL
Edzant, Barry L. ... Encino, CA
Edzant, Jack ... Encino, CA
Edzant, Jack, Law Offices of, A Prof. Law Corp., Law Offices of ... Encino, CA
Eeckhout, Margaret R. ... Dallas, TX
Eeds, Avery A., Jr. ... Clinton, OK
Eee, Aria ... Portland, ME
Eefting, Ronald M. ... Miami, FL
Eelkema, Merlin L. ... Santa Ana, CA
Eells & Dennison, LLC ... Atlanta, GA
Eells, Gregory M. ... Atlanta, GA
Eells, Gwen J. ... La Crescenta, CA
Eells, Lew ... Cedar Rapids, IA
Eells, Rosemary G. ... Upper Darby, PA
Eells & Sovern Law Offices, P.L.C.
Cedar Rapids, IA
Eells, Walter P. ... West Chester, PA
Eenigenburg, John M. ... Los Angeles, CA
Eff, Thomas Allan ... Flushing, NY
Effel, Laura ... New York, NY
Effenbeck, Julie ... Fairbury, NE
Effertz, Steven C. ... Independence, MO
Effinger, George R. ... Paducah, KY
Effinger, J. L. ... New York, NY
Effinger, Joseph M. ... Louisville, KY
Effinger, Montgomery Lee
White Plains, NY
Effken, Matthew J. ... Newport Beach, CA
Omaha, NE
Effland, James N. ... Green Bay, WI
Effland, Janet G. ... Palo Alto, CA
Efflandt, Charles P. ... Wichita, KS
Effler, Fanny P., II ... Toledo, OH
Effler, Stephen Corry ... Rye Brook, NY
Effman, Ingrid Agneta ... Troy, NY
Effman, Norman P. ... Attica, NY
Effman, Richard J. ... Scarsdale, NY
Effman, Steven W. ... Fort Lauderdale, FL
Effner, Robert O. ... Terre Haute, IN
Effrain, Craig H. ... New York, NY
Effrain, Jack ... Herndon, VA
Effren, Jerry C. ... Ashland, MA
Effres & Associates ... Calabasas, CA
Los Angeles, CA
Effres, Steven B. ... Calabasas, CA
Effron, Andrew S.
United States Court Of Appeals For The Armed Forces, GV
Effron, Dawn Dweir ... Boston, MA
Effron, Ellen J. ... Mountain Lakes, NJ
Effron, Gary L. ... Los Angeles, CA
Effron, Joshua J. ... Delmar, NY
Effron Law Firm, The ... Delmar, NY
Effron, Lynn ... East Hanover, NJ
Effron, Wayne D. ... Greenwich, CT
Effron, Wayne D., P.C. ... Greenwich, CT
Stamford, CT
Effros, Erik A. ... New York, NY
Effros, Gail Hochman ... Milwaukee, WI
Effros, Robert C. ... Washington, DC
Efird, Paul H., III ... Charlotte, NC
Efird, Tom D. ... Gastonia, NC
Efkeman, Edward J. ... Alexandria, VA
Efman, Martin I. ... Central Islip, NY
Efman & Obedin ... Central Islip, NY
Efremoff, Anthony E. ... Canton, OH
Efremoff, Sarah K. ... Canton, OH
Efremsky & Nagel ... Pleasanton, CA
Efremsky, Roger L. ... Pleasanton, CA
Efron, Amanda J. ... Minneapolis, MN
Efron, Barry L. ... San Antonio, TX
Efron, Boris E. ... Menlo Park, CA
Efron, Boris E., A Professional Corporation
Menlo Park, CA
Efron, David ... Miami, FL
San Juan, PR
Efron, David J. ... New York, NY
Efron & Efron, A Professional Corporation
Hammond, IN
Efron, Jack A. ... San Antonio, TX
Efron, Jack A., Inc., Law Office of
San Antonio, TX
Efron, Marc F. ... Washington, DC
Efron, Miles E. ... Minneapolis, MN
Efron, Morton L. ... Hammond, IN
Efron, Muriel C. ... West Palm Beach, FL
Efron, Stanley ... Minneapolis, MN
Efron, Steve S. ... New York, NY
Efron, Yael ... Irvine, CA
Efronson, Sidney ... Miami, FL
Efros, Edwin ... New York, NY
Efros, Ellen A. ... Washington, DC
Efros, Lisa B. ... Bloomfield Hills, MI
Efros, M. Nicholas Daniel ... Long Beach, CA
Efros, Peter A. ... Red Bank, NJ
Efroymson, Daniel R. ... Indianapolis, IN
Efroymson, Henry A. ... Indianapolis, IN
Efroymson, Jeremy D. ... Indianapolis, IN
Efroymson, Kevin C. ... Las Vegas, NV
Efroymson, Robert ... Brooklyn, NY
Efroymson, Sarah E. ... New York, NY
Efroymson, Stephen W. ... San Diego, CA
Efrusy, Michael ... Washington, DC
Efstratiades, Anastasius ... Haddonfield, NJ
Philadelphia, PA
Efstration, Gary G. ... Lancaster, PA
Efstration, Gary G., The Legal Works of
Lancaster, PA
Efta, Dennis J. ... Anchorage, AK
Efta, Ronald S. ... Wibaux, MT
Efta, Thomas J. ... Columbus, OH
Efthimiou, Gus, Jr. ... Coral Gables, FL
Efthimiou, Marcus P. ... Corning, NY
Eftimoff, Katerina M. ... Columbus, OH
Efting, James ... Sunnyvale, CA
Eftink, Gerard D. ... Raymore, MO
Efurd Law Firm ... Charleston, AR
Efurd, Paul A. ... Charleston, AR
Efurd, Robt. T., Jr. ... Atlanta, GA
Egan, Alece B. ... Belen, NM
Egan, Ann C. ... Boston, MA
Egan, Ann Marie ... New York, NY
Egan & Associates, P.C. ... Washington, DC
Egan, Barbara M. ... Wakefield, MA
Egan, Becky A. ... West Palm Beach, FL
Egan, Betty L. ... Omaha, NE
Egan, Brendan E. ... New York, NY
Egan, Brian Douglas ... Fresno, CA
Egan, Brian T. ... Melville, NY
Egan, Byron F. ... Dallas, TX
Egan, Catherine P. ... Columbia, SC
Egan, Cecilia E. ... Richmond, TX
Egan, Charles K. ... San Diego, CA
Egan, Charles M., III ... East Rutherford, NJ
Egan, Charles N. ... Green Bay, WI
Egan, Christina ... Chicago, IL
Egan, Christine A. ... Plymouth Meeting, PA
Egan, Christine Louise ... Woonsocket, RI
Egan, Christopher J. ... Lexington, MA
Egan, Claudia ... Milwaukee, WI
Egan, Clifford A. ... Walnut Creek, CA
Egan & Cook ... Shreveport, LA
Egan, D. Shane ... Powell, OH
Egan, Dan W. ... Salt Lake City, UT
Egan, Daniel F., Jr. ... Southborough, MA
Egan, Daniel L. ... Sacramento, CA
Egan, Daniel R. ... Chicago, IL
Egan, David B. ... La Mesa, CA
Egan, David D. ... Rochester, NY
Egan, David F. ... Milford, CT
Egan, Dennis C. ... Department of Justice, Civil Division, GV
Egan, Dennis E. ... Kansas City, MO
Egan, Dennis K. ... Troy, MI
Egan, Donald E. ... Chicago, IL
Egan, Donald E. Jr. ... Binghamton, NY
Egan, Donald J. ... Buffalo, NY
Egan, Donald R. ... Victorville, CA
Egan, Edward J. ... Chicago, IL
Egan, Edward J. ... Chicago, IL
Egan, Eileen M. ... Louisville, KY
Egan, Eileen M. ... Fairfield, NJ
Egan, Elizabeth A. ... San Francisco, CA
Egan, Elizabeth A. ... Boca Raton, FL
Egan, Erin M. ... Washington, DC
Egan, Eugene J. ... Los Angeles, CA
Egan, Flanagan and Cohen, P.C.
Springfield, MA
Egan, Gene Paul ... Santa Ana, CA
Egan, Gerald O. ... San Bernardino, CA
Egan, Gerard P. ... Blue Bell, PA
Egan, Gordon W. ... Sacramento, CA
Egan, Gregory J. ... La Crosse, WI
Egan, J. Michael ... Minneapolis, MN
Egan, J. Murray ... Pittsburgh, PA
Egan, Jacqueline L. ... Baton Rouge, LA
Egan, James C. ... Albany, OR
Egan, James C., Jr. ... Washington, DC
Egan, James E. ... Joliet, IL
Egan, James E. ... Kennewick, WA
Egan, James E., (Chtd.) ... Westmont, IL
Egan, James J. ... North Chicago, IL
Egan, James J., Jr. ... Livingston, NJ
Egan & Jamiolkowski ... Pittsburgh, PA
Egan, Jean M. ... Long Beach, CA
Egan, Jerome William ... Universal City, CA
Egan, John ... Boston, MA
Egan, John C. ... Chicago, IL
Egan, John C., Jr. ... Albany, NY
Egan, John E. ... Franklin, PA
Egan, John F. ... New York, NY
Egan, John J. ... Springfield, MA
Egan, John L., Jr. ... Buffalo, NY
Egan, John S. ... Louisville, KY
Egan, John W. ... Chicago, IL
Egan, Joseph A. ... Pittsburgh, PA
Egan, Joseph, Jr. ... Orlando, FL
Egan, Joseph O., Jr. ... Sacramento, CA
Egan, Joseph R. ... Washington, DC
Egan, Judith A. ... Cambridge, MA
Egan, Judith E. ... Charlotte, NC
Egan, Kathleen T. ... Frederick, MD
Egan, Kevin J. ... Chicago, IL
Egan, Kevin J. ... New York, NY
Egan, Kimberly K. ... Washington, DC
Egan, Lev & Siwica, P.A. ... Orlando, FL
Egan, Lewis Taylor ... Seattle, WA
Egan, Lisa Brett ... Portland, OR
Egan, Lynn C. ... Nashville, TN
Egan, M. Michael ... Atlanta, GA
Egan, Margaret C. ... Chicago, IL
Egan, Margaret Mary ... Pittsburgh, PA
Egan, Mark ... Phoenix, AZ
Egan, Mark H. ... Bartlesville, OK
Egan, Mary ... Staten Island, NY
Egan, Mary Ann ... Santa Rosa, CA
Egan, Matthew J. ... Chicago, IL
Egan, Maureen Nora ... Chicago, IL
Egan & Mazzara, PLLC ... Detroit, MI
Troy, MI
Egan, Michael ... New York, NY
Egan, Michael Aloysius
Department of the Army, U.S. Army Legal Services Agency, GV
Egan, Michael B. ... Media, PA
West Chester, PA
Egan, Michael E. ... Hendersonville, NC
Egan, Michael J. ... Los Angeles, CA
Egan, Michael J. ... Atlanta, GA
Egan, Michael J., III ... Atlanta, GA
Egan, Michael T. ... Las Vegas, NV
Reno, NV
Egan, Michelle A. ... Minneapolis, MN
Egan, Mike F. ... West Palm Beach, FL
Egan, Nancy E. ... Mountain View, CA
Egan, Nancy Jean ... Baltimore, MD
Egan, Patricia S. ... Ramsey, NJ
Egan, Patrick J. ... Philadelphia, PA
Egan, Patrick L. ... Boston, MA
Egan, Patrick S. ... Rochester, NY
Egan, Patrick T. ... Boston, MA
Egan, Paul E. ... Burbank, CA
Egan, Paul V. ... Babson Park, FL
Egan, Raymond R., III ... Mandeville, LA
Metairie, LA
Egan, Richard D. ... Austin, TX
Egan, Richard J. ... Akron, OH
Egan, Richard T. ... Boston, MA
Egan, Robert A. ... Chicago, IL
Egan, Robert J. ... Orlando, FL
Egan, Robert J. ... New York, NY
Egan, Robert J. ... New York, NY
Egan, Robert R. ... Chicago, IL
Egan, Robert T. ... Haddonfield, NJ
Egan, Russell J. ... Houston, TX
Egan, Sallie ... Englewood, CO
Egan, Sara J. ... San Diego, CA
Egan, Sarabeth ... Lawrenceville, NJ
Egan, Sean N. ... Salt Lake City, UT
Egan, Shane M. ... Dallas, TX
Egan, Shannon O'Connell ... Louisville, KY
Egan, Shirley K. ... Ithaca, NY
Egan, Stephen J. ... Sacramento, CA
Egan, Stephen James ... Denver, CO
Egan, Susan Mary ... New York, NY
Egan, Susan S. ... New York, NY
Egan, Theresa L. ... Albany, NY
Egan, Thomas A. ... Apple Valley, MN
Egan, Thomas A. ... New York, NY
Egan, Thomas C., III ... Norristown, PA
Egan, Thomas F. ... Orlando, FL
Egan, Thomas F. ... Albuquerque, NM

Egan, Thomas F. ....New York, NY
Egan, Thomas F., P.A. ....Orlando, FL
Egan, Thomas J. ....Brooklyn, CT
Egan, Thomas J. ....Washington, DC
Egan, Thomas J. ....Monroe, NY
Egan, Thomas J., Jr. ....Washington, DC
Egan, Thomas M. ....Ocala, FL
Egan, Thomas P. ....Chicago, IL
Egan, Thomas P., Jr. ....Omaha, NE
Egan, Timothy O. ....Boston, MA
Egan, Timothy S. ....Boston, MA
Egan and Trapp ....Chicago, IL
Egan, Wayne Jay ....East Dundee, IL
Rochester, NY
Egan, William A., Jr. ....White Plains, NY
Egan, William H. ....Chalmette, LA
Egan, William J. ....Hartford, CT
Egan, William J. ....New Haven, CT
Egan, William J. ....Edina, MN
Egan, William J. ....New York, NY
Egan, William J., III ....Menlo Park, CA
Egan, William T. ....Minneapolis, MN
Eganhouse, Kristian R. ....Kansas City, MO
Eganhouse, Michael E. ....Cedar Rapids, IA
Egar, James S. ....Woodland, CA
Egar, Valerie L. ....Trenton, NJ
Egawa, Tad T. ....Hermosa Beach, CA
Egbarts, Christine J. ....Kansas City, MO
Egber, Mitchell Alan ....Severna Park, MD
Egbers, Daniel F. ....Frankfort, KY
Egbers, Greg A. ....Davenport, IA
Egbert, James Emerson ....Pennsauken, NJ
Philadelphia, PA
Egbert, James P. F. ....Tucson, AZ
Egbert, John J. ....Phoenix, AZ
Egbert, John S. ....Houston, TX
Egbert, Karen L. ....Department of Justice, Environment and Natural Resources Division, GV
Egbert, Kenneth H., Jr. ....Tiffin, OH
Egbert, L. Sharon ....Dothan, AL
Egbert, Margaret Ann ....Massillon, OH
Egbert, Richard M. ....Boston, MA
Egbert, Walter M., III ....New York, NY
Egbert, William M. ....Westerville, OH
Egbune, Chuck O. ....Denver, CO
Egdorf, Eugene R. ....Houston, TX
Ege, A. Andrew, Jr. ....Virginia Beach, VA
Ege, Karl J. ....Tacoma, WA
Ege, Stephen M. ....Washington, DC
Egea, Ana ....Los Angeles, CA
Egel, David J. ....Stoughton, MA
Egel, Dennis E. ....Cedar Rapids, IA
Egel, Dorothy Bacskai ....Sacramento, CA
Egel, Jack ....Clayton, MO
Egeland, Edgar ....Belton, TX
Egeland, Walter A. ....Two Harbors, MN
Egelanian, Nick A. ....Reston, VA
Egeler, Daniel W. ....Ann Arbor, MI
Egeler, David W. ....Saline, MI
Egelhof, Michael J. ....Larchmont, NY
Egelhoff, Michael D. ....Milwaukee, WI
Egeli, Matthew A. ....Annapolis, MD
Egelko, Robert A. ....San Francisco, CA
Egelston, Rebecca A. ....Dallas, TX
Egenberger, Louis B. ....Omaha, NE
Egendorf, Andrew ....Lincoln, MA
Egenes, Jay C. ....Riverside, CA
San Bernardino, CA
Egenhauser, Barbara ....White Plains, NY
Egenhofer, Alfred J. ....Ridgefield Park, NJ
Egenolf Associates, LLP
Santa Barbara, CA
Egenolf, Robert F. ....Santa Barbara, CA
Eger, Alex B., Jr. ....Sewaren, NJ
Eger, Charles L. ....Libertyville, IL
Eger, Elena Marie ....Oakland, CA
Eger, Harold V. ....Sherman Oaks, CA
Eger, Harvey J. ....Jeannette, PA
Eger, Jeffrey Lawrence, Law Offices of
Pawtucket, RI
Eger, John M. ....La Jolla, CA
Egerer, Timothy E. ....Southfield, MI
Egerman, Gary D. ....White Plains, NY
Egerman, William M. ....Beverly Hills, CA
Egermeier, R. P. ....Canoga Park, CA
Egers, Mitchell W. ....Los Angeles, CA
Egers, Ronald R. ....New York, NY
Egert, Bruce ....Tenafly, NJ
Egert, Eli S. ....Ramsey, NJ
Egert, Howard E. ....Lakewood, OH
Egert, Mark A. ....Chicago, IL
Egert, Schneider, Mayer & Hack
Lakewood, OH
Egerton, Anne H. ....Burbank, CA
Egerton & Brenner ....Greensboro, NC
Egerton, Charles H. ....Orlando, FL
Egerton, Lawrence, Jr. ....Greensboro, NC
Egerton, McAfee, Armistead & Davis, P.C.
Knoxville, TN
Egerton, Stuart L. ....Wilmington, NC
Egertson, Jon K. ....Irvine, CA
Egesdal, Steven M. ....Honolulu, HI
Eget, Margie M. ....Atlanta, GA
Egeth & Wallach ....New York, NY
Egg, Thomas C. ....Short Hills, NJ
Eggan, Andrew M. ....Ann Arbor, MI
Ypsilanti, MI
Eggan, Christine A. ....Normal, IL
Eggan, Eric J. ....Lansing, MI
Eggart, R. Brownlee ....Pensacola, FL
Egge, George V., Jr. ....Washington, DC
Egge, George V., Jr., P.C. ....Washington, DC
Egge, Huis M. Coy, (Mrs.) ....Corsicana, TX
Egge, T. Farrell ....Alexandria, VA
Egge, Trygve A. ....Arden Hills, MN
Eggebraaten, Toni ....Palm Desert, CA
Eggeling, William S. ....Providence, RI

Eggeman, James L. ....Treasury Department, Internal Revenue Service, GV
Eggemeier, Thomas B. ....Columbus, OH
Eggemeyer, Gerald A. ....Littleton, CO
Eggemeyer, Teresa C. ....Santa Barbara, CA
Eggen, Brad C. ....Minneapolis, MN
Eggen, Eric C. ....Pensacola, FL
Eggen, Jean M ....Wilmington, DE
Eggena, Eric Karel ....Downey, CA
Eggenberger, Robert E. ....Detroit, MI
Eggenberger, Tod R. ....St. Paul, MN
Eggenberger, William D. ....Detroit, MI
Eggenschwiler, James E., Jr. ....Columbus, OH
Egger, Amy S. ....New York, NY
Egger Betts Austin, PLLC ....Bellevue, WA
Seattle, WA
Egger, Jan P. ....Rochester, NY
Egger & Leegant ....Rochester, NY
Egger, Mary H. ....Department of Energy, Office of the General Counsel, GV
Egger, Matt E. ....Washington, DC
Egger, Michael R. ....Palo Alto, CA
San Francisco, CA
Egger, Patrick R. ....Fresno, CA
Pleasant Hill, CA
Salinas, CA
San Diego, CA
Egger, Phillip E. ....Bellevue, WA
Egger, Richard T. ....Ontario, CA
Egger, Robert C. ....Sandusky, OH
Egger, Susan W. ....Louisville, KY
Egger & Talmadge ....Fresno, CA
Pleasant Hill, CA
Salinas, CA
San Diego, CA
Egger, William C., Jr. ....San Antonio, TX
Egger, William C., Jr., A Professional Corporation ....San Antonio, TX
Eggers, Arthur N. ....Tampa, FL
Eggers, Arthur R. ....Seattle, WA
Eggers, Arthur W. ....Moline, IL
Eggers & Baldwin ....Franklin, IN
Eggers, David A. ....Atlanta, GA
Eggers, Eggers & Eggers ....Boone, NC
Eggers, George H. ....Silver Spring, MD
Eggers, Harmon R.
General Services Administration, Office of the General Counsel, GV
Eggers, Jeffrey C. ....Franklin, IN
Eggers, Jennifer K. ....Minneapolis, MN
Eggers, Jerome E. ....San Diego, CA
Eggers, Kathleen M. ....Chicago, IL
Eggers, Kenneth P., (P.C.) ....Anchorage, AK
Eggers, Laurel Olson ....Sioux Falls, SD
Eggers, Lisa Strauch ....Seattle, WA
Eggers, Paul W. ....Dallas, TX
Eggers, Rebecca E. ....Boone, NC
Eggers, Robert J. ....Springfield, IL
Eggers, Ronald L. ....Omaha, NE
Eggers, Scott A. ....New York, NY
Eggers, Stacy C., Jr. ....Boone, NC
Eggers, Susan E. ....Chicago, IL
Eggers, William D. ....Corning, NY
Eggers, William J., III ....Crow Agency, MT
Eggers-Gryder, Rebecca ....Boone, NC
Eggert, Charles A., Jr. ....New Haven, CT
Eggert, David S. ....Washington, DC
Eggert, Dean B. ....Manchester, NH
Eggert, Edgar H., Jr. ....Mathis, TX
Eggert, Elizabeth P. ....Boston, MA
Eggert, Erb, Frye and Von AH, P.L.C.
Charles City, IA
Eggert, Francis J. ....Winsted, MN
Eggert, Fred. W. ....East Hampton, NY
Eggert, James S. ....Tampa, FL
Eggert, Joan D. ....Thousand Oaks, CA
Eggert, John C. ....Chicago, IL
Eggert, Kurt ....Orange, CA
Eggert Law Office, P.A. ....Winsted, MN
Eggert, Mark W. ....Mathis, TX
Eggert, Michael D. ....Boston, MA
Eggert, Michael L. ....Altoona, PA
Eggert, Paul H. ....Oakland, CA
Eggert, Robert J. ....Charles City, IA
Eggert, Russell R. ....Chicago, IL
Eggert, Steven L. ....Sacramento, CA
Eggert, Stewart C. ....Tampa, FL
Eggert, Waldemar Edmund ....San Diego, CA
Eggerth, Lucy W. ....San Francisco, CA
Eggerth, Richard A. ....San Francisco, CA
Eggertsen, Arly W. ....Chicago, IL
Eggertsen, John H. ....Detroit, MI
Eggie, Herbert A. ....New Berlin, WI
Eggimann, Steven C. ....Minneapolis, MN
Eggink, Anthony G. ....St. Paul, MN
Eggleson, Shari ....Madison, WI
Eggleston, Alan P. ....Lake Success, NY
Eggleston, B. Purnell ....Roanoke, VA
Eggleston & Briscoe ....Houston, TX
Eggleston & Chambers, L.L.P. ....Dallas, TX
Eggleston, Craig A. ....Dallas, TX
Eggleston, Cynthia R. ....Memphis, TN
Eggleston, Duke ....Durango, CO
Eggleston, Ellen K. ....Denver, CO
Eggleston, Fred, Jr.
United States Postal Service, Law Department, GV
Eggleston, James F. ....Memphis, TN
Eggleston, Janis E. ....San Francisco, CA
Eggleston, Jeffrey S., (P.C.) ....Amarillo, TX
Eggleston, John D. ....Saratoga Springs, NY
Eggleston, Jon R. ....Burlington, VT
Eggleston, Joseph L. ....San Diego, CA
Eggleston, Joseph S. ....Hampton, NH
Eggleston, Mark J. ....Sacramento, CA
Eggleston, Matthew K. ....Memphis, TN
Eggleston, Michael Wilson ....Liberty, MO
Eggleston, Michelle Alcon ....Amarillo, TX

Eggleston, Peter M., P.C. ....Denver, CO
Monte Vista, CO
Eggleston, R. Dale ....Dallas, TX
Eggleston, Robert D. ....Dallas, TX
Eggleston, Sam D., III ....Lovingston, VA
Eggleston, Sam D., Jr. ....Lovingston, VA
Eggleston Smith, P.C. ....Newport News, VA
Eggleston & Sperandio, P.C.
San Francisco, CA
Eggleston, Steven B. ....San Francisco, CA
Eggleston & Thelen, A Professional Corporation ....Lovingston, VA
Eggleston, Thomas J. ....White Cloud, MI
Eggleston, Tracy L. ....Charlotte, NC
Eggleston, W. Neil ....Washington, DC
Eggleston, Warren N. ....New York, NY
Eggleston, William J. ....Houston, TX
Eggleston, W. T., Jr. ....Phoenix, AZ
Eggleton, Keith E. ....Palo Alto, CA
Eggmann, Becky Rowe ....St. Louis, MO
Eggmann, Robert E. ....St. Louis, MO
Eggspuehler, Jay B. ....Columbus, OH
Eggum, Susan K. ....Portland, OR
Eggum, Susan K., P.C. ....Portland, OR
Eghrari, Mark S. ....Smithtown, NY
Eghrari, Mark S., and Associates, PLLC
Smithtown, NY
Egidi, David J. ....New York, NY
Egielski, Robert J. ....Phoenix, AZ
Egielski, Robert J. ....New York, NY
Eginton, Warren W. ....Bridgeport, CT
Egitto, Joseph A. ....Poughkeepsie, NY
Egitton, Amy B. ....Syracuse, NY
Egizii, Mary Jo ....Springfield, IL
Eglash, Howard J. ....La Crosse, WI
Eglash, Jeffrey Craig ....Los Angeles, CA
Eglash, Louis R. ....Los Angeles, CA
Egle, Gilbert R. ....Denver, CO
Egle, James B. ....Madison, WI
Egler, Frederick N. ....Pittsburgh, PA
Egler, Frederick N., Jr. ....Pittsburgh, PA
Egler, Garrett & Egler ....Pittsburgh, PA
Egler, Margaret M.
Federal Communications Commission, Common Carrier Bureau, GV
Egler, Margaret Webb ....San Diego, CA
Egler, Theresa Donahue ....Morristown, NJ
New York, NY
Egler, Thomas E. ....San Diego, CA
Egleston, Drew D. ....Youngstown, OH
Egleston, Gregory M. ....Hartford, CT
Egleston, James D. ....Cleveland, OH
Egleston, Mary K. ....Englewood, CO
Egleston, Russell L. ....Mattydale, NY
Eglet Prince, LLP ....Las Vegas, NV
Eglet, Robert T. ....Las Vegas, NV
Egley, James G. ....Madison, NE
Norfolk, NE
Egli, Carol Hayes ....Corona, CA
Egli, Charles G. ....Appleton, WI
Egli, David T. ....San Pedro, CA
Egli, Steven M. ....Waverly, IA
Eglick, Peter J. ....Seattle, WA
Eglin, Connor B. ....Baton Rouge, LA
Eglin, Eileen B. ....Hawthorne, NY
Eglin, Stephen C. ....Philadelphia, PA
Eglinski, Georgann H. ....Lawrence, KS
Eglinton, Donalt J. ....New Bern, NC
Raleigh, NC
Wilmington, NC
Eglinton, Margaret M. ....Meadville, PA
Eglit, Howard C. ....Chicago, IL
Eglitis, Astrid M. ....Minneapolis, MN
Eglitis-Francis, Inga Anna ....Boykins, VA
Egloff, John L. ....Indianapolis, IN
Egloff, Susan J. ....Buffalo, NY
Eglseder, John M. ....St. Michaels, MD
Egly, Jane H. ....Irvine, CA
Egly, Patricia S. ....Woodland Hills, CA
Egly, Paul ....Laguna Beach, CA
Egmond, Lee Van ....Charleston, WV
Egnal, John D. ....Springfield, MA
Egnatchik, Michael R. ....Stamford, CT
Stamford, CT
Egnatuk, Ivan W. ....Marshall, MI
Egner, Carol A. ....Lexington, MA
Egner, Charles A. ....Rockford, IL
Egner, John B. ....Glenside, PA
Egner, Richard, Jr. ....Gresham, OR
Egner, Sylvia Matthews ....Houston, TX
Egner, Theodore K. ....Fort Lauderdale, FL
Egner, Theodore K., Law Offices of
Fort Lauderdale, FL
Egner, Thomas G. ....Ambler, PA
Egnor, Dan W. ....Huntington, WV
Egnor, Lionel D. ....Huntington, WV
Egnor, Ronald William ....Ypsilanti, MI
Egnor, Susan T. ....Salem, OR
Ego, Marian J. ....Boston, MA
Egol, Allana Yoelson ....New York, NY
Egolf, Barbara A. ....Orlando, FL
Egolf, Christopher ....Gulph Mills, PA
Egorov, Puginsky, Afanasiev & Marks, L.L.C. ....Philadelphia, PA
Egosi, Richard S. ....Sag Harbor, NY
Egoville, Gary R. ....Conshohocken, PA
Egozi, Bernard L. ....Miami, FL
Egr & Birkel, P.C. ....David City, NE
Egr, James M. ....David City, NE
Egre, Jack H. ....Garden City, NY
Egren, Michael R. ....Auburn Hills, MI
Egseth, Andrew O., Jr. ....Honolulu, HI
Eguina De LaRosa, Ivelisse ....Ponce, PR
Egurbide, Jose A. ....Los Angeles, CA
Egusquiza, John E. ....Bradenton, FL
Miami, FL
Egusquiza, Mitchell L. ....Mountain Home, ID
Ehalt, Mary Beth ....Montclair, NJ

Ehard, Andrew S. ....Department of Commerce, Patent and Trademark Office, GV
Ehardt, Gregory J. ....Salt Lake City, UT
Ehas, Joan T. ....Cincinnati, OH
Ehat, Joanna Litvak ....Washington, DC
Ehat, Stephen Kent ....Roseville, CA
Eheman, Kenneth E., Jr. ....Raleigh, NC
Eheman, Michael W. ....Houston, TX
Eherenman, Robert W. ....Fort Wayne, IN
Ehinger, James O. ....Phoenix, AZ
Ehinger, Ronald J. ....Fort Wayne, IN
Ehl, Emily C. ....Boston, MA
Ehle, Gary J. ....Hartford, CT
Ehle, Laurie O. ....St. Paul, MN
Ehle, Thomas L. ....Albany, NY
Ehlenbach, Jeffrey E. ....San Rafael, CA
Ehlenbach, Kenneth J. ....New Berlin, WI
Ehlenbach, Paul J. ....Seattle, WA
Ehlenberger, Carol Lynne ....Reston, VA
Ehlenberger, Mona E. ....Washington, DC
Ehler, Anthony L. ....Columbus, OH
Ehler, Chad S. ....Santa Barbara, CA
Ehler, Edward T. ....Glen Rock, NJ
Ehler, Rebecca Whisner ....Alamogordo, NM
Ehler, Renae Lynn ....Marshall, MO
Ehler, Trisha M. ....Dayton, OH
Ehlers, Alix T. ....Riverhead, NY
Ehlers, Carla J. ....Belleville, IL
Ehlers, D. Todd ....Sturgeon Bay, WI
Ehlers, David R. ....Sarasota, FL
Ehlers, Dawn L. ....Stamford, CT
Ehlers, Denny R. ....Durango, CO
Ehlers, Edward J. ....Baltimore, MD
Ehlers & Ehlers ....Riverhead, NY
Ehlers, Elizabeth R. Bacon ....Chicago, IL
Ehlers, Glenn H. ....Sacramento, CA
Ehlers, Gosch L., III ....Bassett, VA
Ehlers, J. Kenneth ....Baltimore, MD
Ehlers, James G. ....San Diego, CA
Ehlers, Kathleen ....Laguna Niguel, CA
Ehlers, Kevin L. ....Lakewood, CO
Ehlers, Kristin M. ....Richfield, OH
Ehlers, Mark J. ....Philadelphia, PA
Ehlers, Michael G. ....Davenport, IA
Ehlers, Randall B., Law Office of
Bloomington, IL
Ehlers, Richard A. ....Riverhead, NY
Ehlers, Richard E. ....Minneapolis, MN
Ehlers, Robert L. ....Minneapolis, MN
Ehlers, Roger D. ....San Francisco, CA
Ehlers, Stephen E. ....Poughkeepsie, NY
Ehlert & Betts, P.C. ....Brenham, TX
Ehlert, Charles E. ....Seattle, WA
Ehlert, David B. ....Neenah, WI
Ehlert, Elizabeth ....Hillsboro, OR
Ehlert, Paul A. ....Brenham, TX
Ehlert, Richard Todd ....Wichita, KS
Ehlert, Shauna Martin ....Seattle, WA
Ehlert, W. Dirker ....Seattle, WA
Ehlert, William J. ....Brenham, TX
Ehli, Phil C. ....Kansas City, MO
Ehlies, William H., II ....Greenville, SC
Ehlies, William H., P.A. ....Greenville, SC
Ehling, Dennis M. P. ....Los Angeles, CA
Ehling, Ernest H., Jr. ....Blue Bell, PA
Ehling, Michael J. ....Media, PA
Ehling, Robert D. ....Santa Monica, CA
Ehlinger, John J., Jr. ....Philadelphia, PA
Ehlinger, Jon D. ....Phoenix, AZ
Ehlinger & Krill, S.C. ....Milwaukee, WI
Ehlinger, Ralph J. ....Milwaukee, WI
Ehlinger, Ross H. ....Austin, TX
Ehlinger, Timothy J. ....Winston-Salem, NC
Ehlis, Kirk A. ....Yakima, WA
Ehlke, Douglas B. M., Law Offices of
Federal Way, WA
Ehlke, Richard C. ....Library of Congress, Congressional Research Service, GV
Ehlke, Stephen E. ....Madison, WI
Ehlman, Paul M. ....Mount Prospect, IL
Ehlmann, Patrick K. ....Lansing, MI
Ehlmann, Steven E. ....St. Charles, MO
Ehman, Dale A. ....Buffalo, NY
Ehmann, Anthony V. ....Phoenix, AZ
Ehmann, Carl G. ....Lake Arrowhead, CA
Ehmann, Frederick H. ....Philadelphia, PA
Ehmann & Hiller, P.C. ....Phoenix, AZ
Ehmann, John ....Cherry Hill, NJ
Philadelphia, PA
Ehmann, Richard S. ....Pittsburgh, PA
Ehmann, Robert L. ....Phoenix, AZ
Ehmann, Robert Norman ....Pendleton, OR
Ehmann, Van Denbergh & Trainor, A Professional Corporation
Philadelphia, PA
Ehmcke, Lance D. ....Sioux City, IA
Ehmke, Andrew S. ....Dallas, TX
Ehmke, John E. ....Shelby Township, MI
Ehmling, M. Allen ....Gallatin, TN
Ehn, Warren R. ....Arlington, TX
Ehney, Charlotte L. K. ....Greenwood, SC
Ehr Law Office, S.C. ....Milwaukee, WI
Ehr, Raoul R. ....Milwaukee, WI
Ehr, Thomas G. ....Department of Commerce, Office of the General Counsel, GV
Ehr, Thomas P. ....Milwaukee, WI
Ehrbar, Christian M. ....Boston, MA
Ehren, Charles A., Jr. ....East Hampton, NY
Ehrenbard, Robert ....New York, NY
Ehrenberg, Alan I. ....Chicago, IL
Ehrenberg, Betsy L. ....Boston, MA
Ehrenberg, Daniel S. ....Vienna, VA
Ehrenberg, Dawn E. ....Chicago, IL
Ehrenberg & Frost, P.C. ....Chicago, IL
Ehrenberg, Howard M. ....Los Angeles, CA
Ehrenberg, Judy L. Peterson ....San Diego, CA
Ehrenberg, Lance ....New York, NY
Ehrenberg, Mitchell ....Cleveland, OH

Ehrenberg, Peter H. ... **Roseland, NJ**
Ehrenberg, Robert J. ... **St. Joseph, MI**
Ehrenberg, Robin J. ... Treasury Department, Internal Revenue Service, GV
Ehrenberg, Suzanne ... Chicago, IL
Ehrenclou, Alfred M. ... North Palm Beach, FL
Ehrenclou, John O. ... Columbia, SC
Ehrenfreund, Norbert ... San Diego, CA
Ehrenhaft, Peter D. ... **Washington, DC**
Ehrenkranz & Ehrenkranz LLP **New York, NY**
Ehrenkranz, Gil ... Bethesda, MD
Ehrenkranz, Gilbert, (A Professional Corporation) ... Bloomfield, NJ
Ehrenkranz, Ilyse Braun ... Manhasset, NY
Ehrenkranz, Joel S. ... **New York, NY**
Ehrenkranz, Pamela ... **New York, NY**
Ehrenkranz, Sanford B. ... **New York, NY**
Ehrenpreis, Charles L. ... Denver, CO
Ehrenpreis, Ralph ... **Los Angeles, CA**
Ehrenpreis, Ralph, A Professional Law Corporation ... **Los Angeles, CA**
Ehrenreich, Arthur D. ... **Phoenix, AZ**
Ehrenreich & Associates ... Cleveland, OH
Ehrenreich Eilenberg & Krause LLP **New York, NY**
Ehrenreich Eilenberg Krause & Zivian LLP Chicago, IL
Ehrenreich, Eric J. ... San Francisco, CA
Ehrenreich, Joseph ... **Chicago, IL** **New York, NY**
Ehrenreich, Leonard ... Cleveland, OH
Ehrenreich, Linda G. ... Pittsburgh, PA
Ehrenreich, Mona Halprin ... Los Angeles, CA
Ehrenreich, Nancy S. ... Denver, CO
Ehrenreich, Richard F. ... Northfield, IL
Ehrenreich, Robert ... **Los Angeles, CA**
Ehrenreich, Todd R. ... **Miami, FL**
Ehrenstamm, Faye S. Department of Justice, Criminal Division, GV
Ehrenstein, Michael D. ... **Miami, FL**
Ehrentreu, Harold J. ... Bedford Hills, NY
Ehrenwerth, David H. ... **Pittsburgh, PA**
Ehrenworth, Cheryl A. ... Hauppauge, NY
Ehrenworth, Douglas J. ... Florham Park, NJ
Ehrenworth, Robert B. ... Los Angeles, CA
Ehresman, Colleen E. ... Harrisburg, PA
Ehresman, Kurt L. ... **Harrisburg, PA**
Ehresman, May S. ... Indianapolis, IN
Ehresman, Walter W. ... Austin, TX
Ehret, Chester E., Jr. ... Austin, TX
Ehret, John B. ... **Chicago, IL**
Ehret, Leslie Weill ... New Orleans, LA
Ehret, Richard Biddle ... **New Orleans, LA**
Ehret Greenfield, Julie ... Sioux Falls, SD
Ehrgood, Daniel G. ... Lebanon, PA
Ehrgood & Enck ... Lebanon, PA
Ehrgood, Horace M. ... Lebanon, PA
Ehrgood, Thomas A. ... Lebanon, PA
Ehrgood, Thomas A., Jr. ... **Washington, DC**
Ehrgott, Catherine A. ... **Los Angeles, CA**
Ehrhard, Lawrence R. ... Springfield, MA
Ehrhardt, Charles L., III ... Houston, TX
Ehrhardt, Charles W. ... Tallahassee, FL
Ehrhardt, Glen R. ... **Columbia, MO**
Ehrhardt, Herbert C. ... **Jackson, MS**
Ehrhardt, James T. ... Melville, NY
Ehrhardt, L. J. ... Elkader, IA
Ehrhardt, Peter R. ... Soldotna, AK
Ehrhardt, Thomas H. ... Haddonfield, NJ
Ehrhardt, Thomas S. ... **Crown Point, IN**
Ehrhart, Amy E. W. ... York, PA
Ehrhart, Diane Karp ... **Chicago, IL**
Ehrhart, John H. ... **Cedar Rapids, IA**
Ehrhart, Kevin M. ... **Los Angeles, CA**
Ehrhart, Richard D. ... Charlotte, NC
Ehrhorn, Robert M., Jr. ... **Honolulu, HI**
Ehrich, Delmar R. ... **Minneapolis, MN**
Ehrich, Lisa ... **Norfolk, VA** **Virginia Beach, VA**
Ehrich, Manfred W., Jr. ... Bennington, VT
Ehrich, Neal B. ... Kingsley, IA
Ehrich, Sandra K. Inkster **South Sioux City, NE**
Ehrick, Richard V. ... **Rochester, MN**
Ehrig, James G. ... **Washington, DC**
Ehrig, Kristen A. ... **Los Angeles, CA**
Ehrig, Lenore G. ... Washington, DC
Ehrig, Robert W. ... St. Louis, MO
Ehrig, Robert W., P.C. ... St. Louis, MO
Ehring, Howard A. ... Stamford, CT
Ehringhaus, Susan H. ... Chapel Hill, NC
Ehrke, William W. ... **Milwaukee, WI**
Ehrle, Frank L. ... Dallas, TX
Ehrle, William L. ... Austin, TX
Ehrler, Robert J. ... Louisville, KY
Ehrlich, A. Joshua ... Bronx, NY
Ehrlich, Abraham ... Encino, CA
Ehrlich, Alan ... **Newark, NJ**
Ehrlich, Alan Gordon ... Plantation, FL
Ehrlich, Alan M. Environmental Protection Agency, Office of the General Counsel, GV
Ehrlich, Albert ... Westbury, NY
Ehrlich, Alvin ... Bethesda, MD
Ehrlich, Anat ... Los Angeles, CA
Ehrlich, Andrew L. ... Washington, DC
Ehrlich, Arthur R. ... Chicago, IL
Ehrlich and Baird, LLP ... Troy, NY
Ehrlich, Barbara J. ... Los Angeles, CA
Ehrlich, Bernard G. ... New York, NY
Ehrlich, Burton S. ... Chicago, IL
Ehrlich, Charles G. ... **Manchester, NH**
Ehrlich, Charles W. ... **St. Petersburg, FL**
Ehrlich, Dana A. ... **San Angelo, TX**
Ehrlich, David ... Chicago, IL
Ehrlich, David W. ... **New York, NY**
Ehrlich, Devri Anne ... Parsippany, NJ
Ehrlich, Edward B. ... New York, NY
Ehrlich and Ehrlich ... Reading, PA
Ehrlich, Elizabeth G. ... Reading, PA
Ehrlich, Emlen Hall ... San Francisco, CA
Ehrlich, Francia E. ... Bradley Beach, NJ
Ehrlich, Frank ... Kansas City, MO
Ehrlich, Frazer & Feldman **Garden City, NY** **Mineola, NY** **Riverhead, NY**
Ehrlich, Fred ... New York, NY
Ehrlich, Fred, P.C. ... New York, NY
Ehrlich, Gary A. ... Trenton, NJ
Ehrlich, Gayle P. ... **Boston, MA**
Ehrlich, Gerald F. ... **Phoenix, AZ**
Ehrlich, Gerd W. ... Baltimore, MD
Ehrlich & Gordon ... Rockville, MD
Ehrlich, Henry L. ... **Houston, TX**
Ehrlich, Henry L. ... Fairfax, VA
Ehrlich, Herbert, (P.C.) ... El Paso, TX
Ehrlich, Howard J. ... **West Orange, NJ**
Ehrlich, Howard S. ... Pompano Beach, FL
Ehrlich, Hyman ... Forest Hills, NY
Ehrlich, Isaac ... Sacramento, CA
Ehrlich, Jack ... **Chicago, IL**
Ehrlich, James ... Lincoln City, OR
Ehrlich, Jeffrey ... **Fort Lauderdale, FL**
Ehrlich, Jeffrey I. ... **Claremont, CA**
Ehrlich, Jeffrey, P.A. ... **Fort Lauderdale, FL**
Ehrlich, Jeffrey Paul ... Washington, DC
Ehrlich, Jerome H. ... **Garden City, NY**
Ehrlich, Jerome L. ... Los Angeles, CA
Ehrlich, Jerrold I. ... **New York, NY**
Ehrlich, John G. ... Little River, SC
Ehrlich, John H. ... Chicago, IL
Ehrlich, Jonathan A. ... **New York, NY**
Ehrlich, Joseph ... **San Francisco, CA**
Ehrlich, Joseph ... **New York, NY**
Ehrlich, Joseph H. ... **Birmingham, MI**
Ehrlich, Joseph L. ... **New York, NY**
Ehrlich, Julian David ... **New York, NY**
Ehrlich, Julie O. ... **Chicago, IL**
Ehrlich, Karen Lynn ... **Bethesda, MD**
Ehrlich, Kenneth A. ... **Los Angeles, CA**
Ehrlich, Kenneth F. ... **Boston, MA**
Ehrlich, Larry D. ... **Wichita, KS**
Ehrlich, Lawrence D. ... **Chicago, IL**
Ehrlich, Leon ... Reading, PA
Ehrlich, Linda J. ... Boca Raton, FL
Ehrlich, Lori ... New York, NY
Ehrlich, Louis H., Jr. ... Kansas City, MO
Ehrlich, M. Gordon ... **Boston, MA**
Ehrlich, Marc Alan ... Poughkeepsie, NY
Ehrlich, Marc S. ... Troy, NY
Ehrlich, Maria T. ... **New York, NY**
Ehrlich, Mark H. ... **Chicago, IL**
Ehrlich, Marvin W. ... Washington, DC
Ehrlich, Melvin L. ... **Bakersfield, CA**
Ehrlich, Michael F. ... Los Angeles, CA
Ehrlich, Miles F. ... Department of Justice, Criminal Division, GV
Ehrlich, Mitchell ... **Perryton, TX**
Ehrlich, Morris ... New York, NY
Ehrlich, Nathaniel E.P. ... **Philadelphia, PA** Reading, PA
Ehrlich, Paul ... Portland, OR
Ehrlich, Paul R. ... **Beaverton, OR**
Ehrlich, Paul S. ... Mineola, NY
Ehrlich, Peter N. ... Denver, CO
Ehrlich, Peter N., P.C. ... Denver, CO
Ehrlich, Philip H. ... **New York, NY**
Ehrlich, Philip S., Jr. Belvedere-Tiburon, CA
Ehrlich, Rachel ... New York, NY
Ehrlich, Randie L. ... **Princeton, NJ**
Ehrlich, Raymond ... **Jacksonville, FL**
Ehrlich, Renee D. ... Kansas City, MO
Ehrlich, Richard ... **New York, NY**
Ehrlich, Richard D. ... Burlington, NJ
Ehrlich, Richard E. ... Coral Springs, FL
Ehrlich, Richard S. ... Rockville, MD
Ehrlich, Robert E. ... New York, NY
Ehrlich & Samis ... **St. Petersburg, FL**
Ehrlich, Scott Brian ... San Diego, CA
Ehrlich, Scott R. ... **Washington, DC** **New York, NY**
Ehrlich, Sherri Mae ... Brooklyn, NY
Ehrlich, Sherwyn L. ... Chicago, IL
Ehrlich, Shirley A. ... San Antonio, TX
Ehrlich, Stacy L. ... **Washington, DC**
Ehrlich, Stephen P. ... Denver, CO
Ehrlich, Stephen R. ... Denver, CO
Ehrlich, Steven A. ... Newport Beach, CA
Ehrlich, Steven E. ... **Chicago, IL**
Ehrlich, Susan A. ... Phoenix, AZ
Ehrlich, Susan C. ... Santa Barbara, CA
Ehrlich, Terry Lynne ... **Littleton, CO**
Ehrlich, Thomas J. ... San Jose, CA
Ehrlich, Tricia Specter ... Holbrook, NY
Ehrlich, Wendy I. ... Tucson, AZ
Ehrlich, William A. ... **Allentown, PA**
Ehrlicher, Matthew A. ... New Orleans, LA
Ehrlicher, Rhonda F. ... **Metairie, LA** **New Orleans, LA**
Ehrlichman, Jeffrey ... Southfield, MI
Ehrlichman, Peter S. ... **Seattle, WA**
Ehrlichman, Thomas J. ... Seattle, WA
Ehrlich-Price, Merrilee ... Fort Lauderdale, FL
Ehrlich-White, Joan F. ... New York, NY
Ehrlinger, David B. ... **Troy, MI**
Ehrlinspiel, Jason S. ... **Jackson, MS**
Ehrlinspiel, Kathryn Thomas ... Richmond, VA
Ehrman, Christopher C. ... Washington, DC
Ehrman, Debra ... Salem, OR
Ehrman, James S. ... **Pittsburgh, PA**
Ehrman, James W. ... **Youngstown, OH**
Ehrman, Joseph S. ... **Chicago, IL**
Ehrman, Kathryn Murray ... **San Jose, CA**
Ehrman, Keith A. ... **San Francisco, CA**
Ehrman, Kurt G. Department Of Veterans Affairs, Board of Veterans Appeals, GV
Ehrman, Mark L. ... Newton, MA
Ehrman, Richard L. ... **Palo Alto, CA**
Ehrman, Rita I. ... **Denver, CO**
Ehrman, Ronald P. ... Sherman Oaks, CA
Ehrmann, Calder D., III ... **Atlanta, GA**
Ehrmann, Frances ... **Los Angeles, CA**
Ehrmann Gehlbach Beckman Badger & Lee **Dixon, IL**
Ehrmann, Herbert Z. ... Beverly Hills, CA
Ehrmann, Mark T. ... **Milwaukee, WI**
Ehrmann, Rolfe F. ... **Dixon, IL**
Ehrmann, Sanford M. ... Beverly Hills, CA
Ehrmann, Thomas W. ... **Milwaukee, WI**
Ehrmantraut, Jennifer ... Waukegan, IL
Ehrmantraut, William A. ... **Annapolis, MD** **Baltimore, MD**
Ehrnfelt, Walter F., III ... Cleveland, OH
Ehrnst, Norman H. ... Turner, MI
Ehrnstein, Lyn B. ... Englewood, CO
Ehrsam, Frederick F., Jr. ... Bridgeport, CT
Ehrsam, Michael E. ... **La Crosse, WI**
Ehrsam-Holland, Anne E. Department of the Army, Office of the Secretary, GV
Ehrstine, William H. ... **Dayton, OH**
Ehudin, Barbara Kreinik ... **New York, NY**
Ehudin, Stephen M. ... Towson, MD
Eia, Cheryl L. ... **Fargo, ND**
Eib, Christopher D. ... Richmond, VA
Eibel, Andrew H. ... Brooklyn, NY
Eiben, Gary ... **Erie, PA**
Eiben, Lawrence A. ... **Chicago, IL**
Eiber, Bernard M. ... Great Neck, NY
Eiber, Bruce ... Fresh Meadows, NY
Eiber, Geraldine T. ... Brooklyn, NY
Eiber, Keven Drummond ... **Cleveland, OH**
Eiberger, Carl F. ... Denver, CO
Eiberson, Arthur M. ... Hempstead, NY
Eiberson, M. Arthur ... Mineola, NY
Eibert, Mark Donald ... Burlingame, CA
Eibl, Carlton J. ... San Diego, CA
Eich, Edwin W., Jr. ... **Chicago, IL** Waukegan, IL
Eich, Jeffrey W. ... **Chicago, IL**
Eich Law Firm, P.C. ... Carroll, IA
Eich, Ronald F. ... Carroll, IA
Eich, William F. ... Madison, WI
Eichbauer, Paul R. ... Highland Park, MI
Eichbaum, June A. ... **New York, NY**
Eichbaum, William M., Jr. Glen Echo Heights, MD
Eichberg, Ross E. ... **Washington, DC**
Eichberger, Joseph M. ... **Chicago, IL**
Eiche & Frakes, S.C. ... Milwaukee, WI
Eiche, Stuart B. ... Milwaukee, WI
Eichel, Charles R. ... **Manchester, VT**
Eichel, Charles R., P.C., Law Offices of **Manchester, VT**
Eichel, Daniel G. ... Hamilton, OH
Eichel & Krone Co., L.P.A. **Cincinnati, OH**
Eichel, Roger M. ... New York, NY
Eichel, Steven B. ... **New York, NY**
Eichel, Steven P. ... **Boston, MA**
Eichel, Steven R. ... **New York, NY**
Eichelbaum, Dennis J. ... **Austin, TX** Plano, TX
Eichelbaum, Melvin N. ... San Antonio, TX
Eichelbaum, Robert F. ... San Antonio, TX
Eichelberg, Martha Jean **Deerfield Beach, FL**
Eichelberger, Dean A. ... Columbia, SC
Eichelberger, Glen T. ... **Houston, TX**
Eichelberger, Jack W. ... Dayton, OH
Eichelberger, James A. ... **Atlanta, GA**
Eichelberger, John R. ... **Muscatine, IA**
Eichelberger, Karl Joseph ... **Atlanta, GA**
Eichelberger Law Firm, The ... **Atlanta, GA**
Eichelberger, R.A. ... Baytown, TX
Eichelberger, Stephen ... Salem, OR
Eichelberger, Theodore B. ... **Atlanta, GA**
Eichelburg, Robert J. ... **Washington, DC**
Eichelhardt, Brian G. ... Fort Lauderdale, FL
Eichelman, Greg W. ... Morristown, TN
Eichelmann, Norman F. ... Millbrae, CA
Eichelzer, Philip Kent, III ... **Atlanta, GA**
Eichen, Barry R. ... Edison, NJ
Eichen, George P. ... New York, NY
Eichen, Jeffrey L. ... Doylestown, PA
Eichen, Jeffrey L., P.C., Law Offices of Doylestown, PA
Eichen, Kuhn & Cahn, PC ... Edison, NJ
Eichen, Linda Ann ... Bronx, NY
Eichen, Naomi G. ... Hackensack, NJ
Eichen, Patrice M. ... Fort Lauderdale, FL
Eichen, Richard L. ... Portland, OR
Eichen, Robin E. ... New York, NY
Eichenauer, Sharon ... Cruz Bay, St. John, VI
Eichenbaum, Bernard L. ... Leesburg, FL
Eichenbaum, Heather M. **Philadelphia, PA**
Eichenbaum, Howard J. ... **Trenton, NJ**
Eichenbaum, Kantrowitz, Leff & Gulko, L.L.C. ... **Englewood Cliffs, NJ** **Jersey City, NJ**
Eichenbaum, Liles & Heister, P.A. **Little Rock, AR**
Eichenbaum, Richard E. ... **San Jose, CA**
Eichenbaum, Richard S. **Englewood Cliffs, NJ**
Eichenberg, Gena Rae ... Eureka, CA
Eichenberg, Tim R. ... Agoura Hills, CA
Eichenberg, Timothy K. ... Washington, DC
Eichenberger, Jerry A. ... **Columbus, OH**
Eichenberger, John C. ... **Washington, DC**
Eichenberger, Richard B. ... Denver, CO
Eichenberger, Robert H. ... **New Albany, IN**
Eichenblatt, Steven S. ... **Winter Park, FL**
Eichenholtz, Leonard Lester ... Lynbrook, NY
Eichenholz, Leon M. ... Louisville, KY
Eichenlaub, Janet M. ... McLean, VA
Eichenwald, Carl J. Environmental Protection Agency, Office of the General Counsel, GV
Eichenwald, Jill A. ... Duluth, MN
Eichenwald, Rachelle ... Overland Park, KS
Eicher, Benjamin J. ... **Rapid City, SD**
Eicher, Donald E., III ... **Jackson, MS**
Eicher, James S. ... Albuquerque, NM
Eicher, Jeffrey D. ... Pittsburgh, PA
Eicher, Lana Grace ... **Jacksonville, FL**
Eicher, Robert E. ... **Richmond, VA**
Eicher, Sandra Marie ... Coshocton, OH
Eicher, Thomas E. ... Iowa City, IA
Eicher, Thomas J. ... Philadelphia, PA
Eichert, Robert P. ... North Brunswick, NJ
Eichfeld, Richard A. ... Brookfield, WI
Eichhold, Paul R., Sr. ... Fairfield, OH
Eichholtz, Steven R. ... Indianapolis, IN
Eichholz, Benjamin Sheftall **Savannah, GA**
Eichholz, Benjamin Sheftall, P.C., The Law Office of ... **Savannah, GA**
Eichholz, James J. ... **Gastonia, NC**
Eichhorn, Charles L. ... Powhatan, VA
Eichhorn, Daniel S. ... **Hackensack, NJ**
Eichhorn, Donald P. ... San Francisco, CA
Eichhorn & Eichhorn ... **Chicago, IL** **Hammond, IN**
Eichhorn, Frederick F., Jr. ... **Hammond, IN**
Eichhorn, George A., III ... Baltimore, MD
Eichhorn, George S. ... **Stratford, IA**
Eichhorn, John C. ... West Des Moines, IA
Eichhorn, Joseph R. ... Oakland, CA
Eichhorn Law Office ... **Stratford, IA**
Eichhorn, R. Scott ... **Springfield, NJ**
Eichhorn, William H. ... **Hammond, IN**
Eichhorn-Hicks & Associates ... **Edina, MN**
Eichhorn-Hicks, Mary H. ... **Edina, MN**
Eichhorn-Hicks, Tracy R. ... **Edina, MN**
Eichhorst, John E. ... **San Francisco, CA**
Eichhorst, Thomas E. ... St. Louis, MO
Eichin, Earl S., Jr. ... **New Orleans, LA**
Eichinger, Charles G. ... Islandia, NY
Eichinger, Charles G., P.C. ... Islandia, NY
Eichinger, David C. ... Downey, CA
Eichinger, Katja M. ... Tulsa, OK
Eichleay, John W., Jr. ... **Pittsburgh, PA**
Eichler, A. Albert ... Chatham, NJ
Eichler, Burton L. ... **Roseland, NJ**
Eichler, Frank M. ... **Englewood, CO**
Eichler, Gregg Alastair ... Glendale, CA
Eichler, Henry J. ... Davie, FL
Eichler, John A. ... Richmond, VA
Eichler, John F., & Assocs. ... Chicago, IL
Eichler, John W. ... Raleigh, NC
Eichler, Jon P. ... Norfolk, VA
Eichler, Lawrence S. ... West Orange, NJ
Eichler, Lawrence S., P.C. ... West Orange, NJ
Eichler, Mark ... **New York, NY**
Eichler, Peter M. ... **Los Angeles, CA**
Eichler, Peter P. ... Rochester, NY
Eichler, Sol A. ... Verona, NJ
Eichler, Steven H. ... **Philadelphia, PA**
Eichlersmith, Jann M. ... **Minneapolis, MN**
Eichling, William H. ... Metuchen, NJ
Eichling, William H., P.A. ... Metuchen, NJ
Eichman, Carmen Cristini ... Middletown, PA
Eichman, John A., (IV) ... Philadelphia, PA
Eichman, John C. ... **Dallas, TX**
Eichman, Rita M. ... Philadelphia, PA
Eichman, Thomas E. ... Springfield, PA
Eichman, William R., II ... **Lubbock, TX**
Eichmann, Erwin P. ... **New York, NY**
Eichmann, John J. ... Westmont, NJ
Eichmeier, Roger W. ... Geneva, IL
Eichna, Michael J. ... Jamaica, NY
Eichner, Adam H. ... Ann Arbor, MI
Eichner, Andrew D. ... **Chicago, IL** **Lake Forest, IL**
Eichner, Claire Seltz ... Chicago, IL **Cincinnati, OH**
Eichner, Deborah J. ... **Dallas, TX**
Eichner, Gregg B. ... **Oklahoma City, OK**
Eichner, James ... Department of Justice, Environment and Natural Resources Division, GV
Eichner, James A. ... Petersburg, VA
Eichner, Jeffrey M. ... Hallandale Beach, FL
Eichner, Jeffrey P. ... Rochester, NY
Eichner, Jill Martin Department of Education, Office of the General Counsel, GV
Eichner, John C. ... Hartford, CT
Eichner, Kenneth F. ... Upper Marlboro, MD
Eichner, Paula Diane ... **Boston, MA**
Eichner, Richard A. ... **Washington, DC**
Eichner, Roland F. ... **Dayton, OH**
Eichner, Stanley J. ... Boston, MA
Eichner, Stewart E. ... **New York, NY**
Eichor, Rick J. ... **Honolulu, HI**
Eichorn, John Carl ... Mountaintop, PA
Eichorn, John F. ... Rockingham, NC
Eichorn, Julie A. ... Austin, TX
Eichorn, L. Mark ... Federal Trade Commission, Bureau of Consumer Protection, GV
Eichorst, Shawn M. ... Milwaukee, WI
Eichstadt, Craig M. ... Pierre, SD
Eichstadt, John R. ... Houston, TX
Eichstadt, Kent E. ... Englewood, CO
Eichstaedt, Richard K. ... Lapwai, ID

Eichten, David R. .... **Irvine, CA**
San Diego, CA
Eick, Charles F. .... Los Angeles, CA
Eick, Heidi K. .... **Los Angeles, CA**
Eick, Tina M. .... **Des Moines, IA**
Eick, William E. .... La Crescenta, CA
Eickelberg & Fewel .... Corvallis, OR
Eickelberg, Henry C. .... **Falls Church, VA**
Eickelberg, James .... Corvallis, OR
Eickelberger, Scott D. .... **Zanesville, OH**
Eickemeyer, John H. .... **New York, NY**
Eickemeyer, Rachel K. .... Northville, MI
Eicken, Darren M.
United States Tax Court, GV
Eickenroht, Marvin B. .... **Houston, TX**
Houston, TX
Eickhoff, Richard P. .... Springfield, IL
Eickholt, William C. .... Toledo, OH
Eickhorst, Anson G. .... St. Louis, MO
Eickman, Tad D. .... Wilber, NE
Eickmeyer, Eric K. .... **St. Louis, MO**
Eickmeyer, Evan .... **Sacramento, CA**
Eicksteadt, Richard W. .... **Marengo, IL**
Eid, Gordon L. .... **Minneapolis, MN**
Eid, John Francis .... Annapolis, MD
Eidahl, Douglas D. .... Pierre, SD
Eidam, Bradford S. .... Boise, ID
Eide, Allen J. .... Pierre, SD
Eide, Allen J., P.C. .... Pierre, SD
Eide, Bert M. .... St. Louis, MO
Eide, D. Mark .... Federal Way, WA
Eide, David A. .... **Chicago, IL**
Eide, David B. .... **Minneapolis, MN**
Eide, Eric J. .... **Fort Dodge, IA**
Eide, Eric R. .... **Orlando, FL**
Eide, Kevin W. .... **Eagan, MN**
Eide, Larry S. .... **Mason City, IA**
Eide & Miller .... Anchorage, AK
Eide, Peter J. .... Washington, DC
Eide, Phillip J. .... Anchorage, AK
Eide, Randolph S. .... Cleveland, OH
Eide, Ronald J. .... Clearwater, FL
Eide, Stephen R. .... **Minneapolis, MN**
Eide, Vogel & Peacock .... Federal Way, WA
Eidel, Michael Lee .... **Los Angeles, CA**
Eidelberg, David L. .... **Columbus, OH**
Eidelberg, Ilana S. .... Columbus, OH
Eidelberg, Lee J. .... Baltimore, MD
Eidelberg, Lisa Dopkin .... Baltimore, MD
Eidelhoch, Arthur M. .... **San Francisco, CA**
Eidelman, Edward R. .... Allentown, PA
Eidelman & Eidelman, P.C. .... Allentown, PA
Eidelman, Gary B. .... **Baltimore, MD**
Eidelman, Mary J. B. .... Allentown, PA
Eidelman, Michael M. .... **Chicago, IL**
Eidelman, Rachel Reby .... St. Louis, MO
Eidelstein, Gary P. .... Miami, FL
Eidemueller, John G., Jr. .... Pittsburgh, PA
Eiden, Carol Ann .... **Minneapolis, MN**
Eiden, Eckert & O'Donnell, Ltd.
Chicago, IL
Vernon Hills, IL
Eiden, Kristine L. .... Woodbury, MN
Eiden, Mark C. .... Chicago, IL
Vernon Hills, IL
Eiden, Max A. .... **Boise, ID**
Eiden, Melvin A. .... **Lafayette, LA**
Eiden, Raymond A. .... Waukegan, IL
Eiden, Robert A. .... **Chicago, IL**
Eiden, Thomas W. .... Raleigh, NC
Eiden, Timothy J. .... **St. Paul, MN**
Eiden, Vincent J. .... Crestwood, KY
Eidenberg, Judith N. .... New York, NY
Eidens & Dickson .... Schenectady, NY
Eidens, Michael C. .... Schenectady, NY
Eidler, Alan D. .... New York, NY
Eidler, Bernard M. .... Brooklyn, NY
Eidler, Daniel .... Rockville Centre, NY
Eidler, Harold .... Brooklyn, NY
Eidlin, Michael B. .... Portland, OR
Eidman & Fox, L.L.P. .... Houston, TX
Eidman, Jack E., Jr. .... Houston, TX
Eidman, K. Greg, Jr. .... Houston, TX
Eidman, Mark W. .... **Austin, TX**
Eidman, Michael K. .... New York, NY
Eidman, Seymour H. .... New York, NY
Eidmann, Maryann .... Wilmette, IL
Eidnier, Robert J. .... **Cleveland, OH**
Eidsmoe, Daniel C. .... Bloomington, IL
Eidsmoe, John .... Montgomery, AL
Eidsmoe, Robert R. .... **Sioux City, IA**
Eidsness, Alan C. .... **Minneapolis, MN**
Eidsness, Paul T. .... **Minneapolis, MN**
Eidson & Associates, P.C. .... **Atlanta, GA**
Eidson, Brad .... Houston, MO
Eidson, Derian D. .... Yorba Linda, CA
Eidson, Frank M. .... **Orlando, FL**
Eidson, Frank M., P.A. .... **Orlando, FL**
Eidson, Gary C. .... **Minneapolis, MN**
Eidson, George T., Jr. .... Orlando, FL
Eidson, James A. .... **Atlanta, GA**
Eidson, James M. .... Abilene, TX
Eidson, Mike .... **Miami, FL**
Eidson, Patrick S. .... **Albany, GA**
Eidson, Richard L. .... Canyon Country, CA
Eidson, Sandra N. .... **Houston, TX**
Eidson, Timothy Lee .... Adel, GA
Eidson, Walter J., Jr. .... **Washington, DC**
Ashburn, VA
Eidt, Gerald A. .... Howell, MI
Eidt, Thomas D. .... Washington, DC
Eidt-hyat, Adrienne V.
Securities and Exchange Commission,
Division of Enforcement, GV
Eidukas, Theodore T. .... **Chicago, IL**
Eielson, Rodney S. .... Bridgeport, CT
Eiesland, Gregory A. .... **Rapid City, SD**
Eiesland, Kenneth R. .... Vancouver, WA

Eiferman, Jack A. .... **Boston, MA**
Eifert, Cheryl Ann .... Charleston, WV
Eiffert, James L. .... Ozark, MO
Eifler, Robin G. .... Orange, CA
Eifler, Timothy J. .... **Louisville, KY**
Eifort, Joseph D. .... Chapel Hill, NC
Eifrid, S. Michael .... Chicago, IL
Eig, Larry M. .... Library of Congress,
Congressional Research Service, GV
Eig and Schwartz, Chartered
Washington, DC
Bethesda, MD
Eig, Wayne D. .... **Bethesda, MD**
Eigen, Walter B. .... Sunrise, FL
Eigenbrodt, Stanton P. .... **Dallas, TX**
Eigenhauser, George J., Jr. .... San Diego, CA
Eiger, Leonard L. .... Scarsdale, NY
Eiger, Marley F., (Miss) .... Painesville, OH
Eiger, Rhonda J. .... Moorestown, NJ
Eiger, Victoria B. .... New York, NY
Eigerman, Daniel A. .... New York, NY
Eigerman, Jared J. .... San Francisco, CA
Eigerman, Joel Z. .... **Boston, MA**
Eighan, Margaret T. .... Philadelphia, PA
Eighmey, George V. .... Portland, OR
Eighmie, James W., Jr. .... Department of State,
Foreign Service Officers (Overseas), GV
Eiglarsh, Mark R. .... **Miami, FL**
Eigles, Henry .... Baltimore, MD
Eigles, William P. .... Denver, CO
Eigner, Richard M. .... **San Francisco, CA**
Eigner, William W. .... **San Diego, CA**
Eiguren, Roy Lewis .... **Boise, ID**
Eihacker, Orrie, (Ms.) .... Albany, NY
Eike, Douglas D. .... Fremont, CA
Eike, Erik D. .... **Honolulu, HI**
Eiken, Dwight C. .... **Williston, ND**
Eikenberry, Colton D. .... Scott City, KS
Eikenberry, Dale W. .... **Indianapolis, IN**
Eikenberry, J. Michael .... Louisville, CO
Eikenberry, Peter G. .... **Brooklyn, NY**
Eikenberry, Peter G. .... **New York, NY**
Eikenberry, Peter G. .... **White Plains, NY**
Eikenberry, William H. .... **Denver, CO**
Eikenburg & Stiles, P.C. .... **Houston, TX**
Eiker, Carmen Elaine .... **Midland, TX**
Eikermann, Douglas R. .... Kansas City, KS
Eikleberry, Jane L. .... **Tucson, AZ**
Eikner, Paola Parra .... **Jacksonville, FL**
Eikner, Reid V. .... Lutherville, MD
Eikner, Tod B. .... **Jacksonville, FL**
Eil, Adele Geffen .... Providence, RI
Eiland, A. Craig .... Galveston, TX
Eiland & Bennett .... **Logan, WV**
Eiland, Edward I. .... **Logan, WV**
Eiland, Gary W. .... **Houston, TX**
Eiland, Mark Pickett .... **Mobile, AL**
Eilbacher, Leonard E. .... **Fort Wayne, IN**
Eilbacher, Paul G. .... Westfield, NJ
Eilbacher Scott, A Professional Corporation
Decatur, IN
Fort Wayne, IN
Eilberg, Joshua .... Jenkintown, PA
Eilberg, William H. .... Jenkintown, PA
Eilbott, Don A. .... **Pine Bluff, AR**
Eilbott, Eli D. .... **Washington, DC**
Eilbott Law Firm .... **Pine Bluff, AR**
Eile, Martin D. .... **New York, NY**
Eilefson, Brent G. .... **St. Paul, MN**
Eilen, Howard S. .... **Uniondale, NY**
Eilenberg, Adam D. .... Chicago, IL
New York, NY
Eilender, Jeffrey M. .... **New York, NY**
Eiler & Aicklen, LLP .... **Long Beach, CA**
Los Angeles, CA
San Francisco, CA
Santa Rosa, CA
Eiler, James O. .... **Long Beach, CA**
Eiler, Janis E. .... Cincinnati, OH
Eiler, Kathleen H. .... **Jackson, MS**
Eiler, Kenneth S. .... Seaside, OR
Eileraas, Anne-Marie .... **San Francisco, CA**
Eilerman, Robert J. .... Dayton, OH
Eilermann, Kenneth W. .... Jacksonville, FL
Eilers, Carl W. .... Kingsport, TN
Eilers & Chiles .... Kingsport, TN
Eilers, Christa Stern .... **Irvine, CA**
Eilers, Dana D. .... **St. Louis, MO**
Eilers, Jennifer .... **Boston, MA**
Eilers, John W., Jr. .... **Cincinnati, OH**
Eilers, Lisa S. .... Chicago, IL
Eilers, Rey .... Clayton, MO
Eilers, Robert E. .... Burr Ridge, IL
Eilers, S. Stuart .... **Cleveland, OH**
Eilers, Theresa G. .... **Austin, TX**
Eilert, Anita M. .... **Los Angeles, CA**
San Diego, CA
Eilert, Benn E. G. .... Geneva, IL
Eilert, Elton L. .... Seattle, WA
Eilertson, Darrin Lloyd .... Minneapolis, MN
Eills, Andrew B. .... **Concord, NH**
Eilman, James R. .... Milwaukee, WI
Eilman & Sakar .... Milwaukee, WI
Eilmes, Kevin G. .... Yakima, WA
Eilperin, Stephen F. .... Washington, DC
Eils, Robert C. .... Elmhurst, IL
Eiman, John F. .... Houston, TX
Eimbeck, Carl V. .... St. Louis, MO
Eimer, Eugene E. .... St. Louis, MO
Eimer, Eugene E., P.C. .... St. Louis, MO
Eimer, Jonna Daleiden .... **Chicago, IL**
Eimer, Nathan P. .... **Chicago, IL**
Eimert, Steven D. .... **Boston, MA**
Eimicke, Robert C. .... **East Brunswick, NJ**
Einarson, Baldvin .... New York, NY
Einarson, Darcie M. .... Grafton, ND
Einarson & Gaustad .... Grafton, ND
Einaudi, Carol P. .... **Washington, DC**

Einbinder, Cheri .... Jericho, NY
New York, NY
Einbinder, Hillard .... New Haven, CT
Einbinder, Howard .... New York, NY
Einbinder, Irving M. .... Hagerstown, MD
Einbinder, Leanna B. .... **Los Angeles, CA**
Einbinder, Michael .... **New York, NY**
Einbinder, Michael P. .... **Newark, NJ**
Einbinder, Robin Stone .... **New York, NY**
Einbinder, Stuart .... Palo Alto, CA
Einboden, Ronald J. .... Los Angeles, CA
Einboden, Suzanne Dorn .... Leonardtown, MD
Einbund, Lewis .... **Cleveland, OH**
Einck, Dean R. .... **Cedar Rapids, IA**
Eindorf, Candace Kaiser .... **Houston, TX**
Eineman, Thomas R. .... **Brooksville, FL**
Eineman, Thomas R. .... **Spring Hill, FL**
Einerson, Roger D. .... Department of Justice,
Civil Division, GV
Einfalt, Mark George .... **Austin, TX**
Houston, TX
Einfeldt, Christian J., Law Offices of
San Francisco, CA
Eingoren, Julius J. .... Kew Gardens, NY
Einhart, V. Jay .... Brecksville, OH
Einhaus, David L. .... **Owatonna, MN**
Einholz, Wendel J. .... Franklin Lakes, NJ
Einhorn, Alan H. .... **Boston, MA**
Einhorn, Ann Adler .... Urbana, IL
Einhorn, Barbara .... Warren, NJ
Einhorn, Brian D. .... **Southfield, MI**
Einhorn, Bruce J. .... Los Angeles, CA
Einhorn, Darren A. .... Glendale, AZ
Einhorn, David .... Bar Harbor, ME
Einhorn, David A. .... **New York, NY**
Einhorn, David M. .... **New York, NY**
Einhorn, Deborah Lee .... Vista, CA
Einhorn, Diane M. .... **Stamford, CT**
Einhorn, Edgar R. .... **Philadelphia, PA**
Einhorn, Eric .... **Seattle, WA**
Einhorn, Eric N.
Federal Communications Commission,
Common Carrier Bureau, GV
Einhorn, Fredric J. .... Rockville, MD
Einhorn, Gerald .... Salt Lake City, UT
Einhorn, Gordon A. .... **Harrisburg, PA**
Einhorn, Harold .... **New York, NY**
Einhorn, Harold .... Philadelphia, PA
Einhorn, Harris, Ascher, Barbarito, Frost & Ironson, A Professional Corporation
Denville, NJ
Morristown, NJ
Einhorn, Irving M., Law Offices of
Los Angeles, CA
Einhorn, Jaymie L. .... **New York, NY**
Einhorn, Joel J. .... Woodbury, CT
Einhorn, John S. .... Vista, CA
Einhorn, Jonathan J. .... New Haven, CT
Einhorn, Kathleen Barnett
Liberty Corner, NJ
Einhorn, Lawrence M. .... Oakland, CA
Einhorn, Randall .... San Diego, CA
Einhorn, Robert M. .... **Miami, FL**
Einhorn, Samuel M. .... Rosemont, IL
Einhorn, Steven .... East Rockaway, NY
Einhorn, Sylvia .... **New York, NY**
Einhorn, Theodore .... Cleveland, OH
Einhorn, Theodore E. B. .... **Denville, NJ**
Einhorn, Theresa A. .... **Houston, TX**
Einhorn, Walter M., Jr. .... **Philadelphia, PA**
Einiger, Scott I. .... **New York, NY**
Einowski, Edward D. .... **Portland, OR**
Einreinhofer, John, Law Offices of
Newfoundland, NJ
Charleston, WV
Einschlag, Michael B. .... Los Altos Hills, CA
Einsel, Carlton E., III .... New York, NY
Einset, Peter O. .... Geneva, NY
Einsiedler, Charles S., Jr. .... **Portland, ME**
Einsohn, Gerald A. .... **Las Vegas, NV**
Einsohn, Ira D. .... **Dallas, TX**
Einspahr, Jan L. .... Norfolk, NE
Einspahr, Leroy .... **Costa Mesa, CA**
Einspanier, Laura A. .... **Dallas, TX**
Einspar-Wayne, Susan E. .... Hinsdale, IL
Einstandig, David E. .... Birmingham, MI
Einstein, Carol Wind .... Crystal Lake, IL
Einstein, Dianne D. .... **Columbus, OH**
Einstein, Edwin F. .... **San Antonio, TX**
Einstein, Gary .... Los Angeles, CA
Einstein, Gloria A. .... Orange Park, FL
Einstein, Jaime .... **Deerfield, IL**
Einstein, Jean M. .... **Chicago, IL**
Einstein, John Lewis, IV .... **Columbus, OH**
Einstein, Joseph H. .... **New York, NY**
Einstein, Nancy .... Lenoir, NC
Einstein, Robert .... **New York, NY**
Einstein & Spiegel .... Los Angeles, CA
Einstein, Stephen .... New York, NY
Einstein, Steven H. .... New York, NY
Einstman, John C. .... Department of the Army,
U.S. Army Legal Services Agency, GV
Einterz, Michael L. .... Indianapolis, IN
Einum, Daniel R. .... McFarland, WI
Einziger, Ronald S. .... New York, NY
Eippert, Tonya L. .... **Cleveland, OH**
Eirich, Jeanette S. .... **Denver, CO**
Eirinberg, James A. .... Sioux Falls, SD
Eirinberg, Julia L.
Office of Government Ethics,
Office of General Counsel and Legal Policy,
GV
Eirinberg, Keith W. .... Washington, DC
Eisaguirre, Lynne .... Golden, CO
Eisan, Daniel H. .... San Mateo, CA
Eisan, Jeannette A. .... Indianapolis, IN
Eisbach, Robert J. .... St. Paul, MN
Eisberg, Howard L. .... Kansas City, MO

Eisberg, James S. .... **New York, NY**
Eisberg, John F. .... **Minneapolis, MN**
Eisbergmoin, Cheryl R. .... New York, NY
Eisbrouch, Antoniewicz & Marsh, A
Professional Corporation .... River Edge, NJ
Eisbrouch, David L. .... River Edge, NJ
Eisbruck, Stuart H. .... New York, NY
Eischeid, Lisa A. .... Murfreesboro, TN
Eischeid, Ronald J. .... Murfreesboro, TN
Eischen, Dana Edward .... Spencer, NY
Eischen, James J., Jr. .... **La Jolla, CA**
Eischens, Joseph K. .... **Kansas City, MO**
Eisdorfer, Raymond .... Union, NJ
Eisdorfer, Stephen M. .... **Princeton, NJ**
Eisel, John L. .... **Chicago, IL**
Eisel, Timothy D. .... **Oklahoma City, OK**
Eisele, Ashburn, Greene & Chapman, P.A.
Statesville, NC
Eisele, Brent J. .... Lexington, KY
Eisele, Clifton M., Jr. .... Hyattsville, MD
Eisele, Douglas G. .... **Statesville, NC**
Eisele, Edward A., Jr. .... **Cleveland, OH**
Eisele, Emily W. .... **Raleigh, NC**
Eisele, Frank L. .... Miami, FL
Eisele, G. Thomas .... Little Rock, AR
Eisele, Hermann H. .... St. Louis, MO
Eisele, John C. .... Prairie Village, KS
Eisele, John E. .... Anderson, IN
Eisele, John M. .... Anderson, IN
Eisele, Joseph T. .... New York, NY
Eisele, Karen L. .... **Cherry Hill, NJ**
Eisele, Laura J. .... **Detroit, MI**
Eisele, Lori Jo Payne .... Frankfort, KY
Eisele, Matthew D. .... **Houston, TX**
Eisele, Michael J. .... Hartford, CT
Eisele, Philip McDowell .... St. Louis, MO
Eisele, R. Joseph .... Hayden Lake, ID
Eisele, Thomas D. .... Cincinnati, OH
Eisele, Thomas Lee .... Elkhart, IN
Eiselein, Albert C., Jr. .... Cincinnati, OH
Eiselein, Jane B. .... Washington, DC
Eiselein, Michael G. .... **Billings, MT**
Eiselman, Robert .... Sacramento, CA
Eiselstein, William P. .... **Atlanta, GA**
Eiselt, Erich R. .... Bethesda, MD
Eiseman, Betty Louise
Westlake Village, CA
Eiseman, Byron M., Jr. (P.A.)
Little Rock, AR
Eiseman, David .... **Palo Alto, CA**
Eiseman, David J. .... **New York, NY**
Eiseman, James, Jr. .... **Philadelphia, PA**
Eiseman, Janice H. .... **White Plains, NY**
Eiseman, Jay H. .... Philadelphia, PA
Eiseman, Jeffrey H. .... Philadelphia, PA
Eiseman, Jonathan .... **New York, NY**
Eiseman, Marvin .... Hackensack, NJ
Eiseman, Matthew C. .... Addison, TX
Eiseman, Neal M. .... **Glen Rock, NJ**
New York, NY
Eiseman, Sharon L. .... Chicago, IL
Eisemann, Alexander E. .... **New York, NY**
Eisemann, Christine M. .... Bethpage, NY
Eisemann, Lisa M. L. .... Baltimore, MD
Eisemann, Mark D. .... **Kansas City, MO**
Eisen, Alan L. .... Concordville, PA
Eisen, Bernard .... **Pittsburgh, PA**
Eisen, Brent A. .... Denver, CO
Eisen, Brian .... Cortlandt Manor, NY
Eisen, Brian N. .... Cleveland, OH
Eisen, Bruce Alan .... **Washington, DC**
Eisen, Bruce M. .... Cambridge, MA
Eisen, Charles Lee .... **Washington, DC**
Eisen, Cheryl R. .... **Boca Raton, FL**
Eisen, D. Glen .... Houston, TX
Eisen, David .... Houston, TX
Eisen, David A. .... New York, NY
Eisen, David S. .... **Los Angeles, CA**
Eisen, David S. .... Chicago, IL
Eisen, Deborah H. .... **Los Angeles, CA**
Eisen, Edwin R. .... New York, NY
Eisen, Ellis .... **Philadelphia, PA**
Eisen, Eric A. .... **Bethesda, MD**
Eisen, George A. .... Milwaukee, WI
Eisen, Gerald .... Park Ridge, IL
Eisen & Gross, LLP .... **Boca Raton, FL**
Fort Lauderdale, FL
Weston, FL
West Palm Beach, FL
Eisen, Hermine G. .... Cleveland, OH
Eisen, Hershcopf & Schulman
New York, NY
Eisen, Jack L. .... Joplin, MO
Eisen, James J. .... San Francisco, CA
Eisen, Jason M. .... **New York, NY**
Eisen, Jay-Allen .... **Sacramento, CA**
Eisen, Jeffrey K., (A Professional Corporation) .... **Los Angeles, CA**
Eisen, Jeffrey M. .... Evansville, IN
Eisen, Jesse M. .... Yonkers, NY
Eisen & Johnston .... **Sacramento, CA**
Eisen, Judith A. .... **Great Neck, NY**
Eisen, Karen H. .... New York, NY
Eisen, Lauren Peretz .... **Pleasantville, NY**
Eisen, Lawrence D. .... **McLean, VA**
Eisen, Lloyd P. .... **Atlantic City, NJ**
Eisen, Marion G. .... St. Louis, MO
Eisen, Mynde S. .... Houston, TX
Eisen, Mynde S., P.C., Law Offices of
Houston, TX
Eisen, Norman L. .... **Washington, DC**
Eisen, Rebecca D. .... **San Francisco, CA**
Eisen, Richard C. .... Washington, DC
Eisen, Richard J. .... **St. Louis, MO**
Eisen, Robert L. .... **New York, NY**
Eisen, Robt. L. .... Chicago, IL
Eisen & Rome, P.C. .... Washington, DC
Eisen, Ruth I. .... **Fountain Valley, CA**

Eisen, S. Sidney ... Flushing, NY
Eisen, Saul ... Cleveland, OH
Eisen, Scott ... Miami, FL
Eisen, Scott J. ... Chicago, IL
Eisen, Steven J. ... Nashville, TN
Eisen, William J. ... Boston, MA
Eisen, Yale B. ... Hoffman Estates, IL
Eisenach, Gretchen ... Richmond, VA
Eisenbach, Arthur ... Boston, MA
Eisenbach, Robert L., III
San Francisco, CA
Eisenbarth, Louis F. ... Topeka, KS
Eisenbaum, Michael S. ... Los Angeles, CA
Eisenbeis, Janet C. ... Sacramento, CA
Eisenbeis, Kevin R. ... Overland Park, KS
Eisenberg, Alan D. ... New York, NY
Eisenberg, Alan D. ... Milwaukee, WI
Eisenberg, Allen M. ... New York, NY
Eisenberg, Alvin H. ... Milwaukee, WI
Eisenberg, Amy Felice ... Washington, DC
Eisenberg, Anderson, Michalik & Lynch, L.L.P. ... Hartford, CT
New Britain, CT
Eisenberg, Andrew D. ... Rockville, MD
Eisenberg, Andrew L. ... Boston, MA
Eisenberg, Anne ... White Plains, NY
Eisenberg, Arnee J. ... Chicago, IL
Eisenberg, Arnold ... Long Beach, CA
Eisenberg, Barry L. ... Roseland, NJ
Eisenberg, Barry R. ... White Plains, NY
Eisenberg, Bernard S. ... Baltimore, MD
Eisenberg, Bertram W. ... Liberty, NY
Eisenberg, Brian M. ... Cleveland, OH
Eisenberg, Bruce A. ... Cherry Hill, NJ
Trenton, NJ
Philadelphia, PA
Eisenberg, Bruce Alan ... Baltimore, MD
Eisenberg & Bruckman, P.C.
White Plains, NY
Eisenberg, Burt E., (P.A.) ... Naples, FL
Eisenberg, Calvin ... Chicago, IL
Eisenberg, Carol I. ... Portland, ME
Eisenberg, Carol S. ... Garden City, NY
Eisenberg, Cindy B. ... New York, NY
Eisenberg, Curtis ... Chicago, IL
Eisenberg, Daniel ... New York, NY
Eisenberg, Daniel S. ... New York, NY
Eisenberg, David ... Beverly Hills, CA
Eisenberg, David ... Richmond Hill, NY
Eisenberg, David A. ... Allentown, PA
Eisenberg, David C. ... Atlanta, GA
Eisenberg, David H. ... Hauppauge, NY
Eisenberg, David M. ... Kansas City, MO
Eisenberg, David M. ... New York, NY
Eisenberg, David S. ... Phoenix, AZ
Eisenberg, Deborah R. ... Glastonbury, CT
Eisenberg, Donald S. ... Glendora, CA
Eisenberg, Dorothy D. T. ... Westbury, NY
Eisenberg, Douglas R. ... Hackensack, NJ
Eisenberg, Eleanor ... Phoenix, AZ
Eisenberg, Elena J. ... Denver, CO
Eisenberg, Elisa A. ... Washington, DC
Baltimore, MD
Rockville, MD
Eisenberg, Eric F. ... Boston, MA
Providence, RI
Eisenberg, Ernest O. ... Bethesda, MD
Eisenberg, Eugene ... Bellmore, NY
Eisenberg, Everett A., (P.C.) ... New York, NY
Eisenberg & Fink, LLP ... Irvine, CA
Eisenberg, Fredric S. ... Philadelphia, PA
Eisenberg, Gary ... Southfield, MI
Eisenberg, Gary C. ... Los Angeles, CA
Eisenberg, Gary D. ... Albuquerque, NM
Eisenberg, Gary E. ... Monroe, NY
Eisenberg, Gary F. ... New Brunswick, NJ
New York, NY
Eisenberg, Gary M. ... Pleasant View, TN
Eisenberg, Gary P. ... Los Angeles, CA
Eisenberg, Gary, P.C. ... Southfield, MI
Eisenberg, Gerald ... New York, NY
Eisenberg, Gilbert ... San Francisco, CA
Eisenberg, Gold & Cettei, P.C.
Haddonfield, NJ
Eisenberg, Gregg A. ... Cleveland, OH
Eisenberg, Harry M. ... Troy, MI
Eisenberg, Harvey Ellis ... Baltimore, MD
Eisenberg, Harvey M. ... New York, NY
Eisenberg, Henry C. ... Washington, DC
Eisenberg, Herbert ... La Jolla, CA
Eisenberg, Herbert ... New York, NY
Eisenberg, Howard ... Portland, OR
Eisenberg, Howard B. ... Milwaukee, WI
Eisenberg, Hyman ... Cleveland, OH
Eisenberg, Israel N. ... Voorhees, NJ
Eisenberg, Jack C., (P.C.) ... Austin, TX
Eisenberg, Jack D. ... Buffalo, NY
Rochester, NY
Eisenberg, Jacob ... Washington, DC
Eisenberg, James B. ... New York, NY
Eisenberg, James H. ... Santa Ana, CA
Eisenberg, James L. ... West Palm Beach, FL
Eisenberg, James L., P.A.
West Palm Beach, FL
Eisenberg, Jamie B. ... Baltimore, MD
Eisenberg & Janger ... Chicago, IL
Eisenberg, Jay M. ... Rockville, MD
Eisenberg, Jeffrey ... New York, NY
Eisenberg, Jeffrey D. ... Salt Lake City, UT
Eisenberg, Jeffrey F. ... Miami, FL
Eisenberg, Jeffrey S. ... Los Angeles, CA
Eisenberg, Jeffrey S. ... New York, NY
Eisenberg, Jerald ... San Francisco, CA
Eisenberg, Jeremy W.
Department of Justice,
Antitrust Division, GV
Eisenberg, Jerry S. ... Pittsburgh, PA
Eisenberg, Jon B. ... Los Angeles, CA
Eisenberg, Jonathan ... Dover, DE
Eisenberg, Jonathan L. ... Minneapolis, MN
Eisenberg, Jonathan M.
San Francisco, CA
Eisenberg, Jos. L. ... Highland Park, IL
Eisenberg, Joseph A., (P.C.)
Los Angeles, CA
Eisenberg, Judith A. ... Hackensack, NJ
Eisenberg, Karen G. ... New York, NY
Eisenberg, Kenneth A. ... New York, NY
Eisenberg, Kevin M. ... New York, NY
Eisenberg & Kirsch ... Liberty, NY
Eisenberg, Laura E. ... Southfield, MI
Eisenberg Law Offices, S.C. ... Madison, WI
Eisenberg, Lawrence ... Redwood City, CA
Eisenberg, Lawrence D. ... New York, NY
Eisenberg, Lawrence J. ... Washington, DC
Eisenberg, Lawrence S. ... Irvine, CA
Eisenberg, Leonard ... New York, NY
Eisenberg, Lewis C. ... Boston, MA
Quincy, MA
Eisenberg, LLoyd J. ... Silver Spring, MD
Eisenberg, Lloyd J., & Associates, P.A.
Silver Spring, MD
Eisenberg, Lloyd M. ... New York, NY
Eisenberg, Lucy T. ... Los Angeles, CA
Eisenberg, Marc R. ... Chicago, IL
Eisenberg, Marcia R. ... New York, NY
Eisenberg, Margolis & Friedman
New York, NY
Eisenberg, Mark A. ... Brooklyn, NY
Eisenberg, Mark A. ... Madison, WI
Eisenberg, Mark L. ... Hayward, CA
Eisenberg, Mark W. ... Orange, CA
Eisenberg, Marlene McGregor ... Plano, TX
Eisenberg, Marsha Katz ... Troy, MI
Eisenberg, Marshall E. ... Chicago, IL
Eisenberg, Martin ... New York, NY
Eisenberg, Martin L. ... Chicago, IL
Eisenberg, Martin M. ... San Francisco, CA
Eisenberg, Matthew J. ... Napa, CA
Eisenberg, Matthew S. ... Westport, CT
Eisenberg, Maureen ... Washington, DC
Eisenberg, Melissa G. ... Goshen, NY
Eisenberg, Melissa W. ... San Francisco, CA
Eisenberg, Meyer ... New York, NY
Eisenberg, Michael ... San Francisco, CA
Eisenberg, Michael E. ... Buckingham, PA
Doylestown, PA
Eisenberg, Michael E. ... Horsham, PA
Eisenberg, Michael E. ... Norristown, PA
Warrington, PA
Eisenberg, Michael M. ... Los Angeles, CA
Eisenberg, Millicent G. ... Boca Raton, FL
Eisenberg, Milton, (P.C.) ... Washington, DC
Eisenberg, Mitchell S. ... Westport, CT
Eisenberg, Neil D. ... San Francisco, CA
Eisenberg, Neil J. ... Foxboro, MA
Eisenberg, Owen N. ... South Dennis, NJ
Eisenberg, Paul ... Philadelphia, PA
Eisenberg, Peter A. ... New York, NY
Eisenberg, Philip G. ... New Orleans, LA
Eisenberg, Philip J. ... New York, NY
Eisenberg, Philip M. ... Union City, NJ
Eisenberg, Rachel V. ... Cleveland, OH
Eisenberg, Rebecca L. ... San Francisco, CA
Eisenberg, Richard D. ... New York, NY
Eisenberg, Richard D. ... Lyndhurst, OH
Eisenberg, Richard J. ... Great Neck, NY
Eisenberg, Richard P. ... New York, NY
Eisenberg, Robert L. ... Reno, NV
Eisenberg, Robert M. ... Tallahassee, FL
Eisenberg, Robert S. ... Jersey City, NJ
Eisenberg, Rochelle Stutman
Baltimore, MD
Eisenberg, Ronald ... Philadelphia, PA
Eisenberg, Ronald A. ... Minneapolis, MN
Eisenberg, Ronald L. ... Woodmere, NY
Eisenberg, Russell A. ... Milwaukee, WI
Eisenberg, Ruth E. ... Washington, DC
Eisenberg, Sam ... White Plains, NY
Eisenberg, Saul ... Bay Shore, NY
Eisenberg, Sheila M. ... Brooklyn, NY
Eisenberg, Sheldon ... Santa Monica, CA
Eisenberg, Sheryl D. ... Boston, MA
Eisenberg & Specter LLP ... Irvine, CA
San Francisco, CA
Eisenberg & Spilman, P.C. ... Southfield, MI
Eisenberg, Stacey ... New York, NY
Eisenberg, Stanley J., (P.C.)
San Antonio, TX
Eisenberg, Stephen A. J. ... Alexandria, VA
Eisenberg, Stephen J. ... New York, NY
Eisenberg, Stephen J. ... Madison, WI
Eisenberg, Stephen P. ... Chicago, IL
Eisenberg, Stephen W. ... Liberty, NY
Eisenberg, Steven A. ... Cleveland, OH
Eisenberg, Steven D. ... Irvine, CA
Eisenberg, Steven E. ... Fort Lauderdale, FL
Fort Lauderdale, FL
Eisenberg, Steven K. ... Marlton, NJ
Horsham, PA
Eisenberg, Stewart ... Greenfield, MA
Eisenberg, Stewart J. ... Philadelphia, PA
Eisenberg, Stuart ... Detroit, MI
Eisenberg, Stuart A. ... Warminster, PA
Eisenberg, Sue Ellen ... Bloomfield Hills, MI
Eisenberg, Sue Ellen, P.C. ... Ann Arbor, MI
Bloomfield Hills, MI
Detroit, MI
Flint, MI
Mount Clemens, MI
Pontiac, MI
Eisenberg, Susan Levy ... South Plainfield, NJ
Feasterville, PA
Eisenberg, Susan Nadler ... Miami, FL
Eisenberg, Tammy ... New York, NY
Eisenberg Tanchum & Levy
New York, NY
Eisenberg, Theodore ... Ithaca, NY
Eisenberg, Theodore ... Philadelphia, PA
Eisenberg, Theodore M. ... Los Angeles, CA
Roseland, NJ
New York, NY
Eisenberg & Van Horn, LLP
Allentown, PA
Eisenberg, Viviane ... New York, NY
Eisenberg, William V. ... Haddonfield, NJ
Eisenberger, Benjamin P. ... New York, NY
Eisenberger, Chad ... New York, NY
Eisenberger, Jeffrey M. ... New York, NY
Eisenberger, Nicholas Moore ... New York, NY
Eisenbiegler, Frederick F. ... Boston, MA
New York, NY
Eisenbise, C. Warner ... Wichita, KS
Eisenbrandt, Jacqueline ... Madison, WI
Eisenbrandt, James L.
Overland Park, KS
Eisenbraun, Eric C. ... Addison, TX
Eisenbraun, Mark ... Houston, TX
Eisenbrey, Karen Kaunisto
Grand Junction, CO
Eisenbud, Deborah S. ... Philadelphia, PA
Eisenbud, Frederick ... Hauppauge, NY
Eisenbud, Robert E. ... Washington, DC
Eisendrath, Jack N. ... Milwaukee, WI
Eisendrath, Margaret M., (Mrs.)
Evanston, IL
Eisenfeld, Gail H. ... New York, NY
Eisenfeld, Rita A. ... Phoenix, AZ
Eisenhammer, Stanley B.
Arlington Heights, IL
Eisenhardt, Howard A., III ... Cleveland, OH
Eisenhardt, Stephen C.
Charlotte Amalie, St. Thomas, VI
Eisenhart & Eisenhart ... Cambridge, NE
Eisenhart, Eric B. ... Cambridge, NE
Eisenhart, Frank J. ... Washington, DC
Eisenhart, Gary N. ... Encino, CA
Eisenhart, John ... Portland, ME
Eisenhart, John C. ... Chantilly, VA
Eisenhart, William S., Jr. ... York, PA
Eisenhauer & Eisenhauer ... San Antonio, TX
Eisenhauer, Hollie M. ... Dallas, TX
Eisenhauer, James W. ... Wauwatosa, WI
Eisenhauer, Larry J. ... Des Moines, IA
Eisenhauer, Margaret P. ... Atlanta, GA
Eisenhauer, Mark A. ... San Antonio, TX
Eisenhauer, Nancy ... Chicago, IL
Eisenhauer, Robert R. ... Medicine Lodge, KS
Pratt, KS
Eisenhauer, Rod L. ... Kansas City, MO
Eisenhauer, Roland A. ... San Antonio, TX
Eisenhauer, Roscoe A., Jr. ... Watertown, NY
Eisenhauer, Shaun R. ... Harrisburg, PA
Eisenhauer, Shirley M. ... St. Louis, MO
Eisenhauer, Susan C. ... Morristown, NJ
Eisenhaure, Jessica L. ... Roseland, NJ
Eisenhofer, Jay W. ... Wilmington, DE
Eisenhower & Carlson, PLLC
Seattle, WA
Tacoma, WA
Eisenhower, James J. ... Philadelphia, PA
Eisenhower, James S. D., III ... Fairfax, VA
Eisenhower, Tarby & Laufer, P.C.
Fairfax, VA
Eisenhut, Bruce ... Boston, MA
Eisenhut, Keith A. ... Utica, NY
Eisenhut, Suzanne M. ... San Francisco, CA
Eisenhut, Timothy V. ... Flemington, NJ
Eisenhuth, Harold P., Jr. ... Nederland, CO
Eisenkramer, Kathryn P. ... Little Rock, AR
Eisenman, Alan ... Houston, TX
Eisenman, Anne F.F. ... Wethersfield, CT
Eisenman, Brett D. ... New York, NY
Eisenman, Carol L. ... Rochester, NY
Eisenman, Dale C. ... Hilliard, OH
Eisenman, Gerard P. ... Bridgeport, CT
Eisenman, Harold J. ... Houston, TX
Eisenman, James A. ... Jericho, NY
Melville, NY
Eisenman, James M. ... Encino, CA
Eisenman, Ronald ... New York, NY
Eisenman, Ronald L. ... Middlebury, VT
Eisenman, Ronald W. ... Atlanta, GA
Eisenman, Steven A. ... New York, NY
Eisenman, Susan Garner ... Columbus, OH
Eisenmann, Carl D. ... Simsbury, CT
Eisenmann, James M. ... Washington, DC
Eisenmenger & Berry, P.A.
Melbourne, FL
Orlando, FL
Titusville, FL
Vero Beach, FL
Eisenmenger, Gregory W. ... Melbourne, FL
Eisenmesser, Scott ... New York, NY
Eisenpress, Sherri L. ... New York, NY
Eisenrich, Gregory O. ... Los Angeles, CA
Eisenrod, Sandra I. ... Encino, CA
Eisenschenk, Frank Christopher
Department of Commerce,
Patent and Trademark Office, GV
Gainesville, FL
Eisenschmidt, Lori E. ... Weymouth, MA
Eisensmith, Jeffrey R. ... Fort Lauderdale, FL
Eisenstadt, Amy ... Fairfield, CT
Eisenstadt, Anita ... Troy, MI
Eisenstadt, Anita R.
National Science Foundation,
Office of the General Counsel, GV
Eisenstadt, Beverly D. ... Miami, FL
Eisenstadt, Brian B. ... St. Petersburg, FL
Eisenstadt, David G. ... Boston, MA
Eisenstadt, Deborah T. ... Minneapolis, MN
Eisenstadt, Eric ... Hicksville, NY
Eisenstadt & Foundas ... Boston, MA
Eisenstadt, Jodi G. ... Chicago, IL
Eisenstadt, Lester ... Philadelphia, PA
Eisenstadt, Mark M.
Department of Housing and Urban Development,
Office of General Counsel, GV
Eisenstadt, Martin A. ... Southfield, MI
Eisenstadt, Melvin M. ... Corrales, NM
Eisenstadt, Neil Brian ... New York, NY
Eisenstadt, Robert ... New York, NY
Eisenstadt, Theodore D. ... Boston, MA
Eisenstadt, William B. ... Philadelphia, PA
Eisenstaedt, Richard M. ... Wayne, PA
Eisenstark, Gregory ... Newark, NJ
Eisenstat, David H. ... Washington, DC
Eisenstat, Gabage, Berman & Furman, A Professional Corporation ... Vineland, NJ
Eisenstat, Gary D. ... Dallas, TX
Eisenstat, Gerald (Jere) M. ... Vineland, NJ
Eisenstat, Jared Parnell ... Long Beach, CA
Eisenstat, Larry F. ... Washington, DC
Eisenstat, Noel E. ... Philadelphia, PA
Eisenstat, Philip M.
Federal Trade Commission,
Bureau of Competition, GV
Eisenstat, Samuel M. ... New York, NY
Eisenstat, Stefani ... Dallas, TX
Eisenstatt, Leo ... Omaha, NE
Eisenstein & Bower ... State College, PA
Eisenstein, Byron A. ... Chicago, IL
Eisenstein, Daniel B. ... Nashville, TN
Eisenstein, David G. ... Boulder, CO
Eisenstein, David G. ...
Federal Deposit Insurance Corporation, GV
Eisenstein, Douglas K. ... New York, NY
Eisenstein, Eric
Department Of The Interior, GV
Eisenstein, Fredrick C. ... New York, NY
Eisenstein, Gwen M. ... Dallas, TX
Eisenstein, Harold ... Albany, NY
Eisenstein, Herman M. ... Clifton, NJ
Eisenstein, Irving ... Des Plaines, IL
Eisenstein, Jeffrey N. ... Washington, DC
Eisenstein, Jethro M. ... New York, NY
Eisenstein, Joel B. ... St. Charles, MO
Eisenstein, Justine J. ... New York, NY
Eisenstein, Laurence J. ... Washington, DC
Eisenstein, Lois Peel ... New York, NY
Eisenstein, Marci A. ... Chicago, IL
Eisenstein, Martin D. ... Secaucus, NJ
Eisenstein, Martin I. ... Lewiston, ME
Eisenstein, Michael C. ... Baltimore, MD
Eisenstein, Miriam R. ... Department of Justice,
Civil Rights Division, GV
Eisenstein, Moses & Mossman
Nashville, TN
Eisenstein, Nancy L. ... Mineola, NY
Eisenstein, Paul ... Woodbury, NY
Eisenstein, Randi S. ... New York, NY
Eisenstein, Roger M. ... Simsbury, CT
Eisenstein, Ronald I. ... Boston, MA
Eisenstein, Scott L. ... Hillsboro, OR
Eisenstein, Stanley ... Chicago, IL
Eisenstein, Steven J. ... Roseland, NJ
Eisenstein Todt Ryan & Porzenski, L.L.P.
St. Charles, MO
Eisenstein, Victor David ... Kansas City, MO
Eisenstein, Virginia B. ... State College, PA
Eisenzimmer, Andrew J. ... St. Paul, MN
Eiser, George H., III ... Modesto, CA
Eiser, Jay N. ... Long Beach, CA
Eiser, Lawrence ... Silver Spring, MD
Eiserloh, Laurie ... Austin, TX
Eisert, Edward G. ... New York, NY
Eisert, Israel J. ... New York, NY
Eisert, Joseph A. ... Washington, DC
Eisert, Richard K. ... Frankfort, KY
Eisert, Richard S. ... New York, NY
Eisfelder, Bart E. ... Kansas City, MO
Eisfelder, Robert W. ... Los Angeles, CA
Eisfelder, Robert W., P.C., Law Offices of
Los Angeles, CA
Eisgrau, Adam M. ... Washington, DC
Eisin, Walter M., Jr. ... Chicago, IL
Eisinger, Dennis J. ... Hollywood, FL
Eisinger, Diane L. ... Rancho Santa Fe, CA
Eisinger, Irwin J. ... Louisville, KY
Eisinger, Jana ... New York, NY
Eisinger, Jeffrey W. ... Fresno, CA
Eisinger, Paul F. ... Las Vegas, NV
Eisland, Evan M. ... New York, NY
Eisland, Marla ... New York, NY
Eisland, Selby & Berman LLP
New York, NY
Eisler, Alan D. ... Bethesda, MD
Eisler, Barry M. ... Menlo Park, CA
Eisler, Barry S. ... New York, NY
Eisler, M. Douglas ... West Chester, PA
Eisler, Michael J. ... Miami, FL
Eisler, Nathan M. ... New York, NY
Eisler, Riane, (Mrs.) ... Carmel, CA
Eisler, Robert G. ... New York, NY
Eisler, Robert W. ... Deal, NJ
Eisler, Stuart ... New York, NY
Eisler, William O. ... Kansas City, MO
Eisma, Douglas E. ... Luverne, MN
Eisman, Andrew B. ... Collegeville, PA
Eisman, Arthur E. ... Larchmont, NY
Eisman, Clyde Jay ... New York, NY
Eisman, Gerald B. ... Tampa, FL
Eisman, Gerald B., P.A. ... Tampa, FL
Eisman, Martin L. ... Larchmont, NY
Eisman, Robert Bernard ... New York, NY
Eisman, Ronald B. ... Whittier, CA
Eisman, Russell K. ... Northport, NY
Eisman, Steven ... Mineola, NY
Eisman, Steven J. ... Mineola, NY

Eisman, Tina J. ... Stamford, CT
New York, NY
Eismann, Debra L. ... Nampa, ID
Eismann, Kevin L. ... Kaukauna, WI
Eismann, Richard B. ... Nampa, ID
Eismann, Samuel ... Coeur d'Alene, ID
Eismeier, Dana L. ... Denver, CO
Eismont, Diane S. ... Pittsburgh, PA
Eisnaugle & Graham Co., L.P.A.
Columbus, OH
Eisnaugle, R. William ... Columbus, OH
Eisnaugle, Richard L. ... Portsmouth, OH
Eisner, Alan ... Los Angeles, CA
Eisner, Benjamin ... Haddonfield, NJ
Philadelphia, PA
Eisner, Charles I. ... Oakland, CA
Eisner, Daniel J. ... Chicago, IL
New York, NY
Eisner, David ... New York, NY
Eisner, David F. ... New York, NY
Eisner, Donald A. ... Encino, CA
Eisner, Douglas Andrew ... New York, NY
Eisner, Elisabeth ... San Diego, CA
Eisner, Elliott R. ... Las Vegas, NV
Eisner, Emily ... Chicago, IL
Eisner, Eugene G. ... New York, NY
Eisner, Evan S. ... Philadelphia, PA
Eisner, Gregory E. ... Los Angeles, CA
Eisner & Hubbard, P.C. ... New York, NY
Eisner, J. Michael ... New Haven, CT
Eisner, Jamie R. ... New York, NY
Eisner, Jerome ... Fort Lauderdale, FL
Eisner, Jonathan David ... Baltimore, MD
Eisner, Kenneth A. ... Pittsburgh, PA
Eisner, Lori Joy ... Baltimore, MD
Eisner, Michael ... Los Angeles, CA
Eisner, Michael I. ... Staten Island, NY
Eisner, Michael L. ... Cleveland, OH
Eisner, Nancy K. ... New York, NY
Eisner, Nashwa R. ... Encino, CA
Eisner, Neil A. ... Austin, TX
Eisner, Neil R.
Department of Transportation,
Office of the General Counsel, GV
Eisner, Paul D. ... Los Angeles, CA
Eisner, Peter D. ... Tucson, AZ
Eisner, Rebecca S. ... Chicago, IL
Eisner, Richard J. ... Canoga Park, CA
Eisner, Robert A. ... Los Angeles, CA
Eisner, Sara L. ... Palo Alto, CA
Eisner, Seth A. ... Northfield, IL
Eisner, Sheldon M. ... Los Angeles, CA
Eisner, Sheri F. ... Los Angeles, CA
Eisner, Steven G. ... Los Angeles, CA
Eisner, Steven M. ... Haddonfield, NJ
Eisner, Susan G. ... Frederick, MD
Eisner, Thomas S. ... Homewood, IL
Eisner, Todd R. ... New York, NY
Eisner-Moelis, Susan R. ... New York, NY
Eiss, Bernard B. ... Philadelphia, PA
Eiss, Charles Merrill ... Plantation, FL
Eiss, Elliott D. ... New York, NY
Eiss, James D., Law Offices of
Buffalo, NY
Eiss, Michael D. ... Philadelphia, PA
Eissenstat, Eric S. ... Oklahoma City, OK
Eissfeldt, Theodore L. ... Peoria, IL
Eissinger, James R. ... Lubbock, TX
Eissle, R. Joseph, P.C. ... Hayden Lake, ID
Eissler, Ellen R. ... Mill Valley, CA
Eissler, Mark ... West Linn, OR
Eissler, Valarie J. ... Houston, TX
Eissman, Mark Paul ... Northfield, IL
Eissner, Scott G. ... Newburgh, NY
Eiswert & Janes, P.A. ... Oakland, MD
Eiswert, Leonard J. ... Oakland, MD
Eiszner, James R., Jr. ... Kansas City, MO
Eitches, Edward
Department of Housing and Urban
Development,
Office of General Counsel, GV
Eitel, Bela Roongta ... Milwaukee, WI
Eitel, Douglas R. ... Iowa City, IA
Eitel, John A., Jr. ... San Francisco, CA
Eitel, Mitchell S. ... New York, NY
Eitel, Nan Roberts ... New Orleans, LA
Eitel, Robert S. ... New Orleans, LA
Eitel, Robert S., L.L.C. ... New Orleans, LA
Eitelbach, Sarah B., P.S. ... Seattle, WA
Eitelbach, Sarah Butler ... Seattle, WA
Eiteljorg, Roger ... Indianapolis, IN
Eitelman, Dinah W. ... Suffolk, VA
Eiten, Gary R. ... La Salle, IL
Eiten, Karen C. ... La Salle, IL
Eiting, Shirle ... Reno, NV
Eitrheim, Marie K. ... Chicago, IL
Eittreim, Richard M. ... Newark, NJ
Eittreim, Theodore S. ... Atlanta, GA
Eitzen, Lawrence O. ... Eureka, CA
Eitzen, Melinda L. ... Dallas, TX
Eitzen, Tari S. ... Spokane, WA
Eivers, George J. ... Milwaukie, OR
Eizelman, Michael J. ... Bloomfield Hills, MI
Eizen, Bernard ... Philadelphia, PA
Eizen Fineburg & McCarthy, A Professional Corporation ... Haddonfield, NJ
Philadelphia, PA
Eizenman, Amy J. ... Alexandria, VA
Eizenman, David B. ... New York, NY
Eizenstat, Jay L. ... Washington, DC
Ejbeh, Joseph N. ... Detroit, MI
Ejebe, Lilian N. ... St. Paul, MN
Ejercito, Marisol G. ... Chicago, IL
Ejtemai & Focsaneanu, P.C. ... Rockville, MD
Ejtemai, Keyhan Sassan ... Rockville, MD
Ejzak, Richard A. ... Pittsburgh, PA
Ejzak, William M. ... Chicago, IL
Ek, Charles Norman ... Minneapolis, MN
Ek, Dale W. ... Albuquerque, NM
Ek, Jeffrey J. ... Oconomowoc, WI
Ek, Tyna L. ... Seattle, WA
Ekamalian, James G. ... Springfield, MA
Ekart, Sonya S. ... Lincoln, NE
Ekberg, Carleton L. ... Denver, CO
Ekberg, Charles R., (P.S.) ... Seattle, WA
Ekberg, John P., III ... Stamford, CT
Ekberg, Peter J. ... Minneapolis, MN
Ekblom & Ekblom LLC ... Vero Beach, FL
New York, NY
Ekblom, Harry E., Jr. ... Boston, MA
Ekblom, Harry E., Sr. ... Vero Beach, FL
New York, NY
Ekblom, Neil H. ... New York, NY
Ekbom, Jeffrey A. ... Phoenix, AZ
Ekdahl, Brian R. ... Red Bank, NJ
Ekdahl, Jon N. ... Chicago, IL
Ekdahl, Sarah M. ... Chicago, IL
Ekdahl, Terry R. ... Oscoda, MI
Eke, Joseph W. ... Indianapolis, IN
Eke, Nicki N. ... Santa Ana, CA
Ekeanyanwu, Thecla ... Washington, DC
Ekeanyanwu, Thecla, P.C., The Law Offices of,
Washington, DC
Ekechukwu, Ebere ... Chicago, IL
Ekechukwu, Ebere N., & Associates, P.C.
Chicago, IL
Ekeh, Vincent ... Kansas City, KS
Ekeler, Kathryn A. ... Omaha, NE
Ekelman, Daniel L. ... Cleveland, OH
Ekelman, Felice B. ... New York, NY
Ekelund, Virginia L. ... Dixon, CA
Eken, Yasemin ... Chicago, IL
Eke-Nweke, Vincent I. ... Brooklyn, NY
Ekerling, Howard L. ... Sherman Oaks, CA
Ekern, Nigel P. ... New York, NY
Ekern, Stephen G. ... Hartford, CT
Ekery, Laura M. ... Austin, TX
Ekery, Rachel Anne ... El Paso, TX
Ekey, William E. ... Kansas City, MO
Ekimoto, Richard S. ... Honolulu, HI
Ekins, Brett D. ... San Diego, CA
Ekirch, Alice Lee ... Roanoke, VA
Ekiss, William J. ... Clayton, MO
Ekizian, L. Danielle ... North Quincy, MA
Ekker, Angela L. ... Englewood, CO
Ekker, Henry M. ... Hermitage, PA
New Wilmington, PA
Sharon, PA
Ekker, Kuster & McConnell
Hermitage, PA
Mercer, PA
New Wilmington, PA
Sharon, PA
Ekker, Steven B. ... Downers Grove, IL
Ekl, Terry A. ... Clarendon Hills, IL
Eklund, Allison Fabyanske
Minneapolis, MN
Eklund, Carl A. ... Denver, CO
Eklund, Carl A. ... Silver Spring, MD
Eklund, Charles E. ... Chicago, IL
Eklund, Claudia Rieth ... Cleveland, OH
Eklund, John A. ... Easton, MA
Eklund, John J. ... Cleveland, OH
Eklund, Maria E. ... Burr Ridge, IL
Eklund, Mary C. ... Seattle, WA
Eklund, Paul D. ... Cleveland, OH
Eklund, Paul G. ... Seattle, WA
Eklund, Paul R. ... Boston, MA
Eklund, Robert D. ... Montague, MI
Eklund Rockey Stratton, P.S. ... Seattle, WA
Eklund, Roger P. ... Wilmette, IL
Eklund, Susan M. ... Ann Arbor, MI
Eklund, Wally ... Sioux Falls, SD
Eklund, William A. ... Los Alamos, NM
Eklund-Easley, Molly S. ... Detroit, MI
Ekman, Bohrer & Thulin, P.S.
Seattle, WA
Ekman, Christopher D. ... Burlington, VT
Ekman, Christopher L. ... Charlotte, NC
Ekman, Donald J. ... Wilsonville, OR
Ekman, Gershon ... New York, NY
Ekman, John C. ... Minneapolis, MN
St. Paul, MN
Ekman Marks & Holmes, P.S. ... Seattle, WA
Ekman, Mary Ann ... Seattle, WA
Ekman, Michael D. ... Louisville, KY
Ekman, Patricia ... New York, NY
Ekman, Richard A. ... Seattle, WA
Ekman, Ulrika ... New York, NY
Ekola, Virginia K. ... Minneapolis, MN
Ekonomides, Anthony C. ... Tampa, FL
Ekonomides & Associates ... Tampa, FL
Ekonomides, Nickolas C. ... Tampa, FL
Ekonomon, Adam M. ... Akron, OH
Ekonomon, Deborah Ann ... Akron, OH
Ekonomou, Andrew J. ... Atlanta, GA
Lilburn, GA
Ekonomou, Anthony, II ... Houston, TX
Ekperigin, Victor E. ... New York, NY
Ekpiken, Alexandra E. ... New York, NY
Ekren, Christopher W. ... San Jose, CA
Ekroot, Bryn ... Mountain View, CA
Ekroth & Osborne, Ltd. ... Hinsdale, IL
Ekroth, Robert R. ... Hinsdale, IL
Eksler, Alla ... Los Angeles, CA
Ekstrand, Peter D. ... Wabasha, MN
Ekstrand, Roy A. ... Costa Mesa, CA
Ekstrom, Harold E. ... Concord, NH
Ekstrom, Richard C. ... Alexandria, VA
Ekstrom, Susan L. ... Des Moines, IA
Ekstrom, William J., Jr. ... Kingman, AZ
Ekstrum, B. William ... Fridley, MN
Ekvall & Byrne, L.L.P. ... Dallas, TX
Ekvall, Erik E. ... Dallas, TX
Ekvall, Lei Lei Wang ... Costa Mesa, CA
Ekvall, Suzanne C., Law Offices of
Dallas, TX
Ela, William M. ... Hotchkiss, CO
Elacqua, James J. ... Palo Alto, CA
Elakman, Howard Gary ... Atlanta, GA
Elam, B. Lee ... Brandon, FL
Elam, B. Lee, P.A. ... Brandon, FL
Elam & Burke, A Professional Association
Boise, ID
Elam, Charlotte A. E., (Mrs.) ... Memphis, TN
Elam, Elizabeth A. ... Fort Worth, TX
Elam & Glasgow ... Union City, TN
Elam, H. Larry, III ... San Francisco, CA
Elam, Harry J. ... South Weymouth, MA
Elam, Harvey T. ... San Francisco, CA
Elam, H. J., III ... Greensboro, NC
Elam, James D. ... Lexington, KY
Elam, James E., IV ... Cherry Hill, NJ
Philadelphia, PA
Elam, John C. ... Columbus, OH
Elam, John Claibourne ... Greensboro, NC
Elam, John W. ... Columbus, OH
Elam, L. B. ... Sacramento, CA
Elam, Linda C. ... Nashville, TN
Elam, Lori L. ... Houston, TX
Elam, Mark R. ... Washington, DC
Elam, Nancy R. ... Portland, ME
Elam, Michael H. ... Pasadena, CA
Elam, Michael H. ... Chicago, IL
Elam & Miller ... Lexington, KY
Elam, Nancy L. ... Treasury Department,
U.S. Customs Service, GV
Elam, Nevan C. ... Palo Alto, CA
Elam, Pryse Roy ... Brentwood, TN
Elam, Randall H. ... Wichita, KS
Elam, Richard L. ... Versailles, KY
Elam & Robbins ... San Francisco, CA
Elam, Robert Joseph ... Columbia, SC
Elam, Theodore M. ... Oklahoma City, OK
Elam, William H. ... Charlotte, NC
El-Amin, Hassan Ali ... Fort Washington, MD
El-Amin, Judith A. ... Chicago, IL
St. Louis, MO
Elam-Krizan, Amy ... Louisville, KY
Elan, Kenneth A. ... New York, NY
Eland, John R. ... Hoxie, KS
Eland, Kenneth J. ... Hoxie, KS
Eland, Richard L. ... Princeton, NJ
Eland, Stephen H. ... Philadelphia, PA
Eland, Terry P. ... Bloomingdale, IL
Elander, Lisa A. ... Hudson, WI
Elander, William A. ... Worcester, MA
Elarbee, Robert Rache ... Atlanta, GA
Elarbee, Thompson & Trapnell, LLP
Atlanta, GA
Elardo, Donald J. ... Washington, DC
Elardo, John A. ... Phoenix, AZ
Elardo, Robert M. ... Buffalo, NY
Elash, Andrew ... Philadelphia, PA
Elash, John J. ... Mc Keesport, PA
El-Ayouty, Yassin ... New York, NY
Elazar, Donna ... Alexandria, VA
Elbadawi, Sam A. ... Syracuse, NY
Elbaor, David W. ... Washington, DC
Elbaum, David ... Somerset, NJ
Elbaum, David ... New York, NY
Elbaum, Jerome D. ... West Hartford, CT
Elbaum, Richard K. ... New York, NY
Elbaum, Saul ... Adelphi, MD
McLean, VA
Elbaum, Sharon Z. ... New York, NY
Elbaum, Steven L. ... Stamford, CT
El-Bayoumi, Amr A. ... Palo Alto, CA
Elbaz, David J. ... Los Angeles, CA
Elbein, Adam S. ... St. Louis, MO
Elbein, Bradley M. ... Atlanta, GA
Elbein, Michael ... Kansas City, MO
Elber, Bonnie E. ... Phoenix, AZ
Elber, Dennis M. ... Long Beach, CA
Elber, George A. ... Claremont, CA
Elberfeld, Donald N. ... Washington, DC
Elberg, Mitchell ... New York, NY
Elberg, Philip ... Newark, NJ
Elberger, Ronald E. ... Indianapolis, IN
Elbert, Charles S. ... St. Louis, MO
Elbert, John Brendan ... Philadelphia, PA
Elbert, Kenneth P. ... Elizabeth, CO
Elbert, Philip N. ... Nashville, TN
Elbert, Richard L. ... Woodbridge, NJ
Elbert, Rosemary R. ... Wausau, WI
Elberts, Leonard J. ... Chicago, IL
Elbertse, Johanna M. ... Chino, CA
Elbiali, Yasir ... Los Angeles, CA
Elbing, Karen L. ... Boston, MA
Elbing, Kristofer E. ... Wayland, MA
Elbogen, William ... Brooklyn, NY
Elbow, Joseph A. ... Oklahoma City, OK
Elbrecht, Anne Elizabeth ... Sacramento, CA
Elbrecht, Frederick J. ... Sarasota, FL
Elbrecht, George K. ... Monroeville, AL
Elbrecht, Richard A. ... Sacramento, CA
Elby, Shannon E. ... Pittsburgh, PA
Elcano, Mary S.
United States Postal Service,
Law Department, GV
Elcano, Paul D., Jr. ... Reno, NV
Elchert, Kenneth J. ... Mountain View, CA
Elchinoff, Nick L. M.
South San Francisco, CA
Elchoness, David A. ... Boston, MA
Elchuk, Mark D. ... Troy, MI
Elcock, Douglas C. ... Vancouver, WA
Elcock, Thomas M. ... Boston, MA
Providence, RI
Elconin, Gene ... Beachwood, OH
Elconin, Richard C. ... Monroe, MI
Elconin, Robert M. ... Minneapolis, MN
Eld, Peter F. ... Morristown, NJ
Eldan, David K. ... Los Angeles, CA
Las Vegas, NV
Reno, NV
Elden, Barry R. ... Chicago, IL
Elden, Douglas L. ... Chicago, IL
Elden, Gary M. ... Chicago, IL
Elden, John A., Jr. ... Vermilion, OH
Elden, Joyce L. ... West Palm Beach, FL
Elden Law Firm, The ... Chicago, IL
Elden, Robbin C. ... Chicago, IL
Elden, S. J. ... Ann Arbor, MI
Elden, Thomas K. ... Salem, OR
Elder, Albert L., III ... Washington, DC
Elder, Alex C. ... Memphis, TN
Elder, Alice L.
Federal Communications Commission,
Wireless Telecommunications Bureau, GV
Elder, Andrew H. ... Springfield, OH
Elder, Anita Jacobe ... Colorado Springs, CO
Elder, A. T., Jr. ... Oklahoma City, OK
Elder, Billy T. ... Burkburnett, TX
Elder, Brad M. ... Los Angeles, CA
Orange, CA
Elder, Brian K. ... Saginaw, MI
Elder, Charles C. ... Medford, MA
Elder, Charles E. ... Los Angeles, CA
Elder, Daniel M. ... San Antonio, TX
Elder, David F. ... Jacksonville, FL
Elder, David Patrick ... Houston, TX
Elder, David R. ... Miami, FL
Elder, David S. ... Houston, TX
Elder, Debra Oswald ... Park Ridge, IL
Elder, Dennis H. ... Monroe, MI
Elder, Diane G. ... Chicago, IL
Elder, Donald E. ... Chicago, IL
Elder, Dulan D. ... Lubbock, TX
Elder, Edward J. ... Washington, DC
Elder & Elder ... Sullivan, IL
Elder, Elysse A. ... Stuart, FL
Elder, Eugene E. ... Austin, TX
Elder, Fitzhugh, Jr. ... Staunton, VA
Elder, Fredrica B. ... Miami, FL
Elder, George P. ... Pasadena, TX
Elder, Gregory R. ... Toledo, OH
Elder, H. H., Jr. ... Brookfield, WI
Elder, Hope C. ... Citrus Heights, CA
Elder, James C. ... Marquette, MI
Elder, James C. ... Oklahoma City, OK
Elder, James David ... Pittsburgh, PA
Elder, James H., III ... Colorado Springs, CO
Elder, James H., III, Law Firm of
Colorado Springs, CO
Elder, James R. ... Tulsa, OK
Elder, James R. ... Dallas, TX
Elder, Jason T. ... Portland, OR
Elder, Jeffrey A. ... Parkersburg, WV
Elder, Jeffrey Ray ... Wamego, KS
Elder, Jinanne S.J. ... Boston, MA
Elder, John D. ... Van Horn, TX
Elder, John E. ... Charleston, IL
Elder, John F., Jr. ... Dallas, TX
Elder, John H. ... Champaign, IL
Elder, John L. ... Pearland, TX
Elder, John M. ... Springfield, OH
Elder, John W. ... Houston, TX
Elder, Joseph S. ... Hartford, CT
Elder, Joseph S., II ... Louisville, KY
Elder, Joseph S., II, P.S.C. ... Louisville, KY
Elder, Judith L. ... Pepper Pike, OH
Elder, Junior F. ... Topeka, KS
Elder, Keith Frederick ... Los Angeles, CA
Elder, Kenneth M. ... Springfield, OH
Elder, Kevin L. ... Sacramento, CA
Elder, Kevin L. ... Peoria, IL
Elder, Kurzman & Vaccarella, P.A.
Fort Lauderdale, FL
Miami, FL
Elder, Lamar A., Jr. ... Hazlehurst, GA
Elder Law Firm of Marshall & Associates, The
Jersey Shore, PA
Williamsport, PA
Elder, Leonard C. ... Grove City, OH
Elder, Linda Guelker ... Muleshoe, TX
Elder, M. Timothy ... Atlanta, GA
Elder & MacIver ... Boston, MA
Elder, Mark J. ... New York, NY
Elder, Michael S. ... Albany, NY
Elder, Nadine DeLuca ... Columbus, GA
Elder, Oliver D. ... Sullivan, IL
Elder & Phillips, P.C. ... Grand Junction, CO
Elder, Rebecca ... Los Angeles, CA
Elder, Richard A. ... North Chicago, IL
Elder, Richard E., Jr. ... Concord, CA
Elder, Robert C., Jr. ... Dallas, TX
Elder, Robert J., III ... Stuart, FL
Elder, Robert S. ... New York, NY
Elder, Robert V. ... Sullivan, IL
Elder, Roberts & Elder ... Springfield, OH
Elder, Rowland H. ... Houston, TX
Elder, Russell F. ... Farmington Hills, MI
Elder, Samuel J., Jr. ... Bellevue, WA
Elder, Sara E. ... Hoffman Estates, IL
Elder, Scott A. ... Atlanta, GA
Elder, Sherri A.B. ... Indianapolis, IN
Elder, Steve ... Hempstead, TX
Elder, Steven A. ... San Antonio, TX
Elder, Thomas C. ... Staunton, VA
Elder, Toby J. ... Riverside, CA
Elder, Tom E. ... Grand Junction, CO
Elder, Victoria S. ... Beverly Hills, CA
Elder, W. Kelly, Jr. ... Burlington, NC
Elder, William A. ... New York, NY
Elder, William J. ... Omaha, NE
Elder, William L. ... Washington, DC
Elder, William N., Jr. ... Anaheim, CA
Elder, William S. ... Columbia, SC
Eldergill, Kathleen ... Manchester, CT
Elder-Howell, Andrea ... Hicksville, NY

Elderkin, Charles B. ... **Charlotte, NC**
Elderkin, David A. ... **Cedar Rapids, IA**
Elderkin, David M. ... **Cedar Rapids, IA**
Elderkin, Dianne B. ... **Philadelphia, PA**
Elderkin, Helaine Grace
Falls Church, VA
Elderkin, Martin, Kelly & Messina, P.C.
Erie, PA
Elderkin & Pirnie, P.L.C.
Cedar Rapids, IA
Elderkin, Vernon H., Jr. ... **Erie, PA**
Elders, Barney ... Santa Cruz, CA
Elders, Vincent J. ... **Geneva, IL**
Eldien, Lorry C. ... Milwaukee, WI
El Diery, Wendy Hill ... **Miami, FL**
El Dorado Legal Clinic ... Placerville, CA
El Dorrado, Felicia R. ... Washington, DC
Eldred, A. Ney ... Tucson, AZ
Eldred, Cynthia L. ... **San Diego, CA**
Eldred, Ernest R. ... Baton Rouge, LA
Eldred, John S. ... **Washington, DC**
Eldred, Marshall P., Jr. ... **Louisville, KY**
Eldred, Michael H. ... Terre Haute, IN
Eldred, Nina R. ... **Washington, DC**
Eldred, Quentin T. ... West Palm Beach, FL
Eldred, Richard E., Law Office of
Glendale, CA
Eldred, Steven ... Fresno, CA
Eldred & Wells ... **Princeton, KY**
Eldred, Willard G. ... Princeton, NJ
Eldredge, Barbara B. ... Fullerton, CA
Eldredge, Charles M. ... **Portsmouth, NH**
Eldredge, David S. ... Palm Coast, FL
Eldredge, David S., P.A. ... Palm Coast, FL
Eldredge, Debra C. ... Baton Rouge, LA
Eldredge and Eldredge ... Baton Rouge, LA
Eldredge, Gary ... New Orleans, LA
Eldredge, George Badge ... Baton Rouge, LA
Eldredge, Jane M. ... **Lawrence, KS**
Eldredge, Jennifer Gandy ... Dallas, TX
Eldredge, John W. ... **Irvine, CA**
Eldredge, Judy ... **Worcester, MA**
Eldredge, Lloyd C. ... Salt Lake City, UT
Eldredge, Robert O., Jr. ... Pocatello, ID
Eldredge, Roger K. ... **Tulsa, OK**
Eldredge, Scott J. ... **Englewood, CO**
Eldrich, Sarah D. ... **New Haven, CT**
Eldridge, Ann B. ... Boston, MA
Eldridge, Cynthia Lynn ... Jackson, MS
Eldridge, David A. ... Dallas, TX
Eldridge, David M. ... **Knoxville, TN**
Eldridge, David O. ... **Atlanta, GA**
Eldridge, David S. ... Oklahoma City, OK
Eldridge, Deborah A. ... **Sacramento, CA**
Eldridge, Douglas A. ... Delmar, NY
Eldridge & Eldridge ... **Sacramento, CA**
Eldridge & Eldridge, P.A. ... Augusta, AR
Eldridge, Elizabeth C. ... **San Diego, CA**
Eldridge, Frank M. ... Atlanta, GA
Eldridge, Gregory S. ... Oklahoma City, OK
Eldridge, Irvine & Henrricks ... Knoxville, TN
Eldridge, James F. ... **Madison, WI**
Eldridge, Joan ... **Cambridge, MA**
Eldridge, Joan M. ... Stamford, CT
Eldridge, John C. ... Annapolis, MD
Eldridge, John D. ... Augusta, AR
Eldridge, John D., III ... Augusta, AR
Eldridge, John E. ... Knoxville, TN
Eldridge, John R. ... Vancouver, WA
Eldridge, John R., III ... **Fayetteville, AR**
Eldridge, John Rolfe ... **Houston, TX**
Eldridge, Kathleen ... **Oakland, CA**
Eldridge, Kent ... **Oklahoma City, OK**
Eldridge, Kent, P.C. ... **Oklahoma City, OK**
Eldridge, Lisa Carney ... **Philadelphia, PA**
Eldridge, Lisa D. ... **Philadelphia, PA**
Eldridge, Loyal A. ... Marshall, MI
Eldridge, Loyal A., III ... **Kalamazoo, MI**
Eldridge, Lucy E. ... Department of Justice,
Civil Division, GV
Eldridge, Marilyn Allen ... San Antonio, TX
Eldridge, Mark B. ... Addison, IL
Eldridge, Matthew X. ... Columbus, OH
Eldridge, Nina B. ... Duncanville, TX
Eldridge, Patrick E. ... **Phoenix, AZ**
Eldridge, Peter B. ... **New York, NY**
Eldridge, Richard A. ... **Sacramento, CA**
Eldridge, Richard M. ... **Tulsa, OK**
Eldridge, Rose P. ... Los Angeles, CA
Eldridge, S. Paige ... Washington, DC
Eldridge, Sheryl D. ... Belvedere-Tiburon, CA
Eldridge, Tate J. ... **Amarillo, TX**
Eldridge, Thomas R. ... Washington, DC
Eldridge, Truman K., Jr.
Kansas City, MO
Eldridge, W. Phil ... Hartford, AL
Eldridge, Wade H. ... Denver, CO
Eldridge, Wallace B., III ... Allentown, PA
Eldridge, William B. ... Winston-Salem, NC
Eleazarian, John P. ... **Fresno, CA**
Eleazer, L. Holmes, Jr. ... **Charlotte, NC**
Eleazer, W. Rhett ... Columbia, SC
Eleazer, William R. ... St. Petersburg, FL
Eleby, Calvin, Jr. ... Detroit, MI
Eleey, Peter L. ... Quincy, MA
Elefant, Carolyn ... **Washington, DC**
Elefant, David J., Law Offices of
Walnut Creek, CA
Elefant, Fred ... Jacksonville, FL
Elefant, Fred, P.A. ... Jacksonville, FL
Elefant, Kelly ... **Denver, CO**
Elefant, Martin ... Brooklyn, NY
Elefante, Angela M. ... Utica, NY
Elefante & Cacciola ... Scarsdale, NY
Elefante, Charles M. ... New York, NY
Elefante, Jeffrey P. ... **Arlington, VA**
Elefante, Mark B. ... **Boston, MA**
Elefante, Michael B. ... **Boston, MA**
Elefante, Ralph J. ... Scarsdale, NY
Eleff, Stanley H. ... **Tampa, FL**
Eleff, Susan ... **Baltimore, MD**
Eleftheri, Anthony M. ... **Indianapolis, IN**
Elegant, Ira M. ... **Miami, FL**
Elegant, Jeffrey L. ... **Chicago, IL**
Elegant, Justin B. ... **Miami, FL**
Elegante, James M. ... Magna, UT
Elenko, Thomas ... Mount Clemens, MI
Elejalde, Anamaria ... **Chicago, IL**
Elek, Steven, III ... Philadelphia, PA
Elekes, John S. ... Irvine, CA
Elenbaas & Hagan ... **Fullerton, CA**
Elenbaas, Thomas E. ... **Fullerton, CA**
Eleniak, Dale A. ... Manhattan Beach, CA
Eleniak, Dale A., Professional Law Corporation
Manhattan Beach, CA
Elenius, Jon Eric ... Chicago, IL
Elento-Sneed, Anna M. ... **Honolulu, HI**
Eler, John D. ... Trenton, NJ
Eler, Refik W. ... **Jacksonville, FL**
Elerding, Gene R. ... **Los Angeles, CA**
Elessar, Shari J. ... Greenwich, CT
Eletich, Derek A. ... **San Francisco, CA**
Eleuteri, Lawrence A., Sr. ... Mount Holly, NJ
Eleveld, Robert J. ... **Grand Rapids, MI**
Eley, Christopher K. ... Stockton, CA
Eley, Clifford E. ... Denver, CO
Eley, Craig C. ... Denver, CO
Eley, Cynthia M. ... Denver, CO
Eley, Edmond L. ... Melbourne, FL
Eley, Edmond L., P.A. ... Melbourne, FL
Eley & Eley ... Denver, CO
Eley, James P. ... Bronson, MI
Eley, James R. ... **Columbus, OH**
Eley, Kirk Edward ... Durham, NC
Raleigh, NC
Eley Law Offices, PLLC ... Durham, NC
Raleigh, NC
Eley, Michael M. ... **Montgomery, AL**
Eley, Randolph D., Jr. ... Pulaski, VA
Elf, Michael W. ... New York, NY
Elf, Randolph Scott ... Jamestown, NY
Williamsville, NY
Elfant, Noel ... Lincolnshire, IL
Elfbrandt, Barbara ... Tucson, AZ
Elfelt, A. J. ... Anoka, MN
Elfenbaum, Ian J. ... Chicago, IL
Elfenbein, Adam D. ... Arlington, VA
Elfenbein, Arthur ... Woodmere, NY
Elfenbein, Randall M. ... **New York, NY**
Elfenbein, Victor S. ... **Dallas, TX**
Elfers, John R. ... Covington, KY
Elfers, Robert J. ... Portland, OR
Elfert, Dennis John ... **Houma, LA**
Elfin, Rodman M. ... Pullman, WA
Elflein, Frederick P. ... Plainfield, NJ
Elfman, David I. ... Wilmington, MA
Elfman, Eric M. ... **Boston, MA**
Elfman, Marc A. ... **Boston, MA**
Elford, Joseph D. ... **San Francisco, CA**
Elford, Kevin Michael ... Staten Island, NY
Elfring, Betsy A. ... Sedalia, CO
Elfstrom, Susan M. ... Minneapolis, MN
Elftmann, Tracy L. ... Minneapolis, MN
Elfvin & Besser ... Cleveland, OH
Elfvin, Bruce B. ... Cleveland, OH
Elfvin, John T. ... Buffalo, NY
Elfving, William J. ... San Jose, CA
El-Gabri, Hatem H. ... Chicago, IL
El-Gamal, Yasser M. ... **Los Angeles, CA**
Elganzouri, Rasha ... **Chicago, IL**
Elgar, Alanson K. ... **Mt. Pleasant, IA**
Elgar Law Office ... **Mt. Pleasant, IA**
Elgart, Adam R. ... **Wilmington, DE**
Cherry Hill, NJ
Elgart, Allen N. ... Lexington, MA
Elgart, David F. ... Saratoga, CA
Elgart, Fredda S. ... Springfield, MA
Elgart, Ronald H. ... Levittown, PA
Elgart, Vanitha M. ... **Cherry Hill, NJ**
Elgarten, Clifton S. ... **Washington, DC**
Elgee, Joan K. ... Olympia, WA
Elgee, Michael W. ... **Stamford, CT**
Elgee, Robert J. ... Hailey, ID
Elger, John F. ... **Atlanta, GA**
Elggren, C. Allen ... Salt Lake City, UT
Elggren, Stephen B. ... **Salt Lake City, UT**
Elggren & Van Dyke, A Professional Corporation ... **Salt Lake City, UT**
El-Ghazzawy, Karim G. ... **Minneapolis, MN**
El-Ghazzawy Law Offices
Minneapolis, MN
Elgidely, Robert F. ... **Syracuse, NY**
Elgin, Ann C. ... Chicago, IL
Elgin, Arthur C., Jr. ... **Washington, DC**
Baltimore, MD
Rockville, MD
Elgin, Clogg & Patin ... Indianola, IA
Elgin, David R. ... **Madera, CA**
Elgin, P. F. ... Indianola, IA
Elgin, Robert A. ... Grosse Pointe Woods, MI
Elgin, Susan Carol ... **Baltimore, MD**
Elgison, Martin J. ... **Atlanta, GA**
Elgo, Nina F. ... Hartford, CT
Elgort, Victor S. ... **Somerville, NJ**
Elgot, Mark S. ... Seattle, WA
Elguézabal, Teresa M. ... Madison, WI
Elguindy, Joseph M. ... **Santa Monica, CA**
Elhard, Julie Ann ... St. Paul, MN
Elhart & Baird, P.C. ... Traverse City, MI
Elhart, Craig W. ... Traverse City, MI
Elhart, Frits, Knowles & Van Berkem
Bothell, WA
Elhart, Larrie E. ... Bothell, WA
Elhassani, Layth S. ... **Raleigh, NC**
Elhauge, Einer R. ... Berkeley, CA
El Hazin, Mirna Sayegh ... **Riverside, CA**
Elhilow, Joseph M. ... Paramus, NJ
Brooklyn, NY
Elhilow & Maiocchi, LLP ... Paramus, NJ
Brooklyn, NY
El-Hindi, Jamal Laurence
Washington, DC
Eli, Daniel ... **Los Angeles, CA**
Eli, David A. ... Beachwood, OH
Elia, Anthony J., Jr. ... North Haven, CT
Elia, Jim T. ... Fresno, CA
Elia, Michael J. ... **Boise, ID**
Elia, Nancy Angela ... **Brooklyn, NY**
Eliach, Steven ... Great Neck, NY
Eliades, Barbara J. ... Glendale, CA
Eliades & Butterworth ... Hopewell, VA
Richmond, VA
Eliades, Costas M. ... **New York, NY**
Eliades, Daniel M., Jr. ... **Rochelle Park, NJ**
Eliades and Eliades ... Hopewell, VA
Eliades, George C., Jr. ... **Lowell, MA**
Eliades, Homer C. ... Hopewell, VA
Eliades, Mark G. ... **Parsippany, NJ**
Eliades, Paris P. ... Sparta, NJ
Eliades, Peter D. ... Richmond, VA
Eliades, Plato G. ... Hopewell, VA
Eliades, Plato George, II ... Richmond, VA
Eliades, Sherri P. ... Hopewell, VA
Elian, Barkave G. ... West New York, NJ
Elias, A. C. ... New Iberia, LA
Elias, Adrienne A. ... Haddonfield, NJ
Elias, Albert G. ... Monroe, LA
Elias, Bettina ... New York, NY
Elias, Betty L. ... Orange, CA
Elias, Books, Brown, Peterson & Massad, P.C. ... **Oklahoma City, OK**
Elias, Brenley Locke ... **Washington, DC**
Elias, Brian ... **Miami, FL**
Elias, Brian Richard ... **Blue Bell, PA**
Elias, Charles A. ... Rolling Hills Estates, CA
Elias, Clifford E. ... Boston, MA
Elias & Crawford ... Tulsa, OK
Elias, Cynthia K. ... Tulsa, OK
Elias, Cynthia Lee ... Peoria, IL
Elias, Dan ... **Rye, NY**
Elias, Daniel Stuart ... New York, NY
Elias, David T. ... Mount Clemens, MI
Elias, Diane J. ... Glendale, CA
Elias, Dov B. ... **New York, NY**
Elias, Edward G. ... Akron, OH
Elias, Emilie H. ... Los Angeles, CA
Elias, Erasmo E. ... Oakland, CA
Elias, Eric S. ... Woodland Hills, CA
Elias, Erwin A. ... Dallas, TX
Elias, Eugene M. ... Akron, OH
Elias, Francis V. ... **New York, NY**
Elias, Frederick D. ... **West Bloomfield, MI**
Elias, Gary I. ... New York, NY
Elias, George, Jr. ... Miami, FL
Elias, George, Jr., P.A. ... Miami, FL
Elias, George P. ... Barnesboro, PA
Elias, Gregory G. ... **Monroe, LA**
Elias, Harry M. ... Vista, CA
Elias, Herbert E. ... Tulsa, OK
Elias, Herbert E., Jr. ... Tulsa, OK
Elias, Imad Y. ... **Beverly Hills, CA**
Elias, Jack I. ... **Washington, DC**
Elias, James M. ... **Bartlesville, OK**
Elias, Jane ... **West Bloomfield, MI**
Elias, Jay M. ... **Providence, RI**
Wakefield, RI
Elias, Jeanne H. ... Tallahassee, FL
Elias, Joan E. ... **Boston, MA**
Elias, John M. ... **Clearwater, FL**
Elias, John M. ... **Newark, NJ**
Elias, John M., P.A. ... **Clearwater, FL**
Elias, John S. ... **Peoria, IL**
Elias, Karen Lee
National Endowment For The Arts, GV
Elias, Kathryn A. ... **Indianapolis, IN**
Elias, Kenneth J. ... Brockton, MA
Elias, Leonard L. ... Miami, FL
Elias, Marc E. ... **Washington, DC**
Elias, Marcie R. ... New York, NY
Elias, Marguerite M. ... **Chicago, IL**
Elias, Marsha K. ... Andover, MA
Elias, Matz, Tiernan & Herrick L.L.P.
Washington, DC
Elias, Meginnes, Riffle & Seghetti, P.C.
Peoria, IL
Elias, Michael E. ... **Stamford, CT**
Elias, Michael T. ... New Orleans, LA
Elias, Nancy Stapler ... Horsham, PA
Elias, Nicole A. ... **Denver, CO**
Elias, Patricia A. ... **Denver, CO**
Elias, Peter J. ... **San Diego, CA**
Elias, Philip D. ... Owasso, OK
Elias, R. Todd ... Texas City, TX
Elias, Richard H. ... Inglewood, CA
Elias, Robert D. ... Wilkes-Barre, PA
Elias, Robert W. ... **Cherry Hill, NJ**
Philadelphia, PA
Elias, Sandra Gross ... Media, PA
Elias, Stacey E. ... Department of Labor,
Office of the Solicitor, GV
Elias, Steven ... New York, NY
Elias, Steven D. ... **Fort Lauderdale, FL**
Elias, Steven D., P.A.
Fort Lauderdale, FL
Elias, Steven E. ... **San Francisco, CA**
Elias, Theodore J. ... Los Angeles, CA
Elias, Thomas P. ... Lowell, MA
Elías, Vanessa ... **San Juan, PR**
Elias, William A. ... El Paso, TX
Elias, William K. ... **Oklahoma City, OK**
Elias, Youseef ... Oakland, CA
Eliasberg, Edward D., Jr.
Department of Justice,
Antitrust Division, GV
Eliasberg, Kenneth C. ... Canyon Country, CA
Eliasberg, Martin D. ... Woodbury, NY
Eliasberg, Michael J. ... **Los Angeles, CA**
Eliasberg, Phyllis W. ... Southfield, MI
Eliasberg-Fuchs, Abbie L. ... **Millburn, NJ**
New York, NY
Eliasen, Gary R. ... **Seattle, WA**
Eliasen, Lyle D. ... American Falls, ID
Eliaser, James R., The Law Offices of
Los Angeles, CA
Elias-Feliciano, Carmen A. ... Plano, TX
Elias-Garcia, Vanessa ... San Juan, PR
Eliashof, Mark W. ... Honolulu, HI
Eliason, Bruce H. ... Orange, CA
Eliason, Carvel H. ... Santa Ana, CA
Eliason, Deborah ... **Boston, MA**
Eliason, Deborah W. A. ... **Enfield, CT**
Eliason, Harry ... South St. Paul, MN
Eliason, Jean M. ... **Birmingham, AL**
Eliason, John A. ... **New York, NY**
Eliason, John E. ... Arlington, TX
Eliason, John W. ... Madison, WI
Eliason, Larry B. ... Birmingham, AL
Eliason, Lisa Ann ... Athens, OH
Eliason, Lonnie ... Midvale, UT
Eliason, Max D. ... Salt Lake City, UT
Eliason, Randall D. ... Washington, DC
Eliason, Robert G. ... **Fresno, CA**
Eliason, Russell A. ... Winston-Salem, NC
Eliason, Verner L. ... Denver, CO
Eliassen, Craig T. ... **Dover, DE**
Eliassof, Wm. R. ... Dallas, TX
Eliasson, Gwyneth M. ... New York, NY
Elibol, David H. ... **Buffalo, NY**
Elicegui, Shawn M. ... **Reno, NV**
Elick & Elick ... Bellville, TX
Elick, Jamie J. ... Bellville, TX
Elick, John V. ... Bellville, TX
Elicker, C. Robert, Jr. ... West Chester, PA
Elicker, Gordon L. ... **New York, NY**
Elicks, Gerard P. ... **Garden City, NY**
Elie, Joseph M. ... Rancho Cordova, CA
Elie, Mamiani ... Long Island City, NY
Elie, Steven J. ... **Los Angeles, CA**
Elieson, Kurt S. ... Little Elm, TX
Elig, Celeste ... Santa Monica, CA
Elig, Michelle ... San Francisco, CA
Eligator, David A. ... **San Francisco, CA**
San Jose, CA
Eligberg, Jodi S. ... **Woodbridge, NJ**
Elijah, Jill C. ... Flushing, NY
Elijah, Steven M. ... Spokane, WA
Elikan, Jeffrey B. ... **Baltimore, MD**
Elikann, Peter T. ... Hartford, CT
Elin, Catherine A. ... Novato, CA
Elin, Seth J. ... Taunton, MA
Eling, Kenneth J. ... **Cincinnati, OH**
Eling, William J. ... Vancouver, WA
Elinger, Annette D. ... **Atlanta, GA**
Elinger, Suzanne M. ... **Tampa, FL**
Elings, G. Roxanne ... **New York, NY**
Elinoff, Drew M. ... Weymouth, MA
Elinoff, Kallman S. ... Denver, CO
Elinski, Karen M. ... **New York, NY**
Elinski, Richard Michael ... West Covina, CA
Elinski, William W. ... **Chicago, IL**
Elio, Joseph M. ... Denver, CO
Elion, Gary D. ... Mill Valley, CA
Elion, Robert B. ... **Williamsport, PA**
Elion, Wayne, Grieco, Carlucci, Shipman & Irwin, P.C. ... **Williamsport, PA**
Eliopoulos, Elaine M. ... Worcester, MA
Eliopoulos, Elias ... **New York, NY**
Eliopoulos, George P.
Department of Justice, Tax Division, GV
Eliopoulos, Peter J. ... **Middletown, NY**
Eliopoulos, Theodore H. ... Roseville, CA
Eliopoulos, William T. ... **San Jose, CA**
Eliopulos, Alexander J. ... Cheyenne, WY
Eliopulos, Chris J. ... Denver, CO
Eliopulos, Christopher ... **New York, NY**
Eliopulos, Linda S. ... **New York, NY**
Eliopulos, Martin A. ... **San Diego, CA**
Eliot, Anna ... Groton, MA
Eliot, Edward E. ... Boston, MA
Eliot, Jason L. ... **Oklahoma City, OK**
Eliot, Judith Seymour ... Tulsa, OK
Eliot, Kimberly E. ... **Cincinnati, OH**
Eliot, Susan J. ... **Los Angeles, CA**
Eliot, Theodore Q. ... **Tulsa, OK**
Eliot, Traci C. ... **Edmond, OK**
Eliou, Keith L. ... Pittsburgh, PA
Elis, Alan M. ... New York, NY
Elisburg, Donald ... Potomac, MD
Elisco, Dennis A. ... New Castle, PA
Eliseeva, Maria ... **Minneapolis, MN**
Elisha, Ekimoto & Harada ... Honolulu, HI
Elisha, G. Stephen ... Honolulu, HI
Elisha, Kristy Lambert ... Kansas City, MO
Elisofon, Barry ... Brooklyn, NY
Elisofon, Howard R. ... **New York, NY**
Elison, Larry M. ... **Whitefish, MT**
Elison, Rand M. ... **Salt Lake City, UT**
Elison, Stephen D. ... **Houston, TX**
Elisseou, Elaine ... New York, NY
Elitcher, Anthony ... Brooklyn, NY
Elitzer, Michael R. ... Albany, NY
Elizabeth, Gretchen - ... **Tampa, FL**
Elizaga, Karen B. ... **New York, NY**
Elizalde, Chris Garza ... Austin, TX
Elizalde-Daly, Michele M.
Rancho Cucamonga, CA
Elizondo, Candelario ... Houston, TX
Elizondo, Lisa Anne ... **El Paso, TX**
Elizondo, Luis A. ... Corpus Christi, TX
Elizondo, Paul Anthony ... Oakland, CA
Elizondo, Terry Lea ... Houston, TX
Eljaiek, Santiago, III ... **Miami, FL**

Elk, Arthur M. .... Akron, OH
Elk, Bankier, Palmer & Christu
Boca Raton, FL
Palm Beach, FL
West Palm Beach, FL
Elk, David J., (Co., L.P.A.) .... Akron, OH
Elk, Elk & Whittington .... Akron, OH
Elk, Scott A., P.A. .... Boca Raton, FL
Florham Park, NJ
Elkan, Harold A. .... Kalamazoo, MI
Elkan, Matthew J.
Commodity Futures Trading Commission, Division of Enforcement, GV
Elkan, Paul W. .... Cooperstown, NY
Elke, Thomas .... Sausalito, CA
Elken, Cassandra S. .... Pasadena, CA
El-Khouri, Catherine M. .... Charlotte, NC
Elkin, Alice Censoplano .... Ann Arbor, MI
Elkin, Barbara .... Great Neck, NY
Elkin, Barry M. .... St. Petersburg, FL
Elkin, Bradley J. .... Sacramento, CA
Elkin, Craig S. .... Los Angeles, CA
Elkin, David R. .... Des Moines, IA
Elkin, David W. .... Philadelphia, PA
Elkin, Edward .... New York, NY
Elkin, Jeffrey H. .... New York, NY
Elkin, Jeffrey R. .... Houston, TX
Elkin, Joshua A. .... Wantagh, NY
Elkin, Judith .... Dallas, TX
Elkin, Julie-Karel .... Nashville, TN
Elkin, Laurie S. .... Chicago, IL
Elkin, Marjorie S. .... New York, NY
Elkin, Matthew R. .... New York, NY
Elkin, Michael S. .... New York, NY
Elkin, Molly Ann .... Washington, DC
Elkin, Paul F. .... Department of the Army, U.S. Army Legal Services Agency, GV
Elkin, Paul S. .... Fredericksburg, VA
Elkin, Robert .... Dallas, TX
Elkin, Steven C. .... Fort Lauderdale, FL
Elkin, Suzanne Chapman .... Baltimore, MD
Elkin, Sydney W. .... West Hartford, CT
Elkin, Sydney W., LLC .... Hartford, CT
West Hartford, CT
Elkin, Tom C. .... Cardington, OH
Mt. Gilead, OH
Elkin and Zahm, P.A. .... St. Petersburg, FL
Elkind, Darren J. .... DeLand, FL
Elkind, David L. .... Washington, DC
Elkind, David S. .... New York, NY
Elkind and DiMento, A Professional Association .... Cherry Hill, NJ
Elkind, Eric A. .... Honolulu, HI
Elkind, Gary N. .... Cherry Hill, NJ
Elkind, Geoffrey M. .... New York, NY
Elkind, Laura Peterson .... Dallas, TX
Elkind, Michael S. .... Los Angeles, CA
Elkind, Morton D. .... New York, NY
Elkind, Nancy B. .... Denver, CO
Elkind, Peter F. .... Oakland, CA
Elkind, Roger S. .... Coral Gables, FL
Elkind, Scott B. .... Silver Spring, MD
Elkind, Thomas I. .... Boston, MA
Elkington, Lawrence R. .... Walnut Creek, CA
Elkington, Sally J. .... Oakland, CA
Elkins, Augustus B., II .... Raleigh, NC
Elkins, Bettye S. .... Ann Arbor, MI
Elkins, Brian E. .... Ketchum, ID
Elkins, Brittany M. .... Atlanta, GA
Elkins, Charles R., II .... Baton Rouge, LA
Elkins, Clarence E., Jr. .... Smyrna, TN
Elkins, D. Michael .... Tampa, FL
Elkins, Daniel R. .... Baytown, TX
Elkins, David G. .... Houston, TX
Elkins, David S. .... Palo Alto, CA
Elkins, Deborah .... Richmond, VA
Elkins, Don H. .... Hendersonville, NC
Elkins & Elkins .... Mendham, NJ
Elkins & Finegood, P.C. .... Detroit, MI
Elkins, Gary J. .... New Orleans, LA
Elkins & Hart, A Professional Corporation
Lindsay, OK
Elkins, Herschel T. .... Los Angeles, CA
Elkins, James A., Jr. .... Columbus, GA
Elkins, James E. .... Oak Ridge, TN
Elkins, James S., III .... West Palm Beach, FL
Elkins, James W. .... Naples, FL
Elkins, Jeffrey L. .... Norton, VA
Elkins, John E. .... Treasury Department, Office of Regulations and Rulings, GV
Elkins, John W. .... San Francisco, CA
Elkins, Julie D. .... Portland, OR
Elkins, Katherine Abagail .... Rio Rancho, NM
Elkins, Keith D. .... Los Angeles, CA
Elkins, Larry .... Chicago, IL
Elkins, Leah Such .... San Jose, CA
Elkins, Lee H. .... New York, NY
Elkins, Lloyd S., Jr. .... Wilmington, NC
Elkins, Marc E. .... Kansas City, MO
Elkins, Michael D. .... Bloomfield Hills, MI
Elkins, Nathaniel B. .... Boone, NC
Elkins, P.L.C., A Professional Law Corporation .... New Orleans, LA
Elkins, R. Carter .... Huntington, WV
Elkins, Randall C. .... Houston, TX
Elkins, Randall S. .... Charleston, WV
Elkins, Randolph H. .... Alexandria, VA
Elkins, Richard A. .... Charlotte, NC
Elkins, Robert A. .... Mendham, NJ
Elkins, Robert J. .... Sarasota, FL
Elkins, Robert L. .... Charleston, WV
Elkins, Robert N. .... Athens, GA
Elkins, Rodney R., Law Offices of
Dallas, TX
Elkins, Ronald D. .... Indianapolis, IN
Elkins, S. Gordon .... Philadelphia, PA
Elkins, Stanley A. .... Warren, OH
Elkins, Stephen G. .... Washington, DC
Elkins, Stephen L. .... Grand Rapids, MI
Elkins, Steven J. .... Los Angeles, CA
Elkins, Susan L. .... Castle Rock, CO
Elkins, Suzanne .... Santa Ana, CA
Elkins, Thomas C. .... Humacao, PR
Elkins, Thomas James .... Lexington, NC
Elkins, Thomas R. .... Baton Rouge, LA
Elkins, Von B. .... Lindsay, OK
Elkins, William C. .... Burdett, NY
Elkins-Elliott, Kay .... Granbury, TX
Elkins-Richardson, Pamela .... Princeton, NJ
New York, NY
Elkman, Kenneth A. .... West Hills, CA
Elko, Allison L. .... Dallas, TX
Elkouri, David S. .... Wichita, KS
Elkouri, Edna Asper .... Norman, OK
Elkouri, Frank .... Norman, OK
Elkouri, Joe M. .... Oklahoma City, OK
El Kouri, Zahie .... Jacksonville, FL
El Koury, Jaime A. .... New York, NY
Elkovitch, David P. .... Auburn, NY
Elkowitz, Robin S. .... New York, NY
Elks, Shari Danielle .... Nashville, TN
Elkus, Lawrence M. .... Detroit, MI
Elkus, Lawrence M. .... Southfield, MI
Elkwood, Caryn Loft .... New York, NY
Ell, Cary R.
Commodity Futures Trading Commission, Division of Enforcement, GV
Ell, Douglas W. .... Washington, DC
Ell, Peggy N. .... Burlington, IA
Ella, V. John .... Minneapolis, MN
Ella, Vincent G. .... Minneapolis, MN
Ella, Vincent John .... Willmar, MN
Ellahie, Javed Inam .... San Jose, CA
Ellahie Law Firm, The .... San Jose, CA
Ellal, Gary A. .... Alexandria, VA
Ellard, Daniel P. .... Moline, IL
Ellard & Franks, P.L.C. .... Davenport, IA
Ellard, George .... Washington, DC
Ellard, George W. .... San Jose, CA
Ellard, Glenn W. .... Clarkesville, GA
Cornelia, GA
Ellard, Harold A. .... Dallas, TX
Ellard, Jan E. .... San Francisco, CA
Ellard, William M. .... Atlanta, GA
Ellbogen, Andrew D. .... Chicago, IL
Ellbogen, John P. .... Casper, WY
Ellcessor, June E. .... Point Pleasant, WV
Ellcessor, Karl M., III .... Charlottesville, VA
Ellcessor, Steven J. .... Orrville, OH
Ellch, Robert H. .... Chicago, IL
Chicago Heights, IL
Elledge, Barry W. .... Palo Alto, CA
Elledge, Donald R. .... Clinton, TN
Elledge, Ernest Thomas, Law Office of
Modesto, CA
Elledge, F. Judith .... Houston, TX
Elledge, Karl D. .... Sierra Vista, AZ
Elledge and Martin .... Brinkley, AR
Elledge, R. Reaves, Jr. .... San Diego, CA
Elledge, Richard R. .... Chicago, IL
Elledge, Robt. R. .... Modesto, CA
Elledge, Steven W. .... Brinkley, AR
Ellefsen, Suzanna E. .... Philadelphia, PA
Ellefson, Anne S. .... Greenville, SC
Ellefson, James C. .... Marshalltown, IA
Ellefson, Norman, II .... Westby, WI
Ellefson, Theodore R. .... Bentonville, AR
Ellefson, Vance E. .... Metairie, LA
Ellefson, Vance E., A Professional Law Corporation .... Metairie, LA
New Orleans, LA
Ellem, John N. .... Parkersburg, WV
Elleman, James R. .... Columbus, OH
Elleman, Jennifer N. .... Dayton, OH
Elleman, John B. .... Syracuse, NY
Elleman, Lawrence R. .... Cincinnati, OH
Elleman & Newcome .... Columbus, OH
Elleman, Steven J. .... Dayton, OH
Ellen, Benita W. .... Richmond, VA
Ellen, Phillip A. .... Raleigh, NC
Ellena, John C. .... Covina, CA
Ellenbecker, John D. .... St. Cloud, MN
Ellenberg, Adelene Fistedis
Bridgewater, MA
Ellenberg, Andrew L. .... Miami, FL
Ellenberg & Associates, P.C. .... Atlanta, GA
Ellenberg, Deborah V. .... Richmond, VA
Ellenberg & Hutson, LLP .... New York, NY
Ellenberg, Marc .... New Brunswick, NJ
Ellenberg, Mark C. .... Washington, DC
Ellenberg, Martin .... White Plains, NY
Ellenberg, Marvin B. .... San Ramon, CA
Ellenberg, Michael A. .... New York, NY
Ellenberg, Richard D. .... Atlanta, GA
Ellenberg, Robert L. .... New York, NY
Ellenberg, Stanley J. .... Philadelphia, PA
Ellenberg, Steven A. .... San Jose, CA
Ellenberg, William J., II .... Atlanta, GA
Ellenberger, James C. .... Denver, CO
Ellenberger, Laura Lynn .... Ramsey, NJ
Ellenberger, Lynn A. .... Chicago, IL
Ellenberger, Matthew S. .... Chelsea, AL
Ellenberger & Pipher .... Tekamah, NE
Ellenberger, Richard F. .... Toledo, OH
Ellenbogen, Bernard .... Latham, NY
Ellenbogen, Bernard .... New York, NY
Ellenbogen & Goldstein, P.C.
New York, NY
Ellenbogen, Hannah Kit .... Newark, NJ
Ellenbogen, Joan .... Pittsburgh, PA
Ellenbogen, Joan L. .... New York, NY
Ellenbogen, Lawrence .... Bloomfield Hills, MI
Ellenbogen, Nina C. .... Miami Beach, FL
Ellenbogen, Richard I. .... New York, NY
Ellenbogen, Susan .... Nevada City, CA
Ellenbogen, Wayne L. .... Syosset, NY
Ellenburg, Paul J. .... Aventura, FL
Ellenburg, Phillip W. .... Nashville, TN
Ellenby, Alan M. .... Chicago, IL
Ellender, Daniel .... Shreveport, LA
Ellender, Robert L. .... Lafayette, LA
Ellender, Timothy C. .... Houma, LA
Ellender, Van F. .... Houma, LA
Ellenhorn, David A. .... Seattle, WA
Ellenhorn, David N. .... New York, NY
Ellenhorn, Michael A. .... St. Louis, MO
Ellenoff, Douglas S. .... New York, NY
Ellenoff Grossman & Schole, L.L.P.
New York, NY
Ellenoff, Neil E. .... Doylestown, PA
Ellenport, Robert S. .... Clark, NJ
Ellenson, Gary .... Detroit, MI
Ellenson, Louis .... Newport News, VA
Ellenstein, William M. .... Roseville, MI
Ellenthal, Judith .... Stamford, CT
Ellentuch, Elmer I. .... Riverdale, NY
Ellentuck, Albert B. .... Washington, DC
Arlington, VA
Ellentuck, Jeff .... Newark, NJ
Ellentuck, Robert P. .... Washington, DC
Eller, Amanda L. .... Department of Justice, Federal Bureau of Investigation, GV
Eller, Brent R. .... Charlotte, NC
Eller, Brink & Sextro .... Denison, IA
Eller, C. Craig .... West Palm Beach, FL
Eller, Carson F. .... Fox Island, WA
Eller, Christie B. .... St. Paul, MN
Eller, Cynthia L. .... Torrance, CA
Eller, Cynthia W. .... Asheville, NC
Eller, Daniel A. .... St. Cloud, MN
Eller and Detrich, A Professional Corporation .... Tulsa, OK
Eller, Dwight E. .... Tucson, AZ
Eller, Gary S. .... Detroit, MI
Eller, J. Johnson, Jr. .... Altavista, VA
Eller, James F. .... Huntington, NY
Eller, James J. .... Palo Alto, CA
San Jose, CA
Eller, James R., Jr. .... San Francisco, CA
Eller, James T., Jr. .... Falls Church, VA
Eller, Jay J. .... Los Angeles, CA
Eller, Jay J., Inc. .... Los Angeles, CA
Eller, John D., Jr. .... Winston-Salem, NC
Eller, John J. .... Baltimore, MD
Eller, Julie G. .... Sarasota, FL
Eller, Leslie Robert .... Boulder, CO
Eller, Martha O. .... Decatur, IL
Eller, Michael E. .... Torrance, CA
Eller, Philip J. .... Tulsa, OK
Eller, Rayna G. .... Department of Commerce, Office of the General Counsel, GV
Eller, Robert M. .... Los Angeles, CA
Eller, Scott D. .... Minneapolis, MN
Eller, Stan .... Bridgeport, CA
Eller, Stanley W. .... Manchester, ME
Eller, Stratton R. .... Paradise Valley, AZ
Eller, Terry K. .... Boise, ID
Eller, Thomas R. .... Denison, IA
Eller, Thomas R., Jr. .... Salisbury, NC
Eller, Travis S. .... Seattle, WA
Elleraas, Allen W., Jr. .... St. Cloud, MN
Ellerbach, Connie L. .... Palo Alto, CA
Ellerbe, David L. .... Dallas, TX
Ellerbe, Frank R., III .... Columbia, SC
Ellerbe, James M. .... Lexington, KY
Ellerbee Law Firm, The, P.C.
Valdosta, GA
Ellerbee, O. Wayne .... Valdosta, GA
Ellerbee, Sarah B. .... Valdosta, GA
Ellerbrock, Charles H. .... Dearborn, MI
Ellerbrock, Michael J. .... Dayton, OH
Ellerby, H. Thomas .... San Marcos, CA
Ellerby, James Edward, II .... New York, NY
Ellerby, Scott M. .... Seattle, WA
Ellerhoff, Ronald D. .... Burlington, IA
Ellerin & Associates .... Atlanta, GA
Ellerin, Betty Weinberg .... New York, NY
Ellerin, Irwin M., (P.C.) .... Atlanta, GA
Ellerin, Jerome M. .... Cleveland, OH
Ellerin, Jerome M., Co., L.P.A.
Cleveland, OH
Ellerin, Michele P. .... Middletown, NY
Ellerin, Milton H. .... New York, NY
Ellerman, C. Howell .... Sacramento, CA
Ellerman, Christopher S. .... Mineola, NY
Ellerman, Jana .... El Dorado Hills, CA
Ellerman, Troy L. .... Sacramento, CA
Ellerman, William D. .... Dallas, TX
Ellermann, Donald R. .... Tucson, AZ
Ellermann, Marti Anne .... Albany, NY
Ellermeyer, Joseph H. .... Brookville, PA
Ellers, Debra K. .... Boise, ID
Ellers, Edward S. .... Philadelphia, PA
Ellers, Richard F. .... Nevada City, CA
Ellersdorfer, Gerald F. .... San Francisco, CA
Ellersdorfer, Rosemary Langs
Mill Valley, CA
Ellerson, H. Watkins, III .... Orange, VA
Ellerson, Tracey L. .... Orlando, FL
Ellert, Wanda L. .... Newark, NJ
Ellerton, Don R., Jr. .... Cypress, CA
Ellerton, Marie S. .... Las Vegas, NV
Ellerton, William .... New York, NY
Ellery, Michael E. .... Moorestown, NJ
Philadelphia, PA
Ellery, Richard M. .... Indianapolis, IN
Elles, Charles F. .... Rock Island, IL
Ellett, Camp, Magre & Glaser, P.C.
Cameron, TX
Rockdale, TX
Ellett, E. Tazewell .... Washington, DC
Ellett, J. Albert .... Roanoke, VA
Ellett, J. David, Jr. .... New York, NY
Ellett, Kathy L. .... Austin, TX
Ellett, Libby C., Law Offices of
Honolulu, HI
Ellett, Marshall L. .... Farmville, VA
Ellett, Marshall L., P.C. .... Farmville, VA
Ellett, Martha L. .... McLean, VA
Ellett, Robert H., Jr. .... Houston, TX
Ellett, Robert L. .... Cameron, TX
Ellett, Walter R. .... Salt Lake City, UT
Ellexson, Georgia Butcher .... Phoenix, AZ
Ellexson, Randy L. .... Phoenix, AZ
Elley, Bradley Paul .... Incline Village, NV
Ellia-Epple, Khurston Stefan .... Oxford, MA
Ellias, Demetre J. .... West Branch, MI
Ellias & Ellias, P.C. .... Detroit, MI
West Bloomfield, MI
Ellias, Frank J. .... West Bloomfield, MI
Ellias, Lauri .... Southfield, MI
Ellias, Randi L. .... Chicago, IL
Ellick, Jones, Buelt, Blazek & Longo
Omaha, NE
Ellick, Ross J. .... White Plains, NY
Ellickson, Dale R. .... Washington, DC
Ellickson, Julie Zuver .... Seattle, WA
Ellickson, Mike .... Seattle, WA
Ellickson, Robert C. .... New Haven, CT
Ellicott, John L. .... Washington, DC
Ellicott, Kevin N. .... Proctor, VT
Ellicott, Vernon L. .... Westlake Village, CA
Elliff, Brian E. .... Cincinnati, OH
Elliff, Carson W. .... Springfield, MO
Elliff, J. Eric .... Denver, CO
Elliff, Keyser, Oberle & Dancey, P.C.
Pekin, IL
Ellig, Michael L. .... Fort Smith, AR
Ellig, Van R. .... Fergus Falls, MN
Elligers, C. David .... Brooklyn, NY
Elligers, Sandra S.
National Labor Relations Board, Office of Board Members, GV
Elligett, Raymond T., Jr. .... Tampa, FL
Ellin and Baker .... Annapolis, MD
Baltimore, MD
Towson, MD
Ellin, Howard L. .... New York, NY
Ellin, Jennifer M. .... Chicago, IL
Ellin, Martin L. .... Atlanta, GA
Ellin, Marvin .... Baltimore, MD
Elling, S. David .... Gaithersburg, MD
Elling, Terry L. .... Department of the Army, U.S. Army Legal Services Agency, GV
Ellingboe, Deborah A. .... Minneapolis, MN
Ellingboe, Richard K. .... Bronx, NY
Ellingburg, C. Michael .... Jackson, MS
Ellinger, Jeffrey R. .... Raleigh, NC
Ellinger, John W., (P.C.) .... Jefferson City, MO
Ellinger, Marc H. .... Jefferson City, MO
Ellinger, Mark S. .... Minneapolis, MN
Ellinger, Rory .... O'Fallon, MO
Ellinger, Steven .... Houston, TX
Ellinger, Susan Yelton .... Raleigh, NC
Ellinger, William B. .... La Plata, MD
Ellinghausen, Edwin A., III
New Orleans, LA
Ellinghausen, John W. .... New Orleans, LA
Ellinghaus-Jones, Jo Ann .... Westminster, MD
Ellinghouse, Jerry W. .... Woodland Hills, CA
Ellingsen, Catharine D. .... Phoenix, AZ
Ellingsen, Erika Beth .... Colville, WA
Ellingsen, Mark A. .... Coeur d'Alene, ID
Ellingsen, Richard D. .... Los Angeles, CA
Ellingsen, Sharon Robinson .... Pasadena, CA
Ellingson, Burke J. .... St. Paul, MN
Ellingson, C. Polly .... Milwaukee, WI
Ellingson, Carol A. .... St. Paul, MN
Ellingson, David P. .... Des Moines, IA
Ellingson, Donald O. .... Denton, NE
Ellingson, Erik B. .... Milwaukee, WI
Ellingson, Janet Willerman .... Elgin, IL
Ellingson, Jeffrey D. .... Kalispell, MT
Ellingson, John R. .... Newport Beach, CA
Ellingson, Jon E. .... Missoula, MT
Ellingson, Joseph E. .... Spearfish, SD
Ellingson, Karen F. .... St. Paul, MN
Ellingson, Kendall J. .... Bloomington, MN
Ellingson Law Firm .... Butte, MT
Helena, MT
Missoula, MT
Ellingson, Mae Nan .... Missoula, MT
Ellingson, Patricia .... Palo Alto, CA
Ellingson, Robert L. .... Minneapolis, MN
Ellingson, Stephen P. .... Redwood City, CA
Ellingson, Steven C. .... Atlanta, GA
Ellingson, William J. .... Sioux Falls, SD
Ellingstad, Susan E. .... Minneapolis, MN
Ellingsworth, Gioia M. .... New York, NY
Ellingsworth, N. Louise .... Kansas City, MO
Ellington, A. Tonya
Equal Employment Opportunity Commission, Office of Federal Operations, GV
Ellington, Anne L. .... Seattle, WA
Ellington, Billy Joe .... Cushing, OK
Pawnee, OK
Ellington, C. Ronald .... Athens, GA
Ellington, David P. .... St. Louis, MO
Ellington, Douglas J. .... Atlanta, GA
Ellington, Edward .... Jackson, MS
Ellington, Gary D. .... Burbank, CA
Ellington, Gregory S. .... Columbus, GA
Ellington, Jacqueline E.
Federal Communications Commission, Mass Media Bureau, GV
Ellington, James B. .... Augusta, GA
Aiken, SC
Ellington, Jerel L. .... Denver, CO
Ellington, John J. .... Soperton, GA
Ellington, Kay E. .... Dallas, TX
Ellington, Marion E., Jr. .... Buford, GA

Ellington, Marion E., Jr., P.C. ... Buford, GA
Ellington, Owen H. ... El Paso, TX
Ellington, Owen H., Jr. ... Houston, TX
Ellington, R. Hunter ... Denver, CO
Ellington, Randall E. ... Longwood, FL
Ellington, Richard R.
West Palm Beach, FL
Ellington, Scott A. ... Jonesboro, AR
Ellington & Thompson, P.C. ... Houston, TX
Ellingwood, Joshua R. ... Los Angeles, CA
Ellingwood, Kendall, Jr. ... Oak Harbor, WA
Ellinor, Thomas R. ... Panama City, FL
Ellinport, Jeffrey M. ... Arlington, VA
Ellins, Howard A. ... New York, NY
Ellins, Lynn J. ... Erie, CO
Ellinwood & Bates, P.C. ... Tucson, AZ
Deming, NM
Silver City, NM
Ellinwood, John C. ... Tubac, AZ
Ellinwood, Joseph Wells ... Roseville, CA
Ellinwood, Lynne T. ... San Francisco, CA
Ellinwood, Ralph E. ... Tucson, AZ
Deming, NM
Ellinwood, Raymond ... Riverwoods, IL
Ellinwood, Steven R. ... Englewood, CO
Elliot, Carolyn A. ... Department of Justice, Executive Office for Immigration Review, GV
Elliot, D. Scott ... Redlands, CA
Elliot, David ... Forest Hills, NY
Elliot, Elizabeth ... Reno, NV
Elliot, Eugene B. ... San Francisco, CA
Elliot, F. Theodore ... Frederick, MD
Elliot, James S. ... Yakima, WA
Elliot, Jonathan D. ... Southport, CT
Elliot, Kyle L. ... Kansas City, MO
Elliot, Lauren ... New York, NY
Elliot, Lucas T. ... Houston, TX
Elliot, Mary E. ... San Francisco, CA
Elliot & Mayock, LLP ... San Francisco, CA
Washington, DC
Elliot, N. Frank, III ... Cameron, LA
Lake Charles, LA
Elliot, Patricia ... San Jose, CA
Elliot, Pishko, Gelbin & Morgan, P.A.
Winston-Salem, NC
Elliot, Ralph Gregory ... Hartford, CT
Elliot & Richardson ... San Francisco, CA
Elliot, Robert M. ... Winston-Salem, NC
Elliot, Snyder & Reid LLP ... Redlands, CA
Elliot, Steven M. ... Billings, MT
Elliot, Stuart G., (P.A.) ... Miami, FL
Elliot, Thomas A. ... Washington, DC
Elliot, Thomas A. ... Garden City, NY
Elliot, Victoria J. ... Tampa, FL
Elliot, William D. ... Roanoke, VA
Elliott, A. Irene ... Brooklyn, NY
Elliott, A. James ... Atlanta, GA
Elliott, A. Thomas, Jr. ... Denver, CO
Elliott, Albert C. ... Sonora, TX
Elliott, Alexander M. ... Morrisville, VT
Elliott, Andrea ... Wichita, KS
Elliott, Anita M. ... Santa Cruz, CA
Elliott, Ann Zimmerman
Birmingham, AL
Elliott, April P. ... Casa Grande, AZ
Elliott, Archie, Jr. ... Portsmouth, VA
Elliott & Associates ... Bloomington, IN
Elliott, Aubrey, Jr. ... Lubbock, TX
Elliott, Barbara Ann ... New Orleans, LA
Elliott, Betsy S. ... Richmond, VA
Elliott, Billy L. ... Birmingham, AL
Elliott & Blackburn ... Valdosta, GA
Elliott, Bradley A. ... Roanoke Rapids, NC
Elliott, Brady G. ... Richmond, TX
Elliott, Brian J. ... Marietta, GA
Elliott & Brouillette ... North Platte, NE
Elliott, Bruce D. ... Minneapolis, MN
Elliott, Bruce N. ... Ann Arbor, MI
Elliott, Bruce Neil ... Gas City, IN
Elliott, Carl ... Jasper, AL
Elliott, Carol A. ... Ann Arbor, MI
Elliott, Caroline R. ... Providence, RI
Elliott, Cathy ... Indianapolis, IN
Elliott, Charles D. ... Alexandria, LA
Elliott, Charles M. W. ... Los Angeles, CA
Elliott, Charles W. ... San Jose, CA
Elliott, Charles W. ... Denver, CO
Elliott, Charles W. ... Easton, PA
Elliott, Charles W. ... Madison, WI
Elliott, Cheri M. ... San Antonio, TX
Elliott, Chris ... Kansas City, MO
Elliott, Christopher A. ... Minneapolis, MN
St. Paul, MN
Elliott, Christopher R. ... Santa Ana, CA
Elliott, Cindy ... Sandpoint, ID
Elliott, Clifford L., Jr. ... Alva, OK
Enid, OK
Elliott, Clifton L. ... Seattle, WA
Elliott, Clinton J ... Louisville, KY
Elliott, Cynthia Elaine ... Flint, MI
Elliott, D. Scott, (P.A.)
West Palm Beach, FL
Elliott, Daniel R., Jr. ... Cleveland, OH
Elliott, Darrell S. ... Denver, CO
Elliott, Darrell S., P.C. ... Denver, CO
Elliott, David A. ... Birmingham, AL
Elliott, David E. ... Lee's Summit, MO
Elliott, David J. ... Hartford, CT
Elliott, David J. ... Houston, TX
Elliott, David Mayfield ... Chattanooga, TN
Elliott, David O. ... Washington, DC
Chicago, IL
New York, NY
Elliott, Dawn M. ... Leawood, KS
Elliott, Deirdre C. ... Milwaukee, WI
Elliott, Dennis H. ... Portland, OR
Elliott, Diane V. ... Bethlehem, PA
Elliott, Don R., Jr. ... Fayetteville, AR
Elliott, Donald E. ... Seattle, WA
Elliott, Donald F., Jr. ... Indianapolis, IN
Elliott, Donald H. ... New York, NY
Elliott, Donald L. ... Denver, CO
Elliott, Douglas B. ... Thomasville, NC
Elliott, Douglas Clinton ... Houston, TX
Elliott, Douglas H. ... Houston, TX
Elliott, Douglas P. ... San Francisco, CA
Elliott, Douglas R. ... New Orleans, LA
Elliott, Dru S., (Ms.) ... Danville, CA
Elliott, E. Donald ... Washington, DC
Elliott, E. Glenn ... Florence, SC
Elliott, Edgar M., III ... Birmingham, AL
Elliott, Edgar M., IV ... Birmingham, AL
Elliott, Edna ... Tampa, FL
Elliott, Edna, P.A. ... Tampa, FL
Elliott, Edward M. ... Riverhead, NY
Elliott, Eileen E. ... Blue Bell, PA
Elliott, Elaine Brown ... Evansville, IN
Elliott & Elliott ... Jasper, AL
Elliott & Elliott ... Overland Park, KS
Elliott & Elliott ... Boothbay Harbor, ME
Elliott & Elliott ... Cohasset, MA
Elliott & Elliott ... Allentown, PA
Easton, PA
Elliott and Elliott ... Houston, TX
Elliott & Elliott, P.A. ... Columbia, SC
Elliott, Enabnit, Newby & Ezzell, A Prof. Corp. ... Alva, OK
Enid, OK
Elliott, Eugene M., Jr. ... Roanoke, VA
Elliott, Ewell H., Jr. ... Atlanta, GA
Elliott, F. Matlock ... Greenville, SC
Elliott, Forest L., Jr. ... Norwalk, CA
Elliott, Frances Barnes ... Greenville, SC
Elliott, Frances C. ... Hudson, OH
Elliott, Frank W. ... Dallas, TX
Elliott, Frederick B., III ... Pittsburgh, PA
Elliott, George Alan ... Lubbock, TX
Elliott, George H. ... Hamilton, OH
Elliott, George L. ... De Kalb, IL
Elliott, George M. ... Grapevine, TX
Elliott, Gerald R. ... Department of Labor, Office of Secretary, GV
Elliott, Gerald T. ... Olathe, KS
Elliott, Glenn B. ... Milwaukee, WI
Elliott, Glynn J., Jr. ... Chicago, IL
Elliott & Goode ... Cleveland, TN
Elliott, Gregory T. ... St. Petersburg, FL
Elliott, Harry B., Jr. ... North Haven, CT
Elliott, Harry F. ... Hillsboro, OR
Elliott & Haskell, P.A. ... Macon, GA
Elliott, Helen G. ... Houston, TX
Elliott, Helen Jeanne ... Denver, CO
Elliott, Heller, Maas, Moro and Magill Co., L.P.A. ... Warren, OH
Youngstown, OH
Elliott, Herbert ... Tarpon Springs, FL
Elliott, Homer L. ... Philadelphia, PA
Elliott, Howard, Jr. ... St. Louis, MO
Elliott, Howard P., Jr. ... Baton Rouge, LA
Elliott, Hoyt, Jr. ... Jasper, AL
Elliott, Ida Lee H. ... White Plains, NY
Elliott, Ivan A., Jr. ... Carmi, IL
Elliott, J. Bryan ... Hickory, NC
Elliott, J. Jean ... Los Angeles, CA
Elliott, J. Maxton ... Concord, NC
Elliott, J. Robert ... Columbus, GA
Elliott, J. Sewell, Jr. ... Macon, GA
Elliott, J. Sewell, Sr. ... Macon, GA
Elliott, J. Victor ... Silver Spring, MD
Elliott, Jack R., (P.A.) ... Orlando, FL
Elliott, Jack W. ... Pittsburgh, PA
Elliott, James B. ... Bruno, AR
Elliott, James D. ... Washington, DC
Elliott, James E. ... Dallas, TX
Elliott, James E., Jr. ... Arvada, CO
Elliott, James E., Jr. ... Warner Robins, GA
Elliott, James F. ... Los Angeles, CA
Elliott, James F. ... Ottumwa, IA
Elliott, James G. ... Camden, ME
Elliott, James H., Jr. ... Charleston, SC
Elliott, James J. ... Stephenville, TX
Elliott, James L. ... Valdosta, GA
Elliott, James M. ... Bloomington, IN
Elliott, James M., Jr. ... Macon, GA
Elliott, James O. ... Bloomfield Hills, MI
Elliott, James Robert ... Taylor, PA
Elliott, James W. ... Dade City, FL
Elliott, James W. ... Roscoe, NY
Elliott, James W. ... Grafton, VA
Elliott, James Ward ... Lynchburg, VA
Elliott, James Wm., Jr. ... Bristol, VA
Elliott, Janette C. ... Tecumseh, OK
Elliott, Jas. F. ... White Cloud, MI
Elliott & Jasper ... Newport, NH
Elliott, Jay C. ... North Platte, NE
Elliott, Jay Jeffrey ... Los Angeles, CA
Elliott, Jaye Jones
Hilton Head Island, SC
Elliott, Jeffrey C. ... Texarkana, TX
Elliott, Jeffrey M. ... New York, NY
Elliott, Jeffrey R. ... Reading, PA
Elliott, Jennifer L. ... Las Vegas, NV
Elliott, Jennifer Peabody ... Manchester, NH
Elliott, Jerome F. ... Portland, OR
Elliott, Jerome M. ... Beloit, WI
Orfordville, WI
Elliott, Jerry E. ... Westerville, OH
Elliott, Jerry G. ... Topeka, KS
Elliott, Jerry V ... Thibodaux, LA
Elliott, Jesse R. ... New Orleans, LA
Elliott, Jessica G. ... Hartford, CT
Elliott, Joanne P. ... Park Ridge, IL
Elliott, Joel C. ... Mesquite, TX
Elliott, John B. ... East Aurora, NY
Elliott, John C. ... Waldorf, MD
Elliott, John C. ... Houston, TX
Elliott, John F. ... Cohasset, MA
Elliott, John F., Jr. ... Cohasset, MA
Elliott, John J. ... Oswego, NY
Elliott, John M. ... Minneapolis, MN
Elliott, John M. ... Hillsboro, OR
Elliott, John M. ... Blue Bell, PA
Harrisburg, PA
Elliott, John P. ... Scranton, PA
Elliott, John R. ... Phoenix, AZ
Elliott, John R. ... York, PA
Elliott, John W. ... San Jose, CA
Elliott, John W. ... Austin, TX
Elliott, John Y., III ... Chattanooga, TN
Elliott, Jon A. ... Omaha, NE
Elliott, Jon F. ... Oakland, CA
Elliott, Joseph C. ... San Antonio, TX
Elliott, Joseph F. ... Columbus, OH
Elliott, Joseph W. ... St. Joseph, MO
Elliott, Joyce L. ... Fairfield, CA
Napa, CA
Elliott, J. W. ... Sonora, TX
Elliott, Karen E. ... Findlay, OH
Elliott, Karen M. ... Rochester, NY
Elliott, Karen S. ... Richmond, VA
Elliott, Karen U. ... Rochester, NY
Elliott, Karla J. ... Washington, DC
Elliott, Kate Ford ... Pittsburgh, PA
Elliott, Kenneth M. ... Boise, ID
Elliott, Kenneth R. ... Vista, CA
Elliott, Kenneth W. ... Oklahoma City, OK
Elliott, Kevin D. ... Charlotte, NC
Elliott, Kimberly Shaw ... St. Louis, MO
Elliott, Kirk W. ... San Jose, CA
Elliott, Kyle Lynn ... Kansas City, MO
Elliott, L. Lynn, (P.C.) ... Dallas, TX
Elliott, Larry K. ... Pittsburgh, PA
Elliott, Laura Cheatham ... Louisville, KY
Elliott Law Firm, The ... Manchester, GA
Elliott Law Offices, A Professional Corporation ... Addison, TX
Dallas, TX
Richardson, TX
Elliott Law Offices, PA ... Minneapolis, MN
Elliott Law Offices, The ... Arvada, CO
Elliott, Lawrence D. ... Victoria, TX
Elliott, Lawson & Pomrenke, P.C.
Bristol, TN
Johnson City, TN
Kingsport, TN
Abingdon, VA
Bristol, VA
Elliott, Lee R. ... Troy, MO
Elliott, Linda D. ... Miami, FL
Elliott, Lisa C. ... Alachua, FL
Elliott, Lisa E. ... San Francisco, CA
Elliott, Lisa M. ... Minneapolis, MN
Elliott, Lori K. ... Cincinnati, OH
Elliott, Lorraine ... Vista, CA
Elliott, Louie C., Jr. ... Newport, NH
Elliott & Magee, L.L.P. ... Doylestown, PA
Elliott, Mara Woodworth ... Monterey, CA
Elliott, Marc E. ... New York, NY
Elliott, Marc E., P.C. ... New York, NY
Elliott, Marcia L. ... Worcester, MA
Elliott, Margaret Copeland ... Atlanta, GA
Elliott, Margaret M. ... Santa Rosa, CA
Elliott, Maria D. ... Chicago, IL
Elliott, Mark D. ... Arvada, CO
Elliott, Mark Lee ... Atlanta, GA
Elliott, Mark M. ... New York, NY
Elliott, Mary ... Fairfax, VA
Elliott, Mary Beth ... Wayne, NJ
Elliott, Mary Jane M. ... Westland, MI
Elliott, Mary Jane M., P.C. ... Westland, MI
Elliott, Mary M. ... Columbia, SC
Elliott, Maryanne Elrod ... Atlanta, GA
Elliott, Matthew J. ... Fort Wayne, IN
Elliott, Matthew J. ... Cranston, RI
Elliott, Maurice L. ... Sparks, MD
Elliott, Meena Lulla ... St. Louis, MO
Elliott, Meredith S. ... New York, NY
Elliott, Merton ... Fox Island, WA
Elliott, Michael A. ... Corpus Christi, TX
Elliott, Michael E. ... Cleveland, OH
Elliott, Michael J. ... Park Ridge, IL
Elliott, Michael J. ... Akron, OH
Elliott, Michael M. ... Indianapolis, IN
Elliott, Michael P. ... Denver, CO
Elliott, Michael W. ... Schenectady, NY
Elliott, Morris and Parks
Oklahoma City, OK
Elliott, Nancy C. ... Seattle, WA
Elliott, Nancy Gail ... Dallas, TX
Elliott, Nathalie C. ... Kansas City, MO
Elliott, Norman ... Coronado, CA
Elliott, Norman J. ... Solana Beach, CA
Elliott & Park ... Portland, OR
Elliott, Patricia A. ... Abilene, TX
Elliott, Patricia D. ... Sacramento, CA
Elliott, Patrick H. ... Minneapolis, MN
Elliott, Paul R. ... Houston, TX
Elliott, Paul Sidney ... Tampa, FL
Elliott, Paul W. ... Foxboro, MA
Elliott, Peggy A. ... Gardner, KS
Elliott, Permenter & Babb, P.A. ... Ripley, MS
Elliott, Pete C. ... Cleveland, OH
Elliott, Peter L. ... Syracuse, NY
Elliott, Phil, Jr. ... West Allis, WI
Elliott, Philip H., Jr. ... Daytona Beach, FL
Maitland, FL
Elliott, R. Brent ... Chillicothe, MO
Elliott, R. Hollis ... Menlo Park, CA
Elliott, R. Lance ... Chevy Chase, MD
Elliott, R. McKinley ... Mishawaka, IN
Elliott, Ralph E. ... Freeport, IL
Elliott, Ralph E., A Prof. Corp., Law Offices of ... Freeport, IL
Elliott, Ralph E., Jr. (P.A.) ... Jacksonville, FL
Elliott, Randall ... Pryor, OK
Elliott, Randall, P.C. ... Pryor, OK
Elliott, Randolph Lee ... Washington, DC
Elliott, Randy A. ... Indianapolis, IN
Elliott, Ray C. ... Oklahoma City, OK
Elliott, Raymond J. ... Dallas, TX
Elliott, Raymond J., III ... Troy, NY
Elliott, Raymond S. ... Dallas, TX
Elliott, Reed A. ... Longmont, CO
Elliott Reihner Siedzikowski & Egan, P.C.
Blue Bell, PA
Harrisburg, PA
Norristown, PA
Philadelphia, PA
Reading, PA
Scranton, PA
Elliott, Rex H. ... Columbus, OH
Elliott, Richard G., Jr. ... Wilmington, DE
Elliott, Richard H. ... Doylestown, PA
Elliott, Richard H. ... Dallas, TX
Elliott, Richard J. ... San Diego, CA
Elliott, Richard J. ... Rochester, NY
Elliott, Richard K. ... Worthington, OH
Elliott, Richard N. ... Jonesboro, GA
Elliott, Richard S. ... Washington, DC
Elliott, Richard W. ... Boothbay Harbor, ME
Elliott, Richard W. ... Bellevue, WA
Elliott, Richard W., II
Boothbay Harbor, ME
Elliott, Robert ... San Francisco, CA
Elliott, Robert A. ... Lombard, IL
Elliott, Robert C. ... New York, NY
Elliott, Robert C., II ... Colonial Heights, VA
Elliott, Robert F. ... Mineola, NY
New York, NY
White Plains, NY
Elliott, Robert G. ... Midland, TX
Elliott, Robert H., Jr. ... Washington, DC
Elliott, Robert J. ... Washington, DC
Elliott, Robert J. ... Janesville, WI
Elliott, Robert K. ... San Andreas, CA
Elliott, Robert L. ... Lexington, KY
Elliott, Robert L. ... Manchester, NH
Elliott, Robert L. ... Dumas, TX
Elliott, Robert L. ... Milwaukee, WI
Elliott, Robert L., Jr. ... Wilmette, IL
Elliott, Robert M. ... Marlborough, CT
Elliott, Robert M. ... Hillsboro, OR
Elliott, Robert M. ... Bellingham, WA
Elliott, Robert R., III ... New York, NY
Elliott, Robert Raymond, (P.C.)
Washington, DC
Philadelphia, PA
Elliott, Robert S. ... Tucson, AZ
Elliott, Robert W. ... Ross, CA
Elliott, Robert W. ... Ripley, MS
Elliott, Roger L. ... Towson, MD
Elliott, Roger P. ... Liberty, KY
Elliott, Roger S. ... Saco, ME
Elliott, Rosalie S. ... Clarksburg, WV
Elliott, Ross L. ... Breckenridge, TX
Elliott, Ross T. ... San Diego, CA
Elliott, Rufus E., III ... Birmingham, AL
Elliott, Rush E. ... Warren, OH
Youngstown, OH
Elliott, Russell D. ...
Department of Energy, GV
Elliott, S. Lee ... Fairfield Glade, TN
Elliott, Salley Wood ... Columbia, SC
Elliott, Sam D. ... Chattanooga, TN
Elliott, Sandra L.
Federal Energy Regulatory Commission, Office of the General Counsel, GV
Elliott, Sarah J. ... Milwaukee, WI
Elliott, Scott ... Columbia, SC
Elliott, Scott D. ... Menlo Park, CA
Elliott, Seth E. ... Chicago, IL
Elliott, Shawn K. ... Los Angeles, CA
Elliott, Sherri Wilson ... Newton, NC
Elliott, Stanek, Mazzaccaro & Sciota
Southington, CT
Elliott, Stephanie A. ... Overland Park, KS
Elliott, Stephen L. ... Roswell, NM
Elliott, Stephen N. ... Metairie, LA
Elliott, Stephen W. ... Oklahoma City, OK
Elliott, Stern & Calabrese ... Rochester, NY
Elliott, Steven C. ... Indianapolis, IN
Elliott, Steven E. ... Dayton, OH
Elliott, Steven P. ... Sparks, NV
Elliott, Stewart B. ... Owensboro, KY
Elliott & Sugarman ... Washington, DC
Elliott, Susan ... Chicago, IL
Elliott, Susan A.
Commodity Futures Trading Commission, Division of Trading and Markets, GV
Elliott, Susan Langley ... Atlanta, GA
Elliott, Susan M. ... Kansas City, MO
Elliott, Suzanne Lee ... Seattle, WA
Elliott, Tedi Spencer ... San Antonio, TX
Elliott, Thania S. ... New Orleans, LA
Elliott, Theresa M. ... Washington, DC
Elliott, Thomas A. ... San Jose, CA
Elliott, Thomas B. ... Toledo, OH
Elliott, Thomas C., Jr. ... Chicago, IL
Elliott, Thomas E. ... Corvallis, OR
Elliott, Thomas E., Jr. ... Columbia, SC
Elliott, Thomas G. ... Lakewood, CO
Elliott, Thomas J. ... Blue Bell, PA
Harrisburg, PA
Reading, PA
Elliott, Thomas R., Jr. ... Birmingham, AL
Elliott, Thomas R., Jr. ... Easton, PA
Elliott, Timothy B. ... Tallahassee, FL
Elliott, Timothy D. ... Chicago, IL
Elliott, Timothy G. ... Overland Park, KS
Elliott, Timothy G. ... Bend, OR
Elliott, Timothy J. ... Albany, NY

Elliott, Timothy L. St. Louis, MO
Elliott, Timothy S.
Department Of The Interior, Office of the Solicitor, GV
Elliott, Todd M. Seattle, WA
Elliott, Travis Quintin Washington, DC
Elliott, Tyron C. Manchester, GA
Elliott, Vanessa R. Morristown, NJ
New York, NY
Elliott, W. Curtis, Jr. Charlotte, NC
Elliott, W. Gus Valdosta, GA
Elliott, W. Mitchell Gower, MO
Elliott, W. Price Ripley, MS
Elliott, W. Randolph Dallas, TX
Elliott, Walter G., II Valdosta, GA
Elliott, Ward E. Y. Claremont, CA
Elliott, Warren G. Washington, DC
Elliott, Wayne N. Dover, DE
Wilmington, DE
Elliott, Wayne T. Roswell, GA
Elliott, Wendy R. Salinas, CA
Elliott, William A. Irvine, CA
Elliott, William A. La Porte, IN
Elliott, William B. Hill City, KS
Elliott, William B. Trotwood, OH
Elliott, William C. Montgomery, AL
Elliott, William D. Dallas, TX
Elliott, William E. Houston, TX
Elliott, William Forbes Covington, GA
Elliott, William G. University Center, MI
Elliott, William J. Braintree, MA
Elliott, William M. Rancho Santa Fe, CA
Elliott-Dumler, Beth Wheat Ridge, CO
Elliotte, C. Shannon Charlotte, NC
Elliott-Howard, Florence E.
Nacogdoches, TX
Elliott-Pinson, Paige Birmingham, AL
Ellis, A. Charles Greenville, NC
New Bern, NC
Ellis, A. Ralph Pittsburgh, PA
Ellis, A. Richard Mill Valley, CA
Ellis, A. Travis Windsor, NC
Ellis, Abraham New York, NY
Ellis & Aeschliman Columbus, OH
Ellis, Al Dallas, TX
Ellis, Alan Sausalito, CA
Ellis, Alan E. Indian Valley, ID
Ellis, Alan, Law Offices of Sausalito, CA
Ellis, Albert M. Stockton, CA
Ellis, Alfred D., (P.C.) Boston, MA
Ellis, Alice D. Portland, OR
Ellis, Allen B. Boise, ID
Ellis, Amanda R. Arlington, VA
Ellis, Amanda R., P.C. Arlington, VA
Ellis, Andrew D. Livingston, NJ
Ellis, Andrew J., Jr. Richmond, VA
Ellis, Andrew M. Phoenix, AZ
Ellis, Anna Maria O. Miami, FL
Ellis, Anne Andrews San Francisco, CA
Ellis, Anthony G. San Diego, CA
Ellis, Anthony Michael Alhambra, CA
Ellis, Arthur U. Chicago, IL
Ellis, Ashley Dallas, TX
Ellis, Astrid E. Chicago, IL
Ellis, Audrey Alterman, (P.A.) Miami, FL
Ellis, Avery M. Department of Justice, Tax Division, GV
Ellis, B. Craig Laurinburg, NC
Ellis, Barbara J. Boston, MA
Ellis, Barbara J. Harrisburg, PA
Ellis, Barbara M. Austin, TX
Ellis, Barnes H. Portland, OR
Ellis & Barrett, A Professional Law Association Mountain View, CA
Ellis, Ben F. Lancaster, TX
Ellis, Benjamin D. Savannah, GA
Ellis, Bernard M. Chicago, IL
Ellis, Bernie W. Greenville, SC
Ellis, Bill, Jr. McAllen, TX
Ellis, Bobby James Gainesboro, TN
Ellis, Braddock & Dees, Ltd.
Vicksburg, MS
Ellis, Bradley H. Los Angeles, CA
Ellis, Brian C. Tampa, FL
Ellis, Brian M. New York, NY
Ellis, Brian R. Cleveland, OH
Ellis, Brian W. Chicago, IL
Ellis, Brown & Sheils, Chartered
Boise, ID
Ellis, Bruce W. Whitehouse Station, NJ
Ellis, C. Pat Houston, TX
Ellis, Carey J., Jr. Rayville, LA
Ellis, Carl R. Buffalo, NY
Ellis, Carolyn T. New York, NY
Ellis, Carrie S. Montgomery, AL
Ellis, Caryl New York, NY
Ellis, Charles E. Blytheville, AR
Ellis, Charles E., Jr. Tullahoma, TN
Ellis, Charles M. Miamisburg, OH
Ellis, Charles W. Oklahoma City, OK
Ellis, Christian Fort Worth, TX
Ellis, Christine M. Danbury, CT
Ellis, Clyde E. Vicksburg, MS
Ellis, Clyde E., Jr. Erie, PA
Ellis, Colin D. Los Angeles, CA
Ellis, Colita San Francisco, CA
Ellis & Collins San Luis Obispo, CA
Ellis, Courtenay Washington, DC
Ellis, Courtney F. Lexington, KY
Ellis, Craig S. Glen Ellen, CA
Ellis, Cupps & Cole Cassville, MO
Ellis, Cynthia A. Punta Gorda, FL
Ellis, Cynthia E. Westport, CT
Ellis, Damon Michael Tampa, FL
Ellis, Daniel Princeton, NJ
Ellis, Daniel C. Portland, OR
Ellis, Daniel E. Atlanta, GA
Ellis, Daniel T. Toledo, OH
Ellis, Darrel R. Cle Elum, WA
Ellensburg, WA
Ellis, David A. New York, NY
Ellis, David B. Denver, CO
Ellis, David B. Boston, MA
Ellis, David G. Portland, OR
Ellis, David J. El Paso, TX
Ellis, David L. Sherman Oaks, CA
Ellis, David M. Dallas, TX
Ellis, David R. Columbia, SC
Ellis, David Roy Largo, FL
Ellis, David Roy Tampa, FL
Ellis, David W. Chicago, IL
Ellis, David W. Chicago, IL
Ellis, David W. Vicksburg, MS
Ellis, Dean B. Hurricane, UT
Ellis, Dean L. Detroit, MI
Ellis, Deborah A. Newark, NJ
Ellis, Deborah E. Oregon, IL
Ellis, Deborah H. Brownwood, TX
Ellis, Deborah K. St. Paul, MN
Ellis, Del J. Wheat Ridge, CO
Ellis, Dennis Gerard Highland, NY
Ellis, Dennis S. Los Angeles, CA
Ellis, Diane L. Irvine, CA
Ellis, Donald C. Anchorage, AK
Ellis, Donald J. Atlanta, GA
Ellis, Donald L. Tyler, TX
Ellis, Donna Cortlandt Manor, NY
Ellis, Donna S. Grand Junction, CO
Ellis, Dorsey D., Jr. St. Louis, MO
Ellis, Douglas J. Pittsburgh, PA
Ellis, Douglas M. Chicago, IL
Ellis, Douglas N., Jr. Boston, MA
Ellis, Duggan F. New Orleans, LA
Ellis, Durham William Mountain Brook, AL
Ellis, Dwight H., III Milwaukee, WI
Ellis, Dwight W., III New York, NY
Ellis, E. Michael Knoxville, TN
Ellis, Earl Kent Houston, TX
Ellis, Easterlin, Peagler, Gatewood & Skipper, P.C., A Professional Corporation
Americus, GA
Ellis, Eby, Conner & Shaner, P.L.L.C.
Ann Arbor, MI
Ellis, Edward D. Paris, TX
Ellis, Edward J. Windsor, CT
Ellis, Edward P. Atlanta, GA
Ellis, Edward T. Cherry Hill, NJ
Philadelphia, PA
Ellis, Elia M. St. Louis, MO
Ellis & Ellis Rockford, IL
Ellis & Ellis Vicksburg, MS
Ellis & Ellis Nashville, TN
Ellis & Ellis Hurricane, UT
Ellis and Ellis Co., L.P.A. Marietta, OH
Ellis & Fisher, P.A. Tupelo, MS
Ellis, Ellis, Hammons & Johnson, P.C.
Springfield, MO
Ellis, Elmer Douglass Washington, DC
Ellis, Emory N., Jr. Washington, DC
Ellis, E.N., IV New York, NY
Ellis, F. Earl, Jr. Columbia, SC
Ellis, Frank A., III Las Vegas, NV
Ellis, Frank & Associates, Ltd.
Las Vegas, NV
Ellis, Frank C., Jr. Columbiana, AL
Ellis, Fredric L. Boston, MA
Ellis, Funk, Goldberg, Labovitz & Dokson, P.C. Atlanta, GA
Ellis, G. Joe Houston, TX
Ellis, G. Kenner, Jr. Greenville, MS
Ellis, G. Kirk Beverly Hills, CA
Ellis, G. Richard Kokomo, IN
Ellis, Gail E. Santa Monica, CA
Ellis, Gail N. Framingham, MA
Ellis, Gamble & Nolan Kokomo, IN
Ellis, Garrettson Chicago, IL
Ellis, Gary Manhattan, KS
Ellis, George C. Millersburg, OH
Ellis, George D. Benton, AR
Ellis, George H., Law Offices of
Los Angeles, CA
Ellis, George J., Jr. Poughkeepsie, NY
Ellis, George M. Columbus, OH
Ellis, George N. Worcester, MA
Ellis, George R. Trenton, TN
Ellis, George R., Jr. Americus, GA
Ellis, George T. Houston, TX
Ellis, Gerald A. Atlanta, GA
Ellis, Gerald B. Tulsa, OK
Ellis, Glen J. Hurricane, UT
Ellis, Glyn D. Logan, WV
Ellis, Graydon H., Jr. Ann Arbor, MI
Ellis, Gregory D. Atlanta, GA
Ellis, Gregory H. Birmingham, AL
Ellis, Gregory J. Schaumburg, IL
Ellis, Gregory M. San Antonio, TX
Ellis, Gregory R. San Francisco, CA
Ellis, Guy T., Jr. Louisville, KY
Ellis, H. Case Crystal Lake, IL
Ellis, H.E., Jr., P.A. Pensacola, FL
Ellis, H. Reed Newark, NJ
Ellis, H. Scott Parsippany, NJ
Ellis, Hal Wm. Stillwater, OK
Ellis, Harlow J. Chatsworth, CA
Ellis, Harvey D., Jr. Oklahoma City, OK
Ellis, H. E., Jr. Pensacola, FL
Ellis, H. E., Sr. Biloxi, MS
Ellis, Helen Carey Tallahassee, FL
Ellis, Helen H. Tuscaloosa, AL
Ellis, Henry C. Taunton, MA
Ellis, Herbert I. Freehold, NJ
Ellis, Herbert W. Lake City, FL
Ellis, Holly A. Newport Beach, CA
Ellis, Hooper, Warlick & Morgan, LLP
Jacksonville, NC
Ellis, Howard M., Law Offices of
Buffalo, NY
Ellis, Insabella & Hutchison Tulsa, OK
Ellis, Irwin D. Philadelphia, PA
Ellis, J. Nicholas Rocky Mount, NC
Ellis, J. Wiley Savannah, GA
Ellis, Jamellah L. Washington, DC
Ellis, James A. Minneapolis, MN
Ellis, James A., Jr. Dallas, TX
Ellis, James B. San Francisco, CA
Ellis, James B., II Washington, DC
Ellis, James C. Dayton, OH
Ellis, James C., (P.C.) Albuquerque, NM
Ellis, James D. Cleveland, OH
Ellis, James D. San Antonio, TX
Ellis, James H. Scarsdale, NY
Ellis, James H., III Solana Beach, CA
Ellis, James L. Baton Rouge, LA
Ellis, James M. Chicago, IL
Ellis, James M. Tarboro, NC
Ellis, James N. Worcester, MA
Ellis, James R. Portland, OR
Ellis, James R. Dallas, TX
Ellis, James R. Seattle, WA
Ellis, James T. Grosse Pointe Farms, MI
Ellis, James T., & Associates, P.C.
Grosse Pointe Farms, MI
Ellis, James W. Albuquerque, NM
Ellis, Jane Truesdell Lynnfield, MA
Ellis, Janice Hensolt Kilauea, HI
Ellis, Jean San Diego, CA
Ellis, Jeffrey A. Milwaukee, WI
Ellis, Jeffrey B. Los Angeles, CA
Ellis, Jeffrey J. New York, NY
Ellis, Jeffrey L. Jackson, MS
Ellis, Jeffrey M. Minneapolis, MN
Ellis, Jeffrey O. Overland Park, KS
Ellis, Jennifer A. Los Angeles, CA
Ellis, Jennifer L. Lexington, KY
Ellis, Jennifer L. Mechanicsburg, PA
Ellis, Jerold R. Miami, FL
Ellis, Jerome O. Staten Island, NY
Ellis, Jerry M. Farmington Hills, MI
Ellis, Jim Louisville, KY
Ellis, Joan Department of Commerce, Patent and Trademark Office, GV
Ellis, Joana S. Montgomery, AL
Ellis, Joe R. Cassville, MO
Ellis, Joe W. Nashville, TN
Ellis, Joel M. Hartford, CT
Ellis, Joel M. Hackensack, NJ
Ellis, John A. Los Angeles, CA
Ellis, John A. Elgin, IL
Ellis, John B. Vallejo, CA
Ellis, John D. Tucson, AZ
Ellis, John D., Jr. Houston, TX
Ellis, John E. Vicksburg, MS
Ellis, John E. M. St. Petersburg, FL
Ellis, John F. Elkhart, IN
Ellis, John G. Detroit, MI
Ellis, John I. Dover, DE
Ellis, John J. Morehead, KY
Ellis, John J. Boston, MA
Ellis, John N. Worcester, MA
Ellis, John O., Jr. Decatur, GA
Ellis, John P. Oak Lawn, IL
Ellis, John P. Omaha, NE
Ellis, John P. Arlington, VA
Ellis, John R. Tallahassee, FL
Ellis, John R. Cleveland, OH
Ellis, John T., II Tupper Lake, NY
Ellis, John T., II, LLC Malone, NY
Tupper Lake, NY
Ellis, John W. Santa Barbara, CA
Ellis, John W. Bellevue, WA
Ellis, John W., Jr. Sherman, TX
Ellis, Jon K. Springfield, IL
Ellis, Jonathan H. Jenkintown, PA
Ellis, Jonathan J. Tampa, FL
Ellis, Joseph A. Frederick, MD
Ellis, Joseph M. Macon, MO
Ellis, Joy Portland, OR
Ellis, Judith St. Petersburg, FL
Ellis, Julie A. Riverside, CA
San Diego, CA
Ellis, Julie H. Memphis, TN
Ellis, Kaleel M. Terre Haute, IN
Ellis, Karen A. Newport Beach, CA
Ellis, Karen L.C. Nashville, TN
Ellis, Katherine P. Houston, TX
Ellis, Kathleen A. Longmont, CO
Ellis, Kathleen A. Baltimore, MD
Ellis, Kathryn A. Department of Education, Office of the General Counsel, GV
Ellis, Keith H. Washington, DC
Ellis, Kelly C. Metairie, LA
Ellis, Kenneth R. Goldsboro, NC
Ellis, Kermit W., Jr. Henderson, NC
Ellis, Kevin R. Denver, CO
Ellis, Kevin R., P.C. Denver, CO
Ellis, Kianga M. New York, NY
Ellis, Kim Louise San Diego, CA
Ellis, Kimberly A. Tucson, AZ
Ellis, Kimberly Lynne Rockledge, FL
Ellis, Kirk D. Springfield, OH
Ellis, Koeneke & Ramirez, L.L.P.
Brownsville, TX
Harlingen, TX
McAllen, TX
Rio Grande City, TX
Ellis, Korman Dorsey Ventura, CA
Ellis, Kristin L.
Office Of Special Counsel, GV
Ellis & Kustell Buffalo, NY
Ellis, L. Neal, Jr. Raleigh, NC
Ellis, Larry R. Charleston, WV
Ellis, Laura Ann Garden City, NY
Ellis Law Firm Benton, AR
Little Rock, AR
Ellis Law Firm Herald, CA
Ellis Law Offices, Inc. Ketchikan, AK
Ellis Law Offices, L.L.C. Terre Haute, IN
Ellis, Lawhorne & Sims, P.A.
Columbia, SC
Ellis, Lee T., Jr. Washington, DC
Ellis, Leigh A. J. Lancaster, PA
Ellis, Leonard & Buckholts Duncan, OK
Ellis, Leroy J., III Nashville, TN
Ellis, Leroy Johnston, IV Nashville, TN
Ellis, Li & McKinstry PLLC Seattle, WA
Ellis, Linda Evonne Northport, NY
Ellis, Lindsay Phoenix, AZ
Ellis, Lisa P. Ellicott City, MD
Ellis, Lonnie J. Springfield, VA
Ellis, Luke Orinda, CA
Ellis, Luther W. Fort Worth, TX
Ellis, Lynn McMains Marietta, OH
Ellis, Madeline F. Washington, DC
Ellis, Malcolm G. Los Angeles, CA
Ellis, Margaret P. Pascagoula, MS
Ellis, Mark Sacramento, CA
Ellis, Mark A. Omaha, NE
Ellis, Mark S. Washington, DC
Ellis, Martin B. Baltimore, MD
Ellis, Martin L. Knoxville, TN
Ellis, Mary A. McLean, VA
Ellis, Mary C. Bradenton, FL
Ellis, Mary C. University, MS
Ellis, Maryjean Montvale, NJ
Ellis, Maurice N. Anchorage, AK
Ellis, Melissa Langer Boston, MA
Ellis, Melvin C., III Tupelo, MS
Ellis, M. H. Hood Elizabeth City, NC
Ellis, Michael Riverside, CA
Ellis, Michael A. Cleveland, OH
Ellis, Michael H., (Professional Law Corporation) Metairie, LA
Ellis, Michael M. Livonia, MI
Ellis, Michael S. Palo Alto, CA
Ellis, Michael Thomas Terre Haute, IN
Ellis, Michel Byrd Palm Beach, FL
Ellis, Mitchell D. San Francisco, CA
Ellis & Morgan Stillwater, OK
Ellis, Morris W. Chicago, IL
Ellis, Neil R. Washington, DC
Ellis, Painter, Ratterree & Bart LLP
Savannah, GA
Ellis, Pamela K. Washington, DC
Ellis, Paris K. Middletown, OH
Ellis, Patricia A. Los Angeles, CA
Ellis, Patrick T. Minneapolis, MN
Ellis, Paul G. Portland, OR
Ellis, Paul R. Pelham, AL
Ellis, Paul R., III Dallas, TX
Ellis, Pauline New York, NY
Ellis, Peter B. Boston, MA
Ellis, Peter G. Springfield, MA
Ellis, Peter M. Columbus, OH
Ellis, Peter R. Ketchikan, AK
Ellis, Philip C., Jr. Inglewood, CA
Ellis & Prehn, P.C. Corpus Christi, TX
Dallas, TX
Ellis, R. Charles Baton Rouge, LA
Ellis, Rachel Los Alamitos, CA
Ellis, Ralph F. Cincinnati, OH
Ellis, Ralph W. Atlanta, GA
Ellis, Ransom A, III Springfield, MO
Ellis, Ransom A., Jr. Springfield, MO
Ellis & Rapacki Boston, MA
Ellis, Raymond G. San Francisco, CA
Ellis, Rebecca M. Montpelier, VT
Ellis, Rene Stemple Cary, NC
Ellis, Reynolds & Bradley
St. Petersburg, FL
Ellis, Rich Herald, CA
Ellis, Richard B. Kansas City, KS
Ellis, Richard K. Aurora, CO
Ellis, Richard M. Tallahassee, FL
Ellis, Richard N. Beverly Hills, CA
Ellis, Richard V. Sarasota, FL
Ellis, Richard W. Wilmington, DE
Ellis, Richard W. Raleigh, NC
Wilmington, NC
Ellis, Robert Marietta, OH
Ellis, Robert B. Chicago, IL
Ellis, Robert B., Jr. Nashville, GA
Ellis, Robert C. Lansing, MI
Ellis, Robert C. Miamisburg, OH
Ellis, Robert D. Hempstead, NY
Ellis, Robert E. Fresno, CA
Ellis, Robert E. Chicago, IL
Ellis, Robert G. Bettendorf, IA
Ellis, Robert G. Vicksburg, MS
Ellis, Robert L. New York, NY
Ellis, Robert L. Columbus, OH
Ellis, Robert L. Fairfax, VA
Ellis, Robert P., Jr. Lorain, OH
Ellis, Robert R. Toms River, NJ
Ellis, Robert Scott Colts Neck, NJ
Ellis, Robert W. Houston, TX
Ellis, Rodney G., (P.C.) Houston, TX
Ellis, Roger G. Clark, NJ
Ellis, Roger W. Birmingham, AL
Ellis, Ronald D. Los Angeles, CA
Santa Ana, CA
Ellis, Ronald D. Torrance, CA
Ellis, Ronald L. New York, NY
Ellis, Ronald S. Morris, IL
Ellis, Ronda L. Boca Raton, FL
Ellis, Rose A. Chicago, IL
Ellis, Russell E. Norristown, PA
Ellis, Ruth T. Knoxville, TN
Ellis, Samuel D. San Luis Obispo, CA
Ellis, Sean San Francisco, CA
Ellis, Sean Wesley Jackson, MS

Ellis, Sharon Alston .... Williamston, MI
Ellis, Sharon Henderson .... Brookline, MA
Ellis, Sheldon M. .... Hillsdale, MI
Ellis, Sheldon R. .... Hyattsville, MD
Ellis, Sheldon S. .... Los Angeles, CA
Ellis, Shelly Nichols .... Tupelo, MS
Ellis & Simons, LLP .... Atlanta, GA
Ellis, Spencer and Butler
Fort Lauderdale, FL
Hollywood, FL
Miami, FL
Ellis, S. T. .... McDonough, GA
Ellis, Stephen .... Brownwood, TX
Ellis, Stephen A. .... Costa Mesa, CA
Ellis, Stephen A. .... Rockford, IL
Ellis, Stephen C. .... Cleveland, OH
Ellis, Stephen C. .... Seattle, WA
Ellis, Stephen D. .... Cape Coral, FL
Ellis, Stephen D. .... Springfield, VT
Ellis, Stephen F. .... Sarasota, FL
Ellis, Stephen F., P.A. .... Bradenton, FL
Sarasota, FL
Venice, FL
Ellis, Stephen G. .... Waynesville, NC
Ellis, Stephen M. .... Anchorage, AK
Ellis, Stephen P. .... Georgetown, DE
Ellis, Stephen P. .... Las Vegas, NV
Ellis, Steven A. .... Los Angeles, CA
Ellis, Steven D. .... Department of Justice, Environment and Natural Resources Division, GV
Ellis, Steven M. .... Boston, MA
Ellis, Steven R. .... Omaha, NE
Ellis, Steven W. .... Corpus Christi, TX
Ellis, Stuart L. .... Chicago, IL
Ellis, Susan .... Wichita, KS
Ellis, Susan K. .... Wilson, NC
Ellis, Susan Pauline .... New Bern, NC
Ellis, Susan Potter .... New York, NY
Ellis, Suzanne M. .... Chicago, IL
Ellis, T.A. .... McDonough, GA
Ellis, T. C. W. .... New Orleans, LA
Ellis, Terry R. .... Mountain View, CA
Ellis, Thomas Borden .... Roanoke, VA
Ellis, Thomas E. .... Birmingham, AL
Ellis, Thomas F. .... Raleigh, NC
Ellis, Thomas F., III .... Annapolis, MD
Ellis, Thomas F., III, P.A. .... Annapolis, MD
Ellis, Thomas H. .... Wilmington, DE
Ellis, Thomas Jay .... Philadelphia, PA
Ellis, Thomas T. .... Duncan, OK
Ellis, Timothy D. .... Los Angeles, CA
Ellis, Timothy D. .... Jacksonville, FL
Ellis, Timothy N. .... San Diego, CA
Ellis, Todd R. .... Columbia, SC
Ellis, Traci D. .... Elgin, IL
Ellis, Tracy Leigh .... Tampa, FL
Ellis & Trattner, P.C. .... Danbury, CT
Stamford, CT
Ellis, Troy H. .... Atlanta, GA
Ellis, T. S., III .... Alexandria, VA
Ellis, Urchie B. .... Richmond, VA
Ellis, Van W. .... Washington, DC
Ellis, Vanessa H. .... Hazelwood, MO
Ellis, Vernon Dale, Jr. .... Tulsa, OK
Ellis, Victor A. .... Atlanta, GA
Ellis, Victor Law .... Tulsa, OK
Ellis, W. Burrell, Jr. .... Atlanta, GA
Ellis, W. Richard, III .... Houston, TX
Ellis, W. Richard, III, P.C., Law Offices of .... Houston, TX
Ellis, Walter .... Houston, TX
Ellis, Warren H. .... Norman, OK
Ellis, Wayne M. .... Jacksonville, FL
Ellis, Wendy Alice Thomas .... Detroit, MI
Ellis, William B. .... Richmond, VA
Ellis, William D. .... Los Angeles, CA
Ellis, William F. .... Burlington, VT
Ellis, William H., Jr. .... Seattle, WA
Ellis, William J. .... El Paso, TX
Ellis, William R. .... Cincinnati, OH
Ellis, William S. .... New York, NY
Ellis, William T. .... Washington, DC
Ellis, Willis H. .... Albuquerque, NM
Ellis, Winston R. .... Houston, TX
Ellis, Wm. L. .... Aransas Pass, TX
Ellis, Wm. L., P.C. .... Aransas Pass, TX
Ellis, Wm. T. .... Shreveport, LA
Ellis-Brown, Teri .... Stone Mountain, GA
Ellis-Cheek, Imani K.
Federal Communications Commission, Cable Services Bureau, GV
Ellisen, Bruce R. .... Department of Justice, Tax Division, GV
Ellisen, E. Patrick .... Palo Alto, CA
Ellisen, Hays .... New York, NY
Ellis Farrell, Tracee .... Los Angeles, CA
Ellis-Harden, Mary M. .... Omaha, NE
Ellis-Hoyle, C. Suzette .... Decatur, GA
Ellis-Monro, Barbara .... Atlanta, GA
Ellison, Anthony L. .... San Francisco, CA
Ellison, Brenda .... Department of Justice, Civil Division, GV
Ellison, Brooks .... Sacramento, CA
Ellison, Bruce H. .... Rapid City, SD
Ellison, Charles W., II .... Poway, CA
Ellison, Christopher T. .... Sacramento, CA
Ellison, Daniel Martin .... Durham, NC
Ellison, David A. .... Lubbock, TX
Ellison, David H. .... Portola Valley, CA
Ellison, David H., Professional Corporation .... Portola Valley, CA
Ellison, David M., Jr. .... Baton Rouge, LA
Ellison, David R. .... Ventura, CA
Ellison, Dawn A. .... Washington, DC
Ellison, Duane C. .... Fairfax, VA
Ellison, Eddie .... White Plains, NY
Ellison and Ellison .... Baton Rouge, LA
Ellison, Elton A. .... Treasury Department, Departmental Offices, GV
Ellison, Ethel C.
Department of Housing and Urban Development, Office of General Counsel, GV
Ellison, Eugenia D.
General Services Administration, Office of the General Counsel, GV
Ellison, Frank M. .... Charleston, WV
Ellison, Gary E. .... Houston, TX
Ellison, George C. .... Chicago, IL
Ellison, George F. .... White River Junction, VT
Ellison, Heidi K. .... Fort Wayne, IN
Ellison & Hinkle, A Professional Law Corporation .... Ventura, CA
Ellison, Jack B. .... Buffalo, TX
Ellison, James E. .... Harrisburg, PA
Ellison, James O. .... Tulsa, OK
Ellison, James P. .... York, PA
Ellison, James W. .... Augusta, GA
Ellison, James W. .... Gering, NE
Ellison, Jane L. .... Los Angeles, CA
Ellison, Jeffrey J. .... Detroit, MI
Ellison, Jennifer S. .... Silver Spring, MD
Ellison, Jo Ann .... New York, NY
Ellison, John N. .... Philadelphia, PA
Ellison, John P., Jr. .... Ann Arbor, MI
Ellison, Judith R. .... Farmington Hills, MI
Ellison, Kathleen R. .... Houston, TX
Ellison, Kathy L. .... Dayton, OH
Ellison, Keith F. .... Wausau, WI
Ellison, Keith P., Law Office of .... Houston, TX
Ellison, Kenneth Gordon .... New York, NY
Ellison, Leland J. .... Sacramento, CA
Ellison, Linda L. .... Albuquerque, NM
Ellison, Lynn .... Jourdanton, TX
Ellison, Marc L. .... Houston, TX
Ellison, Margaret Bates .... Pinecliffe, CO
Ellison, Marjorie .... New York, NY
Ellison, Mark A. .... Boise, ID
Ellison, Mark C. .... Washington, DC
Burke, VA
Ellison, Maurice F., Jr. .... Capitol Heights, MD
Ellison, Melissa S. .... Mount Vernon, IL
Ellison, Michael H. .... Atlanta, GA
Ellison, Michael W. .... Irvine, CA
Ellison, Michelle .... Atlanta, GA
Ellison, Morris A. .... Charleston, SC
Ellison, Myron K. .... Kansas City, MO
Ellison, Nancy M. .... Kenmore, WA
Ellison, Nathaniel L. .... Cresskill, NJ
Ellison, Nielsen, Lofgren & Knibbs, P.C. .... Chicago, IL
Ellison, Noni L. .... Houston, TX
Ellison, Oliver Scott .... Baton Rouge, LA
Ellison, Patricia L. .... Kingston, NY
Ellison, Paul H. .... Merrillville, IN
Ellison, Paula M.
Federal Communications Commission, Office of the General Counsel, GV
Ellison, Penny Conly .... Cherry Hill, NJ
Philadelphia, PA
Ellison, Peter K. .... Salt Lake City, UT
Ellison, Randy D. .... West Palm Beach, FL
Ellison, Robert A. .... Albany, NY
Ellison, Robert L. .... Rock Island, IL
Ellison, Roger L. .... Los Angeles, CA
Ellison, S. Ronald .... Baltimore, MD
Ellison & Schneider .... Sacramento, CA
Ellison, Scott W. .... Manchester, NH
Ellison, Sheila A. .... Hazel Crest, IL
Ellison, Sherman M. .... Sherman Oaks, CA
Ellison, Stacy Ann .... Knoxville, TN
Ellison, Stephen G. .... Houston, TX
Ellison, Steven .... West Palm Beach, FL
Ellison, Steven J. .... Chicago, IL
Ellison, Susan L. .... Moorhead, MN
Ellison, Thomas A. .... Salt Lake City, UT
Ellison, Tracey N. .... Bellaire, TX
Ellison, Tyler S. .... Minneapolis, MN
Ellison, Virginia Murphy .... Mesa, AZ
Ellison, W. James .... Birmingham, AL
Ellison, Ward F. .... Lansing, MI
Ellison, Wayne R. .... Fresno, CA
Ellison, William .... Yucca Valley, CA
Ellison, William C. .... New Orleans, LA
Ellison, William D. .... Chicago, IL
Ellison, William Lewis, Jr. .... Charlotte, NC
Charleston, SC
Ellison, William N. .... Watkins Glen, NY
Ellisor, Arthur J. .... Marble Falls, TX
Ellisor, James B. .... Columbia, SC
Ellisor, John A., Jr. .... Galveston, TX
Ellisor, Michael R. .... Cayce, SC
Elliston, Belinda S. .... Lamar, MO
Elliston, D Mark .... Dallas, TX
Elliston, Gary D. .... Dallas, TX
Elliston, Jay C. .... Houston, TX
Elliston, Jonathan F. .... Houston, TX
Elliston, L. Thomas .... Webb City, MO
Elliston, Mark A. .... Webb City, MO
Elliston, Mary Margret .... Omaha, NE
Elliston & Ormesher, L.L.P. .... Dallas, TX
Elliston, Patrick M. .... Bisbee, AZ
Elliston, Sharon S. .... Covington, KY
Ellixson, Thomas K. .... Norristown, PA
Ellmaker, Lee A. .... Indian Wells, CA
Ellmaker, Mary Susan .... Leawood, KS
Ellmaker, Michael L. .... Lake Oswego, OR
Ellmaker, Susan .... Overland Park, KS
Ellman, Bruce N. .... Los Angeles, CA
Ellman, Burke, Hoffman & Johnson, A Professional Corporation
San Francisco, CA
Ellman, Dennis B. .... Los Angeles, CA
Ellman, Harry S. .... Bingham Farms, MI
Ellman, Howard N. .... San Francisco, CA
Ellman, James D. .... Chicago, IL
Ellman, Jeffrey B. .... Columbus, OH
Ellman, Mark .... New York, NY
Ellman, Murray J. .... Boca Raton, FL
Ellman, Richard Martin .... Dallas, TX
Ellman, Robert L. .... Phoenix, AZ
Ellman, Stephen B. .... Columbus, OH
Ellman, Stephen F. .... New York, NY
Ellmann, Claudia Roberts .... Ann Arbor, MI
Ellmann, Douglas S. .... Ann Arbor, MI
Ellmann & Ellmann, P.C. .... Ann Arbor, MI
Ypsilanti, MI
Ellmann, Erwin B. .... Southfield, MI
Ellmann, Kevin T. .... Fort Collins, CO
Ellmann, Stephen J. .... New York, NY
Ellmann, William M. .... Ann Arbor, MI
Ellmer & Ellmer .... Garden City, NY
Ellmer, Raymond J. .... Garden City, NY
Ellmer, Raymond Jude .... Garden City, NY
Ellmers, Richard D. .... King Salmon, AK
Ellmore, Karen L. .... Rochester, NY
Ellner, Brian V. .... New York, NY
Ellner, Clifford D. .... New City, NY
Ellner, Erik .... New York, NY
Ellner, Howard M. .... Philadelphia, PA
Ellner, J. Robert .... New York, NY
Ellner, Jill S. .... Jericho, NY
Ellner, Kenneth B. .... Redwood City, CA
Ellner, Laurence K. .... New York, NY
Ellowitz, Jonathan R. .... Newport Beach, CA
Ellquist, Claudia .... Tucson, AZ
Ellrod, Anthony J. .... Los Angeles, CA
Ellrod, Frederick E., III .... Washington, DC
Ellrod, Matthew D. .... New Port Richey, FL
Ellrod, Matthew D., P.A.
New Port Richey, FL
Ellrodt, Tyler B. .... Seattle, WA
Ells, Alan S. .... Detroit, MI
Ells, Allan E. .... Philadelphia, PA
Ells, Christopher E. .... Fort Lauderdale, FL
Ells, Harry A., Jr. .... Denver, CO
Ells, Myron B., III .... Fort Worth, TX
Ells, Stephen F. .... Boston, MA
Ells, Stephen G. .... Hampton, NH
Ells, Theodore F. .... Old Greenwich, CT
New York, NY
Ellsley, Eric Matthew .... Miami, FL
Ellson, Laurel A. .... Cohasset, MA
Ellsworth, Andrew Charles
Uniondale, NY
Ellsworth, Anne M. .... Chicago, IL
Ellsworth, Arthur .... Oklahoma City, OK
Ellsworth, Bradford E. .... Houston, MO
Ellsworth, Brent D. .... Mesa, AZ
Ellsworth, Carl A. .... Columbia, SC
Ellsworth, Carlton & Waldman, P.C.
Philadelphia, PA
Reading, PA
Wyomissing, PA
Ellsworth, Carolyn .... Las Vegas, NV
Ellsworth, Cheryl .... Washington, DC
Ellsworth, David G. .... San Francisco, CA
Ellsworth, David S. .... Yuma, AZ
Ellsworth, Ernie M. .... Laguna Hills, CA
Ellsworth, Franklin R., Jr. .... Richmond, VA
Ellsworth, Gilbert N. .... Beloit, WI
Ellsworth, H. Anderson .... New Castle, DE
Voorhees, NJ
Philadelphia, PA
Wyomissing, PA
Ellsworth, James E. .... Salt Lake City, UT
Ellsworth, Jeffrey M. .... Boston, MA
Ellsworth, Joan B. .... Baltimore, MD
Ellsworth, John D. .... Omaha, NE
Ellsworth, John E. .... San Diego, CA
Ellsworth, Joseph .... Boise, ID
Ellsworth, Joseph C. .... Atlanta, GA
Ellsworth Kallas & Talboy, P.L.L.C.
Boise, ID
Ellsworth, Kathryn C. .... New York, NY
Ellsworth, Keen L. .... Las Vegas, NV
Ellsworth, Kirk C. .... Bridgeport, MI
Ellsworth, Laura E. .... Pittsburgh, PA
Ellsworth Law Office .... Anaheim, CA
Irvine, CA
Ellsworth, Lewis L. .... Tacoma, WA
Ellsworth, Marcia L. .... Laguna Hills, CA
Ellsworth, Marcia P. .... Seattle, WA
Ellsworth, Maurice O. .... Boise, ID
Ellsworth & McDowell, Law Offices of, LLP
Laguna Hills, CA
Ellsworth, Moody & Bennion, Chtd.
Las Vegas, NV
Ellsworth, Paul D. .... Mesa, AZ
Ellsworth, Paul D., PLC .... Mesa, AZ
Phoenix, AZ
Ellsworth, Peter H. .... Lansing, MI
Ellsworth, Peter K. .... San Diego, CA
Ellsworth, Richard M. .... Suffern, NY
Ellsworth, Robert A. .... Berkeley, CA
Ellsworth, Robert J. .... Suffern, NY
Ellsworth, Ronald R. .... San Diego, CA
Ellsworth, Scott M. .... Salt Lake City, UT
Ellsworth, Sean M. .... Miami, FL
Ellsworth, Steven M. .... Mesa, AZ
Ellsworth, Timothy S. .... Omaha, NE
Ellsworth, Todd A. .... Irvine, CA
Ellsworth, Vitek & Associates .... Omaha, NE
Ellsworth, W. Wm., Jr. .... Lakeland, FL
Ellsworth, Wiles, Carlton & Waldman, P.C.
New Castle, DE
Voorhees, NJ
Ellsworth-Ungerman, Betty M. .... Dallas, TX
Ellwanger, Carl F. .... Stuart, FL
Ellwanger, Cyril A. .... Sioux City, IA
Ellwanger, J. David .... Richardson, TX
Ellwanger, Kimberly Thompson
Redmond, WA
Ellwanger, Melinda Kaye .... Des Moines, IA
Ellwanger, Michael W. .... Sioux City, IA
Ellwanger, Thomas J. .... Tampa, FL
Ellwein, Michael A. .... Minneapolis, MN
Ellwood, Daniel L. .... Houston, TX
Ellwood, David A. .... Cambridge, OH
Ellwood, Kevin M. .... Roseland, NJ
Ellwood, Robert J., Jr. .... Phillipsburg, NJ
Ellwood, Scott .... Chicago, IL
Ellwood, Stephen P. .... Pottsville, PA
Ellwood, Susan M. .... Montpelier, VT
Ellwood, Timothy B. .... Houston, TX
Ellwood, William P. .... Cedar Rapids, IA
Ellyatt, Patricia E. .... Upland, CA
Ellyn, Heidi H. .... Malibu, CA
Ellyson, Don E. .... Waxahachie, TX
Ellyson, Roger W. .... Watertown, SD
Ellyson, William Gaines, P.C.
Richmond, VA
Ellyson, William Gaines, (P.C.)
Richmond, VA
Ellzey & Brooks, LLC .... Atlanta, GA
Charlotte, NC
Raleigh, NC
Columbia, SC
Ellzey, G. Daniel .... Atlanta, GA
Charlotte, NC
Raleigh, NC
Columbia, SC
Ellzey, Parker .... Alice, TX
Ellzey, Scott .... Tupelo, MS
Elm, J. Tucker .... Indian Wells, CA
Elmaleh, Joseph S. .... Elkins Park, PA
Elmaleh, Sharon .... New York, NY
Elman, Andrew A. .... Hackensack, NJ
Elman, Anthony R. .... Mundelein, IL
Elman & Associates, A Professional Corporation .... Media, PA
Philadelphia, PA
Elman, Barry D. .... Chicago, IL
Elman, Dianne Clare .... Chicago, IL
Elman & Ehardt, Ltd. .... Harvard, IL
Elman, Fred W. .... Mundelein, IL
Elman, Fred W., P.C., Law Offices of
Mundelein, IL
Elman, Gerry J. .... Media, PA
Elman, Howard I. .... New York, NY
Elman, John L. .... Palo Alto, CA
Elman, Lawrence M. .... Chicago, IL
Elman, Leonard S. .... New York, NY
Elman, Philip .... Bethesda, MD
Elman, Sloane .... New York, NY
Elman, Stanley C. .... Park City, UT
Elman, Stefanie M. .... New York, NY
Elman, Stephan A. .... Washington, DC
Elman, Susan .... New York, NY
Elman, William .... Harvard, IL
Elmendorf, Caroline Gosse
Department of Justice, Civil Division, GV
Elmendorf, Gilbert J. .... Lakeland, FL
Elmendorf, J. Kevin .... Sacramento, CA
Elmendorf, John A. .... Silver Spring, MD
Elmendorf, Stephen P. .... Silver Spring, MD
Elmendorf, Ward W. .... San Antonio, TX
Elmendorf & Windheim .... Sacramento, CA
Elmer, Brian C. .... Washington, DC
Elmer, Charity R. .... Springfield, MO
Elmer, Charles M. .... Birmingham, AL
Elmer, Denise M. .... Roseland, NJ
Elmer, George R. .... Park Ridge, IL
Elmer, James E., (Law Corp)
Sacramento, CA
Elmer, Jerry H. .... Providence, RI
Elmer, Joel R. .... Jefferson City, MO
Elmer, John D. .... Canton, NY
Elmer, Julie S. .... Birmingham, AL
Elmer, Mark C. .... Washington, DC
Elmer, Martin James .... Berkeley, CA
Elmer, Michael C. .... Palo Alto, CA
Elmer, Randy M. .... Salem, OR
Elmer, Robert M. .... Boston, MA
Elmer, Russell S. .... Palo Alto, CA
Elmer, Steven R. .... Monroe, WI
Elmer, Thomas R. .... North Tonawanda, NY
Elmer, Todd B. .... Washington, DC
Elmer, William B. .... Traverse City, MI
Elmiger, Richard S. .... Avon-By-The-Sea, NJ
Summit, NJ
Elmlinger, Jeanie M. .... Dayton, OH
Elmlinger, Paul J. .... New York, NY
Elmlinger, Thomas J. .... Nashville, TN
Elmont, Alan S. .... Culver City, CA
Elmont, David L. .... Washington, DC
Elmore, Allan F. .... Department of Defense, Armed Services Board of Contract Appeals, GV
Elmore, Andrew G. .... Fairfax, VA
Richmond, VA
Elmore, Ann McNellis .... Sanford, FL
Elmore & Associates, P.A.
Severna Park, MD
Elmore, Brant M. .... Oklahoma City, OK
Elmore, Bruce A. .... Asheville, NC
Elmore, Bruce A., Jr. .... Asheville, NC
Elmore, Carol Hope .... Manhattan, KS
Elmore, Celeste S. .... Sterling, VA
Elmore, Damon E. .... Atlanta, GA
Elmore, Danny
Department of Justice, GV
Elmore, David G. .... Oak Brook, IL
Elmore, David R. .... Savannah, GA
Elmore, Debra L. .... Houston, TX
Elmore & DeMichael .... Oak Forest, IL
Elmore, Donald E. .... Murphysboro, IL
Elmore, Donald S. .... Richmond, VA

Elmore, E. Whitehead ....Richmond, VA
Elmore, Edward Whitehead, Jr.
Richmond, VA
Elmore, Elbert F. ....Oak Forest, IL
Elmore, Elizabeth Benston
Charleston, WV
Elmore & Elmore ....Charleston, WV
Elmore, Elmore & Williams, P.A.
Asheville, NC
Elmore, Eric M. ....Greenbelt, MD
La Plata, MD
Elmore, Ernest Eric
Federal Trade Commission,
Offices of Commissioners, GV
Elmore, George T., III ....Richmond, VA
Elmore, Jacquelyn P. ....Louisville, KY
Elmore, James E. ....Springfield, IL
Elmore, Jason J. ....Kansas City, MO
Elmore, Jeff W. ....Lafayette, LA
Elmore, Jeffrey Todd ....Mayfield, KY
Elmore, Jerry L. ....Houston, TX
Elmore, Jocelyn Y. ....New Orleans, LA
Elmore, John F. ....Atlanta, GA
Elmore, John S. ....Sullivan, IN
Elmore, John V., Law Offices of
Buffalo, NY
Elmore, Kathleen M. ....Severna Park, MD
Elmore, Kathy Price ....Florence, SC
Elmore, Kenneth B. ....Eugene, OR
Elmore, L. Franklin ....Greenville, SC
Elmore, M. Jerome ....Atlanta, GA
Elmore, Natasha A. ....Houston, TX
Elmore, O. Gay, Jr. ....Charleston, WV
Elmore, O. E. (Ed) ....College Station, TX
Elmore, R. Scott ....Knoxville, TN
Elmore, Ralph A., III
North Myrtle Beach, SC
Elmore & Reid ....Springfield, IL
Elmore, Richard L. ....Reno, NV
Elmore, Robert C. ....Shalimar, FL
Elmore, Roscoe C. ....Katy, TX
Elmore, Sharon L. ....St. Paul, MN
Elmore, Stephen Henry ....Salem, OR
Elmore, Van ....Denver, CO
Elmore, Virgil J., III ....Birmingham, AL
Elmore, William B. ....Charleston, SC
Elmquist, David W. ....Dallas, TX
Elmquist, H. Richard ....Detroit, MI
Elmquist, Jack D. ....Minneapolis, MN
Elmquist Law Offices ....Minneapolis, MN
Elmquist, Ronald C. ....Minneapolis, MN
Elmquist, Theodore G. ....St. Paul, MN
Elms, Daniel P. ....Dallas, TX
Elms • Harmon, LLC ....San Antonio, TX
Elms, Larry A. ....Lubbock, TX
Elms, Larry A., & Associates, Inc.
Lubbock, TX
Elms, Lee ....San Antonio, TX
Elness, Duane G. ....Cavalier, ND
Elnicki, Jeffrey K. ....St. Louis, MO
Elo, Theodore S. ....St. Joseph, MO
Eloff, Kathryn Gonser
Cleveland Heights, OH
Eloff, Lydia A. ....Columbia, SC
Elofson, Carl E. ....Fargo, ND
Elofson, David A. ....Yakima, WA
Elofson, Howard W. ....Yakima, WA
Elofson, John A. ....New York, NY
Elofson, Margaret A. ....Seattle, WA
Elofson, Paul R. ....Omaha, NE
Elofson & Vincent ....Yakima, WA
Elott, David J. ....Salem, OR
Elovich, Harold S. ....Little Silver, NJ
Elovich, Lawrence E. ....Long Beach, NY
Elovich, Wendie L. ....Little Silver, NJ
Elovitz, Kenneth M. ....Foxboro, MA
Elovitz, Louis ....Chicago, IL
Elovitz, Marc ....New York, NY
Elovitz, Marc E. ....New York, NY
Elovitz, Mark H. ....Birmingham, AL
Elovitz, Mark H., P.C. ....Birmingham, AL
Elovitz, Rachel ....Atlanta, GA
Elovitz, Robert L. ....Edwardsville, IL
Elovitz, Shelley W. ....Pittsburgh, PA
Elowe, Michael L. ....Deerfield, IL
Elowe, Wayne H. ....Atlanta, GA
Elowitt, Andrew N. ....Santa Monica, CA
Elperin, William ....Los Angeles, CA
Elpers, Angela J. ....Temecula, CA
Elpers, Ann M. ....Louisville, KY
Elpers, Frank J. ....Ste. Genevieve, MO
Elphick, Kevin J. ....New York, NY
Elrad, Becky M. ....Glencoe, IL
Elrich, Katherine K. ....Dallas, TX
Elrick, F. Lee ....Lutherville, MD
Elrick, Richard D. ....Centerville, MA
Elrick, Stephen B. ....San Jose, CA
Elrifi, Ivor R. ....Boston, MA
Elrod, Bradley C. ....Toledo, OH
Elrod, Charles E., Jr. ....Atlanta, GA
Elrod, Dan H. ....Nashville, TN
Elrod, Daniel R. ....Siloam Springs, AR
Elrod, David W. ....Dallas, TX
Elrod, Don U. ....Fredericktown, MO
Elrod, Eugene R. ....Washington, DC
Elrod, Georgia ....Siloam Springs, AR
Elrod, Harvey ....Decatur, AL
Elrod, Jack T. ....Lawrenceville, GA
Elrod, James W. ....Brentwood, TN
Elrod, John R. ....Fayetteville, AR
Elrod, John W. ....Rison, AR
Elrod, Jones, Leader & Benson, P.A.
Rock Hill, SC
Elrod Law Firm ....Siloam Springs, AR
Elrod, Linda H. ....Topeka, KS
Elrod, Luther C., III ....Rock Hill, SC
Elrod, Mark D. ....St. Louis, MO
Elrod & Mascher, P.C. ....Indianapolis, IN
Elrod, Michael C. ....San Antonio, TX
Elrod, Richard J. ....Chicago, IL
Elrod, Richard T. ....Appleton, WI
Elrod, Robert G. ....Indianapolis, IN
Elrod, Robert W., Jr. ....Jacksonville, FL
Elrod, Robert W., P.A. ....Jacksonville, FL
Orange Park, FL
Elrod, Robert W., Sr. ....Jacksonville, FL
Elrod, Steven M. ....Chicago, IL
Elrod & Thompson ....Atlanta, GA
Elrod, W. W., II ....Little Rock, AR
El-Saden, Dhiya ....Los Angeles, CA
Elsaesser, Eugene F. ....Clarence, NY
Elsaesser, Ford ....Sandpoint, ID
Elsaesser Jarzabek Anderson Marks &
Elliott, Chartered ....Sandpoint, ID
Elsaesser, John F. ....South Dartmouth, MA
Elsaesser, O'Connell & Cleary
Clarence, NY
Elsas, Herbert R. ....Atlanta, GA
Elsass, Carrolyn M. ....Canton, OH
Elsass, Douglas L. ....Minneapolis, MN
Elsass, Eugene P. ....Sidney, OH
Elsass, Michael W. ....Hartford, CT
Elsass, Susan Hugins ....Tallahassee, FL
Elsass, Wallace, Evans, Schnelle & Co.,
L.P.A. ....Sidney, OH
Wapakoneta, OH
Elsasser, Deborah L. ....Las Vegas, NV
Elsasser, Kay A. ....San Antonio, TX
Elsasser, Mary Anne ....Seattle, WA
Elsasser, William Franklin ....Portland, OR
El-Sayed, Dina F. ....Fresno, CA
Elsberg, David D. ....Alexandria, VA
Elsberg, David L. ....New York, NY
Elsberg, R. Lee ....Longmont, CO
Elsberg, Stuart M. ....Chestertown, MD
Elsbernd, Brian ....Washington, DC
Elsbernd, Stephen J. ....Newport, KY
Elsberry, Anne Westlake ....Lenexa, KS
Elsberry, Brantley E. ....Tulsa, OK
Elsberry, Dale ....Tustin, CA
Elsberry, Knight ....Chicago, IL
Elsberry, Michael J. ....Orange, CA
Elsberry, Michael V. ....Orlando, FL
Elsbree, Eugene V., III ....San Francisco, CA
Elsbree, Hugh L., Jr. ....Library of Congress,
Congressional Research Service, GV
Elsbree, Mary E. McElhinney
San Francisco, CA
Else, Kevin D. ....Department of Commerce,
Patent and Trademark Office, GV
Elsea, Kelly Keimig ....Washington, DC
Elsen, D. Henry ....Seattle, WA
Elsen, Herman J. ....St. Paul, MN
Elsen, Lowell N. ....Burbank, CA
Elsen, Sheldon H. ....New York, NY
Elsener & Cadenhead, P.C. ....Seminole, OK
Elsener, G. Dale ....Seminole, OK
Elsener, George M. ....Chicago, IL
Elsener, Mark E. ....Cincinnati, OH
Elser, Eugene C. ....Virginia Beach, VA
Elser & Fabar ....Miami, FL
Elser, George H. ....Wayne, PA
Elser, John T. ....New York, NY
Elser, Marsha B. ....Miami, FL
Elsesser, Adam ....San Francisco, CA
Elsesser, Charles F., Jr. ....Miami, FL
Elsesser, Evelyn Kahl ....San Francisco, CA
Elsesser, James L. ....Chicago, IL
Elsesser, Janice M. ....New York, NY
Elseth, Annette B. ....Washington, DC
Elsevier, Lisa C. ....Atlanta, GA
Elsey, Ivella M. ....Springfield, MO
Elsey, Joanne E. ....Marietta, GA
Elsey, Robert R., P.C. ....Grosse Pointe, MI
Elsey, William T. ....Cartersville, GA
Elsey, William T., P.C. ....Cartersville, GA
El-Shabazz, Ingram & Ingram
Philadelphia, PA
El-Shabazz, Tariq Karim ....Philadelphia, PA
Elshaer, Amr A. ....New York, NY
Elshawi, Ahmed Z. ....New York, NY
Elshoff, James D. ....Great Falls, MT
Elsing, James ....Lemmon, SD
Elsken, Michael J. ....Lincoln, NE
Elskes, Jennifer M. ....Houston, TX
Elsley, John M. ....Houston, TX
Elsman, James Leonard ....Birmingham, MI
Elsner, Edward P., Jr. ....Seymour, IN
Elsner, Gayle L. ....Chicago, IL
Elsner, George F. ....Castle Rock, CO
Elsner, Michael E. ....Fairfax, VA
Elsner, Morton A. ....Hartford, CT
Elsner, Paul C. ....Portland, OR
Elsner, Rita E. ....Lombard, IL
Elsner, Robert A. ....Atlanta, GA
Elsner, Stephen E. ....Carmel, IN
Elsner, Timmie Erin ....New York, NY
Elsnic, Gregory C. ....Chicago, IL
Elsohn, Nina R. ....Oakland, CA
Elsom and Elsom ....Cody, WY
Elsom, Kristi N. ....Midland, TX
Elsom, Teresa Bolton ....Cody, WY
Elsom, Wm. Daniel ....Cody, WY
Elson, Aimee Kemker ....Largo, FL
Elson, Alex ....Chicago, IL
Elson, Amy L. ....Fort Wayne, IN
Elson, Andrew C., III ....Englewood, CO
Elson, Barry R. ....Philadelphia, PA
Elson, Charles L. ....Leon, IA
Elson, Charles M. ....Tampa, FL
Elson, David ....Los Angeles, CA
Elson, Dean Gerald ....Detroit, MI
Elson, Edward E. ....Atlanta, GA
Elson, Edwin J. ....Westport, CT
Elson, Elizabeth S. ....Los Angeles, CA
Elson and Fulton ....Leon, IA
Elson, Henry M. ....Berkeley, CA
Elson, James J., Chtd. ....Canton, IL
Elson, Jeff S. ....Brookfield, MO
Elson, John, (A Professional Corporation)
Los Angeles, CA
Elson, John S. ....Chicago, IL
Elson, Kenneth H. ....Grand Island, NE
Elson, Martin ....Rego Park, NY
Elson, Martin W. ....Cleveland, OH
Elson, Quin S. ....Fairfax, VA
Elson, Sally T. ....Chicago, IL
Elson, Sol ....Lauderhill, FL
Elson, Vera M. ....Palo Alto, CA
Elson, William B. ....Chicago, IL
Elson, William L. ....Southfield, MI
Elste, Gay M. ....Lexington, KY
Elstead, John C. ....Pleasanton, CA
Elstein, Annette S. ....New York, NY
Elstein, Bruce L. ....Bridgeport, CT
Elstein and Elstein, P.C. ....Bridgeport, CT
Elstein, Henry ....Bridgeport, CT
Elstein, Judah I. ....Newark, NJ
Elstein, Matthew C. ....Los Angeles, CA
Elster, Gary S. ....Kahului, HI
Elster, J. Robert ....Winston-Salem, NC
Elster, Marc A. ....Kansas City, MO
Elster, Marvin ....Montgomery Village, MD
Elston, A. Roger ....Centereach, NY
Elston, Ann M. ....San Francisco, CA
Elston, Calita L. ....Atlanta, GA
Elston, Catherine M. ....Parsippany, NJ
Elston, David M. ....Chicago, IL
Elston, David W. ....Tempe, AZ
Elston, Dawn R. ....New Albany, IN
Elston, Gale P. ....New York, NY
Elston, Gale P., P.C. ....New York, NY
Elston, Gerald L. ....Department of Justice,
United States Marshals Service, GV
Elston, James K. ....Houston, TX
Elston, Jay W. ....Houston, TX
Elston, Judith" Jan " ....Washington, DC
Elston, Michael J. ....Kansas City, MO
Elston, Ralph B. ....Fort Wayne, IN
Elston, Sheila W. ....Chicago, IL
Elston, William E., Jr. ....Chicago, IL
Elswick, Carlene ....Abingdon, VA
Elswick, Carol Williams ....Monrovia, CA
Elswick, Kelly Lee ....Charleston, WV
Elswick, Richard L. ....Pikeville, KY
Elswit, Lawrence S. ....Boston, MA
Elsworth, James M. ....Detroit, MI
Elsworth, Judith M. ....Palm Springs, CA
Elterich, John P. ....Bloomington, IL
Elterman, Leon J. ....Ferndale, NY
Eltgroth, George V. ....Las Vegas, NV
Elting, Kimberley A. ....Dallas, TX
Eltman, Alexander ....Floral Park, NY
Eltman, George S.
Christiansted, St. Croix, VI
Elton, Curtis D. ....Salt Lake City, UT
Elton, Robert W. ....Daytona Beach, FL
Elton, Roger H. ....Reno, NV
Elton, Ronald L. ....Tooele, UT
Eltzroth, Carter W. ....Ballston Spa, NY
Eltzroth, Clyde A. ....Hampton, SC
Eltzroth, Clyde A., Jr. ....Hampton, SC
Elu, David M. ....San Francisco, CA
Elum, Edward J. ....Massillon, OH
Eluwa, John Okezie N. ....Cary, NC
Elve, Daniel L. ....Grand Rapids, MI
Elve, Timothy P. ....Ada, MI
Elver, Abell & Hendry, P.A. ....Immokalee, FL
LaBelle, FL
Elver, Ralph ....LaBelle, FL
Elveris, Idil ....New York, NY
Elverman, Jeffrey L. ....Milwaukee, WI
Elverman, Timothy J. ....Milwaukee, WI
Elvers, John D. ....Raleigh, NC
Elvers, Lauren L. ....New York, NY
Elverson, Todd A. ....Des Moines, IA
Elverson, Vasey & Peterson, L.L.P.
Des Moines, IA
Elvig, Mark F. ....Houston, TX
Elvin, Frances T. ....San Francisco, CA
Elvin, George M. ....New York, NY
Elvin, Kelly J.B. ....New York, NY
Elvin, Matthew S. ....Chicago, IL
Elvin, Michael S. ....Fort Wayne, IN
Elvins, Deborah A. ....Seattle, WA
Elvir, Paul Michael, Jr. ....New Orleans, LA
Elvira, Rafael ....Ponce, PR
Elward, Brad A. ....Peoria, IL
Elward, Francis J. ....Annapolis, MD
Elward, Patrick A. ....Indianapolis, IN
Elward, Paul F. ....Chicago, IL
Elwardani, Renata Hutak ....San Diego, CA
Elwart, Ralph J., Jr. ....Northbrook, IL
Elwell and Albino ....Montclair, NJ
Elwell, Anne W. ....Montclair, NJ
Elwell, Christopher L. ....Los Angeles, CA
Elwell, David A. ....Bakersfield, CA
Elwell, Douglas M. ....Fontana, CA
Elwell, Jerome K. ....Phoenix, AZ
Elwell, Kenneth ....Trenton, NJ
Elwell, Kevin M. ....Atlanta, GA
Elwell, Lisa L. ....Bradenton, FL
Elwell, Maureen B. ....Atlanta, GA
Hamburg, NY
Elwell, Michael S. ....Salem, NH
Elwell, Suzanne E. ....Mountain View, CA
Elwell, Thomas J., Jr. ....Lorain, OH
Elwert, Margaret M. ....New York, NY
Elwick, Don D. ....Weatherford, OK
Elwin, Elizabeth A. ....Augusta, ME
Elwin, Eric Ross ....Union, NJ
Elwin, J. William, Jr. ....Chicago, IL
Elwood, Anne Cole ....Philadelphia, PA
Elwood, Clark D. ....Indianapolis, IN
Elwood, Courtney Simmons
Washington, DC
Elwood, David M. ....Boston, MA
Elwood, Elizabeth A. ....Redding, CA
Elwood, Elwood, Buchanan & Leinen
Marengo, IA
North English, IA
Williamsburg, IA
Elwood, Frank D. ....Cresco, IA
Elwood, George H. ....Hancock, NY
Elwood, H. Philip ....Topeka, KS
Elwood, Henry L. ....Charles City, IA
Cresco, IA
New Hampton, IA
Elwood, John P. ....Washington, DC
Elwood, Katherine M. ....Pasadena, CA
Elwood, Kenneth W. ....Chatham, NJ
Elwood, Mark Stephen ....Birmingham, AL
Elwood, Martin P. ....San Diego, CA
Elwood, Michael J. ....Marengo, IA
North English, IA
Williamsburg, IA
Elwood, O'Donohoe, O'Connor & Stochl
Charles City, IA
Cresco, IA
New Hampton, IA
Elwood, Richard H. ....Marengo, IA
North English, IA
Williamsburg, IA
Elwood, Robert M. ....Philadelphia, PA
Elwood, Thomas H. ....Concord, NH
Elwood, W. Douglas ....Fowler, IN
Elwood, William E. ....Washington, DC
Elworth, Ann C. ....Las Vegas, NV
Elworth, James A. ....Lincoln, NE
Elworth, Robert E. ....Chicago, IL
Elworthy, Bruce Rea ....Sheridan, WY
Elworthy & Marshall, A Professional
Corporation ....Sheridan, WY
Elwyn, Morgan D. ....New York, NY
Ely, Bettini, Ulman, Insana & Turley
Phoenix, AZ
Ely, Brenen G. ....Birmingham, AL
Ely, Brian M. ....Lebanon, VA
Ely, Bruce P. ....Tuscaloosa, AL
Ely, C. Davis ....Jacksonville, FL
Ely, Clausen, Jr. ....Washington, DC
Ely, Daniel J. ....Plymouth Meeting, PA
Ely, Daymon B., Law Offices of
Albuquerque, NM
Ely, Donald E. ....Columbus, OH
Ely, Donna R.
Federal Deposit Insurance Corporation, GV
Ely, Douglas M. ....Washington, DC
Ely, Dwight C. ....Fairfield, CA
Ely, Franklin J. ....Utica, NY
Ely, Fritz & Hogan ....Costa Mesa, CA
Ely & Havelock ....Anchorage, AK
Ely, Herbert L. ....Phoenix, AZ
Ely, Hiram, III ....Louisville, KY
Ely, James S. T. S., Jr. ....Rutherford, NJ
Ely, James W., Jr. ....Claremore, OK
Ely, John E. ....Woodbridge, VA
Ely, John Harlan ....Houston, TX
Ely, John Hart ....Palo Alto, CA
Ely, John I. ....New Haven, CT
Ely, John J., Jr. ....Oklahoma City, OK
Ely, John M. ....Aspen, CO
Ely, John P. ....West Springfield, MA
Ely, Lois J. ....Hackensack, NJ
Ely, M. David ....Baltimore, MD
Ely, Milton ....Baltimore, MD
Ely, Monica Lynn ....Tempe, AZ
Ely, Myron C. ....Knoxville, TN
Ely, Natalia W. ....San Francisco, CA
Ely, Northcutt, (P.C.) ....Redlands, CA
Ely, Peter S. ....Denver, CO
Ely, Rae H. ....Louisa, VA
Ely, Rex E. ....Batavia, OH
Ely, Richard O., II ....Houston, TX
Ely, Richard T. ....Memphis, TN
Ely, Robert C. ....Anchorage, AK
Ely, Robert E. ....Montgomery, AL
Ely, Robt. B. ....Miami, FL
Ely, Sema G. ....Baltimore, MD
Ely, Shattuck ....Atlanta, GA
Ely & Smith ....Erie, PA
Ely, Theodore B., II ....Erie, PA
Ely, Thomas W. ....Costa Mesa, CA
Ely and True ....Batavia, OH
Georgetown, OH
Hillsboro, OH
West Union, OH
Wilmington, OH
Ely, Wayne A. ....Langhorne, PA
Ely, William C. ....Boston, MA
Ely, William Watkins ....Independence, MO
Elyea, Olga S. ....Washington, DC
Ely-Yamin, Alicia ....New York, NY
Elza, Laurie J. ....Corpus Christi, TX
Elza, Slater Chalfant ....Amarillo, TX
Elzeer, Jeffrey M. ....Cleveland, OH
Elzeer, John S. ....Tampa, FL
Elzer, Robert W. ....Indianapolis, IN
Elzerman, Sandra K. ....Houston, TX
Elzey, Philip R. ....Atlanta, GA
Elzi, Chris P. ....Petaluma, CA
Elzi & Gurr ....Denver, CO
Elzi, Kathryn A. ....Denver, CO
Elzinga, Gregory A. ....Marquette, MI
Elzinga, Ronald H. ....Portland, OR
Elzoghby, Ahmed ....New York, NY
Elzufon & Austin, P.A. ....Wilmington, DE
Elzufon, John A. ....Wilmington, DE
Elzweig, Brian P. ....Tallahassee, FL
Ema, Christopher J. ....Pompano Beach, FL
Emacio, James P. ....Spokane, WA
Emalfarb, Hal A. ....Highland Park, IL

Emalfarb, Swan & Bain ....Highland Park, IL
Emami, Shirin ....New York, NY
Emamzadeh, Mäny ....Pittsburgh, PA
Emanuel, Anne S. ....Atlanta, GA
Emanuel, Anthony J. ....Garden City, NY
Emanuel, Benjamin F., III ....New York, NY
Emanuel, Bertram ....Skokie, IL
Emanuel, Craig A. ....Los Angeles, CA
Emanuel, Dennis W. ....Ottumwa, IA
Emanuel, Douglas J. ....Providence, RI
Emanuel and Dunn ....Raleigh, NC
Emanuel, Eric ....Los Angeles, CA
Emanuel, H. Mark ....Atlanta, GA
Emanuel, Helene Rich ....Hackensack, NJ
Emanuel, Ira M. ....New City, NY
Emanuel, Jacqueline G.
Fort Lauderdale, FL
Emanuel, John F. ....Milwaukee, WI
Emanuel, Lazar ....Larchmont, NY
Emanuel, Michael S. ....New York, NY
Emanuel, Peter M. ....Princeton, NJ
Emanuel, Ramona L. ....Shreveport, LA
Emanuel, Reuben M. ....Tucson, AZ
Emanuel, Richard ....Hamden, CT
Emanuel, Robert J. ....Chicago, IL
Emanuel, Robert L. ....Raleigh, NC
Emanuel, Ronald B. ....New York, NY
Emanuel, Ronald M. ....Miami, FL
Emanuel, Steven L. ....Larchmont, NY
Emanuel, Todd P. ....Menlo Park, CA
Palo Alto, CA
Emanuel, Todd P. ....Redwood City, CA
Emanuel, Todd P. ....San Jose, CA
San Mateo, CA
Emanuel, William J. ....Los Angeles, CA
Emanuele, Benedict D. ....Great Neck, NY
Emanuele, Mark A. ....Fort Lauderdale, FL
Emanuelli, Albert J. ....White Plains, NY
Emanuelli-Belaval, Aurelio ....San Juan, PR
Emanuelli Freese, Aurelio ....San Juan, PR
Emanuelli-Rivera, Domingo R.
San Juan, PR
Emanuels, Ann ....Roseville, CA
Emanuels, Eric S. ....Sacramento, CA
Emanuelson, Herbert L., Jr. ....Madison, CT
Emanuelson, Roger A. ....Boston, MA
Quincy, MA
Emard, Bruce A. ....Sacramento, CA
Emard, Wayne F. ....San Francisco, CA
Emas, Ellen Marcie ....Washington, DC
Emas, Jack ....Philadelphia, PA
Emas, Joseph I. ....Miami, FL
Emas, Kevin M. ....Miami, FL
Emas, Marshall J. ....Fort Lauderdale, FL
Emas, Richard H., (P.A.) ....Miami, FL
Ember, Richard H. ....Houston, TX
Embers, Edward D. ....McPherson, KS
Emberton, Thomas D. ....Edmonton, KY
Embery, Joseph R., III ....Rockledge, PA
Embery, Joseph R., IV ....Feasterville, PA
Embery, Outterson & Fuges, P.C.
Rockledge, PA
Embery, Richard J. ....Rockledge, PA
Embick, John R. ....Philadelphia, PA
Embick, Marion B., (Mrs.) ....Salem, OR
Emblem, Thor O. ....Escondido, CA
Embleton, Jeffrey M. ....Cleveland, OH
Embley, Craig M. ....Midvale, UT
Emblidge, G. Scott ....San Francisco, CA
Emboulas, Lawrence A. ....Metairie, LA
Embree, Edward E., II ....Lenexa, KS
Embree, Edward L., III ....Durham, NC
Embree, Eric S. ....Hurricane, WV
Embree, H. David ....Norfolk, VA
Embree, Kenneth H. ....Harper Woods, MI
Embree, Kenneth R. ....Durham, NC
Embree, Mark S. ....New Orleans, LA
Embree, Melvyn C. ....Los Angeles, CA
Embretson, Janet E. ....Minneapolis, MN
Embrey, Arlene M.
Small Business Administration, Office of the General Counsel, GV
Embrey, Bruce C. ....Peru, IN
Embrey, David D. ....Lynchburg, VA
Embrey, Diana L. ....United States Senate, Office of Senate Chief Counsel for Employment, GV
Embrey, Douglas R. ....Tulsa, OK
Embrey, James R., Jr. ....Knoxville, TN
Embrey, Patricia A.
Environmental Protection Agency, Office of the General Counsel, GV
Embroski, Paul A. ....Department of Defense, Defense Legal Services Agency, GV
Embry, Bruce J. ....Cambridge, MA
Embry, Charles S., Jr. ....Little Rock, AR
Embry, D. Jason ....Gulfport, MS
Embry, Edwin P. ....Grenada, MS
Embry, Garcelle M. Jones ....Los Angeles, CA
Embry, James B., Jr. ....Pell City, AL
Embry, Jeffrey T. ....Dallas, TX
Embry, Leland G. ....Alameda, CA
Embry and Neusner ....Groton, CT
Embry, Renna R. ....Dallas, TX
Embry, Shan Fox ....Leitchfield, KY
Embry, Stephen C. ....Groton, CT
Embry, Stephen E. ....Louisville, KY
Embry, Trasha D. ....Chicago, IL
Embs, Victoria A. ....Douglasville, GA
Embser, J. Timothy ....Wellsville, NY
Embser & Woltag, P.C. ....Wellsville, NY
Embury, Andrew ....Rochester, NY
Emch, A. L. ....Charleston, WV
Emch, Christopher G. ....Seattle, WA
Emch, Gregg W. ....Toledo, OH
Emch, Julie P. ....Akron, OH
Emch, Richard D. ....Toledo, OH
Emch, Schaffer, Schaub & Porcello Co., L.P.A. ....Toledo, OH
Emde, John P., (P.C.) ....St. Louis, MO
Emden, Craig A. ....Washington, DC
Emden, Marc R. ....Chevy Chase, MD
Emden, Marc R., P.A. ....Chevy Chase, MD
Emden, Milton M. ....Cincinnati, OH
Emdin, Alan C. ....New York, NY
Emede, Julie A. ....San Jose, CA
Emello, Deborah ....Brookline, MA
Emelo, Lisa Marie ....New York, NY
Emelumadu, Uche ....Bronx, NY
New York, NY
Emen, Michael S. ....New York, NY
Emens, J. Richard ....Columbus, OH
Emens, Patricia Franklin, Mrs.
Tuscaloosa, AL
Emens, Steven C. ....Tuscaloosa, AL
Emens-Butler, Jennifer ....Bethel, VT
Emer, Herman C. ....New York, NY
Emer, Steven D. ....Highland Park, IL
Emer, William H. ....Los Angeles, CA
Emerich, David R. ....Fresno, CA
Emerich, Douglas W. ....Tuscaloosa, AL
Emerich, Guy S. ....Punta Gorda, FL
Emerich, John D. ....Springfield, OH
Emerich, Melvin L. ....San Jose, CA
Emerich Pedreira & Fike, A Professional Corporation ....Fresno, CA
Emerich, Winks, Peifer & Dressel
Springfield, OH
Emerick, Bruce S. ....San Bernardino, CA
Emerick & Diggins, P.C. ....Kendallville, IN
Emerick, Douglas Alan ....Reno, NV
Emerick, Edwin, Jr. ....Seattle, WA
Emerick, Hunter B. ....Salem, OR
Emerick, Jana E. ....Lima, OH
Emerick, Julie T. ....Chicago, IL
Emerick and Kemps Law Offices
Duncansville, PA
Emerick, Merrill G. ....San Mateo, CA
Emerick, Michael ....Duncansville, PA
Emerick, Paul T. ....Alexandria, VA
Emerick, Phyllis J. ....Bloomington, IN
Emerick, R. David ....Indianapolis, IN
Emerick, R. Stan ....Kendallville, IN
Emerick, Richard A. ....Burnsville, MN
Emerick, Steven P. ....Milwaukee, WI
Emerick, Susan Peters ....Redwood City, CA
Emerick, William E. ....Lafayette, IN
Emerick, William F. ....Coarsegold, CA
Emeritz, Robert E. ....Bethesda, MD
Emerling, Sandra G. ....Stamford, CT
Emerling, Stanley J. ....Reston, VA
Emero, Thomas D. ....Bangor, ME
Emershaw, George J. ....Akron, OH
Emershaw, Mushkat & Schneier ....Akron, OH
Emerson, Andrew C. ....Indianapolis, IN
Emerson, Andrew F. ....Dallas, TX
Emerson, Barbara ....Dallas, TX
Emerson, Barry T. ....Delphi, IN
Emerson, Benjamin W. ....Richmond, VA
Emerson, Billy D. ....Richardson, TX
Emerson, Boynton C. ....Baltimore, MD
Emerson, Carter W. ....Chicago, IL
Emerson, Catherine E. ....Detroit, MI
Emerson, Catherine V. ....Department of Justice, Justice Management Division, GV
Emerson, Cecil W. ....Dallas, TX
Emerson, Chad D. ....Knoxville, TN
Emerson, Chas. W. ....Atlanta, GA
Emerson, Christel ....Gulph Mills, PA
Emerson, Corey & Barsotti ....Fresno, CA
Emerson, Craig P. ....Redmond, OR
Emerson, Cynthia S. Law Firm, P.C.
La Grange, TN
Emerson, Cynthia Smith ....La Grange, TN
Emerson, Daniel C. ....Indianapolis, IN
Emerson, Daniel P. ....New York, NY
Emerson, David T. ....Palo Alto, CA
Emerson, David T. ....Douglasville, GA
Emerson, Dian B. ....Pleasanton, CA
Emerson, Don R. ....Amarillo, TX
Emerson, Douglas T. ....Fort Worth, TX
Emerson, E. Angela ....Milledgeville, GA
Emerson, Edwin G. ....Toledo, OH
Emerson, Elizabeth B. ....Dallas, TX
Emerson, Elizabeth L. ....Mill Valley, CA
Emerson & Emerson, P.A. ....Naples, FL
Emerson, Emery H., Jr. ....Storm Lake, IA
Emerson, Eric C. ....Washington, DC
Emerson, Eric J. ....Chicago, IL
Emerson, Eugene ....Boston, MA
Emerson, Forrest M. ....Fort Mill, SC
Emerson, Frank D. ....Cleveland, OH
Emerson, Frederick G. ....Phoenix, AZ
Emerson, George Marvin
Oklahoma City, OK
Emerson, George W., Jr. ....Memphis, TN
Emerson, Gregory S. ....Pasadena, CA
Emerson, H. Truxtun, Jr. ....Cincinnati, OH
Emerson, Irene Dwyer ....Winthrop, MA
Emerson, Irvin D. ....Hillsboro, MO
Emerson, James C. ....San Jose, CA
Emerson, James D. ....Fresno, CA
Emerson, James L. ....Girard, KS
Emerson, James L. ....Salem, OR
Emerson, Jay E., Jr. ....Huntsville, AL
Emerson, Jeffrey R. ....Wichita, KS
Emerson, Jill Deziel ....Tampa, FL
Emerson, John A. ....Lawrence, KS
Emerson, John C. ....Houston, TX
Emerson, John F. ....Columbia, SC
Emerson, John G., Jr. ....Houston, TX
Emerson, John R. ....Kansas City, KS
Emerson, John Russell ....Dallas, TX
Emerson, John W. ....Naples, FL
Emerson, John W. ....Libertyville, IL
Emerson, Joseph A., Jr. ....Milton, MA
Emerson, Joseph E. ....Frederick, MD
Emerson, Karen K. ....Fontanelle, IA
Emerson, Karl Erick ....Harrisburg, PA
Emerson, Laurie E. ....Santa Monica, CA
Emerson, Leon ....Downey, CA
Emerson, Linda ....Napa, CA
Emerson, Louis J., Jr. ....Sherman, TX
Emerson & Manahan ....Delphi, IN
Emerson, Marvin C. ....Oklahoma City, OK
Emerson, Matthew D. ....Tampa, FL
Emerson, Michael J. ....Little Rock, AR
Emerson, Michael W. ....New York, NY
Emerson, Patricia B. ....Brookhaven, MS
Emerson, Patrick Kevin ....Port Huron, MI
Emerson, Paul R. ....Beach, ND
Dickinson, ND
Emerson, Peter G. ....Waltham, MA
Emerson, Philip ....Bend, OR
Emerson, Phillip R. ....Las Vegas, NV
Emerson, Ralph W. ....Cordell, OK
Emerson, Ramona M. ....Seattle, WA
Emerson, Richard L. ....Bethel, CT
Waterbury, CT
Emerson, Richard S., Jr. ....Portland, ME
Emerson, Robert B. ....Carbondale, CO
Emerson, Robert B., P.C. ....Carbondale, CO
Emerson, Robert D. ....Providence, RI
Emerson, Robert W. ....Gainesville, FL
Emerson, Roger D. ....Akron, OH
Emerson, Sally Holt ....Amarillo, TX
Emerson, Sandra L. ....Oklahoma City, OK
Emerson, Sandra M. ....Chicago, IL
Emerson, Scott ....Jonesboro, AR
Emerson, Stan A. ....Columbus, NE
Emerson, Steven G. ....Kansas City, MO
Emerson, Suzanne L. ....Los Angeles, CA
Emerson, Thomas Carl ....Norwich, NY
Emerson, Thomas R. ....Frankfort, KY
Emerson, Todd C. ....Salt Lake City, UT
Emerson, Vernon C. ....Birmingham, MI
Emerson, Warren M. ....Belmont, NY
Emerson, William H. ....Lake Forest, IL
Emerson-Henry, Lavon ....Minneapolis, MN
Emert, Bradford C. ....Clayton, MO
Emert, Laurence T. ....Rancho Cucamonga, CA
Emert, Tim J. ....San Francisco, CA
Emert, Timothy R. ....Independence, KS
Emery, Alfred C. ....Salt Lake City, UT
Emery, Alicia ....Philadelphia, PA
Emery, Ann-Margret R. ....Palm Coast, FL
Emery, Arthur J., Jr. ....Tacoma, WA
Emery, Carol R. ....Rockland, ME
Emery, Chandra ....Washington, DC
Emery, Charles W. ....Villa Park, IL
Emery, Charles W., Ltd. ....Villa Park, IL
Emery Cuti Brinckerhoff & Abady PC
New York, NY
Emery, David C. ....Ozark, AL
Emery, Douglas D. ....Idaho Falls, ID
Emery, Frederick C., Jr ....Portland, ME
Emery, Geoffrey P. ....Knoxville, TN
Emery, Geoffrey W. ....Beverly Hills, CA
Emery, Gordon K. ....Bedford, IN
Emery & Graeber ....Los Angeles, CA
Emery, H. Gene ....Dallas, TX
Emery, J. Scott ....Spokane, WA
Emery, Jack S. ....Sierra Vista, AZ
Emery, James M. ....San Francisco, CA
Emery, Jean M. ....Phoenix, AZ
Emery, Jill N. ....St. Petersburg, FL
Emery, John C. ....Boston, MA
Emery, John C. ....Manchester, NH
Emery, John C., III ....Birmingham, MI
Emery, John D. ....Detroit, MI
Emery, John M. ....New York, NY
Emery, Jonathan W. ....White Plains, NY
Emery, Katherine B. ....Washington, PA
Emery, Kent ....Des Moines, IA
Emery, Lawrence J. ....Lansing, MI
Emery, Lawrence J., P.C. ....Lansing, MI
Emery, Louis E. ....Arlington, VA
Emery, Mark K. ....Harrisburg, PA
Mechanicsburg, PA
Emery, Marlene P. ....Solon, OH
Emery, Mary B. ....Santa Clara, CA
Emery, Mary Payton, (P.C.) ....Dallas, TX
Emery, Melissa Johnson
Myrtle Beach, SC
North Myrtle Beach, SC
Emery, Michael N. ....Salt Lake City, UT
Emery, Michael S. ....San Francisco, CA
Emery, Myron D., P.C. ....Beverly Hills, CA
Emery, N. Beth ....Folsom, CA
Emery, Patrick W. ....Santa Rosa, CA
Emery, Paul R. ....New York, NY
Emery, R. Clinton ....Rochester, NY
Emery, Richard D. ....New York, NY
Emery, Richard L. ....Toledo, OH
Emery, Richard T. ....Lincoln, NE
Emery, Robert E. ....Bayfield, WI
Emery, Ronald W. ....Lansing, MI
Emery, Russell L. ....Broomfield, CO
Emery, Scott R. ....New York, NY
Emery, Stephen, Jr. ....Pittsburgh, PA
Emery, Stephen T. ....Bangor, ME
Emery, Stephenson D. ....Casper, WY
Emery, Steven C. ....Eagle Butte, SD
Emery, Steven K. ....Bloomington, IN
Indianapolis, IN
Emery, Thomas C. ....Omaha, NE
Emery, Thomas J. ....East Lansing, MI
Emery, Thomas W. ....Detroit, MI
Emery, Wayne L. ....Warsaw, VA
Emery, William R. ....La Grange Park, IL
Emery, William V., III ....Ormond Beach, FL
Emery, William V., III Law Offices, P.A.
Ormond Beach, FL
Emery-Mincer, Joan E. ....Buffalo Grove, IL
Emeziem, Kelechi C. ....Oakland, CA
Emfinger, Michael O. ....Union Springs, AL
Emge, Derek J. ....Costa Mesa, CA
San Diego, CA
Emge, Kirk J. ....Washington, DC
Emge, N. Keith, Jr. ....Charleston, SC
Emhardt, C. David ....Indianapolis, IN
Emhardt, Frederick D. ....Indianapolis, IN
Emhoff, Douglas C. ....Los Angeles, CA
Emi, Gregory M. ....Granada Hills, CA
Emick, Dudley J., Jr. ....Fincastle, VA
Emig, Frank J. ....Greenbelt, MD
Emig, Gerard J. ....Rockville, MD
Emig, James M. ....Ponca City, OK
Emig, Michele E. ....Casa Grande, AZ
Emigh, Frederic R. ....Montpelier, VT
Emigh, Laura Izon ....San Francisco, CA
Emigholz, Kirsten ....New York, NY
Emil, Arthur D. ....New York, NY
Emil, Craig Allen ....Dana Point, CA
Emil, David A. ....Albany, NY
Emile, Volel ....Austin, TX
Emilian, John H., Jr. ....Boston, MA
Emilio, Daniel G. ....Garden Grove, CA
Emino, Sarah J. Tripp ....Oxford, MI
Emison, Doolittle, Kolb & Roellgen
Lawrenceville, IL
Princeton, IN
Shoals, IN
Sullivan, IN
Vincennes, IN
Washington, IN
Emison and Emison, P.C. ....Alamo, TN
Emison, J. Kent ....Lexington, MO
Emison, Lucy A. ....Indianapolis, IN
Emison, Nancy J. ....Lorton, VA
Emison, Rabb ....Vincennes, IN
Emison, Spencer A. ....Miami, FL
Emison, Theophilius J. ....Alamo, TN
Emison, Theophilius J., Jr. ....Alamo, TN
Emke, Steven E. ....Kansas City, MO
Emkes, Cynthia S. ....Franklin, IN
Emley, Christopher F. ....San Francisco, CA
Emley, Glenn A. ....Fort Wayne, IN
Emley, Sara E. ....Washington, DC
Emley, William W., Sr. ....Canton, OH
Emling & Associates ....Long Beach, CA
Emling, Michael J. ....Long Beach, CA
Emling, Stephen B. ....Jefferson, LA
Emm, Cheri K. ....Fallon, NV
Emma & Cardillo ....Brooklyn, NY
Emma, Charles J. ....Chicopee, MA
Holyoke, MA
Emma, Charles L. ....Brooklyn, NY
Emma, Daniel J. ....Milwaukee, WI
Emma, Karen ....Irvine, CA
Emma, Michael A. ....Dallas, TX
Emmanuel, Barbara ....Jamaica, NY
Emmanuel, John D. ....Tampa, FL
Emmanuel, John N. ....Hartford, CT
Emmanuel, Karen O. ....Pensacola, FL
Emmanuel, Lennox ....Bloomfield Hills, MI
Emmanuel, Patrick G. ....Navarre, FL
Pensacola, FL
Emmanuel, Patrick G., Jr.
Jacksonville, FL
Emmanuel, Robert A. ....Pensacola, FL
Emmanuel, Sheppard & Condon
Navarre, FL
Pensacola, FL
Emmanuel, Stephen C. ....Tallahassee, FL
Emmanuelli, Dean ....Bronx, NY
Emmanuelli, Robin H. ....New York, NY
Emmanuelli-Perez, Edda
General Accounting Office, Office of the General Counsel, GV
Emmel, Allen D. ....Las Vegas, NV
Emmel, Drew M. ....Irvine, CA
Emmel, Heather ....Dallas, TX
Emmens, David P. ....Mansfield, OH
Emmens, Terrance W. ....Rochester, NY
Emmer, Donald S. ....Van Nuys, CA
Emmer & Emmer ....Van Nuys, CA
Emmer, Fred H. ....Panorama City, CA
Emmer, George H. ....Egg Harbor City, NJ
Emmer, Howard A. ....Woodland Hills, CA
Emmer, Irving I. ....Van Nuys, CA
Emmer, Jamie L. ....Palo Alto, CA
Emmer, Marvin ....Brooklyn, NY
Emmer, Matthew D. ....Washington, DC
Emmer, Maurice S. ....Palo Alto, CA
Emmer, Seth H. ....Braintree, MA
Emmer, Sheldon R. ....Los Angeles, CA
Emmer, Susan C. ....Washington, DC
Emmer, Thomas E. ....Maple Plain, MN
Emmerich, Adam O. ....New York, NY
Emmerich, Frank R., Jr.
Mount Laurel, NJ
Philadelphia, PA
Emmerich, Pamela A.N. ....New York, NY
Emmerling, Frederick C.
East Liverpool, OH
Emmerling, John W. ....Largo, FL
Emmerling, Patrick L. ....Buffalo, NY
Emmerman, Howard C. ....Chicago, IL
Emmerman, Ross D. ....Chicago, IL
Emmerman, Todd J. ....New York, NY
Emmerman, Tricia L. ....Camden, NJ
Emmerson, Frank V., Jr. ....Surry, VA
Emmerson, Fred B., Jr. ....Chapel Hill, NC
Emmerson, Milton Gary ....Milwaukee, WI
Emmert, Andrew C. ....Cincinnati, OH
Emmert, Anne E. K. ....New York, NY
Emmert, D. Wade ....Dallas, TX
Emmert, Duane F. ....Houston, TX
Emmert, L. Steven ....Virginia Beach, VA
Emmert, Lawrence L. ....Wyandotte, MI

Emmert, Leonard J. .... Hyattsville, MD
Emmert, Marianne Scott .... Cincinnati, OH
Emmert, Melody A. .... Phoenix, AZ
Emmert, Steven M. .... Miamisburg, OH
Emmert, Steven R. .... Wheeler, TX
Emmert, William D. .... Rockford, IL
Emmet, Marvin & Martin, LLP
Darien, CT
Morristown, NJ
New York, NY
Emmet, Winthrop S. .... West Stockbridge, MA
Emmet-Miller, Maureen .... Largo, FL
Emmett, Cobb, Waits, Kessenich & O'Neil, A Professional Law Corporation
New Orleans, LA
Emmett, Daniel J. .... La Grange Park, IL
Emmett, Francis .... New Orleans, LA
Emmett & Glander .... Newtown, CT
Stamford, CT
Emmett, James R. .... Chicago, IL
Emmett, John .... Dallas, TX
Emmett, John F. .... New Orleans, LA
Emmett, John R. .... Trenton, GA
Emmett, Kathryn .... Newtown, CT
Stamford, CT
Emmett, M. Lawrence .... State College, PA
Emmett, Marita M. .... San Antonio, TX
Emmett, Marita M., P.C. .... San Antonio, TX
Emmett, Mark R. .... Midvale, UT
Emmett, Richard L. .... Durango, CO
Emmett, Robert A. .... Washington, DC
Emmett, Robert S. .... New Orleans, LA
Emmi, Donna Marie Jones .... Bloomfield, NJ
Emmi, Louis W. .... Pittsburgh, PA
Emmick, Michael W. .... Los Angeles, CA
Emminger, Michael M. .... Albany, NY
Emmings, Judy L. .... Fairfax, MN
Emmings, Steven D. .... Fairfax, MN
Emmitt, Tim J. .... Chicago, IL
Emmons, A. Wayne .... Memphis, TN
Emmons, Adeline .... Kalamazoo, MI
Emmons, Alison Lobb .... Richmond, KY
Emmons, Bertin C. .... Boston, MA
Emmons, B. R. .... Georgetown, IN
Emmons, C. S. (Pat) .... Albany, OR
Emmons, Daniel L. .... Kalamazoo, MI
Emmons, David L. .... Dallas, TX
Emmons, Elizabeth B. .... New York, NY
Emmons, Francis J. .... Chicago, IL
Emmons, Greg B. .... Philadelphia, PA
Emmons, John L. .... Mount Prospect, IL
Emmons, Joseph G. .... Sherman Oaks, CA
Emmons, Keith E. .... Champaign, IL
Emmons, Laurie .... Highland Lakes, NJ
Emmons, Lisa Hayden .... Paducah, KY
Emmons, Marcia Faykus .... Philadelphia, PA
Emmons, Melanie M. .... Miami, FL
Emmons, Melvin L. .... Pearland, TX
Emmons, Michael A. .... Oklahoma City, OK
Emmons, Nathaniel F. .... Washington, DC
Emmons, Patricia A. .... San Francisco, CA
Emmons, Peter R. .... Atlanta, GA
Emmons, Philip T. .... Novato, CA
Emmons, Robert B. .... Torrance, CA
Emmons, Robert D. .... Department of State, Foreign Service Officers (Overseas), GV
Emmons, Robert J. .... Great Falls, MT
Emmons, Robert L. .... Mineola, NY
Emmons, Shannon K.
Oklahoma City, OK
Emmons, Steven L. .... Irvine, CA
Emmons, Stuart W. .... Oklahoma City, OK
Emmons & Sullivan .... Great Falls, MT
Emmons, Walter F. .... Loudon, TN
Emmons, Wm. B. .... Houston, TX
Emmott, Jack H., III .... Houston, TX
Emmott, Jack H. III, & Associates, P.C.
Houston, TX
Emnett, Thomas R. .... Owego, NY
Emnett, William M. .... Washington, DC
Emolo, John C. .... Montclair, NJ
Paterson, NJ
Emond, Clifford, Jr. .... Birmingham, AL
Emond, Howard Earl, Jr. .... Rockville, CT
Emond, Marcel L., Jr. .... Springfield, MA
Emond & Vines .... Birmingham, AL
Emons, Clifford C. .... Alton, IL
Emont, Michael J. .... New York, NY
Emord & Associates, P.C.
Washington, DC
Burke, VA
Emord, Jonathan W. .... Washington, DC
Burke, VA
Emory, C. William .... New Orleans, LA
Emory, Carol A., & Associates
Portland, OR
Emory, Charles W., Jr. .... Greenville, SC
Emory, David T., Law Offices of
San Antonio, TX
Emory, Frank E., Jr. .... Charlotte, NC
Emory, Howard B. .... Miami, FL
Emory, Hugh M. .... Paoli, PA
Emory, James E., Jr. .... New York, NY
Emory, John B. .... Dexter, ME
Emory, Meade .... Seattle, WA
Emory, Richard W., Jr.
Environmental Protection Agency, Office of Enforcement and Compliance Assurance, GV
Emory, Rosemary A. .... St. Maries, ID
Emouna, Matin .... West Babylon, NY
Empeño, Henry, Jr. .... San Bernardino, CA
Emper, Nicholas J. .... Media, PA
Emper, Nicholas J., P.C. .... Media, PA
Empey, Carole S. .... Ann Arbor, MI
Empey & Dartt .... Portland, OR
Empey, Dolores J. .... Portland, OR
Empey, Gordon H. .... Kirkland, WA
Empey, Kenneth W. .... Jackson, MI
Empey, Marc E. .... Palm Springs, CA
Empfield, Don M. .... Gillette, WY
Empie, Robt. Y. .... Oklahoma City, OK
Employment Rights Group, The
Pittsburgh, PA
Empson, G. Raymond, III .... Old Bridge, NJ
Empson, Nicholas C.R. .... Raleigh, NC
Empson, Paul D. .... Chadron, NE
Empson, Stacey Renee .... Shawnee, KS
Emquies, Moise .... Los Angeles, CA
Emrey, Jay C., III .... Elkton, MD
Emrich & Dithmar .... Chicago, IL
Emrich, Edmund M. .... New York, NY
Emrich, Henry S. .... Grand Rapids, MI
Emrich, Jerry K. .... Arlington, VA
Emrich, Linny C. .... Des Moines, IA
Emrich, Michael E. .... New York, NY
Emrich, Susan E. .... La Jolla, CA
Emrick, Charles R., Jr. .... Cleveland, OH
Emrick, Gregg M. .... Belpre, OH
Marietta, OH
Emrick, Lori M. .... Philadelphia, PA
Emrick, Matthew L. .... Turlock, CA
Emrick, Nicholas R. .... Dayton, OH
Emrick, Shannon T. .... Los Angeles, CA
Emrick, Steven P. .... Stockton, CA
Emrick, William P. .... Ashland, KY
Emroch & Kilduff, LLP .... Richmond, VA
Emroch, Walter H., & Associates
Chesterfield, VA
Petersburg, VA
Richmond, VA
Emry, Cynthia J. .... Los Angeles, CA
Emry, Debra A. .... Chicago, IL
Emry, Felicia A. .... Baltimore, MD
Emry, Frederic G., II .... Kennewick, WA
Spokane, WA
Emse, Timothy P. .... Upland, CA
Emshoff, Reginald A. .... Madison, WI
Emsley, Albert P., Jr. .... Bothell, WA
Emslie, George A. .... St. Paul, MN
Emswiller, Diane Parsons
Indianapolis, IN
Emswiller, Kent .... Indianapolis, IN
Emswiller, Williams, Noland & Clarke
Indianapolis, IN
Emuryan & Breen .... Woodlyn, PA
Emuryan, D. Michael .... Woodlyn, PA
Enabnit, Nancy L. .... Enid, OK
Enabnit, Ronald E. .... Sacramento, CA
Enabnit, Ted .... Mason City, IA
Enabnit, Ted, P.C. .... Mason City, IA
Enache Brown, Colleen .... New York, NY
Enander, Nancy F. .... Red Bank, NJ
Enayati, Elizabeth F. .... Atherton, CA
Enbody and Dugaw .... Centralia, WA
Enborg, Kenneth D. .... Detroit, MI
Encarnacion, Benjamin S. .... New York, NY
Encarnacion, Yvette .... Brooklyn, NY
Ence, Derek C. .... Las Vegas, NV
Ence, Erik L. .... Lexington, MA
Ence, Matthew D. .... Las Vegas, NV
Encinas, Donna M. .... Glendale, CA
Encinas, Gary P. .... San Francisco, CA
Encinias, Art .... Santa Fe, NM
Enck, Craig A. .... Baltimore, MD
Enck, Dale R. .... Pueblo, CO
Enck, John D. .... Lebanon, PA
End, J. Michael .... Milwaukee, WI
End, Ralph P. .... Dallas, TX
Endacott, Donald E. .... Lincoln, NE
Endacott, James H. .... Houston, TX
Endacott, Kent E. .... Columbus, NE
Endacott, Richard R. .... Lincoln, NE
Ende, Asher H. .... Washington, DC
Ende, Donald C. .... New York, NY
Ende, Douglas J. .... Seattle, WA
Ende, Howard S. .... Princeton, NJ
Ende, Howard S. .... New York, NY
Ende, James .... Kew Gardens, NY
Ende, Michael J. .... Garden City, NY
Ende, Nathan .... New York, NY
Ende, Neil S. .... Washington, DC
Ende, Pamela Porter .... Philadelphia, PA
Ende, Patrick Francis .... Augusta, ME
Endean, Jeffrey J. .... Saginaw, MI
Endean, Leslie A. .... Hobbs, NM
Endejan, Frank J. .... Fond du Lac, WI
Endejan, Judith A. .... Seattle, WA
Endel, Max .... Houston, TX
Endelicato, Constance A.
Santa Monica, CA
Endelman, Charles R. .... Omaha, NE
Endelman, Earle E. .... Troy, MI
Endelman, Gary E. .... Houston, TX
Endeman, Lincoln, Turek & Heater
San Diego, CA
Endeman, Ronald L. .... San Diego, CA
Ender, Patricia M. .... Augusta, ME
Enderby, B. Lynn .... Philadelphia, PA
Enderby, Lindsey .... Taos, NM
Enderle, Alan G. .... Kalamazoo, MI
Enderle, Debra McPipkin .... Baltimore, MD
Enderle, John R. .... Mansfield, OH
Enderle, Louis E., Jr. .... Clarksburg, WV
Enderle, Robert P. .... Landover, MD
Enders, Camille Siano .... Albany, NY
Enders, John B. .... Erie, PA
Enders, Kelli A. .... Minneapolis, MN
Enders, Kelly L. .... Pittsburgh, PA
Enders, Kimberly K. .... Chicago, IL
Enders, Michael B. .... New Haven, CT
Enders, Richard D. .... Clinton, NY
Enders, Robert A. .... Harrisburg, PA
Enders, Robert J. .... Los Angeles, CA
Enders, Robert J., Jr., Law Offices of
Los Angeles, CA
Enders, Warren M. .... Columbus, OH
Enders, William W. .... Austin, TX
Endersby, Kelly B. .... Los Altos, CA
Endervelt, Jeffrey K. .... Los Angeles, CA
Endick, Adam .... New York, NY
Endick, Barry N. .... San Francisco, CA
Endick, Daniel J. .... New York, NY
Endick, Jeffrey S. .... Washington, DC
Endick, Kenneth J. .... Westwood, NJ
Endick, Marshal S. .... New York, NY
Endick, Stuart W. .... Treasury Department, Internal Revenue Service, GV
Endicott, Eugene F. .... Hingham, MA
Endicott & Finch .... Carmi, IL
Endicott, Gary L. .... United States Senate, Office of the Legislative Counsel, GV
Endicott, James A. .... Springfield, MO
Endicott, John L. .... Los Angeles, CA
Endicott, Lee .... Oklahoma City, OK
Endicott, Michael S. .... Paintsville, KY
Endicott, R. Coleman .... Lexington, KY
Endicott, Richard D. .... Hillsboro, WI
Viroqua, WI
Endicott, Robert J. .... St. Louis, MO
Endicott, Wm. R. .... Carmi, IL
Endictor, W. Baer .... Atlanta, GA
Endieveri, Anne C. .... Washington, DC
Endieveri, Anthony F. .... Camillus, NY
Endieveri, Anthony F. .... Syracuse, NY
Endler, Gerald S. .... Bethesda, MD
Endler, Lara J. .... Kingston, PA
Endler, Michael I. .... Albany, NY
New York, NY
Endler, Paul J., Jr. .... Westfield, NJ
Endler, Richard D. .... Buffalo, NY
Endlich, Ben A. .... El Paso, TX
Endlich, Rona C. .... Washington, DC
Endman, James .... Los Angeles, CA
Endo, Kimiyo Tahira
Pension Benefit Guaranty Corporation, Office of the General Counsel, GV
Endo, Randall H. .... Wailuku, HI
Endo, Russell S. .... Philadelphia, PA
Endom, Adras P. LaBorde .... Lafayette, LA
Endom, Franklin V., Jr. .... New Orleans, LA
Endo-Omoto, Darcy L. .... Honolulu, HI
Endorf, Verlane L. .... Minneapolis, MN
Endow, Gordon I. .... San Francisco, CA
Endrelunas, Richard M. .... Windsor Locks, CT
Endreny, Pamela Lawrence
New York, NY
Endres, Ann E. .... Lebanon, PA
Endres, Barbara Jean .... Washington, DC
Endres, C. Todd .... Eureka, CA
Endres, Charles F., Jr. .... Baltimore, MD
Endres, David J. .... Milwaukee, WI
Endres, Frederick M. .... Nashville, IL
Endres, Ira F., Jr. .... Scarsdale, NY
Endres, John M. .... Beardstown, IL
Endres, Kathy A. .... Minneapolis, MN
Endres, Krista A. .... Chicago, IL
Endres, LeRoy E. .... St. Paul, MN
Endres, Louis P., III .... Columbus, OH
Endres, Martin P. .... New York, NY
Endres, Mary .... Tyler, TX
Endres, Richard .... New York, NY
Endres, Richard S. .... New York, NY
Endres, Stephen M. .... Chantilly, VA
Endreson, Douglas B. L. .... Washington, DC
Endress, Ellen C. .... Upper Marlboro, MD
Endress & Endress .... Cleveland, OH
Endress, Jeffrey C. .... Cleveland, OH
Endress, Jennifer A. .... New York, NY
Endress, Ned R. .... Cuyahoga Falls, OH
Endress, Richard R. .... Cleveland, OH
Endries, Karen H. .... Los Angeles, CA
Endries, Robert A. .... Los Angeles, CA
Endris, Lori Kyle .... Indianapolis, IN
Endriss, Marilyn J. .... Seattle, WA
Endriss, Victoria M. .... Philadelphia, PA
Endrizzi, Laura A. .... Garden City, NY
Endrizzi, Suzanne M. .... New York, NY
Endsley, Harry B., & Associates
San Francisco, CA
Endsley, J. Patrick .... Indianapolis, IN
Endsley, Lionel I. .... Detroit, MI
Endsley, Martha Ewing .... Tulsa, OK
Endsley, Meredith Nelson
San Francisco, CA
Endsley, Nancy G. .... Indianapolis, IN
Endsley, Scott K. .... San Diego, CA
Endy, Alexander .... West Chester, PA
Endy, Bruce E. .... Philadelphia, PA
Endy, Karin R. .... New York, NY
Endyke, Mary Beth .... Secaucus, NJ
Endy Klein, Daryl S. .... Paoli, PA
Enea, Anne L. .... San Jose, CA
Enea, Dione Marie .... New York, NY
Enea, Jack A. .... West Bend, WI
Enea & Piunti, A Professional Corporation
San Jose, CA
Enebo, Daniel J. .... Minneapolis, MN
Eneboe-Braithwaite, Tacey
Cedar Rapids, IA
Enechionyia & Associates, Law Offices
Alexandria, VA
Arlington, VA
Enechionyia, Buchi .... Alexandria, VA
Eneman, Elyssa K. .... New York, NY
Enemark, Anders H. .... New York, NY
Enemark, Christine E. .... Washington, DC
Enemuoh-Trammell, H. Nia .... Madison, WI
Enenbach, John K. .... Kansas City, MO
Enenbach, Mark F. .... Omaha, NE
Enenstein, Darren S. .... Los Angeles, CA
Energy Advocates LLP .... Washington, DC
Portland, OR
Enerio, Patricia L. .... Wilmington, DE
Enerle, Stephen D. .... Glendale, CA
Enersen, Burnham .... San Francisco, CA
Eney, Jaine Elkind .... White Plains, NY
Enfield Brown Collins & Knivila
Salem, OR
Enfield, Lisa Horwitz .... Fort Lauderdale, FL
Enfield, Lisa M. .... Albuquerque, NM
Enfield, Myron L. .... Salem, OR
Enfield, Stephen H. .... Portland, OR
Enfield, William H. .... Bentonville, AR
Enfinger, D. Carlton, II .... Tallahassee, FL
Enfinger, D. Carlton, P.A. .... Tallahassee, FL
Enfinger, Floyd C., Jr. .... Montrose, AL
Enfinger, Russell R., Sr. .... Panama City, FL
Eng, Amelia M. .... Los Angeles, CA
Eng, Anne Lee .... San Francisco, CA
Eng, Bjarne R. .... Bloomington, MN
Eng, Carol L. .... Spokane, WA
Eng, Catharina Chin .... New York, NY
Eng, Chi K. .... New York, NY
Eng, Daniel B. .... Sacramento, CA
Eng, David S. .... Los Angeles, CA
Eng, Donald .... New York, NY
Eng, Donald .... Rochester, NY
Eng, Doris W. .... Albuquerque, NM
Eng, Edward J. .... Los Angeles, CA
Eng, Fern .... Eugene, OR
Eng, Geoffrey J. .... Spokane, WA
Eng, George .... Boston, MA
Eng, Glen W. .... Flandreau, SD
Eng, Goldie L. .... Sacramento, CA
Eng, Gordon K. .... Torrance, CA
Eng, Holly S.A. .... Minneapolis, MN
Eng, Jack S. .... Tacoma, WA
Eng, Jeffrey .... St. Paul, MN
Eng, JoAnn .... New York, NY
Eng, John Jeffrey .... Woodland Hills, CA
Eng, Judy M. .... New York, NY
Eng, Kimton N. .... Seattle, WA
Eng, Laura Victoria .... New York, NY
Eng, Leslie J. .... Los Angeles, CA
Eng, Michael J. .... Uniondale, NY
Eng, Michael Paul .... Jacksonville, FL
Eng, Myron A.
Environmental Protection Agency, Program Office Attorneys, GV
Eng, Nancy Charoen .... Los Angeles, CA
Eng, Newcomb & Bot .... Spokane, WA
Eng, Patrick J. .... Columbia, MO
Eng, Perry J. .... Burbank, CA
Eng, Phoebe S. .... New York, NY
Eng, Randall T. .... Kew Gardens, NY
Eng, Richard K. .... New York, NY
Eng, Sam M. .... Houston, TX
Eng, U. P. Peter .... Palo Alto, CA
Eng, Vincent Patrick .... New York, NY
Eng & Woods .... Columbia, MO
Enga, Laura L. .... Minneapolis, MN
Engbarth, Frederick J. .... Santa Rosa, CA
Engber, Michael D. .... Muncie, IN
Engberg, John G. .... Minneapolis, MN
Engberg, Robert A. .... Burlington, IA
Engberg, Stephen, & Associates, P.C.
Chicago, IL
Engberg, Stephen N. .... Chicago, IL
Engberg, William H. .... Pierre, SD
Engbers, James A. .... Grand Rapids, MI
Engdahl, Brad P. .... Minneapolis, MN
Engdahl, David E. .... Tacoma, WA
Engdahl, Kathryn M. .... Minneapolis, MN
Engdahl, K. C. .... Omaha, NE
Engdahl, Laurie W. .... Boston, MA
Engdahl, Marta .... Charlottesville, VA
Engdahl, Walter A. .... Boca Raton, FL
Engdall, Kirk A. .... Salem, OR
Engdol, Traci M. .... Parker, CO
Engebretson, Andrew P. .... St. Paul, MN
Engebretson & Associates, P.A.
St. Paul, MN
Engebretson, Christopher D. .... Boston, MA
Engebretson, William F. .... Jeffersonville, IN
Engel, Alan R. .... Baltimore, MD
Engel, Albert J. .... Grand Rapids, MI
Engel, Albert J., III .... Grand Rapids, MI
Engel, Alexander .... New York, NY
Engel, Alison G. .... Los Angeles, CA
Engel, Allan D. .... Ada, MI
Engel, Allison M. .... Chicago, IL
Engel, Andrew M. .... Dayton, OH
Engel, Annie H. .... West Hartford, CT
Engel, Arthur R. .... Santa Monica, CA
Engel, Austin G. .... Bismarck, ND
Engel, Barrie .... Oakland, CA
Engel, Barry E. .... Houston, TX
Engel, Barry S. .... Denver, CO
Engel, Benjamin .... Hartford, CT
Engel, Beth A. .... Chicago, IL
Engel, Betsey A. .... Detroit, MI
Engel, Brenda Farr .... Trenton, NJ
Engel, Brett E. .... Portland, OR
Engel, Brian E. .... Kansas City, MO
Engel, Bruce M. .... Inverness, IL
Engel, Charles C. .... Brownsburg, IN
Engel, Charles J., Jr. .... Syracuse, NY
Engel, Charles J. (Tim), III
Washington, DC
Engel, Charles T. .... Topeka, KS
Engel, Daniel A. .... Chicago, IL
Engel, Daniel E. .... Los Angeles, CA
Engel, Daniel W. .... Miami, FL
Engel, David .... Washington, DC
Engel, David .... New York, NY
Engel, David A. .... Albany, NY
Engel, David C. .... Exeter, NH
Engel, David J. .... Pittsfield, MA
Engel, David L. .... Boston, MA

Engel, David Wayne
Department Of Health And Human Services, Social Security Administration, GV
Engel, Debra S.
Nuclear Regulatory Commission, Office of the General Counsel, GV
Engel, Denis A. .... Garden City, NY
Engel & Devlin, P.C. .... Warren, NJ
Engel, Devon S. .... Scottsdale, AZ
Engel, Diana R. .... Washington, DC
Engel, Donald F. .... Glen Ellyn, IL
Engel, Donald S. .... Los Angeles, CA
Engel, Donald W. .... Sunnyside, WA
Engel, Douglas J. .... Seattle, WA
Engel, Douglas R. .... Sycamore, IL
Engel, Drew G. .... Oxford, OH
Engel, Edward I. .... Portland, OR
Engel, Edward W. .... Houston, TX
Engel & Engel .... Syracuse, NY
Engel & Engel, A Professional Corporation
Los Angeles, CA
Engel & Engel, P.A. .... Baltimore, MD
Engel, Eric S. .... Santa Monica, CA
Engel, Franklyn J. .... Woodstock, NY
Engel, Frederick W. .... Madison, NJ
Engel, G. Larry .... San Francisco, CA
Engel, Gearreald & Gardner, Professional Association .... Exeter, NH
Engel, Hairston and Johanson, P.C.
Birmingham, AL
Engel, Harold J. .... Washington, DC
Engel, Harold L. .... North Hollywood, CA
Engel, Harry J. .... Arlington, VA
Engel, Herbert .... New York, NY
Engel, Hope Beth .... Albany, NY
Engel, Jacqueline Y. .... Newport Beach, CA
Engel, James .... Hanover Park, IL
Engel, James J.
National Credit Union Administration, Office of General Counsel, GV
Engel, James J. .... Pepper Pike, OH
Engel, James Joseph
Department of Commerce, Patent and Trademark Office, GV
Engel, Jane F. .... Trenton, NJ
Engel, Jason O. .... Orange, CA
Engel, Joan G. .... Hartford, CT
Engel, John C. .... Pewaukee, WI
Engel, John H. .... Stamford, CT
Engel, John M. .... Washington, DC
Engel, John P. .... New York, NY
Engel, John, (P.C.) .... Washington, DC
Engel, John R. .... San Diego, CA
Engel, Jonathan P. .... New York, NY
Engel, Jones, P.C. .... Houston, TX
Engel, Joseph C., III .... Great Falls, MT
Engel, Joseph G. .... Warren, NJ
Engel, Joshua A. .... Boston, MA
Engel, Judith Edelman .... Los Angeles, CA
Engel, Judy S. .... Minneapolis, MN
Engel, Julius M. .... Sacramento, CA
Engel, Kaaren H. .... Nashville, TN
Engel, Kalene M. .... Rochester, MN
Engel, Kevin Joseph .... East Greenbush, NY
Engel, Kirsten .... Washington, DC
Engel, Lauri Ann .... Toledo, OH
Engel, Lawrence E. .... Baltimore, MD
Engel, Lawrence K. .... Bellevue, WA
Engel, Lawrence K. .... Seattle, WA
Engel, Lester .... North Miami Beach, FL
Engel, Lisa R. .... Los Angeles, CA
Engel, Lon C. .... Baltimore, MD
Engel, Lynda S. .... La Grange, GA
Engel, Lynn M. .... Seattle, WA
Engel, Marc R. .... Baltimore, MD
Engel, Marcy .... New York, NY
Engel, Marcy Renee .... Sweet Home, OR
Engel, Mark A. .... Columbus, OH
Engel, Mark A. .... Oklahoma City, OK
Engel, Mark D. .... Boston, MA
Engel, Matthew .... Northampton, MA
Engel, Maurice .... Hayward, CA
Engel, Max P. .... Fort Myers, FL
Engel & McCarney .... New York, NY
Engel, Melvin M. .... Houston, TX
Engel, Michael D. .... Minneapolis, MN
Engel, Mona C. .... Great Neck, NY
Engel, Monte .... Barrow, AK
Engel, Mylan R. .... Mobile, AL
Engel, Patricia N. .... Brookfield, WI
Engel, Paul B. .... Baltimore, MD
Engel, Paul K. .... Palm Desert, CA
Engel, Peter F. .... Crownsville, MD
Engel, Ralph M. .... New York, NY
Engel Reiman & Lockwood pc
Denver, CO
Engel, Renat .... Hollywood, CA
Engel, Richard C. .... Syracuse, NY
Engel, Richard F. .... Trenton, NJ
Engel, Richard L. .... Syracuse, NY
Engel, Richard W., Jr. .... Belleville, IL
St. Louis, MO
Engel, Rick .... Des Moines, IA
Engel, Robert .... Pittsburgh, PA
Engel, Robert A. .... Santa Fe, NM
Engel, Robert G. .... Walnut Creek, CA
Engel, Robin E. .... Seattle, WA
Engel, Ronald L. .... Chicago, IL
Engel, Roy .... New York, NY
Engel, Sandor .... Allentown, PA
Engel, Scott H. .... Dayton, OH
Engel, Sharon .... Rancho Santa Fe, CA
Engel, Sheldon D. .... Chicago, IL
Engel, Shirley A. .... North Hollywood, CA
Engel & Stern .... Santa Fe, NM
Engel, Steven I. .... Miami, FL
Engel, Steven P. .... Pittsburgh, PA
Engel, Tala .... Washington, DC
Engel, Terry L. .... Chicago, IL
Engel, Thomas E. .... New York, NY
Engel, Thomas S. .... San Diego, CA
Engel, Timothy M. .... Pierre, SD
Engel, Todd S. .... Syracuse, NY
Engel, W. Gregory, Law Offices of
San Rafael, CA
Engel, Walsh & Associates .... Mobile, AL
Engel, William J. .... Pittsburgh, PA
Engel, William V. .... Warren, NJ
Engeland, Claudia J. .... Minneapolis, MN
Engelbart, Joan E. .... Martinez, CA
Engelberg, Allen B. .... Crystal Lake, IL
Engelberg, Burt W. .... Chicago, IL
Engelberg, Cantor, Leone & Milgrim, P.L.
Hollywood, FL
Palm Beach, FL
Engelberg, Claire .... Novato, CA
Engelberg, Michael Joseph .... Boston, MA
Engelberg, Morris .... Hollywood, FL
Palm Beach, FL
Engelberg, Phillip G. .... Miami Beach, FL
Engelberg, Richard A. .... Mineola, NY
Engelberg & Smith .... Chicago, IL
Engelberg, Steven L. .... Washington, DC
Engelbert, Caroline E. .... Ann Arbor, MI
Engelbert, David E. .... Ann Arbor, MI
Engelbert, Matthew T. .... Ann Arbor, MI
Engelberth, Melissa M. .... Chicago, IL
Engelbrecht, Ackerman & Hassman
Clarksville, IA
Readlyn, IA
Tripoli, IA
Waverly, IA
Engelbrecht, Charles W. .... Rome, NY
Engelbrecht, Dale R. .... West Plains, MO
Engelbrecht, David M. .... Waverly, IA
Engelbrecht, Dean R. .... Bloomington, IL
Engelbrecht, John C. .... Syracuse, NY
Engelbrecht, Michael H. .... Palm Beach, FL
Engelbrecht, Richard A. .... Green Bay, WI
Engelbrecht, Stacey E. .... Washington, DC
Engelbrecht, Wm. H. .... Readlyn, IA
Tripoli, IA
Waverly, IA
Engeldinger, Gerald L. .... Neenah, WI
Engeldorf, Roseann M. .... Houston, TX
Engeldrum, Joanne M. .... Uniondale, NY
Engeleiter, Gerald H. .... St. Paul, MN
Engeleiter, Susan S. .... Madison, WI
Engeler, Frank D. .... Fort Wayne, IN
Engeler, Gordon F., Jr. .... Springfield, MO
Engelhard, Patricia .... Chicago, IL
Engelhard, Scott J. .... Seattle, WA
Engelhard, Sharon K. .... Baltimore, MD
Engelhard, Sheldon .... New York, NY
Engelhardt, Brian C. .... Reading, PA
Engelhardt, Bruce H. .... Westlake Village, CA
Engelhardt, Carl F., Jr. .... Lexington, KY
Engelhardt, Carol L. .... Newport Beach, CA
Engelhardt, David L. .... Washington, DC
Engelhardt, Jane .... New York, NY
Engelhardt, Jennifer L. .... Batavia, IL
Engelhardt, Jo Ann .... Palm Beach, FL
Engelhardt, Julia R. .... St. Louis, MO
Engelhardt, Julie A. .... Omaha, NE
Engelhardt, Karen .... Chicago, IL
Engelhardt, Kurt D. .... Metairie, LA
Engelhardt, Martin B., Jr. .... White Plains, NY
Engelhardt, Peter R. .... Summit, NJ
Engelhardt, Richard J. .... Trenton, NJ
Engelhardt, Ruth J., (Mrs.)
Beverly Hills, CA
Engelhardt, Stephan M. .... Denison, IA
Engelhardt, Stephen E. .... Hollister, CA
Engelhardt, Steven W. .... Hutchinson, KS
Engelhardt, Theobald H., Jr.
St. Augustine, FL
Engelhardt, Thomas F. .... Sun City, AZ
Engelhardt, Thomas W. .... Chicago, IL
Engelhart, Eva S. .... Houston, TX
Engelhart, Robert D. .... Rome, GA
Engelhart, Robert G. .... Clinton, NJ
Engelke, Paula Cludray .... Minneapolis, MN
Engelke, Robert A. .... Minneapolis, MN
Engelke, Roy .... Galveston, TX
Engelken, Sheri J. .... Chicago, IL
Engelkes, Carroll E. .... Waterloo, IA
Engelking, Bruce E. .... Port Washington, WI
Engelking, James F. .... Denver, CO
Engelking, James F., P.C. .... Denver, CO
Engelking, Lara D. .... Indianapolis, IN
Engelking, Matthew E. .... Minnetonka, MN
Engell, Douglas M. .... Jackson, MS
Engelland, Arthur E., Jr. .... Chicago, IL
Engellenner, Thomas J. .... Boston, MA
Engelmaier, Christine R. .... Boca Raton, FL
Engelman, Bennett S. .... Portland, MI
Engelman Berger, P.C. .... Phoenix, AZ
Engelman & Cabral .... Juneau, AK
Engelman, David Wm. .... Phoenix, AZ
Engelman, Douglas N. .... Williamsport, PA
Engelman & Engelman .... Southbury, CT
Waterbury, CT
Engelman, Geoffrey P. .... Juneau, AK
Engelman, Jerald L. .... Mayville, ND
Engelman, Jerrold W. .... Miami Beach, FL
Engelman, Karen .... Newton, MA
Engelman, Lawrence H. .... Southbury, CT
Engelman, Richard A. .... Hartford, CT
Engelman, Robert J. .... New Haven, CT
Engelman & Smith .... Skokie, IL
Engelman, Stephen B. .... Skokie, IL
Engelman, Steve T. .... Stamford, CT
Engelman & Welch-Rubin, L.L.P.
New Haven, CT
Engelman, William H. .... Baltimore, MD
Engelmanlado, Marianne L. .... New York, NY
Engelmann, Belinda W. .... Roswell, GA
Engelmann, Cheryl A. .... Dallas, TX
Engelmann, Colleen .... Santa Clara, CA
Engelmann, Glenn M. .... Wilmington, DE
Engelmann, John H. .... Wickliffe, OH
Engelmann, Mark D. .... New York, NY
Engelmann, Therese .... Eugene, OR
Engelmayer, Louis .... New York, NY
Engelmeier, Sheila .... Minneapolis, MN
Engelmeyer, Timothy A. .... Chesterfield, MO
Engelmyer, Steven J. .... Montclair, NJ
Engeln, William M. .... St. Joseph, MI
Engels, Bernard L. .... Mendota, IL
Engels, Christy L. .... Santa Monica, CA
Engels, David A. .... Aurora, OR
Engels, Donna J. .... Dixon, IL
Engels, Iris K. .... New York, NY
Engels, John A. .... Blue Earth, MN
Engels, Kevin D. .... Cedar Falls, IA
Engels, Martin .... Miami, FL
Engels, Martin, P.A. .... Miami, FL
Engels, Richard C. .... Presque Isle, ME
Engels, Robert C. .... Kalamazoo, MI
Engels, Shari .... New York, NY
Engelsher, David L. .... Bronx, NY
Engelskirchen, Adam G. .... Los Angeles, CA
Engelskirchen, Gerard .... Santa Cruz, CA
Engelskirchen, Howard H. .... Fullerton, CA
Engelsma, Fernando L. .... Rockford, IL
Engelsman, Gregory .... Alexandria, LA
Engelsman, Jeffrey Alan .... Englewood, CO
Engelson, Gary S. .... Boston, MA
Engelstad, Kurt .... Portland, OR
Engelstein, Daniel .... New York, NY
Engelstein, Larry .... Washington, DC
Engelthaler, Fred E. .... Chevy Chase, MD
Engelthaler, James R. .... Florence, AL
Engeman, Charles E.
Charlotte Amalie, St. Thomas, VI
Engeman, Floyd B. .... Denver, CO
Engeman, Karl S. .... Sacramento, CA
Engeman, William K. .... Cincinnati, OH
Engemann, William D. .... West Branch, MI
Engen, David A. .... Minneapolis, MN
Engen, Gerald B., Jr. .... Boulder, CO
Enger, Clifford E. .... Thousand Oaks, CA
Enger, Erika Zimmer .... Denver, CO
Enger, J. Michael .... Austin, MN
Enger, William K. .... Los Angeles, CA
Engerman, Allen C. .... Northbrook, IL
Engerman, William George .... Chicago, IL
Engerrand, Kenneth G. .... Houston, TX
Engers, Scott .... Ann Arbor, MI
Engert, Curtis M. .... Sarasota, FL
Engert, Lloyd S. .... Champaign, IL
Engert, Wade G. .... Stanley, ND
Engfelt, Frank A. .... San Diego, CA
Engfer, Victoria L. .... Hoffman Estates, IL
Engh, Anna .... Washington, DC
Engh, Christopher H. .... Stockton, CA
Engh, Elizabeth M. .... Oakland, CA
Engh, Lisa A. .... Woodbury, MN
Engh, Rolf .... Minneapolis, MN
Enghagen, Linda K. .... Northampton, MA
Engin, Mutahare Saritabak
East Hartford, CT
Engineer, Rahul D. .... San Jose, CA
Engineer, Rumi, Law Offices of
Denver, CO
Engisch, Nicole A. .... Minneapolis, MN
England, Adele M. .... Irving, TX
England, Anthony V.S. .... Austin, TX
England, Arthur J., Jr. .... Miami, FL
England, Austin Hinds .... Dallas, TX
England, Blair A. .... New York, NY
England, Boyd A. .... Doylestown, PA
England, Brian L. .... Fort Wayne, IN
England, Catherine T. .... Centereach, NY
England & Cohen, LLP .... Oxnard, CA
Ventura, CA
England, Dale R., Jr. .... Baltimore, OH
England, Daniel L. .... Alliance, OH
England, David M. .... Department of Defense, Defense Commissary Agency, GV
England, Deborah Carol .... San Francisco, CA
England, Deborah Z. .... San Francisco, CA
England, Donna .... Centereach, NY
England, Elaine .... Salt Lake City, UT
England, Elizabeth A. .... San Francisco, CA
England & England, P.C. .... Centereach, NY
England, Gary W. .... St. Petersburg, FL
England & Hodik .... San Diego, CA
England, J. Melvin .... Atlanta, GA
England, J. Scott .... Chicago, IL
England, James .... Boulder, CO
England, James C. .... Springfield, MO
England, James S., Jr. .... Houston, TX
England, Jill S. .... Sacramento, CA
England, John F. .... Jackson, MS
England, John H., III .... Huntsville, AL
England, John H., Jr. .... Tuscaloosa, AL
England, John K. .... Dallas, TX
England, John M., Jr. .... Lincolnshire, IL
England, John W. .... Atlanta, GA
England, Joseph .... Orlando, FL
England, Joshua S. .... Worcester, MA
England, Katherine A.
Securities and Exchange Commission, Division of Market Regulation, GV
England, Kathleen Jane .... Las Vegas, NV
England Law Firm .... Rapid City, SD
England, Lee A. .... Lawrenceburg, TN
England, Lee C. .... Jackson, MS
England, Leslie James .... Rapid City, SD
England, Linda F. .... Irvine, CA
England, Louis C. .... Centereach, NY
England, Lynne L. .... Brandon, FL
England, Margaret C. .... Charlotte, NC
England, Margaret Marie
Santa Rosa, CA
England & McKnight .... Atlanta, GA
England, Michael A. .... Lincoln, NE
England, Morrison C., Jr. .... Sacramento, CA
England, Pamela J. .... Gainesville, FL
England, Patricia I. .... Helena, MT
England, Phillip .... New York, NY
England, Rimfa .... Pleasantville, NY
England, Robert B. .... Oxnard, CA
England, Rudy Alan .... Houston, TX
England, Stephen J. .... Springfield, IL
England, Susan L. .... San Diego, CA
England, Teresa N. .... Denver, CO
England, Theodore J. .... Oxnard, CA
England, Thomas F. .... Martinez, GA
England, Traycee S. .... Appleton, WI
England, Wendy V. E. .... Daytona Beach, FL
England, Whitfield, Schröeder & Tredway, L.L.P. .... Oxnard, CA
Thousand Oaks, CA
Ventura, CA
England, William B. .... St. Louis, MO
England, William Lee .... Ellicott City, MD
England, William R., III
Jefferson City, MO
England, William S. .... Kansas City, MO
England, William T. .... Jupiter, FL
Englande, Sherry .... Irving, TX
Englander, Bradford F.
Silver Spring, MD
Englander & Chicoine .... Boston, MA
Newton, MA
Englander, Craig J. .... Beverly Hills, CA
Englander, David M. .... New York, NY
Englander, Diane .... New York, NY
Englander, Edward S. .... Newton, MA
Englander, Ellwood L. .... Silver Spring, MD
Englander, Ira .... Marina Del Rey, CA
Englander, Jeffrey P. .... New York, NY
Englander, John C. .... Boston, MA
Englander, Jonathan J. .... New York, NY
Englander, Joseph R. .... Clearwater, FL
Englander, Leonard S. .... St. Petersburg, FL
Englander, Malvin .... Miami Beach, FL
Englander, Paul A. .... Phoenix, AZ
Englander, Sidney .... North Miami Beach, FL
Englander, Steven .... San Francisco, CA
Englander, William H. .... Mineola, NY
Englar, John D. .... Greensboro, NC
Engle, Annette M. .... Indianapolis, IN
Engle, Arthur K. .... Stamford, CT
Engle, Barry W. .... Portland, OR
Engle, Benjamin J. .... Ventura, CA
Engle & Bride .... Santa Barbara, CA
Ventura, CA
Engle, Carole Hakala .... Lansing, MI
Engle, Charles E. .... Irvine, CA
Engle, Daniel T. .... St. Louis, MO
Engle, Darryl .... Phoenix, AZ
Engle, David C. .... Akron, OH
Engle, David D. .... State College, PA
Engle, David S. .... Atlanta, GA
Engle, David S. .... Maple Valley, WA
Engle, Dawson R. .... Purcell, OK
Engle, Donald E. .... Minneapolis, MN
Engle, Douglas M. .... Medford, OR
Engle, Earl J. .... Kansas City, MO
Engle, Edward J., Jr. .... Hudson, MI
Engle, Elizabeth Gresham .... Alexandria, VA
Engle, Erik T. .... Charleston, WV
Engle, Howard E., Jr. .... Sacramento, CA
Engle, Howard R. .... New York, NY
Engle, Isadore .... Milwaukee, WI
Engle, J. Michael .... Nashville, TN
Engle, Jeffrey M. .... Huntingdon Valley, PA
Engle, Jerry M. .... Jackson, MI
Engle, John H. .... Cincinnati, OH
Engle, Kandice D. .... Lebanon, KY
Engle, Karla L. .... Pierre, SD
Engle & Lewis .... Hazard, KY
Engle, Mary Koelbel
Federal Trade Commission, Bureau of Consumer Protection, GV
Engle, Matthew J. .... Palo Alto, CA
Engle, Niles S. .... Edmond, OK
Engle, Patrick J. .... Mineola, NY
Engle, Paul D. .... Northampton, MA
Engle, Philip Whitworth .... Alpharetta, GA
Engle, Robert J. .... Okemos, MI
Engle, Robert L. .... Woodburn, OR
Engle, Samuel D. .... Leesburg, VA
Engle, Sara Anne .... Bloomfield Hills, MI
Engle & Schmidtman .... Woodburn, OR
Engle, Stephen Wayne .... San Francisco, CA
Engle, Steven E. .... Tacoma, WA
Engle, Susan Carolyn .... Dover, OH
Engle, Thomas D. .... Alexandria, VA
Engle, Thomas H. .... Indianapolis, IN
Engle, Walter E., III .... Lakeland, FL
Engle, William, III .... Hazard, KY
Engle, Wm. D., Jr. .... San Antonio, TX
Englebardt, Eric Keith .... Greenville, SC
Englebardt, Leland S., II .... New York, NY
Englebert, Candy Yarbray .... Owensboro, KY
Englebright, Harry J. .... Sacramento, CA
Engleby, Linda Nash .... Chevy Chase, MD
Warren, NJ
Engledow, James B. .... Dallas, TX
Englehardt, John C. .... Orlando, FL
Englehardt, John C., P.A. .... Orlando, FL
Englehart, Clinton Andrew .... Honolulu, HI
Englehart, David Alan .... Vienna, VA
Englehart, Fredrick W .... Cleveland, OH
Englehart, J. Mark .... Montgomery, AL
Englehart, Janine Piccione .... Pittsburgh, PA
Englehart, Mary Buchanan .... Towson, MD

Englehart, Robert J.
National Labor Relations Board, Office of the General Counsel, GV
Englehart, Stefan W. ... New York, NY
Englehart, William P., Jr. ... Towson, MD
Engleman, Carl J., Jr. ... Reading, PA
Engleman, Charlotte A. ... Keyport, NJ
Engleman, Danita Gay ... Muskogee, OK
Engleman, Donald J. ... Dallas, TX
Engleman, Hoffman & Engleman
Keyport, NJ
Engleman, Howard ... Salina, KS
Engleman, Michael R. ... Washington, DC
Louisville, KY
Englender, Saml. ... Cincinnati, OH
Engler, Barbara W. ... San Francisco, CA
Engler, Barnet C. ... Scottsdale, AZ
Engler, Bruce M. ... Minneapolis, MN
Engler, David L. ... Canfield, OH
Engler, Dennis D. ... Denton, TX
Engler, Donald B. ... Yuma, AZ
Engler, Eric L. ... Miami, FL
Engler, Geo. F. ... Buffalo, NY
Engler, George J. ... San Francisco, CA
Engler, Gregory T. ... Dayton, OH
Engler, Hibbard H. ... Oshkosh, WI
Engler, James W. ... Westmont, IL
Engler, Jane F. ... Jim Thorpe, PA
Engler, John M. ... Lansing, MI
Engler, Jonathan ... Washington, DC
Engler, Joseph P. ... Arlington, VA
Engler, Joseph P., P.C. ... Arlington, VA
Engler, Katherine A. ... Oakdale, MN
Engler, Kathleen M. ... New York, NY
Engler, Lester ... Scottsdale, AZ
Engler, Mark A. ... Pasadena, CA
Engler, Melvin B. ... Omaha, NE
Engler, Michelle ... Lansing, MI
Engler, Monte ... New York, NY
Engler, Paul B. ... Walnut Creek, CA
Engler, Richard D. ... Yuma, AZ
Engler, Ronald C.
Office Of Special Counsel, GV
Engler, Susan A. ... Milwaukee, WI
Engler, Teri E. ... Chicago, IL
Engler, Terri Serrato ... Los Angeles, CA
Engler, Timothy R. ... Lincoln, NE
Engler, W. Joseph, Jr. ... Indiana, PA
Engler, Wendy Ezor ... Hackensack, NJ
Engler, William D., Jr. ... Chilton, WI
Englert, August H. ... Orlando, FL
Englert, Dennis M. ... Schenectady, NY
Englert, Jack M., Jr. ... Denver, CO
Englert, James J. ... Cincinnati, OH
Englert, John J. ... Princeton, NJ
Englert, John P. ... Pittsburgh, PA
Englert, Leo T. ... Incline Village, NV
Englert, Michael J. ... Independence, MO
Englert, Michael J. ... Poughkeepsie, NY
Englert, Robert H. ... Louisville, KY
Englert, Robt. G. ... Austin, TX
Englert, Roy T. ... Springfield, VA
Englert, Roy T., Jr. ... Washington, DC
Englert, Stephen L. ... San Francisco, CA
Englert, Susan Michelle ... Denver, CO
Engles, Albert M. ... Omaha, NE
Engles, Jack A. ... Lakewood, CO
Englesberg, Robert S. ... Pittsburgh, PA
Englese, Anthony M. ... San Francisco, CA
Englese, James R. ... San Mateo, CA
Englesson, Nicholas E. ... Bethlehem, PA
Englett, Matthew S.
Altamonte Springs, FL
Engling, Robert J. (IBA) ... New York, NY
Engling, Timothy J. ... Chicago, IL
Englis, James G. ... Shelton, CT
Englisby, Barnes & Hennessy, P.C.
Chesterfield, VA
Englisby, Denis C. ... Chesterfield, VA
Englisby, Margaret Ann ... Chesterfield, VA
English, Abigail ... San Francisco, CA
English, Albert O. ... Clayton, GA
English, Alfred B. ... Shelbyville, TN
English, Andrew C., III ... Columbia, SC
English, Barbara J. ... College Park, MD
English, Bill J. ... Norman, OK
English, Brent L., Law Offices of
Cleveland, OH
English, Brian M. ... Newark, NJ
English, Carol Wood ... Tulsa, OK
English, Caroline T. ... Washington, DC
English, Charles E. ... Bowling Green, KY
English, Charles E., Jr.
Bowling Green, KY
English, Charles M., Jr. ... Washington, DC
English, Charles R., Law Office of
Santa Monica, CA
English, Cindy M. ... Little Rock, AR
English, Claudine E. ... New York, NY
English & Clemons, L.L.P.
Corpus Christi, TX
English, Craig S. ... New York, NY
English, Creighton M. ... Norwalk, CT
English, D. Joseph ... Alexandria, VA
English, D. Rex ... Baton Rouge, LA
English, Dale L. ... Appleton, WI
English, Dana K. ... Chesapeake, VA
English, Daniel L. ... Arvada, CO
English, David F. ... Painted Post, NY
English, David L. ... Asheville, NC
English, David M. ... Santa Clara, CA
English, Dearing D. ... San Diego, CA
English, Deborah D. ... Houston, TX
English, Donald A. ... San Diego, CA
English, Donald L. ... Vancouver, WA
English, Edward H. ... Andover, MA
English, Elaine Patton ... Washington, DC
English, Elizabeth B. ... Portland, OR
English & English ... Shelbyville, TN
English, Erica L. ... Miami, FL
English, Frederick ... Princeton, NJ
English, Gary R. ... Seattle, WA
English, Ginger M. ... Costa Mesa, CA
English & Gloven, A Professional Corporation ... San Diego, CA
English, Gregory B. ... Alexandria, VA
English, Gregory J. ... Greenville, SC
English, H. Elwood ... Billings, MT
English, Harry G. ... Brooklyn, NY
English, Howard E. ... Punta Gorda, FL
English, J. Benjamin ... Richmond, VA
English, Jack B. ... Tulsa, OK
English, James D. ... Pittsburgh, PA
English, James H. ... Altoona, PA
English, James L., III ... Ardmore, OK
English, James L. ... San Francisco, CA
Las Vegas, NV
English, James L. ... Colorado Springs, CO
English, James R. ... Tallahassee, FL
English, Jeffrey S. ... Lakewood, CO
English, Jerone J. ... Los Angeles, CA
English, Jerry Fitzgerald ... Summit, NJ
English, Jesse L., III ... Silsbee, TX
English, Jodie Ann ... Richmond, IN
English, Joe G. ... Sterling, KS
English, John ... Houston, TX
English, John D. ... Chicago, IL
English, John E. ... Detroit, MI
English, John M. ... Belleville, IL
English, John M. ... Okemos, MI
English, John W. ... Falls Church, VA
English, Joseph M. ... Atlanta, GA
English, Joseph M., IV ... Baltimore, MD
English, Judith A. ... Charlottesville, VA
English, Julia Dryden ... Washington, DC
English, Katharine ... Portland, OR
English, Katherine R. ... Fort Myers, FL
English, Kathryn A. ... Pittsburgh, PA
English, Katrina M. ... Hilliard, OH
English, Katrina W. ... Abilene, TX
English, K. D. ... Houston, TX
English, Kevin J. ... Buffalo, NY
English, Kurt E. ... Newport Beach, CA
English, Laurie Beth ... Salem, OR
English Lloyd & Armenta ... Palm Desert, CA
English, Lucas, Priest & Owsley
Bowling Green, KY
Franklin, KY
Glasgow, KY
Leitchfield, KY
Morgantown, KY
Russellville, KY
Scottsville, KY
English, Luther W. ... Houston, TX
English, Lynne ... Milwaukee, WI
English, Mark A. ... Billings, MT
English, Mark G. ... Kansas City, MO
English, Mark J. ... Syracuse, NY
English, Marti L. ... Fremont, NE
English, Maureen P.
Board of Governors Of The Federal Reserve System, Division of Consumer and Community Affairs, GV
English, McCaughan & O'Bryan, P.A.
Boca Raton, FL
Fort Lauderdale, FL
English, Michael J. ... Chevy Chase, MD
English, Michael K. ... Brookville, PA
English, Michael L. ... Princeton, IL
English, Michelle L. ... New York, NY
English, Milford T. ... Sun City, AZ
English, Monte J. ... Corpus Christi, TX
English, Neill ... Irving, TX
English, Nicholas Conover ... Newark, NJ
English, Noel Ann ... Hillside, IL
English, Noreen M. ... New York, NY
English & Odom ... Norman, OK
English, Patricia A. ... Austin, TX
English, Patrick C. ... Clifton, NJ
English, Paul ... Concord, MA
English, R. Brent ... New York, NY
English, R. Harold ... Arlington, TX
English, Randolph C. ... Boston, MA
English, Ray ... Moro, OR
English, Richard D. ... Pleasanton, CA
English, Richard G. ... Middlebury, VT
English, Richard J. ... Union City, IN
English, Richard L. ... Kansas City, MO
English, Richard W. ... Asbury Park, NJ
English, Robert C. ... Louisville, KY
English, Robert Conover ... Torrance, CA
English, Robert E. ... Corning, NY
English, Robert J. ... Knoxville, TN
English, Robert L. ... Las Vegas, NV
English, Robert L. ... Springfield, TN
English, Robert T. ... Ellicott City, MD
English, Roy E. ... Mansfield, TX
English, Shane A. ... Anthony, NM
English & Smith ... Alexandria, VA
English, Stephen F. ... Portland, OR
English, Stephen R. ... Los Angeles, CA
English, Steven Gregory ... Crystal Lake, IL
English, Susan H. ... North Dartmouth, MA
English, Susan L. ... Binghamton, NY
Owego, NY
English, Tamra J. ... Lake Jackson, TX
English, Tara Inlow ... Edwardsville, IL
English, Terry L. ... Bloomington, IN
English, Thomas F. ... Springfield, MA
English, Thomas L. ... Albuquerque, NM
English, Timothy Christopher
New York, NY
English, Timothy J. ... New York, NY
English, Tunkle & Smith, P.C.
Clarkesville, GA
Clayton, GA
English & van Horne, P.C. ... Detroit, MI
English, William Andrew ... Irvine, CA
English, William D. ... Anchorage, AK
English, William D. ... Bethesda, MD
English, William H. ... San Francisco, CA
English, William R. ... Clinton, NY
English & Wood, P.C. ... Tulsa, OK
English, Woodrow Douglas ... Ventura, CA
English-Martin, Christine
Cherry Hill, NJ
Linwood, NJ
English-Wilson, Ancheska ... Chicago, IL
Englund, Adam ... Cardiff-By-The-Sea, CA
Englund, Brad L ... Yakima, WA
Englund, Brian M. ... Sacramento, CA
Englund, Craig W. ... Beverly Hills, CA
Englund, Eric ... Middleton, WI
Englund, Gregory J. ... Boston, MA
Englund, Gregory J. ... Portland, OR
Englund, Janet I. ... Miami, FL
Englund, John F. ... Iron Mountain, MI
Englund, Karl J. ... Missoula, MT
Englund, Lara A. ... Washington, DC
Englund, Lizbeth A. ... Seattle, WA
Englund, Mary D. ... Seattle, WA
Englund, Philip J. ... San Diego, CA
Englund, Rudy A. ... Seattle, WA
Englund, Steven R. ... Washington, DC
Engman, John R. ... Irwindale, CA
Engman, Jonathan L. ... Troy, MI
Engman, Kathryn A. ... Minneapolis, MN
Engman, Patricia Hanahan ... Washington, DC
Engman, Philip ... King Of Prussia, PA
Engman, Richard H. ... Miami, FL
Engmann, James W. ... Madison, WI
Engnath, Michele A. ... New Orleans, LA
Engolia, Anthony J., III ... New Orleans, LA
Engolio, Edward N. ... Plaquemine, LA
Engoron, Arthur F. ... New York, NY
Engquist, Martin G. ... Santa Ana, CA
Engram, B. Samuel, Jr. ... Albany, GA
Engram, B. Samuel, Jr., P.C. ... Albany, GA
Engram, Deborah Marie ... Baltimore, MD
Engram, Jonathan M.
Winston-Salem, NC
Engrissei, Lawrence P. ... Mount Laurel, NJ
Engroff, Scott H. ... Milwaukee, WI
Engros, Charles E., Jr. ... New York, NY
Engst, Edward T. ... Wenatchee, WA
Engster, Diane C. ... Alexandria, VA
Engster, Paul R. ... Troy, NY
Engstrand, Craig S. ... San Diego, CA
Engstrand, D. Donald, Jr. ... New York, NY
Engstrand, Paul D. ... El Centro, CA
Engstrom, Alan L. ... Kelso, WA
Engstrom, Allan A. ... Hamilton, WA
Engstrom, Carl L. ... Newport Beach, CA
Engstrom, Carl W. ... Albany, NY
Engstrom, Chris L. ... St. George, UT
Engstrom, David F.
General Accounting Office, Office of the General Counsel, GV
Engstrom, David L. ... North Haven, CT
Engstrom, David W. ... Philadelphia, PA
Engstrom, Elizabeth L. ... Farmington, CT
Engstrom, Elton ... Juneau, AK
Engstrom, Everett R. ... Denver, CO
Engstrom, Harry C. ... Madison, WI
Engstrom, J. Eric ... Wichita, KS
Engstrom, Joan H. ... Minneapolis, MN
Engstrom, John C. ... Detroit, MI
Engstrom, Julie A. ... Prospect Heights, IL
Engstrom, Katrena ... New Haven, CT
Engstrom, Kristin M. ... Sacramento, CA
Engstrom, Leonard E. ... Houston, TX
Engstrom, Lipscomb & Lack, A Professional Corporation ... Los Angeles, CA
Engstrom, Mark W. ... New York, NY
Engstrom, Paul H. ... St. Paul, MN
Engstrom, Paul W. ... Los Angeles, CA
Engstrom, Peter J. ... San Francisco, CA
Engstrom, Rebecca Dockter ... Bozeman, MT
Engstrom, Robert C. ... Hartford, CT
Engstrom, Stephen ... Little Rock, AR
Engstrom, Susan Robinson ... Boston, MA
Engurasoff, Laura Lee M. ... San Jose, CA
Engustian, Christine J. ... East Providence, RI
Engvall, David H. ... Reston, VA
Engvall, John L., Jr. ... Houston, TX
Engvalson, Kinley I. ... Fort Myers, FL
Engwall, Craig L. ... St. Paul, MN
Engwall, Gregory B. ... Winthrop, MN
Engwert-Loyd, Donna M. ... Toledo, OH
Enhada, Carina Yoshiko ... Honolulu, HI
Enholm, Robert A. ... Atlanta, GA
Enich, Steve ... Milwaukee, WI
Enichen, Edward J. ... Rockford, IL
Enichen, Peter J. ... Boulder, CO
Enichen & Stephenson, LLC ... Boulder, CO
Enick, Walter D. ... Pittsburgh, PA
Eniclerico, Richard R. ... New York, NY
Enion, Linda Rhone ... Pittsburgh, PA
Enis, Joe M. ... Austin, TX
Enis, Steven R. ... Woodbridge, NJ
Enis, Thomas J. ... Oklahoma City, OK
Enix, Caleb F. ... White Pigeon, MI
Enix, Melinda B. ... Memphis, TN
Enix-Ross, Deborah Delores ... New York, NY
Enjamio, Juan C. ... Miami, FL
Enke, Alan A. ... Salt Lake City, UT
Enke, William G. ... Fort Dodge, IA
Enkelis, Richard L. ... Palo Alto, CA
Enkelmann, Larry K. ... Gladstone, MO
Enkema, John B. ... Nashville, TN
Enko, Peter J. ... Kansas City, MO
Enloe, Caren Davis ... Raleigh, NC
Enloe, Christopher S. ... Atlanta, GA
Enloe, Douglas A. ... Lawrenceville, IL
Enloe, Gary E. ... Tigard, OR
Enloe, Jay D. ... Portland, OR
Enloe, Julie A. ... Milwaukee, WI
Enloe, Margaret McIntyre ... New York, NY
Enloe, R. Ted, III ... Dallas, TX
Enlow, Bruce D. ... St. Joseph, MO
Enlow, David T. ... Lexington, KY
Enlow, Eugene C. ... Lodi, NJ
Enlow, J. Andrew ... Tulsa, OK
Enlow, James R. ... Springfield, IL
Enlow, John A. ... Ravenna, OH
Enlow, Susan Shiffler ... Minneapolis, MN
Enlow, Tracey S. ... Lexington, KY
Enlow, William R. ... Springfield, IL
Enlund, E. Stanley ... Burr Ridge, IL
Enmark, M. Nelson ... Fresno, CA
Enmark, Maureen A. ... Fresno, CA
Enmark, M. Nelson, Inc. ... Fresno, CA
Enna, Bradley James ... Wilmington, DE
Enneking, Anastasia Henry
Kansas City, MO
Enneking, Patrick J. ... Miamisburg, OH
Ennen, Bruce A. ... Newark, OH
Ennenbach, Joseph P. ... Cherry Valley, IL
Chicago, IL
Ennenga, Peter M. ... Salt Lake City, UT
Enney, Victoria L. ... New York, NY
Ennis, Adam S. ... Pittsburgh, PA
Ennis, Browne & Jensen, P.C.
Kansas City, MO
Ennis, Bruce C. ... Dover, DE
Odessa, DE
Ennis, Bruce J., Jr. ... Washington, DC
Ennis, Bruce L. ... Billings, MT
Ennis, Carolyn K. ... Billings, MT
Ennis, Charles R. ... Fairlawn, OH
Ennis, Charles W. ... Denver, CO
Ennis, Cooper & Paige, P.A.
Fort Lauderdale, FL
Naples, FL
Port Charlotte, FL
Weston, FL
Ennis, Cynthia Dawn ... St. Petersburg, FL
Ennis, David F. ... Naples, FL
Port Charlotte, FL
Weston, FL
Ennis, David G. ... Abington, PA
Ennis, Deitra L. ... Anchorage, AK
Ennis, Donald W. ... Wilmington, NC
Ennis, Edgar W., Jr. ... Macon, GA
Ennis, Felicia S. ... New York, NY
Ennis, Gail Susan ... Baltimore, MD
Ennis, Holly Kelly ... Miami, FL
Ennis, J. Daniel ... Miami, FL
Ennis, Jack ... New York, NY
Ennis, James R. ... Farmville, VA
Ennis, John J. ... Bala Cynwyd, PA
Ennis, John M. ... Tacoma, WA
Ennis, John R. ... Amherst, MA
Ennis, John T., Sr. ... Birmingham, AL
Ennis, Kevin G. ... Los Angeles, CA
Ennis, Kris H. ... Fort Pierce, FL
Ennis, Leslie S. ... Trussville, AL
Ennis, Martha E. Bryan ... Fredericksburg, VA
Ennis, Matthew J. ... Tracy, CA
Ennis, Nancy L. N. ... New York, NY
Ennis, Newton & Baynard, P.A.
Wilmington, NC
Wrightsville Beach, NC
Ennis, Pamela S. ... North Bergen, NJ
Ennis, Patrick J. ... Bloomfield Hills, MI
Ennis, Peter J. ... Pittsburgh, PA
Ennis, Rhonda H. ... Lillington, NC
Ennis, Richard J. ... Spokane, WA
Ennis, Robert J. ... Boise, ID
Ennis, Robert W., IV ... Tuscaloosa, AL
Ennis, Roberts and Fischer ... Harrison, OH
Cincinnati, OH
Ennis, Rudolph L. ... Fort Worth, TX
Ennis, Sean M. ... Boston, MA
Ennis, Suzanne ... St. Petersburg, FL
Ennis, Thomas A., Jr. ... Stamford, CT
Ennis, Trudy A. ... Greensboro, NC
Ennis, William J. ... White Plains, NY
Ennis, William J. ... Cincinnati, OH
Harrison, OH
Ennist, Diane Marshall ... McLean, VA
Ennis-Volcy, Wendy ... Miami, FL
Ennix, Frank M., III ... Oakland, CA
Enns, Jean A. ... Los Angeles, CA
Enns, Rodrick J. ... Winston-Salem, NC
Enns, Ronald E. ... Dalhart, TX
Eno, Arthur L., Jr. ... Lowell, MA
Eno, Boulay & Martin, LLP ... Lowell, MA
Eno, Edward S. ... Clearwater, FL
Enobakhare, Lucky O. ... New York, NY
Enoch, Angela Teresa ... Detroit, MI
Enoch, Barton L. ... Colorado Springs, CO
Enoch, Craig T. ... Austin, TX
Enoch, David W. ... Colorado Springs, CO
Enoch & Enoch, P.C. ... Colorado Springs, CO
Enoch, J. Edward, Jr. ... Augusta, GA
Enoch, John T. ... Baltimore, MD
Enoch, Leslie B., II ... Nashville, TN
Enoch, Lisa Ann ... Chappaqua, NY
Enoch, Mark Charles ... Dallas, TX
Enoch, Nicholas J. ... Phoenix, AZ
Enoch, Sharon Blair ... Augusta, GA
Enochian, Steven R. ... Redding, CA
Enochs, Craig R. ... Houston, TX
Enochs, Duane C. ... Manhattan Beach, CA
Enochs, Elizabeth ... Dobbs Ferry, NY
Enochs & Geers ... Houston, TX
Enochs, Herman G., Jr. ... Greensboro, NC
Enochs, John C. ... New Orleans, LA

Enochs, Leland R. ... Taylor, TX
Enochs, Richmond M.
Overland Park, KS
Enochs, Rodney L. ... New York, NY
Enochs, Wendy M. ... Greensboro, NC
Enockson, Donald L. ... Minneapolis, MN
Enockson, Gene O. ... Mesa, AZ
Enockson, Paul S. ... Denver, CO
Enoex, Robert N., Jr. ... Springfield, IL
Enomoto, Elise L. ... Irvine, CA
Enomoto, Michael A., Jr. ... Los Angeles, CA
Enos, Arthur G. ... Fort Worth, TX
Enos, Brandt K. ... New Orleans, LA
Enos, Brian W. ... Fresno, CA
Enos, Bruce G. ... Santa Rosa, CA
Enos, Christopher J. ... Rochester, NY
Enos, Christopher L. ... Tucson, AZ
Enos, Earl P. ... Duncan, OK
Enos and Enos ... Rochester, NY
Enos, Greg B. ... Houston, TX
Enos, Gregory E. ... Rochester, NY
Enos, John H., III ... Harrisburg, PA
Enos, Joseph H., Jr. ... Woodbury, NJ
Enos, Katherine Davitt ... Clarksburg, WV
Enos, Laura J. ... San Francisco, CA
Enos Law Firm, The, P.C. ... Galveston, TX
Houston, TX
Texas City, TX
Enos, P. Beth ... Portland, OR
Enos, Robert J. ... Carmichael, CA
Enos, Robin W. ... Los Angeles, CA
Enos, William T. ... Arlington, VA
Enow and Imudia, PLC ... New Orleans, LA
Enow, Michael ... New Orleans, LA
Enowitz, Daniel J. ... Los Angeles, CA
Enrich, Peter D. ... Boston, MA
Enrico J. Mirabelli and Associates
Chicago, IL
Enrico, Paul J. ... Hauppauge, NY
Enrico, Phillip J., Jr. ... Tyngsborough, MA
Milford, NH
Enrietti, Anthony A. ... Chicago, IL
Enright, Barbara Ann ... Topeka, KS
Enright, Brian G. ... New Haven, CT
Enright, Catherine I. ... Morris Plains, NJ
Enright, Cheryl A. ... Boston, MA
Enright, Daniel A. ... Eau Claire, WI
Enright, Donald J. ... Washington, DC
Enright, Elizabeth A. ... Bloomington, IL
Enright, Erin S. ... New York, NY
Enright, Frank J. ... Stockton, CA
Enright, J. Scott ... Indianapolis, IN
Enright, James F. ... Milford, NH
Enright, James P. ... Grand Rapids, MI
Enright, Jane Groves ... Bloomfield Hills, MI
Enright, John G. ... St. Louis, MO
Enright, John J. ... Chicago, IL
Enright, John J. ... Baldwin, NY
Enright, John K. ... Philadelphia, PA
Enright, Judith A. ... Beverly Hills, CA
Enright, Kathleen M. ... Andover, MA
Enright, Kevin A. ... San Diego, CA
Enright, Madelyn A. ... Irvine, CA
Enright, Mark E. ... Chicago, IL
Enright, Martin W. ... New York, NY
White Plains, NY
Enright, Maureen ... Washington, DC
Enright, Michael P. ... Weehawken, NJ
Enright, Michael R. ... Hartford, CT
Boston, MA
Enright, Michelle Kathleen
Minneapolis, MN
Enright, Neil D. ... Billings, MT
Enright & Ocheltree, LLP
Beverly Hills, CA
Los Angeles, CA
Enright, Patrick J. ... Milford, NH
Enright, Patrick L. ... Fresno, CA
Enright, Paul M. ... Los Angeles, CA
Enright, Phillip N. ... San Diego, CA
Enright, Richard E., Jr. ... Palm City, FL
Enright, Robert A., III ... Naples, FL
Atlanta, GA
Enright, Robert J. ... Vernon, CT
Enright, Rosemary ... Reston, VA
Enright, Ruth V. ... Chicago, IL
Enright, Shannon H. ... Minneapolis, MN
Enright, Stephen D., Jr. ... Metairie, LA
Enright, Thomas H. ... Milford, NH
Enright, Thomas M. ... Chicago, IL
Enright, William B. ... San Diego, CA
Enright, William J., Jr., (P.C.)
Grosse Pointe Farms, MI
Enriquez, Bill H. ... Tucson, AZ
Enriquez, Carlos A. ... Miami, FL
Enriquez, Joseph A. ... West Bridgewater, MA
Enriquez, Kim A. ... Ventura, CA
Enriquez, M. Armando ... Carmichael, CA
Enriquez, Maria G. ... Chicago, IL
Enriquez, Paul M. ... Beverly Hills, CA
Enriquez, Paul V. ... Dallas, TX
Enriquez, Sally P. ... Irvine, CA
Ens, James A. ... Grand Rapids, MI
Ensalaco, Carol A. ... Los Angeles, CA
Ensberg, Stephen E. ... Covina, CA
Ensbury, Linda K. ... Los Angeles, CA
Enschede, Andrew J. ... Chicago, IL
Enscoe, Jon ... San Francisco, CA
Enselman, Mark A. ... Wausau, WI
Ensenat, Donald B. ... New Orleans, LA
Ensign, Cathryn R. ... Cleveland, OH
Ensign, Craig G. ... Northwood, IA
Ensign, Curtis D. ... Phoenix, AZ
Ensign, Gregory M. ... Cleveland, OH
Ensign, James G. ... Laguna Hills, CA
Ensign, James R. ... Bloomington, IL
Ensign, John S.
Department Of Health And Human Services, Food & Drug Administration, GV
Ensign, Jonathon L. ... Hartford, CT
Ensign, Kristin Wright ... Des Moines, IA
Ensign, Mark R. ... Amarillo, TX
Ensign, Mark R. ... Amarillo, TX
Ensign, Robert N. ... Portola Valley, CA
Ensign, Thomas Decatur ... New York, NY
Ensing, William A. ... Lake Forest, IL
Ensle, John F. ... Houston, TX
Enslein, Jerald S. ... Kansas City, MO
Enslein, Peter T. ... Washington, DC
Enslen, Alan F. ... Birmingham, AL
Enslen, Charles Endicott ... Hammond, IN
Enslen, David M. ... Fayette, AL
Enslen, Enslen & Matthews ... Hammond, IN
Enslen, Frederick T. ... Montgomery, AL
Enslen, Frederick T., P.C.
Montgomery, AL
Enslen, John E. ... Wetumpka, AL
Enslen, Johnston & Pinkston, L.L.P.
Wetumpka, AL
Enslen, Joseph R. ... Grandville, MI
St. Joseph, MI
Enslen, Lowell E. ... Hammond, IN
Enslen, Pamela Chapman ... Kalamazoo, MI
Enslen, Richard A. ... Kalamazoo, MI
Enslen, William T. ... Hammond, IN
Ensler, Henry R. ... Boca Raton, FL
Ensley, Arden K. ... Topeka, KS
Ensley, Bruce M. ... Colfax, WA
Ensley & Eilerman ... Dayton, OH
Ensley, Gerry Lee ... Los Alamitos, CA
Ensley, Michael D. ... Des Moines, IA
Ensley, Theodore M. ... Dayton, OH
Ensley-Stanton, Laura J. ... San Antonio, TX
Enslow, Ray B. ... Los Angeles, CA
Ensminger, D. Randall ... Sacramento, CA
Ensminger, John J. ... New York, NY
Ensminger, Rodman R. ... Columbus, OH
Ensor, Bruce D. ... Fulton, MD
Ensor, Gary A. ... South Hadley, MA
Ensor, John E. ... Parkton, MD
Ensor, Judith C. ... Towson, MD
Ensor, R. Steve ... Atlanta, GA
Ensor, Richard F. ... Vienna, VA
Ensor, Richard J. ... Edison, NJ
Ensor, Stephen R. ... Corvallis, OR
Ensor, Thomas R. ... Brighton, CO
Enste, Susan P. ... Trenton, NJ
Enstrom, Elmer M., Jr. ... Julian, CA
Ensz, James H. ... Kansas City, MO
Ensz and Jester, P.C. ... Bethany, MO
Kansas City, MO
Ensz, Robert B. ... Wayne, NE
Ent, Robert W., (Co., L.P.A.)
Cincinnati, OH
Enteen, Laura Z. ... New Hyde Park, NY
Entel, Gerald ... Lake Placid, FL
Entelis, Joelle ... New York, NY
Entelisano, Carol A. ... Tuscaloosa, AL
Enteman, John H. F. ... New York, NY
Enten, Clifford J. ... Englewood, CO
Enten, D. Robert ... Baltimore, MD
Entenman, John A. ... Detroit, MI
Entenmann, George C. ... Pittsburgh, PA
Entenmann, Richard A. ... Toledo, OH
Enterkin, James E., Jr. ... Boston, MA
Enterline, Bradley K. ... Erie, PA
Enterline, Cathy Stricker ... Tulsa, OK
Enterline, Holly L. ... Memphis, TN
Enterline, Paul G. ... Georgetown, DE
Enterline, Richard J. ... Camp Hill, PA
Enterline, Richard S. ... Ashland, PA
Enterprise Counsel Group The
Irvine, CA
Enterprise Law Group, Inc.
Menlo Park, CA
Palo Alto, CA
San Francisco, CA
San Jose, CA
Enterprise Law Group, LLC
Washington, DC
Enterprise Law Group LLC ... McLean, VA
Entertainment & Intellectual Property Group, The ... Chicago, IL
Entes, Isidore ... Bronx, NY
Entezari, Shirin O., & Associates
Washington, DC
Entin, Alvin E. ... Fort Lauderdale, FL
Entin, David ... Fall River, MA
Entin, Fredric J. ... Chicago, IL
Entin, Jeffrey S. ... Fall River, MA
Entin, Jonathan L. ... Cleveland, OH
Entin & Margules, P.A. ... Fort Lauderdale, FL
Entin, Michael J., (P.A.)
Fort Lauderdale, FL
Entin, Richard C. ... Fort Lauderdale, FL
Entin, Seth J. ... Miami, FL
Entis, Lawrence M. ... Morristown, NJ
Entis, Robert ... Cleveland, OH
Entis, Sara Barr ... Bethesda, MD
Entman, Bruce R. ... Buffalo Grove, IL
Entman, June F. ... Memphis, TN
Entner, Kristina M. ... Chicago, IL
Entrekin, B. Lance ... Phoenix, AZ
Entrekin, Hugh W. ... Nashville, TN
Entrekin, Lance, Law Offices of
Phoenix, AZ
Entrekin, Romney H. ... Laurel, MS
Entrekin, Sarah L. ... Laurel, MS
Entress, Geoffrey R. ... Seattle, WA
Entsminger, Kurt E. ... Sterling, VA
Entwisle, Elizabeth Bradbury ... Pittsburgh, PA
Entwisle, Robert M. ... Pittsburgh, PA
Entwisle, Robert M., III ... Pittsburgh, PA
Entwisle, William B. ... Ellsworth, ME
Entwistle, Andrew J. ... New York, NY
Entwistle, Barbara Jo ... Laurel, MD
Gettysburg, PA
Entwistle & Cappucci LLP ... Princeton, NJ
New York, NY
Entwistle, Frederick M. ... Sioux Falls, SD
Entz & Chanay, P.A. ... Topeka, KS
Entz, F. Harold, Jr. ... Dallas, TX
Entz, J. Michael ... Oklahoma City, OK
Entz, Michael L. ... Topeka, KS
Entz, Stewart L. ... Topeka, KS
Entzeroth, Lyn Suzanne ... Norman, OK
Entzminger, Joe ... Bay City, TX
Enu, Haseena J. ... New York, NY
Enusha, Bruce A. ... Walford, IA
Envall, Ronald R. ... Duluth, MN
Environmental Litigation Group, P.C.
Birmingham, AL
Enwall & Grant, L.L.C. ... Boulder, CO
Enwall, Michael R. ... Boulder, CO
Enwall, Peter C. K. ... Gainesville, FL
Enwright, Kent D. ... Englewood, CO
Enwright, Susan Conner ... Andover, KS
Enyart, James R. ... St. Louis, MO
Enyart, Jay W. ... Denver, CO
Enyart, Mary Theresa ... Philadelphia, PA
Enyart, Stacy K. ... San Bernardino, CA
Enyart & Welch ... Belleville, IL
Enyart, William L. ... Belleville, IL
Enyeart, Catherine R. ... Hot Springs, SD
Enyeart, Curtis W. ... Peoria, IL
Enyeart, Kevin S. ... Logansport, IN
Enz, Jonathan K. ... Philomath, OR
Enz, Stephen D. ... Columbus, OH
Enzel, David H. ... Treasury Department, Office of Thrift Supervision, GV
Enzenberger, Robert F. ... Reno, NV
Enzer, Julie ... Burbank, CA
Enzien, Peter J. ... Troy, NY
Enzinna, James B. ... Washington, DC
Enzinna, Paul F. ... Washington, DC
Enzler, Sherry A. ... St. Paul, MN
Enzminger, David P. ... Los Angeles, CA
Enzor, Brett T. ... Dallas, TX
Enzor, Cynthia W. L. ... Gainesville, GA
Enzor, Leland G., Jr. ... Andalusia, AL
Enzor, T. Lamar ... Rutland, VT
Eoannou, Carol L. ... Bethesda, MD
Eoannou & Lana ... Buffalo, NY
Eoannou, Thomas J. ... Buffalo, NY
Eoff, Michael J. ... Indianapolis, IN
Eory, John S. ... Skillman, NJ
Eovaldi, Thomas L. ... Chicago, IL
Eoyang, Jonathan ... Calabasas, CA
Epel, Joshua B. ... Denver, CO
Epelbaum, Manuel ... Miami, FL
Epes, Christopher R. ... New York, NY
Epes, Travis F. ... Riverdale, NY
Epes, Travis Fredricks ... New York, NY
Epes, Wooten ... Little Rock, AR
Ephraim, Allan M. ... Oklahoma City, OK
Ephraim & Associates, P.C. ... Chicago, IL
Ephraim, Charles ... Harlingen, TX
Ephraim, David A. ... Boston, MA
Ephraim, David M. ... Chicago, IL
Ephraim, Donald M. ... Chicago, IL
Ephraim, Edward H. ... Norwalk, CT
Ephraim, Eliot S. ... Chicago, IL
Ephron, Melissa G. ... New York, NY
Ephron, Susan H. ... Redmond, WA
Ephross, Joel N. ... Houston, TX
Epis, David C. ... Ketchum, ID
Episcope, Paul B. ... Chicago, IL
Episcope, Paul B., Ltd. ... Chicago, IL
Episcopo, Eric Leonard ... New Castle, DE
Episcopo, Joe ... Tampa, FL
Eplen, Rebecca D. ... Waco, TX
Epler, David C. ... Gibbsboro, NJ
Epler, Dennis E. ... Livonia, MI
Epler, Palmer Y. ... New Haven, CT
Epley, Alan D. ... Berryville, AR
Epley, James D. ... Chicago, IL
Epley, Lewis E., Jr. ... Holiday Island, AR
Epley, Lewis E., Jr., Ltd.
Holiday Island, AR
Epley, Linda K. ... San Francisco, CA
Epley, Lloyd A. ... Iowa City, IA
Kalona, IA
Epley, Marion J., III ... New York, NY
Epley, Mark D. ... Richmond, VA
Epley, Michael G. ... Magnolia, AR
Epley, Randal K. ... Russellville, KY
Epley, Robert C. ... Yuba City, CA
Epley-McKenna, Linda K. ... Fairfield, CA
Epling, Benny C., II ... Lexington, KY
Epling, David L. ... Grundy, VA
Epling, John A. ... Cincinnati, OH
Epling, John, Company, L.P.A.
Cincinnati, OH
Epling, Lacey D. ... Lexington, KY
Epling, Richard L. ... New York, NY
Epling, Stella Fey ... San Francisco, CA
Epman, Ronald J. ... Culver City, CA
Epner, Maury S. ... Rockville, MD
Epner, Mitchell E. ... New York, NY
Epolite, Anthony S. ... Sacramento, CA
Epolite, Stephanie Glorioso ... Sacramento, CA
Epp, Daniel L. ... San Francisco, CA
Epp, E. LaVerne ... Lawrence, KS
Epp, Henry C. ... Cleveland, OH
Epp, Jeffrey R. ... Escondido, CA
Epp, Timothy Lee ... Costa Mesa, CA
Epp, Timothy R.
Environmental Protection Agency, Environmental Appeals Board, GV
Epp, Todd D. ... Sioux Falls, SD
Eppard, Julia K. ... Washington, DC
Eppard, Richard T. ... Columbus, IN
Eppen, Ronald S. ... Boston, MA
Eppenauer, Bart ... Redmond, WA
Eppens, Alfred John ... Detroit, MI
Eppenstein, David E., Jr. ... Chicago, IL
Eppenstein and Eppenstein
New York, NY
Eppenstein, Madelaine ... New York, NY
Eppenstein, Theodore G. ... New York, NY
Epperley, Gary C. ... San Francisco, CA
Epperley, Linda A. ... Muskogee, OK
Epperly, Brad ... Des Moines, IA
Epperly, David L., Jr. ... Richmond, VA
Epperly, Donald J. ... Clarksburg, WV
Epperly, Follis & Schork, P.C.
Richmond, VA
Epperly, Janice P. ... Huntington, WV
Huntington, WV
Epperly, John David, Jr. ... Fairfax, VA
Eppers, Donald B. ... Buffalo, NY
Epperson, Christopher D. ... Dallas, TX
Epperson, Craig E. ... San Francisco, CA
Epperson, Curtis N. ... Manson, WA
Epperson, David H. ... Salt Lake City, UT
Epperson, Dwight J. L. ... Salt Lake City, UT
Epperson, Heidi ... Belleville, IL
Epperson, J. Barry ... Tulsa, OK
Epperson, James L. ... Hendersonville, NC
Epperson, Joel R. ... Fort Myers, FL
Epperson, John R. ... San Francisco, CA
Epperson & Johnsen ... Tulsa, OK
Epperson, Kathryn M. ... Phoenix, AZ
Epperson, Kraettli Q. ... Oklahoma City, OK
Epperson, Leigh Ann K. ... Dallas, TX
Epperson, Lia B. ... Palo Alto, CA
Epperson & McClary ... Fort Morgan, CO
Epperson, Myles L. ... Belleville, IL
Epperson, N. Marian ... Little Rock, AR
Epperson & Rencher, A Professional Corporation ... Salt Lake City, UT
Epperson, Robert F., Jr. ... St. Louis, MO
Epperson, Woodrow ... Houston, TX
Eppert, Frank J. ... New York, NY
Eppert, Robert J. ... Tawas City, MI
Eppes, Frank ... Greenville, SC
Eppes, Frank L. ... Greenville, SC
Eppes & Plumblee, P.A. ... Greenville, SC
Eppes, Sharon M. ... Wilmington, DE
Eppes, Walter W., Jr. ... Meridian, MS
Eppich, Robert J. ... Cleveland, OH
Eppig, Franklin J., Jr. ... Finksburg, MD
Epping, Gregory J. ... Cedar Rapids, IA
Epping, Jerome N., Jr. ... Covington, KY
Eppinga, Peter L. ... Saratoga, CA
Eppinga, Peter L., Prof. Corp. ... Saratoga, CA
Eppinger, Frank N. ... Groton, CT
Eppinger, John P. ... Erie, PA
Eppinger, Reingold & Korder ... Bronx, NY
Larchmont, NY
Eppinger, Ronald M. ... Bronx, NY
Larchmont, NY
Eppinger, Theodore F. ... Bronx, NY
Larchmont, NY
Eppink, Thomas G. ... Columbia, SC
Epple, Bruce A. ... Orlando, FL
Epple, Cletus F. ... Hammond, IN
Epple, Richard R., Jr. ... Baltimore, MD
Eppler, Don B. ... Lisbon, ND
Eppler, John W. ... Portsmouth, VA
Eppler, Klaus ... New York, NY
Eppler & Leadbetter ... Lisbon, ND
Eppler, Patrick J. ... Council Bluffs, IA
Eppler, Rita S. ... Worthington, OH
Eppler-Epstein, Amy ... New Haven, CT
Eppler-Epstein, Steven D. ... Meriden, CT
Eppley, Daren R. ... Trenton, NJ
Eppley, Lawrence C. ... Chicago, IL
Eppley, William B. ... Brooksville, FL
Spring Hill, FL
Eppling, Thomas J. ... Covington, LA
Metairie, LA
Eppner, Gerald A. ... New York, NY
Eppolito, Anthony P. ... Oneida, NY
Eppolito, Charles, III ... State College, PA
Epport & Richman, L.L.P. ... Los Angeles, CA
Epport, Victor M., (A Law Corporation)
Los Angeles, CA
Eppright, Charles L. ... Austin, TX
Eppright, Frank D. ... Kansas City, MO
Eppright, James F. S. ... Dallas, TX
Eppright, Kathryn M.
San Luis Obispo, CA
Epp-Rosenthal, Janet ... New York, NY
Epps, A. Glenn ... Flint, MI
Epps, A. C. ... Richmond, VA
Epps, Augustus C., Jr. ... Richmond, VA
Epps, Carl B., III ... Columbia, SC
Epps, Charles K. ... Redwood City, CA
Epps, Claude M., Jr. ... Myrtle Beach, SC
Epps, Darren W. ... San Francisco, CA
San Luis Obispo, CA
Epps, David W. ... San Jose, CA
Epps, Donna Maria ... Arlington, VA
Epps, Ellen P. ... Chappaqua, NY
Epps and Epps, Law Office of
Johnson City, TN
Epps, Jack M. ... Overland Park, KS
Epps, Jacqueline G. ... Richmond, VA
Epps, James H., III ... Johnson City, TN
Epps, James H., IV ... Johnson City, TN
Epps, James R. ... Lake City, SC
Epps, Jerald W. ... Austin, TX
Epps, JoAnne A. ... Philadelphia, PA
Epps, John D. ... Richmond, VA
Epps, Julia D. ... Houston, TX
Epps, Julie A. ... Jackson, MS
Epps, Lisa A. ... Kansas City, MO
Epps, Louis E. ... Milwaukee, WI
Epps, M. Richard ... Virginia Beach, VA

Epps, Melea R. ...Federal Trade Commission,
Bureau of Competition, GV
Epps, Michael C. ...Atlantic City, NJ
Epps, Miles A. ...Great Neck, NY
Epps, M. Richard, P.C. ...Norfolk, VA
Virginia Beach, VA
Epps, Nicholson & Stathakis ...Anderson, SC
Epps, Patricia K. ...Richmond, VA
Epps, Raymond R. ...Houston, TX
Epps, Richard A. ...Bainbridge, GA
Epps, Richard M. ...Columbus, OH
Epps, Tonye Russell ...Washington, DC
Epps, Valerie C. ...Boston, MA
Epps, William N., Jr. ...Anderson, SC
Epps Edwards, Marsha ...Washington, DC
Eppstein, Stanley M. ...Youngstown, OH
Eppstein, Steven D. ...Cincinnati, OH
Eppsteiner, Stuart M. ...San Diego, CA
Woodland Hills, CA
Epright, Michael W. ...Haddam, CT
Epsen, Robert A. ...San Francisco, CA
Epsha, Christopher P. ...Royal Oak, MI
Epshtein, Stan ...Lakewood, CO
Epson, Michael W. ...Palmdale, CA
Epson, Milburn & Kahl ...Palmdale, CA
Epst, Bradley I. ...Alden, IL
Epsteen, Ralph ...Pesotum, IL
Epstein, Adam E. ...New York, NY
Epstein, Adam J. ...New York, NY
Epstein, Adam Jay ...Marina Del Rey, CA
Epstein, Adam Scott ...Knoxville, TN
Epstein, Adelson & Rubin
Los Angeles, CA
Epstein, Alan ...Denver, CO
Epstein, Alan ...New York, NY
Epstein, Alan B. ...Philadelphia, PA
Epstein, Alan I. ...La Jolla, CA
Epstein, Alan J. ...Los Angeles, CA
Epstein, Alan M. ...Parsippany, NJ
New York, NY
Epstein, Alan S. ...New York, NY
Epstein, Alan W. ...Palm Beach Gardens, FL
Epstein, Albert W. ...New York, NY
Epstein, Allan D. ...Orange, CA
Epstein, Amy L. ...Washington, DC
Epstein, Andrew D. ...Boston, MA
Epstein, Andrew M. ...Dover, MA
Epstein, Andrew M. ...Chatham, NJ
Epstein, Andrew S. ...New York, NY
Epstein, Andrew Scott ...Fort Myers, FL
Epstein, Anthony C. ...Washington, DC
Epstein, Ari R. ...Cleveland, OH
Epstein, Arlen Tobias ...New York, NY
Epstein, Arnold M. ...Pittsburgh, PA
Epstein, Barbara ...Austin, TX
Epstein, Barbara J. ...Acton, MA
Epstein, Barbara M. ...Department of Justice,
Civil Division, GV
Epstein, Barnet H. ...Chatham, NJ
Epstein, Barry D. ...Englewood, CO
Epstein, Barry D. ...Rochelle Park, NJ
Epstein, Barry D., P.A. ...Hackensack, NJ
Epstein, Barry H. ...Oakland, CA
Epstein, Barry M. ...Newark, NJ
New York, NY
Epstein, Barry W. ...Columbus, OH
Epstein, Bart Scott ...Washington, DC
Epstein Becker & Green ...Los Angeles, CA
San Francisco, CA
Miami, FL
Stamford, CT
Washington, DC
Baltimore, MD
Boston, MA
Newark, NJ
New York, NY
Dallas, TX
Alexandria, VA
Epstein Beirne, P.A. ...Rochelle Park, NJ
Epstein, Bennett L. ...Chicago, IL
Epstein, Bennett M. ...New York, NY
Epstein, Bernard J. ...Point Lookout, NY
Epstein, Bernard S. ...New York, NY
Epstein, Bette B. ...Oakland, CA
Epstein, Bob J. ...Los Angeles, CA
Epstein, Bonnie M. ...Dallas, TX
Epstein & Boskoff, LLP
San Francisco, CA
Epstein, Bradley J. ...Sacramento, CA
Walnut Creek, CA
Las Vegas, NV
Reno, NV
Epstein, Brooke C. ...Dallas, TX
Epstein, Brown, Markowitz & Gioia, A Professional Corporation ...Chatham, NJ
Elizabeth, NJ
Morristown, NJ
Springfield, NJ
Epstein, Bruce F. ...Golden, CO
Epstein, Bruce Howard ...Pasadena, CA
Epstein, Bruce R. ...Youngstown, OH
Epstein, Buddy ...Los Angeles, CA
Epstein, Burton L. ...Ventura, CA
Epstein, Burton M. ...New York, NY
Epstein, Carl L. ...Indianapolis, IN
Epstein, Carol B.
United States Information Agency,
Office of the General Counsel, GV
Epstein, Carol M. ...New York, NY
Epstein, Carol Paskin ...Washington, DC
Epstein, Carol S. ...Newton, MA
Epstein, Carole ...Merion, PA
Epstein, Carolyn Gilbert ...Coral Gables, FL
Epstein, Cary T. ...Los Angeles, CA
Epstein, Charles ...Hackensack, NJ
Epstein, Charles I. ...Hackensack, NJ
Epstein, Charles S. ...Atlantic City, NJ
Epstein, Constance L. ...Hartford, CT
Manchester, CT
Epstein & Cresci, P.C. ...New York, NY
Epstein, Cy ...Richmond, CA
Epstein, Cynthia E. ...Omaha, NE
Epstein, Dan J. ...Chicago, IL
Epstein, Daniel J. ...New York, NY
Epstein, Daniel M. ...Atlanta, GA
Epstein, Daniel N. ...Chicago, IL
Epstein, Daniel N. ...Woodbridge, NJ
Epstein, Danielle ...New York, NY
Epstein, Darren Jay ...New City, NY
Epstein, Daryl ...Fairfield, NJ
Epstein, David ...Washington, DC
Epstein, David ...Department of Justice,
Civil Division, GV
Epstein, David A. ...Chicago, IL
Epstein, David A., Ltd. ...Chicago, IL
Epstein, David B. ...Los Angeles, CA
Epstein, David B. ...New Orleans, LA
Epstein, David B. ...Brooklyn, NY
Epstein, David G. ...Irvine, CA
Epstein, David G. ...Atlanta, GA
Epstein, David J. ...Los Angeles, CA
Epstein, David J. ...Chicago, IL
Epstein, David L. ...Roseland, NJ
Epstein, David M. ...Laguna Hills, CA
Epstein, David M. ...Red Bank, NJ
Epstein, David M. ...Charlotte, NC
Epstein, David M., (P.C.) ...Laguna Hills, CA
Epstein, Deanna Swagel
Huntington Beach, CA
Epstein, Dena E. ...Livingston, NJ
Epstein, Dena Rosen ...Phoenix, AZ
Epstein, Donald R. ...Southfield, MI
Epstein, Donna Broker ...Bryn Mawr, PA
Philadelphia, PA
Pittsburgh, PA
Epstein, Donna I. ...New York, NY
Epstein, Douglas A. ...Long Island City, NY
Epstein, Edell & Retzer ...Washington, DC
Rockville, MD
Arlington, VA
Epstein, Edmund L. ...Denver, CO
Epstein, Edna Selan, The Law Offices of
Chicago, IL
Epstein, Edward G. ...Syosset, NY
Epstein, Edward L. ...Portland, OR
Epstein, Edward P. ...Pleasantville, NJ
Epstein, Edwin M. ...Moraga, CA
Epstein, Edwin N. ...Washington, DC
Epstein, Eileen M. L. ...Portland, ME
Epstein, Elaine M. ...Boston, MA
Epstein, Elizabeth Darien ...Denver, CO
Epstein, Ellen ...Boston, MA
Epstein, Elliot S. ...Washington, DC
Epstein, Elliott L. ...Lewiston, ME
Epstein, Elliott M. ...New York, NY
Epstein, Emily Bermann ...New York, NY
Epstein, Englert, Staley & Coffey
San Francisco, CA
Epstein & Epstein ...Marblehead, MA
Epstein & Epstein ...Omaha, NE
Epstein & Epstein ...New York, NY
Epstein & Epstein ...Rochester, NY
Epstein & Epstein, P.C. ...Englewood, CO
Epstein, Eric Benjamin ...New York, NY
Epstein, Eric Lee ...New York, NY
Epstein, Eric M. ...Los Angeles, CA
Epstein, Eron H. ...Chattanooga, TN
Epstein, Eugene ...Salinas, CA
Epstein Fogarty Cohen Selby
Greenwich, CT
Epstein, Fred L. ...New York, NY
Epstein & Friedman LLP
San Francisco, CA
Epstein & Frisch ...Indianapolis, IN
Epstein, Gary M. ...Washington, DC
Epstein, Gary M. ...Miami, FL
Epstein, Gregory L. ...Bloomfield Hills, MI
Epstein, H. David ...Staten Island, NY
Epstein, Hal J. ...Silver Spring, MD
Epstein, Harold ...New York, NY
Epstein, Harold D. ...Beacon, NY
Epstein & Harvey ...Van Nuys, CA
Epstein, Harvey A. ...Van Nuys, CA
Epstein, Harvey A. ...Baltimore, MD
Epstein, Harvey S. ...New York, NY
Epstein, Heidi J. ...Baltimore, MD
Epstein, Heitzi D. ...Bethesda, MD
Epstein, Helen T. ...Tulsa, OK
Epstein, Helena H. ...Pearl River, NY
Epstein, Henry A. ...San Francisco, CA
Epstein, Howard B. ...New York, NY
Epstein, Howard M. ...New York, NY
Epstein, Howard N. ...Omaha, NE
Epstein, Howard S. ...Allentown, PA
Epstein, Hymen L. ...Los Angeles, CA
Epstein, Ike Lawrence ...Las Vegas, NV
Epstein, Ira S. ...Beverly Hills, CA
Epstein, Ira S. ...Mequon, WI
Epstein, Irving B., (P.C.) ...Omaha, NE
Epstein, J. David ...Carmel, IN
Epstein, J. Earl ...Philadelphia, PA
Epstein, Jacob J. ...Jeffersonville, NY
Epstein, James A. ...Fort Lauderdale, FL
Epstein, James D. ...Philadelphia, PA
Epstein, James E. ...Newton, MA
Epstein, James M. ...Los Angeles, CA
Epstein, James R. ...Skokie, IL
Epstein, Janet T. ...San Francisco, CA
Epstein, Jason I. ...Knoxville, TN
Epstein, Jeffrey Hal ...New York, NY
Epstein, Jeffrey K. ...Woodbridge, NJ
Epstein, Jeffrey M. ...New York, NY
Epstein, Jeffrey M., & Associates
Los Angeles, CA
Epstein, Jeffrey W. ...Washington, DC
Epstein, Jennifer A. ...Washington, DC
Epstein, Jenny E. ...Washington, DC
Epstein, Jeremy G. ...New York, NY
Epstein, Jerome L. ...Washington, DC
Epstein, Jesse A. ...New York, NY
Epstein, Jill R. ...Mineola, NY
Epstein, Jodi H. ...Washington, DC
Epstein, Jon ...Bellmore, NY
Epstein, Jon A. ...Oklahoma City, OK
Epstein, Jon David (J.D.) ...Houston, TX
Epstein, Jonathan A. ...Boulder, CO
Epstein, Jonathan I. ...Princeton, NJ
Epstein, Jonathan M. ...Washington, DC
Epstein, Joseph G. ...Houston, TX
Epstein, Joseph M. ...Englewood, CO
Epstein, Joseph Z. ...New York, NY
Epstein, Juda J. ...Bronx, NY
Epstein, Jules A. ...Garden City, NY
Epstein, Kathleen Suzanne
Canoga Park, CA
Epstein, Keith A. ...Oakland, CA
Epstein, Keith J. ...San Francisco, CA
Epstein, Kevin M. ...San Francisco, CA
Epstein, Kimberly Cornell
San Francisco, CA
Epstein, Larry A. ...Sherman Oaks, CA
Epstein, Larry D. ...Cut Bank, MT
Epstein, Laurie ...New York, NY
Epstein, Laurie Carver ...Scarsdale, NY
Epstein, Lawrence ...New York, NY
Epstein, Lawrence R. ...Brooklyn, NY
Epstein, Lee M. ...New York, NY
Philadelphia, PA
Epstein, Leon S. ...Atlanta, GA
Epstein, Leonard ...Mansfield, MA
Epstein, Leonard ...New York, NY
Epstein, Leonard A. ...Dallas, TX
Epstein, Lester A. ...New York, NY
Epstein, Levinsohn & Weinstein, P.C.
New York, NY
Epstein, Linda A. ...Naples, FL
Epstein, Lloyd ...New York, NY
Epstein, Louis ...Greenwich, CT
Epstein, Louis ...New York, NY
Epstein, Louis J. ...Chattanooga, TN
Epstein, Louise K. ...Treasury Department,
Departmental Offices, GV
Epstein, Lynn A. ...Fort Lauderdale, FL
Epstein, M. David ...Jacksonville, FL
Epstein, Manuel ...Brooklyn, NY
Epstein, Marc G., P.A.
Fort Lauderdale, FL
Epstein, Marc Gary ...Fort Lauderdale, FL
Epstein, Marc N. ...Morristown, NJ
Epstein, Marc N. ...Fort Worth, TX
Epstein, Marc, (P.C.) ...Los Angeles, CA
Epstein, Marcia ...Acton, MA
Epstein, Margaret Lynn ...Los Angeles, CA
Epstein, Mark ...San Francisco, CA
Epstein, Mark B. ...Chicago, IL
Epstein, Mark B. ...New Brunswick, NJ
Epstein, Mark D. ...San Francisco, CA
Epstein, Mark H. ...Los Angeles, CA
Epstein, Mark H. ...Kansas City, MO
Epstein, Mark J. ...Pasadena, CA
Epstein, Mark Jay ...New York, NY
Epstein, Mark L. ...San Francisco, CA
Epstein, Mark P. ...Oakland, CA
Epstein, Mark S. ...New York, NY
Epstein, Mark W. ...San Francisco, CA
Epstein, Marsha J. ...Wilmington, DE
Epstein, Marvin ...New York, NY
Epstein, Matthew E. ...Boston, MA
Epstein, Matthew J. ...New York, NY
Epstein, Matthew S. ...Concord, NH
Epstein, Maurice ...Boston, MA
Epstein, Melvin ...New York, NY
Epstein, Meryl J. ...Boston, MA
Epstein, Michael A. ...Upper Marlboro, MD
Epstein, Michael A. ...New York, NY
Epstein, Michael D. ...Philadelphia, PA
Epstein, Michael J. ...Boston, MA
Epstein, Michael J. ...Rochelle Park, NJ
Epstein, Michael L. ...Cherry Hill, NJ
Philadelphia, PA
Epstein, Michael M. ...Boston, MA
Epstein, Michael S. ...Oakland, CA
Epstein, Michael T. ...United States Senate,
Senatorial Assistants, GV
Epstein, Michael Y. ...New York, NY
Epstein, Milton A. ...New York, NY
Epstein, Murray B. ...Miami, FL
Epstein, Murray B., P.A. ...Miami, FL
Epstein, N. Sandy ...Atlanta, GA
Epstein, Nancy E. ...Philadelphia, PA
Epstein, Nancy Lynn ...New York, NY
Epstein, Natan ...Culver City, CA
Epstein, Neil G. ...Philadelphia, PA
Epstein, Newman & Lubitz ...Bronx, NY
Epstein, Nina S. ...New York, NY
Epstein, Norman L. ...Los Angeles, CA
Epstein, Patricia J. ...Madison, WI
Epstein, Patricia N. ...New York, NY
Epstein, Paul A. ...San Francisco, CA
Epstein, Paul H. ...New York, NY
Epstein, Peter J. ...Boston, MA
Epstein, Philip D. ...Marblehead, MA
Epstein, Philip E. ...Bowie, MD
Epstein, Philip S. ...Pine Brook, NJ
Epstein, Phyllis Horn ...Philadelphia, PA
Epstein, R. Tali ...New York, NY
Epstein, Rafael ...Albany, NY
Epstein, Rebecca E. ...Department of Justice,
Civil Rights Division, GV
Epstein, Rebecca L. ...San Francisco, CA
Epstein & Reed, A Professional Corporation
Los Angeles, CA
Epstein, Reuven J. ...New York, NY
Epstein, Rhonda L. ...New York, NY
Epstein, Richard A. ...Chicago, IL
Epstein, Richard A. ...St. Louis, MO
Epstein, Richard A. ...Marlboro, NY
Epstein, Richard D. ...Washington, DC
Epstein, Richard H. ...Newark, NJ
Epstein, Richard J. ...Omaha, NE
Epstein, Richard L. ...Chicago, IL
Epstein, Richard L. ...Prairie Village, KS
Epstein, Richard W. ...Fort Lauderdale, FL
Epstein, Richard W. ...New Castle, PA
Sharon, PA
Epstein & Robbins ...Jacksonville, FL
Epstein, Robert ...Rochester, NY
Epstein, Robert ...Paulding, OH
Epstein, Robert ...Norfolk, VA
Epstein, Robert A. ...Greenwich, CT
Epstein, Robert C. ...Morristown, NJ
Epstein, Robert C. ...White Plains, NY
Epstein, Robert D. ...Indianapolis, IN
Epstein, Robert D. ...Boston, MA
New York, NY
Epstein, Robert E. ...Detroit, MI
Epstein, Robert E. ...Cleveland, OH
Epstein, Robert F. ...San Rafael, CA
Epstein, Robert H. ...Rockville, MD
Epstein, Robert H. ...St. Louis, MO
Epstein, Robert J. ...Maplewood, NJ
Brooklyn, NY
Epstein, Robert J. ...New York, NY
Epstein, Robert L. ...New York, NY
Epstein, Robert S. ...San Francisco, CA
Epstein, Roger H. ...Honolulu, HI
Epstein, Roger Mark ...Philadelphia, PA
Epstein, Ronald ...Baldwin, NY
Epstein, Ronald A. ...Portland, ME
Epstein, Ronald A. ...Pennsville, NJ
Epstein, Ronald S. ...Santa Clara, CA
Epstein, Roni F.
Federal Energy Regulatory Commission,
Office of the General Counsel, GV
Epstein, Ross A. ...San Diego, CA
Epstein, Roxanne J. ...El Cerrito, CA
Epstein, Roy A. ...New York, NY
Epstein, Roy F. ...Honolulu, HI
Epstein, Ruth S. ...Washington, DC
Epstein, Samantha ...Woodbury, NY
Epstein, Samuel I. ...Asbury Park, NJ
Epstein, Scott M. ...Los Angeles, CA
Epstein, Scott W. ...New York, NY
Epstein, Sean B. ...Pittsburgh, PA
Epstein, Seymour ...Bronx, NY
Epstein, Shapiro & Epstein
Philadelphia, PA
Epstein, Sheldon L. ...Wilmette, IL
Epstein, Sherry J. ...Geneva, OH
Epstein, Sherwin L., & Associates
Kansas City, MO
Epstein & Simantov ...New York, NY
Epstein, Stanley ...New York, NY
Epstein, Stanley ...New York, NY
Epstein, Stanley A. ...Newark, NJ
Epstein, Stanley H. ...New York, NY
Epstein, Stanley M. ...Weston, MA
Epstein, Stanley O. ...Redondo Beach, CA
Epstein, Stanley O., A Professional Law
Corporation ...Redondo Beach, CA
Epstein, Stefan ...Rochester, NY
Epstein, Stephen G. ...New York, NY
Epstein, Stephen J. ...Schaumburg, IL
Epstein, Stephen P. ...Garden City, NY
Epstein, Steven A. ...New York, NY
Epstein, Steven B. ...Denver, CO
Epstein, Steven B. ...Washington, DC
Epstein, Steven B. ...Raleigh, NC
Epstein, Steven F. ...Beverly Hills, CA
Epstein, Steven H. ...New York, NY
Epstein, Steven M. ...Milwaukee, WI
Epstein, Steven S. ...Marblehead, MA
Epstein, Stewart J. ...New York, NY
Epstein, Stuart A. ...Bridgeport, CT
Stamford, CT
Epstein, Sue ...Los Angeles, CA
Epstein, Susan Landerson ...Englewood, CO
Epstein, Susan T. ...New York, NY
Epstein, Terry Jo ...Denver, CO
Epstein, Theodore, Jr. ...Denver, CO
Epstein, Turner & Song, P.C.
Los Angeles, CA
Epstein, Utan, Wilson & Marsili
Scranton, PA
Epstein, Valerie W. ...Chattanooga, TN
Epstein, Walter M. ...New York, NY
Epstein & Weil ...New York, NY
Epstein, Wendy ...New York, NY
Epstein, William H. ...Neptune, NJ
Epstein, William H. ...Nutley, NJ
Epstein, William W. ...Atlanta, GA
Epstein & Wilsey ...Chicago, IL
Epstein-Plaut, Lori ...Boston, MA
Epstein-Terris, Laurie ...Sacramento, CA
Epsten & Grinnell ...San Diego, CA
Epsten, Jon H. ...San Diego, CA
Epstien, Jay A. ...Washington, DC
Epting, Andrew Kenneth, Jr.
Charleston, SC
Epting, Elaine Folline ...Columbia, SC
Epting & Hackney ...Chapel Hill, NC
Epting, John T. ...Washington, DC
Epting, Joseph M. ...Irmo, SC
Epting, Joseph M., Jr. ...Irmo, SC
Epting Law Firm, LLC ...Irmo, SC
Epting, Randolph B. ...Columbia, SC
Epting, Robert ...Chapel Hill, NC
Epting, Thomas W. ...Greenville, SC
Epton, Michael R. ...Des Plaines, IL
Epton, Saul A. ...Chicago, IL
Equals, Tamara L. ...Fresno, CA

Equels, Mary Kogut ... Orlando, FL
Equels, Thomas K. ... Miami, FL; Orlando, FL
Equi, Glenn C. ... Cherry Hill, NJ; Philadelphia, PA
Equi, Rodney W. ... Wheaton, IL
Equitz, Alfred A. ... San Francisco, CA
Eraca-Cornish, Nancy M. ... Elmira, NY
Eraclides, Hermes ... Sarasota, FL; Tampa, FL
Erale, Alexander B. ... Brentwood, NY
Eramo, Margery J. ... Wakefield, MA
Eramo, Martin P. ... Laguna Beach, CA
Eramus, Edward W. ... Spencerport, NY
Erard, Barbara Hughes ... Detroit, MI
Eras, Giselle ... New York, NY
Eras, Ira Lawrence ... Brooklyn, NY
Erasmus, Gavin M. ... Los Angeles, CA
Eraut, Warren E. ... Watsonville, CA
Erazo, Estelle M. Cabrera ... New York, NY
Erazo, Joseph R. ... New York, NY
Erazo, Martin M., Jr. ... Buffalo, NY
Erb, Brian C. ... Palo Alto, CA
Erb, Calvin J. ... Dillon, MT
Erb, Christian S., Jr. ... Harrisburg, PA
Erb, David W. ... Baltimore, MD
Erb, Dean P. ... Gowrie, IA
Erb, Donald R. ... Fitchburg, MA
Erb, Donna E. ... Dallas, TX
Erb, Elisha W. ... Fitchburg, MA
Erb & Erb ... Fitchburg, MA
Erb, Irvin E. ... Fitchburg, MA
Erb, J. Christopher ... Philadelphia, PA
Erb, James A. ... Charles City, IA
Erb, James J. ... Pittsburgh, PA
Erb, Jason R. ... Los Angeles, CA
Erb, Jeffery B. ... Portland, OR
Erb, Joel Patrick ... New York, NY
Erb, John C. ... Chicago, IL
Erb, John E. ... Marietta, OH
Erb, Jonathan H. ... San Francisco, CA
Erb, Joseph E. ... York, PA
Erb, Joseph E., Jr. ... Hanover, PA
Erb, Kathleen Tobin ... Anchorage, AK
Erb, Nicole ... Washington, DC
Erb, Richard A., Jr. ... Buffalo, WY; Gillette, WY
Erb, Robert Jon ... Savannah, GA
Erb, Robert W. ... New York, NY
Erb & Scott Law Office ... Dillon, MT
Erb, Shawna L. ... Youngstown, OH
Erb, Stephen Thomas ... San Diego, CA
Erb, Thomas A. ... Westborough, MA
Erb, Thomas C. ... St. Louis, MO
Erb, Wendy Elaine ... Naples, FL
Erb, William W. ... Sylvania, OH
Erba, Andrew F., Jr. ... Philadelphia, PA
Erbacci, Anthony G. ... Chicago, IL
Erbacci, Cerone & Moriarty, Ltd. ... Chicago, IL
Erbach & Voss, S.C. ... Madison, WI
Erbach, Walter H. ... Madison, WI
Erbaugh, James M. ... Hudson, OH
Erbe, Bonnie G. ... Washington, DC
Erbe, Nicola ... San Francisco, CA
Erbe, Norman A. ... West Des Moines, IA
Erbeck & Associates ... Las Vegas, NV
Erbeck, James W. ... Las Vegas, NV
Erben, Frederick A. ... Birmingham, AL
Erben, Randall H. ... Austin, TX
Erben, Robert D. ... Fort Lauderdale, FL
Erbey, John R. ... West Palm Beach, FL
Erbeznik, Frank A. ... Canoga Park, CA
Erbin, Eugene F. ... Sacramento, CA; San Francisco, CA
Erbin, Thomas J. ... Salt Lake City, UT
Erbland, Peter C. ... Coeur d'Alene, ID
Erblat, Mark ... Boca Raton, FL
Erblich, Christopher E. ... St. Louis, MO
Erbs & Erbs, P.C. ... St. Louis, MO
Erbs, Laura A. ... United States Senate, Committee Legal Personnel, GV
Erbs, Scott T. ... St. Louis, MO
Erbs, Thomas J. ... St. Louis, MO
Erbsen, Diana Lisa ... New York, NY
Erbstein, Bonita ... New York, NY
Erbstein, Keith S. ... Philadelphia, PA
Erbstoesser, Eugene R. ... Los Angeles, CA
Erburu, Robert F. ... Los Angeles, CA
Erca, Alison A. ... Durham, NC
Erceg, James H. ... Schenectady, NY
Erceg, Marta E. ... United States Postal Service, Law Department, GV
Erck, Dever & Merlin, LLC ... Atlanta, GA
Erck, James A. ... Alice, TX
Erck, John R. ... Department of Defense, Defense Legal Services Agency, GV
Erck, Theodore A. ... Atlanta, GA
Erck & Wright ... Alice, TX
Erckert, Christopher P. B. ... Washington, DC
Ercklentz, Enno W., Jr. ... New York, NY
Ercklentz, Enno W., Jr., P.C. ... New York, NY
Ercolani, Heather R. ... Pittsburgh, PA
Ercole, Charles A. ... Philadelphia, PA
Ercole, Robert M. ... Baltimore, MD
Ercoli, Karen M. ... Chicago, IL
Ercolini, Elaine ... Oakland, CA
Ercolino, Gino F. ... Boston, MA
Erd, Christopher A. ... Roseland, NJ
Erd, Daniel R. ... Rock Springs, WY
Erda, Susan M. ... New York, NY
Erdahl, Clemens A., II ... Washington, IA
Erdahl, H. Elvin ... Monticello, IA
Erdahl, Steven D. ... Dallas, TX
Erdall, Richard M. ... Minneapolis, MN
Erdbacher, W. Scott ... Salinas, CA
Erdberg, Joe S. ... Birmingham, AL
Erdberg, Lisa M. ... San Francisco, CA
Erde & Associates P.C. ... Chicago, IL
Erde, Joanne B., (P.A.) ... Miami, FL
Erde, Michael H. ... Chicago, IL
Erdeky, Susan Pendleton ... Department of Education, Office of the General Counsel, GV
Erdel, Dan K. ... Mexico, MO
Erdelack, Wayne F. ... Solon, OH
Erdely, Peter George ... Philadelphia, PA
Erdely, Steve ... Knoxville, TN
Erdelyi, Gabor ... Los Altos, CA
Erdelyi, Susan Smith ... Jacksonville, FL
Erdenberger, Gordon G. ... Doylestown, PA
Erdenberger, Jane ... Omaha, NE
Erdevig, John D. ... Saginaw, MI
Erdheim, Stacey ... New York, NY
Erdley, Randall G. ... Washington, DC
Erdman, David W. ... Charlotte, NC
Erdman, Hockfield and Burt, L.L.P. ... Charlotte, NC
Erdman, Jeffrey W. ... Los Angeles, CA
Erdman, Joseph ... Boca Raton, FL; New York, NY
Erdman, Kevin R. ... Fort Wayne, IN
Erdman, Michael H. ... Chicago, IL
Erdman, Todd Lawrence ... Homewood, IL
Erdman, Virginia L. ... Wausau, WI
Erdman, William A. ... St. Louis, MO
Erdmann, Carl R. ... Washington, DC
Erdmann, Craig C. ... New York, NY
Erdmann, Don A. ... Bedford, IN
Erdmann, James N. ... Red Wing, MN
Erdmann, John D. ... Cheyenne, WY
Erdmann, John R. ... Iselin, NJ
Erdmann, K. Douglas ... Portland, ME
Erdmann, Richard L. ... Arlington, VA
Erdmann, Richard O. ... Fairview Heights, IL
Erdmann, Robert C. ... Grass Valley, CA
Erdmann, Stephen S. ... Clackamas, OR
Erdmann, Thomas A. ... Red Wing, MN
Erdmier, William W. ... Big Bear Lake, CA
Erdoes, Brenda J. ... Carson City, NV
Erdoes, Peter A. ... Oklahoma City, OK
Erdos, Philip G. ... Houston, TX
Erdos, David C. ... Stamford, CT
Erdos, Harger & Juravich, L.L.P. ... Houston, TX; Richmond, TX; Stafford, TX; Sugar Land, TX
Erdos, Ian L. ... Chicago, IL
Erdos, Jacques ... New York, NY
Erdos, Jillian L. ... Boston, MA
Erdos, Michael E. ... Philadelphia, PA
Erdos, Robt. W. ... York, PA
Erdos, Thomas V., Jr. ... Sugar Land, TX
Erdreich, Ben L. ... Merit Systems Protection Board, Board Members, GV
Erdrich, William E. ... St. Joseph, MO
Erdstein, Janice H. ... Huntington Woods, MI
Ereckson, Stanley, Jr. ... Denver, CO
Erem, Donna M. ... Secaucus, NJ
Eremich, Abbie ... Milford, CT
Eren, Günter ... Norwalk, CT
Erenbaum, Jessica Serell ... Miami, FL
Erenberg, Douglas D. ... Los Angeles, CA
Erenea, Doreen ... San Diego, CA
Ereno, Jennifer Ergina ... San Jose, CA
Erenrich, Alan L. ... Great Neck, NY
Erens, Brad B. ... Chicago, IL
Erens, Jay ... Chicago, IL
Erens, Michael G. ... Chicago, IL; Lincolnwood, IL
Erenstoft, Sean G. ... Los Angeles, CA
Eres, Thomas W. ... Sacramento, CA
Erez, Jeffrey ... Fort Lauderdale, FL
Erf, Stephen D. ... Chicago, IL
Erffmeyer, Steven J. ... Montevideo, MN
Erfle, Nancy M. ... Portland, OR
Erftmier, Donald L., Jr. ... Omaha, NE
Erfurt, Edward W., III ... Columbus, OH
Ergas, Leonard ... New York, NY
Ergas, Martin ... Miami, FL
Ergastolo, Joseph T. ... San Diego, CA
Ergazos, John W. ... Canton, OH
Ergenbright, R. Granville ... Charlottesville, VA
Ergener, Denise ... Environmental Protection Agency, Office of Enforcement and Compliance Assurance, GV
Ergo, Richard A. ... Walnut Creek, CA
Ergo, Richard W. ... Santa Rosa, CA
Ergood, Foster C. ... Cherry Hill, NJ
Ergovich, Wm. H. ... Kansas City, MO
Erhan, Merih Okcuoglu ... Philadelphia, PA
Erhard, G. Daniel ... Dallas, TX
Erhard, Gerald A., Jr. ... Zanesville, OH
Erhard, Michael P. ... Madison, WI
Erhard, Robert T. ... Newark, OH
Erhard, Ruebel & Jennings, A Professional Corporation ... Dallas, TX
Erhardt, Carl J. ... Atlanta, GA
Erhardt, Chris ... Batavia, OH
Erhardt, Chris, Jr. ... Batavia, OH
Erhardt, Chris, Law Offices ... Batavia, OH
Erhardt, Clement D., III ... Baltimore, MD
Erhardt, Elizabeth T. ... San Francisco, CA
Erhardt, Frederick J. ... Madison, WI
Erhardt, John D. ... Batavia, OH
Erhardt, Joseph K. ... Detroit, MI
Erhardt, Kelly A. ... Freehold, NJ
Erhardt, Michael M. ... Benson, MN
Erhardt, Rebecca A. ... Madison, WI
Erhardt, Richard A. ... San Carlos, CA
Erhardt, Samuel K. ... Ottumwa, IA
Erhart, Cheryl A. ... Atlantic City, NJ
Erhart, James N. ... Petoskey, MI
Erhart, Jeffrey ... Phoenix, AZ
Erhart, John J. ... Minneapolis, MN
Erhart, William Alan ... Anoka, MN
Erhart, William W. ... Wilmington, DE
Erhart, William W., P.A. ... Wilmington, DE
Erich, David A. ... Harrisburg, PA
Erich, Janice E. ... Alexandria, VA
Erich, John A. ... Milwaukee, WI
Erich, M. Michelle ... Ventura, CA
Erich, Norwood R. ... Sacramento, CA
Erich, Robert W. ... Concord, CA
Erichsen, David H. ... Boston, MA
Erichsen, Francesca M. ... New York, NY
Erichsen, Peter C. ... Philadelphia, PA
Erichson, Howard M. ... Newark, NJ
Ericksen, Arbuthnot, Kilduff, Day & Lindstrom, Inc. ... Fresno, CA; Los Angeles, CA; Oakland, CA; Riverside, CA; Sacramento, CA; San Francisco, CA; San Jose, CA; Walnut Creek, CA
Ericksen, Craig G. ... Palm Springs, CA
Ericksen, David A. ... San Francisco, CA
Ericksen, David P. ... Rahway, NJ
Ericksen, Gaylen C. ... Encino, CA
Ericksen, George W. ... Tampa, FL
Ericksen, Gregory S. ... Bountiful, UT
Ericksen, Jeffery C. ... Waukegan, IL
Ericksen, Keith C. ... Winnetka, IL
Erickson, Alan C. ... Fargo, ND
Erickson, Alf L. ... Fort Lauderdale, FL
Erickson, Ann E. ... Birmingham, MI
Erickson, Armond G. ... Fargo, ND
Erickson, Arnold A. ... San Francisco, CA
Erickson, Arthur J. ... Minneapolis, MN
Erickson, Arthur W. ... Portland, OR
Erickson, Barbara J. ... Westlake Village, CA
Erickson & Barkshire, P.S. ... Bellevue, WA
Erickson, Beasley, Hewitt & Wilson ... Oakland, CA
Erickson, Becky L. ... Minneapolis, MN
Erickson & Birch, P.C. ... Burwell, NE
Erickson, Brent J. ... Dallas, TX
Erickson, Brian H. ... San Diego, CA
Erickson, Brian L. ... Tillamook, OR
Erickson, Bruce D. ... Seattle, WA
Erickson, Bruce H. ... Spokane, WA
Erickson, Burdette W., (Mr.) ... Portland, OR
Erickson, Carl N. ... Magna, UT
Erickson, Carl R. ... Prospect Heights, IL
Erickson, Carl S. ... Braintree, MA
Erickson, Carol A. ... Lake Orion, MI
Erickson, Charles B. ... Park Ridge, IL
Erickson, Charles E. ... Hopkins, MN
Erickson, Charles N. ... Bloomington, IL
Erickson, Charles P. ... Naples, FL
Erickson, Charles R. ... Houston, TX
Erickson, Christina Maria ... Washington, DC
Erickson, Clarence J., III ... New York, NY
Erickson, Clark ... Kankakee, IL
Erickson, Conrad C. ... Burwell, NE
Erickson, Craig A. ... Minneapolis, MN
Erickson, Craig T. ... Albuquerque, NM
Erickson, Dale A. ... Houston, TX
Erickson, Daniel H. ... Bridgeton, NJ
Erickson, David B. ... Salt Lake City, UT
Erickson, David C. ... Valley, NE
Erickson, David E. ... Sacramento, CA
Erickson, David E. ... Rawlins, WY
Erickson, David E., P.C. ... Rawlins, WY
Erickson, David G. ... Northbrook, IL
Erickson, David H. ... Concord, MA
Erickson, David L. ... Denver, CO
Erickson, David L., LLC ... Denver, CO
Erickson, David M. ... Des Moines, IA
Erickson, David R. ... Kansas City, MO
Erickson, Davis, Murphy, Johnson, Griffith & Walsh, Ltd. ... Decatur, IL
Erickson, Denise A. G. ... Annandale, VA
Erickson, Dennis W. ... Hudson, WI
Erickson, Diane Q. ... Woodridge, IL
Erickson, Don E. ... San Diego, CA
Erickson, Donald C. ... Irvine, CA
Erickson, Donald C. ... Duluth, MN
Erickson, Donald E. ... Lansing, MI
Erickson, Donald E. ... Yankton, SD
Erickson, Donald H. ... Omaha, NE
Erickson, Donald J., Jr. ... Chicago, IL
Erickson, Douglas C. ... Phoenix, AZ
Erickson, Douglas E. ... Schenectady, NY
Erickson, Duane A. ... Seattle, WA
Erickson, Duane E. ... Gig Harbor, WA
Erickson, Edward E. ... Bismarck, ND
Erickson, Elizabeth A. ... San Francisco, CA
Erickson, Eric J. ... Los Angeles, CA
Erickson & Erickson ... Spokane, WA
Erickson, Eugene ... Livonia, MI
Erickson, Frederick P. ... Decatur, IL
Erickson, Gail ... Brooklyn, NY
Erickson, George ... Tucson, AZ
Erickson, George E., Jr. ... Topeka, KS
Erickson, Grant D. ... Northbrook, IL
Erickson, Grant G. ... Stockton, CA
Erickson, Gregory J. ... St. Louis, MO
Erickson, Gregory M. ... Woodbury, MN
Erickson, Gunner ... Santa Monica, CA
Erickson, Harvey ... Spokane, WA
Erickson, Helena T. ... New York, NY
Erickson, Howard C. ... Covina, CA
Erickson, Howard E. ... Denver, CO
Erickson, Ingrid W. ... Grand Rapids, MI
Erickson, J. Gunnar ... Santa Monica, CA
Erickson, J. Steven ... St. Louis, MO
Erickson, J. Steven, Law Office of ... St. Louis, MO
Erickson, Jackie Mahi ... Honolulu, HI
Erickson, James C. ... Minneapolis, MN
Erickson, James C. ... St. Paul, MN
Erickson, James D. ... Moorhead, MN
Erickson, James E. ... San Juan Capistrano, CA
Erickson, James E. ... Bloomington, MN
Erickson, James R. ... Balsam Lake, WI
Erickson, James W. ... Appleton, WI
Erickson, Jan A. ... Madison, WI
Erickson, Jay Marcus ... Helena, MT
Erickson, Jean V. ... Syracuse, NY
Erickson, Jeanne M. Peterson ... St. Cloud, MN
Erickson, Jeffery R. ... Riverside, CA
Erickson, Jeffrey A. ... Treasury Department, Internal Revenue Service, GV
Erickson, Jeffrey E. ... Warsaw, NY
Erickson, Jenny A. ... Boston, MA
Erickson, Jerry L. ... Woodbridge, VA
Erickson, Joel M. ... Minnetonka, MN
Erickson, John C., III ... Indianapolis, IN
Erickson, John F. ... Washington, DC
Erickson, John H. ... Oakland, CA
Erickson, John H. ... Brainerd, MN
Erickson, John L. ... Bellingham, WA
Erickson, John R. ... Danbury, CT
Erickson, John R. ... Las Vegas, NV
Erickson, John R. ... McLean, VA
Erickson, John S. ... Wayzata, MN
Erickson, John V. ... San Francisco, CA
Erickson, John W. ... New York, NY
Erickson, Jon P. ... Minneapolis, MN
Erickson, Jon R. ... Atlanta, GA
Erickson, Jon R. ... Huron, SD
Erickson, Joshua M. ... Milwaukee, WI
Erickson, Karen S. ... Arlington, MA
Erickson, Karl G. ... Kalamazoo, MI
Erickson, Kathryn A. ... Chicago, IL
Erickson, Kenneth R., Jr. ... St. Paul, MN
Erickson, Kenneth W. ... Boston, MA
Erickson, Kent R. ... Kansas City, MO
Erickson, Kevin D. ... Hoffman Estates, IL
Erickson, Kipley B. H. ... Fargo, ND
Erickson, Kristin L. ... Reno, NV
Erickson, Kristine Strom ... Minneapolis, MN
Erickson Law Office ... Postville, IA
Erickson Law Office ... Moorhead, MN
Erickson, Leif B. ... Missoula, MT
Erickson, Leif D. ... Sioux City, IA
Erickson, Lewayne M. ... Brookings, SD
Erickson, Lewayne M., P.C. ... Brookings, SD
Erickson, Lindsey ... Overland Park, KS
Erickson, Louis S. ... Naples, FL
Erickson, Lyn E. ... Boston, MA
Erickson, Lynette L. ... Menominee, MI
Erickson, Lynn E. ... Langdon, ND
Erickson, Marc K. ... Kansas City, MO
Erickson, Margery C. ... Department Of Health And Human Services, Food & Drug Administration, GV
Erickson, Marie Kathryn ... New Orleans, LA
Erickson, Marilee C. ... Seattle, WA
Erickson, Marion E. M. ... Department of Justice, Tax Division, GV
Erickson, Marjorie Lakin ... Los Angeles, CA
Erickson, Mark A. ... Campbell, CA
Erickson, Mark A. ... San Jose, CA
Erickson, Mark D. ... Irvine, CA
Erickson, Mary Fingal ... Westminster, CA
Erickson, Mary S. ... Jefferson City, MO
Erickson, Matthew J. ... Postville, IA
Erickson, Matthew S. ... Bangor, ME
Erickson, Michael J. ... Seattle, WA
Erickson, Morrie, A Professional Corporation ... Bloomington, IN
Erickson, Morris H. ... Bloomington, IN
Erickson, Nancy S. ... New York, NY
Erickson, Neil C. ... Los Angeles, CA
Erickson, Patricia Blackford ... Huron, SD; Mitchell, SD
Erickson, Patricia M. ... Las Vegas, NV
Erickson, Paul ... Hartford, CT
Erickson, Paul B. ... Jupiter, FL
Erickson, Paul C. ... Thousand Oaks, CA
Erickson, Paul J. ... New York, NY
Erickson, Paul L. ... Asheville, NC
Erickson, Paul L., P.A. ... Asheville, NC
Erickson, Paul R. ... Milwaukee, WI
Erickson, Pauline A. ... Lexington, MA
Erickson and Pearson Law Offices ... Brainerd, MN
Erickson, Philip ... Oxnard, CA
Erickson, Philip A. ... Jamestown, NY
Erickson, Philip L. ... St. Paul, MN
Erickson, Philip O. ... Atlanta, GA
Erickson, Ralph E. ... Los Angeles, CA
Erickson, Ralph Hull ... Malibu, CA
Erickson, Ralph R. ... Fargo, ND
Erickson, Randall J. ... Milwaukee, WI
Erickson, Randall L. ... Irvine, CA
Erickson, Randall T. ... Chicago, IL
Erickson, Raymond L. ... Duluth, MN
Erickson, Rex R. ... El Cajon, CA
Erickson, Richard A. ... Kansas City, MO
Erickson, Richard C. ... Staunton, VA
Erickson, Richard G. ... Phoenix, AZ
Erickson, Richard J. ... Department of the Air Force, Office of the Judge Advocate General, GV
Erickson, Richard J. ... Cincinnati, OH
Erickson, Richard M. ... Kansas City, MO

Erickson, Robert C., Jr. ...Alexandria, VA
Erickson, Robert D. ...Philadelphia, PA
Erickson, Robert J. ...Alameda, CA
Erickson, Robert J. ...Denver, CO
Erickson, Robert J. ...Department of Justice, Criminal Division, GV
Erickson, Robert L. ...St. Paul, MN
Erickson, Robert M. ...Pleasanton, CA
Erickson, Robert M. ...Cincinnati, OH
Erickson, Robert S. ...Boise, ID
Erickson, Robert S. ...Tulsa, OK
Erickson, Roger L. ...Reno, NV
Erickson, Roger W. ...San Francisco, CA
Erickson, Ronald A. ...Edina, MN
Erickson, Ronald S. ...Yuba City, CA
Erickson, Roy L. ...Decatur, IL
Erickson, Sally A. ...Washington, DC
Erickson, Sarah Z. ...St. Paul, MN
Erickson Schaffer Peterson & Hempel PC Boston, MA Wellesley, MA
Erickson, Scott A. ...Phoenix, AZ
Erickson, Scott R. ...Minneapolis, MN
Erickson, Scott T. ...Telluride, CO
Erickson, Scott T., P.C. ...Telluride, CO
Erickson & Sederstrom, P.C. ...Lincoln, NE Omaha, NE
Erickson & Snook ...Braintree, MA
Erickson, Sonya F. ...Kirkland, WA
Erickson, Stanley E. ...Tualatin, OR
Erickson, Stanley E. ...Bellevue, WA
Erickson, Stephanie L. ...Schaumburg, IL
Erickson, Stephen E. ...Great Neck, NY
Erickson, Stephen E. ...Austin, TX
Erickson, Stephen K. ...Bloomington, MN
Erickson, Stephen R. ...Albert Lea, MN
Erickson, Steven A. ...Boulder, CO
Erickson, Steven W. ...Minneapolis, MN
Erickson, Susan J. ...Chicago, IL
Erickson, Thomas J. ...Commodity Futures Trading Commission, GV
Erickson, Thomas J. ...Milwaukee, WI
Erickson, Thomas S., (P.A.) Minneapolis, MN
Erickson, Thorpe & Swainston, Ltd. Reno, NV
Erickson, Vincent N. ...Palm Desert, CA
Erickson, Wallace E. ...Golden Valley, MN
Erickson, Warren L. ...Seattle, WA
Erickson, Wayne A. ...Lansing, MI
Erickson, Webb & Scolton Jamestown, NY
Erickson, William E. ...Rye Brook, NY
Erickson, William E. ...Sapulpa, OK
Erickson, William H. ...Englewood, CO
Erickson, William H. ...Hartford, CT
Erickson, William J. ...Plymouth, MN
Erickson, William J. ...Broken Bow, NE
Erickson, William N. ...Boston, MA
Erickson, William W. ...Wellesley, MA
Erickson & Wolf ...Tualatin, OR
Erickson, Yolande P. ...Malibu, CA
Erickson, Zierke, Kuderer & Madsen, P.A. Fairmont, MN
Erickson Ober, Lynn ...Leesport, PA
Erickson-Papanek-Hanson ...Northbrook, IL
Erickstad, Ralph J. ...Bismarck, ND
Ericsen, Arnold J. ...Brookfield, WI
Ericson, Benjamin J. ...Boston, MA
Ericson, Bonnie ...Seminole, TX
Ericson, Britt Marie ...Seattle, WA
Ericson, Bruce A. ...San Francisco, CA
Ericson, Carlton R. ...Boise, ID
Ericson, Christine F. ...Washington, DC
Ericson, David B. ...South St. Paul, MN
Ericson, Donald A. ...Spokane, WA
Ericson, E. Dixon ...Huntington, WV
Ericson, Ivan L. ...Oak Ridge, TN
Ericson, James D. ...Milwaukee, WI
Ericson, Jean E. ...New York, NY
Ericson, John C. ...New York, NY
Ericson, M. Scott ...Renton, WA
Ericson, Mark A. ...Westbury, NY
Ericson, Mary A. ...Des Moines, IA
Ericson, Norman J. ...Olympia, WA
Ericson, R. Peter ...Mechanicsburg, PA
Ericson, Robert B. ...Long Beach, CA
Ericson, Robert T. ...Humble, TX
Ericson, Robert W. ...New York, NY
Ericson, Roger D. ...Naples, FL
Ericson, Scalise, Mangan & Zembko, P.C. New Britain, CT
Ericson, Selina G. ...New York, NY
Ericson, Stuart ...Muskogee, OK
Ericson, Sydney K. ...Brea, CA
Ericson, William W. ...Kirkland, WA
Ericsson & Egan, A Professional Corporation Portland, OR Port Townsend, WA
Ericsson, Ellen F. ...West Chester, PA
Ericsson, Ericsson & Leibel ...Madison, SD
Ericsson, John M. ...Columbus, OH
Ericsson, Lloyd B. ...Portland, OR Port Townsend, WA
Ericsson, Mark Stephen ...Walnut Creek, CA
Ericsson, Richard J. ...Westfield, NJ
Ericsson, Richard L. ...Madison, SD
Ericsson Ridgeway ...Anchorage, AK Portland, OR Seattle, WA
Ericsson, Robert J., P.C. ...Anchorage, AK Portland, OR Seattle, WA
Ericsson, Roland S. ...Las Vegas, NV
Ericsson, Samuel E. ...Fairfax, VA
Ericsson, Thomas A. ...Las Vegas, NV
Erie, David T. ...Chicago, IL
Erie, J. Steven ...Richmond, VA
Erie & Kennedy ...Telluride, CO
Erie, Kenneth R. ...Bemidji, MN
Erie, Leigh D. ...Tacoma, WA
Erie, Robert A. ...Telluride, CO
Erigero, Stephen J. ...Los Angeles, CA
Erike, Ona O. ...Uniondale, NY
Eriks, Mark C. ...Grand Rapids, MI
Eriksen, Arthur W. ...Hightstown, NJ
Eriksen, Christopher O. ...Roseland, NJ
Eriksen, Clarence E. ...Houston, TX
Eriksen, David F. ...Dallas, TX
Eriksen, Donald P. ...Pittsburgh, PA
Eriksen, Greg L. ...Orange, CA
Eriksen, James P. ...San Francisco, CA
Eriksen, Michael D., (P.A.) Lake Worth, FL West Palm Beach, FL
Eriksen, Neil Oswald ...West Orange, NJ
Eriksen, Niels C., Jr. ...Warminster, PA
Eriksen, Peter R. ...Walden, NY
Eriksen, Richard C. ...Pontiac, MI
Eriksen, Richard E. ...Washington, DC
Eriksen, Thomas B. ...Vancouver, WA
Eriksen, Victor S. ...San Diego, CA
Erikson, Brian W. ...Dallas, TX
Erikson, George W. ...Landover, MD
Erikson, George W., Jr. ...Washington, DC
Erikson, J. Lance ...Beverly Hills, CA
Erikson, John L., Jr. ...Los Angeles, CA
Erikson, Karen A. ...Chicago, IL
Erikson, Mark A. ...Vancouver, WA
Erikson, Phyllis A. ...Edison, NJ
Eriksson, Erik A., Jr. ...Houston, TX
Eriksson, John M. ...Salt Lake City, UT
Eriksson, Kirsten M. ...New York, NY
Eriksson, Margaret L. ...Plantation, FL
Eriksson, Peder W. ...Salinas, CA
Eriksson, Ralph E. ...Sanford, FL
Eriksson, Tanya F. ...Houston, TX
Eriksson, Xan Marie ...Portland, OR
Erim, Ahmet M. ...Arlington, VA
Eriole, Joseph P. ...Clifton Park, NY
Eriqat, Victoria Alderman ...San Diego, CA
Erisey, Catherine Kemp ...Akron, OH
Erisman, Caroline K. ...New York, NY
Erisman & Curtin ...Wilmington, DE
Erisman, David H. ...Wilmington, DE
Erisman, Frank ...Denver, CO
Erisman, James A. ...Newark, DE Wilmington, DE
Erisman, Jane M. ...Baltimore, MD
Erisman, Kerry L. ...Fayetteville, NC
Erisman, Otis W. ...Philadelphia, PA
Erjavac, Stanley M. ...Troy, MI
Erjavec, Julie E. ...Grand Forks, ND
Erkel, Albert A., Jr. ...Los Angeles, CA
Erkel, James L. ...Minneapolis, MN
Erkelenz, William F. ...Washington, DC
ErkenBrack, Stephen K. ...Denver, CO Grand Junction, CO
Erker, Barbara A. ...Overland Park, KS
Erker, Christopher E. ...St. Louis, MO
Erker, Norton & Hare, L.L.C. ...Olathe, KS
Erker, Thomas J. ...Olathe, KS
Erkert, Randall G. ...Milwaukee, WI
Erkilla, Jack R. ...Evansville, IN
Erkkila, Linda Kuhel ...Cleveland, OH
Erkonen, Samuel J. ...Chicago, IL
Erl, Gene Alan ...Milwaukee, WI
Erlach, Gregory J. ...San Francisco, CA
Erlach, Michelle Marie ...Reno, NV
Erlach, Raymond N. Stella San Francisco, CA
Erlach, Stephen Peter U. San Francisco, CA
Erlain, Anthony J., Jr. ...Pittsburgh, PA
Erlam, Nelson Alexander ...Cherry Hill, NJ
Erland, Alan S. ...Portland, OR
Erlander, Timothy R. ...Minneapolis, MN
Erlandsen, Dana J. ...Madison, WI
Erlandson, Andrew W. ...Madison, WI
Erlandson, Gregory J. ...Rapid City, SD
Erlandson, Mark A. ...Milwaukee, WI
Erlandson, Nikki ...Westminster, CA
Erlandson, Robert C. ...Baltimore, MD
Erlanger, Howard S. ...Madison, WI
Erlanger, Peri B. ...Palo Alto, CA
Erlanger, Richard J. ...Dallas, TX
Erlanger, Robert K. ...New York, NY
Erlbacher-Anderson, Amy L. ...Omaha, NE
Erlbaum, Paul H. ...East Montpelier, VT
Erlenbach & Erlenbach, P.A. Titusville, FL
Erlenbach, Kurt ...Titusville, FL
Erlenbach, Susan K. W. ...Titusville, FL
Erlenbach, Thomas S. ...Columbus, OH
Erlenborn, John N. ...Issue, MD
Erlenborn, Neal Robert ...Chicago, IL
Erler, Carl W., III ...Toms River, NJ
Erler, John Paul ...South Portland, ME
Erler, Kenneth J. ...Stevens Point, WI
Erler, Margaret Cain ...Plover, WI
Erler, Powers & Nicholson ...Portland, ME South Portland, ME
Erler, Randall K. ...Jacksonville, FL
Erlewine, Christopher ...Washington, DC
Erlewine, David E. ...Baltimore, MD
Erlewine, Gary L. ...Columbus, NE
Erlewine, R. Scott ...San Francisco, CA
Erlich, Alfred S. ...Webster, MA
Erlich, Barry A. ...Chicago, IL
Erlich, Donna ...Tallahassee, FL
Erlich, Fred ...Newton, MA
Erlich, Henry P. ...Los Angeles, CA
Erlich, Jacob N. (Jesse) ...Boston, MA
Erlich, Joshua Mark ...Santa Monica, CA
Erlich, Kenneth P. ...Los Angeles, CA
Erlich, Margot ...New York, NY
Erlich, Mark A. ...Webster, MA
Erlich, Nathan ...Forest Hills, NY
Erlich, Norman A. ...Boston, MA
Erlich, Phyllis J. ...Baltimore, MD
Erlich, Scott E. ...Boston, MA
Erlich, Sheldon D. ...Southfield, MI
Erlich, Stewart I. ...Southfield, MI
Erlichman, Joseph ...Phoenix, AZ
Erlichman, Ron Israel ...Houston, TX
Erlichman, Sheryl ...Columbus, OH
Erlichman, Susan M. ...Baltimore, MD
Erlichson, Frances ...Simsbury, CT
Erlichster, Joe ...New York, NY
Erlick, John P. ...Seattle, WA
Erlinger, James H., III ...St. Louis, MO
Erlinger, Michael J. ...Los Angeles, CA
Erlingson, Mary G. ...Baton Rouge, LA
Erlitz, Gail M. ...Hempstead, NY
Erlitz, Stephen N. ...Brooklyn, NY
Erlsten, Steven J. ...Galion, OH
Erly, John L. ...Prince Frederick, MD
Erly, Peter S. ...Burlington, VT
Erm, Rene, II ...Walla Walla, WA
Erman, Earle I. ...Southfield, MI
Erman, Teicher, Miller, Zucker, Freedman & Gordon, A Professional Corporation Detroit, MI Southfield, MI
Ermel, Karen A. ...West Caldwell, NJ
Ermer, David M. ...Washington, DC
Ermer, Marilyn S. ...Washington, DC
Ermer, Michael G. ...Newport Beach, CA
Ermer, Philip M. ...Baltimore, MD
Ermert, James J. ...Racine, WI
Ermert, Michael D. ...Birmingham, AL
Ermes, Charles E. ...Fullerton, CA
Ermeti, Joseph A. ...Sidney, NY
Ermi, Thomas ...Philadelphia, PA
Ermilin, Igor ...New York, NY
Ermilio, Francis G. ...Worcester, MA
Ermilio, James A. ...Webster, MA
Ermine, David B. ...Philadelphia, PA
Ermlich, Arthur C., Jr. ...Virginia Beach, VA
Ermolovich, Nicholas ...Ephrata, PA
Ermoyan, Eugenie ...United States Senate, Senatorial Assistants, GV
Ermshar, Donald P. ...Riverside, CA
Ermshler, Kristin J. ...Rochester Hills, MI
Ernandes, Jack ...Long Beach, CA
Ernce, Lynn Trinka ...Sacramento, CA
Erne, David A. ...Milwaukee, WI
Erne, Edward G. ...West Cape May, NJ
Ernecoff, Henry N. ...San Diego, CA
Ernecoff & Roche ...San Diego, CA
Ernest, George D., III ...Lafayette, LA
Ernest, Michael J. ...New Philadelphia, OH
Ernest, Robert J. ...Burlington, MA
Ernest, Roland P. ...Chicago, IL
Ernest, Stanton D. ...Mount Carmel, IL
Ernest, Steven E. ...Costa Mesa, CA
Ernest, Van C. ...Richmond, VA
Ernewein, Michael E. ...Cleveland, OH
Erney, Jeffry J. ...Cleveland, OH
Erney, Robert D. ...Columbus, OH
Ernick, David M. ...New York, NY
Ernick, Nicholas R. ...Portsmouth, NH
Ernico, Jeffrey A. ...Harrisburg, PA
Ernouf, W. Sherman ...Anchorage, AK
Ernsberger, Barbara B. ...Pittsburgh, PA
Ernsberger, Daniel W. ...Pittsburgh, PA
Ernsberger, Patricia Clark San Francisco, CA
Ernst, Albert ...Lansing, MI
Ernst, Ameneh K. ...San Bernardino, CA
Ernst, Andrew H. ...Atlanta, GA Savannah, GA
Ernst, Arnold F. ...Atlanta, GA
Ernst, Barbara G. ...Washington, DC
Ernst, Brian L. ...Spokane, WA
Ernst, Charles S. ...New York, NY
Ernst, Christopher M. ...Boulder, CO
Ernst, Christopher M. ...Cleveland, OH
Ernst, Christopher W. ...Montrose, CO
Ernst, Cliff ...Austin, TX
Ernst, Dan W. ...Tulsa, OK
Ernst, Daniel D. ...Dayton, OH
Ernst, Daniel P. ...Kewadin, MI
Ernst, David A. ...Portland, OR
Ernst, David D. ...Santa Monica, CA
Ernst, David D. ...Omaha, NE
Ernst, David E. ...Lebanon, OH
Ernst, Don A. ...San Luis Obispo, CA
Ernst, Douglas E. ...Atlanta, GA
Ernst, Frederick D. ...Overland Park, KS Kansas City, MO
Ernst, Frederick J. ...Kansas City, MO
Ernst, Gerald ...New York, NY
Ernst, Gregory ...Lincoln City, OR
Ernst, Gregory L. ...New Orleans, LA
Ernst, Herbert, Jr. ...Dayton, OH
Ernst, James F. ...Santa Rosa, CA
Ernst, Janis C. ...Durham, NC
Ernst, Jeffrey A. ...Buffalo, NY
Ernst, Jill K. ...San Jose, CA
Ernst, John R. ...Tawas City, MI
Ernst, Joseph A. ...Ann Arbor, MI
Ernst, Joseph H. ...Grandview, MO
Ernst, Julia L. ...Detroit, MI
Ernst, Kirsten N. ...Mount Airy, MD
Ernst, Lawrence J. ...New Orleans, LA
Ernst, Lisa A. ...Philadelphia, PA
Ernst, Marcia McCrory ...Atlanta, GA
Ernst, Marcus A. ...New York, NY
Ernst, Mark S. ...Franklin Park, IL
Ernst, Matthew T. ...Cincinnati, OH
Ernst and Mattison, A Law Corporation San Luis Obispo, CA
Ernst, Maximillian L. ...Philadelphia, PA
Ernst, Michael D. ...Boston, MA
Ernst, Michael J. ...Atlanta, GA
Ernst, Peter W. ...Elmhurst, IL
Ernst, Richard ...Occidental, CA
Ernst, Richard C., (Ltd.) ...Lisle, IL
Ernst, Robert G. J. ...New York, NY
Ernst, Robert J., III ...Salinas, CA
Ernst, Robert L. ...New York, NY
Ernst, Russell J. ...McKees Rocks, PA
Ernst, Ruth A. ...United States Senate, Office of the Legislative Counsel, GV
Ernst, Stephen ...Philadelphia, PA
Ernst, Timothy S. ...San Francisco, CA
Ernst, Trudy A. ...Boston, MA
Ernst, W. Ted, Jr. ...Key West, FL
Ernst, W. Ted, Jr., P.A. ...Key West, FL
Ernst, Ward N. ...Stanford, MT
Ernst, Warren M. S. ...Dallas, TX
Ernst, Wendy Anneke ...Lakewood, WA
Ernst, Yaron ...New York, NY
Ernst & Young, LLP ...Cleveland, OH
Ernstein & Ernstein, P.C. West Bloomfield, MI
Ernstein, Gail M. ...West Bloomfield, MI
Ernstein, Robert S. ...West Bloomfield, MI
Ernster, Cletus P., III ...Houston, TX
Ernster, John H. ...Pasadena, CA
Ernster Law Offices, P.C. ...Pasadena, CA
Ernster, Peter G. ...Rahway, NJ
Ernsthaft, William ...New York, NY
Ernsting, Donna Elaine ...Memphis, TN
Ernstoff, Steven E. ...Boston, MA
Ernstoff, Steven E., P.C. ...Boston, MA
Ernstrom & Dreste, LLP ...New York, NY Rochester, NY
Ernstrom, J. William ...New York, NY Rochester, NY
Ernwine, Joseph C. ...Louisville, KY
Erny, Frederick M. ...Cincinnati, OH
Erny, Gabrielle Gros ...Donaldsonville, LA
Erny, James Christopher ...Houma, LA
Erny, John J., Jr. ...Thibodaux, LA
Ernzen, Yvonne M. ...Lenexa, KS
Eroche, William A. ...Houma, LA
Eromin, Frederick W. ...Boston, MA
Eron, Jonathan, Law Office of Collingswood, NJ
Eron, Thomas G. ...Syracuse, NY
Eronini, Uchendu O. ...Charlotte, NC
Eros, Mary Clare ...Charles Town, WV Martinsburg, WV
Erp, Michael B. ...Chicago, IL
Erpelding, Edward J. ...Naples, FL
Erpelding, John W. ...Pacific Palisades, CA
Erpenbeck, Richard W. ...Covington, KY
Erramouspe, Matthew ...Los Angeles, CA
Errant, Karen ...Phoenix, AZ
Errante, Steven J. ...New Haven, CT
Errante, Vincent A., Jr. ...Hartford, CT
Errea, Larry ...Bakersfield, CA
Erreich, Allen J. ...New York, NY
Errett, Kathleen Walsh ...Punta Gorda, FL
Errichetti, Christopher ...Waterbury, CT
Errichetti, Janis L. ...Goshen, NY
Errichetti, Nancy B. ...New York, NY
Errico, Anthony D. ...New York, NY
Errico, Denise M. ...Springfield, NJ
Errico, Frank A. ...Corpus Christi, TX
Errico, Jos. D. ...White Plains, NY
Errico, Mark C. ...Florham Park, NJ
Errico, Melissa ...Tucson, AZ
Errico, Phyllis A. ...Richmond, VA
Errico, V. Douglas ...Braintree, MA
Errington, C. Margaret ...Charlotte, NC
Errington, Colin E. ...Houston, TX
Errington, H Randall ...Kildeer, IL
Errington, Kathryn E. ...Pensacola, FL
Errington, Michael D. ...Toledo, OH
Ersan, Emel Emel ...New York, NY
Ersek, Donna Nicholson Gaithersburg, MD
Ersek, Gregory J. ...Opa Locka, FL
Ershow-Levenberg, Linda S. ...Clark, NJ
Erskine, Amy E. ...Minneapolis, MN
Erskine, Andrew, (P.C.) ...Los Angeles, CA
Erskine, Blake C. ...Longview, TX
Erskine, Blake C., Jr. ...Austin, TX
Erskine, David G. ...Monroe, LA
Erskine, Elizabeth A. ...San Francisco, CA
Erskine & Erskine ...Worcester, MA
Erskine & Fleisher ...Fort Lauderdale, FL
Erskine, G. Randolph ...New Haven, CT
Erskine, Jack ...Austin, TX
Erskine, John M., Jr. ...Austin, TX
Erskine, John P. ...Irvine, CA
Erskine, Kathryn D. ...Department of Commerce, Patent and Trademark Office, GV
Erskine, Kurt R. ...Atlanta, GA
Erskine, Larry R. ...Big Pine Key, FL
Erskine, Linwood M., Jr. ...Worcester, MA
Erskine, Matthew F. ...Worcester, MA
Erskine & McMahon, L.L.P. ...Gilmer, TX Henderson, TX Longview, TX Marshall, TX
Erskine, Morse ...Millbrae, CA
Erskine, Robert S., Jr. ...New York, NY
Erskine, Scott M. ...Farmington Hills, MI
Erskine, Stanley B. ...Fort Lauderdale, FL
Erskine & Tulley, A Professional Corporation ...San Francisco, CA
Erskine, William R., II ...Memphis, TN
Erskine, Wolfson, Gibbon & Fisher, A Professional Corporation Philadelphia, PA
Ersland, Edith L. ...Middleton, WI

Ersland Law Offices ... Middleton, WI
Ersler, Donald J. ... Brookfield, WI
Ersler, Donald J., S.C. ... Brookfield, WI
Ersoff, Victoria L. ... Los Angeles, CA
Erspamer, David M. ... Amery, WI
Erspamer, Gordon P. ... San Francisco, CA
Walnut Creek, CA
Erspamer Law Office ... Amery, WI
Rice Lake, WI
Erspamer, Michael O. ... Chetek, WI
Erspamer, Paul M. ... Waukesha, WI
Erspamer, Thomas S. ... Santa Monica, CA
Erstad, Leon R. ... Minneapolis, MN
Erstad, Richard G. ... Minneapolis, MN
Erstad & Riemer, P.A. ... Minneapolis, MN
Erstad, Tennes I. ... Stanton, NJ
Ersted, Robert S. ... Boynton Beach, FL
Erstling, Helen T. ... Miami, FL
Erstling, Julius H. ... Albany, GA
Erstling, Morton ... Tallahassee, FL
Erstling, Sheila L. ... Tallahassee, FL
Ertel, Allen E., & Associates
Williamsport, PA
Ertel, Karen L. ... Vienna, VA
Ertel, Patrick D. ... Chicago, IL
Ertel, Peter ... Portland, CT
Ertel, Raymond D. ... Washington, DC
Ertel, Richard R. ... Dallas, TX
Ertel, Richard R., P.C. ... Dallas, TX
Ertel, Ruth Robinson ...
Office Of Special Counsel, GV
Ertel, Stephanie L. ... Dallas, TX
Ertel-Sawasky, Anne ... Appleton, WI
Erter, Jack W., Jr. ... Sumter, SC
Erteschik, Louis ... Honolulu, HI
Erthal, Gregory Paul ... Alton, IL
Erthein, John B. ... Setauket, NY
Ertischek, Mark ... Anchorage, AK
Ertischek, Rodney H. ... Briarcliff Manor, NY
Ertl, Bernadette M. ... San Jose, CA
Ertle, John Beardsley, Jr. ... Cleveland, OH
Ertle, Patrick Jay ... Cleveland, OH
Ertler, Mark ... Chicago, IL
Ertl-Lombardi, Deana R. ... Denver, CO
Ertman, David F. ... East Hartford, CT
Ertman, John C. ... New York, NY
Ertman, Robert A.
Department of Agriculture,
Office of the General Counsel, GV
Ertman, Willis M. ... Boston, MA
Ertmann, John C. ... New York, NY
Ertola, Chadwick C. ... San Francisco, CA
Erton, Linda H. ... Schaumburg, IL
Ertsgaard, Duane R. ... Salem, OR
Ertz, Julian S. ... Newport Beach, CA
Ertz, Michael S. ... Milwaukee, WI
Erulkar, Benjamin ... Washington, DC
Erulkar, Eliab S. ... New York, NY
Erum, Theodorico ... Kapaa, HI
Erusha, Bruce A. ... Tempe, AZ
Ervais, Ronald ... Philadelphia, PA
Ervanian, Gregory G.T. ... Des Moines, IA
Erven, Thomas P. ... Cincinnati, OH
Erville, Pierre ... Washington, DC
Ervin, Brian C. ... Bloomington, IL
Ervin, Burgess F. ... Chicago, IL
Ervin, Carlton C. ... New York, NY
Ervin, Carol Brittain ... Charleston, SC
Ervin, Charles (Chuck) H., Law Offices of
Sacramento, CA
Ervin, Cohen & Jessup LLP
Beverly Hills, CA
Los Angeles, CA
Ervin, Cynthia ... Springfield, IL
Ervin, David J. ... McLean, VA
Ervin, Douglas L. ... Lake Oswego, OR
Ervin, Edie R. ... Little Rock, AR
Ervin & Ervin ... Fairfield, CT
Ervin & Ervin ... McAlester, OK
Ervin, Fletcher L. ... Newport, TN
Ervin, Gates & Kelso ... Charlotte, NC
Ervin, Gena Phillips ... Darlington, SC
Ervin, H., & Associates ... Hempstead, NY
Ervin, Hillary Chassen ... Tallahassee, FL
Ervin, James C., Jr. ... Hartford, CT
Ervin, James L, Jr ... Columbus, OH
Ervin, James Mann, Jr. ... Tallahassee, FL
Ervin, James O. ... Baton Rouge, LA
Ervin, John M., III ... Chesterfield, SC
Ervin, John M., III ... Darlington, SC
Ervin, John W., Jr. ... Morganton, NC
Ervin, Julie Berly ... Florence, SC
Ervin, Mark A. ... Muncie, IN
Ervin, Paul R., Jr. ... Marietta, GA
Ervin, Paul R., Jr., P.C. ... Marietta, GA
Ervin, Peter F. ... Louisville, KY
Ervin, Philip M. ... Austin, TX
Ervin, R. Todd ... Nashville, TN
Ervin, Reid H. ... Norfolk, VA
Ervin, Reid H., P.C. ... Norfolk, VA
Virginia Beach, VA
Ervin, Richard W. ... Tallahassee, FL
Ervin, Richard W., III ... Tallahassee, FL
Ervin, Robert C. ... Morganton, NC
Ervin, Robert M. ... Tallahassee, FL
Ervin, Robert M., Jr. ... Tallahassee, FL
Ervin, Roy H. ... Fairfield, CT
Ervin, Roy H., Jr. ... Fairfield, CT
Ervin, Sam J., III ... Morganton, NC
Ervin, Sam J., IV ... Raleigh, NC
Ervin, Sarah A. ... Detroit, MI
Ervin, Shawn J. ... Saratoga, CA
Ervin, Spencer ... Bass Harbor, ME
Ervin, Susan C. ... Washington, DC
Ervin, Teri L. ... Boston, MA
Ervin, Thomas J. ... Anderson, SC
Ervin, Thomas M., Jr. ... Tallahassee, FL
Ervin, Timothy J. ... Boston, MA
Ervin, Varn, Jacobs and Ervin
Tallahassee, FL
Ervin, Wendi R. ... Houston, TX
Ervin, William E. ... Hartford City, IN
Ervin, William J. ... McAlester, OK
Ervin, William J., Jr. ... McAlester, OK
Ervin, William T. ... Mount Pleasant, MI
Ervin, Winfred R. ... Charlotte, NC
Ervin, Winfred R., Jr. ... Charlotte, NC
Ervolina, Anna J. ... Jericho, NY
Erway, Charles E., III ... Morristown, NJ
New York, NY
Erwin, Anne J. ... St. Louis, MO
Erwin and Bernhardt, P.A. ... Charlotte, NC
Erwin, Bethany M. ... Minneapolis, MN
Erwin, C. Mark ... Mobile, AL
Erwin, Charles E. ... Abilene, TX
Erwin, Charles H. ... Mobile, AL
Erwin, Chesley P., Jr. ... Brookfield, WI
Erwin, Christopher M. ... Baltimore, MD
Erwin, Clyde V., Jr. ... Danbury, CT
Erwin, Dan A. ... Chandler, OK
Erwin, Dan Alan, Jr. ... Brownsville, TX
Erwin, David B. ... Tallahassee, FL
Erwin, David J., (P.C.)
Rancho Mirage, CA
Erwin, David R. ... Tucson, AZ
Erwin, Deborah C.
General Services Administration,
Office of the General Counsel, GV
Erwin, Denise Pino ... Denver, CO
Erwin, Don C. ... Detroit, MI
Erwin, Doran E. ... Washington, DC
Erwin, Drew T. ... Quincy, IL
Erwin, E. Alex, III ... Jacksonville, NC
Erwin, Elizabeth J. ... Olympia, WA
Erwin, Fenton T., Jr. ... Charlotte, NC
Erwin, Frank W. ... Emerald Isle, NC
Jacksonville, NC
Swansboro, NC
Erwin, George B., III ... Wauwatosa, WI
Erwin, Gregory DuBois ... Omaha, NE
Erwin, Gregory S. ... Alexandria, LA
Erwin, H. Robert ... Baltimore, MD
Erwin, Harold S. ... Newport, AR
Erwin Harvey ... Omaha, NE
Erwin, Hyle H. ... Lincoln, NE
Erwin, Ingrid Blackwelder ... Greenville, SC
Erwin, J. Roger ... Cincinnati, OH
Erwin, Jacqueline Rohloff ... Jefferson, WI
Erwin, James E. ... Tulsa, OK
Erwin, James N., Jr. ... Houston, TX
Erwin, James P., Jr. ... Asheville, NC
Erwin, James R. ... Portland, ME
Erwin, James S. ... York, ME
Erwin, James S., III ... Clemson, SC
Easley, SC
Erwin, James W. ... St. Louis, MO
Erwin, John R. ... Raleigh, NC
Erwin, John S. ... New York, NY
Scarsdale, NY
Erwin, Joseph B. ... Philadelphia, PA
Erwin, Joseph M. ... Austin, TX
Erwin, Joseph V. ... Canton, OH
Columbus, OH
Erwin, Judith P. ... Jacksonville, FL
Erwin, K. Gregory ... Houston, TX
Erwin, Katherine A. ... Chicago, IL
Erwin, Kenton L. ... Houston, TX
Erwin, Kevin M. ... West Sacramento, CA
Erwin, Kevin P. ... Houston, TX
Erwin, L. Fallasha ... Detroit, MI
Erwin Law Firm, The, P.A.
Baltimore, MD
Erwin, Lawrence W. ... Bend, OR
Erwin, Martin C. ... Sacramento, CA
Erwin, Martin N. ... Greensboro, NC
Erwin, Martinkus & Cole, Ltd.
Champaign, IL
Erwin, Mary Camille ... Louisville, KY
Erwin, Matthew J. ... Costa Mesa, CA
Erwin, Melissa V. ... Birmingham, AL
Erwin, Nancy L. ... Albany, NY
Erwin, Neil T. ... Shreveport, LA
Erwin, Ott, Clark & Campbell ... York, ME
Erwin, Philip O. ... Santa Monica, CA
Erwin, R. Harding, Jr. ... Houston, TX
Erwin, Ralph C. ... Wichita Falls, TX
Erwin, Richard C. ... Winston-Salem, NC
Erwin, Robert C. ... Anchorage, AK
Erwin, Robert F. ... Los Angeles, CA
Erwin, Robert M., Jr. ... Myrtle Beach, SC
Erwin, Robert P., Jr. ... Kansas City, MO
Erwin, Roberta C. ... Anchorage, AK
Erwin, Salle A. ... Southfield, MI
Erwin, Sam ... Champaign, IL
Erwin, Scott R. ... De Kalb, IL
Erwin, Sharon K. ... Houston, TX
Erwin, Sharon M. ... Philadelphia, PA
Erwin, Sharon M., L.L.C., Law Offices of
Philadelphia, PA
Erwin, Sheila L. ... Anchorage, AK
Erwin, Shon T. ... Lawton, OK
Erwin, Simpson & Stroud, P.L.L.C.
Emerald Isle, NC
Jacksonville, NC
Swansboro, NC
Erwin, Steven Lyle ... Plainview, MN
Erwin, Sue C. ... Columbia, SC
Erwin, Thomas C. ... Albany, NY
Erwin, Thomas P. ... Reno, NV
Erwin Thompson & Hascheff ... Elko, NV
Las Vegas, NV
Reno, NV
Erwin, Van, III ... Galloway, OH
Erwin, Walter C., III ... Lynchburg, VA
Erwin, Wilfred H. ... Howell, MI
Erwin, William A. ... Albany, GA
Erwin, William C. ... Angel Fire, NM
Erwin, William F., Jr. ... Houston, TX
Erwin, William M. ... Anchorage, AK
Erwin, William R. ... Danville, KY
Erwin, Woodrow W. ... Franklinton, LA
Erwine, Richard W. ... New York, NY
Erwood, Brent C. ... Kansas City, MO
Erwood, Richard A. ... Indio, CA
Erzen, Mark D. ... Chicago, IL
Esack, Justine M. ... Los Angeles, CA
Esack, Kathleen O'Connor ... Buffalo, NY
Esades, Vincent Jon ... Minneapolis, MN
Esahak-Gage, George ... Phoenix, AZ
Esaki, Amy Ishii ... Kapaa, HI
Esala, Philip J. ... Dayton, OH
Esanu Katsky Korins & Siger, LLP
New York, NY
Esanu, Warren H. ... New York, NY
Esarove, Elizabeth A. ... Columbus, OH
Esary, Gary S. ... Aspen, CO
Esary, Gary S., P.C. ... Aspen, CO
Esary, Sidney R. ... Griffin, GA
Esatto, Paul J., Jr. ... Garden City, NY
Esau, Donald A. ... Vancouver, WA
Esau, Steven ... Bellevue, WA
Esayian, Lisa G. ... Chicago, IL
Esbeck, Carl H. ... Columbia, MO
Esbenshade, Andrew A. ... Los Angeles, CA
Esbenshade, Helen J. ... Philadelphia, PA
West Chester, PA
Esbenshade, Richard D., (A Professional Corporation) ... Los Angeles, CA
Esbenshade, William D. ... Denver, CO
Esber, Brett M. ... Washington, DC
Esber, Eva Petko ... Washington, DC
Esber, Matthew J. ... Austin, TX
Esberg, Tema Feuer ... New York, NY
Esbin, Barbara S. ... Washington, DC
Esbin & Bedell, LLP ... New City, NY
New York, NY
Esbin, Scott L. ... New City, NY
Esbitt, Wm. ... New York, NY
Esborn, Theodore J. ... Cleveland, OH
Escagedo, Ana Maria ... Miami, FL
Escala, Gerald C. ... Tenafly, NJ
Escalante, Julie K. ... San Antonio, TX
Escalante, Kristin Sherratt
Los Angeles, CA
Escalante, Stanley R. ... Irvine, CA
Escalera, Miguel A., Jr. ... Hartford, CT
Escalera, Nitza Milagros ... New York, NY
Escalera, Steve ... El Centro, CA
Escalera, Steve ... El Centro, CA
Escalera Rodriguez, Rafael ... San Juan, PR
Escallier, Susan Kay ... Los Banos, CA
Escalona, Grace L. ... Miami, FL
Escamilla, Elena L. ... Fort Mitchell, KY
Escamilla, John G. ... McAllen, TX
Escamilla, Pablo ... San Antonio, TX
Escamilla & Poneck, Inc.
San Antonio, TX
Escamilla, Samuel Reyes ... Westminster, CO
Escandon, Bernard P. ... Newark, NJ
Escandon, Paul Xavier ... Allenhurst, NJ
Escanellas Rivera, Anibal ... San Juan, PR
Escarciga, Laura M. ... Chicago, IL
Esce, Nicholas J. ... East Syracuse, NY
Esce, Susan N. ... East Syracuse, NY
Esch, Ben ... Nome, AK
Esch, Bryan C. ... Madison, WI
Esch, John H. ... Madison, WI
Esch, Lee E. ... Phoenix, AZ
Esch, Michael D. ... Washington, DC
Esch, Raymond G. ... Toledo, OH
Eschallier, A. R. ... Doylestown, PA
Eschbach, Jesse E. ... West Palm Beach, FL
Eschbach, Leo H. ... Pottstown, PA
Eschbach, Robert M. ... Ottawa, IL
Eschbacher, George R. ... Anchorage, AK
Eschbacher, Timothy J. ... Columbus, OH
Eschberger, Judith A. ... Harrisburg, PA
Eschedor, Jennifer L. ... Cleveland, OH
Eschelbach, Michael A. ... Lansing, MI
Eschelbacher, Michael J. ... Boston, MA
Eschels, Philip C. ... Louisville, KY
Eschen, Andrew M. ... Department of Justice,
Environment and Natural Resources
Division, GV
Eschen & Frenkel, LLP ... West Orange, NJ
Bay Shore, NY
Mineola, NY
Eschen, Seth A. ... Bay Shore, NY
Eschenasy, Aveeram E. ... Los Angeles, CA
Eschenasy, Avy ... New York, NY
Eschenbacher, Romy D. ... Wichita Falls, TX
Eschenburg, Robert L., II
San Antonio, TX
Eschenfelder, Robert Michael
St. Petersburg, FL
Eschenheimer, Whitney M. ... Tulsa, OK
Escher, Henry Joseph, III
San Francisco, CA
Escher, Jill G. ... San Jose, CA
Escher, John, III ... Tucson, AZ
Escher, Patricia G. ... Tucson, AZ
Eschleman, Lisa L. ... Columbus, OH
Eschmann, Frank S. ... Topeka, KS
Eschmann, Jerome H. ... Topeka, KS
Eschmann, Paul ... New York, NY
Eschrich, Suzanne R. ... Tampa, FL
Eschuk, Cara F. ... Waterbury, CT
Eschuk, Paul D. ... Naugatuck, CT
Eschwege, Emanuel ... Boca Raton, FL
Eschweiler, Mary ... San Francisco, CA
Eschweiler, Thomas G. ... Cleveland, OH
Eschwig, W. W. ... Paso Robles, CA
Esckilsen, Christine ... San Diego, CA
Esco, Benjamin M. ... Miami, FL
Esco, Christopher L. ... Coral Gables, FL
Esco, Paul D. ... Montgomery, AL
Esco, W. Jay ... Wichita, KS
Escobar, Ana Maria ... Los Angeles, CA
Escobar, Benjamin A., Jr. ... El Paso, TX
Escobar, Carlos R. ... El Paso, TX
Escobar, Carlos R. ... Houston, TX
Escobar, Christy Brad ... Las Vegas, NV
Escobar, Dana David ... Irvine, CA
Escobar, David ... El Paso, TX
Escobar, David J. ... Fort Worth, TX
Escobar, Elisabeth Roth ... Washington, DC
Escobar and Escobar ... El Paso, TX
Escobar, Jose ... El Paso, TX
Escobar, Manuel G., Jr. ... San Antonio, TX
Escobar, Patricia J. ... Woodland Hills, CA
Escobar, Paul E. ... Moorestown, NJ
Philadelphia, PA
Escobar, Steven R. ... Washington, DC
Escobar, William A. ... New York, NY
Escobar Chanos, Adriana ... Las Vegas, NV
Escobar-Rodriguez, Elsa ... Harlingen, TX
Escobedo, Albert ... Los Angeles, CA
Escobedo, Elias J., Jr. ... Pontiac, MI
Escobedo & Escobedo, Law Office of
El Monte, CA
Escobedo, Irma ... El Monte, CA
Escobedo, Jose, Jr. ... Edinburg, TX
Escobedo, Mildred ... Los Angeles, CA
Escobedo, R. Rene ... San Antonio, TX
Escobedo, Richard E. ... El Monte, CA
Escobedo, Sylvia Y. ... Houston, TX
Escobosa, Paul ... San Francisco, CA
Escoe, J. Delmas ... Silver Spring, MD
Escoe, Marlin R. ... Toccoa, GA
Escoffery, Richard M. ... Atlanta, GA
Escoriaza, Monika Lahiri
New Haven, CT
Escoriaza, Phillip A. ... New Haven, CT
Escoto-Castiello, Maria I. ... Coral Gables, FL
Escott, Alan N. ... Radnor, PA
Escott, Albert M. ... Boston, MA
Escott, Paul D. ... Lafayette, LA
Escovar, Thomas J. ... Cleveland, OH
Escover, Norman C. ... Pleasanton, CA
Escovitz, James A. ... Pittsburgh, PA
Escribano, Elvira A. ... Miami, FL
Escribá Oliver, Antonio R. ... San Juan, PR
Escudero, G. Monique ... New York, NY
Escudero Bonilla, Rafael A. ... San Juan, PR
Escudero-Viera, Antonio ... San Juan, PR
Escudier, Kristie M. ... New Orleans, LA
Escudier, Michael F. ... Chalmette, LA
Escue, Duke T. ... Merrillville, IN
Escue, Merrili L. ... San Diego, CA
Escue, Michael T. ... New York, NY
Escutia, Martha M. ... Los Angeles, CA
Esdaile, Barrett & Esdaile ... Boston, MA
Esdaile, J. Newton ... Boston, MA
Esdaile, James N., Jr. ... Boston, MA
Esdale, R. Graham, Jr. ... Montgomery, AL
Esdale, Robert G. ... Montgomery, AL
Esdorn, Joerg H. ... New York, NY
Esehak, Kenneth G. ... Yonkers, NY
Eselgroth, Carolyn D. ... Dublin, OH
Esely, William J. ... Bethany, MO
Esenberg, Richard M. ... Milwaukee, WI
Esensten, Jack I.
Rolling Hills Estates, CA
Esensten, Robert L. ... Beverly Hills, CA
Esensten, Robert L., A Professional Law Corporation ... Beverly Hills, CA
Esenwein, Brian D. ... Fort Worth, TX
Esernio, George P. ... Garden City, NY
Esfahani, Houtan Khalili ... Washington, DC
Esfahani, Kathleen Forbath ... Santa Ana, CA
Esgar, Kristine L. ... Columbia, SC
Esgro, Patricia C. ... Sacramento, CA
Esgrow, James A. ... Corning, NY
Eshaghian, George M. ... Los Angeles, CA
Eshaghpour, Farhad ... Princeton, NJ
New York, NY
Esham, Tamela E. ... Mobile, AL
Esham, William E., III ... Ocean City, MD
Eshbach, Roseann S.
Department of Education, GV
Eshbaugh, Carl W. ... Knoxville, TN
Eshbaugh, Simpson and Varner
Knoxville, TN
Eshee, William D., Jr. ... Mississippi State, MS
Eshelman, C. Richard ... Akron, OH
Eshelman, David F. ... Winston-Salem, NC
Eshelman, David R. ... Reading, PA
Eshelman, J. William ... Washington, DC
Eshelman, JoAnn ... Sacramento, CA
Eshelman Legal Group ... Akron, OH
Eshelman, Robert A. ... Redmond, WA
Eshelman, Robert P. ... Canton, OH
Eshelman, Rodney L. ... San Francisco, CA
Eshelman, Ross ... Clinton, MO
Eshelman & Shucker, A Professional Corporation ... Reading, PA
Eshelman, Thomas J. ... Reading, PA
Eshelman, Thomas R. ... Philadelphia, PA
Eshelman, W. Richard ... Reading, PA
Eshelman, William E. ... Stafford, VA
Esher, Jacob Aaron ... Cambridge, MA
Esher, Mark R. ... Shawnee, KS
Esherick, Charles R. ... Naples, FL
Eshleman, Dirk E. ... Fort Worth, TX
Eshleman, Robert T. ... Walnut Creek, CA
Eshman, Dennis ... Arlington, VA
Eshman, Patricia S. ... Columbus, OH
Eshman, Thomas H. ... Homosassa, FL
Eshman, Thomas H., II ... Homosassa, FL
Eshoe, Linda ... Los Angeles, CA
Eshoo, Andrew N. ... Modesto, CA
Eshoo, Edward, Jr. ... Chicago, IL

Eshoo, George P. ....Redwood City, CA
Eshraghi, Sharmin Caroline ....Oakland, CA
Eshuis, Penny Colleen ....Los Angeles, CA
Esinhart, Elizabeth Hoyes ....Norfolk, VA
Eskald, James L. ....Largo, FL
Eskald, James L., P.A. ....Largo, FL
Eskandari, Sepideh Suzette ....Seminole, FL
Eskander, Mark B. ....Beverly Hills, CA
Eskanos & Adler, A Professional Corporation
Oakland, CA
Eskanos, David M. ....Los Angeles, CA
Eskanos, Irwin J. ....Oakland, CA
Eskay, Jacquelyn B. ....Phoenix, AZ
Eskay, Robert L., Jr. ....Phoenix, AZ
Eske, James A. ....Lincoln, NE
Eskelsen, Todd R. ....Washington, DC
Eskelson, Scott P. ....Idaho Falls, ID
Eskelson, Thomas Edward ....Denver, CO
Eskenas & Kaplan, P.C. ....Brockton, MA
Eskenas, Leonard A. ....Brockton, MA
Eskenazi, Alan ....San Francisco, CA
Eskenazi, Bonnie E. ....Los Angeles, CA
Eskenazi, Gregg I. ....Redmond, WA
Eskenazi, Ilene R. ....Los Angeles, CA
Eskenazi, Martin ....Seattle, WA
Eskenazi, Mitchell M.
Monroe Township, NJ
Eskenazi, Nancy J. ....Washington, DC
Eskenazi, Phillip J. ....Los Angeles, CA
Eskenazi, Sidney D. ....Indianapolis, IN
Esker, Christopher C. ....Akron, OH
Eskew, Brent ....Longmont, CO
Eskew, Curtis B. ....Corydon, IN
Eskew, Doren R. ....Austin, TX
Eskew, J. Brand ....Blue Springs, MO
Eskey, Leo J. ....Fremont, NE
Eskey, Michael T. ....Providence, RI
Eskigian, Gina Bozajian
Santa Monica, CA
Eskigian, Merak ....Los Angeles, CA
Eskijian, Nancy L. ....Pasadena, CA
Eskildsen, Paul M. ....Washington, DC
Eskildsen, Robert D., Jr. ....Topeka, KS
Eskilson, James R. ....Los Angeles, CA
Eskilson, John S. ....Chicago, IL
Eskin, Amy ....San Francisco, CA
Eskin, Andrew D. ....Washington, DC
Eskin, Barry S. ....San Bernardino, CA
Eskin, Beth L. ....Philadelphia, PA
Eskin, George C. ....Santa Barbara, CA
Ventura, CA
Eskin, Harold S., (P.A.) ....Cape Coral, FL
Eskin & Jackson ....Santa Barbara, CA
Ventura, CA
Eskin, Jeffrey L. ....Las Vegas, NV
Eskin, Mark R. ....Bala Cynwyd, PA
Eskin, Marla Rosoff ....Wilmington, DE
Eskin, Morton H. ....Troy, MI
Eskin, Otho E. ....Washington, DC
Eskin, Ronald B. ....Midland, MI
Eskins, Bradley Wayne ....Memphis, TN
Eskite, Ralph G. ....Austin, TX
Esko, Irwin W. ....Chicago, IL
Esko, Stephen B. ....New York, NY
Eskola, Richard S. ....Fridley, MN
Eskovitz, Sean ....Washington, DC
Eskow, Lisa R. ....Austin, TX
Eskridge & Associates ....Los Angeles, CA
Torrance, CA
Eskridge, Charles R., III ....Houston, TX
Eskridge, Gayle L. ....Torrance, CA
Eskridge, Jack D. ....Walnut Creek, CA
Eskridge, Janelle R. ....Memphis, TN
Eskridge, Jeremy J. ....Tupelo, MS
Eskridge, Laurin N. ....Dallas, TX
Eskridge, T. Hillis ....Tulsa, OK
Eskridge, William Inge ....Montgomery, AL
Eskridge, William W. ....Abingdon, VA
Eskrigge, John V. ....Jackson, MS
Eskwith, Lawrence A. ....Edwards, CO
Vail, CO
Eskwitt, Scott A. ....Red Bank, NJ
Eslamboly, Bahman ....Los Angeles, CA
Eslami, Shahram A. ....Atlanta, GA
Esleeck, Robert E. ....Winston-Salem, NC
Esler, Brian W. ....Seattle, WA
Esler, C. Marshall, Jr. ....Dayton, OH
Esler, Eric A. ....San Francisco, CA
Esler, Gary A. ....Fort Lauderdale, FL
Esler, John A. ....Kaukauna, WI
Esler & Lindie, P.A. ....Fort Lauderdale, FL
Esler, Michael J. ....Portland, OR
Esler, Robert W. ....Detroit, MI
Esler, Stephens & Buckley ....Portland, OR
Esler, Thomas J. ....Chicago, IL
Eslick, Dennis J. ....Chicago, IL
Eslien, Howard J. ....Oconto Falls, WI
Eslien, Howard W. ....Oconto Falls, WI
Eslinger, Henry J. ....Grand Forks, ND
Eslinger, Larry K. ....Sacramento, CA
Eslinger, Robin D. ....Grand Rapids, MI
Eslinger, Victoria L. ....Columbia, SC
Eslocker, Hodson & Oremus, Co., L.P.A.
Athens, OH
Eslocker, Thomas E. ....Athens, OH
Esmail, Aaftab P. ....Los Angeles, CA
Esmaili, Salah ....San Francisco, CA
Esman, Marjorie R. ....New Orleans, LA
Esman, Marjorie R., A Professional Law Corporation ....New Orleans, LA
Esmay, M. Dennis ....East Lansing, MI
Esmel, Jennifer ....Yarmouth Port, MA
Esmerado, John ....Elizabeth, NJ
Esmon, Gregory K. ....Austin, TX
San Antonio, TX
Esmond, Robert W. ....Washington, DC
Esmont, Donald E. ....South Bend, IN
Esnard, John B., III ....Metairie, LA

Esnard, R. Paul ....Newport Beach, CA
Esnard, Roy A. ....Syracuse, NY
Esner & Chang ....Los Angeles, CA
San Francisco, CA
Esner, Stuart B. ....Los Angeles, CA
Esoian, Mitchell ....Hartford, CT
Eson, J. Cindy ....Miami, FL
Esordi Hornby & Sawicki ....Wyandotte, MI
Esordi, Thomas D. ....Wyandotte, MI
Esp, Douglas J. ....Lisle, IL
Esp, Lynn W. ....Naperville, IL
Espach, Robert W. ....Sag Harbor, NY
Espada-Platet, Luis ....Department of State, Foreign Service Officers (Overseas), GV
Espaldon, Karen M. ....Washington, DC
Espar, John M. ....Joliet, IL
Esparraguera, Maria ....Oceanport, NJ
Esparza, Elaine M. ....Harper, KS
Esparza, James ....Salt Lake City, UT
Esparza, Joseph A. ....San Antonio, TX
Esparza, Mario A. ....Las Cruces, NM
Esparza, Mark ....Brownsville, TX
Esparza, Michele P. ....Bryan, TX
Esparza, Rosemary J. ....San Diego, CA
Esparza, Terri Marie ....San Francisco, CA
Esparza, Valerie R. ....Austin, TX
Espat, K. Mitch ....Orlando, FL
Espedal, John Charles ......San Francisco, CA
Espejo, Barbara Gordon ......Pleasant Valley, NY
Espejo, Pierre M. ....Houston, TX
Espel, Larry D. ....Minneapolis, MN
Espeland, Lynn L. ....Omaha, NE
Espelien, Jill Margaret ....Kansas City, MO
Espenkotter, Alex ....Miami, FL
Espenscheid, Alaine T. ....Geneva, NY
Espenschied, Diana ....Canton, OH
Espenschied, Lenné Eidson ....Atlanta, GA
Espenshade, John W. ....Lancaster, PA
Espenshade, Virginia M. ....Homer, AK
Espenship, Jennifer Katz ......Jacksonville, FL
Espenship, Sean A. ....Jacksonville, FL
Esper, David J. ....Plymouth, MI
Esper, David J., Law Offices of, P.C.
Plymouth, MI
Esper, Dilan A. ....Los Angeles, CA
Esper, James, Jr ....Monongahela, PA
Esper, Joseph U. ....Pittsburgh, PA
Esper Law Office ....El Paso, TX
Esper, Mitchell (Mickey) ....El Paso, TX
Esper, Richard D. ....El Paso, TX
Esper, Thomas L. ....Cleveland, OH
Esperanza, Shirley Jane ....Tampa, FL
Esperian, Joni ....Manchester, NH
Esperian, Joni N. ....Manchester, NH
Esperne, Eric G. P. ....Arlington, VA
Esperon, Rosaria Rodriguez ....New York, NY
Esperson, Thomas R. ....Sunnyvale, CA
Esperti, Peterson & Cahoone, The Law Firm of ....Sarasota, FL
Esperti, Robert A., (P.C.) ....Tucson, AZ
Espeseth, Ross ....Bismarck, ND
Espey, Camille L. ....Austin, TX
Espey, Frederic C. ....San Francisco, CA
Espey, Lowell E. ....Flemington, NJ
Espey, Richard W. ....San Antonio, TX
Espey, Robert H., II ....Austin, TX
Espey & Szabo ....Flemington, NJ
Espey-Francis, Lucille M. ....Tavares, FL
Espey-Romero, Ruth ....Washington, DC
Espiefs, Peter S. ....Keene, NH
Espinales, Kimberly ....Paramus, NJ
Esping, Theodore J. ....Indianapolis, IN
Espino, A. Michael ....Holbrook, AZ
Espino, Alejandro ....Fort Lauderdale, FL
Espino, Luis A. ....Miami, FL
Espino, Ozzy, II ....Lantana, FL
Espino, Salvador ....Arlington, TX
Espinola, Kevin B. ....Costa Mesa, CA
Espinosa * Sitterly * Associates
Albuquerque, NM
Espinosa, A. Greg ....Riverside, CA
Espinosa, Anita L. ....Denver, CO
Espinosa, Catherine R. ....Miami, FL
Espinosa, Daniel R. ....Santa Ana, CA
Espinosa, Eduardo S. ....Dallas, TX
Espinosa, James G. ....Framingham, MA
Espinosa, Jorge ....Miami, FL
Espinosa, Jose A. ....Jamaica Plain, MA
Espinosa, Juan Guillermo ....Weehawken, NJ
Espinosa, Leonard G. ....Albuquerque, NM
Espinosa, Lourdes Rodriguez ....Fresno, CA
Espinosa, Michael A. ....Grand Rapids, MI
Espinosa, Noemi C. ....Palo Alto, CA
Espinosa, Patricia O. ....Miami, FL
Espinosa, Philip G. ....Tucson, AZ
Espinosa, Robert A. ....El Centro, CA
Santa Ana, CA
Espinosa, William H. ....Washington, DC
Espinoza, David J. ....Columbus, OH
Espinoza, Patrick L. ....San Diego, CA
Espinoza, Renelde M. ....Irvine, CA
Espinoza, Richard A. ....Baldwin Park, CA
Espinoza, Richard A. and Virginia Taylor, Law Offices of ....Baldwin Park, CA
Espinoza, Rodney J. ....Baldwin Park, CA
Espinoza, Ron ....Los Angeles, CA
Espinoza, Stephen B. ....Los Angeles, CA
Espinoza, Thomas J. ....Salinas, CA
Esplin, DaLon ....Blackfoot, ID
Esplin, Gordon F. ....Fort Collins, CO
Esplin, Louise ....Salt Lake City, UT
Esplin, Michael D. ....Provo, UT
Espo, Caryn S. ....Pacific Palisades, CA
Espo, Joseph B. ....Baltimore, MD
Espohl, Frank E. ....Cincinnati, OH
Espohl, Frank Eric ....Cincinnati, OH
Espohl, Virginia B. ....Cincinnati, OH
Esposito, Anthony ....Whitestone, NY

Esposito, Anthony S. ....New York, NY
Esposito, Carmine J. ....Whitestone, NY
Esposito, Carol Lynn ....Hempstead, NY
Esposito, Charles A. ....St. Augustine, FL
Esposito, Charles J. ....New York, NY
Esposito, Christopher L. ....Bronx, NY
Esposito, Daniel E. ....Somerville, NJ
Esposito, Daniel R. ....Liberty Corner, NJ
Esposito, David V. ....Hamden, CT
Esposito, Denise ....Washington, DC
Esposito, Dennis H. ....Boston, MA
Providence, RI
Esposito, D. J. ....Richmond, VA
Esposito, Dominick C., Jr. ....Stewartsville, NJ
Esposito, Donald R., Jr. ....Charlotte, NC
Esposito & Esposito ......Hilton Head Island, SC
Logan, WV
Esposito, Eugene ....Chicago, IL
Esposito, Faith Dillow ....Bristol, VA
Esposito, Francine ....Roseland, NJ
Esposito, Francis H.
Department of the Air Force, Office of the Judge Advocate General, GV
Esposito, George R. ....Freehold, NJ
Esposito, Gerard F. ....Derby, CT
Esposito, Grant J. ....New York, NY
Esposito, Heuel & Schramm ....Chicago, IL
Esposito, James ....New York, NY
Esposito, James M. ....Greenwich, CT
Esposito, Jewell Lim ....Washington, DC
Esposito, John C. ....Brooklyn, NY
Esposito, John J., Jr. ....New Haven, CT
Esposito, John J., (P.C.) ....New Haven, CT
Esposito, John M., Law Offices
Cedar Grove, NJ
Newark, NJ
Esposito, John Salvatore ....New York, NY
Esposito, John V. ....Hilton Head Island, SC
Logan, WV
Esposito, Joseph A. ....Spokane, WA
Esposito, Joseph E. ....Liberty Corner, NJ
Esposito, Joseph L. ....Tucson, AZ
Esposito, Joseph P., (P.C.)
Washington, DC
Esposito, Julie A. ....Los Angeles, CA
Esposito, Kathleen C. ....Elmhurst, IL
Esposito, Larry J. ....Hackensack, NJ
Esposito, Lauren ....New York, NY
Esposito, Lesli C. ....Washington, DC
Esposito, Licia A. ....Saratoga Springs, NY
Esposito, Lisa Ann ....Tampa, FL
Esposito, Louis C. ....Cedar Grove, NJ
Esposito, Marc J. ....Atlanta, GA
Esposito, Mario A. ....Chicago, IL
Esposito, Marisa ....New York, NY
Esposito, Mark G. ....Moorestown, NJ
Esposito, Mark L. ....Abingdon, VA
Bristol, VA
Esposito, Mark M. ....Richmond, VA
Esposito, Mary T. ....Cape Elizabeth, ME
Esposito, Michael A. ....Columbus, OH
Esposito, Michael A. ....Logan, WV
Esposito, Michael D. ....Boca Raton, FL
Parsippany, NJ
Esposito, Michael F. ....Murray Hill, NJ
Esposito, Michael R. ....River Forest, IL
Esposito, Michael R. ....Morristown, NJ
Esposito, Nicholas F. ....Chicago, IL
Esposito, Pamela P. ....Philadelphia, PA
Esposito, Paul J. ....Harrisburg, PA
Esposito, Paul V. ....Chicago, IL
Esposito, Peter G. ....Washington, DC
Esposito, Ralph J. ....Paramus, NJ
Esposito, Ralph J. ....Rochester, NY
Esposito, Robert S. ....Blue Bell, PA
Philadelphia, PA
Esposito, Roger L. ....White Plains, NY
Esposito, Ronald F. ....Elizabeth, NJ
Esposito, Ronald K. ....Houston, TX
Esposito, Rose Marie ....Logan, WV
Esposito, Serafina M. ....Dallas, TX
Esposito, Stanley E. ....Pleasantville, NY
Esposito, Stephen C. ....Oak Park, IL
Esposito, Thomas E. ....Logan, WV
Esposito, Thomas R. ....New York, NY
Esposito, Tombari, George, Topliff & Campbell, A Professional Service Corporation ....Spokane, WA
Esposito, Valerie Merti ....Pittsburgh, PA
Esposito, Vincent M.
Huntington Station, NY
Esposito, Vincent P., Jr. ....Albany, NY
Esposito-Marshall, Lynn A. ....Somerset, NJ
Espy, Alan C. ....West Palm Beach, FL
Espy, Alan C., P.A. ....West Palm Beach, FL
Espy, Ben E. ....Columbus, OH
Espy & Benton ....Columbus, OH
Espy, Carolyn A. ....Baltimore, MD
Espy, Collier H., Jr. ....Dothan, AL
Espy, Isaac P. ....Tuscaloosa, AL
Espy, Joseph C., III ....Montgomery, AL
Espy & Metcalf, P.C. ....Dothan, AL
Espy, Mike ....Jackson, MS
Espy, Nettles, Scogin and Brantley, P.C.
Birmingham, AL
Tuscaloosa, AL
Espy, Wilma Grimes ....Atlanta, GA
Esquea & Valenzuela ....New York, NY
Esqueda, Carlos A. ....Salt Lake City, UT
Esquenazi, Salomon B. ....Coral Gables, FL
Esquer, Cecilia D. ....Sacaton, AZ
Esquibel, Floyd A. ....Cheyenne, WY
Esquibel, Thomas C. ....Albuquerque, NM
Esquibias, Bridget A. ....Los Angeles, CA
Esquibias, David A. ....Camarillo, CA
Esquina, Leonard, Jr. ....Lansing, MI
Esquinaldo, Steven B. ....Key West, FL
Esquinaldo, Steven B., P.A. ....Key West, FL

Esquirol, John H., Jr. ....Watertown, MA
Esquirol, Joseph A., Jr. ....Mattituck, NY
Esquiroz, Margaret ....Encino, CA
Esquiroz, Margarita ....Miami, FL
Esquivel, Diana ....Oakland, CA
Esquivel, Ed. H. ....Dallas, TX
Esquivel, Hector F.
Hilton Head Island, SC
Esquivel, John M. ....Houston, TX
Esquivel, Jose A., Jr. ....Brownsville, TX
Esquivel, Julio C. ....Tampa, FL
Esquivel, Magdeline R. ....Dallas, TX
Esquivel, Martin R. ....Albuquerque, NM
Esquivel, Mary Ann ....Morris Plains, NJ
Esquivel, Patricio ....Phoenix, AZ
Esquivel, Roel ....Edinburg, TX
Esquivel, Sylvia R. ....Los Angeles, CA
Esquivel, Teodoro F. ....Novato, CA
Esrael, Sandra L. ....Madison, WI
Esraelian, Robyn L. ....Fresno, CA
Esrey, Denise L. ....Nevada City, CA
Esrick, Edward E. ....Staten Island, NY
Esrick, Jerald P. ....Chicago, IL
Esrig, Jerry A. ....Chicago, IL
Ess, Gerry A. ....Taylorville, IL
Ess, Henry N., III ....New York, NY
Ess, John A. ....Edwardsville, IL
Essa, Daniel F. ....East Lansing, MI
Essad, Ernest J., Jr. ....Bloomfield Hills, MI
Essad, Kenneth M. ....Detroit, MI
Essad, Scott C. ....Youngstown, OH
Essary, Bryan ....Nashville, TN
Essary, Jean ....Dolton, IL
Essary, Kimberly S. ....Benton, MO
Essayan, Gregory J. ....White Plains, NY
Essaye, Anne E. ....Charlotte, NC
Essaye, Anthony F. ....Washington, DC
Esseks, Hefter & Angel ....Riverhead, NY
Water Mill, NY
Esseks, James D. ....New York, NY
Esseks, William Watson ....Riverhead, NY
Water Mill, NY
Esselburne, Peter C. ....New Holland, OH
Esselstein, Lynne E. ....Menlo Park, CA
Esselstein, William D. ....Menlo Park, CA
Esselstein, Wright, Jones & Greenberg, A Professional Corporation
Menlo Park, CA
Essen, Bruce M. ....Fort Myers, FL
Essen, Essen, Susaneck, Canet & Lipson, P.A. ....Fort Lauderdale, FL
Miami, FL
Naples, FL
West Palm Beach, FL
Essen, Jeff Erick ....Raleigh, NC
Essen, Richard ....Miami, FL
West Palm Beach, FL
Essenburg, Jan L. ....Seattle, WA
Essenburg, Julie B. ....Dallas, TX
Essenburg, Reindert J. ....Dallas, TX
Essenburg, Sheryl K. ....Springfield, IL
Essene, Karen A. ....Honolulu, HI
Essenfeld, Ann P.
Equal Employment Opportunity Commission, GV
Essenson, James L. ....Sarasota, FL
Essepian, Charles H. ....Latham, NY
Esser, Bradley & Lundy ....Sedona, AZ
Esser, Carl E. ....Philadelphia, PA
Esser, Christine D. ....Milwaukee, WI
Esser, Darren J. ....New York, NY
Esser, Diane H. ....Greenfield, MA
Esser, Donald E. ....Mason City, IA
Esser, Eric D. ....San Francisco, CA
Esser, Fred R. ....Sedona, AZ
Esser, George H. ....Chapel Hill, NC
Esser, James G. ....Henderson, KY
Esser, James G., P.S.C. ....Henderson, KY
Esser, Jane Gale ....Glencoe, IL
Esser, Karen Rapaport ....Washington, DC
Esser, Mary Anne Mascolino ....Dallas, TX
Esser, Michelle Robertson
Philadelphia, PA
Esser, Peter Joseph Christian
Washington, DC
Esser, Peter V. N. ....Saipan, TT
Esser, Terry P. ....Tucson, AZ
Esser, Timothy H. ....Pullman, WA
Esser, William F. ....Dallas, TX
Esser-Ellicott, Jessica ....Rutland, VT
Esserman, Dean M. ....New York, NY
Esserman, Norman S. ....Highland Park, IL
Esserman, Sander L. ....Dallas, TX
Esserman, Susan G.
Executive Office Of The President, Office of the U.S. Trade Representative, GV
Esses, Craig ....Stamford, CT
Esses, Eli ....New York, NY
Esses, Jeffrey Alan ....Denver, CO
Essex, Kenneth F. ....Charlotte, NC
Essex, Maureen Frances ....Rockville, MD
Essex, Nancy Bentson ....Raleigh, NC
Essex, Paul B. ....Beltsville, MD
Essex, Richards, Morris, Jordan & Matus, P.A. ....Charlotte, NC
Essex, Susan R. ....Burbank, CA
Essex, Thomas ....Lebanon, OH
Essex, Thomas D. ....Fort Wayne, IN
Essey, Mark G. ....North Miami, FL
Essey, Norman A. ....Columbus, OH
Esshaki, Gene J. ....Detroit, MI
Essi, Brian J. ....Cleveland, OH
Essi, David, Jr. ....Lakewood, OH
Essick, Robert J. ....Southfield, MI
Essien, Victor L. K. ....New York, NY
Essig, Beth ....New York, NY
Essig, David R. ....Philadelphia, PA
Essig, Dean R. ....Washington, IL

Essig, Ellen ....Cincinnati, OH
Essig, Fred D. ....Salt Lake City, UT
Essig, Gerald ....Commack, NY
Essig, James E. ....Houston, TX
Essig, Lawrence J. ....Springfield, IL
Essig, Leonard J. ....St. Louis, MO
Essig, Lester K. ....Salt Lake City, UT
Essig, Paul T. ....Reading, PA
Essig, Phillip C. ....Rocky Mount, VA
Essig, Robert D. ....Syracuse, NY
Essig, Sheila Marianne ....Chicago, IL
Essig, William V. ....Chicago, IL
Essin, W. Robert ....Vail, CO
Essington, Michael P. ....Miami, FL
Essique, Christine R. ....Troy, MI
Essis, June J. ....Philadelphia, PA
Essler, Karl S. ....Rochester, NY
Essling, David E. ....St. Paul, MN
Essling, Mark P. ....St. Paul, MN
Esslinger, J. Thomas ....Washington, DC
Essman, James H. ....Midland, TX
Essman, James W. ....Midland, TX
Essmann, Gary A. ....Milwaukee, WI
Essmann, Jeffrey V. ....Billings, MT
Essmyer, Michael M. ....Houston, TX
Essmyer & Tritico, L.L.P. ....Houston, TX
Essner, Allen P., (P.C.) ....New York, NY
Essner, Allison ....New York, NY
Essner, David B. ....Milwaukee, WI
Essner, Gene ....Atlanta, GA
Essner, Howard ....New York, NY
Essner, Howard S. ....Hudson, OH
Essner, Jeffrey E. ....San Jose, CA
Essner, Lee B. ....El Segundo, CA
Esson, R. Christopher ....Dallas, TX
Essrig, C. Lee ....Boston, MA
Essrig, Katherine G. ....Tampa, FL
Esswein, Richard J. ....St. Louis, MO
Estabrook & Associates, A Professional Corporation ....Fairfax, VA
McLean, VA
Estabrook, David Mcc. ....McLean, VA
Estabrook, Gregory ....Sacramento, CA
Estabrook, James K. ....Westfield, NJ
Estabrook, Jennifer O. ....New Britain, CT
Estabrook, Kenneth L. ....Westfield, NJ
Estabrook, Madeleine A. ....Boston, MA
Estabrook, Ray C. ....Santa Rosa, CA
Estabrook, Stanley R. ....Sacramento, CA
Estabrook, Steven H. ....Beverly Hills, CA
Estabrook, Timothy J. ....Houston, TX
Estabrook, William S., III
Department of Justice, Tax Division, GV
Estabrook, William T. ....Gaithersburg, MD
Estabrooks, Kathleen B. ....Cranford, NJ
Estabrooks, Kathleen B., P.C. ....Cranford, NJ
Estacio, Richard A. ....Wilmington, DE
Estadt, John R. ....St. Clairsville, OH
Estall, John ....Eden Prairie, MN
Estate Crafters ....Brooklyn Center, MN
Estate Law Group ....Menlo Park, CA
Palo Alto, CA
Estate Planning Services, A Professional Law Corporation ....Pasadena, CA
Estaver, Phillip M. ....Chicago, IL
Estay Lowery & Cuccurullo ....Phoenix, AZ
Estay Lowery, Laura ....Phoenix, AZ
Esteban, Amor A. ....San Francisco, CA
Estebo, Audrey L. ....Minneapolis, MN
Estebo, Orrin S. ....Redwood Falls, MN
Estebo, Schnobrich, Frank, Solie & Gilk, Ltd.
Redwood Falls, MN
Estee, Charles ....San Antonio, TX
Estee, Cynthia J. ....San Antonio, TX
Estefan, Arthur A. ....San Antonio, TX
Este-Green, Donna ....Hempstead, NY
Estel, C. Vernon, Jr. ....Fairmont, WV
Estela, Emilio ....New York, NY
Estell, Barry D. ....Mission, KS
Estell, Patricia ....Riverside, CA
Estell, Reginald, Jr. ....Jacksonville, FL
Estelle, Stephen D. ....Columbus, OH
Esten, Lawrence D. ....Irvine, CA
Estep, A. Lee ....San Diego, CA
Estep, Brian K. ....New London, CT
Estep, C. Paul ....Morgantown, WV
Estep, David F. ....Monterey Park, CA
Estep & Estep ....Tazewell, TN
Estep, F. Lynn, Jr. ....Dallas, TX
Estep, Garrett M. ....Memphis, TN
Estep, Gary L. ....Columbus, OH
Estep, Ida W. ....Maynard, MA
Estep, James D., III ....Tazewell, TN
Estep, James D., Jr. ....Tazewell, TN
Estep, James M. ....Department of Labor, Office of the Solicitor, GV
Estep, Landon R. ....Bellevue, WA
Estep, Madonna C. ....Charleston, WV
Estep, Michael J. ....San Mateo, CA
Estep, Michael T. ....Mobile, AL
Estep, Robert L. ....Dallas, TX
Estep, Robert M. ....Tazewell, TN
Estep, Ruth L. ....Beverly Hills, CA
Estep, Saml. D. ....Ann Arbor, MI
Estep, Shawn Joseph ....St. Charles, MO
Estep, Steven J. ....Atlanta, GA
Estep, Thomas B., Sr. ....Springfield, IL
Estep & Warren ....San Diego, CA
Ester, Elizabeth K. ....Chicago, IL
Ester, John W. ....Farmington Hills, MI
Esterak, Heath D. ....San Antonio, TX
Esterces, Howard M. ....Garden City, NY
Esterces, Howard M., P.C.
Garden City, NY
Estergren, Frederick B., (P.A.)
Fort Walton Beach, FL
Esterhai, John L. ....Lansdale, PA
Esterkin, James ....Portland, OR
Esterkin, Richard W. ....Los Angeles, CA
Esterle, Mark D. ....Bowling Green, KY
Esterman, David N. ....New York, NY
Esterman, Lester ....New York, NY
Esterman, Marc R. ....Stamford, CT
Esterman, Pamela R. ....New York, NY
White Plains, NY
Esterman & Reich ....New York, NY
Estern, Peter A. ....San Jose, CA
Esters, Cory D. ....Los Angeles, CA
Esterson, Andrea L. ....Los Angeles, CA
Estes, Benjamin G. ....Atlanta, GA
Estes, Carl, II ....Houston, TX
Estes, Carol Ann ....Jackson, MS
Estes, Carol Anne ....Abilene, TX
Estes, Carole J. ....Jackson, MS
Estes, Charee B ....San Clemente, CA
Estes, Charles N., Jr. ....Albuquerque, NM
Estes, Cheryl Rumage ....Memphis, TN
Estes, Christopher B. ....Mobile, AL
Estes, David G. ....San Francisco, CA
Estes, David H. ....Dallas, TX
Estes, David J. ....Scottsdale, AZ
Estes, Dawn ....Dallas, TX
Estes, Doyle D. ....Rapid City, SD
Estes, Edwin W., Jr. ....Vista, CA
Estes, Elizabeth A. ....San Francisco, CA
Estes, Elizabeth M. ....Milwaukee, WI
Estes, Ellen G. ....Woodbridge, CT
Estes, Ernest E. ....Portland, OR
Estes & Estes ....San Clemente, CA
Estes, Estes & Gramling, PLC
Fayetteville, AR
Estes & Estes, P.A. ....Biloxi, MS
Gulfport, MS
Estes, Frank W. ....New Haven, CT
Estes, George E., III ....Gulfport, MS
Estes, George E., Jr. ....Gulfport, MS
Estes, Gerre Denise ....Tulsa, OK
Estes, Harper ....Midland, TX
Estes, Hoyt & Hansen, A Professional Corporation ....San Diego, CA
Estes, J. Michael ....Richmond, VA
Estes, James L., Jr. ....Tampa, FL
Estes, James T., Jr. ....Honolulu, HI
Estes, Jerry C. ....Fort Dodge, IA
Estes, Jerry N. ....Athens, TN
Estes, Jerry S. ....Austin, TX
Estes, Joel C. ....San Diego, CA
Estes, John E. ....New York, NY
Estes, John L. ....Dallas, TX
Estes, John N., III ....Washington, DC
Estes, K. E. ....Houston, TX
Estes, Kelly Hubbard ....Birmingham, AL
Estes Law Firm ....Minneapolis, MN
Estes Law Firm ....Rapid City, SD
Estes Law Offices ....Fort Dodge, IA
Estes, Lee ....West Bloomfield, MI
Estes, Lisa Shaw ....Atlanta, GA
Estes, Lynn E., Jr. ....Shreveport, LA
Estes, M. Reid, Jr. ....Nashville, TN
Estes, M. Todd ....Sherman, TX
Estes, Mark ....Los Angeles, CA
Estes Mask, Smallwood & Smallwood
Tupelo, MS
Estes, Matthew W. S. ....Washington, DC
Estes, Max Eugene ....Dodge City, KS
Estes, Max Eugene, P.A. ....Dodge City, KS
Estes, Michael A. ....Orlando, FL
Estes, Monte D. ....Little Rock, AR
Estes, Pamela K. ....Boston, MA
Estes, Paul C. ....Peoria, IL
Estes, Peter G., Jr. ....Fayetteville, AR
Estes, Phillip Grant ....Anniston, AL
Estes, Polly J. ....San Antonio, TX
Estes, R. Donald ....Minneapolis, MN
Estes, R. Scott ....Lawrenceville, GA
Estes, R. Scott, P.C. ....Lawrenceville, GA
Estes, R. Timothy ....Birmingham, AL
Estes, R. Wayne ....Malibu, CA
Estes, Richard M. ....New York, NY
Estes, Robert K. ....Miami, FL
Estes, Robert L. ....Delhi, NY
Estes, Robert L. (Larry) ....Nashville, TN
Estes, Robert R. ....Fayetteville, AR
Estes, Robin Marie ....Santa Rosa, CA
Estes, Ronald D. ....Wenatchee, WA
Estes, Royce J. ....St. Louis, MO
Estes, Sarah B. ....Atlanta, GA
Estes, Stephen C. ....Houston, TX
Estes, Stephen C., P.C. ....Houston, TX
Estes, Steve ....Moore, OK
Estes, Stewart A. ....Seattle, WA
Estes, T. David ....San Clemente, CA
Estes, Theodore D. ....Orlando, FL
Estes, Thomas B. ....Phenix City, AL
Estes, Thomas Howard, Jr. ....Alexandria, VA
Estes, Todd ....Oklahoma City, OK
Estes, Tommy C. ....Nashville, TN
Estes, Virginia D. ....San Diego, CA
Estes, William ....Richmond, TX
Estes, William, P.C. ....Richmond, TX
Estess, George W. ....Fort Walton Beach, FL
Panama City, FL
Pensacola, FL
Estess, Glenn E., Jr. ....Birmingham, AL
Estess, Rudolph, Jr. ....Baton Rouge, LA
Esteva, Henry ....St. Petersburg, FL
Esteve, Edward V. ....Patchogue, NY
Esteves, Alexander M. ....Boston, MA
Esteves, Elvin ....Newark, NJ
Esteves, Jose A. ....New York, NY
Esteves, Juan F. ....San Juan, PR
Estevez, Ana E. ....Amarillo, TX
Estevez, Anne Marie ....Miami, FL
Estevez, Enrique G. ....Orlando, FL
Estevez, Luisa ....Bayonne, NJ
Estevez, Mareza I. ....New York, NY
Estevez, Oscar J. ....Miami, FL
Estevez, Richard J. ....Arlington, VA
Estey, John H. ....Philadelphia, PA
Estey, John S. ....Philadelphia, PA
Estey, Stephen R. ....Detroit, MI
Estey, Wade ....Palo Alto, CA
Estill, John F. ....Maysville, KY
Estill, John S., Jr. ....Tulsa, OK
Estill, Susan L. ....Burnsville, MN
Estin, Ann Laquer ....Boulder, CO
Estis, Dennis A. ....Woodbridge, NJ
Estis, Nathan ....West Palm Beach, FL
Estis, Warren A. ....New York, NY
Estiverne, Nicolas, & Associates
New Orleans, LA
Estle, Mark D. ....San Diego, CA
Estlinbaum, Craig ....Bay City, TX
Estlund, Cynthia L. ....Washington, DC
Estlund, Tim A. ....Cedar Rapids, IA
Estner, Martin I. ....Boston, MA
Estock, Howard G. ....New York, NY
Estoff, Jonathan D. ....Buffalo, NY
Estok, John J. ....Erie, PA
Estok, Paul J. ....Tucson, AZ
Estolano, Cecilia V. ....Los Angeles, CA
Estolano, Gloria ....San Francisco, CA
Estopinal, Fernando J., III ....Slidell, LA
Estopinal, James D. ....Slidell, LA
Estorge, Leonard F. ....Metairie, LA
Estrada, Adriana ....San Francisco, CA
Estrada, Armand M. ....Livermore, CA
Estrada, Arturo ....Treasury Department, Internal Revenue Service, GV
Estrada, Carlos E. ....Cambridge, MA
Estrada, Carlos R. ....Phoenix, AZ
Estrada, Carolina J. ....New York, NY
Estrada, David J. ....Cupertino, CA
Estrada, Edward J. ....Washington, DC
Estrada, José ....Tampa, FL
Estrada, Jose L. ....Tampa, FL
Estrada, Larry F. ....San Jose, CA
Estrada, Linda M. ....Rockville, MD
Estrada, Lionel C. ....Phoenix, AZ
Estrada, Michael ....Los Angeles, CA
Estrada, Michael J. ....San Francisco, CA
Estrada, Michele U. ....Albuquerque, NM
Estrada, Miguel A. ....Washington, DC
Estrada, Nicolas J. ....Marina Del Rey, CA
Estrada, Peter F. ....Sebring, FL
Estrada, R. George ....Phoenix, AZ
Estrada, Ramoñ ....San Diego, CA
Estrada, Rebecca ....El Paso, TX
Estrada, Robert A. ....Dallas, TX
Estrada, Robert F. ....San Antonio, TX
Estrada, Robert F., P.C. ....San Antonio, TX
Estrada, Robert G. ....Wichita Falls, TX
Estrada, Ruth I. ....Beverly Hills, CA
Estrada, Thelma K. ....San Francisco, CA
Estrada & Thomson ....Livermore, CA
Estradas, Anthony R. ....Los Angeles, CA
Estreen, David J. ....Hudson, WI
Estreich, Sonia S. ....New York, NY
Estreicher, Aleta G. ....New York, NY
Estreicher, Herbert ....Washington, DC
Estreicher, Jane L. ....St. Petersburg, FL
Estreicher, Samuel ....New York, NY
Estrella, Cynthia R. ....Phoenix, AZ
Estrella, Mark P. ....Los Angeles, CA
Estrella, Richard F. ....New York, NY
Estrella, William ....San Juan, PR
Estrella, William, P.S.C., Law Offices
San Juan, PR
Estrella Conesa, Alberto G. ....San Juan, PR
Estrem, Debra K. ....San Francisco, CA
Estremera, Jeanette ....Lawrenceville, NJ
Estrich, Lepardo & Hull, P.C. ....Boston, MA
Estrich, Marc ....Boston, MA
Estrich, Susan ....Los Angeles, CA
Estridge, Ann Smith ....Raleigh, NC
Estridge, Larry D. ....Greenville, SC
Estrin, Barry ....Wilmington, DE
Estrin, Daniel E. ....New York, NY
Estrin, Dianne G. ....San Bruno, CA
Estrin, Melvyn J. ....New York, NY
Estrin & Sackstein ....Port Jefferson, NY
Estrin, Somer ....Port Jefferson, NY
Estrin, Zachary R. ....Malvern, PA
Estroff, Allan D. ....Denver, CO
Estroff, Sanford M. ....Lakeland, FL
Estroff, Stephen E. ....New York, NY
Estroff, Susann Deborah ....Marietta, GA
Estryn, Esther I. ....Department of Justice, Executive Office for United States Trustees, GV
Estuar, Paul J. ....Los Angeles, CA
Estudillo, David G. ....Moses Lake, WA
Estwick, Hazel M. ....West Trenton, NJ
Esty & Buckmir, LLC ....New Haven, CT
Esty, Elizabeth Henderson ....Cheshire, CT
Esty, Miles N. ....New Haven, CT
Esty-Kendall, Judson B.C. ....Bangor, ME
Esworthy, Joseph W. ....Binghamton, NY
Etchart, Mark D. ....Helena, MT
Etchemendy, Jeanne Marie ....Dayton, OH
Etcheverry, Bernard, Jr. ....Hillsborough, CA
Etcheverry, Edward ....Fort Lauderdale, FL
Etcheverry, Louis P. ....Bakersfield, CA
Etcheverry, Raymond J.
Salt Lake City, UT
Etcheverry-Barnes, Paige M.
Bakersfield, CA
Etchevers, John A. ....San Francisco, CA
Etchingham, Gerald M. ....Oxnard, CA
Etchingham, James P. ....Palatine, IL
Etchison, Michael E. ....Austin, TX
Etelson, Arnold P. ....Suffern, NY
Etelson & Fassberg ....Suffern, NY
Etelson, Glenn C. ....Gaithersburg, MD
Etelson, Jesse I.
Federal Labor Relations Authority, Office of the Administrative Law Judges, GV
Etem, Craig E. ....Reno, NV
Etem, Tammy N. ....Kansas City, MO
Etengoff, Loren S. ....Vancouver, WA
Eterovich, Janet M. ....Cleveland, OH
Etess, M. Hank ....Pasadena, CA
Etezadi, David ....Los Angeles, CA
Etezadi, Susan ....Redwood City, CA
Etgen, Robert J. ....Queenstown, MD
Eth, Jordan ....San Francisco, CA
Ethen, Anne L. ....Wichita, KS
Ethen, Wendy Barnhart ....Minneapolis, MN
Etheredge, Alison ....Orlando, FL
Etheredge, Edward D. ....Northampton, MA
Etheredge, H. Muldrow ....New Orleans, LA
Etheredge, James G.
Fort Walton Beach, FL
Etheredge, James G., Chartered, Law Offices of ....Fort Walton Beach, FL
Etheredge, Stacy A. ....Eagan, MN
Etheredge, Stephen T. ....Dothan, AL
Etheredge & Steuer, P.C.
Northampton, MA
Etheridge, Dalby Chandler ....Smyrna, GA
Etheridge, David K. ....Jacksonville, FL
Etheridge, Donald M., Jr. ....Atlanta, GA
Etheridge, E. Ray ....Elizabeth City, NC
Etheridge, Fletcher H. ....Houston, TX
Etheridge, Fred S. ....Oakland, CA
Etheridge, Jack P. ....Atlanta, GA
Etheridge, James L. ....Foster City, CA
Etheridge, John R., Jr. ....Darlington, SC
Florence, SC
Marion, SC
Myrtle Beach, SC
Etheridge, John R., Jr. ....Hartsville, SC
Etheridge, Kennieth S. ....Laurinburg, NC
Etheridge, Mary P. ....New York, NY
Etheridge, Moser, Garner and Bruner, P.A.
Laurinburg, NC
Etheridge, Philip F. ....Atlanta, GA
Etheridge, Randall J. ....Pensacola, FL
Etheridge, Ransom W. ....Virginia Beach, VA
Etheridge, Scott C. ....Asheboro, NC
Etheridge, Sykes, Britt & Hamlett, L.L.P.
Halifax, NC
Nashville, NC
Rocky Mount, NC
Tarboro, NC
Etheridge, Tanji B. ....Asheboro, NC
Etheridge, Traci C. ....Albemarle, NC
Etheridge, V. Alfred, Jr. ....Key West, FL
Etheridge, Virginia A. ....Colorado Springs, CO
Etheridge, Virginia A., P.C.
Colorado Springs, CO
Etheridge, Whitson B. ....Conroe, TX
Etheridge, William D. ....Nashville, NC
Etheriedge, John David ....Atlanta, GA
Etherington, Amy R. ....White Plains, NY
Etherington, Charles A. ....Kansas City, MO
Etherington, David B. ....Chicago, IL
Etherington, Edwin D. ....Old Lyme, CT
Etherington, Geoffrey, III ....New York, NY
Etherington, Loraine L. ....San Diego, CA
Etherington, William F. ....Richmond, VA
Etherton, Rayford L., Jr. ....Mobile, AL
Etherton, Regina Picone ....Chicago, IL
Etherton, Sandra L. ....Phoenix, AZ
Ethier, Mederic J. ....Albany, NY
Ethier, Steven F. ....St. Paul, MN
Ethington, H. Jay ....Dallas, TX
Ethington, Mark T. ....Murray, UT
Ethington, Paul J. ....Troy, MI
Ethredge, David L. ....Mountain Home, AR
Ethridge, Christine R. ....Pittsburgh, PA
Ethridge, Deborah J. ....Dallas, TX
Ethridge, George M., III
Charlotte Amalie, St. Thomas, VI
Ethridge, James B. ....Smithfield, NC
Ethridge, James W., Jr. ....Evansville, IN
Ethridge, John C. ....Elberton, GA
Ethridge, John C., Jr. ....Atlanta, GA
Ethridge, Lani A. ....Evansville, IN
Ethridge, Larry C. ....Louisville, KY
Ethridge, Lisa S.
Department Of Veterans Affairs, Board of Veterans Appeals, GV
Ethridge, Lura C. ....West Roxbury, MA
Ethridge, Paul H. ....Rockville, MD
Ethridge, R. Michael ....Atlanta, GA
Ethridge, Russell F. ....St. Clair Shores, MI
Ethridge, Samuel W. ....Kenner, LA
Ethridge, Thelma D. ....Elberton, GA
Ethridge, Thomas R. ....Oxford, MS
Etienne, Ingrid P. ....Arlington, VA
Etienne, Linda ....Bakersfield, CA
Etienne, Myron E., Jr. ....Monterey, CA
Salinas, CA
Etienne, Peter ....Deerfield, IL
Etienne, Robert P. ....San Jose, CA
Etinger, Seth R. ....La Quinta, CA
Etish, Allen A. ....Cherry Hill, NJ
Etkin, Alan R. ....Richardson, TX
Etkin, Davis M. ....Schenectady, NY
Etkin, Douglas M. ....Southfield, MI
Etkin, Hal ....Springfield, MA
Etkin, Helen B. ....Bingham Farms, MI
Etkin, Michael A. ....Philadelphia, PA
Etkin, Michael S. ....Roseland, NJ
New York, NY
Etkin, Patricia S. ....Plantation, FL
Etkin & Stark ....Schenectady, NY
Etkind, Andrew R. ....Olathe, KS
Etkind, Andrew S. ....Covington, GA
Etkind, Barbara E. ....Washington, DC
Etkind, David A. ....New York, NY

Etkind & Golos ..... Elmira, NY
Etkind, Hyman G. ..... Bridgeport, CT
Etkind, Max ..... Elmira, NY
Etkind, Steven M. ..... New York, NY
Etkowicz, Jacques L. ..... Valley Forge, PA
Etlin, Craig B. ..... San Francisco, CA
Etling, Gretchen Holland ..... Indianapolis, IN
Etling, Joseph K. ..... Terre Haute, IN
Etlinger, Deborah ..... Hartford, CT
Etlinger, Louis ..... Nashua, NH
Etlinger, Robert E. ..... San Antonio, TX
Etmekjian, Garbis D. ..... Glendale, CA
Etna, Daniel A. ..... New York, NY
Etner, Jacob M. ..... Thousand Oaks, CA
Etnier, Nancy Joanne ..... St. Louis, MO
Etnire, Geoffrey C. ..... Palo Alto, CA
Pleasanton, CA
Etnyre, Robert H., Jr. ..... Houston, TX
Etoch Law Firm ..... Helena, AR
Etoch, Louis A. ..... Helena, AR
Etoch, Mike J., Jr. ..... Helena, AR
Etoh, Madoka ..... Seattle, WA
Etoll, Stephen G. ..... Syracuse, NY
Etowski, Earl J., Jr. ..... University Heights, OH
Etpison, Suzanne C. ..... San Diego, CA
Etra, Aaron ..... New York, NY
Etra, Donald, Law Offices of
Los Angeles, CA
Etra & Etra, RLLP ..... New York, NY
Etra, Lionel ..... New York, NY
Etra, Marshall I. ..... New York, NY
Etra, Susan ..... New York, NY
Etri, James E. ..... Dallas, TX
Etrick, Mary B. ..... Peoria, IL
Etringer, Walter J. ..... Eden, NC
Etscorn, James V. ..... Orlando, FL
Etsios, Dean A. ..... Detroit, MI
Ettel, Anna-Marie ..... St. Paul, MN
Ettel, Joseph W. ..... San Mateo, CA
Ettelman, Cheryl ..... Miami, FL
Ettelson, Bruce I. ..... Chicago, IL
Ettelson, Jerome L. ..... Chicago, IL
Ettelson, William S. ..... Chicago, IL
Etten, Nicholas J. ..... Chicago, IL
Etten, Stewart L. ..... Wausau, WI
Ettenberg, Irving ..... Denver, CO
Ettenberg, Peter L. ..... Worcester, MA
Ettenger, Erwin L. ..... Plantation, FL
Ettenger, Mark D. ..... New York, NY
Ettensohn, Richard L. ..... Brea, CA
Ettenson, Alan H. ..... Moorestown, NJ
Ettenson, Bernhard M. ..... Rochester, NY
Etter, Andrew B. ..... Fort Worth, TX
Etter, Andrew B., P.C., Law Offices of
Fort Worth, TX
Etter, Bill D. ..... Jonesboro, AR
Etter, Craig A. ..... Washington, DC
Tysons Corner, VA
Etter, Don D. ..... Denver, CO
Etter, Greg V. ..... Houston, TX
Etter, Jeannie M. ..... Fort Lauderdale, FL
Miami, FL
Etter, John C. ..... Spokane, WA
Etter, John K. ..... New Orleans, LA
Etter, John L. ..... Ann Arbor, MI
Etter, Linda K. ..... Denver, CO
Etter, M. Charles ..... Kalamazoo, MI
Etter, McMahon, Lamberson & Clary, P.C.
A Professional Corporation
Coeur d'Alene, ID
Spokane, WA
Etter, R. Max, Jr. ..... Spokane, WA
Etter, Scott C. ..... Bellefonte, PA
State College, PA
Etter, Terry ..... Columbus, OH
Etter, Thomas C. ..... New York, NY
Etter, Thomas C., Jr.
Securities and Exchange Commission,
Division of Market Regulation, GV
Etter, William F. ..... Coeur d'Alene, ID
Spokane, WA
Etterman, Bruce S. ..... Newark, NJ
Etters, Ronald M.
National Mediation Board, GV
Ettien, J. Chan ..... Havre, MT
Ettin, Frank L. ..... Walnut Creek, CA
Ettin, Martin S. ..... Cherry Hill, NJ
Etting, Carl B. ..... Van Nuys, CA
Etting, Paula Sutton
Department of Labor, GV
Ettinger, Adam T. ..... Palo Alto, CA
Ettinger, Albert F. ..... Chicago, IL
Ettinger, Brian, Law Office of ..... Houston, TX
Ettinger, Constance M. ..... Franklin, MI
Ettinger, Daniel P. ..... Grand Rapids, MI
Ettinger, David A. ..... Detroit, MI
Ettinger, David A. ..... Nashville, TN
Ettinger, David M. ..... Woodmere, NY
Ettinger, David S. ..... Los Angeles, CA
Ettinger, Harlan I. ..... Trenton, NJ
Ettinger, Howard J. ..... Beverly Hills, CA
Ettinger, Jack A. ..... Tucson, AZ
Ettinger, Jack A., P.C. ..... Tucson, AZ
Ettinger, Janis ..... New York, NY
Ettinger, Joan F. ..... Riverside, CA
Ettinger, John R. ..... New York, NY
Ettinger, Jonathan M. ..... Boston, MA
Ettinger, Joseph ..... New York, NY
Ettinger, Joseph A. ..... Chicago, IL
Ettinger, Lainie Keslin ..... Portland, OR
Ettinger Law Firm, The, P.C. ..... Albany, NY
Fishkill, NY
New York, NY
Plattsburgh, NY
Poughkeepsie, NY
Syracuse, NY
Tarrytown, NY
Utica, NY
White Plains, NY
Ettinger, Leonard J. ..... Reno, NV
Ettinger, Marc ..... Irvine, CA
Ettinger, Michael ..... Albany, NY
Fishkill, NY
New York, NY
Syracuse, NY
Tarrytown, NY
Ettinger, Mitchell S. ..... Washington, DC
Ettinger, Nicole L. ..... San Francisco, CA
Ettinger, Patrice S. ..... New York, NY
Ettinger, Robert D. ..... Austin, TX
Ettinger, Stacy J. ..... Department of Commerce,
Office of the General Counsel, GV
Ettinger, Steven Z. ..... Cleveland, OH
Ettinger, Warren ..... Los Angeles, CA
Ettinger, William A. ..... San Francisco, CA
Ettinghoff, Tracy H. ..... Laguna Niguel, CA
Ettingoff, Cindy Cole ..... Memphis, TN
Ettl, Frederick B. ..... South Bend, IN
Ettl, Joseph G. ..... South Bend, IN
Ettl, Madeline G. ..... South Bend, IN
Ettlin, Dennis M. ..... Rockville, MD
Ettlinger, Michael B. ..... New York, NY
Ettlinger, Roger J. ..... Walled Lake, MI
Ypsilanti, MI
Ettman, Bruce D. ..... Woodbridge, NJ
Ettman, David K. ..... Seneca Falls, NY
Ettman, David K. ..... Waterloo, NY
Ettman, Jonathan M. ..... New York, NY
Ettman, Philip ..... Simsbury, CT
Ettman, Sidney J. ..... Bronx, NY
Ettner, Michael J.
General Services Administration,
Office of the General Counsel, GV
Ettore, Michele M. ..... Camden, NJ
Ettredge, Sarah K. ..... Dallas, TX
Ettus, Deirdre ..... Long Beach, NY
Etzel, Brian E. ..... Troy, MI
Etzel, Earl ..... Shreveport, LA
Etzel, Frederick M. ..... San Francisco, CA
Etzel, Gregory Nolan ..... Houston, TX
Etzel, Quinton ..... Del Rio, TX
Etzel, Ronald N. ..... Pasadena, TX
Etzell, Matthew J. ..... Eagan, MN
Etzell, Peter G. ..... Mankato, MN
Etzion, Gail ..... Palo Alto, CA
Etzioni, Michael R. ..... Los Angeles, CA
Etzkorn, Daniel D. ..... Little Rock, AR
Etzkorn, John F. ..... Chicago, IL
Etzler, Gordon A. ..... Valparaiso, IN
Etzler, Mary Ann ..... Orlando, FL
Etzler, Todd A. ..... Merrillville, IN
Valparaiso, IN
Etzrodt, Jennifer Courtney ..... Yardley, PA
Etzrodt, Michael T. ..... New York, NY
Etzweiler & Associates ..... Elizabethville, PA
Harrisburg, PA
Millersburg, PA
Etzweiler, Earl Richard ..... Elizabethville, PA
Harrisburg, PA
Millersburg, PA
Etzweiler, Larry R. ..... Trenton, NJ
Etzweiler & Radebach ..... Harrisburg, PA
Etzwiler, Nancy G. ..... St. Paul, MN
Etzwiler, Rhonda L. ..... Glendale, CA
Eubank, Bobbie Lee ..... Gainesville, FL
Eubank, Bret W. ..... Temecula, CA
Eubank, Carol ..... Asheville, NC
Eubank, David L. ..... Dayton, OH
Eubank, Edwin L. ..... New York, NY
Eubank, Franklin J., Jr. ..... Rockford, IL
Eubank, Hassell & Moorhead, P.A.
Daytona Beach, FL
Eubank, J. Thomas ..... Houston, TX
Eubank, James O., II ..... Daytona Beach, FL
Eubank, Katherine Taylor ..... Denver, CO
Eubank, Robert B. ..... Birmingham, AL
Eubank, Robert B., P.C. ..... Birmingham, AL
Eubank, Stephen Reid ..... Amherst, VA
Eubank, Stephen W. ..... Houston, TX
Eubank, Thomas F. ..... Richmond, VA
Eubank, Wm. E. ..... Glendale, AZ
Eubanks & Barrett ..... Tallahassee, FL
Eubanks & Bond ..... Augusta, GA
Martinez, GA
Eubanks, Bradford H. ..... Las Cruces, NM
Eubanks, Charles A. ..... Santa Rosa, TX
Eubanks, Cheryl D. ..... Fairhope, AL
Eubanks, Clyde V. ..... Jackson, MS
Eubanks, David B. ..... Scottsbluff, NE
Eubanks, Dennis E. ..... Sacramento, CA
Eubanks, Edward L. ..... Columbia, SC
Eubanks, Ernest H. ..... Orlando, FL
Eubanks, Ernest H., Jr. ..... Orlando, FL
Eubanks, Gary, & Associates, P.A.
Little Rock, AR
Eubanks, Gary F. ..... Marietta, GA
Eubanks, Gary L. ..... Little Rock, AR
Eubanks, Herman W. ..... Little Rock, AR
Eubanks, Hilyard & Bogan, P.A.
Orlando, FL
Eubanks, Jo Beth ..... San Antonio, TX
Eubanks, John R., Jr.
West Palm Beach, FL
Eubanks, Larry L. ..... Winston-Salem, NC
Eubanks, Lennie R.
Department Of The Interior,
Bureau of Land Management, GV
Eubanks, L. S., Jr. ..... Dallas, TX
Eubanks, Michael C. ..... Augusta, GA
Eubanks, Michael F. ..... Richmond, KY
Eubanks, Michael R. ..... Purvis, MS
Eubanks, Paul Clayton, P.C.
Oklahoma City, OK
Eubanks, Raymond C., Jr. ..... Spartanburg, SC
Eubanks, Rebekah R. ..... Chicago, IL
Eubanks, Renee ..... Department of Justice,
Antitrust Division, GV
Eubanks, Robert E. ..... Tujunga, CA
Eubanks, Robert M., III ..... Little Rock, AR
Eubanks, Rodney L. ..... New York, NY
Eubanks, Sharon Y. ..... Department of Justice,
Civil Division, GV
Eubanks, Silas R. ..... Tallahassee, FL
Eubanks, Tracy L. ..... Mount Vernon, IL
Eubanks, W. Scott, Jr. ..... Live Oak, FL
Eubanks, William S. ..... Black Mountain, NC
Euben, Donna R. ..... Washington, DC
Eucher, Ralph C. ..... Minneapolis, MN
Euchler, M. Jefferson ..... Chesapeake, VA
Euclide, Kristine A. ..... Madison, WI
Eudene, Deborah ..... Menlo Park, CA
Eudey, Scott R. ..... Broken Arrow, OK
Eudy, Clinton, Jr. ..... Greensboro, NC
Eudy, Ron K. ..... Austin, TX
Eufinger, Charlotte Coleman ..... Marysville, OH
Eufinger, Gregory E., Jr. ..... Kansas City, MO
Eufinger, John M. ..... Marysville, OH
Eufusia, Linda M. ..... Redwood City, CA
Eugene, John ..... Metuchen, NJ
Eugeni, Anthony L. ..... Buffalo, NY
Eugenides, Alexander Angelo
West Des Moines, IA
Eugenio, Anthony W. ..... San Antonio, TX
Eugenio, Lawrence A. ..... Los Angeles, CA
Eugenio-Meléndez, Ramón ..... San Juan, PR
Eugenios, Demetrious ..... Campbell, CA
Eugster & Grimes, P.S.C. ..... Spokane, WA
Eugster, Stephen K. ..... Spokane, WA
Euken, James E. ..... Belmont, NY
Eulau, Milton B. ..... New York, NY
Eulberg, Chris H. ..... Oklahoma City, OK
Eulberg, Jane S. ..... Oklahoma City, OK
Eulberg, Jeff A. ..... Oklahoma City, OK
Eulberg Law Offices ..... Oklahoma City, OK
Eule, Avram S. ..... Hackensack, NJ
Eule, Norman L. ..... Bethesda, MD
Eulenstein, Howard R. ..... Williamsville, NY
Euler, Curtis W. ..... Asheville, NC
Euler, Jack R. ..... Troy, KS
Euler, J. D. ..... Hiawatha, KS
Euler, Joel ..... Troy, KS
Euler, John L. ..... Department of the Navy,
Office of the Judge Advocate General, GV
Euler, Mary E. ..... Asheville, NC
Euler & McQuillan ..... Troy, KS
Euler, Sharon K. ..... Kansas City, MO
Eulert, Max A. ..... Manhattan, KS
Eulgen, Lee J. ..... Chicago, IL
Euliss, Wade C. ..... Greensboro, NC
Euller, Steven ..... Minneapolis, MN
Eulo, James R. ..... Novato, CA
Eum, David ..... Los Angeles, CA
Eure, Delman H. ..... Richmond, VA
Eure, Geraldine R. ..... New York, NY
Eure, John D. ..... Roanoke, VA
Eure, John D., Jr. ..... Suffolk, VA
Eure, Kincer & Bell, P.C. ..... Richmond, VA
Eure, Mary F. ..... Reston, VA
Eure, Philip K. ..... Department of Justice,
Civil Rights Division, GV
Eure, Rosemary B. ..... Sarasota, FL
Eurek, Allan J. ..... Lincoln, NE
Eurek, Allan J., P.C. ..... Lincoln, NE
Eurek, Mark L. ..... Loup City, NE
Eurek, Mark L., P.C., The Law Offices of
Loup City, NE
Eurell, John B. ..... Philadelphia, PA
Euren, Gary E. ..... Grand Forks, ND
Euresti, Benjamin, Jr. ..... Brownsville, TX
Euretig, Joseph G. ..... Sacramento, CA
Eurich, Gregory A. ..... Denver, CO
Eurich, Richard R. ..... Boston, MA
Eurie, Stacy Boulware ..... Sacramento, CA
Euripides, Charles C. ..... Charlotte, NC
European Business Law Firm, The, P.C.
Palm Springs, CA
Eury, C. Howard ..... Rock Hill, SC
Eusanio, David M. ..... West Palm Beach, FL
Eusebi, Christopher A. ..... Troy, MI
Eusey, Charles J. ..... Leominster, MA
Eusner and Hardwick ..... Hampton, VA
Eusner, Kenneth A. ..... Hampton, VA
Euson, Richard A. ..... Wichita, KS
Eustace, Edward M. ..... Uniondale, NY
Eustace & Furey ..... Uniondale, NY
Eustace, Joseph A., Jr. ..... Tampa, FL
Eustace, Joseph W. ..... Lawrenceville, NJ
Eustace, Loni N. ..... Greenwood, MS
Eustace, Timothy M. ..... Burlington, VT
Eustace, William C. ..... New Haven, CT
Euster, Mark D. ..... Tucker, GA
Eustice, Benjamin R. ..... Tampa, FL
Eustice, Francis J. ..... Sun Prairie, WI
Eustice, James S. ..... New York, NY
Eustice, Robert C. ..... Washington, DC
Eustice, W. Gordon ..... Los Altos, CA
Eustice, William F. ..... Omaha, NE
Eustis, Albert A. ..... Charlottesville, VA
Eustis, Frederic A., III ..... Westport, MA
Eustis, Geoffrey E. ..... Mobile, AL
Eustis, James R., Jr. ..... New York, NY
Eustis, Jeffrey M. ..... Seattle, WA
Eustis, June E. ..... Window Rock, AZ
Eustis & O'Keefe, LLC ..... New Orleans, LA
Eustis, Richard A. ..... Braintree, MA
Eustis, Richmond M. ..... New Orleans, LA
Eustis, Robert D. ..... Westwood, MA
Eustis, Thomas S. ..... Fort Lauderdale, FL
Eustis, Truman W., III ..... Washington, DC
Euston, Jeffrey M. ..... Leawood, KS
Euston, Michael K. ..... Kansas City, MO
Euto, Jeremy J. ..... Columbus, OH
Eutsler, Robert W. ..... Houston, TX
Euvrard, LeRoy E., Jr. ..... Miamisburg, OH
Euwema, John B. ..... Schaumburg, IL
Eva, W. Allan, III ..... Cleveland, OH
Evain, Eric J. ..... Wilmington, DE
Evale, Colleen M. ..... Washington, DC
Evall, Clay M. ..... New York, NY
Evall, Joseph ..... New York, NY
Evall, Mitchell, (P.C.) ..... Beverly Hills, CA
Evan, David J. ..... New York, NY
Evan, George M. ..... Pittsburgh, PA
Evan, Lior ..... New York, NY
Evanchan, Nicholas L. ..... Akron, OH
Evanchan & Palmisano ..... Akron, OH
Cleveland, OH
Evancho, Ellen M. ..... Knoxville, TN
Evander, G. Mitch ..... Melbourne, FL
Evander, Kerry I. ..... Melbourne, FL
Evangelakos, John ..... New York, NY
Evangelatos, Andrew ..... Los Angeles, CA
Evangelidis, Lewis George ..... Bedford, MA
Evangelist, Frank J., Jr. ..... Jericho, NY
Evangelist, Gregg R. ..... New York, NY
Evangelista, Alessio D. ..... Washington, DC
Evangelista, Alfredo G. ..... Honolulu, HI
Evangelista, Angela M. ..... New York, NY
Evangelista, Dominick F.
Florham Park, NJ
New York, NY
Evangelista, Donato A. ..... Vero Beach, FL
Evangelista, Enrico B.
Santa Fe Springs, CA
Evangelista, James J. ..... Tampa, FL
Evangelista, James P. ..... Cleveland, OH
Evangelista, Janet R. ..... Cleveland, OH
Evangelista, Julio N. ..... Winchester, MA
Evangelista, Karen E. ..... Troy, MI
Evangelista & Keith, P.L.L.C. ..... Troy, MI
Evangelista, Lisa R. ..... Boston, MA
Providence, RI
Evangelista, Margret Jonnson
New York, NY
Evangelista, Mark B. ..... Hyannis, MA
Evangelista, Paul J. ..... Albany, NY
Evangelista and Quiban ..... Honolulu, HI
Evangelista, Renee A.R. ..... Providence, RI
Evangelisti, Celeste ..... Dallas, TX
Evangelisti, John S. ..... Denver, CO
Evangelisti, Michael T. ..... Memphis, TN
Evangelo, Nicholas ..... Orlando, FL
Evangelos, Melisa D. ..... Seattle, WA
Evangelou, Alina M. ..... Chicago, IL
Evangelou, Angelo ..... Chicago, IL
Evangilidis, Lewis ..... Boston, MA
Evani, Carolyn Balster ..... Phoenix, AZ
Evanich, Jeanette M. ..... Elyria, OH
Evanich, Kevin R. ..... Chicago, IL
Evanick, Barbara A. ..... Cleveland, OH
Evanick, Robert B. ..... New Orleans, LA
Evanina, Gunther J. ..... Grand Rapids, MI
Evanko, Ann E. ..... Buffalo, NY
Evanko, Patricia M.
Department of Commerce,
Patent and Trademark Office, GV
Evankovich, Andrew F. ..... Pittsburgh, PA
Evankovich, Thea G. ..... Pittsburgh, PA
Evanns, Joseph R. ..... Beverly Hills, CA
Evanns & Walsh ..... Beverly Hills, CA
Los Angeles, CA
Evanoff, John M. ..... Allentown, PA
Evanoff, Michael B. ..... Chicago, IL
Evans, Aaron L. ..... Denver, CO
Evans, A. H. ..... Houston, TX
Evans, Akosua Barthwell ..... Atlanta, GA
Evans, Albert G. ..... San Francisco, CA
Evans, Albert V. ..... Denver, CO
Evans, Alfred L. ..... Clarksville, TN
Evans, Alfred L., Jr. ..... Atlanta, GA
Evans, Alison B. ..... Seattle, WA
Evans, Allen D. ..... Oklahoma City, OK
Evans, Andre ..... Virginia Beach, VA
Evans, Andrea C. ..... Washington, DC
Evans, Andrea Meshonn ..... Dallas, TX
Evans, Andrew R. ..... Amarillo, TX
Evans, Anne C. ..... Buffalo, NY
Evans, Anne Mayo ..... Fayetteville, NC
Evans Antonelli & Cox, LLC
Washington, DC
Bethesda, MD
Evans, A. O., III ..... Freeport, TX
Evans, April McGandy ..... Los Angeles, CA
Evans, Arleen ..... Griffin, GA
Evans, Arthur H. ..... Chicago, IL
Evans, Arthur W. ..... Utica, NY
Evans & Associates ..... Coral Gables, FL
Miami, FL
Evans & Associates, A Professional
Corporation ..... Las Vegas, NV
Evans & Associates, P.C. ..... Washington, DC
Evans, Audrey R. ..... Little Rock, AR
Evans, Augustus H., Jr. ..... Steubenville, OH
Evans, Barbara B. ..... Atlanta, GA
Evans, Barbara B. ..... Dallas, TX
Evans, Barbara H. ..... Santa Ana, CA
Evans, Barbara J. ..... New York, NY
Evans, Barbara Ryniker ..... New Orleans, LA
Evans, Barbara V. ..... McLean, VA
Evans, Barry ..... New York, NY
Evans, Barry F. ..... Canoga Park, CA
Evans, Barry M. ..... Houston, TX
Evans & Bechtold, P.C.
Bloomfield Hills, MI
Evans and Beier ..... Morristown, TN
Evans, Beverly ..... Des Moines, IA
Evans & Bifferato ..... Wilmington, DE
Evans, Bill J. ..... Champaign, IL
Evans, Billy L. ..... Washington, DC
Evans, Blaine F. ..... Boise, ID
Evans, Blair Beavers ..... Memphis, TN

Evans, Blake S. ... Dallas, TX
Evans, Brent Alan ... Bethlehem, PA
Evans, Brian B. ... Tampa, FL
Evans, Brian J. ... Frederick, MD
Evans, Brian P. ... Walnut Creek, CA
Evans, Brian P. ... Charlotte, NC
Evans, Brian Walsh ... Santa Rosa, CA
Evans, Bruce C. ... Salt Lake City, UT
Evans, Bruce D. ... Pittsburgh, PA
Evans, Bruce L. ... McAlester, OK
Evans, Bryan ... Roswell, NM
Evans & Burrell ... Philadelphia, PA
Evans, C. Carnot, III
Securities and Exchange Commission, Division of Corporation Finance, GV
Evans, C. Dwaine ... Morristown, TN
Evans, C. Kelley ... Sacramento, CA
Evans, C. Thomas, Jr. ... Chicago, IL
Evans, C. Todd ... Atlanta, GA
Evans, Cade A. ... Lafayette, LA
Evans, Cameron J. ... Detroit, MI
Evans, Camille B. ... Treasury Department, Internal Revenue Service, GV
Evans, Camille Henick ... Jackson, MS
Evans, Cari Fusco ... Canton, OH
Evans, Carin S. ... New York, NY
Evans, Carl L. ... Montgomery, AL
Evans, Carl Lenford, Jr.
Montgomery, AL
Evans, Carol A. ... Department of Justice, Civil Division, GV
Evans, Carolyn Wilson ... Bel Air, MD
Evans, Carter, Kunes & Bennett, P.A.
Charleston, SC
Evans, Cassandra Barton ... Santa Fe, NM
Evans, Catherine A. ... Los Angeles, CA
Evans, Catherine B. ... Thomaston, GA
Evans, Catherine E. ... Waterloo, IL
Evans, Catherine L. ... Hamilton, OH
Evans, Cedric E. ... Austin, TX
Evans, Charles A. ... Marietta, GA
Evans, Charles D. ... Manteo, NC
Evans, Charles E. ... Pittsburgh, PA
Evans, Charles G. ... Anchorage, AK
Evans, Charles H. ... Springfield, IL
Evans, Charles H. ... Jackson, MS
Evans, Charles L. ... Raleigh, NC
Evans, Charles N. ... Seattle, WA
Evans, Charles S. ... Portland, OR
Evans, Charles W. ... Austin, TX
Evans, Cherie L. ... Santa Maria, CA
Evans, Chris M. ... Alexandria, VA
Evans, Christina B. ... Quincy, IL
Evans, Christina D'Eramo ... Cleveland, OH
Evans, Christine A. ... Raleigh, NC
Evans, Christopher J. ... Santa Ana, CA
Evans, Christopher L. ... Houston, TX
Evans, Christopher R. ... Honolulu, HI
Evans, Chuck O, P.C. ... Denver, CO
Evans, Clayton E. ... Burnet, TX
Evans and Clesi, A Professional Law Corporation ... New Orleans, LA
Evans & Co. ... Tallahassee, FL
New Orleans, LA
Greensboro, NC
Houston, TX
Evans, Constance G. ... Washington, DC
Evans, Courtney A. ... Washington, DC
Evans, Craig E. ... Worthington, OH
Evans, Craig H. ... Wilmington, DE
Evans, Craig L. ... Kansas City, MO
Evans, Craig V. ... Paris, MO
Evans, Craven & Lackie, P.S.
Coeur d'Alene, ID
Spokane, WA
Evans, Curtis A. ... Alexandria, VA
Evans, Curtis H. ... York, NE
Evans, Cynthia E. ... Charleston, WV
Evans, Cynthia H. ... Washington, DC
Evans, Cynthia J. ... North Grafton, MA
Evans, Cynthia Silas ... Bethlehem, PA
Evans, D. Dean ... Gallipolis, OH
Evans, D. Murphy ... Bellingham, WA
Evans, D. William, Jr. ... Wooster, OH
Evans, Dana W. ... The Woodlands, TX
Evans, Daniel B. ... Philadelphia, PA
Evans, Daniel E. ... Denver, CO
Evans, Daniel F., Jr. ... Indianapolis, IN
Evans, Daniel H. ... Houston, TX
Evans, Daniel J. ... Sewickley, PA
Evans, Daniel K. ... Memphis, TN
Evans, Daniel L. ... Stillwater, OK
Evans, Daniel M. ... Pasadena, CA
Evans, Daniel S.
Treasury Department, GV
Evans, Daniel S. ... Boston, MA
Evans, Daniel W. ... Mesa, AZ
Evans, Danny L. ... London, KY
Evans, Darlene G. ... Glendale, CA
Evans, David A. ... Los Angeles, CA
Evans, David B. ... Clarksville, AR
Evans, David B. ... North English, IA
Evans, David C. ... Washington, DC
Evans, David Cyril ... Farmington, CT
Evans, David E. ... Columbia, MO
Evans, David E. ... Richmond, VA
Evans, David F. ... Cheyenne, WY
Evans, David G. ... Los Angeles, CA
Evans, David H. ... Washington, DC
Evans, David H. ... Ellicott City, MD
Evans, David J. ... Washington, DC
Evans, David J., Jr. ... Guntersville, AL
Evans, David J. D. ... Hartford, CT
Evans, David L. ... Los Angeles, CA
Evans, David L.
National Labor Relations Board, Division of Administrative Law Judges, GV
Evans, David L. ... Orlando, FL
Evans, David L. ... Albany, NY
Evans, David L. ... Federal Way, WA
Evans, David L., P.S., Inc., Law Offices of ... Federal Way, WA
Evans, David Lattimore ... Fort Worth, TX
Evans, David Lee ... Boston, MA
Evans, David M. ... Fremont, NE
Evans, David N. ... Cincinnati, OH
Evans, David P. ... West Seneca, NY
Evans, David P. ... Colleyville, TX
Evans, David R. ... Pasadena, CA
Evans, David R. ... Chattanooga, TN
Evans, David S. ... New Bern, NC
Evans, David W. ... Irvine, CA
Evans, David W. ... San Francisco, CA
Evans, David W. ... Golden Valley, MN
Evans, David W. ... Dallas, TX
Evans, Dawn K. ... Overland Park, KS
Evans, Deanna S. ... Harrison, AR
Evans, Deanna S., P.A. ... Harrison, AR
Evans, Deborah Gale ... Atlanta, GA
Evans, Debra Mosley ... Norfolk, VA
Evans, DeLyle M. ... Ayden, NC
Evans, Dennis P. ... Columbus, OH
Evans, Diane K. ... Cuyahoga Falls, OH
Evans, Diane M. ... Phoenix, AZ
Evans & Dixon, L.L.C. ... Edwardsville, IL
Leawood, KS
Kansas City, MO
St. Louis, MO
Evans, Don ... Rocky Mount, NC
Evans, Don A. ... Nacogdoches, TX
Evans, Don H. ... Jackson, MS
Evans, Don T., Jr. ... Wilmington, NC
Evans, Donald C. ... Tampa, FL
Evans, Donald C., Jr. ... Washington, DC
Evans, Donald C., Jr. ... Atlanta, GA
Evans, Donald D. ... Arlington, VA
Evans, Donald E. ... Pittsburgh, PA
Evans, Donald Elihu ... Wilmington, DE
Evans, Donald J. ... Washington, DC
Evans, Donald J., (P.C.) ... Boston, MA
Evans, Donald W. ... Houston, TX
Evans, Donald William ... Manchester, NH
Evans, Donald York ... Reno, NV
Evans, Donald York, Ltd. ... Reno, NV
Evans, Donna M. ... Boston, MA
Evans, Donna R. ... Los Angeles, CA
Evans, Dorsey ... Silver Spring, MD
Evans, Douglas B. ... San Francisco, CA
Evans, Douglas Hayward ... New York, NY
Evans, Douglas M. ... West Hartford, CT
Evans, Douglas S. ... Springfield, MO
Evans, Duane A.
Charlotte Amalie, St. Thomas, VI
Evans, E. Samuel ... Evans, GA
Evans, Edward Earl ... Oklahoma City, OK
Evans, Edward R. ... Fair Lawn, NJ
Evans, Edward S., III ... Baltimore, MD
Evans, Edwin E. ... Columbia, SC
Evans, Edwin E. ... Sioux Falls, SD
Evans, Eleanor A. ... Boston, MA
Evans, Elena ... Miami, FL
Evans, Eli N. ... New York, NY
Evans, Elizabeth A. ... Houston, TX
Evans, Elizabeth Clydesdale
Poolesville, MD
Evans, Elizabeth Doan ... Vienna, VA
Evans, Elizabeth H. ... New York, NY
Evans, Elliot L. ... New York, NY
Evans, Elwyn, Jr. ... Wilmington, DE
Evans, Emily A. ... Palo Alto, CA
Evans, Eric A. ... Rochester, NY
Evans, Eric V. ... Lexington, KY
Evans, Eric W. ... Granite City, IL
Evans, Ernest E. ... Fort Wayne, IN
Evans, Ernest L. ... Ahoskie, NC
Evans, Ethan C. ... Bloomington, IL
Evans, Eugene ... New York, NY
Evans, Eugene E. ... Rome, GA
Evans, Eugene H. ... West Chester, PA
Evans, Eugene S., Jr. ... Wailuku, HI
Evans, Evan G. ... Corona, CA
Evans & Evans ... Griffin, GA
Evans & Evans ... Topsfield, MA
Evans & Evans ... Beaumont, TX
Evans and Evans, A Professional Association ... Springdale, AR
Evans, Evans & Hoffman L.L.P.
Marion, OH
Richwood, OH
Evans, Eve L. ... Newark, NJ
Evans, F. Birt, Jr. ... Canton, NY
Evans, F. Douglas P. ... Greenville, SC
Evans, F. Owen, III ... Atlanta, GA
Evans, Farber & Cipinko ... San Francisco, CA
Evans, Fatima Brunson ... Oakland, CA
Evans, Feldman & Boyer, L.L.C.
New Haven, CT
Evans & Fox, LLP ... Rochester, NY
Evans, Francis J. ... Englewood, CO
Evans, Frank F. ... Mill Valley, CA
Evans, Frank G. ... Houston, TX
Evans, Frank M., III ... Springfield, MO
Evans, Frederick D. (" Rick "), III
Atlanta, GA
Evans, Frederick R. (Rick)
Chattanooga, TN
Evans, Fredrick W. ... Greensboro, NC
Evans, Freeby & Jennings, LLP
Salem, OR
Evans, Froehlich & Beth ... Champaign, IL
Evans, G. Anne ... Omaha, NE
Evans, G. Daniel ... Birmingham, AL
Evans, G. Marlin ... Greensboro, NC
Evans, Gail S. M. ... Houston, TX
Evans, Gale G. ... Atlanta, GA
Evans, Gandy, Daniel & Moore
Fort Worth, TX
Evans, Gardner A. ... Philadelphia, PA
Evans, Gareth T. ... Los Angeles, CA
Evans, Garvey, Lackey & Ochs
Mercer, PA
Sharon, PA
Evans, Gary Linn ... The Woodlands, TX
Evans, Gary R. ... Oak Brook, IL
Evans, Gary S. ... Pascagoula, MS
Evans, Gary V. ... Mansfield, LA
Evans, Gayle Stutzman ... Kansas City, MO
Evans, Geoffrey C. ... Roseland, NJ
Evans, Geoffrey S.
Department of Commerce, Patent and Trademark Office, GV
Evans, George A., Jr. ... Milwaukee, WI
Evans, George A., Sr. ... Milwaukee, WI
Evans, George Alan ... Meridian, MS
Evans, George C. ... Charleston, SC
Evans, George E. ... Wilmington, DE
Evans, George F., Jr. ... San Antonio, TX
Evans, George K., Jr. ... Charlotte, NC
Evans, George L. ... Portland, OR
Evans, George M. ... Coral Gables, FL
Evans, George Q. ... Jackson, MS
Evans, George S. ... Melville, NY
Evans, George S., Jr. ... New York, NY
Evans, George W. ... New York, NY
Evans, Gerald H. ... Evansville, IN
Evans, Gerald L. ... Salisbury, NC
Evans, Ginny ... Lynnwood, WA
Evans, Glen C. ... Bradenton, FL
Evans, Glория G. ... Oakland, CA
Evans, Godfrey B. ... Glendale, CA
Evans, Gomer A., Jr. ... Tulsa, OK
Evans & González ... Atlanta, GA
Evans, Gordon Alan ... New Haven, CT
Evans, Gordon Alan, & Associates, P.C.
New Haven, CT
Evans, Gordon E. ... Juneau, AK
Evans, Gordon J. ... Portland, OR
Evans, Gordon J., (P.A.) ... Miami, FL
Evans, Gray ... Greenwood, MS
Evans & Green LLP ... Springfield, MO
Evans, Gregory K. ... Houston, TX
Evans, Gregory L. ... Tampa, FL
Evans, Gregory Lawrence
Los Angeles, CA
Evans, Gregory U. ... McLean, VA
Evans, H. Alix ... Los Angeles, CA
Evans, H. Bradley, Jr. ... Falls Church, VA
Evans, H. Duane ... Seattle, WA
Evans, H. Lee ... San Francisco, CA
Evans, H. Lee, Jr. ... Raleigh, NC
Evans, H. Michael ... Clearwater, FL
Evans, H. Thomas ... Eugene, OR
Evans, Hallie Smith ... Tampa, FL
Evans, Harold J. ... Little Rock, AR
Evans, Harry S. ... Ocean Township, NJ
Evans, Henry D., Jr. ... San Francisco, CA
Evans, Henry K. ... Sioux Falls, SD
Evans, Herbert G ... Eugene, OR
Evans, Hill ... Marion, NC
Evans, Hope C. ... Knoxville, TN
Evans, Howard B. ... Oxnard, CA
Evans, Howard R. ... Atlanta, GA
Evans, Hoyte C. ... Richmond Heights, MO
Evans, Hugh C. ... Washington, DC
Evans, Hugh H., Jr. ... Marina Del Rey, CA
Evans, Hugh O. ... Coeur d'Alene, ID
Spokane, WA
Evans, Hugh R., III ... Montgomery, AL
Evans, Iley ... Columbia, LA
Evans, Ingrid Maria ... San Francisco, CA
Evans, Irwin B. ... Sandersville, GA
Evans, Irwin S. ... Los Angeles, CA
Evans • Ivory P.C. ... Pittsburgh, PA
Evans, J. Michael ... Columbus, OH
Evans, J. Randolph ... Atlanta, GA
Evans, J. Scott ... Charlotte, NC
Evans, Jack ... Washington, DC
Evans, Jack David ... Tampa, FL
Evans, Jack E. ... Phoenix, AZ
Evans, Jack G. ... Cincinnati, OH
Evans, Jack H. ... New Haven, CT
Evans, Jack R. ... Houston, TX
Evans, James A. ... Hallettsville, TX
Evans, James A. ... Virginia Beach, VA
Evans, James B., Jr. ... Haddonfield, NJ
Evans, James C. ... Miami, FL
Evans, James C. ... Canfield, OH
Evans, James C. ... Columbia, SC
Evans, James Clarence ... Nashville, TN
Evans, James D. ... Butler, AL
Evans, James D. ... Aurora, CO
Evans, James D., P.C. ... Aurora, CO
Evans, James E. ... Cincinnati, OH
Evans, James E., Jr., (P.A.) ... Springdale, AR
Evans, James F. ... Portland, OR
Evans, James F., III ... Syracuse, NY
Evans, James G., Jr. ... Alexandria, VA
Evans, James H. ... New Canaan, CT
Evans, James H. ... New York, NY
Evans, James Harrace, Jr. ... Irving, TX
Evans, James L. ... Annapolis, MD
Evans, James L. ... Algoma, WI
Evans, James M. ... Columbus, OH
Evans, James M. ... Pittsburgh, PA
Evans, James Michael ... Dearborn, MI
Evans, James P. ... Syracuse, NY
Evans, James P. ... Youngstown, OH
Evans, James R. ... Daytona Beach, FL
Evans, James R., Jr. ... Austin, TX
Evans, James R., Jr., (P.C.)
Los Angeles, CA
Evans, James T. ... Houston, TX
Evans, James W. ... Phoenix, AZ
Evans, James W. ... Harrisburg, PA
Evans, James W. ... Arlington, TX
Evans, James W., (Ltd.) ... Champaign, IL
Evans, Jan R. ... Medford, NJ
Evans, Jan R., P.A. ... Medford, NJ
Evans, Jana L. ... Atlanta, GA
Evans, Jane E. ... Phoenix, AZ
Evans, Jane Faulkner ... Birmingham, AL
Evans, Jane W. ... Wilmington, DE
Evans, Janet C. ... Minneapolis, MN
Evans, Janet L. ... Walnut Creek, CA
Evans, Janet M. ... Federal Trade Commission, Bureau of Consumer Protection, GV
Evans, Janet R. ... Washington, DC
Evans, Janice S. ... Novelty, OH
Evans, Jared Y. ... Shreveport, LA
Evans, J. D. ... Kennewick, WA
Evans, Jeanine C. ... Kitty Hawk, NC
Evans, Jeanne M. ... Irvine, CA
Evans, Jeannie Y. ... Palo Alto, CA
Evans, Jeffrey A. ... Los Angeles, CA
Evans, Jeffrey L. Oglesby ... Atlanta, GA
Evans, Jeffrey Lee ... Richwood, OH
Evans, Jeffrey S. ... Waynesboro, PA
Evans, Jenelle D. ... Birmingham, AL
Evans, Jennifer A. ... King Of Prussia, PA
Evans, Jennifer L. ... Denver, CO
Evans, Jennifer R. ... Chicago, IL
Evans, Jenny L. ... Oklahoma City, OK
Evans, Jeptha A. ... Vienna, VA
Evans, Jeremy H. ... Torrance, CA
Evans, Jerry A. ... Hattiesburg, MS
Evans, Jerry D. ... Uvalde, TX
Evans, Jerry H. ... Charleston, SC
Evans, Jesse P., III ... Birmingham, AL
Evans, J. H. ... Fort Smith, AR
Evans, Jill E. ... Birmingham, AL
Evans, Jim F. ... Dallas, TX
Evans, Joan E. ... Richmond, VA
Evans, Joan Foster ... Boston, MA
Evans, Joe A., III ... Madisonville, KY
Evans, Joe H. ... Hickory, NC
Evans, Joe Scott ... Groveton, TX
Evans, John ... Topsfield, MA
Evans, John A. ... Gloucester City, NJ
Evans, John A. ... Findlay, OH
Evans, John A. ... Green Bay, WI
Evans, John B. ... San Francisco, CA
Evans, John B. ... New York, NY
Evans, John C. ... Troy, MI
Evans, John C. ... Erie, PA
Pittsburgh, PA
Evans, John D., Jr. ... Jacksonville, FL
Evans, John E. ... Hillsboro, IL
Evans, John E. ... Louisville, KY
Evans, John Ford ... Woodstown, NJ
Evans, John Franklin, (P.C.)
Newport Beach, CA
Evans, John G. ... Sebastian, FL
Evans, John H. ... Denver, CO
Evans, John H. ... Titusville, FL
Evans, John H., P.A. ... Titusville, FL
Evans, John J. ... Stamford, CT
Evans, John L., Jr. ... Cincinnati, OH
Evans, John M. ... Englewood, CO
Evans, John M., P.C. ... Englewood, CO
Evans, John P. ... Towson, MD
Evans, John P. ... Seattle, WA
Evans, John R. ... Tucson, AZ
Evans, John R. ... Los Angeles, CA
Evans, John R. ... Santa Rosa, CA
Evans, John R. ... Waterman, IL
Evans, John R. ... Lima, OH
Evans, John R. ... Philadelphia, PA
Evans, John R., III ... Willcox, AZ
Evans, John S. ... Syracuse, NY
Evans, John T. ... Corydon, IN
Evans, John T. ... Mineola, NY
New York, NY
Evans, John T. ... Salt Lake City, UT
Evans, John T., P.C. ... Salt Lake City, UT
Evans, John V. ... Chicago, IL
Evans, John W. ... Huntsville, AL
Evans, John W. ... Los Angeles, CA
Evans, Johnson & Barnes ... Tulsa, OK
Evans & Johnson, LLC ... Silver Spring, MD
Evans, Jon E. ... Pittsburgh, PA
Evans, Jonathan W., & Associates
Los Angeles, CA
Evans, Jonathon P. ... Chardon, OH
Evans, Jones & Reynolds, A Professional Corporation ... Nashville, TN
Evans, Joseph A. ... Detroit Lakes, MN
Evans, Joseph D. ... Washington, DC
Evans, Joseph Lee ... Baltimore, MD
Evans, Joseph W. ... Lincoln, NH
Evans, Joseph W. ... Memphis, TN
Evans, Joy M. ... Cleveland, OH
Evans, Joyce L. ... Alexandria, VA
Evans, Juanita V. ... Highland, CA
Evans, Judy Whalen ... Birmingham, AL
Evans, Judythe A. ... Reading, MA
Evans, Julia Kingsley ... Fairfax, VA
Evans, Julie A. ... Louisville, KY
Evans, Julie A. ... Tulsa, OK
Evans, Julie Kuschner ... New York, NY
Evans, Julie R. ... New York, NY
Evans, Julie Rozanne ... San Bernardino, CA
Evans, K. Stewart, Jr. ... Washington, DC
Evans, Karen ... Miami, FL
Evans, Karen Brown ... Birmingham, AL
Evans, Karen E. ... Fairfax, VA
Evans, Karen J. ... Minneapolis, MN
Evans, Karen, Litigation Resolution, Inc.
Miami, FL
Evans, Karla A. ... Houston, TX
Evans, Katherine E. ... Tabor City, NC
Evans, Kathleen A. ... Salem, OR

Evans, Kathryn P. ... Cincinnati, OH
Evans, Kay L. ... Columbia, MO
Evans, Keane LLP ... Boise, ID
Caldwell, ID
Kellogg, ID
Mountain Home, ID
Nampa, ID
Evans, Kelli M. ... Department of Justice, Civil Rights Division, GV
Evans, Kelly A. ... Denver, CO
Evans, Kenneth E., Jr. ... Columbus, GA
Evans, Kenneth J. ... Mount Vernon, WA
Evans, Kenneth M. ... Bethel, CT
Evans, Kenneth Randall
New Orleans, LA
Evans & Kerr, P.S. ... Kennewick, WA
Evans, Kesha Danyeil ... Washington, DC
Evans, Kevin D. ... Denver, CO
Evans, Kirk W. ... Houston, TX
Evans & Kosut, P.C. ... Houston, TX
Evans, L. Beth ... Nashville, TN
Evans, L. Charles ... Libby, MT
Evans, L. Robert ... Towson, MD
Evans, L. Stanford ... Bloomfield Hills, MI
Evans, Lance ... Fort Worth, TX
Evans, Lance A. ... Maryville, TN
Evans, Lane A. ... Rock Island, IL
Evans, Larry E. ... Tulsa, OK
Evans, Larry G. ... Valparaiso, IN
Evans, Larry H. ... Griffin, GA
Evans, Larry H. ... Fairfax, VA
Evans, Larry Keith ... Griffin, GA
Evans, Larry L. ... Houston, TX
Evans, Latham, Harris and Campisi, A Professional Corporation
San Francisco, CA
Evans, Laurel Paretta ... Towson, MD
Evans, Laurie Pickle ... Coral Gables, FL
Evans, LaVerne ... New York, NY
Evans, LaVerne E. ... Valley Forge, PA
Evans Law Center ... Ponca City, OK
Evans Law Firm ... Waukesha, WI
Evans Law Firm, The, P.C.
Birmingham, AL
Evans Law Group, P.C. ... Atlanta, GA
Evans' Law Office ... Colorado Springs, CO
Evans Law Offices ... Lexington, KY
Evans, Lawrence ... Portland, OR
Evans, Lawrence E. ... Memphis, TN
Evans, Lawrence E., Jr. ... St. Louis, MO
Evans, Lawrence J., Jr. ... Tempe, AZ
Evans, Lawrence S. ... Coral Gables, FL
Evans, Leland B. ... San Mateo, CA
Evans, LeMarr W. ... Biggsville, IL
Evans, Leo F. ... Pittsfield, MA
Evans, Leslie A. ... Sacramento, CA
Evans, Leslie Robert ... Palm Beach, FL
Evans, Leslie Robert, & Associates, P.A.
Palm Beach, FL
Evans, Leslie S. ... Staten Island, NY
Evans, Linda G. ... Holdenville, OK
Evans, Linda S. ... Washington, DC
Evans, Linden R. ... Rapid City, SD
Evans, Linwood S., Jr. ... Sumter, SC
Evans & Lipson ... Denver, CO
Evans, Lisa J. ... San Francisco, CA
Evans, Lisa M. ... Cincinnati, OH
Evans, Lloyd L. ... Sebring, FL
Evans, Loewenstein, Shimanovsky & Moscardini, Ltd. ... Chicago, IL
Evans, Loring P., Jr. ... Miami, FL
Evans, Louis A. ... New York, NY
Evans, Louis D. ... Frankfort, IN
Evans, Louisa P. ... Fishers Island, NY
Evans & Luptak, P.L.C. ... Boca Raton, FL
Detroit, MI
Evans, Lydia V. ... Fredonia, NY
Evans, Lynn S. ... Newtown, PA
Evans, Lynwood P. ... Greenville, NC
New Bern, NC
Evans, Lyris Sue ... Fort Lauderdale, FL
Evans, M. Margaret ... Charleston, WV
Huntington, WV
Evans, Maggie B. ... Mount Dora, FL
Evans & Malter ... Canoga Park, CA
Evans, Margaret ... San Diego, CA
Evans, Margaret A. ... Seattle, WA
Evans, Margaret J. ... St. Paul, MN
Evans, Margaret J. ... New York, NY
Evans, Margo F. ... Charlotte, NC
Evans, Marianne ... Washington, DC
Evans, Maribeth R. ... Alameda, CA
Evans, Marie K. ... Toccoa, GA
Evans, Marie Weston ... Oklahoma City, OK
Evans, Mark C. ... Houston, TX
Evans, Mark D. ... Tustin, CA
Evans, Mark D. ... Bloomfield Hills, MI
Evans, Mark E. ... Dallas, TX
Evans, Mark G. ... Atlanta, GA
Evans, Mark H. ... Los Angeles, CA
Evans, Mark J. ... Lexington, MO
Evans, Mark L. ... Los Angeles, CA
Evans, Mark L. ... Washington, DC
Evans, Mark L. ... Bellevue, WA
Evans, Marquette D. ... Cincinnati, OH
Evans, Martha A. ... Dallas, TX
Evans, Martha C. ... Eugene, OR
Evans, Martin ... New York, NY
Evans, Martin Frederic ... New York, NY
Evans, Marvin D. ... Cleveland, OH
Evans, Marvin L. ... Miami, FL
Evans, Mary Arline ... Nashville, TN
Evans, Mary E. ... Washington, DC
Evans, Mary W. ... Colorado Springs, CO
Evans, Mason, IV ... Columbus, OH
Evans, Mathew D. ... Sacramento, CA
Evans, Matthew J. ... San Diego, CA
Evans, Matthew J. ... Brooklyn, NY
Evans, Matthew J. ... Knoxville, TN
Evans, Matthew L. ... Birmingham, AL
Evans, Matthew N. ... Salt Lake City, UT
Evans, Matthew S., Jr. ... Annapolis, MD
Evans, Maurice L. ... Laguna Hills, CA
Evans, Mechelle ... New York, NY
Evans, Melinda Melhorn ... Rocky Mount, NC
Evans, Melody Brannon ... Topeka, KS
Evans, Melvin H., Jr.
Christiansted, St. Croix, VI
Evans, Melvin I. ... Atlantic Beach, NY
Evans, Melvin J. ... White Plains, NY
Evans, Mercedes Sherrod, (Ms.)
Boston, MA
Evans, Merry C. ... Kansas City, MO
Evans, Mia ... Encino, CA
Evans, Michael D. ... Frederick, OK
Evans, Michael E. ... Canton, IL
Evans, Michael E. ... Nashville, TN
Evans, Michael G. ... Los Angeles, CA
Evans, Michael J. ... Birmingham, AL
Evans, Michael J. ... Salinas, CA
Evans, Michael J. ... Westwood, NJ
Evans, Michael J., P.C. ... Birmingham, AL
Evans, Michael R. ... Washington, DC
Evans, Michael R. ... Houston, TX
Evans, Michael S. ... San Diego, CA
Evans, Michael S. ... Portland, OR
Evans, Michele A. ... White Plains, NY
Evans, Michele A., P.C. ... White Plains, NY
Evans, Michele E. ... New York, NY
Evans, Michelle ... Houston, TX
San Antonio, TX
Evans, Mitchel S. ... Atlanta, GA
Evans, Monica J. ... Santa Clara, CA
Evans, Morgan R. ... Costa Mesa, CA
Evans, Morris M. ... Snellville, GA
Evans & Mullinix, P.A. ... Lenexa, KS
Shawnee, KS
Evans, Mygnon ... Lakeland, FL
Evans, N. Earle ... Syracuse, NY
Evans, Nancy H. ... Cedar Rapids, IA
Evans, Neal D., Jr. (P.A.) ... Jacksonville, FL
Evans, Neil K. ... Cleveland, OH
Evans, Nilene R. ... New York, NY
Evans, Noel K. ... Tampa, FL
Evans & Noll, L.L.P. ... West Chester, PA
Evans, Nolly S. ... Fayetteville, NY
Evans, Nora Ochoa ... Austin, TX
Evans, Noreen M. ... Santa Rosa, CA
Evans, Ollie L., Jr. ... Tallahassee, FL
Evans, Orinda D. ... Atlanta, GA
Evans, Orr, Laffan, Torres & DeMaggio, P.C.
New York, NY
Syosset, NY
Evans, Osborne & Kreizman
Ocean Township, NJ
New York, NY
Evans, Owen T. ... Tulsa, OK
Evans, Parthenia B. ... Kansas City, MO
Evans, Patricia A. ... Boston, MA
Evans, Patricia A. ... Detroit, MI
Evans, Patricia E. ... Alexandria, LA
Evans, Patricia H. ... San Diego, CA
Evans, Patrick J. ... Los Angeles, CA
Evans, Patrick L. ... Watertown, NY
Evans, Patti E. ... New York, NY
Evans, Paul E. ... Independence, MO
Evans, Paul J. ... O'Fallon, IL
Evans, Paul Kemper ... Chatham, NJ
Evans, Paul S. ... Salt Lake City, UT
Evans, Paul V. ... Colorado Springs, CO
Evans, Peggy P. ... Montross, VA
Evans, Peter T. ... Hartford, CT
Evans, Peter V. ... Farmington, CT
Evans, Peter W. ... Huntington Beach, CA
Evans, Peter W. ... Portland, ME
Evans & Petree ... Memphis, TN
Evans, Philip B. ... Boston, MA
Evans, Philip L. ... Utica, NY
Evans, Philip Tucker ... Washington, DC
Evans, Phillips M. ... Largo, FL
Evans & Phipps ... Manassas, VA
Evans, Pletkovic & Rhodes, P.C.
Huntington Woods, MI
Evans, Portnoy & Quinn ... Pittsburgh, PA
Evans, R. Brian ... Louisville, KY
Evans, R. Craig ... Mechanicsville, VA
Evans, R. Hobart, III ... Houston, TX
Evans, R. Leland ... Columbus, OH
Evans, R., P.C. ... Omaha, NE
Evans, R. Wayne ... Tallahassee, FL
Evans, Rachel Cohen ... Washington, DC
Evans, Rachelle L. ... Chicago, IL
Evans, Ralph L. ... Vero Beach, FL
Evans, Ralph T. ... Fullerton, CA
Evans, Randall E. ... Houston, TX
Evans, Randall L. ... Phoenix, AZ
Evans, Randy B. ... Minneapolis, MN
Evans, Raymond S. ... Hauppauge, NY
Mineola, NY
Evans, Rees T. ... Oklahoma City, OK
Evans, Rhys ... Manchester Center, VT
Evans, Richard C. ... Topeka, KS
Evans, Richard G. ... St. Paul, MN
Evans, Richard G. ... Austin, TX
Evans, Richard H. ... Lebanon, NJ
Evans, Richard H. ... Cincinnati, OH
Evans, Richard I. ... Coshocton, OH
Evans, Richard J. ... Ontario, CA
Evans, Richard J. ... Rochester, NY
Evans, Richard J., Jr. ... Rochester, NY
Evans, Richard K. ... Kingston, TN
Evans, Richard L. ... Minneapolis, MN
Evans, Richard L. ... Salt Lake City, UT
Evans, Richard L. ... Bellevue, WA
Evans, Richard M. ... Department of Justice, Civil Division, GV
Evans, Richard M. ... Northampton, MA
Evans, Richard N. ... Beaumont, TX
Evans, Richard N., II ... Beaumont, TX
Evans, Richard T. ... Orlando, FL
Evans, Richard Vernon ... Louisville, KY
Evans, Richard W. ... Palo Alto, CA
Evans, Richard W. ... Washington, DC
Bethesda, MD
Evans, Richard W. ... Salt Lake City, UT
Evans, Richard W., & Associates, P.C.
Salt Lake City, UT
Evans, Robert A. ... Chula Vista, CA
Indianapolis, IN
Evans, Robert B. ... Washington, DC
Evans, Robert B., III ... New Orleans, LA
Evans, Robert B., Jr. ... New Orleans, LA
Evans, Robert C. ... Waukesha, WI
Evans, Robert C., Jr. ... San Francisco, CA
Evans, Robert Collin ... Tallahassee, FL
New Orleans, LA
Greensboro, NC
Houston, TX
Evans, Robert D. ... San Francisco, CA
Evans, Robert D. ... Washington, DC
Evans, Robert D. ... Greenville, MS
Evans, Robert Don, Jr. ... Shreveport, LA
Evans, Robert E. ... Monticello, MS
Evans, Robert E. ... Marietta, OH
Evans, Robert E. ... Lynchburg, VA
Evans, Robert E., Jr. ... Richwood, OH
Evans, Robert F., Jr. ... Orlando, FL
Evans, Robert F., Jr., P.A. ... Orlando, FL
Evans, Robert G. ... Dayton, OH
Evans, Robert G. ... Eau Claire, WI
Evans, Robert, III ... New York, NY
Evans, Robert L. ... Detroit, MI
Evans, Robert M. ... St. Louis, MO
Evans, Robert M., Jr. ... St. Louis, MO
Evans, Robert Michael ... Orlando, FL
Evans, Robert P. ... Wildomar, CA
Evans, Robert S. ... New Haven, CT
Brattleboro, VT
Evans, Robert S. ... Brooklyn, NY
Evans, Robert S., P.C. ... New Haven, CT
Evans, Robert W. ... Long Beach, CA
Evans, Robert W. ... San Jose, CA
Evans, Robert W. ... Pottstown, PA
Evans, Roberta G. ... Chicago, IL
Evans, Robley D. ... Minneapolis, MN
Evans, Roger ... Dallas, TX
Evans, Roger K. ... New York, NY
Evans, Roger K. ... Salem, OR
Evans, Roger R. (IBA) ... Houston, TX
Evans, Roger W. ... Sioux Center, IA
Evans & Rogers ... Shreveport, LA
Evans, Rohde & Criswell ... Silverton, TX
Tulia, TX
Evans, Ronald C. ... Fort Worth, TX
Evans, Ronald K. ... St. Louis, MO
Evans, Ronald R. ... Indianapolis, IN
Evans, Ronald S. ... Richmond, VA
Evans, Ronda Lenise ... Columbus, OH
Evans, Rose Paulnetta ... Montgomery, AL
Evans, Ross M. ... Cincinnati, OH
Evans, Ross S. ... Farmington, CT
Evans & Rowe, P.C. ... San Antonio, TX
Evans, Roy F., Jr. ... Marion, VA
Evans, Roy J. ... Morristown, NJ
Evans, Russell ... Palo Alto, CA
Evans, Ruth Anne ... Omaha, NE
Evans, Ruth B. ... Kansas City, MO
Evans St. Clair & Bainter, L.L.P.
Columbus, OH
Evans, Sandra J. ... Atlanta, GA
Evans, Sara J. ... Dallas, TX
Evans, Sarah ... Norman, OK
Evans, Sarah E. ... Atlanta, GA
Evans, Schnabel & Associates
New Orleans, LA
Evans, Scott ... Charleston, WV
Evans, Scott A. ... Harrisburg, PA
Evans, Scott S. ... Denver, CO
Evans, Scott T. ... Las Vegas, NV
Salt Lake City, UT
Evans, Shannon L. ... Las Vegas, NV
Evans, Sharon L. ... Columbus, OH
Evans, Sharon M. ... West Hazleton, PA
Evans, Sheila T. ... Washington, DC
Evans, Sheldon, P.A. ... Miami Lakes, FL
Evans, Sherri A. ... Houston, TX
Evans, Sonia Malhotra ... Denver, CO
Evans, Stacee E. ... Bloomington, IN
Evans, Stacy J. ... Commack, NY
Evans, Stanley Lewis ... Monterey, CA
Evans, Stanley R. ... Sidney, OH
Evans, Starke M. ... Federalsburg, MD
Evans, Stephanie C. ... Washington, DC
Evans, Stephen ... Palestine, TX
Evans, Stephen B. ... St. Louis, MO
Evans, Stephen G. ... Oquawka, IL
Evans, Stephen L. ... Plant City, FL
Evans, Stephen M. ... Bellevue, WA
Evans, Stephen P. ... Toledo, OH
Evans, Stephen W. ... Greenville, SC
Evans, Steve H. ... Arlington, TX
Evans, Steven C. ... Atlanta, GA
Evans, Steven G. ... Palatine, IL
Evans, Steven L. ... Phoenix, AZ
Evans, Steven L. ... Fuquay-Varina, NC
Evans, Steven L., P.C., Law Offices of
Fuquay-Varina, NC
Evans, Steven R. ... Portland, OR
Evans, Sue Ann Salmon
Palos Verdes Estates, CA
Evans, Sue Mcknight ... Nashville, TN
Evans, Sue Montgomery ... Fredonia, NY
Evans, Sue R. ... Oklahoma City, OK
Evans, Susan A. ... Fairfax, VA
Evans, Susan B. ... Philadelphia, PA
Evans, Susan D. ... Naples, FL
Evans, Susan F. ... Philadelphia, PA
Evans, Susan L. ... Fairbanks, AK
Evans, Susan Lloyd Harrison
Kailua-Kona, HI
Evans, Susan M. ... Cleveland, OH
Evans, Susanne W. ... Houston, TX
Evans, Suzanne A. ... Baltimore, MD
Evans, Suzanne F. ... San Diego, CA
Evans, Suzy ... Palmdale, CA
Evans, T. Oliver ... Clarksville, MD
Evans, Tammy J. ... Los Angeles, CA
Evans, Taz F. ... Mesa, AZ
Evans, Terence T. ... Chicago, IL
Evans, Terrence N. ... Murfreesboro, NC
Evans, Terri L. ... Washington, DC
Evans, Terry M. ... Trenton, MO
Evans, Terry Underwood ... Anniston, AL
Evans, Thomas A. ... Anchorage, AK
Evans, Thomas A., Jr. ... Des Moines, IA
Evans, Thomas B., Jr. ... Washington, DC
Evans, Thomas C. ... McLean, VA
Evans, Thomas C. ... Seattle, WA
Evans, Thomas C., III ... Ripley, WV
Spencer, WV
Evans, Thomas D. ... Findlay, OH
Evans, Thomas E. ... Temple, TX
Evans, Thomas J. ... Holland, MI
Muskegon, MI
Evans, Thomas L. ... Washington, DC
Portland, OR
Evans, Thomas M. ... Garden City, NY
Evans, Thomas M. ... Cincinnati, OH
Evans, Thomas N., Jr. ... Towson, MD
Evans, Thomas P. ... Tampa, FL
Evans, Thomas S. ... Syracuse, NY
Evans, Thomas S. ... Ponca City, OK
Evans, Thomas W. ... Boston, MA
Evans, Thomas W. ... New York, NY
Evans, Tim ... Fort Worth, TX
Evans, Timothy Brian ... Los Angeles, CA
Evans, Timothy J. ... Yuba City, CA
Evans, Timothy J. ... Lenexa, KS
Shawnee, KS
Evans, Timothy Joseph ... Omaha, NE
Evans, Timothy R. ... Waukegan, IL
Evans, Timothy R. ... Hamilton, OH
Evans, Todd & Floyd, PLC ... Nashville, TN
Evans, Todd W. ... New York, NY
Evans, Valerie Weatherford ... Orlando, FL
Evans, Valerie Williams ... Tulsa, OK
Evans, Vaughn E. ... Seattle, WA
Evans, Velma E. ... Silver Spring, MD
Evans, Venci & Camilli ... Green Bay, WI
Evans, Verne H. ... Springfield, IL
Evans, Vernon C. ... Redfield, SD
Evans, Vernon L. ... Fairfax, VA
Evans, Vernon W., Jr. ... Lutz, FL
Evans, Vickie G. ... York, PA
Evans, Victor S. ... Columbia, SC
Evans, Virginia B. ... Baltimore, MD
Evans, Virginia Caroline
Baton Rouge, LA
Evans, W. Hill, P.A. ... Marion, NC
Evans, W. Lawrence ... Denison, TX
Evans, Walter E. ... Dallas, TX
Evans, Walter H., III ... Portland, OR
Evans, Walter Jefferson, Jr. ... New York, NY
Evans, Walter Manning ... San Francisco, CA
Evans, Walter P. (Chip), IV ... Austin, TX
Evans, Walter S. ... Doylestown, OH
Evans, Walter T. ... Rockville, MD
Evans, Warren Cleage ... Detroit, MI
Evans, Warren D. ... Thomson, GA
Evans, Wayne L. ... Bluefield, WV
Evans, Wendell L., Jr. ... Livingston, TX
Evans, Wendy B. ... Elkton, MD
Evans, William A. ... Lakewood, NY
Evans, William B. ... Baton Rouge, LA
Evans, William B. ... Elkton, MD
Evans, William C. ... Washington, DC
Evans, William D. ... Pasadena, CA
Evans, William D. ... Boston, MA
Evans, William D., II ... Akron, OH
Evans, William D., (P.C.)
Long Beach, CA
Evans, William E. ... Monterey, CA
Evans, William E. ... Springfield, MO
Evans, William E. ... Manassas, VA
Evans, William G. ... Topsfield, MA
Evans, William J. ... Anchorage, AK
Evans, William J. ... Salt Lake City, UT
Evans, William L. ... Santa Ana, CA
Evans, William L. ... Ada, OH
Evans, William L. ... Dallas, TX
Evans, William L., Jr. ... Fort Worth, TX
Evans, William M. ... Washington, DC
Evans, William Nole ... Huntington Woods, MI
Evans, William P. ... Atlanta, GA
Evans, William R. ... Soldotna, AK
Evans, William R. ... Baltimore, MD
Evans, William R. ... Mount Morris, MI
Evans, William R. ... New York, NY
Evans, William R. ... Columbus, OH
Evans, William Randall ... Plano, TX
Evans, William T. ... Salt Lake City, UT
Evans, William V. ... Douglas, GA
Evans, William W. ... St. Louis, MO
Evans, Willie ... Boston, MA
Evans & Willock ... Louisville, KY
Evans, Winston S. ... Nashville, TN
Evans, Winthrop S. ... Placentia, CA
Evans, Wm. O. ... Tulsa, OK
Evans, Wm. W. ... Lexington, KY
Evans, Yolanda Perrotta ... Nutley, NJ
Evans, Yvonne Mims ... Charlotte, NC
Evans-Adelman, Denise A ... Blue Bell, PA

Evans-Ervin, Madeline Carol ...... Brooklyn, NY
Evans-Harrell, Valerie D.
Department of Labor, Office of Secretary, GV
Evans III, Merle D. ...... Canton, OH
Evans Klucas, Denise F. ...... Toledo, OH
Evanson, Dennis B. ...... Sandy, UT
Evanson, Joseph George, P.A.
Clearwater, FL
Evans-Orville, J. Keith
San Francisco, CA
Evans-Stanton, Sherri L. ...... Raleigh, NC
Evans-Yosief, Barbara ...... Hampton, VA
Evanusa, Michel S. ...... New York, NY
Evars-Goan, Mary Avis ...... Knoxville, TN
Evarts, Christopher J. ...... Philadelphia, PA
Evarts, Robert A. ...... Lancaster, PA
Evarts, William M., Jr. ...... New York, NY
Evashavik & Evashavik ...... Pittsburgh, PA
Evashavik, G. N. ...... Pittsburgh, PA
Evashavik, Gregory A. ...... Pittsburgh, PA
Evashavik, Nicholas J. ...... Pittsburgh, PA
Evashavik, Susan F. ...... Pittsburgh, PA
Evashevski & Elliott, P.C. ...... Corvallis, OR
Evashevski, Forest, Jr. ...... Corvallis, OR
Evashevski, James A. ...... Ann Arbor, MI
Evashevski, Jean Fee ...... Corvallis, OR
Evashevski, Katherine A. ...... Denver, CO
Evashevski, Tom H. ...... St. Ignace, MI
Evatt, Mary Powell ...... Decatur, GA
Evatt, Timothy G. ...... San Diego, CA
Evatt, Timothy W. ...... Anderson, SC
Evaul, David H. ...... Dallas, TX
Evavold, Dale ...... Rushford, MN
Evavold Law Office, P.A. ...... Rushford, MN
Eve, Leecia Roberta ...... Buffalo, NY
Eve, R. Michael, Jr. ...... Charlotte, NC
Eveillard, Audrey ...... New York, NY
Eveland, Dean S. ...... Department of the Army, Office of the Judge Advocate General, GV
Eveland, Elwood T., Jr. ...... Wilmington, DE
Eveland, Janet L. ...... Columbia, MD
Eveland, Janet L., Chartered, Law Offices of
Columbia, MD
Eveland, Thomas S. ...... Charlotte, MI
Eveld, David J. ...... Seguin, TX
Eveleigh, Cheshire I'Anson
Virginia Beach, VA
Eveleigh, Dennis G. ...... Stamford, CT
Eveleigh, Douglas M. ...... Chicago, IL
Eveleigh, Laurel J. ...... Syracuse, NY
Eveleigh, Robert J. ...... Virginia Beach, VA
Eveler & Eveler ...... York, PA
Eveler, George L., III ...... York, PA
Eveler, George L., Jr. ...... York, PA
Eveler, Kristine K. ...... York, PA
Eveleth, Peter Ames
National Labor Relations Board, Office of the General Counsel, GV
Evelev, David Ross ...... St. Louis, MO
Eveline, Davis & Phillips ...... New Orleans, LA
Eveline, Gregory P. ...... New Orleans, LA
Evelius, John C. ...... Baltimore, MD
Evelius, Karen Gessert ...... Timonium, MD
Evelius, Paul F. ...... Baltimore, MD
Eveloff, Bernard ...... Kansas City, MO
Eveloff, Mark J. ...... Council Bluffs, IA
Eveloff, Philip ...... St. Joseph, MO
Eveloff, Steven ...... Springfield, IL
Evelyn, Aubrey DeLisle ...... Columbia, MD
Even, Chris M. ...... Dubuque, IA
Even, Crandall, Wade, Lowe & Gates, A Professional Corporation ...... Irvine, CA
Rancho Cucamonga, CA
San Diego, CA
Woodland Hills, CA
Even, Francis A. ...... Chicago, IL
Even, James R. ...... Sioux Falls, SD
Even, John B. ...... Phoenix, AZ
Even, John R. ...... Tucson, AZ
Even, John T. ...... Inverness, IL
Even, Kevin B. ...... Muskegon, MI
Even, Leslie A. ...... Madison, WI
Even, Nicholas ...... Dallas, TX
Even, Randolph M. ...... Woodland Hills, CA
Evenchick, Barry H. ...... Newark, NJ
Evendorff, Charles S. ...... San Diego, CA
Evens, Bradley A. ...... Seattle, WA
Evens, Mark Fox ...... Washington, DC
Evens, Muriel G. ...... Sacramento, CA
Evens, Timothy W. ...... Phoenix, AZ
Evensen, Albert W. ...... Kaneohe, HI
Evensen, Dale J. ...... Minneapolis, MN
Evensen, Kerry M. ...... Minneapolis, MN
Evensky, Reid D. ...... Memphis, TN
Evenson, Bryan G. ...... Yakima, WA
Evenson, Carlin & LePage ...... Pineville, MO
Evenson, Christopher H. ...... Appleton, WI
Evenson, Corrine L. ...... St. Cloud, MN
Evenson, Debra M. ...... Chicago, IL
New York, NY
Evenson, Dennis D. ...... Clear Lake, SD
Estelline, SD
Evenson, Donald D. ...... Washington, DC
Evenson, James ...... Baraboo, WI
Evenson, James Albert ...... Boulder, CO
Evenson, Jerry W., P.C. ...... Bismarck, ND
Evenson, Kirk D. ...... Great Falls, MT
Evenson, McKeown, Edwards & Lenahan, P.L.L.C. ...... Washington, DC
Evenson, Peter O. ...... Washington, DC
Greensboro, NC
Evenson, Robert W. ...... Pineville, MO
Evenson, William D. ...... Holland, MI
Everage, Barbara C. ...... Albuquerque, NM
Everage, Charles Ali ...... Montgomery, AL
Everakes, Howard C. ...... Glendale, CA
Everall, Stephen G. ...... Englewood, CO
Everard, Gerald W. ...... Madison, WI
Everard, Jerold T. ...... Seattle, WA
Everard, Scott A. ...... Spokane, WA
Everbach, O. George ...... Dallas, TX
Everberg, Carol J. ...... Woburn, MA
Everdell, William ...... New York, NY
Evered, Donna R. ...... Seattle, WA
Everest, Andrew ...... Chicago, IL
Everest, Mark J. ...... Mobile, AL
Everett, Alan L. ...... Lincoln, NE
Everett, Alicia Glekas ...... New York, NY
Everett, Bernard J. ...... Anaconda, MT
Everett, Bonnie E. ...... Lima, OH
Everett, C. Taylor ...... Waverly, VA
Everett, Camille J. ...... Los Angeles, CA
Everett, Carl B. ...... Wilmington, DE
Philadelphia, PA
Everett, Carmen Zervigon ...... Lawndale, CA
Everett, Charles D. ...... Dallas, TX
Everett, Clifton W., Jr. ...... Greenville, NC
Everett, Cynthia A. ...... Miami, FL
Everett, Dale M. ...... Oklahoma City, OK
Everett, David F. ...... New York, NY
Everett, David R. ...... Albany, NY
Everett, Diana ...... Parkersburg, WV
Everett, Donn J. ...... Manhattan, KS
Everett, Dykes C. ...... Winter Park, FL
Everett, Edward B., III ...... Atlanta, GA
Everett, Edward S. ...... Terre Haute, IN
Everett, Eric R. ...... Boston, MA
Everett & Everett ...... Durham, NC
Everett, Everett & McDonald
Terre Haute, IN
Everett & Everett, P.L.L.C. ...... Elkin, NC
Everett, Fredrick S. ...... Farmington Hills, MI
Everett, Gaskins, Hancock & Stevens, LLP
Raleigh, NC
Everett, Gerald L. ...... Annapolis, MD
Everett, Glennon P. ...... Crowley, LA
Everett, Gregg Brantley ...... Montgomery, AL
Everett, Holly M. ...... Louisville, KY
Everett, J. Mark ...... Austin, TX
Everett, J. Richard ...... Rochester, NY
Everett, James A. ...... Elkin, NC
Everett, James B. ...... Decatur, MS
Everett, James J. ...... Phoenix, AZ
Everett, James J., P.C., Law Offices of
Phoenix, AZ
Everett, James R., Jr. ...... Nashville, TN
Everett, Jeffrey C. ...... Chicago, IL
Everett, Jeffrey M. ...... Phoenix, AZ
Everett, Joe S. ...... Clearwater, FL
Everett, John C. ...... Fayetteville, AR
Everett, John H. ...... Yorba Linda, CA
Everett, John K. ...... Columbus, OH
Everett, John P., Jr. ...... Lake Charles, LA
Everett, Kathy R. ...... Durham, NC
Everett, Kenneth B. ...... Orinda, CA
Everett, Kenneth D. ...... Kingman, AZ
Everett, Kenneth L. ...... New York, NY
Everett, Leonard ...... Tucson, AZ
Everett, Margaret Dodane ...... Cleveland, OH
Everett, Maria J.K. ...... Richmond, VA
Everett, Mark A. ...... New York, NY
Everett & Mars ...... Fayetteville, AR
Everett, Martha ...... San Francisco, CA
Everett, Mary L. ...... Harris, MN
Everett, Mary Lu ...... San Francisco, CA
Everett, Michael ...... Grandview, WA
Everett, Michael T. ...... Dallas, TX
Everett, Mike ...... Marked Tree, AR
Everett, Nancy ...... St. Louis, MO
Everett, Nancy Elizabeth ...... Columbia, MD
Everett, Nora M. ...... Des Moines, IA
Everett, P. David, II ...... Mentor, OH
Everett, Pamela M. ...... San Diego, CA
Everett, Peter, IV ...... Albuquerque, NM
Everett, Peter S. ...... Fairfax, VA
Everett, Preston T., Jr. ...... Port Charlotte, FL
Everett, Ralph B. ...... Washington, DC
Everett, Reid H. ...... Fresno, CA
Everett, Reynolds M., Jr. ...... Galva, IL
Everett, Richard D. ...... Tampa, FL
Everett, Richard H. ...... Clinton, MD
Everett, Robert E. ...... Andover, MA
Everett, Robert W. ...... Russell, KY
Everett, Robinson O. ...... Charlotte, NC
Durham, NC
Raleigh, NC
Everett, Roger D. ...... Yukon, OK
Everett, Sandrea L. ...... Baton Rouge, LA
Everett, Sarah E. ...... New York, NY
Everett, Scott W. ...... Dallas, TX
Everett, Shelley B. ...... Jacksonville, FL
Everett, Stanley E. ...... Akron, OH
Everett, Stephen E. ...... Alexandria, LA
Everett, Stephen, Ltd. ...... Alexandria, LA
Everett, Stephen M. ...... San Francisco, CA
Everett, Terrence A. ...... Los Angeles, CA
Everett, Terry Tumlin ...... Macon, GA
Everett, Thomas H., III ...... Caldwell, NJ
Everett, Thomas Wayne ...... Ailey, GA
Everett, Timothy C. ...... Neenah, WI
Everett, Timothy H. ...... Hartford, CT
Everett, W. Harrell, Jr. ...... Elkin, NC
Goldsboro, NC
Everett, Wade H. ...... Cartersville, GA
Everett, Wade H., P.C. ...... Cartersville, GA
Everett, Warren, Swindell, Kiess & Jones
Greenville, NC
Everett, William ...... Bethlehem, PA
Everett, William C. ...... Mystic, CT
Everett, Womble & Finan, L.L.P.
Goldsboro, NC
Snow Hill, NC
Everett-Church, Ray ...... Hayward, CA
Arlington, VA
Everette, April N. ...... Washington, DC
Everette, Emory B. ...... Atlanta, GA
Everett-Garcia, Jessica L. ...... Phoenix, AZ
Everhard, Conrad E. J. ...... New York, NY
Everhard, John A. ...... Falls Church, VA
Everhardt, Jerry R. ...... Greensboro, NC
Everhardus, John A. ...... Detroit, MI
Everhardus, John C. ...... Chicago, IL
Everhart, Amy J. ...... Nashville, TN
Everhart, Brown & Snyder ...... Kingwood, WV
Everhart, Donald L. ...... Ventura, CA
Everhart, Edward J. ...... West Bloomfield, MI
Everhart, Frank B. ...... Kingwood, WV
Everhart, Jeffrey L. ...... Richmond, VA
Everhart, Lisa A. ...... Arlington, VA
Everhart, M. Daisy ...... El Paso, TX
Everhart, Mirchana S. ...... Lake Charles, LA
Everhart, Pamela D. ...... Boston, MA
Everhart, Robin L. ...... Atlanta, GA
Everhart, Sheila A. ...... Overland Park, KS
Everhart, Stephen M. ...... St. Petersburg, FL
Everheart, William E. ...... Dallas, TX
Everingham, J. Theodore
Grosse Pointe Woods, MI
Everist, Barbara ...... Sioux Falls, SD
Everitt, A. Zachry ...... Augusta, GA
Everitt, Herbert D. ...... Amarillo, TX
Everitt, John R. ...... South Amboy, NJ
Everitt, Keary L. ...... New Orleans, LA
Everitt, Marlene Romano
West Palm Beach, FL
Everitt, Sandra W. ...... Middlebury, VT
Everitt-Emery, Karen ...... Seattle, WA
Everix, Emil T. ...... Lancaster, WI
Everley, Douglas R. ...... Washington, DC
Everlof, Sherman W., Jr. ...... Warrenton, VA
Everlove, Annette M. ...... Tucson, AZ
Everly, Barry E. ...... Columbus, OH
Everly, Carol J. ...... Butte, MT
Everly, Edward E. ...... Signal Hill, CA
Everly, Jon P. ...... Southfield, MI
Everly, Rebecca ...... Department of State, Office of the Legal Adviser, GV
Everly, Robin L. ...... Dallas, TX
Everman, Paul D. ...... Louisville, KY
Everngam, Douglas H. ...... Denton, MD
Everngam, Gary G. ...... Bethesda, MD
Everritt, Christina E. ...... St. Louis, MO
Everroad, Andrew Quinn ...... Phoenix, AZ
Everroad, John D. ...... Phoenix, AZ
Evers, Bradley W. ...... Dayton, OH
Evers, Bruce N. ...... Appleton, WI
Evers, Garrett D. ...... Cleveland, OH
Evers, Geoffrey O. ...... Sacramento, CA
Evers, Gregory W. ...... Charleston, WV
Evers & Hendrickson, LLP
San Francisco, CA
Evers, James F. ...... Honolulu, HI
Evers, James P. ...... Hawthorne, NJ
Evers, Jeffrey W. ...... Hillside, IL
Evers, Joel ...... Wauchula, FL
Evers, John F. ...... Middlebury, VT
Evers, Julie A. ...... Lock Haven, PA
Evers, Kenneth B. ...... Wauchula, FL
Evers, Kim E. ...... Pensacola, FL
Evers, Kristine S. ...... Denver, CO
Evers, Linda R. ...... Morristown, NJ
Evers, Mary F. ...... Cherry Hill, NJ
Evers, Michael D. ...... Evanston, IL
Evers, Michael J. ...... Chicago, IL
Evers, R. Elizabeth ...... Washington, DC
Evers, Randy D. ...... Norman, OK
Evers, Reid A. ...... Los Angeles, CA
Evers, Robert Allen ...... Washington, DC
Evers, Robert Allen, Law Offices, Chartered
Washington, DC
Evers, Robert T. ...... Fairfield, NJ
Evers, Stephen J. ...... Clarks Summit, PA
Evers, William ...... Bronx, NY
Evers, William C., III ...... Collinsville, IL
Evers, William D. ...... San Francisco, CA
Evers, William L. ...... Brooklyn, NY
Eversberg, Andrew W. ...... Baton Rouge, LA
Eversman, Erica L. ...... Cleveland, OH
Eversman, Jay P. ...... Dallas, TX
Eversmeyer, John H. ...... Newport Beach, CA
Eversole, David E. ...... Shelbyville, IL
Eversole, John F., III ...... Boca Raton, FL
Fort Lauderdale, FL
Miami, FL
Eversole, Laura ...... Washington, DC
Eversole, Otis H., Jr. ...... Tulsa, OK
Eversole & Rudd, P.A. ...... Boca Raton, FL
Fort Lauderdale, FL
Miami, FL
Everson, Beverly F. ...... Minneapolis, MN
Everson, David E., Jr. ...... Kansas City, MO
Everson, Donna ...... Houston, TX
Everson, Ernest Lindsey ...... Houston, TX
Everson, Gary B. ...... Billings, MT
Everson, James C. ...... Englewood, CO
Everson, James L. ...... Green Bay, WI
Everson, James R. ...... Denver, CO
Everson, John H. ...... Avon Lake, OH
Everson, Martin J. ...... Walnut Creek, CA
Everson, Mary E. ...... Dallas, TX
Everson, Nanette Rutka ...... Dallas, TX
Everson, P. M. ...... Wymore, NE
Everson, Rodney D. ...... Denver, CO
Everson, Sheri L. ...... Chicago, IL
Everson, Stacey R. ...... Minneapolis, MN
Everson, Steven L. ...... Colorado Springs, CO
Everson, Wayne A. ...... St. Paul, MN
Everson, Whitney, Everson & Brehm, S.C.
Green Bay, WI
Everstine, Richard L. ...... Denver, CO
Evert, C. Michael, Jr. ...... Atlanta, GA
Evert, Charles M. ...... Columbus, GA
Evert, Charles M., P.C. ...... Columbus, GA
Evert, Elisabeth A. ...... Dallas, TX
Evert, James F. ...... Chicago, IL
Evert, Julie German
Charlotte Amalie, St. Thomas, VI
Evert, Julie German, P.C.
Charlotte Amalie, St. Thomas, VI
Evert, Paul F. ...... Eau Claire, WI
Evert, Sharla Leigh ...... Chula Vista, CA
Evert & Weathersby ...... Atlanta, GA
Everton, Angus R. ...... Baltimore, MD
Everton, Glenn D. ...... Memphis, TN
Everton, Harold M. ...... San Jose, CA
Everton & Oliff ...... San Jose, CA
Everts, Alisa M. ...... Washington, DC
Everts, Gregory T. ...... Madison, WI
Everts, Steven H. ...... Mesa, AZ
Everts, William P., Jr. ...... Mill Valley, CA
Evertts, James L. ...... San Jose, CA
Evertz, Barry G. ...... Hackensack, NJ
Evertz, Douglas J. ...... Newport Beach, CA
Evertz, Harry A., III ...... St. Petersburg, FL
Evertz, Wendy G. ...... St. Petersburg, FL
Every, Joel ...... Philadelphia, PA
Every, Joel, & Associates, P.C.
Philadelphia, PA
Every, Judy R. ...... East Hartford, CT
Every & Stack ...... Daytona Beach, FL
Palm Coast, FL
Every, W. Richard ...... Daytona Beach, FL
Eves, G. Christopher ...... Reading, PA
Eves, J. Philip ...... Cedar City, UT
Eves, Mark W. ...... Portland, OR
Eves, S. David ...... Corvallis, OR
Eves, S. David, P.C. ...... Corvallis, OR
Eves, Timothy Richard ...... Annapolis, MD
Eves, Valerie ...... Bend, OR
Eves & Wade ...... Portland, OR
Eves, Walter C. ...... Rochester, NY
Evett, Joshua S. ...... Boise, ID
Evetts, Mark A. ...... Dallas, TX
Evey, Merle K. ...... Hollidaysburg, PA
Evey, Routch, Black, Dorezas, Magee & Levine LLP ...... Altoona, PA
Hollidaysburg, PA
Roaring Spring, PA
Evezich, Craig ...... Seattle, WA
Evich, Dan P. ...... Everett, WA
Evick, Laura S. ...... Harrisonburg, VA
Evidon, James S. ...... Sherman Oaks, CA
Evidon, Norman E. ...... Minneapolis, MN
Evidon & Weisberg, P.A. ...... Minneapolis, MN
Evilsizer, Ivan C. ...... Helena, MT
Evinger, David S. ...... Minneapolis, MN
Evins, Gloria J. ...... Lebanon, TN
Evins, Janie ...... Hot Springs National Park, AR
Evins, Joe B. ...... Edinburg, TX
Evins, Richard Ferrell ...... Smyrna, GA
Evins, Samuel L. ...... Chicago, IL
Evins, T. Alexander ...... Spartanburg, SC
Evitts, J. Leslie, III ...... Fort Smith, AR
Evnen, Robert B. ...... Lincoln, NE
Evnin, Michael D. ...... Chino, CA
Evola, Elizabeth Muraca ...... Chicago, IL
Evola & Evola ...... Chicago, IL
Evola, Maura J. ...... Fresh Meadows, NY
Evola, Robert J. ...... Edwardsville, IL
Evola, Vito M. ...... Chicago, IL
Evora, Carolyn Comeaux ...... Orlando, FL
Evora, Orlando L. ...... Orlando, FL
Evoy, David W. ...... Boca Raton, FL
Evoy, William I. ...... Marlton, NJ
Evrard, David E. ...... Tell City, IN
Evrard, David T. ...... Harrisburg, PA
Evrard, Lisa Lynn ...... Houston, TX
Evrard, Richard J. ...... Overland Park, KS
Evrén, Lisa Ann ...... New York, NY
Evry, Arthur ...... Newbury Park, CA
Evyan, Janelle S. ...... Memphis, TN
Ewald, Charles G. ...... Tehachapi, CA
Ewald, Daniel W. ...... Killington, VT
Ewald, Donald P. ...... Orlando, FL
Ewald, Edward L., Jr. ...... Troy, MI
Ewald, Eugene C. ...... Troy, MI
Ewald, Gregory J. ...... Washington, DC
Baltimore, MD
Ewald, Henry T., Jr. ...... Grosse Pointe, MI
Ewald, John D. ...... Austin, TX
Ewald, Michael J. ...... Hudson, OH
Ewald, Rex A. ...... Monroe, WI
Ewald, Robert C. ...... Louisville, KY
Ewald, Robert F. ...... Riverhead, NY
Ewald, Robert P. ...... Ames, IA
Ewald, Shelly L. ...... McLean, VA
Ewald, Stephen P. ...... Charlotte, NC
Ewald, Steven K. ...... San Diego, CA
Ewald, Timothy J. ...... Minneapolis, MN
Ewald, William J. ...... Grand Rapids, MI
Southfield, MI
Ewald, William J. ...... Green Bay, WI
Ewald-Herrick, Elizabeth Anne
Milwaukee, WI
Ewall & Ewall ...... Huntington, NY
Ewall, Laura E. ...... Dix Hills, NY
Ewall, Merton H. ...... Huntington, NY
Ewall, Steven B. ...... Huntington, NY
Ewalt & Dickinson ...... Houston, TX
Ewalt, Gretchen W. ...... Raleigh, NC
Ewalt, Henry W. ...... Pittsburgh, PA
Ewalt, James H. ...... Annandale, VA
Ewalt, Jeffrey H. ...... Houston, TX
Ewalt, Robert M., Jr. ...... Greensboro, NC
Ewan, David E. ...... Moorestown, NJ
Ewan, James E. ...... Independence, MO
Ewan, Paul D. ...... Lafayette, IN
Ewan, Todd Alan ...... Philadelphia, PA
Ewan, William K. ...... Lawrenceburg, IN
Ewanyshyn, Timothy L. ...... Palm Springs, CA
Ewart, Donald L. ...... Butler, PA

Ewart, John D. ... Tahlequah, OK
Ewart, John P. ... Mattoon, IL
Ewart, Lani L. ... Honolulu, HI
Ewart, Mark ... West Palm Beach, FL
Ewart, Norman D. ... Houston, TX
Ewart, Roy K. ... Sugar Land, TX
Ewart, Stephen C. ... Springfield, IL
Ewashinka, Heather E. ... Cleveland, OH
Ewbank, James B., II ... Austin, TX
Ewbank, John R. ... Southampton, PA
Ewbank and Kramer ... Lawrenceburg, IN
Ewbank, Rhonda G. ... Houston, TX
Ewbank, Robert J. ... Lawrenceburg, IN
Ewbank, Thomas P. ... Indianapolis, IN
Ewel, Dexter ... Washington, DC
Ewell, A. Ben, Jr. ... Fresno, CA
Ewell, Christine C. ... Los Angeles, CA
Ewell, Gary ... San Rafael, CA
Ewell, Gerald L., Jr. ... Tullahoma, TN
Ewell, Gerald L., Sr. ... Manchester, TN
Ewell, Harleigh P.
Consumer Product Safety Commission, Office of the General Counsel, GV
Ewell, James O. ... Dyersburg, TN
Ewell, John F. ... Front Royal, VA
Ewell, Michael W. ... Knoxville, TN
Ewell, Paul C. ... Berlin, MD
Ewell, Paul C., P.A. ... Berlin, MD
Ewell, Raymond W. ... Chicago, IL
Ewell, Taylor A. ... Manhattan Beach, CA
Ewell, Vincent F. ... Houston, TX
Ewell, William L., Jr. ... Sarasota, FL
Ewen, A. Campbell ... Louisville, KY
Ewen, Elaine S. ... Burbank, CA
Ewen, Karen A. ... Pasadena, CA
Ewen & Kinney ... Louisville, KY
Ewen, Linda J. ... McKinney, TX
Ewen, Pamela B. ... Houston, TX
Ewen, Philip ... Los Angeles, CA
Ewenike, Ogbonna ... Anaheim, CA
Ewens, David J. ... Grand Rapids, MN
Ewens, Elizabeth Pridgen ... Denver, CO
Ewer, Phyllis A. ... Chicago, IL
Ewer, Raymond S. ... Newton, MA
Ewers, David A., Law Office of
McAllen, TX
Ewers, Gregory M. ... Dayton, OH
Ewers, Jennifer A. ... Moscow, ID
Ewers, Jennifer P. ... Itasca, IL
Ewers, J. F., Jr. ... McAllen, TX
Ewers, John J. ... Cleveland, OH
Ewers, Lathan M., Jr. ... Richmond, VA
Ewers, Paul J. ... Anchorage, AK
Ewers, Robert E., Jr. ... New York, NY
Ewers, Robt. A. ... Lorain, OH
Ewers, Stephen D. ... Niantic, CT
Ewert, Alfred P. ... New York, NY
Ewert, James W. ... Sacramento, CA
Ewert, Lowell M. ... Portland, OR
Ewert, Quentin A. ... Lansing, MI
Ewert, Russell H. ... Chicago, IL
Ewert, Thomas M. ... Joliet, IL
Ewert, William A., Jr. ... Corpus Christi, TX
Ewert, William G. ... Minneapolis, MN
Ewert Pilchik, Elizabeth
San Francisco, CA
Ewig, Caspar F. ... New York, NY
Ewig, Thelma ... New York, NY
Ewigleben, Donald C. ... Englewood, CO
Ewin, Gordon O. ... New Orleans, LA
Ewin, Nancy Kaupp ... La Mesa, CA
Ewing, Alexander, Jr. ... Media, PA
Philadelphia, PA
West Chester, PA
Ewing, Anthony Phillips ... New York, NY
Ewing, Brenda S. ... Washington, DC
Ewing, Bruce R. ... New York, NY
Ewing, C. David ... Louisville, KY
Ewing, Candyce M. ... Southfield, MI
Ewing, Carey L. ... Durham, NC
Ewing, Caroline Day ... New York, NY
Ewing, Catherine R. ... Sacramento, CA
Ewing, Charles P. ... Buffalo, NY
Ewing, Colin W. ... Indianapolis, IN
Ewing, Cynthia L. ... Virginia Beach, VA
Ewing, David L. ... Columbia, SC
Ewing, David W. ... San Francisco, CA
Ewing, Deborah E. ... El Segundo, CA
Ewing, Diane L. ... Sacramento, CA
Ewing, Dianne L. ... Houston, TX
Ewing, Dietz, Turner & Kehoe, Professional Association ... Cambridge, MD
Centreville, MD
Denton, MD
Easton, MD
Stevensville, MD
Ewing, Douglas A. ... Easton, MA
Ewing, Edward C. ... Oak Brook, IL
Ewing, Eileen Smith ... Boston, MA
Ewing, Eleanor N. ... Philadelphia, PA
Ewing, Elizabeth E. ... Charlottesville, VA
Ewing, Ellen B. ... Louisville, KY
Ewing, Elliott Scott ... Sacramento, CA
Ewing & Ewing, P.C. ... Denver, CO
Ewing, Floyd T., III ... New York, NY
Ewing, Gregory Clyde ... Boston, MA
Ewing Group, The, P.C. ... Atlanta, GA
Ewing, Hickman, Jr. ... Germantown, TN
Ewing & Hoberock ... Nevada, MO
Ewing, J. Darlene ... Dallas, TX
Ewing, J. Michael ... Pittsburgh, PA
Ewing, J. Randolph ... Houston, TX
Ewing, Jack D., Jr. ... Texas City, TX
Ewing, James L., IV ... Atlanta, GA
Ewing, James R. ... Wheeling, WV
Ewing, Jenny ... Cambridge, MA
Ewing, Jerry L., Jr. ... Dallas, TX
Ewing, Jess D. ... Memphis, TN

Ewing, John B., Jr. ... Kansas City, MO
Ewing, John W. ... Lincoln, CA
Ewing, Johnson, Graves & Driskill, Professional Law Corporation
El Centro, CA
Palm Springs, CA
San Diego, CA
Ewing, Joseph Neff, Jr. ... Berwyn, PA
Ewing, Josephine Dorothy ... Brighton, CO
Ewing, Kathleen D. ... Sterling Forest, NY
Ewing, Kenneth P. ... Washington, DC
Ewing, Kent E. ... Cheyenne, WY
Ewing, Kevin A. ... Washington, DC
Ewing, Ky P., Jr. ... Washington, DC
Ewing Law Center, P.C. ... Durham, NC
Ewing, Letitia A. ... Philadelphia, PA
Ewing, Lynn M., III ... Nevada, MO
Ewing, Lynn M., Jr. ... Nevada, MO
Ewing, Malcolm C. ... Glendale, CA
Ewing, Mark ... Vincennes, IN
Ewing, Mary ... Denver, CO
Ewing, Mary M. ... St. Louis, MO
Ewing, Maya K. ... Chicago, IL
Ewing, Michael D. ... Chicago, IL
Ewing, Michael F. ... Bridgeport, CT
Ewing, Michael S. ... Richmond, VA
Ewing, Monet ... Boston, MA
Ewing, Monica E. ... Atlanta, GA
Ewing, Nancy B. ... Chicago, IL
Ewing, Nancy O. ... Atlanta, GA
Ewing, Nelson, II ... Phoenix, AZ
Ewing & Nettles, L.L.P. ... Columbia, SC
Ewing, Noah H., Jr. ... Purcell, OK
Ewing, Palmer W. ... Sacramento, CA
Ewing, Pamina ... Pittsburgh, PA
Ewing, Patricia A. ... Washington, DC
Ewing, Rachel Lilo ... Los Angeles, CA
Ewing, Randy R. ... Council Bluffs, IA
Ewing, Richard S. ... Washington, DC
Ewing, Richard S. ... Indianapolis, IN
Ewing, Richard W., (P.C.) ... Austin, TX
Ewing, Robert B. ... Belvedere-Tiburon, CA
Ewing, Robert C. ... Media, PA
Ewing, Robert Craig ... Denver, CO
Ewing, Robert F. ... Spokane, WA
Ewing, Robert J. ... Joplin, MO
Ewing, Robert P. ... Marlton, NJ
Philadelphia, PA
Plymouth Meeting, PA
Ewing, Robert W. ... Council Bluffs, IA
Ewing, Ron E. ... Colorado Springs, CO
Ewing, Samuel Evans, 3rd
Chester Springs, PA
Ewing & Scott ... Lewistown, IL
Ewing, Scott Ames ... Manchester, NH
Ewing, Shauna ... Portland, OR
Ewing, Steven C. ... Albuquerque, NM
Ewing, Suzanne ... Pittsburgh, PA
Ewing, T. Michael" Mike " ... Lakeport, CA
Ewing, Tamara T. ... Independence, MO
Elmira, NY
Ewing, Thomas C. ... Fort Wayne, IN
Ewing, Thomas D. ... Lafayette, IN
Ewing, Thomas E. ... Salem, OR
Ewing, Thomas L. ... Palo Alto, CA
Ewing, Thomas M. ... Keene, NH
Ewing, Thomas W. ... Pontiac, IL
Ewing, Todd, (P.C.) ... Washington, DC
Ewing, Tom B. ... Lewistown, IL
Ewing, Vincent Carlton ... Pasadena, CA
Ewing, William H. ... Philadelphia, PA
Ewing, William J. ... El Centro, CA
Palm Springs, CA
San Diego, CA
Ewing, William P. ... Atlanta, GA
Ewinger, Curt R. ... Aberdeen, SD
Ewins, Kathleen M. ... San Francisco, CA
Ewoldt, Valerie A. ... Lombard, IL
Ewubare, Roland O. ... New York, NY
Ewy, Barry R. ... Tulsa, OK
Ewy, Richard D. ... Wichita, KS
Ex, Mitchell Craig ... Chicago, IL
Exall, Allison K. ... Dallas, TX
Exall, Henry, IV ... Dallas, TX
Exall, Henry, Jr. ... Dallas, TX
Exall, Marian ... Atlanta, GA
Exar, Eve K. ... Harrisburg, PA
Exarhos, Herbert J. ... San Diego, CA
Exaros, William P. ... Jersey City, NJ
Bethlehem, PA
Exelbert, Robert P. ... New York, NY
Exelby, Donald C. ... Grand Rapids, MI
Exelrod, Alan B. ... San Francisco, CA
Exezidis, Kyriakos T. ... Houston, TX
Exler, Marilyn R. ... Anaheim, CA
Exley, Franc S. ... Macon, GA
Exley, Mark A. ... Arlington, VA
Exley, William M., Jr. ... Savannah, GA
Exley, William T., Jr. ... Amarillo, TX
Exline, Christopher Perry
Winston-Salem, NC
Exline, John D. ... Dallas, TX
Exline, Max I. ... Pueblo, CO
Exner, Cynthia R. ... Danbury, CT
Exner, Donald E. ... Greenbelt, MD
Exner, Melva Marie ... Philadelphia, PA
Exnicios, Hugh B. ... Metairie, LA
Exnicios, James C. ... New Orleans, LA
Exnicios, James R. ... Department of the Navy, Office of the Judge Advocate General, GV
Exnicios, Judith A ... Metairie, LA
Exnicios, Richard M. ... New Orleans, LA
Exnicios, Samuel R. ... New Orleans, LA
Exon, Charles S. ... Irvine, CA
Exon, Rolland J. ... Olathe, KS
Exoo, Diane J., P.C. ... Canton, NY
Exposito, Lorenzo F. ... Washington, DC
Exposito, Patricia A. ... Washington, DC

Ext, Traci L. ... Cleveland, OH
Extavour, N. Kemba ... Los Angeles, CA
Extavour, Winston C. ... Haddonfield, NJ
Extein, Alvin M. ... Chesterfield, MO
Extein, Mark C. ... Orlando, FL
Extein, Susan L. ... Philadelphia, PA
Exton, Kristine J. ... Los Angeles, CA
Extrom, Daniel M. ... Chicago, IL
Exum, Carol Wooten ... Raleigh, NC
Exum, Charles C. ... Jackson, TN
Exum, Darryl L. ... Riverside, CA
Exum, James G., Jr. ... Greensboro, NC
Exum, John B., Jr. ... Rocky Mount, NC
Exum, William T. ... Macon, GA
Ey, Douglas W., Jr. ... Charlotte, NC
Ey, J. Michael ... Columbia, SC
Ey, Robert M. ... Pennington, NJ
Eyal, Omer C. ... Washington, DC
Eyberg, Douglas K. ... Houston, TX
Eychner, David C. ... Woodland Hills, CA
Eydelshteyn, Simon ... Birmingham, MI
Eydt, George J. ... Buffalo, NY
Eye, Charles T. ... Ontario, CA
Eye, Roger N. ... Prior Lake, MN
Eyen, Stephen, Law Offices of
Cambridge, OH
Eyer, Charles P. ... Marshalls Creek, PA
Eyer, John ... Washington, KS
Eyer, Paul K. ... Harrisburg, PA
Eyer, Walter W. ... Seattle, WA
Eyerly, Gloria Ann ... Columbus, OH
Eyerly, Tred R. ... Saipan, TT
Eyerman, Edward L. ... St. Louis, MO
Eyerman, Francis J. ... St. Louis, MO
Eyerman, John R. ... New York, NY
Eyerman, Linda K. ... Portland, OR
Eyerman, Susan E. ... Circleville, OH
Eyestone, Linda L. ... Oak Forest, IL
Eygenhuysen, Robert H. A. ... Chicago, IL
Eyges, Debra Susan ... Hartford, CT
Eyherabide, Dominic P., Jr. ... Bakersfield, CA
Eyhorn, Robert B., Jr. ... Nordheim, TX
Eyhusen, Edward A. ... Twinsburg, OH
Eyke, David H. ... Chicago, IL
Eyland, Jessica ... New York, NY
Eylar, Curtis G. ... Kansas City, MO
Eyler, Bonnie ... West Palm Beach, FL
Eyler, Bridget ... Houston, TX
Eyler, Cynthia A. ... Niagara Falls, NY
Eyler, Dean C. ... Minneapolis, MN
Eyler, Deborah R. ... Pueblo, CO
Westcliffe, CO
Eyler, James R. ... Baltimore, MD
Eyler, JoAnn G. ... Trenton, NJ
Eyler, Kate ... Nashville, TN
Eyler, Richard R. ... Denver, CO
Eyler, Robert W. ... Pittsburgh, PA
Eyles, Thomas H. ... Westerly, RI
Eylward, Elizabeth ... Bayside, NY
Brooklyn, NY
New York, NY
Eyman, Barbara D.A. ... Washington, DC
Eyman, Culver F., III ... Cleveland, OH
Eyman, Donna J. ... San Diego, CA
Eyman, John ... New York, NY
Eyman, Thomas H. ... Brunswick, ME
Eymann, Allison, Hunter & Jones, P.S.
Spokane, WA
Eymann, Kathleen P. ... Bandon, OR
Eymann, Kenneth ... Santa Rosa, CA
Eymann, Richard C. ... Spokane, WA
Eynis, Alexander ... Boca Raton, FL
Eynon, Cynthia O. ... Worcester, MA
Eynon, David G. ... Camden, NJ
Eynon, Ernest A., II ... Cincinnati, OH
Eynon, Gail A. ... Detroit, MI
Eynon, Harmon, Rocker & Glover, P.C.
Columbus, IN
Eynon, Linda W. ... Camden, NJ
Eynon, Richard S. ... Columbus, IN
Eynon-Kokrda, Elizabeth ... Omaha, NE
Eyraud, George V., Jr. ... Birmingham, AL
Eyre, Cynthia G. ... Slaughter, LA
Eyre, Dale P. ... Richfield, UT
Eyre, J. Anthony ... Salt Lake City, UT
Eyre, Kevan C. ... Salt Lake City, UT
Eyre, Melanie C. ... Atlanta, GA
Eyre, Michael J. ... Orange, CA
Eyre, Paul P. ... Cleveland, OH
Eyre, Robert Bruce ... Philadelphia, PA
Eyres, Brian D. ... Torrance, CA
Eyres, Jeffrey A. ... Minneapolis, MN
Eyres & Kohn, P.C. ... Dallas, TX
Eyres, Patricia Stearns ... Long Beach, CA
Eyres, William G. ... Dallas, TX
Eyrich, David J. ... Cincinnati, OH
Eyrich, George C. ... Cincinnati, OH
Eyrich, John F. ... Los Angeles, CA
Eyrich, Lillian E. ... New Orleans, LA
Eyring, Wm. E., Sr. ... Baltimore, MD
Eysie, George M., Jr. ... Norwood, MA
Eysie and O'Donnell ... Norwood, MA
Eysie, Paul W. ... Norwood, MA
Eysman, Harvey A. ... Great Neck, NY
Eyssen, Timothy D. ... Graham, TX
Eyssen, W. H., Jr. ... Fort Worth, TX
Eyster, C. David ... Roseville, CA
Eyster, Charles David ... Santa Monica, CA
Eyster, Charles H., Jr. ... Decatur, AL
Eyster, Charles R. ... San Antonio, TX
Eyster, Chris R. ... Pittsburgh, PA
Eyster, Franklin S., II ... New Castle, DE
Eyster, James P., II ... Ann Arbor, MI
Eyster, John C. ... Decatur, AL
Eyster & Joyce ... Allentown, PA

Eyster, Key, Tubb, Weaver & Roth
Athens, AL
Cullman, AL
Decatur, AL
Florence, AL
Huntsville, AL
Moulton, AL
Eyster, Mary Jo Howard ... Brooklyn, NY
Eyster, Otho ... Mt. Vernon, OH
Eyster, Rodney E. ... Washington, DC
Eytalis, Cecilia M. ... Chicago, IL
Eytalis, Edward C. ... Carterville, IL
Eytan, Eli L. ... Brick, NJ
Eytan, Laura M. ... Trenton, NJ
Eytan, Mattaniah ... San Francisco, CA
Eytan, Mattaniah, A Prof. Corp., Law Offices of
San Francisco, CA
Eytina, Mylo ... Albany, NY
Eyvazzadeh, Blenda ... Los Angeles, CA
Ezalarab, Hamdy A. ... Madison, WI
Ezarik, David B. ... Sugar Land, TX
Ezatoff, Paul R., Jr. ... Tallahassee, FL
Eze, Eze I. ... Camden, NJ
Ezekowitz, D. Zeke ... Midland Park, NJ
Ezell, Andrew B. ... Baton Rouge, LA
Ezell, Boyce F., III, (P.A.) ... Coral Gables, FL
Ezell, Braxton R. ... Bradenton, FL
Ezell & Copeland, LLC ... Butler, AL
Mobile, AL
Ezell, Cynthia E. ... San Diego, CA
Ezell, E. Mark ... Butler, AL
Mobile, AL
Ezell, E. Steven ... Colorado Springs, CO
Ezell, J. Donald ... Wheeling, WV
Ezell, Jeffrey C. ... Phenix City, AL
Ezell, Jeffrey D. ... Greenville, SC
Ezell, Jerome L. ... Hobart, IN
Ezell, John J., Law Office of ... Dallas, TX
Ezell, Julie L. ... Dallas, TX
Ezell, Katherine W. ... Miami, FL
Ezell, Kenneth P., Jr. ... Nashville, TN
Ezell, Kimberly Renee ... Atlanta, GA
Ezell, Mark Edward ... Birmingham, AL
Ezell & Menéndez ... Coral Gables, FL
Ezell, Michael R. ... Harlingen, TX
Ezelle & Evers, P.A. ... Wauchula, FL
Ezelle, Marcus J. ... Wauchula, FL
Ezell Pollzzotto, Julie L. ... Indianapolis, IN
Ezenagu, Samuel O. ... Cincinnati, OH
Ezer, Eric M. ... New York, NY
Ezer, Jim C. ... Houston, TX
Ezer, Jonathan ... Honolulu, HI
Ezer, Mitchel J. ... Los Angeles, CA
Ezer, Renee Ellen ... Longmont, CO
Ezer Williamson Fischbach & Brown LLP
Los Angeles, CA
Ezersky, Jane E. ... Brooklyn, NY
Ezersky, Mark B. ... Burlingame, CA
Ezersky, William M. ... New Hyde Park, NY
Ezgar, Geoffrey M. ... Palo Alto, CA
Ezgar, Michael J. ... Los Gatos, CA
Ezgur, Jerrold J. ... Chicago, IL
Ezgur, Michael H. ... Chicago, IL
Ezhaya, Joseph B. ... Waterville, ME
Ezick, Randall J. ... Albany, NY
Ezickson, Doron F. ... Boston, MA
Ezickson, Elan Z. ... Cambridge, MA
Ezim, Harry W., Jr. & Associates
Baton Rouge, LA
Ezkovich, Alan D. ... New Orleans, LA
Ezold, Nancy O'Mara ... Bala Cynwyd, PA
Ezold, Nancy O'Mara, P.C.
Bala Cynwyd, PA
Philadelphia, PA
Ezolt, Russell A. ... Cleveland, OH
Ezor, A. Edward ... Pasadena, CA
Ezor, Herbert R. ... Clifton, NJ
Ezor, Herbert R., P.C. ... Clifton, NJ
Ezor, Jonathan I. ... Uniondale, NY
Ezor, Robert R. ... Atlanta, GA
Ezra, D. Jeffrey ... St. Louis, MO
Ezra, David A. ... Honolulu, HI
Ezra, David B. ... Irvine, CA
Ezra and Howe ... Elmont, NY
Ezra, Joel S. ... Elmont, NY
Ezra, Robert ... Encino, CA
Ezra, Robert, A Professional Corporation
Encino, CA
Ezra, Scott J. ... Santa Monica, CA
Ezra, Sidney ... Evanston, IL
Ezrati, Lester D. ... Palo Alto, CA
Ezratty, Harry ... San Juan, PR
Ezratty, Ira S. ... Garden City, NY
Ezratty, Jaime D. ... Garden City, NY
Ezrilov, David S. ... Minneapolis, MN
Ezrine, Bruce ... Baltimore, MD
Ezring, Gregory A. ... New York, NY
Ezrol, Kerry L. ... Fort Lauderdale, FL
Ezrol, Lauren B. ... New York, NY
Ezrre Robles, Diana C. ... Tucson, AZ
Ezyk, Barbara Barrows
Breckenridge, CO
Englewood, CO
Ezzard, Martha M. ... Denver, CO
Ezzell, C. Thomas ... Lexington, KY
Ezzell, J. David ... Enid, OK
Ezzell, J. Michael ... San Antonio, TX
Ezzell, Meredith Pierce ... Raleigh, NC
Ezzell, Peter Q., (A Professional Corporation) ... Santa Monica, CA
Ezzell, T. Calder, Jr. ... Roswell, NM
Ezzell Buckley, Deborah Katherine
College Station, TX
Ezzo, Ralph P. ... Miami, FL
Ezzo, Ralph P., P.C. ... Miami, FL
Ezzone, Donald ... Willoughby, OH
Ezzy, Marilyn E. ... Alameda, CA

Faaberg, Vernon E. ....Minneapolis, MN
Faaborg, Karen Kramer ....Cincinnati, OH
Faaborg, Rana L. ....Bloomington, IL
Fáabregas, Ana I. ....Silver Spring, MD
Faal, Edi M. O., (Mr.) ....Los Angeles, CA
Faal, Edirissa Mohammad ....Los Angeles, CA
Faalevao, Aviata Fano ....Pago Pago, TT
Faasse, Ralph E. ....Ridgewood, NJ
Faatz, Clyde A., Jr. ....Denver, CO
Fabacher, Lawrence B. ....New Orleans, LA
Fabar, Laura M. ....Miami, FL
Fabbo, Marylou ....Springfield, MA
Worcester, MA
Fabbri, Frank R., III ....St. Louis, MO
Fabbri, Michael L. ....Framingham, MA
Fabbri & Zotos ....St. Louis, MO
Fabbrini, Richard R. ....Northbrook, IL
Fabbro, Richard M. ....Westport, CT
Fabe, Dana A. ....Anchorage, AK
Fabe, George ....Cincinnati, OH
Fabe, Jacqueline M. ....Los Angeles, CA
Fabel, Thomas L. ....St. Paul, MN
Fabela, Robert ....San Jose, CA
Fabens, Andrew L. ....Cleveland, OH
Faber, Adam ....New York, NY
Faber, Amy M. ....New Bern, NC
Faber, Andrew L. ....San Jose, CA
Faber, Arnold L. ....Laguna Niguel, CA
Faber, Barry M. ....Rockland, ME
Faber, Barry M. ....Baltimore, MD
Faber, Beth Lori ....San Diego, CA
Faber, Brenden C. ....Salt Lake City, UT
Faber, Cameron H. ....Los Angeles, CA
Faber, Carol L. ....Miami, FL
Faber, Christopher J. ....Los Angeles, CA
Faber, David A. ....Bluefield, WV
Faber, Diane L. ....Los Angeles, CA
Faber, Edward M. ....Avon, OH
Faber, Elise M. ....Department of Justice, Executive Office for Immigration Review, GV
Faber, Gerald ....Cherry Hill, NJ
Faber & Gitlitz, P.A. ....Miami, FL
Faber, Glenn Charles ....Seaside, OR
Faber, Irving C. ....Chicago, IL
Faber, Jo Welch ....Philadelphia, PA
Faber, John F., Jr. ....Virginia Beach, VA
Faber, John J. ....Burlingame, CA
Faber, Johnna Lynn ....San Diego, CA
Faber, Joseph L. ....Boston, MA
Faber, Joy ....Camden, NJ
Faber, Keith L. ....Celina, OH
Faber, Louis S. ....Rochester, NY
Faber, Mark Andrew ....Baltimore, MD
Faber, Mark E. ....Irving, TX
Faber, Michael ....Washington, DC
Faber, Michael B. ....Wheeling, IL
Faber, Michael J. ....Los Angeles, CA
Faber, Michael J. ....Santa Monica, CA
Faber, Michael L. ....Elk Grove, CA
Faber, Michael R. ....San Francisco, CA
Faber, Norman L. ....New York, NY
Faber, Pamela J. ....Virginia Beach, VA
Faber, Peter L. ....New York, NY
Faber, Richard Lewis ....Atlanta, GA
Faber, Richard V. ....Dayton, OH
Faber, Richard V., Jr. ....Lewisburg, OH
Faber, Robert C. ....New York, NY
Faber, Robert C. ....Arlington, VA
Faber, Robin W., P.A. ....Miami, FL
Faber, Robin Wilson ....Miami, FL
Faber, Shana S. ....Sacramento, CA
Faber, Sheppard ....Miami, FL
Faber, Stephen W. ....St. Petersburg, FL
Faber, Steven E. ....Columbia, MO
Faber, Steven R. ....Massapequa, NY
Faber, Stuart J. ....Los Angeles, CA
Faber, Wendy A. ....Park City, UT
Faber, William C. ....Decatur, IL
Faberman, Austin S. ....Philadelphia, PA
Faberman, Edward P. ....Washington, DC
Chicago, IL
Faberman, Stephen H. ....Boston, MA
Fabert, Steve R. ....Topeka, KS
Fabi, Keith A. ....Pittsburgh, PA
Fabia, Robert P. ....Department of Education, Office of the General Counsel, GV
Fabian, Albert E. ....Atlanta, GA
Fabian, Anthony John ....Englewood, CO
Fabian, Bill E. ....Los Fresnos, TX
Fabian, Caryn N. ....San Jose, CA
Fabian, Christian W. ....Chicago, IL
Fabian & Clendenin, A Professional Corporation ....Las Vegas, NV
Salt Lake City, UT
Fabian, David Michael ....Morristown, NJ
New York, NY
Fabian, Donald J. ....Geneva, IL
Fabian, Emil M., III ....Omaha, NE
Fabian, Ernest E. ....Cleveland, OH
Fabian, G. Leslie ....New York, NY
Fabian, Gary A. ....Meadville, PA
Fabian, James ....Garden City, NY
Fabian, James J. ....Baltimore, MD
Fabian, Janet M. ....Wexford, PA
Fabian, JoAnne ....San Francisco, CA
Fabian, John, III ....Minneapolis, MN
Fabian, Joseph C. ....Denver, CO
Fabian, Joseph F. ....Haddonfield, NJ
Fabian, Lawrence E. ....New York, NY
New York, NY
Fabian, Linda M. ....San Diego, CA
Fabian, Manuel ....New York, NY
Fabian, Margaret G. ....Riverside, CA
Fabian, Margaret W. ....Los Fresnos, TX
Fabian, Marie-Laurence ....Morristown, NJ
Fabian, Michael H. ....Sacramento, CA
Fabian, Michael H. ....Farmington Hills, MI
Fabian, Nancy W. Department Of Veterans Affairs, Board of Veterans Appeals, GV
Fabian, Patrick H. ....El Cerrito, CA
San Francisco, CA
Fabian, Rudy A. ....Pittsburgh, PA
Fabian, Sharon L. ....Phoenix, AZ
Fabian, Sklar & Davis, P.C. ....Detroit, MI
Farmington Hills, MI
Fabian, Stephen G., Jr. ....Edmond, OK
Fabian, Steven ....Santa Rosa, CA
Fabian & Thielen ....Omaha, NE
Fabian, Virginia R. ....Oakland, CA
Fabiani, Christa A. ....Philadelphia, PA
Fabiani, John V., Jr. ....New York, NY
Fabiani, Kathryn D. ....Southport, CT
Fabiano, Angela ....Mineola, NY
Fabiano, Anthony R. ....Rockford, IL
Fabiano & Associates ....Liverpool, NY
Fabiano, Francesco ....Liverpool, NY
Fabiano, Gerald ....Boston, MA
Fabiano, John G. ....Boston, MA
Fabiano Law Offices ....Rockford, IL
Fabiano, Michael D. ....La Jolla, CA
Fabiano, Philip A. ....Pittsburgh, PA
Fabiano, Salvatore ....Boston, MA
Fabiano, Vincent L. ....Columbia, MD
Fabic, M. Margaret ....Syracuse, NY
Fabien, Marva Claudette ....Salem, OR
Fabietti, A. Steven ....Voorhees, NJ
Fabietti, Carol A. ....Margate City, NJ
Fabina-Abney, Sherry A. ....Indianapolis, IN
Fabio, Anthony W. ....Pittsburgh, PA
Fabio & Merrill ....Houston, TX
Fabio, Thea M. ....Houston, TX
Fabish, Peter M. ....Seattle, WA
Fabiszewski, Karen S. ....Boston, MA
Fabito, Daniel Marc ....Chicago, IL
Fable-Wright, Nicole
West Palm Beach, FL
Fable-Wright, Nicole A. ....Boca Raton, FL
Fabos, Suzanna ....Calabasas, CA
Fabozzi, Dennis F. ....Orange, CA
Fabre, Frank R. S. ....Coral Gables, FL
Fabre, Harold A. ....Pendleton, OR
Fabré, Maria T. ....Orlando, FL
Fabre, Robert B. ....Charlottesville, VA
Fabrega, Luis A. ....Houston, TX
Fabrega, Marelisa Panama Canal Commission, Office of the General Counsel, GV
Fabri, Candace J. ....Chicago, IL
Fabri, William O. ....Boston, MA
Fabriani, Sylvia L. ....Mount Kisco, NY
Fabric, Elliot A. ....Spokane, WA
Fabricant, Alfred R. ....New York, NY
Fabricant, Bernard W. ....Boston, MA
Fabricant, David M. ....New London, CT
Fabricant, Deborah ....Irvine, CA
Fabricant, Elliot N. ....Roseland, NJ
Fabricant, Jonathan S. ....Lakewood, NJ
Fabricant, Judith ....Boston, MA
Fabricant & Lipman ....Goshen, NY
Fabricant, Peter J. ....New York, NY
Fabricant, Richard ....New York, NY
Fabricant & Yeskoo, LLP ....New York, NY
Hoboken, NJ
Fabricius, Raymond P. ....Ottawa, IL
Fabricius, Scott Douglas ....Miami, FL
Fabrick, Howard D. ....Los Angeles, CA
Fabrick, Myrna T. ....Marina Del Rey, CA
Fabrick, Olga ....Upland, CA
Fabrikant, Charles ....New York, NY
Fabrikant, Jay L. ....Fort Lauderdale, FL
Fabrikant, Jay L., P.A. ....Fort Lauderdale, FL
Fabrikant, Marvin ....Washington, DC
Fabrikant, Melinda ....Washington, DC
Fabrikant, Michael R. ....Hollywood, FL
Fabrikant, Robert ....Los Angeles, CA
Fabris, Alfred C. ....Sunnyvale, CA
Fabris, Burgess & Ring, A Professional Corporation ....San Francisco, CA
Fabritz, Deborah J. ....Milwaukee, WI
Fabritz, Henry L. ....Des Moines, IA
Fabrizi, Joseph W. ....Youngstown, OH
Fabrizi, Keith G. ....Houston, TX
Fabrizi, Larry David, (Mr.)
Los Angeles, CA
Fabrizi, Leo T. ....Buffalo, NY
Fabrizio, Eric J. ....Reading, PA
Fabrizio & Fabrizio ....Troy, MI
Fabrizio, James R. ....Joliet, IL
Fabrizio, Joseph J. ....Bloomfield Hills, MI
Fabrizio, Lynn H. ....Washington, DC
Fabrizio, Patricia J. ....Detroit, MI
Fabrizio, Paulette L. ....Troy, MI
Fabrizio, Philip R. ....Troy, MI
Fabrizio, Steven B. ....Washington, DC
Fabrizio, Thomas A. ....Portland, OR
Fabrizio, Vincent A. ....Riverside, CA
Fabrizio, William R. ....New York, NY
Fabro, Kathleen M. ....Columbus, OH
Fabry, John R. ....Houston, TX
Fabry, Scott M. ....Milwaukee, WI
Fabry, Steven F. Executive Office Of The President, Office of the U.S. Trade Representative, GV
Fabrykant, John E. ....Flushing, NY
Faby, Raymond M. ....Baltimore, MD
Fabyan, August E. ....Hartland, WI
Fabyanske, Marvin T. ....Minneapolis, MN
Fabyanske, Westra & Hart, P.A.
Minneapolis, MN
St. Paul, MN
Facaros, Nickolas ....Eugene, OR
Facaros, Nickolas, P.C. ....Eugene, OR
Facca, Patrick A. ....Royal Oak, MI
Faccadio & Dorsey, P.C. ....Middletown, CT
Faccadio, Lisa A. ....Middletown, CT
Faccenda, Michael Anthony ....Chicago, IL
Faccenda, Philip J., Jr. ....South Bend, IN
Faccenda, Philip J., Sr. ....South Bend, IN
Faccenda, Philip L. ....Medford, NJ
Faccenda, Susan M. ....Chicago, IL
Facchina, Bazil ....Washington, DC
Facchini, Gerard A. ....Chicago, IL
Facchini, Michael Dennis ....Springfield, MA
Facchini, Richard A., Jr. ....Springfield, MA
Facciani, Marissa J. ....Fresno, CA
Faccini, Kathleen M. ....New York, NY
Faccinto, Randall M. ....San Francisco, CA
Tahoe City, CA
Facciola, John M. ....
United States District Court For The District Of Columbia, GV
Facciolo, Francis J., III ....Brooklyn, NY
Facciolo, Philip J., Jr. ....Wilmington, DE
Facciolo, Richard J. ....Wilmington, DE
Facciolo, V. James ....Jacksonville, FL
Faccone, Robert D. ....Avon-By-The-Sea, NJ
Facemire, Richard A. ....Sutton, WV
Facemire, Shiela K. ....Huntsville, AL
Facenda, Kristopher J. ....Ocean City, NJ
Facer, Eric F. ....Washington, DC
Facer, Mark S. ....Los Angeles, CA
Facer & Stamoulas ....Washington, DC
Facer, Susan J. ....Williamsville, NY
Facer, Thorpe ....Urbana, IL
Facey, Dale T. ....Longmeadow, MA
Facey, John A., III ....Rutland, VT
Facey, Marcia E. ....Milwaukee, WI
Facey, Peter G. ....Williamsport, PA
Fach, Wesley N. ....San Diego, CA
Facha, Irene H. ....Philadelphia, PA
Facher, Betsy ....Boston, MA
Facher, Irwin L. ....West Orange, NJ
Facher, Jerome P. ....Boston, MA
Faches, Gloe, Quint & Martin
Cedar Rapids, IA
Faches, William G. ....Cedar Rapids, IA
Fachin, Gary M. ....Fresno, CA
Fachini, Denise D. ....Cordele, GA
Fachman, John M. ....Sioux City, IA
Faciane-Small, Elsie A. ....Slidell, LA
Fackel, Joseph F. ....Moline, IL
Fackelman, Dennis M. ....Middlesex, NJ
Fackenthal, Edward ....Norristown, PA
Facklam, Paul M., Jr. ....Boston, MA
Fackler, Benjamin D. ....New York, NY
Fackler, Gregg F. ....Boston, MA
Fackler, Jeff M. ....Walnut Creek, CA
Fackler, Stephen W. ....Palo Alto, CA
Facklis, Margaret L. ....Dallas, TX
Fackrell, Gerald E., III ....Tyler, TX
Fackrell, Gerlad E., III, P.C. ....Tyler, TX
Facktor, Charles E. ....Milwaukee, WI
Facktor, Sheryl ....Chicago, IL
Facter, Jeffrey S. ....San Francisco, CA
Factor, Abe ....Fort Worth, TX
Factor, Abraham ....Providence, RI
Factor, Alfred ....Cranston, RI
Factor, Campbell & Shepherd, L.L.P.
Fort Worth, TX
Factor, Craig H. ....San Jose, CA
Factor & Factor ....Philadelphia, PA
Factor, Gwen E. Federal Deposit Insurance Corporation, Regulation and Legislation Section, GV
Factor, Jason ....New York, NY
Factor, Jeffrey S. ....New York, NY
Factor, Jill Sugar ....Chicago, IL
Factor, Jody L. ....Chicago, IL
Factor, Jonathan D. ....New York, NY
Factor, Kathleen M. ....Philadelphia, PA
Factor, Marvin W. ....Philadelphia, PA
Factor, Max G. ....Tallahassee, FL
Factor, Max, III ....Beverly Hills, CA
Factor, Max, III, P.C. ....Beverly Hills, CA
Factor, Robert E. ....Burlington, MA
Factor, Ruth ....Altadena, CA
Factor, Sandra B. ....New York, NY
Factor, William J. ....Chicago, IL
Factora, Janelle M. ....Tillamook, OR
Fadaol, Robert F., Ltd. ....Gretna, LA
Fadden, Henry C. ....Liverpool, NY
Fadden, Jerome H. ....Buena Park, CA
Fadden, John P. ....Chicago, IL
Fadden, Michael J ....Dracut, MA
Faddick, Colleen ....Houston, TX
Faddis, Eric H. ....Bushnell, FL
Orlando, FL
Tavares, FL
Faddis, Jonathan W. ....Austin, TX
Faddis, Marion W., (Mr.) ....Phoenix, AZ
Faddis, Oldham & Smith, P.A.
Bushnell, FL
Orlando, FL
Tavares, FL
Fadduol, Glasheen & Valles, P.C.
Lubbock, TX
Fadduol, Sam L. ....Lubbock, TX
Fadeff, Jeffery J. ....San Francisco, CA
Fadel, Alfred ....Los Angeles, CA
Fadel Associates ....Bountiful, UT
Fadel, Douglas K. ....Ogden, UT
Fadel, Erika Simone ....Austin, TX
Fadel, George K. ....Bountiful, UT
Fadel, Kim A. ....Roanoke, VA
Fadel, Kristen ....Bountiful, UT
Fadel, Kristin L. ....Bountiful, UT
Fadel, Lynda Wolfson ....Beverly Hills, CA
Fadel, William I. ....Cleveland, OH
Fadeley, Charles N. ....Eugene, OR
Fadeley, Edward N. ....Salem, OR
Fadell, Cheney & Burt, P.L.L.C.
Phoenix, AZ
Fadell, Frederick J. ....Holland, OH
Fadell, Gary A. ....Phoenix, AZ
Fadell, Rita L. ....Louisville, KY
Fadely, Kathlynn G. ....Department of Justice, Civil Division, GV
Fadely, Lewis R. ....Creedmoor, NC
Durham, NC
Greensboro, NC
Raleigh, NC
Fadely, Val R. ....Costa Mesa, CA
Fadem, Barry ....San Francisco, CA
Fadem, BJ, Law Offices of ....San Jose, CA
Fadem, Bruce R. ....Bedminster, NJ
Fadem & Molyneux ....Bedminster, NJ
Faden, Jessica ....Mount Laurel, NJ
Faden, Lisa G. ....Blue Bell, PA
Faden, Neil S. ....New York, NY
Fadenrecht, Anne C. ....Hanford, CA
Fadenrecht, Daniel M. ....Hanford, CA
Fader, Bruce E. ....New York, NY
Fader, Bruce P. ....Ellington, CT
Fader, C. Eric ....Chicago, IL
Fader, Christine ....Roseland, NJ
Fader, Eric D. ....New York, NY
Fader, Henry C. ....Philadelphia, PA
Fader, John F., II ....Towson, MD
Fader, Paul T. ....Roseland, NJ
Fader, Robert S. ....Lake Success, NY
Fader, Theodora B. ....Dearborn, MI
Faderewski, Walter C. ....Pittsburgh, PA
Fadgen, John P. ....Las Vegas, NV
Fadil, Adeeb R. ....New York, NY
Fadim, James B. ....Chicago, IL
Fadini, Lisa M. ....Parsippany, NJ
Fadlovich, Michael R. ....Minneapolis, MN
Fado, John D. ....Springfield, VA
Fadool, Lydia E. ....New York, NY
Fadoul, Thomas J., Jr. ....McLean, VA
Fadum, Nancy F. ....Raleigh, NC
Fadus, Michael J. ....Hamden, CT
Faecher, Marc S. ....Secaucus, NJ
Faegenburg, Glenn Kenneth ....Brooklyn, NY
Faegenburg, Russell W. ....New York, NY
Faeges, Jay ....Cleveland, OH
Faegre & Benson LLP ....Denver, CO
Des Moines, IA
Minneapolis, MN
Faegre, Charles B. ....Minneapolis, MN
Faehner, Michael J. ....Clearwater, FL
Faenza, Heidi Manroe ....Melbourne, FL
Faerber & Cliff ....Naples, FL
Faerber, Fritz G. ....Belleville, IL
Faerber, Jennifer Lee ....Fort Lauderdale, FL
Faerber, Jesse S. ....Plantation, FL
Faerber, Joseph ....Spring Valley, NY
Faerber, Karl G. ....Alpharetta, GA
Faerber, Kent W. ....Amherst, MA
Faerber, Michael A. ....Rockville, MD
Faerber, Mies William ....Kalispell, MT
Faerber, Nelson A., Jr. ....Naples, FL
Faerber, Randolph E. ....Miami, FL
Faerber, Robert E. ....St. Louis, MO
Faerber, William V. ....St. Cloud, MN
Faerber, Yolanda Stefanou ....Bethesda, MD
Faerberg, David B. Federal Energy Regulatory Commission, Office of the General Counsel, GV
Faermark, Byron L. ....Itasca, IL
Faesser, Victor ....Pawnee City, NE
Faeth, George J. ....Brooklyn, NY
Faeth, Steven F. ....Pittsburgh, PA
Faeth, Valerie S. ....Pittsburgh, PA
Faett, Frederick McLain ....Mechanicsburg, PA
Faett, Joshua Joseph ....Naples, FL
Fafarman, Keith R. ....Lafayette, IN
Fafatas, Robert C. ....The Woodlands, TX
Fafenrodt, Alexis A. ....Torrance, CA
Fafinski, Ignatius A. ....Woodhaven, NY
Fafinski, Robert R., Jr. ....Minneapolis, MN
Fafinski, Thomas Michael ....Minneapolis, MN
Fafinski, Timothy W. ....Golden Valley, MN
Faga, Antonio ....Utica, NY
Faga, Enzo A. ....Rochester, NY
Faga, Kevin B. ....Whitestone, NY
Faga, Scott M. ....Washington, DC
Fagalde, Michael A. ....Mariposa, CA
Merced, CA
Fagan, Amy B. ....Detroit, MI
Fagan, Andrew L. ....Palo Alto, CA
Fagan, Barry S. ....Detroit, MI
Fagan, Bernard J., Jr ....Naperville, IL
Fagan, Bruce H. ....San Diego, CA
Fagan, Burton H. ....Bettendorf, IA
Fagan, Charles D. ....Aspen, CO
Fagan, Charles D. ....Waterloo, IN
Fagan, Charles Edward ....Jamestown, NY
Fagan, Christopher B. ....Los Angeles, CA
Fagan, Christopher B. ....Cleveland, OH
Fagan, Christopher J. ....Wethersfield, CT
Fagan, Craig P. ....San Diego, CA
Fagan, D. Michael ....Salem, OR
Fagan, Daniel R. ....Indianapolis, IN
Fagan, Daniel R. ....Grand Rapids, MI
Fagan, David G. ....Portland, OR
Fagan & D'Avino ....New York, NY
Fagan, Debra S. ....Denver, CO
Fagan, Douglas F. ....Riverside, CA
Fagan, Edward D. ....New York, NY
Fagan, Edward T. ....Naples, FL
Fagan & Fagan ....San Diego, CA
Fagan, Gail G. ....Charlotte, NC
Fagan, George D. ....New Orleans, LA
Fagan, Gerry P. ....Billings, MT
Fagan, Goldrick & Segadelli ....Falmouth, MA
Fagan, James D. ....Atlanta, GA
Fagan, James E., III ....Arlington, VA
Fagan, James H. ....Falmouth, MA
Fagan, James W. ....Annandale, VA

Fagan, Janis S. ... San Diego, CA
Fagan, Jas. W. ... Casper, WY
Fagan, Jennifer L. ... Austin, TX
Fagan, Joan M. ... Milwaukee, WI
Fagan, John E. ... Tahoe City, CA
Fagan, John E. ... Fairfax, VA
Fagan, John F. ... The Dalles, OR
Fagan, John P. ... Manchester, NH
Fagan, John Richard ... Doylestown, PA
Fagan, Joseph C. ... Washington, DC
Fagan, Joseph D. ... Chicago, IL
Fagan, Joseph F. ... Department of State, Foreign Service Officers (Overseas), GV
Fagan, Joseph H. ... Washington, DC
Fagan, Joseph M. ... Des Plaines, IL
Fagan, Julian W. ... Amory, MS
Fagan, Kate J. ... Pittsburgh, PA
Fagan, Kathryn A. ... Milton, MA
Fagan, Kathryn Patricia ... Carrboro, NC
Fagan, Keith H. ... Bethesda, MD
Fagan, Lawrence J. ... New Britain, CT
Fagan, Lisa B. ... Somerville, NJ
Fagan, Lisa M. ... St. Paul, MN
Fagan, M. Lee ... Jacksonville, FL
Fagan, Mary Kathleen ... Pawling, NY
Fagan, Maximina Kiko ... San Mateo, CA
Fagan, Michael J. ... Cherry Hill, NJ
Fagan, Michael K. ... St. Louis, MO
Fagan, Osee R. ... Gainesville, FL
Fagan, Patrick V. ... Carson City, NV
Fagan, Paul E. ... Richmond, KY
Fagan, Paul F. ... Pittsburgh, PA
Fagan, Peter J. ... Conyngham, PA
Fagan, Peter L. ... Coronado, CA
Fagan, Peter T. ... Irvine, CA
Fagan, Richard T. ... Atlanta, GA
Fagan, Robert Emmett, Jr. ... Jackson, MS
Fagan, Robert M. ... Fountain Hills, AZ
Freeport, IL
Northbrook, IL
Fagan, Robert M., Ltd., The Law Offices of
Fountain Hills, AZ
Freeport, IL
Northbrook, IL
Fagan, Sean D. ... Baton Rouge, LA
Fagan, Seymour ... Los Angeles, CA
Fagan, Shawn Francis ... Denver, CO
Chicago, IL
Fagan, Sherry ... Billings, MT
Fagan, Shirley A. ... Santa Ana, CA
Fagan, Stanley ... Philadelphia, PA
Fagan, Stuart E. ... San Diego, CA
Fagan, Susan B. ... Clifton, NJ
Fagan, Susan F. ... Malden, MA
Fagan, Terence P. ... Denver, CO
Fagan, Thomas Edward ... St. Louis, MO
Fagan, Thomas L. ... Eugene, OR
Fagan, Thos. J. ... Casper, WY
Fagan, Timothy J. ... Wheaton, IL
Fagan, Timothy M. ... Boston, MA
Fagan, W. Jeffery ... Camden, TN
Fagan, W. Thomas ... Honolulu, HI
Fagan, Wayne I. ... San Antonio, TX
Fagan, William M. ... San Antonio, TX
Fagan, William P. ... Fort Wayne, IN
Fagan-Crawford, Shari Ann ... Wyoming, MN
Fagan-Weber, Susan ... Pittsburgh, PA
Fagel, Allen J. ... Chicago, IL
Fagel, Barry F. ... Cincinnati, OH
Fagel, Brian D. ... Chicago, IL
Fagel, Bruce G., Law Offices of
Beverly Hills, CA
Mission Viejo, CA
Sacramento, CA
San Diego, CA
San Francisco, CA
Fagel & Haber ... Chicago, IL
Fagel, Marc J. ... San Francisco, CA
Fagel, Stephen J. ... Cincinnati, OH
Fagelbaum & Heller, LLP
Los Angeles, CA
Fagelbaum, Jerold ... Los Angeles, CA
Fagella, Robert A. ... Newark, NJ
Fagelman, Jason K. ... Dallas, TX
Fagelman, Samuel ... Shrub Oak, NY
Fagelson, Bernard M. ... Alexandria, VA
Fagelson, Frederick ... Bay Shore, NY
Fagelson, John L. ... Fairfax, VA
Fagelson, Karen C. ... Leesburg, VA
Fagelson, Marilyn B. ... New Haven, CT
Fagelson, Schonberger, Payne and Deichmeister, P.C. ... Alexandria, VA
Fairfax, VA
Fagen, Charles H. ... Dallas Center, IA
Grimes, IA
Fagen, Fran R. ... Newport Beach, CA
Fagen, Herman ... North Woodmere, NY
Fagen, James ... Freehold, NJ
Fagen, Leslie Gordon ... New York, NY
Fagen, Lester J. ... Boston, MA
Fagen, Peter K. ... Escondido, CA
Santa Monica, CA
Fagen, Shari J. ... New York, NY
Fagenson, Lawrence M. ... New York, NY
Fager & Amsler ... East Meadow, NY
New York, NY
Syracuse, NY
Fager, Donald J. ... New York, NY
Fager, Harold W. ... McFarland, WI
Fager, Michael A. ... Boston, MA
Fager-Baldwin, Shirlee ... Hattiesburg, MS
Fagerberg, Richard E.
Overland Park, KS
Fagerberg, Roger R. ... St. Louis, MO
Fagerli, Thomas A. ... Winston-Salem, NC
Fagerlund, Dwain E. ... Crookston, MN
Fagerman, Rodney W. ... Grand Rapids, MI
Fagerman, William M. ... Cadillac, MI
Fagerness, Lawrence W. ... Centralia, WA
Fagerstrom, Donna G. ... Pelham, NY
Fagerstrom, Karen R. ... New York, NY
Fagerstrom, Neil ... Cambridge, MN
Fagg, Brad ... Washington, DC
Fagg, Fred D., III ... Novato, CA
Fagg, George G. ... Des Moines, IA
Fagg, Martha A. ... Dakota City, NE
Fagg, Russell C. ... Billings, MT
Faggard, A. Mark ... Beaumont, TX
Faggen, Edward S. ... Alexandria, VA
Faggert, David Y. ... Chesapeake, VA
Faggert & Frieden, P.C. ... Chesapeake, VA
Norfolk, VA
Virginia Beach, VA
Faggianelli, Nancy J. ... Tampa, FL
Faggiano, John P. ... Boston, MA
Faggiano, Kelly Judge ... Boston, MA
Fagiani, Gabriel F. ... Encino, CA
Fagin, Allen I. ... New York, NY
Fagin, Arnold D. ... Oklahoma City, OK
Fagin, Beth Lauren ... Austin, TX
Fagin, Brown, Bush, Tinney & Kiser, A Professional Corporation
Oklahoma City, OK
Fagin, Charles L. ... Oklahoma City, OK
Fagin, Earl H. ... Granada Hills, CA
Fagin, Fagin, Nixon & Reed, P.C.
Oklahoma City, OK
Fagin, Harold M. ... Riverside, CA
Fagin, Kenneth M. ... Washington, DC
Fagin, Marc K. ... Columbus, OH
Fagin, Melinda R. ... Dallas, TX
Fagin, Michele Berdinis
Colorado Springs, CO
Fagin, Milton I. ... San Antonio, TX
Fagin, Norman ... Columbus, OH
Fagin, Richard A. ... Houston, TX
Fagin, Sarah L. ... Arlington, TX
Fagin, Stuart A. ... Palo Alto, CA
Fagin, Suellen D. ... Orlando, FL
Fagin, Vernon A. ... Los Angeles, CA
Fagiola, Robert W. ... New York, NY
Faglioni, Kelly L. ... Richmond, VA
Fagnani, Louis P., Jr. ... New Haven, CT
Fagnilli, David J. ... Cleveland, OH
Fagnilli, Sara J. ... Lakewood, OH
Fago, Jennifer A. ... Boston, MA
Fagone, Michael A. ... Portland, ME
Fagone, Philip E. ... Belmont, CA
Fagone, Richard S. ... Stoughton, MA
Fagot, Elizabeth L. ... Department of the Army, Office, Chief of Engineers/Headquarters, U.S. Army Corps of Engineers, GV
Fagot-Diaz, Jose G. ... San Juan, PR
Fagre, Nathan E. ... Los Angeles, CA
Fague, Terence L. ... Dayton, OH
Fagundes, Joseph ... Kailua-Kona, HI
Fagundes, Joseph H. ... Stockton, CA
Fagundes, Joseph, III, Atty. at Law, A Law Corp. ... Kailua-Kona, HI
Faherty, Daniel Patrick ... Melbourne, FL
Faherty, Ellen Guglielmo ... Cambridge, MA
Faherty, Genevieve M. ... Los Angeles, CA
Faherty, Jacqueline G. ... Boston, MA
Faherty, Jason P. ... La Plata, MD
Faherty, Kathleen ... New York, NY
Faherty, Lorraine Townsend ... Salinas, CA
Faherty, M. Teresa A. ... New City, NY
Faherty, Michael F. ... Harrisburg, PA
Faherty, Philip J., III ... Lambertville, NJ
Faherty, Philip J., Jr. ... Lambertville, NJ
Fahey, A. Kevin ... Washington, DC
Fahey, Ann S. ... Arlington, MA
Fahey, Brian J. ... Chicago, IL
Fahey, Brian W. ... Springfield, NJ
Fahey, Bruce H. ... Cleveland, OH
Fahey, Craig ... San Diego, CA
Fahey, Donald E. ... St. Louis, MO
Fahey, Douglas A. ... Treasury Department, Internal Revenue Service, GV
Fahey, Edward P. ... San Antonio, TX
Fahey, Eileen K. ... Medford, NJ
Fahey, Eileen M. McGlinchey ... Ithaca, NY
Fahey, Elizabeth M. ... Boston, MA
Fahey, Eugene M. ... Buffalo, NY
Fahey & Fahey ... Springfield, NJ
Westfield, NJ
Fahey, Hallie Miller ... Chicago, IL
Fahey, Helen F. ... Arlington, VA
Fahey, James E. ... Louisville, KY
Fahey, James E., Jr. ... Watertown, MA
Fahey, James G. ... Springfield, IL
Fahey, Jane E. ... Atlanta, GA
Fahey, Janice O'Neill ... Boston, MA
Fahey, John B. ... Somers, CT
Fahey, John F. ... Hartford, CT
Fahey, John J. ... Washington, DC
Fahey, John P. ... Farmington, CT
Fahey, Joseph M. ... Arlington, MA
Fahey, Kathleen A. ... Boston, MA
Fahey, Kevin Paul ... Concord, NH
Fahey, Landolina & Associates, LLC
Windsor Locks, CT
Fahey, Laura E. ... New York, NY
Fahey Law Office ... Weirton, WV
Fahey, Linda R. ... Washington, PA
Fahey, Margaret Hupp ... Chicago, IL
Fahey, Martha Kave ... Pittsfield, MA
Fahey, Mary J. ... Syracuse, NY
Fahey, Michael ... White Plains, NY
Fahey, Michael C. ... New York, NY
Fahey, Patrick ... Hartford, CT
Fahey, Patrick M. ... Pleasanton, CA
Fahey, R. David ... Fort Madison, IA
Fahey, Raymond F. ... Springfield, NJ
Fahey, Richard P. ... Columbus, OH
Fahey, Robert F. ... Peoria, IL
Fahey, Ronald W. ... Santa Rosa, CA
Fahey, Rosalind A. ... New York, NY
Fahey, Sean J. ... Chicago, IL
Fahey, Sean P. ... Philadelphia, PA
Fahey, Stacey O'Haire ... New York, NY
Fahey, Stephen ... Milwaukee, WI
Fahey, T. Kevin ... East Syracuse, NY
Fahey, Thomas J. ... Danville, IL
Fahey, Thomas M. ... Chicago, IL
Fahey, Thomas W., Jr.
Windsor Locks, CT
Fahey, Todd C. ... Concord, NH
Fahey, William ... Wayland, MA
Fahey, William K. ... Lansing, MI
Fahey, William L. ... Belleville, WI
Madison, WI
Fahey, William R. ... Chicago, IL
Fahey, William T. ... Weirton, WV
Fahl, Douglas M. ... Columbia City, IN
Fahl, Glenn J. ... Houston, TX
Fahl & Takeuchi, P.C. ... Metairie, LA
Houston, TX
Fahl, Thomas R. ... Milwaukee, WI
Fahlbusch, Arthur C., Jr. ... New York, NY
Fahle, Becki ... San Antonio, TX
Fahle, John J. ... San Antonio, TX
Fahle Law Firm ... San Antonio, TX
Fahlen, Edwin ... Fountain Valley, CA
Fahleson, Mark A. ... Lincoln, NE
Fahlgren, Daniel J. ... Rolling Meadows, IL
Fahlgren, James W. ... Minneapolis, MN
Fahlgren, Joan J. ... Detroit, MI
Fahlgren, Steven M. ... Orlando, FL
Fahlman, Eric J. ... Seattle, WA
Fahlstedt, A. Gary ... Denver, CO
Fahmi, Muhammad ... New York, NY
Fahmi, Tammy ... Roseland, NJ
Fahmi, Tarek N. ... Sunnyvale, CA
Fahmy, Sami I. ... Houston, TX
Fahmy, Stewart S. ... San Jose, CA
Fahn, Lawrence E. ... San Francisco, CA
Fahn, Meredith L. ... Menlo Park, CA
Fahn, Terence G. ... Los Angeles, CA
Fahndrich, Fred P. ... Chicago, IL
Fahnenbruck, K. Clarke ... Columbus, OH
Fahnenbruck, K. Clarke, Co., L.P.A.
Columbus, OH
Fahner, Sharon A. ... Tallahassee, FL
Fahner, Tyrone C. ... Chicago, IL
Fahnestock, John W. ... Buffalo, NY
Fahnestock, Michael S. ... Columbia, SC
Fahning, Paul W. ... St. Paul, MN
Fahnlander, Vincent J. ... Minneapolis, MN
Fahrenbach, Margaret M. ... Rosemont, IL
Fahrenbacher, Ronald J. ... Milwaukee, WI
Fahrenbruch Law Offices
Plattsmouth, NE
Fahrenbruch, Nanette M.
Plattsmouth, NE
Fahrendorf, Robert P. ... Reno, NV
Fahrenholtz, James E. ... Avon, CO
Fahrenholtz & Riva ... Avon, CO
Fahrenholz, Everett ... Eaton, OH
Fahrenholz, Thomas P. ... San Jose, CA
Fahrenkamp, David M. ... Edwardsville, IL
Fahrenkopf, Frank J., Jr.
Washington, DC
Fahrenkopf, Leslie A. ... New York, NY
Fahrenkopf, Paul E. ... Washington, DC
Fahrenkrog, Eugene H., Jr. ... St. Louis, MO
Fahrenz, Frederick D. ... Nitro, WV
Fahrenz, Richard E. ... Binghamton, NY
Fahrer, Clare ... Cleveland, OH
Fahres, William J. ... Corte Madera, CA
Fahringer, Herald Price ... New York, NY
Fahringer, Philip ... Tucson, AZ
Fahringer, Susan ... Seattle, WA
Fahrlander, Jill A. ... Madison, WI
Fahrmeier, Ruth Newman ... Ellicott City, MD
Fahrnbruch, Dale E. ... Lincoln, NE
Fahrnbruch, Margaret L. ... Lincoln, NE
Fahrner, Karen A. ... Philadelphia, PA
Fahrner, Thomas R. ... San Francisco, CA
Fahrney, Brian J. ... Chicago, IL
Fahrney, John W. ... Colorado Springs, CO
Fahrney, Mary Beth ... Chicago, IL
Fahrney, Richard L., II
Newport Beach, CA
Fahs, Randy C. ... Buffalo, NY
Fahsbender, John J. ... New York, NY
Fahselt, Brian K. ... Denver, CO
Fahy, Albert F., Jr. ... Arlington, VA
Fahy, Edward J. ... Rockford, IL
Fahy, Francis T. ... San Francisco, CA
Fahy, John J. ... Newark, NJ
Fahy, John R. ... Houston, TX
Fahy, Joseph T. ... Boston, MA
Fahy, Laura E. ... New Orleans, LA
Fahy, Margaret M. ... New York, NY
Fahy, Mary ... New York, NY
Fahy, Mary C. ... St. Petersburg, FL
Fahy, Peter B. ... Newport, OR
Fahy, Richard J., Jr. ... Washington, DC
Faia, Carmen R. ... Pleasantville, NJ
Faia, Ronald L., Jr. ... New Orleans, LA
Faia, Salvatore R. ... Philadelphia, PA
Faibish, Laura F. ... Fairfax, VA
Faiella, Christian ... Moberly, MO
Faiella, Elizabeth Hawthorne
Winter Park, FL
Faier & Faier, P.C. ... Chicago, IL
Faier, James M. ... Chicago, IL
Faier, Joan S. ... New Rochelle, NY
Faier, Melinda B. ... Chicago, IL
Faigel, Neil F. ... Methuen, MA
Faigen, Martha S. ... Boston, MA
Faigen, Michael J. ... Florham Park, NJ
Faigenbaum, Bernard D. ... Philadelphia, PA
Faigenblat, Frances Gail ... Miami, FL
Faigin, Alan W. ... Santa Monica, CA
Faigin, Randy A. ... Atlanta, GA
Faignant, John Paul ... Rutland, VT
Faigus, Eugene M. ... Northbrook, IL
Faigus, Martin L. ... Philadelphia, PA
Fail, Christine Dildy ... Petersburg, VA
Faile, William T. ... Selma, AL
Failer, David H. ... San Fernando, CA
Failer, Marvin L. ... Flushing, MI
Failing, Ann C. ... Baltimore, MD
Failing, Martha ... Houston, TX
Failinger, Marie A. ... St. Paul, MN
Failla, John E. ... New York, NY
Failla, Katherine Polk ... New York, NY
Failla, R. Roy ... Caldwell, NJ
Failla, Susan S. ... New York, NY
Faillace, Charles K. ... Mineola, NY
Faillace, Diana Ingallinera ... Princeton, NJ
Faillace, Michael A. ... Armonk, NY
Faille, Christopher C. ... Enfield, CT
Faille, Richard F. ... Springfield, MA
Failmezger and Liegel ... Syracuse, NY
Failmezger, Robert C. ... Syracuse, NY
Failor, Gray L. ... Toledo, OH
Failor, Kenneth G. ... Ada, OH
Fails, Charles H. ... Atlanta, GA
Faiman, Laurence A. ... Framingham, MA
Faimon, James D. ... Lincoln, NE
Faimon, William J. ... Nashville, TN
Fain, Bob ... Billings, MT
Fain, Bruce F. ... Billings, MT
Fain, Constance Frisby ... Houston, TX
Fain, Cynthia M. ... Springfield, IL
Fain, Deidre Susan ... Washington, DC
Fain, Gordon Y. ... New Haven, CT
Fain, Gregory T. ... Fresno, CA
Fain, Harry M. ... Beverly Hills, CA
Fain, Hugh M., III ... Richmond, VA
Fain, Ida Pearl ... Kansas City, MO
Fain, Joel M. ... Hartford, CT
Fain, John W. ... Plano, TX
Fain, Judith ... Erwin, TN
Fain, Katy C. ... Mount Vernon, IL
Fain, Kevin M. ... Rockville, MD
Fain, Major, Wiley & Brennan, P.C.
Atlanta, GA
Decatur, GA
Douglasville, GA
Jonesboro, GA
Lawrenceville, GA
Marietta, GA
Fain, Mike ... Dayton, OH
Fain, Nina J. ... Chicago, IL
Fain, Ralph E. ... Houston, TX
Fain, Renée B. ... Richmond, VA
Fain, Richard L. ... Stanton, KY
Fain, Sheldon, Anderson & Vanderhoef
Seattle, WA
Fain, Suzanne ... Houston, TX
Fain, Thomas H. ... Seattle, WA
Fain, William R., III ... Seymour, TN
Fainberg, Benjamin ... Hackensack, NJ
Fainberg, Bertrand M.
Colorado Springs, CO
Fainberg, Jack H. ... Boston, MA
Fainer, David C., Jr. ... Santa Barbara, CA
Fainer, Margaret A. ... Fresno, CA
Faines, George P. ... Pittsburgh, PA
Fainsbert Mase & Snyder, LLP
Los Angeles, CA
Fainsbert, Stephen B. ... Los Angeles, CA
Faint, Richard Clark, Jr. ... Baltimore, MD
Fainter, John W., Jr. ... Austin, TX
Faintuck, Jeffrey G. ... Franklin, MI
Faintuck & Wolfram ... Franklin, MI
Fair, Andrew J. ... White Plains, NY
Fair, Andrew L. ... New York, NY
Fair, Byron D. ... Cleveland, OH
Fair, C. Roger ... Davenport, IA
Durant, IA
Fair, Catherine T. ... Santa Ana, CA
Fair, Dale ... Wichita, KS
Fair, Diane L. ... Kansas City, MO
Fair, Donald L. ... Upland, CA
Fair, Douglas J. ... Edmonds, WA
Fair, Edward Z. ... Houston, TX
Fair, Eugene L. ... Hattiesburg, MS
Fair, George J. ... Littleton, CO
Fair, George R. ... Jackson, MS
Fair, James R., Jr. ... Natchitoches, LA
Fair, Joseph S. ... Boston, MA
Fair, Joshua D. ... Corona, CA
Fair, Kenneth ... Houston, TX
Fair, Kenneth S. ... Philadelphia, PA
Fair, Lesley Anne
Federal Trade Commission, Bureau of Consumer Protection, GV
Fair, Lisa I. ... Chicago, IL
Fair & Mayo ... Louisville, MS
Fair & Nixon ... Evansville, IN
Princeton, IN
Fair, Paul A. ... Philadelphia, PA
Fair, Randy J. ... Moses Lake, WA
Fair, Robert J. ... Princeton, IN
Fair, Rodney G. ... Jupiter, FL
Fair, Stephen C. ... Encino, CA
Fair, Tamera ... Wilmington, DE
Fair, Ted ... Waco, TX
Fair, Walt ... Waco, TX
Fair, Warren J. ... Columbia, SC
Fair, William E., III ... Augusta, GA
Fair, William J. ... Springfield, PA
Fair, Wilton H. ... Tyler, TX
Fairall, Charles F. ... Marshalltown, IA
Fairall, Loyal S. ... Marshalltown, IA
Fairall, William E., Jr. ... Camp Hill, PA
Fairbairn, David R. ... Minneapolis, MN

Falgoust, David M. ... **Atlanta, GA**
Falgoust, Jerry J. ... **Opelousas, LA**
Falgout, Gregg H. ... Houston, TX
Falgout, Huey P., Jr. ... **Houston, TX**
Falgout, Leroy J. ... Kenner, LA
Falgout, Melinda F. ... New Orleans, LA
Falgout, Nancy A. ... Houston, TX
Falgout, Tilman J., III ... **Houston, TX**
Falgout, Wollen J. ... Raceland, LA
Falgowski, Edmond ... Wilmington, DE
Falhbusch, Patricia ... Miami, FL
Falick, Frederick S. ... Middletown, NY
Falick, Michael C. ... Houston, TX
Falick, Paul ... **New York, NY**
Falik, David E. ... San Francisco, CA
Falik, Joseph L. ... **Detroit, MI**
Falik, Laurie J. ... **San Francisco, CA**
Falik, William A. ... **Berkeley, CA**
Falik, William A., A Professional Corporation ... **Berkeley, CA**
Falin, William H. ... **Cleveland, OH**
Faling, James Richard, Jr.
Oklahoma City, OK
Falis, Melvyn J. ... **New York, NY**
Falis, Neil D. ... **Atlanta, GA**
Falise, Robert A. ... Princeton, NJ
Falish, Thomas J. ... **Charlotte, NC**
Faliszek, David E. ... **San Francisco, CA**
Falivena, Francis D., Jr. ... Newark, NJ
Falivene, Peter Alfonso ... Philadelphia, PA
Falivene, Thomas H. ... **Englewood, CO**
Falk, Alan I. ... **Boston, MA**
Falk, Alan S. ... New Bedford, MA
Falk, Alfred M. ... **Tacoma, WA**
Falk, Allen E. ... Belford, NJ
Falk, Andrew E. ... **Washington, DC**
Falk, Arnold R. ... Keene, NH
Falk, Arthur V. ... Cleveland, OH
Falk, Barry D. ... **Irvine, CA**
Falk, Bennett ... **Miami, FL**
Falk, Bernard B. ... New York, NY
Falk, Beth J. ... New York, NY
Falk, Bradley M. ... **Chicago, IL**
Falk, Bryan H. ... **Cleveland, OH**
Falk, Byron L., (P.C.) ... **Dallas, TX**
Falk, Carol Gundel ... Lancaster, PA
Falk, Charles E. ... Cranford, NJ
Falk, Charles P. ... Pittsburgh, PA
Falk, Christopher R. ... Chicago, IL
Falk, Clifford J. ... Lockport, NY
Niagara Falls, NY
Falk, Conrad E. ... Chicago, IL
Falk, Cynthia A. ... Lockport, NY
Niagara Falls, NY
Falk, David ... College Park, MD
Falk, David ... Houston, TX
Falk, David A. ... Rochester, NY
Falk, Dennis J. ... **Albuquerque, NM**
Falk, Donald M. ... **Washington, DC**
Falk, E. LeRoy ... Kingsburg, CA
Falk, Edward ... **New York, NY**
Falk, Elliot E. ... **New York, NY**
Falk, Eric K. ... **Pittsburgh, PA**
Falk, Erin M. ... Department of Commerce, Patent and Trademark Office, GV
Falk, Ernest H. ... Lauderhill, FL
Falk, Ethan J. ... **Los Angeles, CA**
Falk, Everett H. ... Cookeville, TN
Falk, F. Joe, Jr. ... **Yakima, WA**
Falk & Falk ... Bakersfield, CA
Lockport, NY
Niagara Falls, NY
Falk & Fish, L.L.P. ... Morgan Hill, CA
Dallas, TX
Falk, Glenn P. ... **Coral Gables, FL**
Falk, Gregory A. ... New York, NY
Falk, Gregory P. ... Bakersfield, CA
Falk, Harry J. ... Kentland, IN
Falk, Harry S. ... Greensboro, NC
Falk, Herbert S., Jr. ... **Greensboro, NC**
Falk, I. Lee ... **Philadelphia, PA**
Falk, Jack A., Jr. ... **Miami, FL**
Naples, FL
Palm Beach, FL
Falk, James H., Jr. ... **Washington, DC**
Falk, James H., Sr. ... **Washington, DC**
Falk, James K. ... Louisville, KY
Falk, James W. ... **New York, NY**
Falk, Jeffrey P. ... West Hempstead, NY
Falk, Jennifer Alyse ... **Dallas, TX**
Falk, Jerome B., Jr. ... **San Francisco, CA**
Falk, John A. ... **Rochester, NY**
Falk, John M. ... **Washington, DC**
Falk, Jonathan P. ... **Woodbridge, NJ**
Falk, Julian ... Pittsburgh, PA
Falk, Julie M. ... **Wausau, WI**
Falk, Kathleen M. ... Madison, WI
Falk, Kenneth A. ... New York, NY
Falk, Kenneth B. ... **Woodbridge, NJ**
Falk, Kenneth L. ... New York, NY
Falk, Lauren W. ... Linden, NJ
Falk Law Firm, The, PLLC
Washington, DC
Falk, Lawrence ... New York, NY
Falk, Louis T., Jr. ... Buffalo, NY
Falk, Mark ... **Newark, NJ**
Falk, Mary R. ... Brooklyn, NY
Falk, Mary S. ... Palo Alto, CA
Falk, Matthew R. ... **Milwaukee, WI**
Falk & Mayfield, L.L.P. ... Houston, TX
Falk, Michael ... **Madison, WI**
Falk, Michael G. ... **Chicago, IL**
Falk, Michael J. ... Philadelphia, PA
Falk, Murray H. ... **Los Angeles, CA**
Falk, Nancy Engbers ... **Columbus, OH**
Falk, Neal C. ... **West Palm Beach, FL**
Falk, Nile K." Nick " ... **Rocky Mount, NC**
Falk, Pamela L. ... Dakota City, NE
Falk, Patricia J. ... Cleveland, OH
Falk, Paul T. ... **Chicago, IL**
Falk, R. Joel ... Hartland, WI
Falk, R. Scott ... **Chicago, IL**
Falk, R. H. ... Milwaukee, WI
Falk, Richard A. ... Princeton, NJ
Falk, Robert B. ... Brooklyn, NY
Falk, Robert H. ... New York, NY
Falk, Robert Hardy ... Dallas, TX
Falk, Robert L. ... **San Francisco, CA**
Falk, Robert N. ... **Washington, DC**
Falk, Roger L. ... Wichita, KS
Falk, Roger L., Law Offices of, P.A.
Wichita, KS
Falk, Scott A. ... **Hartford, CT**
Falk, Scott K. ... Indianapolis, IN
Falk & Scrivens ... Cleveland, OH
Falk, Shane ... Wausau, WI
Falk & Sharp, A Professional Corporation
Los Angeles, CA
Falk, Sheryl Anne ... **Houston, TX**
Falk & Siemer, LLP ... Amherst, NY
Buffalo, NY
Lockport, NY
Mayville, NY
Niagara Falls, NY
Falk, Stephanie H. ... Bakersfield, CA
Falk, Stephen S. ... Santa Ana, CA
Falk, Stephen T. ... Philadelphia, PA
Falk, Steven M. ... Miami, FL
Falk, Steven M. ... **Naples, FL**
Falk, Steven M., Professional Association
Miami, FL
Falk, Sydney W., Jr. ... **Austin, TX**
Falk, Theodore C. ... Clackamas, OR
Falk, Theresa Fenelon ... **Washington, DC**
Falk, Thomas E. ... Longmont, CO
Falk, Victor S., III ... Miami, FL
Falk, William E. ... Shenandoah, IA
Falk, William J. ... **St. Louis, MO**
Falke, Anthony J., Jr. ... Lynbrook, NY
Falke, Lee C., & Associates ... **Dayton, OH**
Falke, Lee C., & Associates
Kettering, OH
Falkenbach, John J. ... **Media, PA**
Falkenberg, Charles V., III ... **Chicago, IL**
Falkenberg, Charles V., Jr. ... Palatine, IL
Falkenberg, Denny W. ... Medford, OK
Falkenberg & Isaacson ... Cadott, WI
Falkenberg, Russell R. ... Cadott, WI
Falkenberg, Thomas F. ... **Chicago, IL**
Falkenberry, Eric M. ... **New York, NY**
Falkenberry, John C. ... **Birmingham, AL**
Falkenborg, Marguerite ... Chula Vista, CA
Falkener, Waldo C., Jr. ... **New York, NY**
Falkenhainer, William C., (Professional Corporation) ... **Pasadena, CA**
Falkenham, Eric G. ... **Manchester, NH**
Falkenheiner, Doris ... Baton Rouge, LA
Falkenheiner, Doris, A Prof. Law Corp.
Baton Rouge, LA
Falkenheiner, William C. ... Vidalia, LA
Falkenstein, Alice R. ... New York, NY
Falkenstein, Andrew Lawrence
Washington, DC
Falkenstein, Cynthia J. ... Ypsilanti, MI
Falkenstein, Eric M. ... New York, NY
Falkenstein, Robert H. ... Longview, WA
Falkenstein, Stanley ... Manchester, CT
Falkenthal, Robert J. ... Fontana, CA
Falker, Michael J. ... Hartford, CT
Falker, Robert L. ... New York, NY
Falkides, A. Nicholas ... **Buffalo, NY**
Falkiewicz, Christina Lynn ... San Antonio, TX
Falkin, Gary L. ... Chatham, NJ
Falkin, Jeffrey C. ... **Woodcliff Lake, NJ**
Falkin, Lawrence ... Philadelphia, PA
Falkin, Mark G. ... Dallas, TX
Falkin & O'Toole, L.L.P. ... Dallas, TX
Falkinburg, Thomas ... Tampa, FL
Falkinham, Sara ... **Memphis, TN**
Falkner, Daniel L. ... Norwell, MA
Falkner, Edward W. J. ... Appleton, WI
Falkner, Frank D. ... Brookfield, WI
Falkner, Kelley Kimmel ... **Milwaukee, WI**
Falkner, Rheanne Dodson ... **Louisville, KY**
Falkner, Robert F. ... Schaumburg, IL
Falknor, G. Scott ... **Northbrook, IL**
Falknor, William L. ... Dayton, OH
Falkof, Bradley B. ... **Chicago, IL**
Falkof, Ellen Lubarsky ... Wilmette, IL
Falkoff, Michael I. ... **Boston, MA**
Falkoff, Michelle ... **Palo Alto, CA**
Falkow, Richard S. ... Dallas, TX
Falkowitz, Holly S. ... **New York, NY**
Falkowitz, Tracy M. ... **Tampa, FL**
Falkowski, Anthony J. ... West Simsbury, CT
Falkowski, Charles J. ... Los Angeles, CA
Falkowski, Christopher J. ... Southfield, MI
Falkowski, Colleen A. ... Painesville, OH
Falkowski, Michael P. ... Daytona Beach, FL
DeLand, FL
Falkowski, Michael P., P.A.
Daytona Beach, FL
DeLand, FL
Falkowski, Reginald J. ... Painted Post, NY
Falkson, Susan D. ... **McLean, VA**
Fall, Daniel P. ... Fredericktown, MO
Fall, Don Christophe ... Oxnard, CA
Fall, Janice Leyrer ... **Palo Alto, CA**
Fall, John A. ... **Livingston, NJ**
Fall, John G. ... San Francisco, CA
Fall, Kenneth G. ... **New York, NY**
Fall, Lesa C. ... **Indianapolis, IN**
Fall, Mark S. ... **Los Angeles, CA**
Fall, Pamela K. ... **East Lansing, MI**
Fall, Robert A. ... Toms River, NJ
Fall, Robert A. ... **McLean, VA**
Fall, Robert J. ... Wexford, PA
Fall, Susan M. ... Norfolk, VA
Fall, Timothy L. ... Woodland, CA
Fall, Tristram R., III ... **Philadelphia, PA**
Falla, Charlotte G. ... **Santa Clara, CA**
Falla, James M. ... West Harwich, MA
Fallace & Associates, P.A. ... **Melbourne, FL**
Fallace, James H. ... **Melbourne, FL**
Fallang, Dennis J. ... Dayton, OH
Fallar, Scott William ... Jacksonville, FL
Fallarino, Robert V. ... Great Neck, NY
Fallat, Dale W. ... Maumee, OH
Fallat, George S. ... The Sea Ranch, CA
Fallat, Jennefer Ann ... Viera, FL
Fallat, John L. ... **Kentfield, CA**
Pasadena, CA
San Francisco, CA
Fallat, John L., Law Offices of
Kentfield, CA
Fallat, Judith A. ... Denville, NJ
Fallati, Thomas R. ... **New York, NY**
Fallek, Andrew M. ... Brooklyn, NY
Fallek, Dana M. ... **New York, NY**
Fallek, David ... **San Francisco, CA**
Fallek, Joseph ... Brooklyn, NY
Fallek, Larry ... McAllen, TX
Fallek, Lawrence Lee ... Brooklyn, NY
Fallek, Shari B. ... **Houston, TX**
Faller, Brian V. ... Seattle, WA
Faller, Carl M., Jr. ... Fresno, CA
Faller, Cecile M. ... Green Bay, WI
Faller, Dennis P. ... Wapakoneta, OH
Faller, George B. ... Carlisle, PA
Faller, George B., Jr. ... **Carlisle, PA**
Faller, George R. ... Marinette, WI
Faller, Joel E. ... Barre, VT
Faller, Kenneth R. ... **Cincinnati, OH**
Faller, Morton A. ... **Rockville, MD**
Faller, Pamela N. ... Visalia, CA
Faller, Raymond T. ... **Cincinnati, OH**
Faller, Rhoda Grossberg ... **Louisville, KY**
Faller, Robert A. ... **Garden City, NY**
Faller, Susan Grogan ... **Cincinnati, OH**
Faller, Tammy S. ... **Muncie, IN**
Faller, Virginia L. ... Seattle, WA
Faller, William N. ... Hammond, LA
Faller, William N., Ltd. ... Hammond, LA
Fallert, Thomas M. ... **Pittsburgh, PA**
Fallesen, Byron W. ... Lexington, NE
Fallesen, Byron W., P.C. ... Lexington, NE
Falletta, Charles J. ... **Florham Park, NJ**
Falletta, James A. ... Tonawanda, NY
Falletta & Klein ... San Diego, CA
Falletta, Mae M. ... **Mineola, NY**
Falletta, Salvatore A. ... Rutherford, NJ
Falletta, Salvatore J. ... Canton, OH
Falletta, Stephen N. ... San Diego, CA
Falleur, Michael ... Columbus, OH
Falley, Matthew N. ... **Los Angeles, CA**
Falley, Neil J. ... Whittier, CA
Fallgatter, Curtis S. ... **Jacksonville, FL**
Fallgatter, Curtis S., P.A. ... **Jacksonville, FL**
Fallgatter, Thomas C. ... **Bakersfield, CA**
Fallgren, Burton J. ... Portland, OR
Fallick, Barry ... **New York, NY**
Fallick, Gregg Vance ... **Albuquerque, NM**
Fallick, Shannon S. ... **San Francisco, CA**
Fallico, Fabio ... Nashville, TN
Falligant, J. Daniel ... **Savannah, GA**
Falligant, Robert E., Jr. ... Savannah, GA
Fallik, Alan E. ... Hollywood, FL
Fallin, C. Glenn ... Arcadia, LA
Fallin, Glenna C. ... Baton Rouge, LA
Fallin, Glenna C., A P.L.C.
Baton Rouge, LA
Fallin, Jack F., Jr. ... **San Francisco, CA**
Fallin, Joseph C. ... Tulsa, OK
Fallin, Kathryn O. ... Cordele, GA
Fallin and McIntosh ... **Moultrie, GA**
Fallin, William G. ... **Moultrie, GA**
Fallis, Carol A., (P.C.) ... Fenton, MI
Fallis, Deborah Weisler ... **New Orleans, LA**
Fallis, Harvey D. ... Melville, NY
Fallis, Robert J. ... **Seattle, WA**
Fallis, Russell R. ... Knoxville, TN
Fallis, S. M., Jr. ... **Tulsa, OK**
Fallis, Stephen A. ... Akron, OH
Fallis, Stephen J. ... **New York, NY**
Fallk, David I. ... Scranton, PA
Fallk, Samuel ... Scranton, PA
Fallman, Edward J. ... **Boston, MA**
Fallman, Howard S. ... Los Angeles, CA
Fallman, James ... Oroville, CA
Fallman, Janice M. ... Los Angeles, CA
Fallman, Michael S. ... **Boston, MA**
Fallmer & Friedman ... Skokie, IL
Fallmer, William F. ... Skokie, IL
Fallon, Amanda M. ... **Landover, MD**
Fallon, Ann E. ... Columbus, OH
Fallon, Arthur J. ... Santa Rosa, CA
Fallon, Barbieri & Kissel, P.C. ... Enfield, CT
Fallon, Bixby & Cheng
San Francisco, CA
Fallon, Brett D. ... **Wilmington, DE**
Fallon, Brian M. ... Cleveland, OH
Fallon, Brian M., Co., L.P.A. ... Cleveland, OH
Fallon, Christine A. ... Cleveland, OH
Fallon, Christine Luchok ... Supreme Court Of The United States, GV
Fallon, Christopher C., Jr.
Philadelphia, PA
Fallon, Christopher G. ... Malden, MA
Fallon, Claire ... Department of Justice, Tax Division, GV
Fallon & Cleary ... Buffalo, NY
Fallon, Cynthia L. ... **Manchester, NH**
Fallon, Dana ... **Austin, TX**
Fallon, Dana M. ... **Fairfax, VA**
Fallon, David P. ... Sayville, NY
Fallon, Dominic J. ... Cleveland, OH
Fallon, Eldon E. ... New Orleans, LA
Fallon, Ellen Mercer ... **Middlebury, VT**
Fallon, Eugene A., Jr. ... Florence, SC
Fallon & Fallon ... Cazenovia, NY
Fallon & Fallon ... Sayville, NY
Fallon & Fallon ... Syracuse, NY
Fallon, Francis E. ... New York, NY
Fallon, Francis I. ... Palm Coast, FL
Fallon, Francis X., Jr. ... Minneapolis, MN
Fallon, Gary M. ... **Seattle, WA**
Fallon, Geralyn M. ... Chicago, IL
Fallon, Gerard C. ... Hackensack, NJ
Fallon, Gina E. ... Livingston, NJ
Fallon & Groux ... Warrenton, VA
Fallon, James C. ... **Cleveland, OH**
Fallon, James M. ... Washington, DC
Fallon, James V. ... Sayville, NY
Fallon, James V., Jr. ... Sayville, NY
Fallon, Jeffrey E. ... **Washington, DC**
Fallon, Jim ... **Sherman, TX**
Fallon, John F. ... **Trumbull, CT**
Fallon, John F., Jr. ... Holyoke, MA
Fallon, John J. ... Walden, NY
Fallon, John R., Jr. ... **New York, NY**
Fallon, Joseph D. ... Hinesburg, VT
Fallon, Joseph E. ... Enfield, CT
Fallon, Joseph G. ... Princeton, NJ
Fallon, Joseph P. ... East Hampton, NY
Fallon, Joseph R. ... Westford, MA
Fallon, Joy Kahlenberg ... Newton, MA
Fallon, Kahlman R. ... Atlanta, GA
Fallon, Kathleen ... **New York, NY**
Fallon, Kathleen M. ... Hauppauge, NY
Fallon, Kathryn Michelle ... Malden, MA
Fallon, Kieran J.
Board of Governors Of The Federal Reserve System, Office of the General Counsel, GV
Fallon, Kieran P. ... Miami, FL
Fallon, Kieran P., P.A. ... Miami, FL
Fallon Law Firm, P.A. ... Florence, SC
Fallon, Lawrence J. ... **San Francisco, CA**
Fallon, Leo J. ... Buffalo, NY
Fallon, Lynda Lee ... Spring Lake, NJ
Fallon, Lynnette C. ... **Boston, MA**
Fallon, Martin J. ... **Cleveland, OH**
Fallon, Martin J., Jr. ... **Philadelphia, PA**
Fallon, Mary A. ... **New York, NY**
Fallon, Mary E. ... Akron, OH
Fallon & McKinley ... Seattle, WA
Fallon, Megan Mary ... Syracuse, NY
Fallon, Merle W. ... Warrenton, VA
Fallon, Michael C. ... Santa Rosa, CA
Fallon, Paul E. ... Buffalo, NY
Fallon, Peter B. ... Warren, NJ
Fallon, Peter G. ... Scituate, MA
Fallon, Peter Max ... **Tampa, FL**
Fallon, R. Ann ... **Walnut Creek, CA**
Fallon, R. Scott ... Seattle, WA
Fallon, Richard H., Jr. ... Cambridge, MA
Fallon, Richard J. ... Acton, MA
Fallon, Robert C. ... **Washington, DC**
Fallon, Robert C. ... West Palm Beach, FL
Fallon, Robert J. ... Warwick, RI
Fallon, Sheila M. ... Syracuse, NY
Fallon, Sherry Ruggiero ... **Wilmington, DE**
Fallon, Stephen Gregory ... Monticello, AR
Fallon, Stephen J. ... Taunton, MA
Fallon, Steven P. ... **Chicago, IL**
Fallon, Thomas C. ... Beverly, MA
Fallon, Thomas F. ... Clinton, MA
Fallon, Thomas F. ... Huntington, NY
Fallon, Thomas H. ... Manchester, NH
Fallon, Timothy J. ... Boston, MA
Fallon, Veronica M. ... New Haven, CT
Fallon, Veronica M ... South Burlington, VT
Fallon, W. Gerard, Jr. ... South Hamilton, MA
Fallon, William E. ... Salem, MA
Fallon, William E. ... Springfield, MA
Fallon, William G. ... Santa Ana, CA
Fallon, William H. ... **Grand Rapids, MI**
Fallon, William J. ... Cazenovia, NY
Syracuse, NY
Fallon, William L. ... Mount Airy, MD
Fallon, Yvette Pietruska ... Stamford, CT
Fallone, Edward A. ... Milwaukee, WI
Fallone, Yvette ... **Atlanta, GA**
Fallon-Houle, Nancy ... **Downers Grove, IL**
Fallon-Houle, Nancy, P.C. ... **Chicago, IL**
Downers Grove, IL
Falloon, Elizabeth ... Federal Deposit Insurance Corporation, GV
Fallow, Charles Winston ... **Arlington, VA**
Fallow, Katherine A. ... **Washington, DC**
Fallowfield, Linda J ... Department of Justice, Office of Justice Programs, GV
Fallowfield, Robert I. ... Ketchum, ID
Falls, Brandon K. ... Birmingham, AL
Falls, Dell L. ... Lancaster, CA
Falls, Edward J. ... Phoenix, OR
Falls, Gregory K. ... **Denver, CO**
Falls, Gregory W. ... **Phoenix, AZ**
Falls, H. Naill, Jr. ... Nashville, TN
Falls, J. Craig ... **Dallas, TX**
Falls, John C. ... **Cherry Hill, NJ**
Falls, John Thomas, Jr. ... Columbia, SC
Falls, Josephine F. ... Tucson, AZ
Falls, Kristen Sotnik ... New Haven, CT
Falls, Mia D. ... **New York, NY**
Falls, Michael D. ... Deerfield, IL
Falls, Michael D., Chartered ... Deerfield, IL
Falls, Pamela A. ... Basking Ridge, NJ
Falls, R. Deke ... Charlotte, NC
Falls, Richard Deke ... **Charlotte, NC**
Falls, Robert C. ... Austin, TX
Falls, Thomas C. ... Pomona, CA

Falls, Timothy Berry ... Campbellsville, KY
Falls & Veach, PLC ... Nashville, TN
Fallsgraff, Gary F. ... Cleveland, OH
Fallucca & O'Shea, PLC ... Detroit, MI
Fallucca, Thomas M. ... Detroit, MI
Fallwell, Marion A. ... Houston, TX
Falon, Paul H. ... Washington, DC
Faloni, David A. ... West Caldwell, NJ
Faloni, David A., Jr. ... West Caldwell, NJ
Falor, Tamara Claire ... Eureka, CA
Falotico, John E. ... Woodland Hills, CA
Fals, Mary M. ... Canal Fulton, OH
Falsafi, Shiva ... Boston, MA
Falsani, Balmer, Berglund & Peterson
Duluth, MN
Falsani, Robert C. ... Duluth, MN
Falsetti, Allen A. ... Riverside, CA
Falsetti, Louis P. ... Oklahoma City, OK
Falsetti, Mary Ann ... Milwaukee, WI
Falsetti, Robert D. ... Oakland, CA
Falsey, Edward T., Jr. ... North Haven, CT
Falsey, Marie T. ... Wallingford, CT
Falsgraf, William W. ... Cleveland, OH
Falsioni, Darcie A. ... Syracuse, NY
Falso, Edward D. ... Schenectady, NY
Falsone, G. Jack ... Buffalo, NY
Falsone, N. J. ... Tampa, FL
Falsone, Rico J. ... Cleveland, OH
Falstad, Daniel T. ... Atlanta, GA
Falstad, David Brian ... Orlando, FL
Falstad, Jill N. ... Wausau, WI
Falstad, Robert Eric ... Austin, TX
Falstrault, Jennifer ... Hackensack, NJ
New York, NY
Falstrom, Carl ... San Francisco, CA
Falstrom, Kenneth E. ... Santa Barbara, CA
Faltemier, Valerie ... Wheaton, IL
Faltenovich, Richard A. ... Ambridge, PA
Beaver Falls, PA
Falter, George H., III ... Baltimore, MD
Falter, Karen K. ... Cincinnati, OH
Falter, Lawrence S. ... Denver, CO
Faltischek, Michael L. ... Mineola, NY
Faltys, John H. ... Langley, WA
Falussy, John G. ... White Plains, NY
Falvay, Kirk D. ... Birmingham, MI
Falvay, Kirk D. ... Bloomfield Hills, MI
Falvay, Kirk D. ... Clarkston, MI
Troy, MI
West Bloomfield, MI
Falvello, Anthony C. ... Sugarloaf, PA
Falvello, Conrad A. ... Sugarloaf, PA
Falvey, Anne M. ... New York, NY
Falvey, Brian E. ... Boston, MA
Falvey, Caroline Anne ... Ocala, FL
Falvey, Charles L. ... Brownsburg, IN
Falvey, Cheryl Adams ... Washington, DC
Falvey, Daniel M. ... Dorchester, MA
Falvey, David F. ... Groton, CT
Falvey, Frank J., Jr. ... Lexington, MA
Falvey, James M. ... Northbrook, IL
Falvey, John J., Jr. ... Boston, MA
Falvey, John W. ... Chicago, IL
Falvey, Mary A. ... Canton, OH
Falvey, Patrick J. ... New York, NY
Falvey, Robert E. ... Wakefield, RI
Falvey, Robert V. ... Cherry Hill, NJ
Falvey, Stephen P. ... White Plains, NY
Falvey, Thomas W. ... Pasadena, CA
Falvey, V. H. ... El Paso, TX
Falvey, W. Patrick ... Penn Yan, NY
Falvo, Frank A. ... Pittsburgh, PA
Falvo, Laura A. ... St. Petersburg, FL
Falvo, Mark A. ... Clearfield, PA
Falvo, Peter S., Jr. ... Ocean Township, NJ
Falvo, Steven T. ... Johnston, RI
Falvo, Vincent J., Jr. ... Department of Justice,
Criminal Division, GV
Falvy, Dean G. ... Seattle, WA
Falwell, Jerry Lamon, Jr. ... Forest, VA
Lynchburg, VA
Falwell, Thomas Wray ... Boston, MA
Falzetta, Frank ... Los Angeles, CA
Falzon, Anthony V. ... Miami, FL
Falzon, Joseph K. ... New York, NY
Falzon, Lawrence C. ... Southfield, MI
Falzone, Anthony T. ... San Francisco, CA
Falzone, Clifford A. ... Moberly, MO
Falzone, Frank S. ... Buffalo, NY
Falzone, Gerard A. ... Alameda, CA
Falzone, John M., Jr. ... Colonia, NJ
Falzone, Michael P. ... Richmond, VA
Falzone, Nicholas R. ... Atlanta, GA
Falzone, Paul R. ... Woodland, CA
Falzone, Priscilla J. ... Austin, TX
Falzone, Raymond J., Jr. ... Media, PA
Falzone, Sandra B. ... Department of Labor,
Office of Secretary, GV
Falzone, Stephen T. ... Grosse Ile, MI
Falzone, Todd Robert
Fort Lauderdale, FL
Fam, Samia ... Washington, DC
Fama, Andrew J. ... Rochester, NY
Fama, Anthony ... San Diego, CA
Fama, Arthur F., Jr. ... New York, NY
Fama, David T. ... San Francisco, CA
Fama, James P. ... Washington, DC
New York, NY
Fama, Leo S., II ... Everett, MA
Fama, Patricia M. ... Redwood City, CA
Fama, Paul E. ... San Francisco, CA
Fama, Richard ... New York, NY
Fama, Victor B. ... Tarrytown, NY
Fambrough, Sheryl Deane
Lawrenceville, GA
Fambrough, Talmadge ... Pell City, AL
Fambrough, William S. ... Detroit, MI
Famely, Max ... Bloomfield, CT
Famighetti, Joseph P. ... East Meadow, NY
Famiglietti, Anthony O. ... Plainville, CT
Famiglietti & Carlin, Ltd. ... Providence, RI
Famiglietti, Carolyn N. ... Boston, MA
Famiglietti, Jason S. ... Plainville, CT
Famiglietti, Louis M. ... Manassas, VA
Famiglietti, Matthew T. ... Columbia, SC
Famiglietti, Melissa D. ... Providence, RI
Famiglietti, Michael C. ... Atlanta, GA
Famiglietti, Stephen R. ... Providence, RI
Famiglietti, Thompson & Vollono, LLC
Plainville, CT
Famiglio, George V. ... Broomall, PA
Famiglio, Robert B. ... Media, PA
Familant, Scott B. ... New York, NY
Familo, Edward D. ... Cleveland, OH
Family Law Association, Ltd.
Hickory Hills, IL
Family Law Centers ... Henderson, NV
Las Vegas, NV
Family, Marshall E. ... Moorestown, NJ
Famous, Tracy ... Philadelphia, PA
Famparska, Valentina ... Chicago, IL
Famular, Nan S. ... Pennsauken, NJ
Famularo, R. Anthony ... Dix Hills, NY
Famulari, Anthony C. ... Newark, NJ
Famulari, F. David ... Miami, FL
Famulari, John D. ... Brooklyn, NY
Famulari, Kathleen J. ... Boston, MA
Famulari, Kristin ... Nashville, TN
Famularo, G. A. ... Mount Olivet, KY
Famularo, John M. ... Lexington, KY
Famularo, Joseph L. ... Lexington, KY
Famularo, Robert P. ... Garden Grove, CA
Famulener, Kathleen C. ... Oakland, CA
Fan, Calvin A. ... San Diego, CA
Fan, George ... New York, NY
Fan, Ian ... San Diego, CA
Fan, Jennifer Shiu-Li ... San Francisco, CA
Fan, Peter B. ... Rowland Heights, CA
Fan, Rachelle ... New York, NY
Fanady, Kimberly A., Law Offices of
San Francisco, CA
Fanaff, Jeffrey A. ... Houston, TX
Fanale, Joseph A. ... Danvers, MA
Fanara, Loretta J. ... Canton, MA
Fanarjian, Manuel P. ... Dover, NJ
Fanaro, Ronald S. ... Vero Beach, FL
Fanaroff, Carolyn D. ... Treasury Department,
Internal Revenue Service, GV
Fanaroff, Sheri V.G. ... Owings Mills, MD
Fanburg, John D. ... Roseland, NJ
Fanburg, Robert R. ... Short Hills, NJ
Fancher, Allen P. ... Virginia Beach, VA
Fancher, C. Larry ... La Habra, CA
Fancher, Catherine ... Dallas, TX
Fancher, Darren W. ... Menlo Park, CA
Fancher, Elizabeth L. ... Bend, OR
Fancher, Frederic G. ... Spokane, WA
Fancher, Henry N.
Hot Springs National Park, AR
Fancher, Henry Nolen
Hot Springs National Park, AR
Fancher, James K., Jr. ... Atlanta, GA
Fancher, Joe R., Jr. ... Canton, MS
Fancher, Lisa C. ... Austin, TX
Fancher, Mark P. ... Ann Arbor, MI
Fancher, Paula Conser ... San Francisco, CA
Fancher, Phil M. ... St. Petersburg, FL
Fancher, Richard W. ... Silver Spring, MD
Fancher, Rick ... Corpus Christi, TX
Fancher, Saml. W. ... Tacoma, WA
Fancher, Scott W. ... Richmond, VA
Fancher, Sharon R. ... Dallas, TX
Fancher, Thomas H. ... Saginaw, MI
Fancher & Wickland ... San Francisco, CA
Fancher, William S. ... Walton, NY
Fanchi, Louis A. ... Park Ridge, IL
Fanchi, Peter A. ... St. Louis, MO
Fanciullo, William P. ... Albany, NY
Fancsali, Beth L. ... Dallas, TX
Fancy, Patricia B. ... Detroit, MI
Fandel, John A. ... Seattle, WA
Fandel, K. Michael ... Seattle, WA
Fandel, Mona ... Fort Lauderdale, FL
Fandel, Robert F. ... Brockton, MA
Fandell, Sarah E. ... Chicago, IL
Fandey, Joseph Z.
Truth or Consequences, NM
Fandiño, Berta L. ... Miami, FL
Fandray, Nita M. ... Pittsburgh, PA
Fandre, Scott ... Chicago, IL
Fandrich, Mark H. ... Auburn, NY
Fane, Edward F. ... Fort Edward, NY
Fane, Gerard J. ... Fountain Valley, CA
Faneca, Cy ... Gulfport, MS
Fanego, Carmen L. ... Miami, FL
Fanelli, Anna ... Brooklyn, NY
Fanelli, Cecelia L. ... Philadelphia, PA
Fanelli, Frederick J. ... Pottsville, PA
Fanelli, Joseph C. ... Oak Lawn, IL
Fanelli, Joseph M. ... Newark, DE
Fanelli, Joseph W. ... Bradenton, FL
Fanelli, Lenora Ann ... Utica, NY
Fanelli, Lisa Jo ... Harrisburg, PA
Fanelli, Michael J. ... Washington, DC
Fanelli, Patricia A. ... Media, PA
Fanelli, Robert G. ... New Rochelle, NY
Fanelli, Rosemary ... New York, NY
Fanelli, Thomas F., Jr. ... Hartsdale, NY
Fanelly, Angelo A. ... Akron, OH
Faner, Walter W. ... Canoga Park, CA
Faner, Walter W., A Law Corporation
Canoga Park, CA
Faneuil, Edward J. ... Waltham, MA
Faneuil, Robert A. ... Needham Heights, MA
Fanfera, Jennifer ... Berwyn, PA
Fang, Forrest E. ... San Francisco, CA
Fang, Guanming ... Atlanta, GA
Fang, Helen Haelim ... Minneapolis, MN
Fang, Kenneth T. H. ... Los Angeles, CA
Fang, Melissa ... Boston, MA
Fang, Neil B. ... North Woodmere, NY
Fang, Seymour H. ... New York, NY
Fang, William L. ... Washington, DC
Fang, Zhi-Ying James ... Los Angeles, CA
Fanganello, Joseph M. ... Denver, CO
Fanganello, Joseph M., P.C. ... Denver, CO
Fanger, Irving M. ... Boston, MA
Fanger, Jerome S. ... Troy, MI
Fanger, Katharine Lee Whiteside
Roxbury, MA
Fangio, Mary Lannon ... Syracuse, NY
Fangmeyer, Marsha E. ... Kearney, NE
Fanikos, David W. ... Boston, MA
Fanizza, Joanne ... Fort Lauderdale, FL
Fanizza, Joanne, P.A., Law Offices of
Fort Lauderdale, FL
Fank, Carolyn Leigh, (Ms.)
Pacific Palisades, CA
Fankhanel, K. Jane ... New York, NY
Fankhauser, Allen ... Humboldt, NE
Fankhauser, Ephraim H. ... Salt Lake City, UT
Fankhauser, John T. ... Tinley Park, IL
Fankhauser, Mark A. ... Dallas, TX
Fankhauser, Nelsen & Werts, P.C.
Humboldt, NE
Fann, Donald J. ... Fort Lauderdale, FL
Fann & Rea, P.C. ... Birmingham, AL
Fann, Robert P. ... Birmingham, AL
Fann, Ronald L. ... Crofton, MD
Fann, Terry A. ... Murfreesboro, TN
Fann, Traci Leah ... Kansas City, MO
Fann, Victor H. ... Los Angeles, CA
Fann, William F., Jr. ... Miami Shores, FL
Fannan, John J. ... Roseland, NJ
Fannan, Richard ... Los Angeles, CA
Fannen, Weldon H. Skip ... Overland Park, KS
Fanney, John K. ... Raleigh, NC
Fannig, William C., Jr. ... La Plata, MD
Fannin, David B. ... Austin, TX
Fannin, David C. ... Delray Beach, FL
Fannin, Donald E. ... Cincinnati, OH
Fannin & Fannin ... Fort Worth, TX
Santo, TX
Fannin, Hank ... Talladega, AL
Fannin, Jill C. ... Walnut Creek, CA
Fannin, John F. ... Jacksonville, FL
Fannin, Karen L. ... Houston, TX
Fannin, Linda R. ... Fairfax, VA
Fannin, Lucille Stewart ... Fort Lauderdale, FL
Fannin, Oliver W., Jr. ... Fort Worth, TX
Santo, TX
Fannin, P. Robert ... Phoenix, AZ
Fannin, Patrick K. ... Seattle, WA
Fannin, Richard L. ... Arlington, TX
Fannin, Thomas N. ... East Liverpool, OH
Fannin, William J. ... Petaluma, CA
Fanning, Allan J. ... Kansas City, MO
Fanning, Barry Hedges ... Dallas, TX
Fanning, Charles J. ... McLean, VA
Fanning, David A. ... Palo Alto, CA
Portland, OR
Fanning, Deborah A. ... Hauppauge, NY
Fanning, Deborah S. ... Vista, CA
Fanning, Donald A. ... Beaufort, SC
Fanning, Edward J. ... Woodbridge, NJ
Staten Island, NY
Fanning, Edward J., Jr. ... Newark, NJ
Fanning, Eleanor ... Trevose, PA
Fanning, Eleanor, P.C. ... Trevose, PA
Fanning, Francis G. ... Tempe, AZ
Fanning, Gary L., Jr. ... Topeka, KS
Fanning, Gerald A. ... Tonto Basin, AZ
Fanning & Greer, P.A. ... La Plata, MD
Fanning, Harper & Martinson, A
Professional Corporation ... Dallas, TX
Fanning & Hudson, P.C. ... Newnan, GA
Fanning, H. W. ... Wichita, KS
Fanning, J. Paul ... West Palm Beach, FL
Fanning, James S. ... Buffalo, NY
Eden, NY
Fanning, Joel C. ... Pensacola, FL
Fanning, John J. ... Newark, NJ
Fanning, John P.
Department Of Health And Human Services,
Public Health Service, GV
Fanning, Kent W. ... St. Peters, MO
Fanning, Kevin A. S.
Farmington Hills, MI
Fanning, Kimberly D. ... San Francisco, CA
Fanning, Lofton M. ... Orangeburg, SC
Fanning, Marc Hedges ... Dallas, TX
Fanning, Michael G. ... Gretna, LA
Fanning, Michael R. ... Washington, DC
Fanning, Michaela A. ... Boston, MA
Fanning, Monica ... Kansas City, MO
Fanning, Patrick ... New Orleans, LA
Fanning, Patrick J. ... Des Plaines, IL
Fanning, Patrick N. ... Kansas City, MO
Fanning, Patrick W. ... Boise, ID
Fanning, Paul A. ... Greenville, NC
New Bern, NC
Fanning, Paul T. ... Chicago, IL
Fanning, Paul T., P.C., The Law Offices of
Chicago, IL
Fanning, Philip J. ... Hartford, CT
Fanning, Richard W., Jr. ... Detroit, MI
Fanning, Robert A. ... Indianapolis, IN
Fanning, Robert A. ... Dallas, TX
Fanning, Robin Craig
Hoffman Estates, IL
Fanning, Stephen A. ... Providence, RI
Fanning, Stephen Thomas ... Providence, RI
Fanning, Steven E., (P.C.) ... Newnan, GA
Fanning, Suzanne R. ... Ann Arbor, MI
Fanning, Timothy O'Neil ... West Chester, PA
Fanning, Valerie ... Portland, OR
Fanning, Whitney E. ... Waco, TX
Fanning, William C., Jr. ... La Plata, MD
Fanning, William M. ... Hackensack, NJ
Fannon, Angela L. ... New York, NY
Fannon, David T. ... New York, NY
Fannon, Elizabeth B. ... Hillsborough, CA
Fannon, Francis J. ... Allendale, NJ
Fannon, James G. ... Philadelphia, PA
Fannon, Laura E. ... San Francisco, CA
Fannon, Patrick J. ... Cincinnati, OH
Fannon, Stephen T. ... Mount Laurel, NJ
Fannon, Victoria C. ... Marlton, NJ
Fano, Nicholas J. ... Jersey City, NJ
Fano, Robert M. ... Department of the Army,
Office of the Judge Advocate General, GV
Fano, Ronald L. ... Denver, CO
Fanone, Anthony V. ... Chicago, IL
Fanone, John R. ... Chicago, IL
Fanone, Joseph A. ... Washington, DC
Fanos, Stephanie ... Telluride, CO
Fanos, William R. ... Cleveland, OH
Fanous, Nikki H. ... Fort Worth, TX
Fanshaw, George W., III ... Baltimore, MD
Fanshaw, Gregory Sean ... Baltimore, MD
Fanshaw, Judith L. ... La Jolla, CA
Fanshawe, Frank J. ... Albany, NY
Fanshawe, Helen M. ... Albany, NY
Fansler, Daryl R. ... Knoxville, TN
Fansler, Steven R. ... West Liberty, OH
Fanslow, Heidi ... Missoula, MT
Fansmith, John F., Jr. ... Philadelphia, PA
Fant, Arthur ... Houston, TX
Fant, Brian ... Dallas, TX
Fant, Bruce B. ... Austin, TX
Fant, Carol E. ... St. Petersburg, FL
Fant, Catherine ... Columbia, SC
Fant, Douglas V. ... Midland, TX
Fant & Fant ... Greenville, SC
Fant, Francis R., Jr. ... Anderson, SC
Fant, Gregory C. ... Los Angeles, CA
Fant, John F., Jr. ... Chesterland, OH
Fant, Lester G., III ... Washington, DC
Fant, Patrick C., III ... Greenville, SC
Fant, Patrick C., Jr. ... Greenville, SC
Fant, Philip A. ... San Francisco, CA
Fant, Shannon L. ... Fayetteville, AR
Fant, Simpson Z. ... Columbia, SC
Fant, Traci Dunn ... Chattanooga, TN
Fant, Valerie A. ... Oakton, VA
Fant, William F. ... Metairie, LA
Fanta, Darla K. ... Anaheim, CA
Fanta, John C. ... Chicago, IL
Fantaci, James M. ... New Orleans, LA
Fantaci, Michael L. ... New Orleans, LA
Fantalis, Maryanne ... Springfield, NJ
Fantano, Diana R. ... Melville, NY
Mineola, NY
Fantasia, Emily L. ... Boston, MA
Fantasia, Gina ... Fairmont, WV
Fantasia, Tilia J. ... Westfield, MA
Fantauzzi, David A. ... Youngstown, OH
Fantauzzi, John A. ... Schenectady, NY
Fantauzzi, Kathryn Nolan ... Albany, NY
Fantauzzo, Kevin D. ... St. Petersburg, FL
Fantazzi, Kathleen J. ... Moundsville, WV
Fante, Peter D. ... New York, NY
Fantel, Jane I. ... Seattle, WA
Fanter, Alan R. ... Brooksville, FL
Fanter, Robert L. ... Des Moines, IA
Fanter, William F. ... Des Moines, IA
Fantin, Louis A. ... Lawrenceville, NJ
Fantini, Anthony R. ... Pittsburgh, PA
Fantini Law Firm, The ... Pittsburgh, PA
Fantini, Michael T. ... Philadelphia, PA
Fantl, Nina ... Austin, TX
Fantle, Phillip M. ... Minneapolis, MN
Fanto, James A. ... Brooklyn, NY
Fanton, Joel M. ... Plymouth, MA
Fantoni, Jonathan Bryan ... Louisville, KY
Fantozzi, Martin M. ... Boston, MA
Fantozzi, Michael L. ... Boston, MA
Fantroy, Lloyd N. ... Washington, DC
Fantry, John J., Jr. ... Columbia, SC
Fantuz, Jennifer R. ... Bethesda, MD
Fantuzzi, Catherine Mary ... Newark, NJ
Fanucchi, Charles A. ... Chicago, IL
Fanucchi, Edward D. ... Fresno, CA
Fanucchi, Edward L. ... Fresno, CA
Fanucci, Allan A. ... Washington, DC
New York, NY
Fanucci, Joseph Emil ... San Mateo, CA
Fanucci, Robert M. ... St. Helena, CA
Fanuele, Domenico ... New York, NY
Fanwick, Ernest ... Stamford, CT
Fanwick, Kerry ... Palo Alto, CA
Fanyo, Richard L. ... Denver, CO
Fanzini, James Scott ... Indianapolis, IN
Faoro, Dennis L. ... San Mateo, CA
Faoro, Kelly Louise ... Issaquah, WA
Faoro, Therese Marie ... Dublin, OH
Fapore, Desiree F. ... Bellefonte, PA
Fappiano, Tara C. ... New York, NY
Faquin, Arthur C., Jr. ... Memphis, TN
Fara, Susan L. ... Sarasota, FL
Tallahassee, FL
Fara, Thomas A. ... Indianapolis, IN
Farabaugh, Eugene F. ... White Plains, NY
Farabaugh, Richard J. ... Fremont, MI
Farabaugh, William N. ... South Bend, IN
Farabee, David R. ... San Francisco, CA
Farabee, Kenneth ... Denver, CO
Farabee, Lisa M. ... Washington, DC
Farabee, Ray ... Austin, TX
Farabough, Gary W. ... Ardmore, OK
Farabow, Ford F., Jr. ... Washington, DC

Farabow, Loraine Dillinder
Oklahoma City, OK
Farabow, Sara Beiro ... Washington, DC
Farabow, Stephanie T. ... Greensboro, NC
Farace, Anthony M. ... Chicago, IL
Farace, Suzanne K. ... Baltimore, MD
Farace, Suzanne K., P.A., Law Offices of
Baltimore, MD
Farace, Thomas M. ... Rochester, NY
Farach, Ana V. ... Washington, DC
Farach, Horacio A. ... Columbia, SC
Farach, Juan J., Jr. ... Miami, FL
Farach, Manuel ... West Palm Beach, FL
Faraci, Angelo G. ... Rochester, NY
Faraci, C. Joseph ... Falls Church, VA
Faraci, Dominick D. ... Chicago, IL
Faraci & Lange, LLP ... Rochester, NY
Faraci, Paul A. ... Denver, CO
Faraci, Peter S. ... Chicago, IL
Faraci, Rosanne J. ... Chicago, IL
Faraci, Salvatore ... Haverhill, MA
Faraci, Stephen M. ... Richmond, VA
Faraci, William S. ... Bradford, MA
Farady, John T. ... Ipswich, MA
Farady, Susan E. ... Portland, ME
Farag, Denise M. ... McMinnville, OR
Faragasso, Gregory G.
Securities and Exchange Commission,
Division of Enforcement, GV
Faragasso, Laura Beth ... Tallahassee, FL
Farage, McBride & Ruggieri
Woodbury, NJ
Philadelphia, PA
Faragher, Beth Ann ... Denver, CO
Faragher, Patrick J. ... West Bend, WI
Faragher, Robert V. ... Salem, MA
Faraglia, Annette ... San Francisco, CA
Farago, Vincent J. ... White Plains, NY
Faraguna, Joseph R. ... Hartford, CT
Farah, Anthony E. ... Houston, TX
Farah, Asad S. ... Temperance, MI
Toledo, OH
Farah, Benjamin F. ... Rocky River, OH
Farah, Charlie ... Jacksonville, FL
Farah, David ... Pasadena, CA
Farah, Eddie E. ... Jacksonville, FL
Farah and Farah, P.A. ... Jacksonville, FL
Farah, Joseph J. ... Flint, MI
Farah, Licha H., Jr. ... Lexington, KY
Farah, N. Victor ... Raleigh, NC
Farah, Thomas M. ... Washington, DC
Farah, William J. ... Washington, DC
Farahany, Amanda A. ... Atlanta, GA
Farahany, Amanda A., P.C., Law Offices of
Atlanta, GA
Farahati, Britta ... Treasury Department,
Internal Revenue Service, GV
Faraldo, Dolores F. ... Philadelphia, PA
Faraldo, Joseph A. ... Kew Gardens, NY
Farall, Maria F. ... Atlanta, GA
Faranda, Brian C. ... Long Island City, NY
Farano, Charles M. ... Anaheim, CA
Farano, Dan G. ... Troy, NY
Farano, Gerald P. ... Washington, DC
Farano, Gregg S. ... Washington, DC
New York, NY
Farano, Jeffrey L. ... Anaheim, CA
Farano and Kieviet ... Anaheim, CA
Farano, Richard J. ... Department of Justice,
Civil Rights Division, GV
Faraone, John A. ... Wilmington, DE
Faraone, Joyce A. ... Providence, RI
Faraone, Michael A. ... Lansing, MI
Farar, Donna J. ... Glendale, AZ
Farash, David ... Tampa, FL
Farashahi, Afshin ... Virginia Beach, VA
Farashahi, Ommid C. ... Chicago, IL
Farb, Benjamin ... Jenkintown, PA
Farb, Gail E. ... Atlanta, GA
Farb, Peter M. ... Appleton, WI
Farb, Robert L. ... Chapel Hill, NC
Farb, Samuel L. ... San Jose, CA
Farbarik, Michael A. ... Stuart, FL
Farber, A. Martin ... St. Louis, MO
Farber, Aaron W. ... Neosho, MO
Farber, Alan J. ... Washington, DC
Farber, Alan K., (Inc.) ... San Mateo, CA
Farber, Allen V. ... Washington, DC
Farber, Allyn Ann ... New York, NY
Farber, Amy ... New York, NY
Farber, Anna K. ... Denver, CO
Farber, Anne ... New York, NY
Farber, Barton E. ... New York, NY
Farber, Bernard J. ... Chicago, IL
Farber, Beth M. ... Baltimore, MD
Farber, Braden H. ... Garden City, NY
Farber, Craig R. ... New York, NY
Farber, Curtis Jordan ... New York, NY
Farber, Daniel A. ... Minneapolis, MN
Farber, David I. ... New York, NY
Farber, David J. ... Washington, DC
Farber, Deborah Gerber ... Penfield, NY
Farber, Donald C. ... New York, NY
Farber, Donald L. ... North Miami, FL
Farber, Eugene I. ... White Plains, NY
Farber, Evan R. ... New York, NY
Farber & Farber ... Penfield, NY
Farber & Farber ... Media, PA
Reading, PA
West Chester, PA
Farber, Felicia T. ... Wayne, NJ
Farber & Finder ... New York, NY
Farber, Fredrick ... State College, PA
Farber, Gene A. ... San Francisco, CA
Farber, Gene A. ... Southfield, MI
Farber, George S. ... Seattle, WA
Farber, Gerald ... Victorville, CA
Farber, H. Miriam ... New York, NY
Farber, Harry ... Plainview, NY
Farber, Henry E. ... Seattle, WA
Farber, Herbert G. ... Bellevue, WA
Farber, Herbert, Inc., P.S. ... Bellevue, WA
Farber, Hillary B. ... Chelsea, MA
Farber, Hinda Keller ... White Plains, NY
Farber, Howard ... Media, PA
Reading, PA
West Chester, PA
Farber, Irving ... West Nyack, NY
Farber, Irving O. ... White Plains, NY
Farber, Jacob S. ... Washington, DC
Farber, James A. ... Teaneck, NJ
Farber, Jason A. ... Seattle, WA
Farber, Jason H. ... Los Angeles, CA
Farber, Joanne ... New York, NY
Farber, John W. ... Geneseo, IL
Farber, Joseph ... Rego Park, NY
Farber, Joseph W. ... Oklahoma City, OK
Farber, Joy I. ... Mount Vernon, NY
Farber, Kenneth W. ... Washington, DC
Farber, Larry ... Farmington Hills, MI
Farber, Laura V. ... Pasadena, CA
Farber, Lawrence J. ... Amherst, MA
Farber, Lawrence Z. ... Hackensack, NJ
Farber, M. Jay ... Oklahoma City, OK
Farber, Mark A. ... Los Angeles, CA
Farber, Martin A. ... New York, NY
Farber, Martin A., (P.C.) ... New York, NY
Farber, Martin B. ... Williamsville, NY
Farber, Mia D. ... Los Angeles, CA
Farber, Michael B. ... Los Angeles, CA
Farber, Michael D. ... Washington, DC
Farber, Michael S. ... New York, NY
Farber, Michele A. ... Basking Ridge, NJ
Farber, Mindy G. ... Rockville, MD
Farber, Morton H. ... New York, NY
Farber, Nelson M. ... New York, NY
Farber, Paul ... New York, NY
Farber, Paul S. ... New York, NY
Farber, Peter S. ... Chatham, MA
Farber, Philip M. ... Philadelphia, PA
Farber, Randal S. ... Houston, TX
Farber, Randolph E. ... Nampa, ID
Farber, Rebecca D. ... Atlanta, GA
Farber, Richard ... Department of Justice,
Tax Division, GV
Farber, Richard A. ... Philadelphia, PA
Farber, Robert D. ... Asbury Park, NJ
Farber, Robert H., Jr. ... Columbus, OH
Farber, Roy K. ... Grand Junction, CO
Farber, Sandra R. ... New York, NY
Farber, Scott ... Cambridge, MA
Farber, Segall & Pappalardo ... Roseland, NJ
New York, NY
White Plains, NY
Farber, Seth C. ... New York, NY
Farber, Seth J. ... West Orange, NJ
New York, NY
Farber, Sheldon ... New York, NY
Farber, Sheldon W. ... Pennsburg, PA
Farber, Shelly G. ... Media, PA
Reading, PA
West Chester, PA
Farber, Sidney T. ... Penfield, NY
Farber, Sondra L. ... Hollywood, FL
Farber, Stephen E. ... Philadelphia, PA
Farber, Stephen P. ... New York, NY
Farber, Stephen R. ... New York, NY
Farber, Steven G. ... Santa Fe, NM
Farber, Steven N. ... Boston, MA
Farber, Steven W. ... Denver, CO
Farber, William A. ... North Plainfield, NJ
Farber, William M. ... Chicago, IL
Farber, Zulima V. ... Roseland, NJ
Farberman, Lewis E. ... New York, NY
Farber-Walter, Frances ... Hackensack, NJ
Farbes, Hubert A., Jr. ... Denver, CO
Farbman, David M. ... New York, NY
Farbman, Jay H. ... Glen Burnie, MD
Farbman, Maxilian A. ... Salt Lake City, UT
Farbman, Robin Lori ... Coral Springs, FL
Farbman, Ruth E. ... Chicago, IL
Farbman, Seymour Z. ... Baltimore, MD
Farbman, Steven B.
Department of Transportation,
Federal Highway Administration, GV
Farbman, Steven I. ... Pittsburgh, PA
Farbman, Steven S. ... Hollywood, FL
Farbro, Barry A. ... Claremore, OK
Farbro, Tipton & Shaw, A Professional
Corporation ... Claremore, OK
Farbstein, Ben I. ... Hollywood, FL
Farbstein & Blackman, A Professional
Corporation ... San Mateo, CA
Farbstein, David R. ... Fort Lauderdale, FL
Farbstein, Donald F. ... San Mateo, CA
Farbstein, John F. ... San Mateo, CA
Farbstein, Michael A. ... San Mateo, CA
Farca, Joseph I. ... New York, NY
Farchione, Joseph A., Jr. ... Cleveland, OH
Farchmin, Ralls Wagoner, P.C.
Kansas City, MO
Farchmin, Roy H. ... Kansas City, MO
Farco, Mario V. ... Newark, NJ
Farcus, Joan I. ... Bridgeport, CT
Farcy, Sidney E. ... Seattle, WA
Fard, Sima ... Irvine, CA
Fardal, Harold ... Seattle, WA
Fardal, Patrick M. ... Dublin, OH
Fardella & Feldman ... Smithtown, NY
Fardella, Jess ... New York, NY
Fardella, Robert ... Smithtown, NY
Fardon, D. Alexander ... Nashville, TN
Fardy, Jennifer Kelly ... Chicago, IL
Fardy, P. Stephen ... Chicago, IL
Farek, Marvin J., Jr. ... Rockdale, TX
Farell, Gregory C. ... Toledo, OH
Farella, Alfred A. ... White Plains, NY
Farella Braun & Martel LLP
St. Helena, CA
San Francisco, CA
Farella, Christopher M. ... Roseland, NJ
Farella, Claudia A. ... Somers, NY
Farella, Frank E. ... St. Helena, CA
San Francisco, CA
Farelli, Joseph F. ... New York, NY
Farenga, Andrew A. ... Chicago, IL
Farenga, Cynthia R. ... Chicago, IL
Farenthold, Frances T. ... Houston, TX
Farenthold, R. Blake ... Corpus Christi, TX
Farer, David B. ... Westfield, NJ
Farer Fersko, P.A. ... Elizabeth, NJ
Newark, NJ
Westfield, NJ
Farer, Henry ... Westfield, NJ
Farer, Steven D. ... Albany, NY
Farer, Tom J. ... Camden, NJ
Fareri, James V. ... Stroudsburg, PA
Fares, David J. ... Oak Forest, IL
Farese, Alfred P., III ... Everett, MA
Farese, Alfred P., Jr. ... Everett, MA
Farese, Anthony L. ... Ashland, MS
Farese, Anthony T. ... Ashland, MS
Farese, Farese & Farese, P.A. ... Ashland, MS
Farese, Frank P. ... Warren, NJ
Farese, John Booth ... Ashland, MS
Farese, John Stannard ... Ashland, MS
Farese, Lawrence A. ... Naples, FL
Farese, Robert L. ... Danvers, MA
Farese, Steven E. ... Ashland, MS
Farese, Steven E., Jr. ... Ashland, MS
Farewell, Kevin T. ... New York, NY
Farfalla, Mary Ann K. ... New York, NY
Farfante, Darren D. ... Department of Justice,
Tax Division, GV
Farfour, Leslie A., Jr. ... Shelby, NC
Fargarson, Robert M. ... Brownsville, TN
Memphis, TN
Fargas, Laura V. ... Department of Labor,
Office of the Solicitor, GV
Fargason, Ray ... Lubbock, TX
Fargione, Michael R. ... Minneapolis, MN
Fargis, Edward C. ... New York, NY
Fargo, Alvin W., III ... San Francisco, CA
Fargo, David L. ... Chicago, IL
Fargo, John ... Department of Justice,
Civil Division, GV
Fargo, John Z. ... Columbus, OH
Fargo, Michael D. ... Arcadia, CA
Sherman Oaks, CA
Fargo, Raymond J. ... Los Angeles, CA
Fargotstein, Phillip F. ... Phoenix, AZ
Farha, B.D. Eddie ... Washington, DC
Farha, Gary L. ... Quincy, IL
Farha, Geo. S. ... Oklahoma City, OK
Farha, Mark S. ... Dallas, TX
Farha & Sanders ... Washington, DC
Farhadian, Dorothy J. ... Moraga, CA
Far-hadian, F. Jason ... Los Angeles, CA
Farhang, Ali J. ... Denver, CO
Farhang, Michael M. ... Department of Justice,
Tax Division, GV
Farhart, Elizabeth J. ... Phoenix, AZ
Farhart, Lian & Maxson, P.C. ... Minot, ND
Farhart, Moody M. ... Minot, ND
Farhart, Steven C. ... Minot, ND
Farhat, Ann C. ... Washington, DC
Farhat, David L. ... Lansing, MI
Farhat, Elizabeth S. ... Los Angeles, CA
Farhat, Gabriella Hashem ... Lancaster, PA
Farhat, Joseph, III ... East Lansing, MI
Farhat & Mashhour, Law Offices of
Dearborn, MI
Farhat & Story, P.C. ... East Lansing, MI
Lansing, MI
Farhat, Terese L. ... Detroit, MI
Farhat, Tyler & Associates, P.C.
East Lansing, MI
Farhat, Vince L. ... Los Angeles, CA
Farhat, Yasser K. ... Dearborn, MI
Farhi, Carol R. ... New York, NY
Farhi, Jacques Maurice ... New York, NY
Farhi, Michael ... Lodi, NJ
Long Valley, NJ
Farhi, Nancy Miller ... New York, NY
Farhi, Roberta J. ... Mineola, NY
Faria, Gary W. ... Bloomfield Hills, MI
Faria, Jean M. ... Baton Rouge, LA
Faria, Joseph R., Jr. ... Fremont, CA
Faria, Lee Ann ... Boston, MA
Faria, Manuel A. ... Hayward, CA
Faria, Mark J. ... Providence, RI
Faria, Mary I. ... Rye Brook, NY
Faria, Maureen ... Santa Rosa, CA
Faria, Wendell M. ... Washington, DC
Farias, Cynthia A. ... Honolulu, HI
Farias-Erwin, Veronica ... Brownsville, TX
Faricy, Bridget Nyhan ... St. Paul, MN
Faricy and Dunn ... Golden Valley, MN
St. Paul, MN
Faricy, John H., Jr. ... Minneapolis, MN
Faricy, Megan L. ... St. Paul, MN
Faricy, Raymond W., Jr. ... St. Paul, MN
Faricy & Roen, P.A. ... Minneapolis, MN
Faricy, Roland J., Jr. ... St. Paul, MN
Fariel, Peter T. ... Boston, MA
Faries, Gregory J. ... Jackson, MS
Farin, Frank T. ... Clayton, MO
Farin, Lawrence J. ... Lakewood, CO
Farin, Linda ... Austin, TX
Farin, Susana ... Coral Gables, FL
Farina, Ann Perrin ... Elk Grove, CA
Farina, Anne Judith ... Wellesley Hills, MA
Farina, Benga L. ... Herndon, VA
Farina, Cynthia R. ... Ithaca, NY
Farina, David J. ... Chicago, IL
Des Plaines, IL
Farina, Dennis J. ... Denton, MD
Farina, Dominic J. ... New Buffalo, MI
Farina, Ellen E. ... Philadelphia, PA
Farina, Francis J. ... Devon, PA
Farina and Gross-Farina, P.A. ... Miami, FL
Farina, Guy J. ... Stamford, CT
Farina, John ... West Palm Beach, FL
Farina, John ... Indianapolis, IN
Farina, Joseph A. ... Bellflower, CA
Farina, Joseph A. ... Maywood, IL
Farina, Joseph C. ... Pittsburgh, PA
Farina, Joseph P. ... Miami, FL
Farina, Joseph S. ... Elk Grove, CA
Farina, Julie L. ... Warren, MI
Farina, Kenneth J. ... Brooklyn, NY
Farina, Laura ... Princeton, NJ
Farina, Louis J. ... Lancaster, PA
Farina, Mario G. ... Clark, NJ
Farina, Michael A. ... Westbury, NY
Farina, Nannette ... San Diego, CA
Farina, Philip J. ... Chicago, IL
Farina & Redamak ... New Buffalo, MI
Farina, Richard H. ... Washington, DC
Farina, Robert J. ... San Diego, CA
Farina, Steven M. ... Washington, DC
Farina, Terrance L. ... Grand Junction, CO
Farina, Thomas C. ... Oradell, NJ
Farina, Vincent P. ... Miami, FL
Farinacci, Donald J. ... Garden City, NY
Melville, NY
Farinacci, John G. ... Garden City, NY
Farinaro, James ... San Leandro, CA
Farinas, Guillermo Jose ... South Miami, FL
Farinas, Laureto A. ... Philadelphia, PA
Farinash, Jerrold D. ... Chattanooga, TN
Farinato, Donald J. ... Knoxville, TN
Farine, Cheryl ... Cleveland, OH
Farineau, Shari Lynn ... Concord, CA
Farinella, E. M. ... Huntington, WV
Farinella, Gus Michael ... Flushing, NY
Farinella, Maria ... Washington, DC
Farinella, Mark J. ... Morristown, NJ
Farinella, Susan B. ... Livingston, NJ
Farinholt, Kathryn S. ... Baltimore, MD
Farinholt, L. Whiting ... Gibson Island, MD
Farino, Donald J. ... Hackettstown, NJ
Farino, S. Louis ... Pittsburgh, PA
Farino, Thomas R., Jr. ... Jamesburg, NJ
Farion, George M. ... Philadelphia, PA
Farion, Marta ... Schaumburg, IL
Faris, Barbara Goedeke ... Winchester, TN
Faris, Cheryl J. ... Los Angeles, CA
Faris, D. Vincent ... Batavia, OH
Faris, Dawn E. ... Washington, DC
Faris, Douglas McGruder ... Charlotte, NC
Faris & Faris ... Minneapolis, MN
Faris, Francis W., Jr. ... Wheaton, IL
Faris, Geo. ... Chicago, IL
Faris, George T., IV, Law Offices of
Burlington, VT
Faris, George T., IV, Law Offices of
Shelburne, VT
Faris, James J. ... Washington, DC
Faris, Jean Marie ... Department of Defense,
Defense Legal Services Agency, GV
Faris, Juliana M. ... Columbus, OH
Faris, Lisa M. ... Branford, CT
Faris, Mark A. ... West Palm Beach, FL
Faris, Philip H. ... Colfax, WA
Faris, Priscilla Lord ... Minneapolis, MN
Faris, Robert J. ... Honolulu, HI
Faris, Robert W. ... Arlington, VA
Faris, Sharon L. ... Los Angeles, CA
Faris, Thomas C. ... Winchester, TN
Faris, Thomas H. ... Hayward, CA
Faris, Warren M. ... New Orleans, LA
Faris, Wayne G. ... Minneapolis, MN
Faris, William V. ... Louisville, KY
Farish, Barbara J. ... Midland, TX
Farish, Eugene L. ... Monte Vista, CO
Farish, Eugene L., P.C. ... Monte Vista, CO
Farish, Farish & Romani
Okeechobee, FL
West Palm Beach, FL
Farish, Joseph D., Jr.
West Palm Beach, FL
Farish, Margaret (Peggy) Cantrell ... Jenks, OK
Farish, Robert E., & Associates, PLLC
Biloxi, MS
Farish, Robert E., Jr. ... Biloxi, MS
Farish, Stephen E. ... Libertyville, IL
Fariss, Frank C. ... Houston, TX
Fariss, Renay M. ... Chesterfield, VA
Farivar, Mehrdad ... Los Angeles, CA
Farjami, Farshad ... Newport Beach, CA
Farkas, Alan L. ... Chicago, IL
Farkas, Barry J. ... Hackensack, NJ
Farkas, Daniel S. ... Miami, FL
Farkas, Donald O. ... Los Angeles, CA
Farkas, Drew Eugene ... Chicago, IL
Farkas, Earl E. ... Chicago, IL
Farkas, Evelyn Cadorin ... Morristown, NJ
Farkas, Gregory R. ... Cleveland, OH
Farkas, Ilene S. ... New York, NY
Farkas, Jeffrey Alan ... Forest Hills, NY
Farkas, Jeremy I. ... Burlington, VT
Farkas, Joshua ... Brooklyn, NY
Farkas, Jules ... Princeton, NJ
Farkas, L. Peter ... Washington, DC
Farkas, Lawrence W. ... Great Neck, NY
Farkas & Ledford ... Albany, GA
Farkas, Leonard ... Albany, GA
Farkas, Leslie E. ... Janesville, WI
Farkas & Manelli, P.L.L.C.
Washington, DC
Farkas, Matthew R. ... Trenton, NJ

Farnham, JoEllen .... Tarpon Springs, FL
Farnham, Joseph A. .... Burlington, VT
Farnham, Kristen Potter .... Portland, ME
Farnham, Lloyd .... San Francisco, CA
Farnham, Sheila T. .... Berkeley, CA
Farnham, Sherman .... Rochester, NY
Farnish, Thomas S. .... Hackensack, NJ Philadelphia, PA
Farnoly, Thomas P. .... Vineland, NJ
Farnsley, Douglass C. E. .... Louisville, KY
Farnsworth, A. Randall .... Denver, CO
Farnsworth, Brad T. .... Quantico, VA
Farnsworth, Charles E. .... Oakland, CA
Farnsworth, Daniel J. .... Greenville, SC
Farnsworth, E. Allan .... New York, NY
Farnsworth, Effa G. .... Fairfield, CT
Farnsworth, Eric A. .... Madison, WI
Farnsworth & Ghaowi .... Highland Beach, FL
Farnsworth, James R. .... Washington, DC
Farnsworth, Jo Ann .... Indianapolis, IN
Farnsworth, John P. .... New Orleans, LA
Farnsworth, Joyce Penn .... New York, NY
Farnsworth, Julianne .... Columbia, SC
Farnsworth, Karen L. .... New York, NY
Farnsworth, Peter J. .... Brick, NJ Neptune, NJ
Farnsworth, Scott M. .... Winter Park, FL
Farnsworth, Sidney W., III .... Memphis, TN
Farnsworth, Steven W. .... Los Angeles, CA
Farnsworth, Stuart A. .... San Diego, CA
Farnsworth, Sue Seibert .... Wheeling, WV
Farnsworth, Susan R. .... Hallowell, ME
Farnsworth, T Brooke .... Houston, TX
Farnsworth & vonBerg .... Houston, TX
Farnsworth, William K. .... Hemet, CA
Farnsworth, William Y. .... Alexandria, VA
Farnum, Barbara A. .... Saratoga, CA
Farnum, David M. .... Roanoke, VA
Farnum, Ellen L. .... Charlottesville, VA
Farnum, Gary L. .... Oklahoma City, OK
Farnum, Mark J. .... Beloit, WI
Farnum, Rebecca H. .... Portland, ME
Farnum, Thomas H. .... Kansas City, MO
Farnum, Thomas H., P.C. .... Kansas City, MO
Farnworth, Kevin G. .... Roseville, CA
Farny, Elizabeth Anne .... Santa Monica, CA
Faro, Jeffrey M. .... Union City, NJ
Faro, John H. .... Key Biscayne, FL
Faro, Joseph E. .... Amesbury, MA
Faro and Portanova .... Union City, NJ
Faroldi, Jennifer A. .... New Orleans, LA
Farolino, Shane A. .... Akron, OH
Faron, John Roman .... Buffalo, NY
Farone, Diane Weis .... Nashville, TN
Farone, Nicole L. .... Cleveland, OH
Farouki, Y. Tarek .... New York, NY
Farquer, Thomas L. .... Mundelein, IL
Farquhar, Andrew C. .... Philadelphia, PA
Farquhar, Barron Douglas .... Denver, CO
Farquhar, Carol E. .... Dallas, TX
Farquhar, Christine M. .... Columbus, OH
Farquhar, Douglas B. .... Washington, DC
Farquhar, Elizabeth H. .... Boyds, MD
Farquhar, John L. .... Fort Lauderdale, FL Naples, FL
Farquhar, Martha J. C. .... East Orleans, MA
Farquhar, Michele C. .... Washington, DC
Farquhar, R. Michael .... Dallas, TX
Farquhar, Robert N. .... Dayton, OH
Farquhar, Thomas W. .... Washington, DC
Farquharson, Ernest B. North Little Rock, AR
Farquharson, Ingrid M. .... Bingham Farms, MI
Farquharson, Ivan O. .... Syracuse, NY
Farquharson, Paul N. .... Baltimore, MD
Farqui, Arij S. .... Media, PA
Farr, Alec W. .... Washington, DC
Farr & Bass .... Bohemia, NY
Farr, Brian L. .... Salt Lake City, UT
Farr, Burke, Gambacorta & Wright, A Professional Corporation .... Wilmington, DE Bellmawr, NJ Philadelphia, PA
Farr, C. Sims .... New York, NY
Farr, Charles W. .... Metairie, LA
Farr, Claudia T. .... Richmond, VA
Farr, Daniel A. .... Enumclaw, WA
Farr, David C. .... Eau Claire, WI
Farr, David M. .... Gaithersburg, MD
Farr, Davis & Fitze .... Montrose, PA Tunkhannock, PA
Farr, Donita F. M. .... New York, NY
Farr, Earl Drayton, Jr. .... Punta Gorda, FL
Farr, Evan H. .... Fairfax, VA
Farr, Evan H., P.C., The Law Firm of Fairfax, VA
Farr, Farr, Emerich, Sifrit, Hackett and Carr, P.A. .... Port Charlotte, FL Punta Gorda, FL
Farr, G. Neil .... Bakersfield, CA
Farr & Gustafson .... Enumclaw, WA
Farr, H. Bartow, III .... Washington, DC
Farr, H. Bartow, Jr. .... Winston-Salem, NC
Farr, Herbert R. .... Dallas, TX
Farr • Hickman & Slavin .... Kirksville, MO
Farr, J. Earlene .... Kansas City, MO
Farr, James A. .... Anchorage, AK
Farr, James G. .... Tampa, FL
Farr, Jan R. .... Syracuse, NY
Farr, Jane H. .... Pasadena, CA
Farr, Jesse, & Associates .... Chattanooga, TN
Farr, John B. .... Houston, TX
Farr, Julia M. .... Department of Transportation, Surface Transportation Board, GV
Farr, Julie D. .... Bangor, ME
Farr, Kaufman, Sullivan, Gorman, Jensen, Medsker, Nichols & Perkins .... Ogden, UT
Farr, Keith E. .... Waco, TX
Farr, Ken C. .... Las Vegas, NV
Farr, Lionel M. .... Salt Lake City, UT
Farr, Lloyd G. .... Columbia, SC Greenville, SC
Farr, Louis G. .... Washington, DC
Farr, Lucy W. .... New York, NY
Farr, Mary Ellen Page .... Portland, OR
Farr, Melanie L. .... Fort Wayne, IN
Farr, Michael D. .... Martinez, CA
Farr, Michael J. .... Avon, NY
Farr, Molly E. .... Seattle, WA
Farr, Neal E. .... Miami, FL
Farr, Nell L. .... Stockton, CA
Farr, Norene .... Manchester, NH
Farr & Oosterhouse .... Grand Rapids, MI
Farr, Paul O. .... Americus, GA
Farr, Richard L. .... Melbourne, FL
Farr, Robert .... Hartford, CT
Farr, Robert T. .... Monroe, LA
Farr, Ronald A. .... Bohemia, NY
Farr, Russell O. .... Scottsdale, AZ
Farr, Sarah R. .... Goodland, KS
Farr, Scott A. .... Tampa, FL
Farr, Sidney .... Houston, TX
Farr, Stefan W. .... Portland, OR
Farr, Stephen W. .... Ogden, UT
Farr & Taranto .... Washington, DC
Farr, Thomas A. .... Raleigh, NC
Farr, Thomas C. .... West Des Moines, IA
Farr, Thomas R. .... Green Bay, WI
Farr, Timothy .... Greenville, SC
Farr & Warzecha, The Law Offices of New York, NY
Farr, William E. .... Pana, IL
Farr, William H. .... Rochester, NY
Farr, William R. .... Bellmawr, NJ
Farr, William S. .... Grand Rapids, MI
Farra, George K. .... Duarte, CA
Farra, John L. .... Aberdeen, WA
Farra, John P. .... Houston, TX
Farra, Roxanne L. .... Bend, OR
Farra, Roxanne L., P.C. .... Bend, OR Madras, OR Portland, OR Prineville, OR Redmond, OR
Farragher, Janette E. .... New York, NY
Farragut, James L., Jr. .... Pascagoula, MS
Farragut-Hemphill, Sandra .... Clayton, MO
Farrah, Albert L., Jr. .... Boston, MA
Farrah, Elias G. .... Washington, DC
Farrah, Julie Driscoll .... San Francisco, CA
Farraher, John F., Jr. .... Boston, MA
Farrall, Gary F. .... Everett, WA
Farrall, William P. .... Cleveland, OH
Farran, Jeffrey P. .... Greensboro, NC
Farran, Maria L. Federal Energy Regulatory Commission, Office of the General Counsel, GV
Farran, William N., III .... Cranbury, NJ
Farran, William R. .... Grand Rapids, MI
Farrance, Robert A. .... Bradenton, FL
Farrand Cooper, P.C. .... San Francisco, CA
Farrand, James R. .... Los Angeles, CA
Farrand, Judith A. .... Washington, DC
Farrand, Laura K. .... Los Angeles, CA
Farrand, Stephen R. .... San Francisco, CA
Farrand, Walter F. .... Springfield, IL
Farranto, Peter .... Alpharetta, GA
Farrar, Anne Marie .... Miami, FL
Farrar, Archibald A., Jr. Summerville, GA
Farrar, Bradley T. .... Columbia, SC
Farrar, Brett W. .... Pittsburgh, PA
Farrar, Bruce R. .... Fullerton, CA
Farrar, Bryan R. .... Lake Forest, CA
Farrar, Charles O., Jr. .... Coral Gables, FL
Farrar, Charles R., Jr., Law Offices of Grass Valley, CA
Farrar, Charles R., Jr., Law Offices of Nevada City, CA
Farrar, Clay P., Jr., (P.A.) Hot Springs National Park, AR Hot Springs Village, AR
Farrar & Corbin, P.C. .... Summerville, GA
Farrar, Cristopher Scott .... Boston, MA
Farrar, Darwin E. .... Oakland, CA
Farrar, David D. .... Gorham, ME
Farrar, David W. .... Los Angeles, CA
Farrar, E. Daniel .... Modesto, CA
Farrar, Edward A. .... Fort Worth, TX
Farrar, Elizabeth Turrell .... Columbus, OH
Farrar & Farrar .... Tulsa, OK
Farrar, Frank D. .... Lafayette, TN
Farrar, Frank L. .... Britton, SD
Farrar, Greg A. .... Tulsa, OK
Farrar, Gregory P. .... Pensacola, FL
Farrar, Gus A. .... Tulsa, OK
Farrar & Holliman .... Lafayette, TN
Farrar, James G. .... Minneapolis, MN
Farrar, James P. .... Eastland, TX
Farrar, James S. .... Watsonville, CA
Farrar, Joan L. .... Canoga Park, CA
Farrar, John M. .... New York, NY
Farrar, John P. .... Mount Carmel, IL
Farrar, Joseph L. .... New York, NY
Farrar, Karl L. Nuclear Regulatory Commission, Office of the General Counsel, GV
Farrar, Kenneth W., & Associates Lovingston, VA
Farrar, Lori L. .... Kansas City, MO
Farrar, Mark E. .... Lake Forest, CA
Farrar, Michael .... New York, NY
Farrar, Michael J. .... Houston, TX
Farrar, R. Thomas .... Miami, FL
Farrar, Randal A. .... Boston, MA
Farrar, Reginald W., Jr. .... Ruston, LA
Farrar, Reis, Rowe, Nicolosi & Williams Hot Springs National Park, AR Hot Springs Village, AR
Farrar, Richard G. .... Maumee, OH
Farrar, Robert E. .... St. Albans, VT
Farrar, Sabrina A. .... Washington, DC
Farrar, Sidney C., Jr. .... Fort Worth, TX
Farrar, Stanley F. .... Los Angeles, CA
Farrar, Stephen C. .... Fort Worth, TX
Farrar, Steven E. .... Greenville, SC
Farrar, Stewart E. .... Richmond, VA
Farrar, William D. .... Bryan, TX
Farrar, William G. .... New York, NY
Farrar, William W. .... North Caldwell, NJ
Farrauto, Berman, Fontana & Selznick Yonkers, NY
Farrauto, John P. .... Yonkers, NY
Farrell, A. Hunter .... Palo Alto, CA
Farrell, A. Thomas .... Altoona, PA
Farrell, Alyce Hailstone .... Scranton, PA
Farrell, Angela M. .... Bangor, ME
Farrell, Ann M. .... Olympia, WA
Farrell, Anthony Patrick .... Trenton, MO
Farrell, Antoinette Waters San Francisco, CA
Farrell, April .... Metairie, LA
Farrell & Associates, Ltd. .... Palos Heights, IL
Farrell, Barbara Ann .... Syracuse, NY
Farrell, B. J. .... Westmont, IL
Farrell, Brenda S. .... Indianapolis, IN
Farrell, Brian J. .... Providence, RI
Farrell, Bridget E. .... New York, NY
Farrell, Brien J. .... Santa Rosa, CA
Farrell, Bryan J. .... Atlanta, GA
Farrell, Carmen C. .... Bellaire, TX
Farrell, Catherine L. .... Boston, MA
Farrell, Charles .... Baldwinsville, NY
Farrell, Charles J., Jr. .... Cleveland, OH
Farrell, Christine Gregorak Prineville, OR
Farrell, Christopher F. .... Pittsburgh, PA
Farrell, Christy M. .... Houston, TX
Farrell, C L .... Redlands, CA
Farrell, Clayton F. .... Southfield, MI
Farrell, Clifford M. .... Columbus, OH
Farrell & Croft .... Manassas, VA
Farrell, D. Harmon .... New York, NY
Farrell, Daniel J. .... Palos Heights, IL
Farrell, Daniel R. .... Freeport, TX
Farrell & D'Aniello .... Norristown, PA
Farrell, David C. .... Mountain View, CA
Farrell, David D. .... St. Louis, MO
Farrell, David J. .... Laguna Hills, CA
Farrell, David, Jr. .... Boston, MA South Chatham, MA
Farrell, Diane Klaum .... Hempstead, NY
Farrell, Don E. .... Highlands Ranch, CO
Farrell, Donald F., Jr. .... Boston, MA
Farrell, Donald W. .... Vienna, VA
Farrell, Douglas C. .... Portland, OR
Farrell, Douglas J. .... Sierra Madre, CA
Farrell, E. Beth .... Cincinnati, OH
Farrell, Edgerton & Hatfield West Chicago, IL
Farrell, Edmond D. .... Mineola, NY
Farrell, Edmund G., III .... Los Angeles, CA
Farrell, Edward .... Garden City, NY
Farrell, Edward J. .... Sacramento, CA
Farrell, Edward J. .... Washington, DC
Farrell, Edward J. .... Springfield, MA
Farrell, Edward J., III .... Flint, MI
Farrell, Edward J., Jr. .... Old Saybrook, CT
Farrell, Edward W. .... Barnstable, MA
Farrell, Elise Louise .... Cleveland, OH
Farrell, Ellen A. National Labor Relations Board, Office of the General Counsel, GV
Farrell, Ellen C. .... Falls Church, VA
Farrell, Ellen M. .... New York, NY
Farrell, Eric D. .... Binghamton, NY
Farrell, Erin M. .... Menlo Park, CA
Farrell, Eugene J. .... Minneapolis, MN
Farrell & Farrell .... Redlands, CA
Farrell and Farrell .... Inverness, IL
Farrell, Farrell & Burke .... Mineola, NY
Farrell, Farrell & Farrell, L.C. Charleston, WV Huntington, WV
Farrell, Farrell & Ginsbach, P.C. Hot Springs, SD
Farrell, Frank S. .... Naples, FL
Farrell, Frank S., Jr. .... Minneapolis, MN
Farrell, Frank W. .... Westfield, NJ
Farrell, Fraulob & Brown, A Professional Law Corporation .... Sacramento, CA
Farrell Fritz, Professional Corporation Uniondale, NY
Farrell, Gary A. .... Brooklyn, NY
Farrell, Gary T. .... Spokane, WA
Farrell & Gasparo .... Jacksonville, FL
Farrell, George E. .... Rosslyn, VA
Farrell, George F., Jr. .... Topeka, KS
Farrell, George, III .... Salem, NJ
Farrell, George J., Jr. .... Uniondale, NY
Farrell, Gerald E., Jr. .... Wallingford, CT
Farrell, Gerald E., Sr. .... Wallingford, CT
Farrell, Gerard W. .... Philadelphia, PA
Farrell, Glenn A. .... Rutherford, NJ
Farrell, Goldstein & Seldin .... Englewood, CO
Farrell & Green .... Freehold, NJ
Farrell, Gregory T. .... Temple, TX
Farrell, Guarino & Boccalatte, P.C. Middletown, CT
Farrell, Harry C., III .... Austin, TX
Farrell, Heidi Marie .... Minneapolis, MN
Farrell, Hollyce A. .... Denver, CO
Farrell, Hummel & Constance St. Louis, MO
Farrell, J. Bennett .... Monroe, NY
Farrell, J. David .... Norristown, PA
Farrell, J. Douglas .... Greensburg, PA
Farrell, J. Michael .... Philadelphia, PA
Farrell, J. Paul .... Mc Keesport, PA
Farrell, J. Terrence .... Mc Keesport, PA
Farrell, J. Vincent .... Fairfax, VA
Farrell, James A. .... West Palm Beach, FL
Farrell, James A., Jr. .... Wakefield, RI
Farrell, James B. .... Minneapolis, MN
Farrell, James C. .... Roseburg, OR
Farrell, James C., P.C. .... Roseburg, OR
Farrell, James E. .... Omaha, NE
Farrell, James E., Jr. .... New York, NY
Farrell, James E., Jr. .... New York, NY
Farrell, James F., Jr. .... Hauppauge, NY
Farrell, James H. .... Chepachet, RI
Farrell, James J. .... Los Angeles, CA
Farrell, James J. .... Norwalk, CT
Farrell, James J. .... Edgewater, NJ
Farrell, James M. .... Princeton, NJ
Farrell, James M. .... Burlington, VT
Farrell, James P., Jr. .... Blue Point, NY
Farrell, James R., Jr. .... Rutland, VT
Farrell, James T. .... Atlanta, GA
Farrell, Jan F. .... El Segundo, CA
Farrell, Jane M. .... Hot Springs, SD
Farrell, Jean M. .... New York, NY
Farrell, Jeffrey E. .... Houston, TX
Farrell, Jill E. .... Anchorage, AK
Farrell, Joan Bartels .... Milwaukee, WI
Farrell, Joan S. .... Stamford, CT
Farrell, Jodeane Barlow Rancho Santa Margarita, CA
Farrell, Jodeane Barlow, A Professional Corporation .... Rancho Santa Margarita, CA
Farrell, John .... El Cajon, CA
Farrell, John A. .... Godfrey, IL
Farrell, John B. .... Baltimore, MD
Farrell, John B. .... Grand Blanc, MI
Farrell, John C. .... Philadelphia, PA
Farrell, John E. .... Chicago, IL
Farrell, John E. .... New York, NY
Farrell, John G. .... Albany, NY
Farrell, John J. .... Oakland, CA
Farrell, John L., Jr. .... Tulsa, OK
Farrell, John M. .... San Francisco, CA
Farrell, John M. .... West Palm Beach, FL
Farrell, John M., Jr. .... Great Neck, NY
Farrell, John P. .... Minneapolis, MN
Farrell, John P. .... Houston, TX
Farrell, John R. .... Miami, FL
Farrell, John T., Jr. .... Philadelphia, PA
Farrell, John W. .... Fairfax, VA Leesburg, VA
Farrell, Jonathan D. .... Mineola, NY
Farrell, Joseph .... New York, NY
Farrell, Joseph A. .... Bartlesville, OK
Farrell, Joseph B. .... Costa Mesa, CA
Farrell, Joseph B. .... Kingston, PA
Farrell, Joseph D. .... Marlborough, CT
Farrell, Joseph D. .... New York, NY
Farrell, Joseph H. .... New York, NY
Farrell, Joseph M. .... Palmyra, PA
Farrell, Joseph M., Jr. .... Huntington, WV
Farrell, Joseph P. .... Washington, DC
Farrell, Joseph S. .... Chicago, IL
Farrell, Joseph T. .... Orlando, FL
Farrell, Joseph T., P.A., Law Offices Of Orlando, FL
Farrell, Joseph W. .... Union City, NJ
Farrell, Kathleen A. .... Media, PA
Farrell, Kathleen C. .... Newton, MA
Farrell, Kathleen Latham .... Manassas, VA
Farrell, Kathlyn L. .... Tomball, TX
Farrell, Kathryn Lorch .... Lexington, MA
Farrell, Kelley A. .... Sacramento, CA
Farrell, Kelley Field .... St. Louis, MO
Farrell, Kelly P. .... New York, NY
Farrell, Kenneth J. .... Orchard Park, NY
Farrell, Kevin James .... Denver, CO
Farrell, Kevin M. .... York Harbor, ME
Farrell, Kevin M., P.C. .... York Harbor, ME
Farrell, Kevin P. .... Indianapolis, IN
Farrell, Kevin P. .... Peekskill, NY
Farrell & La Mantia .... Raleigh, NC
Farrell, Laura E. .... New York, NY
Farrell Law Firm, P.C. .... Godfrey, IL
Farrell, Lawrence M. .... Washington, DC
Farrell, Leslie & Grochowski Wallingford, CT
Farrell, Letitia A. .... Houston, TX
Farrell, Lynn P. .... Port Chester, NY
Farrell, M. Catherine .... Troy, MI
Farrell, Marc J. .... Harrisburg, PA
Farrell, Margaret D. .... Boston, MA Providence, RI
Farrell, Margaret G. .... Washington, DC
Farrell, Mark F. .... Mount Kisco, NY
Farrell, Marta Layne .... Palo Alto, CA
Farrell & Martin .... St. Peters, MO
Farrell, Martin .... Research Triangle Park, NC
Farrell, Martin A., Jr. .... Anchorage, AK
Farrell, Martin & Barnett .... Baldwinsville, NY
Farrell, Maureen Sambora .... Denver, CO
Farrell, Megan C. .... Atlantic City, NJ
Farrell, Megan E. .... Pittsburgh, PA
Farrell, Michael .... Jackson, MS
Farrell, Michael A. .... Harrisburg, PA
Farrell, Michael B. .... Lansing, MI
Farrell, Michael F. .... Derry, NH
Farrell, Michael F. .... Cleveland, OH
Farrell, Michael J. .... Phoenix, AZ
Farrell, Michael J. .... Van Nuys, CA
Farrell, Michael J. .... Miami, FL
Farrell, Michael J. .... Portland, OR
Farrell, Michael J. .... Huntington, WV
Farrell, Michael K. .... Cleveland, OH

Fasciana and Associates, P.C. ..... **New York, NY**
Fasciana, John E. ..... **New York, NY**
Fasciano, Paul ..... **New York, NY**
Fase, Kent R. ..... Valparaiso, IN
Faseler, Keri L. ..... **Oakland, CA**
Faseler, Len ..... Austin, TX
Fash, Charles H., III ..... Atlanta, GA
Fashimpaur, Jay Jon ..... Oklahoma City, OK
Fashing, John L. ..... El Paso, TX
Fashing, Laura ..... Albuquerque, NM
Fashing, Peter G. ..... **Fresno, CA**
San Francisco, CA
Fashingbauer, Edward H. ..... St. Paul, MN
Fashjian, Robert G. ..... **Huntington, CT**
Fashjian, Robert G., P.C. ..... **Huntington, CT**
Fashouer, William R., Jr. ..... Department of Transportation, Federal Railroad Administration, GV
Fasi, David F. ..... **Kailua, HI**
Fasi, Gioia M. ..... **Los Angeles, CA**
Fasi, Joseph M., II ..... **Milwaukee, WI**
Fasi, Joseph P. ..... **Hartford, CT**
Fasic, Darlene Marchesani ..... **Philadelphia, PA**
Fasic, G. Kevin ..... **Wilmington, DE**
Fasic, Robert T. ..... Garberville, CA
Fasick, Pamela A. ..... San Francisco, CA
Fasig, Carl E. ..... **Itasca, IL**
Fasig, Donald L. ..... Fort Myers, FL
Fasing, Gregory J. ..... Denver, CO
Fasing, Timothy L. ..... Englewood, CO
Fasinro, Olufela A. ..... Woodland Hills, CA
Fasiska, Barbara C. ..... **Los Angeles, CA**
Faske, Garry Charles ..... Miami, FL
Fasken Martineau DuMoulin ..... **New York, NY**
Fasler, Karen S. ..... San Luis Obispo, CA
Fasman, Irving D. ..... **Chicago, IL**
Fasman, Michael J. ..... **Beverly Hills, CA**
Fasman, Zachary D. ..... **Washington, DC**
Fasnacht, Robert Joseph ..... **Coeur d'Alene, ID**
Faso, Bridget M. ..... **Buffalo, NY**
Faso, John J. ..... **Hudson, NY**
Poughkeepsie, NY
Faso, Salvatore A., II ..... **New Orleans, LA**
Fasold, Edward J., Jr. ..... New York, NY
Fasolo, Krause & Dexter ..... Hackensack, NJ
Fasolo, Valerie J. ..... **Phoenix, AZ**
Fasolo, William A. ..... Hackensack, NJ
Fason, James J., III ..... Atlanta, GA
Fason, John Stewart ..... Houston, TX
Fason, Rita Miller ..... Houston, TX
Fasone, John R. ..... New York, NY
Fasone, Joseph R. ..... Fort Lauderdale, FL
Fasone, Joseph R., P.A. ..... Fort Lauderdale, FL
Fasone, Peter J. ..... Hickory Hills, IL
Fasone, Thomas G., III ..... **Dallas, TX**
Fass, Daniel A. ..... New York, NY
Fass, Florence M. ..... **Garden City, NY**
Fass, Joel S. ..... **Fort Lauderdale, FL**
Fass & Kimack, LLP ..... **Garden City, NY**
Fass, Maxine ..... New York, NY
Fass, Michael G. ..... **Norwalk, CT**
New York, NY
Fass, Peter M. ..... **New York, NY**
Fass, Richard T. ..... **Houston, TX**
Fass, Robyn H. ..... Stockton, CA
Fass, Sarah Moore ..... **Stamford, CT**
Fass, Steven S. ..... Rockville Centre, NY
Fassbender, Charles J. ..... **San Diego, CA**
Fassbender, James H. ..... Kaukauna, WI
Fassbender, Saralee ..... Middleton, WI
Fassberg, Benjamin C. ..... Bethesda, MD
Fassberg, Bruce P. ..... Hempstead, NY
Fassberg, Edith ..... **New York, NY**
Fassberg, Robert ..... Mineola, NY
Fassberg, Wendy J. ..... Encino, CA
Fasse, Cheryl Hotchkiss ..... Waterville, ME
Fasse, J. Peter ..... **Boston, MA**
Fasse, Thomas A. ..... Riverton, WY
Fasse, Walter F. ..... St. Albans, ME
Fasse, Wolfgang G. O. ..... St. Albans, ME
Fasseas, Peter A. ..... Chicago, IL
Fassell, Mary M. ..... Portland, OR
Fassett, Anthony & Taylor, P.A. ..... **Orlando, FL**
Fassett, Brent D. ..... **Boulder, CO**
Denver, CO
Fassett, David W. ..... **Chatham, NJ**
Fassett, Edward C., Jr. ..... Albany, NY
Fassett, John B., II ..... Fort Myers, FL
Fassett, John D. ..... St. Petersburg, FL
Fassett, Ladd H. ..... **Orlando, FL**
Fassett, Mary Jean ..... **Washington, DC**
Fassett, Melissa J. ..... Carpinteria, CA
Fassett, Stephanie A. ..... **Twin Falls, ID**
Fassino, Francis J. ..... Hurley, WI
Fassio, Daniel L. ..... Pittsburgh, PA
Fassler, Allen Lee ..... Yonkers, NY
Fassler, Anne S. ..... **Hartford, CT**
Fassler, Charles ..... **Louisville, KY**
Fassler, Jill S. ..... New York, NY
Fassler, Lawrence J. ..... Santa Rosa, CA
Fassler, Michael R. ..... **San Francisco, CA**
Fassler, Norman ..... **Stamford, CT**
Fassler, Paul C. ..... Montpelier, VT
Fassler, Robert M. ..... Cedar Rapids, IA
Fassnacht, Harold J. ..... **Chicago, IL**
Fassnidge, Warner F. ..... San Antonio, TX
Fassola, John P. ..... Oakbrook Terrace, IL
Fassold, James A. ..... **Scottsdale, AZ**
Fasso-Talley, Jill ..... Los Angeles, CA
Fast, Daniel W. ..... Wise, VA
Fast, David E. ..... Corpus Christi, TX
Fast, Donald J. ..... Baldwin, WI
Fast & Fast ..... Parsippany, NJ
Fast, H. John ..... Akron, OH
Fast, Herman L. ..... Miami Beach, FL
Fast, Kenneth H. ..... **Livingston, NJ**
Fast, Kevin L. ..... **Washington, DC**
Fast, M. Elizabeth ..... **Kansas City, MO**
Fast, Mahlon L. ..... Newark, NJ
Fast, Margaret ..... Portland, ME
Fast, Nancy B. ..... San Antonio, TX
Fast, Robert E. ..... **Boston, MA**
Fast, Scott L. ..... **Philadelphia, PA**
Fast, Sheldon H. ..... Livingston, NJ
Fast, Stanley W. ..... Hot Springs Village, AR
Fast, Steven M. ..... **Hartford, CT**
Fast, Thomas K. ..... Fayetteville, WV
Fast, Thomas M. ..... Parsippany, NJ
Fasteau, Theodore ..... Los Angeles, CA
Fastenau, Robin A. ..... **Washington, DC**
Fastenberg, Andrea ..... New York, NY
Fastenberg, Arthur ..... New York, NY
Fastenberg, Charles ..... **New York, NY**
Fasterling, Charles W. ..... Metairie, LA
Fastiff, Eric B. ..... **San Francisco, CA**
Fastiff, Wesley J. ..... **San Francisco, CA**
Fastiff Ellman, Pamela ..... **Oakland, CA**
Fastman, Lainie R. ..... **Staten Island, NY**
Fastook, Eugene J. ..... Brooklyn, NY
Fastow, Jay N. ..... **New York, NY**
Fastuca, Emilio P. ..... Pittsburgh, PA
Fasula, Gregory G. ..... Port St. Lucie, FL
Fasulis, Maxine ..... Oakland, CA
Fasulo, Albert J., II ..... **Washington, DC**
Fasulo, David J. ..... Pittsburgh, PA
Fasulo, Louis E. ..... Brooklyn, NY
Fasulo, Maria T. ..... **New York, NY**
Fasulo, Salvatore H. ..... **Fort Lauderdale, FL**
Fasy, Richard C. ..... Spokane, WA
Fat, Thomas N. ..... Sacramento, CA
Fata, A. Joseph ..... Hallandale Beach, FL
Fata, Gregory J. ..... Northlake, IL
Fata, Nate ..... Surfside Beach, SC
Fata, Nate, P.A. ..... Surfside Beach, SC
Fata, Paul M. ..... Bishopville, SC
Fatale, Michael T. ..... Boston, MA
Fatall, G. Michael, Law Offices of ..... **Kansas City, MO**
Fatall, Michael G. ..... **Chicago, IL**
Fatcheric, Maureen G. ..... **Syracuse, NY**
Fate, Jennifer L. ..... **Columbus, OH**
Fate, Michael ..... **Culver City, CA**
Fatell, Bonnie Glantz ..... **Philadelphia, PA**
Fatemi, Kayhan M. ..... **Los Angeles, CA**
Fater, Gregory F. ..... Newport, RI
Fater, Joseph F., Jr. ..... Newport, RI
Fates, Megan Geist ..... East Orleans, MA
Fath, Harry J., Jr. ..... Cincinnati, OH
Fathallah, Doaa A. ..... **Los Angeles, CA**
Fathe, Fred C. ..... **Phoenix, AZ**
Fatheree, Larry J. ..... Hitchcock, TX
Fathi, David C. ..... Berkeley, CA
Fathree, Deborah R. ..... Fort Worth, TX
Fathy, Ann T. ..... San Diego, CA
Fatica, Cynthia L. ..... San Diego, CA
Fatica, John A. ..... **Cleveland, OH**
Fatica, Kimberly A. ..... **Phoenix, AZ**
Fatigante, James Michael ..... Tulsa, OK
Fatino, John F. ..... **Des Moines, IA**
Fatka, Stacie L. ..... Washington, DC
Fatkin, Louis A. ..... Westernport, MD
Fato, Gildo E. ..... Libertyville, IL
Fato, Luciana ..... **New York, NY**
Fatolitis, John G. ..... Tarpon Springs, FL
Fatone, Toni M. ..... East Hartford, CT
Fatora, Jerome F. ..... Cincinnati, OH
Fatoullah, Ronald, & Associates, Law Offices of ..... **Brooklyn, NY**
Forest Hills, NY
Great Neck, NY
Fatout, William R. ..... Indianapolis, IN
Fatovic, Robert D. ..... **Miami, FL**
Fatovich, Milica A. ..... **Parsippany, NJ**
Fatse, J. Brian ..... **Trumbull, CT**
Fattahi, Kamran ..... **Woodland Hills, CA**
Fattarsi, William G. ..... Stockton, CA
Fattell, Edward George, III ..... **Florham Park, NJ**
Fattibene, Arthur T. ..... **Southport, CT**
Fattibene & Fattibene ..... **Southport, CT**
Fattibene, Paul A. ..... **Southport, CT**
Fattman, Stephen P. ..... Washington, DC
Fattor, James C. ..... **Denver, CO**
Denver, CO
Fattor, Joseph A. ..... Leadville, CO
Fattor & Kittle ..... Denver, CO
Fattorini, James D. ..... Mount Laurel, NJ
Fattorosi, Michael W. ..... **Encino, CA**
Fatum, Mark E. ..... **Grand Rapids, MI**
Fatum, Stephen M. ..... Park Ridge, IL
Fatzinger, Stephen R. ..... Denver, CO
Fauber, Sue Ann ..... Columbus, OH
Faubion, Catherine K. ..... **Dallas, TX**
Faubion, Charles M. ..... San Jose, CA
Faubion, Kathleen ..... **San Leandro, CA**
Faubion, Marcus E. ..... Houston, TX
Faubion, Thomas K. ..... **Lakewood, WA**
Faubion, William J. ..... Cathlamet, WA
Faubus, Dax O. ..... **Houston, TX**
Faubus, Donald Ellis ..... Diamond Bar, CA
Faubus, Fara E. ..... Little Rock, AR
Faucett, Anne C. ..... Loxahatchee, FL
Faucett, Calvin J. ..... Orlando, FL
Faucett, Mark A. ..... Richmond, TX
Faucette, C. Robert ..... Spartanburg, SC
Faucette, David H. ..... Research Triangle Park, NC
Faucette, Douglas P. ..... **Washington, DC**
Faucette, Gary C. ..... San Luis Obispo, CA
Faucette, Jeffrey E. ..... **San Francisco, CA**
Faucette Law Firm, P.A. ..... Spartanburg, SC
Faucher, Carol I. ..... **Kansas City, MO**
Faucher, Gregory D. ..... **Albany, NY**
Faucher, J. Dennis ..... **Philadelphia, PA**
Faucher, John D. ..... Houston, TX
Faucher, Joseph C. ..... **Los Angeles, CA**
Faucher & Levine LLP ..... Pasadena, CA
Faucher, Mary D. ..... **New York, NY**
Faucher, Rene M. ..... Pasadena, CA
Faucher, Robert A. ..... **Boise, ID**
Faucher, Robert J. ..... Department of State, Foreign Service Officers (Overseas), GV
Faucheux, Patrick J. ..... Panama City, FL
Faucheux, Robert R., Jr. ..... La Place, LA
Faucheux, Robert R., Jr., A Professional Law Corporation ..... La Place, LA
Faucheux, Ronald A. ..... Metairie, LA
Fauci, James R., (P.C.) ..... New York, NY
Fauci, Salvatore A. ..... Endicott, NY
Fauerbach, Michael F. ..... **Ashland, WI**
Faughn, David T. ..... **Lexington, KY**
Faughnan, Elizabeth A. ..... **Mineola, NY**
Faughnan, Eugene D. ..... **Binghamton, NY**
Faughnan, James J. ..... Department of Justice, Civil Division, GV
Faughnan, Joseph E. ..... **New Haven, CT**
Faughnan, Richard T. ..... Brooklyn, NY
Faughnan, Thomas J. ..... Los Angeles, CA
Faughnan, Vincent M. ..... San Francisco, CA
Faught, Ellis R., Jr., P.A. ..... Brandon, FL
Faught, H. Shepherd, Jr. ..... Providence, RI
Faught, Irving L. ..... Oklahoma City, OK
Faught, James J. ..... Chicago, IL
Faught, Jefferson K. ..... Russellville, AR
Faught, John, & Associates, Prof. Corp. ..... Denver, CO
Faught, John D. ..... Denver, CO
Faught, Renee A. ..... **Indianapolis, IN**
Faught, Richard H. ..... St. Louis, MO
Faugno, Paul ..... **Hackensack, NJ**
Faul, Michael J., Jr. ..... **Roseland, NJ**
Faul, Michael M. ..... Phelps, NY
Faul, Regina E. ..... **New York, NY**
Faul, Terence L. ..... Bangor, PA
Stroudsburg, PA
Faulbaum, Otto J. ..... **Waterloo, IL**
Faulconbridge, Jean V. ..... Omaha, NE
Faulconer, Thomas J. ..... Altamonte Springs, FL
Faulconer, Thomas J., IV ..... Fishers, IN
Faulconer, Thos. J., III ..... Indianapolis, IN
Faulders, J. David ..... Richmond, VA
Faulds, Michael J. ..... De Pere, WI
Faulhaber, Charles Daniel ..... Riverside, CA
Faulhaber, Cynthia B. ..... **Lansing, MI**
Faulhaber, Dwight L. ..... Eugene, OR
Faulhaber, Frank R. ..... Forest Lake, MN
Faulise, S. V. ..... Hartford, CT
Faulk, Decanda M. ..... **Florham Park, NJ**
Faulk, Frank F., Jr. ..... Albany, GA
Faulk, J. Robert ..... **Prattville, AL**
Faulk, John E. ..... **Melbourne, FL**
Faulk, Joseph E. ..... **Troy, AL**
Faulk, Karen E. ..... Oklahoma City, OK
Faulk, Martha J. ..... Fort Collins, CO
Faulk, Michael A. ..... **Church Hill, TN**
Faulk, Rabun ..... Jeffersonville, GA
Faulk, Richard O. ..... **Houston, TX**
Faulk, Rodney P., Jr. ..... Cordova, TN
Faulk, Sheldon ..... Baton Rouge, LA
Faulk, Thomas H., Jr. ..... Indian Trail, NC
Faulk, Tron D. ..... Sanford, NC
Faulk, Warren W. ..... **Camden, NJ**
Westmont, NJ
Faulk, W. H., Jr. ..... Houston, TX
Faulk, William A. ..... **Brownsville, TX**
Faulk, William A., Jr. ..... **Brownsville, TX**
Faulk, Winn ..... **Mobile, AL**
Faulken, Bruce C. ..... St. Paul, MN
Faulkes, Gary W. ..... Westlake Village, CA
Faulkingham, John T. ..... Baltimore, MD
Faulkner, Alan R. ..... Hammond, IN
Faulkner, Andrew M. ..... **New York, NY**
Faulkner, Arthur D. ..... Henderson, NC
Faulkner, Audrey H. ..... **Anchorage, AK**
Faulkner, B. Keith ..... Conway, AR
Faulkner Banfield, A Professional Corporation ..... **Juneau, AK**
Ketchikan, AK
Faulkner, Benjamin C. ..... **Tulsa, OK**
Faulkner & Boyce, P.C. ..... **New London, CT**
Westerly, RI
Faulkner, Brian R. ..... **Costa Mesa, CA**
Faulkner, Carole A. ..... Bedford, TX
Faulkner, Charles B. ..... Shell Knob, MO
Faulkner, Charles H. ..... San Gabriel, CA
Faulkner, Cox & Hall ..... Campbellsville, KY
Faulkner, D. Scott ..... Newport Beach, CA
Faulkner, D. Sean ..... **Greenville, SC**
Faulkner, Dale Patrick ..... **New London, CT**
Faulkner, David C. ..... Kenton, OH
Faulkner, David G. ..... **Cleveland, OH**
Faulkner, David L., Jr. ..... **Birmingham, AL**
Faulkner, David P. ..... **New Haven, CT**
Faulkner, David P. ..... **Rockford, IL**
Faulkner, Debora A. ..... Greenville, SC
Faulkner, Donald L. ..... **Lock Haven, PA**
Faulkner, Erin Brown ..... Louisville, KY
Faulkner, Francis F. ..... **Keene, NH**
Faulkner, Fred, Jr. ..... Campbellsville, KY
Faulkner, Garmhausen, Keister & Shenk, A Legal Professional Association ..... Minster, OH
Sidney, OH
Faulkner, George H. ..... **Cleveland, OH**
Faulkner, Gregory F. ..... **Santa Barbara, CA**
Faulkner, Gregory R. ..... **Hartford, CT**
Faulkner, Harry N. ..... **Sidney, OH**
Faulkner, Henry, III ..... Lancaster, PA
Faulkner, Hugh V. ..... Oskaloosa, IA
Faulkner, J. Michael ..... Augusta, GA
Faulkner, J. Robert ..... Macon, GA
Faulkner, J. Todd ..... **Chicago, IL**
Faulkner, James Alsop ..... Miami, FL
Faulkner, James L. ..... **Bakersfield, CA**
Faulkner, James V., Jr. ..... Lake Forest, IL
Faulkner, Jane M. ..... **Little Rock, AR**
Faulkner, Janine ..... Camden, NJ
Faulkner, Joan Simon ..... New York, NY
Faulkner, Joanne S. ..... New Haven, CT
Faulkner, John B. ..... Jarrell, TX
Faulkner, John E. ..... Pomona, CA
Faulkner, John H. ..... **New York, NY**
Faulkner, John W. ..... Pickerington, OH
Faulkner, Kathleen E. ..... **Bakersfield, CA**
Faulkner, Kevin A. ..... Palo Alto, CA
Faulkner, Laurie F. ..... San Jose, CA
Faulkner Law Firm ..... Enid, OK
Faulkner Law Offices ..... **Bakersfield, CA**
Faulkner Law Offices ..... Louisville, KY
Faulkner, Lawrence ..... Albany, NY
Faulkner, LeAnne M. ..... Department of Transportation, Federal Aviation Administration, GV
Faulkner, Lee A. ..... **Henderson, NC**
Faulkner, Lila ..... Philadelphia, PA
Faulkner, Mark S. ..... **Newport Beach, CA**
Faulkner, Mary ..... **Durant, OK**
Faulkner & Maslyn ..... Schenectady, NY
Faulkner, Michael P. ..... Greenbrae, CA
Faulkner, Norman A. ..... Melrose, FL
Faulkner, Patrick K. ..... San Rafael, CA
Faulkner, Paul M. ..... Huntington Woods, MI
Faulkner, Peter D. ..... Springvale, ME
Faulkner, Plaut, Hanna, Freund & Worthen, P.C. ..... **Keene, NH**
Faulkner, R. Mark ..... **State College, PA**
Faulkner, René M. ..... Fairfax, VA
Faulkner, Rex L. ..... Enid, OK
Faulkner, Richard D., Jr. ..... Cleveland, TN
Faulkner, Rick L. ..... Wheelersburg, OH
Faulkner, Rickey L. ..... **Longview, TX**
Faulkner, Robert M. ..... Traverse City, MI
Faulkner, Robert M. ..... Traverse City, MI
Faulkner, Robert P. ..... Department of Justice, Antitrust Division, GV
Faulkner, Robert R. ..... Evansville, IN
Faulkner, Robert W. ..... Sherman, TX
Faulkner, Roland L. ..... Schenectady, NY
Faulkner & Russell, P.C. ..... Macon, GA
Faulkner, Sackett & Muskovitz, LLP ..... **Cleveland, OH**
Faulkner, Shands & Stupar ..... Washington, DC
Faulkner, Sharon M. ..... Wailuku, HI
Faulkner, Sheehan & Wunsch ..... **San Francisco, CA**
Faulkner, Stanley ..... New York, NY
Faulkner, Steven K., Jr. ..... Harahan, LA
Faulkner, Sue Zane M. ..... Lampasas, TX
Faulkner, Sylvia ..... Charlottesville, VA
Faulkner & Tepe, LLP ..... **Cincinnati, OH**
Faulkner, Teresa Stankis ..... Houston, TX
Faulkner, Thomas A. ..... **Denver, CO**
Faulkner, Thomas Wesley ..... Louisville, KY
Faulkner, Walter T. ..... **New York, NY**
Faulkner, William ..... **San Jose, CA**
Faulkner, York Moody ..... **Washington, DC**
Faulks, Robert H., Law Office of ..... **Aberdeen, MS**
Faulks, Tammi L. ..... Santa Maria, CA
Faull, Gary F. ..... Renton, WA
Fauls, Alison Vadnais ..... **Richmond, VA**
Fauls, Thomas E. duB. ..... **Richmond, VA**
Faulstich, James R. ..... Mercer Island, WA
Faulstich, Leo J. ..... Sonora, CA
Faulstich, Lisa D. ..... Fenton, MO
Faulstich, Richard A. ..... St. Louis, MO
Faultless, Scott A. ..... Batesville, IN
Faunce, Edward L. ..... Seal Beach, CA
Faunce, Marisa Gallehr ..... **Washington, DC**
Faunce, Sherman P., II ..... St. Clair, MI
FauntLeRoy, Amber R. ..... **Los Angeles, CA**
FauntLeRoy, Andre ..... Baltimore, MD
Fauntleroy, J. Parker, Jr. ..... **Houston, TX**
Fauntleroy, Richard T. ..... Northfield, NJ
Fauntleroy, Richard T., P.C. ..... Northfield, NJ
Fauntleroy, Veronica Y. ..... Oakland, CA
Faupel & Associates ..... **Ann Arbor, MI**
Birmingham, MI
Southfield, MI
Ypsilanti, MI
Faupel, Marian L. ..... **Ann Arbor, MI**
Faupel, Mary E. ..... Eureka, IL
Faur, Cynthia A. ..... **Chicago, IL**
Faure, David C. ..... **Columbus, OH**
Faure, David E. ..... Houston, TX
Faure, Jean E. ..... **Great Falls, MT**
Faure, John P., (P.A.) ..... Santa Fe, NM
Faure, Karine ..... **San Diego, CA**
Faure, Warren W. ..... Bound Brook, NJ
Faurest, Henry S., Jr. ..... New Albany, IN
Faurholt, Harvey ..... Kennewick, WA
Fauri, Eric J. ..... **Muskegon, MI**
Fauri, Paul F. ..... Frankfort, KY
Faurot, Allen R. ..... Annapolis, MD
Faurot, Jay L. ..... Farmington, NM
Faurot, Jay L., P.A. ..... Farmington, NM
Faurote, Scott P. ..... Huntington, IN
Fausett, Bret A. ..... Boston, MA
Fausett, David L. ..... **Fayetteville, AR**
Fausett, Gaeta & Lund, LLP ..... Boston, MA
Fausett, Nichol L. ..... Springdale, AR
Fausnaugh, Hal A. ..... Rocky River, OH
Fausone, James G. ..... **Northville, MI**
Fausone, Taylor & Bohn, LLP ..... **Detroit, MI**
Northville, MI

Fazzolari, Maria ... **New York, NY**
Fazzone, A. Joseph ... Schenectady, NY
Fazzone, Anthony Angelo ... Schenectady, NY
Fazzone, Anthony J. ... **Cheshire, CT**
Fazzone Baillie Ryan Schmitt & Seadale LLC ... **Cheshire, CT**
Fazzone, David A. ... **Boston, MA**
Fazzone, Rosalia ... **Denver, CO**
Fead, William Alexander ... **Burlington, VT**
Feagan, Charles Mark ... Columbus, NC
Feagan, Cynthia B. ... Kansas City, MO
Feagan and Foster ... Columbus, NC
Feagan, John M. ... Alexandria, VA
Feagan, Jordan C. ... Nashville, TN
Feagan, Phillip R. ... Columbus, NC
Feaganes, David S. ... Lady Lake, FL
Feagans, Derek E. ... **Kansas City, MO**
Feagans, Karen R. ... Kansas City, MO
Feagans, Robert R., Jr. ... Lynchburg, VA
Feagans, Timothy L. ... Worcester, MA
Feagin, John E., Jr. ... Atlanta, GA
Feagin, Robert D. ... **Atlanta, GA**
Feagin, Robert R., III ... **Jacksonville, FL**
Tallahassee, FL
Feagins, Kathryn L. ... Kingsport, TN
Feagins, Ken, Law Office of ... **Norman, OK**
Feagle, James M. ... Decatur, GA
Feagle, Marlin M., (P.A.) ... Lake City, FL
Feagles, Prentiss E. ... **Washington, DC**
Feagles, Shirley L. ... Laguna Niguel, CA
Feagley, Michael R. ... **Chicago, IL**
Feakes, David R. ... Littleton, MA
Feakins, Jeffie W., (Ms.) ... San Mateo, CA
Feakins, Martha S.
Rolling Hills Estates, CA
Fealing, Burt M. ... **Boston, MA**
Fealk, Gary S. ... **Bingham Farms, MI**
Fealk, Marshall ... **Tucson, AZ**
Fealk, Martin N. ... Southfield, MI
Fealk, Martin N., P.C. ... Southfield, MI
Fealk, Sheldon A. ... **Farmington Hills, MI**
Fealko, William L., III ... **Port Huron, MI**
Feal-Nuñez, Moraima ... Miami, FL
Fealy, Glen P. ... Quincy, MA
Feaman, Peter M. ... **Boca Raton, FL**
Feaman, Scott N. ... Chicago, IL
Feamster, Elizabeth S. ... **Lexington, KY**
Feamster, James W., III ... Tulsa, OK
Feamster, Jane M. ... Los Angeles, CA
Feanny, Philip M. ... **Fort Lauderdale, FL**
Fear, Christopher M. ... **Lakeland, FL**
Fear, Heath R. ... **Chicago, IL**
Fear, Ralph J. ... San Diego, CA
Feare, Donald Duffield, Jr ... Fort Worth, TX
Fearen, William ... **Harrisburg, PA**
Fearer, Nye, Ahlberg & Chadwick
Oregon, IL
Rochelle, IL
Fearer, William P., II ... **Oregon, IL**
Fearer, William P., III ... **Oregon, IL**
Fearey, John L. ... New York, NY
Fearey, Margaret S. ... Boston, MA
Fearey, Morton, Jr. ... New York, NY
Fearey, Sharon F. ... **Plymouth, MA**
Fearing, George B. ... **Kennewick, WA**
Fearing, Jill D. ... Flower Mound, TX
Fearing, Renee K. ... **Minneapolis, MN**
Fearn, Colleen Quinn ... San Diego, CA
Fearnley, Gordon ... Boca Raton, FL
Fearnow, Randall R. ... **Indianapolis, IN**
Fearnow, William D. ... **Phoenix, AZ**
Fearns, Alan E. ... Lecanto, FL
Fearns, Geoffrey S. ... Brea, CA
Fearns, John A. ... Parsippany, NJ
Fearnside, Jacqueline M. ... **Boise, ID**
Fearnside, Timothy P. ... **Boise, ID**
Fearon, Flora A. ... Austin, TX
Fearon, George R. ... **New York, NY**
Fearon, James G. ... **Trenton, NJ**
Fearon, John R., Jr. ... Chicago, IL
Fearon, Richard Harold ... San Francisco, CA
Fearon, Stephen J. ... **New York, NY**
Fearon, Stephen J., Jr. ... **New York, NY**
Fearrington, Willa A.
West Palm Beach, FL
Fears, Alfred D. ... Jackson, GA
Fears, Alfred D., Jr. ... Jackson, GA
Fears, Barbara Ann C. ... Columbia, MO
Fears, Daniel F. ... **Irvine, CA**
Fears, Diane Hollis ... Bloomfield Hills, MI
Fears, J. Carroll, Jr. ... **Norfolk, VA**
Fears, Joe M. ... **Tulsa, OK**
Fears, John G. ... Oklahoma City, OK
Fears, John R. ... Phoenix, AZ
Fears, Oscar B., III ... Atlanta, GA
Fears, Robert L. ... Hopkinsville, KY
Fears, Sandra N. ... **Somerset, NJ**
Fears, Thomas D. ... Thornton, CO
Fears, Timothy E. ... **Terre Haute, IN**
Fears, William A. ... Jackson, GA
Fears, William E. ... **Accomac, VA**
Fears, William E., P.C. ... **Accomac, VA**
Feary, Gregory M. ... **Indianapolis, IN**
Fease, Kevin R. ... **Columbus, OH**
Feaster, Jay H. ... Hershey, PA
Feaster, Joseph D., Jr. ... Boston, MA
Feather, David Scott ... Woodmere, NY
Feather and Feather, P.C. ... Annville, PA
Feather, Gerald B., (P.C.)
Grand Junction, CO
Feather, Gregory M. ... **Harrisburg, PA**
Lancaster, PA
Feather, Jean Schwinke
Jefferson City, MO
Feather, John E., Jr. ... Annville, PA
Feather, John R. ... Houston, TX
Feather, Karen M. ... House of Representatives, Congressional Assistants, GV
Feather, Mark R. ... **Louisville, KY**
Feather, Philip H. ... Annville, PA
Feather, Sharon S. ... Lake Forest, IL
Feather, William L. ... North Chicago, IL
Featheringill, Carolyn ... Birmingham, AL
Featherly, Henry F. ... **Oklahoma City, OK**
Featherly, Walter T., III ... **Anchorage, AK**
Featherman, Annie ... San Diego, CA
Featherman, John A., III
West Chester, PA
Featherman, Leland ... San Diego, CA
Featherman, Mark ... **Philadelphia, PA**
Feathers, Lori Ann
Department of Commerce, GV
Feathers, Richard M. ... **Raleigh, NC**
Feathers, Timothy J. ... **Kansas City, MO**
Featherson, Clarence E.
Environmental Protection Agency, Office of Enforcement and Compliance Assurance, GV
Featherston, Brittian A. ... Lufkin, TX
Featherston, D. Elizabeth ... Jackson, MS
Featherston, Daniel F., Jr. ... Boston, MA
Featherston, Jimmy L. ... Murfreesboro, AR
Featherston, Kevin L. ... **Chattanooga, TN**
Featherston, Robert ... San Antonio, TX
Featherston, Thomas M., Jr. ... Waco, TX
Featherston, William S. ... **Houston, TX**
Featherstone, Bruce A. ... **Denver, CO**
Featherstone, D. Michael ... University, MS
Featherstone DeSisto LLP ... **Denver, CO**
Featherstone, Don ... San Bernardino, CA
Featherstone, Harold G. ... Miami, FL
Featherstone, James E. ... Englewood, OH
Featherstone, James W., III
Richmond, VA
Featherstonhaugh, Conway, Wiley & Clyne, L.L.P. ... **Albany, NY**
Saratoga Springs, NY
Schenectady, NY
Featherstonhaugh, James D. ... **Albany, NY**
Featherstun, Donald G.
San Francisco, CA
Featherstun, Glen A. ... **Decatur, IL**
Featherstun, Jeffrey D. ... **Indianapolis, IN**
Feavel, Jonathan T. ... Vincennes, IN
Feavel, Patrick M. ... Monterey, CA
Feaver Law Office, Inc. ... Norman, OK
Feaver, M. Ellen ... Norman, OK
Feaver, Reiko R. ... **Atlanta, GA**
Feazell, Kevin R. ... **Cincinnati, OH**
Feazell, Thomas L. (IBA) ... Covington, KY
Feazell, Victor F. ... Austin, TX
Febbo, Anthony T. ... **Philadelphia, PA**
Febbo, Gary G. ... Easton, PA
Febbraio, Gregg Michael ... White Plains, NY
Febbraio, Samuel, Jr. ... **Westport, CT**
Febbroriello, Conti & Levy ... Torrington, CT
Febbroriello, John P. ... Torrington, CT
Febeo, James F., Jr. ... Arlington, VA
Febeo, Karen L. ... **Boston, MA**
Febles-Gordián, Vanya ... San Juan, PR
Fecher, William B. ... **Cincinnati, OH**
Fechheimer, Fred J. ... **Bloomfield Hills, MI**
Fechhelm, Andrew Lewis ... Fort Belvoir, VA
Fechhelm, Paul L. ... Florham Park, NJ
Fechner, Donovan S. ... Wheaton, IL
Fechter, Adrienne ... **Tampa, FL**
Fechter & Dickson, P.A. ... **Tampa, FL**
Fechter, Gary H. ... **New York, NY**
Fechter, Melvin A. ... Orlando, FL
Fechter, Wendy K. ... Buffalo, NY
Fechtig, C. William ... Robinson, IL
Fechtig, Mary E. ... **Washington, DC**
Fechtmeyer, Kurtis P. ... **New York, NY**
Fecik, Shelley A. ... Hollidaysburg, PA
Fecker, Craig J. ... Carlsbad, CA
Minneapolis, MN
Fecteau, Francis R. ... Boston, MA
Feczko, Albert G., Jr. ... **Bethel Park, PA**
Pittsburgh, PA
Feczko, John J. ... Paramus, NJ
Feczko, Mark D. ... **Pittsburgh, PA**
Feczko and Seymour ... **Bethel Park, PA**
Pittsburgh, PA
Feda, William A. ... Elgin, IL
Fedak, Edward C. ... Newark, NJ
Fedak, K. Dian ... **West Palm Beach, FL**
Fedak, Laurence S. ... Bethesda, MD
Fedalen, Charles H., Jr. ... Irvine, CA
Fedalen, James C. ... **Calabasas, CA**
Fedas, Christine Ann ... Waltham, MA
Fedde, Elisabeth Raag ... Denver, CO
Fedde, G. Bernhard ... Portland, OR
Feddeler, Carl A., III ... **Lakeland, FL**
Fedden, Charles E. ... New York, NY
Fedder, Arthur W. ... Wheaton, IL
Fedder, David M. ... **St. Louis, MO**
Fedder and Garten, Professional Association
Baltimore, MD
Fedder, Joel D. ... **Baltimore, MD**
Fedder, Kenneth P. ... South Bend, IN
Fedder, Martin ... Pikesville, MD
Fedder, Robert J. ... **Asheville, NC**
Fedder, Steven K. ... **Washington, DC**
Baltimore, MD
Fedder, W. J. ... Seneca, SC
Fedderly, Donald P. ... Flanders, NJ
Fedders, Barbara ... Roxbury, MA
Fedders, Gregory A. ... **Madison, WI**
Fedders, John M. ... **Washington, DC**
Fedders, P. Daniel ... Lebanon, OH
Feddersen, Clint W. ... **Pasadena, CA**
Feddersen, James A. ... **Milwaukee, WI**
Fede, Andrew T. ... **Hackensack, NJ**
Fedel, L. Charles ... Pittsburgh, PA
Fedele, Frank ... Brooklyn, NY
Fedele, Jerry J. ... Pittsburgh, PA
Fedele, John E. ... **Dedham, MA**
Fedele and Murray, P.C. ... **Dedham, MA**
Fedele, Thomas D. ... New York, NY
Fedele, Timothy A. ... **Greensburg, PA**
Fedeli, Nicholas C., Jr. ... San Jose, CA
Feder, Alvin B. ... Riverwoods, IL
Feder, Alvin M. ... **New York, NY**
Feder, Ben D. ... Forest Hills, NY
Feder, Benjamin D. ... **New York, NY**
Feder, Bruce ... **Phoenix, AZ**
Feder, Bruce A. ... San Francisco, CA
Feder, Caralyn J. ... Irvington, NY
Feder, Charles E. ... Atlanta, GA
Feder, Daniel E. ... Bloomfield, CT
Feder, Daniel G. ... **St. Louis, MO**
Feder, Daniel, The Law Offices of
San Francisco, CA
Feder, David L.
Federal Labor Relations Authority, Office of the General Counsel, GV
Feder & Della Guardia ... Philadelphia, PA
Feder, Denise H. ... **Princeton, NJ**
Feder, Frank E., (A P.C.)
Los Angeles, CA
New York, NY
Feder, Fred M. ... Philadelphia, PA
Feder, Frederick ... Brooklyn, NY
Feder, Gary Arnold ... Deerfield Beach, FL
Feder, Gary H. ... **St. Louis, MO**
Feder, Gerald M. ... **Washington, DC**
Feder, Gil ... **New York, NY**
Feder, Gregory S. ... **Washington, DC**
Feder, Harold J. ... **Phoenix, AZ**
Feder, Harry B. ... **New York, NY**
Feder, Harvey L. ... Encino, CA
Feder, Helene T. ... Los Angeles, CA
Feder, Irving L. ... New York, NY
Feder, Jack M. ... **Washington, DC**
New York, NY
Feder, James J. ... **Los Angeles, CA**
Feder, Jeffrey S. ... Beachwood, OH
Feder, Jesse M. ... Library of Congress, Copyright Office, GV
Feder, Joan L. ... Metairie, LA
Feder, John M. ... **San Francisco, CA**
Feder, Jon A. ... **Albuquerque, NM**
Feder, Jon C. ... Costa Mesa, CA
Feder, Judith R. ... **New York, NY**
Feder, Judson J. ... Long Beach, CA
Feder, Kaszovitz, Isaacson, Weber, Skala & Bass LLP ... **New York, NY**
Feder Law Office, P.A. ... **Phoenix, AZ**
Feder, Lawrence H. ... Hollywood, FL
Feder, Leonard H. ... Ardsley, NY
Feder, Lynn M. ... **Chicago, IL**
Feder, Melvin ... New York, NY
Feder, Michael Brian ... Santa Monica, CA
Feder, Michael J. ... New York, NY
Feder, Michael N. ... **Philadelphia, PA**
Feder & Mills, A Professional Corporation
Los Angeles, CA
Feder, Milton E. ... Houston, TX
Feder, Milton E., P.C. ... Houston, TX
Feder, Miriam ... Portland, OR
Feder, Morton H. ... Mineola, NY
Feder, Nicole ... Chicago, IL
Feder, Philip G. ... Belleville, IL
St. Louis, MO
Feder, Philip N. ... **Los Angeles, CA**
Feder & Platt ... New York, NY
Feder, Rand A. ... York, PA
Feder, Regina ... Ardsley, NY
Feder, Rhonda C. ... **Collingswood, NJ**
Philadelphia, PA
Feder, Richard G. ... Philadelphia, PA
Feder, Richard Yale ... Miami, FL
Feder, Robert ... **White Plains, NY**
Feder, Robert D. ... **Philadelphia, PA**
Feder, Robert S., (P.A.) ... Union City, NJ
Feder, Robin E. ... Providence, RI
Feder, Ronald M. ... Mobile, AL
Gulfport, MS
Feder, Samuel L. ... **Washington, DC**
Feder, Samuel M. ... **New York, NY**
Feder, Sanford J. ... West Orange, NJ
Feder, Saul E. ... New York, NY
Feder, Scott B. ... **Chicago, IL**
Feder, Scott J. ... **Coral Gables, FL**
Feder, Scott Jay, P.A. ... **Coral Gables, FL**
Feder & Semo, P.C. ... **Washington, DC**
Feder, Sol ... New York, NY
Feder, Stephan J. ... **New York, NY**
Feder, Stephen I. ... Forest Hills, NY
Feder, Steven B. ... Des Moines, IA
Feder, Steven E. ... Rochester, NY
Feder, Steven H. ... Beverly Hills, CA
Feder, Steven J. ... **Philadelphia, PA**
Feder, Steven L. ... Buffalo Grove, IL
Feder, Steven M. ... **Denver, CO**
Feder, Steven S. ... Ventura, CA
Feder, Susan Gelender ... San Rafael, CA
Feder, Tamar ... **Los Angeles, CA**
Feder, Vince D. ... **Chicago, IL**
Federa, Henry A. ... Houston, TX
Federal, Keegan, & Associates
Atlanta, GA
Federal, R. Keegan, Jr. ... **Atlanta, GA**
Federbusch, Susan B. ... **Hackensack, NJ**
Federbusch & Weinstein, A Professional Corporation ... **Hackensack, NJ**
Federbush, Alan M. ... **White Plains, NY**
Federbush, David J. ... Washington, DC
Bethesda, MD
Federbush, Harry ... Bronx, NY
Federer, Federer & Diehl, LLP
St. Charles, MO
St. Louis, MO
Federer, Richard E. ... Skokie, IL
Federer, Richard L. ... St. Louis, MO
Federer, Thomas A. ... **St. Charles, MO**
Federer, Wendy R. ... Southbury, CT
Waterbury, CT
Federgreen, Shepard A. ... **Roseland, NJ**
Federhar, Andrew M. ... **Phoenix, AZ**
Tucson, AZ
Federici, James J. ... Stamford, CT
Federici, Lisa A. ... Falls Church, VA
Federici, Lisa A., P.C. ... Falls Church, VA
Federici, Louis M. ... **New Haven, CT**
Federici, William R. ... **Santa Fe, NM**
Federico, Andrew J. ... **Columbus, OH**
Federico, Daniel G. ... New York, NY
Federico, Domenic ... Dublin, OH
Federico, Dominic M. ... Dallas, TX
Federico, Frank J., Jr. ... Stoneham, MA
Federico, John J. ... Topeka, KS
Federico, Michael A. ... **Las Vegas, NV**
Federico, Philip A. ... St. Petersburg, FL
Federico, Philip C. ... **Washington, DC**
Baltimore, MD
Federico, Phyllis E. ... **Boston, MA**
Federico, Richard E. ... Hagerstown, IN
Federico, Richard M. ... Boston, MA
Federico, Robert A. ... El Segundo, CA
Federico, Thomas C. ... **Boston, MA**
Federico, Thomas M. ... **Nashville, TN**
Federighi, Carol ... Department of Justice, Civil Division, GV
Federizo, Ronald N. ... **Honolulu, HI**
Federle, A. V., Jr. ... Waterville, ME
Federle, Michael W. ... **Newport, KY**
Federle, Richard L. ... Blanchester, OH
Federle, Thomas B. ... Hallowell, ME
Federlein & Keranen, P.C.
Bloomfield Hills, MI
Detroit, MI
Marquette, MI
Sault Ste. Marie, MI
Federlein, Walter J. ... **Bloomfield Hills, MI**
Detroit, MI
Federline, Robert L. ... **Pittsburgh, PA**
Federman, Arthur B. ... Kansas City, MO
Federman, Barbara B. ... Beverly Hills, CA
Federman, David C. ... **Philadelphia, PA**
Federman, David S. ... West Hartford, CT
Federman, Douglas E. ... San Luis Obispo, CA
Federman, Ellen L. ... New York, NY
Federman, Frank ... **Philadelphia, PA**
Federman, Irving L. ... Chicago, IL
Federman, Jerry I. ... Cleveland, OH
Federman, Kenneth D.
West Collingswood, NJ
Bensalem, PA
Federman, Kenneth S. ... **Boston, MA**
Federman, Lynne H. ... **New York, NY**
Federman, Mark I. ... Brooklyn, NY
Federman, Michael K. ... **Washington, DC**
Federman, Pamela R. ... Belmont, CA
Federman, Paul R. ... Bay Shore, NY
Federman and Phelan ... Westmont, NJ
Philadelphia, PA
Federman, Robert J. ... San Luis Obispo, CA
Federman, William B.
Oklahoma City, OK
Federman-Henry, Karen L. ... Rockville, MD
Federoff, Carolyn ...
Department of Housing and Urban Development, GV
Federoff, James A. ... **Fort Wayne, IN**
Federoff, Michael S. ... Kingston, NY
Federoff, Michael S., P.C. ... Kingston, NY
Federoff, Scott M.
Hilton Head Island, SC
Federow, Harold L. ... Seattle, WA
Federowicz, Richard J. ... **Pittsburgh, PA**
Federspiel, Douglas L. ... **Yakima, WA**
Federspiel, Ingrid Lea ... **Louisville, KY**
Federspiel, J. Norbert ... Richmond, VA
Federspiel, Robert W., (P.A.)
Delray Beach, FL
Federspiel, Russell ... Alameda, CA
Fedewa, Tonya A. ... Grand Rapids, MI
Fedick, Thomas J. ... Chicago, IL
Fedigan, John T. ... **Washington, DC**
Fedij, Peter ... **Indianapolis, IN**
Fedinets, Kenneth Alan ... Chicago, IL
Fedirko, Judith E. ... Studio City, CA
Fedirko, Robert J. ... Van Nuys, CA
Fedner, Lee F. ... Baltimore, MD
Fedo, Jason M. ... **West Palm Beach, FL**
Fedo, Stephen ... **Chicago, IL**
Fedock, Michael J., III ... Towson, MD
Fedok, Amy Lynn ... **Wayne, PA**
Fedok, Edward A. ... **Lehigh Valley, PA**
Fedor, Allan J. ... **Largo, FL**
Fedor, Bruce G. ... Tampa, FL
Fedor, David A. ... Columbia, SC
Fedor & Fedor ... **Largo, FL**
Fedor, Franell ... **Largo, FL**
Fedor, Frank P. ... **Sacramento, CA**
Fedor, George E. ... Lakewood, OH
Fedor, Jodi Billehus ... **San Francisco, CA**
Fedor, John M. ... San Diego, CA
Fedor, Robert J., Jr. ... Cleveland, OH
Fedor, Victoria L. ... Cleveland, OH
Fedorchak, James M. ... **Poughkeepsie, NY**
Fedorich, William C. ... Baldwinsville, NY
Fedorko, John M. ... **New York, NY**
Fedorko, John M. ... Morrisville, PA
Fedorko, John P. ... **Pittsburgh, PA**
Fedorochko, Gary D. ... **Washington, DC**
Fedoroff, Gerald P. ... New Orleans, LA
Fedorow, Bradley T. ... Ottawa, IL
Fedors, John, Jr. ... **New York, NY**
Fedota Childers & Rocca, P.C.
Chicago, IL

Feigenbaum, Steven B. ....New York, NY
Feigenbaum & Uddo, P.C. ....Wayland, MA
Feigenbaum, William M. ....Buffalo, NY
Feigenberg, Louis A. ....Chicago, IL
Feigenson, Claire ....Highland, CA
Feigenson, Neal R. ....Hamden, CT
Feiger & Collison, P.C. ....Denver, CO
Feiger, Lynn D. ....Denver, CO
Feiger, Mara W. ....Riverside, CA
Feiger, Robert E. ....Dallas, TX
Feiger, Saul ....Kew Gardens Hills, NY
Feigert, Suzanne Anastos ....McLean, VA
Feigh, Robert J. ....St. Cloud, MN
Feighan, Ann M. ....Cleveland, OH
Feighan, Joseph E., Jr. ....Cleveland, OH
Feighner, John O. ....Fort Wayne, IN
Feighner, Robert D. ....Long Beach, CA
Feighny, Mary Droll ....Topeka, KS
Feighny, Michael Louis ....Kaneohe, HI
Feight, James S., Jr.
Department Of Health And Human Services, Social Security Administration, GV
Feightner Law Firm ....Carmel, IN
Feightner, Robert C. ....Carmel, IN
Feigin, Andrew ....New York, NY
Feigin, Arnold B. ....Hartford, CT
Feigin, Cynthia A. ....New York, NY
Feigin, Laura Beth ....Washington, DC
Feigin, Philip A. ....Denver, CO
Feigin, Samuel E. ....Boston, MA
Feigin, Stephen P. ....Department of Labor, Office of Secretary, GV
Feigles, Heidi ....Horsham, PA
Feijoo, John ....Rego Park, NY
Feikema, Orville A. ....Bradenton, FL
Feikens, Jeffrey ....Detroit, MI
Feikens, John ....Detroit, MI
Feikens, Jon ....Detroit, MI
Feikens, Robert H. ....Detroit, MI
Feikens, Stevens, Kennedy, Hurley & Galbraith, P.C. ....Detroit, MI
Pontiac, MI
Feikes, Michael W. ....Seattle, WA
Feikin, Mark G. ....Stevenson, MD
Feil, Clinton J. ....Chicago, IL
Feil, Clyde Hurt ....Atlanta, GA
Feil, Craig W. ....Champlin, MN
Feil, Frank J., Jr. ....Racine, WI
Feil, Jeffrey J. ....New York, NY
Feil, Joanne ....New York, NY
Feil, Jonathan I. ....Seattle, WA
Feil, Karen A. ....The Dalles, OR
Feil, Matthew J. ....Apopka, FL
Feil, Otto F., III ....Atlanta, GA
Feil, Pettit & Williams, P.L.C.
Charlottesville, VA
Feil, Ralph L. ....Charlottesville, VA
Feil, Randall S. ....Salt Lake City, UT
Feil-Addy, Kelly ....Cincinnati, OH
Feilberg, Deborah J. ....Seattle, WA
Feild, Deborah Love ....Richmond, VA
Feild, Herbert I. L. ....Gloucester, VA
Feild, Robert Benjamin ....Richmond, VA
Feild, Robt. M. ....Little Rock, AR
Feild, Roscoe A., Law Office of
Memphis, TN
Feild, Roscoe Porter ....Memphis, TN
Feild, Webster ....Dallas, TX
Feild, Wendy Coven ....Memphis, TN
Feiler, Alan S. ....San Francisco, CA
Feiler, Eliot R. ....Oklahoma City, OK
Feiler, Eliot R., P.C. ....Oklahoma City, OK
Feiler, Herbert ....New York, NY
Feiler, Michael B. ....Miami, FL
Feiler, Michael E. ....New York, NY
Feiler, P. Diane ....Houston, TX
Feiler, Stanley W. ....Savannah, GA
Feiler, William S. ....New York, NY
Feilmeyer, Franklin J. ....Ames, IA
Feilmeyer, R. E. ....Guthrie Center, IA
Feilmeyer, Ronald W. ....Atlantic, IA
Griswold, IA
Feilzer, Frederick W., Jr. ....Stockton, CA
Feiman, Richd. ....New York, NY
Fein, Alan ....Los Angeles, CA
Fein, Alan H. ....Miami, FL
Fein, Alan H., P.C. ....Suffern, NY
Fein, Albert S. ....Philadelphia, PA
Fein, Albert S., P.C. ....Philadelphia, PA
Fein, Alvin A. ....Cleveland, OH
Fein, Amy Susan ....Arlington, MA
Fein, Andrew K. ....Boca Raton, FL
Fein, Arthur S. ....Monsey, NY
Fein, Benjamin D. ....New York, NY
Fein, Bernard ....New York, NY
Fein, Bonnie L. ....Beverly Hills, CA
Fein, Bradley A. ....New York, NY
Fein, Bruce F. ....Houston, TX
Fein, Bruce F., P.C. ....Houston, TX
Fein, Bruce S. ....Buffalo, NY
Fein, Daniel F. ....Cambridge, MA
Fein, David B. ....Stamford, CT
Fein, David I. ....Chicago, IL
Fein, Dina E. ....Springfield, MA
Fein, Edward K. ....Houston, TX
Fein, Eileen L. ....Oak Park, IL
Fein, Elizabeth V. ....Atlanta, GA
Fein, Eric D. ....Dallas, TX
Fein, Frederick J. ....Miami, FL
Fein & Hameroff, P.C. ....Tucson, AZ
Fein, Harold ....Buffalo, NY
Fein, Harry L. ....Hollywood, FL
Fein, Harvey H. ....Staten Island, NY
Fein, Henry H. ....Parsippany, NJ
Fein, Hyman W. ....Bronx, NY
Fein, Iris W. ....New York, NY
Fein, Irving W. ....New York, NY
Fein & Jakab ....New York, NY

Fein, James A. ....Tucson, AZ
Fein, Joseph M. ....New York, NY
Fein & Kaplan, L.L.P. ....Dallas, TX
Fein, Katherine H. ....Pittsburgh, PA
Fein, Laura E. ....Washington, DC
Fein, Lawrence H. ....Sacramento, CA
Fein, Lee A. ....New York, NY
Fein, Leslie G. ....Washington, DC
Fein, Malcolm ....Brooklyn, NY
Fein, Marshall A. ....San Antonio, TX
Fein, Martin S. ....Fort Lauderdale, FL
Fein, Melvin J. ....Naperville, IL
Fein, Michael B. ....Cherry Hill, NJ
Philadelphia, PA
Fein, Michael S. ....New York, NY
Fein, Pearson, Emond & Fein
Springfield, MA
Fein, Randall J. ....Austin, TX
Fein, Richard Gary ....Alexandria, VA
Fein, Richard S. ....Alexandria, VA
Fein, Robert A. ....Cleveland, OH
Fein, Robert E. ....Springfield, MA
Fein, Robert E. ....New York, NY
Fein, Robert I. ....Miami, FL
Fein, Robert U. ....Cleveland, OH
Fein, Robin D. ....Springfield, MA
Fein, Roger G. ....Chicago, IL
Fein, Ronald J. ....Cincinnati, OH
Fein, Ronald L. ....Los Angeles, CA
Fein, Scott E. ....New York, NY
Fein, Scott N. ....Albany, NY
Fein & Seeskin ....Oak Park, IL
Fein, Sherman E. ....Springfield, MA
Fein, Stephen J. ....Kew Gardens, NY
Fein, Steven A. ....Los Angeles, CA
Fein, Steven A. ....Plantation, FL
Fein, Steven A., P.A. ....Plantation, FL
Fein, Such, Kahn & Shepard, P.C.
Parsippany, NJ
Fein, Terry B. ....Miami, FL
Fein, William S. ....Columbus, OH
Feinartz, David C. ....Chicago, IL
Feinauer, John A. ....Woodburn, OR
Feinbaum, Bart M. ....Detroit, MI
Feinberg, Aaron M. ....Brooklyn, NY
Feinberg, Adam P. ....Washington, DC
Feinberg, Alan ....Richardson, TX
Feinberg & Alban, P.C. ....Brookline, MA
Feinberg, Andrew ....Winter Park, FL
Feinberg, Andrew W. ....Boston, MA
Feinberg, Arnold I. ....Minneapolis, MN
Feinberg, Audrey S. ....Irvington, NY
Feinberg, Barbara L. ....Rockaway, NJ
Feinberg, Barry A. ....Chicago, IL
Feinberg & Barry, P.C. ....Chicago, IL
Orland Park, IL
Feinberg, Charnas & Birmingham, P.C.
Boston, MA
Feinberg, Cheryl H. ....Lawrence, NY
Feinberg, Cheryl Lackman ....Long Beach, CA
Feinberg, Daniel M. ....Oakland, CA
Feinberg, Daniel P. ....Punta Gorda, FL
Feinberg, David ....Chicago, IL
Feinberg, David H. ....Boston, MA
Feinberg, David M. ....Livingston, NJ
Feinberg, Dee & Feinberg ....Bayonne, NJ
Feinberg, Dennis M. ....Chicago, IL
Feinberg, Donald ....Sherman Oaks, CA
Feinberg, Donald J. ....Philadelphia, PA
Feinberg, Donna K. ....Department of Justice, Office of Justice Programs, GV
Feinberg, Donna M. ....East Hills, NY
Feinberg, Douglas ....Fresno, CA
Feinberg, Dyanne E. ....Miami, FL
Feinberg, Edward A. ....Trenton, NJ
Feinberg, Edward R. ....Delmar, NY
Feinberg, Elizabeth H. ....Washington, DC
Feinberg, Ellen Ann, (P.A.)
West Palm Beach, FL
Feinberg, Ellen Bell ....Deal, NJ
Feinberg, Ellen J. ....Philadelphia, PA
Feinberg, Elliot ....Madison, NJ
Feinberg & Feinberg ....South Orange, NJ
Feinberg, Gilbert S. ....Philadelphia, PA
Feinberg, Glen S. ....New York, NY
Feinberg, Gregg M. ....Allentown, PA
Feinberg, Gregory L. ....Camarillo, CA
Feinberg Group, The, LLP
Washington, DC
New York, NY
Feinberg, H. Robert ....Dobbs Ferry, NY
Feinberg, Helen ....Philadelphia, PA
Feinberg, Herbert D. ....East Norwich, NY
Feinberg, Herbert S. ....Pittsburgh, PA
Feinberg, Howard J. ....Miami Shores, FL
Feinberg, Howard J., P.A. ....Miami Shores, FL
Feinberg, Ian N. ....Palo Alto, CA
Feinberg, Ira B. ....Albany, NY
Feinberg, Irwin ....Los Angeles, CA
Feinberg, Jack ....Atlantic City, NJ
Feinberg, Jack E. ....Philadelphia, PA
Feinberg, James L., Law Offices of
Detroit, MI
Feinberg, Jeff D. ....Los Angeles, CA
Feinberg, Jeffrey ....Hollywood, FL
Feinberg, Jeffrey, P.A. ....Hollywood, FL
Feinberg, Jeremy R. ....New York, NY
Feinberg, Jill Kathi ....Melville, NY
Feinberg, Joel D. ....Washington, DC
Feinberg, Joel J. ....Boston, MA
Feinberg, Jonathan L. ....Brookline, MA
Feinberg, Josh ....Newton, MA
Feinberg, Joy M. ....Chicago, IL
Orland Park, IL
Feinberg, Judy Lynn ....Washington, DC
Feinberg, Julius A. ....Newark, NJ
Feinberg & Kamholtz ....Boston, MA

Feinberg, Kenneth R. ....Washington, DC
New York, NY
Feinberg, Kenneth S. ....Akron, OH
Feinberg, Laurence L. ....Brooklyn, NY
Feinberg, Lawrence G. ....Harrisburg, PA
Feinberg, Lee F. ....Charleston, WV
Weirton, WV
Feinberg, Lester H. ....Bel Air, MD
Feinberg, Linda R. ....Lawrenceville, NJ
Feinberg, Lindsay Nicely ....New York, NY
Feinberg, Louis E. ....Maitland, FL
Feinberg, Manley N. ....Louisville, KY
Feinberg, Marc R. ....Bethesda, MD
Feinberg, Margo A. ....Los Angeles, CA
Feinberg, Mark E. ....Brooklyn, NY
Feinberg, Mark J. ....Minneapolis, MN
Feinberg, Mark L. ....Farmington Hills, MI
Feinberg, Mark L., P.C.
Farmington Hills, MI
Feinberg, Martin J. ....New York, NY
Feinberg, Martin L. ....New York, NY
Feinberg, Matthew ....West Hempstead, NY
Feinberg, Matthew H. ....Boston, MA
Feinberg, Melvin E. ....Cleveland, OH
Feinberg, Michael A. ....Boston, MA
Feinberg, Michael H. ....Brooklyn, NY
Feinberg, Michael K. ....Woodbridge, NJ
Feinberg, Michael L. ....West Haven, CT
Feinberg, Michael M. ....Seattle, WA
Feinberg, Michael R. ....Los Angeles, CA
Feinberg, Michael Scott
Newport Beach, CA
Feinberg, Mindel & Kline, LLP
Los Angeles, CA
Feinberg, Mitchell S. ....Chicago, IL
Feinberg, Nancy S. ....South Orange, NJ
Feinberg, Noel J. ....North Miami, FL
Feinberg, Paul C. ....Treasury Department, Internal Revenue Service, GV
Feinberg, Paul H. ....South Orange, NJ
Feinberg, Paul H. ....Cleveland, OH
Feinberg, Paul S. ....East Brunswick, NJ
Feinberg, Paula I. ....New York, NY
Feinberg, Peter D. ....San Jose, CA
Feinberg, Peter H. ....Washington, DC
Feinberg, Raymond J. ....Encino, CA
Feinberg, Rebecca B. ....Chicago, IL
Feinberg, Richard B. ....Tampa, FL
Feinberg, Richard I. ....Pasadena, CA
Feinberg, Richard I., A Law Corporation
Pasadena, CA
Feinberg, Richard J. ....Tamarac, FL
Feinberg, Richard J. ....Bayonne, NJ
Deal, NJ
Feinberg, Robert A. ....Baltimore, MD
Feinberg, Robert A. ....New York, NY
Feinberg, Robert B. ....New York, NY
Feinberg, Robert H. ....Phoenix, AZ
Feinberg, Robert I. ....Boston, MA
Brookline, MA
Feinberg, Robert J. ....Livingston, NJ
Feinberg, Robert J. ....Plattsburgh, NY
Feinberg, Robert, P.A. ....Baltimore, MD
Feinberg, Ronald A. ....Selden, NY
Feinberg, Ross W. ....Newport Beach, CA
Feinberg, Seth J. ....Walnut Creek, CA
Feinberg, Sheldon ....Short Hills, NJ
Feinberg, Shelli Barish ....West Bloomfield, MI
Feinberg & Shelton, P.S.C. ....Louisville, KY
Feinberg, Sidney ....Palo Alto, CA
Feinberg, Sidney ....New York, NY
White Plains, NY
Feinberg & Sigal ....Newton, MA
Feinberg, Stephen D. ....Orlando, FL
Feinberg, Stephen J. ....Chicago, IL
Feinberg, Stephen S. ....Fort Lauderdale, FL
New York, NY
Feinberg, Steven K. ....Andover, MA
Feinberg, Susan B. ....Livermore, CA
Feinberg, Thomas D. ....Minneapolis, MN
Feinberg & Tritsch, P.C. ....Livingston, NJ
Feinberg & Waller, a Professional Corporation
Encino, CA
Feinberg, Wayne R. ....Nyack, NY
Feinberg, Wayne R., P.C. ....Nyack, NY
Feinberg, Wilfred ....New York, NY
Feinberg, William A. ....Encino, CA
Feinberg, William M. ....Bayonne, NJ
Feinblatt, Stuart M. ....Newark, NJ
New York, NY
Feinbloom, Charles R. ....Melville, NY
Feinbloom, Sharyn Faye ....New York, NY
Feinblum, Sherryl A. ....Flushing, NY
Feind, Robert L., Jr. ....Grafton, WI
Feindel, Anneliese ....New York, NY
Feindel, Susan M. ....Sanford, NC
Feindt, Walter G. ....Milford, DE
Feinen, Deborah F. ....Champaign, IL
Feiner, Andrew D. ....New York, NY
Feiner, Edward B. ....Philadelphia, PA
Feiner, John H. ....Costa Mesa, CA
Feiner, Laura Merrideth ....Miami, FL
Feiner, Lisa ....New York, NY
Feiner, Matthew E. ....New York, NY
Feiner, Michael A. ....New York, NY
Feiner, Patricia H. ....Somis, CA
Feiner, Richard ....New York, NY
Feiner, Robert A. ....Hartford, CT
Feiner, Rod A. ....Fort Lauderdale, FL
Feiner, Ronald E. ....New York, NY
Feiner, Thomas M. ....St. Louis, MO
Feiner, Wendy P. ....Fort Lauderdale, FL
Feiner Wolfson LLC ....Hartford, CT
Feinerman, Deborah S. ....Los Angeles, CA
Feinerman, Elliot ....New York, NY
Feinerman, Gary ....Chicago, IL
Feinerman, Jeffrey S. ....White Plains, NY
Feinerman, Neal T. ....Bellevue, WA

Feinerman, Robert ....Pacific Palisades, CA
Feinfield, Kenneth A. ....Los Angeles, CA
Feingerts & Associates, A Professional Law Corporation ....New Orleans, LA
Feingerts, Bruce L. ....New Orleans, LA
Feingerts, Sandra Mills ....New Orleans, LA
Feinglas, Jeffrey K. ....Dallas, TX
Feinglass, Susan B. ....New York, NY
Feingold, Allan S. ....Chicago, IL
Feingold, Allen L. ....Philadelphia, PA
Feingold & Alpert, L.L.P. ....New York, NY
Feingold, Arthur ....San Rafael, CA
Feingold, Bates and Sultze, Law Office
Janesville, WI
Feingold, Benjamin S. ....New York, NY
Feingold, Brandon G. ....Boca Raton, FL
New York, NY
Feingold, Cal R. ....Hackensack, NJ
Feingold, David B. ....Janesville, WI
Feingold, David F. ....San Rafael, CA
Feingold, David J. ....Palm Beach Gardens, FL
Feingold, Erik B. ....Santa Barbara, CA
Feingold, Eugene M., Law Offices of
Hammond, IN
Feingold, Eugene M., Law Offices of
Munster, IN
Feingold, Eugene N. ....Ann Arbor, MI
Feingold, Fred ....New York, NY
Feingold, Harry C. ....Kansas City, MO
Feingold, Herman R. ....Jersey City, NJ
Feingold, Jeffrey M. ....Chicago, IL
Feingold & Jehl, P.A. ....Haddonfield, NJ
Feingold, Jennifer ....Commack, NY
Feingold, Jerald S. ....Department of Labor, Office of the Solicitor, GV
Feingold, Kenneth A. ....Los Angeles, CA
Feingold, Larry E. ....New York, NY
Feingold, Laurence ....Miami Beach, FL
Feingold & Levy ....Chicago, IL
Feingold, Louis R. ....Atlanta, GA
Feingold, Marc D. ....New York, NY
Feingold, Margo R. ....New York, NY
Feingold, Marvin ....South River, NJ
Feingold, Marvin H. ....Charleston, SC
Feingold, Richard I. ....Chicago, IL
Feingold, Richard M. ....Banning, CA
Feingold, Robert A. ....New York, NY
Feingold, Robert B. ....New Bedford, MA
Feingold, Robert B., & Associates, P.C.
New Bedford, MA
Feingold, Robert P. ....Lynn, MA
Feingold, Ronald B. ....New York, NY
Feingold, Russell D. ....Middleton, WI
Feingold, Seymour ....Carteret, NJ
Feingold & Spiegel ....Los Angeles, CA
Feingold, Stanley A. ....San Rafael, CA
Feingold, Stephen W. ....New York, NY
Feingold, William Douglas ....Westfield, NJ
Feingold, William S. ....Lynnfield, MA
Feingold & Youngling, A Prof. Law Corp.
San Rafael, CA
Feinholz, Maryann L. ....Tustin, CA
Feinland, Sandy R. ....Santa Rosa, CA
Feinman, Abby L. T. ....New York, NY
Feinman, Andrew J. ....New York, NY
Feinman, Barbara A. ....Glendale, CA
Feinman, Barbara E. ....New York, NY
Feinman, David ....Brooklyn, NY
Feinman, Heidi A. ....Atlanta, GA
Feinman, Howard F. ....Eugene, OR
Feinman, Howard F., P.C. ....Eugene, OR
Feinman, James B., & Associates
Lynchburg, VA
Feinman, Jay M. ....Camden, NJ
Feinman, Jeff B. ....Cherry Hill, NJ
Philadelphia, PA
Feinman, Martin R. ....Brooklyn, NY
Feinman, Meredith A. ....Bronx, NY
Feinman, Michael B., Law Office of
Andover, MA
Boston, MA
Feinman, Michael J. ....New York, NY
Feinman, Michael S. ....Lauderhill, FL
Feinman, Paul George ....New York, NY
Feinman, Paul J. ....Lynchburg, VA
Feinman, Paul S. ....West Orange, NJ
Feinman, Roger B. ....Jamaica, NY
Feinman, Steven A. ....Davie, FL
Feinman, Steven A. ....Fort Lauderdale, FL
Feinman, Susan L. ....Cheyenne, WY
Feinman, Sylvia J. ....New York, NY
Feinman, Thomas ....Garden City, NY
Feinmark, Phyllis S. Kaplan ....New York, NY
Feinour, J. Stephen ....Harrisburg, PA
Feinrider, Nancy K. ....New York, NY
Feins, Debra Zigelbaum ....Bedford, NH
Feinsand, Howard L. ....San Francisco, CA
Feinschil, Jay M. ....Philadelphia, PA
Feinschreiber, Robert A. ....Key Biscayne, FL
Feinsilver, David ....Millburn, NJ
Feinsmith, Paul L. ....Hollywood, FL
Feinsmith, Todd ....Boston, MA
Feinsod, Herbert M. ....Brooklyn, NY
Feinsod, Paul M. ....Seattle, WA
Feinson, Julius J. ....Nutley, NJ
Feinstein, Adam H. ....Blackwood, NJ
Philadelphia, PA
Feinstein, Allen L. ....Phoenix, AZ
Feinstein, Allen S. ....Boston, MA
Feinstein, Amy P. ....Brooklyn, NY
Feinstein, Andrew A. ....Mystic, CT
Feinstein, Andrew A. ....Washington, DC
Feinstein, Arnold L. ....Atlanta, GA
Feinstein, Arthur W. ....Hartford, CT
Feinstein, Barbara Karen ....New York, NY
Feinstein, Barry A. ....Peabody, MA
Feinstein, Barry L. ....New York, NY
Feinstein, Brett ....Miami Beach, FL

Feldman, David .... Crestline, CA
Feldman, David A. .... New York, NY
Feldman, David B. .... Beverly Hills, CA
Feldman, David B. .... Boston, MA
Feldman, David E. .... Fairfax, VA
Feldman, David H. .... Baltimore, MD
Feldman, David I. .... Chicago, IL
Feldman, David J. .... Las Vegas, NV
Feldman, David M. .... New York, NY
Feldman, David M. .... New York, NY
Feldman, David M. .... New York, NY
Feldman, David M. .... Houston, TX
Feldman, David N. .... New York, NY
Feldman, Deborah G. .... Westwood, MA
Feldman, Deborah Greenberg
West Palm Beach, FL
Feldman, Deborah L.
Woodland Hills, CA
Feldman, Deborah R. .... Bedminster, NJ
Feldman, Debra L. .... Washington, DC
Feldman & Delio, LLP .... New York, NY
Feldman, Dena E. .... Miami, FL
Feldman, Dennie M. .... Houston, TX
Feldman, Donald .... Boca Raton, FL
Feldman, Donald P. .... Worcester, MA
Feldman, Donna J. .... Clearwater, FL
Feldman, Donna Reda .... Matawan, NJ
Feldman, Doreen S.
General Accounting Office,
Office of the General Counsel, GV
Feldman, Dorothy L. .... Harrisburg, PA
Feldman, Douglas M. .... Milwaukee, WI
Feldman, Earl N. .... San Diego, CA
Feldman, Earl N., Inc. .... San Diego, CA
Feldman, Eddy S. .... Beverly Hills, CA
Feldman, Edie A. .... Honolulu, HI
Feldman, Edward G. .... Los Angeles, CA
Feldman, Edward H. .... Highland, IN
Feldman, Edward S. .... Fort Lee, NJ
Feldman, Edward W. .... Chicago, IL
Feldman, Elaine B. .... Littleton, CO
Feldman, Elaine E. .... Miami, FL
Feldman, Elisa G. .... Dallas, TX
Feldman, Ellen S. .... New York, NY
Feldman, Elliot J. .... Washington, DC
Feldman, Elliott R. .... Philadelphia, PA
Feldman, Eric N. .... Wilmington, DE
Feldman, Ethan D. .... Aurora, CO
Feldman, Eugene .... New York, NY
Feldman, Evan J. .... Baltimore, MD
Feldman, Evan M. .... South Miami, FL
Feldman & Feldman .... Moorestown, NJ
Feldman & Feldman .... Huntington, NY
Roslyn, NY
Feldman and Feldman .... Philadelphia, PA
Feldman & Fiorello .... Paterson, NJ
Wayne, NJ
Feldman, Franden, Woodard & Farris
Tulsa, OK
Feldman, Franklin .... New York, NY
Feldman, Frederick M. .... Chicago, IL
Feldman, Frederick Z. .... Fort Lee, NJ
New York, NY
Feldman, Fredric J. .... Highland Park, NJ
Feldman, Fredric J., P.A. .... Highland Park, NJ
Feldman Gale & Weber, P.A. .... Suffield, CT
Fort Lauderdale, FL
Key West, FL
Miami, FL
Naples, FL
Feldman, Gary M. .... Boston, MA
Feldman, George H. .... Morristown, NJ
Feldman, Gerald A., Jr. .... Kansas City, MO
Feldman, Gilbert .... Chicago, IL
Feldman, Glenn M. .... Phoenix, AZ
Feldman, Goldie Jane .... Jackson, MS
Feldman, Gregory L. .... Livingston, NJ
Feldman, H. John .... Tavares, FL
Feldman, H. Leigh .... New York, NY
Feldman, H. Stanley .... Charleston, SC
Feldman, Hadley E. .... East Rutherford, NJ
Feldman & Halprin .... Chicago, IL
Feldman, Harry W. .... West Covina, CA
Feldman, Harvey A. .... Carlisle, PA
Feldman, Harvey I. .... St. Louis, MO
Feldman, Henry Joseph .... Denver, CO
Feldman, Herman L. .... Ellwood City, PA
Feldman, Howard A. .... New York, NY
Feldman, Howard G. .... Bethesda, MD
Feldman, Howard J. .... Washington, DC
Feldman, Howard L. .... Warwick, RI
Feldman, Howard N. .... Washington, DC
Feldman, Howard R. .... Baltimore, MD
Feldman, Howard S. .... Tucson, AZ
Feldman, Howard W. .... Springfield, IL
Feldman, Ian F. .... Bronx, NY
Feldman, Ilene J. .... New York, NY
Feldman, Ira C. .... Chicago, IL
Feldman, Ira R. .... Potomac, MD
Feldman, Ira R. .... New York, NY
Feldman, Irving B. .... Royal Oak, MI
Feldman, Irwin M. .... Cleveland, OH
Feldman, Ivan S. .... Garden City, NY
Feldman, Jack C. .... Chicago, IL
Feldman, Jacob .... Treasury Department,
Internal Revenue Service, GV
Feldman, Jacob S. .... Garden City, NY
Feldman & Jacobson .... Poughkeepsie, NY
Feldman, James A. .... Department of Justice,
Office of the Solicitor General, GV
Feldman, James H. .... Chicago, IL
Feldman, James H. .... Seattle, WA
Feldman, James M. .... Los Angeles, CA
Feldman, James T. .... Myrtle Beach, SC
Feldman, Jan .... Chicago, IL
Feldman, Jason K. .... Portland, OR
Feldman, Jay .... Tamarac, FL
Feldman, Jay, P.A. .... Fort Lauderdale, FL
Tamarac, FL
Feldman, Jeffrey A. .... San Francisco, CA
Feldman, Jeffrey A. .... Las Vegas, NV
Feldman, Jeffrey B. .... New York, NY
Feldman, Jeffrey D. .... Miami, FL
Feldman, Jeffrey H. .... Birmingham, MI
Feldman, Jeffrey H., P.C. .... Birmingham, MI
Feldman, Jeffrey M. .... Anchorage, AK
Feldman, Jeffrey M. .... Fishkill, NY
Feldman, Jeffrey S. .... Schaumburg, IL
Feldman, Jeffrey S. .... Philadelphia, PA
Feldman, Jeffry L. .... New York, NY
Feldman, Jeffry L., P.C. .... New York, NY
Feldman, Jerold
Federal Mine Safety and Health Review
Commission,
Office of the Administrative Law Judges, GV
Feldman, Jerome .... Chicago, IL
Feldman, Jerome I. .... Annapolis, MD
Feldman, Jerome I. .... New York, NY
Feldman, Jesse .... San Francisco, CA
Feldman, Jill .... San Francisco, CA
Feldman, Joan Fishbein .... Baltimore, MD
Feldman, Joan P. .... Pittsburgh, PA
Feldman, Joan W. .... Hartford, CT
Feldman, Jodi L. .... Washington, DC
Feldman, Jody Z. .... Auburn, CA
Feldman, Joel A. .... New York, NY
Feldman, Joel A., (P.S.) .... Tacoma, WA
Feldman, Joel D. .... Philadelphia, PA
Feldman, Joel H. .... Boca Raton, FL
Feldman, Joel H. .... Chicago, IL
Feldman, Joel H. .... Worcester, MA
Feldman, Joel H., P.A. .... Boca Raton, FL
Feldman, Joel M. .... Atlanta, GA
Feldman, Joel S. .... Chicago, IL
Feldman, John P. .... Washington, DC
Feldman, Jon A. .... South Orange, NJ
Feldman, Jonathan .... Rochester, NY
Feldman, Jonathan M.
Marina Del Rey, CA
Feldman, Jonathan R. .... Phoenix, AZ
Feldman, Joseph D. .... Chicago, IL
Feldman, Joshua J. .... New York, NY
Feldman, Joshua Z. .... Los Angeles, CA
Feldman, Joy Anne .... East Aurora, NY
Feldman, Julia Fink .... Boston, MA
Feldman, Julius W. .... Huntington Beach, CA
Feldman, Justin N. .... New York, NY
Feldman, Karen Katz .... Houston, TX
Feldman, Karen M. .... New York, NY
Feldman, Karin S. .... Pittsburgh, PA
Feldman, Kathryn L. .... Seattle, WA
Feldman, Kenneth C. .... Los Angeles, CA
Feldman, Kenneth D. .... Alpharetta, GA
Flower Mound, TX
Feldman, Kenneth H. .... Jersey City, NJ
Feldman, Kenneth N. .... Coral Gables, FL
Feldman, Kenneth N. .... Eugene, OR
Feldman, Kenneth S. .... New York, NY
Feldman, Kieffer & Herman, LLP
Buffalo, NY
Feldman, Kimberly A. .... Las Vegas, NV
Feldman, Kleidman & Coffey, L.L.P.
Fishkill, NY
Poughkeepsie, NY
Feldman, Koenig & Highsmith, P.A.
Key West, FL
Feldman, Kramer & Monaco, P.C.
Hauppauge, NY
New York, NY
Feldman, Kronfeld & Beatty .... New York, NY
Feldman, Lanny M. .... Fort Lauderdale, FL
Feldman, Larry .... Dallas, TX
Feldman, Larry Jason .... Baltimore, MD
Feldman, Larry, Jr. .... Shreveport, LA
Feldman, Larry R. .... Santa Monica, CA
Feldman, Laura A. .... Philadelphia, PA
Feldman, Lawrence .... Hempstead, NY
Feldman, Lawrence E., & Associates
Jenkintown, PA
Feldman, Lawrence E., & Associates
Philadelphia, PA
Feldman, Lawrence S. .... Melville, NY
Feldman, Lee S. .... Los Angeles, CA
Feldman, Leo .... Chicago, IL
Feldman, Leonard .... Boca Raton, FL
Feldman, Leonard .... New York, NY
Feldman, Leonard B. .... Smithtown, NY
Feldman, Leonard J. .... Seattle, WA
Feldman, Leonard P. .... Treasury Department,
Office of Regulations and Rulings, GV
Feldman, Leslie C., P.C. .... New York, NY
Feldman, Lewis G. .... Los Angeles, CA
Feldman, Lewis S. .... South Lake Tahoe, CA
Stateline, NV
Feldman, Linda B. .... Brooklyn, NY
Feldman, Linda I. .... New York, NY
Feldman, Linda S. .... Oakland, CA
Feldman, Lindsey S. .... Los Angeles, CA
Feldman, Lisa A. .... Palo Alto, CA
Feldman, Lisa E. .... Los Angeles, CA
Feldman, Lois S. .... West Orange, NJ
Feldman, Lori B. .... San Francisco, CA
Feldman, Lori G. .... Seattle, WA
Feldman, Lynn A. .... Roseland, NJ
Feldman, Lynn E. .... Allentown, PA
Feldman, Lynne R. .... Champaign, IL
Feldman, Marc E. .... Philadelphia, PA
Feldman, Marc H. .... Bradenton, FL
Feldman, Marc J. .... San Diego, CA
Feldman, Marc S. .... Los Angeles, CA
Feldman, Marina .... New York, NY
Feldman, Mark .... New York, NY
Feldman, Mark .... New York, NY
Feldman, Mark .... Charleston, SC
Feldman, Mark A. .... Los Angeles, CA
Feldman, Mark A. .... Brooklyn, NY
Feldman, Mark B. .... Washington, DC
Feldman, Mark H. .... Carle Place, NY
Feldman, Mark I. .... Chicago, IL
Feldman, Mark Jack .... Miami, FL
Feldman, Mark M. .... Boca Raton, FL
Feldman & Markman, L.L.P. .... New York, NY
Feldman, Martin .... Beechhurst, NY
Feldman, Martin E. .... Hollywood, FL
Feldman, Martin L. C. .... New Orleans, LA
Feldman, Martin S. .... Los Gatos, CA
Feldman, Marvin .... Scarsdale, NY
Feldman, Marvin J. .... Cleveland, OH
Feldman, Matthew A. .... New York, NY
Feldman, Max Craig .... Coraopolis, PA
Feldman, Melvin .... Chicago, IL
Feldman, Melvin M. .... Rockville, MD
Feldman, Melvin S. .... Irvine, CA
Feldman, Michael .... Farmington, CT
Feldman, Michael A. .... San Diego, CA
Feldman, Michael A. .... Naples, FL
Feldman, Michael A., Law Offices of
Brunswick, ME
Feldman, Michael E. .... New York, NY
Feldman, Michael H. .... Washington, DC
Feldman, Michael H. .... Las Vegas, NV
Feldman, Michael J. .... Newark, NJ
Feldman, Michael K.
Bay Harbor Islands, FL
Feldman, Michael R. .... Northbrook, IL
Feldman, Michael S.
Lake Buena Vista, FL
Feldman, Michael S. .... Southfield, MI
Feldman, Michael S. .... Bridgewater, NJ
Feldman, Michael S., (P.C.)
Farmington Hills, MI
Feldman, Michael Scott .... New York, NY
Feldman, Michel J. .... Chicago, IL
Feldman, Michelle S. .... Garden City, NY
Feldman, Midori Hill
San Luis Obispo, CA
Feldman, Miles J. .... Beverly Hills, CA
Feldman, Milton A. .... Philadelphia, PA
Feldman, Mitchell L. .... Miami, FL
Feldman, Monroe J. .... Atlanta, GA
Feldman, Morris S. .... Roslyn, NY
Feldman, Morton .... Atlantic City, NJ
Feldman, Muriel N. .... Department of Labor,
Pension and Welfare Benefits, GV
Feldman, Murray .... New York, NY
Feldman, Murray D. .... Boise, ID
Feldman, Murray R. .... Southfield, MI
Feldman, Murray R., P.C. .... Southfield, MI
Feldman, Myer .... Washington, DC
Feldman, Nancy D. .... New York, NY
Feldman, Nancy G. .... Tulsa, OK
Feldman, Nancy Lee .... Washington, DC
Feldman, Nancy Lee .... Arlington, VA
Arlington, VA
Feldman, Nancy S. .... Diamond Bar, CA
Feldman & Orlansky .... Anchorage, AK
Feldman, Orrin M. .... Los Angeles, CA
Feldman, Oscar H. .... Birmingham, MI
Feldman, Patricia Lulov .... New York, NY
Feldman, Paul J. .... Washington, DC
Arlington, VA
Feldman, Paul J. .... Freehold, NJ
Feldman, Paul K. .... New York, NY
Feldman, Paul L. .... Boston, MA
Feldman, Paul L. .... Moorestown, NJ
Philadelphia, PA
Feldman, Peter L. .... New York, NY
Feldman, Philip B. .... San Francisco, CA
Feldman, Phillip, Law Offices of
Los Angeles, CA
Feldman & Pinto .... Philadelphia, PA
Feldman and Pollak .... New York, NY
Feldman, Randy .... Worcester, MA
Feldman, Ray C. .... Mauston, WI
Feldman, Ray, S.C. .... Mauston, WI
Feldman, Raymond .... Los Angeles, CA
Feldman, Raymond G. .... Tulsa, OK
Feldman, Richard A. .... Coral Gables, FL
Feldman, Richard A., (P.A.) .... Roseland, NJ
Feldman, Richard B. .... New York, NY
Feldman, Richard C. .... New Haven, CT
Feldman, Richard D.
Environmental Protection Agency,
Office of the General Counsel, GV
Feldman, Richard D. .... Great Neck, NY
Feldman, Richard E. .... St. Louis, MO
Feldman, Richard E. .... New York, NY
Feldman, Richard Jay .... Atlanta, GA
Feldman, Richard P. .... Bloomington, IL
Feldman, Richard S. .... Glendale, CA
Feldman, Richard S. .... Uniondale, NY
Feldman, Ricki Ann .... White Plains, NY
Feldman & Roback .... Bradenton, FL
Feldman, Robert .... Freehold, NJ
Feldman, Robert .... New York, NY
Feldman, Robert .... New York, NY
Feldman, Robert A. .... Poughkeepsie, NY
Feldman, Robert A. .... Rochester, NY
Feldman, Robert A. .... Falls Church, VA
Feldman, Robert C. .... Dallas, TX
Feldman, Robert D. .... Montgomery, TX
Feldman, Robert E.
Federal Deposit Insurance Corporation,
Office of the Executive Secretary, GV
Feldman, Robert H. .... Phoenix, AZ
Feldman, Robert J. .... Buffalo, NY
Feldman, Robert Jay .... Baltimore, MD
Feldman, Robert K. .... Chicago, IL
Feldman, Robert L. .... Dallas, TX
Feldman, Robert Lawrence .... Hollywood, FL
Feldman, Robert N. .... Boston, MA
Feldman, Robert N. .... Niles, MI
Feldman, Robert P. .... Palo Alto, CA
Feldman, Robert S. .... Boca Raton, FL
Feldman, Robert T. .... Key West, FL
Feldman, Roberta K. .... Rochester, NY
Feldman, Robin .... Stanford, CA
Feldman, Roger D. .... Washington, DC
Feldman, Roger D. .... Boston, MA
Feldman & Rogers, L.L.P. .... Houston, TX
Feldman, Ronald .... Sherman Oaks, CA
Feldman, Ronald I. .... Chattanooga, TN
Feldman, Rubin .... Cleveland, OH
Feldman, S. Newton .... New York, NY
Feldman, Sammy .... Rochester, NY
Feldman, Samuel .... Roseland, NJ
Feldman, Samuel .... Forest Hills, NY
Feldman, Samuel B. .... West Hartford, CT
Feldman, Samuel F. .... Allentown, PA
Feldman, Samuel L. .... Atlanta, GA
Feldman, Samuel M. .... Bronx, NY
Feldman, Sandra B. .... New York, NY
Feldman, Sandra S. .... Menlo Park, CA
Feldman, Sandy K. .... New York, NY
Feldman, Saul J. .... Boston, MA
Feldman, Scott B. .... New York, NY
Feldman, Scott I. .... King Of Prussia, PA
Feldman, Scott L. .... Doylestown, PA
Feldman, Scott M. .... Chicago, IL
Feldman, Sharon D. .... New York, NY
Feldman, Shaw & Devore, A Law
Corporation .... South Lake Tahoe, CA
Stateline, NV
Feldman, Sheldon .... Washington, DC
Feldman, Shepherd & Wohlgelernter
Haddonfield, NJ
Philadelphia, PA
Feldman, Sherri M. .... Burbank, CA
Feldman, Sidney P. .... New York, NY
Feldman, Solomon .... New York, NY
Feldman, Solomon M. .... Boston, MA
Feldman, Spencer G. .... New York, NY
Feldman, Stacie .... New York, NY
Feldman, Stacie L. .... Santa Monica, CA
Feldman, Stanley C.
Department of Transportation,
National Highway Traffic Safety
Administration, GV
Feldman, Stanley G. .... Phoenix, AZ
Feldman, Stanley G. .... Southfield, MI
Feldman, Stephen A. .... Philadelphia, PA
Feldman, Stephen E. .... Huntington, NY
New York, NY
Feldman, Stephen J. .... New York, NY
Feldman, Stephen L. .... San Francisco, CA
Feldman, Stephen M. .... Washington, DC
Feldman, Stephen M.
Farmington Hills, MI
Feldman, Stephen M. .... Tulsa, OK
Feldman, Stephen M. .... Portland, OR
Feldman, Stephen M. .... Philadelphia, PA
Feldman, Stephen M., Law Offices of
Encino, CA
Feldman, Stephen M., P.C. .... Philadelphia, PA
Feldman, Stephen R. .... Seattle, WA
Feldman, Steven A. .... Roslyn, NY
Feldman, Steven David .... New York, NY
Feldman, Steven E. .... Chicago, IL
Feldman, Steven E., Law Offices of
San Diego, CA
Feldman, Steven H. .... Fort Lauderdale, FL
Feldman, Steven H. .... Portland, OR
Feldman, Steven J. .... El Toro, CA
Feldman, Steven J. .... Long Beach, CA
Feldman, Steven J. .... Pleasantville, NJ
Feldman, Steven L. .... Los Angeles, CA
Feldman, Steven L. .... Boston, MA
Feldman, Steven Mark .... New York, NY
Feldman, Steven W. .... Huntsville, AL
Feldman, Stewart A. .... Houston, TX
Feldman, Stewart A., & Associates, L.L.P.
Houston, TX
Feldman, Stewart L. .... Chicago, IL
Feldman, Stuart A. .... Chicago, IL
Feldman, Stuart A. .... Charleston, SC
Feldman, Stuart F. .... Washington, DC
Feldman, Susan L. .... Baltimore, MD
Feldman, Suzanne Q. .... Boston, MA
Feldman & Talley, LLP .... Los Angeles, CA
Feldman, Ted J. .... Washington, DC
Feldman, Teme T. .... Chicago, IL
Feldman, Theodore F. .... New York, NY
Feldman, Thomas A. .... Denver, CO
Feldman, Todd David .... Philadelphia, PA
Feldman & Troup, P.C. .... New York, NY
Feldman, Waldman & Kline, A Professional
Corporation .... San Francisco, CA
Feldman, Wallace .... Sterling, IL
Feldman, Warren B. .... Hauppauge, NY
New York, NY
Feldman, Warren H. .... Little Falls, NJ
Feldman, Warren L. .... New York, NY
Feldman, Wasser, Draper & Benson
Springfield, IL
Feldman, Wendy M. .... Boston, MA
Feldman, William .... Springfield, NJ
Feldman, William A. .... Wayne, NJ
Feldman, William M. .... Valencia, CA
Feldman, William R. .... Bethesda, MD
Arlington, VA
Feldman, Wm. .... Silver Spring, MD
Feldman, Yacoba Ann, Law Offices of
Sherman Oaks, CA
Feldman, Yacoba Ann, Law Offices of
Woodland Hills, CA
Feldmann, David S. .... Rockville, MD
Feldmann, John A. F. .... Houston, TX
Feldmann, Linda Danielle .... Potomac, MD
Feldmann, Mark C. .... Des Moines, IA
Feldmann, Mark E. .... Roanoke, VA
Feldmann, Mark R. .... Appleton, WI

Feldmann, R. Scott .... Irvine, CA
Feldmann, Robert N. .... St. Louis, MO
Feldmann, Spencer G. .... Oneida, NY
Feldmann, Steven M. .... Cincinnati, OH
Feldman-Rumpler, Leslie .... Boston, MA
Feldmeier, John P. .... Cincinnati, OH
Feldmeier, Mary Sue F. .... Waukesha, WI
Feldmeier, Melissa M. .... Cincinnati, OH
Feldmeier, Robert C. .... Chicago, IL
Feldmesser, Anthony M. .... New York, NY
Feldmiller, Amanda .... Kansas City, MO
Feldmiller, George E. .... Kansas City, MO
Feldmus, Cheryl B.
Branchburg Township, NJ
Feldner, J. Lynn .... San Diego, CA
Feldner, Paul E. .... Milwaukee, WI
Feldner, Rodney K. .... Mandan, ND
Feldpausch, Sherry Miller .... Louisville, KY
Feldscher, Bryan D. .... Cockeysville, MD
Feldscher, Joel .... Cherry Hill, NJ
Feldschreiber, Harvey .... New York, NY
Feldsher, Murray .... Bradbury, CA
Feldshon, Lee Adhemar G. .... New York, NY
Feldsott Lee & Feinberg
Newport Beach, CA
Feldsott, Stanley .... Newport Beach, CA
Feldsted, John F. .... Los Angeles, CA
Feldstein, Alan H. .... Studio City, CA
Feldstein, Alan R. .... Rochester, NY
Feldstein, Alan S. .... New York, NY
Feldstein, Allison L. .... Chicago, IL
Feldstein, Andrew R. .... Farmington Hills, MI
Feldstein, Anthony J. .... San Francisco, CA
Feldstein, David L. .... Towson, MD
Feldstein, Deborah .... Parsippany, NJ
Feldstein, Edward D. .... Providence, RI
Feldstein, Gelpi & Gotay .... San Juan, PR
Feldstein Grinberg Stein & McKee, A Professional Corporation .... Elizabeth, PA
Greensburg, PA
Pittsburgh, PA
Washington, PA
Feldstein, Helen S. .... New York, NY
Feldstein, Hydee R. .... Los Angeles, CA
Feldstein, I. H. .... Skokie, IL
Feldstein, Jay E. .... Toledo, OH
Feldstein, Jay H. .... Elizabeth, PA
Pittsburgh, PA
Feldstein, Joseph .... Trenton, NJ
Feldstein, Merrill D. .... Treasury Department, Internal Revenue Service, GV
Feldstein, Mindy L. .... Philadelphia, PA
Feldstein, Miriam L. .... New York, NY
Feldstein, Rachel E. .... Chicago, IL
Feldstein, Robert Alan .... Brooklyn, NY
Feldstein, Robert Z. .... Troy, MI
Feldstein, S. Peter .... Indian Lake, NY
Feldstein, Scott David .... Washington, DC
Feldstein, Stanley L. .... San Juan, PR
Feldstein, Steven R. .... Palo Alto, CA
Feldstein, Stuart F. .... Washington, DC
Feldstein, Stuart I. .... Ankeny, IA
Feldstein, Susan .... Birmingham, MI
Feldstein, Thomas M. .... San Francisco, CA
Feldstein-Soto, Luis A. .... Washington, DC
Feldstern, Daniel B. .... Calabasas, CA
Feldt, Darlea .... Houston, TX
Feldt, Harrell .... Houston, TX
Feldt, Judith M. .... Washington, DC
Feldt, Robert J. .... Hammond, IN
Feldt, Robert L. .... Great Bend, KS
Feldt & Roth, P.A. .... Great Bend, KS
Feldun, Joseph L. .... Encino, CA
Feldwisch, David L. .... Houston, TX
Feleen, James G. .... Claremont, NH
Felegy, Lorraine .... Albany, NY
Felentzer, Kelli .... Atlanta, GA
Feleppa, Alfred Edward, III .... St. Ignace, MI
Felfe, Peter F. .... New York, NY
Felfe, Sharon .... Austin, TX
Felger, Mark E. .... Wilmington, DE
Felger, Ronald D. .... Fort Wayne, IN
Felger, Thomas R. .... Austin, TX
Dallas, TX
Felgoise, Janet G. .... Bala Cynwyd, PA
Philadelphia, PA
Felhaber, Larson, Fenlon & Vogt, Professional Association
Minneapolis, MN
St. Paul, MN
Feliberti-Cintrón, Roberto .... San Juan, PR
Feliberty, Melba .... Flushing, NY
Felice, Andrew N. .... Washington, DC
Rockville, MD
Vienna, VA
Felice, Charles S., Jr. .... Coral Gables, FL
Felice, David M. .... Wesley Chapel, FL
Felice, Don E. .... Philadelphia, PA
Felice, J. Stephen .... Beverly Hills, CA
Felice, Jon B. .... New York, NY
Felice, Lee P. .... Bakersfield, CA
Felice, Michele R. .... Syracuse, NY
Felice, Peter A. .... Lyons, IL
Felice, Richard D. .... Wheaton, IL
Felice, Robert J. .... Altamonte Springs, FL
Felice, Robert J., P.A.
Altamonte Springs, FL
Felice, Robert L. .... Philadelphia, PA
Felice, Roger A. .... Spokane, WA
Felice, Roger A., P.S. .... Spokane, WA
Felice, Stephen J. .... Othello, WA
Felice, Victor J. .... Spokane, WA
Feliceangeli, Peter S. .... Wilmington, DE
Felicetti, Elinor .... Enfield, CT
Felicetti, Gary F. .... Orland Park, IL
Felicetti, Scott A. .... New York, NY
Felici, Nicholas A. .... Boston, MA
Feliciani, Christopher A. .... Greensburg, PA
Feliciani, Joseph L. .... Norristown, PA
Feliciano, Joel .... New York, NY
Feliciano, José C. .... Cleveland, OH
Feliciano, Julia .... St. Davids, PA
Feliciano, Marta I. .... San Juan, PR
Feliciano, Melanie A. .... Los Angeles, CA
Feliciano, Sahily H. .... Pico-Rivera, CA
Feliciano, Tanya .... New Haven, CT
Feliciano-Guzmán, Javier A.
San Juan, PR
Felicio, David J. .... Danville, PA
Felicione, Paul J. .... Mineola, NY
Felig, Elliot Miles .... New York, NY
Feliks, Deborah .... Washington, DC
Feliksik, James S. .... Chicago, IL
Felinton, Mindy .... Boynton Beach, FL
Felipe, J. Grace .... Los Angeles, CA
Felipe, Ondina .... Boca Raton, FL
Feliton, John R., Jr. .... Los Angeles, CA
Felitti, Rochelle J. .... San Diego, CA
Feliu, Alfred G. .... New York, NY
Feliu, David N. .... Bridgeport, CT
Felix, Alan R. .... Bemidji, MN
Felix, Daniel P. .... Northbrook, IL
Rosemont, IL
Felix, Diane E. .... St. Louis, MO
Felix, Elit R., II .... Philadelphia, PA
Felix, Frederick R. .... Stanwood, MI
Felix, Genevieve A. .... New York, NY
Felix, H. Thomas, II .... Philadelphia, PA
Felix, Harold A. .... New York, NY
Felix, Henry R. .... Department of Justice, Civil Division, GV
Felix, James Clarence .... Washington, DC
Felix, James M. .... Rockville Centre, NY
Felix, Jeffrey A. .... Cincinnati, OH
Felix, Jennings P. .... Seattle, WA
Felix, Jennings P., Inc., Inc., P.S.
Seattle, WA
Felix, John A. .... Phoenix, AZ
Felix, Larry F. .... Phoenix, AZ
Felix, M. Jay .... Phoenix, AZ
Tucson, AZ
Felix, Nadine G. .... Culver City, CA
Felix, Patrick J., III .... San Diego, CA
Pittsburgh, PA
Felix, Patrick J., III P.C. .... Pittsburgh, PA
Felix, Richard .... Valley Stream, NY
Felix, Robert L. .... Columbia, SC
Felix, Robert N. .... New York, NY
Felix, Robert Nicholas Charles
Hilton Head Island, SC
Felix, Robin, Law Office of .... San Diego, CA
Felix, Sarah J. .... Juneau, AK
Felix, Thomas B. .... Crown Point, IN
Felix, Tina Paraskevas
Commodity Futures Trading Commission, Division of Trading and Markets, GV
Felix, Tristram E. .... Wichita, KS
Felix, Victor M. .... San Diego, CA
Felix, Wesley D. .... Salt Lake City, UT
Felixon, Paul J. .... Philadelphia, PA
Felixson, Robert J. .... Los Angeles, CA
Felizmena, Roxanne .... Milwaukee, WI
Felkay, Robert A. .... Pittsburgh, PA
Felkel, Daniel R. .... Portland, ME
Felkel, Shonna Watson .... Greenville, SC
Felker, Barbara Allen .... Treasury Department, Internal Revenue Service, GV
Felker, Carl M. .... Roseburg, OR
Felker, Carol L. .... Exeter, NH
Felker, Daniel K. .... Columbia, SC
Felker, Daniel K. .... Seattle, WA
Felker, Frederic P. .... Superior, WI
Felker, Ish, Ritchie & Geer, P.A.
Santa Fe, NM
Felker, James V. .... Houston, TX
Felker, Kay E. .... Waukesha, WI
Felker, Kenneth B. .... Oklahoma City, OK
Felker & Lazares .... Tacoma, WA
Felker, Lonnie A. .... Los Angeles, CA
Felker, Patti C. .... Los Angeles, CA
Felker, Randolph B. .... Santa Fe, NM
Felker, Robert S. .... Tacoma, WA
Felker, Samuel Lanier .... Nashville, TN
Felker, Sidney L. .... Tucson, AZ
Felker, T. F., Jr. .... Birmingham, MI
Felker, Thomas S. .... Vashon, WA
Felker-Little, Susan Corinne .... Melbourne, FL
Felkins, Jay G. .... Fresno, CA
Felkner, Stacey Haws
Oklahoma City, OK
Felky, William M. .... New Brunswick, NJ
Fell, Alan .... New York, NY
Fell, Arthur M.
Agency for International Development, Other Offices of A.I.D., GV
Fell, Charles E., Jr. .... Louisville, KY
Fell, Charles F. .... Honolulu, HI
Fell, David W. .... Denver, CO
Fell, David W. .... Chicago, IL
Fell, Donna M. .... Denver, CO
Fell, Douglas E. .... Santa Barbara, CA
Fell, Ellis M. .... Lutherville, MD
Fell, Flaster & Eskwitt, LLP
Livingston, NJ
Red Bank, NJ
Fell, George N., II .... Toledo, OH
Fell, Howard L. .... Tucson, AZ
Fell, James F. .... Portland, OR
Fell, Jerry I. .... Wheeling, IL
Fell, John E., Jr. .... Kokomo, IN
Fell, Joseph J. .... Livingston, NJ
Fell, Lloyd C. .... Cheboygan, MI
Fell Marcus & Koder Co., L.P.A.
Toledo, OH
Fell, Marking, Abkin, Montgomery, Granet & Raney, LLP .... Santa Barbara, CA
Fell, Mary Jean .... Washington, DC
Fell, McGarvey, Trauring & Wilson
Kokomo, IN
Fell, Melissa Beth .... Tulsa, OK
Fell, Michael Scott .... Roanoke, VA
Fell, Nicholas J. .... San Francisco, CA
Fell, Norman .... Lansing, MI
Fell, Richard F. .... Hyde Park, MA
Fell, Richard M. .... Newport Beach, CA
Fell, Riley B. .... Tulsa, OK
Fell, Sheila .... Costa Mesa, CA
Fell & Spalding .... Philadelphia, PA
Fell, Thomas H. .... Las Vegas, NV
Fella, Diane Lynn .... Los Angeles, CA
Felland, Garold M. .... St. Paul, MN
Fellas, John .... New York, NY
Felle, Wayne C. .... Kenmore, NY
Niagara Falls, NY
Felleman, Frank .... Woodbourne, NY
Felleman, George P. .... New York, NY
Fellen, Leonard R. .... Manalapan, NJ
Fellen, Linda J. .... Philadelphia, PA
Fellenbaum, Neal .... Hackensack, NJ
New York, NY
Fellenz, Kim A. .... Asbury Park, NJ
Fellenz, Thomas C. .... Sacramento, CA
Feller, Adam P. .... Long Beach, NY
Feller, Andrea B. .... Brooklyn, NY
Feller, David Allan .... Honolulu, HI
Feller, David E. .... Berkeley, CA
Feller, Deena K. .... New York, NY
Feller, Elliot D. .... Atlanta, GA
Feller & Ferrentino .... Albany, NY
Feller, Fred M. .... Berkeley, CA
Feller, Gerald .... New York, NY
Feller, Howard .... Richmond, VA
Feller, Howard J. .... Portland, ME
Feller, Howard J., P.A. .... Portland, ME
Feller, Jeffrey R. .... Phoenix, AZ
Feller, Jerome .... Brooklyn, NY
Feller, Joel J. .... Philadelphia, PA
Feller, John D. .... West Point, NE
Feller, Joseph L. .... Dayton, OH
Feller, Joseph M. .... Sibley, IA
Feller, Katherine Christine .... Madison, OH
Feller, Kristie M. .... Anaheim, CA
Feller Law Office, P.C. .... West Point, NE
Feller, Lawrence J. .... Chicago, IL
Feller, Lloyd H. .... Washington, DC
Feller, Marc A. .... Philadelphia, PA
Feller, Mary Capuano .... Washington, DC
Feller, Maxine E. .... Boca Raton, FL
Feller, Millicent A. .... United States Senate, Senatorial Assistants, GV
Feller, Milton .... Miami Beach, FL
Feller, Mitchell S. .... New York, NY
Feller, Nancy .... New York, NY
Feller, Nathaniel D. .... Far Rockaway, NY
Feller, Peter Buck .... Washington, DC
Feller, Robert C. .... Troy, MI
Feller, Robert H. .... Albany, NY
Feller, S. Frederick .... Olympia, WA
Feller, Sharon Toni .... South Miami, FL
Feller, Susan .... Oakland, CA
Feller, William H. .... Des Moines, IA
Fellerath, Sheila Hogan .... Fairbanks, AK
Fellerhoff, Matthew W. .... Cincinnati, OH
Fellerhoff, William J. .... Chicago, IL
Fellerman, Gregory E .... Wilkes-Barre, PA
Fellerman, Ian P. .... Oakland, CA
Fellers, Carlton E. .... Raleigh, NC
Fellers, Dilver W. .... Pensacola, FL
Fellers, Rhonda G. .... Houston, TX
Fellers, S. L., Jr. .... Roanoke, VA
Fellers, Snider, Blankenship, Bailey & Tippens, A Professional Corporation
Oklahoma City, OK
Tulsa, OK
Felletter, Vincent J., Jr. .... Grand Junction, CO
Fellheimer, Alan S. .... Cherry Hill, NJ
Philadelphia, PA
Fellheimer Braverman & Kaskey, A Professional Corporation
Cherry Hill, NJ
Philadelphia, PA
Fellheimer, Judith Eichen .... Cherry Hill, NJ
Fellheimer Law Firm .... Pontiac, IL
Fellheimer, Mark A. .... Pontiac, IL
Fellheimer & Peters, P.C. .... Doylestown, PA
Fellheimer, Robert M. .... Doylestown, PA
Fellheimer, Ronald K. .... Pontiac, IL
Felli, Martin T. .... New York, NY
Fellig, Thomas J., Law Offices of
Hackensack, NJ
Fellin, Daniel .... Harrisburg, PA
Fellin, John K.
Equal Employment Opportunity Commission, Office of Federal Operations, GV
Felling, Darrell E. .... Terre Haute, IN
Felling, Kirsten J. .... Benton Harbor, MI
Fellinger, John G. .... New York, NY
Fellman, Douglas A. .... Washington, DC
Fellman, Gerry L. .... Pasadena, CA
Fellman, Glenn M. .... Chicago, IL
Fellman, Henry .... Boulder, CO
Fellman, Jonathan .... Omaha, NE
Fellman, Kenneth S. .... Denver, CO
Fellman, Mark J. .... St. Paul, MN
Fellman, Moylan, Natvig & Kelly
Omaha, NE
Fellman, Nancy Fisher .... Dallas, TX
Fellman, Peter J. .... Boston, MA
Fellman, Richard M. .... Omaha, NE
Fellman, Ronald M. .... Waltham, MA
Fellman, Steven John .... Washington, DC
Fellman, Susan B. .... Fanwood, NJ
Fellman, Teri W. .... Los Angeles, CA
Fellmeth, Aaron X. .... San Francisco, CA
Fellmeth, Eugene M. .... Canal Fulton, OH
Fellmeth, Robert C. .... San Diego, CA
Fellmeth, Scott E. .... Massillon, OH
Fellner, Baruch A. .... Washington, DC
Fellner, Daniel S. .... Atlanta, GA
Fellner, Gary M. .... New York, NY
Fellner, Jonathan R. .... San Francisco, CA
Fellner, Morris J. .... Hewlett, NY
Fellom, Nancy Ann .... San Francisco, CA
Fellowes, Frederick Gale, Jr. .... Vienna, VA
Fellows, Adam O. .... Texarkana, AR
Fellows, Anne E. .... Whitewater, WI
Fellows & Blake .... St. Louis, MO
Fellows, Brian J. .... St. Louis, MO
Fellows, Carol J. .... Chicago, IL
Fellows, Charles C. .... Philadelphia, PA
Fellows, D. Tyler .... Manitowoc, WI
Fellows, Damian M. .... Tucson, AZ
Fellows, Donald C. .... Milwaukee, WI
Fellows, Douglas M. .... Portland, OR
Fellows, Elizabeth A. .... Troy, MI
Fellows, G. Robert .... Delray Beach, FL
Fellows, Gage J. .... Commerce City, CO
Fellows, George W. .... Baltimore, MD
Fellows, Gerald L. .... Milwaukee, WI
Fellows, Henry D., Jr. .... Atlanta, GA
Fellows & Hymowitz, P.C. .... New City, NY
Fellows, James E. .... Omaha, NE
Fellows, Jeremy L. .... Portland, OR
Fellows, Jerry K. .... Chicago, IL
Fellows, John L., III .... Torrance, CA
Fellows, Johnson & La Briola, LLP
Atlanta, GA
Fellows, Jonathan B. .... Syracuse, NY
Fellows, Kee & Tymoczko .... Bucksport, ME
Fellows, Leland G. .... Spokane, WA
Fellows, Mary L. .... Iowa City, IA
Fellows, Merrilee .... Santa Barbara, CA
Fellows, Neil R. .... Dearborn, MI
Fellows, Oscar .... Columbia Falls, ME
Fellows, Piper & Schmidt .... Milwaukee, WI
Fellows, Ralph A. .... Reno, NV
Fellows, Richard B. .... Detroit, MI
Fellows, Robert L. .... New City, NY
Fellows, Robert V. .... Jackson Heights, NY
Fellows, Roger .... Brooklyn Park, MN
Fellows, Roger J., P.A. .... Brooklyn Park, MN
Fellows, Steven .... Southfield, MI
Fellows, Thomas R. .... San Jose, CA
Fellrath, Abbie F. .... Elkhart, IN
Fellrath, Charles V. .... Dearborn, MI
Fellrath, Douglas C. .... Oklahoma City, OK
Fellrath, John F. .... Dearborn Heights, MI
Fellrath, Richard F., Law Offices of
Detroit, MI
Fellrath, Richd. A. .... Farmington Hills, MI
Fells, Robert M. .... Reston, VA
Felluca, Ottorino .... Glen Burnie, MD
Fellus, Saul .... New York, NY
Felman, David S. .... Tampa, FL
Felman, Edward L. .... Los Angeles, CA
Felman, H. Marvin .... Dayton, OH
Felman, James E. .... Tampa, FL
Felmeister, Robert A. .... Princeton Junction, NJ
Felmet, L. Holt .... Lillington, NC
Felmly, Bruce W. .... Manchester, NH
Felnagle, Thomas J. .... Tacoma, WA
Felner, Andrew M. .... New York, NY
Felopulos, J. Peter .... Boston, MA
Felos, George J. .... Dunedin, FL
Felper, David M. .... Framingham, MA
Felps, Mary E. .... Austin, TX
Felps, Thomas M. .... Johnson City, TX
Fels, Charles W. B. .... Knoxville, TN
Fels, Gail Pollack .... Miami, FL
Fels, James A. .... Indianapolis, IN
Fels, Jerome L. .... Chicago, IL
Fels, John V. .... Phoenix, AZ
Fels, Leonard R. .... Miami, FL
Fels, Mark C. .... Springfield, MO
Fels, Nicholas W. .... Washington, DC
Fels, Peter .... Vancouver, WA
Fels, Sarah J. .... New York, NY
Felsen, Barry .... Los Angeles, CA
Felsen, Bernard D. .... El Paso, TX
Felsen, Daniel K. .... Washington, DC
Felsen, David .... Rockville, MD
Felsen, Mara F. .... Irvine, CA
Felsen, Marvin Jerome .... Fairfield, CT
Felsen, Michael D. .... Boston, MA
Felsen, Stuart D. .... Randolph, NJ
Felsen, Stuart D., P.A. .... Clifton, NJ
Denville, NJ
Dover, NJ
East Hanover, NJ
Morristown, NJ
Newark, NJ
Randolph, NJ
Felsenburg, Miriam E. (Miki)
Winston-Salem, NC
Felsenfeld, Arthur D. .... New York, NY
Felsenfeld, Howard L. .... Mercerville, NJ
Felsenfeld, Marguerite .... New York, NY
Felsenfeld, Robert .... Lake Forest, CA
Felsenstein, Darrell M. .... Paramus, NJ
Felsenstein, Max .... Bardonia, NY
Felsenstein, Steven M. .... Philadelphia, PA
Felsenthal, Charles L. .... Worcester, MA
Felsenthal, David .... New York, NY
Felsenthal, David B. .... Los Angeles, CA
Felsenthal, Jerry E. .... Chicago, IL
Felsenthal, Peter S. .... Earle, AR
Felsenthal, Steven A. .... Chicago, IL
Felsenthal, Steven A. .... New Orleans, LA
Felsenthal, Steven M. .... New York, NY
Felser, Andrew J. .... Denver, CO
Felser, Andrew J., P.C. .... Denver, CO

Felser, Jeffrey A. ... Savannah, GA
Felser, Paul H. ... Hermosa Beach, CA
Felsher, David P. ... New York, NY
Felsher, Kenneth Allan ... New York, NY
Felsinger, Mortimer N. ... New York, NY
Felsman, Bradley, Gunter & Dillon, LLP
Austin, TX
Fort Worth, TX
Houston, TX
Felsman, Robert A. ... Fort Worth, TX
Felsner, Brigitte J. ... Atlanta, GA
Felson, Cynthia C. ... Cincinnati, OH
Felson, Edgar M. ... Jacksonville, FL
Felson, Edward J. ... Cincinnati, OH
Felson, Ethan J. ... Hartford, CT
Felson & Felson ... Cincinnati, OH
Felson, Howard M. ... New York, NY
Felson, Joseph L. ... Hayward, CA
Felson, Stephen R. ... Cincinnati, OH
Felsted, H. W. ... Pasco, WA
Felsted, Wallace O. ... Salt Lake City, UT
Felsten, Nancy J. ... New York, NY
Felstiner, Reuben ... Venice, CA
Felstiner, Susan Trump ... Portland, OR
Felstiner, William L.F. ... Santa Barbara, CA
Felt, Barbara J. ... St. Paul, MN
Felt, Deborah Perfetti ... Los Angeles, CA
Felt Evans, LLP ... Clinton, NY
Oneida, NY
Utica, NY
Felt, Houghton & Monson, LLC
Colorado Springs, CO
Felt, J. David, Jr. ... Athens, GA
Eatonton, GA
Felt, J. Kay ... Detroit, MI
Felt, James G. ... Colorado Springs, CO
Felt, James H. ... Inverness, IL
Felt, James S. ... Washington, DC
Felt, Jay Bovard ... Sturgis, MI
Felt, Judith M. ... Idaho Falls, ID
Felt, Martin, Frazier, Jacobs & Rapkoch, P.C. ... Billings, MT
Felt, Paul S. ... Salt Lake City, UT
Felt, Russell C. ... St. Paul, MN
Felt, Stanton W., II ... Albuquerque, NM
Feltch, Dava M. ... Boston, MA
Felten-Green, Daphne S.
Department of Justice,
Office of Justice Programs, GV
Feltenstein, Martha ... New York, NY
Felter, Cain & Shurts ... Lebanon, NJ
Felter, Edwin L. ... Santa Fe, NM
Felter, John Kenneth, (P.C.) ... Boston, MA
Feltes, Joseph J. ... Canton, OH
Feltes, Roman ... Arcadia, WI
Feltes, Sandhya M. ... Philadelphia, PA
Feltham, Dudley H. ... New Holland, PA
Feltham, James R. ... Phoenix, AZ
Feltham, Linda D. ... Sacramento, CA
Feltham, Timothy S. ... New York, NY
Felthaus, Todd A. ... Covington, KY
Felthous, Robert A. ... Friday Harbor, WA
Felthouse, Jack C. ... Inglewood, CA
Felthousen, Kris J. ... Kitty Hawk, NC
Feltman, Art ... Hartford, CT
Feltman, Arthur A. ... Melville, NY
Feltman, Gebhardt, Eymann & Jones, P.S.
Coeur d'Alene, ID
Feltman, Gebhardt, Greer & Zeimantz, P.S.
Spokane, WA
Feltman, Jeffrey M. ... Benton, IL
Feltman, Karesh, Major & Farbman
New York, NY
Feltman, Lee ... New York, NY
Feltman, Michael P. ... Hackensack, NJ
Feltman, Nathan J. ... Chicago, IL
Feltman, Paul B. ... Miami, FL
Feltman, Richard C. ... Coeur d'Alene, ID
Spokane, WA
Feltner, David L. ... Akron, OH
Felton, Arnold ... Boston, MA
Felton, Barbara J. ... Princeton, NJ
Felton, Benjamin ... Woodland Hills, CA
Felton, Benjamin, A Law Corp.
Woodland Hills, CA
Felton, Carle A., Jr. ... Jacksonville, FL
Felton & Cave, A Professional Corporation
Richmond, VA
Felton, Cheryl ... Mineola, NY
Felton, Christopher C. ... Denver, CO
Felton, Dale W. ... Katy, TX
Felton, Daniel H., III ... Marianna, AR
Felton, Deborah M. ... Milton, MA
Felton, Duane C. ... Staten Island, NY
Felton & Felton ... Buhl, ID
Felton, Glenn P. ... Chattanooga, TN
Felton, J. Durwood, III ... Richmond, VA
Felton, J. A. (Jay) ... Kansas City, MO
Felton, James R. ... Encino, CA
Felton, Jane J. ... Los Angeles, CA
San Francisco, CA
Felton, John B. ... Philadelphia, PA
Felton, John R. ... Aurora, IL
Felton, John W. ... Gaylord, MI
Felton, Joseph M. ... Rockville, MD
Felton, Kathleen A. ... Department of Justice,
Criminal Division, GV
Felton, Koji E. ... San Francisco, CA
Felton, Margaret L. ... Naples, FL
Felton, Marla J. ... New York, NY
Felton, Michael D. ... Coral Gables, FL
Felton, Michael Harland ... Buhl, ID
Felton, Michael Hoyt ... Buhl, ID
Felton, Murray B. ... New York, NY
Felton, Nicole L. ... New York, NY
Felton, Richard I. ... Los Angeles, CA
Felton, Richard R. ... Anchorage, AK
Felton, Robert J. ... Titusville, PA
Felton, Robert M. ... Salt Lake City, UT
Felton, Thadford A. ... Chicago, IL
Felton, Timothy L. ... Weiser, ID
Felton, Vonda B. ... Columbiana, AL
Felton, W. Raymond ... Woodbridge, NJ
Felton, W. A., Jr. ... Hattiesburg, MS
Felton, Walter S., Jr. ... Williamsburg, VA
Felton, Warren J. ... New Plymouth, ID
Felton-Armouti, Veronica ... Edwardsville, IL
Felton-Elkins, Nancy ... Chicago, IL
Felton-Schnack, Shelby
Colorado Springs, CO
Feltoon, Robert N. ... Mount Laurel, NJ
Philadelphia, PA
Feltovic, Robert J. ... Windsor, CT
Feltri, Joseph V. ... Manville, NJ
Feltrup, Peter J. ... Yakima, WA
Felts, Dan ... Austin, TX
Felts, Everette A. ... Richmond, VA
Felts, Lauren C. ... Dallas, TX
Felts & Mashburn, A Professional Corporation
Austin, TX
Felts, Phillip L. ... Bethesda, MD
Felts, Robert L. ... Visalia, CA
Felts, Robinson & Duval ... Richmond, VA
Felts, Sam L., Jr. ... Sacramento, CA
Felts, Thomas J. ... Fort Wayne, IN
Feltus, James W. ... Tacoma, WA
Feltus, Richard T. ... Memphis, TN
Feltus, Susan S. ... Eden Prairie, MN
Feltus, Todd ... Phoenix, AZ
Felty, B. Kent ... Tulsa, OK
Felty, Keith P. ... Bingham Farms, MI
Felty, Kriss D. ... Cleveland, OH
Felty, Michael C. ... Oklahoma City, OK
Feltz, David A. ... St. Louis, MO
Feltz, Eugene E. ... Portland, OR
Feltz, Firmin Q. ... Ogallala, NE
Feltz, Janet L. ... Phoenix, AZ
Feluren, Mark S. ... Fort Lauderdale, FL
Fort Lauderdale, FL
Miami Beach, FL
Felver, Lloyd W. ... Laguna Niguel, CA
Felzan, John M. ... Chicago, IL
Felzen, Paul ... New York, NY
Felzenberg, Leonard J. ... Livingston, NJ
Felzenberg, Winter & Winkler, P.C.
Livingston, NJ
Felzer, Jordan W. ... Marlton, NJ
Felzer, Lawrence S. ... Philadelphia, PA
Felzer, Todd M. ... Cherry Hill, NJ
Philadelphia, PA
Felzien, Rodney L. ... Boulder, CO
Femal, Michael J. ... Palatine, IL
Feman, Sanford N. ... Palo Alto, CA
Andover, MA
Femano, Richard D. ... New York, NY
Femia, Nicholas R. ... Washington, DC
Femia, Rocco V. ... Washington, DC
Femia, Vincent J. ... Accokeek, MD
Femino, Angela C. ... Kearny, NJ
Femino, Dominic A., Jr.
Department of the Army,
Army Materiel Command, GV
Femino, Leonard F. ... Beverly, MA
Femminineo Attorneys, P.L.L.C.
Detroit, MI
Eastpointe, MI
Mount Clemens, MI
Pontiac, MI
Port Huron, MI
Femminineo, David C. ... Eastpointe, MI
Femminineo, Jacob Michael, Jr.
Eastpointe, MI
Femminineo, Jean Marie ... Eastpointe, MI
Femrite, Jeffrey J. ... Milwaukee, WI
Femrite, Marcia E. ... Birmingham, MI
Fena, Jack R. ... Hibbing, MN
Fenasci, Edward L. ... New Orleans, LA
Fenceroy, Noah A. ... Milwaukee, WI
Fenchel, David L. ... Algona, IA
Fenchel & Doster ... Algona, IA
Fenchel, James R., II ... Pittsburgh, PA
Fenchel, Joel H. ... Chicago, IL
Fenchel, Karen Shore ... Walnut Creek, CA
Fenchel, Marvin S. ... Chicago, IL
Fenchel, Saul R. ... Garden City, NY
Fencik, Joan M. ... Chicago, IL
Fencl, Glenn F. ... Chicago, IL
Fendall, Michael R. ... Portland, OR
Fendel, Frederick A., III ... Denver, CO
Fendell, Charles H. ... St. Louis, MO
Fendell, Jack ... San Francisco, CA
Fendell, Susan ... Boston, MA
Fendelman, James N. ... St. Louis, MO
Fender, Carolyn Tweed ... Elkton, MD
Fender & Fender ... Coeur d'Alene, ID
Fender, G. Steven ... Orlando, FL
Fender, Howard M. ... Fort Worth, TX
Fender, J. Steven ... Coeur d'Alene, ID
Fender, Jane Dowling ... Beaufort, SC
Fender, Jim De ... Colorado Springs, CO
Fender, Joe G. ... Houston, TX
Fender, Lynn D. ... Coeur d'Alene, ID
Fender, Michael ... Maitland, FL
Fender, Michael ... Orlando, FL
Fender, Sherwood N. ... Beaufort, SC
Fenderson, Faun ... New Orleans, LA
Fenderson, Jose W. ... Sanford, ME
Fenderson, Kathryn R.
St. Petersburg, FL
Fenderson, Matthews ... Orlando, FL
Fendia, Sara J. ... Houston, TX
Fendig, Albert, Jr. ... Brunswick, GA
Fendig, John P. ... Louisville, KY
Fendig, McLemore, Taylor, Whitworth & Durham, P.C. ... Brunswick, GA
Saint Marys, GA
Saint Simons Island, GA
Savannah, GA
Waycross, GA
Fendlason, Donald M. ... Covington, LA
Fendler, Frances ... Little Rock, AR
Fendler, Oscar ... Blytheville, AR
Fendler, S. Gene ... New Orleans, LA
Fendler, Stephen J. ... Kingston, PA
Fendley, George W., III ... Camden, AL
Fendley, John C., Jr. (P.A.)
Little Rock, AR
Fendley, John L. ... Houston, TX
Fendley, John R. ... La Grange, KY
Fendley, Mart G. ... Clarksville, TN
Fendley, Stanley G. ... Alexandria, VA
Fendley, Susan Smith ... Knoxville, TN
Fendley, T. A. Harding ... Mobile, AL
Fendon, Don A. ... Phoenix, AZ
Fendon, Don A., P.C. ... Casa Grande, AZ
Phoenix, AZ
Yuma, AZ
Fendrich, Henry M. ... Lake Mary, FL
Fendrich, Roger P. ... Washington, DC
Fendrick, Douglas Adam ... Moorestown, NJ
Fendrick, W. Keith ... Tampa, FL
Fendt, Frederick W. ... DeLand, FL
Fendt, Robert T. ... Philadelphia, PA
Fenech, Craig E. ... Denville, NJ
Fenech, Joseph C. ... Oakbrook Terrace, IL
Fenech, Joseph M. ... Burlingame, CA
Fenelli, Rick J. ... Laguna Hills, CA
Fenello, Carol A. ... Miami Lakes, FL
Fenelon, Christopher R. ... Houston, TX
Fenelon, Kathleen S. ... Houston, TX
Fenelon, Kenneth B. ... Houston, TX
Fenelon, Terence M., Law Office of
Naperville, IL
Fener, Alan R.
National Labor Relations Board,
Office of the General Counsel, GV
Fener, Diane ... Malibu, CA
Feneran, Jeannine R. ... New York, NY
Fenerty, Dennis G. ... Anchorage, AK
Fenerty, Frank B. ... New Orleans, LA
Fenerty, John F. X. ... Huntingdon Valley, PA
Fenerty, Margaret M. ... Philadelphia, PA
Fenerty, Michael Patrick ... Mount Laurel, NJ
Philadelphia, PA
Fenerty, Thomas ... Boston, MA
Fenet, Robert W. ... Baton Rouge, LA
Feng, Felicia Y. ... San Francisco, CA
Feng, Flora W. ... New York, NY
Feng, Hwa-Tsun ... Seattle, WA
Feng & Lee ... San Francisco, CA
Feng, Lillian ... Boston, MA
Feng, Paul Y. ... Los Angeles, CA
Feng, Samuel K. ... San Francisco, CA
Feng, Wendy L. ... San Francisco, CA
Fengya, Harry N., Jr. ... Clifton, NJ
Feniak, John ... Union, NJ
Fenice, Mark S. ... Harrisburg, PA
Fenichel, Abbott S. ... Walpole, MA
Fenichel, David ... New York, NY
Fenichel, Ellen Ruth ... San Francisco, CA
Fenichel, Eric R. ... Atlanta, GA
Fenick, Sharon ... Philadelphia, PA
Fenicle, Linus E. ... Camp Hill, PA
Feniello, Donald C. ... Flushing, NY
Fenig, David H. ... Falls Church, VA
Fenig, Frederick M. ... Chicago, IL
Fenig, Michael M. ... Commerce, CA
Feniger, David R. ... Sacramento, CA
Fenigstein & Kaufman, A Professional Corporation ... Los Angeles, CA
Fenigstein, S. Jack ... Los Angeles, CA
Fenik, Martin L. ... Livingston, NJ
Fenili, Mary Lou ... Denver, CO
Fenili, William J. ... Wheaton, IL
Fenimore, Brian T. ... Kansas City, MO
Fenimore, Chet A. ... Austin, TX
Fenimore, David L. ... New York, NY
Fenimore, George W. ... Beverly Hills, CA
Fenimore, John A. ... Bernardsville, NJ
Far Hills, NJ
Fenimore, Robert G. ... Macon, GA
Fening, M. Brady ... Middletown, OH
Fenix, John H. M. ... Cleveland, OH
Fenkel, Brittany T. ... Philadelphia, PA
Fenkel, David S. ... East Brunswick, NJ
Fenley & Bate, L.L.P. ... Crockett, TX
Groveton, TX
Livingston, TX
Lufkin, TX
Nacogdoches, TX
San Augustine, TX
Fenley, B. C., Jr. ... Houston, TX
Fenley, Curtis W., III ... Lufkin, TX
Fenley, Curtis W., Jr. ... Lufkin, TX
Fenley, David A. ... Kansas City, MO
Fenley, Jule T. ... Diboll, TX
Fenley, Kenneth R., Jr.
Overland Park, KS
Fenlin, Joseph P. ... Philadelphia, PA
Fenlon & Askwith ... Sault Ste. Marie, MI
Fenlon, Brian H. ... Roseland, NJ
Fenlon & Fenlon ... Mexico, MO
Fenlon, Helen B. ... Mexico, MO
Fenlon, Helene S. ... Phoenix, AZ
Fenlon, James F. ... Omaha, NE
Fenlon, Jas. J. ... Sault Ste. Marie, MI
Fenlon, John Martin ... Columbus, OH
Fenlon, Mary Ryan ... Columbus, OH
Fenlon, Mary S. ... San Antonio, TX
Fenlon, Peter C., Jr. ... Charlottesville, VA
Fenlon, Robert J. ... Minneapolis, MN
Fenlon, Robert M. ... Mexico, MO
Fenlon, Thomas B. ... New York, NY
Fenmore, Paul F. ... Rahway, NJ
Fenn, Charles Timothy ... Houston, TX
Fenn, David R. ... Cleveland, OH
Fenn, George K., Jr. ... Amenia, NY
Fenn, Jerry D. ... Salt Lake City, UT
Fenn, John G. ... Sheridan, WY
Fenn, Leonard ... Miami, FL
Fenn, Patrick B. ... New York, NY
Fenn, Paul A. ... Baltimore, MD
Fenn, Peter R. ... Jamaica Plain, MA
Fenn, Thomas O. ... Lexington, MA
Fennebresque, John C. ... Charlotte, NC
Fennegan, J. Garth ... Dallas, TX
Fennel, Scott W. ... Los Angeles, CA
Fennell, Chris F. ... Palo Alto, CA
Fennell, Christopher C. ... Culpeper, VA
Fennell, Darrell ... Vero Beach, FL
Fennell, Darrell K. ... New York, NY
Fennell, David E. ... Bellevue, WA
Fennell, Debra D. ... Rockford, IL
Fennell, Drewry N. ... Wilmington, DE
Fennell, Ervin S., Jr. ... Du Bois, PA
Fennell, F. William ... Sacramento, CA
Fennell, Jeanna G. ... Macon, GA
Fennell, Jerold V. ... Omaha, NE
Fennell, John F. ... Atherton, CA
Fennell, John J., Jr. ... Wheaton, IL
Fennell, Laura D. ... Charlotte, NC
Fennell, Lee Anne ... Washington, DC
Fennell, Mauryne S. ... Santa Fe Springs, CA
Fennell, Melvin ... Pompano Beach, FL
Fennell, Michael J. ... Matteson, IL
Fennell, Michael V. ... Portland, OR
Fennell, Monica A. ... Chicago, IL
Fennell, Patrick T. ... Roanoke, VA
Fennell, Randell T. ... Saipan, TT
Fennell, Richard B. ... Charlotte, NC
Fennell, Stephen A. ... Washington, DC
Fennell, Thomas E. ... Dallas, TX
Fennell, Thomas R. ... Troy, MI
Fennell, Timothy J. ... Oswego, NY
Fennell, Todd W. ... Vero Beach, FL
Fennell, Tommie N. ... Knoxville, TN
Fennell, William A. ... Washington, DC
Fennell, William J. ... Springfield, MA
Fennell, William P. ... San Diego, CA
Fennelly, Jane C. ... Los Angeles, CA
Fennelly, John E. ... Stuart, FL
Fennelly, Kathleen Noonan
Morristown, NJ
Fennelly, Patricia A.
Greenwood Village, CO
Fennelly, Richard P. ... Dobbs Ferry, NY
Fenneman, Rebecca A.
Federal Maritime Commission,
Office of the General Counsel, GV
Fennemore Craig, A Professional Corporation ... Phoenix, AZ
Tucson, AZ
Fenner, Barnhisel, Willis & Barlow, P.C.
Corvallis, OR
Fenner, Bradley S. ... San Francisco, CA
Fenner, David T. ... Columbus, OH
Fenner, Diane ... Bala Cynwyd, PA
Fenner, Edwin H. ... Midland, TX
Fenner, Elizabeth C. ... Northbrook, IL
Fenner, G. Michael ... Omaha, NE
Fenner, Gary A. ... Kansas City, MO
Fenner, George L., Jr. ... Wilkes-Barre, PA
Fenner, Hilary Anne ... New York, NY
Fenner, I. Bernard ... Philadelphia, PA
Fenner, Jesse Lee ... Reston, VA
Fenner, John B. ... Corvallis, OR
Fenner, John Housan, III ... Baton Rouge, LA
Fenner, John Housan, III, A Professional Law Corporation ... Baton Rouge, LA
Fenner, John P. ... Boca Raton, FL
Fenner, Kathryn Braun ... Cleveland, OH
Fenner, Kenneth A. ... Chicago, IL
Fenner, Kimberley P. ... Reno, NV
Fenner, Natalie Stroud ... Towson, MD
Fenner, Paula Martin ... Columbus, OH
Fenner & Quinn ... Bala Cynwyd, PA
Fenner, Randee G. ... Los Altos, CA
Fenner, Robert M.
National Credit Union Administration,
Office of General Counsel, GV
Fenner, Steven Charles ... Springfield, MO
Fenner, Steven J. ... Eastpointe, MI
Fenner, Stewart D., Jr. ... Mount Dora, FL
Fenner, Suzan E. ... Dallas, TX
Fenner, Thomas W. ... Stanford, CA
Fenner, Timothy D. ... Madison, WI
Fennerty, Brian S. ... Indianapolis, IN
Fennerty, Larry L. ... Indianapolis, IN
Fennessey, Dennis J. ... Columbus, OH
Fennessey, Francis B. ... Charlton, MA
Fennessy & Crocker ... Libby, MT
Fennessy, Edward J. ... Rochester, NY
Fennessy, Eileen P.
Department of Transportation,
Board of Contract Appeals, GV
Fennessy, J. F., Jr. ... Libby, MT
Fennessy, Mark J. ... Libby, MT
Fennessy, Michael A. ... Americus, GA
Fennessy, Michelle M. ... Fort Wayne, IN
Fennessy, Timothy B. ... Spokane, WA
Fennie, Bruce W. ... Rochester, NY
Fennie, Dale Graham, (Mrs.) ... Rochester, NY
Fennig, John F. ... Chicago, IL
Fennig, Robt. B. ... Milwaukee, WI
Fenniman, John ... Stuart, FL
Fenniman, John, Chartered ... Stuart, FL
Fenniman, Kathleen Patricia ... New York, NY
Fennimore, C. Thomas ... Charlotte, NC
Fenning, Alan M. ... Los Angeles, CA

Fenning, Anita ... Philadelphia, PA
Fenning, Lisa Hill ... Los Angeles, CA
Fenning, Morton C. ... Palm Springs, CA
Fenninger, Cynthia T. ... Charlotte, NC
Fenningham, John C. ... Marlton, NJ
Trevose, PA
Fenno, Amy ... Morristown, NJ
Fenno, Craig P. ... New York, NY
Fenno, Nathan R. ... Cooperstown, NY
Fenocchio, Bradford R. ... Auburn, CA
Fenoglio, Stephen ... Austin, TX
Fenolio, Ronald L. ... Olympic Valley, CA
Fenollosa, Marilyn M. ... Boston, MA
Fensholt, Edward C. ... Overland Park, KS
Fensin, Scott S. ... Milwaukee, WI
Fenske, Audrey A. ... Cleveland, OH
Fenske, Brian P. ... Houston, TX
Fenske, David R. ... Minneapolis, MN
Fenske, Jeffrey J. ... St. Paul, MN
Fenske, Karl A. ... Morristown, NJ
Fenske, Mark D. ... San Francisco, CA
Fenske, Sandra Lee ... Syracuse, NY
Fenske, Scott A. ... Washington, DC
Fensom, James B. ... Panama City, FL
Fenstemaker, Bill R. ... Elizabeth, NJ
Fenstemaker, Carl R. ... Elizabeth, NJ
Fenstemaker & Fenstemaker, P.A.
Elizabeth, NJ
Fensten, Allan M. ... Encino, CA
Fensten, Julian B. ... Los Angeles, CA
Fenster, Alan ... Beverly Hills, CA
Fenster, Albert M. ... New York, NY
Fenster, Andrew G. ... Memphis, TN
Fenster and Faerber, Professional Association ... Fort Lauderdale, FL
Plantation, FL
Fenster, Fred A. ... Beverly Hills, CA
Fenster, Herbert ... Hackensack, NJ
Fenster, Herbert L. ... Denver, CO
Washington, DC
Fenster, Jay ... New York, NY
Fenster, Jeffrey ... Bethesda, MD
Fenster, Jeffrey H. ... Atlanta, GA
Fenster, Jeffrey M. ... Plantation, FL
Fenster, Jin Park ... Los Angeles, CA
Fenster, Julie R. ... New York, NY
Fenster, Lawrence E. ... New York, NY
Fenster, Leo ... Los Angeles, CA
Fenster, Madeleine ... New York, NY
Fenster, Marc A. ... Los Angeles, CA
Fenster, Martin Brant ... Saratoga, CA
Fenster, Matthew S. ... New York, NY
Fenster, Milford ... Boynton Beach, FL
Fenster, Philip A. ... Paterson, NJ
Fenster, Robert D. ... New City, NY
Fenster, Sidney J. ... Whitestone, NY
Fenster, Simon A. ... Bayside, NY
Fenster, Stephen B. ... Hackensack, NJ
Fenster, Stephen M. ... Beverly Hills, CA
Fenster & Weiss ... New City, NY
Fensterer, Alexandra B. ... Philadelphia, PA
Fensterer, John P. ... Captiva, FL
Fensterheim, Asher ... Purchase, NY
Fensterheim & Bean, P.C.
Washington, DC
Fensterheim, G. David ... Washington, DC
Fensterheim, Robin G. ... New City, NY
Fenstermacher, Adele M. ... San Francisco, CA
Fenstermacher and Associates, P.C.
Ocean City, NJ
Harrisburg, PA
Mechanicsburg, PA
Fenstermacher, David L., Jr. ... Atlanta, GA
Fenstermacher, Donald R.
Albuquerque, NM
Fenstermacher, Donald R., P.C.
Albuquerque, NM
Fenstermacher, John R. ... Ocean City, NJ
Harrisburg, PA
Mechanicsburg, PA
Fenstermacher, O. F. ... Walnut Creek, CA
Fenstermacher, O. F., Professional Corporation ... Walnut Creek, CA
Fenstermacher, Ronald W., Jr.
Plymouth Meeting, PA
Fenstermacher, Susanne M.
Walnut Creek, CA
Fenstermacher, Theodore ... Cortland, NY
Fenstermaker, Eric B. ... Athens, OH
Fenstermaker, Norman K.
Huntington, WV
Fenstermaker, Scott ... New York, NY
Fenstermaker, Scott T. ... Dearborn, MI
Fenstermaker, Sherlynn White ... Provo, UT
Fensterman, Howard S. ... Highland Park, NJ
Fensterman, Judy ... New York, NY
Fensterman, Robert G. ... Lake Success, NY
Fenstersheib, Robert Jay
Hallandale Beach, FL
Fensterstock, Blair C. ... New York, NY
Fensterstock, David ... Great Neck, NY
Fensterstock & Partners LLP
New York, NY
Fensterwald & Alcorn, A Professional Corporation ... Vienna, VA
Fensterwald, Bernard, III ... Vienna, VA
Fenswick, Carla Fiddler ... Nashville, TN
Fent, Jerry R. ... Oklahoma City, OK
Fent, Laura Diane ... Wichita, KS
Fent, Margaret M. ... San Antonio, TX
Fent, Tomme J. ... Oklahoma City, OK
Fente, Manuel F. ... Miami, FL
Fente, Manuel F., P.A. ... Miami, FL
Fenter, Gerard J. ... Greenlawn, NY
Fenter, Marta Gail ... Midland, TX
Fentiman, Linda C. ... White Plains, NY
Fentin, Barry H. ... White Plains, NY
Fentin, Edward M. ... Los Angeles, CA
Fentin, Gary S. ... Springfield, MA
Fentin, Hildy L. ... San Diego, CA
Fentin, Susan G. ... Hartford, CT
Fentis, John ... Long Beach, CA
Fentner, John Benz, Jr. ... Unionville, CT
Fenton, Alan ... Santa Barbara, CA
Fenton, Alan N. ... La Mesa, CA
Fenton, Albert B. ... Dallas, TX
Fenton, Angela M. ... Charleston, WV
Fenton, Ben P. ... Los Angeles, CA
Fenton, Bruce ... New York, NY
Fenton, Bruce K. ... Philadelphia, PA
Fenton, Bruce S. ... Cincinnati, OH
Fenton, Chapman, Fenton, Smith & Kane, P.A. ... Bar Harbor, ME
Ellsworth, ME
Fenton, Charles E. ... Towson, MD
Fenton, Charles F., III ... Kennesaw, GA
Fenton, Daniel B. ... Amherst, NH
Fenton, David J. ... Lowell, MA
Fenton, Diane B. ... Norfolk, VA
Fenton, Diane B. ... Virginia Beach, VA
Fenton, Donald M. ... Margaretville, NY
Fenton, Donna Siobhan ... Falls Church, VA
Fenton, Elliott C. ... Oklahoma City, OK
Fenton & Fenton ... Encino, CA
Fenton, Fenton, Smith, Reneau & Moon
Oklahoma City, OK
Tulsa, OK
Fenton & Fenton, The Firm of
Springfield, MA
Fenton, Georgia Lea ... Richmond, TX
Fenton, Gillian M. ... Cambridge, MA
Fenton, Harry W. ... Lebanon, PA
Fenton, Henry R. ... Los Angeles, CA
Fenton, Jack R. ... Dallas, TX
Fenton, James P. ... Fort Wayne, IN
Fenton, James S. ... Northbrook, IL
Fenton, Jessica Vartanian ... Boulder, CO
Fenton, Joanne ... Beaumont, CA
Fenton, John E., Jr. ... Boston, MA
Fenton, Julia Anne ... Chicago, IL
Fenton, Kathryn M. ... Washington, DC
Fenton & Keller, A Professional Corporation
Monterey, CA
Fenton, Lauren Walker ... Denver, CO
Fenton, Laurence W. ... Wilmington, DE
Fenton, Leslye S. ... Fairfax, VA
Fenton, Lewis L. ... Monterey, CA
San Jose, CA
Fenton, Linda ... Los Angeles, CA
Fenton, Loring I. ... New York, NY
Fenton, M. William ... State College, PA
Fenton, Marc I. ... Chicago, IL
Fenton, Margaret S. ... Muenster, TX
Fenton, Mason L. ... Santa Ana, CA
Fenton, Michael F. ... York, PA
Fenton, Michael J. ... Springfield, MA
Fenton, Milton ... Valley Village, CA
Fenton, Mitchell ... New York, NY
Fenton, Mitchell L. ... Los Angeles, CA
Fenton, Nancy Elizabeth ... Oakland, CA
Fenton, Nathaniel R. ... Bar Harbor, ME
Fenton, Nicole L. ... New York, NY
Fenton, Paul S. ... Seattle, WA
Fenton, Paul S., Inc., Inc., P.S. ... Seattle, WA
Fenton, Paula B. ... New York, NY
Fenton, Peter P. ... Springfield, MA
Fenton, Peter W. ... Marietta, GA
Fenton, Priscilla M. ... Indialantic, FL
Fenton, Ray A. ... Des Moines, IA
Fenton, Richard L. ... Chicago, IL
Fenton, Richard L. ... Timonium, MD
Fenton, Richard T. ... Farmington Hills, MI
Fenton, Robert L. ... Encino, CA
Fenton, Ronald E. ... Marshalltown, IA
Fenton, Scott T. ... Boston, MA
Fenton, Seth M.L. ... New York, NY
Fenton, Stephan H. ... Northampton, MA
Fenton, Stephenie A. ... Dunedin, FL
Fenton, Thaddeus G. ... Dallas, TX
Fenton, Thomas C. ... Louisville, KY
Fenton, Thomas E., A Professional Corporation
Fairbanks, AK
Fenton, Virginia D. ... Lehigh Acres, FL
Fenton, Wendell ... Wilmington, DE
Fenton, William ... Bar Harbor, ME
Fenton, William B. ... Department of Justice,
Civil Rights Division, GV
Fenton, William J. ... Taunton, MA
Fenton-Iler, Ruby D. ... Louisville, KY
Fentonmiller, Keith R. ... Washington, DC
Fentonmiller, Laura C. ... Washington, DC
Fentress, A. Lee ... McLean, VA
Fentress, Irving L. ... Nashville, TN
Fentress, J. Russell, IV ... Norfolk, VA
Fentress, Larry E. ... Frankfort, KY
Fentress, Lisa D. ... Washington, DC
Fentress, Lori J. ... New Orleans, LA
Fentress, Marvin A. ... Savannah, GA
Fentress, Susan Bennett ... Cordova, TN
Fentriss, Anna Cam ... Tallahassee, FL
Fenwick, Ann E. ... Princeton, NJ
Fenwick, Anthony I. ... Menlo Park, CA
Fenwick, Bruce R. ... East Elmhurst, NY
Fenwick, Carrie Goodwin
Charleston, WV
Fenwick, Dennis T. ... Sacramento, CA
Fenwick, Edward C. ... Kosciusko, MS
Fenwick, Francis E. ... Washington, DC
Fenwick, J. David ... Charleston, WV
Fenwick, John B. ... Bronx, NY
Fenwick, Kathleen E. ... Houston, TX
Fenwick, Kimberly S. ... Charleston, WV
Fenwick, Lila Althea ... New York, NY
Fenwick, Lynda Beck ... Aledo, TX
Fenwick, Timothy S. ... Akron, OH
Fenwick & West LLP ... Palo Alto, CA
San Francisco, CA
Washington, DC
Fenwick, William A. ... Palo Alto, CA
Fenyes, Elek A. ... Philadelphia, PA
Fenyes, Richard A. ... New York, NY
Fenyk, Mark B. ... Marion, VA
Fenz, Nicole C. ... Yakima, WA
Fenzel & Associates ... Princeton, NJ
New York, NY
White Plains, NY
Fenzel, H. Jerome ... Ellicott City, MD
Fenzel, Joseph E. ... Milwaukee, WI
Fenzel, Mark S. ... Louisville, KY
Fenzel, Peter D. ... Princeton, NJ
New York, NY
Fenzl, Terry E. ... Phoenix, AZ
Feo, Edwin F. ... Los Angeles, CA
Feofanov, Dmitry ... Naperville, IL
Feola, Dennis L. ... Parma Heights, OH
Feola, Eugene David ... Enfield, CT
Feola, Phil T. ... Washington, DC
Feola, Steven ... Phoenix, AZ
Feola, Thomas P. ... Miami, FL
Feola, Thomas P., P.A. ... Miami, FL
Feola-Guerrieri, Nathalie ... Bridgeport, CT
Feole, Ronald A. ... St. Paul, MN
Feord, Bernard G., Jr. ... McLean, VA
Feore, John R., Jr. ... Washington, DC
Fera, Peter A. ... Orland Park, IL
Fera, Sam Della, Jr. ... Newark, NJ
Ferace, Gene A. ... Greensburg, PA
Ferachi, Michael David ... Baton Rouge, LA
Feran, Amy Rollason ... Cleveland, OH
Ferando, Elizabeth L. ... New York, NY
Ferar, Katherine A. ... Novato, CA
Feraru, Kenneth ... Garden City, NY
Ferazani, Lawrence P., Jr. ... Boston, MA
Ferazzi, Christopher A. ... Houston, TX
Ferb, R J, Law Offices ... Somerville, NJ
Ferb, Robert J. ... Somerville, NJ
Ferbend & Ferbend, Ltd. ... Chicago, IL
Ferber, Alan L. ... Department of Justice,
Justice Management Division, GV
Ferber, Betty N. ... Rockville, MD
Ferber, Brian J. ... Los Angeles, CA
Ferber, David ... Washington, DC
Ferber, David H. ... Concord, NH
Keene, NH
Portsmouth, NH
Ferber, David I. ... New York, NY
Ferber, Elmer ... Ventura, CA
Ferber, Gabriel J. ... Buffalo, NY
Ferber, Gary S. ... Sandusky, OH
Ferber, James M. L. ... Columbus, OH
Ferber, Judith R. ... Washington, DC
Ferber, Laurie R. ... New York, NY
Ferber, Leonard A. ... Chicago, IL
Ferber, Marilyn Sue ... Covington, LA
Ferber, Michelle R. ... Danville, CA
Ferber, Paul R. ... St. Louis, MO
Ferber, Peggy Lynn ... Pittsburgh, PA
Ferber, R. Scott ... Columbus, OH
Ferber, Rachel Best ... Chicago, IL
Ferber, Richard D. ... Hunt Valley, MD
Ferber, Robert A. ... Los Angeles, CA
Ferber, Rosamond S. ... Treasury Department,
Internal Revenue Service, GV
Ferber, Ruth S. ... Philadelphia, PA
Ferber, Stanley ... New York, NY
Ferber, Steven B. ... Hauppauge, NY
Ferber, Tom J. ... New York, NY
Ferchill, Cary A. ... Austin, TX
Ferchland Law Office ... Santa Rosa, CA
Ferchland, William T. ... Santa Rosa, CA
Ferdenzi, Joseph N. ... Bronx, NY
Ferdenzi, Paul J. ... Lyndhurst, NJ
Ferder, Brandt, Casebeer, Cooper, Hoyt and French, L.L.P. ... Salem, OR
Ferder, Paul M. ... Salem, OR
Ferdico, Christopher M. ... Lincoln, NE
Ferdie, Ainslee R. ... Coral Gables, FL
Ferdie & Gouz ... Coral Gables, FL
Ferdinand, Deborah M. ... New York, NY
Ferdinand, Jon J. ... Fort Lauderdale, FL
Ferdinand, Joseph R. ... Hazleton, PA
Ferdinand & Klayman, A Professional Corporation ... Springfield, NJ
Ferdinand, Lane M. ... Springfield, NJ
Ferdinand, Sharon R. Bitzel ... Sugarloaf, PA
Ferdinand & Sullivan, P.A.
Fort Lauderdale, FL
Ferdinand, William V., Jr. ... Augusta, ME
Ferdinandi, Steven J. ... Cranston, RI
Ferdinands, Paul K. ... Atlanta, GA
Ferdman, Michael E. ... Buffalo, NY
Ferdon, Dennis A. ... Norwich, CT
Ferdon, Julie ... Tucson, AZ
Ferdon, Robert E. ... New York, NY
Ferdon, Timothy J. ... San Francisco, CA
Ferdows, Hesam ... Burlingame, CA
Ferdows, Sam ... Burlingame, CA
Ferebee, Claude W. ... Fort Worth, TX
Houston, TX
Ferebee, David B. ... Jacksonville, FL
Ferebee, David B., P.A. ... Jacksonville, FL
St. Augustine, FL
Ferebee, William C. ... Houston, TX
Fereday, Jeffrey C. ... Boise, ID
Feren & Flynn ... New York, NY
Feren, Louis ... New York, NY
Feren, Steven Brian ... Sunrise, FL
Ferenbach, Cam ... Las Vegas, NV
Ferenbach, Gregory ... Alexandria, VA
Ferenc, Neal D. ... Burlington, VT
Ferenc, Richard P. ... Batavia, OH
Ference & Associates ... Pittsburgh, PA
Ference, David ... Ogden, UT
Ference, Ference & Cicirelli, P.C.
Westland, MI
Ference, Gary A. ... Westland, MI
Ference, George R. ... Atlanta, GA
Ference, Michael H. ... New York, NY
Ference, Stanley D., III ... Pittsburgh, PA
Ference, Stanley J. ... Westland, MI
Ferencek, Paul J. ... Milford, CT
Ferenchak, Brett P. ... Washington, DC
Ferencik, Eugene Kirby ... Hempstead, NY
Ferencik, Libanoff, Brandt & Bustamante, P.A. ... Fort Lauderdale, FL
Miami, FL
Ferencik, Robert E., Jr.
Fort Lauderdale, FL
Ferency, Elizabeth M. ... Santa Ana, CA
Ferency, James C. ... Midland, MI
Ferencz, Bradley J. ... New Brunswick, NJ
Ferencz, Glenn E. ... Chicago, IL
Ferencz, Robert A. ... Chicago, IL
Ferenczy, Ilene H. ... Atlanta, GA
Fereno, Gary M. ...
Department of State, GV
Ferens, Donald B. ... Allendale, NJ
Ferens, J. E., Jr. ... Uniontown, PA
Ferenstein, Marvin L. ... Mitchell, OR
Ferentz, Carol A. ... Newark, NJ
Ferentz, Jeff D., (P.C.)
Newport Beach, CA
Ferenz, David G. ... Poughkeepsie, NY
Ferenz, Walter S. ... Half Moon Bay, CA
Ferenzo, André L. ... Roslyn Heights, NY
Ferer, Lyn Jaques ... Omaha, NE
Feres, Jennifer ... Foothill Ranch, CA
Ferestad, Mark Allen ... Cincinnati, OH
Ferester, Philip ... Olympia, WA
Ferestien, Dana A. ... Seattle, WA
Feretic, James J. ... Bronx, NY
Ferg, Bruce E. ... Brockton, MA
Ferg, Bruce M. ... Tucson, AZ
Ferg, Robert A. ... Chippewa Falls, WI
Fergal, James M. ... Milwaukee, WI
Fergang, Julie A. ... New York, NY
Fergason, Jane D. ... Dallas, TX
Fergason, Rodney Dean ... Chickasha, OK
Fergel, Andrew L. ... Pierre, SD
Fergenson, Arthur F. ... Baltimore, MD
Ferger, Kathryn ... Washington, DC
Fergerson, Brandon Beatty ... Kansas City, MO
Fergerson, Monique N. ... Charleston, SC
Fergerson, Ranada R ... New York, NY
Fergeson, James O., Jr. ... Longboat Key, FL
Sarasota, FL
Fergeson, Skipper, Shaw, Keyser, Baron & Tirabassi, P.A. ... Longboat Key, FL
Port Charlotte, FL
Sarasota, FL
Fergestrom, Michael J. ... Southfield, MI
Fergoda, Carolyn M. ... Pasadena, CA
Fergus, Clark ... Santa Ana, CA
Fergus, Dan M. ... Abilene, TX
Fergus, Dan M., Jr. ... Abilene, TX
Fergus, Donald E., Jr. ... Orange, CA
Fergus & Fergus, L.L.P. ... Abilene, TX
Fergus, Gary S. ... San Francisco, CA
Fergus, Harold V., Jr. ... Washington, PA
Fergus, John C., II ... Columbus, OH
Fergus, Kevin B. ... Columbus, OH
Fergus, Margaret ... Kew Gardens, NY
Fergus, Martin and Fergus ... Washington, PA
Fergus, Mary Ann ... Abilene, TX
Fergus, Nellie M. ... Pittsburgh, PA
Fergus, Ronda Hartman ... Columbus, OH
Fergus, Scott H. ... Washington, PA
Fergus, Wm. Lee ... Osceola, AR
Ferguson, Aalon ... Mount Pleasant, TX
Ferguson, Alan E. ... San Diego, CA
Ferguson, Alan E. ... Greensboro, NC
Ferguson, Alfred E. ... Huntington, WV
Ferguson, Alfred L. ... Newark, NJ
Ferguson, Alisia ... Baltimore, MD
Ferguson, Amy H. ... Atlanta, GA
Ferguson, Andrew ... Blair, NE
Ferguson, Andrew M. ... Flint, MI
Saginaw, MI
Ferguson, Andrew R. ... Albany, NY
Ferguson, Angela ... Orlando, FL
Ferguson, Angela J. ... Kansas City, MO
Ferguson, Anna M. ... Visalia, CA
Ferguson, Anne E. ... Sacramento, CA
Ferguson, Anthony B. ... Chicago, IL
Ferguson, Anthony K. ... Lewiston, ME
Ferguson, April R. Wyss ... Memphis, TN
Ferguson, Arthur B., Jr. ... Aspen, CO
Ferguson, Arthur J. ... Arlington, VA
Ferguson, Barbara A. ... Omaha, NE
Ferguson, Barbara B. ... Dallas, TX
Ferguson, Barbara J. ... Santa Ana, CA
Ferguson & Berland, P.C. ... Berkeley, CA
Ferguson, Bernard J. ... Naples, FL
Ferguson & Bernheimer ... Palm Desert, CA
Ferguson, Beth ... Bloomington, IL
Ferguson, Bethel ... Jackson, MS
Ferguson, Blaine R. ... Salt Lake City, UT
Ferguson, Blair Q. ... Wilmington, DE
Ferguson, Boyd A. ... Salt Lake City, UT
Ferguson, Bradford L. ... Chicago, IL
Ferguson, Brenda Renee ... Houston, TX
Ferguson, Brian E. ... Washington, DC
Ferguson, C. Alan ... San Antonio, TX
Ferguson, C. Douglas ... Chicago, IL
Ferguson, C. Hope ... Easton, MD
Ferguson, C. Phillips ... Suffolk, VA
Ferguson, C. Robert ... Claremont, CA
Ferguson, C. Stephen ... Charleston, IL
Ferguson, Cameron M. ... Boone, NC
Ferguson, Candace Chappell ... Irving, TX
Ferguson, Carl G. ... Greenville, SC

Ferguson, Carter L. ....Fort Worth, TX
Ferguson, Case, Orr, Paterson & Cunningham LLP ....Ventura, CA
Ferguson, Catherine A. ....Washington, DC
Ferguson, Charles A. ....San Francisco, CA
Ferguson, Charles M. ....Cuthbert, GA
Ferguson, Charles M. ....Harrisburg, IL
Ferguson, Charles M. ....New York, NY
Ferguson, Charles M., II ....Kansas City, MO
Ferguson, Charles R. ....St. Louis, MO
Ferguson, Charles S. ....Seattle, WA
Ferguson, Charles W. ....Jackson, MS
Ferguson, Charles W., III ....Wayne, WV
Ferguson, Charles W., IV ....Huntington, WV
Ferguson, Chas. W. ....Louisville, KY
Ferguson, Christina Dawn ....Fort Smith, AR
Ferguson, Christopher C. ....St. Petersburg, FL
Ferguson, Cindy A. ....Sarasota, FL
Ferguson, Clarence M. ....Groesbeck, TX
Ferguson, Claud F., Jr. ....Goldsboro, NC
Ferguson, Clifford D. ....West Nyack, NY
Ferguson, Craig C. ....Lyons, CO
Ferguson, Curt W. ....Salem, IL
Ferguson, D. Lynne ....Lancaster, PA
Ferguson, D. Robb ....Munising, MI
Ferguson, Dale C. ....Lake City, FL
Ferguson, Dale E. ....Reno, NV
Ferguson, Dallas E. ....Tulsa, OK
Ferguson, Dana L. ....Atlanta, GA
Ferguson, Daniel C. ....Littleton, CO
Ferguson, Daniel L. ....San Bernardino, CA
Ferguson, Danny T. ....Winston-Salem, NC
Ferguson, David D. ....Kansas City, MO
Ferguson, David E. ....Haddonfield, NJ
Ferguson, David H. ....Akron, OH
Ferguson, David L. ....West Palm Beach, FL
Ferguson, David L. ....Bloomington, IN
Ferguson, David L. ....Westwood, MA
Ferguson, David L. ....Asheville, NC
Ferguson, David R. ....New York, NY
Ferguson, David W. ....Escondido, CA
Ferguson, David W. ....New York, NY
Ferguson, Dean W. ....Dallas, TX
Ferguson, Dennis C. ....Salt Lake City, UT
Ferguson, Dennis R. ....West Hartford, CT
Ferguson, Dennis R. ....Tampa, FL
Ferguson, Dennis V. ....Cincinnati, OH
Ferguson, Dillon J. ....Austin, TX
Houston, TX
Ferguson, Dionne J. ....Brandon, FL
Ferguson & Doctor ....Wellington, KS
Ferguson, Donald ....White Plains, NY
Ferguson, Donald A. ....Denver, CO
Ferguson, Donald L. ....Boca Raton, FL
Ferguson, Donald L. ....Greenville, SC
Ferguson, Donald O. ....San Antonio, TX
Ferguson, Donald P. ....Chickasha, OK
Ferguson, Donald R. ....Redlands, CA
Yucaipa, CA
Ferguson, Donald R. ....Richmond, VA
Ferguson, Dorothy H. ....Rochester, NY
Ferguson, Douglas B. ....Lake Oswego, OR
Ferguson, Douglas K. ....Dayton, OH
Ferguson, Douglas P. ....Mill Valley, CA
Ferguson, Douglas R. ....Denver, CO
Ferguson, Douglas W. ....Meadville, PA
Ferguson & Doyle ....Rocky Hill, CT
Ferguson, Dudley M. ....Gloversville, NY
Ferguson, Dwight D. ....Pittsburgh, PA
Ferguson, E. Grier ....Suffolk, VA
Ferguson, Edward C. ....Edwardsville, IL
Ferguson, Edward L., Jr.
Washington, DC
Ferguson, Edward M.
Department of Housing and Urban Development,
Office of General Counsel, GV
Ferguson, Edward T., III ....New York, NY
Ferguson, Edwin E. ....Bethesda, MD
Ferguson, Edwin H., Jr. ....Concord, NC
Ferguson, Egbert R., Jr.
Chevy Chase, MD
Ferguson, Eileen D. ....Liberty Corner, NJ
Ferguson, Emmet F., III ....Jacksonville, FL
Ferguson, Emmet M. ....United States Senate,
Committee Legal Personnel, GV
Ferguson, Eric H. ....Rocky Mount, VA
Ferguson, Fall ....Palo Alto, CA
Portland, ME
Ferguson & Ferguson ....Huntsville, AL
Ferguson & Ferguson ....Bloomington, IN
Ferguson & Ferguson
North Kansas City, MO
Ferguson Firm ....Beaumont, TX
Ferguson, Floyd E. ....Stone Mountain, GA
Ferguson, Franklin L., Jr. ....Los Angeles, CA
Ferguson, Fred E., Jr. ....Phoenix, AZ
Ferguson, Frederick C. ....Brick Town, NJ
Montclair, NJ
Ferguson, Frost & Dodson, LLP
Birmingham, AL
Ferguson, G. Douglas ....Everett, WA
Ferguson, Gail E. ....Tallahassee, FL
Ferguson, Gary B. ....Salt Lake City, UT
Ferguson, Geoffrey R. ....Austin, TX
Ferguson, George H. ....Elyria, OH
Ferguson, Gerald J. ....Jersey City, NJ
New York, NY
Ferguson, Gerald J., Jr. ....McLean, VA
Ferguson, Gerald P. ....Columbus, OH
Ferguson, Gibbs ....McGehee, AR
Ferguson, Gille & Romaine ....Brick Town, NJ
Montclair, NJ
Ferguson, Glen K. ....Seattle, WA
Ferguson, Glenn R. ....Plainfield, NJ
Ferguson, Gordon S. ....Glastonbury, CT
Ferguson, Gregory ....Rockville, MD
Ferguson & Hanlon ....Akron, OH
Ferguson, Harold L., Jr. ....Birmingham, AL
Ferguson, Harold V., Jr. ....New York, NY
Ferguson, Harvey, Jr. ....Corpus Christi, TX
Ferguson & Hayes ....New York, NY
Ferguson & Heck ....Chickasha, OK
Ferguson, Henry L., III ....Worcester, MA
Ferguson, Herbert H. ....Sarasota, FL
Ferguson & Hix ....Boerne, TX
Ferguson, Howell L. ....Tampa, FL
Ferguson, Hugh W., III ....Dallas, TX
Ferguson, J. Bruce ....New York, NY
Ferguson, Jack N. ....El Paso, TX
Ferguson, Jackie D. ....Huntsville, AL
Ferguson, James ....Washington, DC
Ferguson, James A. ....Washington, DC
Ferguson, James A. ....Clearwater, FL
Ferguson, James B., Jr. ....Bronx, NY
Ferguson, James C. ....Rocky Hill, CT
Ferguson, James C. ....Baton Rouge, LA
Ferguson, James C. ....Oklahoma City, OK
Ferguson, James Cato ....Palm Desert, CA
Ferguson, James E., II ....Charlotte, NC
Ferguson, James E., III ....Birmingham, AL
Ferguson, James E., III ....Charlotte, NC
Ferguson, James F. ....Atlantic City, NJ
Ferguson, James H. ....Bloomington, IN
Ferguson, James H. ....Memphis, TN
Ferguson, James J., Jr. ....Fairfax, VA
Ferguson, James M., III ....Pittsburgh, PA
Ferguson, James P. ....San Diego, CA
Ferguson, James P. ....Springfield, MO
Ferguson, James P. ....Houston, TX
Ferguson, James R. ....Chicago, IL
Ferguson, James Richard ....Brooklyn, NY
Ferguson, James S. ....Missoula, MT
Ferguson, James W. ....Richmond, KY
Ferguson, James W. ....Houston, TX
Ferguson, Jan ....Austin, TX
Ferguson, Jana M. ....Dallas, TX
Ferguson, Janet R. ....Dallas, TX
Ferguson, Janette L. ....Costa Mesa, CA
Ferguson, Janice H. ....Denver, CO
Ferguson, Jas. E. ....Cleburne, TX
Ferguson, Jay A. ....Omaha, NE
Ferguson, Jay H. ....Graham, NC
Ferguson, Jeffrey ....Las Vegas, NV
Ferguson, Jeffrey W. ....Washington, DC
Ferguson, Jeffrey W. ....Toledo, OH
Ferguson, Jeffry D. ....Bethel, OH
Ferguson, Jennifer Clifton
Kansas City, MO
Ferguson, Jennifer Nichols ....Lewiston, ME
Ferguson, Jill ....Durango, CO
Ferguson, Jill Ellen ....Houston, TX
Ferguson, Jo M. ....Louisville, KY
Ferguson, Jodi Lynne ....Newark, NJ
Ferguson, John A., Jr. ....Atlanta, GA
Ferguson, John A., Jr. ....Houston, TX
Ferguson, John A., Jr. ....San Antonio, TX
Ferguson, John A M, Jr. ....Grand Rapids, MI
Ferguson, John B. ....Roanoke, VA
Ferguson, John H.
National Labor Relations Board,
Office of the General Counsel, GV
Ferguson, John J. ....Greenwich, CT
Ferguson, John J. ....Portland, OR
Ferguson, John M. ....Belleville, IL
Ferguson, John M. ....New York, NY
Ferguson, John P. ....Daytona Beach, FL
Ferguson, John R. ....Washington, DC
Ferguson, John R. ....Laurens, SC
Ferguson, John S. ....Syracuse, NY
Ferguson, John T. ....Big Spring, TX
Ferguson, John T., II ....Middlebury, CT
Ferguson, John Tye ....Zebulon, GA
Ferguson, John W., Jr. ....Tyler, TX
Ferguson, Johnathan A. ....Fort Pierce, FL
Ferguson and Johnson, P.A. ....Springvale, ME
Ferguson, Jon David ....San Bernardino, CA
Ferguson, Jon P. ....Seattle, WA
Ferguson, Joseph G. ....Wilkes-Barre, PA
Ferguson, Joseph L. ....New Iberia, LA
Ferguson, Joseph M., III ....Atlanta, GA
Ferguson, Joseph M., III, P.C.
Atlanta, GA
Ferguson, Joseph V., III ....Duluth, MN
Ferguson, Karen L. ....Traverse City, MI
Ferguson, Karen W. ....Washington, DC
Ferguson, Kathi Lee ....Sneads, FL
Ferguson, Kathryn C. ....Trenton, NJ
Ferguson, Katie Seals ....Tuscaloosa, AL
Ferguson, Keith ....Dayton, IA
Ferguson, Keith W. ....St. Joseph, MO
Ferguson, Kenneth ....Stockton, CA
Ferguson, Kenneth D. ....Kansas City, MO
Ferguson, Kenneth J. ....Austin, TX
Ferguson, Kevin L. ....Madison, WI
Ferguson, Kevin M. ....Toledo, OH
Ferguson, L. Kyle ....Dallas, TX
Ferguson, L. Lee ....Medford, OR
Ferguson, Lance ....Cuba, MO
Ferguson, Larry J. ....Ann Arbor, MI
Ferguson, Laura G. ....Washington, DC
Ferguson, Laura M. ....Lexington, KY
Ferguson Law Firm, P.C.
Georgetown, SC
Myrtle Beach, SC
Ferguson Law Offices ....Sacramento, CA
Ferguson, Lawrence W. ....Columbia, MO
Ferguson, Lester L. ....Xenia, OH
Ferguson, Lewis H., III ....Washington, DC
Ferguson, Linda T. ....Los Angeles, CA
Ferguson, Lisa Bucci ....Arlington, VA
Ferguson, Lloyd E. ....Austin, TX
Ferguson, Lori Campione
San Antonio, TX
Ferguson, Luanne Eagle
St. Petersburg, FL
Ferguson, Lucian M. ....Alexandria, VA
Ferguson, M. Carr, Jr. ....New York, NY
Ferguson, M. Eugene ....Tampa, FL
Ferguson, Margaret ....New York, NY
Ferguson, Margaret H. ....Petersburg, VA
Ferguson, Margarita H.
Highland Heights, KY
Ferguson, Marion T. ....Rutland, VT
Ferguson, Mark A. ....Overland Park, KS
Ferguson, Mark A. ....San Antonio, TX
Ferguson, Mark A. ....Charleston, WV
Ferguson, Mark E. ....Denver, CO
Chicago, IL
Ferguson, Mark E. ....Mattoon, IL
Ferguson, Mark E., Ltd. ....Mattoon, IL
Ferguson, Mark G. ....McLean, VA
Ferguson, Mark G., P.C., Law Office of
McLean, VA
Ferguson, Mark M. ....San Antonio, TX
Ferguson, Marvin J. ....North Kansas City, MO
Ferguson, Mary Ann ....Walkersville, MD
Ferguson, Mary B. ....Buffalo, NY
Ferguson, Mary-Olga ....Houston, TX
Ferguson, Matthew C. ....Aspen, CO
Ferguson, Matthew R. ....Glendora, CA
Ferguson, Matthew W. ....Bloomington, IN
Ferguson & McGraw ....Gastonia, NC
Ferguson, Melissa J. ....Atlanta, GA
Ferguson, Melvin D. ....Klamath Falls, OR
Ferguson, Michael ....Lake Success, NY
Ferguson, Michael C. ....Berkeley, CA
Ferguson, Michael D. ....El Paso, TX
Ferguson, Michael L. ....Waterbury, CT
Ferguson, Michael Lambert, (P.A.)
Pensacola, FL
Ferguson, Michael M. ....Elizabethtown, KY
Ferguson, Michael S. ....Boston, MA
Ferguson, Michael S. ....Roanoke, VA
Ferguson, Michael W. ....Nevada City, CA
Ferguson, Nancy C. ....St. Louis, MO
Ferguson, Nancy L. ....San Diego, CA
Ferguson, Nancy Short ....Greensboro, NC
Winston-Salem, NC
Ferguson, Newburn & Weston, A Professional Corporation ....La Jolla, CA
Ferguson, Nohemi Gutierrez ....Pasadena, CA
Ferguson, Pamela Hoke ....Latrobe, PA
Ferguson, Pamela M. ....San Francisco, CA
Ferguson, Pamela P. ....Jonesboro, GA
Ferguson, Patrice L. ....Houston, TX
Ferguson, Patrick A. ....Las Vegas, NV
Ferguson, Patrick H. ....Worcester, MA
Ferguson, Paul ....Arlington, VA
Ferguson, Paul F. ....San Antonio, TX
Ferguson, Paul F. (Chip), Jr.
Beaumont, TX
Ferguson, Paul G. ....Fresh Meadows, NY
Ferguson, Paul H. ....Hilton Head Island, SC
Ferguson, Paula S. ....Prospect Heights, IL
Ferguson, Paulette C. ....Missoula, MT
Ferguson, Peter D. ....La Crosse, WI
Ferguson, Peter James ....Santa Ana, CA
Ferguson, Phillip S. ....Salt Lake City, UT
Ferguson, Priscilla ....Dallas, TX
Ferguson, Ralph A. (Sonny), Jr.
Birmingham, AL
Ferguson, Ralph T. ....Sacramento, CA
Ferguson, Ramona R. ....Plainfield, NJ
Ferguson, Randall C. ....Nashville, TN
Ferguson, Randall L. ....Pearland, TX
Ferguson, Randy W. ....Huntsville, AL
Ferguson, Rawls, MacDonald, Overton & Grissom, P.C. ....Suffolk, VA
Ferguson, Ray Alan ....Rockford, IL
Ferguson, Rebecca J. ....Eaton, OH
Ferguson, Rhonda S. ....Cleveland, OH
Ferguson, Richard ....Columbus, OH
Ferguson, Richard A. ....Palo Alto, CA
Ferguson, Richard C. ....Rochester, NY
Ferguson, Richard G. ....Waco, TX
Ferguson, Richard J. ....Boynton Beach, FL
Ferguson, Richard Y. ....Houston, TX
Ferguson, Richmond H. ....Latrobe, PA
Ferguson, Robert ....Santa Monica, CA
Ferguson, Robert C. ....Dalhart, TX
Ferguson, Robert E. ....Indianapolis, IN
Ferguson, Robert H. M. ....New York, NY
Ferguson, Robert, Jr. ....Hartford, CT
Ferguson, Robert L., Jr. ....Baltimore, MD
Ferguson, Robert Lee ....Jonesboro, GA
Ferguson, Robert R. ....Alpena, MI
Ferguson, Robert Scott ....Big Spring, TX
Ferguson, Robert W. ....Springvale, ME
Ferguson, Robert W. ....Seattle, WA
Ferguson, Robert Warner ....Gastonia, NC
Ferguson, Robin M. ....Treasury Department,
Internal Revenue Service, GV
Ferguson, Rodney A.
South San Francisco, CA
Ferguson, Ron D. ....Tualatin, OR
Ferguson, Roy W., Jr. ....Harrisonburg, VA
Ferguson, Royce A. ....Everett, WA
Ferguson, Ruth H. ....Woodstock, IL
Ferguson, Sally J. ....Minneapolis, MN
Ferguson, Sammons, Olivero & Paraschos
Huntington, WV
Ferguson, Sandra L. ....Taholah, WA
Ferguson, Sandra P. ....North Kansas City, MO
Ferguson, Sanford B. ....Pittsburgh, PA
Ferguson, Sarah Braun ....Cincinnati, OH
Ferguson & Saunders, LLP ....Atlanta, GA
Ferguson and Scarbrough, P.A.
Concord, NC
Ferguson, Schetelich & Heffernan, P.A.
Baltimore, MD
Ferguson & Schieber ....St. Joseph, MO
Ferguson, Scott R. ....San Francisco, CA
Ferguson, Searcy M., Jr. ....Dallas, TX
Ferguson, Shelburne, Jr.
Johnson City, TN
Kingsport, TN
Ferguson, Shelley ....Dallas, TX
Ferguson & Spataro ....Meadville, PA
Ferguson, Stacy C. ....San Antonio, TX
Ferguson, Stanley L. ....Chicago, IL
Ferguson, Stein, Wallas, Adkins, Gresham & Sumter, P.A. ....Chapel Hill, NC
Charlotte, NC
Raleigh, NC
Ferguson, Stephanie A. ....Cumberland, RI
Ferguson, Stephen ....Carmel, IN
Ferguson, Stephen A. ....Worcester, MA
Ferguson, Stephen L. ....Bloomington, IN
Ferguson, Steven E. ....Department of Energy,
Office of the General Counsel, GV
Ferguson, Steven E. ....Oklahoma City, OK
Ferguson, Suellen M. ....Columbia, MD
Ferguson, Susan Copeland ....New York, NY
Ferguson, Susan Hunter ....Crofton, MD
Ferguson, T. Randolph
San Francisco, CA
Ferguson, Terrence J. ....Omaha, NE
Ferguson, Theodore J. ....Bloomington, IN
Ferguson, Thomas G., Jr.
Oklahoma City, OK
Ferguson, Thomas H. ....Chicago, IL
Ferguson, Thomas J. ....Waterloo, IA
Ferguson, Thomas M. ....Pittsburgh, PA
Ferguson, Thomas R. ....Ventura, CA
Ferguson, Thomas S. ....Phillipsburg, NJ
Ferguson, Timothy Dale
Hendersonville, TN
Ferguson, Timothy W. ....Naples, FL
Ferguson, Timothy W. ....Beaumont, TX
Ferguson, Todd C. ....Little Rock, AR
Ferguson, Tom Q. ....Tulsa, OK
Ferguson, Tracy S. ....Charleston, WV
Ferguson, Tricia G. ....Philadelphia, PA
Ferguson, Victor J. ....Columbus, OH
Ferguson, Wallace T. ....Boerne, TX
Ferguson, Walter C. ....Hattiesburg, MS
Ferguson, Ward P. ....McPherson, KS
Ferguson, Warren J. ....Santa Ana, CA
Ferguson & Widmayer, P.C.
Ann Arbor, MI
Ferguson, Wilkie D., Jr. ....Fort Lauderdale, FL
Ferguson, Will ....Albuquerque, NM
Ferguson, Will, & Associates
Albuquerque, NM
Ferguson, William D. ....Atlanta, GA
Ferguson, William E. ....La Jolla, CA
Ferguson, William F., Jr. ....Houston, TX
Ferguson, William G. ....Kansas City, MO
Ferguson, William H. ....Cambridge, OH
Ferguson, William H. ....Medford, OR
Ferguson, William H., (P.C.) ....Atlanta, GA
Ferguson, William I. ....Wheaton, IL
Ferguson, William L. ....Rock Hill, SC
Ferguson, William L. ....Henderson, TX
Ferguson, William M. ....Wellington, KS
Ferguson, William" Marty " ....Addison, TX
Ferguson, William R. ....Akron, OH
Ferguson, William W. ....Raymond, MS
Ferguson, W. J. Thomas ....Seattle, WA
Ferguson-Brey, Harry F. ....Honolulu, HI
Ferguson-Majors, Patricia
Myrtle Beach, SC
Ferguson-Rich, Mary Ann ....Akron, OH
Ferguson-Southard, Denise Rochelle
Baltimore, MD
Fergusson, Colette Y. ....Atlanta, GA
Fergusson, Edgar Bruce
Environmental Protection Agency,
Office of Enforcement and Compliance
Assurance, GV
Ferhadson, Kevin Todd ....Royal Oak, MI
Feria, Sergio ....San Diego, CA
Feria-Cestero, Michelle ....San Juan, PR
Feriancek, J.D. ....Duluth, MN
Feriancek, Jeanine ....Denver, CO
Fericks, Russell C. ....Salt Lake City, UT
Ferikes, Joseph A. ....Asheville, NC
Feringa, Andrew O. ....Los Angeles, CA
Feringa, Peter A., Jr. ....New Orleans, LA
Feringa, Scott D. ....Southfield, MI
Ferington, Karen J. ....Brooklyn, NY
Ferino, Robert J. ....Kew Gardens, NY
Ferioli, William T. ....Glendale, CA
Feriozzi, George S. ....Haddon Heights, NJ
Ferito, D. Stephen ....McMurray, PA
Ferjak, John T. ....Chicago, IL
Ferkich, Roy S. ....Los Angeles, CA
Ferkin, Zori G. ....Washington, DC
Ferkler, Harry W. ....Laurel, MD
Ferko, George ....Hartford, CT
Ferko, Richard T. ....Woodland Hills, CA
Ferko, Sharon ....New York, NY
Ferko, Sharon L. ....Atlanta, GA
Ferkul, Mark E. ....Minneapolis, MN
Ferlaino, John C. ....Garden City, NY
Ferland, Charles P. ....Danielson, CT
Ferland, Niclas A. ....New Haven, CT
Ferland, Roger K. ....Phoenix, AZ
Ferlanti, William J. ....New York, NY
Ferlauto, Thomas M. ....Los Angeles, CA
Ferlazzo, Jean S. ....Danbury, CT
Ferlazzo, Salvatore D. ....Albany, NY
Ferleger & Associates, Ltd. ....Chicago, IL
Ferleger, Daniel S. ....Los Angeles, CA
Ferleger, David ....Philadelphia, PA
Ferleger, Eric P. ....Chicago, IL
Ferleger, Leonard S. ....Pittsburgh, PA
Ferlic, Ann L. ....Omaha, NE
Ferlicca, John J. ....Rochester, NY
Ferlicca, Lawrence N. ....Indianapolis, IN
Ferlin, John R. ....Mount Vernon, WA

Ferlise, Joseph ... Baltimore, MD
Ferlise, Victor J. ... Tinton Falls, NJ
Ferlita, Angelo M. ... Tampa, FL
Ferlita, Frank J. ... Jacksonville, FL
Ferlita, Nutter, Rosello & Newman, P.A. Tampa, FL
Ferlmann, Stephen C. ... Peoria, IL
Ferm, Chas. D. ... Kansas City, MO
Ferm, Daniel W. ... Tacoma, WA
Ferm, Dennis K. ... Honolulu, HI
Ferm, Robert M. ... Denver, CO
Ferm, William N. ... Ellsworth, ME
Ferman, Irving ... Washington, DC
Ferman, Lori ... Cooper City, FL
Ferman, Risa V. ... Norristown, PA
Fermanis, Christopher N. ... New York, NY
Fermann, Robert C. ... New York, NY
Fermelia, Matthew J. ... Cheyenne, WY
Fermelia, Stephen A. ... Denver, CO
Fermin, Maria Luisa (Marisa) Beverly Hills, CA
Fermin, Michael B. ... Riverside, CA
Fermino, David W. ... Los Angeles, CA
Fermoile, Douglas K.M. ... Reno, NV
Fern & Angermayer, L.L.C. ... Pittsburg, KS
Fern, Daniel J. ... Hyannis, MA
Fern, Danielle F. ... Los Angeles, CA
Fern, Donald G. ... Peru, IN
Fern, Frederick H. ... Millburn, NJ
Fern Grund & Grund ... Peru, IN
Fern, Joseph J. ... Los Angeles, CA
Fern, Mark E. ... Pittsburg, KS
Fern, Martin D. ... Los Angeles, CA
Fern, Robert E. ... Elmsford, NY
Fern, Samuel W. ... Cambridge, MA
Fern, Stephen Anthony ... Atlanta, GA
Fernald, Barry P. ... Minneapolis, MN
Fernald, Beth R. ... Keene, NH
Fernald, Brandon C. ... Charlotte, NC
Fernald, Charles E. ... Fort Worth, TX
Fernald, Diane C. ... East Longmeadow, MA
Fernald, Diane L. ... Florence, MA
Fernald, Frances Russell ... Alexandria, VA
Fernald, Gary M. ... Clearwater, FL
Fernald, Graham H. ... Seattle, WA
Fernald, Joseph A., Jr. ... Brookhaven, MS
Fernald, Judy L. ... Houston, TX
Fernald, Lucinda D. ... Seattle, WA
Fernald, Mark D. ... Peterborough, NH
Fernald, Paul C. ... Portland, ME
Fernald, Richard R. ... Peterborough, NH
Fernald, Taft, Falby and Little, Professional Association ... Peterborough, NH
Fernald, W. Tompkins ... Columbus, OH
Fernambucq, George R. ... Birmingham, AL
Fernan, Ann M. ... Mineola, NY
Fernan, John R. ... Ridgway, PA
Fernan, Richard S. ... Southampton, NY
Fernandes, Anthony Curtis ... Sandwich, MA
Fernandes, Anthony M. West Brookfield, MA
Fernandes, Armand, Jr. ... New Bedford, MA
Fernandes, Carl J. ... Wilmington, DE
Fernandes, Christopher J. ... Escondido, CA
Fernandes, Dane K. ... Phoenix, AZ
Fernandes, David A. ... Champaign, IL
Fernandes, Edward F. ... Houston, TX
Fernandes & Finnerty ... New Bedford, MA
Fernandes, Gary L., Sr. ... Gainesville, FL
Fernandes, James ... Tarzana, CA
Fernandes, John V. ... Milford, MA
Fernandes, Joseph L. ... Wilmington, DE
Fernandes, J. P. ... Milwaukee, WI
Fernandes, Ronald D. ... Buffalo, NY
Fernandes, Thomas ... Mineola, NY
Fernandes, Tina B. ... Bethesda, MD
Fernandes, Tracey N. ... Phoenix, AZ
Fernandes-Nakata, D. Lahoma ... Honolulu, HI
Fernandez, Ada ... Washington, DC
Fernandez, Alexander ... Department of Labor, Office of the Solicitor, GV
Fernandez, Alexander E. ... Miami, FL
Fernandez, Alfonso ... San Jose, CA
Fernández, Alfonso, Jr. ... San Juan, PR
Fernandez, Anthony ... Morristown, NJ
Fernandez, Anthony J. ... Phoenix, AZ
Fernandez, Antonio M. ... Los Angeles, CA
Fernandez & Beck, APLC ... Harvey, LA
Fernandez, Ben J. ... Miami, FL
Fernandez, Burstein & Tuczinski, P.C. Albany, NY
Fernandez, Carlos L., (P.A.) ... Miami, FL
Fernandez, Carmen A. ... Hammond, IN
Fernandez, Carol A. ... Chicago, IL
Fernandez, Catherine Livingston Treasury Department, Internal Revenue Service, GV
Fernandez, Charles M. ... Washington, DC
Fernandez, Christina M. ... Ventura, CA
Fernandez, Christine E. ... New York, NY
Fernández, Collins & Rivero-Vergne San Juan, PR
Fernandez, Cristina M. Research Triangle Park, NC
Fernandez, Daniel J. ... Tampa, FL
Fernandez, Daniel J., P.A. ... Tampa, FL
Fernandez, Daniel P. ... Tampa, FL
Fernandez, David ... Newark, NJ
Fernandez, David J. ... New York, NY
Fernandez, David M. ... St. Petersburg, FL
Fernandez, David M. ... Richmond, KY
Fernandez, Dennis S. ... Woodside, CA
Fernandez, Dorothy L. San Francisco, CA
Fernandez, Eduardo ... Miami, FL
Fernandez, Eduardo J. ... New York, NY
Fernandez, Edward A. ... Riverside, CA
Fernandez, Elisa ... Los Angeles, CA
Fernandez, Elizabeth ... Miami, FL
Fernandez, Ellis T., Jr. ... Jacksonville, FL
Fernandez, Emilio ... Miami, FL
Fernandez, Erin L. ... Aspen, CO
Fernandez, E. T., III ... Jacksonville, FL
Fernandez, Fe, (Ms.) ... Evanston, IL
Fernandez, Ferdinand F. ... Pasadena, CA
Fernandez, Ferman M. ... Tallahassee, FL
Fernandez, Fermin J. ... Miami, FL
Fernandez, Frances G. ... Tampa, FL
Fernandez, Francis E. ... Oakland, CA
Fernández, Francisco ... San Juan, PR
San Juan, PR
Fernandez, Francisco M. ... Winter Park, FL
Fernandez, Frank ... Orlando, FL
Fernandez, Frank D. ... Chula Vista, CA
Fernandez, Frank F., III ... Orlando, FL
Fernandez, Frank L. ... Albany, NY
Fernandez Friedman Grossman & Kohn Louisville, KY
Fernandez, Gabriel D. ... Tucson, AZ
Fernandez, Gaston J. ... Tampa, FL
Fernandez, George L. ... Miami, FL
Fernandez, Gerard, Jr. ... New York, NY
Fernandez, Girard J. ... New Orleans, LA
Fernandez, Gonzalo Andres St. Louis, MO
Fernandez, Hermes ... Albany, NY
Fernández & Hertell ... San Juan, PR
Fernandez, Ignacio P. ... San Diego, CA
Fernandez, Irene H. ... Mountain View, CA
Fernandez, Ivan F. ... Miami, FL
Fernandez, J. Michael, Jr. ... Lafayette, LA
Fernandez, Jack E., Jr. ... Tampa, FL
Fernandez, Javier F. ... Pasadena, CA
Fernandez, Jennifer Gentry ... Orlando, FL
Fernandez, Jill Perry ... Longmont, CO
Fernandez, Jim H. ... Mobile, AL
Fernandez, John D. ... Department of State, Foreign Service Officers (Overseas), GV
Fernandez, John D. ... Clearwater, FL
Fernandez, John D., P.A. ... Clearwater, FL
Fernandez, John E. ... Tampa, FL
Fernandez, John P. ... Hillsborough, NC
Fernandez, John Philip Federal Communications Commission, Wireless Telecommunications Bureau, GV
Fernandez, Jorge Luis ... Sarasota, FL
Fernandez, José A. ... New York, NY
Fernandez, Jose C. ... Miami, FL
Fernandez, Jose Ignacio ... Washington, DC
Fernandez, Jose L. ... Miami, FL
Fernandez, Jose W. ... New York, NY
Fernandez, Joseph A. ... Charlotte, NC
Fernandez, Joseph B. ... New York, NY
Fernandez, Joseph M. ... Providence, RI
Fernandez, Joseph W. ... Des Moines, IA
Fernandez, Juan C. ... Roseland, NJ
Fernandez, Julie M. ... Miami, FL
Fernandez, Jun S. ... San Francisco, CA
Fernandez & Knebel, A Professional Corporation ... Dallas, TX
Fernandez, Kristina ... Corpus Christi, TX
Fernandez, Kristopher E. ... Tampa, FL
Fernandez, Laura ... Miami, FL
Fernandez, Lazaro E. ... Riverside, CA
Fernandez, Lazaro, Jr. ... Miami, FL
Fernandez, Leslie Anne ... Raton, NM
Fernandez, Lewis J. ... Treasury Department, Internal Revenue Service, GV
Fernandez, Lillian ... Washington, DC
Fernandez, Lloyd ... Tucson, AZ
Fernandez, Louise Ann ... Los Angeles, CA
Fernandez, Luis ... Miami, FL
Fernandez, Luis F. ... Lansing, MI
Fernandez, Lydia A. ... Miami, FL
Fernandez, Manuel A. Fort Lauderdale, FL
Fernandez, Manuel A. ... Miami, FL
Fernandez, Manuel A. ... Lafayette, LA
Fernandez, Margaret A. ... Atlanta, GA
Fernandez, Maria A. ... Louisville, KY
Fernandez, Maria E. ... White Plains, NY
Fernandez, Maricela C. ... Stockton, CA
Fernández, Marino A., Jr. ... New York, NY
Fernandez, Mark F. ... Dallas, TX
Fernandez, Marta M. ... Los Angeles, CA
Fernandez, Michael ... New York, NY
Fernandez, Miguel C., III ... Fort Myers, FL
Fernandez & Miranda ... Manati, PR
Fernandez, Nancy I. ... Coral Gables, FL
Fernandez, Nicolas ... Miami, FL
Fernandez, Nicolas, P.A. Coral Gables, FL Miami, FL
Fernandez, Noemi ... Buffalo, NY
Fernandez, Norman Gregory Hollywood, CA
Fernandez, Ollinger, Combs & Fontenot, L.L.C. ... Mobile, AL
Fernandez, Orlando ... San Juan, PR
Fernandez, Patricia S. North Andover, MA
Fernandez, Paul E. ... Paterson, NJ
Fernandez, Paul J. ... Poughkeepsie, NY
Fernandez, Pedro C. ... New York, NY
Fernandez, Pedro L., Jr. ... Portland, OR
Fernandez, R. Andrew ... Atlanta, GA
Fernandez, Rafael E. ... Tampa, FL
Fernandez, Raymond R., Jr. ... Dallas, TX
Fernández, Rey ... Conroe, TX
Fernandez, Richard ... Coppell, TX
Fernandez, Richard J. ... Metairie, LA
Fernandez, Richard M. ... Miami, FL
Fernández, Richard M. ... Portland, OR
Fernandez, Richard M., P.A. ... Miami, FL
Fernandez, Robert C. ... Norristown, PA
Fernandez, Robert E. ... Brooklyn, NY
Fernandez, Robert H. ... Miami, FL
Fernandez, Rossana Patricia ... Chicago, IL
Fernandez, Sabrina E.L. ... Anchorage, AK
Fernandez, Santiago ... Los Angeles, CA
Fernandez & Saunders, P.A. Bradenton, FL Pinellas Park, FL St. Petersburg, FL
Fernandez & Seemann ... Lafayette, LA
Fernandez, Segundo J. ... Tallahassee, FL
Fernandez, Shannon L. ... Los Angeles, CA
Fernandez, Sheldon G. ... Harvey, LA
Fernandez, Sherry S. ... Clarksdale, MS
Fernandez, Steven P. ... Anaheim, CA
Fernandez, Susan E. ... Cleveland, OH
Fernandez, Tina Villanueva ... Austin, TX
Fernandez, Tomas J. ... Fort Lauderdale, FL
Fernandez, Traci L. ... Chicago, IL
Fernandez, Victoria Wilson ... New York, NY
Fernandez, Wilfredo ... Miami, FL
Fernandez, William J. ... Menlo Park, CA
Fernandez, William W. ... Winter Springs, FL
Fernandez, Xavier J. ... Pinellas Park, FL
Fernandez, Yolanda B. ... Castro Valley, CA
Fernández-Amy, Gerardo ... San Juan, PR
Fernández-Bared, Manuel ... San Juan, PR
Fernandez-Bigras, Rita ... Toledo, OH
Fernández-Buitrago, Ileana ... San Juan, PR
Fernandez-Caubi, Fernandez & Cancio, P.A. Miami, FL
Fernandez-Caubi, Luis ... Miami, FL
Fernandez-Delgado, Maria de Lourdes San Juan, PR
Fernandez de Zubiria, Jaime New York, NY
Fernandez-Gomez, Maria R. Coral Gables, FL
Fernandez-Gomez, Maria R., P.A. Coral Gables, FL
Fernandez-Gonzalez, Justo ... El Paso, TX
Fernandez-Gray, Carlos A. ... Berkeley, CA
Fernandez-Jaquete, Jose Antonio San Juan, PR
Fernández-Lugo, Carlos J. ... San Juan, PR
Fernández Martínez, Alfredo San Juan, PR
Fernandez-Mendez, Lionel ... San Juan, PR
Fernandez-Paoli, José A. ... San Juan, PR
Fernández-Quincoces, Guillermo J. Miami, FL
Fernandez Ramirez, Luis ... San Juan, PR
Fernández-Reboredo, Jorge A. San Juan, PR
Fernandez Romeu, Camelia San Juan, PR
Fernandez Rundle, Katherine ... Miami, FL
Fernández-Santiago, Evelyn ... Manati, PR
Fernandez-Seebach, Daisy Whitehouse Station, NJ
Fernández-Seín, Jose E. ... San Juan, PR
Fernández-Suárez, Rafael ... San Juan, PR
Fernandez-Valle, Maria ... Coral Gables, FL
Fernandez-Valle, Raul ... Coral Gables, FL
Fernández-Vallejo, Iván R. ... San Juan, PR
Fernandez-Vallejo, Norah E. San Juan, PR
Fernández Villar, José Ramón (IBA) **New York, NY**
Fernandini Sanchez, Arnaldo San Juan, PR
Fernando, Diana Lynn ... Rochester, MI
Fernando, Gihan S. ... Ithaca, NY
Fernando, Raymond M. ... Chicago, IL
Fernands, Anastasia M. ... Boston, MA
Fernbach, Daniel ... Madison, WI
Fernbach, Diane K. ... New York, NY
Ferneau, Philip J. ... Washington, DC
Ferneau, Thomas E., III ... Lincoln, NE
Fernelius, Alice Kronfeld ... Houston, TX
Fernelius, Christopher J. ... Houston, TX
Fernelius, Stephen M. ... Houston, TX
Ferner, Georgia G. ... Albuquerque, NM
Ferner, Raymond F. Department Of Veterans Affairs, Board of Veterans Appeals, GV
Fernety, Michael D. ... Salem, OR
Ferney, Ralph R. ... New York, NY
Ferngren, Lori L. ... Valparaiso, IN
Fernhoff, Michael D. ... Los Angeles, CA
Fernholz, Annette M. ... Chicago, IL
Fernholz & Ehrlich ... Chicago, IL
Fernholz, Frank ... Chicago, IL
Fernholz, Theodore H. ... West Bloomfield, MI
Fernholz, William H. ... Milwaukee, WI
Fernholz, William H. D. San Francisco, CA
Fernich, Marc, Law Office of New York, NY
Fernicola, Gregory A. ... New York, NY
Fernicola, Paul V. ... Middletown, NJ
Fernicola, Robert C. ... Ocean Township, NJ
Fernim, Joseph T. ... Chicago, IL
Fernino, Frank J. ... Reading, MA
Fernino, Kenneth D. ... Hartford, CT
Fernon, Lee P. ... Seymour, TX
Fernos, Antonio ... San Juan, PR
Fernos, Manuel J. ... San Juan, PR
Fernow, James B. ... Fresno, CA
Ferns, Barry W. ... Concord, CA
Ferns, Bridget C. ... Concord, NH
Ferns, Garwacki & Adams, A Professional Corporation ... Concord, CA Pasadena, CA
Ferns, William B. ... Marquette, MI
Fernsler, John P. ... Pittsburgh, PA
Fernsler, Kurt F. ... Pittsburgh, PA
Fernstrom, Robert J. ... Scotch Plains, NJ
Fernstrum, David R. ... Grand Rapids, MI
Fernwood, Raymond F. ... Bodega Bay, CA
Fernwood, Stanley M. ... Modesto, CA
Fero, Dean J. ... Rochester, NY
Fero & Pilato ... Rochester, NY
Feroe, Donald M. ... Minneapolis, MN
Feroleto, John P. ... Buffalo, NY
Feroleto, Paula L. ... Buffalo, NY
Ferolie, Albert F. ... Chicago, IL
Ferolie, Lawrence J. ... Rockford, IL
Ferolie, Perrecone & White, Ltd. Rockford, IL
Ferolie & Stephenson, P.C. ... Chicago, IL
Ferolo, James V. ... Chicago, IL
Feron, Kelly A. ... Buffalo, NY
Ferone & Ferone ... Eastchester, NY
Ferone, Joseph J., Jr. ... Eastchester, NY
Feroze, Zammurad Hyatt ... Dallas, TX
Ferr & Brejcha ... Milwaukee, WI
Ferr, James J. ... Montebello, CA
Ferr, John A. ... Rochester, NY
Ferr, Paul J. ... Milwaukee, WI
Ferracuti, Drew ... Ottawa, IL
Ferracuti, Peter F. ... Ottawa, IL
Ferracuti, Peter F., P.C., Law Offices of Ottawa, IL
Ferradino, Stephanie W. Saratoga Springs, NY
Ferradino, Stephen A. ... Malta, NY
Ferragut, Ulises A., Jr ... Phoenix, AZ
Ferraina, Dominic J. ... Windsor, CT
Ferraioli, Henry G. ... Edison, NJ
Ferraioli, James E. ... Chicago, IL
Ferraiolo, Donald M. ... Hackensack, NJ
Ferraiuoli, Veronica ... San Juan, PR
Ferraiuoli, Zoraida, (Mrs.) ... San Juan, PR
Ferraiuolo, Dominic J. Department of Commerce, Patent and Trademark Office, GV
Ferraiuolo, Peter P. ... New York, NY
Ferrall, Brian L. ... San Francisco, CA
Ferrall, Karen C. ... Florham Park, NJ
Ferrall, Reid D. ... Farmington, MI
Ferrall, Victor E., Jr. ... Beloit, WI
Ferrance, Leon" Pat " ... Roanoke, VA
Ferrand, Frederick Owen ... Atlanta, GA
Ferrand, Timothy S. ... Pontiac, MI Roseville, MI
Ferrandino, Adam C. ... Buffalo, NY
Ferrando, Jonathan P. ... Fort Lauderdale, FL
Ferrán-Pérez Benitoa, Maria T. San Juan, PR
Ferrans, Michael ... Washington, DC
Ferrante, Angelo S. ... Trenton, NJ
Ferrante, Carmen A. ... Paterson, NJ
Ferrante, Christina J. S. Rancho Cucamonga, CA
Ferrante & Cleary ... Bridgeport, CT
Ferrante, Craig ... Fort Myers, FL
Ferrante, David M. ... Los Angeles, CA
Ferrante, Francesco A. ... Dayton, OH
Ferrante, Frank A. ... Clifton, NJ
Ferrante, Frank, Jr. ... New York, NY
Ferrante, Guy J. ... Falls Church, VA
Ferrante, Jennifer A. ... New York, NY
Ferrante and Jingoli ... Trenton, NJ
Ferrante, John J. ... Hartford, CT
Ferrante, Joseph A. ... Passaic, NJ
Ferrante, Joseph A. ... Chagrin Falls, OH
Ferrante, Joseph, Jr. ... Ridgewood, NJ
Ferrante, Joseph M. ... Pasadena, CA
Ferrante, Laura L. ... Jacksonville, FL
Ferrante, Mark V. ... Chicago, IL
Ferrante, Michael A. ... Melville, NY
Ferrante, Michael E. ... Syracuse, NY
Ferrante, Nicholas Joseph Department Of Veterans Affairs, Board of Veterans Appeals, GV
Ferrante, R. William ... Oceanside, CA
Ferrante, Rossana ... Boston, MA
Ferrante, Santino ... Cambridge, MA
Ferrante, Teresa A. ... Washington, DC
Ferrante, Victor M. ... Bridgeport, CT
Ferranti, John A. ... New Haven, CT
Ferranti, Neil J. ... Scarsdale, NY
Ferranty, Robert J. ... Providence, RI
Ferrao, Joaquin Emilio Agency for International Development, Other Offices of A.I.D., GV
Ferrar, Dina M. ... Detroit, MI
Ferrar, Nicholas J. ... Lake Success, NY
Ferrara, A. J. ... Albuquerque, NM
Ferrara, Alan J. ... Farmington Hills, MI
Ferrara, Albert E., Jr. ... Pittsburgh, PA
Ferrara, Alex N. ... Addison, IL
Ferrara, Andrea J. ... Detroit, MI
Ferrara, Anthony J. ... New York, NY
Ferrara, Anthony J. ... New York, NY
Ferrara, Antonio Department of Defense, GV
Ferrara, Barbara N. Securities and Exchange Commission, Division of Market Regulation, GV
Ferrara Belefonte McFadden & Ferrara, L.L.P. ... Media, PA Philadelphia, PA
Ferrara, Benjamin J. ... Syracuse, NY
Ferrara, Brian A. ... New Orleans, LA
Ferrara, C. Thomas ... Altamonte Springs, FL
Ferrara, C. Thomas, P.A. Altamonte Springs, FL
Ferrara, Charles J. ... Metairie, LA
Ferrara, Christopher A. ... Orange, NJ New York, NY
Ferrara, Christopher D. ... Honolulu, HI
Ferrara, Christopher D. ... Morristown, NJ
Ferrara, Daniel A. ... Flushing, NY
Ferrara, David H. ... Cranston, RI
Ferrara, David M. ... Syracuse, NY

Ferrara, David T. .... Shrewsbury, NJ
Ferrara, Dennis M. .... Treasury Department, Internal Revenue Service, GV
Ferrara, Donna .... New York, NY
Ferrara, Fiorenza, Larrison, Barrett & Reitz, P.C. .... East Syracuse, NY
Syracuse, NY
Ferrara, Francis A. .... Media, PA
Ferrara, Francis X. .... Wakefield, MA
Ferrara, Frank J., Jr. .... Walker, LA
Ferrara, Frederick G. .... New York, NY
Ferrara, Haley & Bevis .... Wilmington, DE
Ferrara, James .... Fort Worth, TX
Ferrara, James Leo .... New York, NY
Ferrara, James T. .... Boca Raton, FL
Ferrara, John .... Monticello, NY
Ferrara, John J. .... Danbury, CT
Ferrara, John J. .... North Scituate, MA
Ferrara, John P. .... New Orleans, LA
Ferrara, John S. .... Springfield, MA
Ferrara, Joseph A. .... Coral Gables, FL
Ferrara, Joseph G. .... New York, NY
Ferrara, Joseph J. .... Jersey City, NJ
Ferrara, Joseph Jerome .... Flushing, NY
Ferrara, Kara Lynn S. .... Detroit, MI
Ferrara, Keith M. .... Ballston Spa, NY
Ferrara, Keith M. .... Saratoga Springs, NY
Ferrara, Lesley A. .... Atlanta, GA
Ferrara, Linda Crozier .... Media, PA
Ferrara, Lisa A. .... Boston, MA
Ferrara, Louis B. .... Wilmington, DE
Ferrara, Louis J. .... Washington, DC
Ferrara, Lucas A. .... New York, NY
Ferrara, Lucia A. .... Albany, NY
Ferrara, Mary Byrd .... Nashville, TN
Ferrara, Michael A., Jr. .... Cherry Hill, NJ
Ferrara, Michael J. .... Hackensack, NJ
Ferrara, Michele Dudgeon .... Rochester, NY
Ferrara, Nicholas C. .... New York, NY
Ferrara, Nicole J. .... Orlando, FL
Ferrara, Paul G. .... Syracuse, NY
Ferrara, Peter S. .... St. Louis, MO
Ferrara, Ralph C. .... Washington, DC
Ferrara, Richard P. .... New York, NY
Ferrara, Robert F. .... Media, PA
Ferrara, Rossetti & DeVoto, P.A.
Cherry Hill, NJ
Ferrara, Samuel J. .... Mineola, NY
Ferrara, St. Elmo .... Apache Junction, AZ
Ferrara, Stacy B. .... Providence, RI
Ferrara, Stephen S. .... Allentown, PA
Ferrara & Sullivan .... Monticello, NY
Ferrara, Turitz, Harraka & Goldberg, A Professional Corporation
Hackensack, NJ
New York, NY
Ferrara, Victoria T. .... Westport, CT
Ferrara, Virginia L. .... Albuquerque, NM
Ferraraccio, Blaise Edward .... Clarksville, TN
Ferraraccio, Blaise Joseph .... Clearfield, PA
Ferraraccio & Noble .... Clearfield, PA
Ferrari, Alejandra R. .... Vienna, VA
Ferrari, Andrew B. .... Arlington, VA
Ferrari, Anthony O. .... Yonkers, NY
Ferrari, Bernard T. .... New Orleans, LA
Ferrari, Charles D. .... Sacramento, CA
Ferrari, Clarence J., Jr. .... Menlo Park, CA
San Jose, CA
Ferrari, David G. .... San Jose, CA
Ferrari, Elizabeth Meyer
Overland Park, KS
Ferrari, Erika D. .... Fort Lauderdale, FL
Ferrari & Ferrari, A Law Corporation
Los Altos, CA
Ferrari, Gary J. .... Long Beach, CA
Ferrari, Gary J. .... Peoria, IL
Ferrari, Gerald B. .... Los Altos, CA
Ferrari, Jill E. .... New York, NY
Ferrari, Joan Anne .... Huntington Station, NY
Ferrari, John F. .... Houston, TX
Ferrari, Laura A. .... Dover, MA
Ferrari, Lauren A. .... Morris Plains, NJ
Ferrari, Lauren Boswell .... Sumter, SC
Ferrari, Lisa A. .... New York, NY
Ferrari, Lisa C. .... San Diego, CA
Ferrari, Louis J. .... Framingham, MA
Ferrari, Marcelo A. .... Portland, ME
Ferrari, Maria A. .... Los Altos, CA
Ferrari, Mary .... Hamden, CT
Ferrari, Olsen, Ottoboni & Bebb, LLP
Menlo Park, CA
San Jose, CA
Ferrari, Patricia .... New York, NY
Ferrari, Patricia K. .... New York, NY
Ferrari, Patricia L. .... Miami, FL
Ferrari, Paul L. .... Washington, DC
Ferrari, Philip .... San Francisco, CA
Ferrari, Renata J. .... New York, NY
Ferrari, Robert .... Brooklyn, NY
Ferrari, Robert V. .... New York, NY
Ferrari, Rosenthal & Matusiak
Manhasset, NY
Ferrari, Tammera J. .... Miami, FL
Ferrari, Vicky H. .... Dallas, TX
Ferrarino, D. Benjamin .... Mesa, AZ
Ferrario, Mark E. .... Las Vegas, NV
Ferrario, Raymond W. .... Scranton, PA
Ferrario, Raymond W., P.C. .... Scranton, PA
Ferrario, Remy J. .... New York, NY
Ferraris, Patricia A. .... Frederick, MD
Towson, MD
Westminster, MD
Ferraro, Amedeo F. .... Los Angeles, CA
Ferraro, Anthony B. .... Rosemont, IL
Ferraro, Arthur A. .... Santa Clara, CA
Ferraro, Arthur J. .... Garnerville, NY
Ferraro & Associates, P.A. .... Miami, FL
Ferraro, Carol Ann .... Hartsdale, NY
Ferraro, Carrie .... Kenilworth, NJ
Ferraro, Dennis A. .... Chicago, IL
Ferraro, Dominic J. .... Nazareth, PA
Ferraro, Donald P. .... Washington, DC
Ferraro, Eric K. .... Berkeley, CA
Ferraro, Geraldine A. .... New York, NY
Ferraro, Gregory D. .... Summit, NJ
Ferraro, James K. .... Cambridge, MA
Ferraro, James L. .... Miami, FL
Cleveland, OH
Ferraro, James R. .... Waltham, MA
Ferraro, Joseph .... New Haven, CT
Ferraro, Joseph .... New York, NY
Ferraro, Joseph D. .... New York, NY
Ferraro, Joseph W. .... New York, NY
Ferraro, Joseph W., Jr. .... Jackson, NJ
Ferraro, Joyce M. .... New York, NY
Ferraro, Kenneth C. .... Chicago, IL
Ferraro, Kristi S. .... Aspen, CO
Ferraro, Leigh Greer .... Orange, CA
Ferraro, Lisa E. .... Chattanooga, TN
Ferraro, Madeline R. .... Trenton, NJ
Ferraro, Mark J. .... Bristol, CT
West Hartford, CT
Ferraro, Matthew J. .... Cambridge, MA
Ferraro, Michael S. .... Phoenix, AZ
Ferraro, Neil P. .... Boston, MA
Ferraro, Patricia A. .... Hackensack, NJ
Ferraro, Pete .... Austin, TX
Ferraro, R. Edward .... Brockway, PA
Punxsutawney, PA
Ferraro, Robert A. .... Rutherford, NJ
Ferraro, Ross F. .... Brockway, PA
Punxsutawney, PA
Ferraro, Russell J., Jr. .... Stuart, FL
Ferraro, Russell J., Jr. and Associates, P.A.
Stuart, FL
Ferraro, Thomas .... Perrineville, NJ
Ferraro, V. James .... New Haven, CT
Ferraro, William S. .... Jeannette, PA
Ferraro, William V. .... Cypress, CA
Ferraro & Young .... Brockway, PA
Punxsutawney, PA
Ferraro Zugibe & Albrecht .... Garnerville, NY
Ferrarone, Stephen .... Springfield, MA
Ferrary, Richard .... Santa Fe, NM
Ferras, Deborah Durr .... Vallejo, CA
Ferrate, Alejandro .... Washington, DC
Ferrauiola, Scott E. .... White Plains, NY
Ferrazano, Michael J.
Mountain View, CA
Ferrazi, Karen .... Houston, TX
Ferrazzano, Dennis A. .... Chicago, IL
Ferre, Jeffry F. .... Riverside, CA
Ferre, L. Mark .... Salt Lake City, UT
Ferrebee, Jack E. .... Virginia Beach, VA
Ferrebee, Jack E., P.C.
Virginia Beach, VA
Ferree, Bunn & O'Grady, Chartered
Overland Park, KS
Ferree, David A. .... Ames, IA
Ferree, Donald R. .... Panora, IA
Ferree, Harold C. .... St. Petersburg, FL
Ferree, John N., Jr. .... Phoenix, AZ
Ferree, Lawrence L., III
Overland Park, KS
Ferree, Marcia Jo .... Indianapolis, IN
Ferree, Max F. .... Wilkesboro, NC
Ferree, Roy L. .... Greenville, SC
Ferree, Russell F. .... Wilkesboro, NC
Ferree, W. Kenneth .... Washington, DC
Ferreira, Carmen C. .... Miami, FL
Ferreira, Christopher .... Edina, MN
Ferreira, Cristina M. L. .... Washington, DC
Ferreira, G. Michelle .... San Jose, CA
Ferreira, James H. .... Rochester, NY
Ferreira, Jennifer Renna .... Boston, MA
Ferreira, John G. .... Pittsburgh, PA
Ferreira, Joseph C. .... Easton, MA
Ferreira, Lawrence .... New York, NY
Ferreira, Lawrence S. .... Lakeville, MA
Ferreira, Lisa .... Palo Alto, CA
Ferreira, Louis A., IV .... Portland, OR
Vancouver, WA
Ferreira, Marco P. .... Los Angeles, CA
Ferreira, Michael Ann .... Oakland, CA
Ferreira, Narcie J. .... Claremont, CA
Ferreira, Nelson A. .... New York, NY
Ferreira, Paul R. .... South Orange, NJ
New York, NY
Ferreira, Penelope S. .... Washington, DC
Ferreiro, Nestor A., Jr. .... Bronx, NY
Ferrel, J. Brian .... Department of Justice, Tax Division, GV
Ferrel, Jill S. .... Kansas City, MO
Ferrel, Timothy W. .... Bloomfield Hills, MI
Ferrell, Anne Bowles .... Knoxville, TN
Ferrell, Backus, Sayer & Nicolo, P.C.
Portsmouth, VA
Ferrell, Brian K. .... Nashville, TN
Ferrell & Britton .... Phenix City, AL
Ferrell, Carroll O. .... Portsmouth, VA
Ferrell, Charles S. .... Minneapolis, MN
Ferrell, Clinton F. .... Kirkland, WA
Ferrell, Craig E., Jr. .... Houston, TX
Ferrell, David B. .... Canton, OH
Ferrell, David J. .... El Paso, TX
Ferrell, David P. .... Raleigh, NC
Ferrell, David W. .... Beaumont, TX
Ferrell, Deborah Reib .... El Dorado, KS
Ferrell, Donald V. .... Harrisburg, IL
Ferrell, Donald W. .... Seattle, WA
Ferrell, Edward .... Longview, TX
Ferrell, Elizabeth A. .... Washington, DC
Ferrell, Forrest A. .... Hickory, NC
Ferrell, Gentry R. .... Washington, DC
Ferrell, Gentry R. .... Lynchburg, VA
Ferrell, George A. .... Seattle, WA
Ferrell, Hugh C. .... Sarasota, FL
Ferrell, Iva Johnson .... Philadelphia, PA
Ferrell, J. Pelham .... Phenix City, AL
Ferrell, James C. .... Houston, TX
Ferrell, Joan E. .... Oklahoma City, OK
Ferrell, John A. .... Booneville, MS
Ferrell, John A., P.A. .... Booneville, MS
Ferrell, John D. .... Seattle, WA
Ferrell, John S. .... Palo Alto, CA
Ferrell, John W. .... Richmond, VA
Ferrell, Joseph S. .... Chapel Hill, NC
Ferrell, Kathleen L. .... New York, NY
Ferrell, Kathryn D. .... Fairhope, AL
Ferrell, Kubinski & Smith, P.C. .... El Paso, TX
Ferrell, Larry H. .... Cape Girardeau, MO
Ferrell, Lisa C. .... Little Rock, AR
Ferrell, Mary Alice .... Sarasota, FL
Ferrell, Melissa K. .... Houston, TX
Ferrell, Michael E. .... Olympia, WA
Ferrell, Michael R. .... Raleigh, NC
Ferrell, Michael W. .... Middletown, NY
Ferrell, Michael W. .... Mount Juliet, TN
Ferrell, Milton M., Jr. .... Miami, FL
Ferrell, Paul, Jr. .... Mount Holly, NJ
Ferrell, R. Garth .... Denver, CO
Ferrell, R. Stephen .... Houston, TX
Ferrell, R. Tyson .... North Wilkesboro, NC
Ferrell, Raymond R. .... Roseland, NJ
Ferrell, Richard L., III .... Dayton, OH
Ferrell Schultz Carter & Fertel, P.A.
Miami, FL
Ferrell, Scott J. .... Dallas, TX
Ferrell, Susan .... Tucson, AZ
Ferrell, Thomas W. .... San Diego, CA
Ferrell, Vernon Paul, II .... Parkersburg, WV
Ferrell, Wayne E., Jr. .... Jackson, MS
Ferrell, William H. .... Belleville, IL
Ferrell, William T. .... Anchorage, AK
Ferrell-Bhavsar, Candace .... Nashville, TN
Ferrelle, John R. .... Brunswick, GA
Ferrelle, John R., P.C. .... Brunswick, GA
Ferrelli, Dominick J. .... Mount Holly, NJ
Ferrelli, James J. .... Cherry Hill, NJ
Ferrelli, Joseph Vincent .... Nashville, TN
Ferrelli, Laurel C. .... Providence, RI
Ferren, Andrew J. .... Boston, MA
Ferren, Carol L. .... Philadelphia, PA
Ferren, Edwin T., III .... Haddonfield, NJ
Ferren, Gregory A. .... Honolulu, HI
Ferren, John M. .... Washington, DC
Ferren Law Office .... Ottumwa, IA
Ferren, Norman R. .... New York, NY
Ferren, Philip K. .... Ottumwa, IA
Ferren, William J. .... Blue Bell, PA
Ferrendelli, Lisa M. .... San Diego, CA
Ferrene, Otto W., Jr. .... Hilton Head Island, SC
Ferrentino, Anthony J. .... Santa Ana, CA
Ferrentino, Carl T. .... Albany, NY
Ferrentino, Correen Wiley .... Orange, CA
Ferrentino, David D. .... Tampa, FL
Ferrentino, Joseph A.
Newport Beach, CA
Ferrenz, Andrea Gallimore
Washington, DC
Ferrer, Alberto .... San Juan, PR
Ferrer, Alfred, III .... New York, NY
Ferrer, Barbara J. .... Miami, FL
Ferrer, Eric G. .... Los Angeles, CA
Ferrer, Esteban A. .... Miami, FL
Ferrer, Esteban A., III .... Stamford, CT
Ferrer, Eugene Y. .... New York, NY
Ferrer, F.M. Bud .... Irvine, CA
Ferrer, Francis X. .... San Jose, CA
Ferrer, Geoffrey D. .... Newark, NJ
New York, NY
Ferrer, Gilbert C. .... Round Rock, TX
Ferrer, Jesse F. .... Dallas, TX
Ferrer, Juan Carlos .... Miami, FL
Ferrer, L. Daniel .... Coral Gables, FL
Ferrer Law Offices .... Seattle, WA
Ferrer, Mary A. .... San Francisco, CA
Ferrer, Monica .... New York, NY
Ferrer, Paul A. .... Charlottesville, VA
Ferrer, R. Douglas P. .... Seattle, WA
Ferrer, R. George .... Seattle, WA
Ferrer, Ramon J. .... Wailuku, HI
Ferrer, Sebastian .... Philadelphia, PA
Wayne, PA
Ferrer, Wifredo A. .... Department of Justice, Office of the Attorney General, GV
Ferrera, Charles J. .... Honolulu, HI
Ferrera, Dana K. .... Newark, NJ
Ferrera, David L. .... Boston, MA
Ferrera, Elena .... Brooklyn, NY
Ferrera, G. Daniel .... Dearborn, MI
Ferrera, Gerald R. .... Waltham, MA
Ferrera, Isabelle F. .... Chicago, IL
Ferrera, John M., Jr.
South San Francisco, CA
Ferrera, Sandra M. .... Miami, FL
Ferrera, Tess J. .... Washington, DC
Ferrera, Vinita Chopra .... Boston, MA
Ferrer-Canals, Javier E. .... San Juan, PR
Ferrer-Colon, Pedro .... Flint, MI
Ferrer de Glassberg, María V.
San Juan, PR
Ferrer-Fernández, Javier D.
San Juan, PR
Ferreri, Candyce L. .... Albuquerque, NM
Ferreri, Carlo .... North Hills, CA
Ferreri, Eugene A., Jr. .... Raleigh, NC
Ferreri, Fogle & Picklesimer
Lexington, KY
Louisville, KY
Ferreri, Richard J. .... New York, NY
Ferreri, Thomas A. .... Santa Monica, CA
Ferreri, Thomas L. .... Lexington, KY
Louisville, KY
Ferreri, Timothy J. .... Bartow, FL
Ferreri, V. Richard .... Gibbsboro, NJ
Ferreri, V. Richard, P.C. .... Gibbsboro, NJ
Ferreria, David M. .... Los Angeles, CA
Ferrer-Kerber, Victoria A. .... San Juan, PR
Ferrero, Genevre .... Fort Lauderdale, FL
Ferrero, John D., Jr. .... Massillon, OH
Ferrero, Martin P. .... Harlingen, TX
Ferrero, Ray, Jr. .... Fort Lauderdale, FL
Ferrero, Raymond G., III
Fort Lauderdale, FL
Ferrero, Thomas V. .... Massillon, OH
Ferrero, Vincent M. .... Atlanta, GA
Ferrero-Patten, Rhonda J.
Bloomington, IL
Ferreti, George M. .... Chicago, IL
Ferrette, Joseph Francis .... New York, NY
Ferrette & Slater, A Law Corporation
San Diego, CA
Ferrette, Victor J. .... San Diego, CA
Ferretti, David P. .... Charleston, WV
Ferretti, Jennie Ovrom .... Charleston, WV
Ferretti, John .... Mineola, NY
Ferretti, John S. .... Brooklyn, NY
Ferretti, Joseph J. .... Oklahoma City, OK
Ferretti, Joseph R. .... Martinsburg, WV
Ferretti, Reneé L. .... Allentown, PA
Ferretti, Scott J. .... New York, NY
Ferretti, Vincent E., Jr. .... Rockville, MD
Ferretti Smith, Judith Ann .... Boston, MA
Ferrey, Steven E. .... Boston, MA
Ferri, Carol A. .... Philadelphia, PA
Ferri, Dennis D. .... Wilmington, DE
Ferri, Dennis D., P.A. .... Wilmington, DE
Ferri, Ernest A. .... Burlington, NJ
Ferri, Joseph P., Jr. .... Garden City, NY
Ferri, Karen L. .... Murrysville, PA
Ferri, Lisa M. .... New York, NY
Ferri, Marco .... Miami, FL
Ferri, Michael J. .... Charleston, SC
Ferri, Richard H. .... Chicago, IL
Ferri, Robert .... New York, NY
Ferri, Silvia M. .... Cherry Hill, NJ
Philadelphia, PA
Ferrian, Sandra S. .... Eden Prairie, MN
Ferriby & Houston .... Detroit, MI
Ferriby, Robert L., Jr. .... Detroit, MI
Ferriby, Robin D. .... Birmingham, MI
Ferricci, Brent .... Hinckley, OH
Ferrick, Bryan F. .... Saddle Brook, NJ
Shrewsbury, NJ
Toms River, NJ
Ferrick, Connor .... Ann Arbor, MI
Ferrick, James H., III .... St. Louis, MO
Ferrick & Kurzeja .... Saddle Brook, NJ
Shrewsbury, NJ
Toms River, NJ
Ferrick, Patricia M. .... St. Louis, MO
Ferriell, Bruce Justin .... Louisville, KY
Ferriell, Jeffrey Thomas .... Columbus, OH
Ferrier, Beth B. .... Athens, OH
Ferrier, Cindy Suzanne .... Falls Church, VA
Ferrier, Debra J. .... Los Angeles, CA
Ferrier, Jeffrey P. .... Holmdel, NJ
Ferrier, Jon T. .... Grand Rapids, MI
Ferrier, Joseph H. .... Brunswick, GA
Ferrier, Karl W. .... Ocean Park, WA
Ferrier, Kevin L. .... Tyler, TX
Ferrier, Raymond L. .... Brooklyn, NY
Ferrier, Robert T. .... Conyers, GA
Ferriere, Patrick L. .... New York, NY
Ferrieri, Robert M. .... Providence, RI
Ferriero, Diana .... Hackensack, NJ
Ferriero, Joseph A. .... Hackensack, NJ
Roseland, NJ
Ferries, J. Thomas .... Dearborn, MI
Ferries, Kenneth J. .... Kokomo, IN
Ferriggi, Richard H. .... Garden City, NY
Ferrigno, Anthony A. .... San Clemente, CA
Ferrigno, Cherylann .... Millville, NJ
Ferrigno, Conrad F. .... West Hempstead, NY
Ferrigno, Kevin G. .... Hartford, CT
Ferrigno, Lorraine M. .... New York, NY
Ferrigno, Nicholas W., Jr. .... Covington, KY
Ferrigno, Richard F. .... New York, NY
Ferrigno, Robert Vincent .... Honolulu, HI
Ferrigno, Thomas A. .... Washington, DC
Ferrill, A. Michael .... San Antonio, TX
Ferrill, Donald A. .... Fort Worth, TX
Ferrill, Scott T. .... Hillside, IL
Ferrillo, Paul A. .... New York, NY
Ferriman, David B. .... Columbus, OH
Ferrin, George R. .... Tempe, AZ
Ferrin, George R., P.C. .... Tempe, AZ
Ferrin, J. Michael .... Mesquite, TX
Ferrin, Joel H. .... Lake Bluff, IL
Ferrin, John J. .... Farmington, UT
Ferrin, Mark A. .... Salt Lake City, UT
Ferrin, Martin L. .... New York, NY
Ferrin, Michael J. .... West Palm Beach, FL
Ferrin, Michael K. .... Blackfoot, ID
Ferrin, Michael L. .... Mesa, AZ
Ferrin, Richard P. .... Washington, DC
Ferrin, Shawn C. .... Salt Lake City, UT
Ferrin, William J. .... Tarzana, CA
Ferring, Michael H. .... Seattle, WA
Ferring Nelson LLP .... Seattle, WA
Ferrington, Michael A. .... Santa Rosa, CA
Ferrington, Pamela A. .... Natchez, MS
Ferrini, James T. .... Chicago, IL
Ferrini, Jane Mackin .... Dover, NH
Ferrini, NancyLynn S. .... Fort Edward, NY
Ferrini, Thomas G. .... Dover, NH
Ferrino, Rosemary R.
Plymouth Meeting, PA
Ferriot, Joanne C. .... Thibodaux, LA
Ferris, Alfred G. .... San Diego, CA
Ferris, Andrew M. .... Columbus, OH

Feudale, Barry Francis ..... Sunbury, PA
Feudo, Vincent A. ..... Cleveland, OH
Feuer, Albert ..... Forest Hills, NY
Feuer, Bernard ..... Sun City West, AZ
Feuer, Bradley A. ..... New York, NY
Feuer, Bradley Scott ..... Lake Worth, FL
Feuer, Bruce R. ..... Atlanta, GA
Feuer, Caesar & Fischel
Long Island City, NY
Feuer, Charles E. ..... Cleveland, OH
Feuer, Charles M. ..... White Plains, NY
Feuer, David Z. ..... Chicago, IL
Feuer, Gail Ruderman ..... Los Angeles, CA
Feuer, Harriet D. ..... Albertson, NY
Feuer, Herbert J. ..... Scarsdale, NY
Feuer, I. J. ..... Springfield, IL
Feuer, Jack D. ..... Denver, CO
Feuer, Jeffrey M. ..... Cambridge, MA
Feuer, Jeffrey M., (P.A.) ..... Miami, FL
Feuer, Jerold ..... Boca Raton, FL
Miami, FL
Feuer, Joel A. ..... Los Angeles, CA
Feuer, Joseph M. ..... Atlanta, GA
Feuer, Kurt H. ..... Chicago, IL
Feuer, Lloyd A. ..... Patchogue, NY
Feuer, Marilyn ..... New York, NY
Feuer, Mark S. ..... Dayton, OH
Feuer, Marshall N. ..... Miami, FL
Feuer, Melissa R. ..... Arlington, VA
Feuer, Michael A. ..... St. Louis, MO
Feuer, Michael N. ..... Los Angeles, CA
Feuer, Michael S. ..... New York, NY
Feuer, Paul R. ..... Patchogue, NY
Feuer, Robert A. ..... Stockbridge, MA
Feuer, Robt. W. ..... Fairfax, VA
Feuer, Scott L. ..... Bloomfield Hills, MI
Feuer, Semi ..... Washington, DC
Feuer, Sherri L. ..... Cincinnati, OH
Feuer, Stacey Thomas ..... Chicago, IL
Feuer, Stacy A. ..... Washington, DC
Feuer, Stephen R. ..... Vista, CA
Feuer, Steven Z. ..... Oneonta, NY
Feuer, Wendy S. ..... Anchorage, AK
Feuer, William W. ..... Boston, MA
Feuerbach, Donald E. ..... Vero Beach, FL
Feuerbach, Jerald L. ..... Davenport, IA
Feuerbach, Peter J. ..... Boston, MA
Feuerberg, Stanley C. ..... Manassas, VA
Feuerborn, Paul A. ..... Kansas City, MO
Feuerhake, Herbert G. ..... Wilmington, DE
Feuerhelm, Gerald B. ..... Des Moines, IA
Feuerhelm, Jodi Knobel ..... Phoenix, AZ
Feuerle, Lois M. ..... Montclair, NJ
Feuerle, Peter ..... Washington, DC
Feuerlicht, Brian H. ..... Millburn, NJ
Feuerman, Gary M. ..... New York, NY
Feuerman, Jamie B. ..... San Francisco, CA
Feuerman, Jonathan ..... Miami, FL
Feuerman, Paul ..... Florham Park, NJ
Feuerman, Scott ..... Tavernier, FL
Feuerstein, Abram S. ..... Stockton, CA
Feuerstein, Adam S. ..... Washington, DC
Feuerstein, Alan R. ..... Buffalo, NY
San Juan, PR
Charlotte Amalie, St. Thomas, VI
Feuerstein, Albert I. ..... Wantagh, NY
Feuerstein, Andrew O. ..... New York, NY
Feuerstein, Bernard A. ..... New York, NY
Feuerstein, Daniel A. ..... Park Ridge, NJ
Feuerstein, Donald M. ..... New York, NY
Feuerstein, Eric M. ..... New York, NY
Feuerstein, Gary S. ..... Tampa, FL
Feuerstein, Harvey S., (P.C.)
New York, NY
Feuerstein, Henry I. ..... New York, NY
Feuerstein, Herman ..... Los Angeles, CA
Feuerstein, Howard M. ..... Portland, OR
Feuerstein, Jerold C. ..... Livingston, NJ
New York, NY
Feuerstein, Kim ..... New York, NY
Feuerstein, Michael J. ..... New York, NY
Feuerstein, Morris A. ..... Bay Shore, NY
Feuerstein, Randall J. ..... Denver, CO
Feuerstein, Randy L. ..... New York, NY
Feuerstein, Richard P. ..... San Diego, CA
Feuerstein, Ronald A. ..... Washington, DC
Feuerstein, Sandra J. ..... Mineola, NY
Feuerstein, Sidney A. ..... Memphis, TN
Feuerstein & Smith, LLP ..... Buffalo, NY
Feuerstein & Smith, LLP
Christiansted, St. Croix, VI
Cruz Bay, St. John, VI
Charlotte Amalie, St. Thomas, VI
Feuerzeig, Henry L.
Charlotte Amalie, St. Thomas, VI
Feuille, Frank, IV ..... El Paso, TX
Feuille, Kathleen Day ..... El Paso, TX
Feuille, Richard H. ..... El Paso, TX
Feuille, Robert R. ..... El Paso, TX
Feul, Raymond L. ..... Farmington Hills, MI
Feulner, George J. ..... Tucson, AZ
Feulner, George J., P.C., Law Offices of
Tucson, AZ
Feulner, Gregory J. ..... Wilmington, DE
Feulner, Jeffrey ..... Winter Park, FL
Feulner, Melvin J. ..... Newburgh, IN
Feuquay, Jeffrey P. ..... Perry, OK
Feureisen, David ..... White Plains, NY
Feurer, Deborah A. ..... Baltimore, MD
Feurer, Duane A. ..... Chicago, IL
Feurer, William E. ..... Springfield, IL
Feurey, Edward T. ..... Toms River, NJ
Feury, Kevin C.
Department of Transportation,
Maritime Administration, GV
Feurzeig, Donald L. ..... San Francisco, CA
Feuss, Charles E. ..... Atlanta, GA
Minneapolis, MN
Feuss, Linda U. ..... Minneapolis, MN
Feustel, Bruce G. ..... Madison, WI
Feustel, Richard M., Jr. ..... New York, NY
Feutz, Cheryl L. ..... Kansas City, MO
Feutz, James F. ..... San Francisco, CA
Feutz-Harter, Sheryl ..... Kansas City, MO
Feuvrel, Sidney L., Jr. ..... Orlando, FL
Feuvrel, Sidney L., Jr., P.A. ..... Orlando, FL
Few & Ayala ..... Tampa, FL
Few, J. Kendall ..... Greenville, SC
Few, J. Kendall, P.A. ..... Greenville, SC
Few, John C. ..... Greenville, SC
Few, John C., P.A. ..... Greenville, SC
Few, Molly E. ..... Pittsburgh, PA
Few, Nora Wolfe ..... Conroe, TX
Few, Richard L., Jr. ..... Greenville, SC
Few, W. Crosby ..... Tampa, FL
Few, Wesley Dodgen ..... Columbia, SC
Greenville, SC
Few, William P. ..... Raleigh, NC
Fewel, Harriett M. ..... Lancaster, TX
Fewel, Kathleen R. ..... Ridgeland, MS
Fewel, Scott A. ..... Corvallis, OR
Fewell, Brent A. ..... Pittsburgh, PA
Fewell, Charles K., Jr. (IBA) ..... **New York, NY**
Fewell, D. Michael ..... Winfield, WV
Fewell, Kathryn D. ..... Tacoma, WA
Fewell, Terry G. ..... Indianapolis, IN
Fewell, Victra Lafferty, (Ms.)
Little Rock, AR
Fewell, W. Scott ..... New London, CT
Fewer, Gregory C. ..... Jamaica, NY
Fewer, James K. ..... Glasgow, MT
Fewkes, Daniel S. ..... Naperville, IL
Fewkes, David A. ..... Oak Brook, IL
Fewkes, David A., Jr. ..... Palos Heights, IL
Fewkes Wentz & Strayer ..... Oak Brook, IL
Fewson, George V. ..... Boulder, CO
Fex, Cecilia ..... Washington, DC
Fey, Albert E. ..... New York, NY
Fey, Carol Ann ..... Columbus, OH
Fey, Laura Clark ..... Kansas City, MO
Fey, Lawrence J. ..... Chicago, IL
Fey, Nancy N. ..... Rockville, MD
Fey, Therese M. ..... Anaheim, CA
Fey, W. Benjamin ..... Reno, NV
Fey, Wagner & Sacks ..... Rockville, MD
Feyder, James R. ..... Sioux Falls, SD
Feyder, Robert E. ..... Beverly Hills, CA
Feyen, Mark A. ..... West Olive, MI
Feyer, Robert P. ..... San Francisco, CA
Feyh, Kelly A. ..... Overland Park, KS
Feyko, James ..... Columbus, OH
Feyko, Jeffrey ..... Pickerington, OH
Feyko, John ..... Boca Raton, FL
Fezekas, Michael E. ..... Chicago, IL
Fezer, Stephen J. ..... North Tonawanda, NY
Fezza, Thomas A. ..... Parsippany, NJ
Fezzey, Thomas F. ..... Wheaton, IL
Ffolkes, Brigette A. ..... Tallahassee, FL
Ffolkes, Francine Marie ..... Tallahassee, FL
Ffrench, Robert J. ..... East Hanover, NJ
Ffrench, Thomas ..... Irvine, CA
Fiabane, Louis C. ..... New York, NY
Fiacco, Barbara A. ..... Boston, MA
Fiacco, Violet F. ..... Long Beach, CA
Fiala, Alison T. ..... Paoli, PA
Fiala, Carol Stanton ..... St. Louis, MO
Fiala, David M. ..... Cincinnati, OH
Fiala, Edward M., Jr. ..... Skokie, IL
Fiala, Marie L. ..... San Francisco, CA
Fiala, Robert ..... New York, NY
Fiala, Thomas C. ..... Washington, DC
Fialho, Vincent ..... Fort Worth, TX
Fialho, Vincent F., P.C. ..... Fort Worth, TX
Fialk, Arthur D. ..... Clinton, NJ
Fialko, Christopher C. ..... Charlotte, NC
Fialko, Christopher C., Attorney At Law, PLLC ..... Charlotte, NC
Fialkoff, Jay R. ..... New York, NY
Fialkov, Jay M. ..... Needham, MA
Fialkow, Jay L. ..... Boston, MA
Fialkow, Nadine R. ..... Miami, FL
Fialkowski, Anne E. ..... Philadelphia, PA
Fialkowski, Deborah A. ..... Stockton, CA
Fialkowski, Elise A. ..... Philadelphia, PA
Fialky, Gary L. ..... Springfield, MA
Fialky, Jeffrey Ira ..... Andover, MA
Fiallo, Jesus S. ..... Jackson Heights, NY
Fiamingo, Kathi F. ..... Morristown, NJ
Fiance, Mona C. ..... Bellerose, NY
Fiandaca, Kenneth J. ..... Boston, MA
Fiandach, Edward L. ..... Rochester, NY
Fiandach & Fiandach ..... Rochester, NY
Fiandach, Samuel ..... Rochester, NY
Fiani, Jules N. ..... Brighton, MI
Fiano, Lawrence A. ..... Manchester, CT
Fiano, Sabato P. ..... Southport, CT
Fiarman, Jeffrey A. ..... Washington, DC
Fiasco, William A. ..... Tulsa, OK
Fiasconaro, Betty J. ..... New York, NY
Fiasconaro, Clare D. ..... Shreveport, LA
Fiasconaro & Fiasconaro ..... New Orleans, LA
Fiasconaro, Jos. A., Jr. ..... New Orleans, LA
Fiasconaro, Paul S. ..... New Orleans, LA
Fiazzuddin, Ajaz S. ..... Bangor, ME
Fibich & Garth, P.C. ..... Houston, TX
Fibich, Kenneth T. ..... Houston, TX
Fica, Michael J. ..... Boise, ID
Ficaj, Roman J. ..... Bingham Farms, MI
Ficano, Robert A. ..... Detroit, MI
Ficara, Franne M. ..... San Diego, CA
Ficara, Ignazio ..... Yucca Valley, CA
Ficara, John J. ..... Bellmore, NY
Ficarelli, Anthony ..... Chicago, IL
Ficaretta, Teresa G. ..... Treasury Department,
Bureau of Alcohol, Tobacco and Firearms, GV
Ficaro, Michael A. ..... Chicago, IL
Ficarra, Francis J. ..... Fairfield, CT
Ficarra, Thomas A. ..... Manchester, NH
Ficarra, Troy ..... New York, NY
Ficarro, John R. ..... Youngstown, OH
Ficarrotta, Gasper J. ..... Tampa, FL
Ficarrotta, Joseph H., (P.A.) ..... Tampa, FL
Ficarrotta, Nick ..... Tampa, FL
Ficcadenti, Susan R. ..... Santa Ana, CA
Ficchi, Michael J. ..... Brooklyn, NY
Ficco, Robert E. ..... Franklin, MA
Ficco & Simmler ..... Franklin, MA
Ficek & Buresh, P.C. ..... Dickinson, ND
Ficek, Gary A. ..... Fargo, ND
Ficek, Vince H. ..... Dickinson, ND
Ficenec, James J. ..... San Francisco, CA
Ficerai, Kenneth ..... Greensburg, PA
Ficeto, Anna Carbonaro ..... Hartford, CT
Fichelson, Bruce A. ..... San Francisco, CA
Fichera, A. Philip ..... Ann Arbor, MI
Fichera, Cynthia K. ..... Poughkeepsie, NY
Fichera, Dominic R. ..... Chicago, IL
Fichera, Dominic R., & Associates
Chicago, IL
Des Plaines, IL
Fichera, Lewis C. ..... West Deptford, NJ
Fichera-Burke, Cristina A. ..... Chicago, IL
Fichtel, John W., III ..... Providence, RI
Fichtel, Michael J. ..... Fort Lauderdale, FL
Fichtel, Suzanne E. ..... Dallas, TX
Fichtelman, Carol A. ..... Alexandria, VA
Fichtenbaum, Steven J. ..... Montville, NJ
Fichtenholtz, Theodore ..... Hartford, CT
Fichter, Andrew J. ..... Blue Bell, PA
Fichter, Angela Hawkins ..... Scotland, CT
Fichter, Joel C. ..... Massillon, OH
Fichter, Lawrence R. ..... Decatur, IL
Fichter, Richard E. ..... Alexandria, VA
Fichthorn, Norman W. ..... Washington, DC
Fichtl, Chris J. ..... Uniondale, NY
Fichtner, Carl A. ..... San Diego, CA
Fichtner, Catherine A. ..... Waltham, MA
Fichtner, Jay S. ..... Dallas, TX
Fichtner, Mercedes M. ..... Overland Park, KS
Fichtner, Rae Ann ..... Denton, TX
Fici, Amy Levine ..... Rochester, NY
Fick, Andrew F. ..... Reading, PA
Fick, Barbara J. ..... Notre Dame, IN
Fick, C. Milton ..... Baytown, TX
Fick, James G. ..... Seattle, WA
Fick, John E. ..... Decatur, IL
Fick, John J. ..... St. Paul, MN
Fick, John S. ..... Los Angeles, CA
Fick, Jos. J. ..... Chicago, IL
Fick, Joseph E., Jr. ..... New Orleans, LA
Fick, Matthew L. ..... Seattle, WA
Fick, Nathaniel Crow, Jr. ..... Towson, MD
Fick, Nicholas E. ..... Scranton, PA
Fick & Petty ..... Baltimore, MD
Towson, MD
Fick, Philip J. ..... Washington, DC
Fick, Robert C. ..... Newport Beach, CA
Fick, Rodell R. ..... Orange, CA
Fick, Ronald L. ..... Naples, FL
Palm Beach, FL
Fickbohm, Ronna L. ..... Tucson, AZ
Ficke, Gregory C. ..... Cincinnati, OH
Fickel, David J. ..... Toledo, OH
Fickel, Jenny M. ..... Gold River, CA
Fickel, Keith B. ..... Harrisburg, PA
Fickel, R. Bruce, II ..... Berthoud, CO
Fickel, Randall W. ..... Dallas, TX
Ficken, Bruce W. ..... Philadelphia, PA
Ficken, Bryant, Jr. ..... Corpus Christi, TX
Fickenscher, Carol Ann ..... Castro Valley, CA
Fickenscher, Donald A. ..... Norfolk, VA
Fickenscher, Karl W.
Agency for International Development,
Legal Advisers-Overseas, GV
Ficker, Rodney H. ..... Department of Defense,
Defense Legal Services Agency, GV
Fickes, Clyde R. ..... Des Moines, IA
Fickes, Jeri J. ..... Department of Commerce,
Patent and Trademark Office, GV
Fickes, John C. ..... Akron, OH
Fickes, Karen E. ..... Jacksonville, FL
Fickes, Mark E. ..... Yakima, WA
Fickes, Paul E. ..... Boise, ID
Fickett, Joel A. ..... Washington, DC
Fickett, Lewis P., Jr. ..... Fredericksburg, VA
Fickey, Charles J. ..... Stamford, CT
Fickie, Ward ..... St. Louis, MO
Fickle, Stanley C. ..... Indianapolis, IN
Fickle & Tharp ..... Platte City, MO
Fickle, William D. ..... Platte City, MO
Ficklen, Fielding H. ..... Spokane, WA
Fickler, Arlene ..... Philadelphia, PA
Fickler, Debra F. ..... Villanova, PA
Fickler, Debra J. ..... Chicago, IL
Fickley, R. Bruce ..... Roanoke, VA
Ficklin, Patrice Alexander ..... Washington, DC
Fickling, Craig P., Jr. ..... Cookeville, TN
Fickling, Gregory L. ..... Washington, DC
Fickman, Bruce A. ..... Houston, TX
Fickman, Robert J. ..... Houston, TX
Ficks, Carl R., Jr. ..... New Britain, CT
Ficks, Gregg M. ..... Oakland, CA
Ficksman & Conley ..... Boston, MA
Ficksman, David L. ..... Los Angeles, CA
Ficksman, Max S. ..... Boston, MA
Fico, Gaetano D. ..... Syracuse, NY
Fico, Peter A. ..... Millburn, NJ
Fidalgo, William F. ..... East Providence, RI
Fiddes, Alisa Nicole ..... New York, NY
Fiddes, Richard C. ..... Cincinnati, OH
Fiddler, G. Scott ..... Bellaire, TX
Fiddler González & Rodríguez, LLP
San Juan, PR
Fiddler, Noah D. ..... Kailua, HI
Fiddler, Robert W. ..... Great Neck, NY
Fiddler, Thomas B. ..... Philadelphia, PA
Fidei, Richard J. ..... Fort Lauderdale, FL
Fidel, Arthur G. ..... Pittsburgh, PA
Fidel, Gary S. ..... Kew Gardens, NY
Fidel, Noel A. ..... Phoenix, AZ
Fidel, Stanley J. ..... New York, NY
Fidelibus, Agnes H. ..... Port Chester, NY
Fidell, Eugene R. ..... Washington, DC
Fidell, Jay M. ..... Honolulu, HI
Fidell, Lauri E. ..... Moraga, CA
Fidelman, Morris ..... Washington, DC
Fiden, Joan L. ..... New York, NY
Fides, Peter J., II ..... Orlando, FL
Fidgeon, Timothy F. ..... Boston, MA
Fidis, Marcia Coleman ..... Bethesda, MD
Fidler and Associates, P.C. ..... Houston, TX
Fidler, Christopher D. ..... Columbus, OH
Fidler, Clarence H. ..... Port Angeles, WA
Fidler, Danielle C. ..... Alexandria, VA
Fidler, David A. ..... Los Angeles, CA
Fidler, David P. ..... Bloomington, IN
Fidler, Donald H. ..... Houston, TX
Fidler, Edward ..... Cincinnati, OH
Fidler, G. Craig ..... Denver, CO
Fidler, Gary D. ..... Los Angeles, CA
Fidler, Gayle D. ..... Parker, CO
Fidler, Genine Macks ..... Owings Mills, MD
Fidler, J. Paul ..... Cleveland, OH
Fidler, James G. ..... Canton, OH
Fidler, Jody C. ..... New York, NY
Fidler, Joseph F. ..... Trenton, NJ
Fidler, Joseph F., Jr. ..... Milton, MA
Fidler, Joseph M. ..... Easton, MA
Fidler, Josh E. ..... Owings Mills, MD
Fidler, Larry ..... Los Angeles, CA
Fidler, Lewis A. ..... New York, NY
Fidler, Ray R. ..... Baltimore, MD
Fidler, Roger L. ..... Hackensack, NJ
Fidler, Ronald W. ..... Sherman Oaks, CA
Fidler, Stephanie ..... Philadelphia, PA
Fidler, Walther B. ..... Warsaw, VA
Fidlon, Greg R. ..... New York, NY
Fidlow, Bennett J. ..... Los Angeles, CA
Fidnick, Linda S. ..... Amherst, MA
Fido, Mary E. ..... Woodland Hills, CA
Fido, Silvia Catherine ..... New Bedford, MA
Fidone, Gary P. ..... Los Angeles, CA
San Francisco, CA
Fidone, Kelly Lee ..... Tustin, CA
Fidrych, Robert A. ..... Platteville, WI
Fiducci, Scott E. ..... Milwaukee, WI
Fidurko, William J. ..... Wellesley, MA
Fiebach, H. Robert ..... Philadelphia, PA
Fiebelkorn, Douglas P. ..... Randolph, MA
Fieber, Julie L. ..... Los Angeles, CA
San Francisco, CA
Fieber, Laura ..... New York, NY
Fieber, Samuel L. ..... Grayville, IL
Fieber, Susan E. ..... Omaha, NE
Fiebig, Andre R. ..... Chicago, IL
Fiebig, Glen A. ..... Alliance, NE
Fiebiger, Stephen C. ..... Minneapolis, MN
Fiebiger, Stephen C., & Associates, Chartered
Minneapolis, MN
Fiebiger, Thomas D. ..... Fargo, ND
Fiechter, Michael A. ..... North Bellmore, NY
Fiedel, Mark ..... Miami, FL
Fiedelholtz, Jerald ..... New Windsor, NY
Fiedelholtz, Jerald, P.C. ..... New Windsor, NY
Fiedelman & McGaw ..... Jericho, NY
Fiedelman, Robert I. ..... Jericho, NY
Fiederer, Lee S. ..... Philadelphia, PA
Fiederer, Pamela Rish ..... Madison, OH
Fiedler, Akin, Frank & Carlton, P.C.
Dallas, TX
Fiedler, Alan W. ..... Franklin Lakes, NJ
Fiedler, Anne ..... Chicago, IL
Fiedler, Charles Arthur ..... Bloomfield Hills, MI
Lansing, MI
Fiedler, Charles S. ..... Torrance, CA
Fiedler, Daniel L. ..... Boston, MA
Fiedler, Diane Marie ..... Laramie, WY
Fiedler, Donald B. ..... Omaha, NE
Fiedler, Edward H., Jr. ..... River Forest, IL
Fiedler, frederick Adolph ..... Clinton, TN
Fiedler, James N. ..... Van Nuys, CA
Fiedler, James P. ..... Dodgeville, WI
Fiedler, James S. ..... New York, NY
Fiedler, Jay H. ..... Grand Forks, ND
Fiedler, Julianne M. ..... Minneapolis, MN
Fiedler, Laurie W. ..... Wayne, NJ
Fiedler, Lawrence E. ..... New York, NY
Fiedler, Lawrence E., P.C. ..... New York, NY
Fiedler, Marc ..... Washington, DC
Fiedler, Mary Midkiff ..... Honolulu, HI
Fiedler, Norman D. ..... New York, NY
Fiedler, Paige E. ..... West Des Moines, IA
Fiedler, Patrick J. ..... Madison, WI
Fiedler, Robert Charles ..... Olympic Valley, CA
Fiedler, Robert W., Jr. ..... Toledo, OH
Fiedler, Sara L. ..... Chicago, IL
Fiedler, Susan Birke ..... Hartford, CT
Fiedler, Thomas L. ..... Dallas, TX
Fiege, C. Frederick ..... Chevy Chase, MD
Fiegel, Stephen M. ..... Sacramento, CA
Fiegen, Jon B. ..... Phoenix, AZ
Fiegen Law Firm, P.C. ..... Cedar Rapids, IA
Fiegen, Thomas L. ..... Cedar Rapids, IA
Fieger, Fieger & Schwartz, A Professional Corporation ..... Detroit, MI
Southfield, MI
Fieger, Geoffrey N. ..... Southfield, MI
Fieger, Jason P. ..... Washington, DC
Baltimore, MD
Rockville, MD
Fieger, Joseph L. ..... Highland Park, IL

Fieger, Joseph L., Ltd. ....Highland Park, IL
Fieger, Thomas J., Jr. ....Media, PA
Fieger, Wallace R. ....Findlay, OH
Fiegl, Christopher P. ....Fremont, OH
Fieglein, J. Michael ....Galveston, TX
Fiehler, Alan R. ....Houston, TX
Fiehrer, Jacques J. ....Hamilton, OH
Fiehrer, Lawrence P. ....Hamilton, OH
Fiekowsky, Elisabeth K. ....Brooklyn, NY
Fiel, Martin E. ....New City, NY
Fiel, Stuart D. ....Philadelphia, PA
Fieland, Louis C. ....New York, NY
Field, A. Joseph ....Schaumburg, IL
Field, A. Searle, II ....United States Senate, Senatorial Assistants, GV
Field, Alexandra M.
Federal Communications Commission, International Bureau, GV
Field, Allan S. ....San Diego, CA
Field, Allen David ....Los Angeles, CA
Field, Allen W. ....Portland, OR
Field, Andrea Bear ....Washington, DC
Field, Andrea S. ....Brooklyn, NY
Field, Andrew J. ....Denver, CO
Field, Andrew R. ....Barre, VT
Field, Ann Lederer ....Schaumburg, IL
Field, Ann Thornton ....Philadelphia, PA
Field, Arthur Norman ....New York, NY
Field, Barry H. ....Boston, MA
Field, Benjamin Thomas ....San Jose, CA
Field, Blackshaw & Field, P.C. ....Barre, VT
Field, Bret E. ....Palo Alto, CA
Field, Bridget L. ....Chicago, IL
Field, Catherine R.
Executive Office Of The President, Office of the U.S. Trade Representative, GV
Field, Charles D. ....Riverside, CA
Field, Charles D., Jr. ....Menlo Park, CA
Field, Charles G. ....Washington, DC
Field, Charles H. ....San Diego, CA
Field, Charles W. ....Norcross, GA
Field, Charles W., P.C. ....Norcross, GA
Field, Christine Moriarty ....Wheaton, IL
Field, Christopher ....Falls Church, VA
Field & Cram ....Fairfax, VA
Field & Custer, P.C. ....Syracuse, NY
Field, Dana M. ....Vancouver, WA
Field, Dane S. ....Irving, TX
Field, Daniel G. ....Scottsdale, AZ
Field, Daniel L. ....Fenton, MO
Field, Daniel P. ....Waukegan, IL
Field, David A. ....New York, NY
Field, David B. ....Chicago, IL
Field, David C. ....Lexington, KY
Field, David E. ....Southfield, MI
Field, David Ellis ....Fairfax, VA
Field, David G. ....Hammond, IN
Field, David L. ....Enid, OK
Field, David W. ....Roseland, NJ
Field, Deborah K. ....Syracuse, NY
Field, Denise H. ....San Francisco, CA
Field, Dennis M. ....Waterloo, IL
Field, Diana L. ....Santa Ana, CA
Field, Donald L., Jr. ....San Francisco, CA
Field, Donald S. ....Los Angeles, CA
Field, Douglas L. ....Walnut Creek, CA
Field, Drew ....San Francisco, CA
Field, E. Harper ....Tallahassee, FL
Field, Eliot ....Wiscasset, ME
Field, Ernest R. ....Great Neck, NY
Field, Eva, P.C. ....Chicago, IL
Field, Eva, P.C. ....Chicago, IL
Field, Evan W. ....Santa Rosa, CA
Field & Field, P.C. ....Kalamazoo, MI
Field, Gary L. ....Lansing, MI
Field, Gary P. ....Huntington, NY
Field, Gentry & Benjamin, P.C.
Overland Park, KS
Kansas City, MO
St. Louis, MO
Field, George P. ....Boston, MA
Field, George W. ....Bloomington, MN
Field, Gerald A. ....Hartford, CT
Field, Gerson B. ....Wilmette, IL
Field & Golan ....Chicago, IL
Field, Hal W. ....Columbus, OH
Field, Harlene I. ....Danville, CA
Field, Harold B. ....Seattle, WA
Field, Harold D., Jr., (P.A.)
Minneapolis, MN
Field, Harold G. ....Wheaton, IL
Field, Harold J. ....Bayonne, NJ
Field, Harry B. ....Seal Beach, CA
Field, Harry E. ....Mentor, OH
Field, Henry A., Jr. ....Madison, WI
Field, Henry F. ....Chicago, IL
Field, Howard B., III ....Durham, CT
Field, Hugh M. ....Waterloo, IA
Field, Hurley & Sullivan ....Lowell, MA
Field, Ila L. ....Miami, FL
Field, J. Ritchie, Jr. ....Conroe, TX
Field, James A. ....Chicago, IL
Field, James M. ....Baton Rouge, LA
Field, James M., L.C. ....Baton Rouge, LA
Field, Jeffrey H. ....Beverly Hills, CA
Field, Jere ....Monroe, GA
Field, Jerome N. ....San Francisco, CA
Field, Jerome N., Inc., A Law Corp.
San Francisco, CA
Field, Jesse R. ....Shawnee, OK
Field, Joanne S. ....San Jose, CA
Field, Joel ....New York, NY
Field, John A., Jr. ....Naples, FL
Field, John J. ....Washington, DC
Field, John V. ....Collingswood, NJ
Field, John V., P.A. ....Collingswood, NJ
Field, John W. ....Deerfield Beach, FL
Field, John W., P.A. ....Deerfield Beach, FL
Field, Jon T. ....Ashtabula, OH
Field, Jonathan M. ....Philadelphia, PA
Field, Jonathan W. ....Middletown, CT
Field, Joseph A. ....Hood River, OR
Field, Joseph E. ....New York, NY
Field, Joseph Hooper ....Bath, ME
Field, Joseph M. ....Bala Cynwyd, PA
Field, Julie Kunce ....Fort Collins, CO
Field, Julie Kunce ....Ann Arbor, MI
Field, Karen L. ....Ann Arbor, MI
Field, Karen M.
Treasury Department, GV
Field, Katherine A. ....Taunton, MA
Field, Kathleen C. ....Lynnwood, WA
Field, Larry F. ....Springfield, MA
Field, Larry L. ....Guymon, OK
Field, Larry L., P.C. ....Guymon, OK
Field, Lauren W. ....New York, NY
Field, Laurence ....Boston, MA
Field, Lawrence I. ....Chevy Chase, MD
Field, Lawrence J. ....Minneapolis, MN
Field, Leslie E. ....Chicago, IL
Field, Linda Wheat ....Birmingham, AL
Field, Lomenzo & Turret, P.C.
New York, NY
Field, Lynn M. ....Memphis, TN
Field, Marc D. ....Santa Clara, CA
Field, Marcia K. ....Manhasset, NY
Field, Marjorie Lynn ....Ventura, CA
Field, Mark E. ....Los Angeles, CA
Field, Marshall L. ....Lowell, MA
Field, Martin ....Laguna Hills, CA
Field, Mary L. ....Wheaton, IL
Field, Michael S. ....Boston, MA
Field, Michael W. ....San Francisco, CA
Field, Milton M. ....Alexandria, VA
Field, Milton M., P.C. ....Alexandria, VA
Field, Nancy C., Law Offices of
San Francisco, CA
Field, Nancy L. ....Jackson, MS
Field, Noel M., Jr. ....Boston, MA
Providence, RI
Field, Nora E. ....Boston, MA
Field, O. F., Jr. ....Plano, TX
Field & Olesnycky ....East Hanover, NJ
Field, Pamela J. ....Fayetteville, NY
Field, Paul H. ....Coral Gables, FL
Field, Pecos Bill ....San Francisco, CA
Field, Phyllis J. ....Quincy, MA
Field, R. Jeffrey ....Decatur, GA
Field, R. Louis ....Vicksburg, MS
Field, Richard C. ....Los Angeles, CA
Field, Richard L. ....Cliffside Park, NJ
Field, Richardson & Wilhelmy
Walnut Creek, CA
Field, Rikki Lamatino ....Newark, NJ
Field, Robert ....Fairfax, VA
Field, Robert B., Jr. ....Manchester, NH
Field, Robert C. ....Walnut Creek, CA
Field, Robert C. ....Decatur, GA
Field, Robert E. ....Chicago, IL
Field, Robert F. ....Danbury, CT
Field, Robert M. ....Anniston, AL
Field, Robert Mark ....Memphis, TN
Field, Robert S. ....Washington, DC
Field, Robert S. ....East Hanover, NJ
New York, NY
Field & Roos, LLP ....Boston, MA
Field, S. Randall ....Farmington Hills, MI
Field, Samuel S., III ....Baltimore, MD
Field, Samuel T. ....Kalamazoo, MI
Field, Sandra Gusciora ....Mountain Lakes, NJ
Field, Sarah L. ....Barre, VT
Field & Schultz ....Boston, MA
Field, Scott Douglas ....Bethesda, MD
Field, Scott F. ....Huntington Beach, CA
Field, Scott King ....Austin, TX
Field, Stefanie ....Riverside, CA
Field, Stephen F. ....Vienna, VA
Field, Stephen R., Law Offices of
New York, NY
Field, Stewart E. ....Tulsa, OK
Field, Susan J. ....Los Angeles, CA
Field, T. Mike ....Lubbock, TX
Field, Theodore ....Northridge, CA
Field, Thom G. ....Springfield, MO
Field, Thomas ....New York, NY
Field, Thomas G., Jr. ....Concord, NH
Field, Thomas R. ....Chicago, IL
Field, Thornton Withers
Department of Justice, Environment and Natural Resources Division, GV
Field, Tracy M. H. ....Atlanta, GA
Field, Trojan, Long & Sedbrook, P.C.
Enid, OK
Fairview, OK
Field, William B. ....Barre, VT
Field, William C. ....Charleston, WV
Field, William Douglas, Jr.
Owensboro, KY
Field, William O. ....Frankfort, KY
Fieldcamp, Rochelle B. ....Philadelphia, PA
Fieldcamp, Rochelle B., P.C.
Philadelphia, PA
Fieldcamp, Steven W. ....Corpus Christi, TX
Fielden, Arlen E. ....Oklahoma City, OK
Fielden, Barbara Hebenton ....Seattle, WA
Fielden, Brian K. ....Charlotte, NC
Fielden, Craig A. ....Seattle, WA
Fielden, Harold M. ....Boulder, CO
Fielden, Timothy G. ....Seattle, WA
Fielder, Alan C. ....Lockhart, TX
Fielder, C. David ....Arlington, TX
Fielder, David A. ....Springfield, MO
Fielder, David E. ....Knoxville, TN
Fielder, Elizabeth M. ....Las Vegas, NV
Reno, NV
Fielder, Ernest G., (P.C.) ....Dallas, TX
Fielder, Henry W. ....Waco, TX
Fielder, Hugh B. ....Visalia, CA
Fielder, John R. ....Rosemead, CA
Fielder, Kristi K. ....Detroit, MI
Fielder, Lanny K. ....San Francisco, CA
Fielder, Lynne Hankins ....Key West, FL
Sugarloaf Key, FL
Fielder, Mary L. ....Ventura, CA
Fielder, Mike ....Dayton, TX
Fielder, Richard A. ....Lockhart, TX
Fielder, Robert Lynn ....Dallas, TX
Fielder, Stephanie A. ....Harrisburg, PA
Fielder, Timothy L. ....Girard, KS
Fielder, William C. ....Lockhart, TX
Fieldhack, Randall W. ....Milwaukee, WI
Fieldhouse, Lynn K. ....Louisville, KY
Fielding, Bernard R. ....Charleston, SC
Fielding, Charles L. ....San Diego, CA
Fielding, Cheryl Ann Berlin
Springfield, MO
Fielding, David ....Fort Worth, TX
Fielding, David C. ....Buffalo, NY
Fielding, David H. ....San Francisco, CA
Fielding, Eliot D. ....Treasury Department, Internal Revenue Service, GV
Fielding, Fred F. ....Washington, DC
Fielding & Jacobus, P.A. ....Melbourne, FL
Fielding, Jerry L. ....Talladega, AL
Fielding, John D. ....Melbourne, FL
Fielding, John P. ....McLean, VA
Fielding, John R. ....Pittsburgh, PA
Fielding, Judith L. ....Menlo Park, CA
Fielding, Kenneth ....Tacoma, WA
Fielding, Lois E. ....Detroit, MI
Jasper, TX
Fielding, Lynn ....Kennewick, WA
Fielding, Mary ....East Lansing, MI
Fielding, Nancy E. ....Massapequa, NY
Fielding, Pamela S. ....Hamburg, NJ
Fielding, Parker & Jones, L.L.P.
Fort Worth, TX
Fielding, Thomas C. ....Camden, NJ
Fielding, William J. ....Glendale, NY
Fielding Lopez, Evelyn ....Olympia, WA
Field-Lang, Cheryl A. ....Reno, NV
Fieldman, Arnold ....Washington, DC
Fieldman, Barbara I. ....Los Angeles, CA
Fieldman, Elaine ....Detroit, MI
Fieldman, Eric S. ....New York, NY
Fieldman, Gale Z. ....New York, NY
Fieldman, George M. ....Hackensack, NJ
Fieldman Hay & Ullman, LLP
New York, NY
Fieldman, Henry J. ....New York, NY
Fieldman, Iris E. ....Las Vegas, NV
Fieldman, Leon ....Sonoma, CA
Fieldman, Neil ....Longmeadow, MA
Fieldman, Steven D. ....Altamonte Springs, FL
Fields, Aaron J. ....Brooklyn, NY
Fields, Alan B. ....Naples, FL
Fields, Alan B., Jr. ....Palatka, FL
Fields, Alan M. ....Sherman Oaks, CA
Fields, Aletha V. ....Brooklyn, NY
Fields, Amanda L. ....Greensboro, NC
Fields, Andrew ....Lake Worth, FL
Fields, Andrew J. ....New York, NY
Fields, Arthur A. ....Santa Fe, NM
Fields, August D. ....Dallas, TX
Fields & Bagley, P.C. ....El Paso, TX
Fields, Barry E. ....Chicago, IL
Fields, Benjamin D. ....Philadelphia, PA
Fields, Bernard R. ....New York, NY
Fields, Bertram ....Los Angeles, CA
Fields, Beth Kovitz ....Peekskill, NY
Fields, Beverly Ann ....Washington, DC
Fields & Bible, P.C. ....Chattanooga, TN
Fields, Blaine L. ....San Jose, CA
Fields, Brandon J. ....Washington, DC
Fields, Brent J.
Securities and Exchange Commission, Division of Enforcement, GV
Fields, Brian J. ....Thousand Oaks, CA
Fields, Brian W. ....Kansas City, MO
Fields & Brown ....Kansas City, MO
Fields, C. Kerry ....Anaheim, CA
Fields, C. Russell ....Baltimore, MD
Fields, Candice L. ....Sacramento, CA
Fields, Carla M. ....Kansas City, MO
Fields, Carol Y. ....Detroit, MI
Fields, Carolyn M. ....Kennesaw, GA
Fields, Cathie L. ....Tustin, CA
Fields, Christine S. ....Indianapolis, IN
Fields & Cooper ....Nashville, NC
Rocky Mount, NC
Fields, Craig B. ....New York, NY
Fields, Craig M. ....Beverly Hills, CA
Fields, D. Annette ....Washington, DC
Fields, D. Christopher ....Abingdon, VA
Fields, Darrell A. ....Cleveland, OH
Fields, Darren Charles ....Baltimore, MD
Fields, Dave I. ....New York, NY
Fields, David ....New York, NY
Fields, David Lee ....Dallas, TX
Fields, David M. ....Newport Beach, CA
Fields, Debra E. ....Palm Beach Gardens, FL
Fields, Debra F. ....Washington, DC
Fields, Diana C. ....Denver, CO
Fields, Diana Denman ....Los Angeles, CA
Fields, Donna Lee ....Fort Lauderdale, FL
Fields, Donna M. ....Memphis, TN
Fields, Douglas A. ....Winnetka, IL
Fields, Duncan S. ....Yakutat, AK
Fields, Edward J., Jr. ....Dallas, TX
Fields, Eileen M. ....New York, NY
Fields, Elliot J. ....Philadelphia, PA
Fields, Everett F. ....Pasadena, CA
Fields, F.D. ....Mount Lebanon, PA
Fields & Fields ....Encino, CA
Fields and Fields ....Oxon Hill, MD
Fields, Forrest S., Jr. ....Tallahassee, FL
Fields, Frank J. ....Rochester, NY
Fields, Frederick B. ....Knoxville, TN
Fields, Frederick S. ....San Francisco, CA
Fields & Friedsam, P.A. ....Tampa, FL
Fields, Gary B. ....Mill Valley, CA
Fields, Gary D. ....Long Beach, CA
Fields, Gary D. ....Englewood, CO
Fields, Gary D. ....Palm Beach Gardens, FL
Fields, Gary S. ....Southfield, MI
Fields, Geoffrey A. ....Grand Rapids, MI
Fields, George Andre ....Portland, OR
Fields, George W., Jr. ....Hopewell, VA
Fields, Gerald J. ....New York, NY
Fields, Gordon B. ....Department of Commerce, Office of the General Counsel, GV
Fields, Gregory ....Wilmington, DE
Fields, Guy N., III ....El Paso, TX
Fields, H. Michael ....Seattle, WA
Fields & Hardee ....Athens, TX
Fields, Harry L., Jr. ....Chattanooga, TN
Fields, Heather L. ....Chicago, IL
Milwaukee, WI
Fields, Helen G. ....Beverly Hills, CA
Fields, Helen H. ....Oxon Hill, MD
Fields, Helene L. ....Bayside, NY
Fields, Henry M. ....Los Angeles, CA
Fields & Hopkins, P.C. ....Austin, TX
Fields, Howard A. ....White Plains, NY
Fields, Howard D. ....Hillsboro, OH
Fields, Howard M. ....Calabasas, CA
Fields & Humphrey ....Bakersfield, CA
Fields & Innocenti ....Columbus, OH
Lancaster, OH
Fields, Irwin ....Boca Raton, FL
Fields Israel & Binning LLP
Long Beach, CA
Los Angeles, CA
Santa Ana, CA
Fields, J. Follace, II ....Lexington, KY
Fields, J. Michael ....Greenville, NC
New Bern, NC
Fields, Jack Ceacil ....Bloomington, IL
Fields, Jack E. ....Houston, TX
Fields, Jack H. ....Las Vegas, NV
Fields, Jack M., Jr. ....Humble, TX
Fields, Jackson E., Jr. ....Columbia, SC
Fields, James ....New York, NY
Fields, James A. ....Chattanooga, TN
Fields, James A., Jr. ....Columbus, OH
Lancaster, OH
Fields, James E. ....Evansville, IN
Fields, James H. ....Baltimore, MD
Fields, James P. ....Brunswick, GA
Fields, James P., Jr. ....Columbia, SC
Fields, Jane E. ....Austin, TX
Fields, Jane F. ....Chicago, IL
Fields, Janet ....Encino, CA
Fields, Jeffery William ....Kansas City, MO
Fields, Jeffrey D. ....Garden City, NY
Fields, Jennifer L. ....Huntsville, AL
Fields, Jerome K. ....Los Angeles, CA
Fields, Jerry Douglas, Jr.
Birmingham, AL
Fields, Jim H., Jr. ....Philadelphia, PA
Fields, Jimmie H. ....Meridian, MS
Fields, John C. ....New York, NY
Fields, John H. ....Kansas City, KS
Fields, John N. ....St. Joseph, MI
Fields, John R. ....Glenview, IL
Fields, John W. ....Seneca, SC
Fields, John W., P.A. ....Seneca, SC
Walhalla, SC
Fields & Johnson, A Professional Corporation ....Englewood, CO
Fields, Jonathan A. ....New York, NY
Fields, Jonathan E. ....Newton, MA
Fields, Jordan I. ....Stuart, FL
Fields, Joseph Francis ....Garden City, NY
New York, NY
Fields, Joseph H. ....East Lansing, MI
Fields, Joseph R., Jr. ....West Palm Beach, FL
Fields, Joseph R., P.A.
West Palm Beach, FL
Fields, Julia L. ....Goshen, KY
Fields, Kathy A. ....Boston, MA
Fields, Kenneth L. ....Phoenix, AZ
Fields, Kenneth R. ....New York, NY
Fields, Kenneth S. ....Los Angeles, CA
Fields, Kenneth W. ....Pampa, TX
Fields, Kim Budoff ....Alexandria, LA
Fields, Kimberley R. ....Charleston, WV
Fields, L. Ernestine ....Van Nuys, CA
Fields, Larry G. ....Santa Teresa, NM
El Paso, TX
Fields, Larry G., P.C. ....Santa Teresa, NM
El Paso, TX
Fields, Larry H. ....Glendale, CA
Fields, Larry L. ....Bakersfield, CA
Fields, Laurie B. ....Phoenix, AZ
Fields Law Group ....Anaheim, CA
Fields, Lea Lynn ....San Diego, CA
Fields, Leslie A. ....Denver, CO
Fields, Leslie M. ....Lemoyne, PA
Fields, Leslie T. ....Daphne, AL
Fields, Linda W. ....Frankfort, KY
Fields, Lori A. ....Los Angeles, CA
Fields, Lorraine S. ....New York, NY
Fields, Louise B. ....Tampa, FL
Fields, Marjory D. ....Bronx, NY
Fields, Mark C. ....Torrance, CA
Fields, Marshall G. ....Deerfield, IL
Fields, Marvin L. ....Bayside, NY
Fields, Melissa E. ....Houston, TX
Fields, Melissa J. ....Lexington, MA
Fields, Michael E. ....Birmingham, AL

Fields, Michael J. ... Enid, OK
Fields, Michael R. ... Seattle, WA
Fields, Michael S. ... Artesia, CA
Beverly Hills, CA
Cerritos, CA
Fields, Michael S., Incorporated
Artesia, CA
Beverly Hills, CA
Los Angeles, CA
Fields, Michele McDowell ... Arlington, VA
Fields, Milton P. ... Rocky Mount, NC
Fields, Murray M. ... Los Angeles, CA
Fields, Olivia D. A. ... Los Angeles, CA
Fields, Orval E., II ... Pickerington, OH
Fields, Oscar P., (P.C.) ... Amarillo, TX
Fields, Pamela J. ... Aptos, CA
Fields, Patrick J. ... Los Angeles, CA
Fields, Paul ... New York, NY
Fields, Paul L., Jr. ... Atlanta, GA
Fields, Peter A. ... Los Angeles, CA
Fields, Peter A. ... New York, NY
Fields, Phillip R. ... Wichita, KS
Fields, Preston J.
Palm Beach Gardens, FL
Fields, Randolph H. ... Orlando, FL
Fields, Raymond J., Jr. ... Freeport, TX
Fields, Rebecca D. ... Palo Alto, CA
Fields, Rhodell G.
Federal Energy Regulatory Commission, Office of the General Counsel, GV
Fields, Rhonda C. ... Washington, DC
Fields, Richard B. ... Memphis, TN
Fields, Richard C. ... Boise, ID
Fields, Richard E. ... Charleston, SC
Fields, Richard L. ... Oxon Hill, MD
Fields, Richard S. ... Tucson, AZ
Fields, Richard W. ... Washington, DC
Fields, Richard W. ... Albany, GA
Fields, Robert A. ... Oxon Hill, MD
Fields, Robert C. ... Frankfort, KY
Fields, Robert E., III ... Raleigh, NC
Fields, Robert G. ... Lynn, MA
Fields, Robert H. ... Athens, TX
Fields, Robert J. ... Philadelphia, PA
Fields, Robert M. ... Palatka, FL
Fields, Robert M. ... New York, NY
Fields, Robert W. ... Tampa, FL
Fields, Roberta Browning
Oklahoma City, OK
Fields, Robin F. ... Oklahoma City, OK
Fields, Rodney A. ... Knoxville, TN
Fields, Roger A. ... Rochester, NY
Fields, Ron W. ... Redwood City, CA
Fields, Ronald ... Fort Smith, AR
Fields, Ronald ... New York, NY
Fields, Sally Ann ... Trenton, NJ
Fields, Samuel S. ... Fort Lauderdale, FL
Fields, Scott J. ... Philadelphia, PA
Fields, Shari L. ... Kansas City, MO
Fields, Sidney M. ... Chicago, IL
Fields, Spurgeon, III ... Raleigh, NC
Fields, Stacey B. ... Los Angeles, CA
Fields, Stancy Stribling ... El Paso, TX
Fields, Stanley ... Salem, OR
Fields, Stanley G. ... Jamaica, NY
Fields, Stephen M. ... New York, NY
Fields, Steven D. ... Austin, TX
Fields, Steven J. ... Bothell, WA
Fields, Steven J. ... Seattle, WA
Fields, Stuart J. ... Hackensack, NJ
Fields, Susan E. ... Van Nuys, CA
Fields, Suzanne ... Bethlehem, PA
Fields, T. Elizabeth Fields
Beverly Hills, CA
Fields, Tammy K. ... West Palm Beach, FL
Fields, Taylor ... Kansas City, MO
Fields, Teresa Monica ... Santa Cruz, CA
Fields, Terry R. ... Santa Monica, CA
Fields, Thanda A. ... Boston, MA
Fields, Thisbe Etta ... Gardena, CA
Fields, Thomas R. ... Kansas City, MO
Fields, Thomas R., III ... Hayneville, AL
Fields, Thomas R., III., Attorney at Law P.C.
Hayneville, AL
Fields, Tim L. ... Albuquerque, NM
Fields, Timothy E. ... San Diego, CA
Fields, Toy R., III ... Encino, CA
Fields, Vic ... Austin, TX
Fields, Victor G. ... East Bridgewater, MA
Fields, Virginia S. ... Austin, TX
Fields, W. Lamar ... Savannah, GA
Fields, W. Russell ... Lodi, CA
Fields, Walter D. ... Boise, ID
Fields, Warren J. ... Houston, TX
Fields, W. B. ... Athens, TX
Fields, Wendy L. ... Washington, DC
Fields, Wesley ... Kansas City, MO
Fields & Wilkinson, P.A. ... Stuart, FL
Fields, William A. ... Marietta, OH
Fields, William C., III ... Providence, RI
Fields, William Corbett, Jr. ... Raeford, NC
Fields, William J. ... Wichita, KS
Fields, William S. ... Department of Defense, Defense Legal Services Agency, GV
Fields-Lee, Lori Jean ... Covington, KY
Fieldsteel, Ira ... New York, NY
Fieldsteel, John W. ... Boston, MA
Fieldstein, Jill G. ... New York, NY
Fieldston, Kenneth C. ... Fort Lee, NJ
Fieldstone Lester Shear & Denberg
Aventura, FL
Miami, FL
Fieldstone, Ronald R. ... Aventura, FL
Miami, FL
Fielek, Anthony C. ... Rochester Hills, MI
Fielitz, Alan E ... Hamburg, NY
Fielkow, Arnold D. ... Lincolnwood, IL
Fielkow, Brian L. ... Milwaukee, WI
Fielkow, Colleen ... Chicago, IL
Fiello, Michael A. ... Murphysboro, IL
Fielo, Julius ... East Orange, NJ
Fielo, Michael K. ... West Orange, NJ
Fielstein, William ... Boca Raton, FL
Fiely, Donald E. ... Canton, OH
Fieman, Colin A ... Athens, GA
Fienberg, Jeffrey B. ... Pittsburgh, PA
Fienberg, Lorne M. ... Nashua, NH
Fienberg, Steven D. ... Santa Ana, CA
Fiene, Cynthia ... Madison, WI
Fiene, Laura M. ... Mill Valley, CA
Fien-Helfman, L. Jacob
Securities and Exchange Commission, Division of Corporation Finance, GV
Fieo, Alyssa R. ... Philadelphia, PA
Fier, Elihu ... New York, NY
Fier, Michael H. ... Ronkonkoma, NY
Fier, Robert D. ... New York, NY
Fierberg, Douglas E. ... Washington, DC
Fierberg, Ira M., Law Office of
Los Angeles, CA
Fierberg, Ira M., Law Office of
Manhattan Beach, CA
Fierberg, Ira M., Law Office of
Santa Ana, CA
Fierberg, James Harris ... Miami, FL
Fierce, Allan R. ... Boston, MA
Fierce, Richard A. ... Greenville, SC
Fierce, Robin Kinert ... Richardson, TX
Fierer, Gayle ... West Hartford, CT
Fiergang, Alfred I. ... Fort Washington, PA
Fiergang & Simmons, P.C.
Fort Washington, PA
Fiering, Susan S. ... San Francisco, CA
Fierke, Thomas G. ... New Orleans, LA
Fierman, Gregg H. ... Miami, FL
Fierman, Janet B. ... Boston, MA
Fierman, Martin L. ... Eatonton, GA
Fierman, Robert A., (P.C.) ... Atlanta, GA
Fierman-Cribbs, Stacy ... Los Angeles, CA
Fiero, Anthony W. ... Valley Stream, NY
Fiero, James G. ... Bloomington, IL
Fiero, John D. ... San Francisco, CA
Fierres, Juan Carlos ... San Juan, PR
Fierro, Alfred D. ... Fort Lee, NJ
Fierro, Andrew J. ... Anchorage, AK
Fierro, Arturo N. ... Los Angeles, CA
Fierro, Benjamin, III ... Boston, MA
Fierro, Christian G. ... Santa Rosa, CA
Fierro, Christine M. ... San Francisco, CA
Fierro, Daniel A., Jr. ... Fort Lee, NJ
Fierro, Eugene J. ... Miami, FL
Fierro, Fierro & Izzard, P.C. ... Fort Lee, NJ
Fierro, Frank J. ... Hazleton, PA
Fierro, Gerard A. ... Glendale, CA
Fierro, Gerard A. ... Los Angeles, CA
Fierro, Gerard A. ... Pasadena, CA
Fierro, Henry E. ... Miami, FL
Fierro, Henry E., P.A. ... Miami, FL
Fierro, Herman ... Albuquerque, NM
Fierro, Lara Collins ... Rapid City, SD
Fierro, Mark ... Houston, TX
Fierro, Mark Peter ... Fort Lee, NJ
Fierro, Marylou Gill ... Boston, MA
Fierro, Matthew James ... Fort Lee, NJ
Fierro, Noreen M. ... Short Hills, NJ
Fierro, Patrick H., II ... Rochester, NY
Fierro, Robert J., Jr. ... Norfolk, VA
Fierro, Rocio V. ... Oakland, CA
Fierro, Saverio J. ... Hauppauge, NY
Fierson, Morris ... Arcadia, CA
Fierst, Barry Rueben ... Rockville, MD
Fierst, Bruce P. ... Denver, CO
Fierst, Bruce P., P.C. ... Denver, CO
Fierst, David U. ... Washington, DC
Fierst, Edith U. ... Washington, DC
Fierst, Frederick U. ... Northampton, MA
Fierst, Herbert A. ... Washington, DC
Fierst & Pucci LLP ... Northampton, MA
Springfield, MA
Fierstadt, Edward T. ... Inglewood, CA
Fierstein, Ira ... Chicago, IL
Fierstein, Ronald K. ... New York, NY
Fierstein & Sturman, Law Corporation
Van Nuys, CA
Fierstien, Joel D. ... Livingston, NJ
Fiertz, Beverly F. ... South Woodstock, VT
Fieschko & Associates, P.C. ... Pittsburgh, PA
Fieschko, Craig A. ... Madison, WI
Fieschko, Joseph E. ... Oak Park, CA
Fieschko, Joseph E., Jr. ... Pittsburgh, PA
Fieseler, Robert W. ... Chicago, IL
Fieselman, Lawrence R. ... Long Beach, CA
Fieselmann, Benj. W. ... Eaton, OH
Fiesinger, George G., Jr. ... Little Falls, NY
Fiest, Andrea C. ... New York, NY
Fiest, James E. ... Haverhill, MA
Fiesta, Janine ... Allentown, PA
Fiesta, Jason B ... Orlando, FL
Fiesta, Stephanie ... Pittsburgh, PA
Fiet, Ronald D. ... Rockford, IL
Fiete, Tamara ... New York, NY
Fietkau, August L. ... New York, NY
Fietkau, Carol Dimino ... Staten Island, NY
Fietkiewicz, John M. ... Newark, NJ
Fietz, Jeremy R. ... Santa Rosa, CA
Fietze, David C. ... Manchester, NH
Fieweger, James P. ... Chicago, IL
Fieweger, Michael J. ... Chicago, IL
Fieweger, Peter C. ... Rock Island, IL
Fieweger, Stephen T. ... Rock Island, IL
Fifarek, John R. ... Lansing, MI
Fife, Charles L. ... Denver, CO
Fife, David M. ... Wilmington, OH
Fife, Elaine Harner ... Wilmington, OH
Fife, Eugene M., III ... Indianapolis, IN
Fife & Fife ... Wilmington, OH
Fife, James H., III ... Hammond, IN
Fife, Joan B. Tucker ... Washington, DC
Fife, K. Scott ... Washington, DC
Fife, Kate Wilson ... Charleston, WV
Fife, Kevin J. ... Logan, UT
Fife, Lori R. ... New York, NY
Fife, Lorin M. ... Los Angeles, CA
Fife & McCullough, P.C. ... Denver, CO
Fife, Michael T. ... Portland, OR
Fife, Paul D. ... San Francisco, CA
Fife, Phillip K. ... Seal Beach, CA
Fife, Randall D. ... Moscow, ID
Fife, Robert G. ... Aptos, CA
Fife, Ruth H. ... Atlanta, GA
Fife, W. Randolph ... Charleston, WV
Fifelski, Angela M. ... Indianapolis, IN
Fifer, Anne Bachle ... Grand Rapids, MI
Fifer, C. Gregory ... Clarksville, IN
Fifer, Carson Lee, Jr. ... McLean, VA
Fifer, Diane M. ... Bloomfield Hills, MI
Fifer, Diane M., P.C. ... Bloomfield Hills, MI
Fifer, Gerry Ann ... New York, NY
Fifer, Gregory ... Oak Lawn, IL
Fifer, Harry, Jr. ... Arlington, TX
Fifer, Howard M. ... New York, NY
Fifer, James E. (Jef) ... New Albany, IN
Fifer, Larry W. ... Lewes, DE
Fifer Law Office ... New Albany, IN
Fifer, Michael L. ... Southgate, MI
Fifer, Ronald R. ... Jeffersonville, IN
Fifer, Samuel ... Chicago, IL
Fifer, T. King ... Dallas, TX
Fifer, Vogt & Lanum ... Jeffersonville, IN
Fiffer, James D. ... Chicago, IL
Fiffer, Steven J. ... Evanston, IL
Fiffik, Cristen L. ... Canonsburg, PA
Fiffik, Michael E. ... Pittsburgh, PA
Fifield, Andrew T. ... Dallas, TX
Fifield, Dwight A. ... Portland, ME
Fifield, Harold W. ... El Centro, CA
Fifield, James C. ... Des Moines, IA
Fifield, Jordan A. ... Peoria, IL
Fifield, Sean C. ... Chicago, IL
Fifield, Thomas B. ... Milwaukee, WI
Fifield, William O. ... Dallas, TX
Fifield-Guzman, Barbara ... Albany, NY
Fiflis, Christina A. ... Denver, CO
Fiflis, Michael P. ... Phoenix, AZ
Fiflis, Ted J. ... Boulder, CO
Fifner, David A. ... Temple Terrace, FL
Fifner, David A., P.A. ... Temple Terrace, FL
Fifner, Douglas K. ... Westlake, OH
Fifner, Douglas K., Co., L.P.A.
Westlake, OH
Fifner, Elaine ... Westlake, OH
Fifner, Greta E. ... Cleveland, OH
Fifner & Jeffers, LLC ... Columbus, OH
Fifner, W. Frederick ... Columbus, OH
Fig, William G. ... Portland, OR
Figa, Candace Cole ... Denver, CO
Figa, Phillip S. ... Denver, CO
Figa, Robert J. ... Troy, MI
Figa, S. Fred ... West Orange, NJ
Figard, Wendi Amos ... Charlotte, NC
Figari Davenport & Graves, L.L.P.
Dallas, TX
Figari, Ernest E., Jr., (P.C.) ... Dallas, TX
Figarotta, Robert P. ... New Brunswick, NJ
Figdor, Peter ... New York, NY
Figel, Michael J. ... Houston, TX
Figel, Reid M. ... Washington, DC
Figenshau, Susan Cho ... St. Louis, MO
Figenshaw, Michael H. ... Des Moines, IA
Figetakis, Frances L. ... Columbus, OH
Figg, Beverly J. ... Jefferson City, MO
Figg, E. Anthony ... Washington, DC
Figg, James R. ... Broomfield, CO
Figg, Jill J. ... San Francisco, CA
Figg, Leigh Ann ... Indianapolis, IN
Figge, Jeff D. ... St. Louis, MO
Figg-Hoblyn, W. David
Rancho Cordova, CA
Figgins, Shayne ... Los Angeles, CA
Figiel, Phyllis A. ... Southfield, MI
Figini, Joseph C. ... Washington, DC
Figinski, M. Albert ... Baltimore, MD
Figland, Amanda W. ... Philadelphia, PA
Figler, Dayvid J. ... Henderson, NV
Figler, Jennifer L. ... San Jose, CA
Figler, Paul ... Los Angeles, CA
Figler, Ronald G. ... Canton, OH
Figler, Sue A. ... New York, NY
Figley, Paul F. ... Department of Justice, Civil Division, GV
Figlia, F. Paul ... Bailey, CO
Figlin, Cheryl Rosa ... Philadelphia, PA
Figliola, Anthony A., Jr. ... Wilmington, DE
Figliola & Facciolo ... Wilmington, DE
Figlioli, David ... Chicago, IL
Figliolia, Michael ... Brooklyn, NY
Figliolo, Joseph V. ... New York, NY
Figliomeni, Michael A. ... Cadillac, MI
Figliulo, Donald E. ... Chicago, IL
Figliulo, James R. ... Chicago, IL
Figliulo & Silverman, P.C. ... Chicago, IL
Figman, Alan H. ... New York, NY
Figman, Doris Michelle ... Oakland, CA
Figman, Helene Horn ... Dedham, MA
Figman, Lynne M. ... New York, NY
Fignar, Eugene M. ... Old Greenwich, CT
Figone, Richard P. ... San Francisco, CA
Figore, Gary S. ... Easton, PA
Figore, Tara A. ... Allentown, PA
Figot, Brian D. ... Troy, MI
Figueiredo, Mark R. ... San Jose, CA
Figueras, I. Jaime ... Wilmington, DE
Figueras, Vivian T. ... Coral Gables, FL
Figueredo, Berenice V. ... Weehawken, NJ
Figueredo, Kathryn ... Austin, TX
Figueredo, Luis R. ... Miami, FL
Figueredo, Maribel ... Newark, NJ
Figueroa, Arturo A., Jr. ... San Antonio, TX
Figueroa, Celia ... Houston, TX
Figueroa, Cynthia A. ... Dallas, TX
Figueroa, Diana ... Melbourne, FL
Figueroa, Francisco L. ... Key Biscayne, FL
Figueroa, Gilberto V. ... Florence, AZ
Figueroa, Hector M. ... Tucson, AZ
Figueroa, Leo D. ... San Antonio, TX
Figueroa, Lester J. ... New York, NY
Figueroa, Luis A. ... Coral Gables, FL
Figueroa, Luis A. ... Laredo, TX
Figueroa, Luis G. ... Clearwater, FL
Figueroa, Maria T. ... San Juan, PR
Figueroa, Marta M. ... Oakland, CA
Figueroa, Nicholas ... New York, NY
Figueroa, Rafael S. ... Los Angeles, CA
Figueroa, Raul ... Buffalo, NY
Figueroa, Ricardo ... Roseville, MN
Figueroa, Rosario A. ... Miami, FL
Figueroa, William G. ... Whittier, CA
Figueroa Arus, Ilsa Y. ... San Juan, PR
Figueroa Báez, Elisa ... San Juan, PR
Figueroa Cabán, Felix R. ... San Juan, PR
Figueroa Llinas, Alicia ... San Juan, PR
Figueroa-Llinás, Enrique G.
San Juan, PR
Figueroa-Morales, David ... Fajardo, PR
Figueroa Morales, Jose A. ... San Juan, PR
Figuli, David J. ... Evergreen, CO
Figur, Charles ... Denver, CO
Figur, Lawrence J. ... Prunedale, CA
Figura, David A. ... Chicago, IL
Figura, Mark L. ... Anchorage, AK
Figura, Richard J. ... Flint, MI
Figura, Stanley V. ... Chicago, IL
Figurelli, Daniel M. ... Jersey City, NJ
Figures, Michael A. ... Mobile, AL
Figures, Thomas H. ... Mobile, AL
Figurski, George A. ... Adena, OH
Figurski, Gerald A., P.A. ... Holiday, FL
Figurski, Gerald A., (P.A.) ... Holiday, FL
Figurski, Glenn J. ... Hackensack, NJ
Figus, Thaddeus S. ... Minneapolis, MN
Fihn, Jeffrey G. ... Indianapolis, IN
Fijal, Katherine A. ... Buffalo, NY
Fijal, Robert S. ... Bedford, MA
Fijman, Mark ... Jackson, MS
Fijolek, Richard M. ... Dallas, TX
Fike, Andrea M. ... Minneapolis, MN
Fike, Cascio & Boose ... Johnstown, PA
Somerset, PA
Fike, Charles P. ... Omaha, NE
Fike, David A. ... Fresno, CA
Fike, Dennis H. ... Cleveland, OH
Fike, Edward G. ... Palo Alto, CA
Fike, Eugene E., II ... Somerset, PA
Fike, Geo. T. ... Gilbert, AZ
Fike, Lisa A. ... Cleveland, OH
Fike, Richard D. ... San Francisco, CA
Fike, Sara L. ... Dongola, IL
Fike, Shelby R. ... Houston, TX
Fike, Sheryl Lee Mulliken ... Houston, TX
Fike, Stacy L. ... Shawnee, KS
Fike, Thomas H. ... Baton Rouge, LA
Fike, Thomas L. ... Oakland, CA
Fikes, Horace J., Jr. ... Pine Bluff, AR
Fikes, Richard E. ... Jasper, AL
Fikre, John ... New York, NY
Fikre, Ted ... Los Angeles, CA
Fikry, Eric G. ... Philadelphia, PA
Fikso, Robert B. ... Seattle, WA
Fiktus, Richard D. ... Cleveland, OH
Fil, Richard M. ... Hartford, CT
Fila, Frank A. ... Yuma, AZ
Fila, Sharon G. ... Salt Lake City, UT
Fila, Thomas Charles ... Memphis, TN
Filachek, John M. ... Milwaukee, WI
Filachek, Joseph R. ... Milwaukee, WI
Filak, John J. ... Cleveland, OH
Filak, John J., Jr.
Charlotte Amalie, St. Thomas, VI
Filan, James K., Jr. ... Bridgeport, CT
Filan, Patrick J. ... Stamford, CT
New York, NY
White Plains, NY
Filardi, Charles J., Jr. ... Stamford, CT
Filardi, Constantine B. ... Armonk, NY
Filardi, Edward V. ... New York, NY
Filardi, Joseph J. ... Manhasset, NY
Filardi, Joseph J., P.C. ... Manhasset, NY
Filardi, Maria Frigo ... Baltimore, MD
Filardi, Therese M. ... Manhasset, NY
Filardo, Vincent, Jr. ... New York, NY
Filarowitz, Thomas C. ... Perth Amboy, NJ
Filarski, Thomas J. ... Chicago, IL
Filarsky, Steve A. ... Ojai, CA
Filarsky and Watt ... Ojai, CA
Filas, Jonathan G. ... St. Paul, MN
Filbeck, Tom ... Sapulpa, OK
Filbert, Alvin J., Jr. ... Towson, MD
Filbert, Thomas F. ... Annapolis, MD
Filbert, Walker R. ... Springfield, IL
Filbin, Patrick D. ... Detroit, MI
Filbin, Thomas J. ... Dedham, MA
Filburn, Mark C. ... Orlando, FL
Filce, Richard A. ... New Orleans, LA
Filcher, John E. ... Sioux Falls, SD
Filcik, Jeffrey C. ... Louisville, KY
Filcoff, George, Jr. ... Granite City, IL
Filderman, Jon ... Whitehouse Station, NJ
Fildes, Christopher J.
Grosse Pointe Woods, MI
Fildes, Joan M. ... Buffalo, NY
Fildes, Lisa Sue ... Detroit, MI

Fincher, Robin Kilpatrick ... **Mobile, AL**
Fincher, Roger D. ... Topeka, KS
Fincher, Royce A. ... Sacramento, CA
Fincher, Steven M. ... **Morrow, GA**
Finch-Heuerman, Nancy E. ... **Tustin, CA**
Finchler, Todd M. ... **Wilmington, DE**
Finchum, Travis D. ... **Clearwater, FL**
Finci, Jeffrey R. ... Brisbane, CA
Finci, Richard A. ... **New Carrollton, MD**
Rockville, MD
Finck, Barry Russell ... Denver, CO
Finck, Bruce Alan ... **Ventura, CA**
Finck, Danielle E. ... **Rutland, VT**
Finck, David Laurence ... New York, NY
Finck, Edward R., Jr. ... San Antonio, TX
Finck, Henry W. ... San Antonio, TX
Finck, Kevin W., Law Offices of
San Francisco, CA
Finck, Robert J. ... St. Petersburg, FL
Finck, Robert S. ... Los Angeles, CA
Finckbeiner, John J., Jr. ... **Chalmette, LA**
Fincke, Gerald B. ... Daytona Beach, FL
Fincke, Melvin F. ... Houston, TX
Fincke, Waring R. ... West Bend, WI
Fincun, Jeffrey D. ... **Cleveland, OH**
Findahl, Cynthia G. ... Dallas, TX
Findaro, Joseph T., Jr. ... Washington, DC
Findeiss, Nancy ... Oklahoma City, OK
Findell & Company, Inc. ... Rochester, NH
Findell, George, Jr. ... Rochester, NH
Finder and Cuomo, LLP ... **New York, NY**
Finder, Dolores E. ... New York, NY
Finder, Gary N. ... Oak Park, IL
Finder, Iris Claire ... **New York, NY**
Finder, James A. ... **New York, NY**
Finder, Kenneth A. ... **New York, NY**
Finder, Lawrence D. ... **Houston, TX**
Finder, Michael R. ... New York, NY
Finder Novick Kerrigan & Anderson, LLP
New York, NY
Finder, Sanford S. ... Washington, PA
Finder, Stanley ... Rego Park, NY
Finder, Theodore R. ... Scottsdale, AZ
Finders, Lee ... Portland, OR
Finderson, Roger B. ... Fort Wayne, IN
Findholt, Brian L. ... **Kingston, NY**
Findish, Marie E. ... **Holland, OH**
Findlater, James E. ... Fort Collins, CO
Findlater, John W. ... Los Angeles, CA
Findlay, Berrien H. ... San Bernardino, CA
Findlay, Charles W., III
Department of Justice,
Environment and Natural Resources
Division, GV
Findlay, D. Cameron ... **Chicago, IL**
Findlay, Delano S. ... Salt Lake City, UT
Findlay, Eric H. ... **Tyler, TX**
Findlay, J. Duncan ... Seattle, WA
Findlay, James F. ... Augusta, GA
Findlay, Linda A. ... Bronx, NY
Findlay, R. Bruce ... **Salt Lake City, UT**
Findler, Brett K. ... West Palm Beach, FL
Findler, Lloyd D. ... West Palm Beach, FL
Findler, William E. ... Arlington, VA
Findley, Andrew K. E. ... Erie, PA
Findley, Christopher H. ... **San Diego, CA**
Findley & Ferrier ... **Tyler, TX**
Findley, Gary S. ... Anaheim, CA
Findley, J. Kenneth ... **Tyler, TX**
Findley, Jacquelyn R. ... Spokane, WA
Findley, James Emory ... Clayton, GA
Findley, James L., Jr. ... Natchitoches, LA
Findley, John H. ... Sacramento, CA
Findley, John W. ... San Rafael, CA
Findley, Kevin C. ... **Bakersfield, CA**
Findley, Robert D. ... Bryan, TX
Findley, Robert J. ... Huntington Beach, CA
Findley, Roger W. ... Los Angeles, CA
Findley, Ron L. ... St. Joseph, MO
Findley, Sidney B. ... San Luis Obispo, CA
Findley, Stephen C. ... **Dayton, OH**
Findley, Thomas M. ... **Tallahassee, FL**
Findley, Thomas W. ... **Juneau, AK**
Findling, Anne E. ... Phoenix, AZ
Findling, Darren Martin ... Royal Oak, MI
Findling, David M. ... Royal Oak, MI
Findling, Drew, Law Offices of
Atlanta, GA
Findling, Findling & Findling
Royal Oak, MI
Findling, Fred S. ... Royal Oak, MI
Findling Garau Germano & Pennington, P.C. ... **Indianapolis, IN**
Findling, Janet L. ... Tallahassee, FL
Findling & Johnson ... Portland, OR
Findling, Marlene E. ... Portland, OR
Findling, Martin ... **Canoga Park, CA**
Findling, Martin ... **Los Angeles, CA**
Findling, Mary Arlien ... **Indianapolis, IN**
Findorff, Jean L. ... Minneapolis, MN
Findorff, Karl ... Jefferson City, MO
Fine, A. Kenneth ... St. Petersburg, FL
Fine, Aaron M. ... **Philadelphia, PA**
Fine, Adele M. ... Rochester, NY
Fine, Aden J. ... San Francisco, CA
Fine, Alan S. ... **Miami, FL**
Fine, Alexander ... Great Neck, NY
Fine, Alexander M. ... Marion, IL
Fine, Allan H. ... Louisville, KY
Fine, Andrew S. ... **Virginia Beach, VA**
Fine, Arthur, (A Professional Corporation)
Los Angeles, CA
Fine, Arthur L. ... Denver, CO
Fine & Associates, P.A. ... **Miami, FL**
Fine & Associates, PLC, Professional Law Corporation ... **New Orleans, LA**
Fine, Barbara S. ... West Springfield, MA
Fine, Barry H. ... Miami, FL
Fine, Barry K. ... Huntington, NY
Fine, Betsy L.C. ... Neenah, WI
Fine and Block ... **Atlanta, GA**
Fine, Bonnie N. ... Long Beach, CA
Fine, Bruce ... Seattle, WA
Fine, Burton M. ... New York, NY
Fine, Charles J. ... New York, NY
Fine, Charles L. ... **Phoenix, AZ**
Fine, Cindy G. ... **New York, NY**
Fine, Clark D. ... Montgomery, AL
Fine, Craig S. ... Monticello, NY
Fine, David A. ... **Boston, MA**
Fine, David J. ... **Boston, MA**
Fine, David J. ... Boston, MA
Fine, David R. ... **Denver, CO**
Fine, David R. ... **New Orleans, LA**
Fine, David R. ... **Harrisburg, PA**
Fine, David W. ... Philadelphia, PA
Fine, Deborah M. ... Flagstaff, AZ
Fine, Drew S. ... **New York, NY**
Fine, Edward ... West Palm Beach, FL
Fine, Edward J. ... **New York, NY**
Fine, Edward L. ... Pasadena, CA
Fine, Edward S. ... Beverly Hills, CA
Fine, Eleanor R. J. ... Tacoma, WA
Fine, Elizabeth R. ... Department of Justice,
Office of Policy Development, GV
Fine, Farkash & Parlapiano, P.A.
Gainesville, FL
Fine & Faure ... **Albuquerque, NM**
Santa Fe, NM
Fine, Fine, Legum & Fine ... **Norfolk, VA**
Virginia Beach, VA
Fine, Frances-Ann ... **Las Vegas, NV**
Fine, Fred D. ... New York, NY
Fine, Gary R. ... **Fort Lauderdale, FL**
Fine, Gerald E. ... Miami, FL
Fine, Gerald M. ... Grand Terrace, CA
Fine, Gibbons & MacMeekin, P.A.
Baltimore, MD
Fine, Glenn A. ... Department of Justice,
Office of the Inspector General, GV
Fine, Gordon ... Bronx, NY
Fine, Gordon J. ... San Francisco, CA
Fine, Grant W. ... San Rafael, CA
Fine & Hatfield, A Professional Corporation
Evansville, IN
Henderson, KY
Owensboro, KY
Fine, Helaine S. ... **New York, NY**
Fine, Herbert H. ... Middletown, NJ
Fine, Herbert L. ... Royal Palm Beach, FL
Fine, Howard ... Baltimore, MD
Fine, Howard A. ... **New York, NY**
Fine, Howard F. ... **San Francisco, CA**
Fine, Howard M. ... Everett, MA
Fine, Howard R. ... Vernon Hills, IL
Fine, Irvin ... Youngstown, OH
Fine, Ivy V. ... **San Francisco, CA**
Fine, J. Andrew ... Gainesville, FL
Fine, J. David ... **Ashland, OR**
Fine, J. David ... **Medford, OR**
Fine, Jack D. ... **Beverly Hills, CA**
Fine, Jack J. ... Gainesville, FL
Fine, Jacqueline H. ... **Washington, DC**
Fine, James L. ... Louisville, KY
Fine, Jeffrey A. ... **Chicago, IL**
Fine, Jeffrey E. ... **St. Louis, MO**
Fine, Jeffrey Michael ... Miami, FL
Fine, Jeffrey R. ... **Dallas, TX**
Fine, Jerome L. ... **East Lansing, MI**
Fine, Jerry A. ... Milwaukee, WI
Fine, Joan K. ... **Winchester, VA**
Fine, Joe ... **Russellville, AL**
Fine, Joel H. ... New York, NY
Fine, John C. ... New York, NY
Fine, Jon P. ... **New York, NY**
Fine, Jonathan M. ... **Raleigh, NC**
Fine, Joseph M., (P.A.) ... **Albuquerque, NM**
Fine, Joseph S. ... Newark, NJ
Fine, Julius S. ... Savannah, GA
Fine, Justin D. ... **Philadelphia, PA**
Fine, Kalman E. ... Philadelphia, PA
Fine, Kaplan and Black ... **Philadelphia, PA**
Fine, Karen L.S. ... **Los Angeles, CA**
Fine, Karen M. ... **Chicago, IL**
Fine, Karen R. ... New York, NY
Fine, L. Sandy ... **Atlanta, GA**
Fine, Laura Anne ... Eugene, OR
Fine, Lauri Medwin ... **Warwick, RI**
Fine, Lawrence B. ... **Philadelphia, PA**
Fine, Lawrence H. ... New York, NY
Fine, Lawrence J. ... Winston-Salem, NC
Fine, Leon ... Philadelphia, PA
Fine, Linda Joan ... Denver, CO
Fine, Lisa R. ... **Washington, DC**
Fine, Louis R. ... Chicago, IL
Fine, Louis S. ... Philadelphia, PA
Fine, Lowell ... Springfield, VA
Fine, Lowell S. ... **Atlanta, GA**
Fine, M. Jeffrey ... Sacramento, CA
Fine, Marc D. ... **Evansville, IN**
Fine, Marjorie L. ... **Pleasanton, CA**
Fine, Mark H. ... Northbrook, IL
Fine, Mark S. ... Chicago, IL
Fine, Martin ... **Miami, FL**
Fine, Martin A. ... Los Angeles, CA
Fine, Martin R. ... New York, NY
Fine, Marvin ... Philadelphia, PA
Fine, Michael D. ... **New York, NY**
Fine, Michael E. ... **Washington, DC**
Fine, Michelle F. ... **New York, NY**
Fine, Mickey L. ... Los Angeles, CA
Fine, Mike W. ... Edmond, OK
Fine, Milton ... Pittsburgh, PA
Fine, Morris H. ... **Virginia Beach, VA**
Fine, Naomi R. ... San Leandro, CA
Fine, Neal H.
Government Printing Office, GV
Fine, Ned A. ... **Redwood City, CA**
Fine, Norman J. ... **Boston, MA**
Fine, Paul K. ... Lemon Grove, CA
Fine, Paul R. ... **Los Angeles, CA**
Fine, Peter A. ... Andover, MA
Fine, Philip R. ... Beachwood, OH
Fine, Rachel B. ... **New York, NY**
Fine, Ralph Adam ... Milwaukee, WI
Fine, Raymond ... Youngstown, OH
Fine, Rebecca L. ... **New York, NY**
Fine, Richard ... White Plains, NY
Fine, Richard G. ... **Honesdale, PA**
Scranton, PA
Fine, Richard H. ... Rockville, MD
Fine, Richard I. ... Los Angeles, CA
Fine, Richard I., & Associates, A Prof. Corp., Law Offices of ... Los Angeles, CA
Fine, Richard J. ... **New York, NY**
Fine, Richard W. ... **Houston, TX**
Fine, Rick ... **Austin, TX**
Fine, Risa Schneider ... Providence, RI
Fine, Robert ... Ann Arbor, MI
Fine, Robert B. ... Salisbury, MD
Fine, Robert B. ... St. Louis Park, MN
Fine, Robert D. ... **Providence, RI**
Fine, Robert L. ... Decatur, GA
Fine, Robert M., Jr. ... Los Angeles, CA
Fine, Robert P. ... **Buffalo, NY**
Fine, Robert P. ... Philadelphia, PA
Fine, Robert S. ... **Miami, FL**
Fine, Roberta S. ... Key West, FL
Fine, Robt. G. ... New York, NY
Fine, Roger S. ... New Brunswick, NJ
Fine, Ronald A. ... Los Angeles, CA
Fine, Roy N. ... **Neenah, WI**
Fine, S. Richard ... **Chicago, IL**
Fine, Saminsky, Olin & Stern, P.C.
New York, NY
Fine & Santamaria, Associates
Royal Palm Beach, FL
Fine, Scott J. ... Huntington, NY
Fine, Sharon J. ... Hamburg, NY
Fine, Sharon R. ... Detroit, MI
Fine, Sheldon A. ... Andover, MA
Fine, Sheryl Cohen ... **New York, NY**
Fine, Stanley S. ... **Baltimore, MD**
Fine and Staud ... Philadelphia, PA
Fine, Stephen L. ... Athens, VT
Fine, Stephen R. ... Manchester, NH
Fine, Steven ... Fort Lauderdale, FL
Fine, Steven E. ... **Oak Brook, IL**
Fine, Steven H. ... Chicago, IL
Fine, Steven L. ... Department of Energy,
Office of Hearings and Appeals, GV
Fine, Steven, P.A. ... Fort Lauderdale, FL
Fine, Steven R. ... Randolph, MA
Fine, Susan ... New York, NY
Fine, Susan L. ... **Seattle, WA**
Fine, Thomas F. ... Knoxville, TN
Fine, Thomas H.
Department of Commerce, GV
Fine, Toni M. ... New York, NY
Fine and Veznaian, P.C. ... **Boston, MA**
Fine, William B. ... Baltimore, MD
Fine, William G. ... Oakland, CA
Fine, William I. ... Highland, IN
Fine, William I. ... Minneapolis, MN
Fine & Woliung, A Professional Corporation
Long Beach, CA
Fine, Wyatt & Carey, A Professional Corporation ... **Honesdale, PA**
Scranton, PA
Stroudsburg, PA
Wilkes-Barre, PA
Fineberg, Allen P. ... **Cherry Hill, NJ**
Fineberg, David L. ... Hartford, CT
Fineberg, Douglas A. ... **Boston, MA**
Fineberg & Fineberg ... Syracuse, NY
Fineberg, Jack ... New York, NY
Fineberg, Joel M. ... Dallas, TX
Fineberg, Justin C. ... **Miami, FL**
Fineberg, Lawrence J. ... Iselin, NJ
Fineberg, Leon M. ... Chicago, IL
Fineberg, Leora A. ... Kew Gardens, NY
Fineberg, Leslie J. ... **Chicago, IL**
Fineberg, Lewis H. ... Syracuse, NY
Fineberg, Libo B. ... Pompano Beach, FL
Fineberg, Manuel ... Syracuse, NY
Fineberg, M. J. ... Carmel, IN
Fineberg, Norman ... **New Haven, CT**
Fineberg, Richard ... Simi Valley, CA
Fineberg, Robert A.
Cape May Court House, NJ
Fineberg, Robert A., P.C., A Professional Corporation ... **Avalon, NJ**
Cape May Court House, NJ
Sea Isle City, NJ
Fineberg, Ronald B. ... Phoenix, AZ
Fineberg, Ronald B., P.C. ... Phoenix, AZ
Fineberg, Todd C. ... **Washington, DC**
Fineburg, Herbert R. ... **Philadelphia, PA**
Finefrock, James L. ... **Dayton, OH**
Finefrock, James L., and Associates Co., L.P.A. ... **Dayton, OH**
Finefrock, Jerome Conlan, Law Offices of
Lancaster, PA
Finefrock, Kathleen A. ... **Chicago, IL**
Finefrock, Richd. H. ... Bellefontaine, OH
Finegan, Brian ... Salinas, CA
Finegan, Brian, and Michael D. Cling, A Professional Corporation ... Salinas, CA
Finegan, Byron P. ... Kildeer, IL
Finegan, Cole ... **Denver, CO**
Finegan, Daniel P. ... **Philadelphia, PA**
Finegan, James L. ... **Lakewood, CO**
Finegan, James L., P.C. ... **Denver, CO**
Lakewood, CO
Finegan, James T. ... Bloomington, IL
Finegan, Joanne M. ... Towson, MD
Finegan, Kerry Anne ... **Miami, FL**
Finegan Law Firm ... Bloomington, IL
Finegan, Lawrence E. ... **Frederick, MD**
Finegan, Neil C. ... Rye Brook, NY
Finegan, Pamela A. ... **Englewood Cliffs, NJ**
Finegan, Patrick G. ... Bronx, NY
Finegan, Richard A., Jr. ... Austin, TX
Finegan, Samuel ... Texas City, TX
Finegan, Susan M. ... **Boston, MA**
Finegan, Thomas F., Jr. ... Chicago, IL
Finegan, Thomas S. ... **New York, NY**
Finegan, Timothy D. ... **Birmingham, MI**
Finegan, William P. ... **Dallas, TX**
Finegar, Wayne W, II ... Upper Marlboro, MD
Finegold, Alan H. ... **Pittsburgh, PA**
Finegold, Barry R. ... Andover, MA
Finegold, Daniel W. ... **Boston, MA**
Finegold, Jordan ... Columbus, OH
Finegold, Julius ... Altamonte Springs, FL
Finegold, Laurence B., (P.S.) ... **Seattle, WA**
Finegold Law Firm, The ... **Seattle, WA**
Finegold, Richard L. ... **San Diego, CA**
Finegold, Sharon A. ... **Seattle, WA**
Finegold, Theodore A. ... **Wenatchee, WA**
Finegood, Kenneth D. ... Southfield, MI
Finegood, Ronald L. ... Detroit, MI
Finell, Marvin ... Los Angeles, CA
Finell, Steven ... **Dobbs Ferry, NY**
Finell, Steven, P.C. ... **Dobbs Ferry, NY**
Finelli, Daniel M. ... Cleveland, OH
Finelli, Debra S. ... Albany, NY
Finelli, Domenic ... Revere, MA
Finelli, Philip F., Jr. ... Rockville, MD
Finelli, Philip F., Jr., P.C. ... Rockville, MD
Finelli, Stephanie ... Sacramento, CA
Finelsen, Libbi J. ... Department of Agriculture,
Office of the General Counsel, GV
Fineman, Ana ... San Francisco, CA
Fineman & Bach ... **Haddonfield, NJ**
Philadelphia, PA
Fineman, Bernard ... East Liverpool, OH
Fineman, Bruce L. ... Fort Lauderdale, FL
Fineman, Darrell M. ... **Vineland, NJ**
Fineman, David M. ... **Pittsburgh, PA**
Fineman, Deborah B. ... Orange, NJ
Fineman, Elliott L. ... Kensington, CA
Fineman, Freda S. ... New York, NY
Fineman, Gabriel ... Alexandria, VA
Fineman, Gary L. ... Ann Arbor, MI
Fineman, Joseph E. ... Louisville, KY
Fineman, Joseph I. ... Philadelphia, PA
Fineman, Kimberly S. ... **San Francisco, CA**
Fineman, Lee H. ... Sherman Oaks, CA
Fineman, Marc E. ... **Chicago, IL**
Fineman, Marina ... **Los Angeles, CA**
Fineman, Martha L.A. ... New York, NY
Fineman, Martin L. ... **San Francisco, CA**
Fineman, Nancy Leavitt ... **Burlingame, CA**
Fineman, Neil Burnstein ... Santa Ana, CA
Fineman, Richard A. ... **Philadelphia, PA**
Fineman, Robert A. ... Detroit, MI
Fineman, Robert M. ... **San Francisco, CA**
Fineman, S. David ... **Philadelphia, PA**
Fineman, Samuel B. ... Wayne, PA
Fineman, Samuel M. ... Broad Axe, PA
Fineman & Sotomayor ... San Francisco, CA
Fineman, Stanley J. ... **Washington, DC**
Fineman, Steven E. ... **New York, NY**
Fineman, Teresa Tormey
Newport Beach, CA
Fineman, Thomas J. ... Los Angeles, CA
Finen, C. Michael ... Cameron Park, CA
Finer, Alan R. ... Vineyard Haven, MA
Finer, Barbara Jo ... Tallahassee, FL
Finer, David A. ... Los Angeles, CA
Finer, Dustin K. ... **Los Angeles, CA**
Finer, Jeffry K. ... Spokane, WA
Finer, Joel J. ... Cleveland, OH
Finer, Katherine P. ... **Los Angeles, CA**
Finer, Kim & Stearns ... **Los Angeles, CA**
Newport Beach, CA
Palm Springs, CA
Torrance, CA
Finer, Marc T. ... **Mineola, NY**
Finer & Pugsley, P.S. ... Spokane, WA
Finer, Robert M. ... Treasury Department,
Internal Revenue Service, GV
Finer, Steven A. ... Englewood, CO
Finer, Stuart E. ... Utica, NY
Finer, Teresa Brickman ... **Orlando, FL**
Finer, W. A., (A Professional Corporation)
Torrance, CA
Fineran, Karen D. ... **San Francisco, CA**
Fineran, Robert J. ... Mandeville, LA
Finerfrock, James S. ... Washington, DC
Finerman, Adam W. ... **New York, NY**
Finerman, Scott C. ... Cleveland, OH
Finerty, Brian C. ... **San Jose, CA**
Finerty, Daniel J. ... **Milwaukee, WI**
Finerty, James P. ... Newport Beach, CA
Finerty, John D. ... **Milwaukee, WI**
Finerty, John D., Jr. ... **Milwaukee, WI**
Finerty, Kathryn A. ... Milwaukee, WI
Finerty, Margaret J. ... **New York, NY**
Finerty, Michael Arthur ... Muskogee, OK
Finerty • Rosman, P.C. ... Council Bluffs, IA
Fines, David R. ... **Taylorville, IL**
Fines, L. Anthony ... **Tucson, AZ**
Fines, Michael B. ... West Greenwich, RI
Fines & Oden, P.L.C. ... **Tucson, AZ**
Fineshriber, Howard W. ... Chevy Chase, MD
Finesilver, Michael I. ... Miami Beach, FL
Finesilver, Michael I., P.A., Law Offices of
Miami Beach, FL

Finesilver, Sherman G. ... **Denver, CO**
Finestein, Russell M. ... **Short Hills, NJ**
Finestone, Alan E. ... Beverly Hills, CA
Finestone & Morris ... **Atlanta, GA**
Finestone, Robert Lee ... Westlake Village, CA
Finestone, Stephen D. ... **San Francisco, CA**
Finestone, Stuart ... **Atlanta, GA**
Finestone, William ... **Los Angeles, CA**
Finestrauss, Philip M. ... **Wilmington, DE**
Finestrauss, Philip M., P.A.
Wilmington, DE
Finet, Scott ... Philadelphia, PA
Fine-Trail, Tamera L.
Department of Justice, Tax Division, GV
Finetti, John F. ... San Francisco, CA
Fine-Weinberger, Robin F.
El Dorado Hills, CA
Finfer, Matthew E. ... Haddonfield, NJ
Finfrock, Teri Jo ... Columbus, OH
Finfrock, Wallace P. ... Dallas, TX
Fingal, Christi Stubblefield ... St. Louis, MO
Fingal, Fahrney & Clark, LLP
Newport Beach, CA
Fingal, Stephen L. ... **Newport Beach, CA**
Fingar, Jordon J. ... Surfside, FL
Fingar, Melissa A. ... **Rochester, NY**
Fingar, Michael J. ... North Miami Beach, FL
Fingar, Michael J., P.A.
North Miami Beach, FL
Fingar, Robert D. ... **Tallahassee, FL**
Fingard, Richard A. ... **Chicago, IL**
Finger, Adam G. ... New York, NY
Finger, Barbara S. ... New York, NY
Finger, Charles S. ... Rochester, NY
Finger, Christopher E. ... Bronx, NY
Finger, Craig L. ... **Philadelphia, PA**
Finger, David J. ... Miami, FL
Finger, David L. ... **Wilmington, DE**
Finger, David L., P.A. ... **Wilmington, DE**
Finger, Dorothy M. ... White Plains, NY
Finger, Eric S. ... Lindenhurst, NY
Finger & Finger, A Professional Corporation
White Plains, NY
Finger, George W. ... **El Paso, TX**
Finger, Hochman & Delott, P.C.
Chicago, IL
Finger, Jennifer L. ... **Boston, MA**
Finger, Joe E., Jr. ... Maitland, FL
Finger, Joel L. ... **Parsippany, NJ**
New York, NY
Finger, John W. ... **St. Louis, MO**
Finger, Kenneth J. ... White Plains, NY
Finger, Loretta J. ... **Washington, DC**
Finger, Louis J. ... Wilmington, DE
Finger, M. Neil ... Jonesville, NC
Finger, Parker, Avram, Martin & Roemer, L.L.P. ... Jonesville, NC
Winston-Salem, NC
Finger, Phyllis A. ... Houston, TX
Finger, Robert J. ... Irvine, CA
Finger, Taylor & Andrews, P.A.
Hilton Head Island, SC
Finger, Terry A. ... **Hilton Head Island, SC**
Finger, Timothy L. ... Waynesville, NC
Finger, Todd A. ... **New York, NY**
Finger, William L. ... Jacksonville, FL
Finger, William S. ... Evergreen, CO
Fingeret, Donald J.
Department of Commerce, Patent and Trademark Office, GV
Fingeret, I. Avrum ... Department of Energy, Office of the General Counsel, GV
Fingeret, Ilene H. ... Pittsburgh, PA
Fingeret, Jay L. ... Coraopolis, PA
Pittsburgh, PA
Fingeret, Jonathan M. ... **Denver, CO**
Fingerhood, Karl J. ... Department of Justice, Environment and Natural Resources Division, GV
Fingerhood, Shirley ... New York, NY
Fingerhut, David L. ... New York, NY
Fingerhut, Eric T. ... **Washington, DC**
Fingerhut, H. Scott ... Miami, FL
Fingerhut, Lloyd J. ... Cleveland, OH
Fingerhut, Michael B. ... **Washington, DC**
Fingerhut, Paul M. ... Brooklyn, NY
Fingerhut, Paul M., P.C. ... Brooklyn, NY
Fingerit, Irwin K. ... New York, NY
Fingerman, Albert R. ... **Cincinnati, OH**
Fingerman, Debra Mongan ... Cincinnati, OH
Fingerman, Mark E. ... **Los Angeles, CA**
Fingerman, Michael E. ... Philadelphia, PA
Fingersh, Jack N. ... **Kansas City, MO**
Fingerson, Glenn A. ... Huron, SD
Mitchell, SD
Fingert, Nadine J. ... Chicago, IL
Fingerut, Melvin A. ... Sarasota, FL
Fingold, Brenda J. ... **Boston, MA**
Fingold, Reuben ... Pittsburgh, PA
Fingold, Rona S. ... **Springfield, MA**
Fingold, Ross G. ... **Farmington, CT**
Finguerra-DuCharme, Dyan F.
New York, NY
Fini, Gina R. ... New York, NY
Fini, Rosalina M. ... Medina, OH
Fini, Tom M. ... **New York, NY**
Finical, Scott M. ... **Phoenix, AZ**
Finifter, Michael J. ... Baltimore, MD
Finigan, Barbara J. ... **Pawtucket, RI**
Finigan, Maryanne Huha ... Philadelphia, PA
Finigan, Thomas L. ... Dedham, MA
Finigan, Vincent P., Jr.
San Francisco, CA
Finio, Michael A. ... **Harrisburg, PA**
Finister, Teresa P. ... **Atlanta, GA**
Finitzo, Nicole ... **Lake Forest, IL**
Finizia, Francis E., Jr.
Palm Beach Gardens, FL
Finizio, Michele A. ... **Hicksville, NY**
Finizio, Paul G. ... **Boca Raton, FL**
Fort Lauderdale, FL
Finizio, Ralph A. ... **Pittsburgh, PA**
Finizio, Steven P. ... **Washington, DC**
Finizio-Bascombe, Jamie J.
Boca Raton, FL
Fort Lauderdale, FL
Fink, Adrian B., Jr. ... Cleveland, OH
Fink, Alan ... Towson, MD
Fink, Albert E., (A Prof. Corp.)
Woodland Hills, CA
Fink, Allan L. ... **San Francisco, CA**
Fink, Amy J. ... **Los Angeles, CA**
Fink, Andrew A. ... Worcester, MA
Fink, Andrew A. ... **New York, NY**
Fink, Andrew F. ... Westport, CT
Fink, Arnold H. ... Woodland Hills, CA
Fink, Arnold M. ... Southfield, MI
Fink, Arthur H., Jr. ... Milwaukee, WI
Fink, Barbara Arlene ... Holly Hill, FL
Fink, Baret C. ... Los Angeles, CA
Fink, Barry ... **New York, NY**
Fink, Barry E. ... **Los Angeles, CA**
Fink, Barry M. ... Los Angeles, CA
Fink, Benjamin I. ... **Atlanta, GA**
Fink & Birmingham, P.C. ... **Ludlow, VT**
Fink & Boyle, P.A. ... **Fort Myers, FL**
Fink, Brian L. ... **Miami, FL**
Fink, Bruce R. ... Santa Ana, CA
Fink, Carl M. ... Portland, OR
Fink, Christina M. ... Omaha, NE
Fink, Christopher ... New York, NY
Fink, Christopher C. ... Poplar Bluff, MO
Fink, D. Gene ... Yreka, CA
Fink, David ... **New York, NY**
Wainscott, NY
Fink, David ... Houston, TX
Fink, David A. ... **San Francisco, CA**
Fink, David E. ... **Los Angeles, CA**
Fink, David E. ... **Baltimore, MD**
Fink, David H. ... Atlanta, GA
Fink, David H. ... **Detroit, MI**
Farmington Hills, MI
Lansing, MI
Fink, Dean M. ... **Los Angeles, CA**
Fink, Douglas B. ... **St. Paul, MN**
Fink, Douglas B., Law Offices, P.A.
St. Paul, MN
Fink, Douglas Warren ... **Mobile, AL**
Fink, Edward J. ... Parma, OH
Fink, Edward J. ... Madison, WI
Fink, Edward M. ... **Edison, NJ**
Fink, Edward R. ... Fort Lauderdale, FL
Fink, Elaine E. ... Cincinnati, OH
Fink, Eli H. ... Jacksonville, FL
Fink, Elora C. ... Gretna, LA
Fink, Eric M. ... Philadelphia, PA
Fink & Feldman, LLP ... **Los Angeles, CA**
Fink and Fink ... **Jersey City, NJ**
Fink, Fink and Associates ... Langhorne, PA
Fink Firm, The ... Menasha, WI
Fink, Floran L. ... **Los Angeles, CA**
Fink, Harold B., Jr. ... Port Allegany, PA
Fink, Harold J. ... Trenton, NJ
Fink, Henry Einar ... **Los Angeles, CA**
Fink, Herschel P. ... **Detroit, MI**
Fink & Highmark ... **Hartford, CT**
West Hartford, CT
Fink, Howard Lewis ... Rolling Meadows, IL
Fink, Howard P. ... **Columbus, OH**
Fink, Irving L. ... Indianapolis, IN
Fink, James M. ... Washington, DC
Fink, Janet R. ... New York, NY
Fink, Janie L. ... Minneapolis, MN
Fink, Jeffrey D. ... New York, NY
Fink, Jeffrey H. ... Boca Raton, FL
Fink, Jeffrey N. ... **New York, NY**
Fink, Jeffrey R. ... **St. Louis, MO**
Fink, Jeffrey T. ... Dallas, TX
Fink, Jerold A. ... **Cincinnati, OH**
Fink, Jerrold E. ... **Chicago, IL**
Fink, Jill L. ... Boston, MA
Fink, Joan F. ... Boston, MA
Fink, John W. ... **Little Rock, AR**
Nashville, TN
Fink, Jonathan A. ... New York, NY
Fink, Jonathan D. ... **Los Angeles, CA**
Fink, Jonathan J. ... **New York, NY**
Fink, Joseph A. ... **Lansing, MI**
Fink, Joseph G. ... New York, NY
Fink, Joseph J. ... Cleveland, OH
Middleburg Heights, OH
Fink, Joseph L., III ... Lexington, KY
Fink, Joshua E. ... New York, NY
Fink, Jules ... Silver Spring, MD
Fink, Julie L. ... Charlottesville, VA
Fink, Karl R. ... **Chicago, IL**
Fink, Karl V. ... **Ann Arbor, MI**
Fink, Kathryn Hamilton ... **Chicago, IL**
Fink, Katz & Walz, PLLC ... New York, NY
Fink, Keith A. ... **Los Angeles, CA**
Fink, Kenneth D. ... Miami, FL
Fink, Kenneth E. ... **Wilmington, DE**
Fink, Kenneth N., (P.A.) ... Atlantic Beach, FL
Fink, Kenneth S. ... New York, NY
Fink, Leah S. ... Corydon, IN
Fink, Leonard T. ... **Irvine, CA**
Fink, Lori Anne ... Topeka, KS
Fink, Louis Charles ... New York, NY
Fink, Marc D. ... New York, NY
Fink, Marc J. ... **Washington, DC**
Fink, Mark Andrew ... **Philadelphia, PA**
Fink, Mark H. ... **Southfield, MI**
Fink, Matthew J. ... **Chicago, IL**
Fink, Matthew P. ... Washington, DC
Fink, Melissa S. ... **Santa Monica, CA**
Fink, Melvin D. ... **Ludlow, VT**
Fink, Mendel E. ... Beverly Hills, CA
Fink, Michael F. ... Conshohocken, PA
Fink, Michael F. ... Philadelphia, PA
Fink, Michael G. ... **Fort Myers, FL**
Fink, Michael I. ... Rochester, NY
Fink, Michael J. ... **Reston, VA**
Fink, Michael P. ... **Seattle, WA**
Fink, Mike C. ... Bridgewater, SD
Fink, Myron ... Albuquerque, NM
Fink, N. Leah ... Pittsburgh, PA
Fink, Nancy H ... Brooklyn, NY
Fink, Nathan G. ... Oradell, NJ
Fink, Neal J. ... **Atlanta, GA**
Fink, Neil B. ... **Jersey City, NJ**
Fink, Neil H., Law Offices of
Birmingham, MI
Fink, Norma L. ... Santa Monica, CA
Fink, Paul ... Brooklyn, NY
Fink, Peter W. ... **Boston, MA**
Fink & Platz ... New York, NY
Fink, Rachael ... **New York, NY**
Fink, Raymond L. ... **Buffalo, NY**
Fink, Regina M. ... **Los Angeles, CA**
Fink, Richard A. ... Glendale, CA
Fink, Richard A. ... **Irvine, CA**
Fink, Richard R. ... Langhorne, PA
Fink, Richd. J. ... Park Ridge, IL
Fink, Robert ... San Francisco, CA
Fink, Robert F. ... **New York, NY**
Fink, Robert M., P.C. ... Atlanta, GA
Fink, Robert S. ... **New York, NY**
Fink, Robert S., (A Prof. Corp.)
Los Angeles, CA
Fink, Robert V. ... Ypsilanti, MI
Fink, Robin Y. ... **Atlanta, GA**
Fink, Rodney W. ... Pittsburgh, PA
Fink, Ronald R. ... Port Washington, NY
Fink, Rosalind ... **New York, NY**
Fink, Rosmary Edith ... Omaha, NE
Fink Rosner Ershow-Levenberg, LLC
Clark, NJ
Fink, Russell A. ... Norfolk, VA
Fink, Sally Claire ... Ann Arbor, MI
Fink, Sam F. ... Chicago, IL
Fink, Scott A. ... **San Francisco, CA**
Fink, Sheldon I. ... **Chicago, IL**
Fink, Stanley ... Germantown, TN
Fink, Stanley A. ... Clark, NJ
Fink, Stephanie ... **Rockville, MD**
Fink, Stephanie Lynn ... Landover, MD
Fink, Stephen D. ... Forest Hills, NY
Fink, Stephen F. ... **Dallas, TX**
Fink, Stephen L. ... **Fort Wayne, IN**
Fink, Steven ... **New York, NY**
Fink, Steven A. ... **Irvine, CA**
Fink, Steven B. ... Encino, CA
Fink, Steven D. ... Denver, CO
Fink, Steven H. ... **Mankato, MN**
Fink, Steven M. ... San Jose, CA
Fink, Steven M. ... New York, NY
Fink, Stewart R., (P.C.) ... New York, NY
Fink, Susan B. ... Bridgeport, CT
Fink & Sweet ... Daytona Beach, FL
Fink, Teresa ... **Philadelphia, PA**
Fink, Theresa H. ... Los Alamitos, CA
Fink, Thomas A. ... **Rochester, NY**
Fink, Thomas J. ... Menasha, WI
Fink, Thomas L. ... Tucson, AZ
Fink, Thomas M. ... **Fort Wayne, IN**
Fink, Todd M. ... **Birmingham, MI**
Fink, Tracy ... **New York, NY**
Fink & Travis ... Atlanta, GA
Fink, Vella M. ... Austin, TX
Fink, Wendy Anne ... Garden City, NY
Fink, Wendy L. ... Chicago, IL
Fink, Wesley A. ... Daytona Beach, FL
Fink, William F. ... **Miami, FL**
Fink, Zausmer & Kaufman, P.C.
Detroit, MI
Farmington Hills, MI
Lansing, MI
Finkas, R. Anthony ... **Fairfield, CA**
Finkbeiner and Burnham, P.C.
Marquette, MI
Finkbeiner, James V. ... **Saginaw, MI**
Finkbeiner, Mae L. ... Cincinnati, OH
Finkbeiner, Robert T. ... Marquette, MI
Finkbiner, Aaron C. F., III
Philadelphia, PA
Finkbohner, George W., III ... **Mobile, AL**
Finkbohner, George W., Jr. ... **Mobile, AL**
Finkbohner and Lawler, L.L.C.
Mobile, AL
Finke, A. William ... Milwaukee, WI
Finke, Amy L. ... Vernon, CT
Finke & Associates, P.C. ... **Denver, CO**
Finke, Carl A. ... Joplin, MO
Finke, Carol Murphy ... Boca Raton, FL
Finke, Chad D.S. ... **San Francisco, CA**
Finke, Charles L.
Pension Benefit Guaranty Corporation, Office of the General Counsel, GV
Finke, E. Joe ... Corydon, IN
Finke, Harry J., IV ... **Cincinnati, OH**
Finke, Jeffrey W. ... Chicago, IL
Finke, Nicholas D. ... Cincinnati, OH
Finke, R. Peter ... **Dayton, OH**
Finke, Richard A. ... **Denver, CO**
Finke, Richard C. ... **Columbia, MD**
Finke, Robert A. ... St. Louis, MO
Finke, Robert F. ... **Chicago, IL**
Finke, Robert W. ... **Stamford, CT**
New York, NY
Finke, Robin W. ... Virginia, MN
Finke, Walter W., Jr. ... St. Louis, MO
Finkel, Aaron ... Pomona, NY
Finkel, Alan H. ... **Los Angeles, CA**
Finkel, Alan J. ... New Brunswick, NJ
Finkel, Alan Joel ... Framingham, MA
Finkel, Alan L. ... **Commack, NY**
Finkel, Alan M. ... Los Angeles, CA
Finkel & Altman, L.L.C. ... **Charleston, SC**
Columbia, SC
Finkel, B. Stephan ... Trenton, NJ
Finkel, Barry I. ... Fort Lauderdale, FL
Finkel, Bernard ... Forest Hills, NY
Finkel, Beverly J. ... **Columbia, SC**
Finkel, Bonnie Bazilian ... Philadelphia, PA
Finkel, Charles A. ... Tallahassee, FL
Finkel, Charles M. ... **Beverly Hills, CA**
Finkel, Charles M. ... **Los Angeles, CA**
Finkel, David B. ... Santa Monica, CA
Finkel, David R. ... Northfield, NJ
Finkel, David R. ... New York, NY
Finkel, Debra Paris ... Secaucus, NJ
Finkel, E. Jay ... **Washington, DC**
Finkel, Elliott D. ... Miami, FL
Finkel, Elliott W. ... **Pittsburgh, PA**
Finkel, Eric T. ... **Houston, TX**
Finkel, Evan ... **Los Angeles, CA**
Finkel, Fern J. ... Brooklyn, NY
Finkel, Gerald M. ... **Charleston, SC**
Columbia, SC
Finkel Goldstein Berzow Rosenbloom & Nash, LLP ... **New York, NY**
Finkel, Howard G. ... East Lansing, MI
Finkel, Irving G. ... **Marlton, NJ**
Finkel, J. Maurice, (P.A.) ... Miami, FL
Finkel, James Klee ... New York, NY
Finkel, Jamie ... Culver City, CA
Finkel, Jane E. ... Atlanta, GA
Finkel, Joseph E. ... **Walnut Creek, CA**
Finkel, Joseph J. ... Houston, TX
Finkel, Judith G. ... Houston, TX
Finkel, Kalman ... New York, NY
Finkel, Karen E. ... Springfield, VA
Finkel, Kevin B. ... **Houston, TX**
Finkel, Lee M. ... Scottsdale, AZ
Finkel, Leon I. ... **Chicago, IL**
Lake Forest, IL
Finkel, Leonard L. ... Fresh Meadows, NY
Finkel, Linda K. ... **Chicago, IL**
Finkel, Lonnie ... **San Francisco, CA**
Finkel, Martin D., (P.C.) ... Boston, MA
Finkel, Martwick & Colson, Law Firm of, P.C.
Chicago, IL
Finkel, Melanie ... **New York, NY**
Finkel, Morris S. ... **Pompano Beach, FL**
Finkel, Noah ... **Chicago, IL**
Finkel, Norman D. ... Chicago, IL
Finkel, Norman T. ... **Chicago, IL**
Finkel, Richard A. ... **New York, NY**
Finkel, Richard S. ... Floral Park, NY
Finkel, Robert C. ... **New York, NY**
Finkel, Robert D. ... **Pittsburgh, PA**
Finkel, Robert J. ... **Farmington Hills, MI**
Finkel, Robert Louis ... Encino, CA
Finkel, Robert M. ... **Boston, MA**
Finkel, Robert M. ... **New York, NY**
Finkel, Rosanne A. ... **New York, NY**
Finkel, Sanford N. ... Troy, NY
Finkel, Sharlene K. ... Waltham, MA
Finkel, Sharon E. ... Department of Commerce, Patent and Trademark Office, GV
Finkel, Sidney R. ... Pittsburgh, PA
Finkel, Susan L. ... Austin, TX
Finkel, Suzanne A. ... **New York, NY**
Finkel, Theodore M. ... New York, NY
Finkel, Tomoko Aoyama
Woodland Hills, CA
Finkel, Whitefield, Selik, Raymond, Ferrara & Feldman, Professional Corporation
Detroit, MI
Farmington Hills, MI
Finkelberg, Ellen S. ... Los Angeles, CA
Finkelberg & Finkelberg, A Professional Corporation ... Los Angeles, CA
Finkelberg, Louis I. ... Los Angeles, CA
Finkell, Gregory C. ... Delmar, NY
Finkelman, Daniel P. ... **Boston, MA**
Finkelman, David L. ... **New York, NY**
Finkelman, Eric R. ... Newport, DE
Finkelman, Howard A. ... Ardmore, PA
Finkelman, Jack D. ... **Miami, FL**
Finkelman, Lewis S. ... New York, NY
Finkelman, Natalie A. ... **Jenkintown, PA**
Finkelman & Ross ... Middletown, OH
Finkelmeier & Farrell ... **Cincinnati, OH**
Finkelmeier, Louis J. ... **Cincinnati, OH**
Finkelson, Allen ... **New York, NY**
Finkelson, Ira ... **New York, NY**
Finkelson, Sindy O. ... Linwood, NJ
Finkelstein, Adam D. ... **New York, NY**
Finkelstein, Albert ... Rego Park, NY
Finkelstein, Allen L. ... **New York, NY**
Finkelstein, Andrew G. ... Newburgh, NY
Finkelstein, Anita J. ... **Washington, DC**
Finkelstein, Arlene B. ... **Boca Raton, FL**
Finkelstein, Arnold ... Waterford, MI
Finkelstein, Arthur R. ... Newton, MA
Finkelstein & Associates ... San Diego, CA
Finkelstein, Barry J. ... Treasury Department, Internal Revenue Service, GV
Finkelstein, Ben ... **Washington, DC**
Finkelstein, Bernard ... **New York, NY**
Finkelstein, Beth L. ... Suffern, NY
Finkelstein, Bob ... **New Orleans, LA**
Finkelstein, Brad J. ... **New York, NY**
Finkelstein, Bradley L. ... **Palo Alto, CA**
Finkelstein, Burton H. ... **Washington, DC**
Finkelstein, Charles D. ... Weston, CT
Finkelstein, Daniel ... New York, NY
Finkelstein, David G. ... **San Mateo, CA**
Finkelstein, David N. ... Sarasota, FL
Finkelstein, David S. ... New York, NY
Finkelstein, Diane E. ... San Mateo, CA

Finkelstein, Don B. ....Los Angeles, CA
Finkelstein & Duschaneck .....White Plains, NY
Finkelstein, Edward R. ....New York, NY
Finkelstein, Edward S. ....Harrisburg, PA
Finkelstein, Evelyn M. ....New York, NY
Finkelstein, Fred S. ....Bellevue, WA
Finkelstein, George ....New York, NY
Finkelstein, Henry D. ....Los Angeles, CA
Finkelstein, Herbert L. ....New York, NY
Finkelstein, Howard ....New Rochelle, NY
Finkelstein, Howard D. ....San Diego, CA
Finkelstein, Howard J. ....New York, NY
Finkelstein, Howard M. ....Riverhead, NY
Finkelstein, Howard S., (P.C.)
Newburgh, NY
Finkelstein, Ira A. ....New York, NY
Finkelstein, Ira D. ....Houston, TX
Finkelstein, Irving ....New York, NY
Finkelstein, James N. ....Albany, GA
Finkelstein, Jared T. ....Westport, CT
Finkelstein, Jay Gary ....Washington, DC
Finkelstein, Jay J. ....Pittsburgh, PA
Finkelstein, Jay M. ....Washington, DC
Finkelstein, Jeffrey S. ....Los Angeles, CA
Finkelstein, Jesse A. ....Wilmington, DE
Finkelstein, Joel A. ....Mount Holly, NJ
Finkelstein, Joel M. ....Washington, DC
Finkelstein, Joel S. ....Newburgh, NY
Finkelstein, Johanna ....Asheville, NC
Finkelstein, Jonathan ....Worcester, MA
Finkelstein, Joseph S. ....Philadelphia, PA
Finkelstein, Julius L. ....San Jose, CA
Finkelstein, Kern, Steinberg & Cunningham
Knoxville, TN
Finkelstein, Larry ....Davie, FL
Finkelstein, Laura B. ....Irvine, CA
Finkelstein, Lawrence ....Philadelphia, PA
Finkelstein, Lawrence B. ....New York, NY
Finkelstein, Leo L. ....San Francisco, CA
Finkelstein, Leonard ....Old Bridge, NJ
Finkelstein, Levine, Gittelsohn & Partners
Albany, NY
Newburgh, NY
Finkelstein, Lisa ....San Francisco, CA
Finkelstein, Marc ....Brooklyn, NY
Finkelstein, Marci E. ....Greenwich, CT
Finkelstein, Marcia ....New Orleans, LA
Finkelstein, Marcia Lyn ....Melville, NY
Finkelstein, Mark A. ....Costa Mesa, CA
Finkelstein, Mark A. ....Raleigh, NC
Finkelstein, Mark A. ....Seattle, WA
Finkelstein, Mark R. ....Syracuse, NY
Finkelstein, Mark S. ....Houston, TX
Finkelstein, Matthew M. ....Riverhead, NY
Finkelstein, Mayer ....New Orleans, LA
Finkelstein, Meryl G. ....New York, NY
Finkelstein, Michael ....New York, NY
Finkelstein, Michael O. ....New York, NY
Finkelstein, Nancy Lee ....Seattle, WA
Finkelstein, Nancy R. ....New York, NY
Finkelstein, Nathan I. ....Washington, DC
Finkelstein, Nathan I. ....Bethesda, MD
Finkelstein, Norman M. ....San Diego, CA
Finkelstein, Paul ....Yonkers, NY
Finkelstein, Paul H. ....Vancouver, WA
Finkelstein, Philip M. ....Monsey, NY
Finkelstein, Richard G. ....New York, NY
Finkelstein, Richard S. ....West Orange, NJ
Finkelstein, Robert ....Chinle, AZ
Finkelstein, Robert ....North Miami Beach, FL
Finkelstein, Robert A. ....Los Angeles, CA
Finkelstein, Robert A. ....White Plains, NY
Finkelstein, Robert S. .....Department of Justice, Immigration and Naturalization Service, GV
Finkelstein, Ronald M. ....New York, NY
Finkelstein, Rubi ....New York, NY
Finkelstein, Saul H. ....New York, NY
Finkelstein, Scott J. ....Philadelphia, PA
Finkelstein, Sharyn S. ....New York, NY
Finkelstein, Sheldon M. ....Newark, NJ
Finkelstein, Silvia P. ....New York, NY
Finkelstein, Steven ....Greenwich, CT
Finkelstein, Steven H. ....Cherry Hill, NJ
Finkelstein, Steven J. ....Staten Island, NY
Finkelstein, Steven R. ....New York, NY
Finkelstein, Stuart M. ....New York, NY
Finkelstein, Susan ....Syracuse, NY
Finkelstein, Suzanne M. ....New York, NY
Finkelstein, Tamar ....New York, NY
Finkelstein, Terry Joel ....East Brunswick, NJ
Finkelstein, Thomas ....New York, NY
Finkelstein, Thompson & Loughran
Washington, DC
Finkelstein, Tracy K. ....Beachwood, OH
Finkelstein, Vicki B. ....Columbia, MD
Finkelstein, Victor B. ....Kansas City, MO
Finkelstein, Willard C. ....Austin, TX
Finkelstein, William A. ....Purchase, NY
Finkelstein, William B. ....Dallas, TX
Finkelstein, William M. ....New York, NY
Finkelstein-Fingeret, Rubi ....New York, NY
Finken, Tracy A. ....Philadelphia, PA
Finkenaur, Bridget E. ....Treasury Department, Internal Revenue Service, GV
Finkenberg, Lincoln S. ....New York, NY
Finkenberg, Susan S. ....Montville, NJ
Finker, Jules ....New York, NY
Finkin, Bob M. ....Forest Hills, NY
Finkle, Barbara ....Pleasanton, CA
Finkle, Bruce N. ....Nashua, NH
Finkle, David G., & Associates
Los Angeles, CA
Finkle, David H. ....Chicago, IL
Finkle, Diane ....Providence, RI
Finkle, George A. ....Seattle, WA
Finkle, Harry ....Fresno, CA
Finkle, Isaac ....New York, NY
Finkle, Jason David ....Los Angeles, CA
Finkle, Kenneth S. ....Buffalo Grove, IL
Finkle, Lester W. ....Chicago, IL
Finkle, Michael J. ....Seattle, WA
Finkle, R. Andrew ....Raleigh, NC
Finkle, R. Roy ....Santa Monica, CA
Finkle, Stuart I. ....Chicago, IL
Finkle, Yale S. ....Brea, CA
Finklea, Edward A. ....Portland, OR
Finklea, Gary Ivan ....Florence, SC
Finklea, Robert W. ....Dallas, TX
Finklea, Samuel L., III ....Columbia, SC
Finklea, Wm. B. ....Dallas, TX
Finklehoffe, Carol Lynn ....Miami, FL
Finkleman Booher & Horan Co., L.P.A.
Middletown, OH
Finkler, David J. ....New York, NY
Finkler, Kira L. ....United States Senate, Senatorial Assistants, GV
Finks, Harvey, P.C. ....Sun City, AZ
Finks, Jean M. ....Punta Gorda, FL
Finks, Lisa Janda ....Chicago, IL
Finks, Malcolm D. ....Boston, MA
Finks, Thomas O. ....Shelbyville, IL
Finlan, Patrick H. ....Wausau, WI
Finlator, Martha D. ....Washington, DC
Finlaw, Jack D., Jr. ....Englewood, CO
Finlaw, Kimberly D. ....South Bend, IN
Finlay, Audrea Hyacinth ....New City, NY
Finlay, Campbell H. ....Upland, CA
Finlay, David A. ....Brandon, FL
Finlay, J. Scott ....Syracuse, NY
Finlay, James B. ....Long Beach, WA
Finlay, John A. ....Xenia, OH
Finlay, Joseph B., Jr. ....Philadelphia, PA
Finlay, Luke W. ....Annapolis, MD
Finlay, Robert ....Miami, FL
Finlay, Susan P. ....San Diego, CA
Finlay, T. Robert ....Santa Ana, CA
Finlay, Thomas L. ....San Antonio, TX
Finlay, William H. ....Charlotte, NC
Finlayson, Arnold R. ....Washington, DC
Finlayson, Craig R. ....Fort Wayne, IN
Indianapolis, IN
Finlayson, David A. ....Albuquerque, NM
Finlayson, Dawn Bruner ....San Antonio, TX
Finlayson, Francien R. ....Arlington, VA
Finlayson, Grant ....San Francisco, CA
Finlayson, Jesse S. ....Irvine, CA
Finlayson, Kirsten ....Bozeman, MT
Finlayson, L. Burton ....Atlanta, GA
Finlayson, Mac D. ....Tulsa, OK
Finlayson, Mac D., P.C. ....Tulsa, OK
Finlayson, Mark L. ....Colorado Springs, CO
Finlayson, Ralph L. ....Salt Lake City, UT
Finlayson, Robert M., II ....Atlanta, GA
Finlayson, Stephen D. ....Burns, OR
Finley, Alison K. ....Beverly Hills, CA
Finley, Alt, Smith, Scharnberg, Craig, Hilmes & Gaffney, P.C. .....Des Moines, IA
Finley, Ann H. ....General Accounting Office, Office of the General Counsel, GV
Finley, Anthony L. ....New York, NY
Finley, Arley D., III ....Austin, TX
Finley & Associates, P.A. ....Boca Raton, FL
West Palm Beach, FL
Finley, Barbara K. ....Reno, NV
Finley & Berg, L.L.P. ....San Francisco, CA
Finley, Bonnie S. ....Akron, OH
Finley, Brigitte ....Phoenix, AZ
Finley & Buckley, P.C. ....Atlanta, GA
Finley, Byron C. ....North Hills, CA
Finley, Carol A. ....Colorado Springs, CO
Finley, Carol Turobiner ....New York, NY
Finley, Chandler R. ....Boca Raton, FL
West Palm Beach, FL
Finley, Charles D. ....Houston, TX
Finley, Charles R. ....Albuquerque, NM
Finley, Christine Allgair ....Dallas, TX
Finley, Clarence W. ....San Diego, CA
Finley, Cynthia Cole ....Dallas, TX
Finley, Dale W. ....Russellville, AR
Finley, David G. ....Cleveland, OH
Finley, David G., Co., L.P.A. .....Cleveland, OH
Finley, David Nathan ....Tustin, CA
Finley & Deaton ....San Francisco, CA
Finley, Dee S., Jr. ....Fort Worth, TX
Grapevine, TX
Finley, Edward J., II ....New York, NY
Finley, Edward S., Jr. ....Raleigh, NC
Finley, Eric ....Roanoke, VA
Finley, Felix L., Jr. ....Pickens, SC
Finley & Finley ....Ashdown, AR
Finley, Frances M. ....Little Rock, AR
Finley, Franklin L. ....Treasury Department, Internal Revenue Service, GV
Finley, Gale S. ....Dayton, OH
Finley, George ....Kermit, TX
Finley, George S. ....San Angelo, TX
Finley, George W. ....Los Angeles, CA
Finley, Hugh D. ....San Francisco, CA
Finley, J. Benjamin ....Atlanta, GA
Finley, James F. ....St. Paul, MN
Finley, James W. ....Houston, TX
Finley, Jeffery L. ....Gallipolis, OH
Finley, Jeffrey L. ....Doylestown, PA
Finley, Jeffrey R. ....Phoenix, AZ
Finley, Jennifer J. ....St. Louis, MO
Finley, Jerry ....Baton Rouge, LA
Finley, Joe L., Jr. ....Sparta, TN
Finley, John A. ....Louisville, KY
Finley, John C., III ....Ashdown, AR
Finley, John G. ....New York, NY
Finley, John Jordan, (P.C.) .....New York, NY
Finley, John W., III ....New York, NY
Finley, John W., Jr. ....Goldens Bridge, NY
Finley, Joseph E. ....Atlanta, GA
Finley, Joseph E. ....Baltimore, MD
Finley, Joseph J. ....Trenton, NJ
Finley, Joseph M. ....Minneapolis, MN
Finley, Joseph M. ....St. Paul, MN
Finley, Julie ....San Francisco, CA
Finley, Kathleen A. ....Doylestown, PA
Finley, Kathleen F. ....Berwyn, PA
Finley, Kathleen P. ....San Diego, CA
Finley, Kelly A. ....New York, NY
Finley, Kerry A. ....Des Moines, IA
Finley, Kevin M. ....Louisville, KY
Finley, Kirk H. ....Orange, CA
Finley, L. Terrance Spencer ....Chicago, IL
Finley, Lawrence F. ....Oneida, NY
Finley, Linda S. ....Atlanta, GA
Finley, Lowell ....Berkeley, CA
Finley, Lucinda M. ....Buffalo, NY
Finley, M. Alicia ....Chesterfield, VA
Finley, Michael D. ....North Hills, CA
Finley, Michael D. ....Treasury Department, Internal Revenue Service, GV
Finley, Michael J. ....Akron, OH
Finley, Michael Richard ....Washington, DC
Finley, Miller, Cashman, Weingart, Schmitt & Hill ....Hiawatha, KS
Finley, Myron G. ....New York, NY
Finley, Patricia J. ....Phoenix, AZ
Finley, Patrick J. ....Chicago, IL
Finley, Patrick L. ....Walnut Creek, CA
Finley, Paul A. ....New Braunfels, TX
Finley, Phyllis (Pam) ....Joplin, MO
Finley, Price D. ....Columbus, OH
Finley, Renée M. ....San Francisco, CA
Finley, Robert C. ....Fort Worth, TX
Finley, Robert M. ....Madison, WI
Finley, Robert S. ....New York, NY
Finley, Ron C. ....San Jose, CA
Finley, Sara J. ....Birmingham, AL
Finley, Sarah Hopkins ....Richmond, VA
Finley, Scott ....Roseville, CA
Finley, Stephen M. ....Dallas, TX
Finley, Steven C. ....San Francisco, CA
Finley, Steven R. ....New York, NY
Finley, Steven Z. ....Department of Education, Office of the General Counsel, GV
Finley, Teas and Esser ....Mason City, IA
Finley, Thad R. ....Denton, TX
Finley, Thomas A. ....Des Moines, IA
Finley, Thomas C. ....Chandler, OK
Finley, Thomas P. ....Wausau, WI
Finley, Victoria H. ....Omaha, NE
Finley, W. Thomas ....Dallas, TX
Finley, Warren ....Laguna Beach, CA
Finley, William G. ....St. Paul, MN
Finley, William L. ....Roswell, NM
Finlinson, Fred W. ....Salt Lake City, UT
Finlinson, Scott B. ....Salt Lake City, UT
Finlow, Leslie ....Treasury Department, Internal Revenue Service, GV
Finman, Sheldon E. ....Fort Myers, FL
Finman, Sheldon E., P.A. ......Fort Myers, FL
Finman, Ted ....Madison, WI
Finmann, Victor M. ....Mineola, NY
Finmann, Victor M., P.C. ....Mineola, NY
Finman-Pince, Terry J. ....Janesville, WI
Finn, Andrew L. ....Detroit, MI
Finn, Anne-Marie ....Easton, MA
Finn, Anthony T. ....Detroit, MI
Finn, Aubrey I. ....Los Angeles, CA
Finn, Bernard F. ....Lansing, MI
Finn, Bradley J. ....Billings, MT
Finn, Brian J. ....Daly City, CA
Finn, C. Virginia Regan ....Milwaukee, WI
Finn, Carol Anne Fagen ....Providence, RI
Finn, Catherine H. ....Detroit, MI
Finn, Charles M. ....Knoxville, TN
Finn, Chester E. ....Dayton, OH
Finn, Daniel J. ....Boston, MA
Finn, Daniel J. ....Newton, MA
Finn Dixon & Herling LLP
Bridgeport, CT
Fairfield, CT
Greenwich, CT
New Haven, CT
Norwalk, CT
Stamford, CT
White Plains, NY
Finn, Edward J. ....Washington, DC
Finn, Edward V. ....Bronx, NY
Finn, Eileen E. ....Boston, MA
Finn, Elizabeth (Ellie) R. ....Phoenix, AZ
Finn, Evelynn M. ....Pasadena, CA
Finn, Frank ....Dallas, TX
Finn, Frederick Wells ....Washington, DC
Finn, Gerald F., Jr. ....Albany, NY
Finn, Gerard P. ....Washington, DC
Finn, Herbert H. ....Chicago, IL
Finn & Hurtt ....Dalton, GA
Finn, J. Jerome ....Milwaukee, WI
Finn, James H. ....Brookfield, WI
Finn, James H., Law Office, S.C.
Brookfield, WI
Finn, James M. ....Portland, OR
Finn, Jane A. ....Chevy Chase, MD
Finn, Janet C. ....Cincinnati, OH
Finn, Jeffrey A. ....Los Angeles, CA
Finn, Jerry M. ....Kenilworth, NJ
Finn, John A. ....Miami, FL
Finn, John A. ....Holyoke, MA
Finn, John D. ....Overland Park, KS
Finn, John E. ....Morro Bay, CA
Finn, John F. ....Minneapolis, MN
Finn, John H. (Jack) ....Grand Ledge, MI
Finn, John J. ....Marietta, GA
Finn, John J. ....Hopkinton, MA
Finn, John J. ....Worcester, MA
Finn, John J. ....Norwood, NJ
Finn, John L. ....Peoria, AZ
Santa Fe, NM
Finn, John M. ....Hopkinton, MA
Finn, John S. ....Denver, CO
Finn, John V. ....Stevens Point, WI
Finn, Judith A. ....Tulsa, OK
Finn, Kathryn A. ....Chicago, IL
Finn, Kathy A. ....Los Angeles, CA
Finn, Kelley A., (P.A.) ....Washington, DC
Miami Beach, FL
Finn, Kelley, Law Offices, P.A.
Miami Beach, FL
Finn, Kevin B. ....Los Angeles, CA
Finn, Kevin P. ....Hempstead, NY
Finn, Lawrence B. ....Chicago, IL
Finn, Lawrence F. ....Pocono Pines, PA
Finn, Lynne Stenclik ....Williamsville, NY
Finn, Maloney & Haines, S.C. ......Hartland, WI
Finn, Martin S. ....Albany, NY
Finn, Marvin R. ....Lynn, MA
Finn, Maureen M. ....New York, NY
Finn, Michael J. ....Glastonbury, CT
Finn, Michael J. ....Hartland, WI
Finn, Michael J. ....Rock Springs, WY
Finn, Michael L. ....Columbus, OH
Finn, Michael P. ....Sinton, TX
Finn, Michael S. ....Oak Park, MI
Finn, Natalie K. ....Anchorage, AK
Finn, Newton E. ....Waukegan, IL
Finn, Patrick M. ....Hyannis, MA
Finn, Patrick W. ....Waterbury, CT
Finn, Peter B. ....Boston, MA
Finn, Peter M. ....New York, NY
Finn, R. Donald ....Buffalo, NY
Finn, Raymond S. ....Encino, CA
Finn, Rebecca Elizabeth ....Laurel, MD
Finn, Richard J. ....Oakland, CA
Finn, Richard M. ....Barre, VT
Finn, Robert Joseph ....Concord, NH
Finn, Robert P. ....Long Beach, CA
Kihei, HI
Finn, Robert T. ....Beatrice, NE
Finn, Robert W. ....Tucson, AZ
Finn, Ronald B. ....Coral Springs, FL
Finn, Ronald N. ....New York, NY
Finn, Ruth G. ....Phoenix, AZ
Finn, Stephanie L. ....Eau Claire, WI
Finn, Stephen A. ....Stamford, CT
Finn, Stephen G. ....Salem, MA
Finn, Stephen P. ....Neligh, NE
Finn, Stephen R. ....San Francisco, CA
Finn, Tamar E. ....Washington, DC
Finn, Terrence M. ....Boston, MA
Finn, Terrence S. ....Akron, OH
Finn, Thomas J. ....Department of Commerce, Patent and Trademark Office, GV
Finn, Thomas J. ....Chicago, IL
Finn, Thomas J. ....Syracuse, NY
Finn, Thomas J. ....Hilton Head Island, SC
Myrtle Beach, SC
Finn, Thomas M. ....San Jose, CA
Finn, Thomas M. ....Dalton, GA
Finn, Thomas P. ....Altoona, PA
Finn, Thomas P., Jr. ....New York, NY
Finn, Thomas R. ....Boston, MA
Finn, Thomas S. ....Garden City, NY
Finn, Thomas W. ....Minnetonka, MN
Finn, Timothy A. ....Beaver, PA
Finn, Timothy J. ....Washington, DC
Finn, Timothy J. ....Ames, IA
Finn, Vaughan ....Hartford, CT
Finn, Virginia R. ....Milwaukee, WI
Finn, William M. ....Augusta, ME
Finn, William T. ....New Orleans, LA
Finnan, Fleischut & Associates
Palo Alto, CA
Finnan, George A. ....Charleston, SC
Finnan, Patrick J. ....Rockville, MD
Finnarn, Theodore O. ....Greenville, OH
Finn-DeLuca, Valerie M. ....Dayton, OH
Finne, Bruce J. ....Springfield, IL
Finne, Fredric R. ....Deerfield, IL
Finnegan, B. James ....San Francisco, CA
Finnegan & Barth, P.A. ....Cherry Hill, NJ
Finnegan, Catherine J. ....Washington, DC
Finnegan, Christine ....Washington, NJ
Finnegan, Clinton J. ....Milwaukee, WI
Finnegan, Colleen A. ....New York, NY
Finnegan, Conrad & Peterson, L.C.
Jefferson City, MO
Kansas City, MO
Finnegan, Cornelius T., III
Greenwich, CT
Finnegan, Cornelius T., Jr. ....Lowell, MA
Finnegan, Daniel ....Drexel Hill, PA
Finnegan, Daniel J. ....Springfield, MA
Finnegan, David B. ....Washington, DC
Finnegan, David I. ....Boston, MA
Finnegan, David L. ....Cherry Hill, NJ
Finnegan, Edward F. ....Chelmsford, MA
Finnegan & Finnegan ....Milwaukee, WI
Finnegan, Frank R. ....Rockford, IL
Finnegan, George B., Jr. ....New York, NY
Finnegan, George T. ....Boston, MA
Finnegan, Harold M. ....Houston, TX
Finnegan, Henderson, Farabow, Garrett & Dunner, L.L.P. ....Palo Alto, CA
Washington, DC
Atlanta, GA
Finnegan, Hickey, Dinsmoor & Johnson, P.C.
Boston, MA
Finnegan, Hugh P. ....New York, NY
Finnegan, James J. ....Boston, MA
Finnegan, James P. ....New York, NY
Finnegan, Jeffrey C. ....Newport Beach, CA
Finnegan, Jeremiah D. ....Kansas City, MO
Finnegan, John D. ....Monroeville, PA
Finnegan, John E. ....Stoneham, MA
Finnegan, John E. ....New York, NY
Finnegan, John F. ....New York, NY
Finnegan, John F., Jr. ....Washington, DC

Finnegan, John J. ... Deerfield, IL
Finnegan, John J., III ... Cherry Hill, NJ
Finnegan, John M., Jr. ... Louisville, KY
Finnegan, Karen M. ... Department of Justice, Office of Information and Privacy, GV
Finnegan, Kerian A. ... Mineola, NY
New York, NY
Finnegan, Kevin A. ... New York, NY
Finnegan, Kevin F. ... Chelmsford, MA
Finnegan, Kevin James ... Washington, DC
Finnegan, Kevin S. ... New York, NY
Finnegan, Laura M. ... Chicago, IL
Finnegan, Leslie E. ... San Mateo, CA
Finnegan, Linda A. ... Phoenix, AZ
Finnegan, Lynn Marie ... Los Alamos, NM
Finnegan, Marks & Hampton, A Professional Corporation ... San Francisco, CA
Finnegan, Martin D. ... Philadelphia, PA
Finnegan, Matthew G. ... Washington, DC
Fairfax, VA
Finnegan, Michael J. ... Los Angeles, CA
Finnegan, Michell ... Baton Rouge, LA
Finnegan, Patricia A. ... Media, PA
Finnegan, Patrick C. ... New York, NY
Finnegan, Patrick J. ... St. Paul, MN
Finnegan, Patrick J. ... West Nyack, NY
Finnegan, Patrick T. ... Philadelphia, PA
Finnegan, Paul W. ... Boston, MA
Finnegan, Richard J. ... Phoenix, AZ
Finnegan, Richard N.
Department of Defense, Defense Legal Services Agency, GV
Finnegan, Roger W. ... Milwaukee, WI
Finnegan, Shannon M. ... San Francisco, CA
Finnegan, Sharon O'Neill ... Cherry Hill, NJ
Philadelphia, PA
Finnegan, Sheila M. ... Chicago, IL
Finnegan, Stephen J. ... Boston, MA
Finnegan, Theresa S. ... Springfield, MA
Finnegan, Thomas J. ... Schaumburg, IL
Finnegan, Thomas J., Jr. ... Springfield, MA
Finnegan, Thomas M. ... New York, NY
Finnegan, Timothy M., (P.C.)
New York, NY
Finnegan, Underwood, Ryan & Tierney
Boston, MA
Finnegan, Vincent D. ... Garden City, NY
New York, NY
Finnegan, Walter ... Fort Lauderdale, FL
Finnegan, William F. ... Basking Ridge, NJ
Finnegan, William H. ... Phoenix, AZ
Finnegan, William H. ... Boston, MA
Finnegan, William J. P. ... San Ramon, CA
Finnegan, William N., IV ... Houston, TX
Finnegan, William R. ... Marion, OH
Finnegan, William T., Jr. ... Kingston, PA
Finnegan, Wm. N., III ... Houston, TX
Finnell, Charles A. ... Holliday, TX
Finnell, Conrad ... Cleveland, TN
Finnell, Conrad, P.C. and Associates
Cleveland, TN
Finnell, Gary J. ... Pasadena, CA
Finnell, Gilbert L., Jr. ... Houston, TX
Finnell, James M. ... Tacoma, WA
Finnell, Jeffrey B. ... New York, NY
Finnell, John W. ... Benicia, CA
Finnell, Kelly O. ... Memphis, TN
Finnell, Kevin T. ... Batavia, NY
Finnell, Lisa J. ... New York, NY
Finnell, Matthew J. ... Springfield, IL
Finnell, Robert D. ... Pleasanton, CA
Finnell, Robert K. ... Rome, GA
Finnell, Susan Land ... Dallas, TX
Finnell, Warren J. ... Garden City, NY
Finnelly, Thomas M., Jr. ... Seattle, WA
Finnen, George R. ... Lancaster, OH
Finnen, Malachy W. ... Houston, TX
Finner, Wendell, Law Offices
Jacksonville, FL
Ponte Vedra Beach, FL
Baltimore, MD
Finneran, Adrian Paul ... San Diego, CA
Finneran, Ann M. ... Mountain View, CA
Finneran, Byrne & Drechsler, L.L.P.
Boston, MA
Finneran, Daniel V. ... Brooklyn, NY
Finneran, Ethan V. ... Hackensack, NJ
New York, NY
Finneran & Finneran ... Princeton Junction, NJ
Finneran, John G., Jr. ... Falls Church, VA
Finneran, Lawrence F. ... Coos Bay, OR
Finneran, M. Theresa ... Columbus, OH
Finneran, Michael T. ... St. Louis, MO
Finneran, Michelle L. ... Palo Alto, CA
Finneran, Norma J. N.
Princeton Junction, NJ
Finneran, Robert V. ... Salem, MA
Finneran, Russell D. ... Columbus, OH
Finneran, Séan Paul ... Columbus, OH
Finneran, Susan R. ... Boston, MA
Finneran, Thomas A. ... Concord, MA
Finneran, Thomas John ... Columbus, OH
Finneran, Thomas M. ... Boston, MA
Finneran, Thomas R. ... Princeton Junction, NJ
Finneran, Todd G. ... Athens, OH
Bellefontaine, OH
Chillicothe, OH
Circleville, OH
Finneran, Todd G. ... Columbus, OH
Finneran, Todd G. ... Delaware, OH
Lancaster, OH
Logan, OH
London, OH
Marysville, OH
McArthur, OH
Mt. Vernon, OH
Newark, OH
Pataskala, OH
Pickerington, OH
Sunbury, OH
Finneran, William C., Jr. ... Yonkers, NY
Finnerin, David M. ... Parkersburg, WV
Finnerman, Doris S. ... Department of Justice, Civil Division, GV
Finnerty, Beth A. ... Columbus, OH
Finnerty, Brian P. ... Boston, MA
Finnerty, Catherine E. ... New York, NY
Finnerty, Corinne R. ... North Vernon, IN
Finnerty, Daniel J. ... Long Beach, CA
Finnerty, Edward P. ... Lake Placid, NY
Finnerty & Finnerty ... Boston, MA
Finnerty, Frank A., Jr. ... Syosset, NY
Finnerty, Gail E. ... Boston, MA
Finnerty, James J., Jr. ... New York, NY
Finnerty, John E. ... Paramus, NJ
Finnerty, John F., Jr. ... Boston, MA
Finnerty, John P. ... Bay Shore, NY
Finnerty, Joseph B. ... Lansing, MI
Finnerty, Joseph G., III ... New York, NY
Finnerty, Joseph G., Jr. ... Baltimore, MD
New York, NY
Finnerty, Joseph M. ... Buffalo, NY
Finnerty, Kathleen E. ... Sacramento, CA
Finnerty, Kevin J. ... New Bedford, MA
Finnerty & LaRocca, P.C.
Hackensack, NJ
Paramus, NJ
Finnerty, Marianne ... Department of Justice, Civil Division, GV
Finnerty, Robert W. ... Los Angeles, CA
Finnerty, Terry P. ... Atlanta, GA
Finnerty, Thomas E., Jr. ... Brockton, MA
Finnerty, Thomas H. ... Troy, MI
Finnerty, Timothy E. ... Carnegie, PA
Pittsburgh, PA
Finnerty, Timothy F. ... Garden City, NY
Finnerty, Timothy J. ... Wichita, KS
Finnerty, William J. ... Bayonne, NJ
Finneseth, C. Scott ... Perry, IA
Finney, Barbara ... Houston, TX
Finney, Brian W. ... Decatur, IL
Finney, Charles B. ... Dothan, AL
Finney, Charles E. ... Redwood City, CA
Finney, Charles R. ... Xenia, OH
Finney, Cheryl J. ... Los Angeles, CA
Finney, Christopher P. ... Cincinnati, OH
Finney, Daniel E ... Spokane, WA
Finney, Daniel P., Jr. ... St. Louis, MO
Finney, David R. ... Fort Worth, TX
Finney, Ernest A., III ... Sumter, SC
Finney, Ernest A., Jr. ... Sumter, SC
Finney, Ernest R. (Jud), Jr. ... Amarillo, TX
Finney, Falk & Lawrence-Berrey
Yakima, WA
Finney, Frank H. ... Alamo, CA
Finney, Fred T. ... Albany, GA
Finney, George ... Miami, FL
Finney, Irene Constance ... New Bern, NC
Finney, James H. ... Clinton Township, MI
Detroit, MI
Finney, James N.
Equal Employment Opportunity Commission, Office of Federal Operations, GV
Finney, Jas. W. ... Coshocton, OH
Finney, Jeffrey L. ... Kennewick, WA
Finney, Jervis S. ... Baltimore, MD
Finney, John E. ... Miami, FL
Finney, Josele Arena ... Moorestown, NJ
Finney, Joseph C. ... Maywood, IL
Finney, Joyce E. ... Baltimore, MD
Finney, Kathleen A. ... Rantoul, IL
Finney, Kathleen A. Law Office of, A P.C.
Rantoul, IL
Finney, Kenneth B. ... San Francisco, CA
Finney, Kenneth H. ... San Francisco, CA
Finney, Kristein M. ... Alexandria, VA
Finney, Kristen ... New York, NY
Finney, Lawrence D. ... Philadelphia, PA
Finney, Lee Mills ... Reno, NV
Finney, Lewis, Juneau & Henderson
Clinton Township, MI
Detroit, MI
Finney, Linnes, Jr. ... Fort Pierce, FL
Stuart, FL
Finney, Michael D. ... Yakima, WA
Finney, Michael P. ... Pensacola, FL
Finney, Norman W. ... Nashville, TN
Finney, P. Dustin, Jr. ... Washington, DC
Finney, P. Gray, III ... Boca Raton, FL
Finney, Pelham Gray, III ... Miami, FL
Finney, Robert A. ... Dakota City, NE
Finney, Robert L., (P.C.) ... Pampa, TX
Finney, Stuart L. ... Edina, MN
Finney, Tal Clifton ... Los Angeles, CA
Finney, Valerie A. ... Hamden, CT
Finney, Willard R. ... Rocky Mount, VA
Finnical, Timothy M. ... Jefferson City, MO
Finnican, Lisa A.
Department of Labor, GV
Finnick, John G. ... Walnut Creek, CA
Finnie, Anne Stoddard ... Bridgeport, CT
Finnie, Donald M. ... New York, NY
Finnie, John ... Centerport, NY
Finnigan, James T. ... Boston, MA
Finnigan, John E. ... South Bend, IN
Finnigan, John J., Jr. ... Cincinnati, OH
Finnigan, John M. ... Cocoa, FL
Orlando, FL
Finnigan, Richard A. ... Olympia, WA
Finnigan, Theodore J. ... Williamsville, NY
Finn III, Harold B. ... Stamford, CT
Finning, Richard C. ... New York, NY
Finno, Ralph B. ... Brooklyn, NY
Finnorn, Joanne M. ... Detroit, MI
Finnstrom, John E. ... Sacramento, CA
Fino, Paul A. ... New York, NY
Fino, Paul A., Jr. ... New York, NY
Finocchiaro, David D. ... Smyrna, DE
Finocchiaro, Peter D. ... Deerfield, IL
Finocchio, Carol R. ... New York, NY
Finocchio, English & LaVeck ... Syracuse, NY
Finocchio, Julie M. ... Rochester, NY
Finocchio, Melissa ... Menlo Park, CA
Finocchio, Vincent J., Jr. ... Syracuse, NY
Finocharo, John J. ... Cincinnati, OH
Finoli, Vincent J. ... Greensburg, PA
Finora, Rosemary Frantz ... Milwaukee, WI
Finrow, Thomas M. ... La Mesa, CA
Fins, Theodore S. ... Fox River Grove, IL
Finseth, Carl L. ... Honolulu, HI
Finseth, Eric J. ... Palo Alto, CA
Finseth, Paul A. ... Rochester, MN
Finsilver, Iris Joan ... Beverly Hills, CA
Finson, Hugh ... Monticello, IL
Finson, Lowell W. ... Phoenix, AZ
Finson, Lowell W., P.C. ... Phoenix, AZ
Finstein, Paul M. ... Warwick, RI
Finster, Charles E. ... Walnut Creek, CA
Finster, Evelyn ... New York, NY
Finster, Samuel C., Sr. ... Summerville, GA
Finsterwald, Lori J. ... New York, NY
Finston, Albert L. ... Chicago, IL
Finston, Felicia A. ... Dallas, TX
Finston, Heidi R. ... Burlington, NJ
Finston, John F. ... San Francisco, CA
Portland, OR
Finston, Nina B.
Securities and Exchange Commission, Division of Enforcement, GV
Finston, Steven L. ... Los Angeles, CA
Finston, Susan Kling ... Department of State, Bureau of Economic and Business Affairs, GV
Finstrom, James P. ... Jefferson, TX
Finstrom, Larry ... Dallas, TX
Fint & Associates, Ltd. ... Bloomington, IL
Fint, David G. ... Bloomington, IL
Finta, Monica J ... Las Vegas, NV
Fintel, Edward J., & Associates
Syracuse, NY
Finto, Kevin J. ... Richmond, VA
Finton, Stewart M. ... Albany, NY
Finton, Timothy C. ... Department of State, Bureau of Economic and Business Affairs, GV
Fintonis, Susan L. Beane ... Nahant, MA
Fintor, Susan E. ... Larkspur, CA
Fintz, Alan S. ... Brooklyn, NY
Fintz, Bernard ... Brooklyn, NY
Finucane, Alexandra K. ... Landover, MD
Finucane, Brendan ... Seattle, WA
Finucane, Brian J. ... Kansas City, MO
Finucane, David J. ... Washington, DC
Finucane, Eileen C. ... Chambersburg, PA
Finucane, Hallie A. ... St. Paul, MN
Finucane & Hartzell ... Pittsford, NY
Finucane, Leila Alanna ... New York, NY
Finucane, Leo G. ... Pittsford, NY
Finucane, Michael B. ... Chambersburg, PA
Finucane, Terry R., (A Professional Corporation) ... Los Angeles, CA
Finucane, Thomas J. ... Chambersburg, PA
Finucane, William M. ... Elizabethtown, NY
Finwall, Gordon J. ... San Jose, CA
Finz & Finz, P.C. ... Jericho, NY
New York, NY
Finz, Leonard L. ... Jericho, NY
New York, NY
Finz, Stuart L. ... Jericho, NY
New York, NY
Finzel, Roger A. ... Albuquerque, NM
Finzen, Bruce A. ... Minneapolis, MN
Finzi, David B. ... Long Beach, CA
Fiocca, Carl J. ... Akron, OH
Fiocca, John A., Jr. ... Akron, OH
Fiocca, Joseph V. ... New York, NY
Fiocchi, Richard C. ... Spring Valley, IL
Fiol, Alejandro ... Tampa, FL
Fiol, David L. ... San Francisco, CA
Fiol, Michael ... Portland, ME
Fiola, Anthony J. ... Glassboro, NJ
Vineland, NJ
Fiora, Nancy ... Tucson, AZ
Fioramonti, Frank R. ... New York, NY
Fioravanti, John J., Jr. ... Doylestown, PA
Fioravanti, Joseph M. ... Media, PA
Fioravanti & Knight ... Doylestown, PA
Fioravanti, Michelle A. ... King Of Prussia, PA
Fioravanti, Paul A., Jr. ... Wilmington, DE
Fioravanti, Paul M. ... Rochester, NY
Fioravanti, Perry J. ... Philadelphia, PA
Fioravanti, Raymond R. ... Washington, DC
Fiordalisi, Nicola ... Chicago, IL
Fiordalisi, Vincent E. ... Newark, NJ
Fiordaliso, Robert A. ... Buffalo, NY
Fiore, Albert A. ... Costa Mesa, CA
Fiore, Anthony R. ... Warren, NJ
Fiore, Anthony T. ... Houston, TX
Fiore, Antoinette J ... New York, NY
Fiore, Betsy Ann ... Las Vegas, NV
Fiore, Carol A. ... Hooksett, NH
Fiore, Charles A. ... Norwalk, CT
Fiore, Charles G. ... New York, NY
Fiore, Christopher A. ... Providence, RI
Fiore, Daniel A. ... New York, NY
Fiore, Daniel S., Law Offices of
Arlington, VA
Fiore, Ernest D., Jr. ... Peekskill, NY
Fiore & Fiore, P.C. ... Norwalk, CT
Fiore, Francis ... Boston, MA
Fiore, James V. ... Elizabeth, NJ
Fiore, Joan V. ... New York, NY
Fiore, John R. ... Norwalk, CT
Fiore, Jordan H. F. ... Taunton, MA
Fiore, Joseph E. ... Belmont, MA
Fiore, Kevin J ... Pittsburgh, PA
Fiore, Kevin P. ... Los Angeles, CA
Fiore, Krista Frankina ... Philadelphia, PA
Fiore, Laurie A. ... Pittsburgh, PA
Fiore Law Group, LLP ... San Jose, CA
Fiore, Louis H. ... Melville, NY
Fiore, Marguerite A. ... Staten Island, NY
Fiore, Michael R. ... Franklin, MA
Providence, RI
Fiore, Nicholas J. ... New York, NY
Fiore, Owen G. ... San Jose, CA
Fiore, Peter P., Jr. ... St. Louis, MO
Fiore, Racobs & Powers, A Professional Law Corporation ... Irvine, CA
Palm Desert, CA
Riverside, CA
Fiore, Richard Anthony ... Chicago, IL
Fiore, Richard S. ... Irvine, CA
Fiore, Robert Graham ... Annapolis, MD
Fiore, Robert J. ... Miami, FL
Fiore, Robert J., P.A. ... Miami, FL
Fiore, Ronald A. ... Sun Valley, CA
Fiore, Ronald C. ... New Orleans, LA
Fiore, Rose Marie L. ... Cleveland, OH
Fiore, Salvatore V. ... Fort Lauderdale, FL
Fiore, Salvatore V., P.A.
Fort Lauderdale, FL
Fiore, Samuel J. ... Pawcatuck, CT
Fiore, Thomas G. ... Boston, MA
Fiore, Thomas J. ... Stafford Springs, CT
Fiore, Vincent P. ... Yonkers, NY
Fiore, William J. ... Newark, NJ
Fiorella, Albert J. ... Mineola, NY
Fiorella, Ann ... Seattle, WA
Fiorella, Anthony J., Jr. ... Bronx, NY
Fiorella, Charles J. ... Buffalo, NY
Fiorella, Edward A., Jr. ... Charlotte, NC
Fiorella, John V. ... Haddonfield, NJ
Fiorella, Kenneth S. ... New York, NY
Fiorella, Michael A. ... Owensboro, KY
Fiorella, Palmer & Zakia ... Buffalo, NY
Fiorella, Peter J., Jr. ... Buffalo, NY
Fiorella, Salvatore A. ... New York, NY
Fiorella, Todd M. ... Norfolk, VA
Fiorelli, Paul E. ... Falls Church, VA
Fiorello, Anthony ... Totowa, NJ
Fiorello & Cifelli ... Totowa, NJ
Fiorello, Dominick ... Cherry Hill, NJ
Fiorello, Jeffrey ... Wayne, NJ
Fiorello, John ... Wayne, NJ
Fiorello, Karen L. ... Haverhill, MA
Fiorentini, James J. ... Haverhill, MA
Fiorentini Law Office ... Haverhill, MA
Fiorentino, Antony E. ... Pensacola, FL
Fiorentino, Gilbert J. ... Miami, FL
Fiorentino, James R. ... Bethlehem, PA
Fiorentino, Karen ... New York, NY
Eugene, OR
Fiorentino, Mark H. ... Las Vegas, NV
Fiorentino, Michael D. ... Philadelphia, PA
Fiorentino, Nicholas F. ... Springfield, MA
Fiorentino, Thomas M. ... Jacksonville, FL
Fiorentino, Thomas S. ... Manchester, CT
Fiorenza, Anne Keating ... Harrisburg, PA
Fiorenza, Clare L. ... Mequon, WI
Fiorenza, John A. ... Mequon, WI
Fiorenza, John A., S.C. ... Mequon, WI
Fiorenza, Margaret M. ... Deerfield, IL
Fiorenza, Nicholas J. ... Syracuse, NY
Fiorenza, Robert O. ... Cincinnati, OH
Fiorenza, Ronald J. ... Alexandria, LA
Fiorenzano, Frank J. ... Providence, RI
Fiorenzo, Joseph B. ... Hackensack, NJ
Fioretta, John ... San Jose, CA
Fioretti & Des Jardins, Ltd. ... Chicago, IL
Fioretti, Michael D. ... Cherry Hill, NJ
Philadelphia, PA
Fioretti, Richard C. ... Hicksville, NY
Fioretti, Robert W. ... Chicago, IL
Fioretto, Pasquale A. ... Chicago, IL
Fiori, George, Jr. ... Auburn, WA
Fiori, John D. ... Bedford Hills, NY
Fiori, Nicole C. ... Houston, TX
Fiori, Patricia A. ... Charles Town, WV
Fiori, Robert F. ... Denver, CO
Fiori, Robert F., P.C. ... Denver, CO
Fiori, Rod S. ... San Diego, CA
Fiorica, Jan Paradise ... Tampa, FL
Fiorile, Richard W. ... Poughkeepsie, NY
Fiorilla, John K. ... New Brunswick, NJ
Fiorilla, John Leopoldo ... New York, NY
Fiorillo, Daniel F. ... New York, NY
Fiorillo, Jason P. ... Palo Alto, CA
Fiorillo, John Keenan ... West Chester, PA
Fiorillo, Maddalena F. ... Tucson, AZ
Fiorillo, Michael J. ... Pottsville, PA
Fiorini, Curtis M. ... Modesto, CA
Fiorini, Dante M. ... Miami, FL
Fiorini, Elizabeth Roberts ... Robesonia, PA
Fiorini, John E., III ... Washington, DC
Fiorini, Judith Rose ... New York, NY
Fiorini, Lloyd D. ... Bethesda, MD
Fiorino, Amy Rothfeld ... Boston, MA
Fiorino, Christina M. ... Baltimore, MD
Fiorino, Joan Kelley Fowler
San Antonio, TX
Fiorino, John R., Jr. ... Aberdeen, NJ
Fiorino, Paul ... Fayetteville, NC
Fio Rito, Deborah J. ... Park Ridge, IL
Fiorito, Edward G. ... Dallas, TX
Fiorvento, Sherisse Eddy ... Plymouth, MI
Fioti, John L. ... Maywood, IL
Fioti, Michael P. ... Las Vegas, NV
Fiott, Kenneth J. ... Southfield, MI
Fiotto, Anthony S. ... Boston, MA
Fipp, August B., Jr. ... Rockville, MD

Fipphen, Richard C. ... Rye Brook, NY
Fippinger, Jeffrey D. ... New York, NY
Fippinger, Robert A. ... New York, NY
Fipps, Roger E. ... Fresno, CA
Firch, Tim Joe ... Oakdale, CA
Fire, Patrick Carmen ... Boardman, OH
Firebaugh, Samuel G. ... Dearborn, MI
Firehammer, Richard A., Jr. ... Cypress, CA
Firehock, Gregory R. ... Washington, DC
Firehock, Josephine H. ... Washington, DC
Firehock, Robert A. ... San Francisco, CA
Fireison, Louis ... Bethesda, MD
Fireison, Louis & Associates, P.A.
Bethesda, MD
Fireison, Scott E. ... Washington, DC
Fireman, Payton Despard ... Morgantown, WV
Fireman, Robert N. ... Braintree, MA
Fireman, Steven H. ... Columbus, OH
Fireman, William D. ... New York, NY
Firemark, Gordon Philip ... Los Angeles, CA
Firenze, Don C. ... Boston, MA
Firenze, Laurice ... Melville, NY
Firenze, Lisa F. ... New York, NY
Fireoved, Stephen J. ... Fort Washington, PA
Fires, Paul M. ... Philadelphia, PA
Fireside, Leela Ruth ... Austin, TX
Firestein, Albert I. ... Phoenix, AZ
Firestein, Charles L. ... Phoenix, AZ
Firestein, Charles L., P.C. ... Phoenix, AZ
Firestein & Farruggia, Law Offices of
Los Angeles, CA
Van Nuys, CA
Firestein, Jason Stuart ... Garden City, NY
Firestein, Martin L. ... Los Angeles, CA
Firestein, Michael A. ... Los Angeles, CA
Firester, Robert E. ... Atlanta, GA
Firestone, Adam Brooks ... Los Olivos, CA
Firestone, Alan J. ... Brooklyn, NY
Firestone, Arden E. ... Akron, OH
Firestone, Arnold B. ... Hauppauge, NY
Firestone, Bruce M. ... Seattle, WA
Firestone, Charles M. ... Washington, DC
Firestone, David A. ... San Francisco, CA
Firestone, David B. ... South Royalton, VT
Firestone, Deborah I. ... Portland, ME
Firestone, Dodee ... Fort Lauderdale, FL
Firestone, Edward A. ... San Francisco, CA
Firestone, Eric A. ... Canton, OH
Firestone & Firestone ... Hauppauge, NY
Firestone, Frederic N. ... Virginia Beach, VA
Firestone, Frederick R. ... East St. Louis, IL
Firestone, Gary ... Portland, OR
Firestone, H. Barney ... Evanston, IL
Firestone & Harris ... Brooklyn, NY
Firestone, Hilary P. ... Brooklyn, NY
Firestone, Howard L. ... Beverly Hills, CA
Firestone, Jacob ... Martinez, CA
Firestone, Jeffrey D. ... Washington, DC
Firestone, John R. ... New York, NY
Firestone, Joseph H. ... Southfield, MI
Firestone, Judith M. ... Denver, CO
Firestone, Julie Erkkila
Mayfield Village, OH
Firestone, Keith ... Whitestone, NY
Firestone, Lauren R. ... Los Angeles, CA
Firestone, Louise Ruth ... New York, NY
Firestone, Mark A. ... Kansas City, MO
Firestone, Marvin H. ... Half Moon Bay, CA
Firestone, Matt G. ... Orlando, FL
Firestone, Merrick B. ... Phoenix, AZ
Firestone, Milton I. ... Lansing, MI
Firestone, Nancy ... Washington, DC
Firestone, Nathan N. ... Mc Keesport, PA
Firestone, Richard Donald ... Pittsburgh, PA
Firestone, Richard L. ... Delaware, OH
Firestone, Richard M. ... Washington, DC
Firestone, Robert F. ... Princeton, NJ
Firestone, Scott Craig ... Hauppauge, NY
Firestone, Stephen A. ... Springfield, VA
Firestone, Susan Lorraine
Fort Wayne, IN
Firestone, Thomas ... New York, NY
Firestone & Whitney ... Circleville, OH
Columbus, OH
Delaware, OH
Lancaster, OH
London, OH
Marion, OH
Marysville, OH
Mt. Vernon, OH
Newark, OH
Washington C. H., OH
Firetag, Jules I. ... Phoenix, AZ
Firetog, Theodore W. ... Farmingdale, NY
Firfer, Jodi I. ... Buffalo Grove, IL
Firfer, Marci Ann ... Chicago, IL
Lincolnwood, IL
Firfer, Richard J. ... Chicago, IL
Firgens, Allen J. ... Seal Beach, CA
Firger, Robert A. ... Hartford, CT
Firimonte, Susan J. ... Florence, SC
Firkins, Tyler K. ... Auburn, WA
Firko, Lisa A. ... Roseland, NJ
Firkser, Robert Michael ... Media, PA
Firkser, Steven ... Woodbridge, NJ
Firley, Sean W. ... Miami, FL
Firley, Simone Pappas ... Hollywood, FL
Firmage, Edwin B. ... Salt Lake City, UT
Firman, Fritz J. ... Costa Mesa, CA
Firmani, Paul E. ... New Port Richey, FL
Firment, Paige Dunmire ... Worcester, MA
Firmin, John C. ... Findlay, OH
Firmin, Sprague & Huffman Co., L.P.A.
Findlay, OH
Firn, David A. ... Wayne, PA
Firn, James T. ... Tacoma, WA
Firnrohr, Andrew C. ... Marshfield, MA
Firnschild, George M. ... Phoenix, AZ
Firnschild, Stuart J., (P.C.) ... Wyandotte, MI
Firooz, Jasmine ... Los Angeles, CA
Firoozye, Rod ... Palo Alto, CA
Firpo, Peter A. ... Fairfield, CA
Firriolo, Robert P. ... New York, NY
Firschein, Ben ... Sacramento, CA
Firsching, Ellen F. ... Richmond, VA
Firsel, Michael D. ... Chicago, IL
Firsichbaum, Steven W. ... Livingston, NJ
First, Allison R. ... Boston, MA
First, Blondis, Albrecht, Bangert & Novotnak, S.C. ... Milwaukee, WI
First, Curry ... Milwaukee, WI
First, Dennis A. ... Albany, NY
First, Edward C., Jr. ... Harrisburg, PA
First, Harry ... New York, NY
First, Jeffrey B. ... Philadelphia, PA
First, Jonathan E.
Federal Energy Regulatory Commission,
Office of the General Counsel, GV
First, Jonathan M. ... New York, NY
First Law Group S.C. ... Stevens Point, WI
Wisconsin Rapids, WI
First, Lawrence A. ... New York, NY
First, Lee B. ... New York, NY
First, Mark L. ... Princeton, NJ
First, Mitchell Mark ... New York, NY
First, Patricia A. ... Department of Justice,
Office of Legislative Affairs, GV
First, Penny S. ... West Chester, PA
First, Penny S., The Legal Clinic
West Chester, PA
First, Robin B. ... Washington, DC
First, Samuel M. ... Philadelphia, PA
First, Stanley A. ... Washington, DC
Bethesda, MD
First, Vivian Micznik
Department of Commerce,
Patent and Trademark Office, GV
Firsten, Robert K. ... Bloomfield Hills, MI
Detroit, MI
Firstenberg, Barbara A. ... Cleveland, OH
Firstenberg, Barbara A., & Associates Co., LPA
Cleveland, OH
Firstenberg, JoAnne ... New York, NY
Firstenberg, Paul B. ... New York, NY
Firstenberger, John P. ... Marion, OH
Firstenberger, Lester Wm. ... Middletown, CT
Firstenberger, O. E. ... Detroit, MI
Firstman, Eric J. ... Oakland, CA
Firtch, Susan E. ... Oakland, CA
Firtel, Douglas N. ... West Hartford, CT
Firtell, Ross ... Pompano Beach, FL
Firth, Andrew
Federal Communications Commission,
Common Carrier Bureau, GV
Firth, Charles V. ... Washington, DC
Firth, Douglas A. ... Birmingham, MI
Firth, Jason D. ... San Francisco, CA
Firth, John C. ... South Bend, IN
Firth, Myra A. ... Irvine, CA
Firth, Peter A. ... Glens Falls, NY
Firth, Robert L. ... Green Bay, WI
Firth, Victor M. ... El Paso, TX
Firvida-Oliva, Diana ... Miami, FL
Fisanick, Christian Andrew ... Barnesboro, PA
Fisanick, Solomon & Fisanick
Barnesboro, PA
Ebensburg, PA
Fisanick, Vasil ... Barnesboro, PA
Fiscella, James B. ... Melville, NY
Fiscella, Lynne J. ... Richmond, VA
Fiscella, Paul ... Alexandria, VA
Fiscella, Paul A., P.C. ... Alexandria, VA
Fiscella, Robert A. ... Danbury, CT
Fisch, Alan M. ... Washington, DC
Fisch, Arthur P. ... New York, NY
Fisch, Beth Rachel ... New York, NY
Fisch, Carol ... Los Angeles, CA
Fisch, Edith L. ... New York, NY
Fisch & Fisch ... Brick, NJ
Fisch, Fredrick Lee ... Washington, DC
Fisch, Gregg A. ... Washington, DC
Fisch, James F. ... Burlington, IA
West Point, IA
Fisch, Jeffrey H. ... Roseland, NJ
Fisch, Jerome ... New York, NY
Fisch, Jill E. ... New York, NY
Fisch, Joel S. ... San Francisco, CA
Fisch, John D. ... San Antonio, TX
Fisch, Jordan A. ... Roseland, NJ
Fisch, Joseph ... Kendall Park, NJ
Fisch, Joseph ... Bronx, NY
Fisch, Joseph J. ... San Diego, CA
Fisch, Karin E. ... New York, NY
Fisch, Mark ... Brick, NJ
Fisch, Marla ... Brooklyn, NY
Fisch, Martin R. ... Boston, MA
Fisch, Melanie ... Ontario, CA
Fisch, Paul H. ... Los Angeles, CA
Fisch, Peter E. ... New York, NY
Fisch, Ralph ... Palm Beach Gardens, FL
Fisch, Richard ... Washington, DC
Fisch, Richard L. ... New York, NY
Fisch, Sanford M. ... San Diego, CA
Fisch, Spiegler, Ginsburg, Ladner & Attarian, A Professional Law Corporation
San Diego, CA
Fisch, Steven ... Brick, NJ
Fisch, Susan L. ... Denver, CO
Fisch, Vera ... Scottsdale, AZ
Fisch, William B. ... Columbia, MO
Fischbach, Bernard J. ... Los Angeles, CA
Fischbach, Donald P., Jr.
Oklahoma City, OK
Fischbach, Donald P., P.C.
Oklahoma City, OK
Fischbach, Donald R. ... Fresno, CA
Fischbach, Gregory E. ... Los Angeles, CA
Fischbach, Joseph S. ... Los Angeles, CA
Fischbach, Margaret A. ... Milwaukee, WI
Fischbach, Robert ... Mount Vernon, NY
Fischbarg, Gabriel J. ... New York, NY
Fischbeck, Dean M. ... San Francisco, CA
Fischbeck, Kyra ... United States Senate,
Senatorial Assistants, GV
Fischbeck & Oberndorfer, A Professional Corporation ... El Cajon, CA
La Mesa, CA
San Diego, CA
Fischbeck, Roy S. ... Jacksonville, FL
Fischbeck, William L. ... La Mesa, CA
Fischbein, Alvin M. ... Dix Hills, NY
Fischbein • Badillo • Wagner • Harding
Newark, NJ
Phillipsburg, NJ
New York, NY
Fischbein, Beth W. ... New York, NY
Fischbein, Lewis S. ... New York, NY
Fischbein, Peter D. ... New York, NY
Fischbein, Richard S. ... New York, NY
Fischbein, Stuart M. ... Department of Justice,
Tax Division, GV
Fischbein-Cohen, Ruth Rose ... Cleveland, OH
Fischel, Carolynn N. ... Boston, MA
Fischel, Corrie L. ... Washington, DC
Fischel, Daniel R. ... Chicago, IL
Fischel, Edward B. ... Redlands, CA
Fischel, Elaine B. ... Los Angeles, CA
Fischel, John R. ... Baltimore, MD
Fischel, Jud A. ... Warrenton, VA
Fischel, Jud A., P.C. ... Warrenton, VA
Fischel & Kahn, Ltd. ... Chicago, IL
Fischel, Milton M. ... Long Island City, NY
Fischel, Shelley D. ... New York, NY
Fischel, Stephen K. ... Department of State,
Bureau of Consular Affairs, GV
Fischel, Valerie S. ... Westport, CT
Fischel, William L. ... Troy, MI
Fischer, A. Robert ... Stamford, CT
Fischer, Adam B. ... Sedalia, MO
Fischer, Adam B., Inc. ... Sedalia, MO
Fischer, Alfred ... Indianapolis, IN
Fischer, Alice J. ... Denver, CO
Fischer, Allison L. ... Orange, CA
Fischer, Amy L. ... West Palm Beach, FL
Fischer, Amy Sherry ... Oklahoma City, OK
Fischer, Andrew M. ... Chicago, IL
Fischer, Andrew M. ... Boston, MA
Fischer, Anthony C. ... Santa Barbara, CA
Fischer, Anthony J., Jr. ... Stony Brook, NY
Fischer, Arthur J. ... Lake Forest, IL
Fischer, August W. ... Hackensack, NJ
Fischer, Avery S. ... New York, NY
Fischer, Avrom S. ... Brooklyn, NY
Fischer, Barbara G. ... Escondido, CA
Fischer, Barry ... Chicago, IL
Fischer, Barry R. ... New York, NY
Fischer, Barry S. ... Boston, MA
Fischer, Bennett M. ... Vinton, IA
Fischer, Bernard A. ... Melrose Park, PA
Fischer, Bernard D. ... Los Angeles, CA
Fischer, Bernard D., Inc., A Professional Corporation ... Los Angeles, CA
Fischer, Bessette & Muldowney, L.L.P.
Canton, NY
Lake Placid, NY
Malone, NY
Plattsburgh, NY
Fischer, Betsy A. ... Metairie, LA
Fischer, Blake R. ... Union, MO
Fischer, Brad S. ... Tampa, FL
Fischer, Bradley S. ... Fort Lauderdale, FL
Fischer, Brian E. ... Detroit, MI
Fischer, Brian E., P.C. ... Detroit, MI
Fischer, Brian J. ... Houston, TX
Fischer, Brian M. ... Newark, NJ
Fischer, Brian Scott ... Lake Worth, FL
Fischer, Brian T. ... West Haven, CT
Fischer, Brown & Gunn, P.C.
Fort Collins, CO
Fischer & Burstein, P.C. ... Great Neck, NY
New York, NY
Fischer, C. Michael ... Englewood, FL
Fischer, Caren D. ... St. Helena, CA
Fischer, Carey M. ... Fort Lauderdale, FL
Fischer, Carey M., P.A., Law Offices of
Fort Lauderdale, FL
Fischer, Carmen L. ... Phoenix, AZ
Fischer, Charles ... New York, NY
Fischer, Charlotte J. ... Houston, TX
Fischer, Christine ... Grosse Pointe, MI
Fischer, Christopher J. ... St. Louis, MO
Fischer, Cinthia R. ... Seattle, WA
Fischer, Clinton J. ... Polson, MT
Fischer, Craig S. ... Ventura, CA
Fischer, Cynthia G. ... New York, NY
Fischer, D. Christian ... Syracuse, NY
Fischer, D. Richard ... Astoria, OR
Fischer, Dale L. ... Aurora, CO
Fischer, Dale S. ... Los Angeles, CA
Fischer, Daniel B. ... Hamilton, OH
Fischer, Daniel E. ... Aurora, CO
Fischer, Danielle L. ... Portland, OR
Fischer, Danna Sue ... McLean, VA
Fischer, David A. ... Columbia, MO
Fischer, David B. ... Los Angeles, CA
Fischer, David B. ... Omaha, NE
Fischer, David B. ... Arlington, VA
Fischer, David C. ... New York, NY
Fischer, David J. ... Washington, DC
Fischer, David J. ... Chicago, IL
Fischer, David J. ... Chicago, IL
Fischer, David Jon ... Atlanta, GA
Fischer, David R. ... Martinez, CA
Fischer, David S. ... St. Louis, MO
Fischer, David W., P.A. ... Baltimore, MD
Glen Burnie, MD
Fischer, David William ... Glen Burnie, MD
Fischer, Debra L. ... Los Angeles, CA
Fischer, Dennis A. ... Santa Monica, CA
Fischer, Diane C. ... Chicago, IL
Fischer, Dianne O. ... Miami, FL
Fischer, Donald Lawrence
San Francisco, CA
Fischer, Douglas L. ... New York, NY
Fischer, Dwight David ... Wichita, KS
Fischer, Edward J. ... Toledo, OH
Fischer, Edwin R. ... Williamsburg, VA
Fischer, Edwin W. ... Shell Lake, WI
Fischer, Elia ... New York, NY
Fischer, Elizabeth M. ... Alexandria, VA
Fischer, Ellen S. ... Elkins Park, PA
Fischer, Emeric ... Williamsburg, VA
Fischer, Erby J. ... Tuscaloosa, AL
Fischer, Eric J. ... Jenkintown, PA
Fischer, Eric M. ... Palm Beach Gardens, FL
Fischer, Eric R. ... Boston, MA
Fischer, Erik G. ... Fort Collins, CO
Fischer, Eugene B. ... New York, NY
Fischer, Eugene K., Jr. ... Anaheim, CA
Fischer, Felix L. ... Torrance, CA
Fischer Fiden & Norris, L.L.P.
New York, NY
Fischer & Fischer ... Aurora, CO
Fischer & Fischer ... West Haven, CT
Corpus Christi, TX
Fischer & Fischer, LLP ... Fort Collins, CO
Fischer, Flynn ... Wessington Springs, SD
Fischer, Frank J. ... Manasquan, NJ
Fischer, Franklin & Ford ... Ann Arbor, MI
Detroit, MI
Fischer, Fred E. ... Louisville, KY
Fischer, Frederick Ross ... Austin, TX
Fischer, Frederick W. ... Eau Claire, WI
Fischer, Fredric H. ... Chicago, IL
Fischer, Fritch, Rasche & Fritch ... Jasper, IN
Fischer, G. Timothy ... Akron, OH
Fischer, Gary L. ... Omaha, NE
Fischer, Gary R. ... Des Moines, IA
Fischer, Gene E. ... Fort Collins, CO
Fischer, George H. ... Columbia, SC
Fischer, Gerald D. ... New York, NY
Fischer, Gerald L. ... Jasper, IN
Fischer, Gerard W. ... Department of Justice,
Civil Division, GV
Fischer, Glenn W. ... Chicago, IL
Fischer, Gordon R. ... Des Moines, IA
Fischer and Greene ... Louisville, KY
Fischer, H. Eugene ... Fort Lauderdale, FL
Fischer, H. James ... St. Petersburg, FL
Fischer, H. Robert ... Erie, PA
Fischer, Hannelore D. ... Jefferson City, MO
Fischer, Hans H. ... Columbus, OH
Fischer, Harold E., Jr. ... Kalamazoo, MI
Fischer, Harriet Z. ... New York, NY
Fischer, Harry A., Jr. ... Westchester, IL
Fischer, Harry William ... Alma, MI
St. Louis, MO
Fischer & Hawker ... St. Louis, MO
Fischer, Heike ... Palo Alto, CA
Fischer, Henry A. ... Malone, NY
Fischer, Henry B. ... Cleveland, OH
Fischer, Henry B., Co., L.P.A.
Cleveland, OH
Fischer, Henry G. ... Washington, DC
Fischer, Herbert D. ... West Haven, CT
Fischer, Holly Robinson ... Columbus, OH
Fischer, Howard A. ... New York, NY
Fischer, Howard E. ... New York, NY
Fischer, Ian Ira ... Hastings-On-Hudson, NY
Fischer, Ivy S. ... New York, NY
Fischer, J. Clark ... Winston-Salem, NC
Fischer, J. Michael ... Cincinnati, OH
Fischer, James ... Morris Plains, NJ
Fischer, James E. ... West Haven, CT
Fischer, James H. ... East Hampton, NY
Fischer, James L. ... Hartford, CT
Fischer, James L. ... New York, NY
Fischer, James L., Jr. ... New Albany, IN
Fischer, James M., P.C. ... Jefferson City, MO
Fischer, James M., P.C. ... Jefferson City, MO
Fischer, James N. ... Stockton, CA
Fischer, Jay D. ... New York, NY
Fischer, Jay G. ... Downingtown, PA
Fischer, Jeanne A. ... St. Louis, MO
Fischer, Jeffrey D. ... Tulsa, OK
Fischer, Jenna L. ... Woodland Hills, CA
Fischer, Jennifer K. ... Willmar, MN
Fischer, Jennifer L. ... Chicago, IL
Fischer, Jens ... New York, NY
Fischer, Jerry ... Trenton, NJ
Fischer, Jerry E. ... Corpus Christi, TX
Fischer, Joan Goldstein ... Far Hills, NJ
Fischer, Joan L. ... Boston, MA
Fischer, Joel ... Lake Oswego, OR
Fischer, John A. ... Dayton, OH
Fischer, John C. ... Dayton, KY
Fischer, John D. ... Los Angeles, CA
Fischer, John David ... Houston, TX
Fischer, John E. ... Sacramento, CA
Fischer, John F., II ... Oklahoma City, OK
Fischer, John G. ... Dallas, TX
Fischer, John K. ... Vinton, IA
Fischer, John M. ... Treasury Department,
Internal Revenue Service, GV
Fischer, John P. ... Denver, CO
Fischer, John P. ... Indianapolis, IN
Fischer, John Paul ... San Francisco, CA
Fischer, John R. ... Pasadena, CA
Fischer, John R., A Professional Corporation
Pasadena, CA
Fischer, John W. ... Berwyn, PA
Fischer, John W., II ... Cincinnati, OH

Fishburne, John L., III .... **Jacksonville, FL**
Fishburne & Lewis .... Marion, IN
Fishburne, Raymond P. .... Marion, IN
Fishburne, William S., III
Birmingham, AL
Fishe, Tom E. .... Oroville, CA
Fishel, Alan Gregg .... **Washington, DC**
Fishel, Allegra L. .... **New York, NY**
Fishel, David L. .... Department of Justice, Environment and Natural Resources Division, GV
Fishel & Fishel, Law Office of
Martinez, CA
Fishel, Francine R. .... Chicago, IL
Fishel, Gladys L. .... Arlington, VA
Fishel, Grace J. .... **St. Louis, MO**
Fishel, Gustave, III .... Babylon, NY
Fishel, Gustave, III, P.C. .... Babylon, NY
Fishel & Hoskins, (Not a Partnership)
Marion, IA
Fishel, James Joseph .... Martinez, CA
Fishel, Joan Irwin .... Columbus, OH
Fishel, John L., II .... **Panama City, FL**
Fishel, Marc A. .... Columbus, OH
Fishel, Merle D. .... Marion, IA
Fishel, Ralph J. .... Cleveland, OH
Fishel, Suzyn E. .... Martinez, CA
Fishell, Floyd F. .... Riverside, CA
Fishelman, Bruce C. .... Los Angeles, CA
Fishenfeld, Moses H. .... Calabasas, CA
Fisher, A. Alston, Jr. .... **Naples, FL**
Fisher, Adam, Jr. .... Greenville, SC
Fisher, Adrian S. .... Washington, DC
Fisher, Alan H. .... Baltimore, MD
Fisher, Alan J. .... Elgin, IL
Fisher, Alan Jeffrey .... Boca Raton, FL
Fisher, Alan M. .... Department of Justice, Office of Justice Programs, GV
Fisher, Alice S. .... **Washington, DC**
Fisher, Allan S. .... Toledo, OH
Fisher, Alvan H. .... Banning, CA
Fisher, Amy H. .... **New York, NY**
Fisher, Amy S. .... Phoenix, AZ
Fisher, Amy S., P.C. .... Phoenix, AZ
Fisher, Andrea .... **Miami, FL**
Fisher, Andrew D. .... **New York, NY**
Fisher, Andrew G. .... Houston, TX
Fisher, Andrew J. .... **Denver, CO**
Fisher, Andrew J. .... Atlanta, GA
Fisher, Andrew S., P.C. .... **New York, NY**
Fisher, Ann Bailen .... **New York, NY**
Fisher, Ann Durkin .... Potomac, MD
Fisher, Ann E. .... New Milford, CT
Fisher, Ann Hilton .... Chicago, IL
Fisher, Ann L. .... **Portland, OR**
Fisher, Ann, (P.A.) .... Coral Gables, FL
Fisher, Arnold .... **Roseland, NJ**
Fisher, Arthur E. .... Larkspur, CA
Fisher, Arthur F. .... **Bakersfield, CA**
Fisher, Arthur F., P.C. .... **Bakersfield, CA**
Fisher, Arthur O. .... Dayton, OH
Fisher, Arthur S. .... **Great Neck, NY**
Fisher, Arthur W., III .... **Tampa, FL**
Fisher, Arthur W., III, P.A. .... **Tampa, FL**
Fisher & Associates, A Professional Corporation .... **Newport Beach, CA**
Fisher, Avery, Yawn & Fisher .... Memphis, TN
Fisher, A. W., Jr. .... Tampa, FL
Fisher, Barbara Elaine .... Santa Ana, CA
Fisher, Barbara H. .... Baltimore, MD
Fisher, Barry A. .... Los Angeles, CA
Fisher, Barry J. .... **Mineola, NY**
Fisher, Barry L. .... Morristown, NJ
Fisher, Barry M. .... Chicago, IL
Fisher, Bart S. .... **Washington, DC**
Fisher, Bartley F. .... **New York, NY**
Fisher, Ben C. .... **Washington, DC**
Fisher & Bendeck, P.A.
West Palm Beach, FL
Fisher, Benjamin, Jr. .... Stuart, FL
Fisher, Bennett G. .... Houston, TX
Fisher, Bertram D., (P.C.) .... **New York, NY**
Fisher, Beverly D. .... Clarksville, TN
Fisher, Billy L. .... Houston, TX
Fisher, Bonnie Helfgott .... **Milwaukee, WI**
Fisher, Boyd, Brown, Boudreaux & Huguenard, L.L.P. .... **Houston, TX**
Fisher, Bradford D. .... **Leesburg, FL**
Fisher, Bradley D. .... **Minneapolis, MN**
Fisher, Bradley L. .... **Seattle, WA**
Fisher, Brady .... Paris, TX
Fisher, Brian J. .... Louisville, KY
Fisher, Brian J. .... **New York, NY**
Fisher, Brian M. .... Lima, OH
Fisher, Brian T. .... **Washington, DC**
Fisher, Brook E. .... North Palm Beach, FL
Fisher & Brooker, P.A. .... Fort Pierce, FL
Fisher, Brown, Swartz & Swartz
Steubenville, OH
Fisher, Bruce A. .... San Francisco, CA
Fisher, Bruce Brittin .... San Diego, CA
Fisher, Bryant W. .... Punta Gorda, FL
Fisher, C. Jeffrey .... Fresno, CA
Fisher, Carlos Andrew .... Irvine, CA
Fisher, Carlton D. .... **Chicago, IL**
Fisher, Carole E. Swenson .... Bellevue, WA
Fisher, Carolyn K. .... **Atlanta, GA**
Fisher & Carrasco .... San Luis Obispo, CA
Fisher, Catherine A.
Securities and Exchange Commission, Division of Investment Management, GV
Fisher, Catherine M. .... **Oakland, CA**
Fisher, Cavanaugh, Smith & Lemon, P.A.
Topeka, KS
Fisher, Champe A. .... **Boston, MA**
Fisher, Charles G., VI .... **Chattanooga, TN**
Fisher, Charles J., JR. .... New York, NY
Fisher, Charles M. .... Castro Valley, CA
Fisher, Charles M. .... **Princeton, NJ**
Fisher, Charles O. .... **Westminster, MD**
Fisher, Charles O., Jr. .... **Westminster, MD**
Fisher, Charles S., Jr. .... **Topeka, KS**
Fisher, Charles W. .... **Detroit, MI**
Fisher, Cheryl Francine .... **New York, NY**
Fisher, Cheryl H. .... **Columbia, SC**
Fisher, Cheryl Smith .... **Buffalo, NY**
Fisher, Chester L., III .... **Hartford, CT**
Fisher, Christen & Sabol .... **Washington, DC**
Fisher, Christopher A. .... Houston, TX
Fisher, Christopher B. .... **White Plains, NY**
Fisher, Christopher J. .... **Kansas City, MO**
Fisher, Christopher P. .... **Cleveland, OH**
Fisher, Christy L. .... Plattsburg, MO
Fisher, Claire A. .... Lafayette, LA
Fisher Clinard & Craig, PLLC
High Point, NC
Fisher, Clinton B. .... **New York, NY**
Fisher, Connie L. .... Kenner, LA
Fisher, Conrad J., III .... Clearwater, FL
Fisher, Conrad W. .... Worcester, MA
Fisher, Constance F. .... Chicago, IL
Fisher, Constance J. .... Point Pleasant, WV
Fisher, Cornelia Fuchs .... **Portland, ME**
Fisher, Craig A. .... Los Angeles, CA
Fisher, Craig A. .... **New York, NY**
Fisher, Craig E. .... San Diego, CA
Fisher, Curtis A. .... **Greenville, SC**
Fisher, Curtis W. .... Tulsa, OK
Fisher, Cynthia Dale .... New York, NY
Fisher, Damon R. .... **Los Angeles, CA**
Fisher, Daniel E. .... **Washington, DC**
Fisher, Daniel E. .... **Indianapolis, IN**
Fisher, Daniel E. .... **Louisville, KY**
Fisher, Daniel Scott .... Richmond Hill, GA
Fisher, Darwin .... Provo, UT
Fisher, David .... Norwalk, CT
Fisher, David
Federal Deposit Insurance Corporation, GV
Fisher, David A. .... **La Jolla, CA**
Cincinnati, OH
Fisher, David A. .... Chicago, IL
Fisher, David B. .... Palo Alto, CA
Fisher, David B. .... New York, NY
Fisher, David E. .... New York, NY
Fisher, David F. .... Minneapolis, MN
Fisher, David H. .... **Topeka, KS**
Fisher, David H. .... Hastings, NE
Fisher, David J. .... **Washington, DC**
New York, NY
Fisher, David J. .... Des Moines, IA
Fisher, David J. .... **Frankenmuth, MI**
Saginaw, MI
Fisher, David J. .... **Beaumont, TX**
Silsbee, TX
Fisher, David J. .... **Houston, TX**
Nacogdoches, TX
Fisher, David L. .... San Luis Obispo, CA
Fisher, David M. .... Hartford, CT
Fisher, David N., Jr. .... **Portland, ME**
Fisher, David R. .... **Beverly Hills, CA**
Fisher, David S. .... Woodland Hills, CA
Fisher, David S. .... Woodland Hills, CA
Fisher, David S., A Prof. Corp.
Woodland Hills, CA
Fisher, David T. .... **Denver, CO**
Fisher, David W. .... Park Ridge, NJ
Fisher, David W. .... New York, NY
Fisher, David W. .... Columbus, OH
Fisher, D. E., Law Firm .... Houston, TX
Fisher, Dean R. .... **Williamsport, PA**
Fisher, Deborah A. .... Peoria, IL
Fisher, Deborah E. .... Detroit, MI
Fisher, Deborah K. .... Louisville, KY
Fisher, Deborah P. .... **Birmingham, AL**
Fisher, Dennis D. .... **Moorhead, MN**
Fisher, Dennis L. .... **Milwaukee, WI**
Fisher, Derrick .... Pasadena, CA
Fisher, Diana Panucci .... Charleston, WV
Fisher, Diane .... **Albuquerque, NM**
Fisher, Dianne Coady .... **Philadelphia, PA**
Fisher & DiMonte .... Chicago, IL
Fisher, Dina Schwarz .... **Hartford, CT**
Fisher, Dodd Bryson .... Eastpointe, MI
Fisher, Don .... **Irvine, CA**
Fisher, Donald A. .... **Buffalo, NY**
Fisher, Donald E., Jr. .... Houston, TX
Fisher, Donald J. .... **Cleveland, OH**
Fisher, Donald J., Jr. .... Littleton, CO
Fisher, Donald M. .... Fayetteville, NY
Fisher, Donna .... Tacoma, WA
Fisher, Donna H. .... **Indianapolis, IN**
Fisher, Donna K. .... **Memphis, TN**
Fisher, Donna L. .... **Harrisburg, PA**
Fisher, Douglas A. .... De Kalb, IL
Fisher, Douglas B. .... United States Senate, Committee Legal Personnel, GV
Fisher, Douglas L. .... Fishers, NY
Fisher, Douglas M. .... **Nashville, TN**
Fisher, Duane R. .... **Honolulu, HI**
Fisher, E. Thomas, Jr. .... **St. Petersburg, FL**
Fisher, Earl L. .... Omaha, NE
Fisher, Earl P., Jr. .... Chicago, IL
Fisher, Edgar B., III .... **Charlotte, NC**
Fisher, Edgar B., Jr. .... **Greensboro, NC**
Fisher, Edward J. .... **Chester, IL**
Fisher, Edwin H. .... Brenham, TX
Fisher, Edwin H., Jr. .... Fort Wayne, IN
Fisher, Elisabeth .... **Universal City, CA**
Fisher, Elizabeth .... Worcester, MA
Fisher, Elizabeth M .... Las Cruces, NM
Fisher, Elliot S. .... Ambler, PA
Fisher, Emerson G. .... Portland, OR
Fisher, Emerson G., P.C. .... Portland, OR
Fisher, Emily Estrada .... **Galveston, TX**
Fisher, Eric .... **Denver, CO**
Fisher, Eric A. .... Avon, CO
Fisher, Eric A. .... **San Antonio, TX**
Fisher, Eric B. .... New York, NY
Fisher, Eric H. .... **New York, NY**
Fisher, Eric S. .... **Oklahoma City, OK**
Fisher, Eugene .... Beverly Hills, CA
Fisher, Eugene F. .... Jackson, MS
Fisher, Evangeline L. .... **Claremont, CA**
Fisher & Evans, L.L.P. .... **Austin, TX**
Fisher, Evans W. .... Clemmons, NC
Fisher, Everett .... **Greenwich, CT**
Fisher, Everett E. .... Alameda, CA
Fisher Fallon, LLP .... **Spring Lake, NJ**
New York, NY
Fisher & Fisher .... Chicago, IL
Fisher & Fisher .... **Brattleboro, VT**
Fisher, Fisher & Berger .... **Brooklyn, NY**
New York, NY
Fisher, Fisher & Fisher, P.C. .... Adair, IA
Fisher, Frank A., Jr. .... Harrisburg, PA
Fisher, Frank J. .... San Francisco, CA
Fisher, Frank R. .... Waterloo, NY
Fisher, Fred .... **Southampton, NY**
Fisher, Fred W. .... St. Paul, MN
Fisher, Frederick J. .... **Philadelphia, PA**
Fisher, Frederick L. .... **Rockville, MD**
Fisher, Frederick S. .... Richmond, VA
Fisher, Fredrick L. .... **Columbus, OH**
Fisher, Fritz L. .... **Denver, CO**
Fisher, G. Robert .... **Kansas City, MO**
Fisher, Gail R., (Mr.) .... Champaign, IL
Fisher, Gale .... **Sioux Falls, SD**
Fisher, Gale, P.C. .... **Sioux Falls, SD**
Fisher, Gallagher & Lewis .... Houston, TX
Fisher, Gary A. .... Boulder, CO
Fisher, Gary B. .... Antioch, TN
Fisher, Gary J. .... Department of Justice, Environment and Natural Resources Division, GV
Fisher, Gayle Yeatman .... **Chicago, IL**
Fisher, George A. .... **Washington, DC**
Fisher, George C. .... **Palo Alto, CA**
Fisher, George L. .... Cambridge, MA
Fisher, George M. .... Spartanburg, SC
Fisher, George P. .... Portland, OR
Fisher, George V. .... **Columbus, OH**
Fisher, George W. .... **Princeton, NJ**
Fisher, Gerald A. .... **Farmington Hills, MI**
Fisher, Gerald B. .... San Antonio, TX
Fisher, Gerald F. .... Lincoln, NE
Fisher, Gerald F. .... New York, NY
Fisher, Gerald M. .... **Los Angeles, CA**
Fisher, Gerald M. .... Palo Alto, CA
Fisher, Gillian .... **New York, NY**
Fisher, Girard .... **Los Angeles, CA**
Fisher, Glenn E. .... Webster, SD
Fisher, Gordon D. .... Pittsburgh, PA
Fisher, Gregory H. .... **St. Petersburg, FL**
Fisher, Gregory H., P.A.
St. Petersburg, FL
Fisher, Gregory J. .... **Sacramento, CA**
Fisher, Gregory S. .... Anchorage, AK
Fisher, Guy C. .... **Austin, TX**
Fisher, Guy G. .... **Houston, TX**
Fisher, Hannah Morrison
Department of Commerce, Patent and Trademark Office, GV
Fisher, Harold .... Manchester, TN
Fisher, Harold J. .... Los Altos, CA
Fisher, Harold J. .... Springfield, MO
Fisher, Harold L. .... **New York, NY**
Fisher, Harold R. .... Newton, MA
Fisher, Harry E. .... **Troy, NC**
Fisher, Harry E., P.A. .... **Troy, NC**
Fisher, Harry M., III .... **Dover, DE**
Fisher, Hazel S. .... Downers Grove, IL
Fisher, Hecht & Fisher .... New York, NY
Fisher, Heidi L. .... Coeur d'Alene, ID
Fisher, Heidi M. .... Moorhead, MN
Fisher, Helene S. .... Uniondale, NY
Fisher & Helm Law Offices, P.C.
Memphis, TN
Fisher, Henry M. .... Nashville, NC
Fisher, Herbert .... Columbia, MD
Fisher, Herbert F. .... **New York, NY**
Fisher, Herbert F., PLLC, Law Offices of
New York, NY
Fisher, Herbert H. .... Chicago, IL
Fisher, Howard S. .... Beverly Hills, CA
Fisher, Howard S. .... Boston, MA
Fisher, Howard V. .... **Dallas, TX**
Fisher, Hugh Pearson, III .... Stafford, VA
Fisher, Hugh W. P. .... **Philadelphia, PA**
Fisher, Hugo M. .... San Diego, CA
Fisher, Ian H. .... **Chicago, IL**
Fisher, Ilana R. .... **Washington, DC**
Fisher, Imelda T. .... **Lafayette, LA**
Fisher & Ireland .... Wabash, IN
Fisher, Irene B. .... New York, NY
Fisher, Irene M. .... **Seattle, WA**
Fisher, Isaac K. .... Coral Gables, FL
Fisher, Ivan S. .... New York, NY
Fisher, J. C., P.A., Law Offices of
Altamonte Springs, FL
Fisher, J. Mark .... Mary Esther, FL
Fisher, J. Mark .... **Chicago, IL**
Fisher, J. Matthew .... **Columbus, OH**
Fisher, J. Raymond .... Albany, NY
Fisher, J. Richard, Jr. .... **Chicago, IL**
Fisher, J. Robert .... **Houston, TX**
Fisher, J. Steven .... Granite Quarry, NC
Fisher, Jack .... Chicago, IL
Fisher, Jack D. .... Edmond, OK
Fisher, Jack H. .... Kalamazoo, MI
Fisher, Jack R. .... East Hampton, NY
Fisher, Jacqueline Louise .... Charlotte, NC
Fisher, James A. .... **Battle Creek, MI**
Fisher, James A. .... **Dallas, TX**
Fisher, James B., Jr. .... Memphis, TN
Fisher, James C. .... Altamonte Springs, FL
Fisher, James D. .... San Francisco, CA
Fisher, James E., II .... **Washington, DC**
Fisher, James H. .... Hastings, MI
Fisher, James H. .... Kingston, NY
Fisher, James H., II .... Atlanta, GA
Fisher, James H., P.C. .... Kingston, NY
Fisher, James I. .... Fremont, CA
Fisher, James L. .... Baltimore, MD
Fisher, James L. .... Tecumseh, MI
Fisher, James L. .... **Akron, OH**
Fisher, James M., II .... **Dallas, TX**
Fisher, James P. .... Lima, OH
Fisher, James P. .... Fairfax, VA
Fisher, James Q. .... **Los Angeles, CA**
Fisher, James R. .... Pasadena, CA
Fisher, James R. .... Aurora, CO
Fisher, James R. .... **Indianapolis, IN**
Fisher, James R. .... Dearborn, MI
Fisher, James R. .... New York, NY
Fisher, James W., Jr. .... Goodlettsville, TN
Fisher, Jan L. .... Topeka, KS
Fisher, Jane A. .... Washington, DC
Fisher, Jane L.P. .... St. Paul, MN
Fisher, Janet C. .... **Washington, DC**
Fisher, Janet E. .... Philadelphia, PA
Fisher, Janet L. .... **New York, NY**
Fisher, Janet W. .... Holden, MA
Fisher, Janice V. .... Fort Pierce, FL
Fisher, Jann Iliff .... Coral Gables, FL
Fisher, Jason E. .... **Bethesda, MD**
Frederick, MD
Fisher, Jay M., P.A. .... Maitland, FL
Fisher, Jean Dettmann .... San Diego, CA
Fisher, Jean M. .... Keizer, OR
Fisher, Jeffrey B. .... **Upper Marlboro, MD**
Fisher, Jeffrey D. .... **West Palm Beach, FL**
Fisher, Jeffrey D., (P.C.) .... St. Louis, MO
Fisher, Jeffrey E. .... Las Vegas, NV
Fisher, Jeffrey H., (P.A.) .... Palm Beach, FL
Fisher, Jeffrey L. .... Farmington, CT
Fisher, Jeffrey L. .... Wilmington, IL
Fisher, Jeffrey L. .... **Dallas, TX**
Fisher, Jeffrey M. .... **San Francisco, CA**
Fisher, Jennifer E. .... Los Angeles, CA
Fisher, Jennifer Paganessi .... **Chicago, IL**
Fisher, Jill .... **Westmont, NJ**
Philadelphia, PA
Fisher, Jill L. .... Mineola, NY
Fisher, Jimmy B. .... **Corinth, MS**
Fisher, Joan Marie .... Genesee, ID
Fisher, Joanne Louise .... Troy, MI
Fisher, Jocelyn .... **Washington, DC**
Fisher, Joe J. .... Beaumont, TX
Fisher, Joe J., II .... **Beaumont, TX**
Fisher, Joel A. .... Richfield, MN
Fisher, Joel Hilton .... Washington, DC
Fisher, Joel Hilton, P.C. .... Washington, DC
Fisher, John A. .... **Phoenix, AZ**
Fisher, John B. .... Toledo, OH
Fisher, John B., III .... Waco, TX
Fisher, John B., Jr. .... Waco, TX
Fisher, John C. .... **New York, NY**
Fisher, John Clark .... Longview, TX
Fisher, John E. .... Houston, TX
Fisher, John Edwin .... **Orlando, FL**
Fisher, John F. .... **Lexington, SC**
Fisher, John H. .... **Albany, NY**
Fisher, John H. .... Huntington, NY
Fisher, John H., II .... Clearwater, FL
Fisher, John M. .... Lima, OH
Fisher, John P. .... San Diego, CA
Fisher, John R. .... San Francisco, CA
Fisher, John T., Jr. .... **Tuscaloosa, AL**
Fisher, John W. .... Peru, IL
Fisher, John W. .... Adair, IA
Fisher, John W. .... Dallas, OR
Fisher, John W., II .... Morgantown, WV
Fisher, John W., Jr. .... Lexington, MA
Fisher, Jon E. .... Dallas, TX
Fisher, Jonathan J. .... **Seattle, WA**
Fisher, Jonathan Kirk .... Greenville, SC
Fisher, Joseph A., III .... **Alexandria, VA**
Arlington, VA
Fisher, Joseph Allan .... Muskegon, MI
Fisher, Joseph C. .... Elk Rapids, MI
Traverse City, MI
Fisher, Joseph G. .... **Chicago, IL**
Fisher, Joseph H. .... Hialeah, FL
Fisher, Joseph M. .... Hingham, MA
Fisher, Joshua L. .... Miami, FL
Fisher, Joy .... Sacramento, CA
Fisher, Joy D. .... Buffalo Grove, IL
Fisher, Joy H. .... **Macon, GA**
Fisher, Judith .... **New York, NY**
Fisher, Judith Callison .... **Lexington, SC**
Fisher, Judith M. .... Columbus, OH
Fisher, Julia B. .... **Philadelphia, PA**
Fisher, Julie Bond .... Oskaloosa, IA
Fisher, Kahlia E. .... **New York, NY**
Fisher, Karen A. .... Brooklyn, NY
Fisher, Karen D. Wells .... Joplin, MO
Fisher, Karen L. Buckholz .... Santa Fe, NM
Fisher, Karen S. .... Washington, DC
Fisher, Kathleen A. .... Roswell, GA
Fisher, Kathleen V. .... **San Francisco, CA**
Fisher, Kelly .... **Dallas, TX**
Fisher, Kelly C. .... **Anchorage, AK**
Fisher, Kelly Leigh .... St. Paul, MN
Fisher, Kelly Morgan .... **St. Petersburg, FL**
Fisher, Kellyalexis .... **Miami, FL**
Fisher, Kendall J. .... **Seattle, WA**
Fisher, Kenneth A., Jr. .... **Columbus, OH**
Fisher, Kenneth H. .... Chicago, IL
Fisher, Kenneth H. .... Huntington, WV
Fisher, Kenneth H., L.C. .... Huntington, WV
Fisher, Kenneth J. .... Cleveland, OH

Fishman, Alan S. ....Pompano Beach, FL
Fishman, Alexander S. ....Tamarac, FL
Fishman, Alvin L. ....San Francisco, CA
Fishman, Andrew M. ....Columbus, OH
Fishman, Ankner & Horstmann, LLP
Boston, MA
Fishman, Ann Deborah
West Palm Beach, FL
Fishman, Arnold N. ....Haddon Heights, NJ
Fishman, Arnold N., P.C.
Haddon Heights, NJ
Fishman, Arthur A. ....Bordentown, NJ
Fishman, Aryeh B. ....Washington, DC
New York, NY
Fishman, Barry M. ....Paramus, NJ
Fishman, Barry S. ....Miami Beach, FL
Fishman, Benjamin I. ....Washington, DC
Fishman, Bernard H. ....New York, NY
Fishman, Bradley S. ....Houston, TX
Fishman, Burton J. ....Washington, DC
Fishman & Callahan, P.C. ......East Hanover, NJ
Fishman, Carol H. ....Washington, DC
Fishman, Carrie G. ....Scarsdale, NY
Fishman, Claire ....Dunwoody, GA
Fishman, Clifford C. ....Red Bank, NJ
Fishman, Clifford S. ....Washington, DC
Fishman, Craig ....Washington, DC
Fishman, Craig L. ....Pittsburgh, PA
Fishman, Daniel N. ....Boulder, CO
Fishman, David ....Arlington, VA
Fishman, David A.
Small Business Administration,
Office of the General Counsel, GV
Fishman, David Bennett
South Lake Tahoe, CA
Fishman, David H. ....Baltimore, MD
Fishman, David S. ....Windsor, CT
Fishman, David S. ....North Chicago, IL
Fishman, Deborah E. ....Cupertino, CA
Fishman, Donald A. ....Beverly Hills, CA
Fishman, Donald M. ....Fairfax, VA
Fishman, Edward J. ....Washington, DC
Fishman, Edward M. ....Addison, TX
Fishman, Elaine G. ....Richmond, VA
Fishman, Elizabeth M. ....Los Angeles, CA
Fishman, Ellen B. ....New York, NY
Fishman, Ellen M. ....Jersey City, NJ
Fishman, Ellen S. ....Davis, CA
Fishman, Elliot T. ....Columbus, OH
Fishman, Eric ....Washington, DC
Fishman, Eric ....New York, NY
Fishman, Fay E. ....Minneapolis, MN
Fishman & Fey, Co., L.P.A. ....Columbus, OH
Fishman, Fishman & Saltzberg, P.C.
Chicago, IL
Fishman, Fred N. ....New York, NY
Fishman, Gary S. ....Cleveland, OH
Fishman, George M.
House of Representatives,
Committee Legal Personnel, GV
Fishman, Gerald L. ....Chicago, IL
Fishman, Gregg Richard ....New York, NY
Fishman, Gregory A. ....Chicago, IL
Fishman Group, The .....Bloomfield Hills, MI
Detroit, MI
Fishman, Harriet J. ....Exeter, NH
Fishman Herrmann & Anderson
New York, NY
Fishman, Howard A. ....Los Angeles, CA
Fishman, Howard J. ....Chicago, IL
Fishman, Howard K. ....New York, NY
Fishman, Irving M. ....New York, NY
Fishman, Irving S. ....Chicago, IL
Fishman, Jack B. ....Beloit, WI
Fishman, Jacob ....Miami, FL
Fishman, Jacob D. ....New York, NY
Fishman & Jaklitsch ....Annapolis, MD
Upper Marlboro, MD
Fishman, James B. ....New York, NY
Fishman, James J. ....White Plains, NY
Fishman, James M. ....Miami, FL
Fishman, James M., P.A. ....Miami, FL
Fishman, Jane D. ....Plantation, FL
Fishman, Jarred A. ....Washington, DC
Fishman, Jay B. ....Chicago, IL
Fishman, Jayme M. ....Boston, MA
Fishman, Jeffrey A. ....Worcester, MA
Fishman, Jeffrey Martin ....Norcross, GA
Fishman, Jeremy K. ....Rockville, MD
Fishman, Jerry ....Upper Marlboro, MD
Fishman, Joanne ....Philadelphia, PA
Fishman, Joel H. ....Stoughton, MA
Fishman, Joel L. ....Los Angeles, CA
Los Angeles, CA
Fishman, John ....Merrick, NY
Fishman, Jordan M. ....Los Angeles, CA
Fishman, Joseph ....New York, NY
Fishman, Joseph L. ....Brooklyn, NY
Fishman, Joshua E. ....New York, NY
Fishman, Julius ....Chicago, IL
Fishman, Karen S. ....Beverly Hills, CA
Fishman, Karen S., A Law Corporation
Beverly Hills, CA
Fishman, Kenneth J. ....West Palm Beach, FL
Boston, MA
Fishman, L. William ....New York, NY
Fishman, Lawrence R. ....Cleveland, OH
Fishman, Leonard ....Princeton, NJ
Fishman, Lewis W. ....Miami, FL
Fishman, Lewis W., Professional Association
Miami, FL
Fishman, Libby G. ....Pittsburgh, PA
Fishman, Lois R. ....Torrance, CA
Fishman, Louis Y. ....New Orleans, LA
Fishman, M. Manuel ....San Francisco, CA
Fishman, Marc A. ....Southfield, MI
Fishman, Marc E. ....Newark, NJ
Fishman, Marcia E. ....Atlanta, GA

Fishman, Mark Alan ....New York, NY
Fishman, Mark Andrew ....Albuquerque, NM
Fishman, Mark D. ....Los Angeles, CA
Fishman, Mark I. ....Southport, CT
Fishman, Mark S. ....Cleveland, OH
Fishman, Marshall H. ....Denver, CO
Fishman, Marshall H. ....New York, NY
Fishman, Martin ....New York, NY
Fishman, Martin A. ....Richmond Heights, OH
Fishman, Meryl S. ....Washington, DC
Fishman, Michael D. ....Birmingham, MI
Fishman, Michael D. ......Bloomfield Hills, MI
Fishman, Michael H. ....Olathe, KS
Fishman, Michael L. ....Mineola, NY
Fishman, Michael T. ....Cleveland, OH
Fishman, Mitchell E. ....Union, NJ
Fishman, Mitchell S. ....New York, NY
Fishman & Morgenthal ....Carlisle, PA
Fishman, Nathan ....Long Branch, NJ
Fishman, Neil & Armentrout, LLP
New York, NY
Fishman, Neil G. ....Hartford, CT
Fishman, Nelson I. ....Baltimore, MD
Fishman, Norman W. ....Chicago, IL
Fishman, Patrick M. ....Detroit, MI
Fishman, Paul J. ....Newark, NJ
New York, NY
Fishman, Peter S. ....San Francisco, CA
Fishman, Phillip ....Minneapolis, MN
Fishman, Ralph H. ....New Orleans, LA
Fishman, Richard A. ....Atlanta, GA
Fishman, Richard G. ....Morristown, NJ
Fishman, Richard L. ....Los Angeles, CA
Fishman, Robert A. ....Boston, MA
Fishman, Robert C. ....Los Angeles, CA
Fishman, Robert G. ....Fresno, CA
Fishman, Robert J. ....New York, NY
Fishman, Robert L. ....Richardson, TX
Fishman, Robert M. ....Chicago, IL
Fishman, Robert T. ....Denver, CO
Fishman, Ronald A. ....New York, NY
Fishman, Ronald S. ....Chicago, IL
Fishman, Ross H. ....Highland Park, IL
Fishman, Samuel A. ....New York, NY
Fishman, Saul ....Walnut Creek, CA
Fishman, Seymour J. ....Chicago, IL
Fishman, Shanti A. ....Menlo Park, CA
Fishman, Sheila S. ....St. Paul, MN
Fishman, Stacey K. ....Culver City, CA
Fishman, Stanley P. ....East Hanover, NJ
Fishman, Steven ....Detroit, MI
Fishman, Steven A. ....New York, NY
Fishman, Steven B. ....Laguna Beach, CA
Fishman, Steven J. ....Bloomfield Hills, MI
Detroit, MI
Fishman, Steven J. ....Carlisle, PA
Fishman, Steven M. ....Safety Harbor, FL
Fishman, Steven M., P.A. ....Safety Harbor, FL
Fishman, Stuart D. ....New York, NY
Fishman, Theodore V. ....Trenton, NJ
Fishman, Todd S. ....New York, NY
Fishman, William L. ....Washington, DC
Fishman, William M. ....Minneapolis, MN
Fishman, William R. ....Petaluma, CA
Fishman, William R. ....Denver, CO
Fishman, Yale J. ....Miami, FL
Fishner, Steven Marc ....New York, NY
Fishoff, Donald B. ....New York, NY
Fishwick, John P., Jr. ....Roanoke, VA
Fisichella, Angelo R. ....Lawrence, MA
Windham, NH
Fisk, Arlene D. ....Philadelphia, PA
Fisk, Catherine L. ....Los Angeles, CA
Fisk, Daniel Ward ....United States Senate,
Committee Legal Personnel, GV
Fisk, David P. ....Costa Mesa, CA
Fisk & Fielder, P.C. ....Dallas, TX
Fisk & Fisk ....Fairport, NY
Fisk, George W. ....Savannah, GA
Fisk, Harry J., Law Offices of ....Dallas, TX
Fisk, Hayward D. ....El Segundo, CA
Fisk, Hollye C. ....Dallas, TX
Fisk, Ivan T. ....Mercer Island, WA
Fisk, John R. ....Fairport, NY
Fisk, John W. ....Schaumburg, IL
Fisk, John W. ....Artesia, NM
Fisk Kart and Katz, Ltd. ....Chicago, IL
Fisk, Martin H. ....St. Paul, MN
Fisk, Michael E. ....Bedminster, NJ
Fisk, Robert C. ....Washington, DC
Fisk, Robin J. ....Concord, NH
Fisk, Ronald F. ....Nevada, MO
Fiske, Andrew N. ....Chicago, IL
Fiske, Barbara A. ....Cupertino, CA
Fiske, Colin S. ....Baldwin, NY
Fiske, David G. ....Washington, DC
Fiske, David H. ....Washington, DC
Fiske, Douglas E. ....Hartford, CT
Fiske, Eric K. G. ....Richmond, VA
Fiske, Gregory N. ....Lone Tree, CO
Fiske, J. Peter ....Santa Monica, CA
Fiske, Jeffrey R. ....Denver, CO
Fiske, John A. ....Cambridge, MA
Fiske, Jordan J. ....Syracuse, NY
Fiske, Robert B., Jr. ....New York, NY
Fiske, Ronald N. ....Department of the Navy,
Office of the Judge Advocate General, GV
Fiske, Terry Noble ....Englewood, CO
Fiske, William S. ....Fresno, CA
Fiskey, Leslie A. ....Madison, WI
Fiss, Jan V. ....Belleville, IL
Fiss, Jodi S. ....Highland Park, IL
Fiss, L. LaVerne ....Johnson, KS
Fiss, Owen M. ....New Haven, CT
Fisse, Michael D. ....Covington, LA
Fissel, Barry W. ....Toledo, OH
Fissel, Cynthia A. ....San Diego, CA

Fist, David L. ....Oklahoma City, OK
Tulsa, OK
Fist, Leah Rebecca ....Columbus, OH
Fistel, F. Scott ....Lauderhill, FL
Fistel, F. Scott, P.A. ....Lauderhill, FL
Fistel, Michael K. ....New York, NY
Fister, Alan T. ....Brentwood, TN
Fister, Alan T. ....Nashville, TN
Fister, David L. ....Lexington, KY
Fister, Johanna (Hanna) R. ....Houston, TX
Fister, Jon C. ....Waterloo, IA
Fister, Patrick J. ....St. Louis, MO
Fister, Richard E. ....St. Louis, MO
Fister, Stephen T. ....Chicago, IL
Fisz, Ari Paul ....Chicago, IL
Fiszer, George A. ....Short Hills, NJ
Fiszer, Karen G. ....New York, NY
Fiszer, Michael C. ....Beverly Hills, CA
Fiszman, Sula R. ....Boston, MA
Fitanides, Andrea ....Saco, ME
Fitanides, Selena ....Philadelphia, PA
Fitch, A. Wray, III ....McLean, VA
Fitch, Amy C. ....Colorado Springs, CO
Fitch, Amy J. ....Buffalo, NY
Fitch & Associates ....Malvern, PA
Fitch, Cathleen Gilliland ....San Diego, CA
Fitch, Charles E. ....Houston, TX
Fitch, Christopher N. ....Vienna, VA
Fitch, Colin E. ....Washington, PA
Fitch, Daniel L. ....Harrisonburg, VA
Fitch, Daniel T. ....Philadelphia, PA
Fitch, Daron S. ....Miami, FL
Fitch, David Allan, Law Offices of
Bedford, MA
Fitch, David Allan, Law Offices of
Lexington, MA
Fitch, David P. ....Inver Grove Heights, MN
Fitch, Douglas H. ....Englewood, CO
Fitch, Edward H., IV ....Department of Labor,
Office of the Solicitor, GV
Fitch, Edward P. ....Redmond, OR
Fitch, Elizabeth Savoini ....Phoenix, AZ
Fitch, Even, Tabin & Flannery
Los Angeles, CA
San Diego, CA
Washington, DC
Chicago, IL
Arlington, VA
Fitch, Frank H., III ....New Cumberland, WV
Fitch, Ginger ....Salem, OR
Fitch, Graham ....Seattle, WA
Fitch, Harrison A. ....Boston, MA
Fitch, Howard M. ....Louisville, KY
Fitch, Jack A. ....Conroe, TX
Fitch, James C. ....Portsmouth, OH
Fitch, Janice E. ....Wichita, KS
Fitch, John ....Fresno, CA
Fitch, John H., Jr. ....Washington, DC
Fitch, John K. ....Columbus, OH
Fitch, John L. ....Cambridge, MA
Fitch, John W. ....Greensburg, IN
Fitch, Johnson, Larson, Walsh & Held, P.A.
Minneapolis, MN
Fitch, Jonathan W. ....Boston, MA
Providence, RI
Fitch, Joyce N. ....Columbia, MD
Fitch, Julian M. ....Rochester, NY
Fitch, Kendall, Cecil, Robinson & Magyaros
Co., L.P.A. ....Salem, OH
Fitch, King & Caffentzis
Monmouth Beach, NJ
New York, NY
Fitch, Lee O. ....Portsmouth, OH
Fitch, Lisa Wong ....Washington, DC
Fitch, Lowell H. ....Torrington, WY
Fitch, Lucinda Fluharty ....Wheeling, WV
Fitch & Ludwick ....Seattle, WA
Fitch, Luin P., Jr. ....Department of Justice,
Antitrust Division, GV
Fitch, Marc T.A. ....Santa Ana, CA
Fitch, Mark K. ....Oklahoma City, OK
Fitch, Mary Jane ....Malvern, PA
Fitch, Michael F. ....Seattle, WA
Fitch, Milton F. ....Wilson, NC
Fitch, Morgan L., IV ....Knoxville, TN
Fitch, Morgan L., Jr. ....Chicago, IL
Fitch, Nakata S. ....Atlanta, GA
Fitch, Patrick D. ....Philadelphia, PA
Fitch, Peter J. ....Monmouth Beach, NJ
New York, NY
Fitch, R. Templeton ....Jacksonville, FL
Fitch, Rebecca April ....Washington, DC
Fitch, Richard W., Jr. ....Tampa, FL
Fitch, Robert A. ....New York, NY
Fitch, Ruth E. ....Boston, MA
Fitch, Sharon D. ....Poway, CA
Fitch, Stephen C. ....Columbus, OH
Fitch, Stephen J. ....San Diego, CA
Fitch, Stephen J., & Associates, A Prof. Corp.
San Diego, CA
Fitch, Sue Ann ....Grand Lake, CO
Fitch, Susan Kathleen ....Washington, DC
Fitch, Thomas G. ....Socorro, NM
Fitch, Thomas P. ....Buffalo, NY
Fitch, Valerie L. ....New York, NY
Fitch, W. Lawrence ....Williamsburg, VA
Fitch, Warren Anthony ....Washington, DC
Fitchett, Frederick F., III
Atlantic City, NJ
Fitchett, Leo G. ....White Marsh, VA
Fitchett, Rhonda ....Fort Dodge, IA
Fitchett, Thomas A. ....Farmington Hills, MI
Fitchett, Thomas J. ....Lincoln, NE
Fitch-Schrum, Kara D. ....Spartanburg, SC
Fite, Arthur F., III ....Anniston, AL
Fite, Bill ....Hamilton, AL
Fite, C. Bart ....Muskogee, OK
Fite, Calvin W., Jr. ....Nashville, TN

Fite, Coleman Bartow, Jr. ....Muskogee, OK
Fite, Davis, Atkinson, Guyton & Bentley,
P.C. ....Fayette, AL
Haleyville, AL
Hamilton, AL
Winfield, AL
Fite, Ellen E. ....Memphis, TN
Fite, Frances ....McLean, VA
Fite, Jack P. ....Oklahoma City, OK
Fite, John D. ....Clearwater, FL
Fite, John M. ....Panama City, FL
Fite, Julian K. ....Muskogee, OK
Fite, Kathie Lynn ....Muskogee, OK
Fite & Miller, L.L.C. ....Anniston, AL
Fite & O'Brien, Ltd. ....McLean, VA
Fite & Pierce ....Brookings, SD
Fite, Robert G. ....Brookings, SD
Fite, Robert P. ....Piqua, OH
Fite, William P. ....Seattle, WA
Fitelson, Lasky, Aslan & Couture
New York, NY
Fitelson, Robin ....New York, NY
Fiterstein, Heide ....Brooklyn, NY
Fites, Jennifer Workinger
Jacksonville, FL
Fithian, John F. ....Washington, DC
Fithian, Leslie Ann ....Cupertino, CA
Fithian, William C., III ....Mansfield, OH
Fitkin, Glenn L. ....Saginaw, MI
Fitle, Herbert M. ....Omaha, NE
Fitle, John K. ....Los Alamitos, CA
Fitt, Benjamin J. ....Buffalo, NY
Fitta, Jonathan J. ....Providence, RI
Fittante, Joseph J., Jr. ....Minneapolis, MN
Fittante, Martin F. ....Escanaba, MI
Menominee, MI
Fitter, James C., Jr. ....Kansas City, MO
Fitter, Seth B., (Mr.) ....Chicago, IL
Fitterman, A. ....Atlanta, GA
Fitterman, Mark D. ....Washington, DC
Fitterman, Perri Carol, (Ms.)
East Setauket, NY
Fitterman, Wayne L. ....Beverly Hills, CA
Fitting, Bruce D. ....San Francisco, CA
Fitting, James T. ....Oregon City, OR
Fitting, Lawrence W. ....Fort Smith, AR
Fitting, Lawrence W., P.A. ....Fort Smith, AR
Fitting, Tammy L. ....Harlingen, TX
Fitting, Thomas ....La Jolla, CA
Fittipaldi, Brian D. ....Santa Barbara, CA
Fittipaldi, Frank N., Jr. ....Brecksville, OH
Fittipaldi, Lisa M. ....Englewood, NJ
Fittipaldi, Mark F.
Agency for International Development,
Office of the General Counsel, GV
Fittipaldi, Mary Cocivera ....Norristown, PA
Fittipaldi, Susan M. ....New Brunswick, NJ
Fitton, Pamela J. ....Inverness, IL
Fitton, Pamela J. ....New York, NY
Fitton, Will B. ....San Francisco, CA
Fitts, Barbara Hayden ....Boston, MA
Fitts, Bruce B. ....Wichita, KS
Fitts, Calvert A. ....Cortland, NY
Fitts, Clinton R. ....Amarillo, TX
Fitts, David W. ....Boston, MA
Fitts, Edward M. ....Atlanta, GA
Fitts & Fitts ....Cortland, NY
Fitts, Herman ....Mineral Wells, TX
Fitts, Jane Gale ....Washington, DC
Fitts, John T. ....Mayfield Village, OH
Fitts, Michael A. ....Philadelphia, PA
Fitts, Michael Austin ....Nashville, TN
Fitts, Michael D. ....Beverly Hills, CA
Fitts, Morris C. ....Cortland, NY
Fitts, Olson & Giddings, P.L.C.
Brattleboro, VT
Newfane, VT
Fitts, Renée A. ....Palo Alto, CA
Fitts, Sara A. W. ....New York, NY
Fitts, Stanford P. ....Salt Lake City, UT
Fitts, Stewart C. ....Las Vegas, NV
Fitts, Suzanne R. ....Las Vegas, NV
Fitts, Timothy L. ....Baltimore, MD
Fitz, Elaine F. ....San Francisco, CA
Fitz, Herbert M. ....Glenbrook, NV
Fitz, Kate R. ....San Francisco, CA
Fitz, Michael A. ....Holyoke, MA
Fitz, Robert A. ....Dallas, TX
Fitz, Stephen S. ....Morgantown, WV
Fitz, Terry J. ....Scotts Valley, CA
Fitz, Todd B. ....Newark, OH
Fitz, Victor A. ....Muskegon, MI
Fitz, William H. ....Washington, DC
Fitz, Wm. Lane ....Oklahoma City, OK
Fitze, Dianne Morse ....Tunkhannock, PA
Fitze, Judd B. ....Tunkhannock, PA
Fitzell, Stephen P. ....Chicago, IL
Fitzenhagen, Alexander R. ....Dallas, TX
Fitzenreiter, R. Craig ....Baltimore, MD
Fitzer, Donald N. ....Syracuse, NY
Fitzer, Gretchen J. ....Pittsburgh, PA
Fitzer, Joel M. ....Irvine, CA
Fitzer, John W., Jr. ....Troy, MI
Fitzer, Lynn P. ....San Francisco, CA
Fitzer, Norman B. ....New York, NY
Fitzer, Richard L. ....Long Beach, CA
Fitzer, Stephen R. ....Columbia, SC
Fitzer, Steven F. ....Tacoma, WA
Fitzgeorge, Theodore G. ....Lehigh Acres, FL
Fitzgerald, Abbott & Beardsley LLP
Alameda, CA
Oakland, CA
San Francisco, CA
Fitzgerald, Aguilar, Sherwood & Michner
Visalia, CA
FitzGerald, Alice M. ....Cincinnati, OH
FitzGerald, Amy S. ....Springfield, VT

FitzGibbon, James T. ....Chicago, IL
Fitzgibbon, John E. ....Laredo, TX
Fitz-Gibbon, John H. ....Northampton, MA
FitzGibbon, John J. ....St. Louis, MO
Fitzgibbon, John M. ....Brookline, MA
FitzGibbon, Kathryn A. ....Houston, TX
Fitzgibbon, Lisa M. ....Portland, ME
Fitzgibbon, Matthew F. ....Woodbridge, NJ
Fitzgibbon, Roger H., Jr. ....Little Rock, AR
FitzGibbon, Scott T. ....Boston, MA
FitzGibbon, Susan A. ....St. Louis, MO
Fitz-Gibbon, Thomas D.
Federal Communications Commission, Wireless Telecommunications Bureau, GV
Fitzgibbon, Thomas F. ....Salem, MA
FitzGibbon, Thomas M. ....Kenilworth, NJ
Fitzgibbon, Thomas N. ....Santa Monica, CA
Fitzgibbon, Timothy J. ....Washington, DC
Fitzgibbons, Albert J., Jr. ....Buffalo, NY
Fitzgibbons & Anderson ....Las Vegas, NV
Fitzgibbons Brothers ....Estherville, IA
Fitzgibbons, Dana ....Los Angeles, CA
Fitzgibbons, David A., III
Casa Grande, AZ
Fitzgibbons, Denis M. ....Casa Grande, AZ
Fitzgibbons, Eden M. ....New York, NY
Fitzgibbons, Francis ....Estherville, IA
Fitzgibbons, James J. ....Silver Spring, MD
Fitzgibbons, John Carl ....Los Angeles, CA
Fitzgibbons, John M. ....Sarasota, FL
Tampa, FL
Fitzgibbons, Joseph ....Methuen, MA
Fitzgibbons, Joseph L. ....Estherville, IA
Fitzgibbons Law Offices, P.L.C.
Casa Grande, AZ
Coolidge, AZ
Florence, AZ
Fitzgibbons, Leo E. ....Estherville, IA
Fitzgibbons, Mark J. ....Manassas, VA
Fitzgibbons, Michael Richard ....Olathe, KS
Fitzgibbons, Pat ....Las Vegas, NV
Fitzgibbons, Thomas M. ....Sarasota, FL
Fitzgibbons, W. James ....Troy, MI
Fitz Gibbons, William A. ....Amityville, NY
Fitzgibbons, William F. ....Franklin, NJ
Fitzharris, Gregory R. ....Des Moines, IA
Fitzharris, Kevin K. ....Fort Wayne, IN
Fitzharris, William E., Jr. ....Seattle, WA
Fitzhenry, Edward C., Jr.
Granite City, IL
Fitzhenry, James A. ....Portland, OR
Fitzhenry, Lawrence J. ....Metuchen, NJ
Fitzhenry, Paul E. ....Manchester, NH
Fitzhugh & Associates ....Hartford, CT
Boston, MA
Warwick, RI
Fitzhugh, B. Dewey ....Little Rock, AR
Fitzhugh, Bay ....Augusta, AR
Fitzhugh, Berryman J., III ....Durham, NC
Fitzhugh, C. Craig ....Ripley, TN
Fitzhugh, Elizabeth ....Seattle, WA
Fitzhugh & Elliott, P.C. ....Houston, TX
Fitzhugh, Eugene C. ....Little Rock, AR
Fitzhugh, J. Michael ....Fort Smith, AR
Fitzhugh, John H. ....Montpelier, VT
Fitzhugh, L. Murray ....Venice, FL
Fitzhugh, Margaret S. ....Inglewood, CA
Fitzhugh, Martha (Marty) P. ....Bay City, MI
Fitzhugh, Michael A. ....Hartford, CT
Boston, MA
Warwick, RI
Fitzhugh, Nancy E. ....Los Angeles, CA
Fitzhugh, Nicol Sunrise ....Kansas City, KS
Fitzhugh, Rodney E. ....Montrose, CO
Fitzhugh, Thomas C., III ....Houston, TX
Fitzhugh, Timothy B. ....Costa Mesa, CA
Fitzhugh, Walter P. ....Bay City, MI
Fitzhugh, William M. ....Santa Monica, CA
Fitzhugh, William T. ....Chesterfield, VA
Fitzjarrald, Sheryl L. ....Champaign, IL
Fitzke, C. F. ....Gering, NE
Fitzke, Robert L. ....East Lansing, MI
Fitzke, Tod E. ....Denver, CO
Fitzkee, David E. ....Kennett Square, PA
Fitzkee, Harold N., Jr. ....York, PA
Fitzmahan, Maureen ....Seattle, WA
FitzMaurice & Ambrozaitis ....Waterbury, CT
Fitzmaurice, Cathy L. ....Cedar Rapids, IA
Iowa City, IA
Waterloo, IA
FitzMaurice, Daniel L. ....Hartford, CT
Fitzmaurice, Edmond H., Jr. ....Covington, LA
Fitzmaurice, Edward J., Jr. ....Dallas, TX
Fitzmaurice, Edward L., Jr. ....Milton, MA
FitzMaurice, Eugene M. ....Houston, TX
Fitzmaurice, Evan E. ....Dallas, TX
Fitzmaurice & Freeman ....Stamford, CT
FitzMaurice, Gregory ....Grangeville, ID
FitzMaurice, Gregory, P.A. ....Grangeville, ID
Fitzmaurice, Jack F. ....San Diego, CA
Fitzmaurice, John P. ....Tuckahoe, NY
Fitzmaurice, Joseph L. ....Greenbelt, MD
Fitzmaurice, Karen A. ....Milford, CT
Fitzmaurice, Kevin M. ....Miami, FL
FitzMaurice, Maurice T. ....Hartford, CT
Fitzmaurice, Paul R. ....Haddonfield, NJ
Philadelphia, PA
FitzMaurice, Sean G. ....Waterbury, CT
Fitzmaurice, Shelley A. ....Minneapolis, MN
Fitzmaurice, Therese A. ....Southport, CT
Fitzmaurice & Timone, P.C. ....Tuckahoe, NY
Fitzmaurice, Timothy Robert ....Oakland, CA
Fitzmaurice, Timothy William
Lanham, MD
Fitzmaurice, Victor E. ....Costa Mesa, CA
Fitzmaurice, William T. ....Stamford, CT
FitzMorris, Douglas J. ....New York, NY
Fitzmorris, John D., Jr. ....New Orleans, LA
FitzMorris, Paul E. ....Kings Park, NY
Fitzner, Catherine Hubbard ....Washington, DC
Fitzner, James R. ....Winston-Salem, NC
Fitzner, Linda K. ....Chicago, IL
Fitzner, Peter M. ....Fairfax, VA
Fitzner, R. Jon ....Valley City, ND
Fitzpatrick, Alfred F. ....Carrizo Springs, TX
Fitzpatrick, Alice Ann ....Stamford, CT
Fitzpatrick, Amy R. ....Washington, DC
Fitzpatrick, Anne Baglivo ....Fairfield, NJ
Fitzpatrick, Anne C. ....Pittsburgh, PA
Fitzpatrick, Anne E. ....Mansfield, MA
Fitzpatrick, Anthony J. ....Boston, MA
Fitzpatrick & Associates ....Washington, DC
Bethesda, MD
Fitzpatrick, B. James ....Salinas, CA
Fitzpatrick & Barbieri, A Prof. Law Corp.
San Luis Obispo, CA
Fitzpatrick, Barry C.
Rancho Santa Fe, CA
Fitzpatrick, Barry M. ....Rockville, MD
Fitzpatrick & Bass ....Independence, KS
Fitzpatrick, Beverly T. ....Roanoke, VA
Fitzpatrick, Blackey & Devanie
La Crosse, WI
Fitzpatrick & Bolnick ....Albuquerque, NM
Fitzpatrick, Brendan T. ....Albertson, NY
Fitzpatrick, Brian F. ....Santa Ana, CA
Fitzpatrick, Brian J. ....Ventura, CA
FitzPatrick, Brian T. ....New York, NY
Fitzpatrick, Bridgette ....New York, NY
Fitzpatrick, Broaddus C. ....Roanoke, VA
Fitzpatrick, Burch H. ....Piedmont, CA
Fitzpatrick, Catherine ....Lawrenceville, NJ
Fitzpatrick, Catherine L. ....Chicago, IL
Fitzpatrick, Cella, Harper & Scinto
Costa Mesa, CA
Washington, DC
New York, NY
Fitzpatrick, Charles A., III
Philadelphia, PA
Fitzpatrick, Charles F. ....Hamburg, PA
Reading, PA
Fitzpatrick, Charles J. ....San Antonio, TX
Fitzpatrick, Cheryl B. ....Chicago, IL
Fitzpatrick, Christine ....San Francisco, CA
Fitzpatrick, Christopher M
Clearwater, FL
FitzPatrick, Christopher M.
New York, NY
Fitzpatrick, Christopher R.
Louisville, KY
Fitzpatrick, Colleen A. ....Teaneck, NJ
Fitzpatrick, Collins T. ....Chicago, IL
Fitzpatrick, Cooper & Clark
Birmingham, AL
Fitzpatrick, Curtis M. ....San Diego, CA
Fitzpatrick, Daniel J. ....Teaneck, NJ
Fitzpatrick, Daniel J., Jr. ....New York, NY
FitzPatrick, Daniel M. ....Albuquerque, NM
Fitzpatrick, David C.
San Luis Obispo, CA
Fitzpatrick, David J. ....La Crosse, WI
Fitzpatrick, David W. ....Philadelphia, PA
FitzPatrick, Denise Marie ....Fishkill, NY
Fitzpatrick, Dennis D. ....Chicago, IL
Fitzpatrick, Dennis J. ....Milwaukee, WI
Fitzpatrick, Diane L., P.C. ....Syracuse, NY
Fitzpatrick, Diane Langenmayr
Syracuse, NY
Fitzpatrick, Donald J. ....St. Louis, MO
Fitzpatrick, Donna R. ....Washington, DC
Fitzpatrick, Dora ....Phoenix, AZ
Fitzpatrick, Douglas C. ....Sedona, AZ
Fitzpatrick, Duross ....Macon, GA
Fitzpatrick, E. Joseph, Jr.
Gaithersburg, MD
Fitzpatrick, Edward B., III ....Atlanta, GA
Fitzpatrick, Edward C. ....Chicago, IL
Fitzpatrick, Edward D.
Essex Junction, VT
FitzPatrick, Edward J. ....New York, NY
FitzPatrick, Edward N. ....Teaneck, NJ
Trenton, NJ
Fitzpatrick, E. H. ....Natchez, MS
Fitzpatrick, Eileen M. ....Durham, NH
Fitzpatrick, Elaine M. ....Verona, NJ
Fitzpatrick, Elizabeth A. ....Chicago, IL
Fitzpatrick, Elizabeth A. ....Albertson, NY
Fitzpatrick, Elizabeth O'N. ....Hartford, CT
FitzPatrick, Erik B. ....Burlington, VT
Fitzpatrick, Eugene J. ....Rockville, MD
Fitzpatrick, F. Emmett ....Philadelphia, PA
Fitzpatrick, F. Emmett, III
Philadelphia, PA
Fitzpatrick, F. Emmett, P.C.
Philadelphia, PA
Fitzpatrick, F. Gerald ....Bayonne, NJ
Fitzpatrick, F. Michael ....Knoxville, TN
Fitzpatrick, F. Rodney ....Roanoke, VA
Fitzpatrick, Fidelma L. ....Providence, RI
Fitzpatrick & Fitzpatrick, P.A. ....Inverness, FL
Fitzpatrick & Fitzpatrick, P.A. ....Bayonne, NJ
Fitzpatrick, Francis A., Jr. ....Norwood, MA
Fitzpatrick, Francis G. ....Bayonne, NJ
Fitzpatrick, Francis G.
New Philadelphia, OH
Fitzpatrick, Frank W. ....Dallas, TX
Fitzpatrick, Fray & Bologna LLC
Fairfield, CT
Stamford, CT
Fitzpatrick, Garrett J. ....New York, NY
Fitzpatrick, Gary L. ....Los Angeles, CA
Fitzpatrick, Gary R. ....Auburn, CA
Fitzpatrick, George F., Jr. ....Chicago, IL
Fitzpatrick, Gregory L. ....Philadelphia, PA
Pittsburgh, PA
Fitzpatrick, Harold F. ....Bayonne, NJ
Secaucus, NJ
Fitzpatrick, H. T., Jr. ....Montgomery, AL
Fitzpatrick, Ian C. ....Baltimore, MD
FitzPatrick, James A., Jr. ....New York, NY
Fitzpatrick, James C. ....New York, NY
FitzPatrick, James D. ....Syracuse, NY
Fitzpatrick, James F. ....Washington, DC
Fitzpatrick, James F. ....Washington, DC
Fitzpatrick, James F. ....Westfield, NJ
Fitzpatrick, James K. ....Chicago, IL
Fitzpatrick, James M. V. ....San Diego, CA
Fitzpatrick, James P., Jr. ....Syracuse, NY
Fitzpatrick, James T. ....Rockville, MD
Fitzpatrick, Jane V. ....Lexington, KY
Fitzpatrick, Janet ....Washington, DC
Fitzpatrick, Jas. K. ....Wellesley Hills, MA
Fitzpatrick, Jeanne M. ....Ottawa, IL
Fitzpatrick, Jenny J. ....Gainesville, GA
Fitzpatrick, Joan ....Harrisburg, PA
Fitzpatrick, Johanna L. ....Fairfax, VA
Fitzpatrick, John A. ....Philadelphia, PA
Fitzpatrick, John B. ....New York, NY
Fitzpatrick, John C. ....Salisbury, CT
Fitzpatrick, John C. ....Boston, MA
Fitzpatrick, John C. ....Plattsburgh, NY
Fitzpatrick, John C. ....Burlington, VT
Fitzpatrick, John D. ....Boston, MA
Fitzpatrick, John E., Jr. ....Roselle Park, NJ
Fitzpatrick, John Francis
Washington, DC
Fitzpatrick, John G. ....Brainerd, MN
Fitzpatrick, John J., Jr.
San Francisco, CA
Fitzpatrick, John M. ....Helena, MT
Fitzpatrick, John M. ....Philadelphia, PA
Fitzpatrick, John M. ....Longview, TX
Fitzpatrick, John M. ....Richmond, VA
Fitzpatrick, John R. ....Phoenix, AZ
Fitzpatrick, John R. ....Atlanta, GA
Fitzpatrick, John T. ....Albuquerque, NM
Fitzpatrick, Jon ....Chagrin Falls, OH
Fitzpatrick, Joseph A., Jr. ....Allentown, PA
Fitzpatrick, Joseph F. ....Virginia Beach, VA
Fitzpatrick, Joseph K. ....Brooklyn, NY
Fitzpatrick, Joseph M. ....New York, NY
Fitzpatrick, Josephine A. ....Lakewood, CA
Fitzpatrick, Joyce ....Carlsbad, CA
Fitzpatrick, Julie J. ....Cape Canaveral, FL
Fitzpatrick, Kathy R. ....Dallas, TX
Fitzpatrick, Kaysie A. ....Manhattan Beach, CA
Fitzpatrick, Kenneth R. ....Midland, MI
Fitzpatrick, Kevin M. ....Fairfax, VA
Fitzpatrick, Kevin P. ....White Plains, NY
Fitzpatrick, L. Scott ....Boston, MA
Fitzpatrick, Lane ....Danielsville, GA
Fitzpatrick, Laura Lynn ....Detroit, MI
Fitzpatrick, Lauren E. ....Canton, OH
Fitzpatrick Law Group, P.S. ....Spokane, WA
Fitzpatrick Law Offices ....Chicago, IL
Fitzpatrick, Lee William ....Woodstock, GA
Fitzpatrick Lentz & Bubba, P.C.
Allentown, PA
Bethlehem, PA
Doylestown, PA
Easton, PA
Stroudsburg, PA
Fitzpatrick, Lessie G. ....Houston, TX
Fitzpatrick, Lisa M. ....Anchorage, AK
Fitzpatrick, Lynn M. ....Fairfax, VA
Fitzpatrick, Margaret Doyle ....Seattle, WA
Fitzpatrick, Margaret L.
San Francisco, CA
Fitzpatrick, Margaret M.
New Rochelle, NY
Fitzpatrick, Maria G. ....Hagåtña, GU
Fitzpatrick, Mary C. ....Boston, MA
Fitzpatrick, Matthew P. ....Cincinnati, OH
Fitzpatrick, Maureen F. ....Media, PA
Fitzpatrick & McSherry ....Chagrin Falls, OH
Fitzpatrick, Megan A. ....Chicago, IL
Fitzpatrick, Michael ....Albuquerque, NM
Fitzpatrick, Michael ....Providence, RI
Fitzpatrick, Michael A. ....Bridgeport, CT
Fitzpatrick, Michael C. ....Redding, CA
FitzPatrick, Michael D. ....Troy, MI
Fitzpatrick, Michael D. ....Fairfield, OH
Fitzpatrick, Michael F., Jr. ....New York, NY
Fitzpatrick, Michael G. ....Doylestown, PA
Fitzpatrick, Michael H. ....Knoxville, TN
Fitzpatrick, Michael J. ....San Jose, CA
Fitzpatrick, Michael J. ....Tahoe City, CA
Fitzpatrick, Michael K. ....New Orleans, LA
Fitzpatrick, Michael R. ....Janesville, WI
Fitzpatrick, Michael T. ....Hackensack, NJ
Fitzpatrick, Michael T. ....Milwaukee, WI
Fitzpatrick & Nelson ....Brainerd, MN
Crosslake, MN
Fitzpatrick, Osborne & Sturgill, P.S.C.
Prestonsburg, KY
Fitzpatrick, Patane & Giffen ....Salinas, CA
Fitzpatrick, Patricia A. ....New York, NY
Fitzpatrick, Paul D. ....Spokane, WA
Fitzpatrick, Paul J. ....Santa Rosa, CA
Fitzpatrick, Paul J. ....New York, NY
Fitzpatrick, Paul T. ....Bloomfield Hills, MI
Fitzpatrick, Peter ....Chicago, IL
Fitzpatrick, Peter B. ....McLean, VA
Fitzpatrick, Peter D. ....Gaithersburg, MD
Fitzpatrick, Peter J. ....New York, NY
Fitzpatrick, Philip J. ....Elizabeth, NJ
Fitzpatrick, Philip J. ....Staten Island, NY
Fitzpatrick, Philip J. ....Jeffersonville, VT
Fitzpatrick, Raymond P., Jr.
Birmingham, AL
Fitzpatrick, Richard A. ....Jupiter, FL
Fitzpatrick, Richard C. ....Poplarville, MS
Fitzpatrick, Richard E. ....Prestonsburg, KY
Fitzpatrick, Richard H. ....Chicago, IL
Fitzpatrick, Richard S. ....Inverness, FL
Fitzpatrick, Robert A. ....Sharon, MA
Fitzpatrick, Robert B. ....San Diego, CA
Fitzpatrick, Robert B. ....Washington, DC
Fitzpatrick, Robert F., Jr. ....Boston, MA
Fitzpatrick, Robert J. ....Treasury Department, Internal Revenue Service, GV
Fitzpatrick, Robert J. ....Boston, MA
Fitzpatrick, Robert K. ....New York, NY
Fitzpatrick, Roberta ....Boston, MA
Fitzpatrick, Ronald M. ....La Crosse, WI
FitzPatrick, Rory ....Boston, MA
Fitzpatrick, Ryan Paul ....Plymouth, MI
FitzPatrick, Samuel C. ....Montpelier, VT
Fitzpatrick, Samuel L. ....Chicago, IL
Fitzpatrick, Sean M. ....Simsbury, CT
Fitzpatrick, Shannon M. ....Boston, MA
Fitzpatrick & Showen, LLP
Rancho Santa Fe, CA
San Diego, CA
Fitzpatrick, Stephen R. ....Morristown, NJ
FitzPatrick, T. Kevin ....Norristown, PA
Fitzpatrick, T. Robert ....Los Angeles, CA
Fitzpatrick, Terese L. ....Kennebunk, ME
Fitzpatrick, Terrance J. ....Harrisburg, PA
Fitzpatrick, Thomas ....New York, NY
Fitzpatrick, Thomas A. ....Brainerd, MN
Fitzpatrick, Thomas J. ....Rochester, NY
Fitzpatrick, Thomas J., Jr. ....Irvine, CA
Fitzpatrick, Thomas, Law Office
Brainerd, MN
Fitzpatrick, Thomas M. ....Chicago, IL
Fitzpatrick, Thomas M. ....La Crosse, WI
Fitzpatrick, Thomas S. ....Boston, MA
Fitzpatrick, Timothy D. ....Healdsburg, CA
Fitzpatrick, Timothy D. ....Irvington, VA
Fitzpatrick, Timothy J. ....La Jolla, CA
Fitzpatrick, Toni L. ....Berkeley, CA
Fitzpatrick, Tracy B. ....Boston, MA
Fitzpatrick, V. Vaughan O. ....San Ramon, CA
Fitzpatrick, Vaughan ....New Orleans, LA
FitzPatrick, Vincent R., Jr. ....New York, NY
Fitzpatrick, Walter R., Jr. ....Trophy Club, TX
Fitzpatrick, Walter S., III ....Cookeville, TN
Fitzpatrick, Ward William ....Westbury, NY
Fitzpatrick, Warren L. ....Lynn Haven, FL
Fitzpatrick & Warrenbrand LLP
Boston, MA
Fitzpatrick & Waterman ....Bayonne, NJ
Secaucus, NJ
Fitzpatrick, William D. ....Holyoke, MA
Fitzpatrick, William F. ....Hickory Hills, IL
Fitzpatrick, William J. ....Tower Lakes, IL
Fitzpatrick, William J. ....Independence, KS
Fitzpatrick, William J. ....Syracuse, NY
Fitzpatrick, William J., III ....Fairfield, CT
Fitzpatrick, William M. ....Dedham, MA
Fitzpatrick, William N., Jr. ....Crownsville, MD
Fitzpatrick, William P. ....Redwood City, CA
Fitzpatrick, Zimmerman & Rose Co., L.P.A.
New Philadelphia, OH
FitzRandolph, John A. ....Costa Mesa, CA
FitzRandolph, Laura E. ....Washington, DC
FitzRoy, Forrest S. ....St. Louis, MO
Fitzsimmons, Annette T. ....Tacoma, WA
Fitzsimmons and Associates ....San Diego, CA
Fitzsimmons and Associates
South Yarmouth, MA
Fitzsimmons, Brian P. ....Boston, MA
Fitz-Simmons, C. Douglas ....Pasadena, CA
Fitzsimmons, Carol Anne ....Newark, NJ
New York, NY
FitzSimmons, Catherine ....Oak Park, IL
Fitzsimmons, Debra A. ....Sacramento, CA
Fitzsimmons, DesMarteau, Beale and Nunn
Rochester, NY
Fitzsimmons, Donald Bruce, Jr.
Boston, MA
Fitzsimmons, Donna Congeni
Rocky River, OH
Fitzsimmons, Eileen M. ....Menlo Park, CA
Fitzsimmons, Ellen M. ....Richmond, VA
Fitzsimmons, Erhard ....Colorado Springs, CO
Fitzsimmons, Eve M. ....Seattle, WA
Fitzsimmons, Francis P. ....Lancaster, PA
Fitzsimmons, Frank J. ....Newark, NJ
Fitzsimmons, George Edward ....St. Louis, MO
Fitzsimmons, George L.
North Little Rock, AR
St. Louis, MO
Fitzsimmons, Holly B. ....Bridgeport, CT
Fitzsimmons, J. Michael ....San Jose, CA
Fitzsimmons, J. Michael, (P.C.)
Wheaton, IL
Fitzsimmons, J. Patrick ....Deerfield, IL
Fitzsimmons, James B. ....Churchville, NY
Rochester, NY
Fitzsimmons, James Cody ....New York, NY
Fitzsimmons, James E. ....San Diego, CA
Fitzsimmons, James F. ....Short Hills, NJ
Fitzsimmons, James J. ....Old Field, NY
Fitzsimmons, James N., Jr.
Uniontown, PA
Fitzsimmons, James P. ....New Town, ND
Fitzsimmons, James R. B. ....Garden City, NY
Fitzsimmons, James T. ....Mason City, IA
Fitzsimmons, John A. ....Miami, FL
Fitzsimmons, John B. ....Rochester, NY
Fitzsimmons, John D. ....Marshfield, MA
Fitzsimmons, John E. ....San Diego, CA
Fitzsimmons, John R., Jr. ....San Jose, CA
Fitzsimmons, Kenneth B.
Point Pleasant Beach, NJ
Fitzsimmons, Kevin J. ....Tampa, FL
Fitzsimmons, Laura Wightman
Las Vegas, NV

Fitzsimmons Law Offices ... Boston, MA
Weymouth, MA
Fitzsimmons Law Offices ... Wheeling, WV
Fitzsimmons, Mark ... Weymouth, MA
Fitzsimmons, Mark E. ... Springfield, MO
Fitzsimmons, Mark P. ... Washington, DC
Fitzsimmons, Matthew T. ... Cleveland, OH
Fitzsimmons, Norine P. ... Ocala, FL
Fitzsimmons, Paul ... South Yarmouth, MA
Fitzsimmons, Paul A. ... Washington, DC
Fitzsimmons, Paul E. ... St. Louis, MO
Fitzsimmons, Paul J. ... Dubuque, IA
Fitzsimmons, Philip K. ... Rochester, NY
Fitzsimmons, Rickey A. ... Denver, CO
Fitzsimmons Ringle & Jacobs, P.C.
Hackensack, NJ
Newark, NJ
New York, NY
Fitzsimmons, Robert J. ... Hudson, NY
Fitzsimmons, Robert P. ... Wheeling, WV
Fitzsimmons, Robert V. ... Miami, FL
Fitzsimmons, Robert V. ... Chicago, IL
Fitzsimmons, Roberta ... Boston, MA
Fitzsimmons, Roberts & Paine
Chicago, IL
Wheaton, IL
Fitzsimmons, Stephen ... Denver, CO
Fitzsimmons, Susan ... Des Moines, IA
Fitzsimmons, Thomas F. ... Brooklyn, NY
Fitzsimmons, Thomas R. ... Evansville, IN
Fitzsimmons, Tina ... Cupertino, CA
FitzSimon, Jean K. ... Hoffman Estates, IL
Fitzsimon, Kenneth M. ... Portland, OR
Fitzsimon, Lori M. ... Washington, DC
Fitzsimons & Baylinson ... Northfield, NJ
FitzSimons, Brian W. ... Cleveland, OH
Fitzsimons, David A. ... Harrisburg, PA
Fitzsimons, David R., Jr. ... Northfield, NJ
Fitzsimons, Dennis P. ... Oakland, CA
FitzSimons, Douglas O. ... Kimberton, PA
FitzSimons, Edward J. ... Chicago, IL
Fitzsimons, Hugh F. ... Walters, OK
Fitzsimons, J. David ... Pomona, CA
Fitzsimons, James G. ... Mineola, NY
FitzSimons, James M. ... Shelton, CT
New York, NY
FitzSimons, James Michael, P.C.
Shelton, CT
Fitzsimons, John F. ... Forest Hills, NY
Fitzsimons, John H. ... Laguna Beach, CA
FitzSimons, John H. ... New York, NY
FitzSimons, John H. ... New York, NY
FitzSimons, John V. ... Colorado Springs, CO
Fitzsimons, Joseph B. C. ... San Antonio, TX
Fitzsimons, Kevin W. ... Chicago, IL
Fitzsimons, Louise M. ... New York, NY
FitzSimons, Michael J. ... San Francisco, CA
FitzSimons, Robert C. ... Columbia, SC
Fitzsimons, Thomas R. ... Chicago, IL
Fitzwater, G. Morgan ... Fallbrook, CA
Fitzwater, Kimberly A. ... Oakland, MD
Fitzwater, Lynne E. ... Harrisburg, PA
Fitzwater, Martha A. ... Austin, TX
Fitzwater, Robert L. ... Los Angeles, CA
Fitzwater, Sidney A. ... Dallas, TX
Fitzwater, Wendell D. ... Clackamas, OR
Fitzwater, Wesley D. ... Clackamas, OR
Fitzwilliam, Charles E. ... San Juan, PR
Fiumara, Angelo J. ... Boston, MA
Fiumara, Michael A. ... Santa Rosa, CA
Fiur, Kevin S. ... Houston, TX
Fiveash & Associates, P.A. ... Pensacola, FL
Fiveash, Earnest E., Jr. ... Collierville, TN
Fiveash, Frazer H. ... Norfolk, VA
Fiveash, John L., Jr. ... Pensacola, FL
Fivecoat, Raymond K. ... Midland, TX
Fivehouse, Michele B. ... Falls Church, VA
Fivel, Norman P. ... Albany, NY
New York, NY
Fivel, Steven E. ... Indianapolis, IN
Fiveland, David N. ... New Brunswick, NJ
Fiverson, Stephen B. ... Kearny, NJ
Fiveson, David K. ... New York, NY
Fivey, Daniel B. ... Orinda, CA
Fix, Amy ... Greensboro, NC
Fix, Daniel A. ... Lincoln, NE
Fix, Douglas W. ... Denver, CO
Fix, Gail L. ... Miami Beach, FL
Fix, Julie A. ... East St. Louis, IL
Fix, Melanie ... Norfolk, VA
Fix, Meyer ... Rochester, NY
Fix, Milton S. ... New York, NY
Fix, Raymond F. ... Grand Rapids, MI
Fix, René M. ... Jacksonville, FL
Cleveland, OH
Fix, René Mark ... Cincinnati, OH
Fix, Richard L. ... Des Moines, IA
Omaha, NE
Fix, Robert L. ... Detroit, MI
Fix, Spindelman, Brovitz, Turk, Himelein & Shukoff, P.C. ... Rochester, NY
Fix, Susan M. ... Pittsburgh, PA
Fix, William R. ... Jackson, WY
Fix, William R., P.C. ... Jackson, WY
Fixel, Joe W. ... Orlando, FL
Tallahassee, FL
Fixel & La Rocco ... Fort Lauderdale, FL
Hollywood, FL
Miami, FL
West Palm Beach, FL
Fixel & Maguire ... Orlando, FL
Tallahassee, FL
Fixel, Maurice ... Hollywood, FL
Fixel, Terry Ellen ... Hollywood, FL
Fixler, Arthur I. ... Providence, RI
Fixler & Associates ... Carmel, NY
Fixler, David C. ... Boston, MA
Fixler, Eli Shabsi ... Brooklyn, NY
Fixler, Elliot H. ... New York, NY
Fixler & Gulino, L.L.P. ... New York, NY
Fixler, Herbert B. ... New York, NY
Fixler, Michael A. ... Cleveland, OH
Fixler, Mitchell D. ... New York, NY
Fixsen, Amy R. Pellenberg ... Randolph, MA
Fixx, David W. ... Columbus, OH
Fizzarotti, Ron ... Staten Island, NY
Fizer, Beck, Webster, Bentley & Scroggins, A Professional Corporation ... Houston, TX
Fizer, Don Edward ... Houston, TX
Fizer, Linda S. ... Ashland City, TN
Fizer, Timothy E. ... Baltimore, MD
Fizzarotti, Ronald V. ... East Hartford, CT
Fizzell, J. Tobias ... Chicago, IL
Fizzolio, James M. ... Sherman Oaks, CA
Fizzolio and McLeod ... Sherman Oaks, CA
Fjeld, Carter L. ... Yakima, WA
Fjeldal & Associates, A Professional Corporation ... Houston, TX
Fjeldal, Timothy A. ... Houston, TX
Fjelde, Mark B. ... Fort Wayne, IN
Fjellstrom, Howard G. ... Torrance, CA
Fjelstad, Daniel R. ... Seattle, WA
Fjelstad, Eric B. ... Ketchikan, AK
Fjelstad, Michael M. ... San Jose, CA
Fjelstad, Paul ... Bremerton, WA
Fjelstad, Stephan O. ... Seattle, WA
Tacoma, WA
Fjelstul, Kirk R. ... Atlanta, GA
Fjermedal, Glenn M. ... Rochester, NY
Fjetland, Michael ... Houston, TX
Fjord, Hilliard J. ... Cincinnati, OH
Fjordbeck, Denise G. ... Salem, OR
Flaa, Cynthia J. ... Park Ridge, IL
Flaaen, Diane R. ... Phoenix, AZ
Flaaen, Richard H. ... Glendale, AZ
Flaagan, Elizabeth K. ... Denver, CO
Flaccavento, Frank J. ... Wayne, NJ
Flaccus, Geo. E., Jr. ... Pittsburgh, PA
Flaccus, Janet A. ... Fayetteville, AR
Flach, Charles F., III ... Butler, PA
Flach, Eleanor N. ... New York, NY
Flach, Thomas M. ... St. Charles, MO
Flachbarth, Charles T. P.
Department of the Army, Office, Chief of Engineers/Headquarters, U.S. Army Corps of Engineers, GV
Flachs, Jeremy ... Annandale, VA
Flachs, Patrick M. ... St. Louis, MO
Flachs, Robert J. ... Los Angeles, CA
Flachsbart, William W. ... Chicago, IL
Flack, Charles Haynes ... Macomb, IL
Flack, David G. ... Montgomery, AL
Flack, Donald M. ... East Alton, IL
Flack, Evelyn R. ... Crawfordville, FL
Flack, Gary ... Atlanta, GA
Flack, Gary, and Associates, P.C.
Atlanta, GA
Flack, Hope L. ... Chicago, IL
Flack, Howard I. ... Washington, DC
Flack, Jennifer Schoats ... Southfield, MI
Flack, Jill D. ... Washington, DC
Flack, Joe F., Jr. ... Austin, TX
Flack, McRaven & Stephens ... Macomb, IL
Flack, Michael A. ... Royal Oak, MI
Flack, Milton W. ... Maywood, CA
Flack, Paul D. ... Houston, TX
Flack, Robert A. ... Landover, MD
Flack, Robert D. ... Jackson, MI
Flack, Roy ... Palm Beach Gardens, FL
Flack, Sanford H. ... Springfield, OH
Flack, Stephen P. ... Shawnee, KS
Flack, Steven D. ... Roswell, GA
Flacker, Barbara R. ... Philadelphia, PA
Flacker, William L. ... Elkins Park, PA
Flacks, Franklin L. ... Trenton, NJ
Flacks, Kenneth B. ... Cincinnati, OH
Flacy, Shara A. ... Pulaski, TN
Flad, Diana R. ... Houston, TX
Fladell, Matthew ... Santa Monica, CA
Fladen, Sharon V. ... Canton, OH
Flader, David Matthew ... Beverly Hills, CA
Flader, James A. ... Fond du Lac, WI
Flader, Richard L. ... Chicago, IL
Flader, Ronald F. ... Sugar Land, TX
Fladseth, Douglas C. ... Santa Rosa, CA
Fladung, Hans ... Chicago, IL
Fladung, Richard D. ... Houston, TX
Fladwed, Thor E. ... Coeur d'Alene, ID
Flagel, Gerald P. ... Dayton, OH
Flagel, Mark A. ... Los Angeles, CA
Flagello, Genoveffa ... Wassaic, NY
Flageollet, Ralph J. ... San Francisco, CA
Flager, Randall C. ... Bordentown, NJ
Trevose, PA
Flager & Yockey, A Professional Corporation
Bordentown, NJ
Trevose, PA
Flagg, Brett B. ... Dallas, TX
Flagg, Brett B. and Associates, P.C.
Dallas, TX
Flagg, Brett B. & Associates, P.C.
Frisco, TX
Flagg, Clinton D. ... Miami, FL
Flagg, Cynthia Platt ... Los Angeles, CA
Flagg, Elizabeth A. ... Winston-Salem, NC
Flagg, George E. ... Des Moines, IA
Flagg, Gerald K. ... Farmington Hills, MI
Flagg, Henry W., Jr. ... Houston, TX
Flagg, Jeffrey G. ... Des Moines, IA
Flagg, Jonathan M. ... Hampton, NH
Flagg, Kathryn M. ... Brownsville, TX
McAllen, TX
Flagg Law Corporation, The ... Dallas, TX
Flagg, Lisa M. ... Atlanta, GA
Flagg, Merle R., (P.C.) ... Dallas, TX
Flagg, Neal P. ... Dallas, TX
Flagg, Neal P., P.C., Law Offices of
Dallas, TX
Flagg, Patricia Sharin
Department of Housing and Urban Development, Office of General Counsel, GV
Flagg, Robert F. ... Los Angeles, CA
Flagg, Ronald S. ... Washington, DC
Flagg, Wayne F. ... Cheyenne, WY
Flaggert, James A. ... Seattle, WA
Flaggert, James M. ... Grand Rapids, MI
Flaggman, Daniel J. ... Birmingham, MI
Flaggman, Lawrence S. ... Northville, MI
Flaggman, Steven ... Sun Lakes, AZ
Flagler, Brian D. ... Atlanta, GA
Flagler & Flagler, P.C. ... Norman, OK
Flagler, H. Glen ... Westerville, OH
Flagler, Lynley B. ... Clearwater, FL
Flagler, Nicholas R., Jr. ... Boston, MA
Flagler, Rita M. ... Norman, OK
Flagler, Robert A. ... Norman, OK
Flagsberg, Seth A. ... San Jose, CA
Flagstad, Carl O., Jr. ... Minot, ND
Flaharty, Erin E. ... Phoenix, AZ
Flahavan, Mark ... St. Paul, MN
Flahavan, William F. ... Los Angeles, CA
Flahaven, Roger P. ... Chicago, IL
Flaherty, Alicia E. ... Portland, ME
Flaherty, Amy Archer ... Buffalo, NY
Flaherty, Anne Marie ... Sacramento, CA
Flaherty, Arthur F. ... Boston, MA
Flaherty and Associates ... St. Paul, MN
Flaherty & Associates, P.C. ... Carnegie, PA
Flaherty, B. Frank ... Newark, NJ
Flaherty, Barbara M. ... Washington, DC
Flaherty, Billie S. ... Parsippany, NJ
Flaherty, Bret P. ... Philadelphia, PA
Flaherty, Brian P. ... Philadelphia, PA
Flaherty, Carol A. ... East Aurora, NY
Flaherty, Catherine J. ... Shorewood, WI
Flaherty, Cohen, Grande, Randazzo & Doren, PC ... Buffalo, NY
Flaherty, Daniel K. ... Warwick, RI
Flaherty, Daniel L. ... Des Moines, IA
Flaherty, Daniel T. ... Appleton, WI
Milwaukee, WI
Flaherty, Daniel T. ... La Crosse, WI
Flaherty, David F. ... Wellesley, MA
Flaherty, David M. ... Indianapolis, IN
Flaherty, David T., Jr. ... Lenoir, NC
Flaherty, Dennis M. ... New York, NY
Flaherty, Edw. L., Jr. ... Pittsburgh, PA
Flaherty, Edward F., Jr. ... Riverhead, NY
Flaherty, Edward T. ... Corning, NY
Flaherty, Ethan M. ... Boston, MA
Flaherty, Francis Christopher
Carson City, NV
Flaherty, Francis X. ... Warwick, RI
Flaherty, Francis X. ... Warwick, RI
Flaherty, Griffith F. ... Seattle, WA
Flaherty, Isabelle C. ... Pacific Palisades, CA
Flaherty & Jacobson, P.C. ... Chicago, IL
Flaherty, James ... Seneca, PA
Flaherty, James F. ... Brighton, MA
Flaherty, James G. ... Ottawa, KS
Flaherty, James G. ... Columbus, OH
Flaherty, James G. ... Westerville, OH
Flaherty, James J. ... Carnegie, PA
Flaherty, James J., Jr. ... Southbury, CT
Waterbury, CT
Flaherty, James N. ... Chicago, IL
Flaherty, James T. ... Hartford, CT
Flaherty, James T. ... Cleveland, OH
Flaherty, Jane Sara ... Cleveland, OH
Flaherty, Jeanne Robbins ... Valencia, CA
Flaherty, John A. ... San Jose, CA
Flaherty, John A. ... Stamford, CT
Flaherty, John E. ... Newark, NJ
Flaherty, John E., Jr. ... Philadelphia, PA
Flaherty, John Edward ... Joliet, IL
Flaherty, John F. ... New York, NY
Flaherty, John M. ... Bridgeview, IL
Flaherty, John P. ... Garden City, NY
Flaherty, John T. ... Vancouver, WA
Flaherty, Joseph F. ... Dedham, MA
Flaherty, Joseph R. ... Owensboro, KY
Flaherty, Karen J. ... Brookfield, WI
Flaherty, Kathleen M. ... Evanston, IL
Flaherty, Kathryn A. ... Omaha, NE
Flaherty, Kerry C. ... New York, NY
Flaherty, Kyle P. ... New York, NY
Flaherty, Laurence S. ... Waltham, MA
Flaherty, LeClair L.
Farmington Hills, MI
Flaherty, Leo ... Medford, MA
Flaherty, Margaret A. ... Washington, DC
Flaherty, Margaret P. ... Mineola, NY
Flaherty, Marion Heyna ... Washington, DC
Flaherty, Mark D. ... Boston, MA
Flaherty, Mark F. ... Pittsburgh, PA
Flaherty, Mark G. ... Kansas City, MO
Flaherty, Martin Stephen ... New York, NY
Flaherty, Mary M. ... Boston, MA
Flaherty, Mary Pat ... Oak Brook, IL
Flaherty, Maureen ... Wheaton, IL
Flaherty, Meisler & Courtney
Rockville, CT
Vernon, CT
Flaherty, Melvina Racey
West Palm Beach, FL
Flaherty, Michael ... Brookfield, WI
Flaherty, Michael ... Madison, WI
Flaherty, Michael E. ... Pittsburgh, PA
Flaherty, Michael F. ... Boston, MA
Flaherty, Michael F., Jr. ... Quincy, MA
Flaherty, Michael J. ... Stamford, CT
Flaherty, Michael J. ... Chicago, IL
Flaherty, Michael J. ... Springfield, MA
Flaherty, Michael J. ... Buffalo, NY
Flaherty, Michael J. ... Alexandria, VA
Flaherty, Michael J., Jr. ... Buffalo, NY
Flaherty, Michael, Law Offices of
Sacramento, CA
Flaherty, Michael P. ... Los Angeles, CA
Flaherty, Michael R. ... Chicago, IL
Flaherty, Michael R. ... Rochester, NY
Flaherty, Michael Robert ... Kansas City, MO
Flaherty, Nicole S. ... Warwick, RI
Flaherty, Pamela E. ... New York, NY
Flaherty, Patrick F. ... Minneapolis, MN
Flaherty, Patrick J. ... Hartford, CT
Flaherty, Patrick James ... Newport, OR
Flaherty, Patrick M. ... Aurora, IL
Flaherty, Patrick T. ... Owensboro, KY
Flaherty, Paul E. ... Chicago, IL
Flaherty, Paul R. ... Los Angeles, CA
Flaherty, Paul T. ... Lake Worth, FL
Flaherty, Peter D. ... Madison, WI
Flaherty, Peter J., III ... Richmond, KY
Flaherty, Regina M. ... Stamford, CT
Flaherty, Richard F. ... Newark, NJ
Flaherty, Rita A. ... New Hyde Park, NY
Flaherty, Robert E. ... Warwick, RI
Flaherty, Robert M. ... San Francisco, CA
Flaherty, Robert P. ... Shepherdsville, KY
Flaherty, Robert P. ... Wellesley, MA
Flaherty, Roger P. ... Sanford, ME
Flaherty, Ruth W., (Miss) ... Brookline, MA
Flaherty, Sensabaugh & Bonasso, P.L.L.C.
Charleston, WV
Morgantown, WV
Wheeling, WV
Flaherty, Shawn D. ... Albany, NY
Flaherty, Shawn P. ... Wheaton, IL
Flaherty, Shawn T. ... Pittsburgh, PA
Flaherty & Shea ... Buffalo, NY
Flaherty, Sheila M. ... Westborough, MA
Flaherty, Stephen A. ... Erie, PA
Flaherty, Stephen D. ... Charlotte, NC
Flaherty, Susan L. Q. ... Washington, DC
Flaherty, Thomas A. ... Norwalk, CT
Flaherty, Thomas F. ... Omaha, NE
Flaherty, Thomas J. ... Hillsboro, OR
Flaherty, Thomas J. ... McLean, VA
Flaherty, Thomas V. ... Riverside, CA
Flaherty, Thomas V. ... Charleston, WV
Flaherty, Thos. P. ... Buffalo, NY
Flaherty, Timothy J. ... Astoria, NY
Flaherty, Timothy M. ... San Francisco, CA
Flaherty, Timothy P. ... St. Paul, MN
Flaherty, Timothy R. ... Dedham, MA
Flaherty, Timothy S. ... Peoria, IL
Flaherty, Vincent D. ... Norwalk, CT
Flaherty, Walter T., Jr. ... Stamford, CT
Flaherty, William M. ... Rockford, IL
Flaherty, Wm. J. ... Boston, MA
Flaherty, Yvonne M. ... St. Paul, MN
Flaherty-Dawson, Thomas J. ... Maynard, MA
Flahive, Edward A. ... Delaware, OH
Flahive, Edward F. ... Delaware, OH
Flahive, Katie ... Austin, TX
Flahive, Mark T. ... Westfield, MA
Flahive, Ogden & Latson, A Professional Corporation ... Austin, TX
Flahive, Shawn M. ... Columbus, OH
Flahive, Terrence P. ... Delaware, OH
Flahive, Timothy I. ... Delaware, OH
Flaig, Donald W. ... Los Angeles, CA
Flaig, Joseph L. ... Los Angeles, CA
Flaig, Paul E. ... Maple Glen, PA
Flaigle, Harold E. ... Wichita, KS
Flail, Edward N., Jr. ... Wayne, PA
Flaim, John G. ... Dallas, TX
Flair, Roger N. ... Bozeman, MT
Flaisher, Lynn ... San Francisco, CA
Flake, A. Mark ... New Orleans, LA
Flake, Alan K., Jr. ... Salt Lake City, UT
Flake, Andrew A. ... Fort Smith, AR
Flake, Gail C. ... Decatur, GA
Flake, J. Dee ... Globe, AZ
Flake, Kathleen
Federal Deposit Insurance Corporation, Outside Counsel Section, GV
Flake, Paul Joseph ... Prairie Village, KS
Flake, Richard P. ... Beaumont, TX
Corpus Christi, TX
Houston, TX
Flake, Ronald R. ... Universal City, TX
Flake, Shannon J. ... Midvale, UT
Flakne, Brian R. ... Bloomington, MN
Flakne, Gary W. ... Bloomington, MN
Flakne Law Office, P.A. ... Bloomington, MN
Flam, Carole Gordon ... Tarzana, CA
Flam, Cori ... Washington, DC
Flam, David Rowat ... New York, NY
Flam, Martin H. ... Ventura, CA
Flam, Rachel D. ... New York, NY
Flam, Stewart M. ... Pittsburgh, PA
Flamberg, Gemma ... Rockville, MD
Flame, Andrew J. ... Philadelphia, PA
Flame, Lana S. ... New York, NY
Flame, Philip ... Encino, CA
Los Angeles, CA
Flamen, Stuart M. ... New York, NY
Flamenbaum, Bruce ... Diamond Bar, CA
Flamenbaum, Israel ... Mineola, NY
Flamenbaum, Michael P. ... New York, NY
Flamer, Michelle D. ... Philadelphia, PA
Flamiano, Dominic G. ... Oakland, CA
Flaming, Todd H. ... Chicago, IL
Flaminia, Alinka ... Denver, CO
Flaminio, Joann E. ... Boston, MA
Flamm, Arthur J. ... Palm Beach Gardens, FL
Boston, MA

Flamm, Boroff & Bacine, P.C.
Voorhees, NJ
Blue Bell, PA
Norristown, PA
Philadelphia, PA
Flamm, Brett C. ... New Haven, CT
Flamm, Leonard N., Law Offices of
New York, NY
Flamm, Martin B. ... New Orleans, LA
Flamm, Matthew A. ... Chicago, IL
Flamm, Matthew S. ... Brooklyn, NY
Flamm, Richard C. ... Redmond, WA
Flamm, Richard E. ... Oakland, CA
Flamm, Richard P. ... New York, NY
Flamm & Teilbloom, Ltd. ... Chicago, IL
Flamm, Walter H., Jr. ... Voorhees, NJ
Blue Bell, PA
Flammang, Donna M. ... Cleveland, OH
Flammer, George H. ... Atlantic City, NJ
Flammia, Dayle A. ... Raleigh, NC
Flammia, Kathleen ... Orlando, FL
Flammia, Michael P. ... Boston, MA
Flammia & Solomon ... Coeur d'Alene, ID
Flammia, Sue Solomon ... Coeur d'Alene, ID
Flamporis, Georgia ... Northbrook, IL
Flan, Jeffrey V. ... Marion, IL
Flanagan / Bilton / Brannigan
Phoenix, AZ
Tampa, FL
Chicago, IL
Santa Fe, NM
Hawthorne, NY
Columbus, OH
Houston, TX
Flanagan, Ann Lappen ... Baltimore, MD
Flanagan, Anne S. ... Cincinnati, OH
Flanagan, Anthony Emerson ... Raleigh, NC
Flanagan, Barbara A. ... Orlando, FL
Flanagan, Barbara E. ... Danbury, CT
Flanagan and Benner ... Lancaster, PA
Flanagan, Billy W. ... Mount Pleasant, TX
Flanagan, Blackie & Giffels Co., L.P.A.
Cleveland, OH
Flanagan, Booth, Unger & Moses
Glendale, CA
Los Angeles, CA
Santa Ana, CA
Flanagan, Brendan F. ... Atlanta, GA
Flanagan, Brian G. ... Lawrenceville, NJ
Flanagan, Brian G. ... Rochester, NY
Flanagan, Brian P. ... Boston, MA
Flanagan, Brian T. ... Morristown, NJ
Flanagan, Bridget A. ... San Francisco, CA
Flanagan, Bruce ... Tracy, CA
Flanagan, Bruce A. ... Humble, TX
Flanagan, Catherine Stanton ... Chicago, IL
Flanagan, Charles F. ... Loudonville, NY
Flanagan, Cheryl Turk ... Denver, CO
Flanagan, Christie S. ... San Francisco, CA
Flanagan, Christopher M. ... Boston, MA
Flanagan, Christopher P. ... Lynnfield, MA
Flanagan & Cooke, P.C. ... Morristown, NJ
New York, NY
White Plains, NY
Flanagan, David T. ... Augusta, ME
Flanagan, David T. ... Madison, WI
Flanagan, Dayna A. Kalins
Beverly Hills, CA
Flanagan, Dennis J., Jr. ... Philadelphia, PA
Flanagan, Dennis P. ... Santa Barbara, CA
Flanagan, Donald M. ... Binghamton, NY
Flanagan, Douglas J., & Associates
Augusta, GA
Flanagan, E. Michael ... Washington, DC
Flanagan, Edward J. ... Cleveland, OH
Flanagan, Edward Korb ... Chicago, IL
Flanagan, Edward S. ... Burlington, VT
Flanagan, Eileen M. ... Santa Ana, CA
Flanagan, Elissa A. ... Hartford, CT
Flanagan, Elizabeth C. ... Morristown, NJ
Flanagan, Eugene J. ... Rockaway Park, NY
Flanagan, Eugene J. T. ... Rye, NY
Flanagan, Eugene L., III ... New York, NY
Flanagan, F. Patrick ... Columbus, OH
Flanagan, Fintan M. ... Oshkosh, WI
Flanagan & Flanagan ... Lawton, OK
Walters, OK
Mount Pleasant, TX
Flanagan & Flanagan ... Jackson Hole, WY
Flanagan, Francis D. ... Washington, DC
Flanagan, Francis J. ... Newport, RI
Flanagan, Funston ... Walters, OK
Flanagan, Gary W. ... Denver, CO
Flanagan, Gerald A. ... Milwaukee, WI
Flanagan, Gilbert G. ... Southampton, NY
Flanagan, Gregory S., (P.A.) ... Ocala, FL
Flanagan, Harold J. ... New Orleans, LA
Flanagan, Harold T., Jr. ... Dallas, TX
Flanagan, Heather M. ... Phoenix, AZ
Flanagan, Hugh M. ... Merced, CA
Flanagan & Hunter, P.C. ... Boston, MA
Providence, RI
Flanagan, J. Michael ... Glendale, CA
Santa Ana, CA
Flanagan, J. Michael ... Lancaster, PA
Flanagan, J. Victor ... Beckley, WV
Flanagan, James A. ... Beverly Hills, CA
Flanagan, James F. ... Columbia, SC
Flanagan, James F., III ... Newark, NJ
Flanagan, James H., Jr. ... North Fork, CA
Flanagan, James J. ... Kansas City, MO
Flanagan, James P. ... Woodbury, NY
Flanagan, James T. ... Metairie, LA
Flanagan, James W.
West Palm Beach, FL
Flanagan, Jennifer Z. ... Lincoln, MA
Flanagan, Jeremy J. ... New York, NY
Flanagan, Joanna Scarlata ... Pittsburgh, PA
Flanagan, John A. ... Cincinnati, OH
Flanagan, John C. ... New Haven, CT
Flanagan, John E. ... Middletown, RI
Flanagan, John E. ... Milwaukee, WI
Flanagan, John J. ... Huntington, NY
Flanagan, John K. ... Jackson Hole, WY
Flanagan, John P. ... Bridgeport, CT
Flanagan, John P. ... New York, NY
Flanagan, John R. ... Jackson Hole, WY
Flanagan, Joseph C., Jr.
Chestertown, MD
Flanagan, Joseph F. ... Forty Fort, PA
Flanagan, Joseph M. ... Chicago, IL
Flanagan, Joseph M. ... Lafayette Hill, PA
Flanagan, Joseph P. ... Santa Ana, CA
Flanagan, Joseph P., Jr. ... Flourtown, PA
Flanagan, Katherine E. ... Houston, TX
Flanagan, Kathleen ... Walters, OK
Flanagan, Kathy M. ... Chicago, IL
Flanagan, Kelly M. ... Costa Mesa, CA
San Francisco, CA
Flanagan, Kevin ... Department of Defense,
Office of the General Counsel, GV
Flanagan, L. Martin ... West Palm Beach, FL
Flanagan Law Office ... Merced, CA
Flanagan, Leo M., Jr. ... Elgin, IL
Flanagan, Leonard D. ... Bellevue, WA
Flanagan, Lieberman, Hoffman & Swaim
Dayton, OH
Flanagan, Louise W. ... New Bern, NC
Flanagan, Madeline ... Philadelphia, PA
Flanagan, Maniotis & Berger, P.A.
West Palm Beach, FL
Flanagan, Mari Jo F. ... Darien, CT
Flanagan, Mark D. ... Palo Alto, CA
Flanagan, Mark D. ... Houston, TX
Flanagan, Martin R. ... Elyria, OH
Flanagan, Matthew K. ... Garden City, NY
Flanagan, Maureen ... Portland, OR
Flanagan, Maureen Hope
Philadelphia, PA
Flanagan, Maureen McGlynn ... Madison, WI
Flanagan, Michael C. ... Walters, OK
Flanagan, Michael D. ... Milwaukee, WI
Flanagan, Michael E. ... McAllen, TX
Flanagan, Michael F. ... Washington, DC
Flanagan, Michael F. ... Kansas City, MO
Flanagan, Michael G. ... Altadena, CA
Flanagan, Michael J. ... Sacramento, CA
Flanagan, Michael J. ... Boise, ID
Flanagan, Michael J. ... Philadelphia, PA
Flanagan, Michael J. ... Nashville, TN
Flanagan, Michael J., P.A. ... Boise, ID
Flanagan, Michael L. ... Minneapolis, MN
Flanagan, Michael P. ... Greenville, NC
New Bern, NC
Flanagan, Michael V. ... Rockville Centre, NY
Flanagan, Michelle K. ... Seattle, WA
Flanagan, Nancy M. ... Brooklyn, NY
Flanagan, Norajean M. ... San Francisco, CA
Flanagan, Norman Patrick ... Reno, NV
Flanagan, Patricia A. ... Boise, ID
Flanagan, Patricia Jeanne ... Boston, MA
Flanagan, Patrick A. ... Dayton, OH
Flanagan, Patrick B.
West Palm Beach, FL
Flanagan, Patrick D. ... Chicago, IL
Flanagan, Patrick H ... Raleigh, NC
Flanagan, Patrick J. ... New York, NY
Flanagan, Patrick M. ... Elyria, OH
Flanagan, Patrick W. ... Minneapolis, MN
Flanagan, Paul E. ... Morristown, NJ
Flanagan, Paula ... New Fairfield, CT
Flanagan & Peat ... Danbury, CT
Flanagan, Peter J. ... Augusta, GA
Flanagan, Peter J. ... New York, NY
Flanagan, Peter J. ... New York, NY
Flanagan, Peter J., P.C. ... Augusta, GA
Flanagan, Peter L. ... Washington, DC
Flanagan, Peter M. ... West Lebanon, NH
Flanagan, Pia ... New York, NY
Flanagan, Richard J. ... New York, NY
Flanagan, Robert C. ... East Haven, CT
Flanagan, Robert F. ... San Antonio, TX
Flanagan, Robert J., Jr. ... North Haven, CT
Flanagan, Robert L. ... Columbia, MD
Flanagan, Robert P. ... Chicago, IL
Flanagan, Sarah G. ... San Francisco, CA
Flanagan, Sarah P. ... New York, NY
Flanagan, Sendik & Fahl, LLC
Milwaukee, WI
Flanagan, Sharon R. ... Chicago, IL
Flanagan, Shawn M. ... Charleston, SC
Flanagan, Sheila ... Oakland, CA
Flanagan, Sheila B. ... Hartford, CT
Flanagan, Sherman Edward, III
Richmond, VA
Flanagan, Steven C. ... Sunland, CA
Flanagan, Steven M. ... Washington, DC
Flanagan, Susan A. ... Roslyn Heights, NY
Flanagan, Susan Davis ... Shreveport, LA
Flanagan, T. Mark, Jr. ... Washington, DC
Flanagan, Tara M. ... Costa Mesa, CA
Flanagan, Tavi Claire ... Irvine, CA
Flanagan, Terence R. ... Lansing, MI
Flanagan, Teresa A. ... Springfield, MA
Flanagan, Teresa Maloney ... Atlanta, GA
Flanagan, Terry J. ... St. Louis, MO
Flanagan, Terry J., P.C. ... St. Louis, MO
Flanagan, Thomas D. ... Phoenix, AZ
Tampa, FL
Chicago, IL
Santa Fe, NM
Houston, TX
Flanagan, Thomas F. ... Chicago, IL
Flanagan, Thomas J. ... Bellmore, NY
Flanagan, Thomas J. ... Milwaukee, WI
Flanagan, Thomas M. ... Hartford, CT
Flanagan, Thomas M. ... New Orleans, LA
Flanagan, Thomas M., Jr.
Greenwood, MS
Flanagan, Thomas O. ... Santa Ana, CA
Flanagan, Thomas P. ... Carlsbad, CA
Flanagan, Timothy J. ... Denver, CO
Flanagan, Timothy J. ... Brooklyn, NY
Flanagan, Timothy L. ... Jacksonville, FL
Flanagan, Timothy M. ... Cleveland, OH
Flanagan, Vincent J. ... Mineola, NY
Flanagan, Vincent T. ... Glenwood, NJ
Flanagan, W. Joseph ... Boston, MA
Flanagan, Walter D. ... Danbury, CT
Flanagan, William C. ... Springfield, MA
Flanagan, William J. ... Los Angeles, CA
Flanagan, William J. ... Washington, DC
Flanagan, William K., Jr. ... Darien, CT
Flanagan, William P. ... Washington, DC
Flanagan, William Spencer ... El Reno, OK
Flanagan, Wm. W. ... Miami, FL
Flanagin, Margot ... Winnetka, IL
Flanagin, Neil ... Chicago, IL
Flanary, Bill ... Paris, TX
Flanary, C. V. ... Paris, TX
Flanary, Donald H., Jr., (P.C.) ... Dallas, TX
Flanary, Matthew J. ... Milwaukee, WI
Flanary, Stephanie C. ... Gardiner, ME
Flanary, Walker G. ... Charlotte, NC
Flanary, Walker G., III ... Garden City, NY
Flanary-Smith, Amy ... Charlotte, NC
Flancher, Faye M. ... Racine, WI
Flander and Casper, P.C. ... Winterset, IA
Flander, Leonard M. ... Winterset, IA
Flander, Mervin J. ... Carson City, NV
Flander, Susan R. ... Mason City, IA
Flanders, Albert C. ... Boston, MA
Flanders & Associates ... Salt Lake City, UT
Flanders, Brenda L. ... Salt Lake City, UT
Flanders, Catherine M. ... New York, NY
Flanders, Dale C. ... New Bern, NC
Flanders, Darlene Jonelle
San Francisco, CA
Flanders, David A.
House of Representatives,
Congressional Assistants, GV
Flanders, Douglas A. ... Dallas Center, IA
Grimes, IA
Flanders, Dudley D. ... New Orleans, LA
Flanders, Edward ... New York, NY
Flanders, Flanders & Buhrer
New Orleans, LA
Flanders, Gary C. ... Rockford, IL
Flanders, Gilbert L. ... Downey, CA
Flanders, H. Barrett, Jr. ... Morristown, NJ
Flanders, H. Gibbs ... Dublin, GA
Flanders, Harold H. ... Austin, TX
Flanders, Jackson Kent ... Studio City, CA
Flanders, John C. ... Longmont, CO
Flanders, John R. ... Golden, CO
Flanders, Judith J. ... Lakeland, FL
Flanders, L. B. ... Longmont, CO
Flanders, Lew E. ... Redmond, WA
Flanders, Martha J. ... New York, NY
Flanders + Medeiros Inc. ... Providence, RI
Flanders, Richard ... San Leandro, CA
Flanders, Robert G., Jr. ... Providence, RI
Flanders, Scott A. ... Fairfax, VA
Flanders, Steven M. ... Newton, MA
Flanders, Stover, Elsberg & Ellis, LLP
Longmont, CO
Flanders, Susan Brooks ... Hartford, CT
Flanders, T. Wilson ... Northampton, MA
Flandreau, James R. ... Media, PA
Flandrick, J. Robert ... Camarillo, CA
Los Angeles, CA
Flanery, Lori ... Louisville, KY
Flanery, Sharon O. ... Pittsburgh, PA
Flanery de Tichoc, Kara L. ... Pomona, NY
Flangas, Alex J. ... Reno, NV
Flangas, John A. ... Reno, NV
Flangas, Peter L. ... Las Vegas, NV
Flanigan, Daniel J. ... Kansas City, MO
Flanigan, David A., Jr. ... Atlanta, GA
Flanigan, Donald F. ... Portola Valley, CA
Flanigan, Frank L. ... Edwardsville, IL
Flanigan, George M. ... Carthage, MO
Flanigan, James L. ... Morgantown, WV
Flanigan, James Patrick ... Overland Park, KS
Flanigan, James T. ... Indianapolis, IN
Flanigan, Jas. C. ... Denver, CO
Flanigan, Jayne M. ... Okemos, MI
Flanigan, John C. ... Sacramento, CA
Flanigan, John F. ... West Palm Beach, FL
Flanigan, Lasley & Moore, LLP
Carthage, MO
Joplin, MO
Neosho, MO
Flanigan, Laurence H. ... Carthage, MO
Flanigan Law Firm, The ... Sacramento, CA
Flanigan, Maureen A. ... New York, NY
Flanigan, Monica A. ... Denver, CO
Flanigan, Patrick L. ... Portland, TX
Flanigan, Philip M. ... Laguna Hills, CA
Flanigan, Pierce J. ... Pasadena, MD
Flanigan, Richard C. ... Allenhurst, NJ
Flanigan, Ronald J. ... Lexington, MI
Flanigan, Rose M. ... Denver, CO
Flanigan, Susan S. ... Towson, MD
Flanigan, Terrance W. ... Sacramento, CA
Flanigan, Thomas J. ... Atlanta, GA
Flanigan, Timothy H. ... Sacramento, CA
Flanigan, Traver & Emerson
Port Huron, MI
Flanigan, William B. ... Princeton, WV
Flanigon, Thomas S. ... Chicago, IL
Flaniken, Laure V. ... Indianapolis, IN
Flaningam, DeVon W. ... Crawfordsville, IN
Flank, Arnold M. ... Chicago, IL
Flank, Leonard ... Huntsville, AL
Flann, Christopher ... Billings, MT
Flannagan, Barbara Pope ... Richmond, VA
Flannagan, Benjamin C., IV ... Richmond, VA
Flannagan, Charles B., II ... Bristol, VA
Flannagan, Francis W. ... Bristol, VA
Flannagan, John T. ... Kansas City, KS
Flannagan, Mark B. ... Kansas City, MO
Flannagan, Thomas J. ... Danvers, MA
Flannagan, Thomas M. ... Worcester, MA
Flannell, Danny L. ... Sullivan, IL
Flannelly, Michael W. ... York, PA
Flanner-Strack, Mary C. ... Milwaukee, WI
Flannery, Anne C. ... New York, NY
Flannery, Carolyn ... New Martinsville, WV
Flannery, Caryl Lazzaro ... San Diego, CA
Flannery, Christopher P.
Bala Cynwyd, PA
Philadelphia, PA
Flannery, Colin F. ... Norcross, GA
Flannery, Daniel G. ... Wilkes-Barre, PA
Flannery, David M. ... Charleston, WV
Flannery, Deirdre E ... New York, NY
Flannery, Dennis M. ... Washington, DC
Flannery, Ellen J. ... Washington, DC
Flannery, Francis T. ... Akron, OH
Flannery, Francis T. ... Philadelphia, PA
Flannery, Frank T. ... Washington, DC
Flannery, George P. ... Minneapolis, MN
Flannery, Harry A. ... Akron, OH
Flannery, Hoover & Boyd ... Libertyville, IL
Flannery III, William J., P.C. ... Rockwall, TX
Flannery, Irene M.
Federal Communications Commission,
Common Carrier Bureau, GV
Flannery, J. Harold ... Boston, MA
Flannery, James L. ... Lebanon, OH
Flannery, James P.
Federal Deposit Insurance Corporation,
Professional Liability Section, GV
Flannery, James P., Jr. ... Chicago, IL
Flannery, Jennifer Brinkman
Pittsburgh, PA
Flannery, Jo M. ... Seattle, WA
Flannery, John F. ... Chicago, IL
Flannery, John J., Jr. ... Norristown, PA
Flannery, John M. ... Buffalo, NY
Flannery, John M. ... White Plains, NY
Flannery, John P., II ... Leesburg, VA
Flannery, John W. ... New Castle, PA
Flannery, Joseph W. ... Le Mars, IA
Flannery, Kathleen Berwind ... Claremont, CA
Flannery, Kevin M. ... Philadelphia, PA
Flannery, Kyran J., Jr. ... Albany, NY
Flannery, Mark M. ... Peoria, IL
Flannery, Martin J., Jr. ... New York, NY
Flannery, Matthew C. ... Pittsburgh, PA
Flannery, Michael E. ... Elmhurst, IL
Flannery, Michael F. ... Reading, PA
Flannery, Michael J. ... San Diego, CA
Flannery, Patricia M. ... Boston, MA
Flannery, Patrick D. ... Costa Mesa, CA
Flannery, Patrick J. ... Wilkes-Barre, PA
Flannery, Patrick M. ... Covington, KY
Flannery, Paula Doiron ... Bow, NH
Flannery, Richard E. ... New Castle, PA
Flannery, Richard J. ... Philadelphia, PA
Flannery, Robert H. ... San Francisco, CA
Flannery, Robert M. ... New York, NY
Flannery, Roberta Manda
West Hempstead, NY
Flannery, Rosemary M. ... Bryn Mawr, PA
Flannery, Sandra J. ... Los Angeles, CA
Flannery, Sharon M. ... Hartford, CT
Flannery, Susan N. ... New York, NY
Flannery, Thomas A. ...
United States District Court For The District
Of Columbia, GV
Flannery, W. Gerald, Jr.
Fountain Valley, CA
Flannery, William J. ... Harrisburg, PA
Flannery, William J., III ... Rockwall, TX
Flannery, William O. ... Boston, MA
Flannigan, Betty D. ... Excelsior, MN
Flannigan, Corin Marie ... Brighton, CO
Flannigan, Ellen L. ... Chicago, IL
Flannigan, George E. ... Bedford, TX
Flannigan, John Henry ... Chicago, IL
Flannigan, Justin C. ... Binghamton, NY
Flannigan, Kevin M. ... Hanover, MA
Flannigan, Krista R. ... Georgetown, CO
Flannigan, Marjorie ... New York, NY
Flannigan, Michael F. ... Excelsior, MN
Flannigan, Thomas ... Chicago, IL
Flannigan, Thomas W., Law Offices of
Chicago, IL
Flansburg, Elizabeth ... West Des Moines, IA
Flansburg, Kelli J. ... Albany, NY
Flansburg, Ronald D. ... Anchorage, AK
Flansburg, Stephen C. ... Omaha, NE
Flansburg, Steven M. ... Denver, CO
Flanz, Lou Ann ... Houston, TX
Flanzbaum & Cohen ... Somerville, NJ
Warren, NJ
Flanzbaum, Gerald A. ... Warren, NJ
Flanzenbaum, Karen I. ... New York, NY
Flanzig, Cathy ... Mineola, NY
Flanzig, Daniel ... Mineola, NY
Flanzig, Sheldon ... Mineola, NY
Flanzraich, Neil W. ... Palo Alto, CA
Flapan, Valerie ... New York, NY
Flarity, Thomas F. ... Livingston, NJ
Flartey, Roger W. ... New York, NY
Flasch, Donald A. ... Tulsa, OK
Flaschen, Evan D. ... Hartford, CT
Flaschen, Michael Brett ... New York, NY
Flash, Elena Salerno ... Ithaca, NY
Flash, Malcolm H. ... Boston, MA

Flashenberg, Stephen C. ... Boston, MA
Flashman, Irwin H. ... San Juan, PR
Flashman, Jeffrey S. ... Palm Desert, CA
Flashman, Martin E. ... Arcata, CA
Flashman, Stuart M. ... Oakland, CA
Flashner, Barrish K. ... New York, NY
Flask, Anthony P. ... Hampton, NH
Flask, Jon T. ... Vienna, VA
Flaska, Kenneth A. ... Detroit, MI
Flaskamp, Thomas M. ... Minneapolis, MN
Flaskamp, William D. ... Minneapolis, MN
Flaster, Alan S. ... New York, NY
Flaster Koppel & Bates
Fort Lauderdale, FL
Plantation, FL
Flaster, Lawrence M. ... Plantation, FL
Flaster, Lisa C ... Orinda, CA
Flaster, Neal H. ... Livingston, NJ
Flaster, Richard J. ... Cherry Hill, NJ
Flaster/Greenberg, P.C. ... Camden, NJ
Cherry Hill, NJ
Philadelphia, PA
Flatau, William M. ... Macon, GA
Flate, Ronald A. ... Beverly Hills, CA
Flatebo, James R. ... Long Beach, CA
Flateman, Amy Michelle ... New York, NY
Flateman, Bernard I. ... New York, NY
Flaten, Allen J. ... Grand Forks, ND
Flaten, John P. ... Minneapolis, MN
Flatgard, Spencer J. ... Jackson, MS
Flath, Dennis M. ... Lake City, FL
Flather, Frederick, III ... Andover, MA
Flati, Richard A. ... Harrisburg, PA
Flatley, Brian K. ... Raleigh, NC
Flatley, Catherine M.
Department Of Veterans Affairs,
Board of Veterans Appeals, GV
Flatley, Elizabeth Anne ... Santa Ana, CA
Flatley, Ellen ... Gloucester, MA
Flatley, Francis L. ... Manchester, MA
Flatley, James L. ... Chicago, IL
Flatley, Kevin M. ... Boston, MA
Flatley, Lawrence E. ... Pittsburgh, PA
Flatley, Patrick M. ... Wheeling, WV
Flatley, Robert Hugh ... Green Bay, WI
Flatley, Robert R. ... Green Bay, WI
Flaton, Bernard ... Garden City, NY
Flaton-Origenes, Suzanne ... Madison, NJ
Flatow, Gail M. ... Tampa, FL
Flatow, Jonathan A. ... Westport, CT
Flatow, Stephen M. ... Jersey City, NJ
Flatt, Anita Ann ... Hawley, MN
Flatt, David D. ... Sandy Hook, KY
Flatt, Denise F. ... McLean, VA
Flatt, John C. ... Newport Beach, CA
Flatt, Steven L. ... Cookeville, TN
Flatt, Victor B. ... Atlanta, GA
Flatt, W. Lamar ... Columbia, SC
Flatt, William D. ... Atlanta, GA
Flattau, John W. ... New York, NY
Flatten, Daniel V. ... Houston, TX
Flatten, Gary A. ... Burnsville, MN
Flatten, Gerald R. ... Beaumont, TX
Flatter, Linda ... Houston, TX
Flattery, Chris ... Onaga, KS
Flattery, John T. ... Atlanta, GA
Flattery, Joseph ... Fort Dodge, IA
Flattery, Michael P. ... Los Angeles, CA
Flattmann, Gerald J., Jr. ... New York, NY
Flatto, David C. ... New York, NY
Flatts, Barbara A. ... New York, NY
Flattum, David C. ... Costa Mesa, CA
Flattum, Susan P. ... Los Angeles, CA
Flaugh, Perry L. ... South Bend, IN
Flaugher, Robert A. ... Columbus, OH
Charleston, WV
Flaugher, W. Terry, P.C. ... Oklahoma City, OK
Flaugher, William Terry ... Oklahoma City, OK
Flaum, Alison R. ... New York, NY
Flaum, Delilah B. ... Chicago, IL
Flaum, Douglas H. ... New York, NY
Flaum, Gail P. ... Los Angeles, CA
Newport Beach, CA
Flaum, I. Michael ... Albany, NY
Flaum, Joel M. ... Chicago, IL
Flaum, Jonathan I. ... Chicago, IL
Flaum, Joseph D. ... Los Angeles, CA
Flaum, Keith A. ... Palo Alto, CA
Flaum, Mark A. ... Houston, TX
Flaum, Neil R. ... Garden City, NY
Flaum, Richard P. ... Warren, NJ
Flaum & Verdi, P.C. ... Garden City, NY
Flautt and Allen ... New Lexington, OH
Flautt, David E. ... Tunica, MS
Flautt, J. Gordon ... Baltimore, MD
Flautt, Joseph A. ... New Lexington, OH
Flavell, Robert J. ... Duxbury, MA
Flavin, Chester E. ... Springfield, MA
Flavin, Elizabeth ... New York, NY
Flavin, Francis M. ... Anchorage, AK
Flavin, John E. ... Youngstown, OH
Flavin, Mark C. ... New York, NY
Flavin, Michael M. ... St. Louis, MO
Flavin, Paul K. ... Milton, MA
Flavin, Robert S. ... Alton, IL
Flavin, Sean ... Monterey, CA
Flax, David Allen ... Los Alamitos, CA
Flax, David S. ... San Antonio, TX
Flax, Jeffrey C. ... Virginia Beach, VA
Flax, Jerome B. ... East Brunswick, NJ
Flax, Jessica ... Atlanta, GA
Flax, Joseph D. ... Napa, CA
Flax, Karen H. ... Chicago, IL
Flax, Martin I. ... Boston, MA
Flax, Mary Burke, (Mrs.) ... Helena, MT
Flax, Melissa E. ... Roseland, NJ
Flax, Michael ... Columbus, OH
Flax, Mona Schapiro ... Virginia Beach, VA
Flax, Mona Schapiro, Attorney at Law, P.C.
Virginia Beach, VA
Flax, Richard E. ... London, OH
Flax, Richard L. ... Baltimore, MD
Flax, Robert ... Richmond, VA
Flax, Robert J. ... San Mateo, CA
Flax, Samuel A. ... Washington, DC
Flax, Sherry Hamburg ... Baltimore, MD
Flax & Stout ... Richmond, VA
Flax, Susan D. ... Menlo Park, CA
Flax, Wallace H. ... Plainview, NY
Flax, William E. ... Cincinnati, OH
Flax, Zachary David ... New York, NY
Flax-Davidson, Cheryl ... Washington, DC
Flax-Davidson, Ron H. ... New York, NY
Flaxel, Benton C. ... North Bend, OR
Flaxel & Nylander ... North Bend, OR
Flaxer, David ... Orlando, FL
Flaxer, Jonathan L. ... New York, NY
Flaxer, Pauline N. ... Marblehead, MA
Flaxman & Blakely ... Mill Valley, CA
Flaxman, Carrie Y. ... Philadelphia, PA
Flaxman, Charles ... Hollywood, FL
Flaxman, David ... New York, NY
Flaxman, Howard N. ... Arlington, VA
Flaxman, Howard R. ... Philadelphia, PA
Flaxman, Kenneth D. ... Chicago, IL
Flaxman, Kenneth N. ... Chicago, IL
Flaxman, Kenneth N., P.C. ... Chicago, IL
Flaxman, Lisa J. ... Washington, DC
Flaxman & Lopez, P.A. ... Hollywood, FL
Flaxman, Michelle L. ... New York, NY
Flaxman, Neil ... Miami, FL
Flaxman, Neil, Professional Association
Coral Gables, FL
Miami, FL
Flaxman, Paul S. ... Plainview, NY
Flaxman, Peter F. ... Mill Valley, CA
Flaxman, Shirley ... Boston, MA
Flayhart, Martin A. ... Jersey Shore, PA
Flaynik, Donald G., Jr. ... Chicago, IL
Flayton, Donald ... Chicago, IL
Fleagle, Robert A. ... Minneapolis, MN
Flear, Susan E. ... Alpharetta, GA
Fleary, Geo. M. ... Bayside, NY
Flebbe, Diane Raese ... Denver, CO
Flebotte, Daniel R. ... Creedmoor, NC
Durham, NC
Greensboro, NC
Raleigh, NC
Flechas, Eduardo Alberto ... Madison, MS
Flechtner, Harry M. ... Pittsburgh, PA
Fleck, Aaron H. ... Sarasota, FL
Fleck, Ann M. ... Seattle, WA
Fleck, Arnold V. ... Bismarck, ND
Fleck, Charles A. ... Lansing, MI
Fleck, Charles J. ... Chicago, IL
Lake Forest, IL
Fleck, Conrad L. ... Laurel, MD
Fleck, Daniel J. ... Carnegie, PA
Fleck, David H. ... Milwaukee, WI
Fleck, Deborah D. ... Seattle, WA
Fleck, Donald K. ... Seattle, WA
Fleck, Edward A. ... Garden City, NY
Fleck, Erin Patrice ... Bellevue, WA
Fleck, Fleck & Fleck ... Boca Raton, FL
Garden City, NY
Fleck, Geoffrey C. ... Gainesville, FL
Fleck, Harry M. ... Melbourne, FL
Fleck, J. Larry ... Treasury Department,
Office of Thrift Supervision, GV
Fleck, James R. ... Columbia City, IN
Fleck, Jeffrey B. ... Youngstown, OH
Fleck, Jeffrey B., & Associates
Youngstown, OH
Fleck, Jessica Jackson ... Seattle, WA
Fleck, John D. ... St. Clair Shores, MI
Fleck, John P., Jr. ... Bradenton, FL
Fleck, John R. ... Fort Wayne, IN
Fleck, John W. ... Louisville, KY
Fleck, K. Sean ... Noblesville, IN
Fleck, Mary Ellen ... Washington, DC
Fleck, Mary K. ... Seattle, WA
Fleck, Mather & Strutz, Ltd.
Bismarck, ND
Fleck, Melitta ... San Diego, CA
Fleck, Paul A. ... San Antonio, TX
Fleck, Paul P. ... Philadelphia, PA
Fleck, Paul S. ... Cerritos, CA
Fleck, Paula ... Jackson, WY
Fleck, R. Daniel ... Jackson, WY
Fleck, Raymond A., Jr. ... Boca Raton, FL
Garden City, NY
Fleck, Richard T. ... Milwaukee, WI
Fleck, Robert E. ... Cleveland, OH
Fleck, Robin Margaret ... Dallas, TX
Fleck, Rynold C. ... Seattle, WA
Fleck, Sheldon T. ... Minneapolis, MN
Fleck, Stephen W. ... Louisville, KY
Fleck, William A. ... Jupiter, FL
Fleck-Daneri, Patricia A. ... Garden City, NY
Flecke, J. Bradford ... Evanston, IL
Fleckenstein, Edmund A., Jr. ... Oradell, NJ
Fleckenstein, James B. ... Syracuse, NY
Fleckenstein, Mark A. ... Richmond, VA
Fleckenstein, Robert O. ... New York, NY
Fleckenstein, Thomas J. ... Annapolis, MD
Fleckinger, Clark U., II ... Silver Spring, MD
Fleckman, Dan A. ... Houston, TX
Fleckman & McGlynn ... Austin, TX
Fleckman, Steven A. ... Austin, TX
Fleckner, James O. ... Boston, MA
Fleckner, Magda L. ... Boston, MA
Fleckner, Sarah K. ... Boston, MA
Fledderman, Anne M. ... Cincinnati, OH
Fledderman, H. L. ... Orinda, CA
Fleddermann, Stephen R. ... St. Charles, MO
Fleder, John R. ... Washington, DC
Fleder, Lawrence E. ... Norfolk, VA
Fleder, Mark L. ... Roseland, NJ
Fleder, Robert C. ... New York, NY
Fleece, Jonathan D. ... St. Louis, MO
Fleece, Joseph W. ... St. Petersburg, FL
Fleece, Joseph W., III ... St. Petersburg, FL
Fleece, Steven M. ... Jeffersonville, IN
Fleece, William H. ... Clearwater, FL
Fleegle, Mark C. ... Zanesville, OH
Fleeker, Linda J. ... Manhattan, KS
Fleeman, M. Grace ... Treasury Department,
Internal Revenue Service, GV
Fleeman, Tyrone G. ... Kalamazoo, MI
Fleener, Candace P. ... Atlanta, GA
Fleener, Janlynn R. ... Denver, CO
Fleener, Michael A. ... Indianapolis, IN
Fleener, William Joseph, Jr. ... Lansing, MI
Fleenor, David E. ... Lexington, KY
Fleenor, J. Robert ... Birmingham, AL
Fleenor, James Earnest, Jr.
Birmingham, AL
Fleenor, K. Mike, Jr. ... Pulaski, VA
Fleenor, Phillip E. ... Chattanooga, TN
Fleenor, Stacey S. ... Birmingham, AL
Fleer, Daugherty & Loftis
San Francisco, CA
Orinda, CA
Fleer, John L. ... Orinda, CA
Fleer, Keith G. ... Los Angeles, CA
Fleesler, Gregory J. ... New York, NY
Fleeson, Gooing, Coulson & Kitch, L.L.C.
Wichita, KS
Fleet, Brad Steven ... Miami Beach, FL
Fleet, Brad Steven, P.A. ... Miami, FL
Miami Beach, FL
Fleet, Charles F. ... Memphis, TN
Fleet, David Emory ... Shalimar, FL
Fleet, Erwin ... Shalimar, FL
Fleet, H. Bart ... Fort Walton Beach, FL
Fleet, J. Leonard ... Fort Lauderdale, FL
Fleet, Leslie G. ... Washington, DC
Fleetham, Brian S. ... Grand Rapids, MI
Fleetham, Eric C. ... Grand Rapids, MI
Fleetwood, Bradford S.
Board of Governors Of The Federal Reserve
System,
Office of the General Counsel, GV
Fleetwood, Eric J. ... Los Angeles, CA
Fleetwood, Glen S. ... Woodland Hills, CA
Fleetwood, Judy Lynn ... Oklahoma City, OK
Fleetwood, Martha ... San Francisco, CA
Fleetwood, Patricia Kelley ... Warren, NJ
Fleetwood, Robert M. ... Chicago, IL
Fleetwood, Wilson C., Jr. ... Selma, NC
Fleg, Richard A. ... Los Angeles, CA
Flegal & Associates, P.A. ... Concord, NH
Nashua, NH
Flegal, H. Scott ... Nashua, NH
Flegel, Ann ... San Jose, CA
Flegel, John L. ... Menlo Park, CA
Flegelman, Harold A. ... New York, NY
Flegenheimer, Barry L. ... Seattle, WA
Flegle, Jim L. ... Dallas, TX
Flegm, Stanley E. ... Bucyrus, OH
Fleharty, Bartley S. ... Redding, CA
Flehinger, Kurt ... New York, NY
Flehr Hohbach Test Albritton & Herbert LLP ... Oakland, CA
Palo Alto, CA
San Francisco, CA
Walnut Creek, CA
Fleig, Susan Findling, Law Office of
Washington, DC
Fleig, Susan Findling, Law Office of
Chevy Chase, MD
Fleig, Val J. ... Petersburg, IN
Fleischaker, David S. ... Oklahoma City, OK
Fleischaker, James B. ... Joplin, MO
Fleischaker, Jon L. ... Louisville, KY
Fleischaker, Joseph ... Chicago, IL
Fleischaker, Marc L. ... Washington, DC
Fleischaker, William J. ... Joplin, MO
Fleischauer, Emil, Jr. ... Stevens Point, WI
Fleischauer, J. Eric ... Mansfield, OH
Fleischauer, Marc L. ... Columbus, OH
Fleischauer, Mark A. ... Vancouver, WA
Fleischer, Adam H. ... Chicago, IL
Fleischer, Alan G. ... Richmond, VA
Fleischer, Alfred E., Jr. ... Port St. Lucie, FL
Fleischer, Arnold D. ... New York, NY
Fleischer, Arthur, Jr. (P.C.) ... New York, NY
Fleischer, Bonnie M. ... Reno, NV
Reno, NV
Fleischer, Brian ... New York, NY
Fleischer, Bruce D. ... State College, PA
Fleischer, Cary S. ... Chicago, IL
Fleischer, Charles H. ... Bethesda, MD
Fleischer, David ... New York, NY
Fleischer, David A.
National Labor Relations Board,
Office of the General Counsel, GV
Fleischer, Deborah J. ... Somerville, NJ
Fleischer, Edward Charles ... Lynbrook, NY
Fleischer, Elizabeth B. ... New York, NY
Fleischer, Ernest M. ... Kansas City, MO
Fleischer, Fleischer & Lainer ... Somerville, NJ
Fleischer, Frank N. ... Tampa, FL
Fleischer, Gilbert S. ... Rockville Centre, NY
Fleischer, Henry ... Rochester, NY
Fleischer, Hugh W. ... Anchorage, AK
Fleischer, Ilisa T. ... New York, NY
Fleischer, James S., (P.C.)
Washington, DC
Fleischer, Janice M. ... Miami, FL
Fleischer, Kenneth J. ... Chicago, IL
Fleischer, Kimberly V. ... Walnut Creek, CA
Fleischer, L. Melissa ... New York, NY
Fleischer, Larry L. ... Chicago, IL
Fleischer, Lawrence Marc ... New York, NY
Fleischer, Lisa Kolman ... Voorhees, NJ
Fleischer, Mark ... Los Angeles, CA
Fleischer, Martha H. ... Buffalo, NY
Fleischer, Michael A. ... New York, NY
Fleischer, Michael L. ... New York, NY
Fleischer, Myra Chack ... San Diego, CA
Fleischer, Paul G. ... Somerville, NJ
Fleischer, Randy A. ... Davie, FL
Fleischer, Randy A., P.A. ... Davie, FL
Fleischer, Richard D., (Ltd.) ... Reno, NV
Fleischer, Richard E. ... Somerville, NJ
Fleischer, Richard I. ... Cincinnati, OH
Fleischer, Robert M. ... Norwalk, CT
Fleischer, Roy J. ... Sacramento, CA
Fleischer, S. Hollis ... Washington, DC
Fleischer, Steven D. ... Kings Point, NY
Fleischer, Steven M. ... Somerville, NJ
Fleischer, T. Lynn ... Encino, CA
Fleischer, Theodore E. ... Anchorage, AK
Fleischer, Thomas E. ... Worcester, MA
Fleischer, Walter H. ... Washington, DC
Fleischer, Walter J., Jr. ... Florham Park, NJ
Fleischhacker, Ray J. ... Brooklyn, NY
Fleischhauer, Gene D. ... East Hartford, CT
Fleischhauer, Jeffrey A. ... Roanoke, VA
Fleischhauer, Jeffrey A., P.C.
Christiansburg, VA
Lynchburg, VA
Roanoke, VA
Fleischhauer, Randall ... Mesa, AZ
Fleischli, George R. ... Madison, WI
Fleischli, Steven E. ... Santa Monica, CA
Fleischman, Aaron I. ... Washington, DC
Fleischman, Andrew M. ... Louisville, KY
Fleischman, Bernard ... Chicago, IL
Fleischman & Corenthal ... New York, NY
Fleischman, Dana G. ... New York, NY
Fleischman, Edward H. ... New York, NY
Fleischman, Gail Robin ... New York, NY
Fleischman, Gerald M. ... Middle Village, NY
Fleischman, Grace S. ... Port Washington, NY
Fleischman, Harold S. ... Encino, CA
Fleischman, Herman Israel ... Merrick, NY
Fleischman, Howard S. ... New York, NY
Fleischman, Jay S. ... Great Neck, NY
Fleischman, Jeffrey A. ... Mineola, NY
Fleischman, Jerome B. ... Long Beach, NY
Fleischman, Jerome P. ... Santa Monica, CA
Fleischman, Joseph J. ... Somerville, NJ
Fleischman, Keith M. ... New York, NY
Fleischman, Lawrence H. ... Tucson, AZ
Fleischman, Lisa M. ... Brooklyn, NY
Fleischman, Marc E. ... Santa Barbara, CA
Fleischman Minker & Lopez ... Tucson, AZ
Fleischman, Peter N. ... New York, NY
Fleischman, Richard A. ... Denver, CO
Fleischman, Robert L. ... San Francisco, CA
Fleischman, Robert M. ... Philadelphia, PA
Fleischman, Robert P. ... New York, NY
Fleischman, Steven S. ... Los Angeles, CA
Fleischman and Walsh, L.L.P.
Washington, DC
Fleischman, William O. ... Los Angeles, CA
Fleischmann, Adelbert ... Buffalo, NY
Fleischmann, Amy ... Atlanta, GA
Fleischmann, Arnold ... Towson, MD
Fleischmann, Arnold, P.A. ... Towson, MD
Fleischmann, Brenda M.
Chattanooga, TN
Fleischmann, Charles J. ... Chattanooga, TN
Fleischmann, Charles W. ... Westport, CT
Fleischmann, Craig J. ... Blue Bell, PA
Fleischmann, Darlene A. ... Owings Mills, MD
Fleischmann, Dennis C. ... New York, NY
Fleischmann, Edwin R., Jr. ... Metairie, LA
Fleischmann, Eric ... Hartford, CT
Fleischmann and Fleischmann
Chattanooga, TN
Fleischmann, Frank A. ... East Lansing, MI
Fleischmann, Hartly ... San Francisco, CA
Fleischmann, Karl ... Hartford, CT
Fleischmann, Karl, P.C. ... Hartford, CT
Fleischmann, Kenneth E. ... St. Louis, MO
Fleischmann, Pamela ... Miami, FL
Fleischmann, Roger Justice, Law Offices of
San Francisco, CA
Fleischmann, Samuel J.
Redwood City, CA
Fleischmann, Stuart K. ... New York, NY
Fleischmann, Thomas J., & Associates
Chicago, IL
St. Charles, IL
Fleischmann-Fellowes, Dagmar
Glenview, IL
Fleischner, Benjamin A. ... Red Bank, NJ
New York, NY
Fleischner, Cecelia A. ... Denver, CO
Fleischner, Jeffrey C. ... Denver, CO
Fleischner, Robert D. ... Northampton, MA
Fleischner, Robin A. ... New York, NY
Fleischner, Warren E. ... Wooster, OH
Fleischut, Christopher J. ... Palo Alto, CA
Fleischut, Gretchen M. ... Kansas City, MO
Fleischut, Paul I. J. ... St. Louis, MO
Fleishacker, Alan ... Houston, TX
Fleishaker, Aaron J. ... New York, NY
Fleishaker, Donald J. ... New York, NY
Fleishauer, Frederic W. ... Stevens Point, WI
Fleishell, J. Edw. ... San Francisco, CA
Fleishell, Thomas S. ... New York, NY
Fleisher, Andrew D. ... Fort Lauderdale, FL
Fleisher, Barry C. ... Davie, FL
Fleisher, Cary B. ... Blue Bell, PA
Fleisher, Cary L. ... Greenwich, CT
Fleisher, David Lee, Jr. ... St. Peters, MO
Fleisher, Deborah ... Philadelphia, PA
Fleisher, Douglas J. ... North Bergen, NJ

Fleisher, Hilda W. .... Manchester, NH
Fleisher, James P. .... Dayton, OH
Fleisher, Jay .... Tampa, FL
Fleisher, Jonathan B. .... Chicago, IL
Fleisher, Kenneth J. .... Philadelphia, PA
Fleisher, Leslie .... Philadelphia, PA
Fleisher, Louis .... Birmingham, AL
Fleisher, Lynn D. .... Chicago, IL
Fleisher, Mark E. .... Palo Alto, CA
Fleisher, Marshall A., Law Office of
Philadelphia, PA
Fleisher, Martha Ratnoff .... Dallas, TX
Fleisher, Martin .... Springfield, MA
Worcester, MA
New York, NY
Fleisher, Martin M. .... San Francisco, CA
Fleisher, Neil .... San Juan, PR
Fleisher, Norman .... Miami, FL
Fleisher, Richard S. .... Chicago, IL
Fleisher, Risselle Rosenthal .... Baltimore, MD
Fleisher, Ronald G. .... Chicago, IL
Fleisher, Roslyn .... Bridgeport, CT
Fleisher, Steven M. .... San Francisco, CA
Fleisher, Stewart W. .... Denver, CO
Fleishhacker, Ellen Kaye .... San Francisco, CA
Fleishhacker, William M.
San Francisco, CA
Fleishman, A. Craig .... Denver, CO
Fleishman, Amy T. .... Los Angeles, CA
Fleishman, Barry J. .... Washington, DC
Fleishman, Beth R. .... Raleigh, NC
Fleishman, Beverly A. .... La Crosse, WI
Fleishman, Bobette .... Westlake Village, CA
Fleishman, Charles J. .... Beverly Hills, CA
Fleishman, Charles J., P.C.
Beverly Hills, CA
Los Angeles, CA
Fleishman, David M. .... Paso Robles, CA
Fleishman, David M. .... Baltimore, MD
Fleishman, Fisher & Moest
Los Angeles, CA
Fleishman, Harvey R. .... Cambridge, MA
Fleishman, Howard S. .... Chicago, IL
Fleishman, Irving .... Lanham, MD
Fleishman, Jason Theodore .... Tuscaloosa, AL
Fleishman, Joel L. .... Durham, NC
Fleishman, Joel M. .... Northfield, NJ
Fleishman, Lana C. .... New York, NY
Fleishman, Leon .... Montebello, CA
Fleishman, Lori Farris .... Knoxville, TN
Fleishman, Michael M. .... Louisville, KY
Fleishman, Michael R. .... New York, NY
Fleishman, Michelle Viola .... Newark, NJ
Fleishman, Neill H. .... Richardson, TX
Fleishman, Rachel S. .... New York, NY
Fleishman, Robert S. .... Baltimore, MD
Fleishman, Robert W. .... Washington, DC
Fleishman, Shari L. .... Washington, DC
Fleishman, Sheldon J. .... New York, NY
Fleishman, Stanley .... Los Angeles, CA
Fleishman, Stephen M., (P.C.)
Los Angeles, CA
Fleishman, Sterling, Gregory & Shapiro, P.C. .... Denver, CO
Fleishman, Susan E.
House of Representatives,
Office of Legislative Counsel, GV
Fleishman, Wendy .... Riverwoods, IL
Fleishman, Wendy R. .... New York, NY
Fleisig, Brian E. .... Hackensack, NJ
Fleisig, David H. .... San Francisco, CA
Fleisig & Gavlick .... Providence, RI
Fleisig, Leonard L. .... Washington, DC
Fleisig, Samuel M. .... Providence, RI
Fleisig, Vina .... Forest Hills, NY
Fleiss, Michael E. .... New York, NY
Fleiss, Vicki Share .... Basking Ridge, NJ
Fleissig, Audrey Goldstein .... St. Louis, MO
Fleissig, David A. .... New York, NY
Fleissig, Steven D. .... Roseland, NJ
Fleissner, Michael J. .... Milwaukee, WI
Fleissner, Phillip A. .... Chattanooga, TN
Fleissner, Phillip A., PLLC
Chattanooga, TN
Fleissner, Pierre D. .... Lake Oswego, OR
Fleit, Martin .... Washington, DC
Miami, FL
Fleit, Martin, P.A. .... Miami, FL
Fleitas, Gilbert .... New York, NY
Fleitas, Roberto F., Jr. .... Miami, FL
Fleitman, Peter S. .... Tallahassee, FL
Fleitz, Brett R. .... Indianapolis, IN
Flemenbaum, Arieh M. .... Chicago, IL
Flemer, Lawrence A. .... Cincinnati, OH
Fleming, Alan R. .... Davenport, IA
Fleming, Alfred J. .... Youngstown, OH
Fleming, Alfred J., Co., L.P.A.
Youngstown, OH
Fleming & Allen, L.L.P. .... Irvine, CA
Fleming, Andrew P. .... Blasdell, NY
Fleming, Angel L. .... Miami, FL
Fleming, Anne Delaney .... Jackson, MI
Fleming, Anthony C. .... Jacksonville, FL
Fleming & Associates, L.L.P.
Houston, TX
Fleming, Barry A., (P.C.) .... Augusta, GA
Fleming, Beth Stern .... Cherry Hill, NJ
Philadelphia, PA
Fleming, Bill A. .... St. Augustine, FL
Fleming, Blanchard, Jackson & Durham, A Professional Corporation .... Appling, GA
Atlanta, GA
Augusta, GA
Aiken, SC
Fleming, Bonnie M. .... Minneapolis, MN
Fleming, Brian R. .... Paducah, KY
Fleming, Bruce D. .... Council Bluffs, IA
Fleming, Bruce W. .... Baltimore, MD
Fleming, C. A., III .... Metairie, LA
Fleming, Calvin A., III .... Lafitte, LA
Fleming, Carey William .... Washington, DC
Fleming, Carlton A., Jr. .... Tifton, GA
Fleming, Carol M. .... Warren, MI
Fleming, Carolyn A.
Federal Communications Commission,
Cable Services Bureau, GV
Fleming, Cathy .... New York, NY
Fleming, Charles J. .... Mobile, AL
Fleming, Charles W. .... Cleveland, OH
Fleming, Charles W., Jr. .... Geneva, AL
Fleming, Chester A. .... Eudora, KS
Fleming, Christina V. .... Los Angeles, CA
Fleming, Christopher M. .... Greensburg, PA
Fleming, Christopher T. .... Washington, DC
Fleming, Clarence E., Jr. .... Pasadena, CA
Fleming, Clarence J. .... Hilton Head Island, SC
Fleming, Clark M. .... Laguna Niguel, CA
Fleming, Colleen M. .... Milwaukee, WI
Fleming & Curti .... Tucson, AZ
Fleming, Curtis L. .... Lamar, CO
Fleming, Dalby .... San Antonio, TX
Fleming, Daniel C. .... Edison, NJ
Philadelphia, PA
Fleming, Daniel E., III
Hoffman Estates, IL
Fleming, Daniel J. .... Tampa, FL
Fleming, Daniel J. .... Novi, MI
Fleming, David E. .... Stamford, CT
Fleming, David J. .... Santa Monica, CA
Fleming, David J. .... Garden City, NY
Fleming, David P. .... Arlington, VA
Fleming, David S. .... Chicago, IL
Fleming, David W. .... Indian Wells, CA
Los Angeles, CA
Fleming, David W., P.C. .... Indian Wells, CA
Fleming, Dawn D. .... Newport Beach, CA
Fleming, Dean V. .... San Antonio, TX
Fleming, Deborah A. .... Tampa, FL
Fleming, DeHaven W. .... Boca Raton, FL
Fleming, Denis B., Jr. .... Louisville, KY
Fleming, Dennis M. .... Chicago, IL
Fleming, Donald D. .... Bellevue, WA
Fleming, Donald D., P.S. .... Bellevue, WA
Fleming, Donald J. .... Mattapoisett, MA
Fleming, Donald J. .... Houston, TX
Fleming, Douglas A. .... Boston, MA
Fleming, Douglas E., III .... New York, NY
Fleming, Douglas H. .... Seattle, WA
Fleming, Douglas L., Jr. .... Leesburg, VA
Fleming, DuBois & Trenbeath .... Cavalier, ND
Fleming, Edmund E. .... Newburyport, MA
Fleming, Edward L. .... Downers Grove, IL
Fleming, Edward P., (P.A.) .... Pensacola, FL
Fleming, Edwin D. .... Phoenix, AZ
Fleming, Eli W. .... Beltsville, MD
Ellicott City, MD
Fleming, Emmett L., Jr. .... Fredericksburg, VA
Fleming, Erika M. .... Los Angeles, CA
Fleming, Erin E. .... Raleigh, NC
Fleming & Fleming .... O'Fallon, IL
Fleming & Fleming, P.C. .... Jackson, MI
Fleming, Fletcher .... Pensacola, FL
Fleming, Francis G., Jr. .... New York, NY
Fleming, Francis J. .... Santa Ana, CA
Fleming, Frank C. .... Dallas, TX
Fleming, Frank R., III .... Pittsburgh, PA
Fleming, Frank R., III, P.C.
Pittsburgh, PA
Fleming, Frederick A. .... St. Paul, MN
Fleming, Frederick J. .... Los Angeles, CA
Fleming, Frederick W. .... Tacoma, WA
Fleming, G. Thomas, III .... Los Angeles, CA
Fleming and Galat .... Newburyport, MA
Fleming, Gary L. .... Lakewood, CO
Fleming, Gary W. .... Sedalia, MO
Fleming, George M. .... Houston, TX
Fleming, George R. .... Clarksville, TN
Fleming, George R., Jr. .... Clarksville, TN
Fleming, Gerald B. .... Treasury Department,
Internal Revenue Service, GV
Fleming, Graham K. .... Escondido, CA
Fleming, Grant H. .... State College, PA
Fleming, Gregory C. .... Chesapeake, VA
Fleming, Gregory James .... New York, NY
Fleming, Haile & Shaw, P.A.
North Palm Beach, FL
Palm Beach, FL
Fleming, Harry F. .... Detroit, MI
Fleming, Holloway & Flynn, P.C.
Columbia, TN
Fleming, Horstmeyer & Fleming
Lexington, KY
Fleming, Hoyt A., III .... Boise, ID
Fleming & Ishihara, P.C. .... Mattapoisett, MA
Fleming, J. Carlton .... Charlotte, NC
Fleming, J. Clifton, Jr. .... Provo, UT
Fleming, J. Patrick, Jr. .... Los Angeles, CA
Newport Beach, CA
Fleming, J. S. Lucas, P.A.
St. Petersburg, FL
Fleming, J. William .... Shreveport, LA
Fleming, Jack W. .... Irvine, CA
Fleming, James A. .... Huntsville, AL
Fleming, James A. .... Atlanta, GA
Fleming, James B. .... Jackson, MI
Fleming, James B. .... Monticello, MN
Fleming, James C., P.C. .... Atlanta, GA
Fleming, James Conner .... Bismarck, ND
Fleming, James D. .... Portland, OR
Fleming, James E. .... New York, NY
Fleming, James G. .... Jackson, MI
Fleming, James H. .... Walnut Creek, CA
Fleming, James J. .... Londonderry, NH
Fleming, James M. .... Salem, VA
Fleming, James R. .... Coal City, IL
Fleming, James R. .... Kokomo, IN
Fleming, Jason Shea .... Hopkinsville, KY
Fleming, J. D., Jr. .... Atlanta, GA
Fleming, Jeffrey E. .... Olney, IL
Fleming, Jeffrey M. .... Orlando, FL
Fleming, Jennifer A. Lesny
Cleveland, OH
Fleming, Jerry W. .... Fairfield Bay, AR
Fleming, Jo A. .... Baton Rouge, LA
Fleming, Joan M. .... Chicago, IL
Fleming, Joe W., II (P.C.) .... Washington, DC
Fleming, John .... Augusta, GA
Fleming, John .... Bloomfield Hills, MI
Fleming, John B., Jr. .... Rocky Mount, NC
Fleming, John C. .... Feasterville, PA
Fleming, John C. .... Austin, TX
Fleming, John C., Jr. .... New York, NY
Fleming, John F. .... Fraser, MI
Fleming, John H. .... Atlanta, GA
Fleming, John J., Jr. .... Montrose, CO
Fleming, John N. .... Asheville, NC
Fleming, John P. .... Portola Valley, CA
Fleming, John P. .... Peoria, IL
Fleming, John W. .... Fort Lauderdale, FL
Fleming, John W. .... Pensacola, FL
Fleming, Jonathan W. .... United States Senate,
Senatorial Assistants, GV
Fleming, Joseph .... New York, NY
Fleming, Joseph D. .... Chicago, IL
Fleming, Joseph M. .... Palm Beach, FL
Fleming, Joseph P. .... Trenton, NJ
Fleming, Joseph R. .... Boston, MA
Fleming, Joseph V. .... Staten Island, NY
Fleming, Joseph Z. .... Miami, FL
Tampa, FL
Fleming, Joseph Z., P.A. .... Miami, FL
Fleming, Joshua M.
North Palm Beach, FL
Palm Beach, FL
Fleming, Joycelyn L. .... Atlanta, GA
Fleming, J. S. Lucas .... St. Petersburg, FL
Fleming, Julie .... Los Angeles, CA
Fleming, Julie A. .... Atlanta, GA
Fleming, Juliet Suzanne .... Birmingham, AL
Fleming, Kara C. .... Roswell, GA
Fleming, Karen L. .... Trevose, PA
Fleming, Kate M. .... Milwaukee, WI
Fleming, Kathleen E. .... New Hyde Park, NY
Fleming, Kent .... Chickasha, OK
Oklahoma City, OK
Fleming, Kermin (Ike) E. .... Lexington, KY
Fleming, Kevin J. .... Boston, MA
Fleming, Kim E. .... Whitefish, MT
Fleming, Kyle B. .... Cleveland, OH
Fleming, Kyra M. .... Dayton, OH
Fleming, L. Patrick, Jr. .... Wilson, NC
Fleming, L. Timothy .... Phoenix, AZ
Fleming, La Shon Yvette .... Dallas, TX
Fleming & Langlois .... Quincy, MA
Fleming, Laurel L. .... Chicago, IL
Fleming, Laurence P., II .... Hartford, CT
Fleming, Lawrence J. .... Phoenix, AZ
Fleming, Leslie L. .... Northridge, CA
Fleming, Leslie W. .... Bingham Farms, MI
Fleming, Linda D. .... Boise, ID
Fleming, Linda K. .... Cleveland, OH
Fleming, Linda L. .... Tampa, FL
Fleming, Linda P. .... Washington, DC
Fleming, Linda Rovder .... Johnstown, PA
Fleming, Lisa L. .... Cincinnati, OH
Fleming, Lisa M. .... Boston, MA
Fleming, M. Alex .... Louisville, KY
Fleming, M. Lisa .... Baltimore, MD
Fleming, M. Michele .... Cincinnati, OH
Fleming, Macklin .... Los Angeles, CA
Fleming and MacLeod, P.C.
Londonderry, NH
Fleming, Marcella R. .... Seattle, WA
Fleming, Margaret L. .... Montgomery, AL
Fleming, Margaret M. .... Martinez, CA
Fleming, Marian V. .... Timonium, MD
Fleming, Marie S. .... Savannah, GA
Fleming, Marion Lucas .... St. Petersburg, FL
Fleming, Mark F. .... San Diego, CA
Fleming, Mark J. .... Trenton, NJ
Fleming, Mark L. .... Seattle, WA
Fleming, Mary .... Newark, OH
Fleming, Mary A. .... Woodstock, IL
Fleming, Mary Kay .... Indianapolis, IN
Fleming, Mary L. .... Fairport, NY
Fleming, Mary P. .... Buffalo, NY
Fleming, Matthew Wood .... Fort Smith, AR
Fleming, Maura A. .... New York, NY
Fleming, Messman & O'Connor
Bloomington, IL
Fleming, Michael A. .... Detroit, MI
Fleming, Michael A. .... New York, NY
Fleming, Michael A. .... Philadelphia, PA
Fleming, Michael A., (P.C.) .... Peoria, IL
Fleming, Michael C. .... White Bear Lake, MN
Fleming, Michael E. .... Indianapolis, IN
Fleming, Michael F. .... Minnetonka, MN
Fleming, Michael M. .... Seattle, WA
Fleming, Michael P. .... Washington, DC
Fleming, Michael P. .... Houston, TX
Fleming, Michael R.
Department of Commerce,
Patent and Trademark Office, GV
Fleming, Michael W. .... Washington, DC
Fleming, Michael W.
Whitehouse Station, NJ
Fleming, Michele M. .... New York, NY
Fleming, Michele M. .... New York, NY
Fleming & Miranda .... Wakefield, MA
Fleming, Miriam S. .... Milwaukee, WI
Fleming, Natalie Amann .... Philadelphia, PA
Fleming, Neil W. .... Cavalier, ND
Fleming, Noel C. .... Madison, NJ
Fleming, Norman J. .... New Haven, CT
Fleming, O'Bryan & Fleming, A Professional Association .... Fort Lauderdale, FL
Fleming & Olvera, P.C. .... Brownsville, TX
Fleming & O'Neill, P.C. .... Boston, MA
Fleming, P. Andrew .... Chicago, IL
Fleming, Pamela R. .... Los Angeles, CA
Fleming, Patrice R. .... Austin, TX
Fleming, Patricia E. .... Murray Hill, NJ
Fleming, Patrick J. .... Weatherford, TX
Fleming, Patrick T. .... Butte, MT
Fleming, Pattridge & Runnerstrom, P.C.
Golden, CO
Fleming, Pearce W. .... Columbia, SC
Fleming, Peter C. .... Denver, CO
Fleming, Peter C. .... Washington, DC
Fleming, Peter E., III .... Stamford, CT
Fleming, Peter E., Jr. .... New York, NY
Fleming, Philip A. .... Washington, DC
Fleming & Phillips, LLP
Walnut Creek, CA
Fleming, Porter F. .... New York, NY
Fleming, R. Robert .... Ocean City, NJ
Fleming, Randy K. .... Portage, IN
Fleming & Ray .... Atlanta, GA
Fleming, Raymond J. .... West Orange, NJ
Fleming, Richard A. .... Anaheim, CA
Fleming, Richard N. .... Santa Ana, CA
Fleming, Richard N., P.C. .... Santa Ana, CA
Fleming, Richard W. .... La Jolla, CA
Fleming, Rick A. .... Topeka, KS
Fleming, Rickie Alexander .... Topeka, KS
Fleming, Robben W. .... Ann Arbor, MI
Fleming, Robert A. .... Geneva, IL
Fleming, Robert Alex .... San Juan, PR
Fleming, Robert B. .... Tucson, AZ
Fleming, Robert B. .... Buffalo, NY
Fleming, Robert B., Jr. .... Buffalo, NY
Fleming, Robert E. .... Louisville, KY
Fleming, Robert F. .... Henderson, NC
Fleming, Robert F., Jr. .... Covington, LA
Metairie, LA
Fleming, Robert F., Jr. .... New Orleans, LA
Fleming, Robert G. .... Golden, CO
Fleming, Robert G. .... Southfield, MI
Fleming, Robert J. .... Quincy, MA
Fleming, Robert L. .... Sedalia, MO
Fleming, Robert L. .... Dallas, PA
Fleming, Robert M. .... Franklin, LA
Fleming, Robert O., Jr. .... Atlanta, GA
Fleming, Robert T. .... Bloomington, IL
Fleming, Robert W. .... Lexington, KY
Fleming, Ronald A., Jr. .... New York, NY
Fleming, Ronald G. .... Houston, TX
Fleming & Rosamond, L.L.P. .... Metairie, LA
Fleming, Rose Ann .... Cincinnati, OH
Fleming, Rose Ann, Professoinal Corporation
Cincinnati, OH
Fleming, Roth & Fettweis .... Newark, NJ
Fleming, Russell J. .... Wakefield, MA
Fleming, Sally Dunlap .... New Orleans, LA
Fleming, Scott .... Berkeley, CA
Fleming, Scott A. .... San Diego, CA
Fleming, Scott B. .... Milwaukee, WI
Fleming, Scott D. .... Las Vegas, NV
Fleming, Scott D. .... New York, NY
Fleming, Scott T. .... Salt Lake City, UT
Fleming, Sharon J. .... Albuquerque, NM
Fleming, Sheldon J. .... Irvine, CA
Fleming, Stacey M. .... Garden City, NY
Fleming, Susan A. .... Mount Laurel, NJ
Fleming, T. Clifford .... Merrillville, IN
Valparaiso, IN
Fleming, Tamara Allen .... Mocksville, NC
Fleming, Teresa V. .... Detroit, MI
Fleming, Terrance J.
Department of Transportation,
Surface Transportation Board, GV
Fleming, Terrence J. .... Minneapolis, MN
Fleming, Terry K. .... Fort Worth, TX
Fleming, Thomas F. .... New York, NY
Fleming, Thomas J. .... New York, NY
Fleming, Thomas M. .... Rochester, NY
Fleming, Thomas Mills .... Savannah, GA
Fleming, Thomas P. .... Purchase, NY
Fleming, Timothy L. .... Nampa, ID
Fleming, Timothy P. .... O'Fallon, IL
Fleming, Timothy W. .... Mobile, AL
Fleming, Tom .... Brownsville, TX
Fleming, Victor A. .... Little Rock, AR
Fleming & Vorndran, L.L.C. .... Denver, CO
Fleming, Wendell C. .... Denver, CO
Fleming, Wendy A. .... Cherry Hill, NJ
Philadelphia, PA
Fleming, Whitney Jade .... Austin, TX
Fleming, William B. .... New York, NY
Fleming, William C., Jr. .... Durham, NC
Fleming, William E. .... Naperville, IL
Fleming, William H. .... Cleveland, OH
Fleming, William J. .... East Hampton, NY
Fleming, William L. .... Seattle, WA
Fleming, William N. .... Lawrence, KS
Fleming, William R. .... Boise, ID
Fleming, William R. .... Pittsburgh, PA
Fleming, William S. .... Columbia, TN
Fleming, William T. .... Decatur, GA
Fleming, William T. .... Bellefonte, PA
State College, PA
Fleming, William T., Jr. .... Bryan, TX
Fleming, Willie C. .... Louisville, KY
Fleming, Wm. G. .... North Little Rock, AR
Fleming, Wm. M., Jr. .... Augusta, GA
Fleming-Campbell, Rachel D.
New York, NY
Fleminger, Pauline S. .... Phoenix, AZ
Fleminger, Pauline S., P.C. .... Phoenix, AZ
Fleming-Hughes, David C.
Corpus Christi, TX
Flemings, Tracey E. .... New Orleans, LA

Fliegel, Frederick M. ... Spokane, WA
Fliegel, J. F., Jr. ... Medford, OR
Fliegel, L. Barry ... New York, NY
Fliegel, Lester ... Iselin, NJ
Fliegel, Mary M. ... Tucson, AZ
Fliegel, Melvyn B. ... Los Angeles, CA
Fliegel, Michele L. ... New York, NY
Fliegel, Rod M. ... San Francisco, CA
Fliegelman, Amy M. ... Boca Raton, FL
Fliegelman, Debora C. ... Philadelphia, PA
Fliegelman, Hal ... Norristown, PA
Fliegelman, William ... Bronx, NY
Fliegelman-Olli, Amy M. ... Somers, NY
Fliehler, Schloss & Compton
Strawberry Point, IA
Fliehman, Dennis W. ... Lansing, MI
Flier, Richard S. ... Martinez, CA
Flier, Theodore S. ... Encino, CA
Flierl, Erika T. ... Milwaukee, WI
Flierl, Patricia Leary ... Fresno, CA
Fliés, Elliott M. ... Minneapolis, MN
Flies, Sheri L. ... Puyallup, WA
Fliesler, Dubb, Meyer & Lovejoy LLP
San Francisco, CA
Santa Clara, CA
Fliesler, Martin C. ... San Francisco, CA
Fligel, Kristen E. ... Decatur, IL
Fligeltaub, William H. ... Seattle, WA
Fligg, Jonathon A. ... Atlanta, GA
Fligg, Kenneth L., Jr. ... Kansas City, MO
Fligg, W. Patrick ... Honolulu, HI
Flight, James A. ... Chicago, IL
Flight, Myrtle Ruth ... Canton, MA
Fligsten, Ann M. ... Severna Park, MD
Fligsten, Monte C. ... Los Angeles, CA
Flik, York Milligan ... Miami, FL
Flinchbaugh, John D. ... York, PA
Flinders, Brad A. ... Nyssa, OR
Ontario, OR
Flinders, Ronald J. ... Las Vegas, NV
Flindt, Kyle H. ... Salt Lake City, UT
Fling, James C. ... Shamrock, TX
Fling, Joe C. ... Eagle Lake, TX
Fling, Matthew L. ... Edina, MN
Fling, Virginia R. ... New York, NY
Flink, Alan J. ... New York, NY
Flink, Alan S. ... Providence, RI
Flink, Andrea L. ... New York, NY
Flink, Edward B. ... Latham, NY
Flink, Frank B., Jr. ... Kansas City, MO
Flink, Joel M. ... Philadelphia, PA
Flink, Marc D. ... Denver, CO
Flink, Philip J. ... Boston, MA
Flink, Richard A. ... Murray Hill, NJ
Flink, Robert H. ... New York, NY
Flink, Stephen K. ... Eastchester, NY
Flinker, Jon C. ... Cleveland, OH
Flinkman, Stan ... Santa Monica, CA
Flinn & Beagan ... Fairfax, VA
Vienna, VA
Flinn, Bonnie S. ... Claremont, CA
Flinn, C. Barr ... New York, NY
Flinn, C. Maurice ... Charlottesville, VA
Flinn, Charles A., Jr. ... St. Paul, MN
Flinn, Charles G. ... Arlington, VA
Flinn, David B. ... Martinez, CA
Flinn, Dermod F. ... Brewster, NY
Flinn, Eileen K. ... Harrisburg, PA
Flinn, Eric G. ... Mount Clemens, MI
Flinn, Eric G. ... Sterling Heights, MI
Flinn, Gary L. ... Greenville, OH
Sidney, OH
Flinn, Gloria J. ... Burlington, VT
Flinn, Horace G., Jr. ... Hartford, CT
Flinn, Irvine D. ... New York, NY
Flinn, Jared G. ... San Diego, CA
Flinn, Macdonald ... New York, NY
Flinn, Michael deV. ... Greenwich, CT
Flinn, Michael J. ... Pittsburgh, PA
Flinn and Muntean Co., L.P.A.
Greenville, OH
Sidney, OH
Flinn, Patrick J. ... Atlanta, GA
Flinn, Richd. D. ... Pittsburgh, PA
Flinn, Robert F. ... Vienna, VA
Flinn, T. Michael, Law Offices of
Carrollton, GA
Flinn, Thomas D. ... Montclair, NJ
Flinn, William E. ... Eugene, OR
Flinsch, Suzanne E. ... Apple Valley, MN
Flint, Andrew P. ... Houston, TX
Flint, Anidelle Tomlinson ... Fresno, CA
Flint, Bruce A. ... Dallas, TX
Flint, Bruce A., P.C. ... Dallas, TX
Flint, Bryce A. ... Sturgis, SD
Flint, Chris A. ... Columbus, OH
Flint, Christopher P. ... Albany, NY
Flint, Cort P.A., A Professional Corporation
Greenville, SC
Flint, Cort R., Jr. ... Greenville, SC
Flint, David H. ... Atlanta, GA
Flint, Delos E., Jr. ... New Orleans, LA
Flint, Donald F. ... St. Louis, MO
Flint, Douglas H. ... Canton, GA
Flint, Edward M. ... Garden City, NY
Flint, Elizabeth R. ... Palo Alto, CA
Flint, F. Harlan ... Santa Fe, NM
Flint, George B. ... Dallas, TX
Flint, George B. ... Plano, TX
Flint, George Lee, Jr. ... San Antonio, TX
Flint, George M., III ... Salt Lake City, UT
Flint, George M., Jr. ... Houston, TX
Flint, George S. ... New York, NY
Flint, Henry W. ... Charlotte, NC
Flint, J. Lindsay ... St. Paul, MN
Flint, James F. ... Washington, DC
Flint, James M. ... Gaylord, MI
Flint, Jodee M. ... Washington, DC
Flint, Karen M.
Environmental Protection Agency,
Program Office Attorneys, GV
Flint, Keith G. ... Chatham, NY
Flint, Kelly J. ... Salt Lake City, UT
Flint, Mary M. L. H. ... Farmington, ME
Flint, Michael D. ... Atlanta, GA
Flint, Mitchell L. ... Los Angeles, CA
Flint, Myles E. ... Washington, DC
Flint, Myles E., II ... Department of Justice,
Environment and Natural Resources
Division, GV
Flint, Nancy J. ... Miami, FL
Flint, Richard D. ... Salt Lake City, UT
Flint, Richard E. ... Corpus Christi, TX
Flint, Richard N. ... Minneapolis, MN
Flint, Robert B. ... Anchorage, AK
Flint, Rosemary L. ... Denver, CO
Flint, Sam H. ... Saint Simons Island, GA
Flint, Scott J. ... Tampa, FL
Flint, Susan E. ... Minneapolis, MN
Flint, Wendel Robert ... Galt, CA
Flint, William G. ... Philadelphia, PA
Flintoff, Michael S. ... Okemos, MI
Flintoft, Donald H. ... Houston, TX
Flintoft, Gerald J. ... New York, NY
Flintoft, Peter C. ... Chelsea, MI
Flintrop, William ... Monsey, NY
Flior, B. Edward ... Rancho Palos Verdes, CA
Flippen, Celeste deLorge ... Plano, TX
Flippen, Edward L. ... Richmond, VA
Flippen, James Howard, Jr. ... Norfolk, VA
Flippen, John A. ... Atlanta, GA
Flippen, John T. ... New York, NY
Flippin, Collins, Huey & Webb, P.L.L.C.
Milan, TN
Trenton, TN
Flippin, Densmore, Morse, Rutherford & Jessee ... Roanoke, VA
Flippin, Floyd S. ... Humboldt, TN
Flippin, G. Franklin ... Roanoke, VA
Flippin, Laura L.
Commodity Futures Trading Commission,
Division of Enforcement, GV
Flippin, Michael D. ... Claremont, CA
Flippin, Wilbur H., Jr. ... Mansfield, OH
Flippin, William Jerry ... Milan, TN
Flippo, Dean D. ... Salinas, CA
Flippo & Flippo, Inc. ... Tulsa, OK
Flippo, George W. ... Tulsa, OK
Flippo, Jack ... Independence, MO
Flippo, John W. ... Tulsa, OK
Flippo, Linda G. ... Birmingham, AL
Flipse, Bruce R. ... Colby, KS
Flipse, Cleona ... Colby, KS
Flipse & Flipse Law Office, P.A. ... Colby, KS
Flipse, Kenlyn J. ... Washington, DC
Flis, Edward ... New York, NY
Flis, James S. ... East Islip, NY
Fliss, Kathie J. ... Castle Rock, CO
Fliss, N. John ... Naperville, IL
Flitcraft, Gregg A. ... Northbrook, IL
Flitcroft, David L. ... Oak Ridge, TN
Flitner, John D. ... Santa Rosa, CA
Flitt, Norman ... New York, NY
Flitter, Abigail Lee ... Philadelphia, PA
Flitter, Cary L. ... Cherry Hill, NJ
Narberth, PA
Flitter, Douglas L. ... Philadelphia, PA
Flitter, Jonathan E. ... Boston, MA
Flittie, William J. ... Dallas, TX
Flitton, Edward H. ... Colorado Springs, CO
Flitton, John S. ... Salt Lake City, UT
Flitz, James H. ... Cedar Rapids, IA
Floam, D. Andrew ... Atlanta, GA
Floberg, John F. ... Potomac, MD
Flocco-Hill, Valerie J. ... Philadelphia, PA
Floch & Flock ... Omak, WA
Floch, Fred ... Omak, WA
Flock, Brenda M. ... Philadelphia, PA
Flock, Jack W. ... Tyler, TX
Flock, John ... New York, NY
Flock, John A. ... Playa Del Rey, CA
Flock, Robert V. ... Omak, WA
Flocken, Ann E. ... Westport, CT
Flocken, P. Jay ... Woodcliff Lake, NJ
Flocken, Patricia E. ... Ft. Calhoun, NE
Flockhart, Monica M. ... Los Angeles, CA
Flockhart, Wendy E. ... San Ramon, CA
Flocks, Franklin J. ... Palo Alto, CA
Flocks, Karl W. ... Washington, DC
Flocks, Reed M. ... Santa Cruz, CA
Flocos, Peter N. ... Pittsburgh, PA
Flodman, Steven J. ... Lincoln, NE
Flodstrom, John D. ... Urbana, IL
Floegel, Jody ... Morris Plains, NJ
Floegel, John M., Jr. ... Boca Raton, FL
Floerchinger, David D. ... Anchorage, AK
Floersch, Steven W. ... Omaha, NE
Floersheim, Ray A. ... Raton, NM
Floersheimer, Fred ... Houston, TX
Floersheimer, Rhea ... New York, NY
Floeter, Conrad F. ... Woodstock, IL
Flofting, Henry A. ... Roanoke, VA
Floge, Louis F., Jr. ... Bensalem, PA
Langhorne, PA
Flohr, Arlene ... New York, NY
Flohr, Christopher ... Washington, DC
Flohr, Susan B. ... Washington, DC
Flojo, Raymond B. ... St. Louis, MO
Flom, Barbara M. ... Chicago, IL
Flom, Douglas E. ... Sioux City, IA
Flom, Erik B. ... Chicago, IL
Flom, Gerald T. ... Minneapolis, MN
Flom, Jack T. ... Myrtle Beach, SC
Flom, Jack T., & Associates, P.A.
Myrtle Beach, SC
Flom, Joel A. ... Moorhead, MN
Fargo, ND
Flom, Jonathan P. ... Palm Beach, FL
New York, NY
Flom, Joseph H. ... New York, NY
Flom, Katherine S. ... Minneapolis, MN
Flom, Max H. ... Delray Beach, FL
Flom, Michael C. ... Minneapolis, MN
Flom, Richard A. ... Woodland Hills, CA
Floman, Betsy J. ... New York, NY
Floman, Steven P. ... Orange, CT
Flomenhaft, Fern ... New York, NY
Flomenhaft, Michael ... New York, NY
Flomenhoft, Michael A. ... Chicago, IL
Flood, Ann Meissner ... Manchester, NH
Flood, Annette Englund ... Okemos, MI
Flood and Basile ... Hackensack, NJ
Flood, Charles B., III ... Mission Viejo, CA
Flood, Christopher M. ... Marlborough, MA
Flood, Clifford T. ... Lansing, MI
Flood, Craig B., II ... Memphis, TN
Flood, Daniel B. ... Norfolk, NE
Flood, Douglas F. ... North Andover, MA
Flood, Edward J. ... Wheaton, MD
Flood, Edward P. ... New York, NY
Flood, Emmet T. ... Washington, DC
Flood, Francis C. ... Troy, MI
Flood, Gerard J. ... Elm Grove, WI
Flood & Hartigan ... Lowell, MA
Flood, Henry C., Jr. ... Pittsburgh, PA
Flood, Hindy & Kramer ... Brooklyn, NY
Flood, James A. ... Memphis, TN
Flood, James D. ... Morris, IL
Flood, James J., Jr. ... Washington, DC
Flood, James M. ... Philadelphia, PA
Flood, James P. ... Stamford, CT
Flood, James P. ... Columbus, OH
Flood, James W. ... Norristown, PA
Flood, James W., Jr. ... Lowell, MA
Flood, Joan Healey ... Houston, TX
Flood, John H., III ... New York, NY
Flood, John J. ... Washington, DC
Flood, John J. ... Mount Vernon, IL
Flood, John P. ... New York, NY
Flood, John T. ... Corpus Christi, TX
Flood, John W. ... Wausaukee, WI
Flood Johnston & McShane, P.C.
New York, NY
Flood, Joseph R., Jr. ... Orlando, FL
Flood, Joseph Thomas ... Montgomery, AL
Flood, Kenneth H ... Keaau, HI
Flood, Kevin P. ... Jacksonville, FL
Flood, Kevin Patrick ... Jacksonville, FL
Flood, Linzy & Thigpen ... Temple, TX
Flood, Marc A. ... Philadelphia, PA
Flood, Marianne P. ... Feasterville, PA
Flood, Marilyn J. ... New York, NY
Flood, Mary A. ... Houston, TX
Flood, Mary Patricia ... Chicago, IL
Flood, Michael E. ... Canton, OH
Flood, Michael W. ... Excelsior Springs, MO
Flood, Monica M. ... Coeur d'Alene, ID
Flood, Nicholas A., III ... Temple, TX
Flood, Patricia A. ... St. Louis, MO
Flood, Patrick M. ... Omaha, NE
Flood, Raymond F. ... Hackensack, NJ
Flood, Richard G. ... Crystal Lake, IL
Flood, Scott L. ... New York, NY
Flood, Scott W. ... Manchester, NH
Flood, Stephen B. ... Chappaqua, NY
Flood, Steven P. ... Hays, KS
Flood, Susan E. ... Newark, DE
Flood, T. Patrick ... Phoenix, AZ
Flood, Thomas R. ... Ottawa, IL
Flood, Timothy P. ... Exton, PA
Flood, Vincent P., Jr. ... Chicago, IL
Flood, W. Michael ... Phoenix, AZ
Flood, William F., III ... Annapolis, MD
Floodman, Sheila J. ... Wichita, KS
Flood-Myers, Kelly ... Poughkeepsie, NY
Flood-Smith, Dorothy Ann
Huntington Beach, CA
Flook, Timothy J. ... Liberty, MO
Floor, Richard E., (P.C.) ... Boston, MA
Floors, James E. ... Smithfield, NC
Flor, Albert, Jr. ... Oakland, CA
Flora, Albert J., Jr. ... Wilkes-Barre, PA
Flora, Barry L. ... Roanoke, VA
Flora, Bruce J. ... Trotwood, OH
Flora, Diedra W. ... Grapevine, TX
Flora, Donovan R. ... Seattle, WA
Flora, Ernest Gray, III ... Macon, MS
Flora, James H. ... Mentor, OH
Flora, John J., III ... Moyock, NC
Flora, John M. ... Norfolk, VA
Flora, John W. ... Harrisonburg, VA
Flora, Jonathan R. ... La Jolla, CA
Flora, Kate Clark ... Concord, MA
Flora, Louis M. ... Paterson, NJ
Flora, Lynnae ... Golden, CO
Flora, Mark E. ... Seattle, WA
Flora, Mark R. ... El Paso, TX
Flora, Marsha E. ... Mount Laurel, NJ
Philadelphia, PA
Flora, Matthew E. ... Denver, CO
Flora, Paul E. ... Sun City Center, FL
Flora, Phyllis A. ... Boston, MA
Flora, Robert J. ... Houston, TX
Flora, Ronald J. ... Milton, WV
Flora, Terry L. ... Naples, FL
Flora, William D. ... San Francisco, CA
Flora, William G. ... Independence, MO
Florack, James A. ... New York, NY
Florak, Mark E. ... Columbus, OH
Florance, Cynthia Currey ... Santa Ana, CA
Florance, David B. ... San Diego, CA
Florance, Douglas E. ... Flagstaff, AZ
Florance, Gordon and Brown, A Professional Corporation ... Richmond, VA
Florance, Reynolds G. ... Arlington, VA
Floratos, Loll & Devine, A Professional Law
Corporation ... Irvine, CA
Floratos, William A. ... Irvine, CA
Florczak, Nina R. ... Newark, NJ
Florczak, Thomas J. ... Pueblo, CO
Florczak, Walter E. ... Newark, NJ
Floreani, Michael T. ... Houston, TX
Floreen, Nancy M. ... Rockville, MD
Florek, John A. ... Stratford, CT
Florek, Kenneth F. ... New York, NY
Florek & O'Neill ... Stratford, CT
Florek, Sara E. ... East Chicago, IN
Florek-Birney, Susan ... Amherst, NY
Floren, Arleen ... Springfield, IL
Floren, Charles M. ... Tulsa, OK
Floren, H. Gerald ... Gadsden, AL
Floren, Joseph E. ... San Francisco, CA
Florence, Barry G. ... Los Angeles, CA
Florence, Brian R. ... Ogden, UT
Florence, Craig B. ... Dallas, TX
Florence, Diana J. ... New York, NY
Florence, Elizabeth A. ... Dallas, TX
Florence, Graydon W. ... Atlanta, GA
Florence, Henry J. ... Phoenix, AZ
Florence, Henry J., Ltd. ... Phoenix, AZ
Florence and Hutchison ... Ogden, UT
Florence, Jody M. ... Las Vegas, NV
Florence, Kenneth ... Spring, TX
Florence, Kenneth J. ... Beverly Hills, CA
Florence, Kirk Todd ... Dallas, TX
Florence, Lisa M. ... Detroit, MI
Florence, Louise Marcialis ... Richardson, TX
Florence, M. Taylor ... Gold River, CA
Florence, Mark T. ... Lebanon, OH
Florence, Patricia H. ... Longview, TX
Florence, Phillip, Jr. ... Columbia, SC
Florence & Smith ... Peekskill, NY
Florence, Thad S. ... Milwaukee, WI
Florence, Wanda S. ... Santa Ana, CA
Florence, William B., Jr. ... Atlanta, GA
Florence, William J., Jr. ... Peekskill, NY
Florencourt, W. Louise ... Milledgeville, GA
Florendo, Consuelo S. ... Palmdale, CA
Florendo, David ... New York, NY
Florendo, Joseph P. ... Kealakekua, HI
Florent, Randy D. ... New Orleans, LA
Florentine, Richard T. ... Branford, CT
Florentino, Gregory ... Bay Shore, NY
Florentino, Tonianne ... New York, NY
Florentz, Mary C. ... East Meadow, NY
Florenz, Paul A., (P.C.) ... Bethlehem, PA
Florenzano, Joseph A., II ... Edina, MN
Florenzo, David B. ... Washington, DC
Flores, Abraham A., Jr. ... San Francisco, CA
Flores, Aida S. ... Mission, TX
Flores, Anthony J ... Addison, TX
Flores, Anthony R. ... San Francisco, CA
Flores, Antonio M. ... Jamaica, NY
Flores, Araceli E. ... Houston, TX
Flores, Armando ... Fort Worth, TX
Flores, Armando A. ... Philadelphia, PA
Flores, Armando M. ... Modesto, CA
Flores, Arthur R. ... Guilderland, NY
Flores, Aurelia E. ... San Diego, CA
Flores, Barbara K. ... Durand, IL
Flores, Beatrice P. ... Ventura, CA
Flores, Becky Fitz ... Davenport, IA
Flores, Carmen S., (Ms.) ... Redwood City, CA
Flores, Casso & Pettitt, L.L.P.
McAllen, TX
Flores, Christina ... Montclair, CA
Flores, Cirilo ... Costa Mesa, CA
Flores, Claudio, Jr. ... El Paso, TX
Flores, Craig ... Los Angeles, CA
Flores, Cristina I. ... Baldwin, MD
Flores, Daniel F. ... Hackensack, NJ
Flores, Daniel M. ... Department of Justice,
Environment and Natural Resources
Division, GV
Flores, David ... Fort Worth, TX
Flores, David A. ... Pasadena, CA
Flores, David A. ... Lancaster, PA
Flores, DeAnn M. ... Los Angeles, CA
Flores, Deanna J. ... Washington, DC
Flores, Deborah L. ... Independence, MO
Flores, Dino E., Jr. ... Frederick, MD
Flores, Dorann W. ... Brea, CA
Flores, Dorothy A. ... San Antonio, TX
Flores, Edward A. ... New York, NY
Flores, Edward R. ... Corona Del Mar, CA
Flores, Edwin ... Paterson, NJ
Flores, Edwin S. ... Dallas, TX
Flores, Elizabeth ... New York, NY
Flores, Elizabeth M. ... Denver, CO
Flores, Eric D.
Merit Systems Protection Board,
Office of the General Counsel, GV
Flores, Ernesto, Jr. ... Mercedes, TX
Flores, Gloria P. ... Alameda, CA
Flores, Gregorio, Jr. ... San Antonio, TX
Flores, Guillermo A., Jr. ... San Antonio, TX
Flores, Henry ... Houston, TX
Flores, Henry G. ... Austin, TX
Flores, Jacqueline D. ... Albuquerque, NM
Flores, Jean M. ... Dallas, TX
Flores, Jeanette M. ... Tampa, FL
Flores, Jeffrey Stuart ... Fremont, NE
Flores, Jessica R. ... Santa Rosa, CA
Flores, John R. ... Hartford, CT
Flores, John V. ... Houston, TX
Flores, Joseph A. ... Toledo, OH
Flores, Juan A., Jr. ... Raleigh, NC
Flores, Juan L. ... Albuquerque, NM
Flores, Lisa A. ... San Diego, CA
Flores, Louis F. ... Napa, CA

Flug, James F. .... **Washington, DC**
Flug, Robert K. .... Hillsboro, OR
Flug, Theresa Marie .... Los Altos, CA
Flugaur, Rick A. .... **Stevens Point, WI**
Fluger, Judite P. .... White Bear Lake, MN
Flugge, Valerie V. .... **Los Angeles, CA**
Flugher, Bernard J. .... Harmony, PA
Fluharty, Ann M. .... Cincinnati, OH
Fluharty, E. Stevenson .... Camden, NJ
Fluharty, Robert D. .... **Charleston, WV**
Fluharty, Robert S., Jr. .... **Parkersburg, WV**
Fluharty, Thomas H. .... Clarksburg, WV
Fluharty & Townsend .... **Parkersburg, WV**
Williamstown, WV
Fluhr, Steven S. .... St. Louis, MO
Fluhr, Suzanne .... Philadelphia, PA
Fluhrer, Gary E. .... **Seattle, WA**
Fluk, Gershon H. .... Brooklyn, NY
Fluke, Allan L. .... Pittsburgh, PA
Fluke, Harry S. .... Syracuse, NY
Fluke, Loring Paul .... Lynn, MA
Fluke, Randall L. .... Sherman, TX
Fluke, Stephanie W. .... St. Petersburg, FL
Fluke, Weiers & Schmitt, P.C.
Pittsburgh, PA
Fluker, Brenda A. .... Dorchester, MA
Fluker, James A. .... Gladstone, MO
Flum, Joanna Hamill .... **Philadelphia, PA**
Flum, Joshua M. .... **Washington, DC**
Flum, Paul .... **San Francisco, CA**
Flume, Michael E. .... **San Antonio, TX**
Flume, Richard A. .... Austin, TX
Flumenbaum, Martin .... **New York, NY**
Flummer, James A. .... Cairo, IL
Flunker, Raymond J. .... **St. Louis, MO**
Flurer, Michele E. .... Manhattan Beach, CA
Fluri, James E. .... Waukegan, IL
Flurry, Lillian M. .... Houston, TX
Flury, Carolyn D. .... Bethesda, MD
Flury, Gerald M. .... Southfield, MI
Flury, Lynn M. .... **Boston, MA**
Flury, Michael T. .... **Miami, FL**
Flury, Nancy S. .... **Minneapolis, MN**
Flusche, Marc F. .... **New York, NY**
Flusche, Patricia M. .... **New York, NY**
Flushman, Bruce S. .... **San Francisco, CA**
Fluss, Isaac .... Santa Rosa, CA
Fluxgold, Cindy G. .... Chicago, IL
Fly, Frank M. .... Murfreesboro, TN
Fly, James L. .... **Orlando, FL**
Fly, Jane Mueller .... **Houston, TX**
Fly, Mary .... Beaumont, TX
Fly & Moeller .... **Port Lavaca, TX**
Victoria, TX
Fly, William L. .... San Marcos, TX
Fly, William S. .... **Victoria, TX**
Flyer, Michael R. .... **Washington, DC**
Flyer, Morris .... Brooklyn, NY
Flyer, Steven A. .... New York, NY
Flygare, John A. .... **Lubbock, TX**
Flygare, Schwarz & Closson, PLLC
Exeter, NH
Flygare, Thomas J. .... **Exeter, NH**
Flyger, John .... **Washington, DC**
Flygt, Douglas L. .... **Madison, WI**
Flyke, Martin G. .... **Milwaukee, WI**
Flynn, Alex .... **Milwaukee, WI**
Flynn, Alex, & Associates, S.C.
Milwaukee, WI
Flynn, Allan A. A. .... New York, NY
Flynn, Allison Taylor .... Los Angeles, CA
Flynn, Alvin N. .... Tyler, TX
Flynn, Amie J. .... San Diego, CA
Flynn, Ana M. .... **Chicago, IL**
Flynn, Ann Marie .... **New York, NY**
Flynn, Anne M. .... Ridgefield, CT
Flynn, Anne Macon .... Columbia, SC
Flynn, Anthony G. .... **Wilmington, DE**
Flynn & Associates, P.C. .... **Boston, MA**
Flynn, Barry G. .... **Houston, TX**
Flynn, Benedict D., Jr. .... West Hartford, CT
Flynn, Bernard M. .... **West Trenton, NJ**
Flynn, Bill .... Paducah, KY
Flynn, Blake V. .... **Santa Monica, CA**
Flynn, Blakeslee and Shay, P.C.
Wilton, CT
Flynn, Brendan T. .... **Hartford, CT**
Flynn, Brian C. .... Hammondsport, NY
Flynn, Brian D. .... Summerland, CA
Flynn, Brian M. .... Framingham, MA
Flynn, Brian M. .... East Islip, NY
Flynn, Brian N. .... North Chatham, MA
Flynn, Brian P. .... **New York, NY**
Flynn, Brian T. .... Burlington, NJ
Flynn, Bruce P. .... **Seattle, WA**
Flynn, C. Michael .... Houston, TX
Flynn & Campbell, L.L.P. .... **Southlake, TX**
Flynn, Carol J. .... Anaheim, CA
Flynn, Catherine A. .... **New York, NY**
Flynn, Catherine J. .... **New Providence, NJ**
Flynn, Charles F. .... Washington, DC
Flynn, Charles J. .... Nashua, NH
Flynn, Charles L. .... Orange, CT
Flynn, Charles L.P. .... **Mount Vernon, IL**
Flynn, Charles P. .... **Anchorage, AK**
Flynn, Charles P. .... **Wilton, CT**
Flynn, Charles Patrick .... **Brentwood, TN**
Flynn, Charles W. .... Miami, FL
Flynn, Christopher .... **Washington, DC**
Flynn, Christopher J. .... Orlando, FL
Flynn, Christopher W. .... **Chicago, IL**
Flynn & Clark .... Rittman, OH
Flynn & Clark, P.C. .... **Boston, MA**
Cambridge, MA
Flynn, Claudia J. .... Washington, DC
Flynn, Colin T. .... **Washington, DC**
Flynn, Colleen M. .... Chicago, IL
Flynn, Cournoyer, Hardy & Cohn
Sudbury, MA
Flynn, Cristin L. .... **New York, NY**
Flynn, C. W., IV .... **Dallas, TX**
Flynn, Cynthia Grace .... **Seattle, WA**
Flynn, Cynthia Haney .... **Green Bay, WI**
Flynn, Dan M. .... Winner, SD
Flynn, Daniel Conway
Newport Beach, CA
Flynn, Daniel E. .... Sherman Oaks, CA
Flynn, Daniel F. .... Farmington, CT
Flynn, Daniel J. .... **Milwaukee, WI**
Flynn, Daniel S. .... Warren, NJ
Flynn, Danny .... Glendale, AZ
Flynn, Danny, P.C. .... Glendale, AZ
Flynn, David H. .... Providence, RI
Flynn, David J. .... **Chicago, IL**
Flynn, David K. .... Department of Justice,
Civil Rights Division, GV
Flynn, David M. .... **Philadelphia, PA**
Flynn, David P. .... **Buffalo, NY**
Flynn, Deborah .... Philadelphia, PA
Flynn, Deborah Lassman
Securities and Exchange Commission,
Division of Market Regulation, GV
Flynn, Delich & Wise .... **Long Beach, CA**
San Francisco, CA
Flynn, Dennis P. .... Grand Rapids, MI
Flynn, Diane M. .... **Macon, GA**
Flynn, Diane M. .... **Florham Park, NJ**
Flynn, Dinah I. .... Department of Commerce,
Minority Business Development Agency, GV
Flynn & Dinsmore .... Sioux Falls, SD
Flynn, Donald .... San Francisco, CA
Flynn, Edmund G. .... **Stroudsburg, PA**
Flynn, Edmund J. .... Salt Lake City, UT
Flynn, Edward C. .... North Huntingdon, PA
Flynn, Edward D. (Ned), III, P.C.
Atlanta, GA
Flynn, Edward F. .... Decatur, IL
Flynn, Edward John .... Chicago, IL
Flynn, Eileen F. .... Cleveland, OH
Flynn, Elizabeth Ann .... Markham, IL
Flynn, Ellen Coward .... Bloomfield, CT
Flynn, Ellen L. .... Anaheim, CA
Flynn, Ellen M. .... New York, NY
Flynn, Emily E. .... **San Francisco, CA**
Flynn, Erin L. .... Old Bridge, NJ
Flynn, Errol C. .... Honesdale, PA
Flynn, Eugene J. .... Dallas, TX
Flynn, Eugene J., P.C. .... Dallas, TX
Flynn, Eugene P. .... Sharon, MA
Flynn, F. Jay, Jr. .... **Boston, MA**
Flynn & Flynn .... Jacksonville, IL
Flynn & Flynn .... **Huntington, NY**
Flynn, Francis X. .... **Los Angeles, CA**
Flynn, Frank A. .... **Lafayette, LA**
Flynn, Frank A. .... Boston, MA
Flynn, Frank J. .... Newport, RI
Flynn, Frank L., Jr. .... **Knoxville, TN**
Flynn, Frank M. .... **Portland, OR**
Flynn, Frank P., Jr. .... Richardson, TX
Flynn, Frederick L. .... Arlington, VA
Flynn, Gaiana S. .... **Hackensack, NJ**
Flynn, Gary C. .... Boulder, CO
Flynn, Gary G. .... Newark, NJ
Flynn & Gaskins, L.L.P.
Minneapolis, MN
Flynn, Gayle Montague .... New York, NY
Flynn, George R. .... Bloomington, IL
Flynn, George R., P.C. .... Bloomington, IL
Flynn, George W. .... **Minneapolis, MN**
Flynn, Gerald W. .... Glen Cove, NY
Flynn, Grace .... **Milwaukee, WI**
Flynn, Gregory B. .... Syracuse, NY
Flynn, Gregory C. .... Boston, MA
Flynn, Gregory E. .... **San Diego, CA**
Flynn, Guy E. .... **Baltimore, MD**
Flynn & Guymon .... Belleville, IL
Flynn, H. Joseph
Federal Emergency Management Agency,
Office of the General Counsel, GV
Flynn, Hardy & Cohn .... **Boston, MA**
Waltham, MA
Flynn, Harry C. .... Los Angeles, CA
Flynn, Hoefker & Thayer, P.C.
Houston, TX
Flynn, Hugh J. .... Westfield, MA
Flynn, J. Edward .... Jacksonville, IL
Flynn, Jack W. .... Frankfort, KY
Flynn, James A. .... **Nutley, NJ**
Flynn, James B. .... Westfield, NJ
Flynn, James E. .... Falmouth, MA
Flynn, James F. .... Hinsdale, IL
Flynn, James F. .... Evansville, IN
Flynn, James F. .... Waldorf, MD
Flynn, James F. .... **Columbus, OH**
Flynn, James F., Ltd. .... Hinsdale, IL
Flynn, James G. .... **New York, NY**
Flynn, James J. .... Wilmington, DE
Flynn, James M. .... Williston Park, NY
Flynn, James P. .... **Plainville, CT**
Flynn, James P. .... **Newark, NJ**
Flynn, James R. .... Starke, FL
Flynn, James R. .... Maple Valley, WA
Flynn, James R., P.A. .... Starke, FL
Flynn, James T. .... **Colorado Springs, CO**
Flynn, Jane M. .... **Irvine, CA**
Flynn, Jas. F. .... Waco, TX
Flynn, Jas. P., Jr. .... Cleveland, OH
Flynn, Jas. T. .... Boston, MA
Flynn, Jeanne E. .... **Newton, MA**
Flynn, Jeannine C. .... **Houston, TX**
Flynn, Jeffrey E. .... **San Diego, CA**
Flynn, Jeffrey L. .... Worthington, MN
Flynn, Jeffrey M. .... **Atlanta, GA**
Flynn, Jeffrey P. .... **Newark, NJ**
Flynn, Jennifer B. .... **Salisbury, NC**
Flynn, Jeremiah W. .... Mount Morris, NY
Flynn, Jeri Ann H. .... Baton Rouge, LA
Flynn, Jeri Ann H., A Prof. Corp., Law Offices
of .... Baton Rouge, LA
Flynn, Jerry D. .... Chester, IL
Flynn, Joan .... Cleveland, OH
Flynn, Joan Garrity .... **Boston, MA**
Flynn, Jodi L. .... **Chicago, IL**
Flynn, John .... Townsend, MT
Flynn, John D. .... Grand Rapids, MI
Flynn, John D. .... Research Triangle Park, NC
Flynn, John E. .... Los Angeles, CA
Flynn, John E. .... **La Crosse, WI**
Flynn, John F. .... Scottsdale, AZ
Flynn, John F. .... Halifax, MA
Flynn, John F. .... Melrose, MA
Flynn, John F. .... Salt Lake City, UT
Flynn, John H. .... Detroit, MI
Flynn, John J. .... Manasquan, NJ
Flynn, John J. .... Columbus, OH
Flynn, John J. .... Kent, OH
Flynn, John J. .... Salt Lake City, UT
Flynn, John J., III .... **Irvine, CA**
Flynn, John J., III .... New York, NY
Flynn, John J., Jr. .... **Denver, CO**
Flynn, John L. .... Chicago, IL
Flynn, John L. .... **Dulles, VA**
Flynn, John M. .... **Greensboro, NC**
Flynn, John M. .... Cincinnati, OH
Flynn, John N. .... Boston, MA
Flynn, John P. .... **Los Angeles, CA**
Flynn, John P. .... **Quincy, MA**
Flynn, John P., III .... **Portland, ME**
Flynn, John Patrick .... **Phoenix, AZ**
Flynn, John R. .... **Chicago, IL**
Flynn, John S." Jack " .... Union, SC
Flynn, John T. .... **Atlanta, GA**
Flynn, John T. .... Davenport, IA
Flynn, John T., Jr. .... Montvale, NJ
Flynn, John W. .... Wheaton, IL
Flynn, Jon R. .... Chicago, IL
Flynn, Joseph E. .... **Mendota Heights, MN**
Flynn, Joseph E. .... **St. Paul, MN**
Flynn, Joseph F. .... **Cambridge, MA**
Flynn, Joseph F. .... Lynnfield, MA
Flynn, Joseph F. .... Rockland, MA
Flynn, Joseph P. .... Milford, CT
Flynn, Joseph P. .... Wichita, KS
Flynn, Joseph P. .... **Dallas, TX**
Flynn, Joseph W. .... **Suffield, CT**
Flynn, Karen Marie .... Sacramento, CA
Flynn, Karen P. .... **Philadelphia, PA**
Flynn, Karin Jagel .... **Chicago, IL**
Flynn, Kathleen A. .... Washington, DC
Flynn, Kathleen M. .... Denver, CO
Flynn, Kathleen M. .... Belle Haven, VA
Flynn, Kaufman & Russo .... Newark, NJ
Flynn & Kennedy .... Sharon, MA
Flynn, Kerry A. .... Cambridge, MA
Flynn, Kevin .... Washington, DC
Flynn, Kevin D. .... **Hayward, CA**
Flynn, Kevin E.
Research Triangle Park, NC
Flynn, Kevin G. .... **New York, NY**
Flynn, Kevin J. .... New York, NY
Flynn, Kevin M. .... **New York, NY**
Flynn, Kevin M., & Associates
Chicago, IL
Flynn, Kevin R. .... **Cincinnati, OH**
Flynn, Kristen M. .... **Washington, DC**
Flynn, Kristine L. .... **Newark, NJ**
Flynn, Larry D. .... **Southlake, TX**
Flynn, Larry J. .... Jacksonville, IL
Flynn, Lawrence E., Jr. .... **Spartanburg, SC**
Flynn, Lawrence L. .... **New York, NY**
Flynn, Leo P. .... Milbank, SD
Flynn, Leo T. .... Sioux Falls, SD
Flynn, Leonard T. .... **Champaign, IL**
Flynn, Linda Zappe .... **San Diego, CA**
Flynn, Lisa M.
Department Of Health And Human Services,
Office of the General Counsel, GV
Flynn, Lucy A. .... Boston, MA
Flynn, Lynn Manning .... **Fort Smith, AR**
Flynn, M. Bradley
Department of Agriculture,
Office of the General Counsel, GV
Flynn, Margaret C. .... San Bernardino, CA
Flynn, Margaret Quill .... Nashua, NH
Flynn, Margaret Seely .... Santa Rosa, CA
Flynn, Mark Jude .... Denver, CO
Flynn, Mark S. .... **Newport Beach, CA**
Flynn, Mark S. .... **Stamford, CT**
Flynn, Mark S. .... Department of Labor,
Office of the Solicitor, GV
Flynn, Martin J. .... **Washington, DC**
Flynn, Mary Ann
Department Of Veterans Affairs,
Office of the General Counsel, GV
Flynn, Mary E. .... **New York, NY**
Flynn, Mary Ellen .... **Silver Spring, MD**
Flynn, Mary Ellen .... Boston, MA
Flynn, Mary T. .... **McLean, VA**
Flynn, Matthew J. .... Laguna Hills, CA
Flynn, Matthew J. .... **Milwaukee, WI**
Flynn, Maurice J. .... Huntington, WV
Flynn, Max, Miller & Toney, L.C.
Huntington, WV
Flynn & McGee, P.A. .... **Portsmouth, NH**
Flynn McKenna Wright & Karsh
Colorado Springs, CO
Cripple Creek, CO
Woodland Park, CO
Flynn, Meagan .... Portland, OR
Flynn, Merriman & Palmer .... Kennewick, WA
Flynn, Michael .... Garden City, NY
Flynn, Michael B. .... **Boston, MA**
Flynn, Michael C. .... Chicago, IL
Flynn, Michael D. .... **Kansas City, MO**
Flynn, Michael D. .... Haddonfield, NJ
Flynn, Michael D. .... **New York, NY**
Flynn, Michael D. .... New York, NY
Flynn, Michael D. .... Bethel Park, PA
Flynn, Michael D., Jr. .... **Hagåtña, GU**
Flynn, Michael E. .... **Newport Beach, CA**
Flynn, Michael F. .... Fort Lauderdale, FL
Flynn, Michael F., Jr. .... **Rockville, MD**
Flynn, Michael J. .... **San Francisco, CA**
San Rafael, CA
Flynn, Michael J. .... New Britain, CT
Flynn, Michael J. .... Bloomington, IL
Flynn, Michael J. .... **Boston, MA**
Flynn, Michael J. .... Muskegon, MI
Flynn, Michael L. .... **Charlotte, NC**
Flynn, Michael R. .... **New York, NY**
Flynn, Michael S. .... **New York, NY**
Flynn, Michael T. .... **Milwaukee, WI**
Flynn, Michael W. .... St. Louis, MO
Flynn, Murphy & Ryan .... Chicago, IL
Flynn, Nadine P. .... **New York, NY**
Flynn, Neil F. .... Springfield, IL
Flynn, Nelson D. .... **Madison, WI**
Flynn, Nicholas P. .... Melrose, MA
Flynn, Palmer & Tague .... **Champaign, IL**
Flynn and Paoloni .... Kent, OH
Flynn, Patricia A. .... Orland Park, IL
Flynn, Patricia A. .... Lawrence, MA
Salem, NH
Flynn, Patricia A. .... San Antonio, TX
Flynn, Patricia H. .... Dallas, TX
Flynn, Patricia J. .... Billerica, MA
Flynn, Patrick A. .... Columbia, TN
Flynn, Patrick A. .... Corpus Christi, TX
Flynn, Patrick F. .... San Diego, CA
Flynn, Patrick J. .... **Rock Island, IL**
Flynn, Patrick J. .... **Mendota Heights, MN**
Flynn, Patrick J. .... **Cleveland, OH**
Flynn, Patrick M. .... **Scottsdale, AZ**
Flynn, Patrick M. .... Belleville, IL
Flynn, Patrick M. .... **Haddonfield, NJ**
Flynn, Patrick M. .... Houston, TX
Flynn, Patrick S. .... **Birmingham, AL**
Flynn, Paul G. .... Santa Monica, CA
Flynn, Paul M. .... **Washington, DC**
Flynn, Paulette Kane .... St. Paul, MN
Flynn, Peter E. .... Saugus, MA
Flynn, Peter E., P.C. .... Saugus, MA
Flynn, Peter G. .... Westborough, MA
Flynn, Peter M. .... Department of Justice,
Environment and Natural Resources
Division, GV
Flynn & Phillips, LLP .... **San Francisco, CA**
San Rafael, CA
Flynn, Py & Kruse, A Legal Professional Association .... **Port Clinton, OH**
Sandusky, OH
Flynn, R. Patrick .... **Charleston, SC**
Flynn and Radford, Attorneys, P.C.
Brentwood, TN
Nashville, TN
Flynn, Raymond T. .... White Bear Lake, MN
Flynn, Rebecca M. .... New York, NY
Flynn, Richard J. .... Stratford, CT
Flynn, Richard J. .... Sturbridge, MA
Flynn, Richard M. .... Gloucester City, NJ
Flynn, Richard M. .... New York, NY
Flynn, Richard T. .... San Francisco, CA
Flynn, Robert A. .... Ann Arbor, MI
Flynn, Robert A. .... **Tulsa, OK**
Flynn, Robert Allen .... Houston, TX
Flynn, Robert B. .... **New Haven, CT**
Flynn, Robert D. .... **Memphis, TN**
Flynn, Robert E. .... East Northport, NY
Flynn, Robert H. .... **Boston, MA**
Flynn, Robert H. .... Buffalo, NY
Flynn, Robert J. .... **Englewood, CO**
Flynn, Robert J. .... **Huntington, NY**
Flynn, Robert J., Jr. .... **Huntington, NY**
Flynn, Robert L., III .... Rockville, MD
Flynn, Robert S. .... Sudbury, MA
Waltham, MA
Flynn, Rodney D. .... Cape Coral, FL
Flynn, Ronald P. .... **San Francisco, CA**
Flynn, Rory C.
Securities and Exchange Commission,
Division of Enforcement, GV
Flynn, Rose Ann .... **Fort Lauderdale, FL**
Flynn, Ruth S. .... **Washington, DC**
Flynn, Samantha Francis .... Raleigh, NC
Flynn, Scott A. .... Dallas, TX
Flynn, Sean P. .... **Norristown, PA**
Flynn, Sheridan, Tabb & Stillman
Del Mar, CA
Boston, MA
Flynn, Stanley F. .... San Clemente, CA
Flynn & Steinberg .... San Francisco, CA
Flynn, Stephen G. .... San Francisco, CA
Flynn, Susan Gromis .... **Pittsburgh, PA**
Flynn, Susan J. .... **Burlington, VT**
Flynn, Susan Liess .... Poughkeepsie, NY
Flynn, Tara L. .... Collegeville, PA
Flynn, Tara M. .... Federal Trade Commission,
Bureau of Consumer Protection, GV
Flynn, Taylor .... Los Angeles, CA
Flynn, Tegan M. .... **Washington, DC**
Flynn, Terence E. .... Chicago, IL
Flynn, Terence F. .... **Washington, DC**
Flynn, Terence P. .... Newark, NJ
Flynn, Terrance P. .... **Buffalo, NY**
Flynn, Terrence R. .... Rockaway Beach, NY
Flynn, Terri S. .... **Milwaukee, WI**
Flynn, Therese M. .... **Boston, MA**
Flynn, Thiel, Boutell & Tanis, P.C.
Kalamazoo, MI
Flynn, Thomas A. .... Sun City, AZ
Flynn, Thomas F. .... Naples, FL

Flynn, Thomas J. ... Grand Junction, CO
Flynn, Thomas J. ... Chicago, IL
Flynn, Thomas J. ... Louisville, KY
Flynn, Thomas J. ... Minneapolis, MN
Flynn, Thomas J. ... Elmira, NY
Flynn, Thomas J. ... Cincinnati, OH
Flynn, Thomas L. ... Des Moines, IA
Flynn, Thomas P. ... Hartford, CT
Flynn, Thomas P. ... Bradenton, FL
Flynn, Thomas T. ... Rittman, OH
Flynn, Thomas V. ... Dartmouth, MA
Flynn, Thomas W. ... Department of Justice, Tax Division, GV
Flynn, Thomas W. ... Morton Grove, IL
Flynn, Thomas W. ... Dayton, OH
Flynn, Thomas W., III ... Media, PA
Flynn, Thomas W., III ... Radnor, PA
Flynn, Timothy J. ... Denver, CO
Flynn, Timothy J. ... Buffalo, NY
Flynn, Timothy P. ... Detroit, MI
Flynn, Timothy T. ... Modesto, CA
Flynn, Tracy M. ... New York, NY
Flynn, Vincent J. ... Stamford, CT
Flynn, Vincent J. ... Miami, FL
Flynn, W. Paul ... New Haven, CT
Flynn, Walter A., Jr. ... Bridgeport, CT
Westport, CT
Flynn, Wendell C. ... Romulus, MI
Flynn, William B. ... New York, NY
Flynn, William E. ... Minneapolis, MN
Flynn, William E., III ... Old Bridge, NJ
Flynn, William F. ... Milwaukee, WI
Flynn, William J. ... San Francisco, CA
Flynn, William J. ... Miami, FL
Flynn, William J. ... Tallahassee, FL
Flynn, William J., III ... Tampa, FL
Flynn, William J., III ... New Bedford, MA
Flynn, William J." Jay ", Jr.
Kennewick, WA
Flynn, William J., Jr. ... Hingham, MA
Flynn, William K. ... Cincinnati, OH
Flynn, William M. ... Buffalo, NY
Flynn, William M. ... Charlotte, NC
Flynn, William P., Jr. ... Valley Center, CA
Flynn, William R. ... Pittsfield, MA
Flynn-Antonis, Colleen M. ... Old Bridge, NJ
Flynn-DuPart, Mary Lou ... Houston, TX
Flynn-Hollander, Susan J. ... New York, NY
Flynn Mueller, Mary Anne
Londonderry, NH
Flynn-O'Brien, Judy A. ... Albuquerque, NM
Flynn-O'Brien, Timothy V.
Albuquerque, NM
Flynt, Bobbie L. ... Dayton, OH
Flynt, Crisp B. ... Griffin, GA
Flynt and Flynt ... Griffin, GA
Flynt, Fred P., III ... Winston-Salem, NC
Flynt, John J., III ... Augusta, GA
Flynt, John J., Jr. ... Griffin, GA
Flynt, John M. ... Yazoo City, MS
Flynt, Kimberley S. ... Atlanta, GA
Flynt, Lynda L. ... Montgomery, AL
Flynt, Richard A. ... Washington, DC
Flynt, Teddy L. ... Salyersville, KY
Flynt, Willard Rogers ... Hamburg, NY
Flyntz, Frank J. ... Annapolis, MD
Flythe, Joseph J. ... Burley, ID
Flyzik, Dyan ... San Jose, CA
Foale, William E. ... Chicago, IL
Foard, John H., Jr. ... Kansas City, MO
Foard, Philip O. ... Towson, MD
Foard, Richard M. ... Gloucester, VA
Foard, Richard W., III ... Newark, NJ
Foarde, Mary P. ... Minneapolis, MN
Foarde, Timothy F. ... New York, NY
Foate, Kristine G. ... Milwaukee, WI
Fobbe, Daniel E. ... St. Louis Park, MN
Fobe, Nicholas M. ... Washington, DC
Columbia, MD
Fobert, Dorothy ... Providence, RI
Fobes, David L. ... New York, NY
Fobes, Donald E. ... Chesterfield, MA
Fobes, Duncan K. ... Seattle, WA
Fobes, Ronald L. ... Miamisburg, OH
Focarile, Allan ... White Plains, NY
Focas, Jerry D. ... Towson, MD
Fochler, Craig Steven ... Chicago, IL
Fochler, Stephen H. ... South St. Paul, MN
Focht, A. J." Jack " ... Wichita, KS
Focht, Alan W. ... Plymouth Meeting, PA
Focht, Jack ... Wichita, KS
Focht, Kristine Stockwell
Overland Park, KS
Focht, Richard P. ... Orefield, PA
Focht, Robert M. ... Land O'Lakes, FL
Focht, William Allen, III ... Washington, DC
Fochtman, Kathleen P. ... Grand Rapids, MI
Fochtman, Marjorie S.
San Francisco, CA
Fock, Erich E. ... Santa Barbara, CA
Focke, Robert C., Jr. ... Houston, TX
Fockele, Mark ... Gainesville, GA
Fockler, Edwin B., III ... Elkton, MD
Fockler & Fockler ... Elkton, MD
Fockler, Herbert P. ... Palo Alto, CA
Fockler, John K. ... Memphis, TN
Fockler, Karl H. ... Elkton, MD
Foco, Phillip E. ... Baton Rouge, LA
Focsaneanu, Raluca Cristina ... Rockville, MD
Fodal, Joe R. ... Fairborn, OH
Fodale, Francis J. ... Troy, MI
Foddai, Catherine A. ... Trenton, NJ
Fodeman, Alan B. ... Fairfield, CT
Fodeman & Fodeman ... Fairfield, CT
Fodeman, Leslie J. ... Fairfield, CT
Foden, Maria Luisa de C. ... Hartford, CT
Fodera, L. Richard ... Brooklyn, NY
Fodera, Leonard V. ... Philadelphia, PA
Fodera, Theodore Gaspare
Fresh Meadows, NY
Fodice, Thomas S. ... Jersey City, NJ
Fodiman, Bruce A. ... San Francisco, CA
Fodiman, Todd A. ... Miami, FL
Fodor, Candy S. ... Metairie, LA
Fodor, Janine ... Raleigh, NC
Fodor, Jeffrey W. ... Warren, OH
Fodor, Peter N. ... Tallahassee, FL
Fodor, Salmeh K. ... Phoenix, AZ
Fodor, Susanna S. ... New York, NY
Fodor, Troy A. ... Springfield, IL
Fodrea, Ormond R. ... Sherman Oaks, CA
Fody, Kenneth W. ... Philadelphia, PA
Foe, Alan K. ... Seattle, WA
Foe, Susan E. ... San Francisco, CA
Foeckler, Allan M. ... Milwaukee, WI
Foede, Kaarin K. ... Albert Lea, MN
Foedisch, Victoria L. ... Seattle, WA
Foegen, Celia J ... Denver, CO
Foehl, Angela ... Arlington, VA
Foehl, C. Allen ... Westwood, MA
Foehl, Gene A., & Associates ... Media, PA
Foehl, Susan Sciamanna ... Philadelphia, PA
Foehl, William C. ... Wellesley Hills, MA
Foehr, Megan E. ... Garden City, NY
Foehr, Richard M. ... San Francisco, CA
Foelak, Carol P.
Securities and Exchange Commission, Office of Administrative Law Judges, GV
Foelak, Morton ... Department of Commerce, Patent and Trademark Office, GV
Foelber, David A. ... Valparaiso, IN
Foelber, Richard P.
Commodity Futures Trading Commission, Division of Enforcement, GV
Foell, Darrell W. ... Milwaukee, WI
Foeller, Ann-Jeannine ... Detroit, MI
Foeller, Scott D. ... Sarasota, FL
Foels, Craig S. ... Orlando, FL
Foels, Pamela Lynn ... Orlando, FL
Foeman, Lisa R. ... Fredericksburg, VA
Foeppel, Jerome G. ... Boynton Beach, FL
Foer, Albert A. ... Silver Spring, MD
Foerschler, Ann M. ... Seattle, WA
Foerschler, Robert H. ... Overland Park, KS
Foerst, John J., Jr. ... Belvidere, NJ
Foerst, Lisa R. ... Madison, WI
Foerstel, Jonathan P. ... San Diego, CA
Foerster, Amy C. ... Harrisburg, PA
Foerster, Barrett J., (A P.C.)
San Diego, CA
Foerster, Beth Regier ... Topeka, KS
Foerster, Catherine A. ... Rochester, NY
Foerster, Charles E. ... Pittsburgh, PA
Foerster, Charles J. ... Houston, TX
Foerster, David W. ... Jacksonville, FL
Foerster, G. Cher ... Honolulu, HI
Foerster, Isaac and Yerkes, P.A.
Jacksonville, FL
Foerster, Jerome T. ... Harrisburg, PA
Foerster, Larry L. ... Conroe, TX
Foerster, Mark R. ... Rochester, NY
Foersterling, Fredk. J. ... Palatine, IL
Foerstner, James E., Jr. ... Philadelphia, PA
Foertsch, Ralph A. ... New York, NY
Fog, Jens B. ... Haddonfield, NJ
Fogan, Robert J. ... Fort Lauderdale, FL
Fogarasi, Andre P. ... Washington, DC
Fogarty, Brendan J. ... San Francisco, CA
Fogarty, Brian D. ... West Warwick, RI
Fogarty, Bruce E. ... Clovis, NM
Fogarty, Canice J. (C.J.) ... Dayton, OH
Fogarty Cohen Selby & Nemiroff LLC
Bridgeport, CT
Fairfield, CT
Greenwich, CT
Hartford, CT
Norwalk, CT
Stamford, CT
Fogarty, Dennis R. ... Cleveland, OH
Fogarty, Dolores Gayle ... Unadilla, NY
Fogarty, Edward B. ... Springfield, MA
Fogarty, Edward F. ... Omaha, NE
Fogarty, Edward, Jr. ... New York, NY
Fogarty & Fogarty, P.C. ... Mineola, NY
Fogarty, Frank ... New York, NY
Fogarty and Hara ... Rutherford, NJ
Fogarty, James E. ... New York, NY
Fogarty, James H. ... New Bedford, MA
Fogarty, James R. ... Greenwich, CT
Fogarty, Janet E. ... Burlingame, CA
Fogarty, Janet Souza ... Providence, RI
Fogarty, Jean ... Portland, OR
Fogarty, John A., Jr. ... New York, NY
Fogarty, John E. ... Stamford, CT
Fogarty, John J. ... Clearwater, FL
Fogarty, John, Jr. ... Chicago, IL
Fogarty, John P. ... Smithfield, RI
Fogarty, John P. C.
Environmental Protection Agency, Office of Enforcement and Compliance Assurance, GV
Fogarty, John T. ... Santa Monica, CA
Fogarty, John T. ... Madison, NJ
Fogarty, Joseph P. ... Middletown, NY
Fogarty, Julie S. ... Northbrook, IL
Fogarty, Katherine M. ... Fairfax, VA
Fogarty, Kelly Reynolds
San Francisco, CA
Fogarty, Kevin C. ... Jamaica, NY
Fogarty, Kevin P. ... Kew Gardens, NY
Fogarty, Leo J. ... Atlanta, GA
Fogarty, Lund & Gross ... Omaha, NE
Fogarty, Marianne ... New York, NY
Fogarty, Marie ... Washington, DC
Fogarty, Mark P. ... Neenah, WI
Fogarty, Michael E. ... Washington, DC
Fogarty, Michael J. ... Skokie, IL
Fogarty, Michael J., III ... Dallas, TX
Fogarty, Michael T. ... Sacramento, CA
Fogarty, Neil F. ... Pittsburgh, PA
Fogarty, Neil J. ... Jersey City, NJ
Fogarty, Patricia K. ... Belmont, NY
Fogarty, Patrick J. ... Mineola, NY
Fogarty, Patrick, Jr. ... Charlotte, NC
Fogarty, Patrick V. ... West Palm Beach, FL
Fogarty, Paul E. ... Seattle, WA
Fogarty, Robert E. ... Stamford, CT
Fogarty, Robert J. ... Cleveland, OH
Fogarty, Stephen R. ... Rutherford, NJ
Fogarty, Suzanne Ryder
San Francisco, CA
Fogarty, Timothy J. ... Walnut Creek, CA
Fogarty, Walter J., Jr. ... Napa, CA
Fogarty & Watson ... Burlingame, CA
Fogarty, William A. ... Arlington, VA
Fogarty, William A., Jr. ... Jackson, WY
Fogarty, William M. ... Boca Raton, FL
Fogderude, Eric K. ... Fresno, CA
Fogel, Adelaide F. ... New York, NY
Fogel, Alexis Jill ... North Miami Beach, FL
Boston, MA
Fogel, Baird D. ... Kansas City, MO
Fogel, Barry M. ... Roanoke, VA
Fogel, Barry P. ... Boston, MA
Fogel, Benjamin ... Los Angeles, CA
Fogel & Bluestein ... Denver, CO
Fogel, Bruce M. ... Northampton, MA
Fogel, Daniel H. ... Chicago, IL
Fogel, David ... Northampton, MA
Fogel, David ... Teaneck, NJ
Fogel, David A. ... Denver, CO
Fogel, Deborah M. ... Westport, CT
Fogel, Don ... Houston, TX
Fogel, Edward A. ... New York, NY
Fogel, Elizabeth ... Santa Clara, CA
Fogel, Ellen Kornfield ... New York, NY
Fogel, Eric M. ... Chicago, IL
Fogel, Ethan D. ... Philadelphia, PA
Fogel, Feldman, Ostrov, Ringler & Klevens, A Law Corporation ... Los Angeles, CA
Santa Monica, CA
Fogel, Fogel, Gerard & Ghazey, P.C.
Northampton, MA
Fogel, Frederick H. ... New York, NY
Fogel, Glenn D. ... New York, NY
Fogel, Illyssa I. ... Gardena, CA
Fogel, J. Cathy ... Washington, DC
Fogel, James H. ... Bronx, NY
Fogel, Janet B. ... Somerville, MA
Fogel, Jeffrey I. ... Department of Justice, Criminal Division, GV
Fogel, Jeremy ... San Jose, CA
Fogel, Jo Benson ... Rockville, MD
Fogel, Jo Benson, P.A. ... Rockville, MD
Fogel, Joel D., (P.A.) ... Miami, FL
Fogel, Jonathan J. ... Minneapolis, MN
Fogel, Joseph L. ... Chicago, IL
Fogel, Joseph S. ... Los Angeles, CA
Fogel, Keating & Wagner ... Denver, CO
Fogel, Lamber & Bronnenkant, Professional Association ... Phoenix, AZ
Fogel, Lark H. ... El Paso, TX
Fogel, Louis I. ... New York, NY
Fogel, Mark E. ... Raleigh, NC
Fogel, Mark I. ... Boston, MA
Fogel, Marshall A. ... Denver, CO
Fogel, Maureen Doerner ... New York, NY
Fogel, Nussin S. ... New York, NY
Fogel, Paul D. ... San Francisco, CA
Fogel, Philip B. ... New City, NY
Fogel, Rhonda B. ... Waltham, MA
Fogel, Richard A. ... Melville, NY
Fogel, Richard A. ... Dallas, TX
Fogel, Richard L. ... Chicago, IL
Fogel, Richard M. ... Chicago, IL
Fogel, Richard, (P.A.) ... McAfee, NJ
Fogel, Robert D. ... Charleston, SC
Fogel Rubin & Fogel ... Miami, FL
Fogel, Sam ... Fort Wayne, IN
Grabill, IN
Monroeville, IN
Fogel, Sheldon L. ... Raleigh, NC
Fogel, Sherman D. ... Phoenix, AZ
Fogel, Stefanie J. ... Philadelphia, PA
Fogel, Stephen ... Austin, TX
Fogel, Stephen M. ... New York, NY
Fogel, Terry L., (P.A.) ... Miami, FL
Fogel, Usher ... Albany, NY
Cedarhurst, NY
Fogel & Wachs, LLP ... New York, NY
Fogel, Wm. ... Philadelphia, PA
Fogelberg, Carl R. ... New York, NY
Fogelberg, Jay C. ... Minneapolis, MN
Fogelberg, Marc L. ... Chicago, IL
Fogelberg, Melissa R. ... Minneapolis, MN
Fogelgaren, Eric I. ... New York, NY
Fogelgaren, Ira ... New York, NY
Fogelman, Evan M. ... Dallas, TX
Fogelman, James P. ... Los Angeles, CA
Fogelman, Jerry A. ... Glendale Heights, IL
Fogelman, Leonard M. ... New York, NY
Fogelman, Mark ... San Francisco, CA
Fogelman, Martin ... Huntington, NY
Fogelman, Morton J. ... Dallas, TX
Fogelman, Rita Tavel ... Pearl River, NY
Fogelman, Sheldon ... New York, NY
Fogelsinger, Marilyn Ann ... Saginaw, MI
Fogelson, Joseph ... Trenton, NJ
Fogelson, Lawrence S. ... Paramus, NJ
Fogelson, Matthew A. ... Department of Justice, Environment and Natural Resources Division, GV
Fogelson, Noah T. ... Los Angeles, CA
Fogelson, Richard J. ... Washington, DC
Fogelson, Robert A. ... New York, NY
Fogelson, Robert G. ... Montville, NJ
Fogelson, Steven ... Pendleton, OR
Fogelson, Steven M. ... Burbank, CA
Fogelsong, Marilyn ... Tucson, AZ
Fogerty, Gerald E. ... New York, NY
Fogerty, Kevin T. ... Allentown, PA
Fogerty, Kevin T. ... Easton, PA
Fogerty, Michael J.
National Labor Relations Board, Office of the General Counsel, GV
Fogerty, Sam J. ... Tacoma, WA
Fogerty, Stephen P. ... Westport, CT
Fogg, Alan S., Jr. ... Miami, FL
Fogg, Blaine V. ... New York, NY
Fogg, David N., Sr. ... Minneapolis, MN
Fogg, Fogg & Handley ... El Reno, OK
Fogg, George K. ... Portland, OR
Fogg, Gerald M. ... Philippi, WV
Fogg, Janice ... Los Angeles, CA
Fogg, John M. ... Palo Alto, CA
Fogg, Lois R. ... Philadelphia, PA
Fogg, Margaret L. ... Berlin, NY
Fogg, Mark A. ... Denver, CO
Fogg, Merle N., Jr. ... Ballston Lake, NY
Fogg, R. Lanier ... Memphis, TN
Fogg, Richard E. ... Santa Barbara, CA
Fogg, Richard M. ... El Reno, OK
Fogg, Robert J. ... Princeton, NJ
Fogg, Stephen F. ... Lancaster, NH
Fogg, Stephen K., (P.C.) ... Boston, MA
Fogg, T. Keith ... Richmond, VA
Fogg, Tamara K. ... San Diego, CA
Fogg, Virginia Hewitt ... Palo Alto, CA
Fogg, Virginia K. ... Norfolk, VA
Fogg, William V. ... New York, NY
Foggan, Laura A. ... Washington, DC
Foggie, Cornell, Jr. ... St. Louis, MO
Foggo, James R. ... Oaks, PA
Fogl, Frank C., III ... Erie, PA
Fogl Law Office ... Erie, PA
Fogland, Dennis J. ... Omaha, NE
Fogle, Alice M. ... DeLand, FL
Fogle, Andrew R. ... Libertyville, IL
Fogle, Claudia Everett ... Denton, TX
Fogle & Fogle, P.A. ... DeLand, FL
Fogle & Frazier ... Marietta, OH
Fogle, Fredric D. ... East Orange, NJ
Fogle, Gary L. ... Rock Island, IL
Fogle, H. Glenn, Jr. ... Atlanta, GA
Fogle, Harry W. ... Clearwater, FL
Fogle, J. Dana ... DeLand, FL
Fogle, James G. ... Louisville, KY
Fogle, James L. ... St. Louis, MO
Fogle, John C. ... Mount Sterling, KY
Fogle, John C., III ... Frankfort, KY
Fogle, Lewis H., Jr. ... South Miami, FL
Fogle, Stephen R. ... Fairfield, OH
Fogle, Stephen R. ... San Antonio, TX
Fogle, Toni Mari ... Quantico, VA
Fogle, William H. ... Mount Sterling, KY
Fogleman, Amelia A. ... Tulsa, OK
Fogleman, Amos I. ... New Orleans, LA
Fogleman, Carol Jean ... Rialto, CA
Fogleman, Christopher C. ... Rockville, MD
Fogleman, Dannie B. ... Washington, DC
Fogleman, John A. ... Little Rock, AR
Fogleman, John N. ... Marion, AR
Fogleman, Julian B. ... West Memphis, AR
Fogleman, Krista M. ... Washington, DC
Fogleman, L. Carroll ... Bellaire, TX
Fogleman, Louis H., Jr. ... Fayetteville, NC
Fogleman, Lyle O., Jr. ... Crowley, LA
Fogleman, Paul F., III ... Hickory, NC
Fogleman & Rosenkoetter, P.A.
Sarasota, FL
Fogleman, Ross L., III ... Sarasota, FL
Fogleman, Stephan Wayne, Jr.
Glen Burnie, MD
Fogleman, Stephen C. ... Washington, DC
Fogleman, William A. ... Baton Rouge, LA
Fogler, Holly R. ... Washington, DC
Fogler, Linda M. ... Milford, CT
Fogler, Murray J. ... Houston, TX
Fogler, Robert M. ... Denver, CO
Fogler, Stephen M. ... Haddonfield, NJ
Fogler, Teresa Wiggins ... Houston, TX
Foglesong & Cannon ... Knoxville, TN
Foglesong, James E. ... Knoxville, TN
Foglia, Louis M. ... Upland, CA
Foglia, Maryanne S. ... Scarsdale, NY
Foglia, Matthew G. ... New York, NY
Foglia, Michael A. ... Framingham, MA
Foglia, Philip ... Englewood, NJ
Bronx, NY
White Plains, NY
Foglia, René A. ... Lake Buena Vista, FL
Foglia, Wanda D. ... Philadelphia, PA
Fogliani, Michelle ... Campbell, CA
Fogliani, Michelle L. ... Palo Alto, CA
Fogliani, Theodore J. ... Pasadena, CA
Foglietta, Angelo J. ... Gladwyne, PA
Philadelphia, PA
Fognani, John D. ... Denver, CO
Fognano, Nicholas D., Jr. ... Mays Landing, NJ
Fogo, James Charles ... Houston, TX
Fogt, Howard W., Jr. ... Washington, DC
Fogt & Matheson ... Stuart, FL
Fogt, Thomas A. ... Stuart, FL
Fohn, Gerald A. ... San Angelo, TX
Fohn, Louis J. ... San Angelo, TX
Fohr, Rena J. ... Bradford, PA
Fohrell, Frederick L. ... Huntsville, AL
Fohrman, Darryl ... Key West, FL
Fohrman, Donald W. ... Chicago, IL
Fohrman, Donald W., & Associates, Ltd.
Chicago, IL
Fohrman, Elizabeth P. ... Washington, DC

Fohrman, Jeffrey W. ... Newport Beach, CA
Fohrman, Monica M. ... Chicago, IL
Fohrman, Raleigh S. ... Santa Rosa, CA
Fohrman, Seymour F. ... Skokie, IL
Foianini, Ray A. ... Ephrata, WA
Foil, Frank ... Baton Rouge, LA
Foil, Franklin J. ... Baton Rouge, LA
Foil Law Offices ... Durham, NC
Foil, N. Joanne ... Durham, NC
Foiles, Robert D. ... Redwood City, CA
Foiles, William D. ... Columbia, SC
Foiles, William M. ... Hilton Head Island, SC
Fois, Andrew ... Washington, DC
Fois, Michael T. ... New York, NY
Fois, Sonia (Turcotte) ... Washington, DC
Foissotte, Colette M. ... Chicago, IL
Foister, Michael R. ... Vancouver, WA
Foit, C. Kenneth ... Tonawanda, NY
Fojtik, John D. ... La Mesa, CA
Fojut, Matthew ... Los Angeles, CA
Fokas, Marcia E. ... New York, NY
Fokas, Terry ... Austin, TX
Foker, Eric B. ... Los Angeles, CA
Fokes, W. Robert ... Tallahassee, FL
Fokes, William B. ... Atlanta, GA
Fokkena, Habbo G. ... Clarksville, IA
Fokkena Law Office ... Clarksville, IA
Folami, Akilah N. ... New York, NY
Folan, Gail Y. ... Torrance, CA
Folan, John F. ... New Bedford, MA
Folan, Maureen A. ... San Jose, CA
Folan, McDara P., III ... Beachwood, OH
Folan, Patrick J. ... Torrance, CA
Foland, Arvin R. ... Noblesville, IN
Foland, Brooks R. ... Bethlehem, PA
Harrisburg, PA
Foland, Stephen F. ... Pleasanton, CA
Foland, Theresa C. ... San Francisco, CA
Foland, W. James ... Kansas City, MO
Foland & Wickens, P.C.
Overland Park, KS
Kansas City, MO
Foland-Priver, Laura ... Los Angeles, CA
Foland-Sieck, Jacqueline G. ... Omaha, NE
Folan-Gump, Patricia I.
San Francisco, CA
Folarin, Olufemi O. ... Elgin, IL
Folawn, John ... Portland, OR
Folb, Karen J. ... Newton, MA
Folbe, Amy B. ... Detroit, MI
Folberg, H. Jay ... San Francisco, CA
Folcarelli, John W. ... Boston, MA
Folchetti, Robert W. ... White Plains, NY
Folda, Richard G. ... Schuyler, NE
Foldes, Katherine ... Portland, OR
Foldes, Margaret Y. ... Miami, FL
Foldes, Paul G. ... Alexandria, VA
Folds, Allison E. ... Gainesville, FL
Folds, J. David ... Washington, DC
Folen, Robert A. ... Flint, MI
Folena, Jan M. ... Philadelphia, PA
Foletta, Steven R. ... Palo Alto, CA
Foley, Adrian M., Jr. ... Roseland, NJ
Foley, Albert W. ... Dunkirk, NY
Foley, Amanda L. ... Versailles, KY
Foley, Ann Firestine ... Palmyra, NY
Foley, Anne Higgins ... Boston, MA
Foley, Anne Therese ... Boston, MA
Foley, Arlington J. ... Merrillville, IN
Foley, Arthur J., Jr. ... Vernon, NY
Foley & Associates ... San Diego, CA
Foley, Athena ... New York, NY
Foley, Austin J. ... Chicago, IL
Foley, Barbara Louise Pieti ... Flint, MI
Foley, Bernadette J. ... Seattle, WA
Foley, Bezek & Komoroske, LLP
Burbank, CA
Santa Barbara, CA
Foley, Bowers & Bell ... Knoxville, TN
Foley, Bradley S. ... Milwaukee, WI
Foley, Brian T. ... Greenwich, CT
Foley, Brian T. ... Sterling, MA
Foley, Brian T. ... White Plains, NY
Foley, Bryce E. ... Bothell, WA
Foley & Buddenbohm ... Atchison, KS
Overland Park, KS
Foley, Carlyle, (P.C.) ... Columbia, MO
Fayette, MO
Foley, Carolyn K. ... New York, NY
Foley, Cassandra L. ... Silver Spring, MD
Foley, Catherine A. ... Harrisburg, PA
Foley, Catherine Beltz ... Buffalo, NY
Foley, Charles B. ... Warrenton, VA
Foley, Charles J. ... Bridgewater, NJ
Foley, Cheryl M. ... Cincinnati, OH
Foley, Christopher ... Leonardtown, MD
Foley, Christopher J. ... Hamden, CT
Foley, Christopher P. ... Washington, DC
Foley, Christopher P. ... New York, NY
Foley, Christopher R. ... Orinda, CA
San Francisco, CA
Foley, Christopher R. ... Wauwatosa, WI
Foley, Cognetti, Comerford & Cimini
Scranton, PA
Foley, Colin ... Washington, DC
Foley, Colleen A. ... Newark, NJ
Foley & Colley, P.C. ... Tyler, TX
Foley, Dan ... Richardson, TX
Foley, Daniel F. ... Maplewood, MN
Foley, Daniel J., Jr. ... Framingham, MA
Foley, Daniel Patrick ... Winston-Salem, NC
Foley, Daniel R. ... Honolulu, HI
Foley, Daniel S. ... New Orleans, LA
Foley, Daniel T. ... Las Vegas, NV
Foley, Daniel Thomas ... Greenbelt, MD
Foley, David J. ... Freehold, NJ
Foley, David M. ... North Brunswick, NJ
Foley, David N. ... Henniker, NH
Foley, David R. ... Palo Alto, CA
Foley, David V. ... Olympia, WA
Foley, David W. ... San Diego, CA
Foley, David W. ... Dunkirk, NY
Foley, Dennis ... Baltimore, MD
Foley, Dennis M.
Department Of Veterans Affairs, Office of the General Counsel, GV
Foley, Diana J. ... Las Vegas, NV
Foley, Donald F. ... Indianapolis, IN
Foley, Donald R. ... Oakland, CA
Foley, Dorothy L. ... Department of Justice, Justice Management Division, GV
Foley, Douglas F. ... Vancouver, WA
Foley, Douglas J. ... San Jose, CA
Foley, Douglas M. ... Norfolk, VA
Foley, Dudley C., Jr. ... New Orleans, LA
Foley, E. Tim ... Indianapolis, IN
Foley, Eamonn F. ... Lakeville, CT
New York, NY
Foley, Edmond W. ... South Bend, IN
Foley, Edw. P. ... San Bernardino, CA
Foley, Edward J. ... King City, CA
Foley, Edward M. ... Kennett Square, PA
Foley, Eileen Mary ... North Brunswick, NJ
Foley, Elisabeth K. ... Daly City, CA
Foley, Elizabeth A ... Boston, MA
Foley, Elizabeth A. ... Livonia, MI
Foley, Elizabeth A. ... Minneapolis, MN
Foley, Elizabeth Anne ... Staten Island, NY
Foley, Elizabeth J. ... Las Vegas, NV
Foley, Elizabeth M. ... Toledo, OH
Foley, Elizabeth Pfeiler ... Chicago, IL
Foley, F. James ... Columbus, OH
Foley, F. James, Jr. ... Chicago, IL
Foley, F. James, Jr., Chartered ... Chicago, IL
Foley & Foley ... Washington, DC
Foley & Foley ... Canandaigua, NY
Palmyra, NY
Foley & Foley, A Professional Corporation
Anchorage, AK
Foley & Foley, LLP ... Westbury, NY
Foley, Foley & Passafaro ... Dunkirk, NY
Foley, Foley & Peden ... Martinsville, IN
Foley, Francis C. ... Metuchen, NJ
Foley, Francis H., Jr. ... Alexandria, VA
Foley, Francis J., III ... Hanover, CT
Foley, Francis M., (P.A.)
Lighthouse Point, FL
Foley, Fred A. ... Birmingham, MI
Foley & Freeman, Chartered ... Meridian, ID
Foley, Frye & Foley ... Herkimer, NY
Old Forge, NY
Utica, NY
Foley, George Hamilton ... Lansing, MI
Foley, George Hamilton, P.C. ... Lansing, MI
Foley, George, Jr. ... Las Vegas, NV
Foley, George, Sr. ... Las Vegas, NV
Foley, Gerald S., Jr. ... Canton, MA
Foley, Gerald T., Jr. ... Newark, NJ
Foley, Geraldine M. ... Lexington, MA
Foley, Gerard J. ... Winchester, MA
Foley, H. Thomas ... Cheverly, MD
Foley, Heather Deans ... Baltimore, MD
Foley, Hoag & Eliot LLP
Washington, DC
Boston, MA
Foley and Honigmann ... Phoenix, AZ
Foley, Howard M.
Cumberland Foreside, ME
Foley, Howard R. ... Meridian, ID
Foley, Hugh J. ... Edmond, OK
Foley, Irvin D. ... Louisville, KY
Foley, J. Brian ... Scranton, PA
Foley, J. Dayton ... Jacksonville, FL
Foley, J. Garth ... New York, NY
Foley, J. Mark ... San Francisco, CA
Foley, J. Patrick, III ... Columbus, OH
Foley, Jackson W., Jr. ... Hartford, CT
Foley, James C., Sr. ... Middlebury, VT
Foley, James Charles, Jr. ... Middlebury, VT
Foley, James D. ... Burlington, VT
Foley, James F. ... Palmyra, NY
Foley, James H. ... Albuquerque, NM
Foley, James H., Sr. ... Santa Monica, CA
Foley, James J., Jr. ... Quincy, MA
Foley, James K. ... Silver Spring, MD
Foley, James N. ... Macon, MO
Foley, James R. ... Huntsville, AL
Foley, James R. ... Chicago, IL
Foley, James R. ... Columbus, OH
Foley, James T. ... Bloomington, IL
Foley, James T. ... Chicago, IL
Foley, James T. ... Tyler, TX
Foley, James V. ... Staten Island, NY
Foley, James W. ... Redwood City, CA
Foley, James W. ... Saratoga, CA
Foley, Jani M. ... New York, NY
Foley, Janis E. Susalla ... Ann Arbor, MI
Findlay, OH
Toledo, OH
Foley, Jennifer L. ... Manchester, NH
Foley, Joan B. ... St. Louis, MO
Foley, Joan C. ... Seattle, WA
Tacoma, WA
Foley, Joanne D.C. ... Boston, MA
Foley, John A. ... Los Angeles, CA
Foley, John A. ... West Palm Beach, FL
Foley, John B. ... New York, NY
Foley, John C. ... Farmington, CT
Foley, John D. ... Cape Girardeau, MO
Foley, John D. ... New York, NY
Foley, John D. ... Milwaukee, WI
Foley, John and Elizabeth ... Las Vegas, NV
Foley, John F. ... San Jose, CA
Foley, John F. ... Washington, DC
Foley, John F. ... Kalamazoo, MI
Foley, John F. ... Sandy, UT
Foley, John F. ... Milwaukee, WI
Foley, John F., Jr. ... Towson, MD
Foley, John F., Jr. ... Boston, MA
Foley, John F., Jr. ... Wakefield, MA
Foley, John H., Jr. ... Rockford, IL
Foley, John, III ... Chicago, IL
Foley, John J. ... Chicago, IL
Foley, John J. ... Oklahoma City, OK
Foley, John L. ... Watertown, SD
Foley, John M. ... Chicago, IL
Foley, John M. ... Knoxville, TN
Foley, John P. ... Washington, DC
Foley, John P. ... Las Vegas, NV
Foley, John R. ... Dearborn, MI
Foley, John R., III ... Library of Congress, Congressional Research Service, GV
Foley, John R., Jr. ... Washington, DC
Foley, John R., P.C. ... Dearborn, MI
Foley, John S. ... Providence, RI
Foley, John W. ... Racine, WI
Foley, Jonathan J., Jr. ... Nashville, TN
Foley & Jones ... Las Vegas, NV
Foley, Joseph G. ... Boston, MA
Foley, Joseph L. ... Abington, PA
Foley, Joseph M. ... Las Vegas, NV
Foley, Joseph P. ... Laguna Hills, CA
Foley, Joseph P. ... Natick, MA
Foley, Joseph P. ... White Plains, NY
Foley, Joseph R. ... Seattle, WA
Foley, Joseph W. ... Bloomington, IL
Foley, Joy Guleserian ... Watertown, MA
Foley & Judell, L.L.P. ... Baton Rouge, LA
Metairie, LA
New Orleans, LA
Foley, Judi S. ... San Diego, CA
Foley, K. Michael ... Columbus, OH
Foley, Kandy Heavilin ... Greenville, OH
Foley, Kathleen A. ... San Francisco, CA
Foley, Kathleen Ann ... Concord, MA
Foley, Kathleen D. ... Garden City, NY
Foley, Katrina Anne ... Irvine, CA
Foley, Keith W. ... Beaumont, TX
Foley, Kenneth M. ... San Andreas, CA
Foley, Kerry C. ... New York, NY
Foley, Kevin J. ... New York, NY
Foley, Kevin Jordan ... Southgate, MI
Foley, Kevin M. ... Chicago, IL
Foley, Kevin P. ... Columbus, OH
Foley, Kevin P. ... Scranton, PA
Foley, Kirk J. ... Hurley, WI
Foley, Kristin Dorney ... Milford, CT
Foley & Lardner ... Los Angeles, CA
Sacramento, CA
San Diego, CA
San Francisco, CA
Denver, CO
Washington, DC
Jacksonville, FL
Orlando, FL
Palm Beach, FL
Tallahassee, FL
Tampa, FL
West Palm Beach, FL
Chicago, IL
Annapolis, MD
Madison, WI
Milwaukee, WI
Foley, Leo J. ... South Lyon, MI
Foley, Leo T. ... Minneapolis, MN
Foley, Leo Thomas ... Anoka, MN
Foley, Lorraine S. ... Boston, MA
Foley, Lynn M. ... Livonia, MI
Foley & Mahmood ... Birmingham, AL
Huntsville, AL
Foley & Mansfield ... Bloomfield Hills, MI
Minneapolis, MN
Foley, Margaret E. ... Cambridge, MA
Foley, Margaret M. ... Philadelphia, PA
Foley, Margaret R. ... Cleveland, OH
Foley, Mark A. ... Columbus, OH
Foley, Mark F. ... Milwaukee, WI
Foley, Mark J. ... Philadelphia, PA
Foley, Mark T. ... Upper Marlboro, MD
Foley, Martha C. ... Silver Spring, MD
Foley, Martin J. ... Los Angeles, CA
Foley, Martin J. ... Portland, ME
Foley, Martin J. ... Worcester, MA
Foley, Maryann E. ... Anchorage, AK
Foley, Matthew O., III ... La Jolla, CA
Foley, Matthew T. ... Arlington, VA
Foley McIntosh Frey & Claytor, Professional Corporation ... Albany, CA
Lafayette, CA
Walnut Creek, CA
Foley, McLane, Foley, McDonald & MacGregor ... Hazleton, PA
Scranton, PA
Stroudsburg, PA
Wilkes-Barre, PA
Foley, Meagan M. ... Tacoma, WA
Foley, Michael C. ... Fredonia, NY
Jamestown, NY
Foley, Michael E. ... Hartford, CT
Foley, Michael E. ... New Carrollton, MD
Foley, Michael E. ... Waynesville, OH
Foley, Michael J. ... Key Largo, FL
Foley, Michael J. ... North Chicago, IL
Foley, Michael J. ... Scranton, PA
Foley, Michael L. ... Las Vegas, NV
Foley, Michael P. ... Rochester, MI
Foley, Michael P. ... Cincinnati, OH
Foley, Michael P., Jr. ... Cheshire, CT
Foley, Michael T. ... Chicago, IL
Foley, Miriam F. ... New York, NY
Foley, Molly A. ... Escanaba, MI
Foley, Molly M. ... Phoenix, AZ
Foley and Montalbano ... Clifton, NJ
Foley, Morgan L. ... El Cajon, CA
Foley, Nancy K. ... Newark, NJ
Foley, Nancy Turck ... Lutz, FL
Boston, MA
Foley, Nicholas A. ... Lancaster, TX
Foley, Patricia E. ... Denver, CO
Foley, Patricia K. ... Georgetown, KY
Foley, Patrick F. ... New York, NY
Foley, Patrick J. ... Los Angeles, CA
Foley, Patrick J. ... San Francisco, CA
Foley, Patrick J. ... Miami, FL
New York, NY
Foley, Patrick J. ... Chicago, IL
Foley, Patrick J. ... Buffalo, NY
Foley, Patrick J. ... Dayton, OH
Foley, Patrick J. ... Toledo, OH
Foley, Patrick W. ... Edison, NJ
Foley, Paula W. ... Wellesley, MA
Foley, Pauline ... Morristown, NJ
Foley, Peter A. ... Charlotte, NC
Foley, Peter R. ... Martinsville, IN
Foley, Peter T. ... Concord, NH
Foley, Philip J. ... Tampa, FL
Boston, MA
Foley & Pool, LLP ... Indianapolis, IN
Foley, Ralph M. ... Martinsville, IN
Foley, Raymond I., II
Farmington Hills, MI
Foley, Raymond J. ... Syosset, NY
Foley, Rebecca R. ... Philadelphia, PA
Foley, Rebecca Simmons ... Bloomington, IL
Foley, Regina M. ... Philadelphia, PA
Foley, Richard A. ... Augusta, ME
Foley, Richard H., Jr. ... Anchorage, AK
Foley, Ridgway K., Jr. ... Portland, OR
Foley, Rion Du Bose ... Charleston, SC
Foley, Robert G. ... Sacramento, CA
Foley, Robert G. ... Monroe, LA
Foley, Robert H. ... Bend, OR
Foley, Robert J. ... Orinda, CA
Foley, Robert J. ... Boston, MA
Foley, Robert J. ... St. Louis, MO
Foley, Robert J. ... Plymouth, NH
Foley, Robert J. ... Bridgewater, NJ
Foley, Robert M. ... San Jose, CA
Foley, Robert M. ... Westbury, NY
Foley, Robert Patrick ... West Palm Beach, FL
Foley, Robert Patrick, P.A.
West Palm Beach, FL
Foley, Ruth E. ... Racine, WI
Foley, Sally Lee ... Bloomfield Hills, MI
Foley, Scott W. ... Lanham, MD
Foley, Sean F. ... Treasury Department, Internal Revenue Service, GV
Foley, Shannon M. ... Manhattan Beach, CA
New York, NY
Foley, Shawn P. ... Westfield, NJ
Foley, Sheilah E. ... Minneapolis, MN
Foley, Sherry L. ... Saddle River, NJ
Foley & Small ... South Bend, IN
Foley, Smit, O'Boyle & Weisman
New York, NY
Foley & Sprague ... Boston, MA
Foley, Stephen B. ... Taylor, MI
Foley, Stephen B., P.C. ... Taylor, MI
Foley, Stephen C. ... Cleveland, OH
Foley, Stephen J. ... Minneapolis, MN
Foley, Stephen J. ... Asbury Park, NJ
Foley, Stephen J., Jr. ... Asbury Park, NJ
Foley, Stephen Mark ... Boston, MA
Foley, Stephen P. ... New York, NY
Foley, Stephen P. ... Milwaukee, WI
Foley, Stephen R. ... Buffalo, NY
Foley, Susan Behlke ... Anchorage, AK
Foley, Therese M. ... Bakersfield, CA
Foley, Thomas A. ... Wilmington, DE
Foley, Thomas A. ... Riverwoods, IL
Foley, Thomas C. ... Boston, MA
Foley, Thomas E. ... South Bend, IN
Foley, Thomas F. X. ... Holmdel, NJ
Foley, Thomas G., Jr. ... Santa Barbara, CA
Foley, Thomas J. ... Central Lake, MI
Foley, Thomas J. ... Detroit, MI
Foley, Thomas J. ... Bronxville, NY
Foley, Thomas J. ... Westbury, NY
Foley, Thomas J., III ... Scranton, PA
Stroudsburg, PA
Foley, Thomas J., Jr. ... Scranton, PA
Stroudsburg, PA
Foley, Thomas M. ... Honolulu, HI
Foley, Thomas M. ... McHenry, IL
Foley, Thomas Patrick ... Philadelphia, PA
Foley, Thomas R. ... Los Angeles, CA
Foley, Thomas S. ... Washington, DC
Foley, Thomas W. ... Des Moines, IA
Foley, Thomas W. ... Plymouth, MN
Foley, Timothy D. ... Old Forge, NY
Utica, NY
Foley, Timothy E. ... Oklahoma City, OK
Foley, Timothy E. ... Scranton, PA
Foley, Timothy F. ... Wood Dale, IL
Foley, Timothy J. ... San Francisco, CA
Foley, Timothy J. ... Saddle River, NJ
New York, NY
Foley, Timothy M. ... Treasury Department, United States Secret Service, GV
Foley, Vincent J. ... New York, NY
Foley, Wayne W. ... New Orleans, LA
Foley, William Andrew, III ... Mebane, NC
Foley, William E. ... Chevy Chase, MD
Foley, William J. ... Phoenix, AZ
Foley, William J. ... San Jose, CA
Foley, William J., Jr. ... Albany, NY
Foley, William L., Jr. ... Philadelphia, PA
Foley, William R. ... Lafayette, CA
Foley, William T. ... Omaha, NE
Foley, William T., Jr. ... Staten Island, NY
Foley, W. J. ... Fort Lauderdale, FL
Folfas, Paul A. ... Dayton, OH

Fontana, Frances Chalem ... Denver, CO
Fontana, Frank V. ... Hopewell Junction, NY
Fontana, Gary L. ... San Francisco, CA
Fontana, James C. ... McLean, VA
Fontana, Jane ... Secaucus, NJ
Fontana, Karen M. ... New Orleans, LA
Fontana & Lanier, P.A. ... Durham, NC
Fontana, Lawrence J. ... Houston, TX
Fontana, Louis B., Jr. ... Woodbridge, NJ
Fontana, Louis C. ... Cincinnati, OH
Fontana, Lucille A. ... White Plains, NY
Fontana, Lynn ... Durham, NC
Fontana, Mark A. ... Harrisburg, PA
Fontana, Mia F. ... Los Angeles, CA
Fontana, Nicholas A. ... Flagstaff, AZ
Fontana, Raymond J. ... Springfield, MA
Fontana, Richard G. ... Yonkers, NY
Fontana, Robert C. ... Worcester, MA
Fontana, Tagnia M. ... Beaumont, TX
Fontana, Vincent R. ... New York, NY
Fontana, Wayne J. ... New Orleans, LA
Fontane, M. Matthew ... Dallas, TX
Fontanella, Alfred E. ... Totowa, NJ
Fontanella, Andrew J. ... Hyattsville, MD
Rockville, MD
Fontanella & Benevento ... Totowa, NJ
Fontanella, Bruce A. ... Meriden, CT
Fontanella, David A. ... Alexandria, VA
Fontanella, Doriana ... Denver, CO
Fontanella and Krithades, P.C.
Alexandria, VA
Fontanet-Maldonado, Julio ... San Juan, PR
Fontanetta, Joseph J. ... Garden City, NY
Fontanilla, James J. ... San Francisco, CA
Fonte, Anthony N. ... Buena Park, CA
Fonte, David J. ... Brookline, MA
Fonte, Gina A. ... Boston, MA
Fonte, John P. ... Department of Justice, Antitrust Division, GV
Fonte, Kenneth C. ... Metairie, LA
Fonte, Mark J. ... Staten Island, NY
Fonte, Raul V. ... New Orleans, LA
Fontecchio, Christopher D.
Department Of The Interior, Bureau of Land Management, GV
Fontecchio, Louise R. ... Nashville, TN
Fontecchio, Thomas E. ... Lakewood, CO
Fontein, Douglas J. ... Washington, DC
Fontela, Rogelio J. ... Tallahassee, FL
Fontenelle, Robert E., Jr. ... New Orleans, LA
Fontenot, Allen R. ... New Orleans, LA
Fontenot, Allison ... Billings, MT
Fontenot, Clyde ... Ville Platte, LA
Fontenot, Clyde, A Professional Law Corporation ... Ville Platte, LA
Fontenot, Craig J. ... Baton Rouge, LA
Fontenot, Daniel P. ... Eunice, LA
Fontenot, Elvin C., Jr. ... Leesville, LA
Fontenot, F. Frank, (P.C.)
New Orleans, LA
Fontenot, Gerald J. ... Mamou, LA
Fontenot, Geraldine E. ... Baton Rouge, LA
Fontenot, Gilbert L. ... Mobile, AL
Fontenot, H. Ward ... Cameron, LA
Fontenot, J. Harold ... Ville Platte, LA
Fontenot, J. Jake ... Mamou, LA
Fontenot, J. Jake, A P.L.C. ... Mamou, LA
Fontenot, James E. ... Abbeville, LA
Fontenot, Johanna M. ... Los Angeles, CA
Fontenot, John Brent ... Baton Rouge, LA
Fontenot, John G. ... Eunice, LA
Fontenot, John G., A P.L.C. ... Eunice, LA
Fontenot, Kathy ... Houston, TX
Fontenot, Lisa A. ... San Francisco, CA
Fontenot, Michael J. ... Monroe, LA
Fontenot, Michael W. ... Wellesley Hills, MA
Fontenot, Michelle Daigle ... Baton Rouge, LA
Fontenot, Philip A. ... Lafayette, LA
Fontenot, Timmy J. ... Gonzales, LA
Fontenot, W. Todd ... Lake Charles, LA
Fontenot, Walter P. ... Liberty, TX
Fontes, David A. ... Lakeland, FL
Fontes, J. Mario, Jr. ... Miami, FL
Fontes, Marshall S. ... Bakersfield, CA
Fontes, Silvestre A. ... Boston, MA
Fontes, Zanetta L. ... Renton, WA
Fontg, Ricardo E. ... Kansas City, MO
Fontham, John H. ... New Orleans, LA
Fontham, Michael R., (P.C.)
New Orleans, LA
Fontheim, Claude G.B. ... Washington, DC
Fonti, Edward J. ... Lake Charles, LA
Fonti, Joseph V. ... Wausau, WI
Fontichiaro, James S. ... Detroit, MI
Font Lee, Fernando ... San Juan, PR
Fontoura, Lisa M. ... Roseland, NJ
Fonvielle, C. David ... Tallahassee, FL
Fonvielle Hinkle & Lewis ... Tallahassee, FL
Fonvielle, J. Keaton ... Shelby, NC
Fonvielle, W. Alex, Jr.
Wrightsville Beach, NC
Fonville, Harold W., II ... Memphis, TN
Fonzi, Irene ... Fort Lauderdale, FL
Fonzo, John P. ... Memphis, TN
Fonzone & Ashley ... Allentown, PA
Fonzone, Charles J. ... Allentown, PA
Foo, Josephine ... Philadelphia, PA
Foo, Patrick George ... Los Angeles, CA
Foodim, Lauren ... New York, NY
Foodim, Leslie Ann ... Carle Place, NY
Foodman, Bruce A. ... Westport, CT
Foodman, Marc D. ... Reno, NV
Foody, Alan Michael ... Atlantic Beach, FL
Foody, Ellen K. ... Greenville, SC
Foody, James T. ... Central Square, NY
Foody, Jerome J. ... Central Square, NY
Foody, Richard D. ... Chicago, IL
Foody, Robert J. ... Albany, NY
Foody, Thomas J. ... Columbus, OH
Fooks, Robert H. ... Little Rock, AR
Fooks, Scott Brion ... Santa Barbara, CA
Fooks, William J. ... Lexington, KY
Foon, Ronald H. ... Pontiac, MI
Foonberg, Jay G. ... Santa Monica, CA
Foor, Michael J. ... Stockton, CA
Foor, Steven E. ... West Palm Beach, FL
Foor, Tracy L. ... Norman, OK
Foorman, James L. ... Chicago, IL
Foos, David P. ... Fairfield, CA
Foos, James Reed, Jr. ... Cleveland, OH
Foos, Martin A. ... Dayton, OH
Foosaner, Aaron A. ... Stuart, FL
Foose, Charlene M. ... Carnegie, PA
Foose, K. Donelson ... Mobile, AL
Foose, Nathan T. ... Westfield, NJ
Foose, Robert L., II ... Bethesda, MD
Fooshe, Peter E., Jr. ... St. Paul, MN
Foot, Jonathan T. ... Boston, MA
Foot, Kristine L. ... Missoula, MT
Foot, Silas B., III ... Red Wing, MN
Foote, Alexis G. ... Anchorage, AK
Foote, Anderson M., Jr. ... Jacksonville, FL
Foote & Associates LLP ... New York, NY
Foote, Caleb ... Point Reyes Station, CA
Foote, Carl F. ... Cincinnati, OH
Foote, Charles F. ... Hudson, NY
Foote, Cody W. ... Opelika, AL
Foote, Daniel G. ... Indianapolis, IN
Foote, Debra L. ... Tallahassee, FL
Foote, Douglas D. ... Denver, CO
Foote, Douglas S. ... Dayton, OH
Foote, Edward L. ... Chicago, IL
Foote, Edward T. ... Coral Gables, FL
Foote, Elizabeth Erny ... Alexandria, LA
Foote, Elizabeth V. ... Boston, MA
Foote, Emmerline ... Los Angeles, CA
Foote, Francis W. ... Treasury Department, Office of Regulations and Rulings, GV
Foote, Frank E. ... Sun City, AZ
Foote, Gene C., II ... Hastings, NE
Foote, George E. ... Lexington, MA
Foote, George M. ... Washington, DC
Foote, George M. ... Alexandria, LA
Foote, Gordon T., II ... Dallas, TX
Foote, Gregory B.
Environmental Protection Agency, Office of the General Counsel, GV
Foote, Guy Myrph, Jr. ... Dallas, TX
Foote, Guy Myrph, Jr., P.C. ... Dallas, TX
Foote, Heidi H. ... Indianapolis, IN
Foote, Jack C. ... St. Paul, MN
Foote, Jeffrey P. ... Portland, OR
Foote, John H. ... Tallahassee, FL
Foote, John H. ... Leesburg, VA
Foote, John R. ... San Francisco, CA
Foote, John S. ... Lake Oswego, OR
Foote, Joseph ... Washington, DC
Foote, Kyle E. ... Kansas City, MO
Foote, Orlando B., III ... El Centro, CA
Foote, R. Hale ... San Leandro, CA
Foote, Ralph A. ... Middlebury, VT
Foote, Richard C. ... Shaker Heights, OH
Foote, Richard P. ... Middlebury, VT
Foote, Richard V. ... Wichita, KS
Foote, Richard V., P.A. ... Wichita, KS
Foote, Robert L. ... Chicago, IL
Foote, Robert M. ... Aurora, IL
Foote, Roger R. ... Mesa, AZ
Foote, Roger W. ... Tallahassee, FL
Foote, Sally H. ... Clearwater, FL
Foote, Susan Bartlett ... Washington, DC
Foote & Temple ... Bangor, ME
Foote, Theron A. ... Warsaw, NY
Foote, Thomas R. ... Cleveland, OH
Foote, Thomas W. ... Santa Monica, CA
Foote, W. Penn ... Burlingame, CA
Foote, W. Ross ... Alexandria, LA
Foote, Walter V. ... New York, NY
Foote, Warren G. ... Salem, OR
Foote, Wayne R. ... Bangor, ME
Foote, William C. ... St. Louis, MO
Foote, William D., Jr. ... Rockville, MD
Foote, William J. ... Aurora, IL
Footer, Michael ... Richmond, VA
Footer, Sheila ... Arlington, VA
Footland, Lenard A.
Department of Commerce, Patent and Trademark Office, GV
Footman, Duncan ... Napa, CA
St. Helena, CA
Foottit, Thomas ... Denver, CO
Fopp, Gene P. ... Great Falls, MT
Foppe, Forrest F. ... Shreveport, LA
Foppert, Deborah A. ... Jamestown, NY
Foppiano, C. Houston ... Raleigh, NC
Foppiano, Chas. E. ... Louisville, KY
Foppiano, Christie McCallie ... Raleigh, NC
Foradas, Michael P. ... Chicago, IL
Foradora, John H. ... Ridgway, PA
Foradora, Mary Margaret ... Ridgway, PA
Foraker, David A. ... Portland, OR
Foraker, Peggy S. ... Gresham, OR
Foraker, Scott J. ... Thousand Oaks, CA
Foran, Charles W. ... Shorewood, WI
Foran, David M. ... Hartford, CT
Foran, Elizabeth C. ... Vernon, CT
Foran, J. William ... Milwaukee, WI
Foran, James Edward ... Bronx, NY
Foran, James T. ... Newark, NJ
Foran, John F. ... Sacramento, CA
Foran, John Francis ... Fair Oaks, CA
Foran, John J. ... Chicago, IL
Foran, John R. ... Greenbelt, MD
Foran, Kenneth Lawrence ... Alexandria, VA
Foran, Leo K. ... Dearborn Heights, MI
Foran, Margaret M. ... New York, NY
Foran, Mary Anne ... Los Angeles, CA
Foran, Michael L. ... Chicago, IL
Foran, Nasharr & O'Toole Ltd.
Chicago, IL
Foran, Patrick J. ... Arroyo Grande, CA
Foran, Paul G. ... Danville, IL
Granite City, IL
Foran, Ryan J. ... Greenbelt, MD
Foran & Schultz ... Chicago, IL
Foran, Sheila M. ... Department of Justice, Civil Rights Division, GV
Foran, Terrence J. ... Hartford, CT
Foran, Thomas A. ... Chicago, IL
Foran, Thomas Edward ... Emeryville, CA
San Francisco, CA
Foran, Timothy J. ... Athens, OH
Forastiere, Michael A., III ... New York, NY
Forastieri, Juan José ... San Juan, PR
Forb, Lee B. ... Charleston, WV
Forbath, Brian ... Newport Beach, CA
Forbath, Joseph W. ... Orange, CA
Forbeck, Kenneth W. ... Beloit, WI
Forberg, Lisa B. ... Windham, NH
Forbes, Allen H. ... Boston, MA
Forbes, Amy R. ... Los Angeles, CA
Forbes, Andrew J. ... Media, PA
Forbes, Arthur L., Law Offices ... Houston, TX
Forbes, Ben N. ... Billings, MT
Forbes, Bender, Paolino & DiSanti, P.C.
Media, PA
Forbes & Bowman ... Brunswick, GA
Savannah, GA
Statesboro, GA
Forbes, Brian D. ... Orlando, FL
Forbes, Brian L. ... San Diego, CA
Forbes, Brian R. ... Dallas, TX
Forbes, Cynthia Ann ... Salem, OR
Forbes, Dale ... Great Falls, MT
Forbes, Danielle Marie
Christiansted, St. Croix, VI
Forbes, David L. ... Atlanta, GA
Forbes, David L. ... Michigan City, IN
Forbes, David P.
National Aeronautics And Space Administration, Office of the General Counsel, GV
Forbes, Dean C. ... Federal Trade Commission, Bureau of Consumer Protection, GV
Forbes, Deborah K.
Pension Benefit Guaranty Corporation, Other Lawyers in Staff or Executive Positions, GV
Forbes, Donald R. ... Fresno, CA
Forbes, Donna Shore ... Elizabeth City, NC
Forbes, Douglas ... Del Mar, CA
Forbes, Earl Thomas ... Huntsville, AL
Forbes, Elizabeth G. ... Boston, MA
Forbes, Ernest M., Jr. ... Denham Springs, LA
Forbes, Ernestine ... Plainfield, NJ
Forbes, Eryn E. ... Warren, OR
Forbes, Eugene A. ... Lansing, MI
Forbes, Forbes & Associates ... Cleveland, OH
Forbes, Franklin S. ... Omaha, NE
Forbes, G. Daniel ... Franklin, VA
Forbes, George L. ... Cleveland, OH
Forbes, George T. ... La Jolla, CA
Forbes, Glenn A. ... San Leandro, CA
Forbes, Glenn E. ... Painesville, OH
Forbes, Gordon ... St. Paul, MN
Forbes, Hal E. ... Palo Alto, CA
Forbes, Helen M. ... Cleveland, OH
Forbes, Herbert B. ... Buffalo, NY
Forbes, Holle Bevins ... Boston, MA
Forbes, Ivan M. ... Waterford, MI
Forbes, Ivan M., P.C. ... Waterford, MI
Forbes, J. Randy ... Chesapeake, VA
Forbes, James ... Anchorage, AK
Forbes, James D. ... Kill Devil Hills, NC
Forbes, James, P.C. ... Anchorage, AK
Forbes, James R. ... San Francisco, CA
Forbes, Jane ... Detroit, MI
Forbes, Jay W. ... Carlsbad, NM
Forbes, Jenne S. ... Tucson, AZ
Forbes, Jessica ... New York, NY
Forbes, John A., Jr. ... Bridgeport, CT
Forbes, John G. ... Indianapolis, IN
Forbes, John R. ... Jacksonville, FL
Forbes, Joseph H. ... Gainesville, FL
Forbes, Joseph H., Jr. ... Elizabeth City, NC
Forbes, Joseph H., P.A. ... Gainesville, FL
Forbes, Joseph J. ... Houston, TX
Forbes, Karen L. ... College Park, MD
Forbes, Karyn P. ... Concord, NH
Forbes, Kathleen S. ... Salem, OR
Forbes, Kerrie V. ... Dallas, TX
Forbes, Laurie E. ... Fairfax, VA
Forbes, Lawrence A. ... Los Angeles, CA
Forbes, Layne B. ... Bountiful, UT
Forbes, Lisa Babish ... Cleveland, OH
Forbes, Lisa K. ... Walnut Creek, CA
Forbes, Louise ... Boston, MA
Forbes, Marilyn R. ... Raleigh, NC
Forbes, Martin B. ... Chicago, IL
Forbes, Martin B., Ltd. ... Chicago, IL
Forbes, Mary Jane ... Harrisburg, PA
Forbes, Matthew Edward ... Harrisburg, PA
Forbes & McKelvey ... Franklin, TN
Forbes, Morton G. ... Savannah, GA
Forbes, Nancy E. ... Boston, MA
Forbes, Nicole S. ... Columbus, OH
Forbes, Otis K., III ... Virginia Beach, VA
Forbes, Pamela B. ... Washington, DC
Forbes, Patricia R. ... Arlington, VA
Forbes, Patrick T. ... El Dorado, KS
Forbes, Paula G. ... St. Paul, MN
Forbes, Peter C. ... Steamboat Springs, CO
Forbes, Philip H. ... Boca Raton, FL
Naples, FL
Palm Beach Gardens, FL
Forbes, Randal S. ... Angola, IN
Forbes, Randall J. ... Topeka, KS
Forbes, Richard H. ... Boston, MA
Forbes, Robert G. ... Hartford City, IN
Forbes, Robert H. ... Gastonia, NC
Forbes, Robert S. ... Alton, IL
Forbes, Robin P. ... Fort Lauderdale, FL
Miami, FL
Forbes, Rodney E. ... Lafayette, IN
Forbes & Sommers ... New York, NY
Forbes, Stanley R. ... Davis, CA
Forbes, Steven ... Cleveland, OH
Forbes, Steven H. ... Chicago, IL
Forbes, Stewart W. ... El Paso, TX
Forbes, Terry O. ... Everett, WA
Forbes, Theodore M., Jr. ... Atlanta, GA
Forbes, Thomas A. ... Austin, TX
Forbes, Thomas D. ... New Orleans, LA
Forbes, Timothy George ... Pacific Grove, CA
Forbes, Virginia S. ... Miami, FL
Forbes, W. Ross, Jr. ... Dallas, TX
Forbes, William C. ... Charleston, WV
Forbes, William J. ... New Britain, CT
Forbes, William L. ... Chesapeake, VA
Forbess, John D. ... Beverly Hills, CA
Forbes-Sutherland, Deborah Jean
Ventura, CA
Forbis, Amy Thompson ... Seattle, WA
Tacoma, WA
Forbis, Christopher N. ... Decatur, TX
Forbis, Clinton S., Jr. ... Harrisburg, NC
Kannapolis, NC
Forbis, Glenn E. ... Bloomfield Hills, MI
Forbis & Grossman ... Harrisburg, NC
Kannapolis, NC
Forbis, John T. ... Childress, TX
Forbis, Merwyn C. ... Miami, FL
Forbis, Miriam S. ... Greensboro, NC
Forbis, Patricia L. ... Columbia, SC
Sumter, SC
Forbis & Stegall ... Greensboro, NC
Forbus, Sharon A. ... Indianapolis, IN
Forbush, Audrey J. ... Bloomfield Hills, MI
Forbush, H. S. ... Rexburg, ID
Forbush, Kevin M. ... Colorado Springs, CO
Forbush, Scott R. ... Lansing, MI
Forbush, William B., III ... Boston, MA
Forcade, Bill S. ... Chicago, IL
Force, Alan P. ... New York, NY
Force & Baldwin ... Adrian, MI
Force, F. Duane ... Austin, TX
Force, Frank J. ... Pinehurst, NC
Force, J. Robert ... Los Angeles, CA
Force, Jeffrey L. ... Phoenix, AZ
Force, Jill L. ... Louisville, KY
Force, Joshua S. ... Los Angeles, CA
Force, Margaret ... Raleigh, NC
Force, Melissa K. ... Los Angeles, CA
Towson, MD
Force, Michael A. ... Hillsboro, OR
Force, Michael S. ... Belmar, NJ
Force, Ralph S. ... Atlanta, GA
Force, Raymond C., III ... Walnut Creek, CA
Forcellini, Antonio ... Detroit, MI
Forceno, Hannon & Arangio
Philadelphia, PA
Forceno, Raymond P. ... Philadelphia, PA
Forch, Jeanne Marie ... Washington, DC
Forch, Paul J. ... Charlottesville, VA
Forché, Alison B. ... Columbus, OH
Forchelli, Charles N.
Long Island City, NY
Forchelli, Curto, Schwartz, Mineo, Carlino & Cohn, LLP ... Melville, NY
Mineola, NY
Forchelli & Forchelli ... Tenafly, NJ
Long Island City, NY
Forchelli, Jeffrey D. ... Melville, NY
Mineola, NY
Forchelli, Vincent ... Long Island City, NY
Forchheimer, Jody E. ... Boston, MA
Forcht, Lisa A. ... New York, NY
Forcht, Terry E. ... Corbin, KY
Forcier, Gerald R. ... Elizabethtown, NY
Forcier, Henry E. ... Manchester, NH
Forcier, Hubert V. ... Minneapolis, MN
Forcier, John V. ... Boston, MA
Forcier, Mark S. ... Austin, TX
Forcier, Michael R. ... Westport, NY
Forcier, Richard R. ... Tucson, AZ
Forcier, Ronald A.
Department of the Air Force, Office of the Judge Advocate General, GV
Forcina, Anthony N., Jr. ... Wilmington, DE
Forcino, Scott R. ... White Plains, NY
Forcione, Erika A. ... New York, NY
Forcucci, Glenn D. ... Phoenix, AZ
Forcum and Forbes ... Hartford City, IN
Forcum, James S. ... Hartford City, IN
Forcum, John W. ... Hartford City, IN
Forcum, Mark R. ... Redwood City, CA
Forcum, Richard E. ... Bend, OR
Forcum & Speck ... Bend, OR
Forcum, W. Richard, III ... Lubbock, TX
Ford, Agnes Johnakin ... Pittsburgh, PA
Ford, Alan B. ... Salt Lake City, UT
Ford, Albert Elsworth, II ... Tallahassee, FL
Ford, Alfred G. ... Jamestown, NY
Ford, Alix B. ... New York, NY
Ford, Alvin J. ... Sioux City, IA
Ford, Alvin J., P.C. ... Sioux City, IA
Ford, Amy L. ... Little Rock, AR
Ford, Andrea Shaffer ... Charlotte, NC
Ford, Andrew J. ... New York, NY
Ford, Angela M. ... Lexington, KY

Ford, Walker, Haggerty & Behar, A Professional Law Corporation
Los Angeles, CA
Long Beach, CA
Ford, Wallace L., II ... New York, NY
Ford, Walter J. ... Hampton, VA
Ford & Weaver, P.A. ... Portsmouth, NH
Ford White Wielinski & Salazar P.C.
Dallas, TX
Ford, Will R. ... New Albany, MS
Ford, William D. ... Washington, DC
Ford, William D. ... New York, NY
Ford, William E. ... Allentown, PA
Ford, William E., III ... Charles Town, WV
Ford, William F., Jr. ... Kansas City, MO
Ford, William H. ... San Antonio, TX
Ford, William H., III ... Los Angeles, CA
Ford, William L. ... Hot Springs Village, AR
Ford, William L. ... Saratoga Springs, NY
Ford, William M. ... Alexandria, LA
Ford, William P. ... Montclair, NJ
New York, NY
Ford, William R. ... Joliet, IL
Ford, William T. ... Anchorage, AK
Ford, William W., III ... Cincinnati, OH
Ford, Wm. R. ... Kosciusko, MS
Forde, Barbara J. ... Phoenix, AZ
Forde, Barry V. ... Clearwater, FL
Forde, Benj. F., Jr. ... Scituate, MA
Forde, Brian P. ... Chicago, IL
Forde, C. Douglass, Jr. ... Dallas, TX
Forde, E. Charles ... Irvine, CA
Forde, Eileen ... New York, NY
Forde, George S., Jr. ... Philadelphia, PA
Forde, Hugh A. ... New York, NY
Forde, James E. ... New York, NY
Forde, James L. ... Melville, NY
Forde, Janice R. ... Chicago, IL
Forde, Kevin M. ... Chicago, IL
Forde, Kevin M., Ltd. ... Chicago, IL
Forde, Mark W. ... Bethesda, MD
Forde, Michael ... Minneapolis, MN
Forde, Michael E. ... Woodbury, NY
Forde, Michael K. ... Chicago, IL
Forde, Richard C. ... Lake Oswego, OR
Forde, Timothy J.
Securities and Exchange Commission, Executive Staff, GV
Forde-Mazrui, Kim A. ... Washington, DC
Forden, Nancy T.
United States Postal Service, Law Department, GV
Forder, Anna C. ... St. Louis, MO
Forderhase, Grace M. ... Fort Worth, TX
Forderhase, Greg ... Knoxville, TN
Forderhase, John Stephen ... Seattle, WA
Fordham, Bart W., Jr. ... Columbia, SC
Fordham, Benjamin C. ... Nashville, TN
Fordham, Carris Lee, Jr ... Punta Gorda, FL
Fordham, Dennis A. W. ... Albany, NY
Fordham, Forrest B., III ... Johnstown, PA
Fordham, Gary B. ... Beaufort, SC
Fordham, George F. ... Clarksburg, WV
Fordham, Harriet O. ... Stuart, FL
Fordham, Henry C., Jr. ... Apex, NC
Fordham, James E., Jr. ... Dallas, TX
Fordham, James T. ... Dalton, GA
Fordham, Jefferson B. ... Salt Lake City, UT
Fordham, Laurence S. ... Boston, MA
Fordham, Mark T. Aoki ... Seattle, WA
Fordham, Mary R. ... Atlanta, GA
Fordham, Michael R., Jr. ... New York, NY
Fordham, R. David ... Annapolis, MD
Fordham, Roxanne ... Pittsburgh, PA
Ford-Harder, Jana ... San Diego, CA
Fordiani, Alfred L., Jr. ... Meriden, CT
Fordiani, Martha L. ... Meriden, CT
Fordice, Sylvia M. ... Buffalo, NY
Fordin, Jonathan M. ... Boca Raton, FL
Fording, Thomas E.
Department of the Navy, GV
Fordis, Jean Burke ... Washington, DC
Ford-Livene, Marcelino
Federal Communications Commission, Office of Plans and Policy, GV
Fordney, J. Michael ... Saginaw, MI
Fordney & Prine ... Bay City, MI
Midland, MI
Saginaw, MI
Fordree, Deborah E. ... Mount Clemens, MI
Fordyce, David B. ... Saginaw, MI
Fordyce, Gary K. ... Chicago, IL
Fordyce, Jill A. ... San Jose, CA
Fordyce, Marian C. ... Nashville, TN
Fordyce, Richard A. ... Austin, TX
Fore, Allen G. ... Rockford, IL
Fore, F. Larkin ... Louisville, KY
Fore, Gerri M. ... Houston, TX
Fore, John A. ... Palo Alto, CA
Fore, Marion W., Jr. ... Greenville, SC
Fore, Merritt C., Jr. ... Ocala, FL
Fore, Miller & Schwartz ... Louisville, KY
Fore, Robert M. ... Lakeland, FL
Fore, Robert S. ... San Francisco, CA
Fore, Roy S. ... Wenatchee, WA
Fore, Scott E. ... Elgin, IL
Forecki, Michael H. ... Eau Claire, WI
Foree, Robert H. ... New Castle, KY
Foree, W. Kent ... Tempe, AZ
Forehand, David A., Jr. ... Cordele, GA
Vienna, GA
Forehand, John William ... Tallahassee, FL
Forehand, Jon V. ... Moultrie, GA
Forehand, Karen ... Cary, NC
Forehand, N. Carolyn ... Nashville, TN
Forehand, Ronald C. ... Richmond, VA
Forehand, Sandra L. ... Norfolk, VA
Forehand, Steve R. ... Alexander City, AL
Forehand, Thomas Rex ... George West, TX
Forehand, V. Thomas, Jr. ... Chesapeake, VA
Forehand, Walter Eugene ... Tallahassee, FL
Forehand, William J. ... Tifton, GA
Foreht Last & Katz, LLP ... Fort Lee, NJ
Foreht Last Landau & Katz, LLP
New York, NY
Foreht, Stephen R. ... New York, NY
Forell, Caroline A. ... Eugene, OR
Forelle, John M. ... New York, NY
Foreman, Alan M. ... Columbia, MD
Foreman, Arch, Dodge, Volyn & Zimmerman P.S. ... Chelan, WA
Leavenworth, WA
Moses Lake, WA
Omak, WA
Wenatchee, WA
Foreman, Boudreaux, Smith & Johnson
Dallas, TX
Fort Worth, TX
McKinney, TX
Foreman, Bradley H. ... Chicago, IL
Foreman, Bruce D. ... Harrisburg, PA
Foreman, Carol L. ... Topeka, KS
Foreman, Dale M. ... Wenatchee, WA
Foreman, David M. ... Centralia, IL
Foreman, DeGeurin, Nugent & Gerger
Houston, TX
Foreman, Donald D. ... Naperville, IL
Foreman, Edward D. ... St. Petersburg, FL
Foreman, Edward D., P.A., Law Offices of
St. Petersburg, FL
Foreman, Elaine F. ... Washington, DC
Foreman & Foreman, Ltd. ... Chicago, IL
Foreman, Fred ... Springfield, IL
Foreman, Glenn B. ... Rayne, LA
Foreman, Gregory D. ... Richmond, VA
Foreman, Gregory D., P.C. ... Richmond, VA
Foreman, Ivery D. ... Columbus, OH
Foreman, James H. ... Virginia Beach, VA
Foreman, James L. ... Benton, IL
Foreman, Jeff ... Harrisburg, PA
Foreman, Jeffery M. ... Chicago, IL
Foreman, Jeffrey E. ... Chicago, IL
Foreman, Jeffrey T. ... Miami, FL
Foreman, Jerome ... Chicago, IL
Foreman, Jim ... Dallas, TX
Foreman, John ... Phoenix, AZ
Foreman, John E. ... Burbank, IL
Foreman, John G. ... Joliet, IL
Foreman, Joseph E. ... Wadsworth, OH
Foreman, Keith ... Houston, TX
Foreman, L. Paul ... Lake Charles, LA
Foreman, Lee D. ... Denver, CO
Foreman, LeRoy F.
United States Court Of Appeals For The Armed Forces, GV
Foreman, Lester D. ... Chicago, IL
Foreman, Linda L. ... Seattle, WA
Foreman, Linda S. ... Minneapolis, MN
Foreman, Linda S. ... Oklahoma City, OK
Foreman, Logan N., III ... Minneapolis, MN
Foreman, Marshall L., (A Professional Corporation) ... San Diego, CA
Foreman, Mary Julia ... Chattanooga, TN
Foreman, Michael E. ... New York, NY
Foreman, Michael L. ... Sarasota, FL
Foreman, Michael L. ... Baltimore, MD
Foreman, Paul S. ... Altoona, PA
Foreman, Raellen ... Denver, CO
Foreman, Randall K. ... New Orleans, LA
Foreman, Rawson ... Atlanta, GA
Foreman, Richard M. ... Bellevue, WA
Foreman, Robert L. ... Pittsburgh, PA
Foreman, Robert L., Jr. ... Atlanta, GA
Foreman, Ronald Keith ... Jackson, MS
Foreman, S. Rafe ... Flower Mound, TX
Foreman, Sheldon L. ... Foothill Ranch, CA
Foreman, Stewart H. ... San Francisco, CA
Foreman, Suzanne R. ... Statesville, NC
Foreman, W. Jeffery ... Owensboro, KY
Foreman, Watson, Crone & Shelburne, LLP
Owensboro, KY
Foreman, William ... Phoenix, AZ
Foreman, William P. ... Evansville, IN
Foreman-Harris, Mary E. ... New York, NY
Foremny, Brian ... Hollywood, FL
Foren, William D. ... New Hudson, MI
Forer, Charles F. ... Haddonfield, NJ
Philadelphia, PA
Forer, Herbert L. ... Encino, CA
Forer, Janis R. ... Fort Lauderdale, FL
Forer, Jeffrey ... Los Angeles, CA
Forer, Lois G. ... Philadelphia, PA
Forer, Robert ... Parsons, KS
Forero, Michael A. ... Los Angeles, CA
Fores, Robert P. ... Modesto, CA
Forese, Angela ... South Salem, NY
Foresman, Henry J. ... Lexington, VA
Foresman, James C. ... Detroit, MI
Foresman, John D. ... Traverse City, MI
Foresman, John S. ... DeWitt, MI
Foresman, Pamela S. ... Timonium, MD
Foresman, Raymond J., Jr.
East Lansing, MI
Forest, Adam ... Davis, CA
Forest, Alan John ... Glenview, IL
Forest, Carl A. ... Boulder, CO
Forest, David B., P.C. ... Clinton Township, MI
Forest, Donald K. ... Rockville, MD
Forest, George J. ... Lafayette, LA
Forest, Janet A. ... Washington, DC
Forest, John Paul, II ... McLean, VA
Forest, Joseph A. ... Petaluma, CA
Forest, Lester ... Lynbrook, NY
Forest, Lester, Jr. ... Yorktown Heights, NY
Forest, Lester, Jr. P.C.
Yorktown Heights, NY
Forest, L. R. ... San Diego, CA
Forest, Richard D. ... Asbury Park, NJ
Forest, Warren S. ... Santa Cruz, CA
Foresta, Stephen G. ... New York, NY
Forestell, Stephen E. ... St. Paul, MN
Forester, Charles W. ... Richmond, KY
Forester, Donald W. ... Oak Brook, IL
Forester, G. Yasué ... Washington, DC
Forester, Georgina Y. ... Rockville, MD
Forester, J. Gordon, Jr. ... Washington, DC
Forester, J. Richard ... Portland, OR
Forester, James G. ... Brookfield, WI
Forester, John E. ... Wausau, WI
Forester, John P. ... Grand Haven, MI
Forester, Judy Reese ... Forsyth, MO
Forester, Karl S. ... Lexington, KY
Forester, Laura E. ... Chicago, IL
Forester, Lawson ... Jacksonville Beach, FL
Forester, Richard M. ... Brookfield, WI
Forester, Steven D. ... Miami, FL
Forester, William L. ... Bridgeton, NJ
Forester, William R. ... Lexington, KY
Forester, William Todd ... Logan, WV
Forestier, Thomas J. ... Houston, TX
Forestiere, Nicholas P. ... Fresno, CA
Foret, Charles J. ... Lafayette, LA
Foret, Donald L. ... New Orleans, LA
Foret, J. Burton ... Alexandria, LA
Foret, L. Palmer ... Chevy Chase, MD
Foret, Norman P. ... Lafayette, LA
Forfia, Deborah McCain ... Akron, OH
Forg, E. Farran ... Cincinnati, OH
Forg & Forg ... Cincinnati, OH
Forg, John H. ... Cincinnati, OH
Forgach, John P. ... Columbia, MD
Forgang, Charles S. ... New York, NY
Forgas, Brian James ... Washington, DC
Forgash, Robert J. ... Medford, NJ
Forgays, Janice A. ... Montpelier, VT
Forge, Gregory W. ... Richland, WA
Seattle, WA
Forge, Jason A. ... Los Angeles, CA
Forger, Alexander D. ... New York, NY
Forgeron, Hy Theodore
Battle Mountain, NV
Forget, Guy Gilles ... Ashland, VA
Forgette, Francois X. ... Kennewick, WA
Forgette, Simon H. ... Kirkland, WA
Forgette, Simon H., P.S. ... Bellevue, WA
Kirkland, WA
Seattle, WA
Forgety, Telford E., Jr. ... Dandridge, TN
Forgey, Darrell A. ... Los Angeles, CA
Forgey, Donald G. ... Los Angeles, CA
Forgey, Kimberlie L. ... Muncie, IN
Forgie & Jacobs ... Los Angeles, CA
Westlake Village, CA
Forgie, Kathryn M. ... Santa Monica, CA
Forgie, Peter S. ... Los Angeles, CA
Westlake Village, CA
Forgione, Frank J. ... Branford, CT
Forgione, Henry E., II ... Southington, CT
Forgione, Nicholas ... Andover, MA
Forgione, William J. ... New York, NY
Forgnone, Robert ... Los Angeles, CA
Forgosh, Meredith A. ... Minneapolis, MN
Forgosh, Peter A. ... Morristown, NJ
Forgotson, Elizabeth Nell ... Rockville, MD
Forgotson, Elizabeth, P.C. ... Rockville, MD
Forgotson, Florence F. ... Red Bank, NJ
Forgue, Alvedor J. ... Elmhurst, IL
Forgue, Brian A. ... Elmhurst, IL
Forgue, Charles F. ... Darien, IL
Forgue, David G. ... Chicago, IL
Forgue & Forgue ... Elmhurst, IL
Forgue, Vernon ... Salem, IL
Forgy, Fred, Jr. ... Santa Ana, CA
Forgy, Lawrence E., Jr. ... Lexington, KY
Forhan, Craig G. ... Bloomfield Hills, MI
Forhan, John F. ... Denver, CO
Forhan, John F., P.C. ... Denver, CO
Forhan, John P. ... Santa Barbara, CA
Forhan, Thomas P. ... Chicago, IL
Fori, Thomas J. ... Coxsackie, NY
Forinash, Cecil L. ... Colorado Springs, CO
Forino, Alfred P. ... North Haven, CT
Forizs, Zala L. ... St. Petersburg, FL
Tampa, FL
Forjette, Kevin P. ... Norwich, VT
Forjohn, Steven K. ... Philadelphia, PA
Fork, Allan C. ... Los Angeles, CA
Forker, Dan W., Jr. ... Hutchinson, KS
Forker & Forker ... Sioux City, IA
Forker, Thomas A. ... Minneapolis, MN
Forker, W. Jonathan ... La Porte, IN
Forker, Wil L. ... Sioux City, IA
Forker, Wilford M. ... Sioux City, IA
Forkey, Russell L. ... Fort Lauderdale, FL
Forkey, Russell L., P.A. ... Fort Lauderdale, FL
Forkin, McShane, Manos & Rotz, A Professional Association ... Cherry Hill, NJ
Forkin, Michael J. ... San Francisco, CA
Forkin, Thomas P. ... Philadelphia, PA
Forkins, James M. ... Chicago, IL
Forkins, James M., Jr. ... Lisle, IL
Forkner, Larry F. ... San Antonio, TX
Forkner, Robert L. ... Modesto, CA
Forkner, Thos. F. ... Norcross, GA
Forkosch, Joel A. ... Philadelphia, PA
Forland, Denny R. ... Chico, CA
Forland, Scott T. ... Kansas City, MO
Forlano, Anthony ... Brooklyn, NY
Forlano, Frederick P. ... Houston, TX
Forlano, Lori J. ... New York, NY
Forlenza, Felix G. ... Verona, NJ
Forlenza, Lee A. ... New York, NY
Forlenza, Philip D. ... Middletown, NJ
Forlenza, Philip R. ... New York, NY
Forlidas, Charles W. ... Atlanta, GA
Forlidas, Suzanne Noblit ... Atlanta, GA
Forlines, John A., III ... New York, NY
Forlini, Emidio J., Jr. ... Washington, DC
Forlizzo & Neal, P.A. ... Clearwater, FL
Forlizzo, Robert A. ... Clearwater, FL
Forma, Charles A. ... Bethpage, NY
Forma, Joseph S. ... Buffalo, NY
Formaker, Robin G., (Mr.) ... Ames, IA
Formaker, Steven E. ... Los Angeles, CA
Formaker, Susan L. ... Los Angeles, CA
Formaker, William J. ... Forestville, CA
Forman, A. Jessica ... Canton, OH
Forman, A. A. ... Mineola, NY
Forman, Adam P. ... Boston, MA
Forman, Adam S. ... Detroit, MI
Forman, Alan N. ... New York, NY
Forman, Alan S. ... Glen Burnie, MD
Forman, Andrea E. ... New York, NY
Forman, Andrew S. ... Brandon, FL
Forman, Arthur H. ... Flushing, NY
Forman & Associates, P.C. ... Brooklyn, NY
Forman, Barbara L. ... Holland, MI
Forman, Bernard S. ... Albany, NY
Forman & Bernier, P.A. ... Londonderry, NH
Forman, Charles D. ... Boston, MA
Forman, Charles D. ... Purchase, NY
Forman, Charles M. ... Rochelle Park, NJ
Forman, Charles R. ... Fort Lauderdale, FL
Ocala, FL
Forman, Cindy F. ... Santa Monica, CA
Forman & Crane, L.C. ... Charleston, WV
Forman, Dan ... Los Angeles, CA
Forman, Daniel H. ... Miami, FL
Forman, Daniel H., P.A. ... Miami, FL
Forman, Daniel M. ... Boston, MA
Forman, Daniel R. ... Washington, DC
Forman, David A. ... Boston, MA
Forman, David Copley ... Portland, OR
Forman, David L. ... Austin, MN
Forman, David L. ... New York, NY
Forman, David M. ... Honolulu, HI
Forman, David M. ... Boston, MA
Forman, David S. ... Washington, DC
Forman, Debra S. ... Lambertville, NJ
Forman, Dennis M. ... Chicago, IL
Forman, Dennis M. ... Natick, MA
Forman, Donald J. ... Dallas, TX
Forman, Edward S. ... New York, NY
Forman, Elizabeth ... Philadelphia, PA
Forman, Ellen M. ... San Francisco, CA
Forman, Eric D. ... West Palm Beach, FL
Forman, Erica R. ... New York, NY
Forman, Forman, Cardonsky, Andril & Ungvary
Elizabeth, NJ
Forman, Frank W. ... Alexandria, VA
Forman, Fred J. ... Londonderry, NH
Forman, Gail L. ... New York, NY
Forman, Geoffrey L. ... Baltimore, MD
Forman, George ... San Rafael, CA
Forman, George H. ... Buffalo, NY
Forman, Gerald ... Fort Lauderdale, FL
Forman, Gerald, P.A. ... Fort Lauderdale, FL
Forman, Glenn M. ... New York, NY
Forman, Gregory S. ... Charleston, SC
Forman, Gregory S., P.C. ... Charleston, SC
Forman, Guy Scott ... Reed City, MI
Forman, H. Collins, Jr.
Fort Lauderdale, FL
Forman, H. Collins, Jr., P.A.
Fort Lauderdale, FL
Forman, Harry M. ... Pomona, NY
Forman, Harvey I. ... Philadelphia, PA
Forman, Harvey M. ... Boston, MA
Forman Holt & Eliades LLC
Hackensack, NJ
Newark, NJ
Paramus, NJ
Rochelle Park, NJ
Forman, Howard I. ... Huntingdon Valley, PA
Forman, Howard M. ... New York, NY
Forman, Ian Barry ... New York, NY
Forman, Ina A. ... Hartford, CT
Forman, Ira J. ... Brooklyn, NY
Forman, Jacqueline ... Greensboro, NC
Forman, James, Jr. ... Washington, DC
Forman, James L. ... Minneapolis, MN
Forman, James R., Jr. ... Birmingham, AL
Forman, James Ross, III
Birmingham, AL
Forman, Janette M. ... Chicago, IL
Forman, Jeffrey L. ... Towson, MD
Forman, Jeffrey L. ... Detroit, MI
Forman, Jeffrey S.
General Accounting Office, Office of the General Counsel, GV
Forman, Jerome J. ... Mashpee, MA
Forman, Joel S. ... New York, NY
Forman, Johanna Mendelson
Washington, DC
Forman, Jonathan B. ... United States Senate, Senatorial Assistants, GV
Forman, Jonathan S. ... Cleveland, OH
Forman, Joseph J. ... Omaha, NE
Forman, Judith R. ... Los Angeles, CA
Forman, Judith R., P.C., Law Offices of
Los Angeles, CA
Forman, Kenneth Alan ... North Miami, FL
Forman, Krehl & Montgomery
Fort Lauderdale, FL
Maitland, FL
Ocala, FL
Forman, Larry R. ... Omaha, NE
Forman, Leon S. ... Philadelphia, PA
Forman, Louis L. ... Elizabeth, NJ
Forman, M. Barry ... Cahokia, IL
Forman, M. Donald ... Sewell, NJ

Forman, Marth, Black & Iddings, P.A. **Greensboro, NC**
Forman, Martha P. .... **Grand Rapids, MI**
Forman, Martin L. .... **New York, NY**
Forman, Martin S. .... Miami, FL
Forman, Matthew C. Department of Housing and Urban Development, Office of General Counsel, GV
Forman, Max M. .... Chicago, IL
Forman, Michael C. .... **Philadelphia, PA**
Forman, Michael H. .... **Hackensack, NJ**
Forman, Michael L. .... **Fort Worth, TX**
Forman, Michael R. .... Tecumseh, MI
Forman, Nancy .... **Bala Cynwyd, PA**
Forman, Nancy .... **Philadelphia, PA**
Forman, Neal B. .... Brooklyn, NY
Forman, Paul L. .... Woodinville, WA
Forman, Perry S. .... Horsham, PA
Forman, Perry, Watkins, Krutz & Tardy, PLLC .... **Jackson, MS**
Forman, Peter J. .... **Boca Raton, FL**
Forman, Peter M. .... Poughkeepsie, NY
Forman, Richard .... Boston, MA
Forman, Richard B. .... San Francisco, CA
Forman, Richard C. .... **Greensboro, NC**
Forman, Richard L. .... **Jackson, MS**
Forman, Richard S. .... **Los Angeles, CA**
Forman, Robert A. .... Dallas, TX
Forman, Robert J. .... **Tucson, AZ**
Forman, Robert M. .... Buchanan, NY
Forman, Robert S. .... **Chicago, IL**
Forman, Robert S., (P.A.) Fort Lauderdale, FL
Forman, Robert W. .... **New York, NY**
Forman, Roger D. .... Charleston, WV
Forman, Ronald C. .... Denver, CO
Forman, Samuel S. .... Hollywood, FL
Forman, Scott .... Greensboro, NC
Forman, Seth L. .... **Hagåtña, GU**
Forman, Sheila H. .... Los Angeles, CA
Forman & Steinhardt, P.A. Glen Burnie, MD
Forman, Stephen B. .... **Washington, DC**
Forman, Stephen H. .... **Beaumont, TX**
Forman, Stuart A. .... New York, NY
Forman, Stuart F. .... Potomac, MD
Forman, Terry J. .... Coral Gables, FL
Forman, Thomas M. .... Shaker Heights, OH
Forman, Warren L. .... Brooklyn, NY
Forman, Wayne F. .... **Denver, CO**
Forman, William H. .... Los Angeles, CA
Forman, Willis M. .... St. Paul, MN
Forman-Echols, Liora .... Los Angeles, CA
Formanek, Arthur R. .... **El Paso, TX**
Formanek, Dean J. .... **Phoenix, AZ**
Formanek, Norma G. .... **San Francisco, CA**
Formanek, Roger A. .... Carmichael, CA
Formato, Anthony J. .... **Poughkeepsie, NY**
Formato, Janice G. .... Birmingham, AL
Formby, Daniel M. .... Atlanta, GA
Formby & Mann, L.L.C. .... **Wetumpka, AL**
Formby, Michael D. .... **Honolulu, HI**
Formell, Ross C. .... **Minneapolis, MN**
Formella, Brian G. .... Plover, WI
Formella, Gregg M. .... **Dallas, TX**
Formella, Martha H. .... **Orlando, FL**
Formeller, Daniel R. .... **Chicago, IL**
Forment, Pedro P. .... **Miami, FL**
Formica, Frank J. .... Washington, DC
Formica, Jeffrey N. .... Newton, MA
Formica, John L. .... General Accounting Office, Office of the General Counsel, GV
Formichelli, Robert P. .... Bethpage, NY
Formichi, Robert E. .... San Anselmo, CA
Formicola, Carl A. .... **New York, NY**
Formidoni, Roland R. .... **Trenton, NJ**
Forminard, Elizabeth R. .... **New York, NY**
Forminard, Jared .... **New York, NY**
Formisano, Karen Cornyn .... Somerville, NJ
Formisano, Nicholas A. .... **Atlanta, GA**
Formisano, V. Edward .... **Cranston, RI**
Formoso, Marika Gulyas .... **Miami, FL**
Formoso, Michael E. .... White Plains, NY
Formoso - Murias, A Professional Association Boston, MA
Formoso-Murias, A Professional Association **Miami, FL**
Formoso-Murias, Hector .... **Miami, FL** Boston, MA
Formusa, Lorelyn .... San Jose, CA
Formusa, S. Joseph .... Chicago, IL
Formwalt, Lance J. .... **Kansas City, MO**
Fornaci, Philip J. .... Washington, DC
Fornaciari, Jeffrey L. .... **Santa Fe, NM**
Fornaciari, Joan F. .... Pasadena, CA **San Francisco, CA**
Fornaciari, John R. .... **Washington, DC**
Fornaciari, Linda Cox .... San Francisco, CA
Fornari, James D. .... New York, NY
Fornaris, Carl A. .... **Miami, FL**
Fornaris, Martha D. .... **Fort Lauderdale, FL** **Miami, FL**
Fornaris-Fernández, Fernando J. **San Juan, PR**
Fornaro, Richard D. .... Hamilton, NJ
Fornaro, Susan L. (IBA) .... Boston, MA
Fornary, Giulio J. A. .... Racine, WI
Fornasar, Gregory C. .... **Uniondale, NY**
Fornasero, Joseph M. .... Sacramento, CA
Fornash, F. Theodore .... Alexandria, KY
Fornasier, Donald B. .... **Walnut Creek, CA**
Fornek, Brian M. .... **Chicago, IL**
Fornella, Leonard .... **Pittsburgh, PA**
Fornelli, Anthony J. .... Chicago, IL
Fornelli, Cynthia M. .... Washington, DC
Fornelli, Francis J. .... Mercer, PA
Forner, John F. .... Menands, NY
Forneris, Jeanne M. .... Minneapolis, MN
Fornes, Gerard R. .... **Buffalo, NY**
Fornes, Kirk A. .... New Haven, CT
Fornes, Timothy L. .... **Metropolis, IL**
Forney, Damon B. .... San Diego, CA
Forney, David L. .... **Pittsburgh, PA**
Forney, Dean S. .... Alliance, NE
Forney, Ferdinand A. .... Cincinnati, OH
Forney, Gregory P. .... **Kansas City, MO**
Forney, John P., Jr. (P.C.) .... Houston, TX
Forney, Kent M. .... **Des Moines, IA**
Forney, Marjorie Harrison .... Birmingham, AL
Forney, Paula I. .... Santa Fe, NM
Forney, Susan J. .... Harrisburg, PA
Forni, Fred L. .... New York, NY
Forni, Robert M., Jr. .... **San Francisco, CA**
Fornias, Vincent P. .... **Baton Rouge, LA**
Forno, Lawrence J. .... **Pompano Beach, FL**
Fornoff, Chad D. .... Springfield, IL
Fornoff & Dake, P.C. .... Fremont, NE
Fornoff, Leta F. .... Fremont, NE
Fornos, Mayra M. .... Culver City, CA
Fornshell, William P. .... **New York, NY**
Foronda, Dante .... **Oakland, CA**
Forouhar, Mitra N. .... San Francisco, CA
Forquer, Jennifer A. .... **Tacoma, WA**
Forquer, Robert A. .... Charlotte, NC
Forquer, Robert C., P.C. .... Phoenix, AZ
Forr, Ralph T., Jr. .... Altoona, PA
Forray, Anthony Wayne .... Harrisburg, PA
Forrence, Jennifer L. .... Bridgeport, CT
Forrer, Carl E. .... Orrville, OH
Forrer, David R. .... Annapolis, MD
Forrer, Robert F. .... **Chicago, IL**
Forrest, Alan M. .... New York, NY
Forrest, Audrey P. .... Cleveland, OH
Forrest, Beryl A. .... Houston, TX
Forrest, Bobby L. .... Baton Rouge, LA
Forrest, Bradley A. .... **Minneapolis, MN**
Forrest, Bruce G. .... Department of Justice, Civil Division, GV
Forrest, Carolyn Y. .... **Atlanta, GA**
Forrest, Charles A., Jr. .... Flint, MI
Forrest, Charles O. .... **Omaha, NE**
Forrest, Christopher D. .... Hollywood, FL
Forrest, Christopher J.W. .... **Denver, CO**
Forrest, Clair M. .... Tiffin, OH
Forrest, Clair M., Jr. .... Tiffin, OH
Forrest, Clyde W., Jr. .... Champaign, IL
Forrest, Dallas M. .... **Jefferson City, MO**
Forrest, David A. .... **Cleveland, OH**
Forrest, Davida K. .... Chicago, IL
Forrest, Donald A. .... West Memphis, AR
Forrest, Donald R. .... **New Albany, IN**
Forrest, Douglas E. .... Pelham, NY
Forrest, Ernestine .... Los Angeles, CA
Forrest, Evelyn F. .... Birmingham, MI
Forrest, F. H. (Mike) .... **Des Moines, IA**
Forrest, George L. .... Tiffin, OH
Forrest, George W. .... Kildeer, IL
Forrest, Henderson, Sloan & Davis, A Professional Corporation .... **Fresno, CA**
Forrest, Herbert E. .... Department of Justice, Civil Division, GV
Forrest, H. P. .... Miami, FL
Forrest, James T. .... Del City, OK
Forrest, Jeffrey William House of Representatives, Congressional Assistants, GV
Forrest, John A. .... **Bloomfield Hills, MI**
Forrest, Jonathan I. .... **Washington, DC**
Forrest, Karl J. .... **Atlanta, GA**
Forrest, Katherine B. .... **New York, NY**
Forrest, Katrina Clark .... **Richmond, VA**
Forrest, Kenneth B. .... **New York, NY**
Forrest, Kirk G. .... **Tulsa, OK**
Forrest & Kowalski, P.C. .... Southgate, MI
Forrest, L. Albert .... **Lafayette, LA** **New Iberia, LA**
Forrest, Linda C. .... San Bernardino, CA
Forrest, Loren L., Jr. .... **White Plains, NY**
Forrest, Loyce A. .... **Denver, CO**
Forrest, Mary Anne .... Riverside, CA
Forrest, Mary B. .... Gainesville, GA
Forrest, Mary H. .... Department of Labor, GV
Forrest, Michael .... **Mineola, NY**
Forrest, Neil P. .... **New York, NY**
Forrest, Patrick J. .... Department of Labor, GV
Forrest, Richard D. .... **Boston, MA**
Forrest, Richard M. .... Houston, TX
Forrest, Robert .... Somerville, NJ
Forrest, Robert C. .... Santa Monica, CA
Forrest, Robert E. .... **Southfield, MI**
Forrest & Sirna .... Flint, MI
Forrest, Stephanie Schankerman **Indianapolis, IN**
Forrest, Stephen Paul .... **Phoenix, AZ**
Forrest, Steven W. .... Elmira, NY
Forrest, Tammy D. .... Miami, FL
Forrest, Thelma L. .... Southgate, MI
Forrest, Theodore R., Jr. .... **Fresno, CA**
Forrest, Thomas J. .... **Albany, NY**
Forrest, Tracy L. .... New York, NY
Forrest, Wayne J. .... Somerville, NJ
Forrest, William A., Jr. .... **Richmond, VA**
Forrestal, Francis Tracy .... Falls Church, VA
Forrestal, Jos. B. .... Janesville, WI
Forrestal, Robert P. .... **Atlanta, GA**
Forrestal, Timothy J. .... Cleveland, OH
Forrestel, Richd. E. .... Akron, NY
Forrester, Althea M. Department of Housing and Urban Development, Office of General Counsel, GV
Forrester & Brim .... **Gainesville, GA**
Forrester, Carl Xavier .... Austin, TX
Forrester, Christopher M. **Washington, DC**
Forrester, David C. .... **Baton Rouge, LA**
Forrester, Denise Mariani .... **Princeton, NJ**
Forrester, Denzil H. .... Charlotte, NC
Forrester, Eugene Stone, Jr. **Memphis, TN**
Forrester, G. Nelson .... Tullahoma, TN
Forrester, Geneva .... St. Petersburg, FL
Forrester, Homer W. .... Parker, AZ
Forrester, J. Casey .... **Alexandria, VA**
Forrester, J. Chase .... Louisville, KY
Forrester, J. Owen .... Atlanta, GA
Forrester, J. Paul .... **Chicago, IL**
Forrester, James A. .... Littleton, CO
Forrester, Joe E. .... New York, NY
Forrester, Jordan & Dick, L.L.C. **Baton Rouge, LA**
Forrester, Julia Patterson .... **Dallas, TX**
Forrester, Keith R. .... **Irvine, CA**
Forrester, Kenneth J. .... Little Rock, AR
Forrester, Kevin K. .... **Encinitas, CA**
Forrester and Kovanda .... Cleveland, OH
Forrester, Larry E. .... **Atlanta, GA**
Forrester, Marilynn Franz .... San Diego, CA
Forrester, Mary Beth .... **Naples, FL**
Forrester, Melody .... **Philadelphia, PA**
Forrester, Michael F. .... **Dallas, TX**
Forrester, Michael H. .... New Windsor, NY
Forrester, Michael J. .... Roseland, NJ
Forrester, Michael L. .... **Johnson City, TN** **Kingsport, TN**
Forrester, Michael R. .... Mobile, AL
Forrester, Nathan A. .... Washington, DC
Forrester, Perry M. .... Los Angeles, CA
Forrester, Ray .... San Francisco, CA
Forrester, Richard W. .... High Point, NC
Forrester, Robert A. .... Shrewsbury, NJ
Forrester, Robert A. .... **Dallas, TX** **Plano, TX**
Forrester, Robert A. .... **Richardson, TX**
Forrester, Robert D. .... **Amarillo, TX**
Forrester, S. Cary .... **Phoenix, AZ**
Forrester, Thomas D. .... St. Louis, MO
Forrester, Thomas D. .... Covington, TN
Forrester, Thomas H. .... **Nashville, TN**
Forrester, W. Glenn .... **Cincinnati, OH**
Forrester, W. Howell .... Pulaski, TN
Forrester, Wendy .... Calabasas, CA
Forrester, Weymon H. .... **Gainesville, GA**
Forrester, Whitfield R. .... Cordele, GA
Forrester, William G. .... Lake Havasu City, AZ
Forrester, William R., Jr. **New Orleans, LA**
Forrest-Hoadley, Linda .... Escondido, CA
Forrette, Gerald B. .... Minneapolis, MN
Forristal & Goettsch Law Firm .... Holstein, IA
Forristal, Matthew J. .... Holstein, IA
Forrister, R. M. .... Estes Park, CO
Forro, David R. .... **Minneapolis, MN**
Forro, Lila T. .... Raleigh, NC
Forrow, Brian D. .... Greenwich, CT
Forry, Barbara L. .... St. Paul, MN
Forry, Craig B. .... Manhattan Beach, CA
Forry, Deby L. .... Laramie, WY
Forry, Donna L. .... Ventura, CA
Forry, James R. .... **Norristown, PA** **Reading, PA** Topton, PA
Forry, John H. .... **Norristown, PA** **Reading, PA** Topton, PA
Forry, John I. .... New York, NY
Forry, John T. .... **Reading, PA**
Forry, Robert H., P.C. .... **Atlanta, GA**
Forry, Ullman, Ullman & Forry, P.C. **Norristown, PA** **Reading, PA** Topton, PA
Forry, William R. .... **Reading, PA**
Fors, Elaine R. .... **Bethesda, MD**
Fors, Geoffrey C. .... Monterey, CA
Fors, Jorge L. .... Coral Gables, FL
Fors, Jorge L., P.A. .... Coral Gables, FL
Fors, Judith E. .... **Chicago, IL**
Fors, Kevin A. .... Harcourt, IA
Fors, Luis A., (P.A.) .... Miami, FL
Forsbach, Jack A. .... Los Angeles, CA
Forsberg, Anthony E. .... Mount Pleasant, SC
Forsberg, Carl E. .... **Seattle, WA**
Forsberg, David C. .... **St. Paul, MN**
Forsberg, Eric W. .... **Minneapolis, MN**
Forsberg, Fred N. .... Levittown, PA
Forsberg, Genelle F. .... St. Paul, MN
Forsberg, Lars .... **New York, NY**
Forsberg, Laurel J. .... **Williston, ND**
Forsberg Law Office, P.A. **Minneapolis, MN**
Forsberg, Mark R. .... Carson City, NV
Forsberg, Steven W. .... Santa Rosa, CA
Forsberg, Theodore J. .... Barrington, IL
Forsberg, Thomas G. .... St. Paul, MN
Forsberg & Umlauf, P.S. .... **Seattle, WA**
Forsberg, William R. .... Rexburg, ID
Forsberg, William S. .... **Minneapolis, MN**
Forsblad, David R. .... San Rafael, CA
Forscey, Michael A. .... Washington, DC
Forsch, Daniel E. .... Seattle, WA
Forsch & Harris, P.S. .... Seattle, WA
Forsch, Jennifer M. .... **Seattle, WA**
Forsch, Mark J. .... Houston, TX
Forschein, Scott Lee .... Brooklyn, NY
Forschler, Richard A. .... **Minneapolis, MN**
Forsee, Michael T. .... Jeffersonville, IN
Forsell, Andrew C. .... Princeton, NJ
Forsell, Richard J. .... Kirkland, WA
Forseter, Bernard .... Bethesda, MD Syosset, NY
Forseth, Mark B. .... **Washington, DC**
Forseth, Scott L. .... Washington, DC
Forsey, Stefanie L. .... **Waltham, MA**
Forsgaard, Karl F. .... Snoqualmie, WA
Forsgren, F. Leslie .... Crosby, ND
Forsgren, Matthew D. .... **Minneapolis, MN**
Forsgren, Steven E. .... Noblesville, IN
Forshag, Kurt P. .... Metairie, LA
Forshaw, Joseph, IV .... St. Louis, MO
Forshaw, Liza S. .... **St. Louis, MO**
Forshaw, Mary Beth .... **New York, NY**
Forshay, Paul F. .... **Washington, DC**
Forshee, B. Jason .... **Jackson, MS**
Forshee, Barbara A. .... Taos, NM
Forshee, Richard D. .... **Oklahoma City, OK**
Forsheit, Tanya L. .... **Los Angeles, CA**
Forshey, J. Robert .... **Fort Worth, TX**
Forshey, Michael S. .... Dallas, TX
Forshey, Rhonda L. .... Columbus, OH
Forshey, Timothy Erwin .... Jackson, OH
Forshner, Hugh Craig .... Ridgeland, MS
Forsley, Alan W. .... **Los Angeles, CA**
Forsley & Eggleston, P.A. .... Hampton, NH
Forsley, Lawrence S. .... Hampton, NH
Forsling, Mark W. .... **Atlanta, GA**
Forsling, Susan Barker .... Atlanta, GA
Forslund, James C. .... Denver, CO
Forslund, Mary F. .... Englewood, CO
Forsman, Alpheus E. .... St. Louis, MO
Forsman, Craig H. .... Chanhassen, MN
Forsman, Michael S. .... **Tulsa, OK**
Forsman, Paul J. .... Jersey City, NJ Red Bank, NJ
Forsman, Wade A. .... **Dallas, TX**
Forsman, William F. .... Lewiston, ID
Forson, David A. .... **Houston, TX**
Forspan, Hedy Pollak .... Cedarhurst, NY
Forssberg, Brita J. .... **Portland, ME**
Forssen, Richard E. La Canada Flintridge, CA
Forsstrom, H. Allan, II .... Beverly, MA
Forst, Alan O. .... **Stuart, FL**
Forst, Dana E. .... **Los Angeles, CA**
Forst, David L. .... **Palo Alto, CA**
Forst, Gary .... Coral Springs, FL
Forst, Gayle .... **Washington, DC**
Forst, Harry E. .... **New Orleans, LA**
Forst, John K. Securities and Exchange Commission, Division of Investment Management, GV
Forst, Mary C. .... Portland, OR
Forst, Michael A. .... St. Louis, MO
Forst, Richard J. .... Oak Lawn, IL
Forst, Robert Department Of Health And Human Services, Food & Drug Administration, GV
Forst, Robert L. .... Department of Energy, Office of the General Counsel, GV
Forst, Teresa D. .... **Phoenix, AZ**
Forstadt, Jonathan .... New York, NY
Forstadt, Joseph L. .... **New York, NY**
Forstadt, Matthew J. .... **Stamford, CT**
Forstall, Kweku Dwayne Stone Mountain, GA
Forstall, Molly Brown .... **Palo Alto, CA**
Forstall, Terrence C. .... **New Orleans, LA**
Forstall, Warren A., Jr. .... New Orleans, LA
Forstater, Ira B. .... House of Representatives, Office of Legislative Counsel, GV
Forstein, Ronda S. .... Vineland, NJ
Forstein, Samuel M. .... Washington, DC
Forsten, Richard A. .... Dover, DE **Wilmington, DE**
Forstenzer, Andrew P. .... **New York, NY**
Forstenzer, Edward .... Mammoth Lakes, CA
Forster, Ann .... Irvington, NY
Forster, Annette Williams .... Gulfport, MS
Forster, Arnold .... **New York, NY**
Forster, Carolyn Nipper .... **Nashville, TN**
Forster, Charles M. .... Traverse City, MI
Forster, Clifford .... New York, NY
Forster, Deborah S. .... Marysville, MI
Forster, Denis M., Law Offices of **New York, NY**
Forster, Dudley R. .... **Coeur d'Alene, ID**
Forster, Franz J. .... Pittsfield, MA
Forster, Gary A. .... **Winter Park, FL**
Forster & Iannacone .... **Brooklyn, NY** **Middle Village, NY**
Forster, J. Neil .... Foxboro, MA
Forster, James F. .... Cranford, NJ White Plains, NY
Forster, Jeanne Ellen .... **Middle Village, NY**
Forster, Jeffrey M. .... **San Jose, CA**
Forster, John F., Jr. .... Little Rock, AR
Forster, Jonathan M. .... **Rockville, MD** **McLean, VA**
Forster, Jonathan S. .... **Los Angeles, CA**
Forster, Joy F. .... **New York, NY**
Forster, Lawrence D. .... Ledgewood, NJ
Forster, Louis J. .... New York, NY
Forster, Michael J. .... Saginaw, MI
Forster, Michael W. .... **Belleville, IL** **St. Louis, MO**
Forster, Mitchell L. .... **Walnut Creek, CA**
Forster, Paul S. .... Staten Island, NY
Forster, Peter H. .... Dayton, OH
Forster, Raymond M. Pension Benefit Guaranty Corporation, Office of the General Counsel, GV
Forster, Richard A. .... Falls Mills, VA
Forster, Robert S. .... New Orleans, LA
Forster, Robert S., Jr. .... **Philadelphia, PA**
Forster, Sandra A. .... White Plains, NY
Forster, Sarah A. .... **Boston, MA**
Forster, Scott J. .... Calhoun, GA
Forster & Segal .... **San Jose, CA**
Forster, Sharon S. .... Keizer, OR

Forster, Todd Perry ... Rockville, MD
Forster, William G. ... Bellevue, WA
Forsthoefel, Gregory J. ... Tecumseh, MI
Forsthoefel, Ronald P. ... Loudonville, OH
Forstman, Bryan Keith ... Birmingham, AL
Forstman, James D. ... Birmingham, AL
Forstman, Leigh King ... Birmingham, AL
Forstner, Gerald C., Jr. ... Berea, OH
Forstner, Glenn ... Brooklyn, NY
Forstner, James A. ... Washington, DC
Forstner, Nathaniel E.B.
Grand Rapids, MI
Forstot, Jonathan D. ... Jersey City, NJ
New York, NY
Forsyte, Carol H. ... Schaumburg, IL
Forsyth, Alan Andrews ... Detroit, MI
Forsyth, Allison White ... Neptune Beach, FL
Forsyth, Andrew W., III ... Pittsburgh, PA
Forsyth, Brugger & Bourgeau, P.A.
Naples, FL
Forsyth, C. Benn ... Rochester, NY
Forsyth, Claire Dickie ... Richmond, VA
Forsyth, Daniel P. ... Buffalo, NY
Forsyth, David D. ... Estherville, IA
Forsyth, David L. ... Mesa, AZ
Forsyth, Donald A. ... Rochester, NY
Forsyth, Duncan J. ... Hartford, CT
Forsyth & Forsyth ... Rochester, NY
Forsyth, Gary F. ... Holbrook, AZ
Forsyth, George K. ... Rochester, NY
Forsyth, Gordon J. ... Estherville, IA
Forsyth, Howe, O'Dwyer, Kalb & Murphy, P.C. ... Rochester, NY
Forsyth, Hubert D. ... San Francisco, CA
Forsyth, J. David ... New Orleans, LA
Forsyth, J. Michael ... Fayetteville, NY
Forsyth, James A. ... Owings Mills, MD
Forsyth, James D. ... Leesburg, VA
Forsyth, James W. ... Pittsburgh, PA
Forsyth, Jan D. ... Greenbelt, MD
Forsyth, Janice C. ... St. Louis, MO
Forsyth, Jim ... Anthony, KS
Forsyth, John D. ... Santa Monica, CA
Forsyth, John E. ... Cushing, OK
Stillwater, OK
Forsyth, John F. ... Naples, FL
Naples, FL
Forsyth, Kathleen A. ... Kansas City, MO
Forsyth, Keith B. ... Scottsdale, AZ
Forsyth, Kerry A. ... Minneapolis, MN
Forsyth Law Office ... Estherville, IA
Forsyth, M. McIntosh ... Richton, MS
Forsyth, Marcia A. ... Costa Mesa, CA
Forsyth, Matthew S. ... Boston, MA
Forsyth, Molly ... Lubbock, TX
Forsyth, Patricia M. ... Secaucus, NJ
Forsyth, Priscilla E. ... Spirit Lake, IA
Forsyth, Richard T. ... San Diego, CA
Forsyth, Scott A. ... Santa Clara, CA
Forsyth, Scott A. ... Rochester, NY
Forsyth, Sexton & Teter, P.C.
Cushing, OK
Stillwater, OK
Forsyth, Shaun Spencer ... Boston, MA
Forsyth, Steven G. ... Houston, TX
Forsyth, Stuart A. ... San Francisco, CA
Forsyth, Thomas G., III ... Monroeville, PA
Forsyth, Thomas L. ... Armonk, NY
Forsyth, Timothy ... Staten Island, NY
Forsyth, Tracy C. ... Springfield, NJ
Forsyth, William A. ... Grand Rapids, MI
Forsyth, William F. ... Minneapolis, MN
Forsyth, William H., Jr. ... New York, NY
Forsythe, Amy I. ... Riverwoods, IL
Forsythe, Andrew J. ... Austin, TX
Forsythe, Carl S., III ... New York, NY
Forsythe, Cheryl ... Eden Prairie, MN
Forsythe, Clarke D. ... Chicago, IL
Forsythe, Connie J. ... Las Vegas, NV
Forsythe, Dale K. ... Pittsburgh, PA
Forsythe, David L. ... Manawa, WI
Forsythe, David W. ... Killingworth, CT
Forsythe, Earl A. ... Dallas, TX
Forsythe, Frank E. ... Columbus, OH
Forsythe, Ian D. ... Orlando, FL
Forsythe, J. Michael ... Ann Arbor, MI
Forsythe, James H. ... Memphis, TN
Forsythe, James R. ... Winona, MN
Forsythe, Jennifer S. ... St. Louis, MO
Forsythe, John A. ... Billings, MT
Forsythe, John S. ... Forsyth, MT
Forsythe, John S. ... Alexandria, VA
Forsythe, Joni Louise ... Herndon, VA
Forsythe, L. B. ... Washington, DC
Forsythe, Linda L. ... Kansas City, MO
Forsythe, Marc C. ... Newport Beach, CA
Forsythe, Matthew W. ... Louisville, KY
Forsythe, Patton, Ellis, Lipsett & Savage
New York, NY
Forsythe, Peter W. ... Dover, NH
Forsythe, Reno H., Jr. ... Indianapolis, IN
Forsythe, Robert A. ... Minneapolis, MN
Forsythe, Robert L. ... Muskegon, MI
Forsythe, Robert R. ... Puyallup, WA
Forsythe, Todd P. ... Cedar Rapids, IA
Forsythe, Vandenberg, Judge, Bell & Hamilton
Ann Arbor, MI
Forsythe, Warren ... New York, NY
White Plains, NY
Forsythe, William A. ... Billings, MT
Forszt, Pawlowski & Smith ... Valparaiso, IN
Forszt, Robert P. ... Valparaiso, IN
Fort, Ann G. ... Atlanta, GA
Fort, Bruce J. ... Santa Fe, NM
Fort, Cynthia Morrissey ... Nashville, TN
Fort, D. Stephen ... Dallas, TX
Fort, Frances C. ... San Francisco, CA
Fort, George W. ... New Orleans, LA
Fort, Gilberto V. ... Coral Gables, FL
Fort, J. Franklin ... Delray Beach, FL
Fort, J. Tomlinson ... Pittsburgh, PA
Fort, Jas F. ... Madison, VA
Fort, Jeffrey C. ... Chicago, IL
Fort, Jeffrey E. ... Toledo, OH
Fort, Joanne Doddy ... Washington, DC
Fort, John Kirkland ... Spartanburg, SC
Fort, John L. ... Long Beach, CA
Fort, John T. ... Chattanooga, TN
Fort, Julie Y. ... Dallas, TX
Fort, Linda B. ... Department of Labor, Office of the Solicitor, GV
Fort, Lyman R. ... Stronghurst, IL
Fort, M. Bruce ... Texas City, TX
Fort, M. Bruce, P.C. ... Texas City, TX
Fort, Michael D. ... Nashville, TN
Fort & Neff ... Stronghurst, IL
Fort, P. Edward ... San Diego, CA
Fort, Robert O. ... Sacramento, CA
Fort & Schlefer, L.L.P. ... Washington, DC
Fort, Susan D. ... Castle Rock, CO
Fort, Vance ... Herndon, VA
Fort, W. Howard ... Akron, OH
Fort, William H. ... Washington, DC
Fort & Wirz, L.L.P. ... Dallas, TX
Fortado, Michael G. ... Dallas, TX
Fortain, James M. ... Boca Raton, FL
Fortain, Renee T. ... Bronx, NY
Fortanasce, Frank T., Jr. ... Mineola, NY
Fortay, Bryan P. ... Philadelphia, PA
FortCamp, James R. ... Chicago, IL
Forté, Alexa L. ... Portland, OR
Forté, André M. ... Rockville, MD
Forte, Ann Marie ... New York, NY
Forte, Anthony P. ... Philadelphia, PA
Forte, Booker T., Jr. ... Tuscaloosa, AL
Forte, Carol L. ... Chatham, NJ
Forte, Chris E. ... White Plains, NY
Forte, Danielle F. ... Atlanta, GA
Forte, David F. ... Cleveland, OH
Forte, Denise A. ... Bronx, NY
Forte, Donald, Jr. ... Boston, MA
Forte, Donald N. ... Liberty, NY
Forte, E. Lisa ... Bronx, NY
Forte, Earl M., III ... Philadelphia, PA
Forte, Honoria J. ... Jersey City, NJ
Forte, James H. ... Newark, NJ
Forte, John P. ... Boxborough, MA
Forte, Joseph M. ... South Bend, IN
Forte, Joseph Philip ... New York, NY
Forte & Kaiser, P.C. ... Washington, DC
Forte, Katharine S. ... Kittery, ME
Forte, Laura ... New Haven, CT
Forte Law Office ... Kittery, ME
Forte, Mario R. ... Narragansett, RI
Forte, Michael C. ... Cheshire, CT
Forte, Michelle F. ... Tarrytown, NY
Forte, Palma M. ... Milwaukee, WI
Forte, Patrick ... Antioch, CA
Concord, CA
Fremont, CA
Pleasanton, CA
Richmond, CA
Forte, Patrick A. ... Washington, DC
Forte, Patrick L. ... Oakland, CA
Forte, Stephen M. ... Atlanta, GA
Forte, Stephen P. ... Bend, OR
Forte, Steven J. ... Schaumburg, IL
Forte, Vincent A. ... Eastchester, NY
Forte, Vincent J. ... Washington, DC
Forte, Wesley E. ... New York, NY
Forte, Ydelsy, (P.A.) ... Miami, FL
Forteau, Clement ... South Ozone Park, NY
Fortelka, Lorraine ... Chicago, IL
Fortenbach, Ray T. ... Houston, TX
Fortenbaugh, Samuel B., III
New York, NY
Fortenberry, Amy E. ... Washington, DC
Fortenberry, Davis T. ... Hattiesburg, MS
Fortenberry, Dewitt Langston, Jr.
Mendenhall, MS
Fortenberry, Earl F., Jr. ... Meridian, MS
Fortenberry, Ernest ... Austin, TX
Fortenberry, Jerry P. ... Houston, TX
Fortenberry, Monique Y.
Small Business Administration, Office of the General Counsel, GV
Fortenberry, Parrish ... Jackson, MS
Fortenberry, Rick ... Meridian, MS
Fortenberry, Willie, Jr. ... Jacksonville, FL
Fortenbury, William B. ... St. Louis, MO
Forter, Rodman K. ... Wakefield, MA
Fortes, Melvin F. ... Napa, CA
Fortes, Stacey J. ... Boston, MA
Fortgang, Anna S. ... New York, NY
Fortgang, Bernard ... New York, NY
Fortgang, Brauna E. ... New York, NY
Fortgang, Chaim J. ... New York, NY
Fortgang, Marvin ... New York, NY
Fortgang, Robert, Associates ... Simsbury, CT
Fortgang, Robert M. ... Simsbury, CT
Forth, David R. ... Piketon, OH
Forth, David W. ... St. Louis, MO
Forth, Gordon E. ... Rochester, NY
Forth, Joseph S. ... Costa Mesa, CA
Forth, Lynn Ann ... Rochester, NY
Forth, Michael Christopher ... Brooklyn, NY
Fort-Hood, Karen M. ... Detroit, MI
Forthun-Baldwin, Paula ... Redlands, CA
Forti, David W. ... Philadelphia, PA
Forti, Michael A. ... Chicago, IL
Fortier and Akins ... Ripley, MS
Fortier, Albert M., Jr. ... Boston, MA
Fortier, Allen B. ... Yakima, WA
Fortier, David R. ... Brookings, OR
Fortier, Evelyn Estes ... United States Senate, Senatorial Assistants, GV
Fortier, Joseph K. ... Hartford, CT
Fortier, Joseph N. ... Charlton City, MA
Fortier, Kenneth J. ... Manasquan, NJ
Fortier, M. Angela ... Lafayette, LA
Fortier, Mark L. ... Skowhegan, ME
Fortier, Mark R. ... Yakima, WA
Fortier, Mark R., P.S. ... Yakima, WA
Fortier, Mary A. ... Hartford, CT
Fortier & Mikko, P.C. ... Anchorage, AK
Fortier, Richard A. ... Hartford, CT
Fortier, Robert F. ... Lisle, IL
Fortier, Samuel J. ... Anchorage, AK
Fortier, Terry D. ... Fresno, CA
Fortier, William R. ... Ripley, MS
Forti-Hildreth, Francesca ... Boston, MA
Fortin, Bradford P. ... Chelmsford, MA
Fortin, Glenn M. ... Atlanta, GA
Fortin, Guy S. ... Arlington, VA
Fortin, James E. ... Portland, ME
Fortin, Joan M. ... Anchorage, AK
Portland, ME
Fortin, Julie R. ... Atlanta, GA
Fortin, Kelly A. ... Santa Ana, CA
Fortin, R. Jay ... New York, NY
Fortin, Raymond D. ... Atlanta, GA
Fortin, Robert F. ... Elkins Park, PA
Fortin, Teresa E. ... Andover, MA
Fortin, William L. ... Plymouth, IN
Fortine, Carol A. ... Washington, DC
Fortini, Jack L. ... Kansas City, MO
Fortini, John Louis ... Kansas City, MO
Fortini-Campell, Alan ... Chicago, IL
Fortino, Alfred J. ... Alma, MI
Fortino, Andrea L. ... Gilroy, CA
Fortino, Charles M. ... Alma, MI
Fortino, Micheal A. ... Riverside, CA
Fortino, Paul T. ... Portland, OR
Fortino, Plaxton, Moskal & Costanzo, P.C.
Alma, MI
Fortino, Sara-Jean ... Lakeland, FL
Fortino, Susan R. ... Chicago, IL
Fortinsky, Gila E. ... New York, NY
Fortinsky, Jerome S. ... New York, NY
Fortkiewicz, Victor A. ... Union, NJ
Fortkort, John A. ... Austin, TX
Fortkort, Michael P. ... Washington, DC
Fortkort, Thomas A. ... Fairfax, VA
Fortman, Brian E. ... Los Angeles, CA
Fortman, Donald J. ... Kalamazoo, MI
Fortman, Judith Wilcox ... Columbus, OH
Fortman, Marvin ... Tucson, AZ
Fortmann, Morris K., Jr. ... Seattle, WA
Fortmann, Scott Joseph ... Portland, OR
Fortner, Carl D. ... Milwaukee, WI
Fortner, Charles P., Jr. ... Eupora, MS
Fortner, D. Keith ... Little Rock, AR
Fortner, Douglas B. ... Port Orchard, WA
Fortner, Harmon T., Jr. ... Littleton, CO
Fortner, Hueston G. ... Los Angeles, CA
Fortner, Jack L. ... Farmington, NM
Fortner, Joseph G., Jr. ... Hartford, CT
Fortner, Lloyd B. ... Palm Beach, FL
Fortner, Marjorie ... South Holland, IL
Fortner, Raymond G., Jr. ... Los Angeles, CA
Fortner, Richard L. ... Portland, OR
Fortner, Seymour S. ... Denver, CO
Fortner, Thrower & Whitehead
Farmington, NM
Fortner, W. Ray ... Lakeland, FL
Fortner, W. Ray, P.A. ... Lakeland, FL
Fortney, Andrew D. ... San Jose, CA
Fortney, Anne Price ... Washington, DC
Fortney, David M. ... Houston, TX
Fortney, David S. ... Washington, DC
Fortney, Douglas R. ... Dallas, TX
Fortney, Guy A. ... Tulsa, OK
Fortney & Klingshirn ... Akron, OH
Fortney, Lester N. ... Pittsburgh, PA
Fortney, Michael L. ... Akron, OH
Fortney, Paul B. ... Englewood, CO
Fortney, Rex D. ... Van Wert, OH
Fortney, Thomas R. ... Viroqua, WI
Fortney, Walter S. ... Fort Worth, TX
Fortnow, Matthew J. ... New York, NY
Forton & Forton ... Buffalo, NY
Forton, Gerard Francis ... Buffalo, NY
Forton, Hugh J. ... Columbia, MD
Forton, James F. ... Buffalo, NY
Forton, Sunny K. ... Muskegon, MI
Fortrend International ... New York, NY
Forts, Brian R. ... Holden, MA
Fortsch, Gregory W.
Department Of Veterans Affairs, Office of the General Counsel, GV
Fortson, Alicia K. Glover ... Dallas, TX
Fortson, Arthur M. ... Garden Grove, CA
Fortson, Barbara ... New York, NY
Fortson, Bentley and Griffin, A Professional Association ... Athens, GA
Atlanta, GA
Fortson, E. B. Dick ... Sherman, TX
Fortson, Edwin B. ... Athens, GA
Fortson, Grant E. ... Little Rock, AR
Fortson, Gwendolyn S. ... Savannah, GA
Fortson, H. Brent ... Greenville, SC
Fortson, Helen DeJoice ... San Diego, CA
Fortson, James L., Jr. ... Shreveport, LA
Fortson, Robert D. ... Atlanta, GA
Fortson, Warren C. ... Atlanta, GA
Fortun, Barbara Ekren ... Bothell, WA
Fortun, J. Barton ... Mercer Island, WA
Fortuna, Bert J., Jr. ... Grand Rapids, MI
Fortuna, Carl P. ... Middletown, CT
Fortuna & Cartelli, P.C. ... Middletown, CT
Fortuna, John A. ... Garden City, NY
Fortuna, Nicholas J. ... New York, NY
Fortuna, Roger A., Jr. ... Virginia Beach, VA
Fortuna, Theresa Colangelo ... Atlanta, GA
Fortuna, Victoria Rettberg ... Reston, VA
Fortunate, Robert H. ... Detroit, MI
Fortunati, Frank G., Jr. ... Short Hills, NJ
Fortunato, Annamarie ... Brooklyn, NY
Fortunato, Charles J. ... Dallas, TX
Fortunato, Christopher R. ... Cleveland, OH
Fortunato, David M. ... New York, NY
Fortunato, Farrell & Davenport, Ltd.
Westmont, IL
Fortunato, Francis J. ... Medford, MA
Fortunato, Francis X. ... Princeton, NJ
Fortunato, Gina M. ... Melville, NY
Fortunato, Jeffrey J. ... Spring Valley, NY
Fortunato, John E. ... New York, NY
Fortunato, Joseph A. ... Montclair, NJ
Fortunato, Joseph A. ... Newark, NJ
Fortunato, Joseph R., Jr. ... Westmont, IL
Fortunato, Kim Fremont ... Wilmington, DE
Fortunato, Mark R. ... Youngstown, OH
Fortunato, Michael J. ... Paoli, PA
Fortunato, Michele ... Amarillo, TX
Fortunato, Paul F. ... Medford, MA
Fortunato, Richard K. ... Montclair, NJ
Fortunato, Richard S. ... New York, NY
Fortunato, Robert G. ... Montclair, NJ
Fortunato, S. Joseph ... Morristown, NJ
Fortunato, Samuel F. ... Princeton, NJ
Fortunato, Sweeney & Associates
Princeton, NJ
Fortunato, Theresa A. ... Cleveland, OH
Fortunato, Thomas A. ... Buffalo, NY
Fortune, Anne O. ... Schaumburg, IL
Fortune, Brian H. ... New York, NY
Fortune, Charles W. ... Hartford, CT
Fortune, Diane S. ... Hicksville, NY
Fortune, Drevlow, Schmidt & Nakano
San Francisco, CA
Fortune, James R., Jr. ... Griffin, GA
Fortune, Janet E. ... Norcross, GA
Fortune, Joan A. ... St. Petersburg, FL
Fortune, Johnny A.
Fort Walton Beach, FL
Fortune, Johnny, P.A.
Fort Walton Beach, FL
Fortune, Kimberly D. ... Anderson, IN
Fortune Law Office, S.C. ... Fond du Lac, WI
Fortune, Lowell ... Denver, CO
Fortune, Melody G. ... North Miami, FL
Fortune, Michael A. ... Omaha, NE
Fortune, Mike P. ... Fond du Lac, WI
Fortune, Peter ... San Francisco, CA
Fortune, Philip L. ... Atlanta, GA
Fortune, Richard A. ... Racine, WI
Fortune, Scott Thomas ... Atlantic Beach, FL
Fortune, Terence J. ... Washington, DC
Fortune, William H. ... Lexington, KY
Fortune, William J. ... Englewood, CO
Fortuño, Luis G. ... San Juan, PR
Fortuno, Robert A. ... Tucson, AZ
Fortuno, Robert A., P.C. ... Tucson, AZ
Fortuno, Victor M. ... Washington, DC
Fortuño-Fas, Agustin ... San Juan, PR
Fortunoff, Alan M. ... Old Westbury, NY
Fortuño-Ruiz, Amelia ... San Juan, PR
Fortus, Sidney ... St. Louis, MO
Fortwengler, Richard J., Jr. ... Atlanta, GA
Foruria, Theodore ... Redding, CA
Forve, Frank F. ... Fairfield, CA
Forwalder, Beth A. ... Kansas City, MO
Forward & Dix ... Los Angeles, CA
Forward, Heather Humble ... Dallas, TX
Forward, John F., II ... Eureka, CA
Forward, Richard G. ... Hinsdale, IL
Forward, Rob ... Mandan, ND
Forward, Robert H., Jr. ... Los Angeles, CA
Forward, Stephen A. ... Lafayette, NY
Forwood, Jon R. ... Cheyenne, WY
Fory, Charles E. ... Houston, TX
Forys, Matthew C. ... Neptune, NJ
Foryt, John P. ... Gonzalez, FL
Forzani, Carlo ... Hartford, CT
Torrington, CT
Forzani, Rinaldo, III ... Bernardsville, NJ
Forzano, Michael A. ... Brooklyn, NY
Forzano, Michael J. ... East Hills, NY
Forzley, Michele D. ... Lynnfield, MA
Fos, David S. ... Kenner, LA
Fosaaen, Eric K. ... Moorhead, MN
Fargo, ND
Fosbinder, Jane L. ... Brooklyn, NY
Fosbinder, Julie H. ... Charlotte, NC
Fosbroke, Gerald E. ... Wrentham, MA
Foscarinis, Maria ... Washington, DC
Foschi, Anthony J. ... Harrisburg, PA
Foschini, Charles J. ... Fort Lauderdale, FL
Foschio, Leslie G. ... Buffalo, NY
Fosco, Paul ... Mount Prospect, IL
Fosdick, Geoffrey A.
Department of Commerce, Patent and Trademark Office, GV
Fosdick, Mark W. ... Saline, MI
Fosdick, Patricia A. ... Stroudsburg, PA
Fosdyke, Clyde E. ... Oklahoma City, OK
Foshaug, William M. ... Federal Way, WA
Foshay, William W., III ... New York, NY
Foshee, Clyde H., Jr. ... Louisville, KY
Foshee, David B. ... Atlanta, GA
Foshee, David J. ... New Orleans, LA
Foshee, Deborah Cunningham
New Orleans, LA
Foshee, Elizabeth Y. ... Orlando, FL
Foshee & George, L.L.C. ... Montgomery, AL
Foshee, Jeffery Alan ... Montgomery, AL
Foshee, Jerral Wayne ... Oklahoma City, OK
Foshee, John C. ... Austin, TX
Foshee, Lisa Spooner ... Atlanta, GA

Foshee, Paul E. ... **Albany, NY**
Foshee, Reneé D. ... **Philadelphia, PA**
Foshée, Stanley Kirkland ... Alexandria, VA
Fosheim, Douglas G. ... **Huron, SD**
Fosheim, Haberstick & Hutchinson
Huron, SD
Fosheim, Jon ... **Huron, SD**
Fosher, Michael P. ... Houston, TX
Foskett, John ... **Boston, MA**
Foskey, Preston L. ... Tacoma, WA
Fosland, Jordan A. ... Scobey, MT
Fosler, James E. ... **Anchorage, AK**
Fosler, Lisa C. ... Chicago, IL
Fosmire, Eric G. ... **Columbia, SC**
Fosmire, M. Sean ... **Marquette, MI**
Fosmire, Susan L. ... Brevard, NC
Fosnaught, K. Donald ... Rochester, NY
Fosner, S. Harvey ... Palm Beach, FL
Fosnight, William D. ... Cleveland, OH
Fosnocht, David J. ... Washington, DC
Fosnocht, Thomas A., Jr. ... West Chester, PA
Foss, Arne M. ... **Dothan, AL**
Foss, Candice E. ... New York, NY
Foss, Charlene R. Fisher ... **Chicago, IL**
Foss, Charles M. ... Hartford, CT
Foss, Craig R. ... **Fairfield, IA**
Foss, David M. ... Stafford Springs, CT
Foss, David Nile ... Oklahoma City, OK
Foss, Douglas A. ... **Rochester, NY**
Foss, Forrest R. ... **Baltimore, MD**
Foss, Frederick F. ... San Luis Obispo, CA
Foss, George M. ... Basking Ridge, NJ
Foss, Gerald D. ... Rye, NH
Foss, H. Weston, P.S. ... **Seattle, WA**
Foss, Howard W. ... Pasadena, CA
Foss, James M. ... **Chicago, IL**
Foss, Janet A. ... Norman, OK
Foss, Jim M. ... Rome, GA
Foss, John B. ... Orange, CA
Foss, John T. ... **Coos Bay, OR**
Foss, Joseph E. ... **Los Angeles, CA**
Foss, Kuiken and Gookin, P.C.
Fairfield, IA
Foss, Linda Judd ... Pasadena, CA
Foss, Linda L. ... Ashland, KY
Foss, Marilyn K. ... Bismarck, ND
Foss, Mark D. ... Bismarck, ND
Foss, Mark S. ... Worcester, MA
Foss and Moore ... Bismarck, ND
Foss, Norby L. ... **Newark, NJ**
Foss, Richard E. ... Chicago, IL
Foss, Richard T.
Department Of Veterans Affairs, Board of Veterans Appeals, GV
Foss, Robert F. ... **Los Angeles, CA**
Foss, Roger J. ... Red Bank, NJ
Foss, Stephen J. ... **Troy, MI**
Foss, Stuart M. ... Greenville, NC
Foss, Theodore R. ... Bangor, ME
Foss, Todd W. ... **Moorhead, MN**
Foss, Walter E. ... Portland, ME
Foss, Whitty, Littlefield, McDaniel & Bodkin, LLP ... **Coos Bay, OR**
Foss, William S. ... San Francisco, CA
Fossard, James R. ... Springfield, MO
Fosse, Mark E. ... **Rochester, MN**
Fossee, Burke, III ... Grosse Pointe Woods, MI
Fossee, Carol L. ... **Bingham Farms, MI**
Fossee, Chester S. ... **Pittsburgh, PA**
Fossee, R. Burke ... St. Clair Shores, MI
Fossel, Elizabeth Joy ... **Grand Rapids, MI**
Fosselman, Earl E. ... Sumner, IA
Fossen, Lori Purcell ... **Sioux Falls, SD**
Fossett, Allan J. ... Cincinnati, OH
Fossett, Andrew G. ... **New York, NY**
Fossett, Bruce ... Portland, ME
Fossett & Brugger, Chartered
Greenbelt, MD
La Plata, MD
Fossett, Clarence L. ... **Greenbelt, MD**
La Plata, MD
Fossett, Edward L. ... Frankfort, KY
Fossett, John Jay ... **Fort Wright, KY**
Fossey, Leighton A. ... Mound City, KS
Fossi, Lawrence J. ... **Houston, TX**
Fossier, Mary Barnett ... Burbank, CA
Fossier, Michael P. ... **Pasadena, CA**
Fossland, Jennifer M. ... Chicago, IL
Fosso, Daniel B. ... Mount Vernon, WA
Fosso, Harold C. ... **Seattle, WA**
Fosson, John L. ... Chillicothe, OH
Fosson, Mann & Preston ... Chillicothe, OH
Fossum, Clifford C. ... Cortez, CO
Fossum, Curtis L. ... Sacramento, CA
Fossum, Donna L. ... Washington, DC
Fossum & Hatter ... Cortez, CO
Fossum, James ... Brainerd, MN
Fossum, James P., P.A. ... Brainerd, MN
Fossum, Jeffrey E., P.C. ... Denver, CO
Fossum, John C., (P.C.)
Newport Beach, CA
Fost, Herbert H. ... Elizabeth, NJ
Fost, Kenneth J. ... Morristown, NJ
Fost, Muscio and Caruso, P.A.
Morristown, NJ
Fostel, John H. ... Decatur, TX
Fostel, Michael L. ... **Kermit, TX**
Foster, A. Key, Jr. ... Birmingham, AL
Foster, Abigail K. ... **New York, NY**
Foster, Alan B. ... Pawnee, OK
Foster, Alan T. ... **Mountain View, CA**
Foster, Alan W. ... West Union, OH
Foster, Albert L. ... Jenkintown, PA
Foster, Albert Luscombe, Jr. ... Haverford, PA
Foster, Alex M. ... San Ramon, CA
Foster, Alexander T. ... Rockville, MD
Foster, Alicia Salazar
Board of Governors Of The Federal Reserve System, Office of the General Counsel, GV
Foster, Allen C., II ... Kinston, NC
Foster, Andrea L. ... Atlanta, GA
Foster, Andrew P. ... **Philadelphia, PA**
Foster, Andrew W., Jr. ... Detroit, MI
Foster, Angela Ivy ... Department of Energy, Office of the General Counsel, GV
Foster, Anne C. ... **Wilmington, DE**
Foster, Anne Marie ... Santa Barbara, CA
Foster, Anthony ... Alpine, TX
Foster, Arthur L. ... Chicago, IL
Foster, Aundria D. ... Newport News, VA
Foster, B. Michael ... Santa Ana, CA
Foster, B. Scott ... Santa Rosa, CA
Foster, Barbara
Environmental Protection Agency, Program Office Attorneys, GV
Foster, Barbara Hull ... Baltimore, MD
Foster, Belinda J. ... Wentworth, NC
Foster, Ben F. ... San Antonio, TX
Foster, Ben F., Jr. ... **San Antonio, TX**
Foster, Benjamin R. ... **Chicago, IL**
Foster, Bernard A., III ... **Washington, DC**
Foster, Beverly H. ... Media, PA
Foster & Blair ... Denver, CO
Foster, Braden & Thompson
Stevensville, MD
Foster, Bradley W. ... **Dallas, TX**
Foster, Brett L. ... Wilmington, OH
Foster, Brett L. ... Salt Lake City, UT
Foster, Brian A. ... **San Diego, CA**
Foster, Brian J. ... **Phoenix, AZ**
Foster, Brian M. ... St. Louis, MO
Foster, Brigdon K. ... Tampa, FL
Foster, Bruce ... Spartanburg, SC
Foster, Bruce Evan ... **Midland, TX**
Foster, Bruce M. ... Greenville, SC
Foster, Bruce, P.A. ... Spartanburg, SC
Foster, Bryan F. ... Riverside, CA
Foster, Byron C. ... **San Jose, CA**
Foster, Byron V. ... **Boise, ID**
Foster, Byron V. ... **Pocatello, ID**
Foster, C. Allen ... **Washington, DC**
Foster, C. Bradford, III ... **Memphis, TN**
Foster, Carol ... **Newport Beach, CA**
Foster, Carolyn ... **Abilene, TX**
Foster, Carrie L. ... Edmond, OK
Foster, Catherine Crystal ... Washington, DC
Foster, Cecil G., Jr. ... **Huntington Beach, CA**
Las Vegas, NV
Foster, Charles C. ... **Houston, TX**
Foster, Charles E. ... Los Angeles, CA
Foster, Charles H. ... Aurora, CO
Foster, Charles S. ... **Mayfield, KY**
Foster, Charles W. ... Woodland Hills, CA
Foster, Charles W. ... Gaithersburg, MD
Foster, Charles W. ... Livingston, NJ
Foster, Chase A. ... Gadsden, AL
Foster, Cheryl A. ... Virginia Beach, VA
Foster, Chester H., Jr. ... Homewood, IL
Foster, Chris A. ... Atlanta, GA
Foster, Christie J. ... **Louisville, KY**
Foster, Christopher ... **Boston, MA**
Foster, Christopher F. ... **Overland Park, KS**
Foster, Christopher G. ... **Los Angeles, CA**
Foster, Clare Keefe ... **Philadelphia, PA**
Foster, Clifford D., Jr. ... **Seattle, WA**
Foster, Clifford, III ... Mobile, AL
Foster, Clinton E. ... Panama City, FL
Foster & Colowick ... Nashville, TN
Foster, Constance B. ... **Harrisburg, PA**
Foster, Constance L.
Department Of Health And Human Services, Office of the General Counsel, GV
Foster, Cris Bates ... Melbourne, FL
Foster, Curtis H. ... Minneapolis, MN
Foster, D. Randall ... **Nashville, TN**
Foster, Dan ... **Austin, TX**
Foster, Dana ... **Miami, FL**
Foster, Daniel R. ... **Irvine, CA**
Foster, Daniel W. ... King Of Prussia, PA
Foster, Darryl J. ... **New Orleans, LA**
Foster, David A. ... **Indianapolis, IN**
Foster, David Allen ... **Palo Alto, CA**
Foster, David E. ... **San Jose, CA**
Foster, David J. ... Lemoyne, PA
Foster, David K., Law Office of
San Antonio, TX
Foster, David L. ... Geneva, NY
Foster, David L. ... **New York, NY**
Foster, David M. ... **Washington, DC**
Foster, David M. ... **Jacksonville, FL**
Foster, David M. ... **Farmington Hills, MI**
Foster, David M., P.C.
Farmington Hills, MI
Foster, David R. ... **Portland, OR**
Foster, David S. ... **San Francisco, CA**
Foster, David S. ... **Chicago, IL**
Foster, David S., III ... Cashiers, NC
Foster, David William ... **Denver, CO**
Foster, Davis L. ... **Iowa City, IA**
Foster, Debra Lee ... **Charlotte, NC**
Foster, Denise R. ... Harrisburg, PA
Foster, Dick V. ... Denton, TX
Foster, Dina F. ... Shelby, NC
Foster, Dirks B. ... **San Francisco, CA**
Foster & DiSilvestro, LLP ... Wichita, KS
Foster, Dixon L. ... Irvington, VA
Foster, Doak ... **Little Rock, AR**
Foster, Don A. ... Ridgway, IL
Foster, Don P. ... **Philadelphia, PA**
Foster, Donald ... Department of Justice, Criminal Division, GV
Foster, Donald H. ... Woodland Hills, CA
Foster, Donald R. ... **Jonesboro, GA**
Foster, Douglas B. ... **Manhattan Beach, CA**
New York, NY
Foster, Douglas T. ... **Sacramento, CA**
Foster, Driscoll & Reynolds ... Riverside, CA
Foster, Dulany ... Baltimore, MD
Foster, Dulce Jo ... Minneapolis, MN
Foster, E. Bruce, Jr. ... **Knoxville, TN**
Foster, Edward D. ... Department of Justice, Criminal Division, GV
Foster, Edward G.
Cape May Court House, NJ
Foster, Edward I. ... **Philadelphia, PA**
Foster, Edward J. ... **Memphis, TN**
Foster, Edward N. ... **Kansas City, MO**
Foster, Edward W. ... Waltham, MA
Foster, Edwin A. ... Hilton, NY
Rochester, NY
Foster & Eldridge ... **Boston, MA**
Cambridge, MA
Foster, Elinor J. ... Fullerton, CA
Foster, Elizabeth Tupper ... Omaha, NE
Foster, Elton A. ... **New Orleans, LA**
Foster, Eric C. ... Los Angeles, CA
Foster, Eric J. ... Asheville, NC
Foster, Eric L. ... **New York, NY**
Foster, Erica Mallory ... Beverly, MA
Foster, Erik K., (P.C.) ... **Denver, CO**
Foster, Erin L. ... Malibu, CA
Foster, F. David ... **Washington, DC**
Foster, Florence ... Tampa, FL
Foster & Foster ... Hilton, NY
Rochester, NY
Foster, Foster, Allen & Durrence, P.C.
Chattanooga, TN
Cleveland, TN
Foster, Foster & Heffling, P.A.
Palm Beach, FL
West Palm Beach, FL
Foster & Foster L.L.C. ... Salt Lake City, UT
Foster & Foster, L.L.P. ... **Greenville, SC**
Foster & Foster, P.C. ... **Jonesboro, GA**
Foster & Foster, P.C., Law Office of
Dallas, TX
Foster, Foster & Schaller ... Olympia, WA
Foster, Francis T., (P.C.) ... Chicago, IL
Foster, Frank H. ... **Reynoldsburg, OH**
Foster, Franklin W. ... Monroe, LA
Foster, Fred E. ... Gaylord, MI
Foster, Fred R., Jr. ... Humble, TX
Foster, Frederic C. ... **Westhampton, NY**
Foster, Gale Lauren, P.C. ... New Paltz, NY
Foster, Gary ... Fairbanks, AK
Foster, Geoffrey A. ... Bartow, FL
Foster, George A. ... **La Mesa, CA**
San Diego, CA
Foster, George B. ... **Pittsburgh, PA**
Foster, George H., Jr. ... **Phoenix, AZ**
Foster, George K. ... **Los Angeles, CA**
Foster, George Lane ... **Chattanooga, TN**
Foster, George O. ... **Totowa, NJ**
Foster, George W. ... Chicago, IL
Foster, Glenn B. ... **Red Bank, NJ**
Foster, Glenn H. ... Austin, TX
Foster, Gordon D. ... **Knoxville, TN**
Foster, Gregory Dean ... Richmond, VA
Foster, Gregory James ... **Tucson, AZ**
Foster, Gregory L. ... **Portland, ME**
Foster & Grubschmidt, P.C.
Pittsburgh, PA
Foster & Harmon ... East Lansing, MI
Foster, Harry G. ... Conway, AR
Foster, Harvey J. ... Sacramento, CA
Foster, Helen Currie ... **Austin, TX**
Foster, Helen Goff
Federal Trade Commission, Bureau of Consumer Protection, GV
Foster, Helen M. ... Denver, CO
Foster, Herman ... Bloomfield Hills, MI
Foster, H. F., III ... **New Orleans, LA**
Foster and Hoke ... Sugar Land, TX
Foster, Holly E. ... **Totowa, NJ**
Foster, Hope S. ... **Washington, DC**
Foster, Howard W. ... **Chicago, IL**
Foster, Ivan V. ... Cleveland, OH
Foster, J. Darrell ... **Portsmouth, VA**
Foster, J. Don ... Mobile, AL
Foster, J. Douglas ... **Albuquerque, NM**
Foster, J. Edward ... **Cambridge, MA**
Foster, J. Gail ... **Houston, TX**
Foster, J. Griffin ... **Atlanta, GA**
Foster, J. Holt, III ... **Dallas, TX**
Foster, J. Michael ... **Hopkinsville, KY**
Foster, J. Robert ... Morgan Hill, CA
Foster, Jacquelyn A. ... Irvine, CA
Foster, James A. ... **Chicago, IL**
Foster, James C. ... Bermuda Dunes, CA
Foster, James C. ... Wilmington, MA
Foster, James E. ... **Orlando, FL**
Foster, James E. ... Hammond, IN
Foster, James F. ... Kansas City, KS
Foster, James H. ... **Liberty Corner, NJ**
Foster, James H. ... Harrisburg, PA
Foster, James J. ... **Destin, FL**
Foster, James J. ... **Boston, MA**
Foster, James (Jay) R., II ... Gulfport, MS
Foster, James K. ... Department of Justice, Antitrust Division, GV
Foster, James L. ... Lincoln, NE
Foster, James N., Jr. ... **St. Louis, MO**
Foster, James R. ... Chicago, IL
Foster, James R. ... The Dalles, OR
Foster, James S. ... **Rushville, IN**
Foster, James T. ... Kennewick, WA
Foster, Jane Landes ... **Philadelphia, PA**
Foster, Janell J. ... **Wichita, KS**
Foster, Janice M. ... **New Orleans, LA**
Foster, Janne C. ... Atlanta, GA
Foster, Jason H. ... **Reynoldsburg, OH**
Foster, Jeanne Ann ... Des Moines, IA
Foster, Jeffery G. ... **Jackson, TN**
Foster, Jeffrey B. ... Greenville, NC
Foster, Jeffrey B., P.A. ... Greenville, NC
Foster, Jeffrey P. ... **Cherry Hill, NJ**
Foster, Jennifer C. ... **New York, NY**
Foster, Jennifer Harms ... Madison, WI
Foster, Jensen & Gulley, LLC
Atlanta, GA
Foster, Jerry Ann
General Services Administration, Office of Regional Counsel, GV
Foster, Jerry C. ... Atlanta, GA
Foster, Jerry L. ... Liberty, KY
Foster, Jessica A. ... **Boston, MA**
Foster, Jill F. ... Salem, OR
Foster, Jody M. ... **Washington, DC**
Foster, Joe C., Jr. ... **Lansing, MI**
Foster, Joe D. ... Fort Worth, TX
Foster, John
Pension Benefit Guaranty Corporation, Other Lawyers in Staff or Executive Positions, GV
Foster, John A. ... **Savannah, GA**
Foster, John C. ... Mount Clemens, MI
Foster, John Crandall ... Morgan Hill, CA
Foster, John D. ... **Washington, DC**
Foster, John D. ... Ashland, OR
Foster, John E. ... **Fairfax, VA**
Foster, John Fenn ... **West Palm Beach, FL**
Foster, John J. ... Schaumburg, IL
Foster, John J. ... Hilton, NY
Rochester, NY
Foster, John J., Jr. ... Baltimore, MD
Foster, John K. ... **Pittsburgh, PA**
Foster, John L. ... Detroit, MI
Foster, John L. ... **Austin, TX**
Foster, John Martin ... **Rock Hill, SC**
Foster, John Martin ... **York, SC**
Foster, John P. ... Eastport, ME
Foster, John R. ... **New York, NY**
Foster, John R. ... **Del Rio, TX**
Foster, John S. ... **Atlanta, GA**
Foster, John S. ... **Grand Forks, ND**
Foster, John W. ... **Columbia, SC**
Myrtle Beach, SC
Foster, John W., Jr. ... Tallahassee, FL
Foster, John W., Sr. ... **Orlando, FL**
Foster • Johnson • Harris • McDonald
Albuquerque, NM
Foster, Jonathan P. ... Athens, PA
Foster, Joni K. ... Minneapolis, MN
Foster, Joseph A. ... **Nashua, NH**
Foster, Joseph D. W. ... London, KY
Foster, Joseph E. ... **Orlando, FL**
Foster, Joseph G. ... **Cleveland, OH**
Foster, Joseph H. ... **Philadelphia, PA**
Foster, Joseph L. ... Neptune, NJ
Foster, J. P. ... Nashville, TN
Foster, Judith Ann ... Milton, MA
Foster, Judy E. ... Honolulu, HI
Foster, Julia Anne ... Highland Park, IL
Foster, Julie C. ... **Louisville, KY**
Foster, Julie I. ... Ridgefield, CT
Foster, Julie M.T.W. ... Atlanta, GA
Foster, Justin ... Bloomington, IN
Foster, K. Robert ... **Stockton, CA**
Foster, Karen A. ... Chicago, IL
Foster, Kari L. ... **Jackson, MS**
Foster, Katharine V. ... **Washington, DC**
Foster, Kathleen A. ... Lansing, MI
Foster, Kathleen M. ... Hartford, CT
Foster, Kathleen Weidinger ... Irving, TX
Foster, Kathryn Wilson ... Osterville, MA
Foster, Keith L. ... **De Kalb, IL**
Shabbona, IL
Foster, Keith T. ... Hackensack, NJ
Foster & Kelly, P.A. ... Orlando, FL
Foster, Kennard P. ... Indianapolis, IN
Foster, Kenneth ... **Indianapolis, IN**
Foster, Kent H. ... **San Diego, CA**
Foster, Kent W. ... **Idaho Falls, ID**
Foster, Kerry Anne ... **Southampton, NY**
Foster, Kevin J. ... San Francisco, CA
Foster, Kimball ... Minneapolis, MN
Foster, Kirsten W. ... **Seattle, WA**
Foster, Kristina J. ... **Tampa, FL**
Foster, L. Grant ... Salt Lake City, UT
Foster, L. Hilton
Securities and Exchange Commission, Division of Enforcement, GV
Foster, Lachlan ... Irvine, CA
Foster, Laird C. ... Nashville, TN
Foster, Lance A. ... **Baton Rouge, LA**
Foster, Larry A., Jr. ... **Charleston, SC**
Foster, Larson, Laiche & Griff
Grand Junction, CO
Foster, Laura ... Dallas, TX
Foster, Laura Beth ... **Boston, MA**
Foster, Laura, (P.C.) ... Houston, TX
Foster, Laurie E. ... **New York, NY**
Foster Law Office ... Indianapolis, IN
New Castle, IN
Foster Law Offices ... Ellsworth, ME
Foster, Lawrence C. ... Honolulu, HI
Foster, Leann E. ... **Middletown, NY**
Foster, Leanne ... **Austin, TX**
Foster, Lee Breland ... **Greenville, SC**
Foster, Leila M. ... Evanston, IL
Foster, Lemuel L., Jr. ... Chicago, IL
Foster, Leon H. ... Cookeville, TN
Foster, Leonard A. ... **San Diego, CA**
Foster, Leonard N. ... Chicago, IL
Foster, Leslie T. ... Falls Church, VA
Foster, Lewis C., Jr. ... **Knoxville, TN**
Foster, Linda B. ... **Atlanta, GA**
Foster, Linda L. ... Bayside, NY
Foster, Linda M. ... **Detroit, MI**
Foster, Lisa ... San Diego, CA
Foster, Lisa Ann ... Los Angeles, CA

Foster, Lisa Combs ....Atlanta, GA
Foster, Lisa Lee ....Boston, MA
Foster, Logene L. ....Sugar Land, TX
Foster, Lon, III ....Tulsa, OK
Foster, Lorie S. ....Pittsburgh, PA
Foster, Louise T. ....Washington, DC
Foster, Luke A. ....Sacramento, CA
Foster, Lyle D. ....Hot Springs Village, AR
Little Rock, AR
Pine Bluff, AR
Foster, Lynn ....Little Rock, AR
Foster, Lynn G. ....Salt Lake City, UT
Foster, M. Joan ....Los Angeles, CA
Roseland, NJ
New York, NY
Foster, M. Shannon ....Fort Smith, AR
Foster, Margaret A. ....Santa Fe, NM
Foster, Margaret Marie ....Chicago, IL
Foster, Margaret V.W. ....Charlottesville, VA
Foster, Marion J., (Mr.) ....Raleigh, NC
Foster, Mark A. ....Evansville, IN
Foster, Mark C., (P.C.) ....Denver, CO
Foster, Mark D. ....Dallas, TX
Foster, Mark E. ....Portland, OR
Foster, Mark Edward ....Irvine, CA
Foster, Mark H. ....Minneapolis, MN
Foster, Mark M. ....Washington, DC
Foster, Mark O. ....Minden, LA
Foster, Mark P., Jr. ....Charlotte, NC
Foster, Mark S. ....Kansas City, MO
Foster, Mark S. ....Dayton, OH
Foster, Mark W. ....Washington, DC
Foster, Martin C. ....Cambridge, MA
Foster, Marvin F., Jr. ....Cherokee, TX
Foster, Mary Ann ....San Luis Obispo, CA
Foster, Mary Jo ....Phoenix, AZ
Foster, Maryanne Bridget ....Troy, MI
Foster, Matthew J. ....Tampa, FL
Foster, Matthew K. ....Tallahassee, FL
Foster, Matthew W. ....Indianapolis, IN
Foster & Mazzie ....Paterson, NJ
Totowa, NJ
Foster, Meadows & Ballard, P.C.
Detroit, MI
Foster, Megan L. ....Gulph Mills, PA
Foster, Melinda ....Department of Justice,
Antitrust Division, GV
Foster, Melissa G. ....Charleston, WV
Huntington, WV
Foster, Melody Gunter ....Richmond, VA
Foster, Melvin J. ....Libertyville, IL
Foster, Michael ....Tampa, FL
Foster, Michael C. ....Los Angeles, CA
Foster, Michael C. ....Miami, FL
Foster, Michael D. ....Los Angeles, CA
Foster, Michael D. ....Chicago, IL
Foster, Michael D. ....Charleston, WV
Foster, Michael E. ....Dalton, GA
Foster, Michael E. ....Wichita, KS
Foster, Michael F. ....Wilmington, DE
Foster, Michael G. ....Dallas, TX
Foster, Michael H. ....Princeton, NJ
Foster, Michael J. ....New Canaan, CT
Foster, Michael J. ....Albany, NY
Foster, Michael J. ....Tulsa, OK
Foster, Michael, P.A. ....Tampa, FL
Foster, Michael R. ....Stevensville, MD
Foster, Michael T. ....Indianapolis, IN
New Castle, IN
Foster, Micheal Thomas ....Ottsville, PA
Foster, Michele E. ....Washington, DC
New York, NY
Foster, Mitchell T. ....Lathrup Village, MI
Foster, Monty ....Olympia, WA
Foster, Murphy J., III ....Baton Rouge, LA
Foster, Nancy A. ....Minneapolis, MN
Foster, Nancy R. ....Albuquerque, NM
Foster & Nassar, Law Offices Of
Melbourne, FL
Foster, Neale S. ....Miami, FL
Foster, Orvin W. ....Mena, AR
Foster, Pamela W. ....Sylva, NC
Foster, Patricia A. ....Pleasanton, TX
Foster, Patricia C. ....New York, NY
Foster, Patricia C. ....Knoxville, TN
Foster, Paul L. ....Lincoln, RI
Foster, Paul, Law Offices, P.C. ......Edmond, OK
Foster, Paul M. ....Fairfax, VA
Foster, Paul R. ....Edmond, OK
Foster, Peachey & Young ....The Dalles, OR
Foster Pepper Rubini & Reeves LLC
Anchorage, AK
Foster Pepper & Shefelman LLP
Portland, OR
Foster Pepper & Shefelman PLLC
Seattle, WA
Spokane, WA
Foster, Perry T. ....Treasury Department,
Internal Revenue Service, GV
Foster, Philip A. ....Vancouver, WA
Foster, Philip Carey ....Easton, MD
Foster, Philip E. ....New York, NY
Foster, Philip R. ....Ellsworth, ME
Foster, Phillip J. ....Camden, AR
Foster, Purdy, Allan, Peterson & Dahlin,
LLP ....Medford, OR
Foster, R. Dwight ....Knoxville, TN
Foster, R. Jay ....Columbus, NC
Foster, Ralph ....Wichita, KS
Foster, Randall J. ....Branford, CT
Foster, Randolph C. ....Portland, OR
Foster, Rebecca M. ....Dallas, TX
Foster, Reginald L. ....Spartanburg, SC
Foster, Rex B. ....Jackson, MS
Foster, Rex B. ....Mendenhall, MS
Foster, Rhonda J. ....Peoria, IL
Foster, Richard A. ....East Lansing, MI
Foster, Richard B. ....New Orleans, LA
Foster, Richard B., III ....Chicago, IL
Foster, Richard B., Jr. ....Okemos, MI
Foster, Richard B., P.C. ....Okemos, MI
Foster, Richard C. ....Marietta, GA
Foster, Richard E. B. ....Roanoke, VA
Foster, Richard G. ....Corpus Christi, TX
Foster, Richard H. ....Tulsa, OK
Foster, Richard J. ....Irvine, CA
Foster, Richard J. ....Greenville, SC
Foster, Richard K. ....Lincoln, RI
Foster, Richard L.
Department of Education,
Office for Civil Rights, GV
Foster, Richard M. ....Encino, CA
Foster, Richard M. ....Santa Monica, CA
Foster, Richard M., Jr. ....Denver, CO
Foster, Richard T. ....Wilmington, DE
Foster, Richard T. ....Wichita, KS
Foster, Richard W. ....New Bedford, MA
Foster, Richard W. ....Memphis, TN
Foster, Richard W., Jr. ....Kenedy, TX
Foster, Rita A. ....Tulsa, OK
Foster, Robert A. ....Newport Beach, CA
Foster, Robert A. ....Washington, DC
Foster, Robert A., II ....Irvine, CA
Foster, Robert A., II, A Law Corporation
Irvine, CA
Foster, Robert Allan, Jr. ....Tampa, FL
Foster, Robert Allan, Jr., P.A. ....Tampa, FL
Foster, Robert B. ....Boston, MA
Foster, Robert B. ....Ann Arbor, MI
Foster, Robert C. ....Penn Yan, NY
Foster, Robert G. ....Iron Mountain, MI
Foster, Robert H. ....Columbus, OH
Foster, Robert H. ....Columbia, SC
Foster, Robert J. ....Des Moines, IA
Foster, Robert J. ....Minneapolis, MN
Foster, Robert J. ....Philadelphia, PA
Foster, Robert L. ....Chandler, OK
Foster, Robert M. ....San Diego, CA
Foster, Robert M. ....Jacksonville, FL
Foster, Robert M. ....Gretna, LA
Foster, Robert M. ....Marine City, MI
Foster, Robert N. ....Detroit, MI
Foster, Robert P. ....Atlanta, GA
Foster, Robert P., Jr. ....Dallas, TX
Foster, Robert Paul ....Greenville, SC
Foster, Robert R. ....DeLand, FL
Foster, Robert W. ....Columbia, SC
Foster, Robert W., Jr. ....Columbia, SC
Foster, Robin V.W. ....Kansas City, MO
Foster, Roger C. ....Birmingham, AL
Foster, Roger L. ....Morgantown, WV
Foster, Roger W. ....Clinton, OK
Taloga, OK
Foster, Ronald E. ....Lamar, CO
Foster, Ronald G. ....Liberty Corner, NJ
Foster, Ronald J., Jr ....St. Louis, MO
Foster, Ronald L. ....Grand Rapids, MI
Foster, Rowland B., (P.C.) ....Dallas, TX
Foster, Ruskin C. ....Columbia, SC
Foster, S. Elizabeth ....New York, NY
Foster, Sandra L. ....Lancaster, PA
Foster, Sandra Vinueza ....Perry, GA
Foster, Sarah B. ....Austin, TX
Foster, Scott Evan, (P.A.) ....St. Paul, MN
Foster, Scott R. ....Waltham, MA
Foster, Scott W. ....Springfield, MA
Foster, Seena K. ....Department of Labor,
Office of Secretary, GV
Foster, Sharon E. ....Los Angeles, CA
Foster, Shawn G. ....Kansas City, MO
Foster, Sheila ....Camden, NJ
Foster, Sidney C., Jr. ....Akron, OH
Foster, Stan L. ....Oklahoma City, OK
Foster, Stanbery, Jr. ....Seattle, WA
Foster, Stanley E. ....Atlanta, GA
Foster, Stanley H. ....Lincoln, NE
Foster, Stanley H. ....Cincinnati, OH
Foster, Stephanie M. ....New York, NY
Foster, Stephen A. ....Olympia, WA
Foster, Stephen D. ....Ellsworth, ME
Foster, Stephen Doak ....Little Rock, AR
Foster, Stephen H. ....Denver, CO
Billings, MT
Foster, Stephen H. ....Bristow, OK
Foster, Stephen M. ....Washington, DC
Foster, Stephen P. ....Ozawkie, KS
Foster, Stephen V. ....Perrysburg, OH
Foster, Stephenie
General Services Administration,
Office of the General Counsel, GV
Foster, Steven J. ....Chico, CA
Foster, Steven J. ....Boulder, CO
Foster, Stuart E. ....Medford, OR
Foster, Sullivan & Stephenson
Greenville, SC
Foster, Susan E. ....Seattle, WA
Foster, Susan Johnson ....Dallas, TX
Foster, Susan K. ....New York, NY
Foster, Susan M. ....Syracuse, NY
Foster, Suzanne M. ....Burlington, MA
Foster, Swift, Collins & Smith, P.C.
Farmington Hills, MI
Lansing, MI
Foster, T. Noble ....Seattle, WA
Foster, Tad S. ....Colorado Springs, CO
Foster, Teresa H. ....Phoenix, AZ
Foster, Terry J. ....Metropolis, IL
Foster, Thomas A. ....Burbank, CA
Foster, Thomas A. ....Kansas City, MO
Foster, Thomas B. ....Seattle, WA
Foster, Thomas B., Jr. ....Houston, TX
Foster, Thomas C. ....Irvine, CA
Foster, Thomas C. ....Cincinnati, OH
Foster, Thomas C. ....Richmond, VA
Foster, Thomas Daniel ....Washington, DC
Foster, Thomas E. ....Overland Park, KS
Foster, Thomas E. ....Spartanburg, SC
Foster, Thomas E., III ....Taylor, MI
Foster, Thomas G., Jr. ....Greensboro, NC
Foster, Thomas J. ....Harrisburg, IL
Foster, Thomas J. ....Dallas, TX
Foster, Thomas L. ....Birmingham, AL
Foster, Thomas Michael ....Tampa, FL
Foster, Thomas O., III ....Houston, TX
Foster, Thomas W. ....Tucson, AZ
Foster, Thomas W., P.C. ....Tucson, AZ
Foster, Timothy E. ....Grand Junction, CO
Foster, Todd ....Tampa, FL
Foster, Todd M. ....Dublin, CA
Foster, Tom C. ....Phoenix, AZ
Foster, Tompkins A. ....Orlando, FL
Foster, Toney D. ....Claremore, OK
Foster, Tonita M. ....Roanoke, VA
Foster, Torrey N. ....Beachwood, OH
Foster, Townsend, Jr. ....Covington, OH
Troy, OH
Foster, Tracy McFerrin ......Kansas City, MO
Foster, Troy P. ....Phoenix, AZ
Foster, Twila L. ....San Francisco, CA
Foster, Ty L. ....Cincinnati, OH
Foster, Vicki L. ....Denton, TX
Foster, Vicki Scheer ....Washington, DC
Foster, W. Douglas ....Galveston, TX
Foster, W. Paul ....San Francisco, CA
Foster, W. A., III ....Dallas, GA
Foster Walsh, LLP ....La Mesa, CA
San Diego, CA
Foster, Walter C. ....Rancho Palos Verdes, CA
Foster, Walter E., III ....Daytona Beach, FL
Foster, Walter E., III, P.A.
Daytona Beach, FL
Foster, Walter M. ....Boston, MA
Foster, Walter N. ....Cincinnati, OH
Foster, Walter W. ....Salem, OR
Foster, Wendy B. ....New York, NY
Foster, Wilbur F., Jr. ....New York, NY
Foster, William ....Pittsburgh, PA
Foster, William A. ....Cashiers, NC
Foster, William B., III ....Lynnwood, WA
Foster, William C. ....Stamford, CT
Foster, William C. ....Washington, DC
Foster, William C. ....Collingswood, NJ
Philadelphia, PA
Foster, William C. ....Albany, NY
Foster, William C. ....Findlay, OH
Foster, William D. ....Minneapolis, MN
Foster, William F., II ....Charleston, WV
Foster, William H., III ....Greenville, SC
Foster, William J., III ....Bonita Springs, FL
St. Michaels, MD
Foster, William J., IV ....Greenwich, CT
Foster, William L. ....Syracuse, NY
Foster, William M. ....Chattanooga, TN
Foster, William Scott
Fort Walton Beach, FL
Foster, Wilson Jerry ....Tallahassee, FL
Foster, Winfield W. ....Palo Alto, CA
Foster, Wm. D., & Associates
Minneapolis, MN
Foster, Wood R., Jr. ....Minneapolis, MN
Foster, Yolanda M. ....Broken Arrow, OK
Foster-Au, Renata E. ....Paia, HI
Foster-Morales, Dori ....Miami, FL
Foster-Rice, Angela ....Chicago, IL
Foster-Vargas, Christie Da Lee
San Diego, CA
Fosteson, Grant A. ....St. Paul, MN
Fote, Dominic J. ....Los Angeles, CA
Foteh, Samir J. ....Houston, TX
Fotenos, James F. ....San Francisco, CA
Fotenos & Suttle, P.C. ....Atherton, CA
San Francisco, CA
Foth, Arthur, Jr. ....Middleburg Heights, OH
Foth, Julie Carter ....Overland Park, KS
Foth, Kelly & Urban Co., L.P.A.
Middleburg Heights, OH
Foth, Neil B. ....Lenexa, KS
Fothergill, Kathleen C. ....St. Louis, MO
Fotheringham, Robert C. ....Portland, OR
Fotheringham, Tom J. ....Amarillo, TX
Fotheringill, Linda M ....Towson, MD
Foti, Anthony L. ....Euclid, OH
Foti, Catherine M. ....New York, NY
Foti, Diana B. ....Rochester, NY
Foti, Franco ....Cross River, NY
Foti, John J., Jr. ....Toms River, NJ
Foti, Joseph D., Jr. ....Southington, CT
Foti, Joseph W. ....Montpelier, VT
Foti, Lawrence T. ....Media, PA
Foti, Leola M. ....West Allis, WI
Foti, Margaret M. ....Newark, NJ
Fotiades-Alexander, Speroula P.
Glen Mills, PA
Fotiadis, John ....Bellmore, NY
Fotieo, Themis J. ....Grand Rapids, MI
Fotis, Stephen C. ....Washington, DC
Foto, Charles A. ....Dallas, TX
Foto, Philip J. ....New Orleans, LA
Foto, Tara L. ....New Orleans, LA
Fotopoulos, Dimitrios C. ....New York, NY
Fotopoulos, Gus P. ....Carmel, NY
Fotopoulos, Rosenblatt, Green, & Frasciello
New York, NY
Fotopoulos, Spiros P. ....McLean, VA
Fotopoulos, William ....Hampton Bays, NY
Fotopulos, M. Christine ....Missoula, MT
Fotopulos, Sara ....Tampa, FL
Fotopulos, Spiro A. ....Denver, CO
Fotopulos, Thomas E. ....Tampa, FL
Fotos, Lauren A. ....Westborough, MA
Fotouhi, Shahab E. ....Fresno, CA
San Francisco, CA
San Luis Obispo, CA
Fotsch, Harold R. ....St. Paul, MN
Fotta, Joan T. ....Columbus, OH
Fouassier, James G. ....East Northport, NY
Fouberg, Robert J. ....Washington, DC
Foucek, Oldrich, III ....Allentown, PA
Fouche, Andy M. ....Rockledge, FL
Fouché, William L., Jr. ....Dallas, TX
Foucheaux, Daniel J., Jr.
United States Postal Service,
Law Department, GV
Fouchek, Stephen J. ....McAllen, TX
Foucher, Sherna ....Pasadena, CA
Foudray, Kristina M. ....Minneapolis, MN
Foudree, Bruce W. ....Chicago, IL
Foudy, John P ....Brooklyn, NY
Foudy, Kathleen A. ....Washington, DC
Fougerat, Carol A. ....El Paso, TX
Fougere, Mary Elizabeth ....Portland, ME
Fougeron, Charles E. ....La Mesa, CA
Fougerousse, Philip ....Titusville, FL
Fought, Barbara Croll ....Syracuse, NY
Fought, Bonnie E. ....San Mateo, CA
Foughty, Christianson, White Eagle & Berg
Devils Lake, ND
Foughty, Donovan ....Devils Lake, ND
Foughty, Francis E. ....Devils Lake, ND
Fougner, Ragnhild A. ....Oakland, CA
Fougner, Robert B. ....Foster City, CA
Fouhey, John ....New York, NY
Fouhy, John S. ....Andover, MA
Fouhy, Kevin P. ....Delmar, NY
Fouke, Wertsch & Hayes .....San Francisco, CA
Foulds, Barbara B. ....Novato, CA
Foulds, Carter B. ....Front Royal, VA
Foulds, Gerald ....Pittsburgh, PA
Foulds, Robert J. ....Mayfield Heights, OH
Foulk, Bradley H. ....Erie, PA
Foulk, Gerald C. ....Wilmington, DE
Foulk, Jennifer J. ....Charleston, WV
Foulk, Stephen D. ....Binghamton, NY
Foulke, Cynthia Lee ....Kenilworth, NJ
Foulke, David S. ....Spring House, PA
Foulke, Edwin G., Jr. ....Greenville, SC
Foulke, Maria May ....Irvine, CA
Foulke, Sarah B. ....Saratoga Springs, NY
Foulke, Walter C. ....Auburn, NY
Foulke, Walter L. ....Philadelphia, PA
Foulkes, Andrea Gelman ....Philadelphia, PA
Foulkes, Anne M. ....Pittsburgh, PA
Foulkes, David Michael ....Sacramento, CA
Foulkes, John R. ....Philadelphia, PA
Foulkrod, Andrew H. ....Harrisburg, PA
Foulkrod, Jennifer M. ....Lancaster, PA
Foulkrod, S. Walter, III & Associates
Harrisburg, PA
Foulkrod, S. Walter, IV ....Harrisburg, PA
Foulks, Harry H. ....Sacramento, CA
Foulks, Marsha L. ....Dallas, TX
Foulsham, Linda M. ....Manchester, NH
Foulston Conlee Schmidt & Emerson, LLP
Wichita, KS
Foulston, John E. ....Wichita, KS
Foulston, Nola Tedesco ....Wichita, KS
Foulston, Sidney L., Jr. ....Wichita, KS
Foulston & Siefkin L.L.P. ......Dodge City, KS
Topeka, KS
Wichita, KS
Foulston, Steven L., (P.A.) ....Wichita, KS
Found, Ernest M. ....Batavia, NY
Foundas, Nicholas ....Boston, MA
Foundos, Felice R. ....Chicago, IL
Foung, Cheryl Weisbard ....Palo Alto, CA
Fountain, Allan L. ....Spencer, IN
Fountain, Aubrey W., III ....Richmond, VA
Fountain, Bill D. ....Austin, TX
Fountain, Bryan & Ritter, LLC
Easton, MD
Fountain, C. Wayne ....Lafayette, IN
Fountain, Christina A. Lopez
Newport Beach, CA
Fountain, Christopher C. ....Greenwich, CT
Fountain, Darryl K. ....Wilmington, DE
Fountain, David B. ....Charlotte, NC
Fountain, Dennis F. ....Altamonte Springs, FL
Fountain, Donald R., Jr. (P.A.)
West Palm Beach, FL
Fountain, Edwin L. ....Washington, DC
Fountain, Elizabeth L. ....Washington, DC
Fountain, F. Rayford ....Pasadena, CA
Fountain, Forrest J. ....Los Angeles, CA
Fountain, Galen L. ....United States Senate,
Committee Legal Personnel, GV
Fountain, George L. ....Los Angeles, CA
Fountain, George M. ....Tarboro, NC
Fountain & Goodwyn ....Tarboro, NC
Fountain, Jay M. ....Portland, OR
Fountain, Jennifer N. ....Greensboro, NC
Fountain, John E. ....Mobile, AL
Fountain, John N. ....Raleigh, NC
Fountain, Keith R. ....Altamonte Springs, FL
Fountain, Kenneth R. ....Gulf Breeze, FL
Fountain, L. H. ....Tarboro, NC
Fountain, Lisa L. ....New York, NY
Fountain, P. Burke ....Taunton, MA
Fountain, Reed N. ....Raleigh, NC
Fountain, Richard M. ....Jackson, MS
Fountain, Richard M. Law Offices of, P.A.
Jackson, MS
Fountain, Richard T., III ....Raleigh, NC
Fountain, Richard T., Jr.
Rocky Mount, NC
Fountain, R. M., Jr. ....Washington, NC
Fountain, Ryan M. ....Mishawaka, IN
Fountain, Sharon M. ....Dallas, TX
Fountain, Shirley A. ....Hartford, CT
Fountain, Stanton J., Jr. ....Biloxi, MS
Fountain, Susan T. ....Raleigh, NC
Fountain, Trudy D. ....Minnetonka, MN
Gulfport, MS

Fountain, W. Thomas ... Easton, MD
Fountain, Wendy L. Christensen ... Santa Ana, CA
Fountaine, Cynthia L. ... Cincinnati, OH
Fountas, Christopher N. ... Orlando, FL
Four, Michael D. ... Los Angeles, CA
Fouracre, Rodney D., Sr. ... La Junta, CO
Fouraker, Laura Ann ... Tampa, FL
Fourchy, Patrick L. ... Fresno, CA
Foureman, William C. ... Cincinnati, OH
Fourkas, Roberta M. ... Sacramento, CA
Fourkiller, Lea Gibson ... Tulsa, OK
Fourlas, Debra P. ... Harrisburg, PA
Fournaris, Christina Mesires ... Philadelphia, PA
Fournaris, Constantine T. ... Philadelphia, PA
Fournaris, Emmanuel G. ... Wilmington, DE
Fournaris & Sanet, P.A. ... Coral Gables, FL
Miami, FL
Fournaris, Theodore J. ... Miami, FL
Fournerat, Daniel G. ... Lafayette, LA
Fournet & Adams, Ltd. ... Lafayette, LA
Fournet, M. Michele ... Baton Rouge, LA
Fournet Hoffpauir, Julie ... Lafayette, LA
Fournie, Mary Lindeman ... St. Louis, MO
Fournie, Raymond R. ... Belleville, IL
St. Louis, MO
Fournie, Thomas A. ... Los Angeles, CA
Fournier, Arthur E., Jr. ... Windsor, CT
Fournier, Brian C. ... New Haven, CT
Fournier, Charles W. ... New York, NY
Fournier, Cindy S. ... Environmental Protection Agency, Office of Enforcement and Compliance Assurance, GV
Fournier, David M. ... Wilmington, DE
Fournier, Dean Arthur ... Seattle, WA
Fournier, Emily Haycock ... Boston, MA
Fournier, Gena Danielle ... Fort Lauderdale, FL
Fournier, Gerard O. ... Portland, ME
Fournier, Harry J. ... Oak Brook, IL
Fournier, James D. ... Mount Angel, OR
Fournier, James J. ... Washington, DC
Fournier, Joseph E. ... Boston, MA
Fournier Law Offices, P.C. ... Burlington, MA
Fournier, Michael R. ... Sunnyvale, CA
Fournier, Nicole M. ... New Haven, CT
Fournier, Patricia Bond ... Tallahassee, FL
Fournier, Paul ... East Hartford, CT
Fournier, Paul A. ... Washington, DC
Fournier, Paul C. ... Lewiston, ME
Fournier, Robert M. ... Sarasota, FL
Fournier, Roland O. ... North Smithfield, RI
Fournier, Stephen E. D. ... Madison, CT
Fournier, Teri J. ... Los Angeles, CA
Fournier, Theodore R., Jr. ... Spokane, WA
Fournier, Thomas R. ... Burlington, MA
Fournier Ferrer, Yvonne ... San Francisco, CA
Fouron, Seendy ... New York, NY
Fourqurean, James W. ... Fairfax, VA
Fourr, Robert C. ... Menlo Park, CA
Fourt, Paul L. ... Dallas, TX
Fourt, Paul Lanaux, Jr. ... Dallas, TX
Fourton, Leslie E., Jr. ... New York, NY
Fourton, Leslie E., Jr., Esq., P.C., The Law Offices of ... New York, NY
Fouse, Dale M. ... Aliquippa, PA
Fouse, Ronald L. ... Kansas City, MO
Fousekis, James T. ... San Francisco, CA
Fouser, Scott E. ... Caldwell, ID
Fouser, Trudy Hanson ... Boise, ID
Foushée, Jane C. ... Louisville, KY
Foushee, Rodney L. ... North Myrtle Beach, SC
Foushee, Trudi McCollum ... Washington, DC
St. Louis, MO
Foushee, Wayne H. ... Winston-Salem, NC
Fouss, Daniel A. ... Marietta, OH
Foust, Christopher J. ... Milton, PA
Foust & Clark, P.C. ... McLean, VA
Foust, Cleon H., Jr. ... Indianapolis, IN
Foust, Curt R. ... Denver, CO
Foust, David K. ... Detroit, MI
Foust, Dennis R. ... Benton, KY
Foust, Gene Eric ... Spartanburg, SC
Foust, Jeffrey D. ... Springfield, IL
Foust, Jerry L. ... Cleveland, OH
Foust, John W. ... McLean, VA
Foust, Lawrence L. ... Houston, TX
Foust, Max W. ... Kansas City, MO
Foust, Michael V. ... Goodland, KS
Foust, Pamela W. ... Santa Monica, CA
Foust, Rebecca Jane ... Mill Valley, CA
Foust, Richard T. ... Los Angeles, CA
Foust, Robert A. ... Marion, IN
Foust, Stacey A. ... Pottsville, PA
Foust, William R. ... Newton, IA
Fouste, James E. ... Costa Mesa, CA
Foustoukos, Alexandra P. ... Cambridge, MA
Fout, George D. ... Coronado, CA
Fout, Murray H. ... Frederick, MD
Foutch, David B. ... Lebanon, TN
Foutch, Jack W. ... Colorado Springs, CO
Foutch, James L. ... Oak Ridge, TN
Foutch, James R. ... Houston, TX
Foutch, Louise A. ... Clearwater, FL
Foutch, William O., Jr. ... Morristown, TN
Fouts, Aubrey Jan ... Lubbock, TX
Fouts, Constance A. ... Dallas, TX
Fouts, Daniel W. ... Greensboro, NC
Fouts, Douglas R. ... Solon, OH
Fouts, Fouts & Joplin ... Lubbock, TX
Fouts, James S. ... Waukegan, IL
Fouts, John ... Haskell, TX
Fouts, John D. ... Calistoga, CA
Fouts, Julius P. ... New York, NY
Fouts, Kristen ... Abilene, TX
Fouts, Kurtis G. ... Delphi, IN
Fouts, Leigh Ann ... Lubbock, TX
Fouts, Lindsey, III ... Dallas, TX
Fouts, Louis M., III ... Dallas, TX
Fouts, M. Lindsey, III ... Dallas, TX
Fouts, Michael E. ... Abilene, TX
Fouts, Michael F. ... Oklahoma City, OK
Fouts & Moore, L.L.P. ... Houston, TX
Foutty, David L. ... Indianapolis, IN
Foutty, Stephen L. ... Indianapolis, IN
Foutz, Alan W ... Sacramento, CA
Foutz, Grant L. ... Gallup, NM
Foutz, Samuel T. ... Dallas, TX
Foutz, Stuart R. ... Prescott, AZ
Foutz, Thomas Keasler ... Metairie, LA
Fow, Paula ... Butler, PA
Fowell, Karen S. ... Richland Center, WI
Fowell & Keegan ... Richland Center, WI
Fowerbaugh, Albert E. ... Cleveland, OH
Fowerbaugh, Albert E., Jr. ... Chicago, IL
Fowkes & Birmingham ... Oakmont, PA
Fowkes, George E. ... Oakmont, PA
Fowkes, Richard O. ... Los Angeles, CA
Fowkes, Scott W. ... Chicago, IL
Fowle, A. John ... New York, NY
Fowle, Frank F. ... Winnetka, IL
Fowle, Frederick H. ... Crandon, WI
Fowle, Irene Zorensky ... St. Louis, MO
Fowle, Linda J. ... Centerport, NY
Fowle, Phyllis L. P. ... Bronx, NY
Fowler, Alfred B. ... Larkspur, CA
Fowler, Alfred B. ... San Francisco, CA
Fowler, Alicia Brass ... Sacramento, CA
Fowler, Andrea J. ... Orlando, FL
Fowler, Andrew F. ... New York, NY
Fowler, Andrew S. ... Birmingham, MI
Fowler, Ann G. ... Atlanta, GA
Fowler, Anne B. ... Jeffersonville, IN
Fowler, Arthur Baird, V ... Portland, OR
Fowler, Arthur M. ... Johnson City, TN
Fowler, Aubrey R. ... Madison, WI
Fowler & Ball ... Ukiah, CA
Fowler, Barbara A. ... Houston, TX
Fowler, Barice and Feeney, P.A. ... Orlando, FL
Fowler, Ben A. ... Grand Rapids, MI
Fowler, Betty A. ... Detroit, MI
Fowler, Bradley A. ... Austin, TX
Fowler, Brian F. ... Ridgewood, NJ
Fowler, Brian J. ... Leawood, KS
Kansas City, MO
Fowler, Bruce A. ... Tulsa, OK
Fowler, Byron T. ... Cincinnati, OH
Fowler, C. Edward, Jr. ... Dallas, TX
Fowler, Calvin W. ... Danville, VA
Fowler, Calvin W., Jr. ... Richmond, VA
Fowler, Candace L. ... Atlanta, GA
Fowler, Carlo S. ... San Francisco, CA
Fowler, Carol Ann Kann ... Atlanta, GA
Fowler, Carol F. ... Kansas City, MO
Fowler, Caroline L. ... Santa Rosa, CA
Fowler, Char-La Cain ... Chattanooga, TN
Fowler, Charles Calvin ... Irvine, CA
Fowler, Charles E., III ... Leawood, KS
Fowler, Charles W. ... Laurel, MD
Fowler, Charles W. ... Memphis, TN
Fowler, Clinton H., Jr. ... Torrance, CA
Fowler and Cole ... Lebanon, OH
Fowler, Conrad M., Jr. ... Columbiana, AL
Fowler, Conrad M., Sr. ... Lanett, AL
Fowler, Craig M. ... Dallas, TX
Fowler, Daniel B. ... Merritt Island, FL
Fowler, Daniel J. ... Oklahoma City, OK
Fowler, Daniel L. ... Kansas City, MO
Fowler, Daniel M. ... Denver, CO
Fowler, Daniel P. ... Chicago, IL
Fowler, Darrin F. ... Lansing, MI
Fowler, David A. ... Franklin, GA
La Grange, GA
Fowler, David C. ... Owensboro, KY
Fowler, David E. ... Chattanooga, TN
Fowler, David E. ... Madison, WI
Fowler, David K. ... Fort Myers, FL
Fowler, David L. ... Arlington, VA
Fowler, David M. ... Fernandina Beach, FL
Fowler, David R. ... Salem, OR
Fowler, David T. ... Mineola, NY
Fowler, Dawn E. ... Dallas, TX
Fowler, Deborah L. ... Dallas, TX
Fowler, Debra D. ... Department of Justice, Civil Division, GV
Fowler, Debra-Lynn Gargano ... Washington, DC
Fowler, Don W. ... Chicago, IL
Fowler, Donald A., Jr. ... Kingfield, ME
Fowler, Donald D. ... Folsom, CA
Fowler, Donald W. ... Washington, DC
Fowler, Douglas ... San Francisco, CA
Fowler, Douglas G. ... Cheyenne, WY
Fowler, Earl J., Jr. ... Asheville, NC
Fowler, Edward J. ... Sacramento, CA
Fowler, Edward P. ... Hamilton, AL
Fowler, Elaine H. ... Charleston, SC
Fowler, Emily S. ... Kansas City, MO
Fowler, Felicity A. ... Houston, TX
Fowler, Flora Daun ... Port Orange, FL
Fowler & Fowler ... Key West, FL
Fowler, Frank L. ... Cedar Rapids, IA
Fowler, Frederick J., (P.C.) ... Dallas, TX
Fowler, Frederick L. ... Troy, NY
Fowler, G. William ... Midland, TX
Fowler, G. William ... Odessa, TX
Fowler, Gene D. ... Slidell, LA
Fowler, George J., III ... New Orleans, LA
Fowler, Gerard A. ... St. Louis, MO
Fowler, Gregory L. ... Kansas City, MO
Fowler, Gregory M. ... Washington, DC
Fowler, Griffin, Coyne & Coyne, P.C. ... Winchester, VA
Fowler, H. Gregory ... Savannah, GA
Fowler, Hein, Cheatwood, Passino & Williams, Professional Association ... Atlanta, GA
Fowler, J. Bart ... Austin, TX
Fowler, J. Edward ... Washington, DC
Fowler, J. Kirby, Jr. ... Baltimore, MD
Fowler, J. Robert ... Houston, TX
Fowler, Jack D. ... Mount Carmel, IL
Fowler, James A. ... Orlando, FL
Fowler, James C. ... San Francisco, CA
Fowler, James C. ... Seattle, WA
Fowler, James F. ... Indianola, IA
Fowler, James H., III ... Janesville, WI
Fowler, James M. ... Los Angeles, CA
Fowler, James M. ... Jonesboro, LA
Fowler, James M., Jr. ... Little Rock, AR
Fowler, James R., Jr. ... Hattiesburg, MS
Fowler, James V. ... Livonia, MI
Fowler, Janine R. ... Los Angeles, CA
Fowler, Jay F. ... Wichita, KS
Fowler, Jeffrey S. ... Chicago, IL
Fowler, Jenifer Gaglia ... Cherry Hill, NJ
Fowler, Jennifer Johnson ... Oak Ridge, TN
Fowler, Jennifer M. ... Tampa, FL
Fowler, Jennifer W. ... New York, NY
Fowler, Jennifer W., P.C. ... New York, NY
Fowler, Jerry A. ... Alfred, NY
Fowler, Jill R. ... Berwyn, PA
Philadelphia, PA
Fowler, Joan ... Oviedo, FL
Fowler, Joe L. ... Atlanta, GA
Fowler, Joe W. ... Stillwater, OK
Fowler, Joel A. ... Dunwoody, GA
Fowler, Johanna Searle ... Raleigh, NC
Fowler, John A. ... White Plains, NY
Fowler, John B. ... Knoxville, TN
Fowler, John B., III ... Carlisle, PA
Fowler, John C. ... Toccoa, GA
Fowler, John D. ... Bernardsville, NJ
Fowler, John D., Jr. ... New York, NY
Fowler, John H. ... Sevierville, TN
Fowler, John M. ... Advisory Council on Historic Preservation, GV
Fowler, John P. ... Reno, NV
Fowler, John R. ... Charleston, WV
Fowler, John R., III ... Marietta, GA
Fowler, John R., Jr. ... Troy, MI
Fowler, John T., III ... Louisville, KY
Fowler, John W. ... Palo Alto, CA
Fowler, John W., Jr. ... Philadelphia, PA
Fowler, John W., (P.A.) ... Miami, FL
Fowler, Joseph D., Jr. ... Woodbury, MN
Fowler, Joseph H. ... Douglasville, GA
Fowler, Joseph M. ... Stamford, CT
Fowler, Joseph R. ... Philadelphia, PA
Fowler, Joyce A. ... Southfield, MI
Fowler, Julian L. ... Farmington, NM
Fowler, Kathleen ... Palo Alto, CA
Fowler, Kelesha A. ... Dallas, TX
Fowler, Kelly H. ... Owensboro, KY
Fowler, Kevin D. ... Orlando, FL
Fowler, Kevin J. ... Hagåtña, GU
Fowler, Kevin M. ... Topeka, KS
Fowler, Kim ... Springfield, IL
Fowler & Kirby, P.C. ... Fayetteville, GA
Fowler, L. Buck ... Jacksonville, FL
Fowler, Larkin M., Jr. ... Moultrie, GA
Fowler, Larned B. ... Mission Viejo, CA
Fowler, Larry ... Cleveland, GA
Fowler, Larry L., Jr. ... Arlington, TX
Fowler, Laura J. ... Sacramento, CA
Fowler, Laura S. ... Austin, TX
Fowler, Laurence D. ... Lansing, MI
Fowler, Lea Ellen ... Little Rock, AR
Fowler, Lenora J. ... Palm Beach, FL
Fowler, Lisa Chapman ... Cookeville, TN
Fowler, Louise E. ... Minneapolis, MN
Fowler, Lynn E. ... Atlanta, GA
Fowler, M. Gay ... Houston, TX
Fowler, Margaret J. ... Binghamton, NY
Fowler, Margo Shatz ... Washington, DC
Fowler, Marion S., III ... Columbia, SC
Florence, SC
Fowler, Mark ... Palo Alto, CA
Fowler, Mark A. ... New York, NY
Fowler, Mark S. ... Washington, DC
Fowler, Mark W. ... Union City, TN
Fowler, Mary Katharine A. ... Annapolis, MD
Fowler, Mavis K. ... New York, NY
Fowler & McNair, LLP ... Medford, OR
Fowler, Measle & Bell, L.L.P. ... Lexington, KY
Fowler, Melvin K. ... Santa Maria, CA
Fowler, Michael ... Fayetteville, GA
Fowler, Michael C., (P.C.) ... Atlanta, GA
Fowler, Michael D. ... Fort Pierce, FL
Fowler, Michael R. ... English, IN
Fowler, Michele L. ... Memphis, TN
Fowler, Miles B. ... Clinton, NC
Fowler, Morgan C. ... Atoka, TN
Fowler, Neal I. ... Department of Justice, Tax Division, GV
Fowler, Newton B., III ... Baltimore, MD
Fowler, Pat M. ... Orange Park, FL
Fowler, Pat M., P.A. ... Orange Park, FL
Fowler, Patricia J. ... Kings Beach, CA
Fowler, Patricia L.R. ... New Canaan, CT
Fowler, Patrick X. ... Phoenix, AZ
Fowler, Paul E. ... Portsmouth, OH
Fowler, Paul R. ... Spartanburg, SC
Fowler, Peary S. ... Key West, FL
Fowler, Peter N. ... Department of Commerce, Patent and Trademark Office, GV
Fowler, Peter W. ... Bakersfield, CA
Fowler, Philip J. ... Chicago, IL
Fowler, Phillip J. ... Indianapolis, IN
Fowler, Prince & Webb ... Union City, TN
Fowler, R. Dennis ... Raytown, MO
Fowler, Randall D. ... Monrovia, CA
Fowler, Randolph M. ... Tuscaloosa, AL
Fowler, Rebecca McCarthy ... Tulsa, OK
Fowler, Renn C. ... General Services Administration, Office of the General Counsel, GV
Fowler, Richard J. ... Key West, FL
Fowler, Richard L. ... Knoxville, TN
Fowler, Richard R. ... Mansfield, OH
Fowler, Robert A. ... Ukiah, CA
Fowler, Robert D. ... Austin, TX
Fowler, Robert G. ... Dedham, MA
Fowler, Robert K. ... Houston, TX
Fowler, Robert P. ... Birmingham, AL
Fowler, Robert Penn ... Austin, TX
Fowler, Robert R. ... Chicago, IL
Fowler, Robert V. ... Fond du Lac, WI
Fowler, Ronald K. ... Anderson, IN
Fowler, Roy D. ... Wakefield, RI
Fowler, Roy W., Jr. ... Orangevale, CA
Fowler, Russell A. ... Winchester, VA
Fowler, Russell E., II ... Indianapolis, IN
Fowler, S. Brook ... Greenville, SC
Greer, SC
Fowler, Sam F., Jr. ... Knoxville, TN
Fowler, Samuel A., Jr. ... Thomson, GA
Fowler, Schimberg and Flanagan, Professional Corporation ... Denver, CO
Fowler, Scott R. ... Metairie, LA
Fowler, Sherri Davis ... West Orange, NJ
Fowler, Stacy Hitt ... Portland, OR
Fowler, Stephen J. ... San Francisco, CA
Fowler, Stephen M. ... Charleston, WV
Fowler, Susan ... Atlantic City, NJ
Fowler, Susan D. ... Bloomfield Hills, MI
Fowler, Susan L. ... Burlington, VT
Fowler, Susan Stansfield ... Dayton, OH
Fowler, Teri, (Ms.) ... Oakland, CA
Fowler, Terrell D. ... Lake Charles, LA
Fowler, Terrell D., A Prof. Law Corp. ... Lake Charles, LA
Fowler, Thomas E. ... Lancaster, NY
Fowler, Thomas H., Jr. ... Sherman, TX
Fowler, Thomas K., Jr. ... Columbia, SC
Fowler, Thomas K., Jr., P.A. ... Columbia, SC
Fowler, Timms R. ... Fort Collins, CO
Fowler, Tina Gardner ... Springfield, MO
Fowler, Tracy H. ... Salt Lake City, UT
Fowler, Tuttle, Clark, Coleman & Mannon ... Lansing, MI
Fowler, Vernon E., Jr. ... Selah, WA
Fowler, W. Craig ... Chicago, IL
Fowler, W. Gary ... Dallas, TX
Fowler, W. Howard ... Lawrenceville, GA
Fowler, Walter T., Jr. ... Springfield, MO
Fowler, Wanda McKee ... Houston, TX
Fowler, Wayne J. ... Denver, CO
Fowler, Wayne J., LLC ... Denver, CO
Fowler, Wendell C. ... Little Rock, AR
Fowler, White, Burnett, Hurley, Banick & Strickroot, A Professional Association ... Miami, FL
Fowler, White, Gillen, Boggs, Villareal and Banker, P.A. ... Bradenton, FL
Clearwater, FL
Fort Myers, FL
Lakeland, FL
Naples, FL
New Port Richey, FL
Port Charlotte, FL
St. Petersburg, FL
Sarasota, FL
Tallahassee, FL
Tampa, FL
Fowler & Wiederhoeft ... Madison, WI
Fowler, Wiles & Keith, L.L.P. ... Dallas, TX
Fowler, William G. ... Lebanon, OH
Fowler, William G. ... Salt Lake City, UT
Fowler, William G., II ... Lexington, KY
Fowler, William H. ... Sacramento, CA
Fowler, William H. ... Medford, OR
Fowler, William L. ... Cottonwood Falls, KS
Fowler, William T. ... Conroe, TX
Fowler & Wills ... Thomson, GA
Fowler, Wm. E., Jr. ... National Transportation Safety Board, Office of Administrative Law Judges, GV
Fowler, Wm. Scott ... Youngstown, OH
Fowler-Trinchara, Sharryl E. ... Stockton, CA
Fowles, Dwayne C. ... Spokane, WA
Fowles, Garrett T. ... Richmond, KY
Fowles, James H., III ... Charlotte, NC
Raleigh, NC
Columbia, SC
Fowles, James H., Jr. ... Columbia, SC
Fowles, John C. ... Lincoln, NE
Fowles, Julian ... Los Angeles, CA
Fowles, Neal E. ... Olathe, KS
Fowley & Beckley, P.A. ... Hunt Valley, MD
Fowley, James K. ... Hunt Valley, MD
Fowley, Jeffry ... Boston, MA
Fowlie, Georgina R. ... Albuquerque, NM
Fowlie, Mary M. ... Troy, MI
Fowlkes, C. Edward, Jr. ... Nashville, TN
Fowlkes, Christopher W. ... Minneapolis, MN
Fowlkes, D'Ette L. ... Marfa, TX
Fowlkes, E. Oliver ... Boston, MA
Fowlkes, J. Thomas ... Bristol, VA
Fowlkes, John T., Jr. ... Memphis, TN
Fowlkes, Joseph F. ... Pulaski, TN
Fowlkes, Lisa M. ... Washington, DC

Fowlkes, Norman T., III ... Chicago, IL
Fowlkes, Templeton ... Biloxi, MS
Fowlkes & Whiteside ... Nashville, TN
Fowlkes, Whitman W. ... Mountain View, AR
Fowlkes, W. W. ... San Antonio, TX
Fowlks, Richard E. ... Portland, OR
Fowlston, Tamara R. ... Buffalo, NY
Fox, A. Michael ... New York, NY
Fox, Aaron H. ... Philadelphia, PA
Fox, Adam M. ... New York, NY
Fox, Adam R. ... Cleveland, OH
Fox, Adam T. ... Dallas, TX
Fox, Adrienne M. ... Durham, NC
Fox, Aileen J. ... New York, NY
Fox, Alan C. ... Sherman Oaks, CA
Fox, Alan D. ... New York, NY
Fox, Alan H. ... Saddle Brook, NJ
New York, NY
Fox, Alan L. ... San Juan Capistrano, CA
Fox, Alan P. ... Mount Laurel, NJ
Fox, Alan S. ... New York, NY
Fox, Alashia A. ... Tulsa, OK
Fox, Albert Steven ... Chamberlain, SD
Fox, Alfred L. ... Camarillo, CA
Fox, Allan M. ... Washington, DC
Fox, Allen H. ... Washington, DC
Fox, Allen L. ... Baltimore, MD
Fox, Allyson B. ... Houston, TX
Fox, Alvin B. ... Newport News, VA
Fox, Alvin L. (Peck), Jr. ... Montgomery, AL
Fox, Andrea Harris ... Greensboro, NC
Fox, Angelee ... Los Angeles, CA
Fox, Anita G. ... East Lansing, MI
Fox, Ann Connell ... Boston, MA
Fox, Ann Elizabeth ... Denver, CO
Fox, Anne K. (Katie) ... Oakland, CA
Fox, Anne Marie ... Hackensack, NJ
Fox, Anthony ... Charlotte, NC
Fox, Anthony M. ... San Francisco, CA
Fox, Anthony N. ... Birmingham, AL
Fox, Ariel A. ... New York, NY
Fox & Arnel, P.C. ... Canton, MA
Fox, Arnold ... Athens, NY
Fox, Arthur L. ... Corte Madera, CA
Fox, Arthur L., II ... Washington, DC
Fox, Athena L. ... Hendersonville, NC
Fox, Audrey Braker ... San Mateo, CA
Fox, Autumn L. ... Kansas City, MO
Fox, Barbara N. ... Chicago, IL
Fox, Barbara S. ... Montclair, NJ
Fox, Barry M. ... New York, NY
Fox, Barry S. ... Needham, MA
Fox, Benjamin J. ... Los Angeles, CA
Fox, Bennett & Turner ... Washington, DC
Fairfax, VA
Fox, Bernard C. ... Cincinnati, OH
Fox, Bernard C., Jr. ... Cincinnati, OH
Fox, Beth A. ... Rosemead, CA
Fox, Beverly ... Plantation, FL
Fox, Brendan C.
Securities and Exchange Commission,
Division of Investment Management, GV
Fox, Brian L. ... Ventura, CA
Fox, Brian S. ... Boca Raton, FL
Fox, Bruce A. ... Chicago, IL
Fox, Bruce A. ... Vernon, MI
Fox, Bruce D. ... Clinton, TN
Fox, Bruce R. ... Waltham, MA
Fox, Bruce S. ... Austin, TX
Fox, Byron E. ... Richmond, VA
Fox, Byron Neal, (P.C.) ... Kansas City, MO
Fox, C. LaVaun ... Aiken, SC
Fox, C. Richard ... Columbiana, OH
Fox, Carey J. ... San Diego, CA
Fox, Carl R. ... Chapel Hill, NC
Fox, Caroline Fishburne ... Conway, SC
Fox, Carolyn M. ... Roseburg, OR
Fox, Catherine
Federal Communications Commission,
Wireless Telecommunications Bureau, GV
Fox, Catherine Perez ... Covina, CA
Fox, Catherine Perez ... Los Angeles, CA
Fox, Chandler, Homans, Hicks & McKinnon
Dawsonville, GA
Gainesville, GA
Fox, Charles D., III, The Law Offices of
Roanoke, VA
Fox, Charles D., IV ... Chicago, IL
Fox, Charles F. ... Gainesville, FL
Fox, Charles F., III ... Vandergrift, PA
Fox, Charles M. ... New York, NY
Fox, Charles P. ... Chicago, IL
Fox, Chas. B. ... Dayton, OH
Fox, Cheryl A. ... United States Senate,
Committee Legal Personnel, GV
Fox, Christi Leigh ... Hartford, CT
Fox, Christopher J. ... Philadelphia, PA
Fox, Christopher J. ... Kirkland, WA
Fox, Christopher L. ... Oklahoma City, OK
Fox, Christopher R. ... Lebanon, TN
Fox, Christopher W. ... Syracuse, NY
Fox, Cindy M. ... Hackensack, NJ
Fox, Clenzo B. ... Columbus, OH
Fox & Cotner ... Jeffersonville, IN
New Albany, IN
Fox, Craig A. ... Granada Hills, CA
Fox, Craig H. ... Norristown, PA
Fox, Craig S. ... Fremont, CA
Fox, Cynthia Moseley ... St. Louis, MO
Fox, Cynthia S. ... Dallas, TX
Fox, Cyril A., Jr. ... Pittsburgh, PA
Fox, D. Craig ... Brea, CA
Los Angeles, CA
Fox, Dana A. ... Los Angeles, CA
Fox, Dana Hendricks ... Baltimore, MD
Fox, Dana W. ... San Francisco, CA
Fox, Daniel B. ... Miami, FL
Fox, Daniel E. ... Columbus, OH
Fox, Daniel J. ... Fort Lauderdale, FL
Fox, Daniel L. ... Yankton, SD
Fox, Daniel M. ... Newport Beach, CA
Fox, Daniel N. ... Pomona, CA
Fox, Daniel W. ... San Diego, CA
Fox, David ... New York, NY
Fox, David A. ... Windsor, CT
Fox, David A. ... Gainesville, GA
Fox, David B. ... Haddonfield, NJ
Fox, David E. ... Norwell, MA
Fox, David E. ... Raleigh, NC
Fox, David E., and Associates
Washington, DC
Fox, David F. ... Middletown, RI
Fox, David I. ... Livingston, NJ
Fox, David K. ... New Orleans, LA
Hendersonville, NC
Fox, David L. ... Chicago, IL
Fox, David L. ... New York, NY
Fox, David L. ... Philadelphia, PA
Fox, David L. ... Houston, TX
Fox, David M. ... Los Angeles, CA
Fox, David M. ... Rockville, MD
Fox, David N. ... Oklahoma City, OK
Fox, David S. ... San Francisco, CA
Fox, David S. ... Boston, MA
Fox, David W. ... Chicago, IL
Fox, Deborah ... Fairfax, VA
Fox, Deborah J. ... Los Angeles, CA
Fox, Debra M. ... Haverford, PA
Fox, Deirdre A. ... Chicago, IL
Fox, Dennis J. ... Chicago, IL
Fox, Dennis J. ... Canton, OH
Fox, Dennis M. ... White Plains, NY
Fox, Dennis R. ... Moline, IL
Fox, Dennis W. ... Monterey, CA
Fox, Dennis W. ... St. Louis, MO
Fox, Dewain D. ... Phoenix, AZ
Fox, Diane A. ... Bethesda, MD
Fox, Differ, Callahan, Sheridan & McDevitt
Norristown, PA
Fox, Don W. ... Department of the Air Force,
Office of the General Counsel, GV
Fox, Donald R. ... Rochester, NY
Fox, Donald T. ... New York, NY
Fox, Douglas A. ... Santa Cruz, CA
Fox, Douglas A. ... Wilmington, NC
Fox, Douglas B. ... Philadelphia, PA
Fox, Douglas L. ... Worcester, MA
Fox, Douglas M. ... Baltimore, MD
Fox, Douglas Nathan ... Atlanta, GA
Fox, Douglas T. ... Phillips, WI
Fox, Duane J. ... Kansas City, MO
Fox, E. Frances ... Wilmette, IL
Fox, E. Lee ... Tahoe City, CA
Fox, Earwood & Childers, PLLC
Jackson, MS
Fox, Edgar N., III ... Brooklyn, NY
Fox, Edward A. ... Trevose, PA
Fox, Edward Alexander ... Columbus, OH
Fox, Edward F. ... Minneapolis, MN
Fox, Edward H. ... Rochester, NY
Fox, Edward M. ... Los Angeles, CA
Fox, Edward M. ... New York, NY
Fox, Eileen ... Manchester, NH
Fox, Eileen ... New York, NY
Fox, Eileen ... New York, NY
Fox, Elaine S. ... Chicago, IL
Fox, Eleanor M. ... New York, NY
Fox, Elinor Dibble ... Stockton, CA
Fox, Elizabeth A. ... Phoenix, AZ
Fox, Elizabeth L. R.
Commodity Futures Trading Commission,
Executive Staff, GV
Fox, Elizabeth M. ... Kew Gardens, NY
Fox, Elizabeth W. ... Philadelphia, PA
Fox, Elton A. ... Hackensack, NJ
Fox, Elyse H. ... Newton, MA
Fox, Emilie L. ... Walnut Creek, CA
Fox, Eric C. ... Hartford, CT
Fox, Eric R. ... Washington, DC
Fox, Erika S. ... Kansas City, MO
Fox, Ernest L. ... Garden City, NY
Fox, Etha Beatrice ... Chicago, IL
Fox, Eugene B. ... Youngstown, OH
Fox, Eugene J. ... Yonkers, NY
Fox & Farmer ... Chattanooga, TN
Knoxville, TN
Fox & Fox ... Los Angeles, CA
Fox and Fox ... Mount Pleasant, MI
Fox and Fox ... Doylestown, PA
Media, PA
Norristown, PA
Philadelphia, PA
West Chester, PA
Fox & Fox, A Legal Professional Association
Cincinnati, OH
Fox, Fox, Fitzer & Waterstone ... Troy, MI
Fox & Fox, L.L.P. ... Stamford, CT
Fox and Fox LLP ... Livingston, NJ
Fox & Fox, L.L.P. ... New York, NY
Fox & Fox, P.A. ... Boca Raton, FL
Fox and Fox, P.A. ... Clearwater, FL
Fox & Fox, P.C. ... Phoenix, AZ
Fox and Fox, P.C. ... Ellwood City, PA
Fox & Fox, PLLC ... Tupelo, MS
Fox & Fox, S.C. ... Madison, WI
Fox and Fox, The Law Firm of
Los Angeles, CA
Fox, Francis H. ... Boston, MA
Fox, Frank J. ... San Diego, CA
Fox, Frank M. ... Phoenix, AZ
Fox, Frank O. ... Los Angeles, CA
Fox, Fred ... San Diego, CA
Fox, Fred F. ... Caldwell, OH
Fox, Fred L., II ... Fairmont, WV
Fox, Fred T., Jr. ... Lawton, OK
Fox, Frederic S. ... New York, NY
Fox, Frederick I. ... Glendale, CA
Fox & Frumkin ... Los Angeles, CA
Fox, G. Lawrence (Larry) ... Dallas, TX
Fox, G. Richard ... St. Louis, MO
Fox, G. Richard, P.C. ... St. Louis, MO
Fox, Garrick N. ... Orlando, FL
Fox, Gary ... Small Business Administration,
Office of the General Counsel, GV
Fox, Gary D. ... Miami, FL
Fox, Gary E. ... Allenhurst, NJ
Fox, Gary J. ... Chicago, IL
Fox, Gary L. ... Shreveport, LA
Fox, George F., Jr. ... Lake Providence, LA
Oak Grove, LA
Fox, George M. ... Atlanta, GA
Fox, George Randal, III ... Pittsburgh, PA
Fox, Gerald M., III ... Stamford, CT
Fox, Gerald M., Jr. ... Stamford, CT
Fox, Gerard ... Chicago, IL
Fox, Gerard P. ... Los Angeles, CA
Fox, Gerson I. ... Beverly Hills, CA
Fox, Gilbert E. ... Manchaca, TX
Fox, Glenn D. ... Philadelphia, PA
Fox, Glenn G. ... New York, NY
Fox, Goldblatt & Singer, P.C. ... St. Louis, MO
Fox, Gould ... Kalamazoo, MI
Fox, Grant M. ... Tupelo, MS
Fox, Gregory A. ... Clearwater, FL
Fox, Gregory J. ... Philadelphia, PA
Fox, Gregory M. ... San Francisco, CA
Fox, Gregory S. ... Ellwood City, PA
Fox, Grove, Abbey, Adams, Byelick &
Kiernan ... St. Petersburg, FL
Tampa, FL
Fox & Grove, Chartered
San Francisco, CA
Chicago, IL
Fox, H. Ernest ... Santa Cruz, CA
Fox, H. Ernest ... Santa Cruz, CA
Fox, H. James ... Chicago, IL
Fox, H. Jonathan ... Trenton, NJ
Fox, H. William ... Phoenix, AZ
Fox, Hamilton P., III ... Washington, DC
Fox, Harry ... Owings Mills, MD
Fox, Harry D. ... Whittier, CA
Fox, Harry L. ... Palo Alto, CA
Fox, Harvey ... Carle Place, NY
Fox, Harvey B. ... Washington, DC
Fox, Heather Marie ... Marshfield, MA
Fox, Henry A. ... Los Angeles, CA
Fox, Henry H. (Bucky)
Fort Lauderdale, FL
Fox, Herb ... Santa Barbara, CA
Fox, Hilary A. ... San Francisco, CA
Fox, Horace, Jr. ... Chicago, IL
Fox Horan & Camerini LLP
New York, NY
Fox, Howard ... Washington, DC
Fox, Hugh M. ... Tucson, AZ
Fox, Idee C. ... Philadelphia, PA
Fox, Irving P. ... Newark, NJ
Fox, J. Carlos ... San Diego, CA
Fox, J. Eric ... Conway, SC
Fox, J. Jane ... Ventura, CA
Fox, J. Nixon, III ... Austin, TX
Fox, J. Terence ... Phoenix, AZ
Fox, Jack L. ... New York, NY
Fox, Jack M. ... Orchard Park, NY
Fox, Jack S. ... New York, NY
Fox, Jackson L., Jr. ... Seattle, WA
Fox, Jacob Logan ... Chicago, IL
Fox, Jacqueline ... Los Angeles, CA
Fox, Jacqueline ... Washington, DC
Fox, Jacqueline R. ... Houston, TX
Fox, James ... Buffalo, NY
Fox, James A. ... New York, NY
Fox, James Anthony ... St. Louis, MO
Fox, James B. ... Boston, MA
Fox, James C. ... Boston, MA
Fox, James C. ... Wilmington, NC
Fox, James D. ... Chattanooga, TN
Knoxville, TN
Fox, James E. ... Los Angeles, CA
Fox, James E. ... San Diego, CA
Fox, James E. ... Dayton, OH
Fox, James E. ... Knoxville, TN
Fox, James F. ... Chicago, IL
Fox, James H. ... Westlake Village, CA
Fox, James H. ... Toledo, OH
Fox, James H. ... Allentown, PA
Fox, James Henry ... San Diego, CA
Fox, James J. ... Brooklyn, NY
Fox, James J. ... Port Washington, NY
Fox, James J. ... Stafford, VA
Fox, James L. ... Chicago, IL
Fox, James L. ... Minneapolis, MN
Fox, James L. ... Lockport, NY
Fox, James M. ... Boston, MA
Fox, James M. ... Latrobe, PA
Fox, James P. ... Redwood City, CA
Fox, James P. ... Newton, NJ
Fox, James P. ... Norristown, PA
Fox, James R. ... Winston-Salem, NC
Fox, James R. ... Carlisle, PA
Fox, James R. ... Elkins, WV
Fox, James T., (A P.C.) ... Torrance, CA
Fox, Jamie Beth ... Encino, CA
Fox, Jan L. ... Pittsburgh, PA
Fox, Jan L. ... Charleston, WV
Fox, Jan Woodward ... Houston, TX
Fox, Janet S. ... Los Angeles, CA
Fox, Janice W. ... San Jose, CA
Fox, Jas. ... New Bedford, MA
Fox, Jason D. ... Los Angeles, CA
Fox, Jay ... New York, NY
Fox, Jay Mitchell ... Philadelphia, PA
Fox, Jeanne M. ... St. Louis, MO
Fox, Jeanne M. ... Newark, NJ
Fox, Jeffrey C. ... Aventura, FL
Fox, Jeffrey J. ... Sioux Falls, SD
Fox, Jeffrey M. ... Albany, NY
Fox, Jennifer M. ... Mechanicsville, VA
Fox, Jennifer S. ... Denver, CO
Fox, Jennifer S. ... Atlanta, GA
Fox, Jere L. ... Redlands, CA
Riverside, CA
Yucaipa, CA
Fox, Jeremy B. ... Washington, DC
Fox, Jerome L. ... Two Rivers, WI
Fox, Jim D. ... Belpre, OH
Fox, Joann L. ... Birmingham, AL
Fox, John ... Seattle, WA
Fox, John C. ... Palo Alto, CA
Fox, John C. ... Atlanta, GA
Fox, John C. ... Chicago, IL
Fox, John C. ... Tarrytown, NY
Fox, John C. ... Dallas, TX
Fox, John F. ... Totowa, NJ
Fox, John F., Jr. ... New Orleans, LA
Fox, John F., Jr. ... Philadelphia, PA
Fox, John H., III ... Jackson, MS
Fox, John J. ... Newton, MA
Fox, John J. ... Pearl River, NY
Fox, John J. ... Bismarck, ND
Fox, John Jeffery ... San Antonio, TX
Fox, John L. ... Houston, TX
Fox, John M. ... New York, NY
Fox, John M. ... Madison, WI
Fox, John N., Jr. ... Baltimore, MD
Fox, John O. ... Washington, DC
Fox, John P. ... Houston, MS
Fox, John R. ... Phoenix, AZ
Fox, John R. ... Boston, MA
Fox, John R. ... Kansas City, MO
Fox, John R. ... Santa Fe, NM
Fox, John R. ... Battle Ground, WA
Fox, John W. ... Bakersfield, CA
Fox, John Wayne ... Stamford, CT
Fox Johns Lazar Pekin Treadgold & Wexler
San Diego, CA
Fox, Jon S. ... Bellevue, WA
Fox, Jonathan A. ... Hackensack, NJ
Fox, Jonathan E. ... Syracuse, NY
Fox, Jonathan J. ... Oak Brook, IL
Fox, Jonathan M. ... Washington, DC
Fox, Jonathan M. ... Bethesda, MD
Fox, Jonathan N. ... Hamilton, OH
Fox, Jonathan S. ... Tallahassee, FL
Fox, Jonathon C. ... Moline, IL
Fox, Jordan C. ... New York, NY
Fox, Jordan M. ... Denver, CO
Fox, Joseph ... La Mesa, CA
Fox, Joseph E., Jr. ... Jamesport, NY
Fox, Joseph Holt ... Washington, PA
Fox, Joseph L. ... New York, NY
Fox, Joseph P. ... Chicago, IL
Fox, Joshua J. ... New York, NY
Fox, J.T. ... Los Angeles, CA
Fox, Judith ... Washington, DC
Fox, Judith B. ... Cranston, RI
Fox, Julius I. ... Washington, DC
Fox, Karen ... Danbury, CT
Fox, Karla H. ... Storrs, CT
Fox, Karol Cassell ... Columbus, OH
Fox, Kate M. ... Cheyenne, WY
Sheridan, WY
Fox, Katherine L. ... Chicago, IL
Fox, Kathleen C. ... Alachua, FL
Fox, Kathleen C., P.A. ... Alachua, FL
Fox, Kathleen E. ... Charlestown, MA
Fox, Kathleen M. ... Jericho, NY
Fox, Kathy Pinkstaff ... Chicago, IL
Fox, Kelly J. ... Columbus, OH
Fox, Kenneth ... Bowie, MD
Fox, Kenneth ... New York, NY
Fox, Kenneth A. ... Winnetka, IL
Fox, Kenneth E. ... Ellwood City, PA
Fox, Kenneth H. ... Portland, OR
Fox, Kenneth L. ... Philadelphia, PA
Fox, Kenneth P. ... Bellevue, OH
Fox, Kermit W., Jr. ... San Antonio, TX
Fox, Kevin A. ... New York, NY
Fox, Kevin B. ... Knoxville, TN
Fox, Kevin G. ... Framingham, MA
Fox, Kevin M. ... Hauppauge, NY
Fox, Kevin Nathaniel ... Brooklyn, NY
Fox, Kieran E. ... Towson, MD
Fox, Kraig G. ... New York, NY
Fox, Kristin R. ... South Bend, IN
Fox, Kyle K. ... Austin, TX
Fox, Lance ... Beaumont, TX
Fox, Larry J. ... Walled Lake, MI
Fox, Laura E. ... Philadelphia, PA
Fox, Laura G. ... Richmond, VA
Fox, Laura L. ... Universal City, CA
Fox Law Firm, The, P.C. ... Atlanta, GA
Fox, Lawrence A. ... Stamford, CT
Fox, Lawrence A. ... Lawrenceville, NJ
Fox, Lawrence A. ... New York, NY
Fox, Lawrence B. ... Bethlehem, PA
Fox, Lawrence C. ... New York, NY
Fox, Lawrence H. ... New York, NY
Fox, Lawrence I. ... New York, NY
Fox, Lawrence J. ... Chester, NJ
Fox, Lawrence J. ... Philadelphia, PA
Fox, Lawrence Stewart ... Washington, DC
Fox & Lederer, P.A. ... Greenville, NC
Fox, Lenore B. ... Boulder, CO
Fox, Leo ... New York, NY
Fox, Leo A. ... Boca Raton, FL
Fox, Leo J. ... Boca Raton, FL
Fox, Leon ... Northbrook, IL
Fox, Leon H., Jr. ... Norristown, PA
Fox, Leon M. ... Framingham, MA
Fox, Leon P., Jr. ... San Jose, CA
Fox & Leventon ... Haverford, PA

Fox and Levine, P.A. ... Baltimore, MD
Fox, Linda D. ... San Diego, CA
Fox, Linda M. ... Charlotte, NC
Fox, Lisa Factor ... New York, NY
Fox, Lisa K. ... Albany, NY
Fox, Lisa K. ... Dallas, TX
Fox, Lloyd A. ... Atlanta, GA
Fox, Lori E. ... St. Louis, MO
Fox, Louis B. ... Beverly Hills, CA
Fox, Lynne Pava ... Philadelphia, PA
Fox, M. Lanning ... Stuart, FL
Fox, Margaret L. ... Boulder, CO
Fox, Margaret M. ... Columbia, SC
Fox, Maria C. ... Seattle, WA
Fox, Maria L. ... Houston, TX
Fox, Maria Teresa (Terry) ... Denver, CO
Fox, Marian R.
National Labor Relations Board, Office of Board Members, GV
Fox, Marilyn Murphy ... Phoenix, AZ
Fox, Marjorie J. ... Waynesburg, PA
Fox, Marjorie L. ... Falls Church, VA
Fox, Marjorie Laura ... New York, NY
Fox, Mark D. ... Palo Alto, CA
Fox, Mark D. ... White Plains, NY
Fox, Mark J. ... New York, NY
Fox, Mark R. ... Los Angeles, CA
Fox, Mark R. ... Lansing, MI
Fox, Mark W. ... South Plainfield, NJ
Fox, Mark W., A Professional Corporation
South Plainfield, NJ
Fox, Marley S. ... Los Angeles, CA
Fox, Marshall ... Santa Barbara, CA
Fox, Martha Erwin ... Newton, NC
Fox, Martin ... North Bergen, NJ
Fox, Martin D. ... Seattle, WA
Fox, Martin R. ... Los Angeles, CA
Fox, Martin S. ... Livingston, NJ
Fox, Martin T. ... Redwood City, CA
Fox, Mary E. ... Sycamore, OH
Fox, Mary T. ... Plymouth Meeting, PA
Fox, Mary T. ... Scranton, PA
Fox, Maureen L. ... Los Gatos, CA
Fox, Maurice F. ... Denver, CO
Fox, Melissa J. ... Newport Beach, CA
Fox, Merritt B. ... Bloomington, IN
Fox, Michael ... Indianapolis, IN
Fox, Michael A. ... Los Angeles, CA
Fox, Michael A. ... San Mateo, CA
Fox, Michael A. ... Greenville, NC
Fox, Michael B. ... Olive Hill, KY
Fox, Michael C. ... Camp Hill, PA
Fox, Michael C. ... McLean, VA
Fox, Michael D. ... Pittsburgh, PA
Fox, Michael David ... Santa Barbara, CA
Fox, Michael E. ... Chicago, IL
Fox, Michael E. ... Irving, TX
Fox, Michael J. ... Seattle, WA
Fox, Michael K. ... Los Angeles, CA
Fox, Michael L. ... San Francisco, CA
Fox, Michael P. ... New York, NY
Fox, Michael R. ... Madison, WI
Fox, Michael S. ... New York, NY
Fox, Michael S. ... Greensboro, NC
Fox, Michael T. ... Tarzana, CA
Fox, Michael W. ... Austin, TX
San Antonio, TX
Fox, Michele Mareschi ... Cherry Hill, NJ
Fox, Michelle ... New York, NY
Fox, Michelle A. ... Kansas City, MO
Fox, Michelle Roman ... Martinsburg, WV
Fox, Milton R. ... St. Louis, MO
Fox, Mitchell E. ... Fort Lauderdale, FL
Fox, M. J. Stephen ... Grand Rapids, MI
Fox, Morris B. ... Cape Coral, FL
Fox, Morton Elliot ... Marietta, GA
Fox, Myron J. ... Chestnut Hill, MA
Fox, Nicole L. ... Richmond, VA
Fox, Nina ... New York, NY
Fox, Norman O. ... Bountiful, UT
Fox, Oldt & Brown ... Easton, PA
Fox, O'Neill & Shannon, S.C.
Milwaukee, WI
Fox, Pamela S. ... Washington, DC
Fox, Pamela S. ... Rockford, IL
Fox, Pamela Sarsfield ... Greensboro, NC
Fox, Parnell G. ... Los Angeles, CA
Fox & Partee ... Kansas City, MO
Fox, Patricia A. ... Santa Barbara, CA
Fox, Patricia A. ... Wheaton, IL
Fox, Patricia Elizabeth ... Sunnyvale, CA
Fox, Patrick A. ... Fitchburg, MA
Fox, Patrick J. ... Fayetteville, GA
Fox, Patrick K. ... Dallas, TX
Fox, Patti C.
Federal Deposit Insurance Corporation, Office of the Executive Secretary, GV
Fox, Paul D. ... Grand Rapids, MI
Fox, Paul T. ... Chicago, IL
Fox, Paul W. ... Austin, TX
Fox, Perry W. ... Westminster, CO
Fox, Peter M. ... Cincinnati, OH
Fox, Philip F. ... Minneapolis, MN
Fox, Preston E. ... Aspen, CO
Fox, Priscilla B. ... Montpelier, VT
Fox, Rachel H. ... New York, NY
Fox, Rainey & Buttram ... Houston, TX
Fox, Randall ... Santa Barbara, CA
Fox, Randall M. ... New York, NY
Fox, Randy F. ... Cincinnati, OH
Fox, Raymond J. ... Missoula, MT
Fox, Rebecca A. ... Tacoma, WA
Fox, Rebecca J. ... Austin, TX
Fox, Reeder R. ... Philadelphia, PA
Fox & Reiss, P.C. ... Newport News, VA
Fox, Renee Isla ... Washington, DC
Fox, Richard ... Newark, NJ
Fox, Richard Allen ... Sacramento, CA
Fox, Richard D. ... Bloomington, IL
Fox, Richard D. ... Southfield, MI
Fox, Richard E. ... Fort Wayne, IN
Fox, Richard F. ... Troy, MI
Fox, Richard G. ... Traverse City, MI
Fox, Richard L. ... Chelmsford, MA
Fox, Richard L. ... Strasburg, OH
Fox, Richard L. ... Philadelphia, PA
Fox, Richard P., and Max Gest, A Professional Law Corporation ... Los Angeles, CA
Fox, Richard R. ... New Albany, IN
Fox, Richard S. ... Salt Lake City, UT
Fox, R. K. ... Fullerton, CA
Fox, Robert A. ... Topeka, KS
Fox, Robert A. ... Knoxville, TN
Fox, Robert B. ... Washington, DC
Fox, Robert C. ... St. Paul, MN
Fox, Robert D. ... Bala Cynwyd, PA
Fox, Robert E. ... Newton, MA
Fox, Robert E. ... Grosse Pointe Woods, MI
Fox, Robert E., Jr. ... St. Louis, MO
Fox, Robert J. ... Chicago, IL
Fox, Robert J. ... Waukegan, IL
Fox, Robert J. ... Plainfield, NJ
Fox, Robert L. ... Sherman Oaks, CA
Fox, Robert M. ... Los Angeles, CA
Fox, Robert M. ... Fenton, MO
Fox, Robert O. ... Knoxville, TN
Fox, Robert Payne, Jr. ... Boston, MA
Fox, Robert Roe ... Akron, OH
Fox, Robert T. ... Crystal Lake, IL
Fox, Robert W. ... Merritt Island, FL
Fox, Robert Y. ... White Plains, NY
Fox, Roberta ... Sea Cliff, NY
Fox, Roberta F. ... Miami, FL
Fox, Roberta J. ... Orlando, FL
Fox & Robertson, P.C. ... Denver, CO
Fox, Robin Elizabeth ... Seattle, WA
Fox, Robyn G. ... St. Louis, MO
Fox, Roland ... Clearwater, FL
Fox, Romi T. ... Cincinnati, OH
Fox, Ronald A. ... West Hartford, CT
Fox, Ronald A. ... Montpelier, VT
Fox, Ronald E. ... Belleville, IL
St. Louis, MO
Fox, Ronald W. ... Cambridge, MA
Fox, Ronda ... Los Angeles, CA
Fox, Ronda D. ... Pflugerville, TX
Fox, Rosemary J. ... Madison, WI
Fox, Rothschild, O'Brien & Frankel, LLP
Atlantic City, NJ
Lawrenceville, NJ
Princeton, NJ
Trenton, NJ
Voorhees, NJ
Doylestown, PA
Exton, PA
Harrisburg, PA
Lansdale, PA
Philadelphia, PA
Sellersville, PA
Fox, Russell H. ... Washington, DC
Fox, Samuel J. ... Los Angeles, CA
Fox, Samuel L. ... Washington, DC
Fox, Sara ... Tupelo, MS
Fox, Sarah M.
National Labor Relations Board, Board Members, GV
Fox, Sarah Wesley ... Raleigh, NC
Fox, Saul A. ... Menlo Park, CA
Fox, Scott L. ... Lake Success, NY
Fox, Sean ... Oak Brook, IL
Fox, Seymour, (P.C.) ... Latham, NY
Troy, NY
Fox, Sharon M. ... Tenafly, NJ
Fox, Sharon Moyer ... Calhoun, GA
Fox, Sharon Mullin ... Bloomfield Hills, MI
Fox, Sharon S. ... Houston, TX
Fox, Shayle P. ... Chicago, IL
Fox, Sheila S. ... Palo Alto, CA
Fox, Sheri ... Irvine, CA
Fox, Shjeflo, Wohl, Newkold & Hartley LLP
Daly City, CA
San Francisco, CA
San Mateo, CA
Fox, Sidney ... Reno, NV
Fox, Sidney ... New York, NY
Fox, Sidney N. ... Northbrook, IL
Fox, Sidney N., P.C. ... Northbrook, IL
Fox, Siegler & Spillane, LLP
Los Angeles, CA
Fox, Sigmund, P.C. ... New York, NY
Fox, Sigmund, P.C. ... New York, NY
Fox & Sohagi, LLP ... Los Angeles, CA
Fox, Spencer H. ... Miami, FL
Fox, Stacy L. ... Plymouth, MI
Fox, Stephanie A. ... Frazer, PA
Fox, Stephen D. ... Atlanta, GA
Fox, Stephen E. ... New York, NY
Fox, Stephen E. ... Johnson City, TN
Fox, Stephen E. ... Dallas, TX
Fox, Stephen G. ... Philadelphia, PA
Fox, Stephen K. ... Fairfax, VA
Leesburg, VA
Fox, Stephen L. ... White Plains, NY
Fox, Stephen L. ... Brookfield, WI
Fox, Stephen M. ... Los Angeles, CA
Fox, Stephen P. ... Palo Alto, CA
Fox, Stephen W. ... Mount Pleasant, MI
Fox, Steve ... Lancaster, CA
Fox, Steve E. ... Chattanooga, TN
Knoxville, TN
Fox, Steven A. ... Los Angeles, CA
Fox, Steven B. ... Greensboro, NC
Fox, Steven E. ... Atlanta, GA
Fox, Steven E. ... New York, NY
Fox, Steven I. ... Brooklyn, NY
Fox, Steven I. ... New York, NY
Fox, Steven J. ... Baltimore, MD
Fox, Steven J. ... Minneapolis, MN
Fox, Steven L. ... North Brunswick, NJ
Fox, Steven M. ... Phoenix, AZ
Fox, Steven N. ... Canton, MA
Fox, Steven R. ... Encino, CA
Fox, Steven R. ... Indianapolis, IN
Fox, Steven R. ... Traverse City, MI
Fox, Steven S. ... Buffalo, NY
Fox, Stretz & Quinn, P.C. ... Kansas City, MO
Fox, Stuart E., (P.C.) ... Boyne City, MI
Fox, Susan ... San Diego, CA
Fox, Susan A. ... Springdale, AR
Fox, Susan A. ... Mount Clemens, MI
Fox, Susan B. ... Tucson, AZ
Fox, Susan L.
Federal Communications Commission, Office of the Commissioners, GV
Fox, Susan L. ... Jenkintown, PA
Fox, Susan R. ... Denver, CO
Fox, Susan R. ... Livingston, NJ
Fox, Susan Rae ... Seattle, WA
Fox, Susan W. ... Tampa, FL
Fox, Suzanne S. ... Baltimore, MD
Fox, Swibel & Levin ... Chicago, IL
Fox, Talbert J. ... Florham Park, NJ
Fox, Tamara Marcus ... Boston, MA
Fox, Terence J. ... Haddonfield, NJ
Fox, Terence P. ... Manitowoc, WI
Fox, Terry A. ... Chicago, IL
Wheaton, IL
Fox, Terry E. ... Louisville, KY
Fox, Terry R. ... Des Moines, IA
Fox, Therese P. ... Kalispell, MT
Fox, Thomas A. ... Washington, DC
Fox, Thomas C. ... Washington, DC
Fox, Thomas E. ... New York, NY
Fox, Thomas E., Jr. ... New York, NY
Fox, Thomas E., Jr. ... Mason, OH
Fox, Thomas J. ... Albany, NY
Fox, Thomas P. ... Tampa, FL
Fox, Thomas P., P.A. ... Tampa, FL
Fox, Thomas R. ... Department of Agriculture, Office of the General Counsel, GV
Fox, Thomas W. ... Dover, OH
Fox, Timothy ... Westminster, MD
Fox, Timothy C. ... Helena, MT
Fox, Timothy D. ... North Little Rock, AR
Fox, Timothy E. J. ... Breckenridge, MN
Fox, Timothy J. ... San Francisco, CA
Fox, Timothy J. ... Des Moines, IA
Fox, Timothy M. ... Columbus, OH
Fox, Timothy P. ... Denver, CO
Fox, Todd Harold ... Chicago, IL
Fox, Tracey L. ... Sodus, NY
Fox, Tyler M. ... Cambridge, MA
Fox, V. Michael ... Nashville, TN
Fox, Valerie E. ... Houston, TX
Fox & Verenes ... Aiken, SC
Fox, Vincent L. ... Conneaut, OH
Fox, Warner S. ... Atlanta, GA
Fox, Warren S. ... Beverly Hills, CA
Fox, Wayne C. ... Houston, TX
Fox, W. E. Sam, II ... Charleston, WV
Fox, Willard E. ... Salem, OR
Fox, William A. ... Morristown, NJ
Fox, William B. ... Chicago, IL
Fox, William C. ... Waterford, CT
Fox, William C. ... Schaumburg, IL
Fox, William C. ... Syracuse, NY
Fox, William C., III ... Chicago, IL
Fox, William E. ... Minneapolis, MN
Fox, William F., Jr. ... Washington, DC
Fox, William F., Jr. ... Harleysville, PA
Norristown, PA
Fox, William Fitzhugh ... Milwaukee, WI
Fox, William Gobin ... Canon City, CO
Fox, William J. ... Treasury Department, Bureau of Alcohol, Tobacco and Firearms, GV
Fox, William J. ... Haddonfield, NJ
Philadelphia, PA
Fox, William, Jr. ... Worcester, MA
Fox, William P. ... Fort Wayne, IN
Fox, William Perry ... Erie, PA
Fox, William R. ... Detroit, MI
Fox, William S. ... Philadelphia, PA
Fox, William W. ... La Jolla, CA
Fox, William Z. ... Baltimore, MD
Fox, Wood & Wood ... Maysville, KY
Fox, Yolanda L. ... Fort Lauderdale, FL
Foxall, Roy W. ... Fort Myers, FL
Fox-Butler, Patricia ... Fort Lauderdale, FL
Foxe, Sean M. ... Trenton, NJ
Foxen, Samantha W. ... Burlington, VT
Fox-Finlinson, Christine R.
Salt Lake City, UT
Foxhoven, Jerry R. ... Des Moines, IA
Fox-Isicoff, Tammy ... Miami, FL
Foxley, Griffith W. ... New York, NY
Foxley, John C. ... Chicago Heights, IL
Foxman, Abraham H. ... New York, NY
Foxman, Alan J. ... Fort Lauderdale, FL
Foxman, David H. ... Daytona Beach, FL
Foxman, Diane K. ... Lansdale, PA
Foxman, Michael D. ... West Chester, PA
Foxman, Michelle Pia ... New York, NY
Foxman, Ronald A. ... Dallas, TX
Foxman, S. James ... Daytona Beach, FL
Foxman, Stephen M. ... Philadelphia, PA
Foxman, Susan W. ... Nashville, TN
Fox-Reiter, Nancy Kay ... Shreveport, LA
Fox-Samson, Connie L.
Department of Agriculture, GV
Fox-Snider, John M. ... Boca Raton, FL
Fox-Weingarten, Jo-Ann W.
New York, NY
Foxwell, Robin ... Pennsauken, NJ
Foxwell, Stephen W. ... Tallahassee, FL
Foxworth, Belinda M. ... Dearborn, MI
Foxworth, Billy F. ... Montgomery, AL
Foxworth, John A., Jr. ... Gulfport, MS
Foxworth, R. Andrew ... Columbia, MS
Foxworth, Richard C. ... Decatur, GA
Foxworth, Richard D. ... Columbia, MS
Foxworth, Shepard & Berry, P.A.
Columbia, MS
Jackson, MS
Foxworth, Susan E. ... Atlanta, GA
Foxworthy, Randolph L. ... Indianapolis, IN
Foxx, Jeffrey W. ... Medford, OR
Foxx, Richard A. ... Los Angeles, CA
Foy, Aaron C. ... Denver, CO
Foy, Allan B. ... Los Angeles, CA
Foy, Brett M. ... Los Angeles, CA
Foy, Charles R. ... New York, NY
Foy, Christopher C. ... Waverly, IA
Foy, David M. ... Detroit, MI
Foy, Douglas I. ... Boston, MA
Foy, Edward D., Jr. ... Richboro, PA
Foy, Eric J. ... Roseland, NJ
New York, NY
Foy, Foy & Castillo, P.C. ... Silver City, NM
Foy, George B. ... Barrington, IL
Foy, Henry G. ... Southport, NC
Foy, Jeffery C. ... Los Angeles, CA
Foy, Jim B. ... Las Cruces, NM
Foy, Joe H. ... Houston, TX
Foy, Joe H., Jr. ... Austin, TX
Foy, John N. ... Chattanooga, TN
Foy, Joseph J. ... New York, NY
Foy, Kevin C. ... Chapel Hill, NC
Foy, Leonard W., III ... Nashua, NH
Foy, Linda Q. ... San Francisco, CA
Foy, Louis F., Jr. ... Trenton, NC
Foy, Marykatherine ... Waukegan, IL
Foy, Matthew S. ... Redwood City, CA
Foy, Michael L. ... Springfield, MA
Foy, Michelle Glover ... Norfolk, VA
Foy, Patrick M. ... Cleveland, OH
Foy, Ron E. ... Woodland Hills, CA
Foy, Stacey W. E. ... Honolulu, HI
Foy, Stanley W. ... Montgomery, AL
Foy, Susan Farris ... Brea, CA
Foy, Terrence J. ... Minneapolis, MN
Foy, Thomas F. ... Centereach, NY
Foy, Thomas M. ... Wauwatosa, WI
Foy, Thomas P. ... Trenton, NJ
Foy, Thomas P., Sr. ... Silver City, NM
Foycik, Michael J., Jr. ... Washington, DC
Foye, Anita ... Durham, NC
Foye, Edward ... Boston, MA
Foye, Stephanie A. ... Chicago, IL
Foye, Thomas H. ... Rapid City, SD
Foye, Thomas P. ... Rolling Hills, CA
Foyle, Larry M. ... Tampa, FL
Foyles, Kirsten Ellefson ... Aberdeen, NC
Foynes, John T. ... Boston, MA
Foyt, Brenda R. ... West Fargo, ND
Fozi, Golnar J. ... Solana Beach, CA
Fozzard, Peter A. ... Atlanta, GA
Fraade, Alan P. ... New York, NY
Fraade, Richard D. ... Beverly Hills, CA
Fraade, Robert D. ... Beverly Hills, CA
Fraas, Charles J., Jr. ... Jefferson City, MO
Fraas, H. Charles, Jr. ... Fairfax, VA
Fraas, Kerry Alan ... Pittsburgh, PA
Fraas, Lisa Marie ... Tahoe City, CA
Fraas, Phillip L. ... Washington, DC
Fraas, Richard J. ... Troy, OH
Frase, Mark G. ... Department of Justice, Office of Professional Responsibility, GV
Frase, Mark R. ... Fargo, ND
Frase, Paul H. ... Bismarck, ND
Frabizzio, Anthony M. ... Wilmington, DE
Frabizzio, Samuel J. ... Wilmington, DE
Frabizzio, Veronica ... Philadelphia, PA
Frable, Ralph E. ... Washington, DC
Frabotta, Mia A. ... Framingham, MA
Fracassa, Kelly M. ... Westerly, RI
Fracassa, Philip D. ... Detroit, MI
Fracassa, Russell ... Blue Springs, MO
Fracassa, Terence M. ... Providence, RI
Fracasse, Ronald J. ... New Haven, CT
Fracassi, Donald M. ... Farmington, MI
Fracassi, Frank J. ... Rochester, NY
Fracassi • Mahdavi • LLP ... Washington, DC
New York, NY
Falls Church, VA
Fracassi, Michael A., (P.C.) ... Washington, DC
New York, NY
Falls Church, VA
Fracassi, Roderick J. ... Ann Arbor, MI
Fracassini, Amy L. ... Boston, MA
Fracassini, John P. ... Monroe, CT
Fracasso, Robert G., Jr. ... Miami, FL
Fraccalvieri, Cristina ... Haddonfield, NJ
Philadelphia, PA
Fraccascia, Charrise M. ... Houston, TX
Fracchia, Robert C. ... Vacaville, CA
Frachioni, Michael I. ... Pittsburgh, PA
Fracisco, Betty L. ... Santa Ana, CA
Frackelton, Albert G. ... Grafton, WI
Frackelton, R. Leigh, Jr. ... Fredericksburg, VA
Frackman, Andrew J. ... New York, NY
Frackman, Jeffrey ... New York, NY
Frackman, Lynn Sara ... Chicago, IL
Frackman, Russell J., (A Professional Corporation) ... Los Angeles, CA
Fractenberg, Harry ... New York, NY
Fraczek, Joan E. ... Longmeadow, MA
Fraczkowski, Alfred R. ... Wilmington, DE
Fradelizio, John W. ... San Francisco, CA
Fradella, Frank Thomas ... Metairie, LA
Fradenburg, Susan McNear
Greensboro, NC

Fradette, Nicole H.
Department of Transportation,
National Highway Traffic Safety
Administration, GV
Fradette, Richard E. ... Manchester, NH
Fradin, Alice L. ... New York, NY
Fradin, Gerald E. ... Chicago, IL
Fradin, Joel G. ... Towson, MD
Fradin, Marjorie K. ... Chicago, IL
Fradin, Matthew D. ... Philadelphia, PA
Fradin, Scott R. ... Chicago, IL
Fradkin, Andrew P. ... Roseland, NJ
Fradkin, Edward P. ... Oakhurst, NJ
Fradkin, Elizabeth Berns ... Potomac, MD
Fradkin, Jay A. ... Phoenix, AZ
Fradkin, Jeffery H. ... Deerfield, IL
Fradkin, Lynn ... Chicago, IL
Fradkin, Michael J. ... Towson, MD
Fradkin, Michael J., P.A. ... Towson, MD
Fradkin, Robin A. ... Alexandria, VA
Fradley, Donald S. ... Jupiter, FL
Frado, Edward A. ... Norwood, MA
Frado, William F., Jr. ... Brookline, MA
Fraebel, John F. ... Hillsdale, NJ
New City, NY
Fraedrich, Laura ... Washington, DC
Fraelich, Timothy P. ... Cleveland, OH
Fraenkel, Alice H. ... Dublin, OH
Fraenkel, Charles M. ... Chicago, IL
Fraenkel, Stuart R. ... Los Angeles, CA
Fraerman, Thomas H. ... Wheeling, IL
Fraga, Jose C. ... New York, NY
Fraga, Michelle C. ... Miami, FL
Fraga, Ricardo L. ... Miami, FL
Fragakis, Maria J. ... Staten Island, NY
Fragale, Franklin S., Jr. ... Charleston, WV
Fragale, Robert D. ... Marion, OH
Fragano, Vincent F. ... Staten Island, NY
Fragassi, Maria P. ... New York, NY
Fragasso, Anne E. ... San Diego, CA
Fragel, Patrick S. ... Kalkaska, MI
Traverse City, MI
Frager, Barry L., Law Offices of
Memphis, TN
Frager, Larry N. ... Portland, OR
Frager, Robert ... Kansas City, MO
Frager, Robert D. ... Kingstree, SC
Fragile, Pat C. ... Beckley, WV
Fragner, Mark S. ... New York, NY
Fragner, Matthew C. ... Los Angeles, CA
Fragomen, Austin T., Jr. ... New York, NY
Fragomen, Del Rey, Bernsen & Loewy
Iselin, NJ
Phoenix, AZ
Irvine, CA
Los Angeles, CA
Sacramento, CA
San Francisco, CA
Santa Clara, CA
Stamford, CT
Washington, DC
Coral Gables, FL
Atlanta, GA
Chicago, IL
New York, NY
Dallas, TX
Fragomen, Del Rey & Bernsen, P.L.L.C.
Troy, MI
Fragomeni, Frank L., Jr. ... Boston, MA
Fragos, Frances M. ... New York, NY
Fraher, John Barry ... Menlo Park, CA
Fraher, Richard M. ... Atlanta, GA
Frahm, Charles T. ... Overland Park, KS
Frahm, Christine M. ... San Diego, CA
Santa Barbara, CA
Frahm, Eric S. ... Department of Commerce,
Patent and Trademark Office, GV
Frahm, Fred J. ... Boise, ID
Frahm, Kathy R. ... Richmond, VA
Frahm, Lorna L. ... St. Louis, MO
Frahm, Minda S. ... Baltimore, MD
Frahm, Robert A. ... Houston, TX
Frahm, Robert A., & Associates, A Prof. Corp.
Houston, TX
Frahm, Steven I. ... Department of Justice,
Tax Division, GV
Frahn, Carl A. ... Chatham, NJ
Frahn, Harrison J., IV ... Palo Alto, CA
Fraiberg, Matthew A. ... Southfield, MI
Fraiche, Donna D. ... New Orleans, LA
Fraiden, Norman ... Bronx, NY
Fraiden & Palen ... Bronx, NY
Fraider, M. D. ... Beverly Hills, CA
Fraidin, Matthew I. ... Washington, DC
Fraidin, Stephen, (P.C.) ... New York, NY
Fraigun, Marina Kats ... Sherman Oaks, CA
Frail, John J. ... Charleston, WV
Frail, Lawrence R. ... Beckley, WV
Fraile, Robert J. ... Flint, MI
Frailey, C. Woodrow ... Elizabethtown, IL
Frailey, Tom A. ... Chickasha, OK
Oklahoma City, OK
Frailie, Donald L., II ... Ashland, KY
Frailing, John B. ... Modesto, CA
Fraim, Paul D. ... Norfolk, VA
Fraim, Scott R. ... Flint, MI
Fraiman, Arnold G. ... New York, NY
Fraiman, Genevieve Lam ... New York, NY
Fraiman, Richard B. ... Cambridge, MA
Fraioli, Patrick A., Jr. ... Los Angeles, CA
Fraioli, Ronald M. ... Wood Ridge, NJ
Fraiser, John J., Jr. ... Jackson, MS
Fraiser, John James, III ... Jackson, MS
Fraiser, Leigh A. ... Washington, DC
Fraissinet, Philip ... Houston, TX
Fraizer & Fraizer ... Lincoln, NE
Fraizer, Patricia C. ... Boston, MA
Fraizer, Patrick C. ... Des Moines, IA
Fraizer, Theodore D. ... Lincoln, NE
Fraizer, Theodore J. ... Lincoln, NE
Frake, Barbara J. M. ... Athens, GA
Frake, Diane Faulkner ... Barnard, VT
Fraker, Donald Roy ... Milwaukee, WI
Fraker, French L. ... Champaign, IL
Fraker, Guy C. ... Bloomington, IL
Fraker, J.C. ... Vinton, IA
Fraker, Muriel E. ... Worcester, MA
Fraker, Walter ... Dallas, TX
Frakes, Gary B. ... Woodland Hills, CA
Frakes, Jacqueline E. ... Milwaukee, WI
Frakes, John C., Jr. ... Detroit, MI
Frakes, Michael R. ... McLean, VA
Frakes, Robert J. ... Encino, CA
Frakie, James B. ... Grand Rapids, MI
Frakt, Arthur N. ... Wilmington, DE
Fraleigh, Andrea M. ... Boston, MA
Fraleigh, Michael J. ... Lansing, MI
Fraley, Donald J. ... Wayzata, MN
Fraley, Douglas M. ... Tampa, FL
Fraley, Elizabeth Masters ... Dallas, TX
Fraley, Ernest R. ... San Diego, CA
Fraley, Ernest R., A Professional Corporation
San Diego, CA
Fraley, F. Ronald ... Tampa, FL
Fraley & Fraley ... Sacramento, CA
Fraley & Fraley, L.L.P. ... Dallas, TX
Fraley & Fraley, P.A. ... Tampa, FL
Fraley, Franklin R., Jr. ... Los Angeles, CA
Fraley, Gary Ray ... Sacramento, CA
Fraley, George F., III ... Wilmington, DE
Fraley, Helen P. M. ... Fayetteville, TN
Fraley, James F., Jr. ... Spartanburg, SC
Fraley, Jo Ann Budd ... Reedsville, WV
Fraley, John M. ... Birmingham, AL
Fraley, Lawrence R. ... Endicott, NY
Fraley, Lucinda L. ... Salisbury, NC
Fraley, Margie Irizarry ... Tampa, FL
Fraley, Mark T. ... Nashville, TN
Fraley, McChesney & McChesney
Spartanburg, SC
Fraley, Mitchell L. ... Tampa, FL
Fraley, Nedra A. ... Sacramento, CA
Fraley, Patricia Guthrie ... Birmingham, AL
Fraley, Peter Allen ... Wenatchee, WA
Fraley, Philip K. ... Fair Oaks, CA
Fraley, R. Scott ... Dallas, TX
Fraley, Raymond W., Jr. ... Fayetteville, TN
Fraley, Robert E. ... Orlando, FL
Fraley, Robert L. ... Westmont, NJ
Fraley, Robert Lee ... Phoenix, AZ
Fraley, Roger D., Jr. ... Denver, CO
Fraley, Ronald W. ... Tampa, FL
Fraley, Sandra K. ... Abingdon, VA
Fraley, Vance L. ... Taylorville, IL
Fraley, William B. ... Arlington, VA
Fralick, Cathleen J. ... Palo Alto, CA
Fralicx, Ronald R. ... St. Charles, MO
Fralin, Feinman, Coates & Kinnier, P.C.
Lynchburg, VA
Fralin, George H., Jr. ... Lynchburg, VA
Fralin, W. Heywood ... Roanoke, VA
Fralin, William H., Jr. ... Roanoke, VA
Fralin, William S. ... Arlington, VA
Fralinger, Michael P. ... Vineland, NJ
Fram, Daniel Witt ... St. Paul, MN
Fram, David K.
Equal Employment Opportunity
Commission,
Office of Legal Counsel, GV
Fram, Jeffrey W. ... Painesville, OH
Fram, Kenneth B. ... Los Angeles, CA
Fram, Robert D. ... San Francisco, CA
Fram, Sheldon Karl ... Atlanta, GA
Fram, Steven J. ... Haddonfield, NJ
Frambach, Willis A. ... Culver City, CA
Frame, Bruce C. ... United States Senate,
Senatorial Assistants, GV
Frame, Clarence G. ... St. Paul, MN
Frame, Clark B. ... Morgantown, WV
Frame, D. Allen ... Kinsley, KS
Frame & Frame, P.A. ... Pasadena, MD
Frame, George D., (Ltd.) ... Las Vegas, NV
Frame, James Earl ... Chicago, IL
Frame, Jordan C. ... Baltimore, MD
Frame, Julie A. ... Burlington, VT
Frame, Karen Shoresman ... Boulder, CO
Frame, L. Robert, Jr. ... West Chester, PA
Frame, Lynn Edward ... Tulsa, OK
Frame, Mark R. ... Kinsley, KS
Frame & Matsumoto, A Prtnrshp. incl. A Prof.
Corp. ... Coalinga, CA
Frame, Phillip I. ... Lansing, MI
Frame, Robert G. ... Honolulu, HI
Frame, Tara K. ... Pasadena, MD
Frame, Ted R., (P.C.) ... Coalinga, CA
Frame, Thomas M. ... Sacramento, CA
Frame, Vernon G. ... Pasadena, MD
Frame, William L. ... Morgantown, WV
Frament, Daniel ... Cohoes, NY
Framm, Rhonda I. ... Baltimore, MD
Framme Law Firm, PLC ... Richmond, VA
Framme, Lawrence H., III ... Richmond, VA
Frampton, Christopher P. ... New York, NY
Frampton, George H. ... Des Moines, IA
Frampton, George T. ... Champaign, IL
Frampton, George T., Jr. ... Washington, DC
Frampton, Gregg A. ... San Francisco, CA
Frampton, James H. ... Anadarko, OK
Frampton, John C. ... Richardson, TX
Frampton, John G. ... Summerville, SC
Frampton, Mary Louise ... Fresno, CA
Frampton, Paul E. ... Fairmont, WV
Frampton, Richard K. ... Turlock, CA
Frampton, Sean S. ... Whitefish, MT
Frampton, Thomas T. ... Pittsburgh, PA
Frampton, Williams & Little, A Professional Association ... Fresno, CA
Framson, Jay E. ... San Francisco, CA
Framson, Peter H. ... Sterling, VA
Framularo, Nicholas G. ... Stratford, CT
Frana, Christy A. ... Decorah, IA
Franasiak, David E. ... Washington, DC
Franc, Bradley J. ... Pittsburgh, PA
Franca, James P. ... Fairfax, VA
Francalancia, Nick ... Beaver, PA
Francavilla, Robert J. ... San Diego, CA
France & Associates, P.C. ... Marcellus, MI
France & Associates, P.C. ... Charleroi, PA
France, Belinda T. ... Tallahassee, FL
France, Bonnie M. ... Richmond, VA
France, Connie S. ... Eureka Springs, AR
France, Donald R. ... Marcellus, MI
France, Douglas P. ... York, PA
France, Edward A. ... Philadelphia, PA
France, F. Dennis ... Chicago, IL
France, Floyd L. ... Arlington, VA
France, J. Peter ... Pensacola, FL
France, Jack H. ... Charleroi, PA
France, James W. ... Pittsburgh, PA
France, Jana L. ... Minneapolis, MN
France, Jeffrey A. ... Cambridge City, IN
France, John L. ... Aurora, CO
France, John S. ... Toledo, OH
France, John W. ... Rockford, IL
France, Karen L. ... Topeka, KS
France, Lawrence A., (P.A.)
North Miami Beach, FL
France, Lucy T. ... Missoula, MT
France, Mary D. ... Harrisburg, PA
France, Renay ... Treasury Department,
Internal Revenue Service, GV
France, Robert G. ... St. Louis, MO
France, Thomas M. ... Missoula, MT
France, Thomas W. ... McLean, VA
France, William I. ... Alliance, OH
France, William N., II ... New York, NY
France-Harris, Antoinette ... New York, NY
Francello, Louis P. ... Saugerties, NY
Francello, Robert ... Saugerties, NY
Francello and VanBenschoten, P.C.
Saugerties, NY
Frances, Larry J. ... Annapolis, MD
Frances, Robert J. ... New York, NY
Francescani, David R. ... Great Neck, NY
Francescani, Donna M.
West Palm Beach, FL
Francescani & Hayes, LLP
Great Neck, NY
Francescatti, Darius S., M.D. ... Chicago, IL
Franceschelli, David M. ... Dayton, OH
Franceschi, Ernest J., Jr. ... Los Angeles, CA
Franceschi, John Eric
Farmington Hills, MI
Franceschi, Kristin H. R. ... Baltimore, MD
Franceschi, Robert J. ... Sacramento, CA
Franceschini, Mark C. ... Owings Mills, MD
Franceschini, Michael R. ... Indianapolis, IN
Franceschini, Richard T. ... San Rafael, CA
Francesco, Amy Buchansky
Staten Island, NY
Francesconi, Gary A. ... St. Louis, MO
Francesconi, James L. ... Portland, OR
Francesconi, Michael J. ... Washington, DC
Francesconi-Edward, Susan ... Surf City, NC
Francese, Albert J.
Federal Energy Regulatory Commission,
Office of the General Counsel, GV
Francese, Michael J. ... Washington, DC
Francese, Paula Y. ... Providence, RI
Francese, Peter J. ... Newark, NJ
Francese, Therese K. ... Washington, DC
Franceski, David C., Jr. ... Philadelphia, PA
Franceski, Larry G. ... Washington, DC
Francetic, Judith M. ... Houston, TX
Francez, Robert M. ... Lafayette, LA
Franch, Eileen ... Baltimore, MD
Franch, Jarashow & Howard, P.A.
Washington, DC
Annapolis, MD
Owings Mills, MD
Franch, Richard T. ... Chicago, IL
Franch, William A. ... Washington, DC
Annapolis, MD
Owings Mills, MD
Franchek, James S. ... Boston, MA
Franchek & Porter, LLC ... Boston, MA
Holliston, MA
Franchek, Richard J. ... Houston, TX
Franchetti, Daniel R. ... Chicago, IL
Franchetti, Michael ... San Francisco, CA
Franchetti, Tiffany ... San Francisco, CA
Franchi, Don R. ... San Mateo, CA
Franchi, Donald R. ... Woodland, CA
Franchi, Gregory Michael
San Francisco, CA
Franchi, James J. ... Ilion, NY
Franchi, Peter A. ... Grass Valley, CA
Franchi, Richard M. ... New Haven, CT
Franchina, David A. ... Charlotte, NC
Franchina, Emily F. ... Garden City, NY
Franchina & Giordano, P.C.
Garden City, NY
Franchina, John S. ... Woodbury, NY
Franchini, Eugene J. ... Camillus, NY
Franchini, Gene E. ... Santa Fe, NM
Franchini, John D. ... New York, NY
Franchini, Keith F. ... Albuquerque, NM
Franchini, Nancy J. ... Albuquerque, NM
Franchino & Rawson, P.A. ... Naples, FL
Franchino, Salvatore L. ... Raritan, NJ
Franchino, Thomas W. ... Naples, FL
Franchise Law Team ... Irvine, CA
Los Angeles, CA
Rancho Santa Margarita, CA
Franchot, Douglas W. ... Shaker Heights, OH
Francia, Rosina ... Hartford, CT
Francione, Gary L. ... Newark, NJ
Franciosa, Michael V. ... Easton, PA
Franciose, Anthony R. ... Foxboro, MA
Franciose, James R. ... Montclair, NJ
Franciosi, Michael J. ... Valdez, AK
Franciosi, Steven T. ... Philadelphia, PA
Francipane, Chester ... Metairie, LA
Francis, A. Warren ... Kansas City, MO
Francis, Alan ... Long Beach, CA
Francis, Andrew V. ... Little Rock, AR
Francis, Anna L.
National Labor Relations Board,
Office of the General Counsel, GV
Francis, Anne E. ... Beverly, MA
Francis, Arthur W. ... Charlotte, NC
Francis, Arthur W., Jr.
Redondo Beach, CA
Francis, Arthur W., Jr., A Prof. Corp., Law Offices of ... Los Angeles, CA
Redondo Beach, CA
Francis, August J. ... Chicago, IL
Francis, Bernard E. ... Canton Center, CT
Francis, Blair G. ... Dallas, TX
Francis and Bryant ... Lansdale, PA
Francis, Burton J. ... Fresno, CA
Francis, Byron E., (P.C.) ... St. Louis, MO
Francis, C. Dean ... Lansdale, PA
Francis, Cabell D. ... Stanford, KY
Francis, Cabell D., II ... Stanford, KY
Francis, Camala Collins ... St. Louis, MO
Francis, Carl ... Dayton, OR
Francis, Carol L. ... Palo Alto, CA
Francis, Caryn A. Y. ... Columbus, OH
Francis, C. E." Win " ... Bend, OR
La Pine, OR
Francis, Charlene ... Jacksonville, FL
Francis, Charles A. ... Tallahassee, FL
Francis, Charles T. ... Raleigh, NC
Francis, Connie M. ... Kansas City, MO
Francis, Crystal ... Coolidge, AZ
Francis, Daniel M. ... Waco, TX
Francis, Daniel R. ... North Little Rock, AR
St. Louis, MO
Francis, David R. ... Washington, DC
Francis, David R.
Department of the Air Force,
Office of the Judge Advocate General, GV
Francis, David W. ... Harrisburg, PA
King Of Prussia, PA
Francis, Dennis B. ... Knoxville, TN
Francis, Dennis E. ... Des Moines, IA
Francis, Dennis J. ... Lyndhurst, NJ
Francis, Derek M. ... San Francisco, CA
Francis, DeWitt C., Jr. ... Spokane, WA
Francis, Diana Richards ... St. Louis, MO
Francis, Donald W., Jr. ... Bloomington, IN
Francis, Douglas T. ... Albuquerque, NM
Francis, Douglas Tyler ... Tucson, AZ
Francis, Dwight M. ... Dallas, TX
Francis, Edna E. J., A Professional Corporation
Los Angeles, CA
Francis, Edna E. J. ... Los Angeles, CA
Francis, Elizabeth Pascale
St. Petersburg, FL
Tampa, FL
Francis, Eric S. ... Short Hills, NJ
Francis, Ernest P. ... Arlington, VA
Francis, Ernest P., Ltd. ... Arlington, VA
Francis, Eustace Theodore ... New York, NY
Francis, Flora A. ... Department of Justice,
Federal Bureau of Investigation, GV
Francis, Frances E. ... Washington, DC
Francis & Francis ... Stanford, KY
Francis & Francis ... Tulsa, OK
Francis & Francis ... Boykins, VA
Francis & Francis, P.C. ... Canton Center, CT
Francis, Frank D. ... Nevada City, CA
Francis, Frann G. ... Short Hills, NJ
Francis, Fred G. ... Prestonsburg, KY
Francis, Frederick J. ... Pittsburgh, PA
Francis, Gene W., Jr. ... Austin, TX
Francis, George F. ... Buffalo, NY
Francis, George J. ... Denver, CO
Francis, Gilbert W. ... Boykins, VA
Francis, Gregorio A. ... Orlando, FL
Francis, Harriet F. ... Columbia, MO
Francis, Hugh P. ... Morristown, NJ
Francis, Irene C. ... Fort Worth, TX
Francis, J. Bruce ... Lorain, OH
Francis, J. David ... Bowling Green, KY
Francis, J. Patrick ... Encino, CA
Francis, J. Thomas, Jr. ... Birmingham, AL
Francis, J. Timothy ... Birmingham, AL
Francis, James A. ... Philadelphia, PA
Francis, James B. ... Washington, DC
Francis, James B. ... Dallas, TX
Francis, James C. ... Decatur, AL
Francis, James C., IV ... New York, NY
Francis, James D. ... Jacksonville, FL
Francis, James N., Law Offices of
Dallas, TX
Francis, James W. ... Eastpointe, MI
Francis, James W., P.C. ... Eastpointe, MI
Francis, Jamile J., III ... Greenville, SC
Francis, Jane Oglesby ... Denver, CO
Francis, Jay L. ... Carlsbad, NM
Francis, Jeffrey E. ... Boston, MA
Francis, Jerome L. ... Houston, TX
Francis, Joann H. ... Seattle, WA
Francis, Joe ... Tulsa, OK
Francis, Joe B. ... Tulsa, OK
Francis, John A. ... Denver, CO
Francis, John J., Jr. ... Florham Park, NJ

Francis, John L. ... Dearborn, MI
Francis, John L. ... Columbus, OH
Francis, John R. ... Killeen, TX
Temple, TX
Francis, John W. ... Fullerton, CA
Francis, Joseph G., Jr. ... Greenville, SC
Francis, J. S. ... New Martinsville, WV
Francis, K. Louise ... San Francisco, CA
Francis, Katherine A. ... Columbus, OH
Francis, Kathleen C. ... Princeton, NJ
Francis, Kedric L. ... Los Angeles, CA
Francis, Keith S. ... Tulsa, OK
Francis, Kelly ... San Mateo, CA
Francis, Kendrick and Francis
Paintsville, KY
Pikeville, KY
Prestonsburg, KY
Francis, Kimberly K. ... Chicago, IL
Francis, Kristin G. ... New York, NY
Francis, Kyle M. ... Millburn, NJ
Francis, Lauren L. ... New York, NY
Francis Law Firm, The, Professional Corporation ... San Antonio, TX
Francis Law Group ... Oakland, CA
Francis, Lenzo & Manshel, LLC
Millburn, NJ
Francis, Leonard Bernard, Jr.
Charlotte Amalie, St. Thomas, VI
Francis, Leroy A. ... Terre Haute, IN
Francis, Lewis McKay
Salt Lake City, UT
Francis, Louis D. ... Dallas, TX
Francis, Loyd ... Kimberling City, MO
Francis, Lynn A. ... Terre Haute, IN
Francis & Mailman, A Professional Corporation
Philadelphia, PA
Francis, Marc ... San Francisco, CA
Francis, Marc A. ... Mineola, NY
Francis, Marc D. ... New York, NY
Francis, Martha M. ... Tulsa, OK
Francis & Martin, LLP ... Bend, OR
La Pine, OR
Francis, Marvealavette D. Jackson
Raleigh, NC
Francis, Mary A. ... San Francisco, CA
Francis, Mary Jo ... Miami, FL
Francis, Matthew D. ... Reno, NV
Francis, Melissa ... Seattle, WA
Francis, Meredith S. ... Washington, DC
Francis, Merrill R. ... Los Angeles, CA
Francis, Merrill W. ... Alhambra, CA
Francis, Michael A. ... Los Angeles, CA
Francis, Michael D. ... Fairfield, NJ
Francis, Michael E. ... Topeka, KS
Francis, Michael J. ... Portland, OR
Francis, Michael S. ... Dallas, TX
Francis, Michael S. ... New Martinsville, WV
Francis, Michael T. ... Miami, FL
Francis, Michelle A.H. ... Chicago, IL
Francis, Michelle V. ... Beverly Hills, CA
Francis, Monroe C. ... Oklahoma City, OK
Francis, Nicholas Ward ... Elmwood, CT
Francis, Norman C. ... New Orleans, LA
Francis, Nowell P. ... Gardner, MA
Francis & O'Farrell ... Morristown, NJ
Francis, O'Neil & Del Piano ... Hartford, CT
Francis & Orr, L.L.P. ... Dallas, TX
Francis, Patricia A. ... Washington, DC
Francis, Patricia S. ... Birmingham, AL
Francis, Paul ... Arlington, TX
Francis, Paul A. ... Treasury Department, Internal Revenue Service, GV
Francis, Paul E. ... New York, NY
Francis, Paul M. ... Decatur, IL
Francis, Paul S. ... Houston, TX
Francis, Peter D. ... Seattle, WA
Francis, Philip L. ... Alliance, OH
Francis, Philip M. ... New York, NY
Francis, R. Ford ... Charleston, WV
Francis, Ralph C. ... Oakland, CA
Francis, Randy ... Tulsa, OK
Francis, R. H. ... San Juan, PR
Francis, Richard ... St. Paul, MN
Francis, Richard ... Boykins, VA
Francis, Richard A. ... Denver, CO
Francis, Richard M. ... Charleston, WV
Francis, Richard N., Jr. ... San Antonio, TX
Francis, Rick D. ... Oneonta, AL
Pinson, AL
Francis, Robert A. ... Aspen, CO
Francis, Robert A. ... Wichita, KS
Francis, Robert A., P.C. ... Aspen, CO
Francis, Robert D. ... Belleville, IL
Collinsville, IL
Francis, Robert E. ... Woodbury, NJ
Francis, Robert H. ... Irving, TX
Francis, Robert T. ... Canton Center, CT
Francis, Ronald ... New York, NY
Francis, Ronald L., Jr. ... Pittsburgh, PA
Francis, Samuel A. ... Albuquerque, NM
Francis, Shannon Claire ... Knoxville, TN
Francis, Sheldon M. ... Nashville, TN
Francis, Shirley M. ... Metairie, LA
Francis, Simone R. D.
Charlotte Amalie, St. Thomas, VI
Francis, Stephen J. ... Troy, MI
Francis, Stephen S. ... Marysville, OH
Francis, Steven G. ... Fort Collins, CO
Francis & Sweet ... Tallahassee, FL
Francis, Terryl W. ... Glen Carbon, IL
Francis, Theodore E. ... Greenwich, CT
New York, NY
Francis, Thomas E. ... Irvine, CA
Francis, Thomas E. ... Orlando, FL
Francis, Thomas S., Law Offices of
Boston, MA
Francis, Timothy B. ... New Orleans, LA
Francis, Vernon L. ... Philadelphia, PA
Francis, Victoria L. ... Billings, MT
Francis, W. Bebb, III ... San Antonio, TX
Francis, William ... Newport, OR
Francis, William A. ... Glendale, CA
Francis, William A. ... Grand Island, NE
Francis, William G. ... Prestonsburg, KY
Francis, William H. ... Troy, MI
Francis, William S., Jr. ... Richmond, VA
Francis, William W., Jr. ... Springfield, MO
Francisco, Ana M. ... Boston, MA
Francisco, Brett L. ... Valencia, CA
Francisco, Carolyn M. ... Boston, MA
Francisco, Cecil J., III ... Austin, TX
Francisco, David C. ... Washington, NC
Francisco, Elizabeth R. ... Macon, GA
Francisco, Emilio N. ... Irvine, CA
Francisco & Emison ... Miami, FL
Francisco, George ... Mount Airy, NC
Francisco, Gordon R. ... Simi Valley, CA
Francisco, Gregory W. ... Kingsport, TN
Francisco, Guerra, IV ... San Antonio, TX
Francisco, Jeffrey ... Amsterdam, NY
Francisco, John R. ... Macon, GA
Francisco, John R. ... St. Johnsville, NY
Francisco, John W. ... Charlotte, NC
Francisco, Jose Manuel ... Miami, FL
Francisco, Kelly Allen ... Bakersfield, CA
Francisco, Kelly Allen, A Professional Corporation ... Bakersfield, CA
Francisco, Lizzette M. ... Miami, FL
Francisco, Noel John ... Washington, DC
Francisco, Sammie B., (Mrs.)
Alpharetta, GA
Francisco, William L. ... Johnson City, TN
Francisco, William P. ... San Antonio, TX
Francisconi, Eric P. ... Irvine, CA
Francisconi, JoAnn ... New London, CT
Franciscovich & Associates
Aberdeen, WA
Franciscovich, Frank M. ... Aberdeen, WA
Franciscovich, George ... New Canaan, CT
Franciscovich, Linda E. ... San Francisco, CA
Franciscus, John J. ... Pittsburgh, PA
Franciscy, Bruce ... Stanton, KY
Francish, Dennis R. ... Albuquerque, NM
Franciskato, Brian S. ... Kansas City, MO
Francis-Morrison, Nancy Ann ... Irvine, CA
Francissen, Vernon W. ... Chicago, IL
Francis-Vogelsang, Charee
North Canton, OH
Franck, Donald A.
Department of Housing and Urban Development, Office of General Counsel, GV
Franck, Douglas C. ... Nashville, TN
Franck, D. R. ... Denison, IA
Franck, John M., II ... Nashville, TN
Franck, Lauren E. ... Newark, NJ
Franck, Lawrence J. ... Jackson, MS
Franck, Lewis R. ... New York, NY
Franck, Murray I. ... New York, NY
Franck, Peter, Law Offices of
Tiburon, CA
Franck, Richard L. ... Los Angeles, CA
Franck, Scott L. ... Houston, TX
Franck, Sheldon Mack ... Williamsburg, VA
Franck, Spencer W., Jr. ... New York, NY
Philadelphia, PA
Franck, Victor C. ... Houston, TX
Francka, Benjamin J. ... Springfield, MO
Francka, Brian K. ... Jefferson City, MO
Francke, Albert ... New York, NY
Francke, Catherine Cole ... Henderson, KY
Francke, Claude R.
National Labor Relations Board, Office of the General Counsel, GV
Francke, Harold W. ... Chicago, IL
Francke, Joseph T. ... Carmichael, CA
Francke, Kevin A. ... Henderson, KY
Francke, W. Bradford ... Upland, CA
Franckel, Philip L. ... Roslyn, NY
Franckhauser, Steven P. ... Princeton, NJ
Franckiewicz, Matthew M.
North Versailles, PA
Franckiewicz, Victor J., Jr. ... Gulfport, MS
Franckling, John E. ... Glastonbury, CT
Francklyn, Reginald Endicott
Hartford, CT
Franckowiak, Jason ... Milwaukee, WI
Francks, Heather Coughlan ... Seattle, WA
Francl, Jason K. ... Chicago, IL
Franco, Albert M. ... Seattle, WA
Franco, Alexander S. ... Newport Beach, CA
Franco, Anne M. ... Southfield, MI
Franco, Antonio, Jr. ... El Paso, TX
Franco, Antonio R. ... Washington, DC
Franco & Associates ... New Canaan, CT
Stamford, CT
Franco, Carlos M. ... San Juan, PR
Franco, Christine M. ... Tampa, FL
Franco, Cori ... Miami, FL
Franco, Craig J. ... Fairfax, VA
Franco, Deborah M. ... Brooklyn, NY
Franco, Deborah P. ... Indianapolis, IN
Franco, Elissa Gordet ... Westwood, MA
Franco, Evelia ... Riverside, CA
Franco & Franco ... Roseland, NJ
Franco & Franco, P.A. ... Tampa, FL
Franco, Fred C., Jr. ... Newark, NJ
Franco, Gabriela ... San Francisco, CA
Franco, Gene Allen, Jr. ... Springdale, AR
Franco, Glorene ... San Diego, CA
Franco, Helen R. ... Palm Beach, FL
Franco, Herman B. ... Montgomery, AL
Franco, Hernan R. ... San Juan, PR
Franco, Howard, Jr. ... Pasadena, CA
Franco, J. Thomas ... Huntington Woods, MI
Franco, Jill R. ... New York, NY
Franco, John J., Jr. ... San Antonio, TX
Franco, John L., Jr. ... Burlington, VT
Franco, Jorge, Jr. ... Phoenix, AZ
Franco, José E. ... San Juan, PR
Franco, Joseph A. ... Boston, MA
Franco, Joseph A. ... West Springfield, MA
Franco, Joseph A., Jr ... Jacksonville, FL
Franco, Laura M. ... New York, NY
Franco, Laura S. ... New York, NY
Franco, Lawrence C. ... Buffalo, NY
Franco, Leonard H. ... Hoboken, NJ
Franco, Leonard H., P.A., A Prof. Corp.
Hoboken, NJ
Franco, Leonard L. ... Atlanta, GA
Franco, Lisa M. ... Sacramento, CA
Franco, Lorrie B. ... New York, NY
Franco, Louis J. ... Boston, MA
Franco, Manuel G. ... Tampa, FL
Franco, Mark A. ... Montgomery, AL
Franco, Mark V. ... Portland, ME
Franco, Mary P. ... New York, NY
Franco, Michael ... New Bedford, MA
Franco, Michael D. ... Yorba Linda, CA
Franco, Michael J. ... New Canaan, CT
Franco, Ofelia C. ... Chicago, IL
Franco, Patricia A. ... Washington, DC
Franco, Paul C. ... Fresno, CA
Franco, Paul J. ... Cambridge, MA
Springfield, MA
Franco, Paulo E., Jr. ... Richmond, VA
Franco, Peter James ... Amityville, NY
Franco, Philip A. ... New Orleans, LA
Houston, TX
Franco, Quiles-Mariani & Godinez
San Juan, PR
Franco, R. Kelley ... Stamford, CT
Franco, Ralph A. ... Montgomery, AL
Franco, Ralph P. ... Hempstead, NY
Franco, Randi Kern ... Roseland, NJ
Franco, Richard M. ... San Francisco, CA
Franco, Richard T. ... Derby, VT
Franco, Robert A. ... Roseland, NJ
Franco, Robert J., II ... Chicago, IL
Franco, Ruben ... New York, NY
Franco, Salvatore D. ... New York, NY
Franco, Stephanie B. ... New York, NY
Franco, Thomas M. ... Boston, MA
Francoeur, John P. ... Fall River, MA
Francoeur, Joseph L. ... New York, NY
Francoeur, Laurel J. ... Woburn, MA
Francoeur, Patrick J. ... Lovington, NM
Francoeur, Philip M., Jr. ... Naples, FL
Franco-Feinberg, Felicia ... Chicago, IL
Franco-Gregory, Laura Dennise ... El Paso, TX
François, Anthony L. ... San Francisco, CA
Francois, Denise, (P.C.)
Charlotte Amalie, St. Thomas, VI
Francois, Francis B. ... Bowie, MD
Francois, Judith ... New York, NY
François, Juny E. ... New York, NY
Francois, Linda P. ... New Haven, CT
Francois, Magali M. ... Florham Park, NJ
Francois, Matthew D. ... San Francisco, CA
Francois, Ralph Stanley ... Miami, FL
Francois, Terry A. ... San Francisco, CA
Francois, William A. ... Chicago, IL
Francolini, Eugene R. ... Hampton Bays, NY
Francomano, John R. ... Baltimore, MD
Francomano & Karpook, P.A.
Baltimore, MD
Francomano, Patrick ... North Attleboro, MA
Francomb, Lonn ... Elizabeth, IL
Francone, Bruce E. ... Redlands, CA
Francone, Carol A. ... Los Angeles, CA
Francone, Don ... Scottsdale, AZ
Francone, Stephania ... Aptos, CA
Franco Soto, Carlos M. ... Yauco, PR
Francque, James A. ... Chicago, IL
Francu, Cornel ... Allegan, MI
Francuzenko, Alexander ... Rockville, MD
Francy, Brenna M. ... Denver, CO
Francy, J. Kenton, & Associates
Tulsa, OK
Francy, Thomas L. ... McLean, VA
Franczek, James C., Jr. ... Chicago, IL
Franczek Sullivan P.C. ... Chicago, IL
Franczek, William E. ... Norfolk, VA
Franczyk, John A. ... Chicago, IL
Franczyk, John J., Jr. ... Rosemont, IL
Franczyk, Thomas P. ... Buffalo, NY
Franden, Robert A. ... Tulsa, OK
Frandle, Scott C. ... Milwaukee, WI
Frandsen, Alan D. ... Salt Lake City, UT
Frandsen, Alan Neil ... Columbus, GA
Frandsen, Carl F.
Department of Labor, GV
Frandsen, Carl J. ... Wayne, PA
Frandsen, Duane A. ... Price, UT
Frandsen, Gary G. ... Dallas, TX
Frandsen, Jeffrey H. ... Zionsville, IN
Frandsen, Kent M. ... Indianapolis, IN
Frandsen, Peter A. ... Department of Justice, Criminal Division, GV
Frandsen, Richard A.
House of Representatives, Committee Legal Personnel, GV
Frandsen, Richard B. ... Salt Lake City, UT
Frandsen, Richard B., P.C.
Salt Lake City, UT
Frandsen, Roger K. ... Elgin, IL
Frandsen, Ronald J. ... St. Louis, MO
Frandsen, Russell Mackay
Los Angeles, CA
Frandsen & Wadkins ... Columbus, GA
Frandzel Robins Bloom & Csato, L.C.
Los Angeles, CA
San Francisco, CA
Franecke, Louis S. ... San Francisco, CA
Franecki, Cynthia J. ... Milwaukee, WI
Franek, David M. ... Chicago, IL
Franetovich, Florio N. ... Bel Air, MD
Franey, Leo C. ... Washington, DC
Franey, Martin F. ... Cleveland, OH
Franey, Martin T. ... Cleveland, OH
Frang, James E. ... Jackson, MI
Franges, Anne King ... Montclair, NJ
Frangeš, Christopher S. ... Morristown, NJ
Franges & Thelin ... Montclair, NJ
Frangetis, Anna S. ... New York, NY
Frangiamore, David H. ... Oakland, CA
Frangie, Frederick Paul ... Simsbury, CT
Frangie, Janet M. ... Sherman Oaks, CA
Frangie, Paul D.
Federal Trade Commission, Bureau of Competition, GV
Frangiosa, Christina D. ... Cherry Hill, NJ
Philadelphia, PA
Frangiose, Mario G. ... New York, NY
Frangipane, Noelle L. ... Trenton, NJ
Frangk, Debra M. ... Poughkeepsie, NY
Frangk, Stanley A. ... Poughkeepsie, NY
Frangos, Irene J. ... Spring House, PA
Frangos, James G. ... New York, NY
Frangos, Phillip T. ... East Lansing, MI
Frangos, Phillip T., P.A. ... East Lansing, MI
Frani, Elizabeth C ... Syracuse, NY
Franich, Anthony J. ... Watsonville, CA
Franich, J. John ... Fairbanks, AK
Franich, Mark, (L.C.) ... San Jose, CA
Frank, A. Peter ... Norwell, MA
Frank, Adam L. ... New York, NY
Frank, Alan B. ... Arlington, VA
Frank, Alan G., Jr. ... Lawrenceville, NJ
Frank, Alan H. ... Lincoln, NE
Frank, Alan I W ... Pittsburgh, PA
Frank, Alan L. ... Cherry Hill, NJ
Bethlehem, PA
Blue Bell, PA
Bristol, PA
Feasterville, PA
North East, PA
Philadelphia, PA
Frank, Alfred A. ... Madison, WI
Frank, Alvin M. ... San Jose, CA
Frank, Amy E. ... Westmont, NJ
Frank, Andrew G. ... New York, NY
Frank, Andrew H. ... Janesville, WI
Frank, Ann T. ... Naples, FL
Frank, Anne Doran ... Garrett Park, MD
Frank, Armin ... Loveland, OH
Frank, Arthur D., Jr. ... Fall River, MA
Frank, Arthur D., Jr. ... New Bedford, MA
Rochester, MA
Taunton, MA
Newport, RI
Frank, Arthur J. ... Washington, DC
Frank, Arthur M. ... Baltimore, MD
Frank & Associates, P.C. ... Bethesda, MD
Frank and Ayers ... Del Mar, CA
Frank, Bails, Murcko & Toal, P.C.
Pittsburgh, PA
Frank, Barbara Hoffman ... New York, NY
Frank, Barney ... Newton, MA
Frank, Barry A. ... Parsippany, NJ
Frank, Barry H. ... Philadelphia, PA
Frank, Barry L. ... Clifton, NJ
Frank, Barry N. ... Englewood, NJ
Frank, Barry, (P.A.) ... Miami, FL
Frank, Beatrice S. ... New York, NY
Frank, Ben W. ... Little Rock, AR
Frank, Bernard ... Allentown, PA
Frank, Bernard A. ... Miami Beach, FL
Frank, Bernard A. ... Rochester, NY
Frank, Bernard N. ... St. Louis, MO
Frank, Beverly R. ... New York, NY
Frank, Billy H. ... San Diego, CA
Frank, Bonnie ... Sausalito, CA
Frank and Breads ... Washington, DC
Rockville, MD
Silver Spring, MD
Frank, Brenda J. ... Rockville, MD
Frank, Brenda R. ... Palo Alto, CA
Frank & Breslow, L.L.P. ... Farmingdale, NY
Frank, Brian J. ... Brookfield, WI
Frank, Brian L. ... Sunnyvale, CA
Frank, Brian S. ... Katonah, NY
Frank, Bruce A. ... Chicago, IL
Frank, Bruce S. ... Blooming Grove, NY
Frank, Bryant Marcus ... Detroit, MI
Frank, C. Glendon ... East Petersburg, PA
Frank, Carl J. ... Lombard, IL
Frank, Carl N. ... Wilkes-Barre, PA
Frank, Carl R. ... Washington, DC
Frank, Carolyn B. ... Fort Lauderdale, FL
Frank, Carolyn J. ... Studio City, CA
Frank, Carolyn Moses ... Towson, MD
Frank, Carrie ... Arvada, CO
Frank, Casey ... Denver, CO
Frank, Cathy R. ... Neptune, NJ
Frank, Charles H. ... Pontiac, IL
Frank, Cheryl R. ... Bethesda, MD
Frank, Clarence C. ... Bloomington, IN
Frank, Cletus J. ... Willmar, MN
Frank, Corinne G. ... Dallas, TX
Frank, Cyrus E. ... San Francisco, CA
Frank, Dale S. ... Hermosa Beach, CA
Frank, Dana Beth ... Cherry Hill, NJ
Frank, Daniel B. ... Cheyenne, WY
Frank, Daniel E. ... Washington, DC
Frank, Daniel W. ... San Francisco, CA
Frank, David A. ... Department of Justice, Criminal Division, GV
Frank, David E. ... Los Angeles, CA
Frank, David E. ... Silver Spring, MD
Frank, David E., P.A. ... Silver Spring, MD

Frank, David E., The Law Offices of ... **Auburn, CA**
Frank, David K. ... **Columbus, OH**
Frank, David L. ... House of Representatives, Committee Legal Personnel, GV
Frank, David M. ... Tallahassee, FL
Frank, David Paul ... Sells, AZ
Frank, David R. ... Chico, CA
Frank, David R. ... Rochester, NY
Frank, Debra J. ... Walnut Creek, CA
Frank, Debra S., P.C. ... **Los Angeles, CA**
Frank, Debra Susan ... **Los Angeles, CA**
Frank, Deirdre Barkley ... Ventura, CA
Frank, Donald ... **New York, NY**
Frank, Donald C. ... Okemos, MI
Frank, Douglas B. ... **Los Angeles, CA**
Frank, Edwin H., Jr. ... **Houston, TX**
Frank, Effman, Weinberg & Black, P.A. ... **Fort Lauderdale, FL**; **Plantation, FL**
Frank, Eleanor ... Yuba City, CA
Frank, Eliott S. ... **New York, NY**
Frank, Elisha ... Belmont, MA
Frank, Elizabeth ... Department of Housing and Urban Development, Office of General Counsel, GV
Frank, Ellen ... Woodmere, NY
Frank, Ellen S. ... **Philadelphia, PA**
Frank, Elmore, Lievens, Chesney & Turet, L.L.P. ... **Houston, TX**
Frank, Emily S. ... New York, NY
Frank, Erich ... Loveland, OH
Frank, F. Alex. ... Woodside, NY
Frank & Finger, P.C. ... Evergreen, CO
Frank & Frank ... New York, NY; Janesville, WI
Frank, Frank, Goldstein & Nager ... New York, NY
Frank, Frank, Penn & Frank, P.C. ... **Allentown, PA**
Frank & Frank, PLLC ... **Nashville, TN**
Frank, Frederick J. ... **Detroit, MI**
Frank, Frederick N. ... **Pittsburgh, PA**
Frank and Freedus, A Professional Corporation ... San Diego, CA
Frank, Gabriel B., Jr. ... Wayne, PA
Frank, Garry W. ... Lexington, NC
Frank, Gary Alan ... **Tampa, FL**
Frank, Gary J., (P.C.) ... Phoenix, AZ
Frank, Genevieve M. ... St. Louis, MO
Frank, George A. ... **Wilmington, DE**
Frank, George L. ... Miami, FL
Frank, Gerald ... New York, NY
Frank, Gerald S. ... Tucson, AZ
Frank, Glenn P. ... **Boston, MA**
Frank, Glenn P., P.C. ... **Boston, MA**
Frank, Gloria H. ... Baltimore, MD
Frank, Gloria J. ... **New York, NY**
Frank, Grady C., Jr. ... **Alexandria, VA**
Frank & Gramling ... **Tampa, FL**
Frank, Greenberg & Simone ... **Los Angeles, CA**
Frank & Gryva ... Omaha, NE
Frank, Halsey B. ... Washington, DC
Frank, Hans J. ... **New York, NY**
Frank, Harold L. ... Wayne, PA
Frank, Henry S. ... **Park Ridge, IL**
Frank, Henry W. ... Bay Shore, NY
Frank, Howard B. ... **San Diego, CA**
Frank, Howard B. ... Buffalo, NY
Frank, Ian H. ... **Cleveland, OH**
Frank, Ira L. ... Middle Village, NY
Frank, Irving ... Chicago, IL
Frank, Irving ... New York, NY
Frank, Irwin M. ... Cleveland, OH
Frank, Isabel ... Trenton, NJ
Frank, J. Stephen ... Sebastopol, CA
Frank, J. William, III ... Racine, WI
Frank, Jacob ... **Westborough, MA**
Frank, James E. ... Pueblo, CO
Frank, James H. ... Santa Monica, CA
Frank, James M. ... Spokane, WA
Frank, James S. ... **New York, NY**
Frank, Jamie E. ... Kings Park, NY
Frank, Janette E. ... **Troy, MI**
Frank, Janie L. ... **Fort Worth, TX**
Frank, Jason A., Law Office of ... **Lutherville, MD**
Frank, Jason D. ... **Boston, MA**
Frank, Jason M. ... Los Angeles, CA
Frank, Jay A. ... **Chicago, IL**
Frank, Jay T. ... Chicago, IL
Frank, Jay W. ... Eugene, OR
Frank, Jeffrey G. ... **Seattle, WA**
Frank, Jeffrey H. ... **Chicago, IL**
Frank, Jeffrey M. ... **Troy, MI**
Frank, Jennifer C. ... **Orlando, FL**
Frank, Jennifer K. ... **Syracuse, NY**
Frank, Jerome ... Cincinnati, OH
Frank, Jerome B. ... **Allentown, PA**
Frank, Jerome D. ... **Farmington Hills, MI**
Frank, Jerome D., P.C. ... **Farmington Hills, MI**
Frank, Joanne L. ... Westlake Village, CA
Frank, Joe S. ... **Newport News, VA**
Frank, Joel I. ... **New York, NY**
Frank, Joel L. ... **West Chester, PA**
Frank, John ... Boca Raton, FL
Frank, John B. ... **Los Angeles, CA**
Frank, John C. ... **Madison, WI**; Poynette, WI
Frank, John C. S. ... Newark, DE
Frank, John J. ... **St. Louis, MO**
Frank, John P. ... **Phoenix, AZ**
Frank, John R. ... Canton, OH
Frank, Jon A. ... **Gaithersburg, MD**
Frank, Jonathan Aaron ... **Richmond, VA**
Frank, Jonathan B. ... Troy, MI
Frank, Jonathan B., P.C. ... Troy, MI
Frank, Jonathan D. ... San Diego, CA
Frank, Jonathan H. ... **Southfield, MI**
Frank, Jonathan J. ... Englewood, NJ
Frank, Jonathan L. ... **New York, NY**
Frank, Jonathan S. ... Charlotte, NC
Frank, Jonella J. ... Norman, OK
Frank, Jonny J. ... New York, NY
Frank, Joseph A. ... **St. Louis, MO**
Frank, Joseph D. ... **Chicago, IL**
Frank, Joseph E. ... **Burlington, VT**
Frank, Joseph J. ... **Miami, FL**
Frank, Joseph W., Jr. ... Sea Isle City, NJ
Frank, Joshua B. ... **Washington, DC**
Frank, Joshua B. ... **Boca Raton, FL**
Frank, Joyce F. ... **Boston, MA**
Frank, Judith A. ... Lansing, MI
Frank, Judy E. ... Pittsburgh, PA
Frank, Julianne R. ... **Palm Beach Gardens, FL**
Frank, Julianne R., P.A. ... **Palm Beach Gardens, FL**
Frank, Julie A. ... Omaha, NE
Frank, Karen S. ... **Emeryville, CA**
Frank, Karl C. ... Santa Ana, CA
Frank, Katherine L. ... New York, NY
Frank, Katrin E. ... **Seattle, WA**
Frank, Keith J. ... Brooklyn, NY
Frank, Kenneth B. ... Baltimore, MD
Frank, Kenneth J. ... **Aurora, CO**
Frank, Kenneth J. ... **Goshen, NY**
Frank, Kevin J. ... Carson, CA
Frank, Kevin K. ... **San Leandro, CA**
Frank, Kim R. ... Laguna Beach, CA
Frank, Kirsten, (Ms.) ... Grosse Pointe, MI
Frank & Kraft, A Professional Corporation ... **Indianapolis, IN**
Frank, Lauren D. ... Washington, DC
Frank, Laurie A. ... Buffalo, NY
Frank Law Firm, The, L.L.P. ... **St. Louis, MO**
Frank, Lawrence G., Law Offices of ... Harrisburg, PA
Frank, Lawrence R. ... Hermosa Beach, CA
Frank, Lawrence S. ... Portland, OR
Frank, Lawrence W. ... Redwood Falls, MN
Frank, Leonard J. ... Northbrook, IL
Frank, Lesley R. ... Rockville, MD
Frank, Leslie E. ... **Los Angeles, CA**
Frank, Leslie J. ... **Los Angeles, CA**
Frank & Levin ... Chicago, IL
Frank, Lincoln E. ... New York, NY
Frank, Lionel J. ... **Princeton, NJ**
Frank, L.J., P.C. ... **Southfield, MI**
Frank, Lloyd ... **New York, NY**
Frank, Loraine ... Norman, OK
Frank, Lori J. ... **Southfield, MI**
Frank, Louis L. ... New York, NY
Frank, Lynn H. ... **New Orleans, LA**
Frank, M. Kennith, III ... **Dobbs Ferry, NY**
Frank, Margaret M. ... Salt Lake City, UT
Frank, Mari J. ... Laguna Niguel, CA
Frank, Maria Joy ... Yorktown Heights, NY
Frank, Mark S. ... **Akron, OH**; **Beachwood, OH**
Frank, Mark S. ... **Cleveland, OH**
Frank, Mark S. ... **Pittsburgh, PA**
Frank, Mark W. ... Madison, WI
Frank, Marlene P. ... **Columbus, OH**
Frank, Marshall Jay ... Blacksburg, VA
Frank, Marvin J. ... **Indianapolis, IN**
Frank, Marvin L. ... **New York, NY**
Frank, Marvin R. ... New York, NY
Frank, Mary Kay ... **Lincoln, NE**; **Omaha, NE**
Frank, Maryclaire Donovan ... New York, NY
Frank, Matthew C. ... **St. Louis, MO**
Frank, Matthew G. ... Minneapolis, MN
Frank, Matthew J. ... Madison, WI
Frank, Matthew M. ... Carlsbad, CA
Frank, Matthew W. ... **Washington, DC**
Frank, Maurice A. ... Chicago, IL
Frank, Maurice J. ... Kearny, NJ
Frank, Maxine S. ... Springfield, MA
Frank, Michael ... Canton, OH
Frank, Michael A. ... North Bay Village, FL
Frank, Michael B. ... **New York, NY**
Frank, Michael E. ... **Helena, MT**
Frank, Michael J. ... Anchorage, AK
Frank, Michael M. ... St. Louis, MO
Frank, Michael T. ... **San Francisco, CA**
Frank, Michele Van Patten ... **Washington, DC**
Frank, Michelle H. ... **New York, NY**
Frank, Michelle Tillem ... Atlanta, GA
Frank & Milchen, APC ... **San Diego, CA**
Frank, Milton ... Fair Lawn, NJ; New York, NY
Frank, Milton J. ... Philadelphia, PA
Frank, Milton J., & Associates ... Philadelphia, PA
Frank, Milton, P.A. ... Fair Lawn, NJ
Frank, Miriam J. ... Chicago, IL
Frank, Mitchell A. ... **Englewood Cliffs, NJ**
Frank, Mitchell H. ... Fort Lauderdale, FL
Frank, Mitchell J. ... Orlando, FL
Frank, Monte E. ... **Danbury, CT**
Frank, Morton ... Marina Del Rey, CA
Frank, M. P. ... Fremont, CA
Frank, Nancy A. ... Waynesboro, VA
Frank, Neal M. ... **Hackensack, NJ**
Frank, Neil A. ... New York, NY
Frank, Neil G. ... **Fort Lauderdale, FL**
Frank, Neil M. ... Farmingdale, NY; **Melville, NY**
Frank, Norma R. ... Merion, PA
Frank, Norman Daniel, II ... Mission, TX
Frank, Norman M. ... Columbus, OH
Frank, Norman M., Co., L.P.A. ... Columbus, OH
Frank, Norman S. ... Delray Beach, FL
Frank, Patricia B. ... **St. Louis, MO**
Frank, Patrick C. ... **Dallas, TX**
Frank, Patrick G. ... **Missoula, MT**
Frank, Paul A. ... Longwood, FL
Frank, Paul M. ... Tamarac, FL
Frank, Paul M. ... **New York, NY**
Frank, Paul S. ... **Allentown, PA**
Frank, Phillip B. ... **Indianapolis, IN**
Frank, R. Horton, III ... **Nashville, TN**
Frank, R. Michael ... **Toledo, OH**
Frank, Ralph R. ... Westlake Village, CA
Frank, Renée F. ... **Melville, NY**; New York, NY
Frank, Richard ... New York, NY
Frank, Richard A. ... Washington, DC
Frank, Richard A. ... Dallas, TX
Frank, Richard C. ... Department of the Army, Office, Chief of Engineers/Headquarters, U.S. Army Corps of Engineers, GV
Frank, Richard H. ... **San Francisco, CA**
Frank, Richard H. ... Tampa, FL
Frank, Richard H., Jr. ... **Nashville, TN**
Frank, Richard L. ... **Washington, DC**
Frank, Richard Michael ... Sacramento, CA
Frank, Richard, P.C. ... New York, NY
Frank, Richard T. ... Louisville, KY
Frank, Robert ... Newark, NJ
Frank, Robert ... **Norfolk, VA**
Frank, Robert D. ... Del Mar, CA
Frank, Robert E. ... Menlo Park, CA
Frank, Robert E. ... Norfolk, VA
Frank, Robert G. ... Roanoke, VA
Frank, Robert H., II ... San Francisco, CA
Frank, Robert J. ... Encino, CA
Frank, Robert J. ... **Colorado Springs, CO**
Frank, Robert J. ... **Washington, DC**
Frank, Robert J. ... Concord, NH
Frank, Robert L. ... Reisterstown, MD
Frank, Robert L. ... **Houston, TX**
Frank, Robert M. ... Phoenix, AZ
Frank, Robert P. ... **Philadelphia, PA**
Frank, Robert P. ... Newport News, VA
Frank, Robert R. ... North Bay Village, FL
Frank, Robert S. ... **Portland, ME**
Frank, Robert S., Jr. (P.C.) ... **Boston, MA**
Frank, Robert W. ... **Palm Desert, CA**; **San Diego, CA**
Frank, Robin Jo ... Department of State, Office of the Legal Adviser, GV
Frank, Romayne L. ... Newport News, VA
Frank, Ronald E. ... **Omaha, NE**
Frank, Ronald F. ... **Los Angeles, CA**
Frank, Ronald W. ... **Pittsburgh, PA**
Frank, Rosalynn ... New York, NY
Frank & Rosen ... New Castle, DE; Cherry Hill, NJ; Bethlehem, PA; Blue Bell, PA; Bristol, PA; Feasterville, PA; North East, PA; **Philadelphia, PA**
Frank Rosen Freed Garfinkel & Roberts LLP ... **Seattle, WA**
Frank, Russell L. ... Warren, NJ
Frank, Russell M. ... **Washington, DC**
Frank, Sally Belinkoff ... Des Moines, IA
Frank, Saml. ... Middle Village, NY
Frank, Sanford B. ... Dix Hills, NY
Frank, Sarah M. ... **Indianapolis, IN**
Frank, Scott A. ... Malden, MA
Frank, Scott J. ... **Tampa, FL**
Frank, Scott M. ... Atlanta, GA
Frank, Scott W. ... Daytona Beach, FL
Frank, Seth E. ... **New York, NY**
Frank, Seymour ... Far Rockaway, NY
Frank, Shawn R. ... **Albuquerque, NM**
Frank & Shinglman ... Chicago, IL
Frank, Sidney L. ... **Troy, MI**
Frank, Signe ... Madison, WI
Frank, Stace B. ... New York, NY
Frank, Stacy C., (P.A.) ... **Tampa, FL**
Frank, Stanley C. ... Houston, TX
Frank, Stefani, Haron & Hall, Professional Corporation ... **Detroit, MI**; **Pontiac, MI**; **Troy, MI**
Frank, Stephen A. ... **New York, NY**
Frank, Stephen D. ... **White Plains, NY**
Frank, Stephen I. ... **New York, NY**
Frank, Stephen L. ... Louisville, KY
Frank, Stephen R. ... Urbana, IL
Frank, Stephen R. ... Tulsa, OK
Frank, Stephen R. ... **Portland, OR**
Frank, Stephen T. ... Santa Barbara, CA
Frank, Steve ... Department of Justice, Civil Division, GV
Frank, Steven B. ... **Seattle, WA**
Frank, Steven H. ... Indianapolis, IN
Frank, Steven J. ... **Boston, MA**
Frank, Steven W. ... **San Francisco, CA**
Frank, Stuart J. ... **Boston, MA**
Frank, Stuart J. ... Syracuse, NY
Frank, Susan M. ... **San Diego, CA**
Frank, Terri J. ... White Plains, NY
Frank, Theobald ... Cleveland, OH
Frank, Theodore D. ... **Washington, DC**
Frank, Theodore H. ... **Los Angeles, CA**
Frank, Theodore W. ... **Long Beach, CA**
Frank, Thomas ... Burlington, VT
Frank, Thomas E. ... Evergreen, CO
Frank, Timothy ... Springville, NY
Frank, Todd G. ... Deerfield, IL
Frank, Tram-Anh T. ... **San Francisco, CA**
Frank, Vincent T. ... Jersey City, NJ
Frank, Virginia L. ... Oklahoma City, OK
Frank, Walter M. ... **New York, NY**
Frank, William ... **New City, NY**
Frank, William A. ... **New York, NY**
Frank, William E., Jr. ... Woodsfield, OH
Frank, William H. ... Environmental Protection Agency, Office of Enforcement and Compliance Assurance, GV
Frank, William P. ... **New York, NY**
Frank, William R. ... Fresno, CA
Frank, William S. ... New York, NY
Frankart, Mary E. ... **Long Beach, CA**
Frankart, Robert J. ... Columbus, OH
Franke, Allyn J. ... **Chicago, IL**
Franke, Carolyn Mussio ... Cincinnati, OH
Franke, David S. ... Department of the Army, U.S. Army Legal Services Agency, GV
Franke, Donald S. ... Minneapolis, MN
Franke, Donald T. ... Naples, FL
Franke, E. Philip, III ... **Baltimore, MD**
Franke, Eleanor J. ... Williston Park, NY
Franke, Emily A. ... **Albuquerque, NM**
Franke, Frederick R., Jr. ... **Annapolis, MD**
Franke, Gary F. ... **Cincinnati, OH**
Franke, Hal F. ... **Cincinnati, OH**
Franke, Hal L. ... **Cincinnati, OH**
Franke, Harry F. ... **Milwaukee, WI**
Franke, Janice R. ... Columbus, OH
Franke, Jay R. ... Chicago, IL
Franke, Jerome E. ... Roseville, MN
Franke, John E. ... Overland Park, KS; **Kansas City, MO**
Franke, Kathleen Ann ... **Watsonville, CA**
Franke, Kurt A., Law Offices of ... **Reno, NV**
Franke, Lee Taylor ... Little Rock, AR
Franke, Lisa K. ... **Edwardsville, IL**
Franke, Louis J. ... **Columbia, MD**
Franke, Patrick J. ... **Seattle, WA**
Franke, Paul G. ... **Hamilton, OH**
Franke, Paul M., Jr. ... **Gulfport, MS**
Franke, Paul R., III ... **Denver, CO**
Franke, Paul V. ... **Denver, CO**
Franke, Rainey & Salloum, PLLC ... **Bay St. Louis, MS**; **Biloxi, MS**; **Gulfport, MS**; **Jackson, MS**; **Pascagoula, MS**
Franke & Riach, P.A. ... Roseville, MN
Franke, Robert C. ... Annapolis, MD
Franke, Robert P. ... **Dallas, TX**
Franke & Schultz, A Professional Corporation ... Overland Park, KS; **Kansas City, MO**; **Springfield, MO**
Franke, Scott D. ... Hood River, OR
Franke, William A. ... Phoenix, AZ
Franke, William E. ... St. Louis, MO
Frankel & Abrams ... **New York, NY**
Frankel, Adam B. ... **New York, NY**
Frankel, Allen C. ... **Jericho, NY**
Frankel, Alvin H. ... Collingswood, NJ
Frankel, Amy Jessica ... **Los Angeles, CA**
Frankel, Andrew T. ... **New York, NY**
Frankel, Ann G. ... Highland Beach, FL
Frankel, Ann Posner ... Bloomfield Hills, MI
Frankel, Arthur I. ... New York, NY
Frankel, Arthur I., P.C. ... New York, NY
Frankel, A. S. ... Torrance, CA
Frankel & Associates, LLC ... **Atlanta, GA**
Frankel, B. Harrison ... **New York, NY**
Frankel, Barbara Kamenir ... Pacoima, CA
Frankel, Bare & Assocs. ... York, PA
Frankel, Baron Jay ... Atlanta, GA
Frankel, Barry J. ... Department of the Army, Office, Chief of Engineers/Headquarters, U.S. Army Corps of Engineers, GV
Frankel, Benjamin W. ... **Irvine, CA**
Frankel, Benzion ... **New York, NY**
Frankel, Brian V. ... Escondido, CA
Frankel, Bruce ... **New York, NY**
Frankel, Bruce D. ... **Fort Myers, FL**
Frankel, Bruce H. ... Franklin, MI
Frankel, Bryan E. ... East Islip, NY
Frankel, Caren K. ... Armonk, NY
Frankel, Carl B. ... **Pittsburgh, PA**
Frankel, Cathy J. ... **New York, NY**
Frankel, Charles E. ... **Newburgh, NY**
Frankel, Charles H. ... Sedona, AZ
Frankel & Cohen ... Chicago, IL
Frankel, Craig M. ... **Atlanta, GA**
Frankel, David A. ... New York, NY
Frankel, David C. ... **San Francisco, CA**
Frankel, David J. ... **Chicago, IL**
Frankel, David P. ... Federal Trade Commission, Bureau of Consumer Protection, GV
Frankel, David R. ... Seattle, WA
Frankel, David Robert ... Boulder, CO
Frankel, David S. ... Elmont, NY
Frankel, David S. ... **New York, NY**
Frankel, Dean A. ... **Rosemont, IL**
Frankel, Deborah C. ... Winthrop, MA
Frankel, Diane E. ... Redwood City, CA
Frankel, Donald G. ... Department of Justice, Environment and Natural Resources Division, GV
Frankel, Donald M. ... Cleveland, OH
Frankel, Donna ... **Boston, MA**
Frankel, Douglas K. ... New York, NY
Frankel, Dov Y. ... **Baltimore, MD**
Frankel, Edward M. ... Cincinnati, OH
Frankel, Eli H. ... Tonawanda, NY
Frankel, Emil H. ... **Stamford, CT**
Frankel, Evan M. ... Brooklyn, NY
Frankel, Geoffrey S. ... Cleveland, OH

Frankel, George Robert ... Davis, CA
Frankel, Glenn D. ... Secaucus, NJ
Frankel & Goldware ... Danville, CA
Frankel, Gusti W. ... Winston-Salem, NC
Frankel, I. James ... St. Louis, MO
Frankel, Ira F. ... Suffern, NY
Frankel, Irv ... Oakdale, NY
Frankel, J. Joseph ... Trenton, NJ
Frankel, Jack I. ... Alexandria, VA
Frankel, James B. ... San Francisco, CA
Frankel, James E. ... New York, NY
Frankel, Jan M. ... Cincinnati, OH
Frankel, Janet Lee ... San Francisco, CA
Frankel, Jason ... Beverly Hills, CA
Frankel, Jay N. ... New York, NY
Frankel, Jed L. ... Hollywood, FL
Frankel, Jeffrey ... Augusta, ME
Frankel, Jeffrey A. H. ... Ronkonkoma, NY
Frankel, Jeffrey H. ... Beverly Hills, CA
Frankel, Jerrold B. ... Blue Bell, PA
Frankel, Joan Murtagh ... New York, NY
Frankel, John D. ... Sandusky, OH
Frankel, Jonathan ... Bethesda, MD
Frankel, Jonathan J. ... Washington, DC
Frankel, Judith Ann ... Miami Beach, FL
Frankel, Justin C. ... New York, NY
Frankel, Ken M. ... Pompano Beach, FL
Frankel, Kenneth M. ... Washington, DC
Frankel, Kenneth P. ... Avon Lake, OH
Frankel, Kevin A. ... Santa Monica, CA
Frankel, Lawrence D. ... New York, NY
Frankel, Lawrence M.
Department of Justice, Antitrust Division, GV
Frankel, Lawrence S. ... San Diego, CA
Frankel, Leonard J. ... St. Louis, MO
Frankel, Lionel H. ... Salt Lake City, UT
Frankel, Lisa E. ... Denver, CO
Frankel, Lisa N. ... New York, NY
Frankel, Lois J. ... West Palm Beach, FL
Frankel, Louise, (Mrs.) ... San Francisco, CA
Frankel, Mark A. ... New York, NY
Frankel, Mark A. ... Madison, WI
Frankel, Mark David ... York, PA
Frankel, Mark S. ... Farmington Hills, MI
Frankel, Marsha Diane ... Orlando, FL
Frankel, Marvin E. ... New York, NY
Frankel, Marvin F. ... Oak Park, MI
Frankel, Marvin L. ... Angola, NY
Frankel, Marvin S. ... Anchorage, AK
Frankel, Melvin ... New York, NY
Frankel, Melvin F. ... Miami, FL
Frankel, Merrill A. ... Davis, CA
Frankel, Michael E.S. ... New York, NY
Frankel, Michael G. ... Dallas, TX
Frankel, Michael H. ... Treasury Department, Internal Revenue Service, GV
Frankel, Michael I. ... New York, NY
Frankel, Michael J. ... Springfield, MA
Frankel, Mitchell D. ... New York, NY
Frankel, Morgan J. ... United States Senate, Office of Senate Legal Counsel, GV
Frankel, Nancy S. ... Santa Monica, CA
Frankel, Nat ... Piedmont, CA
Frankel, Patricia H. ... Reading, PA
Frankel, Paul D. ... Toledo, OH
Frankel, Paul H. ... New York, NY
Frankel, Peter A. ... New York, NY
Frankel, Philip ... Syracuse, NY
Frankel, Reneé S. ... Cincinnati, OH
Frankel, Richard A. ... Danville, CA
Frankel, Richard A. ... Albany, NY
Frankel, Richard Gary ... Ardmore, PA
Frankel, Richard M. ... Houston, TX
Frankel, Robert A. ... Philadelphia, PA
Frankel, Robert E. ... Philadelphia, PA
Frankel, Robert F. ... New Haven, CT
Stratford, CT
Frankel, Robert P. ... Miami, FL
Frankel, Robert P., & Associates, P.A.
Miami, FL
Frankel, Robert Perry ... Philadelphia, PA
Frankel, Robin Caryn ... New York, NY
Frankel, Roger ... Washington, DC
Frankel, Ronald S. ... St. Petersburg, FL
Frankel, Rubin, Bond & Dubin, P.C.
St. Louis, MO
Frankel, Samson M. ... New York, NY
Frankel, Samuel N. ... Atlanta, GA
Frankel, Sandor ... New York, NY
Frankel, Scott J. ... Chicago, IL
Frankel, Sheldon S. ... Tacoma, WA
Frankel, Simon J. ... San Francisco, CA
Frankel, Stephen H. ... Kings Point, NY
Frankel, Steven Ami ... New York, NY
Frankel, Steven H. ... San Francisco, CA
Frankel, Steven R. ... Moline, IL
Frankel, Steven R. ... New York, NY
Frankel, Susan Lynn ... San Francisco, CA
Frankel, Susan P. ... Los Angeles, CA
Frankel, Tamar ... Boston, MA
Frankel & Tennant, Professional Corporation ... Irvine, CA
Frankel, Theodore G. ... Atlanta, GA
Frankel, Thomas D. ... Cleveland, OH
Frankel, Thomas H. ... Davis, CA
Frankel, Thomas H., Inc. ... Davis, CA
Frankel & Thornberry ... New Haven, CT
Stratford, CT
Frankel & Thrower ... Boulder, CO
Frankel, William H. ... Chicago, IL
Frankel Bloom, Roberta ... Philadelphia, PA
Franken, Charles D. ... Fort Lauderdale, FL
Franken, Charles D., P.A.
Fort Lauderdale, FL
Franken & Franken ... Carrollton, MO
Franken, Gregory L. ... Wichita, KS
Franken, Jeanne M. ... Department of Justice, Civil Division, GV
Franken, John ... Carrollton, MO
Franken, John C. ... Carrollton, MO
Franken, K. William ... Columbus, OH
Franken, Paul L. ... New York, NY
Franken, Timothy E. ... Youngstown, OH
Frankena, Karl R. ... Ann Arbor, MI
Frankenberg, Don ... Lindsay, OK
Frankenberg, Jeanette ... North Brunswick, NJ
Frankenberger, David J., Jr. ... Fresno, CA
Frankenberger, Glenn F. ... New York, NY
Frankenberger, J. T. ... Gainesville, FL
Frankenberry, Nancy H. ... St. Paul, MN
Frankenburg, Kurt M.
Salt Lake City, UT
Frankenheim, Samuel ... Boston, MA
Frankenheimer, John T., (A P.C.)
Los Angeles, CA
Frankenhoff, Vivian Hamilton
Washington, DC
Frankenstein, Marc C. ... Indianapolis, IN
Frankenstein, Robert R. ... Chicago, IL
Frankenthal, Stuart J. ... Louisville, KY
Frankenthal, Todd S. ... Fort Lauderdale, FL
Frankenthaler, Kohn, Schneider and Katz
New York, NY
Frankenthaler, Marci J. ... New York, NY
Frankewich, Susan K. ... Las Vegas, NV
Frankfater, Samuel ... Whitestone, NY
Frankford, Harold A. ... Philadelphia, PA
Frankfort, Charles E.
Department of Commerce, Patent and Trademark Office, GV
Frankfort, Howard M. ... New York, NY
Frankfort, Philip R. ... Rockford, IL
Frankfort, Robert D. ... Deer Park, NY
Frankfort, Todd M. ... Houston, TX
Frankfurt, Garbus, Klein & Selz, A Professional Corporation ... New York, NY
Frankfurt, Joanne ... San Francisco, CA
Frankfurt, Michael P. ... New York, NY
Frankfurt, Morton A. ... Bellerose, NY
Frankfurt, Shari L. ... Philadelphia, PA
Frankfurter, Jutta ... San Antonio, TX
Frankhauser, Mahlon M.
Washington, DC
Frankhouser, Gary J. ... Uniontown, PA
Frankhouser, Robert M., Jr.
Lancaster, PA
Frankie, Eric Isaac ... Detroit, MI
Frankie & Gentile, P.C. ... Mineola, NY
Frankie, James G. ... Mineola, NY
Frankiewich, Bruce T. ... Rochester, NY
Frankina, Francis J. ... Rochester, NY
Frankino, Stephen M. ... Helena, MT
Frankino, Steven P. ... Villanova, PA
Frankl, Daniel P. ... Roanoke, VA
Frankl, Jesse M. ... Hartford, CT
Frankl, Joseph F.
National Labor Relations Board, Office of the General Counsel, GV
Frankl, Keith E. ... Denver, CO
Frankl, Kenneth R. ... New York, NY
Frankland, Barbara C. ... Leawood, KS
Frankland, David K. ... Albion, IL
Frankland, Kenneth P. ... East Lansing, MI
Frankland, Suzanne J. ... Paramus, NJ
Frankle, Alan B. ... Rockville, MD
Frankle, Almgren & Associates, P.L.L.C.
Bridgman, MI
New Buffalo, MI
Frankle, Diane Holt ... Palo Alto, CA
Frankle, Edward A.
National Aeronautics And Space Administration, Office of the General Counsel, GV
Frankle, Janice Podoll
Federal Trade Commission, Bureau of Consumer Protection, GV
Frankle, Lawrence I. ... New Buffalo, MI
Frankley, Lawrence R. ... Los Angeles, CA
Franklin, Alan M. ... New York, NY
Franklin, Alan M., P.C. ... New York, NY
Franklin, Alfred C.
Department of Defense, GV
Franklin, Alison S. ... Wheaton, IL
Franklin, Angela J. ... Herndon, VA
Franklin, Angela L. ... Salt Lake City, UT
Franklin, Ann Wallis ... Cambridge, MA
Franklin, Anne E. ... Atlanta, GA
Franklin, Annemarie ... New York, NY
Franklin, Arlene S. ... Newton, MA
Franklin, Arnold W. ... Jourdanton, TX
Franklin, Barbara ... Anchorage, AK
Franklin, Barry S. ... North Miami Beach, FL
Franklin, Barry S. & Associates, P.A.
North Miami Beach, FL
Franklin, Ben ... Oklahoma City, OK
Franklin, Benjamin ... Ovid, NY
Franklin, Benjamin C. ... Los Angeles, CA
Franklin, Benjamin, Jr. ... Salisbury, NC
Franklin, Billy A. ... Norfolk, VA
Franklin, Blake T. ... New York, NY
Franklin, Bobbie P. ... Gallup, NM
Franklin, Bruce W. ... Troy, MI
Franklin, Bryce D., Jr. ... Lexington, KY
Franklin, C. Jerry ... Hampton, VA
Franklin, Cardwell & Jones ... Houston, TX
Franklin, Carl H. ... Shreveport, LA
Franklin, Carl J., Jr. ... Concordia, KS
Franklin, Carl M. ... Los Angeles, CA
Franklin, Carla D. ... Gainesville, FL
Franklin, Cassandra S. ... Los Angeles, CA
Franklin, Catherine Troy ... Seattle, WA
Franklin, Charles E. ... Columbus, OH
Franklin, Charles F. ... Coram, NY
Franklin, Charles G., II ... Madisonville, KY
Franklin, Charles P. ... Tempe, AZ
Franklin, Charles R. ... Chicago, IL
Waukegan, IL
Franklin, Charles S. ... Los Angeles, CA
Franklin, Charles S. ... Atlanta, GA
Franklin, Charles W. ... Fulton, MO
Franklin, Christine Pappelis ... Marion, IL
Franklin, Christopher John ... Philadelphia, PA
Franklin, Clarence C. ... Independence, MO
Franklin, Clinton L., III ... Houston, TX
Franklin, Cooper & Marcus, PLLC
Chattanooga, TN
Cleveland, TN
Dayton, TN
Franklin, Daniel M. ... Pana, IL
Franklin, David A. ... Lexington, KY
Franklin, David A. ... Philadelphia, PA
Franklin, David B. ... San Francisco, CA
Franklin, David deN. ... Dallas, TX
Franklin, David E. ... Cincinnati, OH
Franklin, David L. ... Chattanooga, TN
Franklin, David M. ... Palm Desert, CA
Franklin, David N. ... Denver, CO
Franklin, David P. ... Pittsburgh, PA
Franklin, Dean L. ... St. Louis, MO
Franklin, Debra R. ... Wyomissing, PA
Franklin, Denney, Ward & Lawson, PLC
Waynesboro, VA
Franklin, Denson Nauls, III
Birmingham, AL
Franklin, Desiree M. ... Memphis, TN
Franklin, Donald K. ... Seattle, WA
Franklin, Donald R. ... San Bernardino, CA
Franklin, Douglas A. ... Maplewood, NJ
Franklin, Douglas P ... Tacoma, WA
Franklin & Dowling ... Fulton, MO
Franklin, E. Thomas, Jr. ... Goldsboro, NC
Franklin, Earl R. ... Cleveland, OH
Franklin, Eduardo E. ... San Juan, PR
Franklin, Elizabeth A. ... Novato, CA
Franklin, Elizabeth R. ... Boston, MA
Franklin, Eloise A. ... Peoria, IL
Franklin, Eric John ... Washington, DC
Franklin, Eric W. ... Greenwich, CT
Franklin, Ferdie F. ... Orange, CA
Franklin, Francine A. ... Weehawken, NJ
Franklin & Franklin ... Trenton, GA
Franklin, Fred D., Jr. ... Jacksonville, FL
Franklin, Frederick D. ... Omaha, NE
Franklin, Frederick R. ... Unionville, IN
Franklin & Gabriel ... Ovid, NY
Franklin, Gary R. ... Suitland, MD
Franklin, Gary S. ... Miami Beach, FL
Franklin, Geo. W. ... Nashville, TN
Franklin, Gerald ... Miami, FL
Franklin, Gerald ... North Dartmouth, MA
Franklin, Gerald B. ... Larchmont, NY
Franklin, Gerald McC. ... Santa Barbara, CA
Franklin, Giles A. ... Chicago, IL
Franklin, Glenn J. ... Garden City, NY
Franklin, Gordon & Hobgood
Madisonville, KY
Franklin, Gregory A. ... Rochester, NY
Franklin, Gregory W. ... Richmond, VA
Franklin, Gretchen ... Washington, DC
Franklin Gringer, P.C. ... Garden City, NY
Franklin, Guila S. ... New York, NY
Franklin, H. Lehman, Jr. ... Statesboro, GA
Franklin, H. Lehman, Jr., P.C.
Statesboro, GA
Franklin and Hance, P.S.C.
Louisville, KY
Franklin, Harriet ... Wayne, PA
Franklin, Helen E. ... Shaker Heights, OH
Franklin, Henry H. ... Peterborough, NH
Franklin, Herbert E., Jr. ... Trenton, GA
Franklin, Holley Young ... Portland, OR
Franklin, Hugh J. ... Marion, NC
Franklin, Inks ... Oklahoma City, OK
Franklin, J. David ... La Jolla, CA
Franklin, J. Mark, III ... Jackson, MS
Franklin, J. Reese ... Nashville, GA
Franklin, J. Thomas ... Boston, MA
Franklin, Jack ... Sparta, TN
Franklin, Jack B. ... Albuquerque, NM
Franklin, Jack B. ... Memphis, TN
Franklin, Jacky B. ... Houston, TX
Franklin, James Albert, Jr. ... Columbia, SC
Franklin, James B. ... Statesboro, GA
Franklin, James D. ... Trenton, GA
Franklin, James E., II ... Linwood, NJ
Franklin, James E., III ... Shreveport, LA
Franklin, James E., Jr. ... Shreveport, LA
Franklin, James H. ... Lakewood, CO
Franklin, James L. ... Houston, TX
Franklin, James M. ... Colorado Springs, CO
Franklin, James R. ... Bartow, FL
Franklin, Jamie S. ... Chicago, IL
Franklin, Jan C. ... Gainesville, FL
Franklin, Janet M. ... Norwalk, CT
Franklin, Janice P. ... Joplin, MO
Franklin, Jeanette P. ... Columbia, SC
Franklin, Jeanne F. ... Alexandria, VA
Franklin, Jeffrey A. ... Reading, PA
Franklin, Jennifer L. ... New York, NY
Franklin, Jesse Owen, IV ... Seattle, WA
Franklin, Jill A. ... Los Angeles, CA
Franklin, Joel ... Monterey, CA
Franklin & Johansen, P.A. ... Orlando, FL
Franklin, John ... Toledo, OH
Franklin, John B. ... New City, NY
Franklin, John D. ... Toledo, OH
Franklin, John Edward ... Fredericksburg, VA
Franklin, John, III ... Norfolk, VA
Franklin, John L. ... Eugene, OR
Franklin, John N. ... Colorado Springs, CO
Franklin, John O. ... Tucson, AZ
Franklin, Jonathan Derek ... Miami, FL
Franklin, Jonathan S. ... Washington, DC
Franklin, Joni J. ... Wichita, KS
Franklin, Joseph A. ... Bloomington, IN
Franklin, Joseph P. ... Chicago, IL
Franklin, Karla Wolf ... San Francisco, CA
Franklin, Katherine Cooper ... Seattle, WA
Franklin, Kathleen M. ... Albany, NY
New York, NY
Franklin, Kay Tucker ... Philadelphia, PA
Franklin, Keith B. ... Mobile, AL
Franklin, Keith H. ... San Luis Obispo, CA
Franklin, Kelly, Graham & Killough
Houston, TX
Franklin, Kenneth ... Houston, TX
Franklin, Kenneth A. ... Los Angeles, CA
Franklin, Kimberly Lee ... Tampa, FL
Franklin, Kimberly Williams ... Houston, TX
Franklin, Kurt A. ... San Francisco, CA
Franklin, Lair C. ... Los Angeles, CA
Franklin, Larry B. ... Louisville, KY
Franklin Law Firm, The, P.A. ... Brick, NJ
Franklin, Lawr. C. ... Jackson, MS
Franklin, Lee R., (Ms.) ... Detroit, MI
Franklin, Leland K. ... Dallas, TX
Franklin, Leonard L. ... New York, NY
Franklin & Leonard, Professional Corporation
Troy, MI
Franklin, Leslie D. ... St. Petersburg, FL
Franklin, Leslie D., P.A.
St. Petersburg, FL
Franklin, Lester C., Jr. ... Pascagoula, MS
Franklin, Lisa ... Santa Barbara, CA
Franklin, Louis V., Sr. ... Montgomery, AL
Franklin, Lynn G. ... Orlando, FL
Franklin, Malcolm G. ... Branchville, NJ
Franklin & Marbin, P.A.
North Miami Beach, FL
Franklin, Marc A. ... Palo Alto, CA
Franklin, Margaret P. ... Boston, MA
Franklin, Mark R. ... Independence, WI
Franklin, Marlene A. ... Livingston, NJ
Franklin, Marvin E. ... Birmingham, AL
Franklin, Matthew T. ... Birmingham, AL
Franklin, Maurice Edward, Law Offices
Los Angeles, CA
Franklin, Melvin ... Brooklyn, NY
Franklin, Michael ... Ashtabula, OH
Franklin, Michael E. ... St. Louis, MO
Franklin, Michael M. ... Worcester, MA
Franklin, Michael S. ... San Francisco, CA
Franklin, Monica J. ... Atlanta, GA
Franklin, Monica Valencia ... Atlanta, GA
Franklin, Nathan B. ... Midland, MI
Franklin, Neil E. ... Moscow, ID
Franklin, Neil M. ... Montgomery, AL
Franklin, Nick ... Santa Ana, CA
Franklin, Noel M. ... Denver, CO
Franklin & Olson, P.S. ... Seattle, WA
Franklin, Omer W., Jr. ... Duluth, GA
Franklin, Patricia L. ... Minneapolis, MN
Franklin, Patricia M. ... Stamford, CT
Franklin, Patricia S. ... Marietta, GA
Franklin, Peter ... Santa Fe, NM
Franklin, Peter A., III ... Dallas, TX
Franklin, Peter L. ... Lakewood, CO
Franklin, Peter R. ... Atlanta, GA
Franklin, Phil ... Dallas, TX
Franklin, Philip J. ... St. Paul, MN
Franklin, Phillip A. ... St. Louis, MO
Franklin, R. Thomas ... Jourdanton, TX
Franklin, Randy W. ... Chicago, IL
Rosemont, IL
Franklin, Raymond Pierce ... Bronx, NY
Franklin, Rhett Baker ... Hampton, VA
Franklin, Rhonda E. ... Lexington, KY
Franklin, Richard A. ... Philadelphia, PA
Franklin, Richard K. ... San Jose, CA
Franklin, Richard M. ... Chicago, IL
Franklin, Richard S. ... Naples, FL
Franklin, Richard W. ... Mobile, AL
Franklin, Robert A. ... Palo Alto, CA
Franklin, Robert A. ... Greensboro, NC
Franklin, Robert L. ... Philadelphia, PA
Franklin, Robert Michael ... Coral Springs, FL
Franklin, Robert S. ... Morristown, NJ
New York, NY
Franklin, Robert S. ... New York, NY
Franklin, Robert T. ... Baltimore, MD
Franklin, Robert V., Jr. ... Toledo, OH
Franklin, Robert W. ... Greensboro, NC
Franklin, Roberta L. ... Sacramento, CA
Franklin, Roger A. ... Encino, CA
Franklin, Roger Alex ... Newtown, PA
Franklin, Roland M. ... Columbia, SC
Franklin, Ron D. ... New York, NY
Franklin, Ronald G. ... Enid, OK
Franklin, Ronald G. ... Houston, TX
Franklin, Rufus M. ... Holden, MA
Franklin, Russell A. ... Los Angeles, CA
Franklin, Ruth ... Phoenix, AZ
Franklin, Sam B. ... Seattle, WA
Franklin, Samuel H. ... Birmingham, AL
Franklin, Sandra Jo ... Bloomfield Hills, MI
Franklin & Schapiro, Chartered
Baltimore, MD
Franklin, Scott B. ... West Hartford, CT
Franklin, Selim S. ... Costa Mesa, CA
Franklin, Sharon Bradford
Federal Communications Commission, Office of the General Counsel, GV
Bethesda, MD
Franklin, Sheldon R. ... Brick, NJ
Franklin, Sherman Morgan ... Memphis, TN
Franklin & Shipley, Ltd. ... Chicago, IL
Crystal Lake, IL
Waukegan, IL
Franklin, Sidney, Jr. ... Los Angeles, CA
Franklin, Siobhan Anne ... Solana Beach, CA

Franklin, Sloane R. ....Upper Marlboro, MD
Franklin, Stanford H. ....Baltimore, MD
Franklin, Stanley C. ....Van Nuys, CA
Franklin, Stanley C., A Professional Law Corporation ....Van Nuys, CA
Franklin, Stanley M. ....McLean, VA
Franklin, Steven R. ....Menlo Park, CA
Franklin, Talcott J. ....Dallas, TX
Franklin, Taulbee, Rushing & Brogdon, P.C.
Claxton, GA
Statesboro, GA
Franklin, Terrence M. ....Los Angeles, CA
Franklin, Theodore ....Oakland, CA
Franklin, Thomas D. ....Denver, CO
Franklin, Thomas M. ....Kansas City, MO
Franklin, Thomas R. ....Kansas City, MO
Franklin, Timothy S. ....Tallahassee, FL
Franklin, Victor A. ....Aiken, SC
Franklin, W. Heath ....Greenville, MS
Franklin, Webb ....Greenwood, MS
Franklin, Weems L. ....Miami, FL
Franklin, Weinrib, Rudell & Vassallo, P.C.
New York, NY
Franklin, William A. ....Lubbock, TX
Franklin, William C. ....Litchfield, CT
Franklin, William J. ....Washington, DC
Franklin, William P., Jr. ....Savannah, GA
Franklin, William S.
National Labor Relations Board, Office of Board Members, GV
Franklin, Williams & Cowan
Fredericksburg, VA
Franklin, Wm. P. ....Midland, TX
Franklin-Sisson, Victoria
Birmingham, AL
Franklin-Suber, Stephanie L.
Philadelphia, PA
Franklyn, David J. ....Highland Heights, KY
Franklyn, Mary Beth ....Nashville, TN
Frankman, Janice K. ....Minneapolis, MN
Frankman, MaryBeth ....Omaha, NE
Frankman, Thomas M. ....Sioux Falls, SD
Franko, Dennis E. ....Department of Justice, Federal Bureau of Investigation, GV
Franko, Thomas A. ....Jersey City, NJ
Franko, William J. ....Chicago, IL
Frankoff, Richard ....Houston, TX
Frankovic, Charles ....White Oak, PA
Frankovich, George S. ....Cleveland, OH
Frankovich, John J. ....Reno, NV
Frankovich, Kim C. ....Chicago, IL
Frankovich, Thomas E. ....San Francisco, CA
Frankovich, Thomas E., P.C.
San Francisco, CA
Frankovitch, Anetakis, Colantonio & Simon
Pittsburgh, PA
Chester, WV
Weirton, WV
Wheeling, WV
Frankovitch, Carl ....Weirton, WV
Wheeling, WV
Frankovitch, Carl N. ....Pittsburgh, PA
Chester, WV
Weirton, WV
Wheeling, WV
Frankovitch, M. Eric ....Weirton, WV
Wheeling, WV
Frankowski, Jan K. ....New Orleans, LA
Frankowski, Susan E. B. ....Reading, PA
Frankowski, Walter S., Jr. ....Reading, PA
Franks, Anthony L. ....St. Louis, MO
Franks, Audrey J. ....Richmond, VA
Franks & Bodinet, P.C. ....Phoenix, AZ
Franks, Brenda I. ....Dallas, TX
Franks, C. Leon ....Knoxville, TN
Franks, Candace A. Webb ....Little Rock, AR
Franks, Charles K. ....Overland Park, KS
Franks, Clifton H. ....Harrisburg, PA
Franks, Cynthia J. ....Bakersfield, CA
Franks, Daniel L. ....Chicago, IL
Franks, David J. ....Davenport, IA
Franks, David J. ....Southfield, MI
Franks, Dean K., Jr. ....Long Beach, CA
Franks, Dennis B. ....Los Angeles, CA
Franks, E. Ben, Law Offices of
Texarkana, AR
Franks, E. Ben, Law Offices of
Texarkana, TX
Franks, Eli A. ....Chicago, IL
Franks, Eugene A. ....Muskegon, MI
Franks, George J. ....Fayetteville, NC
Franks, Gerkin & McKenna ....Huntley, IL
Marengo, IL
Wonder Lake, IL
Franks, Harry A., Jr. ....Washington, DC
Franks, Harry E., Jr. ....Atlantic City, NJ
Longport, NJ
Northfield, NJ
Franks, Herbert H. ....Huntley, IL
Marengo, IL
Wonder Lake, IL
Franks, Herschel P. ....Chattanooga, TN
Franks, J. Michael ....Nashville, TN
Franks, Jack D. ....Marengo, IL
Franks, James Byron ....Fort Worth, TX
Franks, James D. ....Hernando, MS
Franks, James E. ....Prescott, AR
Franks, James R. ....Alexandria, VA
Franks, Jane C. ....Franklin, TN
Franks, Jerry L., Jr. ....Tulsa, OK
Franks, John R., Jr. ....Tuscaloosa, AL
Franks, Jon Michael ....Grapevine, TX
Franks, Joseph D., Jr. ....Greensboro, NC
Franks, Kelly C. ....Menlo Park, CA
Franks, Leland ....Albuquerque, NM
Franks, Marcus ....New York, NY
Franks, Martha C. ....Santa Fe, NM
Franks and Megias ....West Palm Beach, FL
Franks, Mitchell D. ....Lakeland, FL
Franks, Nancy L. ....Chicago, IL
Franks, Pamela J. ....Phoenix, AZ
Franks, Philip J. ....Ridgefield, CT
Franks, Phyllis M. ....Martinez, CA
Franks, Rae ....West Palm Beach, FL
Franks, Raymond S., II ....Charleston, WV
Franks, Robert A. ....Kenilworth, NJ
Franks, Robert G. ....Davis, CA
Franks, Robert O. ....Orange, CA
Franks, Roger M. ....Irvine, CA
Franks, Stephen F. ....Hendersonville, NC
Franks, Steven L. ....Cleveland, OH
Franks, Timothy J. ....Phoenix, AZ
Franks, Todd H. ....Phoenix, AZ
Franks, William J. ....Uniontown, PA
Franks, William Y. ....Waukegan, IL
Franks, Zachary ....Skamania, WA
Frankston, Arthur ....Carlisle, PA
Frankston, Daniel S. ....San Francisco, CA
Frankston, Jay ....Little River, CA
Frankston, Lawrence ....Skokie, IL
Frankston, Marian E. ....Harrisburg, PA
Frankstone, David R. ....Chapel Hill, NC
Frano, Andrew J. ....Joliet, IL
Frano, Stephen P. ....Palatine, IL
Franowsky, Allan J. ....Burbank, IL
Franquelli, John L. ....Elgin, IL
Franques, Ann Tomino ....Baton Rouge, LA
Franques, Howard L., Jr. ....Lafayette, LA
Franques, Russell ....Baton Rouge, LA
Franqui, Angel Luis, Jr. ....Philadelphia, PA
Frans, Myron L. ....Minneapolis, MN
Franscell, George J. ....Pasadena, CA
Santa Ana, CA
Franscell, Strickland, Roberts & Lawrence, A Professional Corporation
Los Angeles, CA
Pasadena, CA
Santa Ana, CA
Fransdal, Lisa D. ....Inver Grove Heights, MN
Fransdal, Mark W. ....Cedar Falls, IA
Franse, R. Nelson ....Albuquerque, NM
Franseen, Craig J. ....Ponca City, OK
Fransein, Jim ....Tulsa, OK
Fransen, A. Remy, Jr. ....New Orleans, LA
Fransen, Bonnie ....Cheyenne, WY
Fransen, Christopher J. ....New Orleans, LA
Fransen, Curt A. ....Boise, ID
Fransen, David J. ....Gettysburg, SD
Fransen & Hardin, A P.L.C.
New Orleans, LA
Fransen, James W. ....United States Senate, Office of the Legislative Counsel, GV
Fransen, Kenneth J. ....Clovis, CA
Fresno, CA
Fransen, Nels B. ....Stockton, CA
Fransen, Roger C. ....Cheyenne, WY
Fransen, Scott ....Orlando, FL
Fransen, Susan E. ....Chicago, IL
Fransisco, Kerri M. ....Kansas City, MO
Franson, Albert T. ....Jacksonville, FL
Franson, Aldridge and Sands, P.A.
Jacksonville, FL
Franson, Charles J. ....Jacksonville, FL
Franson, Donald R., Jr. ....Fresno, CA
Franson, Kenneth ....Bartlett, IL
Franson, Marc P. ....Chicago, IL
Franson, Marilyn D. ....Chicago, IL
Fransson, Karl A. ....Hartford, CT
Fransway, Paul R. ....Ann Arbor, MI
Fransway, Peter J. ....Minneapolis, MN
Fransz, Helene Zazulak ....Irvine, CA
Frant, Jeffrey A. ....Denver, CO
Frant, Ronald M. ....San Diego, CA
Franta, John N. ....Wabasso, MN
Franta, Richard E. ....Wilmington, DE
Franta, Steven J. ....New Ulm, MN
Franti, Theodore A. ....Rice Lake, WI
Frantin, Joseph G. ....River Vale, NJ
Frantum, Brian Scott ....Elizabethtown, PA
Franty, Elysia ....Houston, TX
Frantz, Anita H. ....Albuquerque, NM
Frantz, Barbara A. ....Encino, CA
Frantz, Barbara Doyle ....Westfield, NJ
Frantz, Benj. D. ....Sacramento, CA
Frantz, C. Gregory ....Somerset, PA
Frantz, Cathryn D. ....Rochester, NY
Frantz, Christopher E. ....Kennett Square, PA
Frantz, David J. ....Washington, DC
Frantz, Edward A. ....Washington, DC
Frantz, Edward J. ....Westfield Center, OH
Frantz, Elizabeth K. ....Boston, MA
Frantz, Ellen M. ....La Crosse, WI
Frantz, Francis X. ....Little Rock, AR
Frantz, Henry D., Jr. ....Decatur, GA
Frantz, Henry D., Jr., P.C. ....Decatur, GA
Frantz, John P. ....Washington, DC
Frantz, Julie E. ....Portland, OR
Frantz, Julie Scroggins ....Greeley, CO
Frantz, Karl F. ....Camp Hill, PA
Frantz, Kenneth G. ....Troy, MI
Frantz, Lora J. ....Frackville, PA
Frantz, Martin H. ....Wooster, OH
Frantz, Mary Ann, P.C. ....Portland, OR
Frantz, McConnell & Seymour, LLP
Knoxville, TN
Frantz, Michael J. ....Cleveland, OH
Frantz, Nancy Sabol ....Philadelphia, PA
Frantz, Paul L. ....Minneapolis, MN
Frantz, Paula F. ....Santa Barbara, CA
Frantz, Philip A. ....Portland, IN
Frantz, Richard C ....Clearwater, FL
Frantz, Robert W. ....Cincinnati, OH
Frantz, Roger C. ....La Jolla, CA
Frantz, Ronald J. ....Grand Haven, MI
Frantz, Sanders & Grattan, LLP ....Atlanta, GA
Frantz, Sandra Hernandez ....Lincoln, NE
Frantz, Stephen H. ....San Diego, CA
Frantz, Steven ....Austin, TX
Frantz, Steven P. ....Washington, DC
Frantz, Thomas R. ....Virginia Beach, VA
Frantz, William E. ....Atlanta, GA
Frantz, William G. ....Akron, OH
Frantze, David W. ....Kansas City, MO
Frantzen, Tamara L. ....Kansas City, MO
Franz, Albert R. ....Milwaukee, WI
Franz, Andrew E. ....Gulfport, MS
Franz, Bernard E. ....Enon, OH
Franz, Catherine M. ....Woodbridge, NJ
Franz, Christopher C. ....Brownsville, TX
Franz, David M. ....Olean, NY
Franz, Deborah M. ....Atlanta, GA
Franz, Donald ....Lake Worth, FL
Franz, Emy Lore ....Owego, NY
Franz, Eric ....Birmingham, AL
Franz, Eric ....Hackensack, NJ
New York, NY
Franz & Franz, P.C. ....Austin, TX
Franz, Gretchen ....Oakland, CA
Franz, Hilary S. ....Seattle, WA
Franz, Holly J. ....Helena, MT
Franz, J. Noland ....Scottsdale, AZ
Franz, J. Noland, P.C. ....Phoenix, AZ
Scottsdale, AZ
Franz, Jack M. ....Selbyville, DE
Franz, James C. ....Woodstock, IL
Franz, James R. ....Binghamton, NY
Franz, John David ....McAllen, TX
Franz, Kathleen A. ....Puyallup, WA
Franz, Keith S. ....Towson, MD
Franz & Kerrick ....Crystal Lake, IL
Franz, Kyleen D. ....Houston, TX
Franz, Maureen McCarthy ....Austin, TX
Franz, Michael T. ....Chicago, IL
Franz, Neil C. ....St. Cloud, MN
Franz, Nicholas R. ....Tacoma, WA
Franz, Patricia L. ....Oklahoma City, OK
Franz, Paul A. ....Cincinnati, OH
Franz, Richard P. ....Atlantic City, NJ
Franz, Robert E., Jr. ....Springfield, OR
Franz, Ronald A. ....Seattle, WA
Franz, Steven J. ....Milwaukee, WI
Franz, Warren L. ....Dallas, TX
Franz, William M. ....Boca Raton, FL
Franz, William M. ....Crystal Lake, IL
Franz, William M. ....Austin, TX
Franza, Arthur J. ....Fort Lauderdale, FL
Franzblau, Deborah A. ....New York, NY
Franzblau Dratch, P.C. ....Morristown, NJ
Newark, NJ
Roseland, NJ
Elizabeth, NJ
Livingston, NJ
Franzblau, Mitchell ....Bronx, NY
Franzblau, Noah ....Morristown, NJ
Franzblau, Richard D. ....Basking Ridge, NJ
Franzblau, Sigrid S. ....Morristown, NJ
Franzblau, S. M. Chris ....Livingston, NJ
Franzblau, William ....Boston, MA
Franze, Anthony J. ....Washington, DC
Franze, Anthony J. ....New York, NY
Franze, Laura M. ....Dallas, TX
Franzel, Brent S. ....Washington, DC
Franzel, Bruce A. ....Philadelphia, PA
Franzel, Clifford B. ....Farmington Hills, MI
Franzel, Frederick J., Jr.
Bloomfield Hills, MI
Franzel, Joanne ....New York, NY
Franzel, Jonathan A. ....Boston, MA
Franzén, David B. ....Charlottesville, VA
Franzen, David D. ....Sioux City, IA
Franzen, Don Erik ....Beverly Hills, CA
Franzen, Douglas J. ....Minneapolis, MN
Franzen, Edwin H., (P.C.)
Los Angeles, CA
Franzen, George E. ....Las Vegas, NV
Franzen, Lisa S. ....McLean, VA
Franzen, Mark V. ....Irvine, CA
Franzén and Salzano, P.C. ....Atlanta, GA
Franzen, Stephen E. ....Lawrenceville, GA
Franzen, Steven J. ....Newport, KY
Franzén, Therese G. ....Atlanta, GA
Franzen, Timothy G. ....Chicago, IL
Franzen, William R. ....Chicago, IL
Franzenburg, Kurt A. ....Endicott, NY
Franzese, Bruce J. ....New York, NY
Franzese, Louis R. ....Park Ridge, NJ
Franzese, Marla G. ....New York, NY
Franzese, Michael R. ....Central Islip, NY
Franzese, Paul N. ....Forest Hills, NY
Franzese, Paula A. ....Newark, NJ
Franzese, Victoria ....La Grange, IL
Franzese, William P. ....Boston, MA
Franzese-Damron, Tonie M.
Los Angeles, CA
Franzetta, Joseph P. ....Culver City, CA
Franzetti, Paul J. ....Houston, TX
Franzetti, Susan M. ....Chicago, IL
Franzinger, Robert J. ....Detroit, MI
Franzini, John D. ....Milwaukee, WI
Franzino, Frank J., Jr. ....Hackensack, NJ
New York, NY
Franzke, A. Allan, (P.C.) ....Portland, OR
Franzke, Richard A. ....Portland, OR
Franzman, Stephen ....Kingston, NY
Franzman, Terry ....Auburn, IN
Franzmann, Christopher J.
Columbus, OH
Franzmann, Michael P. ....Englewood, CO
Franzmathes, Joe E. ....Chevy Chase, MD
Franzoi & Franzoi, S.C. ....Menasha, WI
Franzoi, Joseph F., IV ....Menasha, WI
Franzoi, La Verne, (Mrs.) ....Menasha, WI
Franzoia, John J. ....Walnut Creek, CA
Franzone-Davis, Alisa ....Fort Myers, FL
Franzoni, Dorothy B. ....Atlanta, GA
Franzoni, Henry J., Jr. ....Montclair, NJ
Frapolli, Ted F. ....St. Louis, MO
Frappier, James C. ....Addison, TX
Frappier, Robert F. ....Memphis, TN
Nashville, TN
Houston, TX
Frappier, Ronald J. ....Dallas, TX
Fraps, Anton E." Tony ", IV ....Houston, TX
Frapwell, Dorothy J. ....Bloomington, IN
Frapwell, William H. ....Dayton, OH
Fraraccio, John C. ....Clark, NJ
Frarey, Kimberlee A. ....Rochester, NY
Frarey, Larry C. ....Kansas City, MO
Frary, Brian L. ....San Diego, CA
Frary, John E. ....Valhalla, NY
Frary, Keith M. ....Albany, NY
Frasca & Associates ....Irvine, CA
Frasca, Domenica ....Fort Lauderdale, FL
Frasca, Eugene P. ....New York, NY
Frasca, James J. ....Cincinnati, OH
Frasca, Joanne M. ....Irvine, CA
Los Angeles, CA
Frasca, Joanne M. ....Newark, NJ
Frasca, Peter M. ....Wellesley, MA
Frasca, Stephen J. ....Nashua, NH
Frasca, Susan E. ....Las Vegas, NV
Frascella, Daniel W., III ....Bound Brook, NJ
Frascella, Joseph D. ....Pacific Palisades, CA
Frascella, Thomas M. ....Mountaintop, PA
Frascella, Thomas P. ....Lawrenceville, NJ
Frasch, Brian B. ....San Diego, CA
Frasch, David E. ....Chippewa Falls, WI
Frasch, Joseph F., Jr. ....Columbus, OH
Frasch, Pamela D. ....Portland, OR
Frasch, Richard N. ....Mercer Island, WA
Frasch, William E., Jr. ....Columbus, OH
Frasciello, Giulio S. ....New York, NY
Frasco, John W. ....Bloomfield Hills, MI
Frasco, William A., Jr. ....Southwick, MA
Frascogna Courtney, PLLC ....Jackson, MS
Frascogna, Frank J. ....Depew, NY
Frascogna, J. Patrick ....Jackson, MS
Frascogna, Joseph P. ....Jackson, MS
Frascogna, Xavier M., Jr. ....Jackson, MS
Frascona, Joiner and Goodman, P.C.
Boulder, CO
Frascona, Joseph L. ....Boulder, CO
Frascona, Oliver E. ....Boulder, CO
Frase, Richard S. ....Minneapolis, MN
Frase, Weir, Baker and McCullough Co., L.P.A. ....Coshocton, OH
Fraser, Alexander G. ....New York, NY
Fraser, Alexander P. ....Milwaukee, WI
Fraser & Allen, LLC ....Beaufort, SC
Hilton Head Island, SC
Fraser, Andrea J. ....Boston, MA
Fraser, Andrew A. ....Sparta, NJ
Fraser, Annalisa ....Sacramento, CA
Fraser, Anne H. S., P.C. ....Washington, DC
Fraser, Anne M. ....Falls Church, VA
Fraser, Anne Weston ....Northbrook, IL
Fraser, Antonio Flores ....Waterbury, CT
Fraser, Brenda ....Philadelphia, PA
Fraser, Brian ....Oakland, CA
Fraser, Brian S. ....New York, NY
Fraser, Bruce S. ....Fresno, CA
Fraser, Bruce W. ....Los Angeles, CA
Fraser, C. Jane ....Houston, TX
Fraser, Charles R. ....New York, NY
Fraser, Christie L. ....San Francisco, CA
Fraser, Christopher A. ....New York, NY
Fraser, Cynthia M. ....Salem, OR
Fraser, D. Larry ....Jacksonville, FL
Fraser, Damon Shawn ....Eden Prairie, MN
Fraser, David A. ....Lake Charles, LA
Fraser, David A. ....Syracuse, NY
Fraser, David C. ....Chevy Chase, MD
Fraser, David J. ....Irvine, CA
Fraser, Debra D. ....Tampa, FL
Fraser, Don W. ....Marysville, OH
Fraser, Donald B., Jr. ....Roseland, NJ
Fraser, Donald G. ....Brooklyn, NY
Fraser, Donald H. ....Walterboro, SC
Fraser, Donald M. ....Minneapolis, MN
Fraser, Donald R. ....Perrysburg, OH
Fraser, Donald V., Jr. ....St. Louis, MO
Fraser, Douglas B. ....Austin, TX
Fraser, Douglas W. ....Los Alamos, NM
Fraser, Duncan A., III ....Lido Beach, NY
Fraser, Duncan A., Jr. ....Brooklyn, NY
Fraser, E. Scott ....Los Angeles, CA
Fraser, E. L. ....Los Angeles, CA
Fraser, Elaine Ryzak ....Burlingame, CA
Fraser, Eliza W. ....Fairfield, CT
Fraser, Francis W. ....
Department of Justice, GV
Fraser & Fraser ....Atlanta, GA
Fraser & Fraser ....Brooklyn, NY
Fraser, G. Howden ....Los Angeles, CA
Fraser, G. Knute ....Wichita, KS
Fraser, Gail H. ....Parsippany, NJ
Fraser, George H. ....Portland, OR
Fraser, Georgia M. ....Princeton, NJ
Fraser, Gordon G. ....San Jose, CA
Fraser, Gregory A. ....Tyler, TX
Fraser, Gregory B. ....Warren, PA
Fraser, Henry S. ....Syracuse, NY
Fraser, Hilary T. ....Ithaca, NY
Fraser, J. Kenneth ....Stockton, CA
Fraser, J. Simon ....Hilton Head Island, SC
Fraser, James Andrew
Huntington Beach, CA
Fraser, James C. ....Iowa City, IA
Fraser, James D. ....Los Angeles, CA
Fraser, James M. ....Costa Mesa, CA
Fraser, Janis K. ....Boston, MA
Fraser, Jason Dwight ....New York, NY

Fraser, Jean Skelton ....San Francisco, CA
Fraser, Jeff ....Boston, MA
Fraser, Jeffrey J. ....Grand Rapids, MI
Fraser, Jennifer ....Alexandria, VA
Fraser, J. J., III ....Denver, CO
Fraser, Joan C. ....Baltimore, MD
Fraser, John A., III ....Washington, DC
Fraser, John C. ....Cambridge, MA
Fraser, John D. ....Dallas, TX
Fraser, John J., Jr. ....Houston, TX
Fraser, Judith C. ....Waynesville, NC
Fraser, Keith S. ....Livermore, CA
Fraser & Kretowicz ....Boston, MA
Marlborough, MA
Fraser, Larry M. ....Springfield, MO
Fraser, Leigh R. ....Boston, MA
Fraser, Leo W., III ....New York, NY
Fraser, Leslye M.
Environmental Protection Agency, Office of the General Counsel, GV
Fraser, Lewis L. ....St. Petersburg Beach, FL
Fraser, Linda A. ....Midland, MI
Fraser, Louie Craig ....Dublin, GA
Fraser, Margaret A. ....Phoenix, AZ
Fraser, Margaret A. ....Sacramento, CA
Fraser, Mark J. ....Gainesville, FL
Fraser, Mark S. ....Atlanta, GA
Fraser, Mary Brooks
Securities and Exchange Commission, Division of Corporation Finance, GV
Fraser, Mary Ellen
House of Representatives, Committee on Armed Services, GV
Fraser & McHugh, P.C. .....Mount Clemens, MI
Fraser, Monica C. ....Exeter, NH
Fraser, Morris & Wheeler, L.L.P.
Lake Charles, LA
Fraser, Natascha H. ....Sausalito, CA
Fraser, P. Benedict ....Greenwich, CT
Fraser, Patricia Shukis ....Trenton, NJ
Fraser, Peter ....La Jolla, CA
Fraser, Richard A., III ....New Orleans, LA
Fraser, Robert ....Santa Ana, CA
Fraser, Robert A. ....Brandon, FL
Fraser, Robert B., (P.C.) ....Boston, MA
Fraser, Robert G. ....Boston, MA
Fraser, Robert G. ....Midland, MI
Fraser, Robert G. ....Omaha, NE
Fraser, Robert H. ....Marina Del Rey, CA
Fraser, Robert H. ....Eugene, OR
Fraser, Robert L. ....Ellensburg, WA
Fraser, Robert S. ....New York, NY
Fraser & Rossman ....La Jolla, CA
Fraser, Sara V. Aiken ....Portland, OR
Fraser, Sean A. ....Detroit, MI
Fraser, Shawn W. ....Washington, DC
Fraser, Shelley A. ....Los Angeles, CA
Fraser, Sherman C., Jr. ....Atlanta, GA
Fraser, Stephen C. ....Glendale, CA
Los Angeles, CA
Fraser, Stryker, Vaughn, Meusey, Olson, Boyer & Bloch, P.C. ....Omaha, NE
Fraser, Stuart A. ....Mount Clemens, MI
Fraser, Stuart W. ....New York, NY
Fraser, Tamara Elizabeth ....Troy, MI
Fraser, Thomas E. ....Chicago, IL
Fraser, Thomas J. ....Portland, OR
Fraser, Thomas J., Jr. ....Jacksonville, FL
Fraser, Thomas K. ....Livermore, CA
Fraser, Thomas K. ....Tracy, CA
Fraser, Thomas S. ....Minneapolis, MN
Fraser Trebilcock Davis & Foster, P.C.
Detroit, MI
Lansing, MI
Fraser, William Dean ....Chicago, IL
Fraser, William H. ....Toledo, OH
Fraser, Winston W. ....Newark, NJ
Fraser & Wise, P.C. ....Boston, MA
Fraser-Thomson, Ian A.
San Francisco, CA
Frasher, Gary W. ....Huntington, WV
Frasher, James C. ....Milwaukee, WI
Frasher, Mark William ....Beaumont, TX
Frasher, Marshall C. ....Fresno, CA
Frasher, Michael F. ....Charleston, WV
Frasheski, Katherine A. ....Minneapolis, MN
Frasier, Curtis A. ....Beloit, KS
Frasier, Damion ....Flint, MI
Frasier, Francis J. ....Hampton, NH
Frasier, Frank, III ....Tulsa, OK
Frasier, Frasier & Hickman ....Tulsa, OK
Frasier, George E. ....Seattle, WA
Frasier, Howard E., Jr.
Bowling Green, KY
Frasier, James E. ....Tulsa, OK
Frasier, Jeffrey S. ....Westlake Village, CA
Frasier, Ralph K. ....Columbus, OH
Frasier, Ralph K., Jr. ....Durham, NC
Frasier & Steier ....Beloit, KS
Frasier, Stephen C. ....Stuart, FL
Frasier, Stephen C., P.A. ....Stuart, FL
Frasier, Thomas Dee ....Tulsa, OK
Frasier, T.J. ....Boise, ID
Frasier-Kolligs, Karen ....San Francisco, CA
Frassetto, Eugene A. ....Portland, OR
Frassetto, James M. ....Walnut Creek, CA
Frassetto, Paul ....San Francisco, CA
Frassetto, Robert J. ....San Francisco, CA
Frassetto, Steven J. ....Kaukauna, WI
Frassineti and Glover ....Greensboro, NC
Frassrand, Gregory M. ....Atlanta, GA
Frastai, Robert H. ....New York, NY
Frasure, Bonita C. ....Old Saybrook, CT
Frasure, Bonita C., P.C. ....Old Saybrook, CT
Frasure, Carl C. ....Bakersfield, CA
Frasure, Mark D. ....Canton, OH
Fratangelo, Peter ....Boston, MA
Fratantoni, Sam J. ....Chicago, IL
Fratar & Kern ....Springfield, MA
Fratar, Robert N. ....Springfield, MA
Fratarcangeli, Mark A. ....Warren, MI
Frate, Christina Gene ....Utica, NY
Fratello, Thomas J. ....Hempstead, NY
Frater, Elisabeth A. ....San Francisco, CA
Fraterrigo, Best & Beranek ....Chicago, IL
Wheaton, IL
Fraterrigo, Fredrick J. ....Chicago, IL
Frates, Gregory F. ....Payette, ID
Frates, Kent F. ....Oklahoma City, OK
Frates, Robert A. ....Oakland, CA
Frates, Thomas M. ....Buzzards Bay, MA
Frates, William S., II ....Vero Beach, FL
Frates, William S., II P.A. ....Fort Pierce, FL
Vero Beach, FL
Frateschi, Timothy A. ....Syracuse, NY
Frati, Deborah H. ....New York, NY
Fratianne, Marianne ....Los Angeles, CA
Fratianne, Nicholas J. ....Los Angeles, CA
Fratianne, Robert D. ....Indian Wells, CA
Fratianne, Robert J. ....Los Angeles, CA
Fratianni, Constance A. ....New York, NY
Fratianni, Joann Marie ....Lake Forest, IL
Fraticelli, Thomas M. ....Harrisburg, PA
Fraticelli, Yvonne
Securities and Exchange Commission, Division of Market Regulation, GV
Fraticelli-Torres, Migdalia ....San Juan, PR
Fratini, Pamela J. ....Clarksville, IN
Louisville, KY
Fratino, Donald L. ....Lutherville, MD
Fratkin, Bryan A. ....Richmond, VA
Frattallone, Susan Ann ....East Hartford, CT
Frattallone-Marti, Lillian ....San Juan, PR
Frattarelli, Angelo A. ......Department of Justice, Tax Division, GV
Frattarelli, Peter L. ....Haddonfield, NJ
Frattaroli, Carmen A. ....Salem, MA
Frattini, William L. ....Barre, VT
Fratto, John A. ....Camden, NJ
Fratto, Joseph C., Jr. ....Murray, UT
Frattone, Michael A. ....Philadelphia, PA
Fratus, Charles J. ....Baltimore, MD
Fratus, Donald N. ....Larkspur, CA
Fratzke, Juli C. ....Birmingham, MI
Fraude, Jay P. ....Department of Defense, Defense Legal Services Agency, GV
Frauen, Kurt H. ....Milwaukee, WI
Frauenglass, Lloyd, Law Offices of
Glastonbury, CT
Frauenglass, Lloyd, Law Offices of
Hartford, CT
Frauenhofer, David J. ....Torrington, CT
Frauenshuh, Ronald, Jr. ....Ortonville, MN
Frauenshuh, Ronald R., Sr. ....Paynesville, MN
Frauenshuh, Spooner & Landmark, P.A.
Paynesville, MN
Frau-Escudero, Juan A. ....San Juan, PR
Fraulino, Ellen Ann ....Trenton, NJ
Fraulo, Anthony N. ....Stamford, CT
Fraulob, Donald W. ....Sacramento, CA
Frauman, David C. L. ....New York, NY
Fraumann, Willard G., (P.C.) ......Chicago, IL
Fraumeni, Francis J. ....North Smithfield, RI
Fraunces, Michael G. ....San Diego, CA
Fraunfelder, William A., Jr. ....Cleveland, OH
Frau-Pietri, Manuel A. ....Ponce, PR
Frausto, Carol M. ....San Diego, CA
Frausto, Eulalio ....San Francisco, CA
Frautschi, Timothy C. ....Milwaukee, WI
Fravel, Charlene A. ....Selinsgrove, PA
Fravel, Craig R. ....Del Mar, CA
Frawley, Alfred C., III ....Portland, ME
Frawley, Anne K. ....Elizabeth, NJ
Frawley, Arthur J., Jr. ....Peabody, MA
Frawley, Brian M. ....Boston, MA
Frawley, Brian T. ....New York, NY
Frawley, Denis S. ....New York, NY
Frawley, Frederic L. ....Abilene, TX
Dallas, TX
Frawley, John ....Mountlake Terrace, WA
Frawley, John D. ....Elmira, NY
Frawley, John J. ....Lansing, MI
Frawley, John, P.S. ....Mountlake Terrace, WA
Frawley, John R., Jr. ....Irondale, AL
Frawley, Leonard L. ....Towanda, PA
Frawley, Mark W., Jr. ....New York, NY
Frawley, Michael K ....Ventura, CA
Frawley, Patrick ....Woodland Hills, CA
Frawley, Patrick J. ....Lexington, SC
Frawley, Polly Haight ....North Yarmouth, ME
Frawley, Robert D., Law Offices of
Morristown, NJ
Princeton, NJ
Frawley, Thomas J. ....St. Louis, MO
Fraxedas, Aylin ....Coral Gables, FL
Fraxedas, J. Joaquin ....Maitland, FL
Fray, Carrie C. ....Fresno, CA
Fray, Hudson, Clark & Walker, L.L.P.
Culpeper, VA
Fray, Jennifer H. ....Norwalk, CT
Fray, Joanne C. ....Lexington, MA
Fray, John M. ....Ellwood City, PA
Fray, John P. ....Fairfield, CT
Fray, Robert H. ....Gretna, LA
Fray, William T. ....Bridgeport, CT
Frayer, Dale P. ....Pittsburgh, PA
Frayman, Evan G. ....Jacksonville, FL
Frayman, Susan Z. ....New York, NY
Frayne, Anne M. ....Dayton, OH
Frayne, Anthony J., Jr. ....Philadelphia, PA
Frayne, Clifford G. ....Brick, NJ
Frayne, Gabriel M. ....New York, NY
Frayne, Michael K. ....Sacramento, CA
Frayne, Robert W. ....St. Louis, MO
Frayne, Stephen M. ....San Francisco, CA
Fraysse, Thomas E. ....Oakland, CA
Fray-Witzer, Evan Marc ....Boston, MA
Frazar, Darcy L. ....Carlsbad, CA
Fraze, John H. ....Maryville, MO
Frazee, Bryan W. ....Rosemead, CA
Frazee, Evelyn ....Rochester, NY
Frazee, James H. ....Louisville, KY
Frazee, Mark A. ....Rosemead, CA
Frazee, Michael A. ....Springfield, MA
Frazee, Phillip J. ....Denver, CO
Frazee, Richard O., Sr. ....Santa Ana, CA
Frazee, Robert M. ....Minneapolis, MN
Frazee, Ronald L. ....Dallas, TX
Frazee, Stanley S., Jr. ....Philadelphia, PA
Frazel, Jerome A., Jr. ....Chicago, IL
Frazel, Jerome V. ....Chicago, IL
Frazell, William A. ....San Antonio, TX
Frazelle, Michael J. ....Phoenix, AZ
Frazen, Laurence M. ....Kansas City, MO
Frazen, Mitchell H. ....Chicago, IL
Frazer, A. Danner, Jr. ....Mobile, AL
Frazer, Allen J. ....New York, NY
Frazer, Arthur L. ....Golden, CO
Frazer, Betty S. ....Albany, GA
Frazer, Bradlee R. ....Boise, ID
Frazer, David E. ....New York, NY
Frazer, David R., (P.C.) ....Phoenix, AZ
Frazer, Donald L., Jr. ....San Diego, CA
Frazer, Douglas H. ....Milwaukee, WI
Frazer, Florence T. ....Garden City, NY
Frazer, Greene, Upchurch & Baker, L.L.C.
Mobile, AL
Frazer, Helen Ryan ....Cerritos, CA
Frazer, Hubbard, Brandt & Trask
Dunedin, FL
Frazer, Ira ....Los Alamitos, CA
Frazer, James A. ....Washington, DC
Frazer, James M. ....Somerset, KY
Frazer, James S. ....Garden City, NY
Frazer, Jas. R. ....Garden City, NY
Frazer, John P. ....Dunedin, FL
Frazer, John P., III ....Sterling Heights, MI
Frazer, Lawrence P. ....Boston, MA
Frazer, Leroy, Jr. ....New York, NY
Frazer, Marilee Helen ....Detroit, MI
Frazer, Michael O. ....Battle Creek, MI
Frazer, Molly S. ....Nevada, IA
Frazer, Quin R. ....Chicago, IL
Frazer, Richard S. ....New York, NY
Frazer, Robert B. ....Marion, KY
Frazer, Robert H. ....Cromwell, CT
Frazer, Robert L. ....New York, NY
Frazer, Ryan, Goldberg & Hunter, L.L.P.
Phoenix, AZ
Frazer, S. Stewart ....Dallas, TX
Frazer Schapiro & Rich, S.C.
Milwaukee, WI
Frazer, T. Roe, II ....Jackson, MS
Port Gibson, MS
Frazier, Alison Tam ....Indianapolis, IN
Frazier, Alton Eugene ....Dallas, TX
Frazier, Andrew B., Jr. ....Camden, TN
Frazier, Audria Marie ....Richmond, VA
Frazier, Barney W., Jr. ....Charleston, WV
Frazier, Bill ....Houston, TX
Frazier, Bob ....Malvern, AR
Frazier, Bradley D. ....Carson, CA
Frazier, Brian K. ....Nashville, TN
Frazier, C. Elisia ....Fort Wayne, IN
Frazier, Carey T. ....Brentwood, TN
Frazier, Carl C. ....Jeffersonville, IN
Frazier, Carol Woods ....Chandler, AZ
Frazier, Charles O. ....Keokuk, IA
Frazier, Charles S. ....Wayne, PA
Frazier, Charles T., Jr. ....Dallas, TX
Frazier, Cindy Webb ....Walnut Creek, CA
Frazier, Clarence F. ....Jacksonville, FL
Frazier, Cynthia M. ....Franklin, MA
Frazier, Cyrus Clifford, Jr.
Greensboro, NC
Frazier, Dana S. ....Carbondale, IL
Frazier, Daniel A. ....Winston-Salem, NC
Frazier, David C. ....Pascagoula, MS
Frazier, Donna M. ....St. Louis, MO
Frazier, Douglas Lee ....Chicago, IL
Frazier, Edward A. ....Columbia, SC
Frazier, Edward A., P.A. ....Columbia, SC
Frazier, Eloise J. ....Harrisburg, PA
Frazier, Ernest R., Sr. ....Philadelphia, PA
Frazier & Frazier ....Houston, TX
Frazier & Frazier, Attorneys at Law, P.A.
Jacksonville, FL
Frazier, Frazier & Mahler, LLP
Greensboro, NC
Frazier & Frazier, P.L.L.C. ....Keene, NH
Frazier, French B. ....Lookout Mountain, TN
Frazier, G. Scott ....Tuscaloosa, AL
Frazier, Gail M. .....Department Of The Interior, Office of Hearings & Appeals, GV
Frazier & Garrett ....Omaha, NE
Frazier, Gary E. ....St. Petersburg, FL
Frazier, Gary E., P.A. ....St. Petersburg, FL
Frazier, George ....New Orleans, LA
Frazier, Gerianne Craft ....Newport Beach, CA
Frazier, Gregory G. ....Tampa, FL
Frazier, Harriet C. ....Warrensburg, MO
Frazier, Hotte & Associates, P.A.
Fort Lauderdale, FL
Frazier, J. Anthony ....Jefferson City, MO
Frazier, J. David ....Colfax, WA
Frazier, James A. ....Plano, TX
Frazier, James A., P.C. ....Plano, TX
Frazier, James H., III ....Lexington, KY
Frazier, James Larry ....Washington, DC
Frazier, James Scott ....New York, NY
Frazier, Janet F. ....Marietta, OH
Frazier, Jean M. ....Columbus, OH
Frazier, Jefferson ....Walnut Creek, CA
Frazier, Jeffery D. .....Department of Commerce, Patent and Trademark Office, GV
Frazier, Jeffrey Walker ....Roswell, GA
Frazier, Jerre H. ....Nashville, TN
Frazier, Jessica K. ....Long Beach, CA
Frazier, Jill T. ....Mt. Crested Butte, CO
Frazier, Joan F. ....Chicago, IL
Frazier, John A., Jr. ....Rome, GA
Frazier, John E. ....Fort Worth, TX
Frazier, John M. ....Shreveport, LA
Frazier, John P. ....Martins Ferry, OH
Frazier, John R. ....Wills Point, TX
Frazier, John R. ....Princeton, WV
Frazier, John W., IV ....Philadelphia, PA
Frazier, Joseph G. ....Lockport, NY
Frazier, Karen K. ....Keene, NH
Frazier, Katherine L. ....Memphis, TN
Frazier, Keith D. ....Nashville, TN
Frazier, Kelly A. ....Albany, NY
Frazier, Kelly D. ....Rapid City, SD
Frazier, Kelly K. ....Chicago, IL
Frazier, Kenneth C.
Whitehouse Station, NJ
Frazier, Kenneth R. ....Detroit, MI
Frazier, Kenneth S. ....Billings, MT
Frazier, Kyle ....San Francisco, CA
Frazier, Kyle Allen ....Houston, TX
Frazier Law Firm ....Rapid City, SD
Frazier Law Office ....Indianapolis, IN
Noblesville, IN
Frazier, Lawrence A. ....Lincoln, NE
Frazier, Linda B. ....Houston, TX
Frazier, Linda C. ....Miami, FL
Frazier, Lisa Renee ....Tulsa, OK
Frazier, Loyal D., Sr. ....Ventura, CA
Frazier, Mark B. ....Costa Mesa, CA
Frazier, Marlon W. ....Dallas, TX
Frazier, Melanie T. ....Southfield, MI
Frazier, Melissa M.
North Myrtle Beach, SC
Frazier, Michael J. ....Milwaukee, WI
Frazier, Michael Opie ....Denver, CO
Frazier, Michelle L. ....Raleigh, NC
Frazier, Milton M. ....St. Louis, MO
Frazier, Owsley B. ....Louisville, KY
Frazier & Oxley, L.C. ....Huntington, WV
Frazier, Pamela K. ....Pensacola, FL
Frazier, Patrick W., Jr. ....Hamden, CT
Frazier, Peter A. ....New York, NY
Frazier, Phil ....Tulsa, OK
Frazier, Philip M. ....Benton, IL
Frazier, Randal B. ....Little Rock, AR
Frazier, Rawls H. ....Monterey, CA
Frazier, Reginald B. ....Chesapeake, VA
Frazier, Richard D. ....Springfield, IL
Frazier, Richard T. ....Berwyn, PA
Philadelphia, PA
Frazier, Ricks P. ....Coral Gables, FL
Frazier, Robert A. ....Chattanooga, TN
Frazier, Robert E. ....Cypress, CA
Frazier, Robert F. ....Harrisburg, PA
Frazier, Robert G. ....Kennebunk, ME
Frazier, Robert W., Jr. ....Fort Lauderdale, FL
Frazier & Roberts ....Wayne, PA
Frazier, Roger W. ....Tucson, AZ
Frazier, Ronald F. ....San Diego, CA
Frazier, Ronald W. ....Indianapolis, IN
Noblesville, IN
Frazier, S. Katherine ....Tampa, FL
Frazier, Sam J., III ....Ramona, CA
Frazier, Sam L. ....Birmingham, AL
Frazier, Samuel H. ....Birmingham, AL
Frazier, Sandra J. ....Tulsa, OK
Frazier, Scott E. ....Baton Rouge, LA
Frazier, Seann M. ....Tallahassee, FL
Frazier, Severne A., Jr. ....Montgomery, AL
Frazier, Sharon Mullen ....Huntington, WV
Frazier, Smith & Phillips, P.A. ....Tulsa, OK
Frazier, Soloway & Poorak ....Atlanta, GA
Frazier, Stephen D. ....Springfield, VA
Frazier, Stephen N. ....Paintsville, KY
Frazier, Steven C. ....Church Hill, TN
Frazier, Sydney F., Jr. ....Birmingham, AL
Frazier, T. Rick ....Dallas, TX
Frazier, T. Scott ....Orlando, FL
Frazier, Terry W. ....Jackson, MS
Frazier, Thomas A., Jr. ....Washington, DC
Frazier, Thomas B. ....Dallas, TX
Frazier, Thurston E., Jr. ....Charlotte, NC
Frazier, Timothy M. ....Keene, NH
Frazier, Tina L. ....Raleigh, NC
Frazier, Todd E. ....Omaha, NE
Frazier, W. Edwin, III ....Atlanta, GA
Frazier, W. Michael ....Huntington, WV
Frazier, W. Robinson ....Jacksonville, FL
Frazier & Whitworth ....Camden, TN
Frazier, William D. ....Chicago, IL
Frazier, William F., Jr. ....Big Timber, MT
Frazier, William H. ....Milwaukee, WI
Frazier, William M. ....Huntington, WV
Frazier, William R. ....Jacksonville, FL
Frazier, William S. ....Huffman, TX
Frazier-Clemons, Brenda ....Philadelphia, PA
Frazier-Lyde, Jacquelyn ....Philadelphia, PA
Frazier-Thomas, Avis ....Los Angeles, CA
Frazin, Arthur M. ....Denver, CO
Frazin, Irwin L. ....Chicago, IL
Frazin, James L. ....Libertyville, IL
Frazin, Jennifer B. ....Miami, FL
Frazin, Julian J. ....Chicago, IL
Frazin-Weiner, Barbara ....Chicago, IL
Frazza, George S. ....New York, NY
Frazza, Peter John ....Short Hills, NJ
Frazzetto, Stephen L. ....East Northport, NY
Frazzini, John A. ....Littleton, CO
Frazzini, Madalyn J. ....San Jose, CA
Frazzini, Stephen F. ....Hartford, CT
Frazzitta, Mildred C. ....New York, NY

Frealy, Todd A. ....Riverside, CA
Freamon, Bernard K. ....Newark, NJ
Freaney, Thomas J., Jr. ....Alexandria, VA
Freas, Charles A. ....Amarillo, TX
Freas, Monica A. ....Washington, DC
Frease, Belden A. ....Fort Lauderdale, FL
Freatman, Ellis B., III ....Ypsilanti, MI
Freburg, Cynthia A. ....Evergreen Park, IL
Freburg, Nancy S. ....Kearney, NE
Freccero, Francesca ....Department of Justice, Office of the Inspector General, GV
Portland, OR
Freccero, Stephen P. ....San Francisco, CA
Freccia & Plotkin ....Stamford, CT
Freccia, Vincent J., III ....Stamford, CT
Frecentese, Francis X. ....New York, NY
Frech, Gerard K. ....Skillman, NJ
Frech, Mary Kay Greif
Securities and Exchange Commission, Division of Investment Management, GV
Frechette & Associates, P.C.
Albuquerque, NM
Frechette, Donald E. ....Hartford, CT
Frechette & Frechette ....New Haven, CT
Frechette, John R. ....Elkhart, IN
Frechette, Matthew E. ....New Haven, CT
Frechette, Melinda P. ....Hartford, CT
Frechette, Michelle R. H.
Albuquerque, NM
Frechette, Roderick T. ....Albuquerque, NM
Frechette, Roger J. ....New Haven, CT
Frechtel, Eric A. ....Baltimore, MD
Frechtman, A. Bernard ....New York, NY
Frecia, Graciela ....Atlanta, GA
Frecka, John A. ....Mansfield, OH
Frecker, David L.
General Services Administration, Office of the General Counsel, GV
Frecker, William H. ....Tampa, FL
Frécon, Alain ....Minneapolis, MN
Fred, Alex Denny ....Los Angeles, CA
Freda, Leanne M. ....White Plains, NY
Freda, Michael M. ....Mansfield, OH
Freda, Raymond J. ....New York, NY
Freda, Robert Joseph ....McLean, VA
Freda, Thomas J. ....Medford, MA
Fredbeck, Andrew N. ....New York, NY
Fredbeck, Eric W. ....Franklin, IN
Fredbeck, Melvin N. ....Franklin, IN
Fredd, Anne L. ....Chicago, IL
Fredeking & Fredeking ....Huntington, WV
Fredeking, Robert R., II ....Huntington, WV
Fredel, Ellen A., (P.C.) ....Washington, DC
Fredel, Guy W. ....Mosinee, WI
Fredel Law Offices, S.C. ....Mosinee, WI
Fredella, Anthony M. ....Somerville, MA
Fredeman, Henry F., II ....Groves, TX
Freden, Carol ....Menlo Park, CA
Fredenberg, Mark A. ....Phoenix, AZ
Fredenberger, William E., Jr. ....Stafford, VA
Fredenburg, John M. ....Sacramento, CA
Fredenburg, Lila D. ....Northbrook, IL
Fredenburg, Wesley C.
Fort Lauderdale, FL
Frederici, C. Carleton ....Des Moines, IA
Frederick, Albert, Jr. ....Poughkeepsie, NY
Frederick, Alvin I. ....Baltimore, MD
Frederick, Anne D. ....Youngstown, OH
Frederick, Barry R. ....Los Angeles, CA
Frederick, Barry V. ....Birmingham, AL
Frederick, Becky J. ....Chicago, IL
Frederick, Brent Paul ....Lafayette, LA
Frederick, Brian ....Cle Elum, WA
Ellensburg, WA
Frederick & Brouillette ....Breaux Bridge, LA
Frederick, Calvita J. ....Chicago, IL
Frederick, Carl D. ....Louisville, KY
Frederick, Carl Lee, Jr. ....Rockville, MD
Frederick, Carol L. ....Seattle, WA
Frederick, Charles L. ....Rockville, MD
Frederick, Craig A. ....Grand Rapids, MI
Frederick, Cynthia Marie ....Wexford, PA
Frederick, D. Joleen ....West Liberty, KY
Frederick, David ....Austin, TX
Frederick, David C. ....Department of Justice, Office of the Solicitor General, GV
Frederick, David N. ....Las Vegas, NV
Frederick, Deborah B. ....Okemos, MI
Frederick, Donald A.
Department of Agriculture, Agricultural Cooperative Service, GV
Frederick, Donald B. ....Waverly, NY
Frederick, Edwin ....Great Neck, NY
Frederick, Elizabeth A. ....Fort Wayne, IN
Frederick, Elizabeth M. ....Rapid City, SD
Frederick, Frances A. ....Pittsburgh, PA
Frederick, Francie A. (Patterson) ....Austin, TX
Frederick & Frederick, P.C. ....Livonia, MI
Frederick, George S. ....Wheaton, IL
Frederick, Gordon V. ....Sanford, FL
Frederick, Harold A. ....Phoenix, AZ
Frederick, Harold A. ....Duluth, MN
Frederick, Harry ....Youngstown, OH
Frederick, Howard G. ....White Plains, NY
Frederick, Irving ....Rockville Centre, NY
Frederick, J. Alan ....Burbank, CA
Frederick, J. Dennis ....Salt Lake City, UT
Frederick, Jacqueline Vitti ....Nipomo, CA
Frederick, James A. ....Baltimore, MD
Frederick, James B., Jr. ....Baton Rouge, LA
Frederick, James L. ....Brookline, MA
Frederick, James P. ....Livonia, MI
Frederick, James R. ....Monroe, CT
Frederick, James R. ....Pittsford, NY
Frederick, Jeffrey D. ....Urbana, IL
Frederick, John A. ....Manteca, CA
Frederick, Joyce R. ....Piti, GU
Frederick, Judy ....Austin, TX

Frederick, Kathleen A. ....New York, NY
Frederick, Kathleen A., Law Offices of
Norristown, PA
Frederick, Kathleen A., Law Offices of
Plymouth Meeting, PA
Frederick, Keith I. ....Omaha, NE
Frederick, Kenneth Victor ....Spokane, WA
Frederick, Kent J. ....Baltimore, MD
Frederick, Kevin D. ....Redwood City, CA
Frederick, Kevin S. ....Lafayette, LA
Frederick, L. Barrett ....West Liberty, KY
Frederick, Laura A. ....Austin, TX
Frederick, Loretta M. ....Winona, MN
Frederick, Lynette M. ....Corpus Christi, TX
Frederick, Marilyn K. ....Portland, OR
Frederick, Mark Evan ....Destin, FL
Frederick, Mark Evan, and Assoc., P.A., Law Offices of ....Destin, FL
Frederick, Mary Beth ....New Haven, CT
Frederick, Melvin E. ....Wilmington, MA
Frederick, Michael E. ....Fort Worth, TX
Frederick, Michael J. ....Colorado Springs, CO
Frederick, Nancy A. ....Chicago, IL
Frederick, Patricia M. ....Stockton, CA
Frederick, Paul J. ....Livonia, MI
Frederick, Paula J. ....Atlanta, GA
Frederick, R. Bruce ....Santa Fe, NM
Frederick, R. LaMar ....Toledo, OH
Frederick, Richard A. ....Milwaukee, WI
Frederick, Richard E. ....Tucson, AZ
Frederick, Richmond S., Jr.
Dearborn, MI
Frederick, Robert B. ....Troy, MI
Frederick, Robert E. ....Phillipsburg, NJ
Frederick, Robert G. ....Urbana, IL
Frederick, Robert J. ....Lakin, KS
Frederick, Robert L. ....Richardson, TX
Frederick, Robert O. ....Winterset, IA
Frederick, Robin G. ....Stamford, CT
Frederick, Ronald A. ....Independence, MO
Frederick, Samuel A. (Sam)
King Of Prussia, PA
Frederick, Scott J. ....Hamilton, OH
Frederick, Stanley ....Hollywood, FL
Frederick, Stephen L. ....Breaux Bridge, LA
Frederick, Steven M. ....Stamford, CT
Frederick, Susan S. ....Las Vegas, NV
Frederick, Thomas J. ....Chicago, IL
Frederick, Thomas J. ....Abbeville, LA
Frederick, Timothy P. ....Brooklyn Center, MN
Frederick, W. D., Jr. ....Orlando, FL
Fredericka, James A. ....Warren, OH
Fredericks, Albert G. ....Newark, NJ
New York, NY
Fredericks, Alwyn R. ....Atlanta, GA
Fredericks, Barbara H. ....Beaverton, OR
Fredericks, Barbara S.
Department of Commerce, Office of the General Counsel, GV
Fredericks, Barry I. ....Englewood Cliffs, NJ
New York, NY
Fredericks, Barry I. ....Hackensack, NJ
Fredericks, Carl ....Hiawassee, GA
Fredericks, Charles, Jr. ....Westport, CT
New York, NY
Fredericks, Dale E. ....San Francisco, CA
Fredericks, Diane Ellen
Equal Employment Opportunity Commission, Office of the General Counsel, GV
Fredericks, Douglas ....Norfolk, VA
Fredericks, Frank O. ....Greenwich, CT
Fredericks, Henry J., IV ....St. Louis, MO
Fredericks, James A. ....St. Louis, MO
Fredericks, James M. ....Milwaukee, WI
Fredericks, James W. ....Richland, WA
Fredericks, John D. ....San Francisco, CA
Fredericks, John, III ....Louisville, CO
Fredericks, Jomarie B. ....Evanston, IL
Fredericks, Joseph A. ....Mineola, NY
Fredericks, Karen P. ....New York, NY
Fredericks, Kay M. ....New York, NY
Fredericks, Maurice H. ....Rohnert Park, CA
Fredericks & Melloway, L.L.C.
St. Louis, MO
Fredericks, Michelle A. ....New York, NY
Fredericks, Murray ....Atlantic City, NJ
Fredericks, Pelcyger, Hester & White, LLC
Louisville, CO
Fredericks, Richard L. ....Eugene, OR
Fredericks, Robert B. ....Falmouth, MA
Fredericks, Robert D. ....Raynham, MA
Fredericks, Robert L., Jr. ....Annandale, VA
Fredericks & Stephens, P.C. ....Annandale, VA
Fredericks, Thomas R. ....Covina, CA
Fredericks, Thomas W. ....Louisville, CO
Fredericks, Wendell K. ....Auburn Hills, MI
Fredericks, Wesley C., Jr. ....New York, NY
Fredericks, William Benjamin, Jr.
Bartow, FL
Fredericks, William C. ....New York, NY
Fredericksen, Chris L. ....Peoria, IL
Fredericksen, Eugene D. ....Jerome, ID
Fredericksen, Janel B. ....Wahpeton, ND
Fredericksen, Kenneth S. ....Orlando, FL
Fredericksen, Scott L. ....Seattle, WA
Fredericksen, Williams & Meservy
Jerome, ID
Frederickson, Craig F. ....Toledo, OH
Frederickson, David H. ....Los Angeles, CA
Frederickson, Donald J., Jr. ....Moosic, PA
Frederickson, Frederick O. ....Seattle, WA
Frederickson & Heintschel, Co., L.P.A.
Toledo, OH
Frederickson, Jeanette A.
Minneapolis, MN
Frederickson, John D. ....Fort Lee, NJ
Frederickson, John F. ....Shreveport, LA

Frederickson, John R. ....Deadwood, SD
Frederickson, Roger B. ....St. Paul, MN
Frederickson, Theodore P., II ....Lawrence, KS
Frederico, Donald R. ....Boston, MA
Frederiks, Racquel A. ....Flemington, NJ
Frederiksen, C. Christian, Jr. ....Dallas, TX
Frederiksen, Charles C. ....Dallas, TX
Frederiksen, Karen Nancy
Los Angeles, CA
Frederiksen, Mark D. ....Omaha, NE
Frederiksen, Paul A. ....Parker, CO
Frederiksen, Paul A., P.C. ....Parker, CO
Frederiksen, Stanley A. ....Ferguson, MO
Frederisy, Robert H. ....Inglewood, CA
Frederking, William ....Houston, TX
Fredette, Michael ....Houston, TX
Fredgant, Jane Horswell ....Agoura Hills, CA
Fredgant, Perry R. ....Woodland Hills, CA
Fredgren, Ana Maria Z. ....Los Angeles, CA
Fredgren, Charles T.
Rancho Cucamonga, CA
Fredheim, Timothy ....Augusta, ME
Fredkin, Mark B., (L.C.) ....San Jose, CA
Fredkin, Stephen H. ....Salinas, CA
Fredland, Allan L. ....Boise, ID
Fredland, Daniel R. ....Media, PA
Fredman, Herbert I. ....Olivette, MO
Fredman, Howard S ....Los Angeles, CA
Fredman, I. Jay ....Washington, DC
Fredman, I. Jay, P.C., Law Offices of
Washington, DC
Fredman, James J., III ....Omaha, NE
Fredman, Jane B. ....Colorado Springs, CO
Fredman & Kosan, LLP ....White Plains, NY
Fredman, Mark S. ....St. Louis, MO
Fredman, Michele Wertheimer
New York, NY
Fredman, Milton ....La Jolla, CA
Fredman, Neil A. ....White Plains, NY
Fredman, Richard A. ....St. Louis, MO
Fredman, Samuel G. ....White Plains, NY
Fredman, Steven J. ....New York, NY
Fredman, Stuart A. ....Salt Lake City, UT
Fredregill, Alan E., (P.C.) ....Sioux City, IA
Fredrich, Dolores ....Uniondale, NY
Fredrich, Erwin F. ....San Francisco, CA
Fredrich, Marshall E. ....Milwaukee, WI
Fredrich, Steven R. ....Houston, TX
Fredrick, Bonni D. ....Milwaukee, WI
Fredrick, Carol J. ....McMinnville, OR
Fredrick, Gail L. ....Springfield, MO
Fredrick, Kathleen A. ....Philadelphia, PA
Fredrick, Leonard J. ....Highland Park, NJ
Fredrick, Mark W. ....Santa Ana, CA
Fredrick, Richard J. ....Paris, MO
Fredrick, Rogers & Vaughn, P.C.
Springfield, MO
Fredrick, Thomas W. ....New York, NY
Fredrick, William C. ....Laguna Niguel, CA
Fredricks, Dennis F. ....Los Angeles, CA
Fredricks, Douglas S. ....McMinnville, OR
Fredricks, Josh M. ....Torrance, CA
Fredricks, Nicole L. ....Brainerd, MN
Fredricks, Randall C. ....Boise, ID
Fredricksen, David Scott ....Los Angeles, CA
Fredricksen, Philip R. ....San Diego, CA
Fredricksmeyer, E. Stefan ....Louisville, CO
Fredrickson, Bruce A. ....Washington, DC
Fredrickson, Bruce A. ....Billings, MT
Fredrickson, Bryan T. ....Canon City, CO
Fredrickson, Caroline R.
Executive Office Of The President, GV
Fredrickson, David R.
Securities and Exchange Commission, Office of the General Counsel, GV
Fredrickson, Dennis ....San Diego, CA
Fredrickson, Floyd A. ....Portland, OR
Fredrickson, Hope L. ....Jamestown, NY
Fredrickson, Jas. R. ....Empire, MI
Fredrickson, Jodi K. ....Washington, DC
Fredrickson, John C. ....Greenbelt, MD
La Plata, MD
Fredrickson, John P. ....Milwaukee, WI
Fredrickson & Johnson, P.C.
Canon City, CO
Fredrickson, Jon E. ....Milwaukee, WI
Fredrickson, Kenneth L. ....Conifer, CO
Fredrickson, Kenneth L. ....Denver, CO
Fredrickson, Kirk D. ....Oklahoma City, OK
Fredrickson Law Firm ....Denver, CO
Fredrickson, Leo H. ....Spokane, WA
Fredrickson, Mark A. ....Minneapolis, MN
Fredrickson, Mazeika & Grant
San Diego, CA
Fredrickson, Michael ....Boston, MA
Fredrickson, Richard L. ....Santa Ana, CA
Fredrickson, Robert A. ....Rockford, IL
Fredrickson, Robert G. ....Canon City, CO
Fredrickson, Robin S. ....Houston, TX
Fredrickson, Stephen C. ....Tallahassee, FL
Fredrickson, Terrence L. ....Seattle, WA
Fredrickson, Todd A. ....Denver, CO
Fredrikson & Byron, P.A.
Minneapolis, MN
St. Paul, MN
Fredrikson, Harold M. ....St. Paul, MN
Fredrikson, Mindette R.
Minneapolis, MN
Fredson, Barry ....Passaic, NJ
Fredston, Arthur H. ....New York, NY
Fredston, Dale Carol ....Wilton, CT
Fredyma, John J. ....Cape Coral, FL
Free, Brently W. ....New Braunfels, TX
Free, Brian D. ....Chicago, IL
Free, Charles Richard ....Denver, CO
Free, Dan R. ....Washington, DC
Free, Douglas S. ....Walnut Creek, CA
Free, E. LeBron ....Clearwater, FL

Free, E. LeBron, P.A. ....Clearwater, FL
Free, Edwin W., III ....Indianapolis, IN
Free, Ledger D. ....Menlo Park, CA
Free, Mark A. ....Columbia, TN
Free, Matthew B. ....Tulsa, OK
Free, Melissa P. ....Great Falls, VA
Free, Phillip L., Jr. ....Oklahoma City, OK
Free, Robert A. ....Seattle, WA
Free, Wade H., Jr. ....Anderson, IN
Freeark, Harvey, Mendillo, Dennis, Wuller & Cain, P.C. ....Belleville, IL
Freeark, Ray H., Jr. ....Belleville, IL
Freeberg, Bonnie L. ....Jericho, NY
Freeberg, Bruce W. ....Jefferson, WI
Freeberg, Conrad I. ....Little Falls, MN
Freeberg, Eric O. ....Rancho Santa Fe, CA
Freeberg, Jane M. ....New York, NY
Freebern, Donald J. ....Glens Falls, NY
Freebery & Houghton ....Wilmington, DE
Freebery, Michael P. ....Wilmington, DE
Freeble, Kathleen C. ....Bay Pines, FL
Freeborn, Alison K. ....Dunedin, FL
Freeborn & Freeborn, P.A. ....Dunedin, FL
Freeborn, John B. ....Dunedin, FL
Freeborn, John F. ....Dunedin, FL
Freeborn, Michael D. ....Chicago, IL
Freeborn & Peters ....Denver, CO
Chicago, IL
Springfield, IL
Freeborn, Richard L. ....Clearlake, CA
Freeburg, Dorothy M. ....Westport, CT
Freeburg, Judy & Nettels
Los Angeles, CA
Pasadena, CA
Santa Ana, CA
Tustin, CA
Freeburg, Karen S. ....Pasadena, CA
Freeburg, Karl A. ....Phoenix, AZ
Freeburg, Michelle ....Carlsbad, CA
Freeburg, Philip J. ....Schofield, WI
Freeburg, Steven J. ....Pasadena, CA
Freeburger, Sandra D. ....Henderson, KY
Freeburger, Thomas O. ....Sacramento, CA
Freeburn & Associates ....Harrisburg, PA
Freeburn, Richard E. ....Harrisburg, PA
Freeby, Rose M.Z. ....Salem, OR
Freechack, John E. ....Chicago, IL
Freed, Alan E. ....St. Louis, MO
Freed, Alan, Jr. ....Helena, MT
Freed, Alison R. ....Kew Gardens, NY
Freed, Amy Bowerman ....Baltimore, MD
Freed, Andrew J. ....Beverly, MA
Freed, Ariela ....Emeryville, CA
Freed & Berman, P.C. ....Atlanta, GA
Freed, C. William, Jr. ....Quakertown, PA
Freed, Chad A. ....Phoenix, AZ
Freed, Charles L. ....Washington, DC
Freed, Charles N.
Environmental Protection Agency, Program Office Attorneys, GV
Freed, Cheryl K. ....San Antonio, TX
Freed, Clifford ....Seattle, WA
Freed, D. Scott ....Baltimore, MD
Freed, Daniel J. ....New Haven, CT
Freed, David I. ....Napa, CA
Freed, David I., P.C. ....Napa, CA
Freed, Dean M. ....Wilsonville, OR
Freed, Dennis N. ....Portland, OR
Freed, Diane Susan ....Lakewood, CO
Freed, Ellyn ....San Francisco, CA
Freed, Eric D. ....Philadelphia, PA
Freed, Evan Phillip ....Marina Del Rey, CA
Freed, Floyd W., III ....Houston, TX
Freed, Frederick D. ....Piqua, OH
Freed, Fredric J. ....Encino, CA
Freed, Gary S. ....Atlanta, GA
Freed, Gerald D. ....Baltimore, MD
Freed, Harvey M. ....San Francisco, CA
Freed & Heinemann ....San Francisco, CA
Freed, Helaine B. ....East Norwich, NY
Freed, Helen Dillon ....Atlanta, GA
Freed, Howard A. ....Dickinson, ND
Freed, Howard E. ....Atlantic City, NJ
Freed, James W. ....Salt Lake City, UT
Freed, Jerald Israel ....Silver Spring, MD
Freed, Joanne ....Los Angeles, CA
Freed, Joel M. ....Washington, DC
Freed, Jonathan ....Paducah, KY
Freed, Kelly M. ....Danville, IL
Freed, Kenneth A. ....San Ramon, CA
Freed, Kenneth J. ....Sherman Oaks, CA
Freed Law Firm ....Piqua, OH
Freed, Marc-David ....Franklin, TN
Freed, Marcia H., (Mrs.) ....Albuquerque, NM
Freed, Mark J. ....Santa Rosa, CA
Freed, Mark Landis ....Conshohocken, PA
Freed, Martin J. ....Chicago, IL
Freed, Martin J., Ltd. ....Chicago, IL
Freed, Mayer G. ....Chicago, IL
Freed, Merrill A. ....Chicago, IL
Freed, Michael J. ....Chicago, IL
Freed, Michael J. ....New York, NY
Freed, Michael L., & Associates
Honolulu, HI
Freed, Michael R. ....Jacksonville, FL
Freed, Michael R. ....Pittsburgh, PA
Freed, Michael S. ....San Francisco, CA
Freed, Morton ....Walled Lake, MI
Freed, Myra L. ....New York, NY
Freed, Nancy A. ....Boston, MA
Freed, Owen S. ....Miami, FL
Freed, Peter R. ....Princeton, NJ
Freed, Peter R. ....New York, NY
Freed, Richard G. ....La Mesa, CA
Freed, Richard H. ....Houston, TX
Freed, Robert A. ....Bismarck, ND
Freed, Robert C. ....Minneapolis, MN
Freed, Robert G. ....Fresno, CA

Freed, Robert L. .... Richmond, VA
Freed, Robt. E. .... Cleveland, OH
Freed, Rodney K. .... Shawnee, OK
Freed, Roy N. .... Boston, MA
Freed, Samuel .... Hartford, CT
Freed, Samuel B. .... Forest Hills, NY
Freed, Sanford .... Miami, FL
Freed & Schwartz .... Buffalo, NY
Freed & Shepherd, P.C. .... Richmond, VA
Freed, Sherwood E. .... Buffalo, NY
Freed, Sol .... Brooklyn, NY
Freed, Stanley .... Laredo, TX
Freed, Stephen N. .... West Chester, PA
Freed, Stephen W. .... Manhattan, KS
Freed, Thomas J. .... Stamford, CT
Freed, Todd E. .... New York, NY
Freed, William J. .... Oceanside, CA
Freedberg, Bradley S., Law Offices of
Denver, CO
Freedberg, Debra L. .... New York, NY
Freedberg, Jared M. .... Morristown, NJ
Freedberg, Lucille T. .... New York, NY
Freedberg, Robert A. .... Easton, PA
Freedenberg, Harvey .... Harrisburg, PA
Freedenberg, John P. .... Buffalo, NY
Freedenberg, Oscar .... Oak Park, MI
Freedenberg, Robert .... Harrisburg, PA
Freedenthal, Michele A. .... Los Angeles, CA
Freedheim, Amy J. .... Seattle, WA
Freedland, Arnold I. .... Alhambra, CA
Freedland, Howard M. .... Palo Alto, CA
Freedland, Marvin A. .... Costa Mesa, CA
Freedland, Michael Sean
Fort Lauderdale, FL
Freedland, Sumner .... Los Angeles, CA
Freedlander, Barrett W. .... Baltimore, MD
Freedlander, Mark E. .... Pittsburgh, PA
Freedle, P. Douglas .... Tampa, FL
Freedman, Adam (IBA) .... New York, NY
Freedman, Adele C. .... Mountain View, CA
Freedman, Alan H. .... Silver Spring, MD
Freedman, Alan M. .... Chicago, IL
Freedman, Alan R. .... Santa Monica, CA
Freedman, Alan R. .... Albany, NY
Freedman, Alexandra M. .... New York, NY
Freedman, Allan R. .... Teaneck, NJ
New York, NY
Freedman, Allen R. .... Chicago, IL
Freedman, Allen R. .... Summit, NJ
Freedman, Amy B. .... Salisbury, NC
Freedman, Amy Jo .... Boston, MA
Freedman, Andrew C. .... New York, NY
Freedman, Andrew S. .... Scarsdale, NY
Freedman, Ann Elizabeth .... Camden, NJ
Freedman, Anne L. .... New York, NY
Freedman, Anthony S. .... Washington, DC
Freedman & Areeda, P.C.
Bingham Farms, MI
Freedman, Arthur S. .... Downey, CA
Freedman & Associates, P.A. .... Miami, FL
Freedman, Barry A. .... Boston, MA
Freedman, Barry J. .... Cooper City, FL
Freedman, Bart J. .... Seattle, WA
Freedman, Barton H. .... Louisville, KY
Freedman, Bernard .... Scarsdale, NY
Freedman, Bernard B. .... Kenmore, NY
North Tonawanda, NY
Freedman, Bernard W. .... Laguna Hills, CA
Freedman, Bernard W. .... Santa Monica, CA
Freedman, Beth A. .... Washington, DC
Freedman, Beth S. .... Berkeley, CA
Freedman, Betty O. .... Frankfort, KY
Freedman, Beverly K. .... Bellevue, WA
Freedman & Bornstein, P.C. .... Chicago, IL
Freedman Boyd Daniels Hollander Goldberg & Cline P.A. .... Albuquerque, NM
Freedman, Brenda M. .... Buffalo, NY
Freedman, Brian M. .... Greensboro, NC
Freedman, Bruce G.
Federal Trade Commission, Office of the General Counsel, GV
Freedman, Bruce H. .... Miami, FL
Freedman, Bruce R. .... Akron, OH
Freedman, Bryan Joel .... Los Angeles, CA
Freedman, Callista M. .... Baltimore, MD
Freedman, Carl .... Skokie, IL
Freedman, Carl I. .... Providence, RI
Freedman, Carla B. .... New York, NY
Freedman, Daniel E. .... Garden City, NY
Freedman, Daniel M. .... Los Angeles, CA
Freedman, Dara L. .... Washington, DC
Freedman, Darryl Bowen .... Fresno, CA
Freedman, David A. .... Albuquerque, NM
Freedman, David A., (P.A.) .... Miami, FL
Freedman, David B. .... Winston-Salem, NC
Freedman, David G. .... Los Angeles, CA
Freedman, David H. .... North Miami, FL
Freedman, David H. .... Southfield, MI
Freedman, David H., P.A. .... North Miami, FL
Freedman, David L. .... Ann Arbor, MI
Freedman, David M. .... Houston, TX
Freedman, David Michael .... Albany, NY
Freedman, David P. .... San Juan, PR
Freedman, Debbie .... Los Angeles, CA
Freedman, Deborah .... Philadelphia, PA
Freedman, DeRosa & Rondeau
North Adams, MA
Freedman, Donald E. .... Garden City, NY
Freedman, Donald N. .... Newton, MA
Freedman, Doris S.
Small Business Administration, Office of the General Counsel, GV
Freedman, Douglas A. .... Chicago, IL
Freedman, Edw. .... Boston, MA
Freedman, Edward D. .... Boston, MA
Freedman, Edward R. .... Roslyn, NY
Freedman, Ellis J. .... New York, NY
Freedman, Ellis R. .... Newton, MA
Freedman, Eric .... East Lansing, MI
Freedman, Eric E. .... Everett, WA
Freedman, Eric M. .... New York, NY
Freedman and Fish .... New York, NY
Freedman, Forrest Scott .... Boston, MA
Freedman, Frances F. .... Toluca Lake, CA
Freedman, Frances F. .... Bala Cynwyd, PA
Philadelphia, PA
Freedman, Frank H. .... Springfield, MA
Freedman, Frederick A. .... Hartford, CT
Freedman, Fredrick P. .... Miami, FL
Freedman, Frieda .... New York, NY
Freedman, Gary A. .... Santa Monica, CA
Freedman, Gary B. .... Philadelphia, PA
Freedman, Gary J., (P.C.)
Beverly Hills, CA
Freedman, Gary, Law Offices of
Santa Monica, CA
Freedman, Gary M. .... Miami, FL
Freedman, Gerald A. .... Oak Park, MI
Freedman, Gerald M. .... New York, NY
Freedman, Gilbert P. .... Chicago, IL
Freedman, Helen E. .... New York, NY
Freedman, Henry A. .... New York, NY
Freedman, Herbert D. .... New York, NY
Freedman, Horace N. .... Culver City, CA
Freedman, Howard A. .... White Plains, NY
Freedman, Howard J. .... Chagrin Falls, OH
Freedman, Ira A. .... New York, NY
Freedman, Irving B. .... New York, NY
Freedman, Irving M. .... Chapel Hill, NC
Freedman, Irving S. .... New York, NY
Freedman, Jack E. .... Los Angeles, CA
Freedman, Jack M. .... Indianapolis, IN
Freedman, James D. .... Bedford, MA
Freedman, James J. .... Washington, DC
Freedman, James S. .... Phoenix, AZ
Freedman, Jay .... Boston, MA
Freedman, Jay B. .... Newport Beach, CA
Freedman, Jay W. .... Washington, DC
Freedman, Jeffrey A. .... Tampa, FL
Freedman, Jeffrey Alexander .... Landover, MD
Freedman, Jeffrey C. .... Los Angeles, CA
Freedman, Jeffrey H. .... Sacramento, CA
Freedman, Jeffrey H. .... San Diego, CA
Freedman, Jeffrey J. .... Princeton, NJ
Freedman, Jeffrey M. .... Boston, MA
Freedman, Jeffrey M. .... Buffalo, NY
Freedman, Jeffrey M. .... Philadelphia, PA
Freedman, Jennifer R. .... New York, NY
Freedman, Jerry L. .... Encino, CA
Freedman, Jerry L., Law Offices of
Los Angeles, CA
Freedman, Jerry L., Law Offices of
Sherman Oaks, CA
Freedman, Jessica B. .... Alexandria, VA
Freedman, Joel Andrew .... Atlanta, GA
Freedman, Joel E. .... Stamford, CT
Freedman, Joel F. .... Boston, MA
Freedman, Joel S. .... Boston, MA
Freedman, John A. .... Washington, DC
Freedman, Jon B. .... Fairfield, NJ
Freedman, Jonathan B. .... Cherry Hill, NJ
Freedman, Jonathan J. .... New York, NY
Freedman, Jonathan L. .... New York, NY
Freedman, Jonathan P. .... Denver, CO
Freedman, Jonathan R. .... Simsbury, CT
Freedman, Joseph .... Los Angeles, CA
Freedman, Joseph
Environmental Protection Agency, Office of the General Counsel, GV
Freedman, Karen J. .... New York, NY
Freedman, Karl .... Athens, GA
Freedman, Keith D. .... Rochester, NY
Freedman, Kenneth S. .... Northbrook, IL
Freedman, Krochmal & Goldin, P.C.
Southfield, MI
Freedman, Larry S. .... Chicago, IL
Freedman, Laura .... Sacramento, CA
Freedman, Laurence J.
Department of Justice, Civil Division, GV
Freedman, Lawrence .... New York, NY
Freedman, Lawrence M. .... Chicago, IL
Freedman, Lawrence R. .... Washington, DC
Freedman, Lee J. .... Department of Justice, Civil Rights Division, GV
Freedman, Leland S. .... Cleveland, OH
Freedman, Leo .... Pasadena, TX
Freedman, Leonard L. .... Panorama City, CA
Freedman, Leonard S. .... Baltimore, MD
Freedman, Leora D. .... Santa Monica, CA
Freedman, Levy, Kroll & Simonds
Washington, DC
Freedman, Lewis A. .... Atlanta, GA
Freedman, Linn Foster .... Providence, RI
Freedman, Lisa Snyder .... Elizabethtown, NC
Freedman, Lori H. .... Cambridge, MA
Freedman and Lorry, A Professional Corporation .... Haddonfield, NJ
Freedman, Louis S. .... Naperville, IL
Freedman, Lynn P. .... Dobbs Ferry, NY
Freedman, Marc D. .... Ramsey, NJ
Freedman, Marcia Stander
Mount Laurel, NJ
Freedman, Margo E. .... Los Angeles, CA
Freedman, Mark Franklin .... Ithaca, NY
Freedman, Mark H. .... Pontiac, MI
Freedman, Marshall S. .... Woodland Hills, CA
Freedman, Martin .... Bronx, NY
Freedman, Martin B.
North Miami Beach, FL
Freedman, Marvin A. .... Southfield, MI
Freedman, Marvin S. .... Santa Monica, CA
Freedman, Maryann Saccomando
Buffalo, NY
Freedman & McClosky, P.A.
Fort Lauderdale, FL
Freedman, Melissa L. .... New York, NY
Freedman, Michael A. .... Glen Burnie, MD
Owings Mills, MD
Freedman, Michael A., P.A., Law Offices of
Glen Burnie, MD
Owings Mills, MD
Freedman, Michael E. .... San Francisco, CA
Freedman, Michael H. .... Washington, DC
Freedman, Michael H. .... New York, NY
Freedman, Michael J. .... Tampa, FL
Freedman, Michael J., P.A. .... Tampa, FL
Freedman, Milton L. .... New York, NY
Freedman, Miriam K. .... Boston, MA
Freedman, Mitchell J. .... Camarillo, CA
Freedman, Monroe H. .... Hempstead, NY
Freedman, Morton .... North Adams, MA
Freedman, Nanci Wolf .... Bingham Farms, MI
Freedman, Nancy A. .... New Brunswick, NJ
Freedman, Nancy M. .... Philadelphia, PA
Freedman, Nancy Richards
Santa Monica, CA
Freedman, Neil H. .... Los Angeles, CA
Freedman, Norman P. .... Jacksonville, FL
Freedman, Norman P., P.A. .... Jacksonville, FL
Freedman, Norton A. .... Norristown, PA
Freedman, Norton A., P.C. .... Norristown, PA
Freedman & Paris, Inc. .... Salisbury, NC
Freedman, Paul .... Miami, FL
Freedman, Paul L. .... New York, NY
Freedman, Perry D. .... Mount Kisco, NY
Freedman, Perry Dean .... Mount Kisco, NY
Freedman, Philip .... New York, NY
Freedman, Philip M. .... Newark, NJ
Freedman, Rachel L. .... New York, NY
Freedman, Randall L. .... Dallas, TX
Freedman, Randy R. .... Fort Lauderdale, FL
Freedman, Richard A. .... Boston, MA
Freedman, Richard A. .... Westbury, NY
Freedman, Richard E. .... Chicago, IL
Freedman, Richard L. .... Fort Lauderdale, FL
Freedman, Richard L. .... Collingswood, NJ
Freedman, Richard P. .... Cherry Hill, NJ
Woodbury, NJ
Freedman, Rick, and Associates, P.A.
Miami, FL
Freedman, Robert .... New York, NY
Freedman, Robert .... Philadelphia, PA
Freedman, Robert A. .... Palo Alto, CA
Freedman, Robert A. .... New York, NY
Freedman, Robert B. .... Oakland, CA
Freedman, Robert I. .... New York, NY
Freedman, Robert L. .... Philadelphia, PA
Freedman, Robert L., (P.C.)
Washington, DC
Freedman, Robert M. .... Los Angeles, CA
Freedman, Robert M. .... New York, NY
Freedman, Robert, (P.C.) .... Boston, MA
Freedman, Robert S. .... Tampa, FL
Freedman, Robert W. .... Maple Shade, NJ
Freedman, Roberta, (P.C.)
Washington, DC
Freedman, Robin L. .... New York, NY
Freedman, Robt. P. .... Buffalo, NY
Freedman, Robyn .... San Francisco, CA
Freedman, Sanford A. .... Miami, FL
Freedman, Scott Alan .... Sherman Oaks, CA
Freedman, Scott C. .... Minneapolis, MN
Freedman, Scott J. .... Philadelphia, PA
Freedman, Seth .... Houston, TX
Freedman, Sharri B. .... Rockville, MD
Upper Marlboro, MD
Freedman, Sheldon .... New York, NY
Freedman, Simon J. .... Encinitas, CA
Freedman & Sinowski, A Professional Corporation .... Atlanta, GA
Freedman, Sol .... Rockville Centre, NY
Freedman, Solomon J. .... New York, NY
Freedman, Stanley F., (P.C.) .... Denver, CO
Freedman, Stanley S. .... Stoughton, MA
Freedman, Stephen
National Labor Relations Board, Office of the General Counsel, GV
Freedman, Stephen C. .... Fayetteville, NC
Freedman, Steve F. .... Atlanta, GA
Freedman, Steven L. .... Syosset, NY
Freedman, Stuart D. .... New York, NY
Freedman, Stuart G. .... Detroit, MI
Southfield, MI
Freedman, Stuart J. .... Somerville, NJ
Freedman, Susan .... Stamford, CT
White Plains, NY
Freedman, Susan C. .... Hartford, CT
Freedman, Susan M. .... Los Angeles, CA
Freedman, Susan Rae .... Philadelphia, PA
Freedman, Sylvia L. .... Aberdeen, NJ
Freedman & Taitelman, LLP
Los Angeles, CA
Freedman, Terri Jane .... Roseland, NJ
Freedman, Terry S. .... Atlanta, GA
Freedman, Theodore L. .... Westport, CT
Freedman, Theodore L. .... New York, NY
Freedman, Thomas J. .... Boston, MA
Freedman, Thomas L.
Executive Office Of The President, Office of Policy Development, GV
Freedman, Thomas T., Jr. .... New York, NY
Freedman, Wagner, Tabakman & Weiss
New City, NY
Freedman, Walter .... Washington, DC
Freedman, Warren .... Palm Beach Gardens, FL
Freedman, Wendy C. .... Los Angeles, CA
Freedman, Wendy L. .... New York, NY
Freedman, William .... Philadelphia, PA
Freedman, William D. .... Washington, DC
Freedman, William D. .... New York, NY
Freedman, William E. .... Las Vegas, NV
Freedman, William E., Chartered
Las Vegas, NV
Freedman, William H. .... Los Angeles, CA
Freedman, William M. .... Cincinnati, OH
Freedom, John G. .... Columbus, OH
Freedus, Eric B. .... San Diego, CA
Freedy, Barbara L. .... Winston-Salem, NC
Freefield, Brent Stewart .... Dallas, TX
Freeh, Louis J. .... Department of Justice, Federal Bureau of Investigation, GV
Freehill, George B. .... New York, NY
Freehill Hogan & Mahar .... Stamford, CT
Newark, NJ
Freehill Hogan & Mahar LLP .... Bronx, NY
Brooklyn, NY
New York, NY
White Plains, NY
Freehill, John A. .... Chenoa, IL
Pontiac, IL
Freehling, Paul E. .... Chicago, IL
Freehling, Robert J. .... Boynton Beach, FL
Freehling, Thomas A. .... Hollywood, FL
Freek, William S. .... Belvidere, IL
Freel, Bryan J. .... Chicago, IL
Freel, David E. .... Columbus, OH
Freel & Freel, P.C. .... East Tawas, MI
Freel, John M. .... East Tawas, MI
Freel, Mark W. .... Providence, RI
Freel, Stacy S. .... Chicago, IL
Freel, Timothy R. .... East Tawas, MI
Freeland, Alan C., (Professional Corporation) .... San Francisco, CA
Freeland, Byron L. .... Little Rock, AR
Freeland, C. Joe .... Austin, TX
Freeland, Charles .... Lutherville, MD
Freeland, Charles E. .... Broomfield, CO
Freeland, Charles M. .... Carmel, IN
Freeland, Charles, P.C. .... Lutherville, MD
Freeland Cooper LeHocky & Hamburg, A Professional Corporation
San Francisco, CA
Freeland, Cynthia A. .... San Diego, CA
Freeland, Daniel L. .... Highland, IN
Freeland, Edward M. .... Troy, MI
Freeland, Eric A. .... Chicago, IL
Freeland & Freeland .... Oxford, MS
Freeland, J. Hale .... Oxford, MS
Freeland, James J. .... West Palm Beach, FL
Freeland, James K. .... New Smyrna Beach, FL
Freeland, James K., P.A.
New Smyrna Beach, FL
Freeland, James Walter, Jr. .... Somerville, TN
Freeland, Jeanne A. .... Orange, CA
Freeland, John D. .... Modesto, CA
Freeland, John R. .... McAllen, TX
Freeland, Jorge L. .... Miami, FL
Freeland, Joseph S. .... Paducah, KY
Freeland, Kate Clair .... San Francisco, CA
Freeland & Kronz .... Pittsburgh, PA
Freeland, Mark .... McAllen, TX
Freeland, Meadows & Crabb .... McAllen, TX
Freeland, Michael M. .... San Diego, CA
Freeland, Michael W. .... Bala Cynwyd, PA
Freeland, Ralph L., Jr. .... Menlo Park, CA
Freeland, Rebecca Lynn .... Cumberland, MD
Freeland, Richard R. .... San Diego, CA
Freeland, Robin Page .... Lancaster, SC
Freeland, Rusty W. .... Champaign, IL
Freeland, Samuel Lyles .... Easton, MD
Freeland, Scott A. .... Camp Hill, PA
Freeland, Stephen T. .... Dallas, TX
Freeland, Stuart T. .... Boston, MA
Freeland, T. H., III .... Oxford, MS
Freeland, T. H., IV .... Oxford, MS
Freeland, Timothy A. .... Tampa, FL
Freeland, Verne L. .... Miami, FL
Freeland, Wendell G. .... Pittsburgh, PA
Freeley, Austin J. .... Boston, MA
Freeley & Freeley .... Boston, MA
Freeley, James F., III .... Boston, MA
Freeley, James F., Jr. .... Boston, MA
Freelin, Jason J. .... Reno, NV
Freeling, Kenneth A. .... New York, NY
Freels, Jesse S. (Sandy), Jr. .... Sherman, TX
Freels, John A., (P.C.) .... Lubbock, TX
Freels & Johnston, P.C. .... Sherman, TX
Freemal, Beth .... Chicago, IL
Freeman, A. D., A Law Corporation
New Orleans, LA
Freeman, A. D. .... New Orleans, LA
Freeman, Alan M. .... Washington, DC
Freeman, Alan M. .... Paramus, NJ
Freeman, Alan P. .... Corona Del Mar, CA
Freeman, Alan S. .... Ventura, CA
Freeman, Allen A. .... Chicago, IL
Freeman & Alton, Ltd. .... Minneapolis, MN
Freeman, Alvin L. .... Houston, TX
Freeman, Alvin L., P.C. .... Houston, TX
Freeman, Andrea L. .... South Orange, NJ
Freeman, Andrea Michele .... Novato, CA
Freeman, Andrew D. .... Baltimore, MD
Freeman, Andrew J. .... San Diego, CA
Freeman, Andrew L. .... Windsor, CT
Freeman, Angela R. .... Tulsa, OK
Freeman, Antoinette R. .... Seattle, WA
Freeman, Arthur S. .... Chicago, IL
Freeman Associates .... Marion, VA
Freeman, Barbara .... Hillsborough, CA
Freeman, Barry D. .... Corbin, KY
Freeman, Barry J. .... Highland Park, IL
Freeman, Barry V. .... Los Angeles, CA
Freeman, Barry Y. .... Southfield, MI
Cleveland, OH
Freeman, Barton & Huber, P.A.
Haddonfield, NJ
Freeman, Barton J. .... Dallas, TX
Freeman, Basil J. .... Cocoa, FL
Freeman & Bass, P.A. .... Newark, NJ
Freeman, Ben R. .... Greenville, GA
Freeman, Berkley I., Jr. .... Louisville, CO
Freeman & Berthelsen .... Fairfax, VA

Freeman, Bettye C. ... Boston, MA
Freeman, Beverly Lynne ... Anchorage, AK
Freeman, Bobby L. ... Palestine, TX
Freeman, Bonnie ... Pasadena, CA
Freeman, Bonnie A. ... Santa Rosa, CA
Freeman, Bonnie E. ... Bethesda, MD
Freeman, Bonnie L. Earley
St. Petersburg, FL
Freeman, Brad ... Denton, TX
Flower Mound, TX
Freeman, Brad ... Lewisville, TX
Freeman, Brad C. ... Williamsburg, KY
Freeman, Bradley T. ... Elgin, IL
Freeman, Brandon W. ... Austin, TX
Freeman, Brenda R. ... New Braunfels, TX
Freeman, Brian A. ... Columbus, OH
Freeman, Brian C. ... South Orange, NJ
Freeman, Brian C. S. ... Hartford, CT
Freeman, Brian J. ... Gresham, OR
Freeman, Brien G. ... Corbin, KY
Freeman, Bruce F. ... Rochester, NY
Freeman, Bruce L. ... Charleston, WV
Freeman, Bruce W. ... Tulsa, OK
Freeman, Bryan N. ... Las Vegas, NV
Freeman, Burton M. ... New York, NY
Freeman, Butterman, Haber & Rojas, LLP
Miami, FL
Freeman, Carol A. H. ... Davenport, IA
Freeman, Carol Garfiel ... Rockville, MD
Freeman, Carol R. ... Palo Alto, CA
Freeman, Carolyn B. ... Orlando, FL
Freeman, Carolyn D. ... Denville, NJ
Freeman, Carrie L. ... Tampa, FL
Freeman, Carroll P. ... Lynchburg, VA
Freeman & Castillon ... Laredo, TX
Freeman, Charles ... Houston, TX
Freeman, Charles A. ... Chicago, IL
Freeman, Charles C. ... New York, NY
Freeman, Charles E. ... Chicago, IL
Freeman, Charles E. ... Springfield, VA
Freeman, Charles W. ... Boston, MA
Freeman, Cherylyn ... Washington, DC
Freeman, Chester T. ... Columbus, OH
Freeman, Chester T., Co., L.P.A.
Columbus, OH
Freeman & Chiartas ... Charleston, WV
Freeman, Christine A. ... Nashville, TN
Freeman, Christopher ... North Canton, OH
Freeman, Christopher Dewayne
Dallas, TX
Freeman, Claude C. ... Lubbock, TX
Freeman, Claude H. ... Des Moines, IA
Freeman, Claude Q., Jr. ... Charlotte, NC
Freeman, Clifford M. ... Brookline, MA
Freeman, Clifton M. ... Dallas, TX
Freeman & Connor ... Baltimore, MD
Freeman and Copeland ... Corbin, KY
Williamsburg, KY
Freeman, Corrine M. ... Irvine, CA
Freeman, Craig E. ... New York, NY
Freeman, Craig M. ... Baton Rouge, LA
Freeman, Cyndilee ... New York, NY
Freeman, D. Reed, Jr. ... Washington, DC
Freeman & D'Aiuto, A Professional Law Corporation ... Stockton, CA
Freeman, Dale C. ... San Francisco, CA
Freeman, Dale S. ... San Francisco, CA
Freeman, Daniel A. ... New York, NY
Freeman, Daniel M.
House of Representatives, Committee Legal Personnel, GV
Freeman, Darlene M.
Department of Transportation, Federal Aviation Administration, GV
Freeman, David B. ... Westland, MI
Freeman, David B. ... Greensburg, PA
Freeman, David F. ... Arcadia, CA
Freeman, David F., Jr. ... Washington, DC
Freeman, David H. ... Syracuse, NY
Freeman, David J. ... Bolingbrook, IL
Freeman, David J. ... New York, NY
Freeman, David J. ... White Plains, NY
Freeman, David L. ... Columbus, OH
Freeman, David L. ... Greenville, SC
Freeman, David M. ... Anchorage, AK
Freeman, David M. ... Livingston, NJ
Freeman, David M. ... Philadelphia, PA
Freeman, David R. ... St. Louis, MO
Freeman, David R. ... Austin, TX
Freeman, Deborah A. ... San Francisco, CA
Freeman, Deborah K. ... Naperville, IL
Freeman, Deborah L. ... Denver, CO
Freeman, Deborah Samuels ... Hartford, CT
Freeman, Debra ... New York, NY
Freeman, Debra ... New York, NY
Freeman, Dennis B., (P.A.) ... Miami, FL
Freeman, Dianne C. ... Torrance, CA
Freeman, Don C. ... Forestville, MD
Freeman, Don C. ... Tryon, NC
Freeman, Donald B. ... Jacksonville, FL
Freeman, Donald E. ... Hartford, CT
Freeman, Donald G. ... Carmel, CA
Freeman, Donald J.
West Palm Beach, FL
Freeman, Donald J., P.A.
West Palm Beach, FL
Freeman, Donald R. ... Flint, MI
Freeman, Douglas C. ... Montgomery, AL
Freeman, Douglas C. ... New York, NY
Freeman, Douglas K. ... Irvine, CA
Los Angeles, CA
Freeman, Douglas S. ... Billings, MT
Freeman, Douglas Y. ... Billings, MT
Freeman & Downing, P.C. ... Gresham, OR
Freeman, Dunn, Sweeney & Alexander, A Professional Corporation ... Lynchburg, VA
Freeman, Edgar A. ... Santa Ana, CA
Freeman, Edward C. ... Knoxville, TN

Freeman, Edward J. ... White Plains, NY
Freeman, Edward P. ... High Bridge, NJ
Freeman, Edwin M. ... Larchmont, NY
Freeman, Elizabeth K. ... Raleigh, NC
Freeman, Ellyn ... Brooklyn, NY
Freeman, Emery C. ... East Lansing, MI
Freeman, Eric J. ... Boston, MA
Freeman, Eric O. ... Las Vegas, NV
Freeman, Fleet ... Mount Pleasant, SC
Freeman, Florence E. ... Gloucester, MA
Freeman Forrest & Levy LLP
New York, NY
Freeman, Frank E. ... Miami, FL
Freeman, Frank E. ... Houston, TX
Freeman, Franklin I. ... Baltimore, MD
Freeman, Fred M., Jr. ... Birmingham, AL
Freeman, Fred W. ... Detroit, MI
Freeman, Frederick R. ... Kansas City, MO
Freeman & Freeman ... Encino, CA
Freeman & Freeman ... Woodland Hills, CA
Freeman & Freeman ... St. Petersburg, FL
Freeman & Freeman ... Chicago, IL
Freeman & Freeman ... Brookline, MA
Freeman and Freeman ... Norwalk, OH
Freeman & Freeman ... Mount Pleasant, SC
Freeman, Freeman & Associates, P.C.
Wheaton, IL
Freeman, Freeman & Salzman, P.C.
Chicago, IL
Freeman, Freeman & Smiley, LLP
Irvine, CA
Los Angeles, CA
San Francisco, CA
Freeman, G. Kyle ... Henderson, TX
Freeman, Gail S. ... Chicago, IL
Freeman & Galie ... San Francisco, CA
Freeman, Gary C. ... Houston, TX
Freeman, Gary Michael ... Houston, TX
Freeman, Gary S. ... Washington, DC
Freeman, George ... New York, NY
Freeman, George C., III
New Orleans, LA
Freeman, George C., III ... Richmond, VA
Freeman, George Clemon, Jr.
Washington, DC
Richmond, VA
Freeman, George J. ... Mount Clemens, MI
Freeman, George K., Jr. ... Wilmington, NC
Freeman, George L., Jr. ... Fairfax, VA
Freeman, George T. ... Anchorage, AK
Freeman, Gerald R. ... Minneapolis, MN
Freeman, Geraldine A.
San Francisco, CA
Freeman and Gertner, P.C.
South Orange, NJ
Freeman, Gill Sherryl ... Miami, FL
Freeman, Glenda D. ... Birmingham, AL
Freeman, Glynna W. ... Chicago, IL
Freeman, Gregg D. ... Los Angeles, CA
Freeman, Gregory C. ... Bloomfield, CT
Freeman, Grover C. ... Tampa, FL
Freeman, Gwen ... Glendale, CA
Freeman, H. Crowell, Jr. ... Boston, MA
Freeman & Hankins, L.L.P. ... Palestine, TX
Freeman, Harold J. ... Norwalk, OH
Freeman, Harold S. ... Cincinnati, OH
Freeman, Harris ... Greenfield, MA
Freeman & Hawkins ... Atlanta, GA
Freeman, Helene M. ... New York, NY
Freeman, Henry ... Millburn, NJ
Freeman, Herbert E. ... Cincinnati, OH
Freeman, Homa J., Jr. ... Durham, NC
Freeman, Howard ... Hillsborough, NJ
Freeman, Howard S. ... Oklahoma City, OK
Freeman, Hunter & Malloy ... Tampa, FL
Freeman, Ian W. ... San Francisco, CA
Freeman, Isaac St. C. ... Marion, VA
Freeman, J. Fletcher ... Dallas, TX
Freeman, J Rudy, II ... Los Angeles, CA
Freeman, Jack L. ... Edmond, OK
Freeman, Jamelyn E. ... Warsaw, IN
Freeman, James A., III ... Nashville, TN
Freeman, James Andrew ... Houston, TX
Freeman, James C. ... Mineola, NY
New York, NY
White Plains, NY
Freeman, James E. ... Lubbock, TX
Freeman, James E., Jr. ... Anderson, IN
Freeman, James F., III ... Kansas City, MO
Freeman, James H. ... Blue Bell, PA
Freeman, James J. ... Washington, DC
Freeman, James J., Jr. ... New City, NY
Freeman, James N., Jr. ... Charlotte, NC
Freeman, James R. ... Tampa, FL
Freeman, James R. ... Phoenixville, PA
Freeman, James R., II ... Los Angeles, CA
Freeman, James T. ... Sacramento, CA
Freeman, James W. ... Lexington, KY
Freeman, James W. ... Coshocton, OH
Freeman, Jane E. ... Colorado Springs, CO
Freeman, Jane W. ... New London, CT
Freeman, Janette ... Evanston, IL
Freeman, Janice W. ... Wheaton, IL
Freeman, Jay M. ... Englewood, CO
Freeman, Jayne L. ... Seattle, WA
Freeman, Jeanine M. ... West Des Moines, IA
Freeman, Jeannette E. ... Atlanta, GA
Freeman, Jed S. ... Roseland, NJ
Freeman, Jeffrey L. ... Jeffersonville, IN
Freeman & Jenner, P.C. ... Aspen, CO
Washington, DC
Rockville, MD
Freeman, Jennifer ... New York, NY
Freeman, Jo, (Mr.) ... Brooklyn, NY
Freeman, Joe C. ... Newton, MA
Freeman, Joe C., & Associates, A Professional Corporation ... Newton, MA
Freeman, Joe C., Jr. ... Atlanta, GA

Freeman, John A. ... Cincinnati, OH
Freeman, John C. ... Chicago, IL
Freeman, John D. ... Stamford, CT
Freeman, John E." Ric ", Law Offices of
Tyler, TX
Freeman, John Edward ... Tampa, FL
Freeman, John F. ... Detroit, MI
Freeman, John J. ... Chicago, IL
Freeman, John L. ... New York, NY
Freeman, John L. ... Dallas, TX
Freeman, John M. ... Houston, TX
Freeman, John N. ... Phoenix, AZ
Freeman, John P. ... Columbia, SC
Freeman, John R., Jr. ... Omaha, NE
Freeman, John S. ... Charlotte, NC
Freeman, John S. ... Wyndmoor, PA
Freeman, John T. ... Minneapolis, MN
Freeman, John V. ... Shelbyville, IL
Freeman, John W. ... Boston, MA
Freeman, Jonathan B. ... Dayton, OH
Freeman, Joseph A. ... Charleston, WV
Freeman, Joseph M. ... Los Angeles, CA
Freeman, Joseph M. ... Atlanta, GA
Freeman, Joseph W., Jr. ... Elkin, NC
Freeman, Judd ... Grand Rapids, MI
Freeman, Judson, Jr. ... Jacksonville, FL
Freeman, Judy Anne ... Ashland, KY
Freeman, Judy B. ... Berkeley, CA
Freeman, Karen M. ... San Diego, CA
Freeman, Karen P. ... Houston, TX
Freeman, Karin E. ... Los Angeles, CA
Freeman, Katherine Lynn ... Atlanta, GA
Freeman, Kathleen J. ... Framingham, MA
Freeman, Kelly A. ... Mount Clemens, MI
Freeman, Kenneth D. ... New York, NY
Freeman, Kenneth D. ... Bensalem, PA
Freeman, Kenneth J. ... Cleveland, OH
Freeman, Kenneth L. ... San Francisco, CA
Freeman, Kerry McInerney ... Oakland, CA
Freeman, Kevin C. ... Cleveland, OH
Freeman, Kevin L. ... Chicago, IL
Freeman, Kevin Patrick ... Oklahoma City, OK
Freeman, Kirk B. ... San Francisco, CA
Freeman, Kristy D. ... Dallas, TX
Freeman, Kyle F. ... Tulsa, OK
Freeman, Laura ... Pound Ridge, NY
Freeman, Lauren E. ... Washington, DC
Freeman Law Firm, The ... Billings, MT
Freeman, Lawrence P. ... Encino, CA
Freeman, Lee A., & Associates
Woodland Hills, CA
Freeman, Lee A., Jr. ... Chicago, IL
Freeman, Leo ... Washington, DC
Freeman, Lesley G. ... Los Angeles, CA
Freeman, Leslie V. ... Kirkwood, MO
Freeman, Lewis B. ... Miami, FL
Freeman, Linda S. ... San Diego, CA
Santa Ana, CA
Freeman, Lindsay C. ... San Francisco, CA
Freeman, Linnie A. ... Houston, TX
Freeman, Lisa D. ... Chicago, IL
Freeman, Loftus & Manley ... New City, NY
Freeman, Lorey Huber ... Portland, OR
Freeman, Lori Elison ... Billings, MT
Freeman, Louis J. ... Oklahoma City, OK
Freeman, Louis M. ... New York, NY
Freeman, Louis S. ... Chicago, IL
Freeman, Lynda J. ... Chicago, IL
Freeman, Lynne ... Anchorage, AK
Freeman, Malik Dantala ... Los Angeles, CA
Freeman, Maranda J. ... Raleigh, NC
Freeman, Marcie J. ... Dallas, TX
Freeman, Margaret A. ... Shrewsbury, NJ
Freeman, Marilyn K., Law Offices of
San Marcos, CA
Freeman, Mark ... Beaumont, TX
Freeman, Mark Allan ... Rockville, MD
Freeman, Mark D. ... Miami, FL
Freeman, Mark J. ... Fayetteville, AR
Freeman, Mark J. ... Minneapolis, MN
Freeman, Mark M. ... Boston, MA
Freeman, Mark S. ... Meridian, ID
Freeman, Mark T. ... Cleveland, OH
Freeman, Mark T. ... Nashville, TN
Freeman, Marsha A. ... Minneapolis, MN
Freeman, Marsha Bahl ... St. Petersburg, FL
Freeman, Martin H. ... Aspen, CO
Washington, DC
Rockville, MD
Freeman, Martin J. ... Beverly, MA
Freeman, Martin M.
Department of Commerce, National Oceanic and Atmospheric Administration, GV
Freeman, Marvin G. ... Chicago, IL
Freeman, Mary A. ... Pasadena, CA
Freeman Mathis & Gary, LLP
Atlanta, GA
Decatur, GA
Douglasville, GA
Marietta, GA
Freeman, Matthew J. ... Boise, ID
Freeman, Max E., II ... Dallas, TX
Freeman, Max H. ... Memphis, TN
Freeman, Maxwell M. ... Stockton, CA
Freeman McKenzie, A Professional Corporation ... Mount Clemens, MI
Freeman, M.E. ... New York, NY
Freeman, Melvyn ... New York, NY
Freeman, Mermall & Tubman
Chicago, IL
Freeman, Michael A. ... New York, NY
Freeman, Michael B. ... Greenville, SC
Freeman, Michael D. ... Birmingham, AL
Freeman, Michael D. ... San Jose, CA
Freeman, Michael E. ... Milwaukee, WI
Freeman, Michael H. ... Newark, NJ
Freeman, Michael H. ... Tulsa, OK

Freeman, Michael I. ... Chicago, IL
Freeman, Michael J. ... Miami, FL
Freeman, Michael J. ... Chicago, IL
Freeman, Michael J., P.A. ... Miami, FL
Freeman, Michael L. ... Phoenix, AZ
Freeman, Michael L. ... Troy, MI
Freeman, Michael M. ... New York, NY
Freeman, Michael O. ... Minneapolis, MN
Freeman, Michael S. ... Denver, CO
Freeman, Michelle A. ... New Haven, CT
Freeman, Milton V. ... Washington, DC
Freeman & Mintz, P.A. ... Haddonfield, NJ
Freeman, Monroe E., Jr.
Department of Defense, Armed Services Board of Contract Appeals, GV
Freeman, Nancy S. ... Winter Park, FL
Freeman, Nancy S. ... Haddonfield, NJ
Freeman, Natalie J.
Agency for International Development, Legal Advisers-Overseas, GV
Freeman, Neil M. ... Washington, DC
Freeman, Nicholas D. ... Orlando, FL
Freeman, Nooter & Ginsberg
New York, NY
Freeman, Nora L. ... New York, NY
Freeman, Norman R., II ... Tucson, AZ
Freeman, Norman R., II, P.C. ... Tucson, AZ
Freeman, Orville L. ... Washington, DC
Freeman, P. John ... Rock Hill, SC
Freeman, Palmer ... Columbia, SC
Freeman, Pamela S. ... Brookline, MA
Freeman, Patricia A. ... Jacksonville, FL
Freeman, Patrick O., Jr. ... Thayer, MO
Freeman, Paul H. ... Hialeah, FL
Freeman, Paul M. ... Hudson, NY
Freeman, Paul Wesley, Jr. ... Wilkesboro, NC
Freeman, Paula G. ... Houston, TX
Freeman, Peter B. ... Chicago, IL
Freeman, Peter C. ... Santa Ana, CA
Freeman, Peter L. ... Boston, MA
Freeman, Philip D. ... San Antonio, TX
Freeman, Phyllis K. ... Boston, MA
Freeman & Price, P.C. ... Houston, TX
Freeman, R. Bruce ... Westfield, NJ
Freeman, R. Jack ... Tulsa, OK
Freeman, R. Parrish, Jr.
Salt Lake City, UT
Freeman, Rebecca Jane ... Santa Rosa, CA
Freeman, Regina Gay Slaton ... Checotah, OK
Freeman, Render Crayton ... Atlanta, GA
Freeman, Richard B. ... Atlanta, GA
Freeman, Richard B., P.C. ... Atlanta, GA
Freeman, Richard C. ... Atlanta, GA
Freeman, Richard C., III, P.C. ... Atlanta, GA
Freeman, Richard C., III, P.C. ... Atlanta, GA
Freeman, Richard D. ... Los Angeles, CA
Freeman, Richard G. ... Lakewood, CO
Freeman, Richard H. ... Brooklyn, NY
Melville, NY
Freeman, Richard L. ... Chicago, IL
Freeman, Richard M. ... Diablo, CA
Freeman, Richard M. ... San Diego, CA
Freeman, Richard M. ... New Haven, CT
Freeman, Richard M. ... Knoxville, TN
Freeman, Richard R. ... Jacksonville, IL
Freeman, Richard S. ... Des Moines, IA
Freeman, Richard S. ... Circle Pines, MN
Freeman, Richard W., Jr. ... Santa Rosa, CA
Freeman, Richard W., Jr.
Oklahoma City, OK
Freeman, Richard W., Jr., P.C.
Santa Rosa, CA
Freeman, Richard W., Sr.
Oklahoma City, OK
Freeman, Rick ... Austin, TX
Freeman & Ritchie ... Las Vegas, NV
Freeman, Robert ... Pueblo, CO
Freeman, Robert A. ... Miami, FL
Freeman, Robert A. ... Boston, MA
Freeman, Robert A., III ... Asheville, NC
Freeman, Robert A., P.A. ... Miami, FL
Freeman, Robert E. ... New York, NY
Freeman, Robert J. ... Albany, NY
Freeman, Robert L. ... San Diego, CA
Freeman, Robert L. ... Omaha, NE
Freeman, Robert L., Jr. ... Los Angeles, CA
Freeman, Robert M. ... New York, NY
Freeman, Robert N., II ... Laredo, TX
Freeman, Robert O. ... Jacksonville, FL
Freeman, Robert P. ... Chicago, IL
Freeman, Robert P. ... Chicago, IL
Freeman, Robert P. ... Providence, RI
Freeman, Robert W., Jr. ... Las Vegas, NV
Freeman, Robin F. ... Tallahassee, FL
Freeman, Robin R. ... Springfield, OH
Freeman, Rodney, Jr. ... Huron, SD
Freeman, Roger L. ... Denver, CO
Freeman, Rogers & Loev, P.C.
Blue Bell, PA
Norristown, PA
Freeman, Ronald H. ... Norwalk, OH
Freeman, Ronald J., Law Offices of
Austin, TX
Freeman, Ronald J., P.C. ... Covington, GA
Freeman, Ronald W. ... New York, NY
Freeman, Ronald W., P.C. ... New York, NY
Freeman, Roosevelt H. ... Atlanta, GA
Freeman, Roxane J. ... Portland, OR
Freeman, Ruby Norris ... Alexandria, LA
Freeman, Russell A. ... Los Angeles, CA
Freeman, Russell E. ... Goodlettsville, TN
Freeman, Russell F. ... Fargo, ND
Freeman, S. Kay ... Jackson, MS
Freeman, Saml. H. ... New York, NY
Freeman, Samuel F., II ... Springfield, MO
Freeman, Samuel R. ... Denver, CO
Freeman, Sandra L. ... St. Louis, MO

Freeman, Scott Day ... Las Vegas, NV
Freeman, Scott M. ... New York, NY
Freeman, Scott N., Law Offices of ... Reno, NV
Freeman, Seth ... Forest Hills, NY
Freeman, Shannan L. ... Atlanta, GA
Freeman, Sharon L. ... Succasunna, NJ
Freeman, Shelly L. ... Kansas City, MO
Freeman, Shelton L. ... Phoenix, AZ
Freeman, Sherri Tucker ... Birmingham, AL
Freeman, Sheryl Schaffner ... Sacramento, CA
Freeman, Sidney N. ... Uniontown, OH
Freeman, Southgate B., III ... Cody, WY
Freeman, Stacy G. ... Atlanta, GA
Freeman, Stan ... Woodland Hills, CA
Freeman, Stanley A. ... Washington, DC
Freeman, Stanley E. ... Champaign, IL
Freeman, Stanley G. ... Columbia, SC
Freeman, Stanton D. ... Haddonfield, NJ
Freeman, Stephan J. ... St. Petersburg, FL
Freeman, Stephanie ... New York, NY
Freeman, Stephen A. ... Miami, FL
Freeman, Stephen T. ... Newport Beach, CA
Freeman, Steven A. ... Tarzana, CA
Freeman, Steven D. ... Chicago, IL
Freeman, Steven L. ... Minneapolis, MN
Freeman, Steven M. ... Woodland Hills, CA
Freeman, Steven M. ... New York, NY
Freeman, Steven R. ... Towson, MD
Freeman, Stewart H. ... Lansing, MI
Freeman, Stuart J. ... St. Petersburg, FL
Freeman & Supran, P.A. ... Palatka, FL
West Palm Beach, FL
Freeman, Susan H. ... San Jose, CA
Freeman, Susan M. ... Phoenix, AZ
Freeman, T. Ernest ... Houston, TX
Freeman, Terrence J. ... Barrington, IL
Freeman, Terri L. ... Morristown, NJ
Freeman, Terry ... Dallas, TX
Freeman, Terry E. ... Atlanta, GA
Freeman, Terry N. ... Palatka, FL
West Palm Beach, FL
Freeman, Thaddeus ... St. Petersburg, FL
Freeman, Theodore ... Atlanta, GA
Freeman, Theresa M. ... Waukegan, IL
Freeman, Thom J., III ... Bensenville, IL
Freeman, Thomas Brent ... Clearwater, FL
Freeman, Thomas G., II ... Charleston, WV
Freeman, Thomas G., Jr. ... Sanford, FL
Freeman, Thomas H. ... Norwalk, OH
Freeman, Thomas J. ... Lynnfield, MA
Freeman, Thomas J. ... Cleveland, OH
Freeman, Thomas M. ... Oakland, CA
Freeman, Thomas R. ... Los Angeles, CA
Freeman, Thomas R. ... Washington, DC
Freeman, Timothy D. ... Indianapolis, IN
Freeman, Todd I. ... Minneapolis, MN
Freeman, Tom M. ... San Francisco, CA
Freeman, V. Edward, II ... Bessemer, AL
Freeman, Valli ... San Jose, CA
Freeman, W. Franklin, Jr. ... Forsyth, GA
Freeman, Warren ... Delta, AL
Freeman, Wendi M. ... Mount Pleasant, SC
Freeman, Wilfred J. ... Ventura, CA
Freeman, William Adam ... Lexington, SC
Freeman, William B. ... Los Angeles, CA
Freeman, William E. ... Durham, NC
Freeman, William H. ... Riverside, CA
Freeman, William H. ... Winston-Salem, NC
Freeman, William Howell ... Myrtle Beach, SC
Freeman, William J. ... Birmingham, AL
Freeman, William M. ... San Bernardino, CA
Freeman, William M. ... Cashiers, NC
Freeman, William M., Jr. ... New York, NY
Freeman, William P. ... Haddonfield, NJ
Freeman, William S. ... Palo Alto, CA
Freeman, William T. ... Haddonfield, NJ
Freeman, Wm. Thomas, Jr. ... Wheaton, IL
Freeman, Wm. Tracy ... Houston, TX
Freeman, Wolfe & Greenbaum, P.A. ... Annapolis, MD
Baltimore, MD
Towson, MD
Freeman, Wright & Herman ... Atlanta, GA
Freeman-Burney, Melodie ... Tulsa, OK
Freeman-Caddy, Maureen ... Wahoo, NE
Freeman-Fisher, Berit R. ... New York, NY
Freeman-Gleason, Alison J. ... Seattle, WA
Freeman-Jones, Kathryn ... Glen Allen, VA
Freemann, Richard Z., Jr. ... Philadelphia, PA
Freemann, Scott B. ... Cherry Hill, NJ
Freeman-Wilson, Karen M. ... Gary, IN
Freemas, Ronald E. ... Media, PA
Freemon, Hillhouse & Huddleston ... Lawrenceburg, TN
Freemon, Howard P. ... Lawrenceburg, TN
Freemon, J. Daniel ... Lawrenceburg, TN
Freemon, Robert W. ... Waynesboro, TN
Freemon, Susan H. ... Tampa, FL
Freemond, Ronald H. ... Denver, CO
Freemyer, Allen D.
House of Representatives,
Committee on Resources, GV
Freemyer, Don ... Durango, CO
Freemyer, Howard R. ... Jayton, TX
Freemyer, James Edgar ... Denver, CO
Freemyers, Michele Renee ... Denver, CO
Freeney, Peggy Johnson ... Macon, GA
Freer, Alina M. ... Riverside, CA
Freer, Brant A. ... Detroit, MI
Freer, James G. ... Farmington, MO
Freer, R. Evelyn ... Frankfort, KY
Freer, Rob Walker ... Charlottesville, VA
Freer, Robert E., Jr. ... Washington, DC
Freer & Stevenson ... Farmington, MO
Freer, Todd D. ... Chicago, IL
Freerksen, Gregory N. ... Chicago, IL
Freerksen, Karl W., Jr. ... Hillsboro, OR
Freers, Steven G. ... Warren, MI
Frees, Barbara S. ... Wilton, CT
Frees, David M., III ... Malvern, PA
Phoenixville, PA
Frees, Karen E. ... Columbus, OH
Freese, Chris E. ... Sullivan, IL
Freese, Donald Ralph ... Edgewood, KY
Freese, James A. ... Stuart, FL
Freese, John E. ... DeLand, FL
Freese, John Markham ... Tulsa, OK
Freese, John P. ... Eureka, IL
Freese, Karen H., (P.C.) ... New Orleans, LA
Freese, Kristina Lynn ... Phoenix, AZ
Freese, L. Richard, Jr. ... Denver, CO
Freese, Lois A. Brodhead ... Edmonds, WA
Freese, Lurleen Y. ... Worthington, OH
Freese & March, P.A. ... Tulsa, OK
Freese, Michael Hunter ... Indianapolis, IN
Freese, Paul L. ... Los Angeles, CA
Freese, Paul L., Jr. ... Los Angeles, CA
Freese, Ralph I. ... Edmonds, WA
Freese, Ralph I., Inc., P.S. ... Edmonds, WA
Freese, Richard A. ... Birmingham, AL
Freese, Roger D. ... Clarence, IA
Freese, Scott D. ... Norfolk, NE
Freese, Tad J. ... San Francisco, CA
Freese, William G. ... Yorktown Heights, NY
Freesemann, Penny Haas ... Savannah, GA
Freese Souffront, Henry O. ... San Juan, PR
Freesman, Gordon S. ... Fort Lee, NJ
Freesman, Jacob ... Fort Lee, NJ
Freesman, Steven D. ... Fort Lee, NJ
Freeston, Margaret A. ... Washington, DC
Freestone, Amy R. ... Minneapolis, MN
Freestone, Dianne N. ... Clifton Park, NY
Freestone, Loren G. ... San Diego, CA
Freestone, Mitchell C. ... Boston, MA
Freestone, Wayne A., P.C.
Salt Lake City, UT
Freeswick, James R. ... Wayne, NJ
Freethy, Thomas J. ... Rockford, IL
Freethy, Thomas J., P.C. ... Rockford, IL
Freeto, Peterson & Scoll ... Newton, MA
Freeto, Robert P. ... Newton, MA
Freeze, Janet Gayle ... Baltimore, MD
Freeze, John L. ... Overland Park, KS
Freeze, Lawrence J., III ... Mineola, NY
Freeze, Mark E. ... Columbia, SC
Freeze, R. David ... Texarkana, AR
Freeze, Robert F. ... Timonium, MD
Freeze, Robert F., Jr. ... Baltimore, MD
Freeze, Stephen V. ... Dayton, OH
Freezman, Brad L. ... Trevose, PA
Frega, James J. ... Little Falls, NJ
Fregeau, Jason D. ... Yellow Springs, OH
Freger, Craig J. ... Miami, FL
Fregiato, Frank A. ... Bridgeport, OH
Fregolle, David E. ... Southfield, MI
Fregolle & Fregolle, P.C. ... Southfield, MI
Fregosi, Edward A. ... Rosedale, NY
Fregosi, Edward A., Jr. ... Massapequa, NY
Frehn, Jeffrey L. ... Tallahassee, FL
Frei, Donald F. ... Cincinnati, OH
Frei, Enrika L. ... Muskegon, MI
Frei, Frederick S. ... Washington, DC
Frei, Natalie ... Englewood, CO
Frei, Robert R. ... Chicago, IL
Frei, Steven M. ... Reston, VA
Freiberg, Albert M. ... Cincinnati, OH
Freiberg, Alvin ... Philadelphia, PA
Freiberg, Charles N. ... San Francisco, CA
Freiberg, Craig J. ... New York, NY
Freiberg, Donald H. ... San Jose, CA
Freiberg & Horn, Law Offices
Rapid City, SD
Freiberg, J. Walter, III ... Boston, MA
Freiberg, Jay W. ... New York, NY
Freiberg, Kenneth P.
Executive Office Of The President,
Office of the U.S. Trade Representative, GV
Freiberg, Louis K. ... Rapid City, SD
Freiberg, Margaret B. G. ... Armonk, NY
Freiberg, Peter N. ... New Orleans, LA
Freiberg, Therese M. ... Stevens Point, WI
Freiberg, Thomas A., Jr. ... Los Angeles, CA
Freiberger, Douglas E. ... Red Bank, NJ
Freiberger, Jonathan H. ... Melville, NY
Freiberger, Katie W. ... New Orleans, LA
Freiberger, Marc D. ... Denver, CO
Freiberger, Mary M. ... Dayton, OH
Freiberger, Norman S. ... New Hyde Park, NY
Freiberger, Philip W. ... Indianapolis, IN
Freiberger, Terry J., (A Professional Law Corporation) ... New Orleans, LA
Freibert, Shawn R. ... Louisville, KY
Freibott, Frederick S. ... Wilmington, DE
Freibrun, Eric S. ... Northbrook, IL
Freiburg, James P. ... Chicago, IL
Freiburger, Charles F., IV ... Columbus, OH
Freiburger, Richard ... Chicago, IL
Freiburger, Thomas M. ... San Francisco, CA
Freid, Bernard M. ... Saginaw, MI
Freid, Debra Ann ... Saginaw, MI
Freid and Goldsman, A Professional Law Corporation ... Beverly Hills, CA
Los Angeles, CA
Freid, Jeffrey B. ... Newport Beach, CA
Freid, Joel ... San Francisco, CA
Freid, Manley ... Los Angeles, CA
Freid, Richard M. ... Paterson, NJ
Freid, Stephen H. ... Department of Education,
Office of the General Counsel, GV
Freidberg, Edward ... Sacramento, CA
Freidel, Irene C. ... Boston, MA
Freidel, Martin E. ... Englewood, CO
Freidel, Melvin D. ... Deer Park, NY
Freidel, Melvin D., P.C. ... Deer Park, NY
Freidell, Debra D. ... Kansas City, MO
Freidell, Debra D., P.C. ... Kansas City, MO
Freideman, Irelan, Ward & Lamberton, P.C. ... Washington, DC
Freideman, Robert S. ... Washington, DC
Freidenreich, Stephanie ... Los Angeles, CA
Freidenrich, John ... Palo Alto, CA
Freidheim, Elizabeth A. ... Chicago, IL
Freidig, Dennis R. ... Auburn, CA
Freidin, Aimee F. ... Philadelphia, PA
Freidin & Brown, P.A. ... Miami, FL
Freidin, Ellen C. ... Miami, FL
Freidin, Jay D. ... Chicago, IL
Freidin, Philip ... Miami, FL
Freidl, Kerry S. ... Easton, PA
Freidman, A. David ... Newport Beach, CA
Freidman, Gary B. ... New York, NY
Freidmutter, Cindy L. ... New York, NY
Freidson, Gayle L. ... Newport Beach, CA
Freidson, Jane B. ... New York, NY
Freidson & Joyce, L.L.P. ... New York, NY
Freidson, Mark J. ... Minnetonka, MN
Freidus, Eugene ... Brooklyn, NY
Freidus, Harris B. ... New York, NY
Freie, Rebecca Phillips ... Sacramento, CA
Freier, Elliot G. ... Los Angeles, CA
Freier, Sharon K. ... Minneapolis, MN
Freifeld, Douglas N. ... San Francisco, CA
Freifeld, Harry ... Brooklyn, NY
Freifield, Bruzzese, Wehr, Moreland, Straus & Spahn ... Steubenville, OH
Freiheit, Laurence H.
Department Of Veterans Affairs,
Veterans Benefits Administration, GV
Freiherr, LeRoy A. ... Indianapolis, IN
Freihofer, Charles L. J. ... Fort Mitchell, KY
Freihofer, Victor J. ... Fort Wright, KY
Freihofer, Walter B. ... Grand Rapids, MI
Freihofer, William A. ... Indianapolis, IN
Freihofer, William W., Jr. ... Somers Point, NJ
Freihube, Raimund ... Los Angeles, CA
Freije, Brenda Hacker ... Indianapolis, IN
Freije, Michell J. ... Fort Myers, FL
Freije, Philip C. ... Department of Commerce,
Office of the General Counsel, GV
Freije, Richard T., Jr. ... Indianapolis, IN
Freije, Steven Lance ... Wichita, KS
Freijomil, Derrick R. ... Newark, NJ
Freijy, Leila ... Troy, MI
Freiley, Lisa M. ... Salem, OR
Freilich, Amy E. ... Los Angeles, CA
Freilich, Arthur ... Los Angeles, CA
Freilich, David J. ... Montvale, NJ
Freilich, Diane M. ... West Bloomfield, MI
Freilich, Harold I. ... Washington, DC
Freilich, Hornbaker & Rosen, P.C. ... Los Angeles, CA
Freilich, Irvin M. ... Newark, NJ
Freilich, Leitner & Carlisle ... Kansas City, MO
Freilich, Michael, & Associates, P.A. ... Towson, MD
Freilich, Michael L. ... Towson, MD
Freilich, Morgan, Leitner & Carlisle ... Dallas, TX
Freilich, Myler, Leitner & Carlisle ... Aspen, CO
Freilich, Richard T. ... Bay Shore, NY
Freilich, Robert H., (P.C.) ... Kansas City, MO
Freilich, Seymour ... Brooklyn, NY
Freilich, Sharon Kowal ... Hartford, CT
Freilich, William H. ... New York, NY
Freilicher, David A. ... Denver, CO
Freilicher, Frederic ... McLean, VA
Freilicher & Hoffman, P.C. ... Washington, DC
Freilicher, Ira L. ... New York, NY
Freilicher, Miriam S. ... Washington, DC
Freilicher, Morton ... New York, NY
Freiling, Don Rynn ... Irving, TX
Freiling, Sharon L. ... South St. Paul, MN
Freiman, Arlene O. ... Philadelphia, PA
Freiman, Harold M. ... Monterey, CA
Freiman, Hyson S. ... Lutherville, MD
Freiman, Lawrence H. ... Atlanta, GA
Freiman, Leonard H. ... Boston, MA
Freiman, Leslie Anne ... Washington, DC
Freiman, Lisa A. ... Washington, DC
Freiman, Richard M. ... New York, NY
Freiman, Robert W. ... New York, NY
Freiman, Sharon K. ... Washington, DC
Freimann, Vicki L. ... Los Angeles, CA
Freimark, Jeffrey Philip ... Pompano Beach, FL
Freimark, Linda H. ... Tysons Corner, VA
Freimark, Linda H., P.C., Law Offices of ... Tysons Corner, VA
Freimund, Jeffrey A. O. ... Olympia, WA
Freimuth, Janet L. ... Department of Energy,
Office of Hearings and Appeals, GV
Freimuth, Joseph M. ... Omaha, NE
Freimuth, Marc W. ... Cleveland, OH
Freimuth, Robert S. ... Beverly Hills, CA
Freimuth, Sharon Sager ... Macedonia, OH
Freimuth, Thomas D. ... Lincoln, NE
Freimuth, Victoria S. ... Camp Hill, PA
Freinberg, David C. ... Newark, NJ
Freint, Edw. ... Cranbury, NJ
Freire, Antonio M. ... Silver Spring, MD
Freire, Fernando F. ... Miami, FL
Freire, James ... New York, NY
Freire, Joseph Manuel ... Orlando, FL
Freire, Melanie Tuck, Attorney at Law ... Orlando, FL
Freireich, Gale C. ... New Brunswick, NJ
Freireich, Gale Pritz ... New Brunswick, NJ
Freireich, Jay J. ... Florham Park, NJ
Freireich, Jos. P. ... Tarrytown, NY
Freireich, Lydia Anne ... Palos Heights, IL
Freireich, Robert H. ... Tarrytown, NY
Freireich, Valerie J. ... Lemont, IL
Freireich, Zoe ... New York, NY
Freire Ortiz, Hector L. ... San Juan, PR
Freire-Ortiz Law Offices ... San Juan, PR
Freirich, Evan ... Boulder, CO
Freis, James H. ... Florham Park, NJ
Freis, James H., Jr. ... New York, NY
Freis, Jeffrey Burt ... Harrison, NY
Freise, Eric L. ... Seattle, WA
Freise, Herbert H. ... Seattle, WA
Freise, Kimberly S. ... Seattle, WA
Freise, Mark H. ... Pittsburgh, PA
Freise & Welchman ... Seattle, WA
Freisem, George Hamilton, III ... Atlanta, GA
Freisem, Macon, Swann & Malone, LLP ... Atlanta, GA
Freisen, Maria E. ... West Palm Beach, FL
Freiser, Lawrence M. ... Berkeley, CA
Freiser, Manny ... Northridge, CA
Freiser, Munro I. ... Woodbury, NY
Freishtat, David ... Baltimore, MD
Freishtat, David D. ... Rockville, MD
Freishtat, Harvey W. ... Boston, MA
Freishtat & Sandler ... Baltimore, MD
Freisleben, Alan J. ... Irvine, CA
Freisleben, Amy L. ... Los Angeles, CA
Freistadt, Kathryn V., Law Offices of ... San Francisco, CA
Freistat, Lana L. ... Los Angeles, CA
Freit, Julia M. ... Baltimore, MD
Freitag, Dean M. ... Miami, FL
Freitag, Edward G. ... Washington, DC
Freitag, Julie A. ... Chicago, IL
Freitag, Mark E. ... Atlanta, GA
Freitag, Paul W. ... Sparks, NV
Freitag, Robert H. ... Pana, IL
Freitag, William C. ... Hartford, CT
Freitas, Alfred M. ... Los Angeles, CA
Freitas, David M. ... San Francisco, CA
Freitas, David P. ... San Rafael, CA
Freitas, Joseph, Jr. ... San Francisco, CA
Freitas, Julie K. ... Palo Alto, CA
Freitas, Karen C. ... Los Angeles, CA
Freitas, Mark R. ... Boston, MA
Freitas, McCarthy, MacMahon & Keating, LLP ... Point Reyes Station, CA
San Rafael, CA
Freitas, Paul M. ... Stoughton, MA
Freitas, Robert E. ... Menlo Park, CA
Freitas, Ronald J. ... Stockton, CA
Freitas, Sarah E. ... Department of Justice,
Office of Legal Counsel, GV
Freivogel, William ... Chicago, IL
Freiwald, Aaron J. ... Philadelphia, PA
Freiwald, Hope Seidenberg ... Philadelphia, PA
Freiwald, Susan ... Philadelphia, PA
Freixes, Gonzalo ... Valencia, CA
Freixes, Graciela L. ... Glendale, CA
Frejka, Elise Scherr ... New York, NY
Frejlich, Robert J. ... Elmhurst, IL
Freking, Randolph H. ... Cincinnati, OH
Freling, Richard A. ... Dallas, TX
Frelinghuysen, Peter ... New York, NY
Frelix, Nichelle D. ... Los Angeles, CA
Frels, Jack C. ... McAllen, TX
Frels, Kelly ... Houston, TX
Frels, Mark ... Dallas, TX
Freman, Carl E. ... Mobile, AL
Freman & Kaoui, L.L.C. ... Mobile, AL
Fremantle, Adam ... New York, NY
Frembling, Candice M. ... Houston, TX
Fremder, Edwin J. ... Boston, MA
Freme, Mark S. ... Cedar Rapids, IA
Fremer, Judith A. ... Laguna Hills, CA
Fremgen, Frederick R. ... Jamestown, ND
Fremgen, Jennifer A. ... Flushing, NY
Fremgen, Mark R. ... Oshkosh, WI
Fremgen, Thomas E. ... Oak Brook, IL
Fremgen, William H. ... Chicago, IL
Fremlin, Grace Parke ... New York, NY
Fremlin, Robert ... San Francisco, CA
Fremont, Douglas P. ... West Palm Beach, FL
Fremont, Helen ... Boston, MA
Fremont, Kenneth P. ... Syosset, NY
Fremont-Smith, Marion R., (P.C.) ... Boston, MA
Fremont-Smith, Thayer ... Boston, MA
Fremstad, Joel M. ... Fargo, ND
Fremuth, Michael J. ... Washington, DC
French, Alan W. ... La Jolla, CA
French, Anne W. ... Boston, MA
French & Associates, P.C. ... Albuquerque, NM
French, B. Thomas ... San Francisco, CA
French, Becky R. ... Research Triangle Park, NC
French, Billie C. ... Salinas, CA
French, Bref, (Ms.) ... Sacramento, CA
French, Brian K. ... Boston, MA
French, Bruce Comly ... Ada, OH
French, Camden T. ... Sarasota, FL
French, Carla Maureen ... Salem, OR
French, Cecil P., Jr. ... Hayward, CA
French, Charles Austin ... Sacramento, CA
French, Charles E. ... San Luis Obispo, CA
French, Charles J., III ... Cleveland, OH
French, Charles S. ... Everett, WA
French, Cheryl A. ... Seattle, WA
French, Christopher C. ... Pittsburgh, PA
French, Christopher J. ... Morristown, NJ
French, Colin V. ... Irving, TX

French, Craig A. ....Costa Mesa, CA
French, Curtis M. ....Tallahassee, FL
French, Dahlia M. ....Hyattsville, MD
French, Dale G. ....Houston, TX
French, Dana Bourgeois ....Dallas, TX
French, Daniel H. ....Cassopolis, MI
French, David A. ....Lexington, KY
Nashville, TN
French, David A. ....Ann Arbor, MI
French, David A., Jr. ....New Bedford, MA
French, David E. ....Boca Raton, FL
French, David L. ....Baton Rouge, LA
French, Dennis E. ....Naperville, IL
French, Diane W. ....Lima, OH
French, Diane W., L.P.A. ....Lima, OH
French, Digna ....Miami, FL
French, Dorothy F. ....Lisle, IL
French, Douglas G. ....Milwaukee, WI
French, E. LaVon
United States Court of Federal Claims, Office of Special Masters, GV
French, Edward B., Jr. ....Stowe, VT
French, Elizabeth ....North Chicago, IL
French, Elizabeth A. ....Bluefield, WV
French, Errol R. ....Sherman Oaks, CA
French, Frances Crauser ....Auburn, AL
French & French ....Cleveland, OH
French, G. Dana ....Fresno, CA
French, Gary E. ....Harrisburg, PA
French, George A. ....Louisville, KY
French, George L. ....Atlanta, GA
French, Gregory S. ....Cincinnati, OH
French, H. Dawson ....Dallas, TX
French, H. Louis ....Towson, MD
French & Hamilton, P.C. ....Dallas, TX
French, Harrison & Dickson, P.L.C.
Cassopolis, MI
French, Heather ....Washington, DC
French, Hollis S. ....Anchorage, AK
French, J. Compton ....Daytona Beach, FL
French, J. Davidson ....Nashville, TN
French, J. Kevin ....Benicia, CA
French, James A. ....Chicago, IL
French, James C., Jr. ....Cary, NC
French, James H. ....San Francisco, CA
French, James H. ....Cleveland, OH
French, James M. ....San Francisco, CA
French, Jan H. ....Durham, NC
French, Jed J. ....Freeport, ME
French, Jeffrey A. ....San Diego, CA
French, Joe, & Associates, P.C. ....Dallas, TX
French, Joel K. ....Houston, TX
French, John B. ....Boston, MA
French, John B. ....Boston, MA
French, John D. ....Minneapolis, MN
French, John D. ....Ronan, MT
French, John H. ....Carle Place, NY
French, John H., Jr. ....Tallahassee, FL
French, John, III ....New York, NY
French, John L. ....Freeport, ME
French, John M. ....Council Bluffs, IA
French, John R. ....Greenwich, CT
French, Jos. P. ....Salem, OR
French, Joseph A. ....New York, NY
French, Joseph A. ....Dublin, OH
French, Joseph C. ....Boulder, CO
French, Joseph J., Jr. ....Dallas, TX
French, Judith Kay ....La Grange, IL
French, Karen K. ....Sacramento, CA
French, Karen S. ....Richmond, VA
French, Kevin M. ....Lancaster, PA
French Kezelis & Kominiarek, P.C.
Chicago, IL
Wheaton, IL
French, Kyle G. ....Chicago, IL
French, Laura Jones ....Conyers, GA
French, Linda J. ....Kansas City, MO
French, Linda L. ....Stockton, CA
French, Lloyd S. ....Framingham, MA
French & Lyon, A Professional Corporation
San Francisco, CA
French, Marilyn ....Boston, MA
French, Marion A. ....Alexandria, LA
French, Mark A. ....Columbus, OH
French, Mercer, Grainey & O'Neill
Polson, MT
Ronan, MT
French, Michael Allen ....Tulsa, OK
French, Michael Benton ....Birmingham, AL
French, Michael S. ....Atlanta, GA
French, Nancy N. ....Atlanta, GA
French, Nathan Scott ....Farmington Hills, MI
French, Patricia M. ....Boston, MA
French, Paul E. ....Longview, TX
French, Paul V. ....Loudonville, NY
French, Peter S. ....Indianapolis, IN
French, Philip M. ....Stamford, CT
French, Pilar Cortwright ....Portland, OR
French, Rae Ann ....Waterville, ME
French, Ralph F. ....Cleveland, OH
French, Randal J. ....Boise, ID
French, Raymond E. ....Milwaukee, WI
French, Richard G. ....Chicago, IL
French, Richard H., Jr. ....Cleveland, OH
French, Richard W. ....Columbia, MO
French, Robert A. ....Oklahoma City, OK
French, Robert B., Jr. ....Fort Payne, AL
French, Robert E. ....Los Angeles, CA
French, Robert F. ....Truckee, CA
French, Robert H. S. ....Breckenridge, CO
French, Robert J. ....Rockford, IL
French, Robert S. ....Spartanburg, SC
French, Robin L. ....New York, NY
French, Roger J. ....Chicago, IL
French, Rosemary Rae ....San Francisco, CA
French, Russell R. ....Atlanta, GA
French, Saml. B. ....Austin, TX
French, Saralee B. ....Albany, NY
French, Scott W. ....Racine, WI
French, Sheryl ....New York, NY
French, Stephen B. ....Lakeland, FL
French, Stephen G. ....Albuquerque, NM
French, Stephen W. ....Boise, ID
French, Stephen W. ....Brookville, PA
French & Stone, P.C. ....Boulder, CO
French, Stuart C. ....Everett, WA
French, Stuart P. ....New Castle, NH
French, Susan F. ....Davis, CA
French, Susan J. ....Philadelphia, PA
French, Susan M. ....San Mateo, CA
French, Teresa Ann ....McGehee, AR
French, Thomas A. ....New Orleans, LA
French, Thomas A. ....Harrisburg, PA
French, Thomas C. ....Laguna Niguel, CA
French, Thomas C. ....Atlanta, GA
French, Thomas H. ....New York, NY
French, Thomas M. ....Palo Alto, CA
French, Thomas M. ....Stow, MA
French, Thomas M. ....Brattleboro, VT
French, Thomas R. ....Fort Collins, CO
French, Thomas R. ....Chapel Hill, NC
French, Timothy A. ....Chicago, IL
French, Timothy A. ....Boston, MA
French, Van A. ....Old Hickory, TN
French, Walter ....West Dummerston, VT
French, West, Brown, Huntley & Thompson, P.C. ....Breckenridge, CO
Dillon, CO
Frisco, CO
Silverthorne, CO
Vail, CO
French, William A., III ....Plano, TX
French, William C. ....Newington, CT
French, William C. ....Houston, TX
French, William C. ....Richmond, VA
French, William D. ....New Orleans, LA
French, William G. ....Waco, TX
French, William J. ....Dallas, TX
French, William L. ....Rochester, MN
French, William P. ....Phoenix, AZ
French, William T. ....Rochester, NY
Frenchick, Grady J. ....Madison, WI
Frenchman, Beth M. ....New York, NY
Frenchman, Robert S. ....New York, NY
Frenchmore, Raymond C. ....Westminster, CO
French-Scaggs, Susan K. ....Cleveland, OH
Frenck, Henry C. ....Virginia Beach, VA
Frenden, John A. ....Cleveland, OH
Frenette, David P. ....Brockton, MA
Frenette & Dukess ....Brockton, MA
Frenette, Henry N., Jr. ....Brockton, MA
Frenette, Richard L.
Department of Defense, GV
Frenger, Brian ....Minneapolis, MN
Freni, John J. ....San Diego, CA
Frenier, Diane M. ....Princeton, NJ
Freniere, David J. ....Boston, MA
Freniere, Diane Cabo ....Boston, MA
Frenkel, David ....Bay Shore, NY
Frenkel, David C. ....New York, NY
Frenkel, Douglas N. ....Philadelphia, PA
Frenkel & Frenkel, P.C. ....Dallas, TX
Frenkel & Hershkowitz ....New York, NY
Frenkel, Jacob S. ....Wilmington, DE
Frenkel, John R. ....Miami, FL
Frenkel, Johnathan M. ....Washington, DC
Frenkel, Lisa M. ....Nashville, TN
Frenkel, Mark D. ....Dallas, TX
Frenkel, Martin Scott ....Southfield, MI
Frenkel, Marvin A. ....Detroit, MI
Frenkel, Michael ....New Rochelle, NY
Frenkel, Polly L. ....San Francisco, CA
Frenkel, Robert I. ....New York, NY
Frenkel, Scott B. ....Dallas, TX
Frenkel, Steven I. ....Stamford, CT
Frenkel, Stuart D. ....Arlington, VA
Frenkel, Tally ....Rockville, MD
Frenkel, William G. ....East Rutherford, NJ
Frenkel, Wolf ....Menlo Park, CA
Frenkil, Steven D. ....Baltimore, MD
Frenn, Thomas L. ....Milwaukee, WI
Freno-Engman, Lori L. ....Little Rock, AR
Frensilli, Beth A. ....San Francisco, CA
Frensley, David R. ....Kansas City, MO
Frensley, Jeffrey S. ....Nashville, TN
Frensley, Susan Elizabeth ....Richardson, TX
Frentheway, John E. ....Cheyenne, WY
Frentz & Frentz ....Mankato, MN
Frentz, John C. ....Mankato, MN
Frentz, John C. ....Akron, OH
Frentz, L. Brand ....Mankato, MN
Frentz, Nick A. ....Mankato, MN
Frentz, Stuart Joseph ....Birmingham, AL
Frentz, Thomas W. ....Louisville, KY
Frentzel, Mark J. ....Grand Island, NY
Frenz, Paul D. ....Chicago, IL
Frenz, Robert D. ....Anchorage, AK
Frenze-Donahue, Jenifer ....Wayne, PA
Frenzel, Heidi Honora ....San Francisco, CA
Frenzel, James C. ....Atlanta, GA
Frenzel, James C., P.C. ....Atlanta, GA
Frenzel, Lawrence D. ....Tustin, CA
Frenzel, Mary Naphin ....Evanston, IL
Frenzen, Donald W.
Department of the Army, Office, Chief of Engineers/Headquarters, U.S. Army Corps of Engineers, GV
Frenzen, Niels W. ....Los Angeles, CA
Frenzer, Peter F. ....Columbus, OH
Frenzer, Timothy J. ....Wilmette, IL
Frenznick, David A. ....Sacramento, CA
Frère, Kelly Guyton ....Knoxville, TN
Frère, Matthew B. ....Knoxville, TN
Frere, Raymond G. ....Morgantown, WV
Freret, Douglass V., II ....Mandeville, LA
Freret, Jill E.C. ....Phoenix, AZ
Freret, Julian P. ....Washington, DC
Frerichs, Clarence A. ....Waterloo, IA
Frerichs, Denise McKinney ....Phoenix, AZ
Frerichs, Herbert D., Jr. ....Baltimore, MD
Frerichs Law Office, P.C. ....Waterloo, IA
Frerichs, Myron E., Jr. ....Harriman, NY
Frerichs, Scott F. ....Scottsdale, AZ
Frerichs, Thomas P. ....Waterloo, IA
Frericks and Howard, A Legal Professional Association ....Marion, OH
Frericks, Theodore P. ....Marion, OH
Frericks, Theodore P., IV ....Marion, OH
Frericks, Thomas A. ....Marion, OH
Frericks, Timothy M. ....Marion, OH
Freriks, David R. ....Hinckley, IL
Frering, Mark D. ....Kingston, NY
Frerker, Nicole Christine
Kansas City, MO
Frerking, William A. ....Wichita, KS
Frerks, Harold C. ....Long Beach, CA
Fresard & Associates, P.C.
St. Clair Shores, MI
Fresard, Donn ....St. Clair Shores, MI
Fresard, Fred J. ....Detroit, MI
Fresard, Michael P. ....Troy, MI
Fresch, Elaine K. ....Los Angeles, CA
Fresch, Eric T. ....San Francisco, CA
Freschi, Mark B. ....San Jose, CA
Freschl, Joel H. ....New York, NY
Fresco, Brigitte V. ....Wilmington, DE
Fresco, Ronald A. ....Columbus, OH
Frese, Anthony J. ....Clifton, NJ
Frese, Dana L. ....Jefferson City, MO
Frese, Eugene M. ....Washington, DC
Frese, Gary B. ....Melbourne, FL
Frese, Glenn C. ....Folsom, CA
Frese, Jerome ....South Bend, IN
Frese, Nash & Hansen, P.A.
Melbourne, FL
Frese and Palma, P.C. ....Clifton, NJ
Frese, William E. ....Newark, NJ
Fresh, Douglas ....Jeffersonville, IN
Fresh, John W. ....Atchison, KS
Fresher, Brian L. ....North Haven, CT
Fresher, Charles M. ....New Haven, CT
Freshfields LLP ....Washington, DC
Washington, DC
New York, NY
New York, NY
Freshly, Timothy D. ....Richmond, VA
Freshman Freshman & Traitz, P.A.
Miami, FL
Freshman, Jerald A. ....Miami, FL
Freshman & Kearns, LLC ....Westport, CT
Freshman, Lawrence N. ....Miami, FL
Freshman, Marantz, Orlanski, Cooper & Klein, A Law Corporation
Beverly Hills, CA
Los Angeles, CA
Freshour, Paul D. ....Washington, DC
Freshwater, Maridel S. ....Dallas, TX
Fresia, Bradley D. ....Seattle, WA
Freska, Anna M. ....Monterey, CA
Fresno, Mercedes M. ....Los Angeles, CA
Fresolone, Ralph ....Hauppauge, NY
Freson, Ronald J. ....Evansville, IN
Fresquez, Loretta M. ....Flagstaff, AZ
Fressola, Alfred A. ....Monroe, CT
Freston, Edwin ....Los Angeles, CA
Fretel, Theodore G. ....Madison, CT
Freter, Paul L. ....Chicago, IL
Fretheim, Daniel L. ....Council Bluffs, IA
Fretland, Laura K. ....Minneapolis, MN
Fretland, Millard Lane ....Pensacola, FL
Frets, Timothy S. ....Kansas City, MO
Frett, Eugene J. ....Chicago, IL
Frett, Michael V. ....Brooklyn, NY
Frett, Richard W. ....Elgin, IL
Fretthold, Timothy J. ....San Antonio, TX
Fretwell, Craig B. ....Santa Fe, NM
Fretwell, James L. ....Charlotte, NC
Fretwell, Norman E. ....Kansas City, MO
Fretwell, Susan A. ....Spartanburg, SC
Fretz, David E., Law Offices of
Amherst, NY
Fretz, Donald R. ....Napa, CA
Fretz, Joseph H. ....Denver, CO
Fretzin, Lawrence G. ....Chicago, IL
Freud & Abraham ....Miami, FL
Freud, Edward P. ....Chicago, IL
Freud, Gloria G. ....Detroit, MI
Freud, John S. ....Miami, FL
Freud, Michael S. ....Waterford, MI
Freud, Nicholas S. ....San Francisco, CA
Freudberg, Lee ....Charlottesville, VA
Freudenberg, Benjamin E. ....Grants Pass, OR
Freudenberg, Joan E. ....Philadelphia, PA
Freudenberg, John R. ....Gordon, NE
Rushville, NE
Freudenberg, Joseph B. ....Philadelphia, PA
Freudenberg, Kent L. ....Springfield, MO
Freudenberg, Roger L. ....Boise, ID
Freudenberger, Jodi D. ....Seattle, WA
Freudenberger, Timothy M. ....Irvine, CA
San Diego, CA
Freudenfeld, Bernard N. ....Milwaukee, WI
Freudenheim, Julie ....New York, NY
Freudenrich, Bill G. ....Tulsa, OK
Freudenthal, David D. ....Cheyenne, WY
Freudenthal, Nancy D. ....Cheyenne, WY
Sheridan, WY
Freudenthal, Steven F. ....Cheyenne, WY
Freudiger, David F. ....Memphis, TN
Freudiger, Ray C. ....Dayton, OH
Freuler, Justine Kindley ....Columbus, OH
Freund, Andrea L. ....Bronx, NY
Freund, Andrew T. ....Crystal Lake, IL
Freund, Benni H. ....North Hollywood, CA
Freund, Bernard W. ....Muncie, IN
Freund, Charles G. ....Lincolnshire, IL
Freund, Cynthia A. ....Downers Grove, IL
Freund, Daniel R. ....Eau Claire, WI
Freund, Erin L. ....Columbus, OH
Freund, Fred A. ....New York, NY
Freund, Freeze & Arnold ....Covington, KY
Florence, KY
Greenville, OH
Hamilton, OH
Springfield, OH
Troy, OH
Cincinnati, OH
Dayton, OH
Freund, George R., Jr. ....Keene, NH
Freund, Harold ....Lynbrook, NY
Freund, Henry L., Jr. ....Ashland, OR
Freund, Hugh J. ....New York, NY
Freund, James B. ....Hoffman Estates, IL
Freund, James C. ....New York, NY
Freund, Jeffrey R. ....Washington, DC
Freund, Joanne R. ....Boston, MA
Freund, John E., III ....Allentown, PA
Freund, Jonathan D. ....Beverly Hills, CA
Freund, Lori Lee ....Spokane, WA
Freund, Mark ....Tallahassee, FL
Freund, Mark, P.A. ....Tallahassee, FL
Freund, Max ....New York, NY
Freund, Meir ....New York, NY
Freund, Michelle A. ....Kansas City, MO
Freund, Neil F. ....Dayton, OH
Freund, Richard L. ....Malverne, NY
Freund, Samuel J. ....Montclair, NJ
Freund, Samuel M. ....Los Alamos, NM
Freund, Sandy ....New York, NY
Freund, Sharon B. ....New York, NY
Freund, Susan M. ....Tucson, AZ
Freund, Terry M. ....Chicago, IL
Freund, Todd M. ....Florissant, MO
Freundel, Mark J. ....Oakton, VA
Freundel, William ....New York, NY
Freundlich, Abraham
North Miami Beach, FL
Freundlich, Alisa J. ....Beverly Hills, CA
Freundlich, Gerald M. ....Clifton, NJ
Freundlich, Kenneth D., Law Offices of
New York, NY
Freundlich, Lawrence J. ....Millburn, NJ
Freundlich, Lester G. ....New York, NY
Freundlich, Mc Clear & Reisen, LLP
Millburn, NJ
Freundlich, Robin M. ....New York, NY
Freundlich, Stanley H. ....New York, NY
Freveletti, Jamie S. ....Chicago, IL
Frevert, Lyle R. ....Bloomington, MN
Frevola, Albert L., Jr.
Fort Lauderdale, FL
Frevola, Michael Joseph ....New York, NY
Frew, Charles T. ....Huntsville, AL
Frew, Stephen A. ....Rockford, IL
Frew, Stephen A., Counselor at Law, Ltd.
Rockford, IL
Frew, Stephen B. ....Chicago, IL
Frew, William J., Jr. ....Staten Island, NY
Frewert, William H. ....Western Springs, IL
Frewing, Brooke E. ....McLean, VA
Frewing, H. Kent ....Pasadena, CA
Frewing, Robert L. ....Bellevue, WA
Frewing, Scott H. ....Palo Alto, CA
Frey, A. John, Jr. ....Clinton, IA
Frey, Alan M. ....Washington, DC
Frey, Andrew L. ....Washington, DC
New York, NY
Frey, Ann Luerssen ....Dublin, OH
Frey, Bertram C. ....Chicago, IL
Frey, Bruce M. ....Bloomington, IN
Frey, C. Louis ....St. Paul, MN
Frey, Cecil H. ....Tulsa, OK
Frey, Charles Burton ....Frederick, MD
Frey, Christine E. ....Atlanta, GA
Frey, Christopher G. ....Clearwater, FL
Frey, Clifford J. ....Chandler, AZ
Frey, Cynthia A. ....Albuquerque, NM
Frey, Cynthia M. ....Los Angeles, CA
Frey, Daniel K. ....Chicago, IL
Frey, Daniel M. ....Hanover, PA
Frey, Daniel M., & Associates
Hanover, PA
Frey, David ....New York, NY
Frey, David A. ....Racine, WI
Frey, David G. ....Grand Rapids, MI
Frey, David J. ....Batavia, OH
Frey, David L., Jr. ....Lafayette, CA
Frey, Donald M. ....Seymour, IN
Frey, Donald W. ....Kelso, WA
Frey, Donald W., P.S. ....Kelso, WA
Frey, Douglas A. ....New Haven, CT
Frey, Edward A. ....White Plains, NY
Frey, Edward P. ....Mineola, NY
Frey, Edwin A. ....Soquel, CA
Frey, Elizabeth Jesukiewicz
Washington, DC
Frey, Eric A. ....Terre Haute, IN
Frey, Eric C. ....Lansdale, PA
Frey, Eric D. ....Birmingham, MI
Frey, Ethan E. ....Phoenix, AZ
Frey, Francis C. ....Toledo, OH
Frey & Frey ....New York, NY
Frey & Frey, P.C. ....Chandler, AZ
Frey, George F., Jr. ....Rochester, NY
Frey, H. Edwin, Jr. ....Tecumseh, MI
Frey, Haufe & Current, P.L.C.
Clinton, IA
Frey, Heather A. ....Portland, OR
Frey, Henry C. ....Greeley, CO
Frey, Henry C., L.L.C. ....Greeley, CO
Frey, J. Patrick ....Marina Del Rey, CA
Frey, James R. ....Sacramento, CA

Friedberg, Martha E. .... Oakland, CA
Friedberg, Michael .... Los Angeles, CA
Friedberg, Michael A. .... Newark, DE
Wilmington, DE
Friedberg, Michael R. .... Chicago, IL
Friedberg, Paul M. .... Charleston, WV
Friedberg, Randy M. .... New York, NY
Friedberg, Ronald P. .... Cleveland, OH
Friedberg, Rosalie D. .... New York, NY
Friedberg, Saul .... Brookhaven, NY
Friedberg, Stephen E. .... New York, NY
Friedberg, Stephen M. .... New York, NY
Friedberg, Stephen M. .... Richmond, VA
Friedberg, Steven G. .... New York, NY
Friedberg, Sue .... Wexford, PA
Friedberg, Thomas F. .... San Diego, CA
Friedberg, Wendy E. .... Orlando, FL
Friedberg, William D. .... Somerville, MA
Friede, Arnold I. .... Lisle, IL
Friedeberg, William J. .... West Hartford, CT
Friedel, Howard M. .... McLean, VA
Friedel, Karl W. .... Wichita, KS
Friedel, Patricia A. .... San Francisco, CA
Friedel, Robert A. .... Philadelphia, PA
Friedel, Stuart Lee .... New York, NY
Friedel, Susan P. .... Red Bank, NJ
Friedell, Ellen S. .... Philadelphia, PA
Friedell, Gerald H. .... Minneapolis, MN
Friedell, Katherine A. .... Cleveland, OH
Friedell, Steven F. .... Camden, NJ
Friedeman, John, P.C. .... Phoenix, AZ
Friedeman, Richard L. .... Great Bend, KS
Friedemann, Glenn R. .... Providence, RI
Friedemann, John F. .... Los Angeles, CA
Santa Rosa, CA
Friedemann, Konrad J. .... Minneapolis, MN
Friedemann, O'Brien & Zarian, LLP
Los Angeles, CA
Santa Rosa, CA
Frieden, Alan M. .... Chesapeake, VA
Frieden, André C. .... Chicago, IL
Frieden, Clifford E. .... Costa Mesa, CA
Frieden, Haynes & Forbes .... Topeka, KS
Frieden, James A. .... Santa Monica, CA
Frieden, John C. .... Topeka, KS
Frieden, Jonathan D. .... Fairfax, VA
Frieden, Nancy Mandelker .... New York, NY
Frieden, Paul L. .... Department of Labor, Office of the Solicitor, GV
Friedenberg, David I. .... San Diego, CA
Friedenberg, David J. .... Daly City, CA
Friedenberg, Debra Joy .... Kew Gardens, NY
Friedenberg, Ellen S. .... New York, NY
Friedenberg, Gary H. .... Garden City, NY
Friedenberg, Harold D. .... Cape May, NJ
Friedenberg, Isidor D. .... Suffern, NY
Friedenberg, Jay S. .... Philadelphia, PA
Friedenberg, Jay S., P.C. .... Philadelphia, PA
Friedenberg, Jeffrey .... Washington, DC
Friedenberg, Joann M. .... New York, NY
Friedenberg, Marilyn R. .... Old Westbury, NY
Friedenberg, Mildred M.
Newport Beach, CA
Friedenberg, Peter .... Boston, MA
Friedenberg, Robert L. .... San Diego, CA
Friedenberg, Samuel C. .... Portland, OR
Friedenberg, Stanley .... Old Westbury, NY
Friedenheit, Arthur R. .... New York, NY
Friedensen, Jane T. .... Raleigh, NC
Friedenson, Jay P. .... Morristown, NJ
Friedenthal, Alan H. .... Woodland Hills, CA
Friedenthal, Daniel R. .... Glendale, CA
Friedenthal, Jack H. .... Washington, DC
Friedenthal, Jo Anne .... McLean, VA
Friedenzohn, Daniel Leonardo
Bloomfield Hills, MI
Frieder, Gony .... Lexington Park, MD
Frieder, Helen M. .... Bronx, NY
Frieder, Philip R. .... Rydal, PA
Frieder, Regina .... Encino, CA
Frieder, Thomas M. .... San Francisco, CA
Frieder, William A. .... Tallahassee, FL
Friederich, Blair P. .... Tucson, AZ
Friederich, John A. .... Rock Island, IL
Friederich, Patricia A. .... Yonkers, NY
Friederich, Ralph M. .... Fairview Heights, IL
Friederich & Rollin .... Tucson, AZ
Friederichs, Gerald A. .... Chicago, IL
Friederichs Law Firm, P.L.C.
Minneapolis, MN
Friederichs, N. Paul, III .... Minneapolis, MN
Friederichs, Norman P. .... Minneapolis, MN
Friederichs, Teresa J. .... Los Angeles, CA
Frieders, Jill I. .... Rochester, MN
Friederwitzer, Lisa J. .... Forest Hills, NY
Friedes, David E. .... Toledo, OH
Friedes, Jennifer .... Chicago, IL
Friedewald, James W. .... Marietta, GA
Friedewald, Lynne A. .... Hastings, NE
Friedfeld, Elyce .... New York, NY
Friedfeld, Leon B. .... New York, NY
Friedfertig, Arnold M. .... Brookline, MA
Friedfertig, Richard .... Buffalo, NY
Friedgood, Martin .... Atlanta, GA
Friedgut, Elizabeth H. .... Chicago, IL
Friedheim, Jay Lawrence .... Honolulu, HI
Friedheim-Weis, Lisa J. .... Chicago, IL
Friedhofer, James E. .... San Diego, CA
Friedhoff, Beth Mazur .... River Vale, NJ
Friedhoff, Irven L. .... Jefferson City, MO
Friedhoff, John H. .... Miami, FL
Friedhoff, Nancy J. .... Sacramento, CA
Friedhoff, William R., Jr. .... Seattle, WA
Friedl, John .... Detroit, MI
Friedl, John F. .... Milwaukee, WI
Friedl, Marcia L. .... Chicago, IL
Friedl, Richter & Buri .... Scottsdale, AZ
Friedl, Rick .... California City, CA
Friedl, Robert K. .... Los Angeles, CA
Friedl, William J. .... Scottsdale, AZ
Friedlaender, Howard .... Detroit, MI
Friedlaender, Judith G. .... New York, NY
Friedlaender, Susan Klein
Birmingham, MI
Friedland, Aaron E. .... Los Angeles, CA
Friedland, Allan S. .... Hartford, CT
Friedland, Arthur E. .... New York, NY
Friedland, Barri L. .... Los Angeles, CA
Friedland, Bernard .... Boston, MA
Friedland, Carolyn B. .... Cleveland, OH
Friedland, Charles .... Skokie, IL
Friedland, Dale R. .... Cleveland, OH
Friedland, David K. .... Miami, FL
Friedland, David M. .... Washington, DC
Friedland, Edward A. .... Stamford, CT
Friedland, Gary M. .... Bedford, NY
Friedland, Gary M. .... Philadelphia, PA
Friedland, Gerald B. .... Monsey, NY
Friedland, Harvey .... Plymouth Meeting, PA
Friedland, Harvey K. .... Princeton Junction, NJ
Friedland, Holly M. .... Springfield, NJ
Friedland, Irvin J. ....
Department Of Health And Human Services, GV
Friedland, Jacob .... Staten Island, NY
Friedland, Jay M. .... Boston, MA
Friedland, Jed P. .... Carmel Valley, CA
Friedland, Jennifer M. .... Newport Beach, CA
Friedland, Jerry H. .... Albuquerque, NM
Milwaukee, WI
Friedland, Jerry H., S.C.
Albuquerque, NM
Friedland, Jerry N. .... Roseland, NJ
Friedland, John H. .... New York, NY
Friedland, Jonathan P. .... Chicago, IL
Friedland, Jonathan R. .... Miami, FL
Friedland, Judith B. .... Altamonte Springs, FL
Friedland, Jyoti Mistry .... New York, NY
Friedland, Kenneth .... Titusville, FL
Friedland, Kirk .... West Palm Beach, FL
Friedland Laifer & Robbins, LLP
Woodbridge, NJ
New York, NY
Friedland, Lawrence N. .... New York, NY
Friedland, Lee .... Coral Gables, FL
Friedland, Lesley Ann .... New York, NY
Friedland, Lloyd M. .... Garden City, NY
Friedland, Lori E. .... New City, NY
Friedland, Marcie Sue .... Great Neck, NY
Friedland, Mark .... San Francisco, CA
Friedland, Melvin L. .... San Bernardino, CA
Friedland, Michael .... Nashville, TN
Friedland, Michael K.
Newport Beach, CA
Friedland, Norman M. .... Mineola, NY
Friedland, Patricia A. .... Los Angeles, CA
Friedland, Paul D. .... New York, NY
Friedland, Ralph L. .... Sarasota, FL
Friedland, Ralph L., P.A. .... Sarasota, FL
Friedland, Randy Seth .... McLean, VA
Friedland, Seth D. .... New York, NY
Friedland, Sharon L. .... New York, NY
Friedland, Sheldon, (P.C.)
New Bedford, MA
Friedland, Shelly .... New York, NY
Friedland, Sidney .... Chicago, IL
Friedland, Stephen M. .... Dix Hills, NY
Friedland, Steven D. .... Chicago, IL
Friedland, Steven I. .... Fort Lauderdale, FL
Friedland, Steven L. .... Woodland Hills, CA
Friedland, Stuart R.
Palos Verdes Estates, CA
Friedland, Susan M. .... Bloomfield Hills, MI
Friedland, Todd G. .... Costa Mesa, CA
Friedlander, Alan B. .... Washington, DC
Friedlander, Alan J. .... Waverly, NY
Friedlander, Albert S. .... Agoura Hills, CA
Friedlander, Bernard .... New York, NY
Friedlander, Betty D. .... Ithaca, NY
Friedlander, Bruce D. .... Miami, FL
Friedlander, Carl W. .... Plano, TX
Friedlander, Carl W. .... Richardson, TX
Friedlander, Charles .... Washington, DC
Friedlander, D. Gilbert .... Plano, TX
Friedlander, Dana Allyn .... Tampa, FL
Friedlander, Daniel A. .... Cleveland, OH
Friedlander, David E. .... Worthington, OH
Friedlander, David H. .... White Plains, NY
Friedlander, Donald A. .... Mobile, AL
Friedlander, Earle E. .... Fort Lauderdale, FL
Friedlander, Ezra H. .... Indianapolis, IN
Friedlander & Friedlander, P.C.
Washington, DC
Friedlander & Friedlander, P.C.
Waverly, NY
Friedlander & Friedlander, P.C.
Fairfax, VA
McLean, VA
Friedlander, Gary J. .... Norristown, PA
Friedlander, Gary Scott .... Wood Dale, IL
Friedlander, Gerald A. .... Mobile, AL
Friedlander, Gregory M. .... Mobile, AL
Washington, DC
Friedlander, Gregory M., & Associates, P.C.
Mobile, AL
Friedlander, Gretchen B. .... Phoenix, AZ
Friedlander, Harry P. .... Mesa, AZ
Friedlander, Ian S. .... Tamarac, FL
Friedlander, Itzhak I. .... Richmond, VA
Friedlander, Jack .... Calumet City, IL
Friedlander, Jack L. .... Washington, DC
Friedlander, James S. .... Washington, DC
Friedlander, Jeffrey D. .... New York, NY
Friedlander, Jerome P., II .... McLean, VA
Friedlander, Joel .... Wilmington, DE
Friedlander, Jonathan K. .... Silver Spring, MD
Friedlander, Julia Mary .... San Francisco, CA
Friedlander, Kathleen T.
San Francisco, CA
Friedlander, Lawrence .... Cleveland, OH
Friedlander, Lisa J. .... Windham, ME
Friedlander, Lisa L. .... Washington, DC
Friedlander, Loyd Keith .... Huntington, NY
Friedlander, Marjorie R.
Pacific Palisades, CA
Friedlander, Mark .... New York, NY
Friedlander, Mark C. .... Chicago, IL
Friedlander, Mark P., Jr. .... McLean, VA
Friedlander, Martin E. .... Brooklyn, NY
Friedlander, Martin S. .... Los Angeles, CA
Friedlander, Maury .... Mobile, AL
Friedlander, Michael E. .... Alexandria, VA
Friedlander, Michael I. .... Los Angeles, CA
Friedlander, Misler, Friedlander, Sloan & Herz, PLLC .... Washington, DC
Friedlander, Nathan P. .... Mobile, AL
Friedlander, Neal M. .... Baltimore, MD
Friedlander, Paul S. .... New York, NY
Friedlander, R. B., (Ms.) .... Little Rock, AR
Friedlander, Richard A. .... Phoenix, AZ
Friedlander, Robert L. .... Chicago, IL
Friedlander, Robert S. .... New York, NY
Friedlander, Roberta Burford .... Tampa, FL
Friedlander, Ruth K. .... Fort Lauderdale, FL
Friedlander, S. David .... Boca Raton, FL
Friedlander, Samantha Joy .... Atlanta, GA
Friedlander, Samuel D. .... New York, NY
Friedlander, Scott E. .... Atlanta, GA
Friedlander, Stacey L. .... Los Angeles, CA
Friedlander, Stephen H. .... Washington, DC
Friedlander, Steven L. .... San Francisco, CA
Friedlander, Valerie .... Albany, NY
Friedlander, Wendy Finck
Securities and Exchange Commission, Division of Investment Management, GV
Friedlander, William A. .... Tallahassee, FL
Friedlander, William A. .... Raleigh, NC
Friedlander, William S. .... Waverly, NY
Friedland-Wechsler, Naomi
New York, NY
Friedle, Gary A. .... New Britain, CT
Friedler, Edith .... Los Angeles, CA
Friedler, Ellen B. .... Chicago, IL
Friedler, Frank, III .... New Orleans, LA
Friedler, Lottie .... Baltimore, MD
Friedler, Stephen G. .... New Haven, CT
Friedler, Sydney .... Carle Place, NY
Friedler, William N. .... Boston, MA
Friedli, Helen R. .... Chicago, IL
Friedli, Renee A. .... Houston, TX
Friedlich, Rochelle .... New York, NY
Friedlieb, Bertram .... Jamaica, NY
Friedlieb, Lysa M. .... Miami, FL
Friedline, John J. .... Atlanta, GA
Friedline, Mary Lynch .... Pittsburgh, PA
Friedline, Rodger James .... Jacksonville, FL
Friedling, Richard A. .... San Francisco, CA
Friedling, Richard Anker, Law Offices of
San Francisco, CA
Friedlis, J. Andre .... Lansing, MI
Friedlob, Raymond L. .... Denver, CO
Englewood, CO
Friedlob Sanderson Raskin Paulson & Tourtillott, LLC .... Santa Cruz, CA
Denver, CO
Englewood, CO
Friedly, Jay R. .... Mountain Home, ID
Friedman, Aaron .... Philadelphia, PA
Friedman, Aaron S. .... Los Angeles, CA
Friedman, Abba I. .... Ann Arbor, MI
Friedman, Abbie Green .... Las Vegas, NV
Friedman, Abby B. .... Beverly Hills, CA
Friedman, Abraham .... New York, NY
Friedman, Abraham P. .... Houston, TX
Friedman, Abraham S. .... Brooklyn, NY
Friedman, Adam .... Universal City, CA
Friedman, Adam .... New York, NY
Friedman, Adam H. .... New York, NY
Friedman, Adam P. .... Roseland, NJ
Friedman, Alan E. .... Los Angeles, CA
Friedman, Alan H. .... Napa, CA
Friedman, Alan J.
Federal Trade Commission, Bureau of Competition, GV
Friedman, Alan Jay .... French Lick, IN
Friedman, Alan L. .... New York, NY
Friedman, Alan M. .... New York, NY
Friedman, Alan P. .... Reynoldsburg, OH
Friedman, Alan R. .... Annapolis, MD
Friedman, Alan R. .... New York, NY
Friedman, Alan R. .... New York, NY
Friedman, Alan V., (A Professional Corporation) .... Los Angeles, CA
Friedman, Albert Brooks .... Chicago, IL
Friedman, Albert Brooks, Ltd.
Chicago, IL
Friedman, Albert M. .... Chicago, IL
Friedman, Alissa .... Oakland, CA
Friedman, Allan S. .... Miami Beach, FL
Friedman, Allen D. .... Rochester, NY
Friedman, Allen N. .... Newark, NJ
Friedman, Allen R. .... New York, NY
Friedman, Allison L. .... Coral Gables, FL
Friedman, Alva M. .... Lakewood, CA
Friedman, Alvin .... Washington, DC
Friedman, Alvin E. .... Baltimore, MD
Friedman, Alvin F. .... Chicago, IL
Friedman and Anderson .... Media, PA
Friedman, Andre H. .... New York, NY
Friedman, Andrea E. .... Hoffman Estates, IL
Friedman, Andrea Lee .... New York, NY
Friedman, Andrew .... Los Angeles, CA
Friedman, Andrew C. .... Washington, DC
Friedman, Andrew D. .... Boston, MA
Friedman, Andrew D. .... New York, NY
Friedman, Andrew G. .... Brooklyn, NY
Friedman, Andrew H. .... Venice, CA
Friedman, Andrew H. .... Washington, DC
Friedman, Andrew M. .... Washington, DC
Friedman, Andrew M. .... Washington, DC
Friedman, Andrew M. .... New York, NY
Friedman, Andrew M. .... Richmond Hill, NY
Friedman, Andrew N. .... Washington, DC
Friedman, Andrew R. .... Boca Raton, FL
Friedman, Andrew S. .... Phoenix, AZ
Friedman, Anne Brenner .... Lafayette Hill, PA
Friedman, Anthony A. .... Encino, CA
Friedman, Arnold C. .... Irvington, NJ
Friedman, Arnold M. .... Providence, RI
Friedman, Aron .... Washington, DC
Friedman, Arthur .... St. Louis, MO
Friedman, Arthur .... New York, NY
Friedman, Arthur B. .... Longwood, FL
Friedman, Arthur D. .... Fairfield, CT
Friedman, Arthur D. .... Brooklyn, NY
Friedman, Arthur J. .... San Francisco, CA
Friedman, Arthur N. K. .... Youngstown, OH
Friedman, Arthur R., (P.C.)
Falls Church, VA
Friedman, Arthur S. .... Hauppauge, NY
Friedman, Arthur S. .... New York, NY
Friedman, Arthur S. .... New York, NY
Friedman, Arthur S. .... New York, NY
Friedman, Arthur W. .... Chicago, IL
Friedman, Aryeh S. .... Basking Ridge, NJ
Friedman & Associates .... Houston, TX
Friedman & Atherton .... Boston, MA
Friedman, Avery S. .... Cleveland, OH
Friedman, Avi .... Los Angeles, CA
Friedman & Babbitt Co., L.P.A.
Columbus, OH
Delaware, OH
Lancaster, OH
Newark, OH
Friedman Babcock & Gaythwaite
Portland, ME
Friedman, Bafundo, Ginsberg & Porter
Cherry Hill, NJ
Friedman, Barbara A. .... Washington, DC
Friedman, Barbara K. .... East Hampton, NY
Friedman, Barbara L. .... New York, NY
Friedman, Barbara S. .... La Porte, IN
Michigan City, IN
Friedman, Barbara S. .... New York, NY
Friedman, Barbara T. .... New York, NY
Friedman, Barbara W. .... New York, NY
Friedman, Barry .... Philadelphia, PA
Friedman, Barry A. .... Beverly Hills, CA
Friedman, Barry A. .... Washington, DC
Friedman, Barry A., & Associates
Mobile, AL
Friedman, Barry C. .... New York, NY
Friedman, Barry D. .... Hackensack, NJ
Friedman, Barry E. .... Nashville, TN
Friedman, Barry H. .... Poughkeepsie, NY
Friedman, Barry I. .... Pittsburgh, PA
Friedman, Barry L. .... Los Angeles, CA
Friedman, Barry S. .... Boca Raton, FL
Friedman, Bart .... New York, NY
Friedman, Ben C. .... New York, NY
Friedman, Benjamin A. .... Taunton, MA
Friedman, Benjamin J. .... Oak Park, MI
Friedman, Benjamin S. .... Philadelphia, PA
Friedman, Bennett B. .... Bradford, PA
Friedman, Benson K. .... Chicago, IL
Friedman, Bernard A. .... Detroit, MI
Friedman, Bernard A. .... White Plains, NY
Friedman, Bernard D. .... Manalapan, NJ
New York, NY
Friedman, Bernard E. .... Chicago, IL
Friedman, Bernard L. .... Orange, CT
Friedman, Bernard L. .... Columbia, SC
Friedman, Bernie .... Fort Lauderdale, FL
Friedman, Brad N. .... New York, NY
Friedman, Bradford L. .... Boston, MA
Friedman, Bradley A. .... Denver, CO
Friedman, Bradley A. .... Dallas, TX
Friedman, Brenda A. .... Boca Raton, FL
Friedman, Brent A. .... Miami, FL
Friedman, Brian A. .... Chicago, IL
Friedman, Brian L. .... Troy, NY
Friedman, Brian P. .... New York, NY
Friedman and Briggs .... Taunton, MA
Friedman, Bruce .... Los Angeles, CA
Friedman, Bruce A., (P.C.)
Los Angeles, CA
Friedman, Bruce E. .... Owings Mills, MD
Friedman, Bruce E. .... St. Louis, MO
Friedman, Bruce E. .... Concord, NH
Friedman, Bruce E., P.A. .... Owings Mills, MD
Friedman, Bruce M. .... San Francisco, CA
Friedman, Bruce M. .... Chicago, IL
Friedman, Bruce M. .... New York, NY
Friedman, Bruce P. .... Philadelphia, PA
Friedman, Bruce S. .... Department of Justice, Civil Rights Division, GV
Friedman, Bryan M. .... Irvine, CA
Friedman, Bryce .... New York, NY
Friedman, Bryon L. .... White Plains, NY
Friedman, Burton A. .... Forest Hills, NY
Friedman, Burton S. .... North Andover, MA
Friedman, C. Marshall .... St. Louis, MO
Friedman, C. Marshall, A Professional Corporation .... Clayton, MO
St. Louis, MO
Friedman, Caren Ilene .... Santa Fe, NM
Friedman, Carey M. .... Richmond, VA
Friedman, Carl A. .... New York, NY
Friedman, Carol Ann .... Houston, TX
Friedman, Carol S. .... Philadelphia, PA
Friedman, Carolyn R. .... San Francisco, CA
Friedman, Carolyn R. .... De Witt, NY

Friedman, Carolyn Rose ... Miami, FL
Friedman, Charlene A. ... Palo Alto, CA
Friedman, Charles A. ... Fort Worth, TX
Friedman, Charles B. ... New York, NY
Friedman, Charles E. ... Harrisburg, PA
Friedman, Charles I. ... Phoenix, AZ
Friedman, Charles I., P.C. ... Phoenix, AZ
Friedman, Charles J. ... Denver, CO
Friedman, Charles J., P.C. ... Denver, CO
Friedman, Charles K. ... Arlington, VA
Friedman, Charles L. ... Minneapolis, MN
Friedman, Charles M. ... Louisville, KY
Friedman, Cheryl M. ... Universal City, CA
Friedman, Christine ... Manchester, NH
Friedman, Christine Y. ... San Diego, CA
Friedman, Clayton S. ... Chicago, IL
Friedman, Clifford L. ... Dallas, TX
Friedman, Collard, Cutter & Panneton, Professional Corporation
Sacramento, CA
Friedman, Cory E. ... Crown Point, NY
Friedman, D. Sylvan ... Towson, MD
Friedman, Dale L. ... Hollywood, FL
Friedman, Dan ... Baltimore, MD
Friedman, Dana B. ... New York, NY
Friedman, Dana Eric ... Milford, CT
Friedman, Daniel, (A P.C.)
Thousand Oaks, CA
Friedman, Daniel H. ... Santa Fe, NM
Friedman, Daniel J. ... Los Angeles, CA
Friedman, Daniel J. ... New York, NY
Friedman, Daniel J. ... New York, NY
Friedman, Daniel M.
United States Court Of Appeals For The Federal Circuit, GV
Friedman, Daniel P. ... Oakland, CA
Friedman, Daniel R. ... St. Louis, MO
Friedman, Daniella ... Fort Lauderdale, FL
Friedman, Darren W. ... Miami, FL
Friedman, David ... Beverly Hills, CA
Friedman, David ... Hollywood, FL
Friedman, David ... Atlantic City, NJ
Friedman, David ... Brooklyn, NY
Friedman, David ... Akron, OH
Friedman, David A. ... Miami, FL
Friedman, David A. ... Louisville, KY
Friedman, David A. ... Lawrenceville, NJ
Friedman, David B. ... New York, NY
Friedman, David C. ... Hollywood, CA
Friedman, David C. ... New York, NY
Friedman, David E. ... New York, NY
Friedman, David G. ... New York, NY
Friedman, David I. ... West Bloomfield, MI
Friedman, David J. ... Chicago, IL
Friedman, David J. ... New York, NY
Friedman, David Jon ... Valhalla, NY
Friedman, David K. ... Boca Raton, FL
Friedman, David L. ... Kew Gardens, NY
Friedman, David M. ... Skokie, IL
Friedman, David M. ... New York, NY
Friedman, David P. ... Bridgeport, CT
Friedman, David, P.A. ... Hollywood, FL
Friedman, David R. ... Waltham, MA
Friedman, David R. ... Madison, WI
Friedman, David S. ... New York, NY
Friedman, David Samuel ... Boston, MA
Friedman, Dawn G. ... Beverly Hills, CA
Friedman, Dean I. ... Los Angeles, CA
Friedman, Deborah C. ... Augusta, ME
Friedman, Deborah J. ... Denver, CO
Friedman, Deborah L. ... New York, NY
Friedman, Deborah Lavine
San Francisco, CA
Friedman, Debra S. ... Rockville, MD
Friedman, Debra S. ... Philadelphia, PA
Friedman, Dennis G. ... Chicago, IL
Friedman, Dennis J. ... New York, NY
Friedman, Dennis L. ... Philadelphia, PA
Friedman, Diana S. ... Dallas, TX
Friedman, Dina M. ... New York, NY
Friedman, Dobin ... New Orleans, LA
Friedman, Domiano & Smith Co., L.P.A.
Marco Island, FL
Cleveland, OH
Friedman, Donald ... West Orange, NJ
Friedman, Donald ... Brooklyn, NY
Friedman, Donald ... Aurora, OH
Friedman, Donald B. ... Texarkana, TX
Friedman, Donald J. ... Washington, DC
Friedman, Donald J. ... New York, NY
Friedman, Donald R. ... New York, NY
Friedman, Donald S. ... San Francisco, CA
Friedman, Donna S. ... New York, NY
Friedman, Doris T. ... White Plains, NY
Friedman, Doris T., P.C., Law Offices of
White Plains, NY
Friedman, Douglas ... Los Angeles, CA
Friedman, Douglas E. ... Woodbridge, NJ
Friedman, Douglas I. ... Birmingham, AL
Friedman, Douglas L. ... New York, NY
Friedman, Driegert & Hsueh, P.C., A Professional Corporation ... Dallas, TX
Friedman, Edw. L. ... Scarsdale, NY
Friedman, Edward ... Beverly Hills, CA
Friedman, Edward ... New York, NY
Friedman, Edward A. ... New York, NY
Friedman, Edward A. ... New York, NY
Friedman, Edward A. ... State College, PA
Friedman, Edward D. ... Green Valley, AZ
Friedman, Edward D. ... Jericho, NY
Friedman, Edward I. ... Bedford, NY
Friedman, Edward J. ... Washington, DC
Baltimore, MD
Fairfax, VA
Friedman, Edward L. ... Houston, TX
Friedman, Elaine F. ... New York, NY
Friedman, Elaine R. ... Bronx, NY
Friedman, Elaine Russo ... New York, NY
Friedman, Eli ... West Bloomfield, MI
Friedman, Elizabeth J. ... Granada Hills, CA
Friedman, Ellen A. ... San Francisco, CA
Friedman, Ellen S. ... Nashua, NH
Friedman, Ellen S. ... New York, NY
Friedman, Eric J. ... New York, NY
Friedman, Eric R. ... Portland, OR
Friedman, Eric S. ... Atlanta, GA
Friedman, Eric S. ... Rockville, MD
Friedman, Ernest F. ... Southfield, MI
Friedman, Errol N. ... Texarkana, TX
Friedman, Erwin A. ... Savannah, GA
Friedman, Ethan J. ... Arlington, VA
Friedman, Eugene A. ... Baltimore, MD
Friedman, Eugene F. ... Chicago, IL
Friedman, Eugene F., Ltd. ... Chicago, IL
Friedman, Eugene M. ... Dover, NJ
Friedman, Eugene S. ... Bingham Farms, MI
Friedman, Eugene S. ... New York, NY
Friedman, F. Michael ... Media, PA
Friedman, Faith A. ... New York, NY
New York, NY
Friedman, Felice B.
Securities and Exchange Commission, Office of International Affairs, GV
Friedman & Ferguson ... White Plains, NY
Friedman, Foster S.B. ... Alexandria, VA
Friedman, Frances M. ... New York, NY
Friedman, Frank G. ... Nashville, TN
Friedman, Frank K. ... Roanoke, VA
Friedman, Frank P. ... Freehold, NJ
Friedman & Franks, P.C. ... Fort Worth, TX
Friedman, Fred ... Akron, NY
Friedman, Fred T. ... Duluth, MN
Friedman, Frederic A. ... Cleveland, OH
Friedman, Frederic G. ... Milwaukee, WI
Friedman, Frederick A. ... Garden City, NY
Friedman, Frederick D.
Santa Monica, CA
Friedman & Friedman ... Beverly Hills, CA
Friedman & Friedman ... Towson, MD
Friedman & Friedman ... Jenkintown, PA
Philadelphia, PA
Friedman and Friedman, P.A.
Coral Gables, FL
Miami, FL
Palm Beach, FL
Friedman & Friedman, P.C. ... Southfield, MI
Friedman, G. Robert, (P.C.) ... Houston, TX
Friedman, Gail Tuler ... Chicago, IL
Friedman, Gary A. ... Hawthorne, NY
Friedman, Gary Alan ... Miami, FL
Friedman, Gary B., (Ltd.) ... Chicago, IL
Friedman, Gary D. ... New York, NY
Friedman, Gary D. ... New York, NY
Friedman, Gary David ... Lake Geneva, WI
Friedman, Gary E. ... La Jolla, CA
Friedman, Gary E. ... Jackson, MS
Friedman, Gary H. ... Madison, WI
Friedman, Gary M. ... New York, NY
Friedman, Gary S. ... Las Vegas, NM
Santa Fe, NM
Friedman, Gary S. ... New York, NY
Friedman, Gary S. ... Philadelphia, PA
Friedman, Gary T. ... Bakersfield, CA
Friedman, Gavin ... Los Angeles, CA
Friedman, Gayle C. ... Atlanta, GA
Friedman, Gene ... New Orleans, LA
Friedman, George ... New York, NY
Friedman, George H. ... New York, NY
Friedman, Gerald ... Los Angeles, CA
Friedman, Gerald D. ... Los Angeles, CA
Friedman, Gerald I. ... Bay Shore, NY
Friedman, Gerald Lloyd ... Los Angeles, CA
Friedman, Geri A. ... Uniondale, NY
Friedman & Gilbert ... Cleveland, OH
Friedman, Gilbert B. ... Arcata, CA
Friedman, Gilbert H. ... Los Angeles, CA
Friedman, Gilbert H. ... Santa Monica, CA
Friedman, Gilbert J. ... Palm Desert, CA
Friedman, Gillian E. ... Los Angeles, CA
Friedman, Glenn A. ... San Francisco, CA
Friedman, Glori A. ... Philadelphia, PA
Friedman, Gordon S. ... Cleveland, OH
Friedman & Gotbaum, LLP
New York, NY
Friedman & Greenberg ... Plantation, FL
Friedman, Gregg J. ... Boulder, CO
Friedman, Gregory A. ... Chicago, IL
Friedman, Gregory D. ... Natchitoches, LA
Friedman, Hal D. ... Louisville, KY
Friedman, Hal M. ... New York, NY
Friedman, Harold ... Miami Shores, FL
Friedman, Harold ... Newark, NJ
Friedman, Harold ... Houston, TX
Friedman, Harold A. ... Schenectady, NY
Friedman, Harold, (A Professional Corporation) ... Los Angeles, CA
Friedman, Harold E. ... Cleveland, OH
Friedman, Harold G. ... Oakland, CA
Friedman, Harold J. ... Portland, ME
Friedman, Harold K. ... Walnut Creek, CA
Friedman, Harold L. ... Flushing, NY
Friedman, Harry J. ... Miami, FL
Friedman, Harvey ... New York, NY
Friedman, Harvey D. ... Sunrise, FL
Friedman, Harvey F. ... Manhasset, NY
Friedman, Harvey G. ... Washington, DC
Friedman, Harvey L. ... Amherst, MA
Friedman, Harvey L. ... White Plains, NY
Friedman, Harvey R. ... Los Angeles, CA
Friedman, Heidi F. ... Fort Lauderdale, FL
Friedman, Helene ... Los Angeles, CA
Friedman, Heller & Enriquez, LLP
Beverly Hills, CA
Friedman, Henry ... Los Angeles, CA
Friedman, Henry, A P.C. ... Los Angeles, CA
Friedman, Henry S. ... Department of Justice, Environment and Natural Resources Division, GV
Friedman, Herbert D. ... Boston, MA
Friedman, Herbert J. ... San Francisco, CA
Friedman, Herbert J. ... Lincoln, NE
Friedman, Herbert M. ... Kinderhook, NY
Friedman, Herbert M. ... New York, NY
Friedman, Herbert S. ... Morton Grove, IL
Friedman & Heydasch, P.A. ... Miami, FL
Friedman, Heywood G.
Westlake Village, CA
Friedman, Hirschen, Miller, Coughlin & Campito, P.C. ... Albany, NY
Schenectady, NY
Friedman & Hoch, P.C. ... Harrisburg, PA
Friedman & Hoffman ... Beachwood, OH
Cleveland, OH
Friedman & Holtz, P.C. ... Chicago, IL
Friedman, Howard ... Washington, DC
Friedman, Howard ... Fort Lauderdale, FL
Friedman, Howard ... Chicago, IL
Friedman, Howard ... Boston, MA
Friedman, Howard A. ... Santa Monica, CA
Friedman, Howard D.
Department of Commerce, Patent and Trademark Office, GV
Friedman, Howard D. ... Orlando, FL
Friedman, Howard I., (A P.C.)
Los Angeles, CA
Friedman, Howard M. ... Toledo, OH
Friedman, Hyman ... New York, NY
Friedman, Ian C. ... Washington, DC
Friedman, Ian Jeffrey ... Los Angeles, CA
Friedman, Ian N. ... Cleveland, OH
Friedman, Inez H. ... Boston, MA
Friedman, Ira ... New York, NY
Friedman, Ira J. ... Chicago, IL
Friedman, Ira M. ... Beverly Hills, CA
Friedman, Irvin A. ... St. Louis, MO
Friedman, Irving ... Scottsdale, AZ
Friedman, Irving ... Lewiston, ME
Friedman, Irving I. ... Louisville, KY
Friedman, Irving M. ... Chicago, IL
Friedman, Irving M. ... New York, NY
Friedman, Irwin E. ... Fairfield, CT
Friedman, J. Bennett ... Los Angeles, CA
Friedman, J. Kent ... Houston, TX
Friedman, Jack ... Silver Spring, MD
Friedman, Jack ... Fort Worth, TX
Friedman, Jack A. ... San Francisco, CA
Friedman, Jack B. ... Carle Place, NY
Friedman, Jack O. ... Charleston, WV
Friedman, Jack P. ... Latham, NY
Friedman, Jack R. ... New York, NY
Friedman, Jack T. ... Walnut Creek, CA
Friedman, Jacob I. ... New York, NY
Friedman & James ... Manalapan, NJ
New York, NY
Friedman, James Alan ... Madison, WI
Friedman, James D. ... Boston, MA
Friedman, James D. ... Milwaukee, WI
Friedman, James J. ... Rolling Meadows, IL
Friedman, James J., Law Office of, P.C.
Rolling Meadows, IL
Friedman, James K. ... Southfield, MI
Friedman, James M. ... Cleveland, OH
Friedman, James S. ... Hackensack, NJ
Friedman, James T., (P.C.) ... Chicago, IL
Friedman, Jane ... New York, NY
Friedman, Jane M. ... Detroit, MI
Friedman, Janet ... Davis, CA
Friedman, Janet B. ... Rockville, MD
Friedman, Jason D. ... New York, NY
Friedman, Jason S. ... Denver, CO
Friedman, Jay Fred ... Cordova, TN
Friedman, Jay M. ... Rochester, NY
Friedman, Jeff J. ... Newark, NJ
New York, NY
Friedman, Jeffrey ... Los Angeles, CA
Friedman, Jeffrey ... Washington, DC
Friedman, Jeffrey A. ... Anchorage, AK
Friedman, Jeffrey D. ... Chicago, IL
Friedman, Jeffrey E. ... Birmingham, AL
Friedman, Jeffrey E. ... San Francisco, CA
Friedman, Jeffrey F. ... New York, NY
Friedman, Jeffrey H. ... Laguna Beach, CA
Friedman, Jeffrey H. ... Marco Island, FL
Cleveland, OH
Friedman, Jeffrey L. ... Reisterstown, MD
Friedman, Jeffrey L. ... New York, NY
Friedman, Jeffrey M. ... Fort Lauderdale, FL
Friedman, Jeffrey M. ... Austin, TX
Friedman, Jeffrey S. ... Wilmington, DE
Friedman, Jennifer H. ... Menlo Park, CA
Friedman, Jennifer L. ... Buffalo, NY
Friedman, Jennifer S. ... Atlanta, GA
Friedman, Jerald ... Los Angeles, CA
Friedman, Jere M. ... Phoenix, AZ
Friedman, Jeremiah ... Boston, MA
Friedman, Jeremy D. ... Coral Gables, FL
Friedman, Jeremy L. ... Oakland, CA
Friedman, Jerome B. ... Norfolk, VA
Friedman, Jerome E. ... Metairie, LA
Friedman, Jerome E. ... Columbus, OH
Friedman, Jerome H. ... Benicia, CA
Friedman, Jerry M. ... Cincinnati, OH
Friedman, Jessica ... New York, NY
Friedman, Jessica R. ... New York, NY
Friedman, Jill ... Brooklyn, NY
Friedman, Jill L., Law Offices of
Santa Barbara, CA
Friedman, Jo Anne ... Mercer Island, WA
Friedman, Joan ... Augusta, ME
Friedman, Jodi A. ... Little Silver, NJ
Friedman, Joel ... Media, PA
Friedman, Joel F. ... Phoenix, AZ
Friedman, Joel H. ... Brooklyn, NY
Friedman, Joel L. ... Matawan, NJ
Friedman, Joel M. ... Chicago, IL
Friedman, Joel M. ... Philadelphia, PA
Friedman, Joel Wm. ... New Orleans, LA
Friedman, John A. ... Chicago, IL
Friedman, John A. ... New York, NY
Friedman, John L. ... Baltimore, MD
Friedman, John M. ... Scarsdale, NY
Friedman, Jon L. ... Pittsburgh, PA
Friedman, Jonathan ... Freehold, NJ
Friedman, Jonathan A. ... Washington, DC
Friedman, Jonathan L. ... Los Angeles, CA
Friedman, Jonathan M. ... Portland, OR
Friedman, Jonathan R. ... Atlanta, GA
Friedman, Jonathan S. ... Fort Lauderdale, FL
Friedman, Jonathan Z. ... White Plains, NY
Friedman, Jordan S. ... New York, NY
Friedman, Jos. R. ... Chicago, IL
Friedman, Joseph ... Boston, MA
Friedman, Joseph ... Eastchester, NY
Friedman, Joseph ... Pittsburgh, PA
Friedman, Joseph A. ... Dallas, TX
Friedman, Joseph B., Jr. ... San Antonio, TX
Friedman, Joseph Lee ... Baltimore, MD
Friedman, Joseph N. ... New York, NY
Friedman, Joseph S. ... Olney, MD
Friedman, Josh M. ... Chicago, IL
Friedman, Joshua ... Moorestown, NJ
Friedman, Joshua A. ... Cherry Hill, NJ
Friedman, Joshua T. ... Chicago, IL
Friedman, Joyce F. ... Braintree, MA
Friedman, Joyce G.
Merit Systems Protection Board, Office of the General Counsel, GV
Friedman, Jud J. ... Los Angeles, CA
Friedman, Judi E. ... Meriden, CT
Friedman, Judith E. ... Stamford, CT
Friedman, Judith H. ... Hartford, CT
Friedman, Judith H. ... Department of Justice, Criminal Division, GV
Friedman, Judith L.
Federal Deposit Insurance Corporation, Liquidation Branch, GV
Friedman, Julian R. ... Savannah, GA
Friedman, Julian W. ... New York, NY
Friedman, Julie A. ... Boston, MA
Friedman, Julie Ann ... Seattle, WA
Friedman, Julie Beth ... Binghamton, NY
Friedman, Julie H. ... Chicago, IL
Friedman, K. Betram ... Great Neck, NY
Friedman, K. Bruce ... San Francisco, CA
Friedman Kaplan & Seiler LLP
Newark, NJ
New York, NY
Friedman & Kaplow ... Cleveland, OH
Friedman, Kara M. ... Chicago, IL
Friedman, Karen A. ... New York, NY
Friedman, Karl B. ... Birmingham, AL
Friedman, Karl M. ... El Paso, TX
Friedman, Kate S. ... Los Angeles, CA
Friedman, Kates, Pearlman & Fitzgerald, A Professional Corporation ... Rutherford, NJ
Friedman, Kathleen O'Ferrall
Baltimore, MD
Friedman, Kelley J. ... Sugar Land, TX
Friedman, Kennard N. ... Menasha, WI
Friedman, Kenneth ... Las Vegas, NV
Friedman, Kenneth A.
North Miami Beach, FL
Friedman, Kenneth I. ... Manchester, CT
Friedman, Kenneth J. ... New York, NY
Friedman, Kenneth L., (A Professional Corporation) ... Encino, CA
Friedman, Kenneth P. ... Buffalo, NY
Friedman, Kenneth R. ... Seattle, WA
Friedman, Kent B. ... St. Louis, MO
Friedman, Kerry A. ... Asheville, NC
Friedman & Kessler ... Providence, RI
Friedman, Kevin B. ... Dundalk, MD
Friedman and King, P.C. ... Harrisburg, PA
Friedman & Kline ... Reisterstown, MD
Friedman & Kohut, P.C. ... Detroit, MI
Southfield, MI
Friedman, Krauss & Zlotolow
New York, NY
Friedman, Larry ... Philadelphia, PA
Friedman, Laura A. ... Stamford, CT
Friedman, Lauren ... Ronkonkoma, NY
Friedman, Lauren G. ... Houston, TX
Friedman, Laurence A. ... Cleveland, OH
Friedman, Laurence M. ... New York, NY
Friedman, Laurie S. ... Lutherville, MD
Friedman Law Offices ... Lincoln, NE
Friedman, Lawrence ... Chicago, IL
Friedman, Lawrence ... Boston, MA
Friedman, Lawrence ... Millburn, NJ
Friedman, Lawrence ... Batavia, NY
Friedman, Lawrence A. ... Southfield, MI
Friedman, Lawrence A. ... Somerville, NJ
Friedman, Lawrence B. ... Miami, FL
Friedman, Lawrence B. ... New York, NY
Friedman, Lawrence C. ... St. Louis, MO
Friedman, Lawrence J. ... Stockton, CA
Friedman, Lawrence J. ... Wayne, NJ
Friedman, Lawrence J. ... Dallas, TX
Friedman, Lawrence L. ... New York, NY
Friedman, Lawrence M. ... Palo Alto, CA
Friedman, Lawrence M. ... Chicago, IL
Friedman, Lawrence M. ... Chicago, IL
Friedman, Lawrence Michael ... Toledo, OH
Friedman, Lawrence, P.C. ... Chicago, IL
Friedman, Leak & Bloom, P.C.
Birmingham, AL
Friedman, Lee A. ... Washington, DC
Friedman, Lee M. ... St. Paul, MN
Friedman, Lee S. ... Windermere, FL
Friedman & Leinwand ... Fort Lauderdale, FL
Friedman, Leo H. ... Lansing, MI

Friedman, Leo J. ... Mineola, NY
Friedman, Leon ... East Meadow, NY
Friedman, Leon ... New York, NY
Friedman, Leon, P.C. ... East Meadow, NY
Friedman, Leonard ... Chicago, IL
Friedman, Leonard C. ... New York, NY
Friedman, Leonard E. ... Brooklyn, NY
Friedman, Leonard M. ... Los Angeles, CA
Friedman, Leonard M. ... Sacramento, CA
Friedman, Lesley Szanto ... New York, NY
Friedman, Lester ... San Leandro, CA
Friedman, Lester J., (A Prof. Corp.)
Beverly Hills, CA
Friedman & Levin Associates
Philadelphia, PA
Friedman & Levine ... New York, NY
Friedman, Levy & Goldfarb, P.C.
New York, NY
Friedman, Lewis ... New York, NY
Friedman, Lillian M.
North Miami Beach, FL
Friedman, Lillian S. ... Schenectady, NY
Friedman, Linda ... Orinda, CA
Friedman, Linda A. ... Birmingham, AL
Friedman, Linda Debra ... Chicago, IL
Friedman, Linda E. ... New York, NY
Friedman, Linda Fleisher ... Deerfield, IL
Friedman, Lisa K.
Environmental Protection Agency,
Office of the General Counsel, GV
Friedman, Lisa K. ... New York, NY
Friedman, Lisa Rozett ... Lawrenceville, NJ
Friedman, Lisa S. ... Cleveland, OH
Friedman, Lou & Co., P.A.
Owings Mills, MD
Friedman, Louis A. ... Owings Mills, MD
Friedman, Louis F. ... Towson, MD
Friedman, Louis M. ... Chicago, IL
Friedman, Louis P. ... Los Angeles, CA
Friedman, Lyman G. ... Washington, DC
Friedman, M. Leo ... Schroon Lake, NY
Friedman, M. Ray ... Boca Raton, FL
Friedman & MacFadyen, P.A.
Baltimore, MD
Friedman, Malcolm H. ... Miami, FL
Friedman & Manning, P.C. ... Delmar, NY
Friedman & Marasco ... Bradford, PA
Friedman, Marc ... Rockville, MD
Friedman, Marc ... Linwood, NJ
Friedman, Marc A. ... Northampton, MA
Friedman, Marc B. ... Philadelphia, PA
Friedman, Marc J. ... Parsippany, NJ
Friedman, Marc M. ... Camarillo, CA
Friedman, Marc R. ... Columbus, OH
Friedman, Marc S. ... Roseland, NJ
New York, NY
Friedman, Marci D. ... Los Angeles, CA
Friedman, Marci E. ... Los Angeles, CA
Friedman, Marcie W. ... Philadelphia, PA
Friedman, Margery Sinder
Washington, DC
Friedman, Maria L. ... Atlanta, GA
Friedman, Marilyn F. ... New York, NY
Friedman, Marion S. ... Houston, TX
Friedman, Marjorie Northrop
New York, NY
Friedman, Mark D. ... Beverly Hills, CA
Friedman, Mark E. ... Portland, OR
Friedman, Mark F. ... Hillsboro, OR
Friedman, Mark H. ... Birmingham, AL
Friedman, Mark H. ... Baltimore, MD
Friedman, Mark H. ... Newark, NJ
Friedman, Mark J. ... Los Angeles, CA
Friedman, Mark J. ... Baltimore, MD
Friedman, Mark J. ... Centerville, OH
Friedman, Mark K. ... New York, NY
Friedman, Mark L. ... New York, NY
Friedman, Mark L. ... New York, NY
Friedman, Mark N. ... Hartsdale, NY
Friedman, Mark S. ... Chicago, IL
Friedman, Mark W. ... New York, NY
Friedman, Marsha Harris ... West Hartford, CT
Friedman, Martin ... Homer, AK
Friedman & Martin ... Brunswick, GA
Hinesville, GA
Savannah, GA
Friedman, Martin J. ... Chicago, IL
Friedman, Martin J. ... New York, NY
Friedman, Martin J. ... New York, NY
Friedman, Martin N. ... Lauderhill, FL
Friedman, Martin R. ... Brooklyn, NY
Friedman, Martin S., (P.A.)
Tallahassee, FL
Friedman, Marvin ... Richmond Hill, NY
Friedman, Marvin Ross ... Miami, FL
Friedman, Marvin W. ... San Francisco, CA
Friedman, Mary Lynne ... New Orleans, LA
Friedman, Matthew C. ... Chicago, IL
Friedman, Matthew L. ... Hartford, CT
Friedman, Matthew S. ... Cleveland, OH
Friedman, Max ... New York, NY
Friedman, Melinda A. ... St. Louis, MO
Friedman, Melissa Windham ... Roanoke, VA
Friedman, Mellitz & Newman, P.C.
Bridgeport, CT
Fairfield, CT
Friedman, Melvin I. ... La Jolla, CA
Friedman, Melvin, P.C. ... Virginia Beach, VA
Friedman, Meredith L. ... New York, NY
Friedman, Meryl R. ... Cranbury, NJ
Friedman, Michael ... Torrance, CA
Friedman, Michael ... New York, NY
Friedman, Michael A. ... Phoenix, AZ
Friedman, Michael A. ... Texarkana, TX
Friedman, Michael B.
Belvedere-Tiburon, CA
Friedman, Michael C. ... Washington, DC
Friedman, Michael D. ... New York, NY
Friedman, Michael D. ... New York, NY
Friedman, Michael Dean, (P.A.) ... Miami, FL
Friedman, Michael E. ... Pasadena, CA
Friedman, Michael E. ... New York, NY
Friedman, Michael E. ... Milwaukee, WI
Friedman, Michael G. ... Somerville, NJ
Friedman, Michael H. ... Atlanta, GA
Friedman, Michael H. ... White Plains, NY
Friedman, Michael H. ... Philadelphia, PA
Friedman, Michael J. ... Detroit, MI
Friedman, Michael J. ... Camden, NJ
Friedman, Michael Jeffrey ... Bronx, NY
Friedman, Michael L.
North Miami Beach, FL
Friedman, Michael N. ... Calabasas, CA
Los Angeles, CA
Friedman, Michael P. ... Bangor, ME
Friedman, Michael P. ... Boston, MA
Friedman, Michael P. ... Delmar, NY
Friedman, Michael R. ... Stamford, CT
New York, NY
Friedman, Michael S. ... Chatsworth, CA
Friedman, Michael S. ... Denver, CO
Friedman, Michael S. ... Birmingham, MI
Friedman, Michael S. ... Winchester, VA
Friedman, Michael Scott ... Baltimore, MD
Friedman, Michael T. ... Germantown, MD
Friedman, Michael W. ... Albany, NY
Friedman, Michele L. ... Portland, OR
Friedman, Miles D. ... Laguna Niguel, CA
Friedman, Milton ... New York, NY
Friedman, Milton A. ... Miami, FL
Friedman, Milton H. ... Buffalo, NY
Friedman, Mindy ... Philadelphia, PA
Friedman, Mitchell J. ... San Francisco, CA
Friedman, Mitchell R. ... New York, NY
Friedman, Mitchell R. ... New York, NY
Friedman, Mitchell S., (P.C.)
Great Neck, NY
Friedman, Mona J. ... Columbus, GA
Friedman, Morley ... St. Paul, MN
Friedman, Morris R., (P.C.) ... New York, NY
Friedman, Morris S. ... Franklin, MI
Friedman, Morton ... Greenwich, CT
Friedman, Morton ... Birmingham, MI
Friedman, Morton D. ... Silver Spring, MD
Friedman, Morton L. ... Sacramento, CA
Friedman, Myles F. ... Baltimore, MD
Friedman, Myrna E. ... Vienna, VA
Friedman, Myron ... Northbridgton, ME
Friedman, Myron M. ... Liberty, NY
Friedman, Nancy E. ... New York, NY
Friedman, Nancy L.
Department of Transportation,
Federal Railroad Administration, GV
Friedman, Nansi ... New York, NY
Friedman, Nathan A. ... Deerfield Beach, FL
Cherry Hill, NJ
Friedman, Nathaniel ... Morton Grove, IL
Friedman, Nathaniel J. ... Los Angeles, CA
Friedman, Nathaniel J., P.C.
Los Angeles, CA
Friedman, Natkins & Freedman ... Solon, OH
Friedman, Neal E. ... Newton, MA
Friedman, Neal J. ... Washington, DC
Friedman, Neal S. ... Wantagh, NY
Friedman, Neil H. ... Las Vegas, NV
Friedman, Neile S. ... Baltimore, MD
Friedman, Nelson ... Cleveland, OH
Friedman, Newton S. ... Duluth, MN
Friedman, Nicholas R. ... Miami, FL
Friedman, Nicole L. ... Atlanta, GA
Friedman, Norman ... Atlanta, GA
Dallas, TX
Friedman, Olive, McCubbin, Spalding, Bilter, Roosevelt & Montgomery, A Professional Corporation
San Francisco, CA
Friedman, Orlan S. ... Indian Wells, CA
Friedman, Pachino & Garcia ... Baltimore, MD
Friedman, Pamela S. ... South Salem, NY
Friedman, Pamela Struhl ... Edison, NJ
Friedman, Patricia D. ... Atlanta, GA
Friedman, Paul ... New York, NY
Friedman, Paul A. ... Newark, NJ
Friedman, Paul Alexander
Washington, DC
Friedman, Paul D. ... Phoenix, AZ
Friedman, Paul D. ... Miami, FL
Friedman, Paul D., P.A. ... Miami, FL
Friedman, Paul H. ... Washington, DC
Friedman, Paul J. ... Los Angeles, CA
Friedman, Paul L.
United States District Court For The District
Of Columbia, GV
Friedman, Paul M. ... Cleveland, OH
Friedman, Paul T. ... San Francisco, CA
Friedman, Paula Davis ... Chicago, IL
Friedman, Paula G. ... Washington, DC
Friedman, Paula L. ... Cleveland, OH
Friedman & Pennington, P.C.
Birmingham, AL
Friedman, Penny ... Cincinnati, OH
Friedman, Pepi ... Atlanta, GA
Friedman, Peter B., (P.C.) ... Cleveland, OH
Friedman, Peter C. ... Treasury Department,
Internal Revenue Service, GV
Friedman, Peter M. ... Chicago, IL
Friedman, Peter S. ... Princeton, NJ
Elkins Park, PA
Friedman, Peter S. ... Roseland, NJ
Friedman Peterson & Stroffe, A Professional Law Corporation ... Irvine, CA
Friedman, Philip B. ... Erie, PA
Friedman, Philip J. ... New York, NY
Friedman, Philip L. ... New York, NY
Friedman, Philip S. ... Washington, DC
Friedman, Philip S. ... Evanston, IL
Friedman, Phyllis A. Z. ... Ridgewood, NJ
Friedman, Phyllis C. ... Towson, MD
Friedman, Prizant & Yoffe ... Louisville, KY
Friedman, Ralph D. ... Jenkintown, PA
Friedman, Randi ... Liberty Corner, NJ
Friedman, Randi Diane ... Green Brook, NJ
Friedman, Randolph J. ... Southfield, MI
Friedman & Ranzenhofer, P.C. ... Akron, NY
Friedman & Rau ... Yreka, CA
Friedman, Redina ... Chicago, IL
Friedman, Renée M. ... Chicago, IL
Friedman, Reuben ... Silver Spring, MD
Friedman, Reuben I. ... New Orleans, LA
Friedman, Rhona Wolfe ... Potomac, MD
Friedman, Richard ... Palo Alto, CA
Friedman, Richard ... New York, NY
Friedman, Richard A.
Department of Justice,
Criminal Division, GV
Friedman, Richard A. ... Newark, NJ
Trenton, NJ
Friedman, Richard A. ... New York, NY
Friedman, Richard A. ... Lafayette Hill, PA
Friedman, Richard B. ... Westport, CT
Friedman, Richard B. ... Chicago, IL
Friedman, Richard C. ... Chicago, IL
Friedman, Richard D. ... Ann Arbor, MI
Friedman, Richard E. ... Chicago, IL
Friedman, Richard F. ... Chicago, IL
Friedman, Richard G. ... New York, NY
Friedman, Richard H. ... Anchorage, AK
Friedman, Richard H. ... Albany, NY
Friedman, Richard H. ... Harrisburg, PA
Friedman, Richard I. ... Newark, NJ
Friedman, Richard I. ... New York, NY
Friedman, Richard L. ... Sacramento, CA
Friedman, Richard L. ... Camden, NJ
Friedman, Richard L. ... Middletown, NJ
Friedman, Richard L. ... Cleveland, OH
Friedman, Richard M.
Department Of Health And Human Services,
Office of the General Counsel, GV
Friedman, Richard N. ... Miami, FL
Friedman, Richard S. ... Los Angeles, CA
Friedman, Richard S. ... Harrisburg, PA
Friedman, Richard W. ... Albany, NY
Friedman, RisėA. ... Indianapolis, IN
Friedman, Rita ... Naples, FL
Port Charlotte, FL
Weston, FL
Friedman, Robert ... San Bernardino, CA
Friedman, Robert ... Akron, NY
Friedman, Robert ... New York, NY
Friedman, Robert ... Kirkland, WA
Friedman, Robert Andrew
Coral Gables, FL
Friedman, Robert B. ... Suwanee, GA
Friedman, Robert D. ... Plantation, FL
Friedman, Robert D. ... Boston, MA
Friedman, Robert E. ... Fort Lauderdale, FL
Friedman, Robert E. ... Metairie, LA
Friedman, Robert E. ... New York, NY
Friedman, Robert E. ... Cleveland, OH
Friedman, Robert F. ... Dallas, TX
Friedman, Robert G. ... Cleveland, OH
Friedman, Robert H. ... Atlanta, GA
Friedman, Robert H. ... New York, NY
Friedman, Robert I. ... Canton, OH
Friedman, Robert I. ... Philadelphia, PA
Friedman, Robert I., P.C. ... Phoenix, AZ
Friedman, Robert J. ... Beverly Hills, CA
Friedman, Robert J.
Hallandale Beach, FL
Friedman, Robert J. ... Miami, FL
Friedman, Robert J., P.A.
Hallandale Beach, FL
Friedman, Robert James
White Plains, NY
Friedman, Robert L. ... Southfield, MI
Friedman, Robert M. ... Clinton, NJ
Friedman, Robert M. ... New York, NY
Friedman, Robert M. ... Memphis, TN
Friedman, Robert Mitchel ... Phoenix, AZ
Friedman, Robert P. ... Los Angeles, CA
Friedman, Robert S. ... New York, NY
Friedman, Robert S. ... New York, NY
Friedman, Robert S. ... Kirkland, WA
Friedman, Roberta S. ... New Haven, CT
Friedman, Robin A.
Department Of The Interior,
Office of the Solicitor, GV
Friedman, Robin A. ... Boston, MA
Friedman, Robin C. ... Chicago, IL
Friedman, Rochelle S. ... Doylestown, PA
Friedman & Rodman, P.A. ... Sunrise, FL
Friedman, Roger F. ... Los Angeles, CA
Friedman, Ronald A., Law Offices of
Mineola, NY
Friedman, Ronald Benjamin
Santa Clara, CA
Friedman, Ronald David ... Boston, MA
Friedman, Ronald J. ... Jericho, NY
Friedman, Ronald K. ... Carmel, NY
Friedman, Ronald M. ... Fort Lauderdale, FL
Friedman, Ronald M. ... Chicago, IL
Friedman, Ronald M. ... State College, PA
Friedman, Ronald R. ... Boca Raton, FL
Friedman, Roselyn L. ... Chicago, IL
Friedman, Rosenwasser & Goldbaum
Boca Raton, FL
Friedman, Ross A. ... St. Louis, MO
Friedman, Rubin & White
Anchorage, AK
Friedman, Ruby A. ... San Bernardino, CA
Friedman & Rummell Co., L.P.A.
Youngstown, OH
Friedman, S., & Associates, P.C.
Atlanta, GA
Friedman, S. William ... White Plains, NY
Friedman, Sally B. ... New York, NY
Friedman, Sally Forbes ... Minnetonka, MN
Friedman, Samuel ... New York, NY
Friedman, Samuel J. ... Baltimore, MD
Friedman, Samuel S. ... New York, NY
Friedman, Sandra B. ... Omaha, NE
Friedman, Sandra Liss ... Washington, DC
New York, NY
Friedman, Sandrea ... New York, NY
Friedman, Sanford N. ... St. Louis, MO
Friedman, Sari M. ... Garden City, NY
Friedman, Saul ... Providence, RI
Friedman, Saul B. ... Dallas, TX
Friedman, Saul R. ... Anchorage, AK
Friedman, Scott ... New York, NY
Friedman, Scott ... Seattle, WA
Friedman, Scott B. ... Arlington Heights, IL
Friedman, Scott E. ... Buffalo, NY
Friedman, Scott L. ... New York, NY
Friedman, Scott N. ... Columbus, OH
Friedman, Seth L. ... Jackson Heights, NY
Friedman, Seth M. ... Beverly Hills, CA
Friedman, Seth M. ... San Diego, CA
Friedman, Shari L. ... Chicago, IL
Friedman, Sharon G. ... Los Angeles, CA
Friedman, Sharon S. ... Birmingham, MI
Friedman, Shaw R. ... La Porte, IN
Friedman, Shawn M. ... New York, NY
Friedman, Sheldon E. ... Denver, CO
Friedman, Sheldon E. ... Atlanta, GA
Friedman, Sheldon E. ... Baltimore, MD
Friedman, Shelly S. ... New York, NY
Friedman, Sheri B. ... Philadelphia, PA
Friedman, Sherwin & Scarola, P.C.
Elmwood Park, NJ
Friedman, Shirlee M. ... Philadelphia, PA
Friedman, Sholem ... New York, NY
Friedman, Sidney S. ... Baltimore, MD
Friedman Siegelbaum LLP ... Roseland, NJ
New York, NY
Friedman, Simon ... Los Angeles, CA
Friedman, Simon L. ... Springfield, IL
Friedman, Sinar & Rohlfing ... Chicago, IL
Friedman, Sissman & Heaton, P.C.
Memphis, TN
Friedman & Smith, P.C. ... Chicago, IL
Friedman, Sol ... Yonkers, NY
Friedman, Sol J. ... Baltimore, MD
Friedman, Sol M. ... Detroit, MI
Friedman, Solomon P. ... New York, NY
Friedman, Sonja N. ... New York, NY
Friedman, Stacey R. ... New York, NY
Friedman, Stan Jay ... Oakland, CA
Friedman, Stanley ... Laguna Hills, CA
Friedman, Stanley ... San Jose, CA
Friedman, Stanley D. ... New York, NY
Friedman, Stanley F. ... Florham Park, NJ
Friedman, Stanley H. ... Savannah, GA
Friedman, Stanley M. ... Rochester, NY
Friedman, Stanley R. ... Freehold, NJ
Friedman, Stephen ... New York, NY
Friedman, Stephen A. ... Atlanta, GA
Friedman, Stephen A. ... Greenbelt, MD
Friedman, Stephen A., & Associates, P.C.
Atlanta, GA
Friedman, Stephen J. ... Chicago, IL
Friedman, Stephen J. ... New York, NY
Friedman, Stephen M. ... Southfield, MI
Friedman, Stephen S. ... Savannah, GA
Friedman, Steven ... Pembroke Pines, FL
Friedman, Steven A. ... New York, NY
Friedman, Steven A. ... New York, NY
Friedman, Steven A. ... Cleveland, OH
Friedman, Steven C. ... Baltimore, MD
Friedman, Steven E. ... Washington, DC
Friedman, Steven G. ... Washington, DC
Friedman, Steven H. ... West Palm Beach, FL
Friedman, Steven J. ... Collingswood, NJ
Friedman, Steven J. ... New York, NY
Friedman, Steven L. ... Mission Hills, CA
Friedman, Steven L. ... Princeton, NJ
Friedman, Steven L. ... Philadelphia, PA
Friedman, Steven M. ... Phoenix, AZ
Friedman, Steven M. ... Los Angeles, CA
Friedman, Steven P. ... Houston, TX
Friedman, Steven S. ... Elmwood Park, NJ
Friedman, Steven S. ... New York, NY
Friedman, Stewart H ... Lake Success, NY
Friedman, Stuart A. ... Cleveland, OH
Friedman, Stuart I. ... New York, NY
Friedman, Stuart J. ... Munster, IN
Friedman, Stuart J. ... Arlington, VA
McLean, VA
Friedman, Stuart R. ... New York, NY
Friedman, Susan A. ... Washington, DC
Friedman, Susan E. ... New York, NY
Friedman, Susan Meyers ... Washington, DC
Rockville, MD
Friedman, Susan R. ... New York, NY
Friedman, Susan R. ... Lancaster, PA
Friedman, Susan S. ... Southfield, MI
Friedman, Susannah R. ... Philadelphia, PA
Friedman, Suzan
Federal Communications Commission,
Mass Media Bureau, GV
Friedman, Suzanne C. ... Evanston, IL
Friedman, Sydney S. ... Shaker Heights, OH
Friedman, Tanya Pushnack ... Millburn, NJ
Friedman, Ted S. ... Solon, OH
Friedman, Tedd H. ... Cincinnati, OH
Friedman, Terence D. ... Raleigh, NC
Friedman, Terry A., Law Offices of
Reno, NV
Friedman, Terry K. ... New York, NY
Friedman, Theodore H. ... Southfield, MI
Friedman, Thomas E. ... Columbus, OH
Friedman, Thomas I. ... Woodland Hills, CA

Friedman, Thomas L. ... New York, NY
Friedman, Tod H. ... Columbus, OH
Friedman, Tully M. ... San Francisco, CA
Friedman, Victor ... Mount Holly, NJ
Friedman, Victor S., (P.C.) ... New York, NY
Friedman, Vinson J. ... Garden City, NY
Friedman, Vivian Rivkin ... New York, NY
Friedman, Walker C. ... Fort Worth, TX
Friedman, Wallace ... Burbank, CA
Friedman, Wallace ... Westlake Village, CA
Friedman, Wang & Bleiberg, P.C.
New York, NY
Friedman, Warren W., Law Office of
St. Louis, MO
Friedman & Weddington, Attorneys, L.L.P.
Austin, TX
Friedman Weitzman & Friedman, A Professional Corporation ... St. Louis, MO
Friedman, Wendi ... Houston, TX
Friedman, Wendy B. Gerber
Cross River, NY
Friedman, Wilbur H.
National Labor Relations Board,
Office of the General Counsel, GV
Friedman, Wilbur H. ... New York, NY
Friedman, Wilfred T. ... New York, NY
Friedman, Wilfred T., P.C. ... New York, NY
Friedman, William E. ... Memphis, TN
Friedman, William J. ... Lafayette, LA
Friedman, William J. ... Roseland, NJ
Friedman, William R. ... Pittsburgh, PA
Friedman, William S. ... New York, NY
Friedman, William S. ... Columbus, OH
Friedman, Wittenstein & Hochman, A Professional Corporation ... New York, NY
Friedman, Yamamoto & Eller, L.L.P.
Los Angeles, CA
Torrance, CA
Friedman, Young, Suder & Cooke
Fort Worth, TX
Friedman, Zeev ... Cleveland, OH
Friedman-Blank, Stacey R.
Los Angeles, CA
Friedmann, Alan Raymond
New York, NY
Friedmann, Andrew C. ... Austin, TX
Friedmann, Ellen Taratoot ... Los Angeles, CA
Friedmann, Jonathon D. ... Boston, MA
Friedmann, Kevin ... Los Angeles, CA
Friedmann, Lynda C. ... New Orleans, LA
Friedmann, Peter A. ... Washington, DC
Friedmann, Richard V. ... Cleveland, OH
Friedmann, Roger E. ... Cincinnati, OH
Friedmann, Ronald David ... Arlington, VA
Friedmann, Steven C. ... Chatsworth, CA
Friedmann, Thomas J. ... New York, NY
Friedmann, William D. ... Jamaica, NY
Friedmar, Richard S. ... Holland, OH
Friedmeyer, Joanne B. ... Indianapolis, IN
Friednash, Douglas J. ... Denver, CO
Friedrich, Alexander A. ... Seattle, WA
Friedrich, Alfred A. ... Raleigh, NC
Friedrich, Andrea C. ... Department of Justice,
Executive Office for Immigration Review,
GV
Friedrich, Andrew Ian ... Houston, TX
Friedrich, Andrew J. ... Denver, CO
Friedrich, Bruce R. ... New York, NY
Friedrich, Charles H., III ... Newark, NJ
Friedrich, Chris S. ... San Jose, CA
Friedrich, Craig W. ... Portland, ME
Friedrich, David P. ... Terre Haute, IN
Friedrich, Deborah C. ... Pittsburgh, PA
Friedrich & Friedrich, P.A.
Fort Lauderdale, FL
Friedrich, Gordon R. ... Westlake, OH
Friedrich, Ira S. ... Atlanta, GA
Friedrich, J. Peter ... Fort Lauderdale, FL
Friedrich, J. Peter, Jr.
Fort Lauderdale, FL
Friedrich, Jay Joseph ... Hackensack, NJ
Friedrich, Johnnye L. ... Inverness, FL
Friedrich, Kathleen ... Sacramento, CA
Friedrich, Lisa Marie ... Madison, WI
Friedrich, Lya Tonn ... New York, NY
Friedrich, Matthew I. ... Modesto, CA
Friedrich, Matthew W.
Department of Justice, Tax Division, GV
Friedrich, Penny L. ... Los Angeles, CA
Friedrich, Robert A.
Environmental Protection Agency,
Office of the General Counsel, GV
Friedrich, Robert B. ... New York, NY
Friedrich, Robert E. ... Doylestown, PA
Friedrich, Scott K. ... Harrisonville, MO
Friedrich, Sharon ... Lynnwood, WA
Friedrich & Tholstrup ... Houston, TX
Friedrich, Valerie K. ... Houston, TX
Friedrich, William R. ... San Francisco, CA
Friedrichs, James J. ... Wolfeboro, NH
Friedrichs, John E. ... Los Angeles, CA
Friedrichs, Karl O. ... Mankato, MN
Friedrichs & Marsh, P.A. ... Mankato, MN
Friedrichs, Michael A. ... Escondido, CA
Friedrichsen, Bernard P. ... Madison, WI
Friedrichsen, Fred ... Glenville, MN
Friedrichsen, Gerald L. ... Omaha, NE
Friedrichsen, Tim ... Seattle, WA
Fried-Rubin, Deborah ... New York, NY
Friedsam, Lesley J. ... Tampa, FL
Friedsam, S. Carl ... San Antonio, TX
Friedson, Daniel T. ... St. Louis, MO
Friedt, James P. ... Columbus, OH
Friedwald, Susan B. ... New York, NY
Friefeld, Bruce N. ... Mokena, IL
Friefeld, Sheldon ... Miami, FL
Friel, Alan L. ... Santa Monica, CA
Friel, Bernard P. ... St. Paul, MN
Friel, Brian G. ... Washington, DC
Friel, Carol S. ... Cincinnati, OH
Friel, Coleen ... Washington, DC
Friel, Dennis J. ... Paterson, NJ
Friel, Gregory B. ... Department of Justice,
Civil Rights Division, GV
Friel, James A. ... Orland Park, IL
Friel, John P. ... Gary, IN
Friel, Lisa M. ... New York, NY
Friel, Lorna A. ... Morristown, NJ
Friel, M. Alison ... Mount Kisco, NY
Friel, Nora M. ... Dublin, OH
Friel, Robert ... San Francisco, CA
Friel, Robert H. ... Warwick, RI
Friel, Thomas J., Jr. ... San Francisco, CA
San Jose, CA
Friel, Thomas J., L.P.A. ... Cleveland, OH
Friel, Wallis W. ... Colfax, WA
Frieland, Harry ... Boca Raton, FL
Tampa, FL
Livingston, NJ
New York, NY
Friel-Draper, Theresa ... Sterling, IL
Frieling, Leonard I. ... Boulder, CO
Frieling, Leonard I., P.C. ... Boulder, CO
Frieman, Joshua R. ... Los Angeles, CA
Frieman, Karen S. ... New York, NY
Frieman, Lawrence B. ... Metairie, LA
Frieman, Shlomo R. ... Brea, CA
Frieman, William W. ... South Orange, NJ
Friemel, Russell A. ... Austin, TX
Friend, Andrew H. ... Flagstaff, AZ
Friend & Associates, L.L.P. ... Houston, TX
Friend, Bruce C. ... Denver, CO
Friend, Carol A. ... Bloomfield Hills, MI
Friend and Case ... Pikeville, KY
Friend, Charles E. ... Williamsburg, VA
Friend, Christoffer Carter
New Orleans, LA
Friend, Connie L.C. ... Charlottesville, VA
Friend, Dale, (P.C.) ... Houston, TX
Friend, Daniel K. ... Columbus, OH
Friend, David L. ... Seattle, WA
Friend, David M. ... Chicago, IL
Friend, Donald D., II ... Kansas City, MO
Friend, Edward A. ... San Francisco, CA
Friend, Edward M., III ... Birmingham, AL
Friend, Forman, Jr. ... Cincinnati, OH
Friend, Fred W. ... Cleveland, OH
Friend & Friedman ... Oakland, CA
Friend & Friend ... Clifton, NJ
Friend, Gail N. ... Houston, TX
Friend, Gerald G. ... Clifton, NJ
Friend, Gerald L. ... Los Angeles, CA
Friend, Harlan D. ... Liberty, TX
Friend, James R. ... Kansas City, MO
Friend, Jodi B. ... West Orange, NJ
Friend, Joe J. ... Pikeville, KY
Friend, John ... Tucson, AZ
Friend, Joseph E. ... New Orleans, LA
Friend, Karl E. ... Allentown, PA
Reading, PA
Friend, Kathleen W.R. ... Richmond, KY
Friend, Kelsey E. ... Pikeville, KY
Friend, Kelsey E., Jr. ... Pikeville, KY
Friend, L. Edward, II ... Wheeling, WV
Friend, Mark R. ... Department of Justice,
Tax Division, GV
Friend, Marlyn A. ... Los Angeles, CA
Friend, Martin B. ... Chicago, IL
Friend, Melinda S. ... Washington, DC
Friend, Michael R. ... Coral Gables, FL
Friend, Patricia Lyman ... Baltimore, MD
Friend, Patricia R. ... Dallas, TX
Friend, Paul S. ... New York, NY
Friend, R. Steven ... Cumberland, MD
Friend, Randall J. ... Fullerton, CA
Friend, Rex D. ... Oklahoma City, OK
Friend, Robert H. ... Greensboro, NC
Friend, Ross ... Houston, TX
Friend, Russell L. ... San Dimas, CA
Friend, S. Carter ... Portland, ME
Friend, Shawn ... Apache Junction, AZ
Friend, Sheara F. ... Needham, MA
Friend, Solomon H. ... Great Neck, NY
Friend, Stephen E., (P.C.) ... Dallas, TX
Friend, Susan B. ... Newport Beach, CA
Friend, Teresa Lynn ... Oakland, CA
Friend, Theodore H. ... Yonkers, NY
Friend, Travis S. ... Fort Wayne, IN
Friend, William D. ... Atlanta, GA
Friend, William K. ... Canton, MA
Friend, William M. ... Clifton, NJ
Friend, Zachary S. ... Los Angeles, CA
Friende, Billy D. ... Winston-Salem, NC
Friendly, Deborah ... Department of Education,
Office of the General Counsel, GV
Friends, Nathaniel ... Washington, DC
Friendt, Ronald C. ... San Marino, CA
Santa Monica, CA
Frient, Megan P. ... Cleveland, OH
Frier, Charles Henry ... Smyrna, GA
Frier, Daniel B. ... Morristown, NJ
Frier, J. Randall ... Tallahassee, FL
Frier, Marilyn A. ... New York, NY
Frier, Ronald H. ... New York, NY
Frierdich, Bruce E. ... Chicago, IL
Frierdich, Marcia L. ... Stevens Point, WI
Frierson, Albert M. ... Fort Myers, FL
Frierson, Bobby J. ... Detroit, MI
Frierson, Charles, III ... Jonesboro, AR
Frierson, Katheryn ... Chicago, IL
Frierson, Larry J. ... San Francisco, CA
Frierson, Marvin G. ... Columbia, SC
Frierson, Meade, III ... Mountain Brook, AL
Frierson, Robert deVere
Board of Governors Of The Federal Reserve
System,
Office of the Secretary, GV
Frierson, Robert W. ... Dallas, TX
Frierson, Robin Wesley, (P.A.) ... Stuart, FL
Frierson, Sarah S. ... Mobile, AL
Frierson, Susan Lee ... Los Angeles, CA
Frierson, Thomas J. ... Walker, LA
Frierson, Thomas R., II ... Morristown, TN
Frierson & Watson ... Fort Pierce, FL
Port St. Lucie, FL
Stuart, FL
Frierson, William L. ... Chattanooga, TN
Friery, John J., Jr. ... San Diego, CA
Friery, Mark S. ... Lexington, MA
Friery, Susan ... New York, NY
Fries, Ann C. ... Tulsa, OK
Fries, Anne McGregor ... Kalamazoo, MI
Fries, Arnold Jay ... New Brunswick, NJ
Fries, Brian C. ... Kansas City, MO
Fries, Colleen D. ... Bridgeport, CT
Fries, Daniel R ... Athens, OH
Fries, David K. ... Concord, NH
Fries, David S. ... San Francisco, CA
Fries, David W. ... Cincinnati, OH
Fries, Donald E. ... Worcester, MA
Fries, Donald N. ... Buffalo, NY
Fries, Elizabeth Shea ... Boston, MA
Fries, Janet ... Washington, DC
Fries, Jay R. ... Baltimore, MD
McLean, VA
Fries, John J. ... Phoenix, AZ
Fries, Joseph C. ... Dayton, OH
Fries, Joseph M. ... Washington, DC
Fries, Judith Anne ... Los Angeles, CA
Fries, Karen W. ... St. Louis, MO
Fries, Kenneth E. ... Washington, DC
Fries, Kery A. ... Department of Commerce,
Patent and Trademark Office, GV
Fries, Margaret M. ... Kirkwood, NY
Fries, Maureen L. ... San Francisco, CA
Fries, Michael ... Chicago, IL
Fries, Miles D. ... Zanesville, OH
Fries, Monica L. ... St. Louis, MO
Fries, Patricia L. ... Pittsburgh, PA
Fries, Philip J., Jr. ... San Jose, CA
Fries, Richard D. ... Kalamazoo, MI
Fries, Richard S. ... New York, NY
Fries, Robert J. ... Bartlesville, OK
Fries, Robert T. ... San Francisco, CA
Fries, Thomas M. ... El Centro, CA
Fries, William J. ... Allentown, PA
Friesch, Paulette M. ... Milwaukee, WI
Friese, George R. ... New Castle, NH
Friese, James E. ... Cuthbert, GA
Friese, Robert Charles ... San Francisco, CA
Friese, Ronald E. ... Provincetown, MA
Friesen, Ann K. ... Atlanta, GA
Friesen, Betty A., (P.A.) ... Minneapolis, MN
Friesen, Connie M. ... New York, NY
Friesen, Daniel E. ... Denver, CO
Friesen, Ernest C., Jr. ... Silverthorne, CO
Friesen, Ingrid K. ... Asheville, NC
Friesen, Kandice L. ... Clearwater, FL
Friesen, Keelyn M. ... Minneapolis, MN
Friesen, Lloyd E.
Commodity Futures Trading Commission,
Division of Enforcement, GV
Friesen, Michael J. ... Garden City, KS
Friesen and Wendler, A Professional Association ... Garden City, KS
Friesendorf, Sarah Wills ... San Rafael, CA
Friesenhahn, Ronald J. ... New Braunfels, TX
Friesland, Teddy Craig ... Dallas, TX
Friesler, Perry H. ... Milwaukee, WI
Friesner, Herb ... Miami, FL
Friesner & Salzman, L.L.P. ... Great Neck, NY
Friess, Herman A. ... Rice Lake, WI
Friess, K. Erik ... Irvine, CA
Friess, Katherine Elizabeth ... Washington, DC
Friess & Koehler Law Office, S.C.
Rice Lake, WI
Friess, Richard Daniel ... Farmington Hills, MI
Friess, Toni A. ... Atlanta, GA
Friestad, Christine E. ... San Diego, CA
Friestad, Scott W.
Securities and Exchange Commission,
Division of Enforcement, GV
Friestedt, Betsy Wolf ... Libertyville, IL
Friestedt, Frank C. B. ... Mount Laurel, NJ
Philadelphia, PA
Frietsch, Walter P. ... Yoakum, TX
Frietsche, Susan ... Philadelphia, PA
Friez, Wayde A. ... Atlanta, GA
Frieze, Andrew D. ... Wellesley, MA
Frieze, Cary J. ... Morristown, NJ
Frieze, Cary J., P.C. ... Morristown, NJ
Frieze Cramer Cygelman Rosen & Huber, LLP ... Boston, MA
Wellesley, MA
Frieze, H. Delbert ... Broken Arrow, OK
Frieze, Kenneth W. ... Elk Grove, CA
Frieze, Susan D. ... Dallas, TX
Frigard, Wayne R. ... Boston, MA
Frigerio, Charles S. ... San Antonio, TX
Frigerio, Charles S., A Prof. Corp., Law Offices of ... San Antonio, TX
Frignoca, Ivy L. ... Portland, ME
Frigo, Gregory A. ... Menasha, WI
Frigola, Alfred K. ... Marathon, FL
Frigola, DeVane & Dorl, P.A.
Marathon, FL
Frigoletto, Maria ... Rosemont, PA
Frigon, Bernie D. ... Dodge City, KS
Montezuma, KS
Frigon, Bradley J. ... Dodge City, KS
Frigon, Donald A. ... Dodge City, KS
Frigon Law Firm ... Dodge City, KS
Montezuma, KS
Friia, Jo Ann ... White Plains, NY
Friia, Sam ... Albion, MI
Friis, Belinda A. ... Detroit, MI
Frija, Robert B., Law Offices of
Honolulu, HI
Frijouf, Robert F. ... Tampa, FL
Cleveland, OH
Frijouf, Rust & Pyle, P.A. ... Tampa, FL
Friker, E. Kenneth ... Chicago, IL
Frikert, Laura A. ... Portland, OR
Friley, Keith ... Baton Rouge, LA
Friley, Nancy K. ... St. Petersburg, FL
Frilot, Craig J. ... San Bernardino, CA
Frilot, George A., III (A Professional Law Corp.) ... New Orleans, LA
Frilot, Partridge, Kohnke & Clements, L.C.
New Orleans, LA
Friloux, C. Anthony, Jr. ... Houston, TX
Frim, Gerald S. ... Los Angeles, CA
Frim, Kurt M. ... Boca Raton, FL
Friman, Michael S. ... Chicago, IL
Friman, Paul L. ... New York, NY
Frimann, Nora V. ... San Jose, CA
Frimel, Michael P ... Newbury, OH
Frimel, William J. ... Palo Alto, CA
Frimer, Michael T. ... Bayside, NY
Frimershtein, Aleks S. ... Los Angeles, CA
Frimet, Gilbert M. ... Southfield, MI
Frimet & Rogalski, P.C. ... Detroit, MI
Southfield, MI
Frimmel, Deborah E. ... Orlando, FL
Frimmel, Mark ... Jericho, NY
Frimmer, Paul N., (P.C.) ... Los Angeles, CA
Frimmer, Rick L. ... Philadelphia, PA
Frimodt, Eric C. ... Bellevue, WA
Frimond, Bernard J. ... Laguna Hills, CA
Frind, Denis B. ... New York, NY
Frindell, Sander B. ... Bloomington, IL
Frindt, Ronald J. ... Colorado Springs, CO
Frings-Kolstad, Carole L. ... Washington, DC
Frink, Anthony L. ... Chicago, IL
Frink, Bryan M. ... Detroit, MI
Frink, Carolyn N. ... Sacramento, CA
Frink, D. Michael ... Augusta, ME
Portland, ME
Frink, Daniel N. ... Sacramento, CA
Frink, Foy & Yount, P.A. ... Shallotte, NC
Southport, NC
Frink, Julie A. ... Los Angeles, CA
Frink, Norman W. ... Portland, OR
Frink, Patrick J. ... Seattle, WA
Frink, Sarah E. ... Brookfield, WI
Frink-Hamlett, Katherine ... New York, NY
Frinks-Dixon, Cindylou ... Clifton Park, NY
Frinsko, F. Paul ... Portland, ME
Frio, Francis A. ... Baltimore, MD
Friot, Stephen P. ... Oklahoma City, OK
Friou, Robert E. ... Sleepy Hollow, NY
Frisardi, Thomas ... Boston, MA
Frisbee, Denise S. ... Lake Oswego, OR
Frisbee, Edward ... Hudson, NY
Frisbee, Moore & Olson ... Cut Bank, MT
Frisbee, Robert C. ... Los Angeles, CA
Frisbee, Robert M. ... Minneapolis, MN
Frisbee, Selden S. ... Cut Bank, MT
Frisbie, Charles ... Kansas City, MO
Frisbie, Curtis L., Jr. ... Dallas, TX
Frisbie, Dean R. ... San Francisco, CA
Frisbie, Margaret M. ... Bloomington, IN
Frisbie, Michael F. ... Doylestown, PA
Frisbie, Richard K. ... Berkeley, CA
Frisbie, Shannan L. ... Seattle, WA
Frisbie, Teresa F. ... Chicago, IL
Frisby, Bradford V. ... Washington, DC
Frisby, Dennis E. ... Chicago, IL
Frisby, John D., Jr. ... Cuyahoga Falls, OH
Frisby, Michael L. ... Culver City, CA
Frisby, R. Larson ... Washington, DC
Frisby, Robert M.
Federal Trade Commission,
Bureau of Consumer Protection, GV
Frisch, Andrew J. ... Brooklyn, NY
Frisch, August W. ... Pittsburgh, PA
Frisch, Benjamin ... Olivia, MN
Frisch, Bertrand S. ... New York, NY
Frisch, Brian T. ... Los Angeles, CA
Frisch, Charles J. ... Minneapolis, MN
Frisch, David B. ... Linwood, NJ
Frisch, Donald S. ... Chicago, IL
Frisch, Edward J. ... Westfield, NJ
Frisch, Eric J. ... Atlanta, GA
Frisch, Floyd C. ... Los Gatos, CA
Frisch, Frank R. ... Concord, CA
Frisch & Frisch ... Wilton, CT
Frisch & Frisch, Chartered ... Chicago, IL
Frisch, George H. ... Minneapolis, MN
Frisch, Gerald E. ... St. Paul, MN
Frisch, Harry D. ... New York, NY
Frisch, Jack H. ... Indianapolis, IN
Frisch, James C. ... Tucson, AZ
Frisch, James W. ... Sheboygan, WI
Frisch, Jennifer L. ... Minneapolis, MN
Frisch, Jill A. ... Treasury Department,
Internal Revenue Service, GV
Frisch, John B. ... Baltimore, MD
Frisch, John F. ... Napa, CA
Frisch, Marilyn S. ... Miami, FL
Frisch, Michael S. ... Washington, DC
Frisch, Patricia L. ... Wilton, CT
Frisch, Paul R. ... Portland, OR
Frisch, Randi Gail ... Los Angeles, CA
Frisch, Randy S. ... New York, NY
Frisch, Robert E. ... New York, NY
Frisch, Robert K., Jr. ... Dallas, TX
Frisch, Robert K., P.C. ... Dallas, TX
Frisch, Robert M. ... North Brunswick, NJ
Frisch, Roger ... Wilton, CT
Frisch, Sidney, Jr. ... Chicago, IL

Frisch, Stuart ....Department of Justice, Justice Management Division, GV
Frisch, Tracy Z. ....Philadelphia, PA
Frisch & Waller ....Chicago, IL
Frische, Michael C. ....Indianapolis, IN
Frischer, Harry ....New York, NY
Frischer, Helene J. ....St. Louis, MO
Frischer, Leonard R. ....Overland Park, KS
Frischer & Russell, Chtd. Overland Park, KS
Frischer, Steven ....South Miami, FL
Frischhertz, Lloyd N. ....New Orleans, LA
Frischholz, Barbara J. ....San Jose, CA
Frischknecht, Paul R. ....Manti, UT
Frischkorn, Allen R., Jr. ....Washington, DC
Frischkorn, David M. ....Chicago, IL
Frischkorn, Marci Lynn ....Washington, DC
Frischling, Carl ....New York, NY
Frischling, David Alan Breitbart Boston, MA
Frischling, Gary N. ....Los Angeles, CA
Frischman, Craig E. ....Pittsburgh, PA
Frischmeyer, Linda E. ....Vancouver, WA
Frisch-Winters, Kimberly ....Dallas, TX
Friscia, Edward D. ....New Port Richey, FL
Tampa, FL
Friscia, Francis E. ....Tampa, FL
Friscia, John S. ....Staten Island, NY
Friscia, Michael R. ....Roseland, NJ
Friscia & Nussbaum ....Hackensack, NJ
Friscia, Steven J. ....Mill Valley, CA
Frisco, Charles E. ....Norwalk, CA
Frisco, Nick M. ....Bronx, NY
Friscoe, Lou ....Columbus, OH
Frisella, Barbara Anne ....Hillsboro, OR
Frisenda, Frank, Jr., (A Professional Corporation) ....Los Angeles, CA
Frisenda, Quinton & Nicholson Los Angeles, CA
New York, NY
Frisenda, Robert J. ....White Plains, NY
Frishauf, Holtz, Goodman, Langer & Chick, P.C. ....New York, NY
Frishauf, Stephen H. ....New York, NY
Frishberg, Aaron David ....New York, NY
Frishberg, Neal D. ....Chester, NY
Frishberg, Stephen H. ....Blue Bell, PA
Frishberg, William D. ....White Plains, NY
Frishe, Charles F. ....Cleveland, OH
Frishman, Arnold H. ....Minneapolis, MN
Frishman, David ....Katy, TX
Frishman, David M. ....Los Angeles, CA
Frishman, Deborah H. ....New York, NY
Frishman, Jeffrey B. ....Chicago, IL
Frishman, Lawrence D. ....New York, NY
Frishman, Leigh Zeising ....Chicago, IL
Frishman, Leonard ....Miami, FL
Frishman, Leonard, P.A. ....Miami, FL
Frishman, Richard A. ....Nevada City, CA
Frishman, Ruth I. ....Truckee, CA
Frishman, Sheryl R. ....New York, NY
Frishtick, Jonathan M. ....Boston, MA
Frisius, Edward A. G. ....Tahoe City, CA
Frisk, Arthur W. ....South Bend, IN
Frisk, Frank W., Jr. ....Washington, DC
Frisk, Frank W., Jr., P.C. Washington, DC
Frisk, Judson L. ....Logan, IA
Frisk, Nick A., Jr. ....Ellwood City, PA
Frisk, R. Randall ....Indianapolis, IN
Frisk, Richard M. ....Walnut Creek, CA
Friskney, Stephen H. ....Cincinnati, OH
Frisoli, Carol A. ....Boston, MA
Frisoli, Frank J., Jr. ....Cambridge, MA
Frisoli & Frisoli ....Cambridge, MA
Frisoli, Lawrence M ....Chelmsford, MA
Frisoli, Lawrence W. ....Cambridge, MA
Frisoli, Leonard A. ....Cambridge, MA
Frisoli, Leonard M., Jr. ....Cambridge, MA
Frisone, Deborah Smith ....Hartford, CT
Frisone, Nicholas J. ....Chicago, IL
Friss, Solomon ....Atlantic City, NJ
Frisse, David M. ....Paris, IL
Springfield, IL
Terre Haute, IN
Frisse Law Offices ....Paris, IL
Springfield, IL
Brazil, IN
Terre Haute, IN
Frissell, Anna M. ....Fargo, ND
Fristachi, Mario A. ....Brooklyn, NY
Fristoe, E. Robert ....Olympia, WA
Fristoe, Shelly Clayton ....Austin, TX
Fristoe, Taylor & Schultz, Ltd., P.S. Olympia, WA
Fritch, David P. ....Jasper, IN
Fritch, Kimberly A. ....Sacramento, CA
Fritch, Michael A. ....Jasper, IN
Fritch, Roger A. ....Fountain Valley, CA
Fritch, Stephen A. ....Metairie, LA
Fritch, Stephen A., and Associates, PLC Metairie, LA
Fritchey, John Alden, IV ....Chicago, IL
Fritchie & Cochran, A Professional Law Corporation ....Slidell, LA
Fritchie, Gus A., III ....New Orleans, LA
Fritchie, Gus A., Jr. ....Slidell, LA
Fritchman, Katherine M. ....Eugene, OR
Fritchman, Vernon N. ....Indiana, PA
Frith, Alfred L. ....Orlando, FL
Frith Anderson & Peake PC Roanoke, VA
Frith, Bart R. ....Vermontville, MI
Frith, Douglas K. ....Martinsville, VA
Frith, Douglas K., & Associates, P.C. Martinsville, VA
Frith, Gilbert H. ....Santa Fe, NM
Frith, John W. ....Devils Lake, ND
Frith, Larry P. ....Houston, TX
Frith, Linda Davis ....Roanoke, VA
Frith, Roianne Houlton, & Associates Montgomery, AL
Frith, Ronald M. ....Jackson, MS
Frith, Sara ....Los Angeles, CA
Frith, Schwarz & Steffan ....Devils Lake, ND
Frith, T. Daniel, III ....Roanoke, VA
Frith, Thomas D., Jr. ....Christiansburg, VA
Frith, Tracey N. ....Los Angeles, CA
Fritjofson, Erik M. ....Woodsville, NH
Frits, James W. ....Bothell, WA
Fritsch, Andrew K. ....Sarasota, FL
Fritsch, C. Theodore, Jr. ....Doylestown, PA
Fritsch, Dennis G. ....Washington, PA
Fritsch, Elizabeth Wood ....Bristol, PA
Fritsch, H. Andrew ....Punta Gorda, FL
Fritsch, John J. ....Santa Rosa, CA
Fritsch, Joseph G., Jr. ....Rochester, NY
Fritsch, Regennas E. ....Indianapolis, IN
Fritsch, Ron ....Chicago, IL
Fritsch, Ruth M. ....San Diego, CA
Fritsche, Barbara ....Jacksonville, IL
Fritsche, Deborah J. ....Houston, TX
Fritsche, Deborah J., P.C. ....Houston, TX
Fritsche, Elizabeth T. ....Clifton, VA
Fritsche, Joan M. ....Brighton, CO
Fritsche, R. David, Law Offices of San Antonio, TX
Fritsche, Robert W. ....Garden Grove, CA
Fritsche, Ulrich P. ....Jamaica, NY
Fritschel, Barbara L. ....Beaumont, TX
Fritschie, Bernadette A. ....Manassas, VA
Fritschie, Donald J. ....Overland Park, KS
Fritschler, Alvin H. ....Danbury, CT
Fritschner, Samuel H. ....Hendersonville, NC
Fritton, Gavin ....Overland Park, KS
Fritton, Karl A. ....Philadelphia, PA
Fritts, Brian C. ....Indianapolis, IN
Fritts, David H. ....Savannah, GA
Fritts, David T. ....Dixon, IL
Fritts, Gary N. ....Dayton, TN
Fritts, John F. ....New York, NY
Fritts, John G. ....Seattle, WA
Fritts, Jonathan C. ....Washington, DC
Fritts, Linda A. ....Washington, DC
Fritts, Patricia Rice ....Knoxville, TN
Fritts, Peter H. ....Chicago, IL
Fritts, Richard L. ....Bethesda, MD
Fritts, Robert P. ....Greenacres, FL
Fritts, Robert P., P.A. ....Greenacres, FL
Fritts, Roger M. ....Delmar, NY
Fritts, Sonja D. ....Seattle, WA
Fritts, William F. ....Lexington, NC
Fritz, Abner M. ....Whittier, CA
Fritz, Albert G., Jr. ....Long Beach, CA
Fritz, Amy Vickers ....Beckley, WV
Fritz, Andrew S. T. ....Las Vegas, NV
Fritz, Anne Brafford ....Morristown, NJ
Fritz, Ann-Marie ....Riverside, CA
Fritz, Anthony P. ....San Francisco, CA
Fritz, Arden ....Anoka, MN
Fritz, Arthur A. ....Los Angeles, CA
Fritz, Arthur J., Jr. ....San Francisco, CA
Fritz, Barbara Ann ....Newport Beach, CA
Fritz, Blake T. ....Blue Bell, PA
Fritz, Cassidy C. ....Elkhart, IN
Fritz, Charles E. ....Indianapolis, IN
Fritz, Christian G. ....Albuquerque, NM
Fritz, Christopher J. ....Baltimore, MD
Fritz, Christopher R. ....Ocean City, NJ
Fritz, Clarissa Anne ....Memphis, TN
Fritz, Colin E. ....Syracuse, NY
Fritz, Collin (Marty) ....Honolulu, HI
Fritz, Daniel K. ....Chicago, IL
Fritz, Daniel R. ....Oakland, CA
Fritz, Daniel R. ....Aberdeen, SD
Fritz, Daniel R. ....Sioux Falls, SD
Fritz, David P. ....New York, NY
Fritz, David R. ....Woodcliff Lake, NJ
Fritz, Dennis A. ....La Grange, KY
Fritz, Edw. C. ....Dallas, TX
Fritz, Frank A., III ....Philadelphia, PA
Fritz & Fritz ....San Francisco, CA
Fritz, Gretchen ....New York, NY
Fritz, Hogan & Johnson ....Aberdeen, SD
Fritz, Howard C. ....Thornwood, NY
Fritz, Howard P. ....Mineola, NY
Fritz, James H. ....Costa Mesa, CA
Fritz, James L. ....Harrisburg, PA
Fritz, James W. ....Tempe, AZ
Fritz, Jeffrey C. ....San Diego, CA
Fritz, Jeffrey P. ....Stratford, NJ
Philadelphia, PA
Fritz, Jerald N. ....Washington, DC
Fritz, Joel D. ....Elyria, OH
Fritz, John C. ....Olathe, KS
Fritz, John D. ....Wilbraham, MA
Fritz, Joseph J ....Philadelphia, PA
Fritz, Joseph L. ....East Islip, NY
Fritz, Joseph R., (P.A.) ....Tampa, FL
Fritz, Joseph W., Jr. ....New Orleans, LA
Fritz, Kathryn Jean ....Palo Alto, CA
San Francisco, CA
Fritz, Kenneth O. ....Chattanooga, TN
Fritz, Kevin L. ....St. Louis, MO
Fritz, Kevin Patrick ....Apopka, FL
Fritz, Kurt ....Los Angeles, CA
Fritz, Laura L. ....Las Vegas, NV
Fritz Law Firm, The ....Albuquerque, NM
Austin, TX
Fort Worth, TX
Houston, TX
San Antonio, TX
Fritz Law Offices ....Santa Rosa, CA
Fritz, Lawrence J. ....Metairie, LA
Fritz, Linda C. ....San Diego, CA
Fritz, Lisa A. ....Santa Barbara, CA
Fritz, Lynn C. ....San Francisco, CA
Fritz, Lynne R. ....Lincoln, NE
Fritz, Maranda E. ....New York, NY
Fritz, Mark J. ....Plano, TX
Fritz, Martin A. ....Harrisburg, PA
Fritz, Mary P. ....Minneapolis, MN
Fritz, Michael A., Sr. ....Montgomery, AL
Fritz, Michael David ....Detroit Lakes, MN
Fritz, Michael J. ....Waukegan, IL
Fritz & Miller ....New York, NY
Fritz, Norman C. ....New Berlin, WI
Fritz, Paul D. ....Santa Barbara, CA
Fritz, Peter L. ....Honolulu, HI
Fritz, Randal C. ....Manchester, MA
Fritz, Raymond E., Jr. ....Sunnyvale, CA
Fritz, Raymond N. ....Cleveland, OH
Fritz, Richard ....Dallas, TX
Fritz, Richard D. ....Leonardtown, MD
Fritz, Richard J. ....Detroit, MI
Detroit, MI
Fritz, Richard J. ....Victoria, TX
Fritz, Robert H., III ....Houston, TX
Fritz, Robert J. ....New Orleans, LA
Fritz, Roxane R. ....Sacramento, CA
Fritz, Steven A. ....Sedalia, MO
Fritz, Steven A., P.C. ....Sedalia, MO
Fritz, Ted P. ....Pittsburgh, PA
Fritz, Theresa R. ....Santa Rosa, CA
Fritz, Thomas D. ....Austin, TX
Fritz, Thomas G. ....Rapid City, SD
Fritz, Tina Lynn ....Alexandria, VA
Fritz, William F. ....Santa Rosa, CA
Fritz, William N. ....Grosse Pointe, MI
Fritze, Daniel J. ....Columbia, SC
Fritze, James R. ....Eagle, CO
Fritzel, William J. ....Denver, CO
Fritzemeier, Barbara Mountlake Terrace, WA
Fritzemeier, Jamee C. ....Olathe, KS
Fritzen, Joseph J. ....Denville, NJ
Fritz-Gasteier, Linda ....Sandusky, OH
Fritzhand, Gary I. ....Houston, TX
Fritzinger, John G., Jr. ....New York, NY
Fritz-Klaus, Karri L. ....Milwaukee, WI
Fritzlen, Thomas J., Jr. ....Kansas City, MO
Fritzler, Kenneth C. ....Kearney, NE
Fritzler, Kenneth C. ....Marshfield, WI
Fritzler, Randal B. ....Vancouver, WA
Fritz-Reyes, Angela ....Bettendorf, IA
Fritzsch, Craig R. ....Binghamton, NY
Fritzsch & Nadel ....Binghamton, NY
Fritzsche, Gary R. ....Richardson, TX
Fritzsche, Sybille C. ....Tucson, AZ
Fritzsche, Thomas C. ....Bettendorf, IA
Fritzshall, Albert B. ....Chicago, IL
Fritzshall, Robert S. ....Chicago, IL
Fritzshall, Steven N. ....Chicago, IL
Frix, Dana ....Washington, DC
Frix, Dianne M. ....Buford, GA
Frix, Paige Lane ....Muskogee, OK
Frix, Robert L. ....Worthington, OH
Frix, Richard M., (P.C.) ....Portland, OR
Frizell, David J. ....Metuchen, NJ
Frizell, Edward E., III ....Kansas City, MO
Frizell Goldman & Jaffe ....Metuchen, NJ
Newark, NJ
New Brunswick, NJ
Princeton, NJ
Somerville, NJ
Trenton, NJ
Frizell, Roberta Schwartz San Juan Capistrano, CA
Frizell, Samuel ....Fullerton, CA
Frizelle, Alfred E. ....North Andover, MA
Frizzell, Bill ....Tyler, TX
Frizzell, Blaine G. ....Tulsa, OK
Frizzell, Carol E. ....San Francisco, CA
Frizzell, David G. ....Glen Rock, NJ
Frizzell, David W. ....Albuquerque, NM
Frizzell, Eric F. ....Glen Rock, NJ
Frizzell, Gregory K. ....Tulsa, OK
Frizzell, Jean C. ....Houston, TX
Frizzell, John T. ....Buffalo, NY
Eden, NY
Frizzell, Jonathan S. ....Colebrook, NH
Frizzell, Kent ....Claremore, OK
Frizzell Law Firm ....Tyler, TX
Frizzell, Thomas A. ....Danbury, CT
Frizzell, Thomas A., Jr. ....New York, NY
Frizzell, Thomas R. ....Waterbury, CT
Frizzell, Thomas W. ....Missoula, MT
Frizzi, Daniel L., Jr. ....Bellaire, OH
Frizzi Law Offices ....Bellaire, OH
Frizzie, B. E. ....Sacramento, CA
Frizzie, Scott Bernard ....Sacramento, CA
Frlan-Zovko, Suzana ....Astoria, NY
Frnka, Edward R. ....San Antonio, TX
Froba, David J. ....Modesto, CA
Froba, Frailing & Rockwell ....Modesto, CA
Froberg & Ahern, P.A. ....Minnetonka, MN
Froberg, Andrew D. ....New York, NY
Froberg, Glenn ....Minnetonka, MN
Froberg, James G. ....Chicago, IL
Froberger, Charles A. ....Utica, MI
Frobes, Patricia ....Los Angeles, CA
Newport Beach, CA
Frobish, Harold J. ....Pontiac, IL
Frobish, Jon L. ....Wichita, KS
Froble, Michael E. ....Beckley, WV
Froble, Ronald F. ....Cuyahoga Falls, OH
Frobouck, Stephen C. ....Pittsburgh, PA
Froburg, Alethea L. ....Berlin, NH
Froch, Michael I. ....El Segundo, CA
Frock & Broussard, P.C. ....Houston, TX
Frock, John Brian ....West Chester, PA
Frock, Markwood David ....Houston, TX
Frockt, David S. ....Seattle, WA
Frockt, I. Joel ....Louisville, KY
Frockt & Klingman, L.L.P. ....Louisville, KY
Frockt, Manny H. ....Louisville, KY
Frockt, Stephen S. ....Louisville, KY
Froderman, Troy B. ....Phoenix, AZ
Frodyma, Scott F. ....Cleveland, OH
Froeb, Charles H. ....Tulsa, OK
Froebe, Gerald A. ....Portland, OR
Froeber, James A. ....St. Paul, MN
Froeberg, William R. ....Santa Ana, CA
Froebrich, Alfred W. ....New York, NY
Froede, Joan W. ....Louisville, CO
Froehle, Thomas C., Jr. ....Indianapolis, IN
Froehlich & Associates, P.A. ....Hockessin, DE
Froehlich, Charles W., Jr. ....San Diego, CA
Froehlich, Chas. J., Jr. ....Lutherville, MD
Froehlich, Cheryl A. ....Munster, IN
Froehlich, Daniel J. ....Minneapolis, MN
Froehlich, Francis B. ....Brookville, NY
Froehlich, Harold V. ....Appleton, WI
Froehlich, Jane Elizabeth Federal Energy Regulatory Commission, Office of the General Counsel, GV
Froehlich, Joseph N. ....New York, NY
Froehlich, Kent B. ....Los Angeles, CA
Fröhlich, Kurt P., (Ltd.) ....Champaign, IL
Froehlich, Laurence A. Federal Deposit Insurance Corporation, Office of Inspector General, GV
Froehlich, Mahony & de Bruin Mineola, NY
Froehlich, Marion E. ....Oceanside, CA
Froehlich, Marion R. ....Bartlesville, OK
Froehlich, Mark H. ....Hockessin, DE
Froehlich, Mark S. ....Groveport, OH
Froehlich, Michael J. ....Rockville, MD
Froehlich, Peter B. ....Juneau, AK
Froehlich, Richard M. ....New York, NY
Froehlich, Robert A. ....Syosset, NY
Froehlich, William J. Federal Energy Regulatory Commission, Office of the General Counsel, GV
Froehling, Elizabeth A. ....Chapel Hill, NC
Froehling, Patrick Gerard ....Eagan, MN
Froehling, Ralph ....Canton, IL
Froehling, Taylor, Weber & Evans Canton, IL
Froehlke, Donald F. ....Chicago, IL
Froelich, Alan L. ....Friday Harbor, WA
Froelich and Associates ....Minneapolis, MN
Froelich, Beth A. ....Sheboygan, WI
Froelich, Bruce E. ....Big Rapids, MI
Froelich, Cecilia C. ....New York, NY
Froelich, Cezar M. ....Chicago, IL
Froelich, Edward L. ....Department of Justice, Tax Division, GV
Froelich, F. Edwin ....Washington, DC
Froelich, Gary L. ....Dayton, OH
Froelich, Georgia A. ....Cleveland, OH
Froelich, Jeffrey E. ....Dayton, OH
Froelich, Jerome J., Jr. ....Atlanta, GA
Froelich, Larry R. ....Fayetteville, AR
Froelich, Michael J. ....Minneapolis, MN
Froelich, Raymond R., Jr. ....Cleveland, OH
Froelich & Weprin Co. LPA ....Dayton, OH
Froelicher, Hans, IV ....Annapolis, MD
Froelicher, John Vincent ....Santa Barbara, CA
Froelicher, Peter H. ....Portland, ME
Froelke, D. Richard ....Washington, DC
Froelke, Frank J. ....Hamilton, OH
Froelke, Gerald G. ....Hamilton, OH
Froemel, Jonathan P. ....Chicago, IL
Froemming, John G. ....Washington, DC
Froemming, Robt. H. ....Milwaukee, WI
Froerer, Bryce M. ....Ogden, UT
Froerer, Fredrick (Buck), III ....Ogden, UT
Froerer & Miles, A Professional Corporation Ogden, UT
Froerer, Robert E. ....Ogden, UT
Froerer, Robert L. ....Ogden, UT
Froeschle, Jeffery Allen St. Petersburg, FL
Froeschle, Nina D. ....Los Angeles, CA
Froeschner, Gwendolyn S. ....Columbia, MO
Froeschner, John R. ....Galveston, TX
Froese, Terrance M. ....Anacortes, WA
Froessel, Timothy B. ....New York, NY
Froggatt, Jason T. ....Seattle, WA
Frogge, Gregory ....Oklahoma City, OK
Frogley, Darrel W. ....Kansas City, KS
Frogner, George E. ....Harmony, MN
Froh, Alfred E. ....Suffern, NY
Froh, Walter F. ....Camp Hill, PA
Frohbieter, Gene ....Houston, TX
Frohboese, Robinsue ....Department of Justice, Civil Rights Division, GV
Frohe, Adele N. ....Tonawanda, NY
Frohlich, Anthony W. ....Florence, KY
Frohlich, David ....Washington, DC
Frohlich, Dennis R. ....Boulder, CO
Frohlich, Edward P. ....Grosse Pointe, MI
Frohlich, Elizabeth A. ....San Francisco, CA
Frohlich, Gerhard ....Honolulu, HI
Frohlich, Jack T. ....New York, NY
Frohlich, Julie A ....Boston, MA
Frohlich, W. Cort ....Port Charlotte, FL
Frohlicher, Jean S. ....United States Senate, Committee Legal Personnel, GV
Frohlin, Robyn A. ....Dallas, TX
Frohling, Dana J. ....Britton, SD
Frohling, Daniel D. ....Chicago, IL
Frohling, Hudak & McCarthy, P.C. Roseland, NJ
Frohling, John B. M. ....Roseland, NJ
Frohling, Richard G. ....Milwaukee, WI
Frohlinger, Carol Moran ....Dix Hills, NY
Frohmader, Frederick O. ....Tacoma, WA
Frohman, Jacob ....New York, NY
Frohman, Marc LaPalombara ....Devon, PA

Frohman, Michael C. ... Milwaukee, WI
Frohman, Paul, P.C. ... New York, NY
Frohman, Thomas M. ... Bloomington, IN
Frohn, David R. ... Lake Charles, LA
Frohn & Thibodeaux, L.L.C.
Lake Charles, LA
Frohne, William J. ... Mineola, NY
Frohnmayer, David B. ... Eugene, OR
Frohnmayer, Deatherage, Pratt, Jamieson, Clarke & Moore, P.C. ... Medford, OR
Frohnmayer, John E. ... Bozeman, MT
Frohnmayer, Otto J. ... Medford, OR
Frohock, Joan W., (Mrs.) ... Des Moines, IA
Frohock, Thomas N. ... Arlington, VA
Frohreich, Pamela J. G. ... Los Angeles, CA
Frohsin, Henry I ... Birmingham, AL
Frohsin, Ralph, Jr. ... Alexander City, AL
Frohwein, Robert J. ... Atlanta, GA
Frohwitter ... Houston, TX
Froikin, Stephen D. ... Chicago, IL
Froiland, David J.B. ... Milwaukee, WI
Froiland, Laurel C. ... Eden Prairie, MN
Froimson, Jerome L. ... Phoenix, AZ
Froio, Anthony A. ... Boston, MA
Froio, John A. ... Malden, MA
Frois, Louana H. ... Dallas, TX
Frois, Monica A. ... New Orleans, LA
Frois, Theodore M. ... Houston, TX
Frokjer, Randy L. ... Merrill, WI
Frol, Steven C. ... Walla Walla, WA
Frolich, Evelyn G. ... Manchester, CT
Frolich, John N. ... Encino, CA
Frolich, Lindy ... Denver, CO
Frolich, Terrance J. ... Manchester, CT
Frolik, Ann Ferguson ... Chicago, IL
Frolik, James R. ... San Francisco, CA
Frolik, Lawrence A. ... Pittsburgh, PA
Froling, Bradley Edward
Sterling Heights, MI
Froling, Deborah Schwager
Washington, DC
Frolio, David G. ... Washington, DC
Frolow, Martin J. ... West Palm Beach, FL
Frolow, Martin J., P.A.
West Palm Beach, FL
From, I. Allan ... Raleigh, NC
Froman, Andrew ... Sarasota, FL
Froman, Andrew, P.A., Law Office of
Sarasota, FL
Froman, David ... San Diego, CA
Columbia, MO
Froman, Leroy ... Searcy, AR
Froman, Michael P. ... Atlanta, GA
Froman, Michael S. ... Chicago, IL
Froman, Michael S. ... Skokie, IL
Froman, Sandra S. ... Tucson, AZ
Froman, Thomas E. ... Lansing, MI
Froman & Wagner LLP ... San Diego, CA
Columbia, MO
Froman-Bettencourt, Rachel Jane
Leominster, MA
Fromang, Mark Andrew
Altamonte Springs, FL
Fromang, Stephen D., (P.A.)
Vero Beach, FL
Fromartz, Bernard ... Brooklyn, NY
Fromartz, D. Bunji ... Brooklyn, NY
Fromberg, Douglas M. ... Florham Park, NJ
Fromberg, Jeffrey E. ... Palm Springs, CA
Fromberg, Lynn W. ... Aventura, FL
Fromberg, Malcolm H. ... Aventura, FL
Fromberg, Perlow & Kornik, P.A.
Aventura, FL
Hallandale Beach, FL
Fromberg, Robert M. ... New York, NY
Frome, Bruce M. ... Beverly Hills, CA
Frome, Carolyn Geraci ... Hackensack, NJ
Frome & Frome ... Beverly Hills, CA
Frome, Jacqueline A. ... New York, NY
Frome, Laurelle L. ... Beverly Hills, CA
Frome, Morton J. ... Rockville, MD
Frome, Paula S. ... Garden City, NY
Great Neck, NY
Frome, Richard M. ... New York, NY
Frome, Robert L. ... New York, NY
Frome, Ted C. ... Afton, WY
Fromen, John J. ... Buffalo, NY
Fromen, John J., Jr. ... Buffalo, NY
Fromer, Bruce P. ... Asbury Park, NJ
Fromer, Gary D. ... Newtown Square, PA
Fromer, John J. ... Tannersville, NY
Fromer, Robert L. ... New York, NY
Fromet, Avery H. ... Beachwood, OH
Fromewick, Richard G. ... Mineola, NY
Fromhercz, Stephen ... Cleveland, OH
Fromhold, Fred B. ... Rosemont, PA
Fromhold & Jaffe ... Rosemont, PA
Fromholz, Ann Haley ... San Francisco, CA
Fromholz, Haley J. ... Los Angeles, CA
Fromkes, Otto ... North Plainfield, NJ
Fromkin, David H. ... New York, NY
Fromkin, M. Robert ... Omaha, NE
Fromknecht, Kenneth W., II
Franklin, NC
Fromm, Barbara C. ... Tallahassee, FL
Fromm, Barry H. ... Columbus, OH
Fromm, David Gerard ... Boston, MA
Fromm, David H. ... New York, NY
Fromm, Eva Maria ... Houston, TX
Fromm, Helene ... New York, NY
Fromm, Isaac ... New York, NY
Fromm, Jeffrey A. ... New York, NY
Fromm, Jeffrey B. ... Fort Collins, CO
Fromm, Jennifer S. ... Boston, MA
Fromm, Mark L. ... Chicago, IL
Fromm, Sandra J. ... Phoenix, AZ
Frommann, Walther ... Ridgewood, NY
Fromme, David K. ... Shawnee, KS
Fromme, David K. ... Somerset, PA
Fromme, Douglas L. ... New York, NY
Fromme, Eric F. ... New York, NY
Frommé , Eric J. ... San Francisco, CA
Fromme, J. Thomas, II ... Fairfax, VA
Fromme, Philip M. ... Burlington, KS
Fromme Schwartz Newman & Cornicello, LLP ... New York, NY
Frommelt, James M. ... Minneapolis, MN
Frommelt, Roger H. ... Minneapolis, MN
Frommer, Darío J. ... Los Angeles, CA
Frommer, Henry ... Stamford, CT
Frommer, Hillary Ann ... Chicago, IL
Frommer, John W., III ... Harrisburg, PA
Frommer Lawrence & Haug LLP
New York, NY
Frommer, Peter Joel ... Miami, FL
Frommer, Roger ... Los Angeles, CA
Frommer, Ross A. ... Brooklyn, NY
Frommer, Stephen G. ... Mineola, NY
Frommer, William S. ... New York, NY
Frommeyer, Daniel T. ... Barrington, IL
Frommeyer, Todd A. ... Jacksonville, FL
Fromson, A. Scott ... Beachwood, OH
Fromson, A. Scott ... Cleveland, OH
Fromson, Jeffrey E. ... Columbus, OH
Fromson, Paul D. ... Merced, CA
Fromson, Richard A. ... Cleveland, OH
Fromson, Stephen M. ... Spring Valley, NY
Fromstein, Daniel E. ... Department of Justice, Criminal Division, GV
Fromstein, David M. ... Antigo, WI
Fromstein, Elizabeth H. ... Winnetka, IL
Fron, Michele R. ... Long Beach, CA
Fronabarger, Paige K. ... Washington, DC
Froncek, Frank X.
Research Triangle Park, NC
Froncek, Theodore J. ... Cincinnati, OH
Froncek Rankin, Teresa P. ... Carson City, NV
Fronczak, Stanley W. ... Hinsdale, IL
Frondorf, Shirley H. ... Sonoma, CA
Fronduti, John S. ... New York, NY
Froneberger, David Lee ... Deer Park, TX
Froneberger, Henry D.
Point Reyes Station, CA
Froneberger, J. Douglas
Sulphur Springs, TX
Froneberger, Jennifer ... Atlanta, GA
Fronefield, David ... Fort Lee, NJ
Fronefield and de Furia ... Media, PA
Fronek, David N. ... Minneapolis, MN
Frongillo, Thomas C. ... Boston, MA
Fronheiser, Gary S. ... Boyertown, PA
Fronheiser & Younger ... Boyertown, PA
Fronimos, Gregory L. ... Livonia, MI
Froning, Patricia J. ... Pierre, SD
Froning, Susan Katz ... Dearborn, MI
Fronk, John P. ... Fort Lauderdale, FL
Fronk, John P., P.A. ... Fort Lauderdale, FL
Fronk, Stephen M. ... San Francisco, CA
Fronk, Steven F. ... Milwaukee, WI
Front, Mitchell ... Department of Commerce, Patent and Trademark Office, GV
Frontczak, Mary L. ... St. Louis, MO
Frontczak, Paul R. ... Washington, DC
Frontczak, S. Nicholas ... Hamtramck, MI
Frontczak, Steven R. ... St. Louis, MO
Frontera-Suau, Juan M. ... San Juan, PR
Frontiero, Salvatore J. ... Stoneham, MA
Frontis, Constance E. ... New Haven, CT
Fronzuto, Ernest P. ... Morristown, NJ
Frook, Margaret S. (Peggy) ... Venice, FL
Frooks, George P. ... Mohegan Lake, NY
Frooman, Hilary W. ... Urbana, IL
Frooman, James C. ... Cincinnati, OH
Frooman, Thomas E. ... Cincinnati, OH
Froome, Andrea S. ... Fort Lauderdale, FL
Froot, Steven I. ... New York, NY
Frosch, Craig E. ... Metairie, LA
Frosch, Frederick J., Sr. ... Indianapolis, IN
Frosch & Howard ... Indianapolis, IN
Frosch, Kirk J. ... Metairie, LA
Frosch, Perri E. ... New York, NY
Frosco, Donna E. ... Rye, NY
White Plains, NY
Frosh, Brian E. ... Washington, DC
Bethesda, MD
Frosh, David A. ... Denver, CO
Frosh, Stanley B. ... Bethesda, MD
Fross, Alvin ... New York, NY
Fross, Roger R. ... Chicago, IL
Fross, Stuart E. ... Boston, MA
Fross Zelnick Lehrman & Zissu, P.C.
New York, NY
Frossard, Laura Emily ... Tulsa, OK
Frost, Adam T. ... Bloomfield Hills, MI
Frost, Alan K. ... St. Louis, MO
Frost, Albert W. ... West Hartford, CT
Frost, Allan M. ... New York, NY
Frost, Amanda ... Washington, DC
Frost, Antonia A. ... Washington, DC
Frost, Arthur R. ... Troy, NY
Frost & Associates, Inc. ... Berea, OH
Frost, Barbara S. ... Seattle, WA
Frost, Barry W. ... Trenton, NJ
Frost, Benson R., Jr. ... Rhinebeck, NY
Frost, Billy C. ... Abilene, TX
Frost, Bonnie C. ... Denville, NJ
Frost, Branon R., Jr. ... Charlotte, NC
Frost, Brian ... Topeka, KS
Frost, Bruce E. ... Towson, MD
Frost, Carolyn Melott ... Knoxville, TN
Frost, Charles Estes, Jr. ... Houston, TX
Frost, Charles H. ... Willows, CA
Frost, Christopher ... St. Louis, MO
Frost, Christopher L. ... Los Angeles, CA
Frost, Christopher M. ... Portland, OR
Frost, Christopher P. ... Bellevue, WA
Frost, Ciara Ryan ... Chicago, IL
Frost, Clarence A. ... New Orleans, LA
Frost, Clarence J. ... Salt Lake City, UT
Frost, Claudia W. ... Houston, TX
Frost, Corey Wade ... Cleveland, OH
Frost, Cyrus B., Jr. ... Eastland, TX
Frost & Danchak ... Columbus, OH
Frost, Daniel R. ... Denver, CO
Frost, Daniel S. ... Redding, CA
Frost, David B. ... Englewood, CO
Frost, David B. ... Charleston, WV
Frost, David G. ... Hillsboro, OR
Frost, David M. ... Department of Justice, Federal Bureau of Investigation, GV
Frost, David W. ... Tyler, TX
Frost, Diana R. ... New York, NY
Frost, Don Joaquin, Jr. ... Washington, DC
Frost, Donald F. ... Miami, FL
Frost, Douglas C. ... Ontario, CA
Frost, Earle R., Jr. ... Columbus, OH
Frost, Edmund B. ... Washington, DC
Frost, Elaine ... Grosse Pointe, MI
Frost, Eliot ... Chestnut Hill, MA
Frost, Elsie ... Potomac, MD
Frost, Emily V. ... Birmingham, AL
Frost, F. Daniel ... Los Angeles, CA
Frost, Fisher and Pickett ... Plattsburg, MO
Frost, Frederick Allen ... Houston, TX
Frost, Gary Clayton, Jr. ... Arlington, TX
Frost, Gavin M. ... Billings, MT
Frost, George ... San Francisco, CA
Frost, George E. ... Bloomfield Hills, MI
Frost & Greenblatt ... Chicago, IL
Frost, Gregory D. ... Baton Rouge, LA
Frost, Gregory D. ... New York, NY
Frost, Gregory L. ... Newark, OH
Frost, Gwendolyn S. ... Houston, TX
Frost, H. Turner ... Mc Keesport, PA
Frost & Healy ... Vallejo, CA
Frost, Hugh O., II ... Cincinnati, OH
Frost, Ira M. ... Brooklyn, NY
Frost, Irwin M. ... Miami, FL
Frost, Irwin M., P.A. ... Miami, FL
Frost, J. Edmund ... Bay City, MI
Frost, J. Mitchell, Jr. ... Birmingham, AL
Frost, J. Randall ... Gainesville, GA
Frost, Jack P. ... Highland Park, IL
Frost, Jackson L. ... Albany, OR
Frost & Jacobs ... Lexington, KY
Frost & Jacobs LLP ... Cincinnati, OH
Columbus, OH
Middletown, OH
Frost, James H. ... Mobile, AL
Frost, James J. ... Omaha, NE
Frost, James S. ... Seguin, TX
Frost, James T. ... New York, NY
Frost, James W. ... Federal Trade Commission, Bureau of Competition, GV
Frost, James W. ... Des Moines, IA
Frost, Jeffrey D. ... Los Angeles, CA
Frost, Jeffrey H. ... Houston, TX
Frost, Jeffrey M. ... Baltimore, MD
Frost, Jerome K. ... Troy, NY
Frost, Jerome K., P.C. ... Troy, NY
Frost, Jess B. ... Los Angeles, CA
Frost, Jessica Handley ... Marietta, GA
Frost, Jill ... Kansas City, MO
Frost, John A., Jr. ... New York, NY
Frost, John W., II ... Bartow, FL
Frost, Jonathan M. ... West Palm Beach, FL
Frost, Jonathan M. ... Albany, NY
Frost, Joseph ... New York, NY
Frost, Kathleen A. ... San Francisco, CA
Frost, Kem Thompson ... Houston, TX
Frost, Kimberly A. ... Austin, TX
Frost & Kohl ... Hillsboro, OR
Frost, Krup & Atlas ... Willows, CA
Frost, Laura B. ... Merrillville, IN
Portage, IN
Frost, Laurie A. ... Alexandria, VA
Frost, LeAllen ... Dallas, TX
Frost, Leslie M. ... Minneapolis, MN
Frost, Louis B. ... New York, NY
Frost, Louis Duval ... Atlanta, GA
Frost, Louis O., Jr. ... Jacksonville, FL
Frost, LuAnn Cheyne ... Lansing, MI
Frost, Lynda ... Charlottesville, VA
Frost & Maddox Co., L.P.A.
Columbus, OH
Frost, Marcy R. ... Minneapolis, MN
Frost, Mari Higgins ... Kenosha, WI
Frost, Mark A. ... Columbiana, OH
Frost, Mark B. ... Philadelphia, PA
Frost, Mark E. ... Glens Falls, NY
Frost, Matthew C. ... New York, NY
Frost, Merrie M. ... Cleveland, OH
Mentor, OH
Frost, Meyers, Govier & Milone
Omaha, NE
Frost, Michael A. ... Seattle, WA
Frost, Michael B. ... Tampa, FL
Frost, Michael J. ... Chicago, IL
Frost, Michelle ... New York, NY
Frost, Norbert U. ... Vallejo, CA
Frost, Norman C. ... Naples, FL
Frost, Norman C. ... Atlanta, GA
Frost, Oakley C. ... Costa Mesa, CA
Frost, Otis L., Jr. ... Los Angeles, CA
Frost, Peter F. ... Department of Justice, Civil Division, GV
Frost, Philip ... Philadelphia, PA
Frost, R. Jack ... Sacramento, CA
Frost, Rainer L. C. ... Worcester, MA
Frost, Raymond E. ... Fremont, CA
Frost, Renée E. ... New York, NY
Frost, Robert B., Jr. ... Knoxville, TN
Frost, Robert C. ... Richardson, TX
Frost, Robert E. ... Columbus, OH
Frost, Robert H. ... Dallas, TX
Frost, Robert M. ... Castro Valley, CA
Frost, Robert M., Jr. ... Bridgeport, CT
Frost, Robert R. ... Berea, OH
Frost, Robert S. ... Mobile, AL
Frost, Robert S. ... Columbus, OH
Frost, Roger T. ... Atlanta, GA
Frost, Sarah K. ... Madison, WI
Frost & Saunders, P.A. ... Bartow, FL
Frost, Scott C. ... Chicago, IL
Frost, Sharla J. ... Houston, TX
Frost, Stephen A. ... Chicago, IL
Frost, Stephen F. ... Carnation, WA
Frost, Steven G. ... Chicago, IL
Frost, Susan Hupman ... Raleigh, NC
Frost, Susannah W. ... Orlando, FL
Frost, Thomas B. ... Topeka, KS
Frost, Thomas C. ... San Diego, CA
New York, NY
Frost, Thomas C. ... Boise, ID
Frost, Thomas D. ... Murfreesboro, TN
Frost, Thomas E. ... Arlington, VA
Frost, Warren F. ... Tucumcari, NM
Frost, Warren F., P.C. ... Clovis, NM
Tucumcari, NM
Frost, Wayne N. ... Midland, TX
Frost, William D., II ... Waukegan, IL
Frost, William L. ... Manhattan, KS
Frost, William Peter ... Forest Hills, NY
Frost, Wilson ... Chicago, IL
Frostbaum, Lane R. ... Norcross, GA
Frostbaum, Stephanie D. ... Atlanta, GA
Frost-Davies, Julia ... Boston, MA
Frostic, Dennis L. ... Chicago, IL
Frostick, Randolph D. ... Manassas, VA
Frostrom, Allan M. ... San Diego, CA
Frothingham, Beth A. ... Boston, MA
Frothingham, William R. ... Needham, MA
Frotiner, Elizabeth J. ... Los Angeles, CA
Froug, Robin Kaufman ... Sarasota, FL
Froum, Theodore E. ... Southfield, MI
Frouman, Barbara A. ... Washington, DC
Frowley, Norman E. ... New York, NY
Frownfelter, Darcy Alan ... Austin, TX
El Paso, TX
Froy, Michael M. ... Chicago, IL
Frucchione, Peter A ... Howard Beach, NY
Frucci, A. Michael ... Wheaton, MD
Frucci, Eleanor L. ... Silver Spring, MD
Frucci, Jay M. ... West Bloomfield, MI
Frucci, Steven C. ... Virginia Beach, VA
Frucco, John P. ... White Plains, NY
Fruchler, Michael Y. ... New York, NY
Frucht, Kenneth ... San Francisco, CA
Frucht, Robert G. ... Uniondale, NY
Fruchter, E. Leonard ... Torrance, CA
Fruchter, Harvey ... Kenilworth, NJ
Fruchter, Isla Ann ... Philadelphia, PA
Fruchter, Jack G. ... New York, NY
Fruchter, Joel A. ... New York, NY
Fruchter, Lynn S. ... New York, NY
Fruchter, Michael H. ... New York, NY
Fruchter, Murray ... Chagrin Falls, OH
Fruchter & Twersky ... New York, NY
Fruchterman, James R. ... Pawleys Island, SC
Fruchterman, Richard L., Jr. ... Annandale, VA
Fruchtman, Arthur ... Liberty Corner, NJ
Fruchtman, Cynthia E.
Santa Monica, CA
Fruchtman, David A. ... Chicago, IL
Fruchtman, Jonathan E. ... Minneapolis, MN
Fruchtman, Lawrence D. ... New York, NY
Fruchtman, Susan ... West Orange, NJ
Fruchtman, Tamar ... Santa Clara, CA
Fruda, Ronald J. ... Boynton Beach, FL
Frudden, Sarah A. ... Indianapolis, IN
Frue Law Firm, The, L.L.P.
Asheville, NC
Frue, Michael Calhoun ... Asheville, NC
Frue, William C., Jr. ... Asheville, NC
Fruechte, Kermit N. ... Minneapolis, MN
Fruechtemeyer, A. Scott ... Atlanta, GA
Fruechtenicht, Arthur W. ... Fort Wayne, IN
Fruechtenicht Law Office ... Fort Wayne, IN
Fruechtenicht, Richard C. ... Birmingham, AL
Fruechtenicht, Thomas E. ... Indianapolis, IN
Fruechtenicht, Thomas P. ... Lansing, MI
Frueh, Anne E. ... Lake Forest, IL
Frueh, Edward A. ... Palo Alto, CA
Frueh, Gary L. ... Houston, TX
Frueh, Michael M. ... Austin, TX
Fruehauf, Anne L. ... Washington, DC
Fruehauf, Barbara A. ... Wilmington, DE
Fruehauf, Henry W. ... Chicago, IL
Fruehauf, Richard L. ... Washington, DC
Fruehling, Brian J. ... Madison, WI
Fruehling, Everett E. ... Seattle, WA
Fruehling, Keith E. ... Urbana, IL
Fruehwald, Kristin G. ... Indianapolis, IN
Fruehwald, Michael R. ... Indianapolis, IN
Frugá, Mary Celeste ... The Woodlands, TX
Fruge, Christopher B. ... Ville Platte, LA
Fruge, Don L. ... University, MS
Fruge', Don L., Jr. ... Oxford, MS
Fruge, Jack C. ... Ville Platte, LA
Frugé, M. Celeste ... The Woodlands, TX
Fruge, Melissa P. ... Los Altos, CA
Fruge, Robert E. ... Sunset, LA
Frugé, Scott H. ... Baton Rouge, LA
Fruge & Vidrine ... Ville Platte, LA
Fruhling, Michael A. ... New York, NY
Fruhschein, Jason N. ... Lawrenceville, NJ
Fruhwirth, Frances Ann ... Allentown, PA
Fruin, Garst & Kash ... Paris, IL
Fruin, Peter S. ... Montgomery, AL
Fruin, Richard L., Jr. ... Compton, CA
Fruin, Roger J. ... Paris, IL
Fruin, Stephen F. ... Baltimore, MD

Fruit, Dill, Goodwin and Scholl
Sharon, PA
Fruit, Melvyn H. ... Jacksonville, FL
Fruithandler, Charles M. ... El Paso, TX
Fruitman, Martin ... Millersville, PA
Frulio, Maytel Sorondo ... Jacksonville, FL
Frulla, David E. ... Washington, DC
Frulla, William E. ... Memphis, TN
Frum, Austin P. ... Washington, DC
Frum, Richard D. ... Spencer, WV
Frum, Stuart ... Westport, NY
Frum, Stuart, P.C. ... Westport, NY
Fruman, Harvey B. ... San Diego, CA
Fruman, Lee S. ... Franklin, MI
Frumento, Aegis J. ... New York, NY
Frumer & Etkin ... Philadelphia, PA
Frumer, Jill E. ... Philadelphia, PA
Frumer, John D. ... Boston, MA
Frumer, Marc J. ... Dayton, OH
Frumer, Marshall ... Philadelphia, PA
Frumes, Cheryl B. ... Torrance, CA
Frumes, Larry J. ... Torrance, CA
Frumess, Harry A. ... Denver, CO
Frumin, Jill M. ... Federal Trade Commission, Bureau of Competition, GV
Frumin, Lucille L. ... Brooklyn, NY
Frumkes, Melvyn B. ... Boca Raton, FL
Miami, FL
Frumkes, Melvyn B., & Associates, P.A.
Boca Raton, FL
Miami, FL
Frumkin, Abraham H. ... Philadelphia, PA
Frumkin, Allan R. ... San Leandro, CA
Frumkin, Arthur S. ... Los Angeles, CA
Frumkin, Brian E. ... Charlotte, NC
Frumkin, Elizabeth ... Boston, MA
Frumkin, George J. ... New York, NY
Frumkin, Joseph B. ... New York, NY
Frumkin, Nancy Lee ... Potomac, MD
Frumkin, Paul A. ... West Bloomfield, MI
Frumkin, William D. ... White Plains, NY
Frumm, David B. ... Chicago, IL
Frundt, Charles K. ... Amboy, MN
Blue Earth, MN
Winnebago, MN
Frundt, David F. ... Amboy, MN
Blue Earth, MN
Minnesota Lake, MN
Wells, MN
Winnebago, MN
Frundt, John H. ... Blue Earth, MN
Frundt & Johnson, Ltd. ... Amboy, MN
Blue Earth, MN
Minnesota Lake, MN
Wells, MN
Winnebago, MN
Frunzi, Peter P., Jr. ... Shrewsbury, NJ
Frunzi, Richard L. ... Honolulu, HI
Frunzi & Scarborough ... Shrewsbury, NJ
Frunzi, Susan C. ... New York, NY
Frusciante, John A. ... Fort Lauderdale, FL
Frush, C. James ... Seattle, WA
Tacoma, WA
Frustaci, Aldo G. ... Brooklyn, NY
Frustaglio-Roppo, Anna ... San Diego, CA
Frutchey, Daniel L. ... Pittsburgh, PA
Fruth & Anthony, P.A. ... Minneapolis, MN
Fruth, James W. ... Paulding, OH
Fruth, John L. ... San Francisco, CA
Fruth, Lynn L. ... Toledo, OH
Fruth, Michael H., Jr. ... Buffalo, NY
Fruth, Steven J. ... Chicago, IL
Fruth, Terence M. ... Minneapolis, MN
Frutig, Patricia R. ... Gates Mills, OH
Frutig, Thomas R. ... Gates Mills, OH
Frutiger, Carma L. ... Breese, IL
Frutkin, Harvey L. ... Cleveland, OH
Frutkin, Lawrence D. ... Indianapolis, IN
Frutkin, Reynold F. ... Indianapolis, IN
Frutkin, Robert P. ... Philadelphia, PA
Frutkin, William J. ... Ardmore, PA
Fruto, Richard R. ... Los Angeles, CA
Frutos, Alex ... Dallas, TX
Fry, Candace A. ... Sacramento, CA
Fry, Carl B. ... Columbus, OH
Fry, Cox & Fass LLP ... Houston, TX
Fry, Cynthia A., Law Offices of
Albuquerque, NM
Fry, Daniel P. ... Martins Ferry, OH
Fry, David H. ... San Francisco, CA
Fry, David J. ... Kansas City, MO
Fry, David S. ... Grand Rapids, MI
Fry, Dennis G. ... Los Altos, CA
Fry, Diane ... Dallas, TX
Fry, Donald C. ... Bel Air, MD
Fry, Donald C., P.A., Law Office of
Bel Air, MD
Fry & Elder ... Tulsa, OK
Fry, Elizabeth ... Omak, WA
Fry, Elizabeth A. Livesay ... Irvine, CA
Fry, Elizabeth H. W. ... New York, NY
Fry, Ellen M. ... Escondido, CA
Fry, Frederick R. ... Lansing, MI
Fry, Gary D. ... Haddonfield, NJ
Philadelphia, PA
Fry, Gary H. ... Phoenix, AZ
Fry, Gerald R. ... Houston, TX
Fry, Gloria A. ... Boston, MA
Fry, Howard A. ... Lombard, IL
Fry, Howard M. ... Washington, DC
Fry, J. Marshall ... Clearwater, FL
Fry, J. Wesley ... La Mesa, CA
Fry, James A. ... Pierre, SD
Fry, James A. ... Sherman, TX
Fry, James A., P.C. ... Sherman, TX
Fry, James H. ... Athens, AL
Fry, James R. ... Sherman, TX
Fry, James S. ... Essex Junction, VT
Fry, James W., Jr. ... New York, NY
Fry, Jeffry L. ... Golden, CO
Fry, Jennifer G. ... Irving, TX
Fry, Jennifer L. ... Dallas, TX
Houston, TX
Fry, Joel ... El Paso, TX
Fry, Joel C. ... Columbus, OH
Fry, John J. ... Highland Heights, OH
Fry, John P. ... Atlanta, GA
Fry, John R. ... Chicago, IL
Fry, Jonathan H. ... Covina, CA
Fry, Jude A. ... Cleveland, OH
Fry, Judy A. ... Albuquerque, NM
Fry, Kathy Marie ... Tucson, AZ
Fry, Kristi L. ... Fond du Lac, WI
Fry Law Offices, S.C. ... Fond du Lac, WI
Fry, Lawrence W. ... Indio, CA
Fry, Lee E. ... Greenville, OH
Fry, M. Susanna ... Kenosha, WI
Fry, Mark W. ... Baton Rouge, LA
Fry, Mary Lou ... Houston, TX
Fry, MaryAnn ... Lansing, MI
Fry, Michael R. ... Kansas City, MO
Fry, Morton H. ... New York, NY
Fry, Norman J. ... Washington, DC
Fry, Patricia B. ... Grand Forks, ND
Fry, Patricia Coffin ... New York, NY
Fry, R. Craig ... Omaha, NE
Fry, Randall E. ... Mansfield, OH
Fry, Rebecca R. ... Washington, DC
Fry, Richard D. ... Leawood, KS
Kansas City, MO
Fry, Richard S. ... Cedar Rapids, IA
Fry, Rita A. ... Chicago, IL
Fry, Robert A. ... Findlay, OH
Fry, Robert G, Jr. ... Tulsa, OK
Fry, Robert P. ... Edwards, CO
Fry, Roger N. ... Beaumont, TX
Fry, Ron W. ... Dallas, TX
Fry, Samuel R., II ... Shillington, PA
Fry, Sherry L. ... Cleveland, OH
Fry, Stephen ... Palm City, FL
Fry, Stephen S. ... Menlo Park, CA
Fry, Steven E. ... San Antonio, TX
Fry, Terry G. ... Houston, TX
Fry, Theron E. ... Wichita, KS
Fry, Thomas ... Department Of The Interior, Bureau of Land Management, GV
Fry, Thomas L. ... Tulsa, OK
Fry, Thomas W. ... Los Angeles, CA
Fry, Timothy A. ... Columbus, OH
Fry, Virginia L. ... Springfield, MO
Fry, W. Roger ... Cincinnati, OH
Fry, Waller & McCann Co., L.P.A.
Columbus, OH
Fry, William L. ... Wichita, KS
Fry, William L., P.A. ... Wichita, KS
Fry, William R. ... Washington, DC
Fryar, Etta Davidson ... Houston, TX
Fryar, F. Eric ... Houston, TX
Fryar & Fryar ... Houston, TX
Fryar, Kimberly A. ... San Antonio, TX
Fryar, Michael S. ... Gresham, OR
Fryar, Robert M. ... Troy, MI
Fryar, Scott M. ... Richardson, TX
Fryar, Tina M. ... San Diego, CA
Fryauf, Mark T. ... Rogers, AR
Fryback, John T., (P.A.) ... Bradenton, FL
Fryberger, Buchanan, Smith & Frederick, P.A. ... Iron Mountain, MI
Duluth, MN
St. Paul, MN
Superior, WI
Fryburg, Marc H. ... New York, NY
Fryburger, L. Bruce ... San Antonio, TX
Fryburger, L. Bruce, Inc., A Prof. Corp., Law Offices of ... San Antonio, TX
Frycklund, Robert S. ... Jenkintown, PA
Fryd, Paul A. ... New York, NY
Fryd, Robert ... New York, NY
Fryday, Harold W. ... Santa Clara, CA
Frydman, Abraham C. ... Bronx, NY
Frydman, Ben A. ... Newport Beach, CA
Frydman, David I. ... Concord, NH
Frydman, David S. ... New York, NY
Frydman, Jane ... Lawrence, KS
Frydman, Joel M. ... Dayton, OH
Frydman, John Allen ... Lawrence, KS
Frydman, Robin F. ... Miami, FL
Frydrych, Jack A. ... Los Angeles, CA
Frye, Alan R. ... Melbourne, FL
Frye, Andrew N., Jr. ... Petersburg, WV
Frye, Angela Bonfield ... Chicago, IL
Frye, Anne M. ... Indianapolis, IN
Frye, B. Michael ... Burlington, VT
Frye, Blake H. ... Atlanta, GA
Frye & Booth ... Winston-Salem, NC
Frye & Boyce, P.A. ... Little Rock, AR
Frye, Charles B. ... Houston, TX
Frye, Charles E., III ... Lexington, NC
Frye, Christopher C. ... Kinnelon, NJ
Frye, D. Randall ... Cincinnati, OH
Frye, David D. ... Carmel, IN
Frye, David R. ... Overland Park, KS
Frye, David S.
Securities and Exchange Commission, Division of Enforcement, GV
Frye, David W. ... San Jose, CA
Frye, Dexter A. ... Livermore, CA
Frye, Diane M. ... Indianapolis, IN
Frye, Donald H. ... Towson, MD
Frye, Douglas J., (Professional Corporation)
Malibu, CA
Frye, Emily ... Boulder, CO
Frye, Eric T. ... Washington, DC
Frye, Erik E. ... Sacramento, CA
Frye, F. Kytle, III ... Atlanta, GA
Frye, Frank A., III ... San Diego, CA
Frye, Frank H. ... Portland, ME
Frye, Gary F. ... Marietta, OH
Frye, George M. ... Hopkins, MN
Frye, G. R. Pete ... Greenville, MI
Frye, Harvey L., Jr. ... Fort Worth, TX
Frye, Helen J. ... Portland, OR
Frye, Henry E. ... Raleigh, NC
Frye & Hsieh LLP ... Los Angeles, CA
Malibu, CA
Frye, J. Gregory ... Somerset, KY
Frye, Jack W. ... Charles City, IA
Frye, Jennifer L. ... Lansing, MI
Frye, John N. ... Los Angeles, CA
Frye, John William, III ... Pensacola, FL
Frye, Kimberly A. ... New York, NY
Frye, Kimberly Ruth ... Houston, TX
Frye, Kristin K. ... Austin, TX
Frye, Kristine Corcoran ... Des Moines, IA
Frye, L. Vernon ... Sterling, IL
Frye, Laetitia B. ... Richmond, VA
Frye, Leslie G. ... Winston-Salem, NC
Frye, Lynn Oliver ... Charleston, WV
Frye & Malchow ... Burlingame, CA
Los Angeles, CA
Frye, Mark E. ... Abingdon, VA
Bristol, VA
Frye, Mary Catherine ... Summerdale, PA
Frye, Maurice E., Jr. ... Boston, MA
Frye, Michael A. ... Huntington, WV
Frye, Michael C. ... Denton, TX
Frye, Michael C. ... Fort Worth, TX
Frye, Michael S. ... Fresno, CA
Frye, Miles P. ... Waterville, ME
Frye, Patrick D. ... Denver, CO
Frye, Paul E. ... Albuquerque, NM
Frye, Phyllis Randolph ... Houston, TX
Frye, Rebekah A. ... Palo Alto, CA
Frye, Richard A. ... Old Forge, NY
Utica, NY
Frye, Richard A. ... Columbus, OH
Frye, Robert ... Fort Lauderdale, FL
Frye, Robert D. ... Fort Worth, TX
Frye, Robert D., P.C. ... Fort Worth, TX
Frye, Robert L. ... Denver, CO
Frye, Robert L., P.C. ... Denver, CO
Lakewood, CO
Frye, Robert M. ... Indianapolis, IN
Frye, Robert Owen ... Bay Village, OH
Frye, Rodney B. ... Charleston, WV
Frye, Roger P. ... Hingham, MA
Frye, Roland M., Jr.
Nuclear Regulatory Commission, Office of Commission Appellate Adjudication, GV
Frye, Russell S. ... Washington, DC
Frye, Susan J. ... Iowa City, IA
Frye, Suzanne F. ... Harrisonburg, VA
Frye, Thomas E. ... Euclid, OH
Frye, Todd J. ... Washington, DC
Frye, Tracy D. ... Huntington, WV
Frye, Victor M. ... Bethesda, MD
Frye, Wesley M. ... Anniston, AL
Frye, William C. ... Little Rock, AR
Frye, William C. ... Tampa, FL
Frye, William Davis ... Jackson, MS
Frye, William H. ... Memphis, TN
Frye, William M. ... Charles City, IA
Fryefield, Peter J. ... Jacksonville, FL
Frye-Fowlkes, Vicki L. ... Winchester, TN
Fryer, Brian Michael ... Indio, CA
Fryer, Catherine Brown ... Austin, TX
Fryer, Charles E. ... Boyertown, PA
Fryer, Charles E., P.C. ... Boyertown, PA
Fryer, Christine R. ... New York, NY
Fryer, Clara L. ... Atlanta, GA
Fryer, Douglas J. ... Bloomfield Hills, MI
Fryer, Douglas M. ... Seattle, WA
Fryer, Edwin S. ... St. Louis, MO
Fryer, F. Patrick ... Kansas City, MO
Fryer, Gregory S. ... Portland, ME
Fryer, Hugh N. ... New York, NY
Fryer, J. Stuart ... Hallettsville, TX
Fryer, Joanna ... Kansas City, MO
Fryer, Joel J. ... Atlanta, GA
Fryer, Jonathan ... Dover, MA
Fryer, Judith D. ... New York, NY
Fryer, Keith E. ... Atlanta, GA
Fryer, M. Suzanne ... San Luis Obispo, CA
Fryer, Merrilee A. ... St. Paul, MN
Fryer & O'Brien ... Dover, MA
Fryer, Paul ... Bainbridge, GA
Fryer, R. Alan ... Boston, MA
Fryer, Robert E. ... Ann Arbor, MI
Fryer, Robert H. ... Londonderry, NH
Fryer, Robert N. ... Santa Rosa, CA
Fryer, Robert N., Jr. ... Tamarac, FL
Fryer & Ross ... New York, NY
Fryer, Thomas Henry ... Bellingham, WA
Fryer, William B. ... Atlanta, GA
Fryer, William T., III ... Bethesda, MD
Fryhling, Jennifer S. ... San Francisco, CA
Fryhofer, George W. ... Waynesboro, GA
Fryhofer, George W., III ... Atlanta, GA
Columbus, GA
Fryhoff, Timothy T. ... Bloomfield Hills, MI
Frykberg, Randall ... Minneapolis, MN
Frykberg, Ronald M. ... Omaha, NE
Fryklund, Inge ... Chicago, IL
Fryling, James R. ... Erie, PA
Fryling, Richard, Jr. ... Newark, NJ
Fryling, Robert G. ... Philadelphia, PA
Fryman, David S. ... Philadelphia, PA
Fryman, James Edward ... Chicago, IL
Fryman, Louis W. ... Philadelphia, PA
Fryman, Robert E. ... Hamilton, OH
Fryman, Robert J. ... Rockville Centre, NY
Fryman, Shirley A. ... Dallas, TX
Fryman, V. Thomas, Jr. ... Lexington, KY
Frymire, Evans, Peyton, Teague & Cartwright ... Madisonville, KY
Frymire, Richard L. ... Madisonville, KY
Frymyer, John H., Jr. ... Lancaster, PA
Frysak, Francis M. ... New York, NY
Frysiak, John M.
Federal Communications Commission, Office of Administrative Law Judges, GV
Fryszman, Agnieszka M. ... Washington, DC
Frysztacki, Wesley R. ... Moorestown, NJ
Fryzel, Karl P. ... Boston, MA
Fryzel, Michael E. ... Chicago, IL
Fryzel, Scott R. ... Chicago, IL
Fthenakis, Basil P. ... Palo Alto, CA
Fu, David Dai-Wung ... Sherman Oaks, CA
Fu, Isabella E. ... Santa Clara, CA
Fu, Jingwei Lu ... New York, NY
Fu, K.N. Minnie ... Washington, DC
Fu, Ning ... Portland, OR
Fu, Victor T. ... Los Angeles, CA
Fu, Vivian ... New York, NY
Fuad, Peter H. ... Los Angeles, CA
Fuca, Carrie L. ... Mount Clemens, MI
Fucci, F. Mark ... Hartford, CT
Fucci, Frederick R. ... New York, NY
Fucci, Peter J. ... New York, NY
Fucci, Rick J. ... Miami, FL
Fuccillo, Arthur N. ... North Bethesda, MD
Fuccillo, Thomas J. ... New York, NY
Fuccio, James B. ... Oyster Bay, NY
Fucetola, James Ernest ... Montesano, WA
Fucetola, Ralph, III ... Newton, NJ
Fucheck, Michael W. ... Hunt Valley, MD
Fuchigami, Walter N. ... Citrus Heights, CA
Fuchs, Aaron Leslie ... Atlanta, GA
Fuchs, Alicia A. ... Portland, OR
Fuchs, Altschul, Greenberg & Sapin
Jersey City, NJ
Fuchs, Beatrice G. ... Washington, DC
Fuchs, Bernard ... Brooklyn, NY
Fuchs, Bruce C. ... Pittsburgh, PA
Fuchs, Carol A. ... Schaumburg, IL
Fuchs, Chana G. ... Bronx, NY
Fuchs, Charna L. ... White Plains, NY
Fuchs, Dallin M. ... New York, NY
Fuchs, Daniel J. ... Pittsburgh, PA
Fuchs, Daniel M. ... San Francisco, CA
Fuchs, David ... Phoenix, AZ
Fuchs, David ... Los Angeles, CA
Fuchs, David I. ... Fort Lauderdale, FL
Fuchs, David I., P.A. ... Fort Lauderdale, FL
Fuchs, Dean R. ... Griffin, GA
Fuchs, Dennis M. ... Salt Lake City, UT
Fuchs, Diane J. ... Washington, DC
Fuchs, Donald C. ... Portland, OR
Fuchs, Donald J. ... Evansville, IN
Fuchs, Douglas M. ... Los Angeles, CA
Fuchs, E. Calvin ... Phoenix, AZ
Fuchs, Elsa Theile ... Chicago, IL
Fuchs, Ethan ... Santa Rosa, NM
Fuchs, Frederick Nicholas ... New York, NY
Fuchs, Gerald G. ... Evansville, IN
Fuchs, Gregory C. ... Frankfort, KY
Fuchs, Hanno ... Stamford, CT
Fuchs, Howard ... Boston, MA
Fuchs, Howard M. ... Granada Hills, CA
Fuchs, Irving J. ... Lauderhill, FL
Fuchs, Jack F. ... Cincinnati, OH
Fuchs, Jack S. ... New York, NY
Fuchs, Jacqueline ... Beverly Hills, CA
Fuchs, James L. ... New York, NY
Fuchs, Jan ... Oakland, CA
Fuchs, Jill N. ... Cincinnati, OH
Fuchs, John D. ... Torrance, CA
Fuchs, John F. ... Milwaukee, WI
Fuchs, John P. ... Glendale, CA
Fuchs, John R., (P.C.) ... Los Angeles, CA
Fuchs, Jonathan A. ... Brooklyn, NY
Fuchs, Jonathan N. ... New York, NY
Fuchs, Jones & Morris, P.A.
Royal Palm Beach, FL
Fuchs, Jos. ... New York, NY
Fuchs, Joseph A. ... Chicago, IL
Fuchs, Joseph P. ... Sikeston, MO
Fuchs, Kathleen A. ... Long Beach, CA
Fuchs, Kathleen A., P.C. ... Long Beach, CA
Fuchs, Kenneth ... New York, NY
Fuchs, Kenneth G. ... Conway, AR
Fuchs, Lance Christopher
West Palm Beach, FL
Fuchs, Lawrence M. ... Royal Palm Beach, FL
Fuchs, Lawrence M. ... Red Bank, NJ
Fuchs, Lorrie E. ... Canton, OH
Fuchs, Mark A. ... Portland, OR
Fuchs & Marshall ... Los Angeles, CA
Fuchs, Martin I. ... Washington, DC
Fuchs, Meredith ... Washington, DC
Fuchs, Michael P. ... New York, NY
Fuchs, Michael S.
Securities and Exchange Commission, Division of Enforcement, GV
Fuchs, Nancy E. ... New York, NY
Fuchs, Olivia Morris ... Louisville, KY
Fuchs, Robert ... Jersey City, NJ
Fuchs, Robert B. ... Benton, MO
Fuchs, Robert B. ... Sikeston, MO
Fuchs, Robert F. ... Chicago, IL
Fuchs, Robert H. ... New York, NY
Fuchs, Robert T. ... Brightwaters, NY
Fuchs, Ronald W. ... Washington, DC
Fuchs, Ronni E. ... Philadelphia, PA
Fuchs & Roselli, Ltd. ... Chicago, IL
Wheaton, IL
Fuchs, Sandor C. ... Los Angeles, CA
Fuchs, Shaye J. ... New York, NY
Fuchs, Sidney ... Oceanside, NY
Fuchs, Snow & DeStefanis, S.C.
Milwaukee, WI

Fuchs, Stanley ... Scarsdale, NY
Fuchs, Stephen A. ... Roseland, NJ
New York, NY
Fuchs, Steven L. ... Newton, MA
Fuchs, Stuart ... Chicago, IL
Fuchs, Susan A. ... Scottsdale, AZ
Fuchs, Thomas J. ... San Diego, CA
Fuchsberg, Abraham ... New York, NY
Fuchsberg, Alan L. ... New York, NY
Fuchsberg & Fuchsberg ... New York, NY
Fuchsberg, Jacob D., The Law Firm
New York, NY
Fuchsberg, Lawrence M. ... New York, NY
Fuchsberg, Seymour ... New York, NY
Fuchs-Goldberg, Meryl, (Mrs.) ... Newark, NJ
Fuchsman, David H. ... Dayton, OH
Fuchsman, Jeffrey P. ... Universal City, CA
Fuchsman, Rita S. ... Chillicothe, OH
Fuchsteiner, Peter J. ... St. Cloud, MN
Fucik, Donald E. ... Fort Lauderdale, FL
Fucile, Frank J., Jr. ... St. Louis, MO
Fucile, Mark J. ... Portland, OR
Fucillo, Rocco S. ... Fairmont, WV
Fucillo, Thomas J. ... Syracuse, NY
Fudacz, Frederic A. ... Los Angeles, CA
Fudacz, Paul M. ... Toledo, OH
Fudala, David J. ... Fairfax, VA
Fudala, Muriel ... Lexington, MA
Fudale, William F. ... Willoughby, OH
Fudali, Keefer & Keefer ... St. Paul, MN
Fudali, Peter W. ... Miami, FL
Miami, FL
Fudali, Peter W., P.A. ... Miami, FL
Fudali, Richard H. ... St. Paul, MN
Fudem & Evans ... Santa Rosa, CA
Fudem, Mark Allen ... Santa Rosa, CA
Fudeman, Madelyn S. ... Reading, PA
Fudenna, Keith H. ... Fremont, CA
Fudge, Donna J. ... Tampa, FL
Fudge, Edward W. ... Houston, TX
Fudge & Elder ... Burkburnett, TX
Fudge, Gerald W. ... Atlanta, GA
Fudge, Gregory M. ... Department of Justice, Federal Bureau of Investigation, GV
Fudge, Jack D. ... Los Angeles, CA
Fudge, Jeff D. ... Dallas, TX
Fudge, Reg, Jr. ... Van Nuys, CA
Fudge, Sandi Pearson ... Rowlett, TX
Fudge, Tangla L. ... Atlanta, GA
Fudge, Vonner L., (Miss) ... Atlanta, GA
Fudge, W. Bernard ... Burkburnett, TX
Fudger, Arthur W. ... Dallas, GA
Fudim, Allan ... New York, NY
Fudor, Stanley ... Cranberry Township, PA
Fudurich, Ruth M. ... Sacramento, CA
Fudzie, Patricia C. ... Dallas, TX
Fuechtman, David C. ... Chicago, IL
Fuehr, Ralph V. ... Pittsburgh, PA
Fuehrer, Gloria N. ... Pittsburgh, PA
Fuehrer, J. Alan ... Washington, PA
Fuelberg, Ann Lea ... Austin, TX
Fuelleman, Cheryl ... Palo Alto, CA
Fuelling, Michael L. ... Fort Wayne, IN
Fuente, Jaret J. ... Tampa, FL
Fuente, William ... Tampa, FL
Fuentealba, Victor W. ... Baltimore, MD
Fuentes, Alicia E. ... Chicago, IL
Fuentes & Associates, P.C. ... Rio Rancho, NM
Fuentes, David ... Reston, VA
Fuentes, Ernesto V. ... Los Angeles, CA
Fuentes, Gabriel A. ... Chicago, IL
Fuentes, Grace E. ... St. Charles, MO
Fuentes, Gustavo E. ... Coral Gables, FL
Fuentes, Jorge L. ... Madison, WI
Fuentes, Julio M. ... Newark, NJ
Fuentes and Kreischer ... Tampa, FL
Fuentes, Lawrence E. ... Tampa, FL
Fuentes, Lillian ... Chicago, IL
Fuentes, Lourdes ... Seattle, WA
Fuentes, Mary E. ... San Antonio, TX
Fuentes & McNally ... Glendale, CA
Fuentes, Nicola A. ... Houston, TX
Fuentes, Raymond J. ... Glendale, CA
Fuentes, Robert R. ... Rio Rancho, NM
Fuentes, Rudy ... Washington, DC
Fuentes, Sonia P. ... Potomac, MD
Fuentes-Rivera, Rafael S. ... Guaynabo, PR
Fuentes-Smith, Myrna G. ... Addison, IL
Fuentes-Valentin, Reinaldo ... San Juan, PR
Fuentevilla, Eve J. ... Stockton, NJ
Fuentevilla, William F. ... Bethesda, MD
Fuer, John A. ... Green Valley, AZ
Fuerbringer, Elizabeth M.
Fountain Valley, CA
Fuerch, Stephen M. ... Pleasanton, CA
Fuerman, Robert C. ... Radnor, PA
Fuerman, Ross D. ... Reynoldsburg, OH
Fuerst, Gerald E. ... Cleveland, OH
Fuerst, Harrison M. ... Cleveland, OH
Fuerst, Jack N. ... Houston, TX
Fuerst, Jane R. ... White Plains, NY
Fuerst, John Jacob, III ... Denver, CO
Fuerst, Michael A. ... Claremont, NH
Fuerst, Michael T. ... Houston, TX
Fuerst, Mitchell S. ... Miami, FL
Fuerst, Norman A. ... Cleveland, OH
Fuerst, Randy J. ... Lake Charles, LA
Fuerst, Robert A. ... Cleveland, OH
Fuerst, Robert L. ... Rocky Mount, NC
Fuerst, Russell S. ... Temecula, CA
Fuerst, Sarah L. ... Raleigh, NC
Fuerst, Scott J. ... Fort Lauderdale, FL
Fuerst, Steven B. ... Somerville, NJ
Fuerste, Carew, Coyle, Juergens & Sudmeier, P.C. ... Dubuque, IA
Fuerste, William C. ... Dubuque, IA
Fuerstenberg, James P. ... Argonne, IL
Fuerstman, Elizabeth A. ... New York, NY
Fuertes, Rafael R. ... San Juan, PR
Fuertges, Edmund J. ... Somonauk, IL
Fuerth, Donald S. ... Freehold, NJ
Fuerth, Glenn J. ... New York, NY
Fuerth, Thomas L. ... New York, NY
Fues, Eric J. ... Washington, DC
Fuess, Ruth M. ... Albuquerque, NM
Fuess, William C. ... San Diego, CA
Fuetsch, Franz ... San Francisco, CA
Fueyo, Richard K. ... Tampa, FL
Fufidio, George E., Jr. ... White Plains, NY
Fugal, Jeffrey B. ... Phoenix, AZ
Fugal, John Robert ... Orem, UT
Fugate, Allen L. ... North Platte, NE
Fugate, Andrea A. ... Los Angeles, CA
Fugate, Anthony W. ... Lynn, MA
Fugate, Barbara B.
Department Of The Interior, Office of the Solicitor, GV
Fugate, Charles D., II ... Jonesville, VA
Fugate, Elizabeth F. ... Mill Valley, CA
Fugate, Forrest N. ... San Diego, CA
Fugate, Glenn D. ... Wilmington, DE
Fugate, Ivan D. ... Denver, CO
Fugate, John D. ... Redmond, WA
Fugate, Lee ... Tampa, FL
Fugate, Margaret B. ... Johnson City, TN
Fugate, Rachel E. ... Tampa, FL
Fugate, Robert H. ... Mansfield, TX
Fugate, Sue A. ... Kennett Square, PA
Fugate, Wilbur L. ... Washington, DC
Alexandria, VA
Fugate, William C. ... Jonesville, VA
Fugawa, Michelle ... Sacramento, CA
Fugazi, Robert A. ... Monterey, CA
Fugazy, Amanda M. ... New York, NY
Fugazzi, Fred E., Jr. ... Lexington, KY
Fugazzi, Harold J. ... Mineola, NY
Fuge, Kristine N. ... Forest Lake, MN
Fuge, Lloyd H. ... Clairton, PA
Fuge, Peter L. ... Beaufort, SC
Fuge, Peter L., P.A. ... Beaufort, SC
Fugee, Patricia Brown ... Toledo, OH
Fugelsang, Kathleen ... Melville, NY
Fugelso, William P. ... Watertown, MA
Fuger, Stanley T., Jr. ... Hartford, CT
Fugere, Kathryn Anne ... San Francisco, CA
Fugere, Patricia Mullahy ... Washington, DC
Fuges, Frederick L. ... Philadelphia, PA
Fugett, Anne P. ... Department of Labor, Office of the Solicitor, GV
Fugett, David A. ... Pensacola, FL
Fugh, Jarrett L. ... San Francisco, CA
Fugh, John L. ... Washington, DC
Fugh, Justina C.
Environmental Protection Agency, Office of the General Counsel, GV
Fugina, David J. ... Fountain City, WI
Fugina, Patrick J. ... Anoka, MN
Fugit, Gerald K., (P.C.) ... Odessa, TX
Fugit, Larry F. ... Papillion, NE
Fugit, Lonnie W. ... Austin, TX
Fugitt, F. Andrew ... Oklahoma City, OK
Fuglestad, Nathan P. ... North Branch, MN
Fuglesten, Harlan G. ... Fargo, ND
Fuglsang, Eric J. ... Chicago, IL
Fugolo, Mark J. ... Eastpointe, MI
Fuguet, Evan W. ... Raleigh, NC
Fuguet, Howard K. ... Boston, MA
Fuhr, Edward J. ... Richmond, VA
Fuhr, Frank R. ... Rock Island, IL
Fuhr, Frederick L. ... League City, TX
Fuhr, Joy C. ... Richmond, VA
Fuhr, Mark T. ... Phillips, WI
Fuhr, Mary Lynn ... Rock Island, IL
Fuhr, Piper L. ... Rock Island, IL
Fuhr, Ronald E. ... Effingham, IL
Fuhr, Scott M. ... Green Bay, WI
Fuhrer, Arthur K. ... New York, NY
Fuhrer, Bruce R. ... Ventura, CA
Fuhrer, Flournoy, Hunter & Morton
Alexandria, LA
Fuhrer, Leonard ... Alexandria, LA
Fuhrer, Loriann E. ... Columbus, OH
Fuhrer & Melamed ... New York, NY
Fuhrer, Neil L. ... New York, NY
Fuhrhop, Wm. T. ... Dickinson, TX
Fuhrman, Charles A. ... Toledo, OH
Fuhrman, Harold H. ... Milwaukee, WI
Fuhrman, Hillary Light ... Great Neck, NY
Fuhrman, Howard S. ... Chicago, IL
Fuhrman, Janel M. ... Omaha, NE
Fuhrman, Jeffrey L. ... Minneapolis, MN
Fuhrman, John W. ... Puyallup, WA
Fuhrman, Marc H. ... New York, NY
Fuhrman, Mark H. T. ... Madison, WI
Fuhrman, Mark J. ... Fremont, NE
Fuhrman, Marvin D. ... New York, NY
Fuhrman, Melvin L. ... Narberth, PA
Fuhrman, Paul A. ... Los Angeles, CA
Fuhrman, R. David ... Northport, AL
Fuhrman, Robynne R. ... Los Angeles, CA
Fuhrman, Sandra L. ... Newport Beach, CA
Fuhrman, Sarah A. ... Los Angeles, CA
Fuhrman, Steven M. ... New York, NY
Fuhrman, Timothy J. ... Mobile, AL
Fuhrman, Tom R. ... Miami, FL
Fuhrman, Troy A. ... Tampa, FL
Fuhrman, William A. ... Boise, ID
Fuhrman, William R. ... San Diego, CA
Fuhrmann, Chris C. ... Worcester, MA
Fuhrmann, Maria R. ... Chicago, IL
Fuhrmann, Myron E. ... Springfield, NJ
Fuhrmann, Myron E., P.C. ... Springfield, NJ
Fuhrmann, Stewart M. ... Morristown, NJ
Fuhrmeister, James W. ... Birmingham, AL
Fuhro, Brian D. ... Rutherford, NJ
Fuhry, David L. ... Burton, OH
Fuhry, Kenneth A. ... Burton, OH
Fuimaono, Asaua F. ... Pago Pago, TT
Fuini, John F., Jr. ... San Antonio, TX
Fuire, Dennis P. ... Los Angeles, CA
Fuirst, Alan J. ... Yonkers, NY
Fuisz, Jeffrey A. ... New York, NY
Fuisz, John R. ... Washington, DC
Fuith, David A. ... Eagan, MN
Fuji, Wendell H., (Atty. At Law, A Law Corp.) ... Honolulu, HI
Fujie, Holly J. ... Los Angeles, CA
Fujihira, Donald T. ... Fairfield, NJ
Fujii, Akiyo ... Boston, MA
Fujii, Harold T. ... Sunnyvale, CA
Fujii, Karen ... New York, NY
Fujii, Naoko ... New York, NY
Fujii, Patricia T. ... Honolulu, HI
Fujii, Raymond T. ... Long Beach, CA
Fujii, Rodney A. ... Los Angeles, CA
Fujikawa, David T. ... Honolulu, HI
Fujikawa, Ronald K., (Professional Corporation) ... Los Angeles, CA
Fujikawa & Yasunaga ... Honolulu, HI
Fujiki, Marjorie ... New York, NY
Fujimori, Melody M. ... San Francisco, CA
Fujimoto, Alan S. (IBA) ... **Honolulu, HI**
Fujimoto, Beth K. ... Honolulu, HI
Fujimoto, Daniel K. ... Lake Forest, CA
Fujimoto, James R. ... Chicago, IL
Fujimoto, Kenji ... New York, NY
Fujimoto, Leah ... Fargo, ND
Fujimoto, Marcia K. ... Seattle, WA
Fujimoto, Michelle M. ... Irvine, CA
Fujimoto, Naomi C. ... Honolulu, HI
Fujimoto, Randal T. ... Cambridge, MA
Fujimoto, Randi L. ... Sacramento, CA
Fujimoto, Shirley S. ... Washington, DC
Fujimoto, Stanley S. ... Honolulu, HI
Fujimoto, Ward F. N. ... Honolulu, HI
Fujimoto, Warren S. ... Orange, CA
Fujimoto, Wesley M. ... Honolulu, HI
Fujinaga, Todd Roger ... San Jose, CA
Fujioka, Donna H. ... Oakland, CA
Fujioka, Fred J. ... Los Angeles, CA
Fujioka, Stuart N. ... Honolulu, HI
Fujisaki, Carin T. ... San Francisco, CA
Fujisaki, Hiroshi ... Los Angeles, CA
Fujisaki, Lance S. ... Honolulu, HI
Fujise, Alexa D. M. ... Honolulu, HI
Fujita, Brian Y. ... Orange, CA
Fujita, Deirdre R.
Department of Transportation, National Highway Traffic Safety Administration, GV
Fujita, Garry G. ... Seattle, WA
Fujita, Gerald I. ... Honolulu, HI
Fujita, Sharon M. ... Emeryville, CA
Fujitani, Jay Masa ... Los Angeles, CA
Fujitomi, Irene N. ... San Francisco, CA
Fujiwara, Elizabeth Jubin ... Honolulu, HI
Fujiwara, Ronald T. ... Honolulu, HI
Fujiyama, Duffy & Fujiyama, Attorneys at Law, A Law Corporation ... Honolulu, HI
Fujiyama, Duke T. ... Honolulu, HI
Fujiyama, Rodney M. ... Honolulu, HI
Fujiyama, Sandra S. ... Los Angeles, CA
Fukai, Janice Y. ... Inglewood, CA
Fukano, Russ M. ... Los Angeles, CA
Fukasawa, John K., Jr. ... Campbell, CA
Fukasawa, John K., Jr. ... San Jose, CA
Fukuda, Kenneth ... San Francisco, CA
Fukuda, Kozo ... Chicago, IL
Fukuda, Margaret M. ... Troy, MI
Fukuda, Richard T. ... Honolulu, HI
Fukuda, Steven Ken ... Manchester, NH
Fukuhara, Calvin J. ... Hilo, HI
Fukuhara, Stacy Sachiko ... Hagåtña, GU
Fukuhara, Troy T. ... Honolulu, HI
Fukui, Alexander H. ... Los Angeles, CA
Fukumoto, Bert K. ... Portland, OR
Fukumoto, Leslie S., (Mr.) ... Honolulu, HI
Fukumoto, Russell N. ... Kaneohe, HI
Fukumoto, Scott K.
Department of Defense, GV
Fukumura, Koji F. ... San Diego, CA
Fukunaga, Jill A. ... San Francisco, CA
Fukunaga, John O. ... Culver City, CA
Fukunaga, Kenneth K. ... Honolulu, HI
Fukunaga Matayoshi Hershey & Ching
Honolulu, HI
Fukuoka, S. Geo. ... Wailuku, HI
Fukushima, Paul J. ... Norwalk, CA
Fukushima, Robert K. ... Sacramento, CA
Fukushima, Yasutaka ... Honolulu, HI
Fukuya, Royce F. ... Honolulu, HI
Fularczyk, Kevin P. ... Detroit, MI
Fulbright, Bonnie S. ... Houston, TX
Fulbright & Casselberry ... Lamesa, TX
Fulbright & Jaworski L.L.P.
Los Angeles, CA
Washington, DC
New York, NY
Austin, TX
Dallas, TX
Houston, TX
San Antonio, TX
Fulbright, John W. ... Waco, TX
Fulbright, Michael G. ... Seattle, WA
Fulbright, Paul W. ... Richardson, TX
Fulbright, Shawn C. ... Rockford, IL
Fulbright, William E. ... Lodi, CA
Fulbright, William Ed ... Lamesa, TX
Fulbright, Winniford & Marable, A Professional Corporation ... Waco, TX
Fulbright-Scheyer, Pamela ... Houston, TX
Fulce, Dawn E. ... Laurel, MS
Fulcher, Anthony T. ... Fremont, CA
Fulcher, David H. ... Jackson, MS
Fulcher, Donald R. ... Huntington, WV
Fulcher, H. Clay ... Dardanelle, AR
Fulcher, Hagler, Reed, Hanks & Harper, LLP ... Augusta, GA
Thomson, GA
Waynesboro, GA
Aiken, SC
Fulcher, Henry Clay ... Rogers, AR
Fulcher, James Val ... Teague, TX
Fulcher, Joseph A. C. ... Galveston, TX
League City, TX
Fulcher, Kristin Linette ... Richmond, VA
Fulcher, Laura Phillips ... Columbus, OH
Fulcher, Stacy D. ... Charlotte, NC
Fulco, Dominic, III ... Hartford, CT
Fulco, John Paul ... New York, NY
Fulco, Stacy Dolan ... Chicago, IL
Fuld, Elliot H. ... Bronx, NY
Fuld, James J. ... New York, NY
Fuld, Stanley H. ... New York, NY
Fuld, William H. ... Anchorage, AK
Fulda, Charles J., IV ... Houma, LA
Fuldner, Henry E. ... Milwaukee, WI
Fuleihan, Neville S. ... Rutherfordton, NC
Fuleras, John M. ... Bloomfield Hills, MI
Fulero, Solomon M. ... Dayton, OH
Fulfer, E. Paul ... Modesto, CA
Fulfer, Richard L. ... Modesto, CA
Fulford, Clifford ... Birmingham, AL
Fulford, James E. ... Abbeville, AL
Fulford, Jeffrey C. ... North Palm Beach, FL
Fulford, Mark L. ... Denver, CO
Fulford, Martha S. ... Denver, CO
Fulford, William Patrick ... Orlando, FL
Fulford, Wm. E. ... Norfolk, VA
Fulfree, Richard W. ... Yonkers, NY
Fulfrost, Howard J. ... San Rafael, CA
Fulgency, Robert J. ... Minneapolis, MN
Fulgham, Billy L. ... Jackson, MS
Fulgham, Kay ... Fort Worth, TX
Fulgham, Mischelle R. ... Coeur d'Alene, ID
Spokane, WA
Fulghum, Bernard Eugene ... Moorestown, NJ
Fulghum, Caitlyn T. ... Durham, NC
Fulghum, Gary V. ... Kansas City, MO
Fulghum, James H., Jr. ... Roanoke, VA
Fulghum, Roger J. ... Houston, TX
Fulgieri, Maria A. ... Rye Brook, NY
Fulgieri, Mario ... Uniondale, NY
Fulginiti, Anthony J. ... Wildwood, NJ
Fulginiti, Brian G. ... Princeton, NJ
Fulginiti, Francis R. ... South Weymouth, MA
Fulginiti, John Paul ... Boston, MA
Fulginiti, Kenneth F. ... Philadelphia, PA
Fulginiti & Pessel ... Princeton, NJ
Fulginiti, Rhonda M. ... Philadelphia, PA
Fulgione, Libby G., II ... Boston, MA
Fulgoney, John F. ... Pittsburgh, PA
Fulham, Ellen L. ... Boston, MA
Fulham, Gerarda Marie ... Osterville, MA
Fulk, Baucum ... Little Rock, AR
Fulk, Dwayne A. ... Springfield, MO
Fulk, Jeffrey S. ... New Bern, NC
Fulk, Kirkland A. ... Houston, TX
Fulk, Winton D. ... Skokie, IL
Fulker, Ellen Wilber ... Philadelphia, PA
Fulker, John E. ... Troy, OH
Fulker, William J. ... Troy, OH
Fulkerson, Alan L. ... Chicago, IL
Fulkerson, Andrew ... Paragould, AR
Fulkerson, Beth A. ... Chicago, IL
Fulkerson, Calvin R. ... Lexington, KY
Fulkerson, Donald M. ... Westland, MI
Fulkerson, George J. ... Troy, MI
Fulkerson, Gina V. ... Houston, TX
Fulkerson, Gina Vaccaro, & Associates, P.C.
Houston, TX
Fulkerson, Harold H. ... San Rafael, CA
Fulkerson, Michael Brett
Kansas City, MO
Fulkerson, Ronald D. ... Oklahoma City, OK
Fulkerson, Sam R. ... Oklahoma City, OK
Fulkerson, Sarah Yehle ... Kansas City, MO
Fulkerson, Shawn D. ... Oklahoma City, OK
Fulkerson, Thomas M. ... Houston, TX
Fulkerson, Timothy R. ... Mountain View, CA
Fulkerson & Todd, P.A. ... Paragould, AR
Fulkerson, William C. ... Grand Rapids, MI
Fulkes, Duane S. ... Goldenrod, FL
Fulks, Mark A. ... Memphis, TN
Fulks, Paula J. ... Bellaire, TX
Fulks, Peggy Ann ... Woodland Park, CO
Fulks, Philip A. ... Lapeer, MI
Full, Robert W. ... Parkersburg, WV
Fullagar, William W. ... Chicago, IL
Fullam, John P. ... Philadelphia, PA
Fullam, Nancy H. ... Philadelphia, PA
Fullam, Vincent F., (Rev. Msgr.)
Huntington, NY
Fullan & Fullan ... Birmingham, AL
Fullan, James Guy ... Birmingham, AL
Fullan, James M., Jr. ... Birmingham, AL
Fullan, Margaret Sparks ... Birmingham, AL
Fullana, Isabel M. ... San Juan, PR
Fullano, Genaro G.
Federal Communications Commission, Common Carrier Bureau, GV
Fulle, Floyd F. ... Seattle, WA
Fullem, Gregory D. ... Portland, OR
Fullem, Joseph W., Jr. ... Philadelphia, PA
Fullem, L. Robert ... New York, NY
Fullem, Robert ... Albany, NY
Fullen, Craig M. ... Columbus, OH
Fullen, Tommy L. ... Memphis, TN
FullenKamp, James J. ... Dayton, OH
Fullenkamp, John H. ... Omaha, NE
Fullenkamp, Joseph R. ... South Bend, IN
Fullenweider & Associates ... Houston, TX

Fullenweider, Donn C. ...**Houston, TX**
Fullenweider, Keith R. ...**Houston, TX**
Fullenwider, Sarah J. ...Fort Worth, TX
Fuller, Aaron L.
Hot Springs National Park, AR
Fuller, Albert E. ...**Worcester, MA**
Fuller, Albert G. ...Auburn, NE
Fuller, Alexis J., Jr. ...**Austin, TX**
Fuller, Alfonso ...Detroit, MI
Fuller, Alfonso C., Jr. ...Anaheim, CA
Fuller, Alfred W. ...**Boston, MA**
Fuller, Alison M.
Securities and Exchange Commission, Division of Investment Management, GV
Fuller, Allen D. ...Miami, FL
Fuller, Angela ...**Bridgeport, IL**
Fuller, Anthony ...Bentonville, AR
Fuller, Anthony Edward ...**Boston, MA**
Fuller, A. P. ...**Lead, SD**
Fuller, Becton, Slifkin & Bell, P.A.
Durham, NC
Raleigh, NC
Fuller, Ben A. ...Prattville, AL
Fuller, Bennett B., II ...South Portland, ME
Fuller, Bernard C. ...Miami Beach, FL
Fuller & Berres ...South Barrington, IL
Fuller, Brad D. ...**Tulsa, OK**
Fuller, Brad L. ...Eureka, CA
Fuller, Bradford A. ...Cheshire, CT
Fuller, Brenda P. ...Gaithersburg, MD
Fuller, Bruce ...**Woodland Hills, CA**
Fuller, C. Andrew ...Gainesville, GA
Fuller, Carol A. ...Olympia, WA
Fuller, Caroline C. ...**Denver, CO**
Fuller & Carr ...Idaho Falls, ID
Fuller, Catherine A. ...Phoenix, AZ
Fuller, Catherine N. ...**Houston, TX**
Fuller, Catherine R. ...**Chicago, IL**
Fuller, Chad R. ...San Diego, CA
Fuller, Charles A., Jr. ...**Springfield, MO**
Fuller, Charles F. ...Washington, DC
Bowie, MD
Fuller, Charles L. ...Columbia, MD
Fuller, Chester C. ...Peoria, IL
Fuller, Chlouber, Frizzell & Lehman, L.L.P.
Tulsa, OK
Fuller, Christian A. ...Charlotte, MI
Fuller, Christopher ...**Austin, TX**
Fuller, Christopher C.
Department of Justice, Civil Division, GV
Fuller, Clayton N. ...Springfield, MA
Fuller, Constanze K. ...Pittsburgh, PA
Fuller, D. Ward ...Mill Valley, CA
Fuller, Dale F. ...Palo Alto, CA
Fuller, Daphne A.
Department of Transportation, Federal Aviation Administration, GV
Fuller, David A. ...**Longview, TX**
Fuller, David D. ...Louisville, KY
Fuller, David D., Jr. ...**Daytona Beach, FL**
Fuller, David J. ...Irvine, CA
Fuller, David M. ...Springfield, MA
Fuller, David Otis, Jr. ...**Bronxville, NY**
Fuller, David R. ...**Chico, CA**
Fuller, David R. ...**Washington, DC**
Fuller, David R. ...Rock Island, IL
Fuller, David Ward, II ...**Menlo Park, CA**
Fuller, Dennis A. ...**Dallas, TX**
Fuller, Dennis A. ...**McKinney, TX**
Fuller, Diana C. ...Omaha, NE
Fuller, Diana L. ...**Tampa, FL**
Fuller, Dianna ...Newark, NJ
Fuller, Don E. ...Chillicothe, OH
Fuller, Donald C. ...Bethany, OK
Fuller, Donald L. ...**Casper, WY**
Fuller, Donald O. ...Mesa, AZ
Fuller, Donald R., Jr. ...**Hickory, NC**
Fuller, Donald W. ...Cape Coral, FL
Fuller, Douglas S. ...House of Representatives, Committee on Resources, GV
Fuller, Drew R., Jr. ...**San Antonio, TX**
Fuller, E. Kay ...**Martinsburg, WV**
Fuller, Edwin F. ...Springfield, IL
Fuller, Elisa L. ...**Englewood, CO**
Fuller, Elizabeth ...**Austin, TX**
Fuller, Erin E. ...**St. Louis, MO**
Fuller, Erin L. ...**New York, NY**
Fuller, Ernest F., Jr. ...Aurora, CO
Fuller & Finney ...Edina, MN
Fuller, Frank Lanneau, III ...Wells, VT
Fuller, Frederic J., Jr. ...New York, NY
Fuller & Fuller ...**Los Angeles, CA**
Woodland Hills, CA
Fuller & Fuller ...Olympia, WA
Fuller & Fuller LLP ...**New York, NY**
Fuller, Garrett ...Bethesda, MD
Fuller, Gary B. ...**Vienna, VA**
Fuller, Gary F. ...**Oklahoma City, OK**
Fuller, Gary L., Law Offices of
San Antonio, TX
Fuller, Gary M. ...**Reno, NV**
Fuller, Gayla ...Dallas, TX
Fuller, Gene N. ...**Minneapolis, MN**
Fuller, George C. ...Needham, MA
Fuller, George T. ...Lexington, NC
Fuller, Gerald W. ...Cincinnati, OH
Fuller, Glenn ...**San Diego, CA**
Fuller, Glenn G. ...St. Paul, MN
Fuller, Glenn O. ...**Decatur, IL**
Fuller, G. M. ...**Oklahoma City, OK**
Fuller, Gordon K.
Securities and Exchange Commission, Division of Market Regulation, GV
Fuller, Greg J. ...Twin Falls, ID
Fuller, Gregg G. ...**Tulsa, OK**
Fuller, Grover F., Jr. ...New York, NY
Fuller, Gwendolyn Loretta ...Columbia, SC
Fuller, H. Daniel ...Irvine, CA
Fuller, H. Laurance ...Chicago, IL
Fuller, Harry O. ...Newfane, NY
Fuller, Heather Call ...Department of Justice, Civil Division, GV
Fuller, Henry C., III ...Sacramento, CA
Fuller, Henry C., Jr. ...**Brookfield, WI**
Fuller & Henry Ltd ...**Columbus, OH**
Toledo, OH
Fuller, Herbert H. ...Olympia, WA
Fuller, Hilton M., Jr. ...Decatur, GA
Fuller, Hoffman F. ...New Orleans, LA
Fuller, Holly E. ...**Houston, TX**
Fuller, Holly H. ...**San Antonio, TX**
Fuller Holsonback & Bivins, P.A.
Tampa, FL
Fuller, Hopp, & Quigg ...**Decatur, IL**
Fuller, Irving ...Los Angeles, CA
Fuller, J. Doyle ...**Montgomery, AL**
Fuller, Jack A. ...Long Beach, CA
Fuller, Jack T. ...Phoenix, AZ
Fuller, Jack W. ...Chicago, IL
Fuller, James ...**Northfield, IL**
Fuller, James ...Houston, TX
Fuller, James C., Jr. ...**Raleigh, NC**
Fuller, James P. ...**Palo Alto, CA**
Fuller, James R." Rusty " ...**Midland, TX**
Fuller, James T., III ...**Washington, DC**
Fuller, Janet L. ...**Ocala, FL**
Fuller, Jay ...**Woodland Hills, CA**
Fuller, Jay S. ...Olympia, WA
Fuller, Jeffery M. ...**Tampa, FL**
Fuller, Jeffrey R. ...**St. Petersburg, FL**
Fuller, Jeffrey R. ...**Milwaukee, WI**
Fuller, Jennifer L. ...**Palo Alto, CA**
Fuller, J. H. ...Cleveland, OH
Fuller, Joan D. ...**Boston, MA**
Fuller, John ...Meadville, PA
Fuller, John B. ...**Ocala, FL**
Fuller, John Douglas ...Tallahassee, FL
Fuller, John P. ...**Miami Beach, FL**
Fuller, Johnson & Farrell, P.A.
Pensacola, FL
Tallahassee, FL
Fuller, Joseph C., Jr. ...Fort Myers, FL
Fuller, Joseph C., P.A. ...Fort Myers, FL
Fuller, Joseph L. ...Austin, TX
Fuller, Joseph M. ...Phoenix, AZ
Fuller, Joyce C. ...**Orlando, FL**
Fuller, Judy A. ...Miami, FL
Fuller, Kathryn S. ...Washington, DC
Fuller, Kelli L. ...San Diego, CA
Fuller, Kenneth C. ...Rome, GA
Fuller, Kenneth D. ...**Dallas, TX**
Fuller, Kenneth Lee ...**San Antonio, TX**
Fuller, Kenneth T. ...**Enterprise, AL**
Fuller, Kevin M. ...**Beaumont, TX**
Fuller, Kevin R. ...**Dallas, TX**
Fuller, Kimberly N. ...**Rock Island, IL**
Fuller, Kinnunen, Petruso, Gamble, Fabian, Hall & Johnson ...Meadville, PA
Titusville, PA
Fuller, L. Hayes, III ...**Waco, TX**
Fuller, L. Lynnette ...Chapel Hill, NC
Fuller, Lauren Lea ...Springfield, VA
Fuller Law Firm ...**Rochester, MN**
Fuller Law Office ...Auburn, NE
Fuller Law Offices ...Twin Falls, ID
Fuller, Lawrence A. ...**Miami Beach, FL**
Fuller, Lee C. ...Erie, PA
Fuller, Lee M., Jr. ...**New York, NY**
Fuller, Leonor Rivera ...Olympia, WA
Fuller, Lisa A. ...**Washington, DC**
Fuller, Lisa L. ...Dallas, TX
Fuller, Lori ...**Menlo Park, CA**
Fuller, Louis G. ...**Jackson, MS**
Fuller, Loula M. ...**Tallahassee, FL**
Fuller, Mallah & Associates, P.A.
Fort Lauderdale, FL
Miami Beach, FL
Fuller, Marjorie G. ...Fullerton, CA
Fuller, Mark A. ...Kansas City, MO
Fuller, Mark Andrew ...**Phoenix, AZ**
Fuller, Mark E. ...Enterprise, AL
Fuller, Mark E. ...Edina, MN
Fuller, Mark R. ...Idaho Falls, ID
Fuller, Mark R. ...Chicago, IL
Fuller, Mary E. ...Rancho Cucamonga, CA
Fuller, Marya Carol ...Olympia, WA
Fuller & McKay ...Rome, GA
Fuller, Melody Kay L. ...Boulder, CO
Fuller, Michael J. ...**Glendale, AZ**
Fuller, Michael J. ...**Phoenix, AZ**
Fuller, Michael L. ...**San Diego, CA**
Fuller, Michael R. ...**Los Angeles, CA**
Fuller, Michael R. ...Dedham, MA
Fuller, Michele P
Grosse Pointe Woods, MI
Fuller, Mike D. ...Gillette, WY
Fuller, Millard D. ...Americus, GA
Fuller, Monte L. ...Sacramento, CA
Fuller, Nancy J. ...**Chicago, IL**
Fuller, Nancy M. ...**Longview, TX**
Fuller, Nancy S. ...Austin, TX
Fuller, Nathan C. ...**Charlotte, NC**
Fuller, Ned S. ...**Albuquerque, NM**
Fuller, Ninamaria ...Olympia, WA
Fuller, Norman E. ...Merriam, KS
Fuller, Pamela J. ...Lakin, KS
Fuller, Pamela Wilson ...Treasury Department, Internal Revenue Service, GV
Fuller, Patrick L. ...Okemos, MI
Fuller, Paul D. ...Rochester, NY
Fuller, Paul K. ...Jamaica, NY
Fuller, Pearl E. ...Woodland Hills, CA
Fuller, Peggy S. ...Bakersfield, CA
Fuller, Perry L. ...**Chicago, IL**
Fuller, Randall J. ...**Anoka, MN**
Fuller, Ray Lewis ...Santa Maria, CA
Fuller, Richard G., Jr. ...Fernandina Beach, FL
Fuller, Richard J. ...**Minneapolis, MN**
Fuller, Richard L. ...Denver, CO
Fuller, Richard S. ...Miami, FL
Fuller, Richard T. ...Mesa, AZ
Fuller, Robert ...La Mesa, CA
Fuller, Robert E. ...Burbank, CA
Fuller, Robert E., Jr. ...Goldsboro, NC
Fuller, Robert F. ...Columbia, SC
Fuller, Robert G., Jr. ...Manchester, ME
Fuller, Robert J. ...**Dallas, TX**
Fuller, Robert Lane ...Monroe, LA
Fuller, Robert W. ...**Charlotte, NC**
Fuller, Robert W. ...Midland, TX
Fuller, Robin R. ...**St. Paul, MN**
Fuller, Roger A. ...Dallas, TX
Fuller, Ronald E. ...Denver, CO
Fuller, Ronald J. ...Rolla, MO
Fuller, Rosenberg, Palmer & Beliveau
Boston, MA
Leominster, MA
Springfield, MA
Worcester, MA
Fuller, Roy L. ...**Baytown, TX**
Fuller, S. Wayne ...**Cullman, AL**
Fuller, S. William ...Tallahassee, FL
Fuller, S. William, Jr. ...**Tallahassee, FL**
Fuller, Samuel A. ...**Indianapolis, IN**
Fuller, Samuel W. ...Tallahassee, FL
Fuller, Sarah Betsy ...Syracuse, NY
Fuller, Scott R. ...**New York, NY**
Fuller, Seaver & Ramette, P.A.
Burnsville, MN
Fuller, Shelley L. ...Hillsboro, OR
Fuller, Stacey L. ...**Wilmington, NC**
Fuller, Stacey M. ...Minneapolis, MN
Fuller, Stacy L. ...Washington, DC
Fuller, Stephen P. ...**Duluth, GA**
Fuller, Steven M. ...Bemidji, MN
Fuller, Steven N. ...**Boston, MA**
Fuller, Steven R. ...Preston, ID
Fuller, Steven R. ...North Kansas City, MO
Fuller, Steven S. ...**Rochester, MN**
Fuller & Suarez, P.A. ...Miami, FL
Fuller, Susan Corea ...Harriman, TN
Fuller, Susan K. ...**Seattle, WA**
Fuller, Susan Stieg ...Nashville, TN
Fuller, Susan Straub ...Parsippany, NJ
Fuller, Tania E. (Dee Dee)
Grand Rapids, MI
Fuller, Tellinghuisen, Gordon & Percy, P.C.
Lead, SD
Spearfish, SD
Fuller, Terry R. ...Kinsley, KS
Fuller, Theodore ...Greenwich, CT
Fuller, Thomas A. ...**Arlington, TX**
Fuller, Timothy ...Los Angeles, CA
Fuller, Timothy D. ...**Burnsville, MN**
Fuller, Todd A. ...**Pittsburgh, PA**
Fuller, Trevor M. ...Washington, DC
Fuller, Truman S., III ...Olympia, WA
Fuller, Tubb, Pomeroy & Stokes, A Professional Corporation
Oklahoma City, OK
Fuller, Tyler J. ...**San Francisco, CA**
Fuller, V. Lori ...Raleigh, NC
Fuller, Vanci Y. ...**Los Angeles, CA**
Fuller, Vaughn and Gott ...**Kingsport, TN**
Fuller, Vincent A., Jr.
Charlotte Amalie, St. Thomas, VI
Fuller, Vincent J. ...**Washington, DC**
Fuller, Virginia Hudson ...Raleigh, NC
Fuller, W. Erwin, Jr. ...**Greensboro, NC**
Fuller, W. Scott ...**Raleigh, NC**
Fuller, W. Sidney ...Andalusia, AL
Fuller, Warren R. ...South Barrington, IL
Fuller, Wayne P. ...Weiser, ID
Fuller, William E. ...New York, NY
Fuller, William G. ...Arcadia, LA
Fuller, William H., III ...**Charlotte, NC**
Fuller, William H., III ...Danville, VA
Fuller, William J., III ...Sarasota, FL
Fuller, William P. ...**San Francisco, CA**
Fuller, William P. ...**Sioux Falls, SD**
Fuller, Willie L., (Miss) ...Houston, TX
Fuller & Willingham ...**Cullman, AL**
Fuller, Willis, Jr. ...Charleston, SC
Fuller, Willis, Jr., P.A. ...Charleston, SC
Fuller, W. W., II ...Anna Maria, FL
Fuller-Jacobs, Nancy, & Associates
San Diego, CA
Fullerton, Alexandra P. ...Davis, CA
Fullerton, Arthur C. ...**Greenwich, CT**
Fullerton, Byron F. ...Austin, TX
Fullerton, David S. ...Northbrook, IL
Fullerton, Denise Susan Schwanz
Minneapolis, MN
Fullerton, Donnell R. ...Fairfax, VA
Fullerton, Donnell R., P.C. ...Fairfax, VA
Fullerton, Dwight L. ...Columbus, OH
Fullerton, Frank P. ...El Paso, TX
Fullerton, Gregory L. ...**Albany, GA**
Fullerton, James C. ...Wellesley, MA
Fullerton, James D. ...Clifton, VA
Fullerton, James D., & Associates, P.C.
Clifton, VA
Fullerton, John E. ...**Harrisburg, PA**
Fullerton, John F., III ...**New York, NY**
Fullerton, Jolene D. ...Del Mar, CA
Fullerton, Jon O. ...Coral Gables, FL
Fullerton, Judith A. ...Flint, MI
Fullerton, Laura ...Department of Energy, Office of the General Counsel, GV
Fullerton Law Offices ...Columbus, OH
Fullerton, Lawrence R. ...**Washington, DC**
Fullerton, Lawrence S. ...Denver, CO
Fullerton, Lemann, Schaefer & Dominick, LLP ...Rancho Mirage, CA
San Bernardino, CA
Fullerton, Lorraine K. ...Houston, TX
Fullerton, Lynn E. ...**Palo Alto, CA**
Fullerton, Mark D. ...**Mesa, AZ**
Fullerton, Maryellen ...Brooklyn, NY
Fullerton, Mathew J. ...Clinton, IA
Fullerton, Paul M. ...**Wheaton, IL**
Fullerton, Paul T. ...Grover, MO
Fullerton, Peter V. ...**Miami, FL**
Fullerton & Porfido, P.A. ...Succasunna, NJ
Fullerton, Raymond W. ...Frederick, MD
Fullerton, Richard L. ...Orlando, FL
Fullerton, Robert C. ...Golden, CO
Fullerton, Robert V., (Professional Corporation) ...**San Bernardino, CA**
Fullerton, Robt. P. ...Denver, CO
Fullerton, Samuel C., III ...Miami, OK
Fullerton, Sara E. ...Lincoln, NE
Fullerton, Walter A., III ...Clearwater, FL
Fullerton, William D. ...Columbus, OH
Fullerton, William K. ...Succasunna, NJ
Fullilove, Harold W. ...Newark, NJ
Fullin, Daniel E. ...Columbus, OH
Fullin, James L. ...Tucson, AZ
Fullin, James Lawrence ...Columbus, OH
Fullingim, Dennis L. ...Lubbock, TX
Fullingim, J. Worth ...Lubbock, TX
Fullingim, William E. ...Dallas, TX
Fullington, Mary L. ...**Lexington, KY**
Fullington, Vicki L. ...Ventura, CA
Fullman, Jay D. ...**Brea, CA**
Fullman, Jay D., A Professional Corporation
Brea, CA
Fullmer, Barbara F. ...**Anchorage, AK**
Fullmer, David R. ...**Cleveland, OH**
Fullmer, Harold H. ...**Philadelphia, PA**
Fullmer, Jack A. ...New Orleans, LA
Fullmer, Janet Youtz ...Denver, CO
Fullmer, Jerri A. ...Irvine, CA
Fullmer, John C. ...Honolulu, HI
Fullmer, John D. ...**Minneapolis, MN**
Fullmer, Mark A. ...**New Orleans, LA**
Fullmer, Mark A. ...**Port Huron, MI**
Fullmer, Mark W. ...Anchorage, AK
Fullmer, Robert J. ...**Woodcliff Lake, NJ**
Fullmer, Thomas A. ...Cleveland, OH
Fullmer, William A. ...**Cleveland, OH**
Fullner, Daniel A. ...Madison, NE
Norfolk, NE
Fullum, Karen Yvonne ...**Washington, DC**
Fullwiler, Ruth S. ...Coeur d'Alene, ID
Fullwood, Cynthia M. ...Saginaw, MI
Fullwood, Elizabeth C. ...Lexington, SC
Fullwood, Ernest B. ...Wilmington, NC
Fullwood, Michael D. ...Greenwich, CT
Fullwood, Stanley G. ...Collinsville, CT
Fulman, Arthur S. ...Malden, MA
Fulman & Fulman ...Malden, MA
Fulmer, Allan E., Jr. ...Columbia, SC
Fulmer, Allan E., P.A. ...Columbia, SC
Fulmer, Allan E., Sr. ...Columbia, SC
Fulmer, Ann D. ...Stone Mountain, GA
Fulmer, Arthur C. ...**Lakeland, FL**
Fulmer, Barry F. ...Newark, NJ
Fulmer, Brenda S. ...**Tampa, FL**
Fulmer, C. Richard, Jr.
Fort Lauderdale, FL
Fulmer, Carolyn K. ...Bartow, FL
Fulmer, Christopher T. ...Birmingham, AL
Fulmer, Danny N., Jr. ...**Asheville, NC**
Fulmer, David T. ...Winchester, MA
Fulmer, Frank W. ...Maitland, FL
Fulmer, Frank W., P.A. ...Maitland, FL
Fulmer, Fred L. ...**Fort Lauderdale, FL**
Fulmer, Fred Land, P.A., Law Offices
Fort Lauderdale, FL
Fulmer, James David ...**Palo Alto, CA**
Portland, OR
Fulmer, Jay Lawrence
Huntingdon Valley, PA
Philadelphia, PA
Fulmer, Norman C. ...Sun City West, AZ
Fulmer, Pamela K. ...**San Francisco, CA**
Fulmer, Priscilla S. ...**Denver, CO**
Fulmer, R. Ray, II ...**Fort Smith, AR**
Fulmer, Richard P. ...Greenville, SC
Fulmer, Simone Gosnell
Oklahoma City, OK
Fulmer, Timothy M. ...**Birmingham, AL**
Fulmer, William H., Jr. ...Juno Beach, FL
Fulmer, William K., II ...Erlanger, KY
Fulmer, William W. ...Sierra Madre, CA
Fulmore, Sterling R., Jr. ...Austin, TX
Fulop, Eugene I. ...Portland, OR
Fulop & Gross ...Portland, OR
Fulop, Marcos ...San Antonio, TX
Fulop, Sharon M. ...**Toledo, OH**
Fulp, Carl G., III ...**Valdosta, GA**
Fulp, George T. ...Madison, NC
Fulp, Kenneth E., Jr. ...Beaufort, SC
Fulrath, Logan, Jr. ...New York, NY
Fulreader, John W. ...Rochester, NY
Fulreader, Rosenthal, Sullivan, Clifford, Santoro & Kaul ...Rochester, NY
Fulsher, Allan A. ...Lake Oswego, OR
Fulsher, Theodore F. ...Marquette, MI
Fulsher & Weatherhead, P.C.
Lake Oswego, OR
Fulstone, Lynn S. ...**Las Vegas, NV**
Fulstone, Suellen ...**Reno, NV**
Fulton, A. Jane, Law Offices
Laguna Beach, CA
Fulton, Amy R. ...**Memphis, TN**
Fulton, Andrew, III ...West Palm Beach, FL
Fulton, Andrew, IV ...**West Palm Beach, FL**

Fulton, Angus B. ... Billings, MT
Bozeman, MT
Fulton, Ann Scott ... Raleigh, NC
Fulton, Anne M. ... Tucson, AZ
Fulton, Arthur B. ... Winchester, VA
Fulton & Barr, P.A. ... Greenville, SC
Fulton & Blickensderfer, P.A. ... Eliot, ME
Fulton, Bradford J. ... Seattle, WA
Fulton, Bradley C. ... Madison, WI
Fulton, Burt J. ... Cleveland, OH
Fulton, C. Patrick ... Louisville, KY
Fulton, Carol A. ... West Palm Beach, FL
Fulton, Charles A.
Federal Deposit Insurance Corporation, Resolutions Section, GV
Fulton, Charles L. ... Raleigh, NC
Fulton, Christopher L. ... Hilliard, OH
Fulton, Cynthia L. ... Phoenix, AZ
Fulton, David A. ... Santa Cruz, CA
Fulton, David J. ... Chattanooga, TN
Fulton, David K. ... Eliot, ME
Fulton, David W. ... Department of State, Foreign Service Officers (Overseas), GV
Fulton, Deborah K. ... Chicago, IL
Fulton, Deborah L. ... San Francisco, CA
Fulton, Debra L. ... Knoxville, TN
Fulton, Dennis C. ... Foster City, CA
Fulton, Dennis G. ... Tacoma, WA
Fulton & Devlin ... Louisville, KY
Fulton, Dirk A. ... Benicia, CA
Fulton, Donald T. ... Fort Worth, TX
Fulton, Douglas A. ... Des Moines, IA
Fulton, Douglas C. ... West Palm Beach, FL
Fulton, E. M., Jr. ... Lincoln, IL
Springfield, IL
Fulton, Fred W. ... Dallas, TX
Fulton, George W., Jr. ... Santa Ana, CA
Fulton, Harry J. ... Washington, DC
Fulton, Heck & Silbaugh, P.C.
Bakerstown, PA
Butler, PA
Cranberry Township, PA
Valencia, PA
Fulton, Henry W., Jr. ... Carnegie, PA
Fulton, Holly E. ... Orange Park, FL
Fulton, Hubbard & Hubbard ... Bardstown, KY
Fulton, Jack M. ... Richmond, VA
Fulton, James A. ... Greenwich, CT
Fulton, James F., Jr. ... Menlo Park, CA
Fulton, Janelle E. ... Philadelphia, PA
Fulton, Jerry J. ... San Antonio, TX
Fulton, Jo Ann ... Laramie, WY
Fulton, John M. ... Cleveland, OH
Fulton, Johnnie Dodenhoff ... Greenville, SC
Fulton, Junius Phillip, III ... Norfolk, VA
Fulton, Karen G. ... Kansas City, MO
Fulton, Kathryn M. ... Menlo Park, CA
Fulton and Kee ... Norfolk, VA
Fulton, Kent ... St. Louis, MO
Fulton, Larry C. ... Denver, CO
Fulton, Larry J. ... Tulsa, OK
Fulton, Laurie S. ... Washington, DC
Fulton, Lexi L. ... Pittsburgh, PA
Fulton, Margaret Heiser ... Auburn, CA
Fulton, Martin & Andres, P.C.
Waterloo, IA
Fulton, Michael A. ... Hamilton, OH
Fulton, Michael M., Law Offices of
San Antonio, TX
Fulton, Patsy Sueko ... Dallas, TX
Fulton, Paul ... Boston, MA
Fulton, Philip J., & Associates
Columbus, OH
Fulton, R. Harcourt ... Charlotte, NC
Fulton, Radmila A. ... San Diego, CA
Fulton, Richard A. ... Houston, TX
Fulton, Richard E. ... Santa Ana, CA
Fulton, Richard T. ... Orlando, FL
Fulton, Richard T. ... Atlanta, GA
Fulton, Robert ... Natick, MA
Fulton, Robert D. ... Waterloo, IA
Fulton, Robert E. ... United States Senate, Committee Legal Personnel, GV
Fulton, Robert E., Jr. ... Butler, PA
Fulton, Robert K. ... Philadelphia, PA
Fulton, Robert L. ... Leon, IA
Fulton, Robert M. ... Tampa, FL
Fulton, Robert P. ... Glenside, PA
Fulton, Robert S. ... Youngstown, OH
Fulton, Roberta L. ... Birmingham, AL
Fulton, Robin E. ... Fredericktown, MO
Fulton, Rowe, Hart & Coon
New York, NY
Fulton, Scott Cole
Environmental Protection Agency, Environmental Appeals Board, GV
Fulton, Steven P. ... Pittsburgh, PA
Fulton, Theodore H., Jr.
Fort Lauderdale, FL
Fulton, Thomas H. ... Memphis, TN
Fulton, Thomas Wayne ... Palmyra, VA
Fulton & Tuttle ... Seattle, WA
Fulton, Will H. ... Louisville, KY
Fulton, William H. ... Cleveland, OH
Fulton, William J. ... Carlisle, PA
Fulton, William J. ... Harrisburg, PA
Fulton, William S., Jr. ... Springfield, VA
Fulton, W. R. ... Sulphur, OK
Fults, Marsella Starkey ... Dallas, TX
Fults, Timothy M. ... Dallas, TX
Fultz, Benjamin C. ... Louisville, KY
Fultz, Bernard V. ... Pomeroy, OH
Fultz & Davis ... Navasota, TX
Fultz, Jeffrey Pierce ... Center, TX
Houston, TX
Nacogdoches, TX
Fultz, John M. ... Navasota, TX
Fultz, Karen D. ... Atlanta, GA
Fultz, Palmer ... Columbus, OH
Fultz, Richard D. ... Treasury Department, Internal Revenue Service, GV
Fultz, Robert A. ... Visalia, CA
Fultz, Robert E. ... Columbus, OH
Fultz, William S. ... Washington, DC
Fulvio, George T. ... San Mateo, CA
Fulweiler, Marie-Louise ... New York, NY
Fulwider Patton Lee & Utecht, LLP
Long Beach, CA
Los Angeles, CA
Fulwider, Robert E. ... Indianapolis, IN
Fulwiler, Joe L. ... New York, NY
Fulwood, S. Leigh ... Bellevue, WA
Fulzenloger, Tommy D. ... Mesa, AZ
Fumagalli, Daniel J. ... Chicago, IL
Fumagalli, Rasa E. ... Chicago, IL
Fumagalli, Tecson, Hyman & Brent, Ltd.
Chicago, IL
Fumarolo, Gregory L. ... Fort Wayne, IN
Fumel and Haberman ... Chicago, IL
Fumero, John J. ... West Palm Beach, FL
Fumia, Joan C. ... Bloomfield Hills, MI
Fumich, William M., Jr. ... Cleveland, OH
Fumich, Wm. M. ... Cleveland, OH
Fumo, Michael R. ... Chicago, IL
Fumo, Robert P. ... New York, NY
Fumo, Vincent J. ... Philadelphia, PA
Fumuso, Alan J. ... Hauppauge, NY
Fun, James Lee, Jr. ... Hillsboro, OR
Funada, Albert Takashi ... Torrance, CA
Funahashi, Kenji L. ... San Diego, CA
Funai, Bryan Y. ... Chicago, IL
Cincinnati, OH
Funai, Masaru ... Chicago, IL
Rolling Meadows, IL
Funaki, James T. ... Honolulu, HI
Funaki, Mark A. ... Honolulu, HI
Funamura, Gary M. ... Sacramento, CA
Funamura, Sharyn K. ... Palo Alto, CA
Funaro, Charles D. ... Des Moines, IA
Funaro, Charles W., II ... Pasadena, CA
Funaro, Patricia A. ... Des Moines, IA
Funchess, Jesse R. ... Houston, TX
Funck, W. Michael ... New York, NY
Fund, David, (P.C.) ... New York, NY
Fund, Joan Maffeo ... Wellesley, MA
Fund, Joseph E. ... Livingston, NJ
Fund, Wendy L. ... Costa Mesa, CA
Funda, Joyce E. ... Buffalo, NY
Fundaro, Casey A. ... Naples, FL
Fundaun, Arlie Martin ... Remer, MN
Fundenberg, William C., Jr.
Newport Beach, CA
Funderburg, Erskine R., Jr. ... Pell City, AL
Funderburg, J. Noah ... Tuscaloosa, AL
Funderburg, Judith K.
Colorado Springs, CO
Funderburg, Lisa A. ... St. Louis, MO
Funderburg, Rochelle A. ... Champaign, IL
Funderburg, Steven H. ... Jackson, MS
Funderburk & Andrews
Baton Rouge, LA
Funderburk, Day and Lane ... Opelika, AL
Phenix City, AL
Columbus, GA
Funderburk & Funderburk, L.L.P.
Houston, TX
Funderburk, Harold W., Jr. ... Columbia, SC
Funderburk & Herpin, A Professional Law Corporation ... Abbeville, LA
Funderburk, J. Gregory Guy ... Houston, TX
Funderburk, J. Isaac ... Abbeville, LA
Funderburk, James M. ... Houma, LA
Funderburk, Jim R. ... Gastonia, NC
Funderburk, Kelly L. ... Wichita, KS
Funderburk, Kenneth L. ... Phenix City, AL
Funderburk, Larry B. ... Houston, TX
Funderburk, Michael R. ... Buford, GA
Funderburk, Paul S. ... Tupelo, MS
Funderburk, Raymond ... Chicago, IL
Funderburk, Robert C., Jr.
Baton Rouge, LA
Funderburk, Weldon W. ... Houston, TX
Funderburk, William L., Jr. ... Eden, NC
Funderburk, William W., Jr.
Los Angeles, CA
San Francisco, CA
Funderlich, Gary J. ... Dulles, VA
Fundiller-Zweig, Doreen Lee
West Hartford, CT
Fundingsland, C. Lynne ... Minneapolis, MN
Fundis, John V. ... Dallas, TX
Fundler, Burton L. ... Bradley Beach, NJ
Fundler, Laurence E. ... Paramus, NJ
Fundler, Yevgeny ... New York, NY
Fundling, Julie H. ... Dallas, TX
Fund-Payne, Suzanne ... Basking Ridge, NJ
Fundy, Ira M. ... Springfield, MA
Fung, Allan W. ... Providence, RI
Fung, Elizabeth P.Y. ... San Francisco, CA
Fung, Jean C. ... Hartford, CT
Fung, Ralph ... Oakland, CA
Fung, Richard C. ... Los Angeles, CA
Fung, Robert A. ... San Francisco, CA
Fung, Robert Wai ... Honolulu, HI
Fung, Rodney G. ... Los Angeles, CA
Fung, Roland S. ... Atlanta, GA
Fung, Ronald G. ... Los Angeles, CA
Fung, Russell ... San Francisco, CA
Fung, Stephen G. ... Brooklyn, NY
Funge, Ann M. ... Pittsburgh, PA
Funger & Kirsch ... Washington, DC
Funger, W. Scott ... Washington, DC
Funiciello, Patrick J. ... Euless, TX
Funk, A. Norwood ... Timonium, MD
Funk, A. Peter ... Helena, MT
Funk, Alan J. ... Wood Ridge, NJ
Funk, Alan S. ... Bellevue, WA
Funk, Albert P. ... La Crosse, WI
Funk, Amy Bromberg ... Minneapolis, MN
Funk, Andrew J. ... New York, NY
Funk & Bolton, A Professional Association
Annapolis, MD
Baltimore, MD
Chestertown, MD
Funk, Brian P. ... San Diego, CA
Funk, Bruce C., Law Offices of
San Jose, CA
Funk, C. Alan ... West Lafayette, IN
Funk, Casey S. ... Denver, CO
Funk, Christine ... Stillwater, MN
Funk, Christopher A. ... Brownsville, TX
Funk, D. Richard ... Tulsa, OK
Funk, D. Scott ... Houston, TX
Funk, Dale M. ... Chesterfield, MO
Funk, Daniel J. ... Canton, OH
Funk, Daniel M. ... Newton, MA
Funk, David A. ... Indianapolis, IN
Funk, David A. ... Newberg, OR
Funk, David I. ... Atlanta, GA
Funk, David M. ... Baltimore, MD
Funk, David M., Jr. ... Alpena, MI
Funk, David R. ... Columbus, OH
Funk, Donald H. ... Springfield, IL
Funk & Foster ... Hammond, IN
Funk, Frederick K. ... Newark, DE
Funk, George ... Los Angeles, CA
Funk, Glenn R. ... Nashville, TN
Funk, Harlan J. ... White Plains, NY
Funk, Herman Eugene, Jr.
Baltimore, MD
Funk, J. Stephen ... Bellevue, WA
Funk, James C. ... Marion, OH
Funk, Janis B. ... Indianapolis, IN
Funk, Jerry A. ... Jacksonville, FL
Funk, Joel M. ... Fort Collins, CO
Funk, John ... Falfurrias, TX
Funk, John A. ... Los Angeles, CA
Funk, John C. ... Los Angeles, CA
Funk, John Nelson ... Martinez, CA
Funk, John R. ... Las Cruces, NM
Funk, John W. ... Champaign, IL
Funk, John W. ... Columbus, OH
Funk, John W. ... Oklahoma City, OK
Funk, Jonathan A. ... San Francisco, CA
Funk, Joseph E. ... Londonderry, NH
Funk, Judd ... New York, NY
Funk, Karen M. ... Tulsa, OK
Funk, Katherine I.
Federal Trade Commission, Bureau of Competition, GV
Funk & Kay ... Nashville, TN
Funk, Kenneth W. ... Chicago, IL
Funk, L. Sue ... Austin, TX
Funk, Larry Edward ... Washington, DC
Funk, Linda Matsler ... Gladstone, MO
Funk, Lisa Bossard ... The Woodlands, TX
Funk, Lisa E. ... New York, NY
Funk, Mahlon G., Jr. ... Richmond, VA
Funk, Michael J. ... Charleston, WV
Funk, Mindy C. ... Pembroke Pines, FL
Funk, Norman T. ... Indianapolis, IN
Funk, Peter V. K., Jr. ... New York, NY
Funk, R. Cordell ... Hammond, IN
Funk, Randy D. ... Denver, CO
Funk, Richard H. ... Garden City, NY
Funk, Robert B. ... Logan, UT
Funk, Robert E., Jr. ... Washington, DC
Funk, Robert J. ... Alturas, CA
Funk, Roger L. ... Los Angeles, CA
Funk, Ronald B. ... Laguna Hills, CA
Funk, Ronald P. ... New York, NY
Funk, Rustin J. ... Marietta, OH
Funk, R. V. Terry ... Tulsa, OK
Funk, S. Jeff ... Monticello, IL
Funk, Samuel P. ... Nashville, TN
Funk, Stephen F. ... Atlantic City, NJ
Funk, Stephen W. ... Akron, OH
Funk, Steven J. ... Plano, TX
Funk, Steven R. ... Minneapolis, MN
Funk, Stran J. ... Annapolis, MD
Funk, Susan L. ... Medina, OH
Funk, Thomas E. ... Milwaukee, WI
Funk, Thomas M. ... Dry Ridge, KY
Funk, Thomas W. ... Lincoln, IL
Funk, Vance A., III ... Newark, DE
Funk, W. John ... Concord, NH
Funk, Wendy L. ... Garden City, NY
Funk, William F. ... Portland, OR
Funk, William L., Jr. ... Denver, CO
Funke, James F., Jr. ... Vernon, IN
Funke, Jeffrey J. ... Nebraska City, NE
Funke, Karl A. ... United States Senate, Committee Legal Personnel, GV
Funke, Robert G. ... Taunton, MA
Funke, Rudolph H. ... New York, NY
Funke, Sarah K. ... Indianapolis, IN
Funke-Bilu, Ilan ... San Luis Obispo, CA
Funkenstein, Barbara ... San Diego, CA
Funkey, Michael C., Law Office of
Aurora, IL
Funkhouser, Cameron ... Washington, DC
Funkhouser, Claude, Jr. ... Bethesda, MD
Funkhouser, David E. ... Mason City, IA
Funkhouser, Lindy P., (Mr.) ... Phoenix, AZ
Funkhouser, Paul W. ... Houston, TX
Funkhouser, Robert B. ... Washington, DC
Funkhouser, Robert C. ... Memphis, TN
Funkhouser, William Morry
Costa Mesa, CA
Funkhouser, Wilson P. ... Chicago, IL
Funnekotter, Anna M. ... Monterey Park, CA
Funnell, Donald K. ... Oklahoma City, OK
Funnell, James D., Jr. ... Norwalk, CT
Funnell, Kevin J. ... Dallas, TX
Funnye, Bradley J. ... New York, NY
Funsch, Richard O. ... Princeton, NJ
Funsten & Franzen ... Beverly Hills, CA
Los Angeles, CA
Funsten, James W. ... San Francisco, CA
Funsten, Lawrence D. ... Pittsburgh, PA
Funsten, Melanie F. ... Costa Mesa, CA
Funsten, Peter L. ... Beverly Hills, CA
Funsten, Robert C. ... Corona, CA
Funston, Bob ... Oklahoma City, OK
Funston, Karen Leigh ... Bellingham, WA
Funston, Richard Y. ... Prospect, KY
Funt, Barbra Rachel ... New York, NY
Funt, Barry M. ... New York, NY
Funt, Harold J. ... Bethlehem, PA
Funt, James A. ... Philadelphia, PA
Funt, Norman ... Miami, FL
Funt, Syma B. ... White Plains, NY
Funtowitz, Joel M. ... Chicago, IL
Funyak, Kevin M. ... Billings, MT
Fuoco, Joseph M. ... East Brunswick, NJ
Fuoco, Philip Stephen ... Haddonfield, NJ
Fuoco, Steven ... Chicago, IL
Fuoco, Tina A. ... Flushing, NY
Fuoss, Anita L. ... Murdo, SD
Fuqua, Alexander S. ... Nashville, TN
Fuqua, Amy M. ... Fort Worth, TX
Fuqua, David M. ... Little Rock, AR
North Little Rock, AR
Fuqua, Dawn M. ... Lafayette, LA
Fuqua, Gabriel M. ... Jackson, MS
Fuqua, Harry Matthew ... Marianna, FL
Fuqua, Hudnall & Gappelberg, L.L.P.
Dallas, TX
Fuqua, James A., Jr. ... Georgetown, DE
Fuqua, James B. ... Greenwich, CT
Fuqua, James L., Jr. ... Hendersonville, TN
Fuqua, James R. ... Ozark, AL
Fuqua, Joseph Douglas, Jr. ... Palo Alto, CA
Fuqua, Karen ... Mattoon, IL
Fuqua & Keim, L.L.P. ... Houston, TX
Fuqua, Kenneth W. ... Dallas, TX
Fuqua & Kominos ... Ozark, AL
Fuqua, Morey W. ... Chico, CA
Fuqua, Richard L., (P.C.) ... Houston, TX
Fuqua, Robert S. ... Wichita, KS
Fuqua, William G. ... Bowling Green, KY
Russellville, KY
Fuqua, Winter & Stiles, Ltd.
Libertyville, IL
Waukegan, IL
Fuqua & Yori, P.A. ... Georgetown, DE
Fuquay, Charles S. ... Dallas, TX
Fuquay, Richard W. ... Mobile, AL
Furay, Catherine J. ... Madison, WI
Furay, Joseph F. ... Lakewood, CO
Furbee, Amos, Webb & Critchfield
Clarksburg, WV
Fairmont, WV
Morgantown, WV
Furbee, Bridget D. ... Clarksburg, WV
Furber, Bradley B. ... Seattle, WA
Furber, James A. ... Tacoma, WA
Furber, Philip C. ... Cleveland, OH
Furber, Shirley L. ... Fairmont, MN
Furber, Theodore K. ... Minneapolis, MN
Furber Timmer Zahn, PLLP
Minneapolis, MN
Furber, William E. ... Augusta, ME
Furber, William J., Jr. ... Narberth, PA
Furbish, Robert H. ... Saco, ME
Furbush, David M. ... Palo Alto, CA
Furbush, Michael J. ... Orlando, FL
Furbush, Michael R. ... Reno, NV
Furby, Tommy E. ... Jackson, MS
Furci, Frank C. ... Canton, NC
Furci, Peter A. ... New York, NY
Furcolo, Charles Mark ... Boston, MA
Furcolo, Foster, Jr. ... San Diego, CA
Furcolo, Regan ... San Diego, CA
Furcolow, Robert E. ... Alexandria, VA
Furcron, Wyckliffe S. G.
Department of the Air Force, GV
Furda, Gregory H. ... Chicago, IL
Furda, Michael ... New Brunswick, NJ
Furen, Herman M. ... Los Angeles, CA
Furen, Michael J. ... Sarasota, FL
Furer, Andrew E. ... New York, NY
Furer, Joseph ... Denver, CO
Furer, Julie J. ... Chicago, IL
Furey, Alexander ... Washington, DC
Furey, Barbara Halpern ... Portland, ME
Furey, Charles L. ... Bristol, CT
Furey, Cheryl A. ... Jenkintown, PA
Furey, Danielle R. ... Stamford, CT
Furey, Donovan, Eddy, Kocsis, Tracy & Daly, P.C. ... Bristol, CT
Furey, Doolan & Abell, L.L.P.
Washington, DC
Bethesda, MD
Chevy Chase, MD
Rockville, MD
Furey, Francis S. ... Valley Stream, NY
Furey & Furey, Chartered ... Salmon, ID
Furey & Furey, P.C. ... Hempstead, NY
Furey, Gregory J. ... Stockton, CA
Furey, Jack B. ... Challis, ID
Furey, James F. ... Uniondale, NY
Furey, James M. ... Hempstead, NY
Furey, James M., Jr. ... Hempstead, NY
Furey, Jennifer Bush ... Washington, DC
Furey, John J. ... Camden, NJ
Furey, Joseph M. ... Washington, DC
Furey, Kathleen M. ... New York, NY
Furey, Kerley, Walsh, Matera & Cinquemani, A Professional Corporation
Jamaica, NY
Mineola, NY

Furey, Laura A. ..... Lebanon, NJ
Furey, Margarett Worth ..... Gunnison, CO
Furey, Mark G. ..... Portland, ME
Furey, Michael C. ..... Woodbury, NY
Furey, Michael E. ..... Norristown, PA
Furey, Michael F. ..... Weymouth, MA
Furey, Michael J. ..... Chicago, IL
Furey, Michael K. ..... Chevy Chase, MD
Furey, Michael K. ..... Morristown, NJ
Furey, Neysa A. ..... Bronxville, NY
Furey, Patrick D. ..... Boise, ID
Furey, Raymond J. ..... Mineola, NY
Furey, Richard B. ..... Stamford, CT
Furey, Robert H. ..... Los Gatos, CA
Furey, Roger P. ..... Washington, DC
Furey, Sherman F., III ..... Salmon, ID
Furey, Sherman F., Jr. ..... Salmon, ID
Furey, Thomas R. ..... Toledo, OH
Furey, Timothy W. ..... Bristol, CT
Furey, William J. ..... Chicago, IL
Furey-Tran, Kathleen ..... Staten Island, NY
Furfaro, John P. ..... New York, NY
Furfero, Arlene Joyce ..... New Rochelle, NY
Furfure, Marianne ..... Bath, NY
Furgang & Adwar, LLP ..... New York, NY
West Nyack, NY
White Plains, NY
Furgang, Philip ..... New York, NY
West Nyack, NY
Furgang, Samuel M. ..... Boston, MA
Furgang Adwar, Stephanie ..... New York, NY
West Nyack, NY
Furgason, Barry L. ..... East Lansing, MI
Furgason, David W. ..... Denver, CO
Furgason, Richard M. ..... Aurora, IL
Furgason, Samuel L., Jr. ..... Bellevue, WA
Furgerson, Julie Roberts ..... San Diego, CA
Furgeson, Royal, Jr. ..... Midland, TX
Furgison, Jon C. ..... Hermosa Beach, CA
Furgueson, Stephanie Graham
Hicksville, NY
Furhman, Arthur N. ..... Morristown, NJ
New York, NY
Furia, Arthur J. ..... Miami, FL
Furia, Gina R. ..... Philadelphia, PA
Furia, Mary Beth ..... Providence, RI
Furia, Richard F. ..... Philadelphia, PA
Furia and Turner ..... Philadelphia, PA
Wynnewood, PA
Furiasse, Mary Kay ..... Naperville, IL
Furie, Daniel I. ..... Burbank, CA
Furie, David J. ..... Hartford, CT
Furin, Gary C. ..... Atlanta, GA
Furino, Ralph V. ..... Jamesburg, NJ
Furio, Catherine A. ..... Cleveland, OH
Furio & Plaskow, A Prof. Corp.
Woodland Hills, CA
Furio, Victor F. ..... Woodland Hills, CA
Furjanic, Marie ..... Columbus, OH
Furkin, D. Scott ..... Louisville, KY
Furkiotis, George C. ..... Bridgeport, CT
Furlan, Jesse ..... Hollywood, FL
Furlan, Mark E. ..... Randolph, VT
Furlane, Emil A. ..... Joliet, IL
Furlane, Mark E. ..... Chicago, IL
Furlaud, Eleanor J. ..... New York, NY
Furlaud, Richard M. ..... Princeton, NJ
Furlong & Beitsch, P.C. ..... Fairfax, VA
Furlong, Bradford E. ..... Mount Vernon, WA
Furlong, Christopher G. ..... Springfield, PA
Furlong, Claire Smith ..... Garden City, NY
Furlong, Daniel A. ..... Jamaica, NY
Furlong, Daniel F. ..... Prescott, AZ
Furlong, Daniel J. ..... Elma, NY
Furlong, Douglas J. ..... Baltimore, MD
Furlong, Estelle Gruber ..... Miami Beach, FL
Furlong, Gary C. ..... Seattle, WA
Furlong, John A. ..... Phoenix, AZ
Furlong, John M. ..... Hingham, MA
Furlong, John S. ..... Trenton, NJ
Furlong, Kathleen A. ..... Cincinnati, OH
Furlong and Krasny ..... Trenton, NJ
Furlong, Maria Carroll ..... Boston, MA
Furlong, Matthew F. ..... Boston, MA
Furlong, Michael G. ..... Haverhill, MA
Furlong, Michael G. ..... Burlington, VT
Furlong, Philip D. ..... Sioux City, IA
Furlong, Randall C., Ph.D. ..... Houston, TX
Furlong, Richard D. ..... Cheektowaga, NY
Furlong, Richard D. ..... New Hyde Park, NY
Furlong, Robert W. ..... Wellesley, MA
Furlong, Thaddeus ..... Arlington, VA
Fairfax, VA
Manassas, VA
Furlong, Thomas W. ..... Palo Alto, CA
Furlough, Joette ..... Dallas, TX
Furlough, Joette, A Professional Corporation
Dallas, TX
Furlough, Linda S. ..... Troy, MI
Furlow, Brenda Swierenga ..... Madison, WI
Furlow, Brenda W. ..... Largo, FL
Furlow, Clark W. ..... Wilmington, DE
Furlow, David A. ..... Houston, TX
Furlow, Donald G. ..... Omaha, NE
Furlow, Frances R. ..... La Grange, KY
Furlow, Jon G. ..... Madison, WI
Furlow, Kenneth D. ..... Beaumont, TX
Furlow, Luther C., III ..... Aurora, CO
Furlow, Philip M. ..... Tahoka, TX
Furlow, Terrance Gregory ..... Lexington, KY
Furlow, Thomas M. ..... Corpus Christi, TX
Furlow, Walter S., Jr. ..... Washington, DC
Chevy Chase, MD
Furlow, William M. ..... Tallahassee, FL
Furman, Ann Began ..... Washington, DC
Furman, Ariel Michael ..... New York, NY
Furman, Barry A. ..... Blue Bell, PA
Furman, Bernard ..... Guttenberg, NJ
Furman, C. Dean ..... Louisville, KY
Furman, Cannon & Ross, P.C.
Falmouth, MA
Hyannis, MA
Furman, Daniel L. ..... Boston, MA
Furman, Danielle F. ..... Los Angeles, CA
Furman, Darla T. ..... Huntsville, AL
Furman, David C. ..... Red Bank, NJ
Furman, David D. ..... Bedminster, NJ
Furman, David J. ..... New York, NY
Furman, David M. ..... Louviers, CO
Furman, David M., P.C. ..... Louviers, CO
Furman & Del Core, P.C.
Great Neck, NY
New York, NY
Furman, Denise Wagner
Hastings-On-Hudson, NY
Furman, Diane E. ..... Summit, NJ
Furman, Donald Richard, Jr. ..... Boston, MA
Furman, Donn W. ..... San Francisco, CA
Furman, Eric ..... San Diego, CA
Furman, Harold W., II ..... Las Vegas, NV
Furman, Harry ..... Vineland, NJ
Furman, Henry F. ..... Hanover, MA
Furman, Herbert ..... Farmington Hills, MI
Furman, Howard ..... Birmingham, AL
Furman, Hugh Patrick ..... Boulder, CO
Furman, H. W. C. ..... Camden, SC
Furman, Ira J. ..... Chicago, IL
Furman, Jack J. ..... Hyannis, MA
Furman, James H. ..... Austin, TX
Furman, Jennifer A. ..... Philadelphia, PA
Furman and Jennings ..... Red Bank, NJ
Furman, Jill P. ..... Department of Justice,
Office of Consumer Litigation, GV
Rockville, MD
Furman, Joel M. ..... Patchogue, NY
Furman, John B. ..... Phoenix, AZ
Furman, John P. ..... Mobile, AL
Furman, John P. ..... Bethesda, MD
Furman, Kathryn Mitchem ..... Atlanta, GA
Furman, Kimberly R. ..... Menlo Park, CA
Furman, Leila Saidenberg ..... Los Angeles, CA
Furman, Leonard D. ..... East Brunswick, NJ
Furman, Linda L. ..... Norfolk, VA
Furman, Lizabeth Molly ..... Brooklyn, NY
Furman, Marc ..... Elkins Park, PA
Furman, Mark S. ..... Boston, MA
Furman, Martin S. ..... Randallstown, MD
Furman, Matthew S. ..... New York, NY
Furman, Michael B. ..... San Diego, CA
Furman, Michael J. ..... New Orleans, LA
Furman, Nancy E. ..... Washington, DC
Furman, Pamela J. ..... Washington, DC
Furman, Patrick D. ..... Appleton, WI
Furman & Pitts ..... Huntsville, AL
Furman, Randolph ..... Kelso, WA
Furman, Richard D. ..... Los Angeles, CA
Furman, Richard L. ..... Great Neck, NY
Furman, Rosemary Frankel ..... Miami, FL
Furman, Rumei Clarice ..... Washington, DC
Furman, Scott E. ..... New York, NY
Furman, Speedy & Stegner ..... Camden, SC
Furman, Stanley A. ..... Los Angeles, CA
Furman, Steven M. ..... Fort Morgan, CO
Furman, Stuart ..... Temecula, CA
Furman, Susan S. ..... Stamford, CT
Furman, Suzanne Fechter ..... Rockville, MD
Furman, Terence E. ..... St. Petersburg, FL
Furman, Theodore R., Jr. ..... Skillman, NJ
Furman Usher, Inc. ..... Los Angeles, CA
Furman, Valerie M. ..... Washington, DC
Furman, Wendy L. ..... Boca Raton, FL
Furman, William M. ..... Odessa, TX
Furmidge, Marva L. ..... Oakland, CA
Furnald, Lisa A. ..... Boston, MA
Furnari, Doreen S. ..... Miami, FL
Furnari, Joseph A. ..... Swampscott, MA
Furnari, Stephen T. ..... New York, NY
Furnari, Theresa A. ..... Baltimore, MD
Furnas & Associates, P.C. ..... Indianapolis, IN
Furnas, Larry D. ..... Indianapolis, IN
Furnas, Pamela A. ..... Birmingham, AL
Furnberg, Cynthia A. ..... Torrance, CA
Furne, Holly ..... Kennett Square, PA
Furnell, Terry B. ..... Little Switzeland, NC
Furner, Dean A. ..... Parkersburg, WV
Furner, Walter W. ..... Bessemer, AL
Furness, Amy E. ..... Miami, FL
Furness, Catherine Brown ..... Owatonna, MN
Furness, David K. ..... Owatonna, MN
Furness, John W. ..... San Bernardino, CA
Furness, Kathleen ..... San Diego, CA
Furness, Paulette A. ..... Portland, OR
Furness, Peter J. ..... Providence, RI
Furness, Stephanie A. ..... Lafayette, CA
Furney, Mark A. ..... Houston, TX
Furney, Michael J. ..... Richmond, VA
Furney, Nancy Wyman ..... Dallas, TX
Furnia, Jeffrey C. ..... Downers Grove, IL
Furnier, Robert R. ..... Cincinnati, OH
Furnier & Thomas, LLP ..... Cincinnati, OH
Furnish, Dale Beck ..... Tempe, AZ
Furnish, Davina M. ..... Columbus, OH
Furnish, Erica Webber ..... New Orleans, LA
Furnish, Jeffrey J. ..... Portland, OR
Furnish, Kimberly Boucher ..... Albany, NY
Furnish, Kristin M. ..... Austin, TX
Furnish, Mark F. ..... Louisville, KY
Furnish, William J., Jr. ..... New Orleans, LA
Furniss, Anthony W. ..... Portland, OR
Furniss, C. Thomas ..... Hartford, CT
Furniss, Daniel J. ..... Palo Alto, CA
Furniss, Davis, Rashkind and Saunders, P.C.
Norfolk, VA
Virginia Beach, VA
Furniss, Peter G. ..... New York, NY
Furniss & Quinn, P.C. ..... Hartford, CT
Furniss, Robert F. ..... Wilmette, IL
Furniss, Sally ..... Allentown, PA
Furniss, Shearer & Leineweber
Portland, OR
Furno, Frank J. ..... Utica, NY
Furphy, Geralyn A. ..... Cherry Hill, NJ
Furphy, J. Thomas ..... McLean, VA
Furr, Alan C. ..... Birmingham, AL
Furr, Ann L. ..... Columbia, SC
Furr, Brett P. ..... Baton Rouge, LA
Furr, Carol J. ..... Watonga, OK
Furr, Carter B. S. ..... Norfolk, VA
Furr, Christine R. ..... Findlay, OH
Furr and Cohen, P.A. ..... Boca Raton, FL
Fort Lauderdale, FL
West Palm Beach, FL
Furr, David M. ..... Gastonia, NC
Furr and Henshaw ..... Columbia, SC
Myrtle Beach, SC
Furr, Houghton ..... Lincoln, NE
Furr, J. Cameron, Jr. ..... Charlotte, NC
Furr, Jeffrey L. ..... Winston-Salem, NC
Furr, O. Fayrell, Jr. (P.C.) ..... Columbia, SC
Myrtle Beach, SC
Furr, R. Edward, Jr. ..... Atlanta, GA
Furr, Robert B., Jr. ..... Fairfax, VA
Furr, Robert C. ..... Boca Raton, FL
Furr, Susan W. ..... Baton Rouge, LA
Furr, Warwick R., II ..... Falls Church, VA
Furr, William M. ..... Norfolk, VA
Furrer, Brian P. ..... Everett, WA
Furrer, David E. ..... Baltimore, MD
Cumberland, MD
Towson, MD
Furrer, Patrick J. ..... Tigard, OR
Furrer & Scott LLC ..... Portland, OR
Tigard, OR
Furrer, Urs Broderick ..... Tarrytown, NY
Furrh, Daniel L. ..... Lynnwood, WA
Furrh, John E. ..... San Antonio, TX
Furrh, Paul E., Jr. ..... Nacogdoches, TX
Furrh, Roy H. ..... Jackson, MS
Furrow, Carolyn Handy ..... Bedford, VA
Furrow, Lucian M.
Department of Transportation,
Research and Special Programs
Administration, GV
Furry, Kenneth B. ..... New York, NY
Furry, Richard L. ..... Dayton, OH
Furry & Smith ..... Kansas City, MO
Furry, Thelma C. ..... Munroe Falls, OH
Furry, Theodore J. ..... Kansas City, MO
Furse, Austen H. ..... Austin, TX
Furse, Evelyn J. ..... Washington, DC
Furse, Mark C. ..... Chicago, IL
Furseth, Byron J. ..... Houston, TX
Furseth, Peter L., Jr. ..... Bayport, MN
Furshman, Michael Alan ..... Miami, FL
Furst, Barry W. ..... New York, NY
Furst, Carolyn Frisoli ..... Allentown, PA
Furst, Elliott S. ..... Olympia, WA
Furst, Fred S. ..... Denver, CO
Furst, Gary C. ..... Fort Wayne, IN
Furst, Gelfond & Tolstoi, P.A. ..... Roseland, NJ
Furst, George A. ..... Los Angeles, CA
Furst, Gerald ..... Garden City, NY
Furst, Henry F. ..... West Orange, NJ
Furst, Joel Eric ..... Roseland, NJ
Furst, Julie A. ..... Baltimore, MD
Furst, Larry M. ..... Los Angeles, CA
Furst, Marian J. ..... Boulder, CO
Furst, Marvin R. ..... Upper Saddle River, NJ
Furst, Michael L. ..... Forest Hills, NY
Furst, Mona Lee M. ..... Wichita, KS
Furst Pendergast & Tursi ..... San Francisco, CA
Furst, Peter A. ..... San Francisco, CA
Furst, Robert D., Jr. ..... Chicago, IL
Furst, Robert E. ..... Berkeley Heights, NJ
Furst, Robert G. ..... Phoenix, AZ
Fürst, Roland F. ..... New York, NY
Furst, Thomas ..... New York, NY
Furst, William, (P.A.) ..... Roseland, NJ
Furstenberg, David J. ..... Bloomfield Hills, MI
Furstman, Scott S. ..... Los Angeles, CA
Palo Alto, CA
Furstman, Scott S. ..... Santa Monica, CA
Furtado, Donald A. ..... Charleston, SC
Myrtle Beach, SC
Furtado, Edwin ..... Warwick, RI
Furtado, George E. ..... Providence, RI
Furtado, Jaspovice & Simons ..... Hayward, CA
Furtado, John C. ..... Warwick, RI
Furtado, Lorraine T. ..... Columbus, OH
Furtado, Manuel L. ..... Hayward, CA
Furtado, Michael ..... Seattle, WA
Furtado, Michael J. ..... Riverside, RI
Furtado, Robert A. ..... Hayward, CA
Furtek, Edward C. ..... La Jolla, CA
Furtek, Frank S. ..... Fairfield, CA
Furth, Alexandra D. ..... Boston, MA
Furth, Ben ..... San Francisco, CA
Furth, David L.
Federal Communications Commission,
Wireless Telecommunications Bureau, GV
Furth, Douglas L. ..... New York, NY
Furth, Fahrner & Mason ..... Healdsburg, CA
San Francisco, CA
Furth, Frederick P. ..... Healdsburg, CA
San Francisco, CA
Furth, Glenn D. ..... Chicago, IL
Furth, Helmut F. ..... Santa Monica, CA
Furth, Marlene ..... Inglewood, CA
Furth, Thomas C. ..... Aurora, OH
Furth, Thomas M. ..... New York, NY
Furth, Wynne S. ..... Palo Alto, CA
Furtick, Beverly H. ..... Jacksonville, FL
Ponte Vedra Beach, FL
Furtick, Russell H. ..... Columbia, SC
Furtick, William A. ..... Eugene, OR
Furtney, Gayle L.
Federal Deposit Insurance Corporation,
Outside Counsel Section, GV
Furton, Joseph R., Jr. ..... Detroit, MI
Furton, Katy Kendall ..... Chicago, IL
Furton, Matthew T. ..... Chicago, IL
Furtzaig, Lawrence M. ..... New York, NY
Furukawa, Bruce N. ..... San Francisco, CA
Furukawa, Eri ..... Atlanta, GA
Furukawa, Judith Karen ..... Washington, DC
Furuseth, Peter H. ..... Williston, ND
Furusho, Craig K., Law Offices of
Honolulu, HI
Furuta, Jacqueline H. ..... Honolulu, HI
Furutani, Barbara J. ..... Denver, CO
Furutani, John A. ..... Culver City, CA
Furutani, Miles B. ..... Honolulu, HI
Furutani Sato & Komatsubara ..... Honolulu, HI
Furuya, Russell Y. ..... Hilo, HI
Fury, Andrew Imre ..... Towson, MD
Fury Bailey ..... Seattle, WA
Fury, C. Steven ..... Seattle, WA
Fury Kennedy Griffin & Smith
New City, NY
Pearl River, NY
Fury, Maria L. ..... Harrison, NY
Fury, Michael H. ..... Pearl River, NY
Fury, Michael J. ..... Pearl River, NY
Fury, Torin Lane ..... Greensboro, NC
Fury, William L. ..... Clarksburg, WV
Fury, William M. ..... Gaylord, MI
Furzer, Joyce Helock ..... Glendale, CA
Fus, Elliot A. ..... Morehead City, NC
Fus, Steven Stanley ..... Chicago, IL
Fusaro, Altomare & Ermilio ..... Worcester, MA
Fusaro, Robert F. X. ..... Westport, CT
Fuscaldo, Alfred R. ..... Lansdale, PA
Fuscaldo, James J. ..... Midland, MI
Fuscaldo, Pete A. ..... Pittsburgh, PA
Fusco, A. J. ..... Passaic, NJ
Fusco, Andrew G. ..... Morgantown, WV
Fusco, Andrew S. ..... Auburn, NY
Fusco, Andrew S., P.C. ..... Auburn, NY
Fusco, Anthony J., Jr. ..... Chicago, IL
Fusco, Anthony J., Jr. ..... Passaic, NJ
Fusco, Anthony P. ..... Beverly, MA
Fusco, Anthony Peter ..... Arlington, MA
Fusco, Arthur G. ..... Columbia, SC
Fusco, August John, II ..... Hartford, CT
Fusco & Carlin ..... Yonkers, NY
Fusco, Daniel R. ..... Chicago, IL
Fusco, David M. ..... Cleveland, OH
Fusco, Dino ..... New York, NY
Fusco, Edith M. ..... New York, NY
Fusco, Edward D. ..... Brooklyn, NY
Fusco, Ellen M. ..... New Haven, CT
Fusco, Georgeann R. ..... Bala Cynwyd, PA
Fusco & Giuliano ..... Hartford, CT
Fusco, Holly C. ..... Pensacola, FL
Fusco, Johanna L. ..... Fort Lauderdale, FL
Fusco, John C. ..... Greenwich, CT
Fusco, John J. ..... Yonkers, NY
Fusco, John S. ..... Philadelphia, PA
Fusco, Joseph A. ..... Atlantic City, NJ
Fusco Legal Group, The, L.C.
Morgantown, WV
Fusco, Linda J. ..... Bensalem, PA
Fusco, Louis M. ..... Indianola, IA
Fusco, Mackey, Mathews, Smith & Watkins
Westerville, OH
Fusco, Maria Anita Pamintuan
New York, NY
Fusco, Mark ..... Berea, OH
Fusco, Matthew J. ..... Rochester, NY
Fusco, Mauricio J. ..... Westlake Village, CA
Fusco, Michael ..... Woodbury, NY
Fusco, Michael A., II ..... Ocean City, NJ
Fusco, Michael J. ..... Westerville, OH
Fusco, Otto ..... Bronx, NY
Fusco, Phillip A. ..... Dunn, NC
Fusco, Ralph L. ..... Metuchen, NJ
Fusco, Ralph L. ..... Trenton, NJ
Fusco, Ralph W. ..... Utica, NY
Fusco, Thomas S.
United States International Trade
Commission,
Office of Unfair Import Investigations, GV
Fusco, Victor ..... Brooklyn, NY
Fusco, Victor ..... Woodbury, NY
Fuscoe, John M. ..... Raleigh, NC
Fuselier, Bridget M. ..... Beaumont, TX
Fuselier, Christopher J. ..... Red Bank, NJ
Fuselier, Elizabeth C. ..... Somerville, NJ
Fuselier, Francis A. ..... New York, NY
Fuselier, Louis A. ..... Jackson, MS
Fuselier, Lowell R. ..... San Diego, CA
Fuselier, Perrell ..... Oakdale, LA
Fuselier, Thomas F. ..... Mamou, LA
Fuselier & Walker ..... Mamou, LA
Fusella, Gerald E. ..... Bloomfield, NJ
Fusella, Joseph J. ..... Bloomfield, NJ
Fuseyamore, Michelle T. ..... Boston, MA
Fusfeld, Robert M. ..... Denver, CO
Fusfeld, Steven R. ..... New York, NY
Fusfeld, Warren ..... Philadelphia, PA
Fusfield, Eric A. ..... Washington, DC
Fusfield, Gary ..... New York, NY
Fusha, James E. ..... Columbus, GA
Fusich, Cecelia C. ..... Hayward, CA
Fusilier, Henry L. ..... Boulder, CO
Fusilier, J. Wendel ..... Ville Platte, LA
Fusilier, L. O. ..... Ville Platte, LA
Fusillo, Matthew R. ..... Mineola, NY
Fusner, George R., Jr. ..... Nashville, TN
Fuson, Bradley S. ..... Indianapolis, IN
Fuson, Charles Steven ..... Des Moines, IA
Fuson, Cheryl ..... Kingwood, TX

Fuson, Douglas F. ... Chicago, IL
Fuson, Harold W., Jr. ... La Jolla, CA
Fuson, James E., II ... Decatur, IL
Fuson, James R. ... Oklahoma City, OK
Fuson, Laurel ... Louisville, KY
Fuson, Sandijean ... Portland, OR
Vale, OR
Fuson, Todd A. ... Los Angeles, CA
Fuss, Abraham ... Coral Springs, FL
Fuss, Abraham M. ... New York, NY
Fuss, Daniel N. ... New York, NY
Fuss, David ... Washington, DC
Fuss, David A. ... Washington, DC
Fuss, Gregory C. ... Cleveland, OH
Fuss, Marshall R. ... Los Angeles, CA
Fuss, William H. ... Sellersville, PA
Fussa, Glenda L. ... New York, NY
Fussell, David Dean ... Orlando, FL
Fussell, E. Robert ... Le Roy, NY
Fussell, Herman L. ... Atlanta, GA
Fussell, Howard R. ... Covington, LA
Fussell, Robert F. ... Fayetteville, AR
Fusselman, Christopher A. ... Houston, TX
Fusselman, Ian C. ... Los Angeles, CA
Fusselman, Margo Ornelas ... Houston, TX
Fusselman, Timothy J. ... Houston, TX
Fussinger, Mark C. ... Covington, KY
Fussner, Andrew M. ... Tampa, FL
Fussner, Anthony G. ... St. Louis, MO
Fussner, Eileen Tuhy ... Eugene, OR
Fust, Rebecca Roberson ... Searcy, AR
Fust, Wm. Carl ... Louisville, KY
Fusté, José Antonio ... San Juan, PR
Fuster, Jaime Luis ... Los Angeles, CA
Fuster, Kathleen Dority, (P.C.).
Beverly Hills, CA
Fuster, Maria Luisa B. ... San Juan, PR
Fuster, Peter ... New York, NY
Fuster, Robert M. ... Pittsfield, MA
Fuster-Zalduondo, Maria L.
San Juan, PR
Fustine, Guy C. ... Erie, PA
Fuston, Roger K. ... Birmingham, AL
Fuston, S. Del ... Chattanooga, TN
Fusz, Michael J. ... Waukegan, IL
Futa, Janice T. ... Honolulu, HI
Futami, Norman A. ... Los Angeles, CA
Futch, Delisa J. ... Dallas, TX
Futch, Gregory A. ... Stockbridge, GA
Futch, Gregory S. ... Santa Rosa, CA
Futch, H. Lee ... Ocala, FL
Tallahassee, FL
Futch, Jennifer L. ... Newport Beach, CA
Futch, John Edrington ... Ocala, FL
Futch, Kenneth E. ... Blackshear, GA
Futch, Kenneth E., P.C. ... Blackshear, GA
Futch, Lynn ... Fort Lauderdale, FL
Futch, M. Daniel, Jr. ... Colorado Springs, CO
Futch, Mack S. ... Keystone Heights, FL
Futch, Marjorie Lynn ... Fort Lauderdale, FL
Futch, Michael ... Watsonville, CA
Futch, R. William ... Ocala, FL
Futchko, John J. ... Melbourne, FL
Futerfas, Alan S., Law Offices of
New York, NY
Futerfas, Irwin S. ... Miami, FL
Futerfas, Neal D. ... White Plains, NY
Futerfas, Raye ... Newark, NJ
Futerfas, Rod P. ... Kingston, NY
Woodstock, NY
Futerman, Jerome G. ... Scarsdale, NY
Futerman, Kimberly M. ... Los Angeles, CA
Futerman, Sharon B. ... Sacramento, CA
Futernick, Sheldon M. ... Westland, MI
Futey, Bohdan A.
United States Court of Federal Claims, GV
Futey, Daria S. ... Cleveland, OH
Futey, John R. ... Trenton, NJ
Futhey, Gregory R. ... O'Fallon, MO
Futoran, Herbert S. ... New York, NY
Futorian, Aviva ... Chicago, IL
Futral, Mark ... Bronx, NY
Futrell, Alan ... San Antonio, TX
Futrell, Archie W., III ... Cary, NC
Futrell, C. Michael ... Baton Rouge, LA
Futrell, Elizabeth Jones ... New Orleans, LA
Futrell, F. Alan, P.C. ... San Antonio, TX
Futrell, J. William ... Washington, DC
Futrell, John Maurice ... New Orleans, LA
Futrell, Michael S. ... Metairie, LA
Futrell, Robert E., Jr. ... Raleigh, NC
Futrell, Stephan R. ... Hamlet, NC
Rockingham, NC
Futrovsky, Fred E. ... Bethesda, MD
Futrovsky, Mark Edward ... Rockville, MD
Futscher, David A. ... Covington, KY
Futter, Dror ... Morristown, NJ
Futter, Jeffrey L. ... Hicksville, NY
Futter, Victor ... New York, NY
Futterer, Bruce N. ... Plano, TX
Futterer, Stephen J. ... Willoughby, OH
Futterknecht, Nancy J. ... Indianapolis, IN
Futterman, Craig B. ... Chicago, IL
Futterman, David ... New York, NY
Futterman, Frederic N. ... New York, NY
Futterman & Howard, Chtd. ... Chicago, IL
Futterman, Ira H. ... Kew Gardens, NY
Futterman, Laurence W. ... Newark, NJ
Futterman, Michael A. ... San Francisco, CA
Futterman, Michael M. ... New York, NY
Futterman, Michelle Lynne
Los Angeles, CA
Futterman, Robert M. ... New York, NY
Futterman, Ronald L. ... Chicago, IL
Futterman, Stanley N. ... New York, NY
Futterman, Susan R. ... Las Vegas, NV
Futterman, Virginia Goodman
New York, NY

Futterweit, Marc Allen, Law Offices of
Dover, NJ
Hawthorne, NJ
Futterweit, Marc Allen, Law Offices of
Morristown, NJ
Paterson, NJ
Fuxa Del Cristo, Maria I., P.A. ... Miami, FL
Fuxa Del Cristo, Maria ... Miami, FL
Fuxan, Gregory C. ... New Orleans, LA
Fuyuno, Joy ... San Francisco, CA
Fuzak, John F. ... East Lansing, MI
Fuzak, Mark J. ... Buffalo, NY
Fuzesi, Stephen, Jr. ... Washington, DC
Fuzzell, Cherie M. ... Atlanta, GA
Fybel, Richard D. ... Irvine, CA
Fyda, Kristin Darnell ... Reno, NV
Fye, Alisa B. ... Portland, OR
Fyfe, Douglas M. ... Appleton, WI
Fyfe, Hugh D., Jr. ... White Plains, NY
Fyffe, A. Edward, Jr. ... Honolulu, HI
Fygi, Eric J. ... Department of Energy,
Office of the General Counsel, GV
Fyie & Hawkins ... Fairfield, IL
Fyie, Jay H. ... Fairfield, IL
Fyke, Mary Marvel ... Jackson, MS
Fyke, Tim R. ... Phoenix, AZ
Fyler, Roberta H. ... Tucson, AZ
Fylonenko, Peter ... Southfield, MI
Fylstra, Raymond A. ... Chicago, IL
Fylypovych, Andrew ... Philadelphia, PA
Fynes, Jack G. ... Toledo, OH
Fynes, Pamela Patton ... New York, NY
Fynes, William A. ... Dallas, TX
Fyock, Sheryl A. ... Chicago, IL
Fyvolent, Robert J. ... Culver City, CA

Gaa, Thomas M. ... Palo Alto, CA
Gaal, Barbara S. ... Palo Alto, CA
Gaal, Charlotte K. ... Trenton, NJ
Gaal, Gabriella G. ... Providence, RI
Gaal, John ... Syracuse, NY
Gaal, Richard M. ... Mobile, AL
Gaalema, Richard G. ... Atlanta, GA
Gaalswyk, Richard M. ... Minneapolis, MN
Gaan, Cary A. ... Chicago, IL
Gaar, Dale A. ... Denver, CO
Gaar, Joseph F., Jr. ... Lafayette, LA
Gaar, Norman E. ... Overland Park, KS
Kansas City, MO
Gaar, William E. ... Portland, OR
Gaarde, Ralph E. ... Groveland, CA
Modesto, CA
Gaarder, Conrad C. ... Arlington, VA
Gaarder, Jason W. ... Baltimore, MD
Gaarenstroom, Conrad F. ... Davenport, FL
Sanford, NC
Gaary-Holran, Pamela C.
Washington, DC
Gaas, Patrick E. ... Houston, TX
Gaasedelen, Francis W. ... Minneapolis, MN
Gaass, Klyn & Boehlje ... Pella, IA
Gaass, Peter G. ... Pella, IA
Gab, Helen Paulin ... St. Louis, MO
Gaba, Barbara K. ... Mineola, NY
Gaba, Charles E. ... Chantilly, VA
Gaba, Jeffrey M. ... Dallas, TX
Gaba, Jeffrey N. ... Atlanta, GA
Gaba, Michael M. ... Washington, DC
Gaba, Stephen J. ... Newburgh, NY
Gaba, Steven J. ... Bethesda, MD
Gabage, Charles W. ... Vineland, NJ
Gabai, Joseph ... Los Angeles, CA
Gabala, James A. ... Chicago, IL
Gabalac, Stephan M. ... Toledo, OH
Gabaldon, Adrian ... Auburndale, FL
Gabaldón, Oscar G., Jr. ... El Paso, TX
Gabaldon, Theresa A. ... Washington, DC
Gabaldon, Valentine ... West Palm Beach, FL
Gabauer, Peter A., Jr. ... Washington, DC
Gabay, Carey ... New York, NY
Gabay, David A. ... New York, NY
Gabay, Donald D. ... New York, NY
Gabay, Eli ... Philadelphia, PA
Gabay, Joseph A. ... Wilmington, DE
Gabayan, Shervin I. ... Los Angeles, CA
Gabb, Samuel B. ... Lake Charles, LA
Gabbard, Gregory A. ... Covington, KY
Gabbard, J. Douglas, II ... Atoka, OK
Gabbard, Nanci L. ... Cincinnati, OH
Gabbay, Alan ... Chicago, IL
Gabbay, Carolyn Jacoby ... Boston, MA
Gabbay, Edmond ... New York, NY
Gabbay, Leonard B. ... Austin, TX
Gabbay, Ronen ... Hackensack, NJ
Gabbert, A. Rex ... Liberty, MO
Gabbert, Brian H. ... Houston, TX
Gabbert, Craig V., Jr. ... Nashville, TN
Gabbert, Kay Cooper ... Nashville, TN
Gabbert, Myron Dan ... McCall, ID
Gabbert, Myron Dan, J.D., P.A. ... Boise, ID
McCall, ID
Gabbert, Paul L. ... Santa Monica, CA
Gabbert, Robin C. Jager ... Anchorage, AK
Gabbert, Roy E., Jr. ... West Union, OH
Gabbert, Roy E., Sr. ... West Union, OH
Gabbert, Marjorie P. ... Kensington, MD
Gabbidon, Andrew R. ... Denver, CO
Gabbidon, Jacqueline F. ... Dallas, TX
Gabbrielli, Tina Williams ... Philadelphia, PA
Gabe, Allen S. ... Schaumburg, IL
Gabe & Associates ... Hoffman Estates, IL
Gabe, Caryl Jacobs ... Hoffman Estates, IL
Gabe, Charles H. ... Royal Oak, MI
Gabe, Lawrence M. ... New York, NY
Gabe, Steven Jay ... Brooklyn, NY
Gabe-Cornelius, Jackie ... Miami, FL
Gabehart, James W. ... Charleston, WV

Gabel, Alison ... New York, NY
Gabel, Anthony L. ... Hutchinson, KS
Gabel, Beth S. ... Hudson, NY
Gabel, Clifford D. ... Mineola, NY
Gabel, Dawn R. ... Phoenix, AZ
Gabel, E. Marianne ... Delaware, OH
Gabel, Edward A., III ... Poughkeepsie, NY
Gabel, Eva T. ... Columbus, OH
Gabel, George D., Jr. ... Jacksonville, FL
Gabel, George F., Jr. ... Buffalo, NY
Gabel International Law Firm
Burlington, VT
Gabel, James E. ... Woodbury, NJ
Gabel, Janet Novakowski ... Buffalo, NY
Gabel, Jeffrey ... New York, NY
White Plains, NY
Gabel, Jennifer L. ... Dallas, TX
Gabel, Jody Blouch ... Sarasota, FL
Gäbel, Johannes K. ... New York, NY
Gabel, Kristine L. ... St. Paul, MN
Gabel, Laura J. ... Farmington Hills, MI
Gabel, Megan ... Houston, TX
Gabel, Michael A. ... Decatur, GA
Gabel, Michael E. ... Mobile, AL
Gabel, Michael V. ... Houston, TX
Gabel, Michael Wayne ... Maitland, FL
Gabel, Nancy Shavel ... New York, NY
Gabel, Patricia ... Burlington, VT
Gabel, Roberta D.
Department of Transportation,
Office of the General Counsel, GV
Gabel, Roger L. ... Boise, ID
Gabel, Tamara J. ... San Jose, CA
Gabeler, Battocchi & Griggs, L.L.C.
McLean, VA
Gabeler, Lane R. ... Louisville, KY
McLean, VA
Gabelman, Thomas L. ... Cincinnati, OH
Gaber, Andrew H. ... Philadelphia, PA
Gaber, John J. ... Mount Clemens, MI
Gaber, Kathleen M. ... Chicago, IL
Gaber, Lee ... Philadelphia, PA
Gaber, Lesley A. ... Detroit, MI
Gaberino, John A., Jr. ... Tulsa, OK
Gaberman, Ira H. ... Boston, MA
Gaberman & Parish, P.C. ... Amherst, MA
Northampton, MA
Pittsfield, MA
Springfield, MA
Gaberman, Richard M. ... Springfield, MA
Gaberman, Robert N. ... Findlay, OH
Gabert, Alexander W. ... Rio Grande City, TX
Gabert, Stanley R. ... Appleton, WI
Gabert, Steven C. ... Milwaukee, WI
Gabert, Williams & Farb ... Appleton, WI
Gabhart, Charles M. ... Jeffersonville, IN
Gabhart, Charles Paige ... Jeffersonville, IN
Gabhart, Johnson W. ... Charleston, WV
Gabianelli, David A. ... San Francisco, CA
Gabianelli, Eugene J. ... St. Louis, MO
Gabiati, Gail ... San Francisco, CA
Gabig, A. John ... Washington, DC
Gabig, Jerome S., Jr. ... Washington, DC
Gabiger, Pamela ... Newburgh, NY
Gabilondo, Jose M.
Securities and Exchange Commission,
Office of Compliance Inspections and
Examinations, GV
Gabin, Jan H. ... Yardley, PA
Gabin, Sara L., (P.C.) ... Lake Oswego, OR
Gabin, Vickie L. ... Santa Fe, NM
Gabinet, Arthur S. ... Philadelphia, PA
Gabinet, Leon ... Cleveland, OH
Gabinet, Sarah ... Cleveland, OH
Gabiola, Javier L. ... Pocatello, ID
Gabiola, Julian E. ... Pocatello, ID
Gabis, Elizabeth S. ... Lisle, IL
Gabis, Julia E., & Associates
West Conshohocken, PA
Gabis, Mark A. ... Fort Thomas, KY
Gabis, Ashley G. ... Los Angeles, CA
Gable, Bill ... Los Angeles, CA
Gable, Bill L. ... Irvine, CA
Gable, Elizabeth G. ... Albany, NY
Gable, Erin D. ... Annapolis, MD
Gable, G. Ellis ... Tulsa, OK
Gable, George W. ... Tulsa, OK
Gable, Gordon E. ... Ypsilanti, MI
Gable & Gotwals, A Professional
Corporation ... Oklahoma City, OK
Tulsa, OK
Gable, Hayes H., III ... Sacramento, CA
Gable, J. David, III ... Indian Rocks Beach, FL
Gable, John J. ... Albany, NY
Gable, Karen L. ... Orlando, FL
Gable, Keith A. ... Cranford, NJ
Gable, Marsha A. ... Newport Beach, CA
Gable, Michael P. ... Hollywood, FL
Gable, Patricia Eve ... Hattiesburg, MS
Gable, Patrick C. ... Springfield, MA
Gable, Philip Eugene ... Birmingham, AL
Birmingham, AL
Gable, R. Glenn ... Woodstock, IL
Gable, R. Lewis ... New York, NY
Gable, Richard D., Jr. ... Philadelphia, PA
Gable, Richard W. ... Tulsa, OK
Gable, Thomas D. ... Tulsa, OK
Gablehouse & Epel ... Denver, CO
Gablehouse, Timothy R. ... Denver, CO
Gabler & Associates, P.C. ... Pittsburgh, PA
Gabler, Beth Ann C. ... Chambersburg, PA
Gabler, Bruce G. ... Pittsburgh, PA
Gabler, Charles W. ... Punta Gorda, FL
Gabler, Daniel J. ... Milwaukee, WI
Gabler, Forrest R. ... Baltimore, MD
Gabler, Fred ... Denver, CO
Gabler, H. Edward ... Hopewell, NJ
Gabler, James D. ... Ridgewood, NY

Gabler, Julie S. ... Los Angeles, CA
Gabler, Kathryn ... Greenwich, CT
Gabler, Lisa H. ... New York, NY
Gabler, Mark J. ... Kihei, HI
Gabler, Paul W. ... Chicago, IL
Gabler, Robert C., Law Office of
Boston, MA
Boston, MA
Gabler, Robert E. ... Annapolis, MD
Gabler, Ronald G. ... Beverly Hills, CA
Gabler, William J. ... Olean, NY
Gabler, William M. ... Eau Claire, WI
Gables, Victor A. ... Riverside, CA
Gabliks, Kelly M. ... Salem, OR
Gabor, Arthur M. ... Mount Pocono, PA
Gabor, Brian M. ... Pontiac, IL
Gabor, David R. ... Los Angeles, CA
Gabor, Francis A. ... Memphis, TN
Gabor, Heather L. ... Philadelphia, PA
Gabor, Janell M. ... St. Paul, MN
Gabor, Michael E. ... Algona, IA
Gabor, Renee L. ... Great Neck, NY
Gabor, Richard M. ... Staten Island, NY
Gabor, William G. ... Syracuse, NY
Gaboriault, Andrew L. ... Westport, CT
Gaboriault, Peter W., Law Offices of
Westport, CT
Brewster, NY
Gabourie, Fred W., Jr. ... Post Falls, ID
Gabourie, Fred W., Sr. ... Bonners Ferry, ID
Gaboury, Mario Thomas
Old Saybrook, CT
Fort Lauderdale, FL
Gabovitch, Ellen S. ... Indianapolis, IN
Gabovitch, Michael J. ... Indianapolis, IN
Gabovitch, Steven A. ... Stoughton, MA
Gabovitch, William ... Gloucester, MA
Gabovitch, William N. ... Westborough, MA
Gabowitz-Paxin, Tara J. ... Atlanta, GA
Gabree, Gary A. ... Bath, ME
Gabrellas, Clifford J. ... Philadelphia, PA
Gabrian, Dennis L. ... Bloomfield Hills, MI
Gabrian & Parks ... Bloomfield Hills, MI
Gabric, Millon & Ory, Chtd. ... Wheaton, IL
Gabric, Ralph A. ... Wheaton, IL
Gabric, Ralph J. ... Chicago, IL
Gabriel, Alan L., Law Offices
Fort Lauderdale, FL
Gabriel, Allan ... Los Angeles, CA
Gabriel, Ana Maria G. ... Hagåtña, GU
Gabriel, Andrew S. ... Las Vegas, NV
Reno, NV
Gabriel, Arthur ... Morgantown, WV
Gabriel & Associates ... Long Beach, CA
Gabriel Berry & Weston, L.L.P.
Greensboro, NC
Gabriel, Brian P. ... Pittsburgh, PA
Gabriel, Christina ... Chicago, IL
Gabriel, D. Bruce ... Cleveland, OH
Gabriel, Denise Graves ... Portland, OR
Gabriel, Eberhard J. ... Baltimore, MD
Gabriel, Elizabeth ... Albuquerque, NM
Gabriel, Gail S. ... Cambridge, MA
Gabriel, Gary E. ... Toledo, OH
Gabriel, George ... New York, NY
Gabriel, Grant E. ... Treasury Department,
Internal Revenue Service, GV
Gabriel, Harold J. ... Goldens Bridge, NY
Gabriel, Henry D. ... New Orleans, LA
Gabriel, Herman & Peretz, LLP
Los Angeles, CA
Gabriel, James ... Irvine, CA
Gabriel, James A. ... Ovid, NY
Gabriel, James H. ... Jackson, MS
Gabriel, Jay A. ... Windsor Locks, CT
Springfield, MA
Gabriel, John E. ... Pittsburgh, PA
Gabriel, John F. ... Los Angeles, CA
Gabriel, John F. ... Marlborough, MA
Gabriel, Johnny D., Jr. ... San Antonio, TX
Gabriel, Jonathan G. ... Encino, CA
Gabriel, Joseph M. ... Beverly Hills, CA
Gabriel, Larry W. ... Los Angeles, CA
Gabriel, Laura ... San Francisco, CA
Gabriel, Lee ... Denton, TX
Gabriel, Lori G. ... Chicago, IL
Gabriel & McCartney, P.C. ... St. Louis, MO
Gabriel, Paul R. ... Madison, WI
Gabriel, Richard J. ... Northborough, MA
Gabriel, Richard J. ... St. Paul, MN
Gabriel, Richard L. ... Denver, CO
Gabriel, Richard W. ... Greensboro, NC
Gabriel, Richard W. ... Tullahoma, TN
Gabriel, Robert R. ... Northborough, MA
Gabriel, Robert R., P.C., Law Office of
Northborough, MA
Gabriel, Robert W. ... Great Falls, MT
Gabriel, Ronald W. ... Columbus, OH
Gabriel, Ronnie ... Riverview, FL
Gabriel, Rudolph C. ... Irvine, CA
Gabriel, Sam J. ... Palm Beach Gardens, FL
Gabriel, Samuel E. ... Long Beach, CA
Gabriel, Scot E. ... Methuen, MA
Gabriel, Stacy ... Phoenix, AZ
Gabriel, Steven G. ... Racine, WI
Gabriel, Susan ... New York, NY
Gabriel, Thomas H.
Pension Benefit Guaranty Corporation,
Office of the General Counsel, GV
Gabriel, Todd R. ... San Diego, CA
Gabriel, William ... St. Louis, MO
Gabriel, Ytmar Santiago ... St. Paul, MN
Gabriele, Beverly A. ... Fresno, CA
Gabriele, Emilia ... New York, NY
Gabriele, Guido ... New York, NY
Gabriele, Mark J. ... Niagara Falls, NY
Gabriele, Nicholas A. ... Smithtown, NY
Gabriele, Richard J. ... Mineola, NY

Gabriele, Robert D. ... Fresno, CA
Gabrieli, David C. ... Seattle, WA
Gabrielides, Harry E. ... Chicago, IL
Gabrielides, John T. ... Chicago, IL
Gabrielle, Eric K. ... Fort Lauderdale, FL
Gabrielle, Scott M. ... New York, NY
Gabrielli, Douglas ... Riverside, CA
Gabrielli, John C. ... Davis, CA
Gabrielli, Warren D. ... Nevada City, CA
Gabriels, Catherine B. ... Albany, NY
Gabriels, Thomas J. ... Albany, NY
Gabrielse, Robert J. ... Demotte, IN
Gabrielsen, Allison ... Atlanta, GA
Gabrielski, Robert C. ... Somerville, NJ
Gabrielson, Ann E. ... Montevideo, MN
Gabrielson, Jan C. ... Los Angeles, CA
Gabrielson, Jan C., A Law Corporation
Los Angeles, CA
Gabrielson, Katryn A. ... North Yarmouth, ME
Gabrielson, N. Brooke
Newport Beach, CA
Gabrielson, Stephen D. ... St. Cloud, MN
Gabrielson, W. Scott ... Orlando, FL
Gabrielson, William C. ... San Diego, CA
Gabrik, Michael T. ... San Jose, CA
Gabrio, Gino L. ... Honolulu, HI
Gabron, Christine A. ... Pleasant Prairie, WI
Gabroy, John ... Tucson, AZ
Gabroy, Rollman & Bossé, P.C.
Tucson, AZ
Gabroy-Ayaz, Nicole ... Tucson, AZ
Gabry, Deborah A. ... Nutley, NJ
Gabrys, Matthew E. ... Milwaukee, WI
Gabrysch, Laura A. ... San Antonio, TX
Gabrysh, Celia A. ... Treasury Department, Internal Revenue Service, GV
Gabrysiak, Jeffrey M. ... Madison, WI
Gabrysiak, Walter J. ... West Long Branch, NJ
Gaburo, Virginia H., & Associates
San Diego, CA
Gaby, G. P. ... Greeneville, TN
Gac, Edward J. ... Boulder, CO
Gaca, Giles J. ... Erie, PA
Pittsburgh, PA
Gaca Matis Baum & Rizza, A Professional Corporation ... Erie, PA
Pittsburgh, PA
Wheeling, WV
Gaccione, Courtney ... Livingston, NJ
Gaccione, Paula M. ... New York, NY
Gaccione, Pomaco & Beck, A Professional Corporation ... Belleville, NJ
Gaccione, Robert A. ... Belleville, NJ
Gaccione, Samuel G. ... Greenwich, CT
Gacek, Christopher M.
Federal Communications Commission, Wireless Telecommunications Bureau, GV
Gacek, Stanley A. ... Washington, DC
Gach, Gregory H. ... Charlotte, NC
Gach, Harold I. ... Southfield, MI
Gach, Karen Georgenson
Washington, DC
Gach, Robert M. ... Washington, DC
Gach, Teri-Ellen ... Miami, FL
Gachassin & Hunter, A Professional Law Corporation ... Lafayette, LA
Gachassin, Nicholas, III ... Lafayette, LA
Gachassin, Nicholas, Jr. ... Lafayette, LA
Gaché, Ronald M., (P.A.)
West Palm Beach, FL
Gaché, Russell Carter ... Birmingham, AL
Gaches, Ronald N. ... Topeka, KS
Gachko, Joseph ... Cranford, NJ
Gach Ray, Linda ... Los Angeles, CA
Gacioch, James C. ... Binghamton, NY
Gack, Bruce M. ... Cincinnati, OH
Gacki, Andrea ... Washington, DC
Gacki, Brenda L. ... Harrisburg, PA
Gacki, Thomas P. ... Harrisburg, PA
Gackle, G. Steven ... Los Angeles, CA
Gackle Law Offices ... Kansas City, MO
Gackle, Thomas Edward ... Kansas City, MO
Gacquin, Catherine Anne ... Franklin, NJ
Gacse, Thomas M. ... Youngstown, OH
Gad, Christopher E. ... El Paso, TX
Gad, Lance S. ... New York, NY
Gad, Richard C. ... Mequon, WI
Gad, Robert K., III ... Boston, MA
Gad, Solomon ... Milwaukee, WI
Gadaleto, David M., (P.C.) ... Okemos, MI
Gadanac, Adam, Jr. ... Barberton, OH
Gadarian, Gregory V. ... Tucson, AZ
Gadarowski, James J. ... Hartford, CT
Gadau, John E. ... Champaign, IL
Gadbaw, R. Michael ... Fairfield, CT
Gadberry, Edwin, III ... Richmond, VA
Gadberry, Gavin J. ... Amarillo, TX
Gadbois, Barbara R. ... Los Angeles, CA
Gadbois, David P. ... Marlborough, MA
Gadbois, Richard A. ... Enosburg Falls, VT
Gadbow, Vincent L. ... Tacoma, WA
Gadd, Charles M., Jr. ... Gainesville, FL
Gadd, Lawrence S. ... Bingham Farms, MI
Gadd, Marvin H. ... Farmington Hills, MI
Gadd, Michael S. ... Portland, OR
Gadd, Stephen R. ... Storm Lake, IA
Gadda, David G. ... Boise, ID
Gaddes, Andrew R.C. ... Philadelphia, PA
Gaddes, Kathy Habecker ... Houston, TX
Gaddie, Chad ... St. Joseph, MO
Gaddie, Henry P. ... Louisville, KY
Gaddie, Janette Chase ... San Francisco, CA
Gaddis & Associates ... Houston, TX
Gaddis, Ben ... Hilo, HI
Gaddis, Clifton S. ... Hattiesburg, MS
Gaddis, Howard W., Jr. ... San Antonio, TX
Gaddis, Jan Preece ... Duncan, OK
Gaddis, John W. ... Longmont, CO
Gaddis, Kin & Herd, P.C.
Colorado Springs, CO
Gaddis, Larry D. ... Auburn, CA
Gaddis, Larry R. ... Colorado Springs, CO
Gaddis, Preston G., II
Oklahoma City, OK
Gaddis, Robert P. ... Houston, TX
Gaddis, Robert W. ... Tulsa, OK
Gaddis, Stephen M. ... Seattle, WA
Gaddis, William E. ... Tulsa, OK
Gaddy, Charles P. ... Indianapolis, IN
Gaddy, Clifford F., Jr. ... Greenville, SC
Gaddy, Erin Suzanne ... Washington, NC
Gaddy & Gaddy ... Indianapolis, IN
Gaddy & Hall ... Albuquerque, NM
Gaddy, Martha D. ... Kirkwood, MO
Gaddy, Maureen E. ... Indianapolis, IN
Gaddy, P. Vincent ... Mobile, AL
Gaddy, Philip C. ... Albuquerque, NM
Gaddy, Robert J. ... St. Louis, MO
Gaddy, Rodney E. ... St. Petersburg, FL
Gaddy, Susan M.
Administrative Office Of The United States Courts, GV
Gaddy, W. Brian ... Kansas City, MO
Gade, Alfred E. ... Dearborn, MI
Gade and Cauley ... San Diego, CA
Gade, Elizabeth L. ... Sacramento, CA
Gade, L. Susan ... San Diego, CA
Gade, Mary A. ... Chicago, IL
Gade, Thomas A. ... San Diego, CA
Gadebusch, Rolf V. ... Fresno, CA
Gadek, Deborah S. ... Morristown, NJ
Gadek, Mary Lorr ... Chicago, IL
Gadel, Bradley J. ... Alexandria, LA
Gadell, Patrick H. ... St. Louis, MO
Gaden, Barbara J. ... Richmond, VA
Gaden, Sally I. ... New Orleans, LA
Gadiano, Christina M. ... Arlington, VA
Gadiano, Willem F. ... Washington, DC
Gadient, Janet Y. ... Bethesda, MD
Gadioma, Lourdes ... New York, NY
Gado, Yasmine ... Overland Park, KS
Gadola, Joseph R. ... Wells, MN
Gadola, Paul V. ... Flint, MI
Gadola, Preeti P. ... Haslett, MI
Gadola, Thomas L. ... Flint, MI
Gadon, John H. ... Portland, OR
Gadon, Steven F. ... Philadelphia, PA
Gadoury, Michael J. ... Providence, RI
Gadow, Jan F. ... Jackson, MS
Gadow, Jennifer G. ... Phoenix, AZ
Gadre, Aniruddha (Rudy) ... Bellevue, WA
Gadrix, Edward W., Jr. ... Roswell, GA
Gadsby, C. Norman
Cardiff-By-The-Sea, CA
Gadsby, Edward N., Jr. ... Boston, MA
Gadsby & Hannah LLP ... Washington, DC
Boston, MA
Gadsby, Linda Marcelle ... New York, NY
Gadsby, Richard ... New York, NY
Gadsden, Christopher H. ... Berwyn, PA
Gadsden, Debra R. ... East Point, GA
Gadsden, Donald ... Burbank, CA
Gadsden, Eugene H. ... Savannah, GA
Gadsden, James ... New York, NY
Gadsden, Jessica L. ... Cleveland, OH
Gadsden, M. E. ... Fayetteville, NC
Gadsden, Thomas P. ... Philadelphia, PA
Gadtke, Todd E. ... Minneapolis, MN
Gadue, Michael R. ... Burlington, VT
Gady, N. David ... Anaheim, CA
Gadye, Clifford S. ... San Francisco, CA
Gadzia, William H. ... Phoenix, AZ
Gadziala, Mary Ann
Securities and Exchange Commission, Office of Compliance Inspections and Examinations, GV
Gadzichowski, John M.
Department of Justice, Civil Rights Division, GV
Gaebe, Dana H. ... Providence, RI
Gaebe, Greg M. ... Miami, FL
Gaebe, Harold C. ... St. Louis, MO
Gaebe, John R. ... St. Louis, MO
Gaebe, John S. ... Miami, FL
Gaebe & Kezirian ... Providence, RI
Gaebe, Murphy, Mullen & Antonelli
Coral Gables, FL
Fort Lauderdale, FL
Miami, FL
West Palm Beach, FL
Gaebler, Gordon R. ... Kansas City, MO
Gaebler, Gordon R., P.C. ... Kansas City, MO
Gaebler, Helen Anne ... Department of Justice, Civil Division, GV
Gaebler, John F. ... Milwaukee, WI
Gaebler, Steven G. ... Melville, NY
Mineola, NY
Gaede, A. H., Jr. ... Birmingham, AL
Gaede, Chet F. ... Leadville, CO
Gaede, Heather L. ... Palo Alto, CA
Gaede, Lee A. ... Evanston, IL
Gaede, William G., III ... San Francisco, CA
Gaedeke, Patricia ... Detroit, MI
Gaedke, Gina B. ... San Antonio, TX
Gaegler, Francis X., Jr. ... Riverdale, MD
Gaegler & Hopewell ... Riverdale, MD
Gaegler, Patricia A.
Research Triangle Park, NC
Gaekwad, Ilene Munk ... Salina, KS
Gaelen, Marc M. ... Union, NJ
Gaeng, Gerard J. ... Baltimore, MD
Gaeng, Paul E. ... Belmont, NC
Gaensbauer, John S. ... Denver, CO
Gaenslen, J. Anthony ... Ithaca, NY
Gaenzle, Christopher L. ... Richmond, VA
Gaenzle, Lawrence W. ... Rochester, NY
Gaenzle, Russell E. ... Rochester, NY
Gaer, Eleanor P. ... Cherry Hill, NJ
Gaer, Eugene A. ... New York, NY
Gaer, Seymour L. ... Miami, FL
Gaer, Steven K. ... West Des Moines, IA
Gaerig, Estelle C. ... Memphis, TN
Gaerig, Eugene C. ... Memphis, TN
Gaerig, Eugenia R. ... Jackson, MS
Gaerig, Louise P. ... Memphis, TN
Gaertner, Carl R. ... St. Louis, MO
Gaertner, David P. ... Pittsburgh, PA
Gaertner, Eric J. ... Chicago, IL
Gaertner, Gary J. ... Pittsburgh, PA
Gaertner, Gary M. ... St. Louis, MO
Gaertner, John R., Jr. ... Mesa, AZ
Gaertner, Kent A. ... Naperville, IL
Gaertner, Mark Richard ... St. Paul, MN
Gaertner, Michael J. ... Chicago, IL
Gaertner, Susan E. ... St. Paul, MN
Gaesser, David A. ... Rochester, NY
Gaeta, Angelique Marie ... San Jose, CA
Gaeta, Anthony, Jr. ... Raleigh, NC
Gaeta, Bruce A. ... Hackensack, NJ
Gaeta, Domenic P. ... Lexington, MA
Gaeta, Frank N. ... Boston, MA
Gaeta, Joseph D. ... Concord, CA
Gaeta, Joseph R. ... Fort Myers, FL
Gaeta, Sebastian ... Wyckoff, NJ
Gaeta, Sebastian, Jr. ... Newark, NJ
Gaetani, Salvatore A. ... White Plains, NY
Gaetano, Gerald S. ... Towson, MD
Gaetanos, Christ ... Buffalo, NY
Gaeth, Marilyn R. ... Columbia, MO
Gaetje, Clay E. ... Irvine, CA
Gaetjens, Paul D. ... Los Alamos, NM
Gaetke, Eugene R. ... Lexington, KY
Gaeto, Paul J. ... Nashville, TN
Gaetz, Matthew P. ... Roseville, MN
Gaey, Olga C. ... Coral Gables, FL
Gaff, W. Bennett ... Fitzgerald, GA
Gaffaney, Bernard A. ... Irvine, CA
Gaffaney, George ... Alexandria, MN
Gaffaney, Gerald ... Phoenix, AZ
Gaffaney & Velde Law Firm, Ltd.
Alexandria, MN
Gaffaney, William R. ... Cameron Park, CA
Gaffaney, William R. ... Placerville, CA
Gaffer, Saml. W. ... Randolph, MA
Gaffey, Edward J. ... Concord, MA
Gaffey, James R. ... Towson, MD
Gaffey, Michael J. ... Kew Gardens, NY
Gaffey, Robert W. ... New York, NY
Gaffey, Thomas E. ... West Hartford, CT
Gaffey, William J. ... Wallingford, CT
Gaffield, Diane K. ... Dayton, OH
Gaffigan, Joseph F. ... Beltsville, MD
Gaffigan, Lynn A. ... Lake Forest, IL
Gaffigan, Stephen M. ... Miami, FL
Gaffigan & Zitver ... Beltsville, MD
Gaffin, Dudley ... New York, NY
Gaffin, Gerald E. ... Framingham, MA
Gaffin & Krattenmaker, P.C. ... Boston, MA
Gaffin & Mayo, P.C. ... New York, NY
Gaffin, Michael A. ... Boston, MA
Gaffin, Richard A. ... Grand Rapids, MI
Gaffin & Waldstein ... Framingham, MA
Gaffner, David L. ... Great Neck, NY
Gaffney, Aideen M. ... Portland, OR
Gaffney, Amy L. ... Columbia, SC
Gaffney, Amy Reinhart ... Seattle, WA
Gaffney, Bernard D. ... New Britain, CT
Gaffney, Bernard F. ... Hartford, CT
Gaffney, Bill G. ... Houston, TX
Gaffney, Brian ... Oakland, CA
Gaffney, Brian M. ... Lavallette, NJ
Gaffney, Charles H. ... Kingston, NY
Gaffney, Charles L. ... Belmont, MA
Gaffney, Cherise M. ... Long Beach, CA
Gaffney, Christopher J. ... Houston, TX
Gaffney, Corina Staehle ... Akron, OH
Gaffney, Daniel J. ... Kingston, NY
Gaffney, David C. ... Lexington, SC
Gaffney, Deborah Marie ... Hartford, CT
Gaffney, Dennis F. ... Meriden, CT
Gaffney, Donald F. ... Santa Ana, CA
Gaffney, Donald L. ... Phoenix, AZ
Gaffney, Donna Lynn ... Bethesda, MD
Gaffney, Elizabeth A. ... New York, NY
Gaffney, Francis M. ... Department of State, Office of the Legal Adviser, GV
Gaffney, Frank J. ... Bath, OH
Gaffney, Frank J. ... Pittsburgh, PA
Gaffney, Frederick N.
North Brunswick, NJ
New York, NY
Riverhead, NY
Rockville Centre, NY
Gaffney & Gaffney ... Kingston, NY
Gaffney, Gary R. ... Tonawanda, NY
Gaffney, Gary S. ... Davie, FL
Hollywood, FL
Gaffney, Gary S., P.A. ... Davie, FL
Hollywood, FL
Gaffney, Glenn R. ... Glendale Heights, IL
Gaffney, Heidi Atassi ... Washington, DC
Gaffney, J. Brian ... New Britain, CT
Gaffney, J. Patrick ... New Orleans, LA
Gaffney, James H., Jr. ... Minneapolis, MN
Gaffney, Joan Marie ... St. Louis, MO
Gaffney, John B. ... Paramus, NJ
Gaffney, John C. ... Santa Rosa, CA
Gaffney, John F. ... Fort Washington, PA
Gaffney, John M. ... Anthony, KS
Gaffney, John T. ... New York, NY
Gaffney, John T., Jr. ... Dedham, MA
Gaffney, John T., P.C. ... Dedham, MA
Gaffney, John W. ... Woodstock, IL
Gaffney, Jos. P., Jr. ... Philadelphia, PA
Gaffney, Joseph M. ... Seattle, WA
Gaffney, Joseph P. ... New York, NY
Gaffney Kane, P.C. ... Berlin, CT
Farmington, CT
Hamden, CT
New Britain, CT
Gaffney, Karen O. ... Inverness, FL
Gaffney, Katherine J. ... Glens Falls, NY
Gaffney, Kellylyn ... Roseland, NJ
Gaffney, Kevin J. ... Lowell, MA
Gaffney, Laura P. ... Tallahassee, FL
Gaffney, Margaret A. ... Seattle, WA
Gaffney, Marion L. ... Danvers, MA
Gaffney, Mark W. ... New York, NY
Gaffney, Mark W. ... Oyster Bay, NY
Pelham Manor, NY
Gaffney, Mary Ellen ... Jersey City, NJ
Gaffney, Mary Katherine ... Camas, WA
Gaffney, Mary McCoy ... Sandwich, MA
Gaffney, Maureen C. ... Denver, CO
Gaffney, Michael D. ... Idaho Falls, ID
Gaffney, Michael Dean ... Washington, DC
Gaffney, Michael F. ... Boston, MA
Gaffney, Michael G. ... New Orleans, LA
Gaffney, Michael J. ... Baltimore, MD
Gaffney, Michael J. ... Staten Island, NY
Gaffney, Michelle M. ... St. Louis, MO
Gaffney, Norman M., Jr. ... Lansing, MI
Gaffney, Norman M., Jr., P.C. ... Lansing, MI
Gaffney, Owen J. ... Cambridge, MA
Gaffney, P. Terrence ... Washington, DC
Gaffney, Patrick F. ... Clearwater, FL
Gaffney, Paul B. ... Washington, DC
Gaffney, R. Todd ... Des Moines, IA
Gaffney, Richard C. ... Humble, TX
Gaffney, Robert P. ... San Francisco, CA
Gaffney, Robert T. ... Osage, IA
Gaffney, Ronald L. ... Louisville, KY
Gaffney, S. Asher ... New York, NY
Gaffney, Shannon M. ... Birmingham, AL
Gaffney, Sylvia Polonsky ... La Costa, CA
Gaffney, Terence F. ... Garden City, NY
Gaffney, Teresa M. ... Tampa, FL
Gaffney, Terrence J. ... Hinsdale, IL
Gaffney, Thomas J. ... Buffalo, NY
Gaffney, Thomas J. ... Philadelphia, PA
Gaffney, Thomas P. ... New York, NY
Gaffney-Brown, Mary Ellen ... Spokane, WA
Gaffny, Michael F. ... Amesbury, MA
Gafford, Edward L., III ... La Grange, KY
Gafford, Frank M. ... Lake City, FL
Gafford, George N. ... San Diego, CA
Gafford, George S., II ... Grapevine, TX
Gafford, Gerald A. ... Oxford, MS
Gaffrey, Marc S. ... New Brunswick, NJ
Gafkowski, Frank, Jr. ... South Gate, CA
Gafner, Peter J. ... Maple Grove, MN
Gafney, Thomas J. ... Upland, CA
Gafni, Abraham J. ... Villanova, PA
Gafni, Jonathan M. ... Philadelphia, PA
Gagain, Edward F., III ... Tampa, FL
Gagala, Bruce M. ... Chicago, IL
Gagan, James E. ... Westbrook, ME
Gagan, Kevin ... New York, NY
Gagan, Sarah K. ... Boston, MA
Gagas, Anastasia C. ... New York, NY
Gage, Allen S. ... New York, NY
Gage, Arthur V. ... Tucson, AZ
Gage, Bob ... Fairfield, TX
Gage, Bradley C. ... Woodland Hills, CA
Gage, Carey ... West Orange, NJ
Gage, Charles Q. ... Charleston, WV
Gage, Clint J. ... Detroit, MI
Gage, Colin C. ... Kansas City, MO
Gage, Earl F. ... Berlin, NH
Gage, Edward A. ... Exeter, NH
Gage, Edwin L. ... Muskogee, OK
Gage, G. David ... Phoenix, AZ
Gage, G. Robert, Jr. ... New York, NY
Gage & Gage ... Geneva, NY
El Paso, TX
Gage & Gage, L.L.P. ... Las Vegas, NV
Gage, Gail M. ... Salem, OR
Gage, Gaston H. ... Charlotte, NC
Gage, Henry T. ... Grosse Pointe Farms, MI
Gage, Hilda R. ... Southfield, MI
Gage, Ivy ... Southfield, MI
Las Vegas, NV
El Paso, TX
Gage, Jack D. ... Minneapolis, MN
Gage, Jake W. ... Tulsa, OK
Gage, Jason Aaron ... Detroit, MI
Gage, Jason C. ... Los Angeles, CA
Gage, Jean Kamm ... Tucson, AZ
Gage, Jeffrey L. ... Fort Wayne, IN
Gage, Joe L., Jr. ... Fort Worth, TX
Gage, John B., II ... Overland Park, KS
Gage, John C. ... Mill Valley, CA
Gage, John C. ... Lawrence, KS
Gage, John D. ... San Francisco, CA
Gage, Kelton ... Mankato, MN
Gage, Kenneth W. ... Stamford, CT
Gage, Kevin C. ... Salem, OR
Gage, Kim ... Costa Mesa, CA
Gage, Larry S. ... Washington, DC
Gage, Laura J. ... Milwaukee, WI
Gage, MaryRose ... Chicago, IL
Gage & Mathers, Ltd. ... Phoenix, AZ
Gage, Michael W. ... Appleton, WI
Gage and Moxley ... Cheyenne, WY
Gage, Nancy ... Boston, MA
Gage, Nancy C. ... Landing, NJ
Gage, Nicole E. ... Boston, MA
Gage, Noel A. ... Las Vegas, NV
El Paso, TX
Gage, Patricia S. ... Chevy Chase, MD
Gage & Pavlis ... Southport, CT
New York, NY

Gaither, Elizabeth C. ....San Francisco, CA
Gaither, Gorham & Crone ....Hickory, NC
Gaither, Harold C., Jr. ....Dallas, TX
Gaither, J. Michael ....Charlotte, NC
Gaither, Jack I. ....Tulsa, OK
Gaither, James C. ....San Francisco, CA
Gaither, James M., Jr. ....Hickory, NC
Gaither, Jeffrey R. ....Indianapolis, IN
Gaither, Jennifer P. ....Louisville, KY
Gaither, John F., Jr. ....Deerfield, IL
Gaither, Luther R." Luke " ....Henryetta, OK
Gaither, Mark A. ....San Ramon, CA
Gaither, Marshall V. ....Pewee Valley, KY
Gaither, R. Trent ....Houston, TX
Gaither & Reynolds ....Martinsburg, WV
Gaither, Richard A. ....Nutley, NJ
Gaither, R. M. ....Topeka, KS
Gaither, Roger S. ....San Ramon, CA
Gaither, Ty ....Joplin, MO
Gaither, W. Thomas ....Eufaula, AL
Gaither-Ojeda, Cheryl O. ....New York, NY
Gaitz, Michael A. ....Houston, TX
Gaj, Brian L. ....Cleveland, OH
Gajadharsingh, Adam C. ....Washington, DC
Gajarsa, Arthur J.
United States Court Of Appeals For The Federal Circuit, GV
Gajda, James E. ....Lombard, IL
Gajda, Patricia A. ....Cleveland, OH
Gajdel, John J. ....Des Moines, IA
Gajdos, George J. ....Camarillo, CA
Santa Ana, CA
Sherman Oaks, CA
Gajer, Paul A. ....New York, NY
Gajewski & Baughan ....Culver City, CA
Gajewski, Karen A. ....Culver City, CA
Gajewski, Paul A. ....Chicago, IL
Gaji, Feyisitan Olawale ....Binghamton, NY
Gajo, Sofronio G. ....Flushing, NY
Gakos, Cynthia Terzakis ....Warren, NJ
Gal, Alfred F., Jr. ....Syracuse, NY
Gal, Laura W. ....Boston, MA
Gal, Peter ....Los Angeles, CA
Gala, Andrew R. ....Seattle, WA
Gala, Lori Ann ....Pittsburgh, PA
Galacatos, Theodora ....New York, NY
Galacz, Robert J. ....Bloomfield Hills, MI
Galagaza, Joseph G. ....Houston, TX
Galahad, Giles ....El Paso, TX
Galainena, M. David ....Chicago, IL
Galam, A. Eli ....La Mesa, CA
Galamaga, Paul F. ....Providence, RI
Galamaga, Robert J. ....Miami, FL
Galamaga, Robert J., P.A. ....Miami, FL
Galamba, Susan Saper ....Overland Park, KS
Kansas City, MO
Galambos, L. Denise ....Washington, DC
Galan, Jeffrey J. ....Columbia, SC
Galan, Mary L. ....Clarksburg, WV
Galanaugh, Timothy J. ....Haddonfield, NJ
Philadelphia, PA
Galane, Morton R. ....Las Vegas, NV
Galane, Morton R., A Professional Corporation ....Las Vegas, NV
Galanek, Christopher P. ....Atlanta, GA
Galanes, Joseph C. ....Montpelier, VT
Galanes, Juan C. ....San Juan, PR
Galanes, Philip J. ....New York, NY
Galanides, Theodore M. ....Sandston, VA
Galanis, John ....Milwaukee, WI
Galanis, Michael J. ....Crown Point, IN
Galanis, Pollack & Jacobs, S.C.
Milwaukee, WI
Galanis, Sam J. ....Southgate, MI
Galanis, Thomas J. ....Garrett, IN
Galanits, Richard T. ....Denver, CO
Galanko, Paulette Chernyshev
Virginia Beach, VA
Galanko, William A. ....Norfolk, VA
Galano, Anthony, III ....New York, NY
Galano, Donald J. ....Fort Salonga, NY
Galanopoulos, Helen ....Boston, MA
Galanos, Chris N. ....Mobile, AL
Galanos, George P. ....Crown Point, IN
Galanos, Gus J. ....Merrillville, IN
Galanos, Jean F. ....St. Petersburg, FL
Galant, Daniel G. ....Detroit, MI
Galant, Felice B. ....New York, NY
Galant, Herbert L., (P.C.) ....New York, NY
Galant, Jeffrey A. ....New York, NY
Galant, Luke G. ....Jacksonville, FL
Galante, Andrea M. ....Warrenton, VA
Galante, Anthony L. ....Staten Island, NY
Galante, Edward B. ....Stuart, FL
Galante, Fred ....Costa Mesa, CA
Galante, Gail A. ....Milwaukee, WI
Galante, James L. ....Baltimore, MD
Galante, Jerome A. ....Detroit, MI
Galante, Joanne B. ....Weston, CT
Galante, Joyce M. ....Troy, NY
Galante, Julie A. ....Birmingham, MI
Galante, L. Paul, Jr. ....Medfield, MA
Galante, Linda A. ....Malvern, PA
Galante, Mary Ann F. ....Riverside, CA
Galante and Matthews ....Wayne, NJ
Galante, Nicholas A. ....Wayne, NJ
Galante, Peter A. ....Philadelphia, PA
Galante, Richard A. ....Boston, MA
Galante, Todd Mark ....Newark, NJ
Galanter, David ....New York, NY
Galanter, Douglas F. ....Los Angeles, CA
New York, NY
Galanter, Joel T. ....Nashville, TN
Galanter, Marc ....Madison, WI
Galanter, Pamela R. ....Plymouth, MN
Galanter, Robert A. ....Pittsburgh, PA
Galanter, Sally Joyce ....Albuquerque, NM
Galanter, Seth M. ....Department of Justice, Civil Rights Division, GV
Galanter, Tamara S. ....San Francisco, CA
Galanter, Yale L. ....Miami, FL
Galanthay, Theodore E. ....Carrollton, TX
Galanti, David M. ....Walnut Creek, CA
Galanti, Paul J. ....Indianapolis, IN
Galantino, Michael R. ....Media, PA
Galantino, Nicholas ....Tampa, FL
Galantowicz, Richard E. ....Palatka, FL
Galantucci & Patuto ....Hackensack, NJ
Galantucci, Robert L. ....Hackensack, NJ
Galanty, Caroline C. ....Los Angeles, CA
Galardi, Dino G. ....Miami, FL
Galardi, Gregg M. ....Wilmington, DE
Galardi, Joseph C. ....Montvale, NJ
Galardi, Lawrence J. ....Newport Beach, CA
Galardi, Mary Burns ....Norcross, GA
Galardi, Robert J. ....Scranton, PA
Galardi, Wm. L. ....Andrews, NC
Galaris, Stella T ....Dunedin, FL
Galarneaux, William J. ....Walpole, MA
Galaro, Bruce L. ....Middlebury, CT
Galarowicz, Dennis C. ....Washington, DC
Galarza, Edwin F. ....San Juan, PR
Galas, Lisa A. ....Brockton, MA
Galasek, John N. ....Chicago, IL
Galasi, Ronald S. ....Burlingame, CA
Galaska, Edward J. ....Cleveland, OH
Galasky, Andrew G. ....Tempe, AZ
Galasky, Andrew G., P.C. ....Tempe, AZ
Galassi, Gerard G. ....Duxbury, MA
Galassi, Julie L. ....Peoria, IL
Galassini, Julie ....Lake Forest, IL
Galasso, Christopher D. ....Buffalo, NY
Galasso, John G. ....Grove City, OH
Galasso, John Michael ....Mineola, NY
Galasso, Joseph P., Jr. ....Clawson, MI
Galasso, Langione and Goidell
Garden City, NY
Galasso, Nicholas J. ....Wheaton, IL
Galasso, Peter J. ....Garden City, NY
Galasso, Ralph J. ....New York, NY
Galasso, Raymond M. ....Austin, TX
Galasso, Vincent L. ....Hackensack, NJ
Galasyn, Peter C., Jr. ....Hartford, CT
Galat, Judy D. ....Washington, DC
Galat, Karen ....Newburyport, MA
Galatas, Bob ....Houston, TX
Galati, Daniel T. ....Florham Park, NJ
Galati, Frank T. ....Phoenix, AZ
Galati, Lisa D. ....North Haven, CT
Galati, Scott A. ....Sacramento, CA
Galati, Stephen J. ....Westmont, NJ
Philadelphia, PA
Galati, Vito ....Honolulu, HI
Galatis, Ted P. ....Plantation, FL
Galatis, Ted P., Jr., (P.A.)
Fort Lauderdale, FL
Galatowitsch, Kristin K. ....Wautoma, WI
Galatz, Earl, & Associates ....Las Vegas, NV
Galatz, Eric H. ....Minneapolis, MN
Galatz, Henry F. ....Lincolnshire, IL
Galatz, Neil G. ....Las Vegas, NV
Galatzan, Tamar Ginna ....Los Angeles, CA
Galatzer, Daniel ....Glen Ellyn, IL
Galbally, William J. ....Philadelphia, PA
Galban, John J. ....New York, NY
Galbasini, Donald C. ....Mesa, AZ
Galbato, Riccardo T. ....Syracuse, NY
Galbavy, John N. ....Coeur d'Alene, ID
Galbe, Beatriz C. ....Miami, FL
Galbenski, David J. ....Detroit, MI
Galbi, Elmer W. ....Lake Oswego, OR
Galbo, Andrea ....Larchmont, NY
Galbo, Arnold E. ....Buffalo, NY
Galbo, Richard A. ....Getzville, NY
Galbo, Thomas S. ....Williamsville, NY
Galbraith, Alex T. ....Houston, TX
Galbraith, Allan ....Wenatchee, WA
Galbraith, Allan L. ....Atlanta, GA
Galbraith, Ann ....Kirkland, WA
Galbraith, Anne S. ....Canandaigua, NY
Galbraith & Booms ....Southfield, MI
Galbraith, Brad A. ....Indianapolis, IN
Galbraith, Carrie L. ....St. Petersburg, FL
Galbraith and Cohn, LLP ....Kirkland, WA
Galbraith, Colleen A. ....Philadelphia, PA
Galbraith, David B. ....Houston, TX
Galbraith, Diane L. ....Ithaca, NY
Galbraith, Dirk A. ....Ithaca, NY
Galbraith, Edward H. ....Minneapolis, MN
Galbraith, Gerald C. ....Austin, TX
Galbraith, Glen R. ....Hammond, LA
Galbraith, J. Alan ....Washington, DC
Galbraith, James ....New York, NY
Galbraith, James B. ....Galveston, TX
Galbraith, James M. ....Los Angeles, CA
Galbraith, John A. ....Maumee, OH
Galbraith, John C. ....Tacoma, WA
Galbraith, Katherine L. ....Los Angeles, CA
Galbraith, Linda M. ....Detroit, MI
Galbraith, Lyell G. ....Washington, DC
New York, NY
Rochester, NY
Galbraith, Mark R. ....McLean, VA
Galbraith, Michelle R. ....Sacramento, CA
Galbraith, Milton A., Jr. ....Lake Worth, FL
Galbraith, Moore & Gingrich
Sacramento, CA
Galbraith, Peter A. ....Anchorage, AK
Galbraith, Robert C. ....Des Moines, IA
Galbraith, Robert H. ....Ponca City, OK
Galbraith, Robert L., Jr. ....Rochester, NY
Galbraith, Stephanie D. ....Anchorage, AK
Galbraith, Steven B. ....Southfield, MI
Galbraith, Stewart P. ....Sacramento, CA
Galbraith, Tom ....Phoenix, AZ
Galbraith, Tracy J. ....Indianapolis, IN
Galbraith-Wilson, Lynn M. ....Beloit, WI
Galbreath, Carolyn E.
Department of Justice, Antitrust Division, GV
Galbreath, Charles ....Nashville, TN
Galbreath, David S. ....San Antonio, TX
Galbreath, Gerald H., Jr. ....Columbus, OH
Galbreath, Glenn G. ....Ithaca, NY
Galbreath, James B. ....Newport, KY
Galbreath, Mary E. ....San Francisco, CA
Galbreath, Michael D. ....Columbus, OH
Galbreath, Philip L. ....Washington, DC
Galbreath, R. Ray ....Nashville, TN
Galbreath, Robert L. ....Washington, DC
Galbreath, Roxanna J. ....Los Angeles, CA
Galbreath, Scott E. ....Chicago, IL
Galbreath, William A. ....Portland, OR
Galbut, Abraham A. ....Miami Beach, FL
Galbut and Conant, A Professional Corporation ....Phoenix, AZ
Galbut, Galbut, Menin & Wasserman, P.A.
Miami Beach, FL
Galbut, Howard N. ....Miami Beach, FL
Galbut, Hyman P. ....Miami Beach, FL
Galbut, Martin R. ....Phoenix, AZ
Galbut, Russell W. ....Miami Beach, FL
Galceran, Rafael H., Jr. ....Los Angeles, CA
Galchinsky, Herbert H. ....Denver, CO
Galchus, Donna S. ....Little Rock, AR
Galchus, Kenneth E. ....Little Rock, AR
Galda, Beate ....Helena, MT
Galda, Joseph P. ....Philadelphia, PA
Galdean, Trinidad P. ....Harlingen, TX
Galdi, Francis X. ....New York, NY
Galdieri, James A. ....Jersey City, NJ
Galdston, Joshua ....Boston, MA
Gale, Adam D. ....New York, NY
Gale, Alan S. ....Boston, MA
Gale, Andrew I. ....Boca Raton, FL
Gale, Andrew R. E. ....Santa Ana, CA
Gale, Barbara J. ....Lindale, GA
Gale, Barden N. ....New York, NY
Gale, Barry Lee ....Los Angeles, CA
Gale, Barton D. ....Berkeley, CA
Gale, Benjamin W. ....San Rafael, CA
Gale, Bonnie Tina ....Scarborough, NY
Gale, Brent E. ....Davenport, IA
Gale, Bruce L. ....Houston, TX
Gale, Bruce M. ....Detroit, MI
Gale, Catherine A., & Associates
Fayetteville, NY
Gale, Catherine C. ....Denver, CO
Gale, Catherine F. ....White Plains, NY
Gale, Charles ....Dallas, TX
Gale, Charles C. ....Lowell, MA
Gale, Charles J. ....Chicago, IL
Gale, Charles J., P.C. ....Chicago, IL
Gale, Charles M. ....Long Beach, CA
Gale, Christine ....Pittsburgh, PA
Gale, Christine D. ....Deerfield, IL
Gale, Connie R. ....Bingham Farms, MI
Gale & Corum ....Brattleboro, VT
Gale, David ....Great Neck, NY
Gale, David D. ....Omaha, NE
Gale, David V. ....Grand Junction, CO
Gale, Edward H. ....Redondo Beach, CA
Gale, Edward W. ....St. Paul, MN
Gale, Edwin J. ....Providence, RI
Gale, Eric A. ....San Francisco, CA
Gale, Everett E., III ....Parsippany, NJ
Gale, Fournier J., III ....Birmingham, AL
Gale and Gale ....Syracuse, KS
Gale, Gary H. ....Sacramento, CA
Gale, Gary K. ....Chicago, IL
Gale, Gregory K. ....Atlanta, GA
Gale, Gretchen D. ....Olympia, WA
Gale, J. Jason ....Torrance, CA
Gale, James A. ....Miami, FL
Gale, James H. ....New York, NY
Gale, James L. ....Raleigh, NC
Wilmington, NC
Gale, Jeannette C. ....San Francisco, CA
Gale, Jeffrey B. ....Hazlet, NJ
Gale, Jeffrey J. ....Sacramento, CA
Gale, Jeffry N. ....Mobile, AL
Gale, Jennifer L. ....Boston, MA
Gale, Jerald E. ....Los Angeles, CA
Gale, Joan E. ....Chicago, IL
Gale, John ....Miami, FL
Gale, John A. ....North Platte, NE
Gale, John Q. ....Hartford, CT
Gale, Joseph H.
United States Tax Court, GV
Gale, Kelley Michael ....San Diego, CA
Gale, Kenneth G. ....Wichita, KS
Gale, Kimberley A. ....Kansas City, MO
Gale, Lawrence E. ....Los Angeles, CA
Gale, Lynn M. P. ....Union, NJ
Gale, Mark R. ....St. Louis, MO
Gale, Marla S. K. ....New York, NY
Gale, Martha J. ....Philadelphia, PA
Gale, Mary Ellen ....Costa Mesa, CA
Gale, Max D. ....Washington, DC
Gale, Michael P. ....Coral Gables, FL
Gale, Neal G. ....Brunswick, GA
Gale, Nora Scott ....West Bloomfield, MI
Gale, Norman J., Jr. ....Mobile, AL
Gale, Paul A. ....El Dorado Hills, CA
Gale, Paul L. ....Newport Beach, CA
Gale, Peter L. ....New York, NY
Gale, Ralph A., Jr. ....Bloomington, MN
Gale, Randall G. ....Bethlehem, PA
Harrisburg, PA
Gale, Rhonda ....Los Angeles, CA
Gale, Richard M. ....Miami, FL
Gale, Richard M. ....Brattleboro, VT
Gale, Richard N. ....Washington, DC
Gale, Robert E. ....Syracuse, NY
Gale, Robert F. ....Farmington, CT
Gale, Robert H., Jr. ....Syracuse, KS
Gale, Ronald D. ....Daytona Beach, FL
Gale, Ronald E. ....San Antonio, TX
Gale, Rosemary S. ....Boston, MA
Gale, Russell H. ....New Brunswick, NJ
Gale, S. Warren ....Bloomington, MN
Gale, Shari Kim ....Los Angeles, CA
Gale, Stanley J. ....Fair Oaks, CA
Gale, Stephen P. ....Troy, MI
Gale, Stuart E. ....Bloomington, MN
Gale, Terrie Jean ....Chapel Hill, NC
Gale, Todd A. ....Chicago, IL
Gale, William H., Jr. ....Pleasanton, CA
Galea, Paul D. ....Detroit, MI
Galeano, Ana-Maria ....Albany, NY
Galeano, Judith E. ....Dublin, OH
Galeano, Mara P. ....New York, NY
Galeano, Michael J. ....Groveport, OH
Galebach, Stephen H. ....Burlington, MA
Galef, Deborah ....Cambridge, MA
Galef, Janis Mitsue ....Oceanside, CA
Galego, Nora ....Miami, FL
Galella, Joseph P. ....Peekskill, NY
Galella, Linda A. ....Mount Laurel, NJ
Galella, Marc S. ....Toms River, NJ
Galen, Albert J. ....Los Angeles, CA
Galen, Barry S., & Associates
Dayton, OH
Galen, Jeffrey Michael ....Encino, CA
Galen, Louis J. ....Rancho Mirage, CA
Galen, Michele Beth ....New York, NY
Galen, Morris J., (P.C.) ....Portland, OR
Galen, Richard E. ....Columbia, MD
Galen, Suzanne E. ....North Hollywood, CA
Galena Law Firm, P.A. ....St. Paul, MN
Galena, Richard J. ....St. Paul, MN
Galena, Tracie Ann
Plymouth Meeting, PA
Galenbeck, Scott M. ....Des Moines, IA
Galender, Robin ....Ithaca, NY
Galeno, Janet Ann ....San Mateo, CA
Galeno, Maria T. ....New York, NY
Galeno, Michael L. ....New York, NY
Galenski, Joseph W. ....El Paso, TX
Galeota, Roxanne D. ....Philadelphia, PA
Galeota, William E. ....Morgantown, WV
Galeota, William R. ....Washington, DC
Galeotos, Paul S. ....Cheyenne, WY
Galer, Alison L. ....Somerville, NJ
Galer, Deborah K. ....Encino, CA
Galer, Russell G. ....Washington, DC
Galer, Sally J ....Mio, MI
Galer, Scott D. ....Los Angeles, CA
Galerman, Alan F. ....Philadelphia, PA
Galerston, William A. ....Houston, TX
Gales, Martin ....Spokane, WA
Gales, Robert R. ....Department of Defense, Defense Legal Services Agency, GV
Galesburg, Stuart H. ....Chicago, IL
Galese, John Martin ....Birmingham, AL
Galesi, Morris M. ....Wayne, NJ
GaleWyrick, Molly E. ....Osceola, WI
Galex, Michael H. ....Miami, FL
Galex, Richard ....East Brunswick, NJ
Galey, Charles E. ....Lubbock, TX
Galey, Robert L. ....Costa Mesa, CA
Galey, Shawn P. ....Waterford, NY
Galey, Stefanie N. ....Minneapolis, MN
Galey, Thomas H. ....Boulder, CO
Galey, Thomas S. ....Pittsburgh, PA
Galey-Keith, Bridget Ann ....Hagåtña, GU
Galeziowski, Andrew ....Atlanta, GA
Galeziowski, John A., Jr. ....Hamburg, NY
Galfand Berger, LLP ....Philadelphia, PA
Reading, PA
Galfand & Galfand ....Philadelphia, PA
Galfand, Marvin F. ....Philadelphia, PA
Galfand, Myrna Weiss ....Philadelphia, PA
Galfas, Sandra A. ....Tarzana, CA
Galfin & Passon, LLP ....Irvine, CA
Santa Ana, CA
Galfin, Ted A. ....Irvine, CA
Santa Ana, CA
Galfond, David C. ....Stuart, FL
Galfond, Stephen P. ....Rockville, MD
Galford, Randall Wayne ....Ypsilanti, MI
Galford, Robert M. ....Cambridge, MA
Galfunt, Max H. ....Neponsit, NY
Galfunt, Sheldon I. ....Syosset, NY
Galfy, Joseph J., Jr. ....Clark, NJ
Galgan, Frank S. ....Bloomfield Hills, MI
Galgan, Robert J., Jr. ....Elmhurst, IL
Galgano & Burke ....Hauppauge, NY
Galgano, Kathleen M. ....Garden City, NY
Galgano, Louis J., III ....White Plains, NY
Galgano, Thomas M. ....Hauppauge, NY
Galganski, Paul J. ....Milwaukee, WI
Galganski, P.C. ....St. Louis, MO
Galganski, Terry J. ....St. Louis, MO
Galganski, Thomas R. ....St. Louis, MO
Galgay, Aline D. ....Albany, NY
Galgay, David L., Jr. ....Portland, ME
Galgay, Richard T. ....Department of Labor, Office of the Solicitor, GV
Galiardo, Christopher Deturk
New York, NY
Galiardo, John W. ....Franklin Lakes, NJ
Galiber, Joseph L. ....Bronx, NY
Galiber, Rochelle B. ....Findlay, OH
Galica, Kenneth G. ....Bay City, MI
Farmington Hills, MI
Galich, Andrew A. ....Chicago, IL
Galichon, Christopher M. ....San Diego, CA
Galicia, Esther E. ....Fort Lauderdale, FL
Miami, FL
Galicia, Gilberto M. ....Chicago, IL

Galick, Thomas J. ... Plantsville, CT
Galie, David M. ... San Francisco, CA
Galie, Kevin J. ... Boston, MA
Galien, Kristine J. ... Detroit, MI
Galiette, John V. ... Hartford, CT
Galiette, Robert J. ... Essex, CT
Galifianakis, Nick, & Associates Durham, NC
Galiga, Michael L. ... Wauwatosa, WI
Galiher, Clarke & Galiher ... Rockville, MD
Galiher, Phyllis S. ... Chevy Chase, MD
Galiher, Richard W. ... Rockville, MD
Galiher, Richard W., Jr. ... Rockville, MD
Galik, Albert R. ... Houston, TX
Galik, G. Annette ... Houston, TX
Galin, Douglas M. ... New York, NY
Galin, Gary S. ... Southfield, MI
Galin, M. David ... Cleveland, OH
Galin, Murray A. ... Savannah, GA
Galin, Richard L. ... Las Vegas, NV
Galin, Sharon M. ... Cleveland, OH
Galina, Michael ... Greenlawn, NY
Galinat, Chris ... Madison, WI
Galindez, Peter, Jr. ... Phoenix, AZ
Galindo, Angela ... New York, NY
Galindo & Fox ... Granada Hills, CA
Galindo, Jason Peter ... Lincoln, NE
Galindo, Luis A. ... Fort Worth, TX
Galindo, Marcia ... Granada Hills, CA
Galindo, Mayo J. ... San Antonio, TX
Galindo, Michelle Heron ... Dallas, TX
Galindo, Ofelia E. ... Orlando, FL
Galindo de O, Inocencio E. ... Washington, DC
Galindo-Marrone, Ana ... Office Of Special Counsel, GV
Galindo-Smith, Sylvia E. ... New York, NY
Galine, Donald L. ... San Mateo, CA
Galinet, William G. ... Stanwood, MI
Galinis, David N. ... Gaithersburg, MD
Galinsky, Louis ... Detroit, MI
Galinsky, Marsha D. ... Los Angeles, CA
Galinsky, Marshall S. ... Harrisburg, PA
Galinson, Daniel ... Garden City, NY
Galinson, Murray L. ... San Diego, CA
Galinson, Tracey L. ... Minneapolis, MN
Galioto, Anthony J. ... New York, NY
Galioto, Laurie ... Bronx, NY
Galioto, Lucy Ann ... Bloomfield, NJ
Galiotos, Tasos A. ... Virginia Beach, VA
Galiotto, Nicholas B. ... San Jose, CA
Galip, Ronald G. ... Youngstown, OH
Galis, Denny C. ... Athens, GA
Galis, Mark R. ... Chicago, IL
Galis-Menendez, Isabel B. ... New York, NY
Galis-Menendez, Mitzy ... Secaucus, NJ
Galison, David Phillip ... Mineola, NY
Galison, Edward ... Mineola, NY
Galison & Galison ... Mineola, NY
Galisson, Robert A. ... Whippany, NJ
Galitz, Bernard Edwin ... Temecula, CA
Galitz, Keith G. ... Denver, CO
Galitzer, Joshua S., (P.A.) North Miami Beach, FL
Galivan, Daniel G. ... Chicago, IL
Galizio, Robert A. ... East Brunswick, NJ
Galka, Andrew M. ... Wallington, NJ
Galka, Lawrence S. ... Colorado Springs, CO
Galka, Renee A. ... Beverly Hills, CA
Galker, Andrew L. ... Los Angeles, CA
Galkin, Anne T. ... Chicago, IL
Galkin, David G. ... Norwood, MA
Galkin, Jeffrey M. ... Chicago, IL
Gall, Barbara A. ... Harrisburg, PA
Gall, Barbara Weil ... Denver, CO
Gall, Charles A. ... Dallas, TX
Gall, Charles W., (Atty. At Law, A Law Corp.) ... Honolulu, HI
Gall, Cherie Hill ... Athens, OH
Gall, D. Conrad ... Fairmont, WV
Gall, Dennis J. ... Pearl River, NY
Gall, Douglas Juster ... Stamford, CT
Gall, Duane H. ... Denver, CO
Gall, F. Christian, Jr. ... Charleston, WV
Gall & Gall ... Monterey, CA
Gall, Garrett T. ... St. Marys, OH
Gall, Gary T. ... Lee's Summit, MO
Gall, John C. ... Portland, ME
Gall, John R. ... Columbus, OH
Gall, John U. ... Monterey, CA
Gall, Joseph F., Jr. ... Nashua, NH
Gall, Joseph F., Sr. ... Nashua, NH
Gall, Joseph S. ... Kansas City, MO
Gall, Kenneth Z. ... Dayton, OH
Gall, Lawrence H. ... Houston, TX
Gall, Maryann Baker ... Columbus, OH
Gall, Maty Osborn ... Ballwin, MO
Gall, Phillip ... New York, NY
Gall, Robert J. ... Athens, OH
Gall, Russell B. ... Alamo, CA
Gall, Suzanne M. ... Denver, CO
Gall, Todd A. ... Bakersfield, CA
Gall, Victoria Ann ... Sacramento, CA
Gall, William D. ... Department of Defense, GV
Gall, Yale & Hoy ... St. Marys, OH
Galla, Deeanna M. ... New York, NY
Galla, Karen P. Department Of Veterans Affairs, Office of the General Counsel, GV
Gallacher, Ian ... Baltimore, MD
Gallacher, James M. ... Riverhead, NY
Galla-Dillingham, Tracey L. ... Malden, MA
Gallafent, Dave R. ... Pocatello, ID
Gallaghan, Carolyn M. ... Santa Cruz, CA
Gallagher, Alan L. ... Canby, OR
Gallagher, Amanda J. ... New York, NY
Gallagher, Andrew B. ... Shreveport, LA
Gallagher, Andrew M. ... Manchester, NH
Gallagher, Anne B. ... Annapolis, MD
Gallagher, Anne Stark ... Chicago, IL
Gallagher & Archambeault, A Professional Corporation ... Glasgow, MT
Gallagher, Arthur ... Miami, FL
Gallagher, & Associates ... Honolulu, HI
Gallagher, Barbara Detrich Santa Rosa, CA
Gallagher, Barbara Wetzel ... Elko, NV
Gallagher, Benjamin F. ... St. Paul, MN
Gallagher, Bernard J. ... Charlotte, NC
Gallagher, Bernard P. Department Of Veterans Affairs, Board of Veterans Appeals, GV
Gallagher, Betsy Ellwanger ... Tampa, FL
Gallagher, Boland and Meiburger Washington, DC
Gallagher, Bradigan, Gams, Pryor & Littrell, L.L.P. ... Columbus, OH
Marion, OH
Gallagher & Brady ... De Kalb, IL
Sycamore, IL
Gallagher, Brenda A. ... Cincinnati, OH
Gallagher, Brendan F. ... Garden City, NY
Gallagher, Brennan & Gill ... Wilkes-Barre, PA
Gallagher, Brian A. ... Alexandria, VA
Gallagher, Brian C. ... Hackensack, NJ
Gallagher, Brian D. ... Morgantown, WV
Gallagher, Brian J. ... New York, NY
Gallagher, Brian K. ... New York, NY
Gallagher, Brian P. ... Chicago, IL
Gallagher, Brian P. ... New York, NY
Gallagher, Brian P. ... Allison Park, PA
Gallagher, Brian R. ... New York, NY
Gallagher, Bridget ... Southington, CT
Gallagher Briody & Butler ... Princeton, NJ
Gallagher, Byron P. ... Mount Pleasant, MI
Gallagher, Byron P., Jr. ... Lansing, MI
Gallagher & Calistro ... Hartford, CT
New Haven, CT
Gallagher, Callahan and Gartrell, Professional Association ... Concord, NH
Gallagher, Carl A. ... Kansas City, KS
Gallagher, Casados & Mann, P.C. Albuquerque, NM
Gallagher, Catherine M. ... Paramus, NJ
Gallagher, Catherine S. ... Washington, DC
Gallagher, Cathy Ann ... New York, NY
Gallagher, Charlene A ... St. Davids, PA
Gallagher, Charles A. ... Jersey City, NJ
Gallagher, Charles B. ... Peekskill, NY
Gallagher, Charles E. ... Livonia, MI
Gallagher, Charles E., Jr. ... Lanham, MD
Alexandria, VA
Gallagher, Charles F., III ... Philadelphia, PA
Gallagher, Charles F., Jr. ... New York, NY
Gallagher, Charles P. ... East Haven, CT
Gallagher, Charles W. ... Laconia, NH
Gallagher, Cherlyn Rae ... Gastonia, NC
Gallagher, Christine ... Chico, CA
Gallagher, Christine C. ... Norwich, NY
Gallagher, Christopher C. ... Concord, NH
Gallagher, Claire N. ... New Brunswick, NJ
Gallagher, Clare M. ... Pittsburgh, PA
Gallagher, Cornelius V. ... New York, NY
Gallagher, Craig ... Albany, NY
Gallagher, Daniel A. ... Omaha, NE
Gallagher, Daniel B. ... St. Paul, MN
Gallagher, Daniel D. ... Boston, MA
Gallagher, Daniel E. ... Tampa, FL
Gallagher, Daniel F. ... Chicago, IL
Gallagher, Daniel J. ... Santa Clara, CA
Gallagher, Daniel J. ... Jacksonville, FL
Gallagher, Daniel J. ... Atlantic City, NJ
Pleasantville, NJ
Gallagher, Daniel J. ... New York, NY
Gallagher, Daniel J. ... New York, NY
Gallagher, Daniel J. ... Syracuse, NY
Gallagher, Daniel J. ... Bethlehem, PA
Harrisburg, PA
Gallagher, Daniel M., Jr. ... Washington, DC
Gallagher, Daniel P., Jr. ... Pittsburgh, PA
Gallagher, Daniel Q. ... Winston, OR
Gallagher, Daniel T. ... Department of Justice, Federal Bureau of Investigation, GV
Gallagher, David C. ... Pittsburgh, PA
Gallagher, David J. ... Wakefield, MA
Gallagher, David J. ... Phillipsburg, NJ
Gallagher, David R. ... Albuquerque, NM
Gallagher, David R. ... Alexandria, VA
Gallagher, Deborah S. ... Reno, NV
Gallagher, Deirdre ... Parsippany, NJ
Gallagher, Deirdre C. ... Belleville, IL
St. Louis, MO
Gallagher, Dennis J. ... Department of State, Office of the Legal Adviser, GV
Gallagher, Dennis M. ... Los Angeles, CA
Gallagher, Dennis P. Hot Springs National Park, AR
Gallagher, Dennis R. ... Los Angeles, CA
Gallagher, Dennis V. ... Las Vegas, NV
Gallagher, Donald A., Jr. ... Eugene, OR
Gallagher, Donald Vincent ... Wheaton, IL
Gallagher, Donna Ann ... Washington, DC
Gallagher, Douglas L. ... Tigard, OR
Gallagher Duby, PLC ... Lansing, MI
Gallagher, Edw. F. ... Lincoln, NE
Gallagher, Edward G. ... Washington, DC
Vienna, VA
Gallagher, Edward J. ... Danbury, CT
Gallagher, Edward J., II ... Saginaw, MI
Gallagher, Edward J., III ... Waterloo, IA
Gallagher, Edward J., Jr. ... Waterloo, IA
Gallagher, Edward M. ... Media, PA
Gallagher, Edward R. ... Dayton, OH
Gallagher, Eileen Anna ... Cleveland, OH
Gallagher, Eileen L. ... Jersey City, NJ
Gallagher, Elizabeth Department Of Veterans Affairs, Board of Veterans Appeals, GV
Gallagher, Elizabeth A. ... Dupo, IL
Gallagher, Elizabeth M. ... Cherry Hill, NJ
Gallagher, Ellen M. ... Sacramento, CA
Gallagher, Eoghan G. ... Los Angeles, CA
Gallagher, Eugene G. ... White Plains, NY
Gallagher, Evelius & Jones, LLP Baltimore, MD
Gallagher, Francis ... Glasgow, MT
Gallagher, Francis X. ... Chicago, IL
Gallagher, Frank D. ... Brooklyn, NY
Gallagher, Frank N. ... Doylestown, PA
Gallagher, Frank X. ... Baltimore, MD
Gallagher, Frann Moore ... Reno, NV
Gallagher & Gallagher ... Los Angeles, CA
Gallagher & Gallagher ... Danbury, CT
Gallagher & Gallagher ... Garden City, NY
Gallagher and Gallagher ... Media, PA
Gallagher & Gallagher ... Philadelphia, PA
Gallagher & Gallagher ... Providence, RI
Boston, MA
Gallagher, Garrick L. ... Phoenix, AZ
Gallagher & Gaw, P.C. ... Winston, OR
Gallagher, Gaynell ... St. Louis, MO
Gallagher, George ... Fort Worth, TX
Gallagher, George D. ... Columbia, SC
Gallagher, George P. ... New Hyde Park, NY
Gallagher, George R. ... Washington, DC
Gallagher, George V. ... Palos Park, IL
Gallagher, Gerald B. ... Acton, MA
Gallagher, Gerard B. ... Chicago, IL
Gallagher, Gerard M. ... Mineola, NY
Gallagher, Gerard T. ... South Bend, IN
Gallagher, Geri H. ... Haverford, PA
Gallagher, Gladys Cruz Federal Deposit Insurance Corporation, Regulation and Legislation Section, GV
Gallagher, Gordon E., Jr. (P.C.) Louisville, KY
Gallagher Gosseen Faller Kaplan & Crowley Garden City, NY
New York, NY
Gallagher, Gregory J. ... Pittsburgh, PA
Gallagher, Gregory S. ... Memphis, TN
Gallagher, Gregory W. ... Chicago, IL
Gallagher Harnett & Lagalante New York, NY
Gallagher, Heather A. ... Hackensack, NJ
Gallagher, Helen L. ... Los Angeles, CA
Gallagher, Henry E., Jr. ... Wilmington, DE
Gallagher, Henry M. ... Amherst, MA
Gallagher, Henry T. ... Washington, DC
Gallagher, Herbert F. ... Garden City, NY
Gallagher and Heroux ... Taunton, MA
Gallagher & Howard ... Tampa, FL
Gallagher, Howard J., III ... Media, PA
Gallagher, Hugh B. ... Newark, NJ
Gallagher, Hugh P. ... Sonoma, CA
Gallagher, Hugh R. ... Mayfield Heights, OH
Gallagher, Irene F. ... Chicago, IL
Gallagher, Izah Katherine ... Fort Collins, CO
Gallagher, J. David ... Tampa, FL
Gallagher, J. Michael ... Seattle, WA
Gallagher, J. Patrick ... Honolulu, HI
Gallagher, J. Patrick ... Fort Worth, TX
Gallagher, J. Richard ... Dallas, TX
Gallagher, J. Vincent ... Brooklyn, NY
Gallagher, Jacqueline K. ... Philadelphia, PA
Gallagher, James A. ... Minneapolis, MN
Gallagher, James A., Jr. ... South Bend, IN
Gallagher, James A., Jr. ... Garden City, NY
Gallagher, James C. ... Littleton, NH
St. Johnsbury, VT
Gallagher, James D. ... Boston, MA
Gallagher, James E., Jr. ... Philadelphia, PA
Gallagher, James G. ... St. Petersburg, FL
Gallagher, James J. ... Los Angeles, CA
Gallagher, James J. ... Fort Lauderdale, FL
Gallagher, James J., Law Offices of Fort Lauderdale, FL
Gallagher, James L. ... Washington, DC
Gallagher, James L. ... El Paso, TX
Gallagher, James M. ... Department of Justice, Justice Management Division, GV
Gallagher, James M. ... Minneapolis, MN
Gallagher, James M. ... New York, NY
Gallagher, James M. ... Virginia Beach, VA
Gallagher, James M., Law Office of New York, NY
Gallagher, James N. ... Garden City, NY
Gallagher, James P. ... Memphis, TN
Gallagher, James R. ... Columbus, OH
Gallagher, James W. ... Damariscotta, ME
Gallagher, James W. ... Madison, WI
Gallagher, Janice L. ... Miami, FL
Gallagher, Janis E. ... Greenville, NC
Gallagher, Jas. J., Jr. ... Philadelphia, PA
Gallagher, Jean M. ... Cleveland, OH
Gallagher, Jeanne S. ... San Diego, CA
Gallagher, Jeffrey M. ... Richmond, VA
Gallagher, Jennifer ... Philadelphia, PA
Gallagher, Jennifer A. ... Chicago, IL
Gallagher, Jerome F., Jr. ... Parsippany, NJ
Gallagher, John A. ... Madison Heights, MI
Gallagher, John A. ... Norristown, PA
Gallagher, John B. ... Miami, FL
Gallagher, John C., III ... Boston, MA
Gallagher, John E. ... Hingham, MA
Gallagher, John F. ... Chicago, IL
Gallagher, John F. ... Springfield, MA
Gallagher, John F. ... Cincinnati, OH
Gallagher, John F., III ... New York, NY
Gallagher, John J. ... Santa Rosa, CA
Gallagher, John J. ... Washington, DC
Gallagher, John J. ... Miami, FL
Gallagher, John J. ... Rockville Centre, NY
Gallagher, John J. ... Harrisburg, PA
Gallagher, John J. ... Philadelphia, PA
Gallagher, John J. ... Austin, TX
Gallagher, John J., Jr. ... New York, NY
Gallagher, John J., P.C., Law Offices of Doylestown, PA
Media, PA
Norristown, PA
Philadelphia, PA
Gallagher, John K. ... Reno, NV
Gallagher, John K. ... De Witt, NY
Gallagher, John M. ... Santa Cruz, CA
Gallagher, John M. ... Hazleton, PA
Gallagher, John M., Jr. ... New Orleans, LA
Gallagher, John M., Jr. ... Media, PA
Gallagher, John P. ... Elyria, OH
Gallagher, John P. ... Philadelphia, PA
Gallagher, John P., (P.C.) ... Atlanta, GA
Gallagher, John R. ... San Francisco, CA
Gallagher, John R., III ... Boston, MA
Gallagher, John T. ... Wilmington, DE
Gallagher, John T. ... Kew Gardens, NY
Gallagher, John T. ... New York, NY
Gallagher, John V. ... Los Angeles, CA
Gallagher, John W. ... Lakewood, OH
Gallagher, Joseph A. ... Manassas, VA
Gallagher, Joseph D. ... Rockville, MD
Gallagher, Joseph E. ... Scranton, PA
Gallagher, Joseph G., Jr. New Orleans, LA
Gallagher, Joseph J., Jr. ... Milton, MA
Gallagher, Joseph M. ... Fort Worth, TX
Gallagher, Joseph V. ... Arlington, VA
Gallagher, Joseph W. ... Plymouth Meeting, PA
Gallagher & Joslyn ... Oakbrook Terrace, IL
Gallagher, Joyce Ann ... Pittsburgh, PA
Gallagher, Judee ... Chicago, IL
Gallagher, Julie ... Havana, FL
Gallagher, Julie C. ... Department of Justice, Drug Enforcement Administration, GV
Gallagher, Julie D. ... Dayton, OH
Gallagher, Julie, P.A. ... Havana, FL
Gallagher, Karen ... Madison, WI
Gallagher, Karen A. ... Gloucester, MA
Gallagher, Karen K. ... Bryan, OH
Gallagher, Kari A. ... South Bend, IN
Gallagher, Kate T. ... Morristown, NJ
Gallagher, Kathleen A. ... New York, NY
Gallagher, Kathleen A. ... Houston, TX
Gallagher, Kathleen G. ... McLean, VA
Gallagher, Kathleen J. ... San Francisco, CA
Gallagher, Kathleen R. Port Washington, NY
Gallagher, Kathryn Duhamel Ann Arbor, MI
Gallagher, Katrina L. ... Clarksburg, WV
Gallagher & Kavinsky, A Legal Professional Association ... Columbus, OH
Gallagher, Kendra A. ... Wilmette, IL
Gallagher & Kennedy, P.A. ... Phoenix, AZ
Gallagher, Kent W. ... Severna Park, MD
Gallagher, Kevin C. ... Atlanta, GA
Gallagher, Kevin C. ... Chicago, IL
Gallagher, Kevin E. ... Santa Ana, CA
Gallagher, Kevin M. ... Sarasota, FL
Gallagher, Kevin P. ... Washington, DC
Gallagher, Kevin R. ... Administrative Office Of The United States Courts, GV
Gallagher, Kimberly J. ... West Newton, PA
Gallagher, Kristin V. ... Gladstone, NJ
Gallagher, Langlas & Gallagher, P.C. Waterloo, IA
Gallagher, Larry J. ... Reno, NV
Gallagher & Lathrop, A Professional Corporation ... San Francisco, CA
Gallagher, Laura Bailey ... Lancaster, PA
Gallagher, Laura J. ... Medina, OH
Gallagher, Laurie S. ... Austin, TX
Gallagher, Laurie Vought ... Pittsfield, MA
Gallagher Law Firm ... Mandan, ND
Gallagher Law Office ... Fort Worth, TX
Gallagher, Lawrence G. ... Chicago, IL
Gallagher, Lawrence T. ... Waseca, MN
Gallagher, Leo J. ... Helena, MT
Gallagher, Leslieann ... Denver, CO
Gallagher, Linda ... Chicago, IL
Gallagher, Lisa Coyle ... Boston, MA
Gallagher, Loren V. ... Hemet, CA
Gallagher, Lori Meghan ... Houston, TX
Gallagher, Luke P. ... Conneaut, OH
Gallagher, Lynn Monk ... Washington, DC
Gallagher, Lynne Neely ... Tucson, AZ
Gallagher, M. Colette ... Westlake, OH
Gallagher, M. Leigh-Ann ... Detroit, MI
Gallagher, Mara ... Westmont, NJ
Gallagher, Marie L. ... Buffalo, NY
Gallagher, Mark A. ... Department of Justice, Environment and Natural Resources Division, GV
Gallagher, Mark F. ... Honolulu, HI
Wailuku, HI
Gallagher, Mark J. ... Boston, MA
Gallagher, Mark P. ... Taunton, MA
Gallagher, Mark S. ... New York, NY
Gallagher, Mark T. ... Sacramento, CA
Gallagher, Mark T. ... Philadelphia, PA
Gallagher, Martha Shields ... Haydenville, MA
Gallagher, Martin J. ... East Lansing, MI
Gallagher, Mary Department Of Veterans Affairs, Board of Veterans Appeals, GV
Gallagher, Mary ... Missoula, MT
Gallagher, Mary Hansen ... Baltimore, MD
Gallagher, Mary Jean ... Bloomfield, NJ
Gallagher, Mary K. ... Boston, MA
Gallagher, Mary L. ... Columbus, OH
Gallagher, Mary P. ... Newark, NJ

Gallagher, Mary Patricia ....Wayne, NJ
Gallagher, Maryann ....Scarborough, NY
Gallagher, Maryann P. ....Encino, CA
Gallagher, Mary-Cay ....Irvine, CA
Gallagher, Matthew R. ....Chicago, IL
Gallagher and Matthews
Rockville Centre, NY
Gallagher, Maureen A. ....Newport Beach, CA
Gallagher, Maureen A. ....State College, PA
Gallagher, Megan Ann
Rockville Centre, NY
Gallagher, Michael ....New York, NY
Gallagher, Michael C. ....Philadelphia, PA
Gallagher, Michael D. ....Butler, PA
Gallagher, Michael F. ....Orlando, FL
Gallagher, Michael F. ....New York, NY
Gallagher, Michael G. ....Washington, DC
Gallagher, Michael G. ....Owings Mills, MD
Gallagher, Michael J. ....Denver, CO
Gallagher, Michael J. ....Chicago, IL
Gallagher, Michael J. ....Brighton, MI
Gallagher, Michael J. ....Kansas City, MO
Gallagher, Michael J. ....Buffalo, NY
Gallagher, Michael L. ....Phoenix, AZ
Gallagher, Michael P. ....Grand Rapids, MN
Gallagher, Michael P. ....Berwyn, PA
Gallagher, Michael R. ....Cleveland, OH
Gallagher, Michael S. ....New Orleans, LA
El Paso, TX
Gallagher, Michael T. ....Anoka, MN
Gallagher, Michael T. ....Houston, TX
Gallagher, Michael W. ....Lowell, MA
Gallagher, Michael W. ....King Of Prussia, PA
Gallagher, Michael X. ....Philadelphia, PA
Gallagher, Michele A. ....Washington, DC
Gallagher, Milliken & Stelzer ....Bryan, OH
Gallagher, Molly A. ....San Francisco, CA
Gallagher, M. Shields, & Gallagher
Haydenville, MA
Gallagher, Nancy D. ....Norwalk, CT
Gallagher, Nancy E. ....Mount Pleasant, MI
Gallagher, Owen ....Boston, MA
Providence, RI
Gallagher, Owen L. ....Los Angeles, CA
Gallagher, Patricia ....Huntington, NY
Gallagher, Patricia A. ....Newark, DE
Gallagher, Patricia A.
Postal Rate Commission,
Office of the General Counsel, GV
Gallagher, Patricia C. ....Chicago, IL
Gallagher, Patrick ....San Francisco, CA
Gallagher, Patrick C. ....New York, NY
Gallagher, Patrick E. ....Hingham, MA
Gallagher, Patrick J. ....St. Paul, MN
Gallagher, Patrick J. ....Rockville Centre, NY
Gallagher, Patrick M. ....Vienna, VA
Gallagher, Patrick V., Jr.
Department of Commerce,
Office of the General Counsel, GV
Gallagher, Paul ....Malvern, PA
Gallagher, Paul F. X. ....Philadelphia, PA
Gallagher, Paul H. ....Evanston, IL
Gallagher, Paul J. ....Atlantic City, NJ
Gallagher, Paul J. ....Akron, OH
Gallagher, Paul L. ....Bedminster, NJ
Gallagher, Paul M. ....Sangerfield, NY
Gallagher, Paul T. ....Washington, DC
Gallagher, Paul T. ....Baton Rouge, LA
Gallagher, Paul T. ....Ann Arbor, MI
Gallagher, Peter J. ....Bethesda, MD
Gallagher, Peter J. ....New York, NY
Gallagher, Peter L. ....San Diego, CA
Gallagher & Petrak, Ltd. ....Chicago, IL
Gallagher, Phoebe Sears ....Boston, MA
Gallagher, Phyllis M. ....Wrightwood, CA
Gallagher, Priscilla F. ....Chicago, IL
Gallagher, R. Craig ....Norfolk, VA
Gallagher, R. Louis, II ....Bordentown, NJ
Gallagher, Ralph P., Jr. ....San Francisco, CA
Gallagher, Ralph W. ....Bryan, OH
Gallagher, Raymond E., Jr. ......Washington, DC
Gallagher, Raymond J. ....Woodbridge, VA
Gallagher, Reilly, Lachat & Egbert, P.C.
Wilmington, DE
Colonia, NJ
Pennsauken, NJ
Philadelphia, PA
Gallagher, Richard A. ....Philadelphia, PA
Gallagher, Richard F. ....Chicago, IL
Gallagher, Richard F. ....Great Falls, MT
Gallagher, Richard J. ....Bethesda, MD
Gallagher, Richard J. ....Roswell, NM
Gallagher, Richard J. ....Arlington, VA
Gallagher, Richard S. ....Milwaukee, WI
Gallagher, Richard T., Jr.
New Orleans, LA
Gallagher, Richard W. ....Clarksburg, WV
Gallagher, Robert ....New York, NY
Gallagher, Robert A. ....Williamsport, PA
Gallagher, Robert E., Jr. ....San Diego, CA
Gallagher, Robert E., Jr. ....Miami, FL
Gallagher, Robert E., Jr. ....Albany, NY
Buffalo, NY
Gallagher, Robert H. ....Davenport, IA
Gallagher, Robert J. ....Haydenville, MA
Gallagher, Robert M. ....Gastonia, NC
Gallagher, Robert P. ....Washington, DC
Gallagher, Robert R., Jr.
Greenwood Village, CO
Gallagher, Robert S. ....Davenport, IA
Gallagher, Rosemary
House of Representatives,
Office of Legislative Counsel, GV
Gallagher, Russell J. ....Hayden, ID
Gallagher, Schoenfeld, Surkin & Chupein, A
Professional Corporation ....Media, PA
Gallagher, Sean A. ....Chicago, IL
Gallagher, Sean J. ....Los Angeles, CA

Gallagher, Sean P. ....Louisville, KY
Gallagher, Sean R. ....Denver, CO
Gallagher, Sean W. ....Denver, CO
Chicago, IL
Gallagher, Shannon ....Irvine, CA
Gallagher, Shannon P. ....New York, NY
Gallagher, Sharon A. ....Mandan, ND
Gallagher, Sharon A. ....Oshkosh, WI
Gallagher, Sharon M. ....Los Angeles, CA
Gallagher, Sharp, Fulton & Norman
Cleveland, OH
Gallagher, Shea & Gallagher
Springfield, MA
Gallagher, Sheila ....Anchorage, AK
Gallagher, Shelly A. ....Bradenton, FL
Gallagher, Stacy A. ....St. Petersburg, FL
Gallagher & Stein ....Damariscotta, ME
Gallagher, Stephen B. ....Jacksonville, FL
Gallagher, Stephen C. ....Danbury, CT
Gallagher, Stephen K. ....McLean, VA
Gallagher, Stephen L., Jr. ....Portland, OR
Gallagher, Stephen P. ....Boston, MA
Gallagher, Stephen P. ....Havertown, PA
Philadelphia, PA
Gallagher, Stephen P., & Associates, P.C.
Havertown, PA
Philadelphia, PA
Gallagher, Sue A. ....Conroe, TX
Gallagher, Susan F. ....Chicago, IL
Gallagher, Susan M. ....Houston, TX
Gallagher, T. Jordan ....De Kalb, IL
Sycamore, IL
Gallagher, Terence J. ....Costa Mesa, CA
Gallagher, Terence J. ....Morristown, NJ
Gallagher, Terence J. ....New York, NY
Gallagher, Terence J., III ....New York, NY
Gallagher, Terence L. ....Columbus, OH
Gallagher, Theodore J. ....Columbus, OH
Gallagher & Thierbach ....Santa Ana, CA
Gallagher, Thomas ....Albany, NY
Gallagher, Thomas A. ....San Francisco, CA
Gallagher, Thomas C. ....Minneapolis, MN
Gallagher, Thomas C. ....Media, PA
Gallagher, Thomas E. ....Beverly Hills, CA
Gallagher, Thomas E. ....Schaumburg, IL
Gallagher, Thomas F. ....Philadelphia, PA
Gallagher, Thomas F. ....Tacoma, WA
Gallagher, Thomas H. ....Detroit, MI
Gallagher, Thomas H.A. ....Philadelphia, PA
Gallagher, Thomas J. ....Sarasota, FL
Gallagher, Thomas J. ....Sullivan, IN
Gallagher, Thomas J. ....Columbus, OH
Gallagher, Thomas J. ....Salem, OR
Gallagher, Thomas J. ....Washburn, WI
Gallagher, Thomas J., III
Philadelphia, PA
Gallagher, Thomas J., Jr. ....New York, NY
Gallagher, Thomas K.
West Palm Beach, FL
Gallagher, Thomas L. ....New York, NY
Gallagher, Thomas L., Jr. ....Corvallis, OR
Gallagher, Thomas M.
Department of the Navy, GV
Gallagher, Thomas P. ....Escondido, CA
Gallagher, Thomas P. ....Minneapolis, MN
Gallagher, Thomas P. ....Princeton, NJ
Gallagher, Thomas P. ....Ventnor City, NJ
Gallagher, Thomas P. (Terry)
Albuquerque, NM
Gallagher, Thomas R. ....Charleston, WV
Gallagher, Thomas R., Jr ....Potomac, MD
Gallagher, Thomas S. ....El Cajon, CA
Gallagher, Thomas W. ....Toledo, OH
Gallagher, Timothy D. ....New York, NY
Gallagher, Timothy F. ....Spokane, WA
Gallagher, Timothy J. ....Dubuque, IA
Gallagher, Timothy J.
Richmond Heights, MO
Gallagher, Timothy J. ....Cleveland, OH
Gallagher, Timothy M. ....Chicago, IL
Gallagher, Timothy V.P. ....Los Angeles, CA
Gallagher, Victoria H. ....Tomball, TX
Gallagher, Vincent P. ....Jacksonville, FL
Gallagher, Virginia H. ....Washington, DC
Gallagher, Wade J. ....Washington, DC
Rockville, MD
Gallagher, Walker, Bianco & Plastaras
Mineola, NY
Gallagher, Walter C. ....Lowell, MA
Gallagher, Wilca D. ....San Juan, PR
Gallagher, William A. ....New York, NY
Gallagher, William C. ....Wheeling, WV
Gallagher, William D. ....Santa Ana, CA
Gallagher, William D. ....New York, NY
Gallagher, William E. ....Pittsburgh, PA
Gallagher, William F. ....New Haven, CT
Gallagher, William F., Jr. ....Syracuse, NY
Gallagher, William J. ....Kennett Square, PA
West Chester, PA
Gallagher, William M. ....Sacramento, CA
Gallagher, William R. ....St. Louis, MO
Gallagher, William R. ....Reston, VA
Gallagher, William Scott ....Joplin, MO
Gallagher, William T. ....San Francisco, CA
Gallagher, William T. ....Philadelphia, PA
Gallagher, Young, Lewis, Hampton &
Downey, L.L.P. ....Houston, TX
Gallagher-Alford, Sandra L. ....Tacoma, WA
Gallagher-Duff, Kathleen T.
Washington, DC
Gallagher-Heroux, Susan ....Taunton, MA
Gallaher, Alice L. ....Millington, TN
Gallaher, Caroline D. ....Elkton, MD
Gallaher, D. Clinton, IV ....Fayetteville, WV
Gallaher, D. Patrick ....Buffalo, NY
Gallaher, David D. ....Pendleton, OR
Gallaher, Erin Brynn ....Lexington, KY
Gallaher, Harry E. ....Minneapolis, MN

Gallaher, James W. ....Jefferson City, MO
Gallaher, James W." Jamie ", Jr.
Jefferson City, MO
Gallaher, Kevin M. ....Wheaton, IL
Gallaher, Patricia E. ....Rochester, NY
Gallaher, Richard A. ....Seattle, WA
Gallaher, Stephen G. ....Des Moines, IA
Gallahue, Thomas E. ....Fairfax, VA
Gallahue, Thomas J., Jr. ....Lakehurst, NJ
Gallalee, W. F. Drewry ....Richmond, VA
Gallan, Michael A. ....Long Island City, NY
Gallancy, Jean E. ....New York, NY
Galland, George F., Jr. ....Chicago, IL
Galland, Kharasch, Greenberg, Fellman &
Swirsky, P.C. ....Washington, DC
Galland Legal Clinic, P.C. ......Sioux Falls, SD
Gallanis, James C. ....Milwaukee, WI
Gallanis, Kathryn Ann ....Chicago, IL
Gallanstein, Robert I. ....Maysville, KY
Gallant, Anne C. ....New Haven, CT
Gallant, Bruce D. ....New York, NY
Gallant, Clifford P., Jr. ....Manchester, NH
Gallant, Edward ....New Haven, CT
Gallant, Elisabeth Calhoun ....Columbia, SC
Gallant, Eugene G. ....Providence, RI
Gallant, Gary G., Jr. ....Washington, DC
Gallant, Gerald M. ....Ansonia, CT
Gallant, Howard J. ....Columbus, OH
Gallant, James A. ....Hooper, NE
Scribner, NE
Gallant, Jeffrey Michael
Bloomfield Hills, MI
Gallant, Jonathan Chad ....New York, NY
Gallant, Keith Bradoc ....New Haven, CT
Gallant, Kenneth ....Rochester, NY
Gallant, Kenneth S. ....Moscow, ID
Gallant, Kevin A. ....Ticonderoga, NY
Gallant, Laura R. ....Lynn, MA
Gallant, Leo K. ....Rocklin, CA
Gallant, Mark A. ....Beverly, MA
Gallant, Mark H. ....Philadelphia, PA
Gallant, Mary L. ....Quincy, MA
Gallant, Michael E. ....Washington, DC
Gallant, Michael J. ....Ticonderoga, NY
Gallant, Ronald J. ....York, ME
Gallant, Scott R. ....Philadelphia, PA
Gallant, Stacey Orr ....Atlanta, GA
Gallant, Steven M. ....St. Louis, MO
Gallant, Walter Joseph ....Houston, TX
Gallanter, Peter ....Mineola, NY
Gallanter, Sanford ....San Francisco, CA
Gallanty, Alan T. ....New York, NY
Gallantz, George G. ....New York, NY
Gallard, Elizabeth Schuetz
Philadelphia, PA
Gallardo, Daniel LagosOrtiz ....Santee, CA
Gallardo, Domingo R. ....Garden City, NY
Gallardo, Fernando L. ....San Juan, PR
Gallardo, James E. ....Seattle, WA
Gallardo, Michelle M. ....Miami, FL
Gallarno, Theo. J. ....Frederick, MD
Gallas, Alan B. ....Kansas City, MO
Gallas, George S. ....Independence, OH
Gallas, Jack A. ....Chicago, IL
Gallas, James S. ....Akron, OH
Gallas, Joseph C. ....Santa Maria, CA
Gallas, Joseph C., A Prof. Law Corp.
Santa Maria, CA
Gallas, Philip S. ....Washington, DC
Gallas & Schultz ....Kansas City, MO
Gallas, William E. ....Redondo Beach, CA
Gallaspy, Annette Clayton ....Baton Rouge, LA
Gallaspy, John N. ....Bogalusa, LA
Gallaspy, Leland R. ....Covington, LA
Gallaspy & Paduda ....Bogalusa, LA
Gallaspy, Sara F. ....New Augusta, MS
Gallatin, Howard P. ....Peoria, IL
Gallatin, James P., Jr. ....Washington, DC
Gallatin, Ronald L. ....New York, NY
Gallatin, Thomas G., Jr. ....New York, NY
Gallaudet, Anne M. ....Windsor, CT
Gallaugher, Patrick D., Jr.
Lake Charles, LA
Gallavan, Michael L. ....Upper Marlboro, MD
Gallawa • Brown • Kroesch, A Professional
Corporation ....Sacramento, CA
Gallawa, Gary ....Sacramento, CA
Gallawa, Walter E. ....Sacramento, CA
Gallaway, James W. ....Zephyr Cove, NV
Gallaway, Michael G. ....Pittsburgh, PA
Wheeling, WV
Gallaway, Raymond E., Jr.
San Antonio, TX
Gallaway, Robert L. ....Ventura, CA
Gallay, Mary Jo ....Coral Gables, FL
Gall-Clayton, Nancy J. ....Louisville, KY
Galle, Craig T. ....St. Louis, MO
Galle, J. Thomas ....Louisville, KY
Gallé, Katherine Hammond
White Plains, NY
Galle, Sandra A. ....Newport Beach, CA
Galleano, Paula J. ....Oakland, CA
Galleberg, Paul A. ....Los Angeles, CA
Gallego, David L. ....Columbia, MO
Gallego, Dean R. ....Union, MO
Gallego, Paul D., Law Office of
Laredo, TX
Gallego, Pete P. ....Alpine, TX
Gallegos, Alex Frank ....Del Norte, CO
Gallegos, Andrés J. ....Chicago, IL
Gallegos, Anthony J. ....Albuquerque, NM
Gallegos, Douglas A.
Equal Employment Opportunity
Commission,
Office of the Chairman, GV
Gallegos, Eddie M. ....Albuquerque, NM
Gallegos, Elena M. ....Austin, TX
Gallegos, Esteban G. ....Los Angeles, CA

Gallegos, Gabrielle G. ....Bellingham, WA
Gallegos, George A. ....Costa Mesa, CA
Gallegos, Hector G. ....Los Angeles, CA
Gallegos, James H. ....Denver, CO
Gallegos, Jason E. ....San Diego, CA
Gallegos, J. E. ....Santa Fe, NM
Gallegos, Joan M. ....Eureka, CA
Gallegos, John D. ....Palm Springs, CA
Gallegos, John Joe ....Denver, CO
Gallegos, Larry D. ....Denver, CO
Gallegos, Laurie A. ....Los Alamos, NM
Gallegos Law Firm, P.C. ....Santa Fe, NM
Gallegos Law Offices, The, P.C.
Albuquerque, NM
Gallegos Legal Group ....Albuquerque, NM
Sandia Park, NM
Gallegos, Maclovio ....Pueblo, CO
Gallegos, Mark S. ....Miami, FL
Gallegos, Michael A. ....Sevierville, TN
Gallegos, Paul Varden ....Eureka, CA
Gallegos, R. Ruben ....Albuquerque, NM
Gallegos, Ramon ....Lubbock, TX
Gallegos, Ronald R. ....Glendale, AZ
Gallegos, Thomas R. ....Vacaville, CA
Gallegos, Timoteo ....Montrose, CO
Gallegos, Yolanda R. ....Albuquerque, NM
Sandia Park, NM
Galleher, Watson W. ....Denver, CO
Gallehr, Tracy Ann ....Warrenton, VA
Gallen, David A. ....New York, NY
Gallen, Edward James ....Chester Springs, PA
Gallen, James M. ....Edwardsville, IL
St. Louis, MO
Gallen, John F. ....San Francisco, CA
Gallen, Jonathan ....New York, NY
Gallen, Joseph R. ....Las Vegas, NV
Gallen, Kenneth R. ....Philadelphia, PA
West Chester, PA
Gallen, Kevin P. ....Washington, DC
Gallen, Maureen ....Miami, FL
Gallen, Richard T. ....New York, NY
Gallen, Ross I. ....San Antonio, TX
Gallen, Ross I., A Professional Corporation
San Antonio, TX
Gallen, Thomas M. ....Bradenton, FL
Gallenbeck, James Pendell ....Jackson, MS
Gallender, Eric W. ....Chicago, IL
Gallenson, Mavis S. ....Los Angeles, CA
Gallenson, Stephen M. ....Santa Rosa, CA
Gallenstein, Angila L. ....Phoenix, AZ
Gallent, Amy ....Hartford, CT
Gallent, Judith M. ....New York, NY
Gallent, Martin ....New York, NY
Galler, David E. ....Atlanta, GA
Galler, Debi Evans ....Miami, FL
Galler, Eric S. ....Washington, DC
Baltimore, MD
Galler, Gregory G. ....Stillwater, MN
Galler, Julius ....Marietta, GA
Galler, Linda ....Hempstead, NY
Galler, Perry S. ....New York, NY
Galler, Richard P. ....Hackensack, NJ
Galler, Sheryl ....New York, NY
Gallerani, Tammy-lyn ....Walnut Creek, CA
Gallerano, A.J. ....Dripping Springs, TX
Gallerano, Lisa S. ....Dallas, TX
Gallerizzo, Michael G. ....Baltimore, MD
Gallers, Jackie, (Mr.) ....Brooklyn, NY
Gallerson, Bryan K. ....Allen, TX
Plano, TX
Gallerstein, Edgar ....Mount Kisco, NY
Gallery, Daniel F. ....Sacramento, CA
Gallery, Gary M. ....Sacramento, CA
Gallery, Jennifer G. ....Chicago, IL
Gallery, Michael J. ....Columbia, SC
Gallery, Patrick M. ....Bellingham, WA
Gallery, Thomas F. ....Sacramento, CA
Gallery-Fox, Elizabeth Leslie
Bellingham, WA
Galles, Dale F. ....Billings, MT
Galles, Duane L.C.M. ....Minneapolis, MN
Galles, Kristen M. ....Alexandria, VA
Galles, Patrick C. ....Cedar Falls, IA
Gallese, Paul D. ....Wellesley, MA
Gallese, William F. ....Port St. Lucie, FL
Gallese, William F., P.A.
Port St. Lucie, FL
Galles Lhost, Kathleen ....Appleton, WI
Gallet Dreyer & Berkey, LLP
New York, NY
Gallet, Jeffry H. ....New York, NY
Galletta, Brian K. ....Chatham, MA
Galletti, Joseph ....Orlando, FL
Galletti, Joseph, P.A. ....Orlando, FL
Galley, John R. ....Antioch, IL
Galley, Kelly Ann ....Myrtle Beach, SC
Galley, Kevin R. ....Lacon, IL
Galley, Robert W. ....Twin Falls, ID
Galli, Cesare J., Jr. ....Friendswood, TX
Galli, Craig D. ....Salt Lake City, UT
Galli, Linda Bissett ....Reno, NV
Galli, Mary Ann ....Blue Bell, PA
Galli, Matthew G. ....Pendleton, OR
Galli, Nicholas A. ....Carnegie, PA
Galli, Nicole D. ....Philadelphia, PA
Galli, Reilly & Stellato ....Collingswood, NJ
Philadelphia, PA
Galli, Richard R. ....Philadelphia, PA
Galli, Robert E. ....Farmington, CT
Galli, Robert G. ....New York, NY
Galli, Stacie G. ....Los Angeles, CA
Galli, Susan M. ....Boston, MA
Galli, Thomas ....Washington, DC
Gallia, Garrett F. ....Hershey, PA
Gallia, Jay L. ....Houston, TX
Gallian, Russell J., (PC) ....St. George, UT
Gallian, Westfall, Wilcox & Wright, L.L.C.
St. George, UT

Galliani & Doell, Ltd. .... Chicago, IL
Galliani, Fritzie .... Pasadena, CA
Galliani, William R. .... Chicago, IL
Galliani, William S. .... Palo Alto, CA
Galliano, Gary T. .... San Leandro, CA
Galliart, Lyle R. .... Dubuque, IA
Gallicchio, Joseph J. .... Torrington, CT
Gallicchio, Merati & Griffin .... Torrington, CT
Gallick, Lawrence J. .... Buffalo, NY
Gallie, Picton E. .... Whitestone, NY
Gallien, Mark F. .... Martin, TN
Gallien, Mark F., P.C. .... Martin, TN
Galligan, Anne T. .... Hempstead, NY
Galligan, Arthur J. .... Washington, DC
Galligan & Biscay, P.C. .... San Mateo, CA
Galligan, Colleen D. .... Albany, NY
Galligan, Daniel S. .... Milwaukee, WI
Galligan, Gregory J. .... Rye Brook, NY
Galligan, John P. .... Belton, TX
Galligan, Joseph A. .... San Mateo, CA
Galligan, Kevin M. .... Palo Alto, CA
Galligan, Lawrence W. .... Tucson, AZ
Galligan & Manning .... Houston, TX
Galligan, Mary P. .... Omaha, NE
Galligan, Mary S. .... Houston, TX
Galligan, Matthew G. .... Wallingford, CT
Galligan, Michael D. .... McMinnville, TN
Galligan, Michael F. .... San Mateo, CA
Galligan, Michael J. .... Des Moines, IA
Galligan, Michael W. .... New York, NY
Galligan & Newman .... McMinnville, TN
Galligan, Patricia M. .... San Diego, CA
Galligan, Paul .... New York, NY
Galligan, Robert L. .... Weslaco, TX
Galligan, Susan R. .... New York, NY
Galligan, Terrence J. .... Boston, MA
Galligan, Thomas C. .... Montclair, NJ
Galligan, Thomas Michael
Staten Island, NY
Galligan, Timothy E. .... Detroit, MI
Galligan, Tully, Doyle & Reid, P.C.
Des Moines, IA
Galligan, William C. .... Newington, CT
Galligano, Myrna L. .... Orlando, FL
Galligher, Grace A. .... Sacramento, CA
Galliher, Dennis M. .... Troy, NY
Galliher, James M. .... Fitchburg, MA
Galliher, Keith E., Jr. .... Las Vegas, NV
Galliher, Keith E., Jr., Chartered
Las Vegas, NV
Galliher, Mark R. .... Indianapolis, IN
Galliher, Sean Patrick .... Honeoye Falls, NY
Gallik, Brian K. .... Bozeman, MT
Galliker, Lauren E. .... New York, NY
Galliker, Marie Paulette .... Barnstable, MA
Gallimore, Allan G. .... Altoona, PA
Pittsburgh, PA
Gallimore, Amy E. .... Birmingham, AL
Gallimore, Kim W. .... High Point, NC
Gallin, Dean E.
Department Of Veterans Affairs, Office of the General Counsel, GV
Gallin, Fredric P. .... Rahway, NJ
Gallin, Martin .... Bronx, NY
Gallin & Newman .... Bronx, NY
Gallina, Anthony N. .... Rochelle Park, NJ
Gallina, Dawn M. .... Reston, VA
Gallina, Fred S. .... Rochester, NY
Gallina, Scott D. .... Lewiston, ID
Gallina, William A. .... Bronx, NY
Gallina-Mecca, Jane .... Fair Lawn, NJ
Gallinar, Michael D. .... Miami, FL
Gallinari, Christopher L. .... Chicago, IL
Gallinaro, James J. .... Annandale, VA
Gallin-Dwyer, Alice J. .... Washington, DC
Gallinger, Geoffrey S. .... Detroit, MI
Gallinger, John L., (P.C.) .... Jackson, WY
Gallinger, Susan .... Phoenix, AZ
Gallinghouse, Gerald J. .... New Orleans, LA
Gallinghouse, Robert E., III .... San Diego, CA
Gallinghouse, Scott P. .... New Orleans, LA
Gallington, Debra L. .... La Porte, TX
Gallini, John J. .... Boston, MA
Gallini, Jon C. (Kit) .... Lubbock, TX
Gallini, Ralph W. .... Lovington, NM
Gallion, Baker & Bray, P.S.C.
Lexington, KY
Gallion, Edward R. .... New York, NY
Gallion, Gerald Alan .... Houston, TX
Gallion, Michael L. .... Los Angeles, CA
Gallion, Theresa M. .... Chicago, IL
Gallion, Thomas T., III .... Montgomery, AL
Gallion, William J. .... Lexington, KY
Gallione, John J. .... New York, NY
Gallios, Aris J. .... Phoenix, AZ
Gallios, Barbara J. .... San Francisco, CA
Gallios-Lee, Barbara .... San Francisco, CA
Gallipoli, Marianne J. .... Westbury, NY
Gallipoli, Maurice J. .... Jersey City, NJ
Gallis, Joel .... New York, NY
Gallishen, William Charles .... Pittsburgh, PA
Gallitano, Andrea L. .... Barre, VT
Gallitano, Dennis J. .... Chicago, IL
Gallitano, Joseph R., & Associates
Plymouth, MA
Gallitano, Thomas J. .... Boston, MA
Gallitto, Robyn R. .... Ellwood City, PA
Gallitto, William J. .... Hartford, CT
Gallivan, Bonnie L. .... Indianapolis, IN
Gallivan, Daniel F. .... Central Valley, NY
Gallivan, Erin H. .... Rutland, VT
Gallivan, Gerald M. .... Laramie, WY
Gallivan, Hamilton, Seese & Patterson
Bluffton, IN
Ossian, IN
Gallivan, Henry Mills .... Greenville, SC
Gallivan, Jeremiah P. .... Minneapolis, MN
Gallivan, Joan C. .... Foxboro, MA
Gallivan, John E. .... Rocky Hill, CT
Gallivan, Karen Park .... Minneapolis, MN
Gallivan, Melissa A. .... Boston, MA
Gallivan, Richard S. F. .... Buffalo, NY
Gallivan, Robert H. .... Westminster, CA
Gallivan, Sarah M. .... Natick, MA
Gallman, C. Michael .... Lufkin, TX
Gallman, James R., Jr. .... Texarkana, TX
Gallman, Lawrence F. .... Orlando, FL
Gallman, Leslie L. .... Sugar Land, TX
Gallmeyer, Meg A. .... Fort Wayne, IN
Gallmeyer, Thomas M. .... Fort Wayne, IN
Gallner, Gary M. .... Goodyear, AZ
Gallner, Gary M., P.C. .... Goodyear, AZ
Gallner, Michael .... Council Bluffs, IA
Gallner, Sheldon M. .... Council Bluffs, IA
Gallner, Sheldon, P.C. .... Council Bluffs, IA
Gallner, William .... Coral Gables, FL
Gallo, A. Andrew .... Austin, TX
Gallo, Anthony P. .... Commack, NY
Gallo, Antoinette A., (Ms.) .... New York, NY
Gallo & Associates .... Los Angeles, CA
Gallo & Associates, P.C. .... Seal Beach, CA
Gallo, Barbara H. .... Atlanta, GA
Gallo, Bennett R. .... Coventry, RI
Gallo Brown and Ross, L.L.P.
Washington, DC
Gallo, Bruce Steven .... Columbus, OH
Gallo, Carlene Ruth .... Scranton, PA
Gallo, Catherine .... Simsbury, CT
Gallo, Charles J. .... Cleveland, OH
Gallo, Charles J., Jr. .... Cleveland, OH
Gallo, Charles P. .... Astoria, NY
Gallo, Christopher A. .... Corning, NY
Gallo, Christopher P. .... Montvale, NJ
Gallo, Coby D.
Department of Labor, GV
Gallo, Dana C. .... New York, NY
Gallo & Darmanian .... Flemington, NJ
New York, NY
Gallo, David A. .... Sunnyside, NY
Gallo, David G. .... Greenwich, CT
Rye Brook, NY
Gallo, David J. .... San Diego, CA
Gallo, David R. .... Danbury, CT
Gallo, Diane C. .... Hackensack, NJ
Gallo, Domenick A. .... San Diego, CA
Gallo, Donald J. .... Beacon, NY
Gallo, Donald P. .... Milwaukee, WI
Gallo, Elissa E. .... Philadelphia, PA
Gallo, F. James .... Denver, CO
Gallo, Ferdinand J., III .... Chicago, IL
Gallo, Frank J. .... Philadelphia, PA
Gallo, Frank J. .... Palmyra, VA
Gallo & Gallo .... Cleveland, OH
Gallo Geffner Fenster, P.C.
Hackensack, NJ
Gallo, Geffner, Fenster, Turitz & Harraka
New York, NY
Gallo & Gownley .... Scranton, PA
Gallo, Gregory John .... New York, NY
Gallo, Gregory M. .... Palo Alto, CA
Gallo, James A. .... Los Angeles, CA
Gallo, James A. .... Pasadena, CA
Gallo, James C., Jr. .... Las Vegas, NV
Gallo, James J. .... Jersey City, NJ
Gallo, Joan A. .... Mineola, NY
Gallo, Joan R. .... San Jose, CA
Gallo, John M. .... Grafton, WI
Gallo, John N. .... Chicago, IL
Gallo, John R. .... New York, NY
Gallo, John S. .... Joliet, IL
Gallo, Joie Marie .... Los Angeles, CA
Gallo, Jon J. .... Los Angeles, CA
Gallo, Joseph .... Washington, DC
Gallo, Joseph A. .... Newark, NJ
Gallo, Joseph J. .... Daleville, AL
Gallo, Joseph J. .... Roanoke, VA
Gallo, Joseph P. .... Seal Beach, CA
Gallo, Judith L. .... Park Ridge, IL
Gallo, Katherine L. .... Foster City, CA
Gallo, Kathleen .... Sunnyside, NY
Gallo, Kenneth A. .... Washington, DC
Gallo, Laura A.
Federal Communications Commission, Mass Media Bureau, GV
Gallo, Linda Vellis .... Albany, NY
Gallo, Lori M. .... Cleveland, OH
Gallo, Louis T. .... Ridgewood, NJ
Gallo, Maria C. .... North Miami Beach, FL
Gallo, Matthew J. .... Chicago, IL
Gallo, Michael A. .... Hackensack, NJ
New York, NY
Gallo, Michael A. .... Youngstown, OH
Gallo, Michael A., Jr. .... Roseland, NJ
Gallo, Nicholas A., III .... Flemington, NJ
New York, NY
Gallo, Olivia F. .... Santa Ana, CA
Gallo, Oscar, Jr. .... Chicago, IL
Gallo, Paul J. .... Norcross, GA
Gallo, Paul J. .... Columbia, MD
Gallo, Penny Howe .... Palo Alto, CA
Gallo, Philip W. .... New York, NY
Gallo, Ray A. .... Los Osos, CA
San Luis Obispo, CA
Gallo, Ray Edwin .... Los Angeles, CA
Gallo Reinan & Marek, LLC .... Denver, CO
Gallo, Robert C., II .... Pittsburgh, PA
Gallo, Robert D. .... Hempstead, NY
Gallo, Robert J. .... Hartford, CT
Gallo, Robert J. .... Dover, NH
Gallo, Robert T. .... Valley Stream, NY
Gallo, Ruth .... New York, NY
Gallo, Samuel J. .... Cambridge, MA
Gallo, Stephen A. .... Staten Island, NY
Gallo, Thea Lucy .... Lakewood, OH
Gallo, Thomas J. .... Atlanta, GA
Gallo, Thomas J. .... Hampton, VA
Gallo, Tibor M. .... St. Paul, MN
Gallo, Vincent L., Jr. .... New York, NY
Gallo, Vivian Menge .... Philadelphia, PA
Gallo, Wayne A. .... Miami, FL
Gallo, William F.
Department of Transportation, Federal Aviation Administration, GV
Gallogly, Andrew J. .... Philadelphia, PA
Gallogly, Barry A. .... Brooklyn, NY
Gallogly, Brian P. .... Providence, RI
Gallogly, David A. .... Greenville, PA
Gallogly, David L. .... Boston, MA
Gallogly, John R. .... The Woodlands, TX
Gallogly, Margaret R. .... Phoenix, AZ
Gallogly, Paul V. .... Warwick, RI
Gallogly, Richard J. .... Boston, MA
Gallogly, Stephanie K. .... Meadville, PA
Gallogly, Timothy A. .... Philadelphia, PA
Gallogly, Timothy P. .... Providence, RI
Gallogly, Vincent .... Norwalk, CT
Gallogly, William J. .... Westerly, RI
Gallogly, William W. .... Jacksonville, FL
Gallo-Kotcher, Sharon .... New York, NY
Gallon, E. S., & Associates .... Dayton, OH
Gallon, Jack E. .... Toledo, OH
Gallon, Mark M. .... Manhattan Beach, CA
Gallon, Rosemary .... Tucson, AZ
Gallon, Stanley J. .... Los Angeles, CA
Gallon & Takacs Co., L.P.A. .... Toledo, OH
Gallone, Anthony M. .... Warwick, RI
Gallone, Anthony M., Jr. .... Providence, RI
Gallone, Richard T. .... New Bedford, MA
Gallop, David H. .... Washington, DC
Gallop, Donald P. .... St. Louis, MO
Gallop, Earl G. .... Miami, FL
Gallop, Elizabeth I. .... Chesterfield, MO
Gallop, Jennifer .... Boston, MA
Gallop, Johnson & Neuman, L.C.
St. Louis, MO
Gallop, Jonathan D. .... Minneapolis, MN
Gallop, M. Robert .... New York, NY
Gallop, Marshall Aubrey, Jr.
Rocky Mount, NC
Gallop, Robert J. .... Livingston, NJ
Gallop, Wayne E. .... Pasadena, CA
Gallopoulos, Gregory S. .... Chicago, IL
Gallot, Richard J., Jr. .... Ruston, LA
Gallovic, John G. .... Mentor, OH
Galloway, Albert C., Jr. .... Lake Wales, FL
Galloway, Alexander T., II .... New York, NY
Galloway, Alexander T., III .... Marietta, GA
Galloway, Amy J. .... Fort Lauderdale, FL
Galloway & Associates, P.A. .... Orlando, FL
Galloway, Ball & Cossa, P.L.C.
Fairfax, VA
Galloway, Ben F., III .... Gulfport, MS
Galloway, Bret .... Greenville, SC
Galloway, Bruce C. .... Dallas, TX
Galloway, Bruce C. .... Lake Stevens, WA
Galloway, Bruce H. .... Caruthersville, MO
Galloway, Bruce W. .... Los Angeles, CA
Galloway, Carolyn E. .... Anderson, SC
Galloway, Charles R. .... Gulfport, MS
Galloway, Charles R. .... Jackson, MS
Galloway, Chester S. .... Newark, NJ
Galloway, Clyde W. (Billy), Jr.
Tallahassee, FL
Galloway, Daniel B. .... Denver, CO
Galloway, David H. .... Plant City, FL
Galloway, David K. .... Chesterton, IN
Galloway, Don F. .... Green Bay, WI
Galloway, Donna D. .... Stuttgart, AR
Galloway, Duane L. .... Sandusky, OH
Galloway, E. Dexter .... Hutchinson, KS
Galloway, Edward A. .... Irvine, CA
Galloway, Edward H. .... Greensboro, NC
Galloway, Edward L. .... Louisville, KY
Galloway, Elizabeth A. .... Cincinnati, OH
Galloway, Frances C. .... Scarsdale, NY
Galloway, Frank C., III .... Birmingham, AL
Galloway, Frank C., Jr. .... Birmingham, AL
Galloway, George M. .... Portland, OR
Galloway, George Patrick
Walnut Creek, CA
Galloway, Gerald D. .... Dickinson, ND
Galloway, Graham A. .... Reno, NV
Galloway, Gregory B. .... Orlando, FL
Galloway, H. Harrell .... Mobile, AL
Galloway, Harold L. .... Rochester, NY
Galloway, Harry A. .... Oroville, CA
Galloway, Henry H., Jr. .... Littleton, CO
Galloway, Hunter H., III .... Greensboro, NC
Galloway, J. Scott .... Seattle, WA
Galloway, Jackson B.R. .... Boston, MA
Galloway, James B. .... Gulfport, MS
Galloway, James C., Jr. (A Professional Corporation) .... Los Angeles, CA
Galloway, Jean R. .... Fairfax, VA
Galloway, Jeff H. .... New York, NY
Galloway, Jennifer M.
Mount Pleasant, MI
Galloway & Jensen, A Professional Corporation
Reno, NV
Galloway, Jesse C. .... Rochester, NY
Galloway, John E. .... New Orleans, LA
Houston, TX
Galloway, John H., III .... Scarsdale, NY
Galloway, John L. .... Gulfport, MS
Galloway, John W., Jr. .... Huntsville, TN
Galloway, John W. (Wil), Jr. .... Beeville, TX
Galloway, Johnson, Tompkins & Burr, A Professional Law Corporation
Gulf Breeze, FL
New Orleans, LA
Houston, TX
Galloway, Joseph M. .... Des Moines, IA
Galloway, Judith T. .... Darnestown, MD
Galloway, Judy L. .... Santa Clara, CA
Galloway, Kathleen Vance .... Dallas, TX
Galloway, L. Thomas .... Boulder, CO
Galloway, Lien Dang .... Washington, DC
Galloway, Mark Ellis .... Roxboro, NC
Galloway, Michael C. .... Carmel, IN
Galloway, Michael G. .... Phoenix, AZ
Galloway, Michael M. .... Westminster, MD
Galloway, Michelle Greer .... Palo Alto, CA
Galloway, Morris A. .... Yukon, OK
Galloway, Morris A., P.C. .... Yukon, OK
Galloway & Moss .... Birmingham, AL
Vernon, AL
Galloway, Newton M., & Associates
Griffin, GA
Galloway, Pamela R. .... Highland Park, MI
Galloway, Peter D. .... New York, NY
Galloway, Peter S. .... New Brunswick, NJ
Galloway, Phillip H., Jr. .... Memphis, TN
Galloway, Raymond Forrest .... Helena, AR
Galloway, Richard H. .... Greensburg, PA
Galloway, Robert C. .... Gulfport, MS
Galloway, Robert L. .... Houston, TX
Galloway, Robert M. .... Mobile, AL
Galloway, Robert R. .... Cleveland, OH
Galloway, Robert S., III .... Greenville, SC
Galloway, Robert W. .... Pooler, GA
Galloway, Rocky J. .... Plano, TX
Galloway, Sara E. .... Atlanta, GA
Galloway, Scott D. .... Media, PA
Galloway, Shanda C. .... Macon, GA
Galloway, Sidney B. .... Shreveport, LA
Galloway, Smith, Wettermark & Everest, LLP .... Bay Minette, AL
Mobile, AL
Galloway, Thomas M. .... Mobile, AL
Galloway, Thomas M., Jr. .... Mobile, AL
Galloway, Timothy E. .... Neenah, WI
Galloway, Toby M. .... Dallas, TX
Galloway, Tom F. .... Green Bay, WI
Galloway, Tracy Dale .... Boston, MA
Galloway, Wanzo, Jr. .... Winter Springs, FL
Galloway, Wiegers & Heeney
Blue Rapids, KS
Marysville, KS
Galloway, William D.
Department of Transportation, Surface Transportation Board, GV
Galloway, William E., The Law Offices of
Weirton, WV
Galloway, William F., III .... Maynard, MA
Galloway, William T., Jr. .... Huntsville, AL
Galloway, William Woodson .... Atlanta, GA
Gallozzi, Marialuisa S. .... Washington, DC
Gallt, Leslie W. .... New York, NY
Gallu, Christopher T., Jr. .... Washington, DC
Gallub, Michael B. .... New York, NY
Gallucci, Anita T. .... Madison, WI
Gallucci, Anthony .... Cleveland, OH
Gallucci, Cara L. .... East Providence, RI
Gallucci, Dante R. .... Bridgeport, CT
Gallucci, Frank L. .... Fort Wayne, IN
Gallucci, Hopkins & Theisen, P.C.
Fort Wayne, IN
Gallucci, John A., Jr. .... Piermont, NY
Gallucci, Mario F. .... Staten Island, NY
Gallucci-Davis, Sheila .... Cherry Hill, NJ
Galluccio, Adolph J. .... Paterson, NJ
Galluccio, John V. .... New York, NY
Galluccio, Robert J. .... Paterson, NJ
Galluci, Joseph R. .... San Jose, CA
Gallucio, Anthony S. .... Arlington, VA
Gallucio, Donna D. .... Newark, NJ
Gallun, Frederic P. .... Baltimore, MD
Gallup, Burns & Mills .... Cleveland, OH
Gallup, Charles E. (Bud) .... Vancouver, WA
Gallup, Cynthia L. .... Kansas City, MO
Gallup, Dana H. .... Boston, MA
Gallup, Dana M. .... Miami, FL
Gallup, Daniel .... North Miami, FL
Gallup, David B. .... Cleveland, OH
Gallup, David M. .... Washington, DC
Gallup, Frederick W. .... Bradford, PA
Gallup & Hadley .... Boston, MA
Gallup, J. William .... Omaha, NE
Gallup, John Y. .... Buffalo, NY
Gallup, Joy K. .... New York, NY
Gallup, Nancy L. .... Seattle, WA
Gallup & Schaefer .... Omaha, NE
Gallup, Wallace H., Jr. .... Kailua-Kona, HI
Galluzzo, Gino .... Rockford, IL
Galluzzo, John C., Jr. .... Boston, MA
Galluzzo, John D. .... Fern Park, FL
Galluzzo, Sally Lee .... Pine Ridge, SD
Gallwey Gillman Curtis Vento & Horn, P.A.
Miami, FL
Gallwey, William J., III .... Miami, FL
Gally, Joseph James, Jr. .... Allison Park, PA
Gally, Karen Russell .... Washington, DC
Galm, Sharon .... Treasury Department, Internal Revenue Service, GV
Galman, James J. .... St. Paul, MN
Galnick, Mitchell .... Longmont, CO
Galo, Blanca P. .... San Antonio, TX
Galo, Daniel T. .... West Palm Beach, FL
Galo, Matthew G. .... Chicago, IL
Galo, Michael V., Jr. .... San Antonio, TX
Galonski, John F. .... Ashland, OH
Galonsky, Marc W.F. .... Atlanta, GA
Galoozis, Theofilos G. .... Richmond, VA
Galopin, Gary J. .... Farmington Hills, MI
Galos, Ernest P. .... South Bend, IN
Galos, Jodie-Beth H. .... Salisbury, CT
Galosic, Joseph M. .... Costa Mesa, CA
Galosy, Richard A. .... St. Louis, MO
Galotto, John A. .... Department of Justice, Tax Division, GV
Galow, Jerry .... Austin, TX
Galowich, David H. .... Chicago, IL

Galowich & Galowich ... Chicago, IL
Galowich, Jeffrey A. ... Chicago, IL
Galowich, Lee Ann S. ... Chicago, IL
Galowich, Ronald H. ... Chicago, IL
Galowitz, Sam W. ... New York, NY
Galowitz, Tracey A. ... Lake Elmo, MN
Galpeer, Irving J. ... New York, NY
Galper, Allan S. ... New York, NY
Galper, Howard D. ... Chicago, IL
Galper, Mark S. ... Monessen, PA
Galper, Steven R. ... Tucson, AZ
Galperin, Gary J. ... New York, NY
Galperin, Richard ... Wilmington, DE
Galperin, Robert M. ... Dallas, TX
Galperin, Ron ... Los Angeles, CA
Galpern, Craig S. ... Medford, OR
Galpern, Daniel H. ... New York, NY
Galpern, Michael A. ... Philadelphia, PA
Galpern, Sharon K. ... Mount Laurel, NJ
Galperson, David S. ... Long Beach, CA
Galperson, Herbert I. ... Ontario, CA
Galske, William, III ... Plainville, CT
Galsor, Matt ... Los Angeles, CA
Galst, Jonathan ... Washington, DC
New York, NY
Galstad, Richard D. ... Osseo, WI
Galstad, Ronald Irvin ... Grand Forks, ND
Galstan, Margaret S. ... Omaha, NE
Galstan, William R. ... Antioch, CA
Galsterer, Andrew J., Jr.
Mount Clemens, MI
Galston, Clarence E. ... New York, NY
Galston, Jeffrey L. ... Richmond, VA
Galt, Bonnie Chambless ... Los Angeles, CA
Galt, Frederick B. ... Albany, NY
Galt, George ... Washington, DC
Galt, H. Douglas ... Los Angeles, CA
Galt, Jason ... Encinitas, CA
Galt, Jay M. ... Oklahoma City, OK
Galt, Louise R. ... Helena, MT
Galt, Martin E., III ... St. Louis, MO
Galt, Richard Andrew ... Bennington, VT
Galt, Robert B., III ... Miami, FL
Galt & Siegel ... Rockville, MD
Galt, Stephen H. ... Rockville, MD
Galt & Swanberg ... Helena, MT
Galter, Paul E. ... Lincoln, NE
Galteri, Patricia ... Mineola, NY
Galteri, Stephanie C. ... Riverhead, NY
Galterio, Gregory E. ... Hawthorne, NJ
New York, NY
Galtman, Richard B. ... Fresno, CA
Galtney, David K. ... New Orleans, LA
Galton, Eric R. ... Austin, TX
Galton, Gary M. ... Portland, OR
Galton & Helm LLP ... Los Angeles, CA
Palm Desert, CA
Galton, I. Glenn ... Richardson, TX
Galton, Jeremy ... Plainsboro, NJ
Galton, Scott & Colett ... Portland, OR
Galton, Sidney A. ... Portland, OR
Galton, Stephen H. ... Los Angeles, CA
Galton, Zanley F. ... Portland, OR
Galuchie, Doris M. ... Trenton, NJ
Galumbeck, Robert M. ... Tazewell, VA
Galuppo, Christopher J. ... New Haven, CT
Galuppo, Louis A. ... San Diego, CA
Galusha, Timothy S. ... San Francisco, CA
Galuszka, Paul J. ... Metairie, LA
Galuszka, Paul J., A Professional Law Corporation ... Metairie, LA
Galvagna, Anthony L. ... Boston, MA
Galvan, Armando M. ... Los Angeles, CA
Galvan, Cynthia A. ... Houston, TX
Galvan, Elba-Rose ... New York, NY
Galván, Emilio A. ... New York, NY
Galvan, Ernest J. ... San Francisco, CA
Galvan, Hilda C. ... Dallas, TX
Galvan, Joe H. ... Las Cruces, NM
Galvan, Luis ... Chicago, IL
Galvan, Mary Elizabeth ... Laramie, WY
Galvan, Oscar G. ... San Antonio, TX
Galvan, Patricia Hoon ... Arlington, TX
Galvan, Ramon P. ... Los Angeles, CA
Galvan, Rebecca L. ... San Antonio, TX
Galvan, Rebecca L., P.C., Law Offices of
San Antonio, TX
Galvan, Richard J. ... Phoenix, AZ
Galvan, Robert A. ... El Paso, TX
Galvan, Robt. J. ... El Paso, TX
Galvan, Tanya Vigil ... Riverside, CA
Galvani, Ann M. ... Scarsdale, NY
Galvani, Geraldine P. ... San Francisco, CA
Galvani, Paul B. ... Boston, MA
Galvani, Paul V. ... Framingham, MA
Galvani, Victor H. ... Framingham, MA
Galvano, Douglas Frank
North Tonawanda, NY
Galvano, Joseph ... New York, NY
Galvano, William S. ... Bradenton, FL
Galvão, Susan E. ... White Plains, NY
Galvarro, Sarah R. ... Nashville, TN
Galvas, Walter W. ... West Carrollton, OH
Galves, Fred ... Denver, CO
Galvez, Jason C. ... Bryan, TX
Galvez, Michael L. ... Denver, CO
Galvez, Miguel, Jr. ... Las Vegas, NV
Galvez and Peralta, P.C. ... Denver, CO
Galvez, Sheila R. ... Chicago, IL
Galvez-Lantion Law ... Los Angeles, CA
Galvez-Lantion, Mae R. ... Los Angeles, CA
Galvin & Associates ... North Andover, MA
Galvin, Catherine Buttice ... Olympia, WA
Galvin, Charles J. ... Philadelphia, PA
Galvin, Chas. O. ... Dallas, TX
Galvin, Christine M. ... Latham, NY
Galvin, Clare E., (Mr.)
South Sioux City, NE

Galvin, Dale J. ... Seattle, WA
Galvin, Daniel C. ... Sioux City, IA
Galvin, Daniel J., III ... Santa Rosa, CA
Galvin, Daniel L. ... Naples, FL
Galvin, Daniel W. ... Olympia, WA
Galvin, Deborah L. ... Northfield, IL
Galvin, Dennis M. ... Jackson, NJ
Galvin, Edward F. ... Dover, MA
Galvin, Emmett J. ... Chicago, IL
Galvin, Eugene G. ... Jersey City, NJ
Galvin, Frank J., Jr. ... Rock Island, IL
Galvin, G. Michael ... Alameda, CA
Galvin, Galvin & Leeney
Crown Point, IN
Hammond, IN
Galvin, Harriett ... Miami, FL
Galvin, James R., P.C. ... Chicago, IL
Galvin, James V. ... Middletown, NY
Galvin, Jeanne ... Elmhurst, IL
Galvin, Jeffrey S. ... Sacramento, CA
Galvin, Jodyann ... Buffalo, NY
Galvin, John B. ... Reno, NV
Galvin, John D. ... Des Moines, IA
Galvin, John E. ... Belleville, IL
St. Louis, MO
Galvin, John F. ... Slidell, LA
Galvin, John J. ... New York, NY
Galvin, John Patrick, Sr.
Monarch Beach, CA
Galvin, Joseph F. ... Detroit, MI
Galvin, June R. ... Toledo, OH
Galvin, Kenneth J. ... Chicago, IL
Galvin, Kerry A. ... Houston, TX
Galvin, Kevin P. ... Morristown, NJ
Galvin, Lawrence Francis
Washington, DC
Galvin, Lewis, Watson & Galvin
Chicago, IL
Galvin, Madeline Sheila ... Delmar, NY
Galvin, Malcolm Patrick, III
North Andover, MA
Galvin, Margaret C. ... St. Paul, MN
Galvin, Margaret Royce ... Hammond, IN
Galvin, Mark Gerard ... Lincoln, NE
Galvin, Mark L. ... Providence, RI
Galvin, Martin Jay ... Detroit, MI
Galvin, Martin T. ... Cleveland, OH
Galvin, Mary M. ... Milford, CT
Galvin, Michael B. ... Boston, MA
Galvin, Michael J. ... Rock Island, IL
Galvin, Michael J., Jr. ... St. Paul, MN
Galvin and Mlawski ... New York, NY
Galvin & Morgan ... Delmar, NY
Galvin, Neil P. ... Newport, RI
Galvin, Patricia Jeanne
San Francisco, CA
Galvin, Patrick J. ... Hammond, IN
Galvin, Patrick S. ... Anchorage, AK
Galvin, Paul E., Law Offices of
Dallas, TX
Galvin, Paul F. ... Lowell, MA
Galvin, Paul Timothy ... Fall River, MA
Galvin, Peter D. ... Department of Labor, Office of the Solicitor, GV
Galvin, Robert E. ... Duxbury, MA
Galvin, Robert J. ... Boston, MA
Galvin, Robert M. ... Cupertino, CA
Galvin, Sarah E. ... Oakland, CA
Galvin, Stephen P. ... Merced, CA
Galvin, Thomas F.
Research Triangle Park, NC
Galvin, Timothy P., Jr. ... Hammond, IN
Galvin, Vincent ... North Andover, MA
Galvin, Vincent, Jr. ... San Jose, CA
Galvin, William A. ... Walnut Creek, CA
Galvin, William F. ... Brighton, MA
Galvin, William J., Jr. ... Boston, MA
Galvis, Louis Leonard ... New Orleans, LA
Galvis, Mary Lee White ... New York, NY
Galvis, Sandra J. ... New York, NY
Galvis, Sergio J. ... New York, NY
Galway, Andrew V. ... New York, NY
Galway, Carlyn Froerer ... Aptos, CA
Galway, Richard E., Jr. ... Concord, NH
Galyean, Anthony E. ... Marysville, CA
Galyean, Talley & Wood ... Escondido, CA
Galyean, Thomas E. ... Escondido, CA
Galyen, Jeffrey D. ... New Castle, IN
Galyen, Julia A. ... Chicago, IL
Galyen, Phillip ... Arlington, TX
Bedford, TX
Fort Worth, TX
Granbury, TX
Grand Prairie, TX
Irving, TX
Galyon, David G. ... Jackson, MS
Galyon, Jerry K. ... Sevierville, TN
Galyon, Justin Brent ... Oklahoma City, OK
Galyon Law Firm ... Sevierville, TN
Galysh, Theodore R. ... Centereach, NY
Gam, Gary A. ... Los Angeles, CA
Gama, J. Richard, (P.C.) ... Phoenix, AZ
Gamache, Christina B. ... Seattle, WA
Gamache, David A. ... St. Louis, MO
Gamache, David R. ... St. Louis, MO
Gamache, Eugene R. ... Bay Shore, NY
Gamache, H. Joseph ... Winooski, VT
Gamache, Jerome J. ... Portland, ME
Gamache Law Offices, P.C. ... Winooski, VT
Gamache, Peter C. ... Anchorage, AK
Gamache, Richard E. ... Boston, MA
Gamal, Vincent A. ... Houston, TX
Gamalski, Gregory J. ... Southfield, MI
Gamard, H. A. ... New Orleans, LA
Gamard, Walter T., II ... New Orleans, LA
Gamba, Mark E. ... Philadelphia, PA
Gamba, Paul A. ... Palm City, FL
Gamba, Paul J. ... San Francisco, CA

Gamba, Tomas F. ... Coral Gables, FL
Gamba, Tomas F., P.A. ... Coral Gables, FL
Gamba, Vincent ... New York, NY
Gambaccini, Sue A. ... Trenton, NJ
Gambach, David N. ... Miami, FL
Gambacorta, Bari J. ... Bellmawr, NJ
Gambacorta, Michael P. ... Saddle River, NJ
Gambale, Ganine ... Staten Island, NY
Gambale, Jo Ann ... San Diego, CA
Gambale, Maria C. ... New York, NY
Gambardella, Anthony J., Jr.
Richmond, VA
Gambardella, Anthony R. ... Uniondale, NY
Gambardella, Louis L. ... Winchester, MA
Gambardella, Mary A. ... Stamford, CT
Gambardella, Rosemary ... Newark, NJ
Gambardella, Steven C.
Woodland Hills, CA
Gambardella, Thomas M. ... New York, NY
Gambardella, Tracey ... Fort Lauderdale, FL
Gambaro, Ernest U. ... El Segundo, CA
Gambatese, Roger L. ... Davis, CA
Gambee, W. Scott ... Syracuse, NY
Gambel, Adam F. ... San Francisco, CA
Gambel, Gary J. ... New Orleans, LA
Gambel, Gregory F. ... New Orleans, LA
Gambel, Gregory F., A Professional Law Corporation ... New Orleans, LA
Gambel, William C., (P.C.)
New Orleans, LA
Gambell, Robert L. ... Cherry Hill, NJ
Gambell, Robert L. ... Clementon, NJ
Gambello, Geneen F. ... New York, NY
Gamber, Christopher R. ... Chapel Hill, NC
Gamber, Stephen ... Santa Monica, CA
Gamber, Terry H. ... Mount Vernon, IL
Gamber, Vibeke M. ... Dallas, TX
Gambera-Bentley, Elaina C. ... Riverside, CA
Gamberdell, Joseph V., Jr. ... Norwalk, CT
Gamberdella, Marc J. ... Santa Barbara, CA
Gamberdino, Nello P. ... Maywood, IL
Gamberg, Jay M. ... Hollywood, FL
Miami, FL
Gamberg, Jay M., P.A. ... Hollywood, FL
Miami, FL
Gambert, William N. ... Daytona Beach, FL
Gambescia, John J. ... Philadelphia, PA
Gambill, B. David ... Pawhuska, OK
Gambill, Barbara Fruehling ... Cincinnati, OH
Gambill, Bruce ... Pawhuska, OK
Gambill, Christopher B. ... Terre Haute, IN
Gambill, Gilbert W., Jr. ... Terre Haute, IN
Gambill, John E. ... Rantoul, IL
Gambill, Lawton G. ... Fort Worth, TX
Gambill, M. Arthur ... Atlanta, GA
Gambill, Mark G. ... Indianapolis, IN
Gambill, R. Brent ... Cincinnati, OH
Gambill, Stephen P. ... Gastonia, NC
Gambill, Walter R., P.C. ... Richmond, VA
Gambin, Paul G. ... Boulder, CO
Gambino, Darius C. ... Philadelphia, PA
Gambino, Jerry A. ... Buffalo, NY
Gambino, Jerry J. ... Rochester, NY
Gambino, Joseph A. ... Cleveland, OH
Gambino, Katherine Voskian
Old Tappan, NJ
Gambino, Lawrence F. ... Albany, NY
Gambino, Leonard J. ... Chicago, IL
Gambino, Mary Ellen ... San Francisco, CA
Gambino, Michelle ... Austin, TX
Gambino, Monica ... Pittsburgh, PA
Gambino, Nicholas J. ... Turnersville, NJ
Gamble, Albert R. ... Tucson, AZ
Gamble, Ann H. ... Titusville, PA
Gamble, Beth A. ... Westfield, MA
Gamble, Brent C. ... Houston, TX
Gamble, Bruce ... Washington, DC
Gamble, Cameron C. ... Metairie, LA
Gamble, Cameron C., A Professional Law Corporation ... Metairie, LA
New Orleans, LA
Gamble and Cannata, P.C. ... Houston, TX
Gamble, Carl F.
Federal Deposit Insurance Corporation, GV
Gamble, Carol Abrams ... Palo Alto, CA
Gamble, Charles W. ... Tuscaloosa, AL
Gamble, Christie L. ... Philadelphia, PA
Gamble, Clarence E. ... Las Vegas, NV
Gamble, Clarence E., P.C. ... Las Vegas, NV
Gamble, D. Geoffrey B. ... Wilmington, DE
Gamble, D. Jay ... Salt Lake City, UT
Gamble, Daniel J. ... Kokomo, IN
Gamble, David R. ... Minden, NV
Gamble, David S. ... Houston, TX
Gamble, E. James ... Bloomfield Hills, MI
Gamble, Edward A. ... New Castle, PA
Gamble, F. Page ... Birmingham, AL
Gamble, Frederick G. ... Tempe, AZ
Gamble, Gamble, Calame & Wilson, L.L.C.
Selma, AL
Gamble, Gerald L. ... Oklahoma City, OK
Gamble, Gwendolyn Millicent
Los Angeles, CA
Gamble, Harry W., Jr. ... Selma, AL
Gamble, Harry Whitehead, III ... Selma, AL
Gamble Hartshorn Johnson Co. LPA
Columbus, OH
Gamble, J. Michael ... Amherst, VA
Gamble, Jack R., Jr. ... Mansfield, LA
Gamble, James G. ... New York, NY
Gamble, James P. ... St. Louis, MO
Gamble, John B., Jr. ... Atlanta, GA
Gamble, John C. ... Irvine, CA
San Francisco, CA
Gamble, John E. ... Lisbon, OH
Gamble, Joseph G. ... Birmingham, AL
Gamble, J.Phil ... Austin, TX
Gamble, Kathy L. ... Hillsboro, OH

Gamble, Kenneth A. ... Columbus, OH
Gamble, Kristin L. ... Glendale, CA
Gamble Law Firm, The, P.C. ... Dothan, AL
Gamble, Mary Caroline ... Winston-Salem, NC
Gamble, Michael J. ... Dothan, AL
Gamble, Mojock, Piccione & Palmer, LLP
New Castle, PA
Gamble, Nicole Yvette ... New York, NY
Gamble, Patty S. ... Albany, GA
Gamble, Paul F. ... Bloomfield Hills, MI
Gamble, Ranelle A. ... Cleveland Heights, OH
Gamble, Richard H. ... Appleton, WI
Gamble, Richard O. ... Raleigh, NC
Gamble, Robert A. ... Des Moines, IA
Gamble, Rosenberger & Joswick LLP
Bloomfield Hills, MI
Detroit, MI
Gamble, S. Wayne, III ... Sumter, SC
Gamble, Susan Z. ... St. Louis, MO
Gamble, Thomas J. ... Santa Barbara, CA
Gamble, Thomas R. ... Birmingham, AL
Gamble, Travis S. ... Dallas, TX
Gamble, Wilbur Thomas, III ... Dawson, GA
Gamble, William ... Santa Ana, CA
Gamble, William B. ... Providence, RI
Gamble, William J. ... Selma, AL
Gamble, William J. ... Castroville, TX
Gamble, William J., III ... Purvis, MS
Gamble, William K. ... San Luis Obispo, CA
Santa Maria, CA
Santa Maria, CA
Gamble, William T. ... Kingsport, TN
Gamblin, Bryce David ... Jefferson City, MO
Gamblin, Doris C. ... Lexington, NC
Gamblin, Julie A. ... Omaha, NE
Gamblin, Richard D. ... Jackson, MS
Gamblin, Thomas W. ... San Antonio, TX
Gamboa, Anthony H.
General Accounting Office, Office of the General Counsel, GV
Gamboa, Armando M. ... Chicago, IL
Gamboa, Guadalupe ... Granger, WA
Gamboa, John L. ... Fort Worth, TX
Gamboa, René I., IV ... San Francisco, CA
Gamboa, Salvador A. ... Los Angeles, CA
Gamboa & Stovall ... Reno, NV
Gamboa, Theodore D. ... Reno, NV
Gambol, Robert A. ... Mentor, OH
Gamboli, Michael A. ... Providence, RI
Gamboney, William G., Jr. ... Oak Park, IL
Gamboni, Ciro A. ... New York, NY
Gambourian, A. Ashley ... Beverly Hills, CA
Gambrel, Alexander W. ... Spokane, WA
Gambrel, G. Keith ... Newport, KY
Gambrel, Kimberly ... Dayton, OH
Gambrel, Paul F. ... Youngstown, OH
Gambrell, Charles W. ... Columbia, SC
Gambrell, Charles W., Jr. ... Columbia, SC
Gambrell, Danette P. ... Warren, MI
Gambrell, David H. ... Atlanta, GA
Gambrell, Deborah J. ... Hattiesburg, MS
Gambrell, Elizabeth Reding ... Dallas, TX
Gambrell, Emmett A. ... Milwaukee, WI
Gambrell, Foster L., Jr. ... Anderson, SC
Gambrell, J. Eric ... Dallas, TX
Gambrell, James B. ... Austin, TX
Gambrell, John N., V ... Houston, TX
Gambrell, Lisa L. ... Houston, TX
Gambrell, Melinda J. ... Arlington, TX
Gambrell, Robert, & Associates ... Biloxi, MS
Gambrell & Stolz, L.L.P. ... Atlanta, GA
Gambrell, Todd M. ... Midland, MI
Gambriel, Richard J. ... Landover, MD
Gambril, Gregory L. ... Andalusia, AL
Gambrill, J. Matthew ... Solomons, MD
Gambrill, James H. ... Exeter, NH
Gambro, Michael S. ... New York, NY
Gambs, Charles R., Jr. ... Columbus, OH
Gambs, John R. ... Lafayette, IN
Gambs, Mucker, & Bauman ... Lafayette, IN
Gambucci Law Firm, Ltd. ... Minneapolis, MN
Gambucci, William J. ... Minneapolis, MN
Gamburg, Donald D. ... Philadelphia, PA
Gamburg, Jerome ... Philadelphia, PA
Gamburg, Robert Marc ... Philadelphia, PA
Game, P. Richard ... Atlanta, GA
Game, Paul, Jr. ... Tampa, FL
Game, Rachel ... Portland, OR
Gamel, Gary E. ... Woodside, CA
Gamel, Jason C. ... Orlando, FL
Gamel, Keith E. ... Austin, TX
Gamell, Mark S. ... New York, NY
Gamelson, Lyndon ... Wichita, KS
Gamer, Barbara T. ... San Diego, CA
Gamer, Charles P. ... Cambridge, MA
Gamer, Charles P., P.C. ... Cambridge, MA
Gamer, Daniel A. ... San Rafael, CA
Gamer, Janet G. ... Washington, DC
Gamerman, Berel R., (Mr.)
Treasury Department, GV
Gamerman, Gary E. ... Washington, DC
Gamerman, James P. ... Boston, MA
Gameros, Charles W., Jr. ... Dallas, TX
Gameros, Kathryn Becker ... Dallas, TX
Gamertsfelder, Ann M. ... Columbus, OH
Games, Alene M. ... Los Angeles, CA
Games, Laura V. ... Danville, NH
Games, Lynne J. ... Fairfax, VA
Games, Timothy E. ... Philadelphia, PA
Gamez, Jesse ... Crystal City, TX
Gamez, Jose A. ... San Antonio, TX
Gamez, Jose L. ... McAllen, TX
Gamez, Paul Daniel ... Cedar Rapids, IA
Gamiles, Dorothy A. ... Portland, OR
Gamin, Dean D. ... Cleveland, OH
Gamino, Daniel J. ... Oklahoma City, OK
Gamlen, Tod L. ... Palo Alto, CA
Gamliel, Eyal ... Los Angeles, CA

Gamliel, Martin Nardi ... New York, NY
Gamlin, John P. ... Fort Collins, CO
Gamm, Gordon ... Boulder, CO
Gamm, John R., Law Offices of
Wallingford, CT
Gamm, Morris ... Hamden, CT
Gamma, Frank E. ... Berkeley, CA
Gammage, Bruce W. ... Clinton, IL
Gammage & Burnham, P.L.C.
Phoenix, AZ
Gammage, Earl W. ... Houston, TX
Gammage, Emil Lamar, Jr.
Cedartown, GA
Gammage, Grady, Jr. ... Phoenix, AZ
Gammage, Gregory G. ... Farmer City, IL
Gammage Law Office ... Farmer City, IL
Gammage, Miles L. ... Cedartown, GA
Rome, GA
Gammage, Robert A." Bob " ... Dallas, TX
Gammarano, Paul J. ... Newark, NJ
Gammardella, Elena ... Staten Island, NY
Gammell, Barry R. ... Glendale, CA
Gammell, David D. ... Boston, MA
Gammell & Hoshor ... Dayton, OH
Gammell, Jeffrey W. ... Dayton, OH
Gammello, James M. ... Pequot Lakes, MN
Gammello & Sandelin, P.A.
Pequot Lakes, MN
Gammeltoft, Lisa Wolff ... Knoxville, TN
Gammeltoft, Lise Lotte ... Green Bay, WI
Gammerman, Daniel ... Melville, NY
Gammerman, Ira ... New York, NY
Gammicchia, Gasper J.
Clinton Township, MI
Gammicchia, Joseph A. ... Detroit, MI
Gammick, Richard A. ... Reno, NV
Gammie, John C. ... Tulsa, OK
Gammie, Sandra E. ... Cleveland, OH
Gammill & Gammill ... Hazen, AR
Gammill, J. Stephen ... Grand Junction, CO
Gammill, Kenneth M. ... Greenwich, CT
Gammill, Kenneth M., Jr. ... Greenwich, CT
New York, NY
Gammill, Margaret M. ... Hazen, AR
Gammill, Martha Ann ... Kalamazoo, MI
Gammill, Randall L. ... Hazen, AR
Gammill, Sam Hooper ... Jackson, MS
Gammill, Victor L. ... Newport Beach, CA
Gammill, Warren P. ... Miami, FL
Gammon & Anderson ... Cedartown, GA
Gammon, Elinor W. ... Washington, DC
Gammon, Floyd J. ... Belleair, FL
Gammon, Garry Brent ... Half Moon Bay, CA
Gammon & Grange, P.C.
Washington, DC
McLean, VA
Gammon, James A. ... McLean, VA
Gammon, Juli A. ... San Francisco, CA
Gammon, Julian, III ... New York, NY
Gammon & Matthews ... Houston, TX
Gammon, Nannette ... West Palm Beach, FL
Gammon, Ray E. ... Provo, UT
Gammon, Richard T. ... Raleigh, NC
Gammon, Robert F. ... Indianapolis, IN
Gammon, Timothy E. ... Springfield, MO
Gammon, W. Wright, Jr. ... Cedartown, GA
Gammon, Wayne W. ... Cedartown, GA
Gammon, William G., P.C. ... Houston, TX
Gammon, William H. ... Raleigh, NC
Gammons, Ann C. ... Elyria, OH
Gammons, Debra J. ... Greenville, SC
Gammons, Patrick E. ... Vermilion, OH
Gammons, Robert C. ... Huntsville, AL
Gamoian, Lisa M. ... Fresno, CA
Gamoke, William C. ... Colby, WI
Gamon, Lucy J. ... Waverly, IA
Gamon, Owen J. ... Rochester, MN
Gamoran, Saul ... Seattle, WA
Gamot, Albert J., Jr.
West Palm Beach, FL
Gamot Law Firm, The, P.L.
West Palm Beach, FL
Gamot, Melinda Penney
West Palm Beach, FL
Gamot, N. Nicole ... West Palm Beach, FL
Gamp, Jane L. O'Hara
San Francisco, CA
Gampel, Ross Bennett ... Miami, FL
Gamrat, Theodore ... Schaumburg, IL
Gamrath, Celia G. ... Chicago, IL
Gamrath, Robert L., III ... Chicago, IL
Gams, Ellen Lange ... Thousand Oaks, CA
Gams, Lance S. ... Los Angeles, CA
Gams, Mark H. ... Columbus, OH
Gamse, Alan N. ... Washington, DC
Baltimore, MD
Gamsin, Marc H. ... Los Angeles, CA
Gamsky, Michael J. ... Chicago, IL
Gamso, Jeffrey M. ... Toledo, OH
Gamso, Stanley A. ... Columbus, IN
Gamson, Edward P. ... Chicago, IL
Gamson, Miriam R. ... Washington, DC
Gamson, Paul B. ... Portland, OR
Gamson, Robert M. ... Towson, MD
Gamulka, Daniel K. ... New York, NY
Gamundoy, Marion E. ... Irvine, CA
Gamza, Alan E. ... New York, NY
Gamza, Jonathan R. ... West Orange, NJ
Gan, Cheryl S. ... Tulsa, OK
Gan, David Y. ... Palo Alto, CA
Gan, Deanna M. ... Fremont, CA
Gan, Michael J. ... Washington, DC
Gan, Richard R. ... Lancaster, PA
Gan, Scott H. ... Tucson, AZ
Ganahl, John C. ... Fresno, CA
Ganahl, Mary Catherine ... Los Angeles, CA
Ganan, Clifford I. ... Chicago, IL
Ganan & Shapiro ... Chicago, IL
Ganann, Ross W. ... Austin, TX
Ganassin, Scott J. ... Peru, IL
Ganatra, Avinash V. ... New York, NY
Ganbarg, Susan J. ... Chicago, IL
Gancedo, Hector G. ... Pasadena, CA
Gancer, Donald C. ... Chicago, IL
Ganch, Robert T. ... Verona, WI
Ganchrow, Ari D. ... New York, NY
Ganchrow, Gary ... Los Angeles, CA
Gancz, Ann C. ... Providence, RI
Gandal, Alvin H. ... Washington, DC
Gandal, Larry N. ... Washington, DC
Rockville, MD
Gandal, Robt. ... Cleveland, OH
Gándara, Arturo ... Sacramento, CA
Gandara, Daniel ... Seattle, WA
Gandara, Jaime E. ... El Paso, TX
Gandara, Kathy M. ... Los Angeles, CA
Gándara Sanchez, José L. ... San Juan, PR
Gandarez, Maria F. ... New York, NY
Gandbhir, Una S. ... Anchorage, AK
Gandee, Michael R. ... Irvine, CA
Gandee, Stephen F. ... Clarksburg, WV
Gandel, Debra Ellen ... Columbia, MD
Gandel, Judith R. ... Santa Monica, CA
Gandelman, Perry A. ... Randolph, MA
Lawrenceville, NJ
Gandelot, Jon B. ... Grosse Pointe Woods, MI
Gandelot, Jon B., P.C.
Grosse Pointe Woods, MI
Gandelsman, Julia ... Los Angeles, CA
Gander, David P. ... Brookfield, WI
Gander, Deborah J. ... Miami, FL
Ganderson, Martin J. ... Norfolk, VA
Gandert, William F. ... Mansfield, OH
Gandesbery, Mary A. ... San Francisco, CA
Gandhi, Bharat C. ... Danbury, CT
Gandhi, Indra M. ... Woodland Hills, CA
Gandhi, Jay C. ... Costa Mesa, CA
Gandhi, Mahendra A. ... Union, NJ
Gandhi, Samir A. ... New York, NY
Gandhi, Smita ... Rockville Centre, NY
Gandhi, Swata Jitendra ... Bethesda, MD
Gandia Fabian Law Offices ... San Juan, PR
Gandia, Laura J. ... Salem, NH
Gandia Fabian, Mary Ann ... San Juan, PR
Gandin, Michael I. ... Melville, NY
Gandin, Rachel ... Philadelphia, PA
Gandin, Schotsky, Rappaport, Glass &
Greene, LLP ... Melville, NY
New York, NY
Gandler, Allan E. ... Albany, NY
Gandley, Robert E. ... Erie, PA
Gandolfi, Alan M. ... Gretna, LA
Gandolfi, Stefanie Y. ... San Leandro, CA
Gandolfo, Diego M. ... Kansas City, MO
Gandolfo, Janet A. ... Tarrytown, NY
Gandolfo, Thomas M. ... New York, NY
Gandras-Alperin, Patricia
Los Angeles, CA
Gandrud, Gary L. ... Minneapolis, MN
Gandrud, Ronald G. ... Edina, MN
Gandrup, Bradley F., Jr. ... Boston, MA
Gandy, Charles I. ... Columbia, SC
Gandy, Cheryl M. ... New York, NY
Gandy, Dalton C. ... Fort Worth, TX
Gandy, Donald S. ... Fort Worth, TX
Gandy, Evelyn ... Hattiesburg, MS
Jackson, MS
Gandy, Francis I., Jr. ... Corpus Christi, TX
Gandy, H. Conway ... Denver, CO
Gandy, Harry ... Sutherlin, OR
Gandy, James Dowell, III ... Charleston, SC
Gandy, Kelly O. ... New Orleans, LA
Gandy, Kenneth A. ... Indianapolis, IN
Gandy, Kim A. ... Washington, DC
Gandy Law Offices, P.C. ... Fairfield, IA
Gandy, Leman D. ... Greenwood, MS
Gandy, M. Charles ... College Station, TX
Gandy, Marshall M. ... Dallas, TX
Gandy, Patricia Cox ... Jackson, MS
Gandy, Paul Dwayne ... Fairfield, IA
Gandy, Rice & Sundberg, P.C. ... Atlanta, GA
Gandy, Spencer ... Atlanta, GA
Gandy, William E. ... Tyler, TX
Gandy, William F., Jr. ... Broussard, LA
Gandy, William G. ... Rochester, NY
Ganek, Jeffrey P. ... Atlanta, GA
Ganeles, Alan ... Brooklyn, NY
Ganem, Edward J. ... Victoria, TX
Ganem, Glenda H. ... Boston, MA
Ganem, Joseph J. ... Andover, MA
Ganem, Philip J. ... Wolfeboro, NH
Ganem, Sally Eileen ... Boston, MA
Ganem, Thomas F. ... Tulsa, OK
Ganey, George T., Jr. ... Buffalo, NY
Ganey, Robert S. ... Hanover, VA
Ganey, Timothy L. ... Allentown, PA
Ganezer, David L. ... Santa Monica, CA
Ganfer, Steven R. ... New York, NY
Ganfield, Daniel F. ... Bellevue, WA
Ganfield, David R., II ... Waukegan, IL
Gang, Arthur ... Stamford, CT
Gang, Effie S. ... New York, NY
Gang, Lawrence N. ... Baltimore, MD
Gang, Michael W. ... Harrisburg, PA
Gang, Paulette R. ... Deerfield, IL
Gang, Richard F., Jr. ... Skokie, IL
Gang, Robert C. ... Miami, FL
Gang, Robert J., Jr. ... Marietta, NY
Gang, Tyre, Ramer & Brown, Inc.
Beverly Hills, CA
Los Angeles, CA
Gangadean, Rajendra N. ... Phoenix, AZ
Gange, Arthur F. ... Mineola, NY
Gange, Heather E. ... Washington, DC
Gangei, Gitty D. Samrad ... Greenwich, CT
Gangel, Carl A. ... Kansas City, MO
Gangel, Elaine C. ... New York, NY
Gangel-Jacob, Phyllis B. ... New York, NY
Gangemi, Columbus R., Jr. ... Chicago, IL
Gangemi, Donald P. ... San Mateo, CA
Gangemi, Laura A. ... Miami, FL
Gangemi & Mango, L.L.P. ... New York, NY
Gangemi, Salvatore G. ... New York, NY
Ganger, Milton E., Jr. ... Solon, OH
Ganger, Molly ... Concord, NH
Gangi, Ann ... Riverhead, NY
Gangi, Claudia Barnes
Department of Justice, Civil Division, GV
Gangi, F. Craig ... Parsippany, NJ
Gangi, Jeffrey D. ... Buffalo, NY
Gangi, John F. ... Wilmington, DE
Gangi, Linda Weeks ... Conway, SC
Gangi, Robert C. ... La Crescenta, CA
Gangitano, Nicole E. ... Omaha, NE
Gangl, Walter T. ... Lancaster, PA
Gangle, Karen W. ... Sisseton, SD
Gangle, Margaret E. ... St. Louis, MO
Gangle, Michael L. ... Portland, OR
Gangle, Sandra Smith ... Salem, OR
Gangle, Sandra Smith, P.C. ... Salem, OR
Gangloff, Charles A. ... Long Beach, CA
Gangloff, Charles A. & Associates
Long Beach, CA
Gangloff, Joanne M. ... Long Beach, CA
Gangloff, Joseph E. ... Department of Justice,
Criminal Division, GV
Gangnes, Larry S. ... Seattle, WA
Gangnes, Michele G. ... Austin, TX
Gangolf, Andrew L., III ... New York, NY
Gangsei, Paul A. ... New York, NY
Gangstad, John E. ... Austin, TX
Ganguzza, Carole Kenin ... Miami, FL
Ganguzza, Joseph H. ... Miami, FL
Gangwere, George H., Jr.
Overland Park, KS
Kansas City, MO
Gangwere, Robert L. ... Kansas City, MO
Gangwish, D. Vaughn ... Albuquerque, NM
Gangwish, Richard J., II ... Erlanger, KY
Gani, G. Sal ... Lansing, MI
Gani, G. Sal, P.C. ... Lansing, MI
Gani, Paula ... San Francisco, CA
Gani, Paula ... Washington, DC
Ganiaris, Thomas N. ... Cherry Hill, NJ
Ganiban, Jeffrey T. ... Washington, DC
Ganick, John G. ... Newton, MA
Ganick, O'Brien & Sarin ... Dorchester, MA
Ganieany, Luther L., Jr. ... Manhattan, KS
Ganier, Patricia Kryder ... Nashville, TN
Ganier, Suzanne M. ... Chicago, IL
Ganik & Herbst ... Stamford, CT
Ganim, Davis W. ... Stratford, CT
Ganim, Ganim & Ganim, P.C.
Bridgeport, CT
Ganim, George W., Jr. ... Bridgeport, CT
Ganim, George W., Sr. ... Bridgeport, CT
Ganim, Joseph P. ... Bridgeport, CT
Ganim, Paul J. ... Bridgeport, CT
Ganim, Raymond W. ... Stratford, CT
Ganim, Raymond W., II ... Bridgeport, CT
Ganim, Ronald J. ... Chicago, IL
Ganim, Thomas G. ... Bridgeport, CT
Ganio, Janet ... Melville, NY
Ganion, James M. ... Irvine, CA
Ganis, Stephen L., Law Offices of
Greenwich, CT
Ganis, Stephen L., Law Offices of
Stamford, CT
Ganis, Stephen L., Law Offices of
New York, NY
Ganister, Ruth E. ... West Chester, PA
Ganja, Robert E. ... Chicago, IL
Ganje, David L. ... Albany, NY
Ganje Law Office ... Albany, NY
Ganjon, Frederick K. ... Columbia, MD
Gankendorff, Edgar D. ... Lafayette, LA
Ganley, Charles E., Jr. ... Waynesboro, PA
Ganley, John G. ... Minneapolis, MN
Ganley, John M.
Securities and Exchange Commission,
Division of Investment Management, GV
Ganley, Joseph R. ... Las Vegas, NV
Ganley, Kristin Dwyer ... Newark, NJ
Ganley, Paul Mullin, (A Law Corporation)
Honolulu, HI
Ganly, David M. ... Asheville, NC
Ganly & Ramer ... Asheville, NC
Gann, A. Ann ... Brownsville, TX
Gann, David E. ... Batavia, NY
Gann, Gary T. ... Cedar Knolls, NJ
Gann, Gregg ... Los Angeles, CA
Gann, Gregory S. ... Park Ridge, IL
Gann & Hobbs ... Edwards, CA
Gann, James G., III ... Birmingham, AL
Gann, James G., Jr. ... Birmingham, AL
Gann, James M., P.A. ... Belle Glade, FL
Gann, Jon Bradley
Hot Springs National Park, AR
Gann, Laura L. ... Department of Justice,
Office of Attorney Personnel Management,
GV
Gann, M. Keith ... Birmingham, AL
Gann, Marc Craig ... Carle Place, NY
Gann, Miller & Edwards ... Houston, TX
Gann, Pamela Brooks ... Durham, NC
Gann & Parker, P.C. ... Park Ridge, IL
Gann, Patty R. ... Edwards, CA
Gann, Richard A. ... Tulsa, OK
Gann, Richard D. ... San Diego, CA
Gann, Ronald F. ... Denver, CO
Gann, Stanford G. ... Baltimore, MD
Gann, Stanford G., Jr. ... Baltimore, MD
Gann, Steve D. ... Portland, OR
Gann, Timothy C. ... Birmingham, AL
Gann, Tom R. ... Tulsa, OK
Gann, William S. ... Baltimore, MD
Gann, Wm. Mac ... Houston, TX
Gannam & Gnann ... Savannah, GA
Gannam, Joseph M. ... Savannah, GA
Gannam, Michael J. ... Savannah, GA
Gannam, Philip ... Los Angeles, CA
Gannan, Dennis M.
Macomb Township, MI
Gannan, John W., II ... Blue Springs, MO
Gannascoli, Rudolph ... Washington, DC
Gannaway Fiorella & Cummings
Springfield, MO
Gannaway, James R., Jr. ... Providence, RI
Gannaway, Leland L. ... Springfield, MO
Gannaway, Robert A. ... Muskogee, OK
Gannaway, Sally May ... Topeka, KS
Ganne, Patrick R. ... Austin, TX
Ganner, Christopher N. K. ... Jackson, MS
Gannet, Herbert M. ... West Orange, NJ
Gannett & Associates ... Boston, MA
Gannett, Clifford J. ... Bowie, MD
Gannett, Craig ... Seattle, WA
Gannett, Cynthia S. ... Seattle, WA
Gannett, Damon L. ... Billings, MT
Gannett, David G. ... Portland, OR
Gannett, Deborah Jean ... Newark, NJ
Gannett, Frederick W. ... Basalt, CO
Gannett, Richard W. ... Boston, MA
Gannett, Robert T. ... Brattleboro, VT
Gannett & Sackett, LLC ... Basalt, CO
Gannett, Sarah Sargent ... Washington, DC
Gannett, William B. ... New York, NY
Gannicott, Gordon S. ... Portland, OR
Gannon, Alexia V. ... Houston, TX
Gannon, AnnaMary E. ... San Francisco, CA
Gannon, Brian ... Atlanta, GA
Gannon, Brian Timothy ... Louisville, KY
Gannon, Christian H. ... New York, NY
Gannon, Christopher J.I. ... Cary, NC
Gannon, Christopher R. ... Burlington, VT
Gannon, Cindy A. ... Rancho Cordova, CA
Gannon & Ciyou, P.C. ... Indianapolis, IN
Gannon, Cottrell & Ward, P.C.
Alexandria, VA
Fairfax, VA
Gannon, Curtis E. ... Washington, DC
Gannon, Dana M. ... Austin, TX
Gannon, David A. ... New York, NY
Gannon, David C. ... Albany, NY
Gannon, Deidre E. ... New Egypt, NJ
Gannon, Drew P. ... Harrisburg, PA
Gannon, Edward V. ... Paterson, NJ
Gannon, Eileen R. ... Freehold, NJ
Gannon, Elizabeth M. ... Clearwater, FL
Gannon, Francis L. ... Houston, TX
Gannon, Francis W. ... Mesquite, TX
Gannon, Fred ... Dallas, TX
Gannon, Gannon & Sullivan ... Buffalo, NY
Gannon, Gerald J. ... Detroit, MI
Gannon, Gordon ... Buffalo, NY
Gannon, Gordon, Jr. ... Buffalo, NY
Gannon, Grace Marie ... Marlton, NJ
Gannon, Gregory ... Austin, TX
San Antonio, TX
Gannon, J. Michael ... Concord, NH
Gannon, Jack T. ... Hillsboro, TX
Gannon, James F. ... Huntingdon Valley, PA
Gannon, James P. ... Media, PA
Gannon, James R. ... Chicago, IL
Gannon, John E. ... Saginaw, MI
Gannon, John F. ... Cleveland, OH
Gannon, John G. ... Worcester, MA
Gannon, John J. ... Batavia, NY
Gannon, John L. ... Boise, ID
Gannon, John Russell ... Indianapolis, IN
Gannon, John S. ... Nashville, TN
Gannon, John T. ... Pawtucket, RI
Gannon, Joseph F. ... Haverhill, MA
Gannon, Joseph W., Jr.
Florham Park, NJ
Gannon, Kevin ... Westborough, MA
Gannon, Lawrence J. ... New York, NY
Gannon, Mark S. ... Atlanta, GA
Gannon, Martin A. ... Alexandria, VA
Fairfax, VA
Gannon, Mary T. ... Des Moines, IA
Gannon, Matthew L. ... Washington, DC
Gannon, Michael D. ... Evanston, IL
Gannon, Michael J. ... Oakland, CA
Gannon, Michael J. ... Burlington, VT
Gannon, Michael L. ... Minneapolis, MN
Gannon, Pamela N. ... New York, NY
Gannon, Patrick J. ... Westerville, OH
Gannon, Patrick J., Co., L.P.A.
Westerville, OH
Gannon, Paul J. ... Boston, MA
Gannon, Richard H. ... Los Angeles, CA
Gannon, Robert C., Jr. ... Orange, CA
Gannon, Robert P. ... Butte, MT
Gannon, Ronald G. ... Grand Island, NY
Gannon, Stephen T. ... Richmond, VA
Gannon, Thomas G. ... Toms River, NJ
Gannon, Thomas M. ... Department of Justice,
Criminal Division, GV
Gannon, Thomas M. ... Mineola, NY
New York, NY
Gannon, Thomas P., Jr. ... New York, NY
Gannon, Virginia Baird ... Pikeville, KY
Gannon, William A. ... Rome, NY
Gannon, William J. ... Florham Park, NJ
Gannon, William S. ... Manchester, NH
Gannon-McMurry, Mary E. ... Orlando, FL
Gannott, Peter M. ... Granite City, IL
Gano, Charles H. ... Petoskey, MI
Gano, Donovan & Gano, Inc. ... Houston, TX
Gano, G. Allen ... Wilmington, OH
Gano, Gordon L., Jr. ... Dallas, TX

Gano, Howard H. ....Houston, TX
Gano, John ....Houston, TX
Gano, Judy A. ....Wilmington, OH
Gano, Kenneth R., Jr. ....Charleston, IL
Gano, Stephen M. ....Houston, TX
Gano, Thomas C. ....West Palm Beach, FL
Gano, Wade E. ....Yakima, WA
Ganobsik, Keith J. ....St. Petersburg, FL
Ganon, Neal L. ....Hollywood, FL
West Palm Beach, FL
Ganong, Jas. A., Jr. ....Memphis, TN
Ganong Law Office ....Bakersfield, CA
Ganong, Philip W. ....Bakersfield, CA
Ganong, Robert K. ....Boston, MA
Ganong, William M. ....Klamath Falls, OR
Ganong, Wm., Sr. ....Klamath Falls, OR
Ganoon, Jas. A. ....Guilderland, NY
Ganopole, Deidre S. ....Anchorage, AK
Ganos, John R. ....Southfield, MI
Ganos, Sandra L. ....Farmington Hills, MI
Ganotis, James G. ....Syracuse, NY
Ganotis, John ....Syracuse, NY
Gans, Abbey ....New York, NY
Gans, Adam L. ....Wayne, NJ
Gans, Bernard R. ....Los Angeles, CA
Gans, Bradley Jay ....New York, NY
Gans, David H. ....New York, NY
Gans, Deborah ....Denver, CO
Gans, Edgar H. ....Baltimore, MD
Gans, Edgar H., P.A. ....Baltimore, MD
Gans, Gary E. ....San Francisco, CA
Gans, Ira J. ....Chicago, IL
Gans, Jason Y. ....Bloomfield, CT
Gans, Jeffrey ....Washington, DC
Gans, Jeffrey R. ....Gibbsboro, NJ
Gans, Jerry N. ....Tustin, CA
Gans, Mary W. ....Brockton, MA
Gans, Maurice G. ....Suffern, NY
Gans, Michael J. ....New York, NY
Gans, Mitchell M. ....Hempstead, NY
Gans, Myrna E. ....Bridgeport, CT
Gans, Nancy Freeman ....Boston, MA
Gans, Phillip C. ....Denver, CO
Gans & Reynolds ....Bridgeport, CT
Gans, Richard L. ....New York, NY
Gans, Richard R. ....Sarasota, FL
Gans, Robert E. ....Washington, DC
Gans, Robert H. ....Beverly Hills, CA
Gans, Robert M. ....San Diego, CA
Gans, Robert S. ....New York, NY
Gans, Russell Scott ....Eureka, CA
Gans, Sharon ....Liberty Corner, NJ
Gans & Stedman ....Wellesley, MA
Gans, Steven H. ....Newton, MA
Gans, Susan L. ....Burbank, CA
Gans, Susan L. ....Brooklyn, NY
Gans, Ted M. ....Bloomfield Hills, MI
Gans, Ted M., P.C. ....Bloomfield Hills, MI
Gans, W. Carl ....Goleta, CA
Gans, Walter G. ....New York, NY
Gansa, Sarah Richards
San Francisco, CA
Gansberg, Andrew ....Albany, NY
Gansberg, Eric M. ....Staten Island, NY
Ganschow, C. Michael ....Santa Barbara, CA
Gansell, Jonathan S. ....Dallas, TX
Gansell, Ralph E. ....Brooklyn, NY
Ganser, Marian Molz ....Topeka, KS
Gansinger & Hinshaw, LLP
Los Angeles, CA
Gansinger, James M. ....Los Angeles, CA
Ganske, Lyle G. ....Cleveland, OH
Ganske, Vicki Smith ....Fort Worth, TX
Ganski, Linda S. ....Springfield, IL
Gansl, Evan C. ....Mineola, NY
Ganslaw, Lawrence Steven ....Washington, DC
Gansle, Gary M. ....Palo Alto, CA
Gansler, Douglas F. ....Washington, DC
Gansler, Stephen M. ....Bridgewater, NJ
Gansloser, Quentin H. ....St. Louis, MO
Gansner, Katharine G. ....Madison, WI
Gansner, William L. ....Madison, WI
Ganson, Jeffrey ....Seattle, WA
Ganson, Michael B. ....Cincinnati, OH
Ganson, Michael B., & Kenneth Heuck, Jr.
Cincinnati, OH
Ganson, Norris L. ....Tucson, AZ
Gans-Smith, Susan B. ....Santa Barbara, CA
Gant, Andrew M., Jr. ....Birmingham, AL
Gant, Catherine Adamski ....Fort Worth, TX
Gant, Charles E. ....Millville, NJ
Gant, Christopher I. ....Chalmette, LA
Gant, Craig C. ....Dallas, TX
Gant, David J. ....Cottage Grove, OR
Gant & Gant ....Van Buren, AR
Gant and Gant ....Modesto, CA
Gant & Gant, P.A. ....Millville, NJ
Gant, H. Zed ....Van Buren, AR
Gant, Jack E. ....Independence, MO
Gant, Jesse, III ....Minneapolis, MN
Gant, John W., Jr. ....Birmingham, AL
Gant, Jon L. ....Vista, CA
Gant, Joseph E., III ....Carlsbad, NM
Gant, Leon ....Detroit, MI
Gant, Monica McCullough ....Atlanta, GA
Gant, Nigel F., P.C. ....Fort Worth, TX
Gant, Norma M. ....Detroit, MI
Gant, Paul D. ....Van Buren, AR
Gant, Ralph A. ....New York, NY
Gant, Richard A. ....San Diego, CA
Gant, Scott E. ....Washington, DC
Gant, Tamara J. ....Houston, TX
Gant, Vernon F. ....Modesto, CA
Gant, Warren F. ....Modesto, CA
Gant, William M. ....Owensboro, KY
Gant, William Z. ....Millville, NJ
Gantar & DeMartini ....Antioch, IL
Gantar, Michael W. ....Antioch, IL
Gantcher, Kimberly Kara ....New York, NY
Gantcher, Neal I. ....New York, NY
Gantenbein, Harry W. ....Beloit, KS
Ganter, Daniel D., Jr. ....Minneapolis, MN
Ganther & Fee, P.A. ....Tampa, FL
Ganther, James S. ....Tampa, FL
Gantman, Brian D. ....Sacramento, CA
Gantman & Gantman ....Encino, CA
Gantman, Julius ....New York, NY
Gantman, Lewis I. ....King Of Prussia, PA
Gantman, Morton ....Encino, CA
Gantman, Robert ....Encino, CA
Gantman, Seymour ....Encino, CA
Gantman, Susan Peikes
West Conshohocken, PA
Gantner, Anthony F. ....San Francisco, CA
Gantner, Francis J. ....Goshen, IN
Gantner, Mary Ann ....New York, NY
Gantner, Richard A. ....Somerville, NJ
Gantnier, Cindy L. ....Richmond, VA
Ganton, Robert A. ....Department of the Army,
U.S. Army Legal Services Agency, GV
Gants, Fred ....Madison, WI
Gants, Robert M. ....Alexandria, VA
Gantt, Ben J., Jr. ....Seattle, WA
Gantt, Carroll A., Jr. ....Columbia, SC
Gantt, Charles D. ....Asheville, NC
Gantt, Christine M. ....Greenville, SC
Gantt, Daniel M. ....New York, NY
Gantt, David, Law Offices ....Asheville, NC
Gantt, David W. ....Greenville, SC
Gantt, Gamewell D., III ....Pocatello, ID
Gantt, Gregory M. ....Dayton, OH
Gantt, John B. ....Washington, DC
New York, NY
Gantt, Karen Michelle ....Montgomery, AL
Gantt, Lynn M. ....Columbia, SC
Gantt, William G. ....Birmingham, AL
Gantus, John M. ....Glendale, CA
Gantz, Clayton B. ....San Francisco, CA
Gantz, Curtis F. ....Columbus, OH
Gantz, David A. ....Washington, DC
Gantz, David F. ....Los Angeles, CA
Gantz, Emmett J., Law Office of
Los Angeles, CA
Gantz, Gary W. ....Anchorage, AK
Gantz, Gregory M. ....St. Louis, MO
Gantz, Jule L. ....Washington, DC
Gantz, Mark L. ....Dearborn Heights, MI
Gantz, Neil P. ....Chicago, IL
Gantz, Norman J. ....Chicago, IL
Gantz, William M. ....Chicago, IL
Gantzhorn, Alan ....Atlanta, GA
Ganucheau, Anita H. ....New Orleans, LA
Ganucheau, Charles J. ....Harahan, LA
Ganucheau, Gilbert F., Jr.
New Orleans, LA
Ganucheau, Richard J. ....New Orleans, LA
Ganucheau, Stephanie L. ....Jackson, MS
Ganucheau, Suzanne M. ....Covington, LA
Ganucheau, Thomas E. ....Houston, TX
Ganulin, James E. ....Fresno, CA
Ganulin, Neil ....Cincinnati, OH
Ganus, Charles A. ....El Dorado, AR
Ganus, Gerald A. ....Gardendale, AL
Ganus, Sandra R. ....Atlanta, GA
Ganus, Walter David ....La Jolla, CA
Gany, Alicia M. ....New York, NY
Ganz, Adam ....Las Vegas, NV
Ganz, Alan S. ....Chicago, IL
Ganz, Beth ....Denver, CO
Ganz, Carole I. ....Gloucester, MA
Ganz, Charles D. ....Atlanta, GA
Ganz, David H. ....Somerset, NJ
Ganz, David L. ....Fair Lawn, NJ
New York, NY
Ganz, Denise J. ....Fort Lauderdale, FL
Ganz, Diana ....New York, NY
Ganz, Elliot ....New York, NY
Ganz & Ganz ....Gibbon, NE
Kearney, NE
Ganz & Gorsline, A Law Partnership
Los Angeles, CA
Ganz, Ham & Riley, P.C. ....Boston, MA
Nahant, MA
Ganz & Hollinger, A Professional
Corporation ....New York, NY
Ganz, Howard L. ....New York, NY
Ganz, James R., Jr. ....Kearney, NE
Ganz, James R., Sr. ....Gibbon, NE
Ganz, Jeffrey D. ....Boston, MA
Ganz, Joan ....Sacramento, CA
Ganz, Joseph J., & Associates ....Seattle, WA
Ganz, Judith Ellen ....Oakland, CA
Ganz, Marc D. ....New York, NY
Ganz, Marc David ....Albany, NY
Ganz, Marc P. ....Miami, FL
Ganz, Mark B. ....Portland, OR
Ganz, Mary Keohan ....Seabrook, NH
Ganz, Michael H. ....Hicksville, NY
Ganz, Nicholas T. ....New York, NY
Ganz, Perry ....Boston, MA
Ganz, Peter J. ....Wayne, NJ
Ganz, Philip J., Jr. ....Los Angeles, CA
Ganz, Robert E. ....Albany, NY
Ganz, Sheldon H. ....Boston, MA
Ganz & Sivin, P.A. ....Fair Lawn, NJ
Ganz & Wolkenbreit, LLP ....Albany, NY
Ganzer, James E. ....Stockton, CA
Ganzer, Michael J. ....Milwaukee, WI
Ganzer & Williams ....Stockton, CA
Ganzfried, Jerrold J. ....Washington, DC
Ganzglass, Martin R. ....Washington, DC
Ganzhorn, Lisa A. ....Springfield, NJ
Ganzkow, Gavin M. ....Longwood, FL
Ganzman, Jay A. ....Princeton, NJ
Gao, J. Kevin ....New York, NY
Gao, Tong (Tony) ....St. Louis, MO
Gao, Xiaotian ....Vienna, VA
Gao, Zhun Julie ....Los Angeles, CA
Gaona, David F. ....Phoenix, AZ
Gaona Moore, P.C. ....Phoenix, AZ
Gaouette, David Michael ....Denver, CO
Gaouette, Dudley W. ....San Jose, CA
Gapen, Carol M. ....Madison, WI
Gapinski, Frank A. ....Dayton, OH
Gappa, David ....San Diego, CA
Gappelberg, Rodney J. ....Dallas, TX
Gappen, Tamara L. ....Orlando, FL
Gapstur, James J. ....Duxbury, MA
Gapstur, Lenne A. ....Palm Beach, FL
Gaquin, Daniel O. ....Boston, MA
Gara, Christine A. ....Holland, MI
Gara, Elizabeth E. ....Hartford, CT
Gara, Leslie S. ....Anchorage, AK
Garaas, David ....Fargo, ND
Garaas, John O. ....Detroit Lakes, MN
Garaas, Jonathan T. ....Fargo, ND
Garaas Law Firm ....Fargo, ND
Garabedian, Chas. B. ....Boston, MA
Garabedian, Cynthia E. ....Palo Alto, CA
Garabedian, Deborah ....Fresno, CA
Garabedian, Jeffrey H. ....Providence, RI
Garabedian, Kilbyanne ....Worcester, MA
Garabedian, Michael ....Commack, NY
Garabedian, Mitchell ....Boston, MA
Garabedian, Richard S., (P.C.)
Washington, DC
Garabedian, Todd E. ....New Haven, CT
Garabis, Francisco A. ....Columbus, OH
Garabo, Judith Anne ....Orlando, FL
Garabrant, Mark R. ....Lindenhurst, NY
Garaczkowski, Joan M. ....Portsmouth, OH
Garaffa, John V. ....Department of the Navy,
Office of the Judge Advocate General, GV
Garafola, Frank M. ....Montclair, NJ
Garafola, Joseph S. ....White Plains, NY
Garagiola, Joseph H., Jr. ....Phoenix, AZ
Garagozzo, John J. ....Gibbsboro, NJ
Garahan, James C. ....Palo Alto, CA
Garai, Gabor ....Boston, MA
Garam, Peter P. ....New York, NY
Garamella, Jack D. ....Danbury, CT
Garamella, Sylvester J. ....New York, NY
Garamfalvi, Alexia M. ....New York, NY
Garamone, Patricia L. ....Yuba City, CA
Garan, Lucow, Miller & Seward, P.C.
Adrian, MI
Ann Arbor, MI
Charlotte, MI
Detroit, MI
Flint, MI
Grand Blanc, MI
Grand Haven, MI
Grand Rapids, MI
Howell, MI
Jackson, MI
Lansing, MI
Lapeer, MI
Marquette, MI
Mount Clemens, MI
Muskegon, MI
Pontiac, MI
Port Huron, MI
Saginaw, MI
Traverse City, MI
Troy, MI
Garand, John D. ....Oregon, OH
Garand, Richard C. ....Oregon, OH
Garant, Guy C. ....Port Jefferson, NY
Garant, Lyse M. ....Newark, NJ
New York, NY
Garapetian, Irenna M. ....Saginaw, MI
Garas, John C. ....Buffalo, NY
Garascia, Christian J. ....Troy, MI
Garatoni, Michael R. ....San Antonio, TX
Garau, Jerry A. ....Indianapolis, IN
Garau, Olga H. ....Los Angeles, CA
Garaude, Alfred ....Farmingdale, NY
Garavaglia, Frank L. ....Chicago, IL
Garavaglia, John C. ....St. Louis, MO
Garavaglia, Marco F. ....San Diego, CA
Garavaglia, Mark A. ....Evanston, IL
Garavaglia, Michael J. ....Vero Beach, FL
Garavalia, Anthony R. ....Granite City, IL
Garavalia, David B. ....Benton, IL
Garavi, Behrooz ....Vienna, VA
Garavito, Stephen C. ....Basking Ridge, NJ
Garawski, Michael J.
Commodity Futures Trading Commission,
Office of the General Counsel, GV
Garay, Dana Louise Doss ....Lubbock, TX
Garay, Erica B. ....Uniondale, NY
Garay, Joseph P. ....Warminster, PA
Garay, Joyce-Marie ....Dallas, TX
Garay, Juan Carlos ....San Juan, PR
Garay, Mark M. ....San Francisco, CA
Garay, Mark M., Law Offices of
San Francisco, CA
Garay, Martin R., III ....Hinsdale, IL
Garay, Rufina C. ....Boston, MA
Garay-Aubán, Miguel R. ....San Juan, PR
Garayua Vazquez, Nelson Richard
San Juan, PR
Garazi, Carrie M. ....Kissimmee, FL
Garb, Andrew S., (A P.C.)
Los Angeles, CA
Garb, Ernest L. ....Jamaica, NY
Garb, Fran J. ....Morristown, NJ
Garb, Isaac S. ....Doylestown, PA
Garb, Joel B. ....Kalamazoo, MI
Garb, Robert H. ....San Francisco, CA
Garb, Sarah H. ....Washington, DC
Garb, Sharon ....New York, NY
Garbacik, Denorfia, Foti & Forgione, P.C.
Southington, CT
Garbacik, Roman F. ....Southington, CT
Garbacz, Gregory A. ....Los Angeles, CA
San Diego, CA
Garbade, Jennings B. ....Douglasville, GA
Garbaliauskas, Romas ....New York, NY
Garbanzos, Francis ....Hicksville, NY
Garbar, Marc W. ....New York, NY
Garbar, Marc W., P.C., Law Offices of
New York, NY
Garbarini, Chas. J. ....New York, NY
Garbarini, Paul M. ....Watertown, MA
Garbarini, Richard M. ....New York, NY
Garbarini & Scher, P.C. ....Hackensack, NJ
New York, NY
Garbarino, Arthur ....Livonia, MI
Garbarino, G. Barrett ....Clarion, PA
Garbarino, Linda M. ....Detroit, MI
Garbarino, Robert P. ....Villanova, PA
Garbarino, William F. ....Phoenix, AZ
Garbarino, William R. ....Sayville, NY
Garbee, R. Mitchell ....Lynchburg, VA
Garbee, Wm. C., Jr. ....Richmond, VA
Garbeil, Howard ....Wynnewood, PA
Garbell, Jason ....Westfield, NJ
Garber, Aaron A. ....Wilmington, DE
Garber, Abbey Benjamin ....Dallas, TX
Garber, Adolfo B. ....Los Angeles, CA
Garber, Alan H. ....Atlanta, GA
Garber, Alan S. ....Alameda, CA
Garber, Albert C. ....Los Angeles, CA
Garber, Alice C. ....Palo Alto, CA
Garber, Angus G., Jr. ....Cheshire, CT
Garber & Associates, P.C. ....New York, NY
Garber, Barry L. ....Miami, FL
Garber, Bart K. ....Anchorage, AK
Garber, Bernard J. ....Stockton, CA
Garber, Bonnie D. ....Newton, KS
Garber, Bradley N. ....Irvine, CA
Garber, Bruce S. ....Santa Fe, NM
Garber, Calvin D. ....New York, NY
Garber, David F. ....Naples, FL
Garber, David M. ....Syracuse, NY
Garber, David S. ....Princeton, NJ
Garber, David W. ....Cincinnati, OH
Garber, Deanna R. ....Cincinnati, OH
Garber, Diane M. ....Jefferson City, MO
Garber, Donald L. ....Hackensack, NJ
Garber, Donald L., P.A. ....Hackensack, NJ
Garber, Douglas Jay ....Bradford, PA
Garber, Fern S. ....New York, NY
Garber & Garber ....Los Angeles, CA
Garber & Garber ....New York, NY
Garber & Garber ....York, PA
Garber & Garber, P.C. ....Boston, MA
Garber, Gerald A. ....Great Neck, NY
Garber & Hallmark, P.C. ....Santa Fe, NM
Garber, Harold M. ....Miami, FL
Garber, Harry J. ....Flushing, NY
Garber, Jason S. ....Forest Hills, NY
Garber, Jeffrey B. ....Carle Place, NY
Garber, Jeffrey M. ....El Centro, CA
Garber, Jeffrey M. ....Lake Worth, FL
Garber, Jeremy Simcha ....New York, NY
Garber, Joel ....Voorhees, NJ
Garber, John E. ....Springfield, MA
Garber, John M. ....York, PA
Garber, John R. ....New York, NY
Garber, Judah ....Ann Arbor, MI
Garber, Julie Ann ....Bethesda, MD
Garber, Kasten & Jarve, P.A.
Cherry Hill, NJ
Garber, Katherine T. ....Houston, TX
Garber, Kenneth ....Punta Gorda, FL
Garber, Kenneth E. ....Columbus, OH
Garber, Kenneth N. ....Jenkintown, PA
Garber, Kevin J. ....Pittsburgh, PA
Garber, Kurt H. ....Orlando, FL
Garber, Lance E. ....Los Angeles, CA
Garber, Leonard N. ....Los Angeles, CA
Garber, Linnette M. ....Bethesda, MD
Garber, Lois Seiden ....Cherry Hill, NJ
Garber, Lori L. ....Lawrence, KS
Garber, Marc H. ....Orange, CA
Garber, Marc R. ....Philadelphia, PA
Garber, Margaret E. ....Washington, DC
Garber, Margaret K. ....Roanoke, VA
Garber, Marilyn ....Venice, CA
Garber, Maryanne ....Philadelphia, PA
Garber, Matthew W. ....Washington, DC
Garber, Maurice R. ....New York, NY
Garber & Metcalf ....Minneapolis, MN
Garber, Michael ....Cameron, LA
Lake Charles, LA
Garber, Milton ....Hoboken, NJ
Garber, Milton B. ....Jefferson City, MO
Garber, Mitchell ....New York, NY
Garber, Nancy Matthews ....Los Angeles, CA
Garber, Paul J. ....Delray Beach, FL
Garber, Paul William ....Boston, MA
Garber, Philip C. ....Boston, MA
Garber, Philip E. ....Philadelphia, PA
Garber, Richard ....North Hollywood, CA
Garber & Riskin ....Venice, CA
Garber, Robert D. ....Cherry Hill, NJ
Garber, Robert D. ....Flushing, NY
Garber, Robert E. ....New York, NY
Garber, Robert L. ....Pittsburgh, PA
Garber, Ronald D. ....Beverly Hills, CA
Garber, Ronald H. ....Raleigh, NC
Garber, Ronald J. ....Atlanta, GA
Garber, Ronald L. ....Woodland Hills, CA
Garber, Ross H. ....Hartford, CT
Garber, Samuel B. ....Chicago, IL
Garber, Scott Douglas ....Denver, CO
Garber, Scott J. ....Houston, TX
Garber, Sheldon C. ....Chicago, IL
Garber, Stanley J. ....Chicago, IL
Garber, Stanley N. ....St. Louis, MO

Garcia, Thomas K. ....Fullerton, CA
Garcia, Timothy L. ....Santa Fe, NM
Garcia, Valarie M. ....Tampa, FL
Garcia, Victor Roberto ....Del Rio, TX
Garcia, Victoria Beatrice ....Albuquerque, NM
Garcia, Victoria M. (IBA) ....San Antonio, TX
Garcia, Vincent B., Law Offices of Rancho Cucamonga, CA
Riverside, CA
Garcia, Wendy ....Miami, FL
Garcia, William ....Miami, FL
Garcia, William D., Law Offices of Seattle, WA
Garcia, William F. ....Greeley, CO
Garcia, William F. ....Tampa, FL
Garcia, William J. N. ....Kamuela, HI
Garcia, William O. ....Sherman Oaks, CA
Garcia, William R. ....Montebello, CA
Garcia, William T. ....Arlington, VA
Garcia-Angeli, Gabriel ....Plano, TX
García-Angeli, Samuel ....San Juan, PR
Garcia-Arregui, Andres J. ....San Juan, PR
Garcia-Arregui & Fullana ....San Juan, PR
Garcia-Badillo, Rosa M. ....New York, NY
Garcia-Barron, Gerard L. Los Angeles, CA
Garcia-Benitez, Carla ....San Juan, PR
Garcia-Bokor, Amybeth ....Washington, DC
Garcia C., Elisa D. ....Rye Brook, NY
Garcia-Cardenas, Margarita E. ....San Juan, PR
Garcia-Castillo, Lucinda J. Corpus Christi, TX
Garcia Chamorro, Daniel ....San Juan, PR
Garcia Chamorro, Juan D. ....San Juan, PR
Garcia-Colberg, Mariela ....San Juan, PR
Garcia-Colson, L. Joane Palm Springs, CA
Garcia-Delgado Segues, Vicente New York, NY
Garcia-Diaz, Jorge J. ....San Juan, PR
Garciadiaz, Manuel ....New York, NY
Garcia-Garcia, Emmalind ....San Juan, PR
García-García, Francisco J. ....San Juan, PR
Garcia-Garza, Viola L. ....McAllen, TX
García-Gregory, Jay A. ....San Juan, PR
Garcia-Hirschi, Alba L. ....Delray Beach, FL
García Jiménez, Braulio ....San Juan, PR
Garcia-Jimenez, Gonzalo ....Washington, DC
Garcia-Linares, Manuel A. ....Miami, FL
Garcia-Loper, Yolanda E. ....Trenton, NJ
Garcia Lopez, Noe D. ....San Juan, PR
Garcia-Medina, Ada Angelica, Law Offices San Juan, PR
Garcia-Mendoza, Armando L. ....Miami, FL
Garcia-Mendoza, Eva ....Las Vegas, NV
Garcia-Mendoza & Snavely, Chtd. Las Vegas, NV
Garcia-Montes, Gustavo J. ....Miami, FL
Garcia-Moreno, Pablo A. ....Chicago, IL
Garcia-Moreno, Ricardo ....Houston, TX
Garcia-Mosquera, Gabriel ....Sunrise, FL
Garcia-Mosquera, Walter Gabriel Sunrise, FL
Garcia-Noya, José ....San Juan, PR
Garcia-Oliver, Angel M. ....Miami, FL
Garcia-Pages, Sergio ....Miami, FL
Garcia Palacios, Oscar A. ....San Juan, PR
Garcia-Passalacqua, Juan M. ....San Juan, PR
Garcia-Pedrosa, Jose R. ....Miami, FL
Garcia-Perez, Amarillys E. ....Miami, FL
Garcia-Pérez, Carlos A. ....Miami, FL
García Pérez, José R. ....San Juan, PR
García-Pérez, Michelle M. ....San Juan, PR
Garcia-Pumento, Gilbert J. San Francisco, CA
Garcia-Rodriguez, Carmen M. New York, NY
Garcia-Rodriguez, Sergio ....Orinda, CA
García-Rodríguez, Roberto ....San Juan, PR
García-Rullán, Carlos M. ....San Juan, PR
García-Sánchez, Raúl ....Guaynabo, PR
García-Solá, Arturo J. ....San Juan, PR
Garcia Soto, Jorge ....San Juan, PR
García Tagle, Ricardo Alberto ....Portland, OR
Garcia-Toledo, A. Vicky Leiva ....Miami, FL
Garcia-Vidal & Donet, L.L.P. Coral Gables, FL
Miami, FL
García-Vidal, Raoul ....Miami, FL
Garcia-Vilanova, Apolo ....Mayaguez, PR
Garcia-Villarreal, David ....Philadelphia, PA
Garcia-Zamor, Ruy McEwan Philadelphia, PA
Garcin, Robert A. ....Loveland, CO
Garcin, Robert W. ....Los Angeles, CA
Garcin, Thomas M. ....Los Angeles, CA
Garczynski, Anthony J. ....Northville, MI
Garczynski & Brennan ....Elkhorn, WI
Garczynski, Randall R. ....Elkhorn, WI
Gard, Barbara S. ....Wellesley, MA
Gard, Dawn E. ....Chicago, IL
Gard, Elizabeth A. ....Pleasanton, CA
Gard, John S. ....Newark, OH
Gard, Kevin Matthew ....Chicago, IL
Gard, Robert R. ....Chicago, IL
Gard, S. Richard, Jr. ....Atlanta, GA
Gard, Stephen William ....Cleveland, OH
Gard, Steven J. ....Atlanta, GA
Gard, V. Randall ....Menlo Park, CA
Garda, John E. ....Dallas, TX
Garda, Robert A., Jr. ....Salt Lake City, UT
Gardana, Robert L. ....Miami, FL
Gardana, Robert L., P.A. ....Miami, FL
Gardanier, L. Eric ....Provo, UT
Gardberg, Jerome M. ....Lansing, IL
Gardberg, Jonathan P. ....Mobile, AL
Gardberg & Knopf, P.C. ....Mobile, AL
Garde, Billie Pirner ....Washington, DC
Garde, John C. ....Newark, NJ
Garde, L. Allison ....Morristown, NJ
Garde, Rashmi ....Foster City, CA
Garde, Stephanie ....Brockton, MA
Garde, Tanuja V. ....San Francisco, CA
Chicago, IL
Garde, Thomas C. ....Los Lunas, NM
Gardebring, Sandra S. ....St. Paul, MN
Gardella, Adriana ....New York, NY
Gardella, Daniel A. ....New York, NY
Gardella, Greg H. ....Chicago, IL
Gardella, Jenifer Karen ....Redwood City, CA
Gardella, Lawrence F. ....Montgomery, AL
Gardella, Matthew J. ....Boston, MA
Gardella, Richard E. ....Redwood City, CA
Gardella, Richard M. ....Scarsdale, NY
Gardella, Robert C. ....Brighton, MI
Gardella, Robert C. ....Howell, MI
Gardella, William P. ....New York, NY
Gardella, William S., (P.A.) Fort Lauderdale, FL
Gardels, David E. ....Omaha, NE
Garden, Kevin ....Washington, DC
Garden, Martin L. ....Minneapolis, MN
Garden, Martin L., Chartered, Law Offices of ....Minneapolis, MN
Garden, Richard P., Jr. ....Lincoln, NE
Garden, Warren W. ....Dallas, TX
Gardenal, John ....San Francisco, CA
Gardenal, John, A Professional Corporation San Francisco, CA
Gardener, Diane Levine ....Newton, MA
Gardener, James M. ....Sacramento, CA
Gardener, John R. ....Santa Ana, CA
Gardener, Michael S. ....Boston, MA
Gardener & Riechmann, Inc. ....Santa Ana, CA
Gardener, Yvonne Evadne ....Brooklyn, NY
Gardenhire, Gary W. ....Norman, OK
Gardenhire, Robert D. ....Santa Fe, NM
Gardenswartz, Daniel E. ....San Diego, CA
Gardenswartz, Ted D. ....Aspen, CO
Gardephe, Paul G. ....New York, NY
Gardere & Wynne, L.L.P. ....Tulsa, OK
Dallas, TX
Gardere Wynne Sewell & Riggs, L.L.P. Houston, TX
Gardes, Jeanne Marie ....Alexandria, VA
Gardey, David A. ....Detroit, MI
Gardi, T. David ....New York, NY
Gardieff, Leslie R. ....Winter Park, FL
Gardier, Robert W., Jr. ....Sarasota, FL
Gardill, James C. ....Wheeling, WV
Gardin, Lynn M. ....Minneapolis, MN
Gardiner, A. Theodore, III ....Wickliffe, OH
Gardiner, Ana I. ....Fort Lauderdale, FL
Gardiner, Angela N. ....Louisville, KY
Gardiner, Arthur Z., Jr. ....Hanover, NH
Gardiner, Barry L. ....Fort Lee, NJ
Gardiner, Caroline J., Law Office of Portland, ME
Gardiner, Charles A. ....Metairie, LA
Gardiner, Clinton L. ....Stratford, CT
Gardiner, Craig A. ....Spokane, WA
Gardiner, D. Bruce ....Augusta, GA
Gardiner, Dale F. ....Salt Lake City, UT
Gardiner, David C., Jr. ....Alexandria, VA
Gardiner, Donald B. ....Columbus, OH
Gardiner, Donna duBeth ....Somerset, NJ
Gardiner, Donna M. ....Albany, NY
Gardiner, Edward Donald ....Homewood, IL
Gardiner, Elizabeth A. ....Philadelphia, PA
Gardiner, Gloria ....Portland, OR
Gardiner, Grovetta N.
Federal Deposit Insurance Corporation, Compliance and Enforcement Section, GV
Gardiner, James S. ....Washington, DC
Gardiner, Jan L. ....Sacramento, CA
Gardiner, Joel F. ....Boston, MA
Gardiner, John D. ....Fort Lauderdale, FL
Dulles, VA
Gardiner, John L. ....New York, NY
Gardiner, Kay K. ....New York, NY
Gardiner, Kent A. ....Washington, DC
Gardiner Koch & Hines ....Chicago, IL
Gardiner, L. R., Jr. ....Salt Lake City, UT
Gardiner, Michael A. ....San Diego, CA
Gardiner, Michael B. ....Chicago, IL
Gardiner, Michael J. ....Providence, RI
Gardiner, Nancy Bader ....Brookline, MA
Gardiner, Nathaniel S. ....Boston, MA
Gardiner, Pamela Nan ....Miami Beach, FL
Gardiner, Patrick J. ....Los Angeles, CA
Gardiner, Phyllis ....Augusta, ME
Gardiner, Richard E. ....Fairfax, VA
Gardiner, Robert J. ....Bakersfield, CA
Gardiner, Scott G. ....Hockessin, DE
Gardiner, Stuart K. ....San Francisco, CA
Gardiner, Thomas G. ....Chicago, IL
Gardiner, William A. ....Brooklyn, NY
Gardiner, William C. ....East Orleans, MA
Gardiner, William D. ....Boston, MA
Gardiner, William L., III Fort Lauderdale, FL
Gardiner, William S. ....Indianapolis, IN
Gardis, John E. ....Indianapolis, IN
Gardner, Adrian R. ....Hyattsville, MD
Gardner, Alan J. ....New York, NY
Gardner, Alan M. ....New York, NY
Gardner, Alan R. ....Boise, ID
Gardner, Albert H. ....Kingsville, MD
Gardner, Albert J. ....Springfield, IL
Gardner & Aldrich, A Professional Corporation ....Dallas, TX
Fort Worth, TX
Gardner, Alexander R. ....Roseburg, OR
Gardner, Allen ....Memphis, TN
Gardner, Allen E. ....Bend, OR
Gardner, Allen M. ....Washington, DC
Gardner, Ames, Jr. ....Dayton, OH
Gardner, Andrew M. ....Chicago, IL
Gardner, Andrew R. ....Portland, OR
Gardner, Andrew T. ....Minneapolis, MN
Gardner, Andrew T. ....New York, NY
Gardner, Anne ....Fort Worth, TX
Gardner, Anne C. ....Sedalia, MO
Gardner, Anne E. ....Department of Justice, Office of Justice Programs, GV
Gardner, Anne v.d.L. ....Atherton, CA
Gardner, Anthony Justin ....San Francisco, CA
Gardner, Arnold B., (P.C.) ....Buffalo, NY
Gardner, Arnold E. ....Atlanta, GA
Gardner, Arnold G., Jr. ....Salt Lake City, UT
Gardner, Arthur ....Rancho Palos Verdes, CA
Gardner, Arthur A. ....Marietta, GA
Gardner, Ashley Joel ....Rockville, MD
Gardner & Associates, P.C. Ann Arbor, MI
Gardner, B. Clint ....Brookhaven, MS
Gardner & Balbick ....Batavia, NY
Gardner, Barbara E. ....Hartford, CT
Gardner, Barbara J. ....Houston, TX
Gardner, Barbara K. ....Washington, DC
Gardner, Barrow & Sharpe, A Professional Corporation ....Danville, VA
Gardner, Benjamin R. ....Martinsville, VA
Gardner, Bernard Richard, III ....Tulsa, OK
Gardner, Bill R. ....Ardmore, OK
Gardner, Blair M. ....St. Louis, MO
Gardner Bond Trabolsi St. Louis & Clement, PLLC ....Seattle, WA
Gardner, B. R., Jr. ....Tulsa, OK
Gardner, Bradley D. ....Phoenix, AZ
Gardner, Brant O. ....Indianapolis, IN
Gardner, Brenda L. ....Atlanta, GA
Gardner, Brent C. ....Phoenix, AZ
Gardner, Bret A. ....Salt Lake City, UT
Gardner, Brian C. ....Lexington, KY
Gardner, Brian E. ....Kansas City, MO
Gardner, Brian T. ....Chicago, IL
Gardner, Bruce A. ....Huntsville, AL
Gardner, Bruce A. ....Phoenix, AZ
Gardner, Bruce D. ....Hartford, CT
Gardner, Bruce T. ....New York, NY
Gardner, Buford M., Jr. ....Harrison, AR
Gardner, C. Wesley, Jr. ....Exeter, NH
Gardner, Callie Kennedy ....Camilla, GA
Gardner, Carol A. ....New York, NY
Gardner, Carolanne ....New York, NY
Gardner, Carroll F. ....Mount Airy, NC
Gardner, Carton & Douglas Washington, DC
Chicago, IL
Gardner, Catherine B. ....Washington, DC
Gardner, Cathy A. ....Los Angeles, CA
Gardner, Cecilia L. ....New York, NY
Gardner, Cedric B. ....Topeka, KS
Gardner, Charles A. ....Gouverneur, NY
Gardner, Charles H., Jr. ....Lynchburg, VA
Gardner, Charles J. (Jeff) ....Blytheville, AR
Gardner, Charles R. ....Tallahassee, FL
Gardner & Charney, P.L.L.P. ....Boise, ID
Gardner, Cheryl E. ....Falls Church, VA
Gardner, Christina
Administrative Office Of The United States Courts, GV
Gardner, Christopher H. ....Bend, OR
Gardner, Christopher W. Los Angeles, CA
Gardner, Clifford ....San Francisco, CA
Gardner, Clifford W. ....Janesville, MN
Gardner, Conrad E. ....Golden, CO
Gardner, Conrad E., P.C. ....Golden, CO
Gardner, Craig T. ....Saco, ME
Gardner and Creveling ....Akron, OH
Gardner & Cyrus ....Huntington, WV
Gardner, D. Allen ....Los Angeles, CA
Gardner, D. Max ....Bakersfield, CA
Gardner, Dale Ray ....Sapulpa, OK
Gardner, Dana F. ....Beverly Hills, CA
Gardner, Daniel L. ....Woodland Hills, CA
Gardner, Darrel J. ....Anchorage, AK
Gardner, David B. ....Los Angeles, CA
Gardner, David B. ....Gloucester, MA
Gardner, David C. ....Rockville, MD
Gardner, David Christopher Jonesboro, AR
Gardner, David E. ....Jacksonville, FL
Gardner, David G. ....Boston, MA
Gardner, David H. ....Newport Beach, CA
Gardner, David P. ....Mountain View, CA
Gardner, David P. ....Pocatello, ID
Gardner, David R. ....Bernalillo, NM
Gardner, Dawna Beryl
Department of Commerce, Patent and Trademark Office, GV
Gardner, Debby F. ....Austin, TX
Gardner, Deborah Kantar ....Boston, MA
Gardner, Debra S. ....Richmond, VA
Gardner, Dena W. ....Richmond Hill, GA
Gardner, Denise Shane ....Minnetonka, MN
Gardner, Dennis C. ....Houston, TX
Gardner, Diana R. ....Ann Arbor, MI
Gardner, Diane L. ....La Jolla, CA
Gardner, Dirk R. ....St. Louis, MO
Gardner, Don R. ....Cincinnati, OH
Gardner, Donald D. ....Port Hueneme, CA
Gardner, Donald E. ....Manchester, NH
Gardner, Donald S. ....Grand Rapids, MI
Gardner, Donna DiStefano ....Plaistow, NH
Gardner, Douglas J. ....Las Vegas, NV
Gardner, Douglas Lee ....Concord, CA
Gardner, Douglas R. ....Tampa, FL
Gardner, Douglas W. ....Missouri City, TX
Gardner, Edward W. ....Lexington, KY
Gardner, Eldora A. ....San Francisco, CA
Gardner, Elizabeth ....New York, NY
Gardner, Elizabeth J. ....San Francisco, CA
Gardner, Elizabeth P. ....Philadelphia, PA
Gardner, Eric R. ....Keene, NH
Gardner, Ewing & Souza ....Louisville, KY
Gardner, Francesca ....San Francisco, CA
Gardner, Francis X. ....Cleveland, OH
Gardner, Frank C. ....Pembroke Pines, FL
Gardner, Frank E. ....Chicago, IL
Gardner, Franklin K. ....Woodland, CA
Gardner, Fred ....Huntington, NY
Gardner, Fred L. ....Houston, TX
Gardner, Frederick E. ....Moundsville, WV
Gardner, G. Andrew ....Cleveland, OH
Gardner & Gardner ....Milledgeville, GA
Gardner, Gardner, Barrow & Sharpe, A Professional Corporation Martinsville, VA
Gardner, Gardner & Gardner LLP Sedalia, MO
Gardner, Gardner, Johnson and Mills Mount Airy, NC
Gardner & Gardner, P.C. ....Bend, OR
Gardner, Gary A. ....New York, NY
Gardner, Gary Allen ....Traverse City, MI
Gardner, Gary E. ....Dearborn, MI
Gardner, Gary Edward, P.C. ....Dearborn, MI
Gardner, Gary L. ....Louisville, KY
Gardner, Gary L. ....Somers Point, NJ
Gardner, Gary M. ....Wilmington, DE
Gardner, Gary Thomas ....Akron, OH
Gardner, Gayle W. ....Richmond, IN
Gardner, Gene F. ....Katy, TX
Gardner, Gene M. ....Duncan, OK
Gardner, Gene W. ....Huntington, WV
Gardner, George F., III ....Dover, DE
Gardner, George G. ....Florence, KY
Gardner, Gerald Brian ....San Francisco, CA
Gardner, Gilman J. ....Idaho Falls, ID
Gardner, Grant ....New York, NY
Gardner & Greenwood, LLP ....Atlanta, GA
Gardner, Gregory Scott ....Williamsport, PA
Gardner, Gretchen D. ....Santa Cruz, CA
Gardner & Groff, P.C. ....Atlanta, GA
Marietta, GA
Gardner, H. Daniel ....Milwaukee, WI
Gardner, H. Lawrence, Jr. ....Brenham, TX
Gardner, H. Robert ....New York, NY
Gardner, Hannah ....West Chester, PA
Gardner, Hanun B. ....Cambridge, MA
Gardner & Hardin, P.A. ....Russellville, AR
Gardner, Harrison ....Madison, NJ
Gardner, Henry A., Jr. ....Chicago, IL
Gardner, Howard A. ....New York, NY
Gardner, Howard J. ....Garden City, NY
Gardner, J. Cecil ....Mobile, AL
Gardner, J. Marshall ....Mobile, AL
Gardner, J. Neal ....Cincinnati, OH
Gardner, J. Stephen ....Tampa, FL
Gardner, J. Warren, Jr. ....New Orleans, LA
Gardner, Jack A. ....Bend, OR
Gardner, Jack F. ....Southfield, MI
Gardner, Jack L. ....New York, NY
Gardner & Jackson ....Moundsville, WV
Gardner, Jacqueline D. ....Jersey City, NJ
Gardner, Jacqueline Lisle ....Aspen, CO
Gardner, James A. ....Springfield, MA
Gardner, James A. ....Buffalo, NY
Gardner, James B. ....Shreveport, LA
Gardner, James C. ....Shreveport, LA
Gardner, James E. ....Akron, OH
Gardner, James E., Jr. ....Locust Valley, NY
Gardner, James F. ....San Antonio, TX
Gardner, James G. ....Newark, NJ
Gardner, James K. ....Chicago, IL
Gardner, James K. ....Hillsboro, OR
Gardner, James Knoll ....Allentown, PA
Gardner, James L. ....Richmond, VA
Gardner, James M. ....Blytheville, AR
Gardner, James P. ....Laguna Hills, CA
Gardner, James R. ....Richmond Hill, GA
Savannah, GA
Gardner, James W. ....Lexington, KY
Gardner, James W. ....Gold Beach, OR
Gardner, James W. ....Madison, WI
Gardner, Jamie S. ....Washington, DC
Gardner, Jane W. ....Fairfield, CT
Gardner, Janes, Nakken, Hugo & Nolan Woodland, CA
Gardner, Jared Edgar ....Oakland, CA
Gardner, Jayne E. ....Minneapolis, MN
Gardner, Jean M. ....New York, NY
Gardner, Jeffrey B. ....Newport Beach, CA
Riverside, CA
San Diego, CA
Gardner, Jeffrey C. ....Portland, OR
Gardner, Jeffrey M. ....Morristown, NJ
Gardner, Jeffrey Stuart ....Potomac, MD
Gardner, Jennifer G. ....Washington, DC
Gardner, Jennifer Radding ....New York, NY
Gardner, Jill R. ....New York, NY
Gardner, Joan Marie ....Washington, DC
Gardner, Joel B. ....New York, NY
Gardner, John ....Pearl River, NY
Gardner, John ....Shawnee, OK
Gardner, John A. ....Indianapolis, IN
Gardner, John A., III ....Charlotte, NC
Gardner, John C. ....Clearwater, FL
Gardner, John C. ....Ellicott City, MD
Gardner, John C. W. ....Mount Airy, NC
Gardner, John C. W., Jr. ....Mount Airy, NC
Gardner, John D. ....Lincolnshire, IL
Gardner, John D. ....West Linn, OR
Gardner, John F. ....Walnut Creek, CA
Gardner, John J. ....Olathe, KS
Gardner, John J. ....Boston, MA
Gardner, John J. ....Rye, NY
Gardner, John J., II ....Ponca City, OK
Gardner, John M. ....Denver, CO

Gardner, John M. ..... Gulfport, MS
Gardner, John N. ..... Cleveland, OH
Gardner, John P. ..... Rye, NY
Gardner, John P., Jr. ..... Darlington, SC
Myrtle Beach, SC
Gardner, John R. ..... Shreveport, LA
Gardner, John S. ..... Oklahoma City, OK
Gardner, John W. ..... Brandon, FL
Gardner, Jonathan ..... New York, NY
Gardner, Jonathan H. ..... Buffalo, NY
Gardner, Joseph, III ..... Tucker, GA
Gardner, Joseph M. ..... Vinita, OK
Gardner, Joseph W. ..... Canfield, OH
Gardner, Julie A. ..... Metairie, LA
Gardner, Julie Lingle ..... Missoula, MT
Gardner, K. Van ..... Houston, TX
Gardner, Karey Weeks ..... Texarkana, TX
Gardner, Kathleen E. ..... New York, NY
Gardner, Kathryn ..... Wichita, KS
Gardner, Kathy Woeber
San Francisco, CA
Gardner, Kelly A. ..... Norcross, GA
Gardner, Kenneth E. ..... Dallas, TX
Gardner, Kenneth H. ..... New York, NY
Gardner, Kevin R. ..... Roseland, NJ
Gardner, Kewley & Bisso, A Professional Law Corporation ..... Metairie, LA
New Orleans, LA
Gardner, Kimball ..... Colorado Springs, CO
Gardner, Kit J. ..... San Diego, CA
Gardner, Krystal M. ..... Detroit, MI
Gardner & Kucharski ..... Cleveland, OH
Gardner, Kurt A. ..... Ephrata, PA
Gardner, Lance D. ..... Fairfax, VA
Gardner, Lance D., P.C. ..... Fairfax, VA
Gardner, Lani T. ..... Dallas, GA
Gardner, Larry D. ..... New Orleans, LA
Gardner, Larry F. ..... Windham, NY
Gardner, Larry J. ..... Grand Rapids, MI
Gardner, Laurence ..... Portland, ME
Gardner, Laurence F. ..... Lebanon, NH
Gardner Law Firm ..... Blytheville, AR
Gardner Law Firm, The ..... Conway, SC
Darlington, SC
Florence, SC
Georgetown, SC
Marion, SC
Myrtle Beach, SC
Gardner Law Firm, The, A Professional Corporation ..... San Antonio, TX
Gardner, Lawn B. ..... Oklahoma City, OK
Gardner, Lawrence K., (S.C.) ..... Pewaukee, WI
Gardner, Leonard Levi ..... Miami, FL
Gardner, Leslie K. ..... New York, NY
Gardner, Lewis B. ..... Tysons Corner, VA
Gardner, Lincoln D. ..... San Clemente, CA
Gardner, Linda K. ..... Overland Park, KS
Gardner, Linda M. ..... Washington, DC
Gardner, Linda Ohlemeyer
Jefferson City, MO
Gardner, Linda R. ..... Princeton, NJ
Gardner, Lissa J. ..... Las Cruces, NM
Gardner, Loraine F. ..... New York, NY
Gardner, Lorraine E. ..... Treasury Department, Internal Revenue Service, GV
Gardner, Louis E. ..... Friendswood, TX
Gardner, Luke G. ..... New York, NY
Gardner, Lynn A. ..... Memphis, TN
Gardner, Lynn M. ..... Rosemead, CA
Gardner, M. Ayres ..... Atlanta, GA
Gardner, M. Brent ..... Boise, ID
Gardner, M. Donald ..... Portland, ME
Gardner, Marcie L. ..... Los Angeles, CA
Gardner, Mark ..... Cleveland, OH
Gardner, Mark ..... Hillsboro, OR
Gardner, Mark Douglas ..... Newark, OH
Gardner, Mark E. ..... Springfield, MO
Gardner, Mark H. ..... Exeter, NH
Gardner, Mark J. ..... Cambridge, MA
Gardner, Mark L. ..... Stamford, CT
Gardner, Mark S. ..... Spotsylvania, VA
Gardner, Marshall ..... Florence, AL
Gardner, Marshall C.
Department Of Health And Human Services, Social Security Administration, GV
Gardner, Martin ..... Lincoln, NE
Gardner, Martin J. ..... South Bend, IN
Gardner, Marvin ..... Stamford, CT
Gardner, Mary E. ..... Chicago, IL
Gardner, Matthew D. ..... Des Moines, IA
Gardner, Maupin & Sutton, P.C.
Richmond, VA
Spotsylvania, VA
Gardner, Maureen O'Ferrall ..... Annapolis, MD
Gardner, Max C. ..... St. George, UT
Gardner, Merritt A. ..... Tampa, FL
Gardner, Michael A. ..... Oakland, CA
Gardner, Michael Bruce ..... Cleveland, OH
Gardner, Michael E. ..... Los Altos Hills, CA
Gardner, Michael J. ..... Virginia Beach, VA
Gardner, Michael L. ..... Purcell, OK
Gardner, Michael R. ..... Buena Park, CA
Gardner, Michael R. ..... Oceanside, CA
Gardner, Michael R. ..... Washington, DC
Gardner, Michael R. ..... Wayne, PA
Gardner, Michael R., P.C., The Law Offices of
Washington, DC
Gardner, Michael S. ..... Dallas, TX
Gardner, Middlebrooks, Fleming, Gibbons & Kittrell, P.C. ..... Birmingham, AL
Mobile, AL
Washington, DC
Gardner, Milton F. ..... Milledgeville, GA
Gardner, Milton F., Jr. ..... Milledgeville, GA
Gardner, Minalee E. ..... Stevensville, MI
Gardner, Mitchell ..... New Britain, CT
Gardner, N. Vail ..... Miami, FL
Gardner, Nancy C. ..... New York, NY
Gardner, Naomi C. ..... Brooklyn, NY
Gardner, Naomi C., P.C. ..... Brooklyn, NY
Gardner, Nicholas Berge ..... Eagan, MN
Gardner, O. Max, III ..... Shelby, NC
Gardner, Ohlrich & Vlach
Washington, DC
Gardner, Owen M. ..... Okanogan, WA
Gardner, Pat H. ..... San Antonio, TX
Gardner, Patricia D. ..... Grand Rapids, MI
Gardner, Patricia S. ..... Flemington, NJ
Gardner, Patrick J. ..... Heber Springs, AR
Gardner, Paul A. ..... Boston, MA
Gardner, Paul H. ..... Jefferson City, MO
Gardner, Paul J. ..... Omaha, NE
Gardner, Paul L. ..... Costa Mesa, CA
Gardner, Paulyne A. ..... Norristown, PA
Gardner, Peter C. ..... Philadelphia, PA
Gardner, Peter J. ..... Philadelphia, PA
Gardner, Peter J., A Prof. Corp.
Los Angeles, CA
Gardner, Peter N. ..... Augusta, ME
Gardner, Phil B. ..... Memphis, TN
Gardner, Philip G. ..... Danville, VA
Gardner, Price C., (P.A.) ..... Little Rock, AR
Gardner and Putnam ..... Harrison, AR
Gardner and Quan, Incorporated
Newport Beach, CA
Gardner, R. Kent ..... Olympia, WA
Gardner, R. Scott ..... Washington, DC
Gardner, R. Scott ..... Sedalia, MO
Gardner, Racines & Sheetz
Allentown, PA
Gardner, Racines and Sheetz ..... Emmaus, PA
Gardner, Randall L. ..... Louisville, KY
Gardner, Randy ..... De Soto, KS
Gardner, Randy Steven ..... Memphis, TN
Gardner, Ray D. ..... Anchorage, AK
Gardner, Richard C. ..... San Jose, CA
Gardner, Richard E., Jr. ..... Russellville, AR
Gardner, Richard N. ..... New York, NY
Gardner, Richd. E. ..... Tulsa, OK
Gardner, Robert A. ..... Anadarko, OK
Gardner, Robert A., Jr. ..... Chicago, IL
Gardner, Robert B. ..... Seattle, WA
Gardner, Robert D. ..... Morris Plains, NJ
Gardner, Robert E. ..... Saratoga Springs, NY
Gardner, Robert E. ..... Chesterland, OH
Gardner, Robert F. ..... Columbus, OH
Gardner, Robert H. ..... Overland Park, KS
Gardner, Robert H. ..... Rutherford, NJ
Gardner, Robert I. ..... Bronx, NY
Gardner, Robert L. ..... Sherman Oaks, CA
Gardner, Robert M. ..... Minneapolis, MN
Gardner, Robert M. ..... Las Vegas, NV
Gardner, Robert M., (P.A.)
Ormond Beach, FL
Gardner, Robert R. ..... Raleigh, NC
Gardner, Robert S. ..... Sedalia, MO
Gardner, Robert S. ..... Corvallis, OR
Gardner, Robert T. ..... Birmingham, AL
Gardner, Robert W., Jr. ..... Ayer, MA
Gardner, Robert W., Jr., P.C. ..... Ayer, MA
Devens, MA
Worcester, MA
Gardner, Roland M. ..... Edgewood, MD
Gardner, Ronald C. ..... Seattle, WA
Gardner, Ronald D. ..... Ann Arbor, MI
Gardner, Ronald J. ..... Salt Lake City, UT
Gardner, Ronald K., Jr. ..... Minneapolis, MN
Gardner, Rossie G. ..... High Point, NC
Gardner, Royal C., III ..... St. Petersburg, FL
Gardner, Russell H. ..... Baltimore, MD
Gardner, Russell M. ..... Fort Lauderdale, FL
Gardner, Sally ..... Department of Commerce, Patent and Trademark Office, GV
Gardner, Sam J., Jr. ..... Moultrie, GA
Gardner, Sam R. ..... Monett, MO
Gardner, Samuel C. ..... Detroit, MI
Gardner, Sandra L. ..... Albuquerque, NM
Gardner, Sarah A. ..... New York, NY
Gardner, Sawyer, Gates & Sloan
Providence, RI
Gardner, Scott D. ..... Saco, ME
Gardner, Scott E. ..... Salem, VA
Gardner, Scott L. ..... San Francisco, CA
Gardner, Seth ..... New York, NY
Gardner, Sharon Ann ..... Clarkston, MI
Gardner, Sharon Brand ..... Houston, TX
Gardner, Sheldon ..... Chicago, IL
Gardner, Shelfer, Duggar, Bist & Wiener, P.A. ..... Tallahassee, FL
Gardner & Siringas, P.L.C. ..... Detroit, MI
Gardner & Sosinsky ..... New York, NY
Gardner, Spencer H. ..... Houston, TX
Gardner, Spencer H., P.C. ..... Houston, TX
Gardner, Stanley E. ..... Stockton, CA
Gardner, Stephen ..... Dallas, TX
Gardner, Stephen C. ..... Russellville, AR
Gardner, Stephen D. ..... New York, NY
Gardner, Stephen E. ..... Jackson, MS
Gardner, Stephen K. ..... Washington, DC
Gardner, Steven ..... Ottumwa, IA
Gardner, Steven ..... Winston-Salem, NC
Gardner, Steven A. ..... Idaho Falls, ID
Gardner, Steven D. ..... Charlotte, NC
Gardner, Steven H. ..... Los Angeles, CA
Gardner, Steven L. ..... Cleveland, OH
Gardner, Sue Shaffer ..... Buffalo, NY
Gardner, Susan M. ..... Kansas City, MO
Gardner, Suzanne L. ..... Carol Stream, IL
Gardner, T. Alfred ..... Greensboro, NC
Gardner, T. Allen, Jr. ..... Louisburg, NC
Gardner, T. Truett ..... Tampa, FL
Gardner & Tepper ..... Ormond Beach, FL
Gardner, Terri L. ..... Raleigh, NC
Gardner, Terry ..... Fort Worth, TX
Gardner, Thomas F. ..... Chicago, IL
Gardner, Thomas F. ..... Metairie, LA
Gardner, Thomas J. ..... Milwaukee, WI
Gardner, Thomas J., III ..... Tupelo, MS
Gardner, Todd D. ..... Salt Lake City, UT
Gardner, Todd E. ..... Hagåtña, GU
Gardner, Todd W. ..... Renton, WA
Gardner, W. Franklin, Jr. ..... Austin, TX
Gardner, W. Joseph ..... Carlisle, MA
Gardner, W. Major ..... Lexington, KY
Gardner, W. Stephen ..... Memphis, TN
Gardner, Walter H. ..... Burlington, VT
Gardner, Warner W. ..... Washington, DC
Gardner, Wayne L. ..... Mesa, AZ
Gardner & Weiss ..... New York, NY
Gardner, Wendy D. ..... Newark, NJ
Gardner, Wilkes, Shaheen & Candelora
Tampa, FL
Gardner, William ..... New York, NY
Gardner, William ..... Fairfax, VA
Gardner, William C. ..... Washington, DC
Gardner, William D. ..... New York, NY
Gardner, William D. ..... Milwaukee, WI
Gardner, William F. ..... Birmingham, AL
Gardner, William G. ..... Oak Lawn, IL
Gardner, William H. ..... San Diego, CA
Gardner, William H. ..... Buffalo, NY
Gardner, William L. ..... Washington, DC
Gardner, William R. ..... San Francisco, CA
Gardner, Willis, Sweat & Goldsmith
Atlanta, GA
Albany, GA
Gardner, Winthrop G. ..... New Orleans, LA
Gardner, Wm. L. ..... Millersville, MD
Gardner, Woodford L., Jr. ..... Glasgow, KY
Gardner, Yvette Leerskov ..... Wichita, KS
Gardner-Frum, Miriam ..... New London, CT
Gardner Pearson, Joi ..... Salt Lake City, UT
Gardner-Reese, Pat ..... Marietta, GA
Gardo, William L, II ..... Hendersonville, NC
Gardocki, Christian ..... Lincoln Park, MI
Gardon, Peter L. ..... Madison, WI
Gardstein, Ronnie Kay ..... Red Bank, NJ
Gardunia, Theresa ..... Idaho City, ID
Gardy, Jeffrey L. ..... Suffolk, VA
Gardy, Mark C. ..... New York, NY
Gardy, Rodger Lee, Jr. ..... Chicago, IL
Gardzelewski, Allen ..... Laramie, WY
Gare, Ann-Marie ..... San Rafael, CA
Gare, Henry Eric ..... Jacksonville, FL
Garea, Stephen R. ..... Canfield, OH
Gareau, Bernard H. ..... Longmeadow, MA
Gareau & Dubelko Co., L.P.A.
North Olmsted, OH
Gareau, Michael R. ..... North Olmsted, OH
Gareau, Michael R., Jr. ..... North Olmsted, OH
Gareen, Paul S. ..... New York, NY
Gareis, Robert J. ..... Chicago, IL
Gareis-Smith, Donna L. ..... Harrisburg, PA
Garel, Jules L. ..... Columbus, OH
Garelick, Andrew D. ..... Los Angeles, CA
Garelick, Jared S. ..... Fairfax, VA
Garelick, Jordan R. ..... Chicago, IL
Garelick, Nancy O. ..... San Marino, CA
Garelick, Robert A. ..... Indianapolis, IN
Garelick, Ronna E. ..... Lebanon, NJ
Garelick, Scott Michael ..... Dallas, TX
Garelik, David M. ..... New York, NY
Garelik, Debra L. ..... Pontiac, MI
Garelis, Stephan ..... Berkeley, CA
Garelis, Theodore ..... San Francisco, CA
Garella, Elena Luisa ..... Seattle, WA
Garellek, Steven ..... Boca Raton, FL
Garellek, Steven, P.A., Law Offices of
Boca Raton, FL
Garelli, Theresa Ann ..... New York, NY
Garen, Daniel J. ..... Cleveland, OH
Garett, Jack ..... Shirley, NY
Garetto, Janet M. ..... Chicago, IL
Garewal, E. Kathleen ..... San Antonio, TX
Garey, Eileen C. ..... Kansas City, MO
Garey, Howard B. ..... Los Angeles, CA
Garey, Jack ..... Austin, TX
Garey, John R. ..... Dover, DE
Garey, Kirkland W. ..... Bloomfield Hills, MI
Garey, Lea A. ..... Austin, TX
Garey, Margot Ann ..... San Francisco, CA
Garey, Michael Ian ..... Santa Ana, CA
Garey, Michael J. ..... Los Angeles, CA
Garey, Robert R. ..... Savannah, GA
Garfein, James E. ..... White Plains, NY
Garfein, Mary C. ..... Cupertino, CA
Garfein, Vivian Feist ..... Tallahassee, FL
Garff, Regnal W. ..... Salt Lake City, UT
Garfield, Alan D. ..... New York, NY
Garfield, Alan Evan ..... Wilmington, DE
Garfield, Alan H. ..... Chicago, IL
Garfield, Alice J. ..... Los Angeles, CA
Garfield, Allen M. ..... San Francisco, CA
Garfield, Arthur L. ..... Cheyenne, WY
Garfield, Daniel Jay ..... Denver, CO
Garfield, David R. ..... Minneapolis, MN
Garfield, Dean C. ..... Washington, DC
Garfield, Deborah A. ..... New York, NY
Garfield, Diana ..... Hartford, CT
Garfield, Elizabeth Jo ..... Los Angeles, CA
Garfield, Franklin R. ..... Los Angeles, CA
Garfield, Frederick Mott, Jr.
Birmingham, AL
Garfield, Gary A. ..... Nashville, TN
Garfield, Gerald ..... Hartford, CT
Garfield, Greg S. ..... Santa Clara, CA
Garfield, Harold T. ..... Los Angeles, CA
Garfield & Hecht, P.C. ..... Aspen, CO
Basalt, CO
Garfield, Helen ..... Indianapolis, IN
Garfield, Hollis J. ..... Pittsburgh, PA
Garfield, Howard M. ..... San Francisco, CA
Garfield, J. Brent ..... Naperville, IL
Garfield, Jack C. ..... New York, NY
Garfield, James R. ..... Chicago, IL
Garfield & Lasko, A Legal Prof. Assoc.
Cleveland, OH
Garfield, Martin R. ..... New York, NY
Garfield & Merel, Ltd., A Professional Corporation ..... Chicago, IL
Garfield, Michael A. ..... Jacksonville, FL
Garfield, Michael R. ..... Boston, MA
Garfield, Neil F. ..... Fort Lauderdale, FL
Garfield, Richard T. ..... Fort Lauderdale, FL
Garfield, Robert David ..... Lexington, SC
Garfield, Robert E. ..... Cleveland, OH
Garfield, Robert H. ..... St. Louis, MO
Garfield, Ronald ..... Aspen, CO
Garfield, Roslyn ..... Provincetown, MA
Garfield, Sharyn D. ..... Coral Springs, FL
Garfield & Tepper, P.C. ..... Los Angeles, CA
Garfield, Timothy K. ..... San Diego, CA
Garfin, Jeffrey D., J.D. P.C. ..... Springfield, MA
Garfin, Jeffrey D., P.C. ..... Springfield, MA
Garfing, Karen L. ..... Trenton, NJ
Garfink, Roger K. ..... Baltimore, MD
Garfinkel, Alan A. ..... Pittsburgh, PA
Garfinkel, Barry H. ..... New York, NY
Garfinkel, Bernard J. ..... Memphis, TN
Garfinkel, Catherine L. ..... Pittsburgh, PA
Garfinkel, David A. ..... Jacksonville, FL
Garfinkel, Edward A. ..... New York, NY
Garfinkel, Frances L. ..... New York, NY
Garfinkel, Gregg S. ..... Encino, CA
Garfinkel, Harry ..... Avon, CT
Garfinkel, Howard Ira ..... Yonkers, NY
Garfinkel, Howard M. ..... Cleveland, OH
Garfinkel Immigration Law Firm
Charlotte, NC
Garfinkel, Irwin H. ..... Los Angeles, CA
Garfinkel, Jane E. ..... Cincinnati, OH
Garfinkel, Jill B. ..... Garden City, NY
Garfinkel, Judy ..... Jacksonville, FL
Garfinkel, Louis E. ..... Las Vegas, NV
Garfinkel, Martin ..... Virginia Beach, VA
Garfinkel, Martin S. ..... Seattle, WA
Garfinkel, Marvin ..... Philadelphia, PA
Garfinkel, Michael B. ..... Los Angeles, CA
Garfinkel, Mitchell D. ..... Fort Lauderdale, FL
Garfinkel, Monica S. ..... Phoenix, AZ
Garfinkel, Neil B. ..... New York, NY
Westbury, NY
Garfinkel, Neil M. ..... Palo Alto, CA
Garfinkel, Norman J. ..... Bensenville, IL
Garfinkel, Paul E. ..... Chicago, IL
Garfinkel, Paul W. ..... Charleston, SC
Garfinkel, Philip ..... Charleston, SC
Garfinkel, Roy E ..... Baltimore, MD
Garfinkel, Sandra ..... Houston, TX
Garfinkel, Sandy B. ..... Pittsburgh, PA
Garfinkel, Steven ..... New York, NY
Garfinkel, Steven H. ..... Charlotte, NC
Garfinkel, William I. ..... Bridgeport, CT
Garfinkle, Alan ..... Baltimore, MD
Garfinkle, Allan Jay ..... Omaha, NE
Garfinkle, Allen ..... Oakland, CA
Garfinkle, Ann M. ..... Washington, DC
Garfinkle & Associates, Law Offices of
Washington, DC
Garfinkle, Carla F. ..... Chicago, IL
Garfinkle & Corbman, P.C. ..... Philadelphia, PA
Garfinkle, David D. ..... Irvine, CA
Garfinkle, David L. ..... Chicago, IL
Garfinkle, Debra Lynn ..... San Diego, CA
Garfinkle, Ellie ..... Philadelphia, PA
Garfinkle, Eugene ..... San Francisco, CA
Garfinkle, Gerald D. ..... Philadelphia, PA
Garfinkle, Gerald L. ..... Jamaica, NY
Garfinkle, Irwin P. ..... Wilmington, MA
Garfinkle, Jack R. ..... Philadelphia, PA
Garfinkle, Jeffrey ..... San Diego, CA
Garfinkle, M. Jerry ..... Charleston, SC
Garfinkle, Marc D. ..... Maplewood, NJ
Garfinkle, McLemore & Walker, PLLC
Nashville, TN
Garfinkle, Morris R. ..... Washington, DC
Garfinkle, Robert M. ..... Nashville, TN
Garfinkle, Robin G. ..... New York, NY
Garfinkle, Steven E. ..... Los Angeles, CA
Garfinkle, Vivienne ..... New York, NY
Garfunkel, Alan J. ..... New York, NY
Garfunkel, Aura Sanchez ..... Boston, MA
Garfunkel, David A. ..... Concord, NH
Garfunkel, George M. ..... Great Neck, NY
Garfunkel, Jeffrey A. ..... Ontario, CA
Garfunkel, Kenneth ..... Norwalk, CT
Garfunkel, Steven B. ..... Mayfield Village, OH
Garfunkel, Warren L. ..... New Orleans, LA
Garfunkel, Wild & Travis, P.C.
Great Neck, NY
Garg, Sampak P. ..... House of Representatives, Committee Legal Personnel, GV
Garg, Sunil K. ..... Wayne, NJ
Gargan, John P. ..... Dallas, TX
Gargan, Joseph F. ..... Hyannisport, MA
Gargan, Terence ..... New York, NY
Gargan, William Thomas ..... Rochester, NY
Garganese, Anthony A. ..... Cocoa, FL
Garganigo, Albert D. ..... New York, NY
Gargano, Anthony C.
Hopewell Junction, NY
Gargano, Anthony F. ..... Cambridge, MA
Gargano, Anthony J. ..... Fort Myers, FL
Gargano and Associates ..... Boston, MA
Cambridge, MA
Gargano, Christopher P. ..... Jersey City, NJ
Gargano, Francine A. ..... North Plainfield, NJ
Gargano, Jeffrey R. ..... Chicago, IL
Gargano & Marchewka, L.L.P.
Fort Myers, FL
Gargano, Paul A. ..... Cambridge, MA
Gargano, Roy J. ..... Bakersfield, CA

Gargano, William Roger ......San Francisco, CA
Garganta, Angel A. ....San Francisco, CA
Gargaro, Stephen ....San Francisco, CA
Gargaro, William J., Jr. ....Los Angeles, CA
Gargaro, William J., Jr., A Professional Corporation ....Los Angeles, CA
Gargas, Leonard R. ....Calumet City, IL
Gargas, Melanie J. ....Boston, MA
Gargas, Michael D. ....Salem, MA
Gargasz, Robert J. ....Lorain, OH
Gargasz, Scott Steven ....Akron, OH
Garger, Andrew J. ....New York, NY
Garger, Francis ....Pittsburgh, PA
Garger, Laura Roberts ....Phoenix, AZ
Garger, Melanie M. ....New York, NY
Garger, Walter F. ....Hartford, CT
Gargess, Katherine S. ....Chadds Ford, PA
Garges, Sandra C. ....Grand Rapids, MI
Gargill, Robert M., (P.C.) ....Boston, MA
Gargill, Sassoon & Rudolph LLP
Boston, MA
Manchester, MA
Marblehead, MA
Swampscott, MA
Gargis, C. Lynn ....Winston-Salem, NC
Gargis, H. Alan ....Muscle Shoals, AL
Gargis, Robert S. (Steve) ....Tuscumbia, AL
Gargiulo, Andrea W. ....Boston, MA
Gargiulo, Anthony P. ....Mashpee, MA
Gargiulo, Edward R., Jr. (P.C.)
Boston, MA
Mashpee, MA
Gargiulo, John C. ....Gulfport, MS
Gargiulo, Paul G. ....White Plains, NY
Gargiulo, Richard A., (P.C.) ....Boston, MA
Gargiulo, Robert G. ....Bradenton, FL
Gargiulo, Rudnick & Gargiulo
Boston, MA
Mashpee, MA
Gargiulo, William C. ....Cleveland, OH
Gargotta, Craig A. ....San Antonio, TX
Garguilo, Jerry ....St. James, NY
Gargula, Carl G. ....Chicago, IL
Gargula, Mark C. ....Indianapolis, IN
Gargula, Nancy J. ....Indianapolis, IN
Gargulak, John P. ....Cudahy, WI
Gargulinski, Renee E. ....Worcester, MA
Garhart, John Paul ....Erie, PA
Garhart, Nate A. ....San Francisco, CA
Gari, Ronald F. ....Los Angeles, CA
Garian & Garian ....Royal Oak, MI
Garian, Kalem E. ....Royal Oak, MI
Garian, Marie ....Royal Oak, MI
Garian, Robert L. ....Richmond, VA
Garibaldi, Colette Yoda ....Honolulu, HI
Garibaldi, David J., III ....Costa Mesa, CA
Garibaldi, Donald J. ....San Francisco, CA
Garibaldi & Garibaldi ....Glen Rock, NJ
Garibaldi, John J. ....San Jose, CA
Garibaldi, Marie L. ....Jersey City, NJ
Garibaldi, Mark J. ....Bakersfield, CA
Garibaldi, Oscar M. ....Washington, DC
Garibaldi, Robert L., Jr. ....Glen Rock, NJ
Garibay, Guillermo Ruben ....Pueblo, CO
Garibay, Manuel C. ....Phoenix, AZ
Garibian, Christopher L. ....Morristown, NJ
Garibian, P.C. ....Morristown, NJ
Garick, Jason ....Stamford, CT
Garie, John D. ....Parsippany, NJ
Gariepy, Lloyd R. ....Woonsocket, RI
Gariepy, Paul Francis ....Boston, MA
Gariepy, Richard N. ....Ketchum, ID
Gariepy, Robert L. ....Bloomfield Hills, MI
Gariepy, Roland E. ....Framingham, MA
Gariepy, Stephen H. ....Cleveland, OH
Garigliano, Barbara A. ....Monticello, NY
Garigliano, Walter F. ....Monticello, NY
Gariglietti, John C. ....Pittsburg, KS
Garikian, Ani M. ....Beverly Hills, CA
Garil, Herbert ....Franklin Square, NY
Garil & Meyerson ....Franklin Square, NY
Garin, Joseph P. ....Troy, MI
Garin, Patricia ....Boston, MA
Garin, Peter A. ....Golden, CO
Garing, Robert F. ....Seattle, WA
Garinther, Geoffrey R. ....Baltimore, MD
Towson, MD
Garipay, Kathryn E. ....Chicago, IL
Garippa and Davenport, A Professional Corporation ....Hackensack, NJ
Montclair, NJ
Newark, NJ
Garippa, John E. ....Montclair, NJ
Garippo, Louis B. ....Chicago, IL
Garippo, Louis, Jr. ....West Long Branch, NJ
Garis, George S. ....Livonia, MI
Garis, Jeffrey I. ....Charlotte, NC
Garity, James P. ....Burbank, CA
Garjian, Nelson N. ....Brooklyn, NY
Garjian, Paul G. ....Hackensack, NJ
Garka, Mark W. ....Everett, WA
Garkowski, John J. ....Elmhurst, NY
Garland, Abe J. ....St. Louis, MO
Garland, Alan ....Chicago, IL
Garland, Alec ....Manchester, TN
Garland, Barbara J. ....Hillsboro, OR
Garland, Barbara J., Law Office, P.C.
Hillsboro, OR
Portland, OR
Garland, Benjamin M. ....Macon, GA
Garland, Bruce H. ....Trenton, NJ
Garland, Burton D., Jr. ....St. Louis, MO
Garland, Byrd ....Jackson, GA
Garland, David ....New Orleans, LA
Garland, David A. ....Albany, GA
Garland, David L. ....Arvada, CO
Garland, David W. ....Wellesley, MA
Garland, David W. ....Newark, NJ
Garland, David Wesley ....Richmond, VA
Garland, Dean D. ....Shawnee, KS
Garland and Drum, P.A. ....Charlotte, NC
Gastonia, NC
Lincolnton, NC
Garland, E. Jane ....Brea, CA
Garland, Edward T. M. ....Atlanta, GA
Garland, Felicia L. ....Newark, NJ
Garland, G. Gray, Jr. ....Pittsburgh, PA
Garland, Gary ....Corning, AR
Garland, Gary ....New York, NY
Garland, Gloria J. ....Palo Alto, CA
Garland, Gregory K. ....Omaha, NE
Garland, Gregory S. ....Colorado Springs, CO
Garland, H. Mathews ....Dallas, TX
Garland, Holly G. ....Greensburg, PA
Garland, J. Boyce, Jr. ....Gastonia, NC
Garland, Jack J., Jr. ....Houston, TX
Garland, James B. ....Morristown, NJ
Garland, James B. ....Gastonia, NC
Garland, James C., III ....Tulsa, OK
Garland, James Clinton ....Tulsa, OK
Garland, James E. ....Los Angeles, CA
Garland, James P. ....Baltimore, MD
Garland, Jane ....Columbia, MO
Garland, Jeffrey H. ....Fort Pierce, FL
Garland, Jeffrey N. ....San Diego, CA
Garland, John E. ....Quincy, MA
Garland, John F. ....Fresno, CA
Garland, John G. ....Houston, TX
Garland, John R. ....Denver, CO
Garland, John W. ....Anadarko, OK
Garland, Joseph Christopher
Baltimore, MD
Garland, Joseph P. ....New York, NY
Garland, Karen M. ....Baton Rouge, LA
Garland, L. Brooks ....Nashville, TN
Garland Law Offices, P.C. ....Hillsboro, OR
Garland, Leanne ....Tyler, TX
Garland, M. Spencer ....St. Louis, MO
Garland, Marvin J. ....Hillsboro, OR
Garland, Mary Teresa ....Bel Air, MD
Garland & McCue ....Bradenton, FL
Garland, Merrick B.
United States Court Of Appeals District Of Columbia Circuit, GV
Garland, Michael ....Murfreesboro, NC
Garland, Michael E. ....New Bern, NC
Garland, Michael W. ....Worcester, MA
Garland & Milam, P.C. ....Jackson, GA
Garland, Natalie M. ....Pittsburgh, PA
Garland, Norman M. ....Los Angeles, CA
Garland, Paul Griffith ....Boca Raton, FL
Garland, Peter B. ....Pocasset, MA
Garland, Philip L. ....Garner, IA
Mason City, IA
Garland, Philip O. ....Charlottesville, VA
Garland, R. Scott ....Jackson, WY
Garland, R. C., Jr. ....Pauls Valley, OK
Garland, Rebecca T. ....Brentwood, TN
Garland, Rex A. ....Bremerton, WA
Garland, Richard R. ....Sarasota, FL
Garland, Robert M. ....San Diego, CA
Garland, Robert Wm. ....Greensburg, PA
Garland, Ronald D. ....Knoxville, TN
Garland, Samuel & Loeb, P.C.
Atlanta, GA
Garland, Scott L. ....Portland, OR
Garland, Seth D. ....Washington, DC
Garland, Steven C. ....Winston-Salem, NC
Garland, Sylvia D. ....New York, NY
Garland, Terri A. ....San Francisco, CA
Garland, Thomas J., Jr. ....Greeneville, TN
Garland, Thomas R. ....Port St. Lucie, FL
Garland, Torry ....Omaha, NE
Garland, Walter B. ....Erwin, TN
Garland, William E. ....Newark, NJ
Garland, William H. ....Bradenton, FL
Garland, William Joseph ....Tulsa, OK
Garland, William R. ....Bremerton, WA
Garlanger, James W. ....Palos Heights, IL
Garlasco, Paul James ....New Milford, CT
Garleb, William J., Jr. ....San Diego, CA
Garlepp, Edwin Donnell ....Arlington, VA
Garlett, Philip L. ....Treasury Department, Internal Revenue Service, GV
Garley, R. Scott ....New York, NY
Garley, Richard E. ....Spring Lake, NJ
Garlick, Bruce E. ....Austin, TX
Garlick, Edward E. ....Westport, CT
Garlick, Gerald L. ....Hartford, CT
Garlick, Gordon K. ....Bolton Landing, NY
Garlick, Jason M. ....Palo Alto, CA
Garlick, Michael ....Boca Raton, FL
Garlick, Michael, P.A. ....Boca Raton, FL
Garlick, Thomas B. ....Naples, FL
Garlin, Alexander, (P.C.) ....Boulder, CO
Garlin, Victor A. ....Berkeley, CA
Garling, Ellen J. ....Columbus, OH
Garling, Jerry L. ....Colorado Springs, CO
Garlinger, Donald W. ....Winfield, IL
Garlinger, Lawrence A. ....Columbus, OH
Garlinghouse, Anne P. ....Lawrence, KS
Garlinghouse, David M. ....San Dimas, CA
Garlington, Edward, Jr. ....La Junta, CO
Garlington, Lohn & Robinson, PLLP
Anaconda, MT
Hamilton, MT
Kalispell, MT
Missoula, MT
Polson, MT
Garlington, Monica E. ....Washington, DC
Garlington, Thomas R. ....Olympia, WA
Garlington, W. Conway ....Knoxville, TN
Garlington-Mathews, LaVeeda ....Seattle, WA
Garlinski, Judith E. Basker ....Houston, TX
Garlitz, Janice E. ....Oakton, VA
Garlitz, Janice E., P.C. ....Oakton, VA
Garlitz, Kevin R. ....Los Angeles, CA
Garlitz, Thomas D. ....Charlotte, NC
Garlo, Dolores M. ....Austin, TX
Garlo Ward, L.L.P. ....Austin, TX
Garlock, Barbara B. ....Raleigh, NC
Garlock, David C. ....Washington, DC
Garlock, Edward Sanfern ....El Monte, CA
Garlock, James M. ....San Francisco, CA
Garlock, Peter D. ....Cleveland, OH
Garlock, Steven E. ....St. Louis, MO
Garlock, Timothy G. ....Salem, OR
Garlock, Victor C. ....Fletcher, NC
Garlock, Vincent E.
House of Representatives, Committee Legal Personnel, GV
Garlousky, Hillard ....Skokie, IL
Garlove, Lee K. ....Louisville, KY
Garlove, Louis N. ....Louisville, KY
Garlow, Charles G.
Environmental Protection Agency, Office of Enforcement and Compliance Assurance, GV
Garlow, Janet E. ....Lawrence, KS
Garlow, L. S. ....Lawrence, KS
Garlow, Stephen ....Overland Park, KS
Garlund, Anna W. ....San Francisco, CA
Garlutzo, Carmel A. ....Trinidad, CO
Garm, Kevin J. ....San Francisco, CA
Garmaise, Leslie S. ....Dallas, TX
Garman, Cynthia L. ....Lancaster, PA
Garman, George G. ....San Antonio, TX
Garman, Gill M. ....Danville, IL
Garman, Gregory ....Las Vegas, NV
Garman, Harry L. ....New York, NY
Garman, Harry St.C. ....Lancaster, PA
Garman, Howard P. ....Fort Lauderdale, FL
Garman, Jacquelyn J. ....San Francisco, CA
Garman, John J. ....Brentwood, TN
Garman, Kim M. ....Cherry Hill, NJ
Garman, M. Edwin ....Crystal Lake, IL
Garman, Mary S. ....Sundance, WY
Garman, Morgan G. ....West Sacramento, CA
Garman, Richd. K. ....Dayton, OH
Garman, Rita B. ....Danville, IL
Garman, Robert D. ....Omaha, NE
Garman, Robin L. ....New York, NY
Garman, & White ....Dayton, OH
Garman, William F. ....Irvine, CA
Garmeiser, Dori C.
Department of Housing and Urban Development, Office of Administrative Law Judges, GV
Garmel, Jeffery I. ....Boston, MA
Garment, Leonard ....Washington, DC
Garmer, Benjamin F., III ....Milwaukee, WI
Garmer, John H. ....Towson, MD
Garmer, Richard D., & Associates, Law Firm of ....Des Moines, IA
Garmer, William R. ....Lexington, KY
Garmey, Ronald ....Boston, MA
Garmey, Terrence D. ....Saco, ME
Garmhausen, Charles F. ....Coram, NY
Garmhausen, John M. ....Sidney, OH
Garmil, Richard G. ....North Andover, MA
Garmisa, Gregg A. ....Washington, DC
Garmisa, Steven P. ....Chicago, IL
Garmisa, Thomas ....Chicago, IL
Garmisa, William J. ....Chicago, IL
Garmise, Jason B. ....New York, NY
Garmise, Richard E. ....New York, NY
Garmo, Caroline M. ....Livonia, MI
Garmo, Freddy ....El Cajon, CA
Garmo, Marshal A. ....Southfield, MI
Garmon & Goodman ....Glasgow, KY
Garmon, Hollis D. ....Greenville, TX
Garmon, James H. ....Baton Rouge, LA
Garmon, Jeffrey D. ....Waycross, GA
Garmon, Julie A. ....Calumet City, IL
Garmon, Larry D. ....Glasgow, KY
Garmon, Mary Leslie ....Reston, VA
Garmon, O. L., III ....Jackson, MS
Garmong, Michelle L. ....Temecula, CA
Garms, Janet S. ....Overland Park, KS
Kansas City, MO
Garms, Margaret E. ....Palo Alto, CA
Garmus, Mark A. ....Pasadena, CA
Garn, Katherine Roulhac, (P.C.)
San Francisco, CA
Garn, Marten Neil ....Lansing, MI
Garnaas, Carolyn J. ....Santa Clara, CA
Garnaas, Harold L. ....Missoula, MT
Garnati, Charles R. ....Marion, IL
Garneau, Gregg P. ....White Plains, NY
Garneau, Gregory J. ....Wailuku, HI
Garner, Andrew C., Jr. ....Fort Myers, FL
Garner, Angela Carol
Charlotte Amalie, St. Thomas, VI
Garner, Ann N. ....Atlanta, GA
Garner, B. Allen ....Jefferson City, MO
Garner & Berger ....Crestline, OH
Garner, Beverly D. ....St. Louis, MO
Garner, Brian D. ....Dallas, TX
Garner, Brian F. ....Mashpee, MA
Garner, Bruce E. ....Naperville, IL
Garner, Bruce R. ....Salt Lake City, UT
Garner, Bryan A. ....Dallas, TX
Garner, C.C., P.C. ....Dallas, TX
Garner, Charles C. ....Dallas, TX
Garner, Charles D., Jr. ....Pottstown, PA
Garner, Charles E. ....Staunton, VA
Garner, Charles H. F. ....New York, NY
Garner, Charles R., Jr. ....Fort Smith, AR
Garner, Chas. R. ....Fort Smith, AR
Garner, Christopher J. ....Nashua, NH
Garner, Cicero, Jr. ....Panama City Beach, FL
Garner, Cindy Maria ....Crockett, TX
Garner, Craig Boyd ....Los Angeles, CA
Garner, Craig M. ....San Diego, CA
Garner, Curtis L. ....Salt Lake City, UT
Garner, Cynthia S. ....Alexandria, VA
Garner, D. Eugene ....McCook, NE
Garner, D. Fred ....Bonita Springs, FL
Naples, FL
Garner, Daniel C. ....Dallas, TX
Garner, Daniel T. ....Portland, OR
Garner, Danny C. ....Dallas, TX
Garner, David E. ....Salem, IL
Garner, David E. ....Galveston, TX
Garner, David G. ....Pottstown, PA
Garner, David R. ....Canton, NY
Garner, Dean L. ....Cincinnati, OH
Garner, Donald K. ....Long Beach, CA
Garner, Donald W. ....Carbondale, IL
Garner, Douglas A. ....Cincinnati, OH
Garner, Dwight F. ....Long Beach, CA
Garner, Ebun S. ....New York, NY
Garner, Edward ....Roanoke, VA
Garner, Edward, Jr. ....Raleigh, NC
Garner, Elizabeth A. ....Boston, MA
Garner, Elton R., Jr. ....Willows, CA
Garner, Eric L., (P.C.) ....Riverside, CA
Garner, Eric R. ....Sacramento, CA
Garner, Erika L. ....McMinnville, OR
Garner, Everett H. ....Columbia, SC
Garner, Frederick R., Jr. ....Falls Church, VA
Garner, G. David ....Raleigh, MS
Garner & Garner ....Hernando, MS
Garner, Garner & Kennington, L.L.C.
Ozark, AL
Garner, Gary W. ....Chicago, IL
Garner, Gene M., II ....Washington, DC
Garner, Gerald W. ....Fair Oaks, CA
Garner, Gregory G. ....Wheat Ridge, CO
Garner, Gregory J. ....East Hartford, CT
Garner, Gregory P. ....Centerville, OH
Garner, Gretchen Laurel ....Tulsa, OK
Garner, Guy B., III ....Arlington, TX
Garner, H. Myer ....Shepherdsville, KY
Garner, H. Patterson ....Buford, GA
Garner, Harry Randolph ....Hernando, MS
Garner, Herman E., Jr. ....Lafayette, LA
Garner, Howard G., Jr. ....Huntsville, AL
Garner, Hugh C., Law Offices of
Salt Lake City, UT
Garner, Hugh Griffith ....Whiteville, NC
Garner, Hugh P. ....Chattanooga, TN
Garner, J. Michael ....Atlanta, GA
Garner, J. Michael ....Maryville, TN
Garner, Jacqueline J. ....Dallas, TX
Garner, Jacquelynne ....San Diego, CA
Garner, James E. ....Seattle, WA
Garner, James Gayle ....El Paso, TX
Garner, James L. ....Jackson, MS
Garner, James M. ....New Orleans, LA
Garner, James R. ....Tampa, FL
Garner, James S., III ....Rome, GA
Garner, James W. ....Lawrenceville, GA
Garner, Jean A. ....Laurel, MD
Garner, Jennie B. ....Salt Lake City, UT
Garner, Jennifer B. ....Southern Pines, NC
Garner, Jim ....Coffeyville, KS
Garner, Joan Kaehne ....Philadelphia, PA
Garner, John A. ....Naples, FL
Garner, John C. ....Radnor, PA
Garner, John M. ....Miami, FL
Garner, John N. ....Andover, MA
Garner, John N. ....Seattle, WA
Garner, John P. ....Nashville, TN
Garner, John Steven ....New Orleans, LA
Garner, Joseph P. ....Springfield, MA
Garner, Kathleen B. ....Cheshire, CT
Garner, Kathryn V. ....Houston, TX
Garner, Kenneth A. ....Garland, TX
Garner & Kilgore ....Buford, GA
Garner, Lance B.
Hot Springs National Park, AR
Garner, Larry A. ....Golden, CO
Garner, Lee P. ....Chicago, IL
Garner, Leslie Marion ....Brooklyn, NY
Garner, Lewis & Prickett
Chattanooga, TN
Garner, Lisa K. ....Los Angeles, CA
Garner, Lisa M. ....Chicago, IL
Garner, M. Craig, Jr. ....Columbia, SC
Garner, Mallory J. ....Calabasas, CA
Garner, Margaret Ann ....Newport, NC
Garner, Marilyn D. ....Arlington, TX
Garner, Marviin L. ....Chesterfield, VA
Garner, Mary M. ....Washington, DC
Garner, Max A. ....Troy, NC
Garner, Max D. ....Anchorage, AK
Garner, Melvin C. ....New York, NY
Garner, Michael E. ....Encino, CA
Garner, Michael E. ....Columbus, GA
Garner, Michael E. ....Philadelphia, PA
Garner, Michael H. ....Meredith, NH
Garner, Michael R. ....Seattle, WA
Garner & Minkow, P.A. ....Meredith, NH
Garner, Mitchell E. ....Ann Arbor, MI
Garner & Munoz ....New Orleans, LA
Garner, Nancy, & Associates, P.C.
Albuquerque, NM
Garner, Nancy L. ....Albuquerque, NM
Garner, Nelson ....Crestline, OH
Garner, Paul C. ....New York, NY
Garner, R. Kathy ....Carbondale, IL
Garner, R. Lee, III ....Los Angeles, CA
Garner, Ralph E. ....San Diego, CA
Garner, Raymond M. ....Maryville, TN
Garner, Renatha S. ....Charleston, WV
Garner, Rex W. ....Calhoun, GA
Garner, Richard McLain ....Cleveland, OH
Garner, Robert E. ....Warren, AR
Garner, Robert E. ....Amarillo, TX
Garner, Robert E. Lee ....Birmingham, AL
Garner, Robert H. ....Tulsa, OK

Garrett, Robert D. ... Oklahoma City, OK
Garrett, Robert F., III ... Ocean City, NJ
Garrett, Robert J. ... Cody, WY
Garrett, Robert M. ... St. Louis, MO
Garrett, Robert S. ... Huntington, IN
Warren, IN
Garrett, Robert S. ... Pittsburgh, PA
Garrett, Robert W. ... Benton, AR
Garrett, Robert W. ... Boston, MA
Garrett, Roderick L. ... Houston, TX
Garrett, Roger ... Phoenix, AZ
Garrett, Roger ... Abilene, TX
Garrett, Roy B. ... Escondido, CA
Garrett, Ruby Joyce B. ... Burlington, NC
Garrett, Russell D. ... Vancouver, WA
Garrett, Ryan M. ... Tallahassee, FL
Garrett, S. Jonathan ... Memphis, TN
Garrett, Sam Young ... Richmond, VA
Garrett, Sandra Leach ... Nashville, TN
Garrett, Scott B. ... Columbia, SC
Garrett, Scott E. ... Stamford, CT
White Plains, NY
Garrett, Sharon K. ... Bakersfield, CA
Garrett, Skidmore N. ... Jamestown, TN
Garrett, Stacey A. ... Nashville, TN
Garrett, Stacey Myers ... Long Beach, CA
Garrett, Stacy F., III ... Richmond, VA
Garrett, Stanley ... New York, NY
Garrett, Stanley J. ... Toledo, OH
Garrett, Steffanie N. ... Chicago, IL
Garrett, Stephen P. ... Oklahoma City, OK
Garrett, Steven Carey ... Knoxville, TN
Garrett, Steven Dodd ... Birmingham, AL
Garrett, Steven M. ... Sacramento, CA
Garrett, Steven R. ... College Station, TX
Garrett, Steven W. ... St. Louis, MO
Garrett, Susan Ryan ... Melbourne, FL
Garrett, Susan W. ... San Diego, CA
Garrett, T. Kent ... Montgomery, AL
Garrett, Tammy T. ... Houston, TX
Garrett, Terry J. ... Norman, OK
Garrett, Terry J., & Associates, P.C.
Norman, OK
Garrett, Terry P. ... Irvine, CA
Garrett, Theodore L. ... Washington, DC
Garrett, Thomas B. ... Newport Beach, CA
Garrett, Thomas H., III ... Minneapolis, MN
Garrett, Thomas S. ... Washington, DC
Garrett, Tim K. ... Nashville, TN
Garrett, Tina L. ... Chicago, IL
Garrett, Trent L. ... Indianapolis, IN
Garrett & Tully, A Professional Corporation
Los Angeles, CA
Pasadena, CA
Westlake Village, CA
Garrett, V. Lee ... Wichita, KS
Garrett, Virginia B. ... Douglasville, GA
Garrett & Von Oehsen LLC
Stamford, CT
White Plains, NY
Garrett, Walker Dale ... Fayetteville, AR
Garrett, Wayne E. ... New Orleans, LA
Garrett, W. E. ... Atmore, AL
Garrett, Whiting, & Associates, P.C.
Greenwood, SC
Garrett, William A. ... Temperance, MI
Garrett, William A. ... Columbus, OH
Garrett, William A., Jr. ... Cumming, GA
Garrett, William C. ... Gassaway, WV
Garrett, William E. ... Long Beach, CA
Garrett, William L., Jr. ... Wilmington, DE
Garrett, William M., Jr. ... San Bernardino, CA
Garrett, William R. ... Menlo Park, CA
Garrett, William R. ... Panama City, FL
Garrett, William R. ... Dallas, TX
Garrett-Davis, Cathy Reneé ... Toms River, NJ
Garrette, Merle K. ... Miami, OK
Garrett-Harley, Vanessa ... Philadelphia, PA
Garrett-Nelson, LaBrenda ... Washington, DC
Garrett-Norris, Georgia ... Santa Ana, CA
Garretto, Mark A. ... White Plains, NY
Garrettson, James M. ... Indianapolis, IN
Garrett-Wackowski, Eugenia
San Francisco, CA
Garrety, Paula F. ... Department of Defense, Defense Legal Services Agency, GV
Garrey & Curran, A Professional Corporation
Scottsdale, AZ
Garrey, D. Reid ... Scottsdale, AZ
Garrey, Robert J. ... Richardson, TX
Garrick, Frederick E. ... Birmingham, AL
Garrick, Jan D. ... Jackson, MS
Garrick, John M. ... Los Angeles, CA
Garrick, Joseph D. ... Southfield, MI
Garrick, Laurie V.
Agency for International Development, Other Offices of A.I.D., GV
Garrick, Max C. ... Whittier, CA
Garrick, Robert S. ... Washington, DC
Garrido, Caridad Montero ... Miami, FL
Garrido, Jo-Anne R. ... Philadelphia, PA
Garrido, Jorge L. ... Coral Gables, FL
Garrido, Jose A., Jr. ... Miami, FL
Garrido-Hull, Helia M. ... Orlando, FL
Garrie, Bryan M. ... San Diego, CA
Garrie, Julie L. ... La Jolla, CA
Garrie, Leon J. ... Los Angeles, CA
Garriga, Maria del Carmen
San Juan, PR
Garriga Blanco, Carlos R. ... San Juan, PR
Garrigan, Clyde R. W. ... Concord, NH
Garrigan, Frank E. ... Shamokin, PA
Garrigan, Jeffrey G. ... Jersey City, NJ
Garrigan, John P. ... Norwalk, CT
Garrigan, Kathleen M. ... Staten Island, NY
Garrigan, Michael N. ... Stockton, CA
Garrigan, Peter F. ... Lowell, MA
Garrigan, Raymond C. ... New York, NY
Garrigan & Rosini ... Shamokin, PA
Garrigan, Terrence D. ... Cincinnati, OH
Garrigan, Terrence M. ... Cincinnati, OH
Garrigan, Timothy B. ... Nacogdoches, TX
Garrigan, Timothy J. ... Stockton, CA
Garrigan-Nass, Michele ... Havertown, PA
Garrigle, Palm and Thomasson
Cherry Hill, NJ
Garrigle, William A. ... Cherry Hill, NJ
Garrigo, Silvia M. ... Miami, FL
Garrigues & Andersen ... New York, NY
New York, NY
Garrigues, Gary ... San Francisco, CA
Garrigues, Gayle L. ... Fairbanks, AK
Garringer, Lester A., Jr. ... Tallahassee, FL
Garriott, Gale L., (Mr.) ... Phoenix, AZ
Garriott, James D. ... Omaha, NE
Garriott, Richard E., Jr. ... Norfolk, VA
Garris, Bradley R.
Department of Commerce, Patent and Trademark Office, GV
Garris, Charles E. ... Vero Beach, FL
Garris, Christian J. ... Los Angeles, CA
Garris, Cynthia D. ... Norfolk, VA
Garris, Garris, Garris & Garris, P.C.
Ann Arbor, MI
Garris, Jacalen J. ... Ann Arbor, MI
Garris, Jack J. ... Ann Arbor, MI
Garris, Michael J. ... Ann Arbor, MI
Garris, Steven Z. ... Ann Arbor, MI
Garris, Troy ... Department of Transportation, Surface Transportation Board, GV
Garris, W. Ralph ... Columbia, SC
Garrison, Alan F. ... Staunton, VA
Garrison, Angela D. ... Hamilton, OH
Garrison & Associates PS ... Seattle, WA
Garrison, Bradford T. ... Nicholasville, KY
Garrison, Brown, Carlson, Buchanan & Busby, Incorporated ... Bartlesville, OK
Garrison, Bruce D. ... New York, NY
Garrison, Carolyn A. ... Carmel, CA
Garrison, Charles C. ... Lafayette, LA
New Iberia, LA
Garrison, Charles W., III ... Washington, DC
Garrison, Christopher L. ... Indianapolis, IN
Garrison, Daniel E. ... Salt Lake City, UT
Garrison, David A. ... Aliso Viejo, CA
Garrison, David A. ... Wayne, PA
Garrison, David F. ... Cleveland Heights, OH
Garrison, David H. ... Spring, TX
Garrison, David L. ... Corpus Christi, TX
Garrison, David L. ... Seattle, WA
Garrison, David R. ... Ponca City, OK
Garrison, Debra W. ... Little Rock, AR
Garrison, Denzil D. ... Bartlesville, OK
Garrison, Donald E. ... Nashville, TN
Garrison, Donald W. ... Oklahoma City, OK
Garrison, Douglas S. ... Chicago, IL
Garrison, Eberhard D. ... New Orleans, LA
Garrison, Edward A. ... West Palm Beach, FL
Garrison, Edwin F. ... Oklahoma City, OK
Garrison, Edwin H., Jr. ... Omaha, NE
Garrison, Fabrizio and Hanson, Ltd.
Joliet, IL
Kankakee, IL
Morris, IL
Garrison, F. L. ... Gilmer, TX
Garrison, Frank M. ... Phoenix, AZ
Garrison, Franklin A. ... Memphis, TN
Garrison & Garrison ... Nelson, NE
Garrison, Gary L. ... Oakton, VA
Garrison, George L. ... Clifton, NJ
Garrison, Glen P. ... Seattle, WA
Garrison, Grady M. ... Memphis, TN
Garrison, Gregg S. ... Half Moon Bay, CA
Garrison, Gregory S. ... Galveston, TX
Garrison, Gretchen ... St. Louis, MO
Garrison & Hughes, L.L.P.
Fort Worth, TX
Garrison, J. Gregory ... Indianapolis, IN
Garrison, James D. ... Houston, TX
Garrison, James E. ... Joliet, IL
Garrison, James R. ... Belleville, IL
St. Louis, MO
Garrison, James T. ... Marion, IL
Garrison, James W. ... Los Angeles, CA
Garrison, Jarred Shannon ... Dayton, TN
Garrison, Jay Arthur ... Knoxville, TN
Garrison, Joe T. ... Austin, TX
Garrison, John D., Jr. ... Norfolk, VA
Garrison, John J. ... Columbia, SC
Garrison, John L. ... Boston, MA
Garrison, Joseph D. ... New Haven, CT
Garrison, Julie Ann ... Concord, CA
Garrison, Keech & Downs, P.S.
Kirkland, WA
Garrison & Kiefer, P.C. ... Indianapolis, IN
Garrison, Kimberly Lemmons
Lexington, KY
Garrison, Kristie L. ... Dallas, TX
Garrison, Latasha ... Jacksonville, FL
Garrison Law Corporation, P.C.
Half Moon Bay, CA
Garrison Lawhouse, P.C. ... Dearborn, MI
Garrison, Lee ... Bridgewater, MA
Garrison, Leif ... Colorado Springs, CO
Garrison, Lewis K. ... Memphis, TN
Garrison, Lisa Frye ... Greensboro, NC
Garrison, Lyon H. ... New Orleans, LA
Garrison, Mark H. ... Tampa, FL
Garrison, Mark W. ... Albion, MI
Garrison, Marsha ... Brooklyn, NY
Garrison, Matthew C. ... Annandale, NJ
Garrison, Melissa Lyn ... Aptos, CA
Garrison, Melora M. ... Santa Monica, CA
Garrison, Michael J. ... Fargo, ND
Garrison, Michael S. ... Charleston, WV
Garrison, Michael W. ... Los Angeles, CA
Garrison, Michael W., Jr. ... Honolulu, HI
Garrison, Morris & Haight ... Memphis, TN
Nashville, TN
Garrison, Nancy C. ... Department of Justice, Antitrust Division, GV
Garrison, Nancy E. ... Natchez, MS
Garrison, Pamela S. ... Kansas City, MO
Garrison, Pamela T. ... Kailua, HI
Garrison, Paul C. ... Birmingham, AL
Garrison Phelan Levin-Epstein Chimes & Richardson, P.C. ... New Haven, CT
Garrison, Phillip R. ... Springfield, MO
Garrison, Phyllis J. ... Indianapolis, IN
Garrison, Pitser H. ... Lufkin, TX
Garrison, Randolph Lee ... Roseburg, OR
Garrison, Randolph Lee, P.C.
Roseburg, OR
Garrison, Ray H. ... Flossmoor, IL
Garrison, Richard H. ... West Hartford, CT
Garrison, Robbin Rexroad ... Greer, SC
Garrison, Robert E. ... Woodstock, GA
Garrison, Roger K. ... Sunnyside, WA
Garrison, Ronald D. ... Overland Park, KS
Garrison, Rupert T. ... Helena, MT
Garrison, Sam ... Roanoke, VA
Garrison, Scott B.
Environmental Protection Agency, Office of Enforcement and Compliance Assurance, GV
Garrison, Scott B. ... Boston, MA
Boston, MA
Garrison, Sean D. ... Phoenix, AZ
Garrison, Searcy S., Jr. ... Decatur, GA
Garrison, Serge H. ... Des Moines, IA
Garrison, Sheila C. ... Kansas City, MO
Garrison, Stephen D. ... Minneapolis, MN
Garrison, Stuart H. ... Santa Monica, CA
Garrison & Sumrall, P.C.
Birmingham, AL
Garrison, Susan H. ... Austin, TX
Garrison, Susan K., & Associates ... Media, PA
Garrison, Suzanne L. ... Exeter, NH
Garrison, Theodore E. ... Corona, NY
Garrison, Thomas E. ... Columbia, SC
Garrison, Thomas R., Jr. ... Phoenix, AZ
Garrison, Virginia B. ... Staunton, VA
Garrison, W. Arthur ... Waco, TX
Garrison, W. Lewis, Jr. ... Birmingham, AL
Garrison, Wayne L. ... Nelson, NE
Garrison, William A. ... Rochester, NY
Garrison, William B., Jr. ... Washington, DC
Garrison, William L. ... Danville, IL
Garrison, William N. ... Fort Worth, TX
Garrison, William W. ... Naknek, AK
Garrison-Barrett, Bernadette
Palos Heights, IL
Garriss, James A. ... Irving, TX
Garrity, Avignone, Banick & Whetstone
Bozeman, MT
Garrity, Barbara J. ... Houston, TX
Garrity, Barbara M. ... Quincy, MA
Garrity, Brian T. ... Boston, MA
Garrity, Charles W. ... Orange, CA
Garrity, Cheryl L. ... Boston, MA
Garrity, Christine M.
Palm Beach Gardens, FL
Garrity, Dana Pirone ... Philadelphia, PA
Garrity, Daniel S., II ... Atchison, KS
Garrity, Danielle E. ... Joplin, MO
Garrity, Dennis G. ... De Pere, WI
Garrity, Diane V. ... Woodbridge, NJ
Garrity, Donald A. ... Helena, MT
Garrity, Donald P. ... Boston, MA
Garrity, Francis X. ... Montclair, NJ
Garrity, Garrity & Valvo ... Buffalo, NY
Forestville, NY
Garrity, Graham, Favetta & Flinn
Newark, NJ
Montclair, NJ
Garrity, J.D., & Associates, P.A.
Coral Springs, FL
Garrity, James ... Tallahassee, FL
Garrity, James E. ... Moorhead, MN
Garrity, James J. ... Blue Bell, PA
Garrity, James L. ... New York, NY
Garrity, James L., Jr. ... New York, NY
Garrity, John ... Worcester, MA
Garrity, John A., III ... Chicago, IL
Des Plaines, IL
Garrity, John B. ... Poughkeepsie, NY
Garrity, John J. ... Annapolis, MD
Garrity, John M. ... Joplin, MO
Garrity, John M. ... Buffalo, NY
Garrity, John P. ... Addison, IL
Garrity, Joseph D. ... Coral Springs, FL
Hollywood, FL
Garrity, Joseph T. ... Denver, CO
Garrity, Kuckelman & Kurth ... Atchison, KS
Garrity, Levin & Muir ... Boston, MA
Garrity, Lynn A.
Merit Systems Protection Board, Office of Appeals Counsel, GV
Garrity, Mary E. ... Boston, MA
Garrity, Mary-Elizabeth ... New Brunswick, NJ
Garrity, Melissa L. ... Hacienda Heights, CA
Garrity, Michael E., Jr. ... Boston, MA
Garrity, Michael G. ... Bozeman, MT
Garrity, Patricia A. ... San Juan, PR
Garrity, Patricia E. ... Mandan, ND
Garrity, Patricia J. ... Arlington, MA
Garrity, Patrick J. ... Chicago, IL
Garrity, Patrick S. ... Baton Rouge, LA
Garrity, Patrick T. ... Buffalo, NY
Forestville, NY
Garrity, Paul G. ... Boston, MA
Garrity, Paul J. ... Boston, MA
Londonderry, NH
Garrity, Paul J. ... Hingham, MA
Garrity, Paul W. ... New York, NY
Garrity, Richard E. ... Glen Ellyn, IL
Garrity, Robert A. ... Shawnee, KS
Garrity, Robert J., Jr. ... Dallas, TX
Garrity, Robert P. ... Boston, MA
Garrity, Ronald F. ... San Mateo, CA
Garrity, Ronald W. ... San Francisco, CA
Garrity, Thomas A. ... Williamstown, MA
Garrity, Thomas L. ... Minneapolis, MN
Garrity, Thomas M. ... Blue Bell, PA
Garrity, Timothy P. ... Brookfield, WI
Garrity, Vincent F., Jr. ... Philadelphia, PA
Garrity, W. Arthur, III ... Boston, MA
Garrity, W. Arthur, Jr. ... Boston, MA
Garrity, William J. ... Charlotte, NC
Garrity, Wm. P. ... Washington, DC
Garrity-McNeill, Kathleen M.
Lynnfield, MA
Garrity-Rokous, Frances ... Guilford, CT
Garr-Kraemer, Anne R. ... Chicago, IL
Garro, Alejandro M. ... New York, NY
Garro, Joseph C. ... Oak Brook, IL
Garro, Robert K. ... Chicago, IL
Garrod, David J. ... New York, NY
Garrod, Jeffrey M. ... Roseland, NJ
Garron, Michael E. ... Mineola, NY
Garrot, Louis G., III ... Abbeville, LA
Garrote, Nora E. ... Washington, DC
Garrott, Joan W. ... Los Angeles, CA
Garrou, Douglas M. ... Richmond, VA
Garrou, G. Randall ... Los Angeles, CA
Garrou, John L. W. ... Winston-Salem, NC
Garroussi, Pantea M. ... Denver, CO
Garroutte, Jay ... Des Moines, IA
Garrow, Alan L. ... Aurora, IL
Garrow, George L., Jr ... Washington, DC
Garrow, Heather L. ... McLean, VA
Garrow, Janet E. ... Seattle, WA
Garrow, John F. ... Wheaton, IL
Garrow, Richd. E. ... Manitowoc, WI
Garroway, Nathan Lewis ... St. Louis, MO
Garrubbo, Edwin P. ... West Chester, PA
Garrubbo, Joseph L. ... Westfield, NJ
Garrubbo, Michele ... Westfield, NJ
Garrubbo & Romankow
Berkeley Heights, NJ
Westfield, NJ
Garruto, Andrew F. ... Nutley, NJ
Garruto, Bryan D. ... East Brunswick, NJ
Garry, Bruce S. ... Cincinnati, OH
Garry & Cahill ... Albany, NY
Garry, Elizabeth A. ... Sherburne, NY
Garry & Garry Co., L.P.A. ... Cincinnati, OH
Garry, John R. ... New York, NY
Garry, John R., Jr. ... New Albany, IN
Garry, John T., II ... Albany, NY
Garry, Karen A. ... New York, NY
Garry, Lee A. ... Encino, CA
Garry & Ludwig, P.C. ... Brooklyn, NY
Garry, Mahon B." Buz ", Jr. ... Austin, TX
Garry & Marek, Ltd. ... Crystal Lake, IL
Garry, Michael J. ... Albany, NY
Garry, Paul R. ... Chicago, IL
Garry, Peggy A. ... New York, NY
Garry, Rita M. ... Miamisburg, OH
Garry, Rita W. ... Crystal Lake, IL
Garry, Robert D. ... Cleveland, OH
Garry, Steven E. ... New York, NY
Garry, Thomas John ... Brooklyn, NY
Garry, Thomas L. ... San Gabriel, CA
Garry, Timothy A. ... Cincinnati, OH
Garry, Timothy A., Jr. ... Cincinnati, OH
Garry, Victoria Davidson ... Cincinnati, OH
Garry, William C. ... Sioux Falls, SD
Garry, William J. ... Brooklyn, NY
Garry, William J. ... Brooklyn, NY
Gars, Dixon & Shapiro ... Miami, FL
Gars, Irwin S. ... Miami, FL
Garsaud, Marcel, Jr. ... New Orleans, LA
Garsaud, Monique M. ... New Orleans, LA
Garscia, Mark ... Pasadena, CA
Garsek, Elliott S. ... Fort Worth, TX
Garsh, E. Susan ... Boston, MA
Garshell, Steven E. ... Verona, NJ
Garside, David A. ... Tampa, FL
Garside, Gary A. ... Chicago, IL
Garside, Jonathan H. ... St. Louis, MO
Garside, Mark P. ... Charlotte, NC
Garside, Steven" L " ... Oklahoma City, OK
Garske, Peder A. ... Washington, DC
Garske, Richard D. ... San Diego, CA
Garske, Terrence J. ... Mosinee, WI
Garskof, Deborah M. ... Westport, CT
Garson, Adam G. ... Philadelphia, PA
Garson, Andrew Emery ... Fairfield, CT
Garson, Andrew S. ... New York, NY
Garson & Associates Co., L.P.A.
Cleveland, OH
Garson & Associates, LLC
Washington, DC
Bethesda, MD
Garson, Brent Dale ... Cleveland, OH
Garson, Brian K. ... Cleveland, OH
Garson, Donald M. ... Kearny, NJ
Garson, Edward P. ... San Francisco, CA
Garson, Gary B. ... Cleveland, OH
Garson, Gary W. ... New York, NY
Garson Gerspach DeCorato & Cohen, LLP
New York, NY
Garson, H. Neil ... Fairfax, VA
Garson, Harold M. ... Fairlawn, OH
Garson, Henry K.
Department of Energy, GV
Garson, Jack A. ... Bethesda, MD
Garson, Joel M. ... Santa Ana, CA
Garson, Judith A. ... New York, NY
Garson, Katherine A. ... Hilo, HI
Garson, Michael D. ... Washington, DC

Garson, Peter K. ...Cleveland, OH
Garson, Peter Michael ...Madison, WI
Garson & Slepian ...Fairfield, CT
Garson, Stuart G. ...Southfield, MI
Garson, Stuart I. ...Cleveland, OH
Garson, W. Jeffrey ...Philadelphia, PA
Garsson, Frederic Mark ...New York, NY
Garsson, Ross S. ...Austin, TX
Garst, Claflin, Jr. ...Bradenton, FL
Garst, David Nelson ...Nashville, TN
Garst, Jack L. ...Memphis, TN
Garst, Marcia L. ...Irving, TX
Garst, Marsha L. ...Harrisonburg, VA
Garst, Robert K. ...Blythe, CA
Garst, Serina M. ...Santa Fe, NM
Garst, Steven L. ...Paris, IL
Garstang, Clifford W. ...Chicago, IL
Garstin, Bert N. ...Cumming, GA
Garstka, Kenneth E. ...Rosemont, IL
Gart, Brian K. ...Fort Lauderdale, FL
Gart, Carol A. ...Fort Lauderdale, FL
Gart, David A. ...West Palm Beach, FL
Gart, Paula M. ...Garden City, NY
Gart, Robin G. ...Fort Lauderdale, FL
Gart, Ronald A. ...Encino, CA
Gart, Ronald S. ...Washington, DC
Gartell, Alice Finn ...Phoenix, AZ
Gartell, Edward M. ...Binghamton, NY
Hancock, NY
Windsor, NY
Gartelos, Peter J. ...Waterloo, IA
Gartelos, Wagner & Ament ...Waterloo, IA
Garten, Alan F. M. ...Baltimore, MD
Garten, Alan G. ...New York, NY
Garten, Allan M. ...Portland, OR
Garten, Charles R., Jr. ...Charleston, WV
Garten, David B. ...Houston, TX
Garten, David M.
Palm Beach Gardens, FL
Garten, David M. ...West Palm Beach, FL
Garten, Debbie ...Madison, WI
Garten, Garry E.
Charlotte Amalie, St. Thomas, VI
Garten, Herbert S. ...Baltimore, MD
Garten, Lawrence M. ...Baltimore, MD
Garten, Morris L. ...Baltimore, MD
Garten & Wanek ...Des Moines, IA
Garten, William B. ...Des Moines, IA
Gartenbaum, Peggy ...Westbury, NY
Gartenberg, Amie ...Hackensack, NJ
New York, NY
Gartenberg, Aviva ...Bergenfield, NJ
Gartenberg, Caryn S. ...New York, NY
Gartenberg, Edward ...Los Angeles, CA
Gartenberg, Irving L. ...New York, NY
Gartenberg Jaffe Gelfand & Stein LLP
Los Angeles, CA
Gartenberg, Karen S. ...New York, NY
Gartenlaub, Douglas K. ...Winter Park, FL
Gartenlaub, Evan R. ...Chicago, IL
Gartenstein, Daniel ...Kingston, NY
Gartenstein, David W. ...Brattleboro, VT
Gartenstein, Stanley ...New York, NY
Gartenstein, Victor, (P.C.) ...Brooklyn, NY
Garth, Adam ...South Egremont, MA
Garth, Bryant ...Chicago, IL
Garth, Lance J. ...New Bedford, MA
Garth, Leonard I. ...Newark, NJ
Garth, Natalie P. ...Phoenix, AZ
Garth, S. Tanner ...Houston, TX
Garth, Thomas F. ...Mobile, AL
Garth, William W., IV ...Cambridge, MA
Garthe, David J. ...Oakland, CA
Garthe, Donald W. ...Wyoming, MI
Garthright, James L., III ...Memphis, TN
Garthright Law Firm ...Memphis, TN
Garthwaite, Patricia A. ...Greenville, DE
Gartin, Colby R. ...Palo Alto, CA
Gartin, Edwin V. ...Bentonville, AR
Gartin, John P. ...Bloomington, IL
Gartlan, Michael Joseph ...Vienna, VA
Gartlan, Michael Joseph, P.C. ...Vienna, VA
Gartlan, Peter ...Salem, OR
Gartland, Eugene L. ...San Francisco, CA
Gartland, James M. ...Brooklyn, NY
Gartland, John C. ...Eugene, OR
Gartland, John J., Jr. ...Poughkeepsie, NY
Gartland, John P. ...Columbus, OH
Gartland, Jude T. ...New York, NY
Gartland, Michael G. ...Poughkeepsie, NY
Gartland, Michael J. ...Portland, ME
Gartland, Michele D. ...New York, NY
Gartland, Sheila Nolan ...Columbus, OH
Gartley, Scott C. ...Wilkes-Barre, PA
Gartley, Tina Polachek ...Plains, PA
Gartlir, Bernard ...New York, NY
Gartlir, Kenneth T. ...Treasury Department, Office of the Comptroller of the Currency, GV
Gartlir, Lois ...New York, NY
Gartman, John E. ...La Jolla, CA
Menlo Park, CA
Gartman, Michael R. ...Washington, DC
Gartman, Thomas N. ...Parma Heights, OH
Gartmond, Joy A. ...Stamford, CT
Gartner, Bennett & Schupp, P.C.
Minneapolis, MN
Gartner, Bloom & Greiper, P.C.
New York, NY
Gartner, Brock and Simon
Jacksonville, FL
Gartner, Bruce A. ...Jacksonville, FL
Gartner, Dan M. ...Santa Cruz, CA
Gartner, Daniel D. ...Houston, TX
Gartner, Eve C. ...New York, NY
Gartner, Francis R. ...Blue Bell, PA
Gartner, Gabe B. ...Seattle, WA
Gartner, Gary J. ...New York, NY
Gartner, Greta Sue ...Taylor, MI
Gartner, Harold H., III, (A Professional Corporation) ...Los Angeles, CA
Ventura, CA
Gartner, Henry D. ...Buffalo, NY
Gartner, Janet Hentchel ...East Lansing, MI
Gartner, John C., Sr. ...Glenarm, MD
Gartner, Jon Henry ...Long Beach, NY
Gartner, Judith R. ...St. Paul, MN
Gartner, Kenneth L. ...Mineola, NY
Gartner, Kimberly Willis ...Houston, TX
Gartner, Lawrence J. ...Los Angeles, CA
Gartner, Lee B. ...Coral Springs, FL
Gartner, Lee B., P.A. ...Coral Springs, FL
Gartner, Leonard S. ...Fairfield, OH
Gartner, Ludwig B., Jr. ...Minneapolis, MN
Gartner, Michael C. ...Washington, DC
Gartner, Michael G. ...Ames, IA
Gartner, Michele Lippa ...Merrick, NY
Gartner, Murray ...New York, NY
Gartner, Paul M. ...New York, NY
Gartner, Philip A. ...Lake City, MN
Gartner, Rachel I.
National Labor Relations Board, Office of the General Counsel, GV
Gartner, Richard ...Lansing, MI
Gartner, Richard A. ...St. Charles, MO
Gartner, Robert L. ...Bronx, NY
Gartner, Scott A. ...Los Angeles, CA
Gartner & Shulman, Ltd. ...Lake City, MN
Rochester, MN
Gartner, Steven J. ...New York, NY
Gartner, Stewart I. ...Chicago, IL
Gartner, Stuart F. ...New York, NY
Gartner, Thomas O. ...Milwaukee, WI
Gartner, Winfield A. ...Jacksonville, FL
Gartner & Young, A Professional Corporation ...Los Angeles, CA
Garton, Arthur Andrew ...Warren, MI
Garton, Deborah K. ...Bluefield, WV
Garton, Deirdre Wilson ...Madison, WI
Garton, Jack L. ...Dickson, TN
Garton, Jeffrey P. ...Bristol, PA
Langhorne, PA
Garton, Thomas W. ...Minneapolis, MN
Garton, Vogt & Tomayko, P.C.
Warren, MI
Gartrell & Associates ...Silver Spring, MD
Gartrell, Bernadette ...Silver Spring, MD
Gartrell, Darlene Diane ...Los Angeles, CA
Gartrell, Donald E. ...Concord, NH
Gartrell, Luther S., III ...Ashville, AL
Gartrell, M. Kay ...Washington, DC
Gartrell, P. Garth ...San Diego, CA
Gartrell-Solak, Roxanne ...Antioch, CA
Garts, James R., Jr. ...Memphis, TN
Gartshore, David H. ...San Francisco, CA
Gartside, A. Dru ...Pasadena, CA
Gartside, Frederick W. ...Los Angeles, CA
Gartside, Jeri L. ...Irvine, CA
Gartzke, Dan D. ...Darlington, WI
Monroe, WI
New Glarus, WI
Gartzke, Paul C. ...Madison, WI
Gartzman, Jeffrey S. ...Atlanta, GA
Gartzman, Jeffrey S., P.C. ...Atlanta, GA
Garubba, Alan P. ...Philadelphia, PA
Garubo, Angelo G. ...Florham Park, NJ
Garubo, Philip A., Jr. ...Bridgewater, NJ
Garufi, Carman Michael ...Binghamton, NY
Garufi, Francis A. ...New York, NY
Garufi and Garufy ...Binghamton, NY
Garufy, Sandra J. ...Binghamton, NY
Garvais, William B. ...Pomfret, CT
Garvelink, Todd K. ...New York, NY
Garven, Robert P. ...Coral Springs, FL
Garver, Fred W. ...Indianapolis, IN
Garver, Frederick H. ...Indianapolis, IN
Garver, G. Holdt ...Albuquerque, NM
Garver, G. Holdt, Chartered
Albuquerque, NM
Garver, Geoffrey ...Department of Justice, Environment and Natural Resources Division, GV
Garver, George W., Jr. ...Westlake Village, CA
Garver, James A. ...Harrisburg, PA
Garver, Jeffrey L. ...Portola Valley, CA
Garver, John A. ...New York, NY
Garver, John B., III ...Charlotte, NC
Garver, Julia Amy ...Playa Del Rey, CA
Garver Law Offices, P.C. ...Alexandria, VA
Fairfax, VA
Reston, VA
Garver, Robert B. ...West Des Moines, IA
Garver, Scott A. ...Southington, CT
Garver, Steven M. ...Reston, VA
Garverick, Debra A. ...Galion, OH
Garverick, Grant Bennett ...Galion, OH
Garverick, Lowell B. ...Galion, OH
Garvert, Melinda L. ...Colorado Springs, CO
Garves, Brian R. ...Detroit, MI
Garvett, Fredric M. ...Miami, FL
Garvey, Althea E. ...New York, NY
Garvey, Anderson, Johnson, Gabler & Geraci, S.C. ...Eau Claire, WI
Garvey, Anne E. ...Atlanta, GA
Garvey, Brian L. ...Chicago, IL
Garvey, Carolyn S. ...Concord, NH
Garvey, Catherine L. ...Chicago, IL
Garvey, Catherine N. ...River Ridge, LA
Garvey, Charles C., Jr. ...Metairie, LA
Garvey, Charles P. ...Port Henry, NY
Garvey, Christopher B. ...Roslyn, NY
Garvey, Daniel J. ...Lincoln, RI
Garvey, Darrell D. ...Orlando, FL
Garvey, David T. ...Albany, NY
Garvey, Dennis J. ...Buffalo, NY
Garvey, Dennis N. ...Hilton Head Island, SC
Garvey, Donald B. ...Oak Brook, IL
Garvey, Donald B., & Associates, Ltd., Law Offices of ...Oak Brook, IL
Garvey, Donn E. ...Alexandria, VA
Garvey, Edward R. ...Madison, WI
Garvey, Elizabeth Ann Jenneman
Bloomington, MN
Garvey, Francis B. ...Babylon, NY
Garvey, Francis B., The Firm of
Babylon, NY
Garvey, Francis J. ...Covina, CA
Garvey & Garvey ...Buffalo, NY
Garvey & Garvey ...Lincoln, RI
Garvey, George A. ...Arlington, VA
Garvey, George E. ...Washington, DC
Garvey, George M. ...Los Angeles, CA
Garvey, J. Kevin ...Chicago, IL
Garvey, Jack I. ...Ross, CA
Garvey, James A. ...Buffalo, NY
Garvey, James Andrew, III ...Scarsdale, NY
Garvey, James E. ...Eau Claire, WI
Garvey, James V. ...Chicago, IL
Garvey, Jane R. ...Babylon, NY
Garvey, Jeremiah G. ...Pittsburgh, PA
Garvey, Jill Meier ...Portland, OR
Garvey, Joan ...Omaha, NE
Garvey, Joanne M. ...San Francisco, CA
Garvey, John A. ...Omaha, NE
Garvey, John B. ...Concord, NH
Garvey, John C. ...Washington, DC
Garvey, John C. ...Murray Hill, NJ
Garvey, John H. ...Lexington, KY
Garvey, John J., III ...San Jose, CA
Garvey, John J., III ...Cincinnati, OH
Garvey, John L. ...Washington, DC
Garvey, John P. ...Dallas, TX
Garvey, Joseph J. ...Toms River, NJ
Garvey, Joseph R. ...Lincoln, RI
Garvey, Julie A. ...Chicago, IL
Garvey, Karin E. ...New York, NY
Garvey, Kenneth T. ...Chicago, IL
Garvey, Kevin L. ...Louisville, KY
Garvey, Margaret R. ...Chicago, IL
Garvey, Margaret S. ...Denver, CO
Garvey, Mark
Environmental Protection Agency, Office of Enforcement and Compliance Assurance, GV
Garvey, Mary Ann ...Dallas, TX
Garvey, Mary Anne ...Cleveland, OH
Garvey, MaryAnn Ostroski ...Stroudsburg, PA
Garvey, Mathison & Boggio, P.A.
Bloomington, MN
Garvey, Matthew J. ...Buffalo, NY
Garvey, Maurice J. ...Chicago, IL
Garvey, Michael C. ...Albany, GA
Garvey, Michael D. ...Seattle, WA
Garvey, Michael J. ...Addison, IL
Garvey, Michael J. ...Chicago, IL
Garvey, Michael J., Jr. ...St. Paul, MN
Garvey, Michael W. ...Cleveland, OH
Garvey, Neil E. ...Buffalo, NY
Garvey, Patrick T. ...Chicago, IL
Garvey, Paul T. ...St. Clair Shores, MI
Garvey, Paul T., P.C. ...St. Clair Shores, MI
Garvey, Peter B. ...Ocean City, NJ
Garvey, Peter E. ...Providence, RI
Garvey, Richard A. ...New York, NY
Garvey, Richard J. ...Chicago, IL
Garvey, Richard J., Jr. ...Covington, LA
Garvey, Richd. J. ...New Orleans, LA
Garvey, Robert A. ...Cincinnati, OH
Garvey, Robert F. ...St. Clair Shores, MI
Garvey, Schubert & Barer
Washington, DC
Portland, OR
Seattle, WA
Garvey, Shannon A. ...Fort Lauderdale, FL
Garvey, Shelley N. ...Pittsburgh, PA
Garvey, Smith & Nehrbass ...Metairie, LA
Garvey, Stephen P. ...Ithaca, NY
Garvey & Stoddard, S.C. ...Madison, WI
Garvey, Susan M. ...Oakbrook Terrace, IL
Garvey, Terence Brian ...Gaithersburg, MD
Garvey, Terence Brian ...Greenbelt, MD
Garvey, Thomas J. ...Bellevue, NE
Garvey, Timothy ...Cherry Hill, NJ
Philadelphia, PA
Garvey, Vincent M. ...Department of Justice, Civil Division, GV
Garvey, Vincent R., Jr. ...Hazleton, PA
Garvey, William J. ...Indianapolis, IN
Garvey, William P. ...San Mateo, CA
Garvida, Francine M. ...Milwaukee, WI
Garvie, Pamela Jeanne ...Washington, DC
Garvie, Robert C. ...San Francisco, CA
Garvin, Agee, Carlton & Mashburn
Oklahoma City, OK
Pauls Valley, OK
Garvin, Anthony O. ...San Francisco, CA
Garvin, Arthur H., III ...Summit, NJ
Garvin & Benjamin, LLP
Los Angeles, CA
Garvin, Betsy Morgan ...Kansas City, MO
Garvin, Charles E. ...Burlingame, CA
Garvin, Chas. L., Jr. ...Fayetteville, WV
Garvin, Darryl T. ...Hackensack, NJ
Garvin, David M. ...Miami, FL
Garvin, David M., P.A. ...Miami, FL
Garvin, Deborah K. ...San Diego, CA
Garvin, Dennis E. ...Palo Alto, CA
Garvin, Douglas S. ...Aiken, SC
Garvin, Grace ...San Francisco, CA
Garvin, Gregory M. ...Kansas City, MO
Garvin, Harold T. ...Duncan, OK
Garvin & Hickey, LLC ...Cleveland, OH
Columbus, OH
Garvin, James F. ...Albuquerque, NM
Garvin, James L., Chartered ...Tracy, MN
Garvin, James R. ...Cincinnati, OH
Garvin, James W., Jr. ...Newark, DE
Garvin, Jeffrey R. ...Fort Myers, FL
Garvin, John ...Fresno, CA
Garvin, John C., Jr. ...Huntsville, AL
Nashville, TN
Garvin, John F. ...Van Nuys, CA
Garvin, John H. ...Pleasanton, CA
Garvin, Jonathan F. ...Rochester, NY
Garvin, Kathleen M. ...Cincinnati, OH
Garvin, Kirk S. ...San Bernardino, CA
Garvin, Larry T. ...Tallahassee, FL
Garvin, Leo V., Jr. ...St. Louis, MO
Garvin, Lisa A. ...Palm Desert, CA
Garvin & Maloney ...St. Louis, MO
Garvin, Mark Alan ...Fort Wayne, IN
Garvin, Michael A. ...St. Louis, MO
Garvin, Michael J. ...San Jose, CA
Garvin, Michael J. ...Chicago, IL
Garvin, Michael J. ...Cleveland, OH
Garvin, Michele M. ...Boston, MA
Garvin, Norman R. ...Indianapolis, IN
Garvin, Pamela A. ...Westlake Village, CA
Garvin, Paul M. ...Kansas City, MO
Garvin, Peter F., III ...Washington, DC
Garvin, Preston J. ...Columbus, OH
Garvin, Robert J. ...Pittsburgh, PA
Garvin, Ron H.
Department Of Veterans Affairs, Office of the General Counsel, GV
Garvin, Sylvia E. ...Huntsville, AL
Garvin, Thomas F. R. ...Los Angeles, CA
Garvin & Tripp, A Professional Association
Fort Myers, FL
Garvin, William A. ...Springfield, MA
Garvin, William H., III ...Tallahassee, FL
Beaumont, TX
Garvine, Brian M. ...Toledo, OH
Garvis, Andrew Stanton ...Minneapolis, MN
Garvis, Kerry L. ...Los Angeles, CA
Garvis, Marlene S. ...St. Paul, MN
Garwacki, Ray D., Jr. ...Pasadena, CA
Garwal, Dale A. ...Milwaukee, WI
Garwin, Arthur H. ...Chicago, IL
Garwin, Bronzaft, Gerstein & Fisher, L.L.P.
New York, NY
Garwin, Leo ...Carbondale, IL
Garwood, Calvin B. ...Houston, TX
Garwood, Cynthia L. ...Lafayette, IN
Garwood, David B. ...Red Cloud, NE
Garwood, David B. ...Auburn, NY
Garwood, Frederick L. ...Rochester, NY
Garwood, Harry L. ...San Antonio, TX
Garwood, Harry L., A Prof. Corp., Law Offices of ...San Antonio, TX
Garwood, Heidi E. ...Tallahassee, FL
Garwood, Julia M. ...San Diego, CA
Garwood, M. Lorena ...Honolulu, HI
Garwood, Max ...Huntington, IN
Garwood, McKenna, McKenna & Wolf, P.A.
Cocoa, FL
Orlando, FL
Garwood and Offner, P.C. ...Red Cloud, NE
Garwood, Thomas C., Jr. ...Cocoa, FL
Orlando, FL
Garwood, William L. ...Austin, TX
Garwood, William L., Jr. ...Houston, TX
Gary, Aaron R. ...Madison, WI
Gary, Alice W. ...Baltimore, MD
Gary, Andrew ...Austin, TX
Gary, Andrew ...San Marcos, TX
Gary, Arthur E. ...Department Of The Interior, Office of the Solicitor, GV
Gary, Beall Dozier, Jr. ...Birmingham, AL
Gary, Bob R. ...Tucson, AZ
Gary, Brian Keith ...Dallas, TX
Gary, Bruce J. ...Irvine, CA
Santa Ana, CA
Gary, C. Timothy ...Nashville, TN
Gary, Claudia H. ...Lake Charles, LA
Gary, Corby A. ...Rutland, VT
Gary, David S. ...New York, NY
Gary, Dexter ...Houma, LA
Gary, Donald J., Jr. ...Los Angeles, CA
Orange, CA
Gary, Dytrych & Ryan, P.A.
North Palm Beach, FL
Gary, E. Jean ...Los Angeles, CA
Gary & Goodman Limited
Alexandria, VA
Vienna, VA
Gary, Hope G. ...Chicago, IL
Gary, J. Daniel ...Overland Park, KS
Gary, J. Scott ...Seattle, WA
Gary, James M. ...Louisville, KY
Gary, James M. ...Austin, TX
Gary, James W. ...Corpus Christi, TX
Gary, Jennifer G. ...Lake Charles, LA
Gary, John W., III ...North Palm Beach, FL
Gary, Joseph B. ...Bozeman, MT
Gary, Keisha A. ...Washington, DC
Gary, Kenneth J. ...Huntingdon Valley, PA
Gary, Kevin Michael ...Jericho, NY
Gary, Leon, Jr. ...Baton Rouge, LA
Gary, Loren, II ...Swainsboro, GA
Gary, Marc ...Washington, DC
Gary, Mark C. ...Seattle, WA
Gary, Matthew J. ...Sacramento, CA
Gary, Melvin H. ...Baltimore, MD
Gary, Michael B. ...Denton, TX
Gary, Michelle Kravtin ...Washington, DC
Gary, Naegele & Theado ...Lorain, OH
Gary, Paul R. ...Portland, OR
Gary, Paul R., & Associates, A Prof. Corp.
Portland, OR
Gary, Ray ...Mableton, GA
Gary, Richard A. ...Sacramento, CA

Gary, Richard D. ......Richmond, VA
Gary, Richard N. ......San Francisco, CA
Gary, Robert D. ......Lorain, OH
Gary, Robert N. ......San Diego, CA
Gary, Sally A. ......Beaumont, TX
Gary, Stephan F. ......Mission Hills, CA
Gary, Stuart H. ......Vienna, VA
Gary, Susan N. ......Eugene, OR
Gary, T. Bart ......Atlanta, GA
Gary, Thomas ......Tallahassee, FL
Gary, Thomasson, Hall & Marks, Professional Corporation
Corpus Christi, TX
Gary, Till & Burlingham ......Sacramento, CA
Gary, Todd B. ......San Francisco, CA
Gary, Wendy Alyson ......New York, NY
Gary, William F. ......Eugene, OR
Gary, William L. ......Tallahassee, FL
Gary, Williams, Parenti, Finney, Lewis, McManus, Watson & Sperando
Fort Pierce, FL
Stuart, FL
Gary, Willie E. ......Fort Pierce, FL
Stuart, FL
Gary, Wyndham L. ......New York, NY
Garza, Abelardo ......San Antonio, TX
Garza, Amanda Paquet ......Dallas, TX
Garza, Ana M. ......El Paso, TX
Garza, Baldemar ......Rio Grande City, TX
Garza, Bernardo S. ......Houston, TX
Garza, Carlos ......Galveston, TX
Texas City, TX
Garza, Carlos J. ......Weslaco, TX
Garza, Carlos J., P.C. ......Weslaco, TX
Garza, Carlos R. ......Vienna, VA
Garza, Carmen E. ......Las Cruces, NM
Garza, Cynthia Y. ......Edinburg, TX
Garza, David C. ......Brownsville, TX
Garza, David L. ......Rio Grande City, TX
Garza, Deborah A. ......Washington, DC
Garza, Dennis ......Dallas, TX
Garza, Donna Gunnell ......San Bernardino, CA
Garza, Dori Contreras ......McAllen, TX
Garza, Eduardo G. ......Brownsville, TX
Garza, Edward F. ......Corpus Christi, TX
Garza, Emilio M. ......San Antonio, TX
Garza, F. John ......Dallas, TX
Garza, Fidencio G., Jr. ......Brownsville, TX
Garza, Florentino ......San Bernardino, CA
Garza, Francisco J. ......Harlingen, TX
Garza, Frank ......Dallas, TX
Garza, Frank M. ......Corpus Christi, TX
Garza, G. Jaime ......Edinburg, TX
Garza, G. Rudloph, Jr., P.C.
Corpus Christi, TX
Garza, G. Rudolph, Jr. ......Corpus Christi, TX
Garza & Garza, L.L.P. ......Brownsville, TX
Edinburg, TX
Rio Grande City, TX
Garza, Garza & Pacheco, Law Offices of
San Bernardino, CA
Garza, Guillermo E. ......Jamaica Plain, MA
Garza, Gustavo Ch. ......Raymondville, TX
Garza, Hector F. ......Brownsville, TX
McAllen, TX
Garza, Henry L. ......Belton, TX
Garza, James ......Houston, TX
Garza, Jesus ......Laredo, TX
Garza, Joe A. ......Corpus Christi, TX
Garza, Joe A., Jr. ......Irving, TX
Garza, Joe B., (P.C.) ......Dallas, TX
Garza, John E. ......Slidell, LA
Garza, John R. ......Greenbelt, MD
Rockville, MD
Garza, Jose L. ......Edinburg, TX
Garza, Keith M. ......Salem, OR
Garza & Lazor, P.C. ......San Antonio, TX
Garza, Lisa G. ......Dallas, TX
Garza, Mario M. ......Houston, TX
Garza, Martin E. ......Dallas, TX
Garza, Melissa ......New York, NY
Garza, Omar J. ......Edinburg, TX
Garza, Oscar ......Irvine, CA
Garza, Oscar L. ......Houston, TX
Garza, Regan & Rosenblatt, P.C.
Greenbelt, MD
Rockville, MD
Garza, Reynaldo G. ......Brownsville, TX
Garza, Reynaldo G., Jr. ......Brownsville, TX
Garza, Reynaldo" Trey " ......Edinburg, TX
Garza, Richard G. ......San Antonio, TX
Garza, Richard L. ......San Antonio, TX
Garza, Robert ......Del Rio, TX
Garza, Robert F., Jr. ......Union, MO
Garza, Roberto ......Brownsville, TX
Garza, Roberto ......Laredo, TX
Garza, Roberto M. ......San Angelo, TX
Garza, Rudy A. ......San Antonio, TX
Garza & Staples, A Professional Corporation
Dallas, TX
Garza, Thomas S. ......San Bernardino, CA
Garza, Valerie Ann ......San Angelo, TX
Garza, Vanessa ......Brownsville, TX
Garza, William R. ......McAllen, TX
Garza, Yolanda M. ......San Benito, TX
Garza Anderson, Velma ......San Antonio, TX
Garza-Gongora, Lazaro, Jr. ......Laredo, TX
Garza-Morales, Edgar H. ......New York, NY
Garzia, Mark A. ......Media, PA
Garzia, Samuel A. ......Detroit, MI
Garziglia, John F. ......Washington, DC
Garzilli, Jane B. ......Los Angeles, CA
Garzilli, Richard J. ......Los Angeles, CA
Garzino, Fred R. ......Chicago, IL
Garzoni, Michael J. ......Bingham Farms, MI
Gasalla, Yolanda ......Miami, FL
Gasarch, Mark ......Boca Raton, FL
New York, NY

Gasaway, Anthony S. ......St. Louis, MO
Gasaway, Edwin J. ......Chesterfield, MO
Gasaway, Gary E. ......Tacoma, WA
Gasaway, Gary E., P.S. ......Tacoma, WA
Gasaway, Harold L. ......Enid, OK
Gasaway, Laura N. ......Chapel Hill, NC
Gasaway, Lynn M. ......Houston, TX
Gasaway, Nicholas G., Jr. ......Hillsboro, MO
Gasaway, Patricia M. ......New York, NY
Gasaway, Rankin L. ......Dallas, TX
Gasaway, Robert R. ......Washington, DC
Gasaway, Timothy A. ......Beaumont, TX
Gasbarro, Pasco, Jr. ......Boston, MA
Providence, RI
Gasbarro, William E. ......Absecon, NJ
Gasch, Manning, Jr. ......Richmond, VA
Gasch, Susan Marie ......Spokane, WA
Gasche, Mitchell K. ......Plymouth, MI
Gaschen, Dane A. ......Delaware, OH
Gaschen, Francis A. ......Cumberland, RI
Gaschen Law Offices, A Professional Corporation ......Cumberland, RI
Gaschen, Nancy J. ......Cumberland, RI
Gaschler, Michael ......New York, NY
Gaschler, William B. ......Milwaukee, WI
Gascho, Dean ......Norristown, PA
Gascho, Martha B. ......Noblesville, IN
Gascoigne, Janice M. ......Chicago, IL
Gascoigne, John M. ......Houston, TX
Gascon, Houston C., III ......Covington, LA
Gascon, James J. ......Syracuse, NY
Gascou, Gemmill & Thornton
Los Angeles, CA
Gascou, René J., Jr. ......Los Angeles, CA
Gascoyne & Aylward ......Fort Collins, CO
Gascoyne, Jacques H. ......Florham Park, NJ
Gascoyne, James L. ......Houston, TX
Gascoyne, John P. ......Fort Collins, CO
Gasdia, Brian F. ......Downey, CA
Gasdia, Frank R. ......Downey, CA
Gasdia & Gasdia, A Professional Corporation
Downey, CA
Gasdick, Michael J. ......Orlando, FL
Gase, Gerald R. ......Troy, MI
Gase, Karen Kleiderman ......Los Angeles, CA
Gase, N. Christine ......Wichita, KS
Gase, Williams & Schroeder ......Troy, MI
Gasendo, Leah ......Woodland Hills, CA
Gasery, John L., Jr. ......Slidell, LA
Gasey, Arthur A. ......Chicago, IL
Gasey, Carolyn Eckert ......Chicago, IL
Gash, Barbara A. ......New York, NY
Gash, Gary M. ......White Plains, NY
Gash, Michael E. ......Sacramento, CA
Gash, Richard A. ......New York, NY
Gash, Robert T. ......Brevard, NC
Gashin, Irving ......Brookline, MA
Gashler, Richard A. ......Washington, DC
Gasho, Laura B. ......Washington, DC
Gasick, Gery R. ......Peoria, IL
Gasiel, Erin A. ......Danville, IL
Gasiewski, Stanley J. ......Rutherford, NJ
Gasink, Donald J. ......Augusta, ME
Gasinski, David M. ......Itasca, IL
Gasior, John A. ......North Ridgeville, OH
Gasior, John P. ......New York, NY
Gasior, Joseph J. ......Chicago, IL
Gasiorek, Donald J. ......Southfield, MI
Gasiorkiewicz, Eugene A. ......Racine, WI
Gasiorowski, Beth A. ......Towson, MD
Gasiorowski, Christie A. ......Brick, NJ
Gasiorowski & DeMassi ......Scotch Plains, NJ
Gasiorowski, Frank W. ......Scotch Plains, NJ
Gasiorowski, John A. ......Chicago, IL
Gasiorowski, Ronald S. ......Brick, NJ
Gask, Michael M. ......New York, NY
Gaskamp, Herman ......Caldwell, TX
Gaske, William F. ......New York, NY
Gaskell, George C. ......Austin, TX
Gaskell, George K. ......Tallahassee, FL
Gaskell, Judith A. ......Chicago, IL
Gaskell, Kimbrough ......Houston, TX
Gaskell, Michelle B. ......Pontiac, MI
Gaskey, David J. ......Bloomfield Hills, MI
Gaskie, Richard Kevin ......Denver, CO
Gaskill, Brian S. ......Tulsa, OK
Gaskill, Charles R., II ......Columbus, OH
Gaskill, David C. ......Ocean City, MD
Gaskill, Jay B. ......Oakland, CA
Gaskill, Jay P. ......Lewiston, ID
Gaskill, Raymond J. ......Irvine, CA
Gaskill, Robert F. ......Moorestown, NJ
Gaskill, Timothy W.
North Palm Beach, FL
Gaskill, Valerie Jackson ......Ocean City, MD
Gaskill Sandelin, Margaret ......Camano, WA
Gaskin, D. Erin ......Fort Lauderdale, FL
Gaskin, David C. ......Wewahitchka, FL
Gaskin, David M. ......Birmingham, MI
Grosse Pointe Farms, MI
Gaskin, Deborah J. ......Detroit, MI
Gaskin, George C. ......Poway, CA
Gaskin, John R. ......Indianapolis, IN
Gaskin, Lillian B. ......Washington, DC
Gaskin, Mary J. ......The Woodlands, TX
Gaskin, Ray ......Savannah, GA
Gaskin, Sharon L. N. ......Greensboro, NC
Gaskins, Barbara J. ......Omaha, NE
Gaskins, Charlotte Cooper ......Charlotte, NC
Gaskins, Debra H. ......Washington, NC
Gaskins, Earl J. ......Philadelphia, PA
Gaskins, Eura DuVal (Ed), Jr.
Raleigh, NC
Gaskins and Gaskins, P.A.
Washington, NC
Gaskins, Gregory C. ......Raleigh, NC
Gaskins, Gregory E. ......Bethesda, MD
Gaskins, Herman E., Jr. ......Washington, NC

Gaskins, Johnny S. ......Raleigh, NC
Gaskins, Kenneth D. ......Omaha, NE
Gaskins, M. Gay Caldwell ......Shreveport, LA
Gaskins, Michele R.
Upper Marlboro, MD
Gaskins, Pamela ......New York, NY
Gaskins, Richard C., Jr. ......Charlotte, NC
Gaskins, Roger A. ......San Diego, CA
Gaskins, Steve ......Minneapolis, MN
Gaskins, Tonja M. ......Arlington, VA
Gaslowitz, Adam R., & Associates
Atlanta, GA
Gasman, Gerald B. ......New York, NY
Gasman, Keith A. ......Fort Lauderdale, FL
Gasmer, Harlee M. ......Beverly Hills, CA
Gasner, Geo. E. ......Lackawanna, NY
Gasner, Mary Rose ......New York, NY
Gasner, Stuart L. ......San Francisco, CA
Gasnick, Harry D. ......Lewiston, ID
Gasnier, Philippa T. ......Washington, DC
Gaspar, Christopher J. ......New York, NY
Gaspar, Diane M. ......Hudson, NH
Gaspar, James J. ......Downers Grove, IL
Gaspar, Mark A. ......Baltimore, MD
Gaspar & Ritchie, Law Offices ......Hudson, NH
Gaspar, Russell J. ......Washington, DC
Gaspard & Graves, L.L.P. ......Baton Rouge, LA
Gaspard, James Gerard, II ......Lamar, CO
Gaspard, Scott O. ......Metairie, LA
Gaspard, Scott P. ......Baton Rouge, LA
Gaspardo, Carol A. ......Orland Park, IL
Gasparetti, Lorenzo E. ......Los Angeles, CA
Gaspari, Charles M. ......West Palm Beach, FL
Gaspari, David M. ......West Palm Beach, FL
Gaspari, Paul E. ......San Francisco, CA
Gasparian, Susan A. ......Dearborn, MI
Gasparik, Valerie J. ......Morristown, NJ
Gasparini, Mary E. ......Syracuse, NY
Gasparini, Thomas A. ......Orange, CA
Gasparis, Irene C. ......Crown Point, IN
Gasparo, Frank M. ......New York, NY
Gasparo, Sharon L. ......Jacksonville, FL
Gasparovic, Gary, P.A. ......Bryans Road, MD
Gasparovic, John J. ......Auburn Hills, MI
Gasparri, Rosemarie
West Palm Beach, FL
Gasparrini, Joseph C. ......Stamford, CT
Gasper, Andrew J. ......New York, NY
Gasper, Brent ......Little Rock, AR
Gasper, Carol L. ......Beachwood, OH
Gasper, Francis W. ......Kew Gardens, NY
Gasper, Gary J. ......Washington, DC
Gasper, George E. ......Dallas, TX
Gasper, James A. ......Anchorage, AK
Gasper, Jason R. ......Los Angeles, CA
Gasper, John S. ......Vestal, NY
Gasper, Kateri A. ......Kew Gardens, NY
Gasper, Kerry M. ......Topeka, KS
Gasper, Kym K. ......Salem, OR
Gasper, Robert W. ......Long Beach, CA
Gasperecz, A. Kirk ......New Orleans, LA
Houston, TX
Gasperetti, Barbara Szweda ......Notre Dame, IN
Gasperetti, Joseph E. ......New York, NY
Gasperetti, Joseph E., P.C., Law Offices of
New York, NY
Gasperian, Garee T. ......Woodland Hills, CA
Gasperin, Aldo ......New York, NY
Gasperini, Richard H. ......Richmond, VA
Gaspero, Carmen A. ......Warrenville, IL
Gaspero, Lisa M. ......Hoffman Estates, IL
Gasperson-Justice, Kimberly
Hendersonville, NC
Gaspich, Anthony J. ......Seattle, WA
Gaspich, James G. ......Denver, CO
Gaspich & Williams PLLC ......Seattle, WA
Gasque, B. Pratt, Jr. ......Myrtle Beach, SC
Gasque, B. Pratt, Jr., P.C. ......Myrtle Beach, SC
Gass, Andrew ......Houston, TX
Gass & Associates, P.A. ......Sunrise, FL
Gass, Craig E. ......San Francisco, CA
Gass, Daniel G. ......Sunrise, FL
Gass, Daniel M. ......Knoxville, TN
Gass, David A. ......Chicago, IL
Gass, David B. ......Phoenix, AZ
Gass, David J. ......Grand Rapids, MI
Gass, David O. ......Sheboygan, WI
Gass, Elbert E. ......Boise, ID
Gass, Frank B. ......Melville, NY
Gass, Gillen & Caliendo ......Melville, NY
Gass, Gregg A. ......De Smet, SD
Gass, Henry A. ......Reading, PA
Gass, J. Ric ......Milwaukee, WI
Gass, James A. ......Danvers, MA
Gass, James L. ......Sevierville, TN
Gass, James R. ......Redlands, CA
Gass, John L. ......Denver, CO
Gass, Jonathan J. ......New York, NY
Gass Law Offices ......Boise, ID
Gass and Lewis, Ltd. ......Chicago, IL
Northbrook, IL
Gass, Michael T. ......Boston, MA
Gass, Peter F. ......White Plains, NY
Gass, Raymond W. ......Wilmette, IL
Gass, Richard D. ......Boston, MA
Gass, Ronald S. ......Greenwich, CT
Gass, Ruth A. ......Brookline, MA
Gass, Stanford E. ......Chicago, IL
Northbrook, IL
Gass, Stephen F. ......Portland, OR
Gass, Thomas E. ......New York, NY
Gass, Timothy J. ......Boise, ID
Gassaway, Jim F. ......Tulsa, OK
Gassaway, Kevin T. ......Tulsa, OK
Gassaway, Linda M. ......Waco, TX
Gassaway, Michael B. ......Waco, TX
Gassaway, Rita J. ......Tulsa, OK

Gassaway, Russell
Warrensville Heights, OH
Gassaway, Scott L. ......Sacramento, CA
Gassaway, Terry M. ......Borger, TX
Gassaway, Turner Ford ......Claremore, OK
Gassel, Gary I. ......Sarasota, FL
Gassel, Milton R. ......Boca Raton, FL
Gassel, Philip M. ......New York, NY
Gassenheimer, Emily B. ......Montgomery, AL
Gassenheimer, James D. ......Miami, FL
Gassenheimer, Leandra Lederman
Macon, GA
Gasser, Alexander E. ......Arlington, VA
Gasser, Christine ......Garden City, NY
Gasser, Clark ......Pocatello, ID
Gasser, Edward W. ......Avon, CT
Gasser, Elizabeth ......West Orange, NJ
Gasser, Fred J. ......Wichita, KS
Gasser & Hayes ......Rye, NY
Gasser, Laura E. ......San Francisco, CA
Gasser, Robert A. ......Toms River, NJ
Gasser, Steven O. ......San Francisco, CA
Gassere, Eugene A. ......Mindoro, WI
Gassert, John M. ......Cloquet, MN
Gassett, Christopher T. ......Stratham, NH
Gassett, J. Michael ......Tulsa, OK
Gassett, John D. ......Tulsa, OK
Gassett, Noel B. ......San Jose, CA
Gassett, Perry & Frank ......Oakland, CA
Gassett, Robert A. ......St. Louis, MO
Gassin, Sandra Rice ......Dayton, OH
Gassler, Frank H. ......Tampa, FL
Gassman, Alan S. ......Clearwater, FL
Gassman, Alan S., P.A. ......Clearwater, FL
Gassman, Barry ......Chicago, IL
Gassman, Catherine A. ......Los Angeles, CA
Gassman, Grant Eric ......Denver, CO
Gassman, Stephen ......Garden City, NY
Gassman, Stephen, Law Offices of
Garden City, NY
Gassmann, John T. ......Valley City, ND
Gassmann, Michael L. ......Washington, DC
Gassner, Allison S. ......Chicago, IL
Gassner, Beverly J. ......Ontario, CA
Gassner, Bridget J. ......Framingham, MA
Gassner, Cecelia A. ......Palo Alto, CA
Gassner & Gassner, A Professional Corporation ......Ontario, CA
San Bernardino, CA
Gassner, Helene C. ......Lauderhill, FL
Gassner, Lawrence M. ......Ontario, CA
Gassner, Mark D. ......West Hartford, CT
Gassner, Michael J. ......Ontario, CA
Gassner, Stephen ......Upland, CA
Gast, Amy J. ......Chicago, IL
Gast, B. Elizabeth ......Charlotte, NC
Gast, David A. ......Miami, FL
Gast, John D. ......Naples, FL
Gast, K. Stuart ......Winamac, IN
Gast, Lisa S. ......Washington, DC
Gast, Michael A. ......Edison, NJ
Gast, Nancy S. ......Los Angeles, CA
Gast, Paul F. ......Department of Commerce, Patent and Trademark Office, GV
Gast, Randall Lee ......Green Bay, WI
Gast, Ratz & Gutierrez, P.C. ......Omaha, NE
Gast, Richard Shaeffer ......Fort Collins, CO
Gast, Stephen P. ......Cincinnati, OH
Gast, Theodore E. ......Watchung, NJ
Gast, William E. ......Omaha, NE
Gasteier, Philip A. ......Los Angeles, CA
Gasteiger, Larry D.
Federal Energy Regulatory Commission, Office of the General Counsel, GV
Gastel, Bernard ......Rochester, NY
Gastel, Joseph P. ......Buffalo, NY
Gastelle, Teri J. ......Miami, FL
Gastelo, Elvia Patricia ......Brooklyn, NY
Gaster, Jeffrey N. ......New York, NY
Gastevich, Vladimir, Jr. ......Crown Point, IN
Gasteyer, Philip ......Washington, DC
Gastfreund, Irving ......Santa Monica, CA
Washington, DC
Gasthalter, Edward, P.C. ......New York, NY
Gastilo, J. Carmen
Federal Energy Regulatory Commission, Office of the General Counsel, GV
Gastin, R. Wade ......Savannah, GA
Gastineau, John R. ......LaGrange, IN
Gastineau, Richard Hight
Plymouth Meeting, PA
Gastl, Eugene F. ......Shawnee, KS
Gastler, Debra A. ......Los Angeles, CA
Gastley, Diann M. ......Frederick, MD
Gastley, Harry L. ......Los Angeles, CA
Gastley, Ralph L., Jr. ......Frederick, MD
Gastley, Ralph L., Jr., P.A. ......Frederick, MD
Gastman, Gregory S. ......New York, NY
Gastman, Michael I. ......Closter, NJ
Gaston & Allison ......Greenville, SC
Gaston, André P. ......Visalia, CA
Gaston, Arthur Lee ......Chester, SC
Gaston, Aubra S. ......Philadelphia, PA
Gaston, Colene M. ......Fayetteville, AR
Gaston, D. Anthony ......San Diego, CA
Gaston, Daniel K. ......Pasadena, CA
Gaston, David E. ......Villanova, PA
Gaston, Donald C. ......Woodward, OK
Gaston, Durrance & Fairbanks
Montpelier, VT
Gaston, Erich H. ......Cheshire, CT
Gaston & Gaston ......Mobile, AL
Gaston, Gaston & Marion, P.A.
Chester, SC
Gaston, Geary A. ......Mobile, AL
Gaston, Harley B., Jr. ......Gastonia, NC
Gaston, Hemingway & Thanheiser, P.C.
Houston, TX

Gaston, Hollis Hudson ... Austin, TX
Gaston, Ian F. ... Mobile, AL
Gaston, James Leo, Jr.
Oklahoma City, OK
Gaston, James O. ... Bridgeport, CT
Gaston, John G. ... Houston, TX
Gaston, Judith Y. ... Northbrook, IL
Gaston, Keith A. ... Indianapolis, IN
Gaston Law Office, PLLC
Fayetteville, AR
Gaston Law Offices, Chartered
Overland Park, KS
Gaston, Lawrence W., Jr. ... Indianapolis, IN
Gaston, Lisa Anne ... Atlanta, GA
Gaston, M. Chinta ... New York, NY
Gaston, Marbut Glenn, Jr. ... Nashville, TN
Gaston, Mark H. ... Louisville, KY
Gaston, Mary P. ... Spokane, WA
Gaston, Patrick D. ... Overland Park, KS
Gaston, Paul G., Law Offices of
Washington, DC
Gaston, Paul K. ... Grand Rapids, MI
Gaston, Robert E. ... Las Vegas, NV
Gaston, Robert T. ... Montpelier, VT
Gaston & Ruane ... Bridgeport, CT
Gaston, Vilna Waldron ... Philadelphia, PA
Gaston, W. Clark, Jr. ... Greenville, SC
Gaston, W. Clayton ... Midland, TX
Gaston, W. Frank ... Plainview, TX
Gaston, Wilbert P. ... Newport Beach, CA
Gastwirth, Lloyd S. ... Dallas, TX
Gastwirth, Loretta M. ... Mineola, NY
Gastwirth, Mirsky and Stein ... Manhasset, NY
Gastwirth, Stuart L. ... Manhasset, NY
Gasway, Susan Lake ... Norwalk, CT
Minneapolis, MN
Gaswirth, Mitchell M. ... Los Angeles, CA
Gaswirth, Ronald M. ... Dallas, TX
Gasworth, Dianne Shapiro ... New York, NY
Gat, Nina Sant ... Boston, MA
Gatarz, Craig S. ... Los Angeles, CA
Gatch, Charles D. ... Savannah, GA
Gatch, Lewis G. ... Cincinnati, OH
Gatch, Lewis G., Co., L.P.A. ... Cincinnati, OH
Gatchel, Brian J. ... New Bern, NC
Gatchel, John K. ... Payette, ID
Gatchell, Catherine A. ... Tulsa, OK
Gatchell, David D. ... Kansas City, MO
Gatchell, Margaret A. ... Oklahoma City, OK
Gatdula, Lorena M. ... Oakland, CA
Gatehouse, James B. ... Charlotte, NC
Gatehouse, Rebecca K. ... Charlotte, NC
Gateley, Richard H. ... Fort Worth, TX
Gateley, Wade H. ... Burlington, CO
Gately, Andrew C. ... Kansas City, MO
Gately, Barbara L. ... Ross, CA
Gately, Clifford G. ... Chicago, IL
Gately, Francis A., Jr. ... El Monte, CA
Gately, Gary ... Des Moines, IA
Gately, James A. ... Chicago, IL
Gately, James T. ... Oak Lawn, IL
Gately, John B. ... Norfolk, VA
Gately, John B. ... Virginia Beach, VA
Gately, John P. ... Englewood, CO
Gately, Joseph M. ... Winchester, MA
Gately, Kathryn Elizabeth ... Merrillville, IN
Gately, Manley F. ... Lutherville, MD
Gately, Mark D. ... Baltimore, MD
Gately, Martin J. ... Saugus, MA
Gately, Mary E. ... Washington, DC
Gately, Matthew E., III ... New York, NY
Gately, Noelle ... East Hartford, CT
Gately, S. Jeffrey ... San Antonio, TX
Gately, William E., Jr. ... Braintree, MA
Gately, Wm. F. ... Napa, CA
Gatenby, Karin ... Wilmington, DE
Gater, Bradley N. ... Nome, AK
Gaters, F. Renée ... Charleston, SC
Gaters, F. Renee, LLC, Law Offices of
Charleston, SC
Gates & Adams ... Rochester, NY
Gates, Alexander B. ... Sumner, MS
Gates, Alice E. ... San Francisco, CA
Gates, Andrew L., III ... Lafayette, LA
Gates, Andrew P. ... Clearfield, PA
Gates & Associates, P.C. ... Harrisburg, PA
Lemoyne, PA
Lewistown, PA
Gates, Barry J. ... Ann Arbor, MI
Ypsilanti, MI
Gates, Benton E., Jr. ... Columbia City, IN
Gates, Bert L. ... St. Louis, MO
Gates, Biles, Shields & Ryan, P.A.
Overland Park, KS
Gates, Bob G.
Department Of Veterans Affairs, Office of Employment Discrimination Complaints Adjudication, GV
Gates, Bruce S. ... Bayonne, NJ
Gates, Bryan Emery, Jr. ... Winston-Salem, NC
Gates, C. Donald, Jr. ... Pittsburgh, PA
Gates, C Lynn ... Bloomfield Hills, MI
Gates, Chad L. ... Plantation, FL
Gates, Charles B., Jr. ... Charleston, WV
Gates, Christine Calbert ... Charlotte, NC
Gates, Clayton S.(" SAM ") ... Short Hills, NJ
Gates & Cooper ... Los Angeles, CA
Gates, Cornelia Henderson
Corpus Christi, TX
Gates, Daniel ... Warrendale, PA
Gates, David A. ... Kansas City, MO
Gates, David Allan ... Little Rock, AR
Gates, David H. ... Richmond, VA
Gates, Donald N. ... Los Angeles, CA
Gates, Douglas S. ... Rochester, NY
Gates, Edward R. ... Boston, MA
Gates, Ernest P., Jr. ... Chesterfield, VA
Gates, Ernest P., Sr. ... Chesterfield, VA
Gates, Floyd E., Jr. ... Battle Creek, MI
Gates, G. Thomas ... Lebanon, PA
Gates & Gates ... Hanover, PA
Gates, Gene P. ... Yucca Valley, CA
Gates, George Henry, III ... Los Angeles, CA
Gates, Gerald R. ... Monroe, WA
Gates, Gilbert L. ... High Point, NC
Gates, Glen E. ... Fresno, CA
Gates, Gordon W. ... Springfield, IL
Gates, Greg B. ... Atlanta, GA
Gates, Gregory A. ... Binghamton, NY
Gates, James E. ... Raleigh, NC
Gates, James S. ... Opelousas, LA
Gates, James W. ... Santa Clarita, CA
Gates, Jan E. ... Piedmont, CA
Gates, Jo Angelyn ... Los Angeles, CA
Gates, John C. ... Greenfield, MA
Gates, John D. ... El Paso, TX
Gates, John E. ... Royal Oak, MI
Gates, John E. ... Salt Lake City, UT
Gates, John R. ... Huntingdon, PA
Gates, Kenneth W. ... Spokane, WA
Gates, Kim Boman ... Mundelein, IL
Gates, Lathrop M. ... Kansas City, MO
Gates Law Office ... Columbia City, IN
Gates Law Office, P.S. ... Spokane, WA
Gates, Lawrence C. ... Overland Park, KS
Gates, Lawrence S., Inc. ... Providence, RI
Gates, Lee ... Las Vegas, NV
Gates, Leslie Calvin ... Meridian, MS
Gates, Linda Mandel ... New York, NY
Gates, Lisa B. ... Cleveland, OH
Gates, Lowell R. ... Lemoyne, PA
Gates, Lynn D. ... Buffalo, NY
Gates, Mark F. ... New Orleans, LA
Gates, Mark T., Jr. ... Palo Alto, CA
Gates, Marshall L. ... Succasunna, NJ
Gates, Martha Michael ... Sacramento, CA
Gates, Martin S. ... Cleveland, OH
Gates, Megan N. ... Waltham, MA
Gates, Michael D. ... St. Louis, MO
Gates, Michael L. ... Hollywood, FL
Gates, Michael R. ... Fort Walton Beach, FL
Gates, Nancy E. ... Tonawanda, NY
Gates, Pamela S. ... Phoenix, AZ
Gates, Patricia Finnegan ... Princeton, MA
Gates, Patricia R. ... Sacramento, CA
Gates, Paul H., Jr. ... Dedham, MA
Gates, Peter J. ... Irvine, CA
Gates, Peter P. McN. ... New York, NY
Gates, Peter S. ... Milwaukee, WI
Gates, Philip ... Columbus, TX
Gates, Philomene A., (Mrs.) ... New York, NY
Gates, Raymond R. ... Sacramento, CA
Gates, Richard M. ... Garden City, NY
Gates, Richard O. ... Chesterfield, VA
Gates, Richard W. ... Chula Vista, CA
Gates, Richard W. ... Santa Ana, CA
Gates, Richard W. ... Columbia City, IN
Gates, Robert B. ... Providence, RI
Gates, Robert P. ... San Francisco, CA
Gates, Robert R. ... Boise, ID
Gates, Robt. G. ... Cincinnati, OH
Gates, Roger S. ... Hamilton, OH
Gates, Ronald Kip ... Monroe, LA
Gates, Ronald M. ... Norfolk, VA
Gates, Rose M. ... Santa Ana, CA
Gates, Samuel A. ... Hanover, PA
Gates, Samuel K. ... Hanover, PA
Gates & Seaman ... Clearfield, PA
Gates, Sean P. ... Los Angeles, CA
Gates, Signe S. ... Bristol, CT
Gates, Stacey M. ... Binghamton, NY
Gates, Stein & Prause ... Columbus, TX
Gates, Stephen
Department of Commerce, GV
Gates, Stephen F. ... Chicago, IL
Gates, Susan L. ... Tulsa, OK
Gates, Susan P. ... Akron, OH
Gates, T. Thomas ... Charlotte, NC
Gates, Timothy L. ... Columbus, OH
Gates, Virginia Rayburn ... Springdale, AR
Gates, Walter J., III ... Mankato, MN
Gates, Wendell S. ... Hartford, CT
Gates, William A., III ... Louisville, KY
Gates, William B. ... Friendswood, TX
Gates, William H. ... Seattle, WA
Gates, William L. ... San Jose, CA
Gates, William L. ... Falls Church, VA
Gates, William S. ... Phoenix, AZ
Gates, William T. ... Shreveport, LA
Gates, Wise & Schlosser, P.C.
Springfield, IL
Gates, Wm. W. ... Sioux City, IA
Gates Hildt, Karen A. ... Port Townsend, WA
Gatesman, April P. ... Pittsburgh, PA
Gatesman, Mark A. ... Howell, MI
Gatesman, Valerie A. ... Department of Labor, Pension and Welfare Benefits, GV
Gatewood, Bryan D. ... Louisville, KY
Gatewood, Carol Jean ... Pittsburgh, PA
Gatewood, Diane Ridley ... New York, NY
Gatewood, Evan Blake ... Oklahoma City, OK
Gatewood, Frank C. ... Norman, OK
Gatewood, Harry D., II ... Choctaw, OK
Gatewood, Herbert L., Law Offices of
South Hamilton, MA
Gatewood, Jace C. ... Atlanta, GA
Gatewood, Jack P. ... Department of State, Foreign Service Officers (Overseas), GV
Gatewood, James C. ... Americus, GA
Gatewood, Margaret A. ... Topeka, KS
Gatewood, Sean R. ... New York, NY
Gatewood, Sheryl G. ... St. Louis, MO
Gatewood, Sophia M. ... Monroe, NC
Gatewood, Tela L. ... Dallas, TX
Gatewood, William M., Jr. ... San Antonio, TX
Gath, Neil E. ... Indianapolis, IN
Gathany, Richard S. ... Stone Mountain, GA
Gathings & Associates ... Birmingham, AL
Gathings, Honora M. ... Birmingham, AL
Gathings, John T., Jr. ... Charlotte, NC
Gathings, Jonathan W. ... Moody, AL
Gathings, Lloyd W., II ... Birmingham, AL
Gathings, Susan D. ... Loma Linda, CA
Gathman, J. Edward, Jr.
Cold Spring Harbor, NY
Gathman, Laurel A. ... Hawthorne, NY
Gathman, Laurie E. ... Tarrytown, NY
Gathright, Emmette F. ... El Dorado, AR
Gathright & Hardy ... Louisville, KY
Gathright, Howard T. ... Doylestown, PA
Gathright, Joseph R., Jr. ... Louisville, KY
Gathright, Richard E. ... Springdale, AR
Gatica, Mark A. ... Miami, FL
Gatien, Ralph W. ... Sacramento, CA
Gatier, Edward L. ... Malaga, NJ
Gatins, Patrick C. ... Staten Island, NY
Gatje, Michael A. ... Washington, DC
Vienna, VA
Gatley, Heather L. ... Miami, FL
Gatley, Nancy J. ... Princeton, NJ
Gatley, Steven G. ... Los Angeles, CA
Gatliff II, John E. ... Oklahoma City, OK
Gatlin, Albert E. ... Houston, TX
Gatlin, B. Kenneth ... Tallahassee, FL
Gatlin & Birch, P.A. ... Tampa, FL
Gatlin, C. Elmon ... Tampa, FL
Gatlin, Earl R. ... Rock Hill, SC
Gatlin, Gary H. ... Jasper, TX
Gatlin, Gerald R. ... San Dimas, CA
Gatlin, H. Grady, Jr. ... Bethesda, MD
Gatlin, James P. ... Denver, CO
Gatlin, Joe W. ... Waco, TX
Gatlin, John B. ... Boston, MA
Gatlin, John C. ... Norman, OK
Gatlin, Karen Boe ... Hackensack, NJ
Gatlin, Keith A. ... Rock Hill, SC
Gatlin, Michael G. ... Framingham, MA
Gatlin, Thomas A. ... Fairbanks, AK
Gatlin, Wesley G. ... Louisville, KY
Gatlin, William M. ... Belleville, IL
Gatling, Yvette Vanessa ... Houston, TX
Gatof, Robert Scott ... Newton, MA
Gatoff, Eric ... New York, NY
Gatrell, M. Bryant ... Charlotte, NC
Gatrost, Michael L. ... Kansas City, MO
Gatses, George S. ... Cicero, IL
Lockport, IL
Gatsos, Elaine M., Law Office
Boca Raton, FL
Gatsos, John D. ... New York, NY
Gatt, Frederick W. ... Oakland, CA
Gatta, Douglas J. ... Ocean Township, NJ
Gatta, Michael A. ... Woburn, MA
Gattegno, Mayer ... Coral Springs, FL
Gatterdam, Kort W. ... Columbus, OH
Gatterman, Bruce T. ... Larned, KS
Gattermeyer, Daniel John ... Hamilton, OH
Gattey, James M. ... San Diego, CA
Gattey, James M., Law Offices of
San Diego, CA
Gattey, Scott D. ... Palo Alto, CA
Gatti & Associates ... Haddonfield, NJ
Gatti, Daniel J. ... Salem, OR
Gatti, Francis C., Jr. ... Delran, NJ
Gatti, Frederick, Jr. ... San Diego, CA
Gatti, Gatti, Maier, Jackson & LeDoux
Salem, OR
Gatti, John D. ... Detroit, MI
Gatti, John G. ... Staten Island, NY
Gatti, John M. ... Los Angeles, CA
Gatti, Joseph T. ... New York, NY
Gatti, Joseph V. ... Washington, DC
Gatti, Kathleen M. ... Bloomfield Hills, MI
Gatti, Keltner, Bienvenu & Montesi
Memphis, TN
Gatti, Margaret M. ... Haddonfield, NJ
Gatti, Raymond R. ... Southern Pines, NC
Gatti, Ricco, Jr. ... Memphis, TN
Gatti, Richard D. ... Salem, OR
Gatti, Stefanie ... New York, NY
Gatti, Steven F. ... Washington, DC
Gattine, Andrew M. ... Augusta, ME
Gatting, Carlene J. ... New York, NY
Gattis, David B. ... El Paso, TX
Gattis, Donald L., Jr. ... Orlando, FL
Gattis, Hallowes & Carpenter, Professional Association ... Orlando, FL
Gattis & Kuncz, A P.C. ... San Diego, CA
Gattis, Noel R. ... Dallas, TX
Gattis, Richard E. ... San Diego, CA
Gatto, Elena I. ... Trenton, NJ
Gatto, Gregory D. ... Cleveland, OH
Gatto, James G. ... Washington, DC
Gatto, Janice ... Montvale, NJ
Gatto, John D. ... Waukesha, WI
Gatto, Joseph ... New York, NY
Gatto, Joseph J. ... Winston-Salem, NC
Gatto, Maureen T. ... Newtown, PA
Gatto, Michael E. ... Danville, CA
Gatto, Michael N. ... Blue Bell, PA
Gatto, Michele S. ... Montpelier, VT
Gatto, Nicholas S. ... New York, NY
Gatto, Paul J. ... St. Paul, MN
Gatton, Edwin R. ... Greensboro, NC
Gatton, Robert D., (P.A.) ... Orlando, FL
Gatton, Susanna M. ... Oklahoma City, OK
Gattoni, Todd Andrew ... Milford, MA
Gattoni, Todd Grant ... Oakland, CA
Gattorn, Gerald J. ... Detroit, MI
Gattozzi, Lynn M. ... Cleveland, OH
Gattozzi, Thomas A. ... Cleveland, OH
Gattuso, Christina M. ... Washington, DC
Gattuso, Domenic J. ... Paulsboro, NJ
Gattuso, Dominick T. ... Wilmington, DE
Gattuso, Frank ... Philadelphia, PA
Gattuso, Guy J., Jr. ... Bakersfield, CA
Gattuso, Joseph L.
Department of Commerce, National Telecommunications & Information Administration, GV
Gattuso, Joseph P. ... Chicago, IL
Gattuso, Kimberly L. ... Wilmington, DE
Gattuso, Kummer & Worthing
Bakersfield, CA
Gattuso, Maria ... New York, NY
Gattuso, Philip A. ... Gretna, LA
Gattuso, Roy J. D. ... Gretna, LA
Gaty, Christopher B.
Grand Junction, CO
Gatz, Arthur D., Jr. ... Pittsburgh, PA
Gatz, Carol L. ... Orange, CA
Gatz, C. J. ... Norfolk, NE
Gatz, Cohen, Segal & Koerner, P.A.
Pittsburgh, PA
Gatz, F. Douglas, Jr. ... Lafayette, LA
New Orleans, LA
Gatz, Fitzgerald & Vetter ... Neligh, NE
Norfolk, NE
Pierce, NE
West Point, NE
Gatz, John C. ... Chicago, IL
Gatz, John D. ... Colby, KS
Gatz, Jonathan J. ... Parma, OH
Gatz, Joseph W. ... Parma, OH
Gatz, Kenneth Adam ... Jericho, NY
Gatza, Gary Allen ... New York, NY
Gatzek, Deborah R. ... San Mateo, CA
Gatzert, Norman J.
South San Francisco, CA
Gatziolis, James J. ... Chicago, IL
Gatzke, Dillon & Ballance ... Carlsbad, CA
San Diego, CA
Gatzke, Michael Scott ... Carlsbad, CA
Gau, Suzanne J. ... St. Louis, MO
Gaubatz, George R. ... Georgetown, CO
Gaubatz, John T. ... Coral Gables, FL
Gaube, Ruth E. ... Cupertino, CA
Gaubert, Denis J., III ... Thibodaux, LA
Gaubert, Michael L. ... Dallas, TX
Gauby, Karl M. ... Phoenix, AZ
Gauby, Verne D. ... Nashville, TN
Gauch, Dorothy M.
Nuclear Regulatory Commission, Office of the General Counsel, GV
Gauch, James E. ... Washington, DC
Gauch, John F. ... New York, NY
Gauche, Jerry N. ... United States Senate, Senatorial Assistants, GV
Gaucher, Harry S., Jr. ... Willimantic, CT
Gaucher and Peters ... Willimantic, CT
Gauck, Charles H. ... Hopkins, MN
Gaudaen, Faith M. ... Detroit, MI
Gaudelli, Albert A. ... Forest Hills, NY
Gaudet, Brian L. ... Franklin, MA
Gaudet, Carol A. ... New York, NY
Gaudet, Caroline ... Washington, DC
Falls Church, VA
Gaudet, Denise A. ... Boston, MA
Gaudet, James K. ... Gretna, LA
Gaudet, Matthew C. ... Atlanta, GA
Gaudet, Paul M. ... Las Vegas, NV
Gaudet, Stephen J. ... Boston, MA
Gaudet, Tracy A. ... Hartford, CT
Gaudet, W. Gerald ... Lafayette, LA
Gaudet, William B. ... New Orleans, LA
Houston, TX
Gaudette, Eugene Henri ... Sanford, ME
Gaudette, Gregory ... Boston, MA
Gaudi, Arthur R. ... Santa Barbara, CA
Gaudin, André C. ... Metairie, LA
Gaudin, Andrew M. ... San Francisco, CA
Gaudin, Anne Marie ... New Orleans, LA
Gaudin, Bruce A. ... Opelousas, LA
Gaudin, E. Clark ... Baton Rouge, LA
Gaudin, Gary M. ... Gonzales, LA
Gaudin & Longoria ... New Orleans, LA
Gaudin, Mary Fuchs ... Metairie, LA
Gaudin, Michele ... New Orleans, LA
Gaudin, Pierre F., Jr. ... Gretna, LA
Gaudin, W. Wayne, Jr. ... Baton Rouge, LA
Gaudineer & Comito, L.L.P.
Des Moines, IA
Gaudineer, Lee H., Jr. ... Des Moines, IA
Gaudino, Gregory A. ... Wheeling, WV
Gaudio, Albert C. ... Monessen, PA
Gaudio, Antonio J.
South San Francisco, CA
Gaudio, Arthur R. ... Laramie, WY
Gaudio, Elizabeth A. ... Annapolis, MD
Gaudio, Frank J. ... Western Springs, IL
Gaudio, Frank S. ... Red Bank, NJ
Gaudio, John J. ... Lakewood, CO
Gaudio, John J., P.C. ... Lakewood, CO
Gaudio, John L. ... Window Rock, AZ
Gaudio, Mary Louise ... Bellevue, WA
Gaudio, Michael E. ... Follansbee, WV
Gaudio, Robert Joseph ... Wheeling, WV
Gaudio-Graves, Ginamarie ... Merrillville, IN
Gaudiosi, John P. ... Deerfield Beach, FL
Gaudiosi, Monica Marie ... Danbury, CT
Gaudioso, David A. ... Philadelphia, PA
Gaudioso, Keith R. ... Miami, FL
Gaudioso, Peter A. ... Montclair, NJ
Gaudoin, Ross C. ... Wheeling, WV
Gaudreau, Catherine A. ... Milwaukee, WI
Gaudreau, Donald G. ... Hartford, CT
Gaudreau, Kenneth D. L. ... Salisbury, MD
Gaudreau, Kenneth D.L., P.A.
Ocean City, MD
Salisbury, MD
Gaudreau, Richard D. ... Salem, NH
Gaudreau, Richard D., P.C. ... Salem, NH

Gaudreau, Russell A., III ....Boston, MA
Gaudreau, Russell A., Jr. .....Washington, DC
Gaudry, Thomas L., Jr. ....Gretna, LA
Gauen, Andrew C. ....Seattle, WA
Gauer, Charlotte E. ....Green Valley, AZ
Gauer, Keith A. ....Sioux Falls, SD
Gauer, Paul R. ....Bloomfield, NJ
Gauffreau, Stuart C. ....Charlotte, NC
Gaufin, Samuel O. ....Salt Lake City, UT
Gaug, Joseph M. ....Albany, NY
Gaug, Patricia M. ....Stamford, CT
Gauger, Charles S. ....Portland, OR
Gauger, Christopher F. ....San Francisco, CA
Gauger, Jeffrey A. ....Alexandria, VA
Gauger, Matthew J. ....West Sacramento, CA
Gauger, Timothy G. ....Little Rock, AR
Gaugh, Kenneth Ray ....Torrance, CA
Gaugh, Michael J. ....Washington, DC
Gaughan, Ann M. ....Haddonfield, NJ
Gaughan, Anne M. ....Columbus, OH
Gaughan, Bridget M. ....Phoenix, AZ
Gaughan, Dennis Char ....Hamburg, NY
Gaughan, Dennis J. ....Honolulu, HI
Gaughan, Eugene M. ....Angola, NY
Gaughan, Francis I. ....Chicago, IL
Gaughan, Frank I. ....Chicago, IL
Gaughan, James D. ....Greenwich, CT
Gaughan, James P. ....Chicago, IL
Gaughan, Jeffrey Thomas
Lake Charles, LA
Gaughan, John E., III ....Camden, AR
Gaughan, John J. ....Pittsburgh, PA
Gaughan, John S. ....Tustin, CA
Gaughan, Joseph P. ....Brockton, MA
Gaughan, Lawrence D. ....Fairfax, VA
Gaughan, Martin J. ....Weirton, WV
Gaughan, Mary C. ....Indianapolis, IN
Gaughan, Michael G. ....Scottsdale, AZ
Gaughan, Michael P. ....Kansas City, MO
Gaughan, Mollie B. ....Buffalo, NY
Gaughan, Patricia A. ....Cleveland, OH
Gaughan & Schargorodski ....Fairfax, VA
Gaughan, Thos. J. ....Fargo, ND
Gaughan, Vincent J. ....Trenton, NJ
Gaughan, Vincent M., Jr. ....Hamburg, NY
Gaughen, Gaughen & Gaughen
Weymouth, MA
Gaughen, John R. ....Atlanta, GA
Gaughen, Kevin W. ....Weymouth, MA
Gaughen, Paul L. ....Spokane, WA
Gaughen, Robert H. ....Weymouth, MA
Gaughen, Robert H., Jr. ....Weymouth, MA
Gaughen, Thomas J. ....Omaha, NE
Gaughran, Julie ....Chappaqua, NY
Gaughran, Robert J. ....Middletown, NJ
Gaughran, Robert J., P.A. ....Middletown, NJ
Gaugler, Alexandra Cileone
Philadelphia, PA
Gaugler, Nelson B. ....Warrendale, PA
Gauhan, Dennis P., (A Law Corporation)
Santa Ana, CA
Gauhar, Tashina ....Baltimore, MD
Gaujean, Max G. ....New York, NY
Gaujot, Phillip D. ....Charleston, WV
Morgantown, WV
Gaukel, James F. ....Mapleton, IA
Gaukel, Nevins & Westergaard
Anthon, IA
Mapleton, IA
Onawa, IA
Sloan, IA
Gaukler, Lee A. ....Davenport, IA
Gaukler, Paul A. ....Washington, DC
Gaukrodger, David ....New York, NY
Gaukroger, Robin R. ....Cashmere, WA
Chelan, WA
Wenatchee, WA
Gaul, Annette ....Rochester, NY
Gaul, Brian X. ....Falls Church, VA
Gaul, Carl J. ....Everett, WA
Gaul, Daniel ....Cleveland, OH
Gaul, Dewie J. ....Sioux City, IA
Gaul and Dumont ....San Antonio, TX
Gaul, John F. ....Washington, DC
Gaul, John G. ....Princeton, NJ
Gaul, Kenneth W. ....Department of Justice, Antitrust Division, GV
Gaul, Malinda A. ....San Antonio, TX
Gaul, Marianne ....Newark, NJ
Gaul, Marybeth Z. ....McLean, VA
Gaul, Michael A. ....Stroudsburg, PA
Gaul, Stuart C., Jr. ....Pittsburgh, PA
Gaul, Stuart C., Sr. ....Pittsburgh, PA
Gaul, Timothy J. ....Thousand Oaks, CA
Gaul, Vickie L. ....Washington, DC
Gaulden, David L. ....Baltimore, MD
Gaulden, James C., Jr. ....Duluth, GA
Gaulden, Nadine R. ....Lansing, MI
Gauldin, C. Alan ....Springdale, AR
Gauldin, J. Michael ....Dyersburg, TN
Gauldin, R. Jackson ....Whittier, CA
Gauldin, William H. ....Titusville, FL
Gaulding, James F. ....Dallas, TX
Gaule, John V. ....Arcadia, CA
Gaulin, Edward F. ....Biddeford, ME
Gaulin, Patricia B. ....Greenwich, CT
Gaulin, Robert V., & Associates
Beverly Hills, CA
New York, NY
Gaulke, Kevin C. ....Albany, GA
Gaulke, Paul T. ....Los Angeles, CA
Gaulkin, Geoffrey ....Short Hills, NJ
Gaull, Sharon L. ....Chicago, IL
Gault, Bridget A. ....St. Louis, MO
Gault, Catherine J. ....Gettysburg, PA
Gault, Charles P. ....Knoxville, TN
Gault, Christina L. ....West Des Moines, IA
Gault, Cullen C. ....Lexington, KY

Gault Davison ....Fenton, MI
Lapeer, MI
Owosso, MI
Flint, MI
Gault, Duncan ....Mineral Wells, TX
Gault, E. Nicholson, Jr. ....Lutherville, MD
Gault, Edwin S., Jr. ....Jackson, MS
Gault, Edwin Spivey ....Paducah, KY
Gault & Gault, L.L.P. ....Mineral Wells, TX
Gault, George S. ....Mineral Wells, TX
Gault, Gordon F. ....Chicago, IL
Gault, Harold S. ....Claremont, CA
Gault, James L. ....San Francisco, CA
Gault, Jeffrey P. ....St. Louis, MO
Gault, John C. ....Williamsport, PA
Gault, Marc F. ....Arlington, TX
Gault, Marshall & Miller ....Paducah, KY
Gault, Pamela L. ....Department of Education, Office of the General Counsel, GV
Gault, Patrick W. ....Louisville, KY
Gault, Paul E., Jr. ....Fountain Inn, SC
Gault, Richard S. ....Cumming, GA
Gault, Robert M. ....Boston, MA
Gault, Ronald J. ....Birmingham, AL
Gault, Ross T. ....White Settlement, TX
Gault, William G. ....Pittsburgh, PA
Gault, William H. ....Tulsa, OK
Gault, William I., Jr. ....Jackson, MS
Gault, William R. ....Brownsville, TX
Gaultney, David B. ....Beaumont, TX
Gaulton, David J. ....Canoga Park, CA
Gaum, R. Eric ....Akron, OH
Gaumer, Christie, Law Offices of
Los Angeles, CA
Gaumer, Daniel L. ....Decatur, IL
Gaumer, David D. ....Kingman, KS
Gaumer, Gayle ....Edina, MN
Gaumer, Lynn M. ....Sioux Falls, SD
Gaumer & McClellan ....Kingman, KS
Gaumer, Richard J. ....Ottumwa, IA
Gaumont, R. Robert, Jr. ....Merrimack, NH
Gauna, Eileen ....Los Angeles, CA
Gaunce, Charles W. ....Norman, OK
Gaunt, Dirrim and Coover, P.C.
Brighton, CO
Gaunt, Janet L. ....Seattle, WA
Gaunt, John M. ....York, PA
Gaunt, Leeann Ghazil ....Boston, MA
Gaunt, Pratt & Radford
West Palm Beach, FL
Gaunt, Richard H., Jr. .....West Palm Beach, FL
Gaunt, Robert B. ....Torrance, CA
Gaunt, Stephen F. ....Rolla, MO
Gaunt, William L. ....Reading, PA
Gauntlett & Associates ....Irvine, CA
Gauntlett, Bridget A. ....New York, NY
Gauntlett, David A. ....Irvine, CA
Gauntner, Timothy J. ....Lakewood, OH
Gauntt, John ....Temple, TX
Gauntt, Vernon C. ....San Diego, CA
Gauper, Allen M. ....Spokane, WA
Gaupp, John J. ....Baton Rouge, LA
Gaur, Shanthi V. ....Chicago, IL
Gaura, Patrick A. ....Dunkirk, NY
Gauri, Vineet ....Chicago, IL
Gauron, Paul R., (P.C.) ....Boston, MA
Gaus, Charles F. ....Anderson, IN
Gaus, Conyetta ....Yoakum, TX
Gaus, David S. ....Bernardsville, NJ
Gaus, Elwood ....Yoakum, TX
Gaus, Henry K. ....San Jose, CA
Gaus, Michael C. ....Newton, NJ
Gaus Natho & Gaus ....Yoakum, TX
Gaus, Paula J. ....Irving, TX
Gaus, Stephan M. ....Frankenmuth, MI
Saginaw, MI
Gaus, William ....San Francisco, CA
Gaus, William C. ....Pompano Beach, FL
Gaus, William T. ....Milwaukee, WI
Gausden, Thomas E. ....Milwaukee, WI
Gause, John P. ....Lewiston, ME
Gause, Merritt & Bartirome ....Sarasota, FL
Gause, Randall Kent ....Tulsa, OK
Gause, Stephen D. ....Martinez, CA
Gause, W. Peyton, Jr. ....Sarasota, FL
Gaus Ehning, Michele B. .....Vernon Hills, IL
Gausewitz, Richard L. ....Newport Beach, CA
Gausman, Carlton James ....Seattle, WA
Gausnell, Seth G. ....St. Louis, MO
Gauss, Robert F. ....Evergreen, CO
Gauss, Robert L. ....Indianapolis, IN
Gausselin, Edwin A. ....Chicago, IL
Gaustad, Daniel L. ....Grafton, ND
Gaustad, G. Scott ....Lakeport, CA
Gaustad, G. Scott ....Ukiah, CA
Gaustad, John K. ....Riverside, CA
Gauster, Stephen W. ....New York, NY
Gausvik, Cynthia L. ....Vienna, VA
Gaut, Barton C., (P.C.) ....San Bernardino, CA
Gaut, James R. ....Greensburg, PA
Gaut, Kevin, (A Professional Corporation)
Los Angeles, CA
Gauthier, Andrea M. ....Los Angeles, CA
Gauthier, Angela F. ....Baton Rouge, LA
Gauthier, Anthony P. ....Grand Rapids, MI
Gauthier, Ashley ....Albuquerque, NM
Gauthier, Celeste A. ....Metairie, LA
Gauthier, Daniel J. ....St. Louis, MO
Gauthier, Danny S. ....Baton Rouge, LA
Gauthier, Downing, LaBarre, Beiser & Dean, A Professional Law Corporation
Metairie, LA
New Orleans, LA
Gauthier, Edward P. ....Los Angeles, CA
Gauthier, Frances ....Wilmington, DE
Gauthier, Georgia J. ....Reno, NV
Gauthier, James A. ....Auburn, WA
Gauthier, James D. ....Buffalo, NY

Gauthier, Janice L. ....Milwaukee, WI
Gauthier, John F. ....Pittsford, NY
Gauthier, Jon F. ....San Diego, CA
Gauthier, Joseph T. ....Los Angeles, CA
Gauthier, Lindsey A. ....Wilmington, DE
Gauthier, Lucien P. ....Boston, MA
Gauthier, Madeline (Chott) ....Bellevue, WA
Gauthier, Marybeth C. ....New Haven, CT
Gauthier, Maurice E. ....Boston, MA
Gauthier, Nicole ....Cameron Park, CA
Gauthier, Pamela L. ....Washington, DC
Gauthier, Richard H. ....Arabi, LA
Gauthier, Robert W. ....Newport, RI
Gauthier, Roger L. ....Nashua, NH
Gauthier, Stanford B., II ....Lafayette, LA
Gauthier, Susan D. ....San Diego, CA
Gauthier, Thomas E. ....Fresno, CA
Gauthier, Wendell H. ....Metairie, LA
Gauthreaux, Everette F. ....Gretna, LA
Gautier, Agnes M. ....New York, NY
Gautier, B. Elise ....Portland, OR
Gautier, Emilio P. ....Bronx, NY
Gautier, Harold W., Jr. ....Evanston, IL
Gautier, John H. ....Mishawaka, IN
Gautier, John William
Fort Lauderdale, FL
Miami, FL
Gautier, Juan C. ....Orlando, FL
Gautier & Kavulich, P.A.
Coral Gables, FL
Gautier, Larry F. ....Fort Worth, TX
Gautier, Michael J., Jr ....Alexandria, LA
Gautier, Pamela B. ....Alexandria, LA
Gautier, Russell D. ....Tallahassee, FL
Gautier, Scott ....Chicago, IL
Gautier, Virginia Smith ....Jackson, MS
Gautier, William L. ....Coral Gables, FL
Gautieri, Vincent D. ....Montclair, NJ
Gautney, Donald ....Montgomery, AL
Gautney, John F., Jr. ....Little Rock, AR
Gautreau, Paul N. ....Covina, CA
Gautreau, Raymond B. ....Prairieville, LA
Gautreaux, Bennett J. ....Lafayette, LA
Gautreaux, Jill ....Metairie, LA
Gautreaux, Mark E. ....Oklahoma City, OK
Gautreaux, Rene C. ....Cut Off, LA
Gautschi, Christopher C. ....Ventura, CA
Gautschi, Christopher C. ....Irvine, CA
Gauvey, Susan K. ....Baltimore, MD
Gauvin, Jessica B. ....Hartford, CT
Gauvin, Pamela S. ....Fall River, MA
Gauvin, Shirley A. ....San Diego, CA
Gauvreau, N. Paul ....Lewiston, ME
Gauza, Thaddeus S., Law Office of
Chicago, IL
Gauzza, Michael J. ....Syracuse, NY
Gavagan, M. Anne ....Chicago, IL
Gavagan, Peter J. ....New York, NY
Gavaldon, Joseph A. ....Fort Collins, CO
Gavaletz, Denise M. ....Worcester, MA
Gavan, Glenn T. ....Newton, NJ
Gavan, Henry J. ....Bronx, NY
Gavaris, Helen ....New York, NY
Gavello, Gary A. ....San Francisco, CA
Gaven, Daniel F. ....New York, NY
Gavenchak, Eugenie C. ....New York, NY
Gavend, Richard B. ....Denver, CO
Gavenda, Harris ....Syracuse, NY
Gavenda, John C. ....Albion, NY
Gavenman, Jon E. ....Menlo Park, CA
Gavenus, Gary M. ....Newland, NC
Gaver, Dean A. ....Woodbridge, NJ
Gaver, Donald A. ....Cape May, NJ
Gaver, Eric D. ....Cape May, NJ
Gaver, Frances R. ....Monterey, CA
Gaver and Gaver, P.A. ....Cape May, NJ
Gaver, Mary Catherine Collins
Towson, MD
Gaveras, Peter ....West Roxbury, MA
Gavett and Datt, P.C. ....Rockville, MD
Alexandria, VA
Gavett, Geoffrey S. ....Rockville, MD
Gavia, David R. ....Austin, TX
Gavia, Paul R. ....Austin, TX
Gavic, Diane L. ....Spring Valley, WI
Gavic, Jorv R. ....Spring Valley, WI
Gavic, Robert R. ....Spring Valley, WI
Gavica, Denise ....Miami, FL
Gavigan, Alice Manning ....Charlotte, NC
Gavigan, Anderson & Andrews
Ludington, MI
Gavigan, Brian P. ....Burlington, NC
Gavigan, Grace L. ....Philadelphia, PA
Gavigan, James C. ....Palm Beach, FL
Gavigan, James C., P.A. ....Palm Beach, FL
Gavigan, Kathleen ....Pittsburgh, PA
Gavigan, Leonard J. ....Ludington, MI
Gavigan, Mary Teresa ....Philadelphia, PA
Gavigan, Maura K. ....Raleigh, NC
Gavigan, P. Joan I. ....Frederick, MD
Gavigan, Robert J. ....New York, NY
Gavigan, Robert J. ....New York, NY
Gavigan, Thomas E. ....Dallas, TX
Gavigan, Timothy B. ....Charlotte, NC
Gavigan, Walter F. ....Vineland, NJ
Gavil, Andrew I. ....Washington, DC
Gavilan, David ....New York, NY
Gavilanes, Diego P. ....Everett, WA
Seattle, WA
Gavilanes, Diego P., P.S. ....Everett, WA
Seattle, WA
Gavilondo, Carlos ....Westborough, MA
Gavilondo, Jennifer Brooks ....Phoenix, AZ
Gavin, Alison L. ....Winnetka, IL
Gavin, Barbara S. ....Towson, MD
Gavin, Carol Coghlan ....Lisle, IL
Gavin, Charles A. ....Richmond, VA

Gavin, Cox, Pugh, Etheridge and Wilhoit, L.L.P. ....Asheboro, NC
Gavin & Cunningham ......San Francisco, CA
San Jose, CA
Gavin, Daniel ....Irvine, CA
Gavin, Darryl L. ....Orlando, FL
Gavin, Donald G. ....Washington, DC
Vienna, VA
Gavin, Donald J. ....Department of Justice, Tax Division, GV
Gavin, Edward J. ....Bridgeport, CT
Gavin, F. James ....Yakima, WA
Gavin, Francis X. ....Hackettstown, NJ
Gavin & Gavin, A Professional Corporation
Cranford, NJ
Gavin & Gavin, P.A. ....Cherry Hill, NJ
Gavin, Gayle A. ....New York, NY
Gavin, James C. ....Cherry Hill, NJ
Gavin, James E. ....Reading, PA
Gavin, James G. ....Burlington, NJ
Gavin, James H., Jr. ....Aberdeen, MS
Gavin, James J. ....Oak Brook, IL
Gavin, James M. ....Lodi, CA
Gavin, Jeffrey S. ....St. Louis, MO
Gavin, Jennifer R. ....Lynn, MA
Gavin, John ....Tieton, WA
Gavin, John J. ....New York, NY
Gavin, John L. ....Carson City, NV
Gavin, John N., (P.C.) ....Chicago, IL
Gavin, John R. ....Oil City, PA
Gavin, Joseph M. ....Boston, MA
Gavin, Julie C. ....San Francisco, CA
Gavin, Kenneth M. ....Benton Harbor, MI
Gavin, Kevin P. ....Providence, RI
Gavin, Kristy J. ....Jacksonville, FL
Gavin Law Firm ....Belleville, IL
Gavin, Lawrence M. ....Chicago, IL
Gavin, Linda F. ....Brookline, MA
Gavin, Lynn ....Atlanta, GA
Gavin, Maribeth ....Cleveland, OH
Gavin, Marvin E. ....Markham, IL
Gavin, Mary Kathryn ....San Francisco, CA
Gavin, Meritt B. ....Cranford, NJ
Gavin, Michael J. ....Paoli, PA
Gavin, Michael M. ....Glencoe, MN
Gavin, Michael T. ....Cleveland, OH
Gavin, Mitchell E. ....Alexander City, AL
Gavin, Olson, Conkel & Savre, Ltd.
Glencoe, MN
Gavin, P. David ....Rockville, MD
Gavin, Pamela C. ....Richmond, VA
Gavin, Patrick M. ....Kansas City, MO
Gavin, Paul J. ....New York, NY
Gavin, Paul M. ....White Plains, NY
Gavin, R. Kyle ....Jacksonville, FL
Gavin, Robert A., Jr. ....Brooklyn, NY
Gavin, Robert P. ....Columbus, OH
Gavin, Sandra F. ....Cherry Hill, NJ
Gavin, Sheila M. ....Milwaukee, WI
Gavin, Stephen Diaz ....Washington, DC
Gavin, Steven J. ....Chicago, IL
Gavin, Steven R. ....Atlanta, GA
Gavin, Thomas F. ....Bel Air, MD
Gavin, Thomas G. ....West Chester, PA
Gavin, Tim ....Dallas, TX
Gavin, W. Ed ....Asheboro, NC
Gavin, Walter P. ....Englewood, NJ
Gavin, Wendy Lee ....Philadelphia, PA
Gavin, William E. ....New York, NY
Gavin, William H. ....San Jose, CA
Gavin, William P. ....Belleville, IL
Gavin, William P. ....South Weymouth, MA
Gavin, Wm. F. ....La Jolla, CA
Gavinski, Joseph K. ....Moses Lake, WA
Gavioli, Wayne A. ....Nanuet, NY
Gavioli, Wayne A., P.C. ....Nanuet, NY
Gaviria, Boris ....Chicago, IL
Gaviria, Ivan A. ....Kirkland, WA
Gavis, Alexander C. ....Boston, MA
Gavit, George B. ....Indianapolis, IN
Gavit, Linda ....Arvada, CO
Gavito, Juan E. ....Brownsville, TX
Gavlick, Blase L. ....Reading, PA
Gavlick, Don ....Austin, TX
Gavlick, Jean Gilroy ....Wyomissing, PA
Gavlick, Thomas J. ....Providence, RI
Gavlik, Lisa K. ....Pittsburgh, PA
Gavlik, Robert R. ....Pittsburgh, PA
Gavran, John S. ....Rio Rancho, NM
Gavranovic, Thomas J. ....Houston, TX
Gavras, Chris L. ....Denver, CO
Gavras, Dian L. ....Tulsa, OK
Gavras, Leon C. ....Tulsa, OK
Gavre, W. Mark ....Salt Lake City, UT
Gavriel, Michelle R. ....Glendale, CA
Gavrilik, Joan Susan ....Albany, NY
Gavrilles, Arthur P. ....Norfolk, MA
Gavrilovich, Charles D. ....San Diego, CA
Gavrilovich, Charles D., Jr.
San Diego, CA
Gavrin, Andrew S. ....Philadelphia, PA
Gavrin, Darrell L., (Ms.) ....Kew Gardens, NY
Gavron, Denise H. ....Northridge, CA
Gavron-Ravenelle, Deborah
Marlborough, MA
Gavsie, Brian J. ....New York, NY
Gavtreau, Jennifer Brand ....Baton Rouge, LA
Gavula, John J. ....Roseland, NJ
Gavzy, Ann Bitton ....Wall, NJ
Gavzy, Stuart D. ....Little Falls, NJ
Gaw, David B. ....Fairfield, CA
Napa, CA
Gaw, H. Ralph ....Tipton, MO
Gaw, John G., Jr. ....Kitty Hawk, NC
Gaw, Mary Ellen ....New Canaan, CT
Gaw, Michael James
Board of Governors Of The Federal Reserve

System, Office of the General Counsel, GV
Gaw, Michael Stephen .... Atlanta, GA
Gaw and Opie, P.C. .... Tipton, MO
Gaw, Patricia D. .... Winston, OR
Gaw, R. Steven .... Moberly, MO
Gaw, Van Male, Smith, Myers & Miroglio, A Professional Law Corporation
Fairfield, CA
Napa, CA
Redlands, CA
Gawad, Sam A., Jr. .... Rockville, MD
Gawande, Sumeeta A. .... Newark, NJ
Gawart, Chris K. .... Milwaukee, WI
Gawerc, Jimmie G. .... Houston, TX
Gawinski, Ernest J. .... Buffalo, NY
Gawlas, Robert N., Jr. .... Wilkes-Barre, PA
Gawle, Alphonse .... Seattle, WA
Gawley, Steven .... New York, NY
Gawlik, Leslie W. .... Baltimore, MD
Gawlowski, Richard G. .... Seattle, WA
Gawne, Cathryn S. .... San Francisco, CA
Gawne, Michael S. .... St. Albans, VT
Gawron & Associates, P.A.
Bloomington, MN
Minneapolis, MN
Gawron, Steven L. .... Minneapolis, MN
Gawronski, Frederick J. .... Buffalo, NY
Gawronski, Stacia J. .... San Diego, CA
Gawrych, John A. .... Torrington, CT
Gawryk, Terry R. .... Chicago, IL
Gawryl, Janine .... Nashua, NH
Gawryl & MacAllister .... Nashua, NH
Gawrys, Joseph A. .... Norfolk, VA
Gawthrop, Alfred, Jr. .... Sacramento, CA
Gawthrop, Greenwood & Halsted, A Professional Corporation
West Chester, PA
Gawthrop, Howard E. .... Aptos, CA
Gawthrop, Janet L. .... Lexington, KY
Gawthrop, Robert S., Jr. .... West Chester, PA
Gaxiola, Fernando X. .... Tucson, AZ
Gaxiola, Henry R. .... Santa Ana, CA
Gay, Andrew G. .... Philadelphia, PA
Gay, Andrew G., Jr. .... Philadelphia, PA
Gay, Andy W. .... Zebulon, NC
Gay, Anita J. .... Miami, FL
Gay, Anthony E. .... Philadelphia, PA
Gay, Bonnie Lewis .... Department of Justice, Executive Office for United States Attorneys, GV
Gay, Byron D. .... Orlando, FL
Gay, Carl Lloyd .... Port Angeles, WA
Gay, Cathy A. .... McLean, VA
Gay & Chacker .... Marlton, NJ
Philadelphia, PA
Gay, Charles F., Jr. .... New Orleans, LA
Gay, Clyde S., Jr. .... Franklin, TN
Gay, Darrell S. .... New York, NY
Gay, David T. .... Taunton, MA
Gay, Donald G. .... Dallas, TX
Gay, Donna L. .... Little Rock, AR
Gay, Dorothy P. .... Baltimore, MD
Gay, Douglas F. .... Rock Hill, SC
Gay, E. Laurence .... Honolulu, HI
Gay, E. Phelps .... New Orleans, LA
Gay, Edward J., III .... Covington, LA
Gay, Edward R. .... Orlando, FL
Gay, Edward R., P.A., Law Firm of
Orlando, FL
Gay, Elaine .... Brooklyn, NY
Gay, Eldon L. .... Topeka, KS
Gay, Ernest C. .... Stanley, WI
Gay, Faith E. .... New York, NY
Gay, Francis V. .... Orlando, FL
Gay & Gay, Attorneys, P.C. .... Taunton, MA
Gay, Geoffrey M. .... Austin, TX
Gay, George E. H. .... Montpelier, VT
Gay, Gerald F. .... Baltimore, MD
Gay, Gordon B. .... Falmouth, VA
Gay, Gordon L. .... Roswell, NM
Gay and Gordon, P.A. .... St. Petersburg, FL
Gay, Greeley .... Versailles, IN
Gay, Gregory G. .... New Port Richey, FL
Spring Hill, FL
Gay, Gregory G., P.A.
New Port Richey, FL
Spring Hill, FL
Gay & Hardaway .... Newark, NJ
New York, NY
Gay, Hayward D. .... West Palm Beach, FL
Gay, James .... Seattle, WA
Gay, James L. .... Lexington, KY
Versailles, KY
Gay, Joe Thomas .... Ripley, MS
Gay, John D. .... Versailles, IN
Gay, John E. .... Plano, TX
Gay, John F. .... Houston, TX
Gay, Jonathan L. .... Lexington, KY
Versailles, KY
Gay, Joseph H., Jr. .... Corpus Christi, TX
Gay, Linda .... Charleston, WV
Gay, M. Felicia .... San Francisco, CA
Gay, Mahalie A. .... DeLand, FL
Gay, Marva M. .... Houston, TX
Gay, Mary Ann .... Versailles, IN
Gay, Matthew T. .... Los Angeles, CA
Gay, McCall, Isaacks, Gordon & Roberts, P.C. .... Dallas, TX
McKinney, TX
Plano, TX
Gay and McCombs .... Versailles, IN
Gay, Melisa W. .... Charleston, SC
Gay, M. H. .... Houston, TX
Gay, Michael .... Orlando, FL
Gay, Michael L. .... Cincinnati, OH
Gay, Newell F. .... Houston, TX
Gay, Paul .... El Paso, TX
Gay, Paul C. .... South Dartmouth, MA
Gay, Paul L. .... Westport, MA
Gay, Peter B. .... Taunton, MA
Gay, Prescott H., Sr. .... Lynchburg, VA
Gay, R. Norwood, III .... Orlando, FL
Gay, R. Rex .... Susanville, CA
Gay, Ramsey & Warren, P.A.
West Palm Beach, FL
Gay, Reginald M. .... Anderson, SC
Gay, Remo E. .... Albuquerque, NM
Gay, Richard D. .... Alma, MI
Gay, Richard G. .... Berkeley Springs, WV
Gay, Roy La Barton .... Chippewa Falls, WI
Gay, S. Blair .... Denver, CO
Gay, Sandra Bates .... Bellevue, WA
Gay, Sandra Bates, P.S. .... Bellevue, WA
Gay, Sarah Elizabeth .... Anchorage, AK
Gay, Sharon A. .... Atlanta, GA
Gay, Stephen D. .... Peoria, IL
Gay, Stephen J. .... Sacramento, CA
Gay, Steven F. .... Cincinnati, OH
Gay & Stroud, L.L.P. .... Zebulon, NC
Gay, Susan Jane .... East Walpole, MA
Gay, Terry Christovich .... New Orleans, LA
Gay, Theodore R. .... Miami, FL
Gay, Thomas E. .... Georgetown, DE
Gay, Thomas P. .... Taunton, MA
Gay, Thurman .... O'Neill, NE
Gay, Troy A. .... Metter, GA
Millen, GA
Reidsville, GA
Gay & Walters .... Rock Hill, SC
Gay, William T. .... Irvine, CA
Gayan, Eric M. .... Dublin, OH
Gayathrinath, S. .... Staten Island, NY
Gaybrick, Robert J. .... Washington, DC
Gayda, Michael D. .... Concord, CA
Gayden, Charly .... Princeton, NJ
Gayden, Hamilton, Jr. .... Nashville, TN
Gayden, Vanessa T. .... Miami, FL
Gaydica, J. Stephen, III .... Southern Pines, NC
Gaydos, A. Lawrence, Jr. .... Montclair, NJ
Gaydos, Churnside & Baker, P.C.
Corvallis, OR
Eugene, OR
Gaydos, David P. .... New York, NY
Gaydos, Donald P. .... Mount Holly, NJ
Gaydos, Gaydos and Associates
White Oak, PA
Gaydos, Gerry .... Eugene, OR
Gaydos, John J. .... Elkhart, IN
Gaydos, Joseph, Jr. .... White Oak, PA
Gaydos, Lawrence Andrew
Fort Worth, TX
Gaydos, Mark E. .... Morgantown, WV
Gaydosh, Andrew Michael .... Denver, CO
Gaye, Thomas J. .... Washington, DC
Gayer, Alexander M. .... Melville, NY
Gayer, Anusia .... New York, NY
Gayer, David A.
Department Of The Interior, Office of the Solicitor, GV
Gayer, Gordon K. .... Augusta, ME
Gayer, Harold .... Oak Park, MI
Gayer, Judith S. .... McLean, VA
Gayer, Lee S. .... New York, NY
Gayer, Richard L. .... San Francisco, CA
Gayer, Sarah J. .... Cedar Rapids, IA
Gayheart, M. Andrew .... Culpeper, VA
Gayheart, Melissa .... Owensboro, KY
Gayle, Alana Patrice .... Washington, DC
Gayle, Andrew M. .... Hagåtña, GU
Gayle, Boyles & Culler .... Richmond, VA
Gayle, David M.
National Aeronautics And Space Administration, Office of the General Counsel, GV
Gayle, Dennis A. .... Monterey, CA
Gayle, Gibson, Jr. .... Houston, TX
Gayle, J. Kay .... Round Rock, TX
Gayle, J. Ray, III .... Angleton, TX
Gayle, Jacqueline Marie .... St. Petersburg, FL
Gayle, John Cole, Jr. .... Richmond, VA
Gayle, John Cole, Jr., P.C. .... Richmond, VA
Gayle, Julia .... St. Louis, MO
Gayle, Karalene J. .... New York, NY
Gayle, Kathryn F. .... San Diego, CA
Gayle, Lisa B. .... Mount Juliet, TN
Gayle, Marvin .... Woodland Hills, CA
Gayle, Mary Redus .... Camarillo, CA
Gayle, Mary Redus, A Professional Corporation
Camarillo, CA
Gayle and Neustadt, A Prof. Corp.
Woodland Hills, CA
Gayle, Priscilla P. .... Lake Charles, LA
Gayle, Richard L. .... Chicago, IL
Glenview, IL
Gayle, Robert K. .... Bayside, NY
Gayle, Scott C. .... Greensboro, NC
Gayle & Teker, A Professional Corporation
Hagåtña, GU
Gayle, Thomas J. .... Cameron, LA
Lake Charles, LA
Gayle, Wendy B. .... Fredericksburg, VA
Gayler, Michael L. .... Houston, TX
Gayles, Edw. R. .... Chicago, IL
Gaylinn, Diane K. .... Ramsey, NJ
Gaylo, Mark C. .... Cedar Rapids, IA
Gaylo, Paul J. .... Indianapolis, IN
Gaylock, Stephen L. .... Charleston, WV
Gaylon, Alisa F. .... Chicago, IL
Gaylor, Bruce G. .... Houston, TX
Gaylor, Charles P., III .... Goldsboro, NC
Gaylor, Diane C. .... Washington, DC
Gaylor, Edwards and Vatcher
Jacksonville, NC
Gaylor, Jimmy F. .... Jacksonville, NC
Gaylor, Maren K. .... Seattle, WA
Gaylor, Tony R. .... Jackson, MS
Gaylor, W.E. Chip .... Sarasota, FL
Venice, FL
Gaylord, Amy Moor .... Chicago, IL
Gaylord, Beth A. .... Rosemead, CA
Gaylord, Bruce M. .... New York, NY
Gaylord, Carl R. .... Oakland, CA
Gaylord, Cecil L. .... River Falls, WI
Gaylord, Daniel M. .... Raleigh, NC
Gaylord, Diane .... Silver Spring, MD
Gaylord & Eyerman, P.C. .... Portland, OR
Gaylord, Frank T. .... Eustis, FL
Gaylord & Gaylord .... Eustis, FL
Gaylord, Guilford W. .... New York, NY
Gaylord, Jeffrey R. .... New York, NY
Gaylord, Jennifer M. .... New York, NY
Gaylord, John M. .... Phoenix, AZ
Gaylord, Karen S. .... Phoenix, AZ
Gaylord, Kathleen A. .... St. Paul, MN
Gaylord, Lauri J. .... River Falls, WI
Gaylord Law Offices, S.C. .... River Falls, WI
Gaylord, Leon J., Jr. .... Eatontown, NJ
Gaylord, Louis W., Jr. .... Greenville, NC
Gaylord, Marc R. .... Boca Raton, FL
Gaylord, Mark John .... Schenectady, NY
Gaylord, Mark R. .... Salt Lake City, UT
Gaylord, McNally, Strickland & Snyder, L.L.P. .... Greenville, NC
Gaylord, Ned L. .... Long Beach, CA
Gaylord, Randall K. .... Friday Harbor, WA
Gaylord, Robert E. .... Flagstaff, AZ
Gaylord, Samuel M. .... Princeton, NJ
Gaylord, Shelley J. .... Madison, WI
Gaylord, Stanley Cary, (P.A.) .... Tampa, FL
Winter Park, FL
Gaylord, Thomas Martin, Jr.
Greensboro, NC
Gaylord, William A. .... Portland, OR
Gaylord, William O. .... Rochester, NY
Gayman, Benjamin F. .... Manchester, NH
Gayner, Charles .... New York, NY
Gaynes, Bruce H. .... Atlanta, GA
Gaynes, Martin Jay .... Washington, DC
Gaynes, Seymour J. .... Scottsdale, AZ
Gaynier, Rhonda L. .... New York, NY
Gaynin, Jonathan S. .... New York, NY
Gaynor, Alan S. .... Savannah, GA
Gaynor, Alan S. .... New York, NY
Gaynor, Albert J. .... White Plains, NY
Gaynor, Audrey L. .... Chicago, IL
Gaynor, Audrey L., P.C. Law Offices of
Chicago, IL
Gaynor, Barbara A.
Department of Commerce, Patent and Trademark Office, GV
Gaynor & Bass .... New York, NY
Gaynor, Bertram J. .... Asbury Park, NJ
Gaynor, Bruce E. .... Cleveland, OH
Gaynor, David B. .... Princeton, NJ
Gaynor, David J. .... Miami Beach, FL
Gaynor, Donald A. .... Beachwood, OH
Gaynor, Edward T. .... Tinley Park, IL
Gaynor, Elin A. .... Chicopee, MA
Gaynor, Eric R. .... Milford, CT
Gaynor, Gerald M. .... Monroe, CT
Gaynor, Gilbert .... Santa Barbara, CA
Gaynor, James M., Jr. .... Chicago, IL
Gaynor, Joseph M., Jr. .... Smyrna, GA
Gaynor, Joseph W. .... Clearwater, FL
Gaynor, Kevin A. .... Washington, DC
Gaynor, Lauren Pruzan .... New York, NY
Gaynor, Magdalen .... New York, NY
Gaynor, Magdalen .... White Plains, NY
Gaynor, Malcolm M. .... Chicago, IL
Gaynor, Martin F., III .... Boston, MA
Gaynor, Michael J. .... New York, NY
Gaynor, Mitchell Lee .... Emeryville, CA
Gaynor, Morgan L. .... Jacksonville, FL
Gaynor, Nancy Ina .... Los Angeles, CA
Gaynor, Norman J., III .... Hartville, OH
Gaynor, Paul B. .... New Canaan, CT
Gaynor, Paul Joseph .... Chicago, IL
Gaynor, Philip M. .... Bronx, NY
Gaynor, Robert A. .... Somerville, NJ
Gaynor, Robert H. .... Boston, MA
Gaynor, Robert J. .... Boston, MA
Gaynor, Robert L. .... Succasunna, NJ
Gaynor, Robert M. .... Hollywood, FL
Gaynor, Ronald S. .... Pawleys Island, SC
Gaynor, Ronald S., P.A.
Pawleys Island, SC
Gaynor, Thomas J. .... Morristown, NJ
Gaynus, Deborah M. .... Department of Justice, Criminal Division, GV
Gayo-Guitian, Mariaelena
Fort Lauderdale, FL
Gayoso, Gonzalo Alberto .... Miami, FL
Gayoso, Jay A. .... Miami, FL
Gays, Thomas H., II .... Richmond, VA
Gaytan, Paul A. .... McAllen, TX
Gaythwaite, Martha C. .... Portland, ME
Gayton, Bradley M. .... Dearborn, MI
Gayton, Charles W. .... Columbus, OH
Gayton, Cynthia Marie .... Arlington, VA
Gayton, Gary D. .... Seattle, WA
Gayton, James W. .... San Diego, CA
Gayton, Joseph E. .... Treasure Island, FL
Gayton, Librado .... Bay City, MI
Gayton, Tilton & Endres .... Columbus, OH
Gaza, Copernicus T. .... Hawthorne, NY
Gazala, Richard E. .... Washington, DC
Gazaleh, Fred C. .... Jacksonville, FL
Gazan, Philip L. .... Norristown, PA
Gazaway, Brad A. .... Phoenix, AZ
Gazaway, Hal P. .... Anchorage, AK
Gazaway, Joy .... Cincinnati, OH
Gazaway, R. Lamar, Jr. .... Atlanta, GA
Gazda, Deanna L. .... Department of Labor, Office of Secretary, GV
Gazda, Ernest J., Jr. .... Scranton, PA
Gazda, Karen M. .... Clifton Park, NY
Gazda, Lewis John .... Las Vegas, NV
Gazda & Penetar .... Scranton, PA
Gazda, Peter F. .... San Antonio, TX
Gazdecki, Aloysius F. .... Zumbrota, MN
Gazdo, Michael F., Jr. .... Arlington, VA
Gazdzinski, Robert F. .... San Diego, CA
Gazeley, Barbara J. .... Portland, OR
Gazeley, Lawrence L. .... Green Bay, WI
Gazerro, G. John, Jr. .... Warwick, RI
Gazerro and Richardson .... Warwick, RI
Gazes, Ian J. .... New York, NY
Gazette, Michael E. .... Gilmer, TX
Quitman, TX
Gazette, Michael E. .... Tyler, TX
Gazewood, John A. .... Arlington, TX
Gazi, William H. .... Cranford, NJ
Middlesex, NJ
Gazianis & Herbst .... New York, NY
Gazianis, Thomas L. .... New York, NY
Gaziano, Angelo N. .... Rockford, IL
Gaziano, Cara M. .... Chicago, IL
Gaziano, Frank M. .... Scituate, MA
Gaziano, George G. .... Phoenix, AZ
Gaziano, Mary J. .... Rockford, IL
Gaziano, Paul E. .... Rockford, IL
Gaziano, Todd F. .... Washington, DC
Gazik, L. Martin .... Falls Church, VA
Gazin, Eric D. .... Charlotte, NC
Gazin, Glenn A. .... Stamford, CT
Gazin, Harvey W. .... Van Nuys, CA
Gazin, Harvey W., Inc. .... Van Nuys, CA
Gazin, Michael H. .... Costa Mesa, CA
Gazit, Ophir .... New York, NY
Gazley and Grunow .... Flat Rock, MI
Gazo, Brian B. .... Allentown, PA
Gazourian, Burwick & Dynice, P.C.
Leominster, MA
Gazourian, John .... Leominster, MA
Gazourian, Stephanie .... Leominster, MA
Gaztambide, Elliot .... New York, NY
Gaztambide, Mario F. .... San Juan, PR
Gaztambide & Plaza .... San Juan, PR
Gaztambide Añeses, Jose R.
San Juan, PR
Gaztambide Gomez, Jose R. .... San Juan, PR
Gazur, Wayne M. .... Boulder, CO
Gazza, Beverly A. .... Indiana, PA
Gazza, Joseph F. .... Quogue, NY
Gazza, Michael V .... Brooklyn, NY
Gazzaniga, Suzanne I. .... Auburn, CA
Gazzara, Anthony V. .... Astoria, NY
Gazzera, Stephen P., Jr. .... Mountain View, CA
Gazzigli, Joseph A. .... Redding, CA
Gazzillo, Ralph T. .... Central Islip, NY
Gazzo, Raymond J. .... Coronado, CA
Gazzola, Charles D. .... Portland, OR
Gazzola, Girard .... Roland, OK
Gazzola & Hull .... Portland, OR
Gazzola, Josef John Daniel .... Natick, MA
Gazzola, Mario .... New York, NY
Gazzola, Robert A. .... Washington, DC
Gazzoli, John J., Jr. .... St. Louis, MO
Gbadebo, Brenda .... East Orange, NJ
Gbalazeh, Boniface S. .... Victoria, TX
Gbenjo, Anne Joyin Arinola .... Landover, MD
Gbur, George A. .... Johnstown, PA
Gdanian, Garyn .... Melville, NY
Gdanski, Sam Zalman .... Suffern, NY
Gdowski, Christopher E. .... Denver, CO
Gdula, James M. .... Washington, DC
Geaber, Joseph P., Jr. .... Wakefield, RI
Geach, Anita .... Littleton, CO
Geadelmann, Lori K.
West Des Moines, IA
Geagan, James .... Novato, CA
Geagan, William N. .... Butte, MT
Geaghan, John M. .... Lexington, MA
Geair, Harry F. .... Greenville, SC
Geake, Robert W. .... Phoenix, AZ
Gealow, Jon Carl .... McHenry, IL
Gealy, Grant G. .... Houston, TX
Gealy, Stephen S. .... Lincoln, NE
Gean, David A., III .... Sallisaw, OK
Gean, David C. .... Fort Smith, AR
Gean, Gean & Gean .... Fort Smith, AR
Ozark, AR
Waldron, AR
Sallisaw, OK
Gean, Paul B. .... Fort Smith, AR
Gean, Roy R., III .... Fort Smith, AR
Gean, Roy R., Jr. .... Fort Smith, AR
Gean, Thomas C. .... Fort Smith, AR
Geanacopoulos, David .... Washington, DC
Geanacopoulos, Stephen .... Boston, MA
Providence, RI
Geaney, John F., Jr. .... Elmwood Park, NJ
Geaney, John H. .... Mount Laurel, NJ
Geaney, Kevin P. .... Boston, MA
Geannacopulos, Nick C., Jr.
San Francisco, CA
Geannette, Mark A. .... Fort Lee, NJ
Geannopulos, Timothy N. .... Chicago, IL
Geanuracos, James G. .... Hartford, CT
Gear, Bruce Irving .... Racine, WI
Gear, Gayle Haywood .... Birmingham, AL
Gear, Marguerite G. .... San Francisco, CA
Gearen, John J. .... Chicago, IL
Gearen, Thomas .... Chicago, IL
Gearhardt, Larry R. .... Columbus, OH
Gearhardt, Michelle J. .... Covington, OH
Troy, OH
Gearhart, Camille E. .... Seattle, WA
Gearhart, Donald C.
La Canada Flintridge, CA

Gearhart, Gary L. .... La Salle, IL
Gearhart, Gary L. & Associates .... La Salle, IL
Gearhart, Glenn L. .... Huntington Beach, CA
Gearhart, Jeffrey J. .... Little Rock, AR
Gearhart, Kurt R. .... Chicago, IL
Gearhart, R. Denning .... Clearfield, PA
Gearhart, Richard I. .... Midland, MI
Gearhart, Van A. .... Mountain Home, AR
Gearhart, William W., Jr.
United States International Trade Commission, Office of the General Counsel, GV
Gearheard, Bradley E. .... Bonney Lake, WA
Gearheard, William J. F. .... Mandeville, LA
Gearheart, Ernest T., Jr. .... Leesburg, VA
Gearheart, Mark E. .... Pleasant Hill, CA
Gearheart & Otis, LLP .... Pleasant Hill, CA
Walnut Creek, CA
Gearhiser, Charles J. .... Chattanooga, TN
Gearhiser, Kurt O. .... Columbus, OH
Gearhiser, Peters, Lockaby & Tallant, PLLC
Chattanooga, TN
Geariety, Kimberly K. .... Anchorage, AK
Gearin, Amy L. .... Department of Commerce, Patent and Trademark Office, GV
Gearin, David M.
Federal Deposit Insurance Corporation, Resolutions Section, GV
Gearin, Gail E. .... San Francisco, CA
Gearin, John Miles .... St. Paul, MN
Gearin, Kathleen R. .... St. Paul, MN
Gearin, Kent F. .... Martin, TN
Gearin, Michael J. .... Seattle, WA
Gearin, Robert A. .... St. Paul, MN
Gearin and Shiely, P.A. .... St. Paul, MN
Gearin, Timothy J. .... St. Louis, MO
Gearing, David C. .... Astoria, OR
Portland, OR
Gearing, John K. .... Gaithersburg, MD
Gearinger, Bradford M. .... Akron, OH
Gearinger, Brian .... San Francisco, CA
Gearity, Patricia E., Law Offices of
Rockville, MD
Gearity, Patricia E., Law Offices of
Silver Spring, MD
Gearns, Mary Gail .... New York, NY
Gearon, Jamie H. .... Albany, NY
Gearon, William J. .... Pawtucket, RI
Gearreald, Mark S. .... Manchester, NH
Geartner, J. B. .... Monterey Park, CA
Gearty, Edward J. .... Minneapolis, MN
Gearty, Timothy F. .... Florham Park, NJ
Gearty, William J., (P.C.) .... Spring Lake, NJ
Gearty, William Martin .... Coram, NY
Geary, Adrienne M. .... Chicago, IL
Geary, Brian J. .... Rochester, NY
Geary, Catherine M. .... Lowell, MA
Geary, Charles E. .... Stuart, FL
Geary, Charles E., P.A. .... Stuart, FL
Geary, Christopher R. .... Phoenix, AZ
Geary, Covert J. .... New Orleans, LA
Geary, Daniel W. .... Albany, NY
Geary, Darryl G. .... Somerset, PA
Geary, Donald D. .... New York, NY
Geary, Donna J. .... Pittsburgh, PA
Geary, Edmond F., Jr. .... Oklahoma City, OK
Geary, Francis B., Jr.
West Palm Beach, FL
Geary & Geary .... Lowell, MA
Petersburg, WV
Geary, Gerard M. .... Bayside, NY
Geary, Gillen M. .... Trenton, NJ
Geary, Gregory F. .... Washington, DC
Leesburg, VA
Geary, Harold C. .... Albany, NY
Geary, J. Douglas .... New York, NY
Geary, James F. .... Sacramento, CA
Geary, James H. .... Kalamazoo, MI
Geary, James M., Jr. .... Chelmsford, MA
Geary, James P., II .... Petersburg, WV
Geary, James Paul .... Petersburg, WV
Geary, Jennifer Hill .... Kansas City, MO
Geary, Joel E. .... Dallas, TX
Geary, John C. .... Tulsa, OK
Geary, John E. .... Falmouth, ME
Geary, John F. .... Santa Rosa, CA
Geary, John P. .... Boone, NC
Geary, Johnson & Pfeffer, P.A.
West Palm Beach, FL
Geary, Joseph A. .... Lakeland, FL
Lake Wales, FL
Winter Haven, FL
Geary, Joseph W. .... Dallas, TX
Geary, Katharine, Law Office of
Alexandria, LA
Geary, Kevin M. .... Middlesex, NJ
Geary Law Firm, The, P.C. .... Washington, DC
Geary Law Firm, The, P.C. .... Leesburg, VA
Geary, Lisa Miley .... Metairie, LA
Geary, Lois Witt .... Somerset, PA
Geary & Loperfito .... Vandergrift, PA
Geary, Margaret M. .... Leominster, MA
Geary, Mark F. .... Washington, PA
Geary, Maureen R. .... Grand Rapids, MI
Geary, Michael P. .... Chicago, IL
Geary, Michael P. .... Jefferson, OH
Geary, Michael P. .... Dallas, TX
Geary, Michael Q. .... Lowell, MA
Geary, Michelle K. .... Boston, MA
Geary, Patrick F. .... Grand Rapids, MI
Geary, Paul M. .... Pacifica, CA
Geary, Paul R. .... Southfield, MI
Geary, Porter & Donovan, P.C.
Dallas, TX
Geary, Robert A. .... Culver City, CA
Geary, Robert J. .... Brooklyn, NY
Geary, Robert P. .... Richmond, VA
Geary, Robyn Sherain .... Orange, CA
Geary, Roger C. .... Kansas City, MO
Geary, Ronald G. .... Louisville, KY
Geary, Sean J. .... New York, NY
Geary, Sean T. .... Boston, MA
Geary, Shea, O'Donnell & Grattan, A Professional Corporation .... Petaluma, CA
Santa Rosa, CA
Geary, Stanley R. .... Pittsburgh, PA
Geary, Stephen W. .... Los Angeles, CA
Geary, Steven M. .... Jefferson City, MO
Geary, Susan E. .... Columbus, OH
Geary, Thomas D. .... Santa Rosa, CA
Geary, Timothy J. .... Vandergrift, PA
Geary, Timothy P. .... Vandergrift, PA
Geary, Tracey L. M. .... Westbrook, ME
Geary, William A., Jr. .... St. Louis, MO
Geary, William C. .... Lowell, MA
Geary, William C., III .... Boston, MA
Geary, William D. .... Kansas City, MO
Geary, William E. .... Petaluma, CA
Santa Rosa, CA
Geary, William J. .... Braintree, MA
Geary, William L. .... Circleville, OH
Geary, William L. .... Columbus, OH
Geary, William L. .... Delaware, OH
Geary, William L., Jr. .... Washington, DC
Geasa, Janet .... Mattituck, NY
Geasor, Howard J., Jr. .... Brooklyn, NY
Geauque, Robert E. .... Thousand Oaks, CA
Geb, John .... Santa Barbara, CA
Gebaide, Rachel D. .... Orlando, FL
Gebaide, Robert H. .... Sanford, FL
Geballe, Shelley D. .... Hartford, CT
Gebara, Joseph C. .... Irvine, CA
Gebauer, Alan J. .... Southfield, MI
Gebauer, Albert W. .... Aurora, CO
Gebauer, Gordon C., Jr .... Burlington, VT
Gebauer, Jay A. .... Voorhees, NJ
Gebauer, John A. .... Rochester, NY
Gebauer, Mark E. .... Harrisburg, PA
Gebauer, Marlene C. .... Middlesex, NJ
Gebb, Sheldon A. .... Long Beach, CA
Gebbia, Guy F. .... Austin, TX
Gebbia, Heather W. .... Boston, MA
Gebbia, Karen M. .... Chicago, IL
Gebbie, Gloria .... San Bernardino, CA
Gebbie, William S. .... Rancho Cucamonga, CA
Gebelein, Richard S. .... Wilmington, DE
Gebell, Alan L. .... Schenectady, NY
Gebeloff, Stephen B. .... West Orange, NJ
Geber, David M. .... Treasury Department, Internal Revenue Service, GV
Geberin, Conn & Blackford .... Warsaw, IN
Geberin, John P. .... Warsaw, IN
Gebers, Michael D. .... Davis, CA
Gebert, Daniel L. .... Costa Mesa, CA
Gebert, Kent J. .... Schenectady, NY
Gebert, Robert C. .... Chicago, IL
Gebert, Thomas A. .... Commack, NY
Geberth, Henry E., Jr. .... Springfield, MA
Geberth, Lisa G.
Export-Import Bank of The United States, Office of the General Counsel, GV
Gebetsberger, Leisa Michelle .... Tulsa, OK
Gebhard, Cathy .... Norwell, MA
Gebhard, Robert S. .... San Jose, CA
Gebhard, Theodore A. .... Washington, DC
Gebhardt, Christopher H.
Warrendale, PA
Gebhardt, Dolores .... New York, NY
Gebhardt, Frank J. .... Spokane, WA
Gebhardt, Guy G. .... Atlanta, GA
Gebhardt, Joseph D. .... Washington, DC
Gebhardt, Joseph D., P.C.
Washington, DC
Gebhardt, Kathleen J. .... Boulder, CO
Gebhardt & Kiefer, P.C. .... Bridgewater, NJ
Clinton, NJ
Flemington, NJ
Gebhardt, Lawrence J. .... Baltimore, MD
Gebhardt, Mark J. .... Minneapolis, MN
Gebhardt, Mason R. .... Fayette, MO
Gebhardt, Michael B. .... San Francisco, CA
Gebhardt, Robert A. .... Portland, OR
Gebhardt, Robert C. .... San Francisco, CA
Gebhardt, Robert C. .... Naples, FL
Gebhardt, Shay .... San Antonio, TX
Gebhardt & Smith, LLP .... Baltimore, MD
Gebhart, David E. .... Cincinnati, OH
Gebhart, Donna Riselli .... Tallahassee, FL
Gebhart, James F. .... Madison, WI
Gebhart, Timothy M. .... Sioux Falls, SD
Gebicki, Amanda Bishop .... New York, NY
Gebler, Gary L. .... Irvine, CA
Gebler, Hillary Sloane .... Chicago, IL
Gebler, Howard A. .... Santa Ana, CA
Gebler, Thomas V., Jr. .... Pittsburgh, PA
Gebo, A. Michael .... Ogdensburg, NY
Gebo, Carl A. .... Atlanta, GA
Gebo, Mark G. .... Watertown, NY
Gebo, Stephen W. .... Watertown, NY
Geboy, Scott J. .... Milwaukee, WI
Gebracht, John R. .... Socorro, NM
Gechlik, Stuart .... New York, NY
Gechman, Judy G. .... Houston, TX
Gecht, Robert D. .... Chicago, IL
Gechter, Maureen F. .... Cleveland, OH
Gechter, Ronit .... San Diego, CA
Gechtman, Jeffrey M. .... Union, NJ
Geck, Donna D. .... Santa Barbara, CA
Geck, Duane M. .... San Francisco, CA
Geck, Jay D. .... Olympia, WA
Geck, Timothy R. .... White Bear Lake, MN
Geckeler, Peter M. .... San Francisco, CA
Gecker, Daniel A. .... Richmond, VA
Gecker, Frances .... Chicago, IL
Gecker, James M. .... Chicago, IL
Geckle, Patrick G. .... Philadelphia, PA
Geckle, Robert A., Jr. .... Washington, DC
Geckle, Timothy J. .... Columbia, MD
Geckler, Jack W. .... Miami, FL
Geckos, Marietta I. .... Department of Justice, Criminal Division, GV
Ged, Charles Glen .... Boca Raton, FL
Ged, David Scott .... Boston, MA
Gedan, Barry S. .... Bronx, NY
Gedan, Joseph M. .... Honolulu, HI
Gedanic, Joseph B. .... Albuquerque, NM
Gedanke, Barbara .... Los Angeles, CA
Gedansky, Matthew C. .... Rockville, CT
Geddes, Anthony Ray .... Boise, ID
Geddes, Brian N. .... Colorado Springs, CO
Geddes, Brian N., P.C.
Colorado Springs, CO
Geddes, Daniel .... Elizabeth, NJ
Newark, NJ
Geddes, James F., Jr. .... Wilkes-Barre, PA
Geddes, James McC. .... Wilmington, DE
Geddes, Joan K. .... Boston, MA
Geddes, John D. .... Houston, TX
Geddes, Kenneth W.
Colorado Springs, CO
Geddes, Kenneth W., P.C.
Colorado Springs, CO
Geddes, Margaret .... Sacramento, CA
Geddes, Mary C. .... Anchorage, AK
Geddes, Philip A. .... Decatur, AL
Geddes, Philip A., P.C. .... Decatur, AL
Geddes, Richard J. .... Chicago, IL
Geddes, Robert D. .... Portland, OR
Geddes, Robert W. .... Indianapolis, IN
Geddes, Roger A. .... Coronado, CA
Geddes, Scott R. .... Roanoke, VA
Geddie, Ivan D. .... Oklahoma City, OK
Georgetown, TX
Geddie, John B. .... Houston, TX
Geddie, L. Gray, Jr. .... Raleigh, NC
Greenville, SC
Geddie, Norton M. .... Myrtle Beach, SC
Geddie, Rowland H., III .... Lamar, MO
Geddie, Rowland H., Jr. .... Tupelo, MS
Geddings Law Firm, The .... Manning, SC
Geddings, W.T., Jr. .... Manning, SC
Geddis, J. Clark .... Sparta, NJ
Geddy, Harris, Franck & Hickman, LLP
Williamsburg, VA
Geddy, Vernon M., III .... Williamsburg, VA
Geddy, Vernon M., Jr. .... Williamsburg, VA
Gede, Ellen F. .... Department of Labor, Office of Secretary, GV
Gede, James A. .... Towson, MD
Gede, James A., Jr. .... Baltimore, MD
Gede, Thomas F. .... Sacramento, CA
Gedert, Martha Lee .... Charleston, SC
Gedge, Judy .... West Hartford, CT
Gedgoudas, Michael E. .... Birmingham, AL
Gedicks, Frederick M. .... Provo, UT
Gedid, John L. .... Harrisburg, PA
Gediman, Edwiges B. .... Woodland Hills, CA
Gediman, Nelson .... Boston, MA
Gedlen and Gedlen .... Milwaukee, WI
Gedlen, James M. .... Milwaukee, WI
Gedling, James L. .... Hamilton, OH
Gedmin, Janine .... Key West, FL
Gednalske, Jeffrey D. .... Sioux Falls, SD
Gedney, Seaman & Hilgendorff
Florham Park, NJ
Morristown, NJ
Gedo, Nicholas M. .... Los Angeles, CA
Gedrich, Alan R. .... Philadelphia, PA
Gedrich, Herbert D. .... Philadelphia, PA
Gedrich, Hillel .... New York, NY
Gedrock, David V. .... Litchfield, OH
Gedrose, David I. .... Vancouver, WA
Geduldig, Albert J. .... New York, NY
Geduldig, Howard .... Trenton, NJ
Geduldig, Kenneth L. .... Burlington, VT
Geduldig, Martin .... Hicksville, NY
Geduldig, Stephen E. .... Bethlehem, PA
Harrisburg, PA
Gedvila, Gabriel E. .... Tacoma, WA
Gee, Amy S. .... Campbell, CA
Gee, Andrea Taylor .... Laguna Niguel, CA
Gee, Audrey A. .... Walnut Creek, CA
Gee, Bruce W. .... Hastings, MI
Gee, Byron P. .... Los Angeles, CA
Gee, Carol A. .... San Francisco, CA
Gee, Christopher M. .... Troy, OH
West Milton, OH
Gee, Danielle Ann .... Detroit, MI
Gee, David B. .... San Diego, CA
Gee, David E. .... Salt Lake City, UT
Gee, David W. .... Seattle, WA
Gee, Debra E. .... Shiprock, NM
Gee, Delbert C. .... San Francisco, CA
Gee, Dolly M. .... Los Angeles, CA
Gee, Don P. .... Hot Springs National Park, AR
Gee, Douglas Edmond .... El Centro, CA
Gee, Douglas M. .... Sonora, CA
Gee, Earl J. .... Richmond, VA
Gee, Erin M. .... San Diego, CA
Gee, Everett W., III .... Atlanta, GA
Gee, Gary T. .... Hamburg, IA
Shenandoah, IA
Gee, Gavin M. .... Boise, ID
Gee, Gaylynn .... Dallas, TX
Gee, Ginnifer I. .... Jacksonville, FL
Gee, Gordon D. .... Kansas City, MO
Gee, Harry, Jr. .... Houston, TX
Gee, Harry, Jr., and Associates Law Office of .... Houston, TX
Gee, Henry .... San Jose, CA
Gee, Herbert .... Houston, TX
Gee, Herbert N.F. .... Berkeley, CA
Gee, I. Clark .... Phoenix, AZ
Gee, Ian W. .... Boise, ID
Gee, J. Christopher .... Austin, TX
Gee, Jeffrey J. .... Washington, DC
Gee, Jennifer .... San Francisco, CA
Gee, Judith Boyers .... Covington, KY
Gee, Juliet L. .... San Leandro, CA
Gee, Karen M. .... Pasadena, CA
Gee & Koopman, P.C. .... Houston, TX
Gee, Larry E. .... San Antonio, TX
Gee, Leroy V. .... Fresno, CA
Gee, Lily .... Lansing, MI
Gee, M. Blen, Jr. .... Raleigh, NC
Gee, M. Elizabeth .... Winston-Salem, NC
Gee, Matthew L. .... Oklahoma City, OK
Gee, Maureen Haight .... Santa Monica, CA
Gee, Melanie A. .... Dallas, TX
Gee, Michael G. .... Thibodaux, LA
Gee, Michelle M. .... Oakland, CA
Gee, Nancy Ann .... Mountain View, CA
Gee, Pauline W. .... Marysville, CA
Gee, Raymond W. .... Salt Lake City, UT
Gee, Richard .... Wallingford, CT
Gee, Richard E. .... Grand Island, NE
Gee, Richard M.
Rolling Hills Estates, CA
Gee, Robert C. .... Superior, WI
Gee, Robert N. .... Library of Congress, Law Library, GV
Gee, Robert S. .... Miami, OK
Gee, Ronald .... Troy, MI
Gee, Samme L. .... Charleston, WV
Gee, Steven J. .... San Francisco, CA
Gee & Sunada .... Rolling Hills Estates, CA
Gee, Theresa S. .... San Francisco, CA
Gee, Thomas H. .... San Francisco, CA
Gee, Ty .... Denver, CO
Gee, Ursula C. P. .... Thousand Oaks, CA
Gee, William N., III .... Lafayette, LA
New Orleans, LA
Gee, William N., III, Ltd., A Prof. Law Corp. .... Lafayette, LA
New Orleans, LA
Gee, William S. .... Wilmington, DE
Geeding, Martin D. .... Wichita, KS
Geeding, Wilbur D. .... Wichita, KS
Geedman, Ronald C. .... Houston, TX
Geehern, Joseph J. .... Westfield, MA
Geeker, Marianne .... Dallas, TX
Geeker, Nicholas P. .... Pensacola, FL
Geeker, Van P. .... Tallahassee, FL
Geekie, Eugene J., Jr. .... Chicago, IL
Geekie, Matthew W. .... St. Louis, MO
Geelan, Gregory J. .... San Diego, CA
Geelan, John D. .... New York, NY
Geelan, Sara .... New York, NY
Geelhoed, Thomas A. .... Grand Rapids, MI
Geen, Jeffery S. .... Las Vegas, NV
Geen, John B. .... Grosse Pointe, MI
Geen, Jonathan P. .... San Diego, CA
Geen, Patricia A. .... Danbury, CT
Geen, Stanley .... New York, NY
Geen, William J. .... New York, NY
Geenty, John C. .... Dudley, MA
Geenty, John C., Jr. .... Worcester, MA
Geenty, Julie A. .... San Francisco, CA
Geenty, Susan Perrin .... Middletown, CT
Geer, Bruce R. .... Marysville, IN
Geer, Bryson M. .... Charleston, SC
Geer, Charles A. .... Minneapolis, MN
Geer, Christopher J. .... Columbus, OH
Geer, Edward O. .... Denver, CO
Geer, Elaine .... Chicago, IL
Geer, Eva D. .... Houston, TX
Geer, George R., Jr. .... Georgetown, SC
Geer, H. Stat .... Chicago, IL
Geer & Herman .... New Castle, PA
Geer, Horace G. .... Tacoma, WA
Geer, Hunter L. .... Albuquerque, NM
Geer, Hunter L., P.A. .... Albuquerque, NM
Geer, James H., Jr. .... Dunedin, FL
Geer, John F. .... Boulder, CO
Geer, John F. .... New York, NY
Geer, John J., Jr. .... Washington, DC
Geer, Karen .... New York, NY
Geer, Kurt A. .... Oklahoma City, OK
Geer, Louise A. .... New Castle, PA
Geer, Maria R. Garcia .... Albuquerque, NM
Geer, Mariana Griswold .... Santa Fe, NM
Geer, Martha A. .... Raleigh, NC
Geer, Mary L. .... Port Charlotte, FL
Geer, Norman J. .... Bowling Green, OH
Geer, Paul K. .... Pittsburgh, PA
Geer, Peter Zack, Jr. .... Albany, GA
Geer, Robert L. .... Albany, GA
Geer, Roger C. .... Dallas, TX
Geer, Stacey Kipnis .... Atlanta, GA
Geer, Susan J. .... Denver, CO
Geer, Thomas P. .... Ingomar, PA
Geer, Todd A. .... Waterloo, IA
Geer, William E. .... Ingleside, TX
Geer, Willis .... Gillette, WY
Geer Wissel & Levy, P.A. .... Albuquerque, NM
Geercken, Karl .... New York, NY
Geerdes, Cynthea E. .... Champaign, IL
Geerdes, David B. .... San Diego, CA
Geerdes, Franklin .... Chula Vista, CA
Geerdes & Geerdes .... Chula Vista, CA
Geerdes, Lynn M. .... Chicago, IL
Geerdes, Mary Elizabeth .... Chula Vista, CA
Geerhart, Charles O. .... San Francisco, CA
Geerhart, Donald W. .... Springfield, VA
Geerken, Janet Romano .... New Orleans, LA
Geernaert, Bruce R.
Palos Verdes Estates, CA
Geers, Bonnie A. .... East Lansing, MI
Geers, Christine M. .... Dover, OH
Geers, Mark A. .... St. Louis, MO
Geers, Tammi J. .... Houston, TX
Geers, Torsten M. .... Philadelphia, PA

Geisser, Troy ....New York, NY
Geissinger, Harry E., III ....Hialeah, FL
Geissler, Burkhard ....Rockford, IL
Geissler, Frederick K. ....Ironwood, MI
Geissler, Richard Bryan ....Spokane, WA
Geissler, Stephen J. ....Hartford, CT
Geist, Alan R. ....White Plains, NY
Geist, Andrew J. ....New York, NY
Geist, Bradley B. ....New York, NY
Geist, Carol Berg ....New York, NY
Geist, Debra Velez ....Manhattan Beach, CA
Geist, Edward J. ....Wilkes-Barre, PA
Geist, Gerald K. ....White Plains, NY
Geist, Herman S. ....White Plains, NY
Geist, Laura Leigh ....San Francisco, CA
Geist, Lynn E. ....Detroit, MI
Geist, Melissa A. ....Princeton, NJ
Geist, Michael J. ....Towson, MD
Geist, Nan R. ....Mineola, NY
Geist, Rudolph J. ....Washington, DC
Geist, Stephen D. ....San Francisco, CA
Geist, Tamara ....Villa Park, CA
Geister, Charles E., III Oklahoma City, OK
Geistfeld, Mark ....New York, NY
Geistweidt, A. Gerald ....Mason, TX
Geistweidt, Amy A. ....San Antonio, TX
Geiszler & Newcomer, PLLP ....Missoula, MT
Geiszler, Timothy D. ....Missoula, MT
Geiszler-Ludlum, Joan C. ....Wilmington, NC
Geitgey, Jonna S. ....Oklahoma City, OK
Geithman, Theodore W. ....North Port, FL
Geitner, Charles G. ....Tampa, FL
Geitner, Neal P. ....Northbrook, IL
Geitner, Paul F. ....San Diego, CA
Geittmann, Clay D. ....Jackson, WY
Geitz, Michael M. ....New York, NY
Geiwitz, Cynthia A. ....Minneapolis, MN
Geizhals, Benjamin ....New York, NY
Gekas & Associates, Ltd. ....Chicago, IL
Gekas, Constantine J. ....Bloomington, MN
Gekas, Constantine John (Chris) Chicago, IL
Gekas, JoAnna A. ....San Francisco, CA
Gekoski, Albert C. ....Bala Cynwyd, PA
Gekoski & Bogdanoff, P.C. ....Philadelphia, PA
Gelade, Melvin L. ....Trenton, NJ
Gelade, Richard B. ....Trenton, NJ
Gelander, Jessica L. ....Chicago, IL
Gelardi, James M. ....Valhalla, NY
Gelardi, Vincent ....White Plains, NY
Gelatt, Timothy A. ....New York, NY
Gelb, Aaron R. ....Chicago, IL
Gelb, Alan M. ....New York, NY
Gelb, Andrew S. ....Los Angeles, CA
Gelb & Black ....Brooklyn, NY
Gelb, Bruce L. ....Los Angeles, CA
Gelb, Eunice ....St. Paul, MN
Gelb, F. Gina ....Stamford, CT
Gelb, Fred J. ....Lakewood, NJ
Gelb, Gail Kleven ....Boston, MA
Gelb & Gelb LLP ....Boston, MA
Gelb & Gelb, P.C. ....Washington, DC
Gelb, George Edward ....Miami, FL
Gelb, George Edward, P.A. ....Miami, FL
Gelb, Harry ....Bronx, NY
Gelb, Harvey ....Laramie, WY
Gelb, Howard H. ....St. Paul, MN
Gelb, James I. ....Brooklyn, NY
Gelb, Jeffrey P. ....Houston, TX
Gelb, Jeremy C. ....Philadelphia, PA
Gelb, Johanna L. ....Scranton, PA
Gelb, Jon E. ....Los Angeles, CA
Gelb, Joseph ....Woodmere, NY
Gelb, Joseph D. ....Washington, DC
Gelb, Joseph S. ....Vineland, NJ
Gelb, Joseph W. ....New York, NY
Gelb, Judith A. ....New York, NY
Gelb, Kelley Badger ....Fort Lauderdale, FL
Gelb, Lisa
Federal Communications Commission, Office of the General Counsel, GV
Gelb, Marilyn J. ....Philadelphia, PA
Gelb, Marjorie ....Berkeley, CA
Gelb, Michele R. ....Atlanta, GA
Gelb, Monroe ....Miami, FL
Gelb, Richard M. ....Boston, MA
Gelb, Roger K. ....Washington, DC
Gelb, Sandra Wolk ....Rochester, NY
Gelb, Sarah B. ....Philadelphia, PA
Gelb & Spatz ....Miami, FL
Gelb, Stephen H. ....Teaneck, NJ
Gelband, Barbara ....Tucson, AZ
Gelband, David ....Newark, NJ
Gelband, Glenn Evan ....Cranford, NJ
Gelband, Joseph F., (P.C.) ....Larchmont, NY
Gelband, Miriam ....New Rochelle, NY
Gelband, Robert L. ....Rego Park, NY
Gelband, Scott L. ....Seattle, WA
Gelband, Stephen L. ....Washington, DC
Gelbard, Adrian M. ....Rye Brook, NY
Gelbard, Allan B. ....Encino, CA
Gelbard, Arlen W. ....Arlington, VA
Gelbard, Bernard ....Floral Park, NY
Gelbart, Wendy ....Seattle, WA
Gelber, Bernard M. ....Baltimore, MD
Gelber, Blanche L. ....New York, NY
Gelber, Brian R. ....St. Louis, MO
Gelber, Bruce S. ....Department of Justice, Environment and Natural Resources Division, GV
Gelber, Dale L. ....Millburn, NJ
Gelber, Daniel ....Miami, FL
Gelber, Darling & Robertson Costa Mesa, CA
Gelber, Darren M. ....Woodbridge, NJ
Gelber, Don Jeffrey ....Honolulu, HI
Gelber, Emily R. ....Silver Spring, MD
Gelber & Gelber ....Millburn, NJ
Gelber, Gelber, Ingersoll, Klevansky & Faris, A Law Corporation ....Honolulu, HI
Gelber, Herschel ....Buffalo, NY
Gelber, Irving ....Summit, NJ
Gelber, James J. ....Burlington, VT
Gelber, Jamie P. ....Lake Isabella, CA
Gelber, Joan D. ....Newark, NJ
Gelber, Jonathan Bennett ....Honolulu, HI
Gelber, Jonathan S., P.C. ....Arlington, VA
Gelber, Joseph A. ....Costa Mesa, CA
Gelber, Judith L. ....Miami, FL
Gelber, Lawrence V. ....New York, NY
Gelber, Louise ....Arcadia, CA
Gelber, Martin H. ....New York, NY
Gelber, Martin M. ....Millburn, NJ
Gelber, Rand L. ....Rockville, MD
Vienna, VA
Gelber, Richard S. ....Culver City, CA
Gelber, Robert S. ....Summit, NJ
Gelber, Robert T. ....Los Angeles, CA
Gelber, Seymour ....Miami Beach, FL
Gelber, Sidney L. ....San Gabriel, CA
Gelber, Stephanie S. ....Buffalo, NY
Gelber, Stephen M. ....Honolulu, HI
Gelberg & Associates, P.C. Philadelphia, PA
Gelberg, Frederick ....New York, NY
Gelberg, Jonathan D. ....Montclair, NJ
Gelberg, Stuart P. ....Garden City, NY
Gelberg, Terri N. ....Philadelphia, PA
Gelbert, David R. ....Fort Lee, NJ
Gelbert, Pamela P. ....Lebanon, OH
Gelbfish, Larry J. ....New York, NY
Gelbin, Ellen R. ....Winston-Salem, NC
Gelblum, Michael A. ....Redwood City, CA
Gelblum, Peter B., (A Professional Corporation) ....Los Angeles, CA
Gelblum, Robert R. ....Raleigh, NC
Gelblum, Seth D. ....New York, NY
Gelbman, Alan G. ....Lakewood, OH
Gelbman, Donald R. ....Las Vegas, NV
Gelboin, Tamara R.
Department Of The Interior, GV
Gelbond, Ainard ....Clifton, NJ
Gelbron, Guy G. ....Scottsdale, AZ
Gelbstein, Alan D. ....Brooklyn, NY
Gelburd, Kenneth A. ....Conshohocken, PA
Gelburd, Robin C. ....New York, NY
Gelbwaks, Aaron ....New York, NY
Gelch, Gary D. ....Plantation, FL
Gelch & Taylor, P.A. ....Plantation, FL
Gelczer, Rhonda F. ....Oklahoma City, OK
Geld, Jonathan N. ....Austin, TX
Geldart, Michael D. D. ....St. Petersburg, FL
Geldbart, Jack J. ....Sarasota, FL
Geldenhuys, Mariette ....Ithaca, NY
Gelder, J. Thomas ....Pasadena, CA
Gelder, John W. ....Troy, MI
Gelderman, G. Anthony, III New Orleans, LA
Gelderman, Peter V. ....Fairfield, CT
Gelders, John B., (P.C.) ....Oklahoma City, OK
Geldin, Max ....North Hollywood, CA
Geldmacher, Christopher K. ....St. Louis, MO
Geldmacher, John W. ....Reisterstown, MD
Geldner, JuliAnn Y. ....Chicago, IL
Geldon, Anne W. ....Washington, DC
Geldon, Fred W. ....Herndon, VA
Geldon, Gilbert E. ....Arlington, VA
Geldzahler, Evan
Securities and Exchange Commission, Division of Enforcement, GV
Geldzahler, Janet Thiele ....Washington, DC
Geldzahler, Jonathan S. ....Richmond, VA
Geldzahler, Seth D. ....Springfield, NJ
Gele, Stephen ....Metairie, LA
Geleerd, Guy Delson, Jr. ....Chicago, IL
Gelegan, Timothy R. ....Fresno, CA
Gelenian, Milton C. ....Washington, DC
Gelenitis, James G. ....Roseland, NJ
Gelerman, Cashman & Donahue Boston, MA
Dedham, MA
Gelerman, Richard A. ....Dedham, MA
Gelernt, Karen B. ....New York, NY
Gelernter, Eugene M. ....New York, NY
Gelernter, Sidney A. ....Decatur, GA
Gelety, Michael D. ....Fort Lauderdale, FL
Gelfan, Gregory ....Los Angeles, CA
Gelfand, Andrew ....New York, NY
Gelfand & Arpe, P.A. ....West Palm Beach, FL
Gelfand, Bertram R. ....White Plains, NY
Gelfand, Burton ....Brooklyn, NY
Gelfand, David I. ....Washington, DC
Gelfand, David J. ....Chicago, IL
Gelfand, David R. ....New York, NY
Gelfand, Edith M. ....Palm Beach, FL
Rockville, MD
Gelfand, Edward S. ....Los Angeles, CA
Gelfand, Eugene M. ....Fairfield, OH
Gelfand, Gary B. ....Beverly Hills, CA
Las Vegas, NV
Gelfand and Gelfand, A Law Corporation Beverly Hills, CA
Gelfand, Gerald W. ....Seattle, WA
Gelfand & Glaser ....Los Angeles, CA
Gelfand, Gregory ....Detroit, MI
Gelfand, Joanne ....New York, NY
Gelfand, Jonathan D. ....Los Angeles, CA
Gelfand, Judith Ann ....Beverly Hills, CA
Gelfand, Katherine M. ....New York, NY
Gelfand, M. David ....New Orleans, LA
Gelfand, Mark A. ....Edison, NJ
Gelfand, Mark E. ....Hicksville, NY
Gelfand, Martin N. ....Los Angeles, CA
Gelfand, Marvin, (A Professional Corporation) ....Los Angeles, CA
Gelfand, Michael J. ....West Palm Beach, FL
Gelfand, Mooney & Selem ....Edison, NJ
Gelfand, Murray ....Greenwich, CT
Gelfand, Ross ....Norcross, GA
Gelfand, Scott N. ....New York, NY
Gelfand, Seymour ....New York, NY
Gelfand, Stephen P. ....Smithtown, NY
Gelfand-Chaite, Wendy K. ....Roslyn, NY
Gelfarb, David B. ....New York, NY
Gelfarb, Kenneth A. ....Gaithersburg, MD
Gelfeld, Carole G. ....Rockville, MD
Gelfeld, Mark R. ....Glenview, IL
Gelfer, Florine ....Fullerton, CA
Gelfer, Scott H. ....Newport Beach, CA
Gelfman, Gary Michael ....Sacramento, CA
Gelfman & Gelfman ....Northfield, IL
Gelfman, Lenore R. ....Ellicott City, MD
Gelfman, Mary H. B. ....Ridgefield, CT
Gelfman, Paul M. ....Northfield, IL
Gelfman, Peter T. ....New York, NY
Gelfman, Rhonda F. ....Jacksonville, FL
Gelfman, Rhonda F. North Miami Beach, FL
Gelfman, Richard D. ....Columbia, MD
Gelfman, Robert W. ....New York, NY
Gelfman, Steven M. ....St. Louis, MO
Gelfman, Stuart G. ....Northfield, IL
Gelfon, Jeffrey Neal ....Roxbury, VT
Gelfond, Gordon ....Philadelphia, PA
Gelfond, Judith L. ....New York, NY
Gelfond, Patricia ....New York, NY
Gelfond, Richard B. ....Roseland, NJ
Gelfond, Sheri L. ....New York, NY
Gelfond, Stuart H. ....New York, NY
Gelfound, Craig A. ....Pasadena, CA
Gelfuso, Alan P. ....Cranston, RI
Gelfuso & Lachut, Incorporated Cranston, RI
Gelhaar, Ned M. ....Sacramento, CA
Gelhaar, Patricia Evans ....Norwood, MA
Gelhaar, Peter E. ....Boston, MA
Gelhar, Leslie A. ....Bloomington, MN
Gelhar & Ousky, P.A. ....Bloomington, MN
Gelhard, John C. ....Racine, WI
Gelhaus, Mark J. ....Wilmot, WI
Gelhaus, Robert J. ....San Francisco, CA
Gelhaus, Robert J., A Prof. Corp. San Francisco, CA
Gelin, James Alec ....Decatur, GA
Gelin, Scott ....New York, NY
Gelinas, J. Alexis ....New York, NY
Gelinas, Andre A. ....Fitchburg, MA
Gelinas, Charles A. ....Fitchburg, MA
Gelinas, Daniel Ian ....Philadelphia, PA
Gelinas, James William ....Chicopee, MA
Gelinas, Jason W. ....North Miami, FL
Gelinas, Julia Blackwell ....Indianapolis, IN
Gelinas, Lyn Ann ....Boston, MA
Gelinas, Richard D. ....Chicopee, MA
Gelinas, Robert A. ....Springfield, MA
Gelinas, Robert A. ....Philadelphia, PA
Gelinas & Ward ....Fitchburg, MA
Gelineau, Jill S. ....Portland, OR
Gelineau, Roy F., Jr. ....Salem, MA
Gelineau, Toni Marie ....Bridgeport, CT
Gelini, Thomas S. ....Oakland, CA
Gelinske, Timothy G. ....Minneapolis, MN
Gell, Carl L. ....Sandy Spring, MD
Gell, Harold A. ....New York, NY
Gell, Jane Jensen
Board of Governors Of The Federal Reserve System, Division of Consumer and Community Affairs, GV
Gell, Roland M. ....New York, NY
Gell, Stephen N. ....Washington, DC
Gell, Stephen N., P.C. ....Washington, DC
Gellatly, David A. ....Midlothian, VA
Gellatly, Margaret B. Ponte Vedra Beach, FL
Gellatly, Robert N. ....Seattle, WA
Gellen, David J. ....Atlanta, GA
Gellen, Pamela L. ....Chicago, IL
Gellenbeck, Lynne ....Cincinnati, OH
Gellenthien, T Tom C. ....Washington, DC
Geller, Aaron W. ....Spring Valley, NY
Geller, Albert H. ....Las Vegas, NV
Geller, Alfred ....New York, NY
Geller, Alice ....New York, NY
Geller & Assoc. ....Wilmette, IL
Geller, David J. ....Brookline, MA
Geller, David L. ....Atlanta, GA
Geller, Diane J. ....Fort Lauderdale, FL
Geller, Edward B. ....New York, NY
Geller, Eric D. ....Southfield, MI
Geller, Eric P. ....Chestnut Hill, MA
Geller, Frank W. ....Greenwich, CT
Geller, Geller, Beskin, Shienvold, Fisher & Garfinkel, L.L.P. ....Fort Lauderdale, FL
Geller, Geller, Beskin Shienvold, Fisher & Garfinkel, L.L.P. ....Hollywood, FL
Geller, Geller, Beskin, Shienvold, Fisher & Garfinkel, L.L.P. ....Miami, FL
Geller, Harvey W. ....Universal City, CA
Geller, Irving I. ....Alpine, NJ
Geller, Jack J. ....Clearwater, FL
Geller, Jackie R. ....San Diego, CA
Geller, James A. ....West Caldwell, NJ
Geller, Jan B. ....New York, NY
Geller, Jason A. ....San Francisco, CA
Geller, Jay H. ....Santa Monica, CA
Geller, Jay H., A Professional Corporation Santa Monica, CA
Geller, Jay S. ....Chicago, IL
Geller, Jeffrey S. ....Boca Raton, FL
Geller, Jesse ....Boston, MA
Geller, Joanne McDevitt ....Denver, CO
Geller, John B. ....Detroit, MI
Geller, Jonathan ....Los Angeles, CA
Geller, Joseph D., A Professional Corporation Burlingame, CA
Geller, Joseph S. ....Hollywood, FL
Geller, Karen D. ....Stuart, FL
Geller, Kenneth ....New York, NY
Geller, Kenneth S. ....Washington, DC
Geller, Lance ....Miami, FL
Geller, Larry S. ....Maplewood, NJ
Geller, Laurence H. ....Sacramento, CA
Geller, Lawrence A. ....Norwalk, CT
Geller, Leslie M. ....Paramus, NJ
Geller, Louis ....Baltimore, MD
Geller, Marc B. ....San Diego, CA
Geller, Marc B., A Professional Corporation San Diego, CA
Geller, Marc S. ....Hood River, OR
Geller, Mark B. ....New Albany, IN
Geller, Martin B. ....Morris Plains, NJ
Geller, Marvin N. ....Boston, MA
Geller, Michael L. ....Bloomfield Hills, MI
Geller, Michael Steven ....Moreno Valley, CA
Geller, Mitchell J. ....New York, NY
Geller, Morse ....Forest Hills, NY
Geller, Nathaniel ....Flushing, NY
Geller, Paul Edward ....Los Angeles, CA
Geller, Paul J. ....Boca Raton, FL
Geller, Paul L. ....Toledo, OH
Geller, Randolph ....Moscow, ID
Geller, Richard E. ....New York, NY
Geller, Richard S. ....Orlando, FL
Geller, Robert C., Jr. ....Philadelphia, PA
Geller, Robert M. ....Tampa, FL
Geller, Robert Paul ....Bloomfield Hills, MI
Geller, Roberta ....New Haven, CT
Geller, Sandra R. ....New York, NY
Geller, Scott L. ....Lynnfield, MA
Geller, Seymour A. ....Yonkers, NY
Geller, Shari L. Bunks ....Chester, NJ
Geller, Sheldon M. ....New York, NY
Geller, Sidney H. ....Waterville, ME
Geller, Stanley ....New York, NY
Geller, Stephen E. ....New York, NY
Geller, Stephen R. ....Woodbridge, NJ
Geller, Steven A. ....Hollywood, FL
Geller & Stewart ....Moreno Valley, CA
Geller, Thomas ....Tuckahoe, NY
Geller, Willard ....Kendall Park, NJ
Geller, Willard, P.C. ....Kendall Park, NJ
Geller, William A. ....Wilmette, IL
Geller, William J. ....New York, NY
Gellerman, Marc H. ....Bettendorf, IA
Gellerman, Peter W. ....Santa Monica, CA
Gellersted, Richard H. ....Lake Forest, IL
Gellerstedt, Wright ....Atlanta, GA
Gellert, Arthur L. ....Poughkeepsie, NY
Gellert & Cutler, P.C. ....Poughkeepsie, NY
Purchase, NY
Gellert, David S. ....Reading, PA
Gellert, David S., P.C. ....Reading, PA
Gellert, Donald N. ....New York, NY
Gellert, Karl N. ....Detroit, MI
Gellert, Michael ....New York, NY
Gellert, Michael S. ....Margate, FL
Gellert, Nicholas P. ....Seattle, WA
Gellert, Peter J. ....New York, NY
Gellert & Rodner ....Bronxville, NY
Gellert, Ronald S. ....Philadelphia, PA
Gellert, S. Nina ....New York, NY
Gellert Dunn, Tracy ....Anchorage, AK
Gelles, Jared ....Miami, FL
Gelles, Peter A. ....Los Angeles, CA
Gelles, Richard B. ....New York, NY
Gelles, Richard Marc ....Los Angeles, CA
Gelles, Walter R. ....New York, NY
Gelles, William H., III ....Philadelphia, PA
Gellhaus, Gerdes & Gellhaus, P.C. Aberdeen, SD
Gellhaus, Jay R. ....Aberdeen, SD
Gellhaus, Kenneth L. ....Albany, NY
Gellhaus, Lonald L. ....Aberdeen, SD
Gellhorn, Ernest ....Washington, DC
Gelling, Ralph D. ....Fairfield, CT
Gellis, Alan H. ....Cherry Hill, NJ
Gellis, Ann J. ....Bloomington, IN
Gellis, George A. ....New York, NY
Gellis, Jan I. ....New York, NY
Gellis & Melinger ....New York, NY
Gellman, Alfred B. ....Los Angeles, CA
Gellman, Arnold R., P.A. ....Miami, FL
Gellman, Arnold R., (P.A.) ....Miami, FL
Gellman, Arthur M. ....Amherst, NY
Gellman, David R. ....San Francisco, CA
Gellman, Emanuel ....Monticello, NY
Gellman, Eugene ....Lynbrook, NY
Gellman & Gellman ....Lynbrook, NY
Gellman, George I. ....Amherst, NY
Gellman, Gregg A. ....Los Angeles, CA
Gellman, Jack A. ....Niagara Falls, NY
Gellman, Jack E. ....Amherst, NY
Gellman, James F. ....New York, NY
Gellman, Jason D. ....Phoenix, AZ
Gellman, Jerome I. ....New York, NY
Gellman, Jonathan S. ....New York, NY
Gellman, Lance K. ....New York, NY
Gellman, Melvin H. ....Lynbrook, NY
Gellman, Nancy J. ....Philadelphia, PA
Gellman, Paula ....Cleveland, OH
Gellman, Philip S. ....Niagara Falls, NY
Gellman, Ryan L. ....Buffalo, NY
Gellman, Stephen G. ....New York, NY
Gellman, Stephen K. ....Hartford, CT
Gellman, Stuart A. ....Buffalo, NY
Gellman, Susan B. ....Columbus, OH
Gellman, Tobi K. ....Dallas, TX
Gellman, Wendy P. Rosenthal New York, NY
Gellman, Yale H. ....Great Neck, NY

Genser, David S. .... Quogue, NY
Genser, Erick J. .... Washington, DC
Genser, Jon P. .... Golden, CO
Genser, Joshua G. .... Richmond, CA
Genser, Mitchell S. .... Santa Rosa, CA
Genser, Stanley .... Pacific Palisades, CA
Genshaft, Nelson E .... Columbus, OH
Genshaft, Steven M. .... Canton, OH
Gensheimer, Joseph M. .... Kansas City, MO
Genshlea, Joseph S. .... Sacramento, CA
Gensib, Carl D. .... North Brunswick, NJ
Gensiejewski, Gerald G. .... Philadelphia, PA
Gensini, Gioia A. .... Syracuse, NY
Genske, Gregory B. .... San Francisco, CA
Gensler, Howard .... Costa Mesa, CA
Gensler, Kevin M. .... Naperville, IL
Gensler, Steven S. .... Milwaukee, WI
Gensler, Vicki L. .... Pittsburgh, PA
Gensmer, Timothy W. .... Sarasota, FL
Genson, Edward M. .... Chicago, IL
Genson, Eugene M. .... Los Angeles, CA
Genson & Gillespie .... Chicago, IL
Genson, Melody D. .... Sarasota, FL
Genster, Jane E. .... Washington, DC
Gensweider, Leo T. .... Yates Center, KS
Gent, Douglas H. .... Hanover, PA
Gent, Gent and Snyder .... Franklin, PA
Gent, Henry W., III .... Franklin, PA
Gent, Henry W., Jr. .... Franklin, PA
Gent, John G. .... Erie, PA
Gent, Lisa Gay .... Kaufman, TX
Gent, Patrick W., (P.A.) .... Hollywood, FL
Gent, Thomas W., Jr. .... Vestal, NY
Gent, Wayne .... Kaufman, TX
Gentemann, Evelynn M. .... Washington, DC
Genter, Richard E. .... Philadelphia, PA
Gentes, Eric A. .... Springfield, MA
Gentes, Stephen A. .... San Diego, CA
Gentges, Alan W. .... Tulsa, OK
Gentges, Daniel W. .... Milwaukee, WI
Gentges, Delilah Christine Zarate .... Tulsa, OK
Gentges, Penny G. .... Milwaukee, WI
Genth, Geoffrey H. .... Baltimore, MD
Genther, Christopher R.
Grand Rapids, MI
Genthner, Christine M. .... Racine, WI
Gentilcore, Edward B. .... Pittsburgh, PA
Gentilcore, Laura J. .... Akron, OH
Gentile, Anthony P. .... New York, NY
Gentile, & Associates .... New York, NY
Gentile & Benjamin .... New York, NY
Gentile, Beth-Ann F. .... Washington, DC
Gentile, Bryon A. .... Bridgeport, CT
Gentile, Carmen J. .... Buffalo, NY
Gentile, Carmen L. .... Washington, DC
Gentile, Carmine L., Law Offices of
Framingham, MA
Gentile, Carolyn .... New York, NY
Gentile, Charles R. .... Omaha, NE
Gentile & Chiota .... Fairfield, CT
Gentile and Ciampoli .... Albany, NY
Brooklyn, NY
Mineola, NY
New York, NY
Gentile, Daniel K. .... Hesperia, CA
Gentile, David J. .... Providence, RI
Gentile, Della C. .... Williamson, WV
Gentile, Denise C. .... Philadelphia, PA
Gentile, Diane L. .... Dayton, OH
Gentile & Dickler .... New York, NY
Gentile, Dominic P. .... Las Vegas, NV
Gentile, Dominic P., Ltd. .... Las Vegas, NV
Gentile, Frederick J. .... Philadelphia, PA
Gentile, Gary G. .... Pittsburgh, PA
Gentile, Gary P. .... Fresno, CA
Gentile, Gary T. .... Springfield, MA
Gentile, Geoffrey H. .... Tampa, FL
Gentile, Glen J. .... Mineola, NY
Gentile, Gregory M. .... San Jose, CA
Gentile, James J. .... Fairfield, CT
Gentile, James M. .... San Francisco, CA
Gentile, James P. .... Trenton, NJ
Gentile, James S. .... Youngstown, OH
Gentile, Joan M. .... Hartford, CT
Gentile, Joanne M. .... New York, NY
Gentile, John G. .... Mineola, NY
Gentile, John J. .... Trenton, NJ
Gentile, John J., Jr. .... Westerly, RI
Gentile, Joseph A. .... Worcester, MA
Gentile, Joseph A. .... Jackson, MS
Gentile, Joseph A. .... Mineola, NY
Gentile, Joseph F. .... Los Angeles, CA
Gentile, Laura .... New York, NY
Gentile, Laurie J. .... New York, NY
Gentile, Lawrence, III .... Orlando, FL
Gentile, Leslie A. .... Avon Lake, OH
Gentile, Marc S. .... Charlotte, NC
Gentile, Marion .... Los Angeles, CA
Gentile, Mark J. .... Wilmington, DE
Gentile, Mark L. .... Las Vegas, NV
Gentile, Maury D. .... Pacific Palisades, CA
Gentile, Melinda S. .... Fort Lauderdale, FL
Gentile, Michael A .... New York, NY
Gentile, Michael D. .... South Portland, ME
Gentile, Michael J. .... Augusta, ME
Gentile, Mitchell L. .... Columbus, OH
Gentile, Nicholas T. .... Coral Springs, FL
Gentile, Pasquale D., Jr. .... Pittsburgh, PA
Gentile, Paul T. .... New York, NY
Gentile, Paul V. .... Orland Park, IL
Gentile, Philip G. .... Flemington, NJ
New York, NY
Pleasantville, NY
Gentile, R. Douglas .... Kansas City, MO
Gentile, Ralph E. .... Cold Spring Harbor, NY
Gentile, Richard P. .... Hartford, CT
Gentile, Robert A. .... Providence, RI
Gentile, Robert N. .... Monroeville, PA
Gentile, Susan E. .... Irvine, CA
Gentile, Thomas .... New York, NY
Gentile, Thomas A. .... Chevy Chase, MD
Gentile, Tina L. .... Los Angeles, CA
Gentile & Turpen .... Flemington, NJ
Pleasantville, NY
Gentile, Vernon M. .... Bel Air, MD
Gentile, Vincent E. .... Princeton, NJ
Gentile, Willard J. .... Mount Vernon, NY
Gentili, F. Joseph .... Natick, MA
Gentilli, Richard E. .... Boston, MA
Gentilli, Veronica C. .... Los Angeles, CA
Gentilotti, Jeffrey M. .... Wilmington, DE
Gentilozzi, Traci R. .... Lansing, MI
Gentin, Andrew .... Washington, DC
Gentin, Jennifer L. .... Los Angeles, CA
Gentin, Pierre M. .... New York, NY
Gentinetta, Karina P. .... New Orleans, LA
Gentino, Robert E. .... Universal City, CA
Gentle, Edgar C., III .... Birmingham, AL
Gentle, Mickey Joe .... Huntsville, AL
Gentle, Pickens & Eliason
Birmingham, AL
Gentleman, Joseph T. .... Chicago, IL
Gentleman, Mary Beth .... Boston, MA
Gentlesk, Michael L., II .... Cherry Hill, NJ
Gentner, Brian H. .... San Ramon, CA
Englewood, CO
Gentner, Edward F., Jr. .... New York, NY
Gentner, Frederick J. .... Ann Arbor, MI
Gentner, Joshua D. .... Chicago, IL
Gentner, Marsha G. .... Washington, DC
Gentner, Thomas C. .... Baltimore, MD
Gentner, Virgil R., Chartered .... Las Vegas, NV
Gentry, Ashley Beck .... Shallotte, NC
Conway, SC
Myrtle Beach, SC
Gentry, Bernard H. .... Lakeland, FL
Gentry & Boehm .... Chattanooga, TN
Gentry, Caroline H. .... Dayton, OH
Gentry, Charles A." Chip "
Jefferson City, MO
Gentry, Charles H. .... Fort Scott, KS
Gentry, Cheryl L. .... Tallahassee, FL
Gentry, D. Sharon .... Oklahoma City, OK
Gentry, Dana C. .... Bradenton, FL
Gentry, Daniel J. .... Sidney, OH
Gentry, Deborah B. .... Houston, TX
Gentry, Dianna R. .... Vashon, WA
Gentry, Donald B. .... Denver, CO
Gentry, Edgar C., Jr. .... New York, NY
Gentry, Edwin F. .... Culpeper, VA
Gentry, Eldred A. .... Cleveland, OH
Gentry, Elvin L. .... Colorado Springs, CO
Gentry, Frank W. .... Albuquerque, NM
Gentry, Fred D. .... Olympia, WA
Gentry, Galen .... Los Angeles, CA
Gentry, Gary R. .... Elsah, IL
Gentry, Gavin M. .... Memphis, TN
Gentry & Gentry Co., L.P.A. .... Cleveland, OH
Gentry, Glenn S.
Securities and Exchange Commission,
Division of Enforcement, GV
Gentry, Gretchen Luke .... Jackson, MS
Gentry, H. Clarke .... Oakland, CA
Gentry & Haskins LLP
Colorado Springs, CO
Gentry, Henry L. .... Lisle, IL
Gentry, J. Theodore .... Greenville, SC
Gentry, Jack E. .... Dallas, TX
Gentry, Jacquelyn E. .... Huntington Beach, CA
Gentry, James E. .... Cleveland, OH
Gentry, James Erik .... Bay Minette, AL
Daphne, AL
Foley, AL
Gentry, James O'C. .... Towson, MD
Gentry, James O'Conor, Jr. .... Towson, MD
Gentry, James W., Jr. .... Chattanooga, TN
Gentry, Jean A. .... Treasury Department,
United States Mint, GV
Gentry, Jo Lynn .... Sacaton, AZ
Gentry, John R. .... Clemson, SC
Gentry, Joycean B. .... St. Petersburg, FL
Gentry, K. Anne Gambrill .... Fairfax, VA
Gentry, Kathleen M. .... Los Angeles, CA
Gentry, Kevin S. .... Lansing, MI
Gentry, Larry E. .... Saluda, SC
Gentry, Locke, Rakes & Moore
Roanoke, VA
Gentry, Louis F. .... Pinehurst, NC
Gentry, Mack A. .... Knoxville, TN
Gentry, Mary G. .... Olympia, WA
Gentry, Melinda J. .... Indianapolis, IN
Gentry, Michael Asher .... Houston, TX
Gentry, Michael H. .... College Station, TX
Gentry, Michael J. .... Portland, OR
Gentry, Nicholas R. .... Albuquerque, NM
Gentry, Nicholas R., L.L.C., Law Offices of
Albuquerque, NM
Gentry, Nolden .... Des Moines, IA
Gentry, Patricia V. .... Chicago, IL
Gentry, Phillips and Hodak, P.A.
Jacksonville, FL
Lakeland, FL
Tampa, FL
Gentry, Ray E. .... Stone Mountain, GA
Gentry, Reed O. .... Kansas City, MO
Gentry, Richard E. .... St. Augustine, FL
Gentry, Richard E. .... Tallahassee, FL
Gentry, Richard N., Jr. .... Peoria, IL
Gentry, Sam L. .... Bolivar, MO
Gentry, Sandra M. .... Conyers, GA
Gentry, Stephen M. .... Indianapolis, IN
Gentry, Steven G. .... Dublin, OH
Gentry, Steven H. .... Irvine, CA
Gentry, Susan Campbell .... Charlotte, NC
Gentry, Thomas Lee .... Lexington, KY
Gentry, Tipton, Kizer & McLemore, P.C.
Knoxville, TN
Gentry, Tom .... Little Rock, AR
Gentry, Vanessa L. .... Wyoming, OH
Gentry, W. Michael .... Kansas City, MO
Gentry, W. Richard .... West Chester, PA
Gentry, Walter Neil .... Conyers, GA
Gentry, William C. .... San Diego, CA
Gentry, William C. .... Jacksonville, FL
Gentry, William C. .... Marietta, GA
Gentry, William E. .... Hobart, OK
Gentry, William R., Jr. .... Bardstown, KY
Genty, Philip Michael .... New York, NY
Gentz, Richard D. .... Winsted, MN
Gentz, Susan C. .... Austin, TX
Gentz, William A. .... Mount Clemens, MI
Gentzel, Robert W. .... Norwalk, OH
Genua, Doreen A. .... South River, NJ
Genuardi, Claudia E. .... Lansdale, PA
Genuario & Conover .... Norwalk, CT
Genuario, Robert L. .... Norwalk, CT
Genullis, Erin C. .... Tyler, TX
Genung, Elizabeth A. .... Syracuse, NY
Genung, L. T. .... Tyler, TX
Geny, William O. .... Portland, OR
Genys, Victoria M. .... Pittsburgh, PA
Genz, Edward A. .... Red Bank, NJ
Genz, Michael A. .... Hughesville, MD
Genz, Peter J. .... Atlanta, GA
Genz, Wendy K. .... Los Angeles, CA
Genzano, Joseph L. .... Brooklyn, NY
Genzberger, Earl M. .... Butte, MT
Genzel, George H. .... Rochester, NY
Genzel, Sara E. .... Tallahassee, FL
Genzer, Jeffrey C. .... Washington, DC
Genzer, Marvin D. .... New York, NY
Genzer, Stephen B. .... Newark, NJ
Genzler, Patrick A. .... Kitty Hawk, NC
Norfolk, VA
Genzmer, George V., III .... Los Angeles, CA
Geocaris, Angelo .... Chicago, IL
Geocaris, Diane Fields .... Irvine, CA
Geocaris, James A. .... Newport Beach, CA
Geocaris, James A. .... Palatine, IL
Geocaris, James A. .... Rolling Meadows, IL
Geoffrey, Eugene E., Jr. .... Melbourne, FL
Geoffrey, Michael M. .... Chicago, IL
Geoffrey, Russell J. .... Boston, MA
Geoffrion, Alfred, Jr. .... Springfield, MA
Geoffroy, Elizabeth A. .... Douglasville, GA
Geoffroy, Kate L. .... Portland, ME
Geoffroy, Michael G. .... Narragansett, RI
Geoffroy, Raymond F., III .... Richmond, VA
Geoga, Douglas G. .... Chicago, IL
Geogan, F. Joseph, II .... Rockland, MA
Geogan & Geogan, P.C. .... Boston, MA
Rockland, MA
Geoghan Cohen & Bongiorno
Manalapan, NJ
New York, NY
Geoghan, Dennis P. .... New York, NY
Geoghan, Johanna M. .... New York, NY
Geoghan, Joseph E. .... Danbury, CT
Geoghan, Joseph E., III .... New York, NY
Geoghan, Paul V. .... Jersey City, NJ
Geoghan, Sean J. .... Brooklyn, NY
Geoghan, William F. X., Jr.
New York, NY
Geoghegan, Andrew P. .... Scarborough, ME
Geoghegan & Associates .... Bardstown, KY
Geoghegan, Brian .... Palo Alto, CA
Geoghegan, Brian .... Washington, DC
Geoghegan, Faith J. .... Sacramento, CA
Geoghegan, John A. .... Purchase, NY
Geoghegan, Joseph H. .... Wilmington, DE
Geoghegan, J.T. Terence .... Chicago, IL
Geoghegan, Kimberly J.
Bowling Green, KY
Geoghegan & Ozorowski .... Harleysville, PA
Geoghegan, Patricia .... New York, NY
Geoghegan, Raymond J. .... Brooklyn, NY
Geoghegan, Robert A. .... Jackson, MS
Geoghegan, Terence .... Ventura, CA
Geoghegan, Terry L. .... Bardstown, KY
Geoghegan, Thomas H. .... Chicago, IL
Geohagan, A. Brent .... Lakeland, FL
Geo-Karis, Adeline J., & Assoc., Ltd.
Zion, IL
Geolot, Alan C. .... Washington, DC
Geoly, James C. .... Chicago, IL
Geon, Bryan S. .... Portland, OR
Geonetta, Frederick J. .... San Francisco, CA
Geoppinger, Jean M. .... Cincinnati, OH
Georgakis, Peter U. .... Santa Barbara, CA
Georgalas, Michael .... Pittsburgh, PA
Georgallis, Joann .... Sacramento, CA
Georgantas, Dimitri P. .... Houston, TX
Georgantas, Louis P. .... Boston, MA
Georgantas & Walters, LLP .... Houston, TX
George, Adrienne R.
Federal Deposit Insurance Corporation,
Regulation and Legislation Section, GV
George, Alan B. .... Rutland, VT
George, Alan J. .... Columbia, SC
George, Albert R. .... New York, NY
George, Alexander A. .... Missoula, MT
George, Alisa E. .... Bellevue, WA
George, Allen .... Cleveland, OH
George, Allison C. .... Washington, DC
George, Amy Elizabeth .... Akron, OH
George, Amy Lyn .... Houston, TX
George, Amy R. .... New York, NY
George, Andrea K. .... Minneapolis, MN
George, Andrew W. .... Sacramento, CA
George, Angela S. .... Charlotte, NC
George, Anil Venparampil
Department of Commerce,
Patent and Trademark Office, GV
George, Anne Gibbons .... Bella Vista, AR
George, Anthony D. .... Boston, MA
George, Anthony D., Jr.
Port St. Lucie, FL
George, Anthony D., Jr. .... Stuart, FL
George, Armen L. .... Pacifica, CA
George, Arthur C. .... Randolph, MA
George, Arthur L. .... Chicago, IL
George, Arthur R. .... Sausalito, CA
George, B. Glenn .... Williamsburg, VA
George, B. James .... New York, NY
George, Barbara C. .... Long Beach, CA
George, Barry B. .... Midland, MI
George, Barry B., P.C. .... Midland, MI
George, Bartles & Wallach .... Forest Park, GA
Jackson, GA
George, Bebe .... Timonium, MD
George, Beth V. .... Portland, ME
George, Bonnie M. .... Elk Grove, CA
George, Boyd L. .... Hickory, NC
George, Brett F. .... Franklin Lakes, NJ
George, Brian J. .... Department of the Navy,
Office of the Judge Advocate General, GV
George & Bronstein .... Towson, MD
George, Bryan A. .... Doylestown, PA
George & Buch, A Law Corporation
Los Angeles, CA
George, Buchman & Leigh, P.C.
Houston, TX
George, Burl F. .... Fort Lauderdale, FL
George, Calvin M. .... Glendale Heights, IL
George, Carol G. .... Hempstead, NY
George, Caroline .... Washington, DC
New York, NY
George, Carolyn B. .... Albany, NY
George, Charles .... Raleigh, NC
George, Charles A. .... Randolph, MA
George, Charles D. .... Clearwater, FL
Sarasota, FL
George, Charles D., P.A. .... Clearwater, FL
Sarasota, FL
George, Charles H. .... Glendale, AZ
George, Charles K. .... Fort Lauderdale, FL
Fort Myers, FL
Miami, FL
Orlando, FL
West Palm Beach, FL
George, Charles M.P. .... Miami, FL
George, Charles R., III .... Orlando, FL
George, Charles W. .... Braintree, MA
George, Chris A. .... Pittsburgh, PA
George, Christopher E. .... Washington, DC
George, Christopher Lee .... Mobile, AL
George, Christopher M. .... Louisville, KY
George, Clarence M. .... Spokane, WA
George, Cynthia Coulter .... Greenwich, CT
George, D. Keith .... Richardson, TX
George, Dahlia A. .... Concord, NH
George, Dane .... Austin, TX
George, Daniel .... Sallisaw, OK
George, Daniel C. .... North Miami Beach, FL
George, Danielle .... New York, NY
George, David .... Houston, TX
George, David C. .... Bentonville, AR
George, David C. .... Elyria, OH
George, David C. .... Oklahoma City, OK
George, David Eugene .... Anchorage, AK
George, David J. .... Boca Raton, FL
George, David M. .... Tampa, FL
George, David M., P.A. .... Tampa, FL
George, David R. .... Utica, NY
George, David R. .... Akron, OH
George, David V. .... Juneau, AK
George, Deanne P. .... San Diego, CA
George, Deborah A. .... Pawtucket, RI
George, DeGregorio, Massimiano & McCarthy, A Professional Corporation
Pittsfield, MA
George, Dena G. .... Atlanta, GA
George, Denise C. .... Bellingham, WA
George, Diane F. .... New York, NY
George, Donald L. .... Sandy, UT
George & Donaldson, L.L.P. .... Austin, TX
George, Donna E. .... West Palm Beach, FL
George, Doug .... Alamosa, CO
George, Doughlas M. .... Springfield, KY
George, Duke, Jr .... New Kensington, PA
George, Edmond M. .... Philadelphia, PA
George, Edward, & Associates
Boston, MA
George, Edward F., Jr. .... Boston, MA
George, Edward J. .... Charleston, WV
George, Edward M. .... Montgomery, AL
George, Edward M., III .... Wheeling, WV
George, Edward N., III .... Metairie, LA
George, Edward P., Jr. .... Long Beach, CA
George, Edward P., Jr., Inc., A Prof. Corp.
Long Beach, CA
Los Angeles, CA
Santa Ana, CA
George, Eli J., Jr. .... Louisville, KY
George, Elizabeth .... Bloomfield, CT
George, Elizabeth Anne Parham
Oklahoma City, OK
George, Elmer J. .... Lebanon, KY
George, Emil J. .... Pittsfield, MA
George, Emmit J., Jr. .... Des Moines, IA
George, Eric Albert .... Southampton, PA
George, Eric M. .... United States Senate,
Committee Legal Personnel, GV
George, Erika J. .... Portland, OR
George, Erika R. .... Chicago, IL
George, Eugene O. .... Sarasota, FL
George, Forest N., Jr. .... Richmond, VA
George, Frances H. .... New York, NY
George, Francis J. .... Hartwell, GA
George, Franklin J. .... Grenada, MS
George, Fred W. .... Pittsburgh, PA

George, Frederick A. ....Hermitage, PA
George, Fredk. C. ....Columbus, OH
George, Fredric J. ....Charleston, WV
George, G. Jeffrey ....La Crosse, WI
George, Gary R. ....Dallas, TX
George, Gary R. ....Milwaukee, WI
George, Gene B. ....Cleveland, OH
George, George & Hemsell ....Louisville, KY
George, George J. ....Pittsburgh, PA
George and George, Ltd., A Professional Law Corporation ....Baton Rouge, LA
George & George, P.C. ....Franklin Lakes, NJ
George, Gerald F. ....Houston, TX
George, Gregory T. ....Jefferson City, MO
George, H. Emily ....Forest Park, GA
George, Hal ....Corpus Christi, TX
George & Haldy, A Professional Corporation
Flint, MI
George, Hanna Casper ....Palo Alto, CA
George, Harold W. ....Trenton, NJ
George, Harris James ....Towson, MD
George, Harry Franklyn ....Bellmore, NY
George, Hartz, Lundeen, Flagg & Fulmer
Fort Lauderdale, FL
Fort Myers, FL
Miami, FL
Orlando, FL
Tallahassee, FL
West Palm Beach, FL
George, Helen W. ....New Haven, CT
George, Hilda S., Mrs. ....Suwanee, GA
George, Hulane Evans ....Milledgeville, GA
George, Hull, Porter & Kohli, P.S.
Seattle, WA
George, Ira S. ....Baton Rouge, LA
George, J. K., & Associates ......Los Osos, CA
George, J K., & Associates
Morro Bay, CA
George, J. K., & Associates
Paso Robles, CA
George, J.K., & Associates
San Luis Obispo, CA
George, J. K., & Associates
Santa Maria, CA
George, J. Timothy ....Erie, PA
George, J. Wiley ....Houston, TX
George, James ....Los Angeles, CA
George, James A. ....Baton Rouge, LA
George, James D. ....New York, NY
George, James D. ....San Antonio, TX
George, James E. ....Woodbury, NJ
George, James L. ....Le Mars, IA
George, James Paul ....Fort Worth, TX
George, James R. ....Miami, FL
George, James R. ....Portland, OR
George, James S. ....Monticello, MS
George, James W. ....Oklahoma City, OK
George, James W. ....Austin, TX
George, Jamilia A. ....Anchorage, AK
George, Janet A. ....Seattle, WA
George, Jason L. ....Columbus, OH
George, Jay V. ....Franklin Lakes, NJ
George, Jeff A. ....Los Angeles, CA
George, Jeffrey S. ....Colorado Springs, CO
George, Jennifer Billiet
San Francisco, CA
George, Jennifer M. ....South Barrington, IL
George, J. K. ....Los Osos, CA
San Luis Obispo, CA
George, Joan M. ....Redwood City, CA
George, Jody Ellyn
Federal Judicial Center, GV
George, John ....Louisville, KY
George, John A. ....Victoria, TX
George, John G. ....Fort Lauderdale, FL
George, John J. ....Chicago, IL
George, John J., Law Offices of
Santa Clara, CA
George, John M., Jr. ....Chicago, IL
George, Joseph A. ....Beverly Hills, CA
George, Joseph C. ....Los Angeles, CA
George, Joseph C. ....Sacramento, CA
George, Joseph H. ....White Plains, NY
George, Joseph M. ....Uniontown, PA
George, Joseph M., Jr. ....Uniontown, PA
George, Judith Arnette ....Baton Rouge, LA
George, K. Doyle ....Jacksonville, FL
George, Kathleen A ....Fort Lauderdale, FL
George, Kathy A. ....Midland, TX
George, Keith E. ....Washington, DC
George, Keith J. ....Charleston, WV
George, Kelly A. ....Oklahoma City, OK
George, Kenneth F. ....Kearney, NE
George, Kenneth L. ....Houston, TX
George, Kenneth P. ....New York, NY
George, Kent J. ....Charleston, WV
George, Kevin ....Louisville, KY
George, Kevin C. ....New York, NY
George, Kevin H. ....Houston, TX
George, Kevin O. ....Silver Spring, MD
George, Konstantine P. ....Long Beach, CA
George, Korin, Quattrone, Blumberg & Chant, P.A. ....Woodbury, NJ
George, Kristine A. ....Los Angeles, CA
George, L. Anthony ....Denver, CO
George, LaDale K. ....Chicago, IL
George, Lani A. ....Evansville, IN
George, Larry D. ....Houston, TX
George, Larry W. ....Charleston, WV
George, Laura M. ....Fairfax, VA
George, Lavinia Brown ....Forest Park, GA
George Law Offices ....Missoula, MT
George, Lawrence C. ....Tallahassee, FL
George, Leo I., P.C. ....Washington, DC
George, Leslie M. ....Cleveland, OH
George, Leslie P. ....Atlanta, GA
George, Lina C. ....Englewood, CO
George, Linda S. ....Indianapolis, IN

George, Lisa B. ....Tallahassee, FL
George, Lloyd D. ....Las Vegas, NV
George & Lorensen, P.L.L.C.
Charleston, WV
George, Louis ....Huntington, WV
George, Louis J.
Department Of Veterans Affairs, Board of Veterans Appeals, GV
George, Louis, L.C. ....Huntington, WV
George, Louis N. ....Hartford, CT
George, Margaret R. ....Rockville, CT
George, Margo R. ....Oakland, CA
George, Marion C., Jr. ....Fayetteville, NC
George, Mary Jo ....Washington, DC
George, Maureen R. ....Chandler, AZ
George, Melanie L. ....Wilmington, DE
George, Melisa C. ....Huntsville, AL
George & Meyer Co., L.P.A. ....Columbus, OH
George, Michael A. ....Gettysburg, PA
George, Michael B. ....Flint, MI
George, Michael C., Law Office of
Pittsburgh, PA
George, Michael D. ....Corpus Christi, TX
George, Michael D., P.C.
Corpus Christi, TX
George, Michael F. ....Columbus, OH
George, Michael F., Co., L.P.A.
Columbus, OH
George, Michael J. ....Great Falls, MT
George, Michael P. ....Point Richmond, CA
George, Michael W. ....Denton, TX
George, Micheal G. ....Malakoff, TX
George & Morris, PLLC ....Bella Vista, AR
Bentonville, AR
George & Murphy, P.C. ....Sturbridge, MA
George, Nancy Whorton ....Washington, DC
George, Nancy Whorton, & Associates, P.C.
Washington, DC
George, Natascha Suzanne ....Boston, MA
George, Nicholas A. ....Daytona Beach, FL
George, Nicholas T. ....Akron, OH
George, Nikolaos Charles ....New York, NY
George, Norman ....Brooklyn, NY
George, Patricia A. ....Lockport, NY
George, Paul B. ....Portland, OR
George, Paul E. ....Wellesley, MA
George, Paul F. ....Sterling, VA
George, Paula R. ....New Orleans, LA
George, Peter E. ....Tampa, FL
George, Peter R. ....Chicago, IL
George, Peter R. ....Port Huron, MI
George, Philip S., Jr. ....Lebanon, KY
George, Phillip A. ....Gallatin, TN
George, Phillip M. ....Smyrna, TN
George, R. James, Jr. ....Austin, TX
George, Ralph F., Jr. ....Needles, CA
George, Ralph N. ....Torrance, CA
George, Randall H. ....Oxnard, CA
George, Raymond E. ....Augusta, GA
George, Richard ....New York, NY
George, Richard D. ....Madison, WI
George, Richard M. ....Spokane, WA
George, Richard N. ....Rochester, NY
George, Richard W. ....Cedar Rapids, IA
George, Rick J. ....San Jose, CA
George, Robert A. ....Boston, MA
George, Robert A., and Associates, P.C.
Boston, MA
George, Robert B. ....Media, PA
George, Robert Bruce ....Jacksonville, FL
George, Robert D. ....Cicero, NY
George, Robert D. ....New Castle, PA
George, Robert D., P.C. ....Cicero, NY
George, Robert E. ....Sturbridge, MA
George, Robert E. ....Aurora, MO
George, Robert K. ....Irvine, CA
George, Robert P. ....Detroit, MI
George, Robert Peter ....Charleston, WV
George, Roger Edward ....Palo Alto, CA
George, Ronald J. ....Danbury, CT
George, Ronald M. ....San Francisco, CA
George, Ronald S. ....Pocatello, ID
George, Russell L. ....Rifle, CO
George, Ryan L. ....Vienna, VA
George, Sam ....Madison, IN
George, Samuel M. ....Tyler, TX
George, Sandra ....Hillsdale, MI
George, Schwarz & Rogers ......Des Moines, IA
George, Scott A. ....Philadelphia, PA
George, Shawn P. ....Charleston, WV
George & Shields, LLP ....Irvine, CA
George, Stanley Kaffoglou ....Port Arthur, TX
George, Stephen A. ....Pittsburgh, PA
George, Stephen M. ....Louisville, KY
George, Steve S. ....Dearborn, MI
George, Susan G. ....Pittsburgh, PA
George, Susan M. ....Washington, DC
George, Susan Morale ....Pittsford, VT
George, T. Dennis ....Seattle, WA
George, Terressa E. ....Altoona, PA
George, Terry Lee ....Okmulgee, OK
George, Theodore C., (P.C.) ....Atlanta, GA
George, Thomas ....San Jose, CA
George, Thomas E. ....Naperville, IL
George, Thomas M. ....Toledo, OH
George, Thomas N. ....Yarmouth Port, MA
George, Thomas, P.C. ....Austin, TX
George, Thomas William ....Austin, TX
George, Timothy R. ....Dallas, TX
George & Titus, P.A. ....Tampa, FL
George, Todd S. ....Austin, TX
George, Tom M. ....Harlingen, TX
George, Tom W. ....Des Moines, IA
George, Tracey E. ....Washington, DC
George, Vickery G. ....Bonifay, FL
George, Victor E. ....Chatsworth, CA
George, Virginia E. ....Milwaukee, WI
George, Virginia M. ....Martinez, CA

George, Virginia Storms ....Walnut Creek, CA
George, W. Peyton ....Washington, DC
George, W. Timothy ....Austin, TX
George, Warren E. ....San Francisco, CA
George, Warren S. ....Cleveland, OH
George, William A. ....Media, PA
George, William C. ....Westlake Village, CA
George, William C. ....Baton Rouge, LA
George, William, III ....Aurora, CO
George, William J. ....Gardner, MA
George, William L. ....Tucson, AZ
George, William P. ....Saratoga, CA
George, William V. ....Forest Park, GA
George, Woodrow ....Ardmore, OK
Georgeadis, Philip N. ....Cleveland, OH
Georgeadis, Socrates J. ....Reading, PA
George-Counts, Denise, Law Offices of
Charlotte Amalie, St. Thomas, VI
Georgeff, Gary M. ....Brookings, OR
Georgeff, George C. ....Columbus, OH
Georgelis, Michael A. ....Lancaster, PA
Georgell, Holly Ann ....Chicago, IL
Georgellis, George B. ....Washington, DC
Georgelos, Andrea ....La Grange Park, IL
Georgelos, Debra S. ....Casa Grande, AZ
Georgelos, Demetra V. ....Los Angeles, CA
Georgelos, Pamela G. ....Phoenix, AZ
Georgen, Peter J. ....Richmond, VA
Georgen, Terri A. ....Minneapolis, MN
George, Paul D. ....Buffalo, NY
Georges, Alexander ....Milwaukee, WI
Georges, Carol M. ....Santa Monica, CA
Georges, Elizabeth M. ....Washington, DC
Georges, George Wm. ....Philadelphia, PA
Georges, James ....Huntington Beach, CA
Georges, James A. ....Philadelphia, PA
Georges, Katherine G. ....Portland, OR
Georges, Mara Stacy ....Chicago, IL
Georges, Marie-Helene ....Manchester, NH
Georges, Maurice O. ....Portland, OR
Georges, Melissa ....New York, NY
Georges, Peter J. ....Alexandria, VA
Georges, Richard M. ....St. Petersburg, FL
Georges, Richard M., P.A.
St. Petersburg, FL
Georges, Rudolph ....San Antonio, TX
Georges, Sean M. ....Evansville, IN
Georges, Serge, Jr. ....Boston, MA
Georges, William D. ....Cherry Hill, NJ
Philadelphia, PA
Georges, William H., (Co., L.P.A.)
Canton, OH
Georgeson, Adamont N. ....Mill Valley, CA
Georgeson & Belardinelli ....Fresno, CA
Georgeson, C. James ....Reno, NV
Georgeson, C. Russell ....Fresno, CA
Georgeson, Linda A. M. ....Waukesha, WI
Georgeson, Paul J. ....Reno, NV
Georgeson & Stickel, LLC
Oconomowoc, WI
Georgeson, Thomas D. ....Oconomowoc, WI
Georgeson, Thompson & Angaran, Chartered ....Reno, NV
Georget, Richard P. ....New York, NY
Georgetti, Anthony P. ....Toledo, OH
Georgetti, Dominick J. ....Scranton, PA
Georgetti, Kevin ....Brielle, NJ
Georgetti, Michael A. ....Hartford, CT
Georgevich, Christine M ....Chicago, IL
Georgevich, Margaret M.G. ....Lake Forest, IL
Georgi, Kay ....Washington, DC
Georgi, Richard H. ....Mount Prospect, IL
Georgiades, Peter N. ....Pittsburgh, PA
Georgiades, Peter N., P.C., & Associates
Pittsburgh, PA
Georgiadis, Linda B. ....Richmond, VA
Georgiadis, Paul D. ....Richmond, VA
Georgiana, Joseph S. ....Mount Laurel, NJ
Georgini, Jenevra ....New York, NY
Georgini, Joseph R. ....Casa Grande, AZ
Georgino, Damian C. ....Palm Desert, CA
Georgiopoulos, Constantine P.
New York, NY
Georgiou, Anna L. ....Walden, NY
Georgiou, Byron S. ....San Diego, CA
Georgiou, George ....Oak Park, IL
Georgiou, Nancy ....Martinez, CA
Georgis, Helene ....Brooklyn, NY
Georgis, Thomas J. ....Palos Hills, IL
Georgopoulos, Aurelia A. ....Brooklyn, NY
Georgopoulos, Evan ....Boston, MA
Georgopoulos & Pahlavan
Menlo Park, CA
San Francisco, CA
Georgopoulos, Zach G.
San Francisco, CA
Georgoulakos, Valerie ....New York, NY
Georgoulis, Chris ....New York, NY
Georgouses, Thomas J. ....Fresno, CA
Georis, Fabrice ....Washington, DC
Geosling, Gary ....Bloomington, IL
Geotas, Jordan K. ....Phoenix, AZ
Gepford, Daniel W. ....Basking Ridge, NJ
Gepford, Lawrence F. ....Kansas City, MO
Gepford, Lawrence F., Jr.
Kansas City, MO
Gepford, Monaco & Sanders, L.C.
Kansas City, MO
Gephardt, Richard A. ....St. Louis, MO
Gephart, Ellen Flood ....Spokane, WA
Gephart, John A. ....Baltimore, MD
Gephart, John F. ....Cincinnati, OH
Gephart, John M. ....Wagoner, OK
Gephart, Randall L.
Mammoth Lakes, CA
Gephart, Smith B. ....Harrisburg, PA
Gepp, Randy Charles ....Atlanta, GA
Geppert, Eric J. ....Cincinnati, OH

Geppert, James A. ....Glenview, IL
Geppert, John G., Jr. ....Morristown, NJ
Geppert, McMullen, Paye & Getty
Cumberland, MD
Geppert, William H. ....Cumberland, MD
Gerace, Anthony J., Jr. ....State College, PA
Gerace, Donald R. ....Utica, NY
Gerace, Joseph ....Mayville, NY
Gerace, Michael F. ....Edgewater, MD
Gerace, Michele Kristen ....New York, NY
Gerace, Samuel P. ....Pittsburgh, PA
Gerace, Vincent J. ....Rochester, NY
Gerace, William T. ....Hartford, CT
Gerachis, George M. ....Houston, TX
Geraci, Alan L. ....San Diego, CA
Geraci, Anthony J. ....Penn Yan, NY
Geraci, Carl J. ....St. Louis, MO
Geraci, Caroline R. ....Chicago, IL
Geraci, Jeffrey J. ....San Diego, CA
Geraci, Katherine ....New York, NY
Geraci & LaPerna Co., L.P.A.
Cleveland, OH
Geraci, Leonard J. ....New Rochelle, NY
Geraci, Linda A. ....Hopewell Junction, NY
Geraci, Peter Francis ....Chicago, IL
Geraci, Philip A. ....New York, NY
Geraci, Rudolph J. ....Cleveland, OH
Geraci, Salvatore ....Chattanooga, TN
Geraci, Sebastian J. ....Eau Claire, WI
Geraci, Thomas A.
Department of the Air Force, Office of the Judge Advocate General, GV
Geraci, Victor T. ....Cleveland, OH
Geraci, Vincent ....Newburgh, NY
Geracioti, Michael A. ....Nashville, TN
Geracos, Georgann ....Jacksonville, NC
Gerage, C. Richard ....Metairie, LA
New Orleans, LA
Gerage, Steven D. ....Chicago, IL
Geraghty, Alfred E. ....Gloversville, NY
Geraghty, Andrea ....Pittsburgh, PA
Geraghty, Colleen A. ....Department of Labor, Office of the Solicitor, GV
Geraghty, Daniel B. ....Milwaukee, WI
Geraghty, David P. ....Milwaukee, WI
Geraghty, Diane C. ....Chicago, IL
Geraghty, Diane M. ....Walpole, MA
Geraghty Friedman, P.C. ....Pittsburgh, PA
Geraghty, Gilbert N. ....Mauston, WI
Geraghty, Gwen M. ....Lisle, IL
Geraghty, James A. ....Wheaton, IL
Geraghty, James A. ....New York, NY
Geraghty, James H. ....St. Paul, MN
Geraghty, Jerome G. ....Baltimore, MD
Geraghty, Joanna L. ....New York, NY
Geraghty, John F., Jr. ....Atlantic City, NJ
Geraghty, John J. ....Arlington, VA
Geraghty, John R. ....Hoboken, NJ
New York, NY
Geraghty, Mark D. ....New York, NY
Geraghty, Mark S. ....Los Angeles, CA
Geraghty, Maureen ....Winston-Salem, NC
Geraghty, Michael C. ....Anchorage, AK
Geraghty, Michael C. ....Spokane, WA
Geraghty, Michael F. ....Gloversville, NY
Geraghty, Michael J. ....Newark, NJ
Geraghty, Miriam N. ....Chicago, IL
Geraghty, Molly ....Cambridge, MA
Geraghty, O'Loughlin & Kenney, Professional Association ....St. Paul, MN
Geraghty, Patrick A., Jr. ....Seattle, WA
Geraghty, Patrick E. ....Fort Myers, FL
Geraghty, Patrick E., A Professional Association ....Fort Myers, FL
Geraghty, Patrick G.
National Transportation Safety Board, Office of Administrative Law Judges, GV
Geraghty, Paul M. ....New London, CT
Geraghty, Peter ....Woodbury, NY
Geraghty, Peter H. ....Chicago, IL
Geraghty, Peter R.
Securities and Exchange Commission, Division of Market Regulation, GV
Geraghty, Robert C. ....Northbrook, IL
Geraghty, Robert F. ....Seattle, WA
Geraghty, Terri A. ....Louisville, KY
Geraghty, Thomas A., Jr. ....Denver, CO
Geraghty, Thomas F. ....Chicago, IL
Geraghty, Thomas F., Jr. ......Harbor Springs, MI
Geraghty, Timothy J. ....Kenosha, WI
Geraghty & Van Derhoef ....Seattle, WA
Geraghty, William B. ....Miami, FL
Geraghty, William J. ....New York, NY
Geraghty, William P. ....Fort Lauderdale, FL
Geragos & Geragos ....Los Angeles, CA
Geragos, Mark J. ....Los Angeles, CA
Geragos, Matthew J. ....Los Angeles, CA
Geragos, Paul J. ....Los Angeles, CA
Geragosian, Harold J. ....New Britain, CT
Gerak, Justin A. ....Schaumburg, IL
Gerakitis, Richard ....Atlanta, GA
Gerald & Brand, P.L.L.C. ....Jackson, MS
Newton, MS
Gerald, Dennis M. ....Columbia, SC
Gerald, Jerry D. ....Atlanta, GA
Gerald and Kimpson, L.L.P. ....Columbia, SC
Gerald, Lenora ....Jamaica, NY
Gerald Maglio & Associates ......Las Vegas, NV
Gerald, Patrick S. ....Midland, TX
Gerald, Sandra C. ....Lithonia, GA
Gerald, Sandra C., P.C. ....Lithonia, GA
Gerald, Tilman L. ....Washington, DC
Geraldi, Alan R. ....San Francisco, CA
Geraldi, Daniel J. ....San Francisco, CA
Geraldi, Jerry ....North Miami, FL
Geraldine, Hilaire Ann ....Bakersfield, CA
Geraldo, Manuel R. ....Washington, DC

Geralds, Jones, Sherrow, Schrader & Rice, P.S.C. ....Lexington, KY
Geralds, Oscar H., Jr. ....Lexington, KY
Geraldson, Raymond I. ....Chicago, IL
Geraldson, Raymond I., Jr. ....Chicago, IL
Gerard, Bretton C. ....Addison, TX
Gerard, Bryan E. ....Seattle, WA
Gerard, Carole A. ....Rancho Cordova, CA
Gerard, Christopher C. ....New York, NY
Gerard, Daniel A. ....New York, NY
Gerard, Daniele ....Raleigh, NC
Gerard, David Bradley ....New York, NY
Gerard, Dominique P. ....Houston, TX
Gerard, Donald K. ....St. Louis, MO
Gerard, Egon R. ....New York, NY
Gerard, Francis R. ....Point Pleasant, NJ
Gerard, Ian A. ....New York, NY
Gerard, James P. ....Savannah, GA
Gerard, Jamie Kay ....Westport, CT
Gerard, Joe G. ....United States Senate, Senatorial Assistants, GV
Gerard, John F. ....Los Angeles, CA
Gerard, John F. ....Santa Monica, CA
Gerard, John M. ....Worcester, MA
Gerard, Jules B. ....St. Louis, MO
Gerard, Keith W. ....Madison, WI
Gerard, Kenneth J. ....San Diego, CA
Gerard, Kristine Camron Indianapolis, IN
Gerard, Laura L. ....Wilmington, DE
Gerard, Lester E. ....Riverhead, NY
Gerard & Matthews, Attorneys at Law, P.A. Athens, GA
Gerard, Maurice W. ....Knoxville, TN
Gerard, Melissa K. ....Pasadena, CA
Gerard, Nora S. ....New York, NY
Gerard, Peter Michael ....Northampton, MA
Gerard, Philip C. ....Phoenix, AZ
Gerard, Richard A. ....New York, NY
Gerard, Richard E. ....Lake Charles, LA
Gerard, Richard E., Jr. ....Lake Charles, LA
Gerard, Robert B. ....Las Vegas, NV
Gerard, Robert J., Jr. ....Costa Mesa, CA
Gerard, Ronald ....Lyndhurst, NJ
Gerard, Roy F. ....New York, NY
Gerard Singer & Levick, P.C. Addison, TX; Dallas, TX
Gerard, Stephen C., II ....Iowa City, IA
Gerard, Stephen S. ....Warren, NJ
Gerard, Thomas J. ....Wilmington, DE
Gerard, Timothy F. ....West Burlington, IA
Gerard, Whitney I. ....New York, NY
Gerard, William T. ....Athens, GA
Gerarde, Thomas R. ....Hartford, CT
Gerarden, Ted P. ....Postal Rate Commission, Office of the Consumer Advocate, GV
Gerardi, Greg L. ....San Diego, CA
Gerardi, Jeffrey ....North Charleston, SC
Gerardi, Joseph Lucian ....Stamford, CT
Gerardi, Melissa C. ....New York, NY
Gerardi, Michael M. ....Los Angeles, CA
Gerardi, Richard P. ....Chicago Heights, IL
Gerardi, Robert H. ....Department of Justice, Criminal Division, GV
Gerardi, Theresa ....White Plains, NY
Gerardin, Scott D. ....Oak Creek, WI
Gerardo, Jeffrey S. ....Santa Ana, CA
Gerard-Pateakos, Jenessa Ellen New Bedford, MA
Gerash, Daniel P. ....Denver, CO
Gerash, Gerald A. ....West Los Angeles, CA
Gerash, Karen Mahlman ....Denver, CO
Gerash, Prugh & Gerash, L.L.C. Denver, CO
Gerash, Walter L. ....Denver, CO
Gerasimovich, Kenneth A. ....New York, NY
Gerasimow, Alexander M. ....Racine, WI
Gerasimowicz, George, Jr. ....Pottstown, PA
Geraty, Brent G.T. ....Portland, ME
Geraud, Jos. R. ....Riverton, WY
Geraurd, Lisa R. ....Yorba Linda, CA
Gerb, Bernard ....New York, NY
Gerb, Kalman H. ....Lake Worth, FL
Gerb, Kalman H., P.A. ....Lake Worth, FL
Gerbac, Joseph E. ....Lompoc, CA
Gerbase, Claude J., Jr. ....Billings, MT
Gerbasi, Joseph S. ....Department of Justice, Criminal Division, GV
Gerbasi, Marcella J. ....Uniondale, NY
Gerber, A. Grant ....Elko, NV
Gerber, A. Richard ....Blue Bell, PA
Gerber, Abraham ....Metairie, LA
Gerber, Alan S. ....Tuckerton, NJ
Gerber, Alexandra Malantestinic New York, NY
Gerber, Andrew A. ....Charlotte, NC
Gerber, Andrew J. ....New York, NY
Gerber, Andrew J. ....Winston-Salem, NC
Gerber, Austin J. ....Sacramento, CA
Gerber, Barry K. ....Pittsburgh, PA
Gerber & Bateman, A Professional Association ....Santa Fe, NM
Gerber, Bernard M. ....Atlanta, GA
Gerber, Bernard R. ....Reading, PA
Gerber, Bruce S. ....Fort Myers, FL
Gerber, Carol J. ....New York, NY
Gerber, Charles W. ....New York, NY
Gerber, Christopher P. ....Exton, PA
Gerber, Clifford M. ....San Francisco, CA
Gerber, Daniel J. ....Orlando, FL
Gerber, Daniel W. ....Buffalo, NY
Gerber, Daryl J. ....Palmyra, PA
Gerber, David A. ....Oxnard, CA
Gerber, David J. ....South Windsor, CT
Gerber, David J. ....Chicago, IL
Gerber, David J. ....Chicago, IL
Gerber, David J. ....Edwardsville, IL
Gerber, Dean N. ....Chicago, IL
Gerber, Donna M. ....New York, NY
Gerber, Edward F. ....Syracuse, NY
Gerber, Edward M. ....St. Paul, MN
Gerber, Edward R. ....Sacramento, CA
Gerber, Eliot S. ....New York, NY
Gerber, Ellen W. ....Winston-Salem, NC
Gerber, Eric T. ....Syracuse, NY
Gerber, Ethan B. ....Brooklyn, NY
Gerber, Geoffrey G. ....St. Louis, MO
Gerber & Gerber ....Blue Bell, PA; Norristown, PA; Philadelphia, PA
Gerber & Gerber, P.C. ....Atlanta, GA
Gerber, Glenn I. ....Ambler, PA
Gerber, Gordon W. ....Philadelphia, PA
Gerber, Hal ....Memphis, TN
Gerber, Harriet ....New York, NY
Gerber, Harvey R. ....Rancho Mirage, CA
Gerber, Howard ....Nanuet, NY
Gerber, Howard Richard ....Brooklyn, NY
Gerber, Jack ....Elizabeth, NJ
Gerber, Jack B. ....Miami, FL
Gerber, Jack B., P.A. ....Miami, FL
Gerber, Jay E. ....New York, NY
Gerber, Jeff ....Woodbine, NJ
Gerber, Jeffrey W. ....Florham Park, NJ
Gerber, Jerome ....Philadelphia, PA
Gerber, Jill ....St. Paul, MN
Gerber, Jo Anne C. ....Roseland, NJ
Gerber, Jody N. ....New York, NY
Gerber, Joel United States Tax Court, GV
Gerber, John M. ....Philadelphia, PA
Gerber, Jonathan D. West Palm Beach, FL
Gerber, Jos. S. ....Tucson, AZ
Gerber, Joseph A. ....Philadelphia, PA
Gerber, Joseph E. ....Sacramento, CA
Gerber, Joyce Carolyn ....Cambridge, MA
Gerber, Judith M. ....Buffalo, NY
Gerber, Karen T. ....Cheshire, CT
Gerber, Karl ....Sherman Oaks, CA
Gerber, Katherine I. ....Beech Grove, IN
Gerber, Kelly Matthews ....Washington, DC
Gerber, L. Franklin, Jr. ....Towson, MD
Gerber Law Office ....Memphis, TN
Gerber, Lawrence ....Chicago, IL
Gerber, Lewis ....Wyncote, PA
Gerber, Louis E. ....Columbus, OH
Gerber, Ludwig H. ....Huntington Beach, CA
Gerber, M. Todd ....Virginia Beach, VA
Gerber, Marc J. ....Great Neck, NY
Gerber, Marc S. ....Washington, DC
Gerber, Maria" Mia " ....Lakeland, FL; Lake Wales, FL; Winter Haven, FL
Gerber, Marsha Z. ....Dallas, TX
Gerber, Marshall J. ....Northbrook, IL
Gerber, Marshall L., Law Office of Memphis, TN
Gerber, Mary A. ....Oakland, CA
Gerber, Mary Ann ....Millersville, PA
Gerber, Melanie K. ....Washington, DC
Gerber, Melissa K. Weiler ....Philadelphia, PA
Gerber, Michael A. ....New York, NY
Gerber, Michelle S. ....Roseland, NJ
Gerber, Milton ....New York, NY
Gerber, Neil ....El Centro, CA
Gerber, Nils E. ....Winston-Salem, NC
Gerber, Paul D. ....Santa Fe, NM
Gerber, Peggy A. ....Los Angeles, CA
Gerber, Phillip J. ....Chicago, IL
Gerber, R. Jeffrey ....San Bernardino, CA
Gerber, Ramona L. ....Cleveland, OH
Gerber, Randy S. ....St. Louis, MO
Gerber, Richard E. ....Memphis, TN
Gerber, Richard P. ....Santa Ana, CA
Gerber, Richard S. ....Columbus, OH
Gerber, Robert A. ....Harrington Park, NJ
Gerber, Robert E. ....New York, NY
Gerber, Robert G. ....Chicago, IL
Gerber, Robert P. ....Exeland, WI
Gerber, Robert S. ....San Diego, CA
Gerber, Robin Marla ....Washington, DC
Gerber, Roger ....Salem, OR
Gerber, Roger A. ....New York, NY
Gerber, Ronette Alesia ....Asheville, NC
Gerber, Ross M. ....Valley Stream, NY
Gerber, Rudolph J. ....Phoenix, AZ
Gerber & Samson, L.L.C. ....Paterson, NJ; Wayne, NJ
Gerber, Sandra K. ....Meriden, CT
Gerber, Sanford J. ....Atlanta, GA
Gerber, Sanford K. ....Scottsdale, AZ
Gerber, Steven ....Wayne, NJ
Gerber, Steven K. ....Philadelphia, PA
Gerber, Steven M. ....New York, NY
Gerber, Thomas A. ....Portland, OR
Gerber, Toby L. ....Dallas, TX
Gerber, Victoria ....New York, NY
Gerber, Walter P. ....Portland, OR
Gerber, Wayne S. ....El Paso, TX
Gerber, William A. ....New York, NY
Gerberding, Kent E. ....Traverse City, MI
Gerberding, Miles C. ....Fort Wayne, IN
Frankfort, MI
Traverse City, MI
Gerberg, Joseph K. ....Albany, NY
Gerberry, Robert A. ....Cleveland, OH
Gerbers, Terry J. ....Green Bay, WI
Gerbic, Celina ....Boston, MA
Gerbig, Mary S. ....Green Bay, WI
Gerbing, Joan Poli ....New York, NY
Gerbini, Jean F. ....Albany, NY
Gerbino, Fred W., Jr. ....San Jose, CA
Gerbino, Perry L. ....Brook Park, OH
Gerbino, Vincent F. ....Melville, NY
Gerbitz, Gary D. ....Chattanooga, TN
Gerbitz, Leah M. ....Atlanta, GA
Gerbitz, Sara Mae ....Detroit, MI
Gerbosi, Karen B. ....Chicago, IL
Gerbosi, Paul F. ....Chicago, IL
Gerbracht, John R. ....Socorro, NM
Gerbrandt, Laural ....Fresno, CA
Gerbrecht, Arno E. ....Geneva, IL
Gerbus, David W. ....Cincinnati, OH
Gerch, Edward L. ....Evanston, IL
Gerchak, Michael A. ....Youngstown, OH
Gerchick, Jeffrey S. ....New York, NY
Gerchick, Randy G. ....Irvine, CA
Gercke, Dumser & Feld, A Professional Corporation ....Cherry Hill, NJ
Gercke, John R. ....Cherry Hill, NJ
Gercovich, Lawr. E. ....Carmichael, CA
Gerdano, Michelle Seyman Department of Labor, Office of the Solicitor, GV
Gerde, Cy ....Lafayette, IN
Gerde, Jerry W. ....Panama City, FL
Gerdelman, Bernard W. ....St. Louis, MO
Gerdelman, M. Lee Watson St. Louis, MO
Gerden, Paul ....Northbrook, IL
Gerdes, Andrew J. ....Lansing, MI
Gerdes, C. Edward, Jr. ....Eugene, OR
Gerdes, Charles S. ....Honolulu, HI
Gerdes, David A. ....Pierre, SD
Gerdes, Ellis E. ....Portland, OR
Gerdes, John R. ....Wichita, KS
Gerdes, Kandace C. ....Denver, CO
Gerdes, Mary L. ....New York, NY
Gerdes, Mason, Simpson & Lapham, L.L.P. Charlotte, NC
Gerdes, Michael B. ....Phoenix, AZ
Gerdes, Phillip E. ....Charlotte, NC
Gerdes, Richard S. ....Carmichael, CA
Gerdes, Roger A. ....Seattle, WA
Gerdes, Ronald W. ....Washington, DC
Gerdes, Stephen K. ....Denver, CO; Cheyenne, WY
Gerdes, Stephen L. ....Omaha, NE
Gerdes, Stephen L., Law Firm of Omaha, NE
Gerdes, Steven H. ....Houston, TX
Gerdes, Ted F. ....Los Angeles, CA
Gerdes, Victor ....Middletown, NJ
Gerdes, William D. ....Aberdeen, SD
Gerdevich, Edward F. ....Chicago, IL
Gerdine, Clint A. ....Washington, DC
Gerding, Erik F. ....Washington, DC
Gerding, John M. ....San Francisco, CA
Gerding & O'Loughlin, P.C. Farmington, NM
Gerding, Paul S. ....Phoenix, AZ
Gerding, Paul S., Jr. ....Phoenix, AZ
Gerding, Richard L. ....Farmington, NM
Gerdink, Herbert R. ....Terre Haute, IN
Gerdisch, Matthew P. ....Milwaukee, WI
Gerdts, Charles W., III ....New York, NY
Gerdts, Marlene, Law Offices of Beverly Hills, CA
Gerdy, Harry General Services Administration, Office of Regional Counsel, GV
Gere, Elizabeth Sarah ....Washington, DC
Gerecht, Donald Leon ....Los Angeles, CA
Gerecht, Edwin F., Jr. ....Stirling, NJ
Gerecke, Dale E. ....Cape Girardeau, MO
Gerecke, Edward W. ....Tampa, FL
Gerecke, Sarah Sheon ....Yonkers, NY
Gereighty, Thomas M. ....New Orleans, LA
Gerek, William M. ....Chicago, IL
Gerel, Martin E., (P.C.) ....Rockville, MD
Geremia & De Marco, Ltd. ....Providence, RI
Geremia, Joseph A., Jr. ....Waterbury, CT
Geremia, Lisa A. ....Providence, RI
Geremia, Louis A. ....Providence, RI
Geremia, Todd R. ....New York, NY
Geremonte, Frank M. ....Stoneham, MA
Geren, David K. ....Encino, CA
Geren, Gary A. ....Sacramento, CA
Geren, Gerald S. ....Chicago, IL
Geren, Gerald S., Ltd. ....Chicago, IL
Geren, James B. ....Chicago, IL
Geren, Jeffrey L. ....Encino, CA
Geren, Preston M. (Pete), III Fort Worth, TX
Gerena, Glenn A. ....Boca Raton, FL
Gerena-Méndez, Jorge L. ....San Juan, PR
Gerencser, Alison Eckles ....Gainesville, FL
Gerend, Timothy J. ....Chicago, IL
Gerenraich, Steven ....Chicago, IL
Gerenz, John M. ....St. Paul, MN
Gerepka, Raymond M. ....Parsippany, NJ
Gerety, Christopher J. ....Birmingham, AL
Gerety, Daniel A. ....Anchorage, AK
Gerety, Miles S. ....New Haven, CT
Gerety, Peter L. ....Southport, CT
Gerety, Robert P., Jr. White River Junction, VT
Gerety, Sally C. ....Los Alamos, NM
Gerety, Thomas C. ....Stratford, CT
Geretz, Victor O. ....Canoga Park, CA
Gerez, Alicia M. ....Mineola, NY; New York, NY
Gerg, Ann Marie ....Washington, DC
Gerg, Beth Ammerman ....Brookville, PA; Clearfield, PA
Gergacz, John W. ....Lawrence, KS
Gerganoff, Mark W. ....Denver, CO
Gergel, Nickles & Solomon, P.A. Columbia, SC
Gergel, Richard Mark ....Columbia, SC
Gergely, Alfred J. ....Palm Springs, CA
Gergely, Ernest ....Bridgeport, CT
Gergely, Gabriela S. ....Falls Church, VA
Gergely, Michael C. ....Vicksburg, MI
Gergely, Peter A. ....Boulder, CO; Denver, CO
Gergen, Ann E. ....Bloomington, MN
Gergen, Dawn P. ....Beaver Dam, WI
Gergen, Gergen & Pretto, S.C. Beaver Dam, WI
Gergen, Henry G., Jr. ....Beaver Dam, WI
Gergen, Jennifer A. ....Department of State, Office of the Legal Adviser, GV
Gergen, Mark J. ....Minneapolis, MN
Gergen, Mark P. ....Austin, TX
Gergen, Michael J. ....Washington, DC
Gergen, William H. ....Beaver Dam, WI
Gergen-Mandel, Kathleen M. ....St. Paul, MN
Gergens, Pamela L. ....Milwaukee, WI
Gerger, Alan S. ....Houston, TX
Gerger, David B. ....Houston, TX
Gerges, Abraham G. ....Brooklyn, NY
Gergits, Joseph C. ....Department of Justice, Civil Division, GV
Gergora, Thomas G. ....Orlando, FL
Gergosian, Edward M. ....San Diego, CA
Gergoudis, Paul L. ....Long Island City, NY
Gerhan, Charles F., Jr. ....Manchester, NH
Gerhan, Daniel C. ....Minneapolis, MN
Gerhard, Gerard R. ....Frankfort, KY
Gerhard & Gerhard ....Glenside, PA
Gerhard, Glen R. ....San Francisco, CA
Gerhard, John ....New York, NY
Gerhard, Robert C., III ....Glenside, PA
Gerhard, Robert C., Jr. ....Glenside, PA
Gerhard, Victor J., III ....Albany, NY
Gerhardson, Bruce G. ....Fergus Falls, MN
Gerhardstein, Alphonse A. ....Cincinnati, OH
Gerhardstein, Michael C. ....Chicago, IL
Gerhardstein, Walter J. ....Columbus, OH
Gerhardt, Annette L. ....Sierra Vista, AZ
Gerhardt, Bonnie R. ....Washington, DC
Gerhardt, Bruce R. ....Omaha, NE
Gerhardt, C. William ....Monroe, LA; Shreveport, LA
Gerhardt, Charles H., III ....Cincinnati, OH
Gerhardt, Dan E ....Mansfield, OH
Gerhardt, David J. ....North Miami Beach, FL
Gerhardt, Deborah R. ....Richmond, VA
Gerhardt, Henry ....St. Charles, MO
Gerhardt, Jane E. ....Cincinnati, OH
Gerhardt, John S. ....Campbell, CA
Gerhardt, Kathryn Brook ....Tacoma, WA
Gerhardt, Kathryn Weigand ....Macon, GA
Gerhardt, Laurie B. ....Freehold, NJ
Gerhardt, Maureen Breen Greensboro, NC
Gerhardt, Michael J. ....Cleveland, OH
Gerhardt, Paul ....Portland, OR
Gerhardt, Paul K. ....Indianapolis, IN
Gerhardt, Paul W. ....Newport News, VA
Gerhardt, Richard L. ....Circleville, OH
Gerhardt, Richard L., II ....Circleville, OH
Gerhardt, Robert M. ....San Jose, CA
Gerhart, Christy L. ....Seattle, WA
Gerhart, Donald A. ....Chicago, IL
Gerhart, Eugene C. ....Binghamton, NY
Gerhart, Frederick J. ....Philadelphia, PA
Gerhart, John T. ....Dallas, TX
Gerhart, Leslie C., (Mr.) East Greenville, PA
Gerhart, Peter M. ....Cleveland, OH
Gerharter, James V. ....Minneapolis, MN
Gerhauser, Lisa C. ....San Francisco, CA
Gerhold, Timothy A. G. ....Boston, MA
Gerhold, Wayne D. ....Pittsburgh, PA
Geri, Joseph ....Los Angeles, CA
Geriak, James W., (A Professional Corporation) ....Irvine, CA
Geribon, Hector D. ....New York, NY
Gerich, Michael D. Executive Office Of The President, Office of Management and Budget, GV
Gericke, Douglas N. ....San Bernardino, CA
Gericke, J. Robert ....San Bernardino, CA
Gericke, Robert W. ....Madeira Beach, FL
Gericke, Vernon J. ....Cedar Rapids, IA
Gericke, William E. ....Philadelphia, PA
Gerien, J. Scott ....San Francisco, CA
Gerig, Frank A. ....Colorado Springs, CO
Gerig, Frank A., P.C. ....Colorado Springs, CO
Gerig, Paul J. ....Athens, OH
Gerik, Rodney E. ....Houston, TX
Gerike, Anthony F. ....Medford, NJ
Gerike, Paul A. ....Bridgewater, NJ
Gering, Anne-Marie ....Baltimore, MD
Gering, Charles F., Jr. ....Brooklyn, NY
Gering, Charles M. ....Chicago, IL
Gering, Cheryle Wiedmeier Sioux Falls, SD
Gering, David J. ....Phoenix, AZ
Gering, Richard C. ....Chicago, IL
Gering, Travis L. ....New York, NY
Gering, William J. ....Westminster, MD
Geringer, Aylene M. ....Los Angeles, CA; Sacramento, CA
Geringer & Dolan ....New York, NY
Geringer, Harold I. ....New York, NY
Geringer, James E. ....Portland, OR
Geringer, Robert D. ....Santa Monica, CA
Geringer, Stephen R. ....Tacoma, WA
Geringer, Steven A. ....Sacramento, CA
Gerisch, Alfred W., Jr. ....Los Angeles, CA
Gerish, Jeffrey C. ....Detroit, MI
Gerity, John F. ....Elburn, IL
Gerity, Patrick L. ....Gaithersburg, MD
Gerity, Patrick M. ....Hartford, CT
Gerity, Thomas C. ....Jackson, MS
Gerjuoy, Edward ....Pittsburgh, PA
Gerk, James A. ....Cedar Rapids, IA

Gershfeld, Michelle .... **New York, NY**
White Plains, NY
Gershfeld, Philip .... New York, NY
Gershgorn, Allan S. .... **New York, NY**
Gershik, Gary J. .... **New York, NY**
Gershik, Larry .... La Crescenta, CA
Gershin, Roger Andrew .... Minneapolis, MN
Gershkowitz, Robert J. .... Natick, MA
Gershman, Bennett L .... White Plains, NY
Gershman, Bruce A. .... Minneapolis, MN
Gershman, Cindy Michelle
West Palm Beach, FL
Gershman, David .... **Roseland, NJ**
Gershman, Donald S. .... **West Hartford, CT**
Gershman, Dyan L. .... **New York, NY**
Gershman & Goldstein, P.A.
West Palm Beach, FL
Baltimore, MD
Gershman, Howard .... **Blue Bell, PA**
Gershman, Jeffrey S. .... **St. Louis, MO**
Gershman, Joseph A. .... New York, NY
Gershman, Julie K. .... **New York, NY**
Gershman, Lawrence E. .... Beverly Hills, CA
Gershman, Richard S. .... Garden City, NY
Gershman, Robert Scott
West Palm Beach, FL
Gershman, Stephen A. .... **Los Angeles, CA**
Gershman, Steven L. .... Mount Laurel, NJ
Gershner, Stephen L. .... **Little Rock, AR**
Gershon, A. Arnold .... **New York, NY**
Gershon, A. Arnold, P.C. .... **New York, NY**
Gershon, Andrew J. .... New York, NY
Gershon, Colin Miles .... **Bridgeport, CT**
New Haven, CT
Gershon, Daniel E. .... Santa Fe, NM
Gershon, David J. .... **Columbus, OH**
Gershon, Deborah S. .... **Los Angeles, CA**
Gershon, Fredric B. .... New York, NY
Gershon, Gary N. .... Grand Rapids, MI
Gershon, Harry L. .... **Los Angeles, CA**
Gershon, Holly Gayle .... Boca Raton, FL
Gershon, Holly Gayle, Law Offices of
Boca Raton, FL
Gershon, I. Richard .... St. Petersburg, FL
Gershon, Jules S. .... Chicago, IL
Gershon, Jules S., & Associates .... Chicago, IL
Gershon, Karyn G. .... Wilmette, IL
Gershon, Linda J. .... Dallas, TX
Gershon, Lorry F. .... Agoura Hills, CA
Gershon, Louis .... Chicago, IL
Gershon, Mark A. .... **Chicago, IL**
Gershon, Michael Allan .... San Antonio, TX
Gershon, Neil D. .... **Norwalk, CT**
Gershon, Neil L. .... **Chicago, IL**
Gershon, Nina .... Brooklyn, NY
Gershon, Olim, Katz & Loeb .... Atlanta, GA
Gershon, Richard M. .... **Albany, NY**
Gershon, Robert S. .... Brooklyn, NY
Gershon, Ruth H. .... **Atlanta, GA**
Gershon, Sim .... Pompano Beach, FL
Gershon, Zev T. .... **Baltimore, MD**
Gershonowitz, Aaron .... Melville, NY
Mineola, NY
Gershov, David .... Los Angeles, CA
Gershow, Ellen .... **Gainesville, FL**
Gershowitz, Alan M. .... Bethpage, NY
Gershowitz, Jeffrey A. .... Westport, CT
Gershowitz, Lisa N. .... New York, NY
Gershowitz, Michael S. .... **Chicago, IL**
Gershowitz, Robin Ann .... New York, NY
Gershuni, Gregory B. .... Long Beach, CA
Los Angeles, CA
Gershuni & Imrich, LLP .... Los Angeles, CA
Gershuny, Donald N. .... New York, NY
Gershuny, Douglas E. .... Bridgeton, NJ
Gershuny, Edward S. .... Purchase, NY
Gershuny, Moses M. .... Middletown, NY
Gershuny, Pamela .... **Cincinnati, OH**
Gershuny, William A.
Department Of Health And Human Services, GV
Gershwin, Frances Allou .... **Boston, MA**
Gersich, Bradley J. .... **Palo Alto, CA**
Gersick, Barry A. .... **Minneapolis, MN**
Gerske, Janet F. .... **Chicago, IL**
Gerson, Alan A. .... New Orleans, LA
Gerson, Alan G. .... **St. Louis, MO**
Gerson, Alan H. .... St. Petersburg, FL
Gerson, Alan J. .... **New York, NY**
Gerson, Alfred S. .... Beaumont, TX
Gerson, Allan M. .... Palm Beach Gardens, FL
Gerson, Ann E. .... New York, NY
Gerson, Arthur S. .... Washington, DC
Gerson, Barry L. .... Dayton, OH
Gerson, Beth Merold .... Boston, MA
Gerson, Capek & Voron .... Philadelphia, PA
Gerson, Dan B. .... **Houston, TX**
Gerson, Darlene R. .... Irving, TX
Gerson, David .... Department of Labor,
Office of Secretary, GV
Gerson, David A. .... **Pittsburgh, PA**
Gerson, David H. .... New York, NY
Gerson, David R. .... San Francisco, CA
Gerson, Donna L. .... Pittsburgh, PA
Gerson, Ellen M. .... **Houston, TX**
Gerson, Elliot F. .... Hartford, CT
Gerson, Ervin H. .... **Atlanta, GA**
Gerson, Frederick E. .... **Florham Park, NJ**
Gerson, Frederick Robert .... Richmond, VA
Gerson, Gary E. .... Pittsburgh, PA
Gerson, Gary N. .... **West Palm Beach, FL**
Gerson, Gordon L. .... La Jolla, CA
Gerson, Gordon L., A Professional Corporation
La Jolla, CA
Gerson, Grekin & Wynhoff, Attorneys at Law, A Law Corporation .... **Honolulu, HI**
Gerson, Herbert E. .... **Memphis, TN**
Gerson, James M. .... **Boston, MA**
Gerson, Jeffrey C. .... **Mineola, NY**
Gerson, Jerome H. .... Chicago, IL
Gerson, Jonathon M. .... Albuquerque, NM
Gerson, Leonard H. .... **New York, NY**
Gerson, Lorraine S. .... Newark, NJ
Gerson, Marc J. .... **Washington, DC**
Gerson, Matthew T. .... United States Senate,
Committee Legal Personnel, GV
Gerson, Mervyn S. .... **Honolulu, HI**
Gerson, Michael .... **Miami, FL**
Gerson, Michael G. .... Oakland, CA
Gerson, Milton .... Cumberland, MD
Gerson, Mindy D. .... Coral Gables, FL
Gerson, Mitchell B. .... Newtown, PA
Gerson, Morton M., (A Prof. Law Corp.)
Santa Monica, CA
Gerson, Nancy C. .... Fort Myers, FL
Gerson, Nancy Lee .... Flushing, NY
Gerson, Nicole .... Philadelphia, PA
Gerson, Paul F. .... Bay Harbor Islands, FL
Gerson, Philip B. .... **New York, NY**
Gerson, Philip M., (P.A.) .... Miami, FL
Gerson, Philip S. .... **Las Vegas, NV**
Gerson, Ralph J. .... Washington, DC
Gerson, Rebecca M. .... Youngstown, OH
Gerson, Richard L. .... Philadelphia, PA
Gerson, Rochelle O. .... Studio City, CA
Gerson, Seth J. .... **Chicago, IL**
Gerson, Shari L. .... **Hollywood, FL**
Gerson, Simon .... **New York, NY**
Gerson, Stuart M. .... **Washington, DC**
Gerson, Susan B. .... **Washington, DC**
Gerson, William N. .... Santa Clara, CA
Gerson-Gilfix, Myra .... Palo Alto, CA
Gersowitz, Edward H. .... **New York, NY**
Gersowitz Libo & Korek, P.C.
New York, NY
Gersowitz, Stephen H. .... New York, NY
Gerspach, Thomas J. .... **New York, NY**
Gerspacher, James A. .... Akron, OH
Gerst, Andrew L. .... Rockville, MD
Gerst, Arnold R. .... **Parsippany, NJ**
Gerst, C. Graham .... **Chicago, IL**
Gerst, David M. .... Houston, TX
Gerst, Eric D. .... Newtown Square, PA
Gerst, Morris L. .... Phoenix, AZ
Gerst, Neil .... Garden City, NY
Gerst, Stephen A. .... Phoenix, AZ
Gerst, Toby M. .... Phoenix, AZ
Gerst, William S. .... Forest Park, IL
Gerstein, Allen H. .... **Chicago, IL**
Gerstein, Avery Sheldon .... Chicago, IL
Gerstein, Brian M. .... **West Orange, NJ**
Gerstein, Bruce E. .... **New York, NY**
Gerstein, Caryn Robin .... Woodbury, NY
Gerstein & Churchill, P.C. .... **New York, NY**
Gerstein, David M. .... **New York, NY**
Gerstein, Donald M. .... Cheyenne, WY
Gerstein, Edward L. .... Little Compton, RI
Gerstein Grayson, LLP .... **Haddonfield, NJ**
Gerstein, Joe W. .... **Doraville, GA**
Gerstein, Joe W., P.C. .... **Doraville, GA**
Gerstein, John R. .... **Washington, DC**
Gerstein, Kenneth S. .... **New York, NY**
Gerstein, Leonard J. .... Northbrook, IL
Gerstein, Leonard J., Ltd. .... Northbrook, IL
Gerstein, Manny .... Edison, NJ
Gerstein, Mark D. .... **Chicago, IL**
Gerstein, Marvin I. .... Urbana, IL
Gerstein, Michael A. .... **Haverhill, MA**
Gerstein, Michael D. .... Chicago, IL
Gerstein, Michael J. .... **New York, NY**
Gerstein, Norman S. .... Miami, FL
Gerstein, Rachel L. .... Los Angeles, CA
Gerstein, Ralph M. .... New York, NY
Gerstein, Robert H. .... **Chicago, IL**
Gerstein, Robert M. .... **Chicago, IL**
Gerstein, Robert S. .... **Santa Monica, CA**
Gerstein, Samuel .... **Haddonfield, NJ**
Gerstein, Sherwin A. .... Chicago, IL
Gerstein, Terri E. .... New York, NY
Gerstein, Victor R. .... **New York, NY**
Gerstein, William Gary .... Boca Raton, FL
Gerstel, Bryan R., (A Professional Corporation) .... **San Diego, CA**
Gerstel, Deborah R. .... Washington, DC
Gerstel, Linda .... **New York, NY**
Gerstell, Glenn S. .... **Washington, DC**
Gersten, Aaron L. .... **Hartford, CT**
Gersten, Barry .... Lido Beach, NY
Gersten, Carol R. .... Miami, FL
Gersten, Charles D. .... **Hartford, CT**
Gersten & Clifford .... **Hartford, CT**
Gersten, David M. .... Miami, FL
Gersten, Eliot B. .... **Hartford, CT**
Gersten, Garth A.
Research Triangle Park, NC
Gersten & Gersten .... **Hartford, CT**
Gersten, Judith L. .... Miami, FL
Gersten, Karen S. .... **Hartford, CT**
Gersten, Martin J. .... **Newtown, CT**
Gersten, Marvin .... **New York, NY**
Gersten, Maurice R. .... **Hartford, CT**
Gersten, Peter A. .... Bronx, NY
Gersten, Peter S. .... West Hartford, CT
Gersten, Richard B. .... **Naples, FL**
Gersten, Sandra Pessin
West Hartford, CT
Gersten, Savage & Kaplowitz, LLP
New York, NY
Gersten, Seymour P. .... Lake Worth, FL
Gersten, Tracey Lessen
San Francisco, CA
Gersten, William A. .... Buffalo, NY
Gersten, William J. .... San Diego, CA
Gerstenberger, Katherine L. .... Deerfield, IL
Gerstenberger, Lois W. .... Douglasville, GA
Gerstenberger, Lois W., P.C.
Douglasville, GA
Gerstenblatt, Jeffrey H. .... Lakewood, NJ
Gerstenblatt, Joel K. .... **Providence, RI**
Gerstenblatt, William .... **Providence, RI**
Gerstenblith, Gary .... Baltimore, MD
Gerstenfeld, David K. .... Portland, OR
Gerstenfeld, Gerald F. .... Encino, CA
Gerstenfeld, Phyllis B. .... Turlock, CA
Gerstenfield, Edward H. .... Bethesda, MD
Gerstenfield, Gary H. .... Silver Spring, MD
Gerstenfield, Gary H., P.C.
Silver Spring, MD
Gerstenfield, Jill
Office of Personnel Management,
Compensation Division, GV
Gerstenhaber, Charna L. .... **New York, NY**
Gerstenhaber, Morris B. .... New York, NY
Gerstenhaber, Murray .... Philadelphia, PA
Gerstenhaber, Suzanne .... Houston, TX
Gerstenslager, William E. .... Cleveland, OH
Gerstenzang, Karen O. .... Albany, NY
Gerstenzang, Michael A. .... **New York, NY**
Gerstenzang, O'Hern, Hickey & Gerstenzang
Albany, NY
Gerstenzang, Peter .... Albany, NY
Gerstenzang, William C. .... **Somerville, NJ**
Gerstin, Joshua G. .... Boca Raton, FL
Gerstl, Arthur J. .... Bridgeport, CT
Gerstl & Gorman, Inc. .... Monterey, CA
Gerstl, Hugo N. .... Monterey, CA
Gerstle, Helene .... Newton, MA
Gerstle, John P., II .... Overland Park, KS
Gerstle, Mark R. .... Columbus, IN
Gerstle, Michael B. .... **Dallas, TX**
Gerstler, Elaine .... Orinda, CA
Gerstman, Alan P. .... Buffalo, NY
Gerstman, Alfred M. .... Monticello, NY
Gerstman & Associates, P.C. .... Phoenix, AZ
Gerstman, Barry L .... **New York, NY**
Gerstman, Carol .... New York, NY
Gerstman, Ellis & McMillin, Ltd.
Chicago, IL
Gerstman, Gary D. .... **Chicago, IL**
Gerstman, George H. .... **Chicago, IL**
Gerstman, Ledina & Kelson .... Monticello, NY
Gerstman, Louis .... **Garden City, NY**
Gerstman, Marc S. .... Averill Park, NY
Gerstman, Peter M. .... Sun Lakes, AZ
Gerstman, Renee B. .... Phoenix, AZ
Gerstman, Sharon Stern .... Buffalo, NY
Gerstmann, Elan .... New York, NY
Gerstmayr, John W. .... **Boston, MA**
Gerstner, Cole J. .... **Zanesville, OH**
Gerstner & Gerstner .... Chicago, IL
Gerstner, Gregory S. .... **Kansas City, MO**
Gerstner, John W. .... Chicago, IL
Gerstner, Joseph P. .... New York, NY
Gerstner, Karen S. .... **Houston, TX**
Gerstner, Kurt B. .... **Boston, MA**
Gerstner, Marguerite E. .... Menlo Park, CA
Gerstner, Mary Anne .... Chicago, IL
Gerstner, Neil M. .... **Walnut Creek, CA**
Gerstner, Paul .... New York, NY
Gerstner Prozinski, Jennifer J.
Washington, DC
Gerston, Marcia E. .... San Jose, CA
Gerstung, Robert J. .... Baltimore, MD
Gersz, Steven R. .... **Rochester, NY**
Gersz, Theodore .... Sylvania, OH
Gertel, Barbara P. .... New York, NY
Gertel, Mark S. .... **Cherry Hill, NJ**
Gertel, Michael L. .... Phoenix, AZ
Gerten, John F. .... St. Paul, MN
Gertenbach, Robert F. .... Fort Lee, NJ
Gertenrich, Alan J. .... Chicago, IL
Gertenstein, Brian .... Beverly Hills, CA
Gerth, Mark D. .... **Indianapolis, IN**
Gertler, Cheryl F. .... **Long Beach, CA**
Gertler, Eric J. .... New York, NY
Gertler, Gary B. .... **Los Angeles, CA**
Gertler, Gertler, Vincent & Plotkin
New Orleans, LA
Gertler, Jonathan E. .... **Mill Valley, CA**
Gertler, Joseph B. .... Lynbrook, NY
Gertler, Louis L. .... **New Orleans, LA**
Gertler, Marc .... Brooklyn, NY
Gertler, Meyer" Mike "H.
New Orleans, LA
Gertler, Richard G. .... **Westbury, NY**
Gertler, Robin Tolmas .... Los Angeles, CA
Gertler, Stephen E. .... Wall Township, NJ
Gertler, Steven D. .... Chicago, IL
Gertler, Tamar D. .... Downey, CA
Gertmenian, Alfred N. .... San Francisco, CA
Gertmenian, Russell M. .... **Columbus, OH**
Gertner, A. Allan .... Baltimore, MD
Gertner & Gertner .... **Bexley, OH**
Columbus, OH
Delaware, OH
Dublin, OH
Hilliard, OH
Lancaster, OH
Marion, OH
Marysville, OH
Newark, OH
Springfield, OH
Upper Arlington, OH
Gertner, Jerome A. .... Lakewood, NJ
Gertner, Marc .... **Toledo, OH**
Gertner, Mark .... South Orange, NJ
Gertner, Michael Avey .... Newport Beach, CA
Gertner, Michael D., (Ltd.) .... Chicago, IL
Gertner, Michael H. .... **Columbus, OH**
Gertner, Nancy .... Boston, MA
Gertner, Nancy B. .... Baltimore, MD
Gertner, Robert
Treasury Department, GV
Gertner, Ross D. .... **Lakewood, NJ**
Gertner, Sean D. .... **Lakewood, NJ**
Gerton, Milford D. .... New York, NY
Gerts, Ronald J. .... Bourbonnais, IL
Gertsen, Deborah N. Owings
Dearborn, MI
Gertsmark, Diana .... **Farmington Hills, MI**
Gertson, Richard G. .... Bethany, OK
Gertz, Aaron S. .... Brooklyn, NY
Gertz, Anthony J. .... Reading, OH
Gertz, Benjamin I. .... New York, NY
Gertz, Bette .... Los Angeles, CA
Gertz, Craig M. .... New York, NY
Gertz, Elizabeth .... Van Nuys, CA
Gertz, Elmer .... Chicago, IL
Gertz, Frederick A. .... **Columbia, SC**
Gertz, Gary D. .... Washington, DC
Gertz, Gregory M. .... Minneapolis, MN
Gertz, Gregory M. .... Greensboro, NC
Gertz, Howard .... Los Angeles, CA
Gertz, Marc P. .... **Akron, OH**
Gertz & Moore .... **Columbia, SC**
Gertz, Paul W. .... **Beaumont, TX**
Gertz, Theodore G. .... **Chicago, IL**
Gertzer, Michael K. .... **New York, NY**
Gertzman, Michael E. .... **New York, NY**
Gertzog, Bethany .... New York, NY
Gertzog, Gary M. .... New York, NY
Gertzog, Marvin .... New York, NY
Gervais, Albert T. .... Huntington, NY
Gervais, David R. .... Crystal Lake, IL
Gervais, Debra Bartle .... **Riverside, CA**
Gervais, Eric B. .... Peabody, MA
Gervais, Marc J. .... **Boston, MA**
Gervais, Wilton E. .... **Bayport, MN**
Gervas, Paul A. .... Department of Energy,
Office of the General Counsel, GV
Gervase, Janice E. .... Fullerton, CA
Gervase, Joseph F., Jr. .... **Buffalo, NY**
Gervase, Lisa C. .... Phoenix, AZ
Gervase, Richard G., Jr. .... **New York, NY**
Gervasi, Gerald T. .... Merion, PA
Gervasi, Jay A., Jr. .... **Greensboro, NC**
Gervasi, Joseph A. .... **Liberty Corner, NJ**
Gervasio, Joseph P., Jr.
Department Of Veterans Affairs,
Board of Veterans Appeals, GV
Gervasio, Michael R. .... **Chicago, IL**
Gervasio, Phyllis Jo .... Washington, DC
Gervasoni, Sharon A. .... Department of Justice,
U. S. Parole Commission, GV
Gervelis, Mark S. .... Youngstown, OH
Gerver, Julie Lefkowitz .... New York, NY
Gerver, Kenneth W. .... **New York, NY**
Gerver, Sheldon J. .... Baldwin, NY
Gervich, Sam .... Marshalltown, IA
Gervin, Edward J. .... Studio City, CA
Gervin, Mary Lawrence .... Jackson, MS
Gervino, Eugene F. .... Burbank, CA
Gervinski, Nancy Lee .... Cleveland, OH
Gerwatowski, Ronald T. .... **Providence, RI**
Gerwig, Robert C. .... Atlanta, GA
Gerwig, William B. .... Charleston, WV
Gerwig, William B., III .... Charleston, WV
Gerwin, Ann W. .... **Cincinnati, OH**
Gerwin, Arthur .... New York, NY
Gerwin, Barbara G.
General Services Administration,
Office of Regional Counsel, GV
Gerwin, Beth H. .... Birmingham, AL
Gerwin, Edward F., Jr. .... **Washington, DC**
Gerwin, Leslie E. .... New York, NY
Gery, Erin Quinn .... **Washington, DC**
Gery, Jeffrey V. .... **Indianapolis, IN**
Gery, William L.
Small Business Administration,
Office of the General Counsel, GV
Gery, Yoav Karel .... **Washington, DC**
Gerzog, Ira David .... New York, NY
Gerzog, Jay E. .... **New York, NY**
Gerzog, Lawrence D. .... **New York, NY**
Gesalman, Robert Mark .... Jeannette, PA
Gesas, E. Barney .... **Salt Lake City, UT**
Gesas, Michael L. .... Chicago, IL
Gesas, Pilati & Gesas, Ltd. .... Chicago, IL
Gesch, John C. .... **West Palm Beach, FL**
Gesch, John C., P.A.
West Palm Beach, FL
Gescheidt, Lise J. .... Providence, RI
Gescheidt, Richard A. .... Boca Raton, FL
Geschickter, Charles F., Jr. .... **Fairfax, VA**
Geschke, John .... **Menlo Park, CA**
Geschke, Richard E. .... Philadelphia, PA
Geschwendt, Mark W. .... **Kalamazoo, MI**
Geschwer, Mark S. .... Fort Lee, NJ
Geschwer, Michael J. .... **New York, NY**
Geschwind, Claudia V.
Bingham Farms, MI
Geschwind, Stephanie B. .... Haworth, NJ
Geschwind, Stuart M. .... **Park Ridge, NJ**
Geschwindt, Richard L. .... Reading, PA
Geselbracht, Thomas F. .... **Chicago, IL**
Gesell, Jeffrey N. .... **Irvine, CA**
Gesell, Marvin H. .... Bloomington, IL
Gesell, Robert E. .... **Troy, MI**
Gesell, Scott L. .... Denver, CO
Gesenhues, George W., Jr. .... New Albany, IN
Geshel, Joseph J. .... Howell, MI
Geshell, R. Steven .... Honolulu, HI
Gesicki, Donald M. .... Roseland, NJ
Gesinger, Gerald A. .... Spokane, WA
Gesinsky, Loren M. .... **New York, NY**
Gesk, Mark J. .... **Pittsburgh, PA**
Geske, Alvin J. .... **Washington, DC**
Geske, James A. .... **St. Paul, MN**
Geske, Janine P. .... Milwaukee, WI
Geske, Kurt D. .... **San Jose, CA**
Geske, Michael R. .... **Washington, DC**

Gesler, Alan E. ... Waukesha, WI
Geslewitz, Irving M. ... Chicago, IL
Gesmer, Ellen ... New York, NY
Gesmer, Jason N. ... Rockford, IL
Gesmer, Lee T. ... Boston, MA
Gesmonde, John M. ... Hamden, CT
Gesmonde Pietrosimone Sgrignari & Pinkus LLC ... Hamden, CT
Gesmundo, Cassandra Evans ... Denver, CO
Gesner, Beth Perovich ... Baltimore, MD
Gesner, Cynthia Farrelly ... Los Angeles, CA
Gesner, Lawrence H. ... Washington, DC
Gesoff, Larry ... Pittsburgh, PA
Gespass, Andrew L. ... Pittsburgh, PA
Gess, Albin H. ... Irvine, CA
Gess, E. Joseph ... Alexandria, VA
Gess, Eric A. ... Spring Valley, NY
Gess, Marvin R. ... Spring Valley, NY
Gess Mattingly & Atchison, P.S.C. Lexington, KY
Gess, Nicholas M. ... Department of Justice, Office of the Deputy Attorney General, GV
Gess, Rebecca T. ... Marietta, GA
Gess, Ruth E. ... Alexandria, MN
Gess, Thomas C. ... Toledo, OH
Gesse, Larry J. ... Franklin, IN
Gessel, Louise M. ... Westborough, MA
Gessel, Patricia Sue ... Key Largo, FL
Gessel, Raymond V. ... Bellevue, WA
Gessel, Thomas O. Department Of Veterans Affairs, Office of the General Counsel, GV
Gesser, David P. ... Garden City, NY
Gesser, Herman J., III ... New Orleans, LA
Gessert, Ann L. ... Okemos, MI
Gessert, Gregory L. ... Okemos, MI
Gessesse, Henock F. ... Palo Alto, CA
Gessford, James B. ... Lincoln, NE
Gessford, Marc C. ... Sacramento, CA
Gessin, Joel B. ... Culver City, CA
Gessler, Charles A. ... Los Angeles, CA
Gessler, George W. ... Chicago, IL
Gessler, Hughes & Socol, Ltd. Chicago, IL; Waukegan, IL; Wheaton, IL
Gessner, Brad ... Youngstown, OH
Gessner, Connie R. ... Wheaton, IL
Gessner, Douglas C. ... Chicago, IL
Gessner, George E. ... Cortland, OH; Warren, OH
Gessner, James J. ... Detroit, MI
Gessner, John B. ... Dallas, TX
Gessner, John F. ... Cortland, OH; Warren, OH
Gessner, John J. ... Bel Air, MD
Gessner, Michael M. ... Philadelphia, PA
Gessner & Platt Co., L.P.A. ... Cortland, OH; Warren, OH
Gessner, William J. ... Washington, DC
Gessow, Eugene I. ... Providence, RI
Gesswein, Kyle W. ... Las Cruces, NM
Gest, Alan B. ... Miami, FL
Gest, Darrell D. ... Austin, TX
Gest, Howard D. ... Los Angeles, CA
Gest, Max ... Los Angeles, CA
Gesten, Samuel J. ... Waltham, MA
Gester, Thomas E. (Tom) ... Birmingham, AL
Geston, Mark S. ... Boise, ID
Gesualdi, James F. ... Melville, NY
Gesualdi, Maria ... Fort Lee, NJ
Gesvi-Sharif, & Associates Los Angeles, CA
Geswein, Mary Frances ... Columbus, OH
Getchell, Charles W., Jr. ... Ipswich, MA
Getchell, Earle Duncan, Jr. Richmond, VA
Getchell, Heidi Ann ... Lowell, MA
Getchell, Marlene Pappas ... San Rafael, CA
Getchell, Richard E. ... Miami, FL
Getchell, Robert J. ... Tulsa, OK
Getchell, Robert J., P.C. ... Tulsa, OK
Getchell, Thomas E. ... Portland, ME
Getches, David H. ... Boulder, CO
Getches, Meredith A. ... Seattle, WA
Getchey, Ronald D. ... San Diego, CA
Getchis, Kelli ... North Reading, MA
Getchius, James J. ... Oshkosh, WI
Getelman, Marcie R. ... Aventura, FL
Getelman, Michael J., P.A. ... Miami, FL
Getgen, Todd Dale ... Harrisburg, PA
Gethers, David D. ... Centerville, IN
Gethers, Latasha A. ... Miami, FL
Getka, Gregory G ... Glen Burnie, MD
Getlan, Howard I. ... Baltimore, MD
Getlan, Louis E. ... Baltimore, MD
Getlan, Myles S. ... Washington, DC
Getler, Janine A. ... Woodcliff Lake, NJ
Getman, Charles W. ... Houston, TX
Getman, Daniel Charles ... New Paltz, NY
Getman, Delbert C. ... Bloomington, MN
Getman, Dennis J. ... Coral Gables, FL
Getman, Franchi, Applegate & Roberts, LLP Ilion, NY
Getman, Frank W. ... Oneonta, NY
Getman, G. Stephen ... Ilion, NY
Getman, George H. ... Ilion, NY
Getman, George J. ... Syracuse, NY
Getman, Jack L. ... Buffalo, NY
Getman, Laurence W. ... Bedford, NH
Getman Law Firm ... Oneonta, NY
Getman, Michael F. ... Oneonta, NY
Getman, Morton J. ... New York, NY
Getman, Robert S. ... Los Angeles, CA
Getman, Robert S. ... New York, NY
Getman, Ross E. ... Arlington, VA
Getman & Selcov ... New Paltz, NY
Getman, Stacey, Tamposi & Steere, P.A. Bedford, NH
Getman, Steven J. ... Ovid, NY
Getman, Willard E. ... Jacksonville, FL
Getman, William H. ... Waterville, NY
Getnick & Getnick ... New York, NY
Getnick, Irving M. ... New York, NY
Getnick Livingston Atkinson Gigliotti & Priore, LLP ... Utica, NY
Getnick, Michael E. ... Utica, NY
Getnick, Neil V. ... New York, NY
Getova, Marija ... Burlington, MA
Getraer, Joseph L. ... New York, NY
Getreu, Joel L. ... New York, NY
Getreu, John H. ... McLean, VA
Getreu, Laura ... New York, NY
Getschel, Milton H. ... Floral Park, NY
Getschman, Gregory J. ... Boston, MA
Getschmann, Andreas M. ... Livonia, MI
Getsinger, J. Scott ... Versailles, KY
Getsinger, John W. ... Minneapolis, MN
Getsinger, K. Kirk ... Birmingham, MI
Getson, Allan ... Philadelphia, PA
Getson, Brian H. ... Philadelphia, PA
Getson, Jerilyn G. ... North Wales, PA
Getson, Lisa ... Philadelphia, PA
Getson, Norman B. ... Hollywood, FL
Getson, Norman B., P.A. ... Hollywood, FL
Gette, Christopher R. ... New York, NY
Gette, H. Jerome ... Dallas, TX
Gette, James D. ... Department of Education, Office of the General Counsel, GV
Gette, Joseph R. ... Pittsburgh, PA
Gettel, James J. ... Mequon, WI
Gettelfinger, Dale L. ... New Albany, IN
Gettelman, Michael ... San Francisco, CA
Getten, Thomas F. ... Miami, FL
Gettens, Francis H. ... Leominster, MA
Gettens, James F. ... Worcester, MA
Getter, Douglas L. ... New York, NY
Getter, Frank H. ... Harrisburg, PA
Getter, Matthew M. ... Chicago, IL
Getter, Stephanie ... Silver Spring, MD
Getting, Jeffrey Scott ... Kalamazoo, MI
Gettinger, Daniel K. ... San Marcos, CA
Gettinger, Ellen ... Decatur, GA
Gettinger, John H. ... Mount Kisco, NY
Gettinger, Martin A. ... New York, NY
Gettinger, Matthew ... San Diego, CA
Gettinger, Robert & Martin Gettinger New York, NY
Gettinger, Robert S. ... La Porte, IN
Gettinger, Robt. S. ... New York, NY
Gettis, Dean M. ... North Miami, FL
Gettis, Marc C. ... Gillette, NJ
Gettle, Donald W. ... Atlanta, GA
Gettle, Gregory E. ... York, PA
Gettle, Gregory H. ... York, PA
Gettle, Jeffrey A. ... York, PA
Gettle, Linda Wade ... Marietta, GA
Gettle & Veltri, Attorneys at Law ... York, PA
Gettle, Willard J. ... Oklahoma City, OK
Gettleman, Chad H. ... Chicago, IL
Gettleman, Jeffrey W. ... Chicago, IL
Gettleman, Robert W. ... Chicago, IL
Gettlemen, Carla Reece Fort Lauderdale, FL
Gettler, Benjamin ... Cincinnati, OH
Gettler & Buckley ... Cincinnati, OH
Gettler, Gail A. ... San Francisco, CA
Gettler, Thomas D. ... New York, NY
Gettleson, Franklin D. ... Bloomfield Hills, MI
Gettleson, Franklin D., P.C. Bloomfield Hills, MI
Gettleson, Scott M. ... Chicago, IL
Gettman, Bruce L., Jr. ... Cedar Falls, IA
Gettman, Hilary J. ... Washington, DC
Gettman, Lowell J., Law Offices of New York, NY
Gettner, Alan ... New York, NY
Getto, Cameron R. ... Southfield, MI
Getto, Charles A. ... Kansas City, KS
Getto, Chas. A. ... Chicago, IL
Getto, David R. ... Southfield, MI
Getts, Ernest J. ... Los Angeles, CA
Getts, Philip W. ... Minneapolis, MN
Getty, Carlton A. ... Lamarque, TX
Getty, Charles A. ... Johnstown, PA
Getty, Charles R., Jr. ... Rome, NY
Getty, Eugene Frederick ... New York, NY
Getty, Frederick J. ... Locust Grove, VA
Getty, Gorman E., III ... Cumberland, MD
Getty, Gregory H. ... Cumberland, MD
Getty, Jas. S. ... Cumberland, MD
Getty, Jeffrey S. ... Cumberland, MD
Getty, Joseph M. ... Hampstead, MD
Getty, Keyser & Mayo, LLP Lexington, KY
Getty, Mary Ann ... Lexington, KY
Getty, Michael Brennan ... Chicago, IL
Getty, Michael G. ... Indianapolis, IN
Getty, Michael L. ... Omaha, NE
Getty, Richard A. ... Lexington, KY
Getty, Rita G. ... Albuquerque, NM
Getty, William C. ... San Diego, CA
Getty, William P. ... Pittsburgh, PA
Gettys, Elmer V., (Co., L.P.A.) Perrysburg, OH
Gettys, John Pressly, Jr. ... Rock Hill, SC
Gettys, Lawrence G. ... Baton Rouge, LA
Gettys, Norbert P. ... Covington, KY
Gettys, Robert P. ... Covington, KY
Gettys, Thomas S. ... Rock Hill, SC
Getz, Alan ... Bel Air, MD
Getz, Bettina ... Chicago, IL
Getz, Brenda S. ... Monte Vista, CO
Getz, Brenda S., P.C. ... Del Norte, CO; Monte Vista, CO
Getz, Brian H. ... San Francisco, CA
Getz, Charles W., IV ... San Francisco, CA
Getz & Crosby, LLP ... San Diego, CA
Getz, Daniel B. ... Brooklyn, NY
Getz, David H. ... San Diego, CA
Getz, David R. ... Harrisburg, PA
Getz, Deborah L. ... Windsor, CO
Getz, Edward R. ... Houston, TX
Getz, Edwin A. ... Chicago, IL
Getz, Floyd T. ... Tyler, TX
Getz, Getz & Getz ... Bel Air, MD
Getz, Gregory J. ... New York, NY
Getz, Herbert A. ... Oak Brook, IL
Getz, Howard I. ... Bronx, NY
Getz, Janette R. ... Hartford, CT
Getz, Jerome L. ... St. Paul, MN
Getz, John B. ... Memphis, TN
Getz, John R. ... Glenarm, MD
Getz, Jon Paul ... Rochester, NY
Getz, Joseph Thaddeus ... Memphis, TN
Getz, Karen ... Riverside, CA
Getz, Michael D. ... Beaumont, TX
Getz, Michael I. ... Albany, NY
Getz, Morton H. ... Bel Air, MD
Getz, Pauline H. G. ... San Diego, CA
Getz, Randal D. ... Baltimore, MD
Getz, Randolph H. ... Sacramento, CA
Getz, Richard D. ... East Hartford, CT
Getz, Stanley ... Bel Air, MD
Getz, Stanley H. ... Woodland Hills, CA
Getz, Stanley H., A Law Corporation Woodland Hills, CA
Getz, Stewart H. ... Bel Air, MD
Getz, Tracy M. ... McLean, VA
Getzels, Morris S. ... Beverly Hills, CA
Getzels, Mortimer ... New York, NY
Getzels, Paul D. ... New York, NY
Getzen, Linda R. ... Sarasota, FL
Getzen, William E. ... Sarasota, FL
Getzendanner, Kevin B. ... Atlanta, GA
Getzendanner, Paul H. ... Chicago, IL
Getzendanner, Susan ... Chicago, IL
Getzendanner, Vincent J., Jr. ... Chicago, IL
Getzin, Gerhardt F. ... Wausau, WI
Getzinger, Sheila K. ... Waitsfield, VT
Getzler, Michael J. ... Uniondale, NY
Getzoff, Alan M. ... New York, NY
Getzoff, Deborah A. ... Tampa, FL
Getzoff & Getzoff ... Chicago, IL
Getzoff, Laurence D. ... Los Angeles, CA
Getzoff, Steven B. ... New York, NY
Getzoff, Timothy P. ... Boulder, CO
Getzoff, William M. ... Chicago, IL
Getzov, Harry J. ... New York, NY
Geudtner, Mark C. ... Toledo, OH
Geurin, Stan ... Dallas, TX
Geurin, Wendy A. ... Memphis, TN
Geurink, Allen J. ... Grand Rapids, MI
Geurtsen, David B. ... Watertown, NY
Geuss, Gary ... Van Nuys, CA
Geuther, Gregory K. ... Chicago, IL
Gevarter, Richard Bert ... Rego Park, NY
Gevarter, Steven M. ... Columbia, MD
Gevas, Constantine G. ... Edison, NJ
Geveden, Charles R. ... Paducah, KY; Wickliffe, KY
Geveden, Charles R., Law Offices Wickliffe, KY
Geveden & Zimmerman ... Paducah, KY
Gever, Neil C. ... Philadelphia, PA
Gever, Stanley E. ... Philadelphia, PA
Gevercer, Steven M. ... Sacramento, CA
Gevers, Marcia B. ... Flossmoor, IL
Gevers, Robert W. ... Fort Wayne, IN
Gevertz, David E. ... Atlanta, GA
Gevertz, John N. ... Roseland, NJ
Gevertz, Leonard ... Miami, FL
Gevertz, Michael A. ... San Francisco, CA
Gevlin, Maureen E. ... Washington, DC
Gevurtz, Franklin ... Sacramento, CA
Gevurtz, Irwin S. ... Redondo Beach, CA
Gevurtz, Menashe, Larson & Howe, P.C. Aloha, OR; Gresham, OR; Portland, OR
Gevurtz, Ronald I. ... Portland, OR
Gewald, Anthony J. W. ... Seattle, WA
Gewanter, George ... Silver Spring, MD
Gewanter, Joel B. ... Hempstead, NY
Gewanter, Stanley M. ... New York, NY
Geweke, Barry D. ... Ord, NE
Gewertz, Martin A., P.C. ... San Antonio, TX
Gewertz, Theodore ... New York, NY
Gewin, James W. ... Birmingham, AL
Gewin, Joe C. ... Biloxi, MS
Gewin, Michael E. ... St. Louis, MO
Gewirtz, Daniel S. ... New York, NY
Gewirtz, Edward D. ... Woodmere, NY
Gewirtz, Elliot ... New York, NY
Gewirtz, Evan ... Queens Village, NY
Gewirtz, Gregory S. ... Westfield, NJ
Gewirtz, Jerry M. ... Tampa, FL
Gewirtz, Joel D. ... Washington, DC
Gewirtz, Michael I. ... Indianapolis, IN
Gewirtz, Paul ... New Haven, CT
Gewirtz, Samuel ... Albany, NY
Gewirtz, Seymour ... New York, NY
Gewirtz, Stanley ... New York, NY
Gewirz, Bernard S. ... Washington, DC
Gewurz, Bennett J. ... Garden City, NY
Gewurz, Zev D. ... Boston, MA
Gex and Artigues ... Waveland, MS
Gex, Gerald C. ... Waveland, MS
Gex, Lucien M., Jr. ... Waveland, MS
Gex, Robert B., IV ... San Francisco, CA
Gex, Walter J., III ... Biloxi, MS
Gey, Steven G. ... Tallahassee, FL
Geyelin, Anthony Allen ... Hatboro, PA
Geyer, Aaron David ... Roseville, MI
Geyer, Bradford L. ... Philadelphia, PA
Geyer, Bruce C. ... Los Angeles, CA
Geyer, Catherine Cordial ... Columbus, OH
Geyer, Donald D. ... Harrisburg, PA
Geyer, Douglas W. ... Springfield, OH
Geyer, George P., Jr. ... Pittsburgh, PA
Geyer, John V. ... Sacramento, CA
Geyer, Joseph B. ... Baltimore, MD
Geyer, Kristen N. Securities and Exchange Commission, Division of Market Regulation, GV
Geyer, Laura Talley ... Washington, DC
Geyer, Margery H. ... East Aurora, NY
Geyer, Mark J. ... Seattle, WA
Geyer, Mark M., (A Prof. Law Corp.) Encino, CA
Geyer, Matthew J. ... San Francisco, CA
Geyer, Melvin R. ... Buffalo, NY
Geyer & Pelkofer ... Pittsburgh, PA
Geyer, R. William ... Thornville, OH; Zanesville, OH
Geyer, Rebecca W. ... Indianapolis, IN
Geyer, Robert N. ... Saginaw, MI
Geyer, Sherry L. ... Los Angeles, CA
Geyer, Strozdas, Pedraza LLP Springfield, OH
Geyer, Thomas H. ... Platteville, WI
Geyer, W. Wyndham, Jr. Fort Lauderdale, FL
Geyerhahn, Benjamin E. ... New York, NY
Geyerman, Cheryl A. ... San Diego, CA
Geyer-Smith, Granice ... Charlotte, NC
Geygan, James J. ... Atlanta, GA
Geygan, Thomas J. ... Cincinnati, OH
Geyman, Matthew ... Seattle, WA
Geymann, John F. ... Grosse Pointe Shores, MI
Geyser, Lewis P. ... Los Angeles, CA
Geyser, Lynne M. ... San Clemente, CA
Geyser, M. Joyce ... Phoenix, AZ
Geyso, Anna M. ... Milwaukee, WI
Geyso, Gerald G. ... Racine, WI
Gezelin, E. Pierre ... Carson City, NV
Gezelin, John J., The Law Offices of Reno, NV
Gezelter, Bertram ... Flushing, NY
Gezon, Debbie J. ... Los Angeles, CA
Gfeller, Alena C. ... Hartford, CT
Gfeller, Charles F. ... Hartford, CT
Gfesser, Michael M. Palm Beach Gardens, FL
Gfoeller, Monica S. ... Sanford, NC
Gfroerer, Michael G. ... Concord, NH
Ghadiali, Zohair M. ... St. Petersburg, FL
Ghadimi, René ... Chicago, IL
Ghaffari, Saeed H. ... San Jose, CA
Ghafouri, Noble N. ... Los Angeles, CA
Ghai Law Firm, The, P.C. ... Atlanta, GA
Ghai, Roger K. ... Atlanta, GA
Ghais, Aaron A. ... Washington, DC
Ghajar, Bobby A. ... Menlo Park, CA
Ghaleb, Jhilmil ... Richfield Springs, NY
Ghaly, Deena R. ... New York, NY
Ghan, Dennis W., (A Professional Corporation) ... Irvine, CA
Ghan, Lisa Ann ... Springfield, MO
Ghan, Patrick M. ... Carson City, NV
Ghandchi, Parvine P. ... Dearborn, MI
Ghandour, Rima I. ... Mission Viejo, CA
Ghantous, Karyne T. ... Oakland, CA
Ghaowi, Zikar ... Highland Beach, FL
Gharabegian, Phillip ... Los Angeles, CA
Gharavi, Hamid G. ... New York, NY
Gharrity, Christopher T. ... Denver, CO
Gharrity, Joseph C. ... San Francisco, CA
Ghartey-Tagoe, Kodwo P. ... Richmond, VA
Ghasemian, Shahram ... Bethesda, MD
Ghassemi, Behzad ... Lansing, MI
Ghastin, Jon Jay ... Portland, OR
Ghattas, Ann E. H. ... Miami, FL
Ghattas, David E. ... Marietta, GA
Ghattas, David E., P.C. ... Marietta, GA
Ghattas, Habeeb ... Flint, MI
Ghauri, Shahid ... Houston, TX
Ghazarians, Ann M. ... Los Angeles, CA
Ghazey, Robert G. ... Northampton, MA
Ghazi, Roya A. ... Louisville, KY
Ghecas, Tony ... Houston, TX
Ghee, M. Douglas ... Anniston, AL
Ghee, Peter H. ... New York, NY
Gheen, E. Pennock ... Seattle, WA
Gheesling, W. Earl ... Denver, CO
Gheewala, Parag ... Kirkland, WA
Ghegan, David W. ... Atlanta, GA
Ghelerter, Susan ... Chicago, IL
Gheleta, Michael A. ... Boulder, CO
Ghelli, Robert L. ... Newark, NJ
Ghen, Gregory S. ... Pennsburg, PA
Ghen, Martin N. ... Doylestown, PA
Ghent, Russell D. ... Greenville, SC
Gherardi, Thomas G. ... Washington, DC
Gherardi, Thomas G., P.C. Washington, DC
Gherardini, Gilio ... Belleville, IL
Gherini, Francis ... Oxnard, CA
Gherlein, David G. General Services Administration, Office of Regional Counsel, GV
Gherlein, Gerald L. ... Cleveland, OH
Gherlein, John H. ... Cleveland, OH
Gherlein, John Mills ... Cleveland, OH
Gherlone, David J., Jr. ... Sparta, NJ
Gherman, Ingrid ... Garden City, NY
Ghertner, Douglas N. ... Kansas City, MO
Gherty & Gherty ... Hudson, WI
Gherty, John E. ... St. Paul, MN
Gherty, Mark J. ... Hudson, WI
Gherty, Susan Schleif ... Hudson, WI

Gherty, Terrence M. ... **Hudson, WI**
Ghess, Benjamin ... Chicago, IL
Ghetti, Michelle La Borde
Baton Rouge, LA
Ghetti, Susan A. ... New York, NY
Ghezzi, Frank Christopher ... Long Beach, NY
Ghezzi, Helen Jean ... Albany, NY
Ghezzi, John J. ... Albany, NY
Ghezzi, John W. ... **Houston, TX**
Ghezzi, June K. ... **Chicago, IL**
Ghezzi, Karen B. ... Cleveland, OH
Ghezzi, Sheryl R. ... Chicago, IL
Ghiardi, Giancarlo M. ... Annapolis, MD
Ghiardi, James D. ... Milwaukee, WI
Ghiassi, Ali ... **Los Angeles, CA**
Ghiassi & Associates ... Orange, CA
Ghiassi, Shafagh Z. ... Orange, CA
Ghiden, Reginald J. ... Boston, MA
Ghidina, Douglas R. ... **Charlotte, NC**
Ghiglieri, Bernard J., Jr. ... Peoria, IL
Toluca, IL
Ghigliotti, Jerome J., Jr. ... Novato, CA
Ghiladi, Kathy S. ... **Washington, DC**
Ghilardi, David J. ... Madison, WI
Ghilardi, Joseph J. ... Romeo, MI
Ghilardi, Louis J. ... **Dearborn, MI**
Ghilardi, Melinda C. ... Dunmore, PA
Ghilardi, Ronald S. ... Chicago, IL
Ghilarducci, Lawrence R., Jr.
Tacoma, WA
Ghim, Marianne M. ... **Portland, OR**
Ghingher, John J., III ... **Baltimore, MD**
Ghio, John V. ... Lafayette, LA
Ghio, Matthew J. ... **St. Louis, MO**
Ghio, Rob S. ... Dallas, TX
Ghionis, Christina ... Tampa, FL
Ghirardelli, Albert J. ... **San Fernando, CA**
Ghiroli, Al ... Branford, CT
Ghiselli, Frank V., Jr. ... **Houston, TX**
Ghiselli, James R. ... **Broomfield, CO**
Ghiselli, Kimberly E. ... **Denver, CO**
Ghiselli, Nicholas ... **Denver, CO**
Ghisu, Edmond J. ... **Cherry Hill, NJ**
Philadelphia, PA
Ghitterman, Allan S. ... Santa Barbara, CA
Ghitterman, Russell R. ... Santa Barbara, CA
Ghiz, Leslie E. ... **Cincinnati, OH**
Ghiz, Theodore H. ... Charleston, WV
Ghiz, Theodore H., Jr. ... **Atlanta, GA**
Ghnouly, Nicholes W. ... Orange, CA
Ghobadi, Parand ... New York, NY
Ghods, Mohammed K. ... Santa Ana, CA
Ghogomu, William T. ... Houston, TX
Gholar, John H. ... Evergreen Park, IL
Gholl, Charles T. ... Minneapolis, MN
Gholson, Angela ... McKinney, TX
Gholson, Hicks & Nichols, A Professional Association ... **Columbus, MS**
Gholson, Hunter M. ... **Columbus, MS**
Gholson, Norman W. ... **Los Angeles, CA**
Gholson & Orr, PLLC ... **Bay Springs, MS**
Laurel, MS
Raleigh, MS
Waynesboro, MS
Gholson, Robert D. ... **Laurel, MS**
Gholston, Robert M. ... Franklin, IN
Gholston, Van C. ... Greenville, AL
Gholz, Charles L. ... **Arlington, VA**
Ghoorah, Charles V. ... **Washington, DC**
Ghoorah, Robert R. ... **Palo Alto, CA**
Ghormley, Susan B. ... **Santa Ana, CA**
Ghorra, Danielle ... **New York, NY**
Ghose, Mony R. ... Naperville, IL
Ghose, Rabindra Nath ... Los Angeles, CA
Ghosh, Arpan Bob ... **New York, NY**
Ghosh, Shubha ... Oklahoma City, OK
Ghosh, Sudevi Navalkar ... **Atlanta, GA**
Ghossein, Dominique M. ... Brooklyn, NY
Ghostlaw, Donald K. ... Springfield, MA
Ghougasian, Paul E. ... **Boca Raton, FL**
West Palm Beach, FL
Ghouralal, Mark J. ... New York, NY
Ghrist, Bruce C. ... **Reston, VA**
Ghyka, Alexander George ... Arlington, VA
Giacalone, Anthony T. ... San Jose, CA
Giacalone, Arthur J. ... East Aurora, NY
Giacalone, David A. ... Rochester, NY
Giacalone, Joseph F. ... Staten Island, NY
Giacalone, Joseph J. ... Hoffman Estates, IL
Giacalone, Robert P. ... St. Paul, MN
Giaccherini, Thomas N. ... Del Mar, CA
Giacchetti, Cynthia ... Chicago, IL
Giacchetto, Thomas A. ... **Boston, MA**
Giacchi, Angelo R. ... **Newark, NJ**
Giacci, Edward R. ... Shelton, CT
Giacci, Edward R., P.C. ... Shelton, CT
Giaccia, Andrew A. ... **Washington, DC**
Giaccio, Anthony ... **New York, NY**
Giaccio, Evelyn D. ... **New York, NY**
Giaccio, Wm. G. ... Jamaica, NY
Giacco, Kyle D. ... **Houston, TX**
Giacco, Richard J. ... Newark, DE
Giaccone, C. Francis
Lake Ronkonkoma, NY
Giaccone, Scott D. ... Lake Ronkonkoma, NY
Giachetti, Thomas D. ... **Princeton, NJ**
Giachino, Michael L. ... Oakland, CA
Giachino, Thomas J. ... **Detroit, MI**
Giacinti, Philip J., Jr. ... **San Diego, CA**
Giacobbe, Anthony I. ... Staten Island, NY
Giacobbe, George W. ... Metairie, LA
Giacobbe, Matthew J. ... **Morristown, NJ**
Giacobbe, Paul M. ... Warwick, RI
Giacobbe, Thomas M. ... Bloomingdale, IL
Giacobetti, Alexander B. ... Philadelphia, PA
Giacoia, Joseph D. ... New York, NY
Giacoletto, Steven C. ... Collinsville, IL
Giacoma, James M. ... Louisville, CO
Giacoma, Mary F. ... **Atlanta, GA**
Giacoma, Peter J., Jr. ... Fort Lauderdale, FL
Giacoma, Peter J., Jr., P.A.
Fort Lauderdale, FL
Giacomarra, Arthur J. ... Worcester, MA
Giacomazza, Michael A. ... **Towson, MD**
Giacometti, Harry J. ... **Westmont, NJ**
Philadelphia, PA
Giacomini, Andrew G. ... **San Francisco, CA**
Giacomini, Anthony L. ... Denver, CO
Giacomini, Edward D. ... Mill Valley, CA
Giacomini, Gary T. ... **San Francisco, CA**
Giacomini, J. Anthony ... **Klamath Falls, OR**
Giacomini, J. Anthony, PC
Klamath Falls, OR
Giacomini, Matthew R. ... **Englewood, CO**
Giacomini, Robert W. ... Sterling, CO
Giacomo, Gallo, Feinstein & Naishtut, LLP
Greenwich, CT
Rye Brook, NY
Giacomo, Paul J., Jr., Law Offices of
New York, NY
Giacomo, William J. ... Greenwich, CT
Rye Brook, NY
Giacomuzzi, Sylvia T. ... Chicago, IL
Giacona, Samuel P. ... **Auburn, NY**
Giacone, Gina M. ... **Indianapolis, IN**
Giacone, Ronald J. ... Benton, IL
Giacone, Ronald J., II ... **Springfield, IL**
Giacopelli, Charles T. ... **Manchester, NH**
Giacoppe, Charles M. ... Worcester, MA
Giacoppo, Erin E. ... **San Francisco, CA**
Giacopuzzi, Julie ... **Los Angeles, CA**
Giacosa, Arturo Jorge ... Miami, FL
Giacovas, Robert A. ... **New York, NY**
Giacumbo, Nancy ... Florham Park, NJ
Giagnorio, Joseph D. ... Bloomingdale, IL
Giagnorio & Robertelli, Ltd.
Bloomingdale, IL
Giaimo, Anthony ... New York, NY
Giaimo, Christopher J., Jr.
Baltimore, MD
Giaimo, Edward P. ... New York, NY
Giaimo, Frank P. ... Chicago, IL
Giaimo, Gerald T. ... **North Haven, CT**
Giaimo, Jennifer A. ... Department of Justice, Tax Division, GV
Giaimo, Michael R. ... Livingston, TN
Giaimo, Michael S. ... **Boston, MA**
Giaimo, Thomas J. ... East Haven, CT
Giaimo, Thomas Vincent ... Red Bank, NJ
Giaimo, V. C. ... Wood Ridge, NJ
Giakas, Kristin A. ... **Wilmington, DE**
Gialanella, Earl F., Jr. ... Binghamton, NY
Gialanella, Kathleen M. ... Cranford, NJ
Giali, Dale J. ... **Los Angeles, CA**
Giallanza, Charles P. ... Snellville, GA
Giallanza, Charles P., P.C. ... Snellville, GA
Giallombardo, Robert A. ... **New York, NY**
Giallonardo, Mark ... Pittsburgh, PA
Giallorenzi, Renato C. ... New York, NY
Gialloreto, Benjamin N. ... Philadelphia, PA
Giallourakis, Bill C. ... Eatontown, NJ
Giallourakis, Bill C., P.C. ... Eatontown, NJ
Giamalis, Peter J. ... Palo Alto, CA
Giamalis, Stacey A. ... Burlingame, CA
Giamanco, Thomas A. ... Ridgewood, NJ
Giambalvo, Allyn Myers ... Clearwater, FL
Giambalvo, Charles J., Jr. ... Philadelphia, PA
Giambalvo, Christine M. ... Jericho, NY
Giambalvo, John ... **New York, NY**
Giambalvo, Joseph J. ... Clearwater, FL
Giambalvo, Leonard ... Bangor, ME
Giambalvo, N. A. Jim ... **Chicago, IL**
Giambanco, Deborah L. ... **Boston, MA**
Giambattista, Luigi ... **West Paterson, NJ**
Giambelluca, Ann Craighead
New Orleans, LA
Giambelluca, Lawrence G.
Baltimore, MD
Giamboi, Jos. N. ... Bronx, NY
Giamboi, Joseph J. ... Bronx, NY
Giamboi, Reiss & Squitieri ... Bronx, NY
Giambona, Frank J. ... Daytona Beach, FL
Giambrone, Anthony, Jr. ... Hackensack, NJ
Giambrone, James P., Jr., Law Offices of
Buffalo, NY
Giambrone, Sullivan & Sullivan
Rolling Meadows, IL
Giambroni, Francis R. ... Oakland, CA
Giambroni, Francis R., P.C. ... Oakland, CA
Giambruno, Deborah J. ... San Mateo, CA
Giambusso, Ann ... New York, NY
Giammalvo, Gregory J. ... Massapequa, NY
Giammanco, Joseph ... Garfield, NJ
Giammarco, Anthony ... Mesa, AZ
Giammarco, Dante J. ... **Providence, RI**
Giammichele, Carla N. ... Washington, DC
Giammittorio, E. Robert ... Alexandria, VA
Giammittorio, Gregory M.
Washington, DC
Giammona, Joseph R. ... Solana Beach, CA
Giampa, Frank J. ... **Fairfax, VA**
Giampa, John J. ... Salisbury, MA
Giampa, Kelly A. ... Chicago, IL
Giampa, Richard L. ... Peekskill, NY
Giampa, Richard L., P.C. ... Peekskill, NY
Giampaoli, Matthew D. ... **San Jose, CA**
Giampaolo, Anthony D. ... Philadelphia, PA
Giampaolo, Joseph ... Bronx, NY
Giampapa, Anthony J., (P.C.) ... Clifton, NJ
Giampapa, Joseph A. ... Columbus, OH
Giampapa, Joseph A., (P.C.) ... Clifton, NJ
Giampetro, Nicholas J. ... Towson, MD
Giampetro, Nicholas J., P.A. ... Towson, MD
Giampetroni, Terri L.
Mount Clemens, MI
Giampetruzzi, Gary F. ... **New York, NY**
Giampiccolo, Raphaela M. ... **New York, NY**
Giampiccolo, Salvatore A. ... **Secaucus, NJ**
Giampietro, Gordon P. ... **Milwaukee, WI**
Giampietro, Nicholas L. ... **Louisville, KY**
Giampietro, Wayne B. ... **Chicago, IL**
Giampoli, Frank J. ... Batavia, IL
Giampolo, Charles H. ... La Mirada, CA
Giampolo, Charles H., A Prof. Corp., Law Offices of ... La Mirada, CA
Giamporcaro, David E.
Environmental Protection Agency, Program Office Attorneys, GV
Giamporcaro, Peter F. ... **Philadelphia, PA**
Giamporcaro, Sharon ... Norristown, PA
Giamportone, Philip ... Oxnard, CA
Giamportone, Susan J. ... Cary, NC
Gianacoplos, Peter S. ... **Groton, CT**
Gianakis, James P. ... **Morristown, NJ**
Gianakos, Bradley ... Hastings, NE
Gianakos, Nancy ... Williston Park, NY
Gianarelli, Shari M. ... Minot, ND
Gianaris, Bill ... Kew Gardens, NY
Gianaris, Ted N. ... St. Louis, MO
Gianas, Peter T. ... **Tucson, AZ**
Gianas, Peter T., P.C. ... **Tucson, AZ**
Gianascol, Christine P. ... **Monterey, CA**
Salinas, CA
Giancana, Anthony V. ... **Phoenix, AZ**
Giancana, Kathleen McKay ... **Phoenix, AZ**
Giancarlo, Angela Elizabeth ... Alexandria, VA
Giancarlo & Gnazzo, A Professional Corporation ... **San Francisco, CA**
Giancarlo, J. Christopher ... **New York, NY**
Giancarlo, Susannah Bochenek
Buffalo, NY
Giancaterino, Robert F. ... **Livingston, NJ**
Giancola, Joseph R. ... Euclid, OH
Giancola, Mark G. ... Anoka, MN
Giancola, Paul J. ... **Phoenix, AZ**
Giancotti, John C. ... Birmingham, MI
Giandomenico, Edward ... Walpole, MA
Giandomenico, Frederick C. ... Walpole, MA
Gianelli, David L. ... **Modesto, CA**
Gianelli & Fores, A Professional Law Corporation ... **Modesto, CA**
Gianelli & Gianelli, P.A. ... Winter Park, FL
Gianelli, James A. ... Sonora, CA
Gianelli, Michael L. ... **Modesto, CA**
Gianelli, Paul ... **Hauppauge, NY**
Gianelli, Penelope M. A. ... Winter Park, FL
Gianelli, Peter A. ... Winter Park, FL
Gianelly, Lisa L. ... **Boston, MA**
Gianesin, Bryan A. ... Irvine, CA
Gianforcaro, Gregory G. ... Chester, NJ
Phillipsburg, NJ
Gianforti, Gary J. ... **Rochester, NY**
Gianfortune, John P. ... Lake Success, NY
Gianfortune, John P., P.C., The Law Office of
Lake Success, NY
Gianfrancesco, Anthony J. ... **Providence, RI**
Gianfrancesco, Paul ... Philadelphia, PA
Giangiordano, Ellen C. K. ... Philadelphia, PA
Giangiordano, Gregory M. ... **Malvern, PA**
Giangiorgi, Richard A. ... **Chicago, IL**
Giangiorgi, Ronald L. ... Chicago, IL
Giangiulio, Peter J. ... Unionville, PA
Giangrande, Thomas M.
White Plains, NY
Giangreco, A. Andrew ... Fairfax, VA
Giangreco, Mark G. ... Albany, NY
Buffalo, NY
Giangrieco & Aliano ... Montrose, PA
Giangrieco, Michael J. ... Montrose, PA
Giangrossi, David M. ... **Chicago, IL**
Giangrosso, Salvadore R. ... Covington, LA
Gianguzi, Charles J., Jr. ... Indio, CA
Gianino, John Anthony ... Scituate, MA
Gianino, Peter T. ... Stuart, FL
Gianino, Richard J. ... **Detroit, MI**
Gianna, Dominic J. ... **New Orleans, LA**
Dallas, TX
Giannakouros, James G. ... Brooklyn, NY
Giannamore, Mark J. ... Los Angeles, CA
Giannamore, Michael ... Indianapolis, IN
New York, NY
Giannantonio, Connie Davis
Bakersfield, CA
Giannantonio, Kenneth M. ... Philadelphia, PA
Giannantonio, Rick C. ... Akron, OH
Giannasca, Nicholas A. ... **New York, NY**
Giannascoli, Anthony D. ... **Exton, PA**
Giannasi, Katherine Kelly
Mechanicsville, VA
Giannasi, Robert A.
National Labor Relations Board, Division of Administrative Law Judges, GV
Giannattasio, Brian E. ... **Washington, DC**
Giannattasio, Camillo R. ... Massapequa, NY
Giannattasio, Edward M. ... Massapequa, NY
Giannattasio, Gerard E. ... Hempstead, NY
Giannattasio, Jennifer Britt ... Washington, DC
Giannattasio, Linda R. ... **New York, NY**
Giannella, Andrew R. ... **Cincinnati, OH**
Giannelli, Joseph A. ... **Chicago, IL**
Giannelli, Karen A. ... **Newark, NJ**
Giannelli, Paul Clark ... Cleveland, OH
Giannelli, Vincenza G. ... Chicago, IL
Gianneschi, Lisa V. ... Snellville, GA
Gianneschi, Lois A. ... Morristown, NJ
Giannetta, Andrea J. ... **Morristown, NJ**
Giannetta, Cathleen ... **New York, NY**
Giannetta, Jaime A. ... Wappingers Falls, NY
Giannetta, Michael A. ... **Scranton, PA**
Giannetti, John A., Jr. ... **Greenbelt, MD**
La Plata, MD
Giannetti, Joseph D. ... **Amsterdam, NY**
Giannetti, Paul D. ... Albany, NY
Giannetti, Paul V. ... Hudson, MA
Giannetti, Thomas L. ... New York, NY
Giannetto, Charles ... Valparaiso, IN
Giannetto, Randal J. ... Marshalltown, IA
Gianni, Alice ... **Madison, NJ**
Gianni, Anthony J., Jr. ... Allendale, NJ
Gianni, Christian ... Las Vegas, NV
Gianni, Laura ... **Beverly Hills, CA**
Gianni, Michelle M. ... **Mystic, CT**
Gianni, Monica Brown ... **Seattle, WA**
Gianni, Origoni & Partners
New York, NY
New York, NY
Gianni, Paul F. ... **Dallas, TX**
Fort Worth, TX
Giannico, Annita ... New City, NY
Giannico, Thomas L. ... Bloomfield Hills, MI
Giannini, A. Joseph ... White Plains, NY
Giannini, Alfred F. ... San Francisco, CA
Giannini, Angela Morcone
White Plains, NY
Giannini, Anthony A., Jr. ... Providence, RI
Giannini, Dante H. ... San Jose, CA
Giannini, David T. ... **San Francisco, CA**
Giannini, Frederick D. O. ... Hilo, HI
Giannini, Gary V. ... San Jose, CA
Giannini, Ivo V. ... West Wyoming, PA
Giannini, John J., (P.C.) ... Detroit, MI
Giannini, Louis ... San Francisco, CA
Giannini, Mary R. ... **Spokane, WA**
Giannini, Matthew C. ... Youngstown, OH
Giannini, Michelle F. ... **Silver Spring, MD**
Giannini, Paul L. ... Beverly Hills, CA
Giannini, Peter E. ... Rancho Mirage, CA
Giannini, Peter W. ... Anchorage, AK
Giannini, Regina M. ... **Menlo Park, CA**
Giannini, Richard, Jr. ... Doylestown, PA
Giannini, Valinoti & Dito, A Professional Corporation ... **San Francisco, CA**
Gianniny, Robert V. ... Rochester, NY
Giannola, Joseph G. ... **New York, NY**
Giannonatti, Reathel ... Minneapolis, MN
Giannone, Anthony R. ... Philadelphia, PA
Giannone, Ernest N. ... East Orange, NJ
Giannone, Patricia B. ... Newport Beach, CA
Giannone, Richard J. ... Chatham, NJ
Giannone, Robert A. ... Tinton Falls, NJ
Giannone, Terrence J. ... **Irvine, CA**
Giannoni, Anthony R. ... Davis, CA
Giannotti, David A. ... **Los Angeles, CA**
Giannotto, Michael S. ... **Washington, DC**
Giannotto, Pamela ... Hackensack, NJ
Giannuario, Philip J. ... **Montclair, NJ**
Giannullo, Joseph M.
Department of Justice, Tax Division, GV
Giannuzzi, Ellen Twomey ... Wellesley, MA
Giannuzzi, J. Gregory ... **Tampa, FL**
Giannuzzi, Nicholas ... New York, NY
Gianola, Barnum & Wigal, L.C.
Morgantown, WV
Gianola, Charles M. ... Vallejo, CA
Gianola, Elizabeth C. ... **Monterey, CA**
Gianola, Frank M. ... **Pittsburgh, PA**
Wheeling, WV
Gianola, James A. ... Morgantown, WV
Gianopoulos, Denise A. Pappas
Albuquerque, NM
Gianopulos, James N. ... Beverly Hills, CA
Gianos, Diane ... **Chicago, IL**
Gianotti, E. F. ... Kailua-Kona, HI
Gianoulakis, John ... **St. Louis, MO**
Gianquinto, J. J. ... Bakersfield, CA
Giansante, Louis ... **Mount Laurel, NJ**
Philadelphia, PA
Giansante, Mark P. ... Buffalo, NY
Giansello, John D., III ... **New York, NY**
Gianti, Carmine A. ... Blue Bell, PA
Giantomasi, Francis J. ... Newark, NJ
Giantonio, Brian A. ... **Hartford, CT**
Giantris, Laura A. ... **Baltimore, MD**
Gianturco, Elizabeth Jordan
Department Of Health And Human Services, Office of the General Counsel, GV
Gianturco, Mary Ellen ... New York, NY
Gianuglou, C. Dino ... Dayton, OH
Gianuglou, Dankof, Caras & Skelton
Dayton, OH
Gianulis, James T. ... San Diego, CA
Gianunzio, DeSantis & Schweinberger, LLP
Oakland, CA
Gianunzio, Michael J. ... Everett, WA
Gianunzio, Victor J. ... **Oakland, CA**
Gianvito, Nicholas A. ... **Punxsutawney, PA**
Giappone, Paul ... **New York, NY**
GiaQuinta, Mark E. ... **Fort Wayne, IN**
Giaquinto, Daniel G. ... Trenton, NJ
Giaquinto, Gregg R. ... New York, NY
Giaramita, Joseph, Jr. ... Brooklyn, NY
Giard, David M. ... Winter Park, FL
Giard, Herve J., Jr. ... Palmer, MA
Giardiello, Francis R. ... Paterson, NJ
Giardiello, Jon F. ... Wayne, NJ
Giardiello, Michael C. ... **Wellesley, MA**
Giardina, Anthony ... Albany, NY
Giardina, David C. ... **Chicago, IL**
Giardina, Giovanna Trocchi
Waterbury, CT
Giardina, Jay A. ... Pine Plains, NY
Giardina, Jeffry A. ... Millerton, NY
Giardina, Jerry ... **New York, NY**
Giardina, Lawrence P. ... Brooklyn, NY
Giardina, Lawrence S. ... **Sacramento, CA**
Giardina, Marie J. ... **San Francisco, CA**
Giardina, Michael A. ... Southbury, CT
Giardina, Nancy L. ... Syracuse, NY
Giardina, Scott M. ... New York, NY
Giardini, Anthony B. ... Lorain, OH
Giardino, John J. ... **Buffalo, NY**
Fredonia, NY

Giardino, Richard ... Miami, FL
Pompano Beach, FL
Giardino, Richard C. ... Johnstown, NY
Giardino & Schober ... Fredonia, NY
Buffalo, NY
Giarla, Pamela J. ... Rockville, MD
Giarla, William F. ... Pittsburgh, PA
Giarmarco, Julius H. ... Detroit, MI
Troy, MI
Giarniero, Richard P. ... Stratford, CT
Giarrano, Leonard ... Laurel, FL
Giarratana, Mark D. ... Hartford, CT
Giarratana, Salvatore A. ... Darien, CT
Giarratano, Peter F. ... Norwalk, CT
Giarrusso, Joe, Jr. ... New Orleans, LA
Giarrusso, Lea M. ... New Orleans, LA
Giarrusso, Michael G. ... Milton, MA
Giarrusso, Peter J. ... Baton Rouge, LA
Giarrusso, Robert L. ... Falls Church, VA
Giarrusso, Roy P. ... Quincy, MA
Giasi, Joseph P., Jr. ... New York, NY
Giasullo, Robert J. ... West Orange, NJ
Giatras, Troy N. ... Charleston, WV
Giatras & Webb ... Charleston, WV
Giattina, A. Theodore ... Fair Oaks, CA
Giattina, Anna Lee ... Birmingham, AL
Giauque, Brent J. ... Salt Lake City, UT
Giauque, Crockett, Bendinger & Peterson, A Professional Corporation
Salt Lake City, UT
Giauque, Cyndy ... Fort Collins, CO
Giauque, Richard W. ... Salt Lake City, UT
Giava, John S. ... Newark, NJ
Giba, Paul R. ... Upper St. Clair, PA
Gibaitis, John A. ... Chicago, IL
Gibala, Dennis ... Boise, ID
Gibala, Edw. S. ... Urbana, IL
Gibaldi, Laurel ... White Plains, NY
Gibans, David M ... Denver, CO
Gibart, Joseph G. ... Milwaukee, WI
Gibas, Allen H. ... Minneapolis, MN
Gibas, Allen H., P.A. ... Minneapolis, MN
Gibau-Heyman, Sharyn ... New York, NY
Gibb, Colin R. ... Pearisburg, VA
Gibb, J. Mark ... Salt Lake City, UT
Gibb, Jeffrey B. ... Cherry Hill, NJ
Gibb, Matthew Alan ... Rochester, MI
Gibb, Nancy E. ... Fairfax, VA
Gibb, Robert D. ... Carson City, NV
Gibb, Ryan Edward ... Salem, OR
Gibb, Steven Paul ... Bowie, MD
Gibbar, Kenneth G. ... Fort Collins, CO
Gibbard, Elaine ... Sulphur, OK
Gibbard, Frank ... Sulphur, OK
Gibbard, Gibbard & Wade ... Sulphur, OK
Gibbard, H. Frank, III ... Denver, CO
Gibbel, John R. ... Lancaster, PA
Lititz, PA
Gibbel, Kraybill & Hess ... Lancaster, PA
Lititz, PA
Gibbens, Blackwell & Stevens
New Iberia, LA
Gibbens, Daniel G. ... Norman, OK
Gibbens, Erin ... Dallas, TX
Gibbens, J. Bruce ... Cando, ND
Gibbens, J. Louis ... New Iberia, LA
Gibbens, James C. ... Oklahoma City, OK
Gibbens, Kimberly K. ... Jefferson City, MO
Gibbens Law Office ... Cando, ND
Gibbens, Lisa Beckstrom ... Cando, ND
Gibbens, Michael J. ... Tulsa, OK
Gibbens, Michelle L. ... Tulsa, OK
Gibbens, Wayne ... Washington, DC
Gibbens, William B., III
New Orleans, LA
Gibber, Allan J. ... Baltimore, MD
Gibbert, Floyd V. ... Macon, GA
Gibbes, Asbury H. ... Columbia, SC
Gibbes, C. Denton ... Laurel, MS
Gibbes, Charles W. ... Hilton Head Island, SC
Gibbes, Elizabeth D. ... Charlotte, NC
Gibbes, Frank H., III ... Greenville, SC
Gibbes, Gallivan, White & Boyd, P.A.
Anderson, SC
Greenville, SC
Spartanburg, SC
Gibbes, Garland V. ... Greensboro, NC
Gibbes Graves Mullins Hortman Harlow Martindale & Jones, PLLC ... Laurel, MS
Gibbes, Joseph A. ... Columbia, SC
Gibbes, Laura Limerick ... Jackson, MS
Gibbes Law Firm, P.A. ... Columbia, SC
Gibbes, William H. ... Columbia, SC
Gibbin, James H. ... Springville, NY
Gibbins, Bob ... Austin, TX
Gibbins, Steven, Law Offices of
Austin, TX
Gibble, Sherrie L. ... Trenton, NJ
Gibble, Stephen R. ... Lititz, PA
Gibbon & Associates, P.A. ... Okmulgee, OK
Tulsa, OK
Gibbon, C. Gilpin ... Bryn Mawr, PA
Gibbon, Christopher L. ... Cleveland, OH
Gibbon, Daniel ... Philadelphia, PA
Gibbon, David O. ... Salt Lake City, UT
Gibbon, Denise Hargleroad
Westhampton Beach, NY
Gibbon, E. Johanna ... Newark, NJ
Gibbon, Frederick B. ... Washington, DC
Gibbon, Gibbon & Sheline ... Harlingen, TX
Gibbon, John H. ... Cleveland, OH
Gibbon, John R., Jr. ... Buffalo, NY
Gibbon, John T. ... Portland, OR
Gibbon, John W., II ... Lyons, NY
Gibbon, Kara L. ... Charlotte, NC
Gibbon, Karen L. ... Seattle, WA
Gibbon, Karen L., P.S. ... Seattle, WA
Gibbon, Karl M. (Mac), Jr. ... Harlingen, TX
Gibbon & Lord ... Lyons, NY
Gibbon, Patricia L. ... Palo Alto, CA
Gibbon, Richard D. ... Okmulgee, OK
Tulsa, OK
Gibbon, Thomas R. ... Washington, DC
Gibboney, Allen E. ... Altoona, PA
Gibboney, Margaret A. ... Altoona, PA
Gibbons, A. Joseph ... Ithaca, NY
Gibbons, Adrienne M. ... Boston, MA
Gibbons, Alan Dean ... Boca Raton, FL
Gibbons, Anna M. ... Ware, MA
Gibbons & Associates ... Seattle, WA
Gibbons, Austin J. ... Chicago, IL
Gibbons, Austin R. ... Indian Wells, CA
Walnut Creek, CA
Gibbons, Boyd H., III ... Washington, DC
Gibbons, Bradley V. ... Las Vegas, NV
Gibbons, Brian J. ... Baltimore, MD
Gibbons, Brian M. ... Chester, SC
Gibbons, Buckley & Palmer, P.C.
Media, PA
Gibbons & Burke, P.C. ... Scotia, NY
Gibbons, Carlos W., Jr. ... Columbia, SC
Gibbons, Carol A. ... New York, NY
Gibbons, Carol Rick ... Richmond, VA
Gibbons, Charles B. ... Pittsburgh, PA
Gibbons, Charles G. ... Rockport, TX
Gibbons, Chico F. ... New York, NY
Gibbons, Christopher J. ... Chicago, IL
Gibbons, Cozart, Jones, Hughes, Sallenger & Taylor ... Wilson, NC
Gibbons, Daniel Bay ... Salt Lake City, UT
Gibbons, Daniel J. ... Newark, NJ
Gibbons, David A. ... Washington, DC
Gibbons, David H. ... Columbia, MO
Gibbons, David J. ... Park Ridge, IL
Gibbons, David L. ... Russellville, AR
Gibbons, David T. ... Baltimore, MD
Gibbons & Day ... Decatur, AL
Huntsville, AL
Gibbons, De Grant ... Aiken, SC
Gibbons, Debra Zidich ... Sacramento, CA
Gibbons, Del Deo, Dolan, Griffinger & Vecchione, A Professional Corporation
Newark, NJ
New York, NY
Gibbons, Diane E. ... Doylestown, PA
Gibbons, Earle J. ... Bakersfield, CA
Gibbons, Edward F. ... Williamsville, NY
Gibbons, Edward, Jr. ... Philadelphia, PA
Gibbons, Edward P. ... Chicago, IL
Gibbons, Edward Paul ... Savannah, GA
Gibbons, Elmer G., III, (P.C.)
New Orleans, LA
Gibbons, F. Clifford ... Princeton, NJ
Gibbons, Florence B. ... Uniondale, NY
Gibbons, Francis B. ... Kew Gardens, NY
Gibbons, Francis E., (Mr.) ... Miami, FL
Gibbons, Frederick J. ... Marysville, CA
Gibbons, G. Hunter ... Sarasota, FL
Gibbons, Gary A. ... Tampa, FL
Gibbons, Gerald R. ... Camden, NJ
Gibbons & Gibbons, P.C. ... Kirkwood, MO
Gibbons, Glenn M. ... Santa Barbara, CA
Gibbons, Gregg Clarke ... Scottsdale, AZ
Gibbons, Gregg Clarke, P.C.
Scottsdale, AZ
Gibbons, Gregg M. ... Orange, CA
Gibbons, Harry J., Jr. ... Sacramento, CA
Gibbons, H. F. Thomas ... Little Rock, AR
Gibbons, Hugh ... Concord, NH
Gibbons, Hugh E. ... Clayton, MO
Gibbons, James A. ... Clinton, MA
Gibbons, James A. ... Reno, NV
Gibbons, James A. ... Scranton, PA
Gibbons, James C. ... Treasury Department, Internal Revenue Service, GV
Gibbons, James E. ... Long Beach, CA
Gibbons, James T., (P.C.)
New Brunswick, NJ
Gibbons, Janice Gay ... San Diego, CA
Gibbons, Jason M. ... Cleveland, OH
Gibbons, Jean M. ... Washington, DC
Gibbons, Jeffrey F. ... Cape May, NJ
Gibbons, John B. ... Cleveland, OH
Gibbons, John B. ... Westlake, OH
Gibbons, John Blain ... Tampa, FL
Gibbons, John C. ... San Francisco, CA
Gibbons, John D. ... Mobile, AL
Gibbons, John F. ... Chicago, IL
Gibbons, John F. ... New York, NY
Gibbons, John G. ... Troy, MI
Gibbons, John G., P.C. ... Troy, MI
Gibbons, John J. ... Los Angeles, CA
Gibbons, John J. ... Newark, NJ
Gibbons, John P. ... Edwardsville, IL
Gibbons, John P. ... Dedham, MA
Gibbons, John P. ... New York, NY
Gibbons, John P., Jr. ... Garden City, NY
Gibbons, John T. ... Minnetonka, MN
Gibbons, John W. ... Milton, MA
Gibbons, Johnny O. ... Anchorage, AK
Gibbons, Jon A. ... Fort Lauderdale, FL
Gibbons, Joseph F. ... Albany, NY
Gibbons, Joseph G. ... Philadelphia, PA
Gibbons, Joseph P. ... Needham, MA
Gibbons, Joseph T. ... New York, NY
Gibbons, Joseph T., Jr. ... Santa Ana, CA
Gibbons, Joseph W. ... Springfield, VA
Gibbons, Julia S. ... Memphis, TN
Gibbons, Kathleen ... Washington, DC
Gibbons, Kenneth T. ... Scotia, NY
Gibbons, Kenneth W. ... Schenectady, NY
Gibbons, Kevin M. ... Mesa, AZ
Gibbons, Kirk M. ... Tampa, FL
Gibbons, Kristel G. ... Birmingham, AL
Gibbons, Kristel N. ... Birmingham, AL
Gibbons, Kristen Paulson
Minneapolis, MN
Gibbons, Kristin S. ... Georgetown, DE
Gibbons Law Firm, A Professional Association
Russellville, AR
Gibbons, Lees & Conley ... Indian Wells, CA
Walnut Creek, CA
Gibbons, Lemuel H., III ... Raleigh, NC
Gibbons, Leo M. ... West Chester, PA
Gibbons, Leonard E. ... Holyoke, MA
Gibbons, L. H. ... Wilson, NC
Gibbons, Linda Case ... Scotch Plains, NJ
Gibbons, Lisa M. ... New York, NY
Gibbons, Llewellyn J. ... Toledo, OH
Gibbons, M. Colette ... Cleveland, OH
Gibbons, Margaret M. ... Piscataway, NJ
Gibbons, Maria Etzrodt ... Blue Bell, PA
Gibbons, Marion H. ... Houston, TX
Gibbons, Mark H. ... Tampa, FL
Gibbons, Mark L. ... Dallas, TX
Gibbons, Mark T. ... Cleveland, OH
Gibbons, Mark W. ... Las Vegas, NV
Gibbons, Marlene F. ... Department of Justice, Civil Division, GV
Gibbons, Mary Anne
United States Postal Service, Office of the Deputy General Counsel, GV
Gibbons, Mary E. ... Englewood, CO
Gibbons, Mary Lourdes
Fort Washington, PA
Gibbons, Mary T. ... Boston, MA
Gibbons, Matthew R. ... Miami, FL
Gibbons, Maureen S. ... Philadelphia, PA
Gibbons, Melendi and Garcia
Tallahassee, FL
Gibbons, Melendi, Gibbons and Garcia
Washington, DC
Tampa, FL
Gibbons, Michael ... Kirkwood, MO
Gibbons, Michael C. ... Bloomfield Hills, MI
Gibbons, Michael D. ... Lee's Summit, MO
Gibbons, Michael P. ... Minden, NV
Gibbons, Michael R. ... Orlando, FL
Gibbons, Michael R. ... Kirkwood, MO
Gibbons, Michael T. ... Omaha, NE
Gibbons, Monica H. ... Cary, IL
Gibbons, Nancy A. ... Walnut Creek, CA
Gibbons, Patricia McAdams
Lynchburg, VA
Gibbons, Patrick J. ... Philadelphia, PA
Gibbons, Paul A. ... Baltimore, MD
Gibbons, Paul C. ... Chicago, IL
Gibbons, Paul L. ... Camden, ME
Gibbons, Philip J., Jr. ... Indianapolis, IN
Gibbons, Phillip E. ... Roseville, CA
Gibbons, Phillip E., Inc., A Law Corporation
Roseville, CA
Gibbons, Rachel K. ... Port Washington, NY
Gibbons, Ray D. ... Birmingham, AL
Gibbons, Richard E. ... Berea, OH
Gibbons, Richard F., Jr. ... Stafford, VA
Gibbons, Richard M. ... Boston, MA
Gibbons, Richard S. ... Westport, CT
Gibbons, Robert B. ... Worcester, MA
Gibbons, Robert G. ... New York, NY
Gibbons, Robert J. ... New York, NY
Gibbons, Robert R. ... Dallas, TX
Gibbons, Roger M. ... Osage Beach, MO
Gibbons, Sam M. ... Washington, DC
Tampa, FL
Gibbons, Sean M. ... Richmond, VA
Gibbons, Sheila M. ... Los Angeles, CA
Gibbons, Shelagh A ... Boston, MA
Gibbons, Smith, Cohn & Arnett, A Professional Association ... Tampa, FL
Gibbons, Stephen P. ... San Jose, CA
Gibbons, Steven V. ... Seattle, WA
Gibbons, Susan M. ... San Francisco, CA
Gibbons, Susanna K. ... Raleigh, NC
Gibbons, Theresa ... Seattle, WA
Gibbons, Theresa M. ... Burlington, VT
Gibbons, Thomas ... New York, NY
Gibbons, Thomas A. ... Chicago, IL
Gibbons, Thomas C. ... Wilkes-Barre, PA
Gibbons, Thomas D. ... Bowie, MD
Gaithersburg, MD
Gibbons, Thomas R. ... Hartford, CT
Gibbons, Timothy J. ... Willowick, OH
Gibbons, Timothy M. ... Chattanooga, TN
Gibbons, Toni L. ... Castro Valley, CA
Gibbons, Tucker, Miller, Whatley & Stein, A Professional Association ... Tampa, FL
Gibbons, Virginia L.
Environmental Protection Agency, Office of Congressional and Legislative Affairs, GV
Gibbons, Walter F. ... Bristol, RI
Providence, RI
Gibbons, William E. ... Philadelphia, PA
Gibbons, William E. ... Paris, TX
Gibbons, William J. ... Chicago, IL
Gibbons, William J. ... Winnetka, IL
Gibbons, William J. ... Rockville, MD
Gibbons, William J. ... Cooperstown, NY
Gibbons, William J. ... Portland, OR
Gibbons, William J. ... Caldwell, TX
Gibbons, William J., Jr. ... Decatur, AL
Huntsville, AL
Gibbons, William L. ... Memphis, TN
Gibbons, William M. ... Rancho Cordova, CA
Gibbons, William P. ... Cleveland, OH
Gibbons, William Thomas ... New York, NY
Gibbons, Wyatt N. ... Kew Gardens, NY
Gibbons-Shapiro, James ... San Jose, CA
Gibbs, Ander P. ... Dade City, FL
Tampa, FL
Gibbs, Andrew J. ... Livingston, NJ
Gibbs, Ann S. ... Richmond, VA
Gibbs, Anthony W. ... Redwood City, CA
Gibbs, Arnold J. ... Baton Rouge, LA
Gibbs, Arthur E., III ... Cleveland, OH
Gibbs & Associates, P.A.
St. Petersburg, FL
Gibbs, B. Gray ... St. Petersburg, FL
Gibbs, Barbara ... Westwood, MA
Gibbs, Brad L. ... Woodstock, GA
Gibbs, Brent J. ... St. Petersburg, FL
Gibbs & Bressler ... New York, NY
Gibbs & Bruns, L.L.P. ... Houston, TX
Gibbs, Bud H. ... New York, NY
Gibbs, Carolyn D. ... Detroit, MI
Gibbs, Charles A., III ... Tulsa, OK
Gibbs, Charles F. ... New York, NY
Gibbs, Charles H., Jr. ... Charleston, SC
Gibbs, Charles I. ... Sacramento, CA
Gibbs, Charles R. ... Dallas, TX
Gibbs, Coming B., Jr. ... Charleston, SC
Gibbs, Craig ... Jacksonville, FL
Gibbs & Craze ... Seminole, FL
Menlo Park, CA
Cleveland, OH
Gibbs, Daniel L. ... Peachtree City, GA
Gibbs, Danielle B. ... Wilmington, DE
Gibbs, David C., III ... Seminole, FL
Gibbs, David C., Jr. ... Cleveland, OH
Gibbs, David H., (P.C.) ... Boston, MA
Gibbs, David L. ... San Clemente, CA
Gibbs, David R. ... Lancaster, OH
Gibbs, Deborah P. ... Baton Rouge, LA
Gibbs, Delbert L. ... Dallas, TX
Gibbs, Delinda L. ... Jasper, TX
Gibbs, Edward C., Jr. ... Lanham, MD
Gibbs, Elizabeth A. ... Richmond, VA
Gibbs, Ellen Mills ... Fort Lauderdale, FL
Gibbs, Eppsteiner & Stagg, A P.C.
Irvine, CA
San Diego, CA
Temecula, CA
Gibbs, Eric H. ... San Francisco, CA
Gibbs, Eric P. ... Orlando, FL
Gibbs, Eugene A., Jr ... Corpus Christi, TX
Gibbs, Feyder, Myers, Peters & Hoffman
Sioux Falls, SD
Gibbs, Frank P. ... Sioux Falls, SD
Gibbs, Frederick W. ... Pemberton, NJ
Gibbs, Garry R. ... Federal Trade Commission, Bureau of Competition, GV
Gibbs, Gary E. ... Petaluma, CA
Gibbs, Gary M. ... Henderson, KY
Gibbs, Gary M., P.S.C. ... Henderson, KY
Gibbs, George ... Tulsa, OK
Gibbs, George L. ... Metairie, LA
Gibbs, Gerald R. ... San Clemente, CA
Gibbs, Gerald W. ... Muskegon, MI
Gibbs, Giden, Locher & Turner LLP
Los Angeles, CA
Gibbs, Gregory T., Law Office of
Flint, MI
Gibbs, Greta E. ... Portland, OR
Gibbs & Haller ... Lanham, MD
Gibbs, Hallie H., II ... Jefferson City, MO
Gibbs, Harold J. ... Akron, OH
Gibbs & Holmes ... Charleston, SC
Gibbs Houston Pauw ... Seattle, WA
Gibbs, Howard J. ... El Paso, TX
Gibbs, J. David ... Hartford, CT
Gibbs, J. David ... Boston, MA
Gibbs, J. Gordon, Jr. ... Danville, IN
Gibbs, Jack Gilbert, Jr. ... Columbus, OH
Gibbs, James D. ... Anoka, MN
Gibbs, James David ... Arlington, VA
Gibbs, James F., Jr ... Lawrenceburg, KY
Gibbs, James L., II ... Oklahoma City, OK
Gibbs, James M. ... Chicago, IL
Gibbs, James S., Jr. ... Winston-Salem, NC
Gibbs, Jeanine L. ... Atlanta, GA
Gibbs, Jeffrey J. ... Department of State, Office of the Legal Adviser, GV
Gibbs, Jeffrey L. ... Washington, DC
Gibbs, Jeffrey N. ... Washington, DC
Gibbs, Jo Ann ... Las Vegas, NV
Gibbs, John ... Montgomery, AL
Gibbs, John F. ... Minneapolis, MN
Gibbs, John M. ... Demopolis, AL
Gibbs, John R. ... Honolulu, HI
Gibbs, Joseph A. ... Indian Wells, CA
Gibbs, Joseph A. ... Palm Springs, CA
Gibbs, Joseph C. ... Clarksdale, MS
Gibbs, Joseph W. ... Nashville, TN
Gibbs, Julia D.
Department Of Health And Human Services, GV
Gibbs, Julia P. ... El Dorado Hills, CA
Gibbs, Kaija ... Orinda, CA
Denver, CO
Gibbs, Karen A. ... Cupertino, CA
Gibbs, Kathy Adams ... Miami, FL
West Palm Beach, FL
Gibbs, Kenneth C. ... Los Angeles, CA
Gibbs, Kevin B. ... Orange, CA
Gibbs, Kirk G. ... Salt Lake City, UT
Gibbs, Kirstin E. ... Washington, DC
Gibbs, L. Martin ... New York, NY
Gibbs, Larry W., (P.C.) ... San Antonio, TX
Gibbs Law Firm, The, A Prof. Corp.
San Clemente, CA
Gibbs Law Office, P.C.
Jefferson City, MO
Gibbs, Lawrence A. ... Berkeley, CA
Gibbs, Lawrence A. ... Columbus, OH
Gibbs, Lawrence B. ... Washington, DC
Gibbs, Lendon D. ... Atlanta, GA
Gibbs, Linda F. ... Geneseo, NY
Gibbs, Linda I. ... New York, NY
Gibbs, Margaret R. ... Orange Park, FL
Gibbs, Margaret R. ... Chicago, IL

Gibbs, Marie E. ... Charlotte, NC
Gibbs, Martha E. ... Phoenix, AZ
Gibbs, Mary Catherine H. ... Vienna, VA
Gibbs, Mary M. ... Akron, OH
Gibbs, Max W. ... Broomall, PA
Gibbs, Meredith E. ... Baltimore, MD
Gibbs, Michael C. ... Dallas, TX
Gibbs, Michael T. ... Temecula, CA
Gibbs, Mike D. ... Dallas, TX
Gibbs, Mitchell W. ... New Orleans, LA
Gibbs, Nancy J. ... Naples, FL
Gibbs, Nancy Patricia ... Miami, FL
Gibbs, Pamela A. ... Department of Labor, Office of the Solicitor, GV
Gibbs, Pamela R. ... New Orleans, LA
Gibbs & Parnell, P.A. ... Dade City, FL
Gibbs & Parnell, P.A. ... Tampa, FL
Gibbs, Patricia E. ... Sycamore, IL
Gibbs, Patrick ... Chicago, IL
Gibbs, Patrick J. ... Long Beach, CA
Gibbs, Patrick J. ... Roswell, GA
Gibbs, Patrick J., P.C. ... Roswell, GA
Gibbs, Paula S. ... New York, NY
Gibbs, R. Clifton ... Columbus, OH
Gibbs, R. Nathan ... Las Vegas, NV
Gibbs, Randel B. ... Dallas, TX
Gibbs, Rebecca ... New York, NY
Gibbs, Richard F. ... Wellesley, MA
Gibbs, Richard O. ... Frederick, MD
Gibbs, Richard O., P.A. ... Frederick, MD
Gibbs, Richard P., & Associates
North Canton, OH
Gibbs, Richard S. ... Milwaukee, WI
Gibbs, Robert G. ... Georgetown, DE
Gibbs, Robert H. ... Seattle, WA
Gibbs, Robert L. ... Jackson, MS
Gibbs, Robert L. ... Bedminster, NJ
Gibbs, Robert S. ... Thousand Oaks, CA
Gibbs, Robin C. ... Houston, TX
Gibbs, Ronald W. ... Grand Junction, CO
Gibbs, Sandra G. ... Washington, DC
Gibbs, Sanford M. ... Anchorage, AK
Gibbs and Schwartzman ... San Antonio, TX
Gibbs & Sellers ... Demopolis, AL
Gibbs, Stephen ... San Jose, CA
Gibbs, Stephen M. ... Decatur, GA
Gibbs, Steven G. ... Bakersfield, CA
Gibbs, Steven Howard ... Minneapolis, MN
Gibbs, Susan ... Santa Fe, NM
Gibbs, Susan P. ... San Francisco, CA
Gibbs, Thomas E. ... Irvine, CA
Gibbs, Thomas E. ... Chicago, IL
Gibbs, Thomas E. ... Baton Rouge, LA
Gibbs, Thomas E., Jr.
Rolling Hills Estates, CA
Gibbs, Thomas Edward ... Jacksonville, FL
Gibbs, Timothy J. ... San Clemente, CA
Gibbs, Travis C. ... Los Angeles, CA
Gibbs, Tyrus C. ... Monroe, LA
Gibbs, Vance A. ... Baton Rouge, LA
Gibbs, W. Joseph ... Springfield, IL
Gibbs, W. Tucker ... Miami, FL
Gibbs, William C. ... Salt Lake City, UT
Gibbs, William D. ... Hayward, CA
Gibbs, William D. ... Oakland, CA
Gibbs, William D. ... Treasury Department, Internal Revenue Service, GV
Gibbs, William E. ... Seattle, WA
Gibbs, William G. ... Salt Lake City, UT
Gibbs, William W. ... Miami, FL
Gibbs-Cunningham, Sheila ... Chicago, IL
Gibbs-Roumeliotis, Pamela Elizabeth
Longmeadow, MA
Gibb-Welch, Roberta ... San Diego, CA
Gibby, Daniel J. ... Tampa, FL
Gibby, Daniel J., P.A. ... Tampa, FL
Gibby, Darin J. ... Denver, CO
Gibeau, Randall R. ... Atlanta, GA
Gibeault, Patricia M. ... Madison, WI
Gibeaut, Gary R. ... Los Angeles, CA
Gibeaut, Greg W. ... Los Angeles, CA
Gibeaut, Mahan & Briscoe
Los Angeles, CA
Gibeaut, Randy A. ... Newport Beach, CA
Gibel, Keith S. ... Oceanside, NY
Gibelli, Stephen ... Phoenix, AZ
Giberga, Jill A. ... New Orleans, LA
Giberga, Samuel A. ... New Orleans, LA
Giberson, Jack B. ... Austin, TX
Giberson, Kevin S. ... Watsonville, CA
Giberson, Kirk E. ... Sacramento, CA
Giberson, Laura A. ... Sacramento, CA
Giberstone, Leah E. ... Woodbury, NY
Gibert, Hugh W. ... Atlanta, GA
Gibert, James M., III ... Davidson, NC
Gibert, James Waring ... Kennesaw, GA
Gibian, Craig J. ... Washington, DC
Gibian, Gerald Z. ... New York, NY
Gibian, Roger M.
Federal Energy Regulatory Commission, Office of the General Counsel, GV
Gibilisco, Thomas ... Los Angeles, CA
Gibke, Ladd R. ... Dallas, TX
Giblen, Douglas L. ... Treasury Department, Internal Revenue Service, GV
Gibler, Fred M. ... Kellogg, ID
Gibley, Joseph W. ... Media, PA
Gibley and McWilliams, P.C. ... Media, PA
Giblin, Aaryn E. Kemp ... Beaumont, TX
Giblin & Combs ... Morristown, NJ
Princeton, NJ
Rockaway, NJ
Giblin, Deirdre M. ... Boston, MA
Giblin, Donald F. ... St. Paul, MN
Giblin, Donald J. ... Baltimore, MD
Giblin, E. Burke ... Morristown, NJ
Giblin, Edward P., Jr. ... Gaithersburg, MD
Giblin & Giblin ... Oradell, NJ

Giblin, Gwendolyn R. ... Burlingame, CA
Giblin, James A. ... Berkeley, CA
Giblin, Jennifer A. ... Washington, DC
Giblin, John M. ... Minneapolis, MN
Giblin, John W., Jr., P.C. ... Melville, NY
Giblin, Jon Ann H. ... Baton Rouge, LA
Giblin, Jos. M. ... Bronx, NY
Giblin, L. Thomas ... Tampa, FL
Giblin, Leonard J., Jr. ... Beaumont, TX
Giblin, Mary E. ... Washington, DC
Giblin, Noreen M. ... Roseland, NJ
Giblin, Pamela M. ... Austin, TX
Giblin, Paul J. ... Oradell, NJ
Giblin, Paul J., Jr. ... Oradell, NJ
Giblin, Robert J. ... Beaumont, TX
Giblin, Stephen Q. ... Cleveland, OH
Giblin, Thomas A. ... Boston, MA
Giblin, Thomas G.
Federal Mine Safety and Health Review Commission, Office of the Administrative Law Judges, GV
Giblin, Thomas J. ... Union, NJ
Giblin, Thomas J., III ... Brookline, MA
Giblin, Thomas P., Jr ... New York, NY
Giblin, Vincent M. ... Newark, NJ
Giblin, Walt, & Associates, P.C.
Park Ridge, IL
Giblin, Walter P. ... Park Ridge, IL
Gibney, Alice B. ... Providence, RI
Gibney, Anthony & Flaherty, LLP
New York, NY
Gibney, Charlene Foy ... Salem, MA
Gibney, Edward P., Jr. ... Lakeville, MA
Gibney, John A., Jr. ... Richmond, VA
Gibney, Joy Lynn ... Santa Ana, CA
Gibney, L. Jack ... Jacksonville, FL
Gibney, Michael E. ... Providence, RI
Gibney, Robert E. ... Mobile, AL
Gibney, Robert L., Jr. ... San Francisco, CA
Gibney, Stephen and Barrett ... Xenia, OH
Gibney, Thomas J. ... Columbus, OH
Toledo, OH
Gibney, Tommie Ann ... Medford, NJ
Gibney, Wm. A. ... Phoenix, AZ
Gibofsky, Allan ... New York, NY
Giboney, Michael E. ... Manassas, VA
Gibralter, Susan Feder ... Scarsdale, NY
Gibran, Toni Marie ... San Diego, CA
Gibran-Hesse, M. Ellen ... Belmont, CA
Gibron, J. Kal ... Tampa, FL
Gibron & Quezon, P.A. ... Tampa, FL
Gibson, A. McCampbell ... Atlanta, GA
Gibson, Adele Westmark ... Pensacola, FL
Gibson, Allen D. ... Reno, NV
Gibson, Alvin B. ... Covington, LA
Gibson, Amy E. ... Chicago, IL
Gibson, Amy E. ... Dallas, TX
Gibson, Andrew B., Jr. ... Nashville, TN
Gibson, Angela W. ... Knoxville, TN
Gibson & Associates ... Houston, TX
Gibson, A. T. ... Tulsa, OK
Gibson, Barbara Ann ... Austin, TX
Gibson, Barbara Ann, P.C. ... Austin, TX
Gibson and Behman, P.C. ... Boston, MA
Burlington, MA
New Bedford, MA
Providence, RI
Gibson, Benjamin F. ... Las Vegas, NV
Gibson, Beth A. ... Newberry, MI
Gibson, Beverly Cullen ... Norfolk, VA
Gibson, Beverly K. ... Houston, TX
Gibson, Beverly W. ... Tallahassee, FL
Gibson, Blaine G. ... Yakima, WA
Gibson, Bonnie Kathleen
San Francisco, CA
Gibson, Bradley N. ... Los Angeles, CA
Gibson, Brelo, Ziccarelli & Martello
Cleveland, OH
Gibson, Brett A. ... Anchorage, AK
Gibson, Brian M. ... Goshen, NY
Gibson, Bridgette M. ... San Francisco, CA
Gibson, Bruce A., III ... Orlando, FL
Gibson, Bruce E. ... Kingsport, TN
Gibson, Buck C. ... Little Rock, AR
Gibson, C. Allen, Jr. ... Charleston, SC
Gibson, C. Daniel ... Hillsboro, MO
Gibson, C. Mac, Jr. ... Mount Pleasant, SC
Gibson, C. Martin ... Novato, CA
Gibson, C. Todd ... Pittsburgh, PA
Gibson, C. Vaughan ... Washington, DC
Gibson, Carl G. ... Nowata, OK
Gibson, Carol White ... Buffalo, NY
Gibson, Caroline ... Cape Girardeau, MO
Gibson, Caryn Block ... Great Neck, NY
Gibson, Catherine R. ... Sun City Center, FL
Gibson, Charles Clifford, III
Monticello, AR
Gibson, Charles E., III ... Jackson, MS
Gibson, Charles E., Jr. ... Montpelier, VT
Gibson, Charles M. ... Fairbanks, AK
Gibson, Chas. R. ... Albany, NY
Gibson, Chris ... Sacramento, CA
Gibson, Christopher R. ... Haddonfield, NJ
Gibson, Clare Marie ... Santa Rosa, CA
Gibson & Clark ... Chattanooga, TN
Gibson, C.M. ... Bristow, OK
Gibson, Colin J. ... Los Angeles, CA
Gibson, C.S." Chuck ", II ... Dermott, AR
Gibson, Cynthia L. ... Yorba Linda, CA
Gibson, Cynthia Loren ... Cincinnati, OH
Gibson, D. Barnaby ... Menlo Park, CA
Gibson, D. Randall ... Louisville, KY
Gibson, Dan M. ... Tuscaloosa, AL
Gibson, Dana C. ... Montgomery, AL
Gibson, Daniel E. ... Oakland, CA
Gibson, Daniel J. ... Boston, MA
Gibson, Daniel L. ... Bellingham, WA

Gibson, Daniel P. ... Burlington, MA
New Bedford, MA
Gibson, Darryl S. ... Orange, CA
Gibson, David A. ... Branford, CT
Gibson, David A., Law Office
Brattleboro, VT
Gibson, David G. ... Philadelphia, PA
Gibson, David L. ... San Francisco, CA
Gibson, David S. ... Las Vegas, NV
Gibson, Deal and Fletcher, P.C.
Atlanta, GA
Decatur, GA
Duluth, GA
Lawrenceville, GA
Marietta, GA
Norcross, GA
Gibson, Dennis D. ... Dallas, TX
Gibson, Diane A. ... Kansas City, MO
Gibson, Diane H. ... Carlsbad, CA
Gibson, Diane L. ... San Francisco, CA
Gibson, Diane Larrison ... Kansas City, MO
Gibson, Dianna M. ... Salt Lake City, UT
Gibson, Don C. ... Charleston, SC
Gibson, Donald E. ... Veedersburg, IN
Gibson, Donald H. ... Orlando, FL
Gibson, Donald J., Jr. ... Chicago, IL
Gibson, Donald L. ... Marshfield, MA
Gibson & Donegan ... Branford, CT
Gibson, Dorithea W. ... Los Angeles, CA
Gibson, Douglas G. ... Washington, DC
Gibson, Douglas L. ... Waycross, GA
Gibson, Duane R. ... House of Representatives, Committee on Resources, GV
Gibson & Duffy ... Clackamas, OR
Gibson, Dunn & Crutcher LLP
Irvine, CA
Los Angeles, CA
Newport Beach, CA
Palo Alto, CA
San Diego, CA
San Francisco, CA
Denver, CO
Washington, DC
New York, NY
Dallas, TX
Gibson, E. Paul ... North Charleston, SC
Gibson, Eddie L. ... Jacksonville, FL
Gibson, Edward A. ... Watertown, NY
Gibson, Elise A. ... Chicago, IL
Gibson, Elizabeth Barrowman
Los Angeles, CA
Gibson, Ellen E. ... Chicago, IL
Gibson, Eric ... Oak Park, IL
Gibson, Eric Lynn ... Bardwell, KY
Gibson, Ernest W., III ... Montpelier, VT
Gibson, Eunice ... Madison, WI
Gibson, Everett B. ... Memphis, TN
Gibson, F. Michie, Jr. ... Nashville, TN
Gibson, Ferrin & Riggs, PLC ... Mesa, AZ
Phoenix, AZ
Gibson, Floyd A. ... Charlotte, NC
Gibson, Floyd R. ... Kansas City, MO
Gibson, Francis D., III ... Maryville, TN
Gibson, Frank ... Wichita Falls, TX
Gibson, Frank B., Jr. ... Wilmington, NC
Gibson, Frank C. ... Eugene, OR
Gibson, Frank D. ... Kingsport, TN
Gibson, Franklin K. ... Mesa, AZ
Gibson, Fred D., III ... Las Vegas, NV
Gibson, Fred L., P.C. ... Sterling Heights, MI
Gibson, Frederick W., Jr. ... Washington, DC
Gibson, Gail K. ... St. Paul, MN
Gibson, Garry H. ... Spokane, WA
Gibson, Gary B. ... San Antonio, TX
Gibson, Gary G. ... Redding, CA
Gibson, George C. ... Denver, CO
Gibson, George E. ... Kansas City, MO
Gibson, George K. ... Lodi, CA
Gibson, George M. ... Colorado Springs, CO
Gibson, George M. ... Buffalo, NY
Gibson, George R. ... Houston, TX
Gibson, George W. ... Lakeport, CA
Gibson, Gerry S., (P.A.)
West Palm Beach, FL
Gibson & Gibson ... Bakersfield, CA
Gibson & Gibson ... Stockton, CA
Gibson & Gibson ... Louisville, KY
Gibson & Gibson, Inc. A Law Corporation
Auburn, CA
Roseville, CA
Gibson, Gilchrist M. ... Clarkston, GA
Gibson, Giles ... Portland, OR
Gibson, Gordon R. ... Marion, IA
Gibson & Gregory ... Nashville, TN
Gibson, Gregory C. ... New York, NY
Gibson, Gregory G. ... Fort Worth, TX
Gibson, Gruenert & Hebert, L.L.P.
Lafayette, LA
Gibson, Guy G., Jr. ... Folsom, CA
West Sacramento, CA
Gibson, Guy G., Jr., A Prof. Corp., Law Offices of ... Folsom, CA
West Sacramento, CA
Gibson, Guy R. ... Roseville, CA
Gibson, H. David ... Roanoke, VA
Gibson, H. Martin ... Dallas, TX
Gibson, Haglund & Paulsen ... Irvine, CA
Draper, UT
Gibson & Hamm ... Fayetteville, AR
Gibson, Harold E., Jr. ... Mansfield, OH
Gibson, Harry ... Dearborn, MI
Gibson & Hashem ... Monticello, AR
Gibson, Heather S. ... St. Louis, MO
Gibson, Helen Lee ... Encino, CA
Gibson, Henry H. ... White Plains, NY
Gibson, Herbert C. ... West Palm Beach, FL
Gibson, H. H. C. ... Chicago, IL

Gibson, Hotchkiss, Roach & Davenport
Wichita Falls, TX
Gibson, Hugh ... Eupora, MS
Gibson, Hugh J. ... Beverly Hills, CA
Gibson, Ina Wiesener ... San Diego, CA
Gibson, J. Britton ... Nashville, TN
Gibson, J. Miles ... Columbus, OH
Gibson, J. Ross ... Miami, FL
Gibson, J. Stephen ... Dallas, TX
Gibson, J. William ... Atlanta, GA
Gibson, Jack A., Jr. ... Troy, MI
Gibson, Jack P. ... Lakewood, CO
Gibson, Jacqueline J. ... Irvine, CA
Gibson, James ... Washington, DC
Gibson, James A. B. ... Phoenix, AZ
Gibson, James B. ... Holly Hill, FL
Gibson, James B. ... Henderson, NV
Gibson, James B., III ... Houston, TX
Gibson, James D. ... Sarasota, FL
Gibson, James E. ... Dallas, TX
Gibson, James H. ... Lafayette, LA
Gibson, James J. ... Wexford, PA
Gibson, James L. ... Pasadena, CA
Gibson, James M. ... New York, NY
Gibson, James M. ... Greenville, SC
Gibson, James S., Jr. ... Beaufort, SC
Gibson, James T., Jr. ... Chicago, IL
Gibson, James V. ... Allison, IA
Gibson, James W. ... Bloomfield Hills, MI
Gibson, Jan D. ... Des Moines, IA
Gibson, Janet D. ... Columbus, OH
Gibson, Jason A. ... Houston, TX
Gibson, Jay ... Odessa, TX
Gibson, Jay F. ... Houston, TX
Gibson, Jeffrey G. ... San Francisco, CA
Gibson, Jeffrey L. ... Mesa, AZ
Gibson, Jeffrey M. ... Providence, RI
Gibson, Jeremy A. ... Chicago, IL
Cincinnati, OH
Gibson, Jerry A. ... San Antonio, TX
Gibson, Jerry R., Jr. ... Dallas, TX
Gibson, Jill S. ... Phoenix, AZ
Gibson, Jo Anne ... Princeton, NJ
Gibson, Joan E. ... Pittsburgh, PA
Gibson, Joan W. ... Lynchburg, VA
Gibson, Joe Fred ... Oklahoma City, OK
Gibson, Joe T., Jr. ... Austin, TX
Gibson, John A. C. ... Los Angeles, CA
Gibson, John A. C. ... Encino, CA
Gibson, John B. ... Victorville, CA
Gibson, John B. ... San Antonio, TX
Gibson, John B. ... Seattle, WA
Gibson, John C. ... San Rafael, CA
Gibson, John C. ... Seattle, WA
Gibson, John D. ... Bakersfield, CA
Gibson, John D.
Executive Office Of The President, Council on Environmental Quality, GV
Gibson, John D. ... Johnstown, PA
Gibson, John E. ... Mesa, AZ
Overland Park, KS
Gibson, John Frank, Jr. ... Monticello, AR
Gibson, John H. ... Wichita, KS
Gibson, John L. ... Sacramento, CA
Gibson, John M. ... Lee's Summit, MO
Gibson, John O. ... Loudon, TN
Gibson, John R. ... Kansas City, MO
Gibson, John S. ... Costa Mesa, CA
Gibson, John W. ... Troy, AL
Gibson, John W. ... Ukiah, CA
Gibson, John W. ... Augusta, GA
Gibson, John W. ... Norcross, GA
Gibson, John W. ... Pittsburgh, PA
Gibson, John Wheat ... Dallas, TX
Gibson, Johnson Russell, III
Tuscaloosa, AL
Gibson, Jonathan S., III ... Poquoson, VA
Gibson, Joseph ... Cleveland, OH
Gibson, Joseph E. ... Charlottesville, VA
Gibson, Joseph H. ... House of Representatives, Committee Legal Personnel, GV
Gibson, Joseph L. ... Department of Energy, Office of the General Counsel, GV
Gibson, Joseph M. ... Peoria, IL
Gibson, Joseph Vincent, IV ... Houston, TX
Gibson, Joseph W. ... Uniontown, OH
Gibson, Joseph W., Jr. ... Miami, FL
Gibson, Joseph W., P.A.
Fort Lauderdale, FL
Miami, FL
Gibson, Joy ... Los Angeles, CA
Gibson, Joyce ... Fresno, CA
Gibson, Judith T. ... Orange, CA
Gibson, Julie J. ... Kansas City, MO
Gibson, K. William ... Clackamas, OR
Gibson, Kahala-Ann Trask
San Francisco, CA
Gibson, Katherine H. ... Washington, DC
Gibson, Katherine O. ... Bakersfield, CA
Gibson, Kathleen McIntire ... Philadelphia, PA
Gibson, Kathleen R. ... Moline, IL
Gibson, Keith L. ... Chicago, IL
Gibson, Keith Patrick ... San Luis Obispo, CA
Gibson, Keith R. ... Oklahoma City, OK
Gibson, Kelly ... Miami, FL
Gibson, Kelton Lee ... Ventura, CA
Gibson, Kenneth ... Richmond, VA
Gibson, Kenneth L. ... Arcadia, CA
Gibson, Kenneth L. ... Cuyahoga Falls, OH
Gibson, Kenneth L., Jr. ... Radcliff, KY
Gibson, Kevin D. ... Evansville, IN
Gibson, Kevin William ... Wilmington, DE
Media, PA
Gibson, Kim R. ... Somerset, PA
Gibson, Kirk H. ... Portland, OR
Gibson, Kumiki ... Washington, DC
Gibson, Kurt D. ... Anderson, SC
Gibson, L. Anthony ... Atlantic City, NJ

Gibson, L. Darren ... Memphis, TN
Gibson, Lamar ... Waycross, GA
Gibson, Landon M., III ... Auburn, WA
Gibson, Larry D. ... Mount Vernon, IL
Gibson, Larry D., Law Office of, P.C. Mount Vernon, IL
Gibson, Larry S. ... Baltimore, MD
Gibson, Laura ... Houston, TX
Gibson, Laura Shows ... Andalusia, AL
Gibson, Laurie A. ... Portland, ME
Gibson Law Firm ... Osceola, AR
Gibson, Lawrence ... Toledo, OH
Gibson, Lawrence J. ... Philadelphia, PA
Gibson, L. D. ... Trumann, AR
Gibson, Lefler & Associates ... Beckley, WV
Bluefield, WV
Princeton, WV
Welch, WV
Gibson, Leonard W. ... Norwalk, CA
Gibson, Linda Tilton ... Boston, MA
Gibson, Linda W. ... Belton, TX
Gibson, Lisa M. ... Torrance, CA
Gibson & Loggins, P.A. West Palm Beach, FL
Gibson, Loren F. ... Oklahoma City, OK
Gibson, Lori A. ... Pittsburgh, PA
Gibson, Lori L. ... Grand Rapids, MI
Gibson, Louise ... Albuquerque, NM
Gibson, Lynn H. ... General Accounting Office, Office of the General Counsel, GV
Gibson, Lytton H. ... Fairfax, VA
Gibson, M. Keith ... Lavaca, AR
Gibson, Machree G. ... Austin, TX
Gibson, Mack B. ... Kingsport, TN
Gibson, Mahlon G. ... Fayetteville, AR
Gibson, Mainess ... Houston, TX
Gibson, Malcolm D. ... Houston, TX
Gibson, Margaret A. ... Chicago, IL
Gibson, Marie L. ... New York, NY
Gibson, Marjory F. ... Oakland, CA
Gibson, Mark D. ... Decatur, IL
Gibson, Mark L. ... Perry, OK
Gibson, Mark Monroe ... Montgomery, AL
Gibson, Marshal D. ... New Haven, CT
Gibson, Marshal D., Professional Corporation ... Madison, CT
New Haven, CT
Gibson, Mary R. ... Kansas City, MO
Gibson, Matheson, Weber, Lalliss, Puklin & Freidlander ... Mesa, AZ
Gibson, Maura K. ... Paramus, NJ
Gibson, McAskill & Crosby ... Buffalo, NY
Gibson, McClure & Wallace, L.L.P. Dallas, TX
Gibson, M.D., & Associates, P.C. Houston, TX
Gibson, Melvin E., Jr. ... Charlottesville, VA
Gibson, Merridee P. ... Rocky Mount, NC
Gibson, Michael ... Milton, FL
Gibson, Michael D. ... Bloomfield Hills, MI
Detroit, MI
Gibson, Michael F. ... Princeton, WV
Gibson, Michael G. ... Charlotte, NC
Gibson, Michael J. ... Torrance, CA
Gibson, Michael Lee ... Osceola, AR
Gibson, Michael M. ... Fort Worth, TX
Gibson, Michael M. ... Houston, TX
Gibson, Michael O. ... Springfield, IL
Gibson, Michael P. ... Dallas, TX
Gibson, Michael R. ... El Paso, TX
Gibson, Michael T. ... Oklahoma City, OK
Gibson, Michael W. ... Honolulu, HI
Gibson, Michele ... Woodbridge, NJ
Gibson & Miller ... Hardinsburg, KY
Gibson, Mitchell A. ... St. Louis, MO
Gibson, Monica Derbes ... Washington, DC
Gibson, Murray H., Jr. ... Birmingham, AL
Gibson, Murray T. ... Phoenix, AZ
Gibson, Nancy G. ... Atlanta, GA
Gibson, Nancy P. ... Missoula, MT
Gibson, Nancy S. ... Chicago, IL
Cumberland, ME
Gibson, Nicholas S. ... Alpharetta, GA
Gibson, Nikki Hurst ... Dallas, TX
Gibson, Nora L. ... San Francisco, CA
Gibson, Ochsner & Adkins, LLP Amarillo, TX
Gibson, Ora James, Jr. ... Cape Girardeau, MO
Gibson, Pamela A. ... Denver, CO
Gibson, Pamela V. ... Chicago, IL
Gibson, Patricia M. ... Orlando, FL
Gibson, Patricia M. ... Peoria, IL
Gibson, Patrick J. ... Kingfisher, OK
Gibson, Patrick L. ... New York, NY
Gibson, Paul D. ... Lafayette, LA
Gibson, Paul, Jr. ... New York, NY
Gibson, Paula Lauren ... Los Angeles, CA
Gibson, Phillip ... Huntsville, AL
Gibson, R. Bynum, Jr. ... Dermott, AR
Gibson, R. Peyton ... New York, NY
Gibson, R. Sebastian ... Palm Desert, CA
Gibson, Ralph T. ... Memphis, TN
Gibson, Rankin M. ... Columbus, OH
Gibson, Ray M., Jr. ... Olive Branch, MS
Gibson, Reginald W. United States Court of Federal Claims, GV
Gibson, Requel ... Chicago, IL
Gibson, Rex H. ... Houston, TX
Gibson, Rexanne ... Bellevue, WA
Gibson, Richard A. ... Phoenix, AZ
Gibson, Richard C. ... Louisville, KY
Gibson, Richard D. ... Department of Defense, Defense Legal Services Agency, GV
Gibson, Richard H. ... Los Angeles, CA
Gibson, Richard H., A Prof. Corp., Law Offices of ... Los Angeles, CA
Gibson, Richard J. ... Stockton, CA
Gibson, Richard J., Jr. ... Stockton, CA
Gibson, Richard R. ... Minneapolis, MN
Gibson, Richard W. ... Washington, DC
Gibson, Richard W. ... Edwardsville, IL
Gibson, Richard W., Jr. ... Charlotte, NC
Gibson, Rick J. ... Columbus, OH
Gibson, Ricky L. ... Houston, TX
Gibson and Rivera ... Los Angeles, CA
Pasadena, CA
Gibson & Robb LLP ... San Francisco, CA
Gibson, Robert A. ... Mankato, MN
Gibson, Robert A. ... Cincinnati, OH
Gibson, Robert B. ... Orange, CA
Gibson, Robert E. ... Athens, GA
Gibson, Robert E. ... Chesapeake, VA
Gibson, Robert G. ... Naperville, IL
Gibson, Robert H. ... Montpelier, VT
Gibson, Robert J. ... Jonesboro, AR
Gibson, Robert J. ... Irvine, CA
Gibson, Robert J. ... Norristown, PA
Gibson, Robert J. ... Houston, TX
Gibson, Robert L. ... Paris, IL
Gibson, Robert R. ... Lincoln, NE
Gibson, Robert V. ... Irvine, CA
Gibson, Robert V. ... El Paso, TX
Gibson, Robert W., Jr. Department of Commerce, Patent and Trademark Office, GV
Gibson, Robin, (Mr.) ... Lake Wales, FL
Gibson, Robt. B. ... Dermott, AR
Gibson, Roderick O. ... Houston, TX
Gibson, Ronald L. ... Charlotte, NC
Gibson, S. Elizabeth ... Chapel Hill, NC
Gibson, Sallie P. ... San Francisco, CA
Gibson, Sam Ed ... Benton, AR
Gibson, Sam Ed, P.A. ... Benton, AR
Hot Springs Village, AR
Gibson, Scott B. ... Waukegan, IL
Gibson, Scott B., Ltd. ... Waukegan, IL
Gibson, Scott D. ... Tucson, AZ
Gibson, Scott F. ... Mesa, AZ
Gibson, Sharon Lynn ... Washington, DC
Gibson, Shelly S. ... Louisville, KY
Gibson, Sidney K. ... El Paso, TX
Gibson and Spivey, P.C. ... Waycross, GA
Gibson, Stanley L. ... San Francisco, CA
Gibson, Stanley M. ... Los Angeles, CA
Gibson, Stephanie L. ... Gahanna, OH
Gibson, Stephen L. ... Washington, DC
Gibson, Stephen W. ... Knoxville, TN
Gibson, Steven A. ... Las Vegas, NV
Gibson, Steven H. ... Florham Park, NJ
Gibson, Steven H. ... Seattle, WA
Gibson, Stuart D. ... Department of Justice, Tax Division, GV
Gibson, Sue A. ... Paxton, IL
Gibson, Susan Engelman Department of Justice, United States Marshals Service, GV
Gibson, Susan S. ... Alton, IL
Gibson, Susan W. ... Orlando, FL
Gibson, T. Stewart ... Rocky Mount, NC
Gibson, Terry R. ... Glendale, CA
Gibson, Thad W. ... Americus, GA
Gibson, Theodore P. ... Tulsa, OK
Gibson, Thomas ... Philadelphia, PA
Gibson, Thomas A. ... Toledo, OH
Gibson, Thomas Baron, II ... Macon, GA
Gibson, Thomas E. ... Tyler, TX
Gibson, Thomas F. ... Cambridge, MA
Gibson, Thomas J. ... Denver, CO
Gibson, Thomas R. ... Irvine, CA
Gibson, Thomas S. ... Port St. Joe, FL
Gibson, Timothy X. ... New York, NY
Gibson & Valenti, P.A. ... Lake Wales, FL
Gibson, Virginia L. ... San Francisco, CA
Gibson, W. Clay ... Atlanta, GA
Gibson, Warren W. ... Cuyahoga Falls, OH
Gibson, Wendy J. ... Cleveland, OH
Gibson, Wendy L. ... Fremont, CA
Gibson, William B. ... Whittier, CA
Gibson, William F. ... Cleveland, OH
Gibson, William Frank, II ... Fairfax, VA
Gibson, William L. ... Louisville, KY
Gibson, William L., Jr. ... Binghamton, NY
Gibson, William M. ... Richmond, VA
Gibson, William Russell ... Fayetteville, AR
Gibson, William W. ... Nashville, TN
Gibson, Windel M. ... Midland, TX
Gibson, Wm. W., Jr. ... Austin, TX
Gibson Diehl, Millicent ... Raeford, NC
Gibson-Greene, Cacilla ... New York, NY
Gibson-Gruenert, L.L.P. ... Houston, TX
Gibson-Mason, Virginia A. ... Philadelphia, PA
Gibula, Deborah L ... Chicago, IL
Gichtin, Karen L. ... Los Angeles, CA
Gick, Gary L. Department Of Veterans Affairs, Board of Veterans Appeals, GV
Gick, Thomas A. ... Washington, DC
Gicking, James W. ... Philadelphia, PA
Gidaly, Walter ... New York, NY
Gidari, Albert, Jr. ... Seattle, WA
Gidas, Sam P. ... Pittsburgh, PA
Gidcumb, E. Joseph ... Flint, MI
Gidcumb, Lance E. ... Anchorage, AK
Gidday, Suzanne Lane Grosse Pointe Park, MI
Giddens, Albert Lee ... Pasadena, TX
Giddens, Bert J. ... Jackson, MS
Giddens, Bobby L. ... Atlanta, GA
Giddens, Brent Matthew ... Los Angeles, CA
Giddens, Davidson & Mitchell ... Atlanta, GA
Giddens, Devin J. ... Duncan, OK
Giddens, Elizabeth K. ... Tulsa, OK
Giddens, F. Whitfield ... Santa Ana, CA
Giddens & Garrett, (A Professional Law Corporation) ... Shreveport, LA
Giddens, George" Dave ", Law Office of Carlsbad, NM
Las Cruces, NM
Roswell, NM
Giddens, George" Dave ", Law Office of Albuquerque, NM
Giddens, Gregory P. ... Jackson, MS
Giddens, James W. ... New York, NY
Giddens, Jared D. ... Oklahoma City, OK
Giddens, Twain K., Jr. ... Shreveport, LA
Giddens, William T. ... San Diego, CA
Gidding, Edgar D. ... Sacramento, CA
Gidding, Michael J. Consumer Product Safety Commission, Office of Compliance, GV
Gidding, Robert B. ... Cherry Hill, NJ
Bala Cynwyd, PA
Giddings, Barton W. ... Salt Lake City, UT
Giddings, Caroline D. ... Cedar Rapids, IA
Giddings, Charles E. ... Tucson, AZ
Giddings, Christopher L. Philadelphia, PA
Giddings, Christopher L., P.C. Philadelphia, PA
Giddings, Daniel E. ... Los Angeles, CA
Giddings, James R. ... Lansing, MI
Giddings, James Robert ... Austin, TX
Giddings, Jean Brewster ... Brattleboro, VT
Giddings, Katherine E. ... Tallahassee, FL
Giddings, Kathryn J. ... St. Louis, MO
Giddings, Lawrence D. ... Lebanon, IN
Giddings, Mary K. ... Helena, MT
Giddings, Randolph M. ... Tallahassee, FL
Giddings, Ron ... Arroyo Grande, CA
Giddings, Whitsitt & McClure, P.C. Lebanon, IN
Zionsville, IN
Giddins, Claman & Langs ... New York, NY
Giddins, Paul M. ... New York, NY
Giddon, A. Arthur ... West Hartford, CT
Giddy, James F. ... Jackson, MS
Giddy, Ronald ... Holland, MI
Gide Loyrette Nouel ... New York, NY
New York, NY
Gidel, David D. ... Rockwell City, IA
Gidel, E. Glenn ... Fort Worth, TX
Giden, Joseph M. ... Los Angeles, CA
Giden, Michael I. ... Los Angeles, CA
Gideon, Antoinette F. ... Cleveland, OH
Gideon, C. J. ... Topeka, KS
Gideon, C. J., Jr. ... Nashville, TN
Gideon, Thomas ... Nashville, TN
Gideon, David S. ... Syracuse, NY
Gideon, John J. ... Columbus, OH
Gideon, Kenneth W. ... Washington, DC
Gideon, Kyle L. ... Lafayette, LA
Gideon, Megan E. ... Atlanta, GA
Gideon, Wendell R. ... Forsyth, MO
Gideon & Wiseman ... Nashville, TN
Gidiere, Hinton & Herndon Montgomery, AL
Gidiere, Philip S., III Department Of The Interior, Office of the Solicitor, GV
Gidiere, Philip S., Jr. ... Montgomery, AL
Gidley, Andrew J., Jr. ... San Antonio, TX
Gidley, J. Mark ... Washington, DC
Gidley, James H. ... Portland, OR
Gidley, Michael T. ... Farmington Hills, MI
Gidley, Richard S. ... Bellevue, WA
Gidley, Sarah Heisler ... Detroit, MI
Gidley, Sarli & Marusak ... Providence, RI
Gidley, Thomas D. ... Providence, RI
Gidley, William J. ... Baytown, TX
Gidlow, Catherine S. ... St. Louis, MO
Gidman, Justin V. ... Houston, TX
Gidro, Michael R. ... Tenafly, NJ
Gidron, Leah D. ... Chicago, IL
Gidseg, Barry ... New York, NY
Gidwani, Anita I. ... New York, NY
Gieb, Robert J. ... Fort Worth, TX
Giebel & Gilbert ... St. Paul, MN
Giebel, Kevin E. ... St. Paul, MN
Giebel, Rita D. ... Tustin, CA
Giebelstein, Terry M. ... Davenport, IA
Giebink, Mary Ann ... Sioux Falls, SD
Giebler, Michaelyn Bond ... Temple, TX
Giedgowd, Edward A. ... San Francisco, CA
Giedraitis, Vincent J. ... Vernon, CT
Giedzinski, H.B., P.A. ... Ocala, FL
Giedzinski, H. B. ... Ocala, FL
Giedzinski, Steven P. ... Los Angeles, CA
Giefer, Michael J. ... St. Paul, MN
Gieg, Fred B. ... Altoona, PA
Gieg, Frederick B., Jr. ... Altoona, PA
Gieg, Gieg, Montgomery & Zang Altoona, PA
Gieg, William F. ... Richmond, VA
Gieger, Ernest P., Jr. ... New Orleans, LA
Gieger, Michael E. ... Atlanta, GA
Gieger, Patricia Harrison ... Weatherford, TX
Gieger, Rosemarie Herkert ... Paterson, NJ
Giegerich, Robert A., Jr. ... Cranford, NJ
Giegerich, Thomas W. ... New York, NY
Giel, Frederick G. ... White Plains, NY
Giel, James T. ... Denver, CO
Giele, John C. ... Salina, KS
Gieleghem, J. Neil ... Los Angeles, CA
Gielen, Price O. ... Baltimore, MD
Giella, Catherine R. ... Chicago, IL
Giella, Peter G. ... Hawthorne, NJ
Gielow, Eric R. ... Muskegon, MI
Gielow, G. Roger ... Bloomington, IL
Gielowski, Stephen M. ... Buffalo, NY
Gienapp, David R. ... Madison, SD
Gienapp, Marcia L. ... Valparaiso, IN
Gienapp, Richard K. ... Brighton, MI
Gienko, Gregory A. ... Chicago, IL
Gienko, James R. ... Bloomingdale, IL
Giepert, Gary John ... New Orleans, LA
Giepert, Melvin J. ... New Orleans, LA
Gier, Richard E. ... Overland Park, KS
Kansas City, MO
Gierach, Denice A. ... Naperville, IL
Gierach, Elroy J. ... Orlando, FL
Gierach and Gierach, P.A. ... Orlando, FL
Gierach, James E. ... Oak Lawn, IL
Gierach, John R. ... Orlando, FL
Gierach, Will E. ... Markham, IL
Gierak, John L. ... Troy, MI
Gierasch, Stephen C. ... Harrisburg, PA
Gierasch, William C., Jr. ... York, PA
Gierbolini, Luisette ... Tampa, FL
Gierbolini-Gierbolini, Miguel E. San Juan, PR
Gierbolini-Gonzalez, Fernando J. San Juan, PR
Gierbolini-Ortiz, Gilberto ... San Juan, PR
Giere, John P. ... Laconia, NH
Giere, Rolf A. ... Prescott, WI
Gierhart, Amy Grace ... Caro, MI
Gierhart, Douglas M. ... Shawnee, OK
Gierhart, Roger L. ... Madison, WI
Giering, Edmund J., IV ... Baton Rouge, LA
Giering, Robert E. ... Reading, PA
Gieringer, Janel M. ... Milwaukee, WI
Gieringer, Mark J. ... Friendship, WI
Gieringer, Patricia L. ... Washington, DC
Gieringer, Raymond E. ... Friendship, WI
Gierke, Curwen, Metzler & Erie, P.S. Seattle, WA
Tacoma, WA
Gierke, H. F., III United States Court Of Appeals For The Armed Forces, GV
Gierke, Nora E. ... Milwaukee, WI
Gierke, Scott N. ... Chicago, IL
Gierl, John R. ... Cincinnati, OH
Gierla, Teresa K. ... Toms River, NJ
Gierlach, David J. ... Honolulu, HI
Gierloff, Richard D. ... Phoenix, AZ
Giermann, Edward C. ... Pasadena, CA
Giers, Judith ... Eugene, OR
Giersch, Curtis E. ... Durango, CO
Giersch, E. Paul ... Seattle, WA
Giertz, Robert ... Department of Defense, Armed Services Board of Contract Appeals, GV
Gierum, John E., Jr. ... Park Ridge, IL
Gierum & Mantas ... Park Ridge, IL
Gieryn, Richard T. ... Charlotte, NC
Gieryn, Richard T., Jr. ... Atlanta, GA
Gies, David A. ... Trenton, NJ
Gies, Jill M. ... Southfield, MI
Gies, Scott A. ... Southfield, MI
Gies, Thomas P. ... Washington, DC
Giesa, John P. ... Spokane, WA
Giesa, Timothy J. ... Coeur d'Alene, ID
Spokane, WA
Giesber, Frank W. ... Seguin, TX
Giesber, Rachel S. ... Houston, TX
Giesbrecht, Wayne E. ... Honolulu, HI
Giese, Anne M. ... Sacramento, CA
Giese, Bryan L. ... Mandan, ND
Giese, Darla M. ... Des Moines, IA
Giese, Douglas C. ... Chicago, IL
Giese, Heiner ... Milwaukee, WI
Giese, James W. ... Grand Junction, CO
Giese, James W., P.C. Grand Junction, CO
Giese, Jeffrey W. ... Dallas, TX
Giese, Kay A. ... Athens, GA
Giese, Keith ... Columbia, SC
Giese, Kenneth H. ... Scottsdale, AZ
Giese, Laura ... San Diego, CA
Giese, Michael J. ... Greenville, SC
Giese, Mildred J. ... Clearwater, FL
Giese, Pamela K. ... Giddings, TX
Giese, Paul C. ... Reno, NV
Giese, Robert B. ... Washington, DC
Giese, Sharon ... Westport, CT
Giese, Thomas P. ... Nashville, TN
Giese, William J. ... Madison, WI
Giesecke, Fritz H. ... Fairfax, VA
Giesecke, Karsten P. ... New York, NY
Gieseke, Corinne J. ... Lake Forest, IL
Gieseke, Gordon H. ... New York, NY
Gieseke, James A. ... Houston, TX
Gieseke, Ronald S. ... St. Louis, MO
Gieseking, Kenneth W. ... Fort Lauderdale, FL
Gieseking, Kenneth W., Law Offices of Fort Lauderdale, FL
Gieseking, Weni C. ... Los Angeles, CA
Giesel, Grace McLane ... Louisville, KY
Giesel, James A. ... Louisville, KY
Gieseler, Eugene C. ... Green Valley, AZ
Tucson, AZ
Gieseler, Jeffrey Markus ... New Orleans, LA
Gieseler, Stella Ann United States Tax Court, GV
Gieselman, Walter B. ... Burbank, CA
Gieseman, Albert W., Jr. ... Hollywood, CA
Giesen & Berman, S.C. ... Madison, WI
Giesen, Charles W. ... Madison, WI
Giesen, Hans-Michael ... New York, NY
Giesen, Jennifer E. ... Minneapolis, MN
Giesen, Linda A. ... Dixon, IL
Giesen, Robert P. ... Boca Raton, FL
Giesenschlag, Tom ... College Station, TX
Gieser, Cristin C. ... Tallahassee, FL
Gieser, Susan C. ... Old Bridge, NJ
Gieser, Thomas M. ... San Diego, CA
Santa Ana, CA
Giesler, Ann S. ... Sandusky, OH
Giesler, Ashley N. ... Menlo Park, CA
Giesler, Gary H. ... Los Angeles, CA
Giesler, Greg H. ... Pasadena, CA

Giesler, Mary S. ... **Minneapolis, MN**
Giessel, Barker & Lyman, P.C.
Houston, TX
Giessel, Henry P. ... **Houston, TX**
Giesser, Joanne M.
Whitehouse Station, NJ
Giesser, William R. ... Westlake, OH
Giessmann, Gary L. ... Norman, OK
Gietz, Raymond O. ... **New York, NY**
Gievers, Karen ... **Tallahassee, FL**
Gievers, Karen A., P.A. ... **Tallahassee, FL**
Giezentanner, John P.
Newport Beach, CA
Giffels, John ... Marshall, MI
Giffels, John L. ... Rochester Hills, MI
Giffels, Thomas E. ... Cleveland, OH
Giffen & Barbieri, Inc. ... Wilton, CA
Giffen, Daniel H. ... Kent, OH
Giffen, James Kelly ... **Knoxville, TN**
Giffen, John A. ... Wilton, CA
Giffen, John Gregory ... **Nashville, TN**
Giffen, Jon R. ... **Salinas, CA**
Giffen, K. Franza ... San Rafael, CA
Giffen, Karen L. ... **Cleveland, OH**
Giffen, Kirk S. ... Cohasset, MA
Giffen, Royal B. ... Dumont, NJ
Giffen, Scott E. ... Mission, KS
Giffen, Shavan M. ... Troy, MI
Giffen, William R. ... Stockton, CA
Giffin, Carl J., Jr. ... **Metairie, LA**
Giffin, Donald W. ... **Kansas City, MO**
Giffin, Donald Wm. ... Seminole, FL
Giffin, Donald Wm., P.A. ... Seminole, FL
Giffin, Elizabeth J. ... **Los Angeles, CA**
Giffin, Emily Fisk ... **New York, NY**
Giffin, Gordon D. ... Atlanta, GA
Giffin, James M. ... Federal Trade Commission, Office of the General Counsel, GV
Giffin, John D. ... **San Francisco, CA**
Giffin, Kenna ... Laredo, TX
Giffin, Michael E. ... **Tullahoma, TN**
Giffin, Peter C. ... San Diego, CA
Giffin, Reggie C. ... **Kansas City, MO**
Giffin, Robert ... Honolulu, HI
Giffin, Robert E. ... Columbus, OH
Giffin, Robert E., Co., L.P.A.
Columbus, OH
Giffin, William M. ... Springfield, IL
Giffin, Winning, Cohen & Bodewes, P.C.
Springfield, IL
Gifford, Allan H. ... Honolulu, HI
Gifford, Allison Z. ... **Philadelphia, PA**
Gifford, Anita S. ... **Norcross, GA**
Gifford, Anne K. ... Newport Beach, CA
Gifford, Bret D. ... **Manchester, NH**
Gifford, Brian L. ... **Edwardsville, IL**
Gifford, Brian L. ... **Columbus, OH**
Gifford, Charles H. ... Groton, CT
Gifford, David A. ... **Walnut Creek, CA**
Gifford, David B. ... **Philadelphia, PA**
Gifford & Dearing ... **Los Angeles, CA**
Gifford, Dirk ... **Washington, DC**
Gifford, Donald A. ... **Tampa, FL**
Gifford, Donald G. ... Gainesville, FL
Gifford, Douglas A. ... Souderton, PA
Gifford, Elizabeth Ann ... **Juneau, AK**
Gifford, Ernest I. ... **Birmingham, MI**
Gifford, Eugene B., Jr. ... Booneville, MS
Gifford, Eugenie A. ... **Santa Monica, CA**
Gifford, G. Grant ... **Los Angeles, CA**
Gifford, Geoffrey L. ... **Chicago, IL**
Rockford, IL
Gifford, Gladys P. ... Cambridge, MA
Gifford, Gregory R. ... **Lansdale, PA**
Gifford, Jackson T. ... Oakland, CA
Gifford, James L. ... Yonkers, NY
Gifford, James M. ... Los Gatos, CA
Gifford, Janet L. ... Tallahassee, FL
Gifford, Jean C. ... Davis, CA
Gifford, Jennifer J. ... **Denver, CO**
Gifford, John A. ... Dedham, MA
Gifford, John J. ... Marion, VA
Gifford, John K. ... **Poughkeepsie, NY**
Gifford, Karen E. ... **New York, NY**
Gifford, Keith E. ... **Indianapolis, IN**
Gifford, Krass, Groh, Sprinkle, Anderson & Citkowski, P.C. ... **Venice, FL**
Ann Arbor, MI
Birmingham, MI
Gifford, L. Andrew ... **Los Angeles, CA**
Gifford, Lay & Steele ... **Erie, PA**
Gifford, Leanne A. ... **Omaha, NE**
Gifford, Linda B. ... Augusta, ME
Gifford, Lisa ... **Oklahoma City, OK**
Gifford, M. Elisabeth ... **Walnut Creek, CA**
Gifford, Margaret Rawls ... **Los Angeles, CA**
Gifford, Mark W. ... **Casper, WY**
Gifford, Martha E. ... **New York, NY**
Gifford, Melissa D. ... La Fayette, GA
Gifford, Michael D. ... Peoria, IL
Gifford, Milton E., P.C. ... Cottage Grove, OR
Gifford, Milton Earl ... Cottage Grove, OR
Gifford, Nancy V. ... Hartford, CT
Gifford, Page E. ... Columbus, IN
Gifford, Patricia J. ... Indianapolis, IN
Gifford, Paul E. ... Fort Lauderdale, FL
Gifford, R. Don, II ... Louisville, KY
Gifford, Raymond L. ... Denver, CO
Gifford, Richard E. ... **Edmonds, WA**
Gifford, Richard E., P.L.L.C.
Edmonds, WA
Gifford & Richardson, P.C.
Green City, MO
Kirksville, MO
Gifford, Robert C., Jr. ... **Livingston, NJ**
Gifford, Robert E. ... **Clarksburg, WV**
Gifford, Robert G. ... New York, NY
Gifford, Robert W. ... **Hackensack, NJ**
Gifford, Ronald D. ... **Indianapolis, IN**
Gifford, Ronald D. ... **Plymouth, IN**
Gifford, Seth K. ... Providence, RI
Gifford, Susan W. ... **Clarksburg, WV**
Gifford, Suzanne Balaze ... San Jose, CA
Gifford, Thomas A. ... **Redding, CA**
Gifford, Timothy D. ... **Norristown, PA**
Gifford, Timothy J. ... Norristown, PA
Gifford, Vernon, Barker & Glade, Ltd.
Las Vegas, NV
Gifford, Vicki L. ... Stillwater, MN
Gifford, Wayne D. ... Waynesville, MO
Gifford, Whitney A. ... **Nantucket, MA**
Gifford, William C. ... **New York, NY**
Gifford, William D. ... Macon, GA
Gifford, Yale W. ... Anacortes, WA
Giffords, Norma ... New Hyde Park, NY
Giffune, John P. ... **Boston, MA**
Gifis, Susan P. ... Princeton, NJ
Gift, Douglas A. ... **La Salle, IL**
Giftos, Alexander C. ... **Peoria, IL**
Giftos, P. Michael ... Jacksonville, FL
Gigandet, Michael ... **Nashville, TN**
Gigante, Alexander ... **New York, NY**
Gigante, Carl A. ... **Chicago, IL**
Gigante, John D. ... **New York, NY**
Gigante, Richard ... Chicago, IL
Gigante, Richard, P.C. ... Chicago, IL
Gigante, Robert J. ... Brooklyn, NY
Gigante, Stephen ... **Washington, DC**
Giganti, Adam ... **Springfield, IL**
Giganti, Francis J. ... **Springfield, IL**
Giganti, Karie J. ... Chicago, IL
Gigax, James E. ... **Denver, CO**
Giger, JoAnne Juliano ... **Roseland, NJ**
Giger, Thomas W. ... Berwyn, IL
Giggenbach, Bader C. ... **Morgantown, WV**
Gigger, Helen C. ... Oklahoma City, OK
Gigger, Nathan J. ... Oklahoma City, OK
Giggey, Kempton P. ... Dunstable, MA
Gigl, Robert B., Jr. ... **Livingston, NJ**
Gigler, Douglas W. ... **Fargo, ND**
Gigler, James R. ... Del Mar, CA
Gigler, Robert J. ... Whittier, CA
Gigli, Walter ... Maplewood, NJ
Giglia, Kelly J. ... Viera, FL
Giglio, Aldo L. ... Grosse Pointe Shores, MI
Giglio, Anthony ... **Pittsburgh, PA**
Giglio, Anthony G. ... Chicago, IL
Giglio, Augustine ... **Cincinnati, OH**
Giglio, J. Michael ... Ringgold, GA
Giglio, John D. ... United States Senate, Senatorial Assistants, GV
Giglio, Joseph C., Jr. ... **Lafayette, LA**
Giglio, Paula A. ... Englewood, NJ
Giglio, Raymond W., Jr. ... Key Largo, FL
Giglio, Richard J. ... **New York, NY**
Giglio, Sheila Bond ... Acton, MA
Giglio, Thomas J. ... Utica, NY
Giglio, Valerie E. ... Wakefield, MA
Giglio, Vincent E. ... Tampa, FL
Gigliotti, Anthony J. ... Syracuse, NY
Gigliotti, Carmine D. ... Fort Lauderdale, FL
Gigliotti, Joseph J. ... Fullerton, CA
Gigliotti, Lisa K. ... Lansing, MI
Gigliotti, Louis J., Jr. ... **Akron, OH**
Gigliotti, Louis P. ... **Utica, NY**
Gigliotti, Louis R., Jr.
Fort Lauderdale, FL
Miami, FL
Gigliotti, Paul B. ... Clinton Township, MI
Gigliotti, Robert L. ... Beverly Hills, CA
Gigliotti, Thomas A. ... **Durham, NC**
Gignac, J. Paul ... **Santa Barbara, CA**
Gignilliat, Charles O. ... Gainesville, GA
Gignilliat & Hymen, P.C. ... **Chicago, IL**
Northbrook, IL
Gignilliat, Julian H. ... **Columbia, SC**
Gignilliat, Leigh R., III ... **Northbrook, IL**
Gignilliat, R. Read ... **Atlanta, GA**
Gignilliat, Savitz & Bettis ... **Columbia, SC**
Gignilliat, William R., III ... Atlanta, GA
Gigot, Thomas S. ... **Washington, DC**
Gigounas, John, (A Professional Corporation) ... **Sacramento, CA**
San Francisco, CA
Squaw Valley, CA
Gigowski, William J., Jr. ... Indianapolis, IN
Gigray, Miller & Downen ... Caldwell, ID
Gigray, William F., III ... **Nampa, ID**
Gigray, William F., Jr. ... Caldwell, ID
Giguere, Gary C., Jr. ... **Kalamazoo, MI**
Giguere, Michael J. ... **McLean, VA**
Giguere, Paul G. ... **Washington, DC**
Giguiere, Michele L. ... **Sacramento, CA**
Giguere, William A. ... Manitowoc, WI
Giha, Paul D. ... Toledo, OH
Gijanto, Joseph L. ... Ocean Township, NJ
Gikkas, Nicholas S. ... **Palo Alto, CA**
Giknis, Robert B. ... Endicott, NY
Gikow, David H. ... **New York, NY**
Gil, Adolfo A. ... **Hialeah, FL**
Gil, Anamaria ... **Seattle, WA**
Gil, Andrés V. ... **New York, NY**
Gil, Bertha S. ... **Hialeah, FL**
Gil, Edmund Charles ... Visalia, CA
Gil & Gil, P.A. ... **Hialeah, FL**
Gil, Joseph C. ... **Pittsburgh, PA**
Gil, Patrick R. ... Greenwich, CT
Gilaad, Elana ... **Newark, NJ**
Gilaberte-Marsh, Ana Margarita ... Miami, FL
Gilady, Elizabeth Ilona ... Kew Gardens, NY
Gilan, Ethan A. ... **Southfield, MI**
Gilanians, Alexander ... Glendale, CA
Gilanshah, Bijan
Office of Personnel Management, Merit Systems Division, GV
Gilanshah, Melissa ... Alexandria, VA
Gilardi Cooper & Lomupo, P.A.
Pittsburgh, PA
Gilardi, David ... Gloucester, MA
Gilardi, Richard D. ... Pittsburgh, PA
Gilardi, Richard P. ... Stratford, CT
Gilardi, Richard P. ... Pittsburgh, PA
Gilardi, Richard S. ... **San Francisco, CA**
Gilardy, William H., Jr. ... **Honolulu, HI**
Gilb, Michael E. ... **Findlay, OH**
Gilbane, Donna M. ... **Berlin, CT**
Gilbar, Steven D. ... Santa Barbara, CA
Gilberg, David J. ... **New York, NY**
Gilberg, Donald M. ... **Washington, DC**
Baltimore, MD
Rockville, MD
Boston, MA
New York, NY
Fairfax, VA
Gilberg, Elliott J.
Environmental Protection Agency, Office of Enforcement and Compliance Assurance, GV
Gilberg, Howard L. ... **Dallas, TX**
Gilberg, Jeanne ... New York, NY
Gilberg, Jos. B. ... Mount Vernon, NY
Gilberg, Kenneth R. ... **Philadelphia, PA**
Gilberg & Kiernan ... **Hartford, CT**
Washington, DC
Baltimore, MD
Rockville, MD
Boston, MA
Parsippany, NJ
New York, NY
Providence, RI
Fairfax, VA
Gilberg, Leo ... New York, NY
Gilberg, Michael H. ... Mount Vernon, NY
Gilberg, Richard N. ... **Mineola, NY**
Gilberg, Robert E. ... Philadelphia, PA
Gilbert, A. Kirven, III ... **Atlanta, GA**
Gilbert, A. Spencer, III ... **Jackson, MS**
Gilbert, Adam B. ... New York, NY
Gilbert, Adena S. ... San Francisco, CA
Gilbert, A. J. ... Santa Monica, CA
Gilbert, Alan M. ... **Minneapolis, MN**
Gilbert, Alan S. ... **Chicago, IL**
Gilbert, Albert E. ... Rush, NY
Gilbert, Alice L. ... Pontiac, MI
Gilbert, Alison C. ... **New York, NY**
Gilbert, Allen L. ... Los Angeles, CA
Gilbert, Allison T. ... **Memphis, TN**
Gilbert, Andrea M. ... **Seattle, WA**
Gilbert, Andrew C.
Federal Deposit Insurance Corporation, Professional Liability Section, GV
Gilbert, Andrew M. ... **Dallas, TX**
Gilbert, Andrew P. ... **Princeton, NJ**
Gilbert, Anthony C. ... **San Francisco, CA**
Gilbert, Arch B. ... Fort Worth, TX
Gilbert, Arlene Kohn ... **New York, NY**
Gilbert, B. Eugene ... **Brookville, OH**
Gilbert, B. Eugene ... **Dayton, OH**
Gilbert, Barbara J. ... **Montgomery, AL**
Gilbert, Barbara Snow ... Oklahoma City, OK
Gilbert, Ben M. ... Fort Worth, TX
Gilbert, Benjamin ... Chapel Hill, NC
Gilbert, Blaine L. ... **Baltimore, MD**
Gilbert, Blaine L., & Associates, P.A.
Baltimore, MD
Gilbert & Blaszcyk ... Patchogue, NY
Gilbert, Bradbury ... Saugus, MA
Gilbert, Brenda R. ... **Livingston, MT**
Gilbert, Brett A. ... **Urbana, OH**
Gilbert, Brett D. ... **New York, NY**
Gilbert, Brian B. ... **Chicago, IL**
Gilbert, Bruce A. ... **Santa Monica, CA**
Gilbert, Bruce M. ... Independence, CA
Gilbert, Bruce R. ... **Portland, OR**
Gilbert, Bruce R. ... King Of Prussia, PA
Gilbert, Burton H. ... Fort Worth, TX
Gilbert, C. Coulter ... **Knoxville, TN**
Gilbert, C. Gordon ... Baltimore, MD
Gilbert, C. Gordon, Jr. ... Baltimore, MD
Gilbert, Caroline G. ... San Diego, CA
Gilbert, Cathleen Clark
Salt Lake City, UT
Gilbert, Charles B. ... Kansas City, MO
Gilbert, Charles E., III ... **Bangor, ME**
Gilbert, Charles S. ... **Dallas, TX**
Gilbert, Christine M. ... Germantown, MD
Gilbert, Christopher B. ... **Houston, TX**
Gilbert Coffey Hobson, A Professional Corporation ... **El Paso, TX**
Gilbert, Coit H. ... Columbus, OH
Gilbert & Colvin ... Fort Worth, TX
Gilbert, Craig L. ... **Fort Lauderdale, FL**
Gilbert, Craig R. ... Treasury Department, Internal Revenue Service, GV
Gilbert, Craig S. ... **Bellevue, WA**
Gilbert, Cynthia L. ... Belvedere-Tiburon, CA
Gilbert, Dan L. ... New Orleans, LA
Gilbert, Danita A. ... Norwalk, OH
Gilbert, David A. ... Colorado Springs, CO
Gilbert, David A. ... **Boston, MA**
Gilbert, David B. ... Middletown, NY
Gilbert, David C. ... Belvedere-Tiburon, CA
Gilbert, David G. ... Chicago, IL
Gilbert, David M. ... Saginaw, MI
Gilbert, Dennis V. ... Tillamook, OR
Gilbert, Derek C. ... **Beaufort, SC**
Gilbert, Donald A. ... **Saginaw, MI**
Gilbert, Donald B. ... Sacramento, CA
Gilbert, Donald D. ... American Fork, UT
Gilbert, Donald L. ... **Tampa, FL**
Gilbert, Donald R. ... **Phoenix, AZ**
Gilbert, Dorothy McCabe ... **Wilsonville, OR**
Gilbert, Douglas E. ... **Pittsburgh, PA**
Gilbert, Douglas J. ... Denver, CO
Gilbert, Douglas J. ... **New York, NY**
Gilbert, Douglas M. ... Cupertino, CA
Gilbert, E. Harry, III
Oklahoma City, OK
Gilbert, E. Scott ... **Fairfield, CT**
Gilbert, Edith J. ... Savannah, GA
Gilbert, Edward E. ... Greensburg, PA
Gilbert, Edward H. ... Boca Raton, FL
Gilbert, Edward H., Professional Association
Boca Raton, FL
Gilbert, Edward P. ... **New York, NY**
Gilbert, Elisa T. ... **New York, NY**
Gilbert, Elizabeth ... Iowa Falls, IA
Gilbert, Elizabeth ... New York, NY
Gilbert, Eunice Pennington ... Tucker, GA
Gilbert Firm, The ... Jackson, TN
Gilbert, Floyd H. ... South Yarmouth, MA
Gilbert, Françoise ... **Palo Alto, CA**
Gilbert, Frank J. ... **San Francisco, CA**
Gilbert, Fred A. ... Atlanta, GA
Gilbert, Fred P. ... **Tulsa, OK**
Gilbert, Fredk. C. ... Omaha, NE
Gilbert, G. Timothy ... Ravenna, OH
Gilbert, Galen ... Boston, MA
Gilbert, Gary L. ... **Los Angeles, CA**
Gilbert, Gary M. ... **York, PA**
Gilbert, Geoffrey B. ... Rockville, MD
Gilbert, Geoffrey G. ... **Chicago, IL**
Gilbert, Geoffrey M. ... **St. Louis, MO**
Gilbert, George A. ... **Mount Olive, NJ**
Gilbert, George T. ... **New York, NY**
Gilbert, Gerald D. ... Eugene, OR
Gilbert, Gerald E. ... **McLean, VA**
Gilbert, Gigi A. ... Chicago, IL
Gilbert & Gilbert ... **Angleton, TX**
Gilbert, Gilbert & Bourke
Palm Springs, CA
Gilbert & Gilbert, Inc., P.S.
Mount Vernon, WA
Gilbert, Greg C. ... **Duluth, MN**
Gilbert, Greg D. ... **Wise, VA**
Gilbert, Gregory A. ... **New York, NY**
Gilbert, Gregory F. ... Orangevale, CA
Gilbert, Gregory L. ... Wyandotte, MI
Gilbert, Gregory R. ... **Oswego, NY**
Gilbert, Gregory S. ... **Las Vegas, NV**
Gilbert, Guy J. ... Brea, CA
Gilbert, Gwen E. ... Orlando, FL
Gilbert, Harrell, Gilbert, Sumerford & Martin, P.C. ... **Brunswick, GA**
Gilbert, Harris A. ... **Nashville, TN**
Gilbert, Harry C. ... Walnut Creek, CA
Gilbert, Harvey H. ... Morristown, NJ
Gilbert, Harvey H., P.C. ... Morristown, NJ
Gilbert, Harvey S. ... Beverly Hills, CA
Gilbert, Howard E. ... Skokie, IL
Gilbert, Howard E. ... Melville, NY
Gilbert, Howard N. ... **Chicago, IL**
Gilbert, Howard W., Jr. ... **Hagerstown, MD**
Gilbert, Hugh A. ... Watertown, NY
Gilbert, Ira J. ... **New York, NY**
Gilbert, Irene Casson ... **Garden Grove, CA**
Gilbert, Irene Casson ... **Los Angeles, CA**
Gilbert, Irene D. ... **San Rafael, CA**
Gilbert, Irwin R. ... **West Palm Beach, FL**
Gilbert, J. Lance ... Daytona Beach, FL
Gilbert, J. Parker ... **Atlanta, GA**
Gilbert, J. Phil ... Benton, IL
Gilbert, J. Stephen ... San Antonio, TX
Gilbert, J. Thomas ... **Newport Beach, CA**
Gilbert, Jack F. ... **Oklahoma City, OK**
Gilbert, Jack J. ... Clayton, MO
Gilbert, Jacqueline D. ... **New York, NY**
Gilbert, James A. ... Pasadena, CA
Gilbert, James A. ... Atlanta, GA
Gilbert, James B. ... **Brunswick, GA**
Gilbert, James B., Jr. ... **Brunswick, GA**
Gilbert, James D. ... **Columbus, OH**
Gilbert, James E. ... **Greenbelt, MD**
Silver Spring, MD
Gilbert, James F. ... Dallas, TX
Gilbert, James H. ... St. Paul, MN
Gilbert, James H., Jr. ... Raleigh, NC
Gilbert, James L. ... Arvada, CO
Gilbert, James M. ... **Los Angeles, CA**
Gilbert, James R. ... Cheboygan, MI
Gilbert, James T. ... **Richmond, KY**
Gilbert, Jan R. ... Savannah, GA
Gilbert, Jan S. ... **Washington, DC**
Gilbert, Jane L. ... San Diego, CA
Gilbert, Janet H. ... Rosemont, IL
Gilbert, Janice Gerbaz ... Houston, TX
Gilbert, Janine ... **New York, NY**
Gilbert, Jay ... **Chicago, IL**
Glen Ellyn, IL
Gilbert, Jayne Marsh ... Mount Vernon, WA
Gilbert, Jeffrey B. ... Chicago, IL
Gilbert, Jeffrey C. ... **Fort Lauderdale, FL**
Gilbert, Jeffrey R. ... **Greenville, SC**
Gilbert, Jeffrey T. ... **Chicago, IL**
Gilbert, Jeffry L. ... Allentown, PA
Gilbert, Jennifer ... Boston, MA
Gilbert, Jerold R. ... Englewood, CO
Gilbert, Jerrold ... **New York, NY**
Gilbert, Jerry H. ... Chicago, IL
Gilbert, Jerry W. ... **Richmond, KY**
Gilbert, Jesse W. ... San Diego, CA
Gilbert, Jessie A. ... **Stamford, CT**
Gilbert, John ... **Philadelphia, PA**
Gilbert, John A., Jr. ... **Washington, DC**
Gilbert, John D. ... **San Dimas, CA**
Gilbert, John G. ... Gaithersburg, MD
Gilbert, John J. ... Canandaigua, NY
Gilbert, John L. ... **Edwardsville, IL**
Gilbert, John M. ... Tampa, FL
Gilbert, John Matthew ... Bethesda, MD
Gilbert, John R. ... **Angleton, TX**
Gilbert, John S. ... St. Paul, MN

Gilbert, John T. ... Phoenix, AZ
Gilbert, John T. ... Boston, MA
Gilbert, John W., Jr. ... Rockville, MD
Gilbert, Jon C. ... Burbank, CA
Gilbert, Jonathan B. ... Chicago, IL
Gilbert, Jonathan R. ... Portland, OR
Gilbert, Jonathan S. ... Tampa, FL
Gilbert, Joseph B. ... Jacksonville, NC
Gilbert, Judith Chase ... Boston, MA
Gilbert, Jules M. ... Sacramento, CA
Gilbert, Julie A. ... Los Angeles, CA
Gilbert, Justin S. ... Jackson, TN
Gilbert, Karen L. ... Seattle, WA
Gilbert, Karen Lynn ... Greenbelt, MD
Gilbert, Kathryn Ann ... Hackensack, NJ
Gilbert, Kathryn M. ... La Junta, CO
Gilbert, Kelly, Crowley & Jennett
Los Angeles, CA
Orange, CA
Riverside, CA
San Diego, CA
Gilbert, Kenneth E. ... New York, NY
Gilbert, Keren D. ... San Francisco, CA
Gilbert, Kim Eileen ... Fair Oaks, CA
Gilbert, Kimberly A. ... Greenbelt, MD
Gilbert, Kimmel, Huffman, Prosser and Hewson, Ltd. ... Carbondale, IL
Gilbert, Kurt B. ... Albuquerque, NM
Gilbert, L. Burda ... Sacramento, CA
Gilbert, L. Jay ... Louisville, KY
Gilbert, Lanvil L. ... Austin, TX
Gilbert, Larisa E. Wicklander
Louisville, KY
Gilbert, Larry, (A Law Corporation)
Honolulu, HI
Gilbert, Laura B. ... New York, NY
Gilbert Law Offices, P.A. ... Bangor, ME
Gilbert, Lee Ann ... Cupertino, CA
Gilbert, Lela S. ... Lakewood, CO
Gilbert, Leon P. ... Woodland Hills, CA
Gilbert, Leonard H. ... Tampa, FL
Gilbert, Linda S.
Federal Energy Regulatory Commission, Office of the General Counsel, GV
Gilbert, Lorna A. ... Houston, TX
Gilbert, Louis P. ... New York, NY
Gilbert, Louis R. ... Rockford, IL
Gilbert, M. ... Palm Springs, CA
Gilbert, M. Glenn ... Los Angeles, CA
Gilbert, Margaret J. ... Olympia, WA
Gilbert, Marilyn ... Santa Barbara, CA
Gilbert, Mark A. ... Valdosta, GA
Gilbert, Mark A., P.C. ... Valdosta, GA
Gilbert, Mark E. ... Los Angeles, CA
Gilbert, Mark E. ... St. Paul, MN
Gilbert, Mark J. ... Los Angeles, CA
Gilbert, Marks, Schubel & DiGirolamo, P.A.
Hagerstown, MD
Gilbert, Marlene F. ... Costa Mesa, CA
Gilbert & Marlowe ... Santa Ana, CA
Gilbert, Martin ... Grass Valley, CA
Gilbert, Martin G. ... Bentonville, AR
Gilbert, Martin G. ... Newark, NJ
New York, NY
Gilbert, Mary Beth ... Houston, TX
Gilbert, Mel L. ... Hermitage, MO
Gilbert, Melanie Fess
Administrative Office Of The United States Courts, GV
Gilbert, Melinda R. ... North Little Rock, AR
Gilbert, Melinda R., P.A.
North Little Rock, AR
Gilbert, Melissa W. ... Marietta, GA
Gilbert, Michael A. ... New York, NY
Gilbert, Michael C. ... Louisville, KY
Gilbert, Michael D. ... Chevy Chase, MD
Gilbert, Michael H. ... Palm Springs, CA
Gilbert, Michael L. ... Denver, CO
Gilbert, Michael S. ... Patchogue, NY
Gilbert, Michael T. ... Denver, CO
Gilbert, Michelle J. ... Chicago, IL
Gilbert, Milton E. ... Waltham, MA
Gilbert, Mitchell A. ... New York, NY
Gilbert & Montlick, P.C. ... Atlanta, GA
Gilbert, Nancy B. ... Baton Rouge, LA
Gilbert, Norden S. ... De Kalb, IL
Gilbert, Oscar L. ... Norfolk, VA
Gilbert, Pamela
Consumer Product Safety Commission, Office of Executive Director, GV
Gilbert, Patricia ... Haddonfield, NJ
Gilbert, Paul A. ... Los Angeles, CA
Gilbert, Paul D. ... Dayton, OH
Gilbert, Paul D. ... Nashville, TN
Gilbert, Paul E. ... Phoenix, AZ
Gilbert, Paul N. ... Parsippany, NJ
Gilbert, Paul R. ... Chevy Chase, MD
Gilbert, Paul Terryl ... Baltimore, MD
Gilbert, Paul V. ... Cape Girardeau, MO
Gilbert, Peggy B. ... Bangor, ME
Gilbert, Peter Arey ... Richmond, VA
Gilbert, Peter R. ... Oakland, CA
Gilbert, Peter R. ... Washington, DC
Gilbert, Phil E., Jr. ... New York, NY
Gilbert, Quintress J. ... Macon, GA
Gilbert, Ralf ... Fairless Hills, PA
Gilbert, Ralph J. ... Barrington, IL
Gilbert, Ralph L., III ... Shelby, NC
Gilbert, Ralph W. ... Angleton, TX
Gilbert, Rebecca L. ... Washington, DC
Gilbert & Renton, P.C. ... Andover, MA
Boston, MA
Gilbert, Richard A. ... San Francisco, CA
Gilbert, Richard A. ... Tampa, FL
Gilbert, Richard A. ... New York, NY
Gilbert, Richard Carl ... Santa Ana, CA
Gilbert, Richard E. ... Irvine, CA
Los Angeles, CA
Gilbert, Richard I. ... Boca Raton, FL
Gilbert, Richard I., P.A. ... Boca Raton, FL
Gilbert, Richard J. ... Towson, MD
Gilbert, Richard L. ... Sacramento, CA
Gilbert, Richard M. ... Boston, MA
Gilbert, Risher Smith ... El Paso, TX
Gilbert, Rita K. ... Larchmont, NY
Gilbert, Robert B. ... Schenectady, NY
Gilbert, Robert C. ... Miami, FL
Gilbert, Robert C., P.A. ... Coral Gables, FL
Miami, FL
Gilbert, Robert D. ... New Haven, CT
Gilbert, Robert E. ... Ann Arbor, MI
Gilbert, Robert G. ... El Paso, TX
Gilbert, Robert J. ... Andover, MA
Gilbert, Robert M. ... Greeley, CO
Gilbert, Robert M. ... Whippany, NJ
Gilbert, Robert N. ... West Palm Beach, FL
Gilbert, Robert R. ... Aventura, FL
Gilbert, Robert W. ... Los Angeles, CA
Gilbert, Roberta R. ... Iowa City, IA
Gilbert, Robin H. ... Washington, DC
Gilbert, Robt. E. ... Rio, WI
Gilbert, Robt. L. ... Morrill, NE
Gilbert, Robt. S. ... Saginaw, MI
Gilbert, Roger G. ... Oroville, CA
Gilbert, Roger K. ... Phoenix, AZ
Gilbert, Roger L. ... Knoxville, TN
Gilbert, Roland Thomas ... Columbus, OH
Gilbert, Ronald S. ... Orlando, FL
Gilbert, Ronald W. ... Waukegan, IL
Gilbert, Roy S. ... Hauppauge, NY
Gilbert, Russell ... Yakima, WA
Gilbert, Ruth ... La Jolla, CA
Gilbert, Sabina D. ... Rocklin, CA
Gilbert & Sackman, A Law Corp.
Los Angeles, CA
Gilbert, Sally ... Oklahoma City, OK
Gilbert, Samuel J. ... New York, NY
Gilbert, Sandra F. ... Minneapolis, MN
Gilbert, Sanford D. ... Santa Monica, CA
Gilbert & Schoenstedt ... Joliet, IL
Gilbert, Scott D. ... Washington, DC
Gilbert, Segall and Young LLP
New York, NY
Gilbert, Sheldon S. ... Potomac, MD
Gilbert, Sheri L. ... New York, NY
Gilbert, Shira K. ... Carmichael, CA
Gilbert, Spencer B. ... Fort Pierce, FL
Gilbert, Stanley Leon ... New York, NY
Gilbert & Startzman ... Columbus, OH
Gilbert, Stephen A. ... Paramus, NJ
Gilbert, Stephen C. ... Morristown, NJ
Gilbert, Stephen C., P.C. ... Morristown, NJ
Gilbert, Stephen P. ... New York, NY
Gilbert, Steve ... San Antonio, TX
Gilbert, Steven J. ... Richmond, TX
Gilbert, Steven M. ... Rockville, MD
Gilbert, Steven M. ... Farmington Hills, MI
Gilbert, Susan A. ... Canyon Country, CA
Gilbert, Susan Kass ... Woodbridge, NJ
Gilbert, Suzanne E. ... Orlando, FL
Gilbert, Teal C. ... Scranton, PA
Gilbert, Teresan Wasie ... Cleveland, OH
Gilbert, Terry H. ... Cleveland, OH
Gilbert, Theodore ... Great Neck, NY
Gilbert, Theodore A. ... Chicago, IL
Gilbert, Theresa C. ... Lexington, KY
Gilbert, Thomas B., Jr. ... Atlanta, GA
Gilbert, Thomas J. ... Joliet, IL
Gilbert, Thomas S. ... Traverse City, MI
Gilbert, Tiffany D. ... Atlanta, GA
Gilbert, Timothy ... New York, NY
Gilbert, Timothy W. ... Charlotte, NC
Gilbert, Todd ... Lake Success, NY
Gilbert, Toni E. ... Reston, VA
Gilbert, V. Ann ... Omaha, NE
Gilbert, Vivienne ... New York, NY
Gilbert, Walter H. ... Sturgis, MI
Gilbert, Warren, Jr. ... Mount Vernon, WA
Gilbert, Warren L. ... Pasadena, CA
Gilbert, Warren M. ... Mount Vernon, WA
Gilbert, Wayne H. ... San Francisco, CA
Gilbert, W. G., Jr. ... Dillon, MT
Gilbert, Wil D. ... Hercules, CA
Gilbert, Wilbur G., III ... Dillon, MT
Gilbert, William J. ... Hudson, WI
Gilberti, Lawrence F. ... Philadelphia, PA
Gilberti, Michael V. ... Red Bank, NJ
Gilberti, William J., Jr. ... Albany, NY
Syracuse, NY
Harrisburg, PA
Gilbert-Lurie, Clifford W.
Los Angeles, CA
Gilbert-Rose, Ellen T. ... Fort Lauderdale, FL
Gilbert-Rose, Ellen T., P.A.
Fort Lauderdale, FL
Gilbert Scheer, Suzanne ... McLean, VA
Gilbertsen, Thomas E. ... Washington, DC
Gilbertson, Alfred Gene, Jr. ... Dallas, TX
Gilbertson, Burke S. ... Denver, CO
Gilbertson, Christine K.
West Des Moines, IA
Gilbertson, Cynthia F. ... Minneapolis, MN
Gilbertson, David E. ... Pierre, SD
Gilbertson, David M. ... Clarkfield, MN
Montevideo, MN
Gilbertson, Eric R. ... Johnson, VT
Gilbertson, Francis J. ... Bradley Beach, NJ
Gilbertson, Glen G. ... Cleveland, OH
Gilbertson, Joel W. ... Bismarck, ND
Gilbertson, John R. ... Portland, OR
Gilbertson, John T. ... Washington, DC
Gilbertson, Larry R. ... Washington, DC
Gilbertson, Les ... Tucson, AZ
Gilbertson, Les, P.C. ... Tucson, AZ
Gilbertson, Matthew T. ... Stoneham, MA
Gilbertson, Melvin L. ... Sapulpa, OK
Gilbertson, Michael A. ... Portland, OR
Gilbertson, Robert J. ... Minneapolis, MN
Gilbertson, Rolf E. ... Minneapolis, MN
Gilbertson, Ronald E. ... Washington, DC
Gilbertson, Sherry M. ... Fayetteville, AR
Gilbert-Stanton, Kimberly D. ... Boston, MA
Gilbertz, Jay A. ... Sheridan, WY
Gilboa, Tsach I. ... Santa Monica, CA
Gilboe, Gerard T. ... Southfield, MI
Gilboy, Kevin P. ... Philadelphia, PA
Gilboy, M. Daniel ... Canfield, OH
Gilbreath, Daniel W. ... Fort Smith, AR
Gilbreath, E. C. ... Fort Smith, AR
Gilbreath, Jerry M. ... Laurel, MS
Gilbreath, John S., Jr. ... Ypsilanti, MI
Gilbreath, Karen Griffith ... Washington, DC
Gilbreath Law Firm ... Fort Smith, AR
Gilbreath, Mark B. ... Corpus Christi, TX
Gilbreath, Robert B., (P.C.) ... Dallas, TX
Gilbreath, Timothy P. ... Richardson, TX
Gilbreath, Timothy P., P.C. ... Richardson, TX
Gilbreath, Vicki L. ... San Diego, CA
Gilbreath, William O. ... Lexington, KY
Gilbreath Wells, Shelly ... New Orleans, LA
Gilbreth & Adler ... Houston, TX
Gilbreth, David B. ... Napa, CA
Gilbreth, J. Mark ... Houston, TX
Gilbride, Ann DeBaets ... Washington, DC
Gilbride, Edward F. X.
Federal Deposit Insurance Corporation, Criminal Restitution, GV
Gilbride, Frank J., II ... Greenwich, CT
New York, NY
Gilbride, Gerard A. ... Brooklyn, NY
Gilbride, Gerard A., Jr. ... White Plains, NY
Gilbride, Heller & Brown, P.A.
Miami, FL
Gilbride, J. Thomas ... Whittier, CA
Gilbride, James F. ... Miami, FL
Gilbride, Joan M. ... New York, NY
Gilbride, Mary Callaghan ... Wahoo, NE
Gilbride, Michael P. ... Cleveland, OH
Gilbride, Ronald L. ... Wahoo, NE
Gilbride, Terrence M. ... Buffalo, NY
Gilbride, Tusa, Last & Spellane, LLC
Greenwich, CT
New York, NY
Gilbride, William D.
Grosse Pointe Farms, MI
Gilbride, William D., Jr. ... Detroit, MI
Gilbride, William D., P.C.
Grosse Pointe Farms, MI
Gilburt, Tony ... Washington, DC
Gilby, Adrian Todd ... Olathe, KS
Gilcher, Robert H. ... Wickliffe, OH
Gilchick, Stacey Robin ... New York, NY
Gilchrest, Charles Frederick ... Sharon, PA
Gilchrest, Robert M. ... Los Angeles, CA
Gilchrist, Alan G. ... Detroit, MI
Gilchrist, Andrew M. ... Houston, TX
Gilchrist, Andrew W. ... Albany, NY
Gilchrist, Barbara ... St. Louis, MO
Gilchrist, Brian R. ... Orlando, FL
Gilchrist, Bruce W. ... Washington, DC
Gilchrist, Carol M. ... Boston, MA
Gilchrist, Caroline A. ... Avon, IN
Indianapolis, IN
Gilchrist, David I. ... Southampton, NY
Gilchrist, Denice P. ... West Orange, NJ
Gilchrist, Dennis C. ... Greenville, SC
Gilchrist, Gary C. ... Des Moines, IA
Gilchrist, Gregory S. ... Emeryville, CA
Gilchrist, Gretchen C. ... United States Senate, Senatorial Assistants, GV
Gilchrist, Guy G. ... Des Moines, IA
Gilchrist, Hart D. ... Englewood, CO
Gilchrist, Heather ... Naples, FL
Gilchrist, Henry ... Dallas, TX
Gilchrist, Jack P. ... Oklahoma City, OK
Gilchrist, James H. ... Santa Cruz, CA
Gilchrist, James W., Jr. ... Columbia, SC
Gilchrist, Jane A. ... Raleigh, NC
Gilchrist, Jean M. ... McMinnville, TN
Gilchrist, John E. ... Austell, GA
Gilchrist, John K. ... Springfield, MA
Gilchrist, Jon W. ... Overland Park, KS
Gilchrist, Kathryn Russell ... Jackson, MS
Gilchrist, Kenneth L. ... Chicago, IL
Gilchrist Law Firm, A Professional Association ... Greenville, SC
Spartanburg, SC
Gilchrist, Lee Rodger ... Kirkland, WA
Gilchrist, M. Holly ... Sacramento, CA
Gilchrist, Michael C. ... Des Moines, IA
Gilchrist, Peter Spence, III ... Charlotte, NC
Gilchrist, Ralph W. ... Bolivar, MO
Gilchrist, Richard I. ... Santa Monica, CA
Gilchrist, Robert G. ... Salt Lake City, UT
Gilchrist & Rutter, Professional Corporation
Los Angeles, CA
Santa Monica, CA
Gilchrist, Stewart J. ... Laurel, MS
Gilchrist Sumrall Thaxton Yoder & Boone, PLLC ... Laurel, MS
Gilchrist, Thomas C. ... Cleveland, OH
Gilcrease, Glynn W., Jr., Law Offices of
Tempe, AZ
Gilcreast, Mark S. ... Hartford, CT
Gilcrest, Debra Thatcher ... Eugene, OR
Gilcrest, Roger A. ... Dublin, OH
Gild, Bernard S. ... Annandale, VA
Gild and Pikrallidas, P.C. ... Annandale, VA
Gildan, Herbert L. ... West Palm Beach, FL
Gildan, Laurie Leinwand
West Palm Beach, FL
Gildan, Phillip C. ... West Palm Beach, FL
Gildar, Joel A. ... Scottsdale, AZ
Gildar and Riger ... Bethesda, MD
Gildar, Robert W. ... Bethesda, MD
Gildard, James H., IV ... Salisbury, MD
Gilday, Andrew John ... Kingston, NY
Gilday, Bernard J., Jr. ... Cincinnati, OH
Gilday, Elizabeth A. ... Dallas, TX
Gilday, James K. ... Indianapolis, IN
Gilday, Mark A. ... Bethesda, MD
Gilday, Michael D. ... Cincinnati, OH
Gilday & Morrow ... Poughkeepsie, NY
Gilde, Ann O. ... Brooklyn, NY
Gilde, Thomas F. ... St. Paul, MN
Gildea, Brian D. ... Bedford, MA
Gildea, Brian M. ... New Haven, CT
Gildea, David K. ... Towson, MD
Gildea, Dennis ... San Francisco, CA
Gildea, E. James ... Elmhurst, IL
Gildea, Edward J. ... Battle Creek, MI
Gildea, Fain ... Mashpee, MA
Gildea, Frank S. ... Chicago, IL
Gildea, Gilbert E., Jr. ... Chicago, IL
Gildea, James B. ... Novato, CA
Gildea, James J. ... Newport News, VA
Gildea, John R. ... Elkhart, IN
Gildea, John T. ... White Plains, NY
Gildea, Kevin P. ... New York, NY
Gildea, Larry O. ... Eugene, OR
Gildea, Mark C. ... Brockton, MA
Gildea, Tammie L. ... New London, CT
Gildea, William F. ... Trumbull, CT
Gildehaus, Ralph F. ... Columbus, OH
Gil de Lamadrid-Gautier, E. J. ... San Juan, PR
Gildemeister, G. Daniel ... Sioux City, IA
Gildemeister, Willia, Keane, Stahle & Andreasen, L.L.P. ... Sioux City, IA
Gilden, Carol V. ... Chicago, IL
Gilden, David M. ... Providence, RI
Gilden, Ian L. ... Maitland, FL
Gilden, Jairus M. ... Chicago, IL
Gilden, James W. ... Brookline, MA
Gilden, Lisa J. ... Washington, DC
Gilden, Louis ... St. Louis, MO
Gilden, Richard H. ... New York, NY
Gilden, Robin C. ... Torrance, CA
Gilden, Steve G. ... Baltimore, MD
Gilden, Violet M. ... Baltimore, MD
Gildenhorn, Joseph B. ... Washington, DC
Gildenhorn, Michael S. ... Bethesda, MD
Gildenhorn, Stanton J. ... Rockville, MD
Gilder, Mark A. ... Washington, DC
Gilder, Mark H. ... Los Angeles, CA
Gilder, Robert G. ... Southaven, MS
Gildersleeve, L. Jay ... Lincoln, NE
Gildin, Daniel ... New York, NY
Gildin, Gary S. ... Carlisle, PA
Gildin, Leon H. ... New York, NY
Gildner, Lance A. ... Dayton, OH
Gildner, Michael J. ... Flint, MI
Gildner, Stephen P. ... Bakersfield, CA
Gildroy, Wayne R. ... Knoxville, TN
Gile, C. Merle ... Oklahoma City, OK
Gile, C. Merle, Inc., P.C.
Oklahoma City, OK
Gile, John W. ... Edmond, OK
Gilefsky, Judd ... Los Angeles, CA
Giles, Alexander McKenzie
Baltimore, MD
Giles, Allen E. ... Minneapolis, MN
Giles, Allison C. ... Department of Justice, Civil Division, GV
Giles, Bruce A. ... Phoenix, AZ
Giles, Carol L. ... Anchorage, AK
Giles, Cathy A. ... Mobile, AL
Giles, Charles M. ... Phoenix, AZ
Giles, Charles M. ... Phoenix, AZ
Tucson, AZ
Giles, Chris S. ... Madison, SD
Giles, Clarence A. (Al) ... Mobile, AL
Giles, Clark P. ... Salt Lake City, UT
Giles, Cynthia J. ... Philadelphia, PA
Giles, Daniel L. ... Marshall, MN
Giles, David C. ... San Antonio, TX
Giles, David L. ... Houston, TX
Giles, David M. ... Philadelphia, PA
Giles, David Morgan ... Washington, DC
Giles, Edward M., (P.C.) ... Denver, CO
Giles, Everett L. ... Portland, ME
Giles, F. Michael ... Newark, NJ
Giles, Frederick D. ... Grantville, PA
Giles, Gary T. ... Corpus Christi, TX
Giles, Geoffrey Lynn ... Reno, NV
Giles, Gerald F. ... Portsmouth, NH
Giles and Giles ... Sioux City, IA
Crofton, NE
South Sioux City, NE
Giles, Gordon B. ... Scottsdale, AZ
Giles, Gordon B., P.C. ... Scottsdale, AZ
Giles, Gregory ... Texarkana, AR
Giles, Gregory Gifford ... Sioux City, IA
Giles, H. M., Jr. ... Greensboro, NC
Giles, Irwin F. ... Suffern, NY
Giles, J. Paul H. ... Occoquan, VA
Giles, Jack K. ... Lexington, KY
Giles, James A. ... Des Moines, IA
Giles, James A. ... Mt. Vernon, OH
Giles, James T. ... Philadelphia, PA
Giles, Joel B. ... St. Petersburg, FL
Giles, John C. ... Mesa, AZ
Giles, John E. ... Washington, DC
Giles, John F., Jr. ... Scottsdale, AZ
Giles, Kathleen Carroll ... Groton, MA
Giles, Kathryn Anne ... McLean, VA
Giles, Kelly D. ... Pasadena, CA
Giles, Kenneth M. ... New York, NY
Giles & Lambert, P.C. ... Roanoke, VA
Giles, Laurie B. ... Bridgeport, CT
Giles, Malissa Lambert ... Roanoke, VA
Giles, Marcella ... McLean, VA
Giles, Margaret S. ... Los Angeles, CA

Giles, Mark H. ... Corpus Christi, TX
Giles, Mark H., P.C. ... Corpus Christi, TX
Giles, Marvin M., III ... Richmond, VA
Giles, Melbra J. ... Washington, DC
Giles, Michael D. ... Birmingham, AL
Giles, Michael P. ... Reading, PA
Giles, Molly ... Bloomfield Hills, MI
Giles, Neil E. ... Houston, TX
Giles, Owen M. ... Dallas, TX
Giles, R. David, Jr. ... Atlanta, GA
Giles, Richard C. ... Millburn, NJ
Giles, Richard C. ... Arlington, TX
Giles, Rita L. ... Los Altos, CA
Giles, Robert E. ... Raleigh, NC
Giles, Robert Edward ... Seattle, WA
Giles & Robinson, P.A. ... Orlando, FL
Giles, Rogan B. ... Austin, TX
Giles, Ronald ... Detroit, MI
Giles, Roy A., Jr. ... Raleigh, NC
Giles, Shannon L. ... Tucson, AZ
Giles, Sharon Cummings ... Washington, DC
Giles, Stanley Allen, Jr. ... Albuquerque, NM
Giles, Stephen E. ... Spartanburg, SC
Giles, Stephen R. ... Little Rock, AR
Giles, Susan ... Palm Springs, CA
Giles, Susan Lorraine ... Baltimore, MD
Giles, Terry M. ... Rancho Santa Fe, CA
Giles, Thomas V. ... Bloomfield Hills, MI
Giles, Thomas V. ... Detroit, MI
Giles, Tim W. ... Ventura, CA
Giles, Tracie Butler ... Devon, PA
Giles, Tracy Allen ... Roanoke, VA
Giles, Troy E. ... Milwaukee, WI
Giles, W. Jefferson, III ... Sioux City, IA
Giles, William C., Jr. ... Longmeadow, MA
Giles, William E. ... New York, NY
Giles, William J., IV ... Sioux City, IA
Crofton, NE
Giles-Klein, Bruce H. ... Miami, FL
Giles-Klein, Lisa A. ... Miami, FL
Gilevich, Thomas L. ... Sacramento, CA
Gilezan, Grant P. ... Detroit, MI
Gilfeather, Charles A. ... Saginaw, MI
Gilfeather, Valorie A. ... Midland, MI
Gilfedder, Brian P. ... Lexington, KY
Gilfillan, Charles D. ... Everett, WA
Gilfillan, David G. ... Roseland, NJ
Gilfillan, Douglas W. ... Atlanta, GA
Gilfillan, Gail S. ... Los Angeles, CA
Gilfillan, Gilpin & Brehman
Jenkintown, PA
Gilfillan & Grimm ... Pittsburgh, PA
Gilfillan, Hilda B. ... New York, NY
Gilfillan, Howard T. ... Pittsburgh, PA
Gilfillan, John G., III ... Roseland, NJ
Gilfillan, John Paul ... Gladstone, NJ
Gilfillan, Joseph P. ... Peoria, IL
Gilfillan, Lynn E. ... Chicago, IL
Gilfillan, Paul P. ... Peoria, IL
Gilfillan, Peter S. ... Buffalo, NY
Gilfillan, Sandra Linscott Wagner
Kansas City, MO
Gilfillan, Susan ... Burlington, VT
Gilfix Associates ... Palo Alto, CA
Gilfix & La Poll, Associates ... Palo Alto, CA
Gilfix, Michael ... Palo Alto, CA
Gilfix, Suzanne Glick ... Boston, MA
Gilfoil, F. Robert, Jr. ... Juno Beach, FL
Gilford, Andrew M. ... Los Angeles, CA
Gilford, Anne Johnson ... Evanston, IL
Gilford, Janice L. ... Stockton, CA
Gilford, Ronald M., (Ltd.) ... Chicago, IL
Gilford, Steven J. ... Tionesta, PA
Gilford, Steven R. ... Chicago, IL
Gilford, Tia L. ... New York, NY
Gilfoy, J. R. (Bob) ... Lexington, MS
Gilfoyle, John J. ... Saugus, MA
Gilfoyle, Nathalie F. P. ... Washington, DC
Gilg, Daniel R. ... Ogallala, NE
Gilg, Deborah R. ... Ogallala, NE
Gilg Law Office, P.C. ... Ogallala, NE
Gilges, Walter F. ... Rochester, NY
Gilgor, Edward M. ... Atlanta, GA
Gilgore, Gayle Robin ... Philadelphia, PA
Gilgun, Frederick V. ... Concord, MA
Gilgun, Frederick V., Jr. ... Lexington, MA
Gilgun, Regina M. ... Boston, MA
Gilgus, Mark H. ... Kansas City, MO
Gilham, Carol R. ... Lawrence, KS
Gilham, Charles S. ... St. Louis, MO
Gilham, G. Anthony ... El Cajon, CA
Gilheany, Carolyn-Gail
Securities and Exchange Commission,
Division of Enforcement, GV
Gilheany, Terence F. ... New York, NY
Gilheeney, Shannon ... Providence, RI
Gilhool, Jennifer T. ... Dearborn, MI
Gilhool, John F. ... Southgate, MI
Gilhool, John F., P.C., Law Offices of
Southgate, MI
Gilhool, Kevin M. ... Tampa, FL
Gilhool, Thomas K. ... Philadelphia, PA
Gilhooley, Margaret ... Newark, NJ
Gilhooley, Paul G.
National Labor Relations Board,
Office of Board Members, GV
Gilhooley, Thomas P. ... Cortland, NY
Gilhooly, John E., Jr. ... Chicago, IL
Gilhooly, John V. ... Dallas, TX
Gilhooly, Kathleen
General Accounting Office,
Office of the General Counsel, GV
Gilhooly, Mary C. ... Chicago, IL
Gilhooly, Stephen J. ... Dallas, TX
Gilhooly, Susan H. ... Abingdon, MD
Gilhooly, Susan J. ... West Chester, PA
Gilhousen, Brent J. ... St. Louis, MO
Gilhousen, James R., (P.A.) ... Wichita, KS
Gilhuley, Stephen E. ... Lake Success, NY
Gilhuly, Peter M. ... Los Angeles, CA
Gilhuly, R. Morgan ... San Francisco, CA
Gilhuly, Robert T. ... Greenwich, CT
Gilibert, Sara L. ... Atlanta, GA
Giliberti, Barbara C. ... Annapolis, MD
Giliberti, Ben ... Department of Justice,
Antitrust Division, GV
Giliberti, Catherine T. ... New York, NY
Giliberti, Frank J. ... Uniondale, NY
Giliberti, Mary T. ... Washington, DC
Giliberto, Carol T. ... East Providence, RI
Giliberto, Donna M. Ciaccio ... Albany, NY
Gilida, Laynie B. ... Denver, CO
Gilida, Tamara K.
Greenwood Village, CO
Gilinger, James J. ... Santa Barbara, CA
Gilinsky, Armand ... Fairfield, CT
New York, NY
Gilinsky, Marshall ... New York, NY
Gilio, Ellen J. ... Wood Ridge, NJ
Gilioli, Eric L. ... New York, NY
Gilje, Brent ... Burlington, ND
Gilje, Charles J. ... Jamestown, ND
Gilje & Dalsted, P.C. ... Jamestown, ND
Giljum, Joseph P. ... St. Louis, MO
Gilk, Jennifer L. J. ... Redwood Falls, MN
Gilk, Margaret Epple ... Columbia, MO
Gilker, Daisy D. ... Globe, AZ
Gilker and Jones, A Professional Association
Fayetteville, AR
Fort Smith, AR
Mountainburg, AR
Gilker, Joseph F. ... Mountainburg, AR
Gilker, Paul Alvin ... Mountainburg, AR
Gilker, Robert J. ... Columbus, OH
Gilkers, George E. ... Metairie, LA
Gilkerson, Christopher P.
Securities and Exchange Commission,
Office of the General Counsel, GV
Gilkerson, Edward A. ... St. Louis, MO
Gilkerson, G. Ernest ... Midland, TX
Gilkerson, George E. ... Lubbock, TX
Gilkerson, George E., Attorney-at-Law, P.C.
Lubbock, TX
Gilkerson, George N., Jr. ... Lisle, IL
Gilkes, Arthur G. ... Chicago, IL
Gilkes, Arthur G., Jr. ... Pittsburgh, PA
Gilkeson, John S. ... Claremore, OK
Gilkey, Duane C. ... Albuquerque, NM
Gilkey, Gayle M. ... Huntington Beach, CA
Gilkey, Norman E. ... Pittsburgh, PA
Gilkey, Sara McPeake ... Lynchburg, VA
Gilkey, Stephenson & Weese, P.A.
Albuquerque, NM
Gilkey, William W. ... Clearwater, FL
Gilkison, Frank E. ... Muncie, IN
Gill, Albert Wayne ... Boca Raton, FL
Gill, Amber McLaughlin ... Enid, OK
Gill, Anita A. ... Cleveland, OH
Gill, Anne G. ... New York, NY
Gill, Anne L. ... Kansas City, MO
Gill, Anne W. ... Denver, CO
Gill and Baldwin ... Glendale, CA
Los Angeles, CA
Gill, Barbara P. ... Baton Rouge, LA
Gill & Behnke ... Ocala, FL
Gill, Bernard A., Jr. ... Midlothian, VA
Gill, Betsy ... Overland Park, KS
Gill, Brenda L. ... New York, NY
Gill, Brendan E. ... San Antonio, TX
Gill, Brian F. ... Pacific Grove, CA
Gill, Brian T. ... Grand Rapids, MI
Gill, Brian T., P.C. ... Grand Rapids, MI
Gill, Bryan F., Jr. ... Lake Charles, LA
Gill, C. Clayton ... Boise, ID
Gill, Carmel Cronin ... Denver, CO
Gill, Carolyn Jean ... Riverside, CA
Gill, Carolyn W. ... New Orleans, LA
Gill, Catherine G. ... Mathews, VA
Gill, Celeste R. ... Grand Rapids, MI
Gill, Charles C. ... Tolland, CT
Gill, Charles D. ... Litchfield, CT
Gill, Charles H., Jr. ... Elkton, KY
Gill, Cheryl M. ... La Crosse, WI
Gill, Christine Meagher ... Washington, DC
Gill, Clave E. ... Covington, LA
Gill, Cynthia ... Hackensack, NJ
Gill, Daniel H. ... Los Angeles, CA
Gill, Daren K. ... Wilton, CT
Gill, David A., (A Professional Corporation)
Los Angeles, CA
Gill, David H., II ... San Jose, CA
Gill, David L. ... Sioux City, IA
Gill, David L. ... Cincinnati, OH
Gill, David M. ... San Diego, CA
Gill, Debra Porter ... Overland Park, KS
Gill, Douglas R. ... Southern Pines, NC
Gill & Dow ... Southern Pines, NC
Gill, E. Ann ... New York, NY
Gill, Edward C. ... Georgetown, DE
Gill, Edward J., Jr. ... Washington, DC
Gill, Elizabeth A. ... Overland Park, KS
Gill, Elizabeth S. ... Coronado, CA
Gill, Ellen Beth ... Chicago, IL
Gill, Elliot M. ... Pittsburgh, PA
Gill Elrod Ragon Owen Calhoun Skinner &
Sherman, P.A. ... Little Rock, AR
Gill, Eric J. ... Cincinnati, OH
Gill, Eric V. ... Port Orange, FL
Gill, Frances T. ... Jamaica Plain, MA
Gill, G. William ... Montgomery, AL
Gill, Geoffrey W. ... Long Beach, CA
Gill, George A., Jr. ... Rock Hill, SC
Gill, George E. ... Groton, CT
Gill & Gill, P.C. ... Mathews, VA
Gill & Gill, S.C. ... Appleton, WI
Gill, Glendon K. ... Staunton, VA
Gill, Gordon G. ... Salt Lake City, UT
Gill, Gregory B., Sr. ... Appleton, WI
Gill, Gregory M. ... Baltimore, MD
Greenbelt, MD
Gill, Gregory S. ... Lebanon, TN
Gill, Hallie W. ... Houston, TX
Gill, Harold E., Jr. ... Lawrenceville, GA
Gill, Harold E., Jr., P.C. ... Lawrenceville, GA
Gill, Harry ... Ridgefield, CT
Gill, Harry P. ... Bay City, MI
Gill, Harry W., Jr. ... West Chester, PA
Gill, Henrietta ... Lexington, SC
Gill, Henry A., Jr. ... Atlanta, GA
Gill, Henry F. ... Trenton, NJ
Gill, Herbert C., Jr. ... Chesterfield, VA
Gill, Hubert L. ... Austin, TX
Gill, Hugh W. ... Wichita, KS
Gill, James E., Jr. ... High Point, NC
Gill, James F. ... New York, NY
Gill, James H., Jr. ... Baton Rouge, LA
Gill, James H., Jr. ... Nashville, TN
Gill, James H., Jr., Ltd., A Professional Law
Corporation ... Baton Rouge, LA
Gill, James J. ... Akron, OH
Gill, James T. ... Cedar Knolls, NJ
Gill, Jana L. ... San Francisco, CA
Washington, DC
Gill, Jeffrey M. ... Indianapolis, IN
Gill, Jeffrey M. ... Richmond, VA
Gill, Jeffrey P. ... Pensacola, FL
Gill, Jeremy T. ... Manitowoc, WI
Gill, John D. ... Austin, TX
Gill, John G., Jr. ... Rockville, MD
Gill, John J. ... Washington, DC
Gill, John J. ... Cleveland, OH
Gill, John J. ... Blacksburg, VA
Pulaski, VA
Gill, John J., Jr. ... Wilkes-Barre, PA
Gill, John P. ... Little Rock, AR
Gill, John P. ... Alamo, CA
Gill, John P. ... Yonkers, NY
Gill, John S. ... Mathews, VA
Gill, Jonathan Reed ... Marina, CA
Gill, Joseph P. ... Annapolis, MD
Gill, Joseph S. ... Columbus, OH
Gill, Kathleen E. ... Tarrytown, NY
Gill, Kay Rigling ... Department of Education,
Office of the General Counsel, GV
Gill and Keeley ... Tulsa, OK
Gill, Keith H. ... Woodland Hills, CA
Gill, Kelly ... Abilene, TX
Gill, Kenneth J. ... Peabody, MA
Gill, Kenneth J. ... Minneapolis, MN
Gill, Kennie Lee ... United States Senate,
Committee Legal Personnel, GV
Gill, Kent ... Shreveport, LA
Gill, Kermit A. ... Minneapolis, MN
Gill, Kinloch, III ... Houston, TX
Gill, L. Zane ... Salt Lake City, UT
Gill, Lance Douglas ... Minerva, OH
Gill, Laura B. ... Denver, CO
Gill, Laura Leigh ... Baltimore, MD
Gill, Laurie S. ... Boston, MA
Gill Law Offices, The ... Pacific Grove, CA
Gill Law Practice ... Danbury, CT
Ridgefield, CT
Gill, Lawrence B. ... Los Angeles, CA
Gill, Lawrence D. ... Denver, CO
Gill, Lawrence E. ... Atlanta, GA
Gill, Lawrence M. ... Chicago, IL
Gill, Lee S. ... Houston, TX
Gill, Lyle B. ... Fremont, NE
Gill, L. Zane, A Professional Corporation
Salt Lake City, UT
Gill, M. Michael ... Kansas City, MO
Gill, Manjit ... Tampa, FL
Gill, Manjula ... New York, NY
Gill, Manvinder ... Los Angeles, CA
Gill, Margaret G. ... San Francisco, CA
Gill, Marion S. ... Dumas, AR
Gill, Maris J.W. ... Pittsburgh, PA
Gill, Markley Runyon ... Clarksville, TN
Gill, Mary C. ... Atlanta, GA
Gill, Mary E. ... Greensboro, NC
Gill, Mary Elizabeth ... Columbus, OH
Gill, Mary R. ... Baltimore, MD
Gill, Mellor A. ... Northport, NY
Gill, Michael A. ... Northfield, NJ
Gill, Michael J. ... Los Angeles, CA
Gill, Michael J. ... Chicago, IL
Gill, Michael J. ... Boston, MA
Gill, Michael L. ... Westlake, OH
Gill, Michael Min-Taek ... Los Angeles, CA
Gill, Michael R. ... Dallas, TX
Gill, Michael W. ... La Crosse, WI
Gill, Monty S. ... Santa Maria, CA
Gill, Nancy J. ... Cincinnati, OH
Gill, Ned, III ... Houston, TX
Gill, Nicole R. ... Boston, MA
Gill, P. Dewey ... Ellaville, GA
Gill, Patricia Sjoblom ... Dallas, TX
Gill, Patrick D. ... Washington, DC
New York, NY
Gill, Paul G. ... Department of Justice,
Tax Division, GV
Gill, Peter J. ... New York, NY
Gill Professional Corporation ... Denver, CO
Gill, Rae Farrell ... Provincetown, MA
Gill, Rae Farrell, P.C. ... Barnstable, MA
Provincetown, MA
Gill, Randall A. ... Tulsa, OK
Gill, Raymond ... Pacific Palisades, CA
Gill, Raymond A., Jr. ... Woodbridge, NJ
Gill, Raymond L. ... San Francisco, CA
Gill, Richard H. ... Montgomery, AL
Gill, Richard L. ... Minneapolis, MN
Gill, Richard S.
Federal Deposit Insurance Corporation,
Professional Liability Section, GV
Gill, Robert C., II ... Washington, DC
Gill, Robert D. ... Forest Hills, NY
Gill, Robert E., Jr. ... Houston, TX
Gill, Robert J. ... Sarasota, FL
Gill, Robert T. ... Boston, MA
Gill, Robyn S. ... Austin, TX
Gill, Rockne ... Bend, OR
Portland, OR
Gill, Roger W. ... Hudson, MA
Gill, Ronald H. ... Oxnard, CA
Gill, Ronald W. ... New York, NY
Gill, Roy C., Jr. ... Sacramento, CA
Gill, Russell S. ... Biloxi, MS
Gill, S. Ray, (P.A.) ... Ocala, FL
Gill, S. Sadiq ... Richmond, VA
Gill, Sanjivpal ... Newport Beach, CA
Gill, Scot D. ... Huntingdon, PA
Gill, Scott R. ... Fort Lauderdale, FL
Gill, Scott R., P.A. ... Fort Lauderdale, FL
Gill, Sheila McDonald ... Annapolis, MD
Gill, Sherry L. ... Richmond, VA
Gill & Shinn ... Covington, LA
New Orleans, LA
Gill & Sippel ... Rockville, MD
Gill, Stephanie L. ... Pittsburgh, PA
Gill, Stephen J. ... Boston, MA
Gill, Steven L. ... Nashville, TN
Gill, Susan J. ... San Diego, CA
Gill, Susan Jane ... San Diego, CA
Gill, Susan M. ... Bakersfield, CA
Gill, Susann E. ... Bridgeport, CT
Gill, T. Nicholas ... Washington, DC
Gill, Terence C. ... Denver, CO
Gill, Thomas B. ... Napa, CA
Gill, Thomas D. ... Bethpage, NY
Gill, Thomas D., Jr. ... Boston, MA
Gill, Thomas I. ... Kansas City, MO
Gill, Thomas J. ... San Francisco, CA
Gill, Thomas L. ... Vallejo, CA
Gill, Thomas P. ... Cleveland, OH
Gill, Thomas P., Jr. ... Brandon, FL
Gill, Thomas R. ... San Diego, CA
Gill, Thomas R. ... San Francisco, CA
Gill, Thomas S. ... Buffalo, NY
Gill, Thos. P. ... Honolulu, HI
Gill, Timothy M. ... San Francisco, CA
Gill, Timothy R. ... Rockford, IL
Gill, Tracy L. ... Columbia, MD
Gill, U.S. Mickey ... Arlington, VA
Gill, Vernon S. ... Washington, DC
Gill, W. Brent ... Indianapolis, IN
Seymour, IN
Gill, Wayne T., (P.A.)
West Palm Beach, FL
Gill, William Bobby, III ... Jackson, MS
Gillain, Donald B. ... Warren, MI
Gillam, Anne C. ... Los Angeles, CA
Gillam, Carol L. ... Los Angeles, CA
Gillam, Chad K. ... Denver, CO
Gillam, Christina P. ... Jacksonville, FL
Gillam and Gillam ... Windsor, NC
Gillam, Harry Lee, Jr. ... Marshall, TX
Gillam, M. Braxton, III ... Windsor, NC
Gillam, Marcheta L. ... Cincinnati, OH
Gillam, Moses B., Jr. ... Windsor, NC
Gillam, Robert S. ... Raleigh, NC
Gillam, W. Braxton, IV ... Jacksonville, FL
Gillam, Wiley Braxton, IV
Jacksonville, FL
Gillan, Bradley J. ... Minneapolis, MN
Gillan, Brian P. ... Cincinnati, OH
Gillan, Bruce W. ... Lincoln, NE
Gillan, Charles A. ... San Jose, CA
Gillan, John A. ... Danville, VA
Gillan, Nona K.L. ... St. Albans, VT
Gillan, Paul A., Jr. ... Albany, NY
Gillan, Richard E. ... Rockford, IL
Gillan, Robert B. ... Rancho Cucamonga, CA
Gilland, Dana M. ... Thomaston, CT
Gilland, Michael B. ... Baltimore, MD
Gilland, Richard D. ... Thomaston, CT
Gilland, Richard D., Jr. ... Thomaston, CT
Gilland, Robt. L. ... Lutherville, MD
Gilland, Seabourne and Malley
Thomaston, CT
Gillanders, Robert R. ... Seattle, WA
Gillane, Patricia S. ... New York, NY
Gillane, Timothy E. ... New York, NY
Gillard, Bauer, Mazrum, Florip, Smigelski
and Gulden ... Alpena, MI
Gillard, Cynthia Schaefer ... Elkhart, IN
Gillard & Gillard ... Grand Rapids, MI
Gillard, John F. ... San Antonio, TX
Gillard, Joseph R., III ... Grand Rapids, MI
Gillard, Joseph R., Jr. ... Grand Rapids, MI
Gillard, Patricia ... Commack, NY
Gillard, R. Aloise ... Muskegon, MI
Gillard, Robert H. ... Houston, TX
Gillary, Randall J. ... Troy, MI
Gillary, Randall J., P.C. ... Detroit, MI
Troy, MI
Gillaspia, Lawrence T. ... Houston, TX
Gillaspie, Don G. ... El Dorado, AR
Gillaspie, Julie Ann ... Houston, TX
Gillaspie, Marjean M. ... Omaha, NE
Gillaspie, Michael S. ... Portland, OR
Gillaspie, Thomas J. ... Lincoln, NE
Gillaspie, Tommy W. ... Houston, TX
Gillaspy, Joseph M. ... Carmel, IN
Gill-Austern, Gary L. ... Boston, MA
Gillcrist, Walter E., Jr. ... Bethesda, MD
Gille, Christine D. ... Pasadena, CA
Gille, Grant M. ... Brick Town, NJ
Montclair, NJ
Gille, Lori-jean ... Minneapolis, MN

Gille, Randolph K. .... Pasadena, CA
Gillean, Jack .... Conway, AR
Gillean, Rasa Jucas, Ms. .... Little Rock, AR
Gillease, Dennis B. .... Modesto, CA
Gillece, James P., Jr. .... Baltimore, MD
Gilleece, Anne .... White Plains, NY
Gilleece and Gilleece .... White Plains, NY
Gilleece, Jennifer A. .... New York, NY
Gilleece, Kevin P. .... White Plains, NY
Gilleece, Mary Ann .... Washington, DC
Gillelan, Joshua T., II ...... Department of Labor, Office of the Solicitor, GV
Gilleland, G. Kenneth .... Sevierville, TN
Gilleland, John A. .... Atlanta, GA
Gilleland, John G. .... Houston, TX
Gilleland, Robert B. .... Sanford, NC
Gilleland, Wayne .... Macon, GA
Gillen, Arthur F. .... South St. Paul, MN
Gillen, Christine .... Cliffside Park, NJ
Gillen, Craig A. .... Atlanta, GA
Gillen & Cruz, L.L.C. .... Rock Hill, SC
Gillen Dailey Cromwell & Withers LLC
Atlanta, GA
Norcross, GA
Savannah, GA
Gillen, Daniel M. .... Paramus, NJ
Gillen, Danl. J. .... Boston, MA
Gillen, David M. .... Los Angeles, CA
Gillen, Dennis L. .... Wichita, KS
Gillen, Gary R. .... Chicago, IL
Gillen, James B., Jr. .... Tyler, TX
Gillen, James R. .... Marina Del Rey, CA
Gillen, James R. .... Newark, NJ
Gillen, Jeffrey Dana .... Albany, NY
Gillen, Jill L. .... San Francisco, CA
Gillen, John .... North Andover, MA
Gillen, Karen .... Phoenix, AZ
Gillen, Larry .... Winston-Salem, NC
Gillen, Larry, PLLC .... Winston-Salem, NC
Gillen, Mary D. .... Roselle, NJ
Gillen, Michael Frederick .... Rock Hill, SC
Gillen, Neal P. .... Washington, DC
Gillen, Patricia .... Buffalo, NY
Gillen, Patrick T. .... Charlotte, NC
Gillen, Robert D. .... Naperville, IL
Gillen, Robert D., Ltd., Law Offices of
Naperville, IL
Gillen, Sean M. .... Omaha, NE
Gillen, Stephen E. .... Cincinnati, OH
Gillen, Stephen F. .... Clinton, NJ
Gillen, Teresa .... Philadelphia, PA
Gillen, William A., Jr. .... Tampa, FL
Gillen, Yarbrough & Anderson, P.C.
Tyler, TX
Gillen, Zoe M. .... Baltimore, MD
Gillentine, Billy D. .... Houston, TX
Gillentine, David V. .... Madison, MS
Gillenwater, Bobby Brian ..... Fort Wayne, IN
Gillenwater, Brandy K.
Winston-Salem, NC
Gillenwater, Elba, Jr. .... Wheeling, WV
Gillenwater and Hampton .... Glasgow, KY
Gillenwater, John K. .... Bristol, TN
Gillenwater, Michael A. .... Jeffersonville, IN
Gillenwater, Timothy J. .... Glasgow, KY
Gillenwaters, Charles R. ..... Alexander City, AL
Giller, Brian J. .... Miami, FL
Giller, James .... Oakland, CA
Giller, Jefferson D. .... Houston, TX
Giller, Julia M. .... Boca Raton, FL
Giller, Lee S. .... Macedonia, OH
Giller, Ronald Andrew .... New York, NY
Giller, Ronald K. .... Los Angeles, CA
Giller, Thomas M. .... Elgin, IL
Gilleran, Jeffrey T. .... Washington, DC
Gilleran, Margaret A. .... New York, NY
Gilleran, Marianne .... Boston, MA
Gilleran, Michael C. .... Boston, MA
Gilleran, Paul R. .... Troy, MI
Gilleran, Richard E. .... Spokane, WA
Gilleran-Johnson, Barbara .... Waukegan, IL
Gillerman, Gerald .... Boston, MA
Gillers, Barbara S. .... New York, NY
Gillers, Stephen .... New York, NY
Gillers, William H. .... Treasury Department, Departmental Offices, GV
Gillert, Thomas C. .... Tulsa, OK
Gilles, Albert S. .... Denver, CO
Gilles, Anthony E. .... Santa Fe, NM
Gilles, David J. .... Madison, WI
Gilles, David P. .... Austin, TX
Gilles, George D. .... Midland, TX
Gilles, Herbert J. .... Dallas, TX
Gilles, Hilary Poulsen
Newport Beach, CA
Gilles, Jeffery R. .... Salinas, CA
Gilles, Mark E. .... Princeville, IL
Gilles, Paul Joseph .... Portland, OR
Gilles, Stephen G. .... Hamden, CT
Gilles, Stephen J. .... Dallas, TX
Gilles, Susan M. .... Columbus, OH
Gilles, William F. .... Sun City West, AZ
Gillespie, Alexander H. .... Washington, DC
New York, NY
Gillespie & Allison .... Boca Raton, FL
Gillespie, Amy E. .... Gulfport, MS
Gillespie, Amy R. .... Raleigh, NC
Gillespie, Andrea B. .... Towson, MD
Gillespie & Associates, P.C. .... Phoenix, AZ
Scottsdale, AZ
Tempe, AZ
Gillespie, Bridget M. .... Pittsburgh, PA
Gillespie, Camille O'hara .... Brooklyn, NY
Gillespie, Carl C. .... Tazewell, VA
Gillespie, Carl C., Jr. .... Tazewell, VA
Gillespie, Carol J. .... Miami, FL
Gillespie, Catharine E. .... Philadelphia, PA
Gillespie, Catherine H. .... Cherry Hill, NJ
Philadelphia, PA
Gillespie, C. H., III .... Sherman, TX
Gillespie, Charlotte E. .... Washington, DC
Gillespie, Cheree .... Clemson, SC
Gillespie, Clarke M., III .... Chicago, IL
Gillespie, Colleen P. .... Torrance, CA
Gillespie, Craig C. .... Phoenix, AZ
Gillespie, Craig C., P.C. .... Phoenix, AZ
Gillespie, DeeAn .... Phoenix, AZ
Gillespie, Donald E. .... Richmond, VA
Gillespie, Donald S., Jr. .... Charlotte, NC
Gillespie, Donna S.
United States Postal Service, Law Department, GV
Gillespie, Edmund S. B. .... Boston, MA
Gillespie, Eliza Reyes .... Kenosha, WI
Twin Lakes, WI
Gillespie, Ellen M. .... Somerville, NJ
Gillespie, Eugene J., Jr. .... Short Hills, NJ
Gillespie, Eugenie E. .... Freeport, NY
Gillespie, Frederick L. .... Kearny, NJ
Gillespie, Frederick S. .... Kearny, NJ
Gillespie, G. Rich .... Stockton, CA
Gillespie, Gardner F. .... Washington, DC
Gillespie, Garrett G. .... Boston, MA
Gillespie, George B. .... Springfield, IL
Gillespie, George E., Jr. .... Petal, MS
Gillespie, George J., III .... New York, NY
Gillespie & Gillespie .... Sherman, TX
Gillespie, Gillespie & Jablonski .... Kearny, NJ
Gillespie and Gillespie, P.A.
New Smyrna Beach, FL
Gillespie, Goldman & Kronengold
Fort Lauderdale, FL
Gillespie, Guy T., III .... Oxford, MS
Gillespie, Hal K. .... Dallas, TX
Gillespie, Hart, Altizer & Whitesell, P.C.
Tazewell, VA
Gillespie, Howard L. .... Rockaway Point, NY
Gillespie, Jacqueline D. .... Santa Rosa, CA
Gillespie, James A. .... Roswell, NM
Gillespie, James Bruce .... Houston, TX
Gillespie, James D. .... Elkin, NC
Gillespie, James F. .... Burr Ridge, IL
Gillespie, James F. E. .... Stamford, CT
Gillespie, James F. E., Jr.
Treasury Department, Office of the Comptroller of the Currency, GV
Gillespie, James H. .... Rio Verde, AZ
Gillespie, James J. .... Morristown, NJ
Gillespie, James J. .... Spokane, WA
Gillespie, James P. .... Downey, CA
Gillespie, James P. .... Washington, DC
Gillespie, James R. .... Boise, ID
Gillespie, James R., P.A. .... Boise, ID
Nampa, ID
Gillespie, James W. .... Sterling, IL
Gillespie, Jeffrey Stephen .... Oakland, CA
Gillespie, Jeffrey Warren .... Houston, TX
Gillespie, John A. .... Red Bank, NJ
Gillespie, John Baxter .... Alpharetta, GA
Gillespie, John C. .... Marlton, NJ
Gillespie, John F. .... St. Louis, MO
Gillespie, John F. .... Austin, TX
Gillespie, John L. .... Lansing, MI
Gillespie, John P. .... Secaucus, NJ
Gillespie, John R. .... Dallas, TX
Gillespie, John R., Jr.
Fort Lauderdale, FL
Gillespie, Joseph M. .... Florham Park, NJ
Gillespie, Joseph R. .... Louisville, KY
Gillespie, Judy T. .... Cedar Bluff, VA
Gillespie, Kenneth R. .... New Bern, NC
Gillespie, Kevin F. .... Redlands, CA
Gillespie, Kim D. .... Phoenix, AZ
Gillespie, Laura J.
Department of Commerce, GV
Gillespie, Laurel C. ...... Department of Defense, Defense Legal Services Agency, GV
Gillespie Law Firm, The .... Gulfport, MS
Gillespie, Lawrence G. .... St. Louis, MO
Gillespie, Leonard X. .... Brooklyn, NY
Gillespie, Margaret A. .... Phoenix, AZ
Gillespie, Margaret H. .... Los Angeles, CA
Gillespie, Marie T. .... Garden City, NY
Gillespie, Mary K. .... San Francisco, CA
Gillespie, Mary Schillinger .... Ballwin, MO
Gillespie, Michael C. .... Wichita, KS
Gillespie, Michael D. .... Houston, TX
Gillespie, Michael E. .... Boston, MA
Gillespie, Michael J. .... New York, NY
Gillespie, Michael J. .... Coquille, OR
Gillespie & Murphy, P.A. .... New Bern, NC
Gillespie, Nancy L. .... New York, NY
Gillespie, Norman C. .... Arlington, VA
Gillespie, Norman L. .... Oxford, MS
Gillespie, Patrick R. .... Anoka, MN
Gillespie, Paul J. .... Lynnfield, MA
Gillespie, Paul R. .... Fairfax, VA
Gillespie, Peter A. .... Denver, CO
Gillespie, Peter J. .... Chicago, IL
Gillespie, R. Bowen, III .... Boca Raton, FL
Gillespie, Raymond E. .... Cambridge, MA
Gillespie, Regina Robinson .... Mount Airy, NC
Gillespie, Reginald B., Jr. .... Durham, NC
Gillespie, Richard E. .... Helena, MT
Gillespie, Richard W. .... Larkspur, CO
Gillespie, Robert .... San Francisco, CA
Gillespie, Robert E. .... Springfield, IL
Gillespie, Robert G. .... Unionville, CT
Gillespie, Robert G., Jr. .... Gulfport, MS
Gillespie, Robert J., Jr. .... Wilkes-Barre, PA
Gillespie, Robert M. .... Richmond, VA
Gillespie, Robin Marie .... Dallas, TX
Gillespie, Ronald G. .... White Plains, NY
Gillespie, Roxani .... San Francisco, CA
Gillespie, Rozen & Watsky, P.C.
Dallas, TX
Gillespie, S. Hazard .... New York, NY
Gillespie, Samuel H., III .... Fairfax, VA
Gillespie, S. E. .... Sherman, TX
Gillespie, Sharon .... Austin, TX
Gillespie, Stanley B. .... Kansas City, MO
Gillespie, Stephen D. .... San Francisco, CA
Gillespie, T. David .... Little Rock, AR
Gillespie, Ted C. .... Toledo, OH
Gillespie, Terence P. .... Chicago, IL
Gillespie, Teresa R. .... Seattle, WA
Gillespie, Terrence Alan .... Denver, CO
Gillespie, Thomas .... Cedar Rapids, IA
Gillespie, Thomas E. .... Dallas, TX
Gillespie, Thomas J. .... Miami Beach, FL
Gillespie, Thomas S. .... Berrien Springs, MI
Gillespie, Timothy J. .... Kansas City, MO
Gillespie, Trey .... Austin, TX
Gillespie, Trey, P.C. .... Austin, TX
Gillespie, Veronica M.
Federal Election Commission, Offices of the Commissioners, GV
Gillespie, Victor H. .... Corpus Christi, TX
Gillespie, Vincent Joseph .... Houston, TX
Gillespie, Virgil G. .... Gulfport, MS
Gillespie, William G. .... San Diego, CA
Gillespie, William M.
New Smyrna Beach, FL
Gillespie, Wm. B. .... Clayton, MO
Gillespie & Wysor .... Boston, MA
Lynnfield, MA
Gillespie-Mobley, Ricky L. .... Cleveland, OH
Gillespy, Gerald P. .... Birmingham, AL
Gillespy, Robert H. .... Cleveland, OH
Gillespy, Robert H., III .... Springfield, IL
Gillespy, Rosemary Buntin ...... Birmingham, AL
Gillet, Brian D. .... Trenton, NJ
Gillet, Charles P. .... San Francisco, CA
Gillett, Blaine T. .... North Platte, NE
Gillett, David P. .... New York, NY
Gillett, E. Leigh .... Dallas, TX
Gillett, Eric P. .... Anchorage, AK
Seattle, WA
Gillett, Frank A. .... Fort Myers, FL
Gillett, Gary A. .... Columbus, OH
Gillett, Glenn D. .... Department of Justice, Civil Division, GV
Gillett, Jane Goodnow .... Los Angeles, CA
Gillett, John J. .... Fredonia, KS
Gillett, Judith A. .... La Plata, MD
Gillett, Mark R. .... Norman, OK
Gillett, Mark T. .... Los Angeles, CA
Gillett, Melody Canellis .... Houston, TX
Gillett, Michael B. .... Seattle, WA
Gillett, Michael E. .... Orlando, FL
Gillett, Michael R. .... Dallas, TX
Gillett, S. Christopher .... Houston, TX
Gillett, William J. .... Manchester, NH
Gillette, Battey & Gillette .... Faulkton, SD
Redfield, SD
Gillette, Bert R. .... Brooklyn, IA
Gillette, Brian J. .... Silver Spring, MD
Gillette, Charlie J., Jr. .... Jacksonville, FL
Gillette, Christopher J. .... Seattle, WA
Gillette, Clayton P. .... Charlottesville, VA
Gillette, D. Dale .... Dallas, TX
Gillette, Dane R. .... San Francisco, CA
Gillette, David L. .... Salt Lake City, UT
Gillette, Donald R. .... Tampa, FL
Gillette, Donald R., P.A. .... Tampa, FL
Gillette, Douglas W. .... Hartford, CT
Gillette, E. Peter, Jr. .... Minneapolis, MN
Gillette, Edward C. .... Kansas City, KS
Gillette, Galen G. .... Redfield, SD
Gillette, George C. .... Newport Beach, CA
Gillette, Glenn H. .... Pittsburgh, PA
Gillette, J. Wayne .... New Orleans, LA
Gillette, Jeffrey R. .... Brea, CA
Gillette, Joshua C. .... New York, NY
Gillette, Keith R. .... Pleasanton, CA
Gillette, Leslie .... Minneapolis, MN
Gillette, Margot A. .... Redfield, SD
Gillette, Michele Anne .... Richmond, VA
Gillette, Michelle E. .... San Francisco, CA
Gillette, Nancy Pekkanen .... Hilliard, OH
Gillette, Norman L., Law Offices of
San Bernardino, CA
Gillette, Pamela R. .... Chicago, IL
Gillette, Patricia K. .... San Francisco, CA
Gillette, Paul .... North Hollywood, CA
Gillette, Paul J. .... Redfield, SD
Gillette, Robert E. .... Suffolk, VA
Gillette, Robert H. .... Grand Rapids, MI
Gillette, Robert L. .... Baytown, TX
Gillette, Scott E. .... Mesa, AZ
Gillette, Stephen E. .... Palo Alto, CA
Gillette, Sumner B. .... Quincy, MA
Gillette, Susan .... Baltimore, MD
Gillette, Terry L. .... Jackson, MI
Gilley, Alfonsa .... Baltimore, MD
Gilley, Barry D. .... Edmonton, KY
Gilley, Craig A. .... Washington, DC
Gilley, D. Sandi .... Albuquerque, NM
Gilley, Dennis C. .... South Holland, IL
Gilley, Dewey C., Jr. .... Beaufort, SC
Gilley, Donald A. .... Dallas, TX
Gilley, George D. .... South Holland, IL
Gilley and Gilley .... Shreveport, LA
Gilley, Harold C., Jr. .... Shreveport, LA
Gilley, Harry B. .... Manchester, TN
Gilley, James H., Jr. .... Winston-Salem, NC
Gilley, Jeffrey G. .... Athens, GA
Gilley, Jeffrey G., Law Offices of
Athens, GA
Gilley, Patricia A. .... Shreveport, LA
Gilley, Riley C. .... Naples, FL
Gilley, Smith E. .... Greenville, TX
Gilley, Stephen D. .... Frankfort, KY
Gilley, T. Franklin, III .... Murfreesboro, TN
Gilley, William W. .... Kingsport, TN
Gill Fierro, Marylou .... Boston, MA
Gillham, Fay Cliett .... Austin, TX
Gillham, James L. .... Independence, MO
Gillham, Robert H. .... Santa Ana, CA
Gillia, Beth Ann .... Santa Fe, NM
Gilliam, Anita W. .... Bristol, VA
Gilliam, Annette .... Rosemead, CA
Gilliam, Armistead W., Jr. .... Dayton, OH
Gilliam, Bobby S. .... Shreveport, LA
Gilliam, C. Edgar, Jr. .... Roswell, GA
Gilliam, Carole Currin .... Darien, CT
Gilliam, Charles Phillips .... Stamford, CT
Gilliam, Cockrum & Duren
Goldthwaite, TX
Gilliam, D. Kent .... Richmond, VA
Gilliam, Daniel F. .... Victoria, TX
Gilliam, Earl B. .... San Diego, CA
Gilliam, Fannie H. .... Atlanta, GA
Gilliam, Gary .... Wise, VA
Gilliam, George H. .... Charlottesville, VA
Gilliam, Haywood S., Jr .... San Francisco, CA
Gilliam, J. Duane .... Fayetteville, NC
Gilliam, J. William .... Fairfax, VA
Gilliam, James H. .... Des Moines, IA
Gilliam, John .... Allen, TX
Gilliam, John A. .... Dallas, TX
Gilliam, John B. .... Wichita, KS
Gilliam, Joy B. .... Lexington, KY
Gilliam, Kathryn J. .... Waco, TX
Gilliam, L. Alex, Jr. .... Clarksdale, MS
Gilliam, Latha A. ...... Egg Harbor Township, NJ
Gilliam, Laurie L. .... Orem, UT
Gilliam, Marion G. H. .... New York, NY
Gilliam, Mark E. .... Shreveport, LA
Gilliam, Nancy .... Pensacola, FL
Gilliam, Paul H. .... Tyler, TX
Gilliam, Phillip L. .... Detroit, MI
Gilliam, René Riggs .... Johnson City, TN
Gilliam, Robert L., III .... Richmond, VA
Gilliam, Sanders and Brown, P.L.C.
Fairfax, VA
Gilliam, Steven D. .... Lexington, KY
Gilliam, Steven P. .... Gainesville, GA
Gilliam, Stuart C. .... Walnut Creek, CA
Gilliam, Sue Ballard .... Hendersonville, NC
Gilliam, Theodore N. .... Vancouver, WA
Gilliam, Thomas A. .... Denver, CO
Gilliam, Thomas A. .... Columbus, NC
Gilliam, Thomas J., Jr. .... Pensacola, FL
Gilliam, Vicki Lachney .... Jackson, MS
Gilliam, William C. .... Malvern, AR
Gillian, Earl .... Montgomery, AL
Gillian, Earl, Jr. .... Montgomery, AL
Gillian-Gibson, Kelly E. .... Anchorage, AK
Gilliard, Kirk Emerson .... Augusta, GA
Gilliard, Lori Chambers .... Tulsa, OK
Gilliard, Maryanne G. .... Sacramento, CA
Gilliard, Michael Dee .... Tulsa, OK
Gilliat, Robert L. .... Kensington, MD
Gilliatt, David R. .... New York, NY
Gillice, Thomas A. .... Washington, DC
Gillich, Tina Rose .... Biloxi, MS
Gillick, E. Michael .... Canon City, CO
Gillick, John E. .... Washington, DC
Gillick, Mary F. .... San Diego, CA
Gillick, Michael H. .... Milwaukee, WI
Racine, WI
Gillick, Patrick J. .... Mequon, WI
Milwaukee, WI
Racine, WI
Gillick & Wenner .... Canon City, CO
Gillie, Armon C. .... Bicknell, IN
Gillie, Donna J. .... Indian Hills, CO
Gillie, Kevin J. .... Lafayette, LA
Gillie, William Trescott .... Columbus, OH
Gillies, Bruce D. .... Oakland, CA
Gillies, Cynthia L. .... East Lansing, MI
Gillies, Donald A. .... Chicago, IL
Gillies, James E. .... Houston, TX
Gillies, James L. .... Conifer, CO
Gillies, John E. .... Farmingdale, NY
Gillies, John J., Jr. .... Hartford, CT
Gillies, John M. .... Bradenton, FL
Gillies, Paul S. .... Montpelier, VT
Gillies, Peter W. .... Boston, MA
Gillies, Robert D. .... Walnut Creek, CA
Gillies, W. G., (P.C.) .... Rock Island, IL
Gillies, William S. .... Sacramento, CA
Gillig, Gary L. .... Oxnard, CA
Gillig, Harry .... Fort Lauderdale, FL
Gillig, John S. .... Frankfort, KY
Gillig, Roy W. .... Hingham, MA
Gillig, Susan Cordell .... Los Angeles, CA
Gilligan, Charles W. .... Washington, DC
Gilligan, Daniel F. .... Portland, ME
Gilligan, Erin M. .... Boston, MA
Gilligan, Francis A.
United States Court Of Appeals For The Armed Forces, GV
Gilligan, Gerard J. .... Cedar Grove, NJ
Gilligan, James F. .... San Antonio, TX
Gilligan, James J. .... Department of Justice, Civil Division, GV
Gilligan, James P. .... Lynn, MA
Gilligan, Jane F. .... Wayne, NJ
Gilligan, Jerome P. .... Minneapolis, MN
Gilligan, John J. .... Long Beach, CA
Gilligan, John P. .... Columbus, OH
Gilligan, John W., III .... Chicago, IL
Gilligan, Joseph E. .... Washington, DC
Gilligan, Kathleen M. .... Chicago, IL
Gilligan, Kenneth D. .... Kingston, NY
Gilligan, Kevin M. .... Syracuse, NY
Gilligan, King & Gooding, P.A. .... Ocala, FL
Gilligan, Leigh A. .... Boston, MA

Gilligan, Louis F. ... **Cincinnati, OH**
Gilligan, M. Michele ... Baltimore, MD
Gilligan, Margaret
Department of Transportation, Federal Aviation Administration, GV
Gilligan, Mary Kathleen ... Cincinnati, OH
Gilligan, Matthew J. ... Springfield, VA
Gilligan, Maureen Farquhar ... Morristown, NJ
Gilligan, Michael E. ... **New York, NY**
Gilligan, Michael F. ... Glen Burnie, MD
Gilligan, Nellie ... **New York, NY**
Gilligan, Patrick G. ... Ocala, FL
Gilligan, Paul F., Jr. ... **Cherry Hill, NJ**
Gilligan & Peppelman ... Media, PA
Philadelphia, PA
Gilligan, Philip M. ... Media, PA
Philadelphia, PA
Gilligan, Robert G. ... **Wethersfield, CT**
Gilligan, Robert M. ... Lexington, MA
Gilligan, Robert T. ... Fort Lauderdale, FL
Gilligan, Sean W. ... **Boston, MA**
Gilligan, T. Scott ... **Cincinnati, OH**
Gilligan, Thomas A., Jr. ... **St. Paul, MN**
Gilligan, Thomas M. ... **Boston, MA**
Gilligan-Arendt, Donna-Marie ... Kenosha, WI
Gillihan, Donald E. ... Farmington, MO
Gill II, Sterling E. ... Columbus, OH
Gillikin, Virginia ... New York, NY
Gillilan, David ... **Denver, CO**
Gilliland, Alan D. ... **New York, NY**
Gilliland & Associates ... **Indianapolis, IN**
Covington, KY
Cincinnati, OH
Columbus, OH
Gilliland, Ben D., Jr. ... Memphis, TN
Gilliland, C. Michael ... **Washington, DC**
Gilliland, David H. ... **Austin, TX**
Gilliland, Delton M. ... **Lyndon, KS**
Gilliland, Derek T. ... **Austin, TX**
Gilliland, Donald R. ... Birmingham, AL
Gilliland, Douglas L. ... San Diego, CA
Gilliland, Floyd R., Jr. ... **Montgomery, AL**
Gilliland, Gary ... Greenville, NC
Gilliland and Gilliland ... Wellston, OH
Gilliland & Hayes, P.A. A Professional Association ... **Hutchinson, KS**
Wichita, KS
Kansas City, MO
Gilliland, J. Craig ... **San Francisco, CA**
Gilliland, James G., Jr.
San Francisco, CA
Gilliland, James R. ... **Hutchinson, KS**
Gilliland, Janie S. ... **Montgomery, AL**
Gilliland, Jean E. ... Los Angeles, CA
Gilliland, Jennifer A. ... **Buffalo, NY**
Gilliland, John C., II ... **Indianapolis, IN**
Covington, KY
Gilliland, John M. ... Cranfills Gap, TX
Gilliland, Jonathan ... **Palo Alto, CA**
Gilliland, Joseph F. ... Russellville, AL
Gilliland, Kent A. ... **Oklahoma City, OK**
Gilliland, Kyle R. ... Wellston, OH
Gilliland, Lisa Jeffrey
Research Triangle Park, NC
Gilliland, Lukin ... **San Antonio, TX**
Gilliland, Michael S. ... **Minneapolis, MN**
Gilliland, Robert C., (Co., L.P.A.)
Youngstown, OH
Gilliland, Robert H., Jr.
Oklahoma City, OK
Gilliland, Robert J. ... **Hutchinson, KS**
Gilliland, Roy J. ... Wellston, OH
Gilliland, Scott A. ... **Birmingham, AL**
Gilliland, T. Cullen ... **Atlanta, GA**
Gilliland, William Elton ... Odessa, TX
Gillim, Gaylee W. ... Louisville, KY
Gillin & Alperin ... Santa Monica, CA
Haddonfield, NJ
Philadelphia, PA
Gillin, Andrew R. ... **Orinda, CA**
San Francisco, CA
Gillin, Charles E. ... **St. Paul, MN**
Gillin, Eugene H. ... **Philadelphia, PA**
Gillin, Jacobson, Ellis & Larsen
Orinda, CA
San Francisco, CA
Gillin, Joseph S., Jr. (P.A.) ... Melbourne, FL
Gillin, Leon S. ... Rosemont, IL
Gillin, Lisa Landdeck ... Issaquah, WA
Gillin, Mal ... **Honolulu, HI**
Gillin, Michael F. X., & Associates, Professional Corp. ... Media, PA
Gillin, Michael F. X. ... Media, PA
Gillin, Patricia J. ... **Old Saybrook, CT**
Gillin, Peter G. ... Avon, CT
Gillin, Peter J. ... **Providence, RI**
Gillin, Philip H. ... Santa Monica, CA
Gillin, Scott, Alperstein, Glantz & Simon, A Law Corporation ... **Encino, CA**
Los Angeles, CA
Gillin, Stephen A. ... **Norristown, PA**
Philadelphia, PA
Gilling, Mark R. ... **Phoenix, AZ**
Gillingham, Arthur ... Sacramento, CA
Gillingham, Charles F. ... Media, PA
Gillingham, Paul G. ... Seattle, WA
Gillingham, Stephen T. ... Wayne, NJ
Gillingham, Steven ... Department of Justice, Civil Division, GV
Gillingham, Todd S. ... Minneapolis, MN
Gillings, Frederick L. ... Snohomish, WA
Gillins, Peter W. ... Hillsboro, OR
Gillio & Associates ... Chicago, IL
Gillio, Frank ... Santa Cruz, CA
Gillio, Vickie A. ... Chicago, IL
Gilliom, Michael W. ... Chevy Chase, MD
Gilliom, Richard L. ... Indianapolis, IN

Gillis & Angley ... **Hingham, MA**
Plymouth, MA
Gillis, Angus, III ... **Nashville, TN**
Gillis & Bikofsky, P.C. ... **Newton, MA**
Gillis, Brian A. ... **Boston, MA**
Gillis, Brian J. ... Longwood, FL
Gillis, Catherine ... **Dallas, TX**
Gillis, Charles Michael ... **Houston, TX**
Gillis, Christian D. ... **New York, NY**
Gillis, Colin W. ... Brockton, MA
Gillis, Daniel J. ... Arvada, CO
Gillis, David K. F. ... **New York, NY**
Gillis, David N. ... Jackson, MS
Gillis, Donald D. ... Miami, FL
Gillis, Donald D., P.A. ... Miami, FL
Gillis, Donald H. ... **Troy, MI**
Gillis, Donald W. ... **Dublin, GA**
Gillis, Dwayne H. ... Douglas, GA
Gillis, Dwayne H., P.C. ... Douglas, GA
Gillis, Edward M. ... **New Haven, CT**
Gillis, Eileen King ... **Greensboro, NC**
Gillis, Eileen Sandra ... Sacramento, CA
Gillis, Elizabeth A. ... Newport Beach, CA
Gillis, Geoffrey L. ... **Grand Rapids, MI**
Gillis & Gillis, P.C. ... **New Haven, CT**
Gillis, Gregory A. ... Gary, IN
Gillis, Gregory B. ... Kansas City, MO
Gillis, Gregory P. ... **Phoenix, AZ**
Gillis, H. Lewis ... **Montgomery, AL**
Gillis, Holly B. ... **Walnut Creek, CA**
Gillis, Howard T. ... **New Haven, CT**
Gillis, Jack C., Jr. ... Dallas, TX
Plano, TX
Gillis, James H. ... Orlando, FL
Gillis, James J., Jr. ... Vineyard Haven, MA
Gillis, James P. ... Department of Justice, Criminal Division, GV
Gillis, John B. ... **Clarksdale, MS**
Gillis, John B. ... Kansas City, MO
Gillis, John G. ... **Boston, MA**
Gillis, John H., Jr. ... Detroit, MI
Gillis, John L., Jr., (P.C.) ... **St. Louis, MO**
Gillis, John M. ... Dallas, TX
Gillis, John M., P.C. ... Dallas, TX
Gillis, Joseph L. ... **New Haven, CT**
Gillis, Julie Lynn ... North Quincy, MA
Gillis, Kenneth L. ... Chicago, IL
Gillis, Kevin F. ... **Canton, MA**
Gillis, Kevin M. ... **Portland, ME**
Gillis, Laurence J. ... Rye, NH
Gillis Law Firm ... Columbia, SC
Gillis Law Office, The ... Dallas, TX
Plano, TX
Gillis, Lucian, Jr. ... **Atlanta, GA**
Gillis, Lucinda Kil ... South Bend, IN
Gillis, M. Derek ... Columbia, SC
Gillis, Margaret J. ... **Albany, NY**
Gillis, Mark ... **Boston, MA**
Gillis, Mark H. ... **Columbus, OH**
Gillis, Michael K. ... **Newton, MA**
Gillis, Norman B., & Associates
Nashville, TN
Gillis, Norman B., Jr. ... **Mc Comb, MS**
Gillis, Patricia H., (Mrs.) ... San Antonio, TX
Gillis, Paul J. ... New Bedford, MA
Gillis, Paula Durst ... **Charleston, WV**
Gillis, Philip A. ... Harper Woods, MI
Gillis, R. James ... Van Nuys, CA
Gillis, Ralph J. ... **Hingham, MA**
Gillis, Richard ... Norwalk, CT
Gillis, Richard M., Jr. ... **Philadelphia, PA**
Pocono Pines, PA
Gillis & Slogar ... **Houston, TX**
Gillis, Steven Evan ... Green Bay, WI
Gillis, Susan Fox ... **Chicago, IL**
Gillis, Sylvia Lynn ... **Columbus, OH**
Gillis, Teresa ... Washington, DC
Gillis, Terry D. ... **Fort Payne, AL**
Gillis, Theresa M. ... **New York, NY**
Gillis, Tiffany Anne ... **Burlington, MA**
Gillis, Tom S. ... Houston, TX
Gillis, W. Bruce, Jr. ... Denver, CO
Gillis, Walter C. ... **Alexandria, VA**
Gillis, William A. ... **Santa Rosa, CA**
Gillis, William D., Jr. ... **Boston, MA**
Gillis, William F. ... **Columbus, MS**
Gillison, David F., Jr. ... Lake Village, AR
Gillison, David F., Jr., P.A.
Lake Village, AR
Gillispie, Charles S. ... East Marion, NY
Gillispie, Robert J. ... **New York, NY**
Gillispie, Robert J., Jr. ... **Lakewood, NJ**
Gillispie, Robert R. ... Nicholasville, KY
Gilliss, David D. ... **Baltimore, MD**
Gilliss, Edward J. ... **Towson, MD**
Gilliss, Thomas P. ... San Francisco, CA
Gilliss & Valla ... San Francisco, CA
Gillitzer, Mark A. ... Prairie du Chien, WI
Gillman, Adam J. ... **Irvine, CA**
Gillman, Anthony P. ... Tampa, FL
Gillman, Barry S. ... East Brunswick, NJ
Gillman, Bernard C. ... Rock Island, IL
Gillman, Bruce ... **Madison, WI**
Gillman, Catherine M. ... **Madison, WI**
Gillman, Charles E. ... New York, NY
Gillman, David C. ... Las Vegas, NV
Gillman, Duane H. ... **Salt Lake City, UT**
Gillman, Henry Neal ... Miami, FL
Gillman, J. Scott ... Chicago, IL
Gillman, J. Wayne ... Salt Lake City, UT
Gillman, Jack ... Edgewater, NJ
Gillman, James W. ... Schaumburg, IL
Gillman, Jennifer L. ... **New York, NY**
Gillman, Marvin H. ... Miami, FL
Gillman, Michael E. ... Dallas, TX
Gillman, Michael J. ... **Traverse City, MI**
Gillman, Nancy Sholes ... **Boston, MA**
Gillman, Nina ... **New York, NY**

Gillman, Patricia N. ... **Chicago, IL**
Gillman & Pinto, P.C. ... Philadelphia, PA
Gillman, Richard S. ... St. Paul, MN
Gillman, Ross D. ... **New York, NY**
Gillman, Scott ... Livingston, NJ
Gillman, Seth ... Chicago, IL
Gillman, Stacey S. ... Sarasota, FL
Gillman, Stephen B. ... **Miami, FL**
Gillman, Steven ... Philadelphia, PA
Gillman, Steven L. ... **Chicago, IL**
Gillman, William ... Garden City, NY
Gillmann, Harold E. ... Woodland Hills, CA
Gillmar, Stanley F. ... San Francisco, CA
Gillmeister, William J. ... Buffalo, NY
Gillmor, Helen ... Honolulu, HI
Gillmor, John E. ... **Nashville, TN**
Gillmor, John P. ... Honolulu, HI
Gillmor, Paul E. ... Tiffin, OH
Gillmore, A. James ... **Newton, KS**
Gillmore, Frederick H., Jr. ... **New York, NY**
Gillock, Gerald I. ... **Las Vegas, NV**
Gillock, Markley & Killebrew
Las Vegas, NV
Reno, NV
Gillogly, Daniel W. ... Chicago, IL
Gillombardo, Carl F., Jr. ... Cleveland, OH
Gillon, Brian T. ... New York, NY
Gillon, John Joseph, Jr.
Department of Commerce, Patent and Trademark Office, GV
Gillon, Kara ... Washington, DC
Gillon, Lana E. ... **Jackson, MS**
Gillon, Lepore, & Menefee ... Lancaster, CA
Gillon, Peter M. ... **Washington, DC**
Gillon, Robert ... Lancaster, CA
Gillon, Shelley C. Herman
Silver Spring, MD
Gillon, W. Hugh, IV ... **Jackson, MS**
Gillon, William P. ... Clayton, NJ
Gillon-Alma, Ronit ... New York, NY
Gillooly, Ann F. ... **Fairfax, VA**
Gillooly, Craig Lewis ... La Jolla, CA
Gillooly, Dennis ... **New Haven, CT**
Gillooly, John J. ... **Detroit, MI**
Gillooly, Robert J. ... North Haven, CT
Gillooly, Thomas J. ... **Charleston, WV**
Gilloon, Arthur F. ... **Dubuque, IA**
Gilloon, Frank D., III ... Dubuque, IA
Gilloon, Frank D., Jr. ... Dubuque, IA
Gilloon, Richard J. ... **Omaha, NE**
Gillott, Eloise F. ... Los Angeles, CA
Gillotte, Sylvia Lynn ... Spartanburg, SC
Gillotti, Capristo & Beck, P.C. ... **Beaver, PA**
Butler, PA
Greensburg, PA
Pittsburgh, PA
Gillotti, Chris F. ... **Pittsburgh, PA**
Gillotti, Frank R. ... Des Moines, IA
Gillotti, James J. ... **Scranton, PA**
Gillotti, Joseph M ... **Columbus, OH**
Gillotti, Patrice A. ... **Cherry Hill, NJ**
Philadelphia, PA
Gillow, Louis S. ... Point Pleasant, NJ
Gillow, Paul L. ... **Pleasantville, NY**
Gills, George W., Jr ... Arlington, VA
Gills, Jeanne Marie ... **Chicago, IL**
Gills, Kirk B. ... **Dallas, TX**
Gillum & Gillum ... Somerset, KY
Gillum, James Randolph
Birmingham, AL
Gillum, John M. ... **Nashville, TN**
Gillum, Melinda E. ... Somerset, KY
Gillum, Robert E. ... Somerset, KY
Gillum, Roderick D. ... Detroit, MI
Gillund, Neil T. ... Fargo, ND
Gilly, George M. ... **New Orleans, LA**
Gilly, Kennedy J. ... New Orleans, LA
Gilly, Kennedy J., Jr. ... Raleigh, NC
Gilly, Lionel E. ... Dallas, TX
Gilly, R.P., Intellectual Property Law Offices, P.C. ... **Allentown, PA**
Harrisburg, PA
Norristown, PA
Philadelphia, PA
Gilly, Richard P. ... **Allentown, PA**
Philadelphia, PA
Gilly, Scott B. ... **New York, NY**
Gilly, Stephen L. ... **Kingsport, TN**
Gilman, Aaron A. ... **Andover, MA**
Gilman, Arthur M. ... **Boston, MA**
Gilman & Associates ... **Washington, DC**
McLean, VA
Gilman, Barry J. ... **New York, NY**
Gilman, Benj. A. ... Middletown, NY
Gilman, Berta J. ... **Sacramento, CA**
Gilman, Blaine D., Law Office of
Kenai, AK
Gilman, Bradley D. ... **Arlington, VA**
Gilman, Carol E. ... Littleton, CO
Gilman, Charles A. ... **New York, NY**
Gilman, Christopher M. ... Los Angeles, CA
Gilman, Cindy ... San Francisco, CA
Gilman, Claudia J. ... Princeton, NJ
Gilman, Cyd ... Wichita, KS
Gilman, Cynthia L. ... **Washington, DC**
Gilman, David ... New York, NY
Gilman, David E. ... Indianapolis, IN
Gilman, David R. ... Overland Park, KS
Gilman, Derek ... **Stamford, CT**
Gilman, Doris D. ... New York, NY
Gilman, Earl R. ... La Jolla, CA
Gilman, Edward ... **Austin, TX**
Gilman, Elyse Lubin ... **Rochester, NY**
Gilman, Frances G. ... Quincy, MA
Gilman, Frank Peter ... Overland Park, KS
Gilman, Frederick S. ... **Boston, MA**
Gilman, Gail S. ... Washington, DC
Gilman, Garry L. ... Boise, ID

Gilman, Gary B. ... Newtown, PA
Gilman, George W. ... Houston, TX
Gilman, Gloria M. ... Philadelphia, PA
Gilman, Gregg A. ... **New York, NY**
Gilman, Gregory S. ... **Boston, MA**
Gilman, Holly J. ... Austin, TX
Gilman, James K. ... Albuquerque, NM
Gilman, Jan B. ... **Albuquerque, NM**
Gilman, Jane Prizant ... Middletown, NY
Gilman, Jeffrey L. ... Houston, TX
Gilman, Jeremy ... **Cleveland, OH**
Gilman, John C. ... San Francisco, CA
Gilman, John E. ... Austin, TX
Gilman, John H. ... Washington, DC
Gilman, John I. ... Ventura, CA
Gilman, John S. ... **Rochester, NY**
Gilman, Karen L. ... **Roseland, NJ**
Gilman, Kathleen A. ... San Antonio, TX
Gilman, Keith E. ... **Westfield, NJ**
Gilman, Kenneth G. ... **Boston, MA**
Gilman, Lara N. ... **San Jose, CA**
Gilman, Larry E. ... Rockville, VA
Gilman Law Firm, P.A. ... Albuquerque, NM
Gilman, Lawrence F. ... Pennington, NJ
Gilman, Marilyn E. ... Overland Park, KS
Gilman & Marks ... **East Hartford, CT**
Hartford, CT
Gilman, Matthew Scott ... **Boston, MA**
Gilman, McLaughlin & Hanrahan, LLP
Boston, MA
Gilman, Michael A. ... **Chicago, IL**
Gilman, Michael C. ... **Boston, MA**
Gilman, Michael G. ... **Alexandria, VA**
Gilman, Michael I. ... **Washington, DC**
Gilman, Michael R. ... **Woodbridge, NJ**
Ossining, NY
Gilman, Neil K. ... **Washington, DC**
Gilman, Nicholas ... **Washington, DC**
Gilman, Nichols & Ballard, L.L.P.
Austin, TX
Gilman, Pamela D. ... **Washington, DC**
Gilman, Pamela Slater ... **Boston, MA**
Gilman and Pastor, LLP ... **Boston, MA**
Gilman, Patricia A. ... **Wichita, KS**
Gilman, Paul A. ... **Chicago, IL**
Gilman, Paul C. ... Longmont, CO
Gilman, Peter C. ... Brownsville, TX
Gilman, Peter C., P.C. ... Brownsville, TX
Gilman, Peter M. ... Wynnewood, PA
Gilman, Philip A. ... **New York, NY**
Gilman, Raymond Thompson
Rochester, NY
Gilman, Richard C. ... Oxnard, CA
Gilman, Richard D. ... Malden, MA
Gilman, Richard L. ... Department of Justice, Tax Division, GV
Gilman, Richard L. ... Department of Labor, Office of the Solicitor, GV
Gilman, Ronald Lee ... Memphis, TN
Gilman, Samuel M. ... Rock Island, IL
Gilman, Scott ... East Meadow, NY
Gilman, Scott F. ... **Portland, OR**
Gilman, Sheldon G. ... **Jeffersonville, IN**
Louisville, KY
Gilman, Shelley ... Denver, CO
Gilman, Sherry I. ... **Washington, DC**
Gilman, Sidney ... Beechhurst, NY
Gilman, Steven E. ... Chicago, IL
Gilman, Susan S. Reichman ... **Phoenix, AZ**
Gilman, Thomas L., (P.S.) ... **Seattle, WA**
Gilman, Timothy M. ... **New York, NY**
Gilman, Tom E. ... St. Marks, FL
Gilman, W. Stewart ... Orlando, FL
Gilman, W. Thomas ... **Wichita, KS**
Gilmartin, Anne C. ... Sleepy Hollow, NY
Gilmartin & Associates ... **Cleveland, OH**
Rocky River, OH
Gilmartin, Brian G. ... Washingtonville, NY
Gilmartin, Charles A. ... Chicago, IL
Gilmartin, Craig P. ... **Boston, MA**
Gilmartin, David J. ... Chicago, IL
Gilmartin, David J. ... Southampton, NY
Gilmartin, Eugene H. ... Westwood, NJ
Gilmartin, Fitzsimmons & Ross, P.C.
Boston, MA
Gilmartin, Hugh J. ... Wanaque, NJ
Gilmartin, James H. ... Santa Clarita, CA
Gilmartin, John A. ... College Station, TX
Gilmartin, Karen Baust ... Miami Lakes, FL
Gilmartin, Marianne J. ... **Scranton, PA**
Wilkes-Barre, PA
Gilmartin, Mark B. ... Santa Monica, CA
Gilmartin, Martin R. ... Southampton, NY
Gilmartin, Matthew T. ... **Rocky River, OH**
Gilmartin, Michael J. ... **Chicago, IL**
Gilmartin, Patricia F. ... Oceanside, NY
Gilmartin, Patrick J. ... **New York, NY**
Gilmartin, Poster & Shafto
New York, NY
Gilmartin, Ralph B. ... **New York, NY**
Gilmartin, Robert A. ... Burlingame, CA
Gilmartin, Robert E., III ... **Chicago, IL**
Gilmartin, Robert M., Jr. ... **Hackensack, NJ**
Gilmartin, Stephen P. ... **Atlanta, GA**
Gilmartin, Vincent E. ... Youngstown, OH
Gilmartin, Wayne S. ... **Chicago, IL**
Gilmer, Albert W. ... Philadelphia, PA
Gilmer, Barry W. ... Jackson, MS
Gilmer, Gary C. ... Rocksprings, TX
Gilmer & Gilmer ... Rocksprings, TX
Gilmer, J. Davis ... **Austin, TX**
Gilmer, John B. ... Louisa, VA
Gilmer Law Firm ... Jackson, MS
Gilmer, Lilly F. ... Houston, TX
Gilmer, Lilly Falcon, P.C. ... Houston, TX
Gilmer, Michele D. ... Los Angeles, CA
Gilmer, Robert J., Jr. ... **Toledo, OH**

Gingras, Paul L. .... Minneapolis, MN
Gingras, Robert J. .... Augusta, ME
Gingras, Robert J. .... Madison, WI
Gingrás, Rosario C. .... Washington, DC
Gingras, Steven W. .... Oklahoma City, OK
Gingras, Thomas S. .... Anchorage, AK
Gingrich, Claud L. .... Bethesda, MD
Gingrich, Gary A. .... Oklahoma City, OK
Gingrich, Henry F. .... Elizabethtown, PA
Lancaster, PA
Gingrich, James E. .... Fairfield, CA
Sacramento, CA
Gingrich, Karen .... San Francisco, CA
Gingrich, Kurt R. .... Pittsburgh, PA
Gingrich, Mitchell L. .... Akron, OH
Gingrich, Richard L. .... Belleville, PA
Lewistown, PA
Gingrich, Robert P., Jr. .... Kansas City, MO
Gingrich, Smith, Klingensmith & Dolan
Elizabethtown, PA
Lancaster, PA
Gini, Gerald G. .... San Bernardino, CA
Ginieczki, Michele B. .... Atlantic City, NJ
Giniger, Judith .... Seattle, WA
Ginise, Russell T. .... Beverly Hills, CA
Ginivan, William J. .... Arlington, VA
Ginkel & Gallagher .... St. Paul, MN
Ginkowski, Richard Alan .... Kenosha, WI
Ginley, Gerald P. .... Philadelphia, PA
Ginley, John J., III .... New York, NY
Ginley, Marcia S.
Environmental Protection Agency, Office of Enforcement and Compliance Assurance, GV
Ginley, Richard B. .... Cleveland, OH
Ginn, Alexander .... Chagrin Falls, OH
Ginn, Alexis .... Duluth, GA
Ginn, Bradley R. .... Chicago, IL
Ginn, C. Philip .... Boone, NC
Ginn, David K. .... Alpharetta, GA
Ginn, David W., Law Office of
Walnut Creek, CA
Ginn, Edward B. .... Boston, MA
Needham, MA
Ginn, Glenn .... Tucson, AZ
Ginn, Gordon L. .... Corpus Christi, TX
Ginn, Gregg H. .... Portland, ME
Ginn, James M. .... Southfield, MI
Ginn, John C. .... Sulphur Springs, TX
Ginn Law Offices, The, P.A. .... Boone, NC
Ginn, M. Stanley .... Columbia, MO
Ginn, Neil J. .... Atlanta, GA
Ginn, Raymond E., Jr. .... Wellsboro, PA
Ginn, Robert V. .... Omaha, NE
Ginn, Robert W. .... Omaha, NE
Ginn, Timothy A. .... West Memphis, AR
Ginn & Vickery, P.C. .... Wellsboro, PA
Ginn, Walter P. .... Cleveland, OH
Ginn, William D. .... Cleveland, OH
Ginn, Wm. F. .... Omaha, NE
Ginnaven, Robert A., III .... Bryant, AR
Ginnelly, Paul J. .... Brewerton, NY
Ginnerty, Thomas F. .... Providence, RI
Ginnetti, John P. .... Hartford, CT
Ginnings, C. Michael .... El Paso, TX
Ginnings, Laurence J. .... Missoula, MT
Ginnow, Arnold O. .... St. Paul, MN
Ginns, Deborah E. .... Long Beach, CA
Ginns, Harvey .... Long Beach, CA
Ginns, Ronald L. .... New York, NY
Ginns, Scott A. .... Stockton, CA
Ginns, Steven .... Boca Raton, FL
Ginocchi, James M. .... Pittsburgh, PA
Ginocchio, Alaine T. .... West Palm Beach, FL
Ginocchio, August J. .... Babylon, NY
Ginocchio, Deborah Nellis .... Cincinnati, OH
Ginocchio, James S. .... Cincinnati, OH
Ginocchio, Ralph J. .... Santa Ana, CA
Ginocchio, Ralph P. .... Cincinnati, OH
Ginos, Geoffrey J. .... New York, NY
Ginotti, Carlo P. .... Lansing, MI
Ginoza, Donn .... San Francisco, CA
Ginoza, Lisa M. .... Honolulu, HI
Gins, Albert B. .... Boonton, NJ
Gins & Greenfeld, P.C. .... Washington, DC
Greenbelt, MD
Gins, Richard H. .... Washington, DC
Greenbelt, MD
Ginsbach, Patrick M. .... Hot Springs, SD
Ginsberg, Alan .... North Miami Beach, FL
Ginsberg, Alan R. .... Wayne, NJ
Ginsberg, Albert .... Silver Spring, MD
Ginsberg, Allen L. .... Chicago, IL
Ginsberg, Amy J. .... Lyndhurst, OH
Ginsberg, Ann S. .... New York, NY
Ginsberg, Arnold R., P.A. .... Miami, FL
Ginsberg, Arnold R., P.A. .... Miami, FL
Ginsberg, Barbara J. .... Santa Ana, CA
Ginsberg, Barbara S. .... New York, NY
Ginsberg, Barry P. .... Philadelphia, PA
Ginsberg, Becker & Weaver, L.L.P.
New York, NY
Ginsberg, Benedict, (P.C.) .... New York, NY
Ginsberg, Benjamin L. .... Washington, DC
Ginsberg, Beth M. .... Philadelphia, PA
Ginsberg, Beth S. .... Seattle, WA
Ginsberg & Broome .... New York, NY
Ginsberg, Bruce M. .... New York, NY
Ginsberg, Bruce S. .... New York, NY
Ginsberg and Brusilow, P.C. .... Dallas, TX
Ginsberg, Burton .... North Miami Beach, FL
Ginsberg, Charles E. .... Newburyport, MA
Ginsberg, Cynthia L. .... New York, NY
Ginsberg, Daniel L. .... North Miami Beach, FL
Ginsberg, Daniel P. .... New York, NY
Ginsberg, David Lawrence .... Fairfax, VA
Ginsberg, David M. .... Los Angeles, CA
Ginsberg, David M. .... Marlton, NJ
Philadelphia, PA
Philadelphia, PA
Ginsberg, David M. .... New York, NY
Ginsberg, Eliot H. .... Tampa, FL
Ginsberg, Ellen C. .... Washington, DC
Ginsberg, Elliot A. .... Bloomfield, CT
Ginsberg, Ellsworth W. .... St. Louis, MO
Ginsberg, Ernest .... New York, NY
Ginsberg, Eugene S. .... Garden City, NY
Ginsberg, Fern S. .... New York, NY
Ginsberg, Fred .... Baltimore, MD
Ginsberg, Frederick L. .... Parker, CO
Ginsberg, Gary D. .... Cherry Hill, NJ
Ginsberg, Gary L. .... New York, NY
Ginsberg, Gerry R. .... Rolling Hills, CA
Ginsberg & Ginsberg .... Aurora, CO
Ginsberg, Gordon I. .... Southfield, MI
Ginsberg, Harvey C. .... Minneapolis, MN
Ginsberg, Herbert R. .... Hattiesburg, MS
Ginsberg, Irwin E. .... Buffalo, NY
Ginsberg, Jacob .... Dallas, TX
Ginsberg, Jacob A. .... Gaithersburg, MD
Ginsberg, Jan D. .... Cleveland, OH
Ginsberg, Jason S. .... Los Angeles, CA
Ginsberg, Jay A. .... New Orleans, LA
Ginsberg, Jeffrey S. .... Edison, NJ
New York, NY
Ginsberg, Jerome M. .... Flushing, NY
Ginsberg, Jill Robin .... Hollywood, FL
Ginsberg, Johanna R. .... Brooklyn, NY
Ginsberg, Jonathan .... New York, NY
Ginsberg, Jonathan C. .... Atlanta, GA
Ginsberg, Joseph .... New York, NY
Ginsberg, Karen M. .... Washington, DC
Ginsberg, Katsorhis & Fedrizzi
Flushing, NY
Ginsberg, Kenneth H. .... Dover, NJ
Ginsberg, Kenneth S. .... West Haven, CT
Ginsberg, Lambert L. .... Troy, NY
Ginsberg, Larry A. .... Los Angeles, CA
Ginsberg, Larry F. .... Stamford, CT
Ginsberg, Laurence T. .... Forest Hills, NY
Ginsberg, Laurie .... Philadelphia, PA
Ginsberg Law Offices, P.C. .... Atlanta, GA
Ginsberg, Lawrence A., (A Professional Corporation) .... Los Angeles, CA
Ginsberg, Lawrence N. .... Seal Beach, CA
Ginsberg, Lee A. .... New York, NY
Ginsberg, Leonard .... Somerville, NJ
Ginsberg, Lewis R. .... Chicago, IL
Ginsberg, Louis .... New York, NY
Ginsberg, Lynn Ellen .... Los Angeles, CA
Ginsberg, Major C. .... Dallas, TX
Ginsberg, Mara B. .... Albany, NY
Ginsberg, Marc D. .... Chicago, IL
Ginsberg, Marc R. .... Key West, FL
Miami, FL
Ginsberg, Marcia R. .... Boston, MA
Ginsberg, Marion R. .... New York, NY
Ginsberg, Mark J. .... Portland, OR
Ginsberg, Martin L. .... Kew Gardens, NY
Ginsberg, Michael .... Albany, NY
Ginsberg, Michael D. .... Tampa, FL
Ginsberg, Michael D. .... Dallas, TX
Ginsberg, Michael H. .... Pittsburgh, PA
Ginsberg, Michael L. .... Salt Lake City, UT
Ginsberg, Morton L. .... New York, NY
Ginsberg, Nina J. .... Alexandria, VA
Ginsberg, Norman .... Brooklyn, NY
Ginsberg, Patricia Chen .... Chicago, IL
Ginsberg, Paul D. .... New York, NY
Ginsberg, Perry D. .... Sacramento, CA
Ginsberg, Peter R. .... Washington, DC
Ginsberg, Peter R., P.C. .... Washington, DC
Ginsberg, Phillip H. .... Seattle, WA
Ginsberg, Reuben M. .... Dallas, TX
Ginsberg, Richard E. .... Chicago, IL
Ginsberg, Richard I. .... Jericho, NY
Ginsberg, Robert .... Daytona Beach, FL
Ginsberg, Robert E. .... Chicago, IL
Ginsberg, Robert M. .... New York, NY
Ginsberg, Ronald E. .... Savannah, GA
Ginsberg, Ross D. .... Boston, MA
Ginsberg, Seth .... New York, NY
Ginsberg, Sheara L. .... Philadelphia, PA
Ginsberg, Sheldon K. .... Aurora, CO
Ginsberg, Sidney .... Philadelphia, PA
Ginsberg, Sidney, P.C. .... Philadelphia, PA
Ginsberg, Simon .... New York, NY
Ginsberg, Stephen E. .... Morris Plains, NJ
Ginsberg, Steven F." Sonny "........ Chicago, IL
Ginsberg, Steven I. .... Fort Worth, TX
Ginsberg, Stuart M. .... Washington, DC
Ginsberg, William R. .... Hempstead, NY
New York, NY
Ginsberg-Riesel, Sheila .... New York, NY
Ginsburg, Alan B. .... Albany, NY
Ginsburg, Allen J., (P.C.) .... Chicago, IL
Ginsburg, Alvin B. .... Atlanta, GA
Ginsburg, Alyson J. .... Miami, FL
Ginsburg, Andrew B. .... Hialeah, FL
Ginsburg, Arnold H. .... Chicago, IL
Ginsburg, Arnold R. .... Philadelphia, PA
Ginsburg, Arthur D. .... Sarasota, FL
Ginsburg, Arthur J. .... New York, NY
Ginsburg, Arthur L. .... Flagstaff, AZ
Ginsburg & Associates .... Philadelphia, PA
Ginsburg, Barry S. .... Clayton, MO
Ginsburg & Berkun .... Albany, NY
Ginsburg, Brian M. .... Teterboro, NJ
Ginsburg, Bruce M. .... Philadelphia, PA
Ginsburg, Craig D. .... Philadelphia, PA
Ginsburg, Dana J. .... Burbank, CA
Ginsburg, Daniel H. .... Baltimore, MD
Ginsburg, David .... Washington, DC
Ginsburg, David Brian .... Lanham, MD
Ginsburg, David R. .... Santa Monica, CA
Ginsburg, Dayle S.
Department of Commerce, Economic Development Administration, GV
Ginsburg, Dennis .... Miami, FL
Ginsburg, Don S. .... Philadelphia, PA
Ginsburg, Douglas E.
Department of Justice, Civil Division, GV
Ginsburg, Douglas H.
United States Court Of Appeals District Of Columbia Circuit, GV
Ginsburg, Edward M. .... Concord, MA
Ginsburg, Edward S. .... Cleveland, OH
Ginsburg, Edwin M. .... Miami, FL
Ginsburg, Elizabeth A. .... Herndon, VA
Ginsburg, Frank I. .... Media, PA
Ginsburg, Gary .... New York, NY
Ginsburg, Gilbert J. .... Washington, DC
Ginsburg, Hal R. .... Queens Village, NY
Ginsburg, Howard B. .... Brick, NJ
Ginsburg, Howard I.
Upper Saddle River, NJ
Ginsburg, Jacob .... New York, NY
Ginsburg, James A. .... Beverly Hills, CA
Ginsburg, Jane Carol .... New York, NY
Ginsburg, Janice R. .... Cincinnati, OH
Ginsburg, Jay S. .... Bellaire, TX
Ginsburg, Jay S., P.C. .... Bellaire, TX
Ginsburg, Jennifer .... Worcester, MA
Ginsburg, Jerome M. .... Santa Fe, NM
Ginsburg, Jessica A. .... Department of Justice, Civil Rights Division, GV
Ginsburg, Jonathan .... Fairfax, VA
Ginsburg, Joseph A. .... Chicago, IL
Ginsburg, Julie E. .... Wellesley, MA
Ginsburg, Lawrence D. .... Dallas, TX
Ginsburg, Lawrence L. .... New York, NY
Ginsburg, Lawrence M. .... Atlanta, GA
Ginsburg & Leshin, LLP .... Boston, MA
Wellesley, MA
Ginsburg, Lisa R. .... Miami, FL
Ginsburg, Martin D., (P.C.)
Washington, DC
Ginsburg, Marvin E. .... Chicago, IL
Ginsburg, Matthew J. .... Boston, MA
Ginsburg, Mel B. .... New York, NY
Ginsburg, Neal & Lesage .... Hillsboro, OR
Ginsburg, Paul A. .... Torrance, CA
Ginsburg, Paul A., A Law Corporation
Torrance, CA
Ginsburg, Paul H. .... New York, NY
Ginsburg, Phillip L. .... San Diego, CA
Ginsburg, Rachel D. .... Oakland, CA
Ginsburg, Rachel, The Law Offices of
Oakland, CA
Ginsburg, Reuben .... Los Angeles, CA
Ginsburg, Richard A. .... Dallas, TX
Ginsburg, Richard M. .... Hillsboro, OR
Ginsburg, Robert A. .... Orange, CT
Ginsburg, Robert A. .... Miami, FL
Ginsburg, Robert A., P.C. .... Orange, CT
Ginsburg, Robert G. .... San Rafael, CA
Ginsburg, Robert L. .... Fort Worth, TX
Ginsburg, Roger A. .... Claremont, CA
Ginsburg, Roland E. .... Beverly Hills, CA
Ginsburg, Roy A. .... Minneapolis, MN
Ginsburg, Roy S. .... St. Paul, MN
Ginsburg, Ruth B.
Supreme Court Of The United States, GV
Ginsburg, Samuel J. .... Cincinnati, OH
Ginsburg, Scott K. .... United States Senate, Committee Legal Personnel, GV
Ginsburg, Seymour B. .... Chicago, IL
Ginsburg, Steven D. .... Miami, FL
Ginsburg, Steven D. .... Chicago, IL
Ginsburg, William H. .... Los Angeles, CA
Ginsburg, William S. .... Foster City, CA
Ginsburg, William T. .... Omaha, NE
Ginsburg, Yale M. .... Baltimore, MD
Ginsburgh, Alice R. L. .... Houston, TX
Ginski, Steven J. .... Memphis, TN
Ginsky, Marc S. .... Princeton, NJ
Ginsky, Marvin H. .... Stamford, CT
Ginsparg, Colman .... Chicago, IL
Ginsparg, Norman J. .... Chicago, IL
Ginster, Catherine R. .... Saginaw, MI
Ginster, Thomas A. .... Lansing, MI
Ginster, Wm. J. .... Saginaw, MI
Ginter, Christina A. .... Detroit, MI
Ginter, R. Dale .... Sacramento, CA
Ginther, Fergus M. .... Galena, MO
Ginther, Fergus M., Jr. .... Glendale, CA
Ginther, Jeffrey D. .... Columbus, OH
Ginther, Michael John .... San Francisco, CA
Ginther, Noble C., Jr. .... Houston, TX
Ginther, Robert K. .... Baraboo, WI
Ginther, Sharyl W. .... Cuyahoga Falls, OH
Gintling, Karen J. .... Cambridge, MD
Gintner, Peter P. .... Newport, OR
Gintowt, Daniel R. .... Westfield, MA
Ginty, J. Robert .... Ashland, OH
Ginty, James B. .... Philadelphia, PA
Ginty, Patrick Sean .... Chicago, IL
Ginty, Rosemary .... New York, NY
Ginzberg, David P. .... Boca Raton, FL
Ginzberg, David P. .... Boynton Beach, FL
Ginzberg, David P. .... Delray Beach, FL
Fort Pierce, FL
West Palm Beach, FL
Ginzberg, Ezra J. .... Topeka, KS
Ginzberg, Janet F. .... Haddonfield, NJ
Philadelphia, PA
Ginzberg, Jeffrey D. .... Seymour, CT
Ginzberg, Robert A. .... New York, NY
Ginzburg, Alexander R. .... Los Angeles, CA
Ginzburg, Alexandra .... Los Angeles, CA
Ginzburg, Daniel S. .... Marina Del Rey, CA
Ginzburg, Ezra J. .... Topeka, KS
Ginzburg, Margarita Y. .... Roseland, NJ
Ginzel, Frank .... Colorado City, TX
Ginzel, Jonathan D. .... Peoria, IL
Ginzkey, James P. .... Bloomington, IL
Giobbi, Herbert V. .... Washington, DC
Gioconda, Joseph C. .... New York, NY
Gioeni, Mary Louise .... Albany, NY
Gioffre, Anthony B., III .... Purchase, NY
Gioffre, Anthony Francis .... McLean, VA
Gioffre, Bruno J. .... Purchase, NY
Gioffre & Gioffre, A Professional Corporation .... Scarsdale, NY
Purchase, NY
White Plains, NY
Gioffre, Michael J. .... Hartford, CT
Gioffredi and Associates .... Dallas, TX
Gioffredi, John Michael .... Dallas, TX
Gioia, Allison P. .... New York, NY
Gioia, Anthony M. .... St. Louis, MO
Gioia, Daniel A. .... Merrillville, IN
Gioia, John M. .... Richmond, CA
Gioia, Joseph A. .... Chatham, NJ
Gioia, M. Pat .... Augusta, MI
Gioia, Mary J. .... St. Louis, MO
Gioia, Michael L. .... New York, NY
Gioia, Paul L. .... Albany, NY
Gioia, Randolph .... Boston, MA
Gioia, Rosemary .... Chalmette, LA
Gioia, Veronica A. .... St. Louis, MO
Gioia, Vincent G. .... Irvine, CA
Gioiella, Edward N. .... New York, NY
Gioiella, Russell M. .... New York, NY
Gioiello, John L. .... Panama City, FL
Gioiello, John L., P.A. .... Panama City, FL
Gioimo, Suzzanne J. .... Naperville, IL
Gioino, Charles Anthony .... Livingston, NJ
Gioioso, Dominico J. .... Baltimore, MD
Gioioso, Jacquelin P. .... Montville, NJ
Giokaris, Virginia M. .... Kansas City, MO
Giokas, William J. .... Wilbraham, MA
Giol, Jennifer Lynch .... Lake Worth, FL
Giolito, Laurie A. .... Bronx, NY
Giolito, Robert S. .... Atlanta, GA
Giombetti, Gerald R. .... Minneapolis, MN
Giombetti, Kim A. .... Scranton, PA
Giometti, Gregory R. .... Denver, CO
Gion, James D. .... Regent, ND
Gion Law Office .... Regent, ND
Gionet, Bertrand E. .... Des Moines, IA
Gionfriddo, David P.
Securities and Exchange Commission, Division of Enforcement, GV
Gionfriddo, Jane Kent .... Newton, MA
Gionfriddo, John F. .... Vienna, VA
Gionfriddo, Stephen T. .... Middletown, CT
Gionis, John H. .... East Norwich, NY
Gionis, Kathleen M. .... St. Croix Falls, WI
Giordanella, Frank .... Hartford, CT
Giordanella, John G. .... Hempstead, NY
Giordanella, Robert J. .... New York, NY
Giordani, Frank .... Columbia, SC
Giordani, Leslie C. .... Austin, TX
Giordano, A. Christine .... Philadelphia, PA
Giordano, A. Robert .... White Plains, NY
Giordano, Albert J. .... Cortlandt Manor, NY
Giordano, Angelo A. .... New York, NY
Giordano, Ann Marie, P.A. .... Orlando, FL
Giordano, AnnMarie .... Orlando, FL
Giordano, Anthony L. .... Charlotte, NC
Giordano & Associates, Ltd. .... Chicago, IL
Giordano, Bari Lynn .... Houston, TX
Giordano, Camille J. .... Alexandria, LA
Giordano, Carl A. .... Newark, NJ
Giordano, Carmen S. .... New York, NY
Giordano, Carolyn Gail .... Kew Gardens, NY
Giordano & Champa, P.A. .... Boston, MA
Giordano, Charles A. .... Revere, MA
Giordano, Charles V. .... Metairie, LA
Giordano, Christopher P. .... New York, NY
Giordano, Cynthia A. .... Washington, DC
Giordano, Diego O. .... Fort Worth, TX
Giordano, Elena V. .... Englewood, NJ
Giordano, Emil A. .... Coplay, PA
Giordano, Eva .... San Francisco, CA
Giordano, F. L. .... Brooklyn, NY
Giordano, Frances M. .... Boston, MA
Giordano, Frank J. .... Bronx, NY
Giordano, Gerald F., Jr. .... Phoenix, AZ
Giordano, Gerard .... New York, NY
Giordano, Gerard M. .... Hackensack, NJ
Giordano, Gilbert R.
Upper Marlboro, MD
Giordano & Giordano .... Alexandria, LA
Giordano & Gordon, P.L.L.C. .... Charlotte, NC
Giordano, Gregory A. .... Virginia Beach, VA
Giordano, Gregory J. .... Trenton, NJ
Giordano, Halleran & Ciesla, A Professional Corporation .... Middletown, NJ
Toms River, NJ
Trenton, NJ
Giordano, Jennifer (Meyerhardt)
Menlo Park, CA
Giordano, Jill H. .... Tampa, FL
Giordano, Jill L. .... Princeton, KY
Giordano, John C., Jr. .... Middletown, NJ
Trenton, NJ
Giordano, John L. .... Sacramento, CA
Giordano, John M. .... New York, NY
Giordano, John N. .... Tampa, FL
Giordano, Joseph .... Morristown, NJ
Giordano, Joseph A. .... Hillsborough, CA
Giordano, Joseph F. .... McLean, VA
Giordano, Julie J. .... Brattleboro, VT
Giordano, Kevin C. .... Springfield, MA
Giordano, Kevin H. .... Madison, NJ
Giordano, Laurie A. .... Buffalo, NY
Giordano, Lawrence F. .... Knoxville, TN
Sevierville, TN
Giordano, Lisa .... Pittsburgh, PA

Gitlin, Larry F. ....Woodland Hills, CA
Gitlin, Laura B. ....Princeton, NJ
Gitlin, Leo ....Scarsdale, NY
Gitlin, Martin ....New York, NY
Gitlin, Martin W. ....Denver, CO
Gitlin, Paul ....New York, NY
Gitlin, Paul G. ....Boston, MA
Gitlin, Richard A. ....Hartford, CT
Gitlin, Sheri L. ....New York, NY
Gitlin, Stephanie M. ....Hartford, CT
Gitlin-Petlak, Laura ....Beverly Hills, CA
Gitlin-Petlak, Laura ....Los Angeles, CA
Gitlitz, Carl R. ....Binghamton, NY
Gitlitz, James B. ....Binghamton, NY
Gitlitz, Stuart H. ....Miami, FL
Gitlow, William H. ....
Department Of Health And Human Services, GV
Gitman, David, (Professional Corporation)
Los Angeles, CA
Gitman, Steven D. ....Philadelphia, PA
Gitner, Geoffrey P. ....Washington, DC
Gitnes, Myron J. ....Klamath Falls, OR
Gitnick, Jerry M. ....Scottsdale, AZ
Gitnik, Lisa J. ....New York, NY
Gitnik, Paul J. ....Pittsburgh, PA
Gitnik, Paul J., & Associates ....Pittsburgh, PA
Gitomer, Deborah A. ....Houston, TX
Gitomer, Glenn S. ....Radnor, PA
Gitomer, Jacob ....Queens Village, NY
Gitomer, James J. ....Baltimore, MD
Gitomer, Louis E. ....Washington, DC
Gitomer, Mark L. ....Baltimore, MD
Gitomer, Schwimmer, Berns & Elliot
Forest Hills, NY
Gitomer, Shirley H. ....Floral Park, NY
Gits, Dean R. ....Santa Monica, CA
Gitt, Cynthia E. ....Los Angeles, CA
Gitt, William ....Sherman Oaks, CA
Gittelman, Diana B. ....New York, NY
Gittelman, Janice ....Suffern, NY
Gittelman, Lawrence Eric
Chevy Chase, MD
Gittelman, Mark A. ....Philadelphia, PA
Gittelsohn, David B. ....Framingham, MA
Gittelsohn, Gary ....New York, NY
Gittelsohn, Michael O., (P.C.)
Newburgh, NY
Gittelson, Sidney H. ....Garden City, NY
Gitten, Howard M. ....Boston, MA
New York, NY
Gittens, Noel A.
Securities and Exchange Commission, Division of Enforcement, GV
Gittens, Robert P. ....Boston, MA
Gitter, Alan W. ....New York, NY
Gitter, Allan R. ....Winston-Salem, NC
Gitter, Harvey ....Rockaway Park, NY
Gitter, Henry ....Boston, MA
Gitter, Kenneth H. ....San Antonio, TX
Gitter, Martin ....New York, NY
Gitter, Max ....New York, NY
Gitter, Morton L. ....New York, NY
Gitter, Richard P. ....New York, NY
Gitter, Ronald H. ....New York, NY
Gitter, William ....South Setauket, NY
Gitterman, Frederick ....Philadelphia, PA
Gitterman, Judith B. ....Los Angeles, CA
Gittes, Franklin M. ....New York, NY
Gittes, Frederick M. ....Columbus, OH
Gittes, Marcia F. ....Newton, MA
Gittes, Marvin S. ....New York, NY
Gittess, Leslie E. ....New York, NY
Gittinger, Christopher W. ....Allentown, PA
Gittinger, D. Wayne ....Seattle, WA
Gittinger, Leonard J., Jr. ....San Antonio, TX
Gittinger, Leonard J., Jr., P.C.
San Antonio, TX
Gittinger, L. J., III ....San Antonio, TX
Gittinger, Steven C. ....Cincinnati, OH
Gittings, Thomas Morton, Jr.
Washington, DC
Potomac, MD
Gittins, Charles W. ....Middletown, VA
Gittins, David A., Law Offices of
Clarkston, WA
Gittisriboongul, Alvin ....Sacramento, CA
Gittisriboongul, Jennifer ....Sacramento, CA
Gittleman, Amy ....New York, NY
Gittleman & Barber ....Louisville, KY
Gittleman, Charles S. ....New York, NY
Gittleman, David L. ....Louisville, KY
Gittleman, Eryn P. ....New York, NY
Gittleman, Felicia L. ....Seattle, WA
Gittleman, Gary V. ....Philadelphia, PA
Gittleman, Jeffrey B. ....Philadelphia, PA
Gittleman, Jeffrey M. ....Chappaqua, NY
Gittleman, Marilyn G. ....Fort Lee, NJ
Gittleman, Melvin ....Fort Lee, NJ
Gittleman, Muhlstock, Chewcaskie & Kim, L.L.P. ....Fort Lee, NJ
Gittleman & Paskel, P.C. ....Southfield, MI
Gittleman, Richard M. (IBA)
Washington, DC
Gittleman, Robert ....Southfield, MI
Gittleman, Sharon ....Oak Park, MI
Gittleman, Tracie R. ....Southfield, MI
Gittler, Amy J. ....Phoenix, AZ
Gittler, Amy J., PLC ....Phoenix, AZ
Gittler & Bradford ....Los Angeles, CA
Gittler, Gregg J. ....Los Angeles, CA
Gittler, Jeffrey G. ....Santa Barbara, CA
Gittler, Marvin ....Chicago, IL
Gittler, Sidney J. ....Encino, CA
Gittler, Steven ....Buffalo, NY
Gittleson, Steven L. ....New York, NY
Gittlitz, Sheryl M. ....New York, NY
Gitto, Donald R. ....Binghamton, NY

Gittus, Gary A. ....Rochester, MN
Gitzen, C. Willard ....Southfield, MI
Gitzlaff, James P. ....Chicago, IL
Giudice, Al ....Glenview, IL
Giudice, Daniel L. ....Chicago, IL
Giudice, Daniel L. ....Wheaton, IL
Giudicessi, John D., Jr. ....Minneapolis, MN
Giudicessi, Michael A. ....Des Moines, IA
Giudici, James C. ....Reno, NV
Giuditta, Nicholas A., III ....Somerville, NJ
Giuffra, Robert J. ....New York, NY
Giuffra, Robert J., Jr. ....New York, NY
Giuffra, Thomas P. ....New York, NY
Giuffré, Barbara L. ....San Francisco, CA
Giuffre, Boo J., (Ms.) ....Orange, CA
Giuffre, James D. ....Houston, TX
Giuffre, John B. ....Staten Island, NY
Giuffré, John J. ....Hicksville, NY
Giuffre, Josephine A. ....Boston, MA
Providence, RI
Giuffré & Kaplan, P.C. ....Hicksville, NY
Giuffre, Matthew J. ....Staten Island, NY
Giuffre, Paul J. ....Pittsburgh, PA
Giuffre, Paul L. ....Fort Smith, AR
Giuffre, Susan G. ....Cleveland, OH
Giuffreda, Richard Allen
Fort Lauderdale, FL
Giuffredi-Zaldívar, Anna ....Miami, FL
Giuffrida, Bruno ....San Diego, CA
Giuffrida, Noel P. ....Ridgeland, MS
Giuga, Sheila ....Jackson Heights, NY
Giuggio, John P., Jr. ....Boston, MA
Giugliano, Antoinette G. ....Lexington, MA
Giugliano, Margaret ....Jamaica, NY
Giuliana, Antonia F. ....New York, NY
Giuliana, Cathleen H. ....Morristown, NJ
Giuliana, Christopher N. ....Clearwater, FL
Giuliani, A. Lawrence ....Baltimore, MD
Giuliani, Albert A. ....Cleveland, OH
Giuliani, Alessandro ....New York, NY
Giuliani, Anthony J. ....Columbus, OH
Giuliani & Bernstein ....Hazleton, PA
Giuliani, Elizabeth A. ....Rahway, NJ
Giuliani, Elmer A. ....Cleveland, OH
Giuliani, Emilio R. ....Hopkins, MN
Giuliani, Henry A. ....Hazleton, PA
Giuliani, J. Paul ....Montpelier, VT
Giuliani, Jos. V. ....Long Island City, NY
Giuliani, Mark R. ....Hamden, CT
Giuliani, Matthew T. ....Boston, MA
Giuliani, Richard W. ....Boston, MA
Giuliani, Roger A. ....New York, NY
Giuliani, Rudolph W. ....New York, NY
Giuliano, Anthony F. ....Westbury, NY
Giuliano, Carmine J. ....Hartford, CT
Giuliano, Francis T. ....Ramsey, NJ
Giuliano, Guy G. ....Brooklyn, NY
Giuliano, Judith R. ....Fayetteville, NY
Giuliano, Nicholas P. ....New York, NY
Giuliano, Rachel ....Philadelphia, PA
Giuliano, Rosemary E. ....Woodbury, CT
Giuliano, Sebastian N. ....Middletown, CT
Giuliano, Vincent F. ....North Riverside, IL
Giulianti, Stacey A. ....Plantation, FL
Giulietti, James J. ....North Haven, CT
Giulietti & Morytko, L.L.C.
North Haven, CT
Giulini, Charles A., Jr. ....New York, NY
Giulini, Christine ....New York, NY
Giulini & Giulini ....New York, NY
Giulioli, Thomas C. ....Okmulgee, OK
Giulitto & Berger ....Ravenna, OH
Giulitto, Joseph ....Ravenna, OH
Giulitto, Michael A. ....Ravenna, OH
Giulitto, Paula C. ....Ravenna, OH
Giumarra, Cynthia A. ....Bakersfield, CA
Giumarra, John G., Jr. ....Bakersfield, CA
Giumenti, Katherine Spies
Columbus, OH
Giunco, John A., Jr. ....Middletown, NJ
Giunta, Anthony J. ....Ellsworth, ME
Giunta, Claudia ....Washington, DC
Giunta, Diane T. ....Mashpee, MA
Giunta, Frank ....Dallas, TX
Midland, TX
Giunta, George J., Jr. ....Media, PA
Giunta, House & Romm, P.A.
Fort Lauderdale, FL
Pompano Beach, FL
Giunta, John M. ....Pittsburgh, PA
Giunta, Joseph J. ....Los Angeles, CA
Giunta, Kim Miles ....Phoenix, AZ
Tucson, AZ
Giunta, Mark J. ....Phoenix, AZ
Giunta, Maurice V. ....Gainesville, FL
Giunta, Michael P. ....Boston, MA
Giunta, Patrick B. ....Pompano Beach, FL
Giunta, Richard F. ....Boston, MA
Giunta, Robert G. ....Las Vegas, NV
Giunta, Robert V., Jr. ....Hartford, CT
Giunta, Ronald ....Beverly, MA
Giunta, Rozanne M. ....Bay City, MI
Giunta, Tara Kalagher ....Washington, DC
Giuntini, Charles H. ....Aiken, SC
Giuntini, E. Robert ....White Plains, NY
Giuntini, E. Robert, P.C. ....White Plains, NY
Giuntini, Peter A. ....New York, NY
Giuntini, Russell J. ....Oakland, CA
Giuriceo, Anthony J. ....Somerville, NJ
Giurlani, Emmett J. ....San Francisco, CA
Giusiana, Michele A. ....Seattle, WA
Giusini, Vincent J., Law Offices of
Philadelphia, PA
Giust, John E. ....San Diego, CA
Giusti, Gerald G. ....Mountain View, CA
Giusti, Jay R. ....Chicago, IL
Waukegan, IL

Giusti, John V.
Federal Communications Commission, International Bureau, GV
Giusti, Noreen M. ....New York, NY
Giusti, Peter A. ....Savannah, GA
Giusti, Robert F. ....New York, NY
Giusti, William R. ....New York, NY
Giustina, Ansel J. ....Eugene, OR
Giustina, Arthur D. ....Longmeadow, MA
Giustino, Anthony P. ....Massapequa, NY
Giusto, Blaise Charles ....Cleveland, OH
Giusto, Richard J. ....Miami, FL
Givan, Richard E. ....Richmond, KY
Givan, Richard M. ....Indianapolis, IN
Givan, Timothy G. ....Hutchinson, KS
Givant, Leonard ....New York, NY
Givas, Thomas P. ....Syracuse, NY
Givelber, David S. ....Atlanta, GA
Given, Baron W. ....Sarasota, FL
Given, Bernard R., II ....El Paso, TX
Given, Charles M. ....Mount Vernon, IL
Given, David A. ....Indianapolis, IN
Given, David M. ....San Francisco, CA
Given, J. Randolph ....Naperville, IL
Given, James T. ....Palo Alto, CA
Given, Jeffrey N. ....Chicago, IL
Given, Lynda K. ....Chicago, IL
Given, Robert S. W. ....Birmingham, AL
Given, Ronald B. ....Chicago, IL
Given, Sam Perry ....Birmingham, AL
Given, Samuel Perry, Jr. ....Birmingham, AL
Given, Thomas A. ....Cleveland, OH
Given, Whitney R. ....Boston, MA
Givens, Alice G. ....Richmond, VA
Givens, Andrew ....Washington, DC
Givens, Anne M. ....Milford, MA
Givens, Arthur (Art), Jr. ....Little Rock, AR
Givens and Associates, PLLC
Houston, TX
Givens, Blake R. ....Tulsa, OK
Givens, C. Eugene ....Los Angeles, CA
Givens, Cherie L. ....New Orleans, LA
Givens, David O. ....Mt. Vernon, IN
Givens, David Straley ....Charleston, WV
Givens, David W. ....Indianapolis, IN
Givens, Dermot D. ....Los Angeles, CA
Givens, Donna Seegars ....Lexington, SC
Givens, Edwin D. ....Columbia, SC
Givens, George Franklin ....Raleigh, NC
Givens, Glenn Fishburne ....Florence, SC
Givens, Greg D. ....Oklahoma City, OK
Givens, Hartzell ....Taylorville, IL
Givens, J. Keith ....Dothan, AL
Givens, Jack R. ....Tulsa, OK
Givens, James W. ....Lewiston, ID
Givens, Jimmy D. ....Oklahoma City, OK
Givens, Jon T. ....Anchorage, AK
Givens, Keith F. ....Oklahoma City, OK
Givens, Kelly Seabrook ....Columbia, SC
Givens, Kenneth B. ....Houma, LA
Givens, Kenneth M., Jr. ....Baltimore, MD
Givens, Larry D. ....Gainesville, FL
Givens, Larry E. ....Dothan, AL
Givens, Leonard D. ....Detroit, MI
Givens, M. Stanley ....Johnson City, TN
Givens, Mark S. ....Ocala, FL
Givens, Michael A. ....Sylacauga, AL
Givens, Montia O. ....Washington, DC
Givens, Paul S. ....Sacramento, CA
Givens Pursley LLP ....Boise, ID
Givens, Raymond D. ....Boise, ID
Givens, Rebecca B. ....Denver, CO
Givens, Richard D. ....Redwood City, CA
Givens, Robert T. ....Houston, TX
Givens, Stann W. ....Tampa, FL
Givens, Stephen B. ....Greenwood, IN
Givens, Terry S. ....Birmingham, MI
Givens, Thelma ....Nashville, TN
Givens, Thomas A. ....Rock Hill, SC
Givens, Thomas C., Jr. ....Tazewell, VA
Givens, Thomas P. ....Knoxville, TN
Givens, William D. ....Houston, TX
Givens, Yolanda T. ....North Las Vegas, NV
Giventer, Barnet E. ....Staten Island, NY
Giventer, Lorrie A. ....Washington, DC
Givertz, Lunt, Hambley & Scheffee, P.A.
Portland, ME
Givertz, Phyllis G. ....Portland, ME
Givhan, John B. ....Andalusia, AL
Givhan, Joseph P., Jr. ....Mobile, AL
Givhan, Margaret L. ....Montgomery, AL
Givhan, Mercer A, III ....Washington, DC
New York, NY
Givhan, R. Marcus ....Birmingham, AL
Givhan, Samuel Houston ....Huntsville, AL
Givhan & Spainhour, P.S.C.
Louisville, KY
Shepherdsville, KY
Givhan, Thomas B. ....Louisville, KY
Shepherdsville, KY
Givhan, William B. ....Mobile, AL
Givhan-Brewer, Darvionne J. ....Chicago, IL
Givler & Evers ....Lock Haven, PA
Givler, Mark A. ....Lock Haven, PA
Givner, Bruce ....Los Angeles, CA
Givner, Cheryl G. ....New York, NY
Givner, Jacob J., (P.A.) ....Miami, FL
Givner, Kathleen Graham ....Los Angeles, CA
Givner, Ronald P. ....Los Angeles, CA
Givon, Amiram J. ....San Francisco, CA
Givray, Albert J. ....Tulsa, OK
Giwa, Gabriel I. ....Houston, TX
Giza, David A. ....Lincolnshire, IL
Giza, Laura M.
National Aeronautics And Space Administration, Office of the General Counsel, GV
Gizang, Michael E. ....New York, NY

Gizewski, Theodore M.
San Francisco, CA
Gizinski, Rochelle ....Carteret, NJ
Gizzarelli, John L., Jr. ....Quincy, MA
Gizzi, James F. ....Florham Park, NJ
Gizzi, Keith Wylie ....Columbus, OH
Gizzi, Lisa ....Hartford, CT
Gizzi, Paul G.
Securities and Exchange Commission, Division of Enforcement, GV
Gizzi, Ronald J. ....New York, NY
Gjerde, Ronald L. ....Springfield, IL
Gjerdingen, Kendra Gowdy
Bloomington, IN
Gjersdal, Henry W., Jr. ....Minneapolis, MN
Gjerset, James E. ....Austin, TX
Gjerset & Lorenz L.L.C. ....Austin, TX
Gjertsen, Gary R. ....Scarsdale, NY
Gjertsen, Gerard ....Scarsdale, NY
Gjertsen, O. Gerard ....White Plains, NY
Gjesdahl, Michael L. ....Fargo, ND
Gjevre, Alden H. ....Barnesville, MN
Moorhead, MN
Gjivoje, Larisa V. K. ....Morristown, NJ
Gjording, Jack S. ....Boise, ID
Gjorvad, Robert L. ....Marshall, MN
Gjullin, Kurt O. ....Monitor, WA
Gjurasic, Adrian deF. ....Seattle, WA
Gjurgevich, James L. ....Tucson, AZ
Gjurich, Kenneth N. ....Southampton, PA
Gjurich, Nadine L. ....Washington, DC
Gkonos, James S. ....Plymouth Meeting, PA
Glaab, David A. ....New Boston, MI
Glaab, David A., P.C. ....New Boston, MI
Glabach, Frank C. ....Berkley, MI
Glabach, G. Frank ....Santa Monica, CA
Glaberson, Arnold ....Philadelphia, PA
Glabicki, Jeffrey M. ....Philadelphia, PA
Glabman, Herbert ....Woodmere, NY
Glabman, Scott ....Department of Labor, Office of the Solicitor, GV
Glaccum, Jo Ann Marie ....Montvale, NJ
Glace, John M. ....Harrisburg, PA
Glace, Nivedita ....Napa, CA
Glacken, Claudia C. ....Garden City, NY
Glackin, Charles A. ....Parkesburg, PA
Glackin, Edward J., III ....New York, NY
Glackin, Gerald F. ....Lansdale, PA
Glackin, Maureen A. ....Huntington, NY
Glackin, Michael A. ....Chicago, IL
Glackin, Sheila A. ....Springfield, NJ
Glacy, Cynthia Runge ....Andover, MA
Glad, Amy L. ....Diamond Bar, CA
Glad, Linda G. ....Salt Lake City, UT
Glad, Paul E. B. ....San Francisco, CA
Gladchun, Lawrence L.
Farmington Hills, MI
Gladd, John A. ....Tulsa, OK
Gladd, John S. ....Tulsa, OK
Gladd, Smith, Harris & Rounds, A Professional Association ....Tulsa, OK
Gladden, Brenda W.
Department of Housing and Urban Development, Office of General Counsel, GV
Gladden, C. Scott ....Dallas, TX
Gladden, C. William ....Birmingham, AL
Gladden, Don ....Fort Worth, TX
Gladden, Gregory C. ....Houston, TX
Gladden, James R. ....Oxford, GA
Gladden, James W., Jr. ....Chicago, IL
Gladden, James W., Jr. ....Hattiesburg, MS
Gladden, John B. ....Nags Head, NC
Gladden, John H. ....Joplin, MO
Gladden, Joseph R., Jr. ....Atlanta, GA
Gladden, Kathleen ....Brooklyn, NY
Gladden, Lesley Brackin ....Huntsville, AL
Gladden, Lisa A. ....Baltimore, MD
Gladden, Mark L. ....Healdsburg, CA
Gladden, Randall O. ....Huntsville, AL
Gladden, Robert E. ....Camden, NJ
Gladden & Rose ....Nags Head, NC
Gladden & Sinor, P.C. ....Birmingham, AL
Gladden, Stephen L. ....Voorhees, NJ
Gladden, Thomas D. ....Pittsburgh, PA
Gladden, Thomas D. ....Washington, PA
Gladden, Thomas R., Jr. ....Shelby, NC
Gladden, William E. ....Houston, MO
Gladden, William J. ....Nashville, TN
Gladders, Warren J. ....St. Louis, MO
Glade, J. Richard ....Sacramento, CA
Glade, Kevin G. ....Salt Lake City, UT
Glade, Michael J. ....Denver, CO
Glade, Peter H. ....Portland, OR
Glade, Steven B. ....Las Vegas, NV
Glader, Ralph N. ....Chicago, IL
Glades, Phillip A. ....Joplin, MO
Glades, Phillip A., A Professional Corporation
Joplin, MO
Gladfelter, David D. ....Bordentown, NJ
Gladfelter, Leslie Horton ....Bradenton, FL
Tampa, FL
Gladfelter, Phillip E. ....Bellevue, WA
Gladin, J. Alton ....Macon, GA
Glading, William J. ....Highlands, NJ
Gladis, Jay ....New York, NY
Gladish, David Stephen ....Highland, IN
La Porte, IN
Gladish, Kenneth J. ....Hoffman Estates, IL
Gladish, Scott ....Chicago, IL
Gladke, Lisa Denise ....Hartford, CT
Gladkowski, Mary Ann ....Skokie, IL
Gladner, Albert J. ....Bloomfield Hills, MI
Gladner, Marc S. ....Phoenix, AZ
Gladney, Calvin G. ....Washington, DC
Gladney, Demonica D. ....Houston, TX
Gladney, Jill J. ....Chicago, IL
Gladney, Patrick O. ....Brighton, MI

Glass, Bradley M. ....Dodgeville, WI
Glass & Braus ....Westport, CT
Glass, Bryan C. ....Pittsburgh, PA
Glass, C. Brandon ....Birmingham, AL
Glass, Carson M. ....Lubbock, TX
Glass, Carter, IV ....Richmond, VA
Glass, Charles F. ....Detroit, MI
Harbor Springs, MI
Glass, Charles N. ....Albuquerque, NM
Glass, Colm ....New York, NY
Glass, Connie L. ....Huntsville, AL
Glass, Craig A. ....Van Nuys, CA
Glass, Daniel ....New York, NY
Glass, Daniel B. ....Westport, CT
Glass, Daniel S. ....Citrus Heights, CA
Glass, Danny E. ....Evansville, IN
Glass, David J. ....Philadelphia, PA
Glass, David L. ....New York, NY
Glass, David M. ....Department of Justice, Civil Division, GV
Glass & Dawson, P.A. ....Belfast, ME
Glass, Deborah E. ....Philadelphia, PA
Glass, Denise Webb ....Dallas, TX
Glass, Dennis W. ....Pittsburgh, PA
Glass, Diane ....Trenton, NJ
Glass, Donald E. ....Irvine, CA
Glass, Donald Franklin ....Houston, TX
Glass, Donna Y. ....Detroit, MI
Glass, Douglas Alan ....San Diego, CA
Glass, Ellen Bloom ....Philadelphia, PA
Glass, Elliot H. ....Oxnard, CA
Glass, F. Stephen ....Cary, NC
Glass, Foster A. ....John Day, OR
Glass, Foster A., P.C. ....John Day, OR
Glass, Francis A. ....Juneau, AK
Glass, Fredric J. ....New York, NY
Glass, G. Frederick ....Indianapolis, IN
Glass, Gary B. ....New York, NY
Glass, Gary M. ....Cincinnati, OH
Glass, Geoffrey T. ....Newport Beach, CA
Glass, George W. R. ....Winchester, VA
Glass, Gerald D. ....Baltimore, MD
Glass, Gerard J. ....Orinda, CA
Glass, Gerard J. ....Babylon, NY
Glass, Ginger Gilbert ....Atlantic City, NJ
Glass, Glen A. ....Dallas, TX
Glass & Goldberg, A Law Corporation
Los Angeles, CA
Woodland Hills, CA
Glass, Greg C. ....Columbus, OH
Glass, Gregory W. ....Melbourne, FL
Glass, Harold F. ....Springfield, MO
Glass, Harvey ....Peabody, MA
Glass, Henry R., III ....Charleston, WV
Glass, Howard L. ....Houston, TX
Glass, J. Bennett, P.A. ....Monroe, NC
Glass, J. Luther ....Richmond, VA
Glass, Jacalyn ....Las Vegas, NV
Glass, James A. ....Pomona, CA
Glass, James D., (P.C.) ....New York, NY
Glass, James E. ....Fort Lauderdale, FL
Glass, James Greg ....Houston, TX
Glass, James L., Jr. ....Chicago, IL
Glass, James M. ....Glen Ellyn, IL
Glass, Jane Garrity ....Montclair, NJ
Glass, Jason Lee ....Tulsa, OK
Glass, Jeff ....Austin, TX
Glass, Jeffrey A. ....Fort Lauderdale, FL
Glass, Jeffrey R. ....Belleville, IL
Glass, Jenna K. ....St. Louis, MO
Glass, Jennifer G. ....Washington, DC
Glass, Joanne Wissman ....Cincinnati, OH
Glass, Joel ....New York, NY
Glass, Jonathon C. ....Washington, DC
Glass, Joseph ....New Haven, CT
Glass, Joseph E., Sr. ....Towson, MD
Glass, Joseph F. ....Tulsa, OK
Glass, Joseph G. ....Louisville, KY
Glass, Joseph G. ....Metairie, LA
Glass, Juandell D. ....Norman, OK
Pharr, TX
Glass, Judith R. ....Philadelphia, PA
Glass, Julie P. ....Washington, DC
Glass, K. Wayne ....Staunton, VA
Glass, Keith ....Red Bank, NJ
Glass, Kenneth N. ....Sunnyvale, CA
Glass, Kimberly B. ....Birmingham, AL
Glass, L. Edward ....Albuquerque, NM
Glass, Laura Lee ....Tampa, FL
Glass, Laurie J. ....New York, NY
Glass Law Firm, The ....Houston, TX
Glass, Lebovitz & Kasheta, LLC
Rocky Hill, CT
Glass, Lee S. ....Mercer Island, WA
Glass, Leo ....Jeffersonville, NY
Monticello, NY
Glass, Leonard R. ....Hackensack, NJ
Glass, Linda Cannon
General Accounting Office, Office of the General Counsel, GV
Glass, Lisa A. ....New York, NY
Glass, Lynne M. ....New York, NY
Glass, Marc Jerome ....Rocky Hill, CT
Glass, Margaret S. ....Raleigh, NC
Glass, Maria Leonetti ....Hamburg, NY
Glass, Mark ....East St. Louis, IL
Glass, Martin ....New York, NY
Glass, Martin S. ....Hauppauge, NY
Glass, Melissa ....New York, NY
Glass, Melvin D. ....Kew Gardens, NY
Glass, Michael A. ....Teaneck, NJ
Glass, Michael D. ....Pittsburgh, PA
Glass, Michael E. ....Pikesville, MD
Glass, Michael G. ....Melville, NY
Glass, Michael J. ....Woodland Hills, CA
Glass, Michael L. ....Miami, FL
Glass, Michael L. ....Alexandria, LA
Glass, Michael O. ....Mill Valley, CA
Glass, Morris M. ....Beverly Hills, CA
Glass, Norton ....Avon, CT
Glass, Paul F. ....Los Angeles, CA
Glass, Peter B. ....Atlanta, GA
Glass, Peter M. ....St. Paul, MN
Glass, Philip A. ....Raleigh, NC
Glass & Quintana ....Albuquerque, NM
Glass & Rastatter, P.A. ....Fort Lauderdale, FL
Glass & Reed ....New Orleans, LA
Glass, Reid ....Lexington, KY
Glass, Richard C. ....Atlanta, GA
Glass, Richard W. ....Belfast, ME
Glass, Robert ....New Orleans, LA
Glass, Robert ....Cambridge, MA
Glass, Robert P. ....Dayton, OH
Glass, Robert S. ....Tulsa, OK
Glass, Robert W. ....Tampa, FL
Glass, Robert W. ....Charleston, WV
Glass, Roy L. ....St. Petersburg, FL
Glass, Roy L., P.A., Law Offices of
St. Petersburg, FL
Glass, S. Michael ....Richmond, VA
Glass, Scott A. ....Orlando, FL
Glass & Seebode ....Van Nuys, CA
Glass, Sheldon ....Flushing, NY
Glass, Sidney William ....Oakland, CA
Glass, Stanford L. ....Chicago, IL
Glass, Stefany ....San Jose, CA
Glass, Stephen M. ....Clarksburg, WV
Glass, Steven E. ....Glendale, CA
Glass, Steven M. ....Florence, SC
Glass, Steven R. ....Los Angeles, CA
Woodland Hills, CA
Glass, Stuart E. ....Dallas, TX
Glass, Stuart M. ....Boston, MA
Glass, Stuart M. ....White Plains, NY
Glass, Susan J. ....Irvine, CA
Glass, Susan R. ....Fairfield, CT
Glass, T. Brian ....Atlanta, GA
Glass, Terry Ann Martin ....Piscataway, NJ
Glass, Thomas P. ....Cincinnati, OH
Glass, Thomas Wilson ....New Orleans, LA
Glass, Todd G. ....Seattle, WA
Glass, Todd I. ....Evansville, IN
Glass, Valorie C. ....McAllen, TX
Glass & Vining, LLC ....Cary, NC
Raleigh, NC
Glass, W. Reeder ....Atlanta, GA
Glass, William A. ....Port Jervis, NY
Glass, William G. ....Atlanta, GA
Glass, Wm. P. ....San Antonio, TX
Glass, Woodrow K. ....Oklahoma City, OK
Glassanos, George A. ....Glenmont, NY
Glassband, Rick P.
General Services Administration, Office of the General Counsel, GV
Bethesda, MD
Glassberg, Daniel ....Philadelphia, PA
Glassberg, David E. ....Philadelphia, PA
Glassberg, David L. ....Hazleton, PA
Glassberg, David M. ....Coral Gables, FL
Glassberg, Donald A. ....Chicago, IL
Glassberg, Erica Shiff ....Minneapolis, MN
Glassberg, Frederick W. ....Columbia, MD
Glassberg, Harold B. ....San Francisco, CA
Glassberg and Klemow ....Hazleton, PA
Glassberg, Marc Alan ....St. James, NY
Glassberg, Michael A. ....Brooklyn, NY
Glassberg, Pollak & Associates
San Francisco, CA
Glassberg, Tom A. ....Riverton, WY
Glassburn, John R., III ....Baltimore, MD
Glassburn, Suzanne L. ....Boston, MA
Glassco, Fred A. ....Wichita, KS
Glassco, Kurt G. ....Tulsa, OK
Glasscock, C. Edward ....Louisville, KY
Glasscock, Douglas J. ....Austin, TX
Glasscock, Gardy and Savage ....Suffolk, VA
Glasscock & Glasscock ....San Antonio, TX
Glasscock, J. Samuel ....Suffolk, VA
Glasscock, Kip ....Beaumont, TX
Glasscock, Kip, P.C. ....Beaumont, TX
Glasscock, Lanette H. ....San Antonio, TX
Glasscock, Laurie Patrick ....Boulder, CO
Glasscock, Steven R. ....Atlanta, GA
Glassel, Cheryl L. ....Center City, MN
Glassell, Stephen A. ....Shreveport, LA
Glassen, James W. ....Secaucus, NJ
Glassen, Rhead, McLean, Campbell & Schumacher ....Grand Ledge, MI
Lansing, MI
Glasser, Alan R. ....Santa Clarita, CA
Glasser, Alan R., P.C. ....Santa Clarita, CA
Glasser, Alvin M. ....Valley Stream, NY
Glasser, Brian A. ....Charleston, WV
Glasser, Bruce M. ....San Diego, CA
Glasser, Caryn ....New York, NY
Glasser, Charles E. ....Orinda, CA
Glasser, Charles J., Jr. ....New York, NY
Glasser, Cora J. ....New York, NY
Glasser, Craig R. ....Boca Raton, FL
Glasser, Cynthia B. ....Monterey Park, CA
Glasser, Daniel H. ....Pittsburgh, PA
Glasser, David ....Rye, NY
White Plains, NY
Glasser, David G. ....New York, NY
Glasser, David M. ....Culver City, CA
Glasser, David W. ....Daytona Beach, FL
Glasser, Debra G. ....Panorama City, CA
Glasser, Farrell C. ....New York, NY
Glasser, Francis V. ....Massapequa, NY
Glasser, Gene K. ....Boca Raton, FL
Hollywood, FL
Glasser, George M. ....Toledo, OH
Glasser, Gerald ....Springfield, MA
Glasser and Glasser, P.L.C. ....Norfolk, VA
Glasser, Gregory S. ....Miami, FL
Glasser & Handel ....Daytona Beach, FL
Glasser, Harold A.
Whitehouse Station, NJ
Glasser, Harvey ....New York, NY
Glasser, Henry L. ....San Francisco, CA
Glasser, I. Leo ....Brooklyn, NY
Glasser, Izaak D. ....Chesapeake, VA
Glasser, Jack L. ....Lawrence, NY
Glasser, James I. ....Bridgeport, CT
Glasser, John L. ....Birmingham, AL
Glasser, Jonathan ....New York, NY
Glasser, Kristine F. ....Fort Washington, PA
Glasser, LLoyd S. ....Plantation, FL
Glasser, Lynne
United States Tax Court, GV
Glasser & Macon, P.C. ....Chesapeake, VA
Glasser, Marcie K. ....Garden City, NY
Glasser, Mark K. ....Houston, TX
Glasser, Martin J. ....New York, NY
Glasser, Martin J. ....Charleston, WV
Glasser, Michael A. ....Elmhurst, IL
Glasser, Michael A. ....Norfolk, VA
Glasser, Michael L. ....Charleston, WV
Glasser, Paul N. ....Los Angeles, CA
Glasser, Philip R. ....Overland Park, KS
Glasser, Randa P. ....New York, NY
Glasser, Richard S. ....Norfolk, VA
Richmond, VA
Glasser, Robert ....Washington, DC
Glasser, Robert E. ....Newport Beach, CA
Glasser, Robert J., (P.C.) ....New York, NY
Glasser, Robert L. ....Indianapolis, IN
Glasser & Smith ....Irvine, CA
Newport Beach, CA
Glasser, Stanley M. ....Lake Success, NY
Glasser, Stephen C. ....New York, NY
Glasser, Stuart D. ....Virginia Beach, VA
Glasser, Susanne M. ....River Falls, WI
Glassett, Tim S. ....San Dimas, CA
Glassford, Grant Charles ....Nashville, TN
Glassford, James C. ....Walnut Creek, CA
Glassford, K. Neil ....South Miami, FL
Glasshof, Jacqueline ....Los Angeles, CA
Glassic, Thomas M. ....Washington, DC
Glassie, Jefferson C. ....Washington, DC
Glassl, Norbert ....St. Louis, MO
Glassman, A. J. ....Calabasas, CA
Glassman, Alan B. ....Lakewood, OH
Glassman, Alan C. ....Brooklyn, NY
Glassman, Alan M. ....Dallas, TX
Glassman, Andrew C. ....Hartford, CT
Simsbury, CT
Glassman, Anthony M. ....Beverly Hills, CA
San Jose, CA
Glassman, Arthur A. ....Topeka, KS
Glassman, Arthur J. ....Minneapolis, MN
Glassman, Bernard ....Philadelphia, PA
Glassman, Bird & Braun ....Hays, KS
Glassman, Browning & Saltsman, Inc.
Beverly Hills, CA
Glassman, Bruce R. ....Atlanta, GA
Glassman, Bruce R., P.A. ....Jacksonville, FL
Glassman & Bullock ....Washington, DC
Laytonsville, MD
Vienna, VA
Glassman, Carol ....Boulder, CO
Glassman, Caroline ....Portland, ME
Glassman and Clemens, A Professional Corporation ....Los Angeles, CA
Glassman, Daniel M. ....Costa Mesa, CA
Glassman, David J. ....Atlantic City, NJ
Philadelphia, PA
Glassman, David L. ....Lancaster, PA
Glassman, David S. ....New York, NY
Glassman, Dina S. ....New York, NY
Glassman, Eric J. ....Sacramento, CA
Glassman, Evan ....New York, NY
Glassman, Frederick J., (P.C.)
Los Angeles, CA
Glassman, Frederick Scott ....Chicago, IL
Glassman, Gary M. ....Sarasota, FL
Glassman & Golden Norris ....Sarasota, FL
Glassman, Hilary E. ....New York, NY
Glassman, Howard T. ....Philadelphia, PA
Glassman, Jan A. ....Waltham, MA
Glassman, J. B. ....Jackson, TN
Glassman, Jeffrey L. ....Los Angeles, CA
Glassman, Jeffrey M. ....Department of State, Foreign Service Officers (Overseas), GV
Glassman, Jeffrey R. ....Washington, DC
Glassman, Jeffrey S. ....Boston, MA
Glassman, Jeremiah ....Department of Justice, Civil Rights Division, GV
Glassman, Jerold E. ....Los Angeles, CA
Roseland, NJ
New York, NY
Glassman, Jeter, Edwards & Wade, P.C.
Memphis, TN
Glassman, Joel T. ....Los Angeles, CA
Glassman, John ....Pensacola, FL
Glassman, John, P.A. ....Pensacola, FL
Glassman, Jonathan M. ....New York, NY
Glassman, Julie B. ....Miami, FL
Glassman, Kenneth J. ....New York, NY
Glassman, Laurel W. ....Washington, DC
Glassman, Loren I. ....White Plains, NY
Glassman, Lorna R. ....Department of Justice, Bureau of Prisons, GV
Glassman, M. Katherine ....Hartford, CT
Glassman, M. Melissa ....McLean, VA
Glassman, Margaret M. ....McLean, VA
Glassman, Mark A. ....Fort Lauderdale, FL
Glassman, Mark L. ....Washington, DC
Glassman, Mark P. ....Pepper Pike, OH
Glassman, Martin E. ....Chicago, IL
Glassman, Matthew A. ....Port Jefferson, NY
Glassman, Max ....Florham Park, NJ
Glassman, Mervin B. ....Brooklyn, NY
Glassman, Michael H. ....Morristown, NJ
Glassman, Michael S. ....Los Angeles, CA
Glassman, Michael S. ....Cincinnati, OH
Glassman, Neil B. ....Wilmington, DE
Glassman, Paul R. ....Los Angeles, CA
Glassman, Richard ....Newtown, PA
Philadelphia, PA
Plymouth Meeting, PA
Glassman, Richard ....Memphis, TN
Glassman, Richard A. ....New Haven, CT
Glassman, Richard A. ....Minneapolis, MN
Glassman, Richard S. ....Santa Fe, NM
Glassman, Robert A. ....West Palm Beach, FL
Glassman, Robert B. ....Fresno, CA
Glassman, Robert F. ....Hays, KS
Glassman, Ronald R. ....Akron, OH
Glassman, Ruth A. ....Cranston, RI
Glassman, S. Mitchell ....Houston, TX
Glassman, Sanford ....New London, CT
Glassman, Saul ....Brooklyn, NY
Glassman, Sheldon ....Bronx, NY
Glassman, Sherry A. ....San Francisco, CA
Glassman, Stephen ....Los Angeles, CA
Glassman, Stephen C. ....Washington, DC
Laytonsville, MD
Vienna, VA
Glassman, Stephen M. ....St. Louis, MO
Glassman, Steven B. ....Kansas City, MO
Glassman, Steven J. ....New York, NY
Glassman, Steven S. ....Los Angeles, CA
Roseland, NJ
New York, NY
Glassman, Thomas F. ....Cincinnati, OH
Glassman, Todd J. ....Philadelphia, PA
Glassman & Trickey, P.C. ....Santa Fe, NM
Glassman, Wendi G. ....New York, NY
New York, NY
Glassman, William S. ....Miami, FL
Glassmann, Lawrence A. ....Cincinnati, OH
Glassmeyer, Denise M. ....Troy, MI
Glassmeyer, George S. ....Orangeburg, SC
Glassmire, Daniel F. ....Coudersport, PA
Glassmire & Shaffer Law Offices, P.C.
Coudersport, PA
Glassmith, Scott D. ....Pittsburgh, PA
Glass-Moody, Theresa A. ....Indianapolis, IN
Glassmoyer, Thomas P. ....Philadelphia, PA
Glassner, Bertram J. ....New Brunswick, NJ
Glassner, Bruce M. ....Secaucus, NJ
Glassner, Cary D. ....Santa Monica, CA
Glasson, John A. ....Providence, RI
Glasson, Matthew A. ....Cedar Rapids, IA
Glasson, Richard ....Stateline, NV
Glasson, Sole, McManus & Combs, P.C.
Cedar Rapids, IA
Glasson, Thomas R. ....Charleston, IL
Glasspiegel, Harry H. ....Washington, DC
Glassroth, Stephen R. ....Montgomery, AL
Glassroth & Van Heest, P.C.
Montgomery, AL
Glast, Phillips & Murray, A Professional Corporation ....Dallas, TX
Glast, Sam ....Dallas, TX
Glastetter, Mark D. ....Albany, NY
Glater, David S.
Department of Transportation, Research and Special Programs Administration, GV
Glatman, Arthur L. ....Jersey City, NJ
Glatstein, M. Carl ....Denver, CO
Glatstein & O'Brien, LLP ....Denver, CO
Glatt, Adam J. ....Goshen, NY
Glatt, Andrew M. ....San Diego, CA
Glatt, April Spitzer ....Foster City, CA
Lake Bluff, IL
Glatt, Herman L. ....Los Angeles, CA
Glatt, James E., Jr. ....Orlando, FL
Glatt, Joyce Hiyama ....Berkeley, CA
Glatt, Keith J. ....Bismarck, ND
Glatt, Marjorie B ....Woodmere, NY
Glatt, Michael D. ....New York, NY
Glatter, Denise Rubin ....Philadelphia, PA
Glatter, Eric S. ....Boca Raton, FL
Glatter, Joshua D. ....New York, NY
Glatter & Platt, P.A. ....Boca Raton, FL
Glatter, Susan E. ....Chicago, IL
Glatthaar, James W. ....White Plains, NY
Glatthaar, Joseph B. ....White Plains, NY
Glatthorn, David J. ....West Palm Beach, FL
Glatz, David P. ....Chicago, IL
Glatz, John L. ....Tucson, AZ
Glatz, Robert W. ....Raleigh, NC
Glatzer, Bernard H. ....New York, NY
Glatzer, Bonnie A. ....San Francisco, CA
Glatzer, Jeffrey L. ....New York, NY
Glatzer, Philip E. ....Miami, FL
Glatzer, Sanford B. ....Bronx, NY
Glatzhofer, Gene W. ....Anaheim, CA
Glaub, Michael A. ....Chicago, IL
Glaubensklee, Marilyn ....Fremont, CA
Glauber, Berenson & Salazar
Pasadena, CA
Glauber, David A. ....Memphis, TN
Glauber, Ira N. ....New York, NY
Glauber, Peter J. ....Louisville, KY
Glauber, Russell L. ....Pasadena, CA
Glauberman, Alex J. ....New York, NY
Glauberman, Carol R. ....New York, NY
Glauberman Kessler & Rotmil, LLP
New York, NY
Glauberman, Melvin L. ....New York, NY
Glauberman, Scott P. ....Chicago, IL
Glaubig, Judith C. ....Houston, TX
Glaubiger, Ethan A. ....Santa Rosa, CA
Glaubinger, Wayne R. ....New York, NY
Glauner, Alfred W. ....Cambridge, MA
Glause, Paul Thomas ....Rock Springs, WY
Glause, Paul Thomas, P.C.
Rock Springs, WY

Glauser, Douglas K. ....San Bernardino, CA
Glauser, Gary S. ....El Cajon, CA
Glauser, M. Jane ....Wheeling, WV
Glauser, Richard K. ....Salt Lake City, UT
Glausi, Wallace A. ....Portland, OR
Glavas, Jeannine M. ....Chicago, IL
Glavas, Kosma J. ....Elyria, OH
Glave, Corey W. ....Los Angeles, CA
Glaves, Irby & Rhoads ....Wichita, KS
Glaves, Jack ....Wichita, KS
Glaves, Robert A. ....Chicago, IL
Glaves-Morgan, Sandra D. ....Brooklyn, NY
Glavey, Alfred F. ....Littleton, MA
Glavey, Mattew W. ....New Ipswich, NH
Glaviano, Phillip G ....Los Angeles, CA
Glavin, A. Rita Chandellier ....Waterford, NY
Glavin & Associates, Ltd. ....Chicago, IL
Glavin, Daniel W. ....Hammond, IN
Glavin and Glavin ....Waterford, NY
Glavin, Grace Anne, (P.A.)
Winter Springs, FL
Glavin, James H., III ....Waterford, NY
Glavin, Joanne M. ....Albany, NY
Glavin, John E. ....Detroit, MI
Glavin, John W. ....Rochester, NY
Glavin, Joseph C., Jr. ....Parsippany, NJ
Glavin, Joseph C., Jr., A Professional
Corporation ....Parsippany, NJ
Glavin, Kevin C. ....Providence, RI
Glavin & Kolter ....Los Angeles, CA
Glavin, Kristin Olds ....Rosemont, IL
Glavin, P. Matthew ....Chicago, IL
Glavin, Rita M. ....Department of Justice,
Criminal Division, GV
Glavin, Thomas M. ....Rochester, NY
Glavin, Thomas M. ....Collegeville, PA
Glavin, William P., IV ....Los Angeles, CA
Glavinos, George, Jr. ....Westlake, OH
Glavinovich, Gary Peter ....Oakland, CA
Glavinovich, Mikel A. ....Los Angeles, CA
Glavinskas, Eduard Adam ....Chicago, IL
Glavis & Bloom, PLC ....San Diego, CA
Glavis, Greta ....San Diego, CA
Glawe, Reed H. ....New Ulm, MN
Glaws, Charles T. ....New York, NY
Glaymon, Robert E. ....Linwood, NJ
Glazar, Edward S., Jr. ....Kankakee, IL
Glaze, Catherine ....San Francisco, CA
Glaze, Catherine Reeves ....Birmingham, AL
Glaze, Cynthia L. ....Milwaukee, WI
Glaze, George E. ....Jonesboro, GA
Stockbridge, GA
Glaze & Glaze, P.C. ....Jonesboro, GA
Stockbridge, GA
Glaze, James E. ....Washington, DC
Glaze, Kirby A. ....Jonesboro, GA
Stockbridge, GA
Glaze, Martha K. ....Jonesboro, GA
Glaze, Michael W. ....Cherry Hill, NJ
Glaze, Richard E. ....Winston-Salem, NC
Glaze, Richard E., Jr. ....Winston-Salem, NC
Glaze, Sharron P. ....Batesville, AR
Glaze, Stacie Ann ....Crofton, MD
Glaze, Steven T. ....Washington, DC
Glaze, Thomas A. ....Little Rock, AR
Glaze, Tommy C. ....Arlington, TX
Glazebrook, James G. ....Orlando, FL
Glazek, Patricia W. ....Santa Fe, NM
Glazek, Stephen E. ....Detroit, MI
Glazer, Adam J. ....Chicago, IL
Glazer, Albert A. ....Los Angeles, CA
Glazer, Anne Wheeler ....Portland, OR
Glazer, Ari J. ....Fort Lauderdale, FL
Glazer, Barry ....Chicago, IL
Glazer, Barry R. ....Baltimore, MD
Glazer, Bryan ....Tampa, FL
Glazer, Craig A. ....Columbus, OH
Glazer, Dale Barken ....St. Louis, MO
Glazer, Daryl F. ....Cambridge, MA
Glazer, David A. ....New York, NY
Glazer, David B. ....San Francisco, CA
Glazer, David G. ....Princeton, NJ
Glazer, David L. ....Boca Raton, FL
Miami, FL
Glazer, Debra G. ....Irvine, CA
Glazer, Dennis E. ....New York, NY
Glazer, Diane Pregerson, (Mrs.)
Beverly Hills, CA
Glazer, Donald J. ....Miami, FL
Glazer, Edward L., (P.C.) ....Boston, MA
Glazer, Elizabeth ....New York, NY
Glazer, Eric L. ....Miami Beach, FL
Glazer, Eric L. ....Buffalo, NY
Glazer, Eric M., P.A.
Hallandale Beach, FL
Miami, FL
Glazer, Eric Michael
Hallandale Beach, FL
Glazer, Eugene I. ....Baltimore, MD
Glazer, Gale L., (Ms.) ....Boston, MA
Glazer, George D. ....New York, NY
Glazer & Glazer, P.A. ....Aventura, FL
Glazer & Gottlieb ....New York, NY
Glazer, Gregory S. ....Los Angeles, CA
Glazer, Harry M. ....Tysons Corner, VA
Glazer, Herbert ....Memphis, TN
Glazer, Howard S. ....Boston, MA
Glazer, J. Henry ....San Francisco, CA
Glazer, Jarrold A. ....Houston, TX
Glazer, Jeffrey A. ....New York, NY
Glazer, Jeffrey Stuart ....Cleveland, OH
Glazer, Jenna R. ....New York, NY
Glazer, Joseph A. ....Albany, NY
Glazer, Joseph D. ....Princeton, NJ
Glazer, Kamel & Guberman ....Elizabeth, NJ
Glazer, Keith ....Santa Clarita, CA
Glazer, Kenneth L. ....Atlanta, GA
Glazer, Lawrence M. ....Lansing, MI
Glazer, Leonard ....Boston, MA
Glazer, Leonard, P.C. ....Boston, MA
Glazer, Leven & Sandler ....Calabasas, CA
Glazer, Mark J. ....Bloomfield Hills, MI
Glazer, Mark S. ....Calabasas, CA
Glazer, Marlene L. ....New York, NY
Glazer, Martin ....Louisville, KY
Glazer, Martin A. ....Boston, MA
Glazer, Martin M. ....Elizabeth, NJ
Glazer, Marvin A. ....Phoenix, AZ
Glazer, May ....New York, NY
Glazer, Michael ....Los Angeles, CA
Glazer, Michael B. ....Richardson, TX
Glazer, Michael F. ....Rockville, MD
Glazer, Michael H., (P.C.) ....Boston, MA
Glazer, Michael J. ....Tallahassee, FL
Glazer, Morton A. ....Brookline, MA
Glazer, Myron ....Evanston, IL
Glazer, Natalie ....New York, NY
Glazer, Neal M. ....New York, NY
Glazer, Neil L. ....Philadelphia, PA
Glazer, Neil N. ....Boston, MA
Glazer, Neil S. ....Aventura, FL
Glazer, Neil T. ....Cleveland, OH
Glazer, Peter K. ....Lake Oswego, OR
Glazer, Rachelle H. ....Dallas, TX
Glazer, Reena N. ....Washington, DC
Glazer, Richard C. ....Philadelphia, PA
Glazer, Richard H. ....Cincinnati, OH
Glazer, Richard H., Co., L.P.A.
Cincinnati, OH
Glazer, Robert ....Easton, PA
Glazer, Robert M. ....Hauppauge, NY
Glazer, Robin Kohn ....San Francisco, CA
Glazer, Ronald B. ....Philadelphia, PA
Glazer, Rose Marie Evans ....Dallas, TX
Glazer, Russell I. ....Los Angeles, CA
Glazer, Sharon B. ....Evanston, IL
Glazer, Sharon J. ....Hollywood, FL
Glazer, Stephen G.
Export-Import Bank of The United States,
Office of the General Counsel, GV
Glazer, Steven A.
United States International Trade
Commission,
Office of Unfair Import Investigations, GV
Glazer, Steven D. ....New York, NY
Glazer, Steven M. ....Rockville, MD
Glazer, Steven P. ....Tallahassee, FL
Glazer, Wendy ....Philadelphia, PA
Glazer, William J. ....Los Angeles, CA
Glazerman, Alvin M. ....Boston, MA
Providence, RI
Glazerman, Michael J. ....Boston, MA
Glazier, Alexandra ....Boston, MA
Glazier, Bernard ....Springfield, MA
Glazier, Bradley K. ....Grand Rapids, MI
Glazier, Cynthia J. ....Manchester, NH
Glazier, David L. ....Provo, UT
Glazier, Donald A. ....Rolling Meadows, IL
Glazier, Guy P. ....Los Angeles, CA
Glazier, Herman C., Jr. ....Diamondhead, MS
Glazier, Irwin L. ....Boston, MA
Glazier, J. Lynn ....San Francisco, CA
Glazier, Jonathan Hemenway
Arlington, VA
Glazier, Joshua M. ....Chicago, IL
Glazier, Kenneth M. ....Los Angeles, CA
Glazier, Louis J. ....Syracuse, NY
Glazier, Louis O. ....Fontana, CA
Glazier, Mark A. ....Indianapolis, IN
Glazier, Marvin H. ....Bangor, ME
Glazier, Michael S. ....Overland Park, KS
Glazier, Patricia N. ....Pasadena, CA
Glazier, Penn B. ....Lancaster, PA
Glazier, Richard B. ....Fayetteville, NC
Glazier, Richard L. ....Warrenton, VA
Glazier, Robert S., Law Office of
Miami, FL
Glazier, Sandra D. ....West Bloomfield, MI
Glazier, Sandra D., P.C., Law Offices of
West Bloomfield, MI
Glazier, Scott Allen ....West Palm Beach, FL
Glazier, Scott L. ....Jacksonville, FL
Glazier, Sharon Robles ....Miami, FL
Glazier, Stan Mitchell
House of Representatives,
Committee Legal Personnel, GV
Glazier, Stephen C. ....Washington, DC
Glazier, Steven J. ....Indianapolis, IN
Glazner, Alan L. ....Cranford, NJ
Glazner, Carmen W. ....Fort Worth, TX
Glazner, Larry ....Levelland, TX
Glazov, Burton E. ....Chicago, IL
Glazzard, Charles F. ....Houston, TX
Gleacher, John G. ....New York, NY
Glean, Pamela Stanback ....Durham, NC
Gleaner, Harold P. ....Audubon, NJ
Gleaner, Robert A. ....Audubon, NJ
Gleaner, Robert A., P.C. ....Audubon, NJ
Gleasner, Donald G., Jr. ....New York, NY
Gleason, Andrew D. ....Johnstown, PA
Gleason, Andrew J. ....Harrisburg, PA
Gleason & Barbin, P.C. ....Harrisburg, PA
Gleason, Bruce M. ....North Hills, CA
Gleason, Carolyn B. ....Washington, DC
Gleason, Charles S. ....Tampa, FL
Gleason, Charles T. ....Indianapolis, IN
Gleason, Charles Thomas ....Tampa, FL
Gleason, Cynthia L. ....Atlanta, GA
Gleason, Daniel J. ....Solana Beach, CA
Gleason, Daniel J. ....Boston, MA
Gleason, David L. ....Amarillo, TX
Gleason, David M. ....Houston, TX
Gleason, David R. ....Baltimore, MD
Gleason, Dennis F. ....Roseland, NJ
Gleason, Diane M. ....Houston, TX
Gleason, DiFrancesco, Shahade, Barbin &
Markovitz ....Johnstown, PA
Gleason, Douglas ....Kansas City, MO
Gleason, Dunn, Walsh & O'Shea
Albany, NY
Gleason, Edward A.
Colorado Springs, CO
Gleason, Edward M., Jr. ....Washington, DC
Gleason, Edward W. ....Chicago, IL
Gleason, Eileen ....New Orleans, LA
Gleason, Eugene A., III ....La Mirada, CA
Gleason, Eugene H. ....Interlaken, NJ
Gleason & Ferzola ....Garden City, NY
Gleason, Flynn & Emig, Chartered
Washington, DC
Rockville, MD
Gleason, Francis T., Jr. ....Neshanic Station, NJ
Gleason, Frank M. ....Rossville, GA
Gleason, Gary M. ....Wellsboro, PA
Gleason, Gary R. ....San Mateo, CA
Gleason, George E. ....Tulsa, OK
Gleason, Gerald K.
Environmental Protection Agency,
Office of the General Counsel, GV
Gleason, Gerald M. ....Wichita, KS
Gleason, Gerald W. ....Springfield, MO
Gleason & Gleason ....Solana Beach, CA
Gleason, Gregory ....Pittsburgh, PA
Gleason, Gretchen Bonds ....Greenville, SC
Gleason, Harold Anthony ....New York, NY
Gleason, Harvey G. ....New Orleans, LA
Gleason, Herbert P. ....Boston, MA
Gleason & Hill, LLC ....Darien, CT
Gleason, James A. ....Lexington, NC
Gleason, James D. ....Henniker, NH
Gleason, James E. ....Hamburg, MI
Gleason, James F., Jr. ....New York, NY
Gleason, James J., III ....Covington, LA
Gleason, James M. ....Omaha, NE
Gleason, James P. ....San Jose, CA
Gleason, James P., Jr. ....Rockville, MD
Gleason, James S. ....Binghamton, NY
Gleason, James T., (P.C.) ....Omaha, NE
Gleason, Jan M. ....La Jolla, CA
Gleason, Jean Wilbur ....Washington, DC
Gleason, Jeffrey M. ....Charlottesville, VA
Gleason, Jody A. ....Chicago, IL
Gleason, John A. ....Columbus, OH
Gleason, John D. ....Portland, ME
Gleason, John F. ....Louisville, KY
Gleason, John P. ....New York, NY
Gleason, John S. ....Newport Beach, CA
Gleason, John S. ....Denver, CO
Gleason, Joseph J. ....Lakeland, FL
Gleason, Joseph Matthew
North Andover, MA
Gleason, Judith A. ....Schaumburg, IL
Gleason, Karen M. ....Kansas City, MO
Gleason, Kathryn ....Chicago, IL
Gleason, Kathryn L. ....Washington, DC
Gleason, Kathy A. ....Parsippany, NJ
Gleason, Kathy A. ....Asheville, NC
Gleason, Kenneth P. ....Minneapolis, MN
Gleason, Kenton T. ....Dodge City, KS
Gleason, Kevin C. ....Hollywood, FL
Gleason, Kevin E. ....Naples, FL
Gleason, Kevin M. ....Chicago, IL
Gleason, Kevin, P.A. ....Boca Raton, FL
Fort Lauderdale, FL
Hollywood, FL
Gleason Koatz & Dyer ....New York, NY
Gleason, Laurel S. ....Pittsburgh, PA
Gleason Law Office ....Henniker, NH
Gleason, Leonard G. ....Trenton, NJ
Gleason, Lorna P. ....Minneapolis, MN
Gleason, Lynelle A. ....Newtown, PA
Gleason, M. Bridget ....Grand Rapids, MI
Gleason, Margaret E. ....Kalamazoo, MI
Gleason, Mark L. ....Minneapolis, MN
Gleason, Mary A. ....Doylestown, PA
Gleason, Mary Alana ....Dorchester, MA
Gleason, Mary C. ....New York, NY
Gleason, Michael E. ....Solana Beach, CA
Gleason, Michael P. ....Denver, CO
Gleason, Nancy J. ....Chicago, IL
Gleason, Owen P. ....Eden Prairie, MN
Gleason, Patricia Ecker ....Hollywood, FL
Gleason, Patricia R. ....Tallahassee, FL
Gleason, Patrick M. ....Chicago, IL
Gleason, Paul E. ....Garden City, NY
Gleason, Paul M. ....Austin, TX
Gleason, Philip H. ....Portland, ME
Gleason, Rebecca S. ....Denver, CO
Gleason, Richard A. ....Auburn, NY
Gleason, Richard C. ....Chicago, IL
Gleason, Richard J. ....Denver, CO
Gleason, Richard S. ....Portland, OR
Gleason, Rick A. ....Chicago, IL
Gleason, Rick A., & Associates ....Chicago, IL
Gleason, Robert C. ....Department of Justice,
Drug Enforcement Administration, GV
Gleason, Robert D. ....Johnstown, PA
Gleason, Robert H. ....San Diego, CA
Gleason, Robert J. ....Jacksonville, NC
Gleason, Robert M. ....Edina, MN
Gleason, Scarborough, McNeese, O'Brien &
Barnes, P.C. ....Portland, OR
Gleason, Scot C. ....New York, NY
Gleason, Sean E. ....Rochester, NY
Gleason, Sean F. ....Modesto, CA
Gleason, Sean P. ....Haverhill, MA
Gleason, Sean P., P.C. ....Haverhill, MA
Gleason, Sharon L. ....Anchorage, AK
Gleason, Stephanie A. ....San Francisco, CA
Gleason, Susan Shaw ....Chicago, IL
Gleason, Teresa A. ....Washington, DC
Gleason, Teri Dunaway ....Jackson, MS
Gleason, Theresa ....New York, NY
Gleason, Thomas A. ....Omaha, NE
Gleason, Thomas E. ....Ottawa, KS
Gleason, Thomas F. ....Albany, NY
Gleason, Thomas P. ....Norristown, PA
Philadelphia, PA
Gleason, Thomas W. ....New York, NY
Gleason, Victor E. ....Pacific Palisades, CA
Gleason, Walter J. ....Milton, MA
Gleason, Wilder G. ....Darien, CT
Gleason, Zēb F. ....Santa Monica, CA
Gleason-Groff, Kellie Lynn ....Detroit, MI
Gleaton, Frederick N. ....Atlanta, GA
Gleaton, John E. ....Comanche, TX
Gleaton, Persons, Egan & Jones
Atlanta, GA
Gleave, James Winston, Law Office of
San Diego, CA
Gleaves, A. Frank, III ....Indianapolis, IN
Gleaves, Curt B. ....Portland, OR
Gleaves, James L. ....Wytheville, VA
Gleaves, Kaase & Chitwood ....Wytheville, VA
Gleaves, Karl D. ....Department of Commerce,
National Oceanic and Atmospheric
Administration, GV
Gleaves, R. Leslie ....Richardson, TX
Gleaves Swearingen Larsen Potter Scott &
Smith, LLP ....Eugene, OR
Gleaves, Vernon D. ....Eugene, OR
Gleba, Gary J. ....Buffalo, NY
Glebe, David Curtis ....Wilmington, DE
Gleber, Erich J. ....New York, NY
Gleber, Frederick V. ....New Iberia, LA
Gleberman, Ellen J. ....Cypress, CA
Gleboff, Stephen G. ....Dallas, TX
Glecer, Judy E. ....Demarest, NJ
Gleckman, Maurice A. ....New York, NY
Gleckman, Roger J. ....Los Angeles, CA
Gledhill, Anthony Paul ....Philadelphia, PA
Gledhill, D. Ryan ....New York, NY
Gledhill, Geoffrey E. ....Hillsborough, NC
Gledhill, Karen A. ....Charlotte, NC
Gledhill, Stephen J. ....Boise, ID
Gleekel, Anthony J. ....Minneapolis, MN
Gleekel, Peter J. ....Minneapolis, MN
St. Paul, MN
Gleeman, Mark R. ....Minneapolis, MN
Gleen, Barry H. ....New York, NY
Gleesing, John P. ....Spokane, WA
Gleeson, Albert E. ....Yonkers, NY
Gleeson, Andrew J. ....Belleville, IL
Gleeson, Carrie L. ....San Diego, CA
Gleeson & Corcoran ....Boston, MA
Gleeson & Davis ....Beaverton, OR
Gleeson, Francis E., Jr. ....Philadelphia, PA
Gleeson, Francis M., II ....Cincinnati, OH
Gleeson, Gerald A. ....Philadelphia, PA
Gleeson, Gerald L. ....Stockton, CA
Gleeson, J. Michael ....Beaverton, OR
Gleeson, John ....Brooklyn, NY
Gleeson, John Gerald
Bloomfield Hills, MI
Gleeson, John Gerald, Jr.
Bloomfield Hills, MI
Gleeson, Kathleen A. ....Lansing, MI
Gleeson, Kevin J. ....Southfield, MI
Gleeson, Kevin M. ....Department of State,
Office of the Legal Adviser, GV
Gleeson, Kurt S.
General Services Administration,
Office of Regional Counsel, GV
Gleeson, Marcia J. ....West Hartford, CT
Gleeson, Monica ....San Diego, CA
Gleeson, Paul F. ....Chicago, IL
Gleeson, Richard W. ....Boston, MA
Gleeson, Roger J. ....Jackson, MI
Gleeson, Rosemary K. ....Palo Alto, CA
Gleeson, Timothy P. ....McArthur, OH
Gleeson-Lagace, Kathleen Ann ....Albany, NY
Gleeson-Smith, Jeannine F.
Birmingham, MI
Gleespen, Michael W. ....Columbus, OH
Glegg, Kathryn M. ....Dallas, TX
Gleiberman, Melissa R. ....Beverly Hills, CA
Gleiberman, Paul D. ....Washington, DC
Gleich, Caryn Franklin ....Cincinnati, OH
Gleich, Stephan B. ....Great Neck, NY
Gleichenhaus, Marchese & Falcone, P.C.
Buffalo, NY
Gleichenhaus, Robert B. ....Buffalo, NY
Gleicher, Brian S. ....Washington, DC
Gleicher, Clifford J. ....San Francisco, CA
Gleicher, David W. ....Chicago, IL
Gleicher, Elizabeth ....Detroit, MI
Gleicher, Gary E. ....Beverly Hills, CA
Gleicher, Ilene ....Chicago, IL
Gleicher & Patek, P.C. ....Detroit, MI
Gleicher, Raymond B. ....New York, NY
Gleicher, Warren R. ....New York, NY
Gleichman, Norman M.
Federal Mine Safety and Health Review
Commission,
Office of the General Counsel, GV
Gleichman, Peter A. ....Portsmouth, NH
Gleick, Donen ....New York, NY
Gleim, Holger D. ....St. Petersburg, FL
Gleim, Kristi Ann ....Chicago, IL
Gleim, Lorie M. ....West Palm Beach, FL
Gleim, Michael A. ....San Francisco, CA
Gleimer, Eileen M. ....Washington, DC
Glein, Richard J. ....Seattle, WA
Gleiner, Richard A. B. ....Dallas, TX
Gleiser, Charles C. ....Tacoma, WA
Gleisner, Leslie H. ....Marietta, GA
Gleiss, Elizabeth J. ....Cashton, WI
Sparta, WI
Gleiss, Henry W. ....St. Joseph, MI
Gleiss, Locante & Kaftan, LLP ....Cashton, WI
Sparta, WI

Gleisser, Brian S. ....Cleveland, OH
Gleisser, Marcus D. ....Euclid, OH
Gleissner, John Dewar ....Birmingham, AL
Gleissner, Richard R. ....Columbia, SC
Gleissner, Stallings & Rogers
Birmingham, AL
Gleit & Fair ....New York, NY
Gleit, Howard L. ....Philadelphia, PA
Gleit, Milton R. ....White Plains, NY
Gleit, Stephen P. ....New York, NY
Gleitman, Steven L. ....Los Angeles, CA
Gleitz, George ....Bowling Green, KY
Gleitz, Herbert G. ....Dallas, TX
Gleizer, Guillermo A. ....New York, NY
Glekel, Jeffrey ....New York, NY
Gleklen, Adam M. ....Atlanta, GA
Gleklen, Donald M. ....Plymouth Meeting, PA
Gleklen, Jonathan ....Washington, DC
Glembocki, Christopher R.
Washington, DC
Glembocki, Erica D.B.
Department of Commerce,
Patent and Trademark Office, GV
Glembocki Law Office ....Milwaukee, WI
Glembocki, Linda M. ....Milwaukee, WI
Glembocki, Thomas P. ....Milwaukee, WI
Glembockie, James J. ....Marina Del Rey, CA
Glemby-Pharr, Robyn ....Buffalo, NY
Glen, Alan M. ....Austin, TX
Glen, Bennett R. ....Concord, CA
Glen, George S. ....Chambersburg, PA
Glen and Glen ....Chambersburg, PA
Glen, Jeffrey E. ....New York, NY
Glen, Kristin B. ....Flushing, NY
Glen, Lucinda Cordes ....Lincoln, NE
Glen, Robert A. ....Dover, DE
Glen, Shawn M. ....Great Falls, MT
Glen, Susan C. ....Portland, OR
Glencer, Julia M. ....Harrisburg, PA
Glendening, Alexis A.
Grosse Pointe Farms, MI
Glendening, Bruce B. ....Lowell, MA
Glendening, Dale D., Jr. ....Atlanta, GA
Glendening, George J. ....Hammond, IN
Glendening, Jeffrey A. ....Tulsa, OK
Glendening, John W., Jr. ....Washington, DC
Glendening, R. Bradley ....Dallas, TX
Glendening, Wallace H. ....Detroit, MI
Glendenning, Allen G. ....Great Bend, KS
Glendenning, Carol ....Dallas, TX
Glendenning, Don M. ....Dallas, TX
Glendenning & Jorgensen, Ltd.
St. Paul, MN
Glendenning, W. Gordon ....St. Paul, MN
Glendinning-Johnson, Jane Carol
Niskayuna, NY
Glendon, Andrew J. ....San Jose, CA
Glendon, John B. ....New York, NY
Glendon, Paul E. ....Ann Arbor, MI
Glendon, William R. ....New York, NY
Glen-Grossman, Hilary B. ....Irvine, CA
Glenister, James R. ....Atlanta, GA
Glenn, Alan E. ....Memphis, TN
Glenn, Albert S. ....San Francisco, CA
Glenn, Allen D. ....Abilene, TX
Glenn, Amy L. ....Birmingham, MI
Glenn, Andrea Stacy ....New York, NY
Glenn, Andrew K. ....New York, NY
Glenn, Anne M. ....Richmond, VA
Glenn, Arnold B., Law Offices of
Eastchester, NY
Glenn, Bambi ....Baltimore, MD
Glenn, Barry M. ....Palm Harbor, FL
Glenn, Berg & Blenner ....Palm Harbor, FL
Glenn, Betsy Lee ....Monroe, NC
Glenn, Bill, (P.C.) ....Plano, TX
Glenn, Charles E. B. ....Richmond, VA
Glenn, Colin B. ....Redding, CA
Glenn, Cornish, Hanson & Karns, Chartered
Topeka, KS
Glenn, D. Malcolm ....Rockville, VA
Glenn, D. Roger ....New York, NY
Glenn, D. Woodard ....Dallas, TX
Glenn, Daniel O. ....Olympia, WA
Glenn, David A. ....Orange City, FL
Glenn, David Allen ....Houston, TX
Glenn, David C. ....Madras, OR
Glenn, David M. ....Buffalo, NY
Glenn, David M. ....Dallas, TX
Glenn, David R. ....Chapel Hill, NC
Glenn, Dawn Weekes ....Los Angeles, CA
Glenn, D. L. ....Denver, CO
Glenn, D.L., P.C., Law Offices ....Denver, CO
Glenn, Donald D. ....Jackson, TN
Glenn, Doryn Danner ....Galveston, TX
Glenn, Douglas J. ....Virginia Beach, VA
Glenn, E. Vernon F., Law Offices of
Mount Pleasant, SC
Glenn, Earl F., Jr. ....Phoenix, AZ
Glenn, Edward Holmes, Jr.
New York, NY
Glenn, Edward Vernon Ferrell
Mount Pleasant, SC
Glenn, Elinor B. ....Kingsport, TN
Glenn, Elizabeth A. ....Santa Fe, NM
Glenn, Ernie L. ....San Antonio, TX
Glenn, Feldmann, Darby & Goodlatte, A
Professional Corporation ....Roanoke, VA
Glenn, Gary F. ....New York, NY
Glenn, Gary R. ....Detroit, MI
Glenn, Gene W. ....Ottumwa, IA
Glenn, George A. ....Vero Beach, FL
Glenn, George T., II ....Greensboro, NC
Glenn, Glenn & Glenn, P.C. ....Detroit, MI
Glenn, Gordon H. ....Columbia, MD
Glenn, Grant M. ....Topeka, KS
Wichita, KS
Glenn, Guy M. ....Long Beach, WA

Glenn, Haigler, Maddox & McClain, LLP
Anderson, SC
Seneca, SC
Glenn, Hoff, Hoff & Lambert, S.C.
Appleton, WI
Glenn & Hoffman ....Olympia, WA
Glenn, Hugh M., Jr. ....New Orleans, LA
Glenn, Hugh W. ....Argonne, IL
Glenn, J. Stephen ....Florence, AL
Glenn, James B. ....Vineland, NJ
Glenn, James D., Jr., (Chtd.) ....Twin Falls, ID
Glenn, James G., Jr. ....Newark, NJ
Glenn, James Kenneth ....West Bloomfield, MI
Glenn, James R. ....Mattoon, IL
Glenn, James T. ....Potomac, MD
Glenn, Jane S. ....Roanoke, VA
Glenn, Jeffry M. ....San Francisco, CA
Glenn, Jeremy J. ....Chicago, IL
Glenn, Joe R. ....Phoenix, AZ
Glenn, John A. ....Rochester, NY
Glenn, John F. C. ....Richmond, VA
Glenn, John H. ....Springfield, MA
Worcester, MA
Glenn, John J. ....Fort Lauderdale, FL
Glenn, John M. ....Akron, OH
Glenn, John Patrick ....Denver, CO
Glenn, John R. ....Logan, WV
Glenn, John Wheeler ....Baltimore, MD
Glenn, Jonathan H. ....Baltimore, MD
Glenn, Julie Bailey ....Havelock, NC
Glenn, Kevin J. ....Chicago, IL
Glenn, Kimberly Johnson ....New York, NY
Glenn, Kimette ....Irving, TX
Glenn, Kristi Idell ....Detroit, MI
Glenn, Lana Cece ....Spokane, WA
Glenn, Larry W. ....St. Louis, MO
Glenn, Laura J. ....Woodbury, NJ
Glenn, Laura L. ....Tallahassee, FL
Glenn, Lawrence E. ....Houston, TX
Glenn, Lawrence M. ....Albuquerque, NM
Glenn, Leslie Duberstein ....Boca Raton, FL
Glenn, Leslie Duberstein, P.A.
Boca Raton, FL
Fort Lauderdale, FL
Glenn & Logue ....Mattoon, IL
Glenn, Luther W., Jr. ....Detroit, MI
Glenn, Marcy G. ....Denver, CO
Glenn, Marilyn L. ....Olympia, WA
Glenn, Mark A. ....Albuquerque, NM
Glenn, Martin ....New York, NY
Glenn, Michael A. ....Portola Valley, CA
Glenn, Michael D. ....Anderson, SC
Glenn, Michael J. ....Los Angeles, CA
Glenn, Michael K. ....Kansas City, MO
Glenn, Michael R. ....Nokomis, IL
Glenn, Mills & Fisher, P.A. ....Durham, NC
Glenn Murphy Gray & Stepp, L.L.P.
Columbia, SC
Glenn, Nancy ....Gainesville, GA
Glenn, Neal C. ....Philadelphia, PA
Glenn, Patrick L. ....Boston, MA
Glenn, Patrick M. ....San Francisco, CA
Glenn, Patti G. ....Springfield, MA
Glenn, Paul D. ....Treasury Department,
Office of Thrift Supervision, GV
Glenn, Paul M., Jr. ....Tampa, FL
Glenn, Peggy A. ....Chicago, IL
Glenn, Perman, III ....Springfield, MA
Glenn, Peter G. ....Cleveland, OH
Glenn, Phillip A. ....Wichita, KS
Glenn, Phillip W. ....Casa Grande, AZ
Glenn, Phillip W., P.C. ....Casa Grande, AZ
Glenn, R. Alexander ....St. Petersburg, FL
Glenn, Ralph D. ....Mattoon, IL
Glenn, Randall M. ....Austin, TX
Glenn Rasmussen & Fogarty, P.A.
Clearwater, FL
St. Petersburg, FL
Tampa, FL
Glenn, Richard B. ....Woodland Hills, CA
Glenn, Richard Garland ....Roseville, CA
Glenn, Richard M. C., III ....Providence, RI
Glenn, Richard W. ....West Palm Beach, FL
Glenn, Robert B. ....Tampa, FL
Glenn, Robert B., Jr. ....Durham, NC
Glenn, Robert E. ....Roanoke, VA
Glenn, Robert E., IV ....Falls Church, VA
Glenn, Robert J. ....Chicago, IL
Glenn, Robert R. ....Huntington, IN
Glenn, Robert S., Jr. ....Atlanta, GA
Savannah, GA
Glenn, Robin Day
Rancho Santa Margarita, CA
Glenn, Roger A. ....Appleton, WI
Glenn, Ronda D. Taylor ....Bloomington, IL
Glenn, Sharon M. ....Atlanta, GA
Glenn, Sites & Reeder ....Madras, OR
Glenn, Staci L. ....Dallas, TX
Glenn, Stephen K. ....Richmond, VA
Glenn, Stewart P. ....Newburgh, NY
Glenn, Susan H. ....Morristown, NJ
Glenn, Susan M. ....Columbia, SC
Glenn, Terry K. ....Bryn Athyn, PA
Glenn, Thomas D. ....Conroe, TX
Glenn, Thomas J. ....Tempe, AZ
Glenn, Tracy B. ....Houston, TX
Glenn, W. Lewis, III ....Charlotte, NC
Glenn, Wendy G. ....Los Angeles, CA
Glenn, William L. ....Detroit, MI
Glenn, William P., Jr. ....Houston, TX
Glenn, Wright, Jacobs & Schell, A
Professional Corporation ....San Diego, CA
Glenner, Cary S. ....Chicago, IL
Glenney, Jeffrey W. ....Charlotte, NC
Glenney, Sandra A. ....Leesburg, VA
Glenn-Hart, Chena L. ....State College, PA
Glenn-Joseph, Susan H. ....Eastchester, NY
Glennon, Bert, Jr. ....Van Nuys, CA

Glennon, Charles E. ....Pontiac, IL
Glennon, Edward B. ....Washington, DC
Glennon, Edward M. ....Minneapolis, MN
Glennon, Elizabeth Q. ....Reston, VA
Glennon, Gerald T. ....Clark, NJ
Glennon, Goodman, Lubeley, Vaughn &
Walker, L.L.P. ....Fairfax, VA
Reston, VA
Glennon, Helen L. ....Park Ridge, IL
Glennon, James B. ....Chicago, IL
Glennon, John E. ....Chicago, IL
Glennon, John E. ....Wantagh, NY
Glennon, John P. ....Houston, TX
Glennon, Mark E. ....Chicago, IL
Glennon, Martin K. ....Manchester, NH
Glennon, Martin K., Professional Association
Manchester, NH
Glennon, Marty ....Mineola, NY
Glennon, Michael J. ....Davis, CA
Glennon, Owen G. ....Orland Park, IL
Glennon, Paul W. ....Worcester, MA
Glennon, Philip N. ....Stamford, CT
Glennon, Robert C. ....Ray Brook, NY
Glennon, Robert E., Jr. ....Washington, DC
Glennon, Robert J., Jr. ....Tucson, AZ
Glennon, Robert M. ....Boston, MA
Glennon, Stephanie Martin ....Dedham, MA
Glennon, Theresa ....Philadelphia, PA
Glennon, Thomas E. ....Minneapolis, MN
Glennon, Thomas E., P.A., & Associates
Minneapolis, MN
Glennon, William A., III ....Metairie, LA
Glennon, William A., Jr. ....New Orleans, LA
Glennon, William E. ....Saratoga, CA
Glenns, Barbara J. ....New York, NY
Glenny, Brian S. ....Barnstable, MA
Glenny, David A. ....Ocala, FL
Glenny, Janet E. ....Marina Del Rey, CA
Glenny, Keith P. ....Worcester, MA
Glenny, Raymond C. ....Washington, DC
Glenos, N. Christian ....Birmingham, AL
Glensy, Rex D. ....Pasadena, CA
Glerum, Charles L., (P.C.) ....Boston, MA
Glerum, Glenn M. ....Totowa, NJ
Glerum, Laurence D. ....Santa Barbara, CA
Glerum, Steve M. ....Fort Lauderdale, FL
Glesby, Bruce D. ....Santa Barbara, CA
Glesby, Gary S. ....Houston, TX
Glesener, Robert C. ....Raleigh, NC
Glesius, Amy S. ....Cleveland, OH
Glesner, Richard C. ....Madison, WI
Gless, Alan G. ....Wahoo, NE
Gless, Jason C. ....Riverside, CA
Gless, Maria E. ....Riverside, CA
Gless, Michael M. ....Long Beach, CA
Glessner, Robert D. ....York, PA
Glessner, Ronald E. ....Renton, WA
Glessner, Stephen A. ....Frederick, MD
Glew, Louis Wm. ....Canton, OH
Glew, William B., Jr. ....Washington, DC
Glew, William S. ....Minneapolis, MN
Glewicz, William J. ....Chicago, IL
Glewwe, Leonard W. ....St. Paul, MN
Gleysteen, John W. ....Sioux City, IA
Gleysteen, Nicholas ....Boston, MA
Glezen, John C. ....Hartford, CT
Glezen, Ola Najar ....Birmingham, MI
Gliatta, Paul ....Brooklyn, NY
Gliatta, Stephen ....New York, NY
Gliaudys, George J., Jr. ....Commerce, CA
Glick, Abraham J. ....Sarasota, FL
Glick, Adam D. ....Studio City, CA
Glick, Alvin M. ....Buffalo, NY
Glick, Anna H. ....New York, NY
Glick, Bernard S. ....North Bergen, NJ
Glick, Brian ....Brooklyn, NY
Glick, Brian J. ....Boca Raton, FL
Glick, C. Susan ....LaGrange, IN
Glick, Carol A. ....Westbury, NY
Glick, Carol Nicholson ....Providence, RI
Glick, Charles L. ....Chicago, IL
Glick, Douglas E. ....Chicago, IL
Glick, Earl A. ....Los Angeles, CA
Glick, Elizabeth L. ....St. Clairsville, OH
Glick, Eric S. ....Birmingham, MI
Glick, Evan B. ....Baton Rouge, LA
Glick, Frederick K. ....San Luis Obispo, CA
Glick, Gail A. ....Los Angeles, CA
Glick, Gary A. ....Los Angeles, CA
Glick, Gary D. ....Dallas, TX
Glick, Gregory R. ....Cleveland, OH
Glick, Harry ....Garden City, NY
Glick, Helen L. ....Hillsdale, NJ
Glick, Helene L. ....Washington, DC
Glick, Howard K. ....Birmingham, AL
Glick, Howard W. ....Ashland, OH
Glick, James Bryan ....Staunton, VA
Glick, James M. ....San Bernardino, CA
Glick, Janice L.
Occupational Safety and Health Review
Commission,
Office of the General Counsel, GV
Glick, Jeffrey A. ....Oakland, CA
Glick, Jessica M. ....Department of Labor,
Office of the Solicitor, GV
Glick, Jonathan ....Pittsburgh, PA
Glick, Joseph ....Boca Raton, FL
Glick, Joseph ....Fort Lauderdale, FL
Glick, Joseph A. ....Miami, FL
Glick, Joseph A., P.A., Law Offices of
Miami, FL
Glick, Kenneth J. ....Libertyville, IL
Glick, Kenneth L. ....Detroit, MI
Glick, Kenneth R. ....New York, NY
Glick, Kevin R. ....Miami, FL
Glick, Larry I. ....Garden City, NY
Glick, Larry I., P.C. ....Garden City, NY
Glick, Lawrence E. ....Chicago, IL

Glick, Leonard E. ....Miami, FL
Glick, Leslie Alan ....Washington, DC
Glick, Leslie Ann ....Santa Monica, CA
Glick, Lisa Joy ....New York, NY
Glick, Louis J. ....Towson, MD
Glick, Marc H. ....New York, NY
Glick, Mark A. ....Salt Lake City, UT
Glick, Marshall A. ....Encino, CA
Glick, Martin R. ....San Francisco, CA
Glick, Marvin H. ....Chicago, IL
Glick, Michael ....Chicago, IL
Glick, Mitchell R. ....Great Neck, NY
Glick, Neal B. ....Boston, MA
Glick, Paul M. ....Chicago, IL
Glick, Peter ....Los Angeles, CA
Glick, Peter E. ....Gold River, CA
Glick, Philip J. ....Deerfield, IL
Glick, Philip M. ....Chevy Chase, MD
Glick & Retamar ....Boca Raton, FL
Glick, Richard D. ....Washington, DC
Glick, Richard I ....Tamarac, FL
Glick, Richard M. ....Portland, OR
Glick, Robert A. ....New York, NY
Glick, Robert D. ....Chicago, IL
Glick, Robert Dunn ....Chicago, IL
Glick, Ronald L. ....Haddonfield, NJ
Glick, Ruth V. ....San Francisco, CA
Glick, S. Geoffrey ....Virginia Beach, VA
Glick, S. Mark ....Akron, OH
Glick, Scott J. ....Department of Justice,
Criminal Division, GV
Glick, Shanah D. ....New York, NY
Glick, Sidney A. ....Libertyville, IL
Glick and Simon ....Chicago, IL
Glick, Stephen ....Los Angeles, CA
Glick, Steven P. ....Milwaukee, WI
Glick, Stuart J. ....Newark, NJ
Glick, Thomas E. ....North Miami, FL
Glick, Warren W. ....Washington, DC
Glick & Washburn ....Gold River, CA
Sacramento, CA
Glick & Weintraub, P.C. ....New York, NY
Glick, Yvonne Fisher ....Tulsa, OK
Glickel, Richard A. ....West Nyack, NY
Glicken, Douglas H. ....Orlando, FL
Glicker & Associates ....Encino, CA
Los Angeles, CA
Glicker, Brian I. ....Los Angeles, CA
Glickfeld, Bruce S. ....Los Angeles, CA
Glickfeld, Debra L. ....Silver Spring, MD
Glickfeld, Fields & Jaffe, A Professional
Corporation ....Beverly Hills, CA
Glickfeld, Martin N. ....San Francisco, CA
Glickfeld, Michael L. ....Beverly Hills, CA
Glickfield, Cheryl R. ....Washington, DC
Glickfield, David ....Marion, IN
Glickfield, David ....Marion, IN
Glickfield, Glickfield & Glickfield
Marion, IN
Glickfield, Todd A. ....Marion, IN
Glickler, Cheryl Elyse ....Miami, FL
Glickler, Elliot L. ....Brookline, MA
Glicklich, Peter A. ....New York, NY
Glickman, A.B. ....Cleveland, OH
Glickman, Alan R. ....New York, NY
Glickman, Albert B. ....Beverly Hills, CA
Glickman, Amy ....New York, NY
Glickman, Andrew Z.
Securities and Exchange Commission,
Office of the General Counsel, GV
Glickman, Anne L. ....Suffern, NY
Glickman, Barry D. ....Miami, FL
Glickman, Barry J. ....New York, NY
Glickman, Bruce W. ....New York, NY
Glickman, Daniel R. ....Wichita, KS
Glickman, Daniel S. ....Atlanta, GA
Glickman, David G. ....Dallas, TX
Glickman, David R. ....Beverly Hills, CA
Glickman, David R. ....Baltimore, MD
Glickman, Don E., (Ltd.) ....Chicago, IL
Glickman, Edward M. ....Philadelphia, PA
Glickman, Edward W. ....Edina, MN
Glickman, Ellen J. ....Philadelphia, PA
Glickman, Fred E. ....Miami, FL
Glickman, Fred E., P.A. ....Miami, FL
Glickman, Garry M. ....West Palm Beach, FL
Glickman, Gary S. ....Los Angeles, CA
Glickman, Gladys ....New York, NY
Glickman & Glickman, A Law Corporation
Beverly Hills, CA
Glickman, Harold B. ....Palm Springs, CA
Glickman, Herbert K. ....Trenton, NJ
Glickman, Herbert S. ....Newark, NJ
Glickman, Herlong & Hughes, L.L.P.
Houston, TX
Glickman, I. Henry ....Long Island City, NY
Glickman, Ilene ....Pittsburgh, PA
Glickman, Jacob M. ....San Francisco, CA
Glickman, James ....Boston, MA
Glickman, Jay C. ....Lansdale, PA
Glickman, Jeffrey C. ....Atlanta, GA
Glickman, Julius ....Houston, TX
Glickman, Larry Z. ....Boca Raton, FL
Glickman, Laura L. ....Los Angeles, CA
Glickman, Mark R. ....Chicago, IL
Glickman, Melvyn ....Worcester, MA
Glickman, Michael ....Deerfield, IL
Glickman, Monica S. ....Denver, CO
Glickman, Murray R. ....Elkins Park, PA
Glickman, Norman H. ....Palo Alto, CA
Glickman, Norman H., & Associates, A Prof.
Corp. ....Palo Alto, CA
Glickman, Paul M. ....Department of Justice,
Criminal Division, GV
Glickman, Philip S. ....Rochester, NY
Glickman, Raymond ....San Francisco, CA
Glickman, Richard B. ....San Francisco, CA

Glickman, Richard B., A Professional Corporation ....San Francisco, CA
Glickman, Robert M. ....Longwood, FL
Glickman, Robert P. ....Jenkintown, PA
Glickman, Ronald Carl ....Tampa, FL
Glickman, Roy S. ....Sherman Oaks, CA
Glickman, Sam ....Chicago, IL
Glickman, Stephanie S. ....Dallas, TX
Glickman, Stephen A. ....Chicago, IL
Glickman, Stephen A. ....Pittsburgh, PA
Glickman, Stephen A., P.C. ....Chicago, IL
Glickman, Stephen K. ....Boston, MA
Glickman, Steven C. ....Beverly Hills, CA
Glickman, Steven S. ....Springfield, NJ
Glickman, Stuart I. ....North Hollywood, CA
Glickman, Sugarman, Kneeland & Gribouski ....Worcester, MA
Glickman, Susan ....Washington, DC
Glickman, Witters, Marell & Jamieson West Palm Beach, FL
Glicksberg, Mandell ....Gainesville, FL
Glicksman & Cardoso ....New York, NY
Glicksman, Elliot A. ....Tucson, AZ
Glicksman, Elliot B. ....Lansing, MI
Glicksman, Eugene J. ....New York, NY
Glicksman, Howard J. ....Englewood, CO
Glicksman, John Bruce ....Coudersport, PA
Glicksman, Mitchell S. ....Bay Shore, NY
Glicksman, Paige A. ....Corsicana, TX
Glicksman, Robert L. ....Roseland, NJ
Glickson, Andrew A. ....Norwalk, CT
Stamford, CT
Glickson, Scott L. ....Chicago, IL
Glickstein, Daniel B. ....Northbrook, IL
Glickstein, David ....Chicago, IL
Glickstein & Glickstein, P.A. Jacksonville, FL
Glickstein, Gregg H. ....Boca Raton, FL
Glickstein, Gregg H., P.A. ....Boca Raton, FL
Glickstein, Howard ....Honolulu, HI
Glickstein, Howard A. ....Huntington, NY
Glickstein, Hugh S. ....West Palm Beach, FL
Glickstein, Jill A. ....Chicago, IL
Glickstein, Jon L. ....Chicago, IL
Glickstein, Joseph M., Jr. ....Jacksonville, FL
Glickstein, Karen R. ....Kansas City, MO
Glickstein, Leonard ....New York, NY
Yonkers, NY
Glickstein, Michael R. ....Miami, FL
Glickstein, Richard A. ....Scarsdale, NY
Glickstein, Robert J. ....Emeryville, CA
Glickstein, Steven G. ....Davie, FL
Glickstein, Steven J. ....New York, NY
Glickstein, Steven R. ....Treasury Department, Internal Revenue Service, GV
Glickstein-Hernandez, R. Lynne Pomona, CA
Glidden, Craig B. ....Houston, TX
Glidden, Elizabeth A. ....Minneapolis, MN
Glidden and Glidden, P.C. Nantucket, MA
Glidden, Hollis Porter ....Boston, MA
Glidden, James K. ....Nantucket, MA
Glidden, John R. ....Carthage, IL
Macomb, IL
Glidden, Jonathan D. ....Sacramento, CA
Glidden, Kenneth P. ....Laconia, NH
Glidden, Maribeth L. ....Boston, MA
Glidden, Nancy J. ....Urbana, IL
West Chester, PA
Glidden Partners ....Houston, TX
Glidden, Richard J. ....Nantucket, MA
Glidden, Richard M. ....Benkelman, NE
Glidden, Victoria R. ....Rockford, IL
Glidden, William B. ....Treasury Department, Office of the Comptroller of the Currency, GV
Gliddi, Thomas P. ....Ray Brook, NY
Glidewell, Luann C. ....Louisville, KY
Glidewell, Mark H. ....Savannah, GA
Glidewell, Powell W., IV ....Raleigh, NC
Glidewell, Thomas Jeffery ....Mobile, AL
Glieberman, Herbert A. ....Chicago, IL
Glieberman, Scott L. ....Deerfield, IL
Glieberman, Sheldon L. ....Buffalo Grove, IL
Gliedman, John A. ....New York, NY
Gliedman, Kenneth ....New York, NY
Gliege, Gerhardt J. ....Oak Lawn, IL
Gliege, John G., Law Office of Flagstaff, AZ
Gliha, Gregory L. ....Plymouth, MI
Glik, Marianna ....New York, NY
Glikbarg, A. S., A Professional Corporation Los Angeles, CA
Glikbarg, Allan S. ....Los Angeles, CA
Glikbarg, Andrew S. ....Portland, OR
Glikbarg, William K. ....Santa Monica, CA
Gliko, David V. ....Great Falls, MT
Glimcher, Nancy B. ....Miami, FL
Glimco, Joseph P., III ....Downers Grove, IL
Glimco, Joseph P., III, P.C. Downers Grove, IL
Glime, Raymond G. ....Mount Clemens, MI
Glimis, Al ....New Brunswick, NJ
Glincher, Andrew I., (P.C.) ....Boston, MA
Gline, Gerald H. ....Hackensack, NJ
Gliner, Ray B. ....San Diego, CA
Glinert, David J. ....New York, NY
Glines & Hardy ....Santa Maria, CA
Gliniecki, Patrice Marie ....Washington, DC
Glink, Martin L. ....Arlington Heights, IL
Glink, Marvin J. ....Chicago, IL
Glink, Steven E. ....Chicago, IL
Glinka, Charlotte E. ....Taunton, MA
Glinka, Gleb, Mr. ....Cabot, VT
Glinka & Schwidde ....Cabot, VT
Glinn, Adam R. ....Woodbridge, NJ
New York, NY
Glinn, Franklyn B. ....Miami, FL
Glinn, Matthew Earl ....Reading, PA
Glinos, Demetrios G. ....Apopka, FL
Glinsek, Gerald J. ....Akron, OH
Glinski, Catherine E. ....Olympia, WA
Glinski, David J. ....Stevens Point, WI
Glinski, Herman J. ....Stevens Point, WI
Glinski, John J. ....Madison, WI
Glinski, Mark A. ....Willoughby, OH
Glinski, Robert C. ....Knoxville, TN
Glinsky, Frank J. ....New York, NY
Glinsky, Jennifer B. ....Miami, FL
Glinsmann & Glinsmann, Chartered Gaithersburg, MD
Glinsmann, Maria F. ....Gaithersburg, MD
Glinsmann, Matthew R. ....Gaithersburg, MD
Glionna, Leonard A. ....Medford, MA
Glisich, Gregory ....Chicago, IL
Glissman, David R. ....Hartford, CT
Glisson, Christopher ....Baton Rouge, LA
Glisson, Damon C. ....Apollo Beach, FL
Glisson, Gary W. ....Portland, OR
Glisson, Jackson D., III ....St. Louis, MO
Glisson, Martha McGhee ....Atlanta, GA
Glisson, Michael P. ....Alton, IL
Glisson, Richard C. ....Alton, IL
Glisson, Thomas R. ....Winston, GA
Glisson, William E. ....Batavia, IL
Glist, Paul ....Washington, DC
Glist, Ray ....Miami, FL
Glista, Martin D. ....Kalamazoo, MI
Glitzenstein, Eric R. ....Washington, DC
Glitzenstein, Kurt L. ....Boston, MA
Gliva, Raymond W. ....Chicago, IL
Glivar, Cheryl Ann ....Westminster, CO
Glivar, Daniel J. ....Denver, CO
Gliwa, Kevin A. ....Denver, CO
Gloade, Mark A. ....New York, NY
Global Trade & Development Group Bethesda, MD
Globensky, John L. ....St. Joseph, MI
Glober, George E., Jr. ....Irving, TX
Glober, James ....Jacksonville, FL
Globerman, Ira R. ....Bronx, NY
Globke, Roseanne Ferraro Westborough, MA
Globman, Marcus & Chapple, P.C. Hartford, CT
Globus, Kenneth H. ....Hauppauge, NY
Glock, Earl F. ....Washington, DC
Glock, Earl F. ....Johnstown, PA
Glock, Frank J., Jr. ....Fort Lee, NJ
Glocker, T. William ....Jacksonville, FL
Glocker, Theodore W., Jr. ....Jacksonville, FL
Glockhoff, Roy H. ....Moline, IL
Glockner, Daryl R. ....Mineola, NY
Glockner, David A. ....Chicago, IL
Glockner, Stephen ....Chicago, IL
Glockner, Theodore F. ....Springfield, MA
Glockner-Dow, Katja B. ....Houston, TX
Glockslen, Vincent ....Houston, TX
Glod, Stanley J. ....Reston, VA
Glode, John P. ....Omaha, NE
Glode, Mary Davis T. ....Saratoga, WY
Glodowski, Gregory F. ....Reno, NV
Glodowski, Gregory, Ltd. ....Reno, NV
Gloe, Christopher F. ....Milwaukee, WI
Gloe, Donald H. ....Decorah, IA
Gloe, H. Nick ....Cedar Rapids, IA
Gloe, Steven M. ....Madison, WI
Gloeckner, Linda A. ....Orlando, FL
Gloekler, David P. ....Durham, NC
Gloeser, A. Robert ....Williamstown, NJ
Gloff, Gregory S. ....Department of Justice, Antitrust Division, GV
Glogau, Jonathan A. ....Tallahassee, FL
Gloger, Richard D. ....San Diego, CA
Gloger, Seymour ....New York, NY
Glogiewicz, Barbara H. ....Denver, CO
Glogoff, David ....Princeton, NJ
Glogovac, Scott A. ....Reno, NV
Glogowski, Katrina E. ....Seattle, WA
Glolstein, Robert J. ....San Francisco, CA
Glojek, Gary A. ....West Allis, WI
Glojek Limited ....West Allis, WI
Glomb, Matthew J. Department of Transportation, U. S. Coast Guard, GV
Glomb, Michael B. ....Washington, DC
Glonek, George L. ....Superior, WI
Gloor, Carol L. ....Chicago, IL
Gloor, D. Patterson ....Chicago, IL
Glor, Terry W. ....Birmingham, AL
Glor, Megan E. ....Portland, OR
Glor, Peter J. ....San Diego, CA
Glorch, Robert H., Law Offices of Palatine, IL
Glore, William J. Charlotte Amalie, St. Thomas, VI
Gloria, Daniel C. ....Tucson, AZ
Glorioso, Daryl G. ....Metairie, LA
Glorioso Law Firm, The New Orleans, LA
Glorioso, Maria B. ....New Orleans, LA
Glorioso, Mauro ....Chicago, IL
Glorioso, Russell J. ....Parma, OH
Glorioso, Stacy L. ....Pittsburgh, PA
Glorioso, Vincent J., Jr. ....New Orleans, LA
Glorisi, Vincent R. ....Somerville, NJ
Glos, R. Corbin ....Tampa, FL
Glosband, Daniel M., (P.C.) ....Boston, MA
Glose, Herbert J. ....Hamburg, NY
Glosniak, Ronald G. ....Chicago, IL
Gloss, David R. ....Denver, CO
Gloss, Jeffrey M. ....Merion, PA
Gloss, Jennifer Wysong Redwood City, CA
Gloss, Matthew G. ....Palo Alto, CA
Glosser, Harry J., Jr. ....Morrisville, PA
Glosser, Lawrence S. ....Seattle, WA
Glosser, Mark L. ....Pittsburgh, PA
Glosser & Shreve ....Pittsburgh, PA
Glosserman, Michael J. ....Washington, DC
Glosserman, Robert Luke ....San Antonio, TX
Glosson, Brad C. ....Columbia, SC
Gloster, Dean M. ....San Francisco, CA
Gloster, Loretta Leo ....Bloomfield Hills, MI
Gloster, Thomas F., III (P.C.) ....Boston, MA
Gloth, David Peter ....Towson, MD
Glotta, Ronald D. ....Detroit, MI
Glotzer, Bruce A. ....Boca Raton, FL
Glotzer, Bruce A., P.A. ....Boca Raton, FL
Glotzer, Gilbert S. ....New York, NY
Glotzer, Jeffrey ....Monticello, NY
Glotzer, Mitchell ....Boston, MA
Glotzer, Paul E. ....New York, NY
Glouberman, Steven J. ....Los Angeles, CA
Gloude, Shaun Tara ....Golden, CO
Gloven, Mark M. ....San Diego, CA
Glover, Alan F. ....Brookings, SD
Glover, Alexandra H. ....Boston, MA
Glover, Alice S. ....Raleigh, NC
Glover, Anderson, Lewis & Prebeg P.C., Professional Corporation ....Houston, TX
Glover, Arthur M., Jr. ....Houston, TX
Glover, Barbara A. L. ....Brookline, MA
Glover & Blount ....Augusta, GA
Glover, Carol Ann ....El Segundo, CA
Glover, Carol J. ....Baltimore, MD
Glover, Caryn Scherb ....Minneapolis, MN
Glover, Catherine D. ....New York, NY
Glover, Curtis D. ....Dallas, TX
Glover & Dahnk ....Fredericksburg, VA
Glover, Daniel J. ....Oklahoma City, OK
Glover, David C. ....Clarksburg, WV
Glover, David M. (Mac) ....Malvern, AR
Glover & Davis, P.A. ....Franklin, GA
Greenville, GA
Newnan, GA
Peachtree City, GA
Glover, Dominic W. ....Columbus, IN
Glover, Don E. ....Dermott, AR
Glover, Dorsey D. ....Malvern, AR
Glover, Douglas A. ....Fort Collins, CO
Glover, Durant M. ....Greensboro, NC
Glover, Erica D. ....Tallahassee, FL
Glover, F. Scott, IV ....Houston, TX
Glover, Frederick M. ....Ludlow, VT
Glover, Gary A. ....Augusta, GA
Glover, George H., Jr. ....Brunswick, ME
Glover, Gilbert L., II ....Little Rock, AR
Glover, Greg ....Denver, CO
Glover, Gregory J. ....Washington, DC
Glover, H. Allen, Jr. ....Roanoke, VA
Glover, H. Wingfield, III ....Meridian, MS
Glover, H. Wingfield, Jr. ....Meridian, MS
Glover, Heather A. ....Plainview, TX
Glover, Helsper & Rasmussen, P.C. Brookings, SD
Glover, Irma B. ....Marietta, GA
Glover, J. Littleton ....Newnan, GA
Glover, J. Littleton, Jr. ....Newnan, GA
Glover, Jack M., Jr. ....Bessemer, AL
Glover, James A. ....Portland, OR
Glover, James, III ....Kansas City, MO
Glover, James J. ....Little Rock, AR
Glover, James M. ....Wichita, KS
Glover, James R. ....Chapel Hill, NC
Glover, Jeffrey S. ....Culver City, CA
Glover, Jennifer MacWilliam ....Leverett, MA
Glover, Jerry W. ....Chicago, IL
Glover, Joel A. ....Denver, CO
Glover, John H. ....Houston, TX
Glover, John L. ....Baton Rouge, LA
Glover, John T., Jr. ....Bozeman, MT
Glover, Jonathan Lyman ....Boston, MA
Glover, Julie A. ....Columbus, OH
Glover, Julie C. ....Mobile, AL
Glover, Karen E. ....Seattle, WA
Glover, Kenneth C. ....Lakeland, FL
Glover Law Firm ....Malvern, AR
Glover, Mark Allen ....Charleston, WV
Glover, Marsha Bacon ....Rye Brook, NY
Glover, Martin ....Woodmere, NY
Glover, Max H. ....Webb City, MO
Glover, Melissa Beard ....Little Rock, AR
Glover, Michael C. ....Minneapolis, MN
Glover, Michael E. ....Arlington, VA
Glover, Michael G. ....Santa Ana, CA
Glover, Michael Lakeith ....Houston, TX
Glover, Michael R. ....Phoenix, AZ
Glover, Mildred M. ....Washington, DC
Glover & Miller ....Webb City, MO
Glover & Miller, L.L.C. ....Mobile, AL
Glover, Nancy J. ....El Centro, CA
Glover, Nathaniel ....Santa Ana, CA
Glover, Patricia S. ....Roswell, GA
Glover, Paul L. ....Chicago, IL
Glover & Peterson, P.A. ....Chapel Hill, NC
Glover, R. Allan ....Pueblo, CO
Glover, R. Renee ....Palo Alto, CA
Glover, Randall K. ....Houston, TX
Glover, Randall, (P.C.) ....Albuquerque, NM
Glover, Renee Lewis ....Atlanta, GA
Glover, Reynaldo Preston ....Chicago, IL
Glover, Robert Mark ....Memphis, TN
Glover, Rodney H. ....Washington, DC
Glover, Ronald C. ....Maynard, MA
Glover, Shari Lynn ....Pasadena, TX
Glover, Sharon J. ....Richmond, VA
Glover, Stefanie R. ....Chicago, IL
Glover, Stephen I. ....Washington, DC
Glover, Steven A. ....Houston, TX
Glover, Stuart B. ....New York, NY
Glover, Sylvia L. ....Spokane, WA
Glover, Thomas H. ....Lexington, KY
Glover, Thomas R. ....Cambridge, MA
Glover, Thomas T. ....Seattle, WA
Glover & Van Cott, A Professional Association ....Phoenix, AZ
Glover, Voyle A. ....Merrillville, IN
Glover, Whitney G. ....Anchorage, AK
Glover, William E. ....Fredericksburg, VA
Glover, William H., Jr. ....Jacksonville, FL
Glover, William H., Jr. ....Jackson, MS
Glover, Young, Walton, Phillips & Tucker, PLLC ....Meridian, MS
Glovin, Irving ....Los Angeles, CA
Glovin, Michael H. ....Fair Lawn, NJ
Glovin, Richard A. ....New York, NY
Glovin, Richard M. ....Sacramento, CA
Glovinsky, Eli H. ....Orange, CA
Glovinsky, Jason L. ....Los Angeles, CA
Glovka, John L. ....Monterey Park, CA
Glovka, Richard P. ....Chicago, IL
Glovsky, Alexander S. ....Boston, MA
Glovsky, Bertram ....Beverly, MA
Glovsky, C. Henry ....Beverly, MA
Glovsky & Glovsky ....Beverly, MA
Boston, MA
Glovsky, John E. ....Beverly, MA
Glovsky Law Offices, LLP ....Beverly, MA
Manchester, MA
Rockport, MA
Glovsky, Mark B. ....Beverly, MA
Glovsky, Richard D. ....Washington, DC
Boston, MA
Glovsky, Robert J. ....Cambridge, MA
Glovsky, Roger P. ....Wellesley, MA
Glovsky, Scott C. ....Los Angeles, CA
Glovsky, Steven M. ....Beverly, MA
Glovsky, Susan G. L. ....Lexington, MA
Glovsky & Tarlow LLP ....Washington, DC
Boston, MA
Glow, Lisa L. ....Phoenix, AZ
Glow, Mervin N. ....Long Beach, CA
Glowa, Henry ....Los Angeles, CA
Glowa, Nancy E. ....Cambridge, MA
Glowacki, Brian ....Erie, PA
Glowacki, James L. ....Cleveland, OH
Glowacki, John E. ....Syracuse, NY
Glowacki, Laura ....Lebanon, NJ
Glowacki, Thomas R. ....Madison, WI
Glowicz, Leona M. ....Bethesda, MD
Glowinski, Robert W. ....Washington, DC
Glowinsky, Carol ....Boulder, CO
Glowney, John E. ....Seattle, WA
Glownia, Joseph R. ....Buffalo, NY
Glowski, Daniel T. ....St. Louis, MO
Glowski, Thomas J. ....Glenview, IL
Gloyd, Carol A. ....Batesville, IN
Gloyer, Sharon Blevins ....Louisville, KY
Gloyn, Paul F. ....Bandon, OR
Gloyna, A. Robert, III ....Houston, TX
Glube, Kenneth H. ....Upland, CA
Glubok, David ....Los Angeles, CA
Gluchowski, Francis J. ....Albany, NY
Gluchowski, Paul F. ....Manassas, VA
Gluck, Amy Epstein ....Washington, DC
Gluck, Daniel J. ....Chicago, IL
Gluck, Daniel J. ....New York, NY
Gluck, Daniel S. ....New York, NY
Gluck, David R. ....Boston, MA
Gluck, David T. ....San Diego, CA
Gluck, Diane F. Berney ....New York, NY
Gluck, Elizabeth Brody ....Boston, MA
Gluck, Freema ....New York, NY
Gluck, George ....New York, NY
Gluck, Howard B. ....Los Angeles, CA
Gluck, Jacquelyn N. ....Washington, DC
Gluck, Jason Phillip United States Court of Federal Claims, GV
Gluck, Jeffrey L. T. ....Cliffside Park, NJ
Gluck, Joel M. ....New York, NY
Gluck, Jonathan A. ....New York, NY
Gluck, Lawrence ....Woodland Hills, CA
Gluck, Leonard J. ....Essex Junction, VT
Gluck, Lloyd E. ....Pittsburgh, PA
Gluck, Marshall J. ....New York, NY
Gluck, Matthew ....New York, NY
Gluck, Meryl J. ....New York, NY
Gluck, Michael B. ....Port Jefferson, NY
Gluck, Michael H. ....Trenton, NJ
Gluck, Michelle A. ....Department of Justice, Civil Division, GV
Gluck, Michelle H. ....Fort Lauderdale, FL
Gluck, Mitchell A. ....New York, NY
Gluck, Myriam Waxman ....Columbus, OH
Gluck, Neil N. ....Los Angeles, CA
Gluck, Paul ....New York, NY
Gluck, Peter J. ....Los Angeles, CA
Gluck, Richard D. ....San Diego, CA
Gluck, Richard D. ....Washington, DC
Gluck, Richard E. ....Department of Commerce, Patent and Trademark Office, GV
Gluck, Robert E. ....Fort Lauderdale, FL
Gluck, Robert N., (Co., L.P.A.) Wooster, OH
Gluck, Robert W. ....West Orange, NJ
Gluck, Ronald E. ....Boston, MA
Gluck, Ronald G. ....Department of Justice, Environment and Natural Resources Division, GV
Gluck, Ronda D. ....Boca Raton, FL
Gluck, Ruth R. ....New York, NY
Gluck, Scott E. ....Los Angeles, CA
Gluck, Simon B. ....Cedarhurst, NY
Lawrence, NY
New York, NY
Gluck, Simon B., P.C. ....Cedarhurst, NY
Lawrence, NY
New York, NY
Gluck, Stuart A. ....Coral Springs, FL
Gluck & Tobin ....Elizabeth, NJ

Gluckman, Bruce J. ... Middletown, NY
Gluckman, Casey J. ... Crawfordville, FL
Gluckman, Jeremy E. ... Tampa, FL
Gluckman, Jeremy E., P.A. ... Tampa, FL
Gluckman, Jonathan A. ... Houston, TX
Gluckman, Kenneth I. ... Highland Park, MI
Gluckman, Kenneth Sidney ... Orlando, FL
Gluckman, Leon S. ... Chappaqua, NY
Gluckman, Robert B. ... New York, NY
Gluckow, Paul C. ... New York, NY
Glucksman, Adam W. ... New York, NY
Glucksman, James ... Harrison, NY
Glucksman, Jeffrey ... Bronx, NY
Glucksman, Joel R. ... Roseland, NJ
Glucksman, L. Morris ... Stamford, CT
Glucksman, Mitchell ... Newark, NJ
Glucksman, Philip R. ... Morristown, NJ
Glucksman, Richard H. ... Los Angeles, CA
Glucksman & Weitzman ... Morristown, NJ
Glucksman, William J. ... Beverly Hills, CA
Gluckstern, April Hass ... Baltimore, MD
Gluckstern, Henry A. ... New York, NY
Gluckstern, Michael B. ... Bethesda, MD
Glucoft, Frida Popik, (A Professional Corporation) ... Los Angeles, CA
Glueck, Alan S. ... Fort Lauderdale, FL
Glueck, Daniel S. ... Washington, DC
Glueck, Emily Vrieze ... Seattle, WA
Glueck, Emily Vrieze, P.C. ... Seattle, WA
Glueck, John L. ... New York, NY
Glueck, Lawrence C.
Steamboat Springs, CO
Glueck, Miriam ... Kansas City, MO
Glueck, Neal Jay ... Cincinnati, OH
Glueck, Steven J. ... Hollywood, FL
Glueck, Steven J., P.A., Law Office of
Hollywood, FL
Glueck, Suzan ... Wickliffe, OH
Glueck, William J. ... Seattle, WA
Gluek, Carl H. ... Cleveland, OH
Gluesenkamp, Cary A. ... Hillsboro, OR
Glugover, Jonathon H.
Daytona Beach, FL
Gluntz, Kevin P. ... Cleveland, OH
Gluntz, Maureen P. ... Pittsburgh, PA
Gluntz, Paula ... Columbus, OH
Glusac, Michael M. ... Detroit, MI
Glusac, Rodney M. ... Detroit, MI
Glusband, Steven J. ... New York, NY
Glusgol, Melvin M. ... Boston, MA
Glushak, Solomon P. ... New York, NY
Glushakow, Michael S. ... Baltimore, MD
Glushakow, Robert S. ... Towson, MD
Glushakow-Smith, Fran S.
Baltimore, MD
Glushien, Morris P. ... New York, NY
Glushko, Thomas N. ... New York, NY
Glushon, Eugene E. ... Encino, CA
Glushon, Robert L. ... Los Angeles, CA
Glusing, Benjamin A. ... Kingsville, TX
Glusing, Edward J., Jr. ... Parkville, MD
Glusing, Edward J., Jr., P.A. ... Parkville, MD
Glusker, Daniel J. ... New York, NY
Glusker, Philip ... Los Angeles, CA
Gluski, George ... Dearborn Heights, MI
Gluski, Young & Randall
Dearborn Heights, MI
Gluskin, Michelle Helene ... New York, NY
Glusky, Shon E. ... New York, NY
Glusman, Kenneth A., (P.C.) ... Boston, MA
Glusman, Lawrence J. ... Milwaukee, WI
Glusman, Moore, Arbour, Broyles and Glusman, A Professional Corporation
Baton Rouge, LA
Glusman, Paul ... Berkeley, CA
Glusman, Robert A. ... Chico, CA
Glusman, Stephen W. ... Baton Rouge, LA
Gluss, Norman ... Garden City, NY
New York, NY
Port Washington, NY
Gluss & Pearson ... Garden City, NY
New York, NY
Port Washington, NY
Gluss, Randall R. ... Miami, FL
Glustrom, Robert C. ... Atlanta, GA
Gluszak, Antoinette ... Monticello, NY
Glut, Mark O. ... New York, NY
Glut, Timothy A. ... Nashville, TN
Gluth, Alan D. ... El Paso, TX
Gluth, Renee ... Baton Rouge, LA
Glyer, Grid Riggle ... Treasury Department, Internal Revenue Service, GV
Glyman, Lynda ... Chicago, IL
Glymph, Darrin L. ... Richmond, VA
Glymph, Darrin Lewis ... Washington, DC
Glymph, Stephanie A. ... Marietta, GA
Glyn, David R. ... Philadelphia, PA
Glynias, Stefan J. ... St. Louis, MO
Glynis, Gregory A. ... Tampa, FL
Glynn, Ann ... Spokane, WA
Glynn, Arthur L. ... Natick, MA
Glynn, Astrid C. ... Boston, MA
Glynn, Brian F. ... Sauk City, WI
Glynn, Carolyn ... New York, NY
Glynn, Carolyn M. ... New York, NY
Glynn, Clement L. ... Walnut Creek, CA
Glynn, Crystal Olsen ... Minneapolis, MN
Glynn, Daniel Loras ... Boise, ID
Glynn, David T. ... Phoenix, AZ
Glynn, Dawn E. ... New York, NY
Glynn, Dennis M. ... Chicago, IL
Glynn, Diane M. ... Topeka, KS
Glynn, Donald C. ... Ventura, CA
Glynn, Edward F., Jr. ... Washington, DC
Glynn, Edward J. ... Washington, NJ
Glynn, Elisabeth ... New Haven, CT
Glynn, Elizabeth A. ... Rutland, VT
Glynn, Elizabeth J. ... St. Louis, MO
Glynn & Finley ... Walnut Creek, CA
Glynn, Francis ... Braintree, MA
Glynn, Francis M. ... Hamden, CT
Glynn, Gerald T. ... Department of Commerce, Patent and Trademark Office, GV
Glynn, Gerard F. ... Tallahassee, FL
Glynn, Grant David ... Tulsa, OK
Glynn, Gregory C. ... Los Angeles, CA
Glynn, J. Patrick ... Department of Justice, Civil Division, GV
Glynn, James F. ... Rochester, NY
Glynn, James Martin ... Bronx, NY
Glynn, Jas. L. ... Winsted, CT
Glynn, John ... Norwich, VT
Glynn, John F. ... Chicago, IL
Glynn, John F., Jr. ... Westford, MA
Glynn, John M. ... Natick, MA
Glynn, John M., P.C. ... Norwich, VT
Glynn, John P., Jr. ... Lincoln, NE
Glynn, John W., Jr. ... Menlo Park, CA
Glynn, Joseph P. ... New York, NY
Glynn, Joseph T. ... New York, NY
Glynn, Joyce A. ... Chicago, IL
Glynn, Julie K. ... New York, NY
Glynn, Katherine Piccin ... Ocala, FL
Glynn, Kenneth P. ... Flemington, NJ
Glynn, Kevin E. ... Kansas City, MO
Glynn, Kevin M. ... Boston, MA
Glynn, Laura C., (P.C.) ... Boston, MA
Glynn, Lawrence C. ... New York, NY
Glynn, Lawrence J. ... White Plains, NY
Glynn, Lawrence R. ... Cambridge, MA
Glynn, Liam Davis ... Danbury, CT
Glynn, Margaret A. ... Los Angeles, CA
Glynn, Marilyn ... Office of Government Ethics, Office of General Counsel and Legal Policy, GV
Glynn, Maureen G. ... Providence, RI
Glynn and Mercep ... Riverhead, NY
Stony Brook, NY
Glynn, Michael O., III ... Kensington, MD
Glynn, Patrick J. ... Dallas, TX
Glynn, Raymond J. ... New York, NY
Glynn, Robert B. ... New York, NY
Glynn, Robert J. ... San Francisco, CA
Glynn, Sandy S. ... West Springfield, MA
Glynn, Sean W. ... Washington, DC
Glynn, Stephen M. ... Milwaukee, WI
Glynn, Thomas M. ... Melrose, MA
Glynn, Thomas P. ... Peabody, MA
Glynn, Thomas V. ... New York, NY
Glynn, Timothy B. ... Stony Brook, NY
Glynn, Valerie ... San Francisco, CA
Glynn, William B. ... Deerfield, IL
Glynn, William C. ... Chicago, IL
Glywasky, Donald S. ... Galveston, TX
Gmeiner, Deborah M ... Santa Ana, CA
Gmeiner, James L. ... Littleton, MA
Gmelich, Kathleen M. ... St. Louis, MO
Gmelich, Thomas P. ... Los Angeles, CA
Gmerek, Richard J. ... Harrisburg, PA
Gmitro, George H. ... Edina, MN
Gmora, Barbara S. ... New York, NY
Gmora, Joan E. ... New York, NY
Gmoser, Michael T. ... Hamilton, OH
Gmoser, Olga Faye ... Hamilton, OH
Gnadt, Charlton E., Jr. ... Manassas, VA
Gnadt, Mary Anna ... McLean, VA
Gnaedig, Gerhard ... New York, NY
Gnaedinger, Carolyn A. ... Milwaukee, WI
Gnagy, John D. ... Elkader, IA
Gnall, Gregory P. ... Ho-Ho-Kus, NJ
Gnam, Emily R. ... Madison, WI
Gnann, J. Hamrick, Jr. ... Savannah, GA
Gnapp, Alan B. ... Richmond, VA
Gnass, William E. ... Merced, CA
Gnatek, Catherine A. ... Minneapolis, MN
Gnatt, Sheldon L. ... Upper Marlboro, MD
Gnau, Steven ... San Diego, CA
Gnavi, W. Michael, Jr. ... Collinsville, IL
Gnazzo, Melanie J. ... San Francisco, CA
Gnazzo, Patrick J. ... Washington, DC
Gnefkow, William J. ... Kansas City, MO
Gneiser, Douglas T. ... San Francisco, CA
Gnekow, Kathleen E. ... Sacramento, CA
Gnesin, Raymond ... New York, NY
Gnessin, Alan M. ... Wayne, PA
Gnewkowski, Steven M. ... Kalamazoo, MI
Gniady, John H. ... New Orleans, LA
Gniatkowski, Thomas E. ... Carlsbad, CA
Gnibus, Michael M. ... Phillipsburg, NJ
Gnidovec, Gary F. ... Ottawa, IL
Gniewek, David A. ... Milford, PA
Gniewosz, Felicia M. ... Arlington, VA
Gniffke, Frank L. ... Honolulu, HI
Gnirrep, Jocelyn ... New York, NY
Gnocchi, Thadd A. ... Hartford, CT
Gnocchi-Franco, Antonio ... San Juan, PR
Gnocchi-Franco Law Offices
San Juan, PR
Gnoffo, Vincent J. ... Chicago, IL
Gnoss, George H., Jr. ... San Francisco, CA
Gnoss, Kenneth J. ... Santa Rosa, CA
Gnudi, Dawn J. ... Jersey City, NJ
Gnudi, Robyn M. ... Newark, NJ
Gnuschke, Jerald J. ... Frisco, TX
Gnuse Law Offices, P.C. ... Omaha, NE
Gnuse, Robert F. ... Arlington, VA
Gnuse, Rodney G. ... Omaha, NE
Gnutti, Etalo G. ... Vernon, CT
Gnys, Edward L., III ... Providence, RI
Gnys, Edward L., Jr. ... Providence, RI
Go, Adrienne L. ... San Francisco, CA
Go, Elizabeth C. ... New York, NY
Go, I-Fan C. ... Los Angeles, CA
Go, James Y. ... Kirkland, WA
Go, Jimmy W. ... Portland, OR
Go & Laster ... Portland, OR
Go, Marilyn D. ... Brooklyn, NY
Go, Monique ... San Francisco, CA
Go, Nancy Nearing ... Boston, MA
Go, Phyllis Monique ... San Francisco, CA
Go, William Robert ... Granada Hills, CA
Goad, David L. ... Murfreesboro, TN
Goad, Diane L. ... Ventura, CA
Goad, Frank R. ... Bowling Green, KY
Goad, Frederick A. ... Irving, TX
Goad, Jerry W. ... Denver, CO
Goad, N. Robert, Jr. ... Dayton, OH
Goad, Shelley R. ... Falls Church, VA
Goad, Stephen B. ... Matthews, NC
Goad, Wayne D., Jr. ... Breckenridge, CO
Goad, Wendell W., II ... Schererville, IN
Goade, Ann M. ... Stuart, FL
Goains, Michael D. ... Cameron, TX
Goalwin, John A. ... Los Angeles, CA
Goan, Timothy M. ... Palm Coast, FL
Goan, Timothy M., P.A. ... Palm Coast, FL
Goanos, Larry ... San Francisco, CA
Goar, Dudley C. ... Boston, MA
Goar, H. Thos. ... Dallas, TX
Goar, Lynn Eric ... Tucson, AZ
Goard, Richard L. ... New York, NY
Goas, T. Barry ... Trenton, NJ
Goater, Richard A. ... Troy, OH
Goates, Constance K. ... San Diego, CA
Goates, Kenneth E. ... Pasadena, CA
Goatley, Edward G. ... Springfield, KY
Goatley, Julia A. ... Lansing, MI
Goba, Stephen M. ... Chicago, IL
Gobar, Neal J. ... Del Mar, CA
Gobbel, L. Russell ... College Park, MD
Gobbi, Mark W ... Fort Bragg, CA
Gobble, Wm. Travis ... Lawrenceburg, TN
Gobel & Beisler ... Mc Keesport, PA
Gobel, Dale T. ... Orlando, FL
Gobel, George S. ... Mc Keesport, PA
Gobel & Hollister ... Pittsfield, MA
Gobel, John H. ... Shaker Heights, OH
Gobel, John R. ... Pittsfield, MA
Gobell, Frank A. ... Little Rock, AR
Gobell, Jeffrey A. ... Salinas, CA
Gobelman, Love, Gavin, Blazs & Mathis
Daytona Beach, FL
Gainesville, FL
Jacksonville, FL
Gobelman, Robert C. ... Jacksonville, FL
Gobena, Gejaa Temesgien
Washington, DC
Gobeo, Bruce C. ... Missoula, MT
Gobeo Law Offices, L.C. ... Missoula, MT
Gober, Clyde, Jr. ... Canton, GA
Gober, Frederick ... Los Angeles, CA
Gober, Gary R., The Law Office of
Nashville, TN
Gober, Greg S. ... Fort Worth, TX
Gober, H. Fred ... Atlanta, GA
Gober, James A. ... Atlanta, GA
Gober, James B. ... Chehalis, WA
Gober, Merrilee Aynes ... Atlanta, GA
Gober, Robert ... Baltimore, MD
Goberdhan, Cheddi B. ... New York, NY
Goberdhan, Cheddi B., P.C. ... New York, NY
Gobes, Frank J. ... White Plains, NY
Gobetz, Kenneth C. ... Suffern, NY
Gobeyn, Elena B. ... Chicago, IL
Gobillot, Lori Auray ... Houston, TX
Gobillot, Ted ... Houston, TX
Gobis, Linda J. ... Oshkosh, WI
Goble, Jacqueline M. ... Winston-Salem, NC
Goble, Kenneth R., Jr. ... Clarksville, TN
Goble, Patricia A. ... Deerfield, IL
Goble, Robin A. ... Albuquerque, NM
Goble, Rodney S. ... Waco, TX
Goble, Wayne H., Jr. ... Arlington Heights, IL
Goble, Willis R., Jr. ... Indianapolis, IN
Goblirsch, Timothy G. ... Elgin, IL
Goc, John J. ... Lincoln, NE
Goceljak, George ... West Orange, NJ
Goceljak, John P. ... Paterson, NJ
Goch, David P. ... Washington, DC
Goch, Martin G. ... Philadelphia, PA
Goch, Michael ... Woodland Hills, CA
Gocha, H. Alan ... Bloomfield Hills, MI
Gocha, Lisa E. ... Grand Rapids, MI
Rochester Hills, MI
Gochanour, Gregory M. ... Chicago, IL
Gochanour, Lynne A. ... Chicago, IL
Gochberg, Cheri K. ... Salt Lake City, UT
Gochberg, Lawrence ... Stamford, CT
Gochenour, W. B. ... Salem, VA
Gochfeld, Robert ... New York, NY
Gochis, Djinna M. ... Los Angeles, CA
Gochman, Arthur M. ... Katy, TX
Gochman, Janet A. ... New York, NY
Gochman, John Jay
Croton-On-Hudson, NY
Gochman, John Jay ... White Plains, NY
Gochman, Lisa Sarnoff ... Trenton, NJ
Gochman, Mark A. ... Los Angeles, CA
Gochoel, Karey R. ... Prince Frederick, MD
Gochros, George L. ... Framingham, MA
Gochros, Susan L. ... Honolulu, HI
Gocio, Charles L. ... Bentonville, AR
Gocke, Gregory H. ... Los Angeles, CA
Gocke, James M. ... Ankeny, IA
Gockel, Laura C. ... Cleveland, OH
Gockel, Marie L. ... Kansas City, MO
Gocker, James C. ... Rochester, NY
Gockerman, Bruce C. ... Grand Rapids, MI
Manistee, MI
Gockerman, Wilson, Saylor & Hesslin, P.C.
Beulah, MI
Grand Rapids, MI
Manistee, MI
Gockley, James M. ... Pittsburgh, PA
Gockley, John C., Jr. ... Hoffman Estates, IL
Gockley, Stephen ... Bellingham, WA
Gocyk-Farber, Beata ... New York, NY
Goda, Alan M., (Atty. At Law, A Law Corp.)
Honolulu, HI
Goda, Paul J. ... Santa Clara, CA
Godar, Daniel J. ... St. Louis, MO
Godar, John F. ... St. Louis, MO
Godar, Mary Margaret ... Rockville, MD
Godar, Michael E. ... St. Louis, MO
Godar, Thomas P. ... Madison, WI
Godard, Gary A. ... Fairfax, VA
Godard, Randy E. ... New Brunswick, NJ
Godard, W. Thomas ... Austin, TX
Godard, West & Adelman, P.C.
Rockville, MD
Fairfax, VA
Godat, Peter Eric ... Dallas, TX
Godbe, Douglas E. ... Laguna Hills, CA
Godbe, Mary Lou ... Salt Lake City, UT
Godbersen, Raymond P. ... Kensington, MD
Godbey, Beverly B. ... Dallas, TX
Godbey, David C. ... Dallas, TX
Godbey, James D. ... Toledo, OH
Godbey, Mark E. ... Cincinnati, OH
Godbey, Rebecca G. ... Atlanta, GA
Godbey, Robert Carson ... Honolulu, HI
Godbey, Robert L. ... Huntington, WV
Godbold, Downing, Sheahan & Bill, A Professional Association ... Orlando, FL
Winter Park, FL
Godbold, Gene H. ... Winter Park, FL
Godbold, John C. ... Birmingham, AL
Godbold, John L. ... Camden, AL
Godbold, Leonard W. ... Pine Hill, AL
Godbold, Thomas C. ... Houston, TX
Godbold, Wilford D., Jr. ... Milwaukee, WI
Godbold, William E., III
Chattanooga, TN
Godbold, William H., III ... Rock Hill, SC
Godbolt, Reid A. ... Denver, CO
Godbolt, Sharon A. ... San Jose, CA
Godbout, Amber Lynn ... Butte, MT
Godbout, Blake J. ... Boston, MA
Godbout, Blake J., & Associates
Boston, MA
Godbout, Kevin ... New Haven, CT
Godbout, William H., Jr.
New Brighton, MN
Godbout-Corwin, Kara ... Burbank, CA
Godby, Herbert R. ... Columbus, OH
Goddard, Alexandra M. ... Buffalo Grove, IL
Goddard, Alpheus John, III ... Rockford, IL
Goddard, Arthur B. ... Maryville, TN
Goddard & Blum ... New York, NY
Goddard, Bruce D. ... Washington, IA
Goddard, Charles J. ... Waterbury, CT
Goddard, Charles W. ... Salem, MA
Goddard, Claude P., Jr. ... Washington, DC
Vienna, VA
Goddard, Deborah J. ... Boston, MA
Goddard, Dianne Edmonds
Mount Vernon, WA
Goddard, Edward J. ... Boston, MA
Goddard, Elizabeth ... Prairie Village, KS
Goddard, F. Holt ... New York, NY
Goddard, Frank W. ... St. Petersburg, FL
Goddard, Gabriel L. ... Youngstown, OH
Goddard & Gamble ... Maryville, TN
Goddard, Garry W. ... Allegan, MI
Goddard, Gerald D. ... Burlington, IA
Goddard, Ginger D. ... Norman, OK
Goddard & Goddard, P.C. ... Denver, CO
Goddard, Greg L. ... Buffalo, WY
Goddard, Henry B., Jr. ... Washington, DC
Goddard, J. Andrew ... Nashville, TN
Goddard, James E. ... Dallas, TX
Goddard, James S. ... New York, NY
Goddard, Jennifer M. ... Boston, MA
Goddard, Jo Anna ... Denver, CO
Goddard, Joan M. ... Los Angeles, CA
Goddard, John ... Greensburg, IN
Goddard, Kimber B. ... Sacramento, CA
Goddard, Leigh T. ... Reno, NV
Goddard, Lucy Ellen ... Gainesville, FL
Goddard, Perry & Vogel, P.C.
Buffalo, WY
Goddard, Ralph L. ... Kansas City, MO
Goddard, Ray ... New York, NY
Goddard, Richard P. ... Cleveland, OH
Goddard, Robert E. ... Chicago, IL
Goddard, Robert N. ... Maryville, TN
Goddard, Ross M., Jr. ... Decatur, GA
Goddard, Samuel P., Jr. ... Phoenix, AZ
Tucson, AZ
Goddard, Sara W ... San Clemente, CA
Goddard, Sarah A. ... Chicago, IL
Goddard, Stephen B. ... Hartford, CT
Goddard, Stephen V. ... Boise, ID
Goddard, Susan B. ... Denver, CO
Goddard, Terry ... Phoenix, AZ
Goddard, Timothy L. ... Fort Collins, CO
Goddard, Vanessa L. ... Clarksburg, WV
Goddard, Victor B.
General Accounting Office, Office of the General Counsel, GV
Goddard, Virginia A. ... North Springfield, VT
Goddard, Wendell H. ... Oakland, CA
Goddard, William A., IV ... Irvine, CA
Godderis, Gene ... Tacoma, WA
Godderis, Gene, Inc., P.S. ... Tacoma, WA
Godderz, Eric ... Burlingame, KS
Godderz, Frederick W. ... Burlingame, KS
Godderz, James S. ... Horsham, PA
Goddess, Jeffrey S. ... Wilmington, DE
Goddeyne, Leo P. ... Kalamazoo, MI
Goddin, Cannon Hobson ... Richmond, VA

Goddin, Major, Schubert & Hyman
Richmond, VA
Godding, Bert M. ..... Liberty, MO
Goddu, Christopher R. ..... Boston, MA
Goddu, Peter W. ..... Woodinville, WA
Godduhn, Arnold E. ..... New York, NY
Gode, Jeanne M. ..... St. Paul, MN
Godec, Paul D. ..... Denver, CO
Godek, Laura Moore ..... McHenry, IL
Godek, Stephen M. ..... Rockville, MD
Godeke, Dan A. ..... Fort Bragg, CA
Godel, C. Maria Dill
Commodity Futures Trading Commission, Office of the General Counsel, GV
Godellas, Basil V. ..... Chicago, IL
Godemann, James P. ..... Utica, NY
Goderre, Diane M. ..... Dayton, OH
Goderstad, Lee ..... Minneapolis, MN
Goderstad, Todd M. ..... St. Paul, MN
Godes, James N. ..... Los Angeles, CA
Godes, Scott N. ..... Washington, DC
Godette, Brian O. ..... Washington, DC
Godette, Franklin D. ..... New Bern, NC
Godette, Michelle A.M.
Agency for International Development, Legal Advisers-Overseas, GV
Godfrey, Abby ..... Ashland, MA
Godfrey, Andrea Nuffer ..... Salt Lake City, UT
Godfrey & Associates, Professional Corporation ..... Denver, CO
Godfrey, B.F. (Biff) ..... Orlando, FL
Godfrey, Brace B., Jr. ..... Baton Rouge, LA
Godfrey, Brant H. ..... Winston-Salem, NC
Godfrey, Braun & Frazier
Milwaukee, WI
Godfrey, Brett Marshall ..... Denver, CO
Godfrey, C. Thomas ..... New York, NY
Godfrey, Charles B. ..... Alton, IL
Godfrey, Christopher J. ..... Dakota Dunes, SD
Godfrey, Clarence E. ..... St. Louis, MO
Godfrey and Clase ..... Anderson, IN
Godfrey, Colette Cooper ..... Washington, DC
Godfrey, Cullen M. ..... Plano, TX
Godfrey, Cyrus V. ..... Beverly Hills, CA
Godfrey, David C. ..... St. Louis, MO
Godfrey, David F. ..... Midland, TX
Godfrey, David L. ..... Westport, CT
Godfrey, David R. ..... Apex, NC
Godfrey, Denise G. ..... Los Angeles, CA
Godfrey, Dennis L. ..... Abingdon, VA
Godfrey, Derrick ..... Brooklyn, NY
Godfrey, Douglas W. ..... Chicago, IL
Godfrey, Dudley J., Jr. ..... Milwaukee, WI
Godfrey, Edward S. ..... Portland, ME
Godfrey, Elizabeth B. ..... Raleigh, NC
Godfrey Firm, The, A Professional Law Corporation ..... New Orleans, LA
Godfrey, G. Frank ..... Jacksonville, FL
Godfrey, Gayle L. ..... Pittsburgh, PA
Godfrey, George C., III ..... Atlantic City, NJ
Pleasantville, NJ
Godfrey, G.J. ..... Miami, FL
Godfrey, Gloria S. ..... Sylvania, OH
Godfrey, Gordon L. ..... Montesano, WA
Godfrey, H. Lee, (P.C.) ..... Houston, TX
Godfrey, Jacobs & Porter
Winston-Salem, NC
Godfrey, James E., Jr. ..... St. Louis, MO
Godfrey, James Joseph, Jr. ..... Calverton, NY
Godfrey, Jane A. ..... Culver City, CA
Godfrey, Jane F. ..... Minneapolis, MN
Godfrey, Jarrell E., Jr. ..... New Orleans, LA
Godfrey, John A. ..... Las Vegas, NV
Reno, NV
Godfrey, John A. ..... Seattle, WA
Godfrey, John P., Jr. ..... Frankfort, KY
Godfrey & Kahn, S.C. ..... Appleton, WI
Green Bay, WI
Madison, WI
Milwaukee, WI
Oshkosh, WI
Godfrey, Keith ..... Detroit, MI
Godfrey, L. Allison ..... Kansas City, MO
Godfrey, Lisa A. ..... Kalamazoo, MI
Godfrey, Lisa G. ..... Charlotte, NC
Godfrey, Loretta S. ..... San Diego, CA
Godfrey, Mary Alice H. ..... Greenville, SC
Godfrey, Mary Gager ..... Asheville, NC
Godfrey, Merrill C. ..... Washington, DC
Godfrey, Michael H. ..... Auburn Hills, MI
Godfrey, Morgan A. ..... Minneapolis, MN
Godfrey, Naomi G. ..... Atlanta, GA
Godfrey, Neshek, Worth, Leibsle & Conover, S.C. ..... Delavan, WI
Elkhorn, WI
Fontana, WI
Lake Geneva, WI
Walworth, WI
Whitewater, WI
Godfrey, Otis H., Jr. ..... St. Paul, MN
Godfrey, Paul W. ..... St. Paul, MN
Godfrey, Peter ..... Madill, OK
Godfrey, Peter C. ..... Buffalo, NY
Godfrey, Peter J. ..... Los Angeles, CA
Godfrey, Prentiss ..... Bangor, ME
Godfrey, Rellis P. ..... Shreveport, LA
Godfrey, Richard C. ..... Chicago, IL
Godfrey, Robert ..... Hingham, MA
Godfrey, Robert D. ..... Danbury, CT
Godfrey & Smith, P.L.C. ..... Detroit, MI
Godfrey, Tanya L. ..... Beckley, WV
Godfrey, Ted K. ..... Ogden, UT
Godfrey, Thomas F. ..... New York, NY
Godfrey, Thomas G. ..... Anderson, IN
Godfrey, Thomas J., Jr. ..... Chicago, IL
Godfrey, Thomas W. ..... Milwaukee, WI
Godfrey, Timothy C. ..... St. Paul, MN
Godfrey, Todd J. ..... Salt Lake City, UT

Godfrey, Vandover & Burns, Inc., A Professional Corporation ..... St. Louis, MO
Godfrey, W. Peter ..... Santa Ana, CA
Godfrey, William A. ..... Springfield, MA
Godfroy, William P. ..... Monroe, MI
Godialis, Christopher T. ..... Rocky Hill, CT
Godich, John Paul ..... Indianapolis, IN
Godimis, Andrew A. ..... Worcester, MA
Godin & Baity, LLC ..... Denver, CO
Godin, Edward J. ..... Denver, CO
Godin & Geraghty, S.C. ..... Kenosha, WI
Godin, Jason J. ..... Boston, MA
Godin, Martin Gary ..... Los Angeles, CA
Godin, Philip G. ..... Hopkinton, MA
Godin, Phillip R. ..... Kenosha, WI
Godina, Saundra J. ..... Philadelphia, PA
Godine, Corie W. ..... Towson, MD
Godiner, Clifford A. ..... St. Louis, MO
Godiner, Donald L. ..... St. Louis, MO
Godiner, Lisa Winborn ..... St. Louis, MO
Godinez, Christine A. ..... Los Angeles, CA
Godinez, Cynthia J. ..... La Jolla, CA
Godinez, Fred ..... Irvine, CA
Godinez & Peralez, L.L.P. ..... McAllen, TX
Godinez, Ricardo R. ..... McAllen, TX
Godinez Morales, Enrique ..... San Juan, PR
Godinez-Phillips, Doris ..... Burlingame, CA
Godinger, Isaac ..... New York, NY
Godinho, Douglas F. ..... Buffalo, NY
Godino, James J., Jr. ..... Camden, NJ
Godino, Joseph P. ..... Burlington, MA
Godino, Richard V. ..... Los Angeles, CA
Godkin, David S. ..... Boston, MA
Godkin, Gregory B. ..... Houston, TX
Godkin, Lynda ..... Simsbury, CT
Godkin, Samuel S. ..... San Diego, CA
Godler, Mark D. ..... New York, NY
Godles, Joseph A. ..... Washington, DC
Godles, Michael J. ..... Elyria, OH
Godlesky, C. Eugene ..... Hackensack, NJ
Paterson, NJ
Godlesky & Sywilok ..... Hackensack, NJ
Paterson, NJ
Godlewski & Associates ..... Greensburg, PA
Godlewski, James G. ..... Merrill, WI
Godlewski, Kenneth A. ..... Washington, DC
Godlewski, Kevin T. ..... New York, NY
Godlewski, Paul E. ..... Minneapolis, MN
Godlewski, Paul S. ..... Rockford, IL
Godlewski, Richard J. ..... Naperville, IL
Godlewski, Robert S. ..... Houston, TX
Godlewski, Sally McCarthy ..... Racine, WI
Godlewski, Thomas J. ..... Greensburg, PA
Godlewski, Walter J., III ..... New York, NY
Godley, Barbara A. ..... Kennett, MO
Malden, MO
Godley, Gene E. ..... Washington, DC
Godley, Jeffrey R. ..... Norwich, CT
Godley, Patricia Fry ..... Washington, DC
Godley, T. Michael ..... Mooresville, NC
Godley, Tamerlin J. ..... Los Angeles, CA
Godley, William Lloyd ..... Shreveport, LA
Godlin & Godlin ..... Stamford, CT
Godlin, Harold N. ..... Stamford, CT
Godlin, Paul M. ..... New York, NY
Godlin, Theodore ..... Stamford, CT
Godlove and Carellas ..... Rincon, GA
Godlove, Ernest F. ..... Lawton, OK
Godlove, Mayhall, Dzialo, Dutcher & Erwin, A Professional Corporation ..... Lawton, OK
Godlove, William H. ..... Rincon, GA
Godlstein, Ralph M. ..... Newport News, VA
Godman, Allison Greenhut ..... New York, NY
Godman, James P. ..... New York, NY
Godman, Joseph M. ..... New York, NY
Godnick, Howard O. ..... New York, NY
Godoff, Stan M. ..... Wellesley, MA
Godoff, Stephen W. ..... Baltimore, MD
Godofsky, David R. ..... Nashville, TN
Godofsky, Harvey J. ..... Metairie, LA
Godofsky, Lawrence ..... Miami, FL
Godon, Lisa M. ..... Minneapolis, MN
Godone-Maresca, Lillian ..... San Diego, CA
Godosky, David M. ..... New York, NY
Godosky & Gentile, P.C. ..... New York, NY
Godosky, Richard ..... New York, NY
Godosky, Robert E. ..... New York, NY
Godowsky, Rory Colton ..... Wilmington, DE
Godoy, Edward A. ..... San Juan, PR
Godoy, Jorge C. ..... Camden, NJ
Godoy, Patricia M. ..... New York, NY
Godoy, Ralph ..... Pacifica, CA
Godoy, Roberto A. ..... Miami, FL
Godoy, Teresa Diehl ..... Tucson, AZ
Godre, Cathreen A. ..... Brooklyn, WI
Godre, John K. ..... Dearborn, MI
Godreau, Guillermo J. ..... Salinas, PR
Godreau Zayas, Fausto David ..... San Juan, PR
Godsberg, Steven ..... Garden City, NY
Godsberg Zankel & Golden, P.C.
Garden City, NY
New York, NY
Godschall, Melanie A.
Federal Communications Commission, Mass Media Bureau, GV
Godsey, Gloria Marie ..... Tampa, FL
Godsey, James D. ..... Covington, KY
Godsey, Paula D. ..... Nashville, TN
Godshack, Randy A. ..... Gary, IN
Godshalk, Ernest L. ..... Stuart, FL
Godshalk, Randy A. ..... Gary, IN
Godshall, Brad R. ..... Los Angeles, CA
Godshall, Cathy Carter ..... Akron, OH
Godshall, Craig L. ..... Philadelphia, PA
Godshall, Douglas N. ..... Canton, OH
Godshall, Randolph B. ..... Costa Mesa, CA
Godshall, Scott D. ..... Philadelphia, PA
Godsil, Jennifer K. ..... Boston, MA

Godsil, John P. ..... Whittier, CA
Godsil, Martin A. ..... Seattle, WA
Godson, Anne T. ..... Manassas, VA
Godson, Frank G. ..... Buffalo, NY
Godson, Lloyd David ..... Wakefield, MA
Godsy, Michael M. ..... St. Louis, MO
Godt, Bruce ..... Garden City, NY
Godtland, Janice C. ..... Sioux Falls, SD
Godtland, Paul O. ..... Chamberlain, SD
Goduti, Philip L. ..... Arlington, MA
Goduto, Robert J. ..... Harrisburg, PA
Godward, William W. ..... San Francisco, CA
Godwin, A. Pilston, Jr. ..... Raleigh, NC
Godwin, Arthur F. ..... Turlock, CA
Godwin, A. S., Jr. ..... Roanoke Rapids, NC
Godwin, Billy R., Jr. ..... Dunn, NC
Godwin, Camille ..... Tallahassee, FL
Godwin & Carlton, A Professional Corporation ..... Dallas, TX
Godwin, Charles E. ..... Lake City, SC
Godwin, Charles R. ..... Atmore, AL
Godwin, Christopher B. ..... Fayetteville, NC
Godwin, Clifford ..... Seattle, WA
Godwin, Dana A. ..... San Diego, CA
Godwin, David E. ..... Clarksburg, WV
Godwin, David O., Jr. ..... Frederick, MD
Godwin, Deborah E. ..... Memphis, TN
Godwin, Diana E. ..... Portland, OR
Godwin, Diana L. ..... Aspen, CO
Godwin, Donald E. ..... Dallas, TX
Godwin, Elva Cockrell ..... Houston, TX
Godwin, Fitzhugh Lee, Jr. ..... Arlington, VA
Godwin, Fred E., Jr. ..... Warner Robins, GA
Godwin, Fred R. ..... Lake Charles, LA
Godwin, Frederick H. ..... Memphis, TN
Godwin, G. David ..... San Francisco, CA
Godwin & Godwin ..... Gatesville, NC
Godwin, Howard G., Jr. ..... New York, NY
Godwin, J. Brent ..... Selma, NC
Godwin, J. Henry, III ..... Norfolk, VA
Godwin, James M. ..... Fort Collins, CO
Godwin, James N. ..... Booneville, MS
Godwin, Jenny Phillips ..... New Bern, NC
Godwin, Jeremy H. ..... Charlotte, NC
Godwin, Kimberly A.
Department of State, GV
Godwin, Louanna ..... Richmond, VA
Godwin, Mark ..... Des Moines, IA
Godwin, Maureen A. ..... St. Petersburg, FL
Godwin, Michael C. ..... Pensacola, FL
Godwin, Michael D. ..... Brewton, AL
Godwin, Michael H. ..... Greensboro, NC
Godwin, Michael W. ..... Washington, DC
Godwin, Paul K., Jr. ..... Dearborn, MI
Godwin, Peter C. ..... Chicago, IL
Godwin, Philip P. ..... Gatesville, NC
Godwin, Philip P., Jr. ..... Gatesville, NC
Godwin, Phillip ..... Odessa, TX
Godwin, Phillip, & Associates, P.C.
Midland, TX
Odessa, TX
Godwin, R. Jeffrey ..... Gaithersburg, MD
Godwin, Robert A. ..... Newtown, PA
Godwin, Robert A., and Associates, A Prof. Corp. ..... Newtown, PA
Godwin, Robert E. ..... Coral Gables, FL
Godwin, Robert E. ..... Lafayette, LA
Godwin, Robert L. ..... Stockbridge, GA
Godwin, Robert W. ..... Buffalo, NY
Godwin, Robert W. ..... Knoxville, TN
Godwin, Roger B. ..... Andover, NH
Godwin, Susan Louise ..... Orange, TX
Godwin, Timothy J. ..... Atmore, AL
Godwin, Walter H., Jr. ..... Tarboro, NC
Godwin White & Gruber, A Professional Corporation ..... Dallas, TX
Godwin-Jones, Elizabeth ..... Richmond, VA
Godzala, Thomas A. ..... Little Falls, MN
Godzuk, John S. ..... Buffalo, NY
Goe, Douglas E. ..... Portland, OR
Goe & Forsythe ..... Newport Beach, CA
Goe, Oliver H. ..... Helena, MT
Goe, Pamela L. ..... Bakersfield, CA
Goe, Robert P. ..... Newport Beach, CA
Goe, Steven M. ..... Olathe, KS
Goebel, Adam T. ..... Louisville, KY
Goebel, Amy K. Campin ..... Boston, MA
Goebel, Brian C. ..... Los Angeles, CA
Goebel, Christopher M. ..... New York, NY
Goebel, Dennis M. ..... Troy, MI
Goebel, Don E. ..... Pittsburgh, PA
Goebel, E. Robert ..... Owensboro, KY
Goebel, Edward L., Jr. ..... Indianapolis, IN
Goebel, Edward W., Jr. ..... Erie, PA
Goebel, Gary A. ..... Phoenix, AZ
Goebel, George A. ..... Davenport, IA
Goebel, Heidi G. ..... Indianapolis, IN
Goebel, Heidi L. ..... Cleveland, OH
Goebel, Helen Elizabeth ..... Portland, OR
Goebel, J. Anthony ..... Louisville, KY
Goebel, John J. ..... St. Louis, MO
Goebel, John P. ..... Chicago, IL
Goebel, John W. ..... Lincoln, NE
Goebel, Katherine H. ..... Lubbock, TX
Goebel, Koury & Walker ..... Davenport, IA
Goebel, Linda B. ..... New York, NY
Goebel, Louis E. ..... San Diego, CA
Goebel, Louis E., P.C. ..... San Diego, CA
Goebel, McGaughey & Sosbe
Crawfordsville, IN
Goebel, Monica L. ..... Phoenix, AZ
Goebel, Patrick J. ..... Milwaukee, WI
Goebel, Robert B. ..... New York, NY
Goebel, Robert E., Jr. ..... Escanaba, MI
Goebel, Roger J. ..... New York, NY
Goebel, Scott C. ..... Boston, MA
Goebel, William A. ..... Crawfordsville, IN
Goebel, William H. ..... New York, NY

Goebel, William M. ..... Bloomington, IL
Goebelbecker, William J. ..... New York, NY
Goebels, Paulin C." Mats " ..... New York, NY
Goebert, Donald F. U. ..... West Chester, PA
Goebes, Robert L. ..... Washington, DC
Goecke, Julianne Givens ..... Atlanta, GA
Goecke, Michael Jerome ..... Detroit, MI
Goeckeler, Stephan ..... Palo Alto, CA
Goeckner, Gregory Paul ..... Encino, CA
Goedde, Patricia A. ..... Seattle, WA
Goedde, Thomas J. ..... Miamisburg, OH
Goeddel, Frederic L. ..... Cincinnati, OH
Goeddel, Thomas J. ..... Pittsburg, KS
Goede, John C. ..... Naples, FL
Goeden, Lisa M. ..... San Diego, CA
Goedert, Charles G. ..... Birmingham, MI
Goedert, Huntington & DeBoer
Chicago, IL
Oak Park, IL
Goedert, JoAnn Grozuczak ..... Baltimore, MD
Goedert, John P. ..... Oak Park, IL
Goedert & Michaels ..... Reno, NV
Goedert, Paula Cozzi ..... Chicago, IL
Goedert, Thomas W. ..... Chicago, IL
Wheaton, IL
Goedert, Warren W. ..... Reno, NV
Goedken and Creasey ..... Muscatine, IA
Goedken, Donald D. ..... Falcon Heights, MN
Goedken, Duane J. ..... Muscatine, IA
Goedken, Jeff J. ..... Cedar Rapids, IA
Goedken, Phil L. ..... Bettendorf, IA
Goedken, Rachel J. ..... St. Paul, MN
Goeglein, Andrew M. ..... Fort Wayne, IN
Goeglin, Daniel R. ..... Valparaiso, IN
Goehl, David John ..... Minneapolis, MN
Goehl, Russell R. ..... Quincy, IL
Goehl, Schuering & Cassens ..... Quincy, IL
Goehler, David N. ..... Leawood, KS
Goehler, Richard M. ..... Cincinnati, OH
Goehring, Gregory P. ..... Lodi, CA
Goehring, Jack J., III ..... McLean, VA
Goehring, John R., III ..... Florence, MA
Goehring, Keith A. ..... Parkston, SD
Goehring, Philip A. ..... Anaheim, CA
Goehring, Raymond R., Jr.
Pittsburgh, PA
Goehring, Robert W. ..... Pittsburgh, PA
Goehring, Rutter & Boehm, A Professional Corporation ..... Cranberry Township, PA
Pittsburgh, PA
Wexford, PA
Goehring, Victor ..... Lodi, CA
Goehring, William E. ..... Pittsburgh, PA
Goehringer, Charles W., Jr.
Beaumont, TX
Goehrs, John A. ..... Coldspring, TX
Goehrs, Linda C. ..... Houston, TX
Goeiz, Daniel P. ..... Cleveland, OH
Goeke, Dale E. ..... Waverly, IA
Goeke, Gail A. ..... Kansas City, MO
Goeke & Goeke ..... Cincinnati, OH
Goeke, James A. ..... San Francisco, CA
Goeke, Joseph R. ..... Chicago, IL
Goeke, Judith McLean ..... Golden, CO
Goeke, Michael J. ..... Midland, TX
Goeke, Paul J. ..... San Antonio, TX
Goeke, Reginald R. ..... Washington, DC
Goeken, Richard W. ..... Washington, DC
Goeking, Bryce P. ..... San Francisco, CA
Goekjian, Samuel V. ..... Washington, DC
Goel, Ankur J. ..... Washington, DC
Goel, Asheesh ..... Chicago, IL
Goel, Vinita ..... Fittsford, NY
Goel, Vivek ..... Washington, DC
Goeldner, Christian T. ..... Southaven, MS
Goeller, David H. ..... Terre Haute, IN
Goeller, J. Matthew ..... Macedon, NY
Goeller, Michael C. ..... Wilmington, DE
Goellner, Alfred O. ..... Plano, TX
Goeltz, Thomas A. ..... San Diego, CA
Goeltz, Thomas A. ..... Seattle, WA
Goelz, Christopher A. ..... Seattle, WA
Goelz, Donna M. ..... St. Louis, MO
Goelz, Eric J. ..... Waukesha, WI
Goelz, Robert D. ..... Dayton, OH
Goelz, Virginia G. ..... Westport, CT
Goelzer, Angela C. ..... Washington, DC
Goelzer, Daniel L. ..... Washington, DC
Goemaat, John F. ..... Morristown, NJ
Goemans, John W. ..... Honolulu, HI
Goen, John J. ..... Dyersville, IA
Goen, Timothy G. ..... Dyersville, IA
Goepel, Martha ..... Lambertville, NJ
Goepel, Robert R. ..... Racine, WI
Goepfert, Karen ..... New York, NY
Goeppele, Craighton E. ..... Seattle, WA
Goeppner, Danielle M. ..... San Diego, CA
Goerdt, Charles N. ..... La Crosse, WI
Goeree, Joyce E. ..... Fountain Valley, CA
Goergen, Denise P. ..... Milwaukee, WI
Goergen, Edward M. ..... Henderson, NV
Goergen, Edward M. ..... Las Vegas, NV
Goergen, Glenn N. ..... Milwaukee, WI
Goergen, Jerome J. ..... Berwyn, IL
Goergen, Joseph G., II ..... Hamburg, NY
Goergen, Michael J. ..... Washington, DC
Goergen, Michael J. ..... Chevy Chase, MD
Goergen, Michael S. ..... Glendale, CA
Goergen, Peter J. ..... Richmond, VA
Goergen, Ronald M. ..... Milwaukee, WI
Goerges, Peter Lynn ..... Indianapolis, IN
Goerig & Associates ..... Anchorage, AK
Goerig, George E., Jr. ..... Anchorage, AK
Goering, Alan C. ..... Kiowa, KS
Medicine Lodge, KS
Goering, Ann ..... Minneapolis, MN
Goering, Barbra ..... Chicago, IL
Goering & Belknap, P.A. ..... Phoenix, AZ

Goering, Ellen M. ... **Norfolk, VA**
Goering, Elmer H. ... Moundridge, KS
Goering, Eric W. ... Cincinnati, OH
Goering, Gail M. ... **Chicago, IL**
Goering, George J. ... New York, NY
Goering & Goering ... Cincinnati, OH
Goering, J. Lyn Entrikin ... Topeka, KS
Goering, Jeffrey E. ... **Wichita, KS**
Goering, Jim H. ... **Wichita, KS**
Goering, Kevin W. ... **New York, NY**
Goering, Kurt A. ... **Phoenix, AZ**
Goering & Lehman ... Wichita, KS
Goering, Marlo E. ... Wichita, KS
Goering, Robert A. ... Cincinnati, OH
Goering, Robert Albert ... Cincinnati, OH
Goering, Roberts, Berkman, Rubin & Brogna, P.C. ... **Tucson, AZ**
Goering, Ruth F. ... Cincinnati, OH
Goering, Scott ... **Tucson, AZ**
Goering & Slinkard ... Kiowa, KS
Medicine Lodge, KS
Pratt, KS
Goering, Steven J. ... Department of Energy, Office of Hearings and Appeals, GV
Goering, Susan ... Baltimore, MD
Goering, Teresa W. ... **Phoenix, AZ**
Goering, Wilmer E., II ... Madison, IN
Goeringer, Joan M. ... Rockville, MD
Goerisch, C. David ... **St. Louis, MO**
Goerke, Ariadne
Environmental Protection Agency, Office of the General Counsel, GV
Goerke, Earl E. ... Watonga, OK
Goerke, Joseph K. ... Oklahoma City, OK
Goerke, Steven G. ... Hollywood, FL
Goerl, Conrad H. ... Oakland, CA
Goerler, Ronald B. ... Syosset, NY
Goerlich, Aaron A. ... **Washington, DC**
Goers, Eric R. ... Washington, IA
Goerss, Richard G. ... **Atlanta, GA**
Goertemiller, Benjamin R. ... **Baltimore, MD**
Goerth, Charles R. ... **Wilmette, IL**
Goertz, Bryan C. ... Bastrop, TX
Goertz, Henry A. ... Dodge City, KS
Goertzel, Andrew ... Aurora, CO
Goerwitz, Richard L., Jr. ... Philadelphia, PA
Goerz, Deborah Ann Giddings ... Dayton, OH
Goerz, Gary ... Dallas, TX
Goes, Erik S ... Charleston, WV
Goes, Kelley M. ... **Dallas, TX**
Goeschel, George H., Jr. ... Novi, MI
Goeschko, Norman L. ... Waukesha, WI
Goeser, James R. ... Chicago, IL
Goetcheus, Ann Burton ... New York, NY
Goetcheus, John A. ... United States Senate, Office of the Legislative Counsel, GV
Goethals, James A. ... Sturgis, MI
Goethals, Michael F. ... Clinton Township, MI
Goethals, Patricia A. ... Brooklyn, NY
Goethals, Richard B. ... Glendale, CA
Goethals, Robert K. ... **New York, NY**
Goethals, Thomas M. ... **Laguna Hills, CA**
Goethe, Jeffrey S. ... Bradenton, FL
Goethel, Karl J. ... Durand, WI
Goethel, Stephen B. ... **Ann Arbor, MI**
Goetsch, Alexander E. ... **Cleveland, OH**
Goetsch, Charles C. ... New Haven, CT
Goetsch, Daniel H. ... Milwaukee, WI
Goetsch, Jennifer P. ... **Chicago, IL**
Goetsch, Kathleen ... Howell, MI
Goetsch, Richard J. ... **Chicago, IL**
Goetsch, Scott D. ... **Baltimore, MD**
Goette, Richard A. ... Los Angeles, CA
Goettel, Frederick A., Jr. ... **Syracuse, NY**
Goettel, Gerard L. ... Waterbury, CT
Goettel, Karrsten ... **Elgin, IL**
Goettel, Mark A. ... Port Richey, FL
Goettel, Timothy S. ... **Raleigh, NC**
Goettelman, Scott V. ... **Englewood, CO**
Goetteman, Gary L. ... Miami, AZ
Goetteman, James M. ... Pavillion, WY
Goettemoeller, Duane A. ... Sidney, OH
Goetten, Andrew J. ... Orono, MN
Goetten, Norbert J. ... Jerseyville, IL
Goetting, Ralph W., Jr. ... Tulsa, OK
Goettke, Richard L. ... Blanchester, OH
Goettl, Brian Thomas ... **Lexington, KY**
Goettle, Shane C. ... **Minot, ND**
Goettsch, Becky S. ... Las Vegas, NV
Goettsch, Cecil L. ... Clive, IA
Goettsch, Craig A. ... Des Moines, IA
Goettsch, James G. ... **Kansas City, MO**
Goettsch, Kirk E. ... Holstein, IA
Goettsch, Laura Thompson
Kansas City, MO
Goettsch, Laurilyn Ann ... Kansas City, MO
Goettsch, Raymond H. ... **Long Beach, CA**
Goetz, Amy J. ... Minneapolis, MN
Goetz, Andy J. ... **Long Beach, CA**
Goetz, Angus G., Jr. ... Bloomfield Hills, MI
Goetz, Angus G., Jr., P.C.
Bloomfield Hills, MI
Goetz, Barbara M. ... **Atlanta, GA**
Goetz, Carl J., Jr. ... **Cedar Rapids, IA**
Iowa City, IA
Waterloo, IA
Goetz, Catherine E. ... Bakersfield, CA
Goetz, Cecelia H. ... New York, NY
Goetz, Chad T. ... Arlington, TX
Goetz, Charles J., Jr. ... Pittsburgh, PA
Goetz, Charles M., Jr. ... **Atlanta, GA**
Goetz, Clarence E. ... Baltimore, MD
Goetz, Claude P. ... **New York, NY**
Goetz, Clifford L. ... **St. Louis, MO**
Goetz, Daniel P. ... Cleveland, OH
Goetz, Dean A. ... Solana Beach, CA
Goetz, Donald J. ... South Wellfleet, MA
Goetz, Elizabeth Youse ... **Philadelphia, PA**

Goetz, Ernest A., Jr. ... **Jericho, NY**
Goetz, Eugene F. ... Minneapolis, MN
Goetz Fitzpatrick Most & Bruckman, LLP
Glen Rock, NJ
Manhasset, NY
New York, NY
Goetz, Fleming & Spiegle ... Ocean City, NJ
Goetz, Frances Laughlin ... **St. Louis, MO**
Goetz, Galen F. ... Walker, KS
Goetz, Gallik, Baldwin & Dolan, P.C.
Bozeman, MT
Goetz, Gerould J. ... North Haledon, NJ
Goetz, Gisele ... **Ventura, CA**
Goetz, Gunther ... Austin, TX
Goetz, Harry L. ... Winooski, VT
Goetz, Hartman & Landsteiner
Fort Myers, FL
Goetz, Hirsch & Klimisch ... Hartington, NE
Goetz, J. Erich ... **Troy, MI**
Goetz, James D. ... Wheaton, IL
Goetz, James H. ... **Bozeman, MT**
Goetz, James J. ... Eden Prairie, MN
Goetz, James L., (P.A.) ... **Fort Myers, FL**
Goetz, James T. ... Hartington, NE
Yankton, SD
Goetz, Jane ... **New York, NY**
Goetz, Janet L. ... **Washington, DC**
Goetz, Jeffrey D. ... San Diego, CA
Goetz, John C. ... **Minneapolis, MN**
Goetz, John D. ... **Pittsburgh, PA**
Goetz, John F., Jr. ... **Bloomfield Hills, MI**
Goetz, John R. ... Minneapolis, MN
Goetz, Jon E. ... **Newport Beach, CA**
Goetz, Kathryn L. ... **New York, NY**
Goetz, Kenneth D. ... St. Louis, MO
Goetz & Klimisch ... **Yankton, SD**
Goetz, Laurie H. ... **Cleveland, OH**
Goetz & Mady-Grove ... **Jericho, NY**
Goetz, Mary Therese ... **New York, NY**
Goetz, Matthew D. ... Hartford, CT
Goetz, Matthew D. ... **Fort Worth, TX**
Goetz, Maurice H. ... **New York, NY**
Goetz, Michael S. ... **Tampa, FL**
Goetz, Michael S. ... **New York, NY**
Goetz, Michele R. ... Islip, NY
Goetz, Paul C., III ... Bedford, TX
Goetz, Peter ... **New York, NY**
Goetz, Randy E. ... Eagan, MN
Goetz, Raymond ... Lawrence, KS
Goetz, Raymond T. ... **Chicago, IL**
Goetz, Richard A., (P.A.) ... **Boca Raton, FL**
Goetz, Richard B. ... **Los Angeles, CA**
Goetz, Richard G. ... **Dearborn, MI**
Goetz, Robert I. ... Burlington, VT
Goetz, Sidney M. ... Roslyn Heights, NY
Goetz, Sophie Dagenais ... **Baltimore, MD**
Goetz, Theresa A. ... **Seattle, WA**
Goetz, Thomas J. ... Albany, NY
Goetz, Tibbs & Zahler ... **Atlanta, GA**
Goetz, Tim A. ... Torrance, CA
Goetz, William C. ... Louisville, KY
Goetz, William R. ... **Minneapolis, MN**
Goetze, Andrea J. ... New Orleans, LA
Goetze, Susan L. ... Bend, OR
Goetzel, Dwayne K. ... **Austin, TX**
Goetzinger, Patrick G. ... **Rapid City, SD**
Goetzinger, Robert ... Beaver, OK
Goetzinger, Steven J. ... **Oklahoma City, OK**
Goetzinger, W. M. ... Elbow Lake, MN
Goetzke, Kenneth H., Jr. ... Charlottesville, VA
Goetzke, Paul Garvey ... Annapolis, MD
Goetzl, Katherine Anne ... **Washington, DC**
Goetzl, Robert J. ... Boston, MA
Goetzl, Thomas M. ... San Francisco, CA
Goetzman, H. Mark ... **Arlington, VA**
Goetzman, Robt. R. ... Louisville, KY
Goewert, Bradley J. ... **Tampa, FL**
Goewey, David W. ... **Washington, DC**
Goewey, R. Brian ... Rochester, NY
Gofen, Mary M. ... **Chicago, IL**
Goff, A. Kennon, III ... **Ruston, LA**
Goff, Addison K., IV ... **Ruston, LA**
Goff, Amanda E. ... **Philadelphia, PA**
Goff, Anita Rae ... Los Angeles, CA
Goff, Barry L. ... Orlando, FL
Goff, Ben A. ... Dallas, TX
Goff, Byron H., Jr. ... Scottsdale, AZ
Goff, C. Rose ... **Sacramento, CA**
Goff, Carolyn Warter ... Wallingford, PA
Goff, Caskey, Davis & Fallin ... Arcadia, LA
Goff, Charles A. ... Santa Maria, CA
Goff, Charles A. ... Fort Lauderdale, FL
Goff, Charles E. ... San Francisco, CA
Goff, Christopher L. ... New York, NY
Goff, Christopher M. ... Huntington, IN
Goff, Christopher M. ... **St. Louis, MO**
Goff, Colleen Mullen ... **San Antonio, TX**
Goff, Curtis B. ... Orlando, FL
Goff, Daniel R. ... **Palo Alto, CA**
Goff, Daniel W. ... Eugene, OR
Goff, Daniel W., P.C. ... Eugene, OR
Goff, David C. ... **Gulfport, MS**
Goff, Dennis E. ... Caldwell, ID
Goff, Ernest L. ... Brockton, MA
Goff, Gary ... Oklahoma City, OK
Goff, Gary A. ... Levelland, TX
Goff, Gayle M. ... Virginia, MN
Goff, Greer E. ... New Orleans, LA
Goff, Gregory W. ... **Los Angeles, CA**
Goff, H. Stephen, Jr. ... **Decatur, GA**
Goff, J. Edward ... Naples, FL
Goff, J. Edward ... **Philadelphia, PA**
Goff, J. Rebecca ... Whitehouse, NJ
Goff, Jacquelyn A.
General Accounting Office, Office of the General Counsel, GV
Goff, James R. ... Laguna Hills, CA

Goff, James R. ... Louisville, KY
Goff, John S. ... Phoenix, AZ
Goff, John T. ... **Moorhead, MN**
Fargo, ND
Goff, Joseph A ... Jackson, MS
Goff, Joy Sullivan ... Waltham, MA
Goff, Kathryn J. ... Boulder, CO
Goff, Kenn W. ... **Miami, FL**
Goff, Kenneth H. ... Leitchfield, KY
Goff, Kenneth Harold, II ... Leitchfield, KY
Goff, Lance J. ... Boulder, CO
Goff, Lea Pauley ... **Lexington, KY**
Louisville, KY
Goff, Linda E. ... Pompton Lakes, NJ
Goff, Lionel E., Jr. ... Los Angeles, CA
Goff, Marie Elizabeth ... Conway, AR
Goff, Martin E. ... **Toledo, OH**
Goff, Marvin C., Jr. ... Germantown, TN
Goff, Michael Harper ... **New York, NY**
Goff, Michael S. ... Worcester, MA
Goff, Michelle A. ... **Gold River, CA**
Goff, Neil M. ... **Denver, CO**
Goff, Phillip W. ... Kingsville, TX
Goff, Randall E. ... Annapolis, MD
Goff, Richard D., & Associates
Minneapolis, MN
Goff, Richard James ... Littleton, CO
Goff, Richard James, P.C. ... Littleton, CO
Goff, Richard L. ... **Seattle, WA**
Goff, Robert E., Jr. ... **Dayton, OH**
Goff, Robert K. ... San Diego, CA
Goff, Robert M. ... Memphis, TN
Goff, Robert M., Jr. ... Dover, DE
Goff, Robert Maynard ... **Fairfax, VA**
Goff, Robert W., Jr. ... **Wichita Falls, TX**
Goff, Roger B. ... Los Angeles, CA
Goff, Rose E. ... **Atlanta, GA**
Goff, Sherrie A. Kaiser ... **Oregon City, OR**
Goff, Stacey W. ... Monroe, LA
Goff, Starla Jean ... **Portland, OR**
Goff, Stephanie F. ... **Atlanta, GA**
Goff, Stephen L. ... **Sacramento, CA**
Goff, Steven B. ... **River Falls, WI**
Goff, Susan T. ... Concord, NH
Goff, Tara Kamradt ... **Chicago, IL**
Goff, Thomas H. ... Leitchfield, KY
Goff, Thomas M. ... San Angelo, TX
Goff, Trudy H. ... Kingwood, WV
Goff, V. Barlow ... **Sacramento, CA**
Goff, Warren A. ... **Memphis, TN**
Goff, William M. ... Rockford, IL
Goff & Wilson, P.A. ... Concord, NH
Goffar, John R. ... San Diego, CA
Goff-Crews, Kimberly M. ... Cambridge, MA
Goffe, Peter ... Miami, FL
Goffe, Wendy S. ... **Seattle, WA**
Goffe, William G. ... Washington, DC
Goffen, Howard T. ... Chicago, IL
Goffer, Michael R. ... **Scranton, PA**
Goffigon, Kemper, III ... Cape Charles, VA
Goffin, Cory M. ... **New York, NY**
Goffin, George M. ... Los Angeles, CA
Goffin, Glenn MacRae ... San Francisco, CA
Goffin, Marcia Janice ... New York, NY
Goffin, Sumner J. ... Falmouth, ME
Goffinet, Christopher M. ... **Tell City, IN**
Goffinet, Jeffrey A. ... **Carbondale, IL**
Goffman, Ira S. ... **Cleveland, OH**
Goffman, Jay M. ... **New York, NY**
Goffman, Joseph ... Washington, DC
Goffman, Todd C. ... **Boston, MA**
Goff-Marcil, Joy M. ... Orlando, FL
Goffney, Lawrence J., Jr. ... **Washington, DC**
Goffney, Marcia Marsh ... **Midland, MI**
Goffney, Tara R. ... Bronx, NY
Goffredi, Robert A. ... Portland, OR
Goff Sanders, Leslie B. ... **Nashville, TN**
Goffstein, Adam M. ... **St. Louis, MO**
Goffstein, John H. ... **St. Louis, MO**
Goffstein, Raskas, Pomerantz, Kraus, Sherman, Ruthmeyer & Susman, L.L.C.
St. Louis, MO
Goffstein, Sanford ... **St. Louis, MO**
Gofman, Steven N. ... Culver City, CA
Goforth, Aaron D. ... **Spokane, WA**
Goforth, Calvin T. ... Walnut Creek, CA
Goforth, Cynthia A. ... Piedmont, MO
Goforth, Daniel O. ... **Houston, TX**
Goforth, Ginger D. ... **Spartanburg, SC**
Goforth Group, The, Ltd. ... Aurora, IL
Goforth, Lewis & Williams, L.L.P.
Houston, TX
Goforth and Lucas ... Concord, CA
Goforth, Michael A. ... London, KY
Goforth, Michael D. ... Concord, CA
Goforth, Rebecca M. ... **New Orleans, LA**
Goforth, Richd. E. ... New Philadelphia, OH
Goforth, Richd. E., Co., L.P.A.
New Philadelphia, OH
Goforth, Steven J. L. ... Aurora, IL
Goforth, William H. ... Lafayette, LA
Goforth, William H. ... Sugar Land, TX
Goforth, William H., Professional Law Corporation ... Lafayette, LA
Gofrank, Catherine A. ... Southfield, MI
Gofrank & Kelman ... Southfield, MI
Gofton, Roger K. ... **Oklahoma City, OK**
Goga, Lynn Rose ... Phoenix, AZ
Gogal, David J. ... **Fairfax, VA**
Gogan, Christine Ann ... Englewood, CO
Gogan, Joseph F. ... Hamburg, NY
Gogan, Linda M. ... **Milwaukee, WI**
Gogan, Nancy O. ... Boston, MA
Goganian, Amy E. ... **Boston, MA**
Gogarty, Philip M. ... Pine Brook, NJ
Gogel, Barry L. ... **Baltimore, MD**
Gogel, Barry R. ... **New York, NY**
Gogel, Donald J. ... New York, NY

Gogel, Janet Lynn ... Central Islip, NY
Goger, John J. ... Atlanta, GA
Goger, Kathleen C. ... Newark, NJ
Goger, Thomas J. ... Washington, DC
Gogerty, Gary J. ... **Newburgh, NY**
Goggan, Margaret S. ... Austin, TX
Goggan, Thomas S., III ... Austin, TX
Goggans, James W. ... Abilene, TX
Goggans, Michael D. ... Tupelo, MS
Goggans, Thomas M. ... **Montgomery, AL**
Goggans, Vanessa E. ... **Atlanta, GA**
Goggin, Anne M. ... **Boston, MA**
Goggin and Baker ... Alma, MI
Goggin, Daniel, II ... Neenah, WI
Goggin, Daniel R. ... Neenah, WI
Goggin, Edw. A. ... Oakland, CA
Goggin, Edward P. ... Highland Heights, KY
Goggin, Eileen J. ... Kennett Square, PA
Goggin, James G. ... **Portland, ME**
Goggin, John H. ... Billerica, MA
Goggin, John P. ... **Chicago, IL**
Goggin, Kay E. ... **Richardson, TX**
Goggin, Mary Ellen ... Boston, MA
Goggin, Matthew J. ... **Minneapolis, MN**
Goggin, Michael J. ... Chicago, IL
Goggin, Michael Paul ... **Miami, FL**
Goggin, Richard E. ... Oak Lawn, IL
Goggin, Robert St. Leger
Newtown Square, PA
Goggin, Terrence J. ... Melrose Park, IL
Goggin, William E. ... Alma, MI
Goggins, Alan ... **New York, NY**
Goggins, Bari E. ... **Cleveland, OH**
Goggins, Daria M. ... **New York, NY**
Goggins, Glenn J. ... **Stamford, CT**
Goggins, James O. ... Atlanta, GA
Goggins, John J., III ... New York, NY
Goggins, Michael J. ... St. Paul, MN
Goggins, Renee M. ... Orange, CA
Goggins & Renfrew, Ltd. ... St. Paul, MN
Goggins, Robert J. ... New Prague, MN
Goggins, W. Michael ... Northampton, MA
Goggins, William C. ... **Mattituck, NY**
Goggins, William C. ... **Riverhead, NY**
Gogick, Robert J. ... **West Orange, NJ**
New York, NY
Gogick, Seiden, Byrne & O'Neill, LLP
Stamford, CT
West Orange, NJ
New York, NY
Gogins, Bari E. ... Cleveland, OH
Goginsky, Dennis J. ... Columbia, SC
Goglas, Philip ... Brooklyn, NY
Goglia, Charles A., Jr. ... **Wellesley, MA**
Goglia, Douglas J. ... **New York, NY**
Goglia, Mark T. ... **Austin, TX**
Goglio, Ferdinand R. ... Rockville Centre, NY
Gognat, Richard J. ... **Englewood, CO**
Gogo, Gregory ... Mercerville, NJ
Gogoel, Mary K. ... **Alexandria, VA**
Gogol, Anastasia ... Portland, OR
Gogolin, Elton W., Jr. ... Atlanta, GA
Gogoris, Adda C. ... **New York, NY**
Goguen, Charles J., Jr. ... Alexandria, VA
Goguen, McLaughlin & Stoddard, P.C.
Natick, MA
Goguen, Theodore H., Jr. ... Natick, MA
Gogul, Ronald J. ... Westlake, OH
Goh, Jimmy ... **Denver, CO**
Goh, Richard P. ... **Torrance, CA**
Gohari, Firouzeh Liann
Woodland Hills, CA
Gohari, Nina N. ... Culver City, CA
Gohata, Kim Y. ... **Beverly Hills, CA**
Goheen, Barry ... **Atlanta, GA**
Goheen, DeVere D. ... **South Bend, IN**
Goheen, Gail Hafner ... Hamilton, MT
Goheen, Gregory P. ... **Kansas City, KS**
Goheen, John C. ... **Cleveland, OH**
Goheen, Karen J. ... Detroit, MI
Goheen,, Ronald Richard, Jr. ... Cincinnati, OH
Gohel, Jai Manhar ... San Francisco, CA
Gohil, Sanjay Rasikkumar ... **Charlotte, NC**
Gohl, John P. ... Viera, FL
Gohlke, David E. ... **Houston, TX**
Gohlke, Frances L. ... Waverly, IA
Gohlke, Robin L. ... **Burbank, CA**
Gohl-Noice, Jeane M. ... Champaign, IL
Gohman, Chris ... Radcliff, KY
Gohman, L. Richard ... **Indianapolis, IN**
Gohmann, William A. ... Louisville, KY
Gohmert, Louis B., Jr. ... Tyler, TX
Gohn, Hankey & Stichel, LLP
Baltimore, MD
Gohn, Hankey & Stichel, LLP
Towson, MD
Gohn, Jack L.B. ... **Baltimore, MD**
Towson, MD
Gohn, Sandra P. ... **Baltimore, MD**
Gohr, Lynette M. ... **Buffalo, NY**
Goi, Geo. K. ... Sacramento, CA
Goichman, Jane C. L. ... Los Angeles, CA
Goicoechea, David A. ... **Coeur d'Alene, ID**
Spokane, WA
Goicoechea & Di Grazia, Ltd., A Prof. Corp., Law Offices ... **Elko, NV**
Goicoechea, Jerry J. ... Boise, ID
Goicoechea Law Office ... Idaho Falls, ID
Lewiston, ID
Nampa, ID
Twin Falls, ID
Boise, ID
Goicoechea, Robert B. ... **Elko, NV**
Goidel, Eric M. ... **New York, NY**
Goidel, Jonathan M. ... New York, NY
Goidel & Siegel ... New York, NY
Goidel, Wendy Kaufmann ... New York, NY
Goidell, Mark E. ... **Garden City, NY**

Goidosik, Garold A. ... Kalamazoo, MI
Goidosik & Morse, P.C. ... Kalamazoo, MI
Goimarac, Michael G. ... Sedona, AZ
Goin, David ... Bowling Green, KY
Scottsville, KY
Goin, Yeline ... Tallahassee, FL
Goines, Edward T. ... El Segundo, CA
Goines, M. Douglas ... Atlantic Beach, NC
Goines, William J., (Inc.) ... San Jose, CA
Going, David L. ... Belleville, IL
St. Louis, MO
Going, Eleanor T. ... Columbia, SC
Going, James D., III ... Downey, CA
Going, James P. ... Westhampton Beach, NY
Going, Kimberly K. ... Winston-Salem, NC
Going, Kristin ... Cleveland, OH
Going, Michael P. ... Asheville, NC
Going & Plank ... Lancaster, PA
Going, Robert M. ... Lancaster, PA
Going, Robert M., Jr. ... Lancaster, PA
Going, Robert N. ... Fonda, NY
Going, Stephen M. ... Portland, OR
Going, Thomas M. ... Philadelphia, PA
Going, Walter F., Jr. ... Columbia, SC
Goings, Douglas Richardson ... Carlinville, IL
Goings, Harold H. ... Birmingham, AL
Goings, Hope M. ... Columbus, OH
Goings, Scott R. ... Minneapolis, MN
Goins, Brian L. ... Munster, IN
Goins, C. Douglas ... Oak Ridge, TN
Goins, Carol L. ... Asheville, NC
Goins, Cer Gladwyn
Securities and Exchange Commission, Office of Compliance Inspections and Examinations, GV
Goins, Cynthia L. ... Marshalltown, IA
Goins, Deborah Anne ... Tampa, FL
Goins, E. Eldridge, Jr. ... Dallas, TX
Goins, Frances Floriano ... Cleveland, OH
Goins & Gammon ... Chattanooga, TN
Goins, Jace H. ... Charleston, WV
Goins, Karen ... Tulsa, OK
Goins, Landon H. ... Chattanooga, TN
Goins, Larry E. ... Oklahoma City, OK
Goins, Larry L. ... Boise, ID
Goins Law Firm, The, A Professional Law Corporation ... New Orleans, LA
Goins, Patricia A. ... New York, NY
Goins, Richard A. ... New Orleans, LA
Goins, Ronald E. ... Tulsa, OK
Goins, Susan Reifel ... San Francisco, CA
Goins, Underkofler, Crawford & Langdon, L.L.P. ... Dallas, TX
Goiran, Philip Alexander ... Washington, DC
Goishi, Patricia Tsuyuko ... Sacramento, CA
Goisman, Richard S. ... Milwaukee, WI
Gojio, George T. ... Washington, DC
Gok, Lisa A. ...
Department of Justice, GV
Gokavi, Julia G. ... San Antonio, TX
Goke, Blanche W., (Mrs.) ... Germantown, TN
Goke, Louis P. ... Germantown, TN
Gokel, Ruth L. ... Tallahassee, FL
Gokey, Frank G. ... Fargo, ND
Gokey, Geoffrey J. ... Redmond, OR
Gokhale, Vijay M. ... Livingston, NJ
Gokie, Mark T. ... Lincoln, NE
Goklaney, Anita ... Arlington, VA
Golab, John P. ... Phoenix, AZ
Golab, Michael F. ... Birmingham, MI
Golab, Richard G. ... Chicago, IL
Golabek, Michael J. ... Irving, TX
Golad, Ludmila K. ... New York, NY
Golan, Jeffrey W. ... Philadelphia, PA
Golan, Leonard W. ... Chicago, IL
Golan, Lisa Bodenstein ... Atlanta, GA
Golan, Melissa C. ... Seattle, WA
Golan, Ronald T. ... Palm Desert, CA
Santa Monica, CA
Golan, Stephen L. ... Chicago, IL
Goland, Marina ... New York, NY
Golann, Dwight ... Boston, MA
Golanski, Alani ... New York, NY
Golant, Ben
Federal Communications Commission, Cable Services Bureau, GV
Golant, Joseph H. ... Chicago, IL
Golant, Lisa Allen ... Chicago, IL
Golant, Scott B. ... Chicago, IL
Golanty, Lorriee M. ... Los Alamitos, CA
Golar, Martha L. ... New York, NY
Golas, David A. ... Manchester, CT
Golas, David A., II ... Manchester, CT
Golas & Golas, P.C. ... Manchester, CT
Golay, David C. ... New York, NY
Golay, David E. ... Waldport, OR
Golay, Frank H., Jr. ... Los Angeles, CA
Golay, Yvett ... Cambridge, MA
Golazeski, Gregory ... Philadelphia, PA
Golberg, Aron A.
Environmental Protection Agency, Office of the General Counsel, GV
Golberg, Kenneth ... Tamarac, FL
Golberg, Lynn C. ... Reisterstown, MD
Golbert, Albert S. ... Los Angeles, CA
Golbert & Associates ... Los Angeles, CA
Golbert, Maury D. ... New York, NY
Golbert, Miriam J. ... Los Angeles, CA
Golbey, Anita R. ... New York, NY
Golbranson, Carol Seidler ... San Jose, CA
Golby, Jonathan D. ... New York, NY
Golby, Ralph W. ... Madison, NJ
Gold, Aaron J. ... Tampa, FL
Gold, Adam D. ... Washington, DC
Gold, Adam P. ... Los Angeles, CA
Gold, Alan ... New York, NY
Gold, Alan C. ... Miami, FL
Gold, Alan C., P.A. ... Miami, FL
Gold, Alan L. ... New York, NY
Gold, Alan S. ... Miami, FL
Gold, Alan S. ... Elkins Park, PA
Gold, Allison Clara Goodman
Washington, DC
Gold, Andrew C. ... New York, NY
Gold, Andrew M. ... San Francisco, CA
Gold, Andrew P. ... Fort Lauderdale, FL
Gold, Andrew R. ... Stamford, CT
Gold, Andrew R. ... Warwick, RI
Gold, Andrew S. ... Washington, DC
Gold, Andrew S. ... Dallas, TX
Gold, Ann C. ... Los Angeles, CA
Gold, Anne E. ... New York, NY
Gold, Arnold Barry ... Encino, CA
Gold, Arnold Barry, A P.C. ... Encino, CA
Gold, Arnold H. ... Los Angeles, CA
Gold, Arnold J. ... Clark, NJ
Gold, Arthur D. ... Boston, MA
Gold, Arthur S. ... Wheeling, IL
Gold & Associates ... New York, NY
Gold, Avrom J. ... West Orange, NJ
Gold, Barbara ... Baltimore, MD
Gold, Barbara Stern
Commodity Futures Trading Commission, Division of Trading and Markets, GV
Gold, Barry A. ... Albany, NY
Gold, Barry E. ... Boston, MA
Gold, Barry I. ... Los Angeles, CA
Gold, Barry L. ... Chattanooga, TN
Gold, Barry S. ... New York, NY
White Plains, NY
Gold, Benj. ... Niagara Falls, NY
Gold Bennett Cera & Sidener LLP
San Francisco, CA
Gold, Bernard ... New York, NY
Gold, Bernard ... Staten Island, NY
Gold, Bernard D. ... Los Angeles, CA
Gold, Bonnie M. ... New York, NY
Gold, Brian J. ... Chicago, IL
Gold, Bruce ... New York, NY
Gold, Bryant R. ... Sylmar, CA
Gold, C. Ray ... Washington, DC
Gold, Carl R. ... Baltimore, MD
Gold, Carol D. ... Treasury Department, Internal Revenue Service, GV
Gold, Carolyn A. ... San Francisco, CA
Gold, Carolyn E. ... Erie, PA
Gold, Chas. I. ... Beverly Hills, CA
Gold, Craig Mitchell
Belvedere-Tiburon, CA
Gold, Daniel G. ... Torrance, CA
Gold, Daniel R. ... Downey, CA
Gold, Darren J. ... Manhattan Beach, CA
Gold, Darryl M. ... Albany, NY
Gold, Daryl, Law Offices of
Shreveport, LA
Gold, David A. ... San Francisco, CA
Walnut Creek, CA
Gold, David D. ... New York, NY
Gold, David H. ... Miami, FL
Gold, David J. ... New York, NY
Gold, David Jeffrey ... New York, NY
Gold, David M. ... Monticello, NY
Gold, David M. ... New York, NY
Gold, David Michael ... Covington, LA
Gold, David P. ... Middlefield, CT
Gold, David R. ... Greensburg, PA
Gold, David R. ... Moundsville, WV
Gold, David R., P.C. ... Greensburg, PA
Gold, David S. ... Hollywood, FL
Gold, Denise M. ... Winston-Salem, NC
Gold, Denise S. ... Washington, DC
Gold, Dennis S. ... Naples, FL
Gold, Devon A. ... Los Angeles, CA
Gold, Dina M. ... Washington, DC
Gold, Edward D. ... Birmingham, MI
Gold, Edward I. ... Pasadena, CA
Gold, Edwin ... New York, NY
Gold, Elaine E. ... San Francisco, CA
Gold, Elayne G. ... Albany, NY
Gold, Elise Galler ... Plano, TX
Gold, Elizabeth R. ... Virginia Beach, VA
Gold, Emanuel R. ... New York, NY
Gold, Eric P. ... Oakland, CA
Gold, Eric S. ... Washington, DC
Gold, Estella S. ... Moorestown, NJ
Gold, Farrell & Marks, LLP ... New York, NY
Gold, Farrell & Marks, LLP
New York, NY
Gold, Fern T. ... Setauket, NY
Gold, Frederick B. ... Bingham Farms, MI
Gold, Frederick S. ... Stamford, CT
Gold, G. Richard ... Federal Trade Commission, Office of the General Counsel, GV
Gold, G. Richard ... Harrisburg, PA
Gold, Geoffrey M. ... Los Angeles, CA
Gold, George M. ... Springfield, VA
Gold, Gerald F. ... Brooklyn, NY
Gold, Gerald J. ... New York, NY
Gold, Gerald S. ... Cleveland, OH
Gold, Gerri A. ... New York, NY
Gold and Gold ... Beverly Hills, CA
Gold & Gold ... Newport Beach, CA
Gold & Gold ... Henderson, KY
Gold & Gold ... Plano, TX
Gold, Gordon S. ... Southfield, MI
Gold, Gregory A. ... Englewood, CO
Gold Group, The, Chartered
Washington, DC
Gold, H. Jason ... Silver Spring, MD
Alexandria, VA
Gold, Hadley W. ... Brooklyn, NY
Gold, Haggerty & Adams ... Morristown, NJ
Gold & Hammes ... San Jose, CA
Gold, Hardy R. ... San Diego, CA
Gold, Harold ... Beverly Hills, CA
Gold, Harold ... Washington, DC
Gold, Harold A. ... Pittsburgh, PA
Gold, Harry ... Kingston, NY
Gold, Harry, P.C. ... Kingston, NY
Gold, Harry S. ... Burbank, CA
Gold, Harvey D. ... Baltimore, MD
Gold, Heather ... Boston, MA
Gold, Henry L. ... Southfield, MI
Gold, Howard ... Calabasas, CA
Gold, Howard A. ... Atlanta, GA
Gold, Howard A., P.C. ... Atlanta, GA
Gold, Howard S. ... Worcester, MA
Gold, Ira J. ... New York, NY
Gold, Ivan M. ... San Francisco, CA
Gold, Jack ... Beverly Hills, CA
Gold, Jack ... East Orange, NJ
Gold, Jack A. ... Washington, DC
Bethesda, MD
Gold, Jack J. ... North Hollywood, CA
Gold, Jacob M. ... Plano, TX
Gold, James J. ... San Jose, CA
Gold, Jana G. ... Palo Alto, CA
Gold, Janet L. ... Haddonfield, NJ
Gold, Janet S. ... Irvington, NY
Gold, Jay ... New York, NY
Gold, Jay H. ... Harrington Park, NJ
Gold, Jean McCambridge ... Denver, CO
Gold, Jeanne L. ... Sanford, FL
Gold, Jeff ... Irvine, CA
Long Beach, CA
Gold, Jeffrey L. ... Linwood, NJ
Gold, Jeffrey Lewis ... Los Angeles, CA
Gold, Jeffrey M. ... New York, NY
Gold, Jeffrey M. ... New York, NY
Gold, Jeffrey S. ... East Greenbush, NY
Gold, Jennifer B. ... New York, NY
Gold, Jennifer S. ... Birmingham, MI
Gold, Jerome S. ... Springfield, MA
Gold, Jerrold B. ... New York, NY
Gold, Joel B. ... Pittsburgh, PA
Gold, John A. ... Woody Creek, CO
Gold, Jon M. ... Springfield, MO
Gold, Jonathan C. ... Washington, DC
Gold, Jonathan L. ... Washington, DC
Gold, Joseph ... Monticello, NY
Gold, Joseph M.
Department Of Health And Human Services, Social Security Administration, GV
Gold, Joshua ... New York, NY
Gold, Judith ... Los Angeles, CA
Gold, Judith A. ... Chicago, IL
Gold, Judith Z. ... San Francisco, CA
Gold, Julia Royall ... Corona Del Mar, CA
Gold, Julia S. ... Reno, NV
Gold, Kalman ... Sylvania, OH
Gold, Kate Schneider ... Los Angeles, CA
Gold, Kenneth C. ... Detroit, MI
Gold, Kenneth H. ... Bloomfield Hills, MI
Gold, Kenneth R. ... Livonia, MI
Gold, Kevin M. ... Harrisburg, PA
Gold, Khourey & Turak, L.C.
Moundsville, WV
Gold, Kimberly J. ... Washington, DC
Gold Lange & Majoros, P.C. ... Detroit, MI
Southfield, MI
Gold, Laurence ... Washington, DC
Gold, Laurence E. ... Washington, DC
Gold, Laurie B. ... New York, NY
Gold, Lawrence A. ... Chicago, IL
Gold, Lawrence A. ... Boston, MA
Gold, Lawrence D. ... Monticello, NY
Gold, Lawrence M. ... Atlanta, GA
Atlanta, GA
Gold, Lawrence M., P.C. ... Atlanta, GA
Gold, Lee Andrew ... Hartford, CT
Gold, Leo ... Stamford, CT
Gold, Leon ... New York, NY
Gold, Leon Phillip ... New York, NY
Gold, Leonard S. ... New York, NY
Gold, Leonard W. ... New York, NY
Gold, Leslie J. ... Washington, DC
Gold, Leslie S. ... New York, NY
Gold, Lessing E., (A Professional Corporation) ... Los Angeles, CA
Gold, Lester M. ... Quincy, MA
Gold, Lewis H. ... Philadelphia, PA
Gold, Lila ... Staten Island, NY
Gold, Lisa J. ... Lansing, MI
Gold, Lisa K. ... Dallas, TX
Gold, Loren L. ... Sunrise, FL
Gold, Loren L., P.A. ... Sunrise, FL
Gold, Lori E. ... Atlanta, GA
Gold, Lorne Brian ... Pontiac, MI
Gold, Louis S. ... Pittsburgh, PA
Gold, M. Debra ... Atlanta, GA
Gold, Madeline P. ... Los Angeles, CA
Gold, Maggie ... Boston, MA
Gold, Majer H. ... Kingston, NY
Gold, Marc E. ... New York, NY
Gold, Marc E. ... New York, NY
Gold, Marc E. ... Bala Cynwyd, PA
Gold, Marc I. ... Kinderhook, NY
Gold, Marc J. ... Coral Springs, FL
Gold, Marc S. ... Washington, DC
Gold, Margaret Devra ... Boston, MA
Gold, Mark J. ... New York, NY
Gold, Mark S. ... San Francisco, CA
Gold, Mark S. ... Fort Lauderdale, FL
Gold, Mark S. ... Pittsfield, MA
Williamstown, MA
Gold, Martin ... Bethesda, MD
Gold, Martin ... New York, NY
Gold, Martin B. ... Washington, DC
Gold, Martin E. ... New York, NY
Gold, Martin P. ... Hartford, CT
Gold, Martin R. ... New York, NY
Gold, Marvin H. ... Hatboro, PA
Gold, Matthew A. ... New York, NY
Gold, Matthew Aaron ... New York, NY
Gold, Matthew D. ... San Francisco, CA
Gold, Matthew J. ... New York, NY
Gold, Maurice E. ... Trenton, NJ
Gold, Melissa R. ... New York, NY
Gold, Melvin P. ... Monroeville, PA
Gold, Michael A. ... Los Angeles, CA
Gold, Michael A. ... Washington, DC
Gold, Michael A. ... Tampa, FL
Gold, Michael A. ... Niagara Falls, NY
Gold, Michael Charles ... Tallahassee, FL
Gold, Michael E. ... Ithaca, NY
Gold, Michael H. ... New York, NY
Gold, Michael L. ... Chicago, IL
Gold, Michael S. ... Canton, MA
Gold, Michelle Berk ... Washington, DC
Gold, Miriam V. ... Tarrytown, NY
Gold, Mitchell M. ... Los Angeles, CA
Gold, Morris I. ... Brooklyn, NY
Gold Morrison & Laughlin PC
Washington, DC
Alexandria, VA
Silver Spring, MD
Gold, Morton J., Jr. ... Savannah, GA
Gold, Myron M. ... Coral Gables, FL
Gold, Nancy D. ... Cherry Hill, NJ
Gold, Ned C., Jr. ... Warren, OH
Gold, Neil ... New York, NY
Gold, Norbert L. ... Chicago, IL
Gold, Norman ... Jackson Heights, NY
Gold, Norman M. ... Chicago, IL
Gold, Norton N. ... Chicago, IL
Gold, Pamela Ellen ... New York, NY
Gold, Paul A., (Ltd.) ... Chicago, IL
Gold, Paul Eric ... Hermosa Beach, CA
Gold, Paul N. ... Dallas, TX
Houston, TX
Gold, Paul S. ... Louisville, KY
Gold, Paula S. ... Boca Raton, FL
Gold, Peter A. ... Stamford, CT
Gold, Peter A. ... Cherry Hill, NJ
Trenton, NJ
Philadelphia, PA
Gold, Peter F. ... Washington, DC
Gold, Peter S. ... San Bernardino, CA
Gold, Peter S. ... Dobbs Ferry, NY
Gold, Peter Scott ... New York, NY
Gold, Philip John ... Newport Beach, CA
Gold, Phillip ... Northbrook, IL
Gold, Randall B. ... Chicago, IL
Gold & Resnick, P.A. ... Tampa, FL
Gold, Resnick & Silverman, P.L.
Clearwater, FL
Gold, Richard ... Long Island City, NY
Gold, Richard L. ... Weston, MA
Gold, Richard L. ... New York, NY
Gold, Richard M. ... Washington, DC
Gold, Robert ... Rockville Centre, NY
Gold, Robert B. ... New York, NY
Gold, Robert F. ... Morristown, NJ
Gold, Robert H. ... Hudson, OH
Gold, Robert S. ... Detroit, MI
Gold, Robert S. ... Hackensack, NJ
Gold, Robin Kofsky ... Department of Justice, Criminal Division, GV
Gold, Roger H. ... New York, NY
Gold, Roger Michael ... Cleveland, OH
Gold, Roger N. ... Chicago, IL
Gold, Ronald ... Calabasas, CA
Gold, Ronald ... Hartford, CT
Gold, Ronald E. ... Cincinnati, OH
Gold, Ronald Jay ... New York, NY
Gold, Ronald M. ... Stamford, CT
Gold, Ronald R. ... Southfield, MI
Gold, Ronald T. ... Atlanta, GA
Gold, Ronna Stevens ... Southfield, MI
Gold, Rosalind D. ... Culver City, CA
Gold, Rosemary Grdina ... Cleveland, OH
Gold, Russ T. ... San Diego, CA
Gold, Russell A. ... San Diego, CA
Gold, Sally B., Law Offices of
Baltimore, MD
Gold, Sally B., Law Offices of
Bel Air, MD
Columbia, MD
Towson, MD
Gold, Samuel L. ... Oakland, CA
Gold, Sanford ... New York, NY
Gold, Sarah S. ... New York, NY
Gold, Schwartz & Co., L.P.A.
Cleveland, OH
Gold, Scott A. ... New York, NY
Gold, Seth ... Los Angeles, CA
Gold, Shari S. ... Kingston, NY
Gold, Sharon Cohen ... Braintree, MA
Gold, Sheryl L. ... Universal City, CA
Gold, Sidney ... Wheeling, IL
Gold, Sidney L. ... Morristown, NJ
Philadelphia, PA
Gold, Silverman and Goldenberg
Philadelphia, PA
Gold, Simeon ... New York, NY
Gold, Simon B. ... Des Plaines, IL
Gold, Stanley P. ... Burbank, CA
Gold, Stephan J. ... Hyde Park, NY
Gold, Stephanie H. ... Los Angeles, CA
Gold, Stephanie J. ... Washington, DC
Gold, Stephanie S. ... New York, NY
Gold, Stephen ... Chicago, IL
Gold, Stephen ... Newark, NJ
Gold, Stephen A. ... Oakton, VA
Gold, Stephen H. ... Media, PA
Gold, Stephen M. ... Seattle, WA
Gold, Steve C. ... Department of Justice, Environment and Natural Resources Division, GV
Gold, Steven ... Santa Monica, CA
Gold, Steven ... New York, NY
Gold, Steven A. ... San Francisco, CA

Gold, Steven A. .... New York, NY
Gold, Steven B. .... San Diego, CA
Gold, Steven B. .... Orlando, FL
Gold, Steven D. .... Henderson, KY
Gold, Steven J. .... Atlanta, GA
Gold, Steven M. .... Stamford, CT
Gold, Steven M. .... Brooklyn, NY
Gold, Steven R. .... Henderson, KY
Gold, Steven W. .... New York, NY
Gold, Stuart .... Short Hills, NJ
Gold, Stuart A. .... Southfield, MI
Gold, Stuart H. .... Chicago, IL
Gold, Stuart W. .... New York, NY
Gold, Susan J. .... Chicago, IL
Gold, Thomas R. .... Woburn, MA
Gold, Tod A.
Environmental Protection Agency, Program Office Attorneys, GV
Gold, Tracey E. .... Covington, LA
Gold, Tyler A. .... Fort Lauderdale, FL
Gold & Vanaria, P.C. .... Northampton, MA
Springfield, MA
Gold, Victor J. .... Los Angeles, CA
Gold, W. Robert .... Chicago, IL
Gold, Wayne M. .... New York, NY
Gold, Wayne R.
National Labor Relations Board, Office of Board Members, GV
Gold, Weems, Bruser, Sues & Rundell, A Professional Law Corporation
Alexandria, LA
Gold, William .... Great Neck, NY
Gold, William J. .... Blairstown, NJ
Gold, William L. .... South Orange, NJ
Gold, William T. .... Philadelphia, PA
Golda, G. L., P.A. .... Orlando, FL
Golda, Gail L. .... Orlando, FL
Goldaber, Richard S. .... San Jose, CA
Goldammer, Vance R. C. .... Sioux Falls, SD
Goldammer, Vicki Jaeger
Jefferson City, MO
Goldapp, William A. .... Houston, TX
Goldapp, William A., Jr. .... Houston, TX
Goldasich, Dennis E., Jr.
Birmingham, AL
Goldbach, Aline B. .... Stamford, CT
Goldbach, Anne C. .... Boston, MA
Goldbach, Marc A. .... Whittier, CA
Goldbach, Nancy A. .... New York, NY
Goldban, David R. .... New York, NY
Goldban, Michael .... New York, NY
Goldband, Patricia J. .... Harrisburg, PA
Goldbar, Harry F. .... Alton, MO
Goldbard, Albert B. .... Jamaica, NY
Goldbard, Laura E. .... New York, NY
Goldbarg and Bennett .... Boston, MA
Goldbarg, Irene E. .... Boston, MA
Goldbas, Abbie .... Clinton, NY
Goldbas, David G. .... Utica, NY
Goldbas, Michael B. .... Albany, NY
Goldbas, Moses L. .... Utica, NY
Goldbaum & Gattorn .... Detroit, MI
Goldbaum, Isadore .... Detroit, MI
Goldbaum, Joy Elysium .... Las Cruces, NM
Goldbaum, Keith A. .... Boca Raton, FL
Goldbaum, Robert D. .... New York, NY
Goldbaum, Susan M. .... New York, NY
Goldbeck, Joseph A., Jr. .... Philadelphia, PA
Goldbeck McCafferty & McKeever, A Professional Corporation .... Westmont, NJ
Philadelphia, PA
Goldbeck, Peter E. .... Santa Rosa, CA
Goldbeck, William L. .... Chicago, IL
Goldberg, A. Scott .... Los Angeles, CA
Goldberg, Aaron H. .... Washington, DC
Goldberg, Aaron J., Law Offices of
Burlington, VT
Goldberg, Aaron S. .... San Angelo, TX
Goldberg, Abe D. .... Cincinnati, OH
Goldberg, Abram H. .... Cranbury, NJ
Goldberg, Ada .... Los Angeles, CA
Goldberg, Adam Scott .... Sunrise, FL
Goldberg, Adam W. .... Washington, DC
Goldberg, Adin C. .... New York, NY
Goldberg, Alan .... Eureka, CA
Goldberg, Alan D. .... Chicago, IL
Goldberg, Alan G. .... Lancaster, PA
Goldberg, Alan I. .... Philadelphia, PA
Goldberg, Alan J. .... Albany, NY
Goldberg, Alan J. .... Forest Hills, NY
Goldberg, Alan J. .... Syracuse, NY
Goldberg, Alan L. .... Tucson, AZ
Goldberg, Alan M. .... Winnetka, CA
Goldberg, Alan M. .... Woodland Hills, CA
Goldberg, Alan M. .... Chicago, IL
Goldberg, Alan M. .... New York, NY
Goldberg, Alan N. .... Beverly Hills, CA
Goldberg, Alan P. .... Chicago, IL
Goldberg, Alan S.
General Accounting Office, Office of the General Counsel, GV
Goldberg, Alan S. .... Boston, MA
Goldberg, Alan S. .... Milwaukee, WI
Goldberg, Albert J. .... Mequon, WI
Goldberg, Albert M. .... Phoenix, AZ
Goldberg, Albert M., P.C. .... Phoenix, AZ
Goldberg, Alex A. .... Salt Lake City, UT
Goldberg & Alexander, P.C. .... Dallas, TX
Goldberg, Alfred G. .... Fox Point, WI
Goldberg, Alfred M. .... Washington, DC
Goldberg, Allan .... Chicago, IL
Goldberg, Allen S. .... Chicago, IL
Goldberg, Allison Beth .... Atlanta, GA
Goldberg, Alvin I. .... San Diego, CA
Goldberg & Anderson .... Wilmington, NC
Goldberg, Andrew J. .... Troy, MI
Goldberg, Andrew S. .... Chicago, IL
Goldberg, Anita Meg .... McMinnville, OR

Goldberg, Arthur .... Boston, MA
Goldberg, Arthur A. .... Jersey City, NJ
Goldberg, Arthur H. .... Mineola, NY
Goldberg, Arthur I. .... Hackensack, NJ
New York, NY
Goldberg, Arthur I. .... Garden City, NY
Goldberg, Arthur L. .... Los Angeles, CA
Goldberg, Arthur L. .... Harrisburg, PA
Goldberg, Arthur R. .... Department of Justice, Civil Division, GV
Goldberg & Associates .... Boston, MA
Hyannis, MA
Goldberg & Associates, P.A. .... Tampa, FL
Goldberg & Associates, P.C. .... Houston, TX
Goldberg, Aubrey .... Las Vegas, NV
Goldberg, Audrey L. .... New York, NY
Goldberg, Avrum M. .... Washington, DC
Goldberg, B. Abbott .... Sacramento, CA
Goldberg, Barbara DeCrow
Great Neck, NY
Goldberg, Barbara L. .... Phoenix, MD
Goldberg, Barbara R. .... Phoenix, AZ
Goldberg, Barbara Segal .... Tucson, AZ
Goldberg, Barry D. .... Chicago, IL
Goldberg, Barry D. .... New York, NY
Goldberg, Barry R. .... Bronx, NY
Goldberg, Barth H. .... Chicago, IL
Goldberg, Barton S. .... Miami Beach, FL
Goldberg, Benj. B. .... Evanston, IL
Goldberg, Benjamin .... Charleston, SC
Goldberg, Bernard .... Cambridge, MA
Goldberg, Bernard .... New York, NY
Goldberg, Bernard .... New York, NY
Goldberg, Bernard S. .... Cranston, RI
Goldberg, Beth Karon .... North Attleboro, MA
Goldberg, Billy B. .... Houston, TX
Goldberg, Bob G. .... Hauppauge, NY
Goldberg, Bob J. .... Atlanta, GA
Goldberg, Brett M. .... Boston, MA
Goldberg, Brian M. .... Cincinnati, OH
Goldberg, Bruce A. .... Stamford, CT
Goldberg, Bruce E. .... Los Angeles, CA
Goldberg, Bruce J. .... New Albany, IN
Goldberg, Bruce L. .... Glenview, IL
Goldberg, Bruce Mitchell, P.A. .... Hialeah, FL
Goldberg, Bruce N. .... Rockville, MD
Goldberg, Bruce R. .... Northbrook, IL
Goldberg, C. David .... Woodmere, NY
Goldberg, Caren Berg .... Milwaukee, WI
Goldberg, Carl R. .... San Francisco, CA
Goldberg, Carol Moon .... Elk Grove, CA
Goldberg, Carole E. .... Los Angeles, CA
Goldberg, Cary N. .... Bensenville, IL
Goldberg, Catherine T. .... Albuquerque, NM
Goldberg, Charles .... Denver, CO
Goldberg, Charles .... Houston, TX
Goldberg, Charles L. .... San Diego, CA
Goldberg, Charles N." Boots "
Houston, TX
Goldberg, Charles S. .... Owings Mills, MD
Goldberg, Charles S. .... Charleston, SC
Goldberg, Christine S. .... Baton Rouge, LA
Goldberg & Cohn .... Brooklyn, NY
Goldberg & Connolly .... Mineola, NY
New York, NY
Rockville Centre, NY
Goldberg, Cortney E. .... Detroit, MI
Goldberg, Craig A. .... Stamford, CT
Goldberg, Cy .... Cherry Hill, NJ
Goldberg, Cy, & Assoc. .... Cherry Hill, NJ
Goldberg, Dale Ann .... Columbus, OH
Goldberg, Dan A. .... Birmingham, AL
Goldberg, Daniel E. .... Milwaukee, WI
Goldberg, Daniel I. .... New York, NY
Goldberg, Daniel I. .... New York, NY
Goldberg, Daniel J. .... Washington, DC
Goldberg, Daniel J. .... Boston, MA
Goldberg, Daniel J. .... Minneapolis, MN
Goldberg, Daniel J. .... Houston, TX
Goldberg, Daniel Jay .... Houston, TX
Goldberg, Daniel L. .... Boston, MA
Goldberg, Daniel L. .... St. Louis, MO
Goldberg, Daniel M. .... Garden City, NY
Goldberg, Daniel P. .... New York, NY
Goldberg, Daniel S. .... Washington, DC
Goldberg, Daniel S. .... Minneapolis, MN
Goldberg, Daniel S. .... Westmont, NJ
Philadelphia, PA
Goldberg, Danl. T. .... San Francisco, CA
Goldberg, Darren I. .... Boston, MA
Goldberg, David .... New York, NY
Goldberg, David .... New York, NY
Goldberg, David .... Cleveland, OH
Goldberg, David A. .... Chicago, IL
Goldberg, David A. .... Southfield, MI
Goldberg, David A. .... Kansas City, MO
Goldberg, David A. .... New York, NY
Goldberg, David B. .... Boston, MA
Goldberg, David C. .... Dulles, VA
Goldberg, David H. .... Denver, CO
Goldberg, David J.
Department of Transportation, Office of the General Counsel, GV
Goldberg, David J. .... Princeton, NJ
Goldberg, David Klain .... Atlanta, GA
Goldberg, David M. .... Fort Myers, FL
Goldberg, David M. .... Chicago, IL
Goldberg, David M. .... New York, NY
Goldberg, David M. .... Houston, TX
Goldberg, David Neal .... Fairfax, VA
Goldberg, David R. .... Gaithersburg, MD
Goldberg, David R. .... New York, NY
Goldberg, David S. .... Baltimore, MD
Goldberg, David S. .... Gaithersburg, MD
Goldberg, David S., P.C. .... Gaithersburg, MD
Goldberg, David Thomas .... New York, NY
Goldberg, Dawn E. .... New York, NY
Goldberg, Deborah .... New York, NY

Goldberg, Deborah B. .... Portland, OR
Goldberg, Deborah L. .... Waukegan, IL
Goldberg, Deborah L., P.C., Law Offices of
Waukegan, IL
Goldberg, Deborah R. .... Los Angeles, CA
Goldberg, Debra .... Fort Lauderdale, FL
Goldberg, Debra S. .... Burbank, CA
Goldberg, Diana E. .... New York, NY
Goldberg & Dickman, P.C. .... Philadelphia, PA
Goldberg, Donald Drew .... New York, NY
Goldberg, Donald J. .... Philadelphia, PA
Goldberg, Donald S. .... Beverly Hills, CA
Goldberg, Dorothy P. .... Laguna Beach, CA
Goldberg, Douglas .... Tarrytown, NY
Goldberg, Douglas G.
Colorado Springs, CO
Goldberg & Easterling, P.A.
Bennettsville, SC
Goldberg, Edward .... Hackensack, NJ
Goldberg, Edward .... West Caldwell, NJ
Goldberg, Edward C. .... Charleston, WV
Goldberg, Edward I. .... Pittsburgh, PA
Goldberg, Eli M. .... White Plains, NY
Goldberg, Elizabeth Jo .... New York, NY
Goldberg, Ellen .... New York, NY
Goldberg, Elliot A. .... Falls Church, VA
Goldberg, Elliott D. .... Phoenixville, PA
Goldberg, Eric B. .... Boston, MA
Goldberg, Eric D. .... Los Angeles, CA
Goldberg, Eric L. .... New York, NY
Goldberg, Eric M. .... Washington, DC
Goldberg, Eric Reid .... New York, NY
Goldberg, Eugene H. .... New York, NY
Goldberg, Everett F. .... Baltimore, MD
Goldberg, Faye R. .... Hampton, NH
Goldberg, Felice & Isicrate, Associates, Ltd.
Philadelphia, PA
Goldberg & Finnegan .... Rockville, MD
Washington, DC
Goldberg & Fliegel LLP .... New York, NY
Goldberg, Fred .... Fort Lauderdale, FL
Goldberg, Fred B. .... Washington, DC
Goldberg, Fred M. .... Louisville, KY
Goldberg, Fred T., Jr. .... Washington, DC
Goldberg, Frederick M. .... Van Nuys, CA
Goldberg, Fredric N. .... Grand Rapids, MI
Goldberg, Gabriela Escudero
Los Angeles, CA
Goldberg & Gage .... Woodland Hills, CA
Goldberg, Gail L. .... Columbia, MD
Goldberg, Garth .... Los Angeles, CA
Goldberg, Gary G. .... Riverside, CA
Goldberg, Gary H. .... Worcester, MA
Goldberg, Gary L. .... Lakewood, NJ
Goldberg, Geo. S. .... New York, NY
Goldberg, George .... Tucson, AZ
Goldberg, George Z. .... Miami, FL
Goldberg, Gerald .... Garden City, NY
Goldberg, Gerald .... Cleveland, OH
Goldberg, Gerald A. .... Syracuse, NY
Goldberg, Gerald B. .... Florham Park, NJ
Goldberg, Gerald G. .... Chicago, IL
Goldberg, Gerald N. .... Costa Mesa, CA
Goldberg, Glen Z. .... Miami, FL
Goldberg, Glenn D. .... Newark, NJ
Goldberg, Glenn Evan .... Tampa, FL
Goldberg, Godles, Wiener & Wright
Washington, DC
Goldberg & Goldberg .... Chicago, IL
Goldberg & Goldberg .... Evanston, IL
Goldberg & Goldberg .... San Angelo, TX
Goldberg & Gottheim .... Albany, NY
Goldberg, Gruener, Gentile, Horoho & Avalli, P.C. .... Greensburg, PA
Pittsburgh, PA
Goldberg & Hall .... San Diego, CA
Goldberg, Hank Michael .... Santa Monica, CA
Goldberg, Harly .... Brooklyn, NY
Goldberg, Harold M. .... Yonkers, NY
Goldberg, Harold P. .... Syracuse, NY
Goldberg, Harriet L.
Upper Saddle River, NJ
Goldberg, Harry F. .... Fort Lee, NJ
Newark, NJ
Goldberg, Harry L. .... Columbia, SC
Goldberg, Harry W., P.A. .... Chevy Chase, MD
Goldberg, Harry W., P.A. .... Chevy Chase, MD
Goldberg, Harvey B. .... Fort Myers, FL
Goldberg, Harvey H. .... Framingham, MA
Goldberg, Harwood J. .... Beverly Hills, CA
Goldberg, Helene M. .... Department of Justice, Civil Division, GV
Goldberg, Henry .... Washington, DC
Goldberg, Henry L. .... Rockville Centre, NY
Goldberg, Henry N. .... West Roxbury, MA
Goldberg, Herbert .... New York, NY
Goldberg, Herman M. .... New York, NY
Goldberg & Hirsh, P.A.
Fort Lauderdale, FL
Miami, FL
Goldberg, Holly Lichtenstein .... Trenton, NJ
Goldberg, Honey Lynn .... North Chicago, IL
Goldberg, Howard .... Madison, WI
Goldberg, Howard A. .... Atlantic City, NJ
Goldberg, Howard G. .... Baltimore, MD
Goldberg, Howard P. .... Eatontown, NJ
Goldberg, Howard S. .... Philadelphia, PA
Goldberg, Hyman .... Silver Spring, MD
Goldberg, Hyman S. .... Lorain, OH
Goldberg, I. Andrew .... Boston, MA
Goldberg, I. Elliott .... Baltimore, MD
Goldberg, Idelle A. .... Atlantic City, NJ
Goldberg, Ilana Hoschander
New York, NY
Goldberg, Ilene M. .... Los Angeles, CA
Goldberg, Ilene Verbit .... Lawrenceville, NJ
Goldberg, Ilise S. .... New York, NY
Goldberg & Ingber, P.C. .... Garden City, NY

Goldberg, Ira M. .... Camden, NJ
Goldberg, Ira P. .... Chicago, IL
Goldberg, Irving .... Boston, MA
Goldberg, Irwin A. .... Upper Marlboro, MD
Goldberg, Irwin N. .... Ventnor City, NJ
Goldberg, Israel .... Brooklyn, NY
Goldberg, Israel, PLLC .... Brooklyn, NY
Goldberg, J. Arthur .... Snowmass Village, CO
Goldberg, J. Michael .... Youngstown, OH
Goldberg, Jack G. .... New York, NY
Goldberg, Jack Geddy .... West End, NJ
Goldberg, Jack R. .... Waterbury, CT
Goldberg, Jack R.
Nuclear Regulatory Commission, Office of the General Counsel, GV
Goldberg, Jacob A. .... Philadelphia, PA
Goldberg, Jacqueline M. .... New Orleans, LA
Goldberg, Jacquelyn L. .... Chicago, IL
Goldberg, James .... Los Angeles, CA
San Francisco, CA
Goldberg, James K. .... Pittsburgh, PA
Goldberg, James M. .... Washington, DC
Goldberg, James R. .... Atlanta, GA
Goldberg, James R. .... Cleveland, OH
Goldberg, James S. .... Louisville, KY
Goldberg, James S. .... Attleboro, MA
Goldberg, Janice C. .... Eugene, OR
Florence, OR
Goldberg, Jason S. .... Garden City, NY
Goldberg, Jay .... New York, NY
Goldberg, Jay A. .... Los Angeles, CA
Goldberg, Jay Arthur .... New York, NY
Goldberg, Jay Arthur, P.C. .... New York, NY
Goldberg, Jay D. .... Edina, MN
Goldberg, Jay K. .... New York, NY
Goldberg, Jay L. .... Philadelphia, PA
Goldberg, Jay, P.C. .... New York, NY
Goldberg, Jay Russell .... Chicago, IL
Goldberg, Jeanine Jacobs
Los Angeles, CA
Goldberg, Jeff .... Department of Labor, Office of the Solicitor, GV
Goldberg, Jeffrey A. .... Kingman, AZ
Goldberg, Jeffrey A. .... Chicago, IL
Elgin, IL
Goldberg, Jeffrey A. .... San Antonio, TX
Goldberg, Jeffrey A., Ltd. .... Chicago, IL
Elgin, IL
Goldberg, Jeffrey C. .... New York, NY
Goldberg, Jeffrey D. .... Los Angeles, CA
Goldberg, Jeffrey L. .... Northfield, IL
Goldberg, Jeffrey L. .... Elmhurst, NY
Goldberg, Jeffrey M. .... Chicago, IL
Goldberg, Jeffrey M., & Associates, Ltd.
Chicago, IL
Goldberg, Jeffrey P. .... Malden, MA
Goldberg, Jennifer K. .... New York, NY
Goldberg, Jerold H., (A Professional Corporation) .... San Diego, CA
Goldberg, Jerome D.
Department of Commerce, Patent and Trademark Office, GV
Goldberg, Jerome F. .... Chicago, IL
Goldberg, Jerome F. .... Portland, ME
Goldberg, Jerrold F. .... New York, NY
Goldberg, Jerry S. .... Chicago, IL
Goldberg, Jesse G. .... New York, NY
Goldberg, Jesse S. .... Hicksville, NY
Goldberg, Jill Borin .... Raleigh, NC
Goldberg, Joan E. .... Goshen, NY
Goldberg, Joel A. .... Universal City, CA
Goldberg, Joel A. .... Houston, TX
Goldberg, Joel H. .... New York, NY
Goldberg, Joel J. .... Washington, DC
Goldberg, John A. .... Cincinnati, OH
Goldberg, Jonathan .... Atlanta, GA
Goldberg, Jonathan D. .... Louisville, KY
Goldberg, Jonathan E. .... Baltimore, MD
Goldberg, Jonathan E. .... New York, NY
Goldberg, Jonathan I. J. .... Denver, CO
Goldberg, Jonathan J. .... Chevy Chase, MD
Goldberg, Jonathan L. .... Portland, ME
Goldberg, Jonathan M. .... Southfield, MI
Goldberg, Jonathan, P.C. .... Atlanta, GA
Goldberg, Jordan B. .... Voorhees, NJ
Goldberg, Joseph .... San Diego, CA
Goldberg, Joseph .... Fort Myers, FL
Goldberg, Joseph .... Albuquerque, NM
Goldberg, Joseph .... New York, NY
Goldberg, Joseph .... Philadelphia, PA
Goldberg, Joseph H. .... New Britain, CT
Goldberg, Joseph Keith .... Harrisburg, PA
Goldberg, Joseph L. .... Chicago, IL
Goldberg, Joseph M. .... Washington, DC
Goldberg, Joseph M. .... St. Louis Park, MN
Goldberg, Joseph P. .... New York, NY
Goldberg, Joshua A. .... New York, NY
Goldberg, Joshua B. .... Pittsburgh, PA
Goldberg, Joshua D. .... Cincinnati, OH
Goldberg, Judd J. .... Miami, FL
Goldberg, Judith A. .... Boston, MA
Goldberg, Judith M. .... Danbury, CT
Goldberg, Judy .... Lawrence, NY
Goldberg, Jules E. .... New York, NY
Goldberg, K. Stuart
West Palm Beach, FL
Goldberg, Kamin & Garvin .... Pittsburgh, PA
Goldberg, Karen .... Walnut Creek, CA
Goldberg, Karen B. .... Santa Monica, CA
Goldberg, Karen L. .... New York, NY
Goldberg, Katherine E. .... Chicago, IL
Goldberg, Kathleen .... Irvine, CA
Goldberg, Katie Friedland
Manhasset, NY
Goldberg, Katz & Stansen, P.C.
Fairview Heights, IL
St. Louis, MO

Goldberg, Katzman & Shipman, P.C.
Carlisle, PA
Harrisburg, PA
Hershey, PA
York, PA
Goldberg, Keith A. .... Chicago, IL
Goldberg, Kenneth A. .... New York, NY
Goldberg, Kenneth D. .... Tallahassee, FL
Goldberg, Kenneth D. .... New York, NY
Goldberg, Kenneth J. .... Brockton, MA
Goldberg, Kenneth M. .... Boston, MA
Goldberg, Kenneth Mayer .... Lynnfield, MA
Goldberg, Kenneth R. .... Boston, MA
Goldberg, Kevin I. .... Washington, DC
Goldberg, Kevin M. .... Washington, DC
Goldberg, Knisely & Beyer .... Lancaster, PA
Goldberg, Kohn, Bell, Black, Rosenbloom & Moritz, Ltd. .... Chicago, IL
Goldberg, L. Darren .... Leesburg, VA
Goldberg, Larry .... Pasadena, CA
Goldberg, Larry H. .... Mc Keesport, PA
Goldberg, Larry S. .... Chicago, IL
Goldberg, Laura J. .... Harrisburg, PA
Goldberg, Lauran L. .... Dallas, TX
Goldberg, Lauren .... New York, NY
Goldberg, Laurence A.
San Francisco, CA
Goldberg, Lawrence .... San Francisco, CA
Goldberg, Lawrence .... Santa Monica, CA
Goldberg, Lawrence .... Philadelphia, PA
Goldberg, Lawrence A. .... Los Angeles, CA
Goldberg, Lawrence A. .... New York, NY
Goldberg, Lawrence A. .... West Chester, PA
Goldberg, Lawrence A., A Prof. Law Corp.
Los Angeles, CA
Goldberg, Lawrence B. .... Springfield, MA
Goldberg, Lawrence D.
Walnut Creek, CA
Goldberg, Lawrence H.
Fort Lauderdale, FL
Goldberg, Lawrence R. .... St. Louis, MO
Goldberg, Lawrence S. .... New York, NY
Goldberg, Lazarus H. .... Brookline, MA
Goldberg, Leah S. .... San Francisco, CA
Goldberg, Lee A. .... New York, NY
Goldberg, Lee R. .... Irvine, CA
Goldberg, Lena Genello .... Boston, MA
Goldberg, Leonard .... Bronx, NY
Goldberg, Leonard M. .... West Orange, NJ
Goldberg, Lesley E. .... New York, NY
Goldberg, Leslie E. .... San Diego, CA
Goldberg, Leslie R. .... Chicago, IL
Goldberg, Lester H. .... Chevy Chase, MD
Goldberg, Lewis .... Boston, MA
Goldberg, Lewis S. .... Ardsley, NY
Goldberg, Linda O. .... Ann Arbor, MI
Goldberg, Linda V. .... Chicago, IL
Goldberg, Lisa Beth .... San Francisco, CA
Goldberg, Lisa Gayle .... Fort Lauderdale, FL
Goldberg, Louis .... Norwood, MA
Goldberg, Louis .... New York, NY
Goldberg, Louis E. .... Redondo Beach, CA
Goldberg, Louis L. .... New York, NY
Goldberg, Louis M. .... Garden City, NY
Goldberg, Louis S. .... New York, NY
Goldberg, Louise Koslin .... Houston, TX
Goldberg & Lustig .... Brooklyn, NY
Goldberg, Lyn I. .... San Diego, CA
Goldberg, M. Roy .... Washington, DC
Goldberg, Marc A. .... New York, NY
Goldberg, Marc Evan .... Worcester, MA
Goldberg, Marc H. .... Latham, NY
Goldberg, Marc Stuart .... White Plains, NY
Goldberg, Marci R. .... Woodland Hills, CA
Goldberg, Marcia R. .... Toledo, OH
Goldberg, Margaret T. .... Scarsdale, NY
Goldberg & Marin .... Hoboken, NJ
New York, NY
Goldberg, Marion Kristal .... Baltimore, MD
Goldberg, Mark .... Hopkins, MN
Goldberg, Mark E. .... Bensalem, PA
Goldberg, Mark Edward .... New York, NY
Goldberg, Mark H. .... Phoenix, AZ
Goldberg, Mark H. .... Cooper City, FL
Goldberg, Mark H. .... New York, NY
Goldberg, Mark J. .... Pittsburgh, PA
Goldberg, Mark Jay .... New York, NY
Goldberg, Mark L. .... Washington, DC
Goldberg, Mark R. .... San Francisco, CA
Goldberg, Mark S. .... Southfield, MI
Goldberg, Marlene R. .... New York, NY
Goldberg, Marshall .... Stamford, CT
Goldberg, Marshall F. .... Los Angeles, CA
Woodland Hills, CA
Goldberg, Martin B. .... Miami, FL
Goldberg, Martin B. .... Floral Park, NY
Goldberg, Martin M. .... New York, NY
Goldberg, Martin R. .... Middletown, NY
Goldberg, Martin S. .... Palm Desert, CA
Canfield, OH
Goldberg, Martin S.
Upper Marlboro, MD
Goldberg, Martin S. .... Seattle, WA
Goldberg, Martin S., Co., L.P.A.
Palm Desert, CA
Canfield, OH
Goldberg, Marvin A. .... Philadelphia, PA
Goldberg, Marvin E. .... Bronx, NY
Goldberg, Matthew .... Oakland, CA
Goldberg, Matthew Falk .... Washington, DC
Goldberg, Maureen McKenna
Providence, RI
Goldberg, Max .... Southfield, MI
Goldberg, Max .... Philadelphia, PA
Goldberg, Mechanic & Stuart .... Portland, OR
Goldberg, Melvin A. .... Columbus, OH
Goldberg, Melvin B. .... St. Paul, MN
Goldberg, Melvin J. .... Las Vegas, NV
Goldberg, Meredith S. .... New York, NY
Goldberg, Michael .... Fresno, CA
Goldberg, Michael .... Atlanta, GA
Goldberg, Michael .... Omaha, NE
Goldberg, Michael B. .... Chicago, IL
Goldberg, Michael Craig .... St. Louis, MO
Goldberg, Michael D. .... Philadelphia, PA
Goldberg, Michael E. .... New York, NY
Goldberg, Michael H. .... New York, NY
Goldberg, Michael I.
Fort Lauderdale, FL
Goldberg, Michael J. .... Boston, MA
Goldberg, Michael J. .... New York, NY
Goldberg, Michael L. .... Santa Monica, CA
Washington, DC
McLean, VA
Goldberg, Michael P. .... Brooklyn, NY
Goldberg, Michael R. .... Cambridge, MA
Goldberg, Michael S. .... Houston, TX
Goldberg, Mickey S. .... New York, NY
Goldberg, Minda F. .... Towson, MD
Goldberg, Mindy S. .... Bridgewater, NJ
Goldberg, Miriam G. .... Chevy Chase, MD
Goldberg, Mitchel R. .... Riverside, CA
Goldberg, Mitchell B. .... Cincinnati, OH
Goldberg, Mitchell D. .... New York, NY
Goldberg, Mitchell S. .... Philadelphia, PA
Goldberg, Morton David .... New York, NY
Goldberg, Morton M. .... New York, NY
Goldberg, Morton W. .... Newton, MA
Goldberg, Moses .... San Antonio, TX
Goldberg, Moses, Inc., A Professional Corporation .... San Antonio, TX
Goldberg, Mufson & Spar, A Professional Corporation .... Newark, NJ
West Orange, NJ
Goldberg, Murray .... Garden City, NY
Goldberg, Nancy E. .... Harrisburg, PA
Goldberg, Nathan .... Los Angeles, CA
Goldberg, Nathan H.
Richmond Heights, MO
Goldberg, Nathan M. .... Albany, NY
Goldberg, Nava .... Brooklyn, NY
Goldberg, Neal M. .... Washington, DC
Goldberg, Neil A. .... Buffalo, NY
Goldberg, Nicole .... Menlo Park, CA
Goldberg, Norbert J. .... Southfield, MI
Goldberg, Norman M. .... Boston, MA
Goldberg & Osborne .... Bullhead City, AZ
Casa Grande, AZ
Flagstaff, AZ
Lake Havasu City, AZ
Mesa, AZ
Phoenix, AZ
Prescott, AZ
Sierra Vista, AZ
Tucson, AZ
Goldberg, Oscar .... New York, NY
Goldberg, P.C., Daniel E., Law Offices of
Milwaukee, WI
Goldberg, Pamela H. .... Tulsa, OK
Goldberg, Pamela Procuniar .... Cherry Hill, NJ
Goldberg, Patricia Mitchell .... Bethesda, MD
Goldberg, Patti Woods .... Woodland Hills, CA
Goldberg, Paul .... Delray Beach, FL
Goldberg, Perry .... Chicago, IL
Goldberg, Perry M. .... Los Angeles, CA
Goldberg, Persky, Jennings, White & Hostler
Huntington, WV
Goldberg, Persky, Jennings & White, P.C.
Saginaw, MI
Greensburg, PA
Johnstown, PA
Pittsburgh, PA
Goldberg, Peter H. .... Department of Justice, Antitrust Division, GV
Goldberg, Peter M. .... Boston, MA
Hyannis, MA
Goldberg, Philip L. .... Chicago, IL
Goldberg, Phillip J. .... San Francisco, CA
Goldberg, Phillip M. .... Chicago, IL
Goldberg, Pike & Besche, P.C.
Baltimore, MD
Goldberg & Pines .... New York, NY
Goldberg, R. Marc .... Baltimore, MD
Goldberg, R. Marc, P.C. .... Baltimore, MD
Goldberg, Rachel E. .... Margate, FL
Goldberg, Ralph E. .... New York, NY
Goldberg, Ralph S. .... Decatur, GA
Goldberg, Randy M. .... Plantation, FL
Goldberg, Ray Molly .... Newton, MA
Goldberg, Reuben .... Washington, DC
Goldberg, Rhonda Susan .... Boston, MA
Goldberg, Richard .... Cincinnati, OH
Goldberg, Richard .... Columbus, OH
Goldberg, Richard A. .... Brooklyn, NY
Goldberg, Richard A. .... New York, NY
Goldberg, Richard C. .... New York, NY
Goldberg, Richard D. .... Canfield, OH
Goldberg, Richard D. .... Pittsburgh, PA
Goldberg, Richard H. .... Denver, CO
Goldberg, Richard L. .... Brooklyn, NY
Goldberg, Richard L. .... New York, NY
Goldberg, Richard L. .... Irving, TX
Goldberg, Richard M. .... Westport, CT
Goldberg, Richard M. .... Baltimore, MD
Goldberg, Richard M. .... Hackensack, NJ
Goldberg, Richard M. .... Wilkes-Barre, PA
Goldberg, Richard M. .... Green Bay, WI
Milwaukee, WI
Waukesha, WI
Goldberg, Richard R. .... Camden, NJ
Philadelphia, PA
Goldberg, Richard S. .... Brooklyn, NY
Goldberg, Richard W. .... New York, NY
Goldberg, Richard W. .... Philadelphia, PA
Goldberg, Rita Lynne .... New York, NY
Goldberg, Robert .... North Woodmere, NY
Goldberg, Robert .... Saipan, TT
Goldberg, Robert B. .... Atlanta, GA
Goldberg, Robert B. .... Chicago, IL
Goldberg, Robert C. .... Chicago, IL
Goldberg, Robert D. .... Santa Monica, CA
Goldberg, Robert D. .... Wilmington, DE
Goldberg, Robert D. .... Pawtucket, RI
Goldberg, Robert H. .... New York, NY
Goldberg, Robert J. .... Chicago, IL
Goldberg, Robert L. .... Marlborough, MA
Goldberg, Robert L. .... San Antonio, TX
Goldberg, Robert L., P.C., Law Offices of
San Antonio, TX
Goldberg, Robert M. .... Washington, DC
Goldberg, Robert M. .... Atlanta, GA
Goldberg, Robert M. .... Falls Church, VA
Goldberg, Robert R. .... Harrison, NY
Goldberg, Robert S. .... Santa Ana, CA
Goldberg, Robert S. .... New York, NY
Goldberg, Roberta .... Mineola, NY
Goldberg, Ronald D. .... Seattle, WA
Goldberg, Ronald K. .... Philadelphia, PA
Goldberg, Ronald W. .... New York, NY
Goldberg, Ross .... Philadelphia, PA
Goldberg, Russell M. .... La Jolla, CA
Goldberg, S. David .... Brockton, MA
Goldberg Sager & Associates
Brooklyn, NY
Goldberg, Samuel B. .... Boston, MA
Goldberg, Sandra .... Washington, DC
Goldberg, Sanford B. .... New York, NY
Goldberg, Sanford H. .... New York, NY
Goldberg, Sara A. .... New York, NY
Goldberg, Saul W. .... Pittsburgh, PA
Goldberg, Scot D. .... Fort Myers, FL
Port Charlotte, FL
Goldberg, Scott .... Phoenix, AZ
Goldberg, Scott B. .... New York, NY
Goldberg, Scott, Belfield, Steinberg & Cohen, A Professional Law Corporation
Los Angeles, CA
Goldberg, Scott D. .... Boston, MA
Goldberg, Scott D., P.C., The Law Firm of
Boston, MA
Goldberg, Scott E. .... Cleveland, OH
Goldberg, Scott J. .... Louisville, KY
Goldberg, Selwyn B. .... Palo Alto, CA
Goldberg, Seth .... Washington, DC
Goldberg, Seth M. .... Los Angeles, CA
Goldberg, Seth R. .... Hollywood, FL
Goldberg, Seth Z. .... New York, NY
Goldberg, Seymour .... Garden City, NY
Goldberg, Seymour M. .... Newton, MA
Goldberg, Sheila Bond .... Fort Lauderdale, FL
Goldberg, Sheldon F. .... Denver, CO
Goldberg, Sheri L. .... Livingston, NJ
Goldberg, Sherman I. .... Chicago, IL
Goldberg, Sidney A. .... Miami, FL
Goldberg & Simpson, P.S.C.
Louisville, KY
Goldberg, Sol E. .... Las Vegas, NV
Goldberg, Stacey L. .... Miami, FL
Goldberg, Stan L. .... New York, NY
Goldberg, Stanley J.
United States Tax Court, Special Trial Judges, GV
Goldberg, Stanley M. .... Carle Place, NY
Goldberg, Stanley Z. .... Pittsburgh, PA
Goldberg, Stanton D. .... Dallas, TX
Goldberg, Stephanie B. .... Chicago, IL
Goldberg, Stephen A. .... Baltimore, MD
Goldberg, Stephen B. .... Redondo Beach, CA
Goldberg, Stephen B. .... Chicago, IL
Goldberg, Stephen I. .... New York, NY
Goldberg, Stephen J. .... Los Angeles, CA
Goldberg, Stephen M. .... Baltimore, MD
Goldberg, Stephen M. .... Green Brook, NJ
Goldberg, Stephen N. .... San Francisco, CA
Goldberg, Stephen N. .... Towson, MD
Goldberg, Stephen P. .... New York, NY
Goldberg, Steve .... Washington, DC
Goldberg, Steven .... New York, NY
Goldberg, Steven .... Portland, OR
Goldberg, Steven D. .... Wilmington, DE
Philadelphia, PA
Goldberg, Steven E. .... Charleston, SC
Goldberg, Steven H. .... Sacramento, CA
Goldberg, Steven H. .... New York, NY
Goldberg, Steven H. .... White Plains, NY
Goldberg, Steven J. .... Brookline, MA
Goldberg, Steven J. .... Mount Olive, NJ
Goldberg, Steven M. .... Los Angeles, CA
Goldberg, Steven M. .... Santa Rosa, CA
Goldberg, Steven M. .... Youngstown, OH
Goldberg, Steven R. .... New York, NY
Goldberg, Stinnett, Meyers & Davis, A Professional Corporation .... Oakland, CA
San Francisco, CA
San Jose, CA
Santa Rosa, CA
Walnut Creek, CA
Goldberg, Stuart E. .... Tallahassee, FL
Goldberg, Stuart E. .... Spring Valley, NY
Goldberg, Stuart J. .... Toledo, OH
Goldberg, Stuart M. .... Department of Justice, Criminal Division, GV
Goldberg, Sumner D. .... Boston, MA
Goldberg, Susan A. .... New York, NY
Goldberg, Susan G. .... Washington, DC
Goldberg, Susan L. .... Chester, PA
Goldberg, Suzanne .... New York, NY
Goldberg, Terri L. .... Baltimore, MD
Goldberg, Terry D. .... Philadelphia, PA
Goldberg, Terry M. .... Woodland Hills, CA
Goldberg, Theodore .... Rancho Santa Fe, CA
Goldberg, Theodore .... Pittsburgh, PA
Goldberg, Theodore A. .... Los Angeles, CA
Goldberg, Theodore M. .... Miami, FL
Goldberg, Thomas D. .... Stamford, CT
Goldberg, Thomas D. .... Pawtucket, RI
Goldberg, Todd D. .... Boston, MA
Goldberg, Tom J. .... Bloomfield Hills, MI
Goldberg, Tracy W. .... Los Angeles, CA
Goldberg & Vova .... Miami, FL
Goldberg, Walter .... San Angelo, TX
Goldberg, Weisman & Cairo, Ltd.
Chicago, IL
Goldberg, Weprin & Ustin LLP
New York, NY
Goldberg, William .... Cambridge, MA
Goldberg, William .... Flint, MI
Goldberg, William D. .... Thomasville, PA
Goldberg, William D. .... Thomasville, PA
Goldberg, William Harry .... Seattle, WA
Goldberg, William I. .... Chicago, IL
Goldberg, William R. .... Providence, RI
Goldberg, Yale F., (P.C.) .... Phoenix, AZ
Goldberg, Youngest & Gravenhorst, P.A., Law Offices .... Boca Raton, FL
Fort Lauderdale, FL
North Palm Beach, FL
Goldberg, Zulkie & Frankenstein, Ltd.
Chicago, IL
Goldberger, Alan S. .... Clifton, NJ
Goldberger, Alexis .... Roseland, NJ
Goldberger, Alfred L. .... Albany, NY
Schenectady, NY
Goldberger, Allen S. .... West Orange, NJ
Goldberger, Andrew B. .... Atlanta, GA
Goldberger, Ari .... New York, NY
Goldberger, Bruce N. .... New York, NY
Goldberger, Bryan J. .... Albany, NY
Goldberger, Charles A. .... White Plains, NY
Goldberger, Charles S. .... Pine Bluff, AR
Goldberger, Daniel A. .... New York, NY
Goldberger, David A. .... Columbus, OH
Goldberger and Dubin, P.C.
New York, NY
Goldberger, Elliott I. .... St. Louis, MO
Goldberger, Franklin H. .... Albany, NY
Goldberger, Gary G. .... Studio City, CA
Goldberger & Goldberger .... Clifton, NJ
Goldberger & Goldberger .... Albany, NY
Schenectady, NY
Goldberger, Gustav .... Department of Energy, Office of the General Counsel, GV
Goldberger, Helene G. .... Albany, NY
Goldberger, Howard A. .... Kenilworth, NJ
Goldberger, Jack A.
West Palm Beach, FL
Goldberger, Kim H. .... Golden, CO
Goldberger, Leonard P. .... Philadelphia, PA
Goldberger, M. Norman .... Philadelphia, PA
Goldberger, Marvin L. .... Glenview, IL
Goldberger, Michael J. .... Brooklyn, NY
Goldberger, Paul A. .... New York, NY
Goldberger, Peter .... Ardmore, PA
Goldberger, Peter C. .... La Jolla, CA
Goldberger, Rachael A. .... Minneapolis, MN
Goldberger, Robert R. .... Bridgeport, CT
Goldberger Seligsohn & Shinrod, P.A.
West Orange, NJ
Goldbergh & Spitzer, LLC .... Stamford, CT
Goldbergh, Theodore A. .... New York, NY
Goldberg Rawicz, Jennifer .... Miami, FL
Gold-Bikin, Lynne Z. .... Norristown, PA
Goldblat, Harris C. .... New York, NY
Goldblatt, Ann D. .... Chicago, IL
Goldblatt, Arthur Jacob .... Norwalk, CT
Goldblatt & Associates .... New York, NY
Goldblatt, Bernard .... Minnetonka, MN
Goldblatt, Brett D. .... Los Angeles, CA
Goldblatt, Craig .... Washington, DC
Goldblatt, David I. .... New York, NY
Goldblatt, Dean E. .... Springfield, MA
Goldblatt, Ellen S. .... Oakland, CA
Goldblatt, Gary L. .... Chicago, IL
Goldblatt, Grace R. .... New York, NY
Goldblatt, Greenstein & Rashba, P.C.
Hamden, CT
Goldblatt, Herbert L.
Department of Housing and Urban Development, Office of General Counsel, GV
Goldblatt, Howard I. .... Chicago, IL
Goldblatt, Jay A. .... Cleveland, OH
Goldblatt, Jeffrey W. .... East Brunswick, NJ
Goldblatt, Jonathan R. .... New York, NY
Goldblatt, Kenneth Bruce .... New York, NY
Goldblatt, L. Steven .... St. Louis, MO
Goldblatt, Lester S. .... Metuchen, NJ
Goldblatt, Lipkin & Cohen, P.C.
Norfolk, VA
Virginia Beach, VA
Goldblatt, Lisa A. .... Atlanta, GA
Goldblatt, Lisa Ann .... Washington, DC
Goldblatt, Marjorie .... San Jose, CA
Goldblatt, Marvin .... Yonkers, NY
Goldblatt, Michael L. .... New Orleans, LA
Goldblatt, Richard L. .... Hamden, CT
Goldblatt, Samuel .... Buffalo, NY
Goldblatt, Samuel .... Norfolk, VA
Goldblatt, Samuel A. .... St. Louis, MO
Goldblatt, Stanford J. .... Chicago, IL
Goldblatt, Steven L. .... Boston, MA
Goldblatt, Sylvia .... Florham Park, NJ
Goldblatt, Thomas C. .... Chicago, IL
Goldbloom, Donald S. .... Grantsville, MD
Goldbloom, Irwin .... Washington, DC
Goldbloom, Marcie E. .... Chicago, IL
Goldblum, Bonnie .... New Orleans, LA
Goldblum, Corie M. .... Miami, FL
Goldblum, Joseph A. .... Jenkintown, PA
Goldblum, Keith A. .... Boca Raton, FL
Goldblum, Martin T. .... Los Angeles, CA
Goldblum, Philip A. .... Pittsburgh, PA

Goldblum, Victor .... New York, NY
Goldbrenner, Ronald S. .... New York, NY
Goldbronn, Doreen M. .... Clearwater, FL
Goldbronn, Doreen M., P.A. .... Clearwater, FL
Goldburd, Joseph .... New York, NY
Goldburg, Bonnie B. .... New York, NY
Goldburg, Charles R. .... Kew Gardens, NY
Goldburgh, Lloyd H. .... Miami, FL
Goldby, Glenn S. .... Santa Ana, CA
Goldcamp, Maria Theresa .... Ashland, KY
Goldcamp, Robert T. .... Cincinnati, OH
Golde, Howard R. .... Wilmington, DE
Golde, Lawrence W. .... New York, NY
Golde, Michael J. .... Chicago, IL
Golde, Scott J. .... St. Louis, MO
Goldean, Paul .... Dallas, TX
Goldeen, Barbara .... San Francisco, CA
Goldeen, Sam .... Big Sur, CA
Golden, A. Thomas .... San Diego, CA
Golden, Abraham J. .... Philadelphia, PA
Golden, Adam H. .... New York, NY
Golden, Alan J. .... Shreveport, LA
Golden, Albert J. .... Walla Walla, WA
Golden, Alvin J. .... Austin, TX
Golden, Andrew S. .... Hartford, CT
Golden, Anne .... New York, NY
Golden, Anthony J. .... Daytona Beach, FL
Golden, Anthony T. .... Vero Beach, FL
Golden, Arthur F. .... New York, NY
Golden & Associates, A Professional Corporation .... Houston, TX
Golden, Audrey S. .... New York, NY
Golden Avenue Law Offices
Battle Creek, MI
Golden, Barry M. .... Dallas, TX
Golden, Beth L. .... New York, NY
Golden, Beth R. .... Philadelphia, PA
Golden, Bruce P. .... Chicago, IL
Golden, Byron .... New York, NY
Golden, Caroline P. .... Chicago, IL
Golden, Catherine E. .... San Francisco, CA
Golden, Catherine Filhiol .... Mobile, AL
Golden, Charles .... East Islip, NY
Golden, Charles J. .... Monroe, MI
Golden, Charles M. .... Philadelphia, PA
Golden, Christopher A. .... Elmsford, NY
Garden City, NY
Golden, Colleen Louise .... Atlanta, GA
Golden, Constance .... New York, NY
Golden, Cornelius J., Jr. .... Washington, DC
Golden & Cowan, P.A. .... Miami, FL
Golden, Curtis A. .... Pensacola, FL
Golden, Dale M., The Law Office of
Chicago, IL
Golden, Dale T. .... Tampa, FL
Golden, Daniel B. .... Jersey City, NJ
Golden, Daniel G. .... Plover, WI
Golden, Daniel H. .... New York, NY
Golden, Daniel L. .... South River, NJ
Woodbridge, NJ
Golden, David .... Stuart, FL
Golden, David A. .... Washington, DC
Golden, David A. .... Kingsport, TN
Golden, David B. .... San Francisco, CA
Golden, David E. .... Hartford, CT
Golden, David F. .... Atlanta, GA
Golden, David L. .... Providence, RI
Golden, David S. .... Chicago, IL
Golden, Deborah A. .... Chicago, IL
Golden, Debra R. .... New York, NY
Golden, Diane A. .... Los Angeles, CA
Golden, Donna J. .... Henrietta, NY
Golden, Douglas J. .... Birmingham, MI
Golden, Douglas J., P.C. .... Birmingham, MI
Golden, Douglas W. .... Tulsa, OK
Golden, E. Alexandra .... Needham, MA
Golden, E. Scott .... Fort Lauderdale, FL
Golden, Edmund W., (P.L.C.)
Metairie, LA
Golden, Edward I. .... Miami, FL
Golden, Edward R. .... Atlanta, GA
Golden, Edward R. .... Decatur, GA
Golden, Ellen .... Charleston, WV
Golden, Ellen J. .... Brooklyn, NY
Golden, Elliott .... Bayside, NY
Golden, Eric S. .... Orlando, FL
Golden, Eugene .... Los Angeles, CA
Golden, Eugene T. .... Walla Walla, WA
Golden, Evelyn D. .... Tallahassee, FL
Golden & Fonte .... New Orleans, LA
Metairie, LA
Golden, Francis William .... Chicago, IL
Golden, G. Hawkins, II .... Dallas, TX
Golden, Gary M. .... Toledo, OH
Golden, Gerald A. .... Chicago, IL
Golden & Golden .... Jersey City, NJ
Golden and Golden .... Long Branch, NJ
Golden & Golden .... Fairfax, VA
Golden, Gregg H. S.
Federal Deposit Insurance Corporation, Corporate Affairs Section, GV
Golden, Gregory J. .... Washington, DC
Golden, H. Bruce .... Houston, TX
Golden, Harry G. .... Los Angeles, CA
Golden, Harvey L. .... Columbia, SC
Golden, Henry D. .... Jackson, MS
Golden, Herman .... Short Hills, NJ
Golden, Hershel F. .... Sunnyvale, CA
Golden, Howard G. .... Rahway, NJ
Golden, Howard I. .... New York, NY
Golden, Howard N. .... New York, NY
Golden, Howard S. .... Chicago, IL
Golden, Irvin P. .... Atlantic Beach, FL
Golden, Irwin M. .... East Falmouth, MA
Golden, J. Dale .... Lexington, KY
Golden, Jack .... Santa Ana, CA
Golden, James .... Grand Junction, CO
Golden, James A. .... Hauppauge, NY
Golden, James D. .... Flagstaff, AZ
Golden, James E., Jr.
Oklahoma City, OK
Golden, James, Jr. .... Marlborough, MA
Golden, James P. .... Philadelphia, PA
Golden, James R. .... Middlesboro, KY
Golden, James S. .... San Antonio, TX
Golden, Jane F. .... New York, NY
Golden, Jason A. .... Tampa, FL
Golden, Jason A. .... Columbia, TN
Golden, Jay T. .... Biloxi, MS
Golden, Jean M. .... Chicago, IL
Golden, Jeffrey Benjamin .... New York, NY
Golden, Jeffrey I. .... Costa Mesa, CA
Golden, Jeffrey Stephen .... Mill Valley, CA
Golden, Jennifer K. .... Oklahoma City, OK
Golden, Joe Bob .... Jasper, TX
Golden, Joel S. .... Detroit, MI
Golden, John A. .... Long Branch, NJ
Golden, John A. .... New York, NY
Golden, John D. .... Miami, FL
Golden, John E. .... Northbrook, IL
Golden, John H. .... Pineville, KY
Golden, John M. .... New Orleans, LA
Golden, John M. .... Pittsburgh, PA
Golden, John P. .... San Mateo, CA
Golden, John T. .... Birmingham, AL
Golden, John T. .... Department of Agriculture, Office of the General Counsel, GV
Golden, John T. .... Houston, TX
Golden, Jonathan .... Grand Rapids, MI
Golden, Jonathan K. .... Los Angeles, CA
Golden, Jonathan K. .... New York, NY
Golden, Jonathan, (P.C.) .... Atlanta, GA
Golden, Joseph .... North Miami Beach, FL
Golden, Joseph A. .... Southfield, MI
Golden, Joseph L. .... Los Angeles, CA
Golden, Joseph M. .... Walla Walla, WA
Golden, Joseph W. .... San Diego, CA
Golden, Joseph W. .... Yardley, PA
Golden, Judd .... Boulder, CO
Golden, Karen .... New York, NY
Golden, Kathleen M. .... New York, NY
Golden, Keith E. .... Columbus, OH
Golden, Kelly Jean .... Columbia, SC
Golden, Kenneth B. .... Tacoma, WA
Golden, Kenneth L. .... Valatie, NY
Golden, Kenneth S. .... Durango, CO
Golden and Kernan, P.C. .... Woodbury, NJ
Golden, Kevin C. .... Washington, DC
Golden, Kevin M. .... Worcester, MA
Golden, Kimberly O. .... Monroe, LA
Golden, King, Jr. .... Del Mar, CA
Golden & Knowlton .... Walla Walla, WA
Golden - Kopcke .... San Francisco, CA
Golden & Kunz, P.C. .... Lathrup Village, MI
Golden, L. Warren .... Decatur, IL
Golden, La Quetta M. .... Gulfport, MS
Golden, Larry I. .... Palatine, IL
Golden, Laura S. .... Chicago, IL
Golden, Laurie G. .... Memphis, TN
Golden, Lawrence J. .... Hartford, CT
Golden, Lawrence W. .... Utica, NY
Golden, Lee R. .... Pittsburgh, PA
Golden, Linda P. .... Falls Church, VA
Golden, Linli L. .... San Diego, CA
Golden, Lisa J. .... Santa Monica, CA
Golden, Lisa M. .... New York, NY
Golden, Loren S. .... Elgin, IL
Golden, Louisa A. .... San Diego, CA
Golden, Lucy .... Kansas City, MO
Golden, Mac .... Little Rock, AR
Golden & Mandel .... New York, NY
Golden, Marc A. .... New York, NY
Golden, Marc E. .... Los Angeles, CA
Golden, Marc E. .... West Palm Beach, FL
Golden, Marc L. .... Purchase, NY
Golden, Martin E. .... Baton Rouge, LA
Golden, Mary Pat .... Englewood, CO
Golden & Masano .... Reading, PA
Wyomissing, PA
Golden, Matthew F. .... Williamsport, PA
Golden, Matthew J. .... New York, NY
Golden, Matthew T. .... New York, NY
Golden, Maurene L. .... Medford, MA
Golden, Max .... Arlington, VA
Golden and McClellan, P.C. .... Monroe, MI
Golden & Meizlish, A Legal Professional Association .... Columbus, OH
Golden, Melanie Liebman .... Suffern, NY
Golden, Michael .... Cypress, TX
Golden, Michael .... Cheyenne, WY
Golden, Michael A. .... Basking Ridge, NJ
Golden, Michael B. .... New York, NY
Golden, Michael D. .... Arcata, CA
Golden, Michael D. .... Washington, DC
Golden, Michael D. .... Atlanta, GA
Golden, Michael D. .... New York, NY
Golden, Michael D. .... Oshkosh, WI
Golden, Michael J. .... Santa Fe, NM
Golden, Michael Joseph .... Washington, DC
Fargo, ND
Golden, Michael L., Jr. .... Philadelphia, PA
Golden, Michael M. .... San Francisco, CA
Golden, Michael P. .... Las Vegas, NV
Golden, Michael R.
General Accounting Office, Office of the General Counsel, GV
Golden, Mitchell R. .... St. Petersburg, FL
Golden, Mumby, Summers, Livingston & Kane, LLP .... Grand Junction, CO
Golden, Nancy R. .... Hingham, MA
Golden, Neil D. .... Boston, MA
Golden & Nelson, PLLC .... Washington, DC
Golden, Oliver J. .... Monroe, MI
Golden, Patricia Piper .... Geneva, IL
Golden, Patrick G. .... San Francisco, CA
Golden, Patti C. .... Biloxi, MS
Golden, Paul .... Brooklyn, NY
Golden, Peter G. .... Atlanta, GA
Golden, Peter S. .... New York, NY
Golden, Philip R. .... Merced, CA
Golden, Philip T. .... Houston, TX
Golden, R. Scott .... Wetumpka, AL
Golden, R. Vance, III .... Parkersburg, WV
Golden, Ralph D. .... Memphis, TN
Golden, Randal Louis .... San Ramon, CA
Golden, Randy C. .... Miami, FL
Golden, Renée Wayne .... Los Angeles, CA
Golden, Rex .... St. Petersburg, FL
Golden, Richard .... Lisbon Falls, ME
Golden, Richard A. .... North Miami, FL
Golden, Richard A. .... Fairfax, VA
Golden, Richard B. .... Goshen, NY
Golden, Richard N. .... Forest Hills, NY
Golden, Richard N. .... New York, NY
Golden, Richard W. .... Brooklyn, NY
Golden, Robert .... Sebastian, FL
Vero Beach, FL
Golden, Robert B. .... Scarsdale, NY
Golden, Robert E. .... San Antonio, TX
Golden, Robert E., & Associates, A Prof. Corp. .... San Antonio, TX
Golden, Robert H. .... Boston, MA
Golden, Robert H. .... Lathrup Village, MI
Golden, Robert J. .... Chicago, IL
Des Plaines, IL
Golden, Robert N. .... Bridgewater, NJ
New Brunswick, NJ
Golden, Robert P. .... Cody, WY
Golden, Roger F. .... Niceville, FL
Golden, Roger M. .... Washington, DC
Golden, Ronald D. .... Washington, DC
Golden, Rosalyn M. .... Chicago, IL
Golden, Rothschild, Spagnola, Lundell & Levitt, P.C. .... Bridgewater, NJ
Flemington, NJ
Haddonfield, NJ
Morristown, NJ
Newark, NJ
New Brunswick, NJ
Somerville, NJ
Trenton, NJ
Northport, NY
Golden, Samuel D. .... Chicago, IL
Golden, Samuel H. .... Garden City, NY
Golden, Scott A. .... New York, NY
Golden, Scott M. .... Phoenix, AZ
Golden, Shawn A. .... New York, NY
Golden, Shawn David .... Houston, TX
Golden, Shelby D .... Lima, OH
Golden, Sherman E. .... Atlanta, GA
Golden, SherryLon .... Flagstaff, AZ
Golden, Sidney H. .... Columbus, OH
Golden, Stacey Marian
West Hempstead, NY
Golden, Stefan, Ellenberg & Toby, A P.C.
San Ramon, CA
Golden, Stephanie Lachman .... Fairfax, VA
Golden, Stephen L. .... San Antonio, TX
Golden, Stephen R. .... Pasadena, CA
Golden, Steven R. .... White Plains, NY
Golden, Steven S. .... Atlanta, GA
Golden, Susan E. .... New York, NY
Golden, Susan M. .... Washington, DC
Golden, Sylvia R. .... San Francisco, CA
Golden, Taylor & Potterfield
Columbia, SC
Golden, Thomas F. .... Tulsa, OK
Golden, Thomas H. .... New York, NY
Golden, Thomas J., III .... Upper Darby, PA
Golden, Thomas M. .... Reading, PA
Golden, Thomas R. .... Seattle, WA
Golden, Vicki G. .... Washington, DC
Golden, W. Brian .... Mount Pocono, PA
Golden, W. Eugene .... Shreveport, LA
Golden, Walter B., III .... McLean, VA
Golden, Webster L. .... Lawrence, KS
Golden, Wexler & Sarnese, P.C.
Elmsford, NY
Garden City, NY
Golden, William C. .... Chicago, IL
Golden, William H. .... Miller, SD
Golden, William J. .... Woodbury, NJ
Golden, William P.
Federal Trade Commission, Office of the General Counsel, GV
Golden, William P., Jr. .... La Place, LA
Golden, William R., Jr. .... New York, NY
Golden (Levy), Donna E.
Hewlett Harbor, NY
Goldenberg, Alison E. .... Baltimore, MD
Goldenberg, Andrea B. .... Charlotte, NC
Goldenberg, Bruce .... Norristown, PA
Goldenberg, Charles I. .... Los Angeles, CA
Goldenberg, David .... San Francisco, CA
Goldenberg, David A. .... Farmington Hills, MI
Goldenberg, David Ari .... Miami Lakes, FL
Goldenberg, David H. .... Hermosa Beach, CA
Goldenberg, David M. .... New York, NY
Goldenberg, David M. .... Parkersburg, WV
Goldenberg, David S. .... Kalamazoo, MI
Goldenberg, Debra Ann .... Arlington, VA
Goldenberg, Eva J. .... Oakland, NJ
Goldenberg, Evan M. .... Miami, FL
Goldenberg, Frank J. .... Gaithersburg, MD
Goldenberg, Gary R. .... Philadelphia, PA
Goldenberg, Gloria E. .... New York, NY
Goldenberg & Goldenberg, A Professional Association .... Minneapolis, MN
Goldenberg, Goldenberg & Stealey, PLLC
Parkersburg, WV
Goldenberg, Harry A. .... Atlantic City, NJ
Goldenberg, Ira S. .... White Plains, NY
Goldenberg, Irwin .... Palm Desert, CA
Goldenberg, Jan .... New York, NY
Goldenberg, Jay S. .... Chicago, IL
Goldenberg, Jeffrey S. .... Cincinnati, OH
Goldenberg, Jill Elizabeth
Indianapolis, IN
Goldenberg, John A. .... New York, NY
Goldenberg, Joseph .... New York, NY
Goldenberg, Judith Elena .... Paterson, NJ
Goldenberg, Judy-Lynn .... Towson, MD
Goldenberg, Lisa R. .... New York, NY
Goldenberg, Lorraine G .... Newark, NJ
Goldenberg, Mackler & Sayegh, P.A.
Atlantic City, NJ
Goldenberg, Mark C. .... Granite City, IL
Goldenberg, Marvin A. .... Cazenovia, NY
Goldenberg, Max .... Marina Del Rey, CA
Goldenberg, Michael
Federal Energy Regulatory Commission, Office of the General Counsel, GV
Goldenberg, Michael R. .... Providence, RI
Goldenberg & Muri .... Providence, RI
Goldenberg, Myron .... Brookline, MA
Goldenberg, Natalie Hope .... McLean, VA
Goldenberg, Norman S. .... Santa Monica, CA
Goldenberg, Ralph D. .... Department of Energy, Office of the General Counsel, GV
Goldenberg, Renee .... Fort Lauderdale, FL
Goldenberg, Richard A. .... Boston, MA
Goldenberg, Robert E. .... New York, NY
Goldenberg, Robert S. .... New York, NY
Goldenberg, Robert T. .... Parkersburg, WV
Goldenberg, Sonseere H.
Minneapolis, MN
Goldenberg, Stephen B. .... Brookline, MA
Goldenberg, Stephen F.
Fort Lauderdale, FL
Goldenberg, Stephen F., P.A., Law Offices of .... Fort Lauderdale, FL
Goldenberg, Stephen M. .... New York, NY
Goldenberg, Steven P. .... Valley Stream, NY
Goldenberg, Steven S. .... Woodbridge, NJ
Goldenberg, Stuart E.
Palm Beach Gardens, FL
Goldenberg, Stuart H. .... St. Louis, MO
Goldenberg, Stuart L. .... Minneapolis, MN
Goldenberg, Susan F. .... Birmingham, MI
Goldenberg, Susan L. .... Chicago, IL
Goldenberg, Walters & Lipson
Brookline, MA
Goldenberg, Warren .... Cleveland, OH
Goldenberg, Wayne R. .... Philadelphia, PA
Goldenblum, William J. .... New York, NY
Goldenbogen, Robert L. .... Port Huron, MI
Goldenetz, John P. .... Defiance, OH
Goldenfarb, Craig M.
West Palm Beach, FL
Goldenfarb, Sondra .... Belleair, FL
Goldenhersh, David H. .... East St. Louis, IL
St. Louis, MO
Goldenhersh, Del A. .... Belleville, IL
Goldenhersh, Edward M. .... St. Louis, MO
Goldenhersh & Goldenhersh, P.C.
Belleville, IL
Goldenhersh, Jerold H. .... Belleville, IL
Goldenhersh, Joseph H., and Jerold H. Goldenhersh .... Belleville, IL
Goldenhersh, Lawrence E. .... Los Angeles, CA
Goldenhersh, Marvin W. .... Belleville, IL
Goldenhersh, Richard P. .... Belleville, IL
Goldenhersh, Robert S. .... St. Louis, MO
Goldenkoff, Abbott H. .... Phoenix, AZ
Golden Norris, Sylvia A. .... Sarasota, FL
Goldenring, Ira .... Ventura, CA
Goldenring, Peter A. .... Ventura, CA
Goldenring & Prosser, A Professional Law Corporation .... Ventura, CA
Goldense, David W. .... Cleveland, OH
Goldenstein, Diane .... Longmont, CO
Goldenstein, Joanna .... New York, NY
Goldenthal, Lawrence E. .... Houston, TX
Goldenziel, Gene E. .... Scranton, PA
Golder, Frederick T. .... Lynnfield, MA
Golder, George A. .... Orlando, FL
Golder, James Robert .... Dallas, TX
Golder, Jay P. .... St. Louis, MO
Golder, Mary Noel .... San Angelo, TX
Golder, Michael R. .... Phoenix, AZ
Golder, Morton I. .... Fenton, MO
Golder, Randee J. .... Delray Beach, FL
Golder, Stephen J. .... Huntington, WV
Golderman, William P. .... Albany, NY
Goldetsky, Steven M. .... Bloomington, MN
Goldey, Mark H. .... New York, NY
Goldfaden, Alissa .... Bloomfield Hills, MI
Goldfaden, Louis .... Houston, TX
Goldfaden, Raymond W. .... New York, NY
Goldfaden, Ronald P. .... Chatham, NJ
Goldfarb, Abraham .... New Orleans, LA
Goldfarb & Abrandt .... New York, NY
White Plains, NY
Goldfarb, Alan .... Miami, FL
Goldfarb, Alan .... Minneapolis, MN
Goldfarb, Allan .... New Rochelle, NY
Goldfarb, Allan M. .... El Paso, TX
Goldfarb, Amy Beth .... Baltimore, MD
Goldfarb, Andrew N. .... Washington, DC
Goldfarb and Associates, P.A.
Minneapolis, MN
Goldfarb, Benjamin J. .... Silver Spring, MD
Towson, MD
Goldfarb, Bernard P. .... Miami, FL
Goldfarb, Bernard S. .... Cleveland, OH
Goldfarb, Brooke Deratany
Washington, DC
Goldfarb, Bruce H. .... New York, NY
Goldfarb, Carl E. .... Miami, FL
Goldfarb, Charles .... Brooklyn, NY
Goldfarb, Cynthia R. .... West Bloomfield, MI
Goldfarb, Dale B. .... Los Angeles, CA

Goldfarb, Daniel ... New York, NY
Goldfarb, David ... Department of Labor, GV
Goldfarb, David ... New York, NY
White Plains, NY
Goldfarb, David B. ... Hempstead, NY
Goldfarb, David S. ... Boca Raton, FL
Goldfarb, Eugene L. ... Chicago, IL
Goldfarb, Evan R. ... St. Louis, MO
Goldfarb & Fleece ... New York, NY
Goldfarb, Gail A. ... Detroit, MI
Goldfarb, Gary M. ... Cleveland, OH
Goldfarb, Gold, Gonzalez & Wald, P.A. ... Miami, FL
Goldfarb & Goldfarb ... Brooklyn, NY
Goldfarb & Greenberg ... New York, NY
Goldfarb, Ira H. ... New York, NY
Goldfarb, Jack Maurice ... Los Angeles, CA
Goldfarb, James E. ... Denver, CO
Goldfarb, Jed ... New York, NY
Goldfarb, Jeffrey A. ... Costa Mesa, CA
Goldfarb, Jeffrey L. ... Southfield, MI
Goldfarb, Jeffrey M. ... Middletown, NY
Goldfarb, Jeffrey M. ... Dallas, TX
Goldfarb, Jessie A. ... Denver, CO
Goldfarb, Joan R. ... Department Of The Interior, Office of the Solicitor, GV
Goldfarb, Joanne D. ... South Euclid, OH
Goldfarb, Joel ... Santa Monica, CA
Goldfarb, Jon C. ... Birmingham, AL
Goldfarb, Katrin Doane ... Simsbury, CT
Goldfarb, Kenneth S. ... Ballston Spa, NY
Goldfarb, Lewis H. ... Auburn Hills, MI
Goldfarb, Lewis H. ... Marysville, OH
Goldfarb & Lipman ... San Francisco, CA
Goldfarb, Mark J. ... New York, NY
Goldfarb, Matthew ... New York, NY
Goldfarb, Matthew S. ... Portland, ME
Goldfarb, Max A. ... Miami, FL
Goldfarb, Merrill D. ... Boston, MA
Goldfarb, Michael A. ... Seattle, WA
Goldfarb, Michael J. ... Melville, NY
Goldfarb, Milton P. ... St. Louis, MO
Goldfarb, Neal ... Arlington, VA
Goldfarb, Phyllis ... Newton, MA
Goldfarb, Posner, Beck, DeHaven & Drewitz ... Washington, PA
Goldfarb, Renee G. ... Chicago, IL
Goldfarb, Richard L. ... Seattle, WA
Goldfarb, Robert ... Miami, FL
Goldfarb, Robyn Stacey ... New York, NY
Goldfarb, Ronald C. ... Edison, NJ
Goldfarb, Ronald L. ... Washington, DC
Goldfarb, Ronald S. ... New York, NY
Goldfarb, Sally ... Camden, NJ
Goldfarb, Samuel ... Los Angeles, CA
Goldfarb, Samuel ... New York, NY
Goldfarb, Samuel Z. ... Chicago, IL
Goldfarb, Scott A. ... New York, NY
Goldfarb, Shara ... New York, NY
Goldfarb, Sheldon I. ... Greenwich, CT
Goldfarb, Stephen M. ... Minneapolis, MN
Goldfarb, Steven A. ... Cleveland, OH
Goldfarb, Steven H. ... San Francisco, CA
Goldfarb, Steven M. ... New York, NY
Goldfarb, Sturman & Averbach ... Encino, CA
Los Angeles, CA
Goldfarb, William K., Law Offices of ... Monroe, NC
Goldfarb-Goldner, Shelley R. ... Bala Cynwyd, PA
Goldfeder, Frederick ... Albany, NY
Goldfeder, Gerald ... Bayside, NY
Goldfeder, Jerry H. ... New York, NY
Goldfeder, Michael A. ... Hermosa Beach, CA
Goldfeder, Steven W. ... New York, NY
Goldfein, Adam ... White Plains, NY
Goldfein, Charlotte R. ... Chicago, IL
Goldfein, Fredric L. ... Philadelphia, PA
Goldfein, Jerome ... Westminster, CA
Goldfein & Joseph, A Professional Corporation ... Wilmington, DE
Princeton, NJ
New York, NY
Philadelphia, PA
Goldfein, Joshua Evan ... New York, NY
Goldfein, Laurence ... New York, NY
Goldfein, Michael R. ... Northbrook, IL
Goldfein, Morton ... Secaucus, NJ
Trenton, NJ
Goldfein, Ronda B. ... Merchantville, NJ
Goldfein, Shepard ... New York, NY
Goldfeld, Herbert ... Coral Springs, FL
Goldfeld, Robert ... New York, NY
Goldfield, Alfred S. ... New York, NY
Goldfield, Carl ... New Haven, CT
Goldfield, Frances N., (Mrs.) ... Marblehead, MA
Goldfield, Harold P. ... Washington, DC
Goldfield, Herschel ... New York, NY
Goldfield, H. T. ... Chelsea, MA
Goldfield, Jonathan ... Haverhill, MA
Goldfield, Robert E. ... Oklahoma City, OK
Goldfield, Steven A. ... Philadelphia, PA
Goldfien, Jeffrey H. ... San Rafael, CA
Goldfien, Lisa A. ... Sausalito, CA
Goldfine & Bowles, P.C. ... Peoria, IL
Goldfine, Dan W. ... Phoenix, AZ
Goldfine, David A.J. ... Washington, DC
Goldfine, Henry S. ... Piscataway, NJ
Goldfine, Julienne K. ... New York, NY
Goldfine, Milton E. ... Boca Raton, FL
Goldfine, Morton S. ... Peoria, IL
Goldfinger, Dina ... New York, NY
Goldfinger, Ellen J. ... Clifton, NJ
Goldfinger & Lassar ... New York, NY
Goldfinger, Peter J. ... Brooklyn, NY
Goldfinger, Rea J. ... Department Of Health And Human Services, Social Security Administration, GV
Goldfinger, Roy S. ... Montgomery, AL
Goldfinger, Roy S., P.C. ... Montgomery, AL
Goldfinger, Scott G. ... New York, NY
Goldfischer, Robin L. ... Newark, NJ
Goldfischer, Stephanie A. ... New York, NY
Goldfischer, Susan M. ... Hudson, MA
Goldfisher, Steven J. ... New York, NY
Goldflam & Barth ... Los Angeles, CA
Goldflam, Hal D. ... Los Angeles, CA
Goldflam, Sheldon L. ... Los Angeles, CA
Goldfluss, Bernard H. ... New York, NY
Goldfluss, Howard E. ... New York, NY
Goldfoot, Josh ... Palo Alto, CA
Goldfrank, Joan L. ... Department of Justice, Environment and Natural Resources Division, GV
Goldfried, Daniel A. ... Phoenix, AZ
Goldfried, Robert M. ... Los Angeles, CA
Goldfus, Mark B. ... Princeton, NJ
Goldgar, A. Benjamin ... Chicago, IL
Goldgar, Eugene ... Houston, TX
Goldgar, Harry ... New Orleans, LA
Goldgehn, Mitchell S. ... Chicago, IL
Goldgehn, Seymour R. ... Buffalo Grove, IL
Goldhaber, David Michael ... Chicago, IL
Goldhaber, Douglas R. ... Everett, PA
Goldhaber, Martin E. ... Pittsburgh, PA
Goldhaber, Michael ... New York, NY
Goldhaber, Richard F. ... Farmingdale, NY
Goldhaber, Robert D. ... Farmingdale, NY
Goldhaber, Stanley ... New York, NY
Goldhaber & Weber ... New York, NY
Goldhagen, Jerry C. ... Atlantic City, NJ
Goldhamer, Paul B. ... Montvale, NJ
Spring Valley, NY
Goldhamer, Theresa W. ... Denver, CO
Goldhammer, Earl ... Columbus, OH
Goldhammer, Florie B. ... Pittsburgh, PA
Goldhammer, Harvey L. ... Glendale, CA
Goldhammer, Joel S. ... Philadelphia, PA
Goldhammer, Joseph M. ... Denver, CO
Goldhand, Joanne I. ... Columbus, OH
Goldheim, Laurie B. ... Pearl River, NY
Goldhill, Nancy ... Edison, NJ
Goldhirsch, Lawrence B. ... New York, NY
Goldhirsch, Lawrence B., P.C. ... New York, NY
White Plains, NY
Goldhirsch, Mary B. ... Newark, NJ
Goldhirsh, Dawn R. ... Chicago, IL
Wheaton, IL
Goldhirsh, Michael ... Wilmette, IL
Goldhush, Douglas H. ... Washington, DC
Goldhush, Elliott ... Garden City, NY
Goldi, Robert B. ... Bingham Farms, MI
Goldich, Geoffrey S. ... Chicago, IL
Goldich, Robert M. ... Philadelphia, PA
Goldich, Stanley E. ... Los Angeles, CA
Goldie, James E. ... Harrison, AR
Goldie, Ray R. ... Rancho Mirage, CA
Goldie, Robert H. ... New York, NY
Goldie, Ron R., (A Professional Corporation) ... Los Angeles, CA
Goldie, Scott B. ... Canton, NY
Watertown, NY
Goldie, Susan L. ... Xenia, OH
Goldin, Amy H. ... Miami, FL
Goldin, Arnold ... Memphis, TN
Goldin, Arnold, P.C. ... Memphis, TN
Goldin, Barry L. ... Allentown, PA
Goldin, Claudia Brett ... Denver, CO
Goldin, David L. ... San Diego, CA
Goldin, David N. ... Albany, NY
Goldin, Edward S. ... Providence, RI
Goldin, Elizabeth E. ... Washington, DC
Goldin, Ely ... Philadelphia, PA
Goldin, Gary A. ... Southfield, MI
Goldin, Jared A. ... San Francisco, CA
Goldin, Jonathan B. ... Roseland, NJ
New York, NY
Goldin, Kenneth G. ... San Francisco, CA
Goldin, Larry M. ... Columbus, OH
Goldin, Laura ... San Francisco, CA
Goldin, Laura A. ... New York, NY
Goldin, Laura J. ... Boston, MA
Goldin, Leon ... Los Osos, CA
Goldin, Lori B. ... Boston, MA
Goldin, M. Stuart ... San Diego, CA
Goldin, Marc S. ... Irvine, CA
Goldin, Martha ... Los Osos, CA
Goldin, Martin S. ... North Brunswick, NJ
Goldin, Merolla & Tutalo ... Providence, RI
Goldin, Morris ... Clark, NJ
Goldin, Rochelle M. ... Philadelphia, PA
Goldin • Sharp ... San Diego, CA
Goldin, Sherry A. ... Providence, RI
Goldin, Stefani ... Loveland, CO
Goldin, Sunny Gale ... Miami, FL
Goldin, Theodore ... Mountain View, CA
Golding, Ayala ... Louisville, KY
Golding, David K. ... Long Beach, CA
Golding, Debra M. ... Department of Labor, Pension and Welfare Benefits, GV
Golding, Frank J. ... New York, NY
Golding, Gilbert J. ... Morrisville, PA
Golding, Glenn W. D. ... Washington, DC
Golding, Harold F. ... Silver Spring, MD
Golding, Henrietta U. ... Myrtle Beach, SC
Golding Holden Cosper Pope & Baker, L.L.P. ... Charlotte, NC
Golding, John G. ... Charlotte, NC
Golding, John T. ... Clearwater, FL
Tampa, FL
Golding, Jonathan F. ... Los Angeles, CA
Golding, Mark A. ... Portland, OR
Golding, Marshall Tamor ... Department of Justice, Civil Division, GV
Golding, Michael J. ... Southfield, MI
Golding, Michael L. ... Cleveland, OH
Golding, Mitchell I. ... Philadelphia, PA
Golding, Natasha L. ... San Francisco, CA
Golding, Pete ... Oakland, ME
Golding, Richard N. ... Chicago, IL
Golding, Sheldon ... Fort Lauderdale, FL
Golding, William ... Seattle, WA
Goldinger, Cary Scott ... Garden City, NY
Goldings, Morris M. ... Boston, MA
Goldinov, Frederick Hilary ... Scottsdale, AZ
Goldizen, Bradley Dale ... Alexandria, VA
Goldkin, Scott P. ... Daytona Beach, FL
Goldkind, Leonard D. ... Oroville, CA
Goldklang, Ira C. ... Universal City, CA
Goldklang, Joyce E. ... Scarsdale, NY
Gold-Levy, Meryl S. ... Miami, FL
Goldlist, Glenda G. ... Fort Lauderdale, FL
Goldlust, Perry F. ... Wilmington, DE
Goldmacher, Roslyn D. ... Hicksville, NY
Goldmacher, Sheila L. ... Berkeley, CA
Goldman, A. Leon ... Chestnut Hill, MA
Goldman, Aaron ... Scarsdale, NY
Goldman, Abr. ... Bronx, NY
Goldman, Abraham N. ... Oregon House, CA
Goldman, Aileen R. ... Sherman, TX
Goldman, Akiva E. ... Madison Heights, MI
Goldman, Alan ... Phoenix, AZ
Goldman, Alan B. ... Floral Park, NY
Goldman, Alan J. ... Providence, RI
Goldman, Alan L. ... Chicago, IL
Goldman, Alan L. ... Springfield, IL
Goldman, Alanna J. ... Los Angeles, CA
Goldman, Albert E. ... Rochester, NY
Goldman, Albert L. ... Boston, MA
Goldman, Allan B. ... Los Angeles, CA
Goldman, Alvin J. ... New York, NY
Goldman, Alvin L. ... Lexington, KY
Goldman, Amy L. ... Los Angeles, CA
Goldman, Anastacia W. ... Knoxville, TN
Goldman, Andrea Greene ... New York, NY
Goldman, Andrea Jill ... Newton, MA
Goldman, Andrea Lee ... Farmingdale, NY
Goldman, Andrew J. ... Los Angeles, CA
Goldman, Andrew L. ... Denver, CO
Chicago, IL
Goldman, Andrew N. ... New York, NY
Goldman, Andrew S. ... Philadelphia, PA
Goldman Antonetti & Córdova ... San Juan, PR
Goldman, Arnold B. ... Lakewood, NJ
Goldman, Arnold J. ... Rochester, NY
Goldman, Arren S. ... Woodbridge, NJ
Goldman, Arthur ... Yonkers, NY
Goldman & Associates ... Atlanta, GA
Goldman and Associates ... Meridian, MS
Goldman, Barry A. ... Chicago, IL
Goldman, Barry D. ... Boca Raton, FL
Goldman, Barry G. ... Lancaster, PA
Goldman, Barry I. ... Los Angeles, CA
Goldman, Barry R. ... Atlanta, GA
Goldman & Beninson ... Lakewood, NJ
Goldman, Benjamin E. ... Los Angeles, CA
Goldman, Bernard M. ... Poughkeepsie, NY
Goldman, Beth M. ... San Francisco, CA
Goldman, Bettie E. ... Department of Justice, Drug Enforcement Administration, GV
Goldman & Biafore ... Providence, RI
Goldman, Bob A. ... Albert Lea, MN
Goldman, Bonnie Lynn ... Mount Holly, NJ
Goldman, Bram J. ... Tucson, AZ
Goldman, Brian A. ... Baltimore, MD
Goldman, Brian A. ... Providence, RI
Goldman, Brian S. ... Bayside, NY
Goldman, Bruce ... Boston, MA
Goldman, Bruce E. ... Roseland, NJ
Goldman, Bruce H. ... Rochester, NY
Goldman, Bruce J. ... Coral Gables, FL
Goldman, Bruce J., P.A., Law Offices of ... Coral Gables, FL
Goldman, Bruce L. ... Northbrook, IL
Goldman, Bruce N. ... Southfield, MI
Goldman, C. David ... New York, NY
Goldman, C. Mitchell ... Philadelphia, PA
Goldman, C. Paige ... Birmingham, AL
Goldman, Callahan & Sturtz, Chtd. ... Albert Lea, MN
Goldman, Candace ... Berkeley, CA
Goldman, Carl A. ... Tampa, FL
Goldman, Carlet, Garrison & Klein ... New York, NY
Goldman, Carmen R. Fernandez ... Brooklyn, NY
Goldman, Catherine M. ... Berkeley, CA
Goldman, Charles ... Santa Cruz, CA
Goldman, Charles D. ... Washington, DC
Goldman, Charles J., (P.A.) ... Hollywood, FL
Goldman, Charles M. ... Boston, MA
Goldman, Charles N. ... New York, NY
Goldman, Charles S. ... Walnut Creek, CA
Goldman, Costa, Getman & Biryla ... Buffalo, NY
Goldman, Craig A. ... Burlingame, CA
Goldman, Craig P. ... Minneapolis, MN
Goldman & Curtis, P.C. ... Lowell, MA
Goldman, Cynthia Leap ... Denver, CO
Goldman, Dana M. ... Agawam, MA
Goldman, Daniel B. ... New York, NY
Goldman, Daniel C. ... Boca Raton, FL
Goldman, Daniel E. ... Morristown, NJ
Goldman, Daniel M. ... Danvers, MA
Goldman, Daniel S. ... Chicago, IL
Goldman, Daphne ... Philadelphia, PA
Goldman, David ... Oakland, CA
Goldman, David ... North Bay Village, FL
Goldman, David ... New York, NY
Goldman, David ... Schenectady, NY
Goldman, David ... Pittsburgh, PA
Goldman, David A. ... Chicago, IL
Goldman, David A. ... Lewistown, PA
Goldman, David B. ... Los Angeles, CA
Goldman, David E. ... North Miami Beach, FL
Goldman, David H. ... Des Moines, IA
Goldman, David H., P.C. ... Des Moines, IA
Goldman, David J. ... Minneapolis, MN
Goldman, David M. ... Chicago, IL
Goldman, David M. ... New York, NY
Goldman, David R. ... Los Angeles, CA
Goldman, David W. ... Hamden, CT
Goldman, David W. ... Cincinnati, OH
Goldman, David W. ... Sumter, SC
Goldman, Deborah B. ... Washington, DC
Goldman, Deborah G. ... Rochester, NY
Goldman, Deborah J. ... Torrance, CA
Goldman, Deborah L. ... White Plains, NY
Goldman, Dennis ... Meridian, MS
Goldman, Dennis J. ... Columbus, OH
Goldman, Diane ... Pebble Beach, CA
Goldman, Diane ... Sherman Oaks, CA
Goldman, Dianna Lynn ... Glenview, IL
Goldman, Dolores ... Hammond, IN
Goldman, Donald A. ... Los Angeles, CA
Goldman, Donald H. ... Jupiter, FL
Goldman, Donald J. ... Jericho, NY
Goldman, Donald L. ... Cleveland, OH
Goldman, Donna Bradford ... Baltimore, MD
Goldman, Donna G. ... Plantation, FL
Goldman, Donna Smith ... Silver Spring, MD
Goldman, Dov ... Philadelphia, PA
Goldman, E. Chaim ... Menlo Park, CA
Goldman, Edith A. ... Boston, MA
Goldman, Edward ... Oklahoma City, OK
Goldman, Edward B. ... Ann Arbor, MI
Goldman, Edward R. ... Cincinnati, OH
Goldman, Edward S. ... Chicago, IL
Goldman, Eleanor R. ... New York, NY
Goldman, Eliot ... New York, NY
Goldman, Elisabeth Paris, (P.S.C.) ... Lexington, KY
Goldman, Elizabeth M. ... Boston, MA
Goldman, Ellen ... Pomona, CA
Goldman, Ellen A. ... Fort Lauderdale, FL
Goldman, Ellen S. ... Kansas City, MO
Goldman, Ellen W. ... Trumbull, CT
Goldman, Elliot H. ... Chicago, IL
Goldman, Emanuel ... Chicago, IL
Goldman, Eric ... Berkeley, CA
Goldman, Eric ... Palo Alto, CA
Goldman, Eric S. ... New York, NY
Goldman, Eric Scott ... Boston, MA
Goldman, Erwin R. ... North Bergen, NJ
Goldman, Eugene I. ... Washington, DC
Goldman, Eva J. Csiszar ... San Francisco, CA
Goldman, Evan L. ... Metuchen, NJ
Goldman, Ezra N. ... Madison Heights, MI
Goldman, F. Elliot ... Brea, CA
Goldman & Felcoski, P.A. ... Miami, FL
Naples, FL
Goldman, Fern E. ... Cincinnati, OH
Goldman, Foster S., Jr. ... Pittsburgh, PA
Goldman, Frank G. ... Atlanta, GA
Ithaca, NY
Goldman, Fred B. ... Potomac, MD
Rockville, MD
Goldman, Fred B., P.A. ... Potomac, MD
Rockville, MD
Goldman, Gail G. ... Los Angeles, CA
Goldman, Gary ... New York, NY
Goldman, Gary ... Philadelphia, PA
Goldman, Gary D. ... White Plains, NY
Goldman, Gary R. ... White Plains, NY
Goldman, Gary R., P.C. ... White Plains, NY
Goldman, Gary S. ... Palm Springs, CA
Goldman, Gary S. ... Cincinnati, OH
Goldman, Geoffrey B. ... New York, NY
Goldman, Gerald ... Washington, DC
Goldman, Gerald ... Hackensack, NJ
New York, NY
Goldman, Gerald A. ... Chicago, IL
Goldman, Gilbert Charles ... Atlanta, GA
Goldman, Gilbert M. ... New York, NY
Goldman, Ginny L. ... Boca Raton, FL
Goldman, Ginny L., P.A. ... Boca Raton, FL
Goldman & Gladstone ... New York, NY
Scarsdale, NY
Goldman, Glen B. ... Denver, CO
Goldman, Glen M. ... Wayzata, MN
Goldman, Glenn D. ... Boca Raton, FL
Goldman, Gloria A. ... Tucson, AZ
Goldman, Gloria A., P.C. ... Tucson, AZ
Goldman & Goldman ... Berkeley, CA
Goldman & Goldman ... Chicago, IL
Goldman & Goldman ... Brooklyn, NY
Goldman & Goldman ... Farmingdale, NY
Goldman & Goldman ... Rochester, NY
Goldman & Goldman ... Oklahoma City, OK
Goldman & Goldman ... Philadelphia, PA
Goldman & Greenbaum, P.C. ... New York, NY
Goldman, Greer S. ... Department of Justice, Environment and Natural Resources Division, GV
Goldman, Gregg I. ... New York, NY
Goldman, Gregg P. ... Santa Monica, CA
Goldman & Grossman ... New York, NY
Goldman Gruder Woods & Miller, LLC ... Norwalk, CT
Goldman, H. Shaina ... San Rafael, CA
Goldman & Hafetz ... New York, NY
Goldman, Hailey A. ... Fort Lauderdale, FL
Goldman, Hannah G. ... Roseland, NJ
Goldman, Harold ... Clifton, NJ

Goldman, Harold H., (P.A.) Port St. Lucie, FL
Goldman, Harold L. .... Highland Park, IL
Goldman, Harry H. .... Seattle, WA
Goldman, Harry, Jr. .... Baltimore, MD
Goldman, Harry T., III .... Waterproof, LA
Goldman, Harvey A. .... Miami, FL
Goldman, Henry T. .... Boston, MA
Goldman, Herbert .... Baltimore, MD
Goldman, Herbert C. .... Chicago, IL
Goldman, Herbert C., P.C. .... Chicago, IL
Goldman, Herman, The Firm of New York, NY
Goldman, Hillel .... Danbury, CT
Goldman, Hilton .... West Orange, NJ
Goldman, Horowitz & Cherno, LLP Westbury, NY
Goldman, Howard B. .... Chicago, IL
Goldman, Howard J. .... New York, NY
Goldman, Howard R. .... Brooklyn, NY
Goldman, Howard S. .... Boston, MA
Goldman, Howard S. .... Madison, WI
Goldman, Howard V. Department of the Army, Office, Chief of Engineers/Headquarters, U.S. Army Corps of Engineers, GV
Goldman, Hyman .... Los Angeles, CA
Goldman, Ilan .... New York, NY
Goldman, Ilene Helen .... Metairie, LA
Goldman, Ira H. .... Hartford, CT
Goldman, Ira I .... Staten Island, NY
Goldman, Irve J. .... Norwalk, CT
Goldman, Irving .... Plattsburgh, NY
Goldman, Jack .... Los Angeles, CA
Goldman, Jack H. .... Washington, DC
Goldman, Jacob .... Boston, MA
Goldman, Jacob .... New York, NY
Goldman, Jacob J. .... Bloomfield, CT
Goldman, Jacobson, Kramer & Fradkin, A Professional Corporation .... Roseland, NJ
Goldman, James L. .... Los Angeles, CA
Goldman, Jan D. .... Garden City, NY
Goldman, Janet .... Warwick, RI
Goldman, Jason B. .... Punta Gorda, FL
Goldman, Jay A. .... Valparaiso, IN
Goldman, Jay M. .... Oakland, CA
Goldman, Jay R. .... Upper Marlboro, MD
Goldman, Jay W. .... Newton, MA
Goldman, Jean R. .... New York, NY
Goldman, Jeffrey .... Bordentown, NJ
Mount Holly, NJ
Robbinsville, NJ
Goldman, Jeffrey A. .... Chicago, IL
Goldman, Jeffrey D., (A Professional Corporation) .... Los Angeles, CA
Goldman, Jeffrey E. .... Philadelphia, PA
Goldman, Jeffrey L. .... New York, NY
Goldman, Jeffrey S. .... Plantation, FL
Goldman, Jeffrey S. .... Chicago, IL
Goldman, Jeffrey W. .... Brookline, MA
Goldman, Jennifer E. .... Garden City, NY
Goldman, Jennifer E. .... New York, NY
Goldman, Jennifer S. .... Dallas, TX
Goldman, Jerome E. .... Hallandale Beach, FL
Goldman, Jerome M. .... Melvindale, MI
Goldman, Jerome S. .... Columbus, OH
Goldman, Jerry A. .... Rochester, NY
Goldman, Jerry S. .... New York, NY
Philadelphia, PA
Goldman, Jerry S., & Associates, P.C. Fort Lauderdale, FL
New York, NY
Philadelphia, PA
Goldman, Jessica L. .... Seattle, WA
Goldman, Jill R. .... Media, PA
Goldman, Joan F. .... Chicago, IL
Goldman, Jo-Ann L. .... Little Rock, AR
Goldman, Jodi P. .... Rochester, NY
Goldman, Joel .... Rolling Meadows, IL
Goldman, Joel .... Peabody, MA
Goldman, Joel A. .... Los Angeles, CA
Goldman, Joel J. .... Rochester, NY
Goldman, Joel K. .... Miami, FL
Goldman, Joel K. .... Kansas City, MO
Goldman, Joel L. .... Jacksonville, FL
Goldman, Joel S. .... San Francisco, CA
Goldman, Joel S. .... Atlanta, GA
Goldman, John R. .... Princeton, NJ
New York, NY
Goldman, Jon D. .... Evansville, IN
Goldman, Jos. B. .... New York, NY
Goldman, Joseph .... Beverly Hills, CA
Goldman, Joseph A. .... Washington, DC
Goldman, Joseph B. .... Washington, DC
Goldman, Joseph L. .... New York, NY
Goldman, Joy S. .... Chicago, IL
Goldman, Judith M. .... Sarasota, FL
Goldman, Judith R. .... Washington, DC
Goldman & Kagon, Law Corporation Los Angeles, CA
Goldman & Kaplan, Ltd. .... Mesa, AZ
Phoenix, AZ
Tempe, AZ
Goldman, Karen A. National Science Foundation, Office of Inspector General, GV
Goldman, Karen L. .... Burbank, CA
Goldman, Karin Kunstler .... New York, NY
Goldman, Kathryn Miller .... Baltimore, MD
Goldman, Kenneth A. .... Los Angeles, CA
Goldman, Kenneth J. .... Anchorage, AK
Goldman, Kenneth L. .... Los Angeles, CA
Goldman, Kenneth L., Professional Corporation Los Angeles, CA
Goldman, Kenneth M. .... Atlantic City, NJ
Goldman, Kenneth M. .... Kenilworth, NJ
Goldman, Kenneth S. .... Syracuse, NY
Goldman, Larry J. .... San Antonio, TX

Goldman, Laura S. .... Boston, MA
Goldman, Laurence L. .... Chicago, IL
Goldman, Laurence R. .... Los Angeles, CA
Goldman, Laurence R. Woodland Hills, CA
Goldman Law Firm, The .... San Francisco, CA
Goldman Law Offices .... Columbus, OH
Goldman Law Offices, The .... Allentown, PA
Exton, PA
Quakertown, PA
Goldman, Lawrence A. .... Newark, NJ
Goldman, Lawrence J. .... Charlotte, NC
Goldman, Lawrence M. .... Los Angeles, CA
Goldman, Lawrence S. .... New York, NY
Goldman & LeBrun, Professional Association Concord, NH
Goldman, Lee .... Detroit, MI
Goldman, Leonard A. .... Los Angeles, CA
Goldman, Leonard A. .... Fairfield, IA
Goldman, Leonard A., & Associates Los Angeles, CA
Goldman, Leslie Ann .... Houston, TX
Goldman, Leslie Ayn .... Washington, DC
Goldman, Leslie J. .... Washington, DC
Goldman, Lester H. .... St. Ann, MO
Goldman, Lewis A. .... New York, NY
Goldman, Lewis H. .... Arlington, VA
Goldman, Lewis H., P.C. .... Arlington, VA
Goldman, Linda Ann .... Brooklyn, NY
Goldman, Linda B .... Needham, MA
Goldman, Linda kay Department of Agriculture, Farm Service Agency, GV
Goldman, Linda Marie .... Arlington, VA
Goldman, Linda S. .... Los Angeles, CA
Goldman, Lisa B. .... New York, NY
Goldman, Lisa M. .... Newark, NJ
Goldman, Lonnie .... San Francisco, CA
Goldman, Loretta M. .... Washington, DC
Goldman, Louis B. .... Chicago, IL
Goldman, Louis S. .... Dayton, OH
Goldman, Lowell S. .... Milwaukee, WI
Goldman, Lucille H. .... Miami Beach, FL
Goldman, Lydia D. .... Santa Rosa, CA
Goldman, Lynda B. .... Los Angeles, CA
Goldman, Macey J. .... Shrewsbury, MA
Goldman, Mara K. .... Palo Alto, CA
Goldman, Marc A. .... Farmington Hills, MI
Goldman, Marc A., & Associates, P.C. Farmington Hills, MI
Goldman, Marc L. .... Flint, MI
Goldman, Margie Nan .... Pittsburgh, PA
Goldman, Mari .... Sacramento, CA
Goldman, Mark .... East Orange, NJ
Goldman, Mark A. .... Los Angeles, CA
Goldman, Mark D. .... Southfield, MI
Goldman, Mark E. .... Los Angeles, CA
Goldman, Mark L. .... Farmingdale, NY
Goldman, Mark S. .... Philadelphia, PA
Goldman, Marshall & Muszynski, P.C. Philadelphia, PA
Goldman, Marshall S. .... White Plains, NY
Goldman, Marshall S., P.C. White Plains, NY
Goldman, Martin .... Jamaica, NY
Goldman, Martin B. .... Pasadena, CA
Goldman, Martin C. .... Swampscott, MA
Goldman, Martin F. .... Los Angeles, CA
Goldman, Martin S. .... West Orange, NJ
Goldman, Martin Wm. .... New York, NY
Goldman, Marvin G. .... New York, NY
Goldman, Matt D. .... Coral Gables, FL
Goldman, Matthew J. .... Sacramento, CA
Goldman, Matthew R. .... Cleveland, OH
Goldman & Maurer, P.C. .... Bayside, NY
Goldman, Max .... Philadelphia, PA
Goldman, Max .... San Juan, PR
Goldman, Maxwell H. .... Chicago, IL
Goldman, Melanie P. .... New York, NY
Goldman, Melvin L. .... Bluff, UT
Goldman, Melvin R. .... San Francisco, CA
Goldman, Merton B. .... El Paso, TX
Goldman, Michael .... New York, NY
Goldman, Michael A. .... Durango, CO
Goldman, Michael D. .... Wilmington, DE
Goldman, Michael D. .... Treasury Department, Internal Revenue Service, GV
Goldman, Michael E. .... Trenton, NJ
Goldman, Michael F. .... Washington, DC
Goldman, Michael H. .... Philadelphia, PA
Goldman, Michael J. .... Atlanta, GA
Goldman, Michael K. .... Fairfax, VA
Goldman, Michael L. .... Norwalk, CT
Goldman, Michael L. .... Rochester, NY
Goldman, Michael M. .... Upton, NY
Goldman, Michael P. .... Chicago, IL
Goldman, Michael R. .... Chicago, IL
Goldman, Michael S. .... New York, NY
Goldman, Mitchell A. .... Fort Washington, PA
Goldman, Mitchell M. .... Miami, FL
Goldman, Mitchell S. .... Cocoa, FL
Melbourne, FL
Goldman, Morris .... New York, NY
Goldman, Morris .... Philadelphia, PA
Goldman, Murray .... Miami, FL
Goldman, Myron .... Fort Lauderdale, FL
Goldman, Nadia .... Potomac, MD
Goldman, Nathan .... Louisville, KY
Goldman, Nathan C. .... Houston, TX
Goldman, Nathan D. .... Jacksonville, FL
Goldman, Neal D. .... Cambridge, MA
Goldman, Neal M. .... New York, NY
Goldman, Neil D. .... Washington, DC
Alexandria, VA
Goldman, Newman, Shinder and Franklin, LLP Rochester, NY
Goldman, Norman .... Encino, CA
Goldman, Norman E. .... Chicago, IL

Goldman, Norman H. .... Highland, IN
Goldman, Pam .... Pittsburgh, PA
Goldman, Patrice L. .... San Francisco, CA
Goldman, Paul J. .... Albany, NY
Goldman, Paul M. .... Merritt Island, FL
Goldman, Paul Z. .... Hayward, CA
Goldman, Paula K. .... Bethesda, MD
Goldman, Pearl .... Fort Lauderdale, FL
Goldman, Perry S. .... San Jose, CA
Goldman, Peter A. .... Rye Brook, NY
Goldman, Peter B. .... Tucson, AZ
Goldman, Peter R. .... Fort Lauderdale, FL
Goldman, Philip M. .... Minneapolis, MN
Goldman, Phyllis Lamb .... Evanston, IL
Goldman & Piersma, P.C. .... Highland, IN
Goldman & Presser .... Jacksonville, FL
Goldman, R. Michael .... Jamestown, NY
Goldman, Ralph C. .... Lake Worth, FL
Goldman, Randolph L. .... Philadelphia, PA
Goldman, Rebecca A. .... Washington, DC
Goldman, Renée .... New Haven, CT
Goldman, Richard .... Santa Barbara, CA
Goldman, Richard A. .... Boston, MA
Goldman, Richard B. .... Thousand Oaks, CA
Goldman, Richard C. .... St. Louis, MO
Goldman, Richard G. .... Treasury Department, Internal Revenue Service, GV
Goldman, Richard H. .... Boston, MA
Goldman, Richard J. .... Boca Raton, FL
Goldman, Richard J. .... Kingston, NY
Goldman, Richard L. .... Granby, MA
Goldman, Richard L., (P.C.) New York, NY
Scarsdale, NY
Goldman, Richard M. .... Palo Alto, CA
Goldman, Richard Marc .... Augusta, ME
Goldman, Richard S. .... Princeton, NJ
Goldman, Robbins & Rogers, LLP Durango, CO
Goldman, Robert A. .... San Francisco, CA
Goldman, Robert B. .... Key West, FL
Goldman, Robert B. West Palm Beach, FL
Goldman, Robert C. .... New York, NY
Goldman, Robert E. .... Santa Monica, CA
Goldman, Robert E. .... New York, NY
Goldman, Robert F. .... Nashville, TN
Goldman, Robert G. .... Chicago, IL
Goldman, Robert H. .... Chicago, IL
Goldman, Robert J. .... Palo Alto, CA
Goldman, Robert M. .... Baltimore, MD
Goldman, Robert M. .... Oklahoma City, OK
Goldman, Robert P. .... Rockville, MD
Goldman, Robert P. .... Boston, MA
Goldman, Robert S. .... Wilmington, DE
Goldman, Robert S. .... Tallahassee, FL
Goldman, Robert S. .... Warwick, RI
Goldman, Robert W. .... Naples, FL
Goldman, Robin A. .... Albany, NY
Goldman, Robyn S. .... Beverly Hills, CA
Goldman, Roger A. .... New York, NY
Goldman, Roger L. .... St. Louis, MO
Goldman, Roger O. .... New York, NY
Goldman, Roger S. .... Washington, DC
Goldman, Roger S. .... Miami, FL
Goldman, Ronald A. .... New York, NY
Goldman, Ronald E. .... Oakland, CA
Goldman, Ronald G. .... Garden City, NY
Goldman, Ronald L.M. .... Marina Del Rey, CA
Goldman, Ronald M. .... Torrance, CA
Goldman, Ronald P. .... San Francisco, CA
Goldman, Ronald S. .... Rochester, NY
Goldman, Rori Lisa .... Indianapolis, IN
Goldman & Rosen, Ltd. .... Akron, OH
Goldman & Rosenthal .... Columbus, OH
Goldman & Ross .... Burbank, CA
Goldman, Rothenberg, Estner & Haines, LLP .... Boston, MA
Goldman, Roy L. .... New York, NY
Goldman, Rubin & Shapiro .... Dayton, OH
Goldman, Russell P., (P.C.) .... Eatontown, NJ
Goldman, Ruth .... Chicago, IL
Goldman, S. James .... Pittsburgh, PA
Goldman, Sam .... St. Louis, MO
Goldman, Samuel .... Akron, OH
Goldman, Samuel, & Associates New York, NY
Goldman, Samuel N. .... Pittsburgh, PA
Goldman, Samuel Z. .... Miami Beach, FL
Goldman, Sandra R. .... Denver, CO
Goldman, Sanford M. .... New York, NY
Goldman, Scott .... Bronx, NY
Goldman, Scott David .... Charleston, WV
Goldman, Seth R. .... New York, NY
Goldman, Shane Heather .... Tavernier, FL
Goldman, Sherri Litt .... Newark, NJ
Goldman, Sheryl Powers .... Westbury, NY
Goldman, Sheryl S. .... Lake Success, NY
Goldman, Sidney I. .... Longwood, FL
Goldman, Skeen & Wadler, P.A. Baltimore, MD
Goldman, Solomon .... Bangor, ME
Goldman, Stan .... Boston, MA
Goldman, Stanford N., Jr. .... Boston, MA
Goldman, Stanley A. .... Los Angeles, CA
Goldman, Stanley D. .... Montville, NJ
Goldman, Stanley I. .... Washington, DC
Goldman, Stephen B. .... Westfield, NJ
Goldman, Stephen D. .... Chevy Chase, MD
Goldman, Stephen E. .... Hartford, CT
Goldman, Stephen Mark .... Washington, DC
Goldman, Stephen P. .... Washington, DC
Goldman, Stephen R. .... Concord, NH
Goldman, Steven .... Glencoe, IL
Goldman, Steven .... Allentown, PA
Exton, PA
Quakertown, PA

Goldman, Steven E. .... Fort Lauderdale, FL
Miami, FL
Goldman, Steven F. .... Brooklyn, NY
Goldman, Steven F. .... New York, NY
Goldman, Steven H. .... Newton, MA
Goldman, Steven H. .... Clayton, MO
Goldman, Steven I. .... Atlanta, GA
Goldman, Steven J. .... Warwick, RI
Goldman, Steven M. .... Des Plaines, IL
Goldman, Steven M. .... Newark, NJ
New York, NY
Goldman, Steven M. .... New York, NY
Goldman, Steven Mark .... Washington, DC
Goldman, Stuart B. .... New York, NY
Goldman, Susan Lacy .... Wilton, CT
Goldman, Teri .... Stockton, CA
Goldman, Teri B. .... St. Louis, MO
Goldman, Theodore S. .... New York, NY
Goldman, Thomas F. .... Newtown, PA
Goldman, Thomas F., & Associates Newtown, PA
Goldman, Thomas L. .... Meridian, MS
Goldman, Tyler J. .... Los Angeles, CA
Goldman, Varda A. .... Schaumburg, IL
Goldman & Vetter, P.A. .... Baltimore, MD
Goldman, W. David Hot Springs National Park, AR
Goldman, W. David, P.A. Hot Springs National Park, AR
Goldman & Warshaw, P.C. .... Montville, NJ
Morristown, NJ
Newark, NJ
New York, NY
Goldman & Weintraub .... New York, NY
Goldman, William .... Columbus, GA
Goldman, William .... Auburn, NY
Goldman, William A. .... Columbus, OH
Goldman, William G. .... Palo Alto, CA
Goldman, William J. .... Rochester, NY
Goldman, William L. .... Washington, DC
Goldman, William L. .... Doylestown, PA
Levittown, PA
Goldman, William L., Jr. .... Doylestown, PA
Levittown, PA
Goldman, William L., P.C., Law Offices of Doylestown, PA
Levittown, PA
Goldman, William M. .... New York, NY
Goldman, William S. .... Arlington, VA
Goldmark, Frances .... Princeton, NJ
Goldmeer, Michele .... New York, NY
Goldmeier, Karen E. .... Washington, DC
Goldmeier, Norman P. .... Skokie, IL
Goldner, Abraham B. .... New York, NY
Goldner, Allan .... Cleveland, OH
Goldner, Andrew M. .... New York, NY
Goldner, Anthony M. .... Chicago, IL
Goldner, Arthur P. .... Oxford, OH
Goldner, Barry L. .... Bakersfield, CA
Goldner, Benjamin .... Margate, FL
Goldner, Bruce J. .... New York, NY
Goldner, Charles W., Jr. .... Little Rock, AR
Goldner, David R. .... Newton, MA
Goldner, Eric D., Law Office of Los Angeles, CA
Goldner, Harold M. .... Philadelphia, PA
Goldner, Herman W. .... Tampa, FL
Goldner, Jesse A. .... St. Louis, MO
Goldner, Justin L. .... Beverly Hills, CA
Goldner, Leonard H. .... Bohemia, NY
Goldner, Lester .... Bethesda, MD
Goldner, Lisa McKinney .... Indianapolis, IN
Goldner, Mark .... Pittsburgh, PA
Goldner, Mark A. .... Elm Grove, WI
Goldner, Michael D. .... Minneapolis, MN
Goldner, Michael H. .... Tampa, FL
Goldner, Saren .... New York, NY
Goldner, Seth L. .... Southfield, MI
Goldner, Seth L., P.C. .... Southfield, MI
Goldner, Sidney J. .... Brooklyn, NY
Goldner, Sommers, Scrudder & Bass Atlanta, GA
Marietta, GA
Goldner, Stephen L. .... Atlanta, GA
Goldner, Theresa A., Law Offices of Bakersfield, CA
Goldner, Wendy S. .... Freehold, NJ
Goldoftas, Tobi .... Cleveland Heights, OH
Goldowitz, Israel Pension Benefit Guaranty Corporation, Office of the General Counsel, GV
Goldowitz, Mark Allen .... Oakland, CA
Goldpaugh & Associates, P.C. .... Detroit, MI
Goldpaugh, John J. .... Detroit, MI
Gold-Rand, Anne S. .... Upper Marlboro, MD
Goldrich, David L. .... Harrison, NY
Goldrich, Kenneth S., P.C. Hackensack, NJ
Goldrich, Thomas W., Jr. .... San Diego, CA
Goldrick, Daniel E. .... Falmouth, MA
Goldrick, Janet M. .... Newton, MA
Goldrick, Michael J. .... Chicago, IL
Goldrick, Miles T. .... Santa Barbara, CA
Goldrick, Thomas A. .... Chicago, IL
Goldring, Eric J. .... Red Bank, NJ
Goldring, Esther .... Owings Mills, MD
Goldring, Fred E. .... Beverly Hills, CA
Goldring, Gary F. .... New York, NY
Goldring & Goldring, P.A. .... Red Bank, NJ
Goldring, Irwin D. .... Los Angeles, CA
Goldring, Kalman A. .... Pittsburgh, PA
Goldring, Lee M. .... Torrance, CA
Goldring, Michael W. .... Fresno, CA
Goldring, Stuart J. .... New York, NY
Goldring, Susan L. .... Tinton Falls, NJ
Goldrosen, Donald N. .... Falls Church, VA
Goldrosen, John J. .... Boston, MA
Golds, Howard B. .... Riverside, CA

Golds, Irwin L. ....Palm Desert, CA
Goldsack, John Wood ....North Plainfield, NJ
Goldsamt, Bonnie Blume ....Verona, NJ
Goldsamt, Seth T. ....New York, NY
Goldsand, Corey A. ....Albuquerque, NM
Goldsand, Richard I. ....Brewster, NY
Goldsand, Ronald ....Peekskill, NY
Goldsberry, Francis M., II
Sacramento, CA
Goldsberry, Francis M., III
Sacramento, CA
Goldsberry Freeman & Swanson, L.L.P.
Sacramento, CA
Goldsberry, L. Alan ....Athens, OH
Goldsborough, Charles R., Jr. ....Towson, MD
Goldsborough, John W. ....Philadelphia, PA
Goldsborough, Judith L. ....New York, NY
Goldsborough, Leslie E., III ....Baltimore, MD
Goldsborough, Nicholas ....Annapolis, MD
Goldsborough, Nicholas Ridgely
Encino, CA
Goldsborough, Phillips L., III
Baltimore, MD
Goldsby, Keenan R. ....Fairfax, VA
Goldsby, Larry F. ....Carrollton, MO
Goldsby, Matthew W. ....Los Angeles, CA
Goldscheid, Julie ....New York, NY
Goldscheider, Peter F. ....Palo Alto, CA
Goldscheider, Robert ....New York, NY
Goldscheider, Sidney ....Baltimore, MD
Goldschein, Perry ....Whippany, NJ
Goldschein, Robert D. ....Los Angeles, CA
Goldschein, Scott B. ....Rockville, MD
Goldschlag, Robert A., (P.A.) ....Freehold, NJ
Goldschlager, Carl ....Austin, TX
Goldschmid, Harvey J. ....New York, NY
Goldschmid & Kozma, P.C. ....Detroit, MI
Goldschmid, Michael P. ....New York, NY
Goldschmid, Robert M. ....Detroit, MI
Goldschmid, Vernon ....Los Angeles, CA
Goldschmidt, Aaron R.
Federal Communications Commission,
Common Carrier Bureau, GV
Goldschmidt, Barry
Fort George G. Meade, MD
Goldschmidt, Carolyn B., P.C., The Law Office
of ....Tucson, AZ
Goldschmidt, Carolyn Beth ....Tucson, AZ
Goldschmidt, Daniel Jack ....East Hartford, CT
Goldschmidt, David J. ....New York, NY
Goldschmidt, Diane S. ....Oklahoma City, OK
Goldschmidt & Goldschmidt ....New York, NY
Goldschmidt, Henry J. ....New York, NY
Goldschmidt, Jill H. ....Chicago, IL
Goldschmidt, Joel J. ....New York, NY
Goldschmidt, John W., Jr.
Philadelphia, PA
Goldschmidt, Lawrence E. ....New York, NY
Goldschmidt, Lisa G. ....King Of Prussia, PA
Goldschmidt, Lynn H. ....Chicago, IL
Goldschmidt, Neil ....Portland, OR
Goldschmidt, Stanley H. ....Washington, DC
Goldschmidt, Sylvia ....Elmsford, NY
New York, NY
Pearl River, NY
Goldser, Ronald S. ....Minneapolis, MN
Goldsher & Goldsher ....Chicago, IL
Goldsher, Mark A. ....Chicago, IL
Goldsher, Scott B. ....Chicago, IL
Goldshine, Malcolm S. ....Los Angeles, CA
Goldsholl, Scot P. ....Little Rock, AR
Goldsholle, Gerry H. ....Mill Valley, CA
Goldshore, Lewis P. ....Plainsboro, NJ
Goldshore & Wolf, P.C. ....Plainsboro, NJ
Trenton, NJ
Goldsman, Floyd C. ....East Orange, NJ
Goldsman, Gene ....Santa Ana, CA
Goldsman, Melvin S. ....Los Angeles, CA
Goldsmith, Adam R. ....New York, NY
Goldsmith, Adrianne ....Salt Lake City, UT
Goldsmith, Alan E. ....Department of the Navy,
Office of the Judge Advocate General, GV
Goldsmith, Alvin G. ....Worcester, MA
Goldsmith, Amy B. ....New York, NY
Goldsmith & Anderson ....Radford, VA
Goldsmith, Andrew David
Department of Justice,
Environment and Natural Resources
Division, GV
Goldsmith, Andrew Steven ....New York, NY
Goldsmith, Anthony E. ....Topanga, CA
Goldsmith & Associates, Ltd.
Minneapolis, MN
Goldsmith, Barbara S. ....Newark, NJ
Goldsmith, Barry R. ....Washington, DC
Goldsmith, Barry S. ....Washington, DC
Goldsmith & Bogisch, L.L.P. ....Austin, TX
Goldsmith, Brooks P. ....Lancaster, SC
Goldsmith, Brooks P. ....Rock Hill, SC
Goldsmith, Bruce L. ....Lisle, IL
Goldsmith & Burns ....Los Angeles, CA
Tarzana, CA
Goldsmith, C. Frank, Jr. ....Marion, NC
Goldsmith, C. Oliver ....Glenwood, MD
Goldsmith, Charles J. ....Cincinnati, OH
Goldsmith, Claude O. ....Pasadena, CA
Goldsmith, Claude W. ....Port Arthur, TX
Goldsmith, Dale J. ....Los Angeles, CA
Goldsmith, Daniel S. ....New York, NY
Goldsmith, Dara J. ....Las Vegas, NV
Goldsmith, David H. ....New York, NY
Goldsmith, David J. ....Jericho, NY
Goldsmith, David J. ....New York, NY
Goldsmith, Dawn B. ....Rockville, MD
Goldsmith, Debra L. ....Mount Olive, NJ
Goldsmith, Donald A. ....New York, NY
Goldsmith, Donald W. ....Berkeley, CA
Goldsmith, Earl A. ....Highland Park, IL
Goldsmith, Earl J., Jr. ....Cincinnati, OH
Goldsmith, Edna ....Albany, NY
Goldsmith, Edwin M., III
Philadelphia, PA
Goldsmith, Elaine B. ....New York, NY
Goldsmith, Esten H. ....Concord, NC
Goldsmith, Eugene N. ....Nogales, AZ
Tucson, AZ
Goldsmith, Frederick B. ....Pittsburgh, PA
Goldsmith, Gary W. ....St. Paul, MN
Goldsmith, Gayle S. ....Cincinnati, OH
Goldsmith, Geo. W. ....Carmichael, CA
Goldsmith, Gerald P. ....New York, NY
Goldsmith, Gerson F. ....Portland, OR
Goldsmith, Gilah G. ....Department of Defense,
Defense Legal Services Agency, GV
Goldsmith, Glen R., & Associates
Melbourne, FL
Miami, FL
Goldsmith, Glen R., & Associates, P.A.
Miami, FL
Goldsmith & Goldsmith ....Cincinnati, OH
Goldsmith, Goldsmith & Dews, P.A.
Marion, NC
Goldsmith, Gordon A. ....Duarte, CA
Goldsmith & Grout, P.A. ....Orlando, FL
Tallahassee, FL
Winter Park, FL
Goldsmith & Guymon, P.C.
Las Vegas, NV
Goldsmith, Harry L. ....Memphis, TN
Goldsmith, Harvey S. ....Strongsville, OH
Goldsmith, Herbert A., Jr. ....Arlington, VA
Goldsmith, Herman L. ....New York, NY
Goldsmith, Howard J. ....New York, NY
Goldsmith, Howard M. ....Philadelphia, PA
Goldsmith, Howard M., P.C.
Philadelphia, PA
Goldsmith, Idie R. ....Baltimore, MD
Goldsmith, J. Robert, Jr. ....Austin, TX
Goldsmith, Jack O. ....Monterey Park, CA
Goldsmith, James A. ....Cleveland, OH
Goldsmith, James D. ....New York, NY
Goldsmith, James H. ....Boston, MA
Goldsmith, James L. ....Harrisburg, PA
Goldsmith, James W. ....Marion, NC
Goldsmith, Jan I. ....Poway, CA
Goldsmith, Janet K. ....Sacramento, CA
Goldsmith, Jas. H. ....Decatur, GA
Goldsmith, Jeffrey H. ....Springfield, NJ
Goldsmith, Jeffrey M.
Colorado Springs, CO
Goldsmith, Jeffrey R. ....Columbus, OH
Goldsmith, Jennifer C. ....Columbus, OH
Goldsmith, Jerome B. ....Bangor, ME
Goldsmith, Jessica Galligan
New York, NY
Goldsmith, Jill Susan ....Phoenix, AZ
Goldsmith, Joachim ....Sacramento, CA
Goldsmith, Joan Arbour
Colorado Springs, CO
Goldsmith, John D. ....Newark, NJ
Goldsmith, John Daniel ....Tampa, FL
Goldsmith, John L. ....Gonzales, LA
Goldsmith, John William ....Middletown, NY
Goldsmith, Julie ....Seattle, WA
Goldsmith, Karen L. ....Winter Park, FL
Goldsmith, Karl R. ....Cleveland, OK
Goldsmith, Katherine Doggett
Cincinnati, OH
Goldsmith, Kenneth ....Washington, DC
Goldsmith, Kenneth B. ....Coral Gables, FL
Goldsmith, Laura M. ....Albuquerque, NM
Goldsmith Law Firm, The
Washington, DC
Goldsmith Law Office ....Concord, NC
Goldsmith, Lee S. ....Englewood Cliffs, NJ
New York, NY
Goldsmith, Leigh Jordan
San Francisco, CA
Goldsmith, Leizer Z. ....Washington, DC
Goldsmith, Leo, Jr. ....New York, NY
Goldsmith, Leslie Demaree
Baltimore, MD
Goldsmith, Linn C. ....Hennepin, IL
Goldsmith, Lynn D. ....Newton, MA
Goldsmith, M. Alex ....Birmingham, AL
Goldsmith, Marc H. ....Los Angeles, CA
Goldsmith, Marc L. ....New York, NY
Goldsmith, Marcia Kaplan ....Wellesley, MA
Goldsmith, Mark A. ....Stratford, CT
Goldsmith, Mark A. ....Detroit, MI
Goldsmith, Mark A. ....Princeton, NJ
New York, NY
Goldsmith, Mark E. ....Los Angeles, CA
Goldsmith, Mark J. ....St. James, NY
Goldsmith, Marshall J. ....Chicago, IL
Highland, IN
Goldsmith, Martin N. ....Bedford, TX
Goldsmith, Marvin ....Los Angeles, CA
Goldsmith, Mary A. ....Corpus Christi, TX
Goldsmith, Mason A. ....Greenville, SC
Goldsmith, Mason A., Jr. ....Greenville, SC
Goldsmith, Maurice Alexander
Birmingham, AL
Goldsmith, Max J. ....Louisville, KY
Goldsmith, Michael ....Hicksville, NY
Richmond Hill, NY
Goldsmith, Michael ....White Plains, NY
Goldsmith, Michael B. ....New York, NY
Goldsmith, Michael K. ....New York, NY
Goldsmith, Michael P. ....New York, NY
Goldsmith, Michele M. ....Los Angeles, CA
Goldsmith, Mitchell D. ....Chicago, IL
Goldsmith, Molly H. ....Philadelphia, PA
Goldsmith, Morris ....Northfield, NJ
Goldsmith, Nancy K. ....New York, NY
Goldsmith, Norman S. ....New York, NY
Goldsmith, Pamela B. ....New York, NY
Goldsmith, Patricia ....Los Angeles, CA
Goldsmith, Paul F. ....Oakland, CA
Goldsmith, Paul F. ....Denver, CO
Goldsmith, Paul M. ....Chariton, IA
Goldsmith, Peter A. ....Ida Grove, IA
Goldsmith, Peter D. ....Nashua, NH
Goldsmith, Peter H. ....Emeryville, CA
Goldsmith, Phil ....Portland, OR
Goldsmith, Philip D. ....Monroe, MI
Goldsmith, Rebecca L. ....Washington, DC
Goldsmith, Richard ....Syracuse, NY
Goldsmith, Richard B. ....Livingston, NJ
Goldsmith, Richard E. ....San Antonio, TX
Goldsmith, Richard L., Jr. ....Akron, OH
Goldsmith, Richard N. ....Phoenix, AZ
Goldsmith & Richman, P.A.
Englewood Cliffs, NJ
New York, NY
Goldsmith, Robert D. ....Albany, GA
Atlanta, GA
Goldsmith, Robert M. ....Plainview, NY
Goldsmith, Robert S. ....Southfield, MI
Goldsmith, Robert S. ....Woodbridge, NJ
Goldsmith, Robert W. ....Seattle, WA
Goldsmith, Robin F. ....Needham, MA
Goldsmith, Ross P. ....Denver, CO
Goldsmith, Russell J. ....Portland, ME
Goldsmith, Ruth Harris ....Savannah, GA
Goldsmith, S. Delvalle ....New York, NY
Goldsmith, Scott E. ....New York, NY
Goldsmith, Scott J. ....Department of Justice,
Justice Management Division, GV
Goldsmith, Scott K. ....Minneapolis, MN
Goldsmith, Seth B. ....Worcester, MA
Goldsmith, Stanley A. ....Sarasota, FL
Goldsmith, Stephen ....Indianapolis, IN
Goldsmith, Stephen A. ....New York, NY
Goldsmith, Stephen E. ....Wailuku, HI
Goldsmith, Stephen R. ....San Antonio, TX
Goldsmith, Steven J. ....Pound Ridge, NY
Goldsmith, Steven M. ....Boca Raton, FL
Goldsmith, Steven M., P.A.
Boca Raton, FL
Goldsmith, Stuart O. ....Rochelle Park, NJ
Goldsmith, Susan Okin ....Woodbridge, NJ
Goldsmith, Suzanne ....Whiting, IN
Goldsmith, Tara J. ....New York, NY
Goldsmith, Ted G. ....Chicago, IL
Goldsmith, Thelin, Dickson & Brown
Aurora, IL
Goldsmith, Therese M. ....Baltimore, MD
Goldsmith, Toby ....Fort Worth, TX
Goldsmith, Walter D. ....New York, NY
Goldsmith, Walter J. ....Southfield, MI
Goldsmith & Weiss ....Northfield, NJ
Goldsmith, William A. ....Gallup, NM
Goldsmith, William A., P.A. ....Gallup, NM
Goldsmith, William G. ....New York, NY
Goldsmith, William I., (A Professional
Corporation) ....Los Angeles, CA
Goldsmith, William P. ....Oakland, CA
Goldsmith, William S.
San Juan Capistrano, CA
Goldsmith, Willis J. ....Washington, DC
Goldsobel, Donald G. ....Los Angeles, CA
Goldsobel, Steven Matthew
Los Angeles, CA
Goldson, Amy Robertson ....Washington, DC
Goldson & Goldson ....Commack, NY
Goldson, Howard W. ....Commack, NY
Goldson, Jennifer C. ....Columbus, OH
Goldson, Milton H. ....Commack, NY
Goldson, Robert J., III ....St. Louis, MO
Goldson, Victoria I. ....St. Louis, MO
Goldstaub, David R. ....Phoenix, AZ
Goldstein, Aaron ....New York, NY
Goldstein, Abbe Ellen
Federal Trade Commission,
Bureau of Consumer Protection, GV
Goldstein, Abbey F. ....Kew Gardens, NY
Goldstein, Abe ....Santa Ana, CA
Goldstein, Abraham S. ....New Haven, CT
Goldstein, Adam J. ....Southfield, MI
Goldstein, Aileen N. ....Los Angeles, CA
Goldstein, Aileen N., P.C. ....Los Angeles, CA
Goldstein, Aimee E. ....New York, NY
Goldstein, Aimee H. ....New York, NY
Goldstein, Aiossa & Good, Ltd. ....Chicago, IL
Goldstein, Alan D. ....Succasunna, NJ
Goldstein, Alan D. ....Buffalo, NY
Goldstein, Alan E. ....Nanuet, NY
Goldstein, Alan H. ....Indianapolis, IN
Goldstein, Alan Jay ....Chicago, IL
Goldstein, Alan K. ....St. Louis, MO
Goldstein, Alan P. ....Southfield, MI
Goldstein, Alan S. ....New York, NY
Goldstein, Albert M. ....New York, NY
Goldstein, Alfred French ....Lynn, MA
Goldstein, Allan B. ....Washington, DC
Goldstein, Allan D. ....Houston, TX
Goldstein, Allen ....Treasury Department,
Internal Revenue Service, GV
Goldstein, Allen J. ....New York, NY
Goldstein, Alvin ....Chester, NY
Goldstein, Alvin ....New York, NY
Goldstein, Alvin H., Jr.
San Francisco, CA
Goldstein, Alvin S. ....Boca Raton, FL
Goldstein, Amy C. ....Cherry Hill, NJ
Goldstein, Amy J. ....Buffalo, NY
Goldstein, Amy R. ....Concord, NH
Goldstein, Amy R. ....Columbus, OH
Goldstein, Andrea Katz ....New York, NY
Goldstein, Andrew D. ....Lynn, MA
Goldstein, Andrew E. ....New York, NY
Goldstein, Andrew J. ....Newark, NJ
Goldstein, Andrew Keith ....Boston, MA
Goldstein, Andrew L. ....Chicago, IL
Goldstein, Andrew L. ....Okemos, MI
Goldstein, Andrew L., P.C. ....Okemos, MI
Goldstein, Andrew M. ....Silver Spring, MD
Goldstein, Andrew P. ....Washington, DC
Goldstein, Andrew S. ....Roanoke, VA
Goldstein, Anne B. ....Springfield, MA
Goldstein, Anne T. ....Washington, DC
Goldstein, Arnie E. ....Santa Monica, CA
Goldstein, Arnold D. ....Chicago, IL
Goldstein, Arnold J. ....Brooklyn, NY
Goldstein, Arnold M. ....Scarsdale, NY
Goldstein, Arnold S. ....Deerfield Beach, FL
Goldstein, Arnold V. ....New York, NY
Goldstein, Arthur ....Worcester, MA
Goldstein, Arthur ....Huntington, NY
Goldstein, Arthur ....New York, NY
Goldstein, Arthur ....New York, NY
Goldstein, Arthur D. ....Worcester, MA
Goldstein, Arthur L. ....Scarsdale, NY
Goldstein, Arthur S. ....Roseland, NJ
Goldstein & Ashley ....Los Angeles, CA
Goldstein & Associates, P.C.
Washington, DC
Goldstein, Avery N. ....Birmingham, MI
Goldstein, Ballen, O'Rourke & Wildstein, P.C.
Passaic, NJ
Goldstein, Barbara Allison ....Sylva, NC
Goldstein, Barbara Fisher
Minnetonka, MN
Goldstein, Barbara S. ....New York, NY
Goldstein, Bari L. ....Miami, FL
Goldstein, Barney ....Long Beach, CA
Goldstein, Barney Simeon ....Portland, ME
Goldstein, Barrie L. ....Roxbury, CT
New York, NY
Goldstein, Barry ....Oakland, CA
Goldstein, Barry ....Kenilworth, NJ
Goldstein, Barry ....New York, NY
Goldstein, Barry ....Philadelphia, PA
Goldstein, Barry C. ....Towson, MD
Goldstein, Barry E. ....Fort Lauderdale, FL
Goldstein, Barry H. ....New York, NY
Goldstein, Barry J. ....Denver, CO
Goldstein, Bart S. ....New York, NY
Goldstein, Benjamin ....Sarasota, FL
Goldstein, Benjamin ....Berlin, NJ
Camden, NJ
Goldstein, Bennett H. ....Portland, OR
Goldstein, Benson S. ....Bethesda, MD
Goldstein, Bernard ....Boca Raton, FL
Goldstein, Bernard ....Hempstead, NY
Goldstein, Bernard ....New York, NY
Goldstein, Bernard ....Roslyn Heights, NY
Goldstein, Bernard ....Milwaukee, WI
Goldstein, Bernard L. ....New York, NY
Goldstein, Bershad, Fried & Lieberman,
Professional Corporation ....Detroit, MI
Southfield, MI
Goldstein, Berton Ira ....Chicago, IL
Goldstein, Bertram ....Bronx, NY
Goldstein, Bertram M. ....Baltimore, MD
Goldstein, Bertram M., & Associates, P.A.
Baltimore, MD
Goldstein, Beth ....New York, NY
Goldstein, Beth F. ....New York, NY
Goldstein, Beth R. ....Englewood, CO
Goldstein, Billie Jan ....Pembroke Pines, FL
Goldstein, Blanche K. ....Clifton, NJ
Goldstein, Bonnie L. ....Dallas, TX
Goldstein, Bradley J. ....Tarzana, CA
Goldstein, Brandt J. ....Washington, DC
Goldstein, Brent M. ....Bethesda, MD
Goldstein, Bret R. ....King Of Prussia, PA
Goldstein, Brian D. ....Boston, MA
Goldstein, Brian G. ....Cranston, RI
Goldstein, Brian P. ....Albany, NY
Goldstein, Brian S. ....New York, NY
Goldstein, Brian T. ....Overland Park, KS
Kansas City, MO
Goldstein, Brian T. ....Fairfax, VA
Goldstein, Bruce ....Washington, DC
Goldstein, Bruce A. ....Buffalo, NY
Goldstein, Bruce D. ....Silver Spring, MD
Goldstein, Bruce E. ....Minneapolis, MN
Goldstein, Bruce I. ....Newark, NJ
Goldstein, Bruce S. ....Tampa, FL
Goldstein, Bruce S. ....Akron, OH
Goldstein, Buckley, Cechman, Rice & Purtz,
P.A. ....Cape Coral, FL
Fort Myers, FL
Lehigh Acres, FL
Naples, FL
Port Charlotte, FL
Goldstein, Bulan & Chiari, LLP
Buffalo, NY
Goldstein & Burstein, P.C.
Farmington Hills, MI
Goldstein, Burton B., Jr. ....Atlanta, GA
Goldstein, Burton J. ....San Francisco, CA
Goldstein, Carl ....Wilmington, DE
Goldstein, Carl P. ....Monticello, NY
Goldstein, Carla ....San Jose, CA
Goldstein, Carla ....Chicago, IL
Goldstein, Carol S. ....Monroe, NY
Goldstein, Carol S. ....New York, NY
Goldstein, Carole L. ....Coatesville, PA
Goldstein, Cary W. ....Beverly Hills, CA
Goldstein, Cathy Dobbs ....San Francisco, CA
Goldstein, Charles A. ....New York, NY
Goldstein, Charles H. ....Los Angeles, CA
Goldstein, Charles J. ....Houston, TX
Goldstein, Charles M. ....Minnetonka, MN
Goldstein, Charles R. ....Chicago, IL
Goldstein, Clifford A. ....Jersey City, NJ
Voorhees, NJ
Philadelphia, PA
Pittsburgh, PA

Goldstein, Clifford A.—Continued
Reading, PA
Scranton, PA
Goldstein, Cori L. ... **Alamo, CA**
Goldstein, Corinne A. ... **Washington, DC**
Goldstein, Dana A. ... Worcester, MA
Goldstein, Dana Eve ... Fort Washington, PA
Goldstein, Daniel ... Charleston, SC
Goldstein, Daniel A. ... **Miami, FL**
Goldstein, Daniel A., P.A. ... **Miami, FL**
Goldstein, Daniel F. ... **Baltimore, MD**
Goldstein, Darren H. ... **Voorhees, NJ**
Goldstein, David ... Bronx, NY
Goldstein, David ... Great Neck, NY
Goldstein, David ... **New York, NY**
Goldstein, David A. ... **Los Angeles, CA**
Goldstein, David A. ... **Tampa, FL**
Goldstein, David A. ... **New York, NY**
Goldstein, David A. ... New York, NY
Goldstein, David A. ... **New York, NY**
Goldstein, David A. ... New York, NY
Goldstein, David A. ... **Columbus, OH**
Goldstein, David B. ... **Scottsdale, AZ**
Goldstein, David B. ... **Baltimore, MD**
Goldstein, David B. ... **New York, NY**
Goldstein, David H. ... Minneapolis, MN
Goldstein, David I. ... Portland, ME
Goldstein, David I. ... Ann Arbor, MI
Goldstein, David I., Law Office of
Chestnut Ridge, NY
Goldstein, David J. ... **Minneapolis, MN**
Goldstein, David J. ... Bronx, NY
Goldstein, David L. ... Chicago, IL
Goldstein, David M. ... **Los Angeles, CA**
Goldstein, David M.
Rancho Cucamonga, CA
Goldstein, David M. ... Redwood City, CA
Goldstein, David M. ... **San Francisco, CA**
Goldstein, David M. ... Miami, FL
Goldstein, David S. ... **Washington, DC**
Goldstein, David S. ... Dallas, TX
Goldstein, Dawn ... Department of Energy,
Office of Hearings and Appeals, GV
Goldstein, Dawn B. ... **Los Angeles, CA**
Goldstein, Deborah J. ... **New York, NY**
Goldstein, Deborah L. ... **New York, NY**
Goldstein, Debra E. ... New York, NY
Goldstein, Debra L. ... **Dallas, TX**
Goldstein, Debra Wolf ... Philadelphia, PA
Goldstein, Dennis ... Atlanta, GA
Goldstein, Dennis B. ... San Francisco, CA
Goldstein, Diane Flagg ... **Southfield, MI**
Goldstein & DiGioia, LLP ... **New York, NY**
Goldstein & Dodge ... Denver, CO
Goldstein, Don W. ... **Los Angeles, CA**
Goldstein, Donald A. ... Albany, NY
Goldstein, Donna Fields ... **Los Angeles, CA**
Goldstein, Doris Sussman ... Jacksonville, FL
Goldstein, Douglas J. ... Los Angeles, CA
Goldstein, Edward D. ... **Fullerton, CA**
Goldstein, Edward G. ... **Northfield, NJ**
Goldstein, Edward J. ... **Carlstadt, NJ**
New York, NY
Goldstein, Edward W. ... **Houston, TX**
Goldstein, Eliot Mark ... Bridgewater, NJ
Goldstein, Elise E. ... Encino, CA
Goldstein, Elizabeth J. ... **Harrisburg, PA**
Goldstein, Elliott ... **Atlanta, GA**
Goldstein, Elliott H. ... Chicago, IL
Goldstein, Elliott J. ... Kansas City, MO
Goldstein, Eric A. ... New York, NY
Goldstein, Eric S. ... **Troy, MI**
Goldstein, Eric S. ... **Atlantic City, NJ**
Pleasantville, NJ
Goldstein, Eric S. ... **New York, NY**
Goldstein, Erin F. ... Arlington, VA
Goldstein, Eugene ... New York, NY
Goldstein, Evan S. ... **Scottsdale, AZ**
Goldstein, Eve H. ... Atlanta, GA
Goldstein, Evie C. ... New York, NY
Goldstein, Felice Ann Stern
Birmingham, AL
Goldstein, Felicia F. ... **San Francisco, CA**
Goldstein and Feuer ... Cambridge, MA
Goldstein & Fluxgold, Ltd. ... Chicago, IL
Goldstein, Frank R. ... **Washington, DC**
Goldstein, Franklin ... **Baltimore, MD**
Goldstein, Frederick ... **Boston, MA**
Goldstein, Fredric H. ... New York, NY
Goldstein, Friedberg, Kelly and Dubrow, P.C.
Philadelphia, PA
Goldstein, Garson K. ... Deer Park, NY
Goldstein, Gary ... Bellmore, NY
Goldstein, Gary A. ... **West Palm Beach, FL**
Baltimore, MD
Goldstein, Gary L. ... Johnson City, TN
Goldstein, Gary M. ... **Philadelphia, PA**
Goldstein, Gary S. ... Chester, NY
Goldstein, Gellman, Melbostad, Gibson &
Harris, L.L.P. ... San Francisco, CA
Goldstein, Gerald ... **New York, NY**
Goldstein, Gerald C. ... New York, NY
Goldstein, Gerald D. ... East Brunswick, NJ
Goldstein, Gerald H. ... **San Antonio, TX**
Goldstein, Gerald M.
Equal Employment Opportunity
Commission,
Office of Legal Counsel, GV
Goldstein, Gerald M. ... Brooklyn, NY
Goldstein, Gerard D. ... **Boston, MA**
Goldstein, Gersham ... **Portland, OR**
Goldstein, Gilbert, (P.C.) ... Denver, CO
Goldstein, Glenn A. ... New York, NY
Goldstein, Glenn A. ... **Philadelphia, PA**
Goldstein, Glenn E. ... **Fort Lauderdale, FL**
Goldstein, Glenn S. ... **New York, NY**
Goldstein Goldman Kessler & Underberg
Rochester, NY

Goldstein & Goldstein ... San Francisco, CA
Goldstein & Goldstein ... Jacksonville, FL
Goldstein, Goldstein and Hilley
San Antonio, TX
Goldstein, Goldstein & Rikon ... **Bronx, NY**
Brooklyn, NY
New York, NY
White Plains, NY
Goldstein & Greenberg ... St. Petersburg, FL
Goldstein, Greg R. ... **Los Angeles, CA**
Goldstein, Gurvitz & Silver, LLP
Encino, CA
Goldstein, Hadar Gonen ... Los Angeles, CA
Goldstein Handler & Levine, P.C.
Washington, DC
Bethesda, MD
Rockville, MD
Goldstein, Harley J. ... **Chicago, IL**
Goldstein, Harold ... North Woodmere, NY
Goldstein, Harry ... Warwick, RI
Goldstein, Harry S. ... Columbus, OH
Goldstein, Harvey ... **New York, NY**
Goldstein, Harvey I. ... **Pittsburgh, PA**
Goldstein, Harvey I. ... Miami, FL
Goldstein, Harvey L. ... **New York, NY**
Goldstein, Harvey M. ... Miami, FL
Goldstein, Harvey N. ... **New York, NY**
Goldstein, Hazel H. ... Prince Frederick, MD
Goldstein, Heather R. ... **New York, NY**
Goldstein, Heather Whitaker
Asheville, NC
Goldstein, Heidi B. ... **New York, NY**
Goldstein, Heidi B. ... **Cleveland, OH**
Goldstein, Helen E. ... Cedarhurst, NY
Goldstein, Helyn S. ... **New York, NY**
Goldstein, Henry B. ... **New York, NY**
Goldstein, Henry L. ... **New Canaan, CT**
Goldstein, Henry L. ... **Stamford, CT**
Goldstein, Herbert C. ... Harrisburg, PA
Goldstein & Herst ... Princeton, NJ
Goldstein, Heslop, Steele, Clapper & Oswalt
Tyrone, PA
Goldstein, Heslop, Steele, Clapper, Oswalt &
Stoehr ... **Altoona, PA**
Ebensburg, PA
Goldstein, Hope S. ... **Roseland, NJ**
New York, NY
Goldstein, Howard ... **Las Vegas, NV**
Goldstein, Howard ... New York, NY
Goldstein, Howard I. ... **Newton, MA**
Goldstein, Howard J. ... New York, NY
Goldstein, Howard K. ... Philadelphia, PA
Goldstein, Howard W. ... Beverly Hills, CA
Goldstein, Howard W. ... **New York, NY**
Goldstein, I. Martin ... Trenton, NJ
Goldstein, Ian J. ... West Palm Beach, FL
Goldstein, Ian P. ... **Princeton, NJ**
Goldstein, Ilan ... Brooklyn, NY
Goldstein, Ilene F. ... **Deerfield, IL**
Goldstein, Ira B. ... Joliet, IL
Goldstein, Ira B., Ltd. ... Joliet, IL
Goldstein, Ira J. ... **New York, NY**
Goldstein, Ira J. ... Whitestone, NY
Goldstein, Ira L. ... Glendale, CA
Goldstein, Irena M. ... **New York, NY**
Goldstein, Irving ... Washington, DC
Goldstein, Irving B." Chip "
Newport News, VA
Goldstein, Irving J. ... Danbury, CT
Goldstein, Irwin ... Garden City, NY
Goldstein, Irwin L. ... **Los Angeles, CA**
Goldstein, Irwin M. ... Lawrence, NY
Goldstein, Irwin P. ... Bayonne, NJ
Goldstein, Irwin P., P.A. ... Bayonne, NJ
Goldstein, Jack ... New York, NY
Goldstein, Jack C. ... Wilmington, DE
Goldstein, Jack P. ... Chestnut Hill, MA
Goldstein, Jame S. ... Indianapolis, IN
Goldstein, James A. ... Sherman Oaks, CA
Goldstein, James A. ... **Atlanta, GA**
Goldstein, James A. ... New York, NY
Goldstein, James A. ... Beaverton, OR
Goldstein, James B ... McLean, VA
Goldstein, James E. ... Salinas, CA
Goldstein, Jane D. ... **Boston, MA**
Goldstein, Janet ... New York, NY
Goldstein, Janet A. ... **Park City, UT**
Goldstein, Jared A. ... Department of Justice,
Environment and Natural Resources
Division, GV
Goldstein, Jason ... La Crosse, WI
Goldstein, Jason R. ... **New York, NY**
Goldstein, Jay D. ... Jenkintown, PA
Goldstein, Jay Howard ... Purchase, NY
Goldstein, Jay L. ... **Westport, CT**
Goldstein, Jay M. ... **Charlotte, NC**
Goldstein, Jay R. ... **Philadelphia, PA**
Goldstein, Jayne Arnold
Huntingdon Valley, PA
Goldstein, Jean E. ... **Columbia, MO**
Goldstein, Jeffrey A. ... **New York, NY**
Goldstein, Jeffrey Alan ... Denver, CO
Goldstein, Jeffrey B. ... Worcester, MA
Goldstein, Jeffrey D. ... **Rockville, MD**
Goldstein, Jeffrey I. ... Colts Neck, NJ
Goldstein, Jeffrey I. ... Toledo, OH
Goldstein, Jeffrey N. ... **Burlington, NJ**
Goldstein, Jeffrey S. ... **Baltimore, MD**
Goldstein, Jeffrey S. ... Jersey City, NJ
Goldstein, Jeffrey S. ... **New York, NY**
Goldstein, Jeffrey S. ... Houston, TX
Goldstein, Jennifer A. ... **Washington, DC**
Goldstein, Jennifer Cohen ... Stamford, CT
Goldstein, Jennifer M. ... **San Francisco, CA**
Goldstein, Jennifer S.
Equal Employment Opportunity
Commission,
Office of the General Counsel, GV

Goldstein, Jeremy E. ... **Philadelphia, PA**
Goldstein, Jerold V. ... Encino, CA
Goldstein, Jerome N. ... Huntington, CT
Goldstein, Jerrold D. ... **North Plainfield, NJ**
Goldstein, Jerrold L. ... **Cleveland, OH**
Goldstein, Jerry J. ... Laguna Niguel, CA
Goldstein, Jerry R. ... **Bethesda, MD**
Goldstein, Jill H. ... **Omaha, NE**
Goldstein, Jill N. ... **New York, NY**
Goldstein, Joanne Feinberg ... Boston, MA
Goldstein, Jodi R. ... **Washington, DC**
Goldstein, Joel K. ... St. Louis, MO
Goldstein, Joel M. ... Chicago, IL
Goldstein, John A. ... **Chicago, IL**
Goldstein, John A. ... Rochester, NY
Goldstein, John B. ... **Novato, CA**
Goldstein, Jonah L. ... Elmsford, NY
Goldstein, Jonathan ... **New York, NY**
Goldstein, Jonathan A. ... **La Habra, CA**
Goldstein, Jonathan L. ... **Newark, NJ**
Goldstein, Joni L. ... Winnetka, IL
Goldstein, Jordan B.
Federal Communications Commission,
Common Carrier Bureau, GV
Goldstein, Jordan M. ... New York, NY
Goldstein, Jordana Lee
Fort Lauderdale, FL
Goldstein, Jorge A. ... **Washington, DC**
Goldstein, Joseph ... New Haven, CT
Goldstein, Joseph ... **Carle Place, NY**
Goldstein, Joseph ... New York, NY
Goldstein, Joseph G. ... **Miami, FL**
Goldstein, Joseph I. ... **Washington, DC**
Goldstein, Joseph M.
Fort Lauderdale, FL
Goldstein, Joseph M. ... North Bergen, NJ
Goldstein, Josh D. ... **New York, NY**
Goldstein, Joshua B. ... **New York, NY**
Goldstein, Joshua D. ... **Cleveland, OH**
Goldstein, Joyce ... Cleveland, OH
Goldstein & Joyce, L.L.C. ... **Chicago, IL**
Deerfield, IL
Waukegan, IL
Goldstein, Joyce M. ... Mineola, NY
Goldstein, Judy A., Law Offices of
Mokena, IL
Goldstein, Jules ... Waleska, GA
Goldstein, Jules M. ... Great Neck, NY
Goldstein, Julie Vaccher ... **Somerville, NJ**
Goldstein, Justin B. ... Pittsburgh, PA
Goldstein, Justin M. ... **Los Angeles, CA**
Goldstein, Kaitz & Fellman, LLP
Waltham, MA
Goldstein, Karen ... New York, NY
Goldstein, Karen L. ... Washington, DC
Goldstein, Karen Plave ... **Rockville, MD**
Goldstein, Keith M. ... **Albany, NY**
Goldstein, Kennedy & Petito
Los Angeles, CA
Goldstein, Kenneth A. ... **Chicago, IL**
Goldstein, Kenneth B. ... New York, NY
Goldstein, Kenneth M. ... Brookline, MA
Goldstein, Kenneth R. ... **New York, NY**
Goldstein, Kenneth R. ... New York, NY
Goldstein, Kenneth T. ... **Simsbury, CT**
Goldstein, Kenneth T. ... **Chicago, IL**
Goldstein and Kessler ... Philadelphia, PA
Goldstein, Kevin W. ... **Wilmington, DE**
Goldstein, L. Elliott ... Little Neck, NY
Goldstein, L. Jonathan ... **Birmingham, AL**
Goldstein & LaBue ... Rochester, NY
Goldstein & Lamb, P.C. ... Chicago, IL
Goldstein, Larry D. ... St. Petersburg, FL
Goldstein, Larry R. ... **Chicago, IL**
Goldstein, Laura A. ... **Danbury, CT**
Goldstein, Laurence J. ... Northbrook, IL
Goldstein, Lauri J. ... **Stuart, FL**
Goldstein, Lauri J., & Assoc., P.A., A Law
Office of ... **Fort Pierce, FL**
Stuart, FL
Goldstein, Laurie G., (P.C.) ... Chicago, IL
Goldstein & Law, LLP ... **Atlanta, GA**
Goldstein, Lawr. M. ... Sacramento, CA
Goldstein, Lawrence B. ... Annapolis, MD
Goldstein, Lawrence B. ... **Dallas, TX**
Goldstein, Lawrence E. ... New York, NY
Goldstein, Lawrence I. ... Rochester, NY
Goldstein, Lawrence P. ... Bloomfield, CT
Goldstein, Lee C. ... **Wilmington, DE**
Goldstein, Lee D. ... Cambridge, MA
Goldstein, Lee J. ... Riverside, CA
Goldstein, Lee S. ... **Atlanta, GA**
Goldstein, Leigh A. ... **Pleasanton, CA**
Goldstein Lem, LLC ... **Newark, NJ**
Goldstein, Leo ... Bloomfield Hills, MI
Farmington Hills, MI
Goldstein, Leon ... New York, NY
Goldstein, Leonard ... Newport Beach, CA
Goldstein, Leonard ... Brooklyn, NY
Goldstein, Leonard H.
Consumer Product Safety Commission,
Office of the General Counsel, GV
Goldstein, Leonard M. ... Englewood, CO
Goldstein, Leonard R. ... **Greenbelt, MD**
Rockville, MD
Goldstein, Leslie S. ... Baltimore, MD
Goldstein, Lester L., (P.A.) ... **Miami, FL**
Goldstein & Levy, P.A. ... **Crofton, MD**
Rockville, MD
Goldstein, Linda C. ... **New York, NY**
Goldstein, Linda Gruberger
New York, NY
Goldstein, Lisa B. ... **New York, NY**
Goldstein, Litt, Slinger and Dunwoodie,
P.L.L.C. ... Farmington Hills, MI
Goldstein, L. L. ... Prince Frederick, MD
Goldstein, Lori A. ... **Chicago, IL**
Goldstein, Lori H. ... New York, NY

Goldstein, Louis ... Wilmington, DE
Goldstein, Louis ... Brooklyn, NY
Goldstein, Louis S. ... Chicago, IL
Goldstein, Louisa Horton ... Baltimore, MD
Goldstein, Lynn A. ... Chicago, IL
Goldstein, Lynn L. S. ... Department of Justice,
Drug Enforcement Administration, GV
Goldstein, Lynne S. ... Glendale, CA
Goldstein, M. Robert ... **New York, NY**
Goldstein, Malcolm A. ... **New York, NY**
Goldstein & Manello, P.C. ... **Boston, MA**
Goldstein, Marc ... **Newport Beach, CA**
Goldstein, Marc H. ... Washington, DC
Goldstein, Marc J. ... **Boston, MA**
Goldstein, Marc J. ... **New York, NY**
Goldstein, Marc R. ... Wellington, FL
Goldstein, Marc R., P.A., Law Office of
Wellington, FL
Goldstein, Marcia C. ... **New York, NY**
Goldstein, Marcia J. ... Newark, NJ
Goldstein, Marcia Landweber
New York, NY
Goldstein, Marcie A. ... **New York, NY**
Goldstein, Margaret Frenkel
New York, NY
Goldstein, Marilyn F. ... New York, NY
Goldstein, Mark ... **Burbank, CA**
Goldstein, Mark ... East Brunswick, NJ
Goldstein, Mark ... White Plains, NY
Goldstein, Mark A. ... **Los Angeles, CA**
Goldstein, Mark A. ... Gardner, MA
Goldstein, Mark Adam ... Pittsburgh, PA
Goldstein, Mark B. ... Boca Raton, FL
Goldstein, Mark E. ... Miami, FL
Goldstein, Mark H. ... **Las Vegas, NV**
Goldstein, Mark I. ... Brooklyn, NY
Goldstein, Mark L. ... Northbrook, IL
Goldstein, Mark L. ... **New York, NY**
Goldstein, Mark Lee ... Bronx, NY
Goldstein, Mark S. ... **New Orleans, LA**
Goldstein, Mark S. ... **Bethesda, MD**
Goldstein, Mark S. ... **Uniondale, NY**
Goldstein, Marlo Ann ... Los Angeles, CA
Goldstein, Marsh M. ... Los Angeles, CA
Goldstein, Marsha ... New Rochelle, NY
Goldstein, Marshall L. ... White Plains, NY
Goldstein, Martin E. ... Louisville, KY
Goldstein, Martin E. ... **New York, NY**
Goldstein, Martin J. ... **Garden City, NY**
Goldstein, Marvin J. ... **New York, NY**
Goldstein, Marvin J. ... **New York, NY**
Goldstein, Marvin M. ... **Newark, NJ**
Goldstein, Matthew A. ... **New York, NY**
Goldstein, Matthew N. ... Philadelphia, PA
Goldstein, Maurice A. ... **New Milford, CT**
Goldstein, Maurice W. ... Jacksonville, FL
Goldstein, McGroder & Woods, Ltd. A
Professional Corporation ... **Phoenix, AZ**
Goldstein, Meg D. ... **Charlotte, NC**
Goldstein, Melinda Paige ... Morrison, CO
Goldstein, Melissa B. ... **Wayne, NJ**
Goldstein, Melissa Roselle ... Ann Arbor, MI
Goldstein, Melvin ... **Washington, DC**
Goldstein, Melvin ... **Washington, DC**
Goldstein, Melvin ... Commack, NY
Goldstein, Melvin M. ... **Marietta, GA**
Goldstein, Melvin M., P.C. ... **Marietta, GA**
Goldstein, Melvyn S., P.C.
Birmingham, MI
Goldstein & Metzger, LLP
Poughkeepsie, NY
Goldstein, Meyer B. ... Rockville Centre, NY
Goldstein, Meyer I. ... Portland, OR
Goldstein, Michael ... Cardiff-By-The-Sea, CA
Goldstein, Michael ... **Deerfield Beach, FL**
Goldstein, Michael A. ... **New York, NY**
Goldstein, Michael A. ... Pittsburgh, PA
Goldstein, Michael B. ... **Palm Springs, CA**
Goldstein, Michael B. ... **Washington, DC**
Goldstein, Michael B. ... New York, NY
Goldstein, Michael B. ... Eugene, OR
Goldstein, Michael E. ... **Memphis, TN**
Goldstein, Michael Eric ... Denver, CO
Goldstein, Michael G. ... **St. Louis, MO**
Goldstein, Michael H. ... **Los Angeles, CA**
Goldstein, Michael H. ... **New York, NY**
Goldstein, Michael J. ... **New York, NY**
Goldstein, Michael L. ... **New York, NY**
Goldstein, Michael R. ... **Los Angeles, CA**
Goldstein, Michael R. ... Oakland, CA
Goldstein, Michael R. ... **Miami, FL**
Goldstein, Michael R. ... New York, NY
Goldstein, Michael S. ... Rye Brook, NY
Goldstein, Michael S. ... Cleveland, OH
Goldstein, Michael W., Law Offices of
New York, NY
Goldstein, Michelle ... **Washington, DC**
Goldstein, Michelle E. Gillespy
Cincinnati, OH
Goldstein, Michelle R. ... Greenwich, CT
Goldstein, Milton I. ... **St. Louis, MO**
Goldstein, Miriam J.
Securities and Exchange Commission,
Office of the General Counsel, GV
Goldstein, Miriam L. ... Brooklyn, NY
Goldstein, Mitchell ... New York, NY
Goldstein, Mitchell A. ... **Portland, OR**
Goldstein, Mitchell F. ... Cambridge, MA
Goldstein, Mitchell L. ... Maplewood, NJ
Goldstein, Mitchell P. ... **Fredericksburg, VA**
Goldstein & Morris, LLP ... **New York, NY**
Goldstein, Mort, Law Office, A P.C.
Havre, MT
Goldstein, Morton B. ... Havre, MT
Goldstein, Morton N. ... Silver Spring, MD
Goldstein, Murray ... Encino, CA
Goldstein & Musto, A Professional
Corporation ... **San Francisco, CA**

Goldstein, N. Linda ..... Washington, DC
Goldstein, Nancy Beth ..... New York, NY
Goldstein, Nancy F. ..... Princeton, NJ
Goldstein, Nancy L. ..... Radnor, PA
Goldstein, Natasha R. ..... Golden, CO
Goldstein, Neal ..... Philadelphia, PA
Goldstein, Neal A. ..... New York, NY
Goldstein, Neal M. ..... Los Angeles, CA
Goldstein, Neal T. ..... Chicago, IL
Goldstein, Ned S. ..... Los Angeles, CA
Goldstein, Neil M. ..... San Francisco, CA
Goldstein, Neil S. ..... Great Neck, NY
Goldstein, Neil S. ..... New York, NY
Goldstein, Neil V. ..... Norristown, PA
Goldstein, Noreen Koppelman ..... Perry, OH
Goldstein, Norman
Federal Communications Commission, Mass Media Bureau, GV
Goldstein, Norton A. ..... Needham, MA
Goldstein, Pamela N. ..... New York, NY
Goldstein, Patricia Decicco ..... New York, NY
Goldstein, Paul ..... San Francisco, CA
Goldstein, Paul ..... New York, NY
Goldstein, Paul D. ..... Fort Lauderdale, FL
Goldstein, Paul E. ..... Chicago, IL
Goldstein, Paul H. ..... Palo Alto, CA
Goldstein, Paul I. ..... Fair Haven, VT
Goldstein, Paul I., P.C. ..... Fair Haven, VT
Goldstein, Paul J. ..... Poughkeepsie, NY
Goldstein, Paul L. ..... Rochester, NY
Goldstein, Paul S. ..... Jamaica, NY
Goldstein and Peck, P.C. ..... Bridgeport, CT
Westport, CT
Goldstein & Perakis ..... Sterling Heights, MI
Goldstein, Peter A. ..... Colorado Springs, CO
Goldstein, Peter A., P.C.
Colorado Springs, CO
Goldstein, Peter B. ..... Denver, CO
Goldstein, Peter D. ..... Rye, NY
Goldstein, Philip ..... New York, NY
Goldstein, Philip K. ..... Las Vegas, NV
Goldstein, Philip M. ..... Marietta, GA
Goldstein, Philip T. ..... Phoenix, AZ
Goldstein, Phillip J. ..... Miami, FL
Goldstein, Phillip J., P.A. ..... Miami, FL
Goldstein and Price, L.C.
East St. Louis, IL
St. Louis, MO
Goldstein, R. Stephen ..... San Francisco, CA
Goldstein, Ralph M. ..... Newport News, VA
Goldstein, Ray ..... Cape Coral, FL
Fort Myers, FL
Naples, FL
Port Charlotte, FL
Goldstein, Ray J. ..... Chicago, IL
Goldstein, Raymond R. ..... Culver City, CA
Goldstein, Rayner & Kaplan LLP
New York, NY
Goldstein & Reeves Law Offices ..... Urbana, IL
Goldstein, Richard ..... Boston, MA
Goldstein, Richard ..... Bluefield, WV
Goldstein, Richard A. ..... New York, NY
Goldstein, Richard, (A P.C.)
Los Angeles, CA
Goldstein, Richard D. ..... Decatur, GA
Goldstein, Richard H. ..... Hartford, CT
Goldstein, Richard I. ..... Pleasantville, NJ
Goldstein, Richard J. ..... Cherry Hill, NJ
Philadelphia, PA
Goldstein, Richard Jay ..... Los Angeles, CA
Goldstein, Richard L. ..... Cherry Hill, NJ
Goldstein, Richard M. ..... Miami, FL
Goldstein, Richard M. ..... Flint, MI
Goldstein, Richard M. ..... New York, NY
Goldstein, Richard M. ..... Scarsdale, NY
Goldstein, Richard M., (P.A.) ..... Miami, FL
Goldstein, Richard N. ..... White Plains, NY
Goldstein, Richard P. ..... New York, NY
Goldstein, Richard S. ..... Washington, DC
Goldstein, Richard S. ..... New York, NY
Goldstein, Richard S. ..... West Point, PA
Goldstein, Richard S., P.C., Law Offices of
New York, NY
Goldstein, Richard Scott
Treasury Department, Internal Revenue Service, GV
Goldstein, Robert ..... Jacksonville, FL
Goldstein, Robert ..... New York, NY
Goldstein, Robert A. ..... Oakland, CA
Goldstein, Robert A. ..... Alpharetta, GA
Goldstein, Robert A. ..... Framingham, MA
Goldstein, Robert A. ..... Las Vegas, NV
Goldstein, Robert A. ..... Clinton, NY
Goldstein, Robert A. ..... New York, NY
Goldstein, Robert A., A Professional Corporation ..... Oakland, CA
Goldstein, Robert D. ..... Los Angeles, CA
Goldstein, Robert D. ..... Detroit, MI
Goldstein, Robert D. ..... New York, NY
Goldstein, Robert D. ..... New York, NY
Goldstein, Robert E. ..... San Diego, CA
Goldstein, Robert E. ..... Old Bridge, NJ
Goldstein, Robert G. ..... Chicago, IL
Goldstein, Robert H. ..... Encino, CA
Goldstein, Robert H. ..... Jericho, NY
Goldstein, Robert J. ..... New York, NY
Goldstein, Robert J. ..... White Plains, NY
Goldstein, Robert L. ..... New York, NY
Goldstein, Robert M. ..... Buffalo, NY
Goldstein, Robert M. ..... New York, NY
Goldstein, Robert N. ..... Dallas, TX
Goldstein, Robert N., P.C. ..... Dallas, TX
Goldstein, Robert O. ..... Scarsdale, NY
Goldstein, Robert P. ..... Milwaukee, WI
Goldstein, Robert S. ..... Jenkintown, PA
Goldstein, Robin D. ..... Cupertino, CA
Goldstein, Robin H. ..... Holland, PA
Goldstein, Ronald ..... Phoenixville, PA
Goldstein, Ronald A. ..... Colchester, CT
Goldstein, Ronald A. ..... Sterling Heights, MI
Goldstein, Ronald B. ..... Princeton, NJ
Woodbridge, NJ
Goldstein, Ronald L. ..... Huntington, NY
Goldstein, Ronald L. ..... Dallas, TX
Goldstein, Roy D. ..... Los Angeles, CA
Goldstein, Rubinton, Goldstein & DiFazio P.C. ..... Huntington, NY
Goldstein, Russell ..... Milwaukee, WI
Goldstein, Ryan S. ..... New York, NY
Goldstein, S. William ..... Jacksonville, FL
Goldstein, Samuel ..... Bay Harbor Islands, FL
Goldstein, Samuel E. ..... Walnut Creek, CA
Goldstein, Samuel E. .....
Occupational Safety and Health Review Commission, GV
Goldstein, Samuel S. ..... Hartford, CT
Goldstein, Sandra ..... Los Angeles, CA
Goldstein, Sandra C. ..... New York, NY
Goldstein, Sandra J. ..... Albany, NY
Goldstein, Sara J. ..... New York, NY
Goldstein, Saul ..... Delray Beach, FL
Goldstein, Saul ..... New York, NY
Goldstein, Scott ..... Poughkeepsie, NY
Goldstein, Scott B. ..... Baltimore, MD
Goldstein, Scott H. ..... New York, NY
Goldstein, Scott J. ..... Chicago, IL
Goldstein, Scott J. ..... Kansas City, MO
Goldstein, Seth L. ..... Napa, CA
Goldstein, Seth M. ..... Kew Gardens, NY
Goldstein, Seymour M. ..... Plainview, NY
Goldstein, Seymour R. ..... Baltimore, MD
Goldstein, Shannon McDonald
Palm Desert, CA
Goldstein, Shari L. ..... Houston, TX
Goldstein, Sheldon E. ..... New York, NY
Goldstein, Sheldon M. ..... Mineola, NY
Goldstein, Sherwin ..... Los Angeles, CA
Goldstein, Shirley J. ..... New York, NY
Goldstein, Sidney ..... Silver Spring, MD
Goldstein, Sidney J.
Occupational Safety and Health Review Commission, Administrative Law Judges, GV
Goldstein, Sidney J. ..... Chicago, IL
Goldstein, Sidney M. ..... Bethesda, MD
Goldstein, Sidney S. ..... New York, NY
Goldstein, Simon ..... New York, NY
Goldstein, Sonja ..... New Haven, CT
Goldstein, Sonna F. ..... Jamaica, NY
Goldstein & Stamm, P.A. ..... Greenbelt, MD
Goldstein, Stanley ..... White Plains, NY
Goldstein, Stanley H. ..... Rockville, MD
Goldstein, Stanley M. ..... Trumbull, CT
Goldstein, Stanley M. ..... Miami, FL
Goldstein, Stanley R. ..... New York, NY
Goldstein, Stephan H. ..... Bensalem, PA
Philadelphia, PA
Goldstein, Stephanie J. ..... New York, NY
Goldstein, Stephen B. ..... East Lansing, MI
Goldstein, Stephen J.
Bay Harbor Islands, FL
Goldstein, Stephen L. ..... Fort Lee, NJ
Goldstein, Stephen R. ..... Los Angeles, CA
Goldstein, Stephen R. ..... Waltham, MA
Goldstein, Steven ..... St. Louis, MO
Goldstein, Steven ..... Seattle, WA
Goldstein, Steven A. ..... Everett, WA
Goldstein, Steven B. ..... Upland, CA
Goldstein, Steven B. ..... Philadelphia, PA
Goldstein, Steven I. ..... Asheville, NC
Goldstein, Steven J. ..... Englewood, CO
Goldstein, Steven J. ..... Cincinnati, OH
Goldstein, Steven M. ..... Scottsdale, AZ
Goldstein, Steven M.
Department of Housing and Urban Development, Office of General Counsel, GV
Goldstein, Steven M. ..... Tallahassee, FL
Goldstein, Steven M. ..... New York, NY
Goldstein, Steven R. ..... Garden City, NY
Goldstein, Steven R. ..... New York, NY
Goldstein, Steven S. ..... Cherry Hill, NJ
Goldstein, Stuart ..... Phoenix, AZ
Goldstein, Stuart ..... Farmington Hills, MI
Goldstein, Stuart A. ..... Miami, FL
Goldstein, Stuart M. ..... Voorhees, NJ
Goldstein, Stuart N. ..... New York, NY
Goldstein, Stuart R. ..... Brooklyn, NY
Goldstein, Stuart W. ..... Phoenix, AZ
Goldstein, Stuart W. ..... New York, NY
Goldstein, Susan Cohen ..... Olympia, WA
Goldstein, Susan Jane ..... Cambridge, MA
Goldstein, Susan S. ..... Cleveland, OH
Goldstein, Susan T. ..... Beverly Hills, CA
Goldstein & Tanen, P.A. ..... Miami, FL
Goldstein, Taryn F. ..... Philadelphia, PA
Goldstein, Terry M. ..... Altoona, PA
Tyrone, PA
Goldstein, Theodore N. ..... Orlando, FL
Goldstein, Thomas ..... Miami, FL
Goldstein, Thomas C. ..... Washington, DC
Goldstein, Thomas R. ..... Charleston, SC
Goldstein, Tracey L. ..... Roseland, NJ
Goldstein, Tracy L. ..... Carle Place, NY
Goldstein, Valerie Crown ..... New City, NY
Goldstein, Valerie Hope ..... Salem, MA
Goldstein, Victoria ..... Lake Charles, LA
Goldstein & Vouga, P.C. ..... Clayton, MO
St. Louis, MO
Goldstein, Walter S. ..... Boston, MA
Goldstein & Ward, Inc. ..... La Habra, CA
Goldstein, Warren A. ..... New Orleans, LA
Goldstein, Wendy B. ..... Dallas, TX
Goldstein, Wendy C. ..... New York, NY
Goldstein, William ..... Kingston, NY
Middletown, NY
New Windsor, NY
Poughkeepsie, NY
Goldstein, William ..... Bensalem, PA
Goldstein, William A. ..... New York, NY
Goldstein, William C.E. ..... St. Louis, MO
Goldstein, William I. ..... Encino, CA
Goldstein, William I. ..... Seattle, WA
Goldstein, William M. ..... Urbana, IL
Goldstein, William M. ..... Philadelphia, PA
Goldstein, William N. ..... Newtown, CT
Goldstein, William P. ..... Fairfield, IA
Goldstein, Wynn M. ..... Hackensack, NJ
Goldstein & Young, P.C. ..... Englewood, CO
Goldstein, Zev M. ..... Monsey, NY
Goldstein, Zucker & Flynn ..... New York, NY
Goldstein, Zuzana, Law Offices of
San Francisco, CA
Goldsten, Robert E. ..... Fort Lauderdale, FL
Goldstern, Vladimir ..... New York, NY
Goldstick, Jerome ..... Chicago, IL
Goldstick, Phillip C., & Assoc., Ltd.
Chicago, IL
Goldstick, Weinberger, Feldman & Grossman, P.C. ..... New York, NY
Goldstin, Myron B. ..... Chicago, IL
Goldstine, Robert D. ..... Summit, IL
Goldstine, Skrodzki Russian, Nemec and Hoff, Ltd. ..... Summit, IL
Goldstock, Barry P. ..... Newport Beach, CA
Goldstock, Bruce A. ..... Bronx, NY
Goldstock, Ronald ..... Larchmont, NY
Goldstoff, L. Jack ..... New York, NY
Goldston, Alan M. ..... New York, NY
Goldston, Bruce L. ..... San Antonio, TX
Goldston & Caputo, P.C. ..... Pittsburgh, PA
Goldston, David B. ..... Cleveland, OH
Goldston, Debbi A. ..... Walnut Creek, CA
Goldston, Donald N. ..... Austin, TX
Goldston, Donald N., Law Offices of
Austin, TX
Goldston, Forrest W. ..... Raleigh, NC
Goldston, Linda Leebov ..... Pittsburgh, PA
Goldston, Steven ..... Miami, FL
Goldston, Steven D. ..... Dallas, TX
Goldston, Steven, P.A. ..... Miami, FL
Goldston, William G. ..... Durham, NC
Goldstone, Arthur H. ..... New York, NY
Goldstone, Bernard ..... Sharon, PA
Goldstone, Bruce H. ..... New York, NY
Goldstone, Daniel W. ..... Boston, MA
Goldstone, David J. ..... Department of Justice, Criminal Division, GV
Goldstone, George H. ..... Bloomfield Hills, MI
Goldstone, Hartley A. ..... Denver, CO
Goldstone, Hilary F. ..... Los Angeles, CA
Goldstone, Jason J. ..... West Palm Beach, FL
Goldstone, Mark L. ..... Eldersburg, MD
Goldstone, Michael ..... Houston, TX
Goldstone, Raymond H. ..... Los Angeles, CA
Goldstone, Richard ..... Pompano Beach, FL
Goldstone, Richard, P.A.
Pompano Beach, FL
Goldstone, Richard S. ..... Boston, MA
Goldstone, Shelly B. ..... Boston, MA
Goldstone, Stephanie Stutman ..... Flushing, NY
Goldstone & Sudalter, P.C. ..... Boston, MA
Goldstricker, Herbert S. ..... Oceanside, NY
Goldstrom, Marc J. .....
Federal Deposit Insurance Corporation, GV
Goldstucker, Robert L. ..... Atlanta, GA
Goldsweig, David N. ..... Troy, MI
Goldsweig, Richard ..... Yonkers, NY
Goldsworthy, Donald J. ..... Madison, WI
Goldszer, Ronald Isaac ..... Beverly Hills, CA
Goldthorpe, Christopher J. ..... Alliance, OH
Hartville, OH
Goldthorpe, David R. ..... Amherst, OH
Goldthwaite, Alfred W. ..... Montgomery, AL
Goldthwaite, Alfred Witherspoon
Montgomery, AL
Goldthwaite, Donna L. ..... Shelburne Falls, MA
Goldthwaite, John Randall, Jr. ..... Atlanta, GA
Goldthwaite, Lynn R. ..... Mountain Lakes, NJ
Goldthwaite, Mary A. ..... Montgomery, AL
Goldware, Stuart I. ..... Danville, CA
Goldwasser, Andrew S. ..... Cleveland, OH
Goldwasser, Brian D. ..... Cincinnati, OH
Goldwasser, Charles A. ..... Los Angeles, CA
Goldwasser, Dan L. ..... New York, NY
Goldwasser, Diana J. ..... Brooklyn, NY
Goldwasser, Donald B. ..... Tracy, CA
Goldwasser, Gary H. ..... Cleveland, OH
Goldwasser, Harold F. ..... East Meadow, NY
Goldwasser, Howard M. ..... New York, NY
Goldwasser, Katherine ..... St. Louis, MO
Goldwasser, Richard M. ..... Chicago, IL
Goldwater, Andrew W. ..... New York, NY
Goldwater, Bert M. ..... Reno, NV
Goldwater, David ..... Las Vegas, NV
Goldwater, Deena ..... Los Angeles, CA
Goldwater, James L. ..... New York, NY
Goldwater, Jeffrey A. ..... Chicago, IL
Goldwater Law Offices ..... Phoenix, AZ
Goldwater, Lloyd J. ..... Santa Monica, CA
Goldwater & Richman, A Prof. Corp.
San Pedro, CA
Goldwater, Robert W., III ..... Phoenix, AZ
Goldwater, Vernon ..... San Pedro, CA
Goldweber, Ann L. ..... New York, NY
Goldweber, Elyse S. ..... New York, NY
Goldweber & Hershkowitz ..... Mineola, NY
Goldweber Lauriello and Epstein L.L.P.
New York, NY
Goldweber, Max ..... Mineola, NY
Goldwein, Irwin E. ..... Tamarac, FL
Goldweitz, Julie A. ..... Newton, MA
Goldwich, David S. ..... Miami, FL
Goldwin, David ..... East Meadow, NY
Goldwyn, Brant S. ..... Treasury Department, Internal Revenue Service, GV
Goldwyn, David L. ..... Department of State, U.S. Mission to the United Nations, GV
Goldwyn, Linda F. ..... Short Hills, NJ
Goldwyn, Martin M. ..... Great Neck, NY
Goldy, Donald Chad ..... Denver, CO
Goldy, Jeffery G. ..... Knoxville, TN
Goldy, Jill A. ..... Schaumburg, IL
Goldy, Robert I. ..... Blue Bell, PA
Goldy, Susan E. ..... Philadelphia, PA
Goldzweig, Arthur N. ..... Manalapan, NJ
Goldzweig, Mark Jay ..... Santa Monica, CA
Gole, Gary M. ..... Beverly Hills, CA
Gole, Richard A. ..... Indianapolis, IN
Gole, Rose E. ..... Westbury, NY
Golej, Thomas A. ..... Colorado Springs, CO
Golem, Donna A. ..... Irvine, CA
Golembe, Stephen J. ..... Miami, FL
Golembeck, James G. ..... St. Paul, MN
Golembeski, Dean J. ..... New London, CT
Golembesky, John F. ..... San Diego, CA
Golembiewski, Jeffrey S. ..... Stroudsburg, PA
Golembiewski, Patricia Anne
San Francisco, CA
Golembiewski, Robert M. ..... Okemos, MI
Golemme, Peter M. ..... Boston, MA
Golemon, R. Kinnan ..... Austin, TX
Golen, Amy ..... New York, NY
Golen, Richard F. ..... North Dartmouth, MA
Golenbock, Eiseman, Assor & Bell
New York, NY
Golenbock, Jeffrey T. ..... New York, NY
Goleniak, Doris A. ..... Detroit, MI
Golenor, Richard J. ..... Westlake Village, CA
Goler, Donald S. ..... Miami, FL
Goler, Michael D. ..... Cleveland, OH
Goles, David S. ..... Waukegan, IL
Golesorkhi-Zahedi, Parastoo
Falls Church, VA
Golestaneh, Nader A. ..... Boston, MA
Goletz, Elena Castro ..... Ansonia, CT
Goley, Sharon M. ..... Washington, DC
Golfer, J. Larry ..... Bethesda, MD
Golfinopoulos, George ..... New York, NY
Golger, J. Kevin ..... Fairfield, CT
Golger, Robert G. ..... Fairfield, CT
Golia, Davide ..... San Diego, CA
Golia, James J. ..... Douglaston, NY
Golia, Joseph G. ..... Kew Gardens, NY
Golia, Lorene ..... Nutley, NJ
Golia, Stephen T. ..... Wayne, NJ
Golian, Andrew G. ..... Wilmington, DE
Golian, Gary J. ..... Rockford, IL
Golian, Joseph J. ..... Columbus, OH
Golian, Paul D. ..... Wilmington, DE
Golias, Brian J. ..... Pittsburgh, PA
Golibersuch, Norman G. ..... Lexington, KY
Golick, Maria Bianco ..... Marietta, GA
Golick, Richard M. ..... Atlanta, GA
Golick, Toby ..... New York, NY
Golida, Jay F. ..... Los Angeles, CA
Golieb, Abner J. ..... New York, NY
Golieb, John A. ..... New York, NY
Goliger, Gail ..... New York, NY
Golightly, Kim O. ..... Washington, DC
Golightly, Michael S. ..... Salt Lake City, UT
Golightly, Scott J. ..... Richmond, VA
Golightly-Howell, Velveta P. ..... Denver, CO
Golike, Mary L. ..... St. Paul, MN
Golimbu, Alexander N. ..... Hoboken, NJ
New York, NY
Golin, Charles ..... Lancaster, PA
Golin, Charles David ..... New York, NY
Golin, David A. ..... Chicago, IL
Golin, Elaine P. ..... New York, NY
Golin, Haefner & Bacher ..... Lancaster, PA
Golin, Heather ..... Garden City, NY
Golin, Margery S. ..... New Brunswick, NJ
Golin, Sharon D. ..... Honolulu, HI
Golini, Kathleen A. ..... Providence, RI
Golinkin, Scott G. ..... Chicago, IL
Golino, Santo ..... New York, NY
Golinski, Karen ..... San Francisco, CA
Golinski, Pamela M. ..... New York, NY
Golinski, Paul A. ..... Brooklyn, NY
Golinsky, Dan S. ..... Miami, FL
Golis, Paul R. ..... Boca Raton, FL
Golison, Jennifer Ann ..... Costa Mesa, CA
Goljan, Keith E. ..... Phoenix, AZ
Golkiewicz, Gary J.
United States Court of Federal Claims, Office of Special Masters, GV
Golkin, Jeffrey ..... Warren, NJ
Golkin, Jeffrey ..... New York, NY
Golkin, Lawrence H. ..... Santa Barbara, CA
Golko, Andrew A. ..... Chicago, IL
Golkow, Andrew B. ..... Vienna, VA
Golkow, Curtis L. ..... Cherry Hill, NJ
Philadelphia, PA
Golkow, James D. ..... Philadelphia, PA
Golkow, Michele Berman
Philadelphia, PA
Goll, Geoffrey S. ..... Salem, OH
Goll, Nora H. ..... Tekamah, NE
Goll, Richard K. ..... Wilmington, DE
Golla, Charles E. ..... Minneapolis, MN
Golla, Gregory Charles ..... Minneapolis, MN
Golla, Russell T. ..... Stevens Point, WI
Gollaher, Larry L. ..... Dallas, TX
Gollaher, Larry L., P.C. ..... Dallas, TX
Gollaher, Merton G. ..... New Haven, CT
Golland, Jeffrey P.
Department Of Health And Human Services, Office of the General Counsel, GV
Golland, Michael H. ..... Santa Monica, CA

Gollatz, Alfred A. .... Media, PA
Philadelphia, PA
West Chester, PA
Gollatz, Griffin & Ewing, P.C. .... Media, PA
Philadelphia, PA
Pittsburgh, PA
West Chester, PA
Golle, Eric J. .... **Dallas, TX**
Goller, David R. .... **Jefferson City, MO**
Goller, Diane E. .... Grand Rapids, MI
Goller, Gardner & Feather, Professional Corporation .... **Jefferson City, MO**
Goller, John G. .... **Spokane, WA**
Goller, Karlene Worthington
Los Angeles, CA
Goller, Leslie A. .... **Jacksonville, FL**
Goller, Michael G. .... **Milwaukee, WI**
Goller, Mimi C. .... **North Chicago, IL**
Goller, Nathan .... Los Angeles, CA
Goller, Ronald R. .... Indian Rocks Beach, FL
Gollhofer, Richard A. .... **Washington, DC**
Golliher, Daphne D. .... **Walnut Creek, CA**
Golliher, Kenneth W. .... Louisville, KY
Gollihue, Lisa L. .... **White Plains, NY**
Gollihugh, Susan .... Pittsburgh, PA
Gollin, Adam M. .... Denver, CO
Gollin, Andrew S. .... **Milwaukee, WI**
Gollin, David B. .... **Minneapolis, MN**
Gollin, David L. .... **Philadelphia, PA**
Gollin, Lynn Maynard .... **Miami, FL**
West Palm Beach, FL
Gollin, Mary R. .... Houston, TX
Gollin, Michael A. .... **Washington, DC**
Gollinger, Stuart H. .... Avon, CT
Gollings & Gollings, P.C. .... Decatur, IL
Gollings, James R. .... Decatur, IL
Gollings, Michael L. .... Youngstown, OH
Gollis, Samuel D. .... **Albuquerque, NM**
Gollmitzer, Raymond F. .... Shreveport, LA
Gollnick, Clayton R. .... **Houston, TX**
Gollnick, Theodore A. .... Sarasota, FL
Gollnick, Theodore A., P.A. .... Sarasota, FL
Gollob-Gomez, Jane .... Department of Justice, Civil Division, GV
Gollomp, Jeffrey A. .... **Washington, DC**
Gollomp, Lawrence A.
Department of Energy, Office of the General Counsel, GV
Gollon, Frank R. .... Rochester, NY
Gollop, Scott W. .... Albany, NY
Gollub, Diane .... Rockville Centre, NY
Gollub & Golsan .... **Culver City, CA**
Los Angeles, CA
Gollub, John W. .... Denver, CO
Gollub, Linda J. .... Overland Park, KS
Gollub, Lorraine C. .... **Culver City, CA**
Gollub, Michael S. .... **Uniondale, NY**
Gollub, Myron .... St. Louis, MO
Gollub, Paul N. .... Boston, MA
Gollub, Walter .... Voorhees, NJ
Gollup, Eugenie M. .... North Fort Myers, FL
Gollwitzer, Arthur, III .... **Chicago, IL**
Gollwitzer, Robert .... Richmond, VA
Golm, Jennifer A. .... **Tulsa, OK**
Golman, Mark E. .... **Dallas, TX**
Golman, Sidney J. .... Davis, CA
Golmon, Bradley Truett .... **Greenville, MS**
Golmon, Stacy Woodruff .... Greenville, MS
Golnick, Clare, Professional Corporation
Reno, NV
Golnick, Clare S. .... Reno, NV
Golniewicz, Francis Xavier .... Chicago, IL
Golob, Barry P. .... **Washington, DC**
Golob, Bragin & Sassoe, P.C.
Los Angeles, CA
Golob, Brian C. .... Tacoma, WA
Golob, Dennis E. .... **Los Angeles, CA**
Golob, Gordon A. .... Tacoma, WA
Golob, Howard M. .... Piscataway, NJ
Golob, Michael H. .... **Farmington Hills, MI**
Golob, Nicole I. .... **Los Angeles, CA**
Goloboff, Barry D. .... Cleveland, OH
Golochnik, Lynne M. .... **Palo Alto, CA**
Golod, Lisa Katz .... **Atlanta, GA**
Golodner, Adam M. .... Department of Justice, Antitrust Division, GV
Golodner, Scott M. .... **New York, NY**
Goloff, Carol Niewender .... Marmora, NJ
Golomb, Alan E. .... Garden City, NY
Golomb, Barry .... **New York, NY**
Golomb, Cynthia L. .... Columbia, MD
Golomb, David B., Law Offices of
New York, NY
Golomb, George E. .... **Baltimore, MD**
Golomb, Irving L. .... New York, NY
Golomb, Jeffrey .... **Atlanta, GA**
Golomb, Jonathan I. .... Washington, DC
Golomb, Richard M. .... Philadelphia, PA
Golomb, Samuel J. .... Chicago, IL
Golombeck, Abraham Zev .... Brooklyn, NY
Golonka, Denise Smith .... Columbus, OH
Golonka, Kenneth A., Jr. .... **Columbus, OH**
Golos, Abraham .... Elmira, NY
Golota, Mary Elizabeth .... **Mount Olive, NJ**
Golove, David .... New York, NY
Golovensky, Joel H. (IBA) .... Mineola, NY
Golowich, Joan R. .... **Amherst, MA**
Golowin, Serge A. .... Columbus, OH
Golowski, Anthony J., II .... **Morristown, NJ**
Golper, John B. .... **Universal City, CA**
Golrick, Mary E. .... **Cleveland, OH**
Golrick, Philip D. .... Department of Justice, Office of Intelligence Policy and Review, GV
Golrick, Richard T.
Department of Transportation, Federal Aviation Administration, GV
Golsan, Maryanne .... **Culver City, CA**

Golski, Ann Mayhew .... **Virginia Beach, VA**
Golski, Gregory A. .... St. Clair Shores, MI
Golski, Harry K. .... Charlevoix, MI
Golson, Ari H. .... Chicago, IL
Golson, Jerrold J. .... **Clearwater, FL**
Golson, W. Gregory .... **Tampa, FL**
Golson, William M. .... **Clearwater, FL**
Golson, William M., & Associates, Attorneys at Law, Chartered .... **Clearwater, FL**
Golson-Dunlap, Jenice .... Indianapolis, IN
Golstein, Brad I .... Woodland Hills, CA
Golston Keister & Steen P.L.C.
Tempe, AZ
Golston, Rodger A. .... **Tempe, AZ**
Golter, Harry .... Chicago, IL
Golterman, Anne M. .... **St. Louis, MO**
Golterman, Robert J. .... **St. Louis, MO**
Goltermann, Neil T. .... **Downers Grove, IL**
Goltermann, Robert C. .... Denver, CO
Goltra, Alexis Obolensky .... **Boston, MA**
Goltra, Allen E. .... Stuart, FL
Goltry, Michael W. .... **Phoenix, AZ**
Goltz, Bertram P., Jr. .... Newark, NJ
Goltz, David N. .... Auburn Hills, MI
Goltz, Jeffrey D. .... Olympia, WA
Goltz, Jeffrey Paul .... **Falls City, NE**
Goltz, Jon .... **Anchorage, AK**
Goltz, Paul M. .... Pittsburgh, PA
Goltz, Portor .... Redwood City, CA
Goltz, Susan Ackerman .... Washington, DC
Goltzer & Adler .... **New York, NY**
Goltzer, George R. .... **New York, NY**
New York, NY
Golub, Aaron Richard .... New York, NY
Golub, Alan S. .... **Totowa, NJ**
Golub, Allene H. .... Springfield, PA
Golub, Andrew S. .... **Houston, TX**
Golub, Arnold P. .... Washington, DC
Golub, Benjamin J. .... New York, NY
Golub, Beth Isaacs .... **San Diego, CA**
Golub, Beth T. .... **Chicago, IL**
Golub, Bonnie R. .... **Philadelphia, PA**
Golub, Daniel H. .... **Philadelphia, PA**
Golub, David .... **Wayne, NJ**
Golub, David S. .... **Stamford, CT**
Golub, Errol G. .... Chicago, IL
Golub, Franchot A. S. .... Philadelphia, PA
Golub, Gerald B. .... Canton, OH
Golub & Golub, LLP .... New York, NY
Golub, Howard V. .... **San Francisco, CA**
Golub, I. Jay .... **Houston, TX**
Golub, Ira M. .... **New York, NY**
Golub, J. Richard .... **Kansas City, MO**
Golub, Jeffrey M. .... **Houston, TX**
Golub, Jennifer A. .... **Newark, NJ**
Golub, Jeryl Annette .... **Houston, TX**
Golub, Joel H. .... Walnut Creek, CA
Golub, Larry M. .... **Los Angeles, CA**
Golub, Laurie F. .... **New York, NY**
Golub, Lisa M. .... Newark, NJ
Golub, Marilyn .... Bellaire, TX
Golub, Marjorie E. .... San Francisco, CA
Golub, Martin H. .... Buffalo Grove, IL
Golub, Martin J. .... **Washington, DC**
Golub, Michael E., P.A. .... Tavares, FL
Golub, Michael Edward .... Tavares, FL
Golub, Michael J. .... Washington, DC
Golub, Michael K. .... Worcester, MA
Golub, Mitchell A. .... New York, NY
Golub, Mitchell S., (P.C.) .... **San Diego, CA**
Golub, Norman J. .... **Jersey City, NJ**
Golub, Paul D. .... Compton, CA
Golub, Phillip N. .... Blackshear, GA
Golub, Richard & Allene, The Law Offices of
Springfield, PA
Golub, Richard M. .... Springfield, PA
Golub, Robert .... New York, NY
Golub, Robert L. .... New York, NY
Golub, Rochelle .... Fort Lauderdale, FL
Golub, Sharon J. .... Colorado Springs, CO
Golub, Stanley D. .... Seattle, WA
Golub, Steven M. .... New York, NY
Golub, Todd D. .... **Chicago, IL**
Golub, William W. .... New York, NY
Goluba, David A. .... Ripon, WI
Goluba, Nicholas W., Jr.
Glenwood Springs, CO
Goluba, Todd A. .... **Pleasanton, CA**
Goluban, Joseph J. .... Riverview, MI
Golubchik, David B. .... **Los Angeles, CA**
Golubock, Carol R. .... Washington, DC
Goluboff, Nicole Belson .... Scarsdale, NY
Golubow, Richard H. .... **Newport Beach, CA**
Golum, Gordon J. .... **Woodbridge, NJ**
Golumbic, Court Edward
Treasury Department, Departmental Offices, GV
Golumbic, Lars .... **Washington, DC**
Golup, Janet E. .... **Philadelphia, PA**
Golvach, Steven P. .... Houston, TX
Golwen, John S. .... **Memphis, TN**
Golz, Helmut .... Bellflower, CA
Golz, Thomas Bernard .... **Chicago, IL**
Golzar, Lisa M. .... **Chicago, IL**
Golze, Richard .... Honolulu, HI
Golze, Sandra A. .... **San Francisco, CA**
Golzen, Frank R. .... Mountain View, CA
Gombar, Robert C. .... **Washington, DC**
Gomberg, Arthur S. .... Chicago, IL
Gomberg, Arthur S., Law Offices of, A Professional Corporation .... Chicago, IL
Gomberg, Ira A. .... New York, NY
Gomberg, Jennifer .... **Miami, FL**
Gomberg, Joel .... Oakland, CA
Gomberg Kane & Fischer, Ltd.
Chicago, IL
Gomberg, Robert M. .... **Chicago, IL**

Gomberg, Sharfman, Gold and Ostler, P.C.
Chicago, IL
Gomberg, Sheldon S. .... Chicago, IL
Gomberg, Stanley B. .... Jenkintown, PA
Gomberg, Steven L. .... Akron, OH
Gomberg, Steven P. .... **Chicago, IL**
Gomberg, Steven W. .... West Palm Beach, FL
Gombert, Richard E. .... **Columbus, OH**
Gombinski, Steven J. .... Roseland, NJ
Gombis, Albert T.
Department of the Air Force, Office of the Judge Advocate General, GV
Gombos, Pamela M. .... Miami, FL
Gombos, Steven M. .... **Fairfax, VA**
Gomel & Davis, LLP .... **Atlanta, GA**
Gomel, Jeffrey R. .... **Las Vegas, NV**
Gomel, Walter E. .... **Atlanta, GA**
Marietta, GA
Gomelsky, Victor .... New York, NY
Gomer, Glenn G. .... Tampa, FL
Gomer, Keith G. .... Philadelphia, PA
Gomer, Murray .... Beverly Hills, CA
Gomerman, Adam C. .... Dix Hills, NY
Gomes, Antonio G. .... **Boston, MA**
Gomes, Chandra .... Kew Gardens, NY
Gomes, David A. .... Santa Ana, CA
Gomes, David W. .... Nashua, NH
Gomes, Edward J., Jr. .... Providence, RI
Gomes, Eugene J., Jr. .... New Orleans, LA
Gomes, Gene M. .... Fresno, CA
Gomes, Jackson, Hulse & Klump, An Assn. of Attys. .... Santa Ana, CA
Gomes, Jacqueline L., P.A. .... Lincoln, ME
Gomes, Jacqueline L. .... Lincoln, ME
Gomes, James R. .... Boston, MA
Gomes, Kathleen N. .... Memphis, TN
Gomes, Matthew T. .... **Atlanta, GA**
Gomes, Michael N. .... **Pompano Beach, FL**
Gomes, Michael N., P.A.
Pompano Beach, FL
Gomes, William A. .... Rockville Centre, NY
Gomez, Alberto F., Jr. .... **Tampa, FL**
Gómez, Alexis J. .... **Houston, TX**
Gomez, Alvin M. .... **Chula Vista, CA**
Gomez, Angel G. .... **Chicago, IL**
Gomez, Angel, III .... **Los Angeles, CA**
Gomez, Anna M.
Federal Communications Commission, Common Carrier Bureau, GV
Gomez, Anne M. .... Durham, NC
Gomez, Armando .... **Washington, DC**
Gomez, August L." A.J. "
Donaldsonville, LA
Gomez, Bobbi Acord .... **Atlanta, GA**
Gomez, Carlos M. .... Springfield, MA
Gomez, Carlos M., P.C., Law Offices of
Springfield, MA
Gomez, Cesar .... Key Biscayne, FL
Gomez, Christopher A.
Plymouth Meeting, PA
Gomez, Cristina .... Hialeah, FL
Gómez, Curtis V.
Charlotte Amalie, St. Thomas, VI
Gomez, Dave .... **Phoenix, AZ**
Gomez, David F. .... **Phoenix, AZ**
Gomez, David F., A Professional Corporation
Phoenix, AZ
Gomez, Del Pino & Ruiz, P.A. .... Miami, FL
Gomez, Diana E. .... Santa Ana, CA
Gómez, Diego A.
Federal Energy Regulatory Commission, Office of the General Counsel, GV
Gomez, Edward A. .... San Jose, CA
Gomez, Edward R. .... **New York, NY**
Gomez, Elena Maria .... **Coral Gables, FL**
Gomez, Esteban J. .... Scottsdale, AZ
Gomez, Felipe N. .... Milwaukee, WI
Gomez, Franchesca Rand Fede
McLean, VA
Gomez, Frank A. .... Tampa, FL
Gomez, Frank Thomas .... Roswell, GA
Gomez, Genevieve T. .... Cincinnati, OH
Gomez, German A. .... **New York, NY**
Gomez, Glynda B. .... Los Angeles, CA
Gomez, Gustavo .... Glendale, CA
Gomez, Iris D. .... Boston, MA
Gomez, Irving S. .... **Los Angeles, CA**
Gómez, Ismael .... Jamaica, NY
Gomez, Ivan A., P.A. .... **Miami, FL**
Gomez, Jane G. .... Department of Justice, Civil Division, GV
Gomez, Joel T. .... **Dallas, TX**
Gomez, John B. .... Franklin Square, NY
Gomez, John H. .... San Diego, CA
Gomez, Jorge A. .... **Milwaukee, WI**
Gomez, Joseph R. .... **Miami, FL**
Gomez, Juan R. V. .... Atlanta, GA
Gomez, Julio C. .... **Roseland, NJ**
Gomez, Julio, Jr. .... Edinburg, TX
Gomez, Julio M. .... Miami, FL
Gomez, Ken M. .... Cape May, NJ
Gomez, Kenneth V. .... New York, NY
Gomez, Larry .... Albuquerque, NM
Gomez, Laura L. .... **Laredo, TX**
Gomez, Leo D. .... **Tampa, FL**
Gomez, Lisa A. .... **Chicago, IL**
Gomez, Lisa M. .... **New York, NY**
Gomez, Lisa P. .... **San Diego, CA**
Gomez, Lourdes P., Law Offices of
New York, NY
Gomez, Luis F. .... Orlando, FL
Gomez, Luis F., Jr. .... Upper Marlboro, MD
Gomez, Lynne M. .... **Houston, TX**
Gomez, Manuel A. .... New York, NY
Gomez, Marcelo R. .... Fort Lauderdale, FL
Gomez, Marco .... Oakland, CA
Gomez, Marcus .... Norwalk, CA
Gomez, Marisa A. .... **Washington, DC**

Gomez, Mark A. .... Newnan, GA
Gomez, Mark A. .... New York, NY
Gomez, Matthew P. .... Tulsa, OK
Gomez, Michael W. .... Miami, FL
Gomez, Nicolas J., Jr.
South San Francisco, CA
Gomez, Olga Maria .... Miami, FL
Gómez, Oscar O. .... **McAllen, TX**
Gomez, Patricia .... San Luis Obispo, CA
Gomez, Patricia A. .... **Los Angeles, CA**
Gomez, Paul C. .... Denver, CO
Gomez, Peter .... Orlando, FL
Gomez, Ramon .... Upland, CA
Gomez, Ramon .... New York, NY
Gomez, Raphael O. .... Department of Justice, Civil Division, GV
Gomez, Raymond G. .... Vista, CA
Gomez, Rene .... Brownsville, TX
Gomez, Richard M. .... **Miami, FL**
Gomez, Richard R. .... Rosemead, CA
Gomez, Robert A. .... Sacramento, CA
Gomez, Robert J. .... **Washington, DC**
Gomez, Robert J., Jr. .... Alhambra, CA
Gomez, Rodolfo .... **Miami, FL**
Gomez, Roland H. .... **Miami, FL**
Gomez, Salomon .... Department of Justice, Civil Division, GV
Gomez, Sheila L. .... **New York, NY**
Gomez, Teresita .... **Lilburn, GA**
Gomez, Timoteo E. .... Brownsville, TX
Gómez, Verónica .... **Chicago, IL**
Gomez, Wayne D. .... San Diego, CA
Gomez-Blanchfield, Ana .... Hyannis, MA
Gomez-Colon, Ramon E. .... **San Juan, PR**
Gómez Escarce, Juan Carlos
San Juan, PR
Gomez Getty, Wendy .... Fairfield, CA
Gómez Negrón, César .... **San Juan, PR**
Gomez-Paiewonsky, Amelia Alexandra
Miami, FL
Gomez-Velez, Natalie .... New York, NY
Gomez-Vidal, Alberto .... Miami, FL
Gomien & Harrop Law Offices of
Morris, IL
Gomien, Roger B. .... Morris, IL
Gomila, John G., Jr. .... **New Orleans, LA**
Gomila, Maurice .... New Orleans, LA
Gomlicker, Christopher .... Little Rock, AR
Gomolchak, John E. .... Erie, PA
Gomolinski & Associates, Ltd.
Hickory Hills, IL
Gomolinski, William E. .... Hickory Hills, IL
Gomoll, Gary W. .... Palm Beach Gardens, FL
Gomoll, Jennifer M. .... Elgin, IL
Gomoll, Terry P. .... Lansing, MI
Gomora, Paula A. .... Joliet, IL
Gomory, Paul L. .... Bethesda, MD
Gomoto, Colette H. .... **Honolulu, HI**
Gompers, Geoffrey B. .... Mount Laurel, NJ
Philadelphia, PA
Gompers, Geoffrey B., & Associates, P.C.
Mount Laurel, NJ
Philadelphia, PA
Gompers, John E. .... **Wheeling, WV**
Gompers, Joseph A. .... **Wheeling, WV**
Gompers, McCarthy & McClure
Wheeling, WV
Gomperts, John S. .... Washington, DC
Gompertz, Michael L., Jr.
Treasury Department, Internal Revenue Service, GV
Gompertz, Steven M. .... Arcata, CA
Gompf, Clayton N., Jr. .... Spartanburg, SC
Gompf, Henry L. .... **Dallas, TX**
Gompf, Jean L. .... Seattle, WA
Gomric, Julia R. .... **Belleville, IL**
Gomsrud, Richard G. .... St. Paul, MN
Gomulka, John Kevin .... Mount Olive, NC
Gomulkiewicz, Robert W. .... **Redmond, WA**
Gonakis, Spiros E. .... Euclid, OH
Gonano, Aulo I. .... Wyandotte, MI
Gonano, Aulo I., P.C. .... Wyandotte, MI
Gonano, Douglas E. .... **Fort Pierce, FL**
Gonano, Harrell & Ferguson
Fort Pierce, FL
Stuart, FL
Vero Beach, FL
Gonas, Roy B. .... Miami, FL
Goncalves, Deborah Rupp
Albuquerque, NM
Goncalves, Deborah Rupp, P.C.
Albuquerque, NM
Goncalves, Maria J. R. .... **Boston, MA**
Providence, RI
Goncalves, Solange .... Modesto, CA
Gonce, Robert L. .... **Florence, AL**
Gonce Young Sibley & Moreau
Florence, AL
Tuscumbia, AL
Gonchar, Eric P. .... **New York, NY**
Gonchar, Meryl Ann Greenhause
Woodbridge, NJ
Goncharoff, Jamie W. .... West Chester, PA
Gonciarz, Edward F. .... **Las Vegas, NV**
Goncz, Samuel J. .... **Pittsburgh, PA**
Gonda, Jeffrey J. .... **Sheridan, WY**
Gonda, Richard F. .... Cleveland, OH
Gondak, Cristine E. .... Oakland, CA
Gondek, David F. .... **San Bernardino, CA**
Gondek, Diana S. .... Boston, MA
Gondek, Francis C. .... Wilmington, DE
Gondelman, Harold .... **Pittsburgh, PA**
Gondelman, Larry S. .... **Washington, DC**
Gonden, David Martinez
San Francisco, CA
Gonder, Bridget Tucker .... Kalamazoo, MI
Gonder, Dionne R. .... Winston-Salem, NC
Gonderinger, Robert M. .... **Omaha, NE**

Gonderman, Robert F., Jr. ...South Bend, IN
Gondree, Howard F. ...Buffalo, NY
Gonek, Ben M. ...Detroit, MI
Gonek, Calvin M. ...Bloomfield Hills, MI
Gonella, Carol Samuelian ...Burlingame, CA
Gonella, Robert J. ...Hayward, CA
Goner, Robert David ...New York, NY
Gonet, Richard F. ...Richmond, VA
Gong, Daniel Ling ...Auburn, CA
Gong, Edmond J. ...Miami, FL
Gong, Jennifer H. ...Chicago, IL
Gong, Kevin A. ...Treasury Department, Office of Thrift Supervision, GV
Gong, Lori M. ...Santa Ana, CA
Gong, Mitchell, Combs & Lee, LLP
Oakland, CA
Gong, Raymond G. ...Oakland, CA
Gongora, Michael C. ...Miami Beach, FL
Gonia, Elizabeth M. ...Tustin, CA
Gonias, Ralph ...Brooklyn, NY
Gonick, Denise V. ...Schenectady, NY
Gonick, Harry ...Hayward, CA
Gonick, Jeffrey ...Leola, PA
Gonick, Jerry G. ...San Diego, CA
Gonick, Kathie Shirk ...Lancaster, PA
Gonick, Peter B. ...Seattle, WA
Gonick, Susan ...La Jolla, CA
Goniea, James A. ...San Francisco, CA
Gonillo, Christine M. ...Milford, CT
Gónima, Maureen Strauss
San Antonio, TX
Gonko, Kenneth M. ...Bloomfield Hills, MI
Gonlubol, Ahmet S. ...Des Moines, IA
Gonnella, Carol H. ...Jackson, WY
Gonnella, John A. ...Caldwell, NJ
Gonnella, Joseph C. ...Minneapolis, MN
Gonnella, Louis G. ...Hackensack, NJ
Gonnella, Louis J. ...Winchester, MA
Gonnella & Sullivan, PLLC
Idaho Falls, ID
Ketchum, ID
Bothell, WA
Jackson, WY
Gonnelli, Adam R. ...New York, NY
Gonnerman, Mark A. ...St. Louis, MO
Gonon, Richard B. ...Indianapolis, IN
Gonor, David M. ...Los Angeles, CA
Gonot, Gregory L. ...Sacramento, CA
Gonring, Andrew T. ...West Bend, WI
Gonring, Leroy J. ...West Bend, WI
Gonring, Michael J. ...Milwaukee, WI
Gonring, Michael J., Jr. ...West Bend, WI
Gonsalez, Maximino, Jr. ...New York, NY
Gonsalves, Andrew K. ...New York, NY
Gonsalves, Gregory J. ...Washington, DC
Gonsalves, Howard T. ...Walnut Creek, CA
Gonsalves & Kozachenko ...Fremont, CA
Gonsalves, Linda M. ...Fremont, CA
Gonsalves, Martin T. ...Concord, CA
Gonsalves, Matthew J. ...San Leandro, CA
Gonsalves, Patricia T. ...Alexandria, VA
Gonsalves, Stanislaus Andrew ...Chicago, IL
Gonsalves, Stephanie A. ...Honolulu, HI
Gonsalves, Teresa A. ...New York, NY
Gonsalves, Victor A. ...Modesto, CA
Gonser, Carl A. ...San Anselmo, CA
Gonser, Milo N. ...Denver, CO
Gonser, Pawlowski & Johnson, P.C.
Denver, CO
Gonser, Robert L. ...Lafayette, CA
Gonser, Thomas H. ...Friday Harbor, WA
Gonser, William A., Jr. ...Wilmington, DE
Gonser, William L. ...Walnut Creek, CA
Gonshak, Brett A. ...Miami, FL
Gonshak, David M. ...Miami, FL
Gonshak, Evan J. ...Miami, FL
Gonshorek, Eliot D. ...Brooklyn, NY
Gonski, Dennis M. ...Fairfield, NJ
Carle Place, NY
Gonski, William W., Jr. ...Northampton, MA
Gonsky, Ronald M., (Ltd.) ...Chicago, IL
Gonso, Harry L. ...Indianapolis, IN
Gonson, Benjamin N. ...New York, NY
Gonson, Elise Dawn ...Baldwin, NY
Gonson, Paul ...Washington, DC
Gonson, S. Donald ...Boston, MA
Gonsoulin, Dewey J. ...Beaumont, TX
Gonsoulin, Dewey J., Jr. ...Houston, TX
Gonsowski, Margaret Mary ...Albany, NY
Gonta, John C. ...Redford, MI
Gontar, David P. ...New Orleans, LA
Gontarek, John Jay, (P.A.)
Fort Walton Beach, FL
Gontarek, Paul J. ...Philadelphia, PA
Gontarz, Christopher S. ...Middletown, RI
Gonter, K. Robert, Jr. ...Irvine, CA
Gontovnick, Bernard H. ...Northbrook, IL
Gontownik, I. Joseph ...New York, NY
Gontram, Joseph M. ...
Department of Justice, GV
Gontrum, John B. ...Baltimore, MD
Gonway, John P. ...Birmingham, MI
Gonya, Jeffrey K. ...Baltimore, MD
Gonya, Patrick E., Jr. ...Miami, FL
Gonyea, Patrick H. ...Fort Lauderdale, FL
Gonyea, Sheri L. ...Clarksville, TN
Gonyer, Todd E. ...Overland Park, KS
Gonynor, Francis J. ...Houston, TX
Gonyo, Jeffrey M. ...Slinger, WI
Gonyo, Robert M. ...Berlin, WI
Gonzale, Kenneth Luis Chapman
San Diego, CA
Gonzales, Albert T. ...Santa Fe, NM
Gonzales, Albert V. ...Santa Fe, NM
Gonzales, Alexander J. ...Austin, TX
Gonzales, Alicia J. ...Los Angeles, CA
Gonzales, Andrew G. ...San Jose, CA
Gonzales, Arnold, Jr. ...Corpus Christi, TX
Gonzales, Arthur J. ...Shelby, OH
Gonzales, Brian D. ...Denver, CO
Gonzales, Cal G. ...San Francisco, CA
Gonzales, Cherie L. ...Atlanta, GA
Gonzales, Cheryl J. ...Brooklyn, NY
Gonzales, Claire E. ...
Equal Employment Opportunity Commission, GV
Gonzales, Cynthia E. ...Phoenix, AZ
Gonzales, Cynthia E., P.C. ...Phoenix, AZ
Gonzales, Dan A. ...Las Cruces, NM
Gonzales, Daniel E. ...Portland, OR
Gonzales, Daniel S. ...Palo Alto, CA
San Jose, CA
Gonzales, Debra Lynn ...Los Angeles, CA
Gonzales, Dennis M. ...Los Angeles, CA
Gonzales, Dolores E. ...San Diego, CA
Gonzales, Donald E. ...Spring, TX
Gonzales, Douglas M. ...Baton Rouge, LA
Gonzales, Douglas R. ...Miami, FL
Gonzales, E. Ricardo ...Denver, CO
Gonzales, E. Ricardo, P.C. ...Denver, CO
Gonzales, Edward J., III
Baton Rouge, LA
Gonzales, Edward P. ...Boston, MA
Gonzales, Elizabeth L. ...Waco, TX
Gonzales, Elmira ...Santa Fe, NM
Gonzales, Ernest S. ...Monrovia, CA
Gonzales, Ernesto ...Harlingen, TX
Gonzales, Esteban Huerta ...Dallas, TX
Gonzales, Fernando D. ...New York, NY
Gonzales, Francisco E. ...Edinburg, TX
Gonzales, Frank J. ...El Paso, TX
Gonzales, Gerardo H. ...Houston, TX
Gonzales & Gonzales ...Charleston, SC
Gonzales, Gregory ...Nashville, TN
Gonzales, Gregory M. ...Vancouver, WA
Gonzales, Gustavo E. ...Dallas, TX
Gonzales, Holly Beth ...Fort Collins, CO
Gonzales, Ida Ann ...Austin, TX
Gonzales, Jacquelyn A. ...Birmingham, AL
Gonzales, James E. ...Fremont, CA
Gonzales, James E. ...Charleston, SC
Gonzales, James J. ...Denver, CO
Gonzales, Jeffrey Charles ...Portland, OR
Gonzales, John ...Westbury, NY
Gonzales, John ...San Antonio, TX
Gonzales, John, & Associates, P.C.
San Antonio, TX
Gonzales, John F. ...Department of Commerce, Patent and Trademark Office, GV
Gonzales, John J. ...Feasterville, PA
Gonzales, John M. ...Columbus, OH
Gonzales, John P. ...Norristown, PA
Gonzales, Jon C. ...Palo Alto, CA
Gonzales, Jorge O. ...National City, CA
Gonzales, Jose A. ...San Diego, CA
Gonzales, Juan A. ...Miami, FL
Gonzales, Juan Martinez ...Beeville, TX
Gonzales, Kathleen M. ...Riverside, CA
Gonzales, Kenneth John ...Santa Fe, NM
Gonzales, Larry J. ...Port Richey, FL
Gonzales, Laura E. ...San Francisco, CA
Gonzales Law Firm, The, P.C.
Phoenix, AZ
Tucson, AZ
Gonzales, Leonor C. ...Los Angeles, CA
Gonzales, Leticia L. ...Miami, FL
Gonzales, Liana E. ...Corpus Christi, TX
Gonzales, Louise Michaux ...Baltimore, MD
Gonzáles, Luis A. ...Arlington, VA
Gonzales, Marco E. ...Albuquerque, NM
Gonzales, Margaret H. ...Berkeley Heights, NJ
Gonzales, Martin A. ...Alamosa, CO
Gonzales, Mary ...Silver Spring, MD
Gonzales, Michael ...Rosemead, CA
Gonzales, Nazario A. ...San Jose, CA
Gonzales, Nelva ...Corpus Christi, TX
Gonzales, Norma ...San Antonio, TX
Gonzales, Rafael A. ...Yakima, WA
Gonzales, Ralph E. ...
Department of Housing and Urban Development, GV
Gonzales, Ramon M. ...Albuquerque, NM
Gonzales, Richard ...Denver, CO
Gonzales, Richard A. ...Albuquerque, NM
Gonzales, Richard J. ...Tucson, AZ
Gonzales, Richard M. ...Gilroy, CA
Gonzales, Richard N. ...Denver, CO
Gonzales, Richard O. ...Eagle Pass, TX
Gonzales, Richard R. ...Hebbronville, TX
Gonzales, Richard V
Department of Transportation, U. S. Coast Guard, GV
Gonzales, Robert ...Hayward, CA
Gonzales, Robert E. ...San Francisco, CA
Gonzales, Robert J. ...Nashville, TN
Gonzales, Robert T. ...Baltimore, MD
Gonzales, Ronald R. ...Houston, TX
Gonzales, Rudy, Jr. ...Corpus Christi, TX
Gonzales, Servando H., Jr. ...McAllen, TX
Gonzales, Sherry A. ...Denver, CO
Gonzales, Stephen E. ...Charleston, SC
Gonzales, Steven ...Phoenix, AZ
Gonzales, Thomas L.
Department of Agriculture, Agricultural Research Service, GV
Gonzales, Timothy A. ...Los Angeles, CA
Gonzales, Veronica ...McAllen, TX
Gonzales, Vincent M. ...Long Beach, CA
Gonzales, Virginia C. ...Lamarque, TX
Gonzales, Yvette Jo ...Albuquerque, NM
Gonzales-Kimbrough, Marcia J.
Los Angeles, CA
Gonzales-Madrid, John Eugene
Lafayette, CA
Gonzalez, A. C., Jr. ...El Paso, TX
Gonzalez, Adam N. ...Portland, ME
González, Adán A., III ...Laredo, TX
Gonzalez, Adriano R. ...Port St. Lucie, FL
Gonzalez, Alan F. ...Tampa, FL
Gonzalez, Alan F., P.A. ...Tampa, FL
Gonzalez, Alberto E. ...San Francisco, CA
Gonzalez, Alberto L. ...Sacramento, CA
Gonzalez, Alex M. ...Miami, FL
Gonzalez, Alex R. ...Fort Stockton, TX
Gonzalez, Alexis ...Miami, FL
Gonzalez, Alfonso J. ...Chevy Chase, MD
Gonzalez, Alfonso Z. ...Sacramento, CA
Gonzalez, Alfredo L. ...Miami, FL
Gonzalez, Ana Maria ...Houston, TX
Gonzalez, Ana Maria Mendez
Miami Lakes, FL
Gonzalez, Andres ...Hollywood, FL
Gonzalez, Andres H., Jr. ...McAllen, TX
Gonzalez, Andrew A. ...Staten Island, NY
Gonzalez, Anna Cecilia ...Austin, TX
Gonzalez, Anthony F. ...Tampa, FL
Gonzalez, Arnold G. ...Corpus Christi, TX
Gonzalez, Arnulfo, Jr. ...Laredo, TX
Gonzalez, Arthur I. ...Bakersfield, CA
Gonzalez, Arthur J. ...New York, NY
Gonzalez, Arturo C. ...Del Rio, TX
Gonzalez, Arturo J. ...San Francisco, CA
Gonzalez, Arturo J. ...Houston, TX
Gonzalez, Arturo P. ...Elgin, IL
Gonzalez, Brian C., Law Offices of
Los Angeles, CA
Gonzalez, Brian C., Law Offices of
Manhattan Beach, CA
González, Carlos A. ...Atlanta, GA
Gonzalez, Carlos Antonio ...Birmingham, AL
Gonzalez, Carlos G. ...New York, NY
Gonzalez, Carlos J. ...Chicago, IL
Gonzalez, Carlos M. ...Newark, NJ
Gonzalez, Carmen G. ...San Francisco, CA
Gonzalez, Carmen R. ...Pasadena, CA
González Castañer, Morales & Guzman P.C.
San Juan, PR
Gonzalez, Catherine Jane ...Springfield, IL
Gonzalez, Catherine T. ...Chicago, IL
Gonzalez, Cecilia H. ...Washington, DC
Gonzalez, Celso M. ...Corpus Christi, TX
Gonzalez, Cesar, Jr. ...Bronx, NY
Gonzalez, Charles ...New York, NY
Gonzalez, Charles A. ...San Antonio, TX
Gonzalez, Christina Diaz ...Miami, FL
Gonzalez, Christina E. ...Boston, MA
Gonzalez, Christopher ...Glendale, CA
Gonzalez, Criselda B. ...Fairfield, CA
Gonzalez, Cristina E. ...Boston, MA
Gonzalez, Daniel ...Carrizo Springs, TX
Gonzalez, Daniel E., (P.A.) ...Miami, FL
Gonzalez, Daniel J. ...Los Angeles, CA
Gonzalez, Danielle D. ...Victoria, TX
Gonzalez, David ...Bloomfield, NJ
Gonzalez, David A. ...San Jose, CA
Gonzalez, David O. ...Alice, TX
Gonzalez, Dawn M. ...Chicago, IL
Gonzalez, Donald J. ...Glendale, CA
Gonzalez, Edgardo ...Santa Monica, CA
Gonzalez, Edgardo ...Norristown, PA
Gonzalez, Eduardo A. ...Oakland, CA
Gonzalez, Eduardo W. ...Miami, FL
Gonzalez, Edward ...Washington, DC
Gonzalez, Edward E. ...New York, NY
Gonzalez, Edward, P.C. ...Washington, DC
Gonzalez, Edwin P. ...New York, NY
González, Elizabeth A. ...Denver, CO
Gonzalez, Elizabeth Goff ...Las Vegas, NV
Gonzalez, Elvira M. ...Miramar, FL
Gonzalez, Elvira M., P.A. ...Miramar, FL
Gonzalez, Enrico G. ...Temple Terrace, FL
Gonzalez, Enrico G., P.A.
Temple Terrace, FL
González, Enrique, III ...Coral Gables, FL
Gonzalez, Ervin A. ...Miami, FL
Gonzalez, Estrella F. ...Miami, FL
Gonzalez, Eusebio ...Miami, FL
Gonzalez, Eve Kahao ...Port Allen, LA
Gonzalez, Evelyn ...New York, NY
Gonzalez, Felix P. ...Philadelphia, PA
Gonzalez, Fernando F. ...Philadelphia, PA
Gonzalez, Florentino L. ...Miami, FL
Gonzalez, Floyd A. ...Poughkeepsie, NY
Gonzalez, Francisco J. ...Clewiston, FL
Gonzalez, Frank E. ...San Antonio, TX
Gonzalez, Frederick M. ...Sunnyvale, CA
Gonzalez, George R. ...San Diego, CA
Gonzalez, George Y. ...Houston, TX
Gonzalez, Gerardo (Jerry) H.
Milwaukee, WI
Gonzalez, Gil P. ...San Diego, CA
Gonzalez, Gilbert ...Tucson, AZ
Gonzalez, Gloria M. ...San Francisco, CA
Gonzalez & Gonzalez ...Port St. Lucie, FL
González, González & González, Law Office of
Del Rio, TX
Gonzalez & Gonzalez, L.L.P.
Corpus Christi, TX
Gonzalez, Gonzalo, Jr. ...Detroit, MI
Gonzalez, Graciana ...San Juan, PR
Gonzalez, Gregory ...Roxbury, MA
Gonzalez, Guadalupe ...Irving, TX
Gonzalez, Guillermo J. ...Austin, TX
Gonzalez, Heberto, Jr. ...Laredo, TX
Gonzalez, Hector ...New York, NY
Gonzalez, Henry ...Tampa, FL
Gonzalez, Henry B., III ...San Antonio, TX
Gonzalez, Henry, Jr. ...San Antonio, TX
Gonzalez, Henry P. ...Washington, DC
Gonzalez, Hilda M ...Woodland Hills, CA
Gonzalez, Hiram ...San Juan, PR
Gonzalez, Honey Bee ...West Covina, CA
Gonzalez, Humberto ...Los Angeles, CA
Gonzalez, Idilio A." Ike "
San Luis Obispo, CA
Gonzalez, Irma E. ...San Diego, CA
Gonzalez, Irving Joseph ...Miami, FL
Gonzalez, Ismael, Jr. ...New York, NY
Gonzalez, Jacinto J. ...Miami, FL
Gonzalez, Jacqueline E. ...Miami, FL
Gonzalez, Jason B. ...Tallahassee, FL
Gonzalez, Jason P. ...San Francisco, CA
González, Javier ...Brownsville, TX
Gonzalez, Javier A. ...New York, NY
Gonzalez, Jay ...Boston, MA
Gonzalez, Jeffrey M. ...Trenton, NJ
Gonzalez, Jennifer R. ...Washington, DC
Gonzalez, Jessica L. ...Chicago, IL
Gonzalez, Jim ...Salinas, CA
Gonzalez, Joanne M. ...Port St. Lucie, FL
Gonzalez, Joe M., P.A. ...Tampa, FL
Gonzalez, Joe Manuel ...Tampa, FL
Gonzalez, Joette Marea ...Los Angeles, CA
Gonzalez, John G. ...Alice, TX
Gonzalez, John S. ...Gulfport, MS
Gonzalez, Jorge A. ...Dallas, TX
Gonzalez, Jorge L. ...Coral Gables, FL
González, Jorge R. (IBA) ...San Juan, PR
Gonzalez, Jose ...Purcell, OK
Gonzalez, Jose A. ...Kew Gardens, NY
Gonzalez, Jose A. ...Corpus Christi, TX
Gonzalez, Jose A., Jr. ...Fort Lauderdale, FL
Gonzalez, José E. ...Boca Raton, FL
Gonzalez, Jose Felix ...San Antonio, TX
Gonzalez, Jose L. ...Temple, TX
Gonzalez, Jose Luis ...Dallas, TX
González, José Luis, Jr. ...Enon, OH
Gonzalez, Jose M. ...North Olmsted, OH
Gonzalez, Jose M. ...El Paso, TX
Gonzalez, Jose R. ...New York, NY
Gonzalez, Josie ...Glendale, CA
Gonzalez, Juan A. ...Miami, FL
Gonzalez, Juan A. ...El Paso, TX
Gonzalez, Juan A. ...Harlingen, TX
Gonzalez, Juan A. ...Houston, TX
Gonzalez, Juan DeJesus ...Miami, FL
Gonzalez, Juan F. ...Miami, FL
Gonzalez, Juan M. ...San Antonio, TX
Gonzalez, Julia M. ...Atlanta, GA
San Antonio, TX
Gonzalez, Julian ...Orlando, FL
Gonzalez, Julieta O. ...Los Angeles, CA
Gonzalez, Julius ...Miami, FL
Gonzalez, Karina P. ...Fort Lauderdale, FL
Gonzalez, Kate Jesberg ...Washington, DC
Gonzalez, Katherine ...San Juan, PR
Gonzalez, Kenneth A. ...Staten Island, NY
Gonzalez, Kevin D. ...Palo Alto, CA
Gonzalez, Kevin D. ...Athens, GA
Gonzalez, Laura C. ...New York, NY
Gonzalez Law Office, The ...Dallas, TX
Gonzalez, Lawrence A. ...Tallahassee, FL
Gonzaléz, Leticia ...Berkeley, CA
Gonzalez, Lidia ...San Juan, PR
Gonzalez, Lindy Robin ...San Jose, CA
Gonzalez, Lizel V. ...Miami, FL
González López & López Adames
San Juan, PR
Gonzalez, Louis A., Jr. ...Sacramento, CA
Gonzalez, Madeline I. ...Bronx, NY
Gonzalez, Manuel, Jr. ...Miami, FL
Gonzalez, Manuel, VI ...Newark, NJ
Gonzalez, Marce, Jr. ...Crown Point, IN
Gonzalez, Marce, Jr. ...Merrillville, IN
Gonzalez, Marco A., Jr. ...Newark, NJ
Gonzalez, Margaret M. ...Metairie, LA
Gonzalez, Maria Cristina ...Laredo, TX
Gonzalez, Maria E. ...Fort Myers, FL
Gonzalez, Maria Elena ...Lisle, IL
Gonzalez, Maria M. ...Jacksonville, IL
Gonzalez, Mario ...Black Hawk, SD
Gonzalez, Mario F. ...Los Angeles, CA
Gonzalez, Marissa Ann ...Austin, TX
Gonzalez, Maritza ...Miami, FL
Gonzalez, Maritza ...Pembroke Pines, FL
Gonzalez, Mark A. ...San Jose, CA
Gonzalez, Mark M. ...New Orleans, LA
González, Marta Elisa ...San Juan, PR
Gonzalez, Mary M. ...Detroit, MI
Gonzalez, Michael A. ...Toledo, OH
Gonzalez, Michael D. ...Los Angeles, CA
Gonzalez, Michael Ibs ...San Diego, CA
Gonzalez, Michelle ...Coral Gables, FL
Gonzalez, Miguel A., Jr. ...New York, NY
Gonzalez, Miguel M. ...Miami, FL
Gonzalez, Milton F. ...Gilroy, CA
Gonzalez, Nancy J. ...San Antonio, TX
Gonzalez, Neil M., Jr. ...Hialeah, FL
Gonzalez, Noe ...Edinburg, TX
Gonzalez, Olga ...Miami, FL
Gonzalez, Olga, P.A. ...Miami, FL
Gonzalez, Orlano ...West Palm Beach, FL
Gonzalez, Oscar ...Dallas, TX
Gonzalez, Oscar C. ...Oxnard, CA
Gonzalez, Oscar C. ...San Antonio, TX
González, Oscar, Jr. ...Orlando, FL
Gonzalez, Osualdo ...Union City, NJ
Gonzalez, Patricia E. ...Beverly Hills, CA
Gonzalez, Paul ...Austin, TX
Gonzalez, Paul M. ...San Antonio, TX
Gonzalez, Peter A. ...Coral Gables, FL
Gonzalez, Rachel A. ...Miami, FL
Gonzalez, Raed ...Houston, TX
Gonzalez, Rafael ...Tampa, FL
Gonzalez, Ralph A. ...Voorhees, NJ
Gonzalez, Ralph L. ...Tampa, FL
Gonzalez, Ralph L. ...Richmond, TX
Gonzalez, Ralph R. ...Stamford, CT
Gonzalez, Raquel M. ...San Diego, CA
Gonzalez, Raquel M. ...Miami, FL
Gonzalez, Raul A. ...Austin, TX

Gonzalez, Raul I. ....New Brunswick, NJ
Gonzalez, Raymond G. ....Burbank, CA
Gonzalez & Rembold ....Miami, FL
Gonzalez, Rene ....Houston, TX
Gonzalez, Rene B. ....Brownsville, TX
Gonzalez, Reneé E. ....Houston, TX
Gonzalez, Ricardo ....Edinburg, TX
Gonzalez, Ricardo D. ....El Paso, TX
Gonzalez, Ricardo M. ....New York, NY
Gonzalez, Ricardo N. ....Houston, TX
Gonzalez, Richard ....Hialeah, FL
Gonzalez, Richard J. ....Chicago, IL
Gonzalez, Richard J. ....Laredo, TX
Gonzalez, Richard, Law Offices of
Hialeah, FL
Gonzalez, Robert ....Los Angeles, CA
Gonzalez, Robert A. ....Madison, WI
Gonzalez, Robert J. ....Corpus Christi, TX
Gonzalez, Roberto ....Providence, RI
Gonzalez, Rodrigo A. ....Livingston, NJ
New York, NY
Gonzalez, Roland ....Tampa, FL
Gonzalez, Romualdo, Jr. ....New Orleans, LA
Gonzalez, Ronald A. ....Manchester, CT
Gonzalez, Rosa Elena ....Stanford, CA
Gonzalez, Roy, Jr. ....Miami, FL
Gonzalez, Ruben, Jr. ....Fort Worth, TX
Gonzalez, Saggio, Birdsall & Harlan, LLP
Merrillville, IN
Des Moines, IA
Milwaukee, WI
Gonzalez, Sandra Lee ....Morristown, NJ
González, Sarita Gallardo ....San Juan, PR
Gonzalez, Sergio ....El Paso, TX
González, Sergio J. ....Del Rio, TX
Gonzalez, Sergio M. ....Miami, FL
Gonzalez, Sheila F. ....Sacramento, CA
Gonzalez, Sherry Rudisell
San Antonio, TX
Gonzalez, Silvia Laura ....Washington, DC
Gonzalez, Stephanie A. ....Philadelphia, PA
Gonzalez, Stephen J. ....Tucson, AZ
Gonzalez, Steven C. ....Santa Monica, CA
Gonzalez, Steven M. ....McAllen, TX
Gonzalez, Steven M., & Associates, P.C.
McAllen, TX
Gonzalez, Susana D. ....Tampa, FL
Gonzalez, Sylvia B. ....Miami, FL
Gonzalez, Thomas M. ....Tampa, FL
Gonzalez, Tim ....Dallas, TX
Gonzalez, Tino ....Melbourne, FL
Gonzalez, Valentine M. ....Basking Ridge, NJ
Gonzalez, Vicki M. ....Park Ridge, IL
Gonzalez, Victor J. ....Toledo, OH
Gonzalez, Victoria S. ....Charlotte, NC
Gonzalez, Vincent F. ....Cleveland, OH
Gonzalez, William ....Philadelphia, PA
Gonzalez & Woodrow ....Purcell, OK
Gonzalez, Zoila R. ....Wheeling, IL
Gonzalez-Acevedo, Frank M.
San Juan, PR
Gonzalez-Aranguren, Cynthia M.
San Juan, PR
González-Borgos, José E. ....San Juan, PR
González-Bothwell, Laura ....San Juan, PR
Gonzalez-Buitrago, Ivette ....San Juan, PR
Gonzalez-Burgos, Francisco ....Alma, GA
Gonzalez Calderon, Sila Maria
San Juan, PR
Gonzàlez-Canales, Lucy ....Edinburg, TX
Gonzalez-Carmona, Ivan F. ....San Juan, PR
González Castañer, José Luis
San Juan, PR
González-Díaz, Raúl E. ....San Juan, PR
González-Díaz, Raúl E., P.S.C., Law Firm of
San Juan, PR
Gonzalez-Diez, Lourdes
Securities and Exchange Commission,
Division of Market Regulation, GV
Gonzalez-Falla, Celso M. ....Houston, TX
Gonzalez-Ferrer, Teresa C. ....San Juan, PR
González-Gierbolini, José A.
San Juan, PR
Gonzalez-Goetz, Lisa ....Fort Lauderdale, FL
González-González, Sylvia M.
San Juan, PR
González Hernández, Graciana M.
San Juan, PR
González-Hernández, María Luisa
San Juan, PR
Gonzalez-Heydrich, Alina ....Lakeland, FL
González-Irizarry, José R. ....San Juan, PR
Gonzalez-Isales, Eduardo ....San Juan, PR
González-Llorens, René J. ....Miami, FL
Gonzalez-López, Homero ....San Juan, PR
González-Lugo, José Ramón ....Caguas, PR
Gonzalez-Lugo, Rosa M. ....San Juan, PR
Gonzalez-Maldonado, Armando E.
San Juan, PR
Gonzalez-Mañes, Maria ....New York, NY
Gonzalez Mangual, Victor R. ....San Juan, PR
Gonzalez-Miranda, Noel S. ....San Juan, PR
Gonzalez-Neimeiser, Alma R.
Tallahassee, FL
González-Nieto, Francisco ....San Juan, PR
González-Nieto García Feliciano & Balzac
San Juan, PR
González Nieves, Maribel ....San Juan, PR
González Nogueras, Jose R. ....San Juan, PR
González-Ortiz, Luis Edwin
San Juan, PR
González-Padró, Carlos ....San Juan, PR
González-Pérez, Jeffrey E. ....Arlington, VA
González Riváas, Maria DéL.
San Juan, PR
González-Rivera, Maritza ....San Juan, PR
González-Rivera, Roberto ....San Juan, PR
Gonzalez Romanace, Jose M. ....Ponce, PR
Gonzalez-Santiago, Juan ....San Juan, PR
Gonzalez-Scarano, Frances G.
Washington, DC
González-Sfeir, Javier J. ....San Diego, CA
Gonzalez-Sirgo, J.P., P.A.
Coral Gables, FL
Gonzalez-Sirgo, Juan P. ....Coral Gables, FL
González-Toro, Raúl ....San Juan, PR
Gonzalez-Torres, Edwin
San Francisco, CA
González-Valentín, Katherine
San Juan, PR
Gonzalo, Perez, Jr. ....Coral Gables, FL
Gonzenbach, David S. ....Chattanooga, TN
Gonzo, Barbara D. ....Brooklyn, NY
Gonzo, John Raymond ....Hackensack, NJ
Goo, Colin K. K. ....Honolulu, HI
Goo, Garrick L. H. ....Honolulu, HI
Goo, Gregg M. ....Long Beach, CA
Goo, Lester M. H. ....Honolulu, HI
Goo, Michael L.
Environmental Protection Agency,
Office of the General Counsel, GV
Goo, Rosanne K. ....Honolulu, HI
Goo, Valerie M. ....Los Angeles, CA
Goo, William L. ....Honolulu, HI
Gooby, Steven F. ....Princeton, NJ
New York, NY
Gooch, Ambre Camille
Oklahoma City, OK
Gooch, Anthony C. ....New York, NY
Gooch, Dewayne ....Colorado Springs, CO
Gooch, Edwin J., III ....Creedmoor, NC
Durham, NC
Greensboro, NC
Raleigh, NC
Gooch, Frank, III ....Santa Monica, CA
Gooch, J. Christopher ....Phoenix, AZ
Gooch, James C. ....Nashville, TN
Gooch, Jeffery D. ....Fort Worth, TX
Gooch, Jeffrey ....Salt Lake City, UT
Gooch, Joel E. ....Lafayette, LA
Gooch, John B., Jr. ....New Orleans, LA
Gooch, Judy A. ....Denver, CO
Gooch, Kelly S. ....Memphis, TN
Gooch, Mary Jane ....Omaha, NE
Gooch, Michael V. ....Carmel, IN
Gooch, Neal T. ....Bountiful, UT
Gooch, R. Gordon ....Washington, DC
Gooch, Raymond L. ....Washington, DC
Gooch, Richard H., Jr. ....Crown Point, IN
Gooch, Stephen G. ....Dallas, TX
Gooch, Thomas W., III ....Wauconda, IL
Gooch, W. Kyle ....Dallas, TX
Gooch, Warren L. ....Knoxville, TN
Oak Ridge, TN
Good, Adrian J. ....Elizabethton, TN
Good, Albert E. ....Boston, MA
Good, Albert F. ....Charleston, WV
Good, Amy Schaeffer ....Shelbyville, IN
Good, Andrew H. ....Boston, MA
Good, Andrew S. ....Dallas, TX
Good, Anson B. ....Waynesboro, PA
Good, Ari Benjamin ....Chicago, IL
Good, Barbara S. ....Department of Agriculture,
Office of the General Counsel, GV
Good, Brian M. ....Los Angeles, CA
Good, Bridgid M. ....Reading, PA
Good, C. Edward ....Washington, DC
Good, Carl S. ....Phoenix, AZ
Good, Christina L ....Mount Olive, NJ
Good, Coni Rae ....Phoenix, AZ
Good, Courtney Townes ....Louisville, KY
Good, Darcy M. ....Cleveland, OH
Good, David H. ....Stamford, CT
Good, David L. ....Bethesda, MD
Good, Dennis W., Jr. ....Charlottesville, VA
Good, Douglas J. ....Mineola, NY
Good, Edward F. M. ....Knoxville, TN
Good, Edward P. ....Detroit, MI
Good, Ellen C. ....Hingham, MA
Good, F. Keith ....Perryton, TX
Good, George M. ....Miami, FL
Good, Gerard J. ....Marion, MA
Good & Good, P.C. ....Englewood, CO
Good, Gregory E. ....Tucson, AZ
Good, Gregory E., & Associates, P.C.
Tucson, AZ
Good, Gregory S. ....Los Angeles, CA
Good, James E. ....Riverside, CA
San Bernardino, CA
Good, James G. ....Portland, ME
Good, James W., Jr. ....Southern Pines, NC
Good, Janis C. ....Union, MO
Good, Joan R. ....Hartford, CT
Good, John A. ....Memphis, TN
Good, John Derek ....Cincinnati, OH
Good, John E. ....West Chester, PA
Good, John G., Jr. ....Beaver, PA
Good, Jonathan A. ....Akron, OH
Good, Joseph ....Wantagh, NY
Good, Joseph C., Jr. ....Charleston, SC
Good, Joyce Ann ....Moore, OK
Good, Julian H. ....New Orleans, LA
Good, Katherine A. ....Denver, CO
Good, Kathleen K. ....Downingtown, PA
Good, Ken W. ....Tyler, TX
Good, Kenneth J. ....Chicago, IL
Good, Kevin H. ....Dallas, TX
Good, Marie S. ....Buffalo, NY
Good, Mark A. ....Van Nuys, CA
Good, Martha H. ....Dayton, OH
Good, Mary ....Orchard Park, NY
Good, Michael B. ....Houston, TX
Good, Michael D. ....Irvine, CA
Good, Michael J. ....Brooklyn, NY
Good, Michael R., Law Office of
Santa Maria, CA
Good, Michele W. ....Elkins, WV
Good, Morris F. ....Montoursville, PA
Good, Ned, The Law Offices of
Pasadena, CA
Good, Neil H. ....Palatine, IL
Good, Niel L. ....Lakewood, CO
Good, Otto S. ....San Antonio, TX
Good, Paul A. ....Cambridge, MA
Good, Paul F. ....Wichita, KS
Good, Peter M. ....Harrisburg, PA
Good, R. Douglas ....New Holland, PA
Good, Ralph C., Jr. ....Medfield, MA
Good, Raymond ....Indianapolis, IN
Good, Richard B. ....Buffalo, NY
Good, Robert G. ....Englewood, CO
Good, Robert K. ....Orlando, FL
Good, Robert W. ....Ashland, OR
Good, Samantha B. ....Los Angeles, CA
Good, Sarah Ann ....Palo Alto, CA
Good, Scott Bradley ....Houston, TX
Good, Stephen A. ....Phoenix, AZ
Good, Stephen D. ....Dallas, TX
Good, Stephen G. ....Irving, TX
Good, Stephen H. ....Everett, WA
Good, Steven L. ....Chicago, IL
Good, Suzanne E. ....Berkeley, CA
Good, Teresa M. ....Tyler, TX
Good, Terrance J. ....St. Louis, MO
Good, Thomas G. ....West Des Moines, IA
Good, Timothy D. ....Englewood, CO
Good, Timothy E. ....Gagetown, MI
Good, Warren R. ....Shelbyville, IN
Good, Wildman, Hegness & Walley
Newport Beach, CA
Good, William A. ....Worthington, OH
Good, William E. ....Phoenix, AZ
Good, William J. ....Fort Dodge, IA
Goodale, Eugene C. ....Evanston, IL
Goodale, James C. ....New York, NY
Goodale, Marjorie Elizabeth ....Columbia, SC
Goodale, Paul W. ....Providence, RI
Goodale, Ralph E. ....Winston-Salem, NC
Goodale, Robert L. ....New Bedford, MA
Goodall, Anthony C. ....Austin, TX
Goodall & Associates ....Bellefonte, PA
State College, PA
Goodall, C. Martin ....Little Silver, NJ
Goodall, Charles A. ....Sandy, UT
Goodall, Clifford H. ....Augusta, ME
Goodall, D. Christian ....Columbia, SC
Goodall & Davison, L.L.P. ....Austin, TX
Goodall, Deborah A. ....Dallas, TX
Goodall, Deborah Packer
Fort Lauderdale, FL
Goodall, H. Amos, Jr. ....State College, PA
Goodall, Larry M. ....Richmond, VA
Goodall, Laura Yancey ....Gallatin, TN
Goodall, Mark ....Omaha, NE
Goodall, Nancy Norton ....Topeka, KS
Goodall, Robert B. ....Stafford, VA
Goodall, Robert H. ....Gallatin, TN
Goodall, Sim W. ....Odessa, TX
Goodall & Sooter ....Dallas, TX
Goodall, W. Thomas, Jr. ....Gallatin, TN
Goodart, Nan L. ....Sacramento, CA
Goodbar, C. Lee, Jr.
Colorado Springs, CO
Goodbarn, Barbara Jark ....Omaha, NE
Goodbaum, Samuel ....Westport, CT
Goodbee, Frederick Michael
Breckenridge, CO
Goodbee, Wendell R. ....Colorado Springs, CO
Goodberg, George Barry ....East Hartford, CT
Goodbinder, Robert L. ....Telluride, CO
Goodblatt, Amy E. ....Orlando, FL
Goodbody, Katharine S. ....New Haven, CT
Goodbody, Thomas B. ....McLean, VA
Goodbread, Michael E., Jr.
Jacksonville, FL
Goodbread, Stacy E. ....San Antonio, TX
Goodchild, Alan W. ....Derry, NH
Goodchild, André S. ....Los Angeles, CA
Goodchild, Jack ....Los Angeles, CA
Goodchild, Jack, A Professional Law
Corporation ....Los Angeles, CA
Goodchild, John C., III ....Philadelphia, PA
Goodchild, Kara H. ....Philadelphia, PA
Goodchild, Lester C. ....New York, NY
Goodchild, Phillip E. ....Hoffman Estates, IL
Goodchild, Seth ....New York, NY
Goodding, James K. ....Lincoln, NE
Goode, Allan L. ....Fort Dodge, IA
Goode, Andrew A. ....San Francisco, CA
Goode, Andrew P. ....King Of Prussia, PA
Goode, Barbara A., Law Office of
San Francisco, CA
Goode, Barry P. ....San Francisco, CA
Goode, Carla Alessio ....Joliet, IL
Goode Casseb Jones Riklin Choate &
Watson, A Professional Corporation
San Antonio, TX
Goode, Coralyn ....Washington, DC
Goode, Don H. ....Jackson, MS
Goode, E. Kelly
Equal Employment Opportunity
Commission,
Office of Federal Operations, GV
Goode, Elizabeth Whitener ....Charlotte, NC
Goode, Freddie L. ....Richmond, VA
Goode, Frederick D. ....Concord, NH
Goode & Goode ....Houston, TX
Goode, Grover C. ....Beckley, WV
Goode, Howard C. ....Northbrook, IL
Goode, Irving H. ....Chicago, IL
Goode, J. Philip, Jr. ....Bossier City, LA
Goode, James C. ....Albany, OR
Goode, Jayne E. Costello ....Holliston, MA
Goode, Joe B. ....Cleveland, TN
Goode, John ....Richmond, VA
Goode, Joseph S. ....Milwaukee, WI
Goode, Kenneth E. ....Houston, TX
Goode, Kenneth G. ....Winnsboro, SC
Goode, Lawrence J. ....Morrisville, PA
Goode, M. Jane ....Haddonfield, NJ
Philadelphia, PA
Goode, Maureen ....Morris Plains, NJ
Goode, Michael ....Laguna Niguel, CA
Goode, Paul R., Jr. ....Mullens, WV
Goode, Peter H. ....Marlborough, CT
Goode, Peterson & Weintraub, A
Professional Law Corporation
La Jolla, CA
San Diego, CA
Goode, Richard S. ....Chicago, IL
Goode, Roger M. ....Atlanta, GA
Goode, Scott W. ....Philadelphia, PA
Goode, Thomas B. ....La Jolla, CA
Goode, Thomas E. ....Washington, DC
Goode, Thomas E. ....Boston, MA
Goode, Virgil H., Jr. ....Rocky Mount, VA
Goode, Wendy M. ....Oak Park, IL
Goode, William Kevin ....Houston, TX
Goode, William L. ....Lafayette, LA
Goode, William L., & Associates, A Prof.
Law Corp. ....Bossier City, LA
Lafayette, LA
New Orleans, LA
Shreveport, LA
Goode, William M. ....Sacramento, CA
Goode, William R. ....Portland, OR
Goode, William S. ....Chapel Hill, NC
Good-Earnest, Margaret
West Palm Beach, FL
Goodell, Andrew W. ....Mayville, NY
Goodell, Arthur A. ....Ithaca, NY
Goodell, Charles P., Jr. ....Baltimore, MD
Goodell, Daniel L. ....Tacoma, WA
Goodell, Daniel M. ....San Francisco, CA
Goodell, Deborah Kay ....Austin, TX
Goodell, DeVries, Leech & Gray, LLP
Baltimore, MD
Goodell, Donald J. ....New York, NY
Goodell, Donald P. ....Richmond, VA
Goodell, George S. ....Oxford, OH
Goodell, Gerald L. ....Topeka, KS
Goodell, John L. ....Jamestown, NY
Goodell, John R. ....Pocatello, ID
Goodell, Mary J. ....Los Angeles, CA
Goodell, Rebecca Ellen ....Washington, DC
Goodell, Rick ....Buffalo, NY
Goodell, Robert D. ....Anoka, MN
Goodell, Scott K. ....Seattle, WA
Goodell, Sol ....Dallas, TX
Goodell, Steven P. ....Princeton, NJ
Goodell, Stratton, Edmonds & Palmer,
L.L.P. ....Topeka, KS
Kansas City, MO
Goodell, Timothy B. ....New York, NY
Goodell, William W., Jr.
New Orleans, LA
Goodelman, Jodi ....Rockville Centre, NY
Goodemote, Pamela S. Trapp ....Chicago, IL
Gooden, Alicia A. ....Indianapolis, IN
Gooden, Angelina D.A. ....Houston, TX
Gooden, Deborah M. ....Cleveland, OH
Gooden, Julia L.S. ....Dallas, TX
Gooden, Lonnie J., Jr. ....Houston, TX
Gooden, Mary E. ....Providence, RI
Gooden, Pamela J. ....Montgomery, AL
Gooden, R. Russell ....Columbus, OH
Gooden, William W. ....Indianapolis, IN
Gooden, William W. ....Mt. Vernon, IN
Gooden-Brown, Greta-Ann ....Trenton, NJ
Goodenough, Brian G. ....Lansing, MI
Goodenough, Charles C. ....New York, NY
Goodenough, Daniel J. ....Covington, KY
Goodenough, Fred C. ....Boise, ID
Goodenough, Gene ....Bandera, TX
Goodenough, Jeanne T. ....Boise, ID
Goodenough, Keith F. ....Keswick, VA
Goodenough, Linda B. ....Beverly, MA
Goodenough, Oliver R. ....New York, NY
Goodenough, Robin W. ....Baltimore, MD
Goodenow, Gary Langan ....Miami Shores, FL
Goodenow, J. E. ....Maquoketa, IA
Goodenow, Mark S. ....Marshall, MN
Goodenow, Marsha L. ....Charlotte, NC
Goodenow, Rew R. ....Reno, NV
Gooder, David M. ....Chicago, IL
Gooder, David S. ....San Rafael, CA
Gooderum, Karen A. ....Elmira, NY
Goodfarb, Adam D. ....White Plains, NY
Goodfarb, Stanley Z. ....Phoenix, AZ
Goodfellow, Allan J. ....Johns Island, SC
Goodfellow, Evan Patrick ....Haddonfield, NJ
Goodfellow, James C. ....New York, NY
Goodfellow, James F. ....San Francisco, CA
Goodfellow, Jonathan J. ....Oakland, CA
Goodfellow, Kathleen Koziol ....Del Mar, CA
Goodfellow, Lynn R. ....San Diego, CA
Goodfellow, Mary Beth ....Brockton, MA
Goodfried, Kenneth B. ....Beverly Hills, CA
Goodfried, Marlene D. ....Los Angeles, CA
Goodfried, David R.
Executive Office Of The President, GV
Goodfriend, Douglas E. ....New York, NY
Goodfriend, Gary M. ....Southfield, MI
Goodfriend, Herbert J. ....New York, NY
Goodfriend, Howard M. ....Seattle, WA
Goodfriend, Kathryn A. ....Boston, MA
Goodfriend, Mark E. ....Encino, CA
Goodfriend, Mark F. ....New City, NY
Suffern, NY
Goodfriend, Neal B. ....Chicago, IL
Goodfriend, Robert E. ....Dallas, TX
Goodfriend, Robert E., P.C. ....Dallas, TX

Goodfriend, Saltzman & Newman
New City, NY
Goodfriend, Sam ..... Jacksonville, FL
Goodgal, Paula A. ..... Washington, DC
Baltimore, MD
Goodgame, C. Edward ..... Atlanta, GA
Goodgame, John T., III ..... Houston, TX
Goodgame, Lynda L. ..... Tallahassee, FL
Goodge, Glenn M. ..... Allentown, PA
Goodge & Makoul ..... Allentown, PA
Goodgion, Gilbert ..... Newington, CT
Goodglass, Lawrence B. ..... Portland, ME
Goodgold, Christine M. ..... New York, NY
Goodhand, David B.
Securities and Exchange Commission, Division of Enforcement, GV
Goodhard, Kim A. ..... Miami, FL
Goodhart, Bruce J. ..... Chicago, IL
Goodhart, David Irwin ..... Dallas, TX
Goodhart, James F. ..... Little Rock, AR
Goodhart, James F., P.A. ..... Little Rock, AR
Goodhart, John H. ..... Menlo Park, CA
Goodhart, Philip ..... Las Vegas, NV
Goodheart, Gary R. ..... Las Vegas, NV
Goodheart, Harry G., III, Chartered
Bradenton, FL
Goodheart, Jodi R. ..... Las Vegas, NV
Goodheart, Lisa C. ..... Boston, MA
Goodheart, Marc ..... Cambridge, MA
Goodheart, Michael R. ..... Woodland Hills, CA
Goodheim, Philip ..... Hollywood, FL
Goodhines, James R. ..... Springfield, MA
Goodhope, Andrew C. ..... Wheaton, MD
Goodhope, Samuel M. ..... Sioux Falls, SD
Goodhue Arons and Neary
Mount Kisco, NY
Goodhue, Darrell ..... Carlisle, IA
Goodhue, David L. ..... Westborough, MA
Goodhue, Eldon D. ..... Topsfield, MA
Goodhue, James A. ..... Wellesley, MA
Goodhue, Mary B. ..... Mount Kisco, NY
Goodhue, Mary V. ..... Escondido, CA
Goodhue, Nicholas ..... Santa Monica, CA
Goodhue & Pearl L.L.C. ..... Denver, CO
Goodhue, Steven J. ..... Denver, CO
Goodiel, Nancy J. ..... Fairfax, VA
Goodier, Barbara ..... Yuma, AZ
Goodier, Glenn G. ..... New Orleans, LA
Goodier, Rosemary ..... Wilmington, DE
Goodin, Ben A. ..... Chicago, IL
Goodin, Ben A., & Associates, P.C.
Chicago, IL
Goodin, Charles C. ..... Aiea, HI
Goodin, Charles W. ..... Charleston, WV
Goodin, Eileen S. ..... Columbus, OH
Goodin, Gary P. ..... Indianapolis, IN
Goodin, James A. ..... Indianapolis, IN
Goodin, John D. ..... Johnson City, TN
Goodin, Karen C. ..... Costa Mesa, CA
Goodin, Kenneth E. ..... San Francisco, CA
Goodin & Kraege ..... Indianapolis, IN
Goodin, MacBride, Squeri, Ritchie & Day, LLP ..... San Francisco, CA
Goodin, Mark A. ..... Washington, DC
Baltimore, MD
Rockville, MD
Goodin, Matthew A. ..... San Francisco, CA
Goodin, Michael W. ..... Newport Beach, CA
Goodin, Nelson J. ..... San Diego, CA
Goodin, Patricia Annette ..... Ardmore, OK
Goodin, Robert A. ..... San Francisco, CA
Goodin, Robert L., Jr. ..... Louisville, KY
Goodin, Stephen J. ..... Pasadena, CA
Gooding, Alan Paul ..... Pasadena, CA
Gooding, Chandra L. ..... Los Angeles, CA
Gooding, David M. ..... Jacksonville, FL
Gooding, Denis A. ..... New Brunswick, NJ
Gooding, Denise E. ..... Phoenix, AZ
Gooding & Dodson, P.C. ..... Texarkana, AR
Clarksville, TX
Daingerfield, TX
Jefferson, TX
Linden, TX
Marshall, TX
Mount Pleasant, TX
Paris, TX
Pittsburg, TX
Texarkana, TX
Gooding, Douglas M. ..... San Francisco, CA
Gooding, Douglas R. ..... Boston, MA
Gooding, Elizabeth Kearse ..... Allendale, SC
Gooding and Gooding ..... Allendale, SC
Gooding and Gooding ..... Clarksville, TX
Gooding, Gregory V. (IBA) **..... New York, NY**
Gooding, Gunnar Blaise ..... Aliso Viejo, CA
Gooding, H. Woodrow ..... Allendale, SC
Gooding, Huffman, Kelley & Becker
Lima, OH
Gooding, Jack D. ..... Archbold, OH
Gooding, Jack W. ..... New Boston, TX
Texarkana, TX
Gooding, James ..... Mercer Island, WA
Gooding, John T., II ..... Austin, TX
Gooding, Laurence E., Jr. ..... Milwaukee, WI
Gooding, Martha K. ..... Newport Beach, CA
Gooding, Michele A. ..... West Des Moines, IA
Gooding, Miranda P. ..... Beverly, MA
Gooding, O. Clifton ..... Oklahoma City, OK
Oklahoma City, OK
Gooding, R. Gary ..... Geneva, IL
Gooding, Robert E. ..... Clarksville, TX
Gooding, Robert E., Jr.
Newport Beach, CA
Gooding, Ronald R. ..... Topeka, KS
Gooding, Sandra J. ..... Huntington Beach, CA
Gooding, Theodore J. ..... Hawthorne, CA
Gooding, Thompson H., Jr. ..... Valdosta, GA
Ocala, FL
Gooding, W. James, III C

Gooding, William C. ..... Texarkana, TX
Gooding-Jones, Glorianne
Thousand Oaks, CA
Goodis, Heather C. ..... St. Petersburg, FL
Goodis, Jeffrey M. ..... Orlando, FL
St. Petersburg, FL
Goodis, Randy ..... Miami, FL
Naples, FL
Goodison, Eric ..... New York, NY
Goodkin, Colette A. ..... Roseland, NJ
Goodkin, Daniel L. ..... Santa Monica, CA
Goodkin, Leonard ..... Denville, NJ
Goodkin, Olivia ..... Los Angeles, CA
Goodkin, Richard T. ..... Wildwood, NJ
Goodkin, Stanley J. ..... St. Louis, MO
Goodkin, Stanley J., P.C. ..... St. Louis, MO
Goodkin, Susan L. ..... Ventura, CA
Goodkind, Arthur B. ..... Washington, DC
Goodkind, Brian K. ..... Miami, FL
Goodkind, Conrad G. ..... Milwaukee, WI
Goodkind, E. Robert, (P.C.)
New York, NY
Goodkind, James P. ..... Los Angeles, CA
Goodkind, Kenneth S. ..... Cherry Hill, NJ
Goodkind Labaton Rudoff & Sucharow LLP
Fort Lauderdale, FL
New York, NY
Goodkind, Louis W. ..... Irvington, NY
Goodkind, Maryann L. ..... Los Angeles, CA
Goodland, John S. ..... Chicago, IL
Goodlatte, Maryellen F. ..... Roanoke, VA
Goodlatte, Robert W. ..... Roanoke, VA
Goodlaw, Deene ..... San Francisco, CA
Goodlet, C. William ..... Akron, OH
Goodlett, Collier W. ..... Clarksville, TN
Goodlett, Gwynne Brown ..... Columbia, SC
Goodlett, James Calvin ..... Tallahassee, FL
Goodlette, Coleman & Johnson, P.A.
Naples, FL
Goodlette, J. Dudley ..... Naples, FL
Goodley, Elizabeth ..... Los Altos, CA
Goodley, Samuel A., Jr. ..... Lancaster, PA
Goodliffe, Susan K. ..... Short Hills, NJ
Goodlin, Gary C. ..... Pittsburgh, PA
Goodling, G. Allen ..... Houston, TX
Goodling, Jonathon L., P.C. ..... Portland, OR
Goodloe, Allan McD., Jr. ..... St. Louis, MO
Goodloe, J. W., Jr. ..... Mobile, AL
Goodloe, Martha Bedsole
Los Angeles, CA
Troy, MI
Goodloe, Martha L. ..... Missoula, MT
Goodloe, Peter M. ..... House of Representatives, Office of Legislative Counsel, GV
Goodloe, Stephen H. ..... Atlanta, GA
Goodloe, Wanda N. ..... New York, NY
Goodloe, Wm. C., II ..... Olympia, WA
Goodloe, Wm. D. ..... Louisville, KY
Goodlow, Steven Elza ..... Albia, IA
Goodluck, James R. ..... Cleveland, OH
Goodmacher, Maxine ..... Martinez, CA
Goodmacher, Maxine, Inc., A Professional Corporation ..... Martinez, CA
Goodman, Aaron J. ..... Tulsa, OK
Goodman, Abraham ..... Cape Coral, FL
Goodman Acker, P.C. ..... Southfield, MI
Goodman, Adam ..... Chicago, IL
Goodman, Adam M. ..... New York, NY
Goodman, Adam Matthew ..... Atlanta, GA
Goodman, Adorea S. ..... Glenview, IL
Goodman, Adrienne J. ..... Los Angeles, CA
Goodman, Alan C. ..... Rupert, ID
Goodman, Alan C. ..... Jackson, MS
Goodman, Alan H., (A Professional Law Corp.) ..... New Orleans, LA
Goodman, Alan I. ..... Cleveland, OH
Goodman, Alan L. ..... Boca Raton, FL
Goodman, Alan M. ..... Cleveland, OH
Goodman, Alan P. ..... Garden City, NY
Goodman, Alan R. ..... Chestnut Hill, MA
Goodman, Alan R. ..... Springfield, MA
Goodman, Alfred N. ..... Washington, DC
Goodman, Allan B. ..... Bethlehem, PA
Goodman, Allan H.
General Services Administration, Board of Contract Appeals, GV
Goodman, Allan J. ..... Culver City, CA
Goodman, Allan L. ..... Bethlehem, PA
Goodman, Allen J. ..... Cornwall, NY
Goodman, Alvin ..... Miami, FL
Goodman, Amy Glatter
Federal Communications Commission, Common Carrier Bureau, GV
Goodman, Amy L. ..... Washington, DC
Goodman, Amy L. ..... Columbia, MD
Goodman, Amy O'Connor ..... Pittsburgh, PA
Goodman, Andrew ..... Encino, CA
Goodman, Andrew H. ..... Reston, VA
Goodman, Andrew J. ..... Minneapolis, MN
Goodman, Andrew J. ..... New York, NY
Goodman, Ann F. ..... Jackson, MI
Goodman, Ann Karwacki ..... Easton, MD
Goodman, Ann P. ..... Chicago, IL
Goodman, Anne D. ..... Albuquerque, NM
Goodman, Anthony K.
Fort Lauderdale, FL
Goodman, Arnold N. ..... Little Rock, AR
Goodman, Arnold P. ..... New York, NY
Goodman, Arthur H. ..... Briarcliff Manor, NY
Goodman, Arthur H. ..... Pound Ridge, NY
Goodman, Arthur, Jr. ..... Charlotte, NC
Goodman & Associates, P.C. ..... Atlanta, GA
Goodman, Avery B. ..... Palm Harbor, FL
Goodman, Avery B., P.A. ..... Palm Harbor, FL
Goodman, B. Kenneth ..... Lakeside, CA

Goodman, Ball, Van Bokkelen, Leonard & Kline, Professional Corporation
Chicago, IL
Crown Point, IN
Hammond, IN
Highland, IN
Goodman, Barbara B. ..... Chicago, IL
Goodman, Barbara J. ..... New York, NY
Goodman, Barry ..... Atlanta, GA
Goodman, Barry A. ..... Cincinnati, OH
Goodman, Barry J. ..... Southfield, MI
Goodman, Barry S. ..... Woodbridge, NJ
Goodman, Benj. M. ..... New Orleans, LA
Goodman, Bennet ..... Bronxville, NY
Goodman, Bernard D. ..... Cleveland, OH
Goodman, Bernard E. ..... Vienna, VA
Goodman, Bert M. ..... Colmar, PA
Goodman, Beth ..... Washington, DC
Goodman, Blake ..... El Paso, TX
Goodman & Bollar, Chartered
Rupert, ID
Goodman, Bonnie Sue ..... Huntington, NY
Goodman, Bradley K. ..... Norman, OK
Goodman, Bradley P. ..... Plantation, FL
Goodman & Breen ..... Naples, FL
Goodman, Brett T. ..... New York, NY
Goodman, Brian J. ..... Richmond, VA
Goodman, Brian S. ..... Baltimore, MD
Goodman, Bruce ..... Grand Rapids, MI
Lansing, MI
Goodman, Bruce A. ..... Fort Lauderdale, FL
Goodman, Bruce D. ..... Chicago, IL
Goodman, Bruce D. ..... Schaumburg, IL
Goodman, Bruce E. ..... Baltimore, MD
Goodman, Bruce E. ..... Baltimore, MD
Owings Mills, MD
Goodman, Bruce G. ..... Boston, MA
Providence, RI
Goodman, Bruce S. ..... Chicago, IL
Goodman, Bruce S. ..... Summit, NJ
Goodman, Budd G. ..... New York, NY
Goodman, Carl F. ..... Bethesda, MD
Goodman, Carlos K. ..... Los Angeles, CA
Goodman, Carol ..... San Francisco, CA
Goodman, Carol ..... San Francisco, CA
Goodman, Carol M. ..... New York, NY
Goodman, Carol S. ..... Wellesley, MA
Goodman, Carr, Nixon, Laughrun and Levine
Charlotte, NC
Goodman, Catherine Hendren
Fort Worth, TX
Goodman, Charles A., III ..... Glasgow, KY
Goodman, Charles I. ..... Grundy Center, IA
Goodman, Charles R. ..... Hancock, MI
Goodman, Cheryl S.
Department of Commerce, Patent and Trademark Office, GV
Goodman Chesnoff & Keach, A Professional Corporation ..... Las Vegas, NV
Goodman, Christine Chambers
Los Angeles, CA
Goodman & Clark ..... Arlington, TX
Goodman, Collette C. ..... Washington, DC
Goodman, Craig G. ..... Washington, DC
Goodman, Craig R. ..... Decatur, GA
Goodman, Cronfel & Meurer ..... Laredo, TX
Goodman, Cynthia A. ..... Los Angeles, CA
Goodman, Dale R. F. ..... Atlanta, GA
Goodman, Daniel R. ..... Los Angeles, CA
Goodman, Daniel S. ..... Los Angeles, CA
Goodman, Daniel S. ..... Department of Justice, Criminal Division, GV
Goodman, Daniel S. ..... Florham Park, NJ
Goodman, Darrell Von ..... Cheyenne, WY
Goodman, David ..... Newark, NJ
Goodman, David B. ..... Chicago, IL
Goodman, David C. ..... Jacksonville, FL
Goodman, David H. ..... Austin, TX
Goodman, David M. ..... Buffalo, NY
Goodman, David S. ..... Poughkeepsie, NY
Goodman, David S. ..... Cleveland, OH
Goodman, Davis P. ..... Los Angeles, CA
Goodman, Deana L. Vogel ..... Denver, CO
Goodman, Deanne H. ..... Glendale, CA
Goodman, Debra L. ..... Philadelphia, PA
Goodman, Debra S. ..... Philadelphia, PA
Goodman, Diane A. ..... Albany, NY
Goodman, Diane M. ..... Encino, CA
Goodman, Donald J. ..... Atlanta, GA
Goodman, Donald L. ..... Sparta, WI
Goodman, Donna L. ..... Wilmington, DE
Goodman, Dorothy K. ..... West Des Moines, IA
Goodman, E. Donald ..... Birmingham, MI
Goodman, E. Frank ..... Jackson, MS
Goodman, Earle Gary ..... Beverly Hills, CA
Goodman, Eden, Millender & Bedrosian
Detroit, MI
Goodman, Edgar G. ..... Newkirk, OK
Goodman, Edmund J. ..... Portland, OR
Goodman, Edward ..... New York, NY
Goodman, Edward H. ..... Beverly Hills, MI
Goodman, Edward Seth ..... New York, NY
Goodman, Edward W. ..... Boston, MA
Goodman, Edward W. ..... Tarrytown, NY
Goodman, Eileen H. ..... San Francisco, CA
Goodman, Eklund-Easley & Davis
Detroit, MI
Goodman, Elana B. ..... Fort Lauderdale, FL
Goodman, Elga A. ..... Somerville, NJ
Goodman, Elisabeth C. ..... Pittsfield, MA
Goodman, Elizabeth A.
Department of Labor, Office of the Solicitor, GV
Goodman, Elizabeth A. ..... Minneapolis, MN
Goodman, Ellen Herman ..... Philadelphia, PA
Goodman, Ellen P. ..... Washington, DC
Goodman, Elliot ..... Chappaqua, NY
Goodman, Elliot M. ..... Natick, MA

Goodman, Elliott I. ..... Lombard, IL
Goodman, Ellis H. ..... Baltimore, MD
Goodman, Emily Jane ..... New York, NY
Goodman, Emmett L., Jr. ..... Macon, GA
Goodman, Erik S. ..... Austin, TX
Goodman, Erin Jessica
Virginia Beach, VA
Goodman, Ernest ..... Detroit, MI
Goodman, Ernest B. ..... Universal City, CA
Goodman, Evan Dee ..... Indianapolis, IN
Goodman, Ezra N. ..... New York, NY
Goodman, Farrell J. ..... Cincinnati, OH
Goodman, Fern S. ..... Oyster Bay, NY
Goodman, Frances R. ..... Waco, TX
Goodman, Frank I. ..... Brooklyn, NY
Goodman, Fred Lee ..... Amsterdam, NY
Goodman, Fredric B. ..... Hoboken, NJ
New York, NY
Goodman, Gari W. ..... Seattle, WA
Goodman, Gari W., Inc., Inc., P.S.
Seattle, WA
Goodman, Garth R. ..... St. Petersburg, FL
Goodman, Gary ..... Saginaw, MI
Goodman, Gary A. ..... Chicago, IL
Goodman, Gary A. ..... New York, NY
Goodman, Gary B. ..... Greensboro, NC
Goodman, Geoffrey A. ..... Sacramento, CA
Goodman, George R. ..... Chicago, IL
Goodman, George S. ..... New York, NY
Goodman, George W. ..... McMinnville, OR
Goodman, Gerald ..... Redondo Beach, CA
Goodman, Glazer, Greener & Kremer, P.C.
Marco Island, FL
Naples, FL
Memphis, TN
Goodman, Glenn D. ..... Springfield, MA
Goodman and Goodman ..... Atlanta, GA
Goodman & Goodman ..... Wellesley, MA
Goodman & Goodman, A Legal Professional Association ..... Cincinnati, OH
Goodman Goodman & Jurist
Garden City, NY
Goodman & Goodman, P.A.
Baltimore, MD
Owings Mills, MD
Goodman & Goodman, P.C. ..... Atlanta, GA
Goodman, Gordon E. ..... Houston, TX
Goodman, Grace A. ..... New York, NY
Goodman, Greenzang & Hurwitz
Chestnut Hill, MA
Goodman, Gregory Scott ..... Mount Sinai, NY
Goodman & Guzinski, P.A. ..... Rochester, MN
Goodman, H. Raymond ..... Tupelo, MS
Goodman, Harold I. ..... Philadelphia, PA
Goodman, Harold S. ..... St. Louis, MO
Goodman, Harriet J. ..... Hartford, CT
Goodman, Harvey L. ..... Knoxville, TN
Goodman, Henry A. ..... Braintree, MA
Goodman, Henry L. ..... New York, NY
Goodman, Henry Nicholas ..... New York, NY
Goodman, Herbert ..... New York, NY
Goodman, Herbert H. ..... New York, NY
Goodman & Herman, L.L.C. ..... Baltimore, MD
Goodman, Hilary M. ..... Huntingdon Valley, PA
Goodman, Howard J. ..... New York, NY
Goodman, Howard M. ..... New York, NY
Goodman, Hyman ..... New York, NY
Goodman, I. Wayne ..... Atlanta, GA
Goodman, I. R. ..... Redwood City, CA
Goodman, Irving ..... Braintree, MA
Goodman, Irwin A. ..... Chicago, IL
Goodman, J. Chris ..... Chicago, IL
Goodman, J. David ..... Columbus, OH
Goodman, J. Howard ..... Los Angeles, CA
Goodman, Jack ..... Chicago, IL
Goodman, Jack A. ..... Voorhees, NJ
Goodman, Jack N. ..... Washington, DC
Goodman, Jacob ..... Somers, NY
Goodman & Jacobs LLP ..... New York, NY
White Plains, NY
Goodman, Jacqueline ..... Fullerton, CA
Goodman, Jaimie R., Law Offices of
Detroit, MI
Goodman, James A. ..... Los Angeles, CA
Goodman, James A. ..... Portland, ME
Goodman, James A. ..... Philadelphia, PA
Goodman, James E. ..... Atlanta, GA
Goodman, James E., Jr. ..... Dubuque, IA
Goodman, James L. ..... Marshalltown, IA
Goodman, James M. ..... San Francisco, CA
Goodman, James P. ..... Pottsville, PA
Goodman, James R. ..... Wake Forest, NC
Goodman, James S. ..... San Diego, CA
Goodman, Jan ..... Venice, CA
Goodman, Janice ..... New York, NY
Goodman, Janine F. ..... Washington, DC
Goodman, Jay ..... Santa Fe, NM
Goodman, Jay E. ..... San Francisco, CA
Goodman, Jay S. ..... Providence, RI
Goodman, Jeffrey H. ..... Washington, DC
Goodman, Jeffrey L. ..... Des Moines, IA
Goodman, Jeffrey L. ..... Voorhees, NJ
Goodman, Jeffrey M.
Federal Trade Commission, Bureau of Competition, GV
Goodman, Jeffrey M. ..... Needham, MA
Goodman, Jeffrey S. ..... Cincinnati, OH
Goodman, Jeffrey V. ..... Youngstown, OH
Goodman, Jennifer F. ..... Washington, DC
Goodman, Jerald M. ..... Philadelphia, PA
Goodman, Jerome Daniel
Chestnut Hill, MA
Goodman, Jerry L. ..... Oklahoma City, OK
Goodman, Jim Wade ..... Fayetteville, NC
Goodman, Jimmy ..... Oklahoma City, OK
Goodman, Jody ..... Washington, DC
Goodman, Joe M. ..... Nashville, TN
Goodman, Joel A. ..... Clearwater, FL

Goodman, Joel R. ....Southfield, MI
Goodman, John ....Santa Clara, CA
Goodman, John A. ....Bel Air, MD
Goodman, John D. ....Avon, CO
Goodman, John E. ....Birmingham, AL
Goodman, John F. ....Oakdale, LA
Goodman, John L. ....Cleveland, OH
Goodman, John M. ....Washington, DC
Goodman, John M. ....Miami, FL
Goodman, John M. ....Council Grove, KS
Goodman, John N. ....Oklahoma City, OK
Goodman, John N., A Professional Corporation ....Oklahoma City, OK
Goodman, John P. ....Fort Worth, TX
Goodman, Jon J. ....Philadelphia, PA
Goodman, Jon M. ....Munfordville, KY
Goodman, Jonathan ....Miami, FL
Goodman, Jonathan A. ....Boulder, CO
Goodman, Jonathan H. ....Jacksonville, FL
Goodman, Jonathan H., P.A. Jacksonville, FL
Goodman, Jonathan M. ....New York, NY
Goodman, Jonathan S. ....Chicago, IL
Goodman, Jonathan V. ....Milwaukee, WI
Goodman, Jordan M. ....Chicago, IL
Goodman, Joseph L. ....Portland, ME
Goodman, Joshua D. ....Stamford, CT
Goodman, Joshua R. ....Lake Worth, FL
Goodman, Joshua S. ....San Francisco, CA
Goodman, Joshua S. ....Boston, MA
Goodman, Judith F. ....New York, NY
Goodman, Jules S. ....New York, NY
Goodman, Julie Muth ....Lexington, KY
Goodman • Kang LLP San Francisco, CA
Goodman, Karen M. ....Sacramento, CA
Goodman, Karen R. ....Chicago, IL
Goodman, Karl H. ....Baltimore, MD
Goodman, Katherine E. ....Los Angeles, CA
Goodman, Kennard M. ....Seattle, WA
Goodman & Kenneff ....Millersville, PA
Goodman, Kenneth A. ....Reading, PA
Goodman, Kenneth D. ....Naples, FL
Goodman, Kenneth D. ....Houston, TX
Goodman, Kenneth G. ....New Brunswick, NJ
Goodman, Kenneth I. ....Lexington, MA
Goodman, Kenneth W. ....Duluth, GA
Goodman, Kevin N., Law Offices of Alamo, CA
Danville, CA
Pleasanton, CA
Goodman, Kevin N., Law Offices of San Ramon, CA
Goodman, Kevin N., Law Offices of Walnut Creek, CA
Goodman, Kimberly D. ....Cambridge, MA
Goodman, Larry Bruce ....Pompton Plains, NJ
Goodman, Larry J. ....Oakland, CA
Goodman, Larry L. Federal Deposit Insurance Corporation, Corporate Affairs Section, GV
Goodman, Laura National Labor Relations Board, Office of the General Counsel, GV
Goodman, Laura L. ....San Francisco, CA
Goodman, Lauren B. ....Altamonte Springs, FL
Goodman, Laurence M. ....Philadelphia, PA
Goodman Law Corp. ....Redwood City, CA
Goodman Law Firm, P.C. ....Prescott, AZ
Goodman, Lawrence ....New York, NY
Goodman, Lawrence D. ....Miami, FL
Goodman, Lawrence G. ....Iselin, NJ
Goodman, Lawrence G. ....New York, NY
Goodman, Lawrence I. ....Briarcliff Manor, NY
Goodman, Lawrence S., Ltd. ....Chicago, IL
Northbrook, IL
Goodman, Lee B. ....Prairie Village, KS
Goodman, Leonard ....Baltimore, MD
Goodman, Leonard C. ....Chicago, IL
Goodman, Leonard M. ....Newark, NJ
Goodman, Leonard S. ....Washington, DC
Goodman, Leonard S. ....Rockville, MD
Goodman, Leonard S. ....Philadelphia, PA
Goodman & Levine ....Alameda, CA
Goodman & Levine ....Briarcliff Manor, NY
Goodman, Lewis ....Lansdale, PA
Goodman, Lewis E., Jr. ....Danville, VA
Goodman, Lewis S. ....Baltimore, MD
Goodman, Linda L. ....San Diego, CA
Goodman, Lisa B. ....Wilmington, DE
Goodman, Lois H. ....Newark, NJ
Goodman, Lois R. ....Washington, DC
Goodman, Loren P. ....Fishers, IN
Goodman, Louis A. ....Phoenix, AZ
Goodman, Louis A. ....Boston, MA
Goodman, Louis J. ....Hayward, CA
Goodman, Lynn ....White Plains, NY
Goodman, Lynn C. ....Roslyn Heights, NY
Goodman, M. Leonard ....Chicago, IL
Goodman, M., P.C., & Associates Paramus, NJ
Goodman & Makinen ....Hancock, MI
Goodman, Malcolm L. ....Marion, OH
Goodman, Marc P. ....Los Angeles, CA
Goodman, Marcia B. ....Hartford, CT
Goodman, Marcia E. ....Chicago, IL
Goodman, Marguerite R. ....Paoli, PA
Goodman, Mark A. ....Dallas, TX
Goodman, Mark Alan ....Hayward, CA
Goodman, Mark C. ....San Francisco, CA
Goodman, Mark D. ....Sterling Heights, MI
Goodman, Mark E. ....St. Louis, MO
Goodman, Mark J. ....Atlanta, GA
Goodman, Mark L. ....New Haven, CT
Goodman, Mark L. ....Sparta, WI
Goodman, Mark N. ....Prescott, AZ
Goodman, Mark P. ....New York, NY
Goodman, Mark R. ....Chicago, IL

Goodman, Marsha ....Detroit, MI
Goodman, Martin ....Altoona, PA
Goodman, Martin D. ....San Francisco, CA
Goodman, Martin I. ....Old Greenwich, CT
Goodman, Martin J. ....Albany, NY
Goodman, Martin R. ....Roseland, NJ
Goodman, Marvin I. ....Mineola, NY
Goodman, Max A. ....Los Angeles, CA
Goodman, Maxine D. ....Houston, TX
Goodman, Maxine Graff ....Auburn Hills, MI
Goodman, McGuffey, Aust & Lindsey, LLP Atlanta, GA
Goodman, Meagher & Enoch Baltimore, MD
Goodman, Melanie L. ....Anaheim, CA
Goodman, Melissa M. ....Dallas, TX
Goodman, Melvyn J. ....Fort Myers, FL
Goodman, Meyer F. ....Lake Worth, FL
Goodman, Micah J. ....New York, NY
Goodman, Michael ....Denver, CO
Goodman, Michael ....Brooklyn, NY
Goodman, Michael B. ....Rochester, MN
Goodman, Michael B. ....Norristown, PA
Goodman, Michael B. Plymouth Meeting, PA
Goodman, Michael D. ....Atlanta, GA
Goodman, Michael D. ....Northbrook, IL
Goodman, Michael E. ....Bangor, ME
Goodman, Michael G. ....Omaha, NE
Goodman, Michael J. ....Orlando, FL
Goodman, Michael L. ....Beaverton, OR
Goodman, Michael L. ....Glen Allen, VA
Goodman, Michael M. ....Detroit, MI
Goodman, Michael S. ....San Diego, CA
Goodman, Michael S. ....Miami, FL
Goodman, Michael S. ....Paramus, NJ
Goodman, Michael S. ....Brooklyn, NY
Goodman, Michael S., P.A. ....Miami, FL
Goodman, Milton ....Newark, NJ
Goodman, Milton C. ....Boca Raton, FL
Goodman, Miriam Abrams ....Boulder, CO
Goodman, Miriam Maduro ....Pittsfield, MA
Goodman, Miriam Piwoz Westlake Village, CA
Goodman, Monica ....Tulsa, OK
Goodman, Monica Jo ....Northport, NY
Goodman, Morris H. ....Detroit, MI
Goodman, N. Victor ....Columbus, OH
Goodman, Nancy Barlow ....Clemmons, NC
Goodman, Nancy M. ....Department of Justice, Antitrust Division, GV
Goodman, Neil H. ....Bloomfield Hills, MI
Goodman, Neil M. ....Washington, DC
Goodman and Nekvasil, P.A. ....Clearwater, FL
Goodman & Nichols ....Munfordville, KY
Goodman, Norman ....New York, NY
Goodman, Notopoulos, Silverman, Croyle, Wasovich & Mears ....Altoona, PA
Goodman, Odom, Lacy, Floyd & Midgley, L.L.P. ....Fort Worth, TX
Goodman, Olivia T. ....New York, NY
Goodman, Oscar B. ....Las Vegas, NV
Goodman, Patricia Scott San Francisco, CA
Goodman, Patrick D. ....Monterey Park, CA
Goodman, Paul ....Chicago, IL
Goodman, Paul F. ....Memphis, TN
Goodman, Paul L. ....Greenwood, MS
Goodman, Paul S. ....New York, NY
Goodman, Peter ....San Francisco, CA
Goodman, Peter G. ....New York, NY
Goodman, Peter S. ....New York, NY
Goodman, Philip J. ....Washington, DC
Goodman, Philip J. ....Birmingham, MI
Goodman, Philip J., P.C. Birmingham, MI
Goodman Phillips & Vineberg New York, NY
Goodman, R. Mark ....Cross River, NY
Goodman, R. Mark, P.C. ....Cross River, NY
Goodman, Ramona ....Yonkers, NY
Goodman, Randolph M. ....Irvine, CA
Washington, DC
Goodman, Randy L. ....Midwest City, OK
Goodman, Raymond L. ....Orlando, FL
Goodman, Rebecca R. ....Los Angeles, CA
Goodman, Richard ....West Hartford, CT
Goodman, Richard A. ....Alameda, CA
Goodman, Richard B. ....Uniondale, NY
Goodman, Richard C. Newport Beach, CA
Goodman, Richard I. ....Miami, FL
Goodman, Richard L. ....Sharon, PA
Goodman, Richard Lanahan Cincinnati, OH
Goodman, Richard M. ....Detroit, MI
Goodman, Richard Michael ....Miami, FL
Goodman, Richard S. ....Ferndale, MI
Goodman, Richard S. ....Smithtown, NY
Goodman & Richter, LLP ....San Diego, CA
Goodman, Robert ....New York, NY
Goodman, Robert A. ....Santa Barbara, CA
Goodman, Robert A. ....Aberdeen, NJ
Goodman, Robert A. ....New York, NY
Goodman, Robert A. ....Cleveland, OH
Goodman, Robert A. ....Salt Lake City, UT
Goodman, Robert C., Jr. ....Norfolk, VA
Goodman, Robert Cedric San Francisco, CA
Goodman, Robert D. ....New York, NY
Goodman, Robert E. ....San Mateo, CA
Goodman, Robert E., Jr. ....Dallas, TX
Goodman, Robert F., Jr. ....Atlanta, GA
Goodman, Robert G. ....Woodbridge, NJ
Goodman, Robert I. ....Paterson, NJ
Goodman, Robert J. ....Troy, MI
Goodman, Robert L. ....Pottsville, PA
Goodman, Robert M. ....Newark, NJ

Goodman, Robert S. ....New York, NY
Goodman, Robert T. ....Fort Lauderdale, FL
Goodman, Robert T., A Professional Association ....Fort Lauderdale, FL
Goodman, Robert U. ....Shreveport, LA
Goodman, Robert U., P.L.C. Shreveport, LA
Goodman, Robert W. ....Hackensack, NJ
Goodman, Robert W. ....Charlotte, NC
Goodman, Roberta S. ....Scarsdale, NY
Goodman, Roberta Wilensky ....Deerfield, IL
Goodman, Ron L. ....Little Rock, AR
Goodman, Rona W. ....Quincy, MA
Goodman, Ronald B. ....New York, NY
Goodman, Ronald E. ....Ellendale, ND
Goodman, Ronald H. ....American Fork, UT
Goodman, Ronald J. ....Cincinnati, OH
Goodman, Rosanne ....Princeton, NJ
Goodman, Rosenthal & McKenna, P.C. Hartford, CT
West Hartford, CT
Goodman, Ross M. ....Pensacola, FL
Goodman, S. Mark ....Washington, DC
Goodman, Samuel J. ....Highland, IN
Goodman, Sara ....Parkland, FL
Goodman, Sara B. ....East Hanover, NJ
Goodman, Sarah E. Lyons ....Carlsbad, CA
Goodman, Saul B. ....Washington, DC
Goodman, Scott W. ....Morristown, NJ
Goodman, Selma ....Southgate, MI
Goodman, Sharon McNeilly Washington, DC
Goodman, Sheldon M. ....Eastchester, NY
Goodman, Sheldon S., (A Professional Corporation) ....Laguna Hills, CA
Goodman, Shelley S. ....New York, NY
Goodman, Sheryl L. ....Camden, NJ
Goodman, Shira ....Philadelphia, PA
Goodman, Solomon ....Hopewell, VA
Goodman, Sophia C. Equal Employment Opportunity Commission, Office of the General Counsel, GV
Goodman, Stanley ....Cincinnati, OH
Goodman, Stanley E. ....Hialeah, FL
Goodman, Stanley L. ....Los Angeles, CA
Roseland, NJ
New York, NY
Goodman, Stanley L. ....White Plains, NY
Goodman, Stanley R. ....Garden City, NY
Goodman, Stephanie B. ....Phoenix, AZ
Goodman, Stephanie H. ....New York, NY
Goodman, Stephen E. ....Chicago, IL
Goodman, Stephen H. ....Seattle, WA
Goodman, Stephen J. ....Washington, DC
Goodman, Stephen L. ....Washington, DC
Goodman, Stephen M. ....New York, NY
Goodman, Stephen M. ....Philadelphia, PA
Goodman, Stephen S., IV ....Fort Worth, TX
Goodman, Stephen W. ....New York, NY
Goodman, Steven A. ....Louisville, KY
Goodman, Steven B. ....Philadelphia, PA
Goodman, Steven H. ....Kansas City, MO
Goodman, Steven R. ....New York, NY
Goodman, Steven S. ....Chicago, IL
Goodman, Steven S. ....Woodbury, NY
Goodman, Stuart L. ....Chicago, IL
Goodman, Susan ....Chicago, IL
Goodman, Susan G. Department Of Health And Human Services, GV
Goodman, Susan I. ....Austin, TX
Goodman, Susan J. ....New York, NY
Goodman, Susan Lee ....Marietta, GA
Goodman, Susannah R. ....Houston, TX
Goodman, Terrence L. ....Cincinnati, OH
Goodman, Terri Lynn ....San Diego, CA
Goodman, Terry R. ....Austin, TX
Goodman, Thomas H. ....Minneapolis, MN
Goodman, Thomas J. ....Dubuque, IA
Goodman, Thomas L. ....Millersville, PA
Goodman, Thomas W., Jr. ....Pikeville, KY
Goodman, Toby R. ....Arlington, TX
Goodman, Todd L. ....Wilmington, DE
Goodman, W. Clark ....Charlotte, NC
Goodman and Walker ....Springfield, TN
Goodman, Wayne M. ....Highland Park, IL
Goodman Weiss Miller LLP Cleveland, OH
Goodman, Wendy B. ....Washington, DC
Goodman, West & Filetti, PLLC Charlottesville, VA
Glen Allen, VA
Norfolk, VA
Richmond, VA
Goodman, William B. ....Philadelphia, PA
Goodman, William F. ....San Antonio, TX
Goodman, William F., III ....Jackson, MS
Goodman, William F., Jr. ....Jackson, MS
Goodman, William H. ....Lake Forest, IL
Goodman, William H. ....Detroit, MI
Goodman, William M. ....San Francisco, CA
Goodman, William R., III ....Springfield, TN
Goodman, William S. ....Atlanta, GA
Goodman, William T. ....Rupert, ID
Goodman, Zenia S. ....Chicago, IL
Goodman, Zerline ....New York, NY
Goodman, Zigmund S. ....Chicago, IL
Goodman & Zuchlewski LLP New York, NY
Goodman-Delahunty, Jane ....Los Angeles, CA
Goodman-Guenther, Joyce ....Miami, FL
Goodman-Guenther, Joyce, P.A. Miami, FL
Goodman-Sheikh, Saleema Mount Clemens, MI
Goodmanson, John O. ....Albert Lea, MN

Goodmark & Goodmark, P.A. West Palm Beach, FL
Goodmark, Harry ....West Palm Beach, FL
Goodmark, Jerry J. ....West Palm Beach, FL
Goodmiller, Bruce R. ....Walnut Creek, CA
Goodmon, Raymond H., III ....Raleigh, NC
Goodner, Donald ....Waldron, AR
Goodner, Helaine S. ....Miami, FL
Goodner, John E. ....Macon, GA
Goodner, Richard B. ....Dallas, TX
Goodness, Cindy A. ....Honolulu, HI
Goodnight, David R. ....Seattle, WA
Goodnight, Gaylan ....Dallas, TX
Goodnight, Jane Jacobson ....Minneapolis, MN
Goodnight, Peggy R. ....Atlanta, GA
Goodno, Robin E. General Services Administration, Office of Regional Counsel, GV
Goodnough, Glen Steven ....Lewiston, ME
Goodnough, Roger A. ....New York, NY
Goodnow, Arwe, Ayer, Prigge, Hoppock & Kane, P.C. ....Keene, NH
Goodnow, Donald D. ....Concord, NH
Goodnow, Jannis E. ....Chicago, IL
Goodnow, Jennifer E. ....Los Angeles, CA
Goodnow, John C. ....Minneapolis, MN
Goodnow, John S. ....Keene, NH
Goodnow, Robert J. ....Leominster, MA
Goodove, Michael L. ....Norfolk, VA
Goodovitch, Paul ....Rockville Centre, NY
Goodpaster, Elizabeth ....St. Paul, MN
Goodpaster, Gary S. ....Davis, CA
Goodpaster, Scott A. Department of Commerce, Patent and Trademark Office, GV
Goodpaster, Shawn Cody ....Frankfort, KY
Goodpaster, Sherman, III ....Winchester, KY
Goodpastor, Christopher V. San Francisco, CA
Goodpasture, H. Glenn ....Fredericksburg, VA
Goodpasture, Katherine E. ....Richmond, VA
Goodpasture, Paige E. Hargroves Richmond, VA
Goodpasture, Philip H. ....Richmond, VA
Goodpasture, Purvis & Frackelton, P.C. Fredericksburg, VA
Goodreau, Robert E. ....Chelsea, MA
Goodreid, Thomas Edward ....Denver, CO
Goodrich, Alan O. ....Dallas, TX
Goodrich, Andrea ....Atlanta, GA
Goodrich, Brenton F. ....Los Angeles, CA
Goodrich, Christine A. ....Fresno, CA
Goodrich, Christopher M. ....Houston, TX
Goodrich, Craig N. ....Atlanta, GA
Goodrich & Daffada ....Chicago, IL
Goodrich, David E. ....Chicago, IL
Goodrich, David M. ....Cincinnati, OH
Goodrich, Dennis K. ....Syracuse, NY
Goodrich, Donald W. ....Adams, MA
Goodrich, Edward B. ....Grand Rapids, MI
Goodrich, Ernest W. ....Surry, VA
Goodrich, Frank E. ....Dallas, TX
Goodrich, George D. ....Missoula, MT
Goodrich, George H. ....Washington, DC
Goodrich, Gregory A. ....Houston, TX
Goodrich, Harry L. ....Danville, VA
Goodrich, Herbert F., Jr. Philadelphia, PA
Goodrich, Ira M. ....Austin, TX
Goodrich, James E. ....Baltimore, MD
Goodrich, James H. ....Chicago, IL
Goodrich, Jeffrey J. ....Greenbrae, CA
Goodrich, Jeffrey Mark ....Goffstown, NH
Goodrich, Jennifer A. ....New York, NY
Goodrich, Joan C. United States Postal Service, Law Department, GV
Goodrich, John B. ....Palo Alto, CA
Goodrich, John B. ....Chicago, IL
Goodrich, John H., Jr. ....Hartford, CT
Goodrich, John P. ....Pittsburgh, PA
Goodrich, John Quincy ....San Diego, CA
Goodrich, Julian R. ....Montpelier, VT
Goodrich, Laurence I. ....Tampa, FL
Goodrich, Laurence I., P.A. ....Tampa, FL
Goodrich, Leon R. ....St. Paul, MN
Goodrich, Malcolm H. ....Billings, MT
Goodrich, Mary A. ....Dallas, TX
Goodrich, Mary Warren ....Columbus, OH
Goodrich, Max E. ....Cypress, CA
Goodrich, Michael L. ....Columbus, KS
Goodrich, Michael S. ....Fort Worth, TX
Goodrich, Murray H. ....San Diego, CA
Goodrich, Nancy Z. ....Pittsburgh, PA
Goodrich, Nathaniel H. ....Washington, DC
Goodrich, Paul D. ....Detroit, MI
Goodrich, Paul W. ....Boston, MA
Goodrich, Peter T. ....White Plains, NY
Goodrich, Randy ....Clarksburg, WV
Goodrich, Raymond H. ....Santa Cruz, CA
Goodrich, Robert C., Jr. ....Nashville, TN
Goodrich, Robert D. ....Washington, DC
Goodrich, Robert E. ....Grand Rapids, MI
Goodrich, Robert F. ....Hollywood, FL
Goodrich, Robert L. ....Riverside, CA
Goodrich, Robert R. ....Freeport, ME
Goodrich, Robt. R. ....Fort Worth, TX
Goodrich & Schwartz ....San Diego, CA
Goodrich, Stephen N. ....Laramie, WY
Goodrich, Stephen W. ....Highland Park, MI
Goodrich, Steven C. ....Mesa, AZ
Goodrich, T. Michael ....Birmingham, AL
Goodrich, Thomas M. ....Birmingham, AL
Goodrich, Warren M. ....Tampa, FL
Goodrich, William F. ....Pittsburgh, PA
Goodrich, William K. ....Anoka, MN
Goodrich, William W., Jr. Washington, DC

Goodrick, Harry J. ... Elkton, MD
Goodrick, Michael J. ... Wilmington, DE
Goodridge, Allan D. ... New York, NY
Goodridge, George S.
Research Triangle Park, NC
Goodridge, James P. ... Chicago, IL
Goodridge, Julie Creal ... Milan, MI
Goodridge, Robert P. ... Baltimore, MD
Goodrum, C. Greg ... Houston, TX
Goodrum, Danon D. ... Detroit, MI
Goodrum, Forrest R. ... Boise, ID
Goodrum, Garfield B., Jr.
Washington, DC
Goodrum, Moulton, Jr. ... Houston, TX
Goodrum, Sherry B. ... Columbus, GA
Goodrum, Steven D. ... Lexington, KY
Goodrum, Wayne L. ... Austin, TX
Goods, Robert R. ... Buffalo, NY
Goodsaid, Ira J. ... Department of Commerce, Patent and Trademark Office, GV
Goodsell, Alice Dale ... Jackson, MS
Goodsell, Bradford D. ... Boise, ID
Goodsell, Bruce N. ... Westerly, RI
Goodsell, Daniel V. ... Salt Lake City, UT
Goodsell, David ... Melville, NY
Goodsell, G. Verne ... Rapid City, SD
Goodsell, Gerald W. ... Bakersfield, CA
Goodsell, Patricia A. ... Melville, NY
Goodsell, Robert A. ... Roseland, NJ
Goodsell, Scott L. ... San Jose, CA
Goodsell, Steven A. ... Salt Lake City, UT
Goodside, Robert M. ... Dallas, TX
Goodsill Anderson Quinn & Stifel
Honolulu, HI
Goodsill, Marshall M. ... Honolulu, HI
Goodsir, David V. ... Chicago, IL
Goodsir, Joseph W. ... Romulus, MI
Goodsite, Lawrence M. ... Watertown, NY
Goodsitt, Jack L. ... Milwaukee, WI
Goodsmith, Gregg & Unruh ... Chicago, IL
Goodsmith, Kenneth S. ... Chicago, IL
Goodsnyder, Christopher M. ... Chicago, IL
Goodson, A. C. ... Garrison, TX
Goodson, Andre A.
Federal Energy Regulatory Commission, Office of the General Counsel, GV
Goodson, Andrew Gabriel ... Greenville, SC
Goodson, B. Warren, Jr. ... Galveston, TX
Goodson, Brett C. ... Cincinnati, OH
Goodson, Carl K. ... Washington, DC
Goodson, Carlotta J. ... San Diego, CA
Goodson, Carol Boas ... Los Angeles, CA
Goodson, Caroline ... Chicago, IL
Goodson, Cathy A. ... Seattle, WA
Goodson, Christopher J. ... Hackensack, NJ
Goodson, David M. ... Hinsdale, IL
Goodson, David R. ... Paragould, AR
Goodson, Edward W. ... Coral Gables, FL
Goodson, Ernest, Jr. ... Phoenix, AZ
Goodson, Guy N. ... Beaumont, TX
Goodson, James E. ... Des Moines, IA
Goodson, James, III ... Danville, VA
Goodson, Jerry L. ... Greeneville, TN
Goodson, John C. ... Texarkana, AR
Goodson, John F. ... Phoenix, AZ
Goodson, John W. ... Texarkana, AR
Goodson, Jonathan M. ... Los Angeles, CA
Goodson, L. Aubrey, Jr. ... Danville, VA
Goodson, Manley & Durfee, P.L.C.
Phoenix, AZ
Goodson, Marvin ... Los Angeles, CA
Goodson & Mullins, Ltd. ... Cincinnati, OH
Goodson, Patricia W. ... Raleigh, NC
Goodson, Rhoda Bess ... South Daytona, FL
Goodson, Richard F. ... Boise, ID
Goodson, Robert D. ... San Francisco, CA
Goodson, Robert W. ... Washington, DC
Baltimore, MD
Rockville, MD
Goodson, Scott B. ... Raleigh, NC
Goodson, Stephen M. ... Cincinnati, OH
Goodson, Steven E. ... Houston, TX
Goodson, Suzanne ... New York, NY
Goodson, Vivian B. ... Washington, DC
Goodson, W. Gary ... Idaho Falls, ID
Goodson and Wachtel, A Professional Corporation ... Los Angeles, CA
Goodspeed, E. Givens ... Winter Park, FL
Goodspeed, Ernest L. ... Augusta, ME
Goodspeed, George S., Jr. ... Fairfield, CT
Goodspeed, Norwick R. G. ... Bridgeport, CT
Goodspeed, Patricia E. J. ... Knightstown, IN
Goodspeed, Paul E. ... Denver, CO
Goodspeed, Roger C. ... New York, NY
Goodspeed, Suzanne Sorich ... Denver, CO
Goodstadt, Amanda ... New York, NY
Goodstadt, Andrew S. ... New York, NY
Goodstadt, Craig Marc ... Ramsey, NJ
Goodstadt, Sheldon A. ... Voorhees, NJ
Bensalem, PA
Philadelphia, PA
Goodstein, Aaron E. ... Milwaukee, WI
Goodstein, Abby Beth ... San Francisco, CA
Goodstein, Arnold S. ... Summerville, SC
Goodstein, Barbara M. ... New York, NY
Goodstein, Barnett M. ... Dallas, TX
Goodstein, Clifford S. ... New York, NY
Goodstein, Daniel J. ... Los Angeles, CA
Goodstein, Gary J. ... Los Angeles, CA
Goodstein, Gerald L. ... Salem, MA
Goodstein, Gregory ... Glastonbury, CT
Goodstein, Irving D. ... New York, NY
Goodstein, Judy L. ... Lake Success, NY
Goodstein, Lauren S. ... New York, NY
Goodstein, Lionel ... San Antonio, TX

Goodstein, Michael D.
Department of Justice, Environment and Natural Resources Division, GV
Goodstein, Michael R. ... Washington, DC
Goodstein, Mortimer J. ... New York, NY
Goodstein, Peter E. ... Flint, MI
Goodstein, Peter H. ... New York, NY
Goodstein, Richard F. ... Houston, TX
Goodstein, Robert D. ... New Rochelle, NY
Goodstein, Sanders A. ... Flint, MI
Goodstein, Shari M. ... Stamford, CT
Goodstein, Starr & Pascoe, P.C. ... Dallas, TX
Goodstein, William ... New York, NY
Goodstone, Debra Weiss ... Miami, FL
Goodusky, Amy F. ... Hartford, CT
Goodvin, Grant D. ... Wichita, KS
Goodwell, Karen R. ... New Albany, IN
Goodwill, Betsy M.
Charlotte Amalie, St. Thomas, VI
Goodwill, Frederic C., II ... Chicago, IL
Goodwill, Raymond A., Jr.
Winter Haven, FL
Goodwillie, Eugene W., Jr. ... New York, NY
Goodwillie, Michael J. ... Lincoln, NE
Goodwin, Alan B. ... Davis, CA
Carbondale, IL
Goodwin, Alfred T. ... Pasadena, CA
Goodwin, Allyson D. ... Fort Lauderdale, FL
Goodwin, Amy E. ... San Diego, CA
Goodwin, Andrew B. ... Bridgeport, CT
Goodwin, Andrew J. ... Charleston, WV
Goodwin, Ann R. ... Pittsburgh, PA
Goodwin, Anna E. ... San Francisco, CA
Goodwin, Anne E. ... McLean, VA
Goodwin & Associates ... Livermore, CA
Goodwin, Barbara L. ... Portland, ME
Goodwin, Barry L. ... Tyler, TX
Goodwin, Bernard ... New York, NY
Goodwin, Bethanne Beloff ... Narberth, PA
Goodwin, Beverly B. ... New York, NY
Goodwin, Bill ... Norcross, GA
Goodwin, Bradford K. ... Albuquerque, NM
Goodwin, Brian C. ... San Diego, CA
Goodwin, Brian M. ... Phoenix, AZ
Tucson, AZ
Goodwin & Britain ... Tyler, TX
Goodwin, C. Leon ... Columbia, SC
Goodwin, Camille A. ... Woodstock, IL
Goodwin, Carl B., Jr. ... Seattle, WA
Goodwin, Catharine M.
Administrative Office Of The United States Courts, GV
Goodwin, Cathy J. ... Orlando, FL
Goodwin, C. E. ... Charleston, WV
Ripley, WV
Goodwin, Charles ... Washington, DC
Goodwin, Charles L. ... Grand Rapids, MI
Goodwin, Charles L. ... Clinton, OK
Goodwin, Charles Pearsall
Philadelphia, PA
Goodwin, Charles S. ... Dayton, OH
Goodwin, Charles W. ... Tallahassee, FL
Goodwin, Clifton A. ... Bellaire, TX
Goodwin, Clifton A., Jr. ... Bellaire, TX
Goodwin, Clyde C., Jr. ... Southfield, MI
Goodwin, Dan Luke ... Tulsa, OK
Goodwin, Daniel G. ... Seattle, WA
Goodwin, Daniel R. ... Vienna, VA
Goodwin, Daniel T. ... Commerce City, CO
Goodwin, Darla J. ... Seattle, WA
Goodwin, David ... Sharon, PA
Goodwin, David B. ... San Francisco, CA
Goodwin, David C. ... Miami, FL
Goodwin, David Lawrence ... Huntsville, AL
Goodwin, Deborah ... Oklahoma City, OK
Goodwin, Dodd & Paul ... Wheeling, WV
Goodwin, Elizabeth A. ... Fairview Park, OH
Goodwin, Ellen M. ... New York, NY
Goodwin, Eric ... Coldwater, MI
Goodwin, Eva S. ... Berkeley, CA
Goodwin, F. Lee ... Sioux City, IA
Goodwin, Frances H. ... Dallas, TX
Goodwin, Fred. C., III ... Rochester, NY
Goodwin, Geoffry P. ... Bangor, ME
Goodwin, George E. ... Dallas, TX
Goodwin, George Raymond ... Littleton, CO
Goodwin, George Wayne ... Rockingham, NC
Goodwin, Gerald A. ... Lufkin, TX
Goodwin, Glenn R. ... Greenville, SC
Goodwin and Goodwin ... Tulsa, OK
Goodwin & Goodwin ... Tyler, TX
Goodwin & Goodwin ... Charleston, WV
Parkersburg, WV
Ripley, WV
Goodwin, Gregory J. ... Modesto, CA
Goodwin, Harrison L. ... Auburn, CA
Goodwin & Harrison, L.L.P.
The Woodlands, TX
Goodwin, Herbert N. ... Brookline, MA
Goodwin, Hugh, Jr. ... Palo Alto, CA
Goodwin, Hugh W. ... Fresno, CA
Goodwin, J. Bland, Jr. ... Augusta, GA
Goodwin, J. Jeffries ... Sacramento, CA
Goodwin, J. Jeffries, A Professional Corporation ... Sacramento, CA
Goodwin, J. Miles ... Milwaukee, WI
Goodwin, Jack ... Tehachapi, CA
Goodwin, James ... San Diego, CA
Goodwin, James C. ... Tucson, AZ
Goodwin, James F., Jr. ... Bristol, TN
Goodwin, James M. ... Sharon, PA
Goodwin, James O. ... Tulsa, OK
Goodwin, James O. ... Sisters, OR
Goodwin, James Patrick ... San Jose, CA
Goodwin, James W., II ... Tampa, FL
Goodwin, Jean ... Chicago, IL
Goodwin, Jeffrey B. ... New York, NY

Goodwin, Jennifer L. ... Walnut Creek, CA
Goodwin, Jodi ... Harlingen, TX
Goodwin, John D. ... Shreveport, LA
Goodwin, John H. ... Newtown, PA
Goodwin, John I., III ... Metairie, LA
Goodwin, John J. ... Fairfield, CT
Goodwin, John M., Jr. ... Belleville, IL
Goodwin, Jonathon T. ... Cincinnati, OH
Goodwin, Joseph R. ... Charleston, WV
Goodwin, Joy S. ... Columbia, SC
Goodwin, Julie A. ... Arnold, MD
Goodwin, Julie D. ... Baltimore, MD
Goodwin, Karen L. ... Springfield, MA
Goodwin, Karl ... Salem, OR
Goodwin, Kathleen S. ... Towson, MD
Goodwin, Kenneth A. (Budd)
New Orleans, LA
Goodwin, Kenneth L. ... Tuscaloosa, AL
Goodwin, Kenneth S. ... New York, NY
Goodwin, Kerry B. ... Tullahoma, TN
Goodwin, Kevin A. ... Santa Cruz, CA
Goodwin, Kirby J. ... Allegan, MI
Goodwin, Kristen A. ... Sacramento, CA
Goodwin, Kyle ... Oklahoma City, OK
Goodwin, L. Carey ... Cherry Hill, NJ
Goodwin, L. Todd ... Pittsburgh, PA
Goodwin Law Office, P.C. ... Ames, IA
Goodwin Law Offices ... Rockingham, NC
Goodwin Law Offices, The ... McCook, NE
Goodwin, Lawrence B. ... New York, NY
Goodwin, Lee M. ... Washington, DC
Goodwin, Leonard J. ... Corvallis, OR
Goodwin, Lincoln Hayes ... Lubbock, TX
Goodwin, Linda S. ... West Palm Beach, FL
Goodwin, Linda" Terry " ... Houston, TX
Goodwin, Lisa M. ... New York, NY
Goodwin, Louise M. ... Chicago, IL
Goodwin, Luther A. ... Valley Center, CA
Goodwin, Lynne Browning ... Truckee, CA
Goodwin and Macha ... Bellville, TX
Goodwin, Marion R. ... Bellville, TX
Goodwin, Mark A. ... Shreveport, LA
Goodwin, Mark B. ... Richmond, VA
Goodwin, Mark D. ... New York, NY
Goodwin, Mark S. ... Danville, IL
Goodwin, Mary Jane ... Anderson, SC
Goodwin, Matthew S. ... New Brunswick, NJ
Goodwin, Maureen A. ... Phoenix, AZ
Goodwin, Max E. ... Terre Haute, IN
Goodwin, Michael A. ... Denver, CO
Goodwin, Michael D. ... Washington, DC
Goodwin, Michael S. ... New Britain, PA
Goodwin, Min Choi ... Geneva, IL
Goodwin, Moore, Colbert & Broadaway
Paragould, AR
Goodwin, Nancy J. ... Baton Rouge, LA
Goodwin, Nancy J., A Professional Law Corporation ... Baton Rouge, LA
Goodwin, Neil W. ... Troy, IL
Goodwin, Norris M. ... Oroville, CA
Goodwin, O. David ... Waco, TX
Goodwin, Pamela S. ... Princeton, NJ
New York, NY
Philadelphia, PA
Goodwin, Patricia A. ... Alexandria, LA
Goodwin, Patricia Lynne ... Truckee, CA
Goodwin and Paul ... Tolland, CT
Goodwin, Paul A. ... Salem, OR
Goodwin, Paul L. ... Redlands, CA
Goodwin, Paula Rae ... Cleveland, OH
Goodwin, Perry C., Jr. ... Little Rock, AR
Goodwin, Peter W. ... Fairfax, VA
Goodwin, Preston C. ... The Woodlands, TX
Goodwin, Procter & Hoar LLP
Washington, DC
Boston, MA
New York, NY
Goodwin, Randall D. ... Texarkana, TX
Goodwin Raup PC ... Phoenix, AZ
Tucson, AZ
Goodwin, Ray A. ... Paragould, AR
Goodwin, Raymond ... Newark, NJ
Goodwin, Richard C. ... Fresno, CA
Goodwin, Richard E. ... Aberdeen, WA
Goodwin, Richard K. ... Oklahoma City, OK
Goodwin, Robert A. ... Huntington, NY
Goodwin, Robert A. ... Center, TX
Goodwin, Robert (Booth), II
Charleston, WV
Goodwin, Robert C., Jr. ... Bethesda, MD
Goodwin, Robert E. ... Livermore, CA
Goodwin, Robert E. ... Denver, CO
Goodwin, Robert E., & Associates
Denver, CO
Goodwin, Robert H. ... New Brunswick, NJ
Goodwin, Robert J. ... Birmingham, AL
Goodwin, Robert P. ... Sidney, NE
Goodwin, Robert S. ... Columbia, MD
Goodwin, Robert W. ... Ames, IA
Goodwin, Robert W. ... Newberg, OR
Goodwin, Rolf ... Nashua, NH
Goodwin, Ronald R. ... San Angelo, TX
Goodwin, S. John ... Seattle, WA
Goodwin, Samuel S. ... Monroe, NC
Goodwin, Schult & Goodwin
Huntington, NY
Goodwin and Scieszka, P.C.
Birmingham, MI
Goodwin, Scott A. ... Birmingham, MI
Goodwin, Scott R. ... Washington, DC
Goodwin, Stacey J. ... Albuquerque, NM
Goodwin, Stanley C. ... McCook, NE
Goodwin, Stephen A. ... Dallas, TX
Goodwin, Stephen D. ... Memphis, TN
Goodwin, Stephen P. ... Charleston, WV
Ripley, WV
Goodwin, Steven C. ... Boston, MA
Goodwin, Steven D. ... Richmond, VA

Goodwin, Susan Busby ... Lomita, CA
Goodwin, Susan D. ... Phoenix, AZ
Goodwin, Tara Leigh ... Chicago, IL
Goodwin, Thomas A. ... Wheeling, WV
Goodwin, Thomas B. ... Cheyenne, OK
Goodwin, Thomas J. ... Saddle Brook, NJ
New York, NY
Goodwin, Thomas J. ... Houston, TX
Goodwin, Thomas L. ... Augusta, ME
Goodwin, Thomas M. ... Danville, IL
Goodwin, Thomas P. ... Syracuse, NY
Goodwin, Thomas P. ... Toledo, OH
Goodwin, Thomas R. ... Charleston, WV
Goodwin, Timothy J. ... Atlanta, GA
Goodwin, Timothy J. ... Dallas, TX
Goodwin, Todd M. ... Milwaukee, WI
Goodwin, Tom N. ... Laredo, TX
Goodwin, Traci Marie ... Seattle, WA
Goodwin, V. Glenn, Jr. ... Des Moines, IA
Goodwin, Van A. ... San Diego, CA
Goodwin, W. Bradford ... Tolland, CT
Goodwin, W. Chapman ... Staunton, VA
Goodwin, W. Clark ... Birmingham, AL
Goodwin, Wendy ... Atlanta, GA
Goodwin, Wilfred ... Columbus, OH
Goodwin, William ... New York, NY
Goodwin, William G. ... New Orleans, LA
Goodwin, William K. ... Seattle, WA
Goodwin, William N. ... Omak, WA
Goodwin, William W., Jr. ... Clinton, NJ
Goodwin & Wofford, P.C. ... Norcross, GA
Goodwine, George Earl ... Ormond Beach, FL
Goodwine, J. William, Jr. ... Pasadena, CA
Goodwine, Pamela R. ... Lexington, KY
Goodwine, Paul J. ... New Orleans, LA
Goodwyn, Gardner F., Jr. ... Bessemer, AL
Goodwyn, George A. ... Tarboro, NC
Goodwyn, Lauri K. ... New York, NY
Goodwyn, M. Williams, Jr.
Birmingham, AL
Goodwyn, Maura Reardon ... Birmingham, AL
Goodwyn, Otis J. ... Montgomery, AL
Goodwyn, R. Tyler, IV ... Washington, DC
Goodwyn, S. Bernard ... Norfolk, VA
Goodwyn, Sharon S. ... Norfolk, VA
Goodwyn, Suzanne Spink
Washington, DC
Goodwyn, Ulysses V. ... Birmingham, AL
Goodwyn, Warren H. ... Montgomery, AL
Goodwyn, William V. ... Birmingham, AL
Goodwyn, William Vincent, P.C.
Birmingham, AL
Goodwyne, Jeffrey J. ... Chalmette, LA
Goodwyne, Owen K. ... Tallahassee, FL
Goody, Alycia L. ... Providence, RI
Goody, Jennifer H. ... Albany, NY
Goody, W. Keith ... Jackson, WY
Goodyear, Barbara ... San Francisco, CA
Goodyear, Daniel Lee ... Pittsburgh, PA
Goodyear, Elizabeth B. ... Blue Bell, PA
Goodyear, EllaCortland ... Newark, NJ
Goodyear, Geo. F. ... Buffalo, NY
Goodyear, Lisa Sciullo ... Pittsburgh, PA
Goodyear, Marion M. ... Greenville, SC
Goodyear, Marion M., P.A.
Greenville, SC
Goodyear, Peter Edward ... San Antonio, TX
Goodyear, Robert B. ... Philadelphia, PA
Goodykoontz, J. Greg ... Clarksburg, WV
Goodz, Jeffrey M. ... Aventura, FL
Goodzeit, Carolyn A. ... Raleigh, NC
Goodzeit, David S. ... Bronx, NY
Goodzeit, Margaret ... Woodbridge, NJ
Gooen, Cynthia R. ... New York, NY
Gooen, Michael N. ... Roseland, NJ
Googasian, Dean ... Detroit, MI
Googasian Firm, The, P.C.
Bloomfield Hills, MI
Googasian, George A. ... Bloomfield Hills, MI
Googasian, Steven G. ... Bloomfield Hills, MI
Googe, Charles H., Jr. ... New York, NY
Googe, Earl E., Jr. ... Jacksonville, FL
Googe, Elise Whitaker ... Atlanta, GA
Googe, George Morton ... Jackson, TN
Googe, Howard E., Jr. ... Stuart, FL
Googe, James P., Jr. ... Memphis, TN
Googe, P. Roger, Jr. ... Jackson, MS
Googins, Glen R. ... Chula Vista, CA
Googins, Mark K. ... Portland, ME
Googins, Robert R. ... Hartford, CT
Googooian, Charles L. ... Pasadena, CA
Gooing, Homer ... South Gate, CA
Gookin, Myron L. ... Fairfield, IA
Goold, Barry Stephen ... Las Vegas, NV
Goold, James A. ... Washington, DC
Goold, John J. ... Fairbury, IL
Goold, Linda ... United States Senate, Senatorial Assistants, GV
Goold Patterson DeVore Ales & Roadhouse
Las Vegas, NV
Goold, Richard T. ... Denver, CO
Goold, Richard T., P.C. ... Denver, CO
Gooley, Charles E. ... Meriden, CT
Gooley, Theresa A. ... Minneapolis, MN
Goolie, Jenifer Susan ... Largo, MD
Goolkasian, Gail A. ... Boston, MA
Goolkasian, John T. ... Arlington, VA
Goolnick, Steven B. ... New York, NY
Goolsby, Allen C., III ... Richmond, VA
Goolsby, Barbara Grace ... Miami, FL
Goolsby, Betty Sue ... Dallas, TX
Goolsby, Bryan L. ... Dallas, TX
Goolsby, C. Tolbert, Jr. ... Columbia, SC
Goolsby, Craig W. ... Mobile, AL
Goolsby, George F. ... Houston, TX
Goolsby, James W., Jr. ... Houston, TX
Goolsby, Jo Jenkins ... Topeka, KS
Goolsby, Katherine L. ... Richmond, VA

Goolsby, Kenneth C." Casey " ... Tyler, TX
Goolsby, Michael L. ... Los Angeles, CA
Goolsby, Michelle Parsons ... Dallas, TX
Goolsby, Nolan R. ... Cookeville, TN
Goolsby, Olson & Proctor
Oklahoma City, OK
Goolsby, Richard H. ... Augusta, GA
Goolsby, Robert Todd
Oklahoma City, OK
Goolsby, Thomas C. ... Raleigh, NC
Wilmington, NC
Goolsby, Tonia Suzanne ... Little Rock, AR
Goon, Anne C. ... Santa Monica, CA
Goon, Lyman ... Rockville, MD
Goon, Richard ... Plantation, FL
Goon, Robert H. ... Los Angeles, CA
Goon, Steven John ... Costa Mesa, CA
Goonan, Gregory P. ... San Diego, CA
Goonrey, Charles W. ... Harrisburg, PA
Goor, Richard L. ... Encino, CA
Goore, Hamlet E., Jr. ... Jersey City, NJ
Goorin, Kenneth H. ... Bethpage, NY
Goorjian & McCabe, A Professional Corporation ... San Francisco, CA
Goorjian, Paul M. ... San Francisco, CA
Goorland, Bruce D. ... Fort Lauderdale, FL
Goorley, Richard, (A Professional Law Corporation) ... Shreveport, LA
Goorman, Perry L. ... Englewood, CO
Goos, Stanley ... New York, NY
Goosen, Cynthia Shea ... Dallas, TX
Sherman, TX
Goosen, Frederick D. ... Coral Gables, FL
Goosenberg, David M. ... Los Angeles, CA
Goosenberg, Jennifer B. ... Los Angeles, CA
Goosmann, George F., IV ... Asheville, NC
Goossen, David F. ... Denver, CO
Goossen, Dean H. ... Chicago, IL
Goossen, Levi H. ... Newton, KS
Goossens, Dorit ... Laguna Beach, CA
Goostree, Robert E. ... Reynoldsburg, OH
Goot, Eugene M. ... McLean, VA
Gootee, Jane M. ... Midland, MI
Gootjes, Mary E. ... Chicago, IL
Gootkin, Howard A. ... New York, NY
Gootnick, Margery F. ... Rochester, NY
Goots, John H. ... Ashland, VA
Goots, Thomas R. ... Cleveland, OH
Goott, Alan Franklin ... New York, NY
Goott, Eugene M. ... Washington, DC
Gootzeit, Ronald M. ... Treasury Department, Internal Revenue Service, GV
Goovaerts, Erwin G. ... Franklin, NJ
Goowin, Nancy James ... Jackson, MS
Goozée, King & Horsley ... Birmingham, AL
Goozée, Stevan K. ... Birmingham, AL
Gooze-Miller, Michelle H. ... Chicago, IL
Goozman, Martin L. ... Laurel, MD
GoPaul, Patricia ... New York, NY
Gopen, Richard S. ... Chelsea, MA
Gopin, Albert Jacob ... Beverly Hills, CA
Gopin, Michael J. ... El Paso, TX
Gopin, Robyn N. ... Rockville, MD
Gopin, Steven D. ... Chelsea, MA
Goplen, Susan K. ... Seattle, WA
Goplerud, C. Peter, III ... Tulsa, OK
Goplerud, Harry Christopher ... Tampa, FL
Detroit, MI
Goplerud, Harry Christopher, P.A.
Tampa, FL
Goplerud, J. Barton ... Des Moines, IA
Gopman, Howard Z., & Associates
Skokie, IL
Gopman, Jonathan E. ... Boca Raton, FL
Gopman, Michelle L. ... Atlanta, GA
Gopman, Miles J. ... Miami, FL
Goppert, Ernest J., Jr. ... Cody, WY
Goppert, Olson & Rohrbach ... Cody, WY
Gopstein, Israel ... Alexandria, VA
Gora, Felix J. ... Cincinnati, OH
Gora, Joel M. ... Brooklyn, NY
Gora, Michael H., (P.A.) ... Boca Raton, FL
Gorab, Edward R. ... Longmont, CO
Gorab, Harris G. ... Rehoboth, MA
Gorab, Lisa A. ... Woodbridge, NJ
Gorab, Michele H. ... Rehoboth, MA
Goracke, Bruce J. ... Omaha, NE
Goracke, Max D. ... Kansas City, MO
Goracy, Edward R. ... Pottersville, NJ
Gorai, Jane L. ... San Francisco, CA
Gorak, Mary Jane ... Santa Rosa, CA
Gorak, Thomas C. ... Baltimore, MD
Goral, Brian H. ... Golden, CO
Goraleski, Carl George ... Dayton, OH
Goralewicz, Richard J. ... Oklahoma City, OK
Goralka, John M. ... Sacramento, CA
Goralnick, Howard S. ... Springfield, MA
Goralski, Patricia J. ... Sun City West, AZ
Goralski, Theodore F., Jr. ... Uniondale, NY
Goralski, Zygmunt H. ... Bayonne, NJ
Goran, Jay ... Chicago, IL
Goran, John J. ... Miami, FL
Goran, Mark H. ... St. Louis, MO
Goran, Ruth I. ... Jamaica Plain, MA
Goran, William T. ... Miami, FL
Goranflo, Brenda Grise
Federal Emergency Management Agency, Office of the General Counsel, GV
Goranites, Peter J. ... Portland, ME
Goranson, Bain & Larsen, L.C.
Dallas, TX
Goranson, David L. ... Denver, CO
Goranson, Donald L. ... Clear Lake, IA
Goranson & Goranson ... Toledo, OH
Goranson, James E. ... Toledo, OH
Goranson, Mark D. ... Houston, TX
Goranson & Philibosian, P.C. ... Denver, CO
Goranson, Roger W. ... Toledo, OH
Goranson, Ronald L. ... Dallas, TX
Goranson, Thomas P. ... Dallas, TX
Gorant, Susan J. ... Northbrook, IL
Goray, Caroline Seibert ... Raleigh, NC
Goray, Gerald A. ... Boca Raton, FL
Goraya, Victor S. ... Washington, DC
Gorayeb & Associates, P.C.
New York, NY
Gorayeb, Christopher J. ... New York, NY
Gorayeb, Henry E. ... Flushing, NY
Gorayeb, Joseph G. ... New York, NY
Gorbatoff, Timothy G. ... Detroit, MI
Gorbaty, Dena Gutman ... Baltimore, MD
Gorbaty, Michael A. ... Chalmette, LA
Gorbea, Juan Carlos ... San Juan, PR
Gorbey, Christopher F. ... Media, PA
Gorbey, James H., Jr. ... Media, PA
Gorbey, Leslie ... Lancaster, PA
Gorbey, Timothy J. ... Media, PA
Gorbis, Boris Z. ... Beverly Hills, CA
San Francisco, CA
Gorbis & Liberty, A Legal Corporation, P.C.
Beverly Hills, CA
San Diego, CA
San Francisco, CA
Gorbold, Robert R. ... Joliet, IL
Gorby, Michael J. ... Atlanta, GA
Gorby, Reeves, Peters & Burns, P.C.
Atlanta, GA
Gorchow, Murray A. ... Southfield, MI
Gorcowski, Michael N. ... Joliet, IL
Gorcowski, Pamela Davis ... Joliet, IL
Gorcyca, Jeffrey T. ... Detroit, MI
Gorcyca, S. Gerald ... Bingham Farms, MI
Gorczyca, Diane T. ... San Francisco, CA
Gorczyca, Gary S. ... Orange, CA
Gorczyca, Victoria A. ... Indianapolis, IN
Gorczycki, Henry J.
General Accounting Office, Office of the General Counsel, GV
Gorczynski, Izabelle J. ... Deerfield, IL
Gorczynski, Peter R. ... Hauppauge, NY
Gordan, Cynthia L. ... Fall River, MA
Gordan, John D., III ... New York, NY
Gordan, Stuart S. ... Atlanta, GA
Gordan, Virginia B. ... Ann Arbor, MI
Gordanier, Dean C., Jr. ... Boston, MA
Gorday, Carl L. ... Birmingham, AL
Gorday, T. Gary ... North Miami, FL
Gordee, Alan J. ... Irvine, CA
Gorden, Michelle E. ... Philadelphia, PA
Gorden, William W., Jr. ... Oklahoma City, OK
Gordenev, Brian C. ... San Jose, CA
Gordenker, Hendrik ... Washington, DC
Gorder, Charles F., Jr. ... Portland, OR
Gorder, Charles F., Sr. ... San Diego, CA
Gorder, Gregory ... Seattle, WA
Gordesky, Morton ... Philadelphia, PA
Gordet, Richard E. ... Boston, MA
Gordet, Roy S. ... San Francisco, CA
Gordet, Stephen ... Westwood, MA
Gordian, Carmelo M. ... Austin, TX
Gordian, Nina Lopez ... New York, NY
Gordich, Bernard J. ... Allentown, PA
Gordich, Lawrence Alan ... Miami, FL
Gordillo, Gregory A. ... Cleveland, OH
Gordin, George, Jr. ... Dallas, TX
Gordin, Richard H. ... Washington, DC
Gordin, Robert H. ... Delaware, OH
Gordinier, John K. ... Louisville, KY
Gordinier, Marilyn Low ... Fairfield, CA
Gordinier, Thomas H. ... Fairfield, CA
Gordinier, Todd E. ... Los Angeles, CA
Gordis, Elihu ... New York, NY
Gordner, John R. ... Berwick, PA
Gordnier, John A. ... San Francisco, CA
Gordo, Jose ... Miami, FL
Gordon, A. Matthew ... Rochester, NY
Gordon, A. Pope ... Montgomery, AL
Gordon, A. Reynolds ... Bridgeport, CT
Gordon, Aaron Z., Jr. ... Taylor, MI
Gordon, Abraham I. ... Bridgeport, CT
Gordon, Adam H. ... Washington, DC
Gordon, Adam H. ... Washington, DC
Gordon, Adam K. ... Troy, MI
Gordon, Adam S. ... Naples, FL
Gordon, Adrian J. ... Philadelphia, PA
Gordon, Alan B. ... Pittsburgh, PA
Gordon, Alan C. ... Hillsborough, CA
Gordon, Alan E. ... Oxford, NY
Gordon, Alan H. ... Houston, TX
Gordon, Alan M. ... Parsippany, NJ
Gordon, Alan R. ... Ithaca, NY
Gordon, Alan R. ... Philadelphia, PA
Gordon, Alan S. ... Charlotte, NC
Gordon, Alan S., P.A., Law Offices of
Charlotte, NC
Gordon, Albert A. ... Miami, FL
Gordon, Albert F. ... Westfield, MA
Gordon, Alexander, IV ... Easton, MD
Gordon, Alexander John ... Port Charlotte, FL
Gordon, Alexander N. ... New York, NY
Gordon, Allan H. ... Philadelphia, PA
Gordon, Allen J. ... Chesapeake, VA
Gordon, Allen M. ... Chicago, IL
Gordon Altman Weitzen Shalov & Wein LLP ... New York, NY
Gordon, Alvin ... Washington, DC
Gordon, Alvin A. ... Memphis, TN
Gordon, Alvin Craig ... New York, NY
Gordon, Amanda E. ... Akron, OH
Gordon, Ami ... San Antonio, TX
Gordon, Amy ... Newark, NJ
Gordon, Amy A. ... New York, NY
Gordon, Anat ... Edison, NJ
Gordon, Ana-Valli ... New Orleans, LA
Gordon, Andrew K. ... San Francisco, CA
Gordon, Andrew L. ... Miami, FL
Gordon, Andrew P. ... Las Vegas, NV
Reno, NV
Gordon, Andrew P. ... Roseland, NJ
Gordon, Andrew S. ... Phoenix, AZ
Gordon, Andrew S. ... Boston, MA
Gordon, Andrew S. ... Harrisburg, PA
Gordon, Angel Rochelle ... Charlotte, NC
Gordon, Angus N., Jr. ... Hamden, CT
Gordon, Ann ... Indianapolis, IN
Gordon, Ann C. Wells ... Denver, CO
Gordon, Ann Clary ... Baltimore, MD
Gordon, Ann Vincent ... Charleston, WV
Gordon, Anthony B. ... Woodland Hills, CA
Gordon, Anthony C. ... Las Vegas, NV
Gordon, Anthony R. ... Carson City, NV
Gordon, Arata, McCollam, Duplantis & Eagan, L.L.P. ... Baton Rouge, LA
Lafayette, LA
New Orleans, LA
Gordon, Arnold M. ... Southfield, MI
Gordon, Arnold M. ... Latham, NY
Gordon, Arthur I. ... Plainview, NY
Gordon, A. S. ... Pittsburgh, PA
Gordon & Associates, A Professional Corporation ... Bluffton, IN
Ossian, IN
Gordon, Audrey S ... Peabody, MA
Gordon, Ava ... New York, NY
Gordon, Avery E. ... Farmington, MI
Gordon, Aviva Y. ... Las Vegas, NV
Gordon, Avron L. ... Minneapolis, MN
Gordon & Bales, P.C. ... Jenkintown, PA
Gordon, Bancroft S. ... McLean, VA
Gordon, Barbara ... San Francisco, CA
Gordon & Barnett ... Washington, DC
Gordon, Barry D. ... Boston, MA
Gordon, Barry E. ... Bethesda, MD
Gordon, Barry J. ... Quincy, MA
Gordon Barry J., P.C., Law Offices of
Quincy, MA
Gordon, Barry L. ... Chicago, IL
Gordon, Barry L., & Associates, Prof. Corp.
Chicago, IL
Gordon, Beatriz M. G. ... Irvine, CA
Gordon, Belle Lind ... Chicago, IL
Gordon, Ben W., Jr. ... Pensacola, FL
Gordon, Ben W., Jr., P.A. ... Pensacola, FL
Gordon Bendall Branham McNeely & DeLaney ... Huntington, IN
Roanoke, IN
Warren, IN
Gordon, Bernadette N. ... Newark, NJ
Gordon, Bernard ... Washington, DC
Gordon, Bernard S. ... New York, NY
Gordon, Bert G. ... Bay Shore, NY
Gordon, Beryl ... Department of Transportation, Surface Transportation Board, GV
Gordon, Beverly S. ... Sarasota, FL
Gordon, Bobby Ray ... Honolulu, HI
Gordon, Bonnie C. ... Phoenix, AZ
Gordon, Bonny Kanter ... Chevy Chase, MD
Gordon, Brad M. ... Chicago, IL
Gordon, Bradley Keith ... Pittsfield, MA
Gordon, Bradley M. ... Dallas, TX
Gordon, Bradley P. ... Lead, SD
Gordon & Braiker-Gordon
Woodland Hills, CA
Gordon, Brian A. ... Philadelphia, PA
Gordon, Brian S. ... Brownsburg, IN
Gordon, Brita J. ... Dallas, TX
Gordon, Brock B. ... Mobile, AL
Gordon, Bruce D. ... Fort Lee, NJ
Gordon, Bruce H. ... Tampa, FL
Gordon, Bruce J. ... Morrison, CO
Gordon, Bruce L. ... Birmingham, AL
Gordon, Bruce S. ... Bridgeport, CT
Gordon, Bruce T. ... Canton, OH
Gordon, Bruce W. ... Loveland, OH
Gordon & Bryant ... Washington, DC
Gordon, Burton ... New York, NY
White Plains, NY
Gordon, Burton K. ... New York, NY
Gordon, C. Leonard ... New York, NY
Gordon & Caloccia ... Homewood, IL
Gordon, Calvert J. ... New Lenox, IL
Gordon, Careen M. ... Morris, IL
Gordon, Caren M. ... Trenton, NJ
Gordon, Carlton J. ... New York, NY
Gordon, Carol S. ... San Francisco, CA
Gordon, Carolyn A. ... Pasadena, CA
Gordon, Carolyn Y. S. ... Los Angeles, CA
Gordon, Caruth & Virden, PLC
Conway, AR
Morrilton, AR
Gordon, Caryn Beth ... Boston, MA
Gordon, Cathy R. ... Pittsburgh, PA
Gordon, Cecile L. ... New Orleans, LA
Gordon, Celia A. ... Commack, NY
Gordon, Charles ... San Jose, CA
Gordon, Charles ... Van Nuys, CA
Gordon, Charles ... Powell, TN
Gordon, Charles B. ... Cleveland, OH
Gordon, Charles C. ... Seattle, WA
Gordon, Charles E. ... Winter Park, FL
Gordon, Charles E. ... Columbus, OH
Gordon, Charles M., Jr.
Baton Rouge, LA
Gordon, Charles P. ... Department of Labor, Office of the Solicitor, GV
Gordon, Charles W. ... Easton, PA
Gordon, Charles W., IV
Corpus Christi, TX
Gordon, Charles W., Jr. ... Kansas City, MO
Gordon, Charlie W. ... Louisville, KY
Gordon, Charmaine Baldwin ... Columbia, MD
Gordon, Cheryl Lasris ... Sarasota, FL
Gordon, Chester E. ... Lakewood, OH
Gordon, Chester H. ... Poughkeepsie, NY
Gordon, Christopher A. ... Olathe, KS
Gordon, Christopher Howe
Washington, DC
Gordon, Clarence T., II ... Columbus, OH
Gordon, Claudius A. ... Boston, MA
Gordon, Cliff ... Corpus Christi, TX
Gordon, Clifford ... Monticello, NY
Gordon, Clyde ... Tomball, TX
Gordon, Corbett ... Portland, OR
Gordon, Corey L. ... Minneapolis, MN
Gordon, Craig ... Tucson, AZ
Gordon, Croxton ... Eastville, VA
Gordon, Curtis ... Gretna, LA
Gordon, Curtis D. ... Richmond, VA
Gordon, Curtis W., Jr. ... Birmingham, AL
Gordon, Cutler and Hoffman ... Southfield, MI
Gordon, Cynthia Callendar
Las Vegas, NV
Gordon, Dale C. ... Chicago, IL
Gordon, Dana A. ... Houston, TX
Gordon, Daniel D. ... Chicago, IL
Gordon, Daniel G. ... Chicago, IL
Gordon, Daniel I.
General Accounting Office, Office of the General Counsel, GV
Gordon, Daniel N. ... Eugene, OR
Gordon, Daniel R. ... Miami, FL
Gordon, Daniel R., (P.C.) ... Bluffton, IN
Ossian, IN
Gordon, Danl. ... Baltimore, MD
Gordon, Daryl T. ... Richardson, TX
Gordon, David A. ... Long Beach, CA
Gordon, David A. ... New York, NY
Gordon, David B. ... New York, NY
Gordon, David D. ... Des Moines, IA
Gordon, David D. ... Gig Harbor, WA
Gordon, David E. ... Los Angeles, CA
Gordon, David E. ... Chicago, IL
Gordon, David E. ... Purcellville, VA
Gordon, David J. ... Northbrook, IL
Gordon, David J. ... Rocky Mount, NC
Gordon, David J. ... Cleveland, OH
Gordon, David J. ... Delaware, OH
Gordon, David L. ... Atlanta, GA
Gordon, David L. ... Canton, GA
Gordon, David L. ... Philadelphia, PA
Gordon, David M. ... Newport, OR
Gordon, David P. ... Stamford, CT
Gordon, David P. ... Baltimore, MD
Gordon, David R ... Bangor, PA
Gordon, David S. ... Weatogue, CT
Gordon, David S. ... Princeton, NJ
Gordon, David Stott ... Charlotte, NC
Gordon, David W. ... San Francisco, CA
Gordon, Davidson T. ... New York, NY
Gordon, Dean B. ... Fresno, CA
Gordon, Dean L. ... New Hartford, NY
Gordon, Deborah ... Chicago, IL
Gordon, Deborah L. ... Royal Oak, MI
Gordon, Deborah S. ... Greenwich, CT
Gordon, Deborah S. ... Stamford, CT
Gordon, Debra A. ... Phoenix, AZ
Gordon, Debra G. ... Chicago, IL
Gordon, DeFraga, Watrous & Pezzaglia, A Law Corporation ... Martinez, CA
Gordon, Denis F. ... Washington, DC
Gordon, Denise A. ... West Palm Beach, FL
Gordon, Derek G. ... Lexington, KY
Gordon, Diana ... Department of Justice, Office of the Inspector General, GV
Gordon, Diana Greene ... Santa Monica, CA
Gordon, Diane L. ... Hutchinson, MN
Gordon, Diane R. ... Boston, MA
Gordon, Dodson & Gordon ... Chesterfield, VA
Gordon, Donald H. ... Detroit, MI
Gordon, Donald J. ... Crockett, TX
Gordon, Donald R. ... Los Angeles, CA
Gordon, Donald R. ... Normal, IL
Gordon, Donald Scott ... Santa Monica, CA
Gordon, Donna L. ... Newark, NJ
Gordon, Donna Y. ... Yucca Valley, CA
Gordon, Douglas L. ... Fresno, CA
Gordon, Douglas N. ... Dallas, TX
Gordon, Douglas T. ... Powell, TN
Gordon, Drysdale & Obrand
Newport Beach, CA
Gordon, Edelstein, Krepack, Grant, Felton & Goldstein ... Los Angeles, CA
Gordon, Edgar G. ... Kalamazoo, MI
Gordon, Edward ... Albany, NY
Gordon, Edward Allen ... Morrilton, AR
Gordon, Edward M., III ... Metairie, LA
Gordon, Edward Marshall ... Laconia, NH
Gordon, Edward W. ... Newark, NJ
Gordon, Edwin J. ... Kettering, OH
Gordon, Efrem A. ... Springfield, MA
Gordon, Eileen B. ... New York, NY
Gordon & Einstein, Ltd. ... Chicago, IL
Gordon, Elaine ... New Haven, CT
Gordon, Elizabeth L. ... New Orleans, LA
Gordon, Elizabeth Lynn ... Chicago, IL
Gordon, Ellen Gittel ... Marina Del Rey, CA
Gordon, Ellen L. ... Portsmouth, NH
Gordon, Elliot K. ... Thousand Oaks, CA
Gordon, Eric ... Baltimore, MD
Gordon, Eric A. ... West Palm Beach, FL
Gordon, Eric B. ... Los Angeles, CA
Gordon, Eric L. ... White Plains, NY
Gordon, Eric M. ... Moundsville, WV
Gordon, Eric S. ... Woodland Hills, CA
Gordon, Eric S. ... Cleveland, OH
Gordon, Eric T. ... New York, NY
Gordon, Ernest V., Jr. ... Jackson, MS
Gordon, Errol J. ... Los Angeles, CA
Gordon, Estera F. ... Seattle, WA
Gordon, Eugene A. ... Greensboro, NC
Gordon, Eugene W. ... Chicago, IL
Gord[illegible]n, Ev[illegible]n L. ... New York, NY

Gordon, Feinblatt, Rothman, Hoffberger & Hollander, LLC ... Baltimore, MD
Gordon, Felicia M. ... Miami, FL
Gordon, Felicia S. ... New York, NY
Gordon, Felix F. ... Canoga Park, CA
Gordon, Flem ... Madisonville, KY
Owensboro, KY
Gordon, Forest ... Lauderhill, FL
Gordon, Fournaris & Mammarella, P.A.
Wilmington, DE
Gordon, Frank H. ... Newport, NH
Gordon, Frank J. ... Raleigh, NC
Gordon, Frank X., Jr. ... Phoenix, AZ
Gordon, Franklin D. ... Bakersfield, CA
Gordon, Fred ... Birmingham, MI
Gordon, Fred, Law Offices of, P.C.
Birmingham, MI
Gordon, Frederic L., (P.C.) ... San Diego, CA
Gordon & Freeman, P.C. ... Houston, TX
Gordon, Frieda ... Santa Monica, CA
Gordon & Friedler, P.A. ... Boston, MA
Gordon, G. David ... Tulsa, OK
Gordon, G. David, & Associates, P.C.
Tulsa, OK
Gordon, Gail ... Los Angeles, CA
Gordon, Gail J. ... Seattle, WA
Gordon, Gail K. ... Washington, DC
Gordon, Gail R. ... West Islip, NY
Gordon, Garry ... New York, NY
Gordon, Gary J. ... Minneapolis, MN
Gordon, Gary L. ... Albuquerque, NM
Gordon, Gary P. ... Lansing, MI
Gordon, Geo. W. ... Greensboro, NC
Gordon, George B. ... Tuscaloosa, AL
Gordon, George D. ... Conroe, TX
Gordon, George G. ... Philadelphia, PA
Gordon, George H., Jr. ... Chicago, IL
Gordon, George I. ... Washington, DC
Gordon, George S. ... Philadelphia, PA
Gordon, Gerald ... North Brunswick, NJ
Gordon, Gerald ... New York, NY
Gordon, Gerald M. ... Las Vegas, NV
Gordon, Gerald N. ... Los Angeles, CA
Gordon, Gerald S. ... Houston, TX
Gordon, Gerry R., (P.A.) ... Tampa, FL
Gordon, Gigi ... Santa Monica, CA
Gordon, Gilbert ... Chicago, IL
Gordon, Gilbert W. ... Chicago, IL
Gordon, Gittel ... Marina Del Rey, CA
Gordon, Glen F. ... Boulder, CO
Denver, CO
Gordon, Glenda G. ... Marquette, MI
Gordon, Glenn M. ... Norwich, CT
Gordon, Glenn R. ... Warren, NJ
Gordon, Glenn Stuart ... Miami, FL
Gordon, Glickman, Flesch & Woody
Chicago, IL
Gordon & Glickson LLC ... Chicago, IL
Gordon & Goddard, LLP ... Oakland, CA
Gordon, Goldberg & Juengst ... New York, NY
Gordon & Gordon ... Manhattan Beach, CA
Gordon & Gordon ... Bronx, NY
Gordon & Gordon ... Forest Hills, NY
Mineola, NY
Gordon and Gordon, A Professional Corporation ... West Orange, NJ
Gordon, Gordon & Feldbaum ... Memphis, TN
Gordon & Gordon, P.C. ... Kansas City, MO
Gordon and Gordon, P.C.
Mount Laurel, NJ
Philadelphia, PA
Gordon & Gordon, P.S.C.
Madisonville, KY
Owensboro, KY
Gordon, Gordon & Schnapp, P.C.
New York, NY
Gordon, Grant Gregory ... Bettendorf, IA
Gordon, Gregg S. ... Indianapolis, IN
Gordon, Gregory G. ... Las Vegas, NV
Gordon, Gregory M. ... Dallas, TX
Gordon, H. Stephen ... Silver Spring, MD
Gordon, Harlan M. ... Cleveland, OH
Gordon, Harley ... Boston, MA
Gordon, Harold ... Washington, DC
Kensington, MD
Gordon, Harold ... New York, NY
Gordon, Harold D. ... Latham, NY
Gordon, Harold H. ... Madison Heights, MI
Gordon, Harold K. ... New York, NY
Gordon, Harrison J. ... West Orange, NJ
Gordon, Harry G. ... Greensboro, NC
Gordon, Harry N. ... Athens, GA
Gordon, Harvey C. ... Niles, IL
Gordon, Harvey J. ... Bethesda, MD
Gordon, Heather ... Cleveland, OH
Gordon & Heneson, P.A. ... Baltimore, MD
Gordon, Henry ... Southfield, MI
Gordon, Henry R. ... Las Vegas, NV
Gordon, Henry R., A Prof. Corp., Chartered
Las Vegas, NV
Gordon, Herbert B. ... New York, NY
Gordon, Herbert W. ... Bloomfield Hills, MI
Gordon, Herman ... Houston, TX
Gordon, Herman L. ... Nashville, TN
Gordon and Hiller ... Bridgeport, CT
Gordon, Hiram D. ... New York, NY
Gordon and Hires ... Jesup, GA
Gordon, Horne and Hicks, P.A.
Laurinburg, NC
Gordon, Howard A., P.A. ... West Hartford, CT
Tampa, FL
Gordon, Howard E. ... Norfolk, VA
Gordon, Howard F. ... Fort Lauderdale, FL
Gordon, Howard F. ... East Lansing, MI
Gordon, Howard Jay ... Englewood Cliffs, NJ
Gordon, Howard W. ... Miami, FL
Gordon, Hugh B. ... Ardmore, PA
Gordon, Ilissa S. ... Fort Lauderdale, FL
Gordon, Ilona ... Sherman Oaks, CA
Gordon, Ira R. ... Coral Gables, FL
Gordon, Irvin D. ... Concord, NH
Gordon, Irwin J. ... Trumbull, CT
Gordon, J. Don ... Sherman, TX
Gordon, J. Houston ... Covington, TN
Gordon, J. Houston ... Memphis, TN
Gordon, J. Hugh ... Tifton, GA
Gordon, J. Hugh, P.C. ... Tifton, GA
Gordon, J. Robert ... Laurinburg, NC
Gordon, J. Scott ... Overland Park, KS
Gordon, J. Wyndal ... Baltimore, MD
Gordon, J. Wyndal, P.A., & Associates
Baltimore, MD
Gordon, Jack A. ... New York, NY
Gordon, Jack B. ... Washington, DC
Gordon, Jack D. ... San Jose, CA
Gordon, Jack E. ... Claremore, OK
Tulsa, OK
Gordon, Jack E., Jr. ... Claremore, OK
Tulsa, OK
Gordon, Jackson & Simon
North Woodmere, NY
Gordon, Jacob J. ... North Miami Beach, FL
Gordon, James A. ... Baltimore, MD
Gordon, James A., Jr. ... Los Angeles, CA
Gordon, James B. ... Chestertown, MD
Gordon, James C. ... Fort Worth, TX
Gordon, James D., III ... Provo, UT
Gordon, James E. ... Lincoln, NE
Gordon, James G. ... Pittsburgh, PA
Gordon, James H. ... Columbus, OH
Gordon, James L. ... Memphis, TN
Gordon, James R. ... Englewood, CO
Gordon, James S. ... La Jolla, CA
Gordon, James S., (Ltd.) ... Chicago, IL
Gordon, James Thomas ... Orlando, FL
Gordon, James W. ... Longmeadow, MA
Gordon, Jane A. ... Wayne, NJ
Gordon, Jane H. ... Eugene, OR
Gordon, Jane M. ... West Palm Beach, FL
Gordon, Janet A. ... New York, NY
Gordon, Janice M. ... Sherman Oaks, CA
Gordon, Jason M. ... Cocoa Beach, FL
Gordon, Jay F. ... Garden City, NY
Gordon, Jay I. ... New York, NY
Gordon, Jay R.
Department of Transportation, Maritime Administration, GV
Gordon, Jeanne E. Brown ... Chicago, IL
Gordon, Jeffery K. ... Austin, TX
Gordon, Jeffery K. ... Austin, TX
Gordon, Jeffrey ... Bronx, NY
Gordon, Jeffrey B. ... Washington, DC
Gordon, Jeffrey D. ... Princeton, NJ
Gordon, Jeffrey E. ... Baltimore, MD
Gordon, Jeffrey F. ... West Palm Beach, FL
Gordon, Jeffrey J. ... Los Angeles, CA
Gordon, Jeffrey Lee ... Tampa, FL
Gordon, Jeffrey M. ... Reynoldsville, PA
Gordon, Jeffrey N. ... New York, NY
Gordon, Jeffrey S. ... Los Angeles, CA
Gordon, Jeffry B. ... Birmingham, AL
Gordon, Jennifer ... New York, NY
Gordon, Jennifer L. ... Hempstead, NY
Gordon, Jere C. ... Kenton, TN
Gordon, Jerem M. ... Trenton, NJ
Gordon, Jerry P. ... Sherman Oaks, CA
Gordon, Joan Elbaum ... New York, NY
Gordon, Joan I. ... Rockville, MD
Gordon, Joan Tremblay
Manhattan Beach, CA
Gordon, Jocelyn F. ... Boston, MA
Gordon, Joe K. ... Arlington, TX
Gordon, Joel M. ... Seattle, WA
Gordon, John A. ... Cambridge, MA
Gordon, John A., (A P.L.C.)
New Orleans, LA
Gordon, John B. ... Minneapolis, MN
Gordon, John B. ... Pittsburgh, PA
Gordon, John D. ... Cambridge, MA
Gordon, John E. ... Chicago, IL
Gordon, John J. ... Albuquerque, NM
Gordon, John J. ... Staten Island, NY
Gordon, John R. ... Missoula, MT
Gordon, John R. ... Las Vegas, NV
Gordon, John S. ... Los Angeles, CA
Gordon, John S. ... Kansas City, MO
Gordon, Jon I. ... Miami, FL
Gordon, Jonathan ... Roseland, NJ
New York, NY
Gordon, Jonathan C. ... Falls Church, VA
Gordon, Jonathan Charles ... Cleveland, OH
Gordon, Jonathan D. ... Denver, CO
Gordon, Jonathan M. ... Los Angeles, CA
Gordon, Joseph ... Chicago, IL
Gordon, Joseph ... Millburn, NJ
Gordon, Joseph A. ... Boston, MA
Gordon, Joseph H. ... Rochester, NY
Gordon, Joseph H. ... Tacoma, WA
Gordon, Joseph H., Jr. ... Tacoma, WA
Gordon, Joseph K. ... Philadelphia, PA
Gordon, Joseph P., Jr. ... New Orleans, LA
Gordon, Joseph T. ... Manhattan Beach, CA
Gordon, Joshua A. ... Palo Alto, CA
Gordon, Joshua L. ... Concord, NH
Gordon, Judith A. ... Los Angeles, CA
Gordon, Judith E. ... Los Angeles, CA
Gordon, Judith M. ... Riverhead, NY
Gordon, Judith V. ... Palo Alto, CA
Gordon, Julia R. ... Washington, DC
Gordon, Julie Anne ... Rochester, NY
Gordon & Kanengiser ... Millburn, NJ
Gordon, Karen Hutchinson
Fort Worth, TX
Gordon, Karen L. ... San Diego, CA
Gordon, Karl Herreshoff ... Annapolis, MD
Gordon, Kathryn O. ... Chicago, IL
Gordon, Keara M. ... Washington, DC
Gordon, Kelli Ellen ... Springfield, IL
Gordon, Kelly ... Woodbridge, NJ
Gordon, Kenneth ... New York, NY
Gordon, Kenneth ... Oklahoma City, OK
Gordon, Kenneth A. ... Fort Lauderdale, FL
Gordon, Kenneth E. ... New York, NY
Gordon, Kenneth G. ... Los Angeles, CA
Gordon, Kenneth I. ... Boston, MA
Gordon, Kenneth J. ... Boston, MA
Gordon, Kenneth L. ... Liberty, MS
Gordon, Kenneth M. ... Denver, CO
Gordon, Kenneth W. ... Rochester, NY
Gordon, Kenneth Y.
West Palm Beach, FL
Gordon, Kent H. ... Houston, TX
Gordon, Kevin D. ... Oklahoma City, OK
Gordon, Kevin F. ... Portland, ME
Gordon, Kevin P. ... San Diego, CA
Gordon, Kimberly W. ... Washington, DC
Gordon, Kirby K. ... Pismo Beach, CA
Gordon, L. Gail ... Los Angeles, CA
Gordon, L. James ... Newark, OH
Gordon, Lana ... Houston, TX
Gordon, Lance B. ... Pasadena, CA
Gordon, Larry A. ... Bethesda, MD
Gordon, Larry M. ... Mill Valley, CA
Gordon, Larry S. ... Cleveland, OH
Gordon & Lathum ... Birmingham, AL
Gordon, Laura K. ... Sulphur, OK
Gordon, Laura P. ... Bonita, CA
Gordon, Laurence T. ... Madisonville, KY
Gordon, Laurie L. ... Orlando, FL
Gordon, Laurie Lloyd, P.A. ... Orlando, FL
Gordon Law Firm, The ... Elberton, GA
Hartwell, GA
Gordon Law Office, The
Kansas City, MO
Gordon, Lawrence G., Jr.
Winston-Salem, NC
Gordon, Lawrence H. ... Berkeley, CA
Gordon, Lawrence J. ... St. Charles, MO
Gordon, Lawrence M. ... Boston, MA
Gordon, Lawrence M. ... Glenville, NY
Gordon, Lawrence M. ... Jericho, NY
Gordon, Lawrence M. ... New York, NY
Gordon, Lawrence R. ... Culver City, CA
Gordon, Lawrence R.
Department Of Health And Human Services, Social Security Administration, GV
Gordon, Lawrence S. ... Miami, FL
Gordon, Layne Scott ... Marlton, NJ
Philadelphia, PA
Gordon, Lee ... Baltimore, MD
Gordon, Lee ... Austin, TX
Gordon, Lee A. ... New York, NY
Gordon, Lee B. ... Palm Beach, FL
Gordon, Lee B., P.A. ... Palm Beach, FL
Gordon, Lee M. ... Newport Beach, CA
Gordon, Lelieth L. ... Norwalk, CT
Gordon, Leon L. ... Santa Monica, CA
Gordon, Leonard ... Hewlett, NY
Gordon, Leonard B. ... Philadelphia, PA
Gordon, Leonard L. ... Washington, DC
Gordon, Leonard S. ... North Woodmere, NY
Gordon, Lesley S. ... Beverly Hills, CA
Gordon, Lewis G. ... Coral Gables, FL
Gordon, Lewis Jay ... Philadelphia, PA
Gordon, Leza M. ... Washington, DC
Gordon, Liran A. ... Philadelphia, PA
Gordon, Lisa ... New York, NY
Gordon, Lisa I. ... Chicago, IL
Gordon, Lisa R. ... Los Angeles, CA
Gordon, Lizbeth R. ... San Francisco, CA
Gordon, Lois B. ... New York, NY
Gordon, Lois J. ... Chicago, IL
Gordon, Lori Ann ... New York, NY
Gordon, Lorna Gail ... Los Angeles, CA
Gordon, Louis ... Southfield, MI
Gordon, Lowell J. ... Rockville, MD
Gordon, Lyndi Ann ... Clearwater, FL
Gordon, Lynne M. ... Mattituck, NY
Gordon, M. Kirby, II ... Owensboro, KY
Gordon, M. Scott ... Chicago, IL
Gordon & Macdonald, P.C. ... Denver, CO
Gordon, MacDonnell ... Santa Fe, NM
Gordon, Marc A. ... Fort Lauderdale, FL
Gordon, Marc C. ... Las Vegas, NV
Gordon, Marc E. ... Department of Justice, Environment and Natural Resources Division, GV
Gordon, Marc P. ... Houston, TX
Gordon, Marc R. ... Charlotte, NC
Gordon, Marc R. ... Philadelphia, PA
Gordon, Marci I. ... New York, NY
Gordon, Marcia Z. ... Los Angeles, CA
Gordon, Marcy G. ... Miami, FL
Gordon, Marcy J. ... Golden Beach, FL
Gordon, Marilynn Z. ... Calistoga, CA
Gordon, Maris R. ... Forest Hills, NY
Mineola, NY
Gordon, Mark ... New York, NY
Gordon, Mark ... Pittsburgh, PA
Gordon, Mark A. ... Troy, MI
Gordon, Mark C. ... New York, NY
Gordon, Mark D.
Environmental Protection Agency, Office of Enforcement and Compliance Assurance, GV
Gordon, Mark L. ... Chicago, IL
Gordon, Mark N. ... Cambridge, MA
Gordon, Mark S. ... Hawthorne, CA
Gordon, Marla Meg ... New York, NY
Gordon, Marlene Mitchell ... Miami, FL
Gordon, Marshall K. ... Woodland Hills, CA
Gordon, Martin, Jones & Harris
Nashville, TN
Gordon, Marvene A. ... Sarasota, FL
Gordon, Mary C. ... Salt Lake City, UT
Gordon, Mary Jane A. ... San Francisco, CA
Gordon, Mary Lu T. ... Oklahoma City, OK
Gordon, Mary Rogers ... Webster Groves, MO
Gordon, Mary S. ... Colorado Springs, CO
Gordon, Matthew ... New York, NY
Gordon, Matthew D. ... Denver, CO
Gordon, Matthew Dallas ... Hartford, CT
Gordon, Matthew L. ... Bronx, NY
Gordon, Max ... Albany, NY
Gordon, Max, (P.C.) ... Overland Park, KS
Gordon, Mayer B. ... Southfield, MI
Gordon, Mayer B., & Associates, P.C.
Detroit, MI
Southfield, MI
Gordon, Melvin ... Palm Desert, CA
Gordon, Merrill H. ... Farmington Hills, MI
Gordon, Merrill H., P.C.
Farmington Hills, MI
Gordon, Meryl ... Los Angeles, CA
Gordon, Michael ... West Orange, NJ
Gordon, Michael ... Bronx, NY
Gordon, Michael A. ... Los Angeles, CA
Gordon, Michael A. ... Washington, DC
Gordon, Michael A. ... Chicago, IL
Gordon, Michael A. ... Rockville, MD
Gordon, Michael A. ... St. Louis, MO
Gordon, Michael C. ... Miami, FL
Gordon, Michael D. ... Phoenix, AZ
Gordon, Michael D. ... Kansas City, MO
Gordon, Michael D. ... Raleigh, NC
Gordon, Michael E. ... Washington, DC
Gordon, Michael I. ... Baltimore, MD
Gordon, Michael M. ... New York, NY
Gordon, Michael R. ... Atlanta, GA
Gordon, Michael R. ... Rockville, MD
Gordon, Michael R. ... New York, NY
Gordon, Michael R. ... Raleigh, NC
Gordon, Michael S. ... New York, NY
Gordon, Michael W. ... Gainesville, FL
Gordon, Michaeline ... Chicago, IL
Gordon & Michelson, P.A. ... Miami, FL
Gordon, Miles Z. ... Torrance, CA
Gordon, Millicent E. ... Pikesville, MD
Gordon, Milton H. ... Berkeley, CA
Gordon, Mitchel M. ... Baltimore, MD
Gordon, Mitchell ... Minneapolis, MN
Gordon, Mitchell A. ... Daytona Beach, FL
Gordon, Mitchell A., P.A.
Daytona Beach, FL
Gordon, Mitchell H. ... New York, NY
Gordon, Mitchell H. ... New York, NY
Gordon, Monte S. ... Marina Del Rey, CA
Gordon, Moore, Primason & Bradley
Lynn, MA
Gordon, Morton A. ... Chicago, IL
Gordon, Morton J. ... Hazleton, PA
Gordon, Morton J. ... Wilkes-Barre, PA
Gordon, Muir and Foley, LLP
Hartford, CT
Gordon, Murray B. ... Novelty, OH
Gordon Murray Tilden ... Seattle, WA
Gordon, Myra Miller ... Boston, MA
Gordon, Myron L. ... Milwaukee, WI
Gordon, Nahum L. ... New York, NY
Gordon, Nancy E. ... Atlanta, GA
Gordon, Nancy E. ... Durham, NC
Gordon, Nancy E., P.C., Law Offices of
Durham, NC
Gordon, Nancy J. ... Elk Grove Village, IL
Gordon, Nancy P. ... Coral Gables, FL
Gordon, Nancy R. ... Anchorage, AK
Gordon, Naomi ... New York, NY
Gordon, Nathan ... Morrilton, AR
Gordon, Nathan ... Columbus, OH
Gordon, Nathan W. ... Los Angeles, CA
Gordon, Neal ... Weehawken, NJ
Gordon, Neil ... Baltimore, MD
Gordon, Neil C. ... Atlanta, GA
Gordon, Nicholas ... New York, NY
Gordon, Nicole A. ... New York, NY
Gordon, Nicole L. ... Birmingham, AL
Gordon, Nina S., (P.A.) ... Miami, FL
Gordon, Noceeba Southern ... Detroit, MI
Gordon, Noel H. ... Princeton, NJ
Gordon, Norman ... San Francisco, CA
Gordon, Norman J. ... El Paso, TX
Gordon, Norman P. ... Kansas City, MO
Gordon, Norman R. ... Shreveport, LA
Gordon, Norman W. ... Long Beach, CA
Gordon, Pamela A. ... Denver, CO
Gordon, Pamela I. ... South Boston, VA
Gordon, Patricia ... Newtown, PA
Gordon, Patricia A. ... Scarsdale, NY
Gordon, Patricia Lynn ... Lithonia, GA
Gordon, Patricia S. ... Pasadena, CA
Gordon, Patrick F. ... Chicago, IL
Gordon, Patrick M., P.A. ... Jupiter, FL
Gordon, Patrick R. ... El Paso, TX
Gordon, Paul ... Beverly Hills, CA
Gordon, Paul ... Denver, CO
Gordon, Paul A. ... San Francisco, CA
Gordon, Paul F. ... Kansas City, MO
Gordon, Paul M. ... Oakland, CA
Gordon, Paul M. ... Boston, MA
Gordon, Paul N. ... Dover, OH
Gordon, Paul P. ... Chippewa Falls, WI
Gordon, Paul R.
Federal Communications Commission, Mass Media Bureau, GV
Gordon, Paul R. ... New York, NY
Gordon, Paula N. ... New York, NY
Gordon, Peter C. ... Florham Park, NJ
Gordon, Peter D. ... Los Angeles, CA
Gordon, Peter J. ... Boston, MA
Gordon, Peter J. ... New York, NY
Gordon, Peter S. ... Wilmington, DE

Gordon, Peter S. ... Forest Hills, NY
Mineola, NY
Gordon & Peterson, L.L.C.
Lambertville, NJ
Doylestown, PA
Philadelphia, PA
Gordon, Phil W. ... Chickasha, OK
Gordon, Philip A. ... Boulder, CO
Gordon, Philip J. ... Boston, MA
Gordon, Philip L. ... Denver, CO
Gordon, Philip S. ... Houston, TX
Gordon, Phillip ... Chicago, IL
Gordon, Phillip B. ... Phoenix, AZ
Gordon, Phyllis R. ... Kansas City, MO
Gordon & Polscer ... Seattle, WA
Portland, OR
Gordon & Pont, P.C. ... Southfield, MI
Gordon, R." Bruce " ... Boise, ID
Gordon, R. Kenneth ... Dallas, TX
Gordon, R. Wayne ... Dallas, TX
Gordon, Ralph R. ... Fallbrook, CA
Gordon, Randi E. ... Brooklyn, NY
Gordon, Randolph I. ... Bellevue, WA
Gordon, Randolph M. ... Ottawa, IL
Gordon, Randy D. ... Dallas, TX
Gordon, Randy S. ... Newton, MA
Gordon, Rawson C. ... Atlanta, GA
Gordon, Raymond J. ... Pineville, MO
Gordon, Raymond P. ... Chicago, IL
Gordon, Raymond S., Jr. ... Jesup, GA
Gordon & Rees, LLP ... Los Angeles, CA
San Diego, CA
San Francisco, CA
Gordon, Reginald E. ... Richmond, VA
Gordon, Rena P. ... Potomac, MD
Gordon, Renee H. ... St. Petersburg, FL
Gordon, Rhonda S. ... Stony Brook, NY
Gordon, Richard ... Los Angeles, CA
Gordon, Richard ... Seattle, WA
Gordon, Richard A. ... Westfield, NJ
Gordon, Richard A. ... Memphis, TN
Gordon, Richard A. ... Alexandria, VA
Gordon, Richard C. ... Omaha, NE
Gordon, Richard E. ... Tucson, AZ
Gordon, Richard E. ... Syracuse, NY
Gordon, Richard E. ... Pittsburgh, PA
Gordon, Richard F. ... Morehead City, NC
Gordon, Richard G. ... Fort Lauderdale, FL
Gordon, Richard H. ... Beverly Hills, CA
Gordon, Richard H. ... Farmington, CT
Gordon, Richard H. ... Buffalo, NY
Gordon, Richard H. ... Tiffin, OH
Gordon, Richard Ian ... Cambridge, MA
Gordon, Richard L. ... Wayland, MA
Gordon, Richard L. ... Omaha, NE
Gordon, Richard M. ... Atlanta, GA
Gordon, Richard S. ... Indianapolis, IN
Gordon, Richard S. ... Baltimore, MD
Gordon, Richard S. ... Charlotte, NC
Gordon, Richard S. ... Newport News, VA
Gordon, Richards ... Boston, MA
Gordon, Ricky D., (P.A.) ... Coral Springs, FL
Gordon, Rita W. ... New York, NY
Gordon & Robbins ... Boston, MA
Gordon, Robert ... Salt Lake City, UT
Gordon, Robert A. ... Baltimore, MD
Gordon, Robert A. ... Springfield, MA
Gordon, Robert A., Jr. ... San Francisco, CA
Gordon, Robert B. ... Boston, MA
Gordon, Robert C., III ... San Francisco, CA
Gordon, Robert D. ... Boston, MA
Gordon, Robert D. ... Southfield, MI
Gordon, Robert E. ... Corte Madera, CA
Gordon, Robert E. ... West Palm Beach, FL
Gordon, Robert E. ... Chicago, IL
Gordon, Robert E. ... Chicago, IL
Gordon, Robert J. ... Detroit, MI
Gordon, Robert J. ... New York, NY
Gordon, Robert K. ... Abington, MA
Gordon, Robert K. ... Philadelphia, PA
Gordon, Robert L. ... Forest Hills, NY
Gordon, Robert L. ... Houston, TX
Gordon, Robert L. ... Milwaukee, WI
Gordon, Robert M. ... Washington, DC
McLean, VA
Gordon, Robert M.
House of Representatives, Congressional Assistants, GV
Gordon, Robert M. ... Kailua-Kona, HI
Gordon, Robert M. ... Chicago, IL
Gordon, Robert N. ... Baltimore, MD
Gordon, Robert P. ... Los Angeles, CA
Gordon, Robert S. ... New York, NY
Gordon, Robert T., Jr. ... Jackson, MS
Gordon, Roberta G. ... New York, NY
Gordon, Robin J. ... Nashville, TN
Gordon, Robin Lynn Thompson ... Ruso, ND
Gordon, Rochelle Louise ... Cleveland, OH
Gordon, Roger D. ... Minneapolis, MN
St. Paul, MN
Gordon, Roger L. ... Los Angeles, CA
Gordon, Ronald D. ... Friday Harbor, WA
Gordon, Ronald E. ... Los Angeles, CA
Gordon, Ronald H. ... Teaneck, NJ
Gordon, Ronald H., (Co., L.P.A.)
Lorain, OH
Gordon, Ronald J. ... Jenkintown, PA
Gordon, Rosalind M. ... New York, NY
Gordon, Rosemarie N. ... Tarrytown, NY
Gordon, Rosemary A. ... Grosse Pointe, MI
Gordon, R. T. ... Woodstock, GA
Gordon, Russell L. ... San Bernardino, CA
Gordon, Ruthanne ... Philadelphia, PA
Gordon, S. Ralph ... Nashville, TN
Gordon, Sadie Rose ... Boston, MA
Gordon, Sam ... Los Angeles, CA
Gordon, Sam ... Rancho Palos Verdes, CA
Gordon, Samuel ... Silver Spring, MD
Gordon, Samuel ... Summit, NJ
Gordon, Samuel A. ... Encino, CA
Gordon, Samuel W. ... Encino, CA
Gordon, Samuel Z. ... Chevy Chase, MD
Gordon, Sandi L. ... Homewood, IL
Gordon, Sandra C. ... Orlando, FL
Gordon, Sara ... Broadview, IL
Gordon, Sarah Barringer ... Philadelphia, PA
Gordon, Sarah Groseclose ... Lexington, KY
Gordon, Sarah L. ... Southfield, MI
Gordon, Saul J. ... Dallas, TX
Gordon & Scalo ... Bridgeport, CT
Gordon, Scott B. ... Salt Lake City, UT
Gordon, Scott D. ... Albuquerque, NM
Gordon, Scott E. ... Sarasota, FL
Venice, FL
Gordon, Scott J. ... New York, NY
Gordon, Scott L. ... Red Bank, NJ
Gordon, Scott R. ... Van Wert, OH
Gordon, Scott W. ... Walnut Creek, CA
Gordon, Sean ... Cambridge, MA
Gordon, Seymour A. ... St. Petersburg, FL
Gordon, Seymour N. ... Los Angeles, CA
Gordon, Shari Leigh ... New York, NY
Gordon, Shari Ruth ... Bronx, NY
Gordon, Sharon Gwyn Caldwell
Fort Lauderdale, FL
Gordon, Sharon L. ... Wichita, KS
Gordon, Shea ... Los Angeles, CA
Gordon, Sheila Anne ... Albany, NY
Gordon, Sheila Moore ... Baton Rouge, LA
Gordon, Shelley A. ... Oakland, CA
Gordon, Sherry G. ... Riverside, CA
Gordon, Sherwood ... Bellmore, NY
Gordon, Sherylle A. O. ... Troy, MI
Gordon, Siegel, Mastro, Mullaney, Gordon & Galvin, P.C. ... Albany, NY
Latham, NY
Schenectady, NY
Gordon & Silber, P.C. ... New York, NY
White Plains, NY
Gordon, Silberman, Wiggins & Childs, P.C.
Birmingham, AL
Washington, DC
Gordon & Silver, Ltd. ... Las Vegas, NV
Reno, NV
Gordon & Simmons ... Frederick, MD
Gordon, Stacey Natiss
Roslyn Heights, NY
Gordon, Stacy L. ... Garden City, NY
Gordon, Stanley A. ... Rochester, NY
Gordon, Stanley F. ... Huntington, NY
Gordon, Stanley M. ... Newport Beach, CA
Gordon, Stephen A. ... New York, NY
Gordon, Stephen A. ... Providence, RI
Gordon, Stephen C. ... Department of Justice, Antitrust Division, GV
Gordon, Stephen D. ... St. Paul, MN
Gordon, Stephen F. ... Boston, MA
Gordon, Stephen F. ... Great Neck, NY
Gordon, Stephen J. ... New York, NY
Gordon, Stephen L. ... Saddle Brook, NJ
New York, NY
Gordon, Stephen L. ... New York, NY
Gordon, Stephen M. ... Chicago, IL
Gordon, Stephen M. ... Old Bridge, NJ
Gordon, Stephen R. ... Woodland Hills, CA
Gordon, Steven ... Bronx, NY
Gordon, Steven C. ... Brookline, MA
Gordon, Steven D. ... Washington, DC
Gordon, Steven D. ... New York, NY
Gordon, Steven E. ... Department of Justice, Civil Division, GV
Gordon, Steven J. ... Fort Worth, TX
Gordon, Steven K. ... Salt Lake City, UT
Gordon, Steven L. ... Houston, TX
Gordon, Steven M. ... Salinas, CA
Gordon, Steven M. ... Concord, NH
Gordon, Steven M. ... Pocono Lake, PA
Gordon, Steven M., P.C. ... Salinas, CA
Gordon, Steven Noah ... New York, NY
Gordon, Steven R. ... New York, NY
Gordon, Storrow Moss ... Plano, TX
Gordon, Stuart A. ... New York, NY
Gordon, Stuart D. ... Chicago, IL
Gordon, Stuart I. ... Chicago, IL
Gordon, Stuart I. ... Garden City, NY
Gordon, Stuart J. ... Los Angeles, CA
Gordon, Stuart J. ... Washington, DC
Gordon, Stuart M. ... San Francisco, CA
Gordon, Stuart M. ... Columbus, OH
Gordon, Stuart R. ... Virginia Beach, VA
Gordon, Susan ... Kansas City, MO
Gordon, Susan E. H. ... Scarsdale, NY
Gordon, Susan L. ... Westfield, NJ
Gordon, Susan Lynn ... Seattle, WA
Gordon, Susan M. ... Wilmington, DE
Gordon, Susan M. ... Atlanta, GA
Gordon, Susan W. ... Brownsburg, IN
Gordon, Suzanne ... Irvine, CA
Gordon, Suzanne M. ... West Hartford, CT
Gordon, Sydna H. ... Plano, TX
Gordon, Tamara Farris ... Fort Worth, TX
Gordon, Tamara Steerman ... Narberth, PA
Gordon, Tammy L. ... Malone, NY
Gordon, Teddy B. ... Louisville, KY
Gordon, Tepper & DeCoursey, LLP
Albany, NY
Glenville, NY
Schenectady, NY
Gordon, Terri Ellen ... San Francisco, CA
Gordon, Terry D. ... Denver, CO
Gordon, Terry M. ... San Francisco, CA
Gordon, Theodora ... Chicago, IL
Gordon, Thomas ... Brooklyn, NY
Gordon, Thomas A. ... Portland, OR
Gordon, Thomas C., Jr. ... Richmond, VA
Gordon, Thomas F. ... Kansas City, MO
Gordon, Thomas, Honeywell, Malanca, Peterson & Daheim, P.L.L.C.
Seattle, WA
Tacoma, WA
Gordon, Thomas J. ... Champaign, IL
Gordon, Thomas J. ... Haverhill, MA
Gordon, Thomas J. ... Tiffin, OH
Gordon, Thomas L. ... Chesterfield, VA
Gordon, Thomas Patrick, III
Fort Worth, TX
Gordon, Timothy W. ... Denver, CO
Gordon, Todd A. ... New York, NY
Gordon, Todd I. ... Irvington, NY
Gordon, Tom ... Abilene, TX
Gordon, Tommy J. ... Superior, WI
Gordon, Troy W. ... St. Louis, MO
Gordon, Victor M. ... Woodbridge, CT
Gordon, Walter James ... Hartwell, GA
Gordon, William A. ... Chicago, IL
Gordon, William Alexander ... New York, NY
Gordon, William C. ... Sausalito, CA
Gordon, William C. ... Wilmington, DE
Gordon, William C., A Professional Corporation
Sausalito, CA
Gordon, William F. ... Richardson, TX
Gordon, William H. ... Boston, MA
Gordon, William H., Jr. ... Lubbock, TX
Gordon, William J. ... New York, NY
Gordon, William J., Jr. ... Tampa, FL
Gordon, William J., Jr. ... Cleveland, OH
Gordon, William K. ... Melrose, FL
Gordon, William L. ... Santa Barbara, CA
Gordon, William P. ... Albuquerque, NM
Gordon, William R. ... Montgomery, AL
Gordon, William S. ... Huntington, IN
Gordon, William S. ... Mount Laurel, NJ
Philadelphia, PA
Gordon, William S. ... Orchard Park, NY
Gordon, William S., Jr. ... Huntington, IN
Warren, IN
Gordon, Winston A. ... Fresh Meadows, NY
Gordon & Wise LLP ... Boston, MA
Gordon, Yekaterina A. ... New York, NY
Gordon, Yvette M. ... Newark, NJ
Gordon-Creed, Geoffrey R.
San Francisco, CA
Gordon-Creed, Kelley, Holl & Sugerman, LLP ... San Francisco, CA
Gordon-Reed, Annette ... New York, NY
Gordus, A. Allan, Jr. ... Springfield, MO
Gordy, Emily P.
Securities and Exchange Commission, Division of Enforcement, GV
Gordy, Gretta ... Baltimore, MD
Gordy, Harold B., Jr. ... Berlin, MD
Gordy, John L. ... Humble, TX
Gordy, Scott Atkinson ... La Grange, GA
Gordy, Susan K. ... Chicago, IL
Gore, Andrew M. ... Deerfield, IL
Gore, Arthur E. ... Oceanside, CA
Gore, Barry R. ... Torrance, CA
Gore, Billy L. ... Jackson, MS
Gore, Blinzy L. ... Orangeburg, SC
Gore, Brent S. ... Ferriday, LA
Gore, Bruce W. ... Spokane, WA
Gore, Charles P., III ... Lexington, KY
Gore, Donald E. ... Calabasas, CA
Gore, E. Tucker ... Greenville, MS
Gore, Eloise
Federal Communications Commission, Cable Services Bureau, GV
Gore, George ... Carmel, CA
Gore, George ... Cleveland, OH
Gore, George H. ... Fort Lauderdale, FL
Gore, George R. ... El Dorado Hills, CA
Gore, Gerald B. ... Hartford, CT
Gore, Gregory E.
Federal Deposit Insurance Corporation, Appellate Litigation Section, GV
Gore, Gregory J. ... Sebastian, FL
Gore, Gregory J. ... Doylestown, PA
Gore, Gregory J., P.A. ... Sebastian, FL
Gore, Grover A. ... Southport, NC
Gore, H. Joseph, II ... Torrance, CA
Gore, Harold O. ... Clovis, NM
Gore, Jack H. ... Chicago, IL
Gore, James N., Jr. ... Knoxville, TN
Gore, James S. ... Houston, MS
Gore, Jay, III ... Grenada, MS
Jackson, MS
New Albany, MS
Oxford, MS
Gore, Jeevan ... Costa Mesa, CA
Gore, Jennifer Montgomery ... Houston, TX
Gore, Kenneth B., (Ltd.) ... Chicago, IL
Gore, Lauren E. ... Chicago, IL
Gore, Laurence D. ... Fort Lauderdale, FL
Gore, Lee P. ... Hattiesburg, MS
Gore, Leslie Marie ... Cherry Hill, NJ
Gore, Luke F. ... Austell, GA
Gore, Michael L. ... Orlando, FL
Gore, Morris C. ... Dallas, TX
Gore, Nathaniel S. ... New York, NY
Gore, Nicole L. Reid ... St. Louis, MO
Gore, Paul A. ... Fort Lauderdale, FL
Gore, Paul A., P.A. ... Fort Lauderdale, FL
Gore, Pauline ... Carthage, TN
Gore, Pierce ... San Francisco, CA
Gore, Rebecca M. ... Phoenix, AZ
Gore, Rex ... Bolivia, NC
Gore, Richard J. ... Oklahoma City, OK
Gore, Richard R. ... San Diego, CA
Gore, Robert L. ... Monterey, CA
Gore, Ronald G. ... Houston, TX
Gore, Russell H. ... Washington, DC
Gore, Scott A. ... Chicago, IL
Gore, W. E., Jr. ... Jackson, MS
Gore, William B. ... Akron, OH
Gore, William C., Jr. ... Whiteville, NC
Gore, William E. ... Berkeley, CA
Gorecki, Catherine Herrin ... Boston, MA
Gorecki, John C. ... Boston, MA
Gorecki, John R. ... Vernon, CT
Gorecki, Robert L. ... St. Charles, IL
Gorectke, Donald M. ... Milwaukee, WI
Goreczny, Susan A. ... Chicago, IL
Goree, Brian J. ... Tulsa, OK
Goree, Christopher W. ... Tulsa, OK
Goree, Goree & Goree, P.C. ... Tulsa, OK
Goree, Jack Y. ... Tulsa, OK
Goree, Janace Harvey ... Jackson, MS
Goree, Katharine ... Boston, MA
Gorel, Frazier I. ... El Paso, TX
Gorelick, Barry P. ... Berkeley, CA
Gorelick, Henry ... North Wildwood, NJ
Gorelick, Jacquita R. ... Oklahoma City, OK
Gorelick, Jeff ... Walnut Creek, CA
Gorelick, Michael E. ... Livingston, NJ
New York, NY
Gorelick, Peter J. ... Orange, CA
Gorelick, Peter J., P.C. ... Orange, CA
Gorelick, Philip A. ... Washington, DC
Gorelick, Richard D. ... King Of Prussia, PA
Gorelick, Scott R. ... Charlotte, NC
Gorelick, Sidney J. ... Oklahoma City, OK
Gorelick, Steven D. ... Newark, NJ
Gorelick, Susan M. ... Huntington Beach, CA
Gorelick, Walter L. ... Tulare, CA
Gorelick-Levine, Jo Lynn ... Hayward, CA
Gorell, Stephen G. ... New York, NY
Gorelnik, Marc M. ... San Francisco, CA
Goren, Aaron W. ... Detroit, MI
Goren, Abe S. ... Houston, TX
Goren, Barbara ... New Haven, CT
Goren, Bruce G. ... Los Angeles, CA
Goren, David ... New York, NY
Goren, David J. ... Menlo Park, CA
Goren, Denise L. ... Philadelphia, PA
Goren, Ellen C. ... Houston, TX
Goren & Goren, P.C. ... Birmingham, MI
Goren, John Alan ... Dallas, TX
Goren, Julie A. ... Los Angeles, CA
Goren, Kalman G. ... Detroit, MI
Goren, Leora I. ... Calabasas, CA
Goren, Lisa I. ... Chicago, IL
Goren, Michael E. ... Aliso Viejo, CA
Goren, Miriam S. ... Franklin, MI
Goren, Nicola O.
Corporation for National and Community Service, Office of the General Counsel, GV
Goren, Osias G. ... Los Angeles, CA
Goren, Ralph M. ... Chicago, IL
Goren, Richard A. ... Framingham, MA
Goren, Robert ... Birmingham, MI
Goren, Robert K. ... Washington, DC
Rockville, MD
Goren, Robert L. ... Boston, MA
Goren, Samuel S. ... Fort Lauderdale, FL
Goren, Seth William ... Philadelphia, PA
Goren, Steven C. ... Farmington Hills, MI
Goren, Steven E. ... Birmingham, MI
Goren, William D. ... Jefferson City, MO
Goren, Wolff & Orenstein, L.L.C.
Washington, DC
Rockville, MD
Gorenberg, Carol A. ... Walnut Creek, CA
Gorenberg, David M. ... Moorestown, NJ
Gorenberg, David M., P.C.
Moorestown, NJ
Gorenberg, Donald ... Fort Lauderdale, FL
Gorenberg, Hyman ... Hewlett Bay Park, NY
Gorenberg, Kenneth M. ... Chicago, IL
Gorenberg, Robin ... Brookline, MA
Gorenc, Julie Ann ... Topeka, KS
Gorenc, William, Jr. ... Fairlawn, OH
Gorence, Patricia J. ... Milwaukee, WI
Gorence, Robert J. ... Albuquerque, NM
Gorenfeld, Abraham ... Torrance, CA
Gorenfeld, William R. ... Ventura, CA
Gorenflo, Michael G. ... Aberdeen, NC
Gorenflo, Rachel A. ... Sanford, FL
Gorensek, Thomas F. ... Cleveland, OH
Gorenstein, Charles ... Falls Church, VA
Gorenstein, Edward A. ... Highland Park, IL
Gorenstein, Gabriel W. ... New York, NY
Gorens-Winston, Julie ... Milwaukee, WI
Gores & Blais, P.S. ... Seattle, WA
Gores, Christopher M., (P.C.) ... Dallas, TX
Gores, Guido J. ... Cincinnati, OH
Gores, Hala J. ... Portland, OR
Gores, John J. ... Anoka, MN
Gores, Nancy L. ... Minneapolis, MN
Gores, Thomas C. ... Seattle, WA
Goresen, Thomas Patrick
Oklahoma City, OK
Goresen, Virginia K. ... Oklahoma City, OK
Goret, David L. ... Weehawken, NJ
Goret, Ronald J. ... Cincinnati, OH
Gorevitz, Richard D. ... Newark, NJ
Gorewitz, David J. ... Melbourne, FL
Gorey, Brent S. ... Philadelphia, PA
Gorey, Ellen P. ... Bellevue, WA
Gorey, Hays, Jr. ... Department of Justice, Antitrust Division, GV
Gorey, John J. ... North Riverside, IL
Gorey, Robert C., Jr. ... Fairmont, WV
Gorey, Thomas M. ... Chicago, IL
Gorey, William G. ... North Riverside, IL
Gorfinkel, David B. ... New York, NY
Gorfinkel, M. Paul ... Uniondale, NY
Gorfinkel, Nestor B.
Bay Harbor Islands, FL

Gorfinkel, Nestor B., Chartered
Aventura, FL
Bay Harbor Islands, FL
Miami, FL
Gorfinkle, Robert A. .... Braintree, MA
Gorga, Mary Christa .... Albany, NY
Gorga, Ronald R. .... Troy, MI
Gorgas, Edmund L. .... Sonora, CA
Gorgas and Lamb .... Sonora, CA
Gorgey, Andrew Coleman
Colorado Springs, CO
Gorgone, Christine M. .... Wilmington, DE
Gorgone, William D. .... Saddle Brook, NJ
Gorgone, William S. .... Boston, MA
Providence, RI
Gorgoni, Joseph P. .... Syracuse, NY
Gorgos, Mark S. .... Binghamton, NY
Gorham, A. Dumay, Jr. .... Wilmington, NC
Gorham, Amanda Paige .... Sacramento, CA
Gorham, Anne E. .... Lexington, KY
Gorham, Bradford .... North Scituate, RI
Gorham, Charles B. .... San Antonio, TX
Gorham, Charles W. .... Birmingham, AL
Gorham, Christopher C. .... Boston, MA
Gorham, Claudia J. .... Alameda, CA
Gorham, D. Paige .... Elbridge, NY
Gorham, David S. .... Washington, IA
Gorham, Diarmuid F. .... Baltimore, MD
Gorham, Edwin L., III .... Houston, TX
Gorham, F. Kevin .... Greensboro, NC
Gorham, Gary J. .... Santa Monica, CA
Gorham & Gorham, Incorporated
North Scituate, RI
Gorham, Henry W. .... Raleigh, NC
Gorham, J. Keith .... Universal City, CA
Gorham, J. Samuel, III .... Hickory, NC
Gorham, James B. .... Seattle, WA
Gorham, Jane C. .... Boston, MA
Gorham, J. D. .... Richmond, MO
Gorham, John .... North Scituate, RI
Gorham, Jos. P. .... Bensalem, PA
Gorham, Kathleen Elvins .... Issaquah, WA
Gorham, Marilynne .... Houston, TX
Gorham, Martin .... New York, NY
Gorham, Michael J. .... Hampstead, NH
Gorham, Nicholas .... North Scituate, RI
Gorham, Patricia A. .... Atlanta, GA
Gorham, Patricia A. .... Wichita, KS
Gorham, Robert L. .... Childersburg, AL
Gorham, Robert L. .... Washington, DC
Bethesda, MD
Gorham, Sarah C. .... New York, NY
Gorham, Steven H. .... Salem, OR
Gorham, Timothy N. .... North Scituate, RI
Gorham, Victor A. .... Tustin, CA
Gorham & Waldrep, P.C.
Birmingham, AL
Montgomery, AL
Gorham, William C. .... Denver, CO
Gorham, William H., (P.C.) .... Boston, MA
Gorham, William J., III .... Stockton, CA
Gori, Carole C. .... Pittsburgh, PA
Goria, Charles F. .... San Diego, CA
Goria & Weber, Law Offices Of
San Diego, CA
Gorichan, Bonnie S. .... Dearborn, MI
Goriganti, S. Lata .... New York, NY
Gori-Montanelli, Riccardo .... New York, NY
Gorin, Abbott D. .... New York, NY
Gorin, Alvin .... New York, NY
Gorin, Howard J. .... Beverly Hills, CA
Gorin, Joseph .... Brooklyn, NY
Gorin, Lawrence D. .... Portland, OR
Gorin, Leonard L. .... Waco, TX
Gorin, Robert S. .... New York, NY
Gorin, Steven B. .... St. Louis, MO
Gorin, Tracy Ann .... Norwich, CT
Gorin, William F. .... New York, NY
Gorin, William H. .... Frankfort, KY
Goring, Albert E. .... Winsted, CT
Goring & Dixon .... Winsted, CT
Goring, Geoffrey E. .... San Antonio, TX
Gorini, Richard A. .... San Jose, CA
Gorinson, Barbara J. .... Greenbelt, MD
Gorinson, Stanley M. .... Washington, DC
Goris, Mark D. .... Cazenovia, NY
Gority, Charles R., Jr. .... Hollidaysburg, PA
Gorjanc, Henry A. .... Mentor, OH
Gorka, Paul F. .... Westchester, IL
Gorkin, Mitchell A. .... Brooklyn, NY
Gorla, Michael J. .... St. Louis, MO
Gorland, Emanuel .... Lincoln Park, MI
Gorland, Scott L. .... Detroit, MI
Gorley, David W. .... Scotts Valley, CA
Gorlick, Andrew A. .... New York, NY
Gorlick, Guy J. .... Los Angeles, CA
Gorlick, Jeffrey A. .... Boston, MA
Gorlick, Kravitz & Listhaus, P.C.
Newark, NJ
New York, NY
Gorlick, Saml. .... Burbank, CA
Gorlin, Cathy E. .... Minneapolis, MN
Gorlin, Robert H. .... Auburn Hills, MI
Gorlin, Robert J. .... Emeryville, CA
Gormally, Charles X. .... Roseland, NJ
Gormally, Laura E. .... Wilbraham, MA
Gormam, Frank M. .... Charleston, WV
Gorman, Alan G. .... Minneapolis, MN
Gorman, Albert H. .... New York, NY
Gorman, Andrew G. .... Philadelphia, PA
Gorman, Anna Shedden .... Charlotte, NC
Gorman, Arthur N. .... Phoenix, AZ
Gorman, Ashley .... Troy, MI
Gorman, Audrey Fallon
Rancho Santa Fe, CA
Gorman, Barbara Pugliese .... Dayton, OH
Gorman, Bartle J. .... Utica, NY
Gorman, Bess Beikoussis
Westborough, MA
Gorman, Bradley D. .... Troy, MI
Gorman, Brett K. .... Quincy, IL
Gorman, Bruce M. .... Rio Grande, NJ
Gorman, C. Tyson .... Louisville, KY
Gorman, Cheryl Ann .... New York, NY
Gorman, Clifford .... Fort Lauderdale, FL
Gorman, Dana L. .... Independence, KS
Gorman, Daniel J. .... Angola, NY
Gorman, Daniel L. .... Binghamton, NY
Gorman, David Douglas .... Steubenville, OH
Gorman, David L. .... North Palm Beach, FL
Gorman, David L., P.A.
North Palm Beach, FL
Gorman, David P. .... Albuquerque, NM
Gorman, Deirdre A. .... Ogden, UT
Gorman, Dennis F. .... Worcester, MA
Gorman, Dennis W. .... Quincy, IL
Gorman, E. John .... Houston, TX
Gorman, Earl J., Jr. .... Clarendon Hills, IL
Gorman, Edmund J. .... Boston, MA
Gorman, Edward G. .... Long Beach, CA
Gorman, Edward H., Jr. .... North Chicago, IL
Gorman, Edward J. .... Albany, NY
Gorman, Edward J., III .... Washington, DC
Gorman, Edward J., Jr. .... Rockville, MD
Gorman, Elizabeth J. .... Newark, NJ
Gorman, Ellen A. .... Lewiston, ME
Gorman, Ellen R. .... St. Petersburg, FL
Gorman & Enright, P.C. .... New Haven, CT
Gorman & Epstein .... Point Lookout, NY
Gorman, Eric J. .... Chicago, IL
Gorman, F. Chris .... Louisville, KY
Gorman, Francis J., (P.C.) .... Baltimore, MD
Gorman, Francis L., III .... Rochester, NY
Gorman, Francis X. .... Wilmington, DE
Gorman, Francis X. .... Toledo, OH
Gorman, Frank J. .... Cleveland, OH
Gorman, Frank L. .... Detroit, MI
Gorman, Gary J. .... Madison, WI
Gorman, George C. .... Berkeley, CA
Gorman, Gerald L. .... San Diego, CA
Gorman, Gerald L., A P.C. .... San Diego, CA
Gorman, Gerald P. .... Hamburg, NY
Gorman, Gerald W. .... Kansas City, MO
Gorman and Gorman .... Chicago, IL
Gorman & Gorman, Ltd. .... Red Wing, MN
Gorman & Greenberg .... Dedham, MA
Gorman, Gregory D. .... Los Angeles, CA
Gorman, Gregory D. .... Sherman Oaks, CA
Gorman, Gregory G. .... Los Angeles, CA
Gorman, Gregory P. .... Dallas, TX
Gorman, Gregory P., Law Offices of
Dallas, TX
Gorman, Gregory X. .... Chicago, IL
Gorman, H. Candace .... Chicago, IL
Gorman, Hugh J., III .... Boston, MA
Providence, RI
Gorman, J. Kenneth .... Monterey, CA
Gorman, J. Kenneth .... Stony Brook, NY
Gorman, J. Timothy .... St. Louis, MO
Gorman, James E. .... Chicago, IL
Gorman, James E. .... Edwardsville, IL
Gorman, James F. .... Chicago, IL
Gorman, James H. .... Shrewsbury, NJ
Gorman, James, Law Offices of
San Diego, CA
Gorman, James R. .... Newport Beach, CA
Gorman, Jane A. .... Tustin, CA
Gorman, Jeffrey L. .... Dallas, TX
Gorman, Jennifer Hays .... Cleveland, OH
Gorman, Jerome .... Kansas City, KS
Gorman, Jerry T. .... Champaign, IL
Gorman, John A. .... Peoria, IL
Gorman, John C. .... San Jose, CA
Gorman, John D. .... New York, NY
Gorman, John E. .... Braintree, MA
Gorman, John H. .... Beckley, WV
Gorman, John J. .... Washington, DC
Gorman, John L., III .... Oakdale, CA
Gorman, John R. .... New Haven, CT
Gorman, John R. .... New Brunswick, NJ
Gorman, John T. .... Las Vegas, NV
Gorman, John V. .... Philadelphia, PA
Gorman, Joseph F. .... Akron, OH
Gorman, Joseph G., Jr. .... Los Angeles, CA
Gorman, Joseph M. .... St. Louis, MO
Gorman, Joseph R. .... Punta Gorda, FL
Gorman, Joseph T. .... Greenfield, MA
Gorman, Joseph T. .... Cleveland, OH
Gorman, Joyce J. .... Washington, DC
Gorman, June Hawker .... Boston, MA
Gorman, Karen E. .... Los Angeles, CA
Gorman, Karen Ponton
Office Of Special Counsel, GV
Gorman, Keith C., (Ms.), Law Offices of
El Paso, TX
Gorman, Keith L. .... Philadelphia, PA
Gorman, Keith R. .... Schenectady, NY
Gorman, Kenneth .... Aptos, CA
Gorman, Larry Edward .... Acworth, GA
Gorman, Larry Edward, P.C. .... Acworth, GA
Gorman, Lawrence J. .... New York, NY
Gorman, Lawrence M. .... Bend, OR
Gorman, Lenard H. .... Miami, FL
Gorman, Lenard H., P.A. .... Miami, FL
Gorman, Leo N. .... Washington, DC
Gorman, Leta E. .... Portland, OR
Gorman & Levine, P.C. .... Troy, MI
Gorman, Lisa R. .... Detroit, MI
Gorman, Louis B. .... Phoenix, AZ
Gorman, Lynn K. .... Miami Beach, FL
Gorman, Margaret T. .... Foster City, CA
Gorman, Mark B. .... St. Louis, MO
Gorman, Mark T. .... New York, NY
Gorman, Martin D. .... Rye Brook, NY
Gorman, Mary P. .... Rockford, IL
Gorman & Matthew, P.A. .... Tallahassee, FL
Gorman, Maureen A. .... Chicago, IL
Gorman, Maureen J. .... Chicago, IL
Gorman, Michael .... New York, NY
Gorman, Michael C. .... Riverside, IL
Gorman, Michael J. .... Birmingham, MI
Kansas City, MO
Gorman, Michael P. .... Melville, NY
Gorman, Michael R. .... Royal Oak, MI
Gorman, Michelle L. .... Steubenville, OH
Weirton, WV
Gorman & Miller .... San Jose, CA
Santa Monica, CA
Gorman, Nancy W. .... St. Petersburg, FL
Gorman, Nancy Yaeger .... Washington, DC
Gorman, Patricia Ann .... Dedham, MA
Gorman, Patrick H. .... Bethesda, MD
Gorman, Patrick J. .... Beverly Hills, CA
Gorman, Patrick J. .... Fresno, CA
Gorman, Patrick J. .... Sarasota, FL
Gorman, Patrick J. .... Palatine, IL
Gorman, Paul J. .... Cincinnati, OH
Gorman, Peter J. .... Trenton, NJ
Gorman, R. Barthen
Federal Communications Commission,
Mass Media Bureau, GV
Gorman & Rauh .... Rio Grande, NJ
Gorman, Raymond A. .... Brooklyn, NY
Gorman, Richard D. .... Monterey, CA
Gorman, Richard D. .... Red Wing, MN
Gorman, Richard F., III .... Richmond, VA
Gorman, Richard L. .... Houston, TX
Gorman, Richard M. .... Pleasanton, CA
Gorman, Robert .... Cambridge, MA
Gorman, Robert C. .... Wooster, OH
Gorman, Robert D. .... Birmingham, MI
Gorman, Robert D. .... Albuquerque, NM
Gorman, Robert D., P.A. .... Albuquerque, NM
Gorman, Robert H. .... Cincinnati, OH
Gorman, Robert J. .... Fort Pierce, FL
Gorman, Robert J. .... Chicago, IL
Gorman, Robert J., Jr. .... Hartford, CT
Gorman, Robert J., Jr. .... Atlanta, GA
Gorman, Robert J., P.A. .... Fort Pierce, FL
Stuart, FL
Vero Beach, FL
Gorman, Robert K. .... Chicago, IL
Gorman, Robert L. .... Philadelphia, PA
Gorman, Robert P. .... Princeton, NJ
Gorman, Robert S. .... Department of Defense,
Office of the General Counsel, GV
Gorman, Robert S. M. .... New York, NY
Gorman, Rod E. .... Houston, TX
Gorman, Ruth .... Charlotte, NC
Gorman, Ruth E. .... Charlotte, NC
Gorman, Ruth, Law Firm, P.A.
Charlotte, NC
Gorman, Sarah E. .... Stamford, CT
Gorman, Scott B. .... Philadelphia, PA
Gorman, Sean .... Houston, TX
Gorman, Sean M. .... Hanover, NH
Gorman, Sheatsley & Co., L.C.
Beckley, WV
Gorman, Shirley A. .... Silver Spring, MD
Gorman & Silverman .... New York, NY
Gorman, Stephen A. .... Chicago, IL
Gorman, Stephen B. .... Cameron Park, CA
Gorman, Stephen L. .... Tallahassee, FL
Gorman, Stephen Paul .... Englewood, NJ
Gorman, Susan Yang .... Houston, TX
Gorman, Suzanne M. .... Concord, NH
Gorman, Terrence Charles
Copperopolis, CA
Gorman, Terry P. .... Dallas, TX
Gorman, Tessa M. .... Department of Justice,
Criminal Division, GV
Gorman, Thomas .... New York, NY
Gorman, Thomas E. .... Red Wing, MN
Gorman, Thomas F. .... Escondido, CA
Gorman, Thomas G. .... Chicago, IL
Gorman, Thomas G. .... Cheyenne, WY
Gorman, Thomas J. .... Charlotte, NC
Gorman, Thomas M. .... Miami, FL
Gorman, Thomas O. .... Washington, DC
Gorman, Thomas P. .... Boston, MA
Gorman, Thomas P. .... Alexandria, VA
Gorman, Thomas Ray .... Oakland, CA
Gorman, Thomas W. .... Wilmington, DE
Gorman, Timothy E. .... Baldwinsville, NY
Gorman, Todd .... New York, NY
Gorman, Trienah Meyers .... Albuquerque, NM
Gorman, Veskauf, Henson & Wineberg
Springfield, OH
Gorman, W. Dennis, Jr. .... Tempe, AZ
Gorman, Walter .... Washington, DC
Gorman, Walter T. .... Binghamton, NY
Gorman, Warren E. .... Chevy Chase, MD
Gorman, Waszkiewicz, Gorman & Schmitt
Utica, NY
Gorman, William H., Jr. .... Kenmore, NY
Gorman, William J. .... Vienna, VA
Gorman, William M. .... Valencia, CA
Gorman & Williams .... Washington, DC
Baltimore, MD
Gorman, Wm. F. .... Meadville, PA
Gormanly, Peter D. .... White Plains, NY
Gorman-Stapleton, Odesa .... Fort Worth, TX
Gormezano, Kammie M. .... New York, NY
Gormin, Gary P. .... Seminole, FL
Gormley, Arthur O., III .... Nashua, NH
Gormley, Arthur O., Jr. .... Nashua, NH
Gormley, Barbara H. .... Sarasota, FL
Gormley, Blaise M. .... Dallas, TX
Gormley, Brendan T. .... New York, NY
Gormley, Catherine M.
San Francisco, CA
Gormley, Cathleen Schmidt .... Fairfax, VA
Gormley, Darryl E. .... Westlake, OH
Gormley, David J. .... Foxboro, MA
Gormley, David M. .... Baltimore, MD
Gormley, David M. .... Columbus, OH
Gormley, F. Joseph .... Washington, DC
Baltimore, MD
Gormley, George F. .... Boston, MA
Gormley, George F., P.C. .... Boston, MA
Cambridge, MA
Gormley & Gormley, P.C. .... Nashua, NH
Gormley, Grant E. .... Pierre, SD
Gormley, James H., Jr. .... Milwaukee, WI
Gormley, James J. .... Atlanta, GA
Gormley, James R. .... Linthicum, MD
Gormley, James W. .... Buffalo, NY
Gormley, Jill K. .... New York, NY
Gormley, John E. .... Las Vegas, NV
Gormley, John P. .... Grand Junction, CO
Gormley, John W. .... Syracuse, NY
Gormley, Joseph A. .... Zanesville, OH
Gormley, Joseph K. .... New York, NY
Gormley, Joseph L. .... Washington, DC
Gormley, Kathleen J. .... Denver, CO
Gormley, Kenneth G. .... Pittsburgh, PA
Gormley, Kenneth J. .... New York, NY
Gormley, Kevin T. .... North Haven, CT
Gormley, Lawrence B. .... Portsmouth, NH
Gormley, Lorraine W. .... Trenton, NJ
Gormley, Marilyn .... Cedarhurst, NY
Gormley, Mark E. .... Versailles, KY
Gormley, Mary E. .... Rockville, MD
Gormley, Mary Ellyn .... Oakland, CA
Gormley, Michele J. .... Boston, MA
Gormley, Nancy E. .... Denver, CO
Gormley, Paul .... Department of Justice,
Environment and Natural Resources
Division, GV
Gormley, Paul R., Law Office of
Salem, MA
Gormley, R. James .... Chicago, IL
Gormley, Thomas A., III .... Boston, MA
Gormley, Thomas M. .... Potomac, MD
Gormley, W. Clarke .... Houston, TX
Gormley, W. Paul .... Washington, DC
Gormley, William L. .... Atlantic City, NJ
Pleasantville, NJ
Gormly, Charles F. .... Washington, DC
Gormly, Kenneth N. .... Tacoma, WA
Gormsen, Christine A. .... Garden City, NY
Gormsen, Eric Taylor .... Department of Justice,
Office of Policy Development, GV
Gorn, John W. .... Hilton Head Island, SC
Gorna, Susan L. .... Hartford, CT
Gornall, Jack M. .... Erie, PA
Gornall, Jennifer E. .... Erie, PA
Gornall, John L., Jr. .... Atlanta, GA
Gornall, M. Fletcher .... Erie, PA
Gornbein, Henry S. .... Bloomfield Hills, MI
Gornbein, Henry S. .... Pontiac, MI
Gorney, David I. .... Glendale, CA
Gorney, Howard N., (P.C.) .... Boston, MA
Gorney, James J. .... Oxon Hill, MD
Gornick, Katherine M.
Mendota Heights, MN
Gornick, Lawrence J. .... San Francisco, CA
Gornik, David J. .... Eastlake, OH
Gornik, David Joseph .... Eastlake, OH
Gornik, Gerald A. .... Covina, CA
Gornik, James T. .... Cleveland, OH
Gornish, Gerald .... Philadelphia, PA
Gornstein, Sharon .... Langhorne, PA
Gornstein, Todd M. .... Canton, MA
Gornto, L. A. (Gus), P.A.
Daytona Beach, FL
Gorny, Jack .... Atlantic City, NJ
Gorny, Stephen M. .... Kansas City, MO
Gorny, Stephen T. .... Chicago, IL
Gorny, Timothy D.
Cape May Court House, NJ
Gorodetsky, Sanford H. .... Cranston, RI
Goroff, David B. .... Chicago, IL
Goroff, David E. .... Washington, DC
Gorosh, Bruce M. .... Southfield, MI
Gorosh, Steven J. .... San Francisco, CA
Gorosh, Tamara Rosen .... Farmington, MI
Goroski, Mitchell, Jr. .... Albany, NY
Gorospe, Gregory A. .... Columbus, OH
Gorov, Arthur M. .... Chicago, IL
Gorove, Katherine M .... Washington, DC
Gorovitz, Aaron J. .... Orlando, FL
Gorovitz, Eric K. .... San Francisco, CA
Gorovitz, Jennifer S. .... San Jose, CA
Gorovitz, Sidney .... Lexington, MA
Gorowitz, Francie R. .... Los Angeles, CA
Gorowitz, Suzanne M. .... Miami, FL
Gorowsky, Donald A. .... Minneapolis, MN
Gorr, Arthur R. .... Pittsburgh, PA
Gorr, David D. .... Chicago, IL
Gorr, David D. & Associates .... Chicago, IL
Gorr, Kathleen H. .... Glen Ellyn, IL
Gorr, Moser, Dell & Loughney
Pittsburgh, PA
Gorra, Nicholas J., II .... Old Saybrook, CT
Gorray, Stephen G. .... Westbury, NY
Gorrell, Debra L. .... Columbus, OH
Gorrell, Floyd D. .... Worland, WY
Gorrell, J. Warren, Jr. .... Washington, DC
New York, NY
Gorrell, John T. .... Seattle, WA
Gorrell, Joseph M. .... Roseland, NJ
Gorrell, Michael K. .... Tulsa, OK
Gorrell, Nita R. .... Hammond, LA
Gorrell, Nita R., A Professional Law Corporation .... Hammond, LA
Gorrell, Ralph W. .... Greensboro, NC
Gorrell, Rudy W. .... New Orleans, LA
Gorrell, Teryl R., (P.C.) .... Denver, CO
Gorretta, Laura J. .... Cleveland, OH
Gorrie, Jan Johnson .... Tallahassee, FL

Gorrie, Ronald A. .... **Los Angeles, CA**
San Juan Capistrano, CA
Gorrill, Thomas B. .... San Diego, CA
Gorrin, Erika .... **New York, NY**
Gorrin, Gerald M. .... Livingston, NJ
Gorrin & Gorrin, A Professional Corporation
Livingston, NJ
Gorrin, Jeffrey E. .... Livingston, NJ
Gorrin-Peralta, Carlos I. .... San Juan, PR
Gorrissen, Jeanne E. .... Morristown, NJ
Gorrono, Louie .... Emmett, ID
Gorrow, Diane M. .... **Salem, NH**
Gorry, James A., III .... **Norfolk, VA**
Gorry, James R. .... **Columbus, OH**
Gorry, Kevin R. .... New York, NY
Gorry & Meyer L.L.P. .... **Los Angeles, CA**
Gorry, Timothy J. .... **Los Angeles, CA**
Gors, John A. .... Vermillion, SD
Gors, Max A. .... Pierre, SD
Gorsage, JoAnna D. .... **Rialto, CA**
Gorsalitz, Stephen D. .... Portage, MI
Gorsche, James F., Jr. .... Newton, IA
Gorsché, Ronald C., Jr. .... **Chicago, IL**
Gorsen, Maureen F. .... **Los Angeles, CA**
Gorshein, Doron .... **Littleton, CO**
Gorshel, Donna B. .... Andover, MA
Gorshel, S. Peter .... Andover, MA
Gorske, Robert H. .... Elm Grove, WI
Gorski, Allen I. .... **Trenton, NJ**
Gorski, Anthony G. .... **Annapolis, MD**
Gorski, Brenda L. .... Kankakee, IL
Gorski, Carl A. .... Park Ridge, IL
Gorski, Carl A., Ltd. .... Park Ridge, IL
Gorski, Cheryl A. .... Collingswood, NJ
Gorski, Cheryl B. .... Imperial, PA
Gorski, Edward J. .... Agawam, MA
Gorski, Gerald M. .... Wheaton, IL
Gorski, Gregory M. .... Omaha, NE
Gorski, James M. .... **Anchorage, AK**
Gorski, Janet Weinberg .... Simsbury, CT
Gorski, Jeffrey A. .... **Louisville, KY**
Gorski, Jeffrey A. .... **Cleveland, OH**
Gorski, Jerold M. .... **Orange, CA**
Gorski, Jerome C. .... Buffalo, NY
Gorski, Kenneth W. .... Marshfield, WI
Gorski & Lubiejewski .... Erie, PA
Gorski, Mark S. .... Nashville, TN
Gorski, Mary G. .... Champaign, IL
Gorski, Pamela L. .... **Lakewood, OH**
Gorski, Peter M. .... Tempe, AZ
Gorski, Rachel Mary .... Buffalo, NY
Gorski, Rafal A. .... **Tacoma, WA**
Gorski, Richard D. .... Easton, PA
Gorski, Ronald W. .... **Johnston, RI**
Gorski, Stanley L., II .... Pittsburgh, PA
Gorski, Stephen J. .... **San Francisco, CA**
Gorski, Theodore P., Jr. .... Fort Worth, TX
Gorski, Theresa V. .... Washington, DC
Gorski, Thomas W., Jr. .... Webster, MA
Gorski, Walter J. .... **Canton, MA**
Gorski & Wittman, S.C. .... Marshfield, WI
Gorsky, Betts J. .... **South Portland, ME**
Gorsky, Jeffrey .... Department of State,
Bureau of Consular Affairs, GV
Gorsky, Paul L. .... La Habra, CA
Gorsline, James N. .... **Atlanta, GA**
Gorsline, Laurie Susan .... **Los Angeles, CA**
Gorsline, Monique C. .... **Davenport, IA**
Gorsline, Ronald D. .... **Chattanooga, TN**
Gorsline, Scott J. .... Grand Rapids, MI
Gorson & Gorson .... Northfield, NJ
Philadelphia, PA
Gorson, Matthew B. .... **Miami, FL**
Gorson, Maxwell P. .... Northfield, NJ
Philadelphia, PA
Gorson, Noah .... Northfield, NJ
Philadelphia, PA
Gorss, Frederick G. .... Montgomery, NY
Gorst, Cathy J. .... Marshfield, WI
Gorsuch & Byrd .... **Lubbock, TX**
Gorsuch, Dale E. .... Baltimore, MD
Gorsuch, David R. .... Denver, CO
Gorsuch, Gwynn H. .... Lake Jackson, TX
Gorsuch, James L. .... **Lubbock, TX**
Gorsuch Kirgis LLP .... **Denver, CO**
Gorsuch, Kris Jon .... **Salem, OR**
Gorsuch, Neil M. .... **Washington, DC**
Gorsuch, Norman C. .... Juneau, AK
Gorsuch, Sandra Cardo .... Reedsburg, WI
Gort, Cliffe Lane .... Atlanta, GA
Gort, Randall J. .... Wayne, PA
Gort, Thomas E. .... Winona, MN
Gorte, C. Michael .... Bay City, MI
Gorti, Venkata S. .... Bronx, NY
Gortler, Hugh P. .... Mission Viejo, CA
Gorton, Ann E.
Federal Energy Regulatory Commission,
Office of the General Counsel, GV
Gorton, C. David .... Glasgow, MT
Gorton, David .... Woodland Hills, CA
Gorton, Jacquelyne G. .... San Rafael, CA
Gorton, James .... Oklahoma City, OK
Gorton, James A. .... Pasadena, CA
Gorton, James C. .... New York, NY
Gorton, James E., Jr. .... Anchorage, AK
Gorton, James R. .... Green Bay, WI
Gorton, Janosik & Poxon, LLP
Pasadena, CA
Gorton, John K. .... De Forest, WI
Gorton, John T. .... **Baldwin, NY**
Gorton, Karen E. .... Bridgeport, CT
Gorton, Mark .... **Sacramento, CA**
Gorton, Nathaniel M. .... Worcester, MA
Gorton, Peter A. .... Endicott, NY
Gorton, Thomas P. .... **New York, NY**
Gorton, William T., III .... **Lexington, KY**
Gortsas, Alex .... Cincinnati, OH
Gortych, Joseph E .... Burlington, VT

Gortz, Albert W. .... **Boca Raton, FL**
Gorud, Gail .... Kirkland, WA
Gorup, Geary N. .... **Wichita, KS**
Gorvetzian, Kenneth R. .... **Los Angeles, CA**
Gorvoy, Joseph Martin .... **Greenbelt, MD**
Gorwitz, Carolyn R. .... **Atlanta, GA**
Gorycki, Thaddeus S. .... Jamaica, NY
Goryl, John F. .... Harrisburg, PA
Gorzeck, Rana M. .... **Boca Raton, FL**
Fort Lauderdale, FL
Gorzelany, Robert J. .... **New York, NY**
Gosa, Lewis E. .... Vernon, AL
Gosain, Carol R. .... **Washington, DC**
Gosain, Chetna .... Houston, TX
Gosain, Vikram A. .... Plano, TX
Gosain, Vineet .... **Chicago, IL**
Gosanko, Gary N. .... Mercer Island, WA
Gosanko, Gary N., Inc., P.S., Law Offices of
Mercer Island, WA
Gosar, David M. .... **Jackson, WY**
Gosbee, John J. .... Mandan, ND
Gosch, Cheryl M. .... **Dallas, TX**
Gosch, D. Jeffrey .... Syracuse, NY
Gosch, Daniel F. .... **Grand Rapids, MI**
Gosch, Gerald E. .... **Los Angeles, CA**
Gosch, Kennith L. .... **Aberdeen, SD**
Gosch, Philip A. .... New York, NY
Goschi & Goschi .... Chicago, IL
Goschi, Nicholas P. .... Chicago, IL
Goschi, Peter E. .... Chicago, IL
Goschka, Dennis A. .... Southfield, MI
Goschy, Nicholas P., Jr. .... Knoxville, TN
Goscilo, Jozef K. .... **New York, NY**
Goscinak, Virginia Casey .... **Boston, MA**
Gosda, Douglas T. .... Houston, TX
Gosdeck, Jo Beth .... **Atlanta, GA**
Gosdeck, Thomas J. .... Albany, NY
Gosden, Douglas S. .... **Atlanta, GA**
Gosdick, Robert W. .... Byron, IL
Rockford, IL
Gosdin, Allan L. .... Montvale, NJ
Gosdin, James L. .... Houston, TX
Gose, Donald M. .... Middletown, OH
Gose, Eddie D. .... College Station, TX
Gose, Gregory R. .... Camarillo, CA
Gose, John A. .... **Seattle, WA**
Gose & Lechman .... Camarillo, CA
Gose, Phelps R. .... Spokane, WA
Gose, Thomas M. .... Atlanta, GA
Goseco, Frank E. .... Newport Beach, CA
Goseco, Michelle M. .... Santa Ana, CA
Goselin, John H., II .... **Atlanta, GA**
Gosen, Erik L. .... Los Angeles, CA
Gosewisch, Lawrence S. .... **Chicago, IL**
Gosfield, Alice G. .... Philadelphia, PA
Gosfield, Alice G., & Associates, P.C.
Philadelphia, PA
Gosfield, Gregory G. .... **Philadelphia, PA**
Goshaw, Christina L. .... Chapel Hill, NC
Goshert, Max E. .... Mooresville, IN
Goshgarian, Haig .... Calabasas, CA
Goshgarian, John R. .... Waukegan, IL
Goshgarian, Mark G. .... Calabasas, CA
Goshgarian, Robert N. .... Waukegan, IL
Goshien, David B. .... Cleveland, OH
Goshien, Deborah Purcell .... Cleveland, OH
Goshien, Deborah Purcell, Co., L.P.A.
Cleveland, OH
Goshko, Mark P. .... **Boston, MA**
Goshko, Michael H. .... **Boston, MA**
Goshman, Pamela R. .... Deer Park, NY
Goshorn, Barbara Wright .... Palmyra, VA
Goshorn, Barbara Wright, Ltd. .... Palmyra, VA
Goshorn, Everett E. .... Bluffton, IN
Goshorn, Richard H. .... **Vienna, VA**
Goshorn, Richard W. .... Fort Wayne, IN
Gosier, Carol Zenzel .... **Syracuse, NY**
Gosier, James A. .... Syracuse, NY
Gosin, Barry E. .... Philadelphia, PA
Goska, Matthew L. .... **Grand Rapids, MI**
Goske, Stephen P. .... Youngstown, OH
Goslant, Kim Herman .... **Boston, MA**
Providence, RI
Goslee, David M. .... Rochester, MN
Goslee & Goslee .... **Bellefontaine, OH**
Goslee, William Thomas
Bellefontaine, OH
Goslen, Frank O. .... Greensboro, NC
Goslin, Rich'd W., Jr. .... New York, NY
Gosline, Ann R. .... Augusta, ME
Gosline, Brian G. .... Spokane, WA
Gosline, Brian G., P.C. .... Spokane, WA
Gosline, Robert B. .... Toledo, OH
Gosline, William H. .... **Toledo, OH**
Goslinger, Michael L. .... Washington, DC
Gosling, John G. .... Lebanon, OH
Gosling, Kelcie M. .... **Sacramento, CA**
Gosling, Matthew M. .... **Palo Alto, CA**
Gosling, Tamblyn Fuller .... Goffstown, NH
Goslins, Rachel E. .... Library of Congress,
Copyright Office, GV
Gosma & Gallagher, P.L.C. .... **Moline, IL**
Rock Island, IL
Bettendorf, IA
Davenport, IA
Gosma, John S. .... **Davenport, IA**
Gosman, Jeffrey C. .... Casper, WY
Gosman, Theodore F. .... Roslyn, NY
Gosman, Theodore F., P.C., Law Offices of
Roslyn, NY
Gosnay, Donald R. .... **Cherry Hill, NJ**
Gosnell, Borden, Enloe & Sloss, Ltd.
Lawrenceville, IL
Gosnell, Devon L. .... **Memphis, TN**
Gosnell, Guy R. .... **Charlotte, NC**
Gosnell, Joyce .... Milwaukee, WI
Gosnell, Linda .... **Lexington, KY**
Gosnell, M. Ann .... **Corning, NY**

Gosnell, Maurice E. .... **Lawrenceville, IL**
Gosnell, Michael R. .... Louisville, KY
Gosnell, Ruth A. .... Newburgh, IN
Gosnell, Scott W. .... **Birmingham, AL**
Gosnell, William C. .... Memphis, TN
Gosnell, William F. .... Baltimore, MD
Gosney, Cliff B., Jr. (IBA) .... **Port Orange, FL**
Gosney, J. Wayne .... Oklahoma City, OK
Gosney, Mary Lee .... San Bernardino, CA
Gosney, Steven N. .... **DeLand, FL**
Gosney, Timothy J. .... **Pasadena, CA**
Gosper, Robert L. .... Canandaigua, NY
Gosrisirikul, Vida .... Chicago, IL
Goss, Christopher .... Portland, ME
Goss, Colleen Flynn .... **Cleveland, OH**
Goss, Dahil D. .... Atlanta, GA
Goss, David C. .... Boston, MA
Goss, David D. .... **Boise, ID**
Goss, David P. .... San Mateo, CA
Goss, Dianne .... Columbus, OH
Goss, Donn H. .... Spring Valley, CA
Goss, Douglas A. .... Stockton, CA
Goss, Douglas D. .... Lancaster, PA
Goss, Douglas K. .... Denver, CO
Goss, Douglas L. .... Tulsa, OK
Goss, E. Warren .... Boulder, CO
Goss, Earle D., Jr. .... Bethesda, MD
Goss, Earle D., Jr. .... **Bethesda, MD**
Goss, Edward J. .... Spokane, WA
Goss, Elizabeth .... **Washington, DC**
Goss, Eugene .... Cumberland, KY
Harlan, KY
Goss, Frederick L. .... Oakland, CA
Goss, Geoffrey K. .... San Bernardino, CA
Goss, Geoffrey S. .... **Cleveland, OH**
Goss & Goss .... Cumberland, KY
Harlan, KY
Goss, Gregory S. .... Vista, CA
Goss, Harold M. .... **Kansas City, MO**
Goss, Harry T. .... Coronado, CA
Goss, Hipperson and Sampson
Spokane, WA
Goss, J. Bradford .... St. Peters, MO
Goss, James P. W. .... **Rutland, VT**
Goss, James W. .... Grosse Pointe Farms, MI
Goss, James W., Professional Corporation
Grosse Pointe Farms, MI
Goss, Jay B. .... **Bryan, TX**
Goss, Jeanette .... Milwaukee, WI
Goss, Jeffrey .... **Los Angeles, CA**
Goss, Jeffrey C. .... **Lancaster, PA**
Goss, John C. .... Houston, TX
Goss, Joseph W. .... Leesburg, VA
Goss, Judith A. .... Sacramento, CA
Goss, Kent B. .... **Los Angeles, CA**
Goss, Maisha M. .... **New York, NY**
Goss, Marilynn C. .... Richmond, VA
Goss, Mark David .... Cumberland, KY
Harlan, KY
Goss, Mark P. .... **Phoenix, AZ**
Goss, Michael A. .... Modesto, CA
Goss, Michael D. .... **Lafayette, LA**
Goss, Michael D. .... Tulsa, OK
Goss, Michael M. .... Philadelphia, PA
Goss, Patrick J. .... **Little Rock, AR**
Goss, Patrick L., Law Offices of .... Miami, FL
Goss, Peter J. .... **Minneapolis, MN**
Goss, Philip E., Jr. .... Coral Gables, FL
Goss, Rebecca O. .... **Indianapolis, IN**
Goss, Richard H. .... Chicago, IL
Goss, Robert L. .... Beaverton, OR
Goss, Robert P., Jr. .... Denver, CO
Goss, Roland C. .... **Washington, DC**
Goss, Ronald W. .... **Seattle, WA**
Goss, Scott D. .... **San Jose, CA**
Goss, Sheila M. .... Saratoga Springs, NY
Goss, Stephen S. .... **Albany, GA**
Goss, Steven B. .... **Lancaster, NH**
Goss, Steven D. .... **West Linn, OR**
Goss, Suzanne E. .... **Houston, TX**
Goss, Thomas E. .... Milwaukee, WI
Goss, Thomas E., Jr. .... **Milwaukee, WI**
Goss, Thomas M. .... **Baltimore, MD**
Goss, Tim K., (P.C.) .... **Dallas, TX**
Goss, Tina R. .... **Fort Worth, TX**
Goss, Victoria A. .... New Haven, CT
Goss, William A. .... Atlanta, GA
Goss, William E. .... Stafford, KS
Goss, William W., Jr. .... Spokane, WA
Gossage, Charles R. .... **Irvine, CA**
Gossage, David E. .... San Francisco, CA
Gossage, Kimberly A. .... **Charlotte, NC**
Gossage, Roza .... Belleville, IL
Gossard, David W. .... Seattle, WA
Gossard, Jane G. .... Andover, MA
Gossard, Roger L. .... Coffeyville, KS
Gosse, Thomas A. .... Irvington, VA
Gossé, Thomas J. .... Haddon Heights, NJ
Gosseen, Robert I. .... **New York, NY**
Gossel, Henry G. .... Buffalo, NY
Gossel, Kenneth M. .... **Buffalo, NY**
Gosselar, Barbara J.
Oakbrook Terrace, IL
Gosselin, Craig E. .... Santa Fe Springs, CA
Gosselin, Donald S. .... Winthrop, MA
Gosselin, Dubord & Rabasco, P.A.
Lewiston, ME
Gosselin, Gabrielle A. .... **Batavia, IL**
Gosselin, Jason P. .... **Philadelphia, PA**
Gosselin, John T. .... Winchester, MA
Gosselin, John T., & Associates, P.C.
Winchester, MA
Gosselin, John W. .... **Batavia, IL**
Gosselin, Kathlene F. .... Gainesville, GA
Gosselin, Kenneth .... Carlsbad, CA
Gosselin, Linda P. .... Kingston, MA
Gosselin, Paul R. .... **Lewiston, ME**
Gosselin, Thomas M. .... **San Francisco, CA**

Gosselin, Timothy R. .... **Tacoma, WA**
Gosselink, Margaret L. .... Austin, TX
Gosselink, Paul G. .... **Austin, TX**
Gosselink, Robert G. .... **Washington, DC**
Gossels, C. Peter R. .... **Boston, MA**
Gossen, Ronald J. .... Lafayette, LA
Gossens, Paul J. .... Milwaukee, WI
Gosser, David Alan .... Westminster, CO
Gosser, Francis X. .... Woodstock, IL
Gossett, C. Darrell .... Brunswick, GA
Gossett, David .... Washington, DC
Gossett, David W. .... **Greenville, SC**
Gossett, Denton D. .... Austin, TX
Gossett, F. A., III .... Blair, NE
Gossett, Gary R., Jr. .... **Sebring, FL**
Gossett, George, Jr. .... Philadelphia, PA
Gossett & Gossett, P.A. .... Hollywood, FL
Gossett, Greg .... **San Angelo, TX**
Gossett, Harrison, Reese, Wilson & Millican, P.C. .... **San Angelo, TX**
Gossett, Henry O., Jr. .... Longview, TX
Gossett, Holman C., Jr. .... Spartanburg, SC
Gossett, James Clay .... Henderson, TX
Gossett, James F. .... **Chicago, IL**
Gossett, James M. .... San Marcos, TX
Gossett, Kimberly A. .... Atlantic Beach, FL
Gossett Law Offices, P.A. .... **Sebring, FL**
Wauchula, FL
Gossett, Lewis F. .... **Columbia, SC**
Gossett, Paige Jones .... **Columbia, SC**
Gossett, Randy Dean .... Wheeling, WV
Gossett, Richard B. .... **Chattanooga, TN**
Knoxville, TN
Nashville, TN
Gossett, Richard L. .... McAlester, OK
Gossett, Robert L. .... Hollywood, FL
Gossett, Ronald P. .... Hollywood, FL
Gossett, Stephen E. .... Dallas, TX
Gossett, Tresa G. .... Georgetown, OH
Gossett, Wallace D. .... Brooklyn, NY
Gossett, William A. .... **Duncan, OK**
Gossette, Lois W. .... Greensboro, GA
Gossin, Alex J. .... Rochester, NY
Gossin & Atlas .... Rochester, NY
Gossler, Michael E. .... **Seattle, WA**
Gossman, George W. .... Woodbury, MN
Gossman, Thomas L. .... Kalamazoo, MI
Gossner, Alfred E. .... San Diego, CA
Gossom, David F. .... Wichita Falls, TX
Gossow, Douglas E. .... **St. Louis, MO**
Gossum, Richard B., Jr. .... **Trenton, TN**
Gost, George T. .... **Encino, CA**
Gost, Kimberly J. .... **Philadelphia, PA**
Gostel, Gary S. .... Miami, FL
Gostfrand, Maury Steven .... New York, NY
Gostin, Edgar B. .... Macon, GA
Gostin, Irwin .... San Diego, CA
Gostkowski, Bernard R. .... Hempstead, NY
Gostlow, Gareth A. .... Salinas, CA
Gostyla, Jeffrey F. .... **New Britain, CT**
Gostyla, Tracy L. .... **Houston, TX**
Gostynka Frakt, Agata .... Chicago, IL
Gostynska-Frakt, Agata .... Chicago, IL
Gosule, Alan L. .... **New York, NY**
Goswami, Anuj .... **Cleveland, OH**
Goswami, Debbie .... **Jackson, MS**
Goswami, Virender Kumar
San Francisco, CA
Gosz, William G. .... **Boston, MA**
Gosztonyi, Sylvia .... Landenberg, PA
Gotanco, Lawrence P. .... San Jose, CA
Gotanda, Brenda Hustis
Bala Cynwyd, PA
Gotanda, Neil Tetsu .... Fullerton, CA
Gotaskie, John R., Jr. .... Greensburg, PA
Gotay, Orlando, Jr. .... Gardnerville, NV
Gotay-Barquet, Frank .... **San Juan, PR**
Gotbaum, Irving J. .... **New York, NY**
Gotbetter, Howard .... New York, NY
Gotbetter, Susan .... **New York, NY**
Gotch, Charles F. .... **Omaha, NE**
Gotch, James T. .... **Oakland, CA**
Gotch, Joseph E., Jr. .... **Atlanta, GA**
Gotcher, Deryl L., Jr. .... Tulsa, OK
Gotcher, Deryl Lee .... **Tulsa, OK**
Gotcher, Herman C., Jr. .... Austin, TX
Gotcher, Holly H. .... **Greenville, TX**
Gotcher, James R., III .... Sherman Oaks, CA
Gotcher, Katherine Ann Fekula .... Dallas, TX
Gotcher, Pamela S. .... Dallas, TX
Gotcher, Warren .... McAlester, OK
Goteiner, Neil A. .... **San Francisco, CA**
Gotelli, John E. .... Lake Katrine, NY
Gotenstein, Louis .... Santa Monica, CA
Gotfredson, E. Jay .... Malibu, CA
Gotfredson, Thomas L. .... La Jolla, CA
Gotfredson, William J. .... **Kansas City, MO**
Gotfryd, William T. .... Chicago, IL
Goth, O. A. John .... Menlo Park, CA
Goth & Silvestri .... Redwood City, CA
Menlo Park, CA
Gotha, Frederick .... **Los Angeles, CA**
Gotha, Frederick .... **Pasadena, CA**
Gotham, Roy D. .... Ontonagon, MI
Gothard, Alexander W. .... Chattanooga, TN
Gothard, Crystal .... **Washington, DC**
Gothard, Edward P. .... Metairie, LA
Gothard, James A. .... **Lafayette, IN**
Gothard, Jennifer K. .... Cincinnati, OH
Gothard, John H., Jr. .... Palm Desert, CA
Gothard, Joy Buck .... Cookeville, TN
Gothard, Sol .... Gretna, LA
Gothelf, Aaron M. .... **Chicago, IL**
Gother, Ronald E. .... **Los Angeles, CA**
Gotherman, John E. .... **Cleveland, OH**
Gotimer, William G., Jr.
Rockville Centre, NY
Gotkin, Jerome .... **Boston, MA**

Gotkin, Jonathan S. ....Indianapolis, IN
Gotkin, Martin E. ....Palisades, NY
Gotkin, Michael M. ....New York, NY
Gotkin, Michael S. ....Northbrook, IL
Gotkin, Vicki ....Tucson, AZ
Gotko, Lance J. ....New York, NY
Gotlib, Amir ....New York, NY
Gotlib, Benzion ....Flint, MI
Gotlib, Kerry ....New York, NY
Gotlib, Linda L. ....Metuchen, NJ
Gotlieb, Charles E. ....Palo Alto, CA
Gotlieb, David ....Minneapolis, MN
Gotlieb, Heidi B. ....Los Altos, CA
Gotlieb, Lawrence Barry ....Los Angeles, CA
Gotlieb, William H. ....Minneapolis, MN
Gotlin, Daniel J. ....New York, NY
Gotlin & Jaffe ....New York, NY
Goto, Arthur K. ....Honolulu, HI
Goto, Bruce T. ....Seattle, WA
Goto, Frank K., Jr. ....Honolulu, HI
Goto, Paul R. ....Honolulu, HI
Goto, Roberta Y. ....Boston, MA
Goto, Roy Ai-Ji ....Los Angeles, CA
Goto, Steven L. ....Honolulu, HI
Gotoh, Suko ....Glendale, CA
Gotovich, Walter J. ....Norwood, MA
Gotsch, Allison L. ....New York, NY
Gotsch, Michael Gerald ....South Bend, IN
Gotsch, Theodore T. ....New York, NY
Gotschall, Charles W., Law Offices of
Kansas City, MO
Gotschall, James D. ....O'Neill, NE
Gotschall, Leo C. ....Kansas City, MO
Gotschall, Michael H. ....Orlando, FL
Gotschall, Robert E. ....Marblehead, MA
Gotschall, Sarah E. ....Atlanta, GA
Gotschall, William P. ....Falls Church, VA
Gotsdiner, Gary M. ....Omaha, NE
Gotsdiner, Judy Zaiman ....Omaha, NE
Gotsdiner, Murray B.
West Des Moines, IA
Gotshall, David W. ....Anderson, IN
Gotshall-Maxon, Lee F.
San Francisco, CA
Gott, Dennis C. ....Downers Grove, IL
Gott, Douglas W. ....Bowling Green, KY
Gott, Kimberly Lynn ....Dallas, TX
Gott, Lawrence D. ....Danville, VA
Gott, Michael R. ....Jonesboro, AR
Gott, Michael R., P.A. ....Jonesboro, AR
Gott, Michele C. ....Wilmington, DE
Gott, Ralph E. ....Wolfeboro, NH
Gott, Ronald M. ....Wichita, KS
Gott, Shelby R. ....San Ysidro, CA
Gott, Steven G. ....Kingsport, TN
Gott, Troy H. ....Wichita, KS
Gott, Young & Bogle, P.A. ....Wichita, KS
Gottbetter, Adam Spencer ....New York, NY
Gottbetter, Paul B. ....New York, NY
Gottdiener, I. Scott ....New York, NY
Gottehrer, Gail L. ....Hartford, CT
Gottemoller, Joseph ....Crystal Lake, IL
Gotten, William M. ....Memphis, TN
Gotten, Wilson & Savory ....Memphis, TN
Gottenberg, Karen B. ....Dresher, PA
Gottenborg, David A. ....Englewood, CO
Gottes, John J. ....South Gate, CA
Gottes, John J., Inc. ....South Gate, CA
Gottes, John R. ....South Gate, CA
Gottes, John R., Inc. ....South Gate, CA
Gottesdiener, Eli ....Washington, DC
Gottesfeld, Gary L. ....Denver, CO
Gottesfeld, Matthew W. ....Philadelphia, PA
Gottesfeld, Miriam B. ....New York, NY
Gottesfeld, Sharon P. ....Los Angeles, CA
Gottesfeld, Stephen P. ....Denver, CO
Gottesman, Albert ....New York, NY
Gottesman, Barbara ....New York, NY
Gottesman, Callman ....New York, NY
Gottesman, David J. ....Department of Justice,
Civil Division, GV
Gottesman, David M. ....Nashua, NH
Gottesman, David S. ....Lawrence, NY
Gottesman, Donald ....Chicago, IL
Gottesman, Donald S. ....Los Angeles, CA
Gottesman, Evan R. ....Washington, DC
Gottesman, Gary F. ....Hartford, CT
Gottesman and Hollis, Professional Association ....Manchester, NH
Nashua, NH
Gottesman, J. Michael ....New York, NY
Gottesman, James S. ....San Francisco, CA
Gottesman, Jay F. ....Brooklyn, NY
Gottesman, Joan C. ....Staten Island, NY
Gottesman, Joan K. ....Larchmont, NY
Gottesman, Joel H. ....St. Paul, MN
Gottesman, Josephine C. ....New York, NY
Gottesman & Kircher ....Cincinnati, OH
Gottesman, Larry F. ....Department of Labor,
Office of the Solicitor, GV
Gottesman, Lawrence P. ....New York, NY
Gottesman, Lee D., Law Offices of
Toms River, NJ
Gottesman, Mark A. ....Los Angeles, CA
Gottesman, Michael A. ....Clifton, NJ
Gottesman, Michael H. ....Tucson, AZ
Gottesman, Michael H. ....Washington, DC
Gottesman, Milton M. ....Washington, DC
Gottesman, Nancy S. ....Birmingham, MI
Gottesman, Phyllis R. ....New York, NY
Gottesman & Polito ....Los Angeles, CA
Gottesman, Richard K. ....Dartmouth, MA
Gottesman, Robert S. ....San Francisco, CA
Gottesman, Robert S., Inc.
San Francisco, CA
Gottesman, Shannon ....Seattle, WA
Gottesman, Wolgel, Secunda, Malamy & Flynn, Professional Corporation
New York, NY
White Plains, NY
Gottesman, Zachary ....Cincinnati, OH
Gottesmann, Dennis M. ....Greenbelt, MD
Gottesmann, Dennis M., P.A.
Greenbelt, MD
Gottfred, William E. ....Rockford, IL
Gottfredson, J. Michael, (P.C.)
Salt Lake City, UT
Gottfried, Alona M. ....Phoenix, AZ
Gottfried, Andrew D. ....New York, NY
Gottfried, Barry H. ....Washington, DC
Gottfried, David ....New York, NY
Gottfried, David J.
Environmental Protection Agency,
Office of Enforcement and Compliance
Assurance, GV
Gottfried, David M. ....Austin, TX
Gottfried, David M., A Professional
Corporation ....Austin, TX
Gottfried, Eric Jason ....New York, NY
Gottfried, Gary J. ....Columbus, OH
Gottfried, Gary J., Co., L.P.A.
Columbus, OH
Gottfried, Glenn R. ....Queens Village, NY
Gottfried, Harry J. ....Orinda, CA
Gottfried, Herman E. ....Margaretville, NY
Gottfried, Keith E. ....New York, NY
Gottfried, Linda A. ....Treasury Department,
Office of the Comptroller of the Currency,
GV
Gottfried, Maureen Callahan ....Columbus, GA
Gottfried, Michael ....New York, NY
Gottfried, Michael E. ....Phoenix, AZ
Gottfried, Michael I. ....Los Angeles, CA
Gottfried, Michael R. ....Boston, MA
Gottfried, Paul D. ....Fort Lauderdale, FL
Gottfried, Philip H. ....New York, NY
Gottfried, R. Mark ....Cleveland, OH
Gottfried, R. Mark, Jr. ....Cleveland, OH
Gottfried, Rena Rachel ....Brooklyn, NY
Gottfried, Robert N. ....New York, NY
Gottfried, Roger M. ....Bingham Farms, MI
Gottfried, Theodore A. ....Springfield, IL
Gottfried, William ....Clearwater, FL
Gottheim, Joshua C. ....Los Angeles, CA
Gottheim, Robert M. ....Albany, NY
Gottheim, Robert Marc ....Brooklyn, NY
Gottheiner, Karin J., Law Offices of
Beverly Hills, CA
Gotthelf, Barbara K. ....Cherry Hill, NJ
Gotthelf, Beth S. ....Detroit, MI
Southfield, MI
Gotthoffer, Lance ....New York, NY
Gottilla, Roger R. ....Morristown, NJ
Gotting, Eric P. ....Washington, DC
Gotting, Karl L., (P.C.) ....Lansing, MI
Gottlick, John D. ....Chicago, IL
Gottlieb, Adam J. ....Carle Place, NY
Gottlieb, Alan J. ....East Brunswick, NJ
Gottlieb, Alan P. ....Boston, MA
Providence, RI
Gottlieb, Andrew J. ....Palo Alto, CA
Gottlieb, Arnold ....West Palm Beach, FL
Gottlieb, Arnold N. ....Toledo, OH
Gottlieb, Arthur H. ....Baltimore, MD
Gottlieb, Arthur J. ....Long Beach, CA
Gottlieb, Barry ....New York, NY
Gottlieb, Barry M. ....Montvale, NJ
Nanuet, NY
Gottlieb, Benjamin M. ....Fall River, MA
Gottlieb, Beth M. ....Chicago, IL
Gottlieb, Bruce M. ....Hollywood, FL
Gottlieb, C. Robert, Jr. ....Mobile, AL
Gottlieb, Caryn B. ....Washington, DC
Gottlieb, Charles ....Detroit, MI
Gottlieb, Craig R. ....Department of Justice,
Civil Division, GV
Gottlieb, Daniel M. ....Beverly Hills, CA
Gottlieb, Daniel S. ....Seattle, WA
Gottlieb, David D. ....La Fayette, GA
Gottlieb, David I. ....New York, NY
Gottlieb, Deborah A. ....Houston, TX
Gottlieb, Deborah H. ....Fair Lawn, NJ
Gottlieb, Edward A. ....Boston, MA
Gottlieb, F. Susan ....New York, NY
Gottlieb, Fisher & Andrews, PLLC
Seattle, WA
Gottlieb, Fredric I. ....Boca Raton, FL
Gottlieb, Gail ....Albuquerque, NM
Gottlieb, Gary P. ....Rock Hill, NY
Gottlieb, George ....New York, NY
Gottlieb, Gerald H. ....Los Angeles, CA
Gottlieb, Glenn M. ....Los Angeles, CA
Gottlieb & Gottlieb, P.A. ....Clearwater, FL
Gottlieb & Gottlieb, P.A. ....Hollywood, FL
Gottlieb, Harlan F. ....St. Louis, MO
Gottlieb, Harold E. ....Zanesville, OH
Gottlieb, Howard C. ....Philadelphia, PA
Gottlieb, Ira L. ....Burbank, CA
Gottlieb, Ira L. ....Portland, OR
Gottlieb, Irving J. ....Coral Gables, FL
Gottlieb, James B. ....Chicago, IL
Gottlieb, Janet ....New York, NY
Gottlieb, Jason A. ....Los Angeles, CA
Gottlieb, Jay L. ....New York, NY
Gottlieb, Jay S. ....Philadelphia, PA
Gottlieb, Jeffrey ....Grand Rapids, MI
Gottlieb, Jeffrey H. ....Arlington Heights, IL
Gottlieb, Jeffrey M. ....New York, NY
Gottlieb, Jerome A. ....Hauppauge, NY
Gottlieb, Jerome R. ....Downers Grove, IL
Gottlieb, Jerry ....Clearwater, FL
Gottlieb, Joann ....Arlington, VA
Gottlieb, Joel B. ....Carteret, NJ
Gottlieb, Joel E. ....Columbia, SC
Gottlieb, Johnston, Beam & Dal Ponte, P.L.L. ....Zanesville, OH
Gottlieb, Jon A., P.C. ....Atlanta, GA
Gottlieb, Jonathan ....Los Angeles, CA
Washington, DC
Gottlieb, Jonathan E.
Securities and Exchange Commission,
Division of Corporation Finance, GV
Gottlieb, Jonathan W. ....Washington, DC
Gottlieb, Joseph J. ....Atlanta, GA
Gottlieb, Judah ....Los Angeles, CA
Gottlieb, Judith B. ....Toledo, OH
Gottlieb, Judith Kaplan ....Los Angeles, CA
Gottlieb, Julian H. ....New York, NY
Gottlieb, Karen J. ....New York, NY
Gottlieb, Karen M. ....Miami, FL
Gottlieb, Kenneth A. ....Hollywood, FL
Gottlieb, Kirk A. ....Palo Alto, CA
Gottlieb, Krista ....Buffalo, NY
Gottlieb, Laurie ....Philadelphia, PA
Gottlieb, Lawrence ....Seattle, WA
Gottlieb, Lawrence C. ....New York, NY
Gottlieb, Lawrence M. ....Scarsdale, NY
Gottlieb, Leon S. ....Colorado Springs, CO
Gottlieb, Louis ....New York, NY
Gottlieb, Lynn R. ....Villanova, PA
Gottlieb, Manuel W. ....New York, NY
Gottlieb, Marc J. ....Fort Lauderdale, FL
Gottlieb, Marc S. ....New York, NY
Gottlieb, Marjorie G. ....Clayton, MO
Gottlieb, Mark E. ....Philadelphia, PA
Gottlieb, Mark S. ....Tarzana, CA
Gottlieb, Martin ....Boston, MA
Gottlieb, Michael ....Norristown, PA
Gottlieb, Michael A. ....Van Nuys, CA
Gottlieb, Michael A., P.A.
Fort Lauderdale, FL
Gottlieb, Michael Alan ....Fort Lauderdale, FL
Gottlieb, Michael H. ....Bronx, NY
Gottlieb, Michael R. ....Middletown, NY
Gottlieb, Michael S. ....Washington, DC
Gottlieb, Milton J. ....Miami, FL
Gottlieb, Myron H. ....Mount Holly, NJ
Gottlieb, Nancy R. ....Westwood, MA
Gottlieb, Norman E. ....Hartsdale, NY
Gottlieb, Norman N. ....Flint, MI
Gottlieb, Norman N., P.C. ....Flint, MI
Gottlieb, Paul ....New York, NY
Gottlieb, Paul A. ....Department of Energy,
Office of the General Counsel, GV
Gottlieb, Paul M. ....New York, NY
Gottlieb, Paul S. ....New York, NY
Gottlieb, Peter ....New York, NY
Gottlieb, Rackman & Reisman, P.C.
New York, NY
Gottlieb, Richard ....Clearwater, FL
Gottlieb, Richard E. ....Chicago, IL
Gottlieb, Richard J. ....New York, NY
Gottlieb, Richard L. ....Charleston, WV
Gottlieb, Richard M. ....New York, NY
Gottlieb, Richard N., Law Offices of
Boston, MA
Gottlieb, Richard S. ....Winston-Salem, NC
Gottlieb, Robert C., Law Offices of
Commack, NY
New York, NY
Gottlieb, Robert Gene ....Washington, DC
Gottlieb, Robert S. ....New York, NY
Gottlieb, Robert W. ....New York, NY
Gottlieb, Ronald J. ....Department of Labor,
Office of the Solicitor, GV
Gottlieb, Samuel Joseph ....Great Neck, NY
Gottlieb, Sandra L. ....Los Angeles, CA
Gottlieb, S. B. ....Philadelphia, PA
Gottlieb, Scott C. ....Binghamton, NY
Gottlieb, Scott E. ....Bridgeport, CT
Gottlieb, Seymour ....Los Alamitos, CA
Gottlieb, Sharon E. ....Washington, DC
Gottlieb, Sidney ....New York, NY
Gottlieb & Smith, P.A. ....Columbia, SC
Gottlieb, Solomon ....Pikesville, MD
Gottlieb, Stacey F. ....Phoenix, AZ
Gottlieb, Stephen E. ....Albany, NY
Gottlieb, Stephen P. ....Incline Village, NV
Gottlieb, Stephen S. ....Tell City, IN
Gottlieb, Steven I. ....Kingston, NY
Gottlieb, Stuart M. ....West Palm Beach, FL
Gottlieb, William ....New York, NY
Gottlieb, William A. ....Boston, MA
Gottlieb, William P. ....Brooklyn, NY
Gottlieb, Wilma P. ....New York, NY
Gottlin, Sandra G. ....Stamford, CT
Gottlober, Harold S. ....Philadelphia, PA
Gottman, James F. ....Dayton, OH
Gottner, Robert E. ....Arlington Heights, IL
Gotto, Gary A. ....Phoenix, AZ
Gottovi, Sara L. ....Washington, DC
Gottridge, Marc J. ....New York, NY
Gottron, Denise J. ....Rockville, MD
Gottron, Douglas N. ....Rockville, MD
Gottry, Brian M. ....Bloomfield Hills, MI
Gotts, Ilene Knable ....New York, NY
Gotts, Lawrence J. ....Washington, DC
Gottsch, Alan R. ....Alva, OK
Gottsch, Michael D. ....Haverford, PA
Gottschald, Robert A. ....Indianola, IA
Gottschalk, Andrew S. ....Minneapolis, MN
Gottschalk, Arthur R. ....Frankfort, IL
Gottschalk, Bonita M. ....Boston, MA
Gottschalk, Caroline B. ....New York, NY
Gottschalk, Craig A. ....Lima, OH
Gottschalk, Debbra J. ....Tulsa, OK
Gottschalk, Don E. ....Cedar Falls, IA
Gottschalk, Donald L. ....Hutchinson, KS
Gottschalk, Elizabeth ....Chicago, IL
Gottschalk, Eric L. ....Danbury, CT
Gottschalk, Hugh Q. ....Denver, CO
Gottschalk, J. Michael ....Omaha, NE
Gottschalk, Jack A. ....Livingston, NJ
Gottschalk, James A. ....St. Louis, MO
Gottschalk, Jennifer L. ....Kansas City, MO
Gottschalk, Jennifer Leigh ....Trenton, NJ
Gottschalk, Kim Jerome ....Boulder, CO
Gottschalk, Marc E. ....Palo Alto, CA
Gottschalk, Michael P. ....Hayfork, CA
Gottschalk, Patrick O. ....Richmond, VA
Gottschalk, Randall E. ....Minneapolis, MN
Gottschalk, Robert ....Lake Forest, IL
Gottschalk, Robert M. ....Chicago, IL
Gottschalk, Ronald E. ....Chicago, IL
Gottschalk, Ronald L. ....Greenfield, IN
Gottschalk, Ronald N. ....Arcadia, CA
Gottschalk, Ronald N., Associates
Arcadia, CA
Gottschalk, Stephen E. ....Minneapolis, MN
Gottschalk, Thomas A. ....Detroit, MI
Gottschalk, William S.
Bloomfield Hills, MI
Gottschall, Candace K. ....Pittsburgh, PA
Gottschall, Carl ....Caldwell, NJ
Gottschall, Joan B. ....Chicago, IL
Gottschall, Kurt L. ....Denver, CO
Gottschall, Matthew D. ....Dayton, OH
Gottsche, Steven E. ....Boston, MA
Gottschlich, Gary W. ....Dayton, OH
Gottschlich, Michael H.
Santa Monica, CA
Gottschlich & Portune, LLP ....Dayton, OH
Gottscho, Christopher M. ....Washington, DC
Gottscho, Oscar A. ....New York, NY
Gottsegen, Jonathan M.
Securities and Exchange Commission,
Division of Corporation Finance, GV
New York, NY
Gottsegen, Stanley D. ....Boca Raton, FL
Gottsegen, Thomas Eliot ....Chicago, IL
Gottsfield, Robert L. ....Phoenix, AZ
Gottshall, Julie Helenbrook ....Chicago, IL
Gottshall, Justine Young ....Washington, DC
Gottshall, Kevin L. ....Oklahoma City, OK
Gottshall, Thomas R. ....Columbia, SC
Gottshall-Sayed, Linda ....Los Angeles, CA
Gottstein, James B. ....Anchorage, AK
Gottula, Lisa G. ....Omaha, NE
Gottuso, Deborah C. ....Princeton, NJ
Gottuso, Josephine M. ....Claremont, CA
Gottuso, Richard C. ....Long Branch, NJ
Gottuso, Suzanne C. ....Edison, NJ
Gottwald, Arthur P. ....Alexandria, VA
Gottwald, Jeffrey A. ....Wyncote, PA
Gottwik, Paula J. ....Hyde Park, VT
Gotvald, Christi M. ....San Francisco, CA
Gotwald, Robert Caldwell
Joint Committees And Commissions, GV
Gotwals, Charles P., Jr. ....Tulsa, OK
Gotwals, James R. ....Tulsa, OK
Gotwals, James R., and Associates, Inc., A Prof. Corp. ....Tulsa, OK
Gotwalt, Eric R. ....Savannah, GA
Gotway, Patricia H. ....Indianapolis, IN
Götz, Claudia Botero ....Jersey City, NJ
New York, NY
Gotz, James D. ....Boston, MA
Gotzler, Michael R. ....Chicago, IL
Gouaux, Antoinette C. ....Lockport, LA
Gouaux, Eugene G., Jr. ....Lockport, LA
Goubeaud, Joseph G., Jr.
Mount Vernon, NY
Goubeaux & Goubeaux ....Greenville, OH
Goubeaux, James J. ....Greenville, OH
Goucher Law Offices, P.C. ....Cameron, MO
Goucher, Leigh A. ....Liberty, MO
Goucher, Mark A. ....Cameron, MO
Goucher, Paul B. ....New York, NY
Goudarzi, J. Brent ....Gilmer, TX
Marshall, TX
Goude, C. Reuben ....Georgetown, SC
Goudeau, C. Angelle ....Metairie, LA
Goudeau, Jill B. ....West Monroe, LA
Goudeau, Morgan J., III ....Opelousas, LA
Goudelock, J. Russell, II ....Columbia, SC
Goudey, Elizabeth B. ....Laramie, WY
Goudge, James H. ....Los Angeles, CA
Goudie, Federico ....New York, NY
Goudiss, Alan S. ....New York, NY
Goudiss, Morton R. ....Miami Beach, FL
Goudreau, Elizabeth D. ....Anchorage, AK
Goudreau, Noël P. ....Chicago, IL
Goudsouzian, Steven N. ....Bethlehem, PA
Goudvis, Albert Charles
Briarcliff Manor, NY
New York, NY
Goudy, Craig A. ....Minneapolis, MN
Goudy, Mark D. ....Grand Rapids, MI
Goudy, Robert S. ....Wichita, KS
Gouge, Donald L., Jr. ....Wilmington, DE
Gouge, H. Donald ....Renton, WA
Gouge, Linda K. ....The Dalles, OR
Gouge, M. Gene ....Dalton, GA
Gouge, Marcy A. ....Colorado Springs, CO
Gouge, Ruth L. ....Conifer, CO
Gougeon, Caroline A. ....Minneapolis, MN
Gouger, David H. ....Richmond, VA
Gouger, David H., P.C. ....Richmond, VA
Gouger, William Lee, Jr. ....Jasper, TN
Gough, A. Kenneth ....Eugene, OR
Gough, Aidan R. ....Santa Clara, CA
Gough, Ann R. ....Aiken, SC
Gough, Arnold G., Jr. ....Chicago, IL
Gough, Brian G. ....Santa Barbara, CA
Gough & Cohen ....Oakland, CA
Gough, Denise ....Washington, DC
Gough, Gary C. ....Clifton, VA
Gough, Gayle L. ....San Francisco, CA

Gough, Jerome F. Department Of Veterans Affairs, Board of Veterans Appeals, GV
Gough, John E., Jr. ... **Jackson, MS**
Gough, John Francis ... **Philadelphia, PA**
Gough, Josie M. ... **Chicago, IL**
Gough, Judith Dilley ... Oakland, CA
Gough, Kerry M. ... Oakland, CA
Gough, Kevin R. ... **Brunswick, GA**
Gough, Kevin R. ... **Darien, GA**
Kingsland, GA
Gough, Leroy C. ... Brighton, MI
Gough, Michael P. ... Milford, PA
Gough, Newell, Jr. ... **Helena, MT**
Gough, Patricia A. ... Tallahassee, FL
Gough, Paul T. ... **Los Angeles, CA**
Gough, Peter J. ... **Pittsburgh, PA**
Gough, Robert B., III ... **Tampa, FL**
Gough, Robert E. ... **Rockville, MD**
Gough, Shanahan, Johnson & Waterman **Helena, MT**
Gough, Skipworth, Summers, Eves & Trevett, P.C. ... **Rochester, NY**
Gough, Steven D. ... **Wichita, KS**
Gough, W. Raleigh ... Independence, MO
Goughan, Patricia L. ... **Palo Alto, CA**
Gougis, Lefeba J., Jr. ... Los Angeles, CA
Gougisha, Michael Consumer Product Safety Commission, Commissioners Office, GV
Gouhin, Sean M. ... **Columbus, OH**
Gouig, Steven J. ... Pleasanton, CA
Gouin, Dori Chadbourne ... **Boston, MA**
Gouin, Leon J. ... Wallingford, CT
Gouin, Michelle D. ... **Hartford, CT**
Gouin, Raymond P. ... Melrose, MA
Gouinlock, Susan S. ... Aurora, IL
Goul, Barbara Y. ... Los Angeles, CA
Goul, Dudley J. ... Merced, CA
Goul, Richard M. ... Los Angeles, CA
Goulais, Donald K. ... Escanaba, MI
Goulart, Donald T. ... Boulder, CO
Goulart, Frank ... Hayward, CA
Goulart, John B. ... Modesto, CA
Goulart, Kenneth M. ... Sacramento, CA
Goulart, Paul W. ... **Sacramento, CA**
Goulart, Ronald C. ... Fort Oglethorpe, GA
Goularte, Ronald A. ... Santa Clara, CA
Goulatis, Constance ... Westborough, MA
Gould, A. Sheldon ... Syracuse, NY
Gould, Alan D. ... New York, NY
Gould, Alan I. ... Wildwood, NJ
Gould, Alan I., A Professional Corporation Wildwood, NJ
Gould, Alan J. ... Emeryville, CA
Gould, Alfred R., Jr. ... **Metairie, LA**
Gould, Amy J. ... **Boston, MA**
Gould, Andrew I. ... Londonderry, NH
Gould, Andrew M. ... **Dallas, TX**
Gould, Ann ... **Northbrook, IL**
Gould, Anthony C. ... **Portland, OR**
Gould, Anthony D. ... **Oklahoma City, OK**
Gould, Arnold J. ... New York, NY
Gould, Arthur I. ... **Chicago, IL**
Gould, Barbara J. ... **Stamford, CT**
Gould, Benjamin ... Huntington, NY
Gould, Bertrand F. ... Albany, NY
Gould, Bob ... Lenexa, KS
Gould, Bob, Law Offices, Chartered Lenexa, KS
Gould, Bonnie Brooke ... New York, NY
Gould, Bradley S. ... **Fort Lauderdale, FL**
Gould, Bret Adam ... Sarasota, FL
Gould, Bruce D. ... Great Neck, NY
Gould, Bruce G. ... Seattle, WA
Gould, Bruce H. ... Norfolk, VA
Gould, Bruce Jordan ... New York, NY
Gould, Bruce K. ... Longwood, FL
Gould, Bryan K. ... **Concord, NH**
Lebanon, NH
Gould, Burton D. ... Paia, HI
Gould, C. Joseph ... Newport, RI
Gould, C. Lance ... **Montgomery, AL**
Gould, Calvin ... Salt Lake City, UT
Gould, Carl M. ... **Los Angeles, CA**
Gould, Carole ... Brooklyn, NY
Gould, Carole S. ... **Baltimore, MD**
Gould, Carolyn P. ... **New Haven, CT**
Gould, Charles A., Jr. ... Miami Beach, FL
Gould, Charles E. ... Newton, MA
Gould, Charles K. ... **Huntington, WV**
Gould, Charles N. A. ... Key West, FL
Gould, Charles P. ... **Los Angeles, CA**
Gould, Clifford I. ... San Francisco, CA
Gould & Company ... **Oklahoma City, OK**
Gould & Company, Chartered, Inc. Miami Beach, FL
Gould, Connie Totorica ... **Phoenix, AZ**
Gould, Constance D. ... Seattle, WA
Gould, Cooksey, Fennell, O'Neill, Marine & Carter, Professional Association **Vero Beach, FL**
Gould, Dana L. ... **Washington, DC**
Gould, Daniel W. ... Kankakee, IL
Gould, David ... **Los Angeles, CA**
Gould, David D. ... Bellevue, WA
Gould, David E. ... **Pittsburgh, PA**
Gould, David F. ... Bangor, ME
Gould, David F., III ... Lambertville, NJ
Doylestown, PA
Gould, David J. ... **Wilmington, DE**
Gould, David M. ... Boston, MA
Gould, David S. ... **Brooklyn, NY**
Gould, David S. ... **New York, NY**
Port Washington, NY
Gould, David S., P.C. ... **New York, NY**
Port Washington, NY
Gould, Dean J. ... **Bloomfield Hills, MI**
Gould, Diana S. ... Newton, MA
Gould, Diane B. ... Houston, TX
Gould, Dirk S. ... New York, NY
Gould, Donald B. ... **Boston, MA**
Gould, Donald J. ... Joliet, IL
Gould, Donald W., II ... **Houston, TX**
Gould, Douglas N. ... **Oklahoma City, OK**
Gould, Edward W. ... **Bangor, ME**
Gould, Eli W. ... **Palo Alto, CA**
Gould, Emil Bradley ... **Washington, DC**
Gould, Emily B. ... Chicago, IL
Gould, Emily J. ... **San Francisco, CA**
Gould, Eric ... Houston, TX
Gould, Eric Joel ... **Detroit, MI**
Gould, Eric S. ... Department of Justice, Environment and Natural Resources Division, GV
Gould, Ernest S. ... Los Angeles, CA
Gould & Ettenberg, P.C. ... **Worcester, MA**
Gould, Evan A. ... San Diego, CA
Gould, F. Latimer ... Orange, CA
Gould, Francis J. ... Newark, NJ
Gould, Franklyn ... New York, NY
Gould, Fredric H. ... Great Neck, NY
Gould, Gabrielle L. ... **New York, NY**
Gould, Gaye L. ... Ganado, AZ
Gould, George ... Manhattan Beach, CA
Gould, George D. ... Philadelphia, PA
Gould, George M. ... **Newark, NJ**
Gould, Georgeanne H. ... New York, NY
Gould & Gillin, P.C. ... **Old Saybrook, CT**
Gould, Ginger L. C. ... Chico, CA
Gould, Glenn ... **Oakland, CA**
Gould, Gordon C. ... Redwood City, CA
Gould and Gould ... Dedham, MA
Gould and Gould ... Londonderry, NH
Gould, Gregory G. ... **Helena, MT**
Gould, Harold D., Jr. ... Uxbridge, MA
Gould, Harold I., (A P.C.) Marina Del Rey, CA
Gould, Harold I., A Professional Corporation Marina Del Rey, CA
Gould, Harriet E. ... Dorchester, MA
Gould, Harvey L. ... **San Francisco, CA**
Gould, Henry S. ... Albany, NY
Gould, Howard Jay ... Hampton, VA
Gould, Howard M. ... **Old Saybrook, CT**
Gould, Howard N. ... **Los Angeles, CA**
Gould, Ira P. ... Chicago, IL
Gould, Isabel W. ... Cherry Hills Village, CO
Gould, J. Eric Executive Office Of The President, GV
Gould, J. Samatha ... Wellesley, MA
Gould, Jack A. ... **Fairfax, VA**
Gould, Jack B. ... Newton, MA
Gould, Jack L. ... **Fairfax, VA**
Gould, Jackson A. ... Gloucester, MA
Gould, James C. ... Washington, DC
Gould, James E. ... Grand Rapids, MI
Gould, James E., & Associates, P.C. Grand Rapids, MI
Gould, James M. ... **Kenilworth, NJ**
Gould, James R. ... Dayton, OH
Gould, James W. ... **New York, NY**
Gould, Jane Bilus ... **White Plains, NY**
Gould, Janet Jeter ... Pinetop Lakeside, AZ
Gould, Janet Jeter, P.C. Pinetop Lakeside, AZ
Gould, Jason H. ... **Washington, DC**
Gould, Jay ... New York, NY
Gould, Jay B. ... San Francisco, CA
Gould, Jeffrey R. ... Newton, MA
Gould, Jeffrey S. ... Indianapolis, IN
Gould, Joann E. ... Rochester, NY
Gould, John B. ... Norway, ME
Gould, John C. ... Hopewell, VA
Gould, John D. ... **Minneapolis, MN**
Gould, John E. ... **New York, NY**
Gould, John E. ... Springfield, OH
Gould, John Wiley ... **Portland, OR**
Gould, Jonathan ... **Hartford, CT**
Gould, Jonathan B. ... Beloit, WI
Gould, Jonathan D. ... New York, NY
Gould, Jonathan S. ... New York, NY
Gould, Jonathan S. ... New York, NY
Gould, Judith E. ... New York, NY
Gould, Judson A. ... Washington, DC
Gould, Julian S. ... Los Angeles, CA
Gould, Justin Edward ... Miami Beach, FL
Gould, Karen A. ... **Bloomfield Hills, MI**
Gould, Karen A. ... **Richmond, VA**
Gould, Karlin ... Liberal, KS
Gould, Kenneth B. ... **Boston, MA**
Gould, Kenneth D. ... Toledo, OH
Gould, Kenneth J. ... Londonderry, NH
Gould, Kenneth J. ... **White Plains, NY**
Gould, Kenneth S. ... Little Rock, AR
Gould, Keri A. ... New York, NY
Gould, Kevin L. ... **New York, NY**
Gould, Killian & Wynne ... **Hartford, CT**
Gould, Kimberly I. ... **Exton, PA**
Gould, Kingdon, Jr. ... Washington, DC
Gould, L. Scott ... Portland, ME
Gould, Larson, Bennet, Wells & McDonnell, P.C. ... **Essex, CT**
Middletown, CT
Old Saybrook, CT
Gould, Laura Meyers ... Farmington Hills, MI
Gould, Lauren J. ... **Great Neck, NY**
New York, NY
Gould, Laurie J. ... Palo Alto, CA
Gould Law Office, L.L.C. ... Lenexa, KS
Gould, Lawrence J. ... **Atlanta, GA**
Gould, Lawrence R. ... **New York, NY**
Gould, Lewis F., Jr. ... **Philadelphia, PA**
Gould, Lewis J. ... Rochester, NY
Gould, Linda Flewellen Colorado Springs, CO
Gould, Lisa A. ... Dedham, MA
Gould, Lloyd R. ... Valley Forge, PA
Gould, M. Allison ... Atlanta, GA
Gould, Malcolm Stewart ... **Philadelphia, PA**
Gould, Mark A., Jr. ... **Atlanta, GA**
Gould, Mark T. ... New Haven, CT
Gould, Marshall A. ... **Worcester, MA**
Gould, Martin A. ... **Hartford, CT**
Gould, Marvyn ... Philadelphia, PA
Gould, Michael ... Garden Grove, CA
Gould, Michael A. ... **Kansas City, MO**
Gould, Michael A. ... **New York, NY**
Gould, Michael A. ... Philadelphia, PA
Gould, Michael E. ... Meredith, NH
Gould, Michael L. ... Duluth, GA
Gould, Michael N. ... Garden City, NY
Gould, Michael P. ... **Philadelphia, PA**
Gould, Michael S. ... **Los Angeles, CA**
Gould, Morris Ronald ... Miami Beach, FL
Gould, Morton H. ... Los Angeles, CA
Gould, Nancy E. ... **Hartford, CT**
Gould, Nathaniel J. ... New York, NY
Gould, Neil ... Sacramento, CA
Gould, Norris S. ... **Clearwater, FL**
Gould, Patricia E. ... **San Francisco, CA**
Gould & Peck ... Rochester, NY
Gould, Peter A. ... New York, NY
Gould, Peter C. ... **New York, NY**
Gould, Peter H. Pension Benefit Guaranty Corporation, Office of the General Counsel, GV
Gould, Peter J. ... Santa Fe, NM
Gould, Philip R. ... Miami, FL
Gould & Preziosi, P.C. ... Lambertville, NJ
Doylestown, PA
Gould & Ratner ... **Chicago, IL**
Gould, Richard A. ... Dedham, MA
Gould, Richard B. ... Mission Viejo, CA
Gould, Richard C. ... San Anselmo, CA
Gould, Richard D. ... Boston, MA
Gould, Richard J. ... Green Bay, WI
Gould, Robert B. ... Lowell, MA
Gould, Robert B., The Law Offices of **Seattle, WA**
Gould, Robert D. ... New York, NY
Gould, Robert E. ... Kansas City, MO
Gould, Robert James, Attorney and Counsellor at Law ... **Charleston, WV**
Gould, Robert M. ... **Chicago, IL**
Gould, Robert P." Bob " ... Lenexa, KS
Gould, Rodney United States Postal Service, Law Department, GV
Gould, Rodney E. ... **Framingham, MA**
Gould, Roger W. ... **Coos Bay, OR**
Gould, Roger W., P.C. ... **Coos Bay, OR**
Gould, Ronald ... **Princeton, NJ**
Gould, Ronald I. ... Arroyo Grande, CA
Gould, Ronald M. ... **Seattle, WA**
Gould, Ronald P. ... **Chicago, IL**
Gould, Russell D. ... Kalamazoo, MI
Gould, Scott A. ... **Harrisburg, PA**
Gould, Serra & Flynn ... Boston, MA
Gould, Seth D. ... **Bloomfield Hills, MI**
Gould, Sharon A. ... Elkhart, IN
Gould, Sharon A. ... **Pittsburgh, PA**
Gould, Shelley M. ... **Los Angeles, CA**
Gould, Shepard ... **Chicago, IL**
Gould, Sherri Hallerman ... Minneapolis, MN
Gould, Sherrill R. ... Littleton, MA
Gould, Sidney A. ... Bridgeton, MO
Gould, Sidney A., P.C. ... Bridgeton, MO
Gould, Stacey J. ... Haddonfield, NJ
Gould, Stephen A. ... **Manchester, NH**
Gould, Stephen G. ... **San Francisco, CA**
Gould, Steven C. ... Crystal Lake, IL
Gould, Thad C. ... **Atlanta, GA**
Gould, Thomas D. ... Harrisburg, PA
Gould, Thomas L. ... Chicago, IL
Gould, Thompson, Carr & Bucher, A Professional Corporation ... Kansas City, MO
Gould, Trina Glusenkamp **Fort Wayne, IN**
Gould, Valerie A. ... Arroyo Grande, CA
Gould, W. George ... Brielle, NJ
Gould, Warren H. ... Fort Worth, TX
Gould, Wendy L. ... Bath, NY
Gould & Whitley ... Colorado Springs, CO
Gould & Wilkie LLP ... **Bronxville, NY**
New York, NY
White Plains, NY
Gould, William A. ... **Seattle, WA**
Gould, William A., Jr., (Inc.) **Sacramento, CA**
Gould, William D. ... **Los Angeles, CA**
Gould, William D. ... **Washington, DC**
Gould, William F. ... Washington, DC
Gould, Wm. Dunbar ... Kennedyville, MD
Gould Yaffe & Golden ... Philadelphia, PA
Goulden, Neil L. ... **Chicago, IL**
Goulden, Paula F. ... **Philadelphia, PA**
Goulder, David N. ... **Portland, OR**
Goulder, Diane K. ... **Columbus, OH**
Goulder, Gerald P. ... Greensboro, NC
Goulder, Jeffrey J. ... **Phoenix, AZ**
Goulder, Richard A. ... Cleveland, OH
Goulder, Richard A., Co. L.P.A. Cleveland, OH
Gould-Hilton, Bonnie S. South Berwick, ME
Gouldin, David M. ... **Binghamton, NY**
Gouldin, Robert Alfred ... **Richmond, VA**
Gouldin, Susan Curtin ... Morristown, NJ
Goulding, Allan D., Jr. ... **Morrisville, PA**
Goulding, Cameron C. ... Lake Orion, MI
Goulding, Daniel Joseph ... San Diego, CA
Goulding, Gerald L. ... Afton, WY
Goulding, J. Michael ... **San Francisco, CA**
Goulding, James S. ... **Detroit, MI**
Goulding, Michael Ian ... **Washington, DC**
Goulding, Michael R. ... **Toledo, OH**
Goulding, Regina A. ... Oak Park, IL
Goulding, Ronald K. ... Chicago, IL
Goulding, Suzanne F. ... Glendora, CA
Goulding-Schreck, Barbara J. ... Detroit, MI
Gouldman, Glenda Virginia **Alexandria, VA**
Gouldman, W. Clyde, II ... Charlottesville, VA
Gouldon, Jay T. ... Charleston, SC
Gould-Ross, Bette M. ... **Rochester, NY**
Gould-Saltman, Dianna J. **Los Angeles, CA**
Gould-Saltman Law Offices, LLP **Los Angeles, CA**
Gould-Saltman, Richard F. **Los Angeles, CA**
Goulet, Camille A. ... Los Angeles, CA
Goulet, Cynthia Wagner ... Grafton, ND
Goulet, Gerard R. ... **Boston, MA**
Providence, RI
Goulet, Mark C. ... **Austin, TX**
Goulet, Mary E. ... **Washington, DC**
Goulet, Melissa L. ... **Los Angeles, CA**
Goulet, Michael R. ... Providence, RI
Goulet, Paul C. United States International Trade Commission, Office of Administrative Law Judges, GV
Goulet, Robert G., Jr. ... **Pittsburgh, PA**
Goulet, Robert W. ... Detroit, MI
Goulet, Stephen P. ... **New York, NY**
Goulet, Victor N. ... San Francisco, CA
Goulet, Wallace R., Jr. ... Bismarck, ND
Goulet-Florentin, Suzanne J. Beverly Hills, CA
Goulian, Eric ... Department of Justice, Civil Division, GV
Goulian, Nancy ... New York, NY
Goulka, Joanne L. ... **Boston, MA**
Goulston & Storrs, A Professional Corporation ... **Boston, MA**
Goumas, Gregg P. ... **Westport, CT**
Gounaris, Demetri A. ... **New York, NY**
Gounaris, George J. ... Dayton, OH
Gounaris, Georgia N. ... **New York, NY**
Gounaris, Nicholas G. ... **Dayton, OH**
Gounaris, Nicholas L. ... **Parsippany, NJ**
Gounaris, Thomas L. ... Baltimore, MD
Goundry, Frederick W., III **Frederick, MD**
Gouner, Gregory M. ... Baton Rouge, LA
Gounley, Dennis J. ... Greensburg, PA
Goupillaud, Rene T. ... Los Angeles, CA
Gouraige, Hervé ... Newark, NJ
New York, NY
Gourary, John P. ... **New York, NY**
Gouras, Eckhart K. ... New York, NY
Gouras, Mark S. ... Tukwila, WA
Gourash, Daniel F. ... **Cleveland, OH**
Gourdé, Thomas L. ... **Long Beach, CA**
Gourdin, Deborah T. ... Bloomingdale, IL
Gourdine, Isaac J. ... **Washington, DC**
Gourdouros, Peter T. ... Bethesda, MD
Gourlay, Hugh ... Baltimore, MD
Gourlay, John G., Jr. ... **Jackson, MS**
Gourlay, Thomas H., Jr. ... Cincinnati, OH
Gourley, Alan W.H. ... **Washington, DC**
Gourley, B. Craig ... Snohomish, WA
Gourley, Christine L. ... Vancouver, WA
Gourley, Griffin & Gourley, P.A. **Statesville, NC**
Gourley, J. Britton, Jr. ... King Of Prussia, PA
Gourley, J. Britton, P.C. King Of Prussia, PA
Gourley, Jennifer L. ... Washington, DC
Gourley, John B. ... St. Louis, MO
Gourley, John D. ... Dallas, TX
Gourley, John P. ... Mishawaka, IN
Gourley, Keith D. ... **Allentown, PA**
Gourley, Kimbell D. ... **Boise, ID**
Gourley, Lacey L. ... **Austin, TX**
Gourley, Mary Linn Ketron ... Ottumwa, IA
Gourley, Mills & Bodily, A Professional Corporation ... Las Vegas, NV
Gourley, Nancy Glisan ... **Tulsa, OK**
Gourley, R. Vaughn ... Las Vegas, NV
Gourley, Robert H., Jr. ... **Statesville, NC**
Gourley, Robert H., Sr. ... **Statesville, NC**
Gourley & Sallerson ... St. Louis, MO
Gourley, Sara J. ... **Chicago, IL**
Gourley, Steven ... **Los Angeles, CA**
Gourley, William J. ... Valley, NE
Gournis, Dean ... **Chicago, IL**
Gourrier, Joseph M. ... **Houston, TX**
Gourse, Penelope Ball ... Highland, MD
Gourvitz, Elliot H. ... **Springfield, NJ**
Gourvitz, Elliot H., P.A. ... **Elizabeth, NJ**
Newark, NJ
Springfield, NJ
Gourvitz, Evan ... **San Francisco, CA**
Gourwitz and Barr ... **Detroit, MI**
Southfield, MI
Gourwitz, Howard J. ... **Southfield, MI**
Gouse, Irwin S. ... Bronx, NY
Goushian, Jack C. ... Philadelphia, PA
Goushian, Mooradian & Goldsmith, P.C. Philadelphia, PA
Gousman, Rosemary S. ... **Somerset, NJ**
Goussetis, Harry A. ... Columbus, OH
Goutas, Edward M. ... Bellows Falls, VT
Goutier & Partner GbR ... **New York, NY**
New York, NY
Goutman, Elizabeth M. ... Southfield, MI
Goutman, Philip R. ... Southfield, MI
Goutman, Thomas M. ... **Philadelphia, PA**
Goutras, Gust ... Canton, OH

Gouttiere, John P ... Toledo, OH
Gouttiere, John P, Co LPA ... Toledo, OH
Gouveia, Bill L. ... Bridgeport, CT
Gouveia, D. Robin ... New Bedford, MA
Gouveia, Gordon E. ... Merrillville, IN
Gouveia & Miller ... Merrillville, IN
Gouvin, Eric J. ... Springfield, MA
Gouvis, Olympia ... Islandia, NY
Gouwar, James A. ... New York, NY
Gouwens, Kay E. Maassen
Anchorage, AK
Goux, Marjorie M. ... Palo Alto, CA
Gouy, Jean T. ... Alton, IL
Gouyd, Clayton A., Jr. ... Cool, CA
Gouz, Louis ... Coral Gables, FL
Gouze, Philip J. ... Fort Lauderdale, FL
Gouze, Philip J., P.A. ... Fort Lauderdale, FL
Gouzoules, John C. ... Boston, MA
Govaerts, Clifford M. ... Palo Alto, CA
Govaerts, Elizabeth A. ... Lincoln, NE
Govan, Amelia G. ... Washington, DC
Govan, Cynthia A.
Federal Energy Regulatory Commission, Office of the General Counsel, GV
Govan, Derwin B. ... Greenville, MS
Govan, J. Gardner ... Milwaukee, WI
Govan, Reginald C. ... McLean, VA
Govar, Robert J. ... Little Rock, AR
Gove, Gilbert E. ... Detroit, MI
Gove, Mark E. ... Phoenix, AZ
Govendo, Kenneth L. ... Saipan, TT
Govens, Gordon A. ... New York, NY
Gover, Alan Shore ... Houston, TX
Gover, Annmarie Lantz ... Camp Hill, PA
Gover, Frederic ... Dallas, TX
Gover, Kathryn L. ... Cherry Hill, NJ
Gover, Matthew R. ... Harrisburg, PA
Gover, Melanie G. ... St. Paul, MN
Gover, Thom ... Las Vegas, NV
Goverman, George I. ... Cambridge, MA
Govern, Jodi A. ... Columbus, OH
Govern, McDowell & Becker ... Stamford, NY
Govern, Shawn M. ... Milwaukee, WI
Governale, Jack P. ... New York, NY
Governale, Kathleen T. ... Roseland, NJ
Governali, Joseph P. ... White Plains, NY
Governo, David M. ... Boston, MA
Governo and Kavanagh LLP ... Boston, MA
Govert, Gary R. ... Raleigh, NC
Govett, Brett C. ... Dallas, TX
Govi, John F. ... San Rafael, CA
Govi, Joseph R. ... Greensburg, PA
Govier, Pamela Hogenson ... Omaha, NE
Govin, Yasmi ... Miami, FL
Govindan, S. Jay ... Baltimore, MD
Govindji, Rakesh J. ... Salt Lake City, UT
Govlick, E. Joseph ... East Orange, NJ
Govoni, Jeanne M. ... Boston, MA
Govorchin, Anthony Peter ... Lansing, MI
Govostes, Debra L. ... North Reading, MA
Gow, Finlay W. ... Dallas, TX
Gow, James E. ... Endwell, NY
Gow, Keith L. ... Centerville, MA
Gowa, Andrew ... Philadelphia, PA
Gowan, Amy ... Hattiesburg, MS
Gowan, Bill E. ... Wichita Falls, TX
Gowan, Brelend C. ... Sacramento, CA
Gowan, Dee Dee ... Indianapolis, IN
Gowan, Gregory L. ... Corpus Christi, TX
Gowan, James A. ... Central Islip, NY
Gowan, James G. ... Cleveland, OH
Gowan, John Sherman ... Rochester, MN
Gowan, Jos. A. ... New Orleans, LA
Gowan Law Office ... Hattiesburg, MS
Gowan, Robert E. ... Nashville, TN
Gowan, Sheila M. ... New York, NY
Gowan, Stephen L. ... Hattiesburg, MS
Gowan, Susan W. ... San Diego, CA
Gowan, Thomas W. ... New York, NY
Gowan, Timothy L. ... Macon, MS
Gowan, William A., Jr. ... Jackson, MS
Gowans, Arnold D. ... Santa Barbara, CA
Gowda, Amarnath ... Farmington Hills, MI
Gowder, W. Andrew, Jr. ... Charleston, SC
Gowdey, Peter W. ... Washington, DC
Gowdown, David A. ... Dayton, OH
Gowdy, Franklin Brockway
San Francisco, CA
Gowdy, J. David ... Newport Beach, CA
Irving, TX
Gowdy, J. L. ... Oklahoma City, OK
Gowdy, Jonathan S. ... Washington, DC
Gowdy, Robert L. ... Terre Haute, IN
Gowell, John R., Jr. ... Providence, RI
Gowell, Walter R. ... McMinnville, OR
Gowen, Anne Elizabeth ... Boston, MA
Gowen, Bob James ... Jackson, MO
Gowen, Catherine Kurtz
New Brunswick, NJ
Gowen, Edward M. J. ... Silver Spring, MD
Gowen, Ernest L. ... Oak Forest, IL
Gowen, Francis M., Jr. ... Shreveport, LA
Gowen, George W. ... New York, NY
Gowen, Gregory Scott ... Louisville, KY
Gowen, Laura B. ... San Francisco, CA
Gowen, Orrin M. ... Clearwater, FL
Gowen, Peter J. ... Longmont, CO
Gowen, Philip N. ... Little Rock, AR
Gowen & Spears, P.A. ... Clearwater, FL
Gowen, Terence H. ... Calistoga, CA
Gowen, Thomas L., Jr. ... Norristown, PA
Gowen, William H. ... Hackensack, NJ
Gower, Charles A. ... Columbus, GA
Gower, Edward R. ... Springfield, IL
Gower, Harry ... San Francisco, CA
Gower, Harry T. (Chip) ... San Francisco, CA
Gower, Harry T., III ... San Francisco, CA
Gower, John W. ... Dayton, OH
Gower, Richard S. ... Los Angeles, CA
Gower, Robin A. ... Erie, PA
Gower, Saul A. ... Houston, TX
Gowey, Eric A. ... Los Angeles, CA
Gowey, Roy A. ... Coeur d'Alene, ID
Gowie, Renata A. ... Houston, TX
Gowin, Richard Bryan ... Louisville, KY
Gowing, Delmer C., III ... Delray Beach, FL
Gowing, Delmer C., III, P.A.
Delray Beach, FL
Gowing, Judith E. ... Bloomfield Hills, MI
Gowland, Karen E. ... Boise, ID
Gowland, Kimbal L. ... Boise, ID
Gowling, James R. ... Bloomington, MN
Gown, Carol S. ... Seattle, WA
Gownley, Robert T., Jr. ... Scranton, PA
Gowran, Arthur E.
Federal Deposit Insurance Corporation, Professional Liability Section, GV
Goya, Jo Anne E. ... Hilo, HI
Goya, Kenneth T. ... Honolulu, HI
Goya, Lawrence A. ... Honolulu, HI
Goyak & Associates, P.C. ... McMinnville, OR
Portland, OR
Goyak, Nicholas Ivan ... McMinnville, OR
Portland, OR
Goyal, Praveen ... Washington, DC
Goyco, Jose R. ... Ponce, PR
Goyco Covas, Fernando ... San Juan, PR
Goydan, William E. ... Roseland, NJ
Goyer, James L., III ... Birmingham, AL
Goyer, Wilbur L. ... South St. Paul, MN
Goyette, Anne M. Lawlor ... Palo Alto, CA
Goyette, Daniel T. ... Louisville, KY
Goyette, Diane P. ... Rockville, MD
Goyette, Martin H. ... San Francisco, CA
Goyette, Paul J. ... Flint, MI
Goyette, Paul Q. ... Gold River, CA
Goyette, Randall L. ... Lincoln, NE
Goyette, William A. ... Pittsburgh, PA
Goyke, George B. ... Wausau, WI
Goyne, David Michael ... Monterey, CA
Goyne, Roderick A. ... Dallas, TX
Goza, Claude L., Jr. ... Fayetteville, GA
Goza and Hall, P.A. ... Clearwater, FL
Goza, James R. ... Brownsville, TX
Goza, James R., P.C. ... Brownsville, TX
Goza, John W., Jr. ... Chattanooga, TN
Goza, Kirk J. ... Kansas City, MO
Goza, Robert L. ... Jackson, MS
Goza, Samuel S. ... Jackson, MS
Goza, Shelby Duke ... Grenada, MS
Jackson, MS
New Albany, MS
Oxford, MS
Goza, William Brian ... Fort Worth, TX
Goza, William M. ... Clearwater, FL
Gozansky, Nathaniel E. ... Atlanta, GA
Gozdan, Michael P. ... Mount Laurel, NJ
Gozdecki & Del Giudice ... Chicago, IL
Gozdecki, Eugene E. ... Chicago, IL
Gozdecki, Jeanine M. ... South Bend, IN
Gozdziak, Thomas S. ... Chicago, IL
Gozigian, E.W. Garo ... Cooperstown, NY
Gozigian, Edward ... Cooperstown, NY
Gozigian, Washburn & Clinton
Cooperstown, NY
Gozo, Sara J. ... New York, NY
Gozsa, Kimberly L. ... Forked River, NJ
Gozzi, Joanna ... Syracuse, NY
Gozzi, Paul ... Old Saybrook, CT
Graab, George Allen, Jr. ... Lexington, SC
Graae, Steffen W. ... Washington, DC
Graafstra, Thom H. ... Snohomish, WA
Graass, James H. ... Dallas, TX
Grab, Ann Margaret ... York, PA
Grab, Frederick ... Los Angeles, CA
Grab, Michael S. ... Columbia, PA
Lancaster, PA
Graban, David J. ... Hermitage, PA
Graban, Matthew D. ... Cleveland, OH
Grabar, Joshua H. ... Philadelphia, PA
Grabar, Nicolas ... New York, NY
Grabarek, Christopher ... Valparaiso, IN
Grabarek, Robert L., Jr. ... Washington, DC
Grabarek, William C. ... Elburn, IL
Grabarski, Jodie Leigh ... Stillwater, MN
Grabarsky, Susan B. ... Orange, CA
Grabas, Gary ... Bedminster, NJ
Grabau, Charles M. ... Boston, MA
Grabavoy, Denise ... Joliet, IL
Grabavoy, Marie ... Bolingbrook, IL
Grabavoy, Melanie ... Chicago, IL
Grabb & Durando, P.L.C. ... Tucson, AZ
Grabb, Robert M. ... Tucson, AZ
Grabb, Robt. F. ... Minneapolis, MN
Grabb, Thomas F. ... South Bend, IN
Grabbe, John C. ... Atlanta, GA
Grabbe, William Anthony ... Atlanta, GA
Grabe, Timothy ... Portland, OR
Grabel, Drew N. ... New York, NY
Grabel, Jeffry N. ... Albertson, NY
Grabel, Joshua ... Phoenix, AZ
Grabel, Linda J.
Department Of Health And Human Services, Office of the General Counsel, GV
Grabel, Ralph ... Tulsa, OK
Grabel, Ralph Douglas ... Gainesville, FL
Grabel, Richard J. ... New York, NY
Grabel, Scott ... Santa Monica, CA
Southfield, MI
Grabel, Wendy L. ... New York, NY
Grabell, J. Alison ... Los Angeles, CA
Grabell, Matthew Romain
Hackensack, NJ
Grabell, Neal S. ... West Chester, PA
Grabell, Steven S. ... Pennsauken, NJ
Grabelle, Dean ... Princeton, NJ
Grabelle, Jeffrey E. ... Westfield, NJ
Grabelle, Lisa Nass ... Philadelphia, PA
Grabelle, Paul M.
Department Of Veterans Affairs, Office of the General Counsel, GV
Grabelle, Toby ... Oakhurst, NJ
Grabelsky, Richard H. ... Melville, NY
Grabemann, Karl W. ... Chicago, IL
Grabemann, Robert S. ... Chicago, IL
Graben, Eric K. ... Greenville, SC
Graben, Phillip B. ... Madison, MS
Graben, Stephen R. ... Biloxi, MS
Grabenstein, Stephen J. ... Asheville, NC
Grabenstein-Chandler, Jane ... Lincoln, NE
Graber, Allan L. ... Houston, TX
Graber, Arnold S. ... Fort Lee, NJ
Graber & Baldwin ... Beaufort, SC
Graber, Bernard ... Staten Island, NY
Graber, Brent J. ... Chicago, IL
Graber, C. Scott ... Beaufort, SC
Graber, Charles K. ... Philadelphia, PA
Graber, David F. ... Glendale, CA
Graber, Dennis J. ... Belleville, IL
Graber, Elizabeth A. ... Chicago, IL
Graber, Elysa L. ... Washington, DC
Graber, Gale ... Indianapolis, IN
Graber, Garry M. ... Buffalo, NY
Graber, George M. ... Arvada, CO
Graber, George Moore ... Arvada, CO
Graber, Gordon S. ... Morristown, NJ
Graber & Graber ... Arvada, CO
Graber, Herman I. ... New York, NY
Graber, Howard R. ... Stamford, CT
Graber, Jacqueline ... Fort Lee, NJ
Graber, Joel ... New York, NY
Graber, Kathleen M. ... Washington, DC
Graber, Kenneth E. ... Buffalo, NY
Graber Law Firm ... Middlebury, IN
Graber, Matthew J. ... Greenbelt, MD
Graber, Ned W. ... Houston, TX
Graber, Norman L.
National Labor Relations Board, Office of Board Members, GV
Graber, Patrick M. ... Chicago, IL
Graber, Peter H. ... New York, NY
Graber, Peter H. F. ... Greenbrae, CA
Graber, Richard E. ... San Diego, CA
Graber, Richard J. ... Houston, TX
Graber, Richard W. ... Milwaukee, WI
Graber, Robin S. ... New York, NY
Graber, Ronald B. ... New York, NY
Graber, S. Cameron ... Austin, TX
Graber, Samuel G. ... Louisville, KY
Graber, Samuel W. ... Sherman, TX
Graber, Stanley ... New York, NY
Graber, Steve R. ... New York, NY
Graber, Steven W. ... Hutchinson, KS
Graber, Susan P. ... Salem, OR
Graber, Suzanne E. ... Berkeley, CA
Graber, Thea L. ... St. Petersburg, FL
Graber, Theora E. ... Middlebury, IN
Graber, Thomas D. ... Dallas, TX
Graber, Thomas H. ... Wellington, KS
Graber, Thomas H., II ... Greenville, OH
Graber, Timothy J. ... Tonawanda, NY
Graber, Tony D. ... Elkhart, IN
Middlebury, IN
Graber & Watson, L.L.P. ... Sherman, TX
Graber-Lipperman, Peter J.
West Palm Beach, FL
Grabert, Carla F. ... Bakersfield, CA
Grabicki, Anthony E. ... Spokane, WA
Grabicki, Peter J. ... Spokane, WA
Grabiec, Edwin B. ... Joliet, IL
Grabiec, Sherwood P. ... Avoca, PA
Grabiel, Ann Marlow ... St. Paul, MN
Grabill, David ... Santa Rosa, CA
Grabill, Edward M., Jr. ... Northbrook, IL
Grabill & Grabill ... Woodstock, VA
Grabill, Jon G. ... Chicago, IL
Grabill, Michael R. ... Chicago, IL
Grabill, Philip M. ... Woodstock, VA
Grabill, Philip M., Jr. ... Woodstock, VA
Grabino, Amy M. ... New York, NY
Grabino, Eric H. ... New York, NY
Grabino, Harold ... New York, NY
Grabinski, Douglas R. ... Clear Lake, IA
Grabinski Law Firm ... Clear Lake, IA
Grabinski, Matthew L. ... Naples, FL
Grabinski, Thomas D. ... Phoenix, AZ
Grabish, Frances C. ... Philadelphia, PA
Grable, Amy C. ... Fort Lauderdale, FL
Grable, Andrea F. ... Washington, DC
Boston, MA
Grable, Daniel, Law Offices of
Oconomowoc, WI
Grable, Daniel S. ... Oconomowoc, WI
Grable, Harvey R. ... Atlantic Beach, NY
Grable, J. Lee, Jr. ... Dallas, TX
Grable, James W. ... Buffalo, NY
Grable, James W., Jr. ... Buffalo, NY
Grable, Jeffrey R. ... Fort Worth, TX
Grable, Kirk E. ... Indianapolis, IN
Grable, Michael G. ... Washington, DC
Grable, Michele Hallman ... Pendleton, OR
Grable, Paul R. ... Honolulu, HI
Grable, Phillip Lee ... Miami Shores, FL
Grable, Raúl ... New York, NY
Grable, Robert C. ... Fort Worth, TX
Grable, Roger A. ... Irvine, CA
Grable, Thelma J. ... Las Vegas, NV
Grabler, Edrea M. ... Manchester, NH
Grabler, Michael L. ... Roseland, NJ
Grabler, Peter A. ... Boston, MA
Grabner, Michael Eugene ... Panama City, FL
Graboff, Deborah L. ... Los Angeles, CA
Graboff, Marc J. ... Los Angeles, CA
Grabois, Ellen W. ... Houston, TX
Grabois, Marshall L. ... Ambler, PA
Graboski, Edward T.J. ... Altoona, PA
Grabovac, Greg R. ... Columbus, OH
Grabow, Gary L.
South San Francisco, CA
Grabow, John C. ... Victor, ID
Grabow, Laura M. ... Bethesda, MD
Grabow, Leonard J. ... Sun Valley, ID
Grabow, Lewis A. ... Boca Raton, FL
Grabow, Michael D. ... New York, NY
Grabow, Rachel J. ... Cleveland, OH
Grabow, Raymond J. ... Independence, OH
Grabowski, Anna R. ... Edwardsville, IL
Grabowski Associates, P.C. ... Perkasie, PA
Grabowski, Barbara J. ... Pittsburgh, PA
Grabowski, Bernard F. ... Bristol, CT
Grabowski, David A. ... Cherry Hill, NJ
Grabowski, Donald W. ... Lake Forest, IL
Grabowski, Edward Joseph ... Medina, NY
Grabowski, Francis X. ... Perkasie, PA
Grabowski, J. Elizabeth ... Atlanta, GA
Grabowski, James M. ... Warren, MI
Grabowski, Jeffrey A. ... Atlantic City, NJ
Grabowski, Joan B. ... Elkton, MD
Grabowski, Joe Francis, V ... Alton, IL
Grabowski, John B. ... Arlington Heights, IL
Grabowski, Margaret B. ... Janesville, WI
Grabowski, Marianne ... Chicago, IL
Grabowski, Paul A. ... Evanston, IL
Grabowski, Richard J. ... Irvine, CA
Grabowski, Robert P. ... Trenton, NJ
Grabowski, Theodore J., Jr.
Woodland Hills, CA
Grabowski, Theresa C. ... Haddonfield, NJ
Grabowski, Walter T. ... Wilkes-Barre, PA
Grabowski, Walter T., P.C. ... Scranton, PA
Wilkes-Barre, PA
Grabowsky, Fred ... Arlington, VA
Graboyes, Marc Howard ... Denver, CO
Graboyes, Stephanie A. ... Philadelphia, PA
Graboys, George ... Providence, RI
Graboys, Penelope A. ... New York, NY
Grabs, Kimber S. ... King, NC
Grabstein, Richard M. ... San Francisco, CA
Graca, Gary H. ... Troy, MI
Grace, A. Douglas, Jr. ... Fort Myers, FL
Grace, Adam S. ... New York, NY
Grace, Alan J. ... Boston, MA
Grace, Alicia ... Albany, NY
Grace, Anne Elizabeth ... Albany, NY
Grace, Arthur L. ... Lake Ridge, VA
McLean, VA
Grace & Associates ... Huntsville, AL
Grace, Barbara M. ... Westbury, NY
Grace, Brandon, Hollis and Ramirez
Irvine, CA
San Diego, CA
Grace, Brian G. ... Wichita, KS
Grace, Brian V. ... Belleville, KS
Grace, Bruce R. ... Washington, DC
Grace, Carolyn S. ... Boston, MA
Grace, Cecelia A. ... Pasadena, CA
Grace, Charles A. ... Boston, MA
Grace, Charles B. ... Little Rock, AR
Grace, Charles H. ... Westlake, OH
Grace, Charles W. ... San Antonio, TX
Grace, Christopher T., Jr., A Prof. Law Corp.
Metairie, LA
Grace, Christopher T., Jr. ... Metairie, LA
Grace, Claire S. ... Tacoma, WA
Grace, Connie L.
Hot Springs National Park, AR
Grace, Cynthia Anne ... Seattle, WA
Grace, David A. ... Little Rock, AR
Grace, David J. ... Des Moines, IA
Grace, David L. ... Wisconsin Rapids, WI
Grace, David R. ... Washington, DC
Grace, David W. ... Los Angeles, CA
Grace, Deborah L. ... Bloomfield Hills, MI
Grace, E. Maria ... Lynchburg, VA
Grace, Edward D. ... Chicago, IL
Grace, Elizabeth Cary ... Houston, TX
Grace, Eugene P. ... New York, NY
Grace, Eugene R. ... Los Angeles, CA
Grace, F. Michael ... Catonsville, MD
Grace, Frank H., Jr. ... Fairfax, VA
Grace, Frank, Jr. ... Nashville, TN
Grace, Gary K. ... Huntsville, AL
Grace, Genson, Cosgrove & Schirm, A Professional Corporation
Los Angeles, CA
Grace, Gerald, Jr. ... Buffalo, NY
Grace, Gini G. ... Paducah, KY
Grace, J. Christopher ... Boston, MA
Grace, James F. ... Boston, MA
Grace, James L., Jr. ... Manchester, NH
Grace, James M., Jr. ... Houston, TX
Grace, James P. ... Windsor, CT
Grace, James W. ... Tampa, FL
Grace, Jennifer A.T. ... Boston, MA
Grace, Jo-Ann W. ... Los Angeles, CA
Grace, John Philip ... Phoenix, AZ
Grace, John Philip, P.C. ... Phoenix, AZ
Grace, John R. ... Farmington Hills, MI
Grace, John S. ... Swans Island, ME
Grace, John T. ... Denver, CO
Grace, Joseph M. ... Philadelphia, PA
Grace, Kenneth R. ... Westport, CT
Grace, Kevin A. ... Wichita, KS
Grace, Kevin M. ... New Orleans, LA
Grace, L. Ann ... Huntsville, AL
Grace, Lee W. ... Louisville, KY
Grace, Leo F. ... Boston, MA
Grace, Leo Mark, III ... Austin, TX
Grace, Lisa W. ... Malibu, CA
Grace, Manuel G. ... Burbank, CA
Grace, Marilyn H. ... Laguna Hills, CA
Grace, Mark A. ... Pittsburgh, PA

Grace, Martha P. ... Boston, MA
Grace, Michael A. ... Winston-Salem, NC
Grace, Michael A., Jr. ... Baton Rouge, LA
Grace, Michael J. ... Washington, DC
Grace, Michael J. ... Gurnee, IL
Grace, Michael J. ... Boston, MA
Grace, Michael J. ... Yorktown Heights, NY
Grace, Michael J., (Inc.) ... San Diego, CA
Grace, Michael K. ... Los Angeles, CA
Grace, Michael P. ... Seattle, WA
Grace, Nancy L. ... Raleigh, NC
Grace, Nathan M. ... Holden, MA
Grace, Nicholas A. ... Boston, MA
Grace, Ojay M. ... Houston, TX
Grace, P. Michelle ... Houston, TX
Grace, Patricia A. ... Plymouth, MA
Grace, Patricia N. ... Buffalo, NY
Grace, Phyl ... San Diego, CA
Grace, Richard J. ... Binghamton, NY
Grace, Robert J. ... Brighton, MI
Grace, Robert J., Jr. ... Miami, FL
Tampa, FL
Grace, Robert M., Jr. ... Saddle Brook, NJ
Grace, Roger M. R. ... Los Angeles, CA
Grace, Sarah Olin ... Fort Worth, TX
Grace & Sater, L.L.P. ... Los Angeles, CA
Grace, Stephen S. ... Midland, MI
Grace, Stephen W. ... Nashville, TN
Grace, Terrence P. ... Santa Ana, CA
Grace, Thomas E. ... Hoffman Estates, IL
Grace, Thomas G. ... Lexington, KY
Grace, Thomas H. ... Dallas, TX
Grace, Thomas J. ... Metairie, LA
Grace, Thomas P. ... Philadelphia, PA
Grace, Unruh & Pratt, L.C. ... Wichita, KS
Grace, Valerie S. ... Washington, DC
Grace, W. Charles ... Murphysboro, IL
Grace, Walter J., III ... Tucson, AZ
Grace, Walter, Jr. ... Fort Myers, FL
Grace, Ward P. ... West Palm Beach, FL
Grace, Wiliam J., Jr. ... Yorktown Heights, NY
Grace, William B. ... Atlanta, GA
Grace, William F., Jr. ... New Orleans, LA
Grace, William H., (P.A.) ... Fort Myers, FL
Grace, William Lee, Jr. ... Little Rock, AR
Graceffa, John P. ... Boston, MA
Providence, RI
Graceffo, Anthony J. ... Hackensack, NJ
Graceffo, John P. ... Columbus, OH
Gracer, Jeffrey B. ... Roseland, NJ
Gracey, Cynthia Allen ... Delray Beach, FL
Gracey & Davidson ... Silverton, OR
Gracey, Haven ... Sacramento, CA
Gracey, Hugh C., Jr. ... Nashville, TN
Gracey, Jerome B. ... Granby, CT
Gracey, Judith S. ... Lathrup Village, MI
Gracey, Louise Tanner ... Lawrenceville, GA
Gracey, Paul C. ... Troy, MI
Gracey, Roger W. ... Silverton, OR
Gracey, Ruth, Howard, Tate & Sowell
Nashville, TN
Gracey, Stephen N. ... Austin, TX
Gracey, Taras A. ... Chicago, IL
Gracey, Wayne G. ... Westminster, MD
Grach, Brian S. ... Waukegan, IL
Grachuk, Jeanine L.G. ... Boston, MA
Graci, Angelo ... Jamaica, NY
Graci, Robert A. ... Harrisburg, PA
Gracia, Elizabeth ... Manassa, CO
Gracia, Elizabeth Spears ... Parkersburg, WV
Gracia, Jorge E. ... Coral Gables, FL
Gracia, Luis R. ... Port Orange, FL
Gracia, Stephanie Benanti ... Dallas, TX
Gracianette, Cyril J. ... New Orleans, LA
Graciano, Leo P. ... Concord, NH
Gracie, Brooks B., III ... Bethesda, MD
Gracie, Elizabeth L. ... Chicago, IL
Gracier, Jane Ellen ... Lincoln, NE
Gracin, Hank ... Uniondale, NY
Gracki, Phyllis A. ... Springfield, MA
Gracy, Gregory D. ... Dunedin, FL
Gracyalny, Pamela ... Chicago, IL
Gracyalny, Patricia A. ... Washington, DC
Graczyk, Beverly Joan ... Asbury, NJ
Grad, Catharine A. ... New York, NY
Grad, Frank P. ... New York, NY
Grad, Harvey ... Seattle, WA
Grad, J. Stewart ... Woodbridge, NJ
Grad, Jeffrey S. ... Honolulu, HI
Grad, Jeffrey S., A Law Corporation
Honolulu, HI
Grad, Jonathan ... Minnetonka, MN
Grad, Karen A. ... Lincolnwood, IL
Grad, Laura ... San Francisco, CA
Grad, Logan & Klewans, P.C.
Alexandria, VA
Grad, Mary L. ... Sacramento, CA
Grad, Maxine Jo ... Waterbury, VT
Grad, Michael J. ... New Rochelle, NY
Grad, Neil E. M. ... Reno, NV
Grad, Richard J. ... Los Angeles, CA
Grad, Roger A. ... Irvine, CA
Grad, Ruby Udell ... San Francisco, CA
Grad, Sidney H. ... Trenton, NJ
Gradante, Nancy A. ... New York, NY
Graddick & Belser, P.C. ... Mobile, AL
Montgomery, AL
Graddick, Charles A. ... Mobile, AL
Montgomery, AL
Graddis, Albert H. ... Walnut Creek, CA
Graddis, Richard D. ... Los Angeles, CA
Graddock, Christopher J. ... Atlanta, GA
Graddock, Richard A. ... West Palm Beach, FL
Graddy & Adkisson, P.A. ... Conway, AR
Graddy, Chad D. ... Atlanta, GA
Graddy, Josephine Elizabeth
Pembroke Pines, FL
Homerville, GA
Graddy, Larry E. ... Conway, AR
Graddy, W. Henry, IV ... Versailles, KY
Graddy, William L. ... Fort Myers, FL
Grade, Andrew A. ... Portland, OR
Gradel, James D., (P.C.) ... Seattle, WA
Gradel, John N. ... Bensalem, PA
Gradel, Joyce Ford ... Oak Park, IL
Gradel, Richard K. ... Tulsa, OK
Gradel, Robert ... Lampasas, TX
Graden, Leslie Blair ... Dayton, OH
Graden, William T. ... Bloomington, IL
Grader, George L. ... Seattle, WA
Grader, Samuel G. ... Sacramento, CA
Grader, Scott P. ... New York, NY
Gradert, Melvin M. ... Newton, KS
Gradess, Jonathan E. ... Albany, NY
Gradet, Leslie D. ... Annapolis, MD
Gradia, A. Kenneth ... Washington, DC
Gradinger, Edward B ... Encino, CA
Gradisar, Gilbert J. ... Columbus, OH
Gradisar, Nicholas A. ... Pueblo, CO
Gradisar, Stanley J. ... Denver, CO
Gradisar, Trechter, Ripperger, Roth & Croshal ... Pueblo, CO
Gradisek, W. Michael ... Philadelphia, PA
Gradishar, Rudolph L. ... Newport Beach, CA
Gradisher, Michael R. ... Malibu, CA
Gradison, Helen M. ... St. Augustine, FL
Graditor, Susan Blay ... Calabasas, CA
Gradl, Cindy Algase ... Buffalo, NY
Gradl Polowitz & Schwach, LLP
Buffalo, NY
Gradl, Wayne R. ... Buffalo, NY
Gradle, Brian D. ... Washington, DC
Gradman, Arielle A. ... New York, NY
Gradman, Susan J.
Commodity Futures Trading Commission, Division of Enforcement, GV
Grados, Robert J. ... Pittsburgh, PA
Gradoville, Robert T. ... North Haven, CT
Gradoville, Savery M. ... Washington, DC
Gradoville, Steven J. ... Ames, IA
Gradow, Helene M ... Santa Barbara, CA
Gradowski, Richard C. ... New Milford, CT
Gradstein, Donna Luskin
Los Angeles, CA
Gradstein, Henry D. ... Los Angeles, CA
Gradstein, Luskin & Van Dalsem
Los Angeles, CA
Gradstein, Marc ... Burlingame, CA
Gradus, Karina ... Secaucus, NJ
Gradwohl, Alan J. ... Marina Del Rey, CA
Gradwohl, David A. ... Lansdale, PA
Gradwohl, John M. ... Lincoln, NE
Grady, Albert E. ... Brockton, MA
Hyannis, MA
Grady, Amy Darr ... Minneapolis, MN
Grady, Arey Wilson, III ... New Bern, NC
Grady & Associates ... Rocky River, OH
Grady & Associates, Legal Professional Association ... Naples, FL
Grady, Barbara A. ... Rancho Cucamonga, CA
Grady, Barbara E. ... Providence, RI
Grady, Beverly ... Fort Myers, FL
Grady, Brian ... Plymouth Meeting, PA
Grady, C. Wesley ... Hopewell Junction, NY
Grady, Catherine W. ... Des Moines, IA
Grady, Christine S. ... Hartford, CT
Hartford, CT
Grady, Christopher ... Worcester, MA
Grady, Cynthia S. ... Houston, TX
Grady, David F. ... Washington, DC
Grady, Deena Fraley ... Los Angeles, CA
Grady, Donald R., Jr. ... Boston, MA
Grady, Ellen Canan ... McLean, VA
Grady, Francis J. ... Waterbury, CT
Grady, Francis X. ... Rocky River, OH
Grady, Frank T. ... Elizabethtown, NC
Grady, Frederick J. ... Tampa, FL
Grady, Gary A. ... Elizabethtown, NC
Grady, Gil ... Lincoln, NE
Grady, Graham C. ... Chicago, IL
Grady, Gregory ... Washington, DC
Grady & Hampton, P.A. ... Dover, DE
Grady, Henry W. ... Atlanta, GA
Grady, J. Harold ... Baltimore, MD
Grady, James A. ... Pompano Beach, FL
Grady, James D. ... Craig, CO
Steamboat Springs, CO
Grady, James M. ... San Francisco, CA
Grady, Janessa L.
United States Postal Service, Law Department, GV
Grady, Janet M. ... Burbank, CA
Grady, John C. ... Trenton, NJ
Grady, John F. ... Chicago, IL
Grady, John F. ... Chicago, IL
Grady, John H., III ... Atlanta, GA
Grady, John H., Jr. ... Philadelphia, PA
Grady, John J. ... Boston, MA
Grady, John J. ... Cleveland, OH
Grady, John J., P.C., Law Offices of
Boston, MA
Grady, John S. ... Dover, DE
Grady, John V. ... South Yarmouth, MA
Grady, Karla J. ... Cincinnati, OH
Grady, Kathleen S. ... Cleveland, OH
Grady, Keith ... Houston, TX
Grady, Keith J. ... St. Louis, MO
Grady, Kelley A. ... Philadelphia, PA
Grady, Kenneth A. ... Topeka, KS
Grady, Kevin E. ... Atlanta, GA
Grady, Lance S. ... Milwaukee, WI
Grady, Lawrence J., Jr. ... Silver Spring, MD
Grady, Mary E. ... Rutland, VT
Grady, Maureen F. ... New York, NY
Grady, Medelyian R. ... Redmond, WA
Grady, Michael F. ... Fremont, CA
Grady, Michael F. ... White Plains, NY
Grady, Michael J. ... Barberton, OH
Grady, Patricia S. ... Treasury Department, Office of the Comptroller of the Currency, GV
Grady, Patrick J. ... Irvine, CA
Grady, Patrick R. ... Chicago, IL
Grady, Patrick R. ... Cedar Rapids, IA
Grady, Randall D. ... Clayton, MO
Grady, Richard A. ... Brooklyn, NY
Grady & Riley ... Waterbury, CT
Grady, Robert C. ... Miami, FL
Grady, Robert J. ...
Department Of Health And Human Services, GV
Grady, Robert J. ... Racine, WI
Grady, Ryan A. ... Anaheim, CA
Grady, Sandra K. ... Milwaukee, WI
Grady, Schneider & Newman, L.L.P.
Houston, TX
Grady, Scott F. ... Fort Lauderdale, FL
Grady, Scott J. ... Waukesha, WI
Grady, Scott L. ... Los Angeles, CA
Grady, Stafford R. ... Los Angeles, CA
Grady, Steven T. ... Mundelein, IL
Grady, Susan Brown ... Charlotte, NC
Grady, Susan J. ... Solana Beach, CA
Grady, Susan Phillips ... Amherst, MA
Grady, Terrence A. ... Columbus, OH
Grady, Terrence P. ... Lansing, MI
Grady, Thomas ... San Diego, CA
Grady, Thomas C. ... St. Louis, MO
Grady, Thomas F. ... Philadelphia, PA
Grady, Thomas F., III ... Somerville, MA
Grady, Thomas J. ... Springfield, OH
Grady, Thomas J. ... Westerly, RI
Grady, Thomas M. ... Philadelphia, PA
Grady, Thomas Myers ... Kannapolis, NC
Grady, Thomas R. ... Naples, FL
Grady, Timothy E. ... Columbus, OH
Grady, Victoria Lyn ... Buffalo, NY
Grady, William D. ... East Hampton, CT
Grady, William G. ... Middletown, CT
Grady, William H. ... Seattle, WA
Grady, William V. ... Poughkeepsie, NY
Gradzewicz, Andrew M. ... Lawrence, MA
Grae, Arthur H. ... Hastings-On-Hudson, NY
Grae, Fredric R. ... Staten Island, NY
Grae, Joel B. ... New York, NY
Grae, Rybicki & Partners, P.C.
Staten Island, NY
Grae, Seth H. ... New York, NY
Grae, William Henry ... New York, NY
Graebe, Christopher T. ... Raleigh, NC
Graebe, Frederick ... Sacramento, CA
Graeber, Bruce S. ... Brooklyn, NY
Graeber, Charles C. ... Redlands, CA
Graeber & Davis, P.C. ... Quincy, MA
Graeber, Haviva A. ... Albuquerque, NM
Graeber, Jeffrey M. ... Quincy, MA
Graeber, Kenneth H. ... St. Louis, MO
Graeber, Lawrence O., III ... Los Angeles, CA
Graeber, Michael J. ... Wenatchee, WA
Graebner, Carol F. ... Houston, TX
Graebner, Paul M. ... Eugene, OR
Graef, Russell W. ... Garden Grove, CA
Graefe, Anthony S. ... Chicago, IL
Graefe, Frederick H. ... Washington, DC
Graeff, Bereth K. ... Media, PA
Graeff, Cathy Frances ... Reading, PA
Graeff, David J. ... Columbus, OH
Graeff, Duane R. ... Temple, TX
Graeff, Henigan & Dugan, P.C.
Woodstown, NJ
Philadelphia, PA
Graeff, Paul A., Jr. ... Philadelphia, PA
Graeff, Quinn F. ... Richmond, VA
Graeff, Robert J. ... Lee's Summit, MO
Graeff, Stephen D. ... Washington, DC
Graeler, David ... Los Angeles, CA
Graeser, David A. ... Sidney, IA
Graeser, Suzanne S. ... Palo Alto, CA
Graesser, Maria ... San Francisco, CA
Graessle, William S. ... Jacksonville, FL
Graeter, Don C. ... Louisville, KY
Graeter, Richard A., II ... Cincinnati, OH
Graettinger, John A. ... Milwaukee, WI
Graettinger, John S., Jr. ... Chicago, IL
Graettinger, Robert S. ... Chicago, IL
Graev, Lawrence G. ... New York, NY
Graeve, Shurie R. ... Columbus, NE
Graf, Alan Stuart ... Portland, OR
Graf, Alexandra I. ... Greenwich, CT
Graf, Alfred G. ... Potomac, MD
Graf, Allen V. ... Bowling Green, KY
Graf, Andrew D. ... Cincinnati, OH
Graf, Ann B. ... Columbus, OH
Graf, Bayard H. ... Philadelphia, PA
Graf, Bayard M. ... Devon, PA
Graf, Bayard M., P.C. ... Devon, PA
Graf, Brian R. ... Concord, NH
Graf, Carl N., Jr. ... Morton Grove, IL
Graf, Carl N., Jr. and Associates
Morton Grove, IL
Graf, Catherine S. ... Chicago, IL
Graf, Charles E. ... Washington, DC
Graf, Charles J. ... Mequon, WI
Milwaukee, WI
Racine, WI
Graf, David M., (P.A.) ... Little Rock, AR
Graf, Diane L. ... Norwalk, CT
Graf, Diane L., P.A. ... Norwalk, CT
Graf, Don ... Lubbock, TX
Graf, Edward L., Jr. ... Pittsburgh, PA
Graf, Edwin A. ... Sacramento, CA
Graf, Ernest Robert ... Gaithersburg, MD
Graf, Frederick J. ... Tucson, AZ
Graf, George F. ... Brookfield, WI
Mequon, WI
Racine, WI
Graf, Gregory C. ... Denver, CO
Graf, Gregory C., LLC ... Denver, CO
Graf, Henry L. ... Kansas City, MO
Graf, Jack R., Jr. ... Columbus, OH
Graf, Jerry R. ... Las Vegas, NV
Graf, Jessica A. ... Boston, MA
Graf, John E. ... Pittsburgh, PA
Graf, Joseph C. ... Xenia, OH
Graf, Joseph I. ... New York, NY
Graf, Justin ... North Hollywood, CA
Graf, Karen L. ... Oakland, CA
Graf, Kathleen McIlarky ... Columbia, MD
Graf, Kurt M. ... Whittier, CA
Graf, Laura K. ... Minneapolis, MN
Graf, Margaret G. ... Los Angeles, CA
Graf, Margaret O'Reilly
San Francisco, CA
Graf, Marguerite L. ... Washington, DC
Graf, Mark A. ... Los Angeles, CA
Graf, Paul F. ... St. George, UT
Graf, Paul H. ... Baltimore, MD
Graf, Paul J. ... Salt Lake City, UT
Graf, Paul J. ... Bellevue, WA
Graf, Peter G. ... New York, NY
Graf, Richard J. ... Kitty Hawk, NC
Graf, Richard M. ... Washington, DC
Graf, Robert A. ... Fort Wayne, IN
Graf, Ruth E. ... Los Angeles, CA
Graf, Sandra K. ... Mequon, WI
Milwaukee, WI
Racine, WI
Graf, Sheryl S. ... El Cajon, CA
Graf, Wendy L. ... Raleigh, NC
Graf, William R. ... Cincinnati, OH
Graf, Yvonne ... San Diego, CA
Grafals, Anthony Wayne ... Birmingham, AL
Graf-Caswell, Mary Lynn ... Columbus, OH
Grafe, Darren E. ... Federal Way, WA
Grafe, Donna K. ... Victoria, TX
Grafe, Karl J. ... Cincinnati, OH
Grafe, Rodney H. ... Gladstone, OR
Grafe, Victor Gerald ... Albuquerque, NM
Graff, Aaron G., Jr. ... Atlanta, GA
Graff, Alison M. ... Columbus, OH
Graff, Allan ... New York, NY
Graff, Benjamin C. ... Philadelphia, PA
Graff, Benny A. ... Bismarck, ND
Graff, Beth E. ... Glendale, CA
Graff, Caron P. ... Jenkintown, PA
Graff, Christopher L. ... Austin, TX
Graff, Cindy W. ... Pasadena, CA
Graff, David Allen ... Washington, DC
Graff, Debra J. ... Studio City, CA
Graff, Dena R. ... Oakland, CA
Graff, D. G. ... Rhinelander, WI
Graff, Douglas B. ... Paterson, NJ
Graff, Douglas E. ... Columbus, OH
Graff, Edmund D. ... Washington, DC
Graff, F. Thomas, Jr. ... Charleston, WV
Graff, Gary L. ... San Francisco, CA
Graff, George L. ... New York, NY
Graff, Gil ... Los Angeles, CA
Graff, Glenn A. ... Allentown, PA
Graff, Howard ... New York, NY
Graff & Hunt ... Traverse City, MI
Graff, Ilene K. ... New City, NY
Graff, Jack S. ... Saltville, VA
Graff, James R. ... Redding, CA
Graff, Jeffrey D. ... Clifton Springs, NY
Rochester, NY
Graff, Jeffrey Steven ... Westlake Village, CA
Graff, Joan L. ... Basking Ridge, NJ
Graff, Joan Messing ... San Francisco, CA
Graff, John Paul ... Portland, OR
Graff, John R. ... Alexandria, VA
Graff, Kay S. ... Springfield, MO
Graff & Klevan ... Wayland, MA
Graff & Lahey ... St. Louis, MO
Graff, Lisa J. ... Wayland, MA
Graff, M. Christine ... Chicago, IL
Graff, Matthew T. ... Cedar City, UT
Graff, Michael E. ... Kingston, NY
Graff, Michael P. ... New York, NY
Graff, Michael W., Jr. ... Richmond, VA
Graff, Milton B., IV ... Cincinnati, OH
Graff, N. Walter ... Minneapolis, MN
Graff, Noah ... Los Angeles, CA
Graff & O'Neil ... Portland, OR
Graff, Pnina R. ... Beverly Hills, CA
Graff, Randall W. ... Stillwater, MN
Graff, Rex O., Jr. ... Traverse City, MI
Graff, Robert C. ... Palm Beach Gardens, FL
Graff, Robert L. ... Minneapolis, MN
Graff, Robert M. ... Miami, FL
Graff, Robert S. ... McGregor, MN
Graff, Ronald J. ... Standish, ME
Graff, Steven L. ... Canyon Lake, CA
Graff, Steven L., Inc. ... Canyon Lake, CA
Graff, Stuart I. ... Chicago, IL
Graff, Thomas J. ... Oakland, CA
Graff, Tobi E. ... Lincroft, NJ
Graff, Victoria A. ... Los Angeles, CA
Graff, Wayne L. ... Kingston, NY
Graff, Wilbur L. ... Louisville, KY
Graff, William H., Jr. ... York, PA
Graff, William J. ... White Plains, NY
Graffagnino, Gregg J. ... Houma, LA
Graffagnino, Paul C. ... Mountain View, CA
Graffam & Biaggi ... San Juan, PR
Graffam, Keith A. ... San Juan, PR
Graffam, Stephen W. ... Pittsburgh, PA
Graffam, Ward I. ... Portland, ME
Graffam, William A. ... San Juan, PR
Graffam-Rodríguez, Richard M.
San Juan, PR

Graffe, John C., Jr. ... **Seattle, WA**
Graffeo, C. Anthony ... **Birmingham, AL**
Graffeo, Michael G. ... Birmingham, AL
Graffeo, Michael G., Attorney & Counselor, P.C. ... Birmingham, AL
Graffeo, Victoria A. ... Albany, NY
Graffius, Donald M. ... Bedford, PA
Graffius, Terry L. ... **Johnstown, PA**
Graffunder, Steven M. ... **Minneapolis, MN**
Grafman, Lewis A. ... **Philadelphia, PA**
Grafman, Stephen W. ... **Washington, DC**
Grafmiller, Richard A. ... Upper Sandusky, OH
Grafstein, Fred, P.C. ... Deer Park, NY
Grafstein, Freddie ... Deer Park, NY
Grafstein, Howard S. ... Bohemia, NY
Grafstein, Joan C. ... Atlanta, GA
Grafstein, Lisa ... Raleigh, NC
Graft & Cabaniss ... Clinton, OK
Thomas, OK
Graft, C. B. ... Clinton, OK
Thomas, OK
Graft, Dennis D. ... Kendallville, IN
Graft, Jon S. ... Fairfax, VA
Graft, Linda A. ... **Chicago, IL**
Graft & Owen ... Kendallville, IN
Graft, Robert R. ... **Denver, CO**
Graft and Thomson, P.C. ... **Denver, CO**
Englewood, CO
Graft, William C. ... **Chicago, IL**
Grafton, A. Wallace, Jr. ... **Louisville, KY**
Grafton, B. Craig, (P.C.) ... Moline, IL
Grafton, Edward A. ... Grand Haven, MI
Grafton, Joy R. ... New York, NY
Grafton, K. Susan ... **Washington, DC**
Grafton, Richard H. ... **Austin, TX**
Grafton, Samuel R. ... New York, NY
Gragas, Adrian G. ... Lancaster, CA
Grage, Duana J. ... **Minneapolis, MN**
Grage, Elmer C. ... Chicago, IL
Gragel, Susan L. ... **Cleveland, OH**
Gragert, Hiebert & Gray ... **Wichita, KS**
Gragert, Michael D. ... **Wichita, KS**
Gragg, Billy H. ... **Palestine, TX**
Gragg, David S. ... **San Antonio, TX**
Gragg, Joy L. ... **Asheville, NC**
Gragg, K. Lawrence ... **Miami, FL**
Gragg, Walter L. ... Pasadena, CA
Gragg, Walter L., A Law Corporation
Pasadena, CA
Graglia, Florence Carolyn ... Austin, TX
Graglia, Lino A. ... Austin, TX
Graglia-Kostos, Anne ... Danvers, MA
Gragson, James Phillip ... **Topeka, KS**
Gragson, Keith A. ... Greenwood, MS
Grah, Cynthia J. ... Lafayette, IN
Graham, A. Bruce ... Childersburg, AL
Graham, A. Neal ... **Memphis, TN**
Graham, Alan R. ... Greenville, SC
Graham & Albano, P.C. ... **Amherst, MA**
Hadley, MA
Northampton, MA
Graham, Albert M., Jr. ... Santa Ana, CA
Graham, Alexander C., Jr. ... **Richmond, VA**
Graham, Alexander H., Jr. ... **Durham, NC**
Graham, Alice E. ... **San Antonio, TX**
Graham, Alice M. ... Marina Del Rey, CA
Graham, Allen E. ... **Mobile, AL**
Graham, Alma H. ... **Inglewood, CA**
Graham, Amy R. ... **Alexandria, VA**
Graham, Andrew A. ... **Melbourne, FL**
Vero Beach, FL
Graham, Andrew C. ... **Austin, TX**
Graham, Andrew Jay ... **Baltimore, MD**
Graham, Anthony E. ... Mendocino, CA
Graham, Anthony G. ... **Los Angeles, CA**
Graham, Anthony N. ... Santa Fe, NM
Graham & Arceneaux ... **New Orleans, LA**
Graham, Arnold H. ... Brooklyn, NY
Graham, Arnold K. ... **Glendale, CA**
Graham, Arthur ... **Daytona Beach, FL**
Maitland, FL
Graham, Arthur F. ... Tiffin, OH
Graham & Associates, Ltd. ... **Phoenix, AZ**
Graham, Barbara A. ... **McLean, VA**
Graham, Barbara L. ... **St. Louis, MO**
Graham, Barbara R. ... **Rockville, MD**
Graham, Barry W. ... **Washington, DC**
Graham, Barton D. ... New York, NY
Graham, Bernard J. ... Brooklyn, NY
Graham, Bert ... Houston, TX
Graham, Beverly ... Atlantic City, NJ
Graham, Beverly L. ... Corsicana, TX
Graham, Billie J. ... **Laurel, MS**
Graham, Blake M. ... Roseville, MN
Graham, Bothwell F. ... Columbia, SC
Graham, Boyce L. ... **Dallas, TX**
Graham, Brenton G. ... **Los Angeles, CA**
Graham, Bret ... Los Angeles, CA
Graham, Brian ... **Dallas, TX**
Graham, Brian M. ... **Chicago, IL**
Graham, Bright & Smith ... **Dallas, TX**
Graham, Bruce ... Des Moines, IA
Graham, Bruce J. ... **Los Angeles, CA**
Graham, Bruce M., Jr. ... **Fairfax, VA**
Graham, Bruce N. ... **Los Angeles, CA**
Graham, Bruce N. ... **Ventura, CA**
Graham, Bruce W. ... Lafayette, IN
Graham, Bruce W. ... Seattle, WA
Graham, Bryan D. ... **Raleigh, NC**
Graham, Bryan E. ... Bellaire, MI
Graham, C. Barrett ... Morehead City, NC
Graham, Cameron R. ... **Englewood, CO**
Graham, Campaign, P.C. ... **New York, NY**
Graham, Carla ... Southfield, MI
Graham, Carmen A. ... Dickinson, TX
Graham, Carroll R. ... Dallas, TX
Graham, Charles B., Jr.
Lawrenceville, GA
Graham, Charles B., Jr., P.C.
Atlanta, GA
Lawrenceville, GA
Graham, Charles L. ... Moscow, ID
Graham, Charles L., Jr. ... **Gastonia, NC**
Graham, Charles T. ... **Moline, IL**
Graham, Chas. M. ... Lawrence, NY
Graham, Cheryl K. ... **Leesburg, VA**
Vienna, VA
Graham, Chris S. ... **Palo Alto, CA**
Graham, Christine M.
Overland Park, KS
Kansas City, MO
Graham, Christopher ... Jefferson City, MO
Graham, Christopher B. ... New York, NY
Graham, Christopher D. ... Phoenix, AZ
Graham, Christopher D. ... **Providence, RI**
Graham, Christopher F. ... **New York, NY**
White Plains, NY
Graham, Christopher J. ... **Chicago, IL**
Geneva, IL
Graham, Christopher M. ... **Westport, CT**
Graham, Christopher P. ... **Houston, TX**
Graham, Christopher R. ... **Richmond, VA**
Graham, Clark, Jones, Builder, Pratt & Marks ... **Orlando, FL**
Winter Park, FL
Graham, Claudia M. ... Chicago, IL
Graham, Clay P. ... Zanesville, OH
Graham, Clayton A. ... Indianapolis, IN
Graham, Colleen A. ... **New York, NY**
Graham, Colleen Mary ... St. Paul, MN
Graham, Cone, McKinney & Roberts
Mendocino, CA
Graham, Coretta T. ... Houston, TX
Graham, Courtney J. ... **Chambersburg, PA**
Graham, Croley W., Jr. ... Brentwood, TN
Graham, Curtin & Sheridan, A Professional Association ... **Washington, DC**
Morristown, NJ
Trenton, NJ
Graham, Curtis A. ... **Los Angeles, CA**
Graham, Cynthia Newsome
Cherry Hill, NJ
Graham, Cynthia U. ... Carson, CA
Graham, D. Collier, Jr. ... **Jackson, MS**
Graham, D. Jane ... Dallas, TX
Graham, D. Robert ... Tallahassee, FL
Graham, Daniel M. ... Torrance, CA
Graham, Daniel T. ... **Chicago, IL**
Graham, Darrell Elijah ... **Minneapolis, MN**
St. Paul, MN
Graham, Darrell J. ... **Chicago, IL**
Graham, David A. ... Zanesville, OH
Graham, David B. ... **Cleveland, OH**
Graham, David C. ... Grand Junction, CO
Graham, David C., Jr. ... **Magnolia, AR**
Graham, David Eldridge
Department of the Army,
Office of the Judge Advocate General, GV
Graham, David F. ... **Chicago, IL**
Graham, David L. ... Rehoboth, MA
Graham, David, Law Offices of ... Taos, NM
Graham, David Lawrence ... **Columbia, SC**
Graham, David M. ... Toluca Lake, CA
Graham, David P. ... **Minneapolis, MN**
Graham, David R. ... Milpitas, CA
Graham, David T. ... **Columbus, OH**
Graham, Dean C. ... Washington, DC
Graham, Debra A. ... Charleston, WV
Graham, Dennis A. ... **Denver, CO**
Graham, Dolores ... Santa Ana, CA
Graham, Donald A. ... Burlington, VT
White River Junction, VT
Graham, Donald H. ... Gig Harbor, WA
Graham, Donald J. ... **Indianapolis, IN**
Graham, Donald K. ... **Washington, DC**
Graham, Donald L. ... Miami, FL
Graham, Donald L. ... **Hadley, MA**
Quincy, MA
Graham, Donald M. ... Evanston, IL
Graham, Donald P. ... **Butler, PA**
Cranberry Township, PA
Saxonburg, PA
Graham, Donald S. ... **Denver, CO**
Graham, Donna L. ... Memphis, TN
Graham, Doreen A. ... **St. Louis, MO**
Graham, Dorothy J.
United States Postal Service,
Law Department, GV
Graham, Douglas D. ... **Glendora, CA**
Graham, Douglas W. ... Chicago, IL
Graham, Drew S. ... **Hartford, CT**
Graham, Duane A. ... **Mobile, AL**
Graham & Dunn PC ... **Seattle, WA**
Tacoma, WA
Graham, Dye Ann Griffin ... **Orlando, FL**
Graham, E. Diane ... **Fort Smith, AR**
Graham, Edward C. ... Charleston, MO
Graham, Edward H. ... **Newton, IA**
Graham, Edward L. ... **Florence, SC**
Graham, Edward M. ... **Chicago, IL**
Graham, Edward P. ... **Naperville, IL**
Graham, Edward P., Ltd. ... **Naperville, IL**
Wheaton, IL
Graham, Edward T. ... Wheaton, IL
Graham, Edward T., Jr. ... **Taylorville, IL**
Graham, Elizabeth B. ... **Boston, MA**
Graham, Elizabeth P. ... Birmingham, AL
Graham, Emily ... San Francisco, CA
Graham, Eric E. ... Chicago, IL
Graham, Eric J. ... **Boston, MA**
Graham, Ernest S. ... Tacoma, WA
Graham, E. S., Jr. ... Graham, TX
Graham, Felicia B. ... **Washington, DC**
Graham, Frances H. ... Minneapolis, MN
Graham, Frank P. ... **Asheville, NC**
Graham, Franklin T., Jr. ... Brownsville, TX
Graham, Garrett P. ... San Francisco, CA
Graham, Gary L. ... **Missoula, MT**
Graham, Gayle Elaine ... Martinez, CA
Graham, Gena H. ... **Charlotte, NC**
Graham, Gene P. ... Independence, MO
Graham, Gene P., Jr. ... **Independence, MO**
Graham, Geoffrey A. ... Doylestown, PA
Graham, George A., Jr. ... Artesia, NM
Graham, George E. ... Conway, SC
Graham, George G. ... Eustis, FL
Graham, Gerald B. ... Ravenna, OH
Graham, Gerald T. ... Hart, MI
Graham, Gilbert Terry ... San Francisco, CA
Graham, Gina M. ... **Blue Springs, MO**
Graham, Gordon B. ... **Salem, NH**
Graham, Gordon E. ... Woodstock, IL
Graham, Gordon J. ... Los Angeles, CA
Graham, Gordon L. ... Berkeley, CA
Graham and Graham ... **Chambersburg, PA**
Graham and Graham, Ltd.
Springfield, IL
Graham, Graham & Sbertoli, Ltd.
Libertyville, IL
Graham & Graham, Stubbins, Lewis, Watson & Erhard Co., L.P.A. ... New Lexington, OH
Zanesville, OH
Graham, Gregory B. ... Little Rock, AR
Graham, Gregory S. ... Childersburg, AL
Graham, Gregory S. ... Dallas, TX
Graham, Greta J. ... San Ramon, CA
Graham, Gretchen A. ... **Seattle, WA**
Graham, H. Dillon, III ... **Miami, FL**
Graham, H. Dillon, III, P.A. ... **Miami, FL**
Graham, H. Steven ... **Kansas City, MO**
Graham, Hardy M. ... Union City, TN
Graham, Hardy P. ... Meridian, MS
Graham, Harlan W. ... Manhattan, KS
Graham, Harold G., Jr. ... Birmingham, AL
Graham, Harrell M. ... **Columbia, SC**
Graham, Harry C. ... New Orleans, LA
Graham, Heather Rickett
Los Angeles, CA
Graham, Heather W. ... La Grange, GA
Graham, Heidel E. ... **Chicago, IL**
Graham, Henry H., Jr. ... Jacksonville, FL
Graham, Henry J. ... **Tallahassee, FL**
Graham, Henry T., Jr. ... St. Amant, LA
Graham, Herbert ... Sherman Oaks, CA
Graham, Herta R. ... Philadelphia, PA
Graham, Howard L. ... Tacoma, WA
Graham, Hugh J., III ... **Springfield, IL**
Graham, Hugh Z., Jr. ... Charleston, SC
Graham, J. Douglas ... Campton, KY
Graham, J. Hatcher ... Warner Robins, GA
Graham, J. Mark ... **Houma, LA**
Graham, J. Nicole ... Mountain Home, AR
Graham, J. Patton ... Marion, VA
Graham, J. Susan ... **Los Angeles, CA**
Graham, J. Tyson ... **Columbus, MS**
Graham, Jack H. ... Salem, OR
Graham, James A. ... Barrington, RI
Graham, James C. ... **Hartford, CT**
Southport, CT
Graham, James D. ... **Cleveland, OH**
Graham, James E. ... Brunswick, GA
Graham, James E. ... Ames, IA
Graham, James F. ... **Norristown, PA**
Graham, James J. ... **Washington, DC**
Graham, James K. ... Troy, MI
Graham, James K. ... Arlington, TX
Graham, James K., Inc. ... Arlington, TX
Graham, James L. ... Titusville, FL
Graham, James L. ... Columbus, OH
Graham, James Lee ... Yadkinville, NC
Graham & James LLP ... **Costa Mesa, CA**
Los Angeles, CA
Palo Alto, CA
Sacramento, CA
San Francisco, CA
San Jose, CA
Washington, DC
New York, NY
Graham & James LLP/Riddell Williams P.S.
Seattle, WA
Graham, James M. ... Sacramento, CA
Graham, James M. ... Boston, MA
Graham, James N. ... **Madison, WI**
Graham, James S. ... **San Diego, CA**
Graham, James T. ... Fenwick, CT
Graham, Jamie L. ... Norcross, GA
Graham, Jan ... Salt Lake City, UT
Graham, Jane H. ... **Bellevue, WA**
Graham, Janet A. ... Schenectady, NY
Graham, Janet Capurro ... Pleasanton, CA
Graham, Janet M. ... Lexington, KY
Graham, Jason ... **Dallas, TX**
Graham, Jason W. ... **Atlanta, GA**
Graham, Jeffrey A. ... Santa Monica, CA
Graham, Jeffrey M. ... **Little Rock, AR**
Graham, Jeffrey M. ... Colorado Springs, CO
Graham, Jeffrey M., P.A. ... **Little Rock, AR**
Graham, Jeffrey S. ... Poughkeepsie, NY
Graham, Jeffrey S., P.C. ... Poughkeepsie, NY
Graham, Jeffrey T. ... Lansing, MI
Graham, Jennifer F. ... Washington, DC
Graham, Jerome J., Jr. ... **Morristown, NJ**
Graham, Jesse E. ... **Winter Park, FL**
Graham, Jesse E., Jr. ... **Winter Park, FL**
Graham, Jesse J., II ... **Uniondale, NY**
Graham, Joanne L. ... Lee's Summit, MO
Graham, Joel M. ... **New York, NY**
Graham, John ... Bonita Springs, FL
Graham, John ... Princeton, NJ
Graham, John A. ... **Los Angeles, CA**
Graham, John A. ... Ocala, FL
Graham, John A. ... **Schaumburg, IL**
Graham, John C. ... Zanesville, OH
Graham, John C., III ... **Kitty Hawk, NC**
Graham, John F.
Treasury Department, GV
Graham, John G. ... Parsippany, NJ
Graham, John H. ... Scottsboro, AL
Graham, John J. ... Bridgeport, CT
Graham, John J. ... Boston, MA
Graham, John, Jr. ... Kansas City, MO
Graham, John K. ... Phoenix, AZ
Graham, John K. ... **Boston, MA**
Graham, John L. ... New York, NY
Graham, John M. ... **Birmingham, AL**
Graham, John M., III ... **Rome, GA**
Graham, John M., Jr. ... Lake Success, NY
Graham, John S. ... San Rafael, CA
Graham, John S., III ... **Washington, DC**
Graham, John T. ... **Fairfax, VA**
Graham, John W. ... Canton, NY
Graham, Jonathan P. ... **Washington, DC**
Graham, Joseph M., Jr. ... **Los Angeles, CA**
Graham, Joseph P. ... **Prescott, AR**
Graham, Joseph V. ... Huntsville, OH
Graham, Judith E.
Environmental Protection Agency,
Program Office Attorneys, GV
Graham, Jul Elliot ... New York, NY
Graham, K. Scott ... Chattanooga, TN
Graham, Kate ... Olympia, WA
Graham, Kathleen ... Williamsport, PA
Graham, Kathleen Elizabeth ... Columbus, OH
Graham, Kathleen H.
Oklahoma City, OK
Graham, Kathleen M. ... Highland Park, MI
Graham, Kathleen M. ... Minneapolis, MN
Graham, Kathryn ... **Phoenix, AZ**
Graham, Kathy T. ... Salem, OR
Graham, Keith A. ... **Orlando, FL**
Graham, Keith E. ... Naperville, IL
Graham, Kelsey D. ... **New York, NY**
Graham, Ken J. ... **Lawton, OK**
Graham, Kenneth A. ... Bridgeport, CT
Graham, Kenneth E., Jr. ... Los Angeles, CA
Graham, Kenneth J. ... St. Louis, MO
Graham, Kenneth K. ... Tucson, AZ
Graham, Kent M. ... Cuyahoga Falls, OH
Graham, Kent V. ... **Los Angeles, CA**
Graham, Kevin D. ... **Mobile, AL**
Graham, Kevin H. ... **Tampa, FL**
Graham, Kevin R. ... **San Diego, CA**
Graham, Kimberly Anne ... Hartford, CT
Graham & Krenz, L.L.P. ... Dickinson, TX
Graham, L. Dale ... Taylorsville, NC
Graham, L. Wallace ... **San Rafael, CA**
Graham, L. William ... **Gainesville, FL**
Graham, Larry G. ... Long Beach, CA
Graham, Laura M. ... Topeka, KS
Graham, Laura P. ... Jacksonville, NC
Graham Law Firm, The ... **St. Louis, MO**
Graham Law Firm, The, A Professional Corporation ... **Des Moines, IA**
Graham, Lawrence D. ... Seattle, WA
Graham, Lawrence E. ... **Trenton, NJ**
Graham, Lawrence O. ... Pleasanton, CA
Graham, Lawrence S. ... **New York, NY**
Graham, Lenore Templeton
Oklahoma City, OK
Graham, Leo J. ... **Redding, CA**
Graham, Lewis W. ... Encino, CA
Graham, Linda M. ... Las Vegas, NV
Graham, Linda S. ... Manhattan, KS
Graham, Lindsey O. ... Seneca, SC
Graham, Lisa Howell ... **Athens, GA**
Graham, Lisa M. ... Vancouver, WA
Graham, Liza Shawn ... **Chicago, IL**
Graham, Lloyd R. ... Junction City, KS
Graham, Loren ... Stateline, NV
Graham, Lowell ... Torrance, CA
Graham, Lynsey N. ... **Washington, DC**
Graham, M. Elizabeth ... **San Francisco, CA**
Graham, Margaret A. ... Topeka, KS
Graham, Margaret E. ... **Chicago, IL**
Graham, Marie Elena ... **Richmond, VA**
Graham, Marjorie Gadarian
Palm Beach Gardens, FL
Graham, Marjorie Gadarian, P.A.
Palm Beach Gardens, FL
West Palm Beach, FL
Graham, Mark D. ... **New York, NY**
Graham, Mark E. ... Panama City, FL
Graham, Mark Patrick ... **Vienna, VA**
Graham, Mark R. ... **Abingdon, VA**
Graham, Mark S. ... **Knoxville, TN**
Graham, Marshall P. ... Corpus Christi, TX
Graham, Marvin G. ... Pulaski, VA
Graham, Mary Anne ... **Myrtle Beach, SC**
Graham, Mary B. ... **Wilmington, DE**
Graham, Mary Caryn
Department Of Veterans Affairs,
Board of Veterans Appeals, GV
Graham, Mary Frances ... **Crossville, TN**
Graham, Mary M. ... La Grange, IL
Graham, Mather D. ... **Rome, GA**
Graham, Matthew F. ... **Oakland, CA**
Graham, Matthew T. ... Tacoma, WA
Graham, Maurice ... Oakland Park, FL
Graham, Maurice B. ... **St. Louis, MO**
Graham, Maurice W. ... Minnetonka, MN
Graham, Max W. J., Jr. ... **Lihue, HI**
Graham, Maxine Yvette ... **New York, NY**
Graham & Mayer ... New Orleans, LA
Graham & McCollum, P.C. ... Scottsboro, AL
Graham, Michael A. ... **Phoenix, AZ**
Graham, Michael A. ... **Los Angeles, CA**
Graham, Michael A. ... **Montclair, NJ**
Graham, Michael E. ... **Truckee, CA**
Reno, NV
Graham, Michael H. ... Coral Gables, FL
Graham, Michael H. ... **Savannah, GA**
Graham, Michael J. ... Hartford, CT

Graham, Michael J. ....Camp Springs, MD
Graham, Michael Lynn ....Dallas, TX
Graham, Michael Paul ....Houston, TX
Graham, Michael R. ....Encino, CA
Graham, Michael R. ....Chicago, IL
Graham, Michael R. ....Libertyville, IL
Graham, Michael T. ....Chicago, IL
Graham, Michelle B. ....San Diego, CA
Graham, Michelle M. ....New York, NY
Graham, Moletteire, Tuttle & Torpy, P.A.
Melbourne, FL
Vero Beach, FL
Graham Moody & Sox ....Tallahassee, FL
Graham, Morgan G. ....Buffalo, NY
Graham, Nancy Malley
West Palm Beach, FL
Graham, Nathan G. ....Arapaho, OK
Graham, Neal B. ....Macon, GA
Graham, Neil E. ....Washington, DC
McLean, VA
Graham, Nicholas J. ....Niles, OH
Graham, Norman W. ....Louisville, KY
Graham, Oakley J., Jr. ....Richmond, VA
Graham, P. Jewel ....Yellow Springs, OH
Graham, Patricia D. ....Department of Energy, Office of the General Counsel, GV
Graham, Patricia M. ....Princeton, NJ
New York, NY
Graham, Paul A. ....Salem, OR
Graham, Paul T. ....Jefferson City, MO
Graham, Paula N. ....San Diego, CA
Graham, Peter C. ....Kingston, NY
Graham, Peter D. ....St. Petersburg, FL
Graham, Peter J. ....Port Jefferson, NY
Graham, Philip C. ....St. Louis, MO
Graham, Philip L., Jr. ....New York, NY
Graham, R. Norvell, Jr. ....San Antonio, TX
Graham, R. Van ....Tyler, TX
Graham, R. Van, P.C. ....Tyler, TX
Graham, R. William ....Dayton, OH
Oklahoma City, OK
Graham, Rachel H.
Securities and Exchange Commission, Office of the General Counsel, GV
Graham, Ralph J. ....Corpus Christi, TX
Graham, Raymond A. ....Sarasota, FL
Graham, Rebecca A. ....Clearwater, FL
Graham, Rebecca E. ....Anchorage, AK
Graham, Richard ....Los Angeles, CA
Graham, Richard A.
Pension Benefit Guaranty Corporation, Office of the General Counsel, GV
Graham, Richard C. ....Columbus, OH
Graham, Richard J. ....Lowville, NY
Graham, Richard K. ....Cincinnati, OH
Graham, Richard M. ....Midland, TX
Graham, Richard N. ....Englewood, CO
Graham, Richard N., P.C. ....Englewood, CO
Graham, Richard S. ....Daytona Beach, FL
Graham, Richard W. ....Mill Valley, CA
Graham, Rick J. W. ....Dallas, TX
Graham, Robert ....Denver, CO
Graham, Robert A. ....Washington, DC
Graham, Robert A., Jr. ....Pasadena, CA
Graham, Robert Bruce, Jr. (A Law Corporation) ....Honolulu, HI
Graham, Robert C. ....Las Vegas, NV
Graham, Robert C., III ....St. Louis, MO
Graham, Robert D. ....Stamford, CT
Graham, Robert D. ....Garland, TX
Graham, Robert E. ....Wenatchee, WA
Graham, Robert E., Jr.
Chambersburg, PA
Graham, Robert F. ....San Diego, CA
Graham, Robert H. ....Farmington, NM
Graham, Robert H., P.C. ....Farmington, NM
Graham, Robert L. ....Los Angeles, CA
Graham, Robert L. ....Chicago, IL
Graham, Robert M.
West Palm Beach, FL
Graham, Robert M. ....Florham Park, NJ
Graham, Robert M. ....Salt Lake City, UT
Graham, Robert P. ....Zanesville, OH
Graham, Robert T. ....Pensacola, FL
Graham, Robt. S. ....Jackson, MS
Graham, Roderick D. ....Birmingham, AL
Graham, Roger D. ....Marietta, GA
Graham, Roger D. ....Oklahoma City, OK
Graham, Roland D. ....Minneapolis, MN
Graham, Ron ....Mentor, OH
Graham, Ronald F. ....Bloomfield Hills, MI
Graham, Russell R. ....Austin, TX
Graham, Ruth E. ....Topeka, KS
Graham, Samuel R. ....Austin, TX
Graham & Schewe ....Fairfax, VA
Graham, Scott ....Kalamazoo, MI
Graham, Scott B. ....St. Cloud, MN
Graham, Scott L. ....Broken Arrow, OK
Graham & Segrest ....Columbus, MS
Graham, Seldon B., Jr. ....Austin, TX
Graham, Seymour C. ....Hazleton, PA
Graham, Sharie K. ....New York, NY
Graham, Sharon ....New York, NY
Graham, Shaun E. ....Fort Wayne, IN
Graham, Sherry L. ....Plymouth, MN
Graham, Smith & Lindquist, L.L.P.
Dallas, TX
Graham, Stanford A. ....Ogden, UT
Graham, Stanley E. ....Nashville, TN
Graham, Stanley P. ....Los Angeles, CA
Graham, Stephanie M. ....Evanston, IL
Graham, Stephen B. ....Petoskey, MI
Graham, Stephen M. ....Seattle, WA
Graham, Stephens & McMorrow
Westbury, NY
Graham, Steve R. ....Florence, AL
Graham, Steven A. ....Nashville, NC
Graham, Steven D. ....St. Louis, MO
Graham, Steven J. ....Fort Worth, TX
Graham, Steven T. ....Irvine, CA
Graham, Steven V. ....Birmingham, AL
Graham, Stuart W. ....Boston, MA
Graham, Susan ....Long Beach, CA
Graham, Susan B. ....Irving, TX
Graham, Susan E. ....Irvine, CA
Graham, Susan M. ....Boise, ID
Graham, Susan Weatherford
Birmingham, AL
Graham, T. Andrew ....Atlanta, GA
Graham, T. Malcolm ....Jacksonville, FL
Graham, Tami L. ....Plano, TX
Graham, T. D. ....Chapel Hill, NC
Graham, Terese L. ....Lansing, MI
Graham, Theodore W. ....San Diego, CA
Graham, Thomas A., III
Fort Lauderdale, FL
Graham, Thomas D. ....Jefferson City, MO
Graham, Thomas E. ....Winston-Salem, NC
Graham, Thomas E., Jr. ....Washington, IN
Graham, Thomas H. ....Detroit Lakes, MN
Graham, Thomas J. ....Washington, DC
Graham, Thomas J. ....Westbury, NY
Graham, Thomas J., Jr. ....Eau Claire, WI
Graham, Thomas P. ....Seattle, WA
Graham, Thomas R. ....Washington, DC
Graham, Thomas W. ....Jasper, TN
Graham, Timothy H. ....Charlotte, NC
Graham, Timothy J. ....Seattle, WA
Graham, Timothy R. ....New York, NY
Graham, Tony M. ....Tulsa, OK
Graham, Toya Alek ....Arlington, MA
Graham, V. Ellen ....Dayton, OH
Graham, Vicki Trammell ....Macon, GA
Graham, W. Arthur ....Missoula, MT
Graham, W. Robb ....Cherry Hill, NJ
Graham, W. Thomas ....Monroe, MI
Graham, Walter ....Richmond, VA
Graham, Walter E. ....Boston, MA
Graham, Ward P. ....Amesbury, MA
Graham, Warren D. ....Tulsa, OK
Graham, Warren R. ....New York, NY
Graham, Waylon ....Panama City, FL
Graham, Wayne E., Jr. ....Canton, OH
Graham, William ....Bellevue, WA
Graham, William A. ....Columbia, TN
Graham, William A., III ....Sparta, NC
Graham, William B. ....Tallahassee, FL
Graham, William E., Jr. ....Raleigh, NC
Graham, William G. ....Scotland Neck, NC
Graham, William H. ....Bethlehem, PA
Graham, William J. ....Islandia, NY
Graham, William L. ....Frankfort, KY
Graham, William M. ....Libertyville, IL
Graham, William M. ....Salisbury, NC
Graham, William N. ....Tallahassee, FL
Graham, William Nelson .....Hattiesburg, MS
Graham, William T. ....Raleigh, NC
Graham, William W. ....Des Moines, IA
Graham, William W. ....Manasquan, NJ
Graham, W. K. ....Houston, TX
Graham-Bergin, Anne C. ....Tucson, AZ
Grahame, Christina ....Napa, CA
Grahame, Heather H. ....Anchorage, AK
Graham-Hurd, Melissa ....Akron, OH
Graham-Oliver, Heather D. ....Cleveland, OH
Grahek, David B. ....Baltimore, MD
Grahl, Christine H. ....Chicago, IL
Grahn, Barbara J. ....Minneapolis, MN
Grahn, Charles R. ....Indianapolis, IN
Grahn, David M. ....Napoleon, OH
Grahn, David P. ....Department of Agriculture, Office of the General Counsel, GV
Grahn, Frederick S. ....Chicago, IL
Grahn and Grahn ....Indianapolis, IN
Grahn, Kathleen Mears ....Mount Holly, NJ
Grahn, Raymond J. ....Indianapolis, IN
Grahn, Richard J. ....Boston, MA
Grahn, Thomas B. ....Yakima, WA
Grahovac, John E. ....Brookfield, WI
Racine, WI
Grahovac, Paul T. ....Idaho Falls, ID
Grai, Mark J. ....Memphis, TN
Graif, Jay R. ....Scottsdale, AZ
Graif, Michael R. ....New York, NY
Graifman, Brian D. ....New York, NY
Graifman, Gary S. ....Montvale, NJ
Spring Valley, NY
Grail, Efrem M. ....Pittsburgh, PA
Grain, Jennifer S. ....St. Paul, MN
Grain, Peter S. ....Hoffman Estates, IL
Grain, Peter S., Law Offices of, & Associates, Ltd. ....Hoffman Estates, IL
Graine, Robin L. ....Annandale, VA
Grainer, Caryn S. ....Hollywood, FL
Grainer, Caryn S., P.A. ....Hollywood, FL
Graines, Stuart J. ....Cleveland, OH
Grainey, Bernard F. ....Helena, MT
Grainey, Michael W. ....Salem, OR
Grainey, Philip J. ....Polson, MT
Ronan, MT
Grainger, Amanda R. ....Dallas, TX
Grainger, Andrew R. ....Boston, MA
Grainger, Catherine M. ....Denver, CO
Grainger, Charles E., Jr. ....Montgomery, AL
Grainger, D. W. ....Phoenix, AZ
Grainger, Edmund C., III
White Plains, NY
Grainger, Edmund C., Jr. ....New York, NY
Grainger, Gates E. ....Charlotte, NC
Grainger, Jeffrey D. ....St. Augustine, FL
Grainger, Jeffry J. ....Redwood City, CA
Grainger, Jerald P. ....San Mateo, CA
Grainger, Richard E. ....Wellesley, MA
Grainger, Richard, Law Offices of
Tyler, TX
Grainger, Terri Silver ....Houston, TX
Grainy, Eleanor Jean ....Ottawa, IL
Grais, Adam ....Chicago, IL
Grais, David J. ....New York, NY
Grais, Ronald B. ....Chicago, IL
Graitge, Kathryn ....Las Vegas, NV
Graiwer, Manuel P., Law Offices of
Los Angeles, CA
Grajales, Donald ....Brooklyn, NY
Grajczyk, Gregory P. ....Milbank, SD
Grajeda, Paul F. ....El Paso, TX
Grajeda, Sandra ....Moreno Valley, CA
Grajewski, Sigmund A. ....Staten Island, NY
Grajewski, Wayne S. ....Los Angeles, CA
Grajski, Mark P. ....Sacramento, CA
Grakal, Bruce V. ....Santa Monica, CA
Grakal, Root & Rosenthal
Santa Monica, CA
Gral, Donald J. ....Milwaukee, WI
Gral, Michael A. ....Milwaukee, WI
Grala, Bronislaw E. ....New York, NY
Gralapp, Wesley J. ....Alexandria, LA
Gralen, Donald J. ....Chicago, IL
Gralen, Kimberly Kentra
Western Springs, IL
Gralen, Mark E. ....Chicago, IL
Gralewski, Anthony F. ....Jersey City, NJ
Gralewski, Kelly A. ....San Diego, CA
Gralicer, Richard ....Scarsdale, NY
Gralitzer, Allen M. ....New York, NY
Grall, Bernard F., Jr. ....Vero Beach, FL
Grall, Fanaro & Glenn ....Vero Beach, FL
Grall, Jane ....Trenton, NJ
Grall, John G. ....Binghamton, NY
Gralla, Maurice B. ....Cocoa Beach, FL
Gralley, Kevin G. ....Baltimore, MD
Gralnek, Donald D. ....Los Angeles, CA
Gralnek, Gaelle H. ....Los Angeles, CA
Gralow, William P. ....Albuquerque, NM
Graly, Daniel M. ....Fort Wayne, IN
Gram, Chresten J. ....Portland, OR
Gram, Christopher D. ....Minneapolis, MN
Gram, Frederick J. ....Olean, NY
Gram, H. James ....Grosse Pointe Farms, MI
Gram, John A. ....Gainesville, GA
Gram, Joseph P. ....Greensboro, NC
Gram, Laurence C., Jr. ....Milwaukee, WI
Gram, Mary E. ....Los Angeles, CA
Gram, Richard E. ....Pueblo, CO
Gram, Stacie K. ....Overland Park, KS
Gram, Thomas J. ....Emeryville, CA
Gram, William H. ....Chicago, IL
Gramann, Margaret L. ....Columbus, OH
Grambling & Grambling, L.L.P.
El Paso, TX
Grambling, John A. ....El Paso, TX
Grambling, Randolph H. ....El Paso, TX
Grambow, Martin E. ....Washington, DC
Gramc, Daniel F. ....Pittsburgh, PA
Gramelspacher, Mark B. ....Denver, CO
Gramenopoulos, C. Gregory
Washington, DC
Gramenos, James N. ....Chicago, IL
Gramer, Gary W., & Associates
Lake Grove, NY
Grames, Conan P. ....Princeton, NJ
Gramhofer, Jon L. ....Shaftsbury, VT
Gramigna, Edward A., Jr.
Florham Park, NJ
Gramigna, Elizabeth Watson
Springfield, NJ
Graminski, Gary J. ....McMurray, PA
Gramitt, Jason M. ....Providence, RI
Gramke, Donald J. ....St. Louis, MO
Graml, Charles E. ....Houston, TX
Graml, John A. ....Houston, TX
Graml, John, & Associates, P.C.
Houston, TX
Graml, Nancy ....Houston, TX
Gramley, Lori R. ....Scranton, PA
Gramlich, Charles J. ....Springfield, IL
Gramlich, Dean C. ....Chicago, IL
Gramlich, George A. ....Fort Ann, NY
Gramlich, Harvatin & Lanterman, P.C.
Springfield, IL
Gramlich, Larry E. ....Atlanta, GA
Gramlich, Raymond ....Oklahoma City, OK
Gramlich, Richard C. ....Phoenix, AZ
Gramlich, William E. ....Philadelphia, PA
Gramling, Christopher P.
Kansas City, MO
Gramling, Frank R., (P.A.)
Fort Lauderdale, FL
Gramling, George F., III (P.A.)
Tampa, FL
Gramling, James Douglas
Fayetteville, AR
Gramling, James F., Jr ....Jonesboro, AR
Gramling, Kevin J. ....San Diego, CA
Gramling, Laura A. ....Milwaukee, WI
Gramling, Mitzi Tousman ....St. Paul, MN
Gramling Lopez, Jo Willa ....New York, NY
Gramm, Classen ....San Diego, CA
Gramm, Frank G. ....Lake Forest, IL
Gramm, JoAnn Leigh ....Linwood, NJ
Grammas, George N. ....Washington, DC
Grammas, Peter A. ....Birmingham, AL
Grammatico, Claude N. ....Garden City, NY
Grammer, Bill ....Myrtle Beach, SC
Grammer, David A., III
Albuquerque, NM
Grammer, Elisa J. ....Washington, DC
Grammer, Elizabeth A. ....Waltham, MA
Grammer, Joseph F., III ....Panama City, FL
Grammer Kissel Robbins Skancke & Edwards ....Washington, DC
Grammer Law Firm, P.C.
Myrtle Beach, SC
Grammer, Susan F. ....Bethalto, IL
Grammig, Laurel Lenfestey ....Tampa, FL
Grammig, Robert J. ....Tampa, FL
Gramoglia, Margaret B. ....Kennesaw, GA
Gramovot, Larry I. ....Tampa, FL
Grampp, Glenn A. ....Evansville, IN
Grams, Darrell M., (P.C.) ....Dallas, TX
Houston, TX
Grams, David F. ....Madison, WI
Grams, David F. & Associates, S.C.
Madison, WI
Grams, John F. ....Chicago, IL
Gramstrup, Chris A. ....Superior, WI
Gramzow, Kirsten E. ....Pontiac, MI
Gran, Austin B. ....Pensacola, FL
Gran, James M. ....Newton, IA
Gran, Judith Abbott ....Philadelphia, PA
Gran, Martin R. ....San Francisco, CA
Grana, Diana D. ....Miami, FL
Grana, Paul A. ....St. Louis, MO
Grana, Paul A., P.C. ....St. Louis, MO
Grana, Stephanie E. ....Richmond, VA
Granaada, Michele K. ....San Mateo, CA
Granack, Thomas C. ....Munster, IN
Granade, Fred K. ....Bay Minette, AL
Daphne, AL
Foley, AL
Granade, Gaines C. ....Atlanta, GA
Granade, Ginny S. ....Mobile, AL
Granade, Lars T. ....Mobile, AL
Granade, Phyllis F. ....Atlanta, GA
Granader, Gary ....Southfield, MI
Granader, Jill R. ....Bethesda, MD
Granader, Kevin T. ....Southfield, MI
Granadier, Roberta P.
Bloomfield Hills, MI
Granado, John ....Brookfield, IL
Granado, Rafael E. ....Miami, FL
Granados, Elizabeth ....Chicago, IL
Granados, Luis L., III ....Washington, DC
Granados, Melody ....Dallas, TX
Granados, Michael D. ....San Antonio, TX
Granados, Patricia D. ....Washington, DC
Granados, Raul R. ....Montebello, CA
Granafei, Dinah Lee ....Santa Ana, CA
Granafei, Robert M. ....Orange, CA
Granahan, Colleen M. ....Boston, MA
Granahan, Eileen Francine ....Bradenton, FL
Tampa, FL
Granahan, Kathleen M. ....Philadelphia, PA
Granahan, Patricia ....Cambridge, MA
Granahan, Sean T. ....New York, NY
Granahan, Thomas F.
United States Court Of Appeals For The Armed Forces, GV
Granahan, Thomas F. ....Tampa, FL
Granahan, Thomas F., P.A. ....Tampa, FL
Granas, Justine L. ....Woodland Hills, CA
Granas, Morton A. ....Woodland Hills, CA
Granat, Andrew L. ....St. Louis, MO
Granat, Jeffrey A. ....Garden City, NY
Granat, Jill M. ....Miami, FL
Granat, Kenneth H. ....Riverwoods, IL
Granat & McKee ....St. Louis, MO
Granat, Mitchell W. ....Mineola, NY
Granat, Peter M. ....Kansas City, MO
Granat, Richard S. ....Columbia, MD
Granat, Richard S. & Associates, P.C.
Columbia, MD
Granat, Rochelle F. ....Treasury Department, Office of the General Counsel, GV
Granat, Stephen ....Malta, MT
Granata, Cynthia ....Clinton, NJ
Granata, Fred A. ....Portland, OR
Granata, Linda M. ....Miami, FL
Granata, Louis E. ....Matawan, NJ
Granatelli, Angelo ....Manorville, NY
Granatelli, Lawrence W. ....Palo Alto, CA
Granath, Lars G. ....Portland, OR
Granato, Anthony ....Westmont, NJ
Philadelphia, PA
Granato, Frank D. ....Orange, CA
Granato, Stephanie ....Los Angeles, CA
Granaudo, Maria R. ....Philadelphia, PA
Granberg, Derald E. ....Sacramento, CA
Granberg, Kenneth A. ....San Francisco, CA
Granberg, Kurt M. ....Breese, IL
Granberg, Ronald S. ....Salinas, CA
Granberg, Steven F. ....Albuquerque, NM
Granberry, Henry D., III ....Atlanta, GA
Granberry, Judy ....Houston, TX
Granberry, Melanie D. ....San Antonio, TX
Granberry, William A. ....Raleigh, NC
Granberry, William D.
Corpus Christi, TX
Granberry, William J. (Billy)
Corpus Christi, TX
Granberry Russell, Paulette ....Lansing, MI
Granbery, W. Preston ....Murray Hill, NJ
Granbo, Roger H., Jr. ....Los Angeles, CA
Granbois, Katherine Pandelidis
Lancaster, PA
Granbois, Michael J., Jr. ....New Holland, PA
Granby, James J. ....San Diego, CA
Grancell, Grancell & Marshall, A Professional Corp. ....Los Angeles, CA
Grancell, Norin T. ....Los Angeles, CA
Grancell, Sherman ....Beverly Hills, CA
Grancey, Sharon Anne ....Charlestown, MA
Granchalek, Dale R. ....Chicago, IL
Grancher, Carolyn M. ....New York, NY
Grancio, Joseph P., Jr. ....Brooklyn, NY
Grand, Christine Marie ....Detroit, MI
Grand, Deborah M. ....Baton Rouge, LA
Grand & Grand, P.A. ....Hollywood, FL
Grand, Joel E. ....Farmington Hills, MI
Grand, Joseph L. ....Farmington Hills, MI
Grand, Leonard ....Hollywood, FL
Grand, Mark Steven ....Hollywood, FL

Grand, Michael M. ... Farmington Hills, MI
Grand, Paul R. ... New York, NY
Grand, Paul S. ... Santa Fe, NM
Grand & Pittman, P.C. ... New Orleans, LA
Grand, Richard D. ... Tucson, AZ
Grand, Robert J. ... New York, NY
Grand, Robert T. ... Indianapolis, IN
Grand, Roslyn Dale ... Atlanta, GA
Grand, Sheldon D. ... St. Louis, MO
Grand, Thomas L. ... New Orleans, LA
Grand, Trenton A. ... Baton Rouge, LA
Grand, William D. ... Woodbridge, NJ
Granda, John A. ... Kansas City, MO
Granda, Michele E. ... Boston, MA
Grandaw, Monique ... Redding, CA
Grandchamp, Jeffrey P. ... Adams, MA
Grandchamp, P. Timothy ... Ottawa, IL
Grandchamp, Paul T. ... Downers Grove, IL
Grandchamp, Philip H. ... Adams, MA
Grande, Albert ... West Seneca, NY
Grande, Ana Latour ... Miami, FL
Grande, Anthony D. ... New York, NY
Grande, Corinne P. ... Providence, RI
Grande, Denis E. ... Minneapolis, MN
Grande, Eric T. ... Pawtucket, RI
Grande, Frank A. ... Tracy, CA
Grande, Jane Hille ... Miami, FL
Grande, Karen S. D. ... Providence, RI
Grande, Louis W., Jr. ... Providence, RI
Grande, Richard A. ... Miami, FL
Grande, Stephen E., III ... Sudbury, MA
Grande, Stephen S. ... Orange, CA
Grande, Thomas R., (A Law Corporation)
Honolulu, HI
Grande, Timothy J. ... Minneapolis, MN
Grande, Virginia A. ... New York, NY
Grande, W.G. & E. Vaziri, Law, Inc.
Providence, RI
Grande, William E. ... Buffalo, NY
Kenmore, NY
Grandeau, David M. ... Latham, NY
Grande-Cassell, David D. ... Lansing, MI
Grandefeld, John J. ... New York, NY
Grandell, Erik C. ... Wilmington, DE
Grandelli, Louis ... Brooklyn, NY
Granderson, Kwame J. ... Los Angeles, CA
Grandey, Gerald W. ... Denver, CO
Grandey, James B. ... Greenfield, OH
Grandfield, Fidelis A. ... New York, NY
Grandfield, John D. ... Needham, MA
Grandgenett, Reed A. ... Omaha, NE
Grandgenett, Roger L., II
Beverly Hills, CA
Las Vegas, NV
Grandi, Michael M. ... Lincolnwood, IL
Grandi, Tim S. ... Boca Raton, FL
Grandin, Susan Cobb ... Jacksonville, FL
Grandine, J. Daniel, III ... Medfield, MA
Grandine, Nancy Elizabeth ... Lyme, NH
Grandinette, Anthony Matthew ... Mineola, NY
Grandinetti, Carmin D. ... Louisville, KY
Grandinetti, John F. ... Staten Island, NY
Grandinetti, Joseph D., Jr. ... Rockville, MD
Grandinetti, Lynda M. ... Johnston, RI
Grandinetti, Paul ... Washington, DC
Grandis, Edward S. ... Washington, DC
Grandis, Leslie A. ... Richmond, VA
Grandis, Mary Eve ... Virginia Beach, VA
Grandis, Michael ... New York, NY
Grandison, Sandra E. ... Boston, MA
Grandison, W George ... Washington, DC
Grandjean, Barbara A. ... Denver, CO
Grandjean, Dalma C. ... Dayton, OH
Grandmaison, Real Joseph ... Ambler, PA
Grandoff, J. Bert ... Tampa, FL
Grandoff, John B., III ... Tampa, FL
Grandolfo, James F. ... New York, NY
Grandon, Lana ... Frankfort, KY
Grandon, Pamela ... Columbus, OH
Grandon, Robert M. ... Santa Ana, CA
Grandon, Rodney A. ... Washington, DC
Grandone, Helen F. ... Urbana, IL
Grandone, William J. ... Gillespie, IL
Grandparents Rights Center ... Orange, CA
Grandsaert, John L. ... Redwood City, CA
Grandstaff, Douglas S. ... Peoria, IL
Grandstaff, Sari N. ... Saugerties, NY
Grandstrand, Karen L. ... Minneapolis, MN
Grandy, Benjamin B. ... Lake Oswego, OR
Grandy, C. William ... Charlotte, NC
Grandy, Charles A. ... Indianapolis, IN
Grandy, Edward B. ... Salt Lake City, UT
Grandy, James L. ... Laguna Hills, CA
Grandy, Laura Koeneman ... Belleville, IL
Grandy & Martin ... Charlotte, NC
Grane, Karen M. ... Washington, DC
Granecki, James H. ... Bowling Green, OH
Granelli, James S. ... Los Angeles, CA
Granelli, Laura J. ... Garden City, NY
Granelli, Scott Peter ... Hempstead, NY
Granello, James P. ... Little Silver, NJ
Graner, Jennifer Kujawa
Fort Lauderdale, FL
Graner, Joan Mary ... Media, PA
Graner Root & Libow, P.A.
Boca Raton, FL
Miami, FL
Graner, Thomas U. ... Boca Raton, FL
Granese, Anthony P., P.A. ... Clearwater, FL
Granet, Craig S. ... Santa Barbara, CA
Granet, Harriet Beth ... Baltimore, MD
Granet, Lloyd ... Boca Raton, FL
Granet, Lloyd, P.A. ... Boca Raton, FL
Granet, Nicholas ... Los Angeles, CA
Granett, Gabriel L. ... Mill Valley, CA
Granett, Solomon ... Mamaroneck, NY
Graney, Charles E. ... Buffalo, NY
Graney, Charles F. ... Batavia, NY
Graney, Edward T. ... Chicago, IL
Graney, James J. ... Schaumburg, IL
Graney, John R. ... Le Roy, NY
Graney, Michael P. ... Columbus, OH
Granfield, Debra P. ... Santa Monica, CA
Granfield, Lindsee P. ... New York, NY
Granfield, Patricia G. ... Whittier, CA
Granfors, Ruth E. ... Harrisburg, PA
Granfort, Mary E. ... New York, NY
Grangaard, Bernhard C. ... Sun City, AZ
Grange, David P. ... Waukegan, IL
Grange, George R., II ... McLean, VA
Grange, Jennifer M. ... Sacramento, CA
Grange, Judith L. ... Torrance, CA
Grange, Krista J. ... Paris, IL
Springfield, IL
Terre Haute, IN
Grange, Lori ... Washington, DC
Grange-Holmes, Janet L. ... Glenview, IL
Granger, Andrew L. ... Tallahassee, FL
Granger, Betsy S. ... Pleasanton, CA
Granger, Blair H. ... Collingswood, NJ
Berwyn, PA
Granger, Blair H., P.C. ... Collingswood, NJ
Berwyn, PA
Granger, Bruce R. ... Atlanta, GA
Granger, Bryan T. ... Burlington, VT
Granger, Cecil N. ... Austin, TX
Granger, Chuck D. ... Opelousas, LA
Granger, Cindy A. ... Syracuse, NY
Granger, Darrell R. ... North Bay Village, FL
Granger, David I. ... Washington, DC
Granger, Diana L. ... Austin, TX
Granger, Douglas S. ... Richmond, VA
Granger, Frank ... Lake Charles, LA
Granger, Frank, A Prof. Law Corp.
Lake Charles, LA
Granger, George W. ... Bakersfield, CA
Granger, Greg A. ... Evansville, IN
Granger, Gregory D. ... Los Angeles, CA
Granger, Harvey, IV ... Jacksonville, FL
Granger, Hubert R., Jr. ... Kentfield, CA
Granger, John A. ... Seattle, WA
Granger, Kenton C. ... Kansas City, MO
Granger, Kerry J. ... Hutchinson, KS
Granger, Lisa A. ... Big Pine Key, FL
Granger, Lorna J. ... Milwaukee, WI
Granger, Louis V. ... Cleveland, OH
Granger, Maria D. ... New Albany, IN
Granger, Mark S. ... Boston, MA
Granger, Mark S. ... Columbus, OH
Granger, Matthew W. ... Lompoc, CA
Granger, Michael L. ... Tallahassee, FL
Granger, Michele L. ... Westford, MA
Granger, Patricia A. ... Boston, MA
Granger, Paul H. ... Cambridge, MA
Granger, Raymond R. ... New York, NY
Granger, Robert C. ... Ellsworth, ME
Granger, Robert M. ... Boston, MA
Granger, Santry, Mitchell & Heath, P.A.
Tallahassee, FL
Granger, Terry ... Buffalo, NY
Granger, Theodore C. ... New York, NY
Granger, Theodore G. ... Tallahassee, FL
Granich, Jeff B. ... Chicago, IL
Granich, Joseph A. ... Albany, NY
Granich, Robert J. ... Wayland, MA
Granick, Jennifer Stisa
San Francisco, CA
Granieri, Connie R. ... Puyallup, WA
Graniero, Lisa D. ... Tampa, FL
Graniez, John A. ... Los Angeles, CA
Graniez, Laurie B. ... Los Angeles, CA
Granik, Gary L. ... New York, NY
Granik, Karen G. ... White Plains, NY
Granik, Russell T. ... New York, NY
Granik Silverman Campbell & Hekker
New City, NY
Granik, William R.
Department of Housing and Urban Development,
Office of General Counsel, GV
Graninger, Eric J. ... Louisville, KY
Granison, Henry C. ... St. Paul, MN
Granite, Alvin E. ... Woodbury Heights, NJ
Granite and Heim ... Woodbury Heights, NJ
Granite, Laurence D. ... Marlton, NJ
Granito, A. James ... Boardman, OH
Granito, Frank H., III ... New York, NY
Granito, Frank H., Jr. ... New York, NY
Granito, Gilbert J. ... Riverside, CA
Santa Ana, CA
Granito, Michael B ... Cleveland, OH
Granito & Sondej ... Liverpool, NY
Granito, V. James, Jr. ... Liverpool, NY
Granitsas, James G. ... Cambridge, OH
Granitur, Eric Brett ... Miami Beach, FL
Granlund, Dianne L. ... Philadelphia, PA
Granmayeh, S. John ... Houston, TX
Grann, Henry R., II ... Fort Worth, TX
Grannan, Henry M. ... Chicago, IL
Grannan, Henry M., Chartered ... Chicago, IL
Grannan & Maloy, P.C. ... Arlington, MA
Grannan, William Joseph, Law Office of
Arlington, MA
Granneman, Vernon H. ... San Jose, CA
Granner, Charles W., III ... Paducah, KY
Grannis, Alexander B. ... New York, NY
Grannis, David L., III ... South St. Paul, MN
Grannis, Edward ... Fayetteville, NC
Grannis, Eric ... New York, NY
Grannis, Frederic ... Los Angeles, CA
Grannis & Grannis, P.A.
South St. Paul, MN
Grannis & Hauge, P.A. ... Eagan, MN
Grannis, Joyce M. ... South St. Paul, MN
Grannis, Mark A. ... Washington, DC
Grannis, Priscilla W. ... Naples, FL
Grannis, Vance B., Jr. ... Eagan, MN
Grannon, Elaine Kaplansky ... Miami, FL
Grannum, Colvin W. ... New York, NY
Grano, Ann Kuhn ... Buffalo, NY
Grano, Elisabeth ... Washington, DC
Grano, Joseph D. ... Detroit, MI
Grano, Robert H., Jr. ... Lyndhurst, OH
Granof, Eugene B. ... Herndon, VA
Granof, Gerald H. ... Los Angeles, CA
Granoff, CarolAnne ... Westwood, NJ
Granoff, David P. ... San Jose, CA
Granoff, Gail P. ... Philadelphia, PA
Granoff, Gary C. ... New York, NY
Granoff, Herbert ... Great Neck, NY
Granoff, Jonathan Glenn ... Bala Cynwyd, PA
Granoff & Kessler, P.A. ... Miami, FL
Granoff, Leonard ... Warren, RI
Granoff, Loeb H. ... Kansas City, MO
Granoff, Loren S. ... Miami, FL
Granoff, Nadine ... Washington, DC
Granoff, Peter F. ... Boston, MA
Granoff, Roy E. ... Miami, FL
Granoff, Susan ... Miami, FL
Granoff, Susan N. ... Boston, MA
Granoff, Walker & Forlenza, P.C.
New York, NY
Granofsky, Mark S. ... Dover, MA
Granofsky, Richard ... Millburn, NJ
New York, NY
Granor, Bernard ... Horsham, PA
Granor and Granor, P.C. ... Horsham, PA
Granor, Marshal S. ... Horsham, PA
Granoski, Charles M., Jr. ... Tacoma, WA
Granoski, James A. ... Sarasota, FL
Granovsky, David J. ... Boston, MA
Granovsky, Melissa ... Philadelphia, PA
Granowitz, Richard A., (A P.C.)
San Bernardino, CA
Granowitz White Weber
San Bernardino, CA
Granowsky, Richard T. ... Greensboro, NC
Granquist, Alan D. ... New York, NY
Granquist, Daniel W. ... Valparaiso, IN
Granquist, Deborah Wible ... Weston, VT
Granquist, Frances B. ... New Haven, CT
Granrud, Emily ... New York, NY
Granrud, Robert E. ... St. Paul, MN
Gransee, Kurt W. ... San Antonio, TX
Gransee, Marsha L.
Federal Energy Regulatory Commission,
Office of the General Counsel, GV
Gransee, V. Henry, Jr. ... Raleigh, NC
Granser, Julie M. ... New York, NY
Granski, Edmund W., Jr. ... New York, NY
Granskog, Jason J. ... Walnut Creek, CA
Granstaff, Charles A. ... Kerrville, TX
San Antonio, TX
Granstaff, Charles A., P.C., Law Offices of
Kerrville, TX
San Antonio, TX
Granston, Michael D.
Department of Justice, Civil Division, GV
Grant, A. Gordon, Jr. ... New Orleans, LA
Grant, Adam C., Jr. ... Concord, NC
Grant, Adam D. H. ... Los Angeles, CA
Grant, Adèle G. ... New York, NY
Grant, Alan Bart ... Somerville, NJ
Grant, Alan G., Jr. ... Altamonte Springs, FL
Grant, Alan H. ... Rockville, MD
Grant, Alan H., P.C. ... Rockville, MD
Grant, Alan J. ... Roseland, NJ
Grant, Alex J. ... Department of Justice,
Criminal Division, GV
Grant, Alex M. ... New York, NY
Grant, Alexander M. ... Alhambra, CA
Grant, Alexander R. ... Green Bay, WI
Grant, Allan L. ... Westchester, IL
Grant, Alphonzo A., Jr. ... New York, NY
Grant, Andrea Jill ... Washington, DC
Grant, Andrew P. ... Atlanta, GA
Grant, Ann E. ... Los Angeles, CA
Grant, Ann Ruth ... Downey, CA
Grant, Anthony J. ... Mount Kisco, NY
Grant, Arlene J.M. ... Baltimore, MD
Grant, Arnold ... Fullerton, CA
Grant, Arnold E. ... Chicago, IL
Grant, Artis C., Jr. ... Tacoma, WA
Grant, Barbara K. ... Boulder, CO
Grant & Barrow, A Professional Law
Corporation ... Gretna, LA
Grant, Barry D. ... Springfield, VA
Grant, Barry M. ... Pontiac, MI
Grant, Ben Z. ... Texarkana, TX
Grant, Benjamin I. ... Portland, ME
Grant, Benjamin L. ... Dallas, TX
Grant & Berry ... Little Rock, AR
Grant & Biesinger ... St. Petersburg, FL
Grant, Brad Christian ... Waterville, ME
Grant, Brian P.
Environmental Protection Agency,
Office of the General Counsel, GV
Grant, Brooke ... Salt Lake City, UT
Grant, Bruce J. ... San Francisco, CA
Grant, Burton F. ... Chicago, IL
Northbrook, IL
Grant, C. Randall, Jr.
Department Of The Interior,
Office of Hearings & Appeals, GV
Grant, Cameron A. ... Longmont, CO
Grant, Cannady & Baker, P.A. ... Augusta, KS
Grant, Capper C. ... Lisle, IL
Grant, Carol A. ... Miami, FL
Grant, Carol M. ... Minneapolis, MN
Grant, Carolyn Small ... Indianapolis, IN
Grant, Cary P. ... Rochester, NY
Grant, Catheryne L. ... Nashville, TN
Grant, Celeste Pulju ... Minneapolis, MN
Grant, Charlene ... Salem, NH
Grant, Charles E. ... Detroit, MI
Grant, Charles J. ... Philadelphia, PA
Grant, Charles K. ... Nashville, TN
Grant, Charles L. ... Akron, OH
Grant, Charles M. ... Los Angeles, CA
Grant, Charles W. ... Jacksonville, FL
Grant, Cheryl D. ... Cincinnati, OH
Grant, Cheryl L. ... Washington, DC
Grant, Christine A. ... Department of Justice,
Tax Division, GV
Grant, Christine M. ... Trenton, NJ
Grant, Christopher E. ... Portsmouth, NH
Grant, Christopher L. ... Washington, DC
Grant, Clark J. ... Columbus, NE
Grant, Dale E. ... North Attleboro, MA
Grant, Daniel M. ... Austin, TX
Grant, Danny R. ... San Diego, CA
Grant, Darren D. ... Midland, TX
Grant, David ... Towson, MD
Grant, David A. ... Los Angeles, CA
Grant, David A. ... Cudahy, WI
Grant, David Alistair ... Washington, DC
Grant, David C. ... Houston, TX
Grant, David C., (P.C.) ... Irvine, CA
Grant, David F. ... Rancho Cucamonga, CA
Grant, David F. ... Cottage City, MD
Grant, David L. ... Cleveland, OH
Grant, David M. ... Bellingham, WA
Grant, David M. ... Spokane, WA
Grant, David S. ... Oxnard, CA
Grant, David W.J. ... Houston, TX
Grant, Davida M. ... Washington, DC
Grant, Davison W. ... Austin, TX
Grant, Deandra M. ... Dallas, TX
Grant, Deborah ... Middlebury, VT
Grant, Deirdre Eleanor ... Dallas, TX
Grant, Denise M. ... New York, NY
Grant, Dennis D. ... Columbus, OH
Grant, Dennis M. ... Cheyenne, WY
Grant, Devon D. ... Newport Beach, CA
Grant, Don G. ... Riverside, CA
Grant, Donald G. ... Vancouver, WA
Grant, Donald J. ... Huntington Woods, MI
Grant, Donald K. ... Portland, OR
Grant, Donald M. ... Ventura, CA
Grant, Donald R. ... Lincoln, NE
Grant, Douglas E. ... Salt Lake City, UT
Grant, Douglas L. ... Moscow, ID
Grant, Drayton ... Rhinebeck, NY
Grant, Edmund C. ... Lexington, MA
Grant, Edward I. ... Los Angeles, CA
Grant, Edward J. ... Jackson, MI
Grant, Edward L. ... Cheyenne, WY
Grant, Eileen P. ... Norristown, PA
Grant & Eisenhofer, P.A. ... Wilmington, DE
Grant, Elaine ... New York, NY
Grant, Elinor B. ... San Luis Obispo, CA
Grant, Elizabeth J. ... Burlington, VT
Grant, Elizabeth M. ... Greenwich, CT
Grant, Elizabeth M. ... Department of Defense,
Defense Legal Services Agency, GV
Grant, Elizabeth M.
Federal Trade Commission,
Bureau of Consumer Protection, GV
Grant, Elizabeth R. ... Cleveland, OH
Grant, Ellen G. ... New York, NY
Grant, Ellen R. ... Seattle, WA
Grant, Ellin Wellford ... Columbia, SC
Grant, Eric P. ... Rancho Mirage, CA
Grant, Ernest F. ... Somerville, NJ
Grant, Ervin E. ... Augusta, KS
Grant, Erwin I. ... Woodland Hills, CA
Grant, Eugene F. ... Medford, MA
Grant, Eugene L. ... Portland, OR
Grant, Evelyn S. ... New York, NY
Grant, Florence E. Hill ... Baltimore, MD
Grant, Frederic D., Jr. ... Boston, MA
Grant, Frederick C. ... Baltimore, MD
Grant, Fridkin, Pearson, Athan & Crown,
P.A. ... Key West, FL
Naples, FL
Grant, Garrett ... San Diego, CA
Grant, Gary ... Palo Alto, CA
Grant, Gary D. ... Costa Mesa, CA
Grant, Gary D. ... Florham Park, NJ
Grant, Gayle ... New York, NY
Grant, George C. ... Macon, GA
Grant, Gerald ... Hayward, CA
Grant, Gerald R. ... Phoenix, AZ
Grant, Glenn D. ... Washington, DC
Grant & Gordon, LLP ... Palo Alto, CA
Grant, Gordon M. ... Arlington, VA
Grant and Grant ... Highland Park, IL
Grant & Grant ... Indianapolis, IN
Grant & Grant ... Tacoma, WA
Grant and Grant, A Professional
Corporation ... Chicago, IL
Northbrook, IL
Grant & Grant, A.P.C. ... Salt Lake City, UT
Grant & Grant, LLP ... Denver, CO
Longmont, CO
Grant, Gregg S. ... Troy, NY
Grant, Gregory D. ... Rockville, MD
McLean, VA
Grant, H. Wayne ... Chattanooga, TN
Grant, Hanley & Genovese, LLP
Irvine, CA
Grant, Harriet ... United States Senate,
Committee Legal Personnel, GV
Grant, Harry E., Jr. ... Seattle, WA
Grant, Harvey F. ... Beverly Hills, CA
Grant, Hedy P. ... New Milford, NJ
Grant, Helen Nelson ... Columbia, SC
Grant, Herman ... Chicago, IL
Grant, Herrmann, Schwartz & Klinger, LLP
New York, NY
Grant & Hoeper ... Waupun, WI
Grant, Hugh Jeffrey ... Los Angeles, CA

Grant & Hurlbett ... Santa Barbara, CA
Grant, Ian R. ... Lancaster, CA
Grant, Ilene S. ... Chicago, IL
Grant, Irven L., Jr. ... Concord, CA
Grant, Irvin ... Santa Monica, CA
Grant, Isabella Horton ... San Francisco, CA
Grant, J. Kirkland ... Huntington, NY
Grant, J. Michael ... Charleston, SC
Grant, Jack A. ... Gretna, LA
Grant, Jacqueline D. ... Asheville, NC
Grant, James ... Waupun, WI
Grant, James A. ... Cincinnati, OH
Grant, James B. ... Colorado Springs, CO
Grant, James C. ... Atlanta, GA
Grant, James M. ... Casey, IL
Charleston, IL
Grant, James T. ... Los Angeles, CA
Grant, James W. ... Camano, WA
Grant, Janet Schroeder ... Wetumpka, AL
Grant, Janice M. ... Wausau, WI
Grant, Jay H. ... Los Angeles, CA
Grant, Jay R. ... Los Angeles, CA
Grant, Jeffrey A. ... Oakland, CA
Grant, Jeffrey C. ... Seattle, WA
Grant, Jeffrey D. ... Mamaroneck, NY
Grant, Jeffrey K. ... Orlando, FL
Grant, Jenefer Stenzel ... St. Helens, OR
Grant, Jessica L. ... San Francisco, CA
Grant, Jian H. ... Department of Justice, Tax Division, GV
Grant, Jill Elise ... Washington, DC
Grant, Jill Jenkins ... Topeka, KS
Grant, Jill M. ... Department of the Army, U.S. Army Legal Services Agency, GV
Grant, Jim B., Jr. ... Montgomery, AL
Grant, J. M. ... Miami, FL
Grant, Jo Ellen ... Gretna, LA
Grant, Joan C. ... Chicago, IL
Northbrook, IL
Grant, Joan L. ... San Francisco, CA
Grant, Joan S. ... Upper Saddle River, NJ
Grant, Jodi ... United States Senate, Committee Legal Personnel, GV
Grant, John ... San Francisco, CA
Grant, John A. ... Tallahassee, FL
Grant, John A., Jr. ... Tampa, FL
Grant, John B., Jr. ... New York, NY
Grant, John C. ... Houston, TX
Grant, John C., III ... White Plains, NY
Grant, John H. ... Helena, MT
Grant, John J., Jr. ... Malden, MA
Grant, John K. ... San Diego, CA
Grant, John P. ... Omaha, NE
Grant, John R. ... Grand Rapids, MI
Grant, John T. ... Omaha, NE
Grant, John W. ... Englewood, CO
Grant, John W. ... Lafayette, LA
Grant, Jolyon ... Phoenix, AZ
Grant, Jos. S. ... Chicago, IL
Grant, Joseph B. ... Monroe, LA
Grant, Joseph K. ... Cleveland, OH
Grant, Joseph L. ... Atlanta, GA
Grant, Joseph M. ... Houston, TX
Grant, Joseph W. ... Omaha, NE
Grant, Joshua F., VII ... Wilbur, WA
Grant, Joyce A. ... Denver, CO
Grant, Julia F. ... Stamford, CT
Grant, Julie ... Department of State, GV
Grant, Julie L. ... Department of State, Foreign Service Officers (Overseas), GV
Grant, K. Denise ... Washington, DC
Grant, Kal ... Dallas, TX
Grant, Karen C. ... Westbury, NY
Grant, Karen L. ... Santa Barbara, CA
Grant, Karen S. ... Los Angeles, CA
Grant, Karleen A. ... Key West, FL
Grant, Kathleen E. ... Wausau, WI
Grant, Kathy A. ... Rockville, MD
Grant, Kay Hackney ... San Francisco, CA
Grant, Konvalinka & Harrison, Professional Corporation ... Chattanooga, TN
Grant, Kuyk & Rogers, A Professional Corporation ... Charleston, SC
Grant, Larry F. ... Rock Hill, SC
Grant, Larry L. ... San Jose, CA
Grant & Laughlin, P.C. ... Omaha, NE
Grant, Laura R. ... Palo Alto, CA
Grant, Laurie ... Plymouth, MA
Grant, Lauryn Guttenplan ... Washington, DC
Grant Law Firm, The ... Seattle, WA
Grant, Lawrence E. ... West Chester, PA
Grant, Leatherwood & Pitts, P.A.
Greenville, SC
Grant & Lenneberg ... Portland, OR
Grant, Lisa A. ... Boston, MA
Grant, Louis W., III ... Boise, ID
Grant, Lynda Jacobs ... New York, NY
Grant, Lynn M. ... Billings, MT
Grant & Lyons ... Rhinebeck, NY
Grant, M. Duncan ... Wilmington, DE
Philadelphia, PA
Grant, M. Eugene, Jr. ... Fort Worth, TX
Grant, Margaret Doyle ... Overseas Private Investment Corporation, GV
Grant, Marguerite T. ... Cambridge, MA
Grant, Mario C. ... Arlington, VA
Grant, Mark A. ... San Jose, CA
Grant, Mark D. ... Indianapolis, IN
Grant, Mark F. ... Fort Lauderdale, FL
Grant, Mark S. ... Waterford, MI
Grant, Mark S., Professional Corporation
Waterford, MI
Grant, Marlin J. ... Logan, UT
Tremonton, UT
Grant, Marquerite T. ... Boston, MA
Grant, Marshal S. ... Waltham, MA

Grant, Martha A. ... Fort Fairfield, ME
Grant, Martin C. ... New York, NY
Grant, Marvin F. ... Cincinnati, OH
Grant, Marvin S. ... St. Petersburg, FL
Grant, Mary B.
Research Triangle Park, NC
Grant, Mary Elizabeth ... New York, NY
Grant, Mary W. ... Memphis, TN
Grant, Matthew B. ... Lexington, KY
Grant, Maximilian A. ... Chicago, IL
Grant, Megan ... Washington, DC
Grant, Melinda E. ... Manhattan Beach, CA
Grant, Melissa A. ... Minneapolis, MN
St. Paul, MN
Grant, Merwin D. ... Phoenix, AZ
Grant, Michael ... Tulsa, OK
Grant, Michael E. ... Chicago, IL
Grant, Michael E. ... Oklahoma City, OK
Shawnee, OK
Grant, Michael E. ... Olympia, WA
Grant, Michael J. ... Chicago, IL
Grant, Michael M. ... Phoenix, AZ
Grant, Michael, (P.C.) ... Riverside, CA
Grant, Michael R ... Glendale, CA
Grant, Michael S. ... Fox Lake, IL
Grant, Michael S., Ltd. ... Fox Lake, IL
Grant, Michael W. ... Salem, OR
Grant, Miles D. ... San Diego, CA
Grant, Mindi C. ... Los Angeles, CA
Grant, Mollie A. ... Chicago, IL
Grant & Mullenax, P.C. ... San Antonio, TX
Grant, Nanci J. ... Pontiac, MI
Grant, Nora R. ... Quincy, MA
Grant, Norman L. ... Pawtucket, RI
Grant & O'Malley ... Cleveland, OH
Grant & Osborn ... Cheyenne, WY
Grant, P. Blaine ... Dallas, TX
Grant, Patricia Ann ... Tarrytown, NY
Grant, Patricia E. ... San Antonio, TX
Grant, Patrick A. ... Englewood, CO
Grant, Patrick G. ... Houston, TX
Grant, Patrick J. ... Washington, DC
Grant, Paul ... Parker, CO
Grant, Paul H. ... Juneau, AK
Grant, Paul J. ... Dearborn, MI
Grant, Paul L., Jr. ... Rochester, NY
Grant, Paul M. ... Denver, CO
Grant, Paul R. ... Santa Monica, CA
Grant, Paula DiMeo ... Washington, DC
Grant, Peter E. ... New York, NY
Grant, Peter N. ... San Francisco, CA
Seattle, WA
Grant, Peter R. ... Madison, WI
Grant, Philip G. ... Los Angeles, CA
Grant, Philip H. ... Tucson, AZ
Grant, Philip P. ... Fayetteville, GA
Grant & Popovich ... Santa Monica, CA
Grant, R. David ... Salt Lake City, UT
Grant, R. Jack ... Abilene, TX
Grant, R. Michael, Law Office of
Winchester, KY
Grant, Randall E. ... Salt Lake City, UT
Grant, Rebecca M. ... Seattle, WA
Grant, Richard A. ... Little Rock, AR
Grant, Richard Benjamin
Sherman Oaks, CA
Grant, Richard C. ... Naples, FL
Grant, Richard G. ... Dallas, TX
Grant, Richard L. ... Mission Viejo, CA
Grant, Richard L. ... Danbury, CT
Grant, Richard L. ... Akron, OH
Grant, Richard L. ... Portland, OR
Grant, Richard L. ... Charleston, WV
Grant, Richard M. ... San Rafael, CA
Grant, Richard R. ... Janesville, WI
Grant, Richard S. ... Los Angeles, CA
Grant, Richard W. ... Philadelphia, PA
Grant, Richard W. ... Woodinville, WA
Grant, Robert A. ... South Bend, IN
Grant, Robert D. ... Little Rock, AR
Grant, Robert E. ... Glastonbury, CT
Grant, Robert E. ... Westport, CT
Grant, Robert E. ... Fort Wayne, IN
Grant, Robert E. ... Rockville, MD
Grant, Robert Emmet ... Annandale, VA
Grant, Robert G. ... Indianapolis, IN
Grant, Robert G. ... Dearborn, MI
Grant, Robert H. ... St. Louis, MO
Grant, Robert H. ... Medford, OR
Grant, Robert L. ... Walnut Creek, CA
Grant, Robert L. ... Tupelo, MS
Grant, Robert M., Jr. ... Newton, NC
Grant, Robert N. ... Palo Alto, CA
Grant, Robert N. ... Chicago, IL
Grant, Robert S. ... Brighton, CO
Grant, Robyn B. ... Newport Beach, CA
Grant, Robyn S. ... Burlington, MA
Grant & Roddy ... Boston, MA
Grant, Roger J. ... Las Vegas, NV
Grant, Ronald E. ... Dallas, TX
Grant, Ronald H. ... Topeka, KS
Grant, Ronald J. ... Beverly Hills, CA
Grant, Ronald S. ... Fort Smith, AR
Grant, Ronald V. ... Honolulu, HI
Grant, Rose & Pumphrey
Winchester, KY
Grant, Roslan C. ... Ahoskie, NC
Grant, Ross & Pittman ... Chicago, IL
Grant, Russell E. ... Mulvane, KS
Grant, Russell P., Jr. ... Jackson, MS
Grant, Rusty ... Escondido, CA
Grant, Ruth Ellen ... Paris, TX
Grant, Samuel A. ... Delray Beach, FL
Grant, Samuel M. ... Baltimore, MD
Grant, Sandra J. ... Baltimore, MD
Grant, Sandra P. ... Westbury, NY
Grant, Sarah D. ... Phoenix, AZ
Grant, Scott H. ... Chattanooga, TN

Grant, Scott M. ... Naples, FL
Grant, Scott M., P.A. ... Naples, FL
Grant, Scott S. ... Los Angeles, CA
Grant, Shelley Renée
Securities and Exchange Commission, Division of Enforcement, GV
Grant, Sherry E. ... Los Angeles, CA
Grant & Soden ... San Diego, CA
Grant, Sonya Anne ... Sacramento, CA
Grant, Stefan C. ... New York, NY
Grant, Stephen A. ... New York, NY
Grant, Stephen B. ... Los Angeles, CA
Grant, Stephen Barrett ... New York, NY
Grant, Stephen G. ... Santa Cruz, CA
Grant, Stephen Louis ... Akron, OH
Grant & Sternberg ... Walnut Creek, CA
Grant, Steven R. ... Bedford, VA
Grant, Steven W. ... Chattanooga, TN
Grant, Stewart B. ... Lakewood, CO
Grant, Stuart M. ... Wilmington, DE
Grant, Susan D. ... Westmont, NJ
Grant, Susan E. ... Tallahassee, FL
Grant, Susan H. ... Big Rapids, MI
Grant, Susan I. ... New York, NY
Grant, Susan L. ... Englewood, CO
Grant, Susan L., & Associates, P.C.
Englewood, CO
Grant, Susan M. ... Monument, CO
Grant, Susan M. ... Bethlehem, PA
Grant, T. A., III ... Monroe, LA
Grant, Tamara B. ... Madison, WI
Grant, Teresa Somerfield ... Evanston, IL
Grant, Thomas A. ... Richmond, VA
Grant, Thomas C. ... Atlanta, GA
Grant, Thomas F. ... Seattle, WA
Grant, Thomas W. ... Yorkville, IL
Grant, Timothy J. ... San Diego, CA
Grant, Tina Vicari ... Baton Rouge, LA
Grant, Tone N. ... Chicago, IL
Grant, W. Lawson ... Danville, VA
Grant, Wallace H. ... Longmont, CO
Grant, Walter M. ... Birmingham, AL
Grant, Wayne ... Atlanta, GA
Grant, Weinhaus LLP ... Mamaroneck, NY
New York, NY
White Plains, NY
Grant, Wesley B. ... Concord, NC
Grant, Wesley B., P.A. ... Concord, NC
Grant, William A. ... Bethesda, MD
Grant, William B. ... Oakland, MD
Grant, William E. ... Union, NJ
Grant, William F. ... Boston, MA
Grant, William H. ... Columbus, NE
Grant, William H., III ... Orange Park, FL
Grant, William J. ... Menlo Park, CA
Grant, William J. ... Spokane, WA
Grant, William J., Jr. ... New York, NY
Grant, William L. ... Orlando, FL
Grant, William M., Jr. ... Greenville, SC
Grant, William N. ... Manistee, MI
Grant, William P. ... St. Louis, MO
Grant, William W., (P.A.) ... Oakland, MD
Grant Williams Lake & Dangerfield, P.C.
Phoenix, AZ
Grant, Willie L. ... Fullerton, CA
Grant & Zeko, A Professional Corporation
San Diego, CA
Grant-Cobb, Peggy ... Kansas City, MO
Grantham, Alicia B. ... Valdosta, GA
Grantham, Billy M. ... Donalsonville, GA
Grantham, Brelon E., Jr. ... Jackson, MS
Grantham, C. Ray, Jr.
Winston-Salem, NC
Grantham, Charles W., Jr. ... Grand Prairie, TX
Grantham, David C. ... Madison, MS
Grantham, Gene M. ... Seattle, WA
Grantham & Grantham ... Chattanooga, TN
Grantham, Gregory E.
San Juan Capistrano, CA
Grantham, James A. ... Tuscumbia, MO
Grantham, Jeffrey M. ... Birmingham, AL
Grantham, Judith A. ... Farmers Branch, TX
Grantham, Judson P. ... Columbus, GA
Grantham, Kathleen S. ... Warner Robins, GA
Grantham, Kimberly Martin ... Durham, NC
Grantham, Kirk ... West Palm Beach, FL
Grantham, Kirk, P.A. ... Lake Worth, FL
West Palm Beach, FL
Grantham, Mark E. ... Atlanta, GA
Grantham, Norris Musselwhite
Lumberton, NC
Grantham & Peterson ... Warner Robins, GA
Grantham, Randall C. ... Lutz, FL
Grantham, Randall C., P.A. ... Lutz, FL
Grantham, Robert A. ... Los Angeles, CA
Grantham, Robert E. ... El Reno, OK
Grantham, Russell A. ... St. Louis, MO
Grantham, Susan ... New York, NY
Grantham, Teresa L. ... Springfield, MO
Grantham, Terry L. ... Lubbock, TX
Grantham, Walter E., II
Chattanooga, TN
Grantham, Walter E., III
Chattanooga, TN
Grantham, Walter L., Jr. ... Clearwater, FL
Grantham, Walter L., Jr., P.A.
Clearwater, FL
Grantham, William (Bill)
Beverly Hills, CA
Granthen, Julie L. ... Auburn Hills, MI
Grant-Johnson, Janis (" Jan ") ... Norman, OK
Grantland, Brenda ... Mill Valley, CA
Grantland, Grensky & Blodgett
Medford, OR
Grantland, James L., Jr. ... Medford, OR
Grantland, John M. ... Columbia, SC
Grantmyre, William E. ... Cary, NC

Grant-Wilkinson, Patti L.
Washington, DC
Grantz, David B. ... Newark, NJ
Granucci, Anthony F. ... San Francisco, CA
Granucci, Robert J. ... Sacramento, CA
Granucci, Robert R. ... San Francisco, CA
Granum, Fred M. ... Portland, OR
Granuzzo, Paula T. ... Trenton, NJ
Granville, Elizabeth Elster ... New York, NY
Granville, James F. ... Buffalo, NY
Granville, Patricia A. ... Tarrytown, NY
Granville, Stanley B. ... Inglewood, CA
Granville, Warren J. ... Phoenix, AZ
Granwell, Alan W. ... Washington, DC
Granzier, Paul A. ... Medina, OH
Granzotto, Mark ... Detroit, MI
Granzotto & Nicita, P.C. ... Detroit, MI
Granzow, Andrew S. ... Philadelphia, PA
Granzow, Denise M. ... Grand Blanc, MI
Granzow, Jack Edward ... Smithville, NJ
Granzow, Paul H. ... Dayton, OH
Grape, Jewelie A. ... Minneapolis, MN
Grapek, Harvey ... Long Beach, NY
Grapel, Christian J. ... Freehold, NJ
Graper, Beverly L. ... Gainesville, FL
Graper, Glen E. ... Portsmouth, NH
Graper, Glen E., P.A. ... Portsmouth, NH
Graphia, Gary P. ... Baton Rouge, LA
Graphos, Antonia ... Rancho Mirage, CA
Grapin, Julie ... Hackensack, NJ
Grapp, Wesley G. ... Calabasas, CA
Grappo, Michael A. ... Alameda, CA
Grappotte, Xavier P. ... New York, NY
Grapsas, Diane Curry ... Chicago, IL
Grapsas, Nicholas C. ... Madison, WI
Grasberger, Eric A. ... Portland, OR
Grasberger, John E. ... San Francisco, CA
Grasberger, Robert C. ... Media, PA
Grasch, Albert F., Jr. ... Lexington, KY
Grasch, Walters & Cowen, P.S.C.
Lexington, KY
Graseck, Arthur V., Jr. ... Islip Terrace, NY
Graser, Janet L. ... San Francisco, CA
Grashof, A. Edward ... New York, NY
Grashoff, Philip A., Jr. ... Grand Rapids, MI
Grashow, Murray J., Law Offices of
Williamsville, NY
Grasing, Raymond R. ... Melville, NY
Grasis, Peter I. ... Clifton, VA
Grask, Gerald H. ... Des Moines, IA
Graske, Leslie S. ... Akron, OH
Graski, Diana ... Colorado Springs, CO
Graslie Law Firm ... Rapid City, SD
Graslie, Thomas E. ... Buffalo, SD
Rapid City, SD
Grasmick, T.J. (Mick) ... Los Angeles, CA
Grasmoen, Cheryl L. ... Minneapolis, MN
Grass, Alan B. ... Los Angeles, CA
Grass, Andrew N., Jr. ... New York, NY
Grass, Edward J. ... Washington, DC
Grass & Grass, P.A. ... Melbourne, FL
Grass, Irving ... Melbourne, FL
Grass, Jeffery W. ... Upland, CA
Grass, Jeffrey C. ... Dallas, TX
Grass, John R., (P.A.) ... Pensacola, FL
Grass, Joseph J. ... Dayton, OH
Grass, Mikal ... Melbourne, FL
Grass, Robert ... New York, NY
Grass, Roger Richard ... Bakersfield, CA
Grass, Sharon E. ... Mesquite, TX
Grass, Stuart E. ... Chicago, IL
Grassano, Achilles J. ... Nutley, NJ
Grassbaugh, Stephen P. ... Columbus, OH
Grassby, George E. ... Rapid City, SD
Grassby, John H. ... Steamboat Springs, CO
Grassé, Edward K. ... Chicago, IL
Grassedonio, Roy M. ... Corpus Christi, TX
Grasselena, Gregory C. ... Brooklyn, NY
Grasser, George R. ... Buffalo, NY
Grassgreen, Debra ... Los Angeles, CA
Grassi, Carl J. ... Cleveland, OH
Grassi, David F. ... Hillsdale, MI
Grassi, James D. ... Chicago, IL
Grassi, Joseph C. ... Wildwood, NJ
Grassi, Joseph F. ... New York, NY
Grassi, Joseph J., III ... Washington, DC
Grassi, Lia Silva ... Washington, DC
Grassi, Paolo S. ... New York, NY
Grassi, Robert G. ... New York, NY
Grassi, Ronald M. ... San Francisco, CA
Grassi, Sebastian V., Jr. ... Troy, MI
Grassi & Toering, P.L.C. ... Detroit, MI
Troy, MI
Grassia, Thomas C. ... Natick, MA
Grassick, Harry R. ... West Hartford, CT
Grassie, Charles R. ... Brighton, MI
Grassie, Vernon ... Girard, KS
Grassie, Yvonne G. ... Miami, FL
Grassie, Yvonne G., P.A. ... Miami, FL
Grassini, Lawrence P.
Woodland Hills, CA
Grassini, Stacey N. ... Martinez, CA
Grassini & Wrinkle, A Law Corporation
Los Angeles, CA
Woodland Hills, CA
Grassler, Frank P.
Research Triangle Park, NC
Grasso, Albert L. ... Chicago, IL
Grasso, Alexander A. ... Hastings, NY
Grasso, Alexander A., P.C. ... Hastings, NY
Grasso, Carl T. ... New York, NY
Grasso, Carmen ... Syracuse, NY
Grasso, Christina G. ... Denver, CO
Grasso, David S. ... Syracuse, NY
Grasso, Donald J. ... Toms River, NJ
Grasso, Faith D. ... Topsfield, MA
Grasso, Frank N. ... Schenectady, NY
Grasso, Fred ... Washington, DC

Grasso, Gabriel L. ... Fort Lauderdale, FL
Grasso, Gary A. ... Chicago, IL
Grasso, George A. ... Douglaston, NY
Grasso and Grasso ... Schenectady, NY
Grasso, Jacqueline M. ... Batavia, NY
Grasso, James A. ... Moreland Hills, OH
Grasso, James R. ... Buffalo, NY
Grasso, James V., Jr. ... Portland, ME
Grasso, Jeanne Marie ... Washington, DC
Grasso, John ... Spokane, WA
Grasso, John H. ... Glastonbury, CT
Grasso, Joseph A., Jr. ... Boston, MA
Grasso, Joseph G. ... New York, NY
Grasso, Karen Kelly ... Akron, OH
Grasso, Laura A. ... Washington, DC
Grasso, Leonard L., Jr. ... Mount Holly, NJ
Grasso, Linda M. ... Boston, MA
Providence, RI
Grasso, Lisa M. ... Bridgeport, CT
Grasso, Margaret M. ... Philadelphia, PA
Grasso, Mark F. ... Timonium, MD
Grasso, Maureen ... Newark, NJ
Grasso, Nicholas J. ... Schenectady, NY
Grasso, Randall C. ... Dallas, TX
Grasso, Robert J. ... Las Vegas, NV
Grasso, Robert, Jr. ... Scottsdale, AZ
Grasso, Roberto J. ... San Francisco, CA
Grasso, Rodriguez, Grasso & Zyra
Schenectady, NY
Grasso, Shirley ... Cedar Brook, NJ
Grasso, Thomas A. ... Pawtucket, RI
Grasso, Thomas M. ... New York, NY
Grasso, Tony, III ... St. Louis, MO
Grasso, Vincent J. ... Toms River, NJ
Grassy, John L. ... Mesa, AZ
Graston, Maurice W. ... Greenfield, IN
Grasty, James K. ... Philadelphia, PA
Grasz, L. Steven ... Omaha, NE
Gratch, Ariel ... New York, NY
Gratch Jacobs & Brozman, P.C.
New York, NY
Gratch, Joshua A. ... Los Angeles, CA
Gratch, Karen ... Bingham Farms, MI
Grate, D. Jeffrey ... Atlanta, GA
Grate, Jack R., Jr. ... Independence, MO
Grate, Marshall W. ... Grand Rapids, MI
Grate, Theron B., Jr. ... Des Moines, IA
Grater, Mark O. ... Groton, CT
Grater, Paul T. ... Pittsburgh, PA
Grather, Francis G. ... Morristown, NJ
Grathwohl, Casper O. ... St. Joseph, MI
Grathwohl, J. David ... Belmont, CA
Grathwohl, Linda ... Albert Lea, MN
Grathwohl, Tracy ... New York, NY
Grathwol, James N. ... Excelsior, MN
Grattan, Crary E. ... Okemos, MI
Grattan & Galati ... Sacramento, CA
Grattan, George G., IV ... Earlysville, VA
Grattan, John B. ... Atlanta, GA
Grattan, John P., Jr. ... Sacramento, CA
Grattan, Lisa A. ... Short Hills, NJ
Grattan, Maureen A. ... Goleta, CA
Grattan, Michael J., III ... Elkhart, IN
Grattan, Patrick G. ... Santa Rosa, CA
Grattan, Patrick M. ... Valatie, NY
Gratto, Clarence H. ... Canton, NY
Gratton, David W. ... Boise, ID
Gratton, Gail L. ... Pittsburgh, PA
Gratton, Gaile Pugh ... Birmingham, AL
Gratton, Scott G. ... Billings, MT
Gratton, Stephen A. ... Lakewood, CO
Gratton, Thomas F. ... Boise, ID
Gratton, Vincent J. ... Pueblo, CO
Gratz, Ben ... Tifton, GA
Gratz, Eugene C. ... Laguna Beach, CA
Gratz & Gratz ... Tupelo, MS
Gratz, Marshall L. ... Milwaukee, WI
Gratz, Michael B., Jr. ... Tupelo, MS
Gratz, Michael B., Sr. ... Tupelo, MS
Gratz, Michael J. ... Milwaukee, WI
Gratz, Mitchell J. ... Encino, CA
Gratz, Mitchell J., Law Corp. ... Encino, CA
Gratz, Robert M. ... Bethesda, MD
Gratz, Sally J. ... San Francisco, CA
Gratzer, Thomas R. ... Brockton, MA
Rockland, MA
Grau, Angela B. ... Columbia, MD
Grau & Bassett, A Professional Corporation
Dallas, TX
Midland, TX
Grau, Charles W. ... Concord, NH
Grau, David P. ... Willow Grove, PA
Grau, Glenn A. ... Middlesex, NJ
Grau, James E. ... Madison, WI
Grau, James W. ... Dallas, TX
Grau, John S. ... Dallas, TX
Grau, Jose O. ... Humacao, PR
Grau, Kenneth S. ... New York, NY
Grau, Leonard ... New York, NY
Grau, Paul A. ... Garfield Heights, OH
Grau, Richard ... Fort Wright, KY
Grau, Thomas J. ... Indianapolis, IN
Graub, John W., II ... Indianapolis, IN
Graubard, John J. ... New York, NY
Graubard, M. David ... New York, NY
Graubard Mollen & Miller
New York, NY
Graubard, Myra L. ... Greenwich, CT
Graubard, Myra L. ... Stamford, CT
Graubard, Naomi B. ... New Haven, CT
Graubard, Robert C. ... New York, NY
Graubard, Seymour ... New York, NY
Graubart, Daniel ... White Plains, NY
Graubart, Daniel, P.C. ... White Plains, NY
Graubart, Jeffrey L. ... Los Angeles, CA
Graubart, Tracee A. ... Newark, NJ
Grauberd, Allan ... New York, NY
Grauberger, Albert E. ... Kansas City, KS
Grauberger, Jana L. ... New Orleans, LA
Graubert, David B. ... Los Angeles, CA
Graubert, John D.
Federal Trade Commission,
Office of the General Counsel, GV
Grauel, Douglas ... Auburn, ME
Grauel, Melissa A. ... Danbury, CT
Grauer, Allan L. ... Omaha, NE
Grauer, Brenda L. ... Chicago, IL
Grauer, Corey H. ... Rolling Meadows, IL
Grauer, David ... Columbus, OH
Grauer, David I. ... White Plains, NY
Grauer, Edward ... New York, NY
Grauer, Gregg A. ... New York, NY
Grauer, Joshua J. ... White Plains, NY
Grauer, Marshall Jay ... Syracuse, NY
Grauer, Myron C. ... Columbus, OH
Grauer, Paul W. ... Schaumburg, IL
Grauer, Richard D. ... Bloomfield Hills, MI
Grauer, Robert D. ... Newark, NJ
Grauer, Susan ... Denver, CO
Grauer, Tami Irene ... Rocky River, OH
Grauer, William E. ... San Diego, CA
Grauerholz-Lofton, Stephanie L.
Chicago, IL
Graugnard, George Ann Hayne
La Place, LA
Graugnard, Paul E. ... Shreveport, LA
Graul, David M. ... Coral Gables, FL
Graul, Lisa F. ... San Francisco, CA
Graul, Plimpton L., Jr. ... Greenville, PA
Graul, Robert L., Jr. ... San Antonio, TX
Graul, Walter J. ... Annandale, VA
Graulich, Timothy Edward ... Newark, NJ
New York, NY
Graulty, Reynaldo ... Honolulu, HI
Grauman, Edward ... Helena, AR
Grauman, Nancy E. ... Los Angeles, CA
Grauman, Philip ... Louisville, KY
Grauman, Robert A. ... New York, NY
Graumann, Timothy T. ... Omaha, NE
Graumlich, Betty Sinclaire Wommack
Richmond, VA
Graupensperger, Anthony L. ... Auburn, CA
Graupensperger, Anthony L.
Roseville, CA
Graupensperger, Joseph V. ... Washington, DC
Graupmann Zuckerman, Ann
Los Angeles, CA
Graupner, Charles P. ... Milwaukee, WI
Graus, A. David ... Lakeside, CA
Graus, Stacey L. ... Covington, KY
Grausam, Jeffrey L. ... Los Angeles, CA
Grause, Marie Beatrice ... Washington, DC
Grause, Tara A ... Cincinnati, OH
Graustein, Archibald R., The Firm of
New York, NY
Graustein, John A. ... Portland, ME
Grausz, Daniel S. ... Seattle, WA
Gravallese, David M.
Environmental Protection Agency,
Office of the General Counsel, GV
Gravano, Marialana M. ... Melville, NY
Gravante, Gravante & Looby ... Brooklyn, NY
Gravante, Nicholas A. ... Brooklyn, NY
Gravante, Nicholas A., Jr. ... New York, NY
Gravante, Richard S. ... Brooklyn, NY
Gravatt, Mayo K. ... Blackstone, VA
Gravatt, Stephen A. ... Fords, NJ
Gravatt, William M., III ... Blackstone, VA
Gravatt, W. M., Jr. ... Blackstone, VA
Gravdal, Janet M. ... Portland, OR
Grave de Peralta, Stephen J.
Bradenton, FL
Gravel, Camille F. ... Alexandria, LA
Gravel and Cespiva ... Alexandria, LA
Gravel, Charles G. ... Alexandria, LA
Gravel, Clarke A. ... Burlington, VT
Gravel, Deborah ... Gretna, LA
Gravel, Denis M. ... Gurnee, IL
Gravel, John C. ... Burlington, VT
Gravel & Labovitz ... Gurnee, IL
Gravel, Paul S. ... Baton Rouge, LA
Gravel and Shea, A Professional Corporation
Burlington, VT
Graveley, Michael David ... Wausau, WI
Graveley, William J. ... Aurora, CO
Gravelie, Albert T. ... Cedar Rapids, IA
Graveline, Bradley C. ... Chicago, IL
Graveline, Christopher ... Warner, NH
Gravell, Eve N. ... Truckee, CA
Gravell, Kathy S. ... Odessa, DE
Gravelle, Christine M. ... Lawrenceville, NJ
Gravelle, Douglas A. ... Los Angeles, CA
Gravelle, Howard J. ... Honolulu, HI
Gravelle, James F. ... Department of Defense,
Defense Legal Services Agency, GV
Gravelle, Kent Benedict ... Breckenridge, MN
Gravelle, L. A. ... Tucson, AZ
Gravelle, Louis Alvin ... Tucson, AZ
Gravelle, Michael L. ... Little Rock, AR
Gravelle, Ryan K. ... Houston, TX
Gravely, B. Page, Jr. ... Richmond, VA
Gravely, David R. ... Myrtle Beach, SC
Gravely Law Firm, The, P.A. ... Pickens, SC
Gravely, Marc E. ... San Antonio, TX
Gravely, Perry Hudson ... Pickens, SC
Gravely, Steven D. ... Richmond, VA
Gravelyn, Daniel R. ... Grand Rapids, MI
Gravelyn, Erin E. ... Grand Rapids, MI
Graven and Graven ... Greene, IA
Graven, Irene Kenny ... Owego, NY
Graven, Jim K. ... Early, IA
Sac City, IA
Graven, Joseph C. ... Santa Monica, CA
Graven, Lawrence S. ... Los Angeles, CA
Graven, Marion F., III ... Wooster, OH
Graven, Mark H. ... Wailuku, HI
Graven, Norman R. ... Greene, IA
Graven Perry Block Brody & Qualls, A
Professional Corporation ... Los Angeles, CA
Gravenhorst, Paul S.
Fort Lauderdale, FL
Gravenmier, Stanley A. ... Orlando, FL
Gravenor, John P. ... Crystal Lake, IL
Gravens & Franey Co., L.P.A.
Cleveland, OH
Gravens, Terrance P. ... Cleveland, OH
Graver, Ann C. ... Chicago, IL
Graver, Christopher ... Phoenix, AZ
Graver, Darryl H. ... Woodland Hills, CA
Graver, Julia M. ... Columbus, OH
Graver, Karin J. ... Los Angeles, CA
Graver, Lisa D. ... Chicago, IL
Graver, Wayne A. ... Philadelphia, PA
Graves, A. Julia ... Vero Beach, FL
Graves, Aaron W. ... Harrisonburg, VA
Graves, Alan D. ... Machias, ME
Graves, Albert ... Hope, AR
Graves, Albert, Jr. ... Hope, AR
Graves, Alexander ... Staten Island, NY
Graves & Allen ... Oakland, CA
Graves, Allen L. ... Baton Rouge, LA
Lincoln, NE
Graves, Anna Katherine ... Birmingham, AL
Graves, Anna M. ... Los Angeles, CA
Graves, Anne M. ... New York, NY
Graves, Arthur C. ... Canton, OH
Columbus, OH
Graves, Bernard J., Jr. ... Kingsport, TN
Graves, Bruce ... Des Moines, IA
Graves, Bruce H. ... New York, NY
Graves, Bryant ... West Monroe, LA
Graves, Carla Sue ... Aurora, CO
Graves, Charles B., Jr. ... Tunica, MS
Graves, Charles C., II ... New York, NY
Graves, Charles E. ... Whippany, NJ
Graves, Charles E. ... Cheyenne, WY
Graves, Charles" Tait " ... Oakland, CA
Graves, Cheryl L. ... Anchorage, AK
Graves, Cheryl M. ... Chicago, IL
Graves, Christopher R. ... Norman, OK
Graves, Cody L. ... Oklahoma City, OK
Graves, Daniel B. ... Birmingham, AL
Graves, Daniel B. ... Tulsa, OK
Graves, Daniel H. ... Nashville, AR
Graves, Daniel W. ... Melvin, IA
Graves, Darel A. ... Hamilton, MT
Graves, Darryl W. ... Lawrence, KS
Graves, David A. ... Miami, FL
Graves, David A. ... Dallas, TX
Graves, David G. ... Tulsa, OK
Graves, David W. ... San Diego, CA
Graves, David W., Jr. ... Minneapolis, MN
Graves, Dean L. ... Houston, TX
Graves, Deborah D. ... San Diego, CA
Graves, Debra C. ... Raleigh, NC
Graves, Dennis C. ... Martinez, CA
Graves, Dennis J. ... Salem, OR
Graves, Donet D. ... Washington, DC
Cleveland, OH
Graves, Donet D., Jr. ... Washington, DC
Graves, Dougherty, Hearon & Moody, A
Professional Corporation ... Austin, TX
Kerrville, TX
Graves, E. Allen, Jr. ... Baton Rouge, LA
Graves, E. Wesley, III ... Columbia, SC
Graves, Edward M., Jr. ... Knoxville, TN
Graves, Edward S. ... New York, NY
Graves, Elizabeth ... Gainesville, FL
Graves, Eric L. ... Gold River, CA
Graves, Esther P. ... Teaneck, NJ
Graves, Frank H. ... New Brunswick, NJ
Graves, Frederick ... Jensen Beach, FL
Graves, Freeman P. ... Walnut Creek, CA
Graves, Frierson M., Jr. ... Memphis, TN
Graves, Gene W. ... Oak Harbor, OH
Graves, Geoffrey A. ... Irvine, CA
Graves, George P. ... Decatur, GA
Graves & Graves ... Hope, AR
Graves & Graves ... Nashville, AR
Graves and Graves ... Houston, TX
Graves, Graves & Hanna ... Shreveport, LA
Graves, Greely R., Jr. ... Kennesaw, GA
Graves, Guy A. ... Schenectady, NY
Graves, Guy M. ... Lexington, KY
Graves, H. Brice ... Richmond, VA
Graves, H. Wayne ... Johnson City, TN
Graves, Harmon S. ... Denver, CO
Graves, Harold D. ... Parma, OH
Graves, Herbert M. ... Oklahoma City, OK
Graves, Hideko I. ... Pacific Grove, CA
Graves and Hill, P.A. ... Vero Beach, FL
Graves & Horton, LLC ... Washington, DC
Cleveland, OH
Graves, Irene M. ... Birmingham, AL
Graves, J. Hazen ... Minneapolis, MN
Graves, J. Steven ... Gainesville, FL
Graves, J. Steven, P.A. ... Gainesville, FL
Graves, J. William ... Frankfort, KY
Graves, Jack M. ... Boulder, CO
Graves, Jama Sue ... Prairie Du Sac, WI
Graves, James A. ... Atlanta, GA
Graves, James C. ... Nashville, AR
Graves, James E., Jr. ... Jackson, MS
Graves, James F. ... East Lansing, MI
Graves, James K. ... El Centro, CA
Palm Springs, CA
San Diego, CA
Graves, James M. ... Fayetteville, AR
Graves, James R. ... Billings, MT
Graves, James R., (Co. L.P.A.)
Fairlawn, OH
Graves, James T. ... St. Joseph, MO
Graves, James W., LTD. ... Shreveport, LA
Graves, Jeffery L. ... Albuquerque, NM
Graves, Jeffrey R. ... Los Angeles, CA
Graves, Jennings L., Jr. ... Greenville, SC
Graves, Jerry ... Houston, TX
Graves, Jim I. ... Beaumont, TX
Houston, TX
Graves, John E. ... Duluth, MN
Graves, John J., Jr. ... Las Vegas, NV
Graves, John M. ... Camden, AR
Graves, John P., Jr. ... Sarasota, FL
Graves, John Paul ... Houston, TX
Graves, Jon D. ... Wichita, KS
Graves, Jonathan G. ... Washington, DC
Graves, Joseph Harold ... Clearwater, FL
Graves, Joseph L. ... Monterey Park, CA
Graves, Judson ... Atlanta, GA
Graves, Juliann W. ... Kansas City, MO
Graves, K. Maxwell, Jr. ... Meadville, MS
Graves, Karol A. ... Hawthorne, NJ
Graves, Kathlyn ... Little Rock, AR
Graves, Kathryn A. ... Minneapolis, MN
Graves, Kenneth B. ... Wood River, IL
Graves, Kenneth E. ... Tampa, FL
Graves, Kevin G. ... Salem, MA
White Plains, NY
Graves, L. Page ... East Lansing, MI
Graves, Laurence A. ... Auburn, CA
Graves, Lawrence B., Jr.
Grosse Pointe Farms, MI
Graves, Lawrence D.W.
Northampton, MA
Graves & Leavitt ... Las Vegas, NV
Graves, Lee C. ... Barrington, IL
Graves, Leon B. ... Topeka, KS
Graves, Leslie Theresa ... Detroit, MI
Graves, Linda Richey ... Kansas City, MO
Graves, Lisa R. ... Department of Justice,
Civil Division, GV
Graves, M. Lee ... Clarksdale, MS
Graves, Marco E. ... Cleveland, OH
Graves, Margaret M. ... Lexington, KY
Graves, Marshall W. ... Thousand Oaks, CA
Graves, Matthew J. ... Oklahoma City, OK
Graves, Maureen R. ... Irvine, CA
Graves, Megan E. ... Seattle, WA
Graves, Melinda W. ... Tustin, CA
Graves, Michael A. ... Tavares, FL
Graves, Michael D. ... Tulsa, OK
Graves, Michael K. ... Clarksdale, MS
Southaven, MS
Graves, Michael Lon ... Tulsa, OK
Graves, Miller & Kingston, P.C.
Cheyenne, WY
Graves, N. Warren, P.L.C. ... Shreveport, LA
Graves, Nelson H. ... Boston, MA
Graves & Nicholson ... South Burlington, VT
Graves, Nina Pickett ... Washington, DC
Graves, Palmer M. ... Estes Park, CO
Graves, Patrick H., Jr. ... Huntsville, AL
Graves, Patrick L. ... Riverside, CA
Graves, Paul F. ... Madison, WI
Graves, Paul K. ... Bellevue, WA
Graves, Paul R. ... South Burlington, VT
Graves, Peter E. ... Norman, OK
Graves, Peter K., Jr. ... Santa Monica, CA
Graves, Philip E. ... Saco, ME
Graves, Philip J. ... Los Angeles, CA
Graves, Pleasant F., Jr. ... Houston, TX
Graves, Porter R., Jr. ... Harrisonburg, VA
Graves, Ralph W. ... El Cajon, CA
Graves, Ray ... Tacoma, WA
Graves, Ray Reynolds ... Detroit, MI
Graves & Rethore, P.C. ... Phoenix, AZ
Graves, Richard E. ... Seattle, WA
Graves, Rick E. ... Aberdeen, NC
Wilmington, NC
Graves, Robert ... Boston, MA
Winchester, MA
Graves, Robert J. ... Chicago, IL
Graves, Robert R., Jr. ... Austin, TX
Graves, Robert W. ... Jackson, MS
Graves, Robin Hansen ... Birmingham, AL
Graves, Ronald B. ... Newton, NJ
Graves, Ronald N. ... Boise, ID
Graves, Roy A. ... Visalia, CA
Graves, Sarah E. ... Stamford, CT
Graves, Scott Joseph ... Stoneham, MA
Graves, Sherri M. ... Atlanta, GA
Graves, Silvia R. ... Houston, TX
Graves, Stephanie Balcerzak ... Chicago, IL
Graves, Stephen A. ... Washington, NC
Graves, Stephen A., P.A. ... Washington, NC
Graves, Susan V. Foulk ... Morgantown, WV
Graves, Suzanne M. ... Upland, CA
Graves, T. Henley ... Georgetown, DE
Graves, Tarnisha A. ... Washington, DC
Graves, Terrence L. ... Richmond, VA
Graves, Thomas A. ... Dallas, TX
Graves, Thomas C. ... Kansas City, MO
Graves, Thomas D. ... South Pasadena, FL
Graves, Thomas J. ... Washington, DC
Graves, Thomas W. ... Houston, TX
Graves, Timothy R. ... Los Angeles, CA
Graves, Todd P. ... Platte City, MO
Graves, Toennis & Gustafson, P.C.
Billings, MT
Graves, Vicki Sharron ... Pensacola, FL
Graves, Walter Z. ... Bloomfield Hills, MI
Graves, William C. ... Redmond, WA
Graves, William D. ... Oklahoma City, OK
Graves, William E., Jr. ... Boston, MA
Graves, William S. ... Phoenix, AZ
Graves, William T. ... Charlotte, NC
Graves, Wilson G. ... Milan, TN
Graves, Wm. Griffin, III ... Chapel Hill, NC
Gravesande, Sharon R. ... New York, NY
Gravett & Balcher ... Napa, CA
Gravett, Charles Lewis ... Napa, CA

Gravett, Rebecca B., Law Offices of
Covina, CA
Gravett, Rebecca B., Law Offices of
Pasadena, CA
Pomona, CA
Rancho Cucamonga, CA
Upland, CA
Gravett, Willem H. ..... New York, NY
Gravier, Leonardo ..... Coral Gables, FL
Gravina, John A. ..... Tucson, AZ
Gravina Law Firm ..... Tucson, AZ
Gravina, Peter J. ..... Fort Myers, FL
Gravina, Thomas Joseph ..... Pittsburgh, PA
Graving, Richard J. ..... Houston, TX
Gravini, Stephen M. ..... Alexandria, VA
Gravino, Marc C. ..... Rockford, IL
Gravino, Vittese & Jones ..... Hammonton, NJ
Gravis, Marylinn M. ..... Tulsa, OK
Gravitt, Alan T. ..... Halifax, VA
Gravitt, Carol B. ..... Halifax, VA
Gravitt, Cassius B., Jr. ..... Cincinnati, OH
Gravitt & Gravitt, P.C. ..... Halifax, VA
Gravitt, S. Pilar ..... Beaumont, TX
Gravitt, Timothy A. ..... Irvine, CA
Los Angeles, CA
San Diego, CA
Gravitz, Janet ..... Mays Landing, NJ
Gravitz, Jennifer L. ..... Rochester, NY
Gravley, Adam W. ..... Seattle, WA
Gravley, James R. ..... Abilene, TX
Gravley & Leggett, PLLC ..... Abilene, TX
Gravlin, E. William ..... Los Angeles, CA
Gravo, Debra Colleen ..... Anchorage, AK
Gravois, Diane M. ..... Metairie, LA
Gravois, Jude G. ..... Vacherie, LA
Gravois, Michael L. ..... Birmingham, AL
Gravolet, Margaret S. ..... New Orleans, LA
Graw, Andrew E. ..... Roseland, NJ
Graw, Teresa M. ..... Holmdel, NJ
Grawe, Susan C. ..... West Chester, PA
Grawemeyer, Christine S. ..... Chicago, IL
Grawemeyer, David W. ..... Chicago, IL
Grawey, Richard E. ..... Peoria, IL
Grawl, Robert, Jr. ..... Houston, TX
Grawunder, Leroy, Jr. ..... Irving, TX
Gray, A. Duncan, Jr. ..... Houston, TX
Gray, Abel ..... Spartanburg, SC
Gray, Alan S. ..... Chicago, IL
Gray, Albert W. ..... Salt Lake City, UT
Gray, Alisa J. ..... Scottsdale, AZ
Gray, Alison Leigh ..... Washington, DC
Gray, Alvin J. ..... Bend, OR
Gray, Alyse ..... Albany, NY
Gray, Amy Dickman ..... Chicago, IL
Gray, Andrew J., III ..... Lake Charles, LA
Gray, Andrew J., IV ..... Palo Alto, CA
Gray, Angela Bowden ..... Paragould, AR
Gray, Angela Newell ..... Greensboro, NC
Gray, Anna R. ..... Lake Charles, LA
Gray, Anne M. Heffernan
Shaker Heights, OH
Gray, Annette M. ..... Saginaw, MI
Gray, Anthony L. ..... Boston, MA
Gray, Arnold L. ..... Portland, OR
Gray, Arthur D. ..... New York, NY
Gray, Arthur W., Jr. ..... Anaheim, CA
Gray & Associates ..... Warren, OH
Gray, Austin Richard ..... Philadelphia, PA
Gray, Babetta Ruth ..... Englewood, CO
Gray, Barbara Nelson ..... Houston, TX
Gray & Battey ..... Monterey, CA
Gray & Becker, P.C. ..... Austin, TX
Georgetown, TX
Gray, Ben T. ..... Tigard, OR
Gray, Bernard A., Sr. ..... Washington, DC
Gray Blount & Associates ..... Arlington, VA
Washington, DC
Gray, Bobby G., Jr. ..... Selmer, TN
Gray, Brenda Seale ..... Breckenridge, TX
Gray, Brenda Seale, P.C. ..... Breckenridge, TX
Gray, Brent H. ..... Bala Cynwyd, PA
Gray, Brian D. ..... Overland Park, KS
Gray, Brian E. ..... San Francisco, CA
Gray, Brian M. ..... Palmer, AK
Gray, Brian Mark, A Professional Corporation
Palmer, AK
Gray, Brian V. ..... Itasca, IL
Gray, Bruce D. ..... Atlanta, GA
Gray, Bruce F., Jr. ..... Memphis, TN
Gray, Bruce K. ..... Decatur, GA
Gray, C. Boyden ..... Washington, DC
Gray, C. Michael ..... Huntington, WV
Gray, C. Timothy ..... Tallahassee, FL
Gray, Cameron Davis ..... Dallas, TX
Gray, Carl D. ..... Norfolk, VA
Gray, Carl W. ..... Lexington, NC
Gray, Carol Meyer ..... Valley Forge, PA
Gray, Carole L. ..... Providence, RI
Gray, Carolyn Chapman
Department of Commerce,
Patent and Trademark Office, GV
Gray, Carolyn Doppelt ..... Washington, DC
Gray, Carolyn H. ..... Treasury Department,
Internal Revenue Service, GV
Gray, Carroll D. ..... Spokane, WA
Gray Cary Ware & Freidenrich LLP
El Centro, CA
La Jolla, CA
Palo Alto, CA
Sacramento, CA
San Diego, CA
San Francisco, CA
Austin, TX
Gray, Cecilia Richards
Colorado Springs, CO
Gray, Charles C. ..... Dallas, TX
Gray, Charles D., III ..... Gastonia, NC
Gray, Charles E. ..... St. Louis, MO
Gray, Charles F., Jr. ..... Sacramento, CA
Gray, Charles J. ..... Billerica, MA
Gray, Charles Michael ..... Dallas, TX
Gray, Charles N. ..... Purcell, OK
Gray, Charles S. ..... Parsons, KS
Gray, Cheryl A. ..... New Orleans, LA
Gray, Cheryl E. ..... Mount Pleasant, MI
Gray, Chester L., Jr. ..... Irving, TX
Gray, Christine E. ..... New York, NY
Gray, Christopher D. ..... Palm Harbor, FL
Gray, Christopher J. ..... New York, NY
Gray, Christopher Lee ..... Sacramento, CA
Gray, Christopher R. ..... Allentown, PA
Gray, Cory Mitchell ..... New York, NY
Gray, Cynthia A. ..... Chicago, IL
Gray, Cynthia A. ..... Charlotte, NC
Gray, Cynthia D. ..... Atlanta, GA
Gray, Cynthia P. ..... Moraga, CA
Gray, Cynthia Schroeder ..... Santa Barbara, CA
Gray, Cyril A., Jr. ..... Superior, WI
Gray, D. Lockwood ..... Tampa, FL
Gray, Dale O. ..... St. Johnsbury, VT
Gray, Dan L., Jr. ..... Washington, DC
Gray, Dan T. ..... Oklahoma City, OK
Gray, Daniel Frederick ..... New York, NY
Gray, Daniel L. ..... Washington, DC
Gray, Daniel M. ..... Washington, DC
Gray, David ..... Washington, DC
Gray, David ..... Richfield, MN
Gray, David ..... King Of Prussia, PA
Gray, David B. ..... Louisville, KY
Gray, David B. ..... Portland, OR
Gray, David B. ..... Nashville, TN
Gray, David E. ..... Evansville, IN
Gray, David E. ..... Bangor, ME
Gray, David G. ..... New York, NY
Gray, David G. ..... Asheville, NC
Gray, David H. M. ..... Wichita, KS
Gray, David K. ..... Tucson, AZ
Gray, David L. ..... Toledo, OH
Gray, David N. ..... Houston, TX
Gray, David R. .....
Small Business Administration, GV
Gray, David R. ..... Chicago, IL
Gray, David W. ..... Indianapolis, IN
Gray, David W. ..... Louisville, KY
Gray, David W. ..... Pittsburgh, PA
Gray, Dawn ..... Grass Valley, CA
Gray, Dean L. ..... Salt Lake City, UT
Gray, Deborah Bonarrigo ..... Columbus, OH
Gray, Deborah England ..... Cambridge, MA
Gray, Deborah L. ..... Kalamazoo, MI
Gray, Deborah L. ..... Syracuse, NY
Gray, Denis A. ..... Cherry Hill, NJ
Paoli, PA
Philadelphia, PA
Gray, Dennis H. ..... Oracle, AZ
Tucson, AZ
Gray, Dennis H., P.C. ..... Oracle, AZ
Tucson, AZ
Gray, Dennis M. ..... Council Bluffs, IA
Gray & Dernoga ..... Highland, MD
Gray, Dodd Joseph ..... Indianapolis, IN
Gray, Donald A. ..... Long Prairie, MN
Gray, Donald A., Jr. ..... Waterbury, CT
Gray, Donald L. ..... Whiting, IN
Gray, Donald S. ..... Irvine, CA
Gray, Donald T. ..... San Francisco, CA
Gray, Donna K. ..... Houston, TX
Gray, Donna K., P.C. ..... Houston, TX
Gray, Douglas C. ..... New York, NY
Gray, Douglas G. ..... Providence, RI
Gray, Douglas I. ..... San Leandro, CA
Gray, Douglas R. ..... Rye, NH
Gray, Dudley ..... Torrance, CA
Gray, Dudley, II ..... Torrance, CA
Gray & Duning ..... Lebanon, OH
Gray, E. Crouse, Jr. ..... Kill Devil Hills, NC
Gray, Earl P., & Associates ..... St. Paul, MN
Gray, Edward A. ..... Mount Laurel, NJ
New York, NY
Philadelphia, PA
Gray, Edward J. ..... South Bend, IN
Gray, Edward P. ..... Indianapolis, IN
Gray, Edward W. ..... Baton Rouge, LA
Gray, Edward W. ..... Dallas, TX
Gray, Edward W., Jr. ..... Washington, DC
Gray, Elisabeth Summers ..... Louisville, KY
Gray, Elizabeth Lynn ..... Annandale, VA
Gray, Elizabeth Pickar
Securities and Exchange Commission,
Division of Enforcement, GV
Gray, Elizabeth Van Doren ..... Columbia, SC
Gray & End ..... Milwaukee, WI
Gray, Eric S. ..... Oklahoma City, OK
Gray, Erin ..... Los Angeles, CA
Gray, Ernestine S. ..... New Orleans, LA
Gray, Evan W. ..... New York, NY
Gray, Everett W. ..... Bangor, ME
Gray, F. James ..... St. Louis, MO
Gray, F. William, III ..... Buffalo, NY
Gray, Feldman & Rosenbaum, L.L.P.
Rochester, NY
Gray, Fleig and Biesterveld ..... Petersburg, IN
Gray, Francine H. ..... Portland, OR
Gray, Francis I. ..... Wilsonville, OR
Gray, Frank B. ..... Houston, TX
Gray, Frank J. ..... Fort Wayne, IN
Gray, Frank M., Jr. ..... Washington, DC
Gray, Frank T. ..... Baltimore, MD
Gray, Fred D. ..... Tuskegee, AL
Gray, Fred D., Jr. ..... Tuskegee, AL
Gray, Frederic K. ..... Amarillo, TX
Gray, Frederick (Fritz) C. ..... Tampa, FL
Gray, G. Richard ..... Hunt Valley, MD
Gray, G. Thomas ..... Martinsville, IN
Gray, Garrett L. ..... New York, NY
Gray, Gary D. ..... Treasury Department,
Internal Revenue Service, GV
Gray, Gary E. ..... Monterey, CA
Gray, Gary L. ..... San Francisco, CA
Gray, Gary M. ..... Houston, TX
Gray, Gary S. ..... Los Angeles, CA
Redwood City, CA
Gray, Gene W., Jr. ..... Birmingham, AL
Gray, Gene W., Jr., P.C. ..... Birmingham, AL
Gray, Geoffrey S. ..... Laguna Niguel, CA
Gray, Geoffrey W. .....
Department of Energy, GV
Gray, George Clyde ..... Indianapolis, IN
Gray, George G. ..... Waynesboro, TN
Gray, George H. ..... Rochester, NY
Gray, George H. ..... Chesapeake, VA
Gray, George Spencer ..... Jacksonville, FL
Gray, George W., III ..... Denver, CO
Gray, Gerald ..... San Diego, CA
Gray, Gerald ..... Boston, MA
Gray, Gerald B. ..... Aloha, OR
Gray, Gerald L. ..... Clintwood, VA
Gray, Gerald, Law Firm, A Professional Corporation ..... Clintwood, VA
Gray, Gerald T. ..... San Francisco, CA
Gray, Gerald W. ..... Incline Village, NV
Gray, Gerry ..... Georgetown, DE
Gray & Gidel ..... Rockwell City, IA
Gray & Gilliland, P.C. ..... Atlanta, GA
Gray, Gilson B., III ..... New York, NY
Gray, Glenn O. ..... New York, NY
Gray, Glenn Shelton ..... New York, NY
Gray, Gordon ..... Fort Worth, TX
Gray, Gordon E., III ..... Irvine, CA
Gray & Gray, A Professional Law Corporation
New Orleans, LA
Gray, Gray & Gray ..... Torrance, CA
Gray & Gray, P.C. ..... Kalamazoo, MI
Gray, Grayfred B. ..... Knoxville, TN
Gray, Greg ..... Mesquite, TX
Gray, Gregory A. ..... Tulsa, OK
Gray, Gregory M. ..... Oklahoma City, OK
Gray, Gregory N. ..... Minneapolis, MN
Gray, Guy James ..... Jasper, TX
Gray, H. Steven ..... Arvada, CO
Gray, Harold ..... Palm Beach, FL
Gray, Harris and Robinson, P.A.
Melbourne, FL
Tallahassee, FL
Orlando, FL
Gray, Harry J ..... Hamburg, NY
Gray, Harvey S. ..... Atlanta, GA
Gray & Heard, L.L.C. ..... Tifton, GA
Gray, Hedrick & Edenfield, L.L.P.
Atlanta, GA
Gray, Heiskell R. ..... Washington, DC
Gray, Herbert H., III ..... Atlanta, GA
Gray and Hirrel ..... Pasadena, CA
Gray and Hodnett, P.A. ..... Gastonia, NC
Gray, Humberto R. ..... Los Angeles, CA
Gray, Humberto R., A Professional Law Corporation ..... Los Angeles, CA
Gray, J. Alan ..... Addison, TX
Gray, J. Bowie ..... Tifton, GA
Gray, J. Carter S. ..... Millington, TN
Gray, J. Charles ..... Orlando, FL
Gray, J. Kevin ..... Dallas, TX
Gray, J. Lee ..... Denver, CO
Gray, J. Marie ..... Santa Ana, CA
Gray, J. Michael ..... Kodiak, AK
Gray, J. Reid, III ..... New York, NY
Gray, J. Richard ..... Lancaster, PA
Gray, J. Rockhill ..... Bronxville, NY
Gray, J. Stephen ..... Salisbury, NC
Gray, Jack E. ..... Oklahoma City, OK
Gray, Jack H. ..... Houston, TX
Gray, Jack R. ..... Rockwell City, IA
Gray, Jacqueline R. ..... Santa Ana, CA
Gray, James A. ..... Little Rock, AR
Gray, James A. ..... Caldwell, TX
Gray, James A., II ..... New Orleans, LA
Gray, James A., III ..... Detroit, MI
Gray, James B., Jr. ..... Rochester, NY
Gray, James C. ..... Gastonia, NC
Gray, James C., III ..... Birmingham, AL
Gray, James C., Jr. ..... Columbia, SC
Gray, James Cary ..... Houston, TX
Gray, James D. ..... Cleveland, OH
Gray, James D. ..... Clarksburg, WV
Gray, James E. ..... Baltimore, MD
Gray, James E. ..... Warren, OH
Gray, James F. ..... Gainesville, FL
Gray, James F. ..... Vancouver, WA
Gray, James H. ..... Dallas, TX
Gray, James H., Jr.
Federal Housing Finance Board,
Office of the Board of Directors, GV
Gray, James H., Jr. ..... Woodstock, VT
Gray, James P. ..... Santa Ana, CA
Gray, James P. ..... Springfield, MO
Gray, James R. ..... Athens, GA
Gray, James R. ..... Minneapolis, MN
Gray, James R., P.C. ..... Athens, GA
Gray, James S. ..... Chicago, IL
Gray, James T. ..... Milwaukee, WI
Gray, James W. ..... Indianapolis, IN
Gray, Jan D. ..... Department of Education,
Office for Civil Rights, GV
Gray, Jane Powell ..... Raleigh, NC
Gray, Janet ..... Houston, TX
Gray, Janet ..... Bellevue, WA
Gray, Jason L. ..... Palo Alto, CA
Gray & Jauregui ..... Montgomery, AL
Gray, Jay C. ..... Grapeland, TX
Gray, Jay K. ..... Hurst, TX
Gray, Jeanne P. ..... Chicago, IL
Gray, Jeff ..... Burnsville, MN
Gray, Jefferson M. ..... Baltimore, MD
Gray, Jeffrey ..... Torrance, CA
Gray, Jeffrey B. ..... Boston, MA
Gray, Jeffrey E. ..... North Wilkesboro, NC
Gray, Jeffrey H. ..... Norfolk, VA
Virginia Beach, VA
Gray, Jeffrey M. ..... Hartselle, AL
Gray, Jeffrey P. ..... San Francisco, CA
Gray, Jeffrey P. ..... Chicago, IL
Gray, Jeffrey P. ..... Raleigh, NC
Gray, Jeffrey R. ..... Chicago, IL
Gray, Jeffrey S. ..... Cleveland, OH
Gray, Jeffrey S. ..... Salt Lake City, UT
Gray, Jeffry W. ..... Baton Rouge, LA
Gray, Jennifer K. ..... Houston, TX
Gray, Jennifer L. ..... New York, NY
Gray, Jeremy J. F. ..... Los Angeles, CA
Gray, Jerry C. ..... Jefferson, GA
Gray, Jessica D. ..... Federal Trade Commission,
Bureau of Competition, GV
Gray, Jimmylee, (P.C.) ..... Detroit, MI
Gray, Joan D. ..... New York, NY
Gray, Joanne M. ..... New York, NY
Gray, Joanne S. ..... Middletown, NJ
Gray, Joe ..... Dallas, TX
Gray, Joe S. ..... Sacramento, CA
Gray, Joel W. ..... Huntington Beach, CA
Gray, John A. ..... Plaquemine, LA
Gray, John A. ..... Baltimore, MD
Gray, John A. ..... Salem, MA
Gray, John A. ..... Manchester, NH
Gray, John B. ..... Florissant, MO
Gray, John C. ..... Atlanta, GA
Gray, John C. ..... Sioux City, IA
Gray, John C. ..... Brooklyn, NY
Gray, John D. ..... Oroville, CA
Gray, John D. F. ..... Memphis, TN
Gray, John E. ..... New York, NY
Gray, John F. ..... Fort Worth, TX
Gray, John Fisher ..... Wilmington, DE
Gray, John G., Jr. ..... Boise, ID
Gray, John H. ..... Naples, FL
Gray, John K. ..... Traverse City, MI
Gray, John L. ..... Columbus, OH
Gray, John M. ..... Olympia, WA
Gray, John M., Jr. ..... McMinnville, OR
Gray, John Philip ..... Montgomery, AL
Gray, John S. ..... Huntington Beach, CA
Gray, John S. ..... Newport Beach, CA
Gray, John S. ..... Houston, TX
Gray, John W. ..... Tallahassee, FL
Gray, John W., Jr. ..... Washington, DC
Gray, John W., Jr. ..... Oklahoma City, OK
Gray, John William, Jr. ..... Richmond, VA
Gray, Jon F. ..... Chesterland, OH
Gray, Jon R. ..... Kansas City, MO
Gray, Jonathan ..... New York, NY
Gray, Jonathan W. ..... New York, NY
Gray, Joni L. ..... Santa Maria, CA
Gray, Jordan N. ..... San Bernardino, CA
Gray, Joseph ..... Philadelphia, PA
Gray, Joseph B., Jr. ..... Tifton, GA
Gray, Joseph M., Jr. ..... Pittsburgh, PA
Gray, Joseph R.
Nuclear Regulatory Commission,
Office of the General Counsel, GV
Gray, Judith Bradley ..... Taunton, MA
Gray, Judson C. ..... Tacoma, WA
Gray, Judson, Ford & Seaman, P.C.
Traverse City, MI
Gray, Julia Lea ..... St. Louis, MO
Gray, Julian E. ..... Coraopolis, PA
Pittsburgh, PA
Gray, Karen A. ..... New York, NY
Gray, Karen Scholer ..... San Luis Obispo, CA
Gray, Kari J. ..... Douglas, WY
Gray, Karl R. ..... Oklahoma City, OK
Gray, Karla M. ..... Helena, MT
Gray, Kathleen A. ..... Milwaukee, WI
Gray, Kathleen Ann ..... Chambersburg, PA
Lancaster, PA
Reading, PA
Gray, Kathleen J. ..... Rochester, NY
Gray, Keith P. ..... St. Louis, MO
Gray, Kelly K. ..... Tampa, FL
Gray, Kendall M. ..... Houston, TX
Gray, Kenneth E. ..... Pittsburgh, PA
Gray, Kenneth F., Jr. ..... Birmingham, AL
Gray, Kenneth Fairbanks ..... Portland, ME
Gray, Kenneth H. ..... Helena, MT
Gray, Kenneth P. ..... Millbrae, CA
Gray, Kent R. P. ..... Colorado Springs, CO
Gray, Kerwin L. ..... Atlanta, GA
Gray, Kevin C. ..... Huntsville, AL
Gray, Kevin F. ..... St. Cloud, MN
Gray, Kevin J. ..... San Francisco, CA
Gray, Kimberly S. ..... Pittsburgh, PA
Gray, Kristi L. ..... Pikeville, KY
Gray, Kristin A. .....
Office Of Special Counsel, GV
Gray, Kyle A. ..... Billings, MT
Gray, Langford, Sapp, McGowan, Gray & Nathanson ..... Montgomery, AL
Tuskegee, AL
Gray, Laura A. ..... Chicago, IL
Gray, Laura L. ..... Huntington, WV
Gray, Laura Milliken ..... Salt Lake City, UT
Gray, Laureen J. ..... Santa Ana, CA
Gray, Lauren M. ..... Mineola, NY
Gray, Laurence ..... Chicago, IL
Gray, Laurie Davis ..... Burbank, CA
Gray Law Firm, The, A Professional Law Corporation ..... Lake Charles, LA
Gray, Lawrence A. ..... Chicago, IL
Gray, Lawrence C. ..... Joliet, IL
Gray, Lawrence N. ..... New York, NY
Gray, Lawrence S., Jr. ..... Pasadena, CA

Gray, Layton, Kersh, Solomon, Sigmon, Furr & Smith, P.A. ... Charlotte, NC
Gastonia, NC
Lincolnton, NC
Shelby, NC
Gray, Leonie D. ... Tucson, AZ
Gray, Lil Ann ... Columbia, SC
Gray, Linda L. ... East Troy, WI
Gray, Lisa A. ... Minneapolis, MN
Gray, Llewellyn W. ... Kalamazoo, MI
Gray & Lloyd, LLP ... Kill Devil Hills, NC
Gray, Lois Tabberson ... Westminster, CO
Gray, Lois Tabberson, P.C. ... Westminster, CO
Gray, Loren E. ... Mount Pleasant, MI
Gray, Loring A., Jr. ... Albany, GA
Gray, Louis ... Cleveland, OH
Gray, Louis Patrick, III ... New London, CT
Gray, L. W. ... Caldwell, TX
Gray, Lynette ... Franklin, IN
Gray, Lynn B. ... Fort Worth, TX
Gray, Maria ... San Francisco, CA
Gray, Marita Durkin ... Fall River, MA
Gray, Mark ... Minneapolis, MN
Gray, Mark A., Jr. ... Brookline, MA
Gray, Mark K. ... Louisville, KY
Okolona, KY
Gray, Mark, P.A. ... Minneapolis, MN
Gray, Mark Robert ... Ankeny, IA
Gray, Mark S. ... Indianapolis, IN
Gray, Mark Thaddeus ...
Department of Defense, GV
Gray, Mark William ... Indianapolis, IN
Gray, Marlena" Marnie "
Birmingham, AL
Gray, Martha C. ... Frankfort, KY
Gray, Marvin K. ... Charlotte, NC
Gray, Marvin L., Jr. ... Seattle, WA
Gray, Mary Beth H. ... Philadelphia, PA
Gray, Mary Launa ... Southaven, MS
Gray, Mat M., III ... New Orleans, LA
Gray, Matthew S. ... San Francisco, CA
Gray, Maxwell ... Indianapolis, IN
Gray, Megan E. ... Los Angeles, CA
Gray, Melanie ... Houston, TX
Gray, Melany R. ... New York, NY
Gray, Melissa D., Law Offices of
Towson, MD
Gray, Melissa R. ... Los Angeles, CA
Gray, Melvin ... Homewood, IL
Gray, Melvin N., & Associates
San Angelo, TX
Gray, Michael. ... Dallas, TX
Gray, Michael B. ... Irvine, CA
Gray, Michael D. ... Oklahoma City, OK
Gray, Michael E. ... Sanford, FL
Gray, Michael E., P.A. ... Sanford, FL
Gray, Michael G. ... Perry, GA
Gray, Michael Hall ... Santa Barbara, CA
Gray, Michael J. ... Chicago, IL
Gray, Michael K. ... Vero Beach, FL
Gray, Michael P. ... Kohler, WI
Gray, Michael R. ... Minneapolis, MN
Gray, Michael R. ... Roanoke, VA
Gray, Miller, Patterson & Cody
Lancaster, PA
York, PA
Gray, Milo G., Jr. ... Beech Grove, IN
Gray, Milton ... St. Paul, MN
Gray, Milton H. ... Chicago, IL
Gray & Moore, L.L.P. ... Houston, TX
Gray, Morgan J. ... Burlington, MA
Gray, Morris G. ... Houston, TX
Gray, Moya T. D. ... Honolulu, HI
Gray, N. Dwayne, Jr. ... Orlando, FL
Gray, Nancy M. ... Fitchburg, MA
Gray, Naomi Jane ... New York, NY
Gray, Neil S. ... Hudson, OH
Gray, Oren ... Oswego, KS
Gray, Oscar S. ... Baltimore, MD
Gray & Palmer ... Bangor, ME
Gray, Pamela C. ... Los Angeles, CA
Newport Beach, CA
Gray, Pamela Jean ... Atlanta, GA
Gray, Patricia A. ... Santa Rosa, CA
Gray, Patricia A. ... Westborough, MA
Gray, Patricia D. ... St. Louis, MO
Gray, Patricia L. ... Treasury Department,
Internal Revenue Service, GV
Gray, Patricia, P.C. ... Galveston, TX
Gray, Patrick O. ... Birmingham, AL
Gray, Patrick W. ... Lafayette, LA
Gray, Paul Bryan ... Claremont, CA
Gray, Paul E. ... Wakefield, RI
Gray, Paul L. ... Philadelphia, PA
West Chester, PA
Gray, Paulette Michelle ... Woodstock, IL
Gray, Peter ... Minneapolis, MN
Gray, Peter A. ... Department of Justice,
Antitrust Division, GV
Gray, Peter G. ... Brooklyn, NY
Gray, Peter G., P.C. ... Brooklyn, NY
Gray, Peter L. ... Washington, DC
Gray, Peter S.
Equal Employment Opportunity
Commission,
Office of Federal Operations, GV
Gray, Philip F. ... Harrisburg, PA
Gray, Philip Todd ... Raleigh, NC
Gray, Philip W. ... Honolulu, HI
Gray, Plant, Mooty, Mooty & Bennett, P.A.
Minneapolis, MN
Gray, Priscilla F. ... Cumberland, ME
Gray, R. Benton ... Cleveland, OH
Gray, R. Benton, & Company
Cleveland, OH
Gray, R. Frank ... Raleigh, NC
Gray, R. A., III ... Hattiesburg, MS
Gray, Randal C. ... New Braunfels, TX
Gray, Randal C., P.C. ... New Braunfels, TX
Gray, Randall H. ... Great Falls, MT
Gray, Randall T. ... Blue Springs, MO
Gray, Raymond R. ... Austin, TX
Gray, Raymond W. ... Nashville, IN
Gray, Reuben L. ... Sumter, SC
Gray, Rhonda S. ... Chicago, IL
Gray, Richard A. ... Salem, NH
Fairfax, VA
Gray, Richard A. ... Williamsport, PA
Gray, Richard A., Law Office of, P.C.
Salem, NH
Gray, Richard E., III ... Austin, TX
Gray, Richard H. ... Sacramento, CA
Gray, Richard J. ... Chicago, IL
Gray, Richard L. ... Kansas City, MO
Gray, Richard L. ... Greensboro, NC
Gray, Richard N. ... New York, NY
Gray, Richard O., Jr. ... Bellevue, WA
Gray, Richard R. ... Sacramento, CA
Gray, Richard V. ... Coral Gables, FL
Gray, Richard W. ... Grand Rapids, MI
Gray, Richard Z. ... Elizabethton, TN
Gray & Ritter, P.C. ... North Little Rock, AR
St. Louis, MO
Gray, Robert ... Houston, TX
Gray, Robert B. ... Oakland, CA
Gray, Robert C. ... Melbourne, FL
Gray, Robert C., P.A. ... Melbourne, FL
Gray, Robert D. ... Oklahoma City, OK
Gray, Robert E. ... Troy, NY
Gray, Robert F., Jr. ... Houston, TX
Gray, Robert J. ... Wausau, WI
Gray, Robert L. ... Prince Frederick, MD
Gray, Robert L. ... Mayfield, OH
Gray, Robert Reed ... Washington, DC
Gray, Robert W. ... Fort Myers, FL
Gray, Robert W. ... New York, NY
Gray, Robert W. ... North Ridgeville, OH
Gray, Robert Y. ... Teaneck, NJ
Gray, Robinson, Ryan & Fox, P.C.
Indianapolis, IN
Gray, Rodney D. ... Jefferson City, MO
Gray, Roland, III ... Boston, MA
Gray, Ronald A. ... New York, NY
Gray, Ronald D. ... Dallas, TX
Gray, Ronald L. ... Oregon City, OR
Gray, Rosalie Walker ... Houston, TX
Gray, Roy C., III ... Frankfort, KY
Gray, Russell W. ... Chattanooga, TN
Gray, S. Garrett ... New York, NY
Gray, S. McKinley, III ... New Bern, NC
Gray, S. Zoe ... New York, NY
Gray, Sadow & Hoffman, P.C.
St. Louis, MO
Gray, Samuel O. ... Stamford, CT
Gray, Samuel S., Jr. ... Doylestown, PA
Gray, Sandra ... Atlanta, GA
Gray, Sandra Edwards ... Lancaster, PA
Gray, Saundria Chase ... Houston, TX
Gray, Scott A. ... Norfolk, NE
Gray, Scott W. ... Phoenix, AZ
Gray, Sean ... Trenton, NJ
Gray, Seann Anderson ... Greenville, SC
Gray, Shara L. ... Montgomery, AL
Gray, Sharon D. ... New York, NY
Gray, Sharon T. ... Scotts Valley, CA
Gray, Shawn C. ... Stuart, FL
Gray, Shirley J. ... Harlingen, TX
Gray, Sidney ... Milwaukee, WI
Gray & Slipp ... Newport Beach, CA
Gray, Sowle & Iacco, A Professional Corporation ... Alma, MI
Clare, MI
Midland, MI
Mount Pleasant, MI
Gray, Stanley F. ... Tuskegee, AL
Gray, Stefani & Mitvalsky, P.L.C.
Cedar Rapids, IA
Gray, Stephanie ... Danville, CA
Gray, Stephen C. ... Columbus, OH
Gray, Stephen D. ... Henderson, KY
Gray, Stephen E. ... New York, NY
Gray, Stephen F. ... Chicago, IL
Gray, Stephen G. ... Carver, MA
Gray, Stephen G. ... Essex Fells, NJ
Gray, Stephen Gerald ... Indianapolis, IN
Gray, Stephen H. ... New York, NY
Gray, Stephen M. ... Houston, TX
Gray, Stephen P. ... Tulsa, OK
Gray, Stephen P., P.C. ... Tulsa, OK
Gray, Steven H. ... Ocala, FL
Gray, Steven J. ... Oakland, CA
Gray, Steven J. ... Chicago, IL
Gray, Steven P. ... Kodiak, AK
Gray, Steven R. ... Secaucus, NJ
Trenton, NJ
Gray, Steven W. ... Downey, CA
Gray, Susan Baker ... Highland, MD
Gray, Susan E. ... Buffalo, NY
Gray, Susan G. ... San Antonio, TX
Gray, Susan H. ... Winston-Salem, NC
Gray, Susan L. ... Las Vegas, NV
Gray, Susan M. ... Rocky River, OH
Gray, T. Wayne ... Washington, DC
Gray, Tania Gutman ... Boston, MA
Gray, Terrance M. ... Woodbury, NY
Gray, Terry C. ... Gary, IN
Gray, Terry R. ... Milwaukee, WI
Gray, Thayne D. ... Wilmington, OH
Gray, Theron A.
Department of Transportation,
Federal Aviation Administration, GV
Gray, Thomas ... Menlo Park, CA
Gray & Thomas ... Dallas, TX
Gray, Thomas A. ... Los Angeles, CA
Gray, Thomas A. ... Boston, MA
Gray, Thomas C. ... Petersburg, IN
Gray, Thomas D. ... Anaheim, CA
Gray, Thomas J. ... Wedderburn, OR
Gray, Thomas M. ... Richmond, CA
Gray, Thomas S., Jr. ... Savannah, GA
Gray, Thomas Stewart ... Springfield, IL
Gray, Thomas V. ... Baltimore, MD
Gray, Thomas W. ... Montgomery, AL
Gray, Thomas W. ... Springfield, IL
Gray, Thomas W. ... Kansas City, MO
Gray and Thurn, Inc. ... Sacramento, CA
Gray, Tim ... Jackson, MS
Gray, Timothy J. ... Newport Beach, CA
Gray, Timothy L. ... New Albany, IN
Louisville, KY
Gray, Todd D. ... Washington, DC
Gray, Toni Jo ... Denver, CO
Gray, Toni Jo ... Denver, CO
Gray, Tracy Birnkrant ... Broomfield, CO
Gray, Twyla Mason ... Oklahoma City, OK
Gray, Valerie A. ... New Hyde Park, NY
Gray, Veronica M., (Law Corporation)
Newport Beach, CA
Gray, Victoria Moore ... Cincinnati, OH
Gray, Vykki ... San Diego, CA
Gray, W. Gary ... Bel Air, MD
Gray, W. Robert ... Fort Worth, TX
Gray, Wallace T. ... Indianapolis, IN
Gray, Walter L., III ... Phenix City, AL
Gray, Walter L., Jr. ... Oklahoma City, OK
Gray, Walter Powell ... San Antonio, TX
Gray, Walter Powell, P.C.
San Antonio, TX
Gray, Warren M. ... Department of Energy,
Office of Hearings and Appeals, GV
Gray & Wendell ... Beverly, MA
Boston, MA
Gray, Wendell & Clark, Professional Corporation ... Manchester, NH
Gray, Whitmore ... New York, NY
Gray, William A. ... Atlanta, GA
Gray, William A. ... New York, NY
Gray, William A. ... Pittsburgh, PA
Gray, William Alexander, Jr. ... Mobile, AL
Gray, William C., Jr. ... Wilkesboro, NC
Gray, William E. ... Battle Creek, MI
Gray, William E., II ... Atlanta, GA
Gray, William F. ... West Haven, CT
Gray, William F., Jr. ... New York, NY
Gray, William G. ... Olathe, KS
Gray, William J. ... Miami, FL
Gray, William J. ... Albany, NY
Gray, William O. ... Chattanooga, TN
Gray, William O., III ... New York, NY
Gray, William P., III
West Palm Beach, FL
Gray, William P., Jr. ... Montgomery, AL
Gray, William R. ... Boulder, CO
Denver, CO
Gray, William R. ... Salt Lake City, UT
Gray, William S. ... Ventura, CA
Gray, William S. ... Charlottesville, VA
Gray, William T. ... Irvine, CA
Gray, William T. ... Houston, TX
Gray, Wm. Douglas ... Anderson, SC
Gray, Wm. H. ... Dallas, TX
Gray, Woods & Cooper ... Ashland, KY
Grayson, KY
Greenup, KY
Gray, Wren M. ... Denton, TX
Gray, York & Duffy LLP
Los Angeles, CA
Redwood City, CA
San Francisco, CA
Gray, Zachary S. ... Cleveland, OH
Graybeal, David P. ... New York, NY
Graybeal, David W. ... Norcross, GA
Graybeal Jackson Haley LLP
Bellevue, WA
Graybeal, John F. ... Raleigh, NC
Graybeal, Lee Anne ... Washington, NJ
Graybeal, Lynne E. ... Seattle, WA
Graybehl, Sherry D. ... Santa Ana, CA
Graybill, Barbara G. ... Harrisburg, PA
Graybill, Benjamin R. ... Great Falls, MT
Graybill & English, L.L.C. ... Washington, DC
Graybill, Irvin, Jr. ... Middleburg, PA
Graybill, Jacob S. ... Wichita, KS
Graybill, Jean E. ... Harrisburg, PA
Graybill, Jeffrey H. ... Sacramento, CA
Graybill, Lloyd C. ... Graeagle, CA
Graybill, M. William ... Tampa, FL
Graybill, Nina ... Washington, DC
Graybill, Ostrem & Crotty, PLLP
Great Falls, MT
Graybill, Richard M. ... Ishpeming, MI
Graybill, Turner C. ... Great Falls, MT
Graybill, Wesley M. ... Aiken, SC
Graybill, William J. ... Elkhart, KS
Graybill, Witcher & Ambrosier
Elkhart, KS
Grayburn, Samuel T. ... New York, NY
Grayburn, Susan T. ... New York, NY
Grayck, Marcus D. ... Chicago, IL
Grayden, Margaret Miller ... Davis, CA
Graydon, Elin H. ... Salem, MA
Graydon, G. Galt ... Austin, TX
Graydon, Head & Ritchey ... Florence, KY
Cincinnati, OH
Graydon, J. Nicholas ... New Orleans, LA
Graydon, Marcia Klosk
South Orange, NJ
Graydon, Scot M. ... San Antonio, TX
Grayer, C. David ... Boston, MA
Grayer & Dilday ... Boston, MA
Grayer, Elizabeth L. ... New York, NY
Grayer, Evan Robert ... Washington, DC
Grayer, Frederick R. ... Willingboro, NJ
Grayer, James A. ... New York, NY
Grayer, Julius J. ... Belmar, NJ
Gray-Fuson, Joan ... Sacramento, CA
Gray-Keeler, Karen R. ... Evanston, IL
Gray-Knight, Christine A ... Silver Spring, MD
Graykowski, John E. ... Washington, DC
Grayman, Peter M. ... Playa Del Rey, CA
Graynor, Andrew David ... Mineola, NY
Graynor, Barry A. ... San Francisco, CA
Graynor & Graynor ... Mineola, NY
Graynor, Louis ... Mineola, NY
Grays, Marguerite ... Jamaica, NY
Grays, Taa R. ... Bronx, NY
Graysen, William T. ... Los Angeles, CA
Grayson, Alan M. ... Bronx, NY
Grayson, Andrea ... Springfield, NJ
Grayson, Andrew S. ... Tallahassee, FL
Grayson, Ann S. ... Minneapolis, MN
Grayson, Bette R. ... Springfield, NJ
Grayson, Brad S. ... Chicago, IL
Grayson, Carl E. ... Covington, KY
Grayson, Carole A., Law Office of
Seattle, WA
Grayson, Christopher L. ... Westbury, NY
Grayson, Constance G. ... West Memphis, AR
Grayson, David L. ... Cincinnati, OH
Grayson, Dean L. ... Washington, DC
Grayson, Deborah R. ... Cincinnati, OH
Grayson, Denise M. ... Arlington Heights, IL
Grayson, E. Lynn ... Chicago, IL
Grayson, Eric D., Law Offices of
Greenwich, CT
Stamford, CT
Grayson, Eric D., Law Offices of
Stamford, CT
Grayson, Eric L. ... Wilmington, DE
Grayson, Gary J. ... Walton, NY
Grayson, George ... Binghamton, NY
Grayson, Gerald E. ... New York, NY
Grayson, Glenn S. ... Overland Park, KS
Grayson, Grant S. ... Richmond, VA
Grayson, Grayson & Mansell, A Professional Corporation ... Los Angeles, CA
Grayson & Grayson, P.A. ... Little Rock, AR
North Little Rock, AR
Grayson, Heath H. ... New York, NY
Grayson, James P. ... Bristol, TN
Grayson, Jim G. ... Los Angeles, CA
Grayson, Joel E. ... Portland, OR
Grayson, John A. ... Indianapolis, IN
Grayson, John L. ... Houston, TX
Grayson, John S. ... St. Paul, MN
Grayson, Joni L. ... Jeffersonville, IN
Grayson, Joseph C. ... Chicago, IL
Grayson, Karen N. ... Glen Rock, NJ
Grayson, Keith L. ... North Little Rock, AR
Grayson, Larry D. ... Dallas, TX
Grayson, Laureen B. ... Santa Monica, CA
Grayson, Lee March ... Randolph, NJ
Grayson, Mark ... Los Angeles, CA
Grayson, Mark R. ... New York, NY
Grayson, Martin L. ... Long Beach, CA
Grayson, Martin L. ... Los Angeles, CA
Grayson, Melanie L.
North Little Rock, AR
Grayson, Michael A. ... Beverly Hills, CA
Grayson, Michael B. ... Tucson, AZ
Grayson, Mitchell T. ... Haddonfield, NJ
Grayson, Moises T. ... Miami, FL
Grayson, Myrna N. ... Coronado, CA
Grayson, Neil E. ... Atlanta, GA
Grayson, Nina P. ... New York, NY
Grayson, Patrick H., Jr. ... Greenville, SC
Grayson, Pegine E. ... Pasadena, CA
Grayson, Peter C. ... St. Paul, MN
Grayson, R. Sean ... Worthington, OH
Grayson, Randall D. ... Atlanta, GA
Grayson, Richard A. ... St. Paul, MN
Grayson, Richard E. ... White Plains, NY
Grayson, Robert A. ... Carson City, NV
Grayson, Robert C. ... Seattle, WA
Grayson, Robert J. ... Marietta, GA
Grayson, Robyn J. ... Brooklyn, NY
Grayson, Russell ... Hardeeville, SC
Grayson, Russell W. ... Ridgewood, NJ
Grayson, Russell W., P.C. ... Ridgewood, NJ
Grayson, Sandra L. ... Manhasset, NY
Grayson, Saul ... Los Angeles, CA
Grayson, Smith, Stodghill & Price, P.C.
Greenville, SC
Grayson, Stephen P. ... Los Angeles, CA
Grayson, Steven R. ... Philadelphia, PA
Grayson, Thomas R. ... Mountain City, TN
Grayson, Todd I. ... Beverly Hills, CA
Grayson, Trey ... Covington, KY
Cincinnati, OH
Grayson, Troy L. ... Birmingham, AL
Grayson, V. Elizabeth ... San Francisco, CA
Grayson, Valerie Levy ... Ridgefield, CT
Grayson, Walton G., III ... Dallas, TX
Grayson, Warren B. ... Chicago, IL
Grayson, William E. ... Torrance, CA
Grayson & Wright ... Mountain City, TN
Grayson, Zachary L. ... Philadelphia, PA
Grayston, Charles M. ... Annapolis, MD
Grayton, Lillian M. ... Newburyport, MA
Grazan, Lisa V. ... Pittsburgh, PA
Graze, Lawrence ... La Jolla, CA
Grazi & Gianino, P.A. ... Stuart, FL
Grazi, Leif J. ... Stuart, FL
Graziadei & Cantor, Ltd. ... Las Vegas, NV
Graziadei, Frank M. ... New York, NY
Graziadei, Frank M., P.C., Law Firm of
New York, NY
Graziadei, George E. ... Las Vegas, NV
Graziadei, John B., Jr. ... Brooklyn, NY
Graziadei, John H. ... New York, NY
Grazian, John L. ... Chicago, IL
Grazian, Lawrence L. ... Oak Brook, IL

Grazian, Leonard R. .... Chicago, IL
Graziani, Alfred E. .... Belmont, CA
Graziani, Anthony Eugene
Rockville Centre, NY
Graziani, Joel F. .... Ann Arbor, MI
Graziani, John .... Southgate, MI
Graziani, Regina C. .... Hartford, CT
Graziani, Robert E. .... Detroit, MI
Graziano, Alexander J. .... Livingston, NJ
Graziano, Anthony J. .... Paterson, NJ
Graziano, Bruno L. .... Riverwoods, IL
Graziano, Catherine E. .... Providence, RI
Graziano, Craig F. .... Des Moines, IA
Graziano, Daniel J., Jr. .... Trenton, NJ
Graziano, Dominick J. .... Tampa, FL
Graziano, Gayle .... Daytona Beach, FL
Graziano, James B. .... Middlesex, NJ
Graziano, James M. .... Boulder, CO
Graziano, Jill M. .... New York, NY
Graziano, John W. .... Lee, MA
Graziano, Joseph P. .... Woodland Hills, CA
Graziano, Mark A. .... Tulsa, OK
Graziano, Paul A. .... Santa Barbara, CA
Graziano, Peter .... New York, NY
Graziano, Robert B. .... Columbus, OH
Graziano, Robin M. .... Pittsburgh, PA
Graziano, Ronald A. .... Cherry Hill, NJ
Northfield, NJ
Graziano, Salvatore J. .... New York, NY
Graziano, Sheila G. .... Buffalo, NY
Graziano, William J. .... Thousand Oaks, CA
Grazier, G. Roy, Sr. .... Nowata, OK
Grazioli, Anthony J. .... Tuckahoe, NY
Grazioso, Frank M. .... New Haven, CT
Grazioso, George J. .... Baton Rouge, LA
Grazioso & Hosen .... New Haven, CT
Graziotti, Theodore A.
Dearborn Heights, MI
Grbic, S. Michael .... Cypress, CA
Grbic, Susan M. .... New York, NY
Grcevic, Barbara H. .... Brooklyn, NY
Grden, Thomas R. .... Pontiac, MI
Grdina, Betty .... Washington, DC
Grdina, Michael F. .... Cleveland, OH
Greabe, John M. .... Marion, MA
Greacen, John M. .... Santa Fe, NM
Greagan, William J. .... Albany, NY
Greak, Nolan .... Littlefield, TX
Lubbock, TX
Greak, Nolan .... Muleshoe, TX
Grealis, Thomas V. .... Edison, NJ
Grealis, William J. .... Washington, DC
Grealish, Gerard E. .... Scranton, PA
Grealy, Cornelius J. .... Wilton, CT
Grealy, Mary-Ellen .... Boston, MA
Grean, Michael A. .... Rye, NY
Grean & Ward .... Rye, NY
Greaney, Constance M. .... Columbus, OH
Greaney, Dennis J. .... Dayton, OH
Greaney, E. Michael .... Irvine, CA
New York, NY
Greaney, John F. .... Department of Justice, Antitrust Division, GV
Greaney, John J. .... Bellevue, WA
Greaney, John J., Jr. .... East Durham, NY
Greaney, John M. .... Boston, MA
Greaney, Joseph K. .... Ridgefield Park, NJ
Greaney, Michael E. .... Los Angeles, CA
Greaney, Patrick F. .... Silver Spring, MD
Greaney, Thomas L. .... St. Louis, MO
Greaney, Walter C., Jr. .... Springfield, MA
Greaney, Walter T., Jr. .... Boston, MA
Greaney, William F. .... Washington, DC
Greanias, Basil G. .... Decatur, IL
Greanias, Gus T. .... Decatur, IL
Greanias, John K. .... Decatur, IL
Grear, Craig D. .... Wilmington, DE
Grear, Joan C. Goldenthal .... Hartford, CT
Grear, John Michael .... Greensburg, KS
Grear, Joseph A. .... Chicago, IL
Grear, Kenneth B. .... Philadelphia, PA
Greaser, Bryan D. .... Jackson, MO
Greason, Edward W. .... New York, NY
Greason, Edward W. .... White Plains, NY
Greason, James H. .... Miami, FL
Greason, Katherine .... Augusta, ME
Greason, Murray C. .... Winston-Salem, NC
Greason, Murray C., Jr.
Winston-Salem, NC
Greason, Samuel, IV .... Lafayette, CA
Greathead, R. Scott .... New York, NY
Greathouse, C. Richard, Jr. .... Middletown, OH
Greathouse, Cecil R. .... Boise, ID
Greathouse, Gerald W. .... Dallas, TX
Greathouse, Greg .... Delta, UT
Greathouse, Larry C. .... Cleveland, OH
Greathouse, Larry J. .... Vernon, IN
Greathouse, Larry M. .... Frankfort, KY
Greathouse, Leslie A. .... Kansas City, MO
Greathouse, Michael D.
Fairview Heights, IL
Greathouse, Michael J. .... San Francisco, CA
Greathouse, Paula S. .... Dakota City, NE
Greathouse, Phillip D. .... Joplin, MO
Greathouse, Robert L. .... Lexington, KY
Greathouse, Sidney M. .... Los Angeles, CA
Greaton and Greaton
Fort Lauderdale, FL
Greaton, Wilson B., Jr.
Fort Lauderdale, FL
Greatrex, George C., Jr. .... Philadelphia, PA
Greaud, Stacey L. .... Baton Rouge, LA
Greaves, Bonnie .... New York, NY
Greaves, Burt .... Champaign, IL
Greaves, Catherine M. .... Austin, TX
Greaves, Charles J., (P.C.) .... Pasadena, CA
Greaves, Corin A. .... Philadelphia, PA
Greaves, Deborah E. .... Los Angeles, CA
Greaves, E. Michael .... Des Moines, IA
Greaves, Fiona .... Hartford, CT
Greaves, Jeffrey T. .... New York, NY
Greaves, Jill Renee .... Gainesville, FL
Greaves, John A. .... Los Angeles, CA
Greaves, Josephine M. .... Boston, MA
Greaves, Lawrence H. .... Beverly Hills, CA
Greaves, Linda Kay .... Tulsa, OK
Greaves, Mac B. .... Birmingham, AL
Greaves, Nola Jan Fisher .... Knoxville, TN
Greaves, Robert D. .... Portland, OR
Greaves, Thomas F. .... El Centro, CA
Greaves, Thomas G., III .... Greenville, SC
Greaves, Thomas G., Jr. .... Mobile, AL
Greb, Mitchell J. .... Framingham, MA
Greb, Morris Leo .... Rockaway, NJ
Grebasch, Virginia S.
General Services Administration, Office of Inspector General, GV
Grebber, David L. .... Boston, MA
Grebe, Gregory J. .... Anchorage, AK
Grebe, James R. .... Peoria, IL
Grebe, Jeffrey A. .... Sarasota, FL
Grebe, Katherine H. .... Milwaukee, WI
Grebe, Lynn C. .... Bay City, TX
Grebe, Michael M. .... Milwaukee, WI
Grebe, Michael W. .... Milwaukee, WI
Grebe, Ottmar H., Jr. .... St. Louis, MO
Grebe, Sibylle .... Torrance, CA
Grebe, Walter H. .... Portland, OR
Grebel, Lawrence B. .... St. Louis, MO
Greben & Associates .... Sacramento, CA
Greben, Brian L. .... New York, NY
Greben, Jan Adam .... Sacramento, CA
Grebenar, Tennyson W. .... Denver, CO
Grebene, Alan K. .... Palo Alto, CA
Greber, David S. .... Baltimore, MD
Frederick, MD
Greber, Edmund A. .... Fort Worth, TX
Greber, Forest .... Carlsbad, CA
Greber, Michael J. .... Brooklyn, NY
Greber & Simms .... Baltimore, MD
Frederick, MD
Grebin, Jason Ross .... New York, NY
Grebing, Charles R., (A Professional Corporation) .... San Diego, CA
Grebing, Stephen C. .... San Diego, CA
Las Vegas, NV
Greble, Thomas C. .... Parsippany, NJ
New York, NY
Grebow, Arthur .... Beverly Hills, CA
Grebow, Ralph H. .... Iselin, NJ
Grebow, S. Leonard .... Randallstown, MD
Grebow, Yee & Spiro .... Beverly Hills, CA
Los Angeles, CA
Grec, Mary Ann .... Greensburg, PA
Grecco, David J. .... Pittsburgh, PA
Grecco, Frances E. .... St. Louis, MO
Grecco, Steven R. .... Newport Beach, CA
Grecco & Whaley .... St. Louis, MO
Grech, Christopher A. .... Ocean City, MD
Grech, David A. .... New York, NY
Grech, Jason C. .... Atlanta, GA
Grech, John J. .... Mount Clemens, MI
Grech, Paul, Jr. .... Riverside, CA
Greci, Carl A. .... South Bend, IN
Greco, Albert B., Jr. .... Dallas, TX
Greco, Alfred V. .... New York, NY
Greco, Alfred V., PLLC .... New York, NY
Greco, Amalia G. .... New York, NY
Greco, Amedeo .... Madison, WI
Greco, Angelo F. .... Milwaukee, WI
Greco, Anthony W. .... Columbus, OH
Greco, Carl J. .... Scranton, PA
Greco, Carl J., P.C. .... Scranton, PA
Greco, Carl M. .... Kenosha, WI
Greco, Carmel J. .... Johnstown, NY
Greco, Carmine A. .... Lincoln, MA
Greco, Carrie M. .... Department of the Army, U.S. Army Legal Services Agency, GV
Greco, Catherine V. .... New York, NY
Greco, Claude A. .... Metairie, LA
Greco, Clyde C., Jr. .... San Diego, CA
Greco, Cosmo C. .... Mission Viejo, CA
Greco, Cyrus J. .... Baton Rouge, LA
Greco, David .... Orange, CT
Greco, David F. .... Southfield, MI
Greco, Dawn R. .... Alexandria, VA
Greco, Deanne M. .... Minneapolis, MN
Greco, Dick, Jr. .... Tampa, FL
Greco, Dom W. .... Clarion, PA
Greco, Edward F. .... Front Royal, VA
Greco, Ernest D. .... Spokane, WA
Greco, Frank J. .... Tampa, FL
Greco, Frank J. .... Lansing, MI
Greco, Frank J. .... Cleveland, OH
Greco, Frederick D. .... McLean, VA
Greco, Fredrick T. .... Cleveland, OH
Greco & Gottlieb .... New York, NY
Greco & Greco .... Nesquehoning, PA
Greco & Greco, A Law Corporation
Baton Rouge, LA
Greco & Greco, P.C. .... McLean, VA
Greco, Guy B. .... Newport, OR
Greco, James .... Cheshire, CT
Greco, James A. .... Merrillville, IN
Greco, James J. .... Buffalo, NY
Greco, Jeanne Rose .... Little Silver, NJ
Greco, Joan I. .... New York, NY
Greco, John F. .... New York, NY
Greco, John J. .... Kingston, NY
Greco, John M. .... Annapolis, MD
Greco, Joseph A. .... Palo Alto, CA
Greco, Joseph A. .... Austin, TX
Greco, Joseph D., Jr. .... Hoboken, NJ
Greco, Joseph F. .... Schaumburg, IL
Greco, Joseph G., Jr. .... Nesquehoning, PA
Greco, Joseph P. .... Woodbridge, NJ
Greco, Joseph R. .... Miami, FL
Greco, Josephine A. .... Buffalo, NY
Greco, Karen A. .... Philadelphia, PA
Greco, Karen L. .... Cleveland, OH
Greco, Kevin M. .... Stamford, CT
Greco & Lander, P.C. .... Clarion, PA
Greco, Lara M. .... New York, NY
Greco, Leu Anne Lester .... Baton Rouge, LA
Greco, Louis .... New York, NY
Greco, Mac A., Jr. .... Tampa, FL
Greco, Mac A., Jr., P.A. .... Tampa, FL
Greco, Marc C. .... Norfolk, VA
Richmond, VA
Greco, Maria J. .... Wappingers Falls, NY
Greco, Mario F. .... Chicago, IL
Greco, Matthew P. .... Chula Vista, CA
Greco, Michael A. .... Albany, NY
Greco, Michael J. .... New York, NY
Greco, Michael R. .... Paoli, PA
Greco, Michael S. .... Boston, MA
Greco, Mollis & O'Hara, A Professional Corporation .... Irvine, CA
Greco, Paul .... Atlanta, GA
Greco, Paul A. .... Park Ridge, IL
Greco, Paul J. .... Philadelphia, PA
Greco, Paul V. .... New York, NY
Greco, Paula M. .... New York, NY
Greco, Pera & Bishop .... Merrillville, IN
Greco, Peter M. .... Indianapolis, IN
Greco, Philip A. .... New York, NY
Greco, R. Douglas .... Washington, DC
Greco, R. Raymond .... Cranston, RI
Greco, Richard G. .... New York, NY
Greco, Richard L. .... Worcester, MA
Greco, Rick .... Walnut Creek, CA
Greco, Robert M. .... Chicago, IL
Greco, Robert S. .... Farmingdale, NY
Greco, Rudolph E., Jr. .... Jackson Heights, NY
Greco, Steven .... Suffern, NY
Greco, Susan A. .... Newark, NJ
Greco, Suzette Haynie .... Treasury Department, Office of the Comptroller of the Currency, GV
Greco and Tarallo .... Schaumburg, IL
Greco, Thomas A. .... Irvine, CA
Greco & Traficante, A Professional Corporation .... San Diego, CA
Greco, Victor .... New York, NY
Greco, W. Scott .... McLean, VA
Greco-Buta, Karen L. .... Newton, NJ
Greczek, Elizabeth A. .... Washington, DC
Greczmiel, Horst G. .... North Plainfield, NJ
Gredd, Helen .... New York, NY
Grede, Frederick J. .... Chicago, IL
Greder, Gregory A. .... Lincoln, NE
Greear, Daniel W. .... Charleston, WV
Greear, John Scott .... Bentonville, AR
Greear, Michael D. .... Worland, WY
Greebel & Greebel .... Mineola, NY
Greebel, Lawrence M. .... Mineola, NY
Greebel, Mitchell A. .... Mineola, NY
Greecher, Stephen M., Jr. .... Harrisburg, PA
Greef, Charles E. .... Dallas, TX
Greek, Elaine .... Peoria, IL
Greek, Francis J. .... Philadelphia, PA
Greek, Michael S. .... Lehighton, PA
Greek, Monty L. .... Phoenix, AZ
Greek, Patricia S. .... Houston, TX
Greek, Ronald F. .... Everett, WA
Greek, Susan E. .... Newport Beach, CA
Greelee, Ellen T. .... Philadelphia, PA
Greeley, Alex J. .... New York, NY
Greeley, Burnham H., (A Law Corporation)
Honolulu, HI
Greeley, Carole Speckels .... Fairfield, CA
Greeley, David M. .... San Diego, CA
Greeley, Donald R. .... Washington, DC
Greeley & Futa .... Honolulu, HI
Greeley, Jeanne E. .... New York, NY
Greeley, John M. .... Seattle, WA
Greeley, John P. .... Orlando, FL
Greeley, Kristin M. .... Boston, MA
Greeley, Leland B. .... Rock Hill, SC
Greeley, Leland B., P.A. .... Rock Hill, SC
Greeley, Marcia A. .... Newton, MA
Greeley, Nina Anne M.
San Francisco, CA
Greeley, Patricia M. .... Manasquan, NJ
Greeley, Paul D. .... Stamford, CT
Greeley, Samuel S. .... Winnetka, IL
Greeley & Shea .... Andover, MA
Greeley, Stephen A. .... Boston, MA
Greeley, Thomas F., Jr. .... Boston, MA
Greeley, Timothy P. .... Marquette, MI
Greeley, Todd M. .... New York, NY
Greely, Adam M. .... Irvine, CA
Santa Ana, CA
Greely, Beverly J. .... Houston, TX
Greely, Gail A. .... Alameda, CA
Greely, Kevin B. .... Library of Congress, Congressional Research Service, GV
Greely, Mary-Laura .... Boston, MA
Greely, Michael T. .... Helena, MT
Greely, Mike .... Helena, MT
Greeman, James H. .... St. Paul, MN
Greeman, Kellerman & Koepcke
Batesville, IN
Green, Adam .... Los Angeles, CA
Green & Adams, LLP .... Irvine, CA
Green, Adelbert .... Honolulu, HI
Green, Alan A. .... Hyannis, MA
Green, Alan D. .... Austin, TX
Green, Alan J. .... Marrero, LA
Green, Alan M. .... New York, NY
Green, Alan Marc .... Hollywood, FL
Green, Albert .... Arlington, VA
Green, Albert E. .... Arlington, VA
Green, Alex .... Bolingbrook, IL
Green, Alfred L., Jr. .... Albuquerque, NM
Green, Alison Jennifer .... New York, NY
Green, Alison M. .... Jamaica, NY
Green, Allan .... Boston, MA
Green, Allan M. .... Boston, MA
Green, Allen .... New York, NY
Green, Allen B. .... Washington, DC
Green, Alvin .... New York, NY
Green, Alvin B. .... Encino, CA
Green, Amanda T. .... North Brunswick, NJ
Green, Andrea .... New York, NY
Green, Andrew J. .... New York, NY
Green, Andrew W. .... Lexington, KY
Green, Andrew W. .... West Chester, PA
Green, Angela Brantley .... Tallahassee, FL
Green, Angela K. .... Kansas City, MO
Green, Ann E. .... Swarthmore, PA
Green, Ann McGee .... Vinton, VA
Green, Anna Therese .... Beverly, MA
Green, Anne E. .... Washington, DC
Green, Anne Jorgenson .... Philadelphia, PA
Green, Anne Marguerite .... Hauppauge, NY
Green, Annika .... Montpelier, VT
Green, Arlin S. .... Philadelphia, PA
Green, Arnold B. .... White Plains, NY
Green, Arthur G., Jr. .... Baltimore, MD
Green, Arthur, Jr. .... Bessemer, AL
Green & Ashworth .... Royston, GA
Green, B. Kincey, Jr. .... Selma, AL
Green, B. Regina .... Honolulu, HI
Green, B. Riney .... Nashville, TN
Green & Baker, A Professional Corporation
Phoenix, AZ
Scottsdale, AZ
Green, Barbara F. .... Bridgeport, CT
Green, Barbara J. .... Denver, CO
Green, Barbara L. .... Denver, CO
Green, Barbara McCarthy .... Indianapolis, IN
Green, Barrett Kenneth .... Los Angeles, CA
Green, Barry D. .... Boston, MA
Green, Barry K. .... Austin, TX
Green, Barry L. .... Baltimore, MD
Green, Benjamin C. .... Phoenix, AZ
Green, Benjamin F. .... Inglewood, CA
Green, Benjamin H. .... Stamford, CT
Green, Benouis & McCullar, L.L.P.
Austin, TX
Green, Bernard .... Bridgeport, CT
Green & Berry .... Salt Lake City, UT
Green, Bert B. .... San Francisco, CA
Green, Beth A. .... New York, NY
Green, Beth N. .... New York, NY
Green, Beth Zaro .... New York, NY
Green, Beverly Robin .... San Rafael, CA
Green, Bianca Truitt .... Champaign, IL
Green, Bill F. .... Carbondale, IL
Green & Bivona, P.C. .... Bessemer, AL
Green, Bjorn C. .... Long Beach, CA
Green, Blaine I. .... Los Angeles, CA
Green, Blair F. .... Kittanning, PA
New Bethlehem, PA
Green, Blake A. .... Dothan, AL
Green, Bob McD. .... Johnson City, TN
Green, Bonnie E. .... Gaithersburg, MD
Green, Borden Johnson .... Dallas, TX
Green, Boyd Andrew .... Hillsboro, OR
Green, Brady D. .... Atlanta, GA
Green, Brady L. .... Philadelphia, PA
Green, Brenda M. .... Department of Justice, Civil Division, GV
Green, Brent A. .... Bethlehem, PA
Green, Brent B. (Chris) .... Des Moines, IA
Green, Brent D. .... Springfield, MO
Green, Brent P. .... Tallahassee, FL
Green, Brett H. .... New York, NY
Green, Brian .... Baltimore, MD
Green, Brian D. .... Lincoln City, OR
Green, Brian J. .... Cleveland, OH
Green, Britton B. .... Dallas, TX
Green, Brown & Stark, A Professional Corporation .... Oklahoma City, OK
Green, Bruce .... Springfield, MA
Green, Bruce .... Muskogee, OK
Green, Bruce A. .... Primghar, IA
Green, Bruce A. .... New York, NY
Green, Bruce B. .... Council Bluffs, IA
Red Oak, IA
Green, Bruce D. .... Fort Myers, FL
Green, Bruce David .... Fort Lauderdale, FL
Green, Bruce David, P.A.
Fort Lauderdale, FL
Miami, FL
Green, Bruce M. .... Pelham, AL
Green, Bryan J. .... Chicago, IL
Green, Burl L. .... Wilsonville, OR
Green, Burton J. .... Cocoa Beach, FL
Green, C. Douglas .... Orlando, FL
Green, C. Harry .... Hamilton, AL
Green, Carl A. .... Buffalo, NY
Green, Carl H. .... El Paso, TX
Green, Carl J. .... Washington, DC
Green, Carla A. .... Tallahassee, FL
Green, Carlton M. .... College Park, MD
Green, Carol Gilliam .... Topeka, KS
Green, Carol M. .... Hammond, IN
Green, Carole D. .... Norristown, PA
Green, Carole L. .... Bronx, NY
Green, Carrie A. .... Portland, ME
Green, Caryn Margo .... Orlando, FL
Green, Catherine C. .... Santa Ana, CA
Green, Cathy J. .... Manchester, NH
Green, Charles A. .... Dallas, TX
Green, Charles B. .... Fort Lauderdale, FL
Green, Charles C. .... Oklahoma City, OK
Green, Charles C., Jr. .... Winston-Salem, NC
Green, Charles D. .... Manhattan, KS
Green, Charles E. .... New York, NY
Green, Charles H., III .... Higginsville, MO

Green, Charles H., Jr. ....Higginsville, MO
Green, Charles Kelley ....Houston, TX
Green, Charles L. ....New York, NY
Green, Charles L. ....West Point, NY
Green, Charles O. ....St. Paul, MN
Green, Charles P., Jr. ....Raleigh, NC
Green, Charles R. ....Calabasas, CA
Green, Charles S. ....Wichita, KS
Green, Charles S., Jr. ....New Orleans, LA
Green, Cheney and Hughes, LLP
Jackson, MS
Green, Cheri D. ....Jackson, MS
Green, Cheryl A. ....Buffalo, NY
Green, Cheryl A. ....Providence, RI
Green, Christian B. ....Sacramento, CA
Green, Christine A. ....Ann Arbor, MI
Green, Christine Melucci ....Birmingham, AL
Green, Christopher A. ....Miami, FL
Green, Christopher M. ....Armonk, NY
Green, Christopher R. ....Los Angeles, CA
Green, Christopher R. ....Jackson, MS
Green, Claire H. ....Carbondale, CO
Green, Clarence A. ....Fairfield, CT
Green, Clarence B. ....Shelbyville, KY
Green, Clarence P. ....Oklahoma City, OK
Green, Claudia N. ....New York, NY
Green, Clifford Scott ....Philadelphia, PA
Green, Clifton G. ....Peoria, IL
Green, Colby M. ....Chicago, IL
Green Cordonnier & House, LLP
St. Louis, MO
Green & Countiss ....Honolulu, HI
Green, Cumer L. ....Boise, ID
Green, Cynthia S. ....New Orleans, LA
Green, Cynthia S. ....New Orleans, LA
Green, D. Stewart ....Birmingham, MI
Green, Dale M. ....Spokane, WA
Green, Dana Ann ....Topeka, KS
Green, Dana Bradbury ....Topeka, KS
Green, Dana I. ....Deerfield, IL
Green, Dana Lynn ....San Diego, CA
Green, Daniel ....Westport, CT
Green, Daniel B. ....Philadelphia, PA
Green, Daniel C. ....Pocatello, ID
Green, Daniel H. ....Eldersburg, MD
Green, Daniel H. ....Freehold, NJ
Green, Daniel K. ....Rancho Santa Fe, CA
Green, Daniel R. ....Miami, FL
Green, Daniel R. ....Jefferson City, MO
Green, Daniel R., Jr. ....Hickory, NC
Green, Daniel T. ....Sault Ste. Marie, MI
Green, Danielle ....Chicago, IL
Green, Danny W. ....Santa Maria, CA
Green, D'Arcy Nicole ....Salisbury, MD
Green, Darren M. ....Chicago, IL
Green, David ....St. Louis, MO
Garden City, NY
Green, David A. ....New York, NY
Green, David B. ....San Francisco, CA
Green, David B. ....Providence, RI
Green, David D. ....Morristown, NJ
Green, David E. ....Department of Justice,
Criminal Division, GV
Green, David H. ....Allentown, PA
Green, David Howard ....New York, NY
Green, David L. ....Atlanta, GA
Green, David L. ....New York, NY
Green, David M. ....Atlanta, GA
Green, David M. ....New York, NY
Green, David M. ....Woodmere, NY
Green, David M. ....Hamilton, OH
Green, David M. ....Harrisburg, PA
Green, David M. ....Dumas, TX
Green, David Nathanial ....Albany, NY
Green, David S. ....Seminole, FL
Green, David W. ....De Funiak Springs, FL
Green, David W. ....Grand Rapids, MI
Green, David W. ....Portland, OR
Green, David W. ....Corpus Christi, TX
Green, Deborah A. ....Austin, TX
Green, Deborah G. ....Skokie, IL
Green, Deborah K. ....Department of Labor,
Office of the Solicitor, GV
Green, Deborah L.E. ....Allen Park, MI
Green, Debra L. ....San Diego, CA
Green, Delbert F. ....Flint, MI
Green, Denise Koehler ....Peoria, IL
Green, Dennis B. ....Aspen, CO
Denver, CO
Green, Dennis G. ....Waco, TX
Green, Dennis J. ....Stockton, CA
Green, Dennis J. ....St. Louis, MO
Green, Dennis J. ....Omaha, NE
Green, Dennis P. ....Mount Laurel, NJ
Green, Denslow B. ....Madera, CA
Green, Derek S. ....Houston, TX
Green, Don E. ....Martinez, CA
Green, Donald ....Cleveland, OH
Green, Donald B. ....Kaukauna, WI
Green, Donald C. ....Sacramento, CA
Green, Donald E. ....Boston, MA
Green, Donald H. ....Washington, DC
Green, Donald I. ....Toledo, OH
Green, Donald J. ....Las Vegas, NV
Green, Donald L. ....Washington, DC
Green, Donald M. ....Miami, FL
Green, Donald Ray, Jr. ....Paducah, KY
Green, Donald W., III ....Portland, OR
Green, Donna Powe ....Hattiesburg, MS
Green, Dorcas A. ....Austin, TX
Green, Dori F. ....Philadelphia, PA
Green, Doris ....Washington, DC
Green, Dorothy F. ....Orlando, FL
Green, Dorothy Jean ....Freeport, NY
Green, Dorothy L. ....Pleasanton, CA
Green, Dorothy L. ....New York, NY
Green, Douglas C. ....Minneapolis, MN
Green, Douglas F. ....Keene, NH
Green, Douglas G. ....Washington, DC
Green, Douglas H. ....Washington, DC
Green, Douglas J. ....Seattle, WA
Green, Douglas J. ....Green Bay, WI
Green, Douglas R. ....Cypress, CA
Green, Douglas S. ....Portland, OR
Green, Dove W., Jr. ....Conway, SC
Green, Downey & Black, L.L.P.
Houston, TX
Texas City, TX
Green, Doye E. ....Macon, GA
Green, Doye E., Jr. ....Macon, GA
Green & DuBois, P.C. ....San Antonio, TX
Green, Dwayne M. ....Charleston, SC
Green, E. Hart ....Beaumont, TX
Green, E. C. ....Denison, TX
Green, Edward F. ....Cleveland, OH
Green, Edward G. ....Chicago, IL
Green, Edward H. ....Beaumont, TX
Green, Edward H., III ....Chapel Hill, NC
Green, Edward J. ....Chicago, IL
Green, Edward M. ....Washington, DC
Green, Edward R. ....Springfield, IL
Green, Edward R. ....Winston-Salem, NC
Green, Edward S. ....Syracuse, NY
Green, Edward U., Jr. ....Hauppauge, NY
Green, Edwin A. ....Tallahassee, FL
Green, Edwin A., II, P.A., Law Offices of
Tallahassee, FL
Green, Edwin H. ....Treasury Department,
Internal Revenue Service, GV
Green, Edwin W. ....Los Angeles, CA
Green, Elaine ....McAlester, OK
Green, Elayne Lever ....Boca Raton, FL
Green, Eliot J. ....Cambridge, MA
Green, Eliot P. ....New York, NY
Green, Elissa H. ....Huntsville, AL
Green, Elizabeth Anne ....Baltimore, MD
Green, Elizabeth C. ....Los Angeles, CA
Green, Elizabeth K. ....Los Angeles, CA
Green, Ellen A. ....Philadelphia, PA
Green, Ellen L. ....Wheaton, IL
Green, Eric C. ....Basking Ridge, NJ
Green, Eric D. ....Boston, MA
Green, Eric G. ....Fresno, CA
Green, Eric H. ....New York, NY
Green, Eric N. ....San Antonio, TX
Green, Eric R. ....Philadelphia, PA
Green, Ernest J. ....Fort Worth, TX
Green & Ettinger ....New York, NY
Green, Eunice L. ....Charleston, WV
Green, Eve M. ....Wailuku, HI
Green, F. Gillis ....Baltimore, MD
Green, F. Harrison ....Cincinnati, OH
Green, F. Harrison, Co., L.P.A.
Cincinnati, OH
Green, Fletcher D. ....Clanton, AL
Green and Foushee ....Washington, DC
Green, Frances M. ....Boulder, CO
Green, Frank C., Jr. ....Marshall, TX
Green, Frank W. ....Lancaster, OH
Green, Franklin L. ....New York, NY
Green, Fred B. ....Southfield, MI
Green, Fred D. (Jack) ....Sallisaw, OK
Green, Fred E. ....Las Vegas, NV
Green, Fred K. ....Kansas City, MO
Green, Fred R. ....New York, NY
Green, Frederick D. ....Vail, CO
Green, Frederick H. ....Chardon, OH
Green, Frederick J. ....Copley, OH
Green, Frederick" Rick "N.
Salt Lake City, UT
Green, Frederick S. ....Urbana, IL
Green, Frederick S. ....New York, NY
Green, Frederick W. ....Redmond, WA
Green, Fredric I. ....White Plains, NY
Green & Freedman ....San Francisco, CA
Green, G. Martin ....Dallas, TX
Green, G. Maynard ....Waco, TX
Green, G. Michael ....Washington, DC
Green, G. Michael ....Havertown, PA
Green, G. Richard ....Beverly Hills, CA
Green, G. Scott ....Sevierville, TN
Green, G. Wade ....Chattanooga, TN
Green, Gail S. ....Beverly Hills, CA
Green, Garfield R. ....Staten Island, NY
Green, Garrett D. ....Fairfax, VA
Green, Gary ....Little Rock, AR
Green, Gary ....Philadelphia, PA
Green, Gary B. ....Downey, CA
Green, Gary E. ....Chicago, IL
Green, Gary H., II ....Los Angeles, CA
Green, Gary L. ....El Segundo, CA
Green, Gary L. ....Fresno, CA
Green, Gary L. ....Haddonfield, NJ
Green, Gary L. ....Philadelphia, PA
Green, Gary Layne ....Naples, FL
Green, Gary S. ....Herndon, VA
Green, Gayle ....Delray Beach, FL
Green, Geoffrey D. ....Murray Hill, NJ
Green, Geoffrey F. ....St. Louis, MO
Green, Geoffrey M.
Federal Trade Commission,
Bureau of Competition, GV
Green, George H., Jr. ....Lincoln, NE
Green, George R. ....Washington, DC
Green, George T. ....Miami, FL
Green, Georgia M. ....Annandale, VA
Green, Gerald G. ....Cadillac, MI
Green, Gerald H. ....Jericho, NY
Green, Gerald J. ....Utica, NY
Green, Gerald L. ....Hutchinson, KS
Wichita, KS
Green, Gerald P. ....Oklahoma City, OK
Green, Gerald Stanley ....Memphis, TN
Green, Geri Lynn ....San Francisco, CA
Green, Gillian M. ....Wharton, NJ
Green, Gina L. ....Gary, IN
Green, Glenn ....Riverhead, NY
Green, Glenn P. ....Springfield, MO
Green, Gloria J. ....Atlanta, GA
Green, Gordon B. ....Baton Rouge, LA
Green, Gordon H. ....Muleshoe, TX
Green, Grant D. ....Menlo Park, CA
Green and Green ....Phoenix, AZ
Green and Green ....Rancho Santa Fe, CA
Green & Green ....San Rafael, CA
Green & Green ....De Funiak Springs, FL
Green and Green ....El Dorado, KS
Grenada, MS
Green & Green ....Higginsville, MO
Manchester, NH
Green and Green ....Somerset, NJ
Green & Green ....Scarsdale, NY
Green and Green, A Professional
Corporation ....Beaumont, TX
Conroe, TX
Green, Green, Adams, Palmer & Craig, P.C.
Ann Arbor, MI
Green, Green & Godowsky .....Wilmington, DE
Green, Green & Rigby ....Madera, CA
Green, Gregory ....New York, NY
Green, Griffith L. ....Washington, DC
Green and Gross, P.C. ....Bridgeport, CT
Green, H. Guy ....Marianna, FL
Green, H. Marlow ....Kirkland, WA
Green, H. Walter ....Lakewood, CO
Green, H. Wayne ....Fresno, CA
Green, Haines, Sgambati, Murphy & Macala
Co., L.P.A. ....Akron, OH
Canton, OH
Youngstown, OH
Green & Hale, A Professional Corporation
Bristol, TN
Greeneville, TN
Abingdon, VA
Big Stone Gap, VA
Bristol, VA
Green & Hall, A Professional Corporation
Orange, CA
Green, Harland N. ....Beverly Hills, CA
Green, Harland N., P.C. ....Beverly Hills, CA
Green, Harold ....Tahoka, TX
Green, Harold A. ....Great Neck, NY
Green, Harold H. ....Seattle, WA
Green, Harold N. ....Wilmington, DE
Green, Harold P. ....Boca Raton, FL
Green, Harold W. ....Anchorage, AK
Green, Harry B. ....Encino, CA
Green, Harry C. ....Humble, TX
Green, Heather M. D. ....Pleasanton, CA
Green, Hennings & Henry LLP
St. Louis, MO
Green, Henry A. ....Groveland, MA
Green, Henry D., Jr. ....Marietta, GA
Green, Henry E. ....Brooklyn, NY
Green, Henry E. ....New York, NY
Green, Henry & Green ....Stuttgart, AR
Green, Henry P. ....Ridgefield Park, NJ
Green, Henry S. ....Calumet City, IL
Green, Henry W., Jr. ....Topeka, KS
Green, Herbert G. ....Marianna, FL
Green, Herbert J. ....San Antonio, TX
Green, Hix H., III ....Atlanta, GA
Green, Holcombe T., Jr. ....Atlanta, GA
Green, Horace W. ....San Francisco, CA
Green, Howard Benjamin ....Skokie, IL
Green, Howard C. ....Madera, CA
Green, Howard E. ....Fort Wayne, IN
Green, Howard R. ....Honolulu, HI
Green, Howard W. ....Comstock, MI
Green, Hubert W. ....San Antonio, TX
Green, Hugh E. ....Lebanon, TN
Green, Ian M., (P.C.) ....Los Angeles, CA
Green, Ingram and Anderson, P.C.
Springport, MI
Green, Iris M. ....Washington, DC
Green, Irving ....Albany, NY
Green, Irving A. ....Newburgh, NY
Green, Irving M. ....New Kensington, PA
Green, Isaac H., Jr. ....Philadelphia, PA
Green, J. Bradley ....Stuttgart, AR
Green, J. Bradley ....Houston, TX
Green, J. David ....Irving, TX
Green, J. Frank ....Thomasville, NC
Green, J. Leighton, Jr. ....El Paso, TX
Green, J. Martin ....Beaumont, TX
Conroe, TX
Green, J. Patrick ....Omaha, NE
Green, J. Robert, Jr. ....Fort Worth, TX
Green, J. Russell ....Heber Springs, AR
Green, J. Sterling, Jr. ....Danville, VA
Green, J. William ....Charleston, SC
Green, Jack ....Hempstead, NY
Green, Jack A. ....North Reading, MA
Green, Jack J. ....Nashville, TN
Green, Jack L. ....Missoula, MT
Green, Jack L., II ....Phoenix, AZ
Green, Jack M. ....Tallahassee, FL
Green, Jack M. ....Omaha, NE
Green, Jack, (P.C.) ....Boston, MA
Green, Jack W., Jr. ....Kansas City, MO
Green, Jacob ....Florham Park, NJ
Green, Jacqueline L. Jenkin
Wilmington, DE
Green, Jake ....Memphis, TN
Green, James B. ....Los Angeles, CA
Green, James B. ....Pocatello, ID
Green, James C. ....Delavan, WI
Green, James D. ....Champaign, IL
Green, James D. ....Glen Burnie, MD
Green, James E. ....Covina, CA
Green, James E. ....Bristol, TN
Green, James E., Jr. ....Tulsa, OK
Green, James F.
Federal Communications Commission,
Wireless Telecommunications Bureau, GV
Green, James F. ....Alexandria, VA
Green, James G., Jr. ....Hartford, CT
Green, James H., Jr. ....Paradise Valley, AZ
Green, James K. ....Denver, CO
Green, James K. ....West Palm Beach, FL
Green, James L. ....Jupiter, FL
Green, James L. ....Massapequa, NY
Green, James Lowell ....State College, PA
Green, James M. ....Cranston, RI
Green, James M., Jr. ....High Point, NC
Green, James P. ....Mobile, AL
Green, James Paul ....San Francisco, CA
Green, James R. ....Pensacola, FL
Green, James R. ....Greenwood, IN
Green, James R. ....Columbia, MO
Green, James R., & Associates, P.A.
Pensacola, FL
Green, James S. ....Wilmington, DE
Green, James S.
Office of Personnel Management,
Compensation Division, GV
Green, James V., Jr. ....Alabaster, AL
Green, James W., Jr. ....Chicago, IL
Green, James & Williams
Oklahoma City, OK
Green, Jana W. ....Rancho Santa Fe, CA
Green, Janice L. ....Austin, TX
Green, Jared R. ....Manchester, NH
Green, Jason K. ....Atlanta, GA
Green, Jay B. ....Fort Lauderdale, FL
Green, Jay B. ....Cary, NC
Green, Jay M. ....Philadelphia, PA
Green, Jay N. ....Tyler, TX
Green, Jean B. ....Norristown, PA
Green, Jeanette Drescher ....Dallas, TX
Green, Jeff H. ....Los Angeles, CA
Green, Jeffrey ....Bakersfield, CA
Green, Jeffrey A.
Department Of Veterans Affairs,
Office of the General Counsel, GV
Green, Jeffrey B. ....Pinckney, MI
Green, Jeffrey B. ....Racine, WI
Green, Jeffrey C. ....Somerset, NJ
Green, Jeffrey E. ....Florissant, MO
Green, Jeffrey G. ....Mariposa, CA
Green, Jeffrey K. ....Daytona Beach, FL
St. Augustine, FL
Green, Jeffrey L. ....Lansing, MI
Green, Jeffrey S. ....New York, NY
Green, Jeffrey T. ....Washington, DC
Green, Jennifer ....Garner, NC
Green, Jennifer A. ....San Jose, CA
Green, Jennifer L. ....Chicago, IL
Green, Jennifer Liddy ....New York, NY
Green, Jennifer M. ....New York, NY
Green, Jennifer Miller ....Raleigh, NC
Green, Jerome, & Associates
Little Rock, AR
Green, Jerry A. ....Mill Valley, CA
Green, Jerry H. ....Culver City, CA
Green, Jerry, (P.A.) ....Miami, FL
Green, Jersey M. ....Denver, CO
Green, Jesse D. ....Ada, OK
Green, Jesse J. ....Dallas, TX
Green, Jim R., Jr. ....Norcross, GA
Green, Jim S. ....Sikeston, MO
Green, Joan Carol ....Boston, MA
Green, Joan Corcoran ....Atlanta, GA
Green, Joan M. ....Oklahoma City, OK
Green, Joan Whiteside ....Los Angeles, CA
Green, Jodi B. ....Delray Beach, FL
Green, Jodi B., P.A. ....Delray Beach, FL
Green, Joe L. ....Yuma, AZ
Green, Joel G. ....Seattle, WA
Green, Joel H. ....Minneapolis, MN
Green, Joel Z. ....Bridgeport, CT
Green, John A. ....Oklahoma City, OK
Green, John C. ....Indianapolis, IN
Green, John C. ....Salt Lake City, UT
Green, John D. ....San Francisco, CA
Green, John E. ....Oklahoma City, OK
Green, John F., Jr. ....Fort Worth, TX
Green, John G. ....Mundelein, IL
Green, John G., III ....Mundelein, IL
Green, John Grady ....Grenada, MS
Green, John H. ....Odessa, TX
Green, John, II ....Wilmington, NC
Green, John J., Jr. ....Northampton, MA
Green, John K. ....Omaha, NE
Green, John K. ....Papillion, NE
Green, John L. ....Forest Park, GA
Green, John L. ....Cincinnati, OH
Green, John L. ....Houston, TX
Green, John L., Jr. ....St. Petersburg, FL
Green, John M. ....Chicago, IL
Green, John M. ....Murfreesboro, TN
Nashville, TN
Smyrna, TN
Green, John M. ....Bay City, TX
Green, John M., Jr. ....Ocala, FL
Green, John Mack ....Murfreesboro, TN
Green, John Marshall ....Ocala, FL
Green, John Orne ....San Francisco, CA
Green, John R. ....Minneapolis, MN
Green, John R. ....Duncan, OK
Green, John R., II ....St. Louis, MO
Green, John R., Jr. ....Raleigh, NC
Green, John Stephen ....Conroe, TX
Green, John T. ....Natchez, MS
Green, John W. ....Glendale, CA
Green, John W., Jr. ....Huntsville, AL
Green, Jon A. ....Mobile, AL
Green, Jon W. ....Springfield, NJ
Green, Jonathan Clark ....Chicago, IL
Green, Jonathan D. ....Birmingham, AL

Green, Jonathan D. ....New York, NY
Green, Jonathan H. ....Miami, FL
Green, Jonathan H., P.A. ....Miami, FL
Green, Jonathan J. ....New York, NY
Green, Jonathan S. ....Detroit, MI
Green, Jonathan T. ....Chicago, IL
Green, Jordan ....Phoenix, AZ
Green & Josefiak, P.C. ....Denver, CO
Green, Joseph B. ....Georgetown, DE
Green, Joseph B. ....Lewes, DE
Wilmington, DE
Green, Joseph B. ....Mundelein, IL
Green, Joseph B. ....Boston, MA
Green, Joseph B. ....Spokane, WA
Green, Joseph B., P.S. ....Spokane, WA
Green, Joseph F. ....Santa Barbara, CA
Green, Joseph H., Jr. ....Washington, DC
Green, Joseph J. ....Washington, DC
Green, Joseph L. ....St. Charles, MO
Green, Joseph P. ....Bellefonte, PA
State College, PA
Green, Joseph P., Jr. ....West Chester, PA
Green, Joseph T. ....Minneapolis, MN
Green, Joshua ....Jackson, MS
Green, Joshua, IV ....Bellevue, WA
Green, Joshua L. ....Menlo Park, CA
Green, Joyce A. ....Richmond, VA
Green, Joyce Hens ....
United States District Court For The District Of Columbia, GV
Green, Joyce J. ....Des Moines, IA
Green, Judson Leon, III ....Dublin, GA
Green, Julian C. ....Houston, TX
Green, Julie E. ....Sacramento, CA
Green, June L. ....
United States District Court For The District Of Columbia, GV
Green, Justin Timothy ....New York, NY
Green, J. W., Jr. ....Stuttgart, AR
Green, Kahn & Piotrkowski, P.A.
Miami Beach, FL
Green, Karen ....Mendocino, CA
Green, Karen F. ....Boston, MA
Green, Karen H. ....Bend, OR
Green, Karen L. ....Philadelphia, PA
Green, Karen O. ....Grenada, MS
Green, Karen T. ....Inglewood, CA
Green, Karin L. ....Washington, DC
Green, Karl ....Columbus, WI
Green, Karl T. ....Jacksonville, FL
Green, Kaster & Falvey, P.A. ....Ocala, FL
Green, Katherine M. ....San Diego, CA
Green, Kathryn ....Corpus Christi, TX
Green, Kathy McGrath ....Florham Park, NJ
Green, K. C. ....Cincinnati, OH
Green, Keith A. ....Omaha, NE
Green, Keith S., (Mrs.) ....Charlotte, NC
Green, Kelley ....Houston, TX
Green, Kendall P. ....New Orleans, LA
Green, Kenneth H. ....Atlanta, GA
Green, Kenneth N. ....Van Nuys, CA
Green, Kenneth R. ....San Diego, CA
Green, Kenneth S., Jr. ....Ocala, FL
Green, Kenyatta S. ....Washington, DC
Green, Kevin D. ....Dallas, TX
Green, Kevin I. ....Taylor, MI
Green, Kevin K. ....San Diego, CA
Green, Kevin M. ....New Orleans, LA
Green, Kevin O'C., Law Offices of
Mankato, MN
Green, Kevin S. ....Atlanta, GA
Green, Kevin T. ....Mobile, AL
Green, Kevin W. ....Dallas, TX
Green, Kim ....Los Angeles, CA
Green, Kimberly McCluskey
Houston, TX
Green, Kimberly Sue ....Kansas City, MO
Green, Kristen E. ....Los Angeles, CA
Green & Krupp ....Encino, CA
Green, L. David ....Edwardsville, IL
Green, Lana ....Dayton, OH
Green, Lance M. ....McHenry, IL
Green, Larry J. ....Covington, LA
Green, Larry S. ....Campbell, CA
Green, Larry W. ....Greenville, TX
Green, Larry W., Jr. ....Greenville, TX
Green, Lasser and Smothers, A P.C.
Del Mar, CA
Green, Laura E. ....St. Petersburg, FL
Green, Laurie A. ....Weare, NH
Green, Lauson C. ....Washington, DC
Green Law Offices ....Boise, ID
Green Law Offices, Ltd. ....Milwaukee, WI
Green, Lawrence E. ....Sacramento, CA
Green, Lawrence G. ....Boston, MA
Green, Lawrence J. ....Littleton, CO
Green, Lawrence M. ....Boston, MA
Green, Lawrence R.
Glenwood Springs, CO
Green, Lawrence R. ....New York, NY
Green, Lee E. ....Baldwin City, KS
Green, Leitch & Steelman
College Park, MD
Green, Lemuel R. ....Canton, OH
Green, Leo E. ....Bowie, MD
Green, Leo Edward, Jr. ....Bowie, MD
Green, Leonard ....Cincinnati, OH
Green, Leonard F. ....Austin, TX
Green, Leonard G. ....Smithfield, NC
Green, Leonard S. ....Manchester, NH
Green, Lesley C. ....Los Angeles, CA
Green, Lesley D. ....Wilmette, IL
Green & Levine, LLP ....Farmington, CT
Hartford, CT
Green, Lewis C. ....St. Louis, MO
Green, Lewis P. ....Philadelphia, PA
Green, Lezlie S. ....Emporia, VA
Green, Linda Akoury ....Short Hills, NJ
Green, Linda Lowry ....Paducah, KY
Green, Linda Sommers ....Lakewood, CO
Green, Lisa A. ....St. Louis, MO
Green, Lisa A. ....Weehawken, NJ
Green, Lisa A. ....Huntington, WV
Green, Lisa C. ....Palo Alto, CA
Green, Lisa H. ....Miami, FL
Green, Lisa M. ....Chicago, IL
Green, Lisa R. ....Denver, CO
Green, Lisa S. ....Bakersfield, CA
Green, Lloyd M. ....New York, NY
Green, Lori B. ....Rochester, NY
Green, Louis B. ....Placerville, CA
Green, Louis F. ....Farmington, CT
Green & Luhn, A Professional Corporation
Salt Lake City, UT
Green, Lundgren & Ryan, A Professional Corporation ....Cherry Hill, NJ
Green, Lynda Pegram ....Cleveland, OH
Green, Lynette P. ....Green Bay, WI
Green, Lynn A. ....Melville, NY
Green, Lynn E., Jr. ....Cooperstown, NY
Green, Lynne K. ....Jackson, MS
Green, M. Andree ....Riverdale, MD
Green, Marcella M. ....White Plains, NY
Green, Marci Dana ....Trenton, NJ
Green, Margo L. ....St. Louis, MO
Green, Maria C. ....Glenview, IL
Green, Marilyn G. ....Springfield, MO
Green, Marilyn S. ....Long Beach, CA
Green, Mark ....New York, NY
Green, Mark ....Muskogee, OK
Green, Mark A. ....North Woodmere, NY
Green, Mark Andrew ....Green Bay, WI
Green, Mark M. ....Jacksonville, FL
Green, Mark V. ....Boston, MA
Green, Mark W.
Securities and Exchange Commission, Division of Corporation Finance, GV
Green, Marlon J. ....Laguna Hills, CA
Green, Marshall M. ....New York, NY
Green, Marshall W. ....Bronx, NY
Green, Marti ....Bethpage, NY
Green, Martin ....Springfield, IL
Green, Martin H. ....Framingham, MA
Green, Martin H., P.C. ....Framingham, MA
Green, Martin J. ....Denver, CO
Green, Martin M. ....St. Louis, MO
Green, Marvin ....Chicago, IL
Green, Marvin M. ....Miami Beach, FL
Green, Mary Ann ....Albuquerque, NM
Green, Mary E. ....Fayetteville, AR
Green, Mary E., P.A. ....Bentonville, AR
Fayetteville, AR
Green, Mary H. ....Katonah, NY
Green, Mary Kay ....Omaha, NE
Green, Mary Linn ....Rockford, IL
Green, Mary M. ....Costa Mesa, CA
Green, Mary P., (Mrs.) ....Nashville, TN
Green, Mary Teresa ....San Antonio, TX
Green, Matthew D. ....Seattle, WA
Green, Matthew E. ....Los Angeles, CA
Green, Maureen R. ....Lafayette, CA
Green, Maurice A. ....McCook, NE
Green, Maurice O. ....Charlotte, NC
Green, McMahon and Heed ....Keene, NH
Green, Melanie Joy ....Spokane, WA
Green, Melvyn L. ....Solana Beach, CA
Green, Merritt W., II ....Toledo, OH
Green, Merritt W., III ....Toledo, OH
Green, Micah D. ....Cleveland, OH
Green, Michael ....Washington, DC
Silver Spring, MD
Alexandria, VA
Green, Michael ....New York, NY
Green, Michael A. ....Chula Vista, CA
Green, Michael A. ....Wilmington, NC
Green, Michael A. ....Philadelphia, PA
Green, Michael B. ....Culver City, CA
Green, Michael B. ....San Francisco, CA
Green, Michael B. ....Towson, MD
Green, Michael B. ....Seaford, NY
Green, Michael D. ....Iowa City, IA
Green, Michael E. ....Orange Park, FL
Green, Michael F. ....Cortez, CO
Green, Michael G. ....Department of the Navy, Office of the Judge Advocate General, GV
Green, Michael I. ....Burlington, VT
Green, Michael J. ....Mission Viejo, CA
Green, Michael J. ....Des Moines, IA
Green, Michael J. ....Lansing, MI
Green, Michael Jay ....Tucson, AZ
Green, Michael K. ....Tampa, FL
Green, Michael L. ....Scottsdale, AZ
Green, Michael P. ....Arlington, VA
Green, Michael Preston ....Phoenix, AZ
Green, Michael R. ....Bellevue, WA
Green, Michael S. ....Tucson, AZ
Green, Michael S. ....Royston, GA
Green, Michael S. ....Lansing, MI
Green, Michael S. ....Madison, WI
Green, Michael Z. ....Chicago, IL
Green, Miles & Green ....Daytona Beach, FL
St. Augustine, FL
Green, Miles Lavan, Jr. ....Greenville, SC
Green, Miles, Lipton, White & Fitz-Gibbon
Northampton, MA
Green, Milton ....New York, NY
Green, Mitchell Cutler ....Torrance, CA
Green, Mitchell E. ....Los Angeles, CA
Green, Mitchell F. ....Hollywood, FL
Green, Mitchell J. ....San Francisco, CA
Green, Morris ....Northbrook, IL
Green, Morris L. ....New York, NY
Green and Murphy, P.A.
Fort Lauderdale, FL
Green, Myra J., (P.C.) ....Boston, MA
Green, Nadeen W. ....Atlanta, GA
Green, Nancy A. ....Morgantown, WV
Weirton, WV
Green, Nancy Christine ....Mission Viejo, CA
Green, Nancy Cooper ....Warren, MI
Green, Nancy E. ....Austin, TX
Green, Nancy W. ....Carmel, CA
Green, Nathaniel Edward
Pompano Beach, FL
Green, Nathaniel K. ....Springfield, MA
Green, Nicki Lee ....Cortez, CO
Green, Nicole A. ....Los Angeles, CA
Green, Nino E. ....Escanaba, MI
Green, Norman A. ....Vero Beach, FL
Green, Norman A., P.A. ....Vero Beach, FL
Green, Norman E. ....Beverly Hills, CA
Green, Norman H., (P.C.) ....Glendale, CA
Green, Norris W. ....Montgomery, AL
Green, O. Jerome ....Little Rock, AR
Green & O'Donnell ....Harrisonburg, VA
Green, Oliver F. ....Costa Mesa, CA
Green, Oliver L., Jr. ....Bartow, FL
Green, Ollie M. ....Department of Commerce, Office of the General Counsel, GV
Green, Orville Brent ....Kingsland, GA
Green and Packer ....Boston, MA
Green, Pam Warnock ....Memphis, TN
Green, Pamela K. ....Washington, DC
Green, Pamela L. ....New Hope, MN
Green, Patricia K. ....Miami, FL
Green, Patricia K. ....Houston, TX
Green, Patrick A. ....Conroe, TX
Green, Patrick J. ....Portland, OR
Green, Patrick T. ....Pasadena, CA
Green, Patterson & Schultz, P.C.
Houston, TX
Green, Paul ....Bloomfield Hills, MI
Green, Paul ....New York, NY
Green, Paul A. ....Washington, DC
Green, Paul F., II ....Phoenix, AZ
Green, Paul H. ....Florham Park, NJ
Green, Paul J. ....Brooklyn, NY
Green, Paul M. ....San Antonio, TX
Green, Paul R. ....Milton, FL
Green, Paul W. ....San Antonio, TX
Green, Paula Barach ....New York, NY
Green, Paula J. ....Tampa, FL
Green, Paula J. ....Chicago, IL
Green, P. E. ....Nashville, IL
Green, Percy H. ....Nashville, TN
Green, Peter M. ....Boston, MA
Green, Peter P. ....Cherry Hill, NJ
Green, Philip ....Ann Arbor, MI
Green, Philip B. ....Kansas City, MO
Green, Philip Burton ....Denver, CO
Green, Philip D. ....Washington, DC
Green, Philip L. ....Boaz, AL
Green, Philip P., Jr. ....Chapel Hill, NC
Green, Philip R. ....San Rafael, CA
Green, Philip W. ....Irvine, CA
Green, Phillip C. ....Star City, AR
Green, Phillip J. ....Department of Justice, Civil Division, GV
Green, R.A., P.A. ....Starke, FL
Green, R. Christopher ....Boston, MA
Green, R.A. ....Starke, FL
Green, Rachelle ....Albuquerque, NM
Green, Rachelle ....Providence, RI
Green, Rae Allyson ....Grand Rapids, MI
Green, Randall W. ....East Hartford, CT
Green, Rankin ....Gilbertown, AL
Green, Rayburn W. ....Fayetteville, AR
Green, Raymond B. ....Hartford, CT
Green, Raymond C. ....Flushing, NY
Green, Raymond D.
Rancho Palos Verdes, CA
Green, Raymond P. ....New York, NY
Green, Raymond T. ....Fort Wayne, IN
Green, Raymond W. ....Chicago, IL
Green, Rebecca Mills ....Columbus, OH
Green, Rebecca S. B. ....Wichita, KS
Green, Renner, Weisse, Rettig, Rademacher & Clark ....Escanaba, MI
Green, Rex R. ....Houston, TX
Green, Richard ....Los Angeles, CA
Green, Richard A. ....Washington, DC
Green, Richard A. ....Carbondale, IL
Green, Richard A. ....Syracuse, IN
Green, Richard A. ....Akron, OH
Green, Richard A. ....Brentwood, TN
Green, Richard A., Law Offices of
Birmingham, MI
Green, Richard C. ....Washington, DC
Green, Richard D. ....Department of Justice, Criminal Division, GV
Green, Richard D. ....Clearwater, FL
Green, Richard E. ....Baltimore, MD
Green, Richard Ellett ....Atlanta, GA
Green, Richard F. ....Southport, NC
Green, Richard G. ....New York, NY
Green, Richard J., Jr. ....Johnstown, PA
Green, Richard K ....Santa Ana, CA
Green, Richard L. ....Phoenix, AZ
Green, Richard L. ....Hartford, CT
Green, Richard L. ....Kansas City, MO
Green, Richard M. ....San Francisco, CA
Green, Richard M. ....New York, NY
Green, Richard M. ....Jenkintown, PA
Green, Richard P. ....Omaha, NE
Green, Richard, P.C. ....Jenkintown, PA
Green, Richard, P.C. ....Jenkintown, PA
Green, Richard S. ....New York, NY
Green, Richard W. ....Minnetonka, MN
Green, Rickey A. ....San Jose, CA
Green, Ricky D. ....Austin, TX
Green, Rita ....White Bear Lake, MN
Green, Robert A. ....Los Angeles, CA
Green, Robert A. ....Columbus, NE
Green, Robert A. ....Ithaca, NY
Green, Robert A. ....Seattle, WA
Green, Robert A., Jr.
New Port Richey, FL
Green, Robert B. ....Hartford, CT
Green, Robert B. ....Miami, FL
Green, Robert B. ....Baltimore, MD
Green, Robert B. ....Chatham, NJ
Green, Robert D. ....Houston, TX
Green, Robert E. ....Forest Hills, NY
Green, Robert F. ....Winter Park, FL
Green, Robert F. ....Chicago, IL
Green, Robert F. ....Hackensack, NJ
Green, Robert F. ....Lake Success, NY
Green, Robert G. ....Darien, CT
Green, Robert G. ....Tulsa, OK
Green, Robert H. ....Santa Ana, CA
Green, Robert H. ....Milledgeville, GA
Green, Robert H. ....Knoxville, TN
Green, Robert K. ....Kansas City, MO
Green, Robert L. ....Orange, CA
Green, Robert L. ....Memphis, TN
Green, Robert L., Jr. ....Washington, DC
Green, Robert M. ....Washington, DC
Green, Robert M. ....El Dorado, KS
Green, Robert M. ....Metairie, LA
Green, Robert M., P.C. ....Chicago, IL
Green, Robert M., P.C. ....Chicago, IL
Green, Robert S. ....Tucson, AZ
Green, Robert S. ....San Francisco, CA
Green, Robert S. ....Washington, DC
Green, Robert S. ....Orlando, FL
Green, Robert S. ....New York, NY
Green, Robert W. ....Fairfield, CT
Greenwich, CT
Norwalk, CT
Green, Robert W. ....Stamford, CT
Washington, DC
Green, Robert W. ....Ottawa, KS
Green, Robert W., Chartered ....Ottawa, KS
Green, Roberta F. ....Charleston, WV
Green, Robin Lyn ....Newark, OH
Green, Robin M. ....Lubbock, TX
Green, Robin R. ....Dallas, TX
Green, Roger C. ....El Dorado, KS
Green, Roland D., III ....Austin, TX
Green, Ron C. ....Lower Lake, CA
Green, Ronald J. ....Topeka, KS
Green, Ronald L. ....Lexington, KY
Green, Ronald M. ....Costa Mesa, CA
Palm Springs, CA
San Diego, CA
Green, Ronald M. ....New York, NY
Green, Ronni Sue ....Fort Lauderdale, FL
Green, Ross ....Chicago, IL
Green, Roy E. ....Potomac, MD
Green, Rudolph H. ....Austin, TX
Green, Russell A. ....Milford, CT
Green, Samuel L. ....Buffalo, NY
Green, Samuel T. ....Jeffersonville, IN
Green, Sandor A. ....New York, NY
Green, Sandra Helena ....Washington, DC
Green, Sanford J. ....Phoenix, AZ
Green, Sarah S. ....Memphis, TN
Green & Sasser ....Conway, SC
Green, Schaaf & Jacobson, P.C.
St. Louis, MO
Green, Schulz, Roby, Oviatt, Cummings & Linngren, LLP ....Watertown, SD
Green, Scott A. ....Wilmington, DE
Green, Scott H. ....St. Louis, MO
Green, Scott K. ....Des Moines, IA
Green, Scott M. ....Los Angeles, CA
Green, Scott T. ....Moorpark, CA
Green, Sedgwick W. ....New York, NY
Green & Seifter, Attorneys, P.C.
Geneva, NY
Syracuse, NY
Green, Selma B. ....Scarsdale, NY
Green, Serenea H. ....Paso Robles, CA
Green, Seth M. ....Washington, DC
Green, Shand L. ....Orinda, CA
Green, Sharilyn Maphis ....Washington, DC
Green, Sharmini Nathan ....Menlo Park, CA
Green, Sharon ....Morrisville, VT
Green, Sharon DelFino
San Francisco, CA
San Rafael, CA
Green, Sharon H. ....Las Vegas, NV
Green, Sharon M. ....Johnson City, TN
Green, Sheldon ....Jericho, NY
Green, Sheldon N. ....Memphis, TN
Green, Shelley Z. ....Philadelphia, PA
Green, Sheri ....Towson, MD
Green, Sheri L. ....Hollywood, FL
Green and Siemann ....Carroll, IA
Green & Simon ....Glenside, PA
Green, Stacey M. ....Shelton, CT
Green, Stanley ....Bronx, NY
Green, Stanley ....Cleveland, OH
Green, Stanley B. ....Washington, DC
Green, Stanley B. ....Winston-Salem, NC
Green, Stanley J. ....Washington, DC
Green, Stephanie ....Coral Gables, FL
Green, Stephanie S. ....Chicago, IL
Green, Stephen ....New York, NY
Green, Stephen A. ....Melrose, MA
Green, Stephen H. ....Philadelphia, PA
Green, Stephen H., A Prof. Corp., Law Offices ....Philadelphia, PA
Green, Stephen J. ....Phoenix, AZ
Green, Stephen R. ....Marion, IL
Green, Stephen Ross ....New Castle, PA
Green, Stephen S., (P.C.) ....Los Angeles, CA
Green, Steven J. ....Foster City, CA
Green, Steven Keith ....South Royalton, VT
Green, Steven M. ....Los Angeles, CA
Green, Steven M. ....San Diego, CA

Green, Steven M., Law Firm of
San Diego, CA
Green, Steven Ray .... Athens, TX
Green, Stewart, Farber & Anderson, P.C.
Washington, DC
Chicago, IL
Albany, NY
Green, Stewart M. .... Springport, MI
Green, Stuart H. .... Swarthmore, PA
Green, Stuart P. .... Baton Rouge, LA
Green, Susan .... Newark, NJ
Green, Susan D. .... Leawood, KS
Kansas City, MO
Green, Susan D. .... Blue Springs, MO
Green, Susan H. .... Los Angeles, CA
Green, Susan R. .... Towson, MD
Green, Susan R., P.C. .... Baltimore, MD
Towson, MD
Green, Susan Rose .... Frankfort, KY
Green, Suzanne Worrall
Ponte Vedra Beach, FL
Green, Sydell J. .... New City, NY
Green, Tamara L. .... Ventura, CA
Green, Tamera Lee .... Southfield, MI
Green, Terence C. .... Collegeville, PA
Green, Terry A. .... Los Angeles, CA
Green, Terry Philip .... Somerset, NJ
Green, Theodore .... White Plains, NY
Green, Theodore C. .... Bellevue, WA
Green, Theodore M. .... Atlanta, GA
Green, Theodore M. .... Kansas City, MO
Green, Theodore T. .... Washington, DC
Green, Therese Hagemann .... Mobile, AL
Green, Thomas A. .... Rockford, IL
Green, Thomas B. .... Round Rock, TX
Green, Thomas C. .... Washington, DC
Green, Thomas C., II .... Omaha, NE
Green, Thomas D. .... San Luis Obispo, CA
Green, Thomas D. .... Brooklyn, NY
Green, Thomas E., Jr., (P.C.)
Houston, TX
Green, Thomas H. .... Saline, MI
Green, Thomas H. .... Florham Park, NJ
Green, Thomas H., III .... Boston, MA
Green, Thomas Irvine .... Tequesta, FL
Green, Thomas J. .... St. Louis, MO
Green, Thomas J., (P.C.) .... Watertown, SD
Green, Thomas L. .... San Diego, CA
Green, Thomas M. .... Roberta, GA
Green, Thomas R. .... Las Vegas, NV
Green, Thomas W. .... Irvine, CA
Green, Tim W. .... Guthrie, OK
Green, Tim W., P.C. .... Guthrie, OK
Green, Timothy A. .... Dearborn, MI
Green, Timothy G. .... Houston, TX
Green, Timothy M. .... St. Johns, MI
Green, Tina R. .... Texarkana, AR
Green, Todd A. .... Newport Beach, CA
Green, Todd Douglas .... Bethesda, MD
Green, Todd M. .... San Francisco, CA
Green, Tom L. .... Topeka, KS
Green, Tomie T. .... Jackson, MS
Green, Tracey Colton .... Columbia, SC
Green, Tracy .... Oakland, CA
Green, Tracy .... Pasadena, CA
Green & Utter, P.A. .... Manchester, NH
Green, Valerie E. .... New York, NY
Green, Vanessa C. .... Marrero, LA
Green, Vanessa I. .... Department of Justice,
Civil Division, GV
Green, Vernon N. .... South Glens Falls, NY
Green, Vicki L. .... Monroe, LA
Green, Victoria E. .... Bloomfield Hills, MI
Green, Virginia .... Troy, AL
Green, Virginia D. .... Washington, DC
Green, W. Joseph, Jr. .... Rockville, MD
Green, W. Scott, P.C. .... Billings, MT
Green, W. Travick .... Crystal River, FL
Green, Walker S. .... De Funiak Springs, FL
Green, Wally .... Columbiaville, MI
Green, Walter F., IV .... Harrisonburg, VA
Green, Warren I. .... Stoneham, MA
Green, Warren S. .... New York, NY
Green, Wayne F. .... Lancaster, PA
Green, Wendy A. .... Sacramento, CA
Green, Wendy B. .... Morristown, NJ
Green, William .... San Francisco, CA
Green, William A. .... Colorado Springs, CO
Green, William A., III .... Louisville, KY
Green, William D. .... West Caldwell, NJ
Green, William E. .... San Francisco, CA
San Rafael, CA
Green, William E., Jr. .... Brookneal, VA
Green, William F. .... Cambridge, MA
Green, William G. .... Emeryville, CA
Green, William H. .... Martinez, CA
Green, William H. .... Tallahassee, FL
Green, William H. .... Port Washington, NY
Green, William H. .... Milwaukee, WI
Green, William Howard
De Funiak Springs, FL
Green, William J. .... Washington, DC
Green, William J. .... Pensacola, FL
Green, William L. .... Seattle, WA
Green, William M. .... St. Louis, MO
Green, William O., III
Oklahoma City, OK
Green, William P. .... Pasadena, CA
Green, William R. .... Park Ridge, IL
Green, William S. .... Manchester, NH
Green, William Shalom .... Washington, DC
Green, William T., III .... Houston, TX
Green, William W.
Hot Springs National Park, AR
Green, William W. .... Newport Beach, CA
Green, Williams J. .... Atlanta, GA
Green & Willstatter .... White Plains, NY
Green, Wilson Franklin .... Birmingham, AL
Green, Wilson, III .... Orlando, FL
Green, Wm., Jr. .... Youngstown, OH
Green, Wm. L. .... Mobile, AL
Green, Wood & Howell .... Hamilton, AL
Green, Yvette Chancellor .... Rochester, NY
Green, Zachary C. .... Stamford, CT
Greenacre, Charles R. .... Montrose, CO
Greenan, Gerald J. .... West Seneca, NY
Greenan, Gerald J., III .... Buffalo, NY
Greenan, James M. .... Annapolis, MD
Greenbelt, MD
Greenan, James P. .... Helena, MT
Greenan, James S. .... San Francisco, CA
Walnut Creek, CA
Greenan, Kathleen L. .... Washington, DC
Greenan, Paul .... New York, NY
Greenan, Rebecca L. .... Dallas, TX
Greenan, Thomas J. .... Seattle, WA
Tacoma, WA
Greenan, Walker & Billman, L.L.P.
Annapolis, MD
Greenbelt, MD
Greenapple, Lawrence .... New York, NY
Greenapple, Steven B. .... Morristown, NJ
Greenawalt, Craig N. .... Westfield, NJ
Greenawalt, Kent .... New York, NY
Greenawalt, Leo F. .... Seattle, WA
Greenawalt, Mary Ann .... Euclid, OH
Greenawalt, R Kent .... New York, NY
Greenawalt, Robert L. .... Los Angeles, CA
Greenawalt, William Sloan .... New York, NY
Greenaway, Alicia F. .... Princeton, NJ
Greenaway, Gay & Angier
Port Angeles, WA
Sequim, WA
Greenaway, Joseph A., Jr. .... Newark, NJ
Greenaway, Keith A. .... Princeton, NJ
New York, NY
Greenaway, Sharon P. .... Tampa, FL
Greenaway, Sonia A.
Federal Communications Commission,
Mass Media Bureau, GV
Greenaway, Walter T. .... Port Angeles, WA
Greenbacker, J. E. .... Halifax, VA
Greenbacker, J. E., Jr. .... Halifax, VA
Green-Barnett, Cheryl Delois .... Sylacauga, AL
Greenbaum, Adam R. .... Hackensack, NJ
Greenbaum, Alan
Federal Energy Regulatory Commission,
Office of the General Counsel, GV
Greenbaum, Arthur F. .... Columbus, OH
Greenbaum, Arthur J. .... New York, NY
Greenbaum, Arthur M. .... Woodbridge, NJ
Greenbaum, Bernard S. .... New York, NY
Greenbaum & Champ, LLP
Long Beach, CA
Woodland Hills, CA
Greenbaum, Cheryl B. .... New City, NY
Greenbaum, Cindy B. .... Arlington, VA
Greenbaum, Dana L. .... St. Petersburg, FL
Greenbaum, Daniel A. .... New York, NY
Greenbaum, David .... New York, NY
Greenbaum, David A. .... Towson, MD
Greenbaum, David M. .... New York, NY
Greenbaum, David Roy .... New York, NY
Greenbaum, Don R. .... New York, NY
Greenbaum, Edward .... Scarborough, NY
Greenbaum, Eileen M. .... Washington, DC
Greenbaum, Eli D. .... Troy, MI
Greenbaum, Elise E. .... Hollywood, FL
Highland Park, IL
Greenbaum, Elise M. .... Tallahassee, FL
Greenbaum, Felice G. .... Los Angeles, CA
Greenbaum & Ferentz LLP
Los Angeles, CA
Newport Beach, CA
Palm Springs, CA
San Diego, CA
San Francisco, CA
Greenbaum, Frederick J.
Kansas City, KS
Greenbaum, Gary I. .... Seattle, WA
Greenbaum, Gary M. .... Oakton, VA
Greenbaum & Greenbaum, P.C.
Farmington Hills, MI
Greenbaum, Harry P. .... East Meadow, NY
Greenbaum, Herschel .... Pearl River, NY
Greenbaum, Irving J. .... New York, NY
Greenbaum, Irving L. .... Framingham, MA
Greenbaum, Jack A. .... New York, NY
Greenbaum, James T. .... Montauk, NY
Greenbaum, Jeffrey A. .... New York, NY
Greenbaum, Jeffrey J. .... Newark, NJ
New York, NY
Greenbaum, Jerome B.
Farmington Hills, MI
Greenbaum, Joel W. .... New York, NY
Greenbaum, John A. .... Harrisburg, PA
Greenbaum, Jon M. .... Department of Justice,
Civil Rights Division, GV
Greenbaum, Jonathan W.
Washington, DC
Greenbaum, Joseph A. .... McLean, VA
Greenbaum, Josh M. .... Philadelphia, PA
Greenbaum, Judith Goldstein
Farmington Hills, MI
Greenbaum, Kenneth .... Chicago, IL
Greenbaum, Lawrence D.
Kansas City, KS
Greenbaum, Leslie M. .... Buffalo, NY
Greenbaum, Lewis .... Chicago, IL
Greenbaum, Marc D. .... Boston, MA
Greenbaum, Martin .... Miami, FL
Greenbaum, Martin B., (P.C.)
Newport Beach, CA
Greenbaum, Matt .... New Orleans, LA
Greenbaum, Maurice C. .... New York, NY
Greenbaum, Michael C. .... Washington, DC
Greenbaum, Michael S. .... Los Angeles, CA
Greenbaum, Nagel, Fisher & Hamelburg
Boston, MA
Greenbaum, Nancy B. .... New York, NY
Greenbaum, Nathan J. .... Laurel, MD
Greenbaum, Neil .... Chicago, IL
Greenbaum, Neil S. .... Garden City, NY
Greenbaum, Peter .... East Meadow, NY
New York, NY
Greenbaum, Phoebe K. .... Brooklyn, NY
Greenbaum, Rachel K. .... Glencoe, IL
Greenbaum, Richard E. .... Chatsworth, CA
Greenbaum, Richard W. .... Long Beach, CA
Woodland Hills, CA
Greenbaum, Robert A. .... Springfield, VA
Greenbaum, Robert B. .... Washington, DC
Greenbaum, Robert D. .... Philadelphia, PA
Greenbaum, Robert D., & Associates LLC
Philadelphia, PA
Greenbaum, Robert J. .... Short Hills, NJ
Greenbaum, Robert M. .... Philadelphia, PA
Greenbaum, Robert S. .... Woodbridge, NJ
Greenbaum, Robert S. .... New York, NY
Greenbaum, Roger A. .... San Francisco, CA
Greenbaum, Ronald F. .... Potomac, MD
Greenbaum, Ronald S. .... Kansas City, MO
Greenbaum, Rowe, Smith, Ravin, Davis and Himmel LLP .... Roseland, NJ
Woodbridge, NJ
Greenbaum, Samuel M. .... Washington, DC
Greenbaum, Sheila .... St. Louis, MO
Greenbaum, Sheldon M. .... New York, NY
Greenbaum, Sidney .... Santa Ana, CA
Greenbaum, Stephen A. .... Boston, MA
Greenbaum, Steven E. .... New York, NY
Greenbaum, Steven Marc .... Miami, FL
Greenbaum, Veronica A. .... Boston, MA
Providence, RI
Greenbaum, William I. .... Morris Plains, NJ
Greenberg, A. L., Ltd. .... Newport, RI
Greenberg, Aaron D. .... New York, NY
Greenberg, Aaron G. .... Elizabeth, NJ
Greenberg, Aaron M. .... San Francisco, CA
Greenberg, Aaron S. .... Chicago, IL
Greenberg, Abraham .... New York, NY
Greenberg, Abraham H. .... Brooklyn, NY
Greenberg, Adrianne Susan
Garden City, NY
Greenberg, Alaine S. .... Wilton Manors, FL
Greenberg, Alan .... Aurora, CO
Greenberg, Alan .... Denver, CO
Greenberg, Alan .... Marlton, NJ
Greenberg, Alan .... New York, NY
Greenberg, Alan A. .... Costa Mesa, CA
Greenberg, Alan D. .... Denver, CO
Greenberg, Alan E. .... San Diego, CA
Greenberg, Alan G. .... Waterford, MI
Greenberg, Alan G., P.C. .... Waterford, MI
Greenberg, Alan M. .... New York, NY
Greenberg, Albert L., (M.C.) .... Newport, RI
Greenberg, Alison G. .... Newark, NJ
Greenberg, Allan H. .... New York, NY
Greenberg, Allen .... New York, NY
Greenberg, Allen L. .... Atlanta, GA
Greenberg, Allison Fong
Newport Beach, CA
Greenberg, Amy B. .... Brooklyn, NY
Greenberg, Amy E. .... Los Angeles, CA
Greenberg, Amy J. .... Bridgeport, CT
Greenberg, Andrea J. .... San Francisco, CA
Greenberg, Andrew A. .... New York, NY
Greenberg, Andrew Clifford .... Tampa, FL
Greenberg, Andrew E. .... Philadelphia, PA
Greenberg, Andrew G. .... East Brunswick, NJ
Greenberg, Andrew S. .... Syracuse, NY
Greenberg, Ann Elise .... Austin, TX
Greenberg, Arnold C. .... West Hartford, CT
Greenberg, Arnold L. .... New York, NY
Greenberg, Arnold M. .... Mill Valley, CA
Greenberg, Arthur .... Foster City, CA
Greenberg, Arthur A. .... Encino, CA
Greenberg, Arthur G. .... Peoria, IL
Greenberg, Arthur N. .... Los Angeles, CA
Greenberg, Arthur R. .... Hudson, NY
Greenberg & Associates, A Professional Corporation .... Roanoke, VA
Greenberg, Barbara C. .... Cleveland, OH
Greenberg, Barbara Frances
Roslyn Harbor, NY
Greenberg, Barbara H. .... Rye Brook, NY
Greenberg, Barry C. .... Baltimore, MD
Greenberg, Barry E. .... Dix Hills, NY
Greenberg, Barry M. .... Los Angeles, CA
Greenberg, Barry N. .... Miami, FL
Greenberg, Barry Y. .... Fort Worth, TX
Greenberg, Bart .... Costa Mesa, CA
Greenberg, Barton A. .... New York, NY
Greenberg & Bass .... Encino, CA
Greenberg & Bederman .... Silver Spring, MD
Greenberg, Bennett D. .... Washington, DC
Greenberg, Bernard A. .... Beverly Hills, CA
Greenberg, Bernard L. .... New York, NY
Greenberg, Betty R. .... Newport, RI
Greenberg, Beverly L. .... Miami, FL
Greenberg, Beverly L. (Pevsner) .... Miami, FL
Greenberg, Bradley J. .... Cincinnati, OH
Greenberg, Bruce D. .... Newark, NJ
Greenberg, Bryan S. .... Fort Lauderdale, FL
Greenberg, Burton F. .... Atlantic City, NJ
Greenberg, Burton M. .... St. Louis, MO
Greenberg, Carl .... Short Hills, NJ
Greenberg, Carl P. .... Decatur, GA
Greenberg, Carolyn L. .... Lowell, MA
Greenberg, Cary Mitchel .... New York, NY
Greenberg, Cary S. .... Fairfax, VA
Greenberg, Cassrell .... New York, NY
Greenberg, Cathy A. .... Sylvan Lake, MI
Greenberg, Charles A. .... San Francisco, CA
Greenberg, Charles L. .... Flushing, NY
Greenberg, Charles M. .... Pittsburgh, PA
Greenberg & Cioci .... East Brunswick, NJ
Greenberg, Claudia B. .... Miami, FL
Sarasota, FL
Greenberg, Clayton E. .... Dallas, TX
Greenberg, Clifford L. .... New York, NY
Greenberg & Costa, P.C. .... New Haven, CT
Greenberg, Craig .... Louisville, KY
Greenberg, Craig D. .... Minneapolis, MN
Greenberg & Dallam .... Gretna, LA
Greenberg, Daniel .... Trumbull, CT
Greenberg, Daniel .... Northport, NY
Greenberg, Daniel B. .... Van Nuys, CA
Greenberg, Daniel B. .... Acton, MA
Greenberg, Daniel H. .... New York, NY
Greenberg, Daniel L. .... San Bernardino, CA
Greenberg, Daniel L. .... New York, NY
Greenberg, Daniel, LLC, Law Offices of
Trumbull, CT
Greenberg, Daniel M. .... Homewood, IL
Greenberg, Daniel M., Chartered, Law Offices
Homewood, IL
Greenberg, Danielle B. .... New York, NY
Greenberg Dauber Epstein & Tucker, A Professional Corporation .... Newark, NJ
Greenberg, David .... Los Angeles, CA
Greenberg, David .... Gretna, LA
Greenberg, David .... Spring Valley, NY
Greenberg, David A. .... Westport, CT
Greenberg, David B. .... New Haven, CT
Greenberg, David C. .... Chicago, IL
Greenberg, David H. .... Durango, CO
Greenberg, David H. .... Pompano Beach, FL
Greenberg, David H. .... Columbia, MD
Greenberg, David H. .... Burlington, VT
Greenberg, David H. .... St. Albans, VT
Greenberg, David I. .... Richmond, VA
Greenberg, David J. .... Pittsburgh, PA
Greenberg, David L. .... Atlanta, GA
Greenberg, David M. .... Larkspur, CA
San Francisco, CA
Greenberg, David M .... New York, NY
Greenberg, David M. .... New York, NY
Greenberg, David M., A Professional Corporation .... Larkspur, CA
San Francisco, CA
Greenberg, David P. .... San Diego, CA
Greenberg, David P. .... Martinsburg, WV
Greenberg, David S. .... Englewood Cliffs, NJ
Greenberg, Deborah M. .... New York, NY
Greenberg, Deborah Rockman
Baltimore, MD
Greenberg, Debra I. .... Albany, NY
Greenberg, Debra L. .... Plantation, FL
Greenberg, Diane Stein .... Menlo Park, CA
Greenberg, Dianne .... New York, NY
Greenberg, Dolores H. .... Chicago, IL
Greenberg, Douglas J. .... St. Petersburg, FL
Greenberg, E. Barry .... Oak Brook, IL
Greenberg, Edward A.
Haddon Heights, NJ
Fort Washington, PA
Greenberg, Edward C. .... New York, NY
Greenberg, Edward D. .... Washington, DC
Greenberg, Edward D. .... New York, NY
Greenberg, Eldon V. C. .... Washington, DC
Greenberg, Elena L. .... Garden City, NY
Greenberg, Eli D. .... New York, NY
Greenberg, Eliot L. .... New York, NY
Greenberg, Elizabeth J. .... Woodcliff Lake, NJ
Greenberg, Emanuel .... New York, NY
Greenberg, Eric D. .... Washington, DC
Greenberg, Eric F. .... Chicago, IL
Greenberg, Erwin .... Palm Beach, FL
Greenberg, Erwin H. .... Fort Lauderdale, FL
Greenberg, Felsen & Sargent, L.L.C.
Rockville, MD
Greenberg, Fields & Whitcombe, LLP
Los Angeles, CA
Torrance, CA
Greenberg, Forrest M. .... Stockton, CA
Greenberg, Frank R. .... San Rafael, CA
Greenberg, Fred .... Media, PA
Greenberg, Fred A. .... Yorba Linda, CA
Greenberg, Freddi L. .... Chicago, IL
Greenberg, Freddi L. .... Evanston, IL
Greenberg, Frederick L. .... New Haven, CT
Greenberg, Gail B. .... Beverly Hills, CA
Greenberg, Gary H. .... New York, NY
Greenberg, Gary J. .... New York, NY
Greenberg, Gary L. .... Minneapolis, MN
Greenberg, Gary L. .... Cincinnati, OH
Greenberg, Gary R. .... Boston, MA
Greenberg, Gary S. .... Bloomfield, CT
Greenberg, Gary S. .... Milwaukee, WI
Greenberg, Genell G. .... San Diego, CA
Greenberg, Geoffrey M. .... Red Bank, NJ
Greenberg, Gerald S. .... Cincinnati, OH
Greenberg Glusker Fields Claman & Machtinger LLP .... Los Angeles, CA
Greenberg, Gordon A. .... Los Angeles, CA
Greenberg & Greenberg .... Stockton, CA
Greenberg and Greenberg .... Portland, ME
Greenberg & Greenberg .... Hudson, NY
Greenberg & Halvorsen .... Hauppauge, NY
Greenberg, Harlan Garrett .... New York, NY
Greenberg, Harold .... Los Angeles, CA
Greenberg, Harold .... Indianapolis, IN
Greenberg, Harold .... New York, NY
Greenberg, Harold .... New York, NY
Greenberg, Harvey .... Baltimore, MD
Greenberg, Harvey L. .... New York, NY
Greenberg, Hayley R. .... New York, NY
Greenberg, Helene Migdon .... Hartsdale, NY
Greenberg, Henry I. .... Baltimore, MD
Greenberg, Henry M. .... Albany, NY
Greenberg, Herbert L. .... Culver City, CA

Greenberg, Hilary J. ... Wilkes-Barre, PA
Greenberg, Hindi ... San Francisco, CA
Greenberg & Hofstein, P.C. ... Little Neck, NY
Greenberg, Howard B. ... New York, NY
Greenberg, Howard E. ... Hauppauge, NY
Greenberg, Howard J. ... Philadelphia, PA
Greenberg, Howard N. ... Jenkintown, PA
Greenberg, Howard R. ... Richardson, TX
Greenberg, Howard S. ... Roseland, NJ
Greenberg, Hurwitz, Cooper & Silverman, P.C. New Haven, CT
Greenberg, Illene G. ... Cherry Hill, NJ
Philadelphia, PA
Greenberg, Ira ... Bronx, NY
Greenberg, Ira G. ... New York, NY
Greenberg, Irene S. ... New York, NY
Greenberg, Irving ... Rockville, MD
Greenberg, J. Michael ... Roslyn Harbor, NY
Greenberg, Jack ... New York, NY
Greenberg, Jack M. ... New York, NY
Greenberg, Jacqueline ... Morristown, NJ
Greenberg, James ... Cherry Hill, NJ
Greenberg, James D. ... York, PA
Greenberg, Janice A. ... Cherry Hill, NJ
Philadelphia, PA
Greenberg, Jason Arthur ... Merrick, NY
Greenberg, Jeffrey A. ... Chicago, IL
Greenberg, Jeffrey A. ... New York, NY
Greenberg, Jeffrey B. ... New York, NY
Greenberg, Jeffrey D. ... New York, NY
Greenberg, Jeffrey H. ... Tucson, AZ
Greenberg, Jeffrey M. ... Stockton, CA
Greenberg, Jeffrey P. ... Tampa, FL
Greenberg, Jeffrey P. ... Worcester, MA
Greenberg, Jeremy Moshe ... New York, NY
Greenberg, Jerry ... New York, NY
Greenberg, Jill A. ... Melville, NY
Greenberg, Joan L. ... Jupiter, FL
Greenberg, Joan L. ... New York, NY
Greenberg, Joel E. ... Lake Worth, FL
Greenberg, Joel I. ... New York, NY
Greenberg, Joel M. ... Great Neck, NY
Greenberg, Joel S. ... Pittsfield, MA
Greenberg, Joel S., P.C. ... Pittsfield, MA
Greenberg, John B. ... Belleville, IL
St. Louis, MO
Greenberg, Jonathan A. ... Washington, DC
Greenberg, Jonathan D. ... Cleveland, OH
Greenberg, Jonathan S. ... Newark, NJ
Greenberg, Joseph H. ... Chicago, IL
Greenberg, Joseph H. ... Indianapolis, IN
Greenberg, Joshua F. ... New York, NY
Greenberg, Josiah ... New York, NY
Greenberg, Judi S. ... Boston, MA
Greenberg, Judith G. ... Boston, MA
Greenberg, Jules L. ... Los Angeles, CA
Greenberg, Julie A. ... Birmingham, MI
Greenberg & Kahr ... New York, NY
Greenberg, Karen A. ... St. Louis, MO
Greenberg, Karen K. ... Wellesley Hills, MA
Greenberg, Karen L. ... Los Angeles, CA
Greenberg, Kathryn Olson ... New York, NY
Greenberg, Kenneth L. ... Philadelphia, PA
Greenberg, Kenneth S. ... Santa Barbara, CA
Greenberg & Lanz ... Hackensack, NJ
Greenberg, Larry S. ... Washington, DC
Greenberg, Larry S. ... Bethesda, MD
Greenberg, Lauren A. ... Washington, DC
Greenberg, Laurence A. ... Hollywood, FL
Greenberg, Laurence P. ... Brooklyn, NY
Greenberg, Lawrence A. ... Palm Beach, FL
Greenberg, Lawrence Howell
San Diego, CA
Greenberg, Lawrence J. ... New Haven, CT
Greenberg, Lawrence J. ... New London, CT
Greenberg, Lawrence Steven ... Baltimore, MD
Greenberg, Leibert L. ... New York, NY
Greenberg, Leonard ... New City, NY
Greenberg, Leslie J. ... Washington, DC
Baltimore, MD
Burtonsville, MD
Greenberg, Lester A. ... New York, NY
Greenberg, Lewis ... Jersey City, NJ
Greenberg & Lieberman ... Washington, DC
Takoma Park, MD
Greenberg, Linda Wesson ... La Mesa, CA
Greenberg, Lionel ... St. Paul, MN
Greenberg, Lisa A. ... Danvers, MA
Greenberg, Lori ... Escondido, CA
Greenberg, Lori A. ... San Francisco, CA
Greenberg, Lori C. ... Marlton, NJ
Greenberg, Lorraine M. ... Chicago, IL
Greenberg, Louis Edward ... Natick, MA
Greenberg, Lyle F. ... Woodland Hills, CA
Greenberg, Lynne ... Brooklyn, NY
Greenberg, Malcolm H. ... Virginia, MN
Greenberg, Malcolm H. ... West Orange, NJ
Greenberg & Malick ... Durango, CO
Greenberg, Malin D. ... Minneapolis, MN
Greenberg, Mannes F. ... Baltimore, MD
Greenberg, Manuel H. ... Mays Landing, NJ
Greenberg, Marc H. ... San Francisco, CA
Greenberg, Marc L. ... Cincinnati, OH
Greenberg, Marcia E. ... Brookline, MA
Greenberg, Marcia J. M. ... Bellevue, WA
Greenberg, Margery A. ... New York, NY
Greenberg, Marie-Ann ... Parsippany, NJ
Greenberg, Marilynn R. ... Morristown, NJ
Greenberg, Mark A. ... Walnut Creek, CA
Greenberg, Mark A. ... Miami, FL
Greenberg, Mark B. ... Dallas, TX
Greenberg, Mark D. ... Department of Justice, Office of Policy Development, GV
Greenberg, Mark D. ... Albany, NY
Greenberg, Mark D. ... Hudson, NY
Greenberg, Mark Howard ... Los Angeles, CA
Greenberg, Mark I. ... Chicago, IL
Greenberg, Mark L. ... Houston, TX

Greenberg, Mark M. ... El Paso, TX
Greenberg, Mark S. ... Los Angeles, CA
Greenberg, Mark S. ... Philadelphia, PA
Greenberg, Martin F. ... Boca Raton, FL
Greenberg, Martin J. ... Milwaukee, WI
Greenberg, Martin L. ... Chicago, IL
Greenberg, Martin L. ... Roseland, NJ
Greenberg, Martin R. ... New York, NY
Greenberg, Marvin H. ... Woburn, MA
Greenberg, Matthew M. ... Wilmington, DE
Greenberg, Matthew N. ... New York, NY
Greenberg, Maurice R. ... New York, NY
Greenberg, Max E., Trager, Toplitz & Herbst
West Orange, NJ
New York, NY
Greenberg, Maxwell E. ... Los Angeles, CA
Greenberg, Mayer ... New York, NY
Greenberg, Mead I. ... Los Angeles, CA
Greenberg, Megan Semple
Wilmington, DE
Greenberg, Melvin ... Newark, NJ
Greenberg, Melvin F. ... New York, NY
Greenberg, Melvin J. ... Bensalem, PA
Greenberg, Melvyn H. ... New York, NY
Greenberg & Merola ... New York, NY
Greenberg, Michael ... Miami, FL
Greenberg, Michael D. ... Princeton, NJ
New York, NY
Greenberg, Michael D. ... New York, NY
Greenberg, Michael D., Law Offices of
Cambridge, MA
Greenberg, Michael E. ... Philadelphia, PA
Greenberg, Michael Ellis ... Austin, TX
Greenberg, Michael H. ... New York, NY
Greenberg, Michael J. ... Melville, NY
Mineola, NY
Greenberg, Michael Jay ... New York, NY
Greenberg, Michael L. ... San Francisco, CA
Greenberg, Michael L. ... Takoma Park, MD
Greenberg, Michael S. ... San Francisco, CA
Greenberg, Millicent ... New York, NY
Greenberg, Mitchell B.
San Francisco, CA
Greenberg, Moe ... Providence, RI
Greenberg, Morton I. ... Trenton, NJ
Greenberg, Morton L. ... Beverly Hills, CA
Greenberg, Murray ... East Meadow, NY
Greenberg, Murray ... New York, NY
Greenberg, Murray A. ... Miami, FL
Greenberg, Myron S. ... Larkspur, CA
Greenberg, Myron S. ... Minneapolis, MN
Greenberg, Myron S., A Professional Corporation ... Larkspur, CA
Greenberg, Nancy Gold ... Dedham, MA
Greenberg, Nancy I. ... Wallingford, CT
Greenberg, Nancy R. ... New York, NY
Greenberg, Nathan ... Gretna, LA
Greenberg, Nathan ... Toledo, OH
Greenberg, Neil H. ... Westbury, NY
Greenberg, Neil I. ... Huntington, NY
Greenberg, Neil P. ... Philadelphia, PA
Greenberg, Newton ... New York, NY
Greenberg, Norman ... Wellesley, MA
Greenberg, Norman ... Brooklyn, NY
Greenberg & Panish, A Prof. Corp.
Los Angeles, CA
Greenberg, Paul ... Department of Labor, Office of Secretary, GV
Greenberg, Paul A. ... Chicago, IL
Greenberg, Paul A., Law Offices of
Santa Monica, CA
Greenberg, Paul R. ... Los Angeles, CA
Greenberg, Paul R. ... Boston, MA
Greenberg, Paul R., Inc. ... Los Angeles, CA
Greenberg, Peden, Siegmyer & Oshman, P.C. ... Houston, TX
Greenberg, Penelope Creasey
Burlingame, CA
Greenberg, Peter E. ... New York, NY
Greenberg, Peter E., & Associates, Ltd.
New York, NY
Greenberg, Peter S. ... Philadelphia, PA
Greenberg, Philip A. ... New York, NY
Greenberg, Philip R. ... Miami, FL
Greenberg, Phillip L. ... Horsham, PA
Greenberg & Pleban ... St. Louis, MO
Greenberg, Rachel Ada ... Berkeley, CA
Greenberg, Ralph D. ... Brooklyn, NY
Greenberg, Raymond A. ... Calabasas, CA
Greenberg, Rhonda S. ... New York, NY
Greenberg, Richard ... St. Louis, MO
Greenberg, Richard ... New York, NY
Greenberg, Richard A. ... Tallahassee, FL
Greenberg, Richard A. ... New York, NY
Greenberg, Richard C. ... Torrance, CA
Greenberg, Richard E.
Department of Justice, GV
Greenberg, Richard H. ... Middletown, NJ
Greenberg, Richard H. ... Woodbridge, NJ
Greenberg, Richard I. ... New York, NY
Greenberg, Richard K. ... Hartford, CT
Greenberg, Richard L. ... Roanoke, VA
Greenberg, Richard M. ... New York, NY
Greenberg, Richard S. ... Englewood Cliffs, NJ
Greenberg, Richard T. ... Chicago, IL
Greenberg, Robert ... Berkeley Heights, NJ
West New York, NJ
Greenberg, Robert A. ... Rockville, MD
Greenberg, Robert A. ... Boston, MA
Greenberg, Robert A. ... Rahway, NJ
Greenberg, Robert Aaron ... Mount Laurel, NJ
Greenberg, Robert B. ... Pomona, CA
Greenberg, Robert B. ... Chicago, IL
Greenberg, Robert B. ... Bethesda, MD
Greenberg, Robert B. ... Little Neck, NY
Greenberg, Robert E. ... Washington, DC
Greenberg, Robert E. ... Lake Success, NY
Greenberg, Robert J. ... Forest Hills, NY

Greenberg, Robert L. ... San Francisco, CA
Greenberg, Robert L., A Professional Law Corporation ... San Francisco, CA
Greenberg, Robert M. ... Newtown, PA
Greenberg, Robert M. ... Dallas, TX
Greenberg, Robert S. ... Vineland, NJ
Greenberg, Robt. G. ... St. Louis, MO
Greenberg, Roger B. ... Houston, TX
Greenberg, Roger E. ... Silver Spring, MD
Greenberg, Ronald ... New York, NY
Greenberg, Ronald D. ... New York, NY
Greenberg, Ronald E. ... El Cajon, CA
Greenberg, Ronald M. ... Beverly Hills, CA
Greenberg, Ronald S. ... New York, NY
Greenberg, Rose ... New York, NY
Greenberg, Ross G. ... Washington, DC
Greenberg, Roy E. ... East Hampton, NY
Greenberg, Ruth L. ... Atlanta, GA
Greenberg, Sally Joan ... Washington, DC
Greenberg, Sanford H. ... New York, NY
New York, NY
Greenberg, Sanford N. ... Chicago, IL
Greenberg, Sara B.
Department Of The Interior, Office of Hearings & Appeals, GV
Greenberg, Sari E. ... New York, NY
Greenberg & Scales ... Martinsburg, WV
Greenberg & Schulman ... Woodbridge, NJ
Greenberg, Scott ... Belleville, IL
St. Louis, MO
Greenberg, Scott D. ... New York, NY
Greenberg, Seth M. ... New York, NY
Greenberg, Sheldon J. ... Cleveland, OH
Greenberg, Shmerelson, Weinroth & Miller, P.C. ... Camden, NJ
Greenberg, Sidney ... Bloomfield, CT
Greenberg, Sidney ... Pittsfield, MA
Greenberg, Sidney H. ... Syracuse, NY
Greenberg, Sidney L. ... Pensacola, FL
Greenberg, S. L. ... Beaumont, TX
Greenberg & Soderberg, LLP ... Media, PA
Philadelphia, PA
Greenberg, Sol ... Albany, NY
Greenberg, Stanley F. ... Portland, ME
Greenberg, Stanley I. ... Los Angeles, CA
Greenberg, Stanley J. ... Santa Rosa, CA
Greenberg, Stanley M. ... Philadelphia, PA
Greenberg, Stanley Z. ... Dayton, OH
Greenberg, Stephen ... Austin, TX
Greenberg, Stephen C. ... Atlanta, GA
Greenberg, Stephen F. ... Savannah, GA
Greenberg, Stephen H. ... New York, NY
Greenberg, Stephen M. ... Cherry Hill, NJ
Greenberg, Stephen M. ... Roseland, NJ
Greenberg, Stephen R. ... Pittsburgh, PA
Greenberg, Steven A. ... Chicago, IL
Greenberg, Steven I. ... Oakhurst, NJ
Greenberg, Steven J. ... New York, NY
Greenberg, Steven M.
West Palm Beach, FL
Greenberg, Steven M. ... West Orange, NJ
Greenberg, Steven Morey
Hackensack, NJ
Greenberg, Steven R. ... Sarasota, FL
Greenberg, Steven S. ... New York, NY
Greenberg, Stewart G. ... Miami, FL
Greenberg, Stewart G., P.A. ... Miami, FL
Greenberg, Stuart I. ... Monroe, NY
Greenberg, Stuart J. ... New York, NY
Greenberg, Susan ... New York, NY
Greenberg, Susan E. ... Boca Raton, FL
Greenberg, Susan I. ... Kew Gardens, NY
Greenberg, Susan R. ... Washington, DC
Greenberg, Suzanne F. ... New York, NY
Greenberg, Ted M. ... Bensalem, PA
Greenberg, Terry Goltz ... Addison, TX
Greenberg, Theo. M. ... New York, NY
Greenberg, Theodore S.
Department of Justice, Criminal Division, GV
Greenberg, Thomas ... New York, NY
Greenberg, Thomas M. ... Merrillville, IN
Greenberg, Thomas M., P.C.
Crown Point, IN
Merrillville, IN
Greenberg, Thomas R. ... Los Angeles, CA
Greenberg, Todd D. ... Forest Hills, NY
Greenberg, Todd L. ... Department of Justice, Criminal Division, GV
Greenberg, Toni M. ... Cohoes, NY
Greenberg, Tracy Saffren ... Dallas, TX
Greenberg Traurig ... Washington, DC
Atlanta, GA
Boston, MA
New York, NY
Philadelphia, PA
Tysons Corner, VA
Boca Raton, FL
Fort Lauderdale, FL
Miami, FL
Orlando, FL
Tallahassee, FL
West Palm Beach, FL
Chicago, IL
Greenberg, Tricia L. ... Palo Alto, CA
Greenberg & Walden ... Berkeley Heights, NJ
West New York, NJ
Greenberg, Wanderman & Fromson
Spring Valley, NY
Greenberg, Wilbur ... Philadelphia, PA
Greenberg, William A. ... Fern Park, FL
Greenberg, William G. ... White Plains, NY
Greenberg, William S. ... Newark, NJ
Greenberg, William S. ... West Orange, NJ
Greenberg-Chesnick, Lydia ... Boston, MA
Greenberger, Barry S. ... Brick, NJ
Greenberger, Ellen L. ... Libertyville, IL
Greenberger, Ernest ... Chicago, IL

Greenberger, Feris M., (Ms.)
Beverly Hills, CA
Greenberger, George D. ... Hempstead, NY
Greenberger, Gerald A. ... New York, NY
Greenberger, Howard L. ... New York, NY
Greenberger, I. Michael
Commodity Futures Trading Commission, Division of Trading and Markets, GV
Greenberger, James J. ... Chicago, IL
Greenberger, Jeffrey J. ... Cincinnati, OH
Greenberger, Joseph ... New York, NY
Greenberger, Karen I. ... New York, NY
Greenberger, Karen Kraus ... Cincinnati, OH
Greenberger, Krauss & Tenenbaum
Chicago, IL
Greenberger, Marcia D. ... Washington, DC
Greenberger, Mark Alan ... Cincinnati, OH
Greenberger, Paul M. ... Beachwood, OH
Greenberger, Richard E. ... Stamford, CT
Greenberger, Steven R. ... Chicago, IL
Greenberger, Susan Beale ... Columbus, OH
Greenberger, Tomas ... Brooklyn, NY
Greenberg-Kinne, Susan ... Burlingame, CA
Greenberg-Lewis, Erica
Department Of Veterans Affairs, Veterans Benefits Administration, GV
Greenberg-Maas, Beth I. ... Ventura, CA
Greenblatt, Arthur N. ... Weatogue, CT
Greenblatt, Bruce D. ... Philadelphia, PA
Greenblatt, Bryna S. ... Philadelphia, PA
Greenblatt, Clifford E. ... McLean, VA
Greenblatt, Danny E. ... Roslyn Heights, NY
Greenblatt, David A. ... Dallas, TX
Greenblatt, Deborah ... Raleigh, NC
Greenblatt, Debra Dunitz ... Bethesda, MD
Greenblatt, Edward L. ... Atlanta, GA
Greenblatt, Fredric J. ... Woodland Hills, CA
Greenblatt, Gary E. ... Vineland, NJ
Greenblatt, Gary R. ... Baltimore, MD
Greenblatt, Gershon D. ... Philadelphia, PA
Greenblatt & Greenblatt ... Waukegan, IL
Greenblatt & Greenblatt ... Vineland, NJ
Greenblatt, Hank G. ... Sacramento, CA
Greenblatt, Jacquelyn A. ... San Francisco, CA
Greenblatt, James A. ... Clayton, MO
Greenblatt, Jason D. ... New York, NY
Greenblatt, Jay H. ... Vineland, NJ
Greenblatt, Jay H., & Associates, A Prof. Corp. ... Vineland, NJ
Greenblatt, Jeffrey ... Santa Fe, NM
Greenblatt, Jeffrey ... New York, NY
Greenblatt, Jeffrey A. ... Chicago, IL
Greenblatt, Jeffrey N. ... Gaithersburg, MD
Greenblatt, Jeffrey S. ... Denver, CO
Greenblatt, Joel L. ... Chicago, IL
Greenblatt, Jonathan L. ... Washington, DC
New York, NY
Greenblatt, Judah D. ... Hackensack, NJ
New York, NY
Greenblatt, Larry M. ... Ventura, CA
Greenblatt, Lewis B. ... Chicago, IL
Greenblatt, Lieberman & Conn
Cherry Hill, NJ
Greenblatt, Lyon J. ... Plantation, FL
Greenblatt, Lyon J., P.A. ... Plantation, FL
Greenblatt, Marcia S. ... Houston, TX
Greenblatt, Marilyn D. ... Coral Gables, FL
Greenblatt, Mark B. ... Pittsburgh, PA
Greenblatt, Martin E. ... Boston, MA
Greenblatt, Matthew M. ... Albany, NY
Greenblatt, Michael A. ... Waukegan, IL
Greenblatt, Michael E. ... Cranford, NJ
White Plains, NY
Greenblatt, Michael S. ... Cherry Hill, NJ
Greenblatt, Morton H. ... Branford, CT
Greenblatt, Philip J. ... Northbrook, IL
Greenblatt, Ray H. ... Chicago, IL
Greenblatt, Richard ... Newburgh, NY
Greenblatt, Ronald L. ... Philadelphia, PA
Greenblatt, Russell E., (P.C.) ... Chicago, IL
Greenblatt, Sandra P.
Fort Lauderdale, FL
Greenblatt, Sandra P., P.A.
Fort Lauderdale, FL
Miami, FL
Greenblatt, Seymour ... Newburgh, NY
Greenblatt, Sheldon B. ... Roseville, MI
Greenblatt, Sheldon H. ... New York, NY
Greenblatt, Softness & Lesser, LLP
Hackensack, NJ
Greenblatt, Softness & Lesser, LLP
New York, NY
Greenblatt, Steven J. ... New York, NY
Greenblatt, Steven M. ... Franklin Square, NY
Greenblatt & Winslow, P.C. ... Newburgh, NY
Greenblott, Louis M. ... Rancho Mirage, CA
Greenblum & Bernstein, P.L.C.
Reston, VA
Greenblum, Erika ... Frederick, MD
Lutherville, MD
Greenblum, Neil F. ... Reston, VA
Greenblum, Richard E. ... Austin, TX
Greenblum, Robert F. ... San Antonio, TX
Greenburg, Barry H. ... Chicago, IL
Greenburg, Carl V. ... Clifton, NJ
Greenburg, Daniel E. ... Merrick, NY
Greenburg, David A. ... San Francisco, CA
Greenburg, Douglas H. ... Houma, LA
Greenburg, Douglas L. ... Harrodsburg, KY
Greenburg, Douglas N. ... Washington, DC
Greenburg, Ellen J. ... Bayside, NY
Greenburg, G. Scott ... Seattle, WA
Greenburg, Henry A. ... White Plains, NY
Greenburg, J. Todd ... Bloomington, IL
Greenburg, Jan Crawford ... Chicago, IL
Greenburg, Joel H. ... Chicago, IL
Greenburg, Joel H., Ltd. ... Chicago, IL
Greenburg, Jonathan K. ... New York, NY

Greenburg, Michael M. ... Framingham, MA
Greenburg, Peter A. ... Rockville, MD
Greenburg, Richard L. ... Ithaca, NY
Greenburg, Robert D. ... Bethesda, MD
Greenburg, Rolland E., III ... Columbia, SC
Greenburg, Steven A. ... Santa Cruz, CA
Greenbush, Eric J. ... New York, NY
Greendorfer, Lori ... New York, NY
Greendorfer, Marc A. ... New York, NY
Greendyke, William R. ... Houston, TX
Greene, A. Crawford, Jr. ... San Francisco, CA
Greene, A. Glenn, Jr. ... Dillon, SC
Latta, SC
Greene, A. Kent, (P.C.) ... Las Vegas, NV
Greene, A. Mitchell ... New York, NY
Greene, Abner S. ... New York, NY
Greene, Alan Douglas ... Miami, FL
Greene, Alan I. ... Chicago, IL
Greene, Alan M. ... Bloomfield Hills, MI
Greene, Alan S. ... Dover, NH
Greene, Albert H. ... Orlando, FL
Greene, Alice G. ... Orchard Lake, MI
Greene, Alison ... Vancouver, WA
Greene, Alison E. ... New York, NY
Greene, Alison F. ... Oakland, CA
Greene, Alison K. ... Salem, OR
Greene, Allen S. ... Wheaton, IL
Greene, Allison A. ... Claremont, CA
Greene, Alvin M. ... Buffalo, NY
Greene, Andra Barmash
Newport Beach, CA
Greene, Andrew ... White Plains, NY
Greene, Andrew D. ... New Hyde Park, NY
Greene, Andrew M. ... San Diego, CA
Greene, Andrew N., (P.C.)
Washington, DC
Greene, Andrew R. ... Chicago, IL
Greene, Andrew Robert ... Birmingham, AL
Greene, Angela L. ... Florence, KY
Greene, Arthur A., Jr. ... Manchester, NH
Greene, Arthur G. ... Manchester, NH
Greene, Arthur M. ... Sackets Harbor, NY
Syracuse, NY
Greene, Austin J. ... Palm Coast, FL
Greene, Ava D. ... Washington, DC
Greene & Ayres ... Shreveport, LA
Greene, Baird S. ... Tucson, AZ
Greene, Barbara Bakal ... Concord, MA
Greene, Barbara Z. ... Larkspur, CA
Greene, Barry B. ... Cartersville, GA
Greene, Barry D. ... Hartford, CT
Greene, Barry D. ... Boston, MA
Greene, Barry P. ... Santa Ana, CA
Greene, Barry S. ... Pompano Beach, FL
Greene & Bell, P.A. ... Miami, FL
Greene, Bennett E. ... Burlington, VT
Greene, Bernard H. ... New York, NY
Greene, Bernard W. ... Nashville, TN
Greene, Beth K. ... Bloomington, IN
Greene, Blair C. ... Beverly Hills, CA
Greene, Brian Patrick ... Burlington, MA
Greene, Brian Richard ... Richmond, VA
Greene, Bridgette F. ... Elkhart, IN
Greene, Broillet, Taylor, Wheeler & Panish, LLP ... Los Angeles, CA
Santa Monica, CA
Greene, Browne ... Santa Monica, CA
Greene, Bruce B. ... Savannah, GA
Greene, Bruce H. ... Sandpoint, ID
Greene, Bruce R. ... Los Angeles, CA
Greene, Bruce R. ... Boulder, CO
Greene, Buckley, Jones & McQueen
Atlanta, GA
Greene, C. Claibourne ... Milwaukee, WI
Greene, C. Clay ... San Rafael, CA
Greene, C. Joseph ... Clarksville, IN
Louisville, KY
Greene, C. Reed ... San Antonio, TX
Greene, C. Scott ... Atlanta, GA
Greene, Carlton Eric ... Washington, DC
Greene, Carol ... San Bernardino, CA
Greene, Carolyn Evone ... Brooklyn, NY
Greene, Celeste E. ... San Francisco, CA
Greene, Charles B. ... San Jose, CA
Greene, Charles L. ... Akron, OH
Greene, Charles M. ... Fort Lauderdale, FL
Greene, Charles M. ... Orlando, FL
Greene, Charles R. ... Springfield, MO
Greene, Chauvel, Descalso & Tully, A Professional Corporation
San Francisco, CA
San Jose, CA
San Mateo, CA
Greene, Cheryl A. ... South Bend, IN
Greene, Christopher ... New York, NY
Greene, Christopher A. ... Stockton, CA
Greene, Christopher B. ... Birmingham, AL
Greene, Christopher J. ... Jacksonville, FL
Greene, Christopher T. ... Buffalo, NY
Greene, Clayton, Jr. ... Annapolis, MD
Greene, Clifford H. ... White Plains, NY
Greene, Clifford M. ... Minneapolis, MN
Greene, Clifford T. ... New York, NY
Greene, Colin T. ... Pasadena, CA
Greene & Cooper ... Clarksville, IN
Louisville, KY
Greene, Craig M. ... Hollywood, FL
Greene & Curtis, L.L.P. ... Springfield, MO
Greene, Cynthia L. ... Miami, FL
Greene, Cynthia L., P.A. ... Miami, FL
Greene, Cynthia M. ... Palo Alto, CA
Greene, Cynthia Watts ... Louisville, KY
Greene, Daniel ... Philadelphia, PA
Greene, Darryl E. ... Far Rockaway, NY
Greene, David ... Brooklyn, NY
Greene, David ... New York, NY
Greene, David A. ... Los Angeles, CA
Greene, David A. ... Boca Raton, FL
Greene, David B. ... Greenville, SC
Greene, David E. ... New York, NY
Greene, David F. ... Charleston, WV
Greene, David G. ... Atlanta, GA
Greene, David G. ... Philadelphia, PA
Greene, David K. ... Vernon Hills, IL
Greene, David L. ... Avon-By-The-Sea, NJ
Greene, David M. ... East Brunswick, NJ
Greene, David R. ... Hartford, CT
Greene, David S. ... Rockville, MD
Greene, Deborah L. ... Jacksonville, FL
Greene, Deborah L. ... West Orange, NJ
Greene, Deborah S. ... Atlanta, GA
Greene, Debra A. Shelinsky
Whitehouse Station, NJ
Greene, December ... San Diego, CA
Greene, Dennis I. ... Boston, MA
Greene, Dennis R. ... Oakbrook Terrace, IL
Greene, Diane M. ... Virginia Beach, VA
Greene, Diane Weber ... Houston, TX
Greene, Don H. ... Akron, OH
Greene, Donald B. ... Redondo Beach, CA
Greene, Donald J., (P.C.) ... New York, NY
Greene, Donald L. ... Newport Beach, CA
Greene, Donald R. ... Washington, DC
Greene, Donnelly, Schermer ... Bradenton, FL
Tampa, FL
Greene, Douglas W. ... Springfield, MO
Greene, Douglas W. ... Boone, NC
Greene, Douglas W. ... Seattle, WA
Greene, Douglas W., III ... Springfield, MO
Greene, Earl G., III ... Omaha, NE
Greene, Edith ... Lexington, MA
Greene, Edmund A., II ... Needham, MA
Greene, Edward B. ... Ponte Vedra Beach, FL
Greene, Edward C. ... Mobile, AL
Greene, Edward H. ... Huntington, WV
Greene, Edward J. ... Pittsburgh, PA
Greene, Edward J., Jr. ... Albany, NY
Greene, Edward J., Jr. ... Paoli, PA
Greene, Elizabeth L. B. ... Worcester, MA
Greene, Emanuel L. ... New York, NY
Greene, Enid ... Salt Lake City, UT
Greene, Eric M. ... Hull, MA
Greene, Eric R. ... New York, NY
Greene Espel, P.L.L.P. ... Minneapolis, MN
Greene, Fred ... New York, NY
Greene, Fred G. ... Russellville, KY
Greene, Frederick H., III ... Portland, ME
Greene, Fredrica ... San Rafael, CA
Greene, Gail Armist ... San Diego, CA
Greene, Gail P. ... Virginia Beach, VA
Greene, Gary ... Hartford, CT
Greene, Gary A. ... Basking Ridge, NJ
Greene, Gary A. ... Philadelphia, PA
Greene, Gary S. ... Los Angeles, CA
Greene, Gemma ... Carson City, NV
Greene, George E. ... Atlanta, GA
Greene, George H., Jr. ... Houston, TX
Greene, George Ira ... Chappaqua, NY
Greene, George K. ... New York, NY
Greene, George R. ... Raleigh, NC
Greene, George W. ... Milwaukee, WI
Greene, Gerald ... Los Angeles, CA
Greene, Gerald H. ... Brooklyn, NY
Greene, Gerald L. ... Pineville, KY
Greene, Gerard M. ... Boston, MA
Greene, Gerrie S. ... Washington, DC
Greene, Glenn S. ... Washington, DC
Greene, Gordon C. ... Cincinnati, OH
Greene & Greene ... Cartersville, GA
Greene, Gregory A. ... Chicago, IL
Greene, H. M., Law Office ... Aurora, IN
Greene, Halpern, Dombrowski, Rourke & Hanrahan, P.C. ... Hartford, CT
Greene, Harold A. ... North Miami Beach, FL
Greene, Harold H. ...
United States District Court For The District Of Columbia, GV
Greene, Harold L. ... Simi Valley, CA
Greene, Harold L. ... Miami, FL
Greene and Harris, P.A. ... Jacksonville, FL
Greene, Harvey M. ... Aurora, IN
Greene, Harvey M. ... New York, NY
Greene, Hedley W. ... Spokane, WA
Greene, Henry F. ... Washington, DC
Greene, Henry T. ... Alexandria, VA
Greene, Herbert B. ... Westport, CT
Greene, Herbert I. ... Rockford, IL
Greene, Herman F.
Research Triangle Park, NC
Greene, Hershdorfer & Sharpe
Syracuse, NY
Greene, Horatius A., II ... Newark, NJ
Greene, Howard W. ... New York, NY
Greene & Huggins ... Latta, SC
Dillon, SC
Greene, Hunter V. ... Baton Rouge, LA
Greene, Ira ... Brooklyn, NY
Greene, Ira S. ... New York, NY
Greene, J. Clifford, Jr. ... Chicago, IL
Greene, J. David, P.C. ... Mobile, AL
Greene, J. Michael ... Americus, GA
Greene, J. Thomas ... Salt Lake City, UT
Greene, J. Thomas, Jr. ... Weston, WV
Greene, James A. ... Department of Labor, Office of the Solicitor, GV
Greene, James A. ... Reading, PA
Greene, James C. ... Los Angeles, CA
Greene, James D. ... Las Vegas, NV
Greene, James David, Jr. ... Mobile, AL
Greene, James E. ... Dearborn, MI
Greene, James H. ... Boston, MA
Greene, James N., III ... Charlotte, NC
Greene, James P. ... Boca Raton, FL
Greene, James P. ... Ann Arbor, MI
Greene, James P., Sr. ... Aiken, SC
Greene, James R. ... Springfield, NJ
Greene, James R. ... Albany, NY
Greene, James R., III ... Dayton, OH
Greene, James Robert ... Long Beach, CA
Greene, James S., Jr. ... Harlan, KY
Greene, James W. ... Denver, CO
Greene, James W. ... Washington, DC
Greene, Jamie L. ... Atlanta, GA
Greene, Janet K. ... Houston, TX
Greene, Janet L. ... San Francisco, CA
Greene, Janet M. ... Tampa, FL
Greene, Jason K. ... Atlanta, GA
Greene, Jean Marie ... Houston, TX
Greene, Jeffrey A. ... Goodlettsville, TN
Greene, Jeffrey E. ... Washington, DC
Greene, Jeffrey H. ... New York, NY
Greene, Jennifer K. ... St. Louis, MO
Greene, Jesse J., Jr. ... Webster, NY
Greene, J. F.
Environmental Protection Agency, Office of Administrative Law Judges, GV
Greene, J. H., Jr. ... Raytown, MO
Greene, Jill E. ... Avon-By-The-Sea, NJ
Greene, Joe C. ... Springfield, MO
Greene, Joel L. ... Washington, DC
Greene, Joel P. ... Worcester, MA
Greene, John A. ... Phoenix, AZ
Greene, John B. ... Las Vegas, NV
Greene, John B. ... Seattle, WA
Greene, John D. ... Statesville, NC
Greene, John F. ... New Orleans, LA
Greene, John J. ... New York, NY
Greene, John J. ... Austin, TX
Greene, John R. ... Annapolis, MD
Greene, John R. ... Flint, MI
Greene, John W. ... Covington, LA
Greene, John W. ... White Plains, NY
Greene, Jonathan D. ... Fort Lauderdale, FL
Greene, Jonathan S. ... Towson, MD
Greene, Jones & Brisske ... Wheaton, IL
Greene, Jordan A. ... Miami, FL
Greene, Joseph Christopher
Springfield, MO
Greene, Joseph E., Jr. ... Paoli, PA
Greene, Joseph F., Jr. ... Camden, NJ
Greene, Joseph Patrick ... Boston, MA
Greene, Joyce M. ... Chicago, IL
Greene, Judith ... Roanoke, VA
Greene, Judith B. ... Miami, FL
Greene, Judith B., P.A. ... Miami, FL
Greene, Judith C. ... New York, NY
Greene, Judybeth ... Department of Justice, Tax Division, GV
Greene, Jule B. ... Dublin, GA
Greene, K. Edward ... Raleigh, NC
Greene, Karen B. ... Sacramento, CA
Greene, Karen S. ... Treasury Department, Office of Regulations and Rulings, GV
Greene, Karla D. ... Lawndale, CA
Greene, Katherine A. ... Newport, RI
Greene, Kelley, Tobriner & Farren
San Francisco, CA
Greene, Kenneth A. ... New York, NY
Greene, Kenneth C. ... Greenbrae, CA
Greene, Kenneth C., Jr. ... Dallas, TX
Greene, Kenneth L. ... Department of Justice, Tax Division, GV
Greene, Kenneth M. ... Greensboro, NC
Greene, Ketchum, Bailey & Tweel
Huntington, WV
Greene, Kevin C. ... Atlanta, GA
Greene, Kevin J. ... Hartford, CT
Greene, Kevin K. ... Sacramento, CA
Greene, Kim Elisabeth ... Albany, NY
Greene, Kimberly K. ... Louisville, KY
Greene, Korry Alden ... Pittsburgh, PA
Greene, Kristen Schultze ... Farmington, CT
Greene, L. Hamlin ... Glen, NH
Greene, Lake A., Jr. ... Houston, TX
Greene, Lance Gordon ... Irvine, CA
Greene, Laura Cude ... Rock Hill, SC
Greene Law Firm ... Charleston, SC
Greene Law Firm, The ... Springfield, MO
Greene, Lawrence J. ... New York, NY
Greene, Lawrence M. ... New York, NY
Greene, Lawrence W. ... New York, NY
Greene, Lealand W. ... Snyder, TX
Greene, Leins and Ryan ... Ossining, NY
Greene, Leland L. ... Mineola, NY
Greene, Lesa C. ... Athens, AL
Greene, Leslie M. ... Westport, CT
Greene and Letts ... Chicago, IL
Greene & Lewis ... Middlesboro, KY
Pineville, KY
Greene, Lisa J. ... New York, NY
Greene, Lisa Witt ... Chicago, IL
Greene, Lora B. ... Yadkinville, NC
Greene, Lori G. ... Sacramento, CA
Greene and Lucks, L.P.A. ... Circleville, OH
Greene, Lynn Chapman ... Denver, CO
Greene, M. Howard ... Chicago, IL
Greene, M. Kyle ... Marietta, GA
Greene, M. Michele ... Midland, TX
Greene, Marc Ford ... Washington, CT
Greene, Marcy ... Washington, DC
Greene, Margaret E. ... Detroit, MI
Greene, Margaret H. ... Atlanta, GA
Greene, Marjorie Mitchell
Milwaukee, WI
Greene, Marjorie Reed
Federal Communications Commission, Cable Services Bureau, GV
Greene, Mark C. ... Tampa, FL
Greene, Mark E. ... Minnetonka, MN
Greene, Mark Patrick ... Hanover, MA
Greene, Mark W. ... Woodcliff Lake, NJ
Greene & Markley, P.C. ... Portland, OR
Greene, Martha E. ... Lewiston, ME
Greene, Martin ... New York, NY
Greene, Martin P. ... Chicago, IL
Greene, Marvin, (A P.C.)
Los Angeles, CA
Greene, Mary E. ... Fairbanks, AK
Greene, Mary E. ... Atlanta, GA
Greene, Mary Katherine ... Atlanta, GA
Greene, Matthew A. ... Chicago, IL
Greene, Matthew W. ... Fairfax, VA
Greene, Maura A. ... Boston, MA
Greene & McQuillan Co., L.P.A.
Cleveland, OH
Greene, Meyer & McElroy, P.C.
Boulder, CO
Greene, Michael ... Los Angeles, CA
Greene, Michael ... Miami, FL
Greene, Michael A. ... Los Angeles, CA
Greene, Michael A. ... Chicago, IL
Milwaukee, WI
Greene, Michael A. ... Portland, OR
Greene, Michael E. ... Coral Springs, FL
Greene, Michael E. ... New York, NY
Woodbury, NY
Greene, Michael E., P.A. ... Coral Springs, FL
Greene, Michael J., (A Professional Corporation) ... Irvine, CA
Greene, Michael K. ... Albany, NY
Greene, Michael L. ... Walnut Creek, CA
Greene, Michael R. ... Louisville, KY
Greene, Michael R. ... Liberty Corner, NJ
Greene, Michael R. ... Melville, NY
Greene, Michael S. ... Boca Raton, FL
Greene, Michael S. ... Elkhart, IN
Greene, Michael S. ... Owings Mills, MD
Greene, Mickey W. ... Minneapolis, MN
Greene, Mikel D. ... Palm Beach Gardens, FL
Greene and Millinger ... East Brunswick, NJ
Greene, Mindy H. ... New York, NY
Greene, Mitchell A. ... New York, NY
Greene, Mitchell Amos, III ... Waterloo, IA
Greene, Murray A. ... Houston, TX
Greene, Nancy A. ... Philadelphia, PA
Greene, Nancy D. ... Vienna, VA
Greene, Nancy M. ... Altamont, NY
Greene, Nancy Reva ... Boston, MA
Greene, Natalie Tull ... Philadelphia, PA
Greene, Nathan ... Ellicott City, MD
Greene, Neil B. ... Akron, OH
Greene, Neil J. ... Evanston, IL
Greene, Nelson F. ... Dayton, OH
Greene, Norman L. ... New York, NY
Greene, Pamela B. ... Boston, MA
Greene, Patricia A. ... Spartanburg, SC
Greene, Patricia M. ... Palo Alto, CA
Greene, Patrick ... Circleville, OH
Greene, Patrick J., Jr. ... River Edge, NJ
New York, NY
Greene, Patrick K. ... Albany, NY
Greene, Paul F. ... Providence, RI
Greene, Paul M. ... Park Ridge, IL
Greene, Paula Hobbs ... Elizabethtown, NC
Greene, Peter A. ... Washington, DC
Greene, Peter A. ... West Orange, NJ
Greene, Peter D. ... New York, NY
Greene, Peter E. ... New York, NY
Greene, Philip J. ... Department of Commerce, Office of the General Counsel, GV
Greene, Philip S. ... Houston, TX
Greene, R. Karen ... Raleigh, NC
Greene, R. Thomas, Jr. ... Minneapolis, MN
Greene Radovsky Maloney & Share LLP
San Francisco, CA
Greene, Raleigh" Lee ", III
St. Petersburg, FL
Greene, Raleigh" Lee ", III
St. Petersburg, FL
Greene, Ralph C. ... San Jose, CA
Greene, Ralph N., III ... Jacksonville, FL
Greene, Ralph V. ... Concord, OH
Greene, Randi Yvette ... Nashville, TN
Greene, Randy C. ... Philadelphia, PA
Greene, Raymond A., III
Redwood City, CA
Greene, Raymond John ... St. Petersburg, FL
Greene, Raymond L. ... Mathews, VA
Greene, Raymond T., Jr. ... Sandpoint, ID
Greene, Raymond T., Jr., P.A. ... Sandpoint, ID
Greene, Rebecca E. ... Bellevue, WA
Greene, Rebecca S. ... Newark, NJ
Greene, Regan McCarty ... Atlanta, GA
Greene, Reginald A. ... New York, NY
Greene, Reginald D. ... Los Angeles, CA
Greene and Reid ... Newark, NY
Sackets Harbor, NY
Syracuse, NY
Greene, Renez ... Lombard, IL
Greene, Richard D. ... Wichita, KS
Greene, Richard G. ... Albany, NY
Greene, Richard H. ... New Haven, CT
Greene, Richard J. ... Los Angeles, CA
Greene, Richard L. ... San Francisco, CA
Greene, Richard M. ... Greensboro, NC
Greene, Richard P., P.A.
Fort Lauderdale, FL
Greene, Richard Phillip ... Fort Lauderdale, FL
Greene, Risa B. ... Philadelphia, PA
Greene, Robert ... Nashville, TN
Greene, Robert C. ... Grand Rapids, MI
Greene, Robert D. ... Flagstaff, AZ
Greene, Robert F. ... Bradenton, FL
Greene, Robert F. ... Florence, KY
Greene, Robert G. ... Rochester, NY
Greene, Robert G. ... Columbia, SC
Greene, Robert G., Jr.
North Wilkesboro, NC
Greene, Robert H. ... Brockton, MA
Greene, Robert J., Jr. ... Charlotte, NC
Greene, Robert L. ... Los Angeles, CA
Greene, Robert L. ... Springfield, MO

Greene, Robert M. .... Buffalo, NY
Greene, Robert N. .... Cranston, RI
Greene, Robert T.
Securities and Exchange Commission, Office of the General Counsel, GV
Greene, Robert V. .... Cape Coral, FL
Greene, Robin H. .... Miami, FL
Greene, Robyn .... Ponte Vedra Beach, FL
Greene, Roger S. .... Newport Beach, CA
Greene, Ronald J. .... Washington, DC
Greene, Ronald Louis .... Binghamton, NY
Greene, Roy M. .... Phenix City, AL
Greene, Russell J. .... Syracuse, NY
Greene, Russell T. .... Knoxville, TN
Greene, Ryan W. .... Dallas, TX
Greene, S. Ward .... Portland, OR
Greene, Sally .... Raleigh, NC
Greene, Scott B. .... Chicago, IL
Greene, Sean J. .... Fort Lauderdale, FL
Greene & Seaver, Inc. .... Burlington, VT
Greene, Sheldon L. .... San Francisco, CA
Greene, Shelley L. .... Houston, TX
Greene, Staci H. .... New York, NY
Greene, Stacie .... Orlando, FL
Greene, Stephen A. .... New York, NY
Greene, Stephen C. .... South Plainfield, NJ
Greene, Stephen C. .... Oswego, NY
Greene, Stephen J. .... Sacramento, CA
Greene, Stephen K. .... Birmingham, AL
Greene, Steven C. .... Bedford Hills, NY
Greene, Steven I. .... West Caldwell, NJ
Greene, Steven J. .... New York, NY
Greene, Steven K. .... Denville, NJ
Greene, Steven S. .... Atlanta, GA
Greene, Steven T. .... Boston, MA
Greene, Steven T. .... Newark, OH
Greene, Stewart P. .... New York, NY
Greene, Stuart .... Buffalo, NY
Greene, Susan J. .... New York, NY
Greene, Susan K. .... Houston, TX
Greene, Susanne L. .... Los Angeles, CA
Greene, T. Christopher .... Hardwick, VT
Greene, Tammis F. .... Tacoma, WA
Greene, Tanya .... Palo Alto, CA
Greene, Tanya .... Atlanta, GA
Greene, Terence J. .... Atlanta, GA
Greene, Terence L. .... San Diego, CA
Greene, Theodore J. .... Stamford, CT
New York, NY
White Plains, NY
Greene, Thomas A. .... Manchester, VT
Greene, Thomas A., P.C. .... Manchester, VT
Greene, Thomas E. .... Minneapolis, MN
Greene, Thomas J. .... Los Angeles, CA
Greene, Thomas M. .... Atlanta, GA
Greene, Thomas R. .... Houston, TX
Greene, Thomas W. .... Decatur, GA
Greene, Thomas W. .... Charleston, SC
Greene, Tiffani Wedington .... Atlanta, GA
Greene, Timothy G. .... Washington, DC
Greene, Timothy J. .... Farmington Hills, MI
Greene & Tischler .... Fort Myers, FL
Cape Coral, FL
Greene, Tisha M. .... Los Angeles, CA
Greene, Todd H. .... New York, NY
Greene, Troy L. .... Vidalia, GA
Greene & Tulley Co., L.P.A.
Willoughby, OH
Greene, Victor P. .... New York, NY
Greene, Vincent L., IV .... Providence, RI
Greene, Vincent Tad .... Wheeling, WV
Greene, W. Dale .... Charleston, WV
Greene, W. Michael .... Arlington, TX
Greene, W. Michael, P.C. .... Arlington, TX
Greene, Warren G. .... Los Angeles, CA
Greene, Warren H., Jr. .... Vienna, VA
Greene, William A. .... Anchorage, AK
Greene, William B. .... Cartersville, GA
Greene, William J., III .... New York, NY
Greene, William John .... Flint, MI
Greene, William L. .... Chicago, IL
Greene, William L. .... Minneapolis, MN
Greene, William M. .... Center Sandwich, NH
Greene, William Martin .... Cleveland, OH
Greene, William N. .... Los Angeles, CA
Greene, William P., Jr.
United States Court Of Veterans Appeals, GV
Greene, Wm. M. .... Cleveland, OH
Greene, Yoon Hi .... New York, NY
Greene & Zinner, P.C. .... White Plains, NY
Greenebaum, Ben I., Jr. .... Winnetka, IL
Greenebaum Doll & McDonald PLLC
Covington, KY
Frankfort, KY
Frankfort, KY
Lexington, KY
Louisville, KY
Cincinnati, OH
Nashville, TN
Greenebaum, Edwin H. .... Bloomington, IN
Greenebaum, Eric S. .... Livingston, NJ
Greenebaum, John S. (IBA) **.... Louisville, KY**
Greenebaum, John S., P.S.C.
Louisville, KY
Greenebaum, Leonard C.
Washington, DC
Greene-Buckner, SueCarol
Washington, DC
Greene-Frieden, Charlotte .... Los Angeles, CA
Greene-Gretzinger, Sharon L. .... Bowler, WI
Greenen, Darin R. .... Vancouver, WA
Greenen & Greenen, P.S. .... Vancouver, WA
Greenen, Ronald W. .... Vancouver, WA
Greenen, Therese A. .... Vancouver, WA
Greener, Donald H. .... New York, NY
Greener, Donald H., P.C. .... New York, NY

Greener, Eugene, Jr. .... Marco Island, FL
Naples, FL
Memphis, TN
Greener, Gary J. .... Los Angeles, CA
Greener, Jeffrey S. .... New York, NY
Greener, Marie D. .... Rochester, NY
Greener, Melissa Reiner .... New York, NY
Greener, Michael .... Crown Point, IN
Greener, R. Bertram .... Minneapolis, MN
Greener, Richard H. .... Boise, ID
Greener, William .... Corning, NY
Greenes, Steven R. .... New York, NY
Greenfader, Glenn J. .... New York, NY
Greenfeder, Wayne D. .... Springfield, NJ
Greenfeig, Stuart S. .... Rockville, MD
Greenfeld, Audrey A. .... New York, NY
Greenfeld, Daniel S. .... New York, NY
Greenfeld, Elissa R. .... Schenectady, NY
Greenfeld, Eric M. .... Santa Monica, CA
Greenfeld, Helaine A. .... Department of Justice, Office of Policy Development, GV
Greenfeld, J. Steven .... Los Angeles, CA
Greenfeld, Peggy B. .... Cherry Hill, NJ
Philadelphia, PA
Greenfeld, Peter N. .... Phoenix, AZ
Greenfeld, Rena Hofmann .... Cleveland, OH
Greenfeld, Robert L. .... New York, NY
Greenfeld, Seth Samuel .... Pittsfield, MA
Greenfeld, Steven H. .... Washington, DC
Greenbelt, MD
Greenfelder, Glen E. .... Dade City, FL
Greenfelder, Mander, Hanson, Murphy & Dwyer .... Brooksville, FL
Bushnell, FL
Dade City, FL
New Port Richey, FL
Greenfield, Aaron J .... Baltimore, MD
Greenfield, Adam M. .... New York, NY
Greenfield, Adrienne I. .... Philadelphia, PA
Greenfield, Aimee M. .... Cleveland, OH
Greenfield, Alan E. .... Coral Gables, FL
Greenfield, Alan E., P.A. .... Coral Gables, FL
Greenfield, Alan J. .... Ventura, CA
Greenfield, Albert N. .... Los Angeles, CA
Greenfield, Amy B.
Greenwood Village, CO
Greenfield, Andrew B. .... Washington, DC
Greenfield, Andrew P. .... San Diego, CA
Greenfield, Arthur P. .... Phoenix, AZ
Irvine, CA
Greenfield, Bernard J. .... Falls Church, VA
Greenfield, Bernard S. .... San Jose, CA
Greenfield, Bost & Kliros, P.C.
Atlanta, GA
Greenfield, Brewer, Bailor & Kay
Pittsburgh, PA
Greenfield, Brian J. .... Mineola, NY
Greenfield, Burton D. .... Miami, FL
Greenfield & Cahill .... Mineola, NY
Greenfield, Carol J. .... Baton Rouge, LA
Greenfield, Carol J., A Professional Law Corporation .... Baton Rouge, LA
Greenfield, Charlotte .... Las Cruces, NM
Greenfield, Craig B. .... Melville, NY
Greenfield, Cynthia .... Denver, CO
Greenfield, Dallas D. .... Greeley, CO
Greenfield, David .... Temple, TX
Greenfield, David B. .... New York, NY
Greenfield, David E. .... Bronx, NY
Greenfield, David S. .... New York, NY
Greenfield, David W. .... Troy, MI
Greenfield, Diane E. .... Bridgeport, CT
Greenfield, Douglas C. .... Elizabeth, NJ
Greenfield, Douglas L. .... Washington, DC
Greenfield & DuVal .... North Miami, FL
Greenfield, Edw. J. .... New York, NY
Greenfield, Elizabeth A. .... Maplewood, NJ
Greenfield, Elizabeth S. .... Philadelphia, PA
Greenfield, Ester F. .... Seattle, WA
Greenfield, Faith R. .... Camden, NJ
Greenfield, Francis X. .... Barnegat, NJ
Greenfield, Frank M. .... Chicago, IL
Greenfield, Frank M., & Associates, P.C.
Chicago, IL
Greenfield, Gail Goodman .... Nashville, TN
Greenfield, Gary .... Oakland, CA
Greenfield, Gary A. .... New York, NY
Greenfield, Gary E. .... Library of Congress, Office of the General Counsel, GV
Greenfield, Gary M.
Federal Trade Commission, Office of the General Counsel, GV
Greenfield, Geo. T. .... New York, NY
Greenfield, George L. .... Boston, MA
Greenfield, Gerald .... Columbus, OH
Greenfield & Goodman, LLC .... Paoli, PA
Greenfield, Gregg S. .... Sioux Falls, SD
Greenfield, H. Kent .... Newton, MA
Greenfield, Harry C. .... Merritt Island, FL
Greenfield, Harry C., P.A.
Merritt Island, FL
Greenfield, Harry W. .... Cleveland, OH
Greenfield, Harvey .... New York, NY
Greenfield, James .... Hartford, CT
Greenfield, James A. .... Seattle, WA
Greenfield, James J. .... Radnor, PA
Greenfield, James M. .... Franklin, PA
Greenfield, James Peter .... Washington, DC
Greenfield, James R. .... New Haven, CT
Greenfield, Jane W. .... Boulder, CO
Greenfield, Jay .... New York, NY
Greenfield, Jeffrey O. .... Cherry Hill, NJ
Philadelphia, PA
Greenfield, Jerry R. .... Rochester, NY
Greenfield, Jim .... San Antonio, TX
Greenfield, John F. .... Boise, ID
Greenfield, John F., P.A. .... Boise, ID
Greenfield, John H., Jr. .... Dallas, TX

Greenfield, John M. .... Miami, FL
Greenfield, John W. .... Atlanta, GA
Greenfield, Joseph F. .... Harrisburg, PA
Greenfield, Joyia Z. .... San Diego, CA
Greenfield, Julia Leah .... Irvine, CA
Greenfield, Kelly D. .... Seattle, WA
Greenfield, Kenneth M. .... New York, NY
Greenfield, Kenneth N., Law Offices of
San Diego, CA
Greenfield, Kevin
Department of the Air Force, Office of the Judge Advocate General, GV
Greenfield, Larry S. .... Los Angeles, CA
Greenfield, Laurie H. .... Kansas City, MO
Greenfield Law Firm .... Cameron Park, CA
Sacramento, CA
Greenfield Law Offices .... St. Louis, MO
Greenfield, Lawrence A. .... Los Angeles, CA
Greenfield, Lawrence R.
Federal Energy Regulatory Commission, Office of the General Counsel, GV
Greenfield, Leon B. .... Washington, DC
Greenfield, Leslie H. .... Los Angeles, CA
Greenfield, Louise S. .... Northbrook, IL
Greenfield, Malcolm S. .... Tallahassee, FL
Greenfield, Marc A. .... Providence, RI
Greenfield, Marc F. .... Philadelphia, PA
Greenfield, Marguerite R. .... Newark, NJ
Greenfield, Marjorie E. .... Philadelphia, PA
Greenfield, Mark E. .... New York, NY
Greenfield, Mark R. .... Cleveland, OH
Greenfield, Mark S. .... Los Angeles, CA
Greenfield, Marvin S. .... Houston, TX
Greenfield, Michael C. .... Chicago, IL
Greenfield, Michael H. .... New York, NY
Greenfield, Michael S. .... Chicago, IL
Greenfield, Milton, Jr. .... St. Louis, MO
Greenfield, Murray .... Philadelphia, PA
Greenfield, Neal S. .... New York, NY
Greenfield, Norman E. .... Southfield, MI
Greenfield, Paul .... New York, NY
Greenfield, Peter .... Seattle, WA
Greenfield, Phillip G. .... Kansas City, MO
Greenfield, R. Kevin .... Toledo, OH
Greenfield, Rand L. .... Las Cruces, NM
Greenfield, Richard D. .... Paoli, PA
Greenfield, Richard O. .... Chicago, IL
Greenfield, Robert A. .... Los Angeles, CA
Greenfield, Robert A. .... Oakland, NJ
Greenfield, Robert H. .... Cameron Park, CA
Sacramento, CA
Greenfield, Robert S. .... Chicago, IL
Greenfield, Robin S. .... Brooklyn, NY
Greenfield, Russell R. .... Sioux Falls, SD
Greenfield, Samuel .... Beverly Hills, CA
Greenfield, Scott .... Miami Beach, FL
Greenfield, Scott H. .... New York, NY
Greenfield, Scott I. .... Los Angeles, CA
Greenfield, Sharon .... Overland Park, KS
Greenfield, Stanley W. .... Elizabeth, NJ
Greenfield, Stanley W. .... Pittsburgh, PA
Greenfield Stein & Senior, LLP
New York, NY
Greenfield, Stephen J. .... Philadelphia, PA
Greenfield, Steven .... Great Neck, NY
Greenfield, Steven A. .... Walnut Creek, CA
Greenfield, Steven Brian .... Boca Raton, FL
Greenfield, Steven R. .... Dallas, TX
Greenfield, Stuart B. .... Norwich, CT
Greenfield, Susan Lee .... Auburn Hills, MI
Greenfield, Troy D. .... Seattle, WA
Greenfield, Valory Toni .... Miami, FL
Greenfield-Mandler, Beth A., P.A.
Miami, FL
Greenfield-Sanders, Karin .... New York, NY
Greenfogel, Jane A. .... Cherry Hill, NJ
Greenfogel, Steven J. .... New York, NY
Philadelphia, PA
Greengard, Cara B. .... Denver, CO
Greengard, Richard D. .... Denver, CO
Greenglass, Robert E. .... Plymouth, MA
Greengrass, Andrew R. .... New York, NY
Greengrass, Lawrence S. .... New York, NY
Greengrove-Smith, Wendy S.
Morristown, NJ
Greenhagen, Russell J., Jr.
Jefferson City, MO
Greenhalge, Frederic T. .... Concord, NH
Greenhalge, James W.
Colorado Springs, CO
Greenhalgh, Beckwith, Lemich & Stith, P.C.
Rock Springs, WY
Greenhalgh, Dru .... San Diego, CA
Greenhalgh, Duncan A. .... Boston, MA
Greenhalgh, Gary M. .... Rock Springs, WY
Greenhalgh & Hoffman, S.C.
Baraboo, WI
Madison, WI
Greenhalgh, James D. .... New York, NY
Greenhalgh, Kevin Roy .... Blackstone, MA
Greenhalgh, Mary Beth .... Parsippany, NJ
Greenhalgh, Richard B. .... River Vale, NJ
Greenhalgh, Stephen I. .... Detroit, MI
Greenhalgh, Walter J. .... Newark, NJ
Greenhalgh, William F. .... Baraboo, WI
Greenhall, Audrey L. .... Philadelphia, PA
Greenhall, John A. .... Lawrenceville, NJ
Philadelphia, PA
Greenhall, Richard M. .... St. Louis, MO
Greenham, Candace C. .... Lexington, OH
Greenham, Deborah E.
New Philadelphia, OH
Greenhart, Susan .... Fort Lauderdale, FL
Greenhaus, Bruce W. .... San Diego, CA
Greenhaus, David .... Jericho, NY
Greenhaus, Philip Sherwood .... New York, NY
Greenhaw, Frank P., IV .... Fort Worth, TX
Greenhaw & Greenhaw .... Fayetteville, AR

Greenhaw, John F. .... Fayetteville, AR
Greenhaw, Leigh Hunt .... Harrisburg, PA
Greenhaw, Leonard F. .... Fayetteville, AR
Greenhaw, William K. .... Fayetteville, AR
Greenhawt, Charles E. .... Salt Lake City, UT
Greenheck, Gregory Q. .... Wabasha, MN
Greenheck, Keri L. .... Seattle, WA
Greenheck, Robert A. .... Schofield, WI
Greenhill, Arnold R. .... Shawano, WI
Greenhill, Corey R. .... Phoenix, AZ
Greenhill, Hope L. .... San Francisco, CA
Greenhill, Ira J. .... New York, NY
Greenhill, Joe, Jr. .... Austin, TX
Greenhill, Joe R. .... Austin, TX
Greenhill, Jonathan Seth .... New York, NY
Greenhill, Lorna C. .... Los Angeles, CA
Greenhill, Lorna C. .... Seal Beach, CA
Greenhill Partners, P.C. .... New York, NY
Greenhill, Roy E., Jr. .... Beverly Hills, CA
Greenhill, William D. .... Fort Worth, TX
Greenhill, Zachary Robb .... New York, NY
Greenhood, Bernard L. .... Chestnut Hill, MA
Greenhood, E. J. .... Stoughton, MA
Greenhood, Jane L. .... Boston, MA
Greenhouse, Andrew A. .... New York, NY
Greenhouse, Charles .... Denver, CO
Greenhouse, Elihu A. .... Philadelphia, PA
Greenhouse, Norris J. .... Marksville, LA
Greenhouse, Robin L. .... Washington, DC
Greenhouse-Tiano, Cynthia
Fort Lauderdale, FL
Greenhut, Arnold .... Springfield, MA
Greenhut, Gordon .... Lawrenceville, GA
Greenhut, Miriam Krestul
Jacksonville, FL
Greenhut, Steven B. .... Jacksonville, FL
Greenidge, Alicia D.
Executive Office Of The President, Office of the U.S. Trade Representative, GV
Greenidge, Elizabeth A. .... New York, NY
Greenidge, Stanley E. .... Cambridge, MA
Greenidge-Hoskins, Nicole L.
Department Of Health And Human Services, GV
Greening, Alfred H. .... Williamsville, IL
Greening, David G. .... St. Paul, MN
Greening, Eldridge G. .... Visalia, CA
Greening, Janice M. .... Denver, CO
Greening, Jay E. .... Peoria, IL
Greening, Robert L. .... Dallas, TX
Greening, Ronald G. .... Austin, TX
Greening, Ronald G., & Associates, P.C.
Austin, TX
Greenisen, Charles J. .... Providence, RI
Greenisen, Julie B. .... Washington, DC
Greenker, Jerold A. .... Colorado Springs, CO
Greenland, J. Kingsley, II .... Boston, MA
Greenlaw, Dawn S. .... Simsbury, CT
Greenlaw, Denise M. .... United States Senate, Senatorial Assistants, GV
Greenlaw, Hollis M. .... Washington, DC
Greenlaw, Jane L. .... Rochester, NY
Greenlaw, Kimberly S.
San Francisco, CA
Greenlaw, Rosemary B. .... San Jose, CA
Greenleaf, A. Caroline .... South Portland, ME
Greenleaf, Andree H. .... Gretna, LA
Greenleaf, Christopher J.
Los Angeles, CA
Greenleaf, Clark H. Goodrich
Clearwater, FL
Greenleaf, Frances K. .... Los Angeles, CA
Greenleaf, Jay A. .... Shreveport, LA
Greenleaf, John A. .... Glendale, CA
Greenleaf, John L., Jr. .... Decatur, IL
Greenleaf, John L., Jr., Ltd. .... Decatur, IL
Greenleaf, Lisa Porter .... Lewisville, TX
Greenleaf, Peter W. .... Portland, ME
Greenleaf, Richard F. .... Houston, TX
Greenleaf, Robert J. .... Cambridge, MD
Greenleaf, Stephen H. .... Ashland, OR
Greenleaf, Stephen N. .... Iowa City, IA
Greenleaf, Stewart J. .... Blue Bell, PA
Harrisburg, PA
Greenleaf, Timothy R. .... Anaheim, CA
Greenleaf, W. Frank .... Miami, FL
Greenlee, A. Graham .... Seattle, WA
Greenlee, Barbara F. .... Agawam, MA
Greenlee, Charles C. .... Cheyenne, WY
Greenlee, Cheri N. .... Rockford, IL
Greenlee, Dennis P., Jr. .... Tacoma, WA
Greenlee, Derrico, Posa & Rodgers
Washington, PA
Greenlee, Diane .... Washington, DC
Greenlee, Edward R. .... Baton Rouge, LA
Greenlee, Gary S. .... Cleveland, OH
Greenlee, Gaylord W. .... Washington, PA
Greenlee, G. G." Greg " .... Cheyenne, WY
Greenlee, J. Lane .... Winona, MS
Greenlee, James W. .... Philadelphia, PA
Greenlee, James W. .... Sevierville, TN
Greenlee, Jim M. .... Oxford, MS
Greenlee, John A. .... Raleigh, NC
Greenlee, Lorance L. .... Boulder, CO
Greenlee, Mark B. .... Cleveland, OH
Greenlee, Michael R. .... Atlanta, GA
Greenlee, Peter A.
Department Of Health And Human Services, GV
Greenlee, Peter C. .... Cloquet, MN
Greenlee, Ronald E. .... Ishpeming, MI
Greenlee, Rosalind Anne .... Elkhart, IN
Greenlee, Steven G. .... Denver, CO
Greenlee, Stewart D. .... Fort Worth, TX
Greenlee, Tricia L. .... San Diego, CA
Greenlee, Winner and Sullivan, P.C.
Boulder, CO
Denver, CO

Greenlees, Christine Y.
Securities and Exchange Commission, Division of Investment Management, GV
Greenlees, Lisa Taeko ....Washington, DC
Greenlees, Russell C., Jr. ....Lake Orion, MI
Greenley, Beverly J. ....St. Louis, MO
Greenley, Jennifer Grimes
Philadelphia, PA
Greenley, Joseline L. ....Webster City, IA
Greenley, Kurtis A. ....Minneapolis, MN
Greenley, Ronald L. ....Anoka, MN
Greenlick, Michael A. ....Portland, OR
Greenlief, Joe A. ....Salt Lake City, UT
Greenlief, Magdalen
Department of Commerce, Patent and Trademark Office, GV
Greenlief, Richard D. ....Hardin, IL
Greenlief, Robert S. ....Fairfax, VA
Greenman, Brian M. ....Stamford, CT
Greenman, Charles P. ....Great Neck, NY
New York, NY
Greenman, David W. ....Irvine, CA
Greenman, Donald C. ....Baltimore, MD
Greenman, Elizabeth Bridge ....Buffalo, NY
Greenman, Franklin D. ....Marathon, FL
Greenman, Frederic E. ....Westborough, MA
Greenman, Frederick F., Jr.
New York, NY
Greenman, Gary R. ....New York, NY
Greenman, Gilbert O. ....Washington, DC
Greenman, Goldberg, Raby & Martinez, Professional Corporation ....Las Vegas, NV
Greenman, Harlan T. ....New York, NY
Greenman, Henry B. ....New York, NY
Greenman, Herbert L. ....Buffalo, NY
Greenman, Jacob J. ....Monmouth Beach, NJ
Greenman, Jane F. ....Morristown, NJ
Greenman, Janet E. ....Princeton Junction, NJ
Greenman, Jeffrey M. ....West Haven, CT
Greenman, Jeffrey N. ....Union, NJ
Greenman, John A. ....Las Vegas, NV
Greenman, Joseph A. ....Syracuse, NY
Greenman, Karl ....Boston, MA
Greenman, Kenneth L., Jr., (A P.L.C.)
Oceanside, CA
Greenman, Lacy, Klein, O'Harra & Heffron
La Jolla, CA
Oceanside, CA
Vista, CA
Greenman, Lisa ....
Administrative Office Of The United States Courts, GV
Greenman, Lyle E. ....Boston, MA
Greenman & Manz ....Marathon, FL
Greenman, Milton H. ....Southfield, MI
Greenman, Paula S. ....New York, NY
Greenman, Ronald L., (P.C.)
Portland, OR
Greenman, Roy B. ....Union, NJ
Greenman, Sidney ....New York, NY
Greenman, Steve ....Flushing, NY
Green-Meadows, Leisa V. ....Albany, GA
Upper Marlboro, MD
Greeno, Christopher J. ....Chicago, IL
Greeno, E. Jay ....Wichita, KS
Greeno, John G. ....Pittsburgh, PA
Greeno, Marianne H. ....Boston, MA
Greenough, Charles ....Tulsa, OK
Greenough, Donald M. ....Ipswich, MA
Greenough, Kelly M. ....Tulsa, OK
Greenough, Marc R. ....Seattle, WA
Greenough, Martha A. ....New York, NY
Greenough, Robert K., Jr. ....Camillus, NY
Greenough, Thomas H. ....Las Vegas, NV
Greenough, Walter C. ....Chicago, IL
Green-Rodriguez, George E.
San Juan, PR
Greenseid, David S. ....San Mateo, CA
Greensfelder, Andrew F. ....St. Louis, MO
Greensfelder, Edward B. ....St. Louis, MO
Greensfelder, Edward, Jr. ....Washington, DC
Greensfelder, Harry, III ....St. Louis, MO
Greensfelder, Hemker & Gale
Belleville, IL
St. Louis, MO
Greensfelder, Timothy A. ....New York, NY
Greenside, Myron ....Waltham, MA
Greenslade, Brent C. ....Lihue, HI
Greenslade, George A. ....New York, NY
Greenslade, Joseph L. ....Los Angeles, CA
Greenslade, Maria Marena ....Hartford, CT
Greenslade, Victor F., Jr. ....Independence, OH
Greenspahn, Jill ....Los Angeles, CA
Greenspahn, Melvyn G. ....Miami, FL
Greenspan, Abraham ....New York, NY
Greenspan, Alan N. ....Dallas, TX
Greenspan, Amy L. ....Austin, TX
Greenspan, Andrew B. ....Annapolis, MD
Greenspan, Arthur S. ....New York, NY
Greenspan, Barbara S. ....Palo Alto, CA
Greenspan, Bruce J. ....Jacksonville, FL
Greenspan, Bruce J., P.A. ....Jacksonville, FL
Greenspan, Chester H. ....Garden City, NY
Greenspan, Daniel S. ....Houston, TX
Greenspan, David J. ....New York, NY
Greenspan, Deborah E. ....Washington, DC
New York, NY
Greenspan, Donna M. ....Palm Beach, FL
Greenspan, Edw. J. ....Andover, MA
Greenspan, Elise R. ....New York, NY
Greenspan, Elliott S. ....New York, NY
Greenspan, Eric R. ....Los Angeles, CA
Greenspan & Gaber, P.C. ....Philadelphia, PA
Greenspan & Glasser ....Culver City, CA
Greenspan & Greenspan ....Oradell, NJ
White Plains, NY
Greenspan, Howard L. ....Wellesley, MA
Greenspan, Jane C. ....Philadelphia, PA
Greenspan, Jeffrey D. ....Chicago, IL
Greenspan, Jodi Carpey ....Philadelphia, PA
Greenspan, John P.
Federal Communications Commission, Wireless Telecommunications Bureau, GV
Greenspan, Jonathan H. ....Los Angeles, CA
Greenspan, Judith ....New York, NY
Greenspan & Kane ....Boca Raton, FL
Greenspan, Karen M ....Buffalo, NY
Greenspan, Kenneth J. ....Philadelphia, PA
Greenspan, Leon J. ....Boca Raton, FL
Oradell, NJ
White Plains, NY
Greenspan, Mark D. ....Fort Lauderdale, FL
Greenspan, Marlene A. ....Philadelphia, PA
Greenspan, Michael A. ....Washington, DC
Greenspan, Michael E. ....Oradell, NJ
White Plains, NY
Greenspan, Mitchell S. ....Philadelphia, PA
Greenspan, Morton ....New York, NY
Greenspan, Murray H. ....Garden City, NY
Greenspan, Myron ....Scarsdale, NY
Greenspan, Norman E. ....Philadelphia, PA
Greenspan, Raphael P. ....Carle Place, NY
Greenspan, Richard M. ....Ardsley, NY
Greenspan, Robert M. ....Culver City, CA
Greenspan, Robert M. ....Hingham, MA
Greenspan, Robert S. ....Department of Justice, Civil Division, GV
Greenspan, Ronald B. ....Cleveland, OH
Greenspan, Ronald Fred ....Los Angeles, CA
Greenspan, S. George ....Englewood Cliffs, NJ
Greenspan, Sandra L. ....Riverwoods, IL
Greenspan, Scott D. ....Washington, DC
Greenspan, Stanley M. ....Blue Bell, PA
Greenspan, Steve Zvi ....Corona, CA
Greenspan, Steven A. ....Aventura, FL
Miami, FL
Greenspan, Steven C. ....New York, NY
Greenspan, Steven M. ....Hartford, CT
Greenspan, Steven M. ....Los Angeles, CA
Greenspan, Stewart B. ....New York, NY
Greenspan, Theodore L. ....Mobile, AL
Greenspan, William R. ....Merrick, NY
Greenspon, Burton E. ....Buffalo, NY
Greenspon, Donald B. ....Detroit, MI
Greenspon, Maurice E. ....West Hartford, CT
Greenspon, Robert A. ....New York, NY
Greenspon, Scheff & Washington
Detroit, MI
Greenspon, Susan J. ....Buffalo Grove, IL
Greenspoon, Benjamin ....Washington, DC
Greenspoon, David H. ....Rochester, NY
Greenspoon, Gerald ....Fort Lauderdale, FL
Greenspoon, Lauren R. ....Hartford, CT
Greenspoon, Marder, Hirschfeld, Rafkin, Ross & Berger, P.A.
Fort Lauderdale, FL
Miami, FL
Orlando, FL
West Palm Beach, FL
Greenspoon, Robert P. ....Chicago, IL
Greenspoon and Waknine, P.C. ....Union, NJ
Greenspoon, Yale L. ....Union, NJ
Greenspun, Brian Lee ....Las Vegas, NV
Greenspun, Peter D. ....Fairfax, VA
Greenspun, Peter D., & Associates, P.C.
Fairfax, VA
Greenspun, Scott S. ....New York, NY
Greenstein, Abraham J. ....Washington, DC
Greenstein, Alan J. ....Miami, FL
Greenstein, Allan ....White Plains, NY
Greenstein, Amy ....Atlanta, GA
Greenstein, Andrew M. ....Rochester, NY
Greenstein, Charles A. ....Lincolnwood, IL
Greenstein, Daniel B. ....Minnetonka, MN
Greenstein, Daniel P. ....New York, NY
Greenstein, Daniel S. ....Philadelphia, PA
Greenstein, David H. ....Chicago, IL
Greenstein DeLorme & Luchs, P.C.
Washington, DC
Greenstein, Dennis H. ....New York, NY
Greenstein, Donald L.
United States Postal Service, Law Department, GV
Greenstein, Earl H. ....Beverly Hills, CA
Greenstein, Fred R. ....Kansas City, MO
Greenstein, Garry G. ....Wilmington, DE
Greenstein, Gary L. ....Boston, MA
Greenstein, Gary M. ....Farmington Hills, MI
Greenstein, Gary R. ....Washington, DC
Greenstein, Gary S. ....New York, NY
Greenstein, George ....Hamden, CT
Greenstein, Gregg A. ....Boulder, CO
Greenstein, Guy R. ....Boulder, CO
Greenstein, Guy R., P.C. ....Boulder, CO
Greenstein, Harry J. ....Philadelphia, PA
Greenstein, Ilana E. ....Boston, MA
Greenstein, Ira A. ....New York, NY
Greenstein, J. Richard ....Philadelphia, PA
Greenstein, Jas. F. ....St. Paul, MN
Greenstein, Jonathan E. ....Columbia, MD
Greenstein, Julius ....Pompano Beach, FL
Greenstein, Kenneth I. ....Rochester, NY
Greenstein, Laura S. ....New York, NY
Greenstein, Linda Renee ....Newark, NJ
Greenstein, Mabley & Wall, LLC
St. Paul, MN
Greenstein, Malcolm N. ....Austin, TX
Greenstein, Marci E. ....Washington, DC
Greenstein, Mark A. ....Department of Labor, Pension and Welfare Benefits, GV
Greenstein, Marla N. ....Anchorage, AK
Greenstein, Martin R. ....San Jose, CA
Greenstein, Michael B. ....Pittsburgh, PA
Greenstein, Milton ....Glenview, IL
Greenstein, Neil D. ....San Jose, CA
Greenstein, Paul M. ....Huntington, NY
Greenstein, Rhonda ....New York, NY
Greenstein, Richard G. ....Atlanta, GA
Greenstein, Richard H. ....Union, NJ
Greenstein, Richard K. ....Philadelphia, PA
Greenstein, Robert S. ....Woodland Hills, CA
Greenstein, Scott A. ....New York, NY
Greenstein, Seth D. ....Washington, DC
Greenstein & Solotke ....Chicago, IL
Greenstein Starr Gerstein & Rinaldi LLP
New York, NY
Greenstein, Steven Jay ....Rahway, NJ
Greenstien, Robert E. ....Stuart, FL
Greenstone, Aaron D. ....New Orleans, LA
Greenstone, Adam F.
Executive Office Of The President, Office of Administration, GV
Greenstone, Daniel A. ....New York, NY
Greenstone, Ellen ....Pasadena, CA
Greenstone & Greenstone, A Professional Corporation ....Newark, NJ
Greenstone, Louis ....Newark, NJ
Greenstone, Mark S. ....Los Angeles, CA
Greenstone, Richard J.
San Francisco, CA
Greenstone, Robert F. ....New York, NY
Greenstone, Robert J. ....Birmingham, MI
Greenstone, Samuel J. ....Woodland Hills, CA
Greenstone, Wayne D. ....Newark, NJ
Greenstreet, John R. ....Tulsa, OK
Greenstreet, Mark W.
Department Of Veterans Affairs, Board of Veterans Appeals, GV
Greenstreet, Max L. ....Mission Viejo, CA
Greenstreet, Patricia K. ....Seattle, WA
Greenswag, Douglas B. ....Minneapolis, MN
Greenswag, Richard A. ....Northfield, IL
Greenswag, Richard A., P.C. ....Northfield, IL
Greensweig, Bernard ....Bradenton, FL
Greensweig, Daniel J. ....Minneapolis, MN
Greenthal, David W. ....San Francisco, CA
Greenthal, John L. ....Albany, NY
Greentree, Hugh A. ....Columbus, OH
Greenup, Campbell H. ....El Segundo, CA
Greenup, Carmen S. ....Wichita, KS
Greenup, Edward P. ....St. Clair Shores, MI
Greenup, Geoffrey H. ....Encino, CA
Greenup, George I. ....La Porte, IN
Greenup, Jeff L. ....New York, NY
Greenup, Leo A. ....Detroit, MI
Greenwade, P. Rowland ....Austin, TX
Greenwald, A. Seth ....New York, NY
Greenwald, Alan ....Milford, MA
Greenwald, Alvin G. ....Los Angeles, CA
Greenwald, Alvin G., & Randy Greenwald, A Professional Corporation ....Los Angeles, CA
Greenwald, Andrew E. ....Greenbelt, MD
Greenwald, Barbara D. ....Studio City, CA
Greenwald, Bart L. ....Louisville, KY
Greenwald, Beth Ann ....Wyckoff, NJ
Greenwald, Carol E. ....Troy, OH
Greenwald, Carolyn ....New York, NY
Greenwald, Christoph & Holland, P.C.
New York, NY
Greenwald, Clarence J. ....La Jolla, CA
Greenwald, David J. ....New York, NY
Greenwald, David M. ....Chicago, IL
Greenwald, David N. ....New York, NY
Greenwald, Dennis L. ....Santa Monica, CA
Greenwald, Douglas M. ....Kansas City, KS
Greenwald, Eliot J. ....Washington, DC
Greenwald, Elisabeth Hope ....Winthrop, MA
Greenwald, Eric A. ....New York, NY
Greenwald, Eugene C. ....Jamaica, NY
Greenwald, Gary ....Camp Springs, MD
Greenwald, Gary ....Chester, NY
Greenwald, Gary D. ....Columbus, OH
Greenwald, Gerald B. ....Washington, DC
Greenwald, Glenn ....New York, NY
Greenwald & Gosnell ....Louisville, KY
Greenwald & Greenwald ....Beverly Hills, CA
Greenwald & Greenwald ....Monroeville, PA
Greenwald & Greenwald, P.C.
San Antonio, TX
Greenwald, Greenwald, Powers & Winsor LLP ....Milford, MA
Westborough, MA
Greenwald, Hal B. ....Yonkers, NY
Greenwald, Harold ....New York, NY
Greenwald, Hoffman, Meyer & Montes, L.L.P. ....Glendale, CA
Los Angeles, CA
Greenwald, Howard J. ....East Rochester, NY
Greenwald, Howard R. ....Uniondale, NY
Greenwald, I. Leonard ....Monroeville, PA
Greenwald, Jack ....Denver, CO
Greenwald, James F. ....Syracuse, NY
Greenwald, Jawj E. ....Walnut Creek, CA
Greenwald, Jeffrey L. ....Beverly Hills, CA
Greenwald, Jeffrey L. ....Allentown, PA
Greenwald, Jill ....New York, NY
Greenwald, Joel, and Associates, A Prof. Corp. ....New City, NY
New York, NY
Greenwald, Joel J. ....New City, NY
New York, NY
Greenwald, John D. ....Washington, DC
Greenwald, Joseph W., Jr. ....Shreveport, LA
Greenwald, Joseph W., Sr. ....Baton Rouge, LA
Greenwald, Judith R. ....New York, NY
Greenwald, Kenneth Dana ....New York, NY
Greenwald, Kerry A. ....Boca Raton, FL
Greenwald, Kerry A., & Associates, P.A.
Boca Raton, FL
Greenwald, Laurence ....New York, NY
Greenwald Law Offices ....Chester, NY
Greenwald, Lawrence S. ....Baltimore, MD
Greenwald, Leean Marynchak
Monroeville, PA
Greenwald, Leonard ....New York, NY
Greenwald, Leonard S. ....Cleveland, OH
Greenwald, Leonard S., Co., L.P.A.
Cleveland, OH
Greenwald, Leslie Neil ....Birmingham, MI
Greenwald, Louis D. ....Voorhees, NJ
Greenwald, Marianne W. ....Newark, NJ
Greenwald, Marie E. ....Oklahoma City, OK
Greenwald, Mark David ....Franklin, PA
Greenwald, Mark Evan ....Lyndhurst, NJ
Greenwald, Mark L. ....San Antonio, TX
Greenwald, Marlene M. ....Bronx, NY
Greenwald, Mary E. ....Boston, MA
Greenwald, Melvin L. ....New York, NY
Greenwald, Michael ....Fort Lauderdale, FL
Greenwald, Michael ....Philadelphia, PA
Greenwald, Michael P. ....Chicago, IL
Greenwald, Michael P., Ltd. ....Chicago, IL
Greenwald, Michael R. ....Dallas, TX
Greenwald, Mitchell I. ....Pittsfield, MA
Greenwald, Morton ....New York, NY
Greenwald, Murray J. ....Louisville, KY
Greenwald, Nicole A. ....New York, NY
Greenwald, Paul Evan ....Orange, CA
Greenwald, Paul J. ....Grand Rapids, MI
Greenwald, Peter N. ....New York, NY
Greenwald, Philip C. ....Encino, CA
Greenwald, Randy ....Los Angeles, CA
Greenwald, Robert J.
Commodity Futures Trading Commission, Division of Enforcement, GV
Greenwald, Robert L. ....Jamaica Plain, MA
Greenwald, Robert M. ....Cleveland, OH
Greenwald, Robin L. ....Department of Justice, Environment and Natural Resources Division, GV
Greenwald, Sharon Scharff ....San Antonio, TX
Greenwald, Shelly M. ....Scarsdale, NY
Greenwald, Stephen R. ....New York, NY
Greenwald, Steven A. ....Milford, MA
Greenwald, Steven F. ....San Francisco, CA
Greenwald, Steven I. ....Boca Raton, FL
Greenwald, Steven I., P.A.
Boca Raton, FL
Palm Beach, FL
Greenwald, Steven J. ....Palm Beach, FL
Greenwald, Steven M. ....Wilkes-Barre, PA
Greenwald & Stongin P.C. ....New York, NY
Greenwald, Stuart M. ....Middletown, NY
Greenwald, Susan E. ....New York, NY
Greenwald, Susan G. ....Roseland, NJ
Greenwald, Thomas A. ....Dallas, TX
Greenwald, Thomas E. ....Rockford, IL
Lake Geneva, WI
Greenwald, Thomas H. ....Beverly Hills, CA
Greenwald, Todd A. ....Los Angeles, CA
Greenwald, Tracey M. ....Boston, MA
Greenwald, Wayne M. ....New York, NY
Greenwald, Wendy L. ....Salem, OR
Greenwald, Wendy Lee ....Bronx, NY
Greenwaldt, William E. ....Baltimore, MD
Greenwalt, J. Frank, Jr. ....Stuart, VA
Greenwalt, Karen K. ....Santa Monica, CA
Greenwalt, Paul Edwin, III ....Chicago, IL
Greenwalt, R. Todd ....Houston, TX
Greenwalt, Robert B. ....Baltimore, MD
Greenwalt, Robert D. ....West Chicago, IL
Greenway, Bradley K. ....Rutherfordton, NC
Greenway, Curtis L.
Department of the Army, U.S. Army Legal Services Agency, GV
Greenway, Eugene A. ....Edmonds, WA
Greenway, John S. ....Tucson, AZ
Greenway, John W. ....Austin, TX
Greenway, Lucille M. ....Walnut Creek, CA
Greenway, Pamela Richards
Warner Robins, GA
Greenway, Pamela Richards, P.C.
Warner Robins, GA
Greenway, Paula Coleman
Birmingham, AL
Tuscaloosa, AL
Greenway, S. Jefferson ....Atlanta, GA
Greenway, Teresa Kosla ....Wilmington, IL
Greenway, William P. ....Washington, MI
Greenwell, Amy B. ....Lexington, KY
Greenwell, Andrew M.
Corpus Christi, TX
Greenwell, Charles D. ....Louisville, KY
Greenwell, Ellen R. ....Ellicott City, MD
Greenwell, F. Gerald ....Louisville, KY
Greenwell, Gary L. ....Louisville, KY
Greenwell & Greenwell ....Marion, KY
Greenwell, Henry, III ....Taylorsville, KY
Greenwell, James Zachry ....Marion, KY
Greenwell, Karen J. ....Lexington, KY
Greenwell, Mark A. ....Newport, IN
Greenwell, Mike ....Shelbina, MO
Greenwell, Mike, L.L.C. ....Shelbina, MO
Greenwell, Pamela M. ....Louisville, KY
Greenwell, Patrick B. ....Sonora, CA
Greenwell, Porter, Smaltz & Royal
Wayne, PA
Greenwell, William S. ....Marion, KY
Greenwold, Marcia D. ....San Carlos, CA
Greenwold, Mark E. ....Washington, DC
Greenwood, Allan D. ....Turlock, CA
Greenwood, Amy R. ....Green Bay, WI
Greenwood, Arthur L. ....Alton, IL
Greenwood & Associates Law Group, P.A.
Brandon, FL
Greenwood & Associates, Law Group, P.A.
Tampa, FL
Greenwood, Barbara J. ....Berwyn, PA
Greenwood, Carolyn Diane ....Knoxville, TN
Greenwood & Chambers ....Roswell, GA
Greenwood, Charles ....Providence, RI
Greenwood, Christopher T. ....Bridgeport, CT

Greenwood, Clarence H. ... **Portland, OR**
Greenwood, Craig H. ... Downers Grove, IL
Greenwood, Daniel B. ... Elkhorn, NE
Greenwood, Dann E. ... **Dickinson, ND**
Greenwood, David A. ... **Salt Lake City, UT**
Greenwood, Donald A. ... Syracuse, NY
Greenwood, E. Earl, Jr. ... Salt Lake City, UT
Greenwood, Elizabeth ... **Pinedale, WY**
Greenwood, Elizabeth Carrie ... Dallas, TX
Greenwood, Frederick M., III
Covington, KY
Greenwood, Gail S. ... **San Francisco, CA**
Greenwood, George W., III ... Roswell, GA
Greenwood, Glenn ... Skokie, IL
Greenwood, Gordon D. ... **Oakland, CA**
Greenwood, H. Nadine ... **Memphis, TN**
Greenwood, Henry L. ... Detroit, MI
Greenwood, Herman E. ... Speedway, IN
Greenwood, Howard C. ... Hamilton, MT
Greenwood, James H. ... Atlanta, GA
Greenwood, James, III ... Houston, TX
Greenwood, John E. ... **New York, NY**
Greenwood, John E. ... Jamestown, ND
Greenwood, Jon S. ... **New York, NY**
Greenwood, Judy ... Philadelphia, PA
Greenwood, Kellianne E. ... **New York, NY**
Greenwood, Kelly Leigh ... Dallas, TX
Greenwood, Kenneth ... New York, NY
Greenwood, Kevin J. ... Chicago, IL
Greenwood, Lawrence E. ... Killeen, TX
Greenwood, Lisa E. ... Walnut Creek, CA
Greenwood, Lowell D. ... Charleston, WV
Greenwood, M. Harris ... **Houston, TX**
Greenwood, Mark A. ... **Washington, DC**
Greenwood, Mark L. ... Dickinson, ND
Greenwood, Mary ... Hollywood, FL
Greenwood, Mary J. ... San Jose, CA
Greenwood, Mary L. ... **Brandon, FL**
Greenwood, Michael J. ... **Newark, NJ**
Greenwood, P. Nicholas ... **Birmingham, AL**
Greenwood, Patrick E. ... Council Bluffs, IA
Greenwood, Paul R. ... San Diego, CA
Greenwood & Ramsey, P.L.L.P.
Dickinson, ND
Greenwood, Richard D. ... Twin Falls, ID
Greenwood, Richard G. ... Green Bay, WI
Greenwood, Richard H. ... **Stamford, CT**
Greenwood, Robert H. ... **Wayne, NJ**
Greenwood, Ronald J. ... Walnut Creek, CA
Greenwood, Scott T. ... Cincinnati, OH
Greenwood, Sean F. ... **Houston, TX**
Greenwood, Sharon A. ... Sacramento, CA
Greenwood, Stanley ... Cambridge, MA
Greenwood, Stephen Paul
San Francisco, CA
Greenwood, Steven M. ... Newbury Park, CA
Greenwood, Susan M. ... **New York, NY**
Greenwood, Thomas R. ... Richardson, TX
Greenwood, Tolbert L. ... **Fort Worth, TX**
Greenwood, Truman A. ... **Toledo, OH**
Greenwood, Val D. ... Salt Lake City, UT
Greenwood, Vanessa L. ... **Chicago, IL**
Greenwood, Warren J., Jr. ... New Orleans, LA
Greenwood, William D. ... **Chickasha, OK**
Oklahoma City, OK
Greenzang, Steven S. ... Chestnut Hill, MA
Greer, Alan G. ... **Miami, FL**
Greer, Alcus ... Houston, TX
Greer, Allen Curtis, II ... **New York, NY**
Greer, Amy J. ... **Pittsburgh, PA**
Greer, Anne J. ... Department of Justice, Executive Office for Immigration Review, GV
Greer & Associates, P.C. ... New York, NY
Greer, Ben M. ... McLean, VA
Greer, Benny R. ... Darlington, SC
Greer, Bernard A. ... Beckley, WV
Greer, Bernard L., Jr. ... **Atlanta, GA**
Greer, Beverly Smeal ... Omaha, NE
Greer, Birdia Marie ... Roswell, GA
Greer, Brian E. ... **New York, NY**
Greer, Bridgette A. ... Upper Marlboro, MD
Greer, Bruce G. ... **Lake Worth, FL**
Greer, Bruce W. ... Miami, FL
Greer, Bruce W., P.A. ... Miami, FL
Greer, Burns & Crain, Ltd. ... **Chicago, IL**
Greer, C. Rhodes, II ... Louisville, KY
Greer, Cathy H. ... **Denver, CO**
Greer, Charles E. ... Indianapolis, IN
Greer, Charlotte Morrison ... Little Rock, AR
Greer, Christopher ... New York, NY
Greer, Claudia Russell ... Tupelo, MS
Greer, Curtis Keith ... Del Mar, CA
Greer, Cynthia ... Mamaroneck, NY
Greer, Cynthia D. ... **Washington, DC**
Greer, Daniel ... New Haven, CT
Greer, Daniel J. ... Springfield, IL
Greer, Darrell R. ... **Houston, TX**
Greer, David A. ... **Norfolk, VA**
Greer, David C. ... **Dayton, OH**
Greer, David E. ... Lancaster, PA
Greer, David Keith ... Columbus, OH
Greer, David N. ... Albuquerque, NM
Greer, Dean ... Kingsport, TN
Greer, Dean W. ... San Antonio, TX
Greer, DeEdward ... Houston, TX
Greer, Denise H. ... Los Angeles, CA
Greer, Donald H. ... Kerrville, TX
Greer, Donald K., Jr.
Spring Lake Heights, NJ
Greer, Dora Jean Young ... Tucson, AZ
Greer, Douglas A. ... **Los Angeles, CA**
Greer, Douglas E. ... Indianapolis, IN
Greer, Douglas P. ... Beaumont, TX
Greer, Douglas R. ... Sacramento, CA
Greer, Edward ... **Philadelphia, PA**
Greer, Edward F. ... Beverly Hills, CA
Greer, Edward H. ... Brookline, MA
Greer, Elizabeth S. ... Cupertino, CA
Greer, Elwin H. ... Los Alamitos, CA
Greer, Emily M. ... Brighton, MA
Greer, Ernest LaMont ... **Atlanta, GA**
Greer, Evelyn Langlieb ... **Miami, FL**
Greer, F. Brawner ... Richmond, VA
Greer, G. Carter ... **Martinsville, VA**
Greer, Gabrielle D. ... **Peoria, IL**
Greer, Gary L. ... **Denver, CO**
Greer, Gary R. ... Batavia, OH
Greer, George C. ... Pittsburgh, PA
Greer, George E. ... **Seattle, WA**
Greer, George W. ... Clearwater, FL
Greer, Gina M. ... Sacramento, CA
Greer, Gordon B. ... **Boston, MA**
Greer and Greer ... **Paris, TN**
Greer, Harold E., III ... Richmond, VA
Greer, Harry D. ... Eastsound, WA
Greer, Herz & Adams ... **League City, TX**
Galveston, TX
Houston, TX
Greer, Holly J. ... **Orlando, FL**
Greer, Ida Rae ... New York, NY
Greer, J. Barton, III ... Mobile, AL
Greer, J. Broocks, III ... **Shreveport, LA**
Greer, J. Mark ... Mobile, AL
Greer, J. Mark, P.C. ... Mobile, AL
Greer, J. Scott ... **Poughkeepsie, NY**
Greer, J. Taylor ... **Lincoln, NE**
Greer, J. Willard ... South Boston, VA
Greer, J. Willard, P.C. ... South Boston, VA
Greer, Jack E. ... **Norfolk, VA**
Greer, Jack Kenneth, Jr. ... **Knoxville, TN**
Greer, James A. ... Del Mar, CA
Greer, James A., II (P.C.) ... New York, NY
Greer, James F. ... **Memphis, TN**
Greer, James F. ... Waco, TX
Greer, James H. ... Birmingham, AL
Greer, James H. ... **Dayton, OH**
Greer, James W. ... **Milwaukee, WI**
Greer, Jane Rex ... Phoenix, AZ
Greer, Jeffrey Y. ... **San Diego, CA**
Greer, Jennifer Horan ... **Houston, TX**
Greer, Joel T. S. ... **Marshalltown, IA**
Greer, John B. ... **Boulder, CO**
Greer, John B., III, (P.C.) ... **Texarkana, TX**
Greer, John D., Jr. ... Houston, TX
Greer, John J.
United States International Trade Commission, Office of External Affairs, GV
Greer, John J. ... Spencer, IA
Greer, John L. ... Wayzata, MN
Greer, John P. ... Spencer, IA
Greer, John R. ... Scottsdale, AZ
Greer & Johnson, P.A. ... Roswell, GA
Greer, Jon M. ... **Philadelphia, PA**
Greer, Julia D. ... **San Francisco, CA**
Greer, Julia Lynn Crowder
Richmond, VA
Greer, Kenneth L., Jr. ... San Angelo, TX
Greer, Kevin F. ... **Riverside, CA**
Greer, Kevin L. ... Hillsboro, OH
Greer, Klosik and Daugherty ... **Atlanta, GA**
Greer, L. Edwin ... Shreveport, LA
Greer, Larry A. ... South Bend, IN
Greer Law Office ... Spencer, IA
Greer Law Offices ... **Charleston, WV**
Clarksburg, WV
Greer, Lawrence B. ... **Houston, TX**
Greer, Lawrence G. ... San Bernardino, CA
Greer, Lee M., III ... **Paris, TN**
Greer, Leilan J. ... Oregon City, OR
Greer, Leonard D. ... **Phoenix, AZ**
Greer, Lesley Mason ... Bakersfield, CA
Greer, Leslie B. ... Boston, MA
Greer, Linda R. ... **Atlanta, GA**
Greer, L.K. ... Beaumont, TX
Greer, Marcy Hogan ... **Austin, TX**
Greer, Mark A. ... **Cleveland, OH**
Greer, Mark Charles ... Glastonbury, CT
Greer, Martha J. ... Pittsburgh, PA
Greer & Martin, L.L.P. ... **Houston, TX**
Greer, Mary Adele ... Versailles, MO
Greer, Melinda K. ... **Minneapolis, MN**
Greer, Michael D. ... Tupelo, MS
Greer, Michael J. ... Gladwin, MI
Greer, Michelle L. ... **Atlanta, GA**
Greer, Nora F. ... Phoenix, AZ
Greer, Norris E. ... **Kansas City, MO**
Greer, Patricia B. ... **New York, NY**
Greer, Paul ... Cheltenham, MD
Greer, Paul D. ... Marion, VA
Greer, Phillip B. ... **Irvine, CA**
Greer & Pipkin ... Tupelo, MS
Greer, Ralph S. ... Pasadena, CA
Greer, Randall E. ... **Beverly Hills, CA**
Greer, Randall E. ... **Beverly Hills, CA**
Greer, Randall E. ... **Los Angeles, CA**
Greer, Renee Eva Mumford ... Memphis, TN
Greer, Richard G. ... **Atlanta, GA**
Greer, Robert B. ... Houston, TX
Greer, Robert F. ... **Spokane, WA**
Greer, Robert L. ... **Clarksburg, WV**
Greer, Roger D. ... **Chicago, IL**
Greer, Sara Joanne ... **Miami, FL**
Greer, Scott Allen ... **Atlanta, GA**
Greer, Sharon Soorholtz
Marshalltown, IA
Greer, Sharra Elizabeth ... Somerset, NJ
Greer, Stephen D. ... Port Orchard, WA
Greer, Stephen E. ... Anchorage, AK
Greer, Stephen T. ... Dunlap, TN
Greer, Stephen T., P.C. ... Dunlap, TN
Greer, Steve ... Lawrence, MA
Greer, Steven B. ... **Paris, TN**
Greer, Susan J. ... Denver, CO
Greer, Thomas E. ... **Carrollton, GA**
Greer, Thomas J., Jr. ... Arlington, VA
Greer, Thomas Keister ... Rocky Mount, VA
Greer, Thos. A., Jr. ... Dunlap, TN
Greer, Tim ... Salem, OR
Greer, Tim, P.C. ... Salem, OR
Greer, Todd A. ... Little Rock, AR
Greer, Tracy ... Department of Justice, Antitrust Division, GV
Greer, W. Dan ... Covington, GA
Greer, Wiley, Jr. ... Carlisle, MS
Greer, William H., Jr. ... Washington, DC
Greer, William, Jr. ... Salem, OR
Greer, William R., Jr. ... La Plata, MD
Greer-Stokes, Whitney ... Louisville, KY
Greerty, Thomas P. ... **Martinez, CA**
Greeson & Associates ... **Greensboro, NC**
Greeson, Debra K. ... Buford, GA
Greeson, Harold F. ... **Greensboro, NC**
Greeson, Howard R., Jr. ... High Point, NC
Greeson, Michael R., Jr. ... Greensboro, FL
Greeson, Thomas W. ... **Falls Church, VA**
Greetis, Kathleen Hughes ... Chicago, IL
Greeven, Rainer N. K. P.C.
New York, NY
Greeven, Rainer N. K. ... **New York, NY**
Greever, Anne Gordon ... **Richmond, VA**
Greever, F. Mack ... Claremore, OK
Greeves, Geoffrey J. ... **Washington, DC**
Greeves, Laura L. ... College Park, MD
Greevy & Associates ... **Laporte, PA**
Williamsport, PA
Greevy, Charles F., III ... **Williamsport, PA**
Greevy, Chas. F. ... Williamsport, PA
Greevy, Lester L., Jr. ... **Williamsport, PA**
Greevy, Robert A. ... Harrisburg, PA
Greezicki, Roger J. ... Baltimore, MD
Grefe, Andrea Jane ... **Los Angeles, CA**
Grefé, G. Nicholas ... Naples, FL
Grefe, Rolland E. ... **Des Moines, IA**
Grefe, Ronald D. ... Washington, DC
Grefe & Sidney, P.L.C. ... **Des Moines, IA**
Pella, IA
Grefer, Gregory A. ... **New Orleans, LA**
Grefer, Joseph F. ... Gretna, LA
Grefer, Stephen ... Gretna, LA
Greff, Jacqueline ... Baltimore, MD
Greffenius, A. J. ... **Des Moines, IA**
Grefig, Max E. ... Milwaukee, WI
Grefsheng, L. Robert ... **Columbia, TN**
Grefthen, Daron J. ... Jamestown, ND
Grega, JenniferLynn ... **Los Angeles, CA**
Gregan, David W. ... Mesa, AZ
Gregan, James E. ... Farmington, UT
Gregart, James J. ... Kalamazoo, MI
Greger, Clarke H. ... **Phoenix, AZ**
Greger, Jeffrey H. ... **Alexandria, VA**
Greger, Michael S. ... **Irvine, CA**
Greger, Thomas J. ... Staten Island, NY
Gregersen, Craig M. ... **St. Paul, MN**
Gregerson, Byron A. ... Modesto, CA
Gregerson, David H. ... **Minneapolis, MN**
Gregerson, Eva Heffernan
Department of Justice, GV
Gregerson, Gary L. ... Provo, UT
Gregerson, Gerard L. ... **Indianapolis, IN**
Gregerson, Lloyd G. ... Park Forest, IL
Gregerson, Richard O. ... **Sioux Falls, SD**
Gregg, Aaron C. ... Fullerton, CA
Gregg, Adella J. ... Washington, PA
Gregg, Andrew J. ... **Portland, OR**
Gregg, Bobbie McGee
Hoffman Estates, IL
Gregg, Carol ... Odessa, TX
Gregg, Carol Lees ... Tallahassee, FL
Gregg, Charles N., Jr.
Environmental Protection Agency, Program Office Attorneys, GV
Gregg, Charles R. ... **Houston, TX**
Gregg, Charles R., Jr. ... New York, NY
Gregg, Chester James ... Hudson, MA
Gregg, David D. ... **Chicago, IL**
Gregg, David H., Jr. ... Bethel, VT
Gregg, David Lawrence ... Kirkland, WA
Gregg, Dick H., III ... **Houston, TX**
Gregg, Dick H., Jr. ... **Houston, TX**
Gregg, Donna Coleman ... **Washington, DC**
Gregg, Douglas B. ... Dayton, OH
Gregg, Douglas C., Jr. ... Vista, CA
Gregg, Douglas L. ... **Juneau, AK**
Gregg, Douglas L., A Professional Corporation ... **Juneau, AK**
Gregg, Edward B. ... Palo Alto, CA
Gregg, Ellen M. ... **Winston-Salem, NC**
Gregg, Erica S. ... Providence, RI
Gregg & Farris ... **Batesville, AR**
Gregg, Gabriel G. ... **Los Angeles, CA**
Gregg, Gene E., Jr. (P.C.) ... **Pasadena, CA**
Gregg & Gregg, P.C. ... **Houston, TX**
Gregg, Gregory L. ... Houston, TX
Gregg, Henry A. ... St. Paul, MN
Gregg, Hugh C., II ... Syracuse, NY
Gregg, Isaac D. ... Thorntown, IN
Gregg, James C. ... **Washington, DC**
Gregg, James D. ... Grand Rapids, MI
Gregg, James R. ... Canton, OH
Gregg, James R. ... Vancouver, WA
Gregg, Jameson L. ... **Brunswick, GA**
Gregg, Jamie Vincent ... Torrington, CT
Gregg, Jennifer M. ... **Pasadena, CA**
Gregg, Joan B. ... Anderson, IN
Gregg, John C. ... **Batesville, AR**
Gregg, John P. ... **Washington, DC**
Gregg, John P. ... **Norristown, PA**
Gregg, John R. ... Vincennes, IN
Gregg, John R. ... Bottineau, ND
Gregg, John W. ... **Cincinnati, OH**
Gregg, Jon M. ... **Chicago, IL**
Gregg, Joseph A. ... **Columbus, OH**
Toledo, OH
Gregg, Judd A. ... Concord, NH
Gregg, Kathleen ... **Wellesley, MA**
Gregg, Kathy B. ... Wauchula, FL
Gregg, Kathy B., P.A. ... Wauchula, FL
Gregg, Larry E. ... **Topeka, KS**
Gregg, Larry L. ... Alexandria, VA
Gregg, Lisa R. ... McKinney, TX
Gregg, Lorraine B. ... Cadillac, MI
Gregg, Loyal H. ... **Pittsburgh, PA**
Gregg, Marc A. ... **Fort Lauderdale, FL**
Gregg, Marcia E. ... Boston, MA
Gregg, Mark A. ... **Johnstown, PA**
Gregg, Melissa ... Baton Rouge, LA
Gregg, Michael R. ... **Chicago, IL**
Gregg, Michael S. ... **Reno, NV**
Gregg, Michael S., P.C., Law Offices of
Reno, NV
Gregg, Michael T. ... **New York, NY**
Gregg, Peter T. ... **Beaumont, TX**
Houston, TX
Gregg, Quyona Theone ... Dallas, TX
Gregg, Ralph J. ... **Buffalo, NY**
Gregg, Richard ... **San Jose, CA**
Gregg, Robert E. ... **McLean, VA**
Gregg, Robert E. ... **Madison, WI**
Gregg, Robert M. ... Vancouver, WA
Gregg, Robt. E. ... Kansas City, MO
Gregg, Roger D. ... Phoenix, AZ
Gregg, Russell B. ... Boston, MA
Gregg, Scott A. ... Nashville, TN
Gregg, Sean D. ... **Orange, VA**
Gregg, Sherry L. Biddinger ... Terre Haute, IN
Gregg, Suzanne McIlroy ... San Jose, CA
Gregg, Tammie M. ... **Washington, DC**
Gregg, Tammie M. ... Minneapolis, MN
Gregg, Thomas J. ... Chicago, IL
Gregg, Tom W., Jr. ... San Angelo, TX
Gregg & Valby, L.L.P. ... Houston, TX
Gregg, Valerie S. ... Jefferson City, MO
Gregg, Walter E., Jr. ... Pittsburgh, PA
Gregg, Willard Benton ... **Jackson, MS**
Gregg, William C., III Chartered
Clearwater, FL
Gregg, William J. ... Treasury Department, Internal Revenue Service, GV
Gregg, William J. ... St. Michaels, MD
Endwell, NY
Gregg, William J. ... Cary, NC
Gregg-Capozzola, Theresa A.
Saratoga Springs, NY
Greggo, Robert M. ... Cleveland, OH
Grego, Jennifer A. ... **Albany, NY**
Grego, Lisa A. ... Buffalo, NY
Grego, Paul ... Chicago, IL
Grego, Paul W. ... **Harrisburg, PA**
Grego, Samuel R. A. ... Pittsburgh, PA
Gregoire, Brent J. ... Washington, DC
Gregoire, Calivas, Newman, Morrison & Gray
Dover, NH
Gregoire, Daniel N. ... **Manchester, NH**
Gregoire, David S. ... **Los Angeles, CA**
Gregoire, Gerard ... Dallas, TX
Gregoire, L. Victor ... **Baton Rouge, LA**
Gregoire, Mary Beth ... **Rome, GA**
Gregoire, Nancy ... **Fort Lauderdale, FL**
Gregoire, William J. ... **Great Falls, MT**
Gregor, Bradley S. ... Department of Justice, Federal Bureau of Investigation, GV
Gregor, Douglas J. ... Eveleth, MN
Gregor, Garrett S. ... Santa Ana Heights, CA
Gregor, James P. ... Stroudsburg, PA
Gregor, Jonathan H. ... **Kansas City, MO**
Gregor, Joseph C. ... Baltimore, MD
Gregor, Leah A. ... **Washington, DC**
Gregor, Monia (Monica) C. ... **Troy, MI**
Gregor, Nancy E. ... **Baltimore, MD**
Gregor, Robert J. ... Wickliffe, OH
Gregor, T. Steven ... **San Diego, CA**
Gregor, Vanessa J. ... **Irvine, CA**
Gregora, Peter J. ... **Los Angeles, CA**
Gregoratos, Barbara ... **San Francisco, CA**
Gregorcy, Philip D. ... Oak Brook, IL
Gregorczyk, Florian S. ... **Chicago, IL**
Gregorek, Francis M. ... **San Diego, CA**
New York, NY
Gregorek, Michael John ... New York, NY
Gregorek, Richard James ... Kirkland, WA
Gregores, George J. ... **Portland, OR**
Gregori, Frank L. ... Buffalo, NY
Gregori, Jeannie M. ... Department of Justice, Office of Justice Programs, GV
Gregori, Terri B. ... **Columbus, OH**
Gregoria, Ric ... **Sarasota, FL**
Gregorian, Rima ... Los Angeles, CA
Gregorich, Gregor F. ... **New York, NY**
Gregorich, Joseph E. ... Los Angeles, CA
Gregorich, W. Stephen ... Tacoma, WA
Gregorie, Charles C., Jr. ... Macon, GA
Gregorie, Isaac M., Jr. ... **Baton Rouge, LA**
Gregorie, Nancy Sue ... Baton Rouge, LA
Gregorie, Victor A. ... Vista, CA
Gregoriev, Heidemarie ... **Chicago, IL**
Gregorio, Antone F., (Ltd.) ... Chicago, IL
Gregorio, Arlen ... Burlingame, CA
Gregorio, Carl J. ... **Marlton, NJ**
Gregorio, John F. ... Chicago, IL
Gregorio, Joseph A. ... Bossier City, LA
Gregorio, Ronald J. ... **Morristown, NJ**
Gregorio, Sam N. ... **Shreveport, LA**
Gregorio, Sam N., A Professional Law Corporation ... **Bossier City, LA**
Shreveport, LA
Gregorovic, Peter S. ... San Diego, CA
Gregorowicz, Edward V., Jr. ... **Fairfax, VA**
Gregorowicz, James P. ... Scranton, PA
Gregorowicz, Michael P. ... Bloomsburg, PA

Gregorski, Christine M. ... San Diego, CA
Gregorski, Robert D. ... Manitowoc, WI
Gregorski, Walter F., Jr. ... Manitowoc, WI
Gregory, A. Peter ... Englewood, CO
Gregory and Adams, P.C. ... Wilton, CT
New York, NY
Gregory, Adrienne M.
Grosse Pointe Shores, MI
Gregory, A. J., Jr. ... Natchitoches, LA
Shreveport, LA
Gregory, Alan G. ... Troy, MI
Gregory, Alexander I. ... Portland, OR
Gregory, Amy Lynn ... Louisville, KY
Gregory, Andrew A. ... Houston, TX
Gregory, Angella Whaley ... Dallas, TX
Gregory, Arnold ... Thousand Oaks, CA
Gregory, Arthur ... Atlanta, GA
Gregory, Billy B. ... Gainesville, TX
Gregory, Bion M. ... Sacramento, CA
Gregory, Brent E. ... Milwaukee, WI
Gregory, Buddy W. ... Houston, TX
Gregory, Byron L. ... Chicago, IL
Gregory, C. Ernest ... Los Angeles, CA
Gregory, C. Linwood ... New Kent, VA
Gregory, C. Neil ... Naples, FL
Gregory, Carlton S. ... Richmond, VA
Gregory, Charles C., III ... Houston, TX
Gregory, Charles L. ... Atlanta, GA
Gregory, Charles W. ... Springfield, IL
Gregory, Christy & Maniklal
Cordele, GA
Gregory, Claiborne B. ... San Antonio, TX
Gregory, Claiborne B., Jr.
San Antonio, TX
Gregory, Claire ... Department of Justice,
Civil Rights Division, GV
Gregory, Cleburne E., III ... Atlanta, GA
Gregory, Coleman G. ... New York, NY
Gregory, D. Michael ... Denton, TX
Gregory, Daniel A. ... Durango, CO
Gregory, Danielle L. ... Indianapolis, IN
Gregory, David ... Lansing, MI
Gregory, David ... Geneva, NY
Gregory, David E. ... Riverside, CA
Gregory, David L. ... Jamaica, NY
Gregory, David M. ... Honesdale, PA
Gregory, David M. ... Houston, TX
Gregory, David M., P.A. ... Honesdale, PA
Scranton, PA
Gregory, David Weston ... Centreville, MD
Gregory, Deanie L. ... Madison, TN
Gregory, Derek V. ... Brocton, NY
Gregory, Donald A. ... Washington, DC
Gregory, Donald E. ... Dover, DE
Gregory, Donald W. ... Columbus, OH
Gregory, Douglas S. ... Tampa, FL
Gregory, Draper B. ... Danville, CA
Gregory, Easley and Courtney
Murray, KY
Gregory, Edgar B. ... Wilkesboro, NC
Gregory, Edith M. ... Muskogee, OK
Gregory, Edward G. ... Los Angeles, CA
Gregory, Elizabeth A. ... Chicago, IL
Gregory, Elizabeth V. ... Los Angeles, CA
Gregory, Ellen Davies ... Indianapolis, IN
Gregory, Francis M., III ... Las Vegas, NV
Gregory, Fred ... Farmington Hills, MI
Gregory, Fred F. ... Los Angeles, CA
Gregory, Fred H. ... Bloomington, IN
Gregory, Gary H. ... Manchester, KY
Gregory, Gena ... Little Rock, AR
Gregory, Geo. T., Jr. ... Chester, SC
Gregory, George D. ... Lexington, KY
Gregory, George G. ... Irwindale, CA
Gregory, George W. ... Birmingham, MI
Gregory, George W., Jr. ... Cheraw, SC
Gregory, Gilbert Ernest ... Fort Scott, KS
Gregory, Glenn W. ... Denver, CO
Gregory, Gordon A. ... Detroit, MI
Gregory & Gregory ... Osborne, KS
Gregory & Gregory ... Memphis, TN
Gregory, Gregory P. ... Cudahy, WI
Gregory, Grier J. ... Metairie, LA
Gregory, Gwendolyn H. ... Middleburg, VA
Gregory, H. Watt, III ... Little Rock, AR
Gregory, Hardy, Jr. ... Cordele, GA
Gregory, Harry B., Jr. ... Columbia, SC
Gregory, Heidi Schult ... Rochester, NY
Gregory, Helaine A. ... Hartford, CT
Gregory, Helen A. ... Jamaica, NY
Gregory, Herman Edward, III
Cleveland, OH
Gregory, Holly J. ... New York, NY
Gregory, J. Gordon ... Pittsburg, KS
Gregory, J. Mitchell, Jr.
Oklahoma City, OK
Gregory, J. Scott ... Dallas, TX
Gregory, Jackson V. ... Beaufort, SC
Gregory, Jacob G. ... Los Angeles, CA
Gregory, Jacqueline M. ... Hollywood, FL
Gregory, James D. ... Encino, CA
Gregory, James D., A Professional Corporation
Encino, CA
Gregory, James E. ... Columbus, GA
Gregory, James F. ... Chicopee, MA
Gregory, James G. ... St. Charles, MO
Gregory, James J. ... El Cajon, CA
Gregory, James J. ... Virginia Beach, VA
Gregory, James L., III ... New York, NY
Gregory, James P. ... Denver, CO
Gregory, James P. ... Danbury, CT
Gregory, James R. ... Parsippany, NJ
Gregory, James R. ... Portland, OR
Gregory, James R., A Professional Corporation
Parsippany, NJ
Gregory, James R., Sr. ... Louisville, KY
Gregory, Jana T. ... Portland, OR
Gregory, Jane Dillard ... Baltimore, MD
Gregory, Janet M. ... Grand Forks, ND
Gregory, Janine L. ... Washington, DC
Gregory, Jas. V. ... Fresno, CA
Gregory, Jay S. ... Boston, MA
Gregory, Jeanne Burton ... Nashville, TN
Gregory, Jill S. ... Tahoe City, CA
Gregory, Jimmie R. ... Boynton Beach, FL
Gregory, Joe F. ... Fort Scott, KS
Gregory, John A. ... Okolona, MS
Gregory, John A., Jr. ... Murray, KY
Gregory, John C., Jr. ... Philadelphia, PA
Gregory, John D. ... Hempstead, NY
Gregory, John D. ... Columbia, SC
Gregory, John H. ... Miami, FL
Gregory, John J. ... San Francisco, CA
Gregory, John, Jr. ... Salem, VA
Gregory, John L., III ... Martinsville, VA
Stuart, VA
Gregory, John M. ... Palo Alto, CA
Gregory, Johnny P. ... Little Rock, AR
Gregory & Johnson, P.C. ... Houston, TX
Gregory, Joseph E. ... Uniondale, NY
Gregory, Joseph M., III ... Dallas, TX
Gregory, Joseph W. ... Little Rock, AR
Gregory, Julia O. ... Cambridge, MA
Gregory, Julian A. ... Wilton, CT
New York, NY
Gregory, Julie A. ... Louisville, KY
Gregory, Julie A. ... Middlesex, NJ
Gregory, Karen J. ... Austin, TX
Gregory, Karin A. ... Boston, MA
Gregory, Katherine S. ... Salt Lake City, UT
Gregory, Kathleen Burdic Goshgarian
Pinedale, CA
Gregory, Keith E. ... Henderson, NV
Gregory, Keith M. ... Irvine, CA
Gregory and Kieltyka, P.C. ... Troy, MI
Gregory & Kientz ... Houston, TX
Gregory, Kimbrough ... Memphis, TN
Gregory, Kirsten L. ... Lincoln, NE
Gregory, Kossen ... Roanoke, VA
Gregory, Laura K. ... Northport, AL
Gregory, Laura Meyer ... Boston, MA
Gregory, Laurie Beth ... Anchorage, AK
Gregory, Leo ... Minneapolis, MN
Gregory, Lewis J. ... Indianapolis, IN
Gregory, Lisa M. LeGrand
New York, NY
Gregory, Lois J. ... Trenton, NJ
Gregory, Lois Jane
Commodity Futures Trading Commission,
Division of Trading and Markets, GV
Gregory, Lori A. ... Kansas City, MO
Gregory, Louis P. ... Plano, TX
Gregory, Luther W. ... Centreville, MD
Gregory, Margaret E. ... Colorado Springs, CO
Gregory, Mark C. ... Wilmington, DE
Gregory, Mark S. ... Stamford, CT
Gregory, Mary Jane ... Phoenix, AZ
Gregory, Mary Millwood ... Houston, TX
Gregory, Mary Volk ... Denver, CO
Gregory, Matthew R. ... San Francisco, CA
Gregory, Matthew Theodore ... Saipan, TT
Gregory, Maura N. ... New York, NY
Gregory, Mel ... Wichita, KS
Gregory, Michael E. ... Crestwood, KY
Gregory, Michael H. ... Birmingham, AL
Gregory, Michael L. ... Las Vegas, NM
Gregory, Michael W., Jr. ... Cleveland, OH
Gregory, Michelle D. ... Palo Alto, CA
Gregory, Mike ... Denton, TX
Gregory, Milan K. ... North Brunswick, NJ
Gregory, Moore, Jeakle, Heinen, Ellison &
Brooks, P.C. ... Detroit, MI
Gregory, Myra ... Port Arthur, TX
Gregory, Ned, II ... Lancaster, SC
Gregory, Nicholas A. ... Los Angeles, CA
Gregory, O. Lee ... Conway, NH
Gregory, Oliver W., Jr. ... Chicago, IL
Gregory, Patricia Baldwin ... Deerfield, IL
Gregory, Patrick J. ... Overland Park, KS
Gregory, Patrick L. ... Mt. Orab, OH
Gregory, Paul J. ... Dana Point, CA
Gregory, Paul M. ... Buffalo, NY
Gregory, Paul S. ... Osborne, KS
Gregory, Paul T. ... Houston, TX
Gregory, Peter D. ... Department of Justice,
Immigration and Naturalization Service, GV
Gregory, Ralph Ray, Jr. ... Houston, TX
Gregory, Randall C. ... Baton Rouge, LA
Gregory, Randy A. ... Spokane, WA
Gregory, Randy S. ... Fayetteville, NC
Gregory, Raymond F., Law Offices of
New York, NY
South Salem, NY
Gregory, Raymond G. ... New York, NY
Gregory, Raymond L., II ... Houston, TX
Gregory, Rebecca A. ... Dallas, TX
Gregory, Regina Naylor ... Houston, TX
Gregory, Richard B. ... Las Cruces, NM
Gregory, Richard B., P.C.
Las Cruces, NM
Gregory, Richard F. ... East Islip, NY
Gregory, Richard H., III ... Providence, RI
Gregory, Richard L., Jr. ... Palo Alto, CA
Gregory, Richard W. ... Glen Allen, VA
Richmond, VA
Gregory, Robert A. ... Westfield, NJ
Gregory, Robert B. ... Damariscotta, ME
Gregory, Robert E., Jr. ... Mission, KS
Gregory, Robert F. ... Colchester, CT
Gregory, Robert H. ... North Little Rock, AR
St. Louis, MO
Gregory, Robert H. ... Miami, FL
Gregory, Robert H. ... East Alton, IL
Gregory, Robert J.
Equal Employment Opportunity
Commission,
Office of the General Counsel, GV
Gregory, Robert L. ... Enid, OK
Gregory, Robert Reed ... Louisville, KY
Gregory, Robin N. ... New York, NY
Gregory, Rodney G. ... Jacksonville, FL
Gregory, Rodney G., P.A., Law Office of
Jacksonville, FL
Gregory, Roger L. ... Richmond, VA
Gregory, Rona H. ... Boston, MA
Gregory, Ronald D. ... Lynnwood, WA
Gregory, Ronald W. ... Tampa, FL
Gregory, Russell ... Farmington Hills, MI
Gregory, Russell, Prof. Corp., The Law Offices
of ... Farmington Hills, MI
Gregory, Sandra Eubank ... Birmingham, AL
Gregory, Stephen C. ... Vienna, VA
Gregory, Stephen C., P.C. ... Vienna, VA
Gregory, Steven C. ... Louisville, KY
Gregory, Steven P. ... Tuscaloosa, AL
Gregory, Steven P., P.C. ... Tuscaloosa, AL
Gregory, Sue Ann ... San Antonio, TX
Gregory, Susan B. ... Fishers, IN
Gregory, Susan D. ... Atlanta, GA
Gregory, Susan Lambiase ... Philadelphia, PA
Gregory, Susan Reeves ... Memphis, TN
Gregory, Suzanne ... Buffalo, NY
Gregory, Terry D. ... Tullahoma, TN
Gregory, Theodore C. ... Wilmington, DE
Gregory, Theopalis K. ... Wilmington, DE
Gregory, Theresa Marie ... Jacksonville, FL
Gregory, Thomas Adam ... Richmond, VA
Gregory, Thomas H. ... Canton, OH
Gregory, Thomas J. ... St. Louis, MO
Gregory, Thomas J. ... Philadelphia, PA
Gregory, Toy R., Jr. ... Las Vegas, NV
Gregory, Victoria E. ... Minneapolis, MN
Gregory, W. Stanley ... Montgomery, AL
Gregory, W. Wallace, Jr. ... Charlotte, NC
Gregory, Waldron A. ... Palo Alto, CA
Gregory, Walter E. ... Los Angeles, CA
Gregory, Wayne R. ... Pasadena, CA
Gregory, William A. ... Atlanta, GA
Gregory, William D. ... Mount Vernon, KY
Gregory, William E. ... Miami, FL
Gregory, William H., II ... Albany, GA
Gregory, William L. ... Pana, IL
Gregory, William N., Jr. ... Glen Allen, VA
Gregory, William P. ... Tampa, FL
Gregory, William P., Jr. ... Newark, NJ
Gregory, William S. ... Sacramento, CA
Gregory, William S., A L.C.
Sacramento, CA
Gregson, George O. ... Saugus, MA
Gregson, George O., P.C. ... Saugus, MA
Gregson and Pixler, P.C. ... Denver, CO
Gregson, Richard J. ... Minneapolis, MN
Gregson, Ronald E. ... Denver, CO
Greguras, Fred M. ... Palo Alto, CA
Gregus, Tara Leiby ... Chicago, IL
Grehan, H. Hughes ... New Orleans, LA
Grehan, Kevin J. ... New York, NY
Grehan, Susan M. ... New Orleans, LA
Greher, Lawrence S. ... Albuquerque, NM
Greher, Warren ... New Windsor, NY
Grehlinger, Christine A. ... Cherry Hill, NJ
Greiber, John Ralph, Jr. ... Annapolis, MD
Greider, Deborah S. ... St. Louis, MO
Greider, John K. ... St. Louis, MO
Greidinger, Marc A. ... Columbia, MD
Greif, Alan S. ... New York, NY
Greif, Allen D. ... Towson, MD
Greif, Arthur J. ... DeLand, FL
Greif, Arthur J. ... Bangor, ME
Greif, David D. ... New York, NY
Greif, Edward L. ... New York, NY
Greif, Gary W. ... Austin, TX
Greif, Gary W., P.C. Law Offices of
Austin, TX
Greif, Lisa C. ... Medford, OR
Greif & Litwak, P.C. ... Boston, MA
Greif, Lloyd ... Los Angeles, CA
Greif, Michele S. ... Washington, DC
Greif, Murray Wm. ... Warminster, PA
Greif, Paul Bernard ... Evansville, IN
Greif, Robert C. ... Springfield, MA
Greif, Steven D. ... Baldwin, NY
Greif, Thomas J. ... Portland, OR
Greif, Thomas J., P.C. ... Portland, OR
Greif, William G. ... Washington, DC
Greifer, David ... New York, NY
Greiff, Brenda S. ... New York, NY
Greiff, Murray ... Los Angeles, CA
Greiff, Samuel ... Great Neck, NY
Greiff, Thomas E. ... Valley Village, CA
Greifinger, David R. ... Santa Monica, CA
Greifinger, Richard A. ... Newark, NJ
Greifzu, Carl W. ... Pasadena, CA
Greig, Brian S. ... Austin, TX
Greig, Denise A. ... Baltimore, MD
Greig, Donald A. ... Vancouver, WA
Greig, George A. ... Allegan, MI
Greig, Hal ... Clovis, NM
Greig, Karen K. ... Bellevue, WA
Greig, Richard A. ... Evanston, IL
Greig, Robert T. ... New York, NY
Greig, Ronald B. ... Honolulu, HI
Greig, Tanya C. ... Los Angeles, CA
Greig, William H. ... Clovis, NM
Greigg, Edwin E. ... Falls Church, VA
Greigg & Greigg, P.L.L.C. ... Falls Church, VA
Greigg, Ronald E. ... Falls Church, VA
Greil, Ralph H. ... Atlanta, GA
Greilsheimer, James G. ... New York, NY
Greilsheimer, William H. ... New York, NY
Greilsheimer, Jeffrey M. ... New York, NY
Greim, David M. ... Columbus, OH
Greim, John Karl, Jr. ... Cranston, RI
Greiman, Alan J. ... Chicago, IL
Greiman, Beau T. ... Des Moines, IA
Greiman, Gerald Phillip ... St. Louis, MO
Greiman, Murray ... Jersey City, NJ
Greiman, Virginia A.
Department of Justice, GV
Greimann, Lyndon ... Rochester, MN
Grein, David E. ... Portland, OR
Grein, Frederick H., Jr. ... Boston, MA
Grein, Mary Lavelle ... Carle Place, NY
Grein, Nathan Leonard ... Eau Claire, WI
Greiner, Brett R. ... Edison, NJ
Greiner, Charles R. ... Syracuse, NY
Greiner, Daniel James
Department of Justice, Civil Division, GV
Greiner, Gallagher & Cavanaugh, LLC
Parsippany, NJ
Greiner, Gordon G. ... Denver, CO
Greiner, Gregory F. ... Des Moines, IA
Greiner, James R. ... Sacramento, CA
Greiner, Jeffrey H. ... Sylmar, CA
Greiner, Jill ... Reno, NV
Greiner, John C. ... Cincinnati, OH
Greiner, John K. ... Greensburg, PA
Greiner, Kathryn R. ... Lancaster, PA
Greiner Law Offices, P.C. ... Bethesda, MD
Greiner, Mark L. ... Council Bluffs, IA
Greiner, Mark W. ... Minneapolis, MN
Greiner, Mary L. ... Dallas, TX
Greiner, Mary Lynn, (Law Office Of)
Seattle, WA
Greiner, Matthew B. ... Washington, DC
Greiner, Paul B. ... Ridgway, PA
Greiner, Paul D. ... Ogden, UT
Greiner, Paul H. ... Los Angeles, CA
Greiner, Richard C. ... Yakima, WA
Greiner, Richard G. ... Lancaster, PA
Greiner, Richard R. ... Yakima, WA
Greiner, Robert P. ... Malibu, CA
Greiner, Rodger S. ... Encino, CA
Greiner, Scott P. ... Denver, CO
Greiner, Stephen R. ... Bethesda, MD
Greiner, Stephen W. ... New York, NY
Greiner, Ted R. ... Cleveland, OH
Greiner, Terrence A. ... Buffalo, NY
Greiner, Thomas C., Jr. ... Rochester, NY
Greiner, Timothy R. ... Parsippany, NJ
Greiner, William R. ... Buffalo, NY
Greinert, Jean Graziani ... Grand Island, NY
Greines, Irving H. ... Beverly Hills, CA
Greines, Martin, Stein & Richland LLP
Beverly Hills, CA
Los Angeles, CA
Greinke, Gary A. ... West Bloomfield, MI
Greiper, Ellen H. ... New York, NY
Greisamer, John R. ... Allentown, PA
Greisberger, John L. ... Pittsford, NY
Greisen, Cary P. ... Fair Oaks, CA
Greisen Law Corporation ... Fair Oaks, CA
Greisen, Paul H. ... Fair Oaks, CA
Greisen, Paula D. ... Denver, CO
Greising, Robert A. ... Indianapolis, IN
Greising, Robert M., Law Offices, P.A.
Waterville, MN
Greisler, Nicholas J. ... Albany, NY
Greisman, Jared ... Red Bank, NJ
New York, NY
Greisman, Julius M. ... Washington, DC
Greisman, Kenneth D. ... North Chicago, IL
Greisman, Lois C.
Federal Trade Commission,
Office of the Chairman, GV
Greismann, Zvi ... Rockville, MD
Greiss, Jill B. ... New York, NY
Greiss, Rory A. ... New York, NY
Greissman, Scott ... New York, NY
Greiter, Charles L. ... Briarcliff Manor, NY
Greiter, Gay Lynn ... Minneapolis, MN
Greiter, William Daly ... New York, NY
Greitzer, Betty F. ... Clark, NJ
Greitzer, Dianne ... Philadelphia, PA
Greitzer, Herman S. ... New York, NY
Greitzer, Howard L. ... Fort Lauderdale, FL
Greitzer, Joseph M. ... Philadelphia, PA
Greitzer and Locks ... Cherry Hill, NJ
Philadelphia, PA
Greitzer, Martin ... Philadelphia, PA
Greitzer, Nathan ... Los Angeles, CA
Greitzer, Shirley T. ... Treasury Department,
Office of Regulations and Rulings, GV
Greive, Edward G. ... Akron, OH
Greive, John J. ... Louisville, KY
Greive, R. R." Bob " ... Seattle, WA
Greive, Stacy K. ... Louisville, KY
Greiveldinger, Harold F. ... Racine, WI
Greives, James W. ... Lafayette, IN
Greiwe, Donald G. ... Tampa, FL
Greiwe, Nancy S. ... Cincinnati, OH
Greiwe, Thomas H. ... Tampa, FL
Greiwe, Thomas H., P.A. ... Tampa, FL
Grekin, Joseph K. ... Detroit, MI
Grekin, Nancy Nissen ... Honolulu, HI
Grele, Robert F. ... Greenwich, CT
Grelecki, Carol ... Roseland, NJ
Grelick, Susan J. ... Williamsville, NY
Grell, Barbara Mason ... Babylon, NY
Grell, Christopher E., Law Offices of
San Francisco, CA
Grell, Glen R. ... Harrisburg, PA
Grell, Jeffrey E. ... Minneapolis, MN
Grell, William H. ... Des Moines, IA
Grella, Paul J. ... Boston, MA
Grella, Robert ... Brooklyn, NY
Grella, Thomas C. ... Asheville, NC
Grellas, George ... San Jose, CA
Grelle, Lawrence E. ... Chicago, IL
Hoffman Estates, IL
Grelle, Wm. A. ... Fort Myers, FL

Greller, Barry R. ... St. Paul, MN
Greller, Daniel M. ... Pasadena, CA
Greller, Leonore M. ... New York, NY
Greller, Stephen L. ... Carmel, NY
Poughkeepsie, NY
Grellman, Jack S. ... Reno, NV
Grellmann, Dietmar A. ... Sacramento, CA
Grellner, Cynthia A. ... Tampa, FL
Grellner, John C. ... St. Louis, MO
Grello, Nicholas J., Jr. ... Hartford, CT
Gremel, Andrew Richard ... Ann Arbor, MI
Gremer, John F. ... Chicago, IL
Gremillion, Charles C. ... New Orleans, LA
Gremillion, Charles M. ... Bunkie, LA
Gremillion, Craig D. ... Baton Rouge, LA
Gremillion, Field V., III ... Alexandria, LA
Gremillion, Frank J. ... Baton Rouge, LA
Gremillion, Glenn B. ... Ferriday, LA
Gremillion, Grace Phyllis ... Covington, LA
Gremillion, Gregory G. ... Gretna, LA
Gremillion, L. Todd, (P.C.) ... Houston, TX
Gremillion, Pierre F. ... Metairie, LA
Gremillion, Shannon J. ... Lafayette, LA
Gremillion, William N., Jr. ... San Antonio, TX
Gremillot, Anne M. ... Mineola, NY
Gremmels, L. Berenice ... Chicago, IL
Gremminger, Gary R. ... Moorestown, NJ
Philadelphia, PA
Gremminger, Steven L. ... Washington, DC
Gremo, Michelle Leigh ... Somerville, MA
Grems, Kelly Compton ... Washington, DC
Gremse, Gail R. ... New York, NY
Grenader, Harry B. ... Houston, TX
Grenadier, Ilona Ely Freedman
Alexandria, VA
Grenadier, Simpson & Duffett, P.C.
Alexandria, VA
Fairfax, VA
Grenard, Frank M. ... Des Moines, IA
Grenauer, Regina M. ... Columbus, OH
Grenci, Salvatore A. ... Hauppauge, NY
Grenda, Ronald T. ... Chicago, IL
Grendell, Henry G. ... Cleveland, OH
Greneker, Samuel F. ... Brunswick, GA
Tifton, GA
Greneker, Samuel F. ... Valdosta, GA
Grenell, Barry Alan ... Sacramento, CA
Grenell, David J. ... Wickliffe, OH
Grenen & Birsic, P.C. ... Pittsburgh, PA
Grenen, James F. ... Pittsburgh, PA
Grenen, Mary Dice ... Pittsburgh, PA
Grenert, Gerald T. ... Van Nuys, CA
Grenert, Jennifer G. ... New York, NY
Grenert, Michael E. ... New York, NY
Grenfell, George A., Jr. ... Fresno, CA
Grenfell, James B. ... Jackson, MS
Grenfell, John M. ... San Francisco, CA
Grenfell, Kenneth H. ... Missoula, MT
Grenfell, Robert C. ... Jackson, MS
Grenfell, Sledge & Stevens ... Jackson, MS
Grenga, Paul A. ... Niagara Falls, NY
Grenga, Terry A. ... Canfield, OH
Grenham, E. Bradley ... Portland, OR
Grenham, Robert E. ... Norwood, MA
Grenhart, Robert F. ... Blackwood, NJ
Grenier, Alan L. ... Danvers, MA
Grenier, Antoinette E. ... North Haven, CT
Grenier, Arthur S. ... Dallas, TX
Grenier, Christian A. ... New York, NY
Grenier, Edward J., Jr. ... Washington, DC
Grenier, John B. ... Birmingham, AL
Grenier, John E. ... Birmingham, AL
Grenier, Marc J. ... Norwalk, CT
Grenier & McCarron ... Danvers, MA
Grenier, Normand G. ... Houston, TX
Grenier, Peter C. ... Washington, DC
Grenier, Robert J. ... Burlington, VT
Grenier, Robert J. ... Mercer Island, WA
Grenig, Jay E. ... Milwaukee, WI
Grening, Alan T. ... New Brunswick, NJ
Greninger, Ronald P. ... Orlando, FL
Grenis, Peter S. ... Syracuse, NY
Grenke, John E. ... Bloomfield Hills, MI
Grenker, Adam M. ... New York, NY
Grenko, John J. ... Reading, PA
Grenkowicz, Dennis P. ... Alpena, MI
Grenley, Gary I. ... Portland, OR
Grenley, Henry W. ... Seattle, WA
Grenley, Neal F. ... New York, NY
Grenley, Rotenberg, Evans, Bragg & Bodie, P.C. ... Portland, OR
Grenn, Robert A. ... Dearborn, MI
Grennan & Gossett ... Georgetown, OH
Grennan, James G. ... Oklahoma City, OK
Grennan, Nancy Buanno ... Seattle, WA
Grennan, Philip B. ... Seattle, WA
Grennan, Terry J. ... Omaha, NE
Grennan, Thomas A. ... Omaha, NE
Grennan, Thomas F. ... Georgetown, OH
Grennell, John C. ... Angola, NY
Grenner, William B. ... Irvine, CA
Grenoble, Scott L. ... Lebanon, PA
Grenough, Claudia K. ... Louisville, KY
Grenrock, Susan Paula ... Chicago, IL
Grens, Paul J. ... Manitowoc, WI
Grensky, Ronald D. ... Medford, OR
Grensky, Stephen R. ... Portland, OR
Grenthal, Michael J. ... Tallman, NY
Grenvich, Richard S. ... Chicago, IL
Grenville, Edward S. ... San Francisco, CA
Grenz, Donavin L. ... Linton, ND
Grenz, Eugene Z. ... Albany, NY
Grenzebach, Eric L. ... Springfield, IL
Gres, Viktoria L. ... Key Biscayne, FL
Gresalfi, Richard S. ... New York, NY
Gresback, Timothy Howard
Coeur d'Alene, ID
Gresch, Robert D. ... Houston, TX
Greschler, Ira E. ... Boulder, CO
Greschler, Irwin ... North Woodmere, NY
Greschner, Frederick T., Jr.
New Orleans, LA
Gresek, Dean C. ... Trenton, NJ
Gresens & Gillen LLP ... Buffalo, NY
Gresens, James W. ... Buffalo, NY
Gresens, John J. ... Minneapolis, MN
Gresens, Larry W. ... Mukilteo, WA
Gresens, Michael D. ... Lansing, MI
Gresenz, Kurt G. ... Los Angeles, CA
Greseth, Steven Paul ... Minneapolis, MN
Gresh, Daniel T.
Department of Labor, GV
Gresh, Marlene Triggs ... Brighton, CO
Gresham, A. Brooks ... Los Angeles, CA
Gresham, Allen B. ... Riverside, CA
San Bernardino, CA
Gresham, Claude H. ... Dallas, TX
Gresham, Dan R. ... Atlanta, GA
Gresham, Darryl D. ... Memphis, TN
Gresham, David A. ... Indianapolis, IN
Gresham, David M. ... Quincy, MA
Gresham, Davis, Gregory, Worthy & Moore, A Professional Corporation
San Antonio, TX
Gresham, James E. ... Harrison, AR
Gresham, John A. ... New York, NY
Gresham, John K. ... Richmond, TX
Gresham, John Sanford ... Riverwoods, IL
Gresham, John W. ... Charlotte, NC
Gresham, Katharine B
Securities and Exchange Commission, Office of the General Counsel, GV
Gresham, Kenneth M., Jr. ... Knoxville, TN
Gresham & Kirkpatrick ... Harrison, AR
Gresham, Lowell W. ... Phoenix, AZ
Gresham, Ollie W. ... Tulsa, OK
Gresham, Robert L. ... Centerville, TX
Gresham, Savage, Nolan & Tilden, LLP
Riverside, CA
San Bernardino, CA
Gresham, Spencer A.
Colorado Springs, CO
Gresham, Thomas C. ... Richmond, VA
Gresham, Thomas D.
Colorado Springs, CO
Gresham, Timothy W. ... Abingdon, VA
Gresham, Travis A., Jr. ... Fort Myers, FL
Gresham, W. Lee, III ... Birmingham, AL
Gresham, William B., III
Poplar Bluff, MO
Gresham, William H., Jr. ... Clarksdale, MS
Gresham, Willis E., Jr. ... Lubbock, TX
Gresham, Zane O. ... San Francisco, CA
Greshin, Benjamin ... Smithtown, NY
Greshin, Ziegler & Pruzansky
Smithtown, NY
Gresk, Paul D. ... Indianapolis, IN
Gresko, Gary E. ... Cleveland, OH
Gresko, Janice L. ... Columbus, OH
Grespin, John R. ... Harrisburg, PA
Gress, Alvin D. ... Sacramento, CA
Gress, Gerald K. ... Santa Ana, CA
Gress, James L. ... Portland, OR
Gress, Jodi M. ... Miami, FL
Gressel, Gerry S. ... Cincinnati, OH
Gressel, Lisa V. ... Cincinnati, OH
Gressel, Michele M. ... Fairfield, OH
Gressen, Michael S. ... Philadelphia, PA
Gressen, Shelley Stasson ... Harrisburg, PA
Gresser, James A. ... Department of Justice, Civil Division, GV
Gresser, Julian ... Sausalito, CA
Gresser, Lawrence T. ... Chicago, IL
Gresser, Lawrence T. ... New York, NY
Gresser, Lawrence T., Jr. ... Douglaston, NY
Gressette, Lawrence M., Jr. ... Columbia, SC
Gressin, Seena D.
Federal Trade Commission, Bureau of Consumer Protection, GV
Gressler, Eric A. ... Los Angeles, CA
Gressley, Kaplin & Parker ... Monroe, MI
Toledo, OH
Gressley, Lynn H. ... Toledo, OH
Gressly, Brian K. ... Miamisburg, OH
Gressman, Eric K. ... Miami, FL
Gressman, Eugene ... Washington, DC
Gressman, William E.
Office of Government Ethics, Office of General Counsel and Legal Policy, GV
Greszes, Mario ... Washington, DC
Greszko, Timothy J.
Department of Housing and Urban Development, Board of Contract Appeals, GV
Greta, Carol J. ... Newton, IA
Greta, Richard ... Los Angeles, CA
Gretchko, Lisa Sommers ... Detroit, MI
Gretchko, Steven Michael ... Detroit, MI
Grete, William B. ... Jackson, MS
Greteman, Julie A. ... Carroll, IA
Greten, Richard W. ... Manchester, NH
Gretencord, Laura S. ... Indianapolis, IN
Greth, Phillip A. ... Columbus, OH
Grethen, Charles B. ... Purcell, OK
Grethen, Mary C. ... Arlington, TX
Grether, Henry M., Jr. ... Carlsbad, CA
Grethen, John M. ... Somis, CA
Gretick, Anthony L. ... Bryan, OH
Gretkowski, Susan M. ... Montpelier, VT
Gretler, William E. ... Sterling, IL
Greto, Albert M. ... Media, PA
Gretz, Susan C. ... St. Paul, MN
Gretzinger, John H. ... Grand Rapids, MI
Gretzinger, Norman A. ... New York, NY
Greubel, Michele M. ... Des Moines, IA
Greubel, Stephen J. ... Tulsa, OK
Greul, Mark R. ... Omaha, NE
Greulich, John E. ... Cincinnati, OH
Greuling, Jill Ellen ... Los Angeles, CA
Greuner, John, Law Office of
Grapevine, TX
Greupner, James R. ... Minneapolis, MN
Greusel, Jamie B. ... Marco Island, FL
Grev, Douglas J. ... Minneapolis, MN
Greve, Claire H. ... Sacramento, CA
Greve, Clifford, Wengel & Paras, LLP
Sacramento, CA
Greve, Guy R. ... Bay City, MI
Greve, James T. ... Chicago, IL
Greve, J.E. Barry ... Dallas, TX
Greve, John H. ... Northwood, IA
Greve, Laura G. ... Memphis, TN
Greve, Marlita A. ... Davenport, IA
Greve, Ronald H. ... Roseville, MI
Greve, Thomas F. ... Cleveland, OH
Greve, Wendy E. ... Charleston, WV
Grevelle, James V. ... Dallas, TX
Grevelle, James V., P.C. ... Dallas, TX
Grevemberg, James J., Jr. ... New Orleans, LA
Grevemberg, James T. ... Metairie, LA
Greven, David R. ... Annandale, MN
Grevengoed, Glenn B. ... Chicago, IL
Grever, Mollie K. ... Columbus, OH
Grever, Thomas J. ... Columbus, OH
Grevers, Jean B. ... Somers, NY
Grevey, Bryan G. ... Hamilton, OH
Grevey, Helen A. ... Albuquerque, NM
Grevey, Norman G. ... Hamilton, OH
Grevin, Philippe ... Costa Mesa, CA
Grevior, Arnold, (Chartered)
Fort Lauderdale, FL
Grevior & Jordan ... Fort Lauderdale, FL
Grevior, Jordan & Brannon ... Lake City, FL
Grew, B. Carlton ... Salem, OR
Grew, Frank J. ... Long Beach, CA
Grew, Joseph F. ... Osterville, MA
Grew, Robert R. ... New York, NY
Grewach, Edward J. ... Troy, MO
Grewach, Lawrence D. ... St. Paul, MN
Grewal & Associates, P.C. ... East Lansing, MI
Grewal, Manvir S. ... East Lansing, MI
Grewal, Monica ... Lexington, MA
Grewal, Paul S. ... San Francisco, CA
Grewal, Savi ... Sandpoint, ID
Grewal, Shivbir S. ... Newport Beach, CA
Grewe, Gerald M. ... Englewood, CO
Grewe, Todd M. ... Portland, OR
Grewell, Kevin C. ... Exton, PA
Grewing, Terry Sue ... Houston, TX
Grey & Arsenault, P.C. ... Virginia Beach, VA
Grey, Beth Eiseman ... Highland Park, IL
Grey, Betsy N. ... Tempe, AZ
Grey, Charles E., Jr. ... Baton Rouge, LA
Grey, Christina C. ... Knoxville, TN
Grey, David M. ... Los Angeles, CA
Grey, David M., & Associates ... Irvine, CA
Grey, Erin L. ... Los Angeles, CA
Grey, Francis J., Jr. ... Mount Laurel, NJ
Philadelphia, PA
Grey, Frank I., (P.A.)
New Port Richey, FL
Grey, George R. ... Chicago, IL
Grey, Herbert G. ... Beaverton, OR
Grey, Hyacinth R. ... Washington, DC
Grey, John J. ... San Rafael, CA
Grey, Jordan A. ... Chicago, IL
Grey, Joseph ... Wilmington, DE
Grey, Julie Fairchild ... Hartford, CT
Grey, Kenneth A. ... Frankfort, IL
Joliet, IL
Grey, Kerry Lynn ... Richmond, VA
Grey, Lawrence ... Nelsonville, OH
Grey, Maurice W. ... New York, NY
Grey, Michael E. ... Virginia Beach, VA
Grey, Nathaniel I. ... Chicago, IL
Grey, Nathaniel I., P.C. ... Chicago, IL
Grey, Norman L. ... Enid, OK
Grey, Rebecca ... San Francisco, CA
Grey, Richard ... San Francisco, CA
Grey, Richard E. ... San Diego, CA
Grey, Richard N. ... Encino, CA
Grey, Robert ... Melville, NY
Grey, Robert E. ... Farmingdale, NY
Grey, Robert J. ... Allentown, PA
Grey, Robert J., Jr. ... Richmond, VA
Grey, Robert T., Jr.
Department of State, GV
Grey, Samuel T.
Christiansted, St. Croix, VI
Grey, Sharon Wolf ... San Mateo, CA
Grey, Steven L. ... Buena Park, CA
Grey, Susan P. ... Milpitas, CA
Grey, Teresa A. ... West Chester, PA
Grey, Thomas C. ... Palo Alto, CA
Grey, William L. ... Somers, NY
Greydanus, Aryon ... Okemos, MI
Greydanus, Samuel E., III ... Randolph, MA
Greyf, Jane ... New York, NY
Greyson, Amy ... Anaheim, CA
Greyson, Murray ... Salinas, CA
Greyson, Phoebe Anne ... Boulder, CO
Greystone, Jonathan J. ... Philadelphia, PA
Greytok, John ... Austin, TX
Grezik, Anthony J. ... Daytona Beach, FL
Grezlak, Theodore A., Jr. ... Jersey City, NJ
Grguric, Robert M. ... Orlando, FL
Grguric, Sherry ... Los Angeles, CA
Grib, Philip J. ... Chicago, IL
Gribb, Jeffrey H. ... Harrisburg, PA
Gribbell, Justin J. ... Deshler, OH
Gribbell & Sunderman ... Deshler, OH
Gribben, Gregory W. ... Rochester, NY
Gribben, Thomas E. ... Berwyn, IL
Gribben, Walter P. ... Newport Beach, CA
Gribben, William ... New York, NY
Gribbin, Arthur Joseph, III ... New York, NY
Gribbin, Burns & Eide ... Watertown, SD
Gribbin, D.J., IV ... Washington, DC
Gribbin, Laura L. ... Columbus, OH
Gribbin, Leo E. ... York, PA
Gribble, Bradley J. ... Whittier, CA
Gribble, Charles E. ... Des Moines, IA
Gribble, Don D., II ... Wichita, KS
Gribble, Gayle J. ... San Francisco, CA
Gribble, H. Andrea
Federal Deposit Insurance Corporation, Compliance and Enforcement Section, GV
Gribble, J. Steven ... Port Charlotte, FL
Gribble, Jerry L. ... Bryan, TX
Gribble, Joseph J. ... Farmington, NM
Gribbon, Daniel M. ... Washington, DC
Gribbons, Francis X. ... Holden, MA
Gribbs, Roman S. ... Detroit, MI
Gribens, Jacqueline A. ... Lowell, MA
Gribetz, Judah ... New York, NY
Gribetz, Richard I. ... New York, NY
Gribetz, Uriel E. ... White Plains, NY
Gribin, Michael ... New York, NY
Gribko, R. Joseph ... New York, NY
Gribler, Michael A. ... Cincinnati, OH
Griblin, Monica K. ... Phoenix, AZ
Griboff, Howard
Federal Communications Commission, International Bureau, GV
Gribok, Stephan P. ... Philadelphia, PA
Gribouski, James ... Worcester, MA
Gribouski, James J., Law Offices of
Worcester, MA
Gribow, Dale S. ... Palm Desert, CA
Gricar, Ray Frank ... Bellefonte, PA
Grice, Benning M., Jr. ... Atlanta, GA
Grice, Charles A. ... Nashville, TN
Grice, James W. ... Kansas City, MO
Grice, Kristen Lewis ... Atlanta, GA
Grice, Michael W. ... Auburn Hills, MI
Grice, Randy L. ... North Little Rock, AR
Grice, Richard W. ... Atlanta, GA
Grice, Todd E. ... Elkhart, IN
Grice, Warren C. ... Macon, GA
Gricius, Ronald J. ... Mount Clemens, MI
Gricius, Ronald J., P.C. ... Mount Clemens, MI
Gricks, Thomas C., III ... Pittsburgh, PA
Gricks, Timothy J. ... Pittsburgh, PA
Gridelli, George R. ... Mineola, NY
Gridelli, Paul C. ... Chicago, IL
Oak Park, IL
Grider, C. Alan ... Clarkston, WA
Grider, Hal L. ... Altus, OK
Grider, James A. ... Louisville, KY
Grider, Katrina ... Houston, TX
Grider Law Firm, PLC ... Pocahontas, AR
Grider, M. Joseph ... Pocahontas, AR
Grider, Mark K. ... Sandy, OR
Grider, Mark K., P.C. ... Sandy, OR
Grider, Murrey L. ... Pocahontas, AR
Grider, Ralph H. ... Scottsboro, AL
Grider, Robert C., III ... Jackson, MS
Grider, Sharon D. ... Ada, MI
Grider, Stephen C. ... Tampa, FL
Grider, Steve C., P.A. ... Tampa, FL
Grider, Wm. Jonathan ... Louisville, KY
Gridley, Bruce C. ... Los Angeles, CA
Gridley, Daniel Duke, Jr.
Oklahoma City, OK
Gridley, Doreen J. ... Indianapolis, IN
Gridley, Findley P. ... Layton, UT
Ogden, UT
Gridley, John H. ... Dundee, NY
Gridley, Michael A. ... San Rafael, CA
Gridley, Michael C. ... Houston, TX
Gridley Ward & Shaw ... Layton, UT
Ogden, UT
Gridley, Wendy H. ... Columbus, OH
Gridley, William C. ... Orlando, FL
Grieb, Elizabeth ... Baltimore, MD
Grieb, John T. ... Atlanta, GA
Grieb, Steven E. ... Milwaukee, WI
Griebe, Benjamin G. ... Palo Alto, CA
Griebel, Daniel M. ... Buffalo, NY
Griebel, James B. ... Minneapolis, MN
Griebel, John F. ... Denver, CO
Griebel, Lisa R. ... Minneapolis, MN
Griebel, Pamela D. ... Des Moines, IA
Griebel, Paul ... Sonora, CA
Griebel, R. Nelson ... Boston, MA
Griebel, Stephen P. ... Fort Wayne, IN
Griebling, Eric H. ... Bucyrus, OH
Griebner, Douglas C. ... Sacramento, CA
Griecci, John A. ... Los Angeles, CA
Grieco, Anthony J., II ... Williamsport, PA
Grieco, Charles D. ... Buffalo, NY
Grieco, Daniel J. ... Indian Shores, FL
Grieco, Dennis T., II ... Providence, RI
Grieco, Donald E. ... Bradenton, FL
Grieco, F. Timothy ... Pittsburgh, PA
Grieco, Gloria E. ... Montclair, NJ
Grieco, Jane F. ... San Francisco, CA
Grieco, Jennifer M. ... Southfield, MI
Grieco, Kimberly O. ... Seattle, WA
Grieco, Mark M. ... West Palm Beach, FL
Grieco, Mary L. ... Los Angeles, CA
Grieco, Matthew V. ... New York, NY
Grieco, Michael A. ... Boston, MA
Grieco, Michael H. ... New York, NY
Grieco, Nicholas A. ... West Orange, NJ
Grieco, Oates & Pantano, L.L.C.
West Orange, NJ
Grieco, Paul ... Cleveland, OH
Grieco, Ralph A., (P.A.) ... Short Hills, NJ
Grieco, Robert C. ... Kingston, NY

Grieco & Scalera, P.A. ... West Palm Beach, FL
Grieco, Steven S. ... New York, NY
Grieco, Thomas V. ... Houston, TX
Grieco, Vincent ... Pittsburgh, PA
Grieco, William F. ... Lexington, MA
Grieder, John G. ... New York, NY
Grief, Bus & Blacklidge, P.C. ... West Chicago, IL
Grief, Dalton P. ... West Chicago, IL
Grief, Dottie W. ... Nashville, TN
Grief, Nancy S. ... Durango, CO
Grieff, Edward D. ... Washington, DC
Grieff, Jeffrey Michael ... Seattle, WA
Grieff & Ritchie, Law Offices of ... Seattle, WA
Griege, Mark C. ... Dallas, TX
Grieger, Cynthia H. ... Orange, NJ
Grieger, Gail A. ... Howell, MI
Griego & Associates, P.C. ... Denver, CO
Griego, Gregory D. ... Albuquerque, NM
Griego, Henry C. ... Dallas, TX
Griego, J. Wayne ... Albuquerque, NM
Griego, Michael D. ... Denver, CO
Griego, Michael R. ... Los Lunas, NM
Griego, Patrik M. ... Los Angeles, CA
Griego, Phillip J., and Associates ... San Jose, CA
Griego, Robt. F. ... Omaha, NE
Griego, Thomas J. ... Albuquerque, NM
Griem, David ... Detroit, MI
Mount Clemens, MI
Griem, John M., Jr. ... New York, NY
Grieme, Rosemary E. ... Cincinnati, OH
Grienauer, John V. ... Los Angeles, CA
Grienenberger, Warren F. ... Chicago, IL
Griep, Douglas T. ... West St. Paul, MN
Griepentrog, Mark D. ... Milwaukee, WI
Griepentrog, Paul W. ... Milwaukee, WI
Griepentrog, Richard K. ... Milwaukee, WI
Griepp, Galen F. ... Pasadena, CA
Grier, Benjamin N. ... Detroit, MI
Grier, Bennie L. ... Detroit, MI
Grier, Carol J. ... Barrington, IL
Grier, Cheveda D. ... Atlanta, GA
Grier and Copeland, A Professional Corporation ... Detroit, MI
Grier, David C. ... South Haven, MI
Grier, Donald S. ... Calabasas, CA
Grier, Douglas J. ... Phoenix, AZ
Grier, Eli ... Farmington Hills, MI
Grier, F. Barron, III ... Columbia, SC
Grier & Furr, P.A. ... Charlotte, NC
Grier, Georgina ... Treasury Department, Office of Regulations and Rulings, GV
Grier, J. Michael ... Overland Park, KS
Grier, James F. ... Costa Mesa, CA
Grier, James J. ... Ecorse, MI
Grier, Jean Heilman ... Department of Commerce, Office of the General Counsel, GV
Grier, John B. ... Marshalltown, IA
Grier, John Buford ... York, SC
Grier, John C. ... San Diego, CA
Grier, John H. ... Troy, MI
Grier, John R. ... Chicago, IL
Grier, Joseph L. ... New York, NY
Grier, Joseph W., III ... Charlotte, NC
Grier, Joseph W., Jr. ... Charlotte, NC
Grier, Karlise Y. ... Atlanta, GA
Grier Law Firm, L.L.C. ... Columbia, SC
Grier, Manton M. ... Columbia, SC
Grier, Mark ... Lancaster, SC
Grier, Marshall V. ... Towson, MD
Grier, Mary Mangotich ... Phoenix, AZ
Grier, Melinda W. ... Eugene, OR
Grier, Phillip M. ... Washington, DC
Grier, R. Ann ... Atlanta, GA
Grier, Raymond L. ... Charlotte, NC
Grier, Richard L. ... Richmond, VA
Grier, Sharon L. ... Orange, CA
Grier, Shelby B. ... Atlanta, GA
Grier, Thomas A. ... Bloomfield Hills, MI
Grier, William M. ... Dearborn, MI
Grierson, Kevin W. ... Norfolk, VA
Grierson, Mark ... Saginaw, MI
Grierson, Robert G. ... Mattoon, IL
Gries, Alan R. ... Philadelphia, PA
Gries, Arnold David ... Randallstown, MD
Gries, Donald S. ... Shaker Heights, OH
Gries, James C. ... San Francisco, CA
Gries, John R. ... St. Michael, MN
Gries & Lenhardt, P.L.L.P. ... St. Michael, MN
Gries, Matthew J. ... Atlanta, GA
Griesa, Thomas P. ... New York, NY
Griesar, William H. ... New York, NY
Griesbach, Toni ... St. Louis, MO
Griesbach, William C. ... Green Bay, WI
Griesbauer, Robert C. ... Ballwin, MO
Griesbaum, John M. ... Titusville, FL
Griesbaum, Karl H. ... Barstow, CA
Griesedieck, August L. ... St. Louis, MO
Griesedieck, Edward J., III ... St. Louis, MO
Grieselhuber, Pierre A. ... Strongsville, OH
Griesemer, Elizabeth ... Belleville, IL
Griesemer, Paul G. ... St. Louis, MO
Griesemer, Stephen M. ... Chicago, IL
Griesenbeck, Tim T., Jr. ... San Antonio, TX
Grieser, C. Richard ... Columbus, OH
Grieser, Douglas D. ... Omaha, NE
Griesgraber, Susan M. ... St. Paul, MN
Grieshaber, Al, Jr. ... Albany, GA
Grieshaber, Dominic C. ... New Orleans, LA
Griesheimer & Martin ... Waukegan, IL
Griesheimer, Ronald E. ... Waukegan, IL
Grieshober, Donald W. ... Erie, PA
Grieshober, William E., Jr. ... Buffalo, NY
Grieshop, David B. ... Dayton, OH
Griesing, Francine Friedman ... Philadelphia, PA
Griesinger, Andrew C., (P.C.) ... Boston, MA
Griesinger, Charles Clark, (Co., L.P.A.) ... Medina, OH
Griesinger, Richard C. ... Clearwater, FL
Griesmer, Kelley M. ... Columbus, OH
Griess, Murray W. ... Cincinnati, OH
Griess, Ted S. ... Sutton, NE
Griess, Thomas E., Jr. ... Austin, TX
Griess, Walter A. ... Eutaw, AL
Griesse, Dennis R. ... Little Rock, AR
Griesser, Michael S. ... Dallas, TX
Griest, Himes, Herrold ... York, PA
Griest, Suzanne H. ... York, PA
Grieve, Catherine C. ... Miami, FL
Grieve, Timothy P. ... Sacramento, CA
Grieves, J. W. ... Boston, MA
Grieves, Richard W. ... Hawthorne, CA
Griewahn, Robert D., Jr. ... Pittsburgh, PA
Grifa, Lori E. ... Roseland, NJ
Grife, Jay S. ... Jacksonville, FL
Grife & Walaszek ... Northampton, MA
Griff, Barbara D. ... New York, NY
Griff, David M. ... New York, NY
Griff, Harry ... Grand Junction, CO
Griff, Marvin T. ... Washington, DC
Griffaton, Michael C. ... Columbus, OH
Griffee, J. Mark ... Memphis, TN
Griffee-Ross, Jill R. ... Iowa City, IA
Griffel, Allen M. ... Minnetonka, MN
Griffel, Deborah J. ... New York, NY
Griffel & Dorshow, Chartered ... Minnetonka, MN
Griffel, Ellen ... New York, NY
Griffen, Bruce S. ... Flagstaff, AZ
Griffen, Danl. L., Jr. ... Ames, IA
Griffen, Frederick A. ... Binghamton, NY
Griffen, John P. ... Charleston, SC
Griffen, John W., Jr. ... Birmingham, MI
Griffen, Lorie Soares ... Los Angeles, CA
Griffen, Michael C. ... Washington, DC
Griffen, Robert H. ... Arlington, VA
Griffen, Susan Haberman ... Washington, DC
Griffen, Thomas B. ... Irvine, CA
Griffen, Thomas G. ... Hudson, NY
Griffen, Thomas P. ... New Britain, CT
Griffen, Wendell L. ... Little Rock, AR
Griffen, William W. ... West Chester, PA
Grifferty, Stephen J. ... Albany, NY
Grifferty, Terence J. ... Bronx, NY
Griffeth, George E. ... Phoenix, AZ
Griffeth, Jack D. ... Greenville, SC
Griffeth, Natalie C. Gant ... Kansas City, MO
Griffey, Linda Boyd ... Los Angeles, CA
Griffey, William E. ... Galveston, TX
Houston, TX
Griffie & Associates ... Carlisle, PA
Chambersburg, PA
Griffie, Bradley L. ... Carlisle, PA
Chambersburg, PA
Griffie, Samuel C. ... Amory, MS
Griffin, Alan L. ... New York, NY
Griffin, Alana L. ... Atlanta, GA
Griffin, Albert P. ... Bala Cynwyd, PA
Griffin, Allen ... Dallas, TX
Plano, TX
Griffin, Alton R. ... Lubbock, TX
Griffin, Andrew H., III ... El Cajon, CA
Griffin, Andrew Trost ... Houston, TX
Griffin, Anne Louise ... Norristown, PA
Griffin, Anthony ... San Francisco, CA
Griffin, Arthur James, III ... Madison, WI
Griffin & Associates ... Brandon, FL
Plant City, FL
Tampa, FL
Griffin & Associates ... Jackson, MS
Griffin, Avery Lea ... Baton Rouge, LA
Griffin, B. Franklin, Jr. ... Arlington, VA
Griffin, B. Kendall ... Jackson, MS
Griffin, Barbara J. ... Chelmsford, MA
Griffin, Barbara McDonald ... Lexington, KY
Griffin, Barbara M. L. ... Charlotte, NC
Griffin, Basil W., Jr. ... Bowling Green, KY
Griffin, Benjamin J. ... Washington, DC
Griffin, Bill F., Jr. ... Center, TX
Griffin, Billy D. ... Oklahoma City, OK
Griffin, Bobby H. ... Monroe, NC
Griffin, Brenden ... Tucson, AZ
Griffin, Brian T. ... Windsor Locks, CT
Griffin & Brunson, L.L.P. ... Charlotte, NC
Griffin, Bryan Patrick ... Germantown, TN
Griffin, Bryant W. ... Flemington, NJ
Griffin, Burt W. ... Cleveland, OH
Griffin, Butler, Whisenhunt and Szipl, LLP ... Arlington, VA
Virginia Beach, VA
Griffin, C. Frank ... Monroe, NC
Griffin, Campbell A., Jr. ... Houston, TX
Griffin, Carl R., III ... Boothbay Harbor, ME
Griffin, Carol A. ... Boston, MA
Griffin, Caroline A. ... Baltimore, MD
Griffin, Carolyn L. ... Golden, CO
Griffin Carrick ... Bakersfield, CA
Griffin, Cary S. ... Bluffton, SC
Hilton Head Island, SC
Griffin, Catharine Garbee ... Columbia, SC
Griffin, Catherine A. ... Oak Brook, IL
Griffin, Cathryn D. ... Cleveland, OH
Griffin, Cecilia Hynes ... Chicago, IL
Griffin, Charles A. ... Portsmouth, NH
Griffin, Charles E. ... Jackson, MS
Griffin, Charles E., II ... St. Francisville, LA
Griffin, Charles J. ... Portsmouth, NH
Griffin, Charles J. ... New York, NY
Griffin, Charles J., Jr. ... Chicago, IL
Griffin, Charles L., III ... Sumter, SC
Griffin, Charles N., III ... Raleigh, NC
Griffin, Charles R. ... Bartlesville, OK
Griffin, Charles R., Jr. ... Anderson, SC
Griffin, Charlotte A. Knight ... Memphis, TN
Griffin, Chester B. ... Fort Pierce, FL
Griffin, Christi D. ... Nashville, TN
Griffin, Christian J. ... Winchester, VA
Griffin, Christopher ... Woodland Hills, CA
Griffin, Christopher L. ... Tampa, FL
Griffin, Clift, Everton & Thornton ... Memphis, TN
Griffin Cochrane & Marshall, A Professional Corporation ... Atlanta, GA
Griffin, Colette S. ... Hartford, CT
Griffin, Coogan & Veneruso, P.C. ... Bronxville, NY
Eastchester, NY
Mount Kisco, NY
New Rochelle, NY
New York, NY
Scarsdale, NY
Tarrytown, NY
White Plains, NY
Yonkers, NY
Griffin, Craig L. ... Irvine, CA
Griffin & Crapse, Attorneys, L.L.C. ... Reidsville, NC
Griffin, Dale W. ... Cincinnati, OH
Griffin, Dan G. ... Grand Junction, CO
Griffin, Daniel E. ... Rosemont, IL
Griffin, Daniel J. ... Bronxville, NY
Griffin, Daniel J., Jr. ... Boston, MA
Griffin, Daniel P. ... Atlanta, GA
Griffin, Daniel P. ... Des Moines, IA
Griffin, Danny C. ... Colquitt, GA
Griffin, David C. ... Victoria, TX
Griffin, David D. ... New York, NY
Griffin, David J. ... Chicago, IL
Griffin, David M. ... Bonita Springs, FL
Griffin, David R. ... Bakersfield, CA
Griffin, David W. ... Waterbury, CT
Griffin, David W. ... Clearwater, FL
Griffin, Dawsey and DePaola, P.C. ... Towanda, PA
Griffin, Deborah A. ... Philadelphia, PA
Griffin, Deborah S. ... Boston, MA
Griffin, Deborah S. ... Philadelphia, PA
Griffin, Dennis M. ... San Diego, CA
Griffin, Diane Pomeroy ... Portsmouth, VA
Griffin, Diane S. ... Boone, NC
Griffin, Diane S., P.C., Law Office of ... Boone, NC
Griffin, Dianne ... East Providence, RI
Griffin, Dina White ... Philadelphia, PA
Griffin, Don C., Jr. ... Houston, TX
Griffin, Donna M. ... Tampa, FL
Griffin, Douglas A. ... New York, NY
Griffin, Douglas E. ... Fresno, CA
Griffin, Earl, Jr. ... Childress, TX
Griffin, Edward J. ... Chicago, IL
Griffin, Eileen H. ... Brandon, FL
Griffin, Eileen P. ... Springfield, MA
Griffin, Elizabeth A. ... New Orleans, LA
Griffin, Elizabeth A. ... New York, NY
Griffin, Elizabeth Eddy ... Portland, ME
Griffin, Elizabeth F. ... Denver, CO
Griffin, Eric D., Jr. ... Atlanta, GA
Griffin, Ethel J. ... New York, NY
Griffin, Eugene G. ... Aurora, IL
Griffin, Eugene L. ... Chicago, IL
Griffin, Eurich Z. ... Tampa, FL
Griffin, F. Hastings, Jr. ... Philadelphia, PA
Griffin, F. Heather ... Statesville, NC
Griffin, F. Hollis, Jr. ... Pearl River, NY
Griffin, F. Redmond ... Troy, NY
Griffin & Fletcher ... Cincinnati, OH
Griffin & Foley, P.A. ... Boston, MA
Griffin, Frank E. ... Brownwood, TX
Griffin, Frank H., III ... Media, PA
Philadelphia, PA
West Chester, PA
Griffin, Fred B. ... Los Angeles, CA
Griffin & Freda ... Medford, MA
Griffin, Frederick J. ... Amarillo, TX
Griffin, Frederick J., Jr. ... Concord, NH
Griffin & Gallagher ... Palos Hills, IL
Griffin, Gary L. ... Chicago, IL
Griffin, Gary M. ... Chicago, IL
Griffin, Gary W. ... Paducah, KY
Griffin, Gene C. ... Dallas, TX
Griffin, Gene C. ... Williamsburg, VA
Griffin, Gene R. ... Chattanooga, TN
Griffin, George V. ... Fort Worth, TX
Griffin, Georgia Corbett ... Atlanta, GA
Griffin, Gerald A. ... Los Angeles, CA
Griffin, Gerald A., Jr. ... Medford, MA
Griffin, Gerald A., M.D. ... Indianapolis, IN
Griffin, Gerald M. ... New York, NY
Griffin, Gerald W. ... New York, NY
Griffin, Geraldine ... Boston, MA
Griffin, Gerard P., Jr. ... New York, NY
Griffin, Gleichman & Pudloski, P.L.L.C. ... Portsmouth, NH
Griffin, Gordon ... Brownwood, TX
Griffin, Gordon D. ... Princeton, NJ
Griffin, Gordon H. ... Dysart, IA
Griffin & Goulka ... Boston, MA
Griffin, Gregory ... Middlebury, CT
Griffin, Gregory ... Stamford, CT
Griffin, Gregory A. ... Marietta, GA
Griffin, Gregory O., Sr. ... Montgomery, AL
Griffin and Griffin ... Worcester, MA
Griffin & Griffin ... Kinston, NC
Griffin & Griffin ... Harlingen, TX
Houston, TX
Griffin & Griffin, A Law Corporation ... Ventura, CA
Woodland Hills, CA
Griffin & Griffin, P.C. ... Waterbury, CT
Griffin & Griffin, P.C. ... Randolph, NJ
Griffin, Griffin, Tarby & Murphy, LLP ... Washington, DC
Griffin, Guy W. ... Center, TX
Griffin, H. Flynn, III ... Columbia, SC
Griffin, H. Terrell ... Orlando, FL
Griffin, H. Vaughan, Jr. ... Rutland, VT
Griffin, H Vaughan, Jr., P.C. ... Rutland, VT
Griffin & Hackett, P.A. ... Georgetown, DE
Rehoboth Beach, DE
Griffin, Harold E. ... Santa Monica, CA
Griffin, Harrison D. ... DeLand, FL
Griffin, Harry L., Jr. ... Atlanta, GA
Griffin, Henry M., III ... Owensboro, KY
Griffin, Henry R. F. ... Federal Deposit Insurance Corporation, Resolutions Section, GV
Griffin, Henry V. ... Branson, MO
Griffin, Henry W. ... Lewiston, ME
Griffin, Howard R. ... Department of Justice, Civil Rights Division, GV
Griffin, Hubert P. ... Louisville, KY
Griffin, Hugh C. ... Chicago, IL
Griffin, Hugh P., Jr. ... Reidsville, NC
Griffin, J. Ben ... Ocoee, FL
Griffin, J. David ... West Haven, CT
Griffin, J. David ... Winchester, VA
Griffin, J. Eric ... Charlotte, NC
Griffin, J. Kenneth ... Boston, MA
Griffin, J. Robert ... Tallahassee, FL
Griffin, J. Roger, Jr. ... Virginia Beach, VA
Griffin, J. Ruble ... Jackson, MS
Griffin, J. Timothy ... House of Representatives, Committee Legal Personnel, GV
Griffin, Jacqueline R. ... Daytona Beach, FL
Griffin, James A. ... Oyster Bay, NY
Griffin, James B. ... Randolph, NJ
Griffin, James B., III ... Philadelphia, PA
Griffin, James D. ... Georgetown, DE
Griffin, James D. ... Overland Park, KS
Griffin, James E. ... Portland, OR
Griffin, James H. ... Department Of Health And Human Services, Social Security Administration, GV
Griffin, James J. ... White Plains, NY
Griffin, James M. ... Ventura, CA
Griffin, James M. ... Atlanta, GA
Griffin, James M. ... Bethesda, MD
Rockville, MD
Griffin, James Mixon ... Columbia, SC
Griffin, James N. ... Springfield, OH
Griffin, James P. ... Santa Monica, CA
Griffin, James R. ... Chicago, IL
Griffin, James R. ... Dallas, TX
Griffin, James R. ... Dallas, TX
Griffin, James T. ... Boston, MA
Griffin, James T. ... Manassas, VA
Griffin, James W. ... San Francisco, CA
Griffin, James Wilson ... Lakewood, CO
Griffin, Janet ... Des Moines, IA
Griffin, Janice L. ... Boca Raton, FL
Griffin, J. C. ... North Little Rock, AR
Griffin, Jeanne A. ... Columbus, OH
Griffin, Jeffrey E. ... Houston, TX
Griffin, Jennifer Q. ... Birmingham, AL
Griffin, Jeremy M. ... Washington, DC
Griffin, Jill A. ... National Labor Relations Board, Office of the General Counsel, GV
Griffin, Jimmy ... Houston, TX
Griffin, Joan M. ... Washington, DC
Griffin, Joan M. ... Boston, MA
Griffin, Joanne C. ... Stratham, NH
Griffin, Joe C. ... Ackerman, MS
Griffin, Joe E. ... Texarkana, AR
Griffin, John A. ... Anaheim, CA
Griffin, John C. ... Birmingham, AL
Griffin, John C. ... Palos Hills, IL
Griffin, John C., Jr. ... Bloomfield Hills, MI
Griffin, John D. ... Denver, CO
Griffin, John D. ... Lewiston, ME
Griffin, John D. ... Center, TX
Griffin, John E. ... Modesto, CA
Griffin, John E. ... Tallahassee, FL
Griffin, John E. ... Athens, GA
Griffin, John E. ... Mount Prospect, IL
Griffin, John E., Jr. ... Modesto, CA
Griffin, John F., Jr. ... Amherst, NH
Griffin, John G. ... East Setauket, NY
Griffin, John J. ... Thousand Oaks, CA
Griffin, John J. ... Chicago, IL
Griffin, John J. ... Spring Valley, NY
Griffin, John J. ... Oklahoma City, OK
Griffin, John J. ... Philadelphia, PA
Griffin, John J. ... Towanda, PA
Griffin, John J., Jr. ... Boston, MA
Griffin, John J., Jr. ... Oklahoma City, OK
Griffin, John J., Jr. ... Nashville, TN
Griffin, John (Jack) P. ... Anchorage, AK
Griffin, John Kevin ... Pensacola, FL
Griffin, John Knight ... Lewisville, AR
Griffin, John M. ... Worcester, MA
Griffin, John Mark ... Chattanooga, TN
Griffin, John P. ... Treasury Department, GV
Griffin, John P. ... Tampa, FL
Griffin, John R. (Randy), III ... Fayetteville, NC
Griffin, John T. ... Orange, CA
Griffin, John V., Jr. ... Madison, CT
Griffin, John W. ... Washington, DC
Griffin, John W. ... Atlanta, GA

Griffin, John W. ... Carson City, NV
Griffin, John W., Jr. ... Victoria, TX
Griffin, Johnny L., III ... Sacramento, CA
Griffin, Jon T. ... Des Moines, IA
Griffin, Jos. P. ... Palos Hills, IL
Griffin, Joseph B., Jr. ... Neptune Beach, FL
Griffin, Joseph E. ... Tulsa, OK
Griffin, Joseph F. ... Treasury Department, Office of Thrift Supervision, GV
Griffin, Joseph F. ... Hingham, MA
Griffin, Joseph J. ... Old Greenwich, CT
Griffin, Joseph M. ... Charlotte, NC
Griffin, Joseph P. ... Washington, DC
Griffin, Julie Weston ... Portland, OR
Griffin, Juliet E. ... Nashville, TN
Griffin, Karen E. ... Dallas, TX
Griffin, Katherine M. ... San Francisco, CA
Griffin, Kathleen McAndrew ... Winchester, VA
Griffin, Kathryn Lawson ... Little Rock, AR
Griffin, Keith ... Dallas, TX
Griffin, Ken ... Odessa, TX
Griffin, Kenneth A. ... Charlotte, NC
Griffin, Kenneth G. ... Los Angeles, CA
Griffin, Kenneth M. ... Washington, DC
Griffin, Kevin A. ... Washington, DC
Griffin, Kevin R. ... Newport Beach, CA
Griffin, Kimberly A. ... Hoffman Estates, IL
Griffin, Kimberly Jo. ... San Antonio, TX
Griffin, Kimberly P. ... Prattville, AL
Griffin, Kirk Y. ... Boston, MA
Griffin, Kristin Garner ... Boston, MA
Griffin, L. David ... Salt Lake City, UT
Griffin, L. Robert ... Treasury Department, Office of the Comptroller of the Currency, GV
Griffin, Lance Randall ... New York, NY
Griffin Law Office, S.C. ... Madison, WI
Griffin Law Offices ... Boothbay Harbor, ME
Griffin, Lawrence C. ... North Palm Beach, FL
Griffin, Lawrence P. ... Denver, CO
Griffin, Lee T. ... Jacksonville, FL
Griffin, Linda C. ... Troy, NY
Griffin, Linda Suzzanne ... Clearwater, FL
Griffin, Linda Suzzanne, P.A. ... Clearwater, FL
Griffin & Linder, P.A. ... Kissimmee, FL
Orlando, FL
Griffin, Lisa A. ... Tampa, FL
Griffin, Lissa ... White Plains, NY
Griffin, Lorraine L. ... Columbia, LA
Griffin, M. Lee ... Ruidoso, NM
Griffin, Madeline S. ... Atlanta, GA
Griffin, Malvern U., III ... Atlanta, GA
Griffin, Marc L. ... Indianapolis, IN
Griffin, Marcus R. ... Lubbock, TX
Griffin, Marilyn A. ... West Covina, CA
Griffin, Marilyn Otteman ... Harlingen, TX
Houston, TX
Griffin, Marion L. ... National Labor Relations Board, Office of the General Counsel, GV
Griffin, Mark A. ... Seattle, WA
Griffin, Mark C. ... Seattle, WA
Griffin, Mark D. ... Cleveland, OH
Griffin, Mark Daniel ... Memphis, TN
Griffin, Mark E. ... Washington, DC
Griffin, Mark E. ... Portland, OR
Griffin, Mark F. ... Waterbury, CT
Griffin, Mark F. ... Greensboro, NC
Griffin, Mark G. ... Washington, DC
Griffin, Mark J. ... Salt Lake City, UT
Griffin, Mark V. ... Minneapolis, MN
Griffin, Mark W. ... Ann Arbor, MI
Griffin, Martha W. ... Charlotte, NC
Griffin, Martin L. ... Huntsville, TX
Griffin, Martin R. ... Dallas, TX
Griffin, Mary ... San Francisco, CA
Griffin, Mary B. ... Boston, MA
Griffin, Mary C. ... New York, NY
Griffin, Mary E. ... Nashville, TN
Griffin, Mary (Molly) A. ... Chicago, IL
Griffin, Maryellen C. ... Atlanta, GA
Griffin, Mathew D. ... Everett, WA
Griffin, Matthew John ... Boston, MA
Griffin, Maura E. ... Washington, DC
Griffin, Maureen C. ... Cheshire, CT
Griffin, Maureen O'Brien ... Indianapolis, IN
Griffin, Maxwell, Jr. ... Chicago, IL
Griffin McCandlish ... Portland, OR
Griffin, Melvin E. ... Cameron, MO
Griffin, Michael ... Indianapolis, IN
Griffin, Michael A. ... Port Townsend, WA
Griffin, Michael E. ... Kansas City, MO
Griffin, Michael F. ... New York, NY
Griffin, Michael H. ... Orono, ME
Griffin, Michael H. ... Shelby, NC
Griffin, Michael J. ... Grangeville, ID
Griffin, Michael J. ... Chicago, IL
Griffin, Michael J. ... Boston, MA
Griffin, Michael J., III ... Harlingen, TX
Houston, TX
Griffin, Michael R. ... Carson City, NV
Griffin, Michael S. ... Cleburne, TX
Griffin, Michael T. ... Hartford, CT
Griffin, Mike ... Denton, TX
Griffin, Mitchell S. ... San Francisco, CA
Griffin, M. U., II ... Huntsville, AL
Griffin, Nancy E. Whatley ... Mount Holly, NJ
Griffin, Nancy Hunter ... Hinsdale, IL
Griffin, Nancy K. ... Glendale, CA
Griffin, Nathan K. ... Dallas, TX
Griffin, Norman L. ... Knoxville, TN
Griffin, Omer L. ... Denver, CO
Griffin, Oren R. ... Kalamazoo, MI
Griffin & O'Toole, LLP ... Marietta, GA
Griffin, Pappas & Scarborough ... Portsmouth, VA
Griffin, Patricia A. ... New York, NY
Griffin, Patricia L. ... Santa Ana, CA
Griffin, Patrick B. ... Omaha, NE
Griffin, Patrick Edward, Jr. ... Omaha, NE
Griffin, Patrick J. ... Palos Hills, IL
Griffin, Patrick M. ... St. Charles, IL
Griffin, Patrick M. ... Troy, MI
Griffin, Patrick R. ... West Bend, WI
Griffin, Paul A. ... Atlanta, GA
Griffin, Paul D. ... Groton, MA
Griffin, Paul G. ... Washington, DC
Griffin, Paul M. ... Newark, NJ
Griffin, Paul R. ... San Francisco, CA
Griffin, Paul R. ... Torrington, CT
Griffin, Penelope M. ... Denver, CO
Griffin, Peter P. ... Lock Haven, PA
Griffin, Philip C. ... Los Angeles, CA
Griffin, Phillip E. ... Trenton, NJ
Griffin, Phillip S., II ... Winchester, VA
Griffin, Phillip S., II, P.C. ... Winchester, VA
Griffin, Piper D. ... Metairie, LA
Griffin, R. Gaines ... San Antonio, TX
Griffin, Rainwater & Draper, P.L.C. ... Crossett, AR
Griffin, Ramie H., Jr. ... Beaumont, TX
Griffin, Randall V. ... Wilmington, DE
Griffin, Regina L. ... New York, NY
Griffin, Reynolds & Trout, P.C. ... Oklahoma City, OK
Griffin, Richard A. ... Norwood, MA
Griffin, Richard Allen ... Traverse City, MI
Griffin, Richard Earl ... Crossett, AR
Houston, TX
Griffin, Richard F. ... Washington, DC
Griffin, Richard F. ... Buffalo, NY
Griffin, Richard L. ... Charlotte, NC
Griffin, Richard L. ... Fort Worth, TX
Griffin, Richard T. ... Monrovia, CA
Griffin, Rick E. ... Birmingham, AL
Griffin, Rick L. ... Greenville, NC
Griffin, Rick W. ... Macon, GA
Griffin, Robert C. ... Waterloo, IA
Griffin, Robert C. ... Billings, MT
Griffin, Robert C. ... Randolph, NJ
Griffin, Robert Charles ... Huntsville, TX
Griffin, Robert E. ... Santa Ana, CA
Griffin, Robert E. ... Bartow, FL
Griffin, Robert G. ... Charlotte, NC
Griffin, Robert G. ... Greensboro, NC
Griffin, Robert H. ... Raleigh, NC
Griffin, Robert H., Jr. ... Columbus, OH
Griffin, Robert J. ... Boston, MA
Griffin, Robert J. ... Milwaukee, WI
Griffin, Robert L. ... Anchorage, AK
Griffin, Robert L. ... Columbus, OH
Griffin, Robert Michael ... Boston, MA
Griffin, Robert P. ... Traverse City, MI
Griffin, Robert W. ... Kinston, NC
Griffin, Robert Y., Jr. ... Florence, AL
Griffin, Robin ... Lexington, KY
Griffin, Roland I. ... Palo Alto, CA
Griffin, Ronald C. ... Topeka, KS
Griffin, Royal K. ... San Antonio, TX
Griffin, Rufus, Jr. ... Detroit, MI
Griffin, S. Earl ... Portsmouth, VA
Griffin, S. Samuel ... Atlanta, GA
Griffin, Samuel D., Jr. ... Lufkin, TX
Griffin, Samuel S., III ... Houston, TX
Griffin, Sandra ... Austin, TX
Griffin, Sarah Heck ... Los Angeles, CA
Griffin, Schaune C. ... Atlanta, GA
Griffin, Scot A. ... Palo Alto, CA
Griffin, Sean C. ... Department of Justice, Civil Division, GV
Griffin, Sharon L. ... Toledo, OH
Griffin, Shawn M. ... Rochester, NY
Griffin, Sheila Seig ... Tampa, FL
Griffin, Sheilah A. ... Reading, MA
Griffin, Shelley L. ... Panama City, FL
Griffin & Smith ... Indianapolis, IN
Griffin, Smith, Caldwell, Helder & Lee, P.A. ... Monroe, NC
Griffin, Stephanie J. ... Denver, CO
Griffin, Stephen Barrett ... Birmingham, AL
Griffin, Stephen K. ... Cameron, MO
Griffin, Stephen P. ... Boston, MA
Griffin, Stephen P. ... Canton, OH
Griffin, Stephen R. ... Waterbury, CT
Griffin, Steven D. ... East Alton, IL
Griffin, Steven D. ... Indianapolis, IN
Griffin, Sue ... Tulsa, OK
Griffin & Sullivan ... San Francisco, CA
Griffin, Susan M. ... San Francisco, CA
Griffin, Susanne A. ... Santa Monica, CA
Griffin, Suzanne Kadrie ... Chicago, IL
Griffin, T. McLean ... Salem, MA
Griffin, T. Patrick ... Tucson, AZ
Griffin, Teena ... Bloomington, IL
Griffin, Terrence J. ... Chicago, IL
Griffin, Thomas B. ... Kinston, NC
Griffin, Thomas C. ... Washington, DC
Griffin, Thomas D. ... Long Beach, CA
Griffin, Thomas G. ... Chicago, IL
New York, NY
Griffin, Thomas G. ... Holyoke, MA
Griffin, Thomas J. ... Los Angeles, CA
Griffin, Thomas J. ... Camp Springs, MD
Griffin, Thomas J., Jr. ... Boston, MA
Griffin, Thomas More ... New York, NY
Griffin, Thomas N. ... Watsonville, CA
Griffin, Thomas N., III ... Charlotte, NC
Griffin, Thomas P. ... Sacramento, CA
Griffin, Thomas W. ... West Orange, NJ
Griffin, Thos. D. ... Long Beach, CA
Griffin, Timothy G. ... Norwalk, CT
Griffin, Timothy P. ... Bismarck, ND
Griffin, Timothy S. ... Pittsburgh, PA
Griffin, Timothy W. ... Charlotte, NC
Griffin, Todd Landers ... Little Rock, AR
Griffin, Tom ... Hyattsville, MD
Griffin, Toni L. ... Santa Rosa, CA
Griffin, Tony ... Jonesboro, AR
Griffin, Tony B. ... Tampa, FL
Griffin, Tory E. ... Sacramento, CA
Griffin, W. Bradney ... Lake Placid, NY
Griffin, Walter P. ... Flint, MI
Griffin, Walter R. ... Waterbury, CT
Griffin, Warren L. ... Oklahoma City, OK
Griffin, Wayne E. ... North Platte, NE
Griffin, Whitten & Jones ... Denton, TX
Griffin, William ... St. Petersburg, FL
Griffin, William C. ... Jackson, MS
Griffin, William D., III ... Chicago, IL
Griffin, William E. ... Bronxville, NY
Griffin, William F. ... Port Isabel, TX
Griffin, William F., Jr. ... Boston, MA
Griffin, William H. ... Huntsville, AL
Griffin, William H. ... Columbia, SC
Griffin, William J. ... Chicago, IL
Griffin, William J. ... Arlington, VA
Griffin, William L. ... Washington, DC
Griffin, William Mell, III (P.A.) ... Little Rock, AR
Griffin, William N. ... Memphis, TN
Griffin, William N., Jr. ... Memphis, TN
Griffin, William P., IV ... Nashville, TN
Griffin, William W. ... Atlanta, GA
Griffin, Willie ... Greenville, MS
Griffin, Winona R. ... Texarkana, TX
Griffin, Winston ... London, KY
Griffin, W. L. Hadley ... St. Louis, MO
Griffin, Wm. D. ... Chicago, IL
Griffin, Woodrow H. ... Waynesville, NC
Griffin & Wright, P.A. ... Shelby, NC
Griffin, Yolanda C. ... Washington, DC
Griffin, Yolanda R. ... Irving, TX
Griffin, Yvonne T. ... Charlottesville, VA
Griffing, George ... Jonesville, LA
Griffing, Glenn T. ... Dallas, TX
Griffing, John H. ... Gastonia, NC
Griffing, Juanita C. ... Lancaster, PA
Griffing Law Office ... Centerville, IA
Griffing, Marjorie Jirovec ... St. Paul, MN
Griffing, Meredith R. ... Centerville, IA
Griffing, Roger M. ... Centerville, IA
Griffinger, Michael R. ... Newark, NJ
Griffinger, Theodore A., Jr. ... San Francisco, CA
Griffin-Halliday, Gwendolyn L. ... Spokane, WA
Griffin-Lazerson, Kelly A. ... Bakersfield, CA
Griffis, Andrew B. ... Baytown, TX
Griffis, Anthony E. ... Hilton Head Island, SC
Griffis, Charles B., III ... Lafayette, LA
Griffis, David L. ... Houston, TX
Griffis, Donald W. ... San Angelo, TX
Griffis, Edward A. ... Covington, LA
Griffis, Edward A. ... Mandeville, LA
Griffis, Elbert B., Jr. ... Fort Lauderdale, FL
Griffis, Hilda J. ... Miami, FL
Griffis, Hughes ... New London, CT
Griffis, J. Brandon, Jr. ... Richmond, IN
Griffis, J. Philip ... Houston, TX
Griffis, John Anthony ... Dallas, TX
Griffis, John W., III ... Sarasota, FL
Griffis, Kirby T. ... Washington, DC
Griffis, Larry K. ... Detroit, MI
Griffis, Linda L. ... Los Angeles, CA
Griffis, R. Stephen, (P.C.) ... Hoover, AL
Griffis, Roy W., Jr. ... Macon, GA
Griffis, Samuel L. ... Putney, VT
Griffis, T. Kenneth, Jr. ... Jackson, MS
Griffis, Virgil D. ... Adel, GA
Griffith, Allan T. ... Fort Myers, FL
Griffith, Allan T., P.A. ... Fort Myers, FL
Griffith, Amelia H. ... Decatur, AL
Griffith, Ann M. ... New York, NY
Griffith, Anthony J. ... Clearwater, FL
Griffith & Associates ... Keene, NH
Manchester, NH
Nashua, NH
Wilton, NH
Griffith, Barry E. ... Rutland, VT
Griffith, Barry L. ... Knoxville, IA
Griffith, Battard & Johnson, L.L.C. ... New Orleans, LA
Griffith & Beach ... Fort Collins, CO
Griffith, Benjamin E. ... Cleveland, MS
Griffith and Bennett, P.C. ... Gilmer, TX
Griffith, Beverly H. ... Owensboro, KY
Griffith, Boone and Cruse ... Los Alamos, NM
Griffith, Boulden G. ... Wilsonville, OR
Griffith, Boyce A. ... Charleston, WV
Griffith, Bradford ... Tulsa, OK
Griffith, Brian J. ... Menlo Park, CA
Griffith, C. Drew ... Toledo, OH
Griffith, C. Laurie ... Louisville, KY
Griffith, C. Michael ... Beckley, WV
Griffith, Calvin P. ... Cleveland, OH
Griffith, Carl A. ... Sidney, NY
Griffith, Carl Ray ... Atlanta, GA
Griffith, Carol L. ... Montgomery, AL
Griffith, Carrie R. ... Siloam Springs, AR
Griffith, Charles C. ... Evansville, IN
Griffith, Charles N. ... Winslow, AR
Griffith, Charles N. ... Waverly, TN
Griffith, Charles R. ... Reynoldsburg, OH
Griffith, Charles S., III ... Covington, KY
Griffith, Charles Tayloe ... Richmond, VA
Griffith, Christine Wade ... San Francisco, CA
Griffith, Christopher H. ... Gadsden, AL
Griffith, Christopher T. ... Chicago, IL
Griffith, Clark C. ... Minneapolis, MN
Griffith, Clark C., P.A. ... Minneapolis, MN
Griffith, Craig A. ... Chicago, IL
Griffith, Curtis C. ... Morton, TX
Griffith, Cynthia J. ... San Francisco, CA
Griffith, D. Joe ... Lancaster, OH
Griffith, D. Kendall, (P.C.) ... Chicago, IL
Griffith, Daniel A. ... Cherry Hill, NJ
Griffith, Daniel J. ... Cleveland, MS
Griffith, Daniel L. ... International Falls, MN
Griffith, Darcy L. ... Seattle, WA
Griffith, David B. ... Gilmer, TX
Griffith, David J. ... Cherry Hill, NJ
Philadelphia, PA
Griffith, David L. ... Newington, CT
Griffith, David M. ... Irvine, CA
Irvine, CA
Griffith, David M. ... Warren, OH
Griffith, David P. ... Houston, TX
Griffith, David W. ... Tulsa, OK
Griffith, Deborah A. ... Phoenix, AZ
Griffith, Dodd Sparks ... Concord, NH
Griffith, Don L. ... Las Vegas, NV
Griffith, Donald B. ... Rancho Mirage, CA
Griffith, Donald E. ... Washington, DC
Griffith, Douglas C. ... Los Angeles, CA
Griffith, Douglas E. ... Salt Lake City, UT
Griffith, Douglas J. ... Johnstown, PA
Griffith, Douglas S. ... Houston, TX
Griffith, Dwight J. ... Newport Beach, CA
Griffith, E. Mitchell ... Beaufort, SC
Griffith, Edward ... La Mesa, CA
Griffith, Edward ... New York, NY
Griffith, Edward ... Wayne, PA
Griffith, Edward D. ... New York, NY
Griffith, Edward M., Jr. ... Buffalo, NY
Griffith, Emlyn I. ... Rome, NY
Griffith, Eugene C., Jr. ... Newberry, SC
Griffith, F. Lee, III ... Stamford, CT
Griffith, Frank J., Jr. (P.A.) ... Cocoa, FL
Griffith, Frederick W. ... Cleveland, OH
Griffith, G. Keith ... Van Buren, AR
Griffith, G. Larry, (P.A.) ... Minneapolis, MN
Griffith, G. Sanders, III ... Columbus, GA
Griffith, Gail Elizabeth ... Oak Hill, VA
Griffith, Garth E. ... Richmond, VA
Griffith, Gary R. ... Atlantic City, NJ
Griffith, Gary W. ... Oak Brook, IL
Griffith, George F. ... Chicago, IL
Griffith, George L. ... Arlington, TX
Griffith, George W. ... Madera, CA
Griffith, Gerald M. ... Detroit, MI
Griffith, Gladis Camilien ... Department of State, GV
Griffith, Gregg Holly ... Phoenix, AZ
Griffith, Gregory L. ... Houston, TX
Griffith & Griffith ... Derby, KS
Griffith & Griffith ... Cleveland, MS
Griffith & Griffith, P.C. ... Crockett, TX
Griffith, Gwendolyn ... Eugene, OR
Griffith, H. Morgan ... Salem, VA
Griffith, Harry A. ... Redwood City, CA
Griffith, Harry G. W., Jr. ... Albuquerque, NM
Griffith, J. Leigh ... Nashville, TN
Griffith, J. Paul ... Marianna, FL
Griffith, J. Terry ... San Francisco, CA
Griffith & Jacobson ... Chicago, IL
Griffith, Jacqueline G. ... New Orleans, LA
Griffith, James A. ... Cleveland, OH
Griffith, James D. ... Chicago, IL
Griffith, James E. ... Mt. Pleasant, IA
Griffith, James Lewis ... Philadelphia, PA
Griffith, James Lewis, Jr. ... Philadelphia, PA
Griffith, Jeff ... Westminster, MD
Griffith, Jeff D., Jr. ... Saluda, SC
Griffith, Jefferson D., III ... Charlotte, NC
Griffith, Jeffrey L. ... Derby, KS
Griffith, Jerry L. ... Derby, KS
Griffith, Jerry L. ... Hoisington, KS
Griffith, Jill F. ... Myrtle Beach, SC
Griffith, Joe E. ... Crockett, TX
Griffith, Joe E. (Jody), Jr. ... Crockett, TX
Griffith, John B. ... Riverside, CA
Griffith, John B. ... Chicago, IL
Griffith, John E., Jr. ... Baltimore, MD
Griffith, John Fredrick ... San Francisco, CA
Griffith, John J., Jr. ... Pittsburgh, PA
Griffith, John L., Jr. ... Princeton, NJ
Griffith, John P. ... Wilton, NH
Griffith, John P. ... Anderson, SC
Griffith, John R. ... Lakeland, FL
Griffith, John R. ... Brownsville, TX
McAllen, TX
Griffith, Johnny L. ... Paintsville, KY
Griffith, Jonathan L. ... Washington, DC
Griffith, Jonathan L. ... Nashville, TN
Griffith, Joseph P., Jr. ... Charleston, SC
Griffith, Julia E. ... Securities and Exchange Commission, Division of Corporation Finance, GV
Griffith, Karen A. ... Albuquerque, NM
Griffith, Kevin E. ... Columbus, OH
Griffith, Kevin K. ... Clarksburg, WV
Griffith, Kevin P. ... Indianapolis, IN
Griffith, Kim A. ... Albuquerque, NM
Griffith, Kimberly A. ... Waterloo, IA
Griffith Law Offices ... Rome, NY
Griffith, Lee ... Monticello, IN
Griffith, Leslie Brodhead ... Madison, WI
Griffith, Lewis H. ... Fairfax, VA
Griffith, Lin H., (P.C.) ... Turlock, CA
Griffith, Linda G. ... San Francisco, CA
Griffith, Linda Leann New ... Arlington, TX
Griffith, Lonnie E., Jr. ... Rochester, NY

Grimes & Craytor .... Texarkana, AR
Texarkana, TX
Grimes, Cynthia Day .... San Antonio, TX
Grimes, Cynthia F. .... Lenexa, KS
Grimes, D. Link .... Midland, TX
Grimes, Dana .... Fort Payne, AL
Grimes, David M. .... New York, NY
Grimes, David N. .... Chatham, VA
Grimes, Deborah Frederick
Birmingham, AL
Grimes, Debra Sue .... Rockville, MD
Grimes, Donald M .... Media, PA
Grimes, Donald W. .... Cary, NC
Grimes, Douglas M., (P.C.) .... Gary, IN
Grimes, Douglas M., (P.C.) .... Gary, IN
Grimes, E. B. .... Robstown, TX
Grimes, Elizabeth Glover
Greensboro, NC
Grimes, Ellen Elkins .... Houston, TX
Grimes, Eugene P. .... Elmsford, NY
Grimes, Fay & Gaeth, L.L.C.
Centralia, MO
Columbia, MO
Grimes & Fertitta, P.C. .... Houston, TX
Grimes, Fred H., Jr. .... Paducah, KY
Grimes, G. Douglas .... Waukegan, IL
Grimes, Gary Allmon .... Mesquite, TX
Grimes, Gary D. .... Texarkana, TX
Grimes, Gelders, Anderson & Day
Oklahoma City, OK
Grimes, George E., Jr. .... Austin, TX
San Antonio, TX
Grimes, Gerald E. .... West Bloomfield, MI
Grimes, Gerald W. .... Missoula, MT
Grimes Goebel Grimes Hawkins & Gladfelter, P.A. .... Bradenton, FL
Sarasota, FL
Tampa, FL
Grimes, Gordon F. .... Portland, ME
Grimes & Grimes .... Camden, NJ
Cherry Hill, NJ
Philadelphia, PA
Grimes, Grover S., Jr. .... Houston, TX
Grimes, H. Terry .... Waynesburg, PA
Grimes, Holly A. .... Atlanta, GA
Grimes, Hubert L. .... Daytona Beach, FL
Grimes, J. Geary .... Fort Worth, TX
Grimes, J. Kevin .... Centre, AL
Grimes, J. Randall .... Georgetown, TX
Grimes, J. Stokley .... Berkeley, CA
Grimes, Jacqueline D. .... Lebanon, MO
Grimes, James L., Jr. .... Topeka, KS
Grimes, James R. .... Chicago, IL
Grimes, Jeffrey K. .... Huntsville, AL
Grimes, Jeffry S. .... Clarksville, TN
Grimes, Jerry B. .... Lexington, NC
Grimes, Jimmy, Sr. & Associates
New Orleans, LA
Grimes, Jimmy W. .... Columbia, SC
Grimes, Joan M. .... Walnut Creek, CA
Grimes, Joanne L. .... Honolulu, HI
Grimes, John F. .... Staten Island, NY
Grimes, John J. .... Chappaqua, NY
Grimes, John M. .... New York, NY
Grimes, John Pyatt .... Georgetown, SC
Grimes, John R. .... Atlanta, GA
Grimes, John R. .... Chicago, IL
Grimes, John W. .... Birmingham, AL
Grimes, Joseph P. .... Cherry Hill, NJ
Philadelphia, PA
Grimes, Joshua L. .... Philadelphia, PA
Grimes, Joyce M. .... Nashville, TN
Grimes, Julie M. .... New York, NY
Grimes, Justin Paul .... Natick, MA
Grimes, Kay L. .... San Antonio, TX
Grimes, Kevin .... Kennebunk, ME
Grimes, Kevin D. .... Idaho Falls, ID
Grimes, L. Charles .... Greensboro, NC
Grimes, L. Raymond .... Clarksville, TN
Grimes, Lawrence L. .... Evansville, IN
Grimes, Leonard L. .... Marshalltown, IA
Grimes, Lonnie L. .... North Little Rock, AR
Grimes, Marcia Lucidi .... Pittsburgh, PA
Grimes, Mark A. .... Winter Park, FL
Grimes, Mark E. .... Miami, FL
Grimes, Mel Noble .... Pacific Grove, CA
Grimes, Michael E. .... Round Rock, TX
Grimes, Michael J. .... Minneapolis, MN
Grimes, Michael T. .... Cherry Hill, NJ
Grimes, Michele B. .... Sarasota, FL
Grimes, Nannette G. .... Centreville, MD
Easton, MD
Grimes, Patrick J. .... Cherry Hill, NJ
Philadelphia, PA
Grimes, Perley H., Jr. .... Litchfield, CT
Grimes, Peter O. .... Middletown, RI
Grimes, Philip A. .... Columbia, MO
Grimes, R. Dale .... Nashville, TN
Grimes, Raymond A. .... Warren, NJ
Grimes, Raymond A., P.C. .... Warren, NJ
Grimes & Rebein, L.C. .... Kansas City, KS
Lenexa, KS
Overland Park, KS
Kansas City, MO
Grimes & Reese, P.L.L.C. .... Idaho Falls, ID
Grimes, Regina Temple .... Austin, TX
Grimes, Richard A., (P.C.)
Oklahoma City, OK
Grimes, Richard M. .... Houston, TX
Grimes, Richard V., Jr. .... Pottsville, PA
Grimes, Robert L. .... San Diego, CA
Grimes, Roberta A. .... Sagamore Beach, MA
Grimes, Robt. A. .... Waltham, MA
Grimes, Rodney G. .... Minneapolis, MN
Grimes, Roger M. .... Chicago, IL
Grimes, Russell C., Jr. .... Kenilworth, IL
Grimes, S. Janson .... Asheville, NC
Grimes, S. William .... Chicago, IL

Grimes, Samuel G. .... Washington, NC
Grimes, Samuel L. .... Spring, TX
Grimes, Shell Duncan .... Los Angeles, CA
Grimes & Smith .... Georgetown, SC
Grimes, Stephen H. .... Tallahassee, FL
Grimes, Stewart .... New Bedford, MA
Grimes, Susan M. .... Hempstead, NY
Grimes & Teich .... Asheville, NC
Grimes, Terry N. .... Roanoke, VA
Grimes, Terry N., P.C. .... Roanoke, VA
Grimes, Thomas M. .... Harleysville, PA
Grimes, Warren S. .... Los Angeles, CA
Grimes & Warwick .... San Diego, CA
Grimes, William C. .... Bradenton, FL
Grimes & Winston .... New York, NY
Grimes, Yolanda M. .... Fort Worth, TX
Grimes & Zimet .... Chappaqua, NY
Grimes-Miller, Cathy L.
Department of Education,
Office of the General Counsel, GV
Griminger, Larry B. .... Peoria, IL
Grimit, Robert T. .... Lincoln, NE
Grimland, Andrew M. .... Houston, TX
Grimley, Arthur T.
Department of Commerce,
Patent and Trademark Office, GV
Grimley, Edward J., Jr. .... Lawrence, MA
Grimley, J. Michael, Jr. .... New Orleans, LA
Grimley, Michael J. .... United States Senate,
Senatorial Assistants, GV
Grimley, William D., (A Prof. Law Corp.)
Baton Rouge, LA
Grimm, Allison M. .... Greensboro, NC
Grimm, Andrew E. .... Omaha, NE
Grimm, Bert M., Jr. .... Huntington, WV
Grimm, Beth A. .... Pleasant Hill, CA
Grimm, Beth A., A Professional Law Corporation .... Pleasant Hill, CA
Grimm, Brian T. .... Kent, OH
Grimm, Courtney Kneece
Jacksonville, FL
Grimm, D. Mark, Jr. .... Lancaster, PA
Grimm, Dale L. .... Los Angeles, CA
Grimm, Daniel J. .... Ojai, CA
Grimm, Danielle M. .... Treasury Department,
Internal Revenue Service, GV
Grimm, David M. .... Diboll, TX
Grimm, E. Paul .... Providence, RI
Grimm, Edgar A. .... Auburn, IN
Grimm, Elizabeth A. .... Dallas, TX
Grimm, Elizabeth M. .... Department of Justice,
Executive Office for Immigration Review,
GV
Grimm, Eric C. .... Washington, DC
Grimm, Eugene L. .... Wilmington, DE
Grimm, Frederick W. .... Seattle, WA
Grimm, Fredric A., Jr. .... Muskegon, MI
Grimm & Grimm, P.C. .... Auburn, IN
Grimm, Harper G. .... Fairmont, WV
Grimm, Jeffrey B. .... Atlanta, GA
Atlanta, GA
Grimm, Jeffrey B., P.C. .... Atlanta, GA
Grimm, John C. .... Auburn, IN
Grimm, John F. .... Pleasant Prairie, WI
Grimm, John S. .... Wilmington, DE
Grimm, John W. .... Cape Girardeau, MO
Grimm, Josephine Victoria
North Ridgeville, OH
Grimm, Karen L. .... Washington, DC
Grimm, Kathleen .... New York, NY
Grimm, Kathleen M. .... Aurora, CO
Grimm, Kurt Bentley .... Auburn, IN
Grimm, Kurt R. .... Fort Worth, TX
Grimm Law Office .... Huntington, WV
Grimm, L. F., Jr. .... Pittsburgh, PA
Grimm, M. Sandlin .... Oklahoma City, OK
Grimm, Marcia L. .... Oakland, CA
Grimm, Mark D. .... St. Louis, MO
Grimm, Mark H. .... Providence, RI
Grimm, Matthew J. .... Twinsburg, OH
Grimm, Michael R., Sr. .... Chicago, IL
Grimm, M. Sandlin, P.C.
Oklahoma City, OK
Grimm, Pamela J. .... Pittsburgh, PA
Grimm, Paul D. .... Rockville, MD
Grimm, Paul L. .... Sacramento, CA
Grimm, Paul W. .... Baltimore, MD
Grimm, Peter B. .... Ocean Township, NJ
Grimm, Peter L. .... Fond du Lac, WI
Grimm, Phyllis E. .... Barrington, IL
Grimm, Reed W. .... Jacksonville, FL
Grimm, Richard A., III .... Buffalo, NY
Grimm, Richard A., Jr. .... Buffalo, NY
Grimm, Rita C. .... Sioux City, IA
Grimm, Robert J. .... Pittsburgh, PA
Grimm, Robert W. .... Buffalo, NY
Grimm, Robert W., Jr. .... Buffalo, NY
Grimm, Ronald L. .... Knoxville, TN
Grimm, Stanley A. .... Cape Girardeau, MO
Grimm, Stanley B.
House of Representatives,
Office of Legislative Counsel, GV
Grimm, Stephen L. .... Grand Rapids, MI
Grimm, Steven E. .... Madison, WI
Grimm, Susan Sieger .... New York, NY
Grimm, Terry M. .... Chicago, IL
Grimm, Thomas C. .... Wilmington, DE
Grimm, Thomas H. .... Bellevue, WA
Grimm, Thomas L. .... Bridgeton, NJ
Grimm, Trevor A. .... Los Angeles, CA
Grimm, Victor E. .... Chicago, IL
Grimm, W. Kirk .... Chicago, IL
Grimm, W. Patrick, (Professional Corporation) .... San Diego, CA
Grimm, W. Thomas .... Naples, FL
Grimm, Wayne A. .... Fargo, ND
Grimm, William .... San Francisco, CA
Grimm, William A. .... Orlando, FL

Grimm, William R. .... Boston, MA
Providence, RI
Grimm, William R. .... Tulsa, OK
Grimm, William T. .... Seattle, WA
Grimmelbein, Louis John, IV
Washington, DC
Grimmer, Christopher M. .... Santa Fe, NM
Grimmer, Dan C. .... Fremont, CA
Grimmer, Edward P. .... Crown Point, IN
Grimmer, Gary G. .... Honolulu, HI
Grimmer, John E. .... New York, NY
Grimmer, Judith A. .... Chicago, IL
Grimmer, Kim .... Madison, WI
Grimmer, Maureen Johns .... Hammond, IN
Grimmer, Ronald G. .... Cincinnati, OH
Grimmer, Stephen A. .... Dallas, TX
Grimmer, Thomas M. .... Hyannis, MA
Grimmer, William T. .... South Bend, IN
Grimme-Schilling, Nancy .... Rockford, IL
Grimmett, Cindy Sue .... Cullman, AL
Grimmett, Jeanne J. .... Library of Congress,
Congressional Research Service, GV
Grimmett, Shirley S. .... Morristown, NJ
Grimmett, Thomas T. .... Fort Lauderdale, FL
Grimmett, Thomas T., P.A.
Fort Lauderdale, FL
Grimmick, Noreen DeWire .... Albany, NY
Grimmig, Eugene M. .... Elmsford, NY
New York, NY
Grimminger, Gwyer .... Grand Island, NE
Grimminger, Myrtle E. .... Grand Island, NE
Grimminger, Sam .... Lincoln, NE
Grimms, Linda DeVries .... Salem, OR
Grimsal, A. Gregory .... New Orleans, LA
Grimshaw, Charles M. .... Grosse Pointe, MI
Grimshaw, Eric .... Tulsa, OK
Grimshaw & Harring, A Professional Corporation .... Denver, CO
Grimshaw, Lynn Alan .... Portsmouth, OH
Grimshaw, Randy M. .... Salt Lake City, UT
Grimshaw & Rock, Chartered .... Olathe, KS
Grimshaw, Thomas T. .... Denver, CO
Grimshaw, William .... Olathe, KS
Grimsinger, William O. .... Houston, TX
Grimsley, Charles J. .... Tallahassee, FL
Grimsley, Darrell Wayne, Jr
Birmingham, AL
Grimsley, Donna J. .... St. Johns, AZ
Grimsley, Edward L. .... Columbia, SC
Grimsley, Gregg N. .... Peoria, IL
Grimsley, J. Alex .... Phoenix, AZ
Grimsley, James A., III .... Beaufort, SC
Grimsley, James W., (P.A.)
Fort Walton Beach, FL
Grimsley, John G. .... Jacksonville, FL
Grimsley Marker & Iseley, P.A.
Jacksonville, FL
Grimsley, Michael S. .... Orlando, FL
Grimsley, Ralph W., Jr. .... Jacksonville, FL
Grimsley, Susan M. .... Boca Raton, FL
Grimsley, Woodrow W. .... Atlanta, GA
Grimslid, Gregory .... Ada, OH
Grimslid and Hood .... Ada, OH
Grimson, Jeffrey S. .... Washington, DC
Grimsrud, Richard M. .... Flagstaff, AZ
Grimsrud, Stephen T. .... San Francisco, CA
Grimstad, Charles M. .... Pittsburgh, PA
Grimstad, John A. .... Minneapolis, MN
Grimstad, Paul H. .... Manitowoc, WI
Grimwade, Richard L. .... Newport Beach, CA
Woodland Hills, CA
Grimwood, Helen Perry .... Phoenix, AZ
Grimwood, N. Douglas .... Phoenix, AZ
Grin, S. Spencer .... Rowayton, CT
Grinage, Lauren B. .... Marshall, MI
Grinalds, Julia Clayton Alexander
Trenton, TN
Grinalds, Julie Alexander .... Jackson, TN
Grinalds, Richard Leigh .... Jackson, TN
Grinberg, Edwin I. .... Elizabeth, PA
Pittsburgh, PA
Grinberg, Michele .... Charleston, WV
Grinberg-Funes, George A.
Department of Justice,
Executive Office for Immigration Review,
GV
Grinblat, Tal S. .... Woodland Hills, CA
Grinblatas, Susan Sullivan .... Boston, MA
Grincewich, Katherine G. .... Washington, DC
Grincewicz, Donald E. .... Orlando, FL
Grinch, Jane A. .... Hackensack, NJ
Grinch, John J. .... New York, NY
Grindal, H. Theodore .... Washington, DC
Minneapolis, MN
Grindal, Layne D. .... Houston, TX
Grindall, Lynn .... Nashville, TN
Grindberg, Alan K. .... Bismarck, ND
Grinde, Paul H. .... Rochester, MN
Grinde, William J. .... Schaumburg, IL
Grindell, David L. .... Frederic, WI
Grindell, John .... Frederic, WI
Grindell, Robt. L. .... Frederic, WI
Grinder, Eileen K. .... Irving, TX
Grinder, Jonathan H. .... Tucson, AZ
Grinder, Marcia L. .... Milwaukee, WI
Grindinger, Dennis J. .... Dallas, TX
Grindle, B. Dean, Jr. .... Dahlonega, GA
Grindle, Daniel W. .... San Diego, CA
Grindle, David Jonathan .... Atlanta, GA
Grindle, John, Jr. .... Washington, DC
Grindle, Larry J. .... Mt. Vernon, OH
Grindle, Robert P. .... North Caldwell, NJ
Grindle, Robinson & Goodhue
Wellesley, MA
Grindle, Steven H. .... Wellesley, MA
Grindle, Thomas L. .... San Diego, CA
Grindler, Gary G. .... Department of Justice,
Office of the Deputy Attorney General, GV

Grindol, Wayne W. .... Jewell, KS
Grindon, Tonya Mitchem .... Nashville, TN
Grindrod, Dale E. .... Monterey, CA
Salinas, CA
Grindstaff, Everett J." Ebb " .... Ballinger, TX
Grindstaff & Grindstaff .... Ballinger, TX
Grindstaff, Keith E. .... Indianapolis, IN
Grindstaff, Lorraine .... Monrovia, CA
Grindstaff, Michael J., (P.A.) .... Orlando, FL
Grine, David E. .... Bellefonte, PA
Griner, G. Christopher .... Washington, DC
Griner, Gregg A. .... Boston, MA
Griner, James J. .... Albany, NY
Griner, Jerome M. .... West Hartford, CT
Griner, John A., IV .... Milwaukee, WI
Griner, M. James .... Tallahassee, FL
Griner, Reggie .... San Francisco, CA
Griner, Tammy M. .... Griffin, GA
Grinfas, Dan .... Portland, OR
Grinfeld, Michael J. .... Los Angeles, CA
Gring & Eves .... Reading, PA
Gring, Pamela R. .... Honolulu, HI
Gring, Stephen J. .... Reading, PA
Gringer, Martin .... Garden City, NY
Grinich, Anita H. .... Portland, OR
Grinis, Anita Volgyi .... Kenosha, WI
Grinker, Ronald L. .... Cincinnati, OH
Grinley, A. K. .... Albert Lea, MN
Grinnalds, Robin A. .... Los Angeles, CA
Grinnalds, Terry Noland .... Hampton, VA
Grinnals, R. Daniel .... De Witt, NY
Grinnan, Antonia Fletcher .... Detroit, MI
Grinnan, Danl., IV .... Richmond, VA
Grinnan, Joseph E. .... Southfield, MI
Grinnan, Michael K. .... Burlington, CO
Grinnan-Mitchell, Gloria K.
Indianapolis, IN
Grinnell, Bruce D. .... Pittsfield, MA
Williamstown, MA
Grinnell & Bureau .... Derry, NH
Londonderry, NH
Manchester, NH
Grinnell, Charles M. .... Howell, NJ
Grinnell, Charles W. .... Stamford, CT
Grinnell, Christopher M. .... Hartford, CT
Grinnell, Daniel V. .... Novato, CA
Grinnell, Douglas W. .... San Diego, CA
Grinnell, Dubendorf & Smith LLP
Pittsfield, MA
Williamstown, MA
Grinnell, Ernest D., Jr. .... Frontenac, MO
Grinnell, George H. .... Londonderry, NH
Grinnell, Jeffrey K. .... Redmond, WA
Grinnell, John P. .... Pasadena, CA
Grinnell, Kenneth L. .... Boston, MA
Grinnell, Paul E. .... Moorhead, MN
Fargo, ND
Grinnell, Stephen F. .... Minneapolis, MN
Grinolds, Shawn Arlin .... Grand Forks, ND
Grinols, Elinor I. .... New York, NY
Grinpas, Robert M. .... Kapaa, HI
Grinpas, Robert M., A Law Corporation
Kapaa, HI
Grinsberg, Howard Alan .... New York, NY
Grinsfelder, Lisa .... Columbus, OH
Grinspan, Edward M. .... Ardmore, PA
Grinstead, Angela L. .... New York, NY
Grinstead, Darrel J. .... Washington, DC
Grinstead, E. Mahlian .... Lawrenceburg, KY
Grinstead, Leonard M. .... Hinesville, GA
Grinstead, S. Tevis .... Houston, TX
Grinstead, Yolanda Y. .... New Orleans, LA
Grinsted, Albert .... Fort Walton Beach, FL
Grinsted, Albert H., III .... Shalimar, FL
Grinsted & Grinsted, P.A.
Fort Walton Beach, FL
Grinsted, Patricia S.
Fort Walton Beach, FL
Grinstein, Deborah L. .... Youngstown, OH
Grinstein, Jeffrey M. .... Warren, OH
Grinstein, Joseph S. .... Houston, TX
Grinstein, Peter B. .... Youngstown, OH
Grinvalds, Astra .... Department of Labor,
Office of Secretary, GV
Grinvalds, Edwin Arthur .... Springfield, OH
Grip, Julia Packard .... Chicago, IL
Gripkey, Stephen J. .... Department of Justice,
Civil Division, GV
Gripp, Bert .... Houston, TX
Gripp, David A. .... Leesburg, VA
Gripp, G. Philip .... Hartford, CT
Gripp, Wilbert K. .... Houston, TX
Grippa, Kimberly A. .... Tallahassee, FL
Grippando, Thomas J. .... Chicago, IL
Grippo, Daniel P. .... Uniondale, NY
Grippo & Elden .... Chicago, IL
Grippo, Joanne C. .... Brooklyn, NY
Grippo, Maryann J. .... Scranton, PA
Grippo, Romney L. .... Florham Park, NJ
Grippo, Theodore W. .... Chicago, IL
Grippo, Theodore W., Jr. .... Park Ridge, IL
Grisafi, James Charles .... La Mesa, CA
Grisafi, John P. .... Lake Success, NY
Grisales-Racini, Oscar .... Aventura, FL
Grisamore, C. W. .... Lake Forest, IL
Grisanti, Christopher C. .... New York, NY
Grisanti, Eugene P. .... New York, NY
Grisanti, Joseph D. .... Brick, NJ
Grisanti, Justine .... New York, NY
Grisanti, Maureen A. .... Santa Monica, CA
Grisanti, Richard D. .... Buffalo, NY
Grisanti, Robert C. .... Northfield, OH
Grisaru, Elizabeth A. .... New York, NY
Grischke, Alan E. .... Wausau, WI
Wisconsin Rapids, WI
Grischke & Bremer, S.C. .... Wausau, WI
Wisconsin Rapids, WI
Griscom, Mary Suzanne .... Little Rock, AR

Grogan, David M. ...... **Charlotte, NC**
Grogan, Deborah Marie
Treasury Department, Internal Revenue Service, GV
Grogan, Edward J. ...... Clifton Park, NY
Grogan, Edward Patrick ...... Clifton Park, NY
Grogan, Edward R. ...... San Francisco, CA
Grogan, Eric L. ...... **New Providence, NJ**
Grogan, G. E. ...... Detroit, MI
Grogan, Gerard T. ...... Goshen, NY
Grogan, Graffam, McGinley & Lucchino, P.C. ...... **Pittsburgh, PA**
Grogan, J. Kevin ...... **Springfield, MA**
Grogan, James J. ...... Scottsdale, AZ
Grogan, James J. ...... Chicago, IL
Grogan, Joanne F. ...... Elsmere, KY
Grogan, John M. ...... Traverse City, MI
Grogan, John M., Jr. ...... Milwaukee, WI
Grogan, John T. ...... **Morristown, NJ**
Grogan, Lee R. ...... **Columbus, GA**
Grogan, Lee R., Jr. ...... **Columbus, GA**
Grogan, Lynn L. ...... **Columbus, GA**
Grogan, Michael K. ...... **Jacksonville, FL**
Grogan, Owens D. ...... Malone, NY
Grogan, Philip R. ...... Bowling Green, KY
Grogan, Richard G. ...... Redding, CA
Grogan, R. J., Jr. ...... Dallas, TX
Grogan, Robert A. ...... Los Angeles, CA
Grogan, Robert H. ...... **Miami, FL**
Grogan, Robert J. ...... Lyndhurst, OH
Grogan, Rumer & Gunby ...... **Columbus, GA**
Grogan, Sabrina R. ...... **Charleston, SC**
Grogan, Sean ...... Bayside, NY
Brooklyn, NY
New York, NY
Grogan, Shelley A. ...... Milwaukee, WI
Grogan & Shelor ...... Richmond, VA
Grogan, Souto & Schonberg, P.C.
Goshen, NY
Grogan, Stephanie J. ...... Washington, DC
Grogan, Susan E. ...... **Manassas, VA**
Grogan, Thomas E. ...... Naples, FL
Grogan, Thomas E., P.A. ...... Naples, FL
Grogan, Thomas J. ...... Tigard, OR
Grogan, Thomas R. ...... Oshkosh, WI
Grogan, Timothy M. ...... Mobile, AL
Grogan, Vincent J. ...... **Pittsburgh, PA**
Grogan, Virginia Sollenberger
Costa Mesa, CA
Grogan, William J. ...... Appleton, WI
Grogan, William K. ...... Richmond, VA
Grogan, William P. ...... **Chicago, IL**
Groger, Herbert R. ...... Beachwood, OH
Grogg, Thomas A. ...... Marion, IN
Grogg, Tim A. ...... Columbus, IN
Grogg, Vincent F. ...... Covington, IN
Grogin, Jeffrey P. ...... Pasadena, CA
Grogins, Auden ...... **Fairfield, CT**
Grogins, David L. ...... **Danbury, CT**
Grogins & Grogins ...... **Fairfield, CT**
Grogins, Jack L. ...... Fairfield, CT
Groglio, George M. ...... Port Chester, NY
Grogoza, Stephen M. ...... Naples, FL
Groh, Anthony J. ...... Milwaukee, WI
Groh, Bryan M. ...... **St. Louis, MO**
Groh, Carroll, Stern & Werner, A Professional Corporation ...... Irvine, CA
Groh, Charles M. ...... Ann Arbor, MI
Groh, Charles M., P.C. ...... Ann Arbor, MI
Groh, Clifford J., II ...... Anchorage, AK
Groh, Edward D. ...... Linthicum Heights, MD
Groh Eggers, LLC ...... **Anchorage, AK**
Groh, Ellen G. ...... Greenville, NC
Groh, Gerald R. ...... Dallas, TX
Groh, Irvin L. ...... **Venice, FL**
Groh, James S. ...... **Miami, FL**
Groh, John L.
Federal Deposit Insurance Corporation, GV
Groh, Kirk P. ...... **New Orleans, LA**
Groh, Kitty L. ...... **East Lansing, MI**
Groh, Martin C. ...... **Irvine, CA**
Groh, Robt. T. ...... Jamaica, NY
Groh, Rupert J., Jr. ...... Los Angeles, CA
Groh, Stephen B. ...... Silver Spring, MD
Groh, Stephen Vincent ...... Hagerstown, MD
Groh, Vincent R. ...... Hagerstown, MD
Groh, William C. ...... **Trenton, NJ**
Groh, William Matthew ...... Garden City, NY
Groher, Andrew S. ...... **Hartford, CT**
Groher, Julius ...... New Canaan, CT
Groher & Sullivan ...... New Canaan, CT
Grohl, Renie Yoshida ...... **Washington, DC**
Grohler, Mark C. ...... **Columbus, OH**
Grohman, Joseph M. ...... Fort Lauderdale, FL
Grohman, Michael D. ...... **New York, NY**
Grohman, Thomas F. ...... **Seattle, WA**
Grohmann, James P. ...... **Louisville, KY**
Grohmann, John G. ...... **Louisville, KY**
Grohmann, Richard W. ...... **Paramus, NJ**
Grohmann, Richard W., P.C.
Paramus, NJ
Grohne, Jack A. ...... Chicago, IL
Grohne, James A. ...... Springfield, IL
Grohowski, Alyse Renee ...... Dexter, MI
Grohowski, Robert C. ...... **Washington, DC**
Grohs, Deborah J. ...... Chicago, IL
Grohsgal, Barbara W. ...... Short Hills, NJ
Grohsgal, Bruce ...... **Wilmington, DE**
Groh-Wargo, Frank J. ...... **Cleveland, OH**
Groiss, Fred G. ...... **Milwaukee, WI**
Groisser, Debra S. ...... **Newark, NJ**
Groisser, Suzanne J. ...... New York, NY
Grokenberger, David M.
Santa Barbara, CA
Grokenberger, Smith & Courtney, A Professional Corporation
Santa Barbara, CA
Grolimund, J. Moritz, Jr. ...... Elkhart, IN

Groll, Catherine ...... **Lansing, MI**
Groll, Christina ...... **Denver, CO**
Groll, Christopher J. ...... **Boston, MA**
Groll, Michael ...... **New York, NY**
Groll, William A. ...... **New York, NY**
Grollman, George G. ...... New York, NY
Grolman, Ira H. ...... Boston, MA
Grolnick, Robert T. ...... Philadelphia, PA
Grolock, Ramon C. ...... Sun Valley, CA
Grolz, Edward W. ...... **Garden City, NY**
Gromacki, George P. ...... South Deerfield, MA
Gromacki, Joseph P. ...... **Chicago, IL**
Gromala, John A. ...... Eureka, CA
Groman, Dawn J. ...... **New York, NY**
Groman, Marc M. ...... **Boston, MA**
Groman, Paul B. ...... New York, NY
Groman, Robert H. ...... **Carle Place, NY**
Groman, Ross & Tisman, P.C.
Carle Place, NY
Groman & Segall ...... New York, NY
Groman, Tod P. ...... New York, NY
Gromann, Glenn Eric ...... Newark, NJ
Grombacher, Charles A. ...... **Phoenix, AZ**
Grombala, Carol W.
Farmington Hills, MI
Grombschevsky, Stan A.
Newport Beach, CA
Gromek, Carl L. ...... Lansing, MI
Gromek, Gregory ...... Bloomfield Hills, MI
Gromel, G. H., Jr. ...... Richmond, VA
Gromelski, David J. ...... Wilkes-Barre, PA
Gromelski, Jane A. ...... West Caldwell, NJ
Gromen, Richard John, Jr.
Elizabethtown, PA
Gromer, Paul W. ...... Boston, MA
Gromer, Tracy A. ...... Phoenix, AZ
Gromer & Wittenstrom, P.C. ...... Elgin, IL
Gromet & Associates ...... **Irvine, CA**
Gromet, Stevan J. ...... **Irvine, CA**
Grometer, R. Peter ...... Geneva, IL
Grometstein, Randall ...... Stoneham, MA
Gromfine, Isadore J. ...... Washington, DC
Gromis & Aguirre ...... Fresno, CA
Gromis, David P. ...... Fresno, CA
Gromis, Marc S. ...... Buffalo, NY
Gromley, Colin M. ...... Atlanta, GA
Gromoll, Norda Bardwell ...... Eagle River, WI
Gromowski, JoAnn (IBA) ...... Wauwatosa, WI
Gron, Gary M. ...... Columbus, IN
Gron, Teddy S. ...... Department of Commerce, Patent and Trademark Office, GV
Grona, Sara G. ...... College Station, TX
Gronan, Daphne ...... Ponce, PR
Gronau Choy & Taga
Glenwood Springs, CO
Honolulu, HI
Gronau, Kurt A. ...... **Glenwood Springs, CO**
Honolulu, HI
Gronauer, Robert J. ...... **Las Vegas, NV**
Gronbeck, David ...... **Minneapolis, MN**
Gronbeck, Kelly M. ...... **Pittsburgh, PA**
Gronda, Daniel Amo ...... **New York, NY**
Gronda, John D. ...... Melbourne, FL
Grondahl, Eric E. ...... **Hartford, CT**
Grondin, Belinda B. ...... **New York, NY**
Grondwalski, John H. ...... Tarentum, PA
Gronek, Dennis M. ...... Chicago, IL
Gronek, Robert J. ...... **Orlando, FL**
Groneman, George A. ...... Kansas City, KS
Groneman, Raymond C. ...... Cincinnati, OH
Groneman, Robert T. ...... Houston, TX
Gronemeier & Associates
South Pasadena, CA
Gronemeier, Dale L. ...... South Pasadena, CA
Gronemeyer, Lyman S. ...... Los Angeles, CA
Groner, Arlene Pianko
Department of Justice, Civil Division, GV
Groner, Betty ...... Akron, OH
Groner, Beverly Anne ...... **Chevy Chase, MD**
Groner, David W., (P.C.) ...... New Iberia, LA
Groner, Felicia M. ...... Washington, DC
Groner, Gerald F. ...... Midland, TX
Groner, Gerald T.
Christiansted, St. Croix, VI
Groner and Groner, Chartered
Washington, DC
Chevy Chase, MD
Groner, Irwin H. ...... Woodland Hills, CA
Groner, Isaac N. ...... **Washington, DC**
Groner, Jack C. ...... Baton Rouge, LA
Groner, James M. ...... **Columbus, OH**
Groner, Laurence M.
Department of the Air Force, Office of the General Counsel, GV
Groner, Richard W. ...... **Sarasota, FL**
Groner, Robert ...... Department of Justice, Criminal Division, GV
Groner, Samuel B. ...... **Chevy Chase, MD**
Groner & Schieb ...... **Sarasota, FL**
Groner, Simon ...... Cincinnati, OH
Groner, William H. ...... New York, NY
White Plains, NY
Gronet, Deborah Ann ...... Tucson, AZ
Gronewald, Josephine Renner
Morristown, TN
Gronewold, Stephen J. ...... Minneapolis, MN
Gronfein, Sandra G. ...... Mercer Island, WA
Gronholm, Gregory T. ...... **Atlanta, GA**
Gronhovd, Sheri Lynn ...... Phoenix, AZ
Gronich, Daphne ...... **Beverly Hills, CA**
Gronikowski, Lee A. ...... Trenton, NJ
Groninger, Ann Elizabeth ...... Fayetteville, NC
Groninger, Donald L. ...... Nashville, TN
Beaumont, TX
Groninger, James G. ...... Pittsburgh, PA
Gronke, Robert D. ...... Sacramento, CA
Gronkiewicz, Edmund ...... **Chicago, IL**
Gronkiewicz, Theresa ...... **Chicago, IL**

Gronko, Richard D. ...... Miami, FL
Gronlund, Linda K. ...... Montvale, NJ
Gronlund, Mary ...... Washington, DC
Gronna, Richard D. ...... **Honolulu, HI**
Gronneberg, Gary S. ...... Fargo, ND
Gronniger, Daniel J. ...... Topeka, KS
Gronning, Chris D. ...... **Anchorage, AK**
Gronningsater, Adolphus W. D. ...... Easton, MD
Gronowski, K. Scott ...... **St. Louis, MO**
Gronowski, Katy M. ...... San Francisco, CA
Gronowski, Stephen L. ...... San Francisco, CA
Gronquist, James E. ...... **Charlotte, NC**
Gronquist, Wayne ...... Austin, TX
Gronquist, Wayne, P.C. ...... Austin, TX
Gronseth, Edward C. ...... Treasury Department, Bureau of the Public Debt, GV
Gronseth, Glen B. ...... Lansing, MI
Gronsman, David S. ...... **New York, NY**
Groob, Ressler & Mulqueen, A Professional Corporation ...... New Haven, CT
Groobert, Edward A. ...... **Washington, DC**
Groobert, Paul B. ...... Manchester, CT
Groobey, J. Christopher ...... Washington, DC
Groom, Brit D. ...... Shoshone, ID
Twin Falls, ID
Groom, Brock ...... **Fort Worth, TX**
Groom, Bruce M. ...... Midland, MI
Groom Cave ...... San Jose, CA
Groom, David A. ...... **Denver, CO**
Groom, Donald Lee ...... Louisville, KY
Groom & Groom, P.C. ...... Mabank, TX
Groom, Hammond & Harris, P.C.
Oklahoma City, OK
Groom, John F. ...... San Diego, CA
Groom, Kathleen E. ...... **New York, NY**
Groom Law Group, Chartered
Washington, DC
Groom, M. Thad ...... **Oklahoma City, OK**
Groom, Marshall Hall, Jr. ...... New York, NY
Groom, Michael E. ...... Department of Labor, Office of Secretary, GV
Groom, Michael P. ...... San Jose, CA
Groom, Patrick M. ...... **Greeley, CO**
Groom, Paul W., II ...... **Pensacola, FL**
Groom, Peter E. ...... San Francisco, CA
Groom, Rudy M. ...... Mabank, TX
Groom, Sid M., Jr. ...... **Oklahoma City, OK**
Groom, Steven Evans ...... **Nashville, TN**
Groom, Theodore R. ...... **Washington, DC**
Groom, W. Brad ...... **Muskegon, MI**
Groombridge, Nicholas ...... **New York, NY**
Groome, David K., Jr. ...... **Metairie, LA**
Groome, H. Houston, Jr. ...... **Lenoir, NC**
Groome, Margaret M. ...... New Orleans, LA
Grooms, Alice J. ...... New Orleans, LA
Grooms, Garry K. ...... **Nashville, TN**
Grooms, H. Hobart, Jr. ...... **Birmingham, AL**
Grooms, James E. ...... New York, NY
Grooms, Lloyd W., Jr. ...... **Minneapolis, MN**
St. Paul, MN
Grooms, Odell ...... Washington, DC
Grooms, Stacey Lemley
Lawrenceburg, TN
Grooms, Thomas E., Jr. ...... Indianapolis, IN
Grooms, Thomas J. ...... **Syracuse, NY**
Grooms, Timothy W. ...... **Little Rock, AR**
Grooms-Marvin, Cynthia ...... Fort Pierce, FL
Groon, Gerald H., Jr. ...... **Raleigh, NC**
Groos, Alicia Morris ...... **Austin, TX**
Groos, Richard J. ...... **Austin, TX**
Groose, David F. ...... Wausau, WI
Groot, Gary J. ...... **Wilton, CT**
Groot, Lonnie N. ...... Sanford, FL
Groot, Roger D. ...... Lexington, VA
Groot, S. Robert ...... Whittier, CA
Grooters, David A. ...... **Mason City, IA**
Groothuis, Erik S. ...... **New York, NY**
Groothuis, Kathryn J. ...... **Boston, MA**
Groothuis, Mark L. ...... **Hempstead, NY**
Groover, Arthur (Ike) ...... Hartselle, AL
Groover & Associates, P.C. ...... **Dallas, TX**
Groover, August T. ...... Media, PA
Groover & Childs ...... Macon, GA
Groover, Claramargaret H. ...... **Orlando, FL**
Groover, David E. ...... Anniston, AL
Groover, Denmark, Jr. ...... Macon, GA
Groover, Duke R. ...... Macon, GA
Groover, Jacqueline S ...... Atlanta, GA
Groover, Jennifer ...... **Kansas City, MO**
Groover, Judy L., Law Office of
Jacksonville, FL
Groover, Lewis M., Jr. ...... Atlanta, GA
Groover and Lobos ...... Mifflinburg, PA
Groover, Lona L. ...... Las Vegas, NV
Groover, Madison and Gray, P.C.
Hartselle, AL
Groover, Richard J. ...... Danville, IN
Groover, Robert, III ...... **Dallas, TX**
Gropen, Moss ...... Irvine, CA
Gropen, Sara Lee ...... Charlottesville, VA
Groper, Earle ...... Chestnut Hill, MA
Gropman, Jerome C. ...... **Troy, MI**
Gropp, David L. ...... Beaver, PA
Gropp, Donald W. ...... Naples, FL
Gropp, Mark D. ...... **Atlanta, GA**
Groppe, Charles J. ...... Manhasset, NY
New York, NY
Groppe, Charles P. ...... **Washington, DC**
Gropper, Charles F. ...... Silver Spring, MD
Gropper, Daniel R. ...... Vienna, VA
Gropper, Daniel R., P.C. ...... Vienna, VA
Gropper, Ira F. ...... Pembroke Pines, FL
Gropper, Jane E. ...... Jamaica, NY
Gropper, Jill ...... **Somerville, NJ**
Gropper, Joshua D. ...... New York, NY
Groppi, McNamara & Underhill
Danville, IL
Groppo, Ann Marie ...... Torrington, CT

Grorud, David C. ...... **Minneapolis, MN**
Gros, Helen M. ...... Houston, TX
Gros, Stanley J. ...... Viroqua, WI
Grosbach, Wallace H. ...... Brazil, IN
Grosbard, Alan Z. ...... Los Angeles, CA
Grosberg, A. Hillary ...... Encino, CA
Grosberg, Joel ...... **Washington, DC**
Grosberg, Lawrence M. ...... New York, NY
Grosberg, Lawrence S. ...... Los Angeles, CA
Grosboll, Carolyn Taft ...... Springfield, IL
Grosboll, John E. ...... Petersburg, IL
Grosboll, Richard K. ...... San Francisco, CA
Grosby, Mark J. ...... Waitsfield, VT
Grosby, Robert N. ...... **Westport, CT**
Grosch, Carla A. ...... Elgin, IL
Grosch, Kim J., (Mr.) ...... Coeur d'Alene, ID
Grosch, Nicholas T. ...... Newark, NJ
Grosch, Timothy L. ...... St. Louis, MO
Groschadl, Paul S. ...... **Rochester, NY**
Gros-Cloren, Sara ...... San Diego, CA
Groscup, C. William
Greenwood Village, CO
Groscup, Margaret M. ...... **Denver, CO**
Grosdidier, Kathryn S. ...... New Richmond, WI
Grose, Darla Copeland ...... Spokane, WA
Grose, Douglas L. ...... Tampa, FL
Grose, Douglas L., P.A. ...... Tampa, FL
Grose, James G. ...... Oswego, NY
Grose, John L. ...... Locust Valley, NY
Grose, Peter K. ...... **Washington, DC**
Grose, Scarlett D.
General Services Administration, Office of the General Counsel, GV
Grose, Stephen L. ...... **Harrisburg, PA**
Groseclos, Gene G. ...... Bella Vista, AR
Groseclose, Alan D. ...... Pulaski, VA
Groseclose, Chester A., Jr. ...... **Aberdeen, SD**
Groseclose, David A. ...... Phoenix, AZ
Groseclose, Murry C., III ...... Kingsport, TN
Groseclose, Robert B. ...... **Fairbanks, AK**
Groseclose, Steven J. ...... **Washington, DC**
Grosenheider, Delno J., (P.C.) ...... **Austin, TX**
Groseth, Craig C. ...... **Denver, CO**
Grosfeld, Robert ...... Orange, CA
Grosfeld, Sharon M. ...... **Annapolis, MD**
Grosfield, Norman H. ...... Helena, MT
Grosh, Lisa J. ...... Department of State, Office of the Legal Adviser, GV
Grosh, Susan E. ...... **Lancaster, PA**
Groshek, Michael D. ...... **Denver, CO**
Groshell, Hiram P. ...... Tacoma, WA
Groshens, Thomas E. ...... **Philadelphia, PA**
Groshon, Robert F., Jr. ...... Oklahoma City, OK
Groshong, Donald E. ...... Alton, IL
Groshong, Geoffrey ...... **Seattle, WA**
Groshong, Patrick L. ...... Kansas City, MO
Groshong, W. Ronald ...... Seattle, WA
Grosick, Glenn J. ...... Pittsburgh, PA
Grosjean, Walter C. ...... **Wooster, OH**
Groskaufmanis, Karl A. ...... **Washington, DC**
Groskin, Lawrence J. ...... Tuxedo Park, NY
Groskopf, Aubrey W. ...... Los Angeles, CA
Groskopf, John E. ...... Deerfield, IL
Grosky, David S., Law Office of
Buffalo Grove, IL
Grosky, Mark Brian ...... Albany, NY
Grosman, Alan M. ...... **Millburn, NJ**
Grosman, Albin W. ...... Orlando, FL
Grosman, Christopher A.
Birmingham, MI
Grosman & Grosman ...... **Millburn, NJ**
Grosman, Kurt E. ...... Orlando, FL
Gross, A. David ...... **Dallas, TX**
Gross, Aaron J. ...... Silver Spring, MD
Gross, Abraham J. ...... Great Neck, NY
Gross, Adam E. ...... Chicago, IL
Gross, Alan B. ...... Gaithersburg, MD
Gross, Alan D. ...... Bell Gardens, CA
Gross, Alan D. ...... Cleveland, OH
Gross, Alan M. ...... **St. Petersburg, FL**
Gross, Alan W. ...... Cherry Hill, NJ
Gross, Albert C. ...... **San Diego, CA**
Gross, Albert C. ...... **Solana Beach, CA**
Gross, Albert M. ...... Pembroke Pines, FL
Gross, Allan M. ...... Pittsburgh, PA
Gross, Allen J., (A Professional Corporation)
Los Angeles, CA
Gross, Allison A. ...... **Chicago, IL**
Gross, Amiel S. ...... **Austin, TX**
Gross, Andrea L. ...... Sacramento, CA
Gross, Andrea S. ...... New York, NY
Gross, Andrew J. ...... Seattle, WA
Gross, Andrew M. ...... **Boca Raton, FL**
Gross, Andrew M. ...... Dallas, TX
Gross, Andrew N. ...... **Atlanta, GA**
Gross, Andrew W. ...... **Los Angeles, CA**
Gross, Anita Pellman
Department of Commerce, Patent and Trademark Office, GV
Gross, Anthony G. ...... New York, NY
Gross, Anthony W. ...... Middletown, NY
Gross, Ari Michael ...... **New York, NY**
Gross, Arnold W. ...... Newbury Park, CA
Gross, Arthur ...... Spring Valley, NY
Gross, Avery J. ...... Staten Island, NY
Gross, Avrum M. ...... Juneau, AK
Gross, Baety O., Jr. ...... Fountain Inn, SC
Gross, Barbara A. ...... **New York, NY**
Gross, Barbara R. ...... San Diego, CA
Gross, Barrie ...... San Francisco, CA
Gross, Barry J. ...... Wantagh, NY
Gross, Barry L. ...... Newtown, PA
Gross & Belsky LLP ...... **San Francisco, CA**
Gross, Benjamin ...... Paulsboro, NJ
Gross, Benjamin R. ...... **Savannah, GA**
Gross, Bennett S. ...... Norwalk, CT
Gross, Benton F. ...... Oakland, CA
Gross, Bernard ...... Henderson, NV

Gross, Bernard M. ... Philadelphia, PA
Gross, Bernard M., P.C. ... Philadelphia, PA
Gross, Bert M. ... Minneapolis, MN
Gross, Beverly ... New York, NY
Gross, Brad H. ... Los Angeles, CA
Gross, Bradley J. ... Fort Lauderdale, FL
Gross, Brian D. ... Boston, MA
Gross, Brian J. ... United States Senate, Senatorial Assistants, GV
Gross, Bruce A. ... Manassas, VA
Gross, Bruce F. ... Windom, MN
Gross, Bryon W. ... Ontario, NY
Gross & Burke ... Juneau, AK
Gross, Burton A. ... San Francisco, CA
Gross, Byron J. ... Los Angeles, CA
Gross, Carl P. ... Freehold, NJ
Gross, Carol Sikov ... Pittsburgh, PA
Gross, Charles ... Minneapolis, MN
Gross, Charles H. ... Tecumseh, MI
Gross, Charles R. ... Department of Justice, Civil Division, GV
Gross, Cheryl J. ... Newark, NJ
Gross, Christina ... New York, NY
Gross, Clark D. ... Los Angeles, CA
Gross, Claudia Beth ... New York, NY
Gross, Clifford R. ... Washington, DC
Gross, Craig ... San Diego, CA
Gross, D. Milburn, Jr. ... Andalusia, AL
Gross, Daniel M. ... Wheat Ridge, CO
Gross, David ... Seattle, WA
Gross, David A. ... Washington, DC
Gross, David A. ... Long Beach, NY
Gross, David B. ... Jackson, MS
Gross, David B., (P.C.) ... Austin, TX
Gross, David C. ... Philadelphia, PA
Gross, David E. ... Newburgh, NY
Gross, David F. ... Palo Alto, CA
Gross, David J.F. ... Minneapolis, MN
Gross, David M. ... Brooklyn, NY
Gross, David R. ... Short Hills, NJ
New York, NY
Gross & Davidson, P.A. ... Pensacola, FL
Gross, Deborah J. ... Miami Beach, FL
Gross, Deborah M. ... Hackensack, NJ
Gross, Deborah R. ... Philadelphia, PA
Gross, Debra Lynn ... Monmouth Beach, NJ
Gross, Dennis A. ... Chicago, IL
Gross, Derla R. ... Crown Point, IN
Gross, Diane Arkow ... Los Angeles, CA
Gross, Diane L. ... Washington, DC
Gross, Diane M. ... San Jose, CA
Gross, Dianne G. ... Tehachapi, CA
Gross, Dimitri P. ... Costa Mesa, CA
Gross, Dodi Walker ... Pittsburgh, PA
Gross, Dolores E. ... Southfield, MI
Gross, Donald E. ... St. Paul, MN
Gross, Donald G. ... Department of State, Office of the Secretary, GV
Gross, Donald R. ... Culver City, CA
Gross, Donald W. ... Roseburg, OR
Gross, Douglas ... New York, NY
Gross, Douglas E. ... Des Moines, IA
Gross, Douglas H. ... Dallas, TX
Gross, Douglas M. ... Gaithersburg, MD
Gross, E. Mark ... White Plains, NY
Gross, Edgar F. ... Culver City, CA
Gross, Edmund S. ... Kansas City, MO
Gross, Edward ... New Brunswick, NJ
Gross, Edward ... Fairfax, VA
Gross, Edward, & Associates, P.C.
Fairfax, VA
Gross, Edward F. ... Roseville, MN
Gross, Edward J. ... Nashville, TN
Gross, Edward K. ... Baltimore, MD
Gross, Edward S. ... Boca Raton, FL
Gross, Edward S., P.A. ... Boca Raton, FL
Gross, Edward V. ... New York, NY
Gross, Edwin N. ... West Caldwell, NJ
Gross, Efrom Judah ... New York, NY
Gross, Egon M. ... Warren, MI
Gross, Elizabeth Cari ... Brooklyn, NY
Gross, Elizabeth D. ... Lee, MA
Gross, Ellen Faye ... San Diego, CA
Gross, Elliot S. ... Rockville Centre, NY
Gross, Emily Carol ... Atlanta, GA
Gross, Eric J. ... Aspen, CO
Snowmass Village, CO
Gross, Eric M. ... Bridgeport, CT
Gross, Ernest M. ... San Diego, CA
Gross, Ethan A. ... Huntington Woods, MI
Gross, Evelyn C. ... Oak Park, IL
Gross, Felicia ... New York, NY
Gross, Felix V. ... Pleasant Hill, MO
Gross, Frank H., Jr. ... Westborough, MA
Gross, Frank J. ... Norfolk, MA
Gross, Fred J. ... Dallas, TX
Gross, Fred J., P.C. ... Dallas, TX
Gross, G. Peter ... New York, NY
Gross, G. Raymond F. ... Los Angeles, CA
Gross, Gary E. ... Chicago, IL
Gross, Gary L. ... Cleveland, OH
Gross, Gary Paul ... Washington, DC
Gross, Gene ... Murphysboro, IL
Gross, Geo. W. ... Columbus, OH
Gross, Geoffrey E. ... San Francisco, CA
Gross, George N. ... Salem, OR
Gross, Gerald P. ... New York, NY
Gross, Gerald R. ... St. Paul, MN
Gross, Gerard C. ... Northfield, NJ
Gross, Gerhard R. ... Houston, TX
Gross & Gilbert ... Beverly Hills, CA
Gross, Glen L. ... Arlington, VA
Gross, Gordon R. ... Buffalo, NY
Gross, Gregory A. ... Pittsburgh, PA
Gross, Gregory L. ... Marshfield, WI
Gross & Gross ... River Edge, NJ
Gross & Gross ... Brooklyn, NY
Gross & Gross ... Mount Vernon, NY
Gross, Gross & Gross ... Liberty, NY
Monticello, NY
Gross, Gross & Simon, P.C.
Los Angeles, CA
Gross and Hanlon, P.C. ... Freehold, NJ
Gross, Hannah S. ... Mount Vernon, NY
Gross, Harold J. ... Washington, DC
Gross, Harold M. ... Department of Agriculture, Grain Inspection Packers and Stockyards Administration, GV
Gross, Harris Michael ... Tyler, TX
Gross, Harry A. ... Brooklyn, NY
Gross, Hayim I. ... Southfield, MI
Gross, Heidi Wegryn ... Short Hills, NJ
Gross, Henry ... New York, NY
Gross, Herbert ... Kensington, CA
Gross, Holly Seide ... Miami, FL
Gross, Howard ... Dover, NH
Gross, Howard I. ... Farmington, CT
Gross, Howard P. ... Miami, FL
Gross, Howard R. ... Garden City, NY
Gross, Hyath B. ... Schenectady, NY
Gross, Hyde & Williams ... Hartford, CT
Gross, Hyman ... New York, NY
Gross, Ira K. ... Boston, MA
Gross, Irving M. ... Los Angeles, CA
Gross, Irwin A. ... Chicago, IL
Gross, Irwin Mark ... Brooklyn, NY
Gross, Irwin R. ... Palo Alto, CA
Gross, J. Arthur ... Chicago, IL
Gross, J. Nicholas ... Beverly Hills, CA
Gross, J. Robert ... Centerville, OH
Gross, Jack ... New York, NY
Gross, Jack ... New York, NY
Gross, Jackie L. ... Jamaica, NY
Gross, Jacob N., (Ltd.) ... Chicago, IL
Gross, James A. ... San Jose, CA
Gross, James C. ... Sacramento, CA
San Francisco, CA
Gross, James C. ... Boston, MA
Gross, James E. ... Chicago, IL
Gross, James G. ... Detroit, MI
Gross, James H. ... Columbus, OH
Gross, James J. ... Chevy Chase, MD
Gross, James N. ... Dallas, TX
Gross, Jamie ... New York, NY
Gross, Jamie E. ... Los Angeles, CA
Gross, Jane C.
Federal Communications Commission, Mass Media Bureau, GV
Gross, Janet M. ... Indianapolis, IN
Gross, Janice L. ... San Rafael, CA
Gross, Janice S. ... Boston, MA
Gross, Jared E. ... Los Angeles, CA
Gross, Jason K. ... New York, NY
Gross, Jay N. ... Houston, TX
Gross, Jay S. ... Cedar Rapids, IA
Gross, Jefferson W. ... Salt Lake City, UT
Gross, Jeffrey ... Great Neck, NY
Gross, Jeffrey D. ... Phoenix, AZ
Gross, Jeffrey D. ... Tacoma, WA
Gross, Jeffrey E. ... Philadelphia, PA
Gross, Jeffrey J. ... Poughkeepsie, NY
Gross, Jeffrey S. ... Philadelphia, PA
Gross, Jenny L. ... Los Angeles, CA
Gross, Jerome ... Brooklyn, NY
Gross, Jerome A. ... Baltimore, MD
Gross, Jerry M. ... Houston, TX
Gross, Jessica ... New York, NY
Gross, Jildy H. ... New York, NY
Gross, Jill Israeloff ... New York, NY
Gross, Joan B. ... New York, NY
Gross, Joan M. ... Cleveland, OH
Gross, Joan Robinson ... Elizabeth, NJ
Gross, Joanne ... Cleveland, OH
Gross, Joel H. ... New York, NY
Gross, Joel M. ... Department of Justice, Environment and Natural Resources Division, GV
Gross, John F. ... Allentown, PA
Gross, John H. ... New York, NY
Gross, John H. ... Northport, NY
Gross, John J. ... Omaha, NE
Gross, John Kendall ... Metter, GA
Millen, GA
Reidsville, GA
Gross, John M. ... Atlanta, GA
Gross, John M. ... New York, NY
Gross, John P. ... Somerville, NJ
Gross, John Richard ... Denver, CO
Gross, John S.F. ... Dallas, TX
Gross, Joli Lyn ... Short Hills, NJ
New York, NY
Gross, Jonathan ... San Francisco, CA
Gross, Jonathan M. ... West Orange, NJ
Gross, Jonathan R. ... New York, NY
Gross, Jonathan S. ... Santa Monica, CA
Gross, Joseph A. ... San Francisco, CA
Gross, Joseph F., Jr. ... Omaha, NE
Gross, Joseph H. ... Miami, FL
Gross, Joseph J. ... White Plains, NY
Gross, Joseph N. ... Cleveland, OH
Gross, Judd H. ... Cleveland, OH
Gross, Judith E. ... New York, NY
Gross, Julian Alexander ... San Francisco, CA
Gross, Justin A. ... Woodside, CA
Gross, Kara L. ... New York, NY
Gross, Karen ... New York, NY
Gross, Karen Charal ... New York, NY
Gross, Karin Goldsmith
Treasury Department, Internal Revenue Service, GV
Gross, Karl J. ... Southborough, MA
Gross, Kathleen S. ... Charleston, WV
Gross, Keith H. ... New York, NY
Gross, Keith R. ... Denver, CO
Gross, Kenneth ... Bethesda, MD
Gross, Kenneth A. ... Washington, DC
Gross, Kenneth I. ... Los Angeles, CA
Gross, Kenneth L. ... Beverly Hills, CA
Gross, Kenneth L. ... Birmingham, MI
Gross, Kenneth N. ... Natick, MA
Gross, Kenneth S. ... Baltimore, MD
Gross, Kevin ... Wilmington, DE
Gross, Kevin M. ...
Securities and Exchange Commission, GV
Gross, Kevin M. ... Chicago, IL
Gross, Laddy H. ... Los Altos, CA
Gross, Larry M. ... Buckingham, VA
Gross, Laura A. ... Gainesville, FL
Gross, Laura Geringer ... Norfolk, VA
Gross, Laurel S. ... Macon, GA
Gross, Lawrence A. ... Wayne, PA
Gross, Lawrence J. ... Elmhurst, NY
Gross, Lawrence K., Law Offices of
Forest Hills, NY
Hauppauge, NY
Gross, Leah R. ... Houston, TX
Gross, Lee A. ... Santa Ana, CA
Gross, Lee H. ... Miami, FL
Gross, Lee H., P.A. ... Miami, FL
Gross, Leigh ... New York, NY
Gross, Leon O. ... Wallingford, CT
Gross, Leonard ... Palo Verde, CA
Gross, Leonard ... Carbondale, IL
Gross, Leonard A. ... Oakland, CA
Gross, Leonard A., A Professional Corporation
Oakland, CA
Gross, Leslie Jay ... Miami, FL
Gross, Leslie Marie ... Washington, DC
Gross, Lester ... Columbia, SC
Gross, Lester R. ... Palm Harbor, FL
Gross & Levin LLP ... Elmhurst, NY
Gross, Linda M. ... York, PA
Gross, Linda S. ... Santa Monica, CA
Gross, Lindsay E. ... Bingham Farms, MI
Gross, Lionel G. ... Chicago, IL
Gross, Lisa M. ... Sylvania, GA
Gross, Loren ... Minneapolis, MN
Gross, Louise C. ... Chicago, IL
Gross, Lynn Peterson ... Dallas, TX
Gross, Malcolm ... New York, NY
Gross, Malcolm D. ... Oakdale, CA
Gross, Malcolm J. ... Allentown, PA
Gross, Marc D. ... Los Angeles, CA
Gross, Marc I. ... New York, NY
Gross, Marc Jonathan ... Roseland, NJ
Gross, Marc S. ... New York, NY
Gross, Marcus ... Harlan, IA
Missouri Valley, IA
Gross, Marjorie E. ... New York, NY
Gross, Mark A. ... Mount Vernon, NY
Gross, Mark H. ... New York, NY
Gross, Mark L. ... Department of Justice, Civil Rights Division, GV
Gross, Mark P. ... Encino, CA
Gross, Mark P., A Prof. Corp., Law Offices of ... Encino, CA
Gross, Mark R. ... Lorain, OH
Gross, Marla Baratz ... New York, NY
Gross, Marla Porter ... Boca Raton, FL
Gross, Marlene ... Treasury Department, Internal Revenue Service, GV
Gross, Marlene Anscher ... Farmingdale, NY
Gross, Marta E. ... New York, NY
Gross, Martha V. ... Bellingham, WA
Gross, Martin ... Cherry Hill, NJ
Gross, Martin B. ... Rockville Centre, NY
Gross, Martin L. ... Concord, NH
Gross, Marvin ... Los Angeles, CA
Gross, Marvin S. ... Las Vegas, NV
Gross, Marvin T. ... Milwaukee, WI
Gross, Mary Jo ... Commerce City, CO
Gross, Matthew J. ... Philadelphia, PA
Gross, Maynard A. ... Miami, FL
Gross, McGinley, LaBarre & Eaton, LLP
Allentown, PA
Easton, PA
Gross & McPhail ... Osage, IA
Gross, Melanie ... Woodbridge, CT
Gross, Melissa Beth ... Southfield, MI
Gross, Melvin M. ... Cleveland, OH
Gross, Merrick L. ... Miami, FL
Gross, Meyer A. ... New York, NY
Gross, Michael ... River Edge, NJ
Gross, Michael ... Shirley, NY
Gross, Michael A. ... Tallahassee, FL
Gross, Michael A. ... Albuquerque, NM
Gross, Michael A. ... New York, NY
Gross, Michael A., Law Offices of
St. Louis, MO
Gross, Michael B. ... Landover, MD
Gross, Michael C. ... San Antonio, TX
Gross, Michael D. ... Colorado Springs, CO
Gross, Michael D. ... Lebanon, IN
Gross, Michael D., P.C.
Colorado Springs, CO
Gross, Michael E. ... Chevy Chase, MD
Gross, Michael I. ... Atlantic City, NJ
Gross, Michael J. ... St. Petersburg, FL
Gross, Michael J. ... Kansas City, MO
Gross, Michael J. ... Middletown, NJ
Trenton, NJ
Gross, Michael J. ... Red Bank, NJ
Gross, Michael J., P.A. ... St. Petersburg, FL
Gross, Michael P. ... Santa Fe, NM
Gross, Michael S. ... Fort Lauderdale, FL
Gross, Michael W. ... Denver, CO
Gross, Milton J. ... Brooklyn, NY
Gross, Milton N. ... Spokane, WA
Gross, Minsky, Mogul & Singal, P.A.
Bangor, ME
Ellsworth, ME
Houlton, ME
Machias, ME
Gross, Mitchell S. ... South Euclid, OH
Gross, Monica ... Minneapolis, MN
Gross, Monnye R. ... St. Louis, MO
Gross, Murray ... Wellesley, MA
Gross, Murray B. ... Los Angeles, CA
Gross, Murray J. ... New York, NY
Gross, Neil ... Newark, NJ
Gross, Nemeth & Silverman, P.L.C.
Detroit, MI
Gross, Nina G. ... Washington, DC
Gross, Nina S. ... New York, NY
Gross, Norman ... Chicago, IL
Gross, Norman ... New York, NY
Gross, Norman H. ... Syracuse, NY
Gross, Olivia M. ... New York, NY
Gross, Owen P. ... Los Angeles, CA
Gross, Pamela A ... Sandusky, OH
Gross, Pamela G. ... Los Angeles, CA
Gross, Patricia Moreland ... Darien, CT
Gross, Patricia Tierney ... Mount Dora, FL
Gross, Paul A. ... Pembroke Pines, FL
Gross, Paul R. ... Brooklyn, NY
Gross, Peggy Fraychineaud ... Tacoma, WA
Gross, Peggy L. H. ... Carrollton, TX
Gross, Peter A. ... Washington, DC
Montclair, NJ
Gross, Phil
Securities and Exchange Commission, Division of Enforcement, GV
Gross, Philip S. ... Hackensack, NJ
New York, NY
Gross, Phillip S. ... Fairfax, VA
Gross, Randall S. ... San Francisco, CA
San Jose, CA
Gross, Raymond O. ... Clearwater, FL
Gross, Rhonda Cavin ... Las Vegas, NV
Gross, Richard A. ... Washington, DC
Gross, Richard A. ... Port Orchard, WA
Gross, Richard A., P.S. ... Port Orchard, WA
Gross, Richard B. ... New York, NY
Gross, Richard C. ... Department of the Army, U.S. Army Legal Services Agency, GV
Gross, Richard D. ... Baltimore, MD
Gross, Richard H. ... Osage, IA
Gross, Richard J. ... Bismarck, ND
Gross, Richard L. ... Orange, CT
Gross, Richard W. ... Hialeah, FL
Gross, Robert ... Miami Shores, FL
Gross, Robert ... Manchester, NH
Gross, Robert ... Cleveland, OH
Gross, Robert A. ... Southfield, MI
Gross, Robert C. ... Salt Lake City, UT
Gross, Robert E. ... Shaker Heights, OH
Gross, Robert J. ... Washington, DC
Gross, Robert J. ... Department of Justice, Civil Division, GV
Gross, Robert K. ... New York, NY
Gross, Robert L. ... Joplin, MO
Gross, Robert M. ... West Palm Beach, FL
Gross, Robert S. ... New Orleans, LA
Gross, Robert S. ... White Plains, NY
Gross, Robert W. ... Zionsville, IN
Gross, Robin S.
Securities and Exchange Commission, Division of Investment Management, GV
Gross, Robt. C. ... White Plains, NY
Gross, Roger H. ... Minneapolis, MN
Gross, Roger S. ... San Francisco, CA
Gross, Ron ... Union, NJ
Gross, Ronald J. ... Hanover, PA
Gross, Ronald S. ... New York, NY
Gross, Ronald S. ... Doylestown, PA
Gross, Ronen S. ... Los Angeles, CA
Gross, Ronit ... New York, NY
Gross & Ruderman ... White Plains, NY
Gross, Russell I. ... Edison, NJ
Gross, S. Richard, (P.C.) ... Liberty, NY
Gross, Sandra ... Detroit, MI
Gross, Sanford ... Cleveland, OH
Gross, Sanford, Co., L.P.A. ... Cleveland, OH
Gross, Sanford P. ... Pittsburgh, PA
Gross, Sara Walter ... Louisville, KY
Gross, Saul K. ... Miami Beach, FL
Gross, Scott E. ... Chicago, IL
Gross, Seth D. ... New York, NY
Gross, Seth S. ... Basking Ridge, NJ
Gross, Seymour ... Cleveland, OH
Gross, Sharon P. ... Albuquerque, NM
Gross, Sharon Rae ... Troy, MI
Gross, Sheldon ... Little Neck, NY
Gross, Shirell A. ... Jersey City, NJ
New York, NY
Gross Shuman Brizdle & Gilfillan, P.C.
Buffalo, NY
Niagara Falls, NY
Gross, Simeon F., & Elliot S. Gross
Rockville Centre, NY
Gross, Stanley ... Brooklyn, NY
Gross, Stephen A. ... Carmel, IN
Gross, Stephen J.
National Labor Relations Board, Division of Administrative Law Judges, GV
Gross, Stephen M. ... Bingham Farms, MI
Gross, Steven ... Agoura Hills, CA
Gross, Steven B. ... Bala Cynwyd, PA
Gross, Steven C. ... Truckee, CA
Reno, NV
Gross, Steven E. ... Newark, NJ
New York, NY
Gross, Steven J. ... Chicago, IL
Gross, Steven J., P.C. ... Chicago, IL
Gross, Steven M. ... San Antonio, TX
Gross, Steven R. ... Torrington, CT
Gross, Steven R. ... New York, NY
Gross, Stuart J. ... New York, NY
Gross, Susan English ... Dallas, TX
Gross, Susan L. ... Atlantic City, NJ
Gross, Susan Oman ... Los Angeles, CA
Gross, Susan R. ... Philadelphia, PA

Gross, Suzanne H. ...... **Philadelphia, PA**
Gross & Telisman, P.A. ...... Miami, FL
Gross, Terence A., Law Offices of
Pensacola, FL
Gross, Terry ...... **Oakland, CA**
Gross, Terry ...... **San Francisco, CA**
New York, NY
Gross, Terry ...... Larned, KS
Gross, Theodore M. ...... Schaumburg, IL
Gross, Thomas M. ...... **San Jose, CA**
Gross, Tracey A. ...... Mill Valley, CA
Gross, Virginia C. ...... **Kansas City, MO**
Gross, Vivien ...... Chicago, IL
Gross, Walter C., III
Federal Trade Commission,
Bureau of Consumer Protection, GV
Gross, W. B. Martin ...... **Oak Brook, IL**
Gross & Welch, P.C. ...... **Council Bluffs, IA**
Omaha, NE
Gross, William A. ...... Quakertown, PA
Gross, William F. ...... Santa Barbara, CA
Gross, William F. ...... Columbus, OH
Gross, William J. ...... **Fort Lauderdale, FL**
Gross, William M. ...... Tavares, FL
Gross, Yaacov M. ...... **New York, NY**
Grossack, David ...... Boston, MA
Grossan, Melissa F. ...... Los Angeles, CA
Grossart, Jerry J. ...... **Kearney, NE**
Grossbart, Douglas S. ...... Morristown, NJ
Grossbart, John I. ...... **Chicago, IL**
Grossbart, Kenneth S., (A Law Corporation)
Los Angeles, CA
Grossbart, Robert N., P.A. ...... **Baltimore, MD**
Grossbart, Robert Neil ...... **Baltimore, MD**
Grossbauer, John F. ...... **Wilmington, DE**
Grossbaum, David A. ...... **Boston, MA**
Grossbaum, Debra A. ...... Boston, MA
Grossbaum, John J. ...... Department of Defense,
Armed Services Board of Contract Appeals,
GV
Grossberg, Amy ...... Boston, MA
Grossberg, Bernard M. ...... **Boston, MA**
Grossberg, David ...... New York, NY
Grossberg, David A. ...... **Chicago, IL**
Grossberg, Fredk. S. ...... Houston, TX
Grossberg, Gerald P. ...... **Washington, DC**
Grossberg, Israel ...... Washington, DC
Grossberg, James E. ...... **Washington, DC**
Grossberg, Marc E. ...... **Houston, TX**
Grossberg, Michael W. ...... Atlanta, GA
Grossberg, Scott J. ...... Ontario, CA
Grossberg, Suzan ...... Bridgeport, CT
Grossberg, Yochelson, Fox & Beyda, LLP
Washington, DC
Grossblatt & Booth ...... **Los Angeles, CA**
Grossblatt, Fred J. ...... **Los Angeles, CA**
Grossblatt, Jennifer B. ...... **Los Angeles, CA**
Gross-Bondy, Kerry ...... Monroe, MI
Grosse, A. Barry ...... Jacksonville, FL
Grosse, Alfred C. ...... Dallas, TX
Grosse, C. Kenneth ...... Seattle, WA
Grosse, Charles ...... Smyrna, GA
Grosse, Lowell ...... **Buffalo, NY**
Grosse, Margaret A. ...... Carlsbad, CA
Grosse, Renee D. ...... **Jacksonville, FL**
Grosse, Russell W. ...... Carlsbad, CA
Grosse, W. Jack ...... Highland Heights, KY
Grossel, Jeffrey N. ...... New York, NY
Grosselin, John E., III ...... **Pittsburgh, PA**
Grossenbach, Sharon W. ...... **Denver, CO**
Grossenbacher, Gary M. ...... Austin, TX
Grossenbacher, Julius C., Jr.
San Antonio, TX
Grossenbacher, Karl W.
Rancho Cordova, CA
Grossenbacher, Karla ...... **Washington, DC**
Grossenbacher, Rebecca L. ...... San Diego, CA
Grossenbacher, William L. ...... Tavares, FL
Grossenburg, Bradley C. ...... **Sioux Falls, SD**
Grossenburg, J. M. ...... Winner, SD
Grosser, Frederic M. ...... Champaign, IL
Grosser, Frederick C. ...... Mashpee, MA
Grosser, George E.
Research Triangle Park, NC
Grosser, James M. ...... **Washington, DC**
Grosser, Jonathan M. ...... **Philadelphia, PA**
Grosser, Robert Allen ...... Springfield, MO
Grosser, Ronald C. ...... **New York, NY**
Grosser, Theodore D. ...... **Cincinnati, OH**
Grosserode, Ken ...... **San Francisco, CA**
Grosserode, Kenneth Lee
Department of Justice,
Executive Office for Immigration Review,
GV
Gross-Farina, Sally ...... Miami, FL
Grossfeld, Claudia Zusman
Los Angeles, CA
Grossfeld, Howard M. ...... Baltimore, MD
Grossfeld, Kenneth B. ...... **Sacramento, CA**
Grossfeld, Myer E. ...... Baltimore, MD
Grossfeld, Sandra M. ...... New York, NY
Grossfeld, Scott L. ...... **Los Angeles, CA**
Grossfield, Donald E. ...... Rochester, NY
Grossfield, Sherwin ...... New York, NY
Grosshandler, Seth ...... **New York, NY**
Grosshans, Roland E. ...... Rapid City, SD
Grossheim, E. Ronald ...... Cincinnati, OH
Grossheim, Robert C. ...... **Beaumont, TX**
Grossi, Charles ...... Morganton, NC
Grossi, Colleen Tierney ...... Maywood, IL
Grossi, David P. ...... **Worcester, MA**
Grossi, George J. ...... Warwick, RI
Grossi, Jerome P. ...... **Pittsburgh, PA**
Grossi, John D. ...... Union City, NJ
Grossi, John J., Jr. ...... Jersey City, NJ
Grossi, Patrick S. ...... Orland Park, IL
Grossi, Peter T., Jr. ...... **Washington, DC**
Grossi, Richard J. ...... Princeton, NJ
Grossi, William A. ...... Schaumburg, IL
Grossinger, Gordon & Vatz ...... Pittsburgh, PA
Grossinger, Howard ...... Pittsburgh, PA
Grossi-Perone, Diane A.
Agency for International Development,
Office of the General Counsel, GV
Grossi-Tyson, Laura ...... **Philadelphia, PA**
Grossjung, Mark S. ...... Wappingers Falls, NY
Grossklaus, David D. ...... **Des Moines, IA**
Grossklaus, Timothy A. ...... Grosse Ile, MI
Grosskopf, Myrna E. ...... Seattle, WA
Grosskopf, Peter E. ...... Eau Claire, WI
Grosskreutz, Lisa S. ...... Morristown, NJ
Grosslight, Peter L. ...... Los Angeles, CA
Grossman, Aaron D. ...... Redding, CA
Grossman, Adam B. ...... Riverhead, NY
Grossman, Adrienne R.
Merit Systems Protection Board,
Office of Appeals Counsel, GV
Grossman, Alan ...... Pleasanton, CA
Grossman, Alan Bryce ...... Hollywood, FL
Grossman, Alan Bryce, P.A. ...... Hollywood, FL
Grossman, Alan C. ...... Pennsauken, NJ
Grossman, Alan M. ...... **Denver, CO**
Grossman, Alan N. ...... Chicago, IL
Grossman, Albert ...... Santa Monica, CA
Grossman, Alison E. ...... Washington, DC
Grossman, Allan F. ...... **Encino, CA**
Grossman, Allan I. ...... **Los Angeles, CA**
Grossman, Allan W. ...... Saline, MI
Grossman, Allen, Inc., P.C.
San Francisco, CA
Grossman, Allen R. ...... **Tallahassee, FL**
Grossman, Alysse ...... **New York, NY**
Grossman, Amy C. ...... **Morristown, NJ**
Grossman, Amy M. ...... San Francisco, CA
Grossman, Andrew ...... Department of State,
Foreign Service Officers (Overseas), GV
Grossman, Andrew Scott ...... **Columbus, OH**
Grossman, Anthony C. ...... Los Angeles, CA
Grossman, Arthur D. ...... **Livingston, NJ**
Grossman, Arthur I. ...... Chicago, IL
Grossman & Associates, P.C.
New York, NY
Grossman, Aubery W. ...... San Francisco, CA
Grossman, Audrey K. ...... **Indianapolis, IN**
Grossman, Aviva L. ...... **New York, NY**
Grossman, Barbara F. ...... Detroit, MI
Grossman, Barry I. ...... New York, NY
Grossman, Barry L. ...... **Milwaukee, WI**
Grossman, Barry Scott ...... Omaha, NE
Grossman, Bea ...... **New York, NY**
Grossman, Benjamin B.
Department of Justice,
Antitrust Division, GV
Grossman, Bernard S. ...... Granada Hills, CA
Grossman, Beth M.
Federal Trade Commission,
Bureau of Consumer Protection, GV
Grossman, Brian J. ...... Richmond, VA
Grossman, Brian M. ...... **Los Angeles, CA**
Grossman, Bruce A. ...... **Universal City, CA**
Grossman, Bruce J. ...... **New York, NY**
Grossman, Burton S. ...... Chicago, IL
Grossman, Carl H. ...... **Harrington Park, NJ**
Grossman, Carl L. ...... Cherry Hill, NJ
Grossman, Carole B. ...... **Minneapolis, MN**
Grossman, Charles ...... Providence, RI
Grossman, Charles M. ...... **Newark, NJ**
Grossman, Cindy L. ...... Brockton, MA
Grossman, Colby H. ...... Cherry Hill, NJ
Grossman, Cox & Johnson ...... **Lompoc, CA**
Grossman, Craig A. ...... **Los Angeles, CA**
Grossman, Dale A. ...... Ithaca, NY
Grossman, Dan S. ...... **New York, NY**
Grossman, Daniel ...... Denver, CO
Grossman, Daniel F. ...... Norwich, VT
Grossman, Daniel J. ...... Atlanta, GA
Grossman, Daniel Louis ...... Cranford, NJ
Grossman, Daryn A. ...... **New York, NY**
Grossman, David ...... Chicago, IL
Grossman, David ...... Kenilworth, NJ
Grossman, David A. ...... Jamaica Plain, MA
Grossman, David E. ...... **Boston, MA**
Grossman, David M. ...... Baltimore, MD
Grossman, David M. ...... **Dallas, TX**
Grossman, David S. ...... Brookfield, CT
Grossman, David S. ...... **Seattle, WA**
Grossman, David W. ...... Miami, FL
Grossman, David W. ...... New York, NY
Grossman, Dawn ...... **San Diego, CA**
Grossman, Deborah S. ...... St. Louis, MO
Grossman, Debra ...... **Chelmsford, MA**
Grossman, Debra L. ...... Los Angeles, CA
Grossman, Deidre A. ...... **New York, NY**
Grossman, Dennis A. ...... **New York, NY**
Grossman, Donna Brown ...... Washington, DC
Grossman, E. Michael ...... Dallas, TX
Grossman, Edward ...... North Hollywood, CA
Grossman, Edward ...... Chicago, IL
Grossman, Edward G.
House of Representatives,
Office of Legislative Counsel, GV
Grossman, Edward J. ...... East Northport, NY
Grossman, Eliot Lee ...... San Francisco, CA
Grossman, Elizabeth Anne ...... New York, NY
Grossman, Elizabeth R. ...... **Berkeley, CA**
Grossman, Elizabeth S. ...... **Los Angeles, CA**
Grossman, Ellen S. ...... Wakefield, MA
Grossman, Eric B. ...... Niagara Falls, NY
Grossman, Eric F. ...... **New York, NY**
Grossman, Eric G. ...... **Chicago, IL**
Grossman, Eric P. ...... **Houston, TX**
Grossman, Ernest D. ...... Truckee, CA
Grossman, Erwin ...... Brooklyn, NY
Grossman, Felix T. ...... Los Angeles, CA
Grossman, Floyd G. ...... **Carle Place, NY**
Grossman, Fredric J. ...... **Chicago, IL**
Grossman & Friedman ...... Chicago, IL
Grossman, Gail L. ...... Coral Gables, FL
Grossman, Garry S. ...... **Washington, DC**
Grossman, Gary M. ...... **Boston, MA**
Grossman, Geoffrey F. ...... **Chicago, IL**
Grossman, George ...... Rye, NY
Grossman, George S. ...... Davis, CA
Grossman, Gerald J. ...... New York, NY
Grossman, Glen J. ...... Salinas, CA
Grossman, Glenn M. ...... Crownsville, MD
Grossman & Goldman, P.A. ...... Boca Raton, FL
Grossman, Grant & Cramer
Santa Monica, CA
Grossman, Gregory S. ...... **Miami, FL**
Grossman and Grossman ...... **Denver, CO**
Grossman & Grossman ...... Boston, MA
Needham, MA
Grossman, H. Philip ...... **Louisville, KY**
Grossman, Harman A. ...... New Brunswick, NJ
Grossman, Harris M. ...... Westbury, NY
Grossman, Harvey G. ...... Corpus Christi, TX
Grossman, Harvey M. ...... Los Angeles, CA
Grossman, Harvey M. ...... Chicago, IL
Grossman, Harvey S. ...... West Orange, NJ
Grossman, Heidi ...... Seattle, WA
Grossman, Henry L. ...... **Boston, MA**
Grossman, Herbert ...... Palo Alto, CA
Grossman, Herbert
Federal Energy Regulatory Commission,
Office of the Administrative Law Judges, GV
Grossman, Hindell S. ...... Boston, MA
Needham, MA
Grossman, Hiram S. ...... Flint, MI
Grossman, Howard ...... Boca Raton, FL
Grossman, Howard I. ...... **Philadelphia, PA**
Grossman, Howard Ian ...... **New York, NY**
Grossman, Howard J. ...... **Rochester, NY**
Grossman, Howard L. ...... **New York, NY**
Grossman, Howard R. ...... **Flint, MI**
Grossman, Ira J. ...... **New York, NY**
Grossman, Isaac ...... **New York, NY**
Grossman, J.B., P.A., Law Practice of
Fort Lauderdale, FL
Miami, FL
Grossman, Jack L. ...... Flushing, NY
Grossman, James D.
House of Representatives,
Office of Legislative Counsel, GV
Grossman, James R. ...... **Fort Wayne, IN**
Grossman, James S. ...... Buffalo, NY
Rochester, NY
Grossman, Jan ...... **Phoenix, AZ**
Grossman, Jan C. ...... Levittown, PA
Grossman, Jane H., Law Offices of
St. Petersburg, FL
Grossman, Jason A. ...... **New York, NY**
Grossman, Jay S. ...... New York, NY
Grossman, J.B. ...... **Fort Lauderdale, FL**
Grossman, Jed S. ...... Milford, CT
Grossman, Jeffrey A. ...... **Columbus, OH**
Grossman, Jeffrey C. ...... Chicago, IL
Grossman, Jeffrey O. ...... **New York, NY**
Grossman, Jeffrey T. ...... **Wayne, PA**
Grossman, Jennifer L.
Sterling Heights, MI
Grossman, Jerome B. ...... Livonia, MI
Grossman, Jerome H. ...... Rochester, NH
Grossman, Jerome K. ...... **Wilmington, DE**
Grossman, Jerome P. ...... Omaha, NE
Grossman, Jill B. ...... Bellaire, TX
Grossman, Joanna L. ...... Washington, DC
Grossman, Joanne B. ...... **Washington, DC**
Grossman, Jodie ...... Boston, MA
Grossman, Joel M. ...... Culver City, CA
Grossman, Joel M. ...... **Beaumont, TX**
Houston, TX
Grossman, John L. ...... **Atlantic City, NJ**
Pleasantville, NJ
Grossman, Jon David ...... **Washington, DC**
Grossman, Jonah G. ...... New York, NY
Grossman, Jonathan ...... Jamaica, NY
Grossman, Jonathan C.
Huntington Beach, CA
Grossman, Jonathan D. ...... Stockton, CA
Grossman, Jordan W. ...... Rego Park, NY
Grossman, Julie A. ...... **New York, NY**
Grossman, Juliet D. ...... Riverside, CA
Grossman, Karen Foy ...... **Miami, FL**
Grossman, Katherine A. ...... **Dallas, TX**
Grossman, Kay S. ...... Chicago, IL
Grossman, Keith D. ...... **White Plains, NY**
Grossman, Kenneth M. ...... Paramus, NJ
Grossman, Kenneth S. ...... New York, NY
Grossman Kinney Dwyer & Harrigan, P.C.
Syracuse, NY
Grossman, Kirk J. ...... Ventura, CA
Grossman, Kruttschnitt, Heavey & Jacob, A Professional Corporation ...... **Brick, NJ**
Grossman, Kurt L. ...... **Cincinnati, OH**
Grossman, Kurtiss L. ...... Los Angeles, CA
Grossman, Lance ...... New York, NY
Grossman, Larry S. ...... Philadelphia, PA
Grossman, Laura ...... Great Neck, NY
Grossman, Laura Anne ...... Mineola, NY
Grossman, Laurie S. ...... **New York, NY**
Grossman Law Offices ...... **Columbus, OH**
Grossman, Lawrence A. ...... **New York, NY**
Grossman, Lawrence S. ...... **Bridgeport, CT**
Grossman, Lawrence S., (P.C.)
Morganville, NJ
Grossman, Lee F. ...... Chicago, IL
Grossman, Leonard J. ...... Baltimore, MD
Grossman, Leonard L. ...... Orchard Lake, MI
Grossman, Leonard R. (Bud)
Lubbock, TX
Grossman, Leslie K., (Mr.)
Granada Hills, CA
Grossman, Levine & Civiletto
Niagara Falls, NY
Grossman, Lillian Yvonne ...... Columbus, OH
Grossman & Litchin ...... **Fort Wayne, IN**
Grossman & Logan, LLP ...... San Diego, CA
Grossman, Loren R., (Ms.) ...... Venice, CA
Grossman, Louis ...... New York, NY
Grossman, M. Glenn ...... Acme, MI
Grossman, Madeleine F. ...... **Westport, CT**
Grossman and Mahan ...... Granada Hills, CA
Grossman, Marc David ...... New York, NY
Grossman, Margaret R. ...... Urbana, IL
Grossman, Mark ...... **Miami, FL**
Grossman, Mark ...... **New York, NY**
Grossman, Mark D. ...... **Los Angeles, CA**
Grossman, Mark Jay ...... New Brunswick, NJ
Grossman, Mark M. ...... Newton, MA
Grossman, Mark S. ...... **Oklahoma City, OK**
Grossman, Marla ...... Washington, DC
Grossman, Marnie S. ...... **New York, NY**
Grossman, Marshall B., (P.C.)
Los Angeles, CA
Grossman, Martin E. ...... Villanova, PA
Grossman, Marvin ...... New York, NY
Grossman, Maurice L., (P.A.)
Minneapolis, MN
Grossman, Max L. ...... Playa Del Rey, CA
Grossman, Michael ...... San Dimas, CA
Grossman, Michael B. ...... Mineola, NY
Grossman, Michael E. ...... Roseland, NJ
Grossman, Michael F. ...... New York, NY
Grossman, Michael J. ...... Lexington, KY
Grossman, Michael R. ...... Chicago, IL
Grossman, Michael S. ...... Miami, FL
Grossman, Milton J. ...... **Washington, DC**
Grossman, Mitzenmacher & Schechter
Chicago, IL
Grossman, Morris ...... Flushing, NY
Grossman, N. Matthew ...... **Los Angeles, CA**
Grossman, Nadelle ...... **Houston, TX**
Grossman, Nancy G. ...... New York, NY
Grossman, Nathan M. ...... Chicago, IL
Grossman, Neil D. ...... New York, NY
Grossman, Neil M. ...... Washington, DC
Grossman, Nils F. ...... **Minneapolis, MN**
Grossman, Ofer M. ...... **Santa Monica, CA**
Grossman, Orin G. ...... Las Vegas, NV
Grossman, Patricia A. ...... San Jose, CA
Grossman, Paul ...... **Los Angeles, CA**
Grossman, Paul D. ...... Foster City, CA
Grossman, Paul F. ...... Chicago, IL
Grossman, Paul S. ...... **New York, NY**
Grossman, Peter ...... **Los Angeles, CA**
Grossman, Peter ...... New York, NY
Grossman, Peter G. ...... **Ithaca, NY**
Grossman, Philip J. ...... New York, NY
Grossman, Phillip ...... **Skokie, IL**
Grossman, Randy ...... Jersey City, NJ
Grossman, Randy M. ...... San Diego, CA
Grossman, Raymon A. ...... Lincolnwood, IL
Grossman, Reed S. ...... Brooklyn, NY
Grossman, Rene E. ...... Dallas, TX
Grossman, Rhea P. ...... **Miami, FL**
Miami, FL
Grossman, Richard ...... Miami Beach, FL
Grossman, Richard ...... Lake Forest, IL
Grossman, Richard ...... **St. Louis, MO**
Grossman, Richard A. ...... Los Angeles, CA
Grossman, Richard A. ...... Baltimore, MD
Grossman, Richard A. ...... **Brick, NJ**
Grossman, Richard A. ...... Tarrytown, NY
Grossman, Richard D. ...... **Syracuse, NY**
Waitsfield, VT
Grossman, Richard J. ...... Chicago, IL
Grossman, Richard J. ...... **New York, NY**
Grossman, Richard L. ...... **San Francisco, CA**
Grossman, Richard L. ...... **Norristown, PA**
Grossman, Richard P., Jr. ...... **Edison, NJ**
Grossman, Rick L. ...... **Pasadena, CA**
Grossman, Robert ...... Highlands Ranch, CO
Grossman, Robert ...... **Beaumont, TX**
Houston, TX
Grossman, Robert C. ...... Northbrook, IL
Grossman, Robert C. ...... Rochester, NY
Grossman, Robert D. ...... **Overland Park, KS**
Grossman, Robert D., Jr. ...... Bethesda, MD
Grossman, Robert D., Jr., P.C.
Bethesda, MD
Grossman, Robert E. ...... **New York, NY**
Grossman, Robert J. ...... Los Angeles, CA
Grossman, Robert J. ...... Hopewell Junction, NY
Grossman, Robert L. ...... **Miami, FL**
Grossman, Robert L. ...... **Minneapolis, MN**
Grossman, Robert M. ...... **Chicago, IL**
Grossman, Robert S. ...... **Philadelphia, PA**
Grossman, Roberta Rochelle ...... New York, NY
Grossman, Rochelle B.
Plymouth Meeting, PA
Grossman, Roger Jon ...... Braintree, MA
Grossman, Ronald ...... Chicago, IL
Grossman Roth and Partridge
Sarasota, FL
Grossman and Roth, Professional Association
Boca Raton, FL
Fort Lauderdale, FL
Miami, FL
Grossman, Roxanne ...... Richmond, VA
Grossman, Sally Stolen ...... **Minneapolis, MN**
Grossman, Samuel D. ...... Fresh Meadows, NY
Grossman, Sanford ...... Mount Kisco, NY
Grossman, Scott ...... Riverside, CA
Grossman, Seth ...... Somers Point, NJ
Grossman, Solomon & Fielkow, P.C.
Lincolnwood, IL
Grossman, Stacy J. ...... **New York, NY**
Grossman, Stanley ...... Niagara Falls, NY
Grossman, Stanley M., (P.C.)
New York, NY

Growhoski, Thomas M.
Northampton, MA
Growney, Margaret B. ...St. Petersburg, FL
Growney & McKeown ...St. Petersburg, FL
Growney, Scott Inglis ...Philadelphia, PA
Growney, William E., Jr. ...Menlo Park, CA
Groy, Jeffrey B. ...New York, NY
Grozbean, Stuart H. ...Rockville, MD
Grozindei, John Hopkins ...New York, NY
Grozinger, Stephan B. ...Greenwich, CT
Grskovich, Edward N. ...Chicago, IL
Grua, Remo Mark ...Lansing, MI
Grubacich, Gary Steven
Santa Barbara, CA
Grubaugh, Bruce E., II ...Orange, CA
Grubaugh, Phillip B. ...Kansas City, MO
Grubaugh, Richard H. ...Sea Girt, NJ
Grubb, Bruce R. ...Kalamazoo, MI
Grubb, Charles C. ...Shreveport, LA
Grubb, Colleen M. ...Malvern, PA
Grubb, David K. ...Columbia, PA
Grubb, David L. ...Charleston, WV
Grubb, Derrick A. ...Beloit, WI
Grubb, Earl R. ...Aptos, CA
Grubb, George G., (A Law Corporation)
Honolulu, HI
Grubb, Gerald F. ...Rockford, IL
Grubb, James V., (Inc., P.S.) ...Seattle, WA
Grubb, Janet A. ...Columbus, OH
Grubb, Jay G. ...Baldwin, MD
Grubb, John K. ...Houston, TX
Grubb, Jose Acosta ...San Juan, PR
Grubb, Kevin C. ...Lebanon, NJ
Grubb, Kitty G. ...Seminole, FL
Grubb Law Firm ...Seminole, FL
Grubb, Michael E. ...Janesville, WI
Grubb, Richard L. ...Harrisburg, PA
Grubb, Stephen ...Encino, CA
Grubb, Steven C. ...Memphis, TN
Grubb, Steven E. ...Harrisburg, PA
Grubb, William I., II ...Eufaula, AL
Grubba, Thomas G. ...Detroit, MI
Grubbe, Nelson H. ...Eugene, OR
Grubbe, Richard E. ...Sandusky, OH
Grubber, Karen L. ...Washington, DC
Grubbs, Adele ...Marietta, GA
Grubbs, Cynthia M. ...Silver Spring, MD
Grubbs, Debra Mehl ...Three Rivers, MI
Grubbs, Dee Ellen ...Lewiston, ID
Grubbs, Donald S., Jr. ...Silver Spring, MD
Grubbs, Donell R. ...Columbus, OH
Grubbs, G. Ronald, Jr., (P.C.)
Richmond, VA
Grubbs, Gerald R. ...Cincinnati, OH
Grubbs & Grubbs ...Three Rivers, MI
Grubbs, Irene T. ...Birmingham, AL
Grubbs, J. Keaton ...Wichita Falls, TX
Grubbs, J. Michael ...Indianapolis, IN
Grubbs, James L. ...Los Angeles, CA
Grubbs, Joe F. ...Waxahachie, TX
Grubbs, Julius W., Jr. ...New Iberia, LA
Grubbs, Kelli R. ...Davenport, IA
Grubbs, Larry G. ...Billings, MT
Grubbs, Margo L. ...Covington, KY
Grubbs, Martha L. ...Little Rock, AR
Grubbs, Patricia S. ...Ironton, OH
Grubbs, Philip E. ...Plano, TX
Grubbs, R. Howard ...Winston-Salem, NC
Grubbs, Randall ...Garland, TX
Grubbs, Ronald J. ...Three Rivers, MI
Grubbs, Shelby R. ...Atlanta, GA
Chattanooga, TN
Grubbs, Steven O'Neal ...Houston, TX
Grubbs, Wendy J. ...Washington, DC
Grubbs, Whitney L. ...Portland, OR
Grubbs, William D. ...Louisville, KY
Grubbs, W. K., Sr., (P.A.) ...Eudora, AR
Grube, Alton G. ...Philadelphia, PA
Grube, Brian K. ...Washington, DC
Grube, E. Jeffrey ...San Francisco, CA
Grube, Edwin H. ...Portland, OR
Grube, James R. ...San Jose, CA
Grube, Jeffrey L. ...Warner Robins, GA
Grube, John S. ...Houston, TX
Grube, Karl B. ...St. Petersburg, FL
Grube, Keith S. ...Teterboro, NJ
Philadelphia, PA
Grube, Patsy Matthew ...Bethesda, MD
Grube, Paul A., Jr. ...San Bernardino, CA
Grube, Terrence C. ...Allentown, PA
Grubea, Peter David ...Buffalo, NY
Grubel, Henry M., (P.C.) ...Freeport, NY
Gruben, Catherine M. ...Ottawa, IL
Gruben, Jas. F. ...Wylie, TX
Gruben, Karl T. ...Houston, TX
Grubenhoff, Stephanie L. ...Chicago, IL
Gruber, Alan R. ...Norwich, CT
Gruber, Alice Margaret ...Houston, TX
Gruber, Allen H., (P.A.) ...Miami, FL
Gruber, Andre Wm. ...Kendall Park, NJ
Gruber & Associates, L.L.C.
Bethesda, MD
Gruber, Brian K. ...Washington, DC
Gruber, Burton A. ...Oakland, CA
Gruber, Carolyn ...Denver, CO
Gruber & Colabella ...Hackettstown, NJ
Hopatcong, NJ
Newton, NJ
Gruber, Craig M. ...Roslyn Heights, NY
Gruber & Cunningham ...Alva, OK
Gruber, Daniel S. ...Encino, CA
Gruber, Danna ...New York, NY
Gruber, David ...East Hampton, NY
Gruber, David ...Roslyn Heights, NY
Gruber, David E. ...Milwaukee, WI
Gruber, David J. ...Livingston, NJ
New York, NY
Gruber, Diane L. ...Portland, OR
Gruber, Donald F. ...St. Paul, MN
Gruber, Eric H. ...New York, NY
Gruber, Eric J. ...New York, NY
Gruber, Erik D. ...Chicago, IL
Gruber, F. Gene ...Silver City, NM
Gruber and Fee ...Kendall Park, NJ
Gruber, Frank J. ...Santa Monica, CA
Gruber, Frederick H. ...Southfield, MI
Gruber, G. Michael ...Dallas, TX
Gruber, Gary D. ...Amherst, MA
Greenfield, MA
Gruber, Gregory A. ...Washington, DC
Gruber & Gruber, P.C. ...New York, NY
Gruber, Harry ...San Jose, CA
Gruber, Hermann P. ...Freeport, NY
Gruber, Ilse Lynn ...Albany, NY
Gruber, Ira L. ...Marina Del Rey, CA
Gruber, Irving M. ...New York, NY
Gruber, J. Mark ...Buffalo, NY
Gruber, Jay E. ...Boston, MA
Gruber, Jennifer M. ...Atlanta, GA
Gruber, John J. ...Tonawanda, NY
Gruber, Jon M. ...Lancaster, PA
Gruber, Joseph A. ...New York, NY
Gruber, Joseph C. ...Cincinnati, OH
Gruber, Joseph N. ...Redwood City, CA
Gruber, Julie C. Grollmus
San Francisco, CA
Gruber & Kantor ...Encino, CA
Gruber, Kurt P. ...Orlando, FL
Gruber & Landset ...Amherst, MA
Greenfield, MA
Gruber Law Firm ...North Little Rock, AR
Gruber Law Offices ...Milwaukee, WI
Gruber, Leanora S. ...New York, NY
Gruber, M. Ellen ...Columbus, OH
Gruber, Madelyn S. ...Rochester, NY
Gruber, Mark ...Hackettstown, NJ
Hopatcong, NJ
Newton, NJ
Gruber, Mark H. ...Brooklyn, NY
Gruber, Melodee Laine ...Fort Worth, TX
Gruber, Michael S. ...North Canton, OH
Gruber, Milton E. ...Hidden Hills, CA
Gruber, Misty S. ...Chicago, IL
Gruber, Moia Tamber ...Bethesda, MD
Gruber, Noel M. ...Washington, DC
Bethesda, MD
Gruber, Patricia L. ...Denver, CO
Gruber, Patricia T. ...Plainfield, IL
Gruber, Paul N. ...New York, NY
Gruber, Peter G. ...Miami, FL
Gruber, Peter G., P.A. ...Miami, FL
Gruber & Prescott ...Tonawanda, NY
Gruber, Priscilla H. ...Plainfield, IL
Gruber, Richard J. ...Los Angeles, CA
Gruber, Rita W. ...Little Rock, AR
Gruber, Robert I. ...New York, NY
Gruber, Robert I., P.C. ...New York, NY
Gruber, Robert K. ...Denver, CO
Gruber, Robert L. ...Madison, WI
Gruber, Robert P. ...Raleigh, NC
Gruber, Robert W., (P.C.) ...Bay City, MI
Gruber, Robin Ellyn ...New York, NY
Gruber, Roman F. ...Beachwood, OH
Gruber, Ronald J. ...Ida, MI
Gruber, Samuel S. ...Las Vegas, NV
Gruber, Saul ...Cherry Hill, NJ
Gruber, Sheila G. ...Morristown, NJ
Gruber, Stanley B. ...Haddonfield, NJ
Gruber, Stephen C. ...Los Altos, CA
Gruber, Steven H. ...Marietta, GA
Gruber, Steven M. ...Dallas, TX
Gruber, Susan W. ...Los Angeles, CA
Gruber, Teresa A. ...White Plains, NY
Gruber, Thomas J. ...Cincinnati, OH
Gruber, Thomas W. ...Alva, OK
Gruber, Vicki S. ...Uniondale, NY
Gruber, Walter F. ...Alameda, CA
Gruber, Wayne A. ...North Little Rock, AR
Gruber, Wendy Florence ...Boston, MA
Gruber, William M. Ondrey ...Cleveland, OH
Gruberg, Mark ...Brooklyn, NY
Gruberg, McKay & Stone ...Pleasantville, NY
Grubin, Janice B. ...New York, NY
Grubin, Jerome S. ...New York, NY
Grubin, John F. ...New York, NY
Grubin, Safer & Turner ...New York, NY
Grubin, Sharon E. ...New York, NY
Grubisich, Joseph A. ...Davenport, IA
Grubiss, Randolph H. ...Boulder, CO
Grubiss, Stephen J. ...Boulder, CO
El Prado, NM
Grubler, Gary L. ...Columbus, OH
Grubman, Allen J. ...New York, NY
Grubman, Arnold ...Chicago, IL
Grubman, C. Lawrence ...New York, NY
Grubman, David A. ...Pittsburgh, PA
Grubman, Diana L. ...Fort Lauderdale, FL
Grubman, Don D. ...New York, NY
Grubman Indursky & Schindler, P.C.
New York, NY
Grubman, Jeffrey Scott ...Miami, FL
Grubman & McArthur
Walnut Creek, CA
Grubman, Michael H. ...Walnut Creek, CA
Grubman & Nathan, P.C. ...Chicago, IL
Grubman, Ronald E. ...Monterey, CA
Grubman, Stanley D. ...Morris Plains, NJ
Grubner, Judith L. ...Chicago, IL
Grubner, Steven M. ...Lisle, IL
Grubschmidt, Kurt A. ...Pittsburgh, PA
Gruca, Kathleen M. ...Chicago, IL
Gruca, Terri Paula ...Detroit, MI
Gruccio, James J., Jr. ...Vineland, NJ
Gruccio, James J., Sr. ...Bridgeton, NJ
Vineland, NJ
Woodbury, NJ
Gruccio, Lillian J. ...Medford, NJ
Gruccio, Michael J. ...Vineland, NJ
Gruccio, Pepper, Giovinazzi, DeSanto & Farnoly, P.A. ...Atlantic City, NJ
Avalon, NJ
Bridgeton, NJ
Salem, NJ
Vineland, NJ
Woodbury, NJ
Gruccio, Philip A. ...Wilmington, DE
Gruchot, Thaddeus J. ...Deerfield, IL
Gruchow, Kirby C., Jr. ...Las Vegas, NV
Gruchow, Nancy H. ...Northfield, MN
Grucz, Roman S. ...Traverse City, MI
Grudberg, David T. ...New Haven, CT
Grudberg, Ira B. ...New Haven, CT
Grudberg, Michael J. ...New York, NY
Grude, David G. ...Toledo, OH
Grudem, Dag ...Scottsdale, AZ
Gruder, Bruce ...New York, NY
Gruder, Fredric J. ...New York, NY
Gruder, Glenn B. ...Hauppauge, NY
Gruder, Kenneth M. ...Norwalk, CT
Grudichak, Thomas J. ...Chicago, IL
Grudis, Carol Smith ...Denver, CO
Grudko, Jeffrey ...Cherry Hill, NJ
Grudziecki, Ronald L. ...Alexandria, VA
Grudzien, Lawrence L. ...Chicago, IL
Grudzinskas, Albert J., Jr. ...Oxford, MA
Grudzinski, Chester W., Jr.
Carrollton, TX
Grudzinski, Chester W., Jr.
Fort Worth, TX
Grue, Thomas A. ...Malone, NY
Gruebner, David A. ...Honolulu, HI
Gruel, Grant J. ...Grand Rapids, MI
Gruel, Mills, Nims and Pylman
Grand Rapids, MI
Gruel, Steven F. ...San Francisco, CA
Gruemmer, Brooks B. ...Bannockburn, IL
Gruemmer, Paige Elise ...Chicago, IL
Gruen, Adam S. ...San Francisco, CA
Gruen, Charles A., Law Offices
Hackensack, NJ
Gruen, Evelyn J. ...Simi Valley, CA
Gruen & Farrelly, LLP ...New York, NY
Gruen, Fred R. ...Union, NJ
Gruen & Goldstein ...Union, NJ
Gruen, Jan A. ...Oakland, CA
Gruen, John I. ...Tenafly, NJ
Reston, VA
Gruen, Lisa Parel ...Woodland Hills, CA
Gruen, Lois K. ...Mount Kisco, NY
Gruen, Michael S. ...New York, NY
Gruen, Paul D. ...Los Angeles, CA
Gruen, Peter H. ...New Haven, CT
Gruen, Randy D. ...Glendale, CA
Gruen, Robert D. ...Hackensack, NJ
Gruen, Stanley ...Union, NJ
Gruenbaum, Jerry ...New Milford, CT
Gruenbaum, Samuel H. ...Los Angeles, CA
Gruenbeck, Thomas Stefan ...Irvine, CA
Gruenbeck & Vogeler ...Irvine, CA
Gruenberg, Clover & Holland
Anchorage, AK
Gruenberg, David L. ...Troy, NY
Gruenberg, David M. ...Los Angeles, CA
Gruenberg, Harold ...St. Louis, MO
Gruenberg, Jonas J. ...Dayton, OH
Gruenberg, Joshua D. ...San Diego, CA
Gruenberg, Max F., Jr. ...Anchorage, AK
Gruenberg, Steven P. ...Clinton, NJ
Gruenberger, Peter ...New York, NY
Gruenburg, Dawn Marie ...Center Line, MI
Gruenburg, Roy N. ...Center Line, MI
Gruendel, Clare M. ...Cos Cob, CT
Gruendel, Robert J. ...New York, NY
Gruendel, Yolanda R.
Federal Trade Commission,
Bureau of Competition, GV
Gruender, Daniel F. ...Phoenix, AZ
Gruender, Raymond W. ...St. Louis, MO
Grueneberg, Rudi ...Moorestown, NJ
Grueneberg, Susan ...Los Angeles, CA
Grueneich, Dian M. ...San Francisco, CA
Gruenemeier, Steven A. ...Scottsdale, AZ
Gruener, Arthur P. ...Brooklyn, NY
Gruener, Harry J. ...Pittsburgh, PA
Gruenert, Thomas G. ...Lafayette, LA
Houston, TX
Gruenewald, Barbara ...Reno, NV
Gruenewald, Christopher I. ...Mobile, AL
Gruenewald, John M. ...Anniston, AL
Gruenfeld, Barry J. ...Fort Lauderdale, FL
Gruenglas, Michael H. ...New York, NY
Gruenheck, Katherine S.
Department of Justice, Civil Division, GV
Gruenig, Thomas B. ...Fairbanks, AK
Gruening, Clark S. ...Juneau, AK
Gruening and Spitzfaden, P.C. ...Juneau, AK
Grueninger & Connors ...Belleville, IL
Grueninger, Daniel J. ...Belleville, IL
Gruenisen, Karen K. ...Madison, WI
Gruenisen Law Office, S.C. ...Madison, WI
Gruenke, Dennis J. ...Philadelphia, PA
Gruenloh, Christy ...Charleston, SC
Gruenloh, Wm. Michael ...Charleston, SC
Gruenschlaeger, Jeanne E. ...Cincinnati, OH
Gruenspan, Charles ...Cleveland, OH
Gruenspan, Charles, Co., L.P.A.
Cleveland, OH
Gruenstein, David ...New York, NY
Gruenstein, Debra Lynne ...Bala Cynwyd, PA
Gruenstein & Hickey ...Anchorage, AK
Gruenstein, Peter ...Anchorage, AK
Gruenthal, Barbara ...Boston, MA
Gruentzel, Donald A. ...Cumberland, VA
Gruenwald, Eric W. ...Los Angeles, CA
Gruenwald, Gail S. ...Harbor Springs, MI
Gruenwald Law Offices ...Milbank, SD
Gruenwald, Max ...Milbank, SD
Gruenwald, Robert S. ...Bronx, NY
Gruer, Sharon Kovacs ...Great Neck, NY
Melville, NY
Gruer, Sharon Kovacs, P.C.
Great Neck, NY
Melville, NY
Gruesbeck, Ronald M. ...Lansing, MI
Gruesen, Thomas W. ...Incline Village, NV
Grueskin, Mark G. ...Denver, CO
Grueskin, Ronald J. ...Los Angeles, CA
Gruesner, Mark H. ...Minneapolis, MN
Gruesser, Susan A. ...New York, NY
Grueter, Robert P. ...Aspen, CO
Gruetter, Bryan W. ...Bend, OR
Gruettke, Anita ...Newport Beach, CA
Gruettner, Allison B. ...Los Angeles, CA
Gruettner, Donald W. ...Cleveland, OH
Gruetzmacher, Vance S. ...Stevens Point, WI
Grugel, Roger C. ...St. Cloud, MN
Gruggel, John S., Jr. ...Department of Defense,
Armed Services Board of Contract Appeals,
GV
Grugle, Scott D. ...Cleveland, OH
Gruher, Barry P. ...West Palm Beach, FL
Gruhin & Gruhin ...Nutley, NJ
Gruhin, Lois A. ...Columbus, OH
Gruhin, Louis A. ...Brooklyn, NY
Gruhin, Mark I. ...Washington, DC
Gruhin, Michael H. ...Cleveland, OH
Gruhin, Robert C. ...Nutley, NJ
Gruhin, Stephen W. ...Nutley, NJ
Gruhn, Brian L. ...Cedar Rapids, IA
Gruhn, Robert S. ...Seattle, WA
Gruhn, William Dimmick ...Baltimore, MD
Gruia, Dinu ...Los Angeles, CA
Gruis, Edward G. ...Greenbelt, MD
Gruis, Tracy N. ...Department of the Army,
Office, Chief of Engineers/Headquarters,
U.S. Army Corps of Engineers, GV
Gruitza, Michael C. ...Sharon, PA
Grulke, Robert O. ...Madison, WI
Grum, Robert M. ...Julian, CA
Gruman, Eric S. ...Tampa, FL
Gruman, Perry G. ...Tampa, FL
Gruman, Peter ...Bellingham, WA
Gruman, William V. ...Tampa, FL
Gruman Worldwide, Chartered ...Tampa, FL
Grumbach, Antonia M. ...New York, NY
Grumbach, George J., Jr. ...New York, NY
Grumbach, James E. ...Boston, MA
Grumbach, Leonard ...New York, NY
Grumbacher, John R., (P.C.) ...Boston, MA
Grumbine, D. Allen ...Greenville, SC
Grumbine, David L. ...Benton Harbor, MI
Grumbles, Benjamin H.
House of Representatives,
Committee Legal Personnel, GV
Grumbles, Ernest W., III
Minneapolis, MN
Grumbles, Lisa F. ...Birmingham, AL
Grumbling, Richard David ...Dallas, TX
Grumer, Carl ...Los Angeles, CA
Grumer, Keith T. ...Fort Lauderdale, FL
Grumer & Levin, P.A.
Fort Lauderdale, FL
Grumer, Steve ...Crystal Bay, NV
Grumer, Steve, Ltd., A Prof. Corp.
Crystal Bay, NV
Grumet, Alan M. ...New York, NY
Grumet, Andrew M. ...Hackensack, NJ
Grumet, Auden L. ...Atlanta, GA
Grumet, Jean ...New York, NY
Grumet, Mark L. ...New York, NY
Grumet, Robin ...New York, NY
Grumet, Steven A. ...Merrick, NY
Grumke, Clay L. ...St. Louis, MO
Grumley, George L. ...Chicago, IL
Grumley, James D. ...Joliet, IL
Grumman, Barry Jon ...Newport Beach, CA
Grumman, Fredric R. ...Park Ridge, NJ
Grummer, Dennis E. ...Miami, FL
Grummer, Duane ...San Francisco, CA
Grummer, Kathlene K. ...Deerfield Beach, FL
Grummer, Mark E. ...Washington, DC
Grummon, Scott E. ...New York, NY
Grun, Henry, Jr. & Associates
San Antonio, TX
Grun, Howard ...New York, NY
Grun, Susan Rogers ...Riverhead, NY
Grunat, Joshua G. ...New York, NY
Grunauer, Robert D. ...Beverly Hills, CA
Grunawalt, Karen Cockley ...Wickliffe, OH
Grunbaum, Gustavo ...San Francisco, CA
Grunberg, Adele S. ...San Francisco, CA
Grunberger, Armand ...Cleveland, OH
Grunberger, Armand, Co., L.P.A.
Cleveland, OH
Grunblatt, David ...New York, NY
Grunblatt, Mark ...New Paltz, NY
Grund & Breslau, P.C. ...Denver, CO
Grund, David I. ...Chicago, IL
Grund, David W. ...Bridgton, ME
Lewiston, ME
South Paris, ME
Grund, J. David ...Peru, IN
Grund, James A. ...Peru, IN
Grund, John W. ...Denver, CO
Grund & Starkopf, A Professional Corporation
Chicago, IL
Grunda & Grunda ...Lorain, OH
Grunda, Jay B. ...Lorain, OH
Grunda, Joseph C. ...Lorain, OH
Grunda, Joseph R. ...Lorain, OH
Grundahl, John A. ...West Bend, WI
Grundei, August A. ...Lincolnshire, IL

Grundei, Jacqueline A. ....Westport, CT
Grundei, Michael ....Stamford, CT
Grundeman, Arnold James
Department of Agriculture, Office of the General Counsel, GV
Grundeman, Fredric Edward
Washington, DC
Grundeman, Raymond D.
Department of State, Director General—Foreign Service, GV
Grunden, April S. ....Fort Wayne, IN
Grunden, Ellen Barry ....Easton, MD
Grundfast, Adam S. ....Smithtown, NY
Grundfast & Grundfast ....Centereach, NY
Grundfast, Kim R. ....Boston, MA
Grundfast, Michael K., P.C.
Smithtown, NY
Grundfast & Morrison ....Smithtown, NY
Grundfast, Norman J. ....Centereach, NY
Grundfast, Robert D. ....Centereach, NY
Grundfest, Jack D. ....Little Rock, AR
Grundfestl, Stacy VanAusdall
Little Rock, AR
Grundfossen, Peter ....Portland, OR
Grundhauser, John J. ....Miami, FL
Grundhoefer, Marvin L. ....Northfield, MN
Grundhoefer, Neuville & Ludescher, P.A.
Northfield, MN
Grundhoefer, Peter J. ....Center City, MN
Grundin, Katherine M. ....North Chicago, IL
Grundin, Robert E. ....Chicago, IL
Grundlock, Robert L., Jr. ....Princeton, NJ
Grundman, Frank R. ....Madison, CT
Grundman, James E. ....Concord, CA
Grundman, Mark P. ....Walnut Creek, CA
Grundman, Nancy D. ....Chappaqua, NY
Grundman, Neil ....New York, NY
Grundmann, Catherine M.
San Francisco, CA
Grundmeyer, Douglas L.
New Orleans, LA
Grundner, Charles H. ....Syracuse, NY
Grundon, Traci A. ....Portland, OR
Grundstein, Nathan D. ....Cleveland, OH
Grundstrom, Ed V. ....Novato, CA
Grundstrom, Richard J. ....Jefferson City, MO
Grundvig, Mark ....Department of Justice, Antitrust Division, GV
Grundwerg, Steven Philip ....New York, NY
Grundy, Bradley A. ....Tulsa, OK
Grundy, Charles Albert, Jr ....Lexington, KY
Grundy, David R. ....Reno, NV
Grundy & Hayes LLP ....Houston, TX
Grundy, J. Mark ....Louisville, KY
Grundy, Jana L. ....Phoenix, AZ
Grundy, Janet L. ....Austin, TX
Grundy, Jenifer L. ....Florence, CO
Grundy, John C. ....Warren, OH
Grundy, Karen M. ....Tulsa, OK
Grundy, L. Alan ....Georgetown, TX
Grundy, Richard D. ....Cambridge, MA
Grundy, Thad ....Houston, TX
Grundy, Thad, Jr. ....Houston, TX
Grune, Harold K. ....Stony Point, NY
Grunebach, Georgann Shelby
El Segundo, CA
Grunebaum, David F. ....Boston, MA
Grunebaum, Ernest F. ....New York, NY
Gruneisen, Karen G. ....San Francisco, CA
Gruner, Heidi S. ....Washington, DC
Gruner, Joseph H. ....New York, NY
Gruner, Lawrence ....Fairfield, CA
Grass Valley, CA
Oakland, CA
San Bruno, CA
San Francisco, CA
Gruner, Mitchell ....Philadelphia, PA
Gruner, Paul L. ....Kingston, NY
Gruner, Richard E., Jr. ....New Orleans, LA
Gruner, Richard S. ....Costa Mesa, CA
Gruner, William M. ....New Paltz, NY
Grunert, Carol M. ....Greenville, SC
Grunert, Jim ....Ventura, CA
Grunert, John A. K. ....Boston, MA
Concord, NH
Grunert, Richard E. ....Morganton, GA
Grunert Stout & Bruch
Charlotte Amalie, St. Thomas, VI
Grunes, Allen P. ....Department of Justice, Antitrust Division, GV
Grunes, Susan ....Bala Cynwyd, PA
Grunewald, Carson C. ....Detroit, MI
Grunewald, Edward J. ....Waynesboro, GA
Grunewald, Glen R. ....Oakland, CA
Grunewald and Grunewald ....Waynesboro, GA
Grunewald, Kathy Newman
Waynesboro, GA
Grunewald, Mark H. ....Lexington, VA
Grunewald, Raymond Bernhard
New York, NY
Grunewald, William A. ....Medford, WI
Grunewaldt, Cecelia A. ....Sioux Falls, SD
Grunfeld, Aaron A. ....Los Angeles, CA
Grunfeld, Daniel ....Los Angeles, CA
Grunfeld, David I. ....Norristown, PA
Grunfeld, David I. ....Philadelphia, PA
Grunfeld, Desiderio, Lebowitz & Silverman LLP ....Washington, DC
Atlanta, GA
New York, NY
Houston, TX
Grunfeld, Desiderio, Lebowitz, Silverman & Wright LLP ....Boston, MA
Grunfeld Desiderio LLP ....Los Angeles, CA
Grunfeld, Gideon Y. ....Washington, DC
Grunfeld, Harold M. ....New York, NY
Grunfeld, Jay E. ....Brooklyn, NY
Grunfeld, Raphael S. ....New York, NY
Grunfeld, Thomas B. ....Farmingdale, NY
Grungo, Richard, Jr. ....Haddonfield, NJ
Grunick, Rebecca J. ....Cleveland, OH
Grunin, Barry V. ....Dedham, MA
Grunin, Jay A. ....Toms River, NJ
Grunin & Kalmanowitz, P.A.
Toms River, NJ
Gruning, David W. ....New Orleans, LA
Gruning, John E. ....Brooklyn, NY
Gruning, Peter R. ....Hickory, NC
Grunke, Frederick L. ....St. Cloud, MN
Grunke, Ruth A. ....St. Paul, MN
Grunnet, Roy D. ....Chicago, IL
Grunor, Sylvia A. ....Maitland, FL
Grunow, David P. ....Flat Rock, MI
Grunow, John E. D. ....Stamford, CT
Grunow, Linda M. ....Encinitas, CA
Grunow, Robert A. ....Nashville, TN
Grunschlag, Dov M. ....San Francisco, CA
Grunsfeld, Steven ....Bedminster, NJ
Grunsky, Donald L. ....Watsonville, CA
Grunsky, Ebey, Farrar & Howell, A Professional Corporation ....Monterey, CA
Santa Cruz, CA
Watsonville, CA
Grunspan, Alan M. ....Miami, FL
Grunst, Fred P. ....Naples, FL
Grunstein, Leonard ....New York, NY
Grunther, Rhonda J. ....Brooklyn, NY
Gruntkosky, Jacquelyn K.
Mason City, IA
Gruntkowski, Monica ....Tulsa, OK
Gruntz, Louis G., Jr. ....Jefferson, LA
Grunwald, Barbara Booth ....Fresno, CA
Grunwald, Kristine A. ....Williamston, MI
Grunwald, Milton ....Garden City, NY
Grunwald & Seman, PC
Garden City, NY
Grunwell, Michelle Marie ....Baltimore, MD
Gruny, C. Richard ....Carbondale, IL
Grunzweig, Jonathan H. ....Los Angeles, CA
Grunzweig, Paul S. ....Minneapolis, MN
Grupp, Anne R. ....Los Angeles, CA
Grupp, Charles J., Jr. ....Chicago Heights, IL
Grupp, Edward A. ....Pittsburgh, PA
Grupp, John E. ....Charlotte, NC
Grupp, Leal A. ....Napa, CA
Grupp, Michael C. ....Walnut Creek, CA
Gruppie, Guy R. ....Los Angeles, CA
Gruppo, David M. ....New York, NY
Grusauskas, Kathryn ....Las Cruces, NM
Grusd, Brandon L. ....Los Angeles, CA
Grusd, Gavin C. ....East Meadow, NY
Gruseck, Thomas J. ....Fort Pierce, FL
Grush, Julius S. ....Los Angeles, CA
Grush, Michael J. ....Los Angeles, CA
Grushen, Laurie E. ....Santa Ana, CA
Grushkin, Jay D. ....New York, NY
Grushkin, Mark J. ....Los Angeles, CA
Grushkin, Steven D. ....Stamford, CT
Grushko, Edward M. ....New York, NY
Grushko & Mittman, P.C. ....New York, NY
Grusin, Martin A. ....Memphis, TN
Gruskin, Arnie B. ....Fort Lauderdale, FL
Gruskin, David J. ....St. Petersburg, FL
Gruskin, David S. ....Atlanta, GA
Gruskin, Denis M. ....Reston, VA
Gruskin, Harvey B. ....Springfield, MA
Gruskin & LaBerge, P.A.
St. Petersburg, FL
Gruskin, Mark D. ....Denver, CO
Gruskin, Mark S. ....Glendale, CA
Gruskin, Matthew C. ....New York, NY
Gruskin, Richard E. ....New London, CT
Gruskin, Sanford N. ....San Diego, CA
Gruskin, Steven M. ....Washington, DC
Gruskin, Stuart F. ....New York, NY
Gruskin, Susan A. ....Los Angeles, CA
Gruskos, Alexandra ....Pittsburgh, PA
Grusmark, Milton E. ....North Palm Beach, FL
Gruson, Michael ....New York, NY
Gruss, Albert J. ....Pleasant Ridge, MI
Gruss, Henry Phillip ....Chicago, IL
Rockford, IL
Gruss, Martin D. ....New York, NY
Gruss, Marvin I. ....New Canaan, CT
Gruss, Raymond S. ....Lakewood, OH
Grussel, Susan Ruscitti ....Skokie, IL
Grussendorf, Paul D. ....Washington, DC
Grussing, Bruce D. ....Minneapolis, MN
Grussing, James B. ....Keene, NH
Grussing, Joleen M. ....Mountain View, CA
Grussing, Robert, III ....West Brattleboro, VT
Grussmark, Lori A. ....Coral Gables, FL
Gruszecki, Wilhelm L. ....Philadelphia, PA
Gruszkiewicz, Marjorie R.
New Haven, CT
Grutchfield, Dana ....Tampa, FL
Grutman, Charles A. ....New York, NY
Gruttadaro, Darcy ....Rochester, NY
Gruttadaro, Dennis ....Rochester, NY
Gruttadaro, Gabriel W. ....Rochester, NY
Gruttadaro & Servis ....Rochester, NY
Gruttadaurio, John J. ....South Euclid, OH
Grutz, James A. ....Seattle, WA
Grutz, Scott, Kinney & Fjelstad
Seattle, WA
Grutzmacher, Ralph E.
Upper Marlboro, MD
Grutzner, Edward E., S.C. ....Beloit, WI
Grutzner, Holland & Vollmer, A Prtnrshp. incl. S.C. ....Beloit, WI
Gruver, Charles, III ....Wilmington, DE
Gruver Curtin, Victoria, P.L.C.
Scottsdale, AZ
Gruver, Jonathan A. ....Dallas, TX
Gruver, Lori Diane ....Austin, TX
Gruver, Michael L. ....Panama City, FL
Tallahassee, FL
Gruver, Victoria ....Scottsdale, AZ
Gruvman, Paul S. ....Mineola, NY
Gruwell, Mark A. ....Sarasota, FL
Gruza, Sy ....New York, NY
Gruzen, Ronald L. ....Los Angeles, CA
Gruzmark, Alexander ....Glenview, IL
Gryboski, Thomas S. ....Atlanta, GA
Grybowski, Jeffrey M. ....New York, NY
Grybowski, Keith S. ....Miami, FL
Gryce, David C. ....Washington, DC
Gryczan, Catherine C. ....Chicago, IL
Gryczka, Elizabeth A. ....Syracuse, NY
Gryder, Jana L. E. ....Fort Worth, TX
Gryder, Sandra L. ....Long Beach, CA
Grydyk, Stanley T. ....Richmond, CA
Grygiel, Michael J. ....Albany, NY
Grygiel, Stephen G. ....Portland, ME
Gryk, Anthony J., Jr. ....Manchester, CT
Gryk, Frolich & Frolich ....Manchester, CT
Gryk, Wesley C. ....Manchester, CT
Gryko, Margaret Paluch ....Buffalo, NY
Gryll, Charles R. ....Lincolnwood, IL
Gryll, Charles R., Ltd. ....Lincolnwood, IL
Grylls, Facca, Richter & Pregler, P.C.
Detroit, MI
Royal Oak, MI
Grylls, John K. ....Royal Oak, MI
Grymes, Christie L. ....Washington, DC
Gryniewicz, Victor M. ....Chicago, IL
Gryniewski, Nancy Walker
Myrtle Beach, SC
Grynkewich, Gary S. ....Tucson, AZ
Gryphon, Marie Elizabeth ....Seattle, WA
Grypp, Keith A. ....Union, MO
Grysen & Associates ....Spring Lake, MI
Grysen, Bernard E. ....Spring Lake, MI
Gryska, Mark E. ....Glendale Heights, IL
Grytdahl, Jay L. ....Chicago, IL
Gryte, David M. ....St. Louis, MO
Gryva, Mary Clare ....Omaha, NE
Gryzbek, Thomas J. ....Hammond, IN
Gryzlo, Joseph W. ....New York, NY
Gryzlo, Matthew J. ....Chicago, IL
Gryzmala, Robert J. ....St. Louis, MO
Grzanka, Charles F. ....Grand Rapids, MI
Grzanka, Constance J. ....Grand Rapids, MI
Grzanka Grit ....Grand Rapids, MI
Grzankowski, Joseph A. ....Elizabeth, NJ
Grzeca, Jerome G. ....Milwaukee, WI
Grzeca, Jerome G., S.C. ....Milwaukee, WI
Grzeca, Michael G. ....Green Bay, WI
Grzeca, Michael G., S.C. ....Green Bay, WI
Grzech, Robert W. ....Gaylord, MI
Grzech, Thomas E. ....Baltimore, MD
Grzegorek, Kathleen L. ....Los Angeles, CA
Grzelak, Keith D. ....Spokane, WA
Grzelak, Kevin T. ....Grand Rapids, MI
Grzelakowski, Edward J. ....Oak Brook, IL
Grzenda, Paul W. ....Elizabeth, NJ
Grzeskiewicz, John C.
Securities and Exchange Commission, Division of Investment Management, GV
Grzeskowiak, Colleen B.
Department of Justice, Federal Bureau of Investigation, GV
Grzezinski, Dennis M. ....Milwaukee, WI
Grzybek, John G. ....Detroit, MI
Grzybicki, Daryl S. ....Livermore, CA
Grzybowski, Beth Catherine
North Charleston, SC
Grzybowski, Joseph J. ....Grand Rapids, MI
Grzymek, Kenneth W. ....Chicago, IL
Grzywacz, George M. ....Detroit, MI
Grzywinski, Frank J. ....Pittsburgh, PA
Grzywna, Stanley P. ....Three Rivers, MA
Gsanger, Cecile Foy ....Corpus Christi, TX
Gschwendtner, Susan M. ....Washington, DC
Gschwind, John C. ....Schenectady, NY
Gsell, Greer ....Wichita, KS
Gsovski, Daniel V. ....New York, NY
Gstalder, John M. ....Louisville, CO
Gsteiger, Urs R. ....Winston-Salem, NC
Gsteiger, Yvonne ....Tallahassee, FL
GT Strategies & Solutions ....Potomac, MD
Gu, Wayne Jinwei ....New York, NY
Guadagnino, Frank T. ....Pittsburgh, PA
Guadagnino, Joseph S. ....Rochester, NY
Guadagnino, Peter J., Jr. ....Brooklyn, NY
Guadagno, Anthony F.
Environmental Protection Agency, Office of the General Counsel, GV
Guadagno, Anthony Michael ....Albany, NY
Guadagno, Joann L. ....New York, NY
Guadagno, Kimberly McFadden ....Newark, NJ
Guadagno, Laura M. ....New York, NY
Guadagno, Matthew L. ....New York, NY
Guadagno, Michael A. ....Newark, NJ
Guadagnoli, David A. ....Boston, MA
Guadalupe, Daniel R. ....Somerville, NJ
Guadara, Susanne M. ....Hackensack, NJ
Guaderrama, David C. ....El Paso, TX
Guaderrama, Yvonne R. ....El Paso, TX
Guadiana, James A. ....New York, NY
Guadiz, Grace L. ....Winter Park, FL
Guadnola, John C. ....Tacoma, WA
Guadnolo, Rosemarie J. ....Chicago, IL
Guaetta, Peter V. ....Concord, MA
Guagenty, Michael P. ....Boston, MA
Guaglardi, Barry S. ....Englewood Cliffs, NJ
Guaglianone, Victor F. ....Stamford, CT
Guagliardo, Carl J. ....Kingston, PA
Guagliardo, Paul V. ....Louisville, KY
Guajardo, J. Anthony ....San Antonio, TX
Guajardo, Michael G. ....Dallas, TX
Gualano, Anthony R. ....Verona, NJ
Gualano, Richard L. ....Westmont, IL
Gualco, James A. ....Sacramento, CA
Gualco, Lori J. ....Sacramento, CA
Gualco, Michael O. ....Sacramento, CA
Gualco, Rex-Ann S. ....Sacramento, CA
Gualtier, Vincent L. ....Kansas City, MO
Gualtieri, David S. ....Chicago, IL
Gualtieri, Enrico V. ....Sterling Heights, MI
Gualtieri, John P., Jr. ....Newark, NJ
Gualtieri, Marguerite C. ....Media, PA
Guanci, Matthew J., JR. ....Hartford, CT
Guanciale, Christopher M. ....Akron, OH
Guandolo, John ....Washington, DC
Guaneli, Dean J. ....Juneau, AK
Guanzon, Michael C. ....Danville, VA
Guaragna, John M. ....San Diego, CA
Guararra, Michael ....New York, NY
Guarasci, Daniel J. ....Oklahoma City, OK
Guarascio, Christine ....Wilmington, NC
Guarascio, John A. ....New York, NY
Guarch, Jorge M., Jr. ....Miami, FL
Guarcini, Gerald J. ....Philadelphia, PA
Guard, Danielle M. ....Sacramento, CA
Guard, Lynndon Michael
Oklahoma City, OK
Guard, Pierce J., Jr. ....Lakeland, FL
Guard, Pierce J., Jr., P.A. ....Lakeland, FL
Guardado, Astrid ....Tampa, FL
Guardado, Michelle E. ....Fresno, CA
Guardalabene, John T.
San Francisco, CA
Guardaro, Edw. J. ....New York, NY
Guardaro, Edward J., Jr. ....Mineola, NY
New York, NY
White Plains, NY
Guardi, Noel Edmund ....Lakewood, CO
Guardia, Thos. R., Jr. ....San Antonio, TX
Guardiano, Steven J. ....Daytona Beach, FL
Guardino, Alphonso V. ....Brooklyn, NY
Guardino, Anthony S. ....Uniondale, NY
Guardino, Anthony V. ....Brooklyn, NY
Guardino, Richard V., Jr. ....Mineola, NY
Guardino, Scott F. ....Mineola, NY
Guardo, Marisa ....Summit, NJ
New York, NY
Guare, Michael D. ....Lakeland, FL
Guare, Timothy E. ....Chicago, IL
Guare, Timothy H. ....Richmond, VA
Guari, Jason J. ....West Palm Beach, FL
Guariglia, Dale A. ....St. Louis, MO
Guariglia, Diane M. ....Houston, TX
Guariglia, Kelly Ann ....Newark, NJ
Guariglia, Michael A. ....Newark, NJ
Guariglia, Robert F. ....Deer Park, NY
Guariho, Peter ....East Orange, NJ
Guarini, Frank J. ....Jersey City, NJ
Guarini & Guarini, P.A. ....Jersey City, NJ
Guarino, A. Joseph ....Point Pleasant, NJ
Guarino, Alfred A.
White River Junction, VT
Guarino, Andrew J. ....Mexican Hat, UT
Guarino, Annette L. ....Rye, NY
Guarino, Annette L. ....White Plains, NY
Guarino, Anthony J. ....Glendale, NY
Guarino, Anthony W. ....Irvington, NY
Guarino, Charles P. ....New York, NY
Guarino, Elizabeth Toni ....Washington, DC
Guarino, Gary M. ....Anchorage, AK
Guarino, Glenn A. ....Rochester, NY
Guarino, Joseph D. ....Rochelle Park, NJ
Guarino, Joseph M. ....Houston, TX
Guarino, Joseph S. ....McLean, VA
Guarino, Karen Shedd ....Atlanta, GA
Guarino, Marisa C. ....Las Vegas, NV
Guarino, Matthew M. ....Brooklyn, NY
Guarino, Michael A. ....New York, NY
Guarino, Michael J. ....Walnut Creek, CA
Guarino, Michael J., II ....Galveston, TX
Guarino, Michael J., Jr. ....Morris Plains, NJ
Guarino, Patricia R. ....New York, NY
Guarino, Peter Roserio ....San Francisco, CA
Guarino, Philip L. ....Somerset, NJ
New York, NY
Guarino, Richard ....Davis, CA
Guarino, Robert R., Jr. ....Farmingdale, NY
Guarino and Terino
White River Junction, VT
Guarino, Thomas P. ....Clovis, CA
Guarino, Veronica M. ....Hickory, NC
Guarisco, Annette J. ....Washington, DC
Guarisco, Anthony S., Jr. ....Tallahassee, FL
Guarisco, John W. ....Chicago, IL
Guarisco, Lorie J. ....Metairie, LA
New Orleans, LA
Guarisco, Michael E. ....New Orleans, LA
Guarisco, Paul F. ....Baton Rouge, LA
Guarisco, Peter ....Tallahassee, FL
Guarisco, Peter Phillip ....Baltimore, MD
Guarisco, Weiler & Cordes, L.L.C.
New Orleans, LA
Guarna, Vincent A. ....Haddonfield, NJ
Trevose, PA
Guarna, Vincent A., P.C., Law Offices of
Haddonfield, NJ
Trevose, PA
Guarnaccia, Giacomo J., Jr.
Willimantic, CT
Guarneri, Eugene ....New York, NY
Guarneri, Stephen ....New York, NY
Guarnero, Ricardo ....Seattle, WA
Guarnero, Ricardo A., P.S. ....Seattle, WA
Guarneschelli, P. Nicholas ....Harrisburg, PA
Guarneschelli, Philip G. ....Harrisburg, PA
Guarnieri, Albert E. ....Charlotte, NC
Guarnieri, David J. ....Frankfort, KY
Guarnieri, Debra Ann ....Bronx, NY
Guarnieri, Donald L. ....Warren, OH
Guarnieri, Donald L., Co., L.P.A.
Warren, OH

Guarnieri, Fred R. ...Warren, OH
Guarnieri, James W. ...Brandon, FL
Guarnieri, John A. ...Philadelphia, PA
Guarnieri, Maria T ...New York, NY
Guarnieri, Paul S. ...Wexford, PA
Guarnieri, Richard M. ...Frankfort, KY
Guarnieri and Secrest ...Warren, OH
Guarnieri, William T. ...Cleveland, OH
Guarnuccio, Keith A. ...New York, NY
Guarr, Michael J. ...Houston, TX
Guarrasi, Robert J. ...Eugene, OR
Guarrieri, Frank S. ...Morrisville, PA
Guarton, Gregory B. ...Philadelphia, PA
Guasco, Matthew P. ...Los Angeles, CA
Santa Barbara, CA
Guasco, Matthew P. ...Ventura, CA
Guastaferri, Eugenia M. ...Chelsea, MA
Guastamachio, Wende W. ...Foster City, CA
Guastella, Brendan T. ...New York, NY
Guastella, John ...Massapequa, NY
Guattery, Peter D. ...Baltimore, MD
Guay, Ann E. ...Boston, MA
Guay, Joseph A. ...Stamford, CT
Guay, Joseph M. ...Nantucket, MA
Guay, Kevin H. ...Estacada, OR
Guay, Mark J. ...Newburyport, MA
Guay, Mark J., P.C. ...Boston, MA
Newburyport, MA
Guay, Pauline L. ...Manchester, NH
Guay, Richard F. ...Mineola, NY
Guayante, Mary F. ...La Mirada, CA
Guazzo, Caesar C. ...New York, NY
Guazzo, Delia M. ...Edison, NJ
Guazzo, Robert W. ...New York, NY
Guba, Russell F. ...New York, NY
Gubar, Leonard ...New York, NY
Gubb & Barshay LLP ...San Francisco, CA
Gubb, Ishneila Ingalls ...Richmond, VA
Gubb, Natalie L. ...San Francisco, CA
Gubbe, Robert G. ...Roseville, MN
Gubbels, Darrell J. ...Castle Rock, CO
Highlands Ranch, CO
Gubbins, George C., Jr. ...Hamel, MN
Gubbins, Matthew T., (P.C.) ...Kankakee, IL
Gubbins, Michael D. ...Olympia Fields, IL
Gubbins, Patricia Jane ...Geneva, IL
Gubbins, Roberta M. ...Ann Arbor, MI
Gubbiotti, Christine M. ...Wilkes-Barre, PA
Gubbrud, Dwight A. ...Belle Fourche, SD
Gubbrud, John D. ...Hawarden, IA
Alcester, SD
Gubbrud, Mary A. ...Rapid City, SD
Gubellini, Peter W. ...Wellesley Hills, MA
Guben, Jan K. ...Washington, DC
Baltimore, MD
Guben, Jerrold K. ...Honolulu, HI
Guben, Sue W. ...Baltimore, MD
Guber, Deborah A. ...New York, NY
Guber, Stuart J. ...Philadelphia, PA
Guberman, Barry ...Elizabeth, NJ
Guberman, Daniel A. ...Chicago, IL
Guberman, David A. ...Boston, MA
Guberman, Harold I. ...Centereach, NY
Guberman, Harvey C. ...New York, NY
Guberman, Howard R. ...New York, NY
Guberman, Mark Seth ...
Equal Employment Opportunity Commission, GV
Guberman, Michael H. ...Irving, TX
Guberman, Ross M. ...Washington, DC
Guberman, Theodore ...Hillsboro, MO
Gubernick, Ira C. ...Kennett Square, PA
Gubernick, Jeffrey S. ...Los Angeles, CA
Gubin, Deborah J. ...Chicago, IL
Gubin, Kenneth B. ...Treasury Department, United States Mint, GV
Gubin, Lloyd B. ...St. Louis, MO
Gubinsky, Louis, (P.C.) ...Washington, DC
Gubinsky, Mark K. ...Pittsburgh, PA
Gubitosi, Cleo A. ...Glendale, NY
Gubits, David B. ...Walden, NY
Gubler, E. Warren ...Visalia, CA
Gubler, James L. ...Las Vegas, NV
Gubler, John G., (Ltd.) ...Las Vegas, NV
Gubler, Marion E. ...Burbank, CA
Gubler & Peters ...Las Vegas, NV
Gubman, David S., (A Professional Corporation) ...Beverly Hills, CA
Gubman, Irwin L. ...Torrance, CA
Gubman, Joseph G. ...Bronx, NY
Gubner, Adam I. ...Los Angeles, CA
Gubola, Michelle M. ...Columbus, OH
Gubrud, Kent L. ...McMinnville, OR
Gubser, Véronique ...New York, NY
Gucciardo, Angelo C. ...New York, NY
Gucciardo, Bradford M. ...New York, NY
Gucciardo, Charles S. ...Mineola, NY
New York, NY
Gucciardo, Glenn ...Northport, NY
Gucciardo Law Firm, The ...Mineola, NY
New York, NY
Gucciardo, Maria Laterza ...Mineola, NY
New York, NY
Guccini, Steven R. ...Hawley, PA
Guccione, Loretta A. ...Jackson, MS
Guccione, Thomas P. ...Brooklyn, NY
Guckenberger, Guy C. ...Cincinnati, OH
Guckenberger, Herman J., Jr.
Cincinnati, OH
Guckenberger, Kathie Beirne ...Tampa, FL
Guckenberger, Kenneth A. ...Tampa, FL
Gucker, George A. ...Redwood City, CA
Gucker, George L. ...Ketchikan, AK
Gucker, James R. ...Tiffin, OH
Guckert, Joan M. ...Boston, MA
Gudac, Stephen M. ...Satellite Beach, FL
Gudaitis, Arunas E. ...New York, NY
Gudaitis, Christy Myers ...Durham, NC
Gudal, William C. ...Washington, DC
Gudanowski, Beverly ...Boston, MA
Gudas, Timothy A. ...Concord, NH
Gudbranson, Margaret Ann
Cleveland, OH
Gudbranson, Robert N. ...Cleveland, OH
Gude, Divida ...Atlanta, GA
Gudebski, John J. ...Sacramento, CA
Gudel, Marilyn S. ...San Diego, CA
Gudel, Paul J. ...San Diego, CA
Gudelsky, Joseph W. ...Roswell, GA
Gudeman, Jay M. ...Indianapolis, IN
Gudeman, Leroy D. ...Knox, IN
Gudeman, Stephanie Kilpatrick
Indianapolis, IN
Guden, Jonathan C. ...Department of the Army, U.S. Army Legal Services Agency, GV
Gudenau, Dale Louis ...Southfield, MI
Gudenberg, Harry R. ...Oradell, NJ
Gudenkauf, Bruce P. ...Middletown, OH
Gudgel, Paul D. ...Lexington, KY
Gudgel, Tom H., Jr. ...Tulsa, OK
Gudgel, Trent A. ...Tulsa, OK
Gudgell, K. Heidi ...Lapwai, ID
Gudgeon, John W. ...San Jose, CA
Gudgeon, Le Roy W. ...Prospect Heights, IL
Gudger, Gregory Lamont ...Portland, OR
Gudger & Gudger ...Asheville, NC
Gudger, Lamar ...Asheville, NC
Hendersonville, NC
Gudger, Sally Tickle ...Asheville, NC
Gudger, Vonno Lamar, III ...Asheville, NC
Gudin, Bruce E. ...Newark, NJ
Gudin, Bruce E. ...Bardonia, NY
Gudin, Theresa C. ...New York, NY
Gudino, Alberto C. ...Van Nuys, CA
Gudino, David J. ...Irving, TX
Gudmestad, Terje ...El Segundo, CA
Gudmestad, T. K. ...Windom, MN
Gudmunds, Brenda J. ...Fredericksburg, VA
Gudmunds, S Jon ...Santa Maria, CA
Gudmundsen, Robert F. ...Wilmette, IL
Gudmundsen, Vance C. ...Falls Church, VA
Gudmundsen, Eric ...Detroit Lakes, MN
Gudmundson, Randall J. ...Chicago, IL
Gudmundson, Scott D. ...Schaumburg, IL
Gudmundson, Siggins, Stone & Skinner, LLP
Oakland, CA
San Francisco, CA
Gudmundson, W. W. ...San Francisco, CA
Gudorf, Francis V. ...Miami, FL
Gudorf, Theodore G. ...Dayton, OH
Gudoski, Kristi Lynn ...Los Angeles, CA
Gudsen, Neil A. ...Troy, MI
Gudzy, Michael J. ...New York, NY
Guebert, Terry R. ...Albuquerque, NM
Guebert, Walter C. ...Austin, TX
Guebert & Yeomans, P.C.
Albuquerque, NM
Rio Rancho, NM
Santa Fe, NM
Guecia, Mario ...Gulfport, FL
Gueck, Jay L. ...Dallas, TX
Guedalia, Harris ...Fort Lee, NJ
Guedel, W. Gregory ...Seattle, WA
Guedes, Edward G. ...Miami, FL
Guedri, P. Christopher ...Richmond, VA
Guedry, David N. ...Dallas, TX
Guedry, James W. ...Purchase, NY
Gueft, Esther ...Scarsdale, NY
Guehl, Johanna C. ...Pittsburgh, PA
Guehl Law Offices ...Salem, OH
Guehl, Robert L. ...Lisbon, OH
Salem, OH
Guekguezian, A. Bernard ...Boston, MA
Guelcher, James M. ...Erie, PA
Guelcher, Jeffrey M. ...Bethesda, MD
Gueli, John ...New York, NY
Guelich, Holly B. ...Dallas, TX
Guelpa, E. Jean ...Woodland Hills, CA
Guelzow, Thomas K. ...Eau Claire, WI
Guemmer, Albert M. ...Tampa, FL
Guenaga, Elaine S. ...Reno, NV
Guenard, Glenn S. ...Sacramento, CA
Guendel, Richard T. ...Phoenix, AZ
Guendelsberger, John ...Ada, OH
Guendelsberger, John W. ...Ada, OH
Guendelsberger, Robert J.
New Milford, CT
Guendelsberger and Taylor
New Milford, CT
Guenego, Jacqueline S. ...Haworth, NJ
Guenin, Mark C. ...Wabash, IN
Gueniot, Marcel J., Jr. ...Chalmette, LA
Guensch, Katrina H. ...Orlando, FL
Guentert, Philip A. ...Chicago, IL
Guenther, Annette E. Gustafsson
Chicago, IL
Guenther, Anthony D. ...Las Vegas, NV
Reno, NV
Guenther, Arik J. ...Campbellsport, WI
Guenther, Arthur J., Jr. ...Trenton, NJ
Guenther, Barbara H. ...Bernville, PA
Guenther, Ben L. ...Kansas City, MO
Guenther, Brenda Anne ...Southfield, MI
Guenther, Brian C. ...St. Petersburg, FL
Guenther, Christopher W.
San Luis Obispo, CA
Guenther, Clinton M. ...Greenwood, MS
Guenther, Craig E. ...Costa Mesa, CA
Guenther, David A. ...Mount Pleasant, MI
Guenther, J. Michael ...Grand Rapids, MI
Guenther, Jack ...San Antonio, TX
Guenther, James P. ...Nashville, TN
Guenther, Jerry D. ...Great Falls, MT
Guenther, John F. ...Leucadia, CA
Guenther, John P. ...Bloomfield Hills, MI
Guenther, Jordan & Price, P.C.
Nashville, TN
Guenther, Karin L. ...Portland, OR
Guenther, Mark L. ...Bozeman, MT
Guenther, Pamela E. ...Edna, TX
Guenther, Ralph A. ...Cleveland, OH
Guenther, Ralph P. ...Monterey, CA
Guenther, Rebecca M. ...San Diego, CA
Guenther, Robert S. ...Chicago, IL
Guenther, Scott Michael ...Covington, KY
Guenther, Vanessa L. ...Brookville, OH
Guenther, William H. ...New York, NY
Guenthner, Kenneth S. ...Hamel, MN
Guenthner Law Office, P.A. ...Hamel, MN
Guenthner, Louis R., Jr. ...Louisville, KY
Guenthner, Robert I. ...Wichita, KS
Guenveur, Robert C. ...Flushing, NY
Guenzel, Robert C. ...Lincoln, NE
Guenzel, Steven E. ...Lincoln, NE
Guenzer, Charles S. P. ...Santa Clara, CA
Guerard, Collot ...Federal Trade Commission, Bureau of Consumer Protection, GV
Guerard, Edward P., Jr. ...Charleston, SC
Guerard, Henry W. ...North Charleston, SC
Guerard, Kalina & Butkus ...Wheaton, IL
Guerard, Richard M. ...Wheaton, IL
Guerber, Gaer C. ...Mount Clemens, MI
Guerci, Christine M. ...Staten Island, NY
Guerci, Lloyd S.
Department of Transportation, National Highway Traffic Safety Administration, GV
Guercio, Gregory J. ...Farmingdale, NY
Guercio & Guercio ...Farmingdale, NY
Guercio, Richard J. ...Farmingdale, NY
Guerena, Barbara D. ...Santa Barbara, CA
Guerena, Vance J.I. ...Hagåtña, GU
Guerette, James R. ...New York, NY
Guerette, Susan J. ...Portland, ME
Guerette, Susan M. ...Paoli, PA
Guerin, Cara E. ...Baltimore, MD
Guerin, Charles A. ...Washington, DC
Guerin, Charles A. ...Dallas, TX
Guerin, Cheryl ...Redwood City, CA
Guerin, Christopher D. ...Boston, MA
Guerin, Cynthia C. ...Dallas, TX
Guerin, D. Michael ...Milwaukee, WI
Guerin, Daniel Patrick ...Wheaton, IL
Guérin, Denise M. ...Cambridge, MA
Guerin, Donna Zak ...Chicago, IL
Guerin, Elizabeth L. ...New York, NY
Guerin, Eric J. ...Kalamazoo, MI
Guerin, Geraldine M. ...Charleston, WV
Guerin, James K. ...Somers, NY
Guerin, Jane ...Los Angeles, CA
Guerin, Jeremiah J. ...Merced, CA
Guerin, John ...Huntington Beach, CA
Guerin, John S. ...Paramus, NJ
Guerin, Lisa M. ...San Francisco, CA
Guerin, Marc Andrew ...Boston, MA
Guerin, Marshall W. ...Toledo, OH
Guerin, Regina B. ...Cheltenham, PA
Guerin, Roger J. ...Chicago, IL
Guerin, Sanford M. ...Tempe, AZ
Guerin, T. H., Jr. ...Phoenix, AZ
Guerin, William G. ...Boston, MA
Guerine, George N. ...Melrose Park, IL
Gueringer, Gay ...Austin, TX
San Antonio, TX
Guerini, David W. ...North Ridgeville, OH
Guerini, Rosemarie W. ...Lake Park, FL
Guerino, Anthony M., II ...Houston, TX
Guerino, Jerrel L. ...Pleasanton, CA
Guerinot, Gerard W. ...Houston, TX
Guerke, I. Barry ...Dover, DE
Guerney, Janis ...United States Senate, Committee Legal Personnel, GV
Guernica, Georgina M.
Environmental Protection Agency, Office of Enforcement and Compliance Assurance, GV
Guernica, Mimi
Environmental Protection Agency, Program Office Attorneys, GV
Guernsey, Dan B. ...Miami, FL
Guernsey, Dennis M. ...Waterloo, IA
Guernsey, Donald J. ...Fostoria, OH
Guernsey & Guernsey ...Fostoria, OH
Guernsey, H Sherwood, II ...Pittsfield, MA
Guernsey, J. Thomas ...Lima, OH
Guernsey, Jessica L. ...Miami, FL
Guernsey, Jill ...Tacoma, WA
Guernsey, John (Jack) A.
Mount Laurel, NJ
Philadelphia, PA
Guernsey, Kenneth L. ...San Francisco, CA
Guernsey, Larry B. ...Campbell, CA
Guernsey, Lisle R. ...Seattle, WA
Guernsey, Mary Ann ...Pittsburgh, PA
Guernsey, Paul M. ...Niantic, CT
Guernsey, Sherwood, II ...Pittsfield, MA
Guernsey, Sherwood, II
Williamstown, MA
Guernsey, Thomas F. ...Carbondale, IL
Gueron, Henri M. ...New York, NY
Guerra, Adolph R., Jr. ...Brownsville, TX
Guerra, Alicia ...Walnut Creek, CA
Guerra, Arturo E., Jr. ...Edinburg, TX
Guerra, Bert ...Reno, NV
Guerra, Bobbie Marie ...El Paso, TX
Guerra, Carlos A. ...Scottsdale, AZ
Guerra, Catherine M. ...New York, NY
Guerra, Celeste ...Corpus Christi, TX
McAllen, TX
Guerra, Celinda Baez ...San Antonio, TX
Guerra, David H. ...Mission, TX
Guerra, Donald R. ...Cheektowaga, NY
Guerra, Elizabeth L. ...Marietta, GA
Guerra, Frank, Jr. ...Miami, FL
Guerra, Gina ...Los Angeles, CA
Guerra, Grant ...Walnut Creek, CA
Guerra, Isabel ...New York, NY
Rochester, NY
San Juan, PR
Guerra, Jeanette K. ...Pittsburgh, PA
Guerra, John A. ...San Antonio, TX
Guerra, John B. ...Cleveland Heights, OH
Guerra, Jorge L. ...Miami, FL
Guerra, Joseph M. ...Buffalo, NY
Guerra, Joseph R. ...Washington, DC
Guerra, Juventino, Jr. ...San Antonio, TX
Guerra, Linda ...Los Angeles, CA
Guerra, Luis I. ...Miami, FL
Guerra, Luis Pedro ...Phoenix, AZ
Guerra, M. Daniel ...Austin, TX
Guerra, Mark T. ...Pleasanton, CA
Guerra, Maya S. ...Department of Justice, Civil Division, GV
Guerra, Michael J. ...Louisville, KY
Guerra, Nelson Anthony ...Tampa, FL
Guerra, R. Javier ...San Antonio, TX
Guerra, Rebecca M. ...Dallas, TX
Guerra, Richard A. ...Benson, AZ
Guerra, Robert ...Oxnard, CA
Guerra, Robert J. ...Philadelphia, PA
Guerra, Robert L. ...Brownsville, TX
Guerra, Robert L. ...McAllen, TX
Guerra, Roberto ...San Antonio, TX
Guerra, Roberto (Bobby) D. ...McAllen, TX
Guerra, Rodrigo A., Jr. ...Los Angeles, CA
Guerra, Rolando G., Jr. ...Tampa, FL
Guerra, Ronald G. ...Roseburg, OR
Guerra, Sandra ...Houston, TX
Guerra, Stephanie H. ...Austin, TX
Guerra, Susan C. ...St. Louis, MO
Guerra, Victoria ...Austin, TX
Guerra-Lozano, Crisanta Emma
Brownsville, TX
Guerra-Mondragon, Gabriel
Department of State, Foreign Service Officers (Overseas), GV
Guerrant, Christine E. ...Hingham, MA
Guerrant, Teresa
Equal Employment Opportunity Commission, Office of Legal Counsel, GV
Guerrant, Will ...Austin, TX
Guerrant, William C., Jr. ...Tampa, FL
Guerre, R. Paul ...Grand Rapids, MI
Guerreiro, Manuel G. ...Middletown, NY
Guerrera, Anthony M. ...Stratford, CT
Guerrera, Arthur V. ...Mays Landing, NJ
Guerrera, Joanne M. ...Washington, DC
Guerrera, Mark P. ...Washington, DC
Guerrera, Nicholas S. ...North Andover, MA
Guerrera, Salvatore ...New York, NY
Guerrero, Alberto C. ...San Francisco, CA
Guerrero, Alberto L. ...Edinburg, TX
Guerrero, Ana M. ...Edinburg, TX
Guerrero, Bernard S. ...Department of Justice, Justice Management Division, GV
Guerrero, Bert G., Jr. ...Dallas, TX
Fort Worth, TX
Garland, TX
Guerrero, Daniel C. ...Minneapolis, MN
Guerrero, David J. ...McAllen, TX
Guerrero, David P.
Environmental Protection Agency, Office of the General Counsel, GV
Guerrero, Gregory A. ...Tulsa, OK
Guerrero, J. Richard ...Phoenix, AZ
Guerrero, Jose A. ...San Francisco, CA
Guerrero Law Offices, The ...Dallas, TX
Fort Worth, TX
Garland, TX
Guerrero, Louise Leon ...Daly City, CA
Guerrero, Michael A. ...Montebello, CA
Guerrero, Omar Victor ...Kerrville, TX
Guerrero, Patricia ...San Francisco, CA
Guerrero, Peter A., (P.C.) ...Phoenix, AZ
Guerrero, Rosalinda ...Houston, TX
Guerrero, Roxane M. ...Dallas, TX
Fort Worth, TX
Garland, TX
Guerrero, Ruben ...Houston, TX
Guerrero, Teresita R. ...Newark, NJ
Guerrero, Vincent J. ...Lake Mills, WI
Guerrero, Yalila E. ...Houston, TX
Guerrero-Calderon, Belen M.
San Juan, PR
Guerrero-Noble, Diego ...San Juan, PR
Guerrero-Noble, Perez-Orama & Guerrero-Calderon ...San Juan, PR
Guerrettaz, David A. ...Evansville, IN
Guerri, William G. ...St. Louis, MO
Guerrier, Ernst ...Boston, MA
Guerriere, Terence P. ...White Plains, NY
Guerrieri, Edmond & Clayman, P.C.
Washington, DC
Guerrieri, Joseph, Jr. ...Washington, DC
Guerrieri, Louis M. ...San Francisco, CA
Guerrieri, Susan Giongo ...Philadelphia, PA
Guerriero, Anthony S. ...Stockton, CA
Guerriero, Anthony S. ...Allen Park, MI
Guerriero, Elizabeth J. ...Monroe, LA
Guerriero & Guerriero ...Monroe, LA
Guerriero, Jeffrey Dowling ...Monroe, LA
Guerriero, Joe D. ...Monroe, LA
Guerriero, Michael J. ...Morristown, NJ
Guerriero, Salvatore ...Philadelphia, PA
Guerrini, Bernard A. ...Dallas, TX
Guerrini, Bernard A., P.C. ...Dallas, TX
Fort Worth, TX
Guerrini, Donald P. ...Glastonbury, CT
Guerrini & Guerrini ...Marseilles, IL
Guerrini, John D. ...Encino, CA

Guerrini, Joseph T. ... Marseilles, IL
Guerrini, Timothy J. ... Marseilles, IL
Guerríos-Rodríguez, Rebecca ... San Juan, PR
Guerry, Connie ... Pasadena, CA
Guerry, David L. ... Baton Rouge, LA
Guerry, John D. ... Los Angeles, CA
Guerry, John E., III ... Charleston, SC
Guerry, Leah S., (Mrs.) ... Baton Rouge, LA
Guerry, Lee Bradford ... Alexandria, VA
Guerry, Theodore L., Jr. ... Houston, TX
Guerry, Tucker P. ... Atlanta, GA
Guerry, William M., Jr. ... Washington, DC
Guertin, Debra K. ... St. Paul, MN
Guertin, George P. ... Northford, CT
Guertin, Jack D. ... Cottage City, MD
Guertin, Judith E. ... Milford, MI
Guertin, Richard J. ... Middletown, NY
Guerttman, Dan W. ... Casper, WY
Guervitz, Maurice A. ... Washington, DC
Guesman, James E. ... Las Vegas, NV
Guesnon, Verna R. ... New Orleans, LA
Guess, Carol Y. ... Houston, TX
Guess, Darrell ... Temple, TX
Guess, English & Robinson ... Knoxville, TN
Guess, James D. ... San Antonio, TX
Guess, Joe ... Knoxville, TN
Guess, Joseph D., II ... Knoxville, TN
Guess, Norma J. ... Joliet, IL
Guess, Robert E. ... Union, SC
Guess & Rudd P.C., A Professional Corporation ... Anchorage, AK
Fairbanks, AK
Guess, Samuel Aubrey ... Knoxville, TN
Guess, Sean ... Kansas City, KS
Guess, Sherrie P. ... Detroit, MI
Guest, Alexandra S. H. ... New York, NY
Guest & Associates, A Professional Corporation
Irving, TX
Guest, Austin ... Clarksville, TN
Guest, Beth Connor ... Nashville, TN
Guest, Bill Powell ... Oklahoma City, OK
Guest, Brian M. ... Willingboro, NJ
Guest, Caroline R. ... Portland, OR
Guest, Carolyn R. ... Houston, TX
Guest, Charles L. ... Mississippi State, MS
Guest, David G. ... Tallahassee, FL
Guest, David K. ... Rochelle, IL
Guest, David V. ... Baltimore, MD
Guest, Floyd E., Jr. ... Houston, TX
Guest, George J. ... Chicago, IL
Guest & Hand ... Kenner, LA
Guest, Holly J. ... Glen Allen, VA
Guest, J. Hanson ... Hartford, CT
Guest, James B. ... Kenner, LA
Guest, James H. ... Denver, CO
Guest, James H. ... St. Louis, MO
Guest, James L. ... Houston, TX
Guest, James W., Jr. ... Cleveland, OH
Guest, Jeanne N. ... Myrtle Beach, SC
Guest, John F. ... Rosemead, CA
Guest, John M. ... St. Louis, MO
Guest, John R. ... Houston, TX
Guest, Jonathan C. ... Boston, MA
Guest, Karen J. ... Dallas, TX
Guest, Karl Reed ... San Francisco, CA
San Francisco, CA
Guest, Karl Reed, A Professional Corporation
San Francisco, CA
Guest, Kelley ... Carmel, CA
Guest, Kenneth R. ... Irving, TX
Guest, Kimberly ... Irving, TX
Guest, Kristina L. ... Missoula, MT
Guest, Lance S. ... New Orleans, LA
Guest Legal, P.C. ... Rochelle, IL
Guest, Lemuel S. ... Atlanta, TX
Guest, M. Lou ... Treasury Department, Office of Thrift Supervision, GV
Guest, Michael ... Albuquerque, NM
Guest, Michael K. ... Indianapolis, IN
Guest, Michele B. ... Ponte Vedra Beach, FL
Guest, Pamela G. ... Norcross, GA
Guest, Rex A. ... Chicago, IL
Guest, Robert E., Jr. ... St. Louis, MO
Guest & Savage ... Hartford, CT
Hartsdale, NY
Guest, Steven R. ... Milwaukee, WI
Guest, Suzanne ... Albuquerque, NM
Guest, Thomas D. ... Rochelle, IL
Guest, Thomas D., Jr. ... Surfside Beach, SC
Guest, Victoria Woolworth ... New York, NY
Guest, William F. ... Houston, TX
Guest, William K. ... Glenwood Springs, CO
Guest, William K., P.C. ... Aspen, CO
Glenwood Springs, CO
Guest Sanders, Sandra ... Valdosta, GA
Gutersloh, Kerin M. ... Oakland, CA
Guethlein, Albert ... Cincinnati, OH
Guethlein, William O. ... Louisville, KY
Guetlich, Mark A. ... Redmond, WA
Guetling, Alfred J. ... Sacramento, CA
Guetschow, Bernd C. ... Anchorage, AK
Guetschow, Bernd C., A Professional Corporation ... Anchorage, AK
Guetta, Daniel ... New York, NY
Guettermann, Harlan H. ... Houston, TX
Guettinger, Jeffrey W. ... Eau Claire, WI
Guettler, Heidi ... Portland, OR
Guetz, Burton W. ... San Diego, CA
Guetzkow, Jason S. ... San Francisco, CA
Guevara, Andrew R. ... El Paso, TX
Guevara, Arron ... Portland, OR
Guevara, Daniel L. ... San Diego, CA
Guevara, Delia Y. ... San Francisco, CA
Guevara, Henry Douglas ... Brooklyn, NY
Guevara, Patrick E. ... San Jose, CA
Guevara, Phippard & James, P.C.
San Diego, CA
Guevara, Rebe, Baumann, Coldwell & Reedman, L.L.P. ... Las Cruces, NM
El Paso, TX
Guevara, Ricardo M. ... New Orleans, LA
Guevara, Roger, Law Offices of
San Antonio, TX
Guevin, Jeremiah J. ... Merced, CA
Guevremont, Jane M. ... Boston, MA
Gueymard, Davis A. ... Baton Rouge, LA
Guez, Joseph ... Hackensack, NJ
Guffanti, Albert W., P.A. ... Miami, FL
Guffanti, Albert W., (P.A.) ... Miami, FL
Guffey, Donal D. ... Columbia, MO
Guffey, Jerry W. ... Leitchfield, KY
Guffey, Joseph H. ... St. Louis, MO
Guffey, Larry J. ... Baltimore, MD
Guffey, Nancy E. ... West Palm Beach, FL
Guffey, Wendell Ray ... Oklahoma City, OK
Guffin, Peter J. ... Portland, ME
Guffy, Elizabeth M. ... Houston, TX
Gugala, Anita M. ... Southfield, MI
Gugar, Bernard T. ... New York, NY
Gugelyk, Carolyn K. ... Honolulu, HI
Gugenheim, Lynne ... Chicago, IL
Gugenheim, Paul ... Denver, CO
Gugenheim, Stephen J. ... Dallas, TX
Gugerty, David ... Forest Hills, NY
Gugerty, Michael J. ... Bethesda, MD
Gugerty, Michael J., P.C. ... Bethesda, MD
Guggenheim, Achiezer ... Washington, DC
Guggenheim, Alfred Kim
Los Angeles, CA
Guggenheim, Daniel R.
San Francisco, CA
Guggenheim, David M. ... La Jolla, CA
Guggenheim, Eve B.
Hilton Head Island, SC
Guggenheim, Jana Kay ... Washington, DC
Guggenheim, Marc G. ... Boston, MA
Guggenheim, Miriam J. ... Washington, DC
Guggenheim, Richard E. ... Cincinnati, OH
Guggenheim, Richard R. ... San Jose, CA
Guggenheim, Robert T. ... Lawrenceville, GA
Guggenheim, Robert T., P.C.
Lawrenceville, GA
Guggenheim, Seth M. ... Washington, DC
Guggenheim, Steven D. ... Palo Alto, CA
Guggenheimer, Charles S.
Englewood Cliffs, NJ
Guggenheimer, Joan ... New York, NY
Guggenheimer, Leah Beth ... New York, NY
Guggenhime, Richard J.
San Francisco, CA
Guggenmos, Cheryl C. ... Broken Bow, NE
Guggenmos, Fred A., III ... Stromsburg, NE
Guggino, Laurence P., Jr. ... Los Lunas, NM
Gugig, Darryl E. ... East Rutherford, NJ
Gugig, Michael S. ... New York, NY
Gugino, Cynthia White ... Herndon, VA
Gugino, Frederick R. ... Buffalo, NY
Gugino, Joseph Anthony ... Fort Myers, FL
Gugino, Rand H. ... Amherst, NY
Gugino, Robert L. ... Tucson, AZ
Gugino, Rosanne ... Buffalo, NY
Gugino, Salvatore C. ... Las Vegas, NV
Gugino & Schwartz ... Las Vegas, NV
Gugle, Kathryn R. ... Columbus, OH
Gugleta, James S. ... Austin, TX
Guglielmi, John A. ... Foxboro, MA
Guglielmino, Michael J. ... Novato, CA
Guglielmino, Russell J. ... Rochester, NY
Guglielmo, Angelo A. ... Rye, NY
Guglielmo, Anne Marie ... White Plains, NY
Guglielmo, Carey J. ... Baton Rouge, LA
Guglielmo, Claudia L. ... Woodbridge, NJ
Guglielmo, Daniel A. ... Taunton, MA
Guglielmo, Elizabeth L. ... Lafayette, LA
Guglielmo, James T. ... Opelousas, LA
Guglielmo, John ... Jericho, NY
Guglielmo, Joseph P. ... New York, NY
Guglielmo, Lopez, Tuttle, Hunter & Jarrell
Opelousas, LA
Guglielmo, Marks, Schutte, Terhoeve & Love
Baton Rouge, LA
Guglielmo, Paul D. ... Tucson, AZ
Guglietta, Pasquale ... Cherry Hill, NJ
Gugliotta, John D. ... Akron, OH
Gugliotta, Richard G. ... Bronx, NY
Gugliotti, Thomas A. ... Hartford, CT
Gugni, Gilbert ... Detroit, MI
Guha, Samidh ... New York, NY
Guhin, Tim ... San Bernardino, CA
Guhl, Craig O. ... Clearwater, FL
Guhl, Leslie Dean ... Seabrook, TX
Guhring, Elizabeth ... Silver Spring, MD
Guhring, Elizabeth, Chartered
Silver Spring, MD
Guhring, Eric L. ... New York, NY
Gui, Janice ... Akron, OH
Guia, Lucretia D. ... Greensboro, NC
Guibault, Paula M. ... New York, NY
Guiberson Law Offices, P.L.C. ... Houston, TX
Guiberson, Samuel A. ... Houston, TX
Guibone, Cheryl L. ... New York, NY
Guibord, Barbara B. ... Chicago, IL
Guibord, Scott L. ... Morristown, NJ
Guice, Jacob D. ... Biloxi, MS
Guice, Jon Keith ... Monroe, LA
Guice, Judy ... Biloxi, MS
Guice, Judy M., A Professional Association
Biloxi, MS
Gulfport, MS
Guice, Martha Rebecca ... Houston, TX
Guice, Stacy L. ... Monroe, LA
Guice, Stephen W. ... Barrington, NJ
Guice, Stephen W., P.C. ... Barrington, NJ
Guice, William Lee, III ... Biloxi, MS
Guichard, André P. ... New Orleans, LA
Guichard, Jones & Tarkoff
Sacramento, CA
Lafayette, CA
Walnut Creek, CA
Guichard, Matthew P. ... Sacramento, CA
Walnut Creek, CA
Guichet, Ginger Johnson
New Orleans, LA
Guichet, Joseph P. ... Alexandria, VA
Guida, Anthony J., Jr. ... Pittsburgh, PA
Guida, Carl G. ... New York, NY
Guida, Donald F. ... West Orange, NJ
Guida & Eagan, P.A. ... Columbia, MD
Ellicott City, MD
Guida, Elena Lopez ... Gulfport, MS
Guida, Gail ... Harrisburg, PA
Guida, James J. ... Lyndhurst, NJ
Guida, Joseph F. ... Dallas, TX
Guida, Joseph M., P.A. ... Aberdeen, MD
Guida Law Offices ... Harrisburg, PA
Guida, Patrick A. ... Providence, RI
Guida, Richard E. ... Harrisburg, PA
Guida, Robert F. ... Newark, NJ
Guida, Robert H. ... Beverly, MA
Guida, Robert R. ... Lyndhurst, NJ
Guida, Slavich & Flores, A Professional Corporation ... Dallas, TX
Guida, Thomas A. ... New York, NY
Guida, Toni M. ... White Plains, NY
Guida, Vincent M. ... Columbia, MD
Guida, William C. ... New York, NY
Guidarelli-Wu, Jacqueline M. ... Albany, NY
Guidash, Bryan H. ... Fairfax, VA
Guiddy, Melissa A. ... Greensburg, PA
Guider, Deborah L. ... New York, NY
Guidera, George C. ... Weston, CT
Guidera, John J. ... Union, NJ
Guidera, Kerin Rea ... Southampton, NY
Guidi, Andrew ... Anchorage, AK
Guidi, Dennis E. ... Jacksonville, FL
Guidi, Thomas L. ... Boston, MA
Guidice, Richard J. ... Chicago, IL
Guido, Amy LaVelle ... Hartford, CT
Guido, Anthony S. ... Du Bois, PA
Guido, Catherine ... Pottstown, PA
Guido, Edward E. ... Carlisle, PA
Guido, George Emil, Jr.
Department Of Veterans Affairs, Board of Veterans Appeals, GV
Guido, Kenneth J., Jr. ... Treasury Department, Office of Thrift Supervision, GV
Guido, Michael A. ... New York, NY
Guido, Michael P. ... Cherry Hill, NJ
Guido, Perri Karen Rosenfeld
Syracuse, NY
Guido, Richard A. ... San Diego, CA
Guido, Robert V. ... Uniondale, NY
Guido, Scott R. ... La Salle, IL
Guido, Syndi L. ... Harrisburg, PA
Guidoboni, Edward S. ... York, ME
Lancaster, MA
Guidoboni, Thomas A. ... Washington, DC
Guidorizzi, Douglas D. ... Baltimore, MD
Guidote, Joseph P. ... Appleton, WI
Guidotti, Adrian J. ... Sherman Oaks, CA
Guidotti, Aldo P. ... Orinda, CA
Guidotti, Bernadine Bushman ... Orinda, CA
Guidotti, Joanna R. ... Napa, CA
Guidotti, Karen Marzotto
Redwood City, CA
Guidotti & Lee ... Orinda, CA
Guidroz, Christopher M.
New Orleans, LA
Guidroz, John ... Houston, TX
Guidroz, Lonny E. ... Maringouin, LA
Guidry, Aaron W. ... Lafayette, LA
Guidry, Burton Paul ... Slaughter, LA
Guidry, Calvin T. ... Lafayette, LA
Guidry, Carl A. ... Baton Rouge, LA
Guidry, Charles C. ... Houston, TX
Guidry, Charles C., P.C. ... Houston, TX
Guidry, Daniel G. ... St. Martinville, LA
Guidry, Danny L. ... Lafayette, LA
Guidry, Dean J. ... Lafayette, LA
Guidry, Edmond L., III ... St. Martinville, LA
Guidry, Edmond L., Jr. ... St. Martinville, LA
Guidry, Eric C. ... Washington, DC
Guidry, Frankie L. ... Port Arthur, TX
Guidry, George A. ... New Orleans, LA
Guidry, George A., and Associates, Inc., A Professional Corporation ... New Orleans, LA
Guidry, George H., Jr. ... Baton Rouge, LA
Guidry, Greg ... Lafayette, LA
Guidry & Guidry ... St. Martinville, LA
Guidry, Hervin A. ... New Orleans, LA
Guidry, Jacqueline M. ... Kansas City, MO
Guidry, Jocelyn R. ... Lafayette, LA
Guidry, John M. ... Baton Rouge, LA
Guidry, John R. ... Wayne, NJ
Guidry, Katherine Bess ... Lafayette, LA
Guidry, Kirby J. ... Baton Rouge, LA
Guidry, Kirk A. ... Baton Rouge, LA
Guidry Law Firm ... Slaughter, LA
Guidry, Louis B. ... Lake Charles, LA
Guidry, Michael R. ... New Orleans, LA
Guidry, Randall Lee ... Lafayette, LA
Guidry, Richard J. ... Lafayette, LA
Guidry, Sarah R. ... Corpus Christi, TX
Guidry, Suzanne L. ... New Orleans, LA
Guidry, Victoria A. ... Lafayette, LA
Guidry, Wayne C. ... Grand Isle, LA
Guidry, William D. ... Freehold, NJ
Guidry, William D. ... Nacogdoches, TX
Guidubaldi, David J. ... Cleveland, OH
Guidubaldi, Mark David ... Cleveland, OH
Guiducci, Deborah K. ... Denver, CO
Guiducci, Edward J. ... Denver, CO
Guiducci & Guiducci, P.C. ... Denver, CO
Guiel, Jeffrey M. ... Chicopee, MA
Guier, Lester B. ... Hopkinsville, KY
Guier, Robert ... Troy, KS
Guiffre, Christopher D. T. ... Newton, MA
Guiffre, T. Michael ... Washington, DC
Guiffrida, Grace C. ... Jersey City, NJ
New York, NY
Guiggey, John B. ... Rochester, NY
Guignard, James S. ... Columbia, SC
Guikema, Henry L. ... Grand Rapids, MI
Guikema & Hulbert, P.C.
Grand Rapids, MI
Guil, James L. ... Department of Labor, Office of Secretary, GV
Guilbeau, Benjamin J., Jr.
Lake Charles, LA
Guilbeau, Joseph B. ... Metairie, LA
Guilbeau, Lyle J. ... Richmond, VA
Guilbeau, Thomas E. ... Lafayette, LA
Guilbeaux, Charlotte ... Shreveport, LA
Guilbert, Elizabeth D. ... Roanoke, VA
Guilbert, Elizabeth Douglas ... Lynchburg, VA
Guilbert, Richard J. ... New York, NY
Guilbert, Thomas G. P. ... Portland, OR
Guild, A. Courtney ... Louisville, KY
Guild, A. Courtney, Jr. ... Louisville, KY
Guild, Alden ... Montpelier, VT
Guild, C. Joseph, III ... Reno, NV
Guild, Clark J., Jr. ... Reno, NV
Guild, Donald C. ... Jackson, MS
Guild, Donald E. ... Augusta, ME
Guild, Irene L. ... Boston, MA
Guild, Jeffrey W. ... Chattanooga, TN
Guild, Peter C. ... Phoenix, AZ
Guild, Robert ... Columbia, SC
Guild, Robert B. ... Jacksonville, FL
Guild, Ronald J. ... Chicago, IL
Guild, Russell, Gallagher & Fuller, Ltd.
Carson City, NV
Reno, NV
Guild, William K. ... New York, NY
Guild, William L., III ... Winfield, IL
Guild, William L., III, P.C. ... Winfield, IL
Guilday, Thomas J. ... Tallahassee, FL
Guilde, Karen Johnson ... Wheaton, IL
Guildford, Lizet Acosta
Palm Beach Gardens, FL
Guilds, Ryan D. ... Washington, DC
Guiles, Jon R. ... Oshkosh, WI
Guiley, David D. ... Orlando, FL
Guiley, Richard R. ... Canton, OH
Guilfoil, Micah G. ... Louisville, KY
Guilfoil, Paul ... Ocala, FL
Guilfoil, Paul J., P.A. ... Ocala, FL
Guilfoil Petzall & Shoemake, L.L.C.
St. Louis, MO
Guilfoil, Thomas J. ... St. Louis, MO
Guilfoile, Maureen C. ... Chicago, IL
Guilford, Andrew J. ... Costa Mesa, CA
Guilford, F. W. Mort ... Coral Gables, FL
Guilford, Jeffrey S. ... Oak Ridge, TN
Guilford, Jennifer R. ... Miami, FL
Guilford, John T. ... Houston, TX
Guilford, Laurence M. ... Englewood, CO
Guilford, Michael F. ... Miami, FL
Guilford, Richard A. ... East Lansing, MI
Guilford, Robert E. ... Los Angeles, CA
Guilfoy, Joanna L. ... Boise, ID
Guilfoy, Walter J. ... Quincy, MA
Guilfoyle, Catherine T. ... Cincinnati, OH
Guilfoyle, David T. ... Kansas City, MO
Guilfoyle, J. Charles ... Jeffersonville, IN
Guilfoyle, Joan S. ... Washington, DC
Guilfoyle, John J., Jr. ... Reston, VA
Guilfoyle, Kathleen M. ... Boston, MA
Guilfoyle, Mark A. ... Abilene, KS
Guilfoyle, Mark D. ... Covington, KY
Guilfoyle, Mary L. ... San Francisco, CA
Guilfoyle, Matthew C. ... Houston, TX
Guilfoyle, Michael S. ... Mendota, IL
Guilfoyle, Patrick S. ... Washington, DC
Guilfoyle, Robert J. T. ... Chicago, IL
Guilfoyle, Thomas J. ... Omaha, NE
Guilfoyle, Wendy Mrazek ... Lansing, MI
Guilfoyle, William A. ... Abilene, KS
Guilian, Roger C. ... Mobile, AL
Guilian, William E.
Palm Beach Gardens, FL
Guiliana, Michael A. ... Newport Beach, CA
Arlington, VA
Guiliani, Richard J. ... Stockton, CA
Guiliano, Christine Renee
Philadelphia, PA
Guiliano, J. Jay ... Syracuse, NY
Guiliano, Joseph M. ... New York, NY
Guiliano, Nicholas J. ... Philadelphia, PA
Guiliano, Vincent J. ... New York, NY
Guill, Ann Holton ... Winston-Salem, NC
Guill, Douglas L. ... El Dorado, KS
Guill, Geoffrey C. ... Houston, TX
Guill, John H. ... Chicago, IL
Guill, Theresa Urban ... New Orleans, LA
Guillaume, Patti Reitz ... Boston, MA
Guillemard-Noble, Andres ... San Juan, PR
Guillemard-Noble, Monique
San Juan, PR
Guillén, Elizabeth ... Los Angeles, CA
Guillen, Marin A. ... Montebello, CA
Guillen, Rosalynn D. ... Seattle, WA
Guillen-Bermudez, Isabel M.
San Juan, PR
Guillermety, Rafael ... San Juan, PR
Guillette, Lauren M. ... Boston, MA
Guillien, Michelle M. ... La Crosse, WI
Guilliot, Paul J. ... Lafayette, LA
Guilliot, Paul J., P.L.C. ... Lafayette, LA
Guillorn, Brian W. ... New York, NY
Guillory, Carrie E. ... New York, NY

Guillory, Cynthia Clay ....Lake Charles, LA
Guillory, David J. ....Nacogdoches, TX
Guillory, David L. ....Pineville, LA
Guillory, Dorothy Davis ....Oakland, CA
Guillory, Elbert L. ....Opelousas, LA
Guillory, Jeffery M. ....Joplin, MO
Guillory, John P. ....Lafayette, LA
Guillory, L. Marie ....Washington, DC
Guillory & McCall, L.L.C.
Lake Charles, LA
Guillory, Michael E. ....New Orleans, LA
Guillory, Michael S. ....Metairie, LA
Guillory, Michael S., A Professional Law Corp.
Metairie, LA
Guillory, Phyllis A. ....Houston, TX
Guillory, Robert E., Jr. ....Lake Charles, LA
Guillory, Robert K. ....Eunice, LA
Guillory, Robert L. ....Lewiston, ME
Guillory, Vivian Broussard
Baton Rouge, LA
Guillory-Lee, Lydia Ann ....Lake Charles, LA
Guillot, Brian F. ....New Orleans, LA
Guillot, Dawn N. ....Baton Rouge, LA
Guillot, Gregory H. ....Washington, DC
Guillot, Gregory H., Chartered
Washington, DC
Guillot, Jesse S. ....New Orleans, LA
Guillot, Joseph M. ....New Orleans, LA
Guillot, Patrick C., (P.C.) ....Dallas, TX
Guillot, Robert O. ....Palo Alto, CA
Guillou, Celine M. ....Los Angeles, CA
Guillozet, Thomas L. ....Greenville, OH
Versailles, OH
Guills, Jesse O., Jr. ....Lewisburg, WV
Guimera & Guimera, A Law Corporation
Manhattan Beach, CA
Guimera, Irene M. ....Manhattan Beach, CA
Guimera, Joseph E. ....Manhattan Beach, CA
Guimond, Gene J. ....Norwell, MA
Guimond, Gerard J., Jr ....North Quincy, MA
Guimond, Joseph C. ....Salem, OR
Guimond, Robert W. ....Fall River, MA
Guin, Billy J., Jr. ....Shreveport, LA
Guin, Bouldin & Alexander ....Moulton, AL
Russellville, AL
Guin, David J. ....Birmingham, AL
Guin, David R. ....Louisburg, NC
Guin, David S. ....Chicago, IL
Guin, Don L. ....Tyler, TX
Guin, J. Foy, Jr. ....Birmingham, AL
Guin, Jay F. ....Tuscaloosa, AL
Guin, John H. ....Coeur d'Alene, ID
Spokane, WA
Guin, Sandra C. ....Tuscaloosa, AL
Guin, Shellie L. ....Independence, MO
Guinan, Anne Ward ....Dallas, TX
Guinan, Clark E. ....San Rafael, CA
Guinan, David J. ....Reno, NV
Guinan, Edward D. ....Pittsfield, MA
Guinan, Eric J. ....Wenatchee, WA
Guinan & Guinan ....Dallas, TX
Guinan, James J. ....Reno, NV
Guinan, James L. ....Dallas, TX
Guinan, Joseph A., III ....Philadelphia, PA
Guinan, Kathryn D. ....New London, CT
Guinan, Leslie Anne ....San Francisco, CA
Guinan, Michael D. ....Phoenix, AZ
Guinan, Richard C., Jr. ....Charlotte, NC
Guinan, Richard D. ....Cincinnati, OH
Guinan, Robert C. ....Omaha, NE
Guinan & Scott ....Omaha, NE
Guinan, Terry W. ....Fort Dodge, IA
Guinan, Terry W., P.C. ....Fort Dodge, IA
Guinan, Thomas M. ....Huntingdon Valley, PA
Guinasso, Charles B. ....Portland, OR
Guinasso, John D. ....Portland, OR
Guindi, Salwa ....Detroit, MI
Guindi-Rosenbaum, Magda El
Washington, DC
Guindon, Michele D. ....Tampa, FL
Guinee, Jennifer H. ....Pittsburgh, PA
Guinee, John F. ....Hayward, CA
Guinee, Patrick J. ....Pittsburgh, PA
Guiner, Stephen F. ....San Gabriel, CA
Guiney, Cornelius J., III ....New York, NY
Guiney, Daniel J. ....Belmont, NY
Guiney, Patrick V. ....Greenport, NY
Guiney, Thomas G. ....Boston, MA
Guiney, W. Terrance ....San Diego, CA
Guingona, Michael P. ....San Francisco, CA
Guinivan, James M. ....Washington, DC
Guinn, Charles C. ....Athens, TN
Guinn, David M. ....Waco, TX
Guinn, Donald E. ....Pittsburgh, PA
Guinn, Edward L. ....Columbia, MO
Guinn, Ernest A., Jr. ....El Paso, TX
Guinn, Gammon D. ....San Antonio, TX
Guinn, George R. ....Spokane, WA
Guinn, Guy F. ....Cleveland, OH
Guinn, J. Donald ....Tyler, TX
Guinn, James T. ....Oregon City, OR
Guinn, John ....Copperas Cove, TX
Guinn, Julian P. ....Paris, TN
Guinn, Kirk A. ....Gilbert, AZ
Guinn, Linda A. ....Golden, CO
Guinn, Mark A. ....San Francisco, CA
Guinn, Maurice K. ....Knoxville, TN
Guinn, Rebecca J. ....Atlanta, GA
Guinn, Robert L. ....Dallas, TX
Guinn, Royce D. ....Cleveland, TX
Guinn, Stanley Willis ....San Francisco, CA
Guinn, Steven E. ....Reno, NV
Guinn, Susan Lee ....San Diego, CA
Guinn, Tonya Klutts ....Okemah, OK
Guinness, Robert J. ....St. Charles, MO
Guinot, Luis, Jr. ....Washington, DC
Guinter, Steven D. ....Lancaster, PA
Guiod, Robert D. ....Boston, MA

Guion, Harry E. ....Cleveland, OH
Guion, Neil P. ....Springfield, MO
Guion, Stevens & Rybak ....Litchfield, CT
Guior, Glenn L. ....Whitehouse Station, NJ
Guiou, Shelley J. ....Englewood, CO
Guira, Jorge M. ....Malabar, FL
Guirado, Edward J. ....Capistrano Beach, CA
Guirgis, Ralph A. ....Irvine, CA
Guirl, James N., II ....St. Louis, MO
Guiry, James M. ....Treasury Department,
Internal Revenue Service, GV
Guis, William B. ....Milwaukee, WI
Guisbond, Andrew S. ....Boston, MA
Guisbond, Andrew S. ....Lexington, MA
Guise, Clay A. ....Bloomfield Hills, MI
Guise, Dennis T. ....Harrisburg, PA
Guise, Edward J., III ....Houston, TX
Guise, Heather Lynn ....Columbus, OH
Guise, Jeffrey William ....La Jolla, CA
Guise, Steven L., (A Professional Corporation) ....Los Angeles, CA
Guisinger, Lawrence B. ....Oak Harbor, WA
Guissinger, Lynn G. ....Boulder, CO
Guist, Carolyn L. ....Banks, OR
Guitart, Agustin R. ....Metairie, LA
Guite, Robert J. ....Seattle, WA
Guiter, Steven Wayne ....Knoxville, IA
Guitian, Maria Antonia ....Miami, FL
Guito, Ralph M., III ....Tampa, FL
Guiton, John ....New York, NY
Guittar, Donald J. ....Columbus, OH
Guittard, Charles ....Dallas, TX
Guittard & Hyden, P.C. ....Dallas, TX
Guittard, John R. ....Dallas, TX
Guizan, Julia A. ....Newport Beach, CA
Guizar, Humberto M. ....Los Angeles, CA
Guizar, Ramon L. ....Ventura, CA
Guizlo, Pamela J. ....Wichita, KS
Guizot, Damon ....Los Angeles, CA
Guizot & Mouser ....Los Angeles, CA
Guja, Arthur T. ....New York, NY
Gujarati, Diane ....New York, NY
Gujral, Gautam S. ....New York, NY
Guju, Michael J. ....Clearwater, FL
Gul, Eric I. ....New York, NY
Gula, Joseph M. ....Greenville, PA
Gula, Megan E. ....New York, NY
Gula, Monty ....Phoenix, AZ
Gulack, Robert
Securities and Exchange Commission,
Division of Enforcement, GV
Gulant, Joseph T. ....Philadelphia, PA
Gular, Suzanne R. ....Phoenix, AZ
Gulartie, Louise B. ....Tujunga, CA
Gulas, A. M. ....Treasury Department,
Internal Revenue Service, GV
Gulas, John S. ....Dayton, OH
Gulas, Ruth M. ....Port Clinton, OH
Gulasarian, Mark J.
Newtown Square, PA
Gulash, John R., Jr. ....Bridgeport, CT
Gulash, John R., Jr. & Eugene J. Riccio, Law Offices of ....Bridgeport, CT
Gulati, Anurag ....Minneapolis, MN
Gulatto, Peter C. ....Phoenix, AZ
Gulaya, Krishna ....Santa Ana, CA
Gulaya, Suresh ....Tustin, CA
Gulbankian & Gulbankian ....Racine, WI
Gulbankian, Vartak, (Miss) ....Racine, WI
Gulbin, John F. ....Morristown, NJ
Gulbin, John F. ....Staten Island, NY
Gulbis, Vitauts M. ....Tampa, FL
Gulbrandsen, Carl E. ....Madison, WI
Gulbrandsen, Ole ....Viroqua, WI
Gulbrandsen, Richard M. ....Mesa, AZ
Gulbrandson, Leslie C. ....Tucson, AZ
Guldalian, Bradley T. ....Tampa, FL
Detroit, MI
Guldan, James A. ....St. Paul, MN
Gulde, Jane E. ....Phoenix, AZ
Gulde, John J., Jr. ....Burlington, MA
Gulde, Karen K. ....San Antonio, TX
Gulde, Robert G. ....Rushville, IN
Gulden, A. Spencer ....New Orleans, LA
Gulden, Ashley Spencer ....New Orleans, LA
Gulden, Daniel E. ....Atlanta, GA
Gulden, J. Kenneth ....Deerfield Beach, FL
Gulden, Timothy M. ....Alpena, MI
Guldenschuh, David F. ....Rome, GA
Guldi, George O. ....Westhampton Beach, NY
Guldi, Virginia Whitehill ....Washington, DC
Guldimann, John L. ....Redondo Beach, CA
Guldin, John C. ....Orefield, PA
Guldin, John R. ....Columbus, OH
Guldman, Melanie D. ....Manitou Springs, CO
Guldner, Jeffrey Breck ....Phoenix, AZ
Gulecas, James F. ....Clearwater, FL
Guleke, James O., II ....Austin, TX
Guler, Mary Maichel ....Bismarck, ND
Gulia, Gregory P. ....New York, NY
Gulia, Peter J. ....East Brunswick, NJ
Guliani, Richard J. ....Portland, CT
Guliano, Barry D. ....Manchester, CT
Gulick, Donald L. ....Louisville, KY
Gulick, Glenn R., Jr. ....Joplin, MO
Gulick, James C. ....Raleigh, NC
Gulick, John A., III ....Scottsdale, AZ
Gulick, John N., Jr. ....San Francisco, CA
Gulick, Karen L.
Federal Communications Commission,
Office of the Commissioners, GV
Gulick, Lisa ....Newark, NJ
Gulick, Peter V. ....Bellevue, WA
Gulick, Robert S. ....Boston, MA
Gulick, Robin C. ....Warrenton, VA
Gulick, Robin C., P.C. ....Warrenton, VA
Gulick, Ruth P. ....New Hampton, NH

Gulielmetti & Gesmer, P.C.
New York, NY
Gulielmetti, Paul M. ....New York, NY
Gulig, Michael J. ....Waco, TX
Gulin, Frank C. ....Washington, DC
Gulinello, Joan R. ....Boston, MA
Gulinello, Leo J. ....Boston, MA
Gulino, Charles J. ....Medford, MA
Gulino, Daniel V. ....Atlanta, GA
Allentown, PA
Gulino, Frank ....New York, NY
Gulino, John J. ....Santa Ana, CA
Gulino, Lawrence L. ....New York, NY
Gulino, Leonard M. ....Portland, ME
Gulino, Louis T. ....San Diego, CA
Gulino, Theodore ....Chicago, IL
Gulinson, Gene G. ....Phoenix, AZ
Gulinson, Gene G., Ltd. ....Phoenix, AZ
Gulisano, Philip M. ....Buffalo, NY
Gulish, Nancy L. ....Culver City, CA
Gulitz, Lester M. A. ....Peekskill, NY
Gulker, O. Allan ....Fort Myers Beach, FL
Gulkin, Hock & Lehr, P.A. ....Livingston, NJ
Gulkin, Karen R. ....New York, NY
Gulkin, Stanley J. ....Livingston, NJ
Gulkin, Stephanie M. ....New York, NY
Gulko, Arnold G. ....Silver Spring, MD
Gulko, Paul M. ....Marblehead, MA
Gulko, Ralph ....Englewood Cliffs, NJ
Gulkowitz, Arnold ....New York, NY
Gull, Jason N. ....San Francisco, CA
Gull, Kathryn N. ....New York, NY
Gulla, Deanne Peterson ....Visalia, CA
Gulla, Michael A. ....Visalia, CA
Gullace, Dante ....Rochester, NY
Gullace, John F. ....Bala Cynwyd, PA
Gullace & Weld ....Rochester, NY
Gullage, James T. ....Opelika, AL
Gullahorn & Hare, P.C. ....Albertville, AL
Guntersville, AL
Gullahorn, Jack W. ....Austin, TX
Gullahorn, John C. ....Albertville, AL
Gullahorn, William C., Jr. ....Albertville, AL
Gulland, Eugene D. ....Washington, DC
Gullatt, Dowe D. ....Austin, TX
Gullborg, Peter W. ....St. Louis, MO
Gulledge, Cathleen A. ....Wichita, KS
Gulledge, Jack ....Dallas, TX
Gulledge, John M. ....Greenwood, SC
Gulledge, Linda J. ....Newport Beach, CA
Gulledge, Wayne C. ....Memphis, TN
Gullekson & Daniels ....Tulsa, OK
Gullekson, Larry A. ....Tulsa, OK
Gullen, Christopher R. ....Troy, MI
Gullen, David J., (P.C.) ....Los Angeles, CA
Gullen, John D. ....Dearborn, MI
Gullen, Richard B. ....San Jose, CA
Guller, Arthur Z. ....St. Louis, MO
Guller, Deborah ....Fort Lauderdale, FL
Guller, Jeffrey M. ....Gastonia, NC
Guller, Lisa R. ....West Orange, NJ
Guller, Matthew E. ....Oakland, NJ
Guller, Susan ....St. Louis, MO
Gullet, Michelle Lynne ....Oak Park, MI
Gullett, Asa P., III ....Hazard, KY
Gullett, Combs, Reed & Bowling
Hazard, KY
Hindman, KY
Hyden, KY
Gullett, Gretchen Nunn
Prestonsburg, KY
Gullett, John H. ....Easton, MD
Gullett, Sanford, Robinson & Martin, P.L.L.C. ....Nashville, TN
Gullett, William C. ....Covington, KY
Gullette, John E. ....Woodbridge, VA
Gullette, Richard A. ....Phoenix, AZ
Gullette, Robert L. ....Seattle, WA
Gullette, Robert L., Jr. ....Nicholasville, KY
Gullette, William R. ....Pagosa Springs, CO
Gulley & Calhoun ....Durham, NC
Gulley, Clarke E. ....Atlanta, GA
Gulley, Danelle ....Houston, TX
Gulley, David Wesley ....Hereford, TX
Gulley, George H., Jr. ....Brookhaven, MS
Gulley, Gerald L., Jr. ....Knoxville, TN
Gulley, Gwyn ....Rockford, IL
Gulley, Haygood ....Del Rio, TX
Gulley, Jack Marshall ....Charlotte, NC
Gulley, James L. ....Houston, TX
Gulley, Jeffrey J. ....Fort Wayne, IN
Gulley, Karen Dau ....Little Rock, AR
Gulley, Kenneth G. ....Sedalia, CO
Gulley, Kimberly A. ....Topeka, KS
Gulley, Robert L. ....Washington, DC
Gulley, Roy O. ....Springfield, IL
Gulley, Stacy D. ....San Diego, CA
Gulley, Thomas P. ....Albuquerque, NM
Gulley, Wilbur P. ....Durham, NC
Gullia, Theodore A., Jr. ....Cleveland, OH
Gullick, Lynn G. ....Greensboro, NC
Gullick, Robert H. ....Indianapolis, IN
Gullicksen, Kenneth A. ....Nantucket, MA
Gullickson, Charles D. ....Sioux Falls, SD
Gullickson, Grant Orvis ....Universal City, CA
Gullickson, Gregory B. ....Fargo, ND
Gullickson, Howard M.
Rancho Santa Fe, CA
Gullickson, John C. ....Lawrenceville, GA
Gullickson Law Offices, P.A. ....Kasson, MN
Rochester, MN
Gullickson, Mark W. ....Kasson, MN
Rochester, MN
Gullickson, Randy G. ....Minneapolis, MN
Gullickson, Stuart G. ....Madison, WI
Gulliford, Don M. ....Bellevue, WA
Gulliford & McGaughey, P.L.L.C.
Bellevue, WA

Gullikson, Rosemary L.L. ....Chicago, IL
Gulling, Donald D., Jr. ....Latham, NY
Gullion, Ann Freeman ....Houston, TX
Gullion, Paul D. ....Salinas, CA
Gulliver, Brigitte M. ....Nyack, NY
Gulliver, Carl T. ....New Haven, CT
Gulliver, Gary B. ....Lansing, MI
Gulliver, Gregory B. ....Chicago, IL
Gulliver, John W. ....Portland, ME
Gulliver, Lee S ....Santa Cruz, CA
Gullixson, Conrad F. ....Palo Alto, CA
Gullixson, Janet B. ....Beverly Hills, CA
Gullixson, John M. ....Yorba Linda, CA
Gullixson, Richard L. ....Beverly Hills, CA
Gullo, Benedict S., Jr. ....Uniondale, NY
Gullo, Francis H. ....Turlock, CA
Gullo, George M. ....Deerfield, IL
Gullo, Jack Anthony, Jr. ....New Windsor, MD
Gullo, John P., II ....Dunkirk, NY
Gullo, Michael E. ....Brooklyn, NY
Gullo, Robert J. ....Detroit, MI
Gullotta, Susan C. ....Pleasantville, NY
Gullotti, Daniel T. ....Fredonia, NY
Jamestown, NY
Gullotti, Richard J. ....Waltham, MA
Gullstrand, Gregory R. ....Irvine, CA
Gullufsen, Patrick J. ....Juneau, AK
Gulluni, Maria A. ....Hartford, CT
Gully, Jennifer E. ....Los Angeles, CA
Gully, Russell G. ....Dallas, TX
Gully-Brown, Donna J. ....Worcester, MA
Gulmi, Joseph E. ....New York, NY
Gulo, M. G. ....Streator, IL
Gulo, M. G., and Associates, Ltd.
Streator, IL
Gulo, Michael F. ....Streator, IL
Gulotta, Christina A. ....Hempstead, NY
Gulotta, Christopher ....Carlisle, PA
Gulotta, Christopher J. ....New York, NY
White Plains, NY
Gulotta, Frank A., Jr. ....Williston Park, NY
Gulotta, James C., Jr., (P.C.)
New Orleans, LA
Gulotta, Lawrence ....Calumet City, IL
Gulotta, Peter F. ....Delray Beach, FL
Gulotta, Peter, Jr. ....Kenner, LA
Gulotta, Stephen J., Jr. ....New York, NY
Gulotty, Gina A. ....Albany, NY
Poughkeepsie, NY
Gulovsen, Grant R. ....Champaign, IL
Gulseth, James H. ....Pleasanton, CA
Gulsvig, Pamela H. ....Phoenix, AZ
Gultanoff, Barry F., Law Offices of
Lansdale, PA
Norristown, PA
Pottstown, PA
Gulya, Brigitta Rianna ....Washington, DC
Gulyas, John P. ....Indianapolis, IN
Gulyassy, Anne M. ....Department of Justice,
Office of Attorney Personnel Management,
GV
Gulyassy, Victor J. ....Parma Heights, OH
Gum, Carl D., III ....Cleveland, OH
Gum, Carl D., Jr. ....Belton, MO
Gum & Hillier, P.A. ....Asheville, NC
Gum, Howard L. ....Asheville, NC
Gum, Robert G. ....Oklahoma City, OK
Gum, Scott R. ....Cameron, MO
Kansas City, MO
Gum, Trisha L. ....Los Angeles, CA
Guma, F. Wm., Jr. ....Floral Park, NY
Gumaer, Elliott W., Jr. ....Rochester, NY
Gumaer, Kathleen R. ....Spokane, WA
Gumaer, Matthew D. ....Syracuse, NY
Guman, John D., Jr. ....Bridgeport, CT
Gumataotao, Gary Wayne Francis
Hagåtña, GU
Gumbel, Jon M. ....Atlanta, GA
Gumberg, James K. ....Salinas, CA
Gumbert, James G. ....Houston, TX
Gumbiner & Eskridge LLP
San Francisco, CA
San Rafael, CA
Walnut Creek, CA
Gumbiner, Gary M. ....Buffalo Grove, IL
Gumbiner, Joel P. ....Walnut Creek, CA
Gumbiner, Kenneth J. ....Washington, DC
Greensboro, NC
Gumbiner, Marshall ....Los Angeles, CA
Gumbinger, Aaron M. ....San Francisco, CA
Gumbinger, Walter ....New York, NY
Gumbinner, Fredric R. ....Herndon, VA
Gumble, Morton D. ....Tucson, AZ
Gumble, William C. ....Paupack, PA
Gumbs, Clyde E. ....New York, NY
Gumbs, Etta M. ....New York, NY
Gumbs, Philip N. ....Freehold, NJ
Gumbs, Robina M. ....Rego Park, NY
Gumenick, Robert J ....New York, NY
Gumer, I. R. ....Louisville, KY
Gumer, M. Robert ....Tarzana, CA
Gumer, Sherie B. ....Dunwoody, GA
Gumerove, Saundra M. ....Jericho, NY
Gumersell, John D. ....St. Louis, MO
Gumersell, Walter J. ....Melville, NY
Gumina, Emanuel V. ....Brookfield, WI
Gumina, Frank A. ....Milwaukee, WI
Gumina, Gregory J. ....Rochester, NY
Gumina, James C. ....Chicago, IL
Gumina, John ....Milwaukee, WI
Gumina, Joseph E. ....Milwaukee, WI
Gumina, Julia ....Wheaton, IL
Gumina, Paul L. ....Millbrae, CA
Gumkowski, Joseph J. ....Buffalo, NY
Gumlia, Leonard ....Santa Ana, CA
Gumm, Ada Katherine ....Oklahoma City, OK
Gumm, Janet M. ....Oak Brook, IL
Gumm, Richard W. ....Sarasota, FL

Gunther, John E. ... Summit, NJ
Gunther, John M. ... Hopkinton, MA
Gunther, Laurene Allison
Philadelphia, PA
Gunther, Laurie T. ... Chicago, IL
Gunther, Marilyn R. ... Seattle, WA
Gunther, Mark S. ... Rochester, NY
Gunther, Nicolas L. ... New York, NY
Gunther, Nina L. ... Raleigh, NC
Gunther, Peter C. ... Wausau, WI
Gunther, Robert A. ... Princeton, NJ
Gunther, Robert J. ... Pineville, LA
Gunther, Robert J., Jr. ... New York, NY
Gunther, Robert W. ... Rye, NY
Gunther, Samuel P. ... New York, NY
Gunther, Scott E. ... Brooklyn, NY
Gunther, Stephen D. ... Santa Monica, CA
Gunther, Thomas H. ... Minneapolis, MN
Gunther, Timothy A. ... Raleigh, NC
Gunther, Victoria L. ... Irvine, CA
Gunther-Chung, Karen L. ... New York, NY
Gunti, David K. ... Pine Bluff, AR
Gunton, Judith P. ... San Francisco, CA
Guntren, John W. ... Jerseyville, IL
Gunty & McCarthy ... Chicago, IL
St. Louis, MO
Gunty, Susan ... Chicago, IL
St. Louis, MO
Gunya, Kevin M. ... Kansas City, MO
Gunya, Stacey Janssen ... Olathe, KS
Gunyan, Russell J. ... New York, NY
Gunzburg, Michael B. ... Chicago, IL
Gunzburg, Michael W. ... New York, NY
Gunzburger, Ronald M.
Fort Lauderdale, FL
Günzerodt, Immo C. ... San Francisco, CA
Guokas, Charles R. ... Milwaukee, WI
Guokas, Linda E. ... Sheboygan, WI
Guolee, Michael D. ... Milwaukee, WI
Guolee, Terrence ... Chicago, IL
Guon, Allen J. ... Chicago, IL
Gupp, William R. ... Camp Hill, PA
Gupta, Anand ... Dallas, TX
Gupta, Anirma Rakshpal ... Palo Alto, CA
Gupta, Ankur ... Chicago, IL
Gupta, Archana ... Corona, CA
Gupta, Balaram ... Summit, NJ
Gupta, Barbara Brady ... Houston, TX
Gupta, Gina R. ... Kansas City, KS
Gupta, Krish ... Hopkinton, MA
Gupta, Madhu M. ... Chicago, IL
Gupta, Mona ... Philadelphia, PA
Gupta, Mona ... Addison, TX
Gupta, Neer ... New York, NY
Gupta, Paul R. ... Boston, MA
Gupta, Ragini ... New York, NY
Gupta, Rahul ... Houston, TX
Gupta, Raj K.
Equal Employment Opportunity Commission, Office of the Commissioners, GV
Gupta, Rajat K. ... New Brunswick, NJ
Gupta, Rajiv ... New York, NY
Gupta, Renu K. ... Washington, DC
Gupta, Renuka ... New York, NY
Gupta, R.K. ... Brooklyn, NY
Gupta, Ruth Church ... San Francisco, CA
Gupta, Shilpi ... Chicago, IL
Gupton, Guy W., III ... Atlanta, GA
Gupton, J. Stephen, Jr. ... Valdosta, GA
Gupton, J. Stephen, Jr., P.C. ... Valdosta, GA
Gupton, Janet L. ... Winston-Salem, NC
Gupton, John A., III ... Nashville, TN
Gupton, John B. ... Raleigh, NC
Gura, Alan ... Washington, DC
Gura, Brian C. ... Hermosa Beach, CA
Gura, Charles T. ... New York, NY
Gura, Ian Jay ... New York, NY
Gura, John E., Jr. ... New York, NY
Gura, Lloyd A. ... New York, NY
Gura, Philip Paul ... Atlanta, GA
Gura, Rachelle L. ... New Paltz, NY
Gura, Ruth-Ellen ... Austin, TX
Gura, Stephen A.
Supreme Court Of The United States, GV
Gurahian, Harry ... Southampton, NY
Gurahian, Patricia Wetmore
White Plains, NY
Gurak, Raymond S. ... Newark, NJ
Gurak, Richard J. ... Chicago, IL
Guralnick, Brian D. ... West Palm Beach, FL
Guralnick & Gilliland ... Palm Desert, CA
Guralnick, Ilene H. ... New York, NY
Guralnick, Mark S. ... Broomall, PA
Guralnick, Wayne S. ... Palm Desert, CA
Guran, John M. ... Akron, OH
Guran, Linda S. Lease ... Akron, OH
Gur-Arie, Mira L ... Washington, DC
Gurbacki, Robert H. ... East Aurora, NY
Gurbarg, Jacqueline B. ... Margate City, NJ
Gurber, Kenneth ... Chicago, IL
Des Plaines, IL
Gurbst, Richard ... Cleveland, OH
Gurbuz, Robert B. ... Los Angeles, CA
Gurchik, Stephen J. ... Elyria, OH
Gurczynski, Raymond E., Jr. ... Honolulu, HI
Gurda & Gurda ... Middletown, NY
Gurda, Michael A. ... Middletown, NY
Gurdak, Dianne Schaefer ... Washington, DC
Gurdak, John A. ... Clifton, NJ
Gurdak, Michael P. ... Washington, DC
Gurdak, Natalie M. ... Lakeland, FL
Gurdian, Manuel A. ... Miami, FL
Gurdin, C. Stephen, Jr. ... Wilkes-Barre, PA
Gurdin, Lester J., P.C. ... Sioux City, IA
Gurdin, Steven E. ... Boston, MA
Gurecky, Marcia S. ... Toledo, OH
Gureghian, Tamara C. ... Warrington, PA
Gureghian, Vahan H. ... Philadelphia, PA
Guregian, Richard ... Livonia, MI
Gurell, Marc J. ... New York, NY
Guren, Aliza Karney ... Los Angeles, CA
Guren, Sheldon B. ... Miami, FL
Guresz, Caroline ... Cohoes, NY
Gurev, Elizabeth F. ... Stockton, CA
Gurev, Michael L. ... Stockton, CA
Gurevich, Alexander ... New York, NY
Gurevich, Alexander M. ... Houston, TX
Gurevich, Simona S. ... San Francisco, CA
Gurevitz, Mark S. ... Hartford, CT
Gurewitz, David ... Manhattan Beach, CA
Gurewitz, Harold ... Birmingham, MI
Gurewitz, Marvin L., (Ltd.)
Minneapolis, MN
Gurewitz, Mary Ellen ... Detroit, MI
Gurewitz and Raben, PLC
Birmingham, MI
Detroit, MI
Gurewitz, Thomas M. ... Waukegan, IL
Gurey, Stephen M. ... Murray Hill, NJ
Gurfein, Daniel G. ... New York, NY
Gurfein & Graubard ... New York, NY
Gurfein, Jared L. ... New York, NY
Gurfein, Jay J. ... New York, NY
Gurfein, Peter J. ... Los Angeles, CA
Gurfein, Richard A. ... New York, NY
Gurfinkel, Daniel M. ... Chicago, IL
Gurganus, Alvin E., II ... Bluefield, WV
Gurganus, John C., Jr. ... Scranton, PA
Gurgold, Eric ... Hackensack, NJ
Gurgold & Guadara ... Hackensack, NJ
Guria, Beth Henning ... Chicago, IL
Gurian, Craig ... New York, NY
Gurian, Jeffrey B. ... Highland Park, IL
Gurian, Jonathan ... Columbus, OH
Gurian, Jorge L. ... Miami, FL
Gurian, Jorge L., P.A. ... Miami, FL
Gurian, Robert B. ... Eastchester, NY
Gurican, Barbara Doty ... Milwaukee, WI
Gurich, Noma Diane ... Oklahoma City, OK
Gurien, Michael B. ... Santa Monica, CA
Gurin, Timothy B. ... Highland Heights, OH
Gurion, Henry B. ... Hazel Crest, IL
Guritz, Robert ... Chicago, IL
Guritz, Russlyn Landers
Pension Benefit Guaranty Corporation, Other Lawyers in Staff or Executive Positions, GV
Guritzky, Glenn C. ... Florham Park, NJ
Springfield, NJ
Gurka, Jon W. ... Newport Beach, CA
Gurkin, Larry R. ... Rahway, NJ
Gurkin, William S. ... Rahway, NJ
Gurko, Stephen ... Frisco, CO
Gurland, C. Slowikowski
Department of Transportation, Maritime Administration, GV
Gurland, Harvey W., Jr. ... Miami, FL
Gurland, Jonathan I.
Department Of Veterans Affairs, Office of the General Counsel, GV
Gurland, Robert J. ... New York, NY
Gurley, Charles R. ... Goldsboro, NC
Gurley, Curtis R. ... Farmington, NM
Gurley, David E. ... Sarasota, FL
Gurley, Hilda V. ... Dearborn, MI
Gurley, James B. ... Atlanta, GA
Gurley, James B. ... Roanoke, VA
Gurley, Jane ... San Francisco, CA
Gurley, Joanne G. ... Painesville, OH
Gurley, John C. ... Chicago, IL
Gurley, John Harris ... Columbia, MD
Gurley, John W. ... Albuquerque, NM
Gurley, Joseph M. ... Painesville, OH
Gurley, Kathryn H. ... Friona, TX
Gurley, Michael E. ... Denver, CO
Gurley, Mitchell & Gassaway, L.L.P.
Borger, TX
Panhandle, TX
Gurley Professional Association ... Atlanta, GA
Gurley, Richard A. ... Grove, OK
Gurley, Richard Thomas Damien
Clearwater, FL
Gurley, Roy E. ... Borger, TX
Gurman, Blask & Freedman, Chartered
Washington, DC
Gurman, Louis ... Washington, DC
Gurman, Nancy Schmitt ... Hollidaysburg, PA
Gurmankin, Jay D. ... Salt Lake City, UT
Gurnani, Anita Ramesh ... Edison, NJ
Gurne, Patricia D. ... Washington, DC
Gurnee, Graham F. ... Fayetteville, NC
Gurnee, Steven H. ... Los Angeles, CA
Roseville, CA
Gurnee, Steven H., & Associates, A Law Corporation ... Roseville, CA
Sacramento, CA
Gurney, Annette ... Wichita, KS
Gurney, Brent J. ... Washington, DC
Gurney, D. Scott ... Cincinnati, OH
Gurney, Donald G. ... New York, NY
Gurney, Edward J. ... Winter Park, FL
Gurney & Handley, P.A. ... Orlando, FL
Gurney, Lawrence M. ... Wichita, KS
Gurney, Leanne ... Carmichael, CA
Gurney, Miller & Mamone ... Cleveland, OH
Gurney, Neil W. ... Cleveland, OH
Gurney, Paul C. ... Overland Park, KS
Gurney, Richard L. ... Moreno Valley, CA
Gurney, Sarah Glade ... Santa Rosa, CA
Gurney, W. David ... Corona, CA
Moreno Valley, CA
Gurney, W. David ... Riverside, CA
Gurney, W. David ... Temecula, CA
Gurnham, Roy F. ... Alexandria, VA
Gurnick, David ... Woodland Hills, CA
Gurnick, Ray ... Cleveland, OH
Gurnik, Benjamin C. ... Longwood, FL
Gurnsey, Avery L. ... Bassett, NE
Springview, NE
Gurny, Milton ... Short Hills, NJ
Gurny, Susan Lynn ... Washington, DC
Gurock, Howard M. ... Spring Valley, NY
Guroff, Julia H. ... San Diego, CA
Gurovitsch, James D.
Brooklyn Center, MN
Gurovitsch, Kerry A. ... San Antonio, TX
Guroy, John R., Jr. ... Willoughby, OH
Gurr, Edwin ... Pago Pago, TT
Gurr, Stephen D. ... Denver, CO
Gurren, Jeffrey G. ... New York, NY
Gurrera, Taylor & Makricostas
Weirton, WV
Gurrera, Vincent S. ... Weirton, WV
Gurrieri, Mario C. ... Westfield, NJ
Gurrola, Anthony, III ... Escondido, CA
Gurrola, Barbara ... Inverness, FL
Gurrola, Edward M. ... Farmington, CT
Gurrola, Emilio T. ... Whittier, CA
Gurrola, Robert ... St. Paul, MN
Gurry, Bernard ... Flushing, NY
Gurry, Eric A. ... Chicago, IL
Gursel, Ali R. ... New York, NY
Gursen, Sharon Frida ... Brooklyn, NY
Gurshin, Timothy P. ... Concord, NH
Gurshman, Henry ... Metuchen, NJ
Gursky, Alexis ... Pittsburgh, PA
Pittsburgh, PA
Gursky, Catherine A. ... New York, NY
Gursky & Ederer, P.C. ... New York, NY
Gursky, Irving J. ... Bronx, NY
Gursky, Kenneth D. ... Basking Ridge, NJ
Gursky & Odwak ... Brooklyn, NY
Gursky, Robert J. ... Kew Gardens, NY
Gursky, Ruth M. ... Brooklyn, NY
Gursky, Scott A. ... San Francisco, CA
Gursky, Steven R. ... New York, NY
Gurss, Robert M. ... Washington, DC
Gurstel Law Firm, The, P.A.
Minneapolis, MN
Gurstel, Todd L. ... Minneapolis, MN
Gursten, Lawrence E. ... Southfield, MI
Gursten, Steven M. ... Southfield, MI
Gursten, Wigod, Koltonow & Falzon, P.C.
Southfield, MI
Gurtler, Charles W., Jr.
Bullhead City, AZ
Gurtler, Kelley & Moyer
Bullhead City, AZ
Kingman, AZ
Lake Havasu City, AZ
Gurtler, Paul R. ... Brookfield, WI
Gurtler, Richard W. ... Mesa, AZ
Gurtler, Ronald E. ... Longwood, FL
Gurton, Amy S. ... Juneau, AK
Gurtu, Chat ... New York, NY
Gurtu & McGoldrick, LLP ... New York, NY
Gurule, Agustin T. ... Brentwood, CA
Gurvey, Gary A. ... Chicago, IL
Gurvis, Anthony N. ... Columbus, OH
Gurvitch, Les ... San Francisco, CA
Gurvitch, Neil ... Bethesda, MD
Gurvits, Eugene ... Boston, MA
Gurvitz, Allan R. ... Troy, MI
Gurvitz, Ron F. ... Encino, CA
Gurwell, Karin Easter
Huntington Beach, CA
Gurwicz, Mitchell ... Atlantic City, NJ
Gurwin, David A. ... Pittsburgh, PA
Gurwin, E. Donald ... Southfield, MI
Gurwin, Hanley M. ... Bloomfield Hills, MI
Gurwin, Howard E. ... Farmington Hills, MI
Gurwin, Robert S. ... Cleveland, OH
Gurwin, Steven H. ... Denver, CO
Gurwitch, Arnold A. ... Larchmont, NY
Gurwitch, Lisa D. ... San Francisco, CA
Gurwitz, Adam W. ... Washington, DC
Gurwitz, Barbara L. ... Indianapolis, IN
Gurwitz, Daniel G. ... McAllen, TX
Gurwitz, David P. ... New York, NY
Gurwitz, Gary R. ... McAllen, TX
Gurwitz, Lewis S. ... Winthrop, MA
Gurwitz, Michael D.
Department of Agriculture, Office of the General Counsel, GV
Gurwitz, Michael L. ... Burlingame, CA
Gurwitz, Norman H. ... Indianapolis, IN
Gurwitz, Renee Friend ... Santa Ana, CA
Gury, Elmer F. ... Peoria, IL
Guryan, Barry A. ... Boston, MA
Guryan, Peter S. ... Department of Justice, Antitrust Division, GV
Guryan, Sheppard A. ... Roseland, NJ
Gurza, Renée Ann ... San Jose, CA
Gurzenda, Jane G. ... North Scituate, RI
Gus, Dan ... Dallas, TX
Gusching, Gregory J. ... Sidney, OH
Guschov, Stephen D. ... Danvers, MA
Gusciora, W. Reed ... Trenton, NJ
Gusdorf, Nigel M. ... Austin, TX
Gusdorf, Randall E. ... St. Louis, MO
Guse, Elizabeth Moseley ... Tulsa, OK
Guse, James ... Salem, OR
Guse, Kyle ... Menlo Park, CA
Guse, Randall R. ... Brookfield, WI
Guse, Shawn D. ... Milwaukee, WI
Sheboygan, WI
Gusea, James W. ... Cheyenne, WY
Gusea, James W., P.C. ... Cheyenne, WY
Guseman-Campiz, Margaret M.
New York, NY
Gusenius, William E. ... Lindsborg, KS
Gusenoff, Daniel C. ... Boston, MA
Gusewelle, Anne E. ... Kansas City, MO
Gusfield, Ilene L. ... Berkeley, CA
Gushard, Gary J. ... Pittsburgh, PA
Gushee, Oliver W., Jr. ... Salt Lake City, UT
Gushée, Richard B. ... Detroit, MI
Gushee, Robert L. ... Cold Spring, KY
Gushi, Ross N. ... Department of Commerce, Patent and Trademark Office, GV
Gushiken, Brad K. ... Honolulu, HI
Gushin, Fredric E. ... Lawrenceville, NJ
Gushman, John L. ... Naples, FL
Gushner, Terry J. ... New York, NY
Gushow, Jill M. ... Denver, CO
Gushue, John J. ... New Bedford, MA
Gushue, Michael F. ... Philadelphia, PA
Gushurst, Ann Catherine ... Englewood, CO
Gushurst, David A. ... Brighton, CO
Gusick, Michael S. ... New York, NY
Gusick, Spencer M. ... San Francisco, CA
Gusinsky, Robert ... Rapid City, SD
Gusky, Edward S. ... Detroit, MI
Gusky, Henry ... Pittsburgh, PA
Gusky, Joel D. ... Cherry Hill, NJ
New York, NY
Philadelphia, PA
Gusky, Steven L. ... Pittsburgh, PA
Gusky, Susan Denmon ... Austin, TX
Guslani, Lawrence M. ... Redwood City, CA
Guslani, Lino M. ... Palo Alto, CA
Guslani, Lino M., A Prof. Corp.
Palo Alto, CA
Gusler, Jack S. ... Houston, TX
Gusler, Kathleen Mary ... Trenton, NJ
Gusler, Richard Noel, The Law Offices of
Raleigh, NC
Gusman, George, III ... Honolulu, HI
Gusman, Robert C. ... Calabasas, CA
Gusman, Shane A. ... Sacramento, CA
Gusmano, Joseph M. ... Baltimore, MD
Gusmano, Louis J. ... Highland Beach, FL
Gusmano, Paul C. ... Bridgeport, CT
Gusmorino, Joseph D. ... Richmond Hill, NY
Gusmorino & Marx ... Richmond Hill, NY
Guso, Jordi ... Miami, FL
Gusoff, Arthur H. ... Randolph, NJ
Gusrae, Bert L. ... New York, NY
Gusrae, Kaplan & Bruno ... Bronx, NY
Brooklyn, NY
New York, NY
White Plains, NY
Guss, Amy ... New York, NY
Guss, Bonnie Garland ... Palm Springs, CA
Guss, Debra F. ... Berlin, CT
Guss, Mary E. ... Ketchikan, AK
Guss, Michael B. ... New York, NY
Guss, Michael J. ... Flint, MI
Troy, MI
Guss, Mitchell F. ... Mount Olive, NJ
Guss, Samuel M. ... New York, NY
Guss, Stephen E. ... Fairfax, VA
Guss, Stephen E., P.C. ... Fairfax, VA
Guss, Stewart J. ... Houston, TX
Guss, Suzanne ... Louisville, KY
Gussack, Nina M. ... Philadelphia, PA
Gussaroff, Arthur ... New York, NY
Gusses, George ... Toledo, OH
Gusses, George Co., L.P.A. ... Toledo, OH
Gussett, Sheryl A. ... Houston, TX
Gussin, Alan ... Lincolnwood, IL
Gussin, Arnold M. ... New York, NY
Gussin, Lee E. ... Northbrook, IL
Gussin, Mark A. ... Chicago, IL
Gussin, Zave H. ... Chicago, IL
Gussis, Chrysanthe ... San Francisco, CA
Gussis, Geoffrey G. ... Morristown, NJ
Gussis, George G. ... New Brunswick, NJ
Gussis, George G., P.A. ... New Brunswick, NJ
Gussis, Lloyd E. ... Chicago, IL
Gussis, Randy S. ... Chicago, IL
Gussler, Charles G. ... Seabrook, TX
Gussler, Stephen S. ... Ashville, OH
Circleville, OH
Gussman, John B. ... South Lake Tahoe, CA
Gussman, Marilyn S. ... Kansas City, MO
Gussman, William H., Jr. ... New York, NY
Gussner, J. Walter ... Los Angeles, CA
Gussoff, Jeffrey M. ... Roseland, NJ
Gussoni, Gerald O., Jr. ... New Orleans, LA
Gust, Anne B. ... San Francisco, CA
Gust, Dawn M. ... Pittsburgh, PA
Gust, Gerald N. ... Amery, WI
Gust, Heather A. ... Saginaw, MI
Gust, James B. ... Stratford, CT
Gust, James F. ... Saginaw, MI
Gust, Laverne M. ... Minneapolis, MN
Gust, Morgan M. ... Scottsdale, AZ
Gust, Ralph J., Jr. ... Lombard, IL
Gust, Robert A. ... Minneapolis, MN
Gust, Rockwell T., Jr. ... Naples, FL
Gust Rosenfeld P.L.C. ... Phoenix, AZ
Tucson, AZ
Gust, Terence F. ... Midwest City, OK
Gust, Terence Francis ... Midwest City, OK
Gust, W. William ... Roanoke, VA
Gust & Zerin, PLC ... Minneapolis, MN
Gustad, Susan E. ... Minneapolis, MN
Gustaferro, Barbara-Ann C.
Cleveland, OH
Gustaferro, Mark P. ... Cleveland, OH
Gustafson, Alan P. ... Utica, OH
Gustafson, Albert E. ... Miami, FL
Gustafson, Albert Katsuaki ... Washington, DC
Gustafson, Alice F. ... Seattle, WA
Gustafson, Amy R. ... San Francisco, CA
Gustafson, Andrew B. ... Ventura, CA
Gustafson, Ann M. ... Willmar, MN
Gustafson, Anna M. ... Hartford, CT
Gustafson, Anne-Lise Dirks
Coral Gables, FL

Gutierrez, Terry K. ... Omaha, NE
Gutierrez, Thomas ... Washington, DC
Gutierrez, Thomas A. ... Los Angeles, CA
Gutierrez, Victor T., (P.A.) ... Miami, FL
Gutierrez, Virginia L. ... Philadelphia, PA
Gutierrez, William F. ... San Francisco, CA
Gutierrez, Xavier A. ... Fullerton, CA
Gutierrez, Yahara L. ... El Paso, TX
Gutierrez-Lundquist, Laurelle
San Francisco, CA
Gutillo, Michael Peter ... Albany, NY
Gutin, David ... Bala Cynwyd, PA
Philadelphia, PA
Gutin, Irving ... Jersey City, NJ
Gutin, Robert D. ... Cleveland, OH
Gutjahr, Scott A. ... Santa Ana, CA
Gutke, Robert W. ... Logan, UT
Gutkin, Jerome S. ... Carlsbad, CA
Gutkin, Paula J. ... Rochester, NY
Gutkin, Robert A. ... Washington, DC
Gutknecht, John W. ... Fostoria, OH
Gutknecht, Timothy A. ... Columbia, IL
Gutkoski, John Theodore ... Boston, MA
Gutleber, Edward J. ... Mineola, NY
Gutleber, Jos. F. ... South Ozone Park, NY
Gutleber, Joseph F., Jr. ... New York, NY
Gutmacher, Jon H. ... Orlando, FL
Gutmacher, Jon H., P.A. ... Orlando, FL
Gutmacher, Norman W. ... Cleveland, OH
Gutman, Alan S. ... Beverly Hills, CA
Gutman, Andrew E. ... Mineola, NY
Gutman, Arthur J. ... Jacksonville, FL
Gutman & Bigelman, P.C. ... Southfield, MI
Gutman, Edward J. ... Baltimore, MD
Gutman, Elizabeth A. ... Mineola, NY
Gutman, Elizabeth C. ... Cherry Hill, NJ
Philadelphia, PA
Gutman, Gregory ... Dallas, TX
Gutman & Gutman LLP ... Mineola, NY
Gutman, Harry L. ... Washington, DC
Gutman, Henry B. ... New York, NY
Gutman, Howard W. ... Washington, DC
Gutman, Jack N. ... Tampa, FL
Gutman, Jeffrey K. ... Chicago, IL
Gutman, Jeremiah S. ... New York, NY
Gutman, Jewel A. ... Simsbury, CT
Gutman, Jose ... Fort Lauderdale, FL
Gutman, Julie ... San Francisco, CA
Gutman, Lawrence C. ... Mineola, NY
Gutman, Maxine A. ... Lake Worth, FL
Gutman & Mettee ... Philadelphia, PA
Gutman, Michael Lee ... Freehold, NJ
Gutman, Michele M. ... Pittsburgh, PA
Gutman, Olga ... New York, NY
Gutman, Paul ... Los Angeles, CA
Gutman, Phillip E., Jr. ... Chicago, IL
Gutman, Richard A. ... Philadelphia, PA
Gutman, Richard E. ... Irving, TX
Gutman, Richard M. ... Montclair, NJ
Gutman, Richard, P.C. ... Montclair, NJ
Gutman, Robert ... Brooklyn, NY
Gutman, Robert L. ... Toms River, NJ
Gutman, Ronald Y. ... Southfield, MI
Gutman, Sandra R. ... Baltimore, MD
Gutman, Siegmund Y. ... Chicago, IL
Gutman, Stanley E. ... San Francisco, CA
Gutman, Stephen L. ... Southfield, MI
Gutman, Steven ... New York, NY
Gutmann, Barbara S. ... Houston, TX
Gutmann, David J. ... Rochester, NY
Gutmann, Elizabeth Simms ... Piqua, OH
Gutmann, Gail ... Trenton, NJ
Gutmann, Melvin H. ... Delray Beach, FL
Gutmann, Michael E. ... Piqua, OH
Gutmann, Paul P. ... Piqua, OH
Gutmann, Peter ... Washington, DC
Gutmann, Richard M. ... Morgantown, WV
Gutnick, H. Yale ... Pittsburgh, PA
Gutof, Richard S. ... Skokie, IL
Gutow, Bill ... Dallas, TX
Gutowicz, Theodore S. ... Philadelphia, PA
Gutowitz, Norton ... Toledo, OH
Gutowitz, William M. ... New York, NY
Gutowski, Anthony M. ... Washington, DC
Gutowski, David E. ... Buffalo, NY
Gutowski, Gary ... Granville, NY
Gutowski, Julie Larson ... Hartford, CT
Gutowski, Michael F. ... Omaha, NE
Gutowski, Peter J. ... New York, NY
Gutowsky, Constance M. ... Sacramento, CA
Gutrick, Raynette Rose
Treasury Department,
Office of Thrift Supervision, GV
Gutride, Adam J. ... San Francisco, CA
Gutsch, Kenneth M. ... Anchorage, AK
Gutsche, Allan D. ... San Francisco, CA
Gutsche, Glenn E. ... Chicago, IL
Gutschewski, Bernadette ... Houston, TX
Gutschewski, Bernard R. ... Omaha, NE
Gutsell, Linda M. ... Morgantown, WV
Gutshall, Charles E. ... Harrisburg, PA
Gutshall, Frederick R. ... Huntingdon, PA
Gutshall, Karin Simpson ... Harrisburg, PA
Gutsin, Phillip E. ... New York, NY
Gutsin, Sheri M. ... Miami, FL
Gutstein, Alfred R. ... Angola, IN
Gutstein, Joshua Aaron ... Washington, DC
Gutstein, Solomon ... Chicago, IL
Gutsue, Nicholas C. ... Beverly Hills, CA
Gutt, Ira ... Miami, FL
Gutt, Matthew Moesel ... Philadelphia, PA
Gutt, Morris ... Bronxville, NY
Gutt, Ronald D. ... Cleveland, OH
Guttag, Eric W. ... Cincinnati, OH
Guttas, Charles K. ... Burlingame, CA
Guttell, Steven M. ... Phoenix, AZ
Guttenberg, Alan B. ... San Rafael, CA
Guttenberg, Arnold P. ... Denver, CO
Guttenberg, Aryeh ... Baltimore, MD
Guttenberg, Jeleen ... Los Angeles, CA
Guttenberg, Maria M. ... Englewood, CO
Guttenberg, Rapson & Colvin LLP
Oakland, CA
Guttenberg, Rapson & Colvin, LLP
San Rafael, CA
Guttenmacher & Bohatch
Coral Gables, FL
Key West, FL
Guttenmacher, Edward P.
Coral Gables, FL
Key West, FL
Guttenplan, Kenneth S. ... Great Neck, NY
Guttentag, Jeffrey Lance ... Babylon, NY
Guttentag, Lori D. ... New York, NY
Guttentag, Lucas ... New York, NY
Guttentag, Richard Eric
Fort Lauderdale, FL
Gutter, Louis ... Detroit, MI
Gutter, Marvin C. ... Fort Lauderdale, FL
Gutter, Samuel I. ... Washington, DC
Gutter, Steven J. ... Plantation, FL
Gutteridge, Don J., Jr. ... Oklahoma City, OK
Gutteridge, Georgann
Department of Agriculture,
Office of the General Counsel, GV
Gutterlaite, Andrew L. ... New York, NY
Gutterman, Alan J. ... Westfield, NJ
Gutterman, Alan S. ... San Jose, CA
Gutterman, Alvin H. ... Washington, DC
Gutterman, Andrew M. ... New York, NY
Gutterman, Barry A. ... New York, NY
Gutterman, Barry N., & Associates
New York, NY
Gutterman, Carlton & Heckenbach, L.L.P.
Denver, CO
Lone Tree, CO
Gutterman, David Lewis ... New York, NY
Gutterman, Edward H. ... New York, NY
Gutterman, Janet J. ... White Plains, NY
Gutterman, Joseph L. ... Scottsdale, AZ
Gutterman, Marc J. ... Miami, FL
Gutterman, Melvin ... Atlanta, GA
Gutterman, Meryl J. ... New York, NY
Gutterman, Morris B. ... Norfolk, VA
Gutterman & Oppenheim ... White Plains, NY
Gutterman, Paul G. ... Minneapolis, MN
Gutterman, Robert L. ... Virginia Beach, VA
Gutterman, Sheila M. ... Lone Tree, CO
Gutterman & Speiser ... New York, NY
Gutterman, Susan R. ... Chicago, IL
Gutterman, Wolkstein, Klinger & Yohalem
Westfield, NJ
Guttero, Jeffrey Lee ... Eureka, CA
Gutterridge, Larry G. ... Los Angeles, CA
Gutterson, M. Clea ... Albuquerque, NM
Gutterson, Scott ... New York, NY
Guttikonda, Paresh ... New York, NY
Guttilla, Carla Jo ... Pittsburgh, PA
Guttilla and Murphy, A Professional
Corporation ... Phoenix, AZ
Guttilla, Nicholas C. ... Phoenix, AZ
Guttilla, Nicholas John ... Boston, MA
Guttilla, Phillip P. ... Phoenix, AZ
Gutting, James M. ... Indianapolis, IN
Gutting, Leigh Svetanics ... St. Louis, MO
Guttlein, Jorge De Jesus ... New York, NY
Guttler, Alice J. ... Freehold, NJ
Guttman, Alan J. ... Houston, TX
Guttman, Alan R. ... Belle Vernon, PA
Guttman, Bruce H. ... Melville, NY
Guttman, Charles ... New York, NY
Guttman, Daniel J ... Columbus, OH
Guttman, David S. ... Dallas, TX
Guttman, Gerald ... New York, NY
Guttman, Glenn S. ... Chicago, IL
Guttman & Guttman ... Melville, NY
Guttman, Julia E. ... Washington, DC
Guttman, Lou ... Potomac, MD
Guttman, Mayer E. ... Baltimore, MD
Guttman, Reuben A. ... Washington, DC
Norristown, PA
Guttman, Richard ... Miami, FL
Guttman, Richard T. ... Palatine, IL
Guttman, Robert A. ... San Bernardino, CA
Guttman, Robert M. ... United States Senate,
Committee Legal Personnel, GV
Guttman, Robert S. ... Hoffman Estates, IL
Guttman, Robin Naomi ... Melville, NY
Guttman, Ronald E. ... Los Angeles, CA
Guttman, Rubin ... Cleveland, OH
Guttman, Rubin, Co., L.P.A.
Beachwood, OH
Cleveland, OH
Hudson, OH
Mayfield Heights, OH
Guttman, Steven ... Honolulu, HI
Guttman, W. Charles Julian ... Ithaca, NY
Guttman, Zvi ... Baltimore, MD
Guttman-McCabe, Catherine R.
Washington, DC
Guttman-McCabe, Christopher
Washington, DC
Guttmann, Alesh H. ... Fort Lauderdale, FL
Guttmann, Daniel H. ... Smithtown, NY
Guttmann, J. Michele ... Albuquerque, NM
Guttmann, John S., Jr. ... Washington, DC
New York, NY
Guttmann, Louis B., III ... Orlando, FL
Guttmann, Mary Louise ... New York, NY
Guttmann, Michael L. ... Pensacola, FL
Guttmann, Sheldon M.
Federal Communications Commission,
Office of the General Counsel, GV
Guttmann, Stephen M. ... Pensacola, FL
Guttmann, Susan Taylor ... Pensacola, FL
Gutto, Phyllis ... Newark, NJ
Guttormsen, Gregg N. ... Kenosha, WI
Twin Lakes, WI
Guttormsen, Hartley & Guttormsen
Twin Lakes, WI
Kenosha, WI
Guttormsen, Neil F. ... Kenosha, WI
Twin Lakes, WI
Guttormsson, Paul E. ... Milwaukee, WI
Guttshall, Russell M., III ... Houston, TX
Guttuso, Maria K ... Deerfield Beach, FL
Gutwein, Abraham ... New York, NY
Gutwein, Andrew S. ... Lafayette, IN
Gutwein, Matthew R. ... Indianapolis, IN
Gutwillig, Steven G. ... Joplin, MO
Gutwirth, Carmen ... New York, NY
Gutwirth, Ronald M. ... Orange, NJ
Gutworth, Philip C. ... Hackensack, NJ
Gutworth, Philip C., P.A. ... Hackensack, NJ
Gutz, Larry G. ... Cedar Rapids, IA
Gutzait, Lisa I. ... Foster City, CA
Gutzke, John D. ... Wheaton, IL
Gutzler, Greg G. ... St. Louis, MO
Gutzler & Hudson ... Portland, OR
Gutzler, J. Wallace ... Salem, OR
Gutzler, Michael N. ... Portland, OR
Gutzmer, Alan R. ... Manchester, NH
Gutzmer, Norman E. ... Amarillo, TX
Gutzmer, Peter E. ... Chicago, IL
Gutzwiller, Robert H. ... Cincinnati, OH
Guy, Addeliar D., III ... Las Vegas, NV
Guy, Amy M. ... San Jose, CA
Guy, Andrew A. ... Seattle, WA
Guy, Arthur D. ... Temecula, CA
Guy, Barbara Lamb ... Scottsdale, AZ
Guy, Bert M. ... Tuscaloosa, AL
Guy, Blake M. ... McLean, VA
Guy, Brett Newell ... Annapolis, MD
Guy, Carl F., Jr. ... Syracuse, NY
Guy, Charles B. ... Richardson, TX
Guy, Christopher, Loy & Pherson
Monticello, IN
Guy, Colin ... Palmyra, VA
Guy, Daniel A., Jr.
United States Tax Court, GV
Guy, Daniel S. ... Ada, OH
Guy, Daniel W. ... Pittsboro, NC
Guy, Darrell L. ... Dallas, TX
Guy, David A.
Federal Housing Finance Board,
Office of General Counsel, GV
Guy, David H. ... Afton, NY
Binghamton, NY
Guy, David J. ... Sacramento, CA
Guy, Denine J. ... Aptos, CA
Guy, Don J. ... Tulsa, OK
Guy, Dorothy M. ... Baltimore, MD
Guy, Douglas D. ... San Diego, CA
Guy, Duane D. ... Houston, TX
Guy, Dwight L. ... Seattle, WA
Guy, Edward Gray ... Somers, NY
Guy, Frederick R. ... Syracuse, NY
Guy, G. Hopkins, III ... Menlo Park, CA
Guy, Gary E. ... Washington, DC
Guy, George H., Jr. ... West Point, VA
Guy, Georgina ... Lakewood, CO
Guy, Homa Susan ... Jacksonville, FL
Guy, J. Michael ... Monterey, CA
Guy, James M. ... Wichita, KS
Guy, James O. ... Garden City, NY
Guy, James P., II ... Glen Allen, VA
Richmond, VA
Guy, Jess B. ... San Jose, CA
Guy, John J. ... Akron, OH
Guy, John, Law Office of
Los Angeles, CA
Guy, John, Law Office of
Redondo Beach, CA
Guy, John M. ... Monticello, IN
Guy, Jonathan P. ... Washington, DC
Guy, Joseph R. ... Indianapolis, IN
Guy, Joseph R., P.C. ... Indianapolis, IN
Guy, Kathleen B. ... Lawrenceville, GA
Guy, Kathy Butler ... Dallas, TX
Guy, Kirk N. ... Dayton, OH
Guy, Lammert & Towne ... Akron, OH
Canton, OH
Cleveland, OH
Guy, Laura Breen ... New York, NY
Guy, Leslie Prechtl ... Binghamton, NY
Guy, Loren W. ... Afton, NY
Binghamton, NY
Guy, Martha K. ... San Diego, CA
Guy, Mary E. ... Clarksburg, WV
Guy, Michael S. ... Medford, OR
Guy, Michele L. ... Tallahassee, FL
Guy, N. Gunter, Jr. ... Montgomery, AL
Guy, Patrick W. ... New York, NY
Guy, Peter J. ... New York, NY
Guy, Phelesa M. ... Austin, TX
Guy, Ralph B., Jr. ... Ann Arbor, MI
Guy, Richard D. ... Virginia Beach, VA
Guy, Richard P. ... Olympia, WA
Guy, Richard S. ... Kitty Hawk, NC
Norfolk, VA
Guy, Robert A., Jr. ... Nashville, TN
Guy, Robert D. ... Atlanta, GA
Guy, Robert J. ... Monticello, IN
Guy, Ronald N. ... San Diego, CA
Guy, Stephen J. ... Minneapolis, MN
Guy, Steven R. ... Rusk, TX
Guy, Steven S. ... Phoenix, AZ
Guy, T. Ray ... Dallas, TX
Guy, Terry ... Irvine, CA
Guy, William E., Jr. ... Stuart, FL
Guy, William L. ... Jackson, TN
Guy, William L., III ... Moorhead, MN
Fargo, ND
Guy, William S. ... Mc Comb, MS
Guyder, Daniel J. ... New York, NY
Guydon, Edsel J. ... Washington, DC
Guyer, Charlotte S. ... Keene, NH
Guyer, Edwin L. ... Blue Bell, PA
Guyer & Enichen, P.C. ... Rockford, IL
Guyer, George H. ... Portland, OR
Guyer, J. Dennis ... Greencastle, PA
Guyer, Jennifer P. ... Huntington, WV
Guyer, John C. L. ... Richmond, VA
Guyer, Leah Hamilton ... Glenview, IL
Guyer, Melvin J. ... Ann Arbor, MI
Guyer, Paul M. ... Los Angeles, CA
Guyer, Richard S. ... White Plains, NY
Guyer, Robert A. ... Kailua-Kona, HI
Guyer, Robert L. ... Gainesville, FL
Guyer, Ronald P. ... San Antonio, TX
Guyer, T.M., & Friends, P.C. ... Medford, OR
Guyer, Thad M. ... Medford, OR
Guyer, Thomas J. ... Detroit, MI
Guyett, David F. P. ... Dallas, TX
Guyette, James A. ... Milwaukee, WI
Guyette, Kevin F. ... Binghamton, NY
Guyette & Poehlmann, S.C. ... Milwaukee, WI
Guy-Jackson, Carol ... Washington, DC
Guymon, David E. ... Belleville, IL
Guymon, Marjorie A. ... Las Vegas, NV
Guymon, Paxton ... Salt Lake City, UT
Guynan, Kim M. ... Irving, TX
Guynes, Janet A. ... Marina Del Rey, CA
Guynes, M. Stephen ... Houston, TX
Guynes, Marlene ... Toledo, OH
Guynn & Clemens, P.C. ... Roanoke, VA
Guynn, Douglas L. ... Harrisonburg, VA
Guynn, Elizabeth C. ... Greensboro, NC
Guynn, Jacqueline V. ... Philadelphia, PA
Guynn, Jim H., Jr. ... Roanoke, VA
Guynn, John M. ... Salt Lake City, UT
Guynn, Kevin W. ... Chicago, IL
Guynn, Randall D. (IBA) ... New York, NY
Guynn, Steven D. ... New York, NY
Guynup, Gayle C. ... Sebastopol, CA
Guyol, Deborah S. ... Portland, OR
Guyol, James C. ... St. Louis, MO
Guyon, Peter W. ... Salt Lake City, UT
Guyon, Rudy ... San Jose, CA
Guyot, John F. ... Washington, DC
Guyot, Robert B., III ... Traverse City, MI
Guyot, Robert B., III, P.C.
Traverse City, MI
Guysi, George S. ... Oklahoma City, OK
Guysi, Holt W. ... Albuquerque, NM
Guyther, Oliver R. ... Leonardtown, MD
Guyton, Ada J. ... Belle Vernon, PA
Guyton, Carol ... Southfield, MI
Guyton, Charles A. ... Tallahassee, FL
Guyton, Collins ... Tampa, FL
Guyton, David G. ... Rock Hill, SC
Guyton, Dewuse, Jr. ... Houston, TX
Guyton, Elizabeth Anne ... Broken Arrow, OK
Guyton, Elizabeth L. ... Rocky Ford, CO
Guyton & Frère ... Knoxville, TN
Guyton, Holton Bruce ... Knoxville, TN
Guyton, Jackson W. ... Fairfield, AL
Guyton, Jerry F. ... Hamilton, AL
Guyton, John A., Jr. ... Tampa, FL
Guyton, John A.C., III ... Ocala, FL
Tampa, FL
Guyton, John D. ... Kosciusko, MS
Guyton, Marion E. ... Department of Justice,
Civil Division, GV
Guyton, M.C. Collins ... Tampa, FL
Guyton, Nancy M. ... Wilmington, NC
Guyton, Odell ... Philadelphia, PA
Guyton, Samuel P. ... Denver, CO
Guz, Norman J., Jr. ... Chicopee, MA
Guzda, Thomas G., P.A., Law Office of
Fort Lauderdale, FL
Guzda, Thomas George
Fort Lauderdale, FL
Guze, Jennifer L. ... Newport Beach, CA
Guze, Jonathan David ... Durham, NC
Guzewicz, Blaise J. ... Pittsburgh, PA
Guziak, Edward ... Dallas, TX
Guziak, James J. ... Orange, CA
Guziak, James J., A Professional Corporation
Orange, CA
Guziak, Ronald G. ... Rockville, MD
Guzick, Arlene Horwitz ... Houston, TX
Guzick, Lori A. Schafer ... Pottsville, PA
Guzick, Michael D. ... Birmingham, MI
Guzick, William J. ... Greenville, SC
Guziec, Joan A. ... Springfield, MA
Guziel, Chester P. ... Red Bluff, CA
Guzik & Associates ... Los Angeles, CA
Guzik, John P. ... Roseville, MN
Guzik, Paul C. ... San Diego, CA
Guzik, Robert E. ... Phoenix, AZ
Guzik, Samuel S. ... Los Angeles, CA
Guzikowski, Andrew J. ... Milwaukee, WI
Guzin, Lawrence N. ... Los Angeles, CA
Guzin & Steier ... Los Angeles, CA
Guzinski, Joseph A. ... Department of Justice,
Executive Office for United States Trustees,
GV
Guzinski, Joseph M. ... Rochester, MN
Guzman, Ana M. ... New York, NY
Guzman, Arthur G. ... San Antonio, TX
Guzman, Carlos M. ... Miami, FL
Guzman, Denise M. ... Torrance, CA
Guzman, Eduardo M. ... San Pedro, CA
Guzman, Eloise A. ... Houston, TX
Guzman, Fernando ... Las Vegas, NV
Guzmán, Frank J. ... El Paso, TX
Guzman, Gina M. ... Amherst, NY
Buffalo, NY
Guzman, Gretchen ... Long Beach, CA
Guzman, Hector M. ... Los Angeles, CA

Guzman, Ivan A.
Christiansted, St. Croix, VI
Guzmán, Janine ... **San Juan, PR**
Guzman, Javier M. ... Department of Justice, Civil Rights Division, GV
Guzman, Jeffrey A. ... New York, NY
Guzman, Jill M. ... **Chicago, IL**
Guzman, John J., & Associates, Law Offices of ... **Covina, CA**
Guzman, Jorge ... Los Angeles, CA
Guzman, Jose E. ... **Columbus, GA**
Guzman, Jose E., Jr. ... **San Francisco, CA**
Guzman, Jose G. ... San Jose, CA
Guzman, Leonard T. ... **Palo Alto, CA**
Guzman, Lisa ... Los Angeles, CA
Guzman, Lisa M. ... Tampa, FL
Guzman, Lori Elliott ... **Richmond, VA**
Guzman, Lori L. ... Minneapolis, MN
Guzman, M. Elizabeth ... **Goldsboro, NC**
Guzman, M. Jessie ... Rock Island, IL
Guzmán, Manuel A., Law Offices
San Juan, PR
Guzman, Margaret R. ... Worcester, MA
Guzmán, Maricarmen ... **New York, NY**
Houston, TX
Guzman, Michael ... Beaverton, OR
Guzman, Michael J. ... **Washington, DC**
Guzman, Philip A. ... Silver Spring, MD
Guzman, Raymond ... Bronx, NY
Guzman, Rick ... Austin, TX
Guzmán Valiente, Eduardo R., P.S.C.
San Juan, PR
Guzman, Victor Rene ... Bronx, NY
Guzman, William D. ... Marlborough, CT
Guzmán-Correa, Janine M. ... San Juan, PR
Guzman Lowrey, Carmen
Washington, DC
Guzman Mollet, Efrain ... **San Juan, PR**
Guzman-Nunez, Norma ... Rock Island, IL
Guzmán-Rodríguez, Humberto
San Juan, PR
Guzmán-Rodríguez, Manuel A.
San Juan, PR
Guzmán Valiente, Eduardo R.
San Juan, PR
Guzmán-Wiegert, Chela A.
Minneapolis, MN
Guzov, Debra J. ... New York, NY
Guzovsky, Edward ... Milton, MA
Guzy, Barbara A. ... Sacramento, CA
Guzy, Gary S.
Environmental Protection Agency, Office of the General Counsel, GV
Guzy, Robert A. ... **Minneapolis, MN**
Guzy, Sandra M. ... **San Francisco, CA**
Guzzardi, Robert R. ... Philadelphia, PA
Guzzardi, Robert R., & Associates, P.C.
Philadelphia, PA
Guzzardo, John A. ... **Sterling, IL**
Guzzardo, Joseph M. ... Brooklyn, NY
Guzzardo, Paul A. ... Granite City, IL
Guzzetta, Cynthia R. ... **Fairfield, CA**
Guzzetta, Kathleen S. ... Newark, DE
Guzzetti, William L. ... Dallas, TX
Guzzi, Dawn M. ... **Scranton, PA**
Guzzi, Gary J. ... **Miami, FL**
Guzzi, George D. ... Portland, ME
Guzzo, Carl J., Jr. ... Spring Lake, NJ
Guzzo, Diane R. ... **Akron, OH**
Guzzo, Joseph L. ... Brooklyn, NY
Guzzo, Lori L. ... **Seattle, WA**
Guzzo, Michael ... New York, NY
Guzzo, Susan M. ... **Ridgefield, CT**
Guzzone, Amideo N. ... Centereach, NY
Guzzone, Roberta K. ... Centereach, NY
Guzzy, J. Christian ... **Oklahoma City, OK**
Gvazda, Melvin G. ... Farmington Hills, MI
Gvozdich, Buchan, Svirsko & Kaltenbaugh
Ebensburg, PA
Johnstown, PA
Gvozdich, George, Jr. ... Ebensburg, PA
Gvozdich, Michael A. ... Damascus, MD
Gwadz, Joyce Trimble ... **Washington, DC**
Gwalthney, Bernard J. ... Jacksonville, FL
Gwaltney, Joseph C. ... Arlington, VA
Gwaltney, Richard L. ... Taylorsville, NC
Gwartney, Aaron D. ... **Oklahoma City, OK**
Gwartney, Scott E. ... Tallahassee, FL
Gwartney, Tore Beal ... **Boise, ID**
Gwathmey, Gaines, III ... **New York, NY**
Gwathmey, John Owen ... **Richmond, VA**
Gwathmey, Robert R., III ... Hanover, VA
Gwatkin, Christina M. ... San Francisco, CA
Gwatkin, William E., III
Belvedere-Tiburon, CA
Gwatkin, William E., III
San Francisco, CA
Gweon, Henry ... Los Angeles, CA
Gweon, Judith Wang ... Anaheim, CA
Gwertzman, Lefkowitz, Greenwald & Burman
New York, NY
Gwiazdowski, Leo M. ... Norwich, CT
Gwilliam, Dale R. ... Tempe, AZ
Gwilliam, Ivary, Chiosso, Cavalli & Brewer
San Francisco, CA
San Jose, CA
Oakland, CA
Gwilliam, J. Gary ... **Oakland, CA**
Gwillim, Brent H. ... **Peoria, IL**
Gwillim, Jeffrey E. ... **Traverse City, MI**
Gwin, Arnold F. ... **Greenwood, MS**
Gwin, Doreen S. ... **St. Paul, MN**
Gwin & Gwin ... Bay City, TX
Gwin, H. Sanders, Jr. ... **Minneapolis, MN**
Gwin, Hugh F. ... Hudson, WI
Gwin, Hugh H. ... Hudson, WI
Gwin, Iler and Englebert ... Owensboro, KY
Gwin, James S. ... Akron, OH
Gwin, John T. ... Mount Juliet, TN
Gwin Law Firm, S.C. ... Hudson, WI
Gwin, Lawrence P., Jr. ... Bay City, TX
Gwin, Lewis & Punches, LLP
Natchez, MS
Woodville, MS
Gwin, Lucien C., III ... **Natchez, MS**
Woodville, MS
Gwin, Lucien C., Jr. ... **Natchez, MS**
Gwin, Mark A. ... **Minneapolis, MN**
Gwin, Melbourne N., Jr. ... Merced, CA
Gwin, Michael O. ... **Jackson, MS**
Gwin, Nina J. ... Bay City, TX
Gwin, Robert D. (" Don ") ... **Dallas, TX**
Gwin, Robert H., III ... Conway, SC
Myrtle Beach, SC
Gwin, Robert L. ... Owensboro, KY
Gwin, Robert W., Jr. ... Birmingham, AL
Gwin, Robert Y. ... **Louisville, KY**
Gwin, S. Lawrence, Jr. ... South Hamilton, MA
Gwin, Samuel K. ... Jeffersonville, IN
Gwin, W. Scott ... Canton, OH
Gwin-Lenth, Jere N. ... New Hope, MN
Gwinn, Anne Fowler ... **Paducah, KY**
Gwinn, Casey G. ... San Diego, CA
Gwinn, D. Lee ... **Fort Worth, TX**
Gwinn, Daniel A. ... Birmingham, MI
Gwinn, John ... **Urbana, IL**
Gwinn, Laura J. ... Upper Marlboro, MD
Gwinn, Malcolm S. ... Evansville, IN
Gwinn, Melanie Futrell ... **Johnson City, TN**
Gwinn, Robert A. ... **Dallas, TX**
Gwinn & Roby ... **Dallas, TX**
Fort Worth, TX
Gwinn, Staci B. ... Montgomery, AL
Gwinn, Stephen W. ... Dallas, TX
Gwinn, Susan L. ... Columbus, OH
Gwinn, Walker ... Memphis, TN
Gwinn, Walter E. ... Miami, FL
Gwinn, Yolanda Denise ... Toledo, OH
Gwinnell, Harry J. ... **Kingsport, TN**
Gwire & Frassetto ... **San Francisco, CA**
Gwire, William ... **San Francisco, CA**
Gwizdz, Richard G. ... **Dearborn, MI**
Gworek, Gary M. ... Southington, CT
Gworek, Jonathan D. ... **Waltham, MA**
Gwosdof, Peter M. ... Placentia, CA
Gwydir, Raymond J. ... Greenwich, CT
Gwyn, Allen H., Jr. ... Reidsville, NC
Gwyn, Allen Holt ... **Greensboro, NC**
Gwyn, Gwyn & Farver ... Reidsville, NC
Gwyn, John D. ... Mount Clemens, MI
Gwyn, Julius J. ... Reidsville, NC
Gwyn, Peter D. ... Perrysburg, OH
Gwyn, S. Revelle ... **Huntsville, AL**
Gwyn & Tate ... **Marion, VA**
Gwyn, William B., Jr. ... **Raleigh, NC**
Gwynn, Benita Angel ... **Winston-Salem, NC**
Gwynn, David H. ... Upper Marlboro, MD
Gwynn, Edward R. ... Grand Prairie, TX
Gwynn, Ellen B. ... Tallahassee, FL
Gwynn, George H. ... Tallahassee, FL
Gwynn, Jeffrey T. ... **Riverside, CA**
Gwynn, John C.
Equal Employment Opportunity Commission, Office of Legal Counsel, GV
Gwynn, John S. ... Tallahassee, FL
Gwynn, Kenneth B. ... Wendell, NC
Gwynn, Woodruff C. ... Salt Lake City, UT
Gwynne, J. Robert ... Morgantown, WV
Gwynne, Karl C. ... **Tampa, FL**
Gwynne, Kurt F. ... **Cherry Hill, NJ**
Philadelphia, PA
Gwyther, D.R., Jr. ... **Corpus Christi, TX**
Gyandoh, Samuel O., Jr. ... Philadelphia, PA
Gyarfas, Andrew J. ... Atlanta, GA
Gyarmathy, Joseph A. ... Homewood, IL
Gyben, J. Peter ... **Irvine, CA**
Gydus, Holly G. ... **Bridgeport, CT**
Gyebi, Daniel ... San Ramon, CA
Gyemant, Ina Levin ... San Francisco, CA
Gyepes, David J. ... Los Angeles, CA
Gyer, Connie Lilly ... New Orleans, LA
Gyer, Connie Lilly, and David R. Gyer
New Orleans, LA
Gyer, David R. ... New Orleans, LA
Gyger, Robert G. ... Encino, CA
Gygi, Ann M. ... **Seattle, WA**
Gyimesi, Aladar G. ... Staten Island, NY
Gyler and Gilligan ... **Long Beach, CA**
Gyles, Michelle T. ... Washington, DC
Gyllenborg, Scott C. ... **Olathe, KS**
Gylys, Rita B. ... Boston, MA
Gymer, Ronald G. ... Cleveland, OH
Gyongyos, David G. ... Rosemont, IL
Gyorke, Scott P. ... **Detroit, MI**
Gyorkos, Fenton & Huntington, A Law Corporation ... **Lake Forest, CA**
Gyorkos, John W. ... **Lake Forest, CA**
Gyory, Bruce N. ... **Albany, NY**
Gyory, Richard ... Somers, NY
Gyr, Michael J. ... **Washington, DC**
Gyr, Peter C. ... **New York, NY**
Gysegem, Thomas P. ... Warren, OH
Gysler, Jennifer E ... Westlake Village, CA
Gysler, R. Louis ... Fresno, CA
Gyurci, Robert W. ... Minneapolis, MN
Gyure, Dale A. ... Tampa, FL
Gyves, Alison C. ... Santa Ana, CA
Gyves, William S. ... **New York, NY**
Gyzinski, Irene F. ... Milwaukee, WI
Gzesh & Associates, Ltd. ... **Las Vegas, NV**
Gzesh, David J. ... **Las Vegas, NV**
Gzesh, Irwin I. ... **Chicago, IL**
Gzesh, Morris A. ... Chicago, IL
Gzesh, Susan R. ... **Chicago, IL**
Gzybowski, Michael S. ... **Fort Wayne, IN**
H.D. Yates & Associates ... Houston, TX
Ha, Ellen C. ... Vienna, VA
Ha, Eun (Ellen) G. ... Detroit, MI
Ha, Linh N. ... **San Francisco, CA**
Ha, Martha M. ... Chicago, IL
Ha, Michael Bruce ... **Orange, CA**
Ha, Quang J. ... **New York, NY**
Haab, Eric A. ... **Chicago, IL**
Haac, Gunilla N. ... **New York, NY**
Haack, Cheryl L. ... **Chicago, IL**
Haack, Linda R. ... Jacksonville, FL
Haack, Mark E. ... Carlsbad, CA
Haacke, Leslieann ... **Phoenix, AZ**
Haadsma, James T. ... Muskegon, MI
Haaf, Shannon ... **Philadelphia, PA**
Haaff, Chris S. ... **Woodstock, IL**
Haag, Charles T. ... **Cleveland, OH**
Haag, David Q. ... Houston, TX
Haag, Dennis J. ... **Sayreville, NJ**
Haag, Douglas A. ... **Des Moines, IA**
Haag, E. Lee, III ... **Houston, TX**
Haag, Frederick L. ... **Wichita, KS**
Haag, Gaffney & Wilcox, P.A.
Inverness, FL
Haag, Gary L. ... **Bartlesville, OK**
Haag, Harold A. ... White Plains, NY
Haag, Hellen L. ... **Wichita, KS**
Haag, Jeannette M. ... Inverness, FL
Haag, Jeannine S. ... Fort Collins, CO
Haag, John Randolph ... **Los Angeles, CA**
Haag, Joseph F. ... **Minneapolis, MN**
Haag, Joyce ... Rochester, NY
Haag, Larry M. ... Inverness, FL
Haag, Lloyd H. ... Holton, KS
Haag, Marian E. ... Bridgeton, NJ
Haag, Mark R. ... Department of Justice, Environment and Natural Resources Division, GV
Haag, Michael P. ... San Francisco, CA
Haag, Michael W. ... **Duluth, MN**
Haag, Philip S. ... **Austin, TX**
Haag, Susan White ... Washington, DC
Haage, Lisa A. ... Oakland, CA
Haagen, Paul H. ... Durham, NC
Haagensen, Donald A. ... **Portland, OR**
Haagenson, Roger D. ... Fort Lauderdale, FL
Haagenson, Roger D., P.A.
Fort Lauderdale, FL
Haah, Kevin K. ... **Beverly Hills, CA**
Haahr, J. Tyler ... Storm Lake, IA
Haak, John E. ... Sioux Falls, SD
Haak, Randall A. ... **Kaukauna, WI**
Haak, William H. ... Columbus, OH
Haake, Audrey A. ... **San Antonio, TX**
Haake, Catharine A. ... **Chicago, IL**
Haake, Charles H. ... **Irvine, CA**
Haake, Charles S. ... Cleveland, OH
Haake, Dale G. ... **Rock Island, IL**
Haake, Douglas H. ... Portland, OR
Haake, Floyd D., Jr. ... Carlsbad, NM
Haake, Timothy M. ... Washington, DC
Haakenson, Janet E. ... Janesville, WI
Haakenson, Michael Anthony ... Janesville, WI
Haaker, Christine M. ... **Dayton, OH**
Haakh, Gilbert E. ... **Los Angeles, CA**
Haakonsen, Kate W. ... **Hartford, CT**
Haaland, Dorothy A. ... Bothell, WA
Haan, Debra K. ... **Atlanta, GA**
Haan, Gregson T. ... **Atlanta, GA**
Haan, Jack L. ... Oakbrook Terrace, IL
Haan, Pamela S. ... **Grand Rapids, MI**
Haanpaa, Leo H. ... Nipomo, CA
Haanschoten, Corrie Patricia
Montgomery, AL
Haapa, William M., Jr. ... Tampa, FL
Haapala, John E. ... **Oakland, CA**
Haapala, Michael J. ... **Santa Ana, CA**
Haapoja, Matthew ... Minnetonka, MN
Haar, Carol M. ... Buffalo, NY
Haar, Charles M. ... Cambridge, MA
Haar, David C. ... Myrtle Beach, SC
Haar, H. Jay ... **Surfside Beach, SC**
Haar, James R. ... Tripp, SD
Haar, Paul S., Law Offices of
Washington, DC
Haar, Robert T. ... **St. Louis, MO**
Haar, Susan E. ... Boston, MA
Haar & Woods, LLP ... **St. Louis, MO**
Haara, Brian F. ... **Louisville, KY**
Haara, Laura M. ... **Louisville, KY**
Haaranen, Linda Z. ... New York, NY
Haarer, G. Donald ... Sedona, AZ
Haarer, Jeff G. ... Lansing, MI
Haarlow, John B. ... **Chicago, IL**
Haarmann, Bruce D. ... Wausau, WI
Haarz, David R. ... **Washington, DC**
Haas, Adolph L. ... Chicago, IL
Haas, Al H. ... Durango, CO
Haas, Alfred M. ... **Washington, DC**
Haas & Anderson, P.C. ... **Washington, DC**
Rockville, MD
Fairfax, VA
Leesburg, VA
McLean, VA
Haas, Andrew H. ... Homer, AK
Haas, B. Benjamin ... **Philadelphia, PA**
Haas, Bradley G. ... **Cincinnati, OH**
Haas, Bruce C. ... **New York, NY**
Haas & Castillo, P.A. ... **Clearwater, FL**
Haas, Charla Jo S. ... Nashville, TN
Haas, Christine ... **San Francisco, CA**
Haas, Colleen M. ... **Cincinnati, OH**
Haas, Connie Marie ... Salem, OR
Haas, Daniel S. ... Marietta, GA
Haas, David C. ... **Washington, DC**
Haas, David I. ... **Cherry Hill, NJ**
Philadelphia, PA
Haas, Dennis A. ... Sunrise, FL
Haas, Dennis Charles ... Rockaway, NJ
Haas, Donald F. ... Houston, TX
Haas, Donna E. Goldblum
Bala Cynwyd, PA
Haas, Douglas E. ... Fresno, CA
Haas, Douglas E. ... **Cleveland, OH**
Haas, Douglas L. ... Wheaton, IL
Haas, Edward D. ... **San Francisco, CA**
Haas, Edward J. ... Rhinebeck, NY
Haas, Elizabeth A. ... **Spring Valley, NY**
White Plains, NY
Haas, Elizabeth Corya ... New York, NY
Haas, Elizabeth Gant ... Harrisburg, PA
Haas, Elizabeth Hay ... Houston, TX
Haas, Elizabeth Jane ... San Francisco, CA
Haas, Emanuel ... Tarrytown, NY
Haas, Eric R. ... **Oakland, CA**
Haas, Eric T. ... **New York, NY**
Haas, Erik ... **New York, NY**
Haas, Francis B., Jr. ... **Harrisburg, PA**
Haas, Fredd J. ... Des Moines, IA
Haas, Frederick P. ... North Branford, CT
Haas, Frederick T., III ... **New Orleans, LA**
Haas, G. William ... **New York, NY**
Haas, Gary C. ... **Cleveland, OH**
Haas, Geoffrey J. ... Highland Park, MI
Haas, George A. ... Atlanta, GA
Haas, George E. ... **Milwaukee, WI**
Haas, Gerard R. ... **Buffalo, NY**
Haas, Gina L. ... Newton, MA
Haas, Glenn R. ... Villa Park, IL
Haas & Goffin ... San Francisco, CA
Haas, Gregory F. ... Placerville, CA
Haas, H. Adam ... Mount Laurel, NJ
Haas & Haas ... Mount Prospect, IL
Haas, Harl H. ... Portland, OR
Haas, Henry ... **Tacoma, WA**
Haas, Howard B. ... Philadelphia, PA
Haas, Jacqueline C. ... Weston, MA
Haas, James E. ... **Artesia, NM**
Haas, J. D. ... Minneapolis, MN
Haas, Jeff L. ... Tyler, TX
Haas, Jeffrey D. ... **Washington, DC**
Haas, Jeffrey H. ... Chicago, IL
Haas, Jeremy A. ... Lynnwood, WA
Haas, John ... Tucson, AZ
Haas, John C. ... Mount Prospect, IL
Haas, John Christopher ... **Denver, CO**
Haas, John G. ... Canton, OH
Haas, John M. ... Columbia Station, OH
North Olmsted, OH
Haas, John R. ... **Portsmouth, OH**
Haas, Joseph A. ... Sioux Falls, SD
Haas, Joseph F. ... **Atlanta, GA**
Haas, Karen J. ... Miami, FL
Haas, Karl P. ... **Indianapolis, IN**
Haas, Keith A. ... **Overland Park, KS**
Haas, Kenneth G. ... Seaford, NY
Haas, Kenneth R. ... New York, NY
Haas, Kevin M. ... **Newark, NJ**
Haas, Lawrence F. ... **Chicago, IL**
Haas, Lee L. ... **Clearwater, FL**
Haas, Louis N., (P.C.) ... **San Francisco, CA**
Haas, Mark A. ... Philadelphia, PA
Haas, Mark D. ... Conroe, TX
Haas, Martin A., Jr. ... Covington, KY
Cincinnati, OH
Haas, Mary H. ... **Los Angeles, CA**
Haas & McLennan ... Wheaton, IL
Haas, Michael A. ... Williamsburg, VA
Haas, Michael D. ... Bay St. Louis, MS
Haas, Michael D., Jr. ... Bay St. Louis, MS
Haas, Michael H. ... Hoxie, KS
Haas, Michael J. ... Napa, CA
Haas, Michael J. ... Walker, MN
Haas, Michael J. ... Trenton, NJ
Haas, Michael J. ... **Cleveland, OH**
Haas, Michael R. ... Edgerton, WI
Milton, WI
Haas, Mindy B. ... **New York, NY**
Haas & Najarian ... **San Francisco, CA**
Washington, DC
Haas, Nancy ... **Baltimore, MD**
Haas, Nancy Ellen ... Front Royal, VA
Haas, Nicholas M. ... Waveland, MS
Haas, Patricia J. ... **Cleveland, OH**
Haas, Patricia L. ... **Pittsburgh, PA**
Haas, Patrick Joseph, Jr. ... **Sturgis, MI**
Haas, Peter M.
Commodity Futures Trading Commission, Division of Enforcement, GV
Haas, Ralph R. ... Lakewood, OH
Haas, Ramey & Beik ... Clearwater, FL
Orlando, FL
Tampa, FL
Haas, Raymond A. ... Clearwater, FL
Orlando, FL
Tampa, FL
Haas, Raymond P. ... **San Francisco, CA**
Haas, Rene ... **Corpus Christi, TX**
Haas, Richard ... San Francisco, CA
Haas, Richard H. ... Cuyahoga Falls, OH
Haas, Robert A. ... Pittsburgh, PA
Haas, Robert M. ... Cleveland, OH
Haas, Robert W. ... Houston, TX
Haas, Robert W. ... Leesburg, VA
McLean, VA
Haas, Samuel D. ... **Dallas, TX**
Haas, Sandra J. ... Rochester, VT
Haas, Sandra J., P.C. ... Rochester, VT
Haas, Sandra K. ... Branford, FL
Haas, Scott A. ... **Sarasota, FL**
Haas, Sheila A. ... Fort Thomas, KY
Haas & Spigelmyer ... Homer, AK
Haas, Stanley B., II ... **Houston, TX**
Haas, Stephen C. ... Nevada City, CA
Haas, Stephen C. ... Evansville, IN
Haas, Stephen M. ... New York, NY

Haas, Steven C. ... **Watertown, NY**
Haas, Steven K. ... Harrisburg, PA
Haas, Steven M. ... **Cleveland, OH**
Haas, Steven N. ... **Philadelphia, PA**
Haas, Tamara M. ... Minneapolis, MN
Haas, Teel D. ... Madison, WI
Haas, Thomas G. ... Walnut Creek, CA
Haas, Thomas M. ... **Mobile, AL**
Haas, Virginia Wiggs ... **Mobile, AL**
Haas, W. Melvin, III ... **Macon, GA**
Haas, Warren ... Marion, IN
Haas, Warren C. ... Susanville, CA
Haas, William B. ... Hutchinson, MN
Haas, William C. ... Youngstown, OH
Haas, William K. ... Jefferson City, MO
Haas, William P. ... Bella Vista, AR
Haase, Charles J. ... Colorado Springs, CO
Haase, David K. ... **Chicago, IL**
Haase, David S. ... **Philadelphia, PA**
Haase, Dennis B. ... **Little Rock, AR**
Haase, Dennis M. ... South Orange, NJ
Haase, Donna Marie ... Kew Gardens, NY
Haasé, Edmond C., III ... **New Orleans, LA**
Haase & Eveland ... **Wilmington, DE**
Haase, Frederick T., Jr. ... **Wilmington, DE**
Haase, Glenn R. ... **Nashville, TN**
Haase, Gregory S. ... McLean, VA
Haase & Haase, Inc. ... San Antonio, TX
Haase, Heather ... **Dallas, TX**
Haase, Irene E. ... New York, NY
Haase, John A. ... **Green Bay, WI**
Haase, Karen A. ... **Lincoln, NE**
Haase, Katheleen K. ... Columbus, OH
Haase, Kerryann M. ... **Chicago, IL**
Haase, Leonard J. ... Orlando, FL
Haase, Linda Reed ... Bend, OR
Haase, M. Craig ... **Reno, NV**
Haase, Norman L. ... **Media, PA**
Haase, Richard T. ... San Antonio, TX
Haase, Robert A. ... Oshkosh, WI
Haase, Robert C., Jr. ... **Los Angeles, CA**
Haase, Thomas M. ... **Lincoln, NE**
Haase, Todd D. ... Bridgeport, CT
Haase, William H. ... Rescue, CA
Haase, William S. ... **Albany, NY**
Haase, William X. ... Lakewood, OH
Haaser, James C. ... Fort Smith, AR
Haas-Goldstein, Cheryl L. ... **New York, NY**
Haasis & Goodin ... **San Diego, CA**
Haasis, Regina B. ... Champaign, IL
Haasis, Steven R. ... **San Diego, CA**
Haavisto, Brian F. ... San Francisco, CA
Haaz, Franklin B. ... Holland, PA
Haaz, Richard P. ... **Philadelphia, PA**
Habans, Bologna & Carriere, A Professional Law Corporation ... **New Orleans, LA**
Habans, Robert N., Jr. ... **New Orleans, LA**
Habansky, Ronald J. ... Trumbull, CT
Habas, Christina M. ... Denver, CO
Habas, G. Jay ... **Erie, PA**
Habash, Reasoner & Frazier **Columbus, OH**
Habash, Stephen J. ... **Columbus, OH**
Habat, John L. ... Cleveland, OH
Habbart, Ellisa Opstbaum **Wilmington, DE**
Habberstad, James M., and Associates **The Dalles, OR**
Habbeshaw, Kalmans & Schwartz, P.C. **San Antonio, TX**
Habbeshaw, Penny K. ... **San Antonio, TX**
Habeck, Daniel J. ... **Waukesha, WI**
Habeck, James R. ... Shawano, WI
Habeck, Rollyn J. ... Camarillo, CA
Habecker, Edward T. ... **Peoria, IL**
Habecker, Eugene B. ... New York, NY
Habedank, Cumming, Best & Savage **Sidney, MT** **Williston, ND**
Habedank, Otto T. ... **Sidney, MT**
Habeeb, Michael Elias ... San Francisco, CA
Habeeb, Randal W. ... Hackensack, NJ; New York, NY
Habeeb, Samuel D. ... Vicksburg, MS
Habeebullah, Angela Y. ... Kansas City, MO
Habegger, J. Brittain ... **Oakland, CA**
Habegger, Jane L. ... Olympia, WA
Habein, Peter F. ... **Billings, MT**
Habekost, Martin C. ... Salem, OR
Habekost, Martin C., P.C. ... Salem, OR
Habel, Christopher S. ... **Cincinnati, OH**
Habel, Dennis W. ... **Albany, NY**
Habel, Heidi L. ... Hudson, WI
Habel, James P. ... Studio City, CA
Habel, Kenneth A. ... Brooklyn, NY
Habel, Rayna ... **Dallas, TX**
Habel, Rebecca R. ... Suffolk, VA
Habel, Robert W. ... Asheville, NC
Habelt, William W. ... **Syracuse, NY**
Haben, Ralph H., Jr. ... Tallahassee, FL
Haben & Richmond, P.A. ... Tallahassee, FL
Habenicht, Christopher J. ... **Chester, VA**
Habenicht, Daniel K. ... Houston, TX
Habenicht, Frank W. ... Pittsburgh, PA
Habenicht, Suzanne L. ... Dallas, TX
Habenstreit, David S. National Labor Relations Board, Office of the General Counsel, GV
Haber, Alan B. ... Santa Monica, CA
Haber, Alfred ... Palisades Park, NJ
Haber, Alfred, P.A. ... Palisades Park, NJ
Haber, Allan P. ... New York, NY
Haber, Amy C. ... Mineola, NY
Haber, Andrew H. ... **Chicago, IL**
Haber, Andrew S. ... Albany, NY
Haber, Bernard ... New York, NY
Haber, Bruce I. ... Nyack, NY
Haber, Carol ... Glen Cove, NY
Haber, Carol B. ... Miami, FL
Haber, Corriere & Backenstoe, P.C. Bethlehem, PA
Haber, David B. ... **Phoenix, AZ**
Haber, David B. ... **Miami, FL**
Haber, David C. ... **Glendale, CA**
Haber, David J. ... Red Bank, NJ
Haber, David L. ... **Pittsburgh, PA**
Haber, Dennis ... Miami, FL
Haber, Dennis R., P.A. ... Miami, FL
Haber, Donald D. ... Jamaica Plain, MA
Haber, Edward F. ... **Boston, MA**
Haber, Elaine Fisher ... **White Plains, NY**
Haber, Emanuel ... Kew Gardens, NY
Haber, Eric J. ... **New York, NY**
Haber, Eugene ... New York, NY
Haber, Eugene F. ... Mineola, NY
Haber, Frederic ... Danvers, MA
Haber, George ... Boca Raton, FL
Haber, George ... New York, NY
Haber, Harvey T. ... **New York, NY**
Haber, Herbert M. ... New York, NY
Haber, Irving ... Huntington, NY
Haber, Jeffrey M. ... **New York, NY**
Haber, Jeffrey S. ... **Los Angeles, CA**
Haber, Jennifer Anne ... Sacramento, CA
Haber, Joel A. ... **Chicago, IL**
Haber, Joel M. ... Conyers, GA
Haber, Karin Duchin ... Florham Park, NJ
Haber, Kenneth A. ... Tucson, AZ
Haber, Kenneth I. ... **New York, NY**
Haber, Kenneth J. ... Washington, DC
Haber, Kenneth J., Law Offices of, P.C. Washington, DC
Haber, Larry H. ... New York, NY
Haber, Laura ... Miami, FL
Haber, Laura Dawn ... Pittsburgh, PA; Washington, PA
Haber, Lawrence H. ... **Orlando, FL**
Haber, Lisa B. ... Garden City, NY
Haber, Lisa DiPoala ... Syracuse, NY
Haber, Louis M. ... **Armonk, NY**
Haber, Lynn C. ... Basking Ridge, NJ
Haber, Marc C. ... **San Francisco, CA**
Haber, Marcia E. ... Jersey City, NJ
Haber, Martin David ... **New York, NY**
Haber, Marvin S. ... Bethesda, MD
Haber, Marvin S. ... Philadelphia, PA
Haber, Mary ... **San Francisco, CA**
Haber, Merrill C. ... **San Francisco, CA**
Haber, Michael A. ... Miami, FL
Haber, Michael A. ... Chicago, IL
Haber, Michael A. & Associates, P.C. Chicago, IL
Haber, Michael A., P.A. ... Miami, FL
Haber, Michael S. ... **Atlanta, GA**
Haber, Michael S. ... New York, NY
Haber, Michael W. ... **Tampa, FL**
Haber, Miriam ... New York, NY
Haber, Nancy J. ... Brooklyn, NY
Haber, Neal D. ... New York, NY
Haber, Neal R. ... Warwick, RI
Haber, Norman ... New York, NY
Haber, Patrick J. ... Syracuse, NY
Haber, Patti A. ... **Hollywood, FL**
Haber, Philip A. ... **New York, NY**
Haber, Richard C. ... Cleveland, OH
Haber, Richard J. ... Bethlehem, PA
Haber, Richard M. ... **Tampa, FL**
Haber, Richd. M. ... Cleveland, OH
Haber, Robert Jay ... **New York, NY**
Haber, Robert M. ... **Miami, FL**
Haber, Roger S. ... New York, NY
Haber, Ronald ... **Miami, FL**
Haber & Roth ... **Miami, FL**
Haber, Ruth C. ... **New York, NY**
Haber, Scott R. ... **San Francisco, CA**
Haber & Silver ... Florham Park, NJ
Haber & Slijepcevich ... **San Francisco, CA**
Haber, Stephen D. ... Garden City, NY
Haber, Stephen K. ... New York, NY
Haber, Stephen P. ... White Plains, NY
Haber, Steven A. ... **Philadelphia, PA**
Haber, Steven J. ... Los Angeles, CA
Haber, Steven M. ... **New York, NY**
Haber, Theda R. ... San Francisco, CA
Haber, William ... Los Angeles, CA
Haber, Wolf ... Silver Spring, MD
Haberberger, Susan H. ... Cary, NC
Haberbusch, Carl A. **Rockville Centre, NY**
Haberbush & Campbell, LLP **Long Beach, CA**
Haberbush, David R. ... **Long Beach, CA**
Haberek, Noel B. ... Grosse Pointe Woods, MI
Haberek, Noel B., Jr. ... **Chicago, IL**
Haberer, Miles B. ... **Dallas, TX**
Haberfeld & Haberfeld ... Los Angeles, CA
Haberfeld, Jacqueline N. ... **New York, NY**
Haberfeld, Sharon Burton ... Los Angeles, CA
Haberfeld, Stephen E. ... Los Angeles, CA
Haberfelde, Ann ... Los Angeles, CA
Haberfield, Adam M. ... **Philadelphia, PA**
Habergarten, Charles ... St. Paul, MN
Haberkorn, Gerald ... **Chicago, IL**
Haberkorn, Jeffrey J. ... Aitkin, MN
Haberkorn, Matthew H. ... San Francisco, CA
Haberkorn, Michael S. ... **Carlsbad, CA**
Haberlach, William P. ... **Medford, OR**
Haberlack, Craig J. ... **Minneapolis, MN**
Haberlack, Thomas C. ... **Garden City, NY**
Haberland, Mary E. ... Plant City, FL
Haberle, Christine A. ... **Newark, NJ**
Haberly, M. Karlynn ... Bremerton, WA
Haberman, Alan ... New York, NY
Haberman, Barry A. ... Washington, DC
Haberman, Brook ... New York, NY
Haberman, Carol R. ... San Antonio, TX
Haberman, Christopher L. ... Visalia, CA
Haberman, Daniel Aaron ... Ferndale, MI
Haberman, David P. ... New York, NY
Haberman, David S. ... Syosset, NY
Haberman, F. William ... **Milwaukee, WI**
Haberman, Ian S. ... **Medina, OH**
Haberman, Jay S. ... New York, NY
Haberman, John P. ... **Minneapolis, MN**
Haberman, Keith P. ... Brookfield, WI
Haberman, Kristin K. ... Owatonna, MN
Haberman, Mark A. ... Columbus, OH
Haberman, Melanie ... **New York, NY**
Haberman, Michael H. ... Washington, DC
Haberman, Morton J. ... **Chicago, IL**
Haberman, Neal A. ... Goshen, NY
Haberman, Rick A. ... **Detroit, MI**
Haberman, Simon ... New York, NY
Haberman, Simon, P.C. ... New York, NY
Haberman, Stanley E. ... Encino, CA
Haberman, William E. ... Toledo, OH
Habermann, Frederick E. ... Leesburg, FL
Habermann, Glenn I. ... Jericho, NY
Habermann, Philip S. ... Madison, WI
Habermann, Richard O. ... McAllen, TX
Habermann, Ted. R. ... Gallatin, TN
Habermehl, Alan G. ... Madison, WI
Habermehl, Catherine L. ... **Buffalo, NY**; New York, NY
Habernigg, Ann ... **Palo Alto, CA**
Habernigg, Charles H. ... Portland, OR
Habersaat, Christian W. ... **Boston, MA**
Habersham, Jacqueline R. ... **Houston, TX**
Habershaw, Frank J. ... Daytona Beach, FL
Haberstick, Carl F. ... **Huron, SD**
Haberstock, Simone A. ... **St. Louis, MO**
Haberstock, Simone A., L.L.C. **St. Louis, MO**
Haberstroh, James H. ... Milwaukee, WI
Haberstroh, William J. ... Altoona, PA
Habert, Harriet ... **New York, NY**
Habert, Jack I. ... **New York, NY**
Habert, Natalie M. ... **Media, PA**
Habert, Tricia E. ... **Cherry Hill, NJ**
Habetz, Stephen A. ... **Norwalk, CT**
Habgood, Richard J. ... Morrisville, PA
Habhab, Albert L. ... Fort Dodge, IA
Habhab, Barbara J. ... **Chicago, IL**
Habhab, William H. ... Fort Dodge, IA
Habiague, Steven ... Poughkeepsie, NY
Habian, Bruce G. ... **New York, NY**
Habib, Amy M. ... **Washington, DC**
Habib, David Joseph ... Canoga Park, CA
Habib, Fortuna S. ... Syracuse, NY
Habib, Haim ... Hagåtña, GU
Habib, Jeanne ... **San Juan, PR**
Habib, Jeffrey S. ... **Harrisburg, PA**
Habib, John K. ... **Boston, MA**
Habib, John L. ... **Scottsdale, AZ**
Habib, Mark A. ... **Chico, CA**
Habib, Michael D. ... Fall River, MA
Habib, Perry M. ... Great Neck, NY
Habib, William A. ... Philadelphia, PA
Habibi & Brack ... Marietta, GA
Habibi, Jahan-Geer ... Marietta, GA
Habibi, Joanne L. ... Santa Barbara, CA
Habicht, F. Henry, II ... Elgin, IL
Habicht, Patricia T. ... Chicago, IL
Habicht, William M. ... **Minneapolis, MN**
Habif, Allen J. ... Teaneck, NJ
Habif & Habif ... Atlanta, GA
Habif, Isaac N. ... Atlanta, GA
Habif, Leonard N. ... Atlanta, GA
Habif, Michael A. ... Atlanta, GA
Habiger, Richard J. ... Carbondale, IL
Habinsky, Jason ... **New York, NY**
Habitzreiter, Ronald O. ... Austin, TX
Habjan, Alois V. ... **Roseland, NJ**
Habl, Robert H. ... Brooklyn, NY
Hable, Kevin J. ... **Louisville, KY**
Hable, Martin W. ... North Branch, MI
Hablutzel & Associates ... Chicago, IL
Hablutzel, Margo Lynn ... **Dallas, TX**
Hablutzel, Philip N. ... Chicago, IL
Haboian, Christine ... Aliso Viejo, CA
Haboush, William H. ... Richmond, VA
Habowski, Ronald J. ... Aurora, OH
Habron, Kathy D. ... Mechanicsville, VA
Habtu, Haimanot ... Los Angeles, CA
Haburay, Jane Ellen ... Montclair, NJ
Habush, Habush, Davis & Rottier, S.C. **Appleton, WI** **Green Bay, WI** **Lake Geneva, WI** **Madison, WI** **Milwaukee, WI** **Racine, WI** **Rhinelander, WI** **Stevens Point, WI** **Waukesha, WI** **Wausau, WI**
Habush, Jodi L. ... **Milwaukee, WI**
Habush, Robert L. ... **Milwaukee, WI**
Hacala, Martin G. ... Beachwood, OH
Hacala, Martin J. ... Grosse Pointe Woods, MI
Hach, Gary Lee ... **Dallas, TX**
Hachar, N. David, Jr. ... Laredo, TX
Haché, Rose A. ... Houston, TX
Hachenburg, Barbara L. ... **Beaumont, TX** **Houston, TX**
Hachenburg, Peter H. ... **Johnston, RI**
Hachenburg, Robert ... Philadelphia, PA
Hachey, Donald T. ... Athol, MA
Hachey, Joseph R. ... Kansas City, MO
Hachey, Ronald E. ... St. Paul, MN
Hachigian, Michael M., (A Prof. Law Corp.) Studio City, CA
Hachigian, Nina Executive Office Of The President, National Security Council, GV
Hachiya, Victor K. ... Oakland, CA
Hachler, Dennis A. ... Pendleton, OR
Hachman, Cheryl K. ... Las Vegas, NV
Hachman, Larry W. ... Stanton, MI
Hachman, Timothy J. ... Stockton, CA
Hachmann, H.G. ... New York, NY
Hachmeister, Lydia E. ... **Los Angeles, CA**
Hachmyer, Barry ... Sebastopol, CA
Hack, Andrew W. ... Janesville, WI
Hack, Barbara M. ... New York, NY
Hack, Charles H. ... Redondo Beach, CA
Hack, Charles W. ... Tulsa, OK
Hack, David L. ... **Florham Park, NJ**
Hack, Deborah S. ... Bloomfield Hills, MI
Hack, Edward G. ... Lakewood, OH
Hack, Elizabeth I. ... Department of Justice, Civil Division, GV
Hack, E. W. ... Jenks, OK
Hack, Frances M. ... Lancaster, PA
Hack, Frederick C., Jr. Hilton Head Island, SC
Hack, Jay L. ... **White Plains, NY**
Hack, Julie R. ... Morris Plains, NJ
Hack, Linda ... Dallas, TX
Hack, Lisa A. ... **Boston, MA**
Hack, Lisa B. ... **Annandale, VA** **McLean, VA**
Hack, Lydia L. ... **Mifflintown, PA**
Hack, Marion T. ... **Los Angeles, CA**
Hack, Martin H. ... **New York, NY**
Hack, Mary S. ... Topeka, KS
Hack, Norma ... New York, NY
Hack, Phillip L. ... San Diego, CA
Hack, Piro, O'Day, Merklinger, Wallace & McKenna, P.A. ... **Florham Park, NJ** **Newark, NJ**
Hack, Randall A. ... **Chicago, IL**
Hack, Raymond S. ... Kew Gardens, NY
Hack, Richard R., Jr. ... **Seattle, WA**
Hack, Robert A. ... Greenwich, CT; **New York, NY**
Hack, Robert J. ... **Kansas City, MO**
Hack, Ronald L. ... **St. Louis, MO**
Hack, Stanley F. ... Milwaukee, WI
Hack, Stanley F., & Associates, S.C. Milwaukee, WI
Hack, Susan Moriarty ... **San Diego, CA**
Hackard, Holt & Heller ... **Gold River, CA** **Sacramento, CA**
Hackard, Michael A. ... **Gold River, CA**
Hackathorn, Bill ... Collinsville, OK
Hackathorn, Rod ... Springfield, MO
Hackbart, James W. ... Racine, WI
Hackbart, Rolland R. ... Libertyville, IL
Hackbart, Thomas K. ... Milwaukee, WI
Hackbarth, Alfred E., Jr. ... Chicago, IL
Hackbarth, Cynthia L. ... **Louisville, KY**
Hackbarth & Hudson, P.C. ... Chicago, IL
Hackbarth, Lynn Ellen ... Milwaukee, WI
Hackbarth, Margaret A. ... **Washington, DC**
Hackbarth, Philip M. ... Chicago, IL
Hackbarth, Raymond W., Jr. ... **Irvine, CA**
Hackbert, Andrew J. ... **Los Angeles, CA**
Hackbirth, David W. ... Elizabethton, TN
Hackebeil, Anton E. (Tony) ... Uvalde, TX
Hackel & Hackel ... Waycross, GA
Hackel, Joan M. ... **St. Paul, MN**
Hackel, Kathy D. ... Waycross, GA
Hackel, Lenard P. ... Memphis, TN
Hackel, Richard S. ... **Boston, MA**
Hackel, Thomas M. ... Waycross, GA
Hackel, William H., III **Bloomfield Hills, MI**
Hackeling, C. Steven ... Huntington, NY
Hackeling, John C., Jr. ... Deer Park, NY
Hackenberg, Alan D. ... Findlay, OH
Hackenberg, Anthony W. ... Wadsworth, OH
Hackenberg, Beutler & Rasmussen Findlay, OH
Hackenberg, David A. ... Findlay, OH
Hackenberg, E. Scott ... **Baton Rouge, LA**
Hackenberg, I. James ... Painesville, OH
Hackenberg, Stacey Tsarnas ... **Akron, OH**
Hackenbrach, Joyce K. ... **Philadelphia, PA**
Hackenbracht, Joseph A., Jr. **Fort Washington, PA**
Hackenbracht, Mary E. ... Oakland, CA
Hackenbracht, William N. ... Tucson, AZ
Hacker, Aleta Delong ... Abilene, TX
Hacker, Cheryl R. ... Columbus, OH
Hacker, David A. ... **Cedar Rapids, IA**
Hacker, Donald E., Jr. ... **Seattle, WA**
Hacker, Donald R. ... Greensburg, PA
Hacker, Gary J. ... **Florham Park, NJ**
Hacker, Gary L. ... **Abilene, TX**
Hacker, Henry S. ... Dobbs Ferry, NY
Hacker, Howard B. ... **Houston, TX**
Hacker, Hyman ... **Garden City, NY**
Hacker, James E. ... **Latham, NY**
Hacker, Jeffrey A. ... **Valencia, CA**
Hacker, Jeffrey R. ... **Dallas, TX**
Hacker, John F. ... **Lehigh Valley, PA**
Hacker, Jonathan ... **Washington, DC**
Hacker, Jonathan S. ... **New York, NY**
Hacker, Kanowsky & Braly **Los Angeles, CA** **Valencia, CA**
Hacker, Kerry V. ... Newport Beach, CA
Hacker, Leo V. ... **Albany, NY**
Hacker, Max H. ... **Minneapolis, MN**
Hacker, Michael A. **Whitehouse Station, NJ**
Hacker, Michael S. ... Miami, FL
Hacker, Patrick E. ... **Cheyenne, WY**
Hacker, Patrick E., P.C. ... **Cheyenne, WY**

Hacker, Paul Steven ... Austin, TX
Hacker, Philip A. ... Miami, FL
Chicago, IL
Hacker, Richard ... Honolulu, HI
Hacker, Richard C. ... Juneau, AK
Hacker, Robert A. ... Los Angeles, CA
Hacker, Robert C. ... Washington, DC
Hacker, Ronald J. ... Chicago, IL
Hacker, Susan C. ... Bellevue, WA
Hacker, Suzannah Kirk ... Lowell, MA
Hacker, Teri L. ... Springfield, MO
Hacker, Thomas D. ... Denver, CO
Hacker, William J. ... Chicago, IL
Hacker & Willig, Inc., P.S. ... Seattle, WA
Hackerman, Christopher N. ... Houston, TX
Hackerman Peterson Frankel & Manela, P.C. ... Houston, TX
Hackerman, Richard J. ... Baltimore, MD
Hackerman, Stephen M. ... Houston, TX
Hackerott, Cynthia Lynne ... Riverwoods, IL
Hackert, Timothy J. ... Dayton, OH
Hackethal, Gregg D. ... Santa Barbara, CA
Hackethal McNeill and Aucoin, P.C.
Lakewood, CO
Hackett, Andrew M. ... Columbus, OH
Hackett, Barbara K. ... Ann Arbor, MI
Hackett, Beecher & Hart, Inc., P.S.
Seattle, WA
Hackett, Benjamin F., & Associates
Edmond, OK
Hackett, Beverly R. ... Albany, NY
Hackett, Daniel R. ... Columbus, OH
Hackett, Darrel R. ... Ocala, FL
Hackett, David B. ... Wheaton, IL
Hackett, David L. ... Philadelphia, PA
Hackett, David P. ... Chicago, IL
Hackett, David R. ... Georgetown, DE
Hackett, Emmy B. ... Boston, MA
Austin, TX
Hackett, Florence J. ... Calabasas, CA
Hackett, Fred V. ... Stafford, TX
Hackett, Glenn S. ... Lewiston, NY
Hackett, Grace G. ... Manteca, CA
Hackett, Helen Lucas ... Chicago, IL
Hackett, James ... Edwardsville, IL
Hackett, James M. ... Fairbanks, AK
Hackett, James M. ... Palo Alto, CA
Hackett, James W. ... Boston, MA
Hackett, James W., Jr. ... Boston, MA
Hackett, John A. ... Seattle, WA
Hackett, John Byron ... Flushing, NY
Hackett, John D. ... Chicago, IL
Hackett, John D. ... Boston, MA
Hackett, John J. ... New York, NY
Hackett, John L., Jr. ... Boston, MA
Hackett, Kelly A. ... Chicago, IL
Hackett, Kevin R. ... New York, NY
Hackett, Leo A. ... Media, PA
Hackett, Leonard T. ... Baltimore, MD
Hackett, Lewis E. ... Sacramento, CA
Hackett, Linda S. ... Pittsburgh, PA
Hackett, M. Patricia ... South Bend, IN
Hackett, Mark D. ... Chattanooga, TN
Hackett, Mark J. ... Portland, OR
Hackett, Mary A. (Molly) ... Flanders, NJ
Hackett, Mary Jo ... Pittsburgh, PA
Hackett & Maxwell, P.C. ... Detroit, MI
Lapeer, MI
Pontiac, MI
Troy, MI
Hackett, Michael C. ... Wellesley, MA
Hackett, Michael J. ... Mount Pleasant, MI
Hackett, Montague H., Jr. ... New York, NY
Hackett, Patricia ... New York, NY
Hackett, Patrick E. ... Troy, MI
Hackett, Patrick J. ... Garden City, NY
Hackett, Richard A. ... Minneapolis, MN
Hackett, Richard P. ... Portland, ME
Hackett, Robert C. ... Phoenix, AZ
Hackett, Robert E. ... Milwaukee, WI
Hackett, Robert J. ... Phoenix, AZ
Hackett, Robert L. ... New Orleans, LA
Hackett, Robert N. ... West Mifflin, PA
Hackett, Robert N., Jr. ... Yakima, WA
Hackett, Robert V. ... Bloomfield Hills, MI
Hackett, Stanley H., P.C. ... Atlanta, GA
Hackett, Stephen Beaty ... Norman, OK
Hackett, Stephen R. ... Las Vegas, NV
Hackett, Susan J. ... Washington, DC
Hackett, Sylvia L. ... Catonsville, MD
Hackett, Terry C. ... Newport Beach, CA
Hackett, Terry M. ... Chicago, IL
Hackett, Thomas E. ... Springfield, OH
Hackett, Thomas J. ... Baltimore, MD
Hackett, Thomas P. ... Cheshire, CT
Hackett, Timothy E. ... Fond du Lac, WI
Hackett, Timothy R. ... Youngstown, OH
Hackett, W. Michael ... Tulsa, OK
Hackett, W. Michael, P.C. ... Tulsa, OK
Hackett, Wesley P., Jr. ... Saranac, MI
Hackett, William B. ... Memphis, TN
Hackett, William E.
Department Of Veterans Affairs, Board of Veterans Appeals, GV
Hackett II, Jack O. ... Punta Gorda, FL
Hackim, Marilyn H. ... San Diego, CA
Hacking, Donald G. ... Rio Verde, AZ
Hacking, Earl L. ... Minneapolis, MN
Hacking, Robert M. ... Boston, MA
Hackl, Jo Watson ... Greenville, SC
Hackl, Sylvia Lee ... Cheyenne, WY
Hackleman, James B. ... San Bernardino, CA
Hackleman, Robert S.
Fort Lauderdale, FL
Hackler, Amy E. ... Olathe, KS
Hackler, Amy E., P.A. ... Olathe, KS
Hackler, Deborah L. ... McAlester, OK
Hackler, Donald R. ... McAlester, OK
Hackler, Glen E. ... Pampa, TX
Hackler and Hackler ... McAlester, OK
Hackler, Kenneth P. ... Topeka, KS
Hackler, Kristin S. ... Grass Valley, CA
Hackler, Nolan R. ... Oklahoma City, OK
Hackler, Walter A. ... Newport Beach, CA
Hackley, Brian T. ... San Diego, CA
Hackley, David K. ... Edina, MN
Hackley, John ... Stanford, KY
Hackley, Mary Keiling ... Fort Lauderdale, FL
Hackley, Roger W., II ... San Francisco, CA
Hackman, Anna L. ... Summit, NJ
Hackman, Daniel T. ... Indianapolis, IN
Hackman, Emory E., Jr. ... McLean, VA
Hackman, Florence M. ... Chicago, IL
Hackman, Gordon L. ... Boutte, LA
Hackman, Howard M. ... Worthington, OH
Hackman Hulett & Cracraft, LLP
Indianapolis, IN
Hackman, Jonathan I. ... Encino, CA
Hackman, Karen Lee ... Selinsgrove, PA
Hackman, Kevin A. ... Warwick, RI
Hackman, Mark T. ... Baltimore, MD
Hackman, Marvin L. ... Indianapolis, IN
Hackman, Mary Cook ... Arlington, VA
Hackman, Michael ... Encino, CA
Hackman, Paige E. ... Fort Lauderdale, FL
Hackman, Richard L. ... Baltimore, MD
Hackman, Richard P. ... Philadelphia, PA
Hackman, Robert J. ... Honolulu, HI
Hackman, Stephen J. ... Indianapolis, IN
Hackman, Timothy B. ... Purchase, NY
Hackman, Tracy L. ... Southfield, MI
Hackman, William Henry ... Bloomington, IL
Hackmann, Frank H. ... St. Louis, MO
Hackmann, Glen F. ... Milwaukee, WI
Hackmann, John S. ... Collinsville, IL
Hackmann, Kathy A. ... Millstadt, IL
Hackmann, Tamara K. ... Des Moines, IA
Hackney, Ashby R. ... Richmond, VA
Hackney, Barry A. ... Fredericksburg, VA
Richmond, VA
Hackney, C. Kathryn ... Brunswick, GA
Hackney, Charles D. ... Lansing, MI
Hackney, Clint ... Austin, TX
Hackney, Donald D. ... Spokane, WA
Hackney, Donald L., Jr. ... Atlanta, GA
Hackney, Edward T. ... Kissimmee, FL
Hackney, Elbert R. ... East Point, GA
Hackney, Gar ... Boise, ID
Hackney, Gertrude M. ... Villanova, PA
Hackney, H. Hamilton, III ... Boston, MA
Hackney, Harry T. ... Tavares, FL
Hackney, Harry Thomas, P.A. ... Tavares, FL
Hackney, Hugh Edward ... Dallas, TX
Hackney, J. Patrick ... Tuscaloosa, AL
Hackney, James R., Jr. ... Boston, MA
Hackney, James V. ... Washington, DC
Hackney, James W. ... Austin, TX
Hackney, Joe ... Chapel Hill, NC
Hackney, John G., Jr. ... Charleston, WV
Hackney, Joseph A. ... Miami, FL
Hackney, Joseph, Jr. ... Miami, FL
Hackney, Joseph, Jr., P.A. ... Miami, FL
Hackney, Keith D. ... Washington, NC
Hackney, Laura B. ... Denver, CO
Hackney March & Carroll ... Spokane, WA
Hackney, Melissa McKee
Vineyard Haven, MA
Hackney, Randy J. ... East Lansing, MI
Hackney, Richard C. ... Modesto, CA
Hackney, Robert C.
Palm Beach Gardens, FL
Hackney, S. Fain ... Edgartown, MA
Hackney, S. Fain ... Philadelphia, PA
Hackney, Stephen C. ... Chicago, IL
Hackney, Virginia H. ... Richmond, VA
Hackney, William B. ... Charleston, WV
Hackney, William P. ... Pittsburgh, PA
Hackstaff, James C. ... Denver, CO
Hackworth, Arthur A. ... Menlo Park, CA
Hackworth, Julie Kaye ... Covington, KY
Hackworth, Kime & Bowles, L.L.C.
Piedmont, MO
Hackworth, L. Dwayne ... Piedmont, MO
Hackworth, Michael C. ... Riverside, CA
Hackworth, Michael J. ... Piedmont, MO
Hackworth, Neil S. ... Shelbyville, KY
Hackworth, Paul Kevin ... Olive Hill, KY
Hackworth, Roydera Dolores
Greensboro, NC
Hackworth, Sarah K. ... St. Louis, MO
Hackworth, William M. ... Roanoke, VA
Hacopians, Gerald O. ... Kensington, CA
Hacskaylo, Michael S. ... Golden, CO
Hada, James H. ... Irving, TX
Hada, Rick L. ... Chicago, IL
Hadacek, John D. ... Fostoria, OH
Hadad, Henry S. ... Kenilworth, NJ
Hadar, Ron M. ... Boston, MA
Hadas, David ... Boston, MA
Hadas, Nicole R. ... Boston, MA
Hadaway, Charles R. ... Atlanta, GA
Hadaway, Deborah L. ... Glastonbury, CT
Hadaway, James C. ... Clearwater, FL
Hadaway, James C., P.A. ... Clearwater, FL
Hadaway, Lauralee ... Golden, CO
Hadaway, Shane ... Haskell, TX
Haddad, Amy E. ... Nashville, TN
Haddad, Carl D. ... Houston, TX
Haddad, Charles A. ... Wernersville, PA
Haddad, Charles M. ... Clinton, MI
Haddad, Christine C. ... Glendale, CA
Haddad, Christopher A.
West Palm Beach, FL
Haddad, Christopher Markham
Hartford, CT
Haddad, Christopher A., P.A.
West Palm Beach, FL
Haddad, Deborah Tyler ... Palatine, IL
Haddad, Donna ... Chicago, IL
Haddad, Edward A. ... Omaha, NE
Haddad, Edward S. ... Albany, NY
Haddad, Emily E. ... Minneapolis, MN
Haddad, Ernest M. ... Boston, MA
Haddad, Geoffry Alan ... Charleston, WV
Haddad, George J. ... Southfield, MI
Haddad, Gerard A. ... New York, NY
Haddad, Gil ... Miami, FL
Haddad & Haddad ... Clinton, MI
Haddad, Henry G. ... Los Angeles, CA
Haddad, Jack ... Santa Monica, CA
Haddad, Jack D. ... Bellingham, WA
Haddad, Jack, Inc. ... Santa Monica, CA
Haddad, James G. ... Worcester, MA
Haddad, James M. ... New York, NY
Haddad, Jennifer W. ... Hartford, CT
Haddad, Karen K. ... Elkhart, IN
Haddad, Linda ... Pittsburgh, PA
Haddad, Lisa R. ... Boston, MA
Haddad, Louis ... Brooklyn, NY
Haddad, Mark A. ... New York, NY
Haddad, Mark C. ... Clinton, MI
Haddad, Mark E. ... Washington, DC
Haddad, Mark E. ... Boston, MA
Haddad, Marty J. ... Port Huron, MI
Haddad, Mary Louise ... Chicago, IL
Haddad, Matthew A. ... Richmond, VA
Haddad, Michael J. ... Oakland, CA
Haddad, Michael J. ... Chicago, IL
Haddad, Mitchell D. ... New York, NY
Haddad, Mitchell E. ... Santa Ana, CA
Haddad, Monica N. ... Charleston, WV
Haddad, P. Gregory ... Morgantown, WV
Haddad, Patricia K. ... Millburn, NJ
Haddad, Patrick J. ... Detroit, MI
Haddad, Peter ... Viera, FL
Haddad, Richard ... Department of Defense, Office of the General Counsel, GV
Haddad, Richard G. ... New York, NY
Haddad, Robert ... Louisville, KY
Haddad, Robert J. ... Troy, MI
Haddad, Robert J. ... Virginia Beach, VA
Haddad, Roland J. ... La Mesa, CA
Haddad, Ronald L. ... Chicago, IL
Haddad, Royce C., Jr. ... Clearwater, FL
Haddad, Sam W. ... Grosse Pointe, MI
Haddad & Sherwin ... Oakland, CA
San Francisco, CA
Haddad & Shuttera, P.A. ... Clearwater, FL
Haddad, Susan Christine ... Chicago, IL
Haddad, Tina R. ... Lima, OH
Haddad, Virginia Warneke ... Valparaiso, FL
Haddad, William J. ... Chicago, IL
Haddad, William N. ... Chicago, IL
Haddad, William N. ... New York, NY
Haddad, Wm. C. ... Sutton, MA
Haddad, Yvonne R. ... Philadelphia, PA
Haddan, Jon R. ... Newport Beach, CA
Haddan & Zepfel, LLP ... Newport Beach, CA
Haddaway, Bryan B. ... Towson, MD
Haddaway, Keith G. ... Washington, DC
Hadden, Arthur C. ... Hamden, CT
Hadden, Callender F., Jr.
New Orleans, LA
Hadden, Carlton Maurice
Equal Employment Opportunity Commission, Office of Federal Operations, GV
Hadden, Catherine C. ... Lexington, KY
Hadden, Charles I. ... Washington, DC
Hadden Co., L.P.A. ... Columbus, OH
Hadden, Donnelly W. ... Ann Arbor, MI
Hadden, Donnelly W., P.C. ... Ann Arbor, MI
Hadden, E. Bruce ... Columbus, OH
Hadden, Eddie Raynord
Englewood Cliffs, NJ
Hadden, Francis McGill ... Haddonfield, NJ
Philadelphia, PA
Hadden, Hamilton, Jr. ... Muttontown, NY
Hadden, J. David ... Palo Alto, CA
Hadden, J. Wayne ... La Grange, GA
Hadden, James B. ... Columbus, OH
Hadden, James Patrick ... Philadelphia, PA
Hadden, J. C. David ... Hartford, CT
Hadden, Jeffrey C. ... Boston, MA
Hadden, Joe D. ... Ventura, CA
Hadden, Lawrence D. ... Houston, TX
Hadden, Lee E. ... Odessa, TX
Hadden, Mark C. ... Providence, RI
Hadden, Richard R. ... Cincinnati, OH
Hadden, Richard R., L.P.A. ... Cincinnati, OH
Hadden, Robert Morris ... Johnson City, TN
Kingsport, TN
Hadden, Roby ... Tyler, TX
Hadden, S. Morris ... Johnson City, TN
Kingsport, TN
Hadden, Sally E. ... Tallahassee, FL
Hadden, Will ... Odessa, TX
Hadden, William J. ... Santa Monica, CA
Hadden, Wm. L., Jr. ... New Haven, CT
Haddican, Mary Pat ... Houston, TX
Haddick, Charles E., Jr. ... Camp Hill, PA
Haddigan, John F. ... Quincy, MA
Haddigan, John F., P.C. ... Quincy, MA
Haddix, Kathleen McClary
Louisville, KY
Haddix, Lance ... North Hollywood, CA
Haddix, William E., Jr. ... Haddon Heights, NJ
Haddleton & Collins, P.C. ... Chatham, MA
Hyannis, MA
Nantucket, MA
Haddleton, Frank B. ... Richmond, VT
Haddleton, Russell E. ... Hyannis, MA
Haddock, Bradley E. ... Wichita, KS
Haddock, Diane ... Fort Worth, TX
Haddock, Donald M., Jr.
Fredericksburg, VA
Haddock, Douglas R. ... San Antonio, TX
Haddock, Edward E., Jr.
Winter Park, FL
Haddock, Gary L. ... Pittsfield, IL
Haddock, Gerald R. ... Spokane, WA
Haddock, Gerald W. ... Fort Worth, TX
Haddock, James W. ... Lake Village, AR
Haddock, Jane W. ... Jackson, MS
Haddock, Jas. H. ... Ridgeland, MS
Haddock, Kathleen E. ... Boulder, CO
Haddock, Lawrence Page, Jr.
Jacksonville, FL
Haddock, Matthew E. ... Fort Worth, TX
Haddock & Mazzanti ... Lake Village, AR
Haddock, Peter ... Oklahoma City, OK
Haddock Professional Association
Orlando, FL
Winter Park, FL
Haddock, R. Philip ... Maggie Valley, NC
Haddock, Rand ... Phoenix, AZ
Haddock, Rex J. ... Whittier, CA
Haddock, Robert M. ... Phoenix, AZ
Haddock, Sheila P. ... Houston, TX
Haddock, Steven E. ... Decatur, AL
Haddock, Terence B. ... San Diego, CA
Haddock, Thomas Brian ... Reston, VA
Haddon, Harold A. ... Denver, CO
Haddon, James T., (Ltd.) ... Chicago, IL
Haddon, Jonathan W. ...
Overseas Private Investment Corporation, GV
Haddon, M. Leigh ... Cary, NC
Haddon, Morgan & Foreman, P.C.
Denver, CO
Haddon, Phoebe A. ... Philadelphia, PA
Haddon, Roger S. ... Sunbury, PA
Haddon, Sam E. ... Missoula, MT
Haddon, Steven C. ... Missoula, MT
Haddon, William C. ... Atlanta, GA
Haddow, Howard J. ... Columbus, OH
Haddow, James B. ... Portland, ME
Haddow, Jon A. ... Bangor, ME
Haddox, Benjamin E., Jr. ... Evansville, IN
Haddox, Craig A. ... Columbus, OH
Haddox, D. Michael ... Zanesville, OH
Haddox, Hayes P. ... Louisville, KY
Haddox, Jerome B. ... Columbus, OH
Haddox, Kelley R. ... Dallas, TX
Haddox, Kerry E. ... Zanesville, OH
Haddox, Kimberly L. ... Pittsburgh, PA
Haddox, Ronald D. ... Baytown, TX
Haddy, Larry G. ... Phoenix, AZ
Haddy, Larry G., Ltd. ... Phoenix, AZ
Hade, Sean E. ... Owatonna, MN
St. Paul, MN
Hade, Victor ... New York, NY
Hadeed, Albert J. ... Bunnell, FL
Hadeed, Michael Mitry, Jr.
Springfield, VA
Hadell, Cynthia R. ... Ukiah, CA
Haden, Anne S. ... Oakland, CA
Haden, Brent R. ... Norfolk, VA
Haden, Charles Edward ... Hampton, VA
Haden, Charles H., II ... Charleston, WV
Haden, Charles M. ... Houston, TX
Haden and Dawson, Professional Corporation
Merced, CA
Haden, Fred M. ... Fairfax, VA
Haden and Gabbert ... Houston, TX
Haden, Grant Q. ... Springfield, MO
Haden, Gregory K. ... Johnson City, TN
Kingsport, TN
Haden, Jay D. ... Kansas City, MO
Haden, Jonathan R. ... Kansas City, MO
Haden, Lorri L. ... Lampasas, TX
Haden, Mabel D., P.C. ... Washington, DC
Haden, Mary Elaine G. ... Dallas, TX
Haden, Micah Cade ... Corsicana, TX
Haden, Patrick C. ... Los Angeles, CA
Haden, R. Quentin ... Ava, MO
Haden, Robert E. ... Morgantown, WV
Haden, Robert H. ... Merced, CA
Haden, Robert T. ... Merced, CA
Haden, William H., Jr. ... Louisville, KY
Hadenfeldt, Jerry L. ... Des Moines, IA
Hadenfeldt, Kent A. ... Scottsbluff, NE
Hader, Cheryl E. ... New York, NY
Hader, Geoffrey E. ... New York, NY
Hader, H. Townsend ... Lexington, MO
Hader, Robert E. ... Mount Clemens, MI
Hader, Stephen M. ... Charlotte, NC
Haderlein, Gerard D. ... Chicago, IL
Haderlein, John A. ... Chicago, IL
Haderlein, John F. ... Chicago, IL
Haderlein, Robert Kendall ... Atlanta, GA
Haderlein, Thomas M. ... Chicago, IL
Hadfield, Ben H. ... Brigham City, UT
Hadfield, James D. ... Petaluma, CA
Hadfield, Marnee Lynn ... Charleston, SC
Hadfield, Reed W. ... Brigham City, UT
Hadfield, Robin W. ... Lincoln, NE
Hadfield, Stephen R. ... Brigham City, UT
Hadges, Jason ... Washington, DC
Hadgi & Hadgi ... Boston, MA
Hadgi, Wm. ... Boston, MA
Hadiaris, Peter N. ... San Francisco, CA
Hadican, J. Martin, P.C. ... St. Louis, MO
Hadidi, Frederick F. ... Palo Alto, CA
Hadigian, Carl H. ... Newark, NJ
Hadigian, Dana G. ... Hagerstown, MD
Hadinger, Kristina Pike ... Princeton, NJ
Hadji, Serge B. ... Cleveland, OH
Hadjian, Abbas ... Sherman Oaks, CA
Hadjis, Alexander J. ... Washington, DC
Hadjis, Thomas J., II ... Lake Placid, NY

Hadjiyane, Paul ..... Towson, MD
Hadjiyannis, Cynthia A. ..... Secaucus, NJ
Hadland, Harold L. ..... Columbus, NE
Hadland, Kenneth W. ..... Oak Brook, IL
Hadlen, David A. ..... Los Angeles, CA
Hadler, John W. ..... Westbury, NY
Hadler, Joseph W. ..... Indianapolis, IN
Hadler, Patrick J. ..... Indianapolis, IN
Hadley, Albert P. ..... Sedgwick, ME
Hadley, Beverly A.
Agency for International Development, Office of the General Counsel, GV
Hadley, Bob W. ..... Orem, UT
Hadley, Bruce ..... Louisville, KY
Hadley, Charles D. ..... Scottsdale, AZ
Hadley, Charles S. ..... Avon Park, FL
Hadley, Curtis R. ..... East Lansing, MI
Hadley, Dana V. ..... West Chester, PA
Hadley, David, Jr. ..... Phoenix, AZ
Sun City, AZ
Hadley, David Wm. ..... Hermiston, OR
Hadley, Donald H. ..... Rockville, MD
Hadley, Donald H., LLC ..... Washington, DC
Rockville, MD
Hadley, Duane L. ..... Tawas City, MI
Hadley, Edward Ashley ..... Nashville, TN
Hadley, Edwin W. ..... Boston, MA
Hadley, Elizabeth Harrison .....
Department Of Health And Human Services, GV
Hadley, Ernest C. ..... West Wareham, MA
Hadley, Greg A. ..... Dublin, OH
Hadley, Gregory B. ..... Provo, UT
Hadley & Hadley ..... Baldwin Park, CA
Hadley, Harold D. ..... Marysville, CA
Hadley, Howard ..... Maitland, FL
Hadley, James E. ..... Seattle, WA
Hadley, James F. ..... Columbus, OH
Toledo, OH
Hadley, James F., Co., L.P.A.
Columbus, OH
Toledo, OH
Hadley, Janis T. ..... Seattle, WA
Hadley, Jean Erickson ..... New Harmony, IN
Hadley, Jennifer L. ..... Phoenix, AZ
Hadley, Joseph E., Jr. ..... Washington, DC
Hadley, Joseph P. ..... New York, NY
Hadley, Karl E. ..... Noblesville, IN
Hadley, Katherine G. ..... St. Paul, MN
Hadley, Kathleen D. ..... Wilmington, DE
Hadley, Kenneth C., Jr. ..... Newport, OR
Hadley, Kirk ..... Pocatello, ID
Hadley, Lawrence M. ..... Los Angeles, CA
Hadley, Linda Clifford ..... Hartford, CT
Hadley, Maria K. ..... Buffalo, NY
Hadley, Marshall ..... Baldwin Park, CA
Hadley & McKenna ..... Washington, DC
Fairfax, VA
Hadley, Michael Robert ..... Oil City, PA
Hadley, Milton ..... Baldwin Park, CA
Hadley, Paul A. ..... Danville, IN
Hadley, Poach & Anderson, P.C.
Phoenix, AZ
Sun City, AZ
Hadley, R. Jonathan ..... Phoenix, AZ
Hadley, Ralph V., III ..... Winter Park, FL
Hadley, Reed V. ..... Longview, WA
Hadley, Richard P. ..... New York, NY
Hadley, Robert E. ..... Roanoke, VA
Hadley, Robert J. ..... Farmington Hills, MI
Hadley, Robert J. ..... Dayton, OH
Hadley, Ronald E. ..... Lima, OH
Hadley, Roy E., Jr. ..... Atlanta, GA
Hadley, Russell J. ..... Salt Lake City, UT
Hadley, Scott M. ..... Ogden, UT
Hadley, Sheldon C. ..... Marysville, CA
Hadley, Stephanie Mergel
Florham Park, NJ
Hadley, Stephen J. ..... Washington, DC
Hadley, Stephen M. ..... Bountiful, UT
Hadley, Steven M. ..... New York, NY
Hadley, Sybil C. ..... Atlanta, GA
Hadley, Theodore C. ..... Schaumburg, IL
Hadley, Thomas J. ..... Antlers, OK
Hadley, Timothy D. .....
Department of State, GV
Hadley, W. Mike ..... Santa Ynez, CA
Hadley, William H. ..... New York, NY
Hadley, William L. ..... Reno, NV
Hadley, William P. ..... Springfield, MA
Hadley, William R. ..... Littleton, CO
Hadlock, David F. ..... Framingham, MA
Hadlock, John M. ..... New York, NY
Hadlock, Lorna J.
Federal Energy Regulatory Commission, Office of the General Counsel, GV
Hadlock, Patrick L. ..... Corvallis, OR
Hadlock, Robert J.
Rancho Santa Margarita, CA
Hadlock, Timothy J. ..... San Francisco, CA
Hadlow, Richard B. ..... Tampa, FL
Hadra, Douglas F. ..... Denver, CO
Hadrick, Raymond W. ..... Brooklyn, NY
Hadro, Edward M. ..... Newton, MA
Hadrovic, Peter D. ..... New York, NY
Hadsall, John D. ..... St. Petersburg, FL
Hadsell, Barbara E. ..... Pasadena, CA
Pasadena, CA
Hadsell, Landgraf & Lynch, LLP
Niles, MI
St. Joseph, MI
Hadsell, Philip A., Jr. ..... Niles, MI
Hadsell & Stormer ..... Pasadena, CA
Hadsock, Donald B. ..... Bradenton, FL
Hadwiger, Kyle B. ..... Cherokee, OK
Hadwiger Law Firm P.L.L.C. ..... Alva, OK
Cherokee, OK
Fairview, OK
Medford, OK
Hadwiger, Mickey J. ..... Cherokee, OK
Hadwiger, Ronald R. ..... Cherokee, OK
Hadwiger, William A. ..... Alva, OK
Hadwin, Arden J. ..... Savannah, GA
Hadwyn, Laurie J. ..... Rossville, GA
Hadyniak, Lynn Qualtrough ..... Newark, NJ
Hadzi-Antich, Theodore ..... Buffalo, NY
Hadzima, Joseph G., Jr. ..... Boston, MA
Hadziosmanovic, Nicola R.J.
Roseland, NJ
Haeberle, Raelenne Jensen ..... Richmond, VA
Haeberlin, Jeffrey A. ..... Louisville, KY
Haeckel, Robert W. ..... St. Louis, MO
Haecker, Arthur J., III ..... Marietta, GA
Haeckl, Jenifer ..... Westborough, MA
Haeder, Richard ..... Rapid City, SD
Haeder, Robert V. ..... Huron, SD
Haedicke, Mark E. ..... Houston, TX
Haefele, Richard J. ..... Chaska, MN
Haefele, Robert T. ..... Woodbridge, NJ
Haefeli, Richard T. ..... Southampton, NY
Haefeli, Richard T.
Westhampton Beach, NY
Haefer, Mary Polson ..... Sun Prairie, WI
Haefliger, William W. ..... Los Angeles, CA
Haefliger, William W. ..... Pasadena, CA
Haefner, Bridget A. ..... Minneapolis, MN
Haefner, David A. ..... Buffalo, NY
Haefner & Enzenberger ..... Reno, NV
Haefner, Gail E. ..... Burlington, VT
Haefner, Henry C. ..... Lancaster, PA
Haefner, Marc D. ..... Roseland, NJ
Haefner, Paul E. ..... Reno, NV
Haegele, Gary L. ..... St. Louis, MO
Haegelin, Elizabeth J. ..... Torrance, CA
Haeger, Mary E. ..... Chicago, IL
Haeger, Robert J. ..... Gaithersburg, MD
Haehl, Harry L. ..... San Francisco, CA
Haehnel, Craig W. ..... Grand Rapids, MI
Haehnel, Fred M., Jr. ..... St. Louis, MO
Haehnel, Freeman M. ..... Grand Rapids, MI
Haehnel, Phelan & Liquigli
Grand Rapids, MI
Haemmerle, Jennifer L. Kroos ..... Hailey, ID
Haemmerle, Todd M. ..... Cleveland, OH
Haen, Katherine E. ..... Shelby, NC
Haendiges, Deborah A. ..... Kenmore, NY
Haendiges, Robert L. ..... Whittier, CA
Haenel, Howard M. ..... Denver, CO
Haenggi, Sara Louisa ..... Houston, TX
Haenicke, Christopher T. ..... Kalamazoo, MI
Haenke, Robert S. ..... Mossyrock, WA
Haenle, Alice L. ..... Olympia, WA
Haenn, Michael S. ..... Bangor, ME
Haenni, Scott Alan ..... Charlotte, NC
Haenny, Mark A. ..... Loveland, CO
Haensel, Curt C. ..... House of Representatives, Office of Legislative Counsel, GV
Haensel, Peter C. ..... Milwaukee, WI
Haensly, Sharon Ilene ..... Seattle, WA
Haerens, Paul J. ..... Royal Oak, MI
Haerens, Roger A. ..... Warren, MI
Haerens, Ronald O. ..... Mount Clemens, MI
Haering, Margaret E. ..... Milford, CT
Haerr, Roger C. ..... San Diego, CA
Haerter, Martin W. ..... New York, NY
Haerter, Ursula L. ..... Hartford, CT
Haertling, Tiffany L. ..... Denton, TX
Haertter, Rocco G. ..... Scranton, PA
Haesche, Frederick J. ..... Hartford, CT
Haese, Glenn H. ..... Boston, MA
Haese, LLC ..... Hartford, CT
Boston, MA
Haesemeyer, Richard E. ..... Des Moines, IA
Haesloop, E. Gordon ..... Mineola, NY
New York, NY
White Plains, NY
Haesloop, Mark ..... San Carlos, CA
Haesloop, Martha V. ..... Mineola, NY
Haessler, Eric R. ..... Lake Oswego, OR
Haessler, George W. ..... Wahoo, NE
Haessler, John F. ..... Lincoln, NE
Haessler, Margaret E. ..... Burlington, IA
Haessler, Sullivan, Nygren & Klein, Ltd.
Wahoo, NE
Haet, Donald M. ..... San Francisco, CA
Haettenschwiller, Inez Maria ..... Albany, NY
Haeuber, Douglas H. ..... Kirkland, WA
Haeuser, Alan F. ..... Eastsound, WA
Haeuser, Thomas A. ..... Sonoma, CA
Haeusler, Rita M. ..... Los Angeles, CA
Haeussler, Richard L. ..... Costa Mesa, CA
Haeussler, Timothy J. ..... Savannah, GA
Hafar, Barry L. ..... Oklahoma City, OK
Hafele, Donald W. ..... West Palm Beach, FL
Hafele, James L. ..... Peoria, IL
Hafele, Schmidt, Stephens & Glancy, P.C.
Peoria, IL
Hafeli, Mark W. ..... Bloomfield Hills, MI
Hafeli, Susan M. ..... Washington, DC
Hafemeister, Thomas L. ..... Lincoln, NE
Hafen, Conrad ..... Winnemucca, NV
Hafen, Gregory T. ..... Las Vegas, NV
Pahrump, NV
Hafen, Jonathan O. ..... Salt Lake City, UT
Hafen, Kendrick J. ..... Salt Lake City, UT
Hafen, Mark W. ..... Salinas, CA
Hafen, Talbot, Porter & Cardone, Ltd.
Pahrump, NV
Hafen, Talbot, Porter & Greene, Ltd.
Las Vegas, NV
Hafener, Patricia A. ..... Portland, ME
Hafenstein, Kenneth S. ..... Columbus, OH
Hafenstein, Lance A. ..... Napa, CA
Hafer, Carol B. ..... Brooklyn, NY
Hafer, Douglas R. ..... Dallas, TX
Hafer, F. Eugene ..... Raleigh, NC
Hafer, Henry M. ..... New York, NY
Hafer, Hugh ..... Seattle, WA
Hafer, J. Jeffrey ..... New York, NY
Hafer, Joseph P. ..... Bethlehem, PA
Harrisburg, PA
Hafer, Mark C. ..... Las Vegas, NV
Hafer, McNamara, Caldwell & Curtner, P.A.
Raleigh, NC
Hafer, Price, Rinehart & Robblee
Seattle, WA
Hafer, Randall F. ..... Atlanta, GA
Hafer, Robert A. ..... Department of Commerce, Patent and Trademark Office, GV
Hafer, Stanley J. ..... Fallbrook, CA
Hafer, Thomas F. ..... Reading, PA
Hafer, William L. ..... Naperville, IL
Hafer, William W. ..... Hanover, PA
Haferkamp, Hugh J. ..... Santa Barbara, CA
Haferkamp, Richard E. ..... St. Louis, MO
Haferman & Ilten ..... Stevens Point, WI
Haferman, James T. ..... Stevens Point, WI
Hafertepe, James M. ..... Chicago, IL
Hafets, Richard J. ..... Baltimore, MD
Hafetz, Frederick P. ..... New York, NY
Hafetz, Lawrence L. ..... Los Angeles, CA
Hafey, Amy B. ..... Los Angeles, CA
Hafey, Matthew J. ..... Los Angeles, CA
Hafey, Robert E. ..... Coronado, CA
Hafey, Susan K. ..... Manassas, VA
Haff, Alicia J. ..... San Antonio, TX
Haff, Eric L. ..... Boise, ID
Haff, Jeffery S. ..... Minneapolis, MN
Haff, Tula Michele ..... Winter Haven, FL
Haffeman, Paul R. ..... Great Falls, MT
Haffenden, Philip E. ..... Findlay, OH
Haffenden, Rebecca A. ..... Chicago, IL
Haffer, Edward A. ..... Concord, NH
Manchester, NH
Haffer, Gloria S. ..... Cincinnati, OH
Hafferman, Stanley J. ..... Anchorage, AK
Hafferty, Carole A. ..... Morristown, NJ
Haffey, Bruce W. ..... Detroit, MI
Haffey, Cynthia J. ..... Detroit, MI
Haffey, David A. ..... Dayton, OH
Haffey, Dennis M. ..... Bloomfield Hills, MI
Haffey, Edward H. ..... Denver, CO
Haffey, Gary William ..... Alma, MI
Haffey, J. Ross, Jr. ..... Cleveland, OH
Haffey, John F. ..... Helena, MT
Haffey, Timothy P. ..... Cleveland, OH
Haffke, Christopher W. ..... Atlanta, GA
Haffke, George R. ..... Fort Morgan, CO
Haffke, Haffke and Lebsack
Fort Morgan, CO
Haffke, Julia B. ..... Atlanta, GA
Haffmans, Marcia B. ..... Minneapolis, MN
Haffner, Alfred L., Jr. ..... New York, NY
Haffner, Allan S. ..... Silver Spring, MD
Haffner, David Jeffrey ..... San Antonio, TX
Haffner, F. Kinsey ..... Palo Alto, CA
Haffner, Greg W. ..... Tacoma, WA
Haffner, James F. ..... St. Louis, MO
Haffner, Joshua H. ..... Los Angeles, CA
Haffner, Karri K. ..... Cincinnati, OH
Haffner, Nancy G. ..... Los Angeles, CA
Haffner, Pamela A. ..... Schenectady, NY
Haffner, Paul F. ..... Cincinnati, OH
Haffner, Robin B. ..... Placerville, CA
Haffner, S. Robert ..... Boca Raton, FL
Haffner, Steve R. ..... Bayside, NY
Haffner, Steven B. ..... Farmington Hills, MI
Haffner, Steven B., & Associates, P.C.
Farmington Hills, MI
Haffner, Timothy J. ..... Fort Wayne, IN
Hafford, Arnold A. ..... Reno, NV
Hafford, Roger W. ..... Fremont, OH
Hafif, Herbert ..... Claremont, CA
Newport Beach, CA
Hafif, Herbert, A Professional Corporation
Claremont, CA
Newport Beach, CA
Hafitz, Michael Robert ..... New York, NY
Hafiz, Ishraq A. ..... Canfield, OH
Hafke, Alfred ..... New Paltz, NY
Haflich, Mark R. ..... Department of Commerce, Office of the General Counsel, GV
Hafling, Marilyn Elizabeth ..... Largo, FL
Hafner, Bruce R. ..... Lynbrook, NY
Hafner, Dyann L. ..... Richland Center, WI
Hafner, Elizabeth Cole ..... Washington, DC
Hafner, Phyliss Ann ..... Buffalo, NY
Hafner, Randell J. ..... Largo, FL
Hafner, Robert H. ..... Glens Falls, NY
Hafner, Robert J. ..... Mount Laurel, NJ
Philadelphia, PA
Hafner, Robert R., III ..... Montgomery, AL
Hafner, Thomas M. ..... Atlanta, GA
Hafner, Troy B. ..... Vero Beach, FL
Hafner, Walter W., Jr. ..... Hannibal, NY
Hafron, Norman L. ..... Chicago, IL
Hafsten, Raymond J., Jr. ..... Indianapolis, IN
Haft, James E. ..... Harrison, OH
Haft, James Frederic ..... New York, NY
Haft, James G. ..... Chicago, IL
Haft, Jay M. ..... New York, NY
Haft, Jonathan D. ..... Beverly Hills, CA
Haft, Larry I. ..... Newtown, PA
Haft, Marilyn G. ..... New York, NY
Haft, Phillip ..... San Francisco, CA
Haft, Richard A., Jr. ..... Torrance, CA
Haft, Robert J. ..... Washington, DC
Haft, Robert M. ..... New York, NY
Haft, Robert Stephen ..... Remsenburg, NY
Haft, Scott ..... Brooklyn, NY
Haft, Stuart J. ..... Palm Beach, FL
Haft, William S. ..... New York, NY
Haftel, Benjamin H. ..... Princeton, NJ
Haftel, Richard E. ..... New York, NY
Hafter, Brian T. ..... San Francisco, CA
Hafter, Jerome C. ..... Greenville, MS
Hafter, Matthew I. ..... Chicago, IL
Haga, D. Stephen, Jr. ..... Christiansburg, VA
Haga, David L. ..... Washington, DC
Haga, David L., Jr. ..... Phoenix, AZ
Haga, Eileen Ann ..... Phoenix, AZ
Haga, Robert ..... Washington, DC
Haga, Thomas H. ..... Flint, MI
Haga, William S. ..... Dunwoody, GA
Hagadone, Ronald R. ..... East Point, GA
Hagadorn, Brett W. ..... Orange, CA
Hagaman, David C. ..... Atlanta, GA
Hagaman, Kenzel D. ..... Foster City, CA
Hagaman, Margot G. ..... San Francisco, CA
Hagaman, Robert R. ..... Naples, FL
Hagaman, Robert R., & Associates, Trial Lawyers & Coun. at Law, Chtd.
Naples, FL
Hagan, Alex J. ..... Raleigh, NC
Hagan, Ann P. ..... Mexico, MO
Hagan, Benjamin, Jr. ..... Sacramento, CA
Hagan & Bolt ..... Hartford, KY
Hagan, Brian F. ..... Fairview Park, OH
Hagan, Cara J. ..... Fullerton, CA
Hagan, Carol Westrich ..... Kansas City, MO
Hagan, Cecelia Allen ..... Louisville, KY
Hagan, Charles A. ..... Hartford, KY
Hagan, Charles C., Jr. ..... Louisville, KY
Hagan, Charles Owen, Jr. ..... Bokeelia, FL
Hagan, Charles T., III ..... Greensboro, NC
Hagan, Charles T., Jr. ..... Greensboro, NC
Hagan, Christina ..... Brooklyn, NY
Hagan, Christine ..... New York, NY
Hagan, Christopher J. ..... Washington, DC
Hagan, Coury & Associates ..... Brooklyn, NY
Hagan, Daniel A. ..... Woodbridge, NJ
Hagan, David L. ..... Grover Beach, CA
Hagan, Deborah ..... Springfield, IL
Hagan, Dianne D. ..... Sarasota, FL
Hagan, Gary C. ..... Hutchinson, KS
Hagan, Gregory ..... Valparaiso, IN
Hagan, Hamlett and Maxwell, L.L.C.
Mexico, MO
Hagan, Harry A. ..... San Francisco, CA
Hagan, Henry J. ..... Stamford, CT
Hagan, Herbert E. ..... New York, NY
Hagan, J. Andrew ..... Orlando, FL
Hagan, J. Scott ..... Louisville, KY
Hagan, James ..... Palo Alto, CA
San Francisco, CA
Hagan, James C. ..... Oklahoma City, OK
Hagan, James J., (P.C.) ..... New York, NY
Hagan, James R. ..... Palo Alto, CA
Hagan, James W. ..... Atlanta, GA
Hagan, James W. ..... Francestown, NH
Hagan, Jennifer J. ..... Palo Alto, CA
Hagan, John F., Jr. ..... Chicago, IL
Hagan, John J. ..... Stamford, CT
Hagan, John J., Esq. ..... Fort Washington, PA
Hagan, John L. ..... Houston, TX
Hagan, John Peter ..... Dallas, TX
Hagan, Joseph C. ..... New York, NY
Hagan, Jude A. ..... Lebanon, KY
Hagan, Julia M. ..... Portland, OR
Hagan, Julia P. ..... Louisville, KY
Hagan, Kay Ruthven ..... Greensboro, NC
Hagan, Kelly T. ..... Portland, OR
Hagan, Kera E. ..... West Palm Beach, FL
Hagan, Kevin F. ..... Port Washington, NY
Hagan, Laura M. ..... Bowling Green, KY
Elizabethtown, KY
Hagan, Linda B. ..... Troy, MI
Hagan, Martin J. ..... Pittsburgh, PA
Hagan, Martin W. ..... San Diego, CA
Hagan, Mary Ann ..... Philadelphia, PA
Hagan, Mary Arena ..... Pittsburgh, PA
Hagan, Mary Patricia ..... Boston, MA
Hagan, Matthew Thomas ..... Houston, TX
Hagan, Michael E. ..... Aiken, SC
Houston, TX
Hagan, Michael J. ..... New York, NY
Hagan, Michele E. ..... San Francisco, CA
Hagan, Patrick J. ..... San Francisco, CA
Hagan, Patrick J. ..... Philadelphia, PA
Hagan, Paula M. ..... Dallas, TX
Hagan, Peter A. ..... New York, NY
Hagan, Peter C. ..... Wichita, KS
Hagan, Robert Aubrey ..... Vienna, VA
Hagan, Robert C. ..... Daleville, VA
Hagan, Ronald S. ..... Metairie, LA
Hagan, Rose A. ..... Austin, TX
Hagan, Saca & Hagan, Law Corporation
Palo Alto, CA
San Francisco, CA
Hagan, Sally Ann ..... Albuquerque, NM
Hagan, Samuel J., IV ..... Fort Myers, FL
Hagan, Samuel L. ..... Brooklyn, NY
Hagan, Sheila B. ..... Dakota Dunes, SD
Hagan, Stephanie Frangos ..... Short Hills, NJ
Hagan, Timothy G. ..... Mount Clemens, MI
Hagan, Timothy G., P.C., Law Office of
Detroit, MI
Mount Clemens, MI
Hagan, Timothy M. ..... Houston, TX
Hagan, Timothy W. ..... Dayton, OH
Hagan, W. Carr, Jr. ..... Kingsport, TN
Hagan, William A., Jr. ..... Manhasset, NY
Hagan, William F., Jr. ..... Hernando, MS
Hagan, William H. ..... Needham, MA
Hagan, William J. ..... Bethel, CT
Hagan, William L., III ..... Collierville, TN
Hagani, James A. ..... Tenafly, NJ
Hagans, Ahearn, McLaughlin & Webb
Anchorage, AK
Hagans & Bobb, A Professional Corporation
Houston, TX
Hagans, Charles ..... Anchorage, AK

Hagans, Donald F., II ... El Paso, TX
Hagans, Mark D. ... Archbold, OH
Hagans, Max V. ... Sterling, IL
Hagans, Samuel L., Jr. ... Dayton, OH
Hagans, William Fred ... Houston, TX
Hagar & Cotten ... Vista, CA
Hagar, James L. ... Vista, CA
Hagar, Kelby D. ... Dallas, TX
Hagar, Larry H. ... Nashville, TN
Hagar, Margret MacGaffey Philadelphia, PA
Hagar, Richard L. ... Minot, ND
Hagar, William S. ... Las Vegas, NV
Hagarman, Ronald J. ... Gettysburg, PA McSherrystown, PA
Hagarty, James P. ... Montesano, WA
Hagarty, Lois Sherman ... Harrisburg, PA Philadelphia, PA
Hagarty, Mark ... San Diego, CA
Hagarty, Thomas J. ... West Hartford, CT
Hagarty, Thomas J., Jr. ... Hartford, CT
Hagauer, Ronald William ... San Antonio, TX
Hagberg, Harold G. ... Merrillville, IN
Hagberg, Peter N. ... Oakland, CA
Hagberg, Steven V. ... Minneapolis, MN
Hagberg, Viola Wilgus Department of Defense, Defense Legal Services Agency, GV
Hagburg, Michael ... Bismarck, ND
Hage, Gloria A. ... Ann Arbor, MI
Hage and Hobaica LLP ... Utica, NY
Hage, James D. ... Upper Marlboro, MD
Hage, James J. ... Utica, NY
Hage, Jamie N. ... Manchester, NH
Hage, Jeffrey A. ... Dallas, TX
Hage, Joseph K., III ... Washington, DC Utica, NY
Hage, Michael J. ... Arlington, VA
Hage, Susan Haddad ... Manchester, NH
Hage, Tristam O. ... Minneapolis, MN
Hagedorn, Brenda J. ... Kingston, NY
Hagedorn, Frank M. ... Tulsa, OK
Hagedorn, James C. ... Sacramento, CA
Hagedorn, James C., Inc. Sacramento, CA
Hagedorn, Jeffrey W. ... Indianapolis, IN
Hagedorn, Jennifer G. ... San Francisco, CA
Hagedorn, Michael ... St. Paul, MN
Hagedorn, Michael H. ... Tell City, IN
Hagedorn, Patricia K., (Mrs.) Lexington, MA
Hagedorn, Richard B. ... Salem, OR
Hagedorn, Robert B. ... San Francisco, CA
Hagedorn, William D. ... Washington, DC
Hagedorn, William G. ... Vancouver, WA
Hagee, Robert Joseph ... Martinsville, IN
Hagee, Talmadge M. ... Long Beach, CA
Hagefstration, John E., Jr. Birmingham, AL
Hagel, Bruce J. ... Sacramento, CA
Hagel & Coulter ... Seal Beach, CA
Hagel, Gali L., P.C. ... Atlanta, GA
Hagel, Harry ... Cromwell, CT
Hagel, James A. ... Seal Beach, CA
Hagel, Lawrence B. ... Washington, DC
Hagel, Vicki A. ... Philadelphia, PA
Hagelberg, Frank S. ... Buffalo, NY Rochester, NY
Hagelberg, Michael T. ... Rochester, NY
Hagele, F. John ... Philadelphia, PA
Hagele, Michael J. ... Palo Alto, CA
Hagelgans, James D. ... Lancaster, PA
Hagelin, John H. ... Brooklyn, NY
Hagelin, Michael T., Law Offices of Buffalo, NY
Hagelshaw, R. Lee ... San Francisco, CA
Hagelstein, Marie ... Berkeley, CA
Hagelthorn, Erik R. ... Troy, MI
Hageman, A. Joe ... Laramie, WY
Hageman, Alice L. ... Boston, MA
Hageman, Andrew F. ... Madison, NJ
Hageman, Christopher W. Coto De Caza, CA
Hageman, Cynthia L. ... Dallas, TX
Hageman, E. Charles ... Stockton, KS
Hageman, Edward C. ... Stockton, KS
Hageman, Edward C., P.A. ... Stockton, KS
Hageman, Eric William ... Minneapolis, MN
Hageman, Hans E. ... United States Senate, Committee Legal Personnel, GV
Hageman, Hilary Lee Department of Defense, Defense Legal Services Agency, GV
Hageman, John A. ... Miami, FL
Hageman, Mark R. ... Scarsdale, NY
Hageman, Paul H. K., & Associates, Ltd. Rolling Meadows, IL
Hageman, Paul Henry Kivett Rolling Meadows, IL
Hageman, Peggy K. ... Wilmington, DE
Hagemann, Andrew E., Jr. ... Worthington, MN
Hagemann, Cheryl L. ... Wichita, KS Houston, TX
Hagemann, Don L. ... Waverly, IA
Hagemann, Goeke, Egli & Thalacker Waverly, IA
Hagemann, Heather Scheel ... Denver, CO
Hagemann, Jody L. ... Austin, TX
Hagemann, John F. ... Vermillion, SD
Hagemann, Leroy J. ... Wisconsin Rapids, WI
Hagemann, Thomas A. ... Houston, TX
Hagemeier, Frederick W. ... Union, NJ
Hagemeier, Luisa K. ... New York, NY
Hagemeier, Malaine P. ... St. Charles, MO
Hagemeier, Mark Arnold ... Little Rock, AR
Hagemeister, C. Steve ... Irvine, CA
Hagemeister, Daniel R. ... Norfolk, VA
Hagemeister, Mark W. ... St. Louis, MO
Hagemeyer, David R. ... Boston, MA
Hagemeyer, J. Lyndal ... Lakeside, OH
Hagemeyer, Michael A. ... Long Beach, CA
Hagemeyer, Norman P. ... Memphis, TN
Hagemier, Allen & Smith ... Indianapolis, IN
Hagemier, Robert C. ... Indianapolis, IN
Hagen, Amy C. ... Los Angeles, CA
Hagen, Andrea D. ... Treasury Department, United States Secret Service, GV
Hagen, Bohm, Boyle & Jones, P.C. Phoenix, AZ
Hagen, Catherine Burcham Los Angeles, CA Newport Beach, CA
Hagen, Cathryn C. ... Portland, OR
Hagen, Cheryl A. ... Racine, WI
Hagen, Christopher D. ... Des Moines, IA
Hagen, Christopher H. ... San Diego, CA
Hagen, Dale B. ... Des Moines, IA
Hagen, Dale W. ... Sarasota, FL
Hagen, Daniel C. ... Cleveland, OH
Hagen, David A. ... Coral Gables, FL
Hagen, David R. ... Woodland Hills, CA
Hagen, David S. ... Encino, CA
Hagen, David W. ... Reno, NV
Hagen, Donald J. ... Bothell, WA
Hagen, Douglas D. ... Portland, OR
Hagen, Dye, Hirschy & DiLorenzo, P.C. Portland, OR Salem, OR Vancouver, WA
Hagen, Earl A. ... Milwaukee, WI
Hagen, Earle ... Encino, CA
Hagen, Edward I., Jr. ... Eugene, OR
Hagen, Eric W. ... Los Angeles, CA
Hagen, Glenn W. ... Highlands Ranch, CO
Hagen, Glenn W., P.C. Highlands Ranch, CO
Hagen, Gregory D. ... San Diego, CA
Hagen, Gregory S. ... Fort Myers, FL
Hagen, H. Richard ... Chicago, IL
Hagen & Hagen ... Encino, CA
Hagen & Hagen ... Albion, IN
Hagen, Harold Allen ... San Francisco, CA
Hagen, Henry C. ... Springfield, IL
Hagen, Holly L. ... Treasury Department, Internal Revenue Service, GV
Hagen, Howard O. ... Des Moines, IA
Hagen, James C. N. ... Shingle Springs, CA
Hagen, Jeffrey J ... Encino, CA
Hagen, Jeffrey J. ... Buffalo, NY
Hagen, Jessica J-M ... Macon, GA
Hagen, Jo Anne ... Loveland, CO
Hagen, Joanne Petrone ... Loveland, CO
Hagen, Joel T. ... Sioux Falls, SD
Hagen, Joseph T. ... Portland, OR
Hagen, Katherine ... Washington, DC
Hagen, Kathleen Marie ... Kansas City, MO
Hagen, Kathleen R. ... Minneapolis, MN
Hagen, Laura J. ... Chicago, IL
Hagen, Lee, Law Office, Ltd. ... Fargo, ND
Hagen, Leland F. ... Fargo, ND
Hagen, Leon L. ... Salem, OR
Hagen, Leonard A. ... Eugene, OR
Hagen, Marie Louise ... Department of Justice, Civil Division, GV
Hagen, Mary S. ... Minneapolis, MN
Hagen, Max M. ... Hollywood, FL
Hagen, Max M., P.A. ... Hollywood, FL
Hagen, Melissa A. ... Lansing, MI
Hagen, Melissa L. ... Middletown, OH
Hagen, Michael S. ... Fort Myers, FL
Hagen, Paul E. ... Washington, DC
Hagen, Paulette Bea ... Anchorage, AK
Hagen, Randall L. ... Baltimore, MD
Hagen, Raymond M. ... Beulah, ND
Hagen, Richard A. ... Edgartown, MA
Hagen, Robert W. ... Somerset, KY
Hagen, Rodger A. ... Minneapolis, MN
Hagen, Rolf G. ... Minneapolis, MN
Hagen, Scott A. ... Salt Lake City, UT
Hagen, Stephan M. ... Greenville, NC
Hagen, Stephen A. ... Littleton, CO
Hagen, Stephen E. ... Palo Alto, CA
Hagen, Steven C. ... Albion, IN Ligonier, IN
Hagen, Steven H. ... Miami, FL
Hagen, Terry E. ... Forest City, IA
Hagen, Theresa L. ... Columbus, OH
Hagen, Theresa R. ... Baton Rouge, LA
Hagen, Thomas Kristian ... Waseca, MN
Hagen, Tom J. ... Phoenix, AZ
Hagen, Wayne D., Jr. ... Aberdeen, WA
Hagen, Wilka & Archer, P.C. Sioux Falls, SD
Hagen, William C. ... Columbus, MT
Hagen, William G. ... Sun City, CA
Hagen, Willis W. ... Milwaukee, WI
Hagenah, Henry A. ... Lenox, MA
Hagenah, Jeffrey A. ... Redwood City, CA
Hagenah, Patricia M. ... Independence, MO
Hagenau, Wendy L. ... Atlanta, GA
Hagenbaugh & Murphy ... Glendale, CA Orange, CA San Bernardino, CA
Hagenbuch, Clifton L., Jr. San Clemente, CA
Hagenbuch, Kathryn L. ... St. Johns, MI
Hagenbuch, Lili A. ... Danville, PA
Hagenbuch, William P., Jr. Scottsville, KY
Hagenbush, Christopher L. ... Atlanta, GA
Hagendorf, Stanley ... St. Petersburg, FL New York, NY
Hagendorf, Wayne A. ... Los Angeles, CA
Hagendorn, William H. ... New York, NY
Hagener, Maria N. ... Hoffman Estates, IL
Hagenow, Christopher C. Indianapolis, IN
Hagenow, Laura C. ... Indianapolis, IN
Hagens Berman ... Seattle, WA
Hagens Berman & Mitchell, P.L.L.C. Phoenix, AZ
Hagens, Carl H. ... Seattle, WA
Hagens, David G. ... Grand Rapids, MI
Hagenswold, H. Eric ... Dallas, TX
Hagen-Tucker, Emily M. ... St. Louis, MO
Hager, Andrew J. ... Pontiac, MI
Hager, Andrew J., Jr. ... Mount Vernon, MO
Hager, Ashley Z. ... Atlanta, GA
Hager, Auborn L., III ... Nashville, TN
Hager, Barbara G. ... New London, CT
Hager, Barry E. ... San Diego, CA
Hager, Benjamin M. ... New York, NY
Hager, Brett M. ... Flagstaff, AZ
Hager, C. Eric ... Department Of The Interior, Minerals Management Service, GV
Hager, Charles C. ... Trenton, NJ
Hager, Charles R. ... New York, NY
Hager, Christopher W. ... Woodbridge, NJ
Hager, Don ... Oklahoma City, OK
Hager, Donald ... Larimore, ND
Hager, Douglas Allen ... Topeka, KS
Hager, Douglas E. ... Gibson City, IL
Hager & Dowling, Professional Corporation Santa Barbara, CA
Hager, Earl ... Buckhannon, WV
Hager & Ennis ... Tacoma, WA
Hager, Eric L. ... San Diego, CA
Hager, Eric W. ... New York, NY
Hager, Gabrielle ... Beverly, MA
Hager, George W., Jr. ... Fairfax, VA
Hager, Harold ... Grand Forks, ND
Hager, Harry L. ... Huntington, WV
Hager & Heilman ... Huntington, WV
Hager, Henry G. ... Philadelphia, PA
Hager, Hilary Anne ... San Diego, CA
Hager, James M. ... San Jose, CA
Hager, Jennifer M. ... Northbrook, IL
Hager, Jeremy I. ... New York, NY
Hager, Jerry A. ... Irvine, CA
Hager, Jerry John, Jr. Oklahoma City, OK
Hager, John F. ... Green Bay, WI
Hager, John S. ... Owensboro, KY
Hager, John V. ... Santa Barbara, CA
Hager, Jonathan F. ... Boulder, CO
Hager, Julie-Ann ... Austin, TX
Hager, Julie-Ann, A Prof. Legal Assn., Law Offices of ... Austin, TX
Hager, Karen Halpern ... Hartford, CT
Hager, Kenneth W. ... Minneapolis, MN
Hager, Kimberly L. ... Birmingham, AL
Hager, Lawrence ... Southbury, CT
Hager, Mark E. ... Brandon, FL
Hager, Mark M. ... Washington, DC
Hager, Marvin M. ... Bismarck, ND
Hager, Mary ... Houston, TX
Hager, Mary Marvin ... Minneapolis, MN
Hager, Melissa A. ... New York, NY
Hager, Melissa E. ... Trenton, NJ
Hager, Michael E. ... Boston, MA
Hager, Orval O. ... Portland, OR
Hager, Paul R. ... Fresno, CA
Hager, Phillip T. ... Metairie, LA
Hager, Phillip T., A Professional Law Corporation ... Metairie, LA
Hager, Rachel R. ... Short Hills, NJ
Hager, Richard B. ... Sanford, NC
Hager, Richard B., P.A. ... Sanford, NC
Hager, Rita Merino ... Niagara Falls, NY
Hager, Robert A. ... Washington, DC
Hager, Robert A. ... Cleveland, OH
Hager, Robert E. ... Dallas, TX
Hager, Robert R. ... Reno, NV
Hager, Robert R., Law Offices of ... Reno, NV
Hager, Roger W. ... Johnstown, PA
Hager, Ronald B. ... Carmel, CA
Hager, Ronald M. ... Buffalo, NY
Hager, Sarina Drago ... Richardson, TX
Hager, Sharon K. ... Louisville, KY
Hager, Stephanie Lynn Department of Commerce, GV
Hager, Steven R. ... Bellingham, WA
Hager, Susan Y. ... Portland, OR
Hager, Tamsin J ... Buffalo, NY
Hager, Trippel, Macy & Jensen ... Fresno, CA
Hager, Virginia R. ... Wilmington, NC
Hager, Wallace B. ... Tacoma, WA
Hager, William D. ... Boca Raton, FL
Hager, William D. ... Lexington, VA
Hager, William E., III ... New Bethlehem, PA
Hagerdon, J. Mikeal ... Shawnee, KS
Hagerman, Audrey Sander ... Bristol, NH
Hagerman, Brenda West ... Larned, KS
Hagerman, C. David ... Catlettsburg, KY
Hagerman, Douglas M. ... Chicago, IL
Hagerman, Gary N. ... Honokaa, HI
Hagerman, John D. ... Spring, TX
Hagerman, Michael C. ... Franklin, MA
Hagerman, Nathan J. ... Detroit, MI
Hagerott, Edward C., Jr. ... Los Angeles, CA
Hagerstrand, Eric C. ... Cincinnati, OH
Hagerty & Brady ... Buffalo, NY
Hagerty, Dennis W. ... Southfield, MI
Hagerty, Duane P. ... Des Moines, IA
Hagerty, Edward S. ... Minneapolis, MN
Hagerty, Eileen M. ... Boston, MA
Hagerty, Gail ... Bismarck, ND
Hagerty, George E. ... New York, NY
Hagerty, Jack ... Chicago, IL
Hagerty, James J. ... Buffalo, NY
Hagerty, James R. ... Washington, DC
Hagerty, John B. ... Charleston, SC
Hagerty, Johnson, Albrightson & Beitz, P.A. Minneapolis, MN
Hagerty, Kim ... Traverse City, MI
Hagerty, Lawrence V. ... San Rafael, CA
Hagerty, Marcie A. ... Lincoln, NE
Hagerty, Michael C. ... Minneapolis, MN
Hagerty, Pat ... Pasadena, TX
Hagerty, Patrick J. ... North Little Rock, AR **St. Louis, MO**
Hagerty, Peter R. ... Cleveland, OH
Hagerty, Richard D. ... Yankton, SD
Hagerty, Richard E. ... Rockville, MD
Hagerty, Robert J. ... Mount Laurel, NJ
Hagerty, Shawn D. ... San Diego, CA
Hagerty, Sheila M. ... Cedar Knolls, NJ
Hagerty, Susan M. ... Cranbury, NJ
Hagerty, Thomas G. ... Washington, DC
Hagerty, Thomas V. ... Buffalo, NY
Hagerty, Timothy J. ... Louisville, KY
Hagerup, Eric ... Los Angeles, CA
Hagerup, Stefan A. ... Washington, DC
Hages, Lew J. ... Vienna, VA
HagEstad, G. Patrick ... Missoula, MT
Hagewood, Karen A. ... Pleasanton, CA
Hagey, John W. ... Fairbanks, AK
Hagey, Kristi L. ... Pendleton, OR
Hagg, Brian D. ... Rapid City, SD
Hagg, Kent R. ... Rapid City, SD
Hagg, Rexford A. ... Rapid City, SD
Hagg, Thomas D. ... Weirton, WV
Haggar, Philippa M. ... New York, NY
Haggard, Alan H. ... Cupertino, CA
Haggard, Albert L. ... Temple, TX
Haggard, Carl ... Houston, TX
Haggard, Cora Nell ... Marianna, FL
Haggard, Cora Nell, Law Offices of Marianna, FL
Haggard, Guy S. ... Orlando, FL
Haggard, H. Patrick ... Athens, GA
Haggard, J.M., P.C. ... Huntsville, TX
Haggard, Jerry L. ... Phoenix, AZ
Haggard, J. M. ... Huntsville, TX
Haggard, Joel E. ... Seattle, WA
Haggard, Jolene M. ... Lynn, MA
Haggard, Katherine A. ... Overland Park, KS
Haggard, Kenneth, & Associates Hopkinsville, KY
Haggard, Loretta K. ... St. Louis, MO
Haggard, Mark L. ... Los Angeles, CA
Haggard, Michael Andrew ... Miami, FL
Haggard, Michael L. ... Birmingham, AL
Haggard, Parks & Stone, P.A. Coral Gables, FL Fort Lauderdale, FL Miami, FL
Haggard, Phillip J. ... Durant, OK
Haggard, Robert H. ... Hendersonville, NC
Haggard, Robert M. ... Miami, FL
Haggard, Thomas D. ... Lynn, MA
Haggard, Thomas Ross ... Columbia, SC
Haggard, Tim D. ... Dallas, TX
Haggard, Wm. Andrew ... Miami, FL
Haggart, Richard G. ... Anchorage, AK
Haggart, Richard J. ... St. Paul, NE
Haggart, V. James ... Fort Myers, FL
Haggart, W. Todd ... Fargo, ND
Haggas, Stephen W. ... New York Mills, NY
Hagge, Christopher S. ... Dallas, TX
Hagge, Marty A. ... Anamosa, IA
Haggenjos, Michael S. ... Port Washington, WI
Haggenmiller, Joseph Jon ... Marquette, MI
Haggerty, Ancer L. ... Portland, OR
Haggerty, Barbara ... Chicago, IL
Haggerty, Bernard P. ... Laramie, WY
Haggerty, Brian ... Newport, OR
Haggerty, Colleen ... Wyndmoor, PA
Haggerty, Daniel D. ... Cherry Hill, NJ
Haggerty, Daniel L., III ... Princeton, NJ
Haggerty, Dennis E. ... Drexel Hill, PA
Haggerty, Don M. ... Durant, OK
Haggerty, Donohue & Monaghan, A Professional Association ... Summit, NJ
Haggerty, Edwin R. ... Basking Ridge, NJ
Haggerty, George J. ... Garden City, NY
Haggerty, Haggerty & Maschmeyer Indianapolis, IN
Haggerty, James A., Jr. ... Birmingham, AL
Haggerty, James C. ... Summit, NJ
Haggerty, James C. ... Philadelphia, PA
Haggerty, James E. ... Bloomfield Hills, MI
Haggerty, James J. ... Scranton, PA
Haggerty, James J. ... Wilkes-Barre, PA
Haggerty, James P. ... Mineola, NY
Haggerty, James R. ... Pittsburgh, PA
Haggerty, Jay B. ... Indianapolis, IN
Haggerty, Jay J. ... Indianapolis, IN
Haggerty, John J. ... Philadelphia, PA
Haggerty, John J., III ... Fort Collins, CO
Haggerty, John J., III ... Morristown, NJ
Haggerty, John R. ... Bedminster, NJ
Haggerty, John T. ... Boston, MA
Haggerty, Jon. F. ... Indianapolis, IN
Haggerty, Joseph K. ... Des Moines, IA
Haggerty, Joseph M. ... Boston, MA
Haggerty, Joseph O., Jr. ... Scranton, PA
Haggerty, Judson F. ... Indianapolis, IN
Haggerty, Kathleen A. ... Department of Justice, Justice Management Division, GV
Haggerty, Kathleen M. ... Chicago, IL
Haggerty, Koenig & Hill, Chtd. ... Chicago, IL
Haggerty, Margaret E. ... Sussex, WI
Haggerty, Matthew E. ... Scranton, PA
Haggerty, McDonnell and O'Brien Scranton, PA
Haggerty, Michael ... Chicago, IL
Haggerty, Michael J. ... Southfield, MI
Haggerty, Michael Patrick ... Dallas, TX

Haggerty, Michel P. ... Poughkeepsie, NY
Rhinebeck, NY
Haggerty, Mildred F. ... Chicago, IL
Haggerty, Nancy Leary ... Milwaukee, WI
Haggerty, Patrick F. ... Cleveland, OH
Haggerty, Peter J. ... Fairfax, VA
Haggerty, Philip M. ... Phoenix, AZ
Haggerty, Richard J. ... Dallas, TX
Haggerty, Robert B. ... Woodbridge, NJ
Haggerty, Robert H. ... New York, NY
Haggerty, Robert J. ... Windham, CT
Haggerty, Robert J. ... Washington, DC
Haggerty, Ronald W. ... Houston, TX
Haggerty, Rose Ann ... Summit, NJ
Haggerty, S. Jane ... Salem, MA
Haggerty, Terrence E. ... Detroit, MI
Haggerty, Thomas J. ... Washington, DC
Haggerty, Thomas J. ... Summit, NJ
Haggerty, Thomas M., Jr. ... Skillman, NJ
Haggerty, Timothy E. ... Wall Township, NJ
Haggerty & Urbanski ... Wilkes-Barre, PA
Haggerty, Virginia Brady ... Orlando, FL
Haggerty, Walter E. ... Cincinnati, OH
Haggerty, William C. ... Long Beach, CA
Haggerty, William E. ... Lancaster, PA
Haggerty, William F. ... Lansing, MI
Haggerty, William T. ... Newton, NJ
Haggerty-Foster, Jacqueline ... Salem, OR
Haggestad, Troy E. ... Rockford, IL
Haggin, Mary Estes ... Lexington, KY
Haggins, Edward T. ... Cleveland, OH
Haggitt, John R. ... Clearwater, FL
Hagglund, Clarance E. ... Minneapolis, MN
Hagglund, Clemens ... St. Petersburg, FL
Hagglund, Paul H. ... Tampa, FL
Hagglund, Weimer & Speidel
Minneapolis, MN
Haggstrom, Leslie J. ... Angelica, NY
Haghighi, Dawn L. ... Chicago, IL
Hagie, Leslie E. ... Roanoke, VA
Hagigh, Sara E. ... Baltimore, MD
Hagihara, Yasuhiro ... Los Angeles, CA
Hagin, C. Terry ... Abilene, TX
Hagin, T. Richard ... Bushnell, FL
Hagino, David M. ... Honolulu, HI
Hagins, John A., Jr. ... Greenville, SC
Hagle & Boyle, P.C. ... Dallas, TX
Grand Prairie, TX
Hagle, Diana Woodward ... Sacramento, CA
Hagle, Frank H., Jr. ... Grand Prairie, TX
Hagle, George H. ... Washington, DC
Hagle, James J. ... Urbana, IL
Hagle, Jennifer C. ... Los Angeles, CA
Hagle, Paige ... Houston, TX
Hagle, Timothy M. ... Iowa City, IA
Hagler, Andrew S. ... New York, NY
Hagler, Brooks H. ... Abilene, TX
Hagler, Debra K. ... Truckee, CA
Hagler, Donald B. ... San Marino, CA
Hagler, Gould B. ... Augusta, GA
Hagler, Hyles, Adams & Hix ... Columbus, GA
Hagler, J. Eric ... Bentonville, AR
Hagler, James M. ... Chicago, IL
Hagler, James T. ... Newport Beach, CA
Hagler, John B., Jr. ... Cleveland, TN
Hagler, John H. ... Dallas, TX
Hagler, Joseph W. ... Liberty Lake, WA
Hagler, Kenneth D. ... St. Augustine, FL
Hagler, Kenneth D., P.A. ... St. Augustine, FL
Hagler, Marian M. ... Treasury Department,
Office of the General Counsel, GV
Hagler, Mendel R. ... New York, NY
Hagler, Michael B., (P.C.) ... Augusta, GA
Hagler & Nelson ... Vacaville, CA
Hagler, O. Maynard ... Houston, TX
Hagler, Richard C. ... Columbus, GA
Hagler, Robert A. ... Xenia, OH
Hagler, Robert C., (P.C.) ... Augusta, GA
Hagler, Stanley ... Denver, CO
Hagler, Thomas M. ... Vacaville, CA
Hagler-Gray, Terrie V. ... Garner, NC
Hagley, Judith A.
Federal Labor Relations Authority,
Office of the Solicitor, GV
Hagley, Terence R. ... Chillicothe, OH
Haglin, Cynthia J. ... Chandler, AZ
Haglof, Ronald E. ... St. Louis, MO
Haglund, Alexander L. ... Sterling, IL
Haglund, Benjamin E. ... Morristown, NJ
New York, NY
Haglund, Bruce H. ... Irvine, CA
Haglund, David R. ... Treasury Department,
Internal Revenue Service, GV
Haglund, Deborah Bahn ... Dallas, TX
Haglund and Gretler ... Sterling, IL
Haglund, Heather A. ... Clinton, NY
Haglund, Jacqueline O'Neil ... Tulsa, OK
Haglund, Karen Jan ... Memphis, TN
Haglund, Kirtley, Kelley & Horngren LLP
Portland, OR
Haglund, LeRoy E. ... Wayzata, MN
Haglund, Michael E. ... Portland, OR
Haglund, Norman D. ... Denver, CO
Haglund, Terence G. ... Williamsburg, VA
Haglund, Victor E. ... Everett, WA
Haglund, Wayne D. ... Lufkin, TX
Hagmaier, Jason K. ... Mobile, AL
Hagman, Keith H. ... Cape Coral, FL
Hagmann, David L. ... Orinda, CA
Hagnell, Karen ... Chicago, IL
Hagner, Faye E. ... Orange, CA
Hagner, John D. ... Washington, DC
Hagner, Joseph C. ... Stamford, CT
Hagner, Thomas J. ... Cherry Hill, NJ
Hagness, Robert ... Mondovi, WI
Hagney, James F. ... Hauppauge, NY
Hagny, Matthew Philip ... Salina, KS
Hagood, Ben A., Jr. ... Charleston, SC
Hagood, Daniel K. ... Dallas, TX
Hagood, Elisabeth J. ... Orlando, FL
Hagood, Elisabeth J., P.A. ... Orlando, FL
Hagood, Gene S. ... Alvin, TX
Hagood, George B. ... Savannah, GA
Hagood, George T. ... Charlotte, NC
Hagood, H. Brewton ... Charleston, SC
Hagood, James M. ... Lakewood, CO
Hagood, Jamie R. ... Knoxville, TN
Hagood, Jennifer M. ... Eufaula, AL
Hagood, John P. ... Eufaula, AL
Hagood, Joseph Herrin, III ... Selma, AL
Hagood, L. Jeffrey ... Knoxville, TN
Hagood, Lewis R. ... Knoxville, TN
Hagood & Neumann, L.L.P. ... Alvin, TX
Hagood, Peter P. ... Fort Lauderdale, FL
Hagood, R. J., Jr. ... Denison, TX
Hagood, Tarpy & Cox, PLLC
Knoxville, TN
Hagood, William M., III ... Greenville, SC
Hagoort, Nicholas H., Jr.
Boynton Beach, FL
Hagoort, Nicholas H., Jr., P.A.
Boynton Beach, FL
Hagoort, Thomas H. ... New York, NY
Hagopian, Catia C. ... Riverside, CA
Hagopian, David G. ... Irvine, CA
Hagopian, Gary ... Cincinnati, OH
Hagopian, Gregory Scott ... Bradenton, FL
Hagopian & Hagopian ... Providence, RI
Hagopian, Harry H. ... Granite City, IL
Hagopian, Jacob ... Providence, RI
Hagopian, Jon G. ... Providence, RI
Hagopian, Mark A. ... San Francisco, CA
Hagopian, Mark J. ... Providence, RI
Hagopian, Melanie ... Boston, MA
Hagopian, Michael R. ... Cranston, RI
Hagopian, Robert W. ... Bedford, MA
Hagopian, Sharon F. Dunkin
Winter Park, FL
Hagopian, Suzanne L. ... Madison, WI
Hagopian, Tara A. ... Media, PA
Hagquist, Drew ... Minneapolis, MN
Hagquist, Nancy ... Austin, TX
Hagstette, Eric S. ... Houston, TX
Hagstrom, Anne Cagwin ... Augusta, ME
Hagstrom, David D. ... Poughkeepsie, NY
Hagstrom, Dennis W. ... Fergus Falls, MN
Hagström, Earl L. ... San Francisco, CA
Hagstrom, Gary M. ... Minneapolis, MN
Hagstrom, James A. ... Chicago, IL
Hagstrom, Michael C. ... Mattapoisett, MA
Hagstrom, Richard M. ... Minneapolis, MN
Hagstrom, Ronald G. ... Oak Park, IL
Hague, Charles G. ... Jefferson, OH
Hague, David Charles ... Charleston, WV
Hague, Douglas I. ... Rochester, NY
Hague, Douglas T. ... Newark, NJ
Hague, Eugene T., Jr. ... Parkersburg, WV
Hague, Gregg R. ... Chicago, IL
Hague, Henry R. ... Oceanside, CA
Hague, John H. ... Wayne, NJ
Hague, Margaret Gallagher
Kansas City, MO
Hague, Merrilee C. ... Foster City, CA
Hague, Michael B. ... Coeur d'Alene, ID
Hague, P. Christian ... Pittsburgh, PA
Hague, Paige Stover ... Brockton, MA
Hague, Richard E. ... Franklin, MI
Hague & Simon ... Ashtabula, OH
Hague, Wendy Marie ... Coeur d'Alene, ID
Hague, William F., Jr. ... Johnston, RI
Haguel, Steven H. ... Miami, FL
Haguel, Steven H., P.A. ... Miami, FL
Haguewood, Steven A. ... Newport Beach, CA
Hagwood, L. Carl ... Greenville, MS
Hagy, Colleen Tate ... Martinsville, VA
Hagy, David S. ... Atlanta, GA
Hagy, James C. ... Chicago, IL
Hagy, John, Jr. ... San Antonio, TX
Hagy, Sarah Elizabeth ... Houston, TX
Hah, Mimi K. ... New York, NY
Hahalis & Kounoupis, P.C.
Collingswood, NJ
Bethlehem, PA
Philadelphia, PA
Hahami, Asaf ... Washington, DC
Hahamovitch, Donald E. ... Lauderhill, FL
Hahesy, William C., Sr. ... Tulare, CA
Hahl, James G. ... Ormond Beach, FL
Hahl, Robert W. ... Arlington, VA
Hahm, Eugene L. ... Palo Alto, CA
Hahm, Jeannette ... Los Angeles, CA
Hahm, Kevin K. ... Washington, DC
Hahm, Robert K. ... Berwyn, PA
Hahn, A. Robert, Jr. ... Anchorage, AK
Hahn, Adrienne R. ... Torrance, CA
Hahn, Andrew T. ... New York, NY
Hahn, Arthur W. ... Chicago, IL
Hahn, Ava M. ... Palo Alto, CA
Hahn, B. Scott ... Alliance, OH
Hahn, Benjamin M. ... Poquoson, VA
Hahn, Beth J. ... Irvine, CA
Hahn & Bolson, LLP ... Los Angeles, CA
Hahn, Bradley L. ... Mesa, AZ
Hahn, Bradley S. ... Sun City, AZ
Sun City West, AZ
Hahn, Brian A. ... San Francisco, CA
Hahn, Bruce E. ... Kansas City, MO
Hahn, Buddie J. ... Orange, TX
Hahn & Burnett ... San Diego, CA
Hahn, C. Alexander ... Boston, MA
Hahn, Carl G. ... Jamison, PA
Hahn, Carol W. ... McLean, VA
Hahn, Caroline H. ... New York, NY
Hahn, Charles B. ... Greensboro, NC
Hahn, Charles D. ... Auburn, NE
Hahn, Charles J. ... Buffalo, NY
Hahn, Charles L. ... Warren, MI
Hahn, Charles W. ... Joliet, IL
Hahn, Chihoe ... Santa Clara, CA
Hahn, Christopher E. ... Santa Barbara, CA
Hahn, Christopher H. ... Austin, TX
Hahn, Clayton R. ... Milwaukee, WI
Hahn, Cynthia A. ... Boston, MA
Hahn, Cynthia M. ... Towson, MD
Hahn, Dale A. ... Redwood City, CA
Hahn, David ... Laurel, MD
Hahn, David A. ... San Diego, CA
Hahn, David G. ... Closter, NJ
Hahn, David H. ... Lincoln, NE
Hahn, David J. ... Denver, CO
Hahn, Deborah L. Weston ... Lincoln, NE
Hahn, Derrick J. ... Lincoln, NE
Hahn, Don ... Bellefonte, PA
Hahn, Donald J., Jr. ... Dallas, TX
Hahn, Dorothy Kuhns ... Edwardsville, IL
Hahn, Douglas C. ... Dayton, OH
Hahn, Douglas D. ... Appleton, WI
Hahn, Edmund J. ... Williston Park, NY
Hahn, Eduard J. ... Fairfield, NJ
Hahn, Edward J. ... New York, NY
Hahn, Edward L. ... Manchester, NH
Hahn, Elaine C. ... Palo Alto, CA
Hahn, Elliott J. ... Los Angeles, CA
Hahn, Erich ... Wichita, KS
Hahn, Ermina ... Newark, NJ
Hahn, Eva ... Chicago, IL
Hahn, Ford & Hundertmark
Williston Park, NY
Hahn, Frank E., Jr. ... Philadelphia, PA
Hahn, Fred Joseph ... Idaho Falls, ID
Hahn, Frederic L. ... Chicago, IL
Hahn, Frederick H., V ... Anchorage, AK
Hahn, Frederick J. ... Gunnison, CO
Hahn, Frederick J., III ... Idaho Falls, ID
Hahn, Fredrick W. ... Springfield, IL
Hahn, Gary L., P.C. ... Ann Arbor, MI
Hahn, George A. ... New York, NY
Hahn, Gerald M. ... Bellevue, WA
Hahn, Gilbert, Jr. ... Washington, DC
Hahn, Glenda F. ... Omaha, NE
Hahn, Gregory F. ... Indianapolis, IN
Hahn, Gus W. ... San Antonio, TX
Hahn, H. Blair ... Charleston, SC
Hahn & Hahn ... Los Angeles, CA
Pasadena, CA
Hahn and Hahn Lawyers, P.A.
Phillipsburg, KS
Hahn & Hessen LLP ... New York, NY
Hahn, Howard Fredrick ... Omaha, NE
Hahn, J. Victor ... Columbus, OH
Hahn, James H. ... Denver, CO
Hahn, James H. ... Providence, RI
Hahn, James P. ... Lakeland, FL
Hahn, James W., II ... Cape Girardeau, MO
Hahn, Jane ... San Diego, CA
Hahn, Janet L. ... Fort Worth, TX
Hahn, Janet P. ... San Mateo, CA
Hahn, Jay Todd ... New York, NY
Hahn, Jeffrey A. ... Valparaiso, IN
Hahn, Jeffrey M. ... Raleigh, NC
Hahn, Jeffrey P. ... Leesburg, VA
Hahn, Jennifer R. ... West Dundee, IL
Hahn, Jerome ... Washington, PA
Hahn, John C. ... Lincoln, NE
York, NE
Hahn, John R. ... Gold River, CA
Hahn, John S. ... Washington, DC
Hahn, Joseph J. ... Portland, ME
Hahn, Joseph T. ... Los Angeles, CA
Hahn, Junie ... Roseland, NJ
Hahn, Karen Kelly ... Shrewsbury, NJ
Hahn, Karen L. ... Southfield, MI
Hahn, Katherine M. ... Fremont, CA
Hahn, Kathleen A. ... Waterloo, IA
Hahn, Keith A. ... Livonia, MI
Hahn, Kenneth A. ... Palm Springs, CA
Hahn, Kevin M. ... Hackettstown, NJ
Morristown, NJ
Trenton, NJ
Hahn, L. Allen ... Greenville, NC
Hahn, L. Allen, P.A. ... Greenville, NC
Hahn, Laura J. ... Cedar Rapids, IA
Hahn Law Office, A Professional Corporation
Scottsbluff, NE
Hahn, Lawrence E. ... Columbia, MS
Hahn, Lawrence H. ... Amityville, NY
Hahn, Leibowitz & Associates, P.C.
Denver, CO
Hahn, Leonard Zin-Oogk ... New York, NY
Hahn, Linda L. ... St. Louis, MO
Hahn Loeser & Parks LLP
Cleveland, OH
Columbus, OH
Hahn, Lowell E. ... Auburn, NE
Hahn, Lowell F. ... Phillipsburg, KS
Hahn, Marcy A. ... Detroit, MI
Hahn, Marlene M. ... Fairfax, VA
Hahn, Martin J. ... Washington, DC
Hahn, Mary L. ... Park Ridge, IL
Hahn, MaryLu ... Chicago, IL
Hahn, Maurice ... New York, NY
Hahn, Max ... New York, NY
Hahn, McClurg, Watson, Griffith & Bush, P.A. ... Lakeland, FL
Hahn, Michael F. ... New York, NY
Hahn, Michael J. ... Atlanta, GA
Hahn, Michael L. ... Atlanta, GA
Hahn, Michael L. ... Chicago, IL
Hahn, Moira L. ... Philadelphia, PA
Hahn, Morgan & Lamb, P.A. ... Tampa, FL
Hahn, Nicolette G. ... Kalamazoo, MI
Hahn, Paul A. ... Madison, WI
Hahn, Paul B. ... New York, NY
Hahn, Paul W. ... Jackson, MO
Hahn, Peter K. ... San Diego, CA
Hahn, Peter W. ... Columbus, OH
Hahn, Philip M. ... New York, NY
Hahn, Rachel Shari ... New York, NY
Hahn, Randy R. ... Dallas, TX
Hahn, Reynolds E. ... Rochester, NY
Hahn, Richard ... Sheboygan, WI
Hahn, Richard E. ... New York, NY
Hahn, Richard E. ... Cleveland, OH
Hahn, Richard F. ... Indianapolis, IN
Hahn, Richard F. ... New York, NY
Hahn, Richard H. ... Cleveland Heights, OH
Hahn, Richard J. ... Byron, IL
Hahn, Richard L. ... Bala Cynwyd, PA
Hahn, Richard M. ... Vienna, VA
Hahn, Robert A. ... Washington, DC
Hahn, Robert A. ... Towson, MD
Hahn, Robert A. ... Saginaw, MI
Hahn, Robert C. ... Boston, MA
Hahn, Robert C. ... Sheboygan, WI
Hahn, Robert H. ... Evansville, IN
Hahn, Robert J. ... Charlotte, NC
Hahn, Robert J., III
Farmington Hills, MI
Hahn, Robert S. ... Knoxville, TN
Morristown, TN
Hahn, Roger ... Woodland, CA
Hahn, Ronald E. ... Deerfield, IL
Hahn, Ronald J. ... Denver, CO
Hahn, Roy ... Scottsbluff, NE
Hahn, Russell W. ... Chicago, IL
Hahn, Sally Jo ... Austin, TX
Hahn, Saul ... Boston, MA
Hahn, Steven K. ... Evansville, IN
Hahn, Steven R. ... Lodi, CA
Hahn, Steven R. ... Burlington, IA
Hahn, Susan ... Miami, FL
Hahn, Susan R. ... Denver, CO
Hahn, Susie L. ... Columbus, OH
Hahn, Swadey & Pollock ... Cleveland, OH
Hahn, Thomas G., A Professional Law Corporation ... Newport Beach, CA
Hahn, Thomas S. ... Washington, DC
Hahn, Victor H. ... Cleveland, OH
Hahn, Walz and Knepp, A Professional Association ... South Bend, IN
Hahn, Wendy E. ... Omaha, NE
Hahn, Wilford A. ... Huntington, IN
Hahn, William A. ... Boston, MA
Hahn, William A., Jr. ... Towson, MD
Hahn, William E. ... Tampa, FL
Hahn, Wolfgang F. ... La Jolla, CA
Hahn-Burkett, Tracy ... Washington, DC
Hahner, Mikael G. ... Iron Mountain, MI
Hahni, Veronica Bernice ... Pasadena, CA
Hahn-Saperstein, Marcy ... Boca Raton, FL
Hahon, Nancy Eileen ... New York, NY
Hahs, Andrew D. ... Portland, OR
Hahs, Ilyse D. ... Albuquerque, NM
Hai, Jill I. ... Chicago, IL
Haia, Moses K.N., III ... Honolulu, HI
Haiber, Jayne T. ... Philadelphia, PA
Haiber, Scott R. ... Baltimore, MD
Haic, james R. ... San Diego, CA
Haick, David P. ... Louisville, KY
Haidar, Mark M. ... Northville, MI
Haider, Carissa Freie ... Hannibal, MO
Haider, Thomas E. ... Minneapolis, MN
Haidet, Jeffrey K. ... Atlanta, GA
Haidle, Samuel J. ... Bloomfield Hills, MI
Haidri, Amirali Y. ... Union, NJ
Haidt, David James ... New Bern, NC
Haidt, Harold ... New York, NY
Haidze, Christopher A. ... New Kensington, PA
Haies, Jay W. ... Brooklyn, NY
Haies, Matthew N. ... New York, NY
Haiet, Beth R. ... New York, NY
Haifleigh, Debra G. ... Wichita, KS
Haig, Clyde A. ... Department of the Navy,
Office of the Judge Advocate General, GV
Haig, Elizabeth R. ... Absecon, NJ
Haig, Jerome J. ... Norwalk, CA
Haig, Robert L. ... New York, NY
Haig, Wayne O. S. ... Roanoke, VA
Haigazian, Rosemarie ... Edgartown, MA
Haiges, Robert William ... Edmond, OK
Haigh, Burton S. ... Kansas City, MO
Haigh, Douglas M. ... Long Beach, CA
Haigh, G. David ... Santa Ana, CA
Haigh, James C. ... Burlingame, CA
Haigh, James L. ... Minneapolis, MN
Haigh, Mark W. ... Sioux Falls, SD
Haigh, Michael S. ... Newport News, VA
Haigh, Todd W. ... Chicago, IL
Haigh, William L. ... Raleigh, NC
Haigh, William S. ... Barstow, CA
Haight, Ann L. ... Charleston, WV
Haight, Barry M. ... Milton, MA
Haight, Betty Anne ... Laguna Beach, CA
Haight, Bradley Joseph ... Denver, CO
Lafayette, LA
Haight, Brown & Bonesteel, L.L.P.
Los Angeles, CA
Riverside, CA
San Diego, CA
San Francisco, CA
Santa Ana, CA
Santa Monica, CA
Haight, Carol B. ... Boca Raton, FL
Haight, Carol B., A Professional Association
Boca Raton, FL
Haight, Catherine L. ... Los Angeles, CA
Haight, Charles S., Jr. ... New York, NY
Haight, Donald H. ... Las Vegas, NV
Haight, Edward A. ... Highland Park, IL
Haight, Ehrick K., Jr.
Hilton Head Island, SC

Haight, Fabyan & Langer, S.C. Hartland, WI
Haight Gardner Holland & Knight New York, NY
Haight Gardner Poor & Haven New York, NY
Haight, Geri L. ....Boston, MA
Haight, Gregory D. ....Vienna, VA
Haight, H. Kevin ....St. Joseph, MI
Haight, James C. ....Rockville, MD
Haight, James J. ....San Francisco, CA
Haight, James T. ....Pasadena, CA
Haight, Kathryn ....Denver, CO
Haight, Kevin ....Boulder, CO
Haight, Lloyd E. ....Boise, ID
Haight, Neil ....Helena, MT
Haight, Raymond L., III ....Laguna Beach, CA
Haight, Richard L. ....Ada, OH
Haight, Richard R. ....Gaithersburg, MD
Haight, Robert M., Jr. ....Los Angeles, CA
Haight, Robert M., Law Office of Scotts Valley, CA
Haight, Robert S., Jr. ....Myrtle Beach, SC
Haight, Scott K. ....Memphis, TN
Haight, Timothy V. ....Des Moines, IA
Haight, Tramonte, Siciliano, Flask & Yeonas, P.C. ....Fairfax, VA
Vienna, VA
Haight, Viviane M. ....Atlanta, GA
Haight, William H. ....San Antonio, TX
Haigian, Aris ....New York, NY
Haigis, John W., III ....Philadelphia, PA
Haigler, Charles B., III ....Montgomery, AL
Haigler, Dave ....Abilene, TX
Haigler, Janet B. ....Columbia, SC
Haigler, Kenneth E. ....Greenville, NC
Haigler, Mitchell B. ....Tallahassee, FL
Haigler, Stephen K. ....Anderson, SC
Haignere, E. Franklin ....San Diego, CA
Haigney, John E. ....New York, NY
Haigney, Stacy J. ....New York, NY
Haigney, William F. ....New York, NY
Haigood, Staci A. ....Fort Worth, TX
Haigwood, Thomas D. ....Greenville, NC
Haik and Haik ....New Orleans, LA
Haik, Louis A. ....Minneapolis, MN
Haik, Minvielle & Grubbs New Iberia, LA
Haik, Morris M., Jr. ....New Iberia, LA
Haik, Paul Raymond ....Minneapolis, MN
Haik, Raymond A. ....Minneapolis, MN
Haik, Richard T. ....Lafayette, LA
Haik, Robert B. ....New Orleans, LA
Haik, Robert G. ....New Orleans, LA
Haik, Theodore M., Jr. ....New Iberia, LA
Haikala, Harri J. ....Birmingham, AL
Haikala, Madeline H. ....Birmingham, AL
Haiken, Marvin B. ....Healdsburg, CA
Haiken, Matthew S. ....New York, NY
Hail, Brian D. ....New York, NY
Hail, Brian N. ....Dallas, TX
Hailand, Jeffress B. ....St. Louis, MO
Haile, David C. ....Towson, MD
Haile, Deborah Yalowitz ....Dallas, TX
Haile, Debrai ....Chicago, IL
Haile, Donald R. ....Santa Cruz, CA
Haile, Elster S. ....Palo Alto, CA
Haile, Jeffrey A. ....San Diego, CA
Haile, John, P.A. ....Lake Placid, FL
Haile, John S. ....Lake Placid, FL
Haile, Kimberly Meyer ....San Diego, CA
Haile, Lawrence B. ....Beverly Hills, CA
Haile, Lisa A. ....San Diego, CA
Haile & Peck ....Towson, MD
Haile, Rebecca G. ....New York, NY
Haile, Robert G., Jr. North Palm Beach, FL
Palm Beach, FL
Haile, Suzanne W. ....Brooklyn, NY
Haile, Thomas V. ....Louisville, KY
Haile, Walter R. ....Towson, MD
Haile, Wanda H. ....Columbia, SC
Hailer, Fredk. C. ....Caseville, MI
Hailer, George F. ....Boston, MA
Hailes, Edward A., Jr. ....Washington, DC
Hailey, Anna C. ....Elwood, IN
Hailey, C. David ....Atlanta, GA
Hailey, Gary D. ....Washington, DC
Hailey & Hailey ....San Antonio, TX
Hailey, Hans R. ....Boston, MA
Hailey, James D. ....Seattle, WA
Hailey, James W., III ....Metairie, LA
Hailey, James W., Jr., (P.L.C.) Metairie, LA
Hailey, J. M. ....Walled Lake, MI
Hailey, Joe C. ....Selmer, TN
Hailey, Joel M. ....San Antonio, TX
Hailey, Kara A. ....New York, NY
Hailey, Maureen E. ....Philadelphia, PA
Hailey, McNamara, Hall, Larmann & Papale, L.L.P. ....Metairie, LA
New Orleans, LA
Hailey, R. Douglas ....Indianapolis, IN
Hailey, R. B. ....Sevierville, TN
Hailey, Rennard E. ....Grand Junction, CO
Hailey, Robert P. ....Spokane, WA
Hailey, Rosalie A. ....Boston, MA
Hailey, Roy D. ....Houston, TX
Hailey, Royce Jay, Jr. ....Austin, TX
Hailey & Seaton ....Selmer, TN
Hailey, Tasha M. ....New York, NY
Hailey, William E. ....San Antonio, TX
Hailman, John R. ....Oxford, MS
Hails, Carine J. ....Grand Rapids, MI
Hails, Robert L., Jr. ....Washington, DC
Hailstone, A. James ....Scranton, PA
Hailstone, Andrew ....Scranton, PA
Hailu, Zecharias ....Minneapolis, MN

Haim, Allen A. ....San Rafael, CA
Haim, Patricia Ann ....Portland, OR
Haiman, Arnold J. Agency for International Development, Office of the General Counsel, GV
Haiman, Eric S. ....Saratoga, CA
Haiman, Frederick Owen ....San Antonio, TX
Haiman, Irwin S. ....Cleveland, OH
Haiman, Mark L. ....Carlsbad, CA
Haiman, Robert G. ....Dallas, TX
Haimbaugh, George D., Jr. ....Columbia, SC
Haimes, Burton K. ....New York, NY
Haimes, Perry L. ....Elkhart, IN
Haimes, Rand S. ....Cleveland, OH
Haimm, Neil K. ....Berwyn, PA
Philadelphia, PA
Haimo, Stephan H. ....New York, NY
Haimowitz, Harold B. ....Boca Raton, FL
Haimowitz, Jack ....Albany, NY
Haimowitz, Stephan Joel ....Albany, NY
Haimowitz, Stuart L. ....Philadelphia, PA
Haims, Arnold B. ....Oakland, CA
Haims, Bruce D. ....New York, NY
Haims, Joel C. ....New York, NY
Haims, MacGowan, Valentino & Peebles, L.L.P. ....Oakland, CA
San Francisco, CA
Hain, Benjamin M. ....New York, NY
Hain, Charyn K. ....Muskegon, MI
Hain, Cynthia L. ....Tampa, FL
Hain, Donald C. ....Fort Lauderdale, FL
Hain, Elwood B., Jr. ....Costa Mesa, CA
Hain, Frank E. ....Milwaukee, WI
Hain, Howard A. ....Erie, PA
Hain, Mark H. ....Atlanta, GA
Hain, Mary C. M. ....Portland, OR
Hain, Wendy L. ....Portland, OR
Hain, William C. ....Alna, ME
Hain, William J. ....Erie, PA
Hainbach, Don H. ....Washington, DC
Haine, James M. ....Stevens Point, WI
Haine, John W. ....Minneapolis, MN
Haine, Matthew D. ....Stamford, CT
Haine & Murtagh ....Lexington, VA
Haine, Ross S. ....Lexington, VA
Haine, Susan J. ....Washington, DC
Haine, Thomas ....San Diego, CA
Haine, William R. ....Edwardsville, IL
Hainen, John B. ....De Queen, AR
Hainen, Michael C. ....Chicago, IL
Hainer & Berman, P.C. ....Detroit, MI
Troy, MI
Hainer, Michael J. ....Dearborn, MI
Troy, MI
Haines, Amanda ....Newark, NJ
Haines, Barton A. ....Bala Cynwyd, PA
Haines, Brian S. ....Philadelphia, PA
Haines, Bruce S. ....Cherry Hill, NJ
Philadelphia, PA
Haines Brydon & Lea, A Law Corporation Long Beach, CA
San Francisco, CA
Haines, Brynne L. ....New York, NY
Haines, C. Gordon ....Baltimore, MD
Haines, Candace A. ....Corvallis, OR
Haines, Charlene J. ....Troy, MI
Haines, Charles F. ....San Francisco, CA
Haines, Clifford E. ....Philadelphia, PA
Haines, Cyndee C. ....Eugene, OR
Haines, Dallas W., III ....Boston, MA
Haines, Daniel H. ....Boston, MA
Haines, Daniel N. ....New York, NY
Haines, David I. ....Aberdeen, MD
Haines, Dennis ....Akron, OH
Canton, OH
Youngstown, OH
Haines, Dennis ....Erie, PA
Haines, Franklin M., Jr. ....Rye Brook, NY
Haines, Friedrick C. ....Englewood, CO
Haines, Gerald M., II ....Peabody, MA
Haines, Gregory J. ....South Bend, IN
Haines, Harry A. ....Missoula, MT
Haines, Jack C. ....Pitman, NJ
Haines, Jacque M. ....Cleveland, OH
Haines, James B. ....Boston, MA
Haines, James B., Jr. ....Bangor, ME
Haines, James S., Jr. ....El Paso, TX
Haines, James W., Jr. ....Monongahela, PA
Haines, Jane ....Pacific Grove, CA
Haines, Jeffrey D. ....Cleveland, OH
Haines, Jerry V. ....Washington, DC
Haines, Jill M. ....Dearborn, MI
Haines, John A., Jr. ....Bridgeport, MI
Haines, John D. ....Winter Park, FL
Haines, John G. ....Hartford, CT
Haines, John L., Jr. Panama Canal Commission, Office of the General Counsel, GV
Haines, John M. Department of Housing and Urban Development, GV
Haines, Joseph L. ....Reading, PA
Haines, Kara R. ....Wilmington, DE
Haines, Kenneth P. ....Shreveport, LA
Haines, Kimberley K. ....Columbus, OH
Haines, Kimberly K. ....Hartland, WI
Haines, Laurence Frederick ....San Diego, CA
Haines, Lewis D., II ....Fort Lauderdale, FL
Haines, Lewis J., Jr. ....Tulsa, OK
Haines, Lisa Broman ....Kansas City, MO
Haines, Lisa Mary ....Fort Worth, TX
Haines, Lloyd M. ....Ashland, OR
Haines, Martha Mahan ....Chicago, IL
Haines, Martin L. ....Mount Holly, NJ
Haines, Martin L., III ....Lake Park, FL
Haines, Martin L., III, Chartered Lake Park, FL
Haines, Michael A. ....San Francisco, CA

Haines, Michael C. ....Grand Rapids, MI
Haines, Miriam J. ....New York, NY
Haines & Oeming ....Bridgeport, MI
Haines, Patrick N. ....Houston, TX
Haines, Paul Lowell ....Indianapolis, IN
Haines, Philip E. ....Mount Holly, NJ
Haines, Quentin R. ....Delaware, OH
Haines, Ralph W. ....Romney, WV
Haines, Randolph J. ....Phoenix, AZ
Haines, Richard L. ....Pittsburgh, PA
Haines, Richard M. ....Cincinnati, OH
Haines, Richard S. ....Toms River, NJ
Haines, Robert B. ....Warren, NJ
Haines, Robert H. ....New York, NY
Haines, Robert L. ....Alexandria, VA
Haines, Robert T. ....Littleton, CO
Haines, Roger W., Jr. ....San Diego, CA
Haines, Rush T., II ....Philadelphia, PA
Haines, Sandra F. ....Crownsville, MD
Haines, Sarah Criss ....New Albany, IN
Haines, Scott B. ....Kansas City, MO
Haines, Sigrid C. ....Bethesda, MD
Haines, Susan G. ....Denver, CO
Haines, Susan G., A Prof. Corp., Law Offices of ....Denver, CO
Haines, Susan Q. ....Washington, DC
Haines, Thomas D., Jr. ....Roswell, NM
Haines, Thomas J. ....Philadelphia, PA
Haines, Thomas W. ....Shakopee, MN
Haines, Thomas W. W. ....Baltimore, MD
Haines & Thompson ....Toms River, NJ
Haines, Timothy D. ....Ocala, FL
Haines, Todd F. ....Calabasas, CA
Haines, Victoria M. ....Rockford, IL
Haines, Warren M., II ....Cleveland, OH
Haines, Wilbur H. ....Sacramento, CA
Hainke, Harold J., Esq. ....Whitefield, ME
Hainkel, Alida C. ....New Orleans, LA
Hainkel, John J., III ....New Orleans, LA
Hainkel, John J., Jr. ....New Orleans, LA
Hainline, Dallas D. ....Overland Park, KS
Hainline, Forrest A., III ....Washington, DC
Hainline, Forrest A., III ....Washington, DC
Hainline, Theodore R., Jr. Jacksonville, FL
Hains, Fred R., & Associates ....Elkhart, IN
Hains, Fred R., & Associates South Bend, IN
Hains, Glenn D. ....Newtown, PA
Hains, John P. ....Buffalo, NY
Hains, Timothy G. ....Naples, FL
Hainsfurther, A. Michael ....Dallas, TX
Hair, Barbara ....New York, NY
Hair, Barry W. ....Birmingham, AL
Hair, Charles J. ....Allentown, PA
Hair, Christopher A. ....Colorado Springs, CO
Hair, D. Charles ....San Diego, CA
Hair, Deidra L. ....Cincinnati, OH
Hair, Gregory W. ....McLean, VA
Hair, Jacqueline Carol ....Tulsa, OK
Hair, Lacy S. ....Fayetteville, NC
Hair, Mattox S. ....Jacksonville, FL
Hair, Patricia A. ....Houston, TX
Hair, Penda D. ....Washington, DC
Hair, Roberta Ann ....Cincinnati, OH
Hair, Steven W. ....Clearwater, FL
Hair, Steven W., P.A., Law Office of Clearwater, FL
Hair, William H. ....Oxnard, CA
Hairapetian, Armen ....Los Angeles, CA
Hairapetian, Shahen ....South Pasadena, CA
Hairapetian, Victor ....Pasadena, CA
Haire, Bridgers & Ridenour, P.A. Sylva, NC
Haire, John F. ....Columbia, MD
Haire, L. Ray ....Phoenix, AZ
Haire, Michael T. ....Maitland, FL
Haire, R. Phillip ....Sylva, NC
Haire, Rocky ....Denton, TX
Haire, Rocky ....Frisco, TX
Haire, Stephen A. ....Newport, RI
Haire, Susan L. ....Morganton, NC
Hairelson, Andrea L. ....Tampa, FL
Hairr, John R., III ....Charlotte, NC
Hairrell, Les Bradford ....Los Angeles, CA
Hairrell, Wayne F. ....Lawrenceburg, TN
Hairston, Abbey Gail ....Washington, DC
Baltimore, MD
Hairston, Alonzo P. ....Baltimore, MD
Hairston, Andrew J. ....Atlanta, GA
Hairston & Associates, P.A. ....Baltimore, MD
Hairston, Billy H. ....Inglewood, CA
Hairston, Charles C. ....Houston, TX
Hairston, Charles Rogers ....Taylor, TX
Hairston, Curtis M., Jr. ....Richmond, VA
Hairston, Cynthia M. ....Decatur, GA
Hairston, George E. ....New York, NY
Hairston, George W. ....Columbus, OH
Hairston, James E., Jr. ....Durham, NC
Hairston, Joe B. ....Austin, TX
Hairston, Joseph H. ....Washington, DC
Hairston, Kenneth A. ....Birmingham, AL
Hairston, Kenneth W. Department of Commerce, Patent and Trademark Office, GV
Hairston, Leslie A. ....Springfield, IL
Hairston, Lionel ....Dolton, IL
Hairston, Pamera D. Federal Communications Commission, Compliance and Information Bureau, GV
Hairston, Paula T. ....Department of Commerce, Patent and Trademark Office, GV
Hairston, Peter W. ....Advance, NC
Hairston, Roosevelt, Jr. ....Philadelphia, PA
Hairston, Samuel M. ....Chatham, VA
Hairston, Sandra J. ....Greensboro, NC
Hairston, Tanya N. ....Atlanta, GA
Hairston, Waller S. ....Easton, MD

Hairston, William B., III Birmingham, AL
Hairston, William B., Jr. Birmingham, AL
Hairston-Anderson, Toye ....Miami, FL
Hais, Samuel J. ....Clayton, MO
Hais, Susan M. ....Clayton, MO
Haisch, Anthony A. ....Southfield, MI
Haisch, Boyda & Summers, P.C. Detroit, MI
Southfield, MI
Haiser, James A. ....Chicago, IL
Haislet, Gerald S. ....Lafayette, CA
Haisley, James R. ....Salt Lake City, UT
Haislip, A. Lee, Jr. ....Temple Hills, MD
Haislip, Gene R. ....Leesburg, VA
Haislip, Janet M. ....Newburgh, NY
Haislip, John L. ....Scottsboro, AL
Haislip, Lawrence F. ....Towson, MD
Haislmaier, Jason D. ....Pittsburgh, PA
Haislup, Marshall A., III ....Philadelphia, PA
Haist, Dennis P. (IBA) ....Pleasanton, CA
Haist, Thomas R. ....Harrisburg, PA
Hait, Fred H. ....Carlisle, PA
Hait, Lawrence W. ....Beverly Hills, CA
Hait, Les ....Chico, CA
Hait, Louis J. ....New York, NY
Haitbrink, Richard F. ....Shawnee, KS
Haith, Aaron E. ....Indianapolis, IN
Haith, Scott C. ....Los Angeles, CA
Haithcock, W. Timothy ....Goldsboro, NC
Haithcox, Kevin M. ....San Francisco, CA
Haitsuka, Edmund W.K. ....Kailua-Kona, HI
Haitsuka, Jon M. Small Business Administration, GV
Haivala, Robert A. ....Buffalo, SD
Haizlip, Wilson W. ....Chattanooga, TN
Hajda, Thomas A. ....Jacksonville, FL
Hajdar, Esther L. ....Austin, TX
Hajdu, Lyle T. ....Jamestown, NY
Hajdu, Mary Speedy ....Jamestown, NY
Hajdu, Robert ....New York, NY
Hajduk, J. Lawrence ....Markleysburg, PA
Hajdukiewicz, Leo P. ....Pittsburgh, PA
Haje, Peter R. ....New York, NY
Hajek, Anne C. ....Sioux Falls, SD
Hajek, Christopher A. ....Flint, MI
Hajek, David H. ....Indianapolis, IN
Hajek, David W. ....Seymour, TX
Hajek, Douglas J. ....Sioux Falls, SD
Hajek, Francis P. ....Virginia Beach, VA
Hajek, Lynn C. ....Mineola, NY
Hajek, Monika D. ....Dearborn, MI
Hajek, Robert J. ....Minneapolis, MN
Hajewski, Cyril M. ....West Allis, WI
Hajian, Susan Tamar ....Waltham, MA
Hajinian, Christopher V. ....Philadelphia, PA
Hajjak, Paul S. ....Quincy, MA
Hajjak, Paul S. ....Quincy, MA
Hajjar, Albert J. ....Harrisburg, PA
Hajjar, Anton G. ....Washington, DC
Hajjar, David R. ....Washington, DC
Hajjar, Geo. J. ....Paterson, NJ
Hajjar, James G. ....Lawrence, MA
Hajjar, Paul S. ....Quincy, MA
Hajjar, S. John ....Quincy, MA
Hajjar, William A. ....Boston, MA
Hajnosz, Patricia J. ....Bronx, NY
Hajny, Jonathan M. ....Oregon, WI
Hajost, Theresa W. ....Washington, DC
Hajovsky, Patrick C. ....Houston, TX
Hajra, Neelav ....Dearborn, MI
Hak, Brian M. ....Parsippany, NJ
Hak, Kelly L. ....Grand Rapids, MI
Haka, John J. ....Stevens Point, WI
Hakak, Lev ....Los Angeles, CA
Hakala, Leslie A. Supreme Court Of The United States, GV
Hakamaki, Michaele A. ....St. Paul, MN
Hakanson, Jeffrey C. ....Tampa, FL
Hakanson, John R. ....Alamogordo, NM
Ruidoso, NM
Hakanson & Pruett, P.C. Alamogordo, NM
Hake, Bruce A. ....Silver Spring, MD
Hake, Bruce A., P.C. ....Silver Spring, MD
Hake, Carol C. ....Batavia, OH
Hake, Kelvin (Kelly) ....Bristow, OK
Hake, Linda C. R. ....Stuart, FL
Hake, Richard A. ....San Diego, CA
Hake, Steven Ray ....Austin, TX
Hake, Theodore C. ....Edinburg, TX
Hake, William Murray ....Long Beach, CA
San Francisco, CA
Hakeem, Ellis, Simonelli & Marengo, A Professional Corporation ....Stockton, CA
Hakeem, Michael D. ....Stockton, CA
Hakel, Karen E. ....Department of Education, Office for Civil Rights, GV
Haken, Jack E. ....Tarrytown, NY
Hakenen, Carl A., Jr. ....Suisun, CA
Haker, Keith D. ....Miles City, MT
Hakes, Harold L. ....Willowbrook, IL
Hakes, James E. ....Solon, OH
Hakes, John M. ....Lake Forest, IL
Hakes, John M. ....Indianapolis, IN
Hakes, Patricia Jones ....Atlanta, GA
Hakes, Steven C. ....San Diego, CA
Hakes, William D. ....St. Louis, MO
Hakim, Afshin ....Los Angeles, CA
Hakim, Anat ....Madison, WI
Hakim, David C. ....Southfield, MI
Hakim, Frank ....Los Angeles, CA
Hakim, George P. ....Winnetka, CA
Hakim, Lawrence J. ....Batesville, MS
Hakim, Louis G. ....Clifton, NJ
Hakim, Mark A. ....New York, NY
Hakim, Maroun J. ....St. Clair Shores, MI

Hakim, Richard J. ... Rockville, MD
Hakim, Ronald G. ... Eastpointe, MI
Hakim, Sana ... Chicago, IL
Hakim, Shazmah ... Washington, DC
Hakim, Veronique G. ... Brooklyn, NY
Hakimi, Shahryar ... Washington, DC
Hakimian, Rina ... Chicago, IL
Hakken, Andrew D. ... Grand Rapids, MI
Hakki, Adam S. ... New York, NY
Hakl, Anthony R., III ... Sacramento, CA
Haklar, Thomas D. ... San Diego, CA
Hakman, Deborah R. ... Los Angeles, CA
Hakman, Gary Allen ... Los Angeles, CA
Hakoda, Harvey ... Honolulu, HI
Hakomaki, James R. ... Minneapolis, MN
Hakun, Joseph ... Malvern, PA
Hakura, Dima S. ... Washington, DC
Haky, Lowell H. ... San Francisco, CA
Hala, Theresa Gilhooly
West Springfield, MA
Halaas, Eugene T., Jr. ... Pueblo, CO
Halabi, Christian I. ... New York, NY
Halabu, Shamil E. ... Southfield, MI
Halaby, Alexa ... Dickerson, MD
Halaby, Andrew Foster ... Phoenix, AZ
Halaby Cross & Schluter ... Denver, CO
Halaby, Dennis E. ... Cincinnati, OH
Halaby, Edward K. ... Cincinnati, OH
Halaby, Julie ... Denver, CO
Halaby, Samuel A., Jr. ... Rochester, NY
Halaby, Theodore S. ... Denver, CO
Halachian-Kritzer, Elena ... Houston, TX
Haladyna, Gregg S. ... Chelmsford, MA
Haladyna, Ruth H. ... Beaumont, TX
Halagan, Robert S. ... Minnetonka, MN
Halagao, Avelino G. ... Vienna, VA
Halak, John J. ... St. Petersburg, FL
Halal, Robert S. ... Westminster, CA
Halama, William A. ... Los Angeles, CA
Halamandaris, Val J. ... United States Senate, Committee Legal Personnel, GV
Halamka, Dagmar V. ... Los Angeles, CA
Halamka, John E. ... Torrance, CA
Halan, Ann E. ... Redding, CT
Halan, John M. ... Southfield, MI
Halanski, Roman ... Warren, MI
Halas, Anthony ... Phoenix, AZ
Halas, Daniel F. ... Toledo, OH
Halas, Monica ... Boston, MA
Halas, Paul J. ... Waltham, MA
Halas, Robert S. ... Independence, MO
Halasz, Carlos H. ... Miami, FL
Halasz, Michelle M. ... Richmond, VA
Halasz, Paul J. ... Morristown, NJ
Halasz, Peter J. ... New York, NY
Halasz, Stephen G. ... Trenton, NJ
Halatyn, Susan M. ... New York, NY
Halavi, Vida B. ... Los Angeles, CA
Halayko, Robert H. ... Fairfax, VA
Halbach, Edward C., Jr. ... Berkeley, CA
Halbach, Joseph J. ... Houston, TX
Halbach, Joseph" Tad ", Jr. ... Houston, TX
Halbach, Maren H. ... Devils Lake, ND
Halbach, Patrice H. ... Minneapolis, MN
Halbach, Peter K. ... Devils Lake, ND
Halbach, Steven J. ... Waterloo, IA
Halbach, Susan T. ... Houston, TX
Halbach, Victor M., Jr. ... Jacksonville, FL
Halbardier, Suzanne M. ... New York, NY
Halbe, Shailendra N. ... Los Angeles, CA
Halbeisen, Stephen M. ... Dallas, TX
Halber, Eric P. ... Washington, DC
Halber, Lori E. ... Philadelphia, PA
Halber, Shelley R. ... White Plains, NY
Halberg & Associates Co., L.P.A.
Northfield, OH
Halberg, Blake Dexter ... Atlanta, GA
Halberg, Charles ... Apple Valley, MN
Halberg, Charles C. ... St. Paul, MN
Halberg, David J. ... Miami, FL
West Palm Beach, FL
Halberg, David J., P.A. ... Miami, FL
West Palm Beach, FL
Halberg, Herbert B. ... New York, NY
Halberg, Marsh J. ... Minneapolis, MN
Halberg, Samuel S. ... Brooklyn, NY
Halberg, William S. ... Northfield, OH
Halberstadt, Bertram S. ... Wilmington, DE
Halberstadt, Bertram S., P.A.
Wilmington, DE
Halberstadt, Bradley J. ... Minneapolis, MN
Halberstadt, Ethan N. ... Cherry Hill, NJ
Harrisburg, PA
King Of Prussia, PA
Halberstadter, David ... Los Angeles, CA
Halberstadter, Jo Ann ... Philadelphia, PA
Halberstadter, Sanford ... Clark, NJ
Halberstam, David ... New York, NY
Halberstam, Malvina ... New York, NY
Halberstam, Michael J. ... New York, NY
Halberstam, Saundra R. ... New York, NY
Halberstein & Byrne ... Washington, DC
Halberstein, Richard ... Washington, DC
Halbert, Charles, Jr. ... Helena, AR
Halbert, David M. ... Houston, TX
Halbert & Dunn ... Falls City, NE
Halbert, Gregory T. ... Minneapolis, MN
Halbert, Lisa L. ... Northampton, MA
Halbert, Mark N. ... Little Rock, AR
Halbert, Marvin R. ... Philadelphia, PA
Halbert, Mary ... San Rafael, CA
Halbert, Michael J. ... San Jose, CA
Halbert, Randi L. ... Stamford, CT
Halbert, Richard L. ... Falls City, NE
Halbert, Shawn ... San Francisco, CA
Halbert, Stanley E. ... Orlando, FL
Halbert, Todd M. ... Southfield, MI
Halbkat, Fredk. W. ... Houston, TX
Halbleib, Brent W. ... St. Louis, MO
Halbleib, Irvin J., Jr. ... Louisville, KY
Halbleib, John F. ... Chicago, IL
Halbleib, W. Thomas, Jr. ... Louisville, KY
Halbleib, Wayne T. ... Richmond, VA
Halbo, Karen E. ... Sacramento, CA
Halbohn, Donald F. ... Massapequa, NY
Halbower, Matthew Charles ... Muskegon, MI
Halbower, Norman C. ... Muskegon, MI
Halbower, Norman C., P.C. ... Muskegon, MI
Halbreich, David M. ... Los Angeles, CA
Halbreich, Eva S. ... Irvine, CA
Halbreich, Jeffrey W. ... Baldwin, NY
Halbreich, Michael M. ... Atlanta, GA
Halbritter, Marc A. ... Cleveland, OH
Clarksburg, WV
Halbritter, Robert C. ... Kingwood, WV
Halbrook, Allen, Jr. ... Austin, TX
Halbrook, Donald E. ... Moore, OK
Halbrook, Karen J. ... Kansas City, MO
Halbrook, Rebecca Thacker
White Plains, NY
Halbrook, Robert L. ... Georgetown, DE
Halbrook, Stephen P. ... Fairfax, VA
Halbrook, Wm. M. ... Little Rock, AR
Halbrooks, David R. ... Madison, WI
Halbrooks, James W., Jr.
Minneapolis, MN
Halbrooks, Jill Flaskamp ... St. Paul, MN
Halbrooks, William H. ... Birmingham, AL
Halbruner, Mark E. ... Lemoyne, PA
Halbur, Joseph E. ... Carroll, IA
Halbur, Paul J. ... Omaha, NE
Halby, Karen L. ... Purchase, NY
Halby, William G. ... Larchmont, NY
Halcarz, John J. ... Highland, IN
Halchak, Alyce Cesare ... Newark, NJ
Halcom, H. F. ... Columbus, TX
Halcomb, J. Christopher ... Cumming, GA
Halcomb, J. Christopher, P.C.
Cumming, GA
Halcomb, Larry L. ... Birmingham, AL
Halcomb, Roy S., Jr. ... Alexandria, LA
Halcomb, Tina Marie Crow
Jefferson City, MO
Halcomb, W. McCollum ... Birmingham, AL
Halcomb & Wertheim, P.C.
Birmingham, AL
Haldan, Dwight S. ... Redwood City, CA
Haldane, Douglas A. ... Houston, TX
Haldane, Elise ... Washington, DC
Haldeman & Associates ... Rockford, IL
Haldeman, Charles E., Jr. ... Philadelphia, PA
Haldeman, E. Barry ... Hollywood, CA
Haldeman, Gene A. ... New York, NY
Haldeman, George P. ... Seattle, WA
Haldeman, Harold W. ... Westport, CT
Haldeman, Richard R. ... Rockford, IL
Haldeman, Susan W. ... San Francisco, CA
Halden, Ann E. ... New York, NY
Halden, Peter M. ... Haddonfield, NJ
Haldenstein, Michael K.
United States International Trade Commission, Office of the General Counsel, GV
Halderman, Berton F. ... Syracuse, NY
Halderman, Daphne R. ... Kansas City, MO
Halderman, John C. ... Philadelphia, PA
Halderson, Clark A. ... Dallas, TX
Haldi, Glenville, (P.C.) ... Atlanta, GA
Haldiman, Robert C. ... Collinsville, IL
Haldin, William C., Jr. ... Ocala, FL
Haldorsen, Thomas M. ... San Bernardino, CA
Haldrup, Neil S. ... Charleston, SC
Haldusiewicz, Joseph J. ... Newark, NJ
Haldy, Ronald L. ... Flint, MI
Hale, A. Craig ... Salt Lake City, UT
Hale, Alan N. ... Bellefontaine, OH
Hale, Allan L. ... Denver, CO
Hale, Allan M. ... Boston, MA
Hale, Allen W. ... Tacoma, WA
Hale, Alton C., Jr. ... Fort Pierce, FL
Stuart, FL
Hale, Andrew M. ... Chicago, IL
Hale, Angela Clark ... Indianapolis, IN
Hale, Audrey A. ... Newark, NJ
Hale, B. Don ... Cullman, AL
Hale, Ben W., Jr. ... Columbus, OH
Hale, Bradley ... Atlanta, GA
Hale, Bradley M. ... Tuscaloosa, AL
Hale, Brenda Franks ... Franklin, TN
Hale, Bruce M. ... Los Angeles, CA
Hale, Bruce M., Jr. ... Salt Lake City, UT
Hale, Candace ... Sausalito, CA
Hale, Catherine H. ... Wallace, NC
Hale, Charles F. ... Philadelphia, PA
Hale, Charlotte Bentley ... Tuscaloosa, AL
Hale, Chris A. ... Austin, TX
Hale, Christopher D.
Fort Lauderdale, FL
Hale, Christopher T. ... Milwaukee, WI
Hale, Clayton H., Jr. ... Syracuse, NY
Hale, Damone K. ... San Francisco, CA
Hale, Daniel C. ... Boulder, CO
Hale, Daniel G. ... Philadelphia, PA
Hale, Daniel J. ... Dallas, TX
Hale, Darryl ... Hartford, CT
Hale, David J. ... Louisville, KY
Hale, Dayton F. ... Tuscaloosa, AL
Hale, Dayton F., Jr. ... Tuscaloosa, AL
Hale, Debora L. ... Hannibal, MO
Hale, Donald A. ... Steelville, MO
Hale, Donald J. ... Everett, WA
Hale and Dorr LLP ... Washington, DC
Boston, MA
Hale, Douglas A. ... Raynham, MA
Hale, Douglas S. ... Franklin, TN
Hale, Douglas V. ... Huntsville, AL
Hale, Earl F., Jr. ... Dallas, TX
Hale, Earle T. ... Williamsburg, VA
Hale, Edward William
West Palm Beach, FL
Hale, Eileen M. ... Burbank, CA
Hale, Eileen M. ... Cherry Hill, NJ
Hale, Ellen M. ... Forked River, NJ
Hale, Eugene B., Jr. ... Prescott, AR
Hale, Eugene G. ... Athens, TN
Hale, F. Sheffield ... Atlanta, GA
Hale, Floyd ... Las Vegas, NV
Hale, Fogleman & Rogers ... Marion, AR
West Memphis, AR
Hale, Frank ... Olympia, WA
Hale, Frank A. ... Pasadena, TX
Hale, Frederick D. ... Los Angeles, CA
Hale, G. Gregory ... Gainesville, FL
Hale, G. Robert, (P.C.) ... Los Angeles, CA
Hale, Garvin W. ... Fresno, CA
Hale, Gary D. ... Lawrence, KS
Hale, Gary J. ... Denver, CO
Hale, Geoffrey B. ... Palo Alto, CA
Hale, George E. ... Lake Forest, IL
Hale, Gerald G. ... Brownwood, TX
Hale, Gina L. ... Vancouver, WA
Hale, Goodwin ... Lubbock, TX
Hale, Grayson S. ... Dallas, TX
Hale, Gregory A. ... Westborough, MA
Hale, Gregory D. ... Allegan, MI
Hale, H. DeWayne" Cooter " ... Dallas, TX
Hale Hackstaff Tymkovich & ErkenBrack, L.L.P. ... Denver, CO
Grand Junction, CO
Hale, Hal Davis, Jr. ... Houston, TX
Hale and Hale ... Franklin, TN
Austin, TX
Hale, Hale & McInturff ... Chattanooga, TN
Hale & Hale, P.A. ... Beaufort, SC
Hilton Head Island, SC
Hale & Hall, P.L.L.C. ... Williamsburg, VA
Hale & Hamlin ... Ellsworth, ME
Hale, Harland Hanna ... Columbus, OH
Hale Headrick Dewey & Wolf, PLLC
Memphis, TN
Hale, Headrick, Dewey & Wolf, PLLC
Nashville, TN
Hale, Hunter D. ... Arlington, VA
Hale, Hunter, International ... Arlington, VA
Hale, J. Kevin ... Farmington, NM
Hale, J. Scott ... Greensboro, NC
Hale, J. Thomas ... Reno, NV
Hale, James C., Jr. ... West Memphis, AR
Hale, James Chapman ... Roanoke, VA
Hale, James O. ... Hilton Head Island, SC
Hale, James R. ... San Antonio, TX
Hale, James S. ... Kailua-Kona, HI
Hale, James T. ... Minneapolis, MN
Hale, James W. ... Leakey, TX
San Antonio, TX
Hale, James W., P.C. ... Leakey, TX
San Antonio, TX
Hale, Janet ... Austin, TX
Hale, Jeannie L. ... Seattle, WA
Hale, Jeannine ... Oklahoma City, OK
Hale, Jeffrey D. ... Minneapolis, MN
Hale, Jeffrey F. ... Tacoma, WA
Hale, Jennifer Ansbro ... Chicago, IL
Hale, Jerald V. ... Salt Lake City, UT
Hale, Jess O., Jr. ... Nashville, TN
Hale, Jim Pete ... Brownfield, TX
Hale, Jim Pete, P.C. ... Brownfield, TX
Hale, John A., Jr. ... Houston, TX
Hale, John B. ... Palo Alto, CA
Hale, John C. ... Fairfax, VA
Hale, John E. ... Tallahassee, FL
Hale, John P. ... Dearborn, MI
Hale, John P. ... New York, NY
Hale, John Rudy ... Nogales, AZ
Hale, John S. ... McLean, VA
Hale, Joseph L. ... Portsmouth, OH
Hale, Karen L. ... Louisville, KY
Hale, Kathleen M. ... Chagrin Falls, OH
Hale, Kelly ... Newport Beach, CA
Hale, Kenneth D. ... Bristol, TN
Hale, Kenneth M. ... Houston, TX
Hale, Kenneth W. ... Fort Worth, TX
Hale, Kent D. ... Lubbock, TX
Hale, Kincaid & Skinner, P.C.
Kansas City, MO
Liberty, MO
Hale, L. DeWitt ... Austin, TX
Hale, Lance M., & Associates ... Roanoke, VA
Hale Lane Peek Dennison Howard and Anderson ... Carson City, NV
Elko, NV
Incline Village, NV
Las Vegas, NV
Reno, NV
Hale, Larry D. ... St. Louis, MO
Hale, Laura Gaughan ... Roanoke, VA
Hale Law Firm ... St. Louis, MO
Hale, Lee L. ... Mobile, AL
Hale, Linda A. ... Dallas, TX
Hale, Lisa T. ... Atlanta, GA
Hale, Lola Miranda ... Chicago, IL
Hale, Louis H. ... Kanab, UT
Hale, M. Kevin ... Los Angeles, CA
Hale, Marian F. ... Washington, DC
Hale, Marilyn F. ... Washington, DC
Hale, Marion ... Clearwater, FL
Hale, Mark J. ... Brooklyn, NY
Hale, Mary Arens ... Columbus, OH
Hale, Mary L. ... Washington, DC
Hale, Matthew R. ... Kansas City, MO
Hale, Matthew S. ... Williamsburg, VA
Hale, Matthew T. ... Seattle, WA
Hale, Mercedes Gonzalez ... Tampa, FL
Hale, Michael E. ... Little Rock, AR
Hale, Michael S. ... Detroit, MI
Hale, Michael T. ... Baton Rouge, LA
Hale, Milas H., III ... North Little Rock, AR
Hale, Milas H., (P.A.)
North Little Rock, AR
Hale, Nancy W. ... Treasury Department, Internal Revenue Service, GV
Hale, Nathan ... New York, NY
Hale, Nina B. ... Department of Justice, Antitrust Division, GV
Hale, Olin R. ... Phoenix, AZ
Hale, Oscar J., Jr. ... Laredo, TX
Hale, Pat B. ... Grundy, VA
Hale, Philip Doubleday ... Annapolis, MD
Hale, R. Alan ... Fort Lauderdale, FL
Hale, R. William ... Silver Spring, MD
Hale, Rand S. ... East Alton, IL
Hale, Raymond S. ... Fort Collins, CO
Hale, Rebecca Hendricks
Hilton Head Island, SC
Hale, Rebecca M. ... San Francisco, CA
Hale, Richard L. ... Pacifica, CA
Hale, Richard N. ... Princeton, NJ
Hale, Robert B. ... Dallas, TX
Hale, Robert B.C. ... Memphis, TN
Hale, Robert D. ... Chattanooga, TN
Hale, Robert H. ... Boston, MA
Hale, Robert J. ... Los Angeles, CA
Hale, Robert J. ... Granby, CT
Hale, Robert M. ... Boston, MA
Hale, Roderick N. ... Minneapolis, MN
Hale, Russell B. ... Orlando, FL
Hale, S. Edward, Jr. ... Rockwall, TX
Hale, S. Jerome, II ... Chattanooga, TN
Hale, Samuel D. ... Sacramento, CA
Hale, Sanderson, Byrnes & Morton, A Professional Association ... Boston, MA
Hale & Schenkman ... Princeton, NJ
Hale, Scott A. ... Denver, CO
Hale, Shadonna E. ... Washington, DC
Hale, Skemp, Hanson, Skemp & Sleik
La Crosse, WI
Hale, Stephanie J. Weber ... Cookeville, TN
Knoxville, TN
Hale, Stephen B. ... Tulsa, OK
Hale, Stephen E. W. ... Salt Lake City, UT
Hale, Stephen L. ... Bolivar, TN
Hale, Stephen P. ... Memphis, TN
Hale, Steven A. ... Michigan City, IN
Hale, Steven P. ... Glendale, CA
Hale, Steven W. ... Lake Charles, LA
Hale, Steven W. ... Seattle, WA
Hale, Tarin Stuart ... New Philadelphia, OH
Hale, Theodore G. ... Carolina Beach, NC
Hale, Thomas A. ... Chicago, IL
Hale, Thomas F. ... Highland Heights, KY
Hale, Thomas M. ... Knoxville, TN
Hale, Thomas S. ... Birmingham, AL
Hale, Timothy C. ... Palo Alto, CA
Hale, Timothy C. ... Santa Barbara, CA
Hale, Timothy S. ... Albuquerque, NM
Hale, Todd E. ... Phoenix, AZ
Hale, Veronica S. ... Fort Irwin, CA
Hale, Vivian C. ... Tulsa, OK
Hale, W. Michael, Jr. ... Atlanta, GA
Hale & Wagner, S.C. ... Milwaukee, WI
Hale, William E. ... Sacramento, CA
Hale, William Kenneth ... Raleigh, NC
Hale, William L. ... Washington, GA
Hale, William W. ... Stockton, CA
Hale, Wright Williams ... Tuscaloosa, AL
Hale & Young ... North Little Rock, AR
Haleas & Haleas ... Bridgeview, IL
Haleas, James W. ... Bridgeview, IL
Haleas, Peter E. ... Bridgeview, IL
Haleas, Peter J. ... Bridgeview, IL
Halebian, John ... New York, NY
Halebian, Michael, Jr. ... Hackensack, NJ
Halecky, Janet ... New York, NY
Halem, Daniel R. ... New York, NY
Halem, Sydney ... Encino, CA
HaleMcFadden, LLP, Law Offices of
Annapolis, MD
Hale-Milliken, Amy Beth
Bowling Green, KY
Halen, Barbara J. ... Pittsburgh, PA
Halen, John T. ... Elizabeth City, NC
Halencak, Daryl R. ... Crowell, TX
Hales, Brent J. ... Temecula, CA
Hales, Bryan S. ... Chicago, IL
Hales, Daniel B. ... Chicago, IL
Hales, David K. ... Cleveland, OH
Hales, Edwin B. ... Redlands, CA
Hales, H. Edward, Jr. ... Atlanta, GA
Hales, H. Lee, Jr. ... Logan, UT
Hales, Hales & Etienne ... San Jose, CA
Hales, Hales & George ... Saratoga, CA
Hales, James R. ... Minden, NV
Hales, Jan Marie ... Saratoga, CA
Hales, Janet E. ... Ann Arbor, MI
Findlay, OH
Toledo, OH
Hales, Kelly Wilson ... Chicago, IL
Hales, Lawrence C. ... Lancaster, CA
Hales, Michele Elizabeth ... San Jose, CA
Hales, Myrt T., Jr. ... Rayville, LA
Hales, Nat E., Jr. ... San Jose, CA
Hales, Nicholas E. ... Salt Lake City, UT
Hales, Paul R. ... St. Louis, MO
Hales, Robert E. ... Orange, CA
Hales, Robert E. ... Saratoga, CA
Hales, Roger J. ... Boise, ID
Hales, Tiffany ... Nampa, ID
Hale-Smith, Ann ... Atlanta, GA
Haleva, Aaron S. ... New York, NY
Halevy, Amy Karff ... Houston, TX
Halevy, Beth M. ... Chicago, IL
Halevy, Daniel E. ... Philadelphia, PA

Hall, David and Joseph, P.A.
Fort Lauderdale, FL
Key West, FL
Miami, FL
West Palm Beach, FL
Hall, David K. ... Baltimore, MD
Hall, David L. ... Palo Alto, CA
Hall, David L. ... Winston-Salem, NC
Hall, David L. ... Dayton, OH
Wilmington, OH
Hall, David M. ... Los Angeles, CA
Hall, David M. ... Waukegan, IL
Hall, David M. ... Anthony, KS
Hall, David M. ... Fairfax, VA
Hall, David P. ... Sacramento, CA
Hall, David R. ... Las Vegas, NV
Hall, David S. ... New York, NY
Hall, David V. ... Chicago, IL
Hall, David W. ... Orlando, FL
Hall, David W. ... Honolulu, HI
Hall, David W., Attorney At Law, A Law Corporation ... Honolulu, HI
Hall, David W., Jr. ... Springfield, MO
Hall, Dean W. ... Brea, CA
Hall, Deborah J. ... Boston, MA
Hall, Deborah J. Thiel ... Berwyn, PA
Hall, Debra ... San Antonio, TX
Hall, Debra Dison ... Los Angeles, CA
Hall, Debra J. ... Washington, DC
Hall, Debra Tedeschi ... Elkins, WV
Hall, Denise ... San Antonio, TX
Hall, Dennis James ... Golden, CO
Hall, Dennis L. ... Dayton, OH
Hall, Diana Drinkwater ... Atlanta, GA
Hall, Diana Jeannine ... Atlanta, GA
Hall Dickler Kent Friedman & Wood LLP
Los Angeles, CA
New York, NY
White Plains, NY
Hall, Don L. ... Birmingham, AL
Hall, Don T. ... Arcadia, FL
Hall, Donald C., Jr. ... Tustin, CA
Hall, Donald D., (P.C.) ... Fairfield, CT
Hall, Donald E. ... Bethesda, MD
Hall, Donald H. ... Riverton, WY
Hall, Donald J. ... Nashville, TN
Hall, Donald L. ... Charleston, WV
Hall, Donald L., Jr. ... Tulsa, OK
Hall, Donald M. ... San Juan, PR
Hall, Donald O. ... Waco, TX
Hall, Donald R. ... Irvine, CA
Hall, Donald R. ... Clearwater, FL
Hall, Donald R. ... Fort Lauderdale, FL
Hall, Donna E. ... San Diego, CA
Hall, Donna Joyce ... Norfolk, VA
Hall, Donna L. ... Millbrae, CA
Hall & Doran, P.L.C. ... Pontiac, MI
Hall, Douglas ... Minneapolis, MN
Hall, Douglas ... White Plains, NY
Hall, Douglas L. ... Newland, NC
Hall, Douglas Lee ... Tallahassee, FL
Hall, Douglas W. ... Washington, DC
Hall, Dwight R. ... Elkins, WV
Hall & Dwyer ... Winchester, MA
Hall, E. Harold ... Ada, OK
Hall, E. C. Kirk ... Perkasie, PA
Hall, Edison H., Jr. ... Cleveland, OH
Hall, Edmon G. ... McAllen, TX
Hall, Edward M. ... Irvine, CA
Hall, Edward N. ... Madison, WV
Hall, Edward S. ... Barre, VT
Hall, Edward W. ... Santa Ana, CA
Hall, Eileen ... Dallas, TX
Hall, Elaine D'Amico ... Tallahassee, FL
Hall, Eldon J. ... Ely, MN
Hall, Eldon L., Jr. ... Gahanna, OH
Hall, Elizabeth A. ... Houston, TX
Hall, Elizabeth A. ... McLean, VA
Hall, Elizabeth J. ... Maumee, OH
Hall, Elizabeth K. ... Tulsa, OK
Hall, Elizabeth Peterson ... Danville, PA
Hall, Elizabeth R. ... Houston, TX
Hall, Elizabeth T. ... Irvine, CA
Hall, Elkin & Howland ... Mt. Gilead, OH
Cardington, OH
Hall, Ellsworth, III ... Macon, GA
Hall, Emmett V., Jr. ... Irving, TX
Hall, Eric B. ... Houston, TX
Hall, Eric D. ... Prestonsburg, KY
Hall, Eric R. ... Albuquerque, NM
Hall, Erika M.
Department of Housing and Urban Development, GV
Hall, Estill, Hardwick, Gable, Golden & Nelson, A Professional Corporation
Fayetteville, AR
Washington, DC
Oklahoma City, OK
Tulsa, OK
Hall, Eugene ... Los Angeles, CA
Hall, Eugene C. ... Kansas City, MO
Hall, Eugene M. ... Wilmington, DE
Hall & Evans, L.L.C.
Colorado Springs, CO
Denver, CO
Washington, DC
Hall, Everett I. ... Indianapolis, IN
Hall, F. Kennedy ... Macon, GA
Hall, F. Richard ... Charleston, WV
Parkersburg, WV
Hall, F. Riley ... Marion, OH
Hall, Farley, Oberrecht & Blanton, P.A.
Boise, ID
Caldwell, ID
Coeur d'Alene, ID
Idaho Falls, ID
Ketchum, ID
Lewiston, ID
Pocatello, ID
Sun Valley, ID
Twin Falls, ID
Hall, Forrest C. ... Graham, NC
Hall, Fox and Atlee, P.C. ... Hampton, VA
Newport News, VA
Hall, Frances H. ... Raleigh, NC
Hall, Francis L. ... Washington, DC
Hall, Frank D. ... Arcadia, FL
Hall, Frank W. ... Asheville, NC
Hall, Franklin P. ... Richmond, VA
Hall, Franklin R. ... Bullhead City, AZ
Flagstaff, AZ
Lake Havasu City, AZ
Prescott, AZ
Hall, Franklin W. ... Chicago, IL
Hall, Franklin W. ... New Orleans, LA
Shreveport, LA
Hall, Fred ... Wallace, NC
Hall, Fred L. ... Springfield, MO
Hall, Fred W., Jr. ... Rochester, NH
Hall, Frederick" Rick "I., III, P.A.
Columbia, SC
Lexington, SC
Hall, Frederick G. ... Los Angeles, CA
Hall, Frederick L., III ... Honolulu, HI
Hall, Frederick" Rick "I., III
Lexington, SC
Hall, Frederick S. ... Concord, NH
Hall, Friedly & Ward
Mountain Home, ID
Hall, G. Kennedy, Jr. ... Louisville, KY
Hall, G. Rick ... Tuscumbia, AL
Hall, Garland C., III ... Decatur, AL
Hall, Gary ... Chicago, IL
Hall, Gary A. ... Syracuse, NY
Hall, Gary A., Attorney at Law
Corpus Christi, TX
Hall, Gary B. ... Richardson, TX
Hall, Gary E. ... Seattle, WA
Hall, Gary L. ... Cincinnati, OH
Hall, Gary L., Law Office of ... Roseville, CA
Hall, Gary T. ... Newark, NJ
Hall, Gene H. ... Brandon, FL
Hall, Geoffrey C. ... Omaha, NE
Hall, George ... Mansfield, OH
Hall, George Atwater, Jr. ... Cambridge, MA
Hall, George B., Jr. ... New Orleans, LA
Hall, George E. ... Riverside, CT
Hall, George H. ... Chelsea, MA
Hall, George H. G. ... Jacksonville, FL
Hall, George R. ... Augusta, GA
Aiken, SC
Hall, George V. ... Manhattan Beach, CA
Hall, George W. ... Pawhuska, OK
Hall, Gina M. ... Bridgeport, CT
Hall, Glade L. ... Reno, NV
Hall, Glen W. ... Jackson, MS
Hall, Glenn Allen ... Lee's Summit, MO
Hall, Glenn D. ... Las Cruces, NM
Hall, Glenn O., Jr. ... Kensington, MD
Hall, Gloretta H. ... Stuart, FL
Hall, Gordon R. ... Salt Lake City, UT
Hall, Gordon T. ... Garden City, NY
Hall, Gordon W. ... Houston, TX
Hall, Gregory A. ... Denver, CO
Hall, Gregory B. ... Pensacola, FL
Hall, Gregory J. ... Glenwood Springs, CO
Hall, Gregory J. ... Portland, OR
Hall, Gregory L. ... Pikeville, KY
Hall, Gregory R. ... Phoenix, AZ
Hall, Gregory T. ... Tampa, FL
Hall, Gretchen Ann ... Milaca, MN
Hall, Guy C. ... Champaign, IL
Hall, H. Craig ... Salt Lake City, UT
Hall, H. Dean ... Anderson, SC
Hall, H. Glen ... Ossining, NY
Hall, H. Glenn, Jr. ... Austin, TX
Hall, H. Gordon ... New Haven, CT
Hall, H. Jack ... Costa Mesa, CA
Hall, H. John ... Chehalis, WA
Hall, H. Leslie ... Phoenix, AZ
Hall, H. Lowell ... Milwaukee, WI
Hall, H. Robert ... Pleasanton, CA
Hall & Hagan ... Collierville, TN
Hall & Hall ... Hawkinsville, GA
Hall & Hall ... Anthony, KS
Hall & Hall ... New York, NY
Hall & Hall ... Southold, NY
Hall & Hall ... Staten Island, NY
Hall & Hall ... Cleveland, OH
Hall & Hall ... Marion, OH
Hall & Hall ... Richmond, VA
Hall & Hall, Attorneys at Law, P.C.
Newland, NC
Hall & Hall, LLC, Law Offices of
Birmingham, AL
Hall, Harold A. ... Brooklyn, NY
Hall, Harold E. ... Madison, WI
Hall, Harold G. ... Raleigh, NC
Hall, Harold L. ... Jacksonville, AR
Hall, Harry E. ... Decatur, GA
Hall, Harry L. ... Denton, TX
Hall, Harry P. ... Atlanta, GA
Hall, Harry P., II ... Dothan, AL
Hall, Haynes, Lusk & Foster
Chattanooga, TN
Hall, Hazel A. ... Detroit, MI
Hall & Hedrick ... Miami, FL
Hall, Helena L. ... Anchorage, AK
Hall Hemhauser ... Fair Haven, NJ
Hall, Henderson S., Jr. ... Jackson, MS
Hall, Henry J. ... Compton, CA
Hall, Henry L., Jr. ... Boston, MA
Hall, Hess, Stewart, Murphy & Brown, P.A.
Manchester, NH
Hall & Hieatt ... San Luis Obispo, CA
Hall, Hilary R. ... Merrillville, IN
Hall, Holly Peck ... New York, NY
Hall, Horace C., III ... Laredo, TX
Hall, Howard C. ... Oakland, CA
Hall, Howard D. ... Orange, CA
Hall, Howard E. ... Cardington, OH
Mt. Gilead, OH
Hall, Howard H. ... Paramount, CA
Hall, Howard H., Inc. ... Paramount, CA
Hall, Howard J. ... Chelmsford, MA
Hall, Howard Keith ... Pikeville, KY
Hall, Howard (Terry) ... Seattle, WA
Hall, Howell A. ... Atlanta, GA
Hall, Hugh B., Jr. ... Pikeville, KY
Hall, Hunter A. ... Orlando, FL
Hall, Idaline L. ... St. Louis, MO
Hall, Ina M. ... Rochester, NY
Hall, Ira B. ... Norfolk, VA
Hall, Isaac D., Jr. ... Wailuku, HI
Hall, J. Andre ... Charlotte, NC
Hall, J. Christopher ... Chattanooga, TN
Hall, J. Clifton, III ... Houston, TX
Hall, J David ... Austin, TX
Hall, J. Diana ... Tulsa, OK
Hall, J. Edward ... Milledgeville, GA
Hall, J. Ellsworth, IV ... Macon, GA
Hall, J. Fay, Jr. ... Wynnewood, PA
Hall, J. Frank ... Memphis, TN
Hall, J. Johnson ... Hawkinsville, GA
Hall, J. Lewis, Jr. ... Tallahassee, FL
Hall, J. Michael ... Statesboro, GA
Hall, J. Randal ... Augusta, GA
Hall, J. Richard ... Houston, TX
Hall, J. Robert ... Chicago, IL
Hall, J. Scott ... Santa Fe, NM
Hall, J. Tiffin ... Missoula, MT
Hall, Jack A. ... Galveston, TX
Hall, Jack H. ... Elgin, IL
Hall, Jack J. ... Birmingham, AL
Hall, Jack J., Jr. ... Birmingham, AL
Hall, Jacqulyn Kay ... Amarillo, TX
Hall, James ... Anchorage, AK
Hall, James ... Groton, CT
Hall, James ... Library of Congress, Office of the General Counsel, GV
Hall, James A. ... Chelmsford, MA
Hall, James A. ... Akron, OH
Hall, James A. ... Columbus, OH
Hall, James A. ... San Antonio, TX
Hall, James A., Jr. ... Tuscaloosa, AL
Hall, James C. ... Albuquerque, NM
Hall, James C. ... Oak Ridge, TN
Hall, James Christopher ... Chattanooga, TN
Hall, James D. ... South Bend, IN
Hall, James D. ... Bossier City, LA
Hall, James E. ... Los Angeles, CA
Hall, James E. ... Redford, MI
Hall, James E., II ... Florence, AL
Hall, James E., P.C., Law Offices of
Redford, MI
Hall, James F., II ... Austell, GA
Hall, James H., Jr. ... Milwaukee, WI
Hall, James L., Jr. ... Pine Bluff, AR
Hall, James L., Jr. ... Oklahoma City, OK
Hall, James M. ... Fayetteville, AR
Hall, James M. ... Lompoc, CA
Hall, James M. ... San Diego, CA
Hall, James M. ... Boston, MA
Hall, James M. ... Wiggins, MS
Hall, James M., Jr. ... Cincinnati, OH
Hall, James P. ... Wilmington, DE
Hall, James P. ... Wells, ME
Hall, James R. ... Lakeville, MN
Hall, James R. ... Doniphan, MO
Hall, James R. ... Oak Grove, MO
Hall, James R. ... Ambler, PA
Lansdale, PA
Hall, James Rogers (Josh), Jr.
Jackson, MS
Memphis, TN
Hall, Jan C. ... Cincinnati, OH
Hall, Jane Beaumont ... Santa Monica, CA
Hall, Jane G. ... Birmingham, AL
Hall, Jane S. ... San Antonio, TX
Hall, Janet C. ... Bridgeport, CT
Hall, Janet L. ... Elk Grove Village, IL
Hall, Janice L. ... Huntington, WV
Hall, Jas. S., Jr. ... Philadelphia, PA
Hall, Jay A. ... Hawkinsville, GA
Hall, Jean ... South Yarmouth, MA
Hall, Jean A. ... Indianapolis, IN
Hall, Jeffery M. ... Phoenix, AZ
Hall, Jeffrey A. ... Santa Cruz, CA
Hall, Jeffrey A. ... Denver, CO
Chicago, IL
Hall, Jeffrey A.
Department of Housing and Urban Development, Office of General Counsel, GV
Hall, Jeffrey L. ... Hattiesburg, MS
Hall, Jeffrey L. ... Wadsworth, OH
Hall, Jeffrey L. ... Webster Springs, WV
Hall, Jeffrey L., (P.C.) ... Jacksboro, TN
Hall, Jeffrey M. ... Pasadena, CA
Hall, Jeffrey M., Law Offices ... Princeton, NJ
Hall, Jeffrey R. ... Walnut Creek, CA
Hall, Jeffrey W. ... Salt Lake City, UT
Hall, Jeffry H. ... Charleston, WV
Hall, Jennelle ... Portland, OR
Hall, Jennifer ... Harleysville, PA
Hall, Jennifer Anne ... Denver, CO
Hall, Jennifer C. ... San Jose, CA
Hall, Jennifer M. ... Chicago, IL
Hall & Jensen, Ltd. ... Waukegan, IL
Hall, Jerilynn Ono ... Kamuela, HI
Lihue, HI
Hall, Jerome L. ... Fort Lauderdale, FL
Hall, Jerome L., P.A. ... Fort Lauderdale, FL
Hall, Jerry D. ... Stockton, CA
Hall, Jerry L., Jr. ... Vienna, VA
Hall, Jerry W. ... Vancouver, WA
Hall, Jess, Jr. ... Houston, TX
Hall, Jill ... Austin, TX
Hall, Jill Cernuda ... Marysville, CA
Hall, Jill Pedigo ... Milwaukee, WI
Hall, Jimmy Alan ... Austin, TX
Hall, J. M. Dryden, Jr. ... Baltimore, MD
Hall, Joan M., (Ltd.) ... Chicago, IL
Hall, Joel C. ... Oklahoma City, OK
Hall, Joel R. ... San Bruno, CA
Hall, John ... Jackson, MS
Hall, John A. ... Austin, TX
Hall, John A. F. ... Harrisburg, PA
Hall, John B. ... Newark, NJ
Hall, John B. ... Houston, TX
Hall, John C., III ... Birmingham, AL
Hall, John C., Law Offices of
Bakersfield, CA
Hall, John E. ... St. Louis, MO
Hall, John E. ... Wilkesboro, NC
Hall, John E. ... Pittsburgh, PA
Hall, John E. ... Huntington, WV
Hall, John E., Jr. ... Atlanta, GA
Hall, John F. ... Easton, MD
Hall, John F. ... Fremont, OH
Hall, John F. ... Seattle, WA
Hall, John F., Jr.
National Aeronautics And Space Administration, Office of the General Counsel, GV
Hall, John G. ... Staten Island, NY
Hall, John H. ... San Francisco, CA
Hall, John H. ... New York, NY
Hall, John H. ... Dallas, TX
Hall, John H., Jr. ... Garden City, NY
Hall, John H., Jr. ... Elizabeth City, NC
Hall, John H., Jr.
Research Triangle Park, NC
Hall, John Henry ... Gary, IN
Hall, John J. ... St. Louis, MO
Hall, John Joseph ... Los Angeles, CA
Hall, John L. ... West Chester, PA
Hall, John M. ... Boston, MA
Hall, John M. ... North Syracuse, NY
Hall, John M. ... Seattle, WA
Hall, John P. ... Dallas, TX
Hall, John R. ... Washington, DC
Hall, John R. ... Seattle, WA
Hall, John R., II ... Stamford, CT
Hall, John T., III ... Raleigh, NC
Hall, John W. ... Portsmouth, VA
Hall, John W., Jr. ... Plainsboro, NJ
Hall, John Wendell ... Encino, CA
Hall, John Wesley, Jr. ... Little Rock, AR
Hall, John Wesley, Jr., A Professional Corporation ... Fayetteville, AR
Fort Smith, AR
Little Rock, AR
Hall, Jon ... Winter Haven, FL
Hall, Jon C., (P.A.) ... Miami, FL
Hall, Jonathan E. ... Raleigh, NC
Hall & Joneth, P.C. ... Raleigh, NC
Hall, Joseph A. ... New York, NY
Hall, Joseph E. ... Los Angeles, CA
Hall, Joseph K. ... Fort Lauderdale, FL
Hall, Joseph M. ... Newport, RI
Hall, Judith A. ... San Francisco, CA
Hall, Judy A. ... Hopkinsville, KY
Hall, Julie Gamburg ... Chester, SC
Hall, Julie L. ... Sunnyvale, CA
Hall, Justin K. ... Albuquerque, NM
Hall, K. Mark ... Pittsburgh, PA
Hall, Karen A. ... San Francisco, CA
Hall, Karen B. ... Memphis, TN
Hall, Karen Kimbrell ... Huntsville, AL
Hall, Karl E., Jr ... Miami, FL
Hall & Karz ... Canandaigua, NY
Hall, Katherine A. Killen
Minneapolis, MN
Hall, Katherine C. ... Pittsburgh, PA
Hall, Katherine E. ... Sacramento, CA
Hall, Katherine Rounsborg
North Platte, NE
Hall, Katherine Weeks ... Santa Fe, NM
Hall, Kathleen J. ... Bismarck, ND
Hall, Kathleen S. ... Kansas City, MO
Hall, Keith A. ... Rye Brook, NY
Hall, Keith B. ... New Orleans, LA
Hall, Keith E. ... Los Angeles, CA
Hall, Keith R. ... Dayton, OH
Hall, Kelley M. ... Greenville, SC
Hall, Kellyn A. ... Palm Beach Gardens, FL
Hall, Ken R. ... Minneapolis, MN
Hall, Kendra J. ... Los Angeles, CA
San Diego, CA
Hall, Kenneth F. ... New York, NY
Hall, Kenneth H.
Securities and Exchange Commission, Division of Enforcement, GV
Hall, Kenneth H. ... East Aurora, NY
Hall, Kenneth L. ... Las Vegas, NV
Hall, Kenneth N. ... Mountain Home, AR
Hall, Kenneth R. ... Park Ridge, IL
Hall, Kenneth R. ... Minneapolis, MN
Hall, Kenneth R. ... Jackson, MS
Hall, Kenneth S. ... Norristown, PA
Hall & Kent ... Long Beach, CA
Hall, Kenton M. ... Jackson, MO
Hall, Kevin ... New York, NY
Hall, Kevin A. ... Columbia, SC
Hall, Kevin P. ... Los Angeles, CA
Hall, Kevin R. ... Marion, OH
Hall, Kevin W. ... Macon, GA
Hall, Kim ... Knox, IN
Hall, Kim Majors ... Tulsa, OK
Hall, Kimberly M. ... Boca Raton, FL
Hall, Kirk R. ... Lake Oswego, OR

Hall & Kleeman, PLLC ... Austin, TX
Hall, Kristin Karls ... Everett, WA
Hall, Kristina M. ... Sacramento, CA
Hall, Kyle M. ... Broomfield, CO
Hall, Kyle S. ... Raleigh, NC
Hall, L. Michael ... St. Cloud, MN
Hall, L. Nelson ... Corpus Christi, TX
Hall, Lance ... Sweetwater, TX
Hall & Lane, L.L.P. ... San Angelo, TX
Hall, Larik M. ... St. Paul, MN
Hall, Larry C. ... Laurel, MD
Hall, Larry D. ... Lakewood, CO
Hall, Larry D. ... Orlando, FL
Hall, Larry G. ... Chicago, IL
Hall, Laura Louise ... Concord, NH
Hall, Laura R. ... Atlanta, GA
Hall, Laurence C.
Palos Verdes Estates, CA
Hall, Laurie J. ... Boston, MA
Hall, Lavinia E. ... Boston, MA
Hall Law Office, The ... Rockwall, TX
Hall, Lawrence A. ... Tulsa, OK
Hall, Lawrence J. ... Silverton, OR
Hall, Lawrence R. ... Bremerton, WA
Hall, Lee Murray ... Huntington, WV
Hall, Leo ... Ashville, OH
Circleville, OH
Hall, Leonard A. ... Olathe, KS
Hall, Leonard D. ... Youngstown, OH
Hall, Lestage & Landreneau
De Ridder, LA
Lake Charles, LA
Hall, Lester Leonard ... Tustin, CA
Hall, Levy, DeVore, Bell, Ott & Kritz,
Professional Association ... Coffeyville, KS
Hall and Lewis, P.C. ... Mount Pleasant, MI
Hall, Linda A. ... Waterloo, IA
Hall, Linda A. ... Tulsa, OK
Hall, Linnea K. ... Starkville, MS
Hall, Lisa Boylan ... Baltimore, MD
Hall, Lisa Comber ... West Chester, PA
Hall, Lisa Jellison ... Knoxville, TN
Hall, L. Michael, P.A. ... St. Cloud, MN
Hall, Lori L. ... Chicago, IL
Hall, Louis ... New York, NY
Hall & Lunn ... Bangor, ME
Hall, Lyman J. ... Missoula, MT
Hall, Lynn E. ... Los Angeles, CA
Hall, Lysle G., Jr. ... Jackson, MI
Hall, Lyssa Eileen ... Department of Labor,
Pension and Welfare Benefits, GV
Hall, M. Brent ... Elizabethtown, KY
Hall, M. Chapin ... Eden Prairie, MN
Hall, M. Christopher ... New York, NY
Hall, M. Craig ... Atlanta, GA
Hall, M. Lewis, III ... Miami, FL
Sarasota, FL
Hall, M. Lewis, Jr. ... Miami, FL
Hall, M. Scott ... Fort Wayne, IN
Hall, M. Wesley, III ... Madison, TN
Hall, Margaret Cunnane ... Milford, NH
Hall, Margaret Donahue ... Dallas, TX
Hall, Margaret Yowell ... Fairfax, VA
Hall, Marianne Mele ... Vineland, NJ
Hall, Marilyn K. ... Lansing, MI
Hall, Marion H., Mr. ... Macon, GA
Hall, Mark C. ... Lubbock, TX
Hall, Mark E. ... Tempe, AZ
Hall, Mark G. ... Burlington, VT
Hall, Mark Gabriel ... Prospect, KY
Hall, Mark R. ... New Smyrna Beach, FL
Hall, Mark R. ... Dallas, TX
Hall, Mark R., P.A.
New Smyrna Beach, FL
Hall, Mark S. ... Austin, TX
Hall, Mark Spencer ... Santa Ana, CA
Hall, Marlene D. ... New York, NY
Hall, Marshall King ... Fort Myers, FL
Hall, Martha M. ... San Diego, CA
Hall, Martin ... Boston, MA
Hall & Martin ... North Syracuse, NY
Hall, Martin E. ... Lexington, KY
Hall & Martin, Inc.
Palos Verdes Estates, CA
Hall, Martin S. ... Barrington, IL
Hall, Mary Anne ... Atlanta, GA
Hall, Mary Anne ... Alexandria, VA
Hall, Mary Elaine ... Cleveland, OH
Hall, Mary Elizabeth ... Jackson, MS
Hall, Mary Jane ... Norfolk, VA
Hall, Mary M. ... Chicago, IL
Hall, Mary T. ... Department of the Navy,
Office of the Judge Advocate General, GV
Hall & Mathis, P.C. ... Denver, CO
Hall, Matthew F. ... Washington, DC
Hall, Matthew S. ... Cheshire, CT
Hall, Matthew W. ... Philadelphia, PA
Hall, Maureen L. ... Missoula, MT
Hall, Maureen R. ... Charlotte, NC
Hall, Maurice H., Jr. ... Meridian, MS
Hall, Maurice J. ... West Palm Beach, FL
Hall, Melissa Beth ... Waukesha, WI
Hall, Melvin C. ... Oklahoma City, OK
Hall, Michael ... Commack, NY
Hall, Michael A. ... Peoria, IL
Hall, Michael C. ... Albany, GA
Hall, Michael C. ... Richmond, VA
Hall, Michael D. ... Reston, VA
Hall, Michael E. ... Traverse City, MI
Hall, Michael E., P.C. ... Traverse City, MI
Hall, Michael J. ... Albany, NY
Hall, Michael J. ... Southold, NY
Hall, Michael L. ... Birmingham, AL
Hall, Michael L. ... Seattle, WA
Hall, Michael M. ... Saginaw, MI
Hall, Michael P. ... Manchester, NH
Hall, Michael R. ... Tallahassee, FL
Hall, Michael R. ... Las Vegas, NV
Hall, Michael S. ... Cincinnati, OH
Hall, Michael Seth ... New York, NY
Hall, Michael T. ... Dayton, OH
Hall, Michael W. ... Menlo Park, CA
Hall, Michael W. ... Palo Alto, CA
Hall, Michael W. ... Washington, DC
Hall, Michael W. ... Fulton, NY
Hall, Michael Wayne ... Edmonds, WA
Hall, Molly E. ... Milwaukee, WI
Hall, Mona M. ... San Anselmo, CA
Hall, Monahan, Engle, Mahan & Mitchell
Leesburg, VA
Winchester, VA
Hall, Monica M. ... Newport Beach, CA
Hall, Monica N. ... Crownsville, MD
Hall, Monte ... Las Vegas, NV
Hall, Monty ... Elizabethtown, KY
Hall, Morse, Anderson, Miller & Spinella,
P.C. ... Concord, NH
Hall, Moses S. ... Fullerton, CA
Hall & Mullins, P.C. ... Atlanta, GA
Augusta, GA
Hall, Munford Page, II ... Washington, DC
Hall, Myron J. ... Waukegan, IL
Hall, Nancy J. ... El Segundo, CA
Hall, Nancy L. ... Cambridge, MA
Hall, Naneaster F. ... New York, NY
Hall, Narrvel E. ... Salt Lake City, UT
Hall, Ned ... Vancouver, WA
Hall, Nelson R. ... Portland, OR
Hall, Nicholas B. ... Grafton, ND
Hall, Nicole C. ... Atlanta, GA
Hall, Nikki ... San Francisco, CA
Hall, Norman D., Jr. ... Phoenix, AZ
Hall, O. Wendell, Jr. ... Benton, AR
Hall & O'Donnell, L.L.P. ... Raleigh, NC
Hall, O. Z., Jr. ... Birmingham, AL
Hall, Pamela ... New York, NY
Hall, Pamela Loftin ... Amory, MS
Tupelo, MS
Hall, Partenheimer & Kinkle
Evansville, IN
Princeton, IN
Hall, Pat ... El Dorado, AR
Hall, Pat ... San Angelo, TX
Hall, Patricia A. ... Durango, CO
Hall, Patricia A. ... Paramus, NJ
Hall, Patricia B. ... Raleigh, NC
Hall, Patricia D. ... Ventura, CA
Hall, Patricia Winston ... Mobile, AL
Hall, Patrick C. ... Winchester, MA
Hall, Patrick C. ... Troy, MI
Hall, Patrick Q. ... San Diego, CA
Hall, Patrick Talbot ... San Francisco, CA
Hall, Patrick W. ... Carroll, IA
Glidden, IA
Hall, Paul J. ... San Francisco, CA
Hall, Paula S. ... Santa Rosa, CA
Hall, Peggy Kubicz ... St. Paul, MN
Hall, Perce ... Mountain Home, ID
Hall, Peter C. ... Doylestown, PA
Hall, Peter W. ... Rutland, VT
Hall, Philip H. ... Chicago, IL
Hall, Philip J. ... Tucson, AZ
Hall, Philip Lyle ... Yuma, AZ
Hall, Philip M. ... Corpus Christi, TX
Hall, Phillip R. ... San Antonio, TX
Hall, Philo I. ... Aberdeen, SD
Hall, Phoebe P. ... Richmond, VA
Hall and Piazza ... Jamestown, NY
Hall, Pike, Jr. ... Shreveport, LA
Hall, Pinckney & Kintner, P.S.
Bremerton, WA
Hall & Pittman ... Chester, SC
Rock Hill, SC
Hall, Priddy & Myers ... Washington, DC
Potomac, MD
Hall, Quintanilla & Alarcon, L.C.
Laredo, TX
Hall, R. Brian ... Gladstone, MO
Hall, R. Bruce ... Dothan, AL
Hall, R. Eric ... Allentown, PA
Hall, Rachel Brown ... Greensboro, NC
Hall, Rafe Robert ... Altus, OK
Hall, Ralph C. ... Corpus Christi, TX
Hall, Ralph E., Jr. ... Vero Beach, FL
Hall, Ralph F. ... St. Paul, MN
Hall, Ralph M. ... Rockwall, TX
Hall, Randall I. ... Springdale, AR
Hall, Randall J. ... Camden, AR
Hall, Randall R. ... Bloomfield Hills, MI
Hall, Randolph Warren ... El Sobrante, CA
Hall, Randy J. ... Fort Worth, TX
Hall, Randy J. ... Fort Worth, TX
Hall, Raymond G. ... Vista, CA
Hall, Raymond W. ... Bloomington, MN
Hall, Reed E. ... Marshfield, WI
Hall, Render, Killian, Heath & Lyman,
Professional Services Corporation
Indianapolis, IN
Louisville, KY
Hall, Ricardo A. ... Merrillville, IN
Hall, Richard ... New York, NY
Hall, Richard ... Houston, TX
Hall, Richard A. ... Auburn, CA
Hall, Richard D. ... Los Angeles, CA
Hall, Richard D. ... Atlanta, GA
Hall, Richard D., Jr. ... Greensboro, NC
Hall, Richard D., Jr., P.A. ... Greensboro, NC
Hall, Richard E. ... Boise, ID
Hall, Richard E. ... North Syracuse, NY
Hall, Richard F., Jr. ... Accomac, VA
Hall, Richard G. ... Long Beach, CA
Hall, Richard G. ... Reston, VA
Hall, Richard J. ... Indianapolis, IN
Hall, Richard L., (P.C.) ... Pasadena, CA
Hall, Richard M. ... Capistrano Beach, CA
Hall, Richard M. ... Indianapolis, IN
Hall, Richard P. ... Littleton, CO
Hall, Richard S., Law Offices of
Riverside, CA
Hall, Richard T. ... Chelmsford, MA
Hall, Richard V. ... Colorado Springs, CO
Hall, Richard W. ... Park Forest, IL
Hall, Richard W. ... Bangor, ME
Hall, Rick J. ... Salt Lake City, UT
Hall, Ricketts, Marky & Gurbacki
East Aurora, NY
Hall, Ridgway M., Jr. ... Washington, DC
Hall, Risa L. ... Central Point, OR
Hall, Robert ... Wichita, KS
Hall, Robert A. ... Oakbrook Terrace, IL
Hall, Robert A. ... Houston, TX
Hall, Robert A. ... Lake Kiowa, TX
Hall, Robert A., Jr. ... Wasilla, AK
Hall, Robert B. ... Spartanburg, SC
Hall, Robert C. ... Peoria, IL
Hall, Robert C. ... Elmsford, NY
Hall, Robert C. ... Philadelphia, PA
Hall, Robert Charles
Dearborn Heights, MI
Hall, Robert D. ... Ankeny, IA
Hall, Robert D. ... Harwich Port, MA
Hall, Robert D. ... Columbia, MO
Hall, Robert D., Jr. ... Tampa, FL
Hall, Robert E. ... Los Angeles, CA
Hall, Robert E. ... Houston, TX
Hall, Robert E." Ted " ... Atlanta, GA
Hall, Robert F. ... Southold, NY
Hall, Robert G. ... Fairlawn, OH
Hall, Robert G., Jr. ... Norwalk, CT
Hall, Robert H. ... Newtown, CT
Hall, Robert J. ... Aurora, CO
Hall, Robert J. ... Chicago, IL
Hall, Robert J. ... Seattle, WA
Hall, Robert John ... Garden City, NY
Hall, Robert M. ... El Segundo, CA
Hall, Robert M. ... Washington, DC
Hall, Robert M. ... Williamsport, IN
Hall, Robert M. ... Albuquerque, NM
Hall, Robert P. ... Oklahoma City, OK
Hall, Robert P., Jr. ... Greenbrae, CA
Hall, Robert Price, III ... United States Senate,
Senatorial Assistants, GV
Hall, Robert R. ... Phoenix, AZ
Hall, Robert R. ... Lafayette, CA
Hall, Robert S., Jr. ... Washington, DC
Hall, Robert Stephen ... Denver, CO
Hall, Robert T. ... Springfield, IL
Hall, Robert T. ... Reston, VA
Hall, Robert T., III ... Washington, DC
Hall, Robert Trent ... Dyersburg, TN
Hall, Robert W. ... Harlan, IA
Hall, Robin Ann ... Dobbs Ferry, NY
Hall, Robin L. ... Department of the Army,
U.S. Army Legal Services Agency, GV
Hall & Rochelle ... Texarkana, TX
Hall, Rochelle S. ... St. Louis, MO
Hall, Roderick R. ... Boise, ID
Hall, Roger R. ... Madison, WI
Hall, Roger W. ... Phoenix, AZ
Hall, Roger W. ... Ashland, KY
Hall, Roger W., P.C. ... Phoenix, AZ
Hall, Roland F. ... Atlanta, GA
Hall, Ronald E., Jr. ... Detroit, MI
Hall, Ronald J. ... Aberdeen, SD
Hall, Ronald L. ... Kansas City, MO
Hall, Ronald L. ... Burlington, NC
Hall, Ronald M. ... Downey, CA
Hall, Rosanne M. ... Denver, CO
Hall, Rosemarie A. ... Canton, OH
Hall, Roy A. ... Orange Beach, AL
Hall, Roy G., Jr. ... Winston-Salem, NC
Hall, Roy J. D., Jr. ... Pago Pago, TT
Hall & Runnels, P.A. ... Destin, FL
Hall, Rupert A., Jr. ... Moorestown, NJ
Hall, Russell D. ... Buffalo, NY
Hall, Russell D. ... Midwest City, OK
Hall, Russell E. ... Valhalla, NY
Hall, Russell W. ... Escanaba, MI
Hall, Ruth ... Ovid, NY
Hall, Ruth A. ... Union, NH
Hall, Ruth Ann ... Huntsville, AL
Hall, Ruth Ann ... Tuscaloosa, AL
Hall, Ryan J. ... Seattle, WA
Hall, S. Jeanne ... New York, NY
Hall, Sam J., Jr. ... Pensacola, FL
Hall, Sam W., Jr. ... Martinez, CA
Hall, Samuel A., Sr. ... Brookings, OR
Hall, Samuel H., Jr.
Charlotte Amalie, St. Thomas, VI
Hall, Samuel L., Jr. ... Richmond, VA
Hall, Samuel M. ... Pensacola, FL
Hall, Samuel M. ... Canandaigua, NY
Hall, Sara L. ... Memphis, TN
Hall, Sara N. ... Welch, WV
Hall, Sarah Alexander
Oklahoma City, OK
Hall, Sarah E. ... Jacksonville, FL
Hall, Sarah E. ... Seattle, WA
Hall, Sarah Elizabeth ... Fairfax, VA
Hall, Sarah Kent ... Saco, ME
Hall & Savarese, P.C. ... Danbury, CT
Newtown, CT
Hall and Schlenker ... Indianola, IA
Hall & Schwartz ... Baltimore, MD
Hall, Scott A. ... Cranford, NJ
Marlton, NJ
Hall, Scott D. ... Sevierville, TN
Hall, Scott Middleton ... Orange, CA
Hall, Scott R. ... Idaho Falls, ID
Hall, Scott R. ... Tulsa, OK
Hall, Sharon L. ... Treasury Department,
Internal Revenue Service, GV
Hall, Sharon L. ... Elk River, MN
Hall, Shawn D. ... Milpitas, CA
Hall, Shelley ... Seattle, WA
Hall, Shelvin Louise Marie, (Ms.)
Chicago, IL
Hall, Sherry Grant ... Destin, FL
Hall and Sickels, P.C. ... Fairfax, VA
Reston, VA
Hall, Sidney W. ... Baton Rouge, LA
Hall, Smith & Conaway ... Dothan, AL
Hall, Sophia H. ... Chicago, IL
Hall, Spencer ... Seattle, WA
Hall, Stefanie M. ... Santa Monica, CA
Hall, Stephanie McClain ... San Antonio, TX
Hall, Stephen A. ... Indianola, IA
Hall, Stephen C. ... Louisville, KY
Hall, Stephen C. ... Portland, OR
Hall, Stephen C. ... Richmond, VA
Hall, Stephen D. ... Idaho Falls, ID
Hall, Stephen E. ... Chicago, IL
Hall, Stephen E. ... Meadville, PA
Hall, Stephen H. ... Huntsville, AL
Hall, Stephen K. ... San Luis Obispo, CA
Hall, Stephen K. ... Hendersonville, NC
Hall, Stephen M. ... Redwood City, CA
Hall, Stephen P. ... New Orleans, LA
Hall, Stephen W. ... Washington, DC
Hall, Stephen W. ... Lake Worth, FL
Hall, Stephen W., P.A. ... Lake Worth, FL
Hall, Steven E. ... Farmington Hills, MI
Hall, Steven G. ... Atlanta, GA
Hall, Steven K. ... Destin, FL
Hall, Steven R. ... Indianapolis, IN
Hall, Stewart K. ... Hudson, NH
Hall, Stuart A. ... Portland, OR
Hall, Stuart C. ... Anchorage, AK
Hall, Stuart H. ... Gaffney, SC
Hall, Stuart L. ... Lock Haven, PA
Hall, Sue M. ... San Antonio, TX
Hall, Susan ... Newland, NC
Hall, Susan B. ... Los Angeles, CA
Hall, Susan Joyce ... Fayetteville, NC
Hall, Susan L. ... Totowa, NJ
Hall, Suzanne L. ... Huntington Beach, CA
Hall, Suzanne L. ... Evanston, IL
Hall, Suzanne T. ... Detroit, MI
Hall, Suzy T. ... Milford, OH
Hall, T. Max ... Muncy, PA
Williamsport, PA
Hall, Teresa Dawn ... Williamson, WV
Hall, Terrance A. ... Hillsboro, OR
Hall, Terrance W. ... Fairbanks, AK
Hall, Terrence L. ... Pontiac, MI
Hall, Terry E. ... Newport News, VA
Hall, Terry F. ... Phoenix, AZ
Hall, Terry F. ... Baltimore, MD
Hall, Thelma E. ... Houston, TX
Hall, Theodore L. ... Mobile, AL
Hall, Theodore L. ... Cloquet, MN
Hall, Theresa M. ... Bethesda, MD
Hall, Theresa Shean ... Kansas City, MO
Hall, Theron M., Jr. ... Phoenix, AZ
Hall, Thomas ... Ocean Township, NJ
Hall, Thomas C. ... Troy, NY
Hall, Thomas D. ... Tallahassee, FL
Hall, Thomas D. ... Atlanta, GA
Hall, Thomas D. ... Pittsburgh, PA
Hall, Thomas F. ... Santa Ana, CA
Hall, Thomas G. ... Seattle, WA
Hall, Thomas George, Jr. ... Fort Worth, TX
Hall, Thomas J. ... Palo Alto, CA
Hall, Thomas J. ... South Bend, IN
Hall, Thomas J. ... Reno, NV
Hall, Thomas J. ... Stateline, NV
Hall, Thomas J. ... New York, NY
Hall, Thomas J. ... New York, NY
Hall, Thomas J. ... Staten Island, NY
Hall, Thomas J. ... Roanoke, VA
Hall, Thomas J. ... Wausau, WI
Hall, Thomas Jay ... Newark, NJ
Hall, Thomas K., II ... Beattyville, KY
Hall, Thomas L. ... Bardstown, KY
Hall, Thomas Lee ... Austin, TX
Hall, Thomas P. ... Punta Gorda, FL
Hall, Thomas R. ... Okemos, MI
Hall, Thomas W. ... Lancaster, PA
Hall, Thomas W., Jr. ... Mount Pleasant, MI
Hall, Tiffany J.L. ... Detroit, MI
Hall, Tim D. ... Helena, MT
Hall, Timothy C. ... Sheboygan, WI
Hall, Timothy C., Jr. ... Columbus, OH
Hall, Timothy K. ... Macon, GA
Hall, Timothy S. ... Highland Heights, KY
Hall, Tina A. ... Baltimore, MD
Hall, Tina A. ... Enid, OK
Hall, Tom ... San Antonio, TX
Hall, Tom Brice ... Chester, SC
Hall, Tom, Law Offices of ... Fort Worth, TX
Hall, Toxey, Jr. ... Canton, MS
Hall, Troy A. ... San Diego, CA
Hall, Tucker, FullenKamp and Singer
Dayton, OH
Hall, Veronica Archederra
Las Vegas, NV
Hall, Vic ... China Spring, TX
Hall, Vincent T. ... Arcadia, FL
Hall and Vogler, L.L.P. ... Mocksville, NC
Hall, Vonda G. ... Denver, CO
Hall, W. Bromley ... Greenlawn, NY
Hall, W. Bryan ... Cumberland, MD
Hall, W. Douglas ... Tallahassee, FL
Hall, W. James, III ... Miami, FL
Hall, W. Leland ... Dayton, OH
Hall, W. Marvin, (P.L.C.) ... Metairie, LA
Hall, W. Perry ... Mobile, AL
Hall, W. Wendell ... San Antonio, TX
Hall, Wade ... Asheville, NC
Hall, Wade M. ... Greenville, SC
Hall, Wallace H. ... Sanford, FL
Hall, Walter A., II ... New Orleans, LA

Hall, Walter M. .... Austin, TX
Hall, Walter R., II .... Stamford, CT
Hall, Warren R., Jr. .... Atlanta, GA
Hall, Wayne C. .... Venice, FL
Hall, Wendel V. .... Bethesda, MD
Hall, Wendell F. .... Los Angeles, CA
Hall, Willard, Firm, The .... Beaumont, TX
Hall, Willard J., Jr. .... Beaumont, TX
Hall, William Craig .... Tampa, FL
Hall, William D. .... Greenwood, IN
Hall, William D. .... Shreveport, LA
Hall, William D. .... Potomac, MD
Hall, William D. .... Ponca City, OK
Hall, William D., Jr. .... Tallahassee, FL
Hall, William Douglas .... Blakely, GA
Hall, William Duane .... Marina Del Rey, CA
Hall, William E. .... Vernon, CT
Hall, William E. .... Saint Simons Island, GA
Hall, William E. .... Mocksville, NC
Hall, William E., Jr. .... De Ridder, LA
Hall, William E., Jr. .... Conroe, TX
Hall, William E., Law Offices of, Jr., P.C.
Conroe, TX
Hall, William F. .... Greensboro, NC
Hall, William F., Jr. .... Philadelphia, PA
Hall, William G., Jr. .... Fort Lauderdale, FL
Hall, William H. .... Los Angeles, CA
Hall, William H. .... Soddy-Daisy, TN
Hall, William H., Jr. .... Richmond, VA
Hall, William J. .... Scranton, PA
Hall, William L. .... Independence, MO
Hall, William M., Jr. .... Campbellsville, KY
Hall, William Mitchell .... Ashland, KY
Hall, William N. .... Washington, DC
Hall, William P. .... Houston, TX
Hall, William S. .... Indianapolis, IN
Hall, William S. .... Concord, NH
Hall, William T., & Associates .... Austin, TX
Hall, William V., Jr. .... Decatur, GA
Hall, William W. .... Grand Rapids, MI
Hall, William W., & Associates
Metairie, LA
Hall, William W., & Associates
New Orleans, LA
Hall, Willie Earl, (P.A.)
Fort Lauderdale, FL
Hall, Willis B. .... Spring Valley, CA
Hall, W. M. .... Campbellsville, KY
Hall, Wm. Craig .... Collierville, TN
Hall, Wm. Gregory, Jr. .... Knoxville, TN
Hall, W. Q. .... Huntsville, AR
Hall, Wright & Baker, P.A. .... Fayetteville, AR
Hall, Wynne duMariau Caffey
Knoxville, TN
Hall Zanzig Widell PLLC .... Seattle, WA
Halla, F. Johnson .... Minneapolis, MN
Halla, Trudy J. .... Minneapolis, MN
Halla, Walter R. .... Birmingham, MI
Hallab, Charles Salem .... Chicago, IL
Hallabrin, Scott J. .... Sacramento, CA
Hallacher, Lester L. .... Princeton, NJ
Hallack, Dennis W. .... Monroe, LA
Hallack, Robert W. .... Baton Rouge, LA
Hallack, Robert W., A Professional Law Corporation .... Baton Rouge, LA
Hallack, William H., Jr. .... Monroe, LA
Hallacy, John Adrian .... Battle Creek, MI
Halladay, Angela K. .... Little Rock, AR
Orlando, FL
Halladay, Emilie D. .... Tempe, AZ
Halladay, Michael B. .... Tucson, AZ
Halladay, Roberta L. .... Washington, DC
Hallagan, James .... Chicago, IL
Hallagan, John B. .... Washington, DC
Hallagan, Kevin J. .... Racine, WI
Hallagan, Stuart D., III .... Providence, RI
Hallahan, Felicia Koprowicz
Woodbridge, NJ
Hallahan, James C. .... Geneva, IL
Hallahan, Janet V. .... Philadelphia, PA
Hallahan, Laura M. .... Bloomfield Hills, MI
Hallahan, Maureen F. .... San Diego, CA
Hallahan, Sheila A. .... Somers, NY
Hallahan, Susan .... Reno, NV
Hallahan, William J. .... Chevy Chase, MD
Hallajian, Andrew H .... Huntington, NY
Hallak, Anthony G. .... Clinton, NY
Hallake, Marcello (IBA) .... **New York, NY**
Hallal, George L. .... Uniontown, PA
Hallal, John R. .... Boston, MA
Hallal, Thomas J., Jr. .... Fall River, MA
Hallam, Charles Richard .... Phoenix, AZ
Hallam, Jeffrey C. .... San Francisco, CA
Hallam, Kirk M. .... Beverly Hills, CA
Hallam, Linda .... Oceanside, CA
Hallam, Michael .... Phoenix, AZ
Hallam, Peter G. .... Chicago, IL
Hallam, Robert G. .... Dallas, TX
Hallam, William L. .... Baltimore, MD
Hallanan, Elizabeth V. .... Beckley, WV
Hallanan, Sharon M. .... Trenton, NJ
Hall-App, Robert P. .... New York, NY
Hallas, Charles C. .... Bridgeport, CT
Hallas, Herbert C. .... Malone, NY
Hallas, Linda M. .... Largo, FL
Hallas, Louise L. .... Hartford, CT
Hallas, Maria E. .... Raleigh, NC
Hallauer, Debra Davis .... Leawood, KS
Kansas City, MO
Hallbauer, John A. .... Cleveland, OH
Hallbauer, John B. .... Walnut Creek, CA
Hallbauer, Miriam .... Chicago, IL
Hallberg, Charles A. .... Oelwein, IA
Hallberg, Ernest V., Jr. .... Falls Church, VA
Hallberg, Kathleen .... Los Angeles, CA
Hallberg, Krista S. .... Chicago, IL
Hallberg, Mark A. .... Minneapolis, MN
Hallberg, V. Rodney .... Estes Park, CO
Hallberlin, Cynthia J.
United States Postal Service, Law Department, GV
Hallborg, Robert Babcock, Jr. .... Buffalo, NY
Hallcom, Danielle D. .... Washington, DC
Halldorson, Burke M. .... Midland, MI
Halle, April I. .... Fort Lauderdale, FL
Halle, Barbara W. .... Portland, OR
Halle, Edward .... Boca Raton, FL
Halle, Edward A., Jr. .... Hunt Valley, MD
Halle, Edward J. .... Chicago, IL
Halle, Ernest W. .... Cheyenne, WY
Halle, John J. .... Portland, OR
Halle, M. Henry .... Seattle, WA
Halle, Marla B. .... New City, NY
Halle, Oliver G. .... Atlanta, GA
Halle, Peter E. .... Washington, DC
Halle, William E. .... Irvine, CA
Halleck & Beaver .... Rensselaer, IN
Halleck & Geer .... Bowling Green, OH
Halleck & Halleck .... Bowling Green, OH
Halleck, John C. .... Bowling Green, OH
Halleck, Lisa E. .... Norfolk, VA
Halleck, Michael J. .... Bowling Green, OH
Halleck, Nancy H. .... Albany, NY
Halleck, Peter T. .... Bowling Green, OH
Halleck, Roger R. .... Des Moines, IA
Halleen, Michelle L. .... Omaha, NE
Halleen, Otis H. .... Des Plaines, IL
Halleen, Toni L. .... Minnetonka, MN
Halleland, Keith J. .... Minneapolis, MN
Halleland Lewis Nilan Sipkins & Johnson P.A. .... Minneapolis, MN
Hallem, James .... Flint, MI
Hallem, Jeffrey P. .... Pierre, SD
Hallem, Timi Anyon .... Los Angeles, CA
Hallemann, Michelle .... Manchester, MO
Hallen, C. Bradley .... Carlsbad, CA
Hallen, C. Bradley .... Encinitas, CA
Hallen, Shelley Odin .... Miami, FL
Hallenbeck, Alfred M. .... Rochester, NY
Hallenbeck, John H. .... Dunkirk, NY
Hallenbeck, Julianne M. .... Pittsburgh, PA
Hallenbeck, Lascell, Norris & Heller
Rochester, NY
Hallenbeck, Lisa Anne .... Butte, MT
Hallenbeck, Mark D. .... Atlanta, GA
Hallenbeck, Prentiss W., Jr.
Cincinnati, OH
Hallenbeck, Robert M. .... Franklin Lakes, NJ
Hallenbeck, Stephen M. .... Oak Lawn, IL
Hallenberg, Robert L. .... Louisville, KY
Hallenborg, Mary Ann .... Upper Nyack, NY
Haller, Albert J. .... St. Louis, MO
Haller, Alexis .... San Francisco, CA
Haller, Alice Milmed .... Summit, NJ
Haller, Andrew P. .... Philadelphia, PA
Haller, Anthony B. .... Philadelphia, PA
Haller, Carol M. .... Greeley, CO
Haller, Colin K. .... Arlington, VA
Haller & Colvin, P.C. .... Fort Wayne, IN
Haller, Daniel L. .... Pittsburgh, PA
Haller, David .... Harrisburg, PA
Haller, David K. .... Mount Pleasant, SC
Haller, David W. .... New York, NY
Haller, Diane M. .... Phoenix, AZ
Haller, Don H., III .... Astoria, OR
Haller, Donald B. .... Arlington, VA
Haller, Fred T., III .... Glendale, NY
Haller, James R. .... Minneapolis, MN
Haller, Jo Ann .... Pittsburgh, PA
Haller, John D. .... New York, NY
Haller, John E. .... Columbus, OH
Haller, John L. .... San Diego, CA
Haller, John R. .... Weston, WV
Haller, John T., Jr. .... Cranberry Township, PA
Haller, Judith L. .... San Diego, CA
Haller, Judith Mellon .... Hobart, IN
Haller, Judy A. .... Colorado Springs, CO
Haller, Karen S. .... Las Vegas, NV
Haller, Karl .... Georgetown, DE
Haller, Kathryn .... Columbus, OH
Haller, Laura K. .... San Francisco, CA
Haller, Leon P. .... Harrisburg, PA
Haller, Linda L.
Federal Communications Commission, International Bureau, GV
Haller, Marcia H. .... Erie, PA
Haller, Martin R. .... Boston, MA
Haller, Mary Beth .... Baltimore, MD
Haller, Maryanne B. .... Cleveland, OH
Haller, Michael J., Jr. .... Omaha, NE
Haller, Mitchell .... San Anselmo, CA
Haller, Natalie Dwyer .... Erie, PA
Haller, Nina J. .... Palo Alto, CA
Haller, Paul H. .... Colorado Springs, CO
Haller, Peter E. .... New York, NY
Haller, Peter H. .... Seattle, WA
Haller, Philip L. .... Louisville, KY
Haller, R. Gregory .... Colorado Springs, CO
Haller, Rebecca R. .... Chicago, IL
Haller, Robert W. .... Fort Wayne, IN
Haller, Sonja M. .... Richfield, OH
Haller, Stephen K. .... Xenia, OH
Haller, Stephen P. .... Livingston, NJ
Haller, Susan C. .... Washington, DC
Haller, Susan Z. .... McLean, VA
Haller, Thomas B., Jr. .... Cary, NC
Haller, Thomas H. .... Lanham, MD
Haller, Timothy J. .... Chicago, IL
Haller & Wagoner, L.C. .... Weston, WV
Haller, Wendy A. .... New York, NY
Haller, William B. .... Ballwin, MO
Halleran, James H. .... Dublin, OH
Halleran, John R. .... Middletown, NJ
Halleran, Michael A. .... Olathe, KS
Halleran, Richard C. .... Pittsburgh, PA
Halleran, Vincent E., Jr. .... Freehold, NJ
Hallerdin, Gail I. .... Buffalo, NY
Halleron, John J., III .... East Islip, NY
Halleron, L. Timothy .... New York, NY
Hallert & Hallert, A Law Corporation
Walnut Creek, CA
Hallert, Marc E. .... Walnut Creek, CA
Hallert, Steven D. .... Walnut Creek, CA
Hallerud, John C. .... Chicago, IL
Hallerud, Michael C. .... San Francisco, CA
Hallett, Bruce H. .... Dallas, TX
Hallett, Bruce R. .... Irvine, CA
Hallett, Corinne .... Hinsdale, IL
Hallett, Darrell D. .... Seattle, WA
Hallett, David J. .... Boston, MA
Provincetown, MA
Hallett, Denise M. .... Hobart, IN
Hallett, Erma R., (Miss) .... St. Petersburg, FL
Hallett, Eugene R. .... San Bernardino, CA
Hallett, Hallett & Nagel .... Wauseon, OH
Hallett, Ingrid .... Minneapolis, MN
Hallett, James M. .... Manhattan Beach, CA
Hallett, Kenneth V. .... Milwaukee, WI
Hallett, Lawrence J., Jr. .... Mobile, AL
Hallett, Lester S. .... Wauseon, OH
Hallett, Mark S. .... Princeton, NJ
Hallett & McCormick .... Woodland Hills, CA
Yorba Linda, CA
San Bernardino, CA
Hallett & Perrin, P.C. .... Dallas, TX
Hallett, R. F. .... Irvine, CA
Hallett, Steve .... Trenton, NJ
Hallett, Terrence E. .... Swanton, OH
Hallett, Thomas F. .... Portland, ME
Hallett, Timothy W. .... Wauseon, OH
Halley, Calkins & Avallone, P.C. .... Miami, FL
New York, NY
Halley, D. Gunnar .... Washington, DC
Halley, David H. .... El Reno, OK
Halley, Duke .... Woodward, OK
Halley, Francis W. .... Modesto, CA
Halley, James J. .... Reno, NV
Halley, James R., Jr. .... New York, NY
Halley, Joanne M. .... Seal Beach, CA
Halley, John A. .... Pittsburgh, PA
Halley, Joyce J. Green .... Treasury Department, Internal Revenue Service, GV
Halley, Mesonie T., Jr. .... Lake Charles, LA
Halley, Michael K. .... Reno, NV
Halley, Philip J. .... Milwaukee, WI
Halley, Thomas P., Jr. .... Poughkeepsie, NY
Halley, Thomas V. .... Miami, FL
Halley, Van M. .... Wichita, KS
Hallford, David C. .... Glenwood Springs, CO
Hallgren, Carl R. .... Lancaster, PA
Hallgren, Peter S. .... Sitka, AK
Hallgren, Wendy A. Learmont .... Irvine, CA
Hallgrimson, Gerald P. .... Anchorage, AK
Hallgrimson McNichols, LLP
Pleasanton, CA
San Jose, CA
Hallgrimson, Steven L. .... Pleasanton, CA
San Jose, CA
Halliburton, Christian M. .... Seattle, WA
Halliburton, David V. .... Las Cruces, NM
Halliburton, Grover C. .... Orange, TX
Halliburton, Jack L. .... Memphis, TN
Halliburton, John R. .... Richardson, TX
Halliburton, Mary L. .... Denver, CO
Halliburton, Richard F. .... Kansas City, MO
Halliburton, Roy W. .... Austin, TX
Halliburton-Cohen, Kim M. .... Columbus, OH
Halliday, Andrew W. .... Albany, NY
Halliday, Bruce K. .... Price, UT
Halliday, Culver V. .... Lexington, KY
Louisville, KY
Halliday, David E. .... Salt Lake City, UT
Halliday, David E., P.C. .... Salt Lake City, UT
Halliday & Gorman, LLP .... Albany, NY
Halliday, Gregory H. .... Irvine, CA
Halliday & Halliday .... Salt Lake City, UT
Halliday, Herbert H., Jr. .... Salt Lake City, UT
Halliday, James Bailey .... Gulfport, MS
Halliday, Joanne A. .... Glendale, CA
Halliday, John M. .... Marietta, OH
Halliday, John T. .... Arlington, VA
Halliday, Joseph W. .... New York, NY
Halliday, Lana .... New York, NY
Halliday, Max G. .... San Diego, CA
Halliday, Michael .... Greenville, PA
Halliday & Monroe .... Canton, NY
Potsdam, NY
Halliday, Paul M. .... Salt Lake City, UT
Halliday, Robert H. .... Canton, NY
Potsdam, NY
Halliday, Ronald E. .... Peoria, IL
Halliday, S. Grant .... Tampa, FL
Halliday, Sheets & Saunders .... Gallipolis, OH
Halliday, Stephen D. .... Washington, DC
Halliday, Susan M. .... Fairfax, VA
Halliday, Walter J. .... Rockville Centre, NY
Halliday, Walter S., Jr.
North Palm Beach, FL
Halliday, William J., Jr.
Grand Rapids, MI
Hallie, Michelena .... New York, NY
Hallifax, Peter .... Oakland, CA
Halligan, Brendan Patrick .... Boston, MA
Halligan, Brian J. .... Tenafly, NJ
Halligan, Brian J. .... Ashland, OH
Halligan, Caitlin J. .... New York, NY
Halligan, Christopher E. .... New York, NY
Halligan, Francis X., Jr. .... Toms River, NJ
Halligan & Ginty .... Ashland, OH
Mansfield, OH
Halligan, James E., Jr. .... Bremerton, WA
Halligan, John Patrick .... Golden, CO
Halligan, Kelly A. .... Ashland, VA
Halligan, Kevin L. .... Davenport, IA
Halligan, Margaret M. .... New York, NY
Halligan, Michael G. .... Portland, OR
Halligan, Mike .... Missoula, MT
Halligan, Patrick D. .... Milwaukee, WI
Halligan, R. Mark .... Chicago, IL
Halligan, Rosemary .... New York, NY
Halligan, Rosemary D. .... Ashland, VA
Halligan, Thomas S. .... Baton Rouge, LA
Halligan, Timothy M. .... Atlanta, GA
Halligan, William F. .... Columbia, SC
Halligan, William G. .... Media, PA
Halligan-Brown, Julie A. .... Des Moines, IA
Halliman, Colleen Leonie .... Chicago, IL
Hallin, Andrew J. .... Walnut Creek, CA
Hallin, David B. .... Longview, WA
Hallin, Jeane Lorraine .... San Bernardino, CA
Hallin, Thomas A. .... Dearborn, MI
Hallinan, C. Joseph, Jr. .... New York, NY
Hallinan & Camche .... New York, NY
Hallinan, David J. .... Salem, MA
Hallinan, Jacqueline A. .... Charleston, WV
Hallinan, Kathleen M. .... Culver City, CA
Hallinan, Lauren Poplack
San Francisco, CA
Hallinan Law Office .... Charleston, WV
Hallinan, Michael R. .... San Francisco, CA
Hallinan, Patrick S. .... San Francisco, CA
Hallinan, Paul G. .... Dayton, OH
Hallinan, Robert E. .... New York, NY
Hallinan, Terence K. .... San Francisco, CA
Hallinan, Thomas J. .... Lincoln, NE
Hallinan, Thomas N. .... Oakdale, CA
Hallinan, Thomas P. .... New York, NY
Hallinan, William J. .... Phoenix, AZ
Hallinan & Wine .... San Francisco, CA
Halline, Janet C. .... San Francisco, CA
Halling, Bruce E. .... Houston, TX
Halling & Cayo, S.C. .... Milwaukee, WI
Halling, Chris W. .... Los Angeles, CA
Halling, Dale B. .... Colorado Springs, CO
Halling, David B. .... Milwaukee, WI
Halling, Gary L. .... San Francisco, CA
Halling, Susan S. .... San Francisco, CA
Hallingby, Jo Davis .... New York, NY
Hallinger, Robert W. .... Lancaster, PA
York, PA
Hallisey, Dennis L. .... Dover, NH
Hallisey, Jas. V. .... New York, NY
Hallisey, Jeremiah F. .... San Francisco, CA
Hallisey, John D. .... Orleans, MA
Hallisey and Johnson .... San Francisco, CA
Hallisey, Peta Lewis .... Mountain View, CA
Hallisey, Robert J. .... Boston, MA
Hallisey, Russell J. .... Medfield, MA
Hallisey, Wade Nolan .... Tyler, TX
Hallissey, Francis J. .... Machias, ME
Hallissey, John J. .... Garden City, NY
Hallissy, Erin B. .... Los Angeles, CA
Hallissy, John P. .... Sacramento, CA
Halliwell, Thomas L. .... Los Angeles, CA
Hall-Justice, Susannah Machin
Logansport, IN
Hall-Keith, Jacqueline Y. .... Detroit, MI
Hall-Lewis, Lynnette .... Metairie, LA
Hallman, Carol A. .... Pocahontas, IA
Pomeroy, IA
Hallman, Christopher J. .... San Diego, CA
Hallman, Clinton H., Jr. .... Greensboro, NC
Hallman, David A. .... Chiefland, FL
Hallman, David A., P.A. .... Chiefland, FL
Hallman, F. Edwin, Jr. .... Atlanta, GA
Hallman, Glen .... Phoenix, AZ
Hallman, Harry W. .... Falmouth, MA
Hallman, Hugh L. .... Phoenix, AZ
Hallman, James E. .... Cleburne, TX
Hallman, Jonathan .... Irvine, CA
Hallman, Larry .... Dallas, TX
Hallman, Leroy .... Dallas, TX
Hallman, Mary K. .... Duluth, GA
Hallman, Michael O. .... Greenville, SC
Hallman, Paul W., Jr. .... Great Falls, VA
Hallman, Robert L. .... Columbia, SC
Hallman, Robert M. .... New York, NY
Hallman, Ronald S. .... Chesapeake, VA
Hallman, Samuel J. .... Dallas, TX
Hallman, Shelley Anne .... Dallas, TX
Hallman, W. Eugene .... La Grande, OR
Hallman, W. Eugene .... Pendleton, OR
Hallman, William H., III .... Brooksville, FL
Hallman, William H., III .... Bushnell, FL
Hallman, William P., Jr. .... Fort Worth, TX
Hallmark, B. Cullen .... Santa Fe, NM
Hallmark, Bob .... Houston, TX
Hallmark, Bruce .... El Paso, TX
Hallmark, James B. .... Dallas, TX
Hallmark, Kadhrann J. .... Brady, TX
Hallmark, Kenzy D. .... Lufkin, TX
Hallmark, Linda Saoud .... Pontiac, MI
Hallmark, M. F. .... Lafayette, CA
Hallmark, R. Elaine .... Portland, OR
Hallmark, Sandra W. .... Washington, DC
Hallmark, William L. .... Portland, OR
Hallock, Alan D. .... Wichita, KS
Hallock, David D., Jr. .... Lakeland, FL
Hallock, David H., Jr. .... Richmond, VA
Hallock, Douglas J. .... Lexington, KY
Hallock, Gary M. .... Steubenville, OH
Hallock & Hallock .... Logan, UT
Hallock, Houghton R., Jr.
Securities and Exchange Commission, Division of Investment Management, GV
Hallock, Jeffrey M. .... Norfolk, VA
Hallock, John W. .... Rockford, IL
Hallock, Joseph A. .... Wayne, NJ
Hallock, Joseph A. .... New York, NY
Hallock, Joseph E. .... Gillette, WY
Hallock, Kurt D. .... El Segundo, CA
Hallock, Kurt W. .... San Diego, CA

Halstead, R. Stewart ... Glendale, AZ
Halstead, Rodney A. ... Omaha, NE
Halstead, Roland W., Jr.
Department Of Veterans Affairs, Office of the General Counsel, GV
Halstead, Sherman O., Jr. ... Irvine, CA
Halstead, Stephen P. ... Winston-Salem, NC
Halstead & Whiddon ... Headland, AL
Halstead, William J. ... Olympia, WA
Halstead-White, Melissa J. ... Atlanta, GA
Halsted, Douglas L. ... Hilo, HI
Halsted, John S. ... West Chester, PA
Halsted, Kellie S. ... Chicago, IL
Halsted, Patricia A. ... Nantucket, MA
Halstenberg, Deborah K. ... Chicago, IL
Halston, Daniel W. ... Boston, MA
Halstrom, Douglas R. ... Garden City, NY
Halstrom, Frederic N. ... Boston, MA
Carlisle, MA
Lowell, MA
Halstrom Law Offices, P.C. ... Boston, MA
Carlisle, MA
Halstrom, Timothy C. ... Montgomery, AL
Halt, Gerald B., Jr. ... Philadelphia, PA
Halter, Brenda W. ... Champaign, IL
Halter, Edwin C., Jr. ... Yorktown Heights, NY
Halter, Julie Anne ... Seattle, WA
Halter, Mark K. ... Little Rock, AR
North Little Rock, AR
Halter, Milton F. ... North Little Rock, AR
Halter, Richard F. ... San Antonio, TX
Halter, Thomas Edwin ... Phoenix, AZ
Halter, William C., Jr. ... New York, NY
Halterman, Carlin W. ... Aptos, CA
Halterman, Charles D. ... Kansas City, MO
Halterman, Dennis D. ... Rapid City, SD
Halterman, H. Lee ... Oakland, CA
Haltom, B. Reid ... Albuquerque, NM
Haltom, Brent ... Lewisville, AR
Haltom, E. B., Jr. ... Florence, AL
Haltom, Hal V., Jr. ... Houston, TX
Haltom, James N., (P.C.) ... Texarkana, TX
Haltom, John T. ... Indianola, MS
Haltom, Lynn ... Seminole, TX
Haltom, Matthew ... Dallas, TX
Haltom, Steve D. ... Elberton, GA
Haltom, William H., Jr. ... Memphis, TN
Halton, Ann F. ... Phoenix, AZ
Haltrecht, Carol E. ... West Chester, PA
Haluck, John R. ... Sacramento, CA
Haluck, William L. ... Irvine, CA
Halula, John F. ... Miami, FL
Halushka, James J. ... Pontiac, MI
Haluska, James E. ... Fairfax, VA
Haluszczak, Thomas, Jr. ... Roseland, NJ
Haluza, Thomas J. ... La Jolla, CA
Halva, Allen Keith ... St. Paul, MN
Halva, Donald P. ... New Brighton, MN
Halva, Robert E. ... Columbia Heights, MN
Halva, Robert E., P.A.
Columbia Heights, MN
Halvachs, Kenneth L. ... Belleville, IL
St. Louis, MO
Halverhout, Winn W. ... Kansas City, MO
Halversen, George C. ... Glendale, CA
Halverson & Andreasen ... Mankato, MN
Halverson & Applegate, P.S. ... Yakima, WA
Halverson, Charles D. ... Brainerd, MN
Halverson, Chris G. ... Racine, WI
Halverson, Craig E. ... Dallas, TX
Halverson, Elizabeth A. ... Billings, MT
Halverson, Frederick N. ... Yakima, WA
Halverson, G. W. ... Duluth, MN
Halverson, J. Scott ... Phoenix, AZ
Tempe, AZ
Halverson, James G. ... Madison Heights, MI
Halverson, James R. ... Billings, MT
Halverson, James T. ... Washington, DC
Halverson, Jan Douglas ... Minneapolis, MN
Halverson, Jerry F. ... Los Angeles, CA
Halverson, Joel L. ... San Francisco, CA
Halverson, Karen ... Chicago, IL
Halverson, Keith E. ... Menomonie, WI
Halverson, Lowell K., Law Offices of
Mercer Island, WA
Halverson, Mark B. ... United States Senate, Senatorial Assistants, GV
Halverson, Mark C. ... Mankato, MN
Halverson, Mark D. ... Atlanta, GA
Halverson, Nancy ... St. Paul, MN
Halverson, Philip J. ... San Francisco, CA
Halverson, Philip R. ... Duluth, MN
Halverson, Sheehy & Plath, P.C.
Billings, MT
Halverson, Steven T. ... Denver, CO
Halverson, Sue ... Minneapolis, MN
Halverson, Victor R. ... Billings, MT
Halverson, Watters, Downs, Reyelts & Bateman, Ltd. ... Duluth, MN
Halverstadt, Peter B. ... Nashville, TN
Halvey, John K. ... New York, NY
Halvey, Kristin ... Ridgewood, NJ
Halvey, Thomas J. ... Woodside, NY
Halvonik, Paul N. ... Berkeley, CA
Halvordson, Martha A. ... Kansas City, MO
Halvorsen, Allan Laugen ... Albert Lea, MN
Halvorsen & Buesing, S.C.
Sheboygan, WI
Halvorsen, Charles D. ... Buffalo, NY
Halvorsen, Daniel O. ... Chicago, IL
Halvorsen, Deborah S.
Winston-Salem, NC
Halvorsen, Jack R. ... Chicago, IL
Halvorsen, John H. ... Manchester, NH
Halvorsen, John Paul ... Scarsdale, NY
Halvorsen, Kathi Busch ... Sarasota, FL
Halvorsen, Kristin Jennie ... Ashford, CT
Halvorsen & O'Connell ... Manchester, NH
Halvorsen, Robert H. ... Sheboygan, WI
Halvorsen, Victoria A. ... Hauppauge, NY
Halvorson, Bridget C. ... Sacramento, CA
Halvorson, David R. ... Mountain View, CA
Halvorson, David T. ... New York, NY
Halvorson, Eric H. ... Camarillo, CA
Halvorson, Larry E. ... Seattle, WA
Halvorson, Neil A. ... Macon, GA
Halvorson, Neil J. ... West Bend, WI
Halvorson, Newman T., Jr.
Washington, DC
Halvorson, Omar W. ... Portland, OR
Halvorson, Sarah D. ... Minneapolis, MN
Halvorson & Saunders, P.L.L.C. ... Seattle, WA
Halvorson, Steven W.
West Palm Beach, FL
Halvorson & Venable, P.C. ... Phoenix, AZ
Haly, Lisa M. ... Media, PA
Halyard, Leslie L. ... Morristown, NJ
Ham, Albert S. ... Monterey, CA
Ham, Benny E. ... Somerset, KY
Ham, C. Keith ... Bristow, OK
Sapulpa, OK
Ham, Chad B. ... Metairie, LA
Ham, Charles Wright ... Fairhope, AL
Ham, David J. ... Indianapolis, IN
Ham, David L. ... Madison, WI
Ham, Donald R. ... Amarillo, TX
Ham, Edwin C. ... Charlotte, NC
Ham, Eldon L. ... Chicago, IL
Ham, Ellen C. ... Atlanta, GA
Ham, Floyd Russell ... Austin, TX
Ham, Glen ... Pauls Valley, OK
Ham, H. Ray ... Cayce, SC
Ham, Harold A. ... Gladstone, MO
Ham, James H., III ... Indianapolis, IN
Ham, James I. ... Los Angeles, CA
Ham, Jason J. ... Harrisonburg, VA
Ham, John Charles ... Auburn, AL
Ham, John E. ... Las Vegas, NV
Ham, Kathleen O'Brien
Federal Communications Commission, Wireless Telecommunications Bureau, GV
Ham, Kathryn R. ... Edgartown, MA
Ham, Lamar, III ... Birmingham, AL
Ham, Linda DiLorenzo ... Greensboro, NC
Ham, Marti Anne ... Monterey, CA
Ham, Richard J. ... Crofton, MD
Mitchellville, MD
Ham, Richd. C. ... San Francisco, CA
Ham, Rose Mary ... Tulsa, OK
Ham, Scott W. ... San Diego, CA
Ham, Seungsook ... Department of Commerce, Patent and Trademark Office, GV
Ham, Stephen L., III ... Southampton, NY
Ham, Willburt D. ... Lexington, KY
Ham, William R. ... Atlanta, GA
Ham, W. J. ... Austin, TX
Ham, Yoon S. ... Washington, DC
Ham & Zundel, L.L.C. ... Fairhope, AL
Hamacher, David M. ... Hammond, IN
Hamacher, Shawn D. ... Grand Rapids, MI
Hamack, Keith H. ... Rolling Bay, WA
Hamack, Robt. A. ... Edmonds, WA
Hamada, Cindy R. ... Woodbury, NY
Hamada, Darolyn Y. ... Irvine, CA
Hamada, Edwin C. ... Boston, MA
Hamada, Edwin C., P.C., The Law Office of
Boston, MA
Hamada, Herbert Y. ... Honolulu, HI
Hamada, Irving ... New York, NY
Hamada, Linda ... Nashua, NH
Hamada, Paul I. ... Long Beach, CA
Hamaker, Charles L. ... Monroe, LA
Hamaker, Donald W. ... New York, NY
Hamaker, Mary M. ... Palo Alto, CA
Hamala, Richard L. ... Austin, TX
Hamamoto, Kenji ... Irvine, CA
Haman, Douglas A. ... Arlington, TX
Haman, Edward A. ... Clearwater, FL
Haman, Gary M. ... Coeur d'Alene, ID
Haman, Michael L. ... Coeur d'Alene, ID
Haman, W. Douglas ... Cincinnati, OH
Hamann, Ardath A. ... Chicago, IL
Hamann, Charles M. ... Boston, MA
Hamann, Daniel E. ... Kansas City, MO
Hamann, Deryl F. ... Omaha, NE
Hamann, Ingrid ... Miami, FL
Hamann, Kim ... Santa Fe, NM
Hamann, Kristine ... New York, NY
Hamann, Lee H. ... Omaha, NE
Hamann, Leigh Kirkwood ... Kansas City, MO
Hamann, Malinda C. ... Atlanta, GA
Hamann, Richard ... Gainesville, FL
Hamann, Richard G. ... Lewiston, ME
Hamann, Robert L. ... Overland Park, KS
Hamann, Steven Louis ... Chicago, IL
Hamann, Thos. J. ... Parma, OH
Hamann, Timothy W. ... Waterloo, IA
Hamann, Walter C. ... Lake Forest, IL
Hamann, Warren D. ... Miami, FL
Hamann, William J. ... Canton, OH
Hamar, Maria Rivas ... Beverly Hills, CA
Hamar, Michael B. ... Norfolk, VA
Hamar, Richard A. ... Beverly Hills, CA
Hamasaki, James S. ... Lafayette, CA
Hamasaki, Lisa C. ... Oakland, CA
Hamasaki, Marsha Michiko
Los Angeles, CA
Hamasaki, Peter J. ... Honolulu, HI
Hamaty, Christopher J. ... Washington, DC
Hamaty, Gail J. ... Pittsburgh, PA
Hamaway, Michael P.
Fort Lauderdale, FL
Hamb, Christopher L. ... Charleston, WV
Hamb, Roosevelt, Jr. ... Atlanta, GA
Hamb, William E., Law Offices
Charleston, WV
Hambach, Geoffrey G. ... Brookhaven, MS
Hambel, John J. ... Washington, DC
Hambelton, H. Charles ... Burlington, MA
Hamberg, Gilbert L. ... Yardley, PA
Hamberger, Catherine M.
Philadelphia, PA
Hamberger, Douglas P. ... Buffalo, NY
Hamberger, Edward R. ... Washington, DC
Hamberger, Jeffrey M. ... Washington, DC
Hamberger, Mark W. ... Buffalo, NY
Hamberger, Robert S. ... Washington, DC
Hamberger & Weiss ... Buffalo, NY
Rochester, NY
Hambidge, Timothy J. ... Evansville, IN
Hamble, Frederick J. ... Washington, DC
Hamblen, Clayton R. ... Mesa, AZ
Hamblen, David L. ... Union City, TN
Hamblen, Joe D. ... Chattanooga, TN
Jackson, TN
Hamblen, L. Jane ... New York, NY
Hamblen, Lapsley W., Jr.
United States Tax Court, GV
Hamblen, Michael G. ... Richardson, TX
Hamblen & Teague ... Houston, TX
Hamblen, William D. ... Manassas, VA
Hamblet, Gary A. ... Los Angeles, CA
Hamblet, Michael J. ... Chicago, IL
Hamblet, Oremus & Little ... Chicago, IL
Hambleton, David P. ... New Haven, CT
Hambleton, Debby R. ... Los Angeles, CA
Hambleton, Douglas M. ... Chicago, IL
Hambleton, Eric P. ... New York, NY
Hambleton, Evan K. ... West Chester, PA
Hambleton, James E. ... Fort Worth, TX
Hambleton, Karen S. ... Taunton, MA
Hambleton, Kaye E. ... La Mesa, CA
Hambleton, Neal ... Rockville, MD
Hamblett, Frank S. ... Boston, MA
Hamblett & Kerrigan, P.A. ... Nashua, NH
Hamblett, Robert M. ... San Francisco, CA
Hambley, Clarke C., Jr. ... Portland, ME
Hambley, Gwyneth E. ... Washington, DC
Hambley, William C. ... Cincinnati, OH
Hamblin, B. Dale, Jr. ... Louisville, KY
Hamblin, Janice K. ... Chicago, IL
Hamblin, Joseph M. ... Burlingame, CA
Hamblin, Laura J. ... Fort Worth, TX
Hamblin, Pierce W. ... Lexington, KY
Hamblin, Ramona J. ... Boston, MA
Hamblin, Randolph L. ... Albuquerque, NM
Hamblin, R. L. ... Safford, AZ
Hamblin, Rodney H. ... Daly City, CA
Hamblin, Terry D. ... Topeka, KS
Hamblin, William H. ... Chicago, IL
Hambly, Charles A., Jr. ... Providence, RI
Hambly, Michael R. ... Los Angeles, CA
Hamborg, Carla Jensen ... Des Moines, IA
Hamborg, Kelly D. ... Des Moines, IA
Hamborg, Robert C. ... Simsbury, CT
Hambourger, David R. ... Chicago, IL
Hambrecht, Patricia G. ... New York, NY
Hambrick, David W. ... Lewisburg, WV
Hambrick, E. L. ... Washington, DC
Hambrick, Harry F., Jr. ... Roanoke, VA
Hambrick, J. Reid ... McLean, VA
Hambrick, J. C., Jr. ... Kansas City, MO
Hambrick, Jonathan H. ... Washington, DC
Hambrick, Kenton Warden ... McLean, VA
Hambrick, Robert L. ... Clearwater, FL
Hambrick, Todd H. ... Casper, WY
Hambrick-Stowe, Elizabeth Anne
Lancaster, PA
Hambright, James W. ... Beaumont, TX
Hambright, Joseph A. ... Grand Junction, CO
Washington, DC
Hambright, Robert J. ... Beaumont, TX
Hambro, Steven M. ... New Brunswick, NJ
Hambsch, Michael P., Law Offices of
South Lake Tahoe, CA
Hambuechen, James P.
Department of Justice, Drug Enforcement Administration, GV
Hamburg, Ben I. ... San Francisco, CA
Hamburg, Brian E. ... Springfield, MO
Hamburg, C. Bruce ... New York, NY
Hamburg, Donald A. ... New York, NY
Hamburg, Donald H.
Glenwood Springs, CO
Hamburg, Gerald ... Lansdale, PA
Hamburg & Golden ... Philadelphia, PA
Hamburg, Hanover, Edwards & Martin LLP
Los Angeles, CA
Hamburg, Jeanne M. ... New York, NY
Hamburg, Jeffrey A. ... Chicago, IL
Hamburg, Louise E. ... Philadelphia, PA
Hamburg, M. Michael ... Troy, MI
Hamburg, Mervyn ... Department of Justice, Criminal Division, GV
Hamburg, Neil J. ... Philadelphia, PA
Hamburg, Rubin, Mullin, Maxwell & Lupin, A Professional Corporation
Lansdale, PA
Hamburg, Sidney A. ... Los Angeles, CA
Hamburg, Steven D. ... New York, NY
Hamburg, Steven M. ... St. Louis, MO
Hamburg, Susan H. ... Silver Spring, MD
Hamburg, Toni C. ... New York, NY
Hamburger, Amanda G. ... New Orleans, LA
Hamburger, Annette C. ... Bethesda, MD
Hamburger, Brian S. ... Princeton, NJ
Hamburger, Calvin I. ... Towson, MD
Hamburger, David A. ... Los Angeles, CA
Hamburger, Edmund A. ... Los Angeles, CA
Hamburger, Edmund A., A Professional Corporation ... Los Angeles, CA
Hamburger Green & Haber ... New York, NY
Hamburger, Henry I. ... Leonia, NJ
Hamburger, John A. ... Southfield, MI
Hamburger, Lon D. ... Jackson, CA
Hamburger, Martin A. ... Pittsburgh, PA
Hamburger, Maxson & Yaffe, LLP
Melville, NY
Hamburger, Paul M. ... Washington, DC
Hamburger, Philip A. ... Washington, DC
Hamburger, Richard ... Melville, NY
Hamburger, Robert L. ... West Bloomfield, MI
Hamburger, Robert L., P.C.
West Bloomfield, MI
Hamburger, Sol ... Phoenix, AZ
Hamburger, Weinschenk, Molnar and Fisher
New York, NY
Hamburgh, Mark S. ... New York, NY
Hamby, David A., Jr. ... Mobile, AL
Hamby, Donna S. ... Orlando, FL
Hamby, E. Lee ... Denver, CO
Hamby, Ferriel C., Jr. ... Harlingen, TX
Hamby, Gene M., Jr. ... Sheffield, AL
Hamby & Hamby, A Professional Corporation ... Big Spring, TX
Hamby, Jane Obee ... Wilmington, DE
Hamby, Jeffrey D. ... Marietta, GA
Hamby, Joey ... Phoenix, AZ
Hamby, Kathi Gale ... Denver, CO
Hamby, L. Ellen ... Sugar Hill, GA
Hamby, Lanny ... Big Spring, TX
Hamby, Louis L., III ... Palm Beach, FL
Hamby, Michael J. ... Greenwood, AR
Hamby, Paul J. ... Maspeth, NY
Hamby, Penelope E. Joyner
Granite Falls, NC
Hamby, R. Kevin ... Farmers Branch, TX
Hamby, Rick W. ... Big Spring, TX
Hamby, Roger D. ... Nashville, TN
Hamby, Ruben Irvin ... Savage, MD
Hamby, S. Todd ... St. Louis, MO
Hamby, Sally A. ... Troy, MI
Hamby, William G., Jr. ... Concord, NC
Hamby, William H. ... Wilmington, DE
Hamdan, Alexis Smith ... Boston, MA
Hamdan, Lawrence A. ... New York, NY
Hamdan, Maha Abbas ... San Francisco, CA
Hamdy, Dina ... San Francisco, CA
Hamed, Michael R. ... Cleveland, OH
Hameed, Azim Q. ... Phoenix, AZ
Hameetman, Christopher
Los Angeles, CA
Hamel, Charles ... Los Angeles, CA
Hamel, Denise M. ... Seattle, WA
Hamel, Douglas ... Southgate, MI
Hamel, Douglas E. ... Houston, TX
Hamel, E. Anne ... Baltimore, MD
Hamel, Fred M. ... Denver, CO
Hamel, Gregory J. ... Toledo, OH
Hamel, Howard N. ... Orange, CA
Hamel, Hubert O. ... Hayward, CA
Hamel, James W. ... Dallas, TX
Hamel, Judy G. ... Palo Alto, CA
Hamel, Karl Anthony ... Sterling Heights, MI
Hamel, Kevin R. ... Philadelphia, PA
Hamel Law Firm, The ... Amesbury, MA
Haverhill, MA
Lawrence, MA
Methuen, MA
Newburyport, MA
Topsfield, MA
Hamel Law Firm, The, P.A.
Charlotte, NC
Hamel, Lee, Law Offices of ... Houston, TX
Hamel, Linda L. ... Auburn, CA
Hamel, Louis H., Jr. ... Boston, MA
Hamel, Mark E. ... Minneapolis, MN
Hamel, Martha L. ... Pawleys Island, SC
Hamel, Matthew E. ... New York, NY
Hamel, Matthew J. ... Troy, MI
Hamel, Melody A. ... Pittsburgh, PA
Hamel, Michael A. ... Methuen, MA
Hamel, Paul G. ... New Bedford, MA
Hamel, Reginald S. ... Charlotte, NC
Hamel, Richard P. ... Amesbury, MA
Hamel, Robert D. ... Zurich, KS
Hamel, Robert E. ... Frankfort, MI
Hamel, Robert R., Jr. ... Boston, MA
Hamel, Rodolphe ... New York, NY
Hamel, Scott ... Ocala, FL
Hamel, Stephen D. ... Oak Ridge, TN
Hamel, Stephen G. ... Denver, CO
Hamel, Thomas J. ... Pittsfield, MA
Hamel, Vicki L. ... Midwest City, OK
Hamel, W. Warren ... Baltimore, MD
Hamel, Waxler, Allen & Collins
Providence, RI
Fall River, MA
New Bedford, MA
Hamel, William B., Sr. ... Charlotte, NC
Hamel, William F. ... Charlotte, NC
Hamel, William J. ... Philadelphia, PA
Hamelburg, Barbara S. ... Boston, MA
Hamelburg, Gerald A. ... Boston, MA
Hamelburg, Jay S. ... New York, NY
Hamelburg, Mark E. ... Washington, DC
Hameline, H. Joseph ... Boston, MA
Hamell, John A., Jr. ... Milwaukee, WI
Hamelsky, Andrew I. ... Paramus, NJ
Hamel-Smith, M. Glenn ... Miami, FL
Hament, Andrew S. ... Melbourne, FL
Hament, Carrol ... Baltimore, MD
Hament, John M. ... Fort Myers, FL
Sarasota, FL
Tampa, FL
Hamer, Anne E.S. ... Nashville, TN
Hamer, Anne-Marie Storey ... Bangor, ME
Hamer, Brian A. ... Chicago, IL
Hamer, Chris Carol ... Arcata, CA
Hamer, David R. ... Indianapolis, IN
Hamer, Donald L. ... Hartford, CT
Hamer, Eric T. ... Jackson, MS

Hamer, John Kenneth ... Amherst, NH
Hamer, Judy P. ... Birmingham, AL
Hamer, Kelly Gardner ... Ocala, FL
Hamer, Lissa L. ... Wheaton, IL
Hamer, Mark H. ... San Diego, CA
Hamer, Mark T. ... Iowa City, IA
Hamer, Paul ... Northbrook, IL
Hamer, Robert E. ... Hackensack, NJ
Hamer, Robert L. ... Worcester, MA
Hamer, Robert M. ... Dayton, OH
Hamer, Schuh & Cuda ... Woodstock, IL
Hamer, Sean P. ... Kansas City, MO
Hamer, Shelli C. ... Whitinsville, MA
Hamer, Spencer ... Los Angeles, CA
Hamer, Ted J. ... Atkinson, IL
Geneseo, IL
Hamer, Theresa M. ... Escondido, CA
Hamer, Thomas E. ... Anderson, IN
Hamera, Jeffrey L. ... Chicago, IL
Hamerlik, Michael F. ... Fargo, ND
Hamerlinck & Besk, PLLC ... Bellevue, WA
Hamerlinck, Thomas G. ... Bellevue, WA
Hamerling, Dale A. ... San Francisco, CA
Hamerling, Jeffrey M. ... San Francisco, CA
Hamerly, Paul M. ... Monterey, CA
Salinas, CA
Hamerman, Debra A. ... Great Neck, NY
Hamermesh, Frances W. ... Austin, TX
Hamermesh, Lawrence A. ... Wilmington, DE
Hamermesh, Matthew A. ... Bala Cynwyd, PA
Hamernik, Robert ... Tulsa, OK
Hamernik, Ronald H. ... Camarillo, CA
Hameroff, Anne Holt ... Tucson, AZ
Hameroff, David E. ... Tucson, AZ
Hamers, James ... Salem, OR
Hamerschlag, Elizabeth Barba
Bernardsville, NJ
Hamerslag, Peter S. ... New Brunswick, NJ
Hamerslough, David M. ... San Jose, CA
Hamersmith, Harold E. ... Los Angeles, CA
Hamersmith, Minda ... Miami, FL
Hames, Anderson & Whitlow, P.S.
Kennewick, WA
Pasco, WA
Richland, WA
Hames, David L. ... Ojai, CA
Hames, Eugene S. ... Denver, CO
Hames, Joanne I. ... San Jose, CA
Hames, John Duncan ... Chico, CA
Hames, Laurence C. ... Orlando, FL
Hames, Llewellyn Hiott ... Columbia, SC
Hames, Mark B. ... San Jose, CA
Hames, Orville A. ... Remsen, IA
Hames, Richard L. ... Richland, WA
Seattle, WA
Hames, Thomas E. ... Englewood, CO
Hames, William L. ... Kennewick, WA
Hames, William M. ... Atlanta, GA
Hametz, Ivan W. ... Merrick, NY
Hamid, Ferhan ... Chicago, IL
Hamideh, Khalid Y. ... Garland, TX
Hamidi, Ali Pasha ... Menlo Park, CA
Hamidi, Frank ... Detroit, MI
Hamiel, Norman J. ... Tipton, IA
Hamil, J. Lawrence ... Denver, CO
Hamil Professional Corporation
Denver, CO
Hamil, Richard T. ... Cumming, GA
Hamili, Ruby A. ... Wailuku, HI
Hamill, Bernard J. ... Quincy, MA
Hamill, Cheryl Urbanski ... Chicago, IL
Hamill, Christopher G. ... Phoenix, AZ
Hamill, David R. ... Treasury Department,
Office of the General Counsel, GV
Hamill, Donald E., Jr. ... Lynnfield, MA
Hamill, Dorothy Anne ... Philadelphia, PA
Hamill, Edward K. ... Woodbridge, NJ
Hamill, Eugene ... Philadelphia, PA
Hamill, Gail J. ... Treasury Department,
Office of Regulations and Rulings, GV
Hamill, James C.
Federal Trade Commission,
Office of the Chairman, GV
Hamill, James G. ... Oklahoma City, OK
Hamill, James J. ... Chicago, IL
Hamill, Jill D. ... Chicago, IL
Hamill, John F., Jr. ... Jersey City, NJ
Hamill, John J. ... Chicago, IL
Hamill, John P. ... Boston, MA
Hamill, John R., III ... St. Louis, MO
Hamill, Joseph J., Jr. ... Philadelphia, PA
Hamill, Katherine M. ... Boston, MA
Hamill, Kathleen M. ... Collegeville, PA
Hamill, Luanna L. ... Tulsa, OK
Hamill, Mark A. ... Chicago, IL
Hamill, Mary R. ... Trenton, NJ
Hamill, Nancy Greenan
San Francisco, CA
Hamill, Norman J. ... San Francisco, CA
Hamill, Patricia M. ... Philadelphia, PA
Hamill, Raymond L. ... Honesdale, PA
Hamill, Robert P. ... Owensboro, KY
Hamill, Robert W. ... Meridian, MS
Hamill & Schloesser ... Honesdale, PA
Hamill, S. F., Jr. ... Oakland, MD
Hamill, Stephen A. ... Walnut Creek, CA
Hamill, Steven Owen ... Evergreen Park, IL
Hamill, Susan Pace ... Tuscaloosa, AL
Hamill, Thomas A. ... Overland Park, KS
Hamill, Thomas G. ... Chicago, IL
Hamill, Thomas J. ... Florham Park, NJ
Hamill, Thomas R. ... Indianapolis, IN
Hamilton, A. Patrick ... Columbus, OH
Hamilton, Alan D. ... San Francisco, CA
Hamilton, Alan R. ... Elmira, NY
Hamilton, Alexander E. ... San Francisco, CA
San Mateo, CA
Hamilton, Alexander R. ... New York, NY

Hamilton, Amy E. ... Indianapolis, IN
Hamilton, Andrew ... Philadelphia, PA
Hamilton, Andrew J. ... Atlanta, GA
Hamilton, Andrew L. ... Oklahoma City, OK
Hamilton, Angela Humphreys
Brentwood, TN
Hamilton, Ann D. ... Toledo, OH
Hamilton, Ann Elizabeth ... St. Louis, MO
Hamilton, Ann M. ... Western Springs, IL
Hamilton, Anne M. ... West Hartford, CT
Hamilton, Anne M. ... Washington, DC
Hamilton, Anthony B. ... Bay City, TX
Hamilton, Arthur J. ... Harrisonburg, VA
Hamilton, Audra K. ... Tulsa, OK
Hamilton, B. Forest ... Tallahassee, FL
Hamilton, Bailey, Way & Brothers
Morehead City, NC
Hamilton, Barbara Kadish ... Media, PA
Hamilton, Barbara L. ... Los Angeles, CA
Hamilton, Benjamin N. ... Waco, TX
Hamilton, Beth L. ... San Jose, CA
Hamilton, Brad H. ... Denver, CO
Hamilton, Bradley D. ... Kokomo, IN
Lafayette, IN
Hamilton, Brenda G. ... Kansas City, MO
Hamilton, Brent B. ... Plainview, TX
Hamilton, Brett L. ... Houston, TX
Hamilton, Brian E. ... New York, NY
Hamilton, Brian G. ... Dallas, TX
Hamilton, Brian K. ... Hamilton, OH
Hamilton, Brian Y. ... Des Plaines, IL
Hamilton, Brook, Smith & Reynolds, P.C.
Boston, MA
Lexington, MA
Hamilton, Brooks ... Dallas, TX
Hamilton, Bruce Alan ... Raleigh, NC
Hamilton, Burgess, Young & Pollard, P.L.L.C. ... Beckley, WV
Fayetteville, WV
Oak Hill, WV
Hamilton, Butler, Riddick, Tarlton & Sullivan, P.C. ... Mobile, AL
Hamilton, Byron A., Jr. ... Fort Worth, TX
Hamilton, C. Bruce ... Menlo Park, CA
Hamilton, Calvin K. ... Kansas City, MO
Hamilton, Camille ... San Francisco, CA
Hamilton, Carl D. ... Nampa, ID
Hamilton, Carol ... Glendale, CA
Hamilton, Carol J. ... St. Louis, MO
Hamilton, Carole K. ... Dallas, TX
Hamilton, Carolyn Chew ... San Francisco, CA
Hamilton, Carrie E. ... Chicago, IL
Hamilton & Carroll ... Monroe, LA
Oak Grove, LA
Hamilton, Charles C. ... Atlanta, GA
Hamilton, Charles E. ... Belleville, IL
Hamilton, Charles E. ... Brownsville, TX
Hamilton, Charles E. ... Riverton, WY
Hamilton, Charles E., III
New Orleans, LA
Hamilton, Charles E., Ltd. ... Belleville, IL
Hamilton, Charles E., P.C.
Brownsville, TX
Hamilton, Charles E. L., Sr. ... Cleveland, OH
Hamilton, Charles F. ... Melville, NY
Hamilton, Charles J., Jr. ... New York, NY
Hamilton, Charles K. ... Birmingham, AL
Hamilton, Charles L. ... San Francisco, CA
Hamilton, Charles M. ... Dallas, TX
Hamilton, Charles R. ... Clearwater, FL
Hamilton, Charlotte A. ... Gillette, WY
Hamilton, Christina S. ... Phoenix, AZ
Hamilton, Christopher ... Atlanta, GA
Hamilton, Christopher E. ... Walnut Creek, CA
Hamilton, Christopher P. ... Boston, MA
Providence, RI
Hamilton, Christopher S. ... Durango, CO
Hamilton, Clifford E., Jr. ... Fulton, MO
Hamilton, Clovia Ann
Department of Commerce,
Patent and Trademark Office, GV
Hamilton, Clyde H. ... Columbia, SC
Hamilton, Cristina Navarro
Department of Justice,
Immigration and Naturalization Service, GV
Hamilton & Cumare, LLP ... Pasadena, CA
Valencia, CA
Hamilton, Curtis J., III ... Henderson, KY
Hamilton, Cynthia ... St. Louis, MO
Hamilton, D. Kaye ... Whittier, CA
Hamilton, D. Ross, Jr. ... Greensboro, NC
Hamilton, D. Wesley ... Exeter, CA
Hamilton & Dahmen, LLP ... Boston, MA
Hamilton, Dale ... Longview, TX
Hamilton, Dana ... Red Oak, TX
Hamilton, Daniel H. ... Key West, FL
Hamilton, Daniel O'C. ... St. Louis, MO
Hamilton, Daniel W. ... Augusta, GA
Hamilton, Darrin T. ... Newton, IA
Hamilton, David ... Reno, NV
Hamilton, David A. ... Pasadena, CA
Hamilton, David A. ... Baton Rouge, LA
Hamilton, David B. ... Baltimore, MD
Hamilton, David B. ... Charlotte, NC
Hamilton, David F. ... Indianapolis, IN
Hamilton, David J. ... Valencia, CA
Hamilton, David Ley ... Wilmington, DE
Hamilton, David M. ... Paris, TX
Hamilton, David R. ... Ogden, UT
Hamilton, David S. ... Agoura Hills, CA
Hamilton, David T. ... St. Charles, MO
Hamilton, David W. ... Indianapolis, IN
Hamilton, Dawn F. ... San Diego, CA
Hamilton, Deanna Jo ... Slidell, LA
Hamilton, Deborah L. ... Cleveland, OH
Hamilton, Debra A. ... Armonk, NY
Hamilton, Debra I. ... Los Angeles, CA

Hamilton, Delleney & Gibbons, P.A.
Chester, SC
Great Falls, SC
Lancaster, SC
Union, SC
Winnsboro, SC
Hamilton, Dennis P. ... Getzville, NY
Hamilton, Dexter R. ... Philadelphia, PA
Hamilton, Dolton & Sauers, LLP
Menlo Park, CA
Hamilton, Don F. ... Little Rock, AR
Hamilton, Donald ... Melrose Park, IL
Hamilton, Donald J. ... Great Falls, MT
Hamilton, Donis B. ... Paragould, AR
Hamilton, Donna Harper
Winston-Salem, NC
Hamilton, Donna J. ... Phoenix, AZ
Hamilton, Donna J. ... Phoenix, AZ
Hamilton, Douglas M. ... Portland, OR
Hamilton, Douglass M. ... Portland, OR
Hamilton, Drew S. ... San Diego, CA
Hamilton, Duncan ... Prospect Heights, IL
Hamilton, Dwight Alan ... Denver, CO
Hamilton, Dwight K. ... Grand Rapids, MI
Hamilton, E. Bentley, Jr. ... Durango, CO
Hamilton, E. Duncan ... Birmingham, AL
Hamilton, E. James ... Portland, ME
Hamilton, Earl L. ... Columbus, OH
Hamilton, Edward J., Jr. ... Greenville, SC
Hamilton, Edwin L. ... Atlanta, GA
Hamilton, Eileen F.S. ... Sacramento, CA
Hamilton, E. L. (Max) ... San Saba, TX
Hamilton, Elizabeth A. ... Columbus, OH
Hamilton, Elizabeth A. ... San Antonio, TX
Hamilton, Ellen M. ... Houston, TX
Hamilton, Eric E. ... Bellevue, NE
Hamilton, Ernest ... Greenville, SC
Hamilton, Eugene N. ... Washington, DC
Hamilton, Everett N. ... Immokalee, FL
Hamilton, F. Cooper ... Jacksonville, NC
Hamilton and Faatz, A Professional Corporation ... Denver, CO
Hamilton, Francis M. (Trey), III
Nashville, TN
Hamilton, Francis P. ... Jacksonville, FL
Hamilton, Frank, & Associates, P.A.
Tampa, FL
Hamilton, Frank E., III ... Tampa, FL
Hamilton, Frank I., Jr. ... Greensburg, IN
Hamilton, Frank M. ... Fort Lauderdale, FL
Hamilton, Frank O. ... Oklahoma City, OK
Hamilton, Franklin T. ... Sparks, NV
Hamilton, Frederick D. ... Dallas, TX
Hamilton, Frederick N. ... Cincinnati, OH
Hamilton, Fulton S. ... Huntsville, AL
Hamilton, G. Alexander ... Louisville, KY
Hamilton & Gardner ... Huntsville, AL
Hamilton, Gary ... Rome, GA
Hamilton, Gary W. ... Austin, TX
Hamilton, Gayle K. ... Shreveport, LA
Hamilton, Gene E. ... Spokane, WA
Hamilton, Geoffrey ... Honolulu, HI
Hamilton, Geoffrey R.
General Accounting Office,
Office of the General Counsel, GV
Hamilton, George A. ... Shreveport, LA
Hamilton, George D. ... Gallatin, TN
Hamilton, George M., III ... Richardson, TX
Hamilton, George O. ... Columbus, IN
Hamilton, Gerard H. ... Pittsburgh, PA
Hamilton, Gibson, Nickelsen, Rush & Moore
Honolulu, HI
Hamilton, Glenn S. ... London, OH
Hamilton, Gregg, Barker & Johnson
Topeka, KS
Hamilton, Gregory C. ... Troy, MI
Hamilton, Gregory W. ... Providence, RI
Hamilton, Gretchen Kendall ... Boston, MA
Hamilton, H. Bruce ... Phoenix, AZ
Hamilton, H. Robert ... Salem, OR
Hamilton, H. Trevor ... Napa, CA
Hamilton, Hal A. ... St. Louis, MO
Hamilton & Hamilton ... Hamburg, AR
Hamilton & Hamilton ... Melrose Park, IL
Hamilton and Hamilton, LLP
Washington, DC
Hamilton, Harold C., II ... Bangor, ME
Hamilton, Harriet Homsher ... Belleville, IL
Hamilton, Harry S. ... Ithaca, NY
Hamilton & Hartfield ... Dallas, TX
Hamilton, Heather G. ... Phoenix, AZ
Hamilton, Heather R. ... Kansas City, MO
Hamilton, Henry K. ... Seattle, WA
Hamilton, Henry L. ... Columbia, SC
Hamilton, Herbert W. ... Rock Hill, SC
Hamilton, Herman H., Jr. ... Montgomery, AL
Hamilton, Herman L., Jr. ... Hamburg, AR
Hamilton, Howard D. ... Fort Dodge, IA
Hamilton, Howard D., Jr. ... Plano, TX
Hamilton, Hubert E., III
Chattanooga, TN
Hamilton, Hubert E., III
Chattanooga, TN
Hamilton, Imy ... St. Petersburg, FL
Hamilton, J. Clark, Jr. ... Jacksonville, FL
Hamilton, J. Gregory ... Baltimore, MD
Hamilton, J. Richard ... Cleveland, OH
Hamilton, J. Robert ... Lebanon, TN
Hamilton, J. Roger ... Portland, OR
Hamilton, J. Scott ... Montgomery, AL
Hamilton, J. Scott, P.C. ... Montgomery, AL
Hamilton, Jack T. ... Charlotte, NC
Hamilton, Jackson D. ... Asheville, NC
Hamilton, Jacqueline ... Pleasanton, CA
Hamilton, James ... Washington, DC
Hamilton, James A. ... Hamburg, AR
Hamilton, James A. ... Los Angeles, CA
Hamilton, James A., III ... Philadelphia, PA

Hamilton, James A., III ... Dyersburg, TN
Hamilton, James A. G. ... Boston, MA
Hamilton, James B., Jr. ... Harwood, MD
Hamilton, James C. ... Boston, MA
Hamilton, James D. ... Arlington, VA
Hamilton, James D., Jr. ... Camden, NJ
Hamilton, James E. ... Poteau, OK
Hamilton, James L. ... Pikeville, KY
Hamilton, James L. ... Westlake, OH
Hamilton, James P. ... North Little Rock, AR
Hamilton, James P., Jr. ... Lithonia, GA
Hamilton, James T. ... St. Paul, MN
Hamilton, James W. ... Costa Mesa, CA
Hamilton, James W. ... Harleysville, PA
Hamilton, Jan ... Topeka, KS
Hamilton, Jane Ellen ... Aspen, CO
Hamilton, Janet L. ... Jackson, MI
Hamilton, Janet L. ... Austin, TX
Hamilton, Jas. W. ... Citrus Heights, CA
Hamilton, Jay W. ... Iowa Falls, IA
Hamilton, Jay W. ... Seattle, WA
Hamilton, Jean C. ... St. Louis, MO
Hamilton, Jeanette L. ... Little Rock, AR
Hamilton, Jeanne M. ... Greenfield, IN
Hamilton, Jefferi ... San Diego, CA
Hamilton, Jeffrey A. ... Louisville, KY
Hamilton, Jeffrey G. ... Dallas, TX
Hamilton, Jeffrey S. ... Gate City, VA
Hamilton, Jeffrey W. ... Celebration, FL
Hamilton, Jeffrey Y., Jr. ... Fresno, CA
Hamilton, Jeffries M. ... Lexington, KY
Hamilton, Jennifer J. ... Hartford, CT
Hamilton, Jerry D. ... Miami, FL
Hamilton, Jerry J. ... Houston, TX
Hamilton, Jim D. ... Houston, TX
Hamilton, Jim T. ... Columbia, TN
Hamilton, Joan M. ... Topeka, KS
Hamilton, Joanne ... Chico, CA
Hamilton, Jody K. ... Spokane, WA
Hamilton, Joe Clay ... Meridian, MS
Hamilton, John A. ... Evansville, IN
Hamilton, John A. ... Pierre, SD
Hamilton, John Arthur ... Caro, MI
Hamilton, John C. ... Tampa, FL
Hamilton, John C. ... South Bend, IN
Hamilton, John Clay ... Oak Grove, LA
Hamilton, John D. ... Tawas City, MI
Hamilton, John D., Jr. ... Boston, MA
Hamilton, John E., Jr. ... Tappahannock, VA
Hamilton, John E., Jr., A Professional Corporation ... Tappahannock, VA
Hamilton, John F. ... Garden City, NY
Hamilton, John J. ... New York, NY
Hamilton, John L. ... South Hamilton, MA
Hamilton, John M. ... Los Angeles, CA
Hamilton, John M. ... Indianapolis, IN
Hamilton, John M. ... Dallas, TX
Hamilton, John M. ... Moorefield, WV
Hamilton, John N. ... Melbourne, FL
Hamilton, John R. ... Orlando, FL
Hamilton, John R. ... Topeka, KS
Hamilton, John R., III ... Atlanta, GA
Hamilton, John R., Jr. ... Media, PA
Hamilton, John T. ... Lexington, KY
Hamilton, John T., Jr. ... Delhi, NY
Hamilton, John W. ... Indianapolis, IN
Hamilton, John W. ... Dallas, TX
Hamilton, John W., Jr. ... Costa Mesa, CA
Hamilton, John Wallace ... St. Petersburg, FL
Hamilton, Joni ... Atlanta, GA
Hamilton, Joseph E. ... Minneapolis, MN
Hamilton, Joseph L. ... Louisville, KY
Hamilton, Joseph L. ... Salem, NH
Hamilton, Joseph M. ... Worcester, MA
Hamilton, Joshua G. ... Los Angeles, CA
Hamilton, Joyce A. ... Raleigh, NC
Hamilton, Judith Marie ... Baltimore, MD
Hamilton, Judy E. ... Charleston, WV
Hamilton, Judy E., Law Offices of
San Diego, CA
Hamilton, K. Scott ... Detroit, MI
Hamilton, Karen J. ... Hollister, CA
Hamilton, Karen L. ... Sacramento, CA
Hamilton, Katherine M. ... Knoxville, TN
Hamilton, Kathleen A. ... Conroe, TX
Hamilton, Kathleen R. ... Rosemead, CA
Hamilton, Kathryn DeVane ... Miami, FL
Hamilton & Keegan ... San Francisco, CA
Hamilton, Kelly J. ... Daly City, CA
Hamilton, Ken, Law Office of ... Austin, TX
Hamilton, Kenneth F. ... Fort Wayne, IN
Hamilton, Kevin J. ... Seattle, WA
Hamilton, Kimberly ... Bellefonte, PA
Hamilton, Kramer, Morris & McLeod
Columbus, OH
Hamilton, Kristin L. ... Houston, TX
Hamilton, L. Walter ... Idabel, OK
Hamilton, Lance J. ... Swainsboro, GA
Hamilton, Laura D. ... Amarillo, TX
Hamilton, Laura Wilburn ... Huntsville, AL
Hamilton Law Firm, A Professional Corporation ... South Bend, IN
Hamilton Law Firm, P.C. ... Storm Lake, IA
Hamilton Law Offices, P.S.C.
Lexington, KY
Hamilton, Lawrence J., II
Jacksonville, FL
Hamilton, Lawrence R. ... Chicago, IL
Hamilton, Lawrence R.
Saratoga Springs, NY
Hamilton, Leah L. ... Tucson, AZ
Hamilton, Lee ... Abilene, TX
Hamilton, Leo C. ... Baton Rouge, LA
Hamilton, Lewis S. ... Greenville, AL
Hamilton, Liisa V. ... Boothbay Harbor, ME
Hamilton, Linda M. ... Landover, MD
Hamilton, Linda M., P.C. ... Landover, MD
Hamilton & Linder ... Meridian, MS

Hamilton, Lisé .... **Los Angeles, CA**
Hamilton, Lise C. .... **Rochester, NY**
Hamilton, Lloyd B. .... Placerville, CA
Hamilton, Lloyd W. .... McLean, VA
Hamilton, Lorentz C., Jr. .... Grantsville, WV
Hamilton, Louis G. .... Cincinnati, OH
Hamilton, Lowell D. .... Mesa, AZ
Hamilton, Lynnwood Hale
Chattanooga, TN
Hamilton, Lysette .... Newark, NJ
Hamilton, Madge M.
Commodity Futures Trading Commission, Executive Staff, GV
Hamilton, Marcella T. .... **Tampa, FL**
Hamilton, Marci A. .... New York, NY
Hamilton, Margaret R.
Whitehouse Station, NJ
Hamilton, Mari Anne T. .... Bethesda, MD
Hamilton, Maria Prats .... Miami, FL
Hamilton, Marianne S. .... **San Diego, CA**
Hamilton, Mark Bradley .... Kalamazoo, MI
Hamilton, Mark D. .... Madison, WI
Hamilton, Mark E. .... Glenwood Springs, CO
Hamilton, Mark G.
House of Representatives, Office of Legislative Counsel, GV
Hamilton, Mark R. .... **Pittsburgh, PA**
Hamilton, Mark Scott .... San Francisco, CA
Hamilton, Mark T. .... Grayslake, IL
Hamilton, Mark T. .... **New York, NY**
Hamilton, Marvin J. .... Torrance, CA
Hamilton, Mary C. .... **Storm Lake, IA**
Hamilton, Mary Chapman .... Norfolk, VA
Hamilton, Mary F. .... Wilmette, IL
Hamilton, Mary J. .... Bloomington, IN
Hamilton, Mary K. .... Toledo, OH
Hamilton, Mary McCrory .... **Lafayette, LA**
Hamilton, Mary P. .... Boston, MA
Hamilton, Matthew J. .... **Philadelphia, PA**
Hamilton, Maurice K. .... San Bruno, CA
Hamilton and McDonald, P.C.
Ann Arbor, MI
Ypsilanti, MI
Hamilton & McMahon, Ltd.
Nevada City, CA
Quincy, CA
South Lake Tahoe, CA
Susanville, CA
Carson City, NV
Elko, NV
Gardnerville, NV
Incline Village, NV
Minden, NV
Reno, NV
Winnemucca, NV
Hamilton Mediation and Arbitration
Portland, OR
Hamilton, Melanie Martin
Greensboro, NC
Hamilton, Melissa .... **Los Angeles, CA**
Hamilton, Melissa .... **Austin, TX**
Hamilton, Meriam E. .... **Los Angeles, CA**
Hamilton, Michael A. .... Columbus, OH
Hamilton, Michael A. .... **Philadelphia, PA**
Hamilton, Michael D.
Department of Commerce, Patent and Trademark Office, GV
Hamilton, Michael G. .... Hastings, MN
Hamilton, Michael J. .... Redding, CA
Hamilton, Michael T. .... **Philadelphia, PA**
Hamilton & Michaelson .... Nampa, ID
Hamilton, Michele Claire .... Washington, DC
Hamilton, Michelle .... **Phoenix, AZ**
Hamilton, Michelle C. .... **Atlanta, GA**
Hamilton, Milton E. .... **Chester, SC**
Hamilton, Milton H., Jr. .... McLean, VA
Hamilton & Mitchell LLP .... **Paragould, AR**
Hamilton, M. J. .... Davis, CA
Hamilton & Mueller, S.C. .... **Dodgeville, WI**
Hamilton, Nancy E. .... St. Louis, MO
Hamilton, Nancy L. .... Houston, TX
Hamilton, Nancy Wells .... **Houston, TX**
Hamilton, Narcisse E. .... New Rochelle, NY
Hamilton, Nathan C. .... **Columbus, OH**
Hamilton, Nathan H. .... Sacramento, CA
Hamilton, Neal Jay .... Fairmont, WV
Hamilton, Neil D. .... Des Moines, IA
Hamilton, Neil E. .... **Milwaukee, WI**
Hamilton, Neil W. .... St. Paul, MN
Hamilton, O. Lee, III .... **Montgomery, AL**
Hamilton, O. C., Jr. .... **McAllen, TX**
Hamilton, Oliver G. .... Madison, WI
Hamilton, Oliver T. .... Tucson, AZ
Hamilton, Orlando N., Jr. .... **Oak Grove, LA**
Hamilton, Orman L. .... Sylva, NC
Hamilton, Orris L. .... Olympia, WA
Hamilton, P. Andrew .... **Bangor, ME**
Hamilton, Palmer C. .... **Mobile, AL**
Washington, DC
Hamilton, Pat R. .... **Oak Hill, WV**
Hamilton, Patricia C. .... Nevada City, CA
Hamilton, Patricia E. .... **Overland Park, KS**
Hamilton, Patricia M. .... Long Beach, NY
Hamilton, Patrick A. .... Overland Park, KS
Hamilton, Patrick M. .... Boston, MA
Hamilton, Paul E. .... Okemos, MI
Hamilton, Paul E. .... **Dallas, TX**
Hamilton, Paul F. .... **Reno, NV**
Hamilton, Paul R. .... **Los Angeles, CA**
Hamilton, Paul R. .... Austin, TX
Hamilton, Paul V. .... Colonial Heights, VA
Hamilton, Peatross, Wright & Pou
Shreveport, LA
Hamilton, Percival B. .... Bradenton, FL
Hamilton, Perrin C. .... **Philadelphia, PA**
Hamilton, Peter B. .... Columbus, IN
Hamilton, Peter M. .... **Denver, CO**
Hamilton, Peterson & Keeshan .... Topeka, KS

Hamilton, Philip K. .... Boston, MA
Hamilton, Philip L. .... Naples, FL
Hamilton, Phillip D. .... **Costa Mesa, CA**
Hamilton, Phillip H. .... **Belleville, IL**
Hamilton, Phillip J. .... Holt, MI
Hamilton & Quigley, PLC .... St. Paul, MN
Hamilton, R. Alston .... **Chattanooga, TN**
Hamilton, R. Andrew (Andy)
Houston, TX
Hamilton, R. Dickey .... **Chicago, IL**
Hamilton, R. Lee .... Grand Forks, ND
Hamilton, Rachael A. .... **Louisville, KY**
Hamilton, Randall R., P.C. .... Winchester, VA
Hamilton, Ray F., III .... Tulsa, OK
Hamilton, Ray F., P.C. .... Tulsa, OK
Hamilton, Raymond Wesley .... Richmond, CA
Hamilton, Rebecca B. .... Okeechobee, FL
Hamilton, Rebecca E. .... **Rockwall, TX**
Hamilton, Regina N. .... **Baton Rouge, LA**
Hamilton, Reginald O. .... Southfield, MI
Hamilton, Reid H. .... Kansas City, MO
Hamilton, Richard A. .... Flint, MI
Hamilton, Richard A. .... Toledo, OH
Hamilton, Richard D. .... Laguna Niguel, CA
Hamilton, Richard E. .... **Morristown, NJ**
Hamilton, Richard F. .... **Princeton, NJ**
Hamilton, Richard K. .... Richardson, TX
Hamilton, Richard L. .... Sacramento, CA
Hamilton, Richard P. .... Drexel Hill, PA
Hamilton, Richard T., Jr.
Department of Justice, Antitrust Division, GV
Hamilton, Richard W. .... Pascagoula, MS
Hamilton, Rita D. .... **Dallas, TX**
Hamilton, Robert A. .... San Francisco, CA
Hamilton, Robert C. .... Holland, MI
Hamilton, Robert D. .... **Harrisburg, PA**
Hamilton, Robert E. .... **Chicago, IL**
Hamilton, Robert F. .... Atlanta, GA
Hamilton, Robert L. .... Orlando, FL
Hamilton, Robert L. .... Chicago, IL
Hamilton, Robert M. .... **Irvine, CA**
Hamilton, Robert N. .... **St. Louis, MO**
Hamilton, Robert O. .... **Marysville, OH**
Hamilton, Robert P. .... **San Francisco, CA**
Hamilton, Robert P. .... New Albany, IN
Hamilton, Robert P. .... Battle Creek, MI
Hamilton, Robert P. .... Lebanon, TN
Hamilton, Robert R. .... Huntsville, AL
Hamilton, Robert S. .... Klamath Falls, OR
Medford, OR
Hamilton, Robert W. .... Cumberland, MD
Hamilton, Robert W. .... New York, NY
Hamilton, Robert W. .... **Columbus, OH**
Hamilton, Robert W. .... Buckley, WA
Hamilton, Robt. B. .... Jackson, MS
Hamilton, Robyn J. .... Eagle, CO
Hamilton, Roger .... Worcester, MA
Hamilton, Roland G. .... **Galveston, TX**
Hamilton, Ronald B. .... **Philadelphia, PA**
Hamilton, Russel T. .... **New York, NY**
Hamilton, Ruth R. .... **Juneau, AK**
Hamilton, Sally S. .... New York, NY
Hamilton, Samuel C. .... **Washington, DC**
Hamilton, Samuel C. .... **Silver Spring, MD**
Hamilton, Samuel Stephen .... Tampa, FL
Hamilton, Sandra A. .... Defiance, OH
Hamilton, Sandra B. .... Lafayette, CA
Hamilton, Sandra S. .... Grand Rapids, MI
Hamilton, Sarah J. .... New York, NY
Hamilton, Scot Gordon .... New York, NY
Hamilton, Scott .... Kalispell, MT
Hamilton, Scott .... Tulsa, OK
Hamilton, Scott B. .... Naperville, IL
Hamilton, Scott Cameron .... Lexington, MO
Hamilton, Scott J. .... Newtown, CT
Hamilton, Scott T. .... Pontiac, MI
Hamilton, Shane T. .... **Washington, DC**
Hamilton, Shannon Antle .... **Louisville, KY**
Hamilton, Sharon I. .... **Marathon, FL**
Hamilton, Shawna Lynn .... **Houston, TX**
Hamilton, Shelby G. .... **Washington, DC**
Hamilton, Stephanie L. .... **Fresno, CA**
Hamilton, Stephen D. D. .... **Philadelphia, PA**
Hamilton, Stephen E. .... **Houston, TX**
Hamilton, Stephen G. .... St. Louis, MO
Hamilton, Stephen J. .... Auburn Hills, MI
Hamilton, Stephen K. .... **Houston, TX**
Hamilton, Stephen M. .... Chelmsford, MA
Hamilton, Stephen S. .... **Santa Fe, NM**
Hamilton, Stephen W. .... **Washington, DC**
Hamilton, Steven A. .... **Chevy Chase, MD**
Hamilton, Steven D. .... **Storm Lake, IA**
Hamilton, Steven D. .... **Kansas City, MO**
Hamilton, Steven G. .... West Des Moines, IA
Hamilton, Steven J. .... **West Covina, CA**
Hamilton, Steven J., A Professional Corporation .... **West Covina, CA**
Hamilton, Steven M. .... **Butte, MT**
Hamilton, Stuart J. .... **Boston, MA**
Hamilton, Sue A. .... Howell, MI
Hamilton, Susan O. .... Jacksonville, FL
Hamilton, Tamara L. .... **Chicago, IL**
Hamilton, Teresa D. .... Sacramento, CA
Hamilton, Terrance J. .... **Boston, MA**
Hamilton, Terry M. .... Houston, TX
Hamilton, Theodore C. .... Irvine, CA
Hamilton, Theodore Jay .... **Tampa, FL**
Hamilton, Thomas .... **Richmond, VA**
Hamilton, Thomas A. .... **Cleveland, OH**
Hamilton, Thomas E. .... **Plainview, TX**
Hamilton, Thomas H. .... Riverside, CA
Hamilton, Thomas I. .... **Los Angeles, CA**
Hamilton, Thomas M. .... Santa Barbara, CA
Hamilton, Thomas M., Jr. .... **Chicago, IL**
Hamilton, Thomas P., Jr. .... Media, PA
Hamilton, Thomas R. .... **South Bend, IN**
Hamilton, Timothy M. .... **San Francisco, CA**

Hamilton, Todd .... **Birmingham, AL**
Hamilton, Tom .... Spirit Lake, IA
Hamilton, Tracy L. .... **Richmond, VA**
Hamilton, Trudie Ross .... **Waterbury, CT**
Hamilton, Valerie A. .... **Trenton, NJ**
Hamilton, Vanzetti M. .... Ann Arbor, MI
Hamilton, Vene M. .... Pembroke Pines, FL
Hamilton, Vene M., Law Offices of, P.A.
Pembroke Pines, FL
Hamilton, Vicki L. .... Carlsbad, CA
Hamilton, Victor .... Grantsville, WV
Hamilton, Victoria .... **New York, NY**
Hamilton, W. Andrew .... Tampa, FL
Hamilton, W. James .... Indianapolis, IN
Hamilton, W. Michael .... **Nashville, TN**
Hamilton, W. Russell, III .... **Miami, FL**
Hamilton, Walter H. .... Geneva, IL
Hamilton, Walter K. .... Ann Arbor, MI
Hamilton, Warren & Bovos, A Professional Corporation .... **Poteau, OK**
Hamilton, Wayne A. .... **Philadelphia, PA**
Hamilton, Wayne A.S. .... **Troy, MI**
Hamilton, Wesley F. .... Zelienople, PA
Hamilton, Westby, Marshall & Antonowich
Atlanta, GA
Hamilton, William A. .... Tucker, GA
Hamilton, William A., III .... Orange Park, FL
Hamilton, William C. .... San Antonio, TX
Hamilton, William F. .... **Miami, FL**
Tampa, FL
Hamilton, William G., Jr. .... Buffalo, NY
Hamilton, William H. .... Clemmons, NC
Hamilton, William J. .... **Lowell, MA**
Hamilton, William J., III .... Charleston, SC
Hamilton, William J., Jr.
New Brunswick, NJ
Hamilton, William N. .... San Diego, CA
Hamilton, William N. .... **Dallas, TX**
Hamilton, William R. .... Paw Paw, MI
Hamilton, William Roderick
Los Angeles, CA
Hamilton, William Scott .... **Bradenton, FL**
Hamilton, Willis J. .... **Storm Lake, IA**
Hamilton, Wm. A. .... Reedley, CA
Hamilton, Wm. C. .... Hagerstown, MD
Hamilton, W. P., (P.A.) .... Little Rock, AR
Hamilton-Day, Ala .... Philadelphia, PA
Hamilton-Dewitt, Lori I. .... Mocksville, NC
Hamister, Kenneth C. .... Elyria, OH
Hamity, Karen L. .... Highland Park, IL
Hamje, John F., III .... Austin, TX
Hamje, Paula J. .... Austin, TX
Hamker, William D. .... Amarillo, TX
Hamlar, Portia Y. T. .... Southfield, MI
Hamlen, Herschel H., Jr. .... Marietta, GA
Hamler, Sonya Zoe .... Brooklyn, NY
Hamlet, Bill .... Marietta, GA
Richmond, VA
Hamlet, Brenton A. .... **Newport Beach, CA**
Hamlet, Fred T. .... **Greensboro, NC**
Wilmington, NC
Hamlet, Glaidell D. .... Irmo, SC
Hamlet, H. Mark .... **Wilmington, NC**
Hamlet, J. Rachael .... Falls Church, VA
Hamlet-Cox, Diana .... Palo Alto, CA
Hamlett, Carson E., Jr. .... Richmond, VA
Hamlett, J. Richard, II .... **Nashville, NC**
Hamlett, James D. .... **Montgomery, AL**
Hamlett, James K. .... Mexico, MO
Hamlett, Jeffrey M. .... Edmonds, WA
Hamlett, John R. .... Buffalo, NY
Hamlett, Laurie R. .... McAllen, TX
Hamlett, Leroy R., Jr. .... **Charlottesville, VA**
Hamlett, Michael R. .... Princeton, NJ
Hamlett, Robert M. .... **Indianapolis, IN**
Hamlett, Stephanie L. .... **Richmond, VA**
Hamley, James P. .... **Seattle, WA**
Hamley, Jerald R. .... Ephrata, WA
Hamlin, Barney T. .... Washington, DC
Hamlin, Bret T. .... **Tampa, FL**
Hamlin, Bruce C. .... **Portland, OR**
Hamlin, C. Judson .... **Bedminster, NJ**
Hamlin, Charles F. .... Fresno, CA
Hamlin, Christopher L. .... **Greenbelt, MD**
Hamlin, Curtis D. .... **Bradenton, FL**
Hamlin, David O. .... Seattle, WA
Hamlin, Deborah A. .... Great Neck, NY
Hamlin, Donald R. .... Pell City, AL
Hamlin, Edward .... New York, NY
Hamlin, Edwin J. .... Raleigh, NC
Hamlin, Elizabeth H. .... Washington, DC
Dunkirk, MD
Hamlin, Elizabeth H., P.C., Law Offices of
Washington, DC
Dunkirk, MD
Hamlin, Frank S. .... Bentonville, AR
Fort Smith, AR
Little Rock, AR
Hamlin, George W., IV .... Canandaigua, NY
Hamlin, Gregory A. .... **Utica, NY**
Hamlin, H. Ward, Jr. .... Buffalo, NY
Hamlin, Harold W. .... **Little Rock, AR**
Hamlin, J. Reuben .... Tallahassee, FL
Hamlin, Jack B. .... San Diego, CA
Hamlin, James B., (P.C.) .... **Washington, DC**
Hamlin, Jeffrey R. .... **Troy, MI**
Hamlin, Jennifer J. .... **Beverly Hills, CA**
Hamlin, Jerry W. .... Ashland City, TN
Hamlin, Joe W. .... Lawton, OK
Hamlin, John C. .... **Miami, FL**
Miami, FL
Hamlin, John C., P.A. .... **Miami, FL**
Hamlin, John W. .... **Stamford, CT**
Hamlin, Judson M. .... Bedminster, NJ
Hamlin, Julie Meck .... Southport, CT
Hamlin Law Office, L.C. .... Huntington, WV
Hamlin, M. Helene .... Ilion, NY
Hamlin, Mary K. Viegelahn .... Kalamazoo, MI

Hamlin, Matthew E. .... **Utica, NY**
Hamlin, Michael D. .... **Johnson City, TN**
Hamlin, Neil H. .... Milo, ME
Hamlin, Richard .... Los Angeles, CA
Hamlin, Richard .... Sacramento, CA
Hamlin, Richard C. .... **New York, NY**
Hamlin, Robert G. .... **Boise, ID**
Hamlin & Sasser, P.A. .... **Boise, ID**
Coeur d'Alene, ID
Hamlin, Susan M. .... Clinton, NY
Hamlin, Susan R. .... Sacramento, CA
Hamlin, Thomas L. .... **Minneapolis, MN**
Hamlin, W. Kent .... Fresno, CA
Hamlin, W. Robert .... Huntington, WV
Hamlin, Ward S., Jr. .... Paw Paw, MI
Hamlin, Wilbur Gordon, Jr. .... **Atlanta, GA**
Hamlin, William J. .... New Orleans, LA
Hamling, Jeff C. .... Roswell, GA
Hamlish, Richard .... Westlake Village, CA
Hamlyn, John J., III .... **Santa Cruz, CA**
Hamlyn, John J., Jr. .... **Sacramento, CA**
Hamm, D. Michael .... Houston, TX
Hamm, Daniel G. .... Montgomery, AL
Hamm, David B. .... **New York, NY**
Hamm, Donovan M., Jr.
Christiansted, St. Croix, VI
Hamm, Gene A., II .... **Dallas, TX**
Hamm, George M. .... Houston, TX
Hamm, H. Evins .... Florence, AL
Hamm & Hanna, Ltd. A Professional Corporation .... **Peoria, IL**
Hamm, Janet Williams .... Houston, TX
Hamm, Jimmy D. .... Beaumont, TX
Hamm, John Patrick .... **Louisville, KY**
Hamm, John W. .... United States Senate, Senatorial Assistants, GV
Hamm, Kathleen M.
Securities and Exchange Commission, Division of Enforcement, GV
Hamm, Kimberly M. .... Chicago, IL
Hamm, Laura Ellen .... **Richmond, VA**
Hamm, Leisa J. .... **Chicago, IL**
Hamm, M. Allison .... Worcester, MA
Hamm, Macy M. .... Lafayette, LA
Hamm, Maureen Skates .... Livermore, CA
Hamm, Milby & Ridings .... **London, KY**
Manchester, KY
Somerset, KY
Hamm, Nancy L. .... Fayetteville, AR
Hamm, Nathan A. .... Albany, NY
Hamm, O. Kelly .... Alexandria, LA
Hamm, Richard F., Jr. .... Bradenton, FL
Hamm, Robert A. .... Florence, KY
Hamm, Robert J. .... Houston, TX
Hamm, Roberta M. .... Detroit, MI
Hamm, Ronald L. .... **Peoria, IL**
Hamm, Scott .... San Jose, CA
Hamm, Sharon .... Denver, CO
Hamm, Steven W. .... **Columbia, SC**
Hamm, Valerie J. .... **Elizabethtown, KY**
Hamm, W. Gerald .... Panama City, FL
Hamm, W. Jeff .... Jackson, MS
Hamm, William C., Jr. .... **Lake Alfred, FL**
Hamm, William R. .... Philadelphia, PA
Hamma, Melissa .... Des Moines, IA
Hammack, Albert D. .... **Dallas, TX**
Hammack, Alex L. .... **Claremore, OK**
Hammack & Armata .... Bristol, CT
Hammack, E. Eugene .... Oklahoma City, OK
Hammack, Henry A. .... Albany, GA
Hammack, Larry C. .... **Medford, OR**
Hammack, Lorenza J., Jr. .... Lawrenceville, VA
Hammack, Marsha C. .... Beaverton, OR
Hammack, Paul W., Jr. .... **Washington, DC**
Hammack, Paul W., Jr. .... **Fairfax, VA**
Hammack, Robert K. .... **Lafayette, LA**
Hammack, Timothy L. .... Bristol, CT
Hammack, Wayne H. .... **Sherman Oaks, CA**
Hammack, William C. .... **Meridian, MS**
Hammack, William F. .... Dallas, TX
Hammad, Michael .... **Newport Beach, CA**
Hammaker, Charles Aldine .... **Houston, TX**
Hammaker, Jeffrey B. .... **Virginia Beach, VA**
Hammaker, John L. .... Atlanta, GA
Hammaker, John L., P.C. .... Atlanta, GA
Hammalian, John B. .... **New York, NY**
Hamman & Benn .... **Chicago, IL**
Hamman, Christopher Leif
Jonesboro, AR
Hamman, Donald J. .... **Newport Beach, CA**
Hamman, George W. .... **Chicago, IL**
Hamman, James S. .... Chicago, IL
Hamman, James S., Jr. .... Chicago, IL
Hamman, K. Douglas .... Belleville, IL
Hamman Law Firm .... **Jonesboro, AR**
Hamman, Rodd A. .... **Billings, MT**
Hamman, Timothy C. .... Lima, OH
Hammann, Chester A. .... San Antonio, TX
Hammann, William A. .... Superior, WI
Hammans, Tania Rae .... Des Moines, IA
Hammant, Elizabeth A. .... New Orleans, LA
Hammar, John C. .... **Seattle, WA**
Hammar, Kevin D. .... **Albuquerque, NM**
Hammarback, Bernt J. .... River Falls, WI
Hammarback Law Offices, S.C.
River Falls, WI
Hammarberg, Jon K. .... **Minneapolis, MN**
Hammargren, David D. .... Minneapolis, MN
Hammargren & Meyer, P.A.
Minneapolis, MN
Hammarlund, John T.
Department Of Health And Human Services, Public Health Service, GV
Hammarstrom, B. David .... **Warwick, RI**
Hammatt, Matthew P. .... **Chicago, IL**
Hammatt, Meryle G. .... Fountain Valley, CA
Hammatt & Still .... Chatham, MA
Hammatt, William R. .... Chatham, MA

Hammond, Mikini M. ... San Diego, CA
Hammond, Nancy D. Washington C. H., OH
Hammond, P. Theodore ... Pasadena, CA
Hammond, Pamela W. ... New Orleans, LA
Hammond, Patricia Flood ... Manassas, VA
Hammond, Paul F. ... Buffalo, NY
Hammond, Paula Biggs ... Portland, OR
Hammond, Peirce A., II ... New Orleans, LA
Hammond, Phil B. ... Phoenix, AZ
Hammond, Randall J. ... Fort Wayne, IN
Hammond, Reidar O. ... Greeley, CO
Hammond, Richard E. ... San Francisco, CA
Hammond, Richard H. ... Beavercreek, OH
Hammond, Richard W. ... Cleveland, OH
Hammond, Rick A. ... Jackson, MS
Hammond, Rick L. ... Chicago, IL
Hammond, Robert L. ... Blue Earth, MN
Hammond, Robert L. Washington C. H., OH
Hammond, Robert M. ... Youngstown, OH
Hammond, Robert M., Associates Doylestown, PA
Hammond, Robert N. ... Grand Rapids, MI
Hammond, Robin M. ... Raleigh, NC
Hammond, Roy J. ... Camden, NC
Hammond, S. Robert, Jr. Hattiesburg, MS
Hammond, Sandra Barr ... Louisville, KY
Hammond, Scott D. ... Department of Justice, Antitrust Division, GV
Hammond & Sewards ... Cambridge, OH
Canton, OH
Chillicothe, OH
Circleville, OH
Columbus, OH
Delaware, OH
Lancaster, OH
London, OH
Mansfield, OH
Marysville, OH
Newark, OH
Portsmouth, OH
Zanesville, OH
Hammond, Shawn P. ... Augusta, GA
Hammond and Smith, P.A. ... Vero Beach, FL
Hammond, Stephen V. ... Decatur, AL
Hammond, Steven A. ... New York, NY
Hammond, Steven P. Department of the Navy, Office of the Judge Advocate General, GV
Hammond & Stier Law Offices Beavercreek, OH
Hammond, Susan K. ... Portland, OR
Hammond, Susan Lynette ... Lubbock, TX
Hammond, Terry W. ... El Paso, TX
Hammond, Thomas Brittan ... Thomson, GA
Hammond, Thomas E. ... Wichita, KS
Hammond, Thomas J. ... Denver, CO
Hammond, Thomas M. ... New York, NY
Hammond, Thomas W., Jr. ... Boston, MA
Hammond, Timothy ... Washington, DC
Hammond & Tobler, P.C. ... Phoenix, AZ
Hammond, Todd S. ... Salem, OR
Hammond, V. Paige ... Orlando, FL
Hammond, Warren L., Jr. ... Mobile, AL
Hammond, Wesley J. ... Fresno, CA
Hammond, Whitney D. ... Vernal, UT
Hammond, William D. ... Houston, TX
Hammond, William E. ... New York, NY
Hammond, William F. ... Augusta, GA
Aiken, SC
Hammond, William G. ... Olathe, KS
Hammond, William S. ... Detroit, MI
Hammond, Zongker & Farris, L.L.C. Wichita, KS
Hammond-Carroll, Jennifer Sacramento, CA
Hammonds, Chad Wyatt ... Maxton, NC
Hammonds, E. C. ... Lexington, KY
Hammonds, Glen D. ... Oklahoma City, OK
Hammonds, Kevin B. ... Greenville, SC
Hammonds, Oliver W. ... Dallas, TX
Hammonds, Pat ... El Paso, TX
Hammonds, Robert L. ... Baton Rouge, LA
Hammonds, Samuel F. ... Fostoria, OH
Hammonds & Sills ... Baton Rouge, LA
Hammonds, Stephanie L., Law Office of Detroit, MI
Hammonds, William E. ... San Francisco, CA
Hammons, Allen J., Jr. ... Brownfield, TX
Hammons, Brian K. ... Stockton, MO
Hammons, Erik L. ... Bryan, TX
Hammons, Hal V., Jr. ... Ventura, CA
Hammons, James H., Jr. ... Boston, MA
Hammons, John D., Jr. ... Springfield, MO
Hammons, John L. ... Shreveport, LA
Hammons, Joseph L. ... Pensacola, FL
Hammons, Mark E. ... Oklahoma City, OK
Hammons, Michael J. ... Covington, KY
Hammons, Mills & Spickerman ... Eugene, OR
Hammons, Robert E. ... Cobleskill, NY
Hammons, Robert P. ... Corbin, KY
Hammons, S. Paul ... Oklahoma City, OK
Hammons, Samuel G. ... Edmond, OK
Hammons, Terence J. ... Eugene, OR
Hammons, Teresa N. ... Virginia Beach, VA
Hammons, Troy D. ... Amarillo, TX
Hammons & Whittaker, P.A. Pensacola, FL
Hammontree, Jack D. ... Enid, OK
Okeene, OK
Seiling, OK
Hammoud, Abed E. ... Detroit, MI
Hamner, Frank A. ... Orlando, FL
Hamner, Gordon J. ... Houma, LA
Hamner, Herschel T., Jr. ... Tuscaloosa, AL
Hamner, Holly J. ... Tuscaloosa, AL
Hamner, Joan G. ... Nashville, TN
Hamner, Joel R. ... Huntsville, AL
Hamner, John Alton, II ... La Grande, OR
Hamner, John L. ... Butte, MT
Hamner, Julie G. ... New Orleans, LA
Hamner, Lewis H., Jr. ... Roanoke, AL
Hamner, Philip E. ... San Antonio, TX
Hamner, Reginald T. ... Montgomery, AL
Hamner, Scott E. ... Toledo, OH
Hamner, William S. ... Houston, TX
Hamner, W. J. Dyson ... Cullman, AL
Hamnett, Iam ... Princeton, NJ
Hamo, George R., and Associates Flint, MI
Charlotte, NC
Hamon, Colleen ... Fort Worth, TX
Hamon, Richard G. ... Dallas, TX
Hamood, Jamal John ... Dearborn, MI
Hamood, Jamal John ... Troy, MI
Troy, MI
Hamor, Lillian M. ... Tulsa, OK
Hamor, Steven D. ... San Diego, CA
Hamor, Steven D., Law Office of San Diego, CA
Hamoudi, Haider Ala ... New York, NY
Hamovit, Jerry M. ... Chevy Chase, MD
Hamovitz, Glenn D. ... Los Angeles, CA
Hamp, Richard G. ... Salt Lake City, UT
Hampar, Armen ... Los Angeles, CA
Hampar, Arthur E. ... Visalia, CA
Hampar, Berge ... Frederick, MD
Hampar, Gary W. ... Beverly Hills, CA
Hamparyan, Robert ... Irvine, CA
Hampden, Brenda Saunders ... Newark, NJ
Hampden, Michael D. ... White Plains, NY
Hampe, Carl W. ... Washington, DC
Hampe, David E., Jr. ... Birmingham, AL
Hampe, Kevin F. ... Dedham, MA
Hampe, Rachel A. ... Manchester, NH
Hampe, Richard A. ... Concord, NH
Hampe, Robert A. ... Cheyenne, WY
Hampe, Robert A., P.C. ... Cheyenne, WY
Hampel, Elizabeth M. ... Springfield, OH
Hampel, Larry ... Washington, DC
Hampel, Leonard A., Jr. ... Costa Mesa, CA
Hamper, Sidney C. ... Chicago, IL
Hampers, L. Joyce, (Mrs.) Chestnut Hill, MA
Hampf, Carol J. ... Boulder, CO
Hampilos, George P. ... Rockford, IL
Hampilos, Gus Theodore ... Danbury, CT
Hampl, Lisa S. ... Columbus, OH
Hampo, Adrianne E. ... Chicago, IL
Hampole, Gowri V. ... Avon Lake, OH
Hampsch, Robert J. ... Peoria, IL
Hampsey, Bernard J., Jr. ... Jaffrey, NH
Hampshire & Associates, P.C. Fort Wayne, IN
Hampshire, Gifford R. ... Fairfax, VA
Hampshire, Melissa V. Consumer Product Safety Commission, Office of the General Counsel, GV
Hampshire, Sherie L. ... Fort Wayne, IN
Hampshire, Thomas R. ... Belvidere, NJ
Hampson, Bruce ... Springer, NM
Hampson, Colin Cloud ... Washington, DC
Hampson, Debra A. ... Simsbury, CT
Hampson, Gary T. ... Fullerton, CA
Hampson, H. Robert ... Warren, PA
Hampson, J. Jay ... Bremen, OH
Lancaster, OH
Hampson, Robert F. ... Philadelphia, PA
Hampson, Robert G. ... Somerset, NJ
Hampson, Theresa L. ... Walla Walla, WA
Hampson, Thomas M. ... Rochester, NY
Hampton, Albert ... Calabasas, CA
Hampton, Amy Spear ... Houston, TX
Hampton, André ... Austin, TX
Hampton, Anthony R. ... San Francisco, CA
Hampton, Audris G. ... Denver, CO
Hampton, Bernard ... Baton Rouge, LA
Hampton, Bill ... Elizabethton, TN
Hampton, Bill V., Jr. ... Pratt, KS
Hampton, Bradley P. ... Seattle, WA
Hampton, Brett G. ... Los Angeles, CA
Hampton, Bruce E. ... Farmerville, LA
Hampton, Carolyn A. ... Universal City, CA
Hampton, Cathy D. ... Atlanta, GA
Hampton, Charisse L. ... Chicago, IL
Hampton, Charles B. ... Houston, TX
Hampton, Charles E. ... Austin, TX
Hampton, Charles J. ... Atlanta, GA
Hampton, Clyde R. ... Aurora, CO
Hampton, Daniel H. ... Warsaw, IN
Hampton, Daniel K. ... Boston, MA
Hampton, David A. ... Rock Springs, WY
Hampton, David M. ... San Francisco, CA
Hampton, Deann ... Los Angeles, CA
Hampton, Dorothy A. ... San Diego, CA
Hampton, Douglas D. ... Detroit, MI
Hampton, Douglas D., & Associates, P.C. Detroit, MI
Hampton, Douglas W. ... Brandon, FL
Hampton, Elizabeth J. ... Cherry Hill, NJ
Hampton, Elizabeth S. ... Little Rock, AR
Hampton & Facemire ... Huntsville, AL
Hampton, Frances H. ... Virginia Beach, VA
Hampton, Gail Ingram ... Montgomery, AL
Hampton, Geoffrey A. ... Utica, NY
Hampton, George L., IV ... Irvine, CA
Hampton, Gilbert L. ... Dallas, TX
Hampton, Glen L. ... Vista, CA
Hampton, Glenn W. ... Norfolk, VA
Hampton, Gray Watson, III ... New York, NY
Hampton, Gregory J. ... San Francisco, CA
Hampton & Hampton ... Pratt, KS
Hampton & Hampton ... Ashland, PA
Hampton, Hartley ... Houston, TX
Hampton, J. David ... Oklahoma City, OK
Hampton, Jack ... Horseshoe Bay, TX
Hampton, James R. ... Hazard, KY
Hampton, Jeffrey C. ... Philadelphia, PA
Hampton, Jennifer ... New York, NY
Hampton, Jennifer L. ... Atlanta, GA
Hampton, Joe M. ... Oklahoma City, OK
Hampton, John ... Pendleton, OR
Hampton, John C. ... Bryan, TX
Hampton, John E. ... Dallas, TX
Hampton, John L. ... Overland Park, KS
Hampton, John M. ... Ashland, PA
Hampton, Joseph D. ... Seattle, WA
Hampton, Joy S. ... Placerville, CA
Hampton, Karen R. ... Portland, OR
Hampton, Kenneth D. ... Huntsville, AL
Hampton, Kenneth R. ... Bayonne, NJ
Hampton, Kent B. ... Findlay, OH
Hampton, Kimberly C. ... Dallas, TX
Hampton, L. Winton ... Houston, TX
Hampton Law Office ... Overland Park, KS
Hampton Law Offices ... Canton, CT
Hampton, Leslie B. ... Salem, OR
Hampton, Lewis B. ... Portland, OR
Hampton, Lloyd R. ... Ashland, PA
Hampton, Lynn Wolgamott ... Pendleton, OR
Hampton, M. Michele ... Indianapolis, IN
Hampton & Mallers, P.C. ... Dallas, TX
Hampton, Maria L. ... Collinsville, CT
Hampton, Mark I. ... Jamestown, NY
Hampton and Milligan Oklahoma City, OK
Hampton, Patricia G. Department of Housing and Urban Development, GV
Hampton, Peter W. ... Elizabethton, TN
Hampton, Philip G., II ... Washington, DC
Hampton, Ray L., II ... Huntington, WV
Hampton, Richard A. ... Holmes Beach, FL
Hampton, Richard D. ... Oklahoma City, OK
Hampton, Rick Dean ... Oklahoma City, OK
Hampton, Robert J. ... Tulsa, OK
Hampton, Robert Morgan ... Wichita Falls, TX
Hampton, Ronald L. ... Glasgow, KY
Hampton, Roy ... Atlanta, GA
Hampton & Royce, L.C. ... Salina, KS
Hampton, Scott A. ... Calabasas, CA
Hampton, Stephen A. ... Dover, DE
Hampton, Steven J. ... Chicago, IL
Hampton, Stoddard, Griffin & Runnells Brandon, FL
Hampton & Street ... Elizabethton, TN
Hampton, Suzanne M. ... Fort Wayne, IN
Hampton, Teresa M. ... Lincoln, NE
Hampton, Thomas A. ... Barnesville, OH
Hampton, Van Z. ... Dodge City, KS
Hampton, Verne C., II ... Detroit, MI
Hampton, Wade McK. ... Jacksonville, FL
Hampton, Wallis M. ... Houston, TX
Hampton, Walter R., Jr. ... Canton, CT
Hampton, Wardell ... Gary, IN
Hampton, Wayne ... San Antonio, TX
Hampton, William P. Farmington Hills, MI
Hampton, Wm. W. ... Gainesville, FL
Hampton-York Law Center, P.C. Hampton, VA
Hamra, H. Dean ... Pekin, IL
Hamra, H. Dean, P.C. ... Pekin, IL
Hamra, Jacqueline K. Commodity Futures Trading Commission, Division of Enforcement, GV
Hamra, Michael ... Washington, DC
Hamra, Sam F. ... Springfield, MO
Hamre, Austin C. ... Denver, CO
Hamre, Curtis B. ... Minneapolis, MN
Hamre, Mareta C. ... Los Angeles, CA
Hamren, Nancy H. ... Houston, TX
Hamric, B. Rebecca ... Houston, TX
Hamric, Bryan D. ... Richardson, TX
Hamric, Fred L. ... Dallas, TX
Hamric, Laurence M. ... New Orleans, LA
Hamric, Louis D. ... Memphis, TN
Hamrick, A. Raymond, III Los Angeles, CA
Hamrick, Anna R. ... Asheville, NC
Hamrick & Associates ... High Point, NC
Hamrick, Ben W. ... San Diego, CA
Hamrick, Bowen, Nanney & Dalton, L.L.P. Forest City, NC
Rutherfordton, NC
Hamrick, C. Page, III ... Charleston, WV
Hamrick, Cameron S. ... Washington, DC
Hamrick, Claude A. S. ... Palo Alto, CA
Hamrick, Claude M. ... Winston-Salem, NC
Hamrick, Daniel D. ... Christiansburg, VA
Hamrick, Daniel D., P.C. ... Christiansburg, VA
Hamrick, David Edgar ... Englewood, CO
Hamrick, Diane Q. ... High Point, NC
Hamrick, Ellen P. ... Greensboro, NC
Hamrick & Evans LLP ... Los Angeles, CA
Universal City, CA
Hamrick, Gayle B. ... Augusta, GA
Hamrick, George N. ... Knightdale, NC
Hamrick, George W. ... Shelby, NC
Hamrick, Henry Pope, Jr. Daytona Beach, FL
Hamrick, J. Thomas, Jr. New Orleans, LA
Hamrick, Joanna V. ... Houston, TX
Hamrick, John M., Jr. ... Bethlehem, PA
Hamrick, Katrina L. ... Deer Park, TX
Hamrick, Kent L. ... Winston-Salem, NC
Hamrick, Lillian F. ... San Francisco, CA
Hamrick, Lloyd A. ... Kansas City, MO
Hamrick, Martha F. ... Jackson, MS
Hamrick, Mary ... Washington, DC
Hamrick, Mauney, Flowers, Martin & Moore ... Shelby, NC
Hamrick, Melissa L. ... Fort Worth, TX
Hamrick, Michael M. ... Bradenton, FL
Hamrick, Patricia ... Oakland, CA
Hamrick, Perrey, Quinlan & Smith, P.A. Bradenton, FL
Hamrick, Richard D. ... Tampa, FL
Hamrick, Roy E. ... San Leandro, CA
Hamrick, Roy E., & Associates San Leandro, CA
Hamrick, S. Dean ... Charlotte, NC
Hamrick, Stanley S. ... Fairfax Station, VA
Hamrick, Steven J. ... Washington, DC
Hamrick, Terry D. ... Cissna Park, IL
Urbana, IL
Hamrick, W. Samuel, Jr. ... Asheville, NC
Hamrick, William G., III ... Carrollton, GA
Hamrick, William G., Jr. ... Smyrna, GA
Hamrick, Winn C. ... Dayton, OH
Hamrin, Donald C. ... Chicago, IL
Hamrin, Donald C., Ltd. ... Chicago, IL
Hamrock, Kurt J. ... Washington, DC
Hamrock, William F. ... Kennebunkport, ME
Hamroff, Marc L. ... Garden City, NY
Hamrum, Kenneth L. ... Morris, MN
Hams, Thomas P. ... Simsbury, CT
Hamsher, F. Bernard ... Buffalo, NY
Hamson, Jack C. ... Ukiah, CA
Hamstead & Associates Charles Town, WV
Hamstead, Braun A. ... Charles Town, WV
Hamstead, Hamstead & Williams Fairmont, WV
Kingwood, WV
Morgantown, WV
Hamstra, Nancy LeBlanc ... Center, TX
Hamud, Randall B. ... San Diego, CA
Hamula, James J. ... Phoenix, AZ
Hamula, Steven ... Charleston, WV
Hamwi, Joseph F. ... Los Angeles, CA
Hamwi, Susan L. ... Santa Monica, CA
Hamza, Beatrice Aisha ... New York, NY
Han, Alenka Jana ... Denver, CO
Han, Andrew ... Los Angeles, CA
Han, Arlene Lloyd ... Fort Myers, FL
Han, Chung H. ... Santa Monica, CA
Han, David T. ... Los Angeles, CA
Han, Edward ... San Francisco, CA
Han, Edward ... Washington, DC
Han, Grace H. ... Plainville, CT
Han, Grace J. ... Seattle, WA
Han, Ittah ... Las Vegas, NV
Han, James W. ... Irvine, CA
Han, Jennifer Yulin ... Piscataway, NJ
Han, Joanna S. ... Washington, DC
Han, John K. ... New York, NY
Han, Karen R. ... New York, NY
Han, Kathy K. ... Houston, TX
Han, Lisa G. ... Columbus, OH
Han, Marjorie ... New York, NY
Han, Moon-Young ... New York, NY
Han, Sang Jin ... New York, NY
Han, Sook F. ... Detroit, MI
Han, Su Lin ... Glastonbury, CT
Han, Terry H. ... Pittsburgh, PA
Hanafi, Alex G. ... San Francisco, CA
Hanafin, John C. ... Litchfield, IL
Hanaford, Robert H. ... Chicago, IL
Hanafourde, Bradley K. ... Miami, FL
Hanafourde, Bradley K., P.A. ... Miami, FL
Hanagami, Steven S. ... Irvine, CA
Hanagami, William K. ... Los Angeles, CA
Hanagan & Dousman ... Mount Vernon, IL
Hanagan, Michael J. ... Mount Vernon, IL
Hanagan, Sean G. ... White Plains, NY
Hanagan, Steven F. ... Mount Vernon, IL
Hanagan, William D. ... Mount Vernon, IL
Hanaghan, Dennis M. ... Dayton, OH
Hanaghan, Ralph J. ... Kettering, OH
Hanahan, Geoffrey C. ... Painesville, OH
Hanahan, Michael J. ... Chicago, IL
Hanahan, Robert P. ... Waterbury, CT
Hanahan, Thomas M. ... Indianapolis, IN
Hanahan, William O., III ... Charleston, SC
Hanaike, Dona L. ... Honolulu, HI
Hanak, Elmer W., III Department of Commerce, Patent and Trademark Office, GV
Hanak, Guido & Taladay ... Du Bois, PA
Hanak, Nicole J. ... Denver, CO
Hanak, Robert M. ... Du Bois, PA
Hanamirian, A. Arthur, P.C. Philadelphia, PA
Hanamirian, John M. ... Pennsauken, NJ
Hanamirian, Mark C. ... Philadelphia, PA
Hanamirian, Michael Albert Philadelphia, PA
Hanamirian, Robert A. ... Philadelphia, PA
Hanan, Albert ... Seattle, WA
Hanan, Andrew C. ... Mount Laurel, NJ
Philadelphia, PA
Hanan, Benjamin Ross ... Sarasota, FL
Hanan, Beth E. ... Milwaukee, WI
Hanan, Catherine B. ... Los Angeles, CA
Hanan, Catherine B., A Prof. Corp. Los Angeles, CA
Hanan, Ellis D. ... Montgomery, AL
Hanan, Mary B. ... Oklahoma City, OK
Hanan, Mindy Bradford ... Montgomery, AL
Hanan, Timothy A. ... Washington, DC
Hananel, Sam R. ... Washington, DC
Hanania, Maher H. ... Department of Labor, Office of the Solicitor, GV
Hanania, Mitri ... Redwood City, CA
Hanano, Scott ... Wailuku, HI
Hanaoka, Louise O. ... Port Charlotte, FL

Hanas, Stephen M.
Federal Deposit Insurance Corporation, GV
Hanasono, Theodore Y. ... Torrance, CA
Hanau, Helen ... Janesville, WI
Hanau, Paul E. ... New York, NY
Hanau, Rosalinda Laguna ... Chula Vista, CA
Hanauer, Charles T. ... Santa Ana, CA
Hanauer, Maurice K. ... San Francisco, CA
Hanauer, Richd. H. ... Cincinnati, OH
Hanavan, James M. ... San Francisco, CA
Hanavan, Taylor W. ... Wilmington, DE
Hanavan, Thomas L. ... Oakland, CA
Hanawalt, Richard W. ... Ventura, CA
Hanaway, Charles T. ... Green Bay, WI
Hanaway, David P. ... Green Bay, WI
Hanaway, Susan D. ... Chicago, IL
Hanaway, Weidner, Bachhuber, Woodward & Maloney, S.C. ... Green Bay, WI
Hanba, Lawrence J. ... Flint, MI
Hanba & Lazar, P.C. ... Flint, MI
Hanback, Christopher B.
Washington, DC
Hanberry, Joel ... Cut Off, LA
Hanbery, Donna E. ... Minneapolis, MN
Hanbery, Neumeyer & Carney, P.A.
Minneapolis, MN
Hanberry, William L. ... Florence, AL
Hanbey, Michael ... Olympia, WA
Hanbury, David R. ... Birmingham, AL
Hanbury, Doyle ... Dalhart, TX
Hanbury, George L., III ... Washington, DC
Hanbury, John L. ... Ashland, KY
Hanbury, Kevin P. ... Southfield, MI
Hanbury, Marshall E. ... Chicago, IL
Hanbury, Potter, Hall & Winans, P.S.C.
Ashland, KY
Hanby, Blake Patrick ... Springdale, AR
Hanby, Clinard J. ... The Woodlands, TX
Hanby, William F.E., III
Huntingdon Valley, PA
Hance, Bryan S. ... Malibu, CA
Hance, C. Eric ... Batesville, AR
Hance, Catherine A. ... Denver, CO
Hance, Elvin D. ... Des Moines, IA
Hance & Hance, P.A. ... Batesville, AR
Hance & Iverson, Ltd. ... Fridley, MN
Hance, Jeffrey E., (Mrs.) ... Batesville, AR
Hance, John P. ... Eden, NC
Hance, John P. ... Martinsville, VA
Hance, Kenneth G., Jr. ... Washington, DC
Hance, Kent R. ... Washington, DC
Austin, TX
Hance, Larry ... Dallas, TX
Hance, Michael R. ... Louisville, KY
Hance, Scarborough, Wright, Keiffer, Woodward & Weisbart, L.L.P.
Washington, DC
Hance, Scarborough, Wright, Keiffer, Woodward & Weisbart, L.L.P.
Austin, TX
Hance, Scarborough, Wright, Keiffer, Woodward & Weisbart, L.L.P.
Dallas, TX
Hance, Stephen W. ... Minneapolis, MN
Hance, Terence C. ... Flagstaff, AZ
Hancey, Christian ... Rochester, NY
Hanchak, Carl M. ... Pittsburgh, PA
Hancher, Darla J. ... Zelienople, PA
Hancher, George H. ... Zelienople, PA
Hanchet, Markham G. ... New York, NY
Hanchett, Karen M.
Administrative Office Of The United States Courts, GV
Hanchett, Kevin P. ... Seattle, WA
Hanchett, Paul E. ... Chicago, IL
Hanchett, Richard M. ... Tampa, FL
Hanchey, Ben R. ... Monroe, LA
Hanchey, Carl H. ... Lake Charles, LA
Hanchey, David H. ... Lake Charles, LA
Hanchey, Frederick L. ... Houston, TX
Hanchey, James C. ... Lake Charles, LA
Hanchey, Lisa D. ... Lafayette, LA
Hanchuk, Walter G. ... New York, NY
Hanchulak, Gerald J. ... Scranton, PA
Hanchuruck, Stephen P. ... Branford, CT
Hancks, Derek L. ... Moline, IL
Hancks, Gregory B. ... Kansas City, MO
Hancks, Marvin L. ... Moline, IL
Hanclich, Charles M.
Merit Systems Protection Board, Office of Appeals Counsel, GV
Hancock, A. Van W. ... Syracuse, NY
Hancock, Aaron ... Walnut Creek, CA
Hancock, Alan R. ... Coupeville, WA
Hancock, Alice J. ... Madison, AL
Hancock, Amy E. ... Washington, DC
Hancock, Anthony J. ... Phoenix, AZ
Hancock, Bobbie ... Jackson, GA
Hancock, Burnace M., Jr. ... Siler City, NC
Hancock, C. Hattie ... Longmont, CO
Hancock, Cameron M.
Salt Lake City, UT
Hancock & Canada, P.C. ... Amarillo, TX
Hancock, Catherine ... Easthampton, MA
Hancock, Charles R. ... Houston, TX
Hancock, Christopher H.
Bowling Green, KY
Hancock, Claire D. ... Tampa, FL
Hancock, Claire Shows ... Little Rock, AR
Hancock, Clarence L. ... South Pasadena, CA
Hancock, D. Michael ... Dale City, VA
Hancock, Darrell D. ... Kingwood, TX
Hancock, David C. ... San Francisco, CA
Hancock, David G. ... Seattle, WA
Hancock, David J. ... Riverside, CA
Hancock, David J. ... Elizabeth, NJ
Hancock, David L. ... Fort Pierce, FL
Hancock, David L. ... Stuart, FL
Hancock, Don R. ... Austin, TX
Hancock, Donald C. ... Boston, MA
Hancock, Douglas D. ... Portland, OR
Hancock, Dudley S. ... Duluth, GA
Hancock, E. Reginald ... Atlanta, GA
Hancock, Earl C. ... Boulder, CO
Hancock & Echols ... Forest Park, GA
Hancock, Ed W. ... Frankfort, KY
Hancock, Edward L., Jr. ... New York, NY
Hancock & Estabrook, LLP ... Albany, NY
Syracuse, NY
Hancock, Frank J. ... Forest Hills, NY
Hancock, Franklin S. ... Monroe, NC
Hancock, Gary C. ... Blacksburg, VA
Pulaski, VA
Hancock, George L., Jr. ... Dayton, OH
Hancock, Glenn G. ... New Albany, IN
Hancock, Graeme ... Phoenix, AZ
Hancock, Gregory P. ... Boston, MA
Hancock, Gregory S. ... Lebanon, VA
Hancock & Hancock ... Jackson, MS
Hancock, Harriet D. ... Columbia, SC
Hancock, Helen U. ... Biloxi, MS
Hancock, Hellar-Ann C. ... Los Angeles, CA
Hancock, Henry H. ... Memphis, TN
Hancock and Hundley ... Salisbury, NC
Hancock, I. Lionel, III ... Norfolk, VA
Hancock, J. Anne ... Fort Lauderdale, FL
Hancock, J. Vance ... New Haven, CT
Hancock, Jaci S. ... Baltimore, MD
Hancock, Jack R. ... Forest Park, GA
Hancock, James ... Prescott, AZ
Hancock, James B. ... New Albany, IN
Hancock, James H. ... Birmingham, AL
Hancock, James H. ... New York, NY
Hancock, James H., Jr. ... Birmingham, AL
Hancock, James Pryor ... Louisville, KY
Hancock, James T. ... Bath, NY
Hancock, James W., Jr. ... Rock Hill, SC
Hancock, J. D. ... Rexburg, ID
Hancock, Jeffrey H. ... Santa Cruz, CA
Hancock, Jerry L. ... Madison, WI
Hancock, Jo Weathers ... Montgomery, AL
Hancock, Joan T. ... Topeka, KS
Hancock, John B. ... Palo Alto, CA
Hancock, John B. ... Spokane, WA
Hancock, John D. ... Boston, MA
Hancock, John P., Jr. ... Detroit, MI
Hancock, John S. ... Syracuse, NY
Hancock, Jonathan C. ... Memphis, TN
Hancock, Jonathan H. ... Sebring, FL
Hancock, Joseph E. ... Dallas, TX
Hancock, Judith L. ... Shawnee, KS
Hancock, Kelly D. ... Fort Lauderdale, FL
Hancock, Kelly, P.S. ... Omak, WA
Hancock, Kristina A.
Rancho Santa Fe, CA
Hancock, L. Ben ... Kodiak, AK
Hancock, L. Bradley ... Houston, TX
Hancock, Laura L. ... Worcester, MA
Hancock, Laurence W. ... Ravenswood, WV
Hancock, Lisa Milner ... Guntersville, AL
Hancock, Mackey K. ... Lubbock, TX
Hancock, Manuella ... San Francisco, CA
Hancock, Mark E. ... Ventura, CA
Hancock, Mark J. ... San Francisco, CA
Hancock, Mary Ann ... Washington, DC
Hancock, Matthew Wade ... Fort Worth, TX
Hancock & McGill, L.L.P. ... Austin, TX
Hancock Meininger & Porter LLP
Portland, OR
Hancock, Melanie J. ... Hartford, CT
Hancock, Michael F. ... Tampa, FL
Hancock, Morris W. ... Indianapolis, IN
Hancock, Nancy A. D. ... Bridgeport, CT
Hancock, Nancy L. ... Santa Barbara, CA
Hancock, Nicole B. ... Los Angeles, CA
Washington, DC
Hancock, Pamela L. ... Jackson, MS
Hancock, Patricia Almon ... Jackson, MS
Hancock, Patricia Ann ... Houston, TX
Hancock, Patricia B. ... Tampa, FL
Hancock, Patricia J. ... Orlando, FL
Hancock, Paul D. ... Findlay, OH
Hancock, Quinlan H. ... Fairfax, VA
Hancock, R. Darrell ... Salisbury, NC
Hancock, Reuben L. ... Amarillo, TX
Hancock, Robert D., Jr. ... Atlanta, GA
Hancock, Robert I., III ... Omaha, NE
Hancock, Robert W. ... Pasadena, CA
Hancock, Ronald T. ... Houston, TX
Hancock Rothert & Bunshoft LLP
Los Angeles, CA
San Francisco, CA
Tahoe City, CA
Hancock, S. Lee ... Irvine, CA
San Diego, CA
Hancock, Scott ... Santa Fe, NM
Hancock, Scott A. ... South Pasadena, CA
Hancock & Sears ... Ravenswood, WV
Hancock, Shelly P. ... Houston, TX
Hancock and Skinner ... Lebanon, VA
Hancock, Stewart F., Jr. ... Syracuse, NY
Hancock, Taylor ... Montgomery, TX
Hancock, Ted W. ... Santa Ana, CA
Hancock, Terry C. ... Des Moines, IA
Hancock, Terry L. ... Santa Cruz, CA
Hancock, Thomas C. ... Waco, TX
Hancock, Thomas F.
Federal Trade Commission, Bureau of Competition, GV
Hancock, Thomas F., III ... Richmond, VA
Hancock, Tim ... Jackson, MS
Hancock, W. Robert, Jr.
Peachtree City, GA
Hancock, Warren E., Jr. ... Houston, TX
Hancock, Wayne ... Dallas, TX
Hancock, William A. ... Chesterland, OH
Hancock, William B., Jr. ... Fort Worth, TX
Hancock, William D. ... New York, NY
Hancock, William F., Jr. ... Fresno, CA
Hancock, William G. ... Richmond, VA
Hancock, William G. (Gerry), Jr.
Raleigh, NC
Hancock, William J. ... Indianapolis, IN
Hancock, William J. ... Des Moines, IA
Hancock, William K. ... Birmingham, AL
Hancock, William N. ... San Francisco, CA
Hancock, William W. ... Dallas, TX
Hancock, Wm. Caldwell ... Nashville, TN
Hancox, Bradford Scott ... Fayetteville, NC
Hancox, Ellen B. ... Fayetteville, NC
Hancuch, Thomas G. ... Chicago, IL
Hanculak, Thomas M. ... Cleveland, OH
Hanczor, Peter J. ... Bronxville, NY
Hanczor, Theresa Rose ... Garrison, NY
Hand, Albert C. ... Highland, IN
Hand, Albert M., Jr. ... Shreveport, LA
Hand, Albert P. ... New York, NY
Hand, Alice ... Los Angeles, CA
Hand, Amy C. ... Grand Junction, CO
Hand, Apryl E. ... New York, NY
Hand Arendall, L.L.C. ... Birmingham, AL
Foley, AL
Mobile, AL
Washington, DC
Hand, Arlene Dolores ... Columbia, SC
Hand, Ben C., Jr. ... Auburn, AL
Hand, Brian M. ... New York, NY
Hand, Bruce G. ... Bellevue, WA
Hand, Carla L. ... Wichita, KS
Hand, David N. ... Sarasota, FL
Hand, Debra Heller ... New York, NY
Hand, Dent N., Jr. ... Palm Springs, CA
Hand, Donald J. ... San Antonio, TX
Hand, Donald J., P.C. ... San Antonio, TX
Hand, Donald W. ... Allenspark, CO
Hand, Douglas W. ... Lincoln, NE
Hand, Drew, Showalter, Mercier, Kelly & McCaulie, Professional Association
Jacksonville, FL
Hand, Edward L. ... Deming, NM
Hand, Edward P. ... Pound Ridge, NY
Hand, Edward T. ... Department of Justice, Antitrust Division, GV
Hand, Elisabeth J. ... Washington, DC
Hand, Francis C. ... New York, NY
Hand, Fred B., Jr. ... Pelham, GA
Hand, G. Patrick, III ... Gretna, LA
Hand, Gary R. ... Albany, NY
Hand, Gary S. ... San Francisco, CA
Chicago, IL
Hand, George F., Jr. ... Mineola, NY
Hand, Gregg A. ... Washington, DC
Hand, Gregory A. ... Pittsburgh, PA
Hand, I. B. ... Weatherford, TX
Hand, J. Patrick ... Douglas, WY
Hand, J. Patrick, P.C. ... Douglas, WY
Hand, Jack G., Jr. ... Jacksonville, FL
Hand, Jacqueline P. ... Detroit, MI
Hand, James F. ... Laramie, WY
Hand, James H. ... Austin, TX
Hand, James L. ... Piedmont, CA
Hand, James R. ... Birmingham, MI
Hand, James R. ... Newark, OH
Hand, James S. ... Grand Forks, ND
Hand, Jeffrey J. ... Gretna, LA
Hand, Jehu ... Dana Point, CA
Hand, Jennifer A. ... New York, NY
Hand, John ... Boston, MA
Hand, John C. ... Indianapolis, IN
Hand, John H. ... Lake Mary, FL
Hand, John M. ... Waco, TX
Hand, John R. ... Dearborn, MI
Hand, John T. ... White Plains, NY
Hand, John T., Jr. ... Bethlehem, PA
Hand, Judson L. ... East Brunswick, NJ
Hand, Julianne Platz ... Hillsboro, MO
Hand, Kathryn E. ... Boston, MA
Hand, Kenneth E. ... St. Louis, MO
Hand, Kevin L. ... Newtown, PA
Hand, Laurie A. ... Alexandria, VA
Hand, Lawrence J., Jr. ... New Orleans, LA
Hand, Leslie F. ... Tallahassee, FL
Hand, Linda Marie ... Birmingham, AL
Hand, Lloyd N. ... Washington, DC
Hand, Lynwood E. ... Houlton, ME
Hand, Margaret J. ... Lafayette, IN
Hand, Margaret M. ... Oakland, CA
Hand, Marian B. ... Boston, MA
Hand, Marilyn Frison
Manchester Center, VT
Hand, Mary Ann ... Chalmette, LA
Hand, Matthew H. ... Amarillo, TX
Hand, Melissa H. ... Columbus, OH
Hand, Michael A. ... Santa Monica, CA
Hand, Michael J. ... Kenner, LA
Hand, Michael J. ... Farmington, MI
Hand Muenich Wilk & Reid ... Highland, IN
Hand, N. Shelton, Jr. ... Jackson, MS
Hand, Nathan G ... Monticello, NY
Hand, Patrick T. ... Washington, DC
Hand, Pattie L. ... New York, NY
Hand, Penny R. ... Los Angeles, CA
Hand, Philip J. ... Woodburn, OR
Hand & Quinn, S.C. ... Racine, WI
Hand, Randall E. ... Plano, TX
Hand, Raymond W. ... St. Louis, MO
Hand, Richard C. ... Babylon, NY
Hand, Robert C. ... Winter Park, FL
Hand, Robert E. ... New York, NY
Hand, Robert J., Jr. ... Casper, WY
Hand, Robert Jerry ... Casper, WY
Hand, Ronald G. ... Covington, LA
Hand, Ronald M. ... Kissimmee, FL
Hand, Ronald M., P.A. ... Kissimmee, FL
Hand, Saundra S. ... Palo Alto, CA
Hand, Sheila R. ... Albany, NY
Hand, Stephanie A. ... New York, NY
Hand, Stephen B. ... Garden City, NY
Hand, Thomas G. ... Weehawken, NJ
Hand, Thomas J. ... Yonkers, NY
Hand, William D. ... New York, NY
Hand, Wm. Brevard ... Mobile, AL
Handa, Brent ... Columbus, OH
Handa, Brent, Co., L.P.A. ... Columbus, OH
Handa, Jennifer A. ... Chicago, IL
Handal, Anthony H. ... Norwalk, CT
Handal, Jason R. ... Milwaukee, WI
Handal, Kenneth V. ... New York, NY
Handal & Morofsky ... Norwalk, CT
Handal, Phillip C. ... New York, NY
Handal, Terre W. ... Miami, FL
Handal, Vincent J., Jr. ... New York, NY
Handal, Virginia M. ... New York, NY
Handberg, Roger B., III ... Atlanta, GA
Handel, Allison R. ... Boston, MA
Handel, Arthur Mark ... Newport Beach, CA
Handel, Bernard ... Poughkeepsie, NY
Handel, Diego ... Daytona Beach, FL
Handel, Harold G. ... Trenton, NJ
Handel, Haya Miriam ... Los Angeles, CA
Handel, Joel M. ... New York, NY
Handel, Jonathan L. ... Los Angeles, CA
Handel, Lyn Niswander ... Okemos, MI
Handel, Richard C. ... Columbia, SC
Handel, Richard T. ... Los Altos, CA
Handel, Rodney R. ... Corpus Christi, TX
Handel, Stephen E. ... Houston, TX
Handel, Susan ... Coronado, CA
Handel, Ted M. ... Los Angeles, CA
Handel, William W. ... Beverly Hills, CA
Handeli, Ira D ... Forest Hills, NY
Handelman, Albert G. ... Petaluma, CA
Santa Rosa, CA
Handelman, Arthur Z. ... Chicago, IL
Handelman, David Y. ... Los Angeles, CA
Handelman, Eric David ... Albany, NY
Handelman, Frank ... New York, NY
Handelman, Gwen T. ... Lexington, VA
Handelman, Howard M. ... Wilmington, DE
Handelman & Jacobs ... Dunellen, NJ
Handelman, James M. ... Beachwood, OH
Handelman, Jarad W. ... Hershey, PA
Handelman, Jay B. ... Greenlawn, NY
Handelman, Jeffery A. ... Chicago, IL
Handelman, Joel L. ... Chicago, IL
Handelman, Joseph H. ... New York, NY
Handelman & Kilroy ... Columbus, OH
Handelman, Leigh R. ... Chicago, IL
Handelman, Marc ... New York, NY
Handelman, Martin S. ... Rochester, NY
Handelman, Robert B. ... Newark, OH
Handelman, Robert K. ... Columbus, OH
Handelman, Scott F. ... Walnut Creek, CA
Handelman, Seymour N. ... New York, NY
Handelman & Stainbrook, LLP
Santa Rosa, CA
Handelman, Stephen E. ... Southfield, MI
Handelman, Stuart B. ... Chicago, IL
Handelman, Stuart B. Law Offices of, P.C.
Chicago, IL
Handelman, Susan H. ... Redwood City, CA
Handelman, Todd S. ... Albany, GA
Handelman, Walter J. ... White Plains, NY
Handelman, Walter J., Law Offices of
New York, NY
White Plains, NY
Handelman & Witkowicz ... Rochester, NY
Handelsman, Dan G. ... Briarcliff Manor, NY
Handelsman, David A. ... Southfield, MI
Handelsman, George B. ... Pittsburgh, PA
Handelsman, George B., P.A., Law Offices of
Pittsburgh, PA
Handelsman, Harold S." Hank "... Chicago, IL
Handelsman, Lawrence M. ... New York, NY
Handelsman, Norman A. ... Chicago, IL
Handelsman, S. George ... Marietta, GA
Hander, Howard B. ... Paramus, NJ
Handevidt & Anderson ... Jackson, MN
Handevidt, Steven L. ... Jackson, MN
Handfelt, Mark J. ... Chicago, IL
Kirkland, WA
Handford, Lee A. ... Norfolk, VA
Handfuss, Robert J. ... Aberdeen, NJ
Handin, Gary I. ... Coral Springs, FL
Handin, Gary I., P.A. ... Coral Springs, FL
Handin, Phillip E. ... San Francisco, CA
Handlan, Allen L. ... Columbus, OH
Handlan, Joseph M. ... Wilmington, NC
Handleman, Aaron L. ... Washington, DC
Handleman, Claiborne P., (Ms.)
St. Louis, MO
Handleman, Paul F. ... Treasury Department, Internal Revenue Service, GV
Handler, Adam M. ... Los Angeles, CA
Handler, Alan B. ... Woodbridge, NJ
Handler, Alan D. ... Syosset, NY
Handler, Allyson B. ... Washington, DC
Handler, Arthur M. ... New York, NY
Handler, Barry James ... Mesa, AZ
Handler, Betsy ... Pacific Palisades, CA
Handler, Bradley A. ... San Jose, CA
Handler, Bruce ... New York, NY
Handler, Carole E. ... Los Angeles, CA
Handler, Carolyn B. ... New York, NY
Handler, David A. ... Chicago, IL
Handler, David P. ... Washington, DC
Handler, Edward J., III ... New York, NY
Handler, Elizabeth A. ... Treasury Department, Internal Revenue Service, GV
Handler, Eric P. ... Greensboro, NC
Handler, Geoffry R. ... New York, NY
Handler & Goodman LLP ... New York, NY

Handler, Harold R., (P.C.) ... New York, NY
Handler, Heidi D. ... Boston, MA
Handler, Henning & Rosenberg
Harrisburg, PA
Lancaster, PA
Handler, Henry B. ... Boca Raton, FL
New York, NY
Handler, James H. ... San Francisco, CA
Handler, James M. ... Cedar Rapids, IA
Handler, Janice ... New York, NY
Handler, Jeffrey ... Atlanta, GA
Handler, Jeffrey P. ... Tucson, AZ
Handler, Jody Lynne ... Newton, MA
Handler, Joel F. ... Chicago, IL
Handler, Joel F. ... Madison, WI
Handler, Jonathan I. ... Boston, MA
Handler, Lauren E. ... Brick, NJ
Morristown, NJ
New York, NY
Handler, Leslie B. ... Harrisburg, PA
Handler, Lester ... Edison, NJ
Handler, Lloyd E. ... Los Angeles, CA
Handler, Louise A. ... Boston, MA
Handler, Marcia S. ... Washington, DC
Handler, Michael ... Indiana, PA
Handler, Michael D. ... Seattle, WA
Handler, Michael H. ... Manchester, CT
Handler, Morris ... New York, NY
Handler & Nachman, P.A. ... Towson, MD
Handler, Norman B. ... Bethesda, MD
Handler, R. Arnold ... New York, NY
Handler, Richard G. ... Amityville, NY
Handler, Rick W. ... Milwaukee, WI
Handler, Roanne ... Baltimore, MD
Handler, Robert B. ... Towson, MD
Handler, Robert L. ... Los Angeles, CA
Santa Monica, CA
Handler, Robert L., Law Office of
Santa Monica, CA
Handler, Robert P. ... Chicago, IL
Handler, Sharon J. ... New York, NY
Handler, Stephen E. ... Department of Justice,
Civil Division, GV
Handler, Steven P. ... Chicago, IL
Handler, Susan L. ... Seattle, WA
Handler, T. Richard ... Dallas, TX
Handler, Wallace M. ... Southfield, MI
Handler, William L. ... West Orange, NJ
Handler, William Neil ... West Palm Beach, FL
Handler-Menahem, Susan ... Newark, NJ
Handley, Andrea L. ... Lamesa, TX
Handley, Barbara A. ... Birmingham, AL
Handley, Bobby J. ... Pataskala, OH
Handley, David A. ... Atlanta, GA
Handley, E. Lee ... Anderson, IN
Handley, Earl L. ... Wilmington, DE
Handley, F. James
Environmental Protection Agency,
Office of Enforcement and Compliance
Assurance, GV
Handley, Fletcher Dal, Jr. ... El Reno, OK
Handley, G. Kenneth, Jr. ... White Plains, NY
Handley, Gerald M. ... Kansas City, MO
Handley, Harvey L., III
Department of Justice,
Civil Rights Division, GV
Handley, Hugh T. ... Tallahassee, FL
Handley, James E. ... Olympia, WA
Handley, Larry J. ... Ankeny, IA
Handley, Laura A. ... Salt Lake City, UT
Handley, Leon H. ... Orlando, FL
Handley, Mark W., (P.C.) ... Dallas, TX
Handley, Mary E. ... St. Louis, MO
Handley, Randall ... Jefferson, IA
Handley, Robert ... Carol Stream, IL
Handley, Robert H. ... Springfield, MO
Handley, Siobhan ... New York, NY
Handley, Thomas A. ... Montgomery, AL
Handley-Dee, Garrett ... Chicago, IL
Handlin & Associates ... Houston, TX
Handlin, Jay S. ... Burbank, CA
Handlin, Joseph J. ... New York, NY
Handlin, Patrick L. ... Andover, MA
Handlin, Terry J. ... Houston, TX
Handlon, Eastman & DeWitt, P.C.
Gladwin, MI
Midland, MI
Handlon & Handlon ... Portage, IN
Handlon, Michael C. ... Portage, IN
Handlon, Richard M. ... Midland, MI
Handlon, Steven W. ... Portage, IN
Handlos, Bryan G. ... Omaha, NE
Handlos, Michael D. ... San Francisco, CA
Handlovics, Steve J. ... Seven Hills, OH
Handly, Kevin J. ... Boston, MA
Handly, Ned Kinkler ... Beeville, TX
Handmacher, James V. ... Tacoma, WA
Handmacher, Leonard E. ... Chicago, IL
Handmaker, Kenneth S. ... Louisville, KY
Handmaker, Margaret A. ... Louisville, KY
Handmaker, Stuart Allen ... Louisville, KY
Handman, Daniel H. ... Rockville, MD
Handman, Laura R. ... Washington, DC
New York, NY
Handman, Martha L. ... Gaithersburg, MD
Handman, Stanley H. ... Beverly Hills, CA
Handorf, Edmund R. ... Palestine, TX
Handorf, Karen L. ... Department of Labor,
Office of the Solicitor, GV
Handorff, Thomas F. ... Minneapolis, MN
Handrinos, Peter N. ... Boston, MA
Handros, Joseph ... New York, NY
Hands, Iliaura ... New Orleans, LA
Hands, John M. ... Cincinnati, OH
Handsaker, Jerrold L. ... Algona, IA
Swea City, IA
Handschu, Barbara E. ... Buffalo, NY
Handschuch, Elizabeth Ann ... Dallas, TX
Handschuh, G. Gregory ... Sunnyvale, CA
Handscomb, John Joseph ... Baltimore, MD
Handsman, David S. ... New York, NY
Handweiler, Martin C. ... Newport Beach, CA
Handweiler, Martin C., Inc.
Newport Beach, CA
Handwerger, Barry ... Columbia, PA
Lancaster, PA
Lititz, PA
Quarryville, PA
Handwerger, Jay R. ... Delmar, NY
Handwerger, Stephanie A.
Washington, DC
Handwerker, Barry A. ... Chicago, IL
Handwerker, David J. ... New York, NY
Handwerker, Isidore J. ... New York, NY
Handwerker, Jeffrey L. ... Washington, DC
Handwerker, Michael H. ... New York, NY
Handwerker, Neil Evan ... New York, NY
Handwork and Associates ... Perrysburg, OH
Handwork, B. Thomas, Jr. ... Perrysburg, OH
Handwork, Peter M. ... Toledo, OH
Handy, Algernon L., Jr. ... Arlington, VA
Handy, Charles E. ... Dallas, TX
Handy, Cheryl A. ... Champaign, IL
Handy, Chie M. ... Detroit, MI
Handy, Christopher M. ... Washington, DC
Chicago, IL
Handy, Edna Wells ... Hempstead, NY
Handy, Edward O., Jr. ... Barnstable, MA
Handy, Eric S. ... Detroit, MI
Handy, Eugene V., Jr. ... Sparkill, NY
Handy, Frank H., Jr. ... Boston, MA
Handy, George B. ... Ogden, UT
Handy, Gretchen M. ... Crookston, MN
Handy, Grey ... Santa Fe, NM
Handy, James E. ... Folsom, CA
Handy, James R. ... Hurst, TX
Handy, James S. ... Saratoga, CA
Handy, Janet Bush ... Baltimore, MD
Handy, Jeremiah ... San Antonio, TX
Handy, Jody DePree ... Holland, MI
Handy, John B., Jr. ... Bethesda, MD
Handy, Mary Z. ... New Bern, NC
Handy, Michael ... Fort Worth, TX
Handy & Morgan ... Hurst, TX
Handy, Nelson J. ... Los Angeles, CA
Handy, Patricia L. ... Doylestown, PA
Handy, Robert M. ... Scottsdale, AZ
Handy & Robinson, P.C. ... Fort Worth, TX
Handy, Seth H. ... Providence, RI
Handy, Sharon R. ... Louisville, KY
Handy, Susan B. ... New London, CT
Handy, Timothy D. ... Big Rapids, MI
Handy, Tom ... London, KY
Handy, Valerie R. Lape ... Albany, NY
Handy, Veronica J.
Cruz Bay, St. John, VI
Charlotte Amalie, St. Thomas, VI
Handy, William H. ... Magnolia, AR
Handzel, Henry J., Jr. ... Madison, WI
Handzel, Joan C. ... Agoura Hills, CA
Handzlik, Anthony J. ... Milwaukee, WI
Handzlik, Jan Lawrence ... Los Angeles, CA
Handzo, David A. ... Washington, DC
Handzo, Robert S. ... Towson, MD
Hane, Curtis A. ... Washington, DC
Hane, Jeffrey W. ... Hallock, MN
Hane, John Keitt, III ... Atlanta, GA
Hane, Laurie S. ... San Francisco, CA
Hane, Raymond E., III ... Los Angeles, CA
Haneberg, Bradley A. ... Richmond, VA
Hanebutt, Pamela R. ... Chicago, IL
Hanefeld, Stacy L. ... Indianapolis, IN
Hanegan, Herbert M. ... Atlanta, GA
Hanek, Wendy Noelle ... Wayne, NJ
Hanekamp, Thomas K. ... Chicago, IL
Haneke, G. Donald ... Newark, NJ
Haneline, Kenneth M. ... Cleveland, OH
Hanemann, Albert H., Jr.
New Orleans, LA
Hanemann, Bateman & Jones ... Olympia, WA
Hanemann, Carl C. ... New Orleans, LA
Hanemann, Charles ... Houma, LA
Hanemann, Jack W. ... Olympia, WA
Hanen, Alexander, Johnson & Spalding, L.L.P. ... Houston, TX
Hanen, Andrew S. ... Houston, TX
Hanenberg, Samuel ... Beaufort, SC
Hanenburg, Kathleen M.
Grand Rapids, MI
Hanenian, Keith M. ... Hollywood, FL
Haner, Alexandra ... New York, NY
Haner, Annemarie Spadaro ... Wilmington, DE
Haner, Eric J. ... Louisville, KY
Haner, John W. F. ... Roanoke, VA
Hanes, Arthur J. ... Birmingham, AL
Hanes, Arthur J., Jr. ... Birmingham, AL
Hanes, Gary L. ... Metairie, LA
New Orleans, LA
Hanes, Grayson P. ... Falls Church, VA
Hanes, Heather R. ... Greensboro, NC
Hanes, James H. ... Midland, MI
Hanes, Jeffrey P. ... Towson, MD
Hanes, Jeffrey W. ... Neenah, WI
Hanes, John G. ... Cheyenne, WY
Hanes, L. Thompson ... Roanoke, VA
Hanes, Leigh B., Jr. ... Roanoke, VA
Hanes, Patrick D. ... East Lansing, MI
Hanes, Patrick R. ... Richmond, VA
Hanes, Paul L. ... Atlanta, GA
Hanes, Paul L., P.C. ... Atlanta, GA
Hanes, Richard W. ... Colorado Springs, CO
Hanes, Ronald P. ... Tampa, FL
Hanes, Schipfer, Hurley, McClurg, Cooper & Graber, A Prtnshp. incl. Prof. Corps.
Versailles, OH
Greenville, OH
Hanes & Schutz, P.C.
Colorado Springs, CO
Denver, CO
Hanes, Thomas B. ... Birmingham, AL
Hanes, Thomas C., (Co., L.P.A.)
Greenville, OH
Hanes, William B. ... Leesburg, VA
Hanesian, Shavasp ... Niagara Falls, NY
Hanessian & Clarke ... Fullerton, CA
Hanessian, Edward J. ... Fullerton, CA
Hanessian, Grant ... New York, NY
Hanesworth, L. Michael ... Atlanta, GA
Hanewich, Mark C. ... Plainville, MA
Hanewicz, Christopher ... Madison, WI
Hanewicz, Nancy Y. T. ... Madison, WI
Hanewicz, Wayne Omar ... Madison, WI
Hanewinckel, Dean ... Englewood, FL
Hanewinckel, Dean, P.A. ... Englewood, FL
Port Charlotte, FL
Haney, Akers & Segura ... New Iberia, LA
Haney, Angela D. ... Pittsburgh, PA
Haney, Beverly J. ... Stafford, VA
Haney, Buchanan & Patterson
Los Angeles, CA
Haney, C. Kent ... Clarksdale, MS
Haney, Cecelia E. ... Teaneck, NJ
Haney, Cynthia L. ... Washington, DC
Haney, Deborah Lee ... Louisville, KY
Haney, Dennis R. ... Las Vegas, NV
Haney, Diane P. ... Olive Branch, MS
Haney, Don D. ... Las Vegas, NV
Haney, Douglas C. ... Carmel, IN
Haney, F. Michael ... Gadsden, AL
Haney, G. Lee ... Brownwood, TX
Haney, Gail Grunditz ... Trenton, NJ
Haney, Gerald J. ... Oak Lawn, IL
Haney, Gloria D. ... Anaheim, CA
Haney, Gregory Scott R. ... Tampa, FL
Haney, Hays T. ... Dallas, TX
Haney, J. Donald ... Colorado Springs, CO
Haney, J. Mark ... East Sandwich, MA
Haney, J. Phil ... New Iberia, LA
Haney, Jack ... Huntsville, TX
Haney, James E. ... Seattle, WA
Haney, James Kevin ... Parsippany, NJ
New York, NY
Haney, James S. ... Madison, WI
Haney, Janell Duncan ... Cincinnati, OH
Haney, Jeffrey N. ... Emeryville, CA
San Francisco, CA
Haney, John D. ... Doylestown, OH
Haney, John L., Jr. ... Hilliard, OH
Haney, John M. ... Miami, FL
Haney, Kevin W. ... Fort Worth, TX
Haney & Kraemer ... Huntsville, TX
Haney Law Firm ... Clarksdale, MS
Haney, Mae Elizabeth
Executive Office Of The President, GV
Haney, Marian C. ... Chicago, IL
Haney, Mark A. ... Peoria, IL
Haney, Mary Fagan ... Littleton, CO
Haney, Mary M. ... Detroit Lakes, MN
Haney, Michael H. ... Columbus, OH
Haney, Michael Jack ... Dallas, TX
Haney, Michael P. ... Philadelphia, PA
Haney, Patti M. ... Marshfield, WI
Haney, Philip S. ... Tulsa, OK
Haney, Philip S., Associates ... Tulsa, OK
Haney, Phyllis D. ... Treasury Department,
Internal Revenue Service, GV
Haney, R. T., & Associates
Sacramento, CA
Haney, Reed Park ... Lakewood, CO
Haney, Richard D. ... Cincinnati, OH
Haney, Robert E. ... Chicago, IL
Northfield, IL
Milwaukee, WI
Haney, Robert G., (Inc.) ... Miami, OK
Haney, Robert J. ... West Trenton, NJ
Haney, Robert P., Jr. ... New York, NY
Haney, Robert Reid ... Tampa, FL
Haney, Rosanne Cannon ... Alexandria, VA
Haney, R. T., & Associates ... Roseville, CA
Haney, Steven C. ... Joliet, IL
Haney, Steven H. ... Los Angeles, CA
Haney, Stuart A. ... Middleburg, VA
Haney, Susan J. ... Austin, TX
Haney, Tammy K. ... Indianapolis, IN
Haney, Thomas D. ... Topeka, KS
Haney, Thomas E. ... Phoenix, AZ
Haney, Thomas E., P.C. ... Phoenix, AZ
Haney, Thomas M. ... Chicago, IL
Haney, Thomas M. ... Wilmington, NC
Haney, Thomas W. ... Herrin, IL
Haney, Troy Westley ... Grand Rapids, MI
Haney, William D., III ... New York, NY
Haney, William E. ... Pawhuska, OK
Haney, William P., Jr. ... Malibu, CA
Haney, Woloson & Mullins, Ltd.
Las Vegas, NV
Hanf, Noel E. ... New Haven, CT
Hanf, Russell Scott ... Portland, OR
Hanf, Scott E. ... Charlotte, NC
Hanflig & Banash ... Boston, MA
Hanflig, Louis S. ... Boston, MA
Hanflik, Henry M. ... Flint, MI
Hanflik, Henry M., P.C., Law Offices of
Flint, MI
Hanfling, Brent D. ... Chicago, IL
Hanfling, Norman, & Associates
Chicago, IL
Hanfling, Phyllis A. ... Department of Energy,
Office of the General Counsel, GV
Hanfling, Scott A. ... Chicago, IL
Hanflink, Jason ... St. Petersburg, FL
Hanfman, Charles P. ... Atlanta, GA
Hanford, Andrew H. ... Graham, NC
Hanford, Anne ... Boston, MA
Hanford, Donald W. ... Seattle, WA
Hanford, Eleanor B. ... Bridgeton, NJ
Hanford, M. Shae ... Rochester, NY
Hanford, Thomas R. ... San Jose, CA
Hanford, Timothy L.
House of Representatives,
Committee on Ways & Means, GV
Hanford, Walter D. ... Miami, FL
Hanford-Beach, Sharon ... Salem, OR
Hanft, Burton H. ... New York, NY
Hanft, Fride, O'Brien, Harries, Swelbar & Burns, P.A. ... Duluth, MN
Superior, WI
Hanft, James E. ... New York, NY
Hanft, John K., Jr. ... San Francisco, CA
Hanft, Michael J. ... Carlisle, PA
Hanft, Noah J. ... Purchase, NY
Hanft, Richard A. ... Troy, NY
Hanft, William Gary ... Parsippany, NJ
Hangarter, Franc, Jr. ... Dallas, TX
Hangarter, Joseph C. ... Greenbelt, MD
Hangartner, Jonathan ... San Diego, CA
Hanger, Chris ... Austin, TX
Hanger, Elizabeth E. ... Columbus, OH
Hanger, Eric W.
Department of the Navy, GV
Hanger, JauNae M. ... Indianapolis, IN
Hanger, Levine & Steinberg, A Law Corporation ... Woodland Hills, CA
Hanger, Lisa E. ... Columbus, OH
Hanger, Robert T. ... Woodland Hills, CA
Hanger, Teresa S. ... Richmond, VA
Hanger, Willard M. ... Hilton Head Island, SC
Hangley Aronchick Segal & Pudlin, A Professional Corporation
Cherry Hill, NJ
Philadelphia, PA
Hangley, William T. ... Philadelphia, PA
Hango, David J. ... Belford, NJ
Hanhan, Isam A. ... San Francisco, CA
Hanhart, David M. ... Dover, OH
Hanhart, Gwendolyn M.
New Orleans, LA
Hanhart, Richard M. ... Dover, OH
Hani, George A. ... Washington, DC
Hani, Tiffany Heitzenrader ... Washington, DC
Hanifan, Michael J. ... Newton, NJ
Hanifen, Pershing D. ... Roche Harbor, WA
Hanifen, Robert E., Jr. ... Torrance, CA
Hanifen, William H., IV ... Collingswood, NJ
Hanifin, David S. ... Boston, MA
Hanifin, James M., Jr. ... Boston, MA
Hanifin, Jerome F. ... Binghamton, NY
Hanifin, Jerome L. ... New York, NY
Hanifin, John F. ... Poughkeepsie, NY
Hanifin, Patrick W. ... Honolulu, HI
Hanifin, Sean M. ... Washington, DC
Hanifin, Thomas J. ... Buffalo, NY
Hanifin, Timothy J. ... San Jose, CA
Hanify, Brian J. ... Cheyenne, WY
Hanify, Edward B. ... Boston, MA
Hanify, Francis V. ... Belmont, MA
Hanify, John D. ... Boston, MA
Hanify, Joseph E., Jr. ... Fall River, MA
Hanify & King, Professional Corporation
Boston, MA
Hanig, Joel D. ... Poughkeepsie, NY
Hanig, Laurie R. ... Rockville, MD
Hanig, Lynn ... Poughkeepsie, NY
Hanigan, Amy Elizabeth
Saratoga Springs, NY
Hanigan, Edward J. ... Las Vegas, NV
Hanigan, George F. ... Cathlamet, WA
Hanigan, George F., P.S. ... Cathlamet, WA
Hanigan, Timothy R. ... Woodland Hills, CA
Hanigan, William E. ... Des Moines, IA
Haniger, Julie Fabian ... Palo Alto, CA
Hanin, Daniel ... La Canada Flintridge, CA
Haning, Zerne P., III ... San Francisco, CA
Hanington, Paula Taylor ... Albany, GA
Hanis, David W. ... West Paterson, NJ
Hanis, Michael M. ... Renton, WA
Hanis & Olson ... Renton, WA
Hanisch, Douglas L. ... Wichita, KS
Hanisch, Gary E. ... Walsenburg, CO
Hanisch, Jane D. ... Wichita, KS
Hanisch, Mark C. ... Grand Rapids, MI
Tallmadge, MI
Hanisee, Michele A. ... Los Angeles, CA
Hanish, John P. ... New York, NY
Hanish, Marc S. ... San Jose, CA
Hanish, Sidney ... Louisville, KY
Hanisko-Greenberg, Lana ... San Diego, CA
Hanjani, Julie ... Loretto, MN
Hank, Sheri Kasper ... Minneapolis, MN
Hanka, William W., Jr. ... Washington, DC
Hankal, John E. ... Lakeland, FL
Hanke, G. F. Robert ... New York, NY
Hanke, Gunther O. ... Long Beach, CA
Hanke, Harold C. ... St. Louis, MO
Hanke, Maria Hilakos ... Sacramento, CA
Hanke, Paul A. ... Columbus, OH
Hankel, Robert E. ... Racine, WI
Hankel, Therese M. ... Mammoth Lakes, CA
Hanken, Garrett L. ... Los Angeles, CA
Hanken, James C. ... Seattle, WA
Hanken, W. Scott ... Springfield, IL
Hankens, Don R. ... Cherokee, IA
Hankens, R. Stephen ... Cherokee, IA
Hankerson, Cheryl Renee ... Columbus, OH
Hankerson, James A., Jr. ... Dallas, TX
Hankerson, Jeanne ... Owatonna, MN
Hankes, Jim ... St. Paul, MN
Hankes, L. Michael ... Boston, MA
Hanket, Dominic J. ... Burbank, CA
Hanket, Mark J. ... Southfield, MI
Hankey, Charles D. ... Indianapolis, IN
Hankey, David Lawrence ... Baltimore, MD

Hankin, Albert M. ... Philadelphia, PA
Hankin, Arthur W. ... Philadelphia, PA
Hankin, Barbara L. ... Westport, CT
Hankin, Bernard J. ... Whitefish Bay, WI
Hankin, David Lee ... Culver City, CA
Hankin, Donna M. Walsh ... Gainesville, FL
Hankin, Hanig, Stall, Caplicki, Redl & Curtin, LLP ... LaGrangeville, NY
Newburgh, NY
Poughkeepsie, NY
Hankin & Hankin ... Gainesville, FL
Hankin, Jerard S. ... Poughkeepsie, NY
Hankin, Joe ... Hollywood, FL
Hankin, Lawrence M. ... Sarasota, FL
Hankin, Lowen K. ... Rye Brook, NY
Hankin, Marc B. ... Los Angeles, CA
Hankin, Marc E. ... Los Angeles, CA
Hankin, Mark L. ... New York, NY
Hankin, Nancy L. ... Department of Commerce, Patent and Trademark Office, GV
Hankin, Persson & Darnell ... Sarasota, FL
Hankin, Robert L. ... Chicago, IL
Hankin, Robert M. ... Baltimore, MD
Hankin, Rockell N. ... Los Angeles, CA
Hankin, Samuel ... Gainesville, FL
Hankin, Sandra H. ... Miami, FL
Hankin, Sandson & Sandman
Atlantic City, NJ
Hankin, Stephen ... Atlantic City, NJ
Hankin, Steven J. ... Treasury Department, Internal Revenue Service, GV
Hankin, T. Jonathan ... Philadelphia, PA
Hankin, Theodore M.
Newport Beach, CA
Hankin-Birke, Susan ... New London, NH
Hankins, A. B. ... Amarillo, TX
Hankins, Angie M. ... New York, NY
Hankins, Dan E. ... Okemos, MI
Hankins, Dana H., P.A. ... Orlando, FL
Hankins, Dana Harden ... Orlando, FL
Hankins, Don B. ... Huntsville, AL
Hankins & Flanigan, P.C. ... Okemos, MI
Hankins, G. William ... Kansas City, MO
Hankins, Grover G. ... Houston, TX
Hankins, Hicks, Madden & Blackwood
North Little Rock, AR
Hankins, Irvin W., III ... Charlotte, NC
Hankins, Jack F. ... Martinsville, VA
Hankins, James D. ... Palestine, TX
Hankins, James L. ... Enid, OK
Hankins, James M. ... Boca Raton, FL
Hankins, John A. ... Washington, DC
Hankins, John H. ... Huntington, WV
Hankins, Joseph M. ... Philadelphia, PA
Hankins, Kenneth E., Jr. ... Chambersburg, PA
Hankins, Kenneth L. ... Olympia Fields, IL
Hankins, Kimyotta P.
Cape May Court House, NJ
Hankins, Leonard B. ... San Luis Obispo, CA
Hankins, Linda C. ... Orlando, FL
Hankins, Mark ... Coral Gables, FL
Hankins, Mark, P.A. ... Coral Gables, FL
Hankins, Melissa Andrews ... Atlanta, GA
Hankins, Michael A. ... Belleville, IL
Hankins, Michele R. ... Phoenix, AZ
Hankins, Mitchell D. ... Lubbock, TX
Hankins, Nadolyn J. ... Milwaukee, WI
Hankins, Pauline ... Shallotte, NC
Hankins, R. Brent ... Kansas City, MO
Hankins, Richard B. ... Atlanta, GA
Hankins, Robert B. ... Springfield, MO
Hankins, Robyn S. ... Fort Lauderdale, FL
Hankins, S. Ellis ... Raleigh, NC
Hankins, Sara M. ... Phoenix, AZ
Hankins, Scott H. ... Cincinnati, OH
Hankins, Shawn K. ... Orland Park, IL
Hankins, Stephen M. ... San Francisco, CA
Hankins, Stuart W., (P.A.)
North Little Rock, AR
Hankins, Suzanne M. ... Newport Beach, CA
Hankins & Taylor ... Huntington, WV
Hankins, Thomas E. ... Kansas City, MO
Hankins, Thomas E., P.C.
Kansas City, MO
Hankins, Timothy H. ... Newport News, VA
Hankins, Trent A. ... Boston, MA
Hankins, Vernon L. ... Porter, TX
Hankins, W. Paul ... Dallas, TX
Hankins, Wendy J. ... Charlotte, NC
Hankins, William ... Kansas City, MO
Hankins, William T., III ... Decatur, GA
Hankins, Winston ... San Antonio, TX
Hankinson, Bruce A. ... Chattanooga, TN
Hankinson, D'Andra Askew ... Irving, TX
Hankinson, James C. ... Tallahassee, FL
Hankinson, Maurice W. ... Kerrville, TX
Hankinson, Nancy J. ... Ventura, CA
Hankinson, Tommy R. ... Thomaston, GA
Hankinson, William T. ... Dallas, TX
Hankison, J. E. ... Maumee, OH
Hankla, Brian W. ... Minot, ND
Hankla, Peter B. ... Minot, ND
Hankla, Sharon Lee ... Albuquerque, NM
Hankla, W. Carl ... Department of Justice, Tax Division, GV
Hankla, Walfrid B. ... Minot, ND
Hankle, James R. ... Pittsburgh, PA
Hanko, Kenneth J. ... Mount Arlington, NJ
Hanko, Kenneth J., P.C.
Mount Arlington, NJ
Hankovszky, Zoltan ... New York, NY
Hanks, Andre' Pierre ... Jersey City, NJ
Hanks, Ann E. ... High Point, NC
Hanks, Arlene D. ... Durham, NC
Hanks, Charles E. ... Fayetteville, AR
Hanks, Cheryl Love ... Houston, TX
Hanks, Curtis W. ... Lemmon, SD
Hanks, Dale K. ... Beaumont, TX
Hanks, David H., (P.C.) ... Augusta, GA
Hanks, Eugene ... Los Angeles, CA
Hanks, George C., Jr. ... Houston, TX
Hanks, Gregg ... Phoenix, AZ
Hanks & Hanks ... Brockport, NY
Hanks, J. Larry ... Orlando, FL
Hanks, J. Larry, P.A. ... Orlando, FL
Hanks, Jack W. ... Dallas, TX
Hanks, Jackson, P.C. ... Palestine, TX
Hanks, Jackson R. ... Palestine, TX
Hanks, James B. ... Salt Lake City, UT
Hanks, James C. ... Des Moines, IA
Hanks, James J., Jr. ... Baltimore, MD
Hanks, Jerald R. ... Atlanta, GA
Hanks, John Conrad ... Washington, DC
Hanks, John H. ... West Hartford, CT
Hanks, Joseph B. ... Memphis, TN
Hanks, Judith A. ... Fremont, CA
Hanks, Kimberley A. ... Portland, OR
Hanks, Leslie M. ... San Francisco, CA
Hanks, Linda M. ... La Jolla, CA
Hanks, Mark S. ... St. Petersburg, FL
Hanks, Mary Diversi ... Jonesboro, GA
Hanks, Michael L. ... Gold River, CA
Hanks, Minnie E. ... Plattsburg, MO
Hanks, Patricia R. ... Little Rock, AR
Hanks, Paul B., Jr. ... Brockport, NY
Hanks, Robert P. ... Rochester, NY
Hanks & Rooker, A Professional Corporation
Salt Lake City, UT
Hanks, Sara P. ... Washington, DC
Hanks, Stephen G. ... Boise, ID
Hanks, Stephen W. ... Houston, TX
Hanks, William J. ... Indio, CA
Hanks, William L. ... Fairview Heights, IL
Hankus, David S. ... Troy, MI
Hanlan, Ronald H. ... Clarksburg, WV
Hanle, Steven M. ... Newport Beach, CA
Hanley, Andrew ... Wilmington, NC
Hanley & Andrews, P.A. ... South Paris, ME
Hanley, Ann Strader ... Raleigh, NC
Hanley, Anthony L. ... Kilauea, HI
Hanley, Anthony R. ... Syracuse, NY
Hanley, Bruce H. ... Minneapolis, MN
Hanley, Cecilia M. ... Boston, MA
Hanley, Charles C. ... Binghamton, NY
Hanley, Christen E. ... Royal Oak, MI
Hanley, Christine D.
West Palm Beach, FL
Hanley, Christine D., & Associates, P.A.
West Palm Beach, FL
Hanley, Cynthia A. ... Lisbon, OH
Hanley, Cynthia L. ... Mansfield, MA
Hanley, Dana C. ... South Paris, ME
Hanley, Daniel A. ... Vero Beach, FL
West Palm Beach, FL
Hanley, Daniel E., Law Offices of
San Jose, CA
Hanley, Daniel J. ... Towson, MD
Hanley, David F. ... Fort Lauderdale, FL
Hanley, David J., Jr. ... Saddle Brook, NJ
New York, NY
Hanley, Dean F. ... Boston, MA
Hanley & Dejoras, P.A. ... Minneapolis, MN
Hanley, Edward T., Jr. ... Chicago, IL
Hanley, Edward T., Jr. ... Pittsford, NY
Rochester, NY
Hanley, Edward W., Jr. ... Belmont, MA
Hanley, Elizabeth A. ... Boston, MA
Hanley, George T. ... Parsippany, NJ
Hanley, Gregory D. ... Royal Oak, MI
Hanley and Hanley ... Towson, MD
Hanley, Harold T., Jr. ... Toledo, OH
Hanley, Henry Joseph ... Boston, MA
Hanley, J. Frank, II ... Indianapolis, IN
Hanley, J. Russell ... Stratford, CT
Hanley, James A. ... Milwaukee, WI
Hanley, James J. ... Wilmington, DE
Hanley, James L. ... Anchorage, AK
Hanley, James M. ... Oakland, CA
Hanley, James Patrick ... Anchorage, AK
Hanley, Jennifer L. ... Cleveland, OH
Hanley, Joanne E. ... Jersey City, NJ
Hanley, John C. ... Department of Commerce, Patent and Trademark Office, GV
Hanley, John E., II ... Louisville, KY
Hanley, John F. ... Indianapolis, IN
Hanley, John J. ... Omaha, NE
Hanley, John J. ... Glen Cove, NY
Hanley, John M. ... Sunnyvale, CA
Hanley, John V. ... Los Angeles, CA
Hanley, John V. ... Louisville, KY
Hanley, John W., Jr. ... Seattle, WA
Hanley, Julian ... Naples, FL
Hanley, Kathleen A. ... Columbus, OH
Hanley, Kenneth T. ... Kenilworth, NJ
Hanley, Kevin M. ... Coraopolis, PA
Hanley, Kim A. ... Carmel, NY
New York, NY
Hanley, Marianne ... Nantucket, MA
Hanley, Marianne E. ... Buffalo, NY
Hanley, Mark A. ... Tampa, FL
Hanley, Mark J. ... Spokane, WA
Hanley, Mark P., Jr. ... Towson, MD
Hanley, Marshall S. ... Indianapolis, IN
Hanley, Martin S. ... Oakbrook Terrace, IL
Hanley, Mary C.
Environmental Protection Agency, Program Office Attorneys, GV
Hanley, Mary Ellen ... Seattle, WA
Hanley, Mary Smith ... Metuchen, NJ
Hanley, Michael F.
White River Junction, VT
Hanley, Michael J. ... San Francisco, CA
Hanley, Michael J. ... Vero Beach, FL
Hanley, Michael L. ... Indianapolis, IN
Hanley, Michael L. ... Rochester, NY
Hanley, Nancy M. ... Natick, MA
Hanley, Neil ... Mobile, AL
Hanley, Patrick ... Detroit, MI
Hanley, Patrick D. ... Towson, MD
Hanley, Patrick J. ... Cincinnati, OH
Hanley, Paul J. ... Denver, CO
Hanley, Paul J. ... Towson, MD
Hanley & Radmacher ... Louisville, KY
Hanley, Raphael F. J. ... Topeka, KS
Hanley, Robert J. ... Waco, TX
Hanley, Robert L. ... Milwaukee, WI
Hanley, Robert L., Jr. ... Towson, MD
Hanley, Robert R. ... Carmel, NY
Hanley, Robt. R. ... Monrovia, CA
Hanley, Ruth Ann ... Indianapolis, IN
Hanley, Scott R. ... Los Angeles, CA
Hanley, Sharon E. ... Department of Labor, Office of the Solicitor, GV
Hanley, Sheryl D. ... Bethesda, MD
Hanley & Spadoro ... Chicago, IL
Hanley, Steven C. ... Charleston, WV
Hanley, T. Bruce ... Towson, MD
Hanley, Terence ... Port Orchard, WA
Hanley, Thomas F., III ... Los Angeles, CA
Hanley, Thomas L. ... Washington, DC
Hanley, Thomas P., Jr. ... New York, NY
Hanley, Tracey Gibbons
Rockville Centre, NY
Hanley, Vincent O. ... Buffalo, NY
Hanley, Vincent P., Jr. ... New York, NY
Hanley, Walter E., III ... Wayne, NJ
Hanley, Walter E., Jr. ... New York, NY
Hanley, William B. ... Irvine, CA
Hanley, William B. ... Chicago, IL
Hanley, William J. ... Minneapolis, MN
Hanley, William J. ... Livingston, NJ
Hanley, William R. ... Tallahassee, FL
Hanley, William S. ... Springfield, IL
Blue Hill, ME
Hanley-Wu, Terri R. ... Menlo Park, CA
Hanlin, George Harold ... Columbia, SC
Hanlin, James R. ... Clayton, MO
Hanlin, Jared L. ... Kansas City, MO
Hanlin, William K. ... Indian Wells, CA
Hanlin, William M. ... Birmingham, AL
Hanlon, Adriene Lepiane
Department of Commerce, Patent and Trademark Office, GV
Hanlon, Arthur M. ... Saginaw, MI
Hanlon & Barber ... Galesburg, IL
Hanlon, Bonnie H. ... Edison, NJ
Hanlon, Brian E. ... Washington, DC
Hanlon, Brian T. ... Coconut Creek, FL
Hanlon, Carrie Ann ... Atlanta, GA
Hanlon, Carrie McCrea ... Las Vegas, NV
Hanlon, Charles J., Jr. ... Ocean City, NJ
Hanlon, Christine Giordano ... Edison, NJ
Hanlon, Christopher J. ... Freehold, NJ
Hanlon, Christopher M. ... Chicago, IL
Hanlon, Clay E. ... Grand Junction, CO
Hanlon, Colleen M. ... Burbank, CA
Hanlon, Daniel J., Jr. ... Clearwater, FL
Hanlon, Daniel M. ... San Francisco, CA
Hanlon, Daniel P. ... Pasadena, CA
Hanlon, David G. ... Tampa, FL
Hanlon, David G. ... Harrisville, WV
Hanlon, Dee A. ... Akron, OH
Hanlon, Deidre A. ... Akron, OH
Hanlon, Dolores M. ... Los Angeles, CA
Hanlon, Donna Stoehr ... Boston, MA
Hanlon, Duff, Paleudis & Estadt Co., LPA
St. Clairsville, OH
Hanlon & Dunn ... Morristown, NJ
Hanlon, Francis X. ... Boston, MA
Hanlon, Garry Stephen ... Rochester, NY
Hanlon, Gerard E. ... Morristown, NJ
Hanlon, Grace M. ... Jamestown, NY
Hanlon & Greene, A Professional Corporation ... Pasadena, CA
Hanlon, J. Robert, Jr. ... Pittsburgh, PA
Hanlon, J. Roger ... Hartford, CT
Hanlon, James A. ... Springfield, IL
Hanlon, James E. ... Buffalo, NY
Syracuse, NY
Hanlon, James E., Jr. ... Chicago, IL
Hanlon, James J. ... Anchorage, AK
Hanlon, James Patrick ... Chicago, IL
Hanlon, Jennifer ... Olympia, WA
Hanlon, Jill S. ... Las Vegas, NV
Hanlon, John C. ... Wellesley Hills, MA
Hanlon, John F. ... St. Louis, MO
Hanlon, John F., III ... Park City, UT
Hanlon, John F., Jr. ... Fort Lauderdale, FL
Hanlon, John J. ... Springfield, IL
Hanlon, John M. ... Galesburg, IL
Hanlon, John R. ... Minneapolis, MN
Hanlon, John W. ... Galesburg, IL
Hanlon, Joseph A. ... Boston, MA
Hanlon, Joseph C. ... Tampa, FL
Hanlon, Joseph E. ... Princeton, NJ
Hanlon, Karl J. ... Glenwood Springs, CO
Hanlon, Kay M. ... Chicago, IL
Hanlon & Lane, P.L.L.P. ... Minneapolis, MN
Hanlon, Laura L.H. ... Boston, MA
Hanlon & Lavigne, A Professional Corporation ... Edison, NJ
New York, NY
Hanlon Lavigne Topchik, A Professional Corporation ... Marysville, PA
Hanlon, Leah L. ... Basking Ridge, NJ
Hanlon, Lodge L. ... St. Clairsville, OH
Hanlon, M. Timothy ... Palm Beach, FL
Hanlon, Margaret Elizabeth ... Vail, CO
Hanlon, Mark Douglas ... Rochester, NH
Hanlon, Mark J. ... Jericho, NY
Hanlon, Martin J. ... San Francisco, CA
Hanlon, Mary Katherine ... Kingston, PA
Hanlon, Mary Kathleen ... Los Angeles, CA
Hanlon, Maureen A. ... New York, NY
Hanlon, Maureen J. ... Chicago, IL
Hanlon, Michael G. ... Portland, OR
Hanlon, Michael J. ... Media, PA
Philadelphia, PA
Hanlon, Michelle L.D. ... Reston, VA
Hanlon, Morton J. ... Tampa, FL
Hanlon, Neal B. ... Naugatuck, CT
Hanlon, Pamela J. ... Seattle, WA
Hanlon, Patrick M. ... Washington, DC
Hanlon, Paul M. ... Jersey City, NJ
Hanlon, Paul P. ... Montpelier, VT
Hanlon, Peter J. ... New York, NY
Hanlon, R. Timothy, (P.C.)
Washington, DC
Hanlon, Richard J. P. ... Syracuse, NY
Hanlon, Robert E. ... New York, NY
Hanlon, Robert M. ... Edison, NJ
Marysville, PA
Hanlon, Robert Michael, Jr. ... Edison, NJ
Hanlon, Roger M. ... Sandpoint, ID
Hanlon, Roger Michael ... Hillsboro, OR
Hanlon, Russell J., Law Offices of
San Jose, CA
Hanlon, Sherry Gunn ... St. Louis, MO
Hanlon, Stephen F. ... Tallahassee, FL
Hanlon, Stuart D. ... San Francisco, CA
Hanlon, Susan L. ... Jacksonville, FL
Hanlon, Suzanne M. ... Fort Washington, PA
Hanlon, Sydney ... Dorchester, MA
Hanlon, Thomas John ... Dade City, FL
Hanlon, Thomas Ward, Jr. ... New York, NY
Hanlon, William F. ... Madras, OR
Hanlon, William J. ... Boston, MA
Hanlon, William J. ... Irving, TX
Hanlon, William M., Jr. ... Ann Arbor, MI
Troy, MI
Hanlon, William R. ... Washington, DC
Hanlon, William W. ... Tampa, FL
Hanlon-Leh, Natalie ... Denver, CO
Hanly, Kevin ... Edgewater, NJ
Hanly, Patrick K. ... Sacramento, CA
Hanly, Paul J., Jr. ... New York, NY
Hanly, Timothy J. ... Santa Ana, CA
Hanmer, Don R. ... Dallas, TX
Hanmer, Susan B. ... Boston, MA
Hann, Carole ... San Francisco, CA
Hann, Charles R. ... Newtown Square, PA
Hann, Daniel P. ... Warsaw, IN
Hann, Donald H. ... Holland, MI
Hann, G. Marshall ... Valencia, CA
Hann, James F. ... Palo Alto, CA
Hann, Jennifer ... Dayton, OH
Hann, Persinger, Knoll, Bedevia & Hamilton, P.C. ... Holland, MI
Hann, Steven A. ... Lansdale, PA
Hann, Steven H. ... Kansas City, MO
Hann, Thelma E. ... Santa Rosa, CA
Hanna, Adam Keith ... Chicago, IL
Hanna, Albert C. ... Chicago, IL
Hanna, Albert R. ... El Dorado, AR
Hanna, Anita J. ... Lancaster, PA
Lititz, PA
Hanna, Anne O. ... San Jose, CA
Hanna, Bob ... Abilene, TX
Hanna, Bret M. ... Salt Lake City, UT
Hanna, Brett T. ... Raleigh, NC
Hanna, Brophy, MacLean, McAleer & Jensen
Bakersfield, CA
Fresno, CA
Oakland, CA
Redding, CA
Sacramento, CA
Salinas, CA
San Bernardino, CA
San Francisco, CA
Santa Rosa, CA
Stockton, CA
Hanna, Bruce A. ... Daytona Beach, FL
Hanna, Carol A. ... Clymer, PA
Indiana, PA
Hanna, Carol L. ... Bethel Park, PA
Hanna, Catherine L. ... Austin, TX
Hanna, Charles W. ... Salt Lake City, UT
Hanna, Christopher H. ... Dallas, TX
Hanna, Claire E. Sanderson
Albuquerque, NM
Hanna, Cody A. ... Buffalo, MO
Hanna, Cynthia ... Cedar Rapids, IA
Hanna, Dane M. ... Bellefontaine, OH
Hanna, Daryl K. ... Dallas, TX
Hanna, David H., Sr. ... Spartanburg, SC
Hanna, David J. ... Akron, OH
Hanna, Denise E. ... Los Angeles, CA
Hanna, Dolores K. ... Chicago, IL
Hanna, Donald B., (P.C.) ... Decatur, GA
Hanna, Douglas B. ... Manasquan, NJ
Hanna, Drew A. ... Bowling Green, OH
Hanna, E. Mark ... Fresno, CA
Hanna, Edward A., Jr. ... Miami, FL
Hanna, Edwin R., Jr. ... Placida, FL
Hanna, Faith ... Federal Way, WA
Hanna, Florence M. ... Oakland, CA
Hanna, Forest W. ... Kansas City, MO
Hanna, Forest W. (Trey), III
Jefferson City, MO
Hanna, Francis M. ... Kansas City, MO
Hanna, Fred ... Marietta, GA
Hanna, Fred T. ... Portland, OR
Hanna, Frederick B. ... Logansport, IN
Hanna, Gary D. ... West Palm Beach, FL
Hanna, Gary Edward ... New York, NY
Hanna, George B. ... Atlanta, GA
Hanna, George K. ... Washington, PA
Hanna, George L. ... Lafayette, IN
Hanna, George R. ... Keene, NH
Hanna, George V., III ... Charlotte, NC
Hanna, Gerarda Anne ... Pittsburgh, PA
Hanna & Gerde ... Lafayette, IN

Hanna, Gigi ... **Livingston, NJ**
Hanna, Glen Gary ... Cumberland, MD
Hanna, Gordon R. ... Portland, OR
Salem, OR
Hanna & Hanna ... **Bowling Green, OH**
Hanna & Hanna ... Clymer, PA
Indiana, PA
Hanna, Hanna Z. ... New York, NY
Hanna, Harold C. ... Woodruff, SC
Hanna, Harold M. ... **Bowling Green, OH**
Hanna, Harry A. ... Cleveland, OH
Hanna, Harry M. ... **Portland, OR**
Hanna, H. B. (Jerry) ... East Wenatchee, WA
Hanna, James R. ... **Washington, DC**
Hanna, Jan McDonald ... Houston, TX
Hanna, Jeanie E. ... Tampa, FL
Hanna, Jefferson, III ... Middletown, CT
Hanna, Jeffery ... Warrensburg, MO
Hanna, Jerry F. ... **Stroudsburg, PA**
Hanna, Jett ... Austin, TX
Hanna, John A. ... Clymer, PA
Indiana, PA
Hanna, John F. ... **Towson, MD**
Hanna, John H. ... Napoleon, OH
Hanna, John, Jr. ... **Albany, NY**
Hanna, John P. ... **Chicago, IL**
Hanna, John Paul ... **Palo Alto, CA**
Hanna, John R. ... **Santa Ana, CA**
Hanna, John T. ... **Cleveland, OH**
Hanna, John V. ... Stuart, FL
Hanna, Jon ... Abilene, TX
Hanna, Joseph E. ... Akron, OH
Hanna, Joseph J., Jr. ... **Portland, OR**
Hanna, Joseph M. ... **Santa Ana, CA**
Hanna, Julian Z. ... Pawleys Island, SC
Hanna, Juliet M. ... **Denver, CO**
Hanna, Katherine M. ... **Manchester, NH**
Hanna, Kerns & Strader, A Professional Corporation ... **Portland, OR**
Hanna, L. Lynn ... Marietta, GA
Hanna, Lanette M ... Prescott, AZ
Hanna, Lauren J. ... San Diego, CA
Hanna, Lawrence D., P.A. ... **Hobbs, NM**
Hanna, Lawrence Edward ... Los Alamitos, CA
Hanna, Lawrence J. ... Van Nuys, CA
Hanna, Linda C. ... **Tampa, FL**
Hanna, Linda C., Professional Association
Tampa, FL
Hanna, Lucy W. ... **Los Angeles, CA**
Hanna, M. Nicole ... **Virginia Beach, VA**
Hanna, Marion O. ... Columbia, SC
Hanna, Mark E. ... Kenton, OH
Hanna, Mark Emerson ... **Metairie, LA**
Hanna, Mark J. ... Austin, TX
Hanna, Mark J., P.C. ... Austin, TX
Hanna, Martin J. ... Pompano Beach, FL
Hanna, Martin Shad ... **Bowling Green, OH**
Hanna, Mary Ann ... **Philadelphia, PA**
Hanna, Mary K. ... Philadelphia, PA
Hanna, Matthew ... Media, PA
Hanna, Michael D. ... Green Bay, WI
Hanna, Michael J. ... **Beverly Hills, CA**
Hanna, Michael K. ... **Lock Haven, PA**
Hanna, Michael R. ... Boston, MA
Hanna, Michael W. ... Raytown, MO
Hanna, Michelle M. ... **Miami, FL**
Hanna, Mitchell J. ... Modesto, CA
Hanna, Mona Z. ... **Irvine, CA**
Hanna and Morton ... **Los Angeles, CA**
Hanna, Myron A. ... **Belleville, IL**
St. Louis, MO
Hanna, Nicola T. ... **San Diego, CA**
Hanna, Patrick J. ... Lafayette, LA
Hanna, Peter N. ... Fort Lauderdale, FL
Hanna, Philip E. ... **Springfield, IL**
Hanna & Plaut, L.L.P. ... **Austin, TX**
Hanna, Ralph Emerson, III ... **Augusta, GA**
Aiken, SC
Hanna, Ramsey ... **Palo Alto, CA**
Hanna, Randall W. ... **Tallahassee, FL**
Hanna, Ray L. ... Washington, DC
Hanna, Raymond A. ... Prescott, AZ
Hanna, Raymond A., P.C. ... Prescott, AZ
Hanna, Reed & Neville ... Kenton, OH
Hanna & Reyes Law Firm, L.L.P.
Abilene, TX
Hanna, Richard D. ... Dallas, TX
Hanna, Richard K. ... Mount Clemens, MI
Hanna, Richard L. ... **Amarillo, TX**
Hanna, Richard W. ... **Danbury, CT**
Hanna, Robert ... Shreveport, LA
Hanna, Robert C. ... Albuquerque, NM
Hanna, Robert G., Jr. ... **Harrisburg, PA**
Hanna, Robert J. ... **San Diego, CA**
Hanna, Robert J. ... **Cleveland, OH**
Hanna, Robert K. ... Sacramento, CA
Hanna, Robert S. ... **Mammoth Lakes, CA**
Monterey, CA
Hanna, Ronald ... **Peoria, IL**
Hanna, Ross D. ... Albany, NY
Hanna, Sean T. ... Webster, NY
Hanna, Shane L. ... **Salt Lake City, UT**
Hanna, Small, Sabatini, Becker & Murray, P.A.
Logansport, IN
Hanna, Steven E. ... **Oklahoma City, OK**
Hanna, Steven W. ... Moline, IL
Hanna, Tania W. ... **Washington, DC**
Hanna, Terry R. ... **Oklahoma City, OK**
Hanna, Thomas H., Jr. ... New York, NY
Hanna, Thomas, Jr. ... Brooklyn, NY
Hanna, Thomas L. ... **Beaumont, TX**
Hanna, Thomas L. ... **Nederland, TX**
Hanna, Thomas M. ... **St. Louis, MO**
Hanna, Thomas M. ... **Dayton, OH**
Hanna, Thomas P. ... **Philadelphia, PA**
Hanna, Thomas R. ... Carson City, NV
Hanna, Thomas R. ... **Keene, NH**
Hanna, Timothy H. ... Akron, OH

Hanna, Valerie M. ... **Cleveland, OH**
Hanna & Van Atta ... **Palo Alto, CA**
San Francisco, CA
Hanna, W. Clark ... Blue Bell, PA
Hanna, W. Michael ... **Cleveland, OH**
Hanna, Willard D., Jr. ... **Myrtle Beach, SC**
Surfside Beach, SC
Hanna, William C. ... Burton, SC
Hanna, William E. ... **Kansas City, MO**
Hanna, William J. ... **Charleston, WV**
Hanna, Young, Upright & Catina, LLP
Jim Thorpe, PA
Milford, PA
Stroudsburg, PA
Hanna, Zaher N. ... Orange, CA
Hannabach, Paul F.
Rancho Santa Margarita, CA
Hannafan, Blake T. ... **Chicago, IL**
Hannafan, Brent A. ... **Chicago, IL**
Hannafan, Kay Pierce ... North Chicago, IL
Hannafan, Michael T. ... **Chicago, IL**
Hannafan, Michael T., & Associates, Ltd.
Chicago, IL
Hannafey, Mark P. ... **New York, NY**
Hannafin, Edward J. ... **Danbury, CT**
Hannaford, John L. ... St. Paul, MN
Hannaford, Jule M., IV ... **Minneapolis, MN**
Hannaford, Leon E., Jr. ... **Senatobia, MS**
Hannah, Carrie Grace ... **Montauk, NY**
Hannah, Colvin & Pipes, L.L.P.
Baton Rouge, LA
Hannah, David A. ... **Houston, TX**
Hannah, David W., Jr. ... **Houston, TX**
Hannah, Estes & Ingram, P.A.
Orlando, FL
Hannah, H. W. ... Texico, IL
Hannah, J. Richard ... Phoenix, AZ
Hannah, James B. ... Hopkins, MN
Hannah, Jan Jordan ... Baton Rouge, LA
Hannah, Jeffrey A. ... Atlanta, GA
Hannah, Jennifer Marie ... **Kansas City, MO**
Hannah, Jerry W. ... **Vail, CO**
Hannah, Joanna B. ... Hartwell, GA
Hannah, John R. ... **Phoenix, AZ**
Hannah, Julie ... Rockport, TX
Hannah, Larry W. ... Woodland Hills, CA
Hannah, Lawrence B. ... **Bellevue, WA**
Hannah, Lewis P., III ... Philadelphia, PA
Hannah, Mark ... **Santa Cruz, CA**
Hannah, Mark A. ... Olathe, KS
Hannah, Mitchell Blinn ... Irvine, CA
Hannah, Nancy Edmunds ... **Raleigh, NC**
Hannah, Nathan B. ... Tucson, AZ
Hannah, O. B. ... Frankfort, KY
Hannah, Patricia ... Searcy, AR
Hannah, Paul F.
Board of Governors Of The Federal Reserve System,
Office of the General Counsel, GV
Hannah, Paul R. ... St. Paul, MN
Hannah, R. Craig ... Searcy, AR
Hannah, Randal P. ... **Upland, CA**
Hannah, Rita G. ... Tucson, AZ
Hannah, Robert A. ... **Orlando, FL**
Hannah, Roderick V.
Fort Lauderdale, FL
Hannah, T. Jeffrey ... Indianapolis, IN
Hannah, Thomas N. ... Hickory, NC
Hannah, Walter L. ... **Greensboro, NC**
Hannah, Wayne R., Jr. ... **Chicago, IL**
Hannah, William R. ... **Chattanooga, TN**
Hannaher, Michael J. ... **Barnesville, MN**
Moorhead, MN
Hannahs, Fred C. ... Albuquerque, NM
Hannahs, Kenneth R., Jr. ... **Atlanta, GA**
Hannah-White, C. M. ... Cortland, NY
Hannam, Jack R. ... Portland, OR
Hannam, Kenneth R. ... Corpus Christi, TX
Hannan, B. Miles ... **Valdosta, GA**
Hannan, C. R. ... **Council Bluffs, IA**
Hannan, Daniel A. ... **Mobile, AL**
Hannan, David C. ... **Mobile, AL**
Hannan, David F. ... **Baltimore, MD**
Hannan, Denise R. ... **San Francisco, CA**
Hannan, Edward A. ... **Milwaukee, WI**
Hannan, Edwin Y. ... Jackson, MS
Hannan, Gregg M. ... Wallingford, CT
Hannan, Haripriya M. ... **Hartford, CT**
Hannan, J. Thomas ... **San Francisco, CA**
Hannan, James M. ... Chicago, IL
Hannan, Joan E.
Equal Employment Opportunity Commission,
Office of Federal Operations, GV
Hannan Law Firm, The, LLC
Wallingford, CT
Hannan, Michael D. ... Metairie, LA
Hannan, Michael J., III ... **Atlanta, GA**
Hannan, Myles ... **Silver Spring, MD**
Hannan, Nancy H. ... Hyde Park, MA
Hannan, Patrick J. ... Huntington Station, NY
Hannan, Raymond T., Jr. ... **Simsbury, CT**
Hannan, Richard C., Jr. ... Wallingford, CT
Hannan, Robert A. ... Camas, WA
Hannan, Siesennop & Sullivan
Milwaukee, WI
Hannan, Sonya Kazazian ... Baltimore, MD
Hannan, Stephen J. ... **Beaver Dam, WI**
Hannan, Susan F. ... **Los Angeles, CA**
Hannan, Terrance D. ... **Vancouver, WA**
Hannan, Timothy J. ... **Santa Rosa, CA**
Hannan, Wendy C. ... Washington, DC
Hannan, William E., III
San Francisco, CA
Hannan, William J. ... North Branford, CT
Hannan-Anton, Laurie ... **Fort Myers, FL**
Hannapel, Timothy B.
Office Of Special Counsel, GV

Hannasch, Richard A. ... St. Louis, MO
Hannawalt, James F. ... San Francisco, CA
Hannawalt, Vivian ... San Francisco, CA
Hannawalt, Willis D. ... San Francisco, CA
Hannaway, E.L., P.C. ... **Philadelphia, PA**
Hannaway, John J., The Law Offices of
New York, NY
Hannaway, Lawrence ... **Philadelphia, PA**
Hannay, Felicity ... Denver, CO
Hannay, William M. ... **Chicago, IL**
Hannebaum, Nancy Hall ... Mount Vernon, IL
Hannegan, Garret B. ... **New Albany, IN**
Hannegan, John C. ... St. Louis, MO
Hanneken, D. V. ... Escondido, CA
Hanneman, Brian G. ... **Los Angeles, CA**
Hanneman, Donna Pfouts ... Toledo, OH
Hanneman, Heather R. ... Denver, CO
Hanneman, James A. ... Columbus, OH
Hanneman, James F. ... **Minneapolis, MN**
Hanneman, Jennifer J. ... Milwaukee, WI
Hanneman, Paul W. ... Sweetwater, TX
Hanneman, Richard A. ... **Denver, CO**
Hannemann, Frederick C.
San Francisco, CA
Hannemann, Mark ... **New York, NY**
Hannen, George, & Company, A Prof. Corp.
Newport Beach, CA
Hannen, George M. ... Newport Beach, CA
Hannen, J. Mark ... Castle Rock, CO
Hannen, Justin D. ... Denver, CO
Hannen, Robert J. ... **Wheeling, WV**
Hannen and Tomassetti ... **Weirton, WV**
Wheeling, WV
Hanner, Clelland J. ... Rockville, IN
Hanner, Gary G. ... Rockville, IN
Hanner, Hanner and Hanner ... Rockville, IN
Hanner, James O. ... Rockville, IN
Hanner, Jerome S. ... **Chicago, IL**
Hanner, Karl Tiger ... Austin, TX
Hanner, Melanie Davies ... Brentwood, TN
Hanner, Patricia L. ... **Chicago, IL**
Hanner, Robert P., II ... **Charlotte, NC**
Hanner, Willard K., Jr. ... Dover, OH
Hanners, Michael J. ... **Dallas, TX**
Hannes, Steven P. ... **Washington, DC**
Hannesson, John D. ... Irvine, CA
Hannett, George Foster
Albuquerque, NM
Hannett, Gordon E., Jr. ... Christiansburg, VA
Hannett, Hannett & Cornish, A Professional Association ... **Albuquerque, NM**
Hanney, Laura M. ... Redwood City, CA
Hanni, Clint M. ... **Salt Lake City, UT**
Hanni, Don L. ... Youngstown, OH
Hanni, Glenn C. ... **Salt Lake City, UT**
Hanni, Kenneth J. ... Salt Lake City, UT
Hanni, Teresa Gerlock ... Marlton, NJ
Hannibal, Julie I. ... Pittsburgh, PA
Hannibal, Richard A.
Securities and Exchange Commission,
Office of Compliance Inspections and Examinations, GV
Hannifan, James M. ... **Springfield, MA**
Hannifan, Rebecca D. ... **Lexington, KY**
Hannifin, Bret ... Los Angeles, CA
Hannifin, Dorothy M. ... Butte, MT
Hannig & Ellison, P.A. ... Moorhead, MN
Hannig, Frank L. ... Woodside, CA
Hannig, Jack F. ... Los Angeles, CA
Hannig, Jean P. ... Moorhead, MN
Hannig, Jeffrey R. ... Moorhead, MN
Hannig Law Firm LLP
Redwood City, CA
San Francisco, CA
San Jose, CA
Walnut Creek, CA
Hannig, Ted J. ... **Redwood City, CA**
Hannigan, Barbara B.
Securities and Exchange Commission,
Office of the General Counsel, GV
Hannigan, Charles J. ... Lockport, NY
Hannigan, David ... Florida, NY
Hannigan, Donald E. ... Springfield, MA
Hannigan, Henry Jay ... Peru, IL
Hannigan, J. Gregory, (P.A.)
Hagerstown, MD
Hannigan, John F. ... Allen, TX
Hannigan, John P. ... **White Plains, NY**
Hannigan, Keith C. ... **Chicago, IL**
Hannigan, Michael J. ... **New York, NY**
Hannigan, Michael P. ... **Chicago, IL**
Hannigan, Michelle Therese ... Lakewood, CO
Hannigan, Patricia C. ... Wilmington, DE
Hannigan, Penelope J. ... Portland, OR
Hannigan, Raymond N. ... **Princeton, NJ**
New York, NY
Hannigan, Richard D. ... Mundelein, IL
Hannigan, Richard D., Ltd. ... Mundelein, IL
Hannigan, Robert F. ... Cape Elizabeth, ME
Hannigan, Susan Marzec ... Chicago, IL
Hannigan, Terence S. ... **Albany, NY**
Hannigan, Thomas H., Jr. ... **Boston, MA**
Hannigan, Thomas M. ... Mundelein, IL
Hannigan, Thomas M. P. ... Mundelein, IL
Hannigan, Vince ... Houston, TX
Hanninen, John H. ... Cleveland, OH
Hanning, Elizabeth A. ... **Grand Rapids, MI**
Hanning, Richard A. ... Hammond, IN
Hanning, Rolf A. ... Aurora, CO
Hannink, James T. ... **San Diego, CA**
Hanno, Diana J. ... Chicago, IL
Hannon, Andrew J. ... Hot Springs Village, AR
Hannon, Ann L. ... Kalamazoo, MI
Hannon, Barry T. ... Braintree, MA
Hannon, Bonnie Spaccarelli ... Barrington, IL
Hannon, Bonnie Spaccarelli, P.C.
Barrington, IL
Hannon, Brian J. ... San Jose, CA

Hannon, Brian W. ... **Washington, DC**
Hannon, Cynthia A. ... Berkeley, CA
Hannon, David F. ... **Boston, MA**
Hannon, Debra S. ... Baltimore, MD
Hannon, Dennis P. ... Wheaton, IL
Hannon, Donald H. ... **Troy, MI**
Hannon, Edward E. ... Lincoln, NE
Hannon, Edward J. ... **Chicago, IL**
Hannon, Edward R. ... **Indianapolis, IN**
Hannon, Edwin F., Jr. ... Braintree, MA
Hannon, Eugene M. ... Walnut Creek, CA
Hannon, Gerard V. ... **New York, NY**
Hannon, Gregory John ... **Philadelphia, PA**
Hannon, J. Kemp ... **Uniondale, NY**
Hannon, J. Michael ... **Washington, DC**
Rockville, MD
Hannon, James E., Jr. ... **Pittsburgh, PA**
Hannon, James P. ... Coeur d'Alene, ID
Hannon, James R. ... **Oak Brook, IL**
Hannon, James T. ... **Denver, CO**
Hannon, Jeffrey ... **Rockville, MD**
Hannon, John F. ... Castro Valley, CA
Hannon, John T.
Environmental Protection Agency,
Office of the General Counsel, GV
Hannon, Jos. J. ... Jamaica, NY
Hannon, Joseph P. ... South Dartmouth, MA
Hannon & Joyce ... **Woodbury, NJ**
Philadelphia, PA
Hannon, J.P. ... New York, NY
Hannon, Kathleen M. ... Hartford, CT
Hannon, Kathleen M. ... Scarsdale, NY
Hannon, Kevin S. ... **Denver, CO**
Pine, CO
Hannon Law Firm, The, LLC
Denver, CO
Pine, CO
Hannon, Lerner, Cowhig, Scully and Bell
Lee, MA
Hannon & Lisoni ... Castro Valley, CA
Hannon, Marc S. ... **Miami, FL**
Hannon, Mary E. ... Department of Commerce,
Patent and Trademark Office, GV
Hannon, Mary E. ... Minneapolis, MN
Hannon, Maureen E. ... **New York, NY**
Hannon, Maureen O. ... Chicago, IL
Hannon, Michael B. ... Los Angeles, CA
Hannon, Michael J. ... Honolulu, HI
Hannon, Michael John ... Pittsburgh, PA
Hannon, Neill Edward ... San Francisco, CA
Hannon, Park and Lennon ... Los Angeles, CA
Hannon, R. Daniel ... Batavia, OH
Hannon, Richard C., Jr. ... Columbus, OH
Hannon, Robert C. ... **Nashville, TN**
Hannon, Robert E. ... Macon, GA
Hannon, Robert J. ... Farmington, CT
Hannon, Robt. E. ... Alamo, CA
Hannon, Samuel J. ... Miami, FL
Hannon & Scalzo ... **Chicago, IL**
Oak Brook, IL
Hannon, Sean P. ... Pittsburgh, PA
Hannon, T. Patrick ... Campbell, CA
Hannon, Tara ... **New City, NY**
Hannon, Terrance W. ... Coeur d'Alene, ID
Hannon, Theodore B. ... Arcata, CA
Hannon, Thomas ... Edina, MN
Hannon & Trepel ... Silver Spring, MD
Hannon, William P., Jr. ... Atlanta, TX
Hannoy, Ann Bartlett ... Indianapolis, IN
Hannoy, Douglas J. ... **Indianapolis, IN**
Hannuksela, Jane S.
Department of Commerce,
National Oceanic and Atmospheric Administration, GV
Hannula, Daniel D. ... Superior, WI
Hannula, Daniel L. ... **Tacoma, WA**
Hannum, Charles J. ... Dunkirk, NY
Hannum, Christopher E. ... **Charlotte, NC**
Hannum, David C. ... North Chicago, IL
Hannum, John B., Jr. ... **Media, PA**
Philadelphia, PA
West Chester, PA
Hannum, John E. ... Stony Point, NY
Hannum, Karl Eric ... **Southfield, MI**
Hannum, Margo R. ... Southfield, MI
Hannum, Matthew E. ... **Santa Rosa, CA**
Hannum, Richard P. S. ... Wilmington, DE
Hannum, Wendy J. ... **San Francisco, CA**
Hannums, Peter J.
Department of Transportation,
Federal Aviation Administration, GV
Hannusch, Laura E. ... **San Francisco, CA**
Hanny, James M. ... **Washington, DC**
Hanofee, Joseph A. ... Northampton, MA
Hanoian, Louis R. ... El Cajon, CA
Hanoka, Lenore ... **Boston, MA**
Hanold, Terrance ... Minneapolis, MN
Hanold, Wayne L. ... **Peoria, IL**
Hanoman, Robert H ... Jamaica, NY
Hanophy, Robert J. ... Jamaica, NY
Hanophy, Robert J., Jr. ... Kew Gardens, NY
Hanor, Charles W., (P.C.)
San Antonio, TX
Hanover, G. Norden ... Harbor City, CA
Hanover, George M. ... Palm Desert, CA
Hanover, Hollis H. ... Kansas City, MO
Hanover, Jay Alan ... **Memphis, TN**
Hanover, John D. ... **Los Angeles, CA**
Las Vegas, NV
Hanover, Lawrence J. ... New York, NY
Hanover, Mark L. ... **Chicago, IL**
Hanover, Norman L. ... **San Bernardino, CA**
Hanover, Pamela Iddings ... **Cleveland, OH**
Hanover, Pamela M. ... Westlake Village, CA
Hanover, Pamela M., P.C.
Westlake Village, CA
Hanover, Richard ... New York, NY

Hanover & Schnitzer ....**Riverside, CA**
San Bernardino, CA
Hanover, Stanley Ira ....Chesterland, OH
Hanover, Walsh, Jalenak & Blair, PLLC
Memphis, TN
Hanower, L. David ....**Houston, TX**
Hanower, Patricia L. ....Department of Justice, Civil Division, GV
Hanpeter, Edward C. ....Detroit, MI
Hanrahan, Ann Marie ....**Minneapolis, MN**
Hanrahan, Audrey S. ....Chicago, IL
Hanrahan, Catherine A. ....**Washington, DC**
Baltimore, MD
Rockville, MD
Hanrahan, Curtis G. ....Jefferson City, MO
Hanrahan, David G. ....**Boston, MA**
Hanrahan, Dennis J. ....Leesburg, VA
Hanrahan, Donald J. ....Springfield, IL
Hanrahan, Edward V. ....Oak Park, IL
Hanrahan, Eileen M.
Department of Education, Office for Civil Rights, GV
Hanrahan, G. Michael ....Pelham, NY
Hanrahan, Grabowski & Hayes, P.C.
Bristol, CT
Hanrahan, Gretchen C. ....Harrisburg, PA
Hanrahan & Hanrahan ....Pelham, NY
Hanrahan, Hugh H. ....Albany, NY
Hanrahan, James D. ....**Framingham, MA**
Hanrahan, James J. ....**Arcadia, CA**
Hanrahan, James R., Jr. ....Chicago, IL
Woodstock, IL
Hanrahan, Jeffrey R. ......**The Woodlands, TX**
Hanrahan, Jeremiah J. ....**New York, NY**
Hanrahan, Joan C. ....San Francisco, CA
Hanrahan, John A. ....Boston, MA
Hanrahan, John C. ....**Frederick, MD**
Hanrahan, John H., III ....**Ithaca, NY**
Hanrahan, John James ....Salem, MA
Hanrahan, John K. ....**Unionville, CT**
Hanrahan, Katharine ....San Francisco, CA
Hanrahan, Louis F. ....**Bristol, CT**
Hanrahan, Marc P. ....**New York, NY**
Hanrahan, Mark E. ....Cedar Rapids, IA
Hanrahan, Mark V. ....**Atlanta, GA**
Hanrahan, Michael ....**Wilmington, DE**
Hanrahan, Michael G. ....Pelham, NY
Hanrahan, Michael J. ....**Milwaukee, WI**
Hanrahan, Michael V. ....**Jericho, NY**
Hanrahan, Patrick L. ....**Los Angeles, CA**
Hanrahan, Patrick R. ....**Mentor, OH**
Hanrahan, Patrick T. ....**Kansas City, MO**
Hanrahan, Paul M. ....**Syracuse, NY**
Hanrahan, Philip L. ....Lexington, KY
Hanrahan, Phillip J. ....**Milwaukee, WI**
Hanrahan, Renee K. ....**Cedar Rapids, IA**
Hanrahan, Sheila M. ....Milwaukee, WI
Hanrahan, Thomas B. ....Hackensack, NJ
Hanrahan, Thomas J. ....Whittier, CA
Woodland Hills, CA
Hanrahan, Thomas J. ....Glendive, MT
Hanrahan, Thomas J. ....Glen Rock, NJ
Hanrahan, Thomas P. ....Los Angeles, CA
Hanrahan, Thomas P. ....Chicago, IL
Hanrahan, Thomas S. ....**Milwaukee, WI**
Hanrahan, Vincent M. ....Des Moines, IA
Hanrahan, William F. ....**Washington, DC**
Hanrath, James P. ....**Barrington, IL**
Hanratty, James P. ....**Canton, OH**
Hanratty, Joseph M. ....Ocala, FL
Hanratty, Kevin Joseph ....Artesia, NM
Hanratty, Kevin P. ....**Houston, TX**
Hanratty, Richard R., Jr. ....**Berlin, CT**
Hanratty, Susan DeRitis ....Philadelphia, PA
Hans, Allen A. ....Ramsey, NJ
Hans, Jason M. ....**Kansas City, MO**
Hans, Lynne ....Springfield, IL
Hans, Peter E. ....Oregon, WI
Hans, Richard F., Jr. ....**New York, NY**
Hans, Rupinder ....**New York, NY**
Hans, William E. ....Kansas City, MO
Hansa, Kathleen J. ....**Portland, OR**
Hansan, Heidi A. ....**Baltimore, MD**
Hansard, George H. ....Lamesa, TX
Hansard, Wade M. ....**Fresno, CA**
Hansbarger, William H. ......**Falls Church, VA**
Hansberger, Sandra A ....Portland, OR
Hansberry, Barbara J. ....Boston, MA
Hansberry, Charles E. ....**Billings, MT**
Hansberry, Denise ....Baltimore, MD
Hansberry, John C. ....**Pittsburgh, PA**
Hansberry, Scott B. ....**Grand Rapids, MI**
Hansberry, W. J. ....Royal Oak, MI
Hansbro, Kevin R. ....Houston, TX
Hansbrough, Nancy L.
Securities and Exchange Commission, Office of Compliance Inspections and Examinations, GV
Hansbrough, W. Ann ....**Overland Park, KS**
Kansas City, MO
Hansburg, Daniel ....**New York, NY**
Hansburg, Stephen B. ....New York, NY
Hansbury, John W. ....New York, NY
Hansbury, Stephan C. ....**Summit, NJ**
Hansch, Dennis L. ....**Janesville, WI**
Hansche, Heather L. ....**Chicago, IL**
Hanschen, David J. ....Dallas, TX
Hanschen, Peter W. ....**San Francisco, CA**
Hanschu, James L. ....**Sacramento, CA**
Hanscom, Douglas R. ....**Arlington, VA**
Hanscom, Richard J. ....San Diego, CA
Hanscom, Stephen W. ....**Rockland, ME**
Hanscom, Ward T. ....Sanford, ME
Hanscom, Warren K. ....Westfield, NJ
Hanscom, Weston W. ....Chicago, IL
Hanscom-Bolton, Chris ....**Garden City, NY**
Hanscum, Arthur T. ....Laramie, WY
Hanscum, Jerry D. ....**Southfield, MI**

Hanse, Brian W. ....Wayne, NJ
Hanse & Hanse ....Wayne, NJ
Hanse, William C. ....Wayne, NJ
Hanseen, Tawni ....**Salt Lake City, UT**
Hansel, Anthony A. ....Washington, DC
Hansel, Austin ....Munfordville, KY
Hansel, Benjamin H., II ....Roanoke, VA
Hansel, Gregory P. ....**Portland, ME**
Hansel, Helen S. ....St. Petersburg, FL
Hansel, Sarah E. ....**Tulsa, OK**
Hansel, Stephen E. ....Santa Rosa, CA
Hansell, Churita H. ....**New Orleans, LA**
Hansell, David A. ....New York, NY
Hansell, Dean ....**Los Angeles, CA**
Hansell, Edgar F. ....**Des Moines, IA**
Hansell, Herbert J. ....**Washington, DC**
Hansell, Lawton Henry ....**Seattle, WA**
Hansell & Post ....**Atlanta, GA**
Hansell, R. Stephen ....Indianapolis, IN
Hansell, Sanford I. ....Southfield, MI
Hansell, Walter W. ....**San Francisco, CA**
Hanselman, David L. ....Bluffton, IN
Hanselman, David L., Jr. ......**Indianapolis, IN**
Hanselman, Suzanne K. ....**Cleveland, OH**
Hanselman, Theodore F. ....**Boston, MA**
Hanselmann, Fredrick C.
Philadelphia, PA
Hanselmann, Thomas G. ....Greeley, CO
Hansemann, René M. L. ....**Detroit, MI**
Hansen, Adrian Nathan ....**Phoenix, AZ**
Hansen, Albert ....Kingston, NH
Hansen, Amy J. ....**Irvine, CA**
Hansen, Amy K. ....**Kansas City, MO**
Hansen, Amy L. ....**Roanoke, VA**
Hansen, Amy Oatfield ....**Portland, OR**
Hansen, Andrea ....**Lansing, MI**
Hansen, Andrew S. ....**Minneapolis, MN**
Hansen, Angela J. ....**San Diego, CA**
Hansen, Ann M. ....Oakland, CA
Hansen, Ardene L. ....Bloomington, UT
Hansen, Arne ....San Diego, CA
Hansen, Barbara J. ....Bloomfield Hills, MI
Hansen, Barry C. ....**Washington, DC**
Hansen, Bax & Schiffer, P.C. ....Houston, TX
Hansen, Bennett J. ....**Seattle, WA**
Hansen, Bernard M. ....**San Diego, CA**
Hansen, Bernt" Al " ....McMinnville, OR
Hansen, Beth E. ....**Waterloo, IA**
Hansen, Blake ....**Odessa, TX**
Hansen, Borah R. ....Inverness, CA
Hansen, Boyd, Culhane & Watson, LLP
Sacramento, CA
Hansen, Bradley Brydon ....Lake Zurich, IL
Hansen, Brenda E. ....**Los Angeles, CA**
Hansen, Brian F. ....**Atlanta, GA**
Hansen, Brian L. ....**Norcross, GA**
Hansen, Brian L., (P.S.) ....**Bellingham, WA**
Hansen, Brian N. ....Denver, CO
Hansen, Bruce E. ....**Rochester, NY**
Hansen, C. LeRoy ....Albuquerque, NM
Hansen, C. Russel, Jr. ....Lincoln, MA
Hansen, Camille ....**Washington, DC**
Hansen, Camille L. ....**Garden City, NY**
Hansen, Carl Douglas ....Tulsa, OK
Hansen, Carlton W., Jr. ....Metuchen, NJ
Hansen, Carol M. ....Oklahoma City, OK
Hansen, Cary L. ....Waynesville, MO
Hansen, Charles ....**St. Louis, MO**
Hansen, Charles A. ....**Oakland, CA**
Hansen, Chris H. ....**Boise, ID**
Hansen, Christian B. ....**Washington, DC**
Hansen, Christian W.
Fort Lauderdale, FL
Hansen, Christina Flores ....Des Moines, IA
Hansen, Christine K. ....**Minneapolis, MN**
Hansen, Christine M. ....Wilmington, DE
Hansen, Christopher A. ....**Washington, DC**
Towson, MD
Hansen, Christopher F. ....Albany, NY
Hansen, Christopher Ilum ....Lincoln, NE
Hansen, Christopher P. ....**Dallas, TX**
Hansen, Clark A. ....Victorville, CA
Hansen, Clark A., III ....San Bernardino, CA
Hansen & Connolly, P.C. ....Denver, CO
Hansen, Conrad A. ....**Minneapolis, MN**
Hansen, Courtenay C. ....**Princeton, NJ**
Hansen, Craig A. ....St. Louis, MO
Hansen, Craig D. ....**Phoenix, AZ**
Hansen, Curtis A. ....Columbus, OH
Hansen, Cynthia L. ....**Washington, DC**
Hansen, Cynthia L. ....Plymouth, MI
Hansen, D. Thomas ....Bloomington, IL
Hansen, Dale Allen ....Fairmont, MN
Hansen, Dale R. ....**Sturgis, SD**
Hansen, Dale T. ....**Salt Lake City, UT**
Hansen, Dale W. ....Union, NJ
Hansen, Daniel J. ....Albertson, NY
Hansen, Daniel P. ....Atlanta, GA
Hansen, Daniel R. ....**Palo Alto, CA**
Hansen, Daniel R. ....**Charlotte, NC**
Hansen, Darwin C. ....Salt Lake City, UT
Hansen, Daryl D. ....Orange, CA
Hansen, David Altan ....Dearborn, MI
Hansen, David B. ....**Salt Lake City, UT**
Hansen, David B. ....**Seattle, WA**
Hansen, David G. ....Spokane, WA
Hansen, David I. ....**Des Moines, IA**
Hansen, David Oman ....Littleton, CO
Hansen, David P. ....**Seattle, WA**
Hansen, David R. ....Denver, CO
Hansen, David R. ....Cedar Rapids, IA
Hansen, David W. ....**Palo Alto, CA**
Hansen, Dean N. ....Edgar, NE
Hansen, Deborah A. ....Tucson, AZ
Hansen, Dennis B., (P.C.)
Los Angeles, CA
Hansen, Dennis Ronald ....Little Rock, AR
Hansen, Dianne M. ....Kansas City, MO

Hansen, Donald ....Medford, OR
Hansen, Donald B. ....**Newcastle, WY**
Hansen, Donald G. ....Montello, WI
Hansen, Donald R. ....**Fargo, ND**
Hansen, Donald W. ....Quincy, MA
Hansen, Donald W. ....Fairfax, VA
Hansen, Dordell, Bradt, Odlaug & Bradt, P.L.L.P ....**St. Paul, MN**
Hansen, Douglas L. ....Kansas City, MO
Hansen, Douglas R. ....Alta, IA
Hansen, Douglas W. ....**Storm Lake, IA**
Hansen, Douglas W. ....**Scotch Plains, NJ**
Hansen, E. Lewis ....Atlanta, GA
Hansen, Edward C. ....Baldwin, NY
Hansen, Edward D. ....Wheaton, IL
Hansen, Edward D. ....Everett, WA
Hansen, Edward J. ....**New York, NY**
Hansen, Edwin R., Jr.
Department of Education, Office of the General Counsel, GV
Hansen, Eggers & Blakely ....Beloit, WI
Hansen, Eileen A. ....Omaha, NE
Hansen, Eileen M. ....**San Francisco, CA**
Hansen, Elizabeth ....San Francisco, CA
Hansen, Elizabeth A. ....Burlington, NC
Hansen, Ellen Lynne ....Boston, MA
Hansen, Engles & Locher, P.C.
Council Bluffs, IA
Omaha, NE
Papillion, NE
Hansen, Eric L. ....**Prairie Village, KS**
Hansen, Eric M.
Securities and Exchange Commission, Division of Enforcement, GV
Hansen, Eric P. ....**St. Paul, MN**
Hansen, Eric R. ....Federal Way, WA
Hansen, Eric W. ....**Green Bay, WI**
Hansen, Ernest R. ....Temple City, CA
Hansen, Erwin H. ....Manning, IA
Hansen, Eugenia S. ....Dallas, TX
Hansen, Evan M. ....**Portland, ME**
Hansen, F. Mark ....Las Vegas, NV
Salt Lake City, UT
Hansen, F. Mark, P.C. ....Las Vegas, NV
Salt Lake City, UT
Hansen, Frederick J. ....Wichita, KS
Hansen, G. Olaf ....**Seattle, WA**
Hansen, G. Olaf, Inc., P.S., Law Offices of
Seattle, WA
Hansen, Gary ....**Minneapolis, MN**
Hansen, Gene H. ....Park Ridge, IL
Hansen, Geoffrey K. ....**Redding, CA**
Hansen, George A. ....Corvallis, OR
Hansen, George I. ....Tigard, OR
Hansen, Gerald B. ....San Jose, CA
Hansen, Gerald H. ....**Denver, CO**
Hansen, Gerald J. ....New Orleans, LA
Hansen, Glen C. ....**Sacramento, CA**
Hansen, Glenn S. ....Akron, OH
Hansen, Gordon O.
Department Of The Interior, Bureau of Land Management, GV
Hansen, Gregg A. ....Greensboro, NC
Hansen, Gregory C. ....**Salem, OR**
Hansen, Gregory M. ....**Honolulu, HI**
Hansen, Gregory S. ....**Melbourne, FL**
Hansen, H. James ....Alexandria, VA
Hansen, H. Reese ....Provo, UT
Hansen, H. Ted ....Yuba City, CA
Hansen, H. Victor, (P.C.) ....**Atlanta, GA**
Hansen, Hans C. ....Wichita, KS
Hansen, Hans R. ....Midland, TX
Hansen, Harold J. ....Treasury Department, Office of the Comptroller of the Currency, GV
Hansen, Hartley T., (Inc.)
Sacramento, CA
Hansen, Heather ....**Plymouth Meeting, PA**
Hansen, Henrik H. ....Lockport, NY
Hansen, Henry ....**Spring House, PA**
Hansen, Herb ....Seattle, WA
Hansen, Herbert E. ....Houston, TX
Hansen & Herrick, P.C. ....Grand Rapids, MI
Hansen, Holly L. ....**Rochester, NY**
Hansen, Howard W. ....Yakima, WA
Hansen, Hubbard & Swanson
Deadwood, SD
Sturgis, SD
Hansen, Hubert J. ....Shreveport, LA
Hansen, Hugh C. ....New York, NY
Hansen, Ingrid K ....Austin, TX
Hansen, J. Gordon ....**Salt Lake City, UT**
Hansen, J. Mark ....**Memphis, TN**
Hansen, J. Mark, (P.C.) ....**Dallas, TX**
Hansen, J. Michael ....**Salt Lake City, UT**
Hansen, Jacobson, Teller & Hoberman
Beverly Hills, CA
Hansen, James A. ....Longmont, CO
Hansen, James A. ....**St. Louis, MO**
Hansen, James C. ....**New York, NY**
Hansen, James D. ....Boise, ID
Hansen, James J. ....**Houston, TX**
Hansen, James K. ....Albuquerque, NM
Hansen, James L. ....Salinas, CA
Hansen, James L. ....Des Moines, IA
Hansen, James M. ....**Tustin, CA**
Hansen, James M. ....Oskaloosa, IA
Hansen, James Tucker ....Pleasant Grove, UT
Hansen, Jane D. ....Omaha, NE
Hansen, Janet Pignataro ....**Houston, TX**
Hansen, Jason Dax ....**Seattle, WA**
Hansen, Jay D. ....**Palo Alto, CA**
Hansen, Jean M. ....Bloomfield Hills, MI
Hansen, Jean Marie, P.C.
Bloomfield Hills, MI
Hansen, Jeffrey E. ....**Arlington, TX**
Hansen, Jeffrey L. ....**Scottsbluff, NE**
Hansen, Jeffrey R. B. ....Hastings, NE

Hansen, Jeffrey W. ....**Portland, OR**
Hansen, Jens ....Chicago, IL
Hansen, Jill Thompson ....**Des Moines, IA**
Hansen, Jim Michael ....Golden, CO
Hansen, Joan ....Los Angeles, CA
Hansen, Joan E. ....Seattle, WA
Hansen, Joan E., Inc., P.S. ....Seattle, WA
Hansen, Joel F., & Associates
Las Vegas, NV
Hansen, John Bill ....Fargo, ND
Hansen, John C. ....**Chicago, IL**
Hansen, John Clyde ....Salt Lake City, UT
Hansen, John D. ....**Idaho Falls, ID**
Hansen, John D. ....Rutland, VT
Hansen, John Edward ....**Salt Lake City, UT**
Hansen, John F. ....Soulsbyville, CA
Hansen, John G. ....**Kansas City, MO**
Hansen, John Joel ....St. Paul, MN
Hansen, John Joseph ....Twin Falls, ID
Hansen, John M. ....Solana Beach, CA
Hansen, John P. ....**Boston, MA**
Hansen, John R., Jr. ....Boise, ID
Hansen, John T. ....**San Francisco, CA**
Hansen, John T. ....**San Francisco, CA**
Hansen, John W., Jr. ....San Diego, CA
Hansen, Johnna Jane ....**Torrance, CA**
Hansen, Jon R. ....Wichita, KS
Hansen, Joseph D. ....**New York, NY**
Hansen, Joy E. ....**Denver, CO**
Hansen, Joyce M. ....**New York, NY**
Hansen, Judith K ....Stockton, CA
Hansen, Judith L. ....Grosse Pointe Farms, MI
Hansen, Julian R. ....Barrington, IL
Hansen, Julie M. ....Redwood City, CA
Hansen, Karen A. Ciegler
Minneapolis, MN
Hansen, Karen I. ....**New York, NY**
Hansen, Karen M. ....**Washington, DC**
Hansen, Karl E. ....Department of Defense, Defense Legal Services Agency, GV
Hansen, Karl M., Jr. ....Metairie, LA
Hansen, Karla J. ....Colorado Springs, CO
Hansen, Katherine A. ....Denver, CO
Hansen, Katherine L. ....Lansing, MI
Hansen, Katherine M. ....San Francisco, CA
Hansen, Kathleen ....Coronado, CA
Hansen, Kathleen (Cuffaro) ....Coronado, CA
Hansen, Keith E. ....Washington, DC
Hansen, Kenneth A. ....Grand Forks, ND
Hansen, Kenneth J. ....**Madison, WI**
Hansen, Kenneth W. ....**Washington, DC**
Hansen, Kent A. ....**Corona, CA**
Hansen, Kent W. ....Salt Lake City, UT
Hansen, Keri S. ....St. Paul, MN
Hansen and Kerr ....San Francisco, CA
Hansen, Kevin A. ....Grand Rapids, MI
Hansen, Kevin B. ....**Seattle, WA**
Hansen, Kevin C. ....**Pittsburgh, PA**
Hansen, Kevin D. ....**Fresno, CA**
Hansen, Kimberly A. ....Silverado, CA
Hansen, Kindra L. ....**Boise, ID**
Hansen, Kristie A. ....Denver, CO
Hansen, Kristopher M. ....**New York, NY**
Hansen, Kurt F. ....**Portland, OR**
Hansen, Kurt N. ....Gladwin, MI
Hansen, Lamonte L. ....Williams, AZ
Hansen, Laura J. ....**Walker, MN**
Hansen, Laurence A. ....**Chicago, IL**
Hansen Law Firm ....**Ephrata, WA**
Hansen Law Office, Ltd. ....Winona, MN
Hansen, Lawrence M. ....**Indianapolis, IN**
Hansen, Lee A. ....**Portland, OR**
Hansen, Leith B. ....**Fresno, CA**
Hansen, Leland G. ....**Chicago, IL**
Hansen, Leo H. ....Beloit, WI
Hansen, Leroy R. ....Willowbrook, IL
Hansen, Leslie C. ....**Denver, CO**
Hansen, Leslie M. ....**Houston, TX**
Hansen, Lewis D. ....**Denver, CO**
Hansen, Linda E. B. ....**Milwaukee, WI**
Hansen, Linda M. ....Los Angeles, CA
Hansen, Lisa Bradford ....McIntosh, AL
Hansen, Lisa J. ....**Kansas City, MO**
Hansen, Lisa Kralik ....**Los Angeles, CA**
Hansen, Lona J. ....Des Moines, IA
Hansen, Loren P., (P.C.)
Newport Beach, CA
Hansen, Lorentz W. ....White Plains, NY
Hansen, Lori D. ....Bellevue, WA
Hansen, Lorraine L. ....Portsmouth, NH
Hansen, Lorraine L., P.A. ....Portsmouth, NH
Hansen, Lotte Rose ....**St. Cloud, MN**
Hansen, Louis Jerry ....Sacramento, CA
Hansen, Louise E.
Department of Defense, GV
Hansen, Lynelle M. ....Price, UT
Hansen, Lynn M. ....**Las Vegas, NV**
Hansen, Marc ....Eugene, OR
Hansen, Marc P. ....Rockville, MD
Hansen, Marcelle F. ....Groton, CT
Hansen, Marcia ....Sherman Oaks, CA
Hansen, Mark B. ....Oak Harbor, WA
Hansen, Mark B., P.S. ....Oak Harbor, WA
Hansen, Mark C. ....**Washington, DC**
Hansen, Mark C. ....Omaha, NE
Hansen, Mark D. ....**Chicago, IL**
Hansen, Mark D. ....**Peoria, IL**
Hansen, Mark F. ....Wadena, MN
Hansen, Mark T. ....**Los Angeles, CA**
Hansen, Mark W. ....**San Diego, CA**
Hansen, Marlene Nagel ....Vancouver, WA
Hansen, Martin E. ....**Bend, OR**
Hansen, Mary D. ....Daytona Beach, FL
Hansen, Mary K. ....Lincoln, NE
Hansen, Max A. ....**Dillon, MT**
Hansen, Max A., & Associates, P.C.
Dillon, MT

Hansen, McClintock & Riley
Des Moines, IA
Hansen, M. D. ......Santa Cruz, CA
Hansen, Meagher, Shambeau & Maroney, S.C. ......Iola, WI
Waupaca, WI
Wausau, WI
Hansen, Melvin C., Jr. ......Omaha, NE
Hansen, Merrill G. ......Salt Lake City, UT
Hansen, Michael D. ......Houston, TX
Hansen, Michael E. ......Des Moines, IA
Hansen, Michael J. ......Lincoln, NE
Hansen, Michael J. ......Salem, OR
Hansen, Michael W. ......Joliet, IL
Hansen, Michelle ......Joliet, IL
Hansen, Mildred Havard ......Little Rock, AR
Hansen, Miles J. ......Selma, CA
Hansen, Milton C. ......Monona, WI
Hansen, Molly C. ......Venice, CA
Hansen, Monica A. ......Wooster, OH
Hansen, Myles R. ......Washington, DC
Hansen, Nadine R. ......Cupertino, CA
Hansen, Nels A. ......Ephrata, WA
Hansen, Nicholas Paul ......Denver, CO
Hansen, Niels Eric ......Troy, MI
Hansen, Norman P. ......Yuba City, CA
Hansen, Olivia Widmeyer ......Mequon, WI
Hansen, Orval ......Washington, DC
Hansen, Pamela Van Geffen
New Orleans, LA
Hansen, Patricia Isela ......Austin, TX
Hansen, Paul D. ......Everett, WA
Hansen and Peck ......Newcastle, WY
Hansen & Pederson, P.A. ......Wadena, MN
Hansen, Peter O. ......Denver, CO
Hansen, Peter O. ......Portland, OR
Hansen, Peter T. ......Washington, DC
Hansen, Peter W. ......Burlington, IA
Hansen, Phillip P. ......Winona, MN
Hansen, Rachel E. ......Cincinnati, OH
Hansen, Ralph H. ......Johnson City, NY
Hansen, Ralph L. ......Orange, CA
Hansen, Raphael K. R. ......Houston, TX
Hansen, Raymond L. ......Los Angeles, CA
Hansen, Raymond L. ......Wheaton, IL
Hansen, Rebecca S. ......Milwaukee, WI
Hansen, Reid J. ......Rosemount, MN
Hansen, Richard ......Boise, ID
Hansen, Richard ......Cedar Falls, IA
Hansen, Richard A. ......Seattle, WA
Hansen, Richard C. ......Duluth, MN
Hansen, Richard G. ......Moss Landing, CA
Hansen, Richard K. ......Torrance, CA
Hansen, Richard K. ......Portland, OR
Hansen, Richard N. ......Laredo, TX
Hansen, Richard R. ......Minneapolis, MN
Hansen, Richard W. ......Seattle, WA
Hansen, Robert B. ......San Leandro, CA
Hansen, Robert C. ......Eugene, OR
Hansen, Robert D. ......San Jose, CA
Hansen, Robert J. ......Monrovia, CA
Hansen, Robert L. ......Palm Springs, CA
Hansen, Robert L. ......New London, IA
Hansen, Robert M. ......Ottawa, IL
Hansen, Robert W. ......Nashotah, WI
Hansen, Robt. B. ......Salt Lake City, UT
Hansen, Robt. W. ......Milwaukee, WI
Hansen, Robyn ......St. Paul, MN
Hansen, Robyn Hylton
Newport News, VA
Hansen, Rochelle Feder ......New York, NY
Hansen, Roger A. ......Dallas, TX
Hansen, Roger A., P.C. ......Dallas, TX
Hansen, Ronald L. ......Forest City, IA
Hansen, Ronald W. ......Merced, CA
Hansen, Ross D. ......San Diego, CA
Hansen, Royal I. ......Salt Lake City, UT
Hansen, Rupert P., Jr. ......San Francisco, CA
Hansen, Russell A. ......Gillette, WY
Hansen, Russell C. ......Los Angeles, CA
Hansen, Russell J. ......Des Moines, IA
Hansen, Russell W. ......Ellensburg, WA
Hansen, Sandra ......Vernal, UT
Hansen, Scott E. ......Memphis, TN
Hansen, Scott Hillam ......Blackfoot, ID
Hansen, Scott R. ......Los Angeles, CA
Hansen, Scott W. ......Salt Lake City, UT
Hansen, Scott W. ......Milwaukee, WI
Hansen, Shane B. ......Grand Rapids, MI
Hansen, Shannon M. ......Los Angeles, CA
Hansen, Sharon L. ......Cortez, CO
Hansen, Sherma ......Tremonton, UT
Hansen, Stanley B. ......Oxnard, CA
Hansen, Stefanie Alexis ......Westbrook, CT
Hansen, Stephen A. ......Fresno, CA
Hansen, Stephen C. ......Clarkson, NE
Columbus, NE
Hansen, Stephen C. ......Pittsburgh, PA
Hansen, Stephen C. ......Bellevue, WA
Hansen, Stephen F. ......Waupaca, WI
Hansen, Stephen M. ......Tacoma, WA
Hansen, Stephen W. ......Seattle, WA
Hansen, Sterling L. ......Cody, WY
Hansen, Steven A. ......Monroe, LA
Hansen, Steven K. ......San Diego, CA
Hansen, Steven R. ......Los Angeles, CA
Hansen, Steven W. ......Lakewood, CA
Hansen, Steven W. ......Boston, MA
Hansen, Stierberger, Downard, Melenbrink & Schroeder ......Union, MO
Hansen, Sue C. ......San Francisco, CA
Hansen, Susan D. ......Richmond, VA
Hansen, Susan K. ......Plymouth, MN
Hansen, Susan M. ......Minneapolis, MN
Hansen, Susan Taylor ......Portsmouth, VA
Hansen, Theodore E. ......Scottsdale, AZ
Hansen, Therese M. ......Seattle, WA
Hansen, Thomas A. ......Dayton, OH
Hansen, Thomas G. ......Lincoln City, OR
Hansen, Thomas J. ......Chicago, IL
Hansen, Thomas M. ......Beverly Hills, CA
Hansen, Thomas M. ......Bellevue, WA
Hansen, Thomas P. ......San Jose, CA
Hansen, Thomas R. ......Oak Park, IL
Hansen, Timothy J. ......Rochester, MN
Hansen, Timothy L. ......Boise, ID
Hansen, Tina Lynn ......Los Angeles, CA
Hansen, Tracy Lynn ......Nashville, TN
Hansen, Victor C. ......San Diego, CA
Hansen, W. Brett ......Elko, NV
Hansen, W. Eugene ......Salt Lake City, UT
Hansen, W. Karl ......St. Paul, MN
Hansen, Walter D. ......Washington, DC
Manassas, VA
Hansen, Walter L. ......Ishpeming, MI
Hansen, Wayne W. ......Seattle, WA
Hansen, William A. ......Forked River, NJ
Hansen, William C. ......Silver Spring, MD
Hansen, William J. ......Denver, CO
Hansen, William J. ......Salt Lake City, UT
Hansen, William M. ......Chicago, IL
Hansen, William R. ......New York, NY
Hansen, William R. ......Cleveland, OH
Hansen-Corona, Inger Christine
St. Paul, MN
Hansen-Stamp, Catherine ......Golden, CO
Hanser, Frederick O., (P.C.)
St. Louis, MO
Hanser, Harold F. ......Billings, MT
Hanser, Leonard ......West Palm Beach, FL
Hanser, Russell P. ......Boston, MA
Hanses, Joseph J. ......St. Louis, MO
Hansfield, Paul ......Chicago, IL
Hansford, Bridget H. ......Jackson, MS
Hansford, Jeffrey L. ......New Albany, IN
Hansford, Nathaniel ......Tuscaloosa, AL
Hansgen, Shirley C. ......London, OH
Hanshaw, A. Alan ......Tucson, AZ
Hanshaw, Lance L. ......Lonoke, AR
Hanshaw, Mark E.
Department of Commerce, GV
Hanshaw, Randal ......Reno, NV
Hanshaw, William ......Warren, OH
Hanshe, Joseph Arthur ......East Meadow, NY
Hanshumaker, Rita Lane ......Raleigh, NC
Hansing, James T. ......Minneapolis, MN
Hansing, Mark D. ......Des Moines, IA
Omaha, NE
Hanski, Adam S. ......Los Angeles, CA
Hansler, John F. ......Tacoma, WA
Hansler, Joy H. ......Los Angeles, CA
Hansler, Mark W. ......Philadelphia, PA
Hanslick, Jeffrey D. ......Kansas City, MO
Hanslik, Christopher P. ......Houston, TX
Hanslovsky, Julius I. ......Okemos, MI
Hansmann, Arthur J. ......Racine, WI
Hansmann, Dale L. ......Parkersburg, IA
Hansmeier, Gordon H. ......St. Cloud, MN
Hansom, Thomas E. ......Memphis, TN
Hanson, Alan ......Pratt, KS
Hanson, Alan G. ......Salem, OR
Hanson, Alan J. ......New York, NY
Hanson, Alan R. ......Birmingham, AL
Hanson, Alan V. ......Park Ridge, IL
Hanson, Alfred R. ......Sun City, AZ
Hanson, Allan E. ......Providence, RI
Hanson, Allegra A. ......Albuquerque, NM
Hanson, Allegra A., P.C. ......Albuquerque, NM
Hanson, Amanda G. ......Cherry Hill, NJ
Hanson, Amy N.L. ......Seattle, WA
Hanson, Andre T. ......Minneapolis, MN
Hanson, Andrew P. ......Newport Beach, CA
Hanson, Andrina A. ......Woodland Hills, CA
Hanson, Arnold P. ......Berlin, NH
Hanson, Arnold P., Jr. ......Dallas, TX
Hanson & Associates ......Minneapolis, MN
Hanson, Avarita L. ......Atlanta, GA
Hanson Baker Ludlow Drumheller P.S.
Bellevue, WA
Seattle, WA
Hanson, Barbara R. ......Fergus Falls, MN
Hanson, Belinda ......San Mateo, CA
Hanson, Benjamin G. ......Tacoma, WA
Hanson, Bill ......Bozeman, MT
Hanson, Bjork & Russell, L.L.P.
Des Moines, IA
Hanson, Bradley W. ......St. Cloud, MN
Hanson, Brian E. ......Sitka, AK
Hanson, Brian R. ......Boulder, CO
Hanson, Bridgett, Marcus, Vlahos & Rudy, LLP ......San Francisco, CA
Hanson, Britt W. ......St. Johns, AZ
Hanson, Bruce E. ......Minneapolis, MN
Hanson, Bruce G. ......Seattle, WA
Hanson, Bruce P. ......Yakima, WA
Hanson, Calvin T. ......Denver, CO
Hanson, Candice S. ......Beverly Hills, CA
Hanson, Caren Lock ......Dallas, TX
Hanson, Carl D. ......Claremont, NH
Hanson, Carl P. ......Homestead, FL
Hanson & Cartwright, LLC ......Chicago, IL
Hanson, Catherine I. ......San Francisco, CA
Hanson, Chad A. ......Minneapolis, MN
Hanson, Charles E. ......La Crosse, WI
Hanson, Charles O. ......Tulsa, OK
Hanson, Cheryl J. ......Denver, CO
Hanson, Cindy D. ......Atlanta, GA
Hanson, Clinton E., Jr. ......Eagle River, AK
Hanson, Colette M. ......Washington, DC
Hanson, Craig A. ......Olympia, WA
Hanson, Craig W. ......Olympia, WA
Hanson, Curran, Parks & Whitman
Providence, RI
Hanson, Daniel J. ......Des Moines, IA
Hanson, Daniel P. ......Overland Park, KS
Hanson, David A. ......Topeka, KS
Hanson, David C. ......Pittsburgh, PA
Hanson, David F. ......Columbus, OH
Hanson, David G. ......Cambridge, MA
Hanson, David G. ......Milwaukee, WI
Hanson, David J. ......Merrillville, IN
Hanson, David J. ......Fayette, IA
Hanson, David J. ......Madison, WI
Hanson, David K. ......Brighton, MI
Hanson, David P. ......Pittsburgh, PA
Hanson, David S. ......Lincolnshire, IL
Hanson, Dayten P. ......Milwaukee, WI
Hanson, Denise L. ......Columbus, OH
Hanson, Dennis A. ......Denver, CO
Hanson, Diane E. ......Dayton, OH
Hanson, Diane M. ......El Dorado Hills, CA
Hanson, Diann M. ......Irving, TX
Hanson & Dionne ......Olympia, WA
Hanson, Donald E. ......San Mateo, CA
Hanson, Donald E., Jr. ......Burbank, CA
Hanson, Donald S. ......Chicago, IL
Hanson, Donald W. ......Washington, DC
Hanson, Douglas A. ......Evanston, IL
Hanson, E. Daniel, II ......Chicago, IL
Hanson, Earl J. ......Billings, MT
Hanson, Earl L. ......Los Angeles, CA
Hanson, Edward J., Jr. ......York, PA
Hanson, Edward M., Jr. ......Rockville, MD
Hanson, Edward W., Jr. ......Virginia Beach, VA
Hanson & Egers ......Los Angeles, CA
Hanson, Einar E. ......Red Wing, MN
Hanson, Elaine B. ......Jacksonville, FL
Hanson, Ellen Chamberlain ......Morris, IL
Hanson, Ellen D.
Department of Transportation, Surface Transportation Board, GV
Hanson, Elroy E. ......Mahnomen, MN
Hanson, Eric A. ......Santa Barbara, CA
Hanson, Eric C. ......Los Angeles, CA
Hanson, Eric C. ......Council Bluffs, IA
Hanson, Eric C. ......Seattle, WA
Hanson, Eric J. ......Atlanta, GA
Hanson, Eric P. ......Joliet, IL
Hanson, Ernest O. ......La Crosse, WI
Hanson, Eugene N. ......Ada, OH
Hanson, Eugene P. ......Chester, NJ
Hanson, Eugene P., P.C., Law Offices of
Chester, NJ
Hanson, F. Michael ......Walnut Creek, CA
Hanson Family Law Group, LLP
San Mateo, CA
Hanson, Francine M. ......San Francisco, CA
Hanson, Frank O., Jr. ......Birmingham, AL
Hanson, Franklin C. ......South Haven, MI
Hanson, Fred B. ......Northbrook, IL
Hanson, Gail A. ......Boston, MA
Hanson, Gail I. ......South Haven, MI
Hanson, Gary A. ......Malibu, CA
Hanson, Gary H. ......Topeka, KS
Hanson & Gasiorkiewicz, S.C. ......Racine, WI
Hanson, George A. ......Kansas City, MO
Hanson, Gerard H. ......Princeton, NJ
Hanson, Gordon N. ......Palo Alto, CA
Hanson, Gregory H. ......San Francisco, CA
Hanson, Gregory L. ......Missoula, MT
Hanson, Guy A. ......Phoenix, AZ
Hanson, H. Bruce ......Philadelphia, PA
Hanson, H.E., P.C. ......Western Springs, IL
Hanson, H. Eldon, (P.C.) ......Phoenix, AZ
Hanson & Hanson ......McCook, NE
Hanson & Hanson ......Cherry Hill, NJ
Hanson and Hanson, Attorneys at Law, P.C.
Morris, IL
Hanson & Hanson, P.A. ......Orlando, FL
Hanson, Harold C. ......Albany, NY
Hanson, Harry A., III (P.C.) ......Boston, MA
Hanson, Harry A., Jr. ......San Mateo, CA
Hanson, Harry W. ......Washington, IN
Hanson, Heidi E. ......Western Springs, IL
Hanson Holmes Snider & Shipley
Tulsa, OK
Hanson, Howard E. ......Hayward, WI
Hanson, Howard F. ......Kendallville, IN
Hanson, Hugh Kristian ......Salisbury, MD
Hanson, Jack L., Jr. ......Towson, MD
Hanson, Jack W. ......Minneapolis, MN
Hanson, James H. ......Indianapolis, IN
Hanson, James R. ......Wichita, KS
Hanson, James R. ......Columbus, OH
Hanson, James S. ......Ellicott City, MD
Hanson, James S. ......Midland, MI
Hanson, Jane Ann ......Fort Bragg, CA
Hanson, Jane H. ......South Plainfield, NJ
Hanson, Jane L. ......New York, NY
Hanson, Jane M. ......Newark, NJ
Hanson, Janet C. ......San Francisco, CA
Hanson, Jared P. ......San Diego, CA
Hanson, Jarrod ......Cleveland, OH
Hanson, Jason D. ......Waukesha, WI
Hanson, Jay D. ......San Diego, CA
Hanson, Jay M. ......Cambridge, IL
Hanson, Jean E. ......New York, NY
Hanson, Jean M. ......St. Paul, MN
Hanson, Jeanne M. ......Wilmington, DE
Hanson, Jeanne M., Attorney at Law, LLC
Wilmington, DE
Hanson, Jeffrey A. ......Rochester, MN
Hanson, Jeffrey B. ......Macon, GA
Hanson, Jeffrey K. ......Portland, OR
Hanson, Jennifer L. ......Chicago, IL
Hanson, Jennifer L. ......Charlestown, MA
Hanson, Jerry C. ......Houston, TX
Hanson, Jerry H. ......Green Bay, WI
Hanson, Jill A. ......Nashville, TN
Hanson, John C., II ......Miami, FL
Hanson, John D. ......St. Cloud, MN
Hanson, John D. ......Madison, WI
Hanson, John E. ......Bellevue, WA
Hanson, John F. ......McCook, NE
Hanson, John F., Jr. ......Alameda, CA
Hanson, John H. ......Chicago, IL
Hanson, John H. ......Park Ridge, IL
Hanson, John J. ......Los Angeles, CA
Hanson, John K. ......South Bend, IN
Hanson, John L., Jr. ......Chantilly, VA
Hanson, John N. ......Washington, DC
Hanson, John R. ......Santa Ana, CA
Hanson, John R. ......Medford, OR
Hanson, John T. ......Washington, DC
Hanson, John V. ......Morris, IL
Hanson, John W. ......Brooklyn Center, MN
Hanson, Jon A. ......Minneapolis, MN
Hanson, Jon S. ......Elm Grove, WI
Hanson, Jon S. B. C. ......Wolfeboro, NH
Hanson, Jonathan R. ......Owatonna, MN
Hanson, Joseph D. ......Los Angeles, CA
Hanson, Joseph L. ......Emmetsburg, IA
Hanson, Karen M. ......Minneapolis, MN
Hanson, Karen Reynolds ......Davisburg, MI
Hanson, Karl B., III ......Jacksonville, FL
Hanson, Karl B., Jr. (P.C.)
Jacksonville, FL
Hanson, Karl G. A. L. ......St. Paul, MN
Hanson, Kathy ......Baltimore, MD
Hanson, Keith A. ......Chicago, IL
Hanson, Keith A. ......Minneapolis, MN
Hanson, Kenn Martin ......Glendale, AZ
Hanson, Kenneth C. ......Columbia, SC
Hanson, Kenneth M. ......Fort Worth, TX
Hanson, Kent B. ......Minneapolis, MN
Hanson, Kent B. ......Reno, NV
Hanson, Kent E. ......Denver, CO
Hanson, Kirk D. ......San Diego, CA
Hanson, Kristie Halloran ......Schenectady, NY
Hanson, Kristin ......San Antonio, TX
Hanson, Kurt E. ......Chicago, IL
Hanson, Kurt M. ......Houston, TX
Hanson, Kyle L. ......Kearney, NE
Hanson, L. Eugene ......Goldendale, WA
Hanson, L. Reid, Jr. ......Wheatland, CA
Hanson, L. Thaxton ......Northridge, CA
Hanson, Lamberth & Kiatta, LLP
Houston, TX
Hanson, Lance Eugene ......Kansas City, MO
Hanson, Larry A. ......St. Paul, MN
Hanson, Laura J. ......Minneapolis, MN
Hanson, Lawrence I. ......Madison, WI
Hanson, Lawrence P. ......Cheboygan, MI
Hanson, Lawrence W. ......Houston, TX
Hanson, Lee, (Ms.) ......New York, NY
Hanson, Lee W. ......St. Cloud, MN
Hanson, Leslie James ......Mount Vernon, IL
Hanson, Letitia J. ......New York, NY
Hanson, Linscott R. ......Park Ridge, IL
Hanson, Lon R. ......Stockton, CA
Hanson, Loren Q. ......Fort Worth, TX
Hanson, Lori W. ......San Antonio, TX
Hanson, Loyal M. ......Fallbrook, CA
Hanson, Lulic & Krall ......Minneapolis, MN
St. Paul, MN
Hanson, Lyle O. ......Bellingham, WA
Hanson, Lynne M. ......Denver, CO
Hanson, Mahlon F. ......St. Paul, MN
Hanson Marek Bolkcom & Greene, Ltd.
Minneapolis, MN
Hanson, Margaret ......Lihue, HI
Hanson, Marilee ......Sacramento, CA
Hanson, Mark A. ......Englewood, CO
Hanson, Mark A. ......Sarasota, FL
Hanson, Mark C. ......Chicago, IL
Hanson, Mark D. ......Fort Collins, CO
Hanson, Mark E. ......Joliet, IL
Hanson, Mark E. ......Vienna, VA
Hanson, Mark Graham ......Fort Lauderdale, FL
Hanson, Mark J. ......Minneapolis, MN
Hanson, Mark L. ......Atlanta, GA
Hanson, Mark R. ......Fargo, ND
Hanson, Mark Richard
West Palm Beach, FL
Hanson, Mark V. ......Des Moines, IA
Hanson, Marvin B. ......Hallock, MN
Hanson, Mary ......Oklahoma City, OK
Hanson, Mary M. ......Torrance, CA
Hanson, Matthew D. ......Crete, NE
Wilber, NE
Hanson, Melinda M. ......Washington, DC
Hanson, Melissa O. ......Jacksonville, FL
Hanson, Michael A. ......Orlando, FL
Hanson, Michael C. ......Norwell, MA
Hanson, Michael F. ......Atlanta, GA
Hanson, Michael J. ......Anchorage, AK
Hanson, Michael W. ......Sioux Falls, SD
Hanson, Milton L. ......Avoca, IA
Hanson, Mitchell A. ......Orlando, FL
Hanson & Molloy ......Washington, DC
Hanson, Monte R. ......Sioux Falls, SD
Hanson, Murlie C. ......Salinas, CA
Hanson, Myrna A. ......Jacksonville, FL
Hanson, Norman ......Billings, MT
Hanson, Norman D. ......New York, NY
Hanson, Patricia J. ......Oklahoma City, OK
Hanson, Patricia M. ......Chicago, IL
Hanson, Patricia M. ......Houston, TX
Hanson, Paul E. ......Fort Worth, TX
Hanson, Paul G., III ......Lynnwood, WA
Hanson, Paul T. ......Los Angeles, CA
Hanson, Per K. ......Northbrook, IL
Hanson, Peter D. ......Boston, MA
Hanson, Peter G. ......San Francisco, CA
Hanson & Peters ......Chicago, IL
Hanson, Ralph D. ......Irvine, CA
Hanson, Randall A. ......Greensboro, NC
Hanson, Randall C. ......Omaha, NE
Hanson, Randall S. ......Grand Forks, ND
Hanson, Rebecca J. ......Fort Dodge, IA
Hanson, Rebecca J. ......McLean, VA
Hanson, Rebecca S. ......Boston, MA

Hanson, Richard A. ... **Chicago, IL**
Hanson, Richard E. ... Wichita Falls, TX
Hanson, Robert B. ... Treasury Department, Internal Revenue Service, GV
Hanson, Robert B. ... **Des Moines, IA**
Hanson, Robert C. ... Seattle, WA
Hanson, Robert D. ... **Harrisburg, PA**
Hanson, Robert E. ... Indianapolis, IN
Hanson, Robert E. ... Columbia, KY
Hanson, Robert E. ... **Albuquerque, NM**
Hanson, Robert E. ... **Columbus, OH**
Hanson, Robert F. ... **Portland, ME**
Hanson, Robert P. ... Treasury Department, Departmental Offices, GV
Hanson, Robert T. ... **Mount Morris, IL**
Hanson, Robert W. ... **Albertville, AL**
Hanson, Rodney C. ... **Willmar, MN**
Hanson, Rodney D. ... **Bridgeport, OH**
Hanson, Roger S. ... Santa Ana, CA
Hanson, Rolfe E. ... Madison, WI
Hanson, Ronald M. ... **Dallas, TX**
Hanson, Ronald W. ... **Chicago, IL**
Hanson, Ronald Windell ... Gadsden, AL
Hanson, Rondell B. ... Newport Beach, CA
Hanson, Rory A. ... Eureka, CA
Hanson, Ross D. ... Houston, TX
Hanson, Roybal, Lee & Todd, P.C. **Billings, MT**
Hanson, Russell L. ... Westby, WI
Hanson, Samuel L. ... **Minneapolis, MN**
Hanson, Sandy K. ... **Los Angeles, CA**
Hanson, Scott K. ... Marquette, MI
Hanson, Shane A. ... **Bismarck, ND**
Hanson, Shannon Thee Department of Justice, Criminal Division, GV
Hanson, Sharon Lindley ... Wilmington, MA
Hanson, Shawn E. ... **San Francisco, CA**
Hanson, Stephen P. ... **New York, NY**
Hanson, Steven A. ... Billings, MT
Hanson, Stewart M., Jr., P.C. **Salt Lake City, UT**
Hanson, Stuart A. ... Sacramento, CA
Hanson & Sulhoff ... Avoca, IA
Hanson, Susan K. ... Cherry Hill, NJ
Hanson, Susan R. ... **South Bend, IN**
Hanson, T. Philip, Jr. ... **Dade City, FL**
Hanson, Theodore J. ... Orange, CA
Hanson, Thomas A. ... **West Palm Beach, FL**
Hanson, Thomas D. ... **Des Moines, IA**
Hanson, Thomas E., Jr. ... **Philadelphia, PA**
Hanson, Thomas J. ... Manchester, IA
Hanson, Thomas M. ... **San Francisco, CA**
Hanson, Thomas William ... Evergreen, CO
Hanson, Timothy R. ... Salt Lake City, UT
Hanson, Tom S. ... **Portland, ME**
Hanson, Tonya R. ... **Spokane, WA**
Hanson & Vandlik, L.L.C. ... **Chicago, IL** **Park Ridge, IL**
Hanson, Victor G. ... Detroit, MI
Hanson, Victor L., III ... Dallas, TX
Hanson, Vivian L. ... **New York, NY**
Hanson & Werger ... Manchester, IA
Hanson, William C. ... **Bloomfield Hills, MI**
Hanson, William F. ... New York, NY
Hanson, William G. ... Lafayette, CA
Hanson, William H. ... **Bangor, ME**
Hanson, William L. ... Seattle, WA
Hanson, William P., Jr. ... **Richmond, VA**
Hanson, Wm. P. ... Richmond, VA
Hanson-Lebihan, Rachel ... **Houston, TX**
Hansotte, Louis B. ... San Diego, CA
Hansra, Paul S. ... **Denver, CO**
Hanss, Mary Beth ... Newtown Square, PA
Hanssen, Dennis L. ... **Des Moines, IA**
Hanssen, Henry R., Jr. ... **Bellevue, WA**
Hanssen, William A. ... **Santa Monica, CA**
Hanssens, Francis J., Jr. ... Philadelphia, PA
Hanssler, Scott William ... Orange, CA
Hansson, Beth K. ... **Greenwich, CT**
Hansson, Christine E ... San Francisco, CA
Hansson, Kurt W. ... **Stamford, CT**
Hansson, Leigh T. ... **McLean, VA**
Hansson, Petur O. ... **Plainsboro, NJ**
Hanst, Dale E. ... Santa Barbara, CA
Hanstad, Susan M. ... Minneapolis, MN
Hanstad, Timothy M. ... Seattle, WA
Hanstein, Brian Kyle ... **Philadelphia, PA**
Hanstein, Walter E., III ... Farmington, ME Mexico, ME
Hansult, William G. ... Santa Barbara, CA
Hansum, Richard V. ... **Houston, TX**
Hanswirth, Dori Ann ... **New York, NY**
Hansz, Gary A. ... **Farmington Hills, MI**
Hantel, Gina Baker ... Nashville, TN
Hantel, John L. ... **Metairie, LA**
Hantel, Michael P. ... **Sugar Land, TX**
Hantel, Philip E. ... Gretna, LA
Hanten, Linda K. ... Washington, DC
Hanthorn, Gregory Russell ... **Atlanta, GA**
Hanthorn, Jack E. ... Vista, CA
Hantke, David W. ... Tillamook, OR
Hantke, Frank J. ... New York, NY
Hantke, Meighan M. ... Milwaukee, WI
Hantla, G. Bradley ... Litchfield, IL
Hantla, G. Bradley, Ltd. ... Litchfield, IL
Hantler, Steven B. ... Highland Park, MI
Hantman, Alfred ... Silver Spring, MD
Hantman, Allen ... Denville, NJ
Hantman, Arnold ... Miami, FL
Hantman & Associates ... **New York, NY**
Hantman, Daniel ... Riverside, CA
Hantman, David S. ... United States Senate, Senatorial Assistants, GV
Hantman, Debra S. ... **Marlton, NJ**
Hantman, Howard ... Tucson, AZ
Hantman, Lawrence W. ... **Randolph, MA**
Hantman, Robert J. ... **New York, NY**
Hantman, Sue-Ellen W. ... Columbia, MD
Hanton, Mary E. ... Somers, NY
Hanton, Rena C. ... Tulsa, OK
Hantz, Anna Barbara ... **Nashua, NH**
Hantz, Steven A. ... **New York, NY**
Hantzes, Nicholas H. ... Reston, VA
Hantzes, Savas ... North Falmouth, MA
Hantzmon, Richard V. ... Middleburg, VA
Hantzos, Elizabeth G. ... Chicago, IL
Hanudel, Robert A. ... Roanoke Rapids, NC
Hanula, Robert Walter ... Phoenix, AZ
Hanuman, Shashi K. ... **Los Angeles, CA**
Hanus, David J. ... **Milwaukee, WI**
Hanus, George D. ... Chicago, IL
Hanus, Richard ... **Berwyn, IL** **Chicago, IL** Elgin, IL
Hanus, Richard, Law Offices of **Berwyn, IL** **Elgin, IL**
Hanus, Ronald B. ... Chardon, OH
Hanusa, Julie M. ... **Chicago, IL**
Hanusek, Michael S. ... Hackensack, NJ
Hanusik, Thomas A. ... Department of Justice, Criminal Division, GV
Hanusz, Richard W. ... Toledo, OH
Hanuszczak, Michael L. ... Syracuse, NY
Hanvey, Frank W. ... Monroe, LA
Hanvey, J. Scott ... **Hickory, NC**
Hanvik, James T. ... Edina, MN
Hanvy, Kevin L. ... Simpsonville, SC
Hanway, Kevin L. ... Lake Oswego, OR
Hanwell, Jerry W. ... Pittsburgh, PA
Hanwell, Robert M. ... Medina, OH
Hany, Frederick C., II ... Oak Harbor, OH
Hanyak, Anne M. ... Phoenix, AZ
Hanyen, Clyde K., Jr. ... **Brockton, MA**
Hanyon, Joseph P. ... Mount Pocono, PA
Hanz, Gayle C. ... **Houston, TX**
Hanz, Patricia M. ... Milwaukee, WI
Hanzawa, Karen ... Bridgeton, NJ
Hanzawa & Melnicove ... Bridgeton, NJ
Hanzawa, Yoshitaka ... Bridgeton, NJ
Hanze, Carlos L. ... New York, NY
Hanzel, A. Keith ... St. Paul, MN
Hanzel, John F. ... Mooresville, NC
Hanzel, Matthew J. ... **St. Paul, MN**
Hanzel, Michael C. ... Pittsburgh, PA
Hanzelik, Carl H. ... **Philadelphia, PA**
Hanzelik, Fred T. ... **Chattanooga, TN**
Hanzelik & James ... **Chattanooga, TN**
Hanzen, William E. ... Bothell, WA
Hanzlick, Glenn P. ... **Torrance, CA**
Hanzlik, Paul F. ... **Chicago, IL**
Hanzman Criden Chaykin Ponce & Heise, P.A. ... **Miami, FL**
Hanzman, Michael A. ... **Miami, FL**
Hao, James P. ... San Jose, CA
Hao, Mei-Ying ... **Chicago, IL**
Hao, Rita A. ... **San Francisco, CA**
Hap, Jeffrey ... Brooklyn, NY
Hapgood, Clifford F. ... Rocky Mount, VA
Hapgood, Cyrus S. ... New York, NY
Hapgood, Larry L. ... Topeka, KS
Hapgood, Mark Wayne ... Eureka, CA
Hapgood, Molly ... St. Paul, MN
Hapka, Gerald A. ... **Wilmington, DE**
Hapka, Susan M. ... **Albuquerque, NM**
Hapke, Daniel S. ... St. Louis, MO
Hapke, Daniel S., Jr. ... **Salt Lake City, UT**
Hapke & Donovan ... **Norwalk, CT** **Stamford, CT**
Hapke, Kenneth A. ... **Norwalk, CT**
Hapner, Elizabeth L. ... Tampa, FL
Hapner and Hapner ... Hillsboro, OH
Hapner, James D. ... Hillsboro, OH
Hapner, Jon C. ... Hillsboro, OH
Hapner, Kathryn ... Hillsboro, OH
Hapner, Priscilla ... **Columbus, OH**
Happ, Gregory W. ... Medina, OH
Happas, Jamie D. ... **New Brunswick, NJ**
Happe, Dale J. ... Burnsville, MN
Happe, Elizabeth Bandoli ... Des Moines, IA
Happe, Joseph A. ... **Des Moines, IA**
Happe, Judith ... **New York, NY**
Happe, Michael J. ... **Eau Claire, WI**
Happel, David E. ... Vinton, IA
Happel, Dennis W. ... Perham, MN
Happel, Douglas I. ... Pittsburgh, PA
Happel, Henry H., III ... **Seattle, WA**
Happel, Jana L. ... Cedar Rapids, IA
Happel, Jason P. ... Ames, IA
Happel, Michael A. ... New York, NY
Happell, Perry R. ... **Nashville, TN**
Happeney, Randy L. ... **Lancaster, OH**
Happer, M. Marshall, III ... **Raleigh, NC**
Happy, J. Nelson ... Newport News, VA
Hapward, Curt M. ... **Morristown, NJ**
Hapworth, Peter J. ... Aldie, VA
Haq, Arif S. ... **Atlanta, GA**
Haque, Bradley O. ... **Washington, DC**
Haque, Elizabeth M. ... Johnstown, PA
Haque, Ruma ... Jackson, MS
Har, T. Steven ... **New York, NY**
Hara, Cheryl K. ... Denver, CO
Hara, Colin ... **Chicago, IL** **Cincinnati, OH**
Hara, Gilbert K. ... Hilo, HI
Hara, Glenn S. ... Hilo, HI
Hara, Izumi ... Morris Plains, NJ
Hara, Larry S. ... Honolulu, HI
Hara, Max ... Fullerton, CA
Hara, Michael E. ... Treasury Department, Internal Revenue Service, GV
Hara, Rodney T. ... Rutherford, NJ
Hara, Thomas I. ... Brooklyn Center, MN
Harab, Jeffrey W. ... Chevy Chase, MD
Harab, Jeffrey W., Law Offices of, P.C. Chevy Chase, MD
Haraburd, Suzanne ... River Forest, IL
Haracz, David ... Chicago, IL
Haracz, Stephen M. ... **New York, NY**
Harad, Charles A. ... **Philadelphia, PA**
Harad, Deborah N. ... Warminster, PA
Harad, Gittleman, Greenberg, Brunner & Love ... **Philadelphia, PA**
Harada, Arlette S. ... Honolulu, HI
Harada, Jon T. ... San Jose, CA
Harada, Karilee Endow ... Honolulu, HI
Harada, Kenneth W. ... Honolulu, HI
Harada, Lyle Y., (Atty. At Law, A Law Corp.) ... **Honolulu, HI**
Harada, Mitchell T. ... Seattle, WA
Harada, Stanley D. ... Albuquerque, NM
Harada-Stone, David R. ... **Honolulu, HI**
Haradhvala, Adil N. ... Detroit, MI
Haraguchi, Ben I. ... New York, NY
Haraguchi, Bruce K. ... Oak Park, IL
Haraguchi, John P. ... Honolulu, HI
Harak, Charles ... Boston, MA
Harak, David A. ... Baltimore, MD
Harak, David A., L.L.C. ... Baltimore, MD
Harak, Paul J. ... Bethlehem, PA
Harakal, Randall ... **Honolulu, HI**
Harakas, Andrew J. ... **New York, NY**
Harakas, Dean ... Chicago, IL
Haralambides, Alexandros J. ... **Miami, FL**
Haralambie, Ann M. ... Tucson, AZ
Haralambie, John P. ... Youngstown, OH
Haralampu, Evelyn A. ... **Boston, MA**
Haraldsen, Gary A. ... Aptos, CA
Haraldson, Comet H. ... **Sioux Falls, SD**
Haraldson, Deborah ... Newark, NJ
Haraldson, John O. ... **West Des Moines, IA**
Haralson, Brad ... San Antonio, TX
Haralson, Dale, P.C. ... **Tucson, AZ**
Haralson, Howard R. ... Oklahoma City, OK
Haralson, Howard R., P.C. Oklahoma City, OK
Haralson, J. David ... **Atlanta, GA**
Haralson, Miller, Pitt & McAnally, P.L.C. **Tucson, AZ**
Haralson, Paul ... **Coral Gables, FL**
Haralson, Regina ... **Little Rock, AR**
Haralson, Shannon L. ... United States Senate, Committee Legal Personnel, GV
Haralson, Steve W. ... Little Rock, AR
Haralson, Steven W., PLC ... Little Rock, AR
Haralson, W. W. ... Scottsboro, AL
Haramis, Lee Stathis ... **Jacksonville, FL**
Haran, Gerald ... San Pablo, CA
Haran, Mary-Ann P. ... New Haven, CT
Haran, Michael M. ... Phoenix, AZ
Haran, Sean T. ... **New York, NY**
Haran, Thomas O. ... **Emeryville, CA** San Francisco, CA
Haranas, Mark R. ... **Framingham, MA**
Harang, Bruce E. ... Asheville, NC
Harang, Donald F., Jr. ... Larose, LA
Harang, Jack W. ... Metairie, LA
Harang Law Firm, A Professional Law Corporation ... Larose, LA Thibodaux, LA
Harang, Linda S. ... **New Orleans, LA**
Harant, Linda L. ... Florence, AZ
Harants, Stephen J. ... **Fort Wayne, IN**
Haranzo, James J. ... Wheeling, WV
Haranzo, Mark E. ... **Iselin, NJ** **New York, NY**
Haranzo & McGuane ... Wheeling, WV
Harari, David ... New York, NY
Harari, Jack A. ... Washington, DC
Harari, Peggy-Jean ... Manhattan Beach, CA
Harari, Rachel M. ... Uniondale, NY
Harary, Alice Sardell ... New York, NY
Harary, David S. ... New York, NY
Harary, Joel T. ... **New York, NY**
Harary, Joseph M. ... **New York, NY**
Harary, Morris ... New York, NY
Harasek, Craig ... Placerville, CA
Harasti, Gina M. ... **Baltimore, MD**
Harasty, Zoltan A." Walt " Santa Barbara, CA
Harasym, Bohdan M. ... Buffalo, NY
Harasym, Leslie A. ... **New York, NY**
Harasz, Katherine ... Viera, FL
Haratani, Joan M. ... **Oakland, CA**
Haratsis, George C. ... **Fort Worth, TX**
Haratz, Michael S. ... **Roseland, NJ**
Haraughty Sanna, Patricia ... Madison, WI
Haray, Jonathan W. ... **New Haven, CT**
Haray, Richard J. ... New York, NY
Harazin, William D. ... Raleigh, NC
Harb, Albert J. ... **Knoxville, TN**
Harb, Kimberly ... Department Of The Interior, Bureau of Land Management, GV
Harb, Mariam M. ... **Detroit, MI**
Harb, Omar J. ... **Troy, MI**
Harb, Rifat A. ... New York, NY
Harb, Robert D. ... Haverhill, MA
Harbach, David V., II ... **Houston, TX**
Harbage, Paula Adix ... **Chicago, IL**
Harball, Charles A. ... Kalispell, MT
Harball, Charles A., P.C. ... Kalispell, MT
Harband, Martin E. ... San Mateo, CA
Harband, Vida Buchalter ... Sausalito, CA
Harbanuk, Roger A. ... Wolcott, CT
Harbarger, David R. ... **Cleveland, OH**
Harbart, Michael D. ... San Antonio, TX
Harbaugh, Audrey Woloshin ... York, PA
Harbaugh and Bloom, P.S. ... Spokane, WA
Harbaugh, Claudia ... San Diego, CA
Harbaugh, Daniel P. ... Spokane, WA
Harbaugh, David L. ... **Philadelphia, PA**
Harbaugh, Gary B. ... St. Clair, MI
Harbaugh, Gregory A. ... **Pittsburgh, PA**
Harbaugh, Joseph D. ... Fort Lauderdale, FL
Harbaugh, Karen R. ... **Vienna, VA**
Harbaugh, Mark ... Tacoma, WA
Harbaugh, Richard A. ... **Chicago, IL**
Harbaugh, Russell H., Jr. ... **Tulsa, OK**
Harbeck, David A. ... **Minneapolis, MN**
Harbeck, Dorothy A. ... **Trenton, NJ**
Harbeck, Karen M. ... Malden, MA
Harbeck, Stephen P. ... **Washington, DC**
Harbeck, William H. ... **Milwaukee, WI**
Harbecke, Fred R. ... Chicago, IL
Harben, Emily Bagwell ... Gainesville, GA
Harben & Hartley ... Gainesville, GA
Harben, Jeb ... **New York, NY**
Harben, Ralph E., Jr. ... Atlanta, GA
Harben, Sam S., Jr. ... Gainesville, GA
Harber, Carolyn Lee ... Atlanta, GA
Harber, Everett Edsel ... Blytheville, AR
Harber & Freesman ... Fort Lee, NJ
Harber, John K. ... **Knoxville, TN**
Harber, Kandyce Morgan ... **Knoxville, TN**
Harber, Kevin R. Small Business Administration, Office of the General Counsel, GV
Harber, Melanie T. ... El Paso, TX
Harber, Sofia ... **Austin, TX**
Harber, Stephen M. ... **Los Angeles, CA**
Harber, Steven R. ... New York, NY
Harberg, Allen, Jr. ... **Philadelphia, PA**
Harberg, David B. ... Houston, TX
Harberg, Franklin J., Jr. ... Houston, TX
Harberg, Joseph L. ... Dallas, TX
Harbers, Kirsten S. ... Los Angeles, CA
Harbers, Michael J. ... **Nashville, TN**
Harberson, James C., Jr. ... Watertown, NY
Harbert, David A. ... Redwood City, CA
Harbert, Guy M., III ... **Roanoke, VA**
Harbert, James ... **Chicago, IL**
Harbert, Mary L. ... **Vineland, NJ**
Harbert, Robert P., II ... **North Canton, OH**
Harbert, Ronald A. ... **Orlando, FL**
Harbert, Thomas R. ... **Orlando, FL**
Harbert, Walter C. ... Littleton, CO
Harberts, Helen ... Oroville, CA
Harbeson, Joseph R. ... **Mineola, NY**
Harbeson, Pamela A. ... **Boston, MA**
Harbeson, Robert G. ... **Haddonfield, NJ**
Harbeson, Timothy D. ... Columbia, SC
Harbeson, William P. ... Austin, TX
Harbin, Alisa A. ... **Emeryville, CA**
Harbin, Anthony L. ... **Anderson, SC**
Harbin, Bruce A. ... Santa Ana, CA
Harbin, Carolyn Bell ... Detroit, MI
Harbin, Cynthia C. ... Asheville, NC
Harbin, Eddie R. ... Greenville, SC
Harbin, Harry S. ... Department of Justice, Criminal Division, GV
Harbin, John A. ... Los Angeles, CA
Harbin, John W. ... **Atlanta, GA**
Harbin, Lawrence ... **Washington, DC**
Harbin, Marty ... Akron, OH
Harbin, Reid Hamilton ... **Atlanta, GA**
Harbin, Robin H. ... Birmingham, AL
Harbin-Forte, Brenda F. ... Oakland, CA
Harbinger, Bonny ... **Washington, DC**
Harbinger, Richard ... Los Angeles, CA
Harbinson, Ann ... Minneapolis, MN
Harbinson, Barbara N. ... Ross, CA
Harbinson, Joel C. ... **Taylorsville, NC**
Harbinson, Thomas J. ... **San Francisco, CA**
Harbinson, Thomas J. ... Shakopee, MN
Harbinson, Tune, Mangold & Kasselik, A Professional Corporation **San Francisco, CA**
Harbison, Brenda Houck ... **Richmond, VA**
Harbison, Finley W. ... Lebanon, TN
Harbison, Gregory Owen ... Richmond, VA
Harbison, James M., Jr. ... **Houston, TX**
Harbison, James W., Jr. ... **New York, NY**
Harbison, Jeffrey T. ... Ft. Calhoun, NE
Harbison, Joseph F., III ... **Sacramento, CA**
Harbison, Katherine A. ... **Birmingham, AL**
Harbison, Kent G. ... **Minneapolis, MN**
Harbison, Kessinger, Lisle & Bush **Lexington, KY**
Harbison, Kip Andrew ... **Norfolk, VA**
Harbison, Mark P. ... **Paoli, PA**
Harbison, Rick ... **Guymon, OK**
Harbison, Sam B. ... Medford, OR
Harbison, Stephen F. ... **Los Angeles, CA**
Harbison, William L. ... **Nashville, TN**
Harbison, William R. ... **Columbia, SC**
Harbison, William T., II ... Tulsa, OK
Harbist, Nicholas C. ... **Cherry Hill, NJ**
Harbold, R. Chris, and Associates **Columbus, OH**
Harbolt, James B. ... Portland, OR
Harbolt, John L. ... **Louisville, KY**
Harbor, Marla A. ... Jackson, MS
Harbor, William S. ... Troy, OH
Harbottle, C.D. ... Visalia, CA
Harbottle, Michelle R. ... **Palo Alto, CA**
Harbottle, Nancy S. ... **Hoffman Estates, IL**
Harbottle, S. Daniel ... **Costa Mesa, CA**
Harbottle, Scott A. ... Cleveland, OH
Harbour, Bryan C. ... Mc Comb, MS
Harbour, Clifford P. ... Durham, NC
Harbour, Cori Ann ... El Paso, TX
Harbour, David M. ... Oklahoma City, OK
Harbour, Francine D., Law Offices of Anchorage, AK
Harbour, John W. ... New Brunswick, NJ
Harbour, John W., Jr. ... Oklahoma City, OK
Harbour, Kathleen P. ... Summit, MS
Harbour, M. Dave ... Meridian, MS
Harbour, Michael H. ... **Albuquerque, NM**
Harbour, Nancy Caine ... Southfield, MI

Harbour, Pamela Jones ....New York, NY
Harbour, Randall L. ....Southfield, MI
Harbour, Smith, Harris & Merritt, P.C. Longview, TX
Harbour, Steven E. ....Norcross, GA
Harbour, Ted I. ....Arlington, TX
Harbour, Vicki L. ....Boston, MA
Harbourt, Boyd ....Phillipsburg, NJ
Harbourt, Clifford M. ....Treasury Department, Internal Revenue Service, GV
Harbourt, Maureen N. ....Baton Rouge, LA
Harbrecht, Grant A. ....Charlotte, NC
Harbron, Garrett Lee, Jr. ....Indianapolis, IN
Harbsmeier, Curt L. ....Lakeland, FL
Harbst, John W. ....Chicago, IL
Harbuck, Jonathan S. ....Birmingham, AL
Harbulak, Stephen J. ....New York, NY
Harbur, Marilyn J. ....Salem, OR
Harbur, Nathan C. ....Leawood, KS
Harbur, Nathan C., Chartered ....Leawood, KS
Harburg, Richard D. ....Philadelphia, PA
Harburg, Stephen J. ....Washington, DC
Harbus, Richard ....New York, NY
Harbutte, Alice M. ....San Diego, CA
Harby, Shawn R. ....Baltimore, MD
Harcar, Mary V. ....Washington, DC
Harcar, Richard J. ....Trenton, NJ
Harcha, Howard H., III ....Portsmouth, OH
Harcha, Howard H., Jr. ....Portsmouth, OH
Harchenhorn, V. Lanny ....Westminster, MD
Harchenko, Elizabeth ....Salem, OR
Harchut, Robert F. ....Philadelphia, PA
Harckham, Finley T. R. ....New York, NY
Harcleroad, F. Douglass ....Eugene, OR
Harclerode, Judith L. ....Baltimore, MD
Harcourt, Barbara Arnold ....Rushville, IN
Harcourt, Bernard ....Montgomery, AL
Harcourt, Caroline A. ....New York, NY
Harcourt-Hearring, Cynthia ....St. Louis, MO
Harcrow, E. Earl ....Fort Worth, TX
Harcus, Sinclair J. ....Bloomfield Hills, MI
Hard, Eric C. ....Hartford, CT
Hard, James H., IV ....Birmingham, AL
Hard, James H., Jr. ....Houston, TX
Hard, Judith Ann ....Albany, NY
Hard, Lawrence E. ....Seattle, WA
Hard, Stephen T. ....Salt Lake City, UT
Hardacker, William J. ....Prior Lake, MN
Hardacre, David W. ....Los Angeles, CA
Hardacre, Edwin Grantley Los Angeles, CA
Hardacre, Elizabeth A. ....Milwaukee, WI
Hardacre, Lynn L. ....Hudson, OH
Hardacre, Stephen R. ....Anderson, IN
Hardacre-Fergus, Jean ....New York, NY
Hardage, A. Carter ....Little Rock, AR
Hardage, J. Milton ....Austin, TX
Hardaman, Donna M. ....Atlanta, GA
Hardamon, Donald L. ....Indianapolis, IN
Hardaway, Charles R. ....Philadelphia, PA
Hardaway, Christopher Lee ....Denver, CO
Hardaway, Eddie, Jr. ....Livingston, AL
Hardaway, John B., III ....Greenville, SC
Hardaway, John Frank ....Columbia, SC
Hardaway, Larry D. ....Lakeland, FL
Hardaway, Patricia L. ....Newark, NJ New York, NY
Hardaway, Richard A. ....Denver, CO
Hardaway, Robert M. ....Denver, CO
Hardaway, Roger D. ....Alva, OK
Hardaway, Samantha L. ....San Francisco, CA
Hardaway, Thomas C. ....Enfield, NC
Hardberger, J. Derek ....Oklahoma City, OK
Hardberger, Melissa L. ....Albuquerque, NM
Hardberger, Phil ....San Antonio, TX
Hardcastle, A., Jr. ....Dallas, TX
Hardcastle, Allan D. ....Santa Rosa, CA
Hardcastle, C. J. ....Bentonville, AR
Hardcastle, Gerald W. ....Las Vegas, NV
Hardcastle, Heath E. ....Tulsa, OK
Hardcastle, Ian ....Palo Alto, CA
Hardcastle, J. B., Jr. ....Nashville, TN
Hardcastle, Joseph F. ....Boston, MA
Hardcastle, Kathleen ....Moscow, ID
Hardcastle, Kathy A. ....Las Vegas, NV
Hardcastle Law Firm, P.A. ....Bentonville, AR
Hardcastle, Lloyd A. ....Farmington, UT
Hardcastle, Marianne S. ....Tulsa, OK
Hardcastle, Mark J. ....Baltimore, MD
Hardcastle, Patricia Ann ....Mobridge, SD
Hardcastle, Richard R., III ....St. Louis, MO
Hardcastle, Robert T. ....Greeley, CO
Hardcastle, V. Wayne ....Hanford, CA Visalia, CA
Hardee, Britannia Hobbs ....San Antonio, TX
Hardee, Cary A., II ....Madison, FL
Hardee, Charles J., III ....Tallahassee, FL
Hardee, Charles R. ....Greenville, NC
Hardee, Covington ....Washington, CT
Hardee, Daniel R. ....Boise, ID
Hardee, David ....Jackson, TN
Hardee, Felicity ....Springfield, MA
Hardee, G. Wayne ....Greenville, NC
Hardee & Hardee ....Greenville, NC
Hardee, Jack Y. ....Athens, TX
Hardee, James A. ....Douglas, WY
Hardee, John H. ....Whittier, CA
Hardee, Kathleen A. ....Kansas City, MO
Hardee Law Offices ....Tyler, TX
Hardee, Lee R., III ....Kansas City, MO
Hardee, Marcy S. ....Franklin, TN
Hardee, Mark W. ....Columbia, SC
Hardee, Martin, Jaynes & Ivy Brownsville, TN Dyersburg, TN Jackson, TN Lexington, TN Memphis, TN Savannah, TN Somerville, TN
Hardee, Marynelle ....Gainesville, FL
Hardee, N. Christopher ....Washington, DC
Hardee, Nathan A. ....Houston, TX
Hardee, Richard Brooks ....Tyler, TX
Hardee, Roya R. ....Jefferson City, MO
Hardee-Thomas, Marva A. ....Summerville, SC
Hardegree, A. Lee, III ....Birmingham, AL
Hardegree, Arthur L. ....Ashland, AL
Hardegree, Craig ....Carrollton, GA
Hardegree, Henry B. ....Montgomery, AL
Hardegree, Howard L. General Services Administration, Office of Regional Counsel, GV
Hardegree, Joe H. ....Mena, AR
Hardegree, Joe, P.A. ....Mena, AR
Hardegree, William B. ....Anniston, AL
Hardegree, William B. ....Columbus, GA
Hardek, Scott M. ....Lisle, IL
Hardeman, Anita B. ....Chattanooga, TN
Hardeman, Dale F. ....Tustin, CA
Hardeman, Donald W., Jr. ....Miami, FL
Hardeman, Hunter D. ....Colorado Springs, CO
Hardeman, J. Greg. ....Nashville, TN
Hardeman, John T. ....Oklahoma City, OK
Hardeman, Robert K. ....Savannah, GA
Hardeman & Scruggs ....Nashville, TN
Hardeman & Suarez, P.A. ....Miami, FL
Hardeman, Thomas D. ....Lafayette, LA
Harden, Charles W. G. ....Greensboro, NC
Harden, Claude M., III ....Lakeland, FL
Harden, Connie K. ....San Francisco, CA
Harden, Curtis L. ....Casper, WY
Harden, Curtis R., Jr. ....Plano, TX
Harden, Davina F. ....Cerritos, CA
Harden, Debbie Weston ....Charlotte, NC
Harden, Donald B., (P.C.) ....Atlanta, GA
Harden, Gary M. ....Toledo, OH
Harden, Hass, Haag & Hallberg, P.C. Estes Park, CO Fort Collins, CO
Harden, Hobart B., Jr. ....Casper, WY
Harden, Holmes P. ....Raleigh, NC
Harden, J. David, Jr. ....Tucson, AZ
Harden, Jane A. ....Roanoke, VA
Harden, Jill D. ....Charlotte, NC
Harden, Joseph N. ....Birmingham, AL
Harden, Kate E. ....Bartow, FL
Harden, Kathleen B. ....Florham Park, NJ
Harden, Kenneth E. ....Chillicothe, MO
Harden, L. Theresa ....Jacksonville, FL
Harden, Lanae M. ....Indianapolis, IN
Harden, Paul M. ....Monroeville, AL
Harden, Paul M. ....Jacksonville, FL
Harden, Quentin F. ....Bonners Ferry, ID
Harden, R. David Agency for International Development, Office of the General Counsel, GV
Harden, Ralph B. ....Fort Collins, CO
Harden, Richard J. ....Oakdale, MN
Harden, Richard L. ....New York, NY
Harden, Richard L. ....Casper, WY
Harden, Richard R. ....Champaign, IL
Harden, Ronald E. ....Terrell, TX
Harden, R. U. ....Waynesboro, GA
Harden, Timothy, III ....Macon, GA
Harden, Timothy M. ....Indianapolis, IN
Harden, Vicki L. ....Plano, TX
Harden, William W. ....Casper, WY
Hardenbrook, Kristin A. Department Of Health And Human Services, Office of the General Counsel, GV
Hardenburg, Lance M. ....Dallas, TX
Harder, Carl W. ....Boise, ID
Harder, Charles J. ....Little Rock, AR
Harder, Charles J. ....Los Angeles, CA
Harder, Daniel C. ....Albany, NY
Harder, Danille Lynn ....Aurora, CO
Harder, David L. ....Topeka, KS
Harder, David W. ....Denver, CO
Harder, George W. ....Albany, NY
Harder, Janice A. ....Columbia, MO
Harder, Jeffrey R. ....Houston, TX
Harder, Jennifer ....Sacramento, CA
Harder, John R. ....Albany, NY
Harder, Kenneth J. ....Brownsville, TX Houston, TX
Harder, Lawrence J. ....Baltimore, MD
Harder, Mark E. ....Mount Clemens, MI
Harder, Mark K. ....Holland, MI
Harder, Michelle C. ....Phoenix, AZ
Harder, Patrick D. ....Pasadena, CA
Harder, Paul R. ....Fullerton, CA
Harder, Rick A. ....Eugene, OR
Harder, Robert C. ....Fayetteville, AR
Harder, Robert L. ....Albany, NY
Harder Silber and Bergan ....Albany, NY
Harder, Terri S. ....Kearney, NE
Harder, Thomas A. ....Minneapolis, MN
Harder, Julie K. ....Fort Dodge, IA
Harders, R. Terrence ....Carbondale, IL
Harders, W. Scott ....Cleveland, OH
Harders-Chen, Gretchen ....New York, NY
Hardester, Jennifer L. ....St. Louis, MO
Hardesty, Alonzo H., III ....Orange City, FL
Hardesty, Alonzo H., III, P.A. Orange City, FL
Hardesty, Bruce R. ....Austin, TX
Hardesty, C. Howard, Jr. ....Washington, DC
Hardesty, Danny L. ....Austin, TX
Hardesty, David A. ....Detroit, MI
Hardesty, Derek J. ....Atlanta, GA
Hardesty, George N., Jr. ....Mobile, AL
Hardesty and Hardin, PC ....Austin, TX
Hardesty, James W. ....Reno, NV
Hardesty, Jo ....Lawrence, KS
Hardesty, Joseph L. ....Louisville, KY
Hardesty, Kenneth W. ....Lima, OH
Hardesty, Randall L. ....Madisonville, KY
Hardesty, Rebecca B. ....Boise, ID
Hardesty, Ronald C. ....Bellingham, WA
Hardesty, Stephen C. ....Boise, ID
Hardesty, Stephen D. ....Akron, OH
Hardesty, Theresa Rahe ....Peoria, IL
Hardesty, Thomas F. ....Owensboro, KY
Hardesty & Tyde, P.A. ....Jacksonville, FL
Hardesty, W. Marc ....Jacksonville, FL
Hardesty, Willard B. ....Wheat Ridge, CO
Hardesty, Willard B., P.C. ....Wheat Ridge, CO
Hardeway, Grant U., Sr. ....Houston, TX
Hardey, Chas. O. ....Shreveport, LA
Hardge, Andrew ....East St. Louis, IL
Hardgrave, Meredith E., (Mr.) ....Antlers, OK
Hardgrove, James A. ....Chicago, IL
Hardgrove, James A. ....Reynoldsburg, OH
Hardgrove, Jennifer Anne ....Chicago, IL
Hardgrove, Kenneth M. ....Los Angeles, CA
Hardgrove, Nicholas A. ....Woodridge, IL
Hardgrove, Sarah C. ....Chicago, IL
Hardick, Daniel ....Mineola, NY
Hardick, Deborah Lynne ....Albany, NY
Hardie & Baxter, P.C. ....El Paso, TX
Hardie, Brooke ....Dallas, TX
Hardie, Donald M. ....New York, NY
Hardie, Geo. B., Jr. ....Miami, FL
Hardie, J. Keith, Jr. ....New Orleans, LA
Hardie, James H. ....Pittsburgh, PA
Hardie, Jeffrey B. ....Washington, DC
Hardie, John R. ....San Jose, CA
Hardie, Les Glenn ....Calabasas, CA Santa Monica, CA
Hardie, Les Glenn ....Los Angeles, CA
Hardie, Lisa D. ....Austin, TX
Hardie, M. Susan ....Houston, TX
Hardie, Rebecca C. ....San Francisco, CA
Hardie, Roderick D. ....Houston, TX
Hardie, Thornton, III ....Dallas, TX
Hardie, William B., Jr. ....El Paso, TX
Hardie, William H., Jr. ....Mobile, AL
Hardig, Edward W. ....South Bend, IN
Hardig, Joseph L., III Bloomfield Hills, MI
Hardig, Joseph L., Jr. Bloomfield Hills, MI
Hardig, Julianne R. ....South Bend, IN
Hardig, Lee and Groves, Professional Association ....South Bend, IN
Hardig, Mark N. ....Hamilton, OH
Hardig Parsons Pedersen & Stout, PLLC Bloomfield Hills, MI Charlevoix, MI Detroit, MI Pontiac, MI Pawleys Island, SC
Hardigree, Christian E. ....Las Vegas, NV
Hardiman, A. J., (Ltd.) ....Chicago, IL
Hardiman, Alexander D. ....Los Angeles, CA
Hardiman & Carroll, A Law Partnership San Francisco, CA
Hardiman, Charles Edward, Jr. ....Madison, TN
Hardiman, Edward J. ....Pocono Pines, PA
Hardiman, Edward J., and Associates, P.C. Pocono Pines, PA
Hardiman, Eugene C. ....Chicago, IL
Hardiman, James L. ....Cleveland, OH
Hardiman, Jason E. ....New York, NY
Hardiman, John L. ....New York, NY
Hardiman, Johnette L. ....Miami, FL
Hardiman, Joseph R. ....Washington, DC
Hardiman, Kevin G. ....New York, NY
Hardiman, Lori Z. ....Pittsburgh, PA
Hardiman, Mark S. ....Los Angeles, CA
Hardiman, Mary B. ....Concord, NH
Hardiman, Megan ....Chicago, IL
Hardiman, Michael D. ....Philadelphia, PA
Hardiman, Michael F. ....San Francisco, CA
Hardiman, Morgan P. ....United States Senate, Senatorial Assistants, GV
Hardiman, P. Michael ....Arlington, VA
Hardiman, Patricia A. ....Chicago, IL
Hardiman, Patricia A., Ltd., Law Offices of Chicago, IL
Hardiman, Patricia A., Ltd., Law Offices of Chicago, IL
Hardiman, Patrick M. ....Chicago, IL
Hardiman, Paula Lynch ....Providence, RI
Hardiman, Roy Charles South San Francisco, CA
Hardiman, Therese Anne ....Pocono Pines, PA
Hardiman, Thomas M. ....Pittsburgh, PA
Hardimon, John C. ....Dallas, TX
Hardin, A. Edward ....Baton Rouge, LA
Hardin, A. Edward, Jr. ....Baton Rouge, LA
Hardin, A. Edward, PLC ....Baton Rouge, LA
Hardin, Adlai S., Jr. ....White Plains, NY
Hardin, Allain F. ....New Orleans, LA
Hardin, Allison Cahill ....Columbia, SC
Hardin, Barry L., (P.C.) ....Dallas, TX
Hardin, Ben ....Angleton, TX
Hardin, Carl C., Jr. ....Austin, TX
Hardin, Charles A. ....Tuscaloosa, AL
Hardin, Charles L. ....Cookeville, TN
Hardin, Charles R., Jr. ....Basking Ridge, NJ
Hardin, Charles V. ....Shamrock, TX
Hardin, Charles W., Jr. ....Cleveland, OH
Hardin, Charles William ....Mount Vernon, KY
Hardin, Cindy Ann ....Lakeland, FL
Hardin, Claude E., Jr. ....Columbia, SC
Hardin & Coffin, LLP San Luis Obispo, CA Santa Barbara, CA Ventura, CA
Hardin, David A. ....San Jose, CA
Hardin, David C. ....Fort Lauderdale, FL
Hardin, David E. ....Cincinnati, OH
Hardin, David G. ....Summit, NJ
Hardin, Dawson & Terry ....Fort Smith, AR
Hardin, Donald E. ....Cincinnati, OH
Hardin, Edward J. ....Atlanta, GA
Hardin, Edward L., Jr. (P.C.) Birmingham, AL
Hardin, Edward R. ....Banner Elk, NC
Hardin, Edwin C. ....Leakesville, MS
Hardin, Elaine C., Law Office of Tucson, AZ
Hardin, Eric W. ....Greensboro, NC
Hardin, F. Caroline ....Orlando, FL
Hardin, G. Robert ....Little Rock, AR
Hardin, G. Timothy ....Dallas, TX
Hardin, George R. ....Springfield, NJ
Hardin, Gina B. ....Denver, CO
Hardin, Gordon W. ....Austin, TX
Hardin, Grace A. Department Of Health And Human Services, Social Security Administration, GV
Hardin & Grace, A Professional Association Little Rock, AR
Hardin, Gregory Kevin ....Knoxville, TN
Hardin, Guy S. ....Shamrock, TX
Hardin, Hal D. ....Nashville, TN
Hardin & Hardin ....Hopkinsville, KY
Hardin & Hardin Associates, P.C. Dallas, TX
Hardin, Harry S., III ....New Orleans, LA
Hardin, Harry T., III ....Harvey, LA
Hardin & Hawkins, P.C. Birmingham, AL
Hardin, Henry T., III ....Chattanooga, TN
Hardin, Hess & Walsh ....Garnerville, NY
Hardin, Hord W. ....St. Louis, MO
Hardin, Irene C. ....Indianapolis, IN
Hardin, J. Scott ....Fort Smith, AR
Hardin, J. Thomas ....Inez, KY
Hardin, Jack F. ....Bellaire, TX
Hardin, James C., III ....Rock Hill, SC
Hardin, James K. ....Houston, TX
Hardin, James R. ....Sonora, CA
Hardin, James R., Jr. ....Washington, DC
Hardin, James T. ....Montgomery, AL
Hardin, Jane H. ....Morristown, NJ
Hardin, Janet Vest ....Johnson City, TN
Hardin, Jason Todd ....Louisville, KY
Hardin, Jay A. ....Mount Vernon, IL
Hardin, Jeffry L. ....Washington, DC
Hardin, Jesson & Terry ....Fort Smith, AR
Hardin, Joe K. ....Benton, AR
Hardin, John Charles ....McKinney, TX
Hardin, John O., III ....Hopkinsville, KY
Hardin, John T. ....Little Rock, AR
Hardin, John W., III ....River Forest, IL
Hardin, Julia P. ....Winston-Salem, NC
Hardin, Kelly A. ....St. Louis, MO
Hardin, Keyes C. ....New York, NY
Hardin, Kundla, McKeon, Poletto & Polifroni, P.A., A Professional Corporation Elizabeth, NJ Newark, NJ Springfield, NJ
Hardin, Lefton, Lazarus & Marks, LLC Cincinnati, OH
Hardin, Leslie M. ....New York, NY
Hardin, Lloyd T., Jr. ....Oklahoma City, OK
Hardin, Lu ....Russellville, AR
Hardin, M. Guy, Jr. ....Castroville, TX
Hardin, Mark A. ....Washington, DC
Hardin, Mark Edward ....Tulsa, OK
Hardin, Matthew S. ....Pittsburgh, PA
Hardin, Maxie Duran ....Dallas, TX
Hardin, Parkes & Kettering, PLLC Columbia, TN
Hardin, Patrick H. ....Knoxville, TN
Hardin, Paul, III ....Chapel Hill, NC
Hardin, Pauline F. ....New Orleans, LA
Hardin, Peter James ....Birmingham, AL
Hardin, P. H. ....Fort Smith, AR
Hardin, R. Jay ....Traverse City, MI
Hardin, Ray I. ....Short Hills, NJ
Hardin, Richard D. ....Chico, CA
Hardin, Rick D. ....Santa Barbara, CA
Hardin, Robert ....Department of Labor, Employment Standards Administration, GV
Hardin, Robert E., Sr. ....Rome, GA
Hardin, Robert N. ....Benton, AR
Hardin, Robert W. ....Russellville, AR
Hardin, Roseanne ....Boise, ID
Hardin, Roy W. ....Dallas, TX
Hardin, Rusty ....Houston, TX
Hardin, Rusty, & Associates, P.C. Houston, TX
Hardin & Schaffner, LPA Cambridge, OH Canton, OH **Carrollton, OH Dover, OH Millersburg, OH New Philadelphia, OH**
Hardin, Stacey L. ....Lebanon, KY
Hardin, Steven D. ....Indianapolis, IN
Hardin, Susan G. ....Columbus, GA
Hardin, Terrence J. ....Pasadena, CA
Hardin, Thomas W. New Philadelphia, OH
Hardin, Thomas W. ....Columbia, TN
Hardin, Walton ....Washington, GA
Hardin, William Andy ....Nashville, TN
Hardin, William D. ....Short Hills, NJ
Hardin, William M. ....Phoenix, AZ
Hardin, William W. ....Knoxville, IA
Hardin Curry, H.D. ....Covington, KY
Hardine, Kimberly A. ....McHenry, IL
Harding, Alan F. ....Presque Isle, ME
Harding, Ann Lea ....Department of Justice, Antitrust Division, GV

Hare, Bruce E. ....Amarillo, TX
Hare, C. Michael ....Honolulu, HI
Hare, Carol N. ....Norfolk, VA
Hare & Chaffin ....Boston, MA
Hare, Charles R., Jr. ....Albertville, AL
Hare, Claire Roberta ....Brooklyn, NY
Hare, Constance M. ....Baltimore, MD
Hare, Cornelius C., Jr. ....Southfield, MI
Hare, David B. ....Akron, OH
Hare, David B. ....Medina, OH
Hare, Dawn Wiggins ....Monroeville, AL
Hare, Deborah Frome ....Dallas, TX
Hare, Diana S. ....Philadelphia, PA
Hare, Elgart, Bryant, Stamm & Nassar
Springfield, MA
Hare, Francis H., Jr., (P.C.)
Birmingham, AL
Hare, George W. (Ben) ....Lansing, MI
Hare, Glenn P. ....Martinsburg, WV
Hare, Gregory J. ....Atlanta, GA
Hare, Hair & White, P.C.
Birmingham, AL
Hare and Hare ....Monroeville, AL
Hare & Hare ....Washington, DC
Hare, I. Edmund, Jr. ....Wethersfield, CT
Hare, J. Ryan ....Olathe, KS
Hare, James I., II ....Redfield, SD
Hare, J. C. ....Charleston, SC
Hare, Jeffrey L. ....Charleston, WV
Hare, John P. ....Pasadena, CA
Hare, Jon C. ....Oakville, WA
Hare, Joseph C. ....Philadelphia, PA
Hare, Kai Tamara ....San Jose, CA
Hare, Karen Queen ....Little Rock, AR
Hare, Kimberly A. ....Portland, OR
Hare, Kirsten B. ....Philadelphia, PA
Hare, Lynn Etheridge ....Birmingham, AL
Hare, Mark L. ....Springfield, MA
Hare, Michael B. ....Annapolis, MD
Hare, Neil E. ....Washington, DC
Hare, Nicholas D. ....Nashville, TN
Hare, Nicholas S. ....Monroeville, AL
Hare, Nicholas S., Jr. ....Monroeville, AL
Hare, Philip J. ....Washington, DC
Hare, Richard C. ....Trenton, NJ
Hare, Ronald ....Fillmore, UT
Hare, Scott M. ....Pittsburgh, PA
Hare, Verlanteree, (Ms.) ....Chicago, IL
Hare, Warren Evan ....Red Bank, NJ
Hare, William D. ....Washington, DC
Hare, Wynn, Newell and Newton
Birmingham, AL
Hareid, John T. ....Albert Lea, MN
Harel, Nir ....New York, NY
Harelick, Maxine E. ....Pearl River, NY
Harelick, Norman R. ....Mineola, NY
Harelson, Douglas E. ....Orinda, CA
Harelson, Gilbert ....La Mesa, CA
Haremski, Louis A. ....Buffalo, NY
Haren, Kimberly A. ....Philadelphia, PA
Haren, Mary Anne ....Dallas, TX
Haren, Sheila A. ....Philadelphia, PA
Haren, Stanley ....Calabasas, CA
Harens, John M. ....Minneapolis, MN
Harenza, Charles F. ....Reading, PA
Harenza, John A. ....Reading, PA
Harenza, Joseph M. ....Reading, PA
Harenza, Katherine L. ....Chicago, IL
Harenza, Kathryn K. ....Reading, PA
Hares, David I. ....St. Louis, MO
Harewood, Francesca D. ....Los Angeles, CA
Hareza, Randy K. ....Pittsburgh, PA
Harf, Cynthia M. ....San Diego, CA
Harfeld, David I.
Federal Energy Regulatory Commission,
Office of the Administrative Law Judges, GV
Harfenist, Kenneth ....Nanuet, NY
Harfenist, Stephen ....Jericho, NY
Harff, Charles H. ....Sewickley, PA
Harfield, Henry ....New York, NY
Harford, Russell W. ....Chadron, NE
Harfst, James A. ....St. Louis, MO
Harfst, Linda ....Madison, WI
Hargadon, Sean T. ....San Diego, CA
Hargadon, D. Scott ....Chicago, IL
Hargadon, Harry L., Jr. ....Louisville, KY
Hargadon, Lenihan, Harbolt & Herrington
La Grange, KY
Louisville, KY
Hargadon, Patrick C. ....Austin, TX
Hargadon & Wise, P.C. ....Austin, TX
Hargan, Eric D. ....Chicago, IL
Hargan, Mark C. ....Newport Beach, CA
Hargarten, James P. ....San Francisco, CA
Hargas, Katherine ....New York, NY
Hargate, Edwin V., III
Highland Heights, OH
Hargens, William F. ....Omaha, NE
Harger, Dale R. ....Worcester, MA
Harger, David N. ....McPherson, KS
Harger, Gary D. ....Sweetwater, TX
Harger, Horace N. ....Sebring, OH
Harger, J. Randolph
Indian Rocks Beach, FL
Harger, William G. ....Sugar Land, TX
Harges, Bobby Marzine ....New Orleans, LA
Hargesheimer, Elbert, III ....Hamburg, NY
Hargesheimer, Philip K. ....Lewiston, ME
Hargest, Robert F. ....Arlington, VA
Harget, Matthew E. ....Spokane, WA
Hargett, Bernard Coughlin ....Maysville, KY
Hargett, Charles B. ....Mount Olive, NJ
Hargett, Christopher W. ....Russellville, AL
Hargett, Jeffrey B. ....Charlotte, NC
Hargett, Paul R., Jr. ....Rock Hill, SC
Hargett, Robert L. ....Austin, TX
Hargett, Robert T. ....Raleigh, NC
Hargett, Thomas A. ....Indianapolis, IN
Hargett-Robinson, Deborah ....York, PA
Hargis, B. Newton ....Alexandria, LA
Hargis, Barbara E. ....Fort Worth, TX
Hargis, David M. ....Little Rock, AR
Hargis, David Michael ....Little Rock, AR
Hargis, Ed ....Miami, FL
Hargis, Hal ....Sugar Land, TX
Hargis & Harpold, L.L.P. ....Houston, TX
Hargis, J. Richard ....Houston, TX
Hargis, John A. ....Rockport, IN
Hargis, Lynn N. ....Washington, DC
Hargis, Michael S. ....Lexington, KY
Hargis, Michael T. ....Santa Ana, CA
Hargis, Rudolph D., Jr. ....Houston, TX
Hargis, Susan C. ....Fort Worth, TX
Hargis, V. Burns ....Oklahoma City, OK
Hargis, William J. ....Woodbury, MN
Hargiss, William S. ....Woodland Hills, CA
Hargitai, Peter P. ....Jacksonville, FL
Hargleroad, Jewell J. ....Oakland, CA
Hargleroad, Susan M. ....Denver, CO
Hargrafen, William J. ....Muscatine, IA
Hargrave, Alexander D. ....Rochester, NY
Hargrave, Allison C. ....Newport Beach, CA
Hargrave, Caryn L. M. ....Princeton, NJ
New York, NY
Hargrave, Dennis W. ....Sacramento, CA
Hargrave, Doris D. ....Gainesville, FL
Hargrave, Douglas ....Hillsborough, NC
Hargrave, John R. ....Oklahoma City, OK
Wewoka, OK
Hargrave, John W., & Associates
Westmont, NJ
Hargrave, Louis W. ....Baltimore, MD
Hargrave, Mark ....Kansas City, MO
Hargrave, Robert C. ....Steubenville, OH
Hargrave, Rudolph ....Oklahoma City, OK
Hargrave, W. Lee ....Baton Rouge, LA
Hargraves, Charles N. ....Los Angeles, CA
Hargraves, Daniel A. ....New York, NY
Hargraves, Dirck A. ....Silver Spring, MD
Hargraves, Karb, Wilcox & Galvani, LLP
Boston, MA
Framingham, MA
Hargraves, Kathryn M. ....Frankfort, KY
Hargraves & McCrary
Hot Springs National Park, AR
Hargraves, Robert S.
Hot Springs National Park, AR
Hargreaves, Carol Jacobson ....Toledo, OH
Hargreaves, Harry ....San Diego, CA
Hargreaves, J. William, Law Offices of
San Diego, CA
Hargreaves, Jeanette ....Cincinnati, OH
Hargreaves, Kelly A. ....Sacramento, CA
Hargreaves, Michael S. ....Waltham, MA
Hargreaves, Robert C. ....Olympia, WA
Hargreaves, Robert W.
Rancho Mirage, CA
Hargreaves-Heald, Geoffrey ....Boston, MA
Hargrove, Bedelia C ....Atlanta, GA
Hargrove, Beth Woodland ....Towson, MD
Hargrove, Brant L. ....Tallahassee, FL
Hargrove & Costanzo ....Fresno, CA
Hargrove, Danielle L. ....San Antonio, TX
Hargrove, David L. ....Mayfield, KY
Hargrove, Earl L., Jr. ....Richmond, VA
Hargrove, Edward ....Cotulla, TX
Hargrove, Frank D., Jr. ....Ashland, VA
Hargrove, Gayle D. ....Englewood, NJ
Hargrove, Gerry ....Detroit, MI
Hargrove, Greg S. ....Fort Worth, TX
Hargrove, J. Clayton ....Eatonton, GA
Hargrove, Jacko ....Houston, TX
Hargrove, James E. ....Lexington, KY
Hargrove, James L. ....El Dorado, KS
Hargrove, James T. ....Boston, MA
Hargrove, John J. ....San Diego, CA
Hargrove, John L. ....Washington, DC
Hargrove, John R. ....Fort Lauderdale, FL
Hargrove, John R. ....Trenton, NJ
Hargrove, John R., Jr. ....Glen Burnie, MD
Hargrove, John William ....Birmingham, AL
Hargrove, Joseph J. ....New York, NY
Hargrove, Joseph L., Jr. ....Shreveport, LA
Hargrove, Judith A. ....Austin, TX
Hargrove, Kathryn Koons ....Dallas, TX
Hargrove, Keith L. ....Salt Lake City, UT
Hargrove, Lorrie L. ....Birmingham, AL
Hargrove, Nancy Wilson ....Houston, TX
Hargrove, Nelson S. ....Houston, TX
Hargrove, Pesnell & Wyatt, A P.L.C.
Bossier City, LA
Shreveport, LA
Hargrove, Richard H. ....Fresno, CA
Hargrove, Robert H., III ....Sacramento, CA
Hargrove, Roger T. ....Phoenix, AZ
Hargrove, Stephen E. ....Odessa, TX
Hargrove, Susan E. ....Torrance, CA
Hargrove, Theodore A., III ....San Angelo, TX
Hargrove, Thomas W. ....Chicago, IL
Merrillville, IN
Hargrove, Todd R. ....Seattle, WA
Hargrove, Trent ....Harrisburg, PA
Hargrove, W. Richard ....Beaumont, TX
Hargrove, Wade H. ....Greensboro, NC
Raleigh, NC
HargroveBaker, PSC ....Lexington, KY
Hargrow, Craig ....Clarksville, TN
Hargus, Curtis D. ....Tecumseh, OK
Harhai, Stephen J. ....Denver, CO
Harhut, Chester T. ....Scranton, PA
Hariani, Hari M. ....Philadelphia, PA
Hariani, Hari M., P.C. ....Philadelphia, PA
Hariani, Sunil S. ....New York, NY
Haridakis, Paul M. ....Akron, OH
Haried, John M. ....Denver, CO
Harig, Lisa A. ....Washington, DC
Harig, Robert E. ....Oakbrook Terrace, IL
Harimoto, Ken ....Honolulu, HI
Harimoto, Ryan K. ....Honolulu, HI
Haring, Brian J. ....Cuyahoga Falls, OH
Haring, Christina L. ....Portland, OR
Haring, D. Brett ....Westwood, KS
Haring, David N. ....Mansfield, OH
Haring, Eugene M. ....Newark, NJ
Haring, Ruth Pinkham ....Chicago, IL
Haring, Sherri S. ....Richmond, VA
Haring, Thomas F. ....Wayne, NJ
Haring, William H. ....Denver, CO
Haring, William H., P.C. ....Denver, CO
Harinski, James M. ....Uniondale, NY
Hariri, Mahshid M. ....Los Angeles, CA
Hariri, Perry P. ....Pacific Palisades, CA
Hariri, Ronald D. ....Manhattan Beach, CA
New York, NY
Haris, Kim N. ....Department of Defense,
Defense Legal Services Agency, GV
Haritchabalet, Muriel C. ....Los Angeles, CA
Hariton, Carolyn J. ....Englewood, CO
Hariton, Carolyn Jane ....Englewood, CO
Hariton, David P. ....New York, NY
Hariton, Frank J. ....New York, NY
White Plains, NY
Hariton, Ira M. ....Bay Shore, NY
Hariton, Nicholas T. ....Los Angeles, CA
Haritos, Gus P. ....New York, NY
Harjani, Savita ....St. Paul, MN
Harjehausen, John D. ....Anchorage, AK
Harjo, Jennifer ....Wilmington, NC
Harjo, Yvette ....Ada, OK
Hark Andrucki ....Lewiston, ME
Hark, Clifford B. ....Miami, FL
Hark, Clifford B., P.A. ....Miami, FL
Hark, Jeffrey S. ....Cherry Hill, NJ
Hark, Ned ....Philadelphia, PA
Hark, Richard Q. ....Philadelphia, PA
Hark, Robert S. ....Lewiston, ME
Harkavy, Abraham I. ....West Orange, NJ
Harkavy, Alan M. ....Memphis, TN
Harkavy, Dennis G. ....Woodland Hills, CA
Harkavy, Goldman, Goldman & Caprio,
P.A., A Professional Corporation
Newark, NJ
West Orange, NJ
Harkavy, Harriet ....New York, NY
Harkavy, Ira B. ....Brooklyn, NY
Harkavy, John A. ....Oakland, CA
Harkavy, John B. ....Boston, MA
Harkavy, Jonathan R. ....Greensboro, NC
Harkavy, Lee A. ....Memphis, TN
Harkavy, Martin R. ....Sarasota, FL
Harkavy, Michelle S. ....Memphis, TN
Harkavy, Mitchell & Stewart, P.A.
Sarasota, FL
Harkavy, Nahomi ....Greensboro, NC
Harkavy, Neil ....Memphis, TN
Harkavy, Ronald M. ....Memphis, TN
Harkavy, Roy ....Breinigsville, PA
Harkavy, Shainberg, Kosten, Kaplan &
Dunstan, PC ....Memphis, TN
Harkavy, Steven Jeffrey ....New York, NY
Harkavy, Susan H. ....Brooklyn, NY
Harkaway, Aaron A. ....Nashua, NH
Harkaway, Barry I. ....Nashua, NH
Harkaway, William I. ....Washington, DC
Harkawik, Dennis P. ....Buffalo, NY
Harkcom, David I. ....Long Lake, MN
Harkcom, Gary V.
Department of Commerce,
Patent and Trademark Office, GV
Harke, Alison C. ....Miami, FL
Harke, Lance A. ....Miami, FL
Harkel-Rumford, Lynne ....Houston, TX
Harken, Grant L. ....Burien, WA
Harkenrider, Lawrence E. ....Cleveland, OH
Harker, Albert C. ....Marion, IN
Harker, Catherine A. ....Bellevue, WA
Harker, Donald F., III ....Dayton, OH
Harker, Drew A. ....Washington, DC
Harker, Edward W. ....Hackensack, NJ
Harker, Edward W. ....Carlisle, PA
Harker, James F. ....Wilmington, DE
Harker, James G. ....Newport Beach, CA
Harker, Jay D. ....Newport Beach, CA
Harker, Kenneth R., Jr. ....Richardson, TX
Harker, Michael ....Las Vegas, NV
Harker, R. Charles ....Alexandria, VA
Harker, Timothy L. ....Potomac, MD
Harkey, Averill C. ....Charlotte, NC
Harkey, Byron E., Jr. ....Oklahoma City, OK
Harkey, Christine S. ....Washington, DC
Harkey, Haynes L., Jr. ....Monroe, LA
Harkey, Henry A. ....Charlotte, NC
Harkey, Joanna L. ....Lubbock, TX
Harkey, John D., Jr. ....Dallas, TX
Harkey, John Norman ....Batesville, AR
Harkey, Lambeth, Nystrom, Fiorella &
Morrison, L.L.P. ....Charlotte, NC
Harkey, Michael J. ....Oklahoma City, OK
Harkey, Paul ....Dallas, TX
Harkey, Robert S. ....Atlanta, GA
Harkey, William T. ....Pascagoula, MS
Harkiewicz, Erin O'Brien
Philadelphia, PA
Harkiewicz, Steven N. ....San Antonio, TX
Harkin, Douglas G. ....Missoula, MT
Harkin, Edward C. ....Collingdale, PA
Harkin, George F. ....Hauppauge, NY
Harkin, Ruth R. ....Washington, DC
Harkins, Ann M. ....Department of Justice,
Office of the Attorney General, GV
Harkins & Associates ....Springfield, OH
Urbana, OH
Harkins, Brian J. ....Boston, MA
Harkins, Charles J., Jr. ....Washington, DC
Harkins, Christopher A. ....Chicago, IL
Harkins, Clinton Alan ....Atlanta, GA
Harkins Cunningham ....Washington, DC
Philadelphia, PA
Harkins, Daniel C. ....Springfield, OH
Harkins, Daniel M. ....Newport Beach, CA
Harkins, Daniel S. ....Danville, CA
Harkins, Deborah Duplechin
Baton Rouge, LA
New Orleans, LA
Harkins, Donald D. ....Lexington, KY
Harkins, Elizabeth ....Alexandria, VA
Harkins, Francis J., Jr.
West Palm Beach, FL
Harkins and Harkins ....Philadelphia, PA
Harkins, Harold L., Jr. ....Tampa, FL
Harkins, Harry H., Jr. ....Atlanta, GA
Durham, NC
Harkins & Hunte ....Mohegan Lake, NY
Harkins, J. Daniel ....San Antonio, TX
Harkins, James A. ....Niantic, CT
Harkins, James A. ....Tampa, FL
Harkins, James C., IV ....Irvine, CA
Harkins, Jane E. ....Beckley, WV
Harkins, Jas. L., Jr. ....Shaker Heights, OH
Harkins, Jim Neil ....Buffalo, OK
Laverne, OK
Harkins, John D. ....St. Louis, MO
Harkins, John G., Jr. ....Philadelphia, PA
Harkins, Joseph P. ....Washington, DC
Harkins, Kathleen M. ....New London, CT
Harkins, Kenneth R.
United States Court of Federal Claims, GV
Harkins, Kenneth V. ....New York, NY
Harkins, Kevin C. ....Pittsburgh, PA
Harkins, Kevin P. ....Ridgewood, NJ
Harkins, Kimberly K. ....Glendale, CA
Harkins, Kristin Jordan ....Dallas, TX
Harkins, L. James ....Akron, OH
Harkins, Latimer & Dahl, P.C.
San Antonio, TX
Harkins, Laurie N. ....Cleveland, OH
Harkins, Luke B. ....Kansas City, KS
Harkins, Malcolm J., III ....Washington, DC
Harkins, Mary Abbott ....Birmingham, AL
Harkins, Mary Anne M. ....Mohegan Lake, NY
Harkins, Mary E. ....Rocky Mount, VA
Harkins, Michael Jerome ....Houston, TX
Harkins, P. Nicholas, III ....Jackson, MS
Harkins, Patrick R. ....Washington, DC
Harkins, Paul F. ....Wyckoff, NJ
Harkins, Peter Codyre ....New York, NY
Harkins, Richard A. ....Bethesda, MD
Harkins, Richard O. ....Ekalaka, MT
Harkins, Richard S. ....Philadelphia, PA
Harkins, Robert F. ....Colorado Springs, CO
Harkins, Robert M., Jr. ....San Diego, CA
Harkins, Robert Wm. ....Middlebury, CT
Harkins & Sargent ....Danville, CA
Walnut Creek, CA
Harkins, Susan B. ....Marietta, GA
Harkins, Susan E. ....New York, NY
Harkins, Thad ....San Antonio, TX
Harkins, Thomas F., Jr. ....Fort Worth, TX
Harkins, Thomas S. ....Melville, NY
Harkins, Thos. I. ....Waltham, MA
Harkins, Tracy J. ....Mount Sinai, NY
Harkins, Vernon W. ....Tacoma, WA
Harkins, William D. ....Indianapolis, IN
Harkins, William H., Jr. ....Huntington, WV
Harkinson, Daniel J. ....Rochester, NH
Harkleroad, Donald R. ....Atlanta, GA
Harkleroad & Hermance, A Professional
Corporation ....Atlanta, GA
Harkleroad, Roy E. ....Douglas, GA
Harkless, Angela ....Chicago, IL
Harkless, James M. ....Washington, DC
Harkness, Andrew M. ....Rochester, NY
Harkness, Angela ....Westford, MA
Harkness, Dawn FitzGerald
Framingham, MA
Harkness, Diana K. ....Columbus, OH
Harkness, Donna S. ....Pensacola, FL
Harkness, Gwendolyn C. ....Alexandria, VA
Harkness, Harvey D. ....Marietta, GA
Harkness, James A. ....Trenton, NJ
Harkness, James S. ....Chicago, IL
Harkness, John F., Jr. ....Tallahassee, FL
Harkness, Karen S. ....Miami, FL
Harkness, Loring E., III ....Denver, CO
Harkness, Richard M. ....Muncie, IN
Harkness, Robert H. ....Southfield, MI
Harkness, Scott A. ....Indianapolis, IN
Harkness, Thomas R. ....Austin, TX
Harkness, Timothy P. ....New York, NY
Harkness, Wanda J. ....Austin, TX
Harkov, Anderson D. ....East Brunswick, NJ
Harkow, Lincoln D. ....Forest Hills, NY
Harkrader, Carleton A. ....Washington, DC
Harkrader, Clyde M. B. ....Mineral, VA
Harkrader, Fletcher W., III ....Louisa, VA
Harkrader, F. W., Jr. ....Louisa, VA
Harkrader, Trent Lloyd Bruce ....
Federal Communications Commission, GV
Harkrider, John D. ....New York, NY
Harl, Neil E. ....Ames, IA
Harla, Harlan A. ....Belleville, IL
Harla, William ....Teaneck, NJ
Harlamert, Irvin H., Jr. ....Dayton, OH
Harlan, Alan J. ....Dallas, TX
Harlan, Barry T. ....Encino, CA
Harlan, Bruce L. ....Littlefield, TX
Lubbock, TX
Harlan, Bruce M., P.A. ....Clearwater, FL
Harlan, Bruce O. ....Blytheville, AR
Harlan, Catherine M. ....Clearwater, FL
Harlan, Daniel J. ....St. Louis, MO
Harlan, Danielle ....Lexington, KY

Harmon, Susan S. ....New York, NY
Harmon & Sutter ....Alva, OK
Harmon, T. Craig ....Richmond, VA
Harmon, Teresa Wilton ....Chicago, IL
Harmon, Thomas D. ....Minneapolis, MN
Harmon, Thomas E. ....Coldwater, MI
Harmon, Thomas H. ....Pierre, SD
Harmon, Thomas K. ....Omaha, NE
Harmon, Thomas M. ....Long Beach, CA
Harmon, Thomas S. ....Tampa, FL
Harmon, Thomas S. ....San Antonio, TX
Harmon, Thomas W. ....Anniston, AL
Harmon, Timothy J. ....San Francisco, CA
Harmon, Timothy R. ....Portland, OR
Harmon, Timothy S. ....Tulsa, OK
Harmon & Tootell ....Lafayette, CA
San Francisco, CA
Harmon, Vanessa R. ....Columbus, OH
Harmon, William B. ....Baltimore, MD
Harmon, William J. ....Los Angeles, CA
Harmon, William J. ....Chicago, IL
Harmon, William J., III
San Francisco, CA
Harmon, William R. ....Pasadena, CA
Harmon & Wilmot, L.L.P.
Washington, DC
Harmon, Yvette ....New York, NY
Harmon, Zachary J. ....Washington, DC
Harmond, George M., Jr. ....Price, UT
Harmonis, Michael P.
Department of Justice, Antitrust Division, GV
Harmon-McQueen, M. Kathlene
Charleston, WV
Harms, Allan L. ....Cedar Rapids, IA
Harms, Brian G. ....Roseland, NJ
Harms, Bruce L. ....Madison, WI
Harms, Charles D. ....Portland, OR
Harms, Charles F., Jr. ....New York, NY
Harms, Christina L. ....Boston, MA
Harms, Clark Allen ....Salt Lake City, UT
Harms, David B. ....New York, NY
Harms, Donald C. ....Farmington Hills, MI
Harms, Donn K. ....San Diego, CA
Harms, Edward C., Jr. ....Springfield, OR
Harms, Gus ....Waterloo, WI
Harms, Jeanette S. ....San Jose, CA
Harms, Jeffrey C. ....Houston, TX
Harms, Joe G., II ....St. Louis, MO
Harms, Julie A. ....Chicago, IL
Harms, Julius F. ....New Brunswick, NJ
Harms Law Offices, Ltd. ....Bismarck, ND
Harms, Lisa M. ....Springfield, IL
Harms, Mark R. ....Lake Bluff, IL
Harms, Michael S. ....Mission Viejo, CA
Harms, Richard ....Melville, NY
Harms, Richard A. ....Oakland, CA
Harms, Robert G. ....Bowling Green, OH
Harms, Robert J. ....Atlanta, GA
Harms, Robert W. ....Bismarck, ND
Harms, Sally M. ....San Francisco, CA
Harms, Samuel D., III ....Arlington, VA
Harms, Stephen J. ....Indianapolis, IN
Harms, Steven A. ....Birmingham, MI
Harms, Thomas E. ....Minneapolis, MN
Harms, Wendell J. ....Des Moines, IA
Harmsen, Carpenter, Sidell & Olson, A Law Corporation ....San Diego, CA
Harmsen, Harlan F. ....San Diego, CA
Harmsen, Stephen ....Salt Lake City, UT
Harmsen, William R. ....Los Angeles, CA
Harmssen, Robert H. ....San Jose, CA
Harmsworth, Esmond V. ....Boston, MA
Harmuth, Raymond J., Jr. ....Pittsburgh, PA
Harn, Joy M. Fernbach ....Los Angeles, CA
Harn, Terry G. ....Chapel Hill, NC
Harn, William Davis ....Rosemead, CA
Harnack, Don S. ....Chicago, IL
Harnage, Henry H. ....Miami, FL
Harnagel, Breke J. ....Lakewood, CO
Harnden, Edwin A. ....Portland, OR
Harnden, Ernest F., Jr. ....Sarasota, FL
Harnden, Ron H. ....Wichita, KS
Harnden, Thomas L. ....Barberton, OH
Harned & Associates ....Sacramento, CA
Harned, Bachert & Denton
Bowling Green, KY
Harned, Kenneth ....Lansing, MI
Harned & McMeen ....Marengo, IA
Harned, Michael L. ....Frankfort, KY
Harned, Nicholas S. ....Madison, WI
Harned, Norman E. ....Bowling Green, KY
Harned, Pete ....Sacramento, CA
Harned, Price ....Mountain Home, AR
Harned, W. Price ....Mountain Home, AR
Harnedy, Edmund R. ....New York, NY
Harner, Harry E. ....Columbia, SC
Harner, Heather J.
Department Of Veterans Affairs, Board of Veterans Appeals, GV
Harner, Heather J. Mumma ....Mount Joy, PA
Harner, Janet G. ....Pittsburgh, PA
Harner, Paul E. ....Columbus, OH
Harner, Timothy R. ....Le Roy, NY
Harnes, Joan T. ....New York, NY
Harnes, John F. ....New York, NY
Harness, Charles Byan ....Clarksville, MD
Harness, Charles L. ....Clarksville, MD
Harness, Dickey & Pierce, P.L.C.
Washington, DC
Ann Arbor, MI
Detroit, MI
Troy, MI
Harness, Gordon A. ....New Castle, OK
Harness, Hugh G. ....Detroit, MI
Harness, Inona Jane ....Oklahoma City, OK
Harness, Melody L. ....Gainesville, FL
Harness, Philip S. ....Olathe, KS

Harness, Suzanne ....Washington, DC
Harness, Walter W., Jr. ....Atlanta, GA
Harnetiaux, Bryan P. ....Spokane, WA
Harnett, Andrea L. ....Washington, DC
Harnett, Bertram ....Boca Raton, FL
Harnett, Christopher J. ....New York, NY
Harnett, Christopher M., Jr.
Oakland, CA
Harnett, Cynthia L. ....Cheyenne, WY
Harnett, Daniel J. ....Los Angeles, CA
Harnett, Doris A. ....Augusta, ME
Harnett, Jack A. ....Quincy, FL
Harnett, James D. ....Madison, WI
Harnett, John M. ....Providence, RI
Harnett, Lawrence M. ....Pittsfield, MA
Harnett Lesnick & Ripps, P.A.
Boca Raton, FL
Harnett, Matt ....Rutland, VT
Harnett, Melissa M. ....Los Angeles, CA
Harnett, Nancy M. ....New York, NY
Harnett, Nicole T. ....Los Angeles, CA
Harnett & Slay ....Quincy, FL
Harnett, Thomas A. ....Augusta, ME
Harnett, Thomas A. ....New York, NY
Harney, Darlene H. ....Denver, CO
Harney, David T. ....Los Angeles, CA
Harney, Edward F., Jr. ....Indianapolis, IN
Harney, Francis J. ....Boston, MA
Harney, Gerard P. ....San Diego, CA
Harney, James J. ....Fairfax, VA
Harney, Jeanne M. ....Boston, MA
Harney, John R. ....Washington, DC
Harney, John W. ....Boston, MA
Harney, Julie A. ....Los Angeles, CA
Harney Law Offices, A Legal Corporation
Los Angeles, CA
Harney, Michael J. ....Boston, MA
Harney, Naomi R. ....Amarillo, TX
Harney, Peter P. ....Natick, MA
Harney, Stephen M. ....Millis, MA
Harney, Thomas C. ....Atlanta, GA
Harney, Thomas Roy ....Palm Desert, CA
Harney, Timothy L. ....Chicago, IL
Harnice, Paul C. ....Frankfort, KY
Harnick, Ellen A. ....New York, NY
Harnick & Harnick ....New York, NY
Harnick, Robert M. ....New York, NY
Harnik, Brian S. ....Indian Wells, CA
Harnik, Stephen M., Law Offices of
New York, NY
Harnisch, Alan C. ....Bingham Farms, MI
Harnisch & Associates, P.C.
Bingham Farms, MI
Detroit, MI
Harnisch, Elizabeth K. ....New York, NY
Harnisch, Kevin J.
Securities and Exchange Commission, Division of Enforcement, GV
Harnisch, Linda L. ....New York, NY
Harnisch, Ronald F. ....New York, NY
Harnisch, Thomas W. ....Madison, WI
Harnisch, William O'C. ....Stamford, CT
Harnish, David L. ....Pittsburgh, PA
Harnish, Jenney, Mitchell and Resh
Boston, MA
Waltham, MA
Harnish, Jonathan T. ....Portland, OR
Harnish, Sara L. ....Boston, MA
Harnishfeger, John G. ....Washington, DC
Harnois, Albert J., Jr. ....Pasadena, CA
Harnois, Deborah L. ....Lincoln, RI
Harnsberger, Richard S. ....Lincoln, NE
Harnsberger, Thomas L. ....Los Angeles, CA
Haro, Cindy W. ....Wausau, WI
Haroche, Bob ....Sebastopol, CA
Haroff, Kevin T. ....Palo Alto, CA
Haroian, John D. ....Cambridge, MA
Haroian, Richard ....San Diego, CA
Harokopus, Mary L. ....Plano, TX
Harold, Christopher ....White Plains, NY
Harold, Douglas W., Jr. ....Washington, DC
Manassas, VA
Stephens City, VA
Harold, Edward F. ....New Orleans, LA
Harold, Elliotte M., Jr. ....New Orleans, LA
Harold, John T. ....Garden City, NY
Harold, Leahy, Trudeau & Kieran
Eugene, OR
Springfield, OR
Harold, Michael D. ....Metairie, LA
New Orleans, LA
Harold, Patricia Ann ....Garden City, NY
Harold, Paul D. ....Quincy, MA
Harold, Rosemary C. ....Washington, DC
Harold, Salant, Strassfield & Spielberg
White Plains, NY
Harold, Susan Kott ....Schaumburg, IL
Harold, Timothy J. ....Springfield, OR
Haroldsen, Orvil O. ....Canoga Park, CA
Haroldson, Delwyn G. ....Denver, CO
Haroldson, Thomas E. ....New York, NY
Haron, David L. ....Troy, MI
Haron, Rodney C. ....Fresno, CA
Haronian, Howard R. ....Warwick, RI
Haronian, Paquin, Bramley & Harrington, Inc.
Warwick, RI
Haroonian, Alexander ....Los Angeles, CA
Harootunian, John P. ....Treasury Department, Office of Thrift Supervision, GV
Harootunian, Sarkis L. ....Syracuse, NY
Harootunian, Shant J. ....Westwood, NJ
Haros, Nicholas Charles ....Stroudsburg, PA
Harounian, Debra D. ....New York, NY
Harounian, Jacqueline ....Great Neck, NY
Harouse, David Kyle ....Pittsburgh, PA
Haroutunian, Krista Licata ....Southfield, MI
Haroutunian, Lucy ....Houston, TX
Haroutunian, Susan Licata ....Detroit, MI

Harowitz, David J. ....Tempe, AZ
Harowitz, David J., P.C. ....Phoenix, AZ
Tempe, AZ
Harowitz, Filmore S. ....Philadelphia, PA
Harowitz, Steven M. ....San Francisco, CA
Haroz, Audrey E. ....New York, NY
Haroz, Michael J. ....Boston, MA
Harp, Aaron ....San Diego, CA
Harp, B. Seth, Jr. ....Columbus, GA
Harp, Chadwick Allen ....Norristown, PA
Harp, Charles H., II ....Denton, NC
Lexington, NC
Harp, Charles L., Jr. ....Haddonfield, NJ
Harp, Darrell W. ....Clifton Park, NY
Harp, David K. ....Fort Smith, AR
Harp, Heidi P. ....Gadsden, AL
Harp, Hilary ....Atlanta, GA
Harp, J. Anderson ....Columbus, GA
Harp, James H. ....San Angelo, TX
Harp, Jason G. ....Chicago, IL
Harp, Jay Andrew ....Indianapolis, IN
Harp, Jeri G. ....Marietta, GA
Harp & Johnson, P.C. ....Columbus, GA
Harp, Malinda Dexter ....Cleveland, OH
Harp, Marilyn M. ....Wichita, KS
Harp, Osa Jackson, III ....Brooksville, FL
Harp, R. Kymn ....Chicago, IL
Harp, Reno S., III ....Richmond, VA
Harp, Robert D. ....Chico, CA
Harp, Robert L. ....New Paltz, NY
Harp, Wendell D. ....New Paltz, NY
Harp, William R. ....Atlanta, GA
Harpe, Clifford W., Jr. ....Cordele, GA
Harpel, Joanne L. ....New York, NY
Harpell, Cherie L. ....Oakland, CA
Harpen, Shawn M. ....Los Angeles, CA
Harper, A. John, II ....Houston, TX
Harper, Alan ....Medford, OR
Harper, Alan J. ....Cheyenne, WY
Harper, Albert B. ....Hartford, CT
Harper, Albert L., Jr. ....Little Rock, CA
Harper, Alex A. ....San Diego, CA
Harper, Anne C. ....San Francisco, CA
Harper, Anne C. ....Seattle, WA
Harper, Anne T. ....Tucson, AZ
Harper, Ashley A. ....Houston, TX
Harper, Aubrey L. ....McMinnville, TN
Harper, Belle ....New York, NY
Harper, Benita F. ....San Antonio, TX
Harper, Blake M. ....San Diego, CA
Harper, Blaney ....Washington, DC
Harper & Blocker ....Springdale, AR
Harper, Bonnie C. ....New York, NY
Harper, Brian D., Law Office of
Twin Falls, ID
Harper, Burch A. ....Palo Alto, CA
Harper & Burns, L.L.P. ....Orange, CA
Harper, C. David ....Tampa, FL
Harper, Candice B. ....Sacramento, CA
Harper, Catherine M.
Fort Washington, PA
Harper, Charles C. ....Fort Lauderdale, FL
Harper, Charles Edward ....Jackson, MS
Harper, Charles L. ....Reno, NV
Harper, Charles N. ....Lake Charles, LA
Harper, Charles W., II ....Junction City, KS
Harper, Cheryl Lee ....Atlanta, GA
Harper, Chris ....Oklahoma City, OK
Harper, Chris B. ....Dallas, TX
Harper, Connye Y. ....Detroit, MI
Harper, Conrad K. ....New York, NY
Harper, Daniel R. ....Downers Grove, IL
Harper, David ....Stuart, FL
Harper, David A. ....Saratoga Springs, NY
Harper, David C. ....Bridgeton, NJ
Harper, David H. ....Dallas, TX
Harper, David S. ....Chicago, IL
Harper, David W. ....Louisville, KY
Harper, David W. ....Portland, OR
Harper, David W., P.C. ....Portland, OR
Harper, Dennis J. ....Sterling Heights, MI
Harper, Derry ....Atlanta, GA
Harper, Donald A. ....Greenville, SC
Harper, Donald W. ....Rock Hill, SC
Harper, Dorothy J. ....St. Louis, MO
Harper, Douglas B. ....Chicago, IL
Harper, Douglas B. ....West Des Moines, IA
Harper, Douglas J. ....Newark, NJ
Harper & Driver ....Philadelphia, PA
Harper, Duncan M. ....Sioux City, IA
Harper, Eddie ....McAlester, OK
Harper, Edward J., II ....Greenville, NC
Harper, Edwin A. ....Richmond, VA
Harper, Elisabeth J. ....Washington, DC
Harper, Elizabeth Ann ....Carrollton, TX
Harper, Emery W. ....Washington, DC
Harper, Ernest H., Jr. ....Little Rock, AR
North Little Rock, AR
Harper, Eugene W., Jr. ....Hartwell, GA
Harper, Eugene W., Jr. ....New York, NY
Harper, Eugene W., Jr., P.C.
Hartwell, GA
Harper, Evans & Schneider
Columbia, MO
Harper, F. Mikell ....Beaufort, SC
Harper, Ferguson & Davis ....Louisville, KY
Harper, Frampton L., II ....Beaufort, SC
Harper, Franklin M. ....Broken Arrow, OK
Harper, Fred P., Jr. ....New Orleans, LA
Harper, G. Thomas ....Jacksonville, FL
Harper, Gail Ellen ....San Francisco, CA
Harper, Geoffrey S. ....Dallas, TX
Harper, George ....Upper Marlboro, MD
Harper, George A. ....Little Rock, AR
Harper, George A. ....Atlanta, GA
Harper, George E. ....Fresno, CA
Harper, George R., (P.A.) ....Miami, FL
Harper, Georgia K. ....Austin, TX

Harper, Gerard E. ....New York, NY
Harper, Glenda ....Columbus, GA
Harper, Godfrey W., III ....Princeton, NJ
Harper, Gregory L. ....Jackson, MS
Harper, Gregory L. ....Bellevue, WA
Harper, Gregory Lee ....Emeryville, CA
Harper, H. Don ....Sparta, GA
Harper, H. Lon ....Houston, TX
Harper, Harlan, Jr. ....Dallas, TX
Harper, Harold C. ....Valparaiso, IN
Harper, Harold Thomas ....Valparaiso, IN
Harper and Harper ....Hartford, CT
Harper & Harper ....Beaufort, SC
Harper & Harper, Ltd. ....Reno, NV
Harper, Harry C. ....Carpinteria, CA
Harper, Harry L. ....Panama City, FL
Harper, Herbert C. ....Department of Defense, Armed Services Board of Contract Appeals, GV
Harper, Hornbaker, Altenhofen & Opat, Chartered ....Junction City, KS
Harper, J. Bruce ....Clearwater, FL
Harper, J. Frank ....Santa Fe Springs, CA
Harper, J. Glen ....Anchorage, AK
Harper, J. Lavell ....Lakeside, AZ
Harper, Jack C. ....St. Louis, MO
Harper, Jack H. ....Allentown, PA
Harper, Jack H. ....Tyler, TX
Harper, Jack R. ....Helena, MT
Harper, Jake Richey ....New York, NY
Harper, James ....Duluth, MN
Harper, James A. ....Moline, IL
Harper, James, Jr. ....Old Greenwich, CT
Harper, James L. ....Nashville, TN
Harper, James L., Jr. ....Northbrook, IL
Harper, James R. ....Redlands, CA
Harper, James R. ....Beaver City, NE
Harper, James R., Jr. ....Mobile, AL
Harper, James T.
United States Court Of Appeals For The Armed Forces, GV
Harper, James W. ....House of Representatives, Committee Legal Personnel, GV
Harper, James W. ....Cincinnati, OH
Harper, James W. ....Fort Worth, TX
Harper, Jane V. ....Charlotte, NC
Harper, Jason B. ....Kansas City, MO
Harper, Jeanne Schick ....Glencoe, IL
Harper, Jeff C. ....Springdale, AR
Harper, Jeffrey A. ....Fairfield, CA
Oakland, CA
Harper, Jeffrey R. ....Wolcott, NY
Harper, Jennifer L. ....Richmond, VA
Harper, Jerald R. ....Shreveport, LA
Harper, Jerry L. ....Topeka, KS
Harper, Jerry W., Jr. ....Chattanooga, TN
Harper, Jessica J. ....Atlanta, GA
Harper, Joanne Esposito ....New York, NY
Harper, John A. ....Green Valley, AZ
Harper, John B. ....Birmingham, AL
Harper, John Dean ....Las Vegas, NV
Harper, John G. ....Orlando, FL
Harper, John E., Jr. ....Tulsa, OK
Harper, John G. ....Orlando, FL
Harper, John I., (P.C.) ....Augusta, GA
Harper, John, III (P.A.) ....Minneapolis, MN
Harper, John J. ....Morristown, NJ
Harper, John O. ....Springfield, OH
Harper, John R. ....Orange, CA
Harper, John S. ....Washington, DC
Harper, John V. ....Americus, GA
Harper, John W. ....New York, NY
Harper, John Y., Jr. ....San Antonio, TX
Harper, Jon V. ....Salt Lake City, UT
Harper, Jonathan J. ....Morristown, NJ
Harper, Joseph A. ....Big Rapids, MI
Harper, Joseph John, Jr. ....Tarboro, NC
Harper, Joyce W. ....Marietta, GA
Harper, Kathleen M. ....Santa Ana, CA
Harper, Keith C. ....Port Townsend, WA
Harper, Keith M. ....Washington, DC
Harper, Kenneth A. ....Scottsdale, AZ
Harper, Kenneth A. ....Monticello, AR
Harper, Kenneth L. ....Jonesboro, LA
Harper, Kenneth W. ....Yakima, WA
Harper, Kevin P. ....Cherry Hill, NJ
Harper, Kevin R. ....Tucson, AZ
Harper, Kim L. ....DeSoto, TX
Harper, Kimberly A. ....Jefferson City, MO
Harper, Kimberly D. ....Chicago, IL
Harper, K. P. Dean ....Walnut Creek, CA
Harper, Krista Pool ....Doylestown, PA
Harper, Kurt A. ....Wichita, KS
Harper, Kynes, Geller, Watson & Buford, P.A. ....Clearwater, FL
Harper, Larry W. ....Birmingham, AL
Harper, Laura C. ....Santa Fe, NM
Harper, Laura S. ....Washington, DC
Harper Law Firm, P.C. ....Billings, MT
Bridger, MT
Harper Law Firm, The, P.A.
Greenville, SC
Harper Law Office ....Big Rapids, MI
Harper, Leigh O. ....San Bernardino, CA
Harper, Lesly Robyn ....East Orange, NJ
Harper, Lisa Fivars ....Atlanta, GA
Harper, Lubbie, Jr. ....New Haven, CT
Harper, Lynne L. ....Henderson, NV
Harper, M. Bruce ....Norfolk, VA
Harper, Mark N. ....Augusta, GA
Harper, Marlin J. ....St. Clairsville, OH
Harper & Marti ....Warren, PA
Harper, Marty ....Phoenix, AZ
Tucson, AZ
Harper, Matthew D. ....Toledo, OH
Harper, Meaghan E. ....Lakeville, MN
Harper, Melissa A. ....Menlo Park, CA
Harper, Meredith A. ....Orlando, FL
Harper, Michael F. ....Franklin, IN

Harper, Michael G. ... Sacramento, CA
Harper, Michael H. ... Denver, CO
Harper, Michael H., Jr. ... Minneapolis, MN
Harper, Michael J. ... Fountain Hills, AZ
Harper, Michael S. ... Tallassee, AL
Harper, Michael S. ... Lafayette, LA
Harper, Milton E., Jr., P.C.
Columbia, MO
Harper, Mitchell T. ... Knoxville, TN
Harper, Monica Lafferty ... Hartford, CT
Harper, Nolan S. ... Jackson, MS
Harper, P. Bruce, P.C. ... Billings, MT
Bridger, MT
Harper, Paige A. ... Miami, FL
Harper, Pamela R. ... Minden, LA
Harper & Paul ... Philadelphia, PA
Harper, Paul A. ... Fallston, MD
Harper Peterson Rogers & Reno, P.A.
Rock Hill, SC
Harper, Phyllis C. ... Baytown, TX
Harper, & Pitts ... Fort Worth, TX
Harper & Pozefsky ... Saratoga Springs, NY
Harper, R. Victor ... Star City, AR
Harper, Rachael Kearse ... Beaufort, SC
Harper, Ralph A. ... San Fernando, CA
Harper, Ralph A. ... Houston, TX
Harper, Ralph E. ... Rochester, NY
Harper, Randall W. ... Walnut Creek, CA
Harper, Richard A. ... New Castle, PA
Harper, Richard B. ... Sylva, NC
Harper, Richard B. ... Richmond, VA
Harper, Richard C. ... Hayward, CA
Harper, Rita I. ... Hayward, CA
Harper, Robert Augustus, Jr.
Tallahassee, FL
Harper, Robert C. ... Brunswick, GA
Harper, Robert C., Jr.
Treasury Department, GV
Harper, Robert E. ... Coraopolis, PA
Pittsburgh, PA
Harper, Robert F. ... Garden City, NY
Harper, Robert G. ... Washington, DC
Chevy Chase, MD
Harper, Robert H. ... Memphis, TN
Harper, Robert P. ... Valparaiso, IN
Harper, Robert T. ... Philadelphia, PA
Pittsburgh, PA
Harper, Roeliff E. ... Mansfield, OH
Harper, Roger C. ... New York, NY
Harper, Ronald J. ... Philadelphia, PA
Harper, Ronald L. ... Memphis, TN
Harper, Ronnie L. ... Natchez, MS
Harper, Roy Ellis ... Nevada City, CA
Harper, Roy W. ... St. Louis, MO
Harper, Royce N. ... Lincoln, NE
Harper, Ruth Milner ... Utica, NY
Harper, Sara J. ... Cleveland, OH
Harper, Sarah Shuman ... Macon, GA
Harper, Scott ... Aspen, CO
Harper, Scott C. ... St. Louis, MO
Harper, Scott L. ... Bakersfield, CA
Harper, Scott L. ... Dallas, TX
Harper, Scott, P.C. ... Aspen, CO
Harper, Spencer E., Jr. ... Louisville, KY
Harper, Stephen D. ... Houston, TX
Harper, Stephen J. ... Albertville, AL
Harper, Stephen L. ... Dublin, OH
Harper, Stephen S. ... Orinda, CA
Harper, Steven J., (P.C.) ... Chicago, IL
Harper, Steven K. ... Hotchkiss, CO
Harper, Steven M. ... Conway, AR
Harper, Susan Ritz ... Uniontown, PA
Harper, Tara L. ... New York, NY
Harper, Terry D. ... Fayetteville, AR
Harper, Theodore Raymond ... Raleigh, NC
Harper, Thomas A. ... Moline, IL
Harper, Thomas B., III ... Philadelphia, PA
Harper, Thomas D. ... Atlanta, GA
Harper, Thomas D. ... Las Vegas, NV
Harper, Thomas D., Ltd. A Prof. Corp.
Las Vegas, NV
Harper, Thomas F. ... Phoenix, AZ
Harper, Thomas L., Jr. ... Charleston, SC
Harper, Thomas O., III ... Durham, NC
Harper, Thomas R. ... Indianapolis, IN
Harper, Tom, Jr., (PLC) ... Fort Smith, AR
Harper, Troy J. ... Brookville, PA
Harper, Vesta T. ... Dallas, TX
Harper, Virginia A. ... Saddle Brook, NJ
Harper, W. Wayne ... Butte, MT
Harper, Waldon & Craig ... Atlanta, GA
Harper, Walter G. ... Cleveland, OH
Harper, Ward ... Salt Lake City, UT
Harper, Wesley E. ... Williamston, MI
Harper, William B., Jr. ... Miami, FL
Harper, William Beach, II ... Castlewood, VA
Harper, William D. ... St. Paul, MN
Harper, William L. ... Atlanta, GA
Harper, William L. ... Reno, NV
Harper, William R., Jr. ... Coraopolis, PA
Harper, Willis H., Jr. ... Whiteville, NC
Harper, Wm. Bruce, Jr. ... Miami, FL
Harper, Young, Smith & Maurras, PLC
Fort Smith, AR
Van Buren, AR
Harper, Zenola ... Farmington, CT
Harper-Hunter, Kimberly ... Charlotte, NC
Harpham, Elisabeth W. ... Kennett Square, PA
Harpham, Sarah L. ... San Francisco, CA
Harpham, Wilfred J. ... Kelseyville, CA
Harpin, William C. ... Boxford, MA
Harpold, David L. ... Kent, WA
Harpold, Grant P. ... Houston, TX
Harpold, Lew W. ... Houston, TX
Harpold, Robert R., Jr. ... Charleston, WV
Harpold, Stephen B. ... Houston, TX
Harpold, Stephen K. ... Kent, WA
Harpole, J. Marinda ... Washington, DC
Harpole, John W. ... Louisville, KY
Harpole, Myron E. ... Pasadena, CA
Harpool, M. Douglas ... Springfield, MO
Harpootian, John M. ... Providence, RI
Harpootlian, Richard A. ... Columbia, SC
Harpring, James George ... Vero Beach, FL
Harpring, Michael R. ... Indianapolis, IN
Harps, Joseph P. ... Roswell, GA
Harpst, Carlton L. ... Orange, CA
Harpst, Ronald J. ... Middleburg Heights, OH
Harpst, Todd A. ... Canton, OH
Harpster, Dawn R. ... Kansas City, MO
Harpster, James E. ... Memphis, TN
Harpster, Pamela S. ... Topeka, KS
Harpster, Russell L. ... Ashland, OH
Harr, Brian L. ... Omaha, NE
Harr, Donald J. ... Oklahoma City, OK
Harr, E. David ... Greensburg, PA
Harr, J. Ernest ... Rock Hill, SC
Harr, James J. ... Hemet, CA
Harr, Jennifer K. ... Los Angeles, CA
Harr, Josie Olsvig ... Dayton, OH
Harr, Karl G., Jr. ... Washington, DC
Harr, Kevin M. ... Los Angeles, CA
Harr, Lawrence F. ... Omaha, NE
Harr, Michael E. ... Denver, CO
Harr, Nancy Stallard ... Knoxville, TN
Harr, Randall L. ... Redding, CA
Harr, Steven A. ... Dallas, TX
Harr, Thomas Alan ... Prairie Village, KS
Harr, Timothy A. ... Washington, DC
Harr, W. Clyde ... Andalusia, AL
Harr, W. Clyde, III, P.C. ... Andalusia, AL
Harradine, David A. ... Rochester, NY
Harragan, Edwin J., Jr. ... New York, NY
Harragarra Waters, Deana J. ... Boulder, CO
Harrah, Eugene ... Carmel, CA
Harrah, Michael K. ... Oklahoma City, OK
Harrahy, Thomas F. ... Auburn, MA
Harraka, Dennis G. ... Hackensack, NJ
Harraka, Joseph G., Jr. ... Irvine, CA
Harral, John M. ... Biloxi, MS
Harral, John M. ... Gulfport, MS
Harral, Larry S. ... Tulsa, OK
Harrall, Eldon R., Jr. ... Houma, LA
Harralson, Daniel L. ... Fresno, CA
Harralson, James G. ... Birmingham, AL
Atlanta, GA
Harralson, John H., III ... Louisville, KY
Harraman, Brent M. ... Marion, OH
Harrang, James P. ... Eugene, OR
Harrang, Kevin J. ... Redmond, WA
Harrang Long Gary Rudnick P.C.
San Jose, CA
Eugene, OR
Roseburg, OR
Salem, OR
Harrar, Peter C. ... New York, NY
Harras, John A. ... Melville, NY
Harras, Steven ... Melville, NY
Harray & Linker ... Monterey, CA
Santa Cruz, CA
Harray, Richard K. ... Monterey, CA
Harre, Gary L. ... Long Beach, CA
Harre, John A. ... Boston, MA
Harrel, Alan D. ... Texarkana, TX
Harrel, Celo ... Elk City, OK
Harrel, Leon J., Jr. ... Baton Rouge, LA
Harrel, Linda Cohen ... Los Angeles, CA
Harrel, P. Arley ... Seattle, WA
Harrel, Susan K. ... Ellensburg, WA
Harreld, Mary Gillilan ... Denver, CO
Harrell, Adam N., Jr. ... Richmond, VA
Harrell, Alec ... Los Angeles, CA
Harrell, Alfred C. ... Denver, CO
Harrell, Allen W. ... Wilson, NC
Harrell, Alvin C. ... Oklahoma City, OK
Harrell, Alvin M., III ... Fresno, CA
Harrell, Amy M. ... Charleston, SC
Harrell, Arlan La Monte ... Fresno, CA
Harrell, Bernard A. ... Raleigh, NC
Harrell, Brett R. ... Salinas, CA
Harrell, Broderick W. ... Durham, NC
Harrell, Bruce A. ... Omaha, NE
Harrell, Bruce B. ... Ashland, OR
Harrell, C. Ed ... Houston, TX
Harrell, C. Kendall ... San Antonio, TX
Harrell, C. Miner ... Pensacola, FL
Harrell, Charles C. ... Memphis, TN
Harrell, Charles E. ... Houston, TX
Harrell, Chris ... Morehead, KY
Harrell, Colleen R. ... Topeka, KS
Harrell, Dana L. ... Portsmouth, RI
Harrell, Daniel B. ... Fort Pierce, FL
Harrell, Daren S. ... Dallas, TX
Harrell, David ... Ventura, CA
Harrell, David E., Jr. ... Houston, TX
Harrell, David L. ... Brandon, MS
Harrell, Dennis O. ... Cincinnati, OH
Harrell, Donald J. ... Sarasota, FL
Harrell, Dorothy J. ... Washington, DC
Harrell, Edward J. ... Macon, GA
Harrell, Fred M., Jr. ... Brandon, MS
Harrell, Gary ... Albuquerque, NM
Harrell, Gary P. ... Portland, OR
Harrell, George L., II ... Jacksonville, FL
Harrell, George W., Jr. ... Bluffton, SC
Harrell, Glenn T., Jr. ... Upper Marlboro, MD
Harrell, Gregory Carter ... Tallahassee, FL
Harrell, Harold A. ... Bloomington, IN
Harrell and Harrell ... Trenton, TN
Harrell, J. Alan ... Baton Rouge, LA
Harrell, J. Hayden ... Charlotte, NC
Harrell, J. Kirby ... Atascadero, CA
Harrell, Jack E., Jr. ... Lawrenceville, GA
Harrell, Jack F. ... Pasadena, CA
Harrell, James E., Jr. ... Cleveland, TX
Harrell, James S. ... St. Peters, MO
Harrell, Jeffrey ... Palo Alto, CA
Harrell, John D. ... Charleston, SC
Harrell, John G. ... Birmingham, AL
Harrell & Johnson, P.A. ... Jacksonville, FL
Atlanta, GA
Harrell, Jonathan E. ... Granada Hills, CA
Harrell, Katie Quinn ... Beulaville, NC
Harrell, Kay Mary Kober ... Boerne, TX
Harrell, Kenneth W. ... North Charleston, SC
Harrell, Kimbara Graham ... Olney, IL
Harrell, Kyle A. ... Charlotte, NC
Harrell, L. Christian, III ... Memphis, TN
Harrell & Leake ... Asheville, NC
Marshall, NC
Harrell, Limmie Lee, Jr. ... Trenton, TN
Harrell & Lindsey, P.A. ... Camden, AR
Harrell, Louise ... Jackson, MS
Harrell, M. Jerald ... Syracuse, NY
Harrell, Marlise O. ... Hammond, LA
Harrell, Marshall A. ... Caldwell, TX
Harrell, Mary Elizabeth ... San Antonio, TX
Harrell, Mary Hunter ... Montgomery, AL
Harrell, Mary L. ... Houston, TX
Harrell, Mason D., Jr. ... San Bernardino, CA
Harrell, Maurice ... Irving, TX
Harrell, Maynard A., Jr. ... Plymouth, NC
Harrell, Michael E. ... Englewood, CO
Harrell, Michael P. ... New York, NY
Harrell, Michael S. ... Raleigh, NC
Harrell, Morris ... Dallas, TX
Harrell & Nester, LLP ... Portland, OR
Harrell, P. Kent ... Nashville, TN
Harrell, Prentiss G. ... Hattiesburg, MS
Harrell, Renee Daigle ... Jacksonville, FL
Harrell & Rester ... Brandon, MS
Harrell, Richard D. ... San Antonio, TX
Harrell, Richard K. ... Burgaw, NC
Harrell, Richard O., III ... South Boston, VA
Harrell, Richard S. ... Washington, DC
Harrell, Robert E. ... Asheville, NC
Harrell, Robert S. ... Houston, TX
Harrell, Robison R., & Associates
Shalimar, FL
Harrell, Robison Ronald ... Shalimar, FL
Harrell, Roy G., Jr. ... St. Petersburg, FL
Harrell, S. Frank ... Santa Ana, CA
Harrell, Searcy W., Jr. ... Camden, AR
Harrell, Shawn E. ... Oklahoma City, OK
Harrell, Sidney M. ... Mobile, AL
Harrell, Steven ... Perry, GA
Harrell, Steven ... Warner Robins, GA
Harrell, Steven D. ... Springfield, MO
Harrell, Susan W. ... Pensacola, FL
Harrell, T. Michael ... Dallas, TX
Harrell, Terry L. ... Indianapolis, IN
Harrell, Thomas A. ... Baton Rouge, LA
Harrell, Thomas R. ... San Francisco, CA
Harrell, Veronica Vanessa ... Miami, FL
Harrell, W. Hugh ... Lubbock, TX
Harrell, Wallace E. ... Brunswick, GA
Harrell, Wallace E., III ... Brunswick, GA
Harrell, William A. ... Phoenix, AZ
Harrell, William A., P.C., Law Office of
Phoenix, AZ
Harrell, William B. ... Texarkana, TX
Harrell, William C. ... La Quinta, CA
Harrell, William G., Jr. ... Tazewell, TN
Harrell, William H. ... Jacksonville, FL
Harrell, William H., Jr. ... Tampa, FL
Harrell Wiltshire, P.A. ... Pensacola, FL
Harrell-James, Veronica Vanessa ... Miami, FL
Harrell Jr., C. Lydon ... Norfolk, VA
Harrelson, Edward L. ... Hendersonville, NC
Harrelson, F. Daniel ... Pine Bluff, AR
Harrelson, Gene ... Texarkana, AR
Harrelson, George I. ... Marshall, MN
Harrelson, Hayes and Guyton, L.L.C.
Rock Hill, SC
Harrelson, Hugh L., Sr. ... Rock Hill, SC
Harrelson, Jeffrey S. ... Texarkana, AR
Harrelson, Laura Goehring ... Dayton, OH
Harrelson, Michael J. ... Gaylord, MI
Harrelson, Paula M. ... Santa Ana, CA
Harrelson, Robert M. ... Troy, OH
Harrelson, Robert Victor
West Columbia, SC
Harrelson, Thomas M. ... San Francisco, CA
San Mateo, CA
Harrelson, Wallace C. ... Greensboro, NC
Harrelson, William C.
Belvedere-Tiburon, CA
Harrelson, Wm. Jay ... Nashville, TN
Harrelson, Yulee E. ... Columbia, SC
Harren, Jos. A. ... Red Lake Falls, MN
Harren, Kevin ... Albany, NY
Harren, Michael T. ... Rochester, NY
Harren, Richard L. ... Wasilla, AK
Harren, Richard L., Law Office of, A Prof. Corp. ... Wasilla, AK
Harrer, Richard G. ... Scottsdale, AZ
Harri, Edward J. ... Salem, OR
Harri, JoAnn P. ... Albany, NY
Harrian, Robert F. ... Glendale, AZ
Harrie, William P. ... Fargo, ND
Harriel, Kyla L. ... San Francisco, CA
Harrienger, Tracy ... Amherst, NY
Harries, Gilbert W. ... Duluth, MN
Harries, James H. ... Phoenix, AZ
Harries, James R. ... Minneapolis, MN
Harriett, Kathleen M. ... St. Charles, IL
Harriett and Sproull, P.A. ... Palatka, FL
Harrigal, Rebecca L. ... Treasury Department, Internal Revenue Service, GV
Harrigan, Anne B. ... San Francisco, CA
Harrigan, Arthur W., Jr. ... Seattle, WA
Harrigan & Associates ... Chicago, IL
Harrigan, Bernadette ... Northampton, MA
Harrigan, Brenda Coville ... Providence, RI
Harrigan, C. Frank ... Syracuse, NY
Harrigan, Cecil C., II ... Washington, DC
Harrigan, Cecil C., II, P.C. ... Washington, DC
Harrigan, Christopher ... Austin, TX
Harrigan, Clifford T. ... Schenectady, NY
Harrigan, Daniel J. ... Ventura, CA
Harrigan, Daniel J. ... Kokomo, IN
Harrigan, David L. ... Concord, NH
Harrigan, Dennis F. ... Waterbury, CT
Harrigan, Donna R. ... Chicago, IL
Harrigan, Edward D. ... Miami, FL
Harrigan, James F. ... San Francisco, CA
Harrigan, James G. ... San Diego, CA
Harrigan, John F. ... Glen Arbor, MI
Harrigan, John M. ... Oakland, CA
Harrigan, John W. ... Minneapolis, MN
Harrigan, Judith A. ... Minneapolis, MN
Harrigan, Kenneth H. ... Atlanta, GA
Harrigan, Kenneth L. ... Albuquerque, NM
Harrigan, Kristina E. ... San Francisco, CA
Harrigan, Marie G. ... Chicago, IL
Harrigan, Marjorie A. ... Fairfax, VA
Harrigan, Nancy Stafford ... Albany, NY
Harrigan, Patricia Driscoll ... Stamford, CT
Harrigan, Patrick F. ... Portsmouth, NH
Harrigan, Robert
Department of Housing and Urban Development, GV
Harrigan Ruff, A Professional Corporation
San Diego, CA
Harrigan, Shane P. ... San Diego, CA
Harrigan, Terence D.
Department Of Veterans Affairs, Board of Veterans Appeals, GV
Harrigan, Terence M. ... Bangor, ME
Harrigan, Thomas G. ... Minneapolis, MN
Harrigan, Thomas J. ... Fairfax, VA
Harrigan, Thomas Q. ... Philadelphia, PA
Harrigan, Timothy M. ... Needham, MA
Harriger, Bill ... Lubbock, TX
Harriger, Gary C. ... Baltimore, MD
Harriger, Harold O. ... Lubbock, TX
Harrigfeld, Karna E. ... Stockton, CA
Harrigfeld, William G. ... Boise, ID
Harrigian, Mark W. ... Los Angeles, CA
Harrill, James A., Jr. ... Winston-Salem, NC
Harrill, James F. ... Akron, OH
Harrill, Paul Daniel ... Columbia, SC
Harrill, Raymond A., (P.A.) ... Little Rock, AR
Harrill, Roy B. ... Chicago, IL
Harriman, Charles J. ... Secaucus, NJ
Harriman, Darrell C. ... Downey, CA
Harriman, David P. ... Charlottesville, VA
Harriman, Edward R., Jr. ... Holden, MA
Harriman, Erin M. ... Washington, DC
Harriman, Guy L., Jr. ... Columbia, MD
Towson, MD
Harriman, Harold C. ... Newport Beach, CA
Harriman, Jansak, Levy & Wylie
Washington, DC
Columbia, MD
Towson, MD
Harriman, J. D., II ... Los Angeles, CA
Harriman, John H. ... Los Angeles, CA
Harriman, Jordon E. ... Los Angeles, CA
Harriman, Malory N. ... Chicago, IL
Harriman, Martha Miller ... Van Buren, AR
Harriman, Morril H., Jr. ... Van Buren, AR
Harriman, Richard L. ... Chico, CA
Fresno, CA
Harriman, Susan J. ... San Francisco, CA
Harriman, William M. E. ... Mill Valley, CA
Harring, Michael A. ... Moline, IL
Harring, Richard L. ... Denver, CO
Harrington, Afton L. ... Roseville, CA
Harrington, Alan L. ... Paducah, KY
Harrington, Alden C. ... Providence, RI
Harrington, Anderson & DeBlasio
Portland, OR
Harrington, Andrew R. ... Fairbanks, AK
Harrington, Ann A. ... Oakland, CA
Harrington, Anthony S. ... Washington, DC
Harrington, Arthur J. ... Milwaukee, WI
Harrington, Barrett, Law Offices of
Crowley, LA
Harrington, Benedict W. ... Carteret, NJ
Harrington, Billy J. ... Natchitoches, LA
Harrington, Bonnie ... Albany, NY
Harrington, Braddy & Romary
Greenville, NC
Harrington, Brian C., (P.A.)
St. Petersburg, FL
Harrington, Brian D. ... Springfield, MA
Harrington, Brian K. ... Worcester, MA
Harrington, Bridget Fitzgibbons
Phoenix, AZ
Harrington, Brooks ... Fort Worth, TX
Harrington, Bruce C. ... Topeka, KS
Harrington, Bruce E. ... Newport Beach, CA
Harrington, Bruce M. ... Houston, TX
Harrington, C. Michael ... Houston, TX
Harrington, C. Rodney ... Natchitoches, LA
Harrington & Caldwell, P.C.
Philadelphia, PA
Harrington, Carol A. ... Chicago, IL
Harrington, Carole J. ... Denver, CO
Harrington, Carter D. ... Charleston, SC
Harrington, Catherine A. ... New York, NY
Harrington, Cathryn L. ... Van Wert, OH
Harrington, Chantal J. ... Jacksonville, FL
Harrington, Charles F. ... Buffalo, NY
Harrington, Charles J., III ... Montclair, NJ
Harrington, Charles J., Jr. ... Jersey City, NJ
Harrington, Charles L. ... Moraga, CA
Harrington, Charles L. ... Butte, MT
Harrington, Charles L. ... Marion, VA
Harrington, Charles Tiffin ... San Diego, CA
Harrington, Charles V. ... Tucson, AZ

Harrington, Cheryl ....Augusta, ME
Harrington, Chris ....Hartford, CT
Harrington, Christine ....Treasury Department, Office of Thrift Supervision, GV
Harrington, Christopher J. ....Dallas, TX
Harrington, Christopher Mark ....Dulce, NM
Harrington, Clair A. ....Richmond, VA
Harrington, Clayton F., Jr. ....Spokane, WA
Harrington, Clifford M. ....Washington, DC
Harrington, Colleen Anne ....Pullman, WA
Harrington, Corbit S. ....Roundup, MT
Harrington, Cornelius J., III ....Chicago, IL
Highland, IN
Harrington, Cornelius J., Jr.
Olympia Fields, IL
Harrington, Curtis L., & Associates
Long Beach, CA
Harrington, Cynthia M. ......Kansas City, MO
Harrington, Daniel G. ....Delray Beach, FL
Champaign, IL
Harrington, Daniel P. ....Boston, MA
Harrington, Daniel Q. ....Westmont, NJ
Philadelphia, PA
Harrington, Danny A. ....Greenville, NC
Harrington, David A. ....Washington, DC
Harrington, David L. ....Murray, KY
Harrington, David L. ....Springville, UT
Harrington, Dean A. ....St. Louis, MO
Harrington, Dennis ....Marietta, OH
Harrington, Dennis C. ....Pittsburgh, PA
Harrington, Diantha C., (Mrs.)
Framingham, MA
Harrington, Don L. ....San Diego, CA
Harrington, Donald F. ....Miami, FL
Harrington, Donald G. ....Philadelphia, PA
Harrington, Donald J. ....Southfield, MI
Harrington, E. Jackson, Jr.
Greensboro, NC
Harrington, Edw. F. ....New Bedford, MA
Harrington, Edward F. ....Boston, MA
Harrington, Edward F., Jr. ....Louisville, KY
Harrington, Edward J., Jr.
North Dartmouth, MA
Harrington, Edward P. ....Boston, MA
Harrington, Elisabeth D. ....New Orleans, LA
Harrington, Elizabeth M. ....Hauppauge, NY
Harrington, Ellen M. ....Boston, MA
Harrington, Emmett F. ....San Francisco, CA
Harrington, Eric R. ....Natchitoches, LA
Harrington, Eugene M. ....Houston, TX
Harrington & Fowler ....Owensboro, KY
Harrington, Foxx, Dubrow & Canter
Los Angeles, CA
Orange, CA
San Diego, CA
San Francisco, CA
Harrington, Francis E. ....Portland, OR
Harrington, Frank B. ....Princeton, NJ
Harrington, Freddie N., Jr.
Birmingham, AL
Harrington, Gary P. ....Eden Prairie, MN
Harrington, Gene ....Warner Robins, GA
Harrington, George C. ....Framingham, MA
Harrington, George S., Jr. ......Port Orchard, WA
Harrington, Gerald Michael
San Francisco, CA
Harrington, Gerald T. ....Providence, RI
Harrington, Gerald W. ....Providence, RI
Harrington and Graham ....Marion, VA
Harrington, Greg ....Los Angeles, CA
Harrington & Harrington ....Natchitoches, LA
Harrington, Harrington & Nabb
Cambridge, MD
Harrington, Helise ....New York, NY
Harrington Henry LLP ....New York, NY
Harrington, Hoppe & Mitchell, Ltd.
Warren, OH
Youngstown, OH
Harrington, Hub ....Birmingham, AL
Harrington, Irvin C. (Todd)
Los Angeles, CA
Harrington, J. Allen ....Sanford, NC
Harrington, J. Cort, Jr. ....Helena, MT
Harrington, J. Patrick ....Queens Village, NY
Harrington, Jack ....Rutherford, NJ
Harrington, James C. ....Austin, TX
Harrington, James D. ....Chicago, IL
Harrington, James D. ....Winthrop, ME
Harrington, James D. ....Cohoes, NY
Harrington, James E. ....Glenview, IL
Harrington, James F. ....Miami, FL
Harrington, James F. ....Syosset, NY
Harrington, James F. ....Wausau, WI
Harrington, James H. ....Gualala, CA
Harrington, James J. ....Stamford, CT
Harrington, James J. ....New York, NY
Harrington, James J., III, Law Offices of
Novi, MI
Harrington, James M. ......Redwood City, CA
Harrington, James P. ....Butte, MT
Harrington, James P. ....Buffalo, NY
Harrington, James S. ....Boston, MA
Harrington, James T. ....Chicago, IL
Harrington, Jana Therese ....Sacramento, CA
Harrington, Jane P. ....Goshen, NY
Harrington, Jas. M., Jr. ....Houston, TX
Harrington, Jay L. ....Oklahoma City, OK
Harrington, Jean A. ....Westwood, MA
Harrington, Jennifer C. ....Clearwater, FL
Harrington, Jennifer L. ....Hillsboro, OR
Harrington, Jesse M. ....Jackson, MS
Harrington, J.G. ....Washington, DC
Harrington, Joan C. ....Westport, CT
Harrington, Joe D. ....Orlando, FL
Harrington, John ....Dublin, CA
Harrington, John C. ....Tulsa, OK
Harrington, John C., Jr.
Oklahoma City, OK

Harrington, John D. ....Portland, OR
Harrington, John Dolan, P.A.
Hackensack, NJ
Harrington, John F. ....Washington, DC
Harrington, John F. ....Memphis, TN
Harrington, John H. ....Atlanta, GA
Harrington, John J. ....Warwick, RI
Harrington, John J. ....Nashville, TN
Harrington, John L.
House of Representatives, Committee on Ways & Means, GV
Harrington, John L. ....Saugus, MA
Harrington, John M. ....Winston-Salem, NC
Harrington, John M., Jr. ....Boston, MA
Harrington, John P. ....Eastman, GA
Harrington, John P. ....Liberty Corner, NJ
Harrington, John P. ....Cincinnati, OH
Harrington, John P. ....Salt Lake City, UT
Harrington, John P., Co., L.P.A.
Cincinnati, OH
Harrington, John R. ....Hollywood, FL
Harrington, John R. ....Chicago, IL
Harrington, John Ray ....Concord, NH
Harrington, John T. ....Milwaukee, WI
Harrington, John W. ....Chicago, IL
Harrington, Joseph B. ....Wakefield, MA
Harrington, Joseph B., P.C. ....Wakefield, MA
Harrington, Joseph Lawrence
Washington, DC
Harrington, Joseph M. ....McLean, VA
Harrington, Joseph P. ....New Bedford, MA
Harrington, Joseph P. ....White Plains, NY
Harrington, Joseph P., P.C.
New Bedford, MA
Harrington, Josephine H. ....Sugar Land, TX
Harrington, Kady & Gottlieb, P.A.
Carteret, NJ
Harrington, Kathleen ....Emeryville, CA
Harrington, Kelly Robbins
Flower Mound, TX
Harrington, Kenneth J. ....San Francisco, CA
Harrington, Kenneth R. ....Nashville, TN
Harrington, Kevin F. ....New York, NY
Harrington, Kevin J. ....White Plains, NY
Harrington, Kevin M. ....White Plains, NY
Harrington, Kevin P. ....North Haledon, NJ
Harrington, Larry E. ....Monroe, NC
Harrington, Larry K. ....Owensboro, KY
Harrington, Larry W. ....Casper, WY
Harrington, Laurence
General Services Administration, Office of the General Counsel, GV
Harrington, Laurence P. ....Boston, MA
Harrington Law Office ....Nashville, TN
Harrington, Lee K. ....Los Angeles, CA
Harrington, Louis D. ....Rockville, MD
Harrington, Lucy E. ....Cedar Rapids, IA
Harrington, M. Eileen
Federal Trade Commission, Bureau of Consumer Protection, GV
Harrington & Mahoney ....Buffalo, NY
Harrington, Maley, Gardner, Sayre & Weikart ....Richmond, IN
Harrington & Mann ....Oklahoma City, OK
Tulsa, OK
Harrington, Margaret M. ....Philadelphia, PA
Harrington, Mark E.
House of Representatives, Committee on Science, GV
Harrington, Mark Ellis ....Los Angeles, CA
Harrington, Mark F. ....Fairfield, CT
Harrington, Mark T. ....Syracuse, NY
Harrington, Marla R. ....Aiken, SC
Harrington, Mary J. ....Rochester, NY
Harrington, Mary K. ....Fayetteville, NY
Harrington, Mary Piemonte ....Salem, MA
Harrington, Matthew P. ....Walnut Creek, CA
Harrington, Maxine M. ....Fort Worth, TX
Harrington and Merryweather
Cambridge, MD
Harrington, Michael B. ....Tacoma, WA
Harrington, Michael C. ....Hartford, CT
Harrington, Michael E. ....Boston, MA
Harrington, Michael F. ....Cedar Rapids, IA
Harrington, Michael F. ....Boston, MA
Harrington, Michael J. ....Davis, CA
Harrington, Michael J. ....Palm Springs, CA
Harrington, Michael J. ....San Francisco, CA
Harrington, Michael J. ....Indianapolis, IN
Harrington, Michael J. ....Salem, MA
Harrington, Michael J. ....Stewart Manor, NY
Harrington, Michael K. ....Boston, MA
Harrington, Michael P. ....Cleveland, OH
Harrington, Michael R. ....Boston, MA
Harrington, Michael Scott ....Exton, PA
Harrington, Michael V. ....Butte, MT
Harrington, Michele A. ....Springdale, AR
Harrington, Michele Sasse ....McLean, VA
Harrington, Michelle T. ....Beverly Hills, CA
Harrington, Mickki L. ....Troy, NY
Harrington, Miller, Neihouse & Krug, P.A.
Bella Vista, AR
Fayetteville, AR
Rogers, AR
Siloam Springs, AR
Springdale, AR
Harrington, Moira cm ....Pittsburgh, PA
Harrington, Molly C. ....Oakland, CA
Harrington, Nancy Jane ....Boston, MA
Harrington, Neil J. ....Phoenix, AZ
Harrington, Ocko & Monk, LLP
Brooklyn, NY
New York, NY
Scarsdale, NY
White Plains, NY
Harrington, Overton T., Jr. ....Gretna, LA
Harrington, Patrick ....Boise, ID
Harrington, Patrick H. ....Fall River, MA

Harrington, Patrick J. ....Chicago, IL
Harrington, Patrick J. ....Cleveland, OH
Harrington, Patrick L. ....Lansing, MI
Harrington, Patrick W. ....Hackensack, NJ
Harrington, Paul David
Department of the Army, Army Materiel Command, GV
Harrington, Paul H. ....Washington, DC
Harrington, Paul H., Jr. ....Fairfax, VA
Harrington, Paul J. ....Braintree, MA
Harrington, Paul K. ....Shelburne Falls, MA
Harrington, Paul M. ....Treasury Department, Internal Revenue Service, GV
Harrington, Paul T. ....Raquette Lake, NY
Harrington, Paula L. ....San Diego, CA
Harrington, Pauline M. ....Duxbury, MA
Harrington, Penny ....Nashville, TN
Harrington, Peter F. ....White Plains, NY
Harrington, Peter F., Jr. ....Newton, MA
Harrington, Peter P., Jr. ....Boston, MA
Harrington, Philip E. ....Park Ridge, IL
Harrington, Phillip H. ....Washington, DC
Harrington, Porter, Ermentrout & Tock
Delray Beach, FL
Champaign, IL
Urbana, IL
Harrington, R. Cole
Research Triangle Park, NC
Harrington, R. Lee ....Chandler, AZ
Harrington, Raymond ....St. James, NY
Harrington, Richard ....San Francisco, CA
Harrington, Richard D. ....Cambridge, MD
Harrington, Richard L. ....Milwaukee, WI
Harrington, Richard W. ....Costa Mesa, CA
Harrington, Rick A. ....Houston, TX
Harrington, Robert E., Jr. ....Chicago, IL
Harrington, Robert E., (P.C.)
New Orleans, LA
Charlotte, NC
Harrington, Robert J. ....Stockton, CA
Harrington, Robert J. ....Boston, MA
Harrington, Robert L. ....Oregon City, OR
Harrington, Robert P. ....Boston, MA
Harrington, Robert T. ....Lowell, MA
Harrington, Robert T., III ....Branford, CT
Harrington, Robert W. ....Boston, MA
Harrington, Roger J. ....Philadelphia, PA
Harrington, Ronald G. ....Ventura, CA
Harrington, Ryan J. ....Chicago, IL
Harrington, Sara Duval ....Palo Alto, CA
Harrington, Sarah L. ....Lexington, KY
Harrington, Schweers, Dattilo & McClelland
Erie, PA
Pittsburgh, PA
Washington, PA
Harrington, Scott D. ....Los Angeles, CA
Harrington, Scott L. ....Spring, TX
Harrington, Scott M. ....Stamford, CT
Harrington, Sheila A. ....Providence, RI
Harrington, Sheila C. ....Harvard, MA
Harrington & Spaulding, P.L.L.C.
Roundup, MT
Harrington, Susan D. ....New York, NY
Harrington, Terence D. ....Seattle, WA
Harrington, Terri ....Denver, CO
Harrington, T. F., Jr. ....Greenbrae, CA
Harrington, Thomas D., Jr. ....Tampa, FL
Harrington, Thomas E. ....Delray Beach, FL
Champaign, IL
Harrington, Thomas J. ....Boston, MA
Harrington, Thomas J. ....Dayton, OH
Harrington, Thomas M. ....Stockton, CA
Harrington, Thomas N. ....Milwaukee, WI
Harrington, Thomas R. ....Philadelphia, PA
Harrington, Thomas S. ....Eden, NC
Wentworth, NC
Harrington, Thomas W. ....Worland, WY
Harrington, Thompson, Acker & Harrington, Ltd. ....Chicago, IL
Harrington, Timothy J. ....Southfield, MI
El Paso, TX
Harrington, Timothy J., Jr.
Fort Worth, TX
Harrington, Timothy W. ....Miami, FL
Harrington, Tommy K. ....Houston, TX
Harrington, Travers R., Jr. ....Fayetteville, WV
Harrington, Vernon D. ....Chicago, IL
Harrington, Vincent A. ....North Quincy, MA
Harrington, Vincent A., Jr. ....Oakland, CA
Harrington, Walter E., Jr.
Warner Robins, GA
Harrington, Walter H., Jr.
Redwood City, CA
Harrington, Ward, Gilleland & Winstead
Sanford, NC
Harrington, William A. ....Tulsa, OK
Harrington, William D. ....Buffalo, NY
Harrington, William D. ....Jamaica, NY
Harrington, William F. ....White Plains, NY
Harrington, William J. ....Chicago, IL
Harrington, William K. ....Philadelphia, PA
Harrington, William P. ....White Plains, NY
Harrington, Wilton D. ....Eastman, GA
Harrington-McBride, Catherine C.
Federal Trade Commission, Bureau of Consumer Protection, GV
Harriott, Rex K. ....Newark, NJ
Harris, A. Lee ....Hillsboro, TX
Harris, Adam C. ....New York, NY
Harris, Addie M. ....Raleigh, NC
Harris, Alan ....Bangor, ME
Harris, Alan B. ....Bakersfield, CA
Harris, Alan E. ....San Francisco, CA
Harris, Alan E. ....Baltimore, MD
Harris, Alan M. ....Los Angeles, CA
Harris, Alan N. ....Ann Arbor, MI
Harris, Alan R. ....Philadelphia, PA
Harris, Alan S. ....Rochester, NY

Harris, Alan W. ....Dallas, TX
Harris, Alexander E. ....Brooklyn, NY
Harris, Alfred J.
Department Of Health And Human Services, Office of Community Services, GV
Harris, Alfreda T. ....Franklin, VA
Harris, Alice Price ....Columbia, SC
Harris, Alice V. ....Columbia, SC
Harris, Alison L. ....Los Angeles, CA
Harris, Allan F. ....Sarasota, FL
Harris, Allan M. ....Chicago, IL
Harris, Allan M. ....Roseland, NJ
Harris, Allen ....New York, NY
Harris, Allen F. ....Atlanta, GA
Harris, Allen I. ....St. Louis, MO
Harris, Allen L. ....Whitehouse Station, NJ
Harris, Allen and Yoder, P.C.
Lynchburg, VA
Harris, Alton B. ....Chicago, IL
Harris, Alvin L. ....Nashville, TN
Harris, Amethyst ....West Point, MS
Harris, Amy S. ....Dallas, TX
Harris, Amy Stokes ....Ripley, MS
Harris, Ana Cela ....Miami, FL
Harris, Andrew B. ....Chicago, IL
Harris, Andrew M. ....New York, NY
Harris, Angela ....Berkeley, CA
Harris, Ann Bethune ....Marietta, GA
Harris, Ann C. ....San Diego, CA
Harris, Ann C., A Professional Law Corporation ....San Diego, CA
Harris, Annabelle M. ....Newport Beach, CA
Harris, Anna-Liza B. ....Washington, DC
Harris, Anne A. ....Seminole, FL
Harris, Anne R. ....Greensboro, NC
Harris, Anthony E. ....Department of Justice, Antitrust Division, GV
Harris, April D. ....New York, NY
Harris, Archie L., Jr. ....Washington, DC
Harris, Arlene ....New York, NY
Harris, Arnold S. ....Chicago, IL
Harris, Arthur B. ....Milwaukee, WI
Harris, Arthur Claborn ....Stamford, CT
Harris, Arthur I. ....Cleveland, OH
Harris, Arthur R. ....Warrington, PA
Harris & Associates ....Dallas, TX
Harris, Audrey ....Jupiter, FL
Harris, Aurora D. ....Orange, CA
Harris, Baird & Abraham ....Los Angeles, CA
Harris, Barbara ....Barnstable, MA
Harris, Barbara ....Providence, RI
Harris, Barbara A. ....Atlanta, GA
Harris, Barbara J. ....Kansas City, MO
Harris, Barbara L. ....San Francisco, CA
St. Louis, MO
Harris & Bar-Levav ....New York, NY
Harris & Bar-Levav LLP ....Newark, NJ
Harris, Barrett Howard ....Stilwell, OK
Harris, Barrett, Mann & Dew .....Ruskin, FL
St. Petersburg, FL
Sun City Center, FL
Tampa, FL
Harris, Barry P., IV ....Charlotte, NC
Harris, Bayard E. ....Roanoke, VA
Harris, B.C. ....Shawnee, OK
Harris Beach & Wilcox, LLP
San Francisco, CA
Washington, DC
Hackensack, NJ
Albany, NY
Buffalo, NY
Hamburg, NY
Ithaca, NY
New York, NY
Rochester, NY
Syracuse, NY
Harris, Belvin R. ....Gainesville, TX
Harris, Ben H., III ....Mobile, AL
Harris, Ben H., Jr. ....Mobile, AL
Harris, Benjamin J. ....Franklin, WI
Milwaukee, WI
Harris, Benjamin K. ....Wayne, PA
Harris, Benjamin P., III ....Providence, RI
Harris & Berlin ....Chicago, IL
Harris, Bert J., III ....Lake Placid, FL
Sebring, FL
Harris, Beth A. ....San Diego, CA
Harris, Beth A. ....Chicago, IL
Harris, Beth Jacobi ....North Palm Beach, FL
Harris, Beverly ....Blairsville, GA
Harris, Beverly A. ....Cleveland, OH
Harris, Beverly K. ....Evansville, IN
Harris, Billy E. ....Quitman, MS
Harris & Bixby ....Albany, NY
Harris & Block ....Miami, FL
Harris, Bob L. ....Tallahassee, FL
Harris, Bonnie E. ....Anchorage, AK
Harris & Bowker, LLP ....Portland, OR
Harris, Brad ....Austin, TX
Harris, Bradford J. ....Lancaster, PA
Harris, Bradley J. ....Oak Brook, IL
Harris, Bradley J. ....Grundy Center, IA
Harris, Brantly ....Houston, TX
Harris, Brenda Valentine ....Baltimore, MD
Harris, Brent A. ....Indianapolis, IN
Harris, Brett Ian ....New York, NY
Harris, Brett R. ....Woodbridge, NJ
Harris, Brian ....Reno, NV
Harris, Brian C. ....Livingston, NJ
New York, NY
Harris, Brian P. ....Boston, MA
Harris, Bridget McInerney ....Oakland, CA
Harris, Britton B. ....Houston, TX
Harris, Bruce A. ....Boca Raton, FL
Harris, Bruce A. ....Morristown, NJ
Harris, Bruce G. ....Baltimore, MD
Harris, Bruce M. ....Orlando, FL

Harris, Bruce R. ....Department Of The Interior, Office of Hearings & Appeals, GV
Harris, Bryan K. ....Corpus Christi, TX
Harris & Burdick ....Boulder, CO
Harris & Burgin ....Cincinnati, OH
Harris, Burton H. ....Logan, UT
Harris, Burton M. ....Boston, MA
Harris, C. Anthony ....Cheraw, SC
Harris, C. Anthony, Jr. ....Cheraw, SC
Harris, C. Eiland ....Jackson, MS
Harris, C. Marcus ....Charlotte, NC
Harris, C. Wayne ....Fort Smith, AR
Harris, Caddell & Shanks, P.C.
Athens, AL
Decatur, AL
Moulton, AL
Harris & Callaghan ....Missoula, MT
Harris, Calvin ....Phoenix, AZ
Harris & Cargill, P.A. ....Minneapolis, MN
Harris, Carl A. ....Upper Marlboro, MD
Harris, Carl A. & Assocs., P.C.
Upper Marlboro, MD
Harris, Carl L. ....Fayetteville, WV
Harris, Carol A. ....San Francisco, CA
Harris, Carole C. ....Washington, DC
Harris, Caroline G. ....New York, NY
Harris, Carolyn ....San Diego, CA
Harris, Carolyn A. ....
General Services Administration, GV
Harris, Carrie Tyrrell ....Marietta, GA
Harris, Carroll James ....Baltimore, MD
Harris, Cassandra D. ....Charlotte, NC
Harris, Catherine C. ....Sacramento, CA
Harris, Cathy A. ....Washington, DC
Harris, Cathy S. ....Denver, CO
Harris, Cecelia ....Canton, GA
Harris, Celeste M. ....Winston-Salem, NC
Harris, Chad A. ....Los Angeles, CA
Harris, Charles ....San Diego, CA
Harris, Charles ....Chicago, IL
Harris, Charles B. ....Fort Worth, TX
Harris, Charles B. ....Baldwin, WI
Harris, Charles Bradford ....Lexington, KY
Harris, Charles E. ....Los Angeles, CA
Harris, Charles E. ....Sonoma, CA
Harris, Charles E. ....Des Moines, IA
Harris, Charles E. ....Philadelphia, PA
Harris, Charles E., III ....Atlanta, GA
Harris, Charles E., III ....Pittsburgh, PA
Harris, Charles E.C. ....San Francisco, CA
Harris, Charles Edison ....Orlando, FL
Harris, Charles F. ....Morrow, GA
Harris, Charles F. ....Wichita, KS
Harris, Charles F. ....Princeton, NJ
Harris, Charles L. ....Irvine, CA
Harris, Charles M. ....Daytona Beach, FL
Harris, Charles M. ....Fort Myers, FL
Harris, Charles M., Jr. ....Tampa, FL
Harris, Charles T. ....Bloomfield Hills, MI
Harris, Charles W. ....Indianapolis, IN
Harris, Charlie J., Jr. ....Kansas City, MO
Harris, Charlotte Aline ....Alpine, TX
Harris, Chas. A. ....Beach Haven, NJ
Harris, Chas. J. ....Baltimore, MD
Harris, Cherie Erickson
Laguna Beach, CA
Harris, Cherie Erickson, P.C.
Laguna Beach, CA
Los Angeles, CA
Harris, Cheryl A. ....New York, NY
Harris, Cheryl B. ....Portland, OR
Harris, Cheryl I. ....Chicago, IL
Harris, Cheryl K. ....Lexington, KY
Harris, Chesworth & O'Brien
Rochester, NY
Harris, Chris, & Associates, P.C.
Arlington, TX
Harris, Chris J. ....Arlington, TX
Harris, Christian R. ....Williamson, WV
Harris, Christina M. ....Jonesboro, GA
Harris, Christine ....Milwaukee, WI
Harris, Christopher ....Bozeman, MT
Harris, Christopher ....Brentwood, TN
Harris, Christopher P. ....Cleveland, OH
Harris, Christopher R. ....New York, NY
Harris, Christy F., (Mr.) ....Lakeland, FL
Harris, Claude W. ....Raleigh, NC
Harris, Cleckler & Hollis
Birmingham, AL
Harris, Clifford W. ....Chandler, AZ
Harris, Clifton G. ....Fresno, CA
Harris, Clint J. ....Manchester, KY
Harris, Colin G. ....Denver, CO
Harris, Constance S. ....New York, NY
Harris, Craig A. ....Dallas, TX
Harris, Craig C. ....Richmond, VA
Harris, Craig H. ....Denver, CO
Harris, Craig Randall ....Newark, NJ
Harris & Currens, Professional Corporation
Mooresville, IN
Harris, Cynthia A. ....San Francisco, CA
Harris, Cynthia Barnes ....Chicago, IL
Harris, D. Alan ....Los Angeles, CA
Chicago, IL
Harris, D. Neil ....Pascagoula, MS
Harris, D. Patrick ....Montgomery, AL
Harris, D. Steve ....San Francisco, CA
Harris, Dahl L. ....Santa Fe, NM
Harris, Dale H. ....Lynchburg, VA
Harris, Dale R. ....Denver, CO
Harris, Dalton D., III ....Dallas, TX
Harris & Damashek ....New York, NY
Harris, Dana M. ....Overland Park, KS
Kansas City, MO
Harris and Daniel ....Fayetteville, WV
Harris, Daniel A. ....New York, NY
Harris, Daniel B. ....San Francisco, CA
Harris, Daniel E. ....Portland, ME
Harris, Daniel J. ....New Hyde Park, NY
Harris, Daniel, Jr. ....Omaha, NE
Harris, Daniel M. ....Chicago, IL
Harris, Daniel M., The Law Offices of
Chicago, IL
Harris, Daniel P. ....Seattle, WA
Harris, Daniel R. ....Palo Alto, CA
Harris, Daniel S. ....San Rafael, CA
Harris, Dara D. ....New York, NY
Harris, Darcy R. ....Los Angeles, CA
Harris, Darlene D. ....Hempstead, NY
Harris, Darren M. ....Tustin, CA
Harris, Darrin W. ....Indianapolis, IN
Harris, David ....Jefferson, IA
Harris, David ....Stilwell, OK
Harris, David A. ....San Francisco, CA
Harris, David A. ....Wilmington, DE
Harris, David A. ....Louisville, KY
Harris, David A. ....Reno, NV
Harris, David A. ....Brooklyn, NY
Harris, David A. ....Dallas, TX
Harris, David B. ....Trenton, NJ
Harris, David C. ....Philadelphia, PA
Harris, David E. ....Walnut Creek, CA
Harris, David E. ....Indianapolis, IN
Harris, David E. ....Issaquah, WA
Harris, David F. ....Washington, DC
Harris, David G. ....Chicago, IL
Harris, David G. ....Evansville, IN
Harris, David G. ....New York, NY
Harris, David G. ....Tulsa, OK
Harris, David H. ....Department of Agriculture, Office of the General Counsel, GV
Harris, David H., Jr. ....Waukegan, IL
Harris, David J. ....Washington, DC
Harris, David J. ....St. Louis, MO
Harris, David J. ....Wilkes-Barre, PA
Harris, David J. ....Memphis, TN
Harris, David J., (P.C.) ....Atlanta, GA
Harris, David K. ....Springfield, IL
Harris, David L. ....Roseland, NJ
Harris, David L. ....Graham, NC
Harris, David M. ....Los Angeles, CA
Harris, David M. ....Belleville, IL
St. Louis, MO
Harris, David M. ....Collinsville, IL
Harris, David N. ....Peabody, MA
Harris, David O. ....Tulsa, OK
Harris, David O., Inc. ....Tulsa, OK
Harris, David S. ....Miami, FL
Harris, David W. ....New York, NY
Harris, Dawn L. Stewart ....Nutley, NJ
Harris, Dawn Marie ....La Crosse, WI
Harris, Dawn-Carole ....Denver, CO
Harris, Dean M. ....Los Angeles, CA
Harris, Dean M. ....Raleigh, NC
Harris, Deborah ....Philadelphia, PA
Harris, Deborah A. ....Rockville, MD
Harris, Deborah Ashmore ....Amarillo, TX
Dallas, TX
Harris, Debra Jean ....Brooklyn, NY
Harris, Debra Moseley ....Houston, TX
Harris, Dee R. ....Phoenix, AZ
Harris, Denise ....Philadelphia, PA
Harris, Dennis L. ....Kansas City, KS
Harris, Dick ....Abilene, TX
Harris, Dick, P.C. ....Abilene, TX
Harris, Dina O. ....Riverside, CA
Harris, Don V., Jr. ....Washington, DC
Harris, Donald C., Sr. ....Round Rock, TX
Harris, Donald L. ....Idaho Falls, ID
Harris, Donald L. ....Billings, MT
Harris, Donald M. ....New York, NY
Harris, Donald P. ....Franklin, TN
Harris, Donald R., (Ltd.) ....Chicago, IL
Harris, Donald Ray ....Memphis, TN
Harris, Donald W. ....Phoenix, AZ
Harris, Donna Adams ....Houston, TX
Harris, Donna J. ....Garland, TX
Harris, Donna J., P.C. ....Garland, TX
Harris, Donna L. ....San Diego, CA
Harris, Donna M. ....Atlanta, GA
Harris, Douglas B. ....Warrensburg, MO
Harris, Douglas D. ....Missoula, MT
Harris, Douglas E., Sr. ....Norman, OK
Harris, Douglas W. ....Bellevue, WA
Harris, Dowell, Fisher & Harris, L.C.
St. Louis, MO
Harris, Drexel B. ....New York, NY
Harris, Duke C. ....Sycamore, IL
Harris, Duncan G. ....Chicago, IL
Harris, E. Ray ....Bartlesville, OK
Harris, Earl D. ....Atlanta, GA
Harris & Ebert ....Marion, OH
Harris, Eddie J. ....Los Angeles, CA
Harris, Edgar M. ....Marietta, GA
Harris, Edgar Y. ....Media, PA
Harris, Edward A. ....New York, NY
Harris, Edward B., Jr. ....Baltimore, MD
Harris, Edward I. ....Van Nuys, CA
Harris, Edward J. ....Galveston, TX
Harris, Edward L., Jr. ....New York, NY
Harris, Edward R. ....Denver, CO
Harris, Edward S. ....Baltimore, MD
Harris, Edward W. ....Cheyenne, WY
Harris, Edward W., III ....Indianapolis, IN
Harris, Edwin C. ....Madisonville, TN
Harris, Edwin L., III ....Fayetteville, NC
Harris, Elaine ....South Orange, NJ
Harris, Elihu M. ....Oakland, CA
Harris, Elise ....Atlanta, GA
Harris, Elizabeth A. ....Pleasanton, CA
Harris, Elizabeth A. ....Washington, DC
Harris, Elizabeth B. ....Bennettsville, SC
Harris, Elizabeth E. ....New York, NY
Harris, Elizabeth Leigh ....Boulder, CO
Harris, Elizabeth P. ....Philadelphia, PA
Harris, Elizabeth S. ....Birmingham, MI
Harris, Elizabeth Siano ....Titusville, FL
Harris, Ella P.
National Labor Relations Board, Office of the General Counsel, GV
Harris, Ellen W. ....New York, NY
Harris, Elliott ....Miami, FL
Harris Ellsworth & Levin
Washington, DC
Harris, Emily Sue ....Montrose, CO
Harris, Enid W. ....Wilkes-Barre, PA
Harris, Eric A. ....Richmond, VA
Harris, Eric C. ....Park Hills, MO
Harris, Eric I. ....New Brunswick, NJ
Harris, Eric M. ....New York, NY
Harris, Eric W. ....Chesapeake, VA
Harris, Erica L. ....Chicago, IL
Harris, Erica W. ....Houston, TX
Harris, Ernest L. ....Newburgh, NY
Harris, Ernest V. ....Athens, GA
Harris, Eugene S. ....Pine Bluff, AR
Harris, Eugene W. ....Lakeland, FL
Harris, Evelyn S. ....Harrisburg, PA
Harris, F. Epperson ....Jacksonville, FL
Harris, F. Michael, Jr. ....California, MD
Harris, Fannie Jordan ....Nashville, TN
Harris, Faye C. ....Kerrville, TX
Harris, Fears, Davis, Lynch & McDaniel
Norfolk, VA
Virginia Beach, VA
Harris, Feldman Law Offices ....Omaha, NE
Harris, Finley & Bogle, A Professional Corporation ....Dallas, TX
Fort Worth, TX
Grapevine, TX
Harris, Flora A. ....Los Angeles, CA
Harris, Floyd A. ....Milwaukee, WI
Harris, Franca E. ....New York, NY
Harris, Frances Ann ....Dallas, TX
Harris, Francesca C. ....Wichita, KS
Harris, Frank D. ....South Hill, VA
Harris, Frank J. ....Charlestown, MA
Harris, Frank Philips ....Marietta, GA
Harris, Frank W. ....Mineola, NY
Harris, Franklin ....Fremont, CA
Harris, Fred Damon ....Charlotte, NC
Harris, Fred F., Jr. ....Tallahassee, FL
Harris, Fred L., (A Professional Corporation)
Rancho Cordova, CA
Harris, Frederic C. ....Arlington, MA
Harris, Frederick L. ....Farmington, MI
Harris, Frederick L. ....Myrtle Beach, SC
Surfside Beach, SC
Harris, Frederick S. ....Baltimore, MD
Harris, Frederick S. ....New York, NY
Harris, Frederick T. ....Omaha, NE
Harris, Fredrick G. ....Walnut Creek, CA
Harris, G. Bernard ....Uniontown, OH
Harris, G. Ray ....Spartanburg, SC
Harris, G. Ray, Attorney at Law, P.A.
Spartanburg, SC
Harris, Gail B. ....New York, NY
Harris, Gail W. ....Tulsa, OK
Harris, Gale I. ....East Lansing, MI
Harris, Gary K. ....Orlando, FL
Armonk, NY
Harris, Gary T. ....Williamsport, PA
Harris Geno & Dunbar, P.A. ....Jackson, MS
Oxford, MS
Harris, George A. ....Pasadena, CA
Harris, George A., III ....Richmond, CA
Harris, George Bryan ....Birmingham, AL
Harris, George C. ....Salt Lake City, UT
Harris, George E.
Palm Beach Gardens, FL
Harris, George E., Jr. ....Salt Lake City, UT
Harris, George F. ....East Rochester, NY
Honeoye Falls, NY
Harris, George I. ....New York, NY
Harris, George N., Jr. ....Washington, DC
Harris, George P. ....Las Vegas, NV
Harris, George R. ....Montclair, NJ
Harris, George W. ....Pinson, AL
Harris, Gerald ....New York, NY
Harris, Gerald L. ....Baytown, TX
Harris, Gerry L. ....Lexington, KY
Harris, Ginger ....Millburn, NJ
New York, NY
Harris • Ginsberg LLP ....Los Angeles, CA
Harris, Glenn A. ....North Miami Beach, FL
Harris, Glenn A. ....Voorhees, NJ
Harris, Glenn E. ....Marble, NC
Harris, Glenn P.
Small Business Administration, Office of the General Counsel, GV
Harris, Gordon H." Stumpy "
Orlando, FL
Harris, Gordon K., Jr. ....Troy, MI
Harris, Gordon, McMahan, Peters & Thompson, P.C. ....Claremore, OK
Tulsa, OK
Harris and Graves, P.A. ....Columbia, SC
Greenville, SC
Harris & Greenwell, L.L.P.
Corpus Christi, TX
Harris, Greg C. ....Kearney, NE
Harris, Greg E. ....Boston, MA
Harris, Gregg W. ....Washington, DC
Harris, Gregory A. ....Maywood, IL
Harris, Gregory E. ....Portland, OR
Harris, Gregory G. ....Albany, NY
Harris, Gregory J. ....Leesburg, VA
Harris, Gregory J., P.C., Law Offices of
Leesburg, VA
Harris, Gregory K. ....Springfield, IL
Harris, Gregory L. ....New York, NY
Harris, Gregory M. ....Middletown, CT
Harris, Gregory P. ....Columbia, SC
Harris, Gregory R. ....Seattle, WA
Harris, Gregory W. ....Little Rock, AR
Harris, Gregory Y. ....Phoenix, AZ
Harris, Gretchen Grover
Oklahoma City, OK
Harris, Guidi, Rosner & Mordecai, P.A.
Jacksonville, FL
Harris, Gwendolyn D. ....Huntsville, AL
Harris, Gwendolyn W. ....Brattleboro, VT
Harris, Gwynne E. ....Topeka, KS
Harris, H. Anthony ....Solana Beach, CA
Harris, H. Donald ....El Macero, CA
Harris, H. Elizabeth ....Los Angeles, CA
Harris, H. Stanley, Jr. ....Charlotte, NC
Harris, H. Stephen, Jr. ....Atlanta, GA
Harris, Haig Arsen, Jr.
San Francisco, CA
Harris & Hanna, P.A. ....Myrtle Beach, SC
Surfside Beach, SC
Harris, Harley R. ....Solana Beach, CA
Harris, Harold ....Thiensville, WI
Harris, Harold A. ....Chicago, IL
Harris, Harold F. ....Temple, TX
Harris & Harris ....Lincoln, IL
Harris & Harris ....Warsaw, IN
Harris & Harris ....Austin, TX
Harris & Harris ....Issaquah, WA
Harris and Harris, A Professional Corporation ....Warrington, PA
Harris, Harris & Harris ....San Diego, CA
Harris, Harris & King ....Florence, AL
Harris & Harris, LLP ....Birmingham, AL
Harris & Harris, Ltd. ....Chicago, IL
Harris & Harris, P.C. ....Fredericksburg, VA
Harris & Harris, P.S.C. ....Columbia, KY
Harris, Harry L. ....Evanston, WY
Harris, Harry N. ....Fort Worth, TX
Harris, Harvey A. ....St. Louis, MO
Harris, Hedy A. ....Townshend, VT
Harris, Heidi ....New York, NY
Harris, Helen C. ....Department of Agriculture, Office of the General Counsel, GV
Harris, Henry ....Ventura, CA
Harris, Henry B., III ....Atlanta, GA
Harris, Henry G. ....Massillon, OH
Harris, Herbert E., II ....Washington, DC
Harris, Herbert E., Jr. ....Providence, RI
Harris, Holly A. ....San Francisco, CA
Harris, Holly K. ....Marshfield, MA
Harris, Holly L. ....Dallas, TX
Harris, Homer B., Jr. ....Lincoln, IL
Harris, Homer L. ....New York, NY
Harris, Howard A. ....New York, NY
Harris, Howard Dane, Jr. ....Houston, TX
Harris, Howard R. ....San Diego, CA
Harris, Howard S. ....Woodcliff Lake, NJ
Harris, Howard Y., Jr. ....Englewood, CO
Harris, H. S., III ....Austin, TX
Harris, Huel ....Decatur, AL
Harris, Hugh C. ....Cullman, AL
Harris & Hull, pllc ....Seattle, WA
Harris, I. Alan ....New York, NY
Harris, I. Robert ....New York, NY
Harris, I. Ron ....Mount Kisco, NY
Harris, Ian F. ....New York, NY
Harris, Imogene H. ....Tulsa, OK
Harris, Ira G. ....Southfield, MI
Harris, Ira J. ....Walnut Creek, CA
Harris, Irving ....Sunrise, FL
Harris, Irving ....Cincinnati, OH
Harris, Irwin ....Phoenix, AZ
Harris, Irwin H. ....St. Louis, MO
Harris, Ivan D., Jr. ....Collierville, TN
Harris, Ivy Cream ....Jacksonville, FL
Harris, J. Barton ....Houston, TX
Harris, J. Calhoun, Jr. ....Atlanta, GA
Harris, J. Colter ....Dallas, TX
Harris, J. Edward ....San Diego, CA
Harris, J. Gates ....Red Springs, NC
Harris, J. Joe ....San Antonio, TX
Harris, J. Kenneth ....Haddonfield, NJ
Moorestown, NJ
Harris, J. Lamont ....Crawfordsville, IN
Harris, J. Malcolm ....Austin, TX
Harris, J. Pierce ....San Diego, CA
Harris, J. Richard
Palm Beach Gardens, FL
Harris, J. Robert ....Houston, TX
Harris, J. Robert, III ....Hampton, VA
Harris, J. Thadieu, III ....Wise, VA
Harris, Jack C. ....Jacksonville, FL
Harris, Jack C. ....Canfield, OH
Harris, Jack L. ....Richmond, VA
Harris, Jack P. ....Baton Rouge, LA
Harris, Jack W. ....Sweetwater, TX
Harris, Jackson B. ....Rome, GA
Harris, Jackson B. ....Rome, GA
Harris & James ....Macon, GA
Harris, James A. ....Glastonbury, CT
Harris, James A. ....Washington, DC
Harris, James A. ....Hammond, IN
Harris, James A. ....Clarksburg, WV
Harris, James A., III ....Birmingham, AL
Harris, James A., Jr. ....Birmingham, AL
Harris, James A., Jr. ....Paducah, KY
Harris, James Alan ....Marion, OH
Harris, James B. ....Columbus, OH
Harris, James B. ....Dallas, TX
Harris, James D. ....Houston, TX
Harris, James D., (A Professional Corporation)
Pasadena, CA
Harris, James D., Jr. ....Bowling Green, KY
Harris, James D., Jr. ....Oxford, MS
Harris, James E. ....Birmingham, AL
Harris, James E. ....Sacramento, CA
Harris, James E. ....Martinsville, IN
Harris, James E. ....Omaha, NE
Harris, James E. ....Portland, OR
Harris, James E., (P.A.) ....Little Rock, AR

Harris, James G. ..... Roanoke Rapids, NC
Harris, James H. ..... Lutz, FL
Harris, James H. ..... Loudon, TN
Harris, James H., III ..... Nashville, TN
Harris, James Jeffrey ..... Columbus, OH
Harris, James L. ..... Fayetteville, AR
Harris, James L. ..... Chicago, IL
Harris, James L. ..... New York, NY
Harris, James L., Jr. ..... Salt Lake City, UT
Harris, James M. ..... Los Angeles, CA
Harris, James M. ..... San Antonio, TX
Harris, James M., Jr. ..... Beaumont, TX
Harris, James P. ..... Montgomery, NY
Harris, James P. ..... Wilkes-Barre, PA
Harris, James P., III ..... Wilkes-Barre, PA
Harris, James P., Jr. ..... Miami, FL
Harris, James R. ..... Lincoln, NE
Harris, James R. ..... Corpus Christi, TX
Harris, James S. ..... Springhill, LA
Harris, James T. ..... Atlanta, GA
Harris, James T. ..... New York, NY
Harris, James T. ..... Dallas, TX
Harris, James W.
Hot Springs National Park, AR
Harris, James W. ..... Atlanta, GA
Harris, James W. ..... Mineral Point, WI
Harris, James Warden ..... Washington, DC
Harris, Jamie O. ..... San Francisco, CA
Harris, Jana J. ..... Oklahoma City, OK
Harris, Jana K. ..... Little Rock, AR
Harris, Jane E. ..... Joliet, IL
Harris, Jane R. ..... Tallahassee, FL
Harris, Janet N. ..... Denver, CO
Harris, Janie Greenwood ..... St. Louis, MO
Harris, Janine D. ..... Alexandria, VA
Harris, Janna D. ..... Charlotte, NC
Harris, Jared M. ..... Blackfoot, ID
Harris, Jasper G., Jr. ..... Houston, TX
Harris, Jay ..... Toledo, OH
Harris, Jay Barry ..... Philadelphia, PA
Harris, Jay G. ..... Las Vegas, NM
Harris, Jay J. ..... Baton Rouge, LA
Harris, Jay R. ..... Dallas, TX
Harris, Jay S. ..... New York, NY
Harris, Jean E. ..... Phoenix, AZ
Harris, Jeff D. ..... Chicago, IL
Harris, Jeff T. ..... Charlotte, NC
Harris, Jeffery D. ..... Sacramento, CA
Harris, Jeffrey ..... Washington, DC
Harris, Jeffrey B. ..... Los Angeles, CA
Harris, Jeffrey C. ..... Houston, TX
Harris, Jeffrey J. ..... New York, NY
Harris, Jeffrey L. ..... Rockford, IL
Harris, Jeffrey M. ..... Fort Lauderdale, FL
Harris, Jeffrey M., P.A.
Fort Lauderdale, FL
Harris, Jeffrey P. ..... Cincinnati, OH
Harris, Jeffrey S. ..... Honolulu, HI
Harris, Jeffrey W. ..... Atlanta, GA
Harris, Jennifer ..... Los Angeles, CA
Harris, Jerald David ..... Cincinnati, OH
Harris, Jermaine ..... Philadelphia, PA
Harris, Jerome J. ..... Baton Rouge, LA
Harris, Jerome M. ..... Houston, TX
Harris, Jerrold D. ..... Ephrata, PA
Harris, Jerry L. ..... San Diego, CA
Harris, Jerry L. ..... Austin, TX
Harris, Jerry S. ..... Longview, TX
Harris, Jesse S. ..... Tulsa, OK
Harris, Jessica Zeller ..... Lawrenceville, NJ
Harris, Jessie M. ..... Washington, DC
Harris, Jet ..... Atlanta, GA
Harris, Jill M. ..... Beverly Hills, CA
Harris, Jim C. ..... Boise, ID
Harris, Jimmie ..... Beverly Hills, CA
Harris, Jo Ann ..... New York, NY
Harris, Jo Ann ..... Akron, OH
Harris, Joan A. ..... Cincinnati, OH
Harris, Joan Bannan ..... New Providence, NJ
Harris, Joan Elizabeth West ..... Macon, GA
Harris, Joe Frank, Jr. ..... Cartersville, GA
Harris, Joe Frank, Jr., & Associates, P.C.
Cartersville, GA
Harris, Joe H. ..... Washington, DC
Harris, Joe H. ..... Cedar Rapids, IA
Harris, Joe M., Jr. ..... Jonesboro, GA
Harris, Joel A. ..... Antioch, CA
Harris, Joel B. ..... New York, NY
Harris, Johanna ..... Boston, MA
Harris, John ..... New York, NY
Harris, John A. ..... Carrollton, GA
Columbus, GA
Harris, John A. ..... West Allis, WI
Harris, John Anthony ..... Phoenix, AZ
Harris, John B. ..... New York, NY
Harris, John Burke, III ..... Macon, GA
Harris, John C. ..... Sells, AZ
Harris, John C. ..... Russellville, AR
Harris, John C. ..... Arlington, TX
Harris, John C., Jr. ..... Florence, AL
Harris, John D. ..... Los Angeles, CA
Harris, John D. ..... Orlando, FL
Harris, John D. ..... San Antonio, TX
Harris, John D., P.C. ..... Phoenix, AZ
Harris, John David ..... Phoenix, AZ
Harris, John David ..... Little Rock, AR
Harris, John Duke ..... Phoenix, AZ
Harris, John E. ..... Minneapolis, MN
Harris, John E., III ..... Department of Justice,
Criminal Division, GV
Harris, John F. ..... Los Angeles, CA
Harris, John F. ..... Tallahassee, FL
Harris, John F., P.C. ..... Los Angeles, CA
Harris, John G. ..... Wilmington, DE
Harris, John H., Jr. ..... Memphis, TN
Harris, John I., III ..... Nashville, TN
Harris, John J. ..... Victorville, CA
Harris, John Joseph ..... Los Angeles, CA

Harris, John K. ..... Brighton, MI
Harris, John K., Jr. ..... Danielson, CT
Harris, John M. ..... Stockton, CA
Harris, John M. ..... Titusville, FL
Harris, John M. ..... Morehead City, NC
Harris, John M., P.A. ..... Morehead City, NC
Harris, John O. ..... St. Louis, MO
Harris, John O. ..... Ashland, VA
Harris, John P. ..... Moline, IL
Harris, John P. ..... Millburn, NJ
New York, NY
Harris, John P. ..... Seattle, WA
Harris, John P., III ..... Fredericksburg, VA
Harris, John R. ..... Atlanta, GA
Harris, John R. ..... Austin, TX
Harris, John S. ..... Albany, NY
New York, NY
Harris, John T. ..... Gridley, CA
Harris, John T. ..... Hartford, CT
Harris, John T. ..... Drummond Island, MI
Harris, John T. ..... East Rochester, NY
Honeoye Falls, NY
Harris, John W. ..... Los Angeles, CA
Harris, John W. ..... Dallas, TX
Harris, John W. ..... Victoria, TX
Harris, John W., Jr. ..... San Antonio, TX
Harris, John Wallis ..... San Antonio, TX
Harris, Johnny Ray ..... Paintsville, KY
Harris, Jon R., Jr. ..... Atlanta, GA
Harris, Jonathan ..... Oklahoma City, OK
Harris, Jonathan A. ..... Los Angeles, CA
Harris, Jonathan A. ..... Hartford, CT
Harris, Jonathan C. ..... Baton Rouge, LA
Harris, Jonathan C. ..... New York, NY
Harris, Jonathan D. ..... Los Angeles, CA
Harris, Jonathan M. ..... New York, NY
Harris, Jonathan M. ..... Richmond, VA
Harris, Jonathan N. ..... Hackensack, NJ
Harris, Jonathan R. ..... Boston, MA
Harris, Jonathan T. ..... San Diego, CA
Harris, Jonathan T. ..... Portland, ME
Harris, Jonathan T. ..... Houston, TX
Harris, Jonathan W. ..... Chicago, IL
Harris, Jonathon ..... Houston, TX
Harris, Jos. B. ..... Randallstown, MD
Harris, Joseph ..... Los Angeles, CA
Harris, Joseph ..... Albany, NY
Harris, Joseph B. ..... Los Angeles, CA
Harris, Joseph R. ..... Houston, TX
Harris, Josh A. ..... Albuquerque, NM
Harris, Joshua G. ..... Yuba City, CA
Harris, Joy M. ..... Los Angeles, CA
St. Louis, MO
Harris, Joyce B. ..... Government Printing Office,
Office of General Counsel, GV
Harris, J. P., II ..... Salem, OR
Harris, Judah J. ..... Hartford, CT
Harris, Judd M. ..... Chicago, IL
Harris, Judith E. ..... Philadelphia, PA
Harris, Judith L. ..... Washington, DC
Harris, Judith Lynn ..... Irving, TX
Harris, Julian A., Jr. ..... Pensacola, FL
Harris, Julie A. ..... Glastonbury, CT
Harris, Julie A. ..... Cleveland, OH
Harris, Julie E. ..... Charlotte, NC
Harris, June A. ..... Cambridge, MA
Harris, June Lorraine ..... Fullerton, CA
Harris, Justin D. ..... Fresno, CA
Harris, Justine A. ..... New York, NY
Harris, Karen K. ..... Chicago, IL
Harris, Kari K. ..... Boston, MA
Harris, Karl R. ..... Hamilton, OH
Harris, Karstaedt, Jamison & Powers, P.C.
Colorado Springs, CO
Englewood, CO
Harris, Katherine L. ..... St. Louis, MO
Harris, Katherine M. ..... Washington, DC
Harris, Kathleen ..... Lexington, KY
Harris, Kathleen F. ..... Houston, TX
Harris, Kathleen Gay ..... Richmond, VA
Harris, Kathleen M. ..... Forest Grove, OR
Harris, Kathleen N. ..... Lansing, MI
Harris, Kathryn Toub ..... Vienna, VA
Harris, Kathy C. ..... Fort Lauderdale, FL
Harris, Keith ..... Livingston, NJ
Harris, Keith E. ..... Palatine, IL
Harris, Keith E. ..... New York, NY
Harris, Keith E., P.C. ..... Palatine, IL
Harris, Kelley Dee ..... Edmond, OK
Harris, Kelly Crowell ..... Morehead City, NC
Harris, Kelly J. ..... Washington, DC
Harris, Ken ..... Lawton, OK
Harris, Kenneth D. ..... San Francisco, CA
Harris, Kenneth E. ..... Columbus, OH
Harris, Kenneth E., Jr. ..... Westminster, CO
Harris, Kenneth J. ..... Department of Justice,
Criminal Division, GV
Harris, Kenneth L. ..... Chicago, IL
Harris, Kenneth L. ..... Southfield, MI
Harris, Kenneth L. ..... Charlotte, NC
Harris, Kent D. ..... Sacramento, CA
Harris, Kenward K. ..... Alexandria, VA
Harris Kessler & Goldstein LLC
Chicago, IL
Waukegan, IL
Harris, Kevin C. ..... Shawnee, KS
Harris, Kevin D. ..... Indianapolis, IN
Harris, Kevin F. ..... Springfield, IL
Harris, Kevin W. ..... Sacramento, CA
Harris, Kimberley D. ..... New York, NY
Harris, Kimberly Cofer ..... Macon, GA
Harris, Kimberly J. ..... Bellevue, WA
Harris, Kimberly Paige ..... Odessa, TX
Harris, Kimkea L. ..... Memphis, TN
Harris, Kirk E. ..... San Diego, CA
Harris, Kirstan Brooks ..... Boston, MA
Harris, Kristen A. ..... Chicago, IL

Harris, Kristen S. ..... Cerritos, CA
Riverside, CA
Harris, Kukey & Helgesen, P.A.
Palm Beach, FL
Palm Beach Gardens, FL
West Palm Beach, FL
Harris, Kurt K. ..... Las Vegas, NV
Harris, L. Archie ..... Sacramento, CA
Harris, L. Christopher ..... Dallas, TX
Harris, L. Craig ..... Jersey Shore, PA
Harris, L. Douglas ..... New York, NY
Harris, L. Lee ..... Blythewood, SC
Harris, L. Randolph ..... Oakland, CA
Harris, Lambert, Howerton & Dorris
Carbondale, IL
Harrisburg, IL
Marion, IL
Murphysboro, IL
Harris, Lara Drino ..... Los Angeles, CA
Harris, L. Archie, Professional Law Corporation
Sacramento, CA
Harris, Larry C., Jr. ..... Asheville, NC
Harris, Larry D. ..... Washington, DC
Harris, Larry E. ..... Concord, NC
Harris, Larry K. ..... St. Louis, MO
Harris, Larry N. ..... Littleton, CO
Harris, Laura Berry ..... Dearborn, MI
Harris, Laura H. ..... Columbia, KY
Harris, Laura J. ..... Houston, TX
Harris, Laura M. ..... Syracuse, NY
Harris, Laureen C. ..... Mineola, NY
Harris, Lauren K. ..... Bedminster, NJ
Harris, Laurie S. ..... Santa Barbara, CA
Harris, Lavern D. ..... Kerrville, TX
Harris, Lavern D., Attorney at Law, P.C.
Kerrville, TX
Harris Law Firm ..... Sacramento, CA
Harris Law Firm ..... Alexandria, LA
Harris Law Firm, L.L.P.
Baton Rouge, LA
Harris Law Firm, P.C. ..... Billings, MT
Harris Law Firm, P.C. ..... Evanston, WY
Harris Law Firm, The ..... East Rochester, NY
Honeoye Falls, NY
Harris Law Firm, The ..... Carthage, TX
Harris Law Offices ..... Lincoln, NE
Harris, Lee ..... Chicago, IL
Harris, Lee A., Jr. ..... Richmond, VA
Harris, Lee Blair ..... Louisville, KY
Harris, Lee G. ..... Kokomo, IN
Harris, Lee S. ..... San Francisco, CA
Harris, Lee S. ..... Department of Education,
Office of the General Counsel, GV
Harris, Leodis ..... Cleveland, OH
Harris, Leon R., III ..... Bakersfield, CA
Harris, Lesley B. ..... San Francisco, CA
Harris, Leslie J. ..... New York, NY
Harris, Leslie J. ..... Eugene, OR
Harris, Levanche T. ..... Houston, TX
Harris & Liken ..... Athens, GA
Atlanta, GA
Harris, Lillian E. ..... Red Bank, NJ
Harris, Lillian Smith ..... Harrisburg, PA
Harris, Linda Chaplik ..... Chicago, IL
Harris, Linda L. ..... Billings, MT
Harris, Linda M. ..... Oklahoma City, OK
Harris, Linda S. ..... Chicago, IL
Harris, Lisa Dawn ..... Clayton, MO
Harris, Lisa K. Wells
Department of Education,
Office of the General Counsel, GV
Harris, Lisa L. ..... Atlanta, GA
Harris, Lisa L. ..... Grosse Pointe Park, MI
Harris, Lisa M. ..... Orlando, FL
Harris, Lisa M. ..... Baltimore, MD
Harris, Lisa Rochelle ..... Miami, FL
Harris & Literski ..... Brighton, MI
Harris, Lively & Duesler, L.L.P.
Beaumont, TX
Harris, Lloyd G. ..... New York, NY
Harris, Lon ..... El Segundo, CA
Harris, Lonnie W. ..... Kansas City, MO
Harris, Lori E. ..... Boston, MA
Harris, Lori R. ..... New York, NY
Harris, Lorinda B. ..... Costa Mesa, CA
Harris, Louis ..... San Francisco, CA
Harris, Louis A. ..... St. Paul, MN
Harris, Louise E. ..... Winston-Salem, NC
Harris, Lowell W. ..... Sacramento, CA
Harris, Lyman H. ..... Birmingham, AL
Harris, Lynda J. ..... West Palm Beach, FL
Harris, Lynn C. ..... Provo, UT
Harris, Lynn Maynard ..... Miami, FL
Harris, M. June ..... Whiteriver, AZ
Harris, M. Taylor, Jr. ..... Nashville, TN
Harris, M. Teresa ..... Buena Vista, VA
Harris, Malcolm A. ..... Metamora, MI
Harris, Malcolm E. ..... Raleigh, NC
Harris, Malcolm E. ..... Wake Forest, NC
Harris, Malcolm H. ..... Los Angeles, CA
Harris, Malcolm S. ..... Port Townsend, WA
Seattle, WA
Harris, Marc S. ..... Los Angeles, CA
Harris, Marcia J. ..... Los Angeles, CA
Harris, Marcy L. ..... Eden Prairie, MN
Harris, Marcy Ressler ..... New York, NY
Harris, Margaret A. ..... Greensboro, NC
Harris, Margaret A. ..... Houston, TX
Harris, Margaret Carol ..... San Antonio, TX
Harris, Marged G.
Environmental Protection Agency,
Office of Enforcement and Compliance
Assurance, GV
Harris, Maria Englert ..... New York, NY
Harris, Marjorie A. ..... Champaign, IL
Harris, Marjory ..... San Francisco, CA
Harris, Mark A. ..... Chicago, IL

Harris, Mark D. ..... Treasury Department,
Internal Revenue Service, GV
Harris, Mark E. ..... Kansas City, MO
Harris, Mark G. ..... Costa Mesa, CA
Harris, Mark H., Law Offices of
Sacramento, CA
Harris, Mark J. ..... New York, NY
Harris, Mark L. ..... Indianapolis, IN
Harris, Mark M. ..... Chicago, IL
Harris, Mark P. ..... Arcata, CA
Harris, Mark Randal ..... Griffith, IN
Harris, Mark S. ..... Blue Bell, PA
Harris, Mark W. ..... Dallas, TX
Harris, Mark W. ..... Evanston, WY
Harris, Marshall S. ..... Miami, FL
Harris, Martha ..... Dallas, TX
Harris, Martha J. ..... Bangor, ME
Harris, Martha M. ..... Buffalo, NY
Harris, Martin ..... Chicago, IL
Harris, Mary A. ..... San Luis Obispo, CA
Harris, Mary Ann Spangler ..... Chicago, IL
Harris, Mary DePoy ..... Evanston, IL
Harris, Mary Mell ..... Beaverton, OR
Harris, Mary W. ..... Jefferson City, MO
Harris, Matthew R. ..... Seattle, WA
Harris, Matthew S. ..... San Jose, CA
Harris, Matthew Thompson ..... Nashville, TN
Harris, Matthews & Warren, P.C.
Bracey, VA
Kenbridge, VA
South Hill, VA
Harris, Maureen Finnegan ..... Albany, NY
Harris, Max D. ..... St. Paul, MN
Harris, Maxwell D. ..... Oklahoma City, OK
Harris, McCausland & Schmitt, P.C.
Overland Park, KS
Kansas City, MO
Harris, McClellan, Binau & Cox, P.L.L.
Columbus, OH
Harris, Mel E. ..... Brooklyn, NY
Harris, Mel S. ..... New York, NY
Harris, Melanie W. ..... Jacksonville, FL
Harris, Melody ..... San Diego, CA
Harris, Mericle & Wakayama
Port Townsend, WA
Seattle, WA
Harris, Micalyn S. ..... Ridgewood, NJ
Harris, Michael ..... Los Angeles, CA
Harris, Michael B. ..... San Diego, CA
Harris, Michael C. ..... Chesterton, IN
Harris, Michael D. ..... Los Angeles, CA
Harris, Michael D. ..... West Palm Beach, FL
Harris, Michael D., (P.C.)
Rancho Mirage, CA
Harris, Michael F. ..... St. Louis, MO
Harris, Michael F. ..... Cleveland, OH
Harris, Michael F. R. ..... Philadelphia, PA
Harris, Michael G. ..... Encinitas, CA
Harris, Michael G. ..... Oklahoma City, OK
Harris, Michael J. ..... Burlington, VT
Harris, Michael John ..... McLean, VA
Harris, Michael K. ..... Lodi, CA
Harris, Michael L. ..... Columbia, KY
Harris, Michael L. ..... Baton Rouge, LA
Harris, Michael L. ..... Chickasha, OK
Harris, Michael P. ..... Seattle, WA
Harris, Michael Paul ..... St. Joseph, MO
Harris, Michael Paul, P.C. ..... St. Joseph, MO
Harris, Michael R. ..... Philadelphia, PA
Harris, Michael Ray ..... Los Angeles, CA
Harris, Michael Richard ..... Los Angeles, CA
Harris, Michael S. ..... Beverly Hills, CA
Las Vegas, NV
Harris, Michael S. ..... Stamford, CT
Harris, Michael S. ..... Houston, TX
Harris, Michael T. ..... Foster City, CA
Harris, Michael T. ..... Margate, FL
Harris, Michael T. ..... Lansing, MI
Harris, Michael W. ..... Syracuse, NY
Harris, Michele Silva ..... Denver, CO
Harris, Mickey E. ..... Springfield, MA
Harris, Midyette & Darby, P.A.
Lakeland, FL
Harris, Mildred ..... San Francisco, CA
Harris, Mindy ..... Englewood, CO
Harris, Mindy A. ..... Norristown, PA
Harris, Mitchell, Burns & Brewer PLLC
Fayetteville, NC
Harris, Mitchell R. ..... Hartford, CT
Harris, Monica R. ..... New York, NY
Harris, Monica Y. ..... Pasadena, CA
Harris, Morgan D. ..... Las Vegas, NV
Harris, Morgan & Parson, LLC
Marietta, GA
Harris, Morran D. ..... Clinton, MO
Osceola, MO
Harris, Morton A. ..... Columbus, GA
Harris, Morton J. ..... Northfield, IL
Harris & Muchow ..... Santa Rosa, CA
Harris, Muriel Yates ..... Kansas City, KS
Harris, Myra A. ..... Phoenix, AZ
Harris, Myra Lou ..... Washington, DC
Harris, Myron ..... Philadelphia, PA
Harris, Nancy ..... San Francisco, CA
Harris, Nancy E. ..... Oberlin, OH
Harris, Nancy Hutcheson ..... Tampa, FL
Harris, Nancy Hutcheson, P.A.
Tampa, FL
Harris, Nathan H. ..... Los Angeles, CA
Harris, Neil A. ..... Chico, CA
Harris, Nelda F. ..... Dallas, TX
Harris, Nelson G. ..... Raleigh, NC
Harris, Nelson G. ..... Philadelphia, PA
Harris, Nicholas C. ..... New York, NY
Harris, Nicole D. ..... San Francisco, CA
Harris, Norma ..... Orinda, CA
Harris, Norman ..... Burlingame, CA
Harris & Offner, LLP ..... San Diego, CA

Harris, O. H. (Ike) ... Dallas, TX
Harris, Oliver H., 3rd ... Stuart, FL
Harris, Oliver III, P.A. ... Stuart, FL
Harris, P. Shawn ... Forest, MS
Harris, P. Stephen ... Kansas City, MO
Harris, Palumbo, Powers & Cunningham, P.L.L.C. ... Phoenix, AZ
Harris, Pamela Lee ... Crookston, MN
Harris, Pamela M. ... Minneapolis, MN
Harris, Pamela W. ... Lancaster, TX
Harris, Patrice J. ... Chicago, IL
Harris, Patricia A. ... Louisville, KY
Harris, Patricia Ann ... Bethesda, MD
Harris, Patricia M. ... Moline, IL
Harris, Patricia M. ... New Orleans, LA
Harris, Patrick E. ... New York, NY
Harris, Paul A. ... San Francisco, CA
Harris, Paul A. ... Oklahoma City, OK
Harris, Paul A. ... Madison, WI
Harris, Paul Clinton, Sr.
Charlottesville, VA
Harris, Paul E. ... Houston, TX
Harris, Paul F. ... Glen Burnie, MD
Harris, Paul F., Jr. ... Glen Burnie, MD
Harris, Paul J. ... St. Louis, MO
Harris, Paul J. ... Abilene, TX
Harris, Paul Marshall ... Boston, MA
Harris, Paul N. ... New Brunswick, NJ
Harris, Paul N. ... Cleveland, OH
Harris, Paul R. ... St. Cloud, MN
Harris, Perisho & Woodson ... Stockton, CA
Harris, Peter F. ... Los Angeles, CA
Harris, Peter H. ... Boca Raton, FL
Harris, Peter J. ... Seattle, WA
Harris, Peter L. ... Minneapolis, MN
Harris, Peter R. ... Santa Rosa, CA
Harris, Peter T. ... Denville, NJ
Harris, Phil B. ... Greenfield, TN
Harris, Phil M. ... Weslaco, TX
Harris, Philip E. ... Madison, WI
Harris, Philip H. ... New York, NY
Harris, Philip J. ... Warsaw, IN
Harris, Philip L. ... San Antonio, TX
Harris, Philip Lee ... Chicago, IL
Harris, Philip S. ... Portland, OR
Harris, Phillip G. ... Memphis, TN
Harris, Phillip H. ... Chicago, IL
Harris, Phillips & Harris, A Professional Corporation ... Atlanta, GA
Harris, Pierce Jackson, Jr. ... Guntersville, AL
Harris, Polly J. ... Columbus, OH
Harris, Preston & Chambers, A Professional Corporation ... Logan, UT
Harris, Priscilla Norwood ... Orange Park, FL
Harris, R. Andrew ... Morehead City, NC
Harris, R. Barton, II ... Dallas, TX
Harris, R. Britt, Jr. ... Atlanta, GA
Harris, R. Everett ... Mesa, AZ
Harris, R. Jeffrey ... Kansas City, MO
Harris, R. Jeffrey ... Milwaukee, WI
Harris, R. Kennedy ... Greensboro, NC
Harris, R. Lawrence ... Norwood, MN
Waconia, MN
Harris, R. Lynne ... Department of Justice, Civil Division, GV
Harris, R. Robert ... Ogden, UT
Harris, R. Thomas ... Stockton, CA
Harris, Ralph C., Jr. ... Charlotte, NC
Harris, Ralph D. ... Phoenix, AZ
Harris, Ralph E. ... El Paso, TX
Harris, Rand F. ... Los Angeles, CA
Harris, Rand F., A Prof. Corp., Law Offices of ... Los Angeles, CA
North Hollywood, CA
Harris, Randall G. ... Los Angeles, CA
Harris, Randall M. ... Clovis, NM
Harris, Randall P. B. ... Trimble, TN
Harris, Ray F. ... Tucson, AZ
Harris, Ray K. ... Phoenix, AZ
Harris, Raymond I. ... St. Louis, MO
Harris, Raymond P., Jr. ... Amarillo, TX
Dallas, TX
Harris, Reginald L. ... St. Louis, MO
Harris, Reid W. ... Saint Simons Island, GA
Harris, Reid W., P.C.
Saint Simons Island, GA
Harris, Renée G. ... Doylestown, PA
Harris, Rhonda F. ... Philadelphia, PA
Harris, Rhonda R. ... Newport Beach, CA
Harris, Rhonda W. ... Memphis, TN
Harris, Richard ... Detroit, MI
Harris, Richard A. ... Fresno, CA
Harris, Richard A., (A Professional Corporation) ... Las Vegas, NV
Harris, Richard Bates ... Leominster, MA
Harris, Richard C. ... Washington, DC
Harris, Richard C. ... Wichita, KS
Harris, Richard C. ... Georgetown, TX
Harris, Richard D. ... Hartford, CT
Harris, Richard D. ... Chicago, IL
Harris, Richard D. ... Tacoma, WA
Harris, Richard D., Jr. ... Midlothian, VA
Harris, Richard E. ... Atlanta, GA
Harris, Richard E. ... Bethesda, MD
Harris, Richard E. ... Salt Lake City, UT
Harris, Richard E. V. ... Oakland, CA
Harris, Richard F., III ... Charlotte, NC
Harris, Richard G. ... Los Angeles, CA
Harris, Richard G. ... Santa Monica, CA
Harris, Richard H., III ... Akron, OH
Harris, Richard H., Jr.
San Francisco, CA
Harris, Richard J. ... San Francisco, CA
Harris, Richard J. ... Savannah, GA
Harris, Richard J. ... Oklahoma City, OK
Harris, Richard K. ... Louisville, KY
Harris, Richard L. ... Caldwell, ID
Harris, Richard L. ... Claremore, OK
Tulsa, OK
Harris, Richard M. ... Fairfield, CA
Harris, Richard M. ... United States Senate, Committee Legal Personnel, GV
Harris, Richard M. ... Orlando, FL
Harris, Richard M. ... Chicago, IL
Harris, Richard N. ... Richmond, VA
Harris, Richard O. ... Urbana, OH
Harris, Richard S. ... Los Angeles, CA
Harris, Richard S. ... Flint, MI
Harris, Richard S., P.C. ... Flint, MI
Harris, Richard W. ... College Park, MD
Harris, Richard W. ... Reno, NV
Harris, Rick E. ... Montgomery, AL
Harris, Rick J. ... Pampa, TX
Harris, Rick J., P.C., A Professional Corporation ... Pampa, TX
Harris, Ricky ... Spartanburg, SC
Harris, Rita H. ... Los Angeles, CA
Harris, Rita Reed ... Forrest City, AR
Harris, Robert ... Miami, FL
Harris, Robert A. ... Bridgeport, CT
Harris, Robert A. ... Columbus, OH
Harris, Robert A., II ... Bethesda, MD
Harris, Robert A., IV ... McLean, VA
Harris, Robert B. ... Bryan, TX
Harris, Robert B., P.C. ... Bryan, TX
Harris, Robert C. ... San Francisco, CA
Harris, Robert C. ... New York, NY
White Plains, NY
Harris, Robert D. ... Lawrence, KS
Harris, Robert D. ... White Plains, NY
Harris, Robert E. ... Boulder, CO
Harris, Robert E. ... Warrensburg, MO
Harris, Robert E. ... Albany, NY
Harris, Robert F. ... Santa Barbara, CA
Harris, Robert G. ... San Jose, CA
Harris, Robert G. ... Deerfield Beach, FL
Harris, Robert H. ... Decatur, AL
Harris, Robert I. ... Sacramento, CA
Harris, Robert I. ... Wheatley Heights, NY
Harris, Robert J. ... Florence, AL
Harris, Robert J. ... Chicago, IL
Harris, Robert J. ... Minneapolis, MN
Harris, Robert J. ... Raleigh, NC
Harris, Robert J. ... Hillsboro, OR
Harris, Robert J. ... Winchester, VA
Harris, Robert Jonathan ... Durham, NC
Harris, Robert K. ... Department of State, Office of the Legal Adviser, GV
Harris, Robert K. ... Atlanta, GA
Harris, Robert L. ... San Francisco, CA
Harris, Robert L. ... Denver, CO
Harris, Robert L. ... Forsyth, GA
Harris, Robert L. ... Sioux City, IA
Harris, Robert L. ... New York, NY
Harris, Robert L. ... Nashville, TN
Harris, Robert L. ... Vancouver, WA
Harris, Robert L., Jr. ... Richmond, VA
Harris, Robert L., Sr. ... Richmond, VA
Harris, Robert M. ... Jacksonville, FL
Harris, Robert M., P.C. ... Scottsbluff, NE
Harris, Robert N. ... Glendale, CA
Harris, Robert O. ... Washington, DC
Harris, Robert O. (Buck), III ... Killeen, TX
Harris, Robert P. ... Phoenix, AZ
Harris, Robert P. ... Chicago, IL
Harris, Robert R. ... Bethesda, MD
Harris, Robert R. ... Philadelphia, PA
Harris, Robert R., The, Law Firm, P.C.
Philadelphia, PA
Harris, Robert S. ... Chesterfield, MO
Harris, Robert T. ... South Pasadena, CA
Harris, Robert W. ... Englewood, CO
Harris, Robert W. ... Kansas City, KS
Harris, Robert W. ... Albuquerque, NM
Harris, Roberta A. ... Milwaukee, WI
Harris, Roberta M. ... Houston, TX
Harris, Robin D. ... Los Angeles, CA
Harris, Robt. J. ... Cincinnati, OH
Harris, Rodger Craig ... Jacksonville, NC
Harris, Rogena ... McLean, VA
Harris, Roger B. ... Twin Falls, ID
Harris, Roger B. ... Chicago, IL
Harris, Roger I. ... New York, NY
Harris, Roger K. ... Portland, OR
Harris, Roger K. ... Houston, TX
Harris, Roger K., P.C. ... Portland, OR
Harris, Roger L. ... Chicago, IL
Harris, Roger L. ... Beatrice, NE
Harris, Roland V. ... Dallas, TX
Harris, Ronald ... Birmingham, AL
Harris, Ronald B. ... Washington, DC
Harris, Ronald C. ... Laguna Beach, CA
Harris, Ronald D. ... Jeffersonville, IN
Harris, Ronald E. ... Arroyo Grande, CA
Harris, Ronald F. ... Jefferson City, MO
Harris, Ronald G. ... Albuquerque, NM
Harris, Ronald G. ... Nashville, TN
Harris, Rosemary L. ... Santa Fe, NM
Harris & Ruble ... Los Angeles, CA
Chicago, IL
Harris & Rufty, L.L.C. ... New Orleans, LA
Harris, Rufus C., III ... New Orleans, LA
Harris, Rufus C., Jr. ... Metairie, LA
Harris, Russell B. ... Charles City, VA
Harris, Russell W. ... Lakewood, OH
Harris, Ruth Jensen ... St. Paul, MN
Harris, Ruth M. ... La Jolla, CA
Harris, S. Ranchor, III
Winston-Salem, NC
Harris, Sally H. ... Overland Park, KS
Harris, Samantha Anne ... Columbia, MO
Harris, Samuel J. ... Washington, DC
Harris, Samuel Lowe, Jr.
Hot Springs Village, AR
Harris, Sandra J. ... Los Angeles, CA
Harris, Sandra Young ... Little Rock, AR
Harris, Sanford A. ... Baltimore, MD
Harris, Sanford & Baggett ... Gridley, CA
Harris, Sara Dineen ... Los Angeles, CA
Harris, Sarah Stevenson ... Macon, GA
Harris, Sarah T. ... Houston, TX
Harris, Scott Blake ... Washington, DC
Harris, Scott C. ... La Jolla, CA
Harris, Scott G. ... Minneapolis, MN
Harris, Scott H. ... Manchester, NH
Harris, Scott K. ... Atlanta, GA
Harris, Scott M. ... Scottsdale, AZ
Harris, Scott S. ... San Diego, CA
Harris, Seth A. ... New York, NY
Harris, Seymour B. ... Longmeadow, MA
Harris, Seymour N. ... Mineola, NY
Harris, Sheldon A. ... Chicago, IL
Harris, Sheldon J. ... Washington, DC
Harris, Sheldon J. ... Omaha, NE
Harris, Shelton, Dunlap and Cobb, P.L.L.C.
Memphis, TN
Harris, Shevon L. ... St. Louis, MO
Harris, Shields, Creech and Ward, P.A.
New Bern, NC
Harris, Shipp D. ... Columbia, SC
Harris, Shirley M. ... Memphis, TN
Harris, Sidney
United States International Trade Commission, Office of Administrative Law Judges, GV
Harris & Smith ... Media, PA
Harris, Sondra I. ... Woodmere, NY
Harris, Stacy J. ... Aliquippa, PA
Harris, Stacy Kerns ... Evansville, IN
Harris, Stacy Pilgreen ... Montgomery, AL
Harris, Stan N. ... Albuquerque, NM
Harris, Stanley E., Jr. ... Savannah, GA
Harris, Stanley S.
United States District Court For The District Of Columbia, GV
Harris, Stephanie ... Louisville, KY
Harris, Stephanie H. ... Tyler, TX
Harris, Stephen B. ... Hartford, CT
Harris, Stephen B. ... Warrington, PA
Harris, Stephen C. ... Louisa, VA
Harris, Stephen D. ... Colorado Springs, CO
Harris, Stephen D. ... Williamsburg, VA
Harris, Stephen E. ... Baltimore, MD
Harris, Stephen H. ... Los Angeles, CA
Harris, Stephen H. ... Savannah, GA
Harris, Stephen J. ... Bloomfield Hills, MI
Harris, Stephen J. ... Pittsburgh, PA
Harris, Stephen M. ... Glendale, CA
Harris, Stephen P. ... Warsaw, IN
Harris, Stephen R. ... Reno, NV
Harris, Stephen R. ... Malvern, PA
Harris, Stephen W. ... Austin, TX
Harris, Steven A. ... Tequesta, FL
Harris, Steven B. ... Houston, TX
Harris, Steven C. ... Pleasantville, NJ
Harris, Steven D. ... Atlanta, GA
Harris, Steven D. ... Overland Park, KS
Harris, Steven E. ... Boulder, CO
Harris, Steven E. ... Kansas City, MO
Harris, Steven I. ... Los Angeles, CA
Harris, Steven L. ... Mooresville, IN
Harris, Steven M. ... Miami, FL
Harris, Steven M. ... Chicago, IL
Harris, Steven M. ... Columbus, OH
Harris, Steven M. ... Tulsa, OK
Harris, Steven R., & Associates
New York, NY
Harris, Steven W. ... Alexandria, LA
Harris, Steven W. ... Albany, NY
Harris, Stewart L. ... Orange Park, FL
Harris, Stuart C. ... Portland, OR
Harris, Stuart H. ... Washington, DC
Harris, Sue Elizabeth ... Marblehead, MA
Harris, Susan ... Stillwater, MN
Harris, Susan A. ... Detroit, MI
Harris, Susan Banes ... Washington, DC
Harris, Susan Feigin ... Houston, TX
Harris, Susan L. ... Los Angeles, CA
Harris, Susan L. ... New York, NY
Harris, Susan Lauren ... Oak Brook, IL
Harris, Susan R. ... Denver, CO
Harris, Susan Schild ... Rush, NY
Harris, Susan V. ... Chicago, IL
Harris, Susan Ward ... Phoenix, AZ
Harris & Sutton ... Boise, ID
Harris, Suzanne ... Los Angeles, CA
Harris, Sylvia ... Naugatuck, CT
Harris & Synakowski ... Wellsville, NY
Harris, T. Alan ... Houston, TX
Harris, T. Michael ... Irvine, CA
Harris, T. Randolph ... New York, NY
Harris, T. Wayne ... Houston, TX
Harris, Tamsen H. ... Brooklyn, CT
Harris, Tanya J. ... Santa Cruz, CA
Harris, Tarlow & Stonecipher, P.L.L.C.
Bozeman, MT
Harris, Ted W. ... San Francisco, CA
Harris, Tedd B., Jr. ... Gardena, CA
Harris, Teresa Lynn ... Greenville, NC
Harris, Teresa V. ... Austin, TX
Harris, Terrance R. ... Phoenix, AZ
Harris, Terrell L. ... Memphis, TN
Harris, Terri ... Hot Springs National Park, AR
Harris, Terri L. ... Treasury Department, Internal Revenue Service, GV
Harris, Terrill Johnson ... Greensboro, NC
Harris, Terry E. ... Crawfordsville, IN
Harris, Terry J. ... Cheyenne, WY
Harris, Theodore ... Marlboro, NJ
Harris, Theodore A. ... Niantic, CT
Harris, Theodore P. ... New York, NY
Harris, Theophilus I., IV ... Miami, FL
Harris, Theresa M. ... Minneapolis, MN
Harris, Thomas A. ... Fresno, CA
Harris, Thomas A. ... Winston-Salem, NC
Harris, Thomas A. ... Chattanooga, TN
Harris, Thomas D. ... Valley Center, KS
Harris, Thomas E. ... New Bern, NC
Harris, Thomas E. ... Conneaut, OH
Harris, Thomas F., III
Department of Agriculture, Farm Service Agency, GV
Harris, Thomas G. ... Philadelphia, PA
Harris, Thomas J. ... Carthage, TX
Harris, Thomas K. ... Baltimore, MD
Harris, Thomas L. ... Miami, FL
Harris, Thomas M. ... St. Petersburg, FL
Harris, Thomas M. ... Lincoln, IL
Harris, Thomas M., Jr. ... Bloomington, IL
Chicago, IL
Harris, Thomas Osa ... Houston, TX
Harris, Thomas R. ... Sarasota, FL
Harris, Thomas R. ... Eden Prairie, MN
Harris, Thomas V. ... Seattle, WA
Harris, Thorne D., III ... New Orleans, LA
Harris, Thorne D., III ... New Orleans, LA
Harris, T. I., III ... DeLand, FL
Harris, Tim L. ... Charlotte, NC
Gastonia, NC
Monroe, NC
Harris, Tim L., and Associates
Charlotte, NC
Concord, NC
Gastonia, NC
Monroe, NC
Harris, Timothy ... New York, NY
Harris, Timothy B. ... Dallas, TX
Harris, Timothy H. ... Tulsa, OK
Harris, Timothy J. ... Los Angeles, CA
Harris, Timothy J. ... Palo Alto, CA
Harris, Timothy J. ... Chicago, IL
Harris, Timothy J. ... Springfield, MO
Harris, Timothy S. ... Los Angeles, CA
Harris, Timothy S. ... Chicago, IL
Harris, Tina L. ... Kansas City, MO
Harris, Todd A. ... West Monroe, LA
Harris, Todd R. ... Hawthorne, NY
Harris, Tom B., Jr. ... Ashland City, TN
Harris, Tom D., Jr. ... Dallas, TX
Harris, Tommy David ... Stilwell, OK
Harris, Tracy B. ... Wickliffe, OH
Harris, Trester S., Jr. ... Corona, CA
Harris, Trimmer & Thompson
Las Vegas, NV
Reno, NV
Harris, Turano & Mazza ... Columbus, OH
Harris, Tyree B., IV ... Nashville, TN
Harris, Urlin G., Jr. ... Columbus, OH
Harris & Van Jura ... Wilkes-Barre, PA
Harris, Vernon A. ... San Francisco, CA
Harris, Vernon L., Jr. ... Phoenix, AZ
Harris, Victor ... San Rafael, CA
Harris, Victor L. ... Sugar Land, TX
Harris, Victoria Ann ... Bedford, TX
Harris, Virginia H. ... Issaquah, WA
Harris, W. Gibson ... Richmond, VA
Harris, W. Hensell, Jr. ... Atlanta, GA
Harris, W. Larry ... Jackson, MS
Harris, W. Noel ... Greenville, MS
Harris, W. Stanworth ... Jackson, TN
Harris, W. Stokes, Jr. ... Lexington, KY
Harris, W. Theodore, Jr. ... Worcester, MA
Harris, W. Thomas ... Salt Lake City, UT
Harris, Walter Baker ... Jackson, TN
Harris, Walter D. ... Saint Simons Island, GA
Harris, Warren E. ... Springfield, MO
Harris, Warren L. ... Tampa, FL
Harris, Warren L., & Associates, P.A.
Tampa, FL
Harris, Warren O. F. ... Santa Fe, NM
Harris, Warren T. ... New York, NY
Harris, Warren Wayne ... Houston, TX
Harris & Watts, P.C. ... Brownsville, TX
Corpus Christi, TX
Harris, Wayne A. ... Indianapolis, IN
Harris, Wayne E. ... Portland, OR
Harris, Wayne I. ... Brooklyn, NY
Harris, Wayne M. ... Rochester, NY
Harris, Wayne R. ... McMinnville, OR
Harris, Wayne T., Jr. ... Raleigh, NC
Harris, W. C., Jr. ... Raleigh, NC
Harris, Welsh & Lukmann
Chesterton, IN
Valparaiso, IN
Harris, Wendy B. ... Fairfax, VA
Harris, Wendy S. ... Las Vegas, NV
Harris, Wesley N. ... Fort Worth, TX
Harris, Weston L. ... Salt Lake City, UT
Harris, Whitney R. ... St. Louis, MO
Harris, Willard H., Jr. ... Lockport, NY
Harris, William A. ... Killeen, TX
Harris, William C. ... Tallahassee, FL
Harris, William C. ... Macon, GA
Harris, William D. ... Philadelphia, PA
Harris, William D., Jr. ... Dallas, TX
Harris, William E. ... Los Angeles, CA
Harris, William E. ... Fort Wayne, IN
Harris, William G. ... San Francisco, CA
Harris, William G. ... Hampton, NJ
Harris, William H. ... Tempe, AZ
Harris, William H. ... Norwood, NC
Harris, William H. ... Fredericksburg, VA
Harris, William H., Jr. ... Washington, DC
Harris, William J. ... Solana Beach, CA
Harris, William J., Jr. ... Campbell, CA
Harris, William L., Jr.
Equal Employment Opportunity Commission, Office of Federal Operations, GV
Harris, William M. ... Lynn Haven, FL
Harris, William M. ... Albany, NY

Harris, William M. ... Norfolk, VA
Harris, William N. ... Charlotte, NC
Harris, William P. ... High Point, NC
Harris, William P. ... Lynchburg, VA
Harris, William P., III ... San Diego, CA
Harris, William P., Jr. ... Miami, FL
Harris, William P., (P.C.) ... Seattle, WA
Harris, William R. ... Irvine, CA
Harris, William R. ... Franklin, KY
Harris, William R. ... San Antonio, TX
Harris, William S. ... Pasadena, CA
Harris, William S. ... Fort Worth, TX
Harris & Williams ... San Diego, CA
Harris, Willie ... Gary, IN
Harris, Wilmer J. ... Venice, CA
Harris, Wilmot L., Jr. ... Greenwich, CT
Harris, Wiltshire & Grannis LLP
Washington, DC
Harris, Wyatt & Amala ... Salem, OR
Harris, Zelda B. ... Chicago, IL
Harris-Humphrey, Karen ... Des Moines, IA
Harris III, Elsey A. ... Norton, VA
Harrisingh, Frances E. R.
New Rochelle, NY
Harrisingh, John L. ... White Plains, NY
Harris-Jenkins, Pamela R. ... Atlanta, GA
Harris-Joplin, Jane I. ... Houston, TX
Harrison, A. Wayne ... Greensboro, NC
Harrison, Aaron ... Los Angeles, CA
Harrison, Adam C. ... Towson, MD
Harrison, Akinyale S. ... Washington, DC
Harrison, Alleda ... San Diego, CA
Harrison, Allen H., Jr. ... Washington, DC
Harrison, Alvin (Al) ... Houston, TX
Harrison, Amy L. ... East Longmeadow, MA
Harrison, Andrew M. ... New York, NY
Harrison, Andrew Thomas ... Bayside, NY
Harrison, Ann E. ... Philadelphia, PA
Harrison, Anne H. ... Washington, DC
Harrison, Anthony L., P.C. ... Brunswick, GA
Harrison, Anthony L., (P.C.) ... Brunswick, GA
McDonough, GA
Harrison, Arnold M. ... Winter Park, FL
Harrison, Arnold S., (P.C.) ... Chicago, IL
Harrison, Arthur A. ... Redlands, CA
Harrison, Barbara E. ... Department of Justice, Justice Management Division, GV
Harrison, Baya, III ... Monticello, FL
Harrison, Benis & Spence, LLP
La Conner, WA
Seattle, WA
Harrison, Benjamin C. ... Spartanburg, SC
Harrison, Benjamin N. ... Washington, DC
Harrison, Bernard ... Brooklyn, NY
Harrison, Bernard P. ... Chicago, IL
Harrison, Betsy M. ... Double Springs, AL
Harrison, Bettis & Staff, L.L.P.
Houston, TX
Harrison, Bob D. ... Dallas, TX
Harrison, Bonnie Bakeman ... Seattle, WA
Harrison, Boyd (Michael) ... Visalia, CA
Harrison, Breck ... Austin, TX
Harrison, Brennecke, Moore, Smaha & McKibben ... Marshalltown, IA
Harrison, Brian D. ... San Francisco, CA
Harrison, Bruce F. ... Okeechobee, FL
Harrison, Bruce, Jr. ... Pittsburgh, PA
Harrison, Bruce L. ... Mount Laurel, NJ
Harrison, Bruce S. ... Baltimore, MD
Harrison, Bryan G. ... Atlanta, GA
Harrison, Burton ... Miami, FL
Harrison, C. Bennett, Jr. ... Nashville, TN
Harrison, C. Gerard ... Houston, TX
Harrison, C. Lash ... Atlanta, GA
Harrison, C. Paul ... Knoxville, TN
Harrison, Casby, III ... Providence, RI
Harrison, Catherine B. ... Atlanta, GA
Harrison, C. B., Jr. ... Dallas, TX
Harrison, Cecil W., Jr. ... Raleigh, NC
Harrison, Charles A. ... Riverside, CA
Harrison, Charles A., III ... Detroit, MI
Harrison, Charles D. ... Tulsa, OK
Harrison, Charles E. ... Fayette, AL
Harrison, Charles R. ... Winter Park, FL
Harrison, Charles T., III ... Atlanta, GA
Harrison, Chason Lash, Jr. ... Atlanta, GA
Harrison, Christian ... Austin, TX
Harrison, Christopher T. ... Honolulu, HI
Harrison, Christy J. ... Chicago, IL
Harrison, Clarence W. ... Granite City, IL
Harrison, Clifford J. ... Nashville, TN
Harrison, Clifford L. ... Houston, TX
Harrison, Clifford L. ... Radford, VA
Harrison & Coman ... Pasadena, TX
Harrison, Craig S. ... Washington, DC
Harrison, Curtis W. ... Frisco, TX
Harrison, Curtis W., Law Office of, PLLC
Frisco, TX
Harrison, D. Marie ... Woodbury, NJ
Harrison, Dallas R. ... Richmond, MI
Harrison, Daniel A. ... Los Angeles, CA
Harrison, Darren L. ... Cherry Hill, NJ
Philadelphia, PA
Harrison, Darryl ... New Orleans, LA
Harrison, David A., III ... Hopewell, VA
Harrison, David A., IV ... Hopewell, VA
Harrison, David B. ... Boulder, CO
Harrison, David C. ... La Grange, IL
Harrison, David C. ... Hartsburg, MO
Harrison, David C. ... White Plains, NY
Harrison, David C., Law Offices of
Philadelphia, PA
Harrison, David E. ... Fairfield, IL
Harrison, David E. ... Gloucester, MA
Harrison, David E. ... Chattanooga, TN
Harrison, David G. ... Upton, MA
Harrison, David G. ... Roanoke, VA
Harrison, David H. ... New York, NY
Harrison, David L. ... Boulder, CO
Harrison, David L. ... Grand Rapids, MI
Harrison, David L. ... Rochester Hills, MI
Harrison, David M. ... Jasper, AL
Harrison, David M. ... Little Rock, AR
Harrison, David M. ... Irvine, CA
Harrison, David R. ... San Francisco, CA
Harrison, David R. ... Pickens, SC
Harrison, David Scott ... Lincoln, NE
Harrison, Dawn A. ... Flanders, NJ
Harrison, Dawn M. ... Sanford, FL
Harrison, Dean W. ... San Francisco, CA
Harrison, Debra A. ... Washington, DC
Harrison, Dennis ... Tucson, AZ
Harrison, Donald ... Washington, DC
Harrison, Donald C. ... Seattle, WA
Harrison, Donald G. ... Detroit, MI
Harrison, Donald M. ... Philadelphia, PA
Harrison, Donald R. ... Dadeville, AL
Harrison, Donna L. ... New York, NY
Harrison, Douglas A. ... Miami, FL
Harrison, Douglas A. ... Portland, OR
Harrison, Douglas A. ... Dallas, TX
Harrison, Douglas J. ... Worcester, MA
Harrison, E. Eugene ... Kansas City, MO
Harrison, E. Nicole ... Norcross, GA
Harrison & Edmondson, L.L.C.
Dadeville, AL
Harrison, Edward J. ... Scottsdale, AZ
Harrison & Egbert ... Houston, TX
Harrison, Eichenberg & Murphy
Agoura Hills, CA
Harrison, Eileen ... Little Rock, AR
Harrison, Elaine G. ... Dallas, TX
Harrison, Elaine J. ... Alameda, CA
Harrison, Elaine M. ... New York, NY
Harrison, Elizabeth
Department of Defense, GV
Harrison, Elizabeth E. ... Sacramento, CA
Harrison, Elizabeth H. ... Boston, MA
Harrison, Elizabeth L. ... Placerville, CA
Harrison, Elizabeth Newbill
Washington, DC
Harrison, Ellen ... Department of Justice, Drug Enforcement Administration, GV
Harrison, Ellen K. ... Washington, DC
Harrison, Emily D. ... Gastonia, NC
Harrison, Evette E. ... New York, NY
Harrison, Faye M. ... Saginaw, MI
Harrison, Fenton F. ... Buffalo, NY
Harrison Firm, The, P.C. ... Roanoke, VA
Harrison & Fisher ... Manchester, TN
Harrison, Frank E. ... McCormick, SC
Harrison, Frank G. ... San Antonio, TX
Harrison, Frank J. ... Streator, IL
Harrison, Frank R. (Randy)
Missoula, MT
Harrison, Frank T. ... Des Moines, IA
Harrison, Franklin R. ... Panama City, FL
Harrison, Fred A., Jr. ... Fort Lauderdale, FL
Harrison, Fred A., Jr., P.A.
Fort Lauderdale, FL
Harrison, Fred H. ... Little Rock, AR
Harrison, Fred L., Jr. ... Augusta, GA
Harrison, Fred W. ... Kinston, NC
Harrison, Frederick J. ... Rawlins, WY
Harrison, G. Gordon ... Fort Myers, FL
Harrison, G. Hughel ... Lawrenceville, GA
Harrison, G. Joseph ... Bradenton, FL
Harrison, Garnett ... Saint Marys, GA
Harrison, Garnett, P.C. ... Saint Marys, GA
Harrison, Gary L. ... Palmer, TX
Harrison, Gary L., P.C. ... Palmer, TX
Harrison, Gayla R. ... Ottumwa, IA
Harrison, Genie ... San Diego, CA
Harrison, Geoffrey D. ... Lansing, MI
Harrison, Geoffrey L. ... Houston, TX
Harrison, George A. ... Aztec, NM
Harrison, George H. ... Bradenton, FL
Harrison, George W. ... San Angelo, TX
Harrison, Gerald ... Golden, CO
Harrison, Gilbert W. ... New York, NY
Harrison, Glen Neil ... Sweetwater, TX
Harrison, Glenda J. ... Covington, KY
Harrison, Glenn ... Lakewood, NJ
Harrison & Goin ... Bowling Green, KY
Scottsville, KY
Harrison, Gordon J. ... Encino, CA
Harrison, Gregg ... Beverly Hills, CA
Harrison, Gregory A. ... Cincinnati, OH
Harrison, Gregory H. ... Knoxville, TN
Harrison, Guy N. ... Longview, TX
Harrison, Gwendolyn R. ... Costa Mesa, CA
Harrison, Hal G., (P.A.) ... Spruce Pine, NC
Harrison, Haldon R. ... Culver City, CA
Harrison, Harlan R. ... Albany, NY
Harrison, Harold C. ... Forest Hills, NY
Harrison, Harold H. ... Helena, MT
Harrison & Harrison ... Gilroy, CA
Harrison & Harrison ... Los Angeles, CA
Harrison & Harrison ... Lawrenceville, GA
Harrison & Harrison ... McDonough, GA
Harrison & Harrison ... Wayne, WV
Harrison, Hartwell ... Baltimore, MD
Harrison, Harvey E. ... Westlake Village, CA
Harrison, Harvey L. ... Des Moines, IA
Harrison, Hendrickson, Douglass & Kirkland, P.A. ... Bradenton, FL
Harrison, Holly A. ... Chicago, IL
Harrison, Holmes C. ... Harrisonburg, VA
Harrison, Holt B. ... Baton Rouge, LA
Harrison, Howard F. ... Irvine, CA
Harrison, Howard H., Jr. ... Delray Beach, FL
Harrison, Howard R. ... Skokie, IL
Harrison, Howard W., Jr. ... Sedgwick, ME
Harrison, Hugh R. ... Los Angeles, CA
Harrison, Hugh T., II ... Richmond, VA
Harrison, Hugh W., Jr. ... Jonesboro, AR
Harrison & Hughes, P.C. ... Alexandria, VA
Harrison, Hunter C., Jr. ... McLean, VA
Harrison, Irwin J. ... Palm Beach, FL
Harrison, J. Clifford ... Jackson, MS
Harrison, J. Eric ... Knoxville, TN
Harrison, J. Michael ... Atlanta, GA
Harrison, J. Michael ... Baltimore, MD
Harrison, J. Wade ... Burlington, NC
Harrison, Jack B. ... Cincinnati, OH
Harrison, Jack H. ... Hoover, AL
Harrison, Jack L. ... Oakland, CA
Harrison, Jack L. ... Tucker, GA
Harrison, James A. ... Dallas, TX
Harrison, James B. ... Sullivan, MO
Harrison, James B. ... Cincinnati, OH
Harrison, James B. ... Herndon, VA
Harrison, James C. ... San Francisco, CA
Harrison, James C. ... Circleville, NY
Harrison, James C. ... Seattle, WA
Harrison, James C., Jr. ... Columbia, SC
Harrison, James C., Jr., P.C. ... Columbia, SC
Harrison, James D. ... Indianapolis, IN
Harrison, James G. ... Huntsville, AL
Harrison, James G., III ... Richmond, VA
Harrison, James H. ... Orlando, FL
Harrison, James H. ... Columbia, SC
Harrison, James J. ... Rutherford, NJ
Harrison, James L. ... Denver, CO
Harrison, James L. ... Jacksonville, FL
Harrison, James L. ... Burnsville, MN
Harrison, James L., Jr. ... Jacksonville, FL
Harrison, James P. ... Irvine, CA
Harrison, James R. ... Phoenix, AZ
Harrison, James T., Jr. ... Helena, MT
Harrison, James W. ... Morristown, TN
Harrison, James William ... Stamford, CT
Harrison, Jamie King ... Dallas, TX
Harrison, Jane C. ... Hartford, CT
Harrison, Jane F. ... Salt Lake City, UT
Harrison, Janet DeLaura ... Raleigh, NC
Harrison, Janet M. ... Metairie, LA
New Orleans, LA
Harrison, Jeanne D. ... Augusta, GA
Harrison, Jeff A. ... Los Angeles, CA
Harrison, Jeffrey B. ... San Francisco, CA
Harrison, Jeffrey H. ... Springfield, MO
Harrison, Jeffrey T. ... Troy, MI
Harrison, Jeffrey W. ... Dallas, TX
Harrison, Jeremy T. ... Honolulu, HI
Harrison, Jerry L. ... Beloit, KS
Harrison, Jill ... Phoenix, AZ
Harrison, Jill Morgan ... Abingdon, VA
Harrison, Joan A. ... Gilroy, CA
Harrison, Jodi ... Bozeman, MT
Harrison, Joe ... Fairfield, IL
Harrison, Joe B. ... Dallas, TX
Harrison, Joe J., Jr. ... Chattanooga, TN
Harrison, John C. ... Shalimar, FL
Harrison, John C. ... Chattanooga, TN
Harrison, John C., Jr. ... Helena, MT
Harrison, John C., P.A. ... Shalimar, FL
Harrison, John E. ... Rochester, NY
Harrison, John Edwards ... Alexandria, VA
Harrison, John G. ... Dallas, TX
Harrison, John L. ... Crystal Falls, MI
Harrison, John L., Jr. ... Philadelphia, PA
Harrison, John M. ... Shreveport, LA
Harrison, John R. ... Monroe, LA
Harrison, John R. ... Oklahoma City, OK
Harrison, John R. ... Pasadena, TX
Harrison, John R., Jr. ... Sacramento, CA
Harrison, John R., Jr. ... San Antonio, TX
Harrison, John S. ... Oakland, CA
Harrison, John S. ... Decatur, GA
Harrison, John S. ... Henderson, KY
Harrison, John S. ... Saddle River, NJ
Harrison, John S. ... Winston-Salem, NC
Harrison, John S. ... Bethlehem, PA
Harrison, John S., P.C. ... Decatur, GA
Harrison, John W., Jr. ... Louisville, KY
Harrison, John Wyly ... Huntsville, AL
Harrison & Johnston ... Winchester, VA
Harrison, Jonathan G. ... Chicago, IL
Harrison, Joseph ... Boca Raton, FL
Harrison, Joseph F. ... Bristol, TN
Harrison, Joseph G., Jr. ... Ocean City, MD
Harrison, Joseph H. ... Evansville, IN
Harrison, Joseph H., Jr. ... Chicago, IL
Harrison, Joseph H., Jr. ... Evansville, IN
Harrison, Joseph M., IV ... Dallas, TX
San Antonio, TX
Harrison, Joseph R. ... Akron, OH
Harrison, Joseph R., Company, L.P.A.
Akron, OH
Harrison, Joseph S. ... Saginaw, MI
Harrison, Joseph S., P.C., Law Office of
Saginaw, MI
Harrison, Joshua M. ... The Woodlands, TX
Harrison, Julian E. ... Bushnell, FL
Harrison, Julian E., P.A. ... Bushnell, FL
Harrison, Julie ... Satellite Beach, FL
Harrison, Julie ... Rye Brook, NY
Harrison, Julie A. ... Traverse City, MI
Harrison, Karen E.
Environmental Protection Agency, Office of Enforcement and Compliance Assurance, GV
Harrison, Kathleen A. ... San Pablo, CA
Harrison, Keith ... New York, NY
Harrison, Keith J. ... Washington, DC
Harrison, Keith Michaele ... De Kalb, IL
Harrison, Kelli P. ... Houston, TX
Harrison, Kemp & Jones, Chartered
Las Vegas, NV
Harrison, Kendall W. ... Madison, WI
Harrison & Kennedy ... Bristol, TN
Harrison, Kenneth C. ... Plymouth, MI
Harrison, Kenneth C., P.C. ... Plymouth, MI
Harrison, Kenneth G. ... Penndel, PA
Harrison, Kimberly Ann ... Bear, DE
Harrison, Kimberly E.
Department Of Veterans Affairs, Board of Veterans Appeals, GV
Harrison, Kirk R. ... Las Vegas, NV
Harrison, L. Wade, Jr. ... Bartlett, TN
Memphis, TN
Harrison & Lamar ... Augusta, GA
Harrison, Larry W. ... Sugar Land, TX
Harrison, LaTonya R., Mrs. ... Mesa, AZ
Harrison, LaVonne ... Sunset Beach, CA
Harrison Law Office ... Missoula, MT
Harrison Law Office, P.C. ... Houston, TX
Harrison, Lee R. ... Cartersville, VA
Harrison, Lemuel E., Jr. ... Columbus, OH
Harrison, Leslie A. ... Seattle, WA
Harrison, Lien Ski ... Costa Mesa, CA
Harrison, Linda Ciske ... New Baltimore, MI
Harrison, Linda Frances ... Atlanta, GA
Harrison, Lisa Erb ... Indianapolis, IN
Harrison & Llop, P.C. ... Eastman, GA
Harrison, Loendorf, Poston & Duncan, P.C.
Helena, MT
Harrison, Lolla M. ... Evanston, IL
Harrison, Louis S. ... Chicago, IL
Harrison, Lowell Winston
Fort Worth, TX
Harrison, L. Wade, Jr., P.C. ... Bartlett, TN
Memphis, TN
Harrison, Lynn P., III ... New York, NY
Harrison, Lynne L. ... Poughkeepsie, NY
Harrison, M. Lillie ... Washington, DC
Harrison, M. Ruth ... Florence, AZ
Harrison, Marc I. ... Philadelphia, PA
Harrison, Marc L. ... Atlanta, GA
Harrison, Marcie B. ... New York, NY
Harrison, Marian F. ... Nashville, TN
Harrison, Marian T. ... Gretna, LA
Harrison, Marion Edwyn
Washington, DC
Falls Church, VA
Harrison, Marion Edwyn, The Law Firm of
Washington, DC
Harrison, Mark B. ... Washington, DC
Harrison, Mark D. ... Sacramento, CA
Harrison, Mark E. ... Boston, MA
Harrison, Mark I. ... Phoenix, AZ
Harrison, Mark I. ... Woodbridge, CT
Harrison, Mark I., P.C. ... Woodbridge, CT
Harrison, Mark S. ... Lakewood, NJ
Harrison, Marlon ... Baton Rouge, LA
Harrison, Martha Blair ... Bowling Green, KY
Scottsville, KY
Harrison, Martin W. ... Whitewater, WI
Harrison, Mary Anne ... Beverly Hills, CA
Harrison, Mary T. ... Arlington, TX
Harrison & Massey, LLC ... Rawlins, WY
Harrison & Matsuoka ... Honolulu, HI
Harrison, Matthew R. ... Boise, ID
Harrison, Matthew W. ... Flagstaff, AZ
Harrison, Maureen C. ... Palo Alto, CA
Harrison, Maurice E., III
Sherman Oaks, CA
Harrison, Max B. ... Blytheville, AR
Harrison & Mecklenburg, Inc.
Kingfisher, OK
Oklahoma City, OK
Harrison, Melinda J. ... Wellesley, MA
Harrison, Michael A. ... Price, UT
Harrison, Michael D. ... Los Angeles, CA
Harrison, Michael E. ... Brunswick, GA
Harrison, Michael G. ... Mason, MI
Harrison, Michael, III ... Stamford, CT
Harrison, Michael J.
United States Postal Service, GV
Harrison, Michael James
Bloomfield Hills, MI
Harrison, Michael L.
House of Representatives, Congressional Assistants, GV
Harrison, Michael N. ... Phoenix, AZ
Harrison, Michael T. ... Los Angeles, CA
Harrison, Michele Holovak ... Gloucester, MA
Harrison, Michelle Jackowski ... Detroit, MI
Harrison, Mike D. ... Marietta, GA
Harrison & Million ... Irvine, CA
Harrison, Milton ... Eastman, GA
Harrison, Milton G. ... Hackensack, NJ
Harrison, Milton M. ... Baton Rouge, LA
Harrison, Milton S. ... White Plains, NY
Harrison, Mina M. ... Northampton, MA
Harrison, Miriam E. ... Glenview, IL
Harrison & Moberly ... Carmel, IN
Indianapolis, IN
Harrison, Moses W. ... Fairview Heights, IL
Harrison, N. Sean
Securities and Exchange Commission, Division of Corporation Finance, GV
Harrison, Nancy C. ... Sarasota, FL
Harrison, Nancy J. ... Indianapolis, IN
Harrison, Nancy L. ... Annapolis, MD
Harrison, Nancy S. ... Fort Lauderdale, FL
Harrison, Newt P. ... Jackson, MS
Harrison, North, Cooke & Landreth
Greensboro, NC
Harrison, Orrin L., III ... Dallas, TX
Harrison, Orval C. ... Salt Lake City, UT
Harrison, Otis W. ... Augusta, GA
Harrison, Paige E. ... Rockville, MD
Harrison, Pamela A. ... Eugene, OR
Harrison, Pamela Karr ... Philadelphia, PA
Harrison, Patricia L. ... Columbia, SC
Harrison, Patrick W. ... Columbus, IN
Harrison, Pattie Sue ... Roxboro, NC
Harrison, Paul E. ... Little Rock, AR
Harrison, Paul E. ... New Orleans, LA
Harrison, Pegram ... Atlanta, GA

Harrison, Penny H. ... Portland, OR
Harrison, Peter B. ... Arlington Heights, IL
Harrison, Peter M. ... Philadelphia, PA
Harrison, Peter N. ... Doylestown, PA
Harrison, Philip B. ... Cassopolis, MI
Harrison, Philip B. ... West Orange, NJ
Harrison & Poore ... Spruce Pine, NC
Harrison, R. Craig ... Sarasota, FL
Harrison, R. Gregory ... Liberty, MO
Harrison, R. Louis, Jr. ... Bedford, VA
Harrison, R. Louis, Jr., P.C. ... Bedford, VA
Harrison, R. Ross ... Houston, TX
Harrison, Ralph E. ... Kingfisher, OK
Oklahoma City, OK
Harrison, Ralph K. ... The Woodlands, TX
Harrison, Randall P. ... Macon, GA
Harrison, Raymond M. ... Warwick, RI
Harrison, Reese L., Jr. ... San Antonio, TX
Harrison, Reginald W., Jr. ... Wilson, NC
Harrison, Renate ... Boston, MA
Harrison & Rial, L.L.P. ... Austin, TX
Harrison, Richard A. ... Eufaula, AL
Harrison, Richard A. ... Tampa, FL
Harrison, Richard D. ... Fall River, MA
Harrison, Richard D. ... Oklahoma City, OK
Harrison, Richard E. ... Dallas, TX
Harrison, Richard E., Law Offices of
Bonham, TX
Denton, TX
Gainesville, TX
McKinney, TX
Harrison, Richard E., Law Offices of
Sherman, TX
Harrison, Richard F. ... Garden City, NY
Harrison, Richard H. ... Manchester, TN
Harrison, Richard S. ... Gilroy, CA
Harrison, Richard V. ... Sarasota, FL
Harrison, Richard W. ... Austin, TX
Harrison, Robert, & Associates
Bloomfield Hills, MI
Detroit, MI
Harrison, Robert B., III ... Baltimore, MD
Harrison, Robert C. ... Florham Park, NJ
Harrison, Robert C. ... New York, NY
Harrison, Robert D. ... Ridgeland, MS
Harrison, Robert E. ... Bowling Green, KY
Scottsville, KY
Harrison, Robert E. ... New York, NY
Harrison, Robert G. ... Los Angeles, CA
Harrison, Robert H., Jr.
Denham Springs, LA
Harrison, Robert L. ... San Rafael, CA
Harrison, Robert L. ... Albany, NY
Harrison, Robert M. ... New York, NY
Harrison, Robert N. ... Venice, FL
Harrison, Robert R. ... Salt Lake City, UT
Harrison, Robert S. ... Los Angeles, CA
Harrison, Robert S. ... Bloomfield Hills, MI
Harrison, Robert S. ... New York, NY
Harrison, Robert W. ... San Diego, CA
Harrison, Robin L. ... Houston, TX
Harrison, Robin T. ... Claremont, CA
Harrison, Roddy L. ... Pecos, TX
Harrison, Rodney A. ... St. Louis, MO
Harrison, Roger E. ... Marshalltown, IA
Harrison, Ronald D. ... Fort Smith, AR
Harrison, Ronald I. ... Sacramento, CA
Harrison, Ronnie Ellen Gidseg ... Houston, TX
Harrison, Rosalie B. ... Detroit, MI
Harrison, Roslyn S. ... Newark, NJ
Harrison, Ruth A. ... East Brunswick, NJ
Harrison, S. David ... New York, NY
Harrison, S. Malcolm O. ... Jackson, MS
Harrison, S. Michael ... Agoura Hills, CA
Harrison, Sale, McCloy, Thompson &
Harrison, Chartered ... Panama City, FL
Harrison, Samuel H. ... Lawrenceville, GA
Harrison & Scott, P.C. ... Lansing, MI
Harrison, Scott R. ... New York, NY
Harrison, Shari L. ... Livingston, NJ
Harrison, Shawn E. ... Tallahassee, FL
Tampa, FL
Harrison, Shawn M. ... Austin, TX
Harrison, Simon M. ... Fort Myers, FL
Harrison and Simpson, P.A. ... Kinston, NC
Harrison, Spencer L. ... New York, NY
Harrison Steck Hoover & Drake, P.C.
Fort Worth, TX
Harrison, Stephen A. ... Brooklyn, NY
Harrison, Stephen D. ... Fort Worth, TX
Harrison, Stephen E., II ... Jackson, MS
Waco, TX
Harrison, Stephen J. ... Albany, NY
Harrison, Stephen J. ... Canton, OH
Harrison, Stephen L. ... Monroe, LA
Harrison, Stephen P., (P.C.)
McDonough, GA
Harrison, Steven E. ... Phoenix, AZ
Harrison, Steven F. ... Tuscaloosa, AL
Harrison, Steven M. ... Los Angeles, CA
Harrison, Steven M. ... Eastman, GA
Harrison, Stewart S. ... Los Angeles, CA
Harrison, Sue Ellen ... Boulder, CO
Harrison, Susan G. ... Tampa, FL
Harrison, Susan M. ... Seattle, WA
Harrison, Susan R. ... New York, NY
Harrison, Suzanne A. ... Atlanta, GA
Harrison, Sylvia L. ... Las Vegas, NV
Reno, NV
Harrison, Sylvia P. ... Greenville, SC
Harrison, Taylor & Bazile ... Oakland, CA
Harrison, Ted W. ... San Francisco, CA
Harrison, Teresa Harshman, (P.A.)
Sarasota, FL
Harrison, Terri J. ... Short Hills, NJ
Harrison, Theodore E. ... Tallahassee, FL
Harrison, Thomas E. ... Mobile, AL
Harrison, Thomas F. ... Hartford, CT

Harrison, Thomas George ... Bel Air, MD
Harrison, Thomas J. ... New York, NY
Harrison, Thomas M. ... Columbia, MO
Harrison, Thomas W. ... Bradenton, FL
Harrison & Thompson ... Macon, GA
Harrison, Thumma & Carr, P.C.
Harrisonburg, VA
Harrison, Timothy P. ... Memphis, TN
Harrison, Todd A. ... Washington, DC
Harrison, Todd R. ... New York, NY
Harrison, Tom ... Austin, TX
Harrison, Tom M. ... Corpus Christi, TX
Harrison, Tracy Leigh ... Dallas, TX
Harrison, Travenia A. ... Nashville, TN
Harrison, Travis J. ... New Orleans, LA
Harrison, Tucker & Hyde, LLP
Springfield, MO
Harrison, Van D., Jr. ... Herndon, VA
Harrison, Vicki B. ... Marietta, GA
Harrison, Victoria Ann ... Oklahoma City, OK
Harrison, W. Chris ... Memphis, TN
Harrison, W.J., & Associates, P.C.
Tucson, AZ
Harrison, W. James ... Tucson, AZ
Harrison, Wade E. ... Columbus, OH
Harrison & Wall ... Dublin, GA
Eastman, GA
Harrison, Walter J., Jr. ... Wilmington, DE
Harrison, Walter L. ... Grand Rapids, MI
Harrison, Wayne A. ... Lansing, MI
Harrison, Wendy J. ... Phoenix, AZ
Harrison, White, Smith, Hayes & Coggins,
P.A. ... Spartanburg, SC
Harrison, William A. ... Stamford, CT
Harrison, William A. ... Honolulu, HI
Harrison, William A. (Tex) ... Houston, TX
Harrison, William C. ... Fairfield, CA
Harrison, William C. ... Memphis, TN
Harrison, William C. ... Spokane, WA
Harrison, William C., Jr.
New Orleans, LA
Harrison, William D. ... Atlanta, GA
Harrison, William E. ... The Woodlands, TX
Harrison, William E. ... The Woodlands, TX
Harrison, William G., Jr.
Panama City, FL
Harrison, William K., Jr. ... Cincinnati, OH
Harrison, William P. ... Baltimore, MD
Harrison, William R. ... Los Angeles, CA
Harrison, William S. ... Baltimore, MD
Harrison, William T. ... Columbiana, AL
Harrison, William T. ... Wayne, WV
Harrison, William T., III ... Tampa, FL
Harrison, William T., Jr. ... Sarasota, FL
Harrison, William W., Jr. ... Norfolk, VA
Virginia Beach, VA
Harrison, William W., Law Offices of
Sparks, NV
Harrison, Wm. S. ... Minneapolis, MN
Harrison, W. O. (Bill) ... Corpus Christi, TX
Harrison, Zoe Elise ... Memphis, TN
Harrison-Bennett, Olivia Tanyel
Houston, TX
Harrison-Jolly, Emily ... Fort Lauderdale, FL
Harrison-Kahler, Jennifer Lynn ... Tiffin, OH
Harrison-Smith, Denise Arlene
El Cerrito, CA
Harris-Pearson, Colleen A.
Minneapolis, MN
Harris-Pearson, P.A. ... Minneapolis, MN
Harris-Ransom, Lori K. ... Caldwell, NJ
Harris-Ritter, Bilenda ... Sacramento, CA
Harriss, Alan G. ... Ironton, MO
Harriss, Donald G. ... Topsfield, MA
Harriss, Gail C. ... Durango, CO
Harriss, Hartman, Aaron, Wharton, Boyd &
Secord, P.C. ... Rossville, GA
Harriss, Lowell Gordon ... New York, NY
Harriss & Marion, P.L.L.C. ... Durham, NC
Harriss, Martha A. ... New York, NY
Harriss, Nancy ... Seattle, WA
Harriss, Robert J. ... Rossville, GA
Harriss, William G. ... Durham, NC
Harris-Starks, Cassandra L. ... Detroit, MI
Harrist, Richard C. ... San Antonio, TX
Harristhal, Christopher J.
Minneapolis, MN
Harriton, Keith S., P.C. ... Tarrytown, NY
Harriton & Mignano, LLP
Tarrytown, NY
Harriton, Norman ... Los Angeles, CA
Harriton, Paul J. ... East Hampton, NY
Harritt, Melissa A. ... St. Paul, MN
Harritt, Susan R. ... Montpelier, VT
Harritt, William L., Jr. ... Sumter, SC
Harrity, Bernadine T. ... University Park, PA
Harrity, John E. ... Arlington, VA
Harrity, Laura Fitch ... New Berlin, WI
Harrity, Martin F. ... Worcester, MA
Harrity, Paul A. ... Arlington, VA
Harrity & Snyder, L.L.P. ... Arlington, VA
Harroch, Richard D. ... San Francisco, CA
Harrod, Carole Novak
Corpus Christi, TX
Harrod, Chet ... Monroe, LA
Harrod, Daniel M. ... Eureka, IL
Harrod, Dave W. ... Heber Springs, AR
Harrod, David F. ... Athens, TN
Harrod, David Warner ... Hamburg, AR
Harrod & Harrod ... Peabody, MA
Harrod, Jean T. ... Louisville, KY
Harrod, Jennifer T. ... Greensboro, NC
Harrod, Katie Nichols ... Buffalo, NY
Harrod Law Firm, P.C. ... Eureka, IL
Harrod Law Offices ... Hamburg, AR
Harrod, Marsha Dee Debord
Oklahoma City, OK
Harrod, Michael W. ... Shelbyville, KY

Harrod, Rebecca H. ... Oakridge, LA
Harrod, Robert C. ... Cincinnati, OH
Harrod, Robert T. ... Frankfort, KY
Harrod, Samuel G., IV ... Schaumburg, IL
Harrod, Shelby Reid, Jr. ... Hamburg, AR
Harrod, Walter D. ... Valley Stream, NY
Harrod, William T., III ... Peabody, MA
Harrold, Bernard ... Chicago, IL
Harrold, Daniel J.
Federal Communications Commission,
Office of the General Counsel, GV
Harrold, Dennis E. ... Shelbyville, IN
Harrold, Dianne Barker ... Tahlequah, OK
Harrold, Gregory J. ... Minocqua, WI
Harrold, Jeffrey S. ... Fenton, MO
Harrold, Joseph Laurence ... Norwood, MA
Harrold, Linda Hauserman
Cleveland, OH
Harrold, M. Bradley ... Raleigh, NC
Harrold, Nancy J. ... Philadelphia, PA
Harrold, Scrobell & Danner, S.C.
Minocqua, WI
Harrold, Steven E. ... Sacramento, CA
Harrold, Thomas J., Jr. ... Atlanta, GA
Harrold, Wayne H., Jr. ... Kenosha, WI
Harrold, William H., Jr. ... Tallahassee, FL
Harrold, William S. ... New London, NH
Harron, Denise M. ... Milwaukee, WI
Harron, Edwin J. ... Wilmington, DE
Harron, Susan Graham ... Wilmington, DE
Harron, Thomas J. ... Spring Valley, CA
Harron, Thomas J. ... White Plains, NY
Harrop, Blake L. ... Chicago, IL
Harrop, Caldwell ... Department of Justice,
Antitrust Division, GV
Harrop, Donald E., Jr. ... Dunn, NC
Harrop, Grenville W., Jr. ... Buffalo, NY
Harrop, Joan N. ... Morris, IL
Harrop, John K. ... Washington, DC
Harrop, Robert J. ... Kansas City, MO
Harrop, Ronald L. ... Orlando, FL
Harroun, Bernard M. ... Tryon, NC
Harroun, Charles R. ... Bloomfield Hills, MI
Harrover, Stephen J. ... San Francisco, CA
Harrow, Arthur L. ... New York, NY
Harrow, Clay S. ... Palm Beach Gardens, FL
Harrow, Ellen A. ... New York, NY
Harrow, Gustave ... Forest Hills, NY
Harrow, Howard S. ... New York, NY
Harrow, Seth D. ... Saco, ME
Harroz, Joseph, Jr. ... Norman, OK
Harrsch, Keith A. ... Madison, WI
Harry, C. Daniel ... Clarkston, MI
Harry, Donald S. ... Wilmington, VT
Harry, Eric L. ... Houston, TX
Harry, G. Blair ... Suffolk, VA
Harry, Joseph James ... Bridgeport, CT
Harry, Lisa Garrett ... Pittsburgh, PA
Harry, Marina Matlin ... Houston, TX
Harry, Peter J. ... Dallas, TX
Harry, Randolph H. ... Norfolk, VA
Harry, Robert H. ... Denver, CO
Harry, Robert H. ... Oklahoma City, OK
Harry, Samuel C. ... Harrisburg, PA
Harry, Venus V. ... Springfield, MO
Harry, Virgil M., III ... Oklahoma City, OK
Harry, Virgil M., Jr. ... Oklahoma City, OK
Harryman, Julie L. ... San Leandro, CA
Harryman, William R., Jr.
Department Of Veterans Affairs,
Board of Veterans Appeals, GV
Harsany, Danielle M. ... Austin, TX
Harsch, David R. ... Barnstable, MA
Harsch, J. William W. ... Providence, RI
Harsch, Michael A. ... Northbrook, IL
Harsch, Roy M. ... Chicago, IL
Harsell, Maralee D. ... Beverly Hills, CA
Harsh & Glasser ... Birmingham, AL
Harsh, Janet K. ... Adrian, MI
Harsh, Joe D. ... Gallatin, TN
Harsh, Nathan J. ... Gallatin, TN
Harsh, Parks & Harsh ... Gallatin, TN
Harsh, R. Stanley ... Winchester, VA
Harsha, E. Houston ... Winnetka, IL
Harsha, H. Vincent ... Chicago, IL
Harsha, Mary Ruth ... St. Paul, MN
Harsha, Shelly ... Circleville, OH
Harsha, William C. ... Bingham Farms, MI
Harsha, William C., P.C., Law Offices of
Bingham Farms, MI
Harsha, William H. ... Portsmouth, OH
Harsham, Brenda Davis ... Boston, MA
Harshaw, James W. ... Princeton, NJ
Harshbarger, Benjamin S. ... Boston, MA
Harshbarger, Kelli L. ... Princeton, WV
Harshbarger, Kimberly ... Dayton, OH
Harshbarger, Laura H. ... Syracuse, NY
Harshbarger, Scott ... Boston, MA
Harshe, Maria T. ... Bingham Farms, MI
Harshman, Beth B. ... Greensboro, NC
Harshman, David J. ... Irvine, CA
Harshman & Gervelis ... Warren, OH
Youngstown, OH
Harshman, John G. ... Pittsburgh, PA
Harshman, Mark ... Chinook, MT
Harshman & McBee ... Grand Junction, CO
Harshman, Michael S. ... Warren, OH
Harshman, R. Brent ... Dallas, TX
Harshman, Scott ... Irvine, CA
Harshman, T. J. ... Grand Junction, CO
Harsip, Barry S. ... Acton, MA
Harson, Linn S. ... Dayton, OH
Harson, Michael ... Lafayette, LA
Harsoyo, Rubin ... Los Angeles, CA
Harstad, C. Blaine ... Minneapolis, MN
Harstad, Clifford A. ... Chicago, IL
Harstad, Clifford A., Ltd. ... Chicago, IL
Harstad, Keith T. ... St. Paul, MN

Harste, Richard R. ... Gainesville, GA
Harston, Bryan G. ... Dallas, TX
Hart, A. Gene, Jr. ... Charlottesville, VA
Hart, Albert E., Jr. ... Philadelphia, PA
Upper Darby, PA
Hart, Albert M. ... Los Angeles, CA
Hart, Alexander ... Philadelphia, PA
Hart, Allison S. ... Beverly Hills, CA
Hart, Andrew D. ... Winston-Salem, NC
Hart, Angela J. ... Portland, OR
Hart, Angela Katherine ... Rockville, MD
Hart, Ann Marie ... Washington, DC
Hart, Anne ... Corunna, MI
Hart, Anthony S., III ... Ann Arbor, MI
Hart, Anthony W. ... Los Angeles, CA
Hart, Arthur L. ... Vincennes, IN
Hart & Associates ... Salt Lake City, UT
Hart, Austin D. ... Burlington, VT
Hart, Avely ... New York, NY
Hart, Barbara Jane ... New York, NY
Hart, Barry H. ... Scottsdale, AZ
Hart, Barry J. ... Washington, DC
Hart, Baxley, Daniels & Holton
New York, NY
Hart, B. C. ... Minneapolis, MN
Hart & Beisher ... Gillette, WY
Sheridan, WY
Hart, Bell, Cummings, Ewing & Stuckey
Lawrenceville, IL
Olney, IL
Robinson, IL
Shoals, IN
Vincennes, IN
Washington, IN
Hart, Bennett F. ... Chicago, IL
Hart, Berne C. ... Irvine, CA
Hart, Bill, Jr. ... Houston, TX
Hart, Bradley G. ... Cedar Rapids, IA
Hart, Bradley S. ... Houston, TX
Hart, Brenda Ayres ... Richmond, VA
Hart, Brett J. ... Chicago, IL
Hart, Brian A. ... Miami, FL
Hart, Brian A. ... Freeport, IL
Hart, Brian S. ... Chicago, IL
Hart, Brian T. ... Kinderhook, NY
Hart, Brook ... Honolulu, HI
Hart, Brook, Attorney At Law, A Law
Corporation ... Honolulu, HI
Hart, Bruce ... Philadelphia, PA
Hart, Bruce B. ... Dallas, TX
Hart, Bruce G., Jr. ... Miami, FL
Hart, Bruce L. ... Cozad, NE
Eustis, NE
Hart, Buckley & Wallace, P.C. ... Dallas, TX
Hart, C. Allan, Jr. ... Portland, OR
Hart, C. Michael ... Baton Rouge, LA
Hart & Calley, P.C. ... Alexandria, VA
Hart, Carl K., Jr. ... Seward, NE
Hart, Carl W., Jr. ... Delano, CA
Hart, Carol B., (P.L.C.) ... Metairie, LA
Hart, Caryl ... Sebastopol, CA
Hart, Charles C. ... Gadsden, AL
Hart, Charles M. ... El Dorado, KS
Hart, Charles M. ... Philadelphia, PA
Hart, Charles R. ... Gillette, WY
Sheridan, WY
Hart, Charles R., Jr. ... Los Angeles, CA
Hart, Charles W., III ... Eufaula, AL
Hart, Christopher A.
Department of Transportation,
Federal Aviation Administration, GV
Hart, Christopher H. ... San Francisco, CA
Hart, Christopher J. ... Washington, DC
Hart, Christopher R. ... Houston, TX
Hart, Clifford H., Law Offices of
Flint, MI
Hart, Craig A. ... New York, NY
Hart, Daniel ... San Diego, CA
Hart, Daniel J. ... Philadelphia, PA
Hart, Daniel W. ... Des Moines, IA
Hart, Dannie L. ... Winter Park, FL
Hart, Darrell M. ... St. Paul, MN
Hart, Darren M. ... Richmond, VA
Hart, Darryl A. ... San Francisco, CA
Hart, David B. ... Roanoke, VA
Hart, David C. ... Evanston, IL
Hart, David E. ... Southfield, MI
Hart, David G. ... Bedford, TX
Hart, David J. ... Simi Valley, CA
Hart, David J. ... Miami, FL
Hart, David J. ... Lowell, MA
Hart, David J. ... Cary, NC
Hart, David J., P.A. ... Miami, FL
Hart, David Jonathan ... Hanover, PA
Hart, David Sean ... Beckley, WV
Hart, Dean, Jr. ... Pauls Valley, OK
Hart, Deborah D. ... Tampa, FL
Hart, Demaris A. ... Texarkana, TX
Hart, Dennis C. ... Boston, MA
Hart, Dennis M. ... Washington, DC
Hart, Don, Jr. ... Pleasanton, TX
Hart, Donald S., Jr. ... Tampa, FL
Hart, Donald Willard ... Phoenix, AZ
Hart, Donna M. ... New York, NY
Hart, Douglas E. ... Cincinnati, OH
Hart, Douglas J. ... Columbus, OH
Hart, Douglas R. ... Los Angeles, CA
Hart, Duane A. ... Jamaica, NY
Hart, Edward F. X. ... New York, NY
Hart, Edward J. ... Mineola, NY
Hart, Edward J., Jr. ... Mineola, NY
Hart, Edward Standish ... Boston, MA
Hart, Edwin M. ... Huntsville, AL
Hart, Eileen M. ... Brooklyn, NY
Hart, Elizabeth ... Secaucus, NJ
Hart, Emmett C. ... Albuquerque, NM
Hart, Emmett D., Jr. ... La Grange, GA
Hart, Eric D. ... El Cajon, CA

Hart, Erich O. ...... Department of the Air Force, Office of the Judge Advocate General, GV
Hart, Erik A. ...... Los Angeles, CA
Hart, Erin M. ...... New Orleans, LA
Hart, Ernest Francis ...... New York, NY
Hart, Eugene F., Jr. ...... Medford, OR
Hart, F. Michael ...... Albuquerque, NM
Hart, F. Theresa ...... Denver, CO
Hart, Falk & Huebner ...... Edgerton, WI
Hart, Frank L. ...... Tulsa, OK
Hart, Frank L. ...... El Paso, TX
Hart, Frederick M. ...... Albuquerque, NM
Hart, Gary ...... Denver, CO
Hart, Gary W. ...... St. Louis, MO
Hart, Gary W. ...... Charleston, WV
Hart, George E. ...... Buffalo, NY
Hart, George W. ...... Atlanta, GA
Hart, George W., P.C. ...... Atlanta, GA
Hart, Gordon E. ...... San Francisco, CA
Hart, Gordon E. ...... Tacoma, WA
Hart, Gordon L. ...... Stamford, CT
Hart & Gray ...... Miami, FL
Ocala, FL
Hart, Gregory C. ...... Franklin Lakes, NJ
Hart, Harold C. ...... Portland, OR
Hart, Harris, II ...... Tazewell, VA
Hart, Harry P. ...... Alexandria, VA
Hart & Hart ...... Los Angeles, CA
Hart and Hart ...... Benton, IL
Du Quoin, IL
Herrin, IL
Marion, IL
McLeansboro, IL
Mount Vernon, IL
Pinckneyville, IL
West Frankfort, IL
Hart & Hart ...... Pauls Valley, OK
Hart & Hart, Attorneys, Ltd. ...... Roanoke, VA
Hart Hart & Ruderman ...... New York, NY
Hart, Heather R. ...... St. Louis, MO
Hart, Heidi Susan ...... Rancho Cordova, CA
Santa Monica, CA
Hart, Henry ...... Midland, MI
Hart, Henry ...... Abilene, TX
Hart, Henry A. ...... Washington, DC
Hart, Henry R. ...... Granger, IN
Hart, Herbert D., III ...... Chicago, IL
Hart, Hollie H. ...... Charlotte, NC
Hart, Holly ...... Portland, OR
Hart & Horan, P.C. ...... Fairfax, VA
Hart, Howard F. ...... Los Angeles, CA
Hart, Hubert M. ...... Eagle Grove, IA
Hart & Hume, LLP ...... New York, NY
Hart, J. Larry ...... New Port Richey, FL
Hart, J. Mark ...... Birmingham, AL
Hart, J. Michael ...... Monroe, LA
Hart, J. Myles ...... Mineola, NY
Hart, J. Philip ...... Richmond, VA
Hart, J. Steven ...... Washington, DC
Hart, J. William ...... Rupert, ID
Hart, Jack ...... New York, NY
Hart, Jack L. ...... Dallas, TX
Hart, Jacob P. ...... Philadelphia, PA
Hart, Jacquelyn A. ...... New York, NY
Hart, James A. ...... Coronado, CA
Hart, James A. ...... Kansas City, MO
Hart, James A., III ...... Elizabeth, NJ
Hart, James D. ...... Estherville, IA
Hart, James E. ...... Corning, NY
Hart, James E., III ...... San Jose, CA
Hart, James F. ...... Clovis, NM
Hart, James H. ...... Perrysburg, OH
Hart, James R. ...... Mesa, AZ
Hart, James R. ...... Fairfax, VA
Hart, James W. ...... Kissimmee, FL
Hart, James W. ...... Orlando, FL
Hart, James W. ...... Sanford, FL
Hart, James W. ...... Sandusky, OH
Hart, Jana L. ...... Los Angeles, CA
Hart, Jane E. ...... Kansas City, MO
Hart, Jane R. ...... Durham, NC
Hart, Janet K. ...... Los Angeles, CA
Hart, Janet Marie ...... Upper Marlboro, MD
Hart, Janice G. ...... Springfield, VA
Hart, Jas. P., Jr. ...... Roanoke, VA
Hart, Jeffery L. ...... Austin, TX
Hart, Jeffrey ...... Spokane, WA
Hart, Jeffrey C. ...... Chicago, IL
Hart, Jeffrey C. ...... Charlotte, NC
Hart, Jeffrey P. ...... Boston, MA
Hart, Jeffrey W. ...... Eau Claire, WI
Hart, Jennifer Collins ...... Philadelphia, PA
Hart, Jennifer L. ...... Los Angeles, CA
Hart, Jeremy J. ...... Miami, FL
Hart, Jerold ...... Fort Lauderdale, FL
Hart, Jerold, P.A. ...... Fort Lauderdale, FL
Hart, Jerry B. ...... McMinnville, OR
Hart, Jerry W. ...... Tustin, CA
Hart, Jim S. ...... Houston, TX
Hart, JoAnn M. ...... Madison, WI
Hart, John C. ...... New York, NY
Hart, John C. ...... Rochester, NY
Hart, John C. ...... Fort Worth, TX
Hart, John D. ...... Poway, CA
Hart, John David ...... Fort Worth, TX
Hart, John E. ...... Atlanta, GA
Hart, John E. ...... West Trenton, NJ
Hart, John E. ...... Dayton, OH
Hart, John E. ...... Portland, OR
Hart, John J. ...... New York, NY
Hart, John J. ...... Patchogue, NY
Hart, John J. ...... Morrisville, PA
Hart, John J. ...... Johnston, RI
Hart, John K. ...... Los Angeles, CA
Hart, John K. ...... Arlington Heights, IL
Hart, John M., Jr. ...... Olean, NY
Hart, John R. ...... Yuma, AZ
Hart, John R. ...... West Palm Beach, FL
Hart, John S., Jr. ...... Harrisonburg, VA
Hart, John S., Jr., P.C. ...... Harrisonburg, VA
Hart, John W. ...... Missoula, MT
Hart, John W. ...... Virginia Beach, VA
Hart, John W. ...... Waupaca, WI
Hart, John Webb ...... Birmingham, AL
Hart, Jonathan D. ...... Washington, DC
Hart, Joseph F. ...... Beverly Hills, CA
Hart, Joseph H. ...... Austin, TX
Hart, Joseph H., IV ...... New Orleans, LA
Hart, Joseph K., Jr. ...... Bloomfield Hills, MI
Hart, Joseph L., Jr. ...... Marlborough, MA
Hart, Joseph P. ...... San Francisco, CA
Hart, Joseph P. ...... Annapolis, MD
Fort Washington, MD
Waldorf, MD
Hart, Joseph T. C. ...... New York, NY
Hart, Joseph W. ...... Atlanta, GA
Hart, Judith A. ...... Westport, CT
Hart, Judith L. ...... Lisle, IL
Hart, Julia D. ...... Boston, MA
Hart, Julianne M. ...... Lansing, MI
Hart, Julie M. ...... Chicago, IL
Hart, Karen ...... New York, NY
Hart, Karl V. ...... Miami, FL
Ocala, FL
Hart, Katherine L. ...... Fresno, CA
Hart, Kathleen ...... Gunnison, CO
Hart, Kathleen M. ...... St. Louis, MO
Hart, Kenneth H., Jr. ...... Tallahassee, FL
Hart, Kenneth M. ...... West Palm Beach, FL
Hart, Kenneth N. ...... New York, NY
Hart, Kenneth R. ...... Tallahassee, FL
Hart, Kenneth W. ...... Seattle, WA
Hart, Kevin C. ...... Lubbock, TX
Hart, Kevin D. ...... Fairport, NY
Hart, Kevin M. ...... Fort Collins, CO
Hart, Kevin M. ...... Princeton, NJ
Hart, Kevin R. ...... Westminster, MA
Hart, Kim Patrick ...... Fort Myers, FL
Hart, Kimberly D.
Department of Agriculture, Office of the General Counsel, GV
Hart, King & Coldren, A Professional Law Corporation ...... Santa Ana, CA
Hart & Kohler ...... Idaho Falls, ID
Hart, Kyle E. ...... Minneapolis, MN
Hart, Ladson F. ...... Brevard, NC
Hart, Larry C. ...... Los Angeles, CA
Hart, Laura Callaway ...... Columbia, SC
Hart, Laurel L. ...... Schaumburg, IL
Hart, Laurie S. ...... Salt Lake City, UT
Hart, Lauryn J. ...... New York, NY
Hart Law Firm, The ...... Bedford, TX
Hart Law Office, P.C. ...... Cozad, NE
Eustis, NE
Hart, Leigh D. ...... Tallahassee, FL
Hart, Leon T. ...... Jacksonville, NC
Hart, Leslie Bryan ...... Reno, NV
Hart, Leslie J. ...... Melbourne, FL
Hart, Leslie K. ...... Torrance, CA
Hart, Liam E. ...... Detroit, MI
Hart, Lillie Currington ...... Columbia, SC
Hart, Linda C. ...... Leawood, KS
Hart, Lisa J. ...... New York, NY
Hart, Lori B. ...... Maumee, OH
Hart, Louis I. ...... Denver, CO
Hart, Lynn C. ...... Salt Lake City, UT
Hart, Lynn Leary ...... Atlanta, GA
Hart, Lynn P. ...... Del Mar, CA
Hart, M. Scott ...... Virginia Beach, VA
Hart, Marcy Newman ...... Philadelphia, PA
Hart, Mark ...... Minneapolis, MN
Hart, Mark L., Jr. ...... Fort Worth, TX
Hart, Mark M. ...... Oklahoma City, OK
Hart, Martin G. ...... Tulsa, OK
Hart, Marvin E. ...... Washington, DC
Hart, Mary Jo ...... San Francisco, CA
Hart, Mary N. Moy ...... Needham, MA
Hart, Maurice ...... Waukon, IA
Hart, Maurice A. ...... Los Angeles, CA
Hart, Melissa A. ...... Pittsburgh, PA
Hart, Michael A. ...... Pittsburgh, PA
Hart, Michael Allan ...... Suwanee, GA
Hart, Michael D. ...... St. Louis, MO
Hart, Michael D. ...... Roanoke, VA
Hart, Michael D., P.C. ...... Roanoke, VA
Hart, Michael F. ...... Milwaukee, WI
Hart, Michael J. ...... Haverhill, MA
Hart, Michael Jos. ...... St. Louis, MO
Hart, Michael T. ...... Milwaukee, WI
Hart, Michele E. ...... Middletown, NJ
Hart, Michele Lynnette ...... Baltimore, MD
Hart, Micras, Morris & Peale ...... Pasadena, CA
Hart, Milby A. ...... Houston, TX
Hart, Miles D. ...... Bloomfield Hills, MI
Hart, Miles M. ...... Montgomery, AL
Hart, Murphy C. ...... Benton, IL
Hart, Nancy Elizabeth ...... Manchester, NH
Hart, Nancy L. ...... Midland, TX
Hart, Nathan W. ...... St. Paul, MN
Hart, Neal G. ...... Salt Lake City, UT
Hart, Neal L. ...... Little Rock, AR
Hart, Newton N., Jr. ...... Seal Beach, CA
Hart, P. Brennan ...... Pittsburgh, PA
Hart, Patricia A. ...... St. Louis, MO
Hart, Patricia Pelz ...... New York, NY
Hart, Patrick J. ...... Point Richmond, CA
Hart, Patrick J. ...... Libertyville, IL
Hart, Patrick J. ...... Akron, OH
Hart, Patrick M. ...... Marlborough, MA
Hart, Patrick S. ...... Des Plaines, IL
Hart, Patrick V. ...... Wells, MN
Hart, Paul ...... Portland, OR
Hart, Paul E. ...... Sunnyside, WA
Hart, Paul J. ...... Atlanta, GA
Hart, Paul R. ...... Elmira, NY
Hart, Peter ...... West Chester, PA
Hart, Peter C. ...... Emmetsburg, IA
Hart, Peter M. ...... San Francisco, CA
Hart, Peter M. ...... Santa Monica, CA
Hart, Philip D. ...... Oklahoma City, OK
Hart, Philip Matthew ...... New Haven, CT
Hart, R. Jonathan ...... Savannah, GA
Hart, R. Laird ...... Washington, DC
Hart, Rachel A. ...... Chicago, IL
Hart, Rachelle R. ...... Milwaukee, WI
Hart, Ralph V. ...... St. Louis, MO
Hart, Randall E. ...... Lake Charles, LA
Hart, Randy B. ...... Murray, UT
Hart, Randy J. ...... Cleveland, OH
Hart & Raphael ...... Chicago, IL
Hart & Regan ...... Bath, ME
Hart, Richard B. ...... Nashville, TN
Hart, Richard E. ...... Springfield, IL
Hart, Richard H. ...... Eagle, CO
Hart, Richard H., Jr., Law Offices ...... Milwaukee, WI
Hart, Richard H., Law Office of ...... Sacramento, CA
Hart, Richard K. ...... Seattle, WA
Hart, Richard O. ...... Benton, IL
Hart, Richard Thomas ...... Los Angeles, CA
Hart, Richard W. ...... San Francisco, CA
Hart, Richd. C. ...... Beverly Hills, CA
Hart, Richd. T. ...... Moose Lake, MN
Hart, Robert B. ...... Berkley, MI
Hart, Robert B. ...... Salt Lake City, UT
Hart, Robert C. ...... Racine, WI
Hart, Robert D. ...... Cleveland, OH
Hart, Robert D. ...... Tulsa, OK
Hart, Robert D., Jr. ...... Pensacola, FL
Hart, Robert G. ...... Fremont, OH
Hart, Robert H. ...... Portland, OR
Hart, Robert I. ...... Lansing, MI
Hart, Robert L., Jr. ...... Pine Bluff, AR
Hart, Robert M. ...... New York, NY
Hart, Robert M. ...... Columbus, OH
Hart, Robert M. ...... Alexandria, VA
Hart, Robert P. ...... Chicago, IL
Hart, Robert T. ...... St. Louis, MO
Hart, Robin D. ...... San Francisco, CA
Hart, Robin Sobo ...... Fort Lauderdale, FL
Hart, Roger C. ...... Dallas, TX
Hart, Ronald A. ...... Bath, ME
Hart, Ronald M. ...... Soda Springs, ID
Hart, Ronald Paul ...... Ithaca, NY
Hart, Ronald Paul, P.C. ...... Ithaca, NY
Hart, Rosemary ...... Department of Justice, Office of Legal Counsel, GV
Hart, Ross C. ...... Roanoke, VA
Hart, Ross R. ...... Los Angeles, CA
Hart, Roy E. ...... Lancaster, OH
Hart, Royal ...... San Angelo, TX
Hart, Russell H. ...... Lafayette, IN
Hart, Sally ...... Tucson, AZ
Hart, Samuel L. ...... Woodland Hills, CA
Hart, Scott C. ...... New Bern, NC
Hart, Sean M. ...... Allentown, PA
Hart and Seibert, P.C. ...... Lawrence, MA
Lowell, MA
Salem, MA
Hart, Severns & Lynch, L.L.P.
Texarkana, TX
Hart, Seward L. ...... Omaha, NE
Hart, Shane A. ...... Tampa, FL
Hart, Shannon B. ...... La Crosse, WI
Hart, Shawna G. ...... Altadena, CA
Hart, Shellie H., Jr. ...... New York, NY
Hart, Shireen T. ...... Burlington, VT
Hart, Shirley Kay ...... Orlando, FL
Hart, Southworth & Witsman
Springfield, IL
Hart, Stephanie J. ...... Newark, NJ
Hart, Stephen A. ...... Richmond, VA
Hart, Stephen E. ...... Treasury Department, Office of Thrift Supervision, GV
Hart, Stephen E. ...... Houston, TX
Hart, Stephen J. ...... Iselin, NJ
Hart, Stephen M. ...... Phoenix, AZ
Hart, Stephen O. ...... Edgerton, WI
Hart, Stephen S. ...... Idaho Falls, ID
Hart, Stephen S. ...... New York, NY
Hart, Steven A. ...... Chicago, IL
Hart, Steven A. ...... Nashville, TN
Hart, Susan B. ...... New York, NY
Hart, T. Alan ...... Jasper, TX
Hart, Tamara K. ...... New York, NY
Hart, Tamara K. ...... Nashville, TN
Hart, Terence J. ...... Dallas, TX
Hart, Terry A. ...... Pueblo, CO
Hart, Theodore M. ...... Bel Air, MD
Hart, Thomas A., Jr. ...... Washington, DC
Hart, Thomas B. ...... Fort Myers, FL
Hart, Thomas B., Jr. ...... Chicago, IL
Hart, Thomas C. ...... Dallas, TX
Hart, Thomas F. ...... Coral Gables, FL
Hart, Thomas G. ...... Weston, CT
Hart, Thomas H. ...... Lindsay, OK
Hart, Thomas H., III
Christiansted, St. Croix, VI
Hart, Thomas J. ...... Washington, DC
Hart, Thomas M. ...... New Hartford, CT
Hart, Thomas M. ...... Salem, OR
Hart, Thomas M., III ...... Houston, TX
Hart, Thomas M., IV ...... Minneapolis, MN
St. Paul, MN
Hart, Thomas P. ...... Mobile, AL
Hart, Thomas S. ...... Daytona Beach, FL
Hart, Timothy ...... Kent, OH
Hart, Timothy J. ...... Los Angeles, CA
Hart, Timothy R. ...... Visalia, CA
Hart, Timothy S. ...... Houston, TX
Hart, Trevor L. ...... Boise, ID
Hart and Trinen, L.L.P. ...... Denver, CO
Hart, Trip ...... Enumclaw, WA
Hart, Veronica M. ...... Phoenix, AZ
Hart, W. Christopher ...... Destin, FL
Pensacola, FL
Hart, W. Stephen ...... Atlanta, GA
Hart, Walter D. ...... Pauls Valley, OK
Hart, Walter L., IV ...... Charlotte, NC
Hart, Walter M., III ...... Albuquerque, NM
Hart, Walter T. ...... Des Moines, IA
Hart & Watters, A Professional Law Corporation ...... Los Angeles, CA
Hart, Wayne A. ...... Fort Wayne, IN
Hart, Webster A. ...... Eau Claire, WI
Hart, William C. ...... Duxbury, MA
Hart, William C. ...... Washington, PA
Hart, William D., III ...... Shelton, CT
Hart, William D., Jr. ...... New York, NY
Hart, William E. ...... Amherst, MA
Hart, William G., Jr. ...... Frankfort, KY
Hart, William H. ...... Dallas, TX
Hart, William J. ...... Springfield, MO
Hart, William, Law Offices of
New York, NY
Hart, William M. ...... Minneapolis, MN
Hart, William M. ...... New York, NY
Hart, William R. ...... Santa Ana, CA
Hart, William Ryan, Jr. ...... Exeter, NH
Hart, William S. ...... Los Angeles, CA
Hart, William S. ...... Lakewood, CO
Hart, William S. ...... Waukon, IA
Hart, William T. ...... Denver, CO
Hart, William T. ...... Chicago, IL
Hart, William Troy ...... Marietta, GA
Hart, William W., Jr. ...... Trenton, NJ
Hart and Winfree ...... Sunnyside, WA
Hart & Wren, L.L.P. ...... Little Rock, AR
Hartary, Joseph W.
Department of Commerce, Patent and Trademark Office, GV
Hartburg, Michael ...... Huntington, IN
Hartch, Sophia S. ...... New York, NY
Hartch, Thomas F. ...... Greenwich, CT
Harte, Alisan ...... New York, NY
Harte, Amy Edwards ...... Surry, VA
Harte, J. Bernard ...... Bennington, VT
Harte, John W. ...... Aiken, SC
Harte, Phyllis K. ...... Miami, FL
Harte, Robert J. ...... Aiken, SC
Harte, Sandy, III ...... Seal Beach, CA
Harte, William J. ...... Chicago, IL
Harte, William J., Ltd. ...... Chicago, IL
Hartel, Arthur J., III ...... Liberty, TX
Hartel, Arthur P., Jr. ...... Wayne, PA
Hartel, Arthur P., Jr., P.C. ...... Wayne, PA
Hartel, John W. ...... Lanham, MD
Hartel & Kenny, P.L.C. ...... Metairie, LA
Hartel, Stephen C., Jr. ...... Metairie, LA
Hartelius, Channing J. ...... Lakeside, MT
Hartelius, Howard, Crosswhite & Baker, L.L.D.
Lakeside, MT
Hartell, Cheryl A. ...... Garden City, NY
Harten, James C. ...... St. Paul, MN
Harten, Marvin A. ...... Los Angeles, CA
Harten, Stephen P. ...... Providence, RI
Hartenau, Christopher H.
Department of Housing and Urban Development, Office of General Counsel, GV
Hartenbach, James R. ...... Clayton, MO
Hartenbach, John H. ...... Kansas City, MO
Hartenberger, Werner K.
Washington, DC
Hartenstein, Eric ...... Wichita, KS
Hartenstein, Geoffrey R. ...... Greenville, PA
Hartenstein, John M. ...... San Francisco, CA
Hartenstein, Mark, Law Offices of ...... Boise, ID
Hartenstine, Ernest E. ...... Denham Springs, LA
Hammond, LA
Hartenstine, J. Michael ...... Sarasota, FL
Harter, Alan R. ...... Las Vegas, NV
Harter, Ava Askenazi ...... Dayton, OH
Harter, Benedict T. ...... New York, NY
Harter, Christine ...... Salinas, CA
Harter, Christine L. ...... Ocala, FL
Harter, David James ...... Santa Ana, CA
Harter, Deborah Jo L. ...... Endicott, NY
Harter, Diana ...... St. Louis, MO
Harter, Edward A., Jr. ...... Columbia, SC
Harter, Elizabeth D. ...... Charleston, WV
Harter, Franklin C. ...... Benton Harbor, MI
Harter, Gary R. ...... Belleville, IL
Mascoutah, IL
Harter, Gene G. ...... Los Angeles, CA
Harter, Jay A. ...... Lansing, MI
Harter, Joe A. ...... Kansas City, MO
Harter, John L. ...... Stamford, CT
Harter, Kenneth S. ...... Carpinteria, CA
Harter, Lafayette G., III ...... Washington, DC
Harter & Larson ...... Belleville, IL
Mascoutah, IL
Harter Law Offices, P.C. ...... Plattsmouth, NE
Harter, Mathew P. ...... Las Vegas, NV
Harter, Patricia S. ...... Fresno, CA
Harter, Paul S. ...... Phoenix, AZ
Harter, Paul S., P.C. ...... Phoenix, AZ
Harter, Philip J. ...... Washington, DC
Harter, Phillip E. ...... Battle Creek, MI
Harter, Ralph M. Peter ...... Rochester, NY
Harter, Richard J. ...... Farmingdale, NJ
Harter, Richard M. ...... Boston, MA
Harter, Richard W. ...... Plattsmouth, NE
Harter, Robert J., Jr. ...... Los Angeles, CA
Harter, Russell W., Jr. ...... Greenville, SC
Harter, Scott A. ...... Huntington, IN
Harter, Secrest & Emery LLP
Fort Myers, FL
Naples, FL
Albany, NY
Buffalo, NY

Rochester, NY
Harter, Simon ... New York, NY
Harter, Stanley A. ... Redlands, CA
San Bernardino, CA
Temecula, CA
Harter, William M. ... Huntington, WV
Hartert, Gerald D. ... Glenwood Springs, CO
Hartert, Thomas J. ... Glenwood Springs, CO
Hartert and Wilson ... Glenwood Springs, CO
Hart-Esposito, Nancy L. ... Cherry Hill, NJ
Philadelphia, PA
Hartfeldt, Will ... Minneapolis, MN
Hartfield, Richard A. ... Denver, CO
Hartford & Ackerman ... Los Alamitos, CA
Hartford, Carolyn R. ... Stow, MA
Hartford, Donald M., Jr. ... Lakeport, CA
Hartford, James ... East Palestine, OH
Hartford, John J. ... Redwood City, CA
Hartford, Phyllis K. ... Stamford, CT
Hartford, Richard S. ... Chicago, IL
Hartford, Robert L. ... Buffalo, NY
Hartford, Robert S., Jr. ... Youngstown, OH
Hartford, Stanley R. ... Los Alamitos, CA
Hartford, Steven ... Westerly, RI
Hartford, Thomas J., III ... Salt Lake City, UT
Hartford, Vera K. ... Pleasanton, CA
Hart-Franklin, Cassandra D.
Los Angeles, CA
Hartgens, Amber N. ... Burbank, CA
Hartglass, Lori R. ... Fort Lauderdale, FL
Harth, Charles C. ... Park Ridge, IL
Harth, Danita Y. ... Chicago, IL
Harth, David J. ... Madison, WI
Harth, William F. ... Newark, NJ
Harth, William T., Jr. ... Woodbridge, NJ
Harthcock, Tammy Green ... Jackson, MS
Harthill, Susan ... Washington, DC
Harthoorn, Ruth ... Washington, DC
Harthun, Annemarie Scanlon
Federal Trade Commission,
Bureau of Consumer Protection, GV
Harthun, Luther A. ... Willoughby, OH
Hartig, Alan R. ... Barrow, AK
Hartig, Bjelajac, Swanson & Koenen
Racine, WI
Hartig, Douglas W. ... St. Louis, MO
Hartig, Francis E. ... Norwood, MA
Hartig, Helene Wasserheit ... New York, NY
Hartig, Lawrence L. ... Anchorage, AK
Hartig, Rhodes, Norman, Mahoney & Edwards, A Professional Corporation
Anchorage, AK
Hartig, Sue Ann ... Evansville, IN
Hartigan, Bruce ... Minneapolis, MN
Hartigan, Cecile Blakeslee ... Concord, NH
Hartigan, Daniel E. ... Newton, IL
Hartigan, David M. ... Chicago, IL
Hartigan, Gerard F. ... Boston, MA
Hartigan, John D. ... Rye, NY
Hartigan, John D., Jr. ... Omaha, NE
Hartigan, John F. ... Los Angeles, CA
Hartigan, John J. ... Lowell, MA
Hartigan, John M. ... Chicago, IL
Hartigan, Mary K. ... Los Angeles, CA
Hartigan, Maurice H., III ... New York, NY
Hartigan, Melissa A. ... Hackensack, NJ
Hartigan, Michael D. ... Boston, MA
Hartigan, Michael J., Jr. ... Riverwoods, IL
Hartigan, Michele L. ... Philadelphia, PA
Hartigan, Neil F. ... Chicago, IL
Hartigan, Russell W., & Associates
Chicago, IL
Hartigan, Thomas J. ... St. Paul, MN
Hartigan, Thomas L. ... Sacramento, CA
Hartigan, Timothy J. ... King Of Prussia, PA
Hartigan, Vicki E. ... Carson City, NV
Hartigan, William F., Jr. ... Trenton, NJ
Hartig-Osanka, Judith M. ... Racine, WI
Hartin, David P. ... Marietta, GA
Hartin, Sara ... Copperas Cove, TX
Hartin, Timothy A. ... Madison, WI
Harting, Carolyn E. ... Bedford, NY
Harting, David B. ... New Castle, OK
Harting, Marta D. ... Baltimore, MD
Harting, Michael G. ... Portland, OR
Harting, Richard A. ... Long Beach, CA
Harting, Thomas E. ... Lancaster, PA
Hartinger, Arthur A. ... San Leandro, CA
Hartinger, Harold T. ... Tacoma, WA
Hartinger, Lawrence W. ... Lafayette, CA
Hartinger, Scott M. ... Rockville, MD
Hartje, Dana Lynn ... Denver, CO
Hartje, George F. ... Conway, AR
Hartje, Jeffrey H. ... Spokane, WA
Hartje, John ... New York, NY
Hartje, Keith D. ... Council Bluffs, IA
Hartje, Michael E., Jr. ... Little Rock, AR
North Little Rock, AR
Hartjen & Hudanich ... Johnson City, NY
Waverly, NY
Hartjen, Lee C. ... Johnson City, NY
Waverly, NY
Hartka, Margaret ... Catonsville, MD
Hartke & Hartke ... Falls Church, VA
Hartke, J. Alan ... Falls Church, VA
Hartke, James R. ... Cincinnati, OH
Hartke, Paul V. ... Falls Church, VA
Hartke, Phyllis A. ... Anchorage, AK
Hartke, Vance ... Falls Church, VA
Hartke, Wayne R. ... Falls Church, VA
Hartker, Gregory J. ... Palo Alto, CA
Hart-Klein, Deborah J. ... Chestnut Hill, MA
Hartkop, Jeffrey W. ... Sterling Heights, MI
Hartl, Colleen A. ... Seattle, WA
Hartl, Donna F. ... Chicago, IL
Hartland, Christine Ann ... Phoenix, AZ
Hartland, Michelle L. ... Washington, DC
Hartland, Robert W. ... Pittsburgh, PA
Hartland, Thomas J., Jr. ... Atlanta, GA
Hartlaub, Dotten, Terry & Townsend, P.C.
Summit, NJ
Hartlaub, Joseph V. ... Columbus, OH
Hartlaub, Lawrence P. ... Winter Park, CO
Hartlaub, Lawrence P. ... Chicago, IL
Hartlaub, Lawrence P., P.C.
Winter Park, CO
Hartlaub, R. Jeffrey ... Summit, NJ
Hartle, Daniel J. ... Bradford, PA
Hartle, John W. ... Juneau, AK
Hartleb, David F. ... Cincinnati, OH
Hartley, Alton G. ... Decatur, GA
Hartley, Andrea Stone ... Miami, FL
Hartley, Angela Hibbard ... Baltimore, MD
Hartley, Ann ... Austin, TX
Hartley, Brett ... Daytona Beach, FL
Hartley, Carl E. ... Chattanooga, TN
Johnson City, TN
Nashville, TN
Hartley, Carl W. ... Paola, KS
Hartley, Carl W., Jr. ... Orlando, FL
Hartley, Carla J. ... San Francisco, CA
Hartley & Chidester, P.C. ... Pearisburg, VA
Hartley, Christian H. ... Charleston, SC
Hartley, Crystal K. ... Centreville, AL
Hartley, Daniel R. ... Hampton, NH
Hartley, Daryl K. ... Union, MO
Hartley, David V. ... Lillington, NC
Hartley, Deborah K. ... Arlington, TX
Hartley, Dennis W. ... Colorado Springs, CO
Hartley, Dennis W., P.C., Professional Corporation ... Colorado Springs, CO
Hartley, Diane J. ... St. Louis, MO
Hartley, Donald V. ... Irwindale, CA
Hartley, Edon V. ... Denver, CO
Hartley, Edward E. ... San Francisco, CA
Hartley and Edwards ... Lillington, NC
Hartley, Floyd R., Jr. ... Dallas, TX
Hartley, G. Michael ... Douglasville, GA
Hartley, George R. ... Irwindale, CA
Hartley, Gerald W. ... Montgomery, AL
Hartley, H. James ... Boston, MA
Hartley & Hartley ... Los Angeles, CA
Santa Monica, CA
Hartley & Hickman ... Greenville, AL
Hayneville, AL
Hartley, James A. ... Pearisburg, VA
Hartley, James E. ... Denver, CO
Hartley, James E., Jr. ... Waterbury, CT
Hartley, Jason S. ... San Diego, CA
Hartley, Jayne ... Oak Brook, IL
Hartley, Jeffery J. ... Mobile, AL
Hartley, Jennifer A. ... Savannah, GA
Hartley, Jill ... Hartford, CT
Hartley, Jill M. ... Milwaukee, WI
Hartley, Jocelyn B. ... Lock Haven, PA
Hartley, John P. ... Arlington, VA
Hartley, John W., Jr. ... Montgomery, AL
Hartley & Jones ... Vinita, OK
Hartley, Joseph C., Jr. ... Natchez, MS
Hartley, Joseph M. ... Santa Monica, CA
Hartley, Judy L. ... Los Angeles, CA
Hartley, Karen, & Associates ... Eugene, OR
Hartley, Kathleen H. ... San Francisco, CA
Hartley, Kevin F. ... Herndon, VA
Hartley, Kirk T. ... Chicago, IL
Hartley, Larry S. ... Charlotte, NC
Hartley, Les J. ... Newport Beach, CA
Las Vegas, NV
Hartley, Linda D. ... Tampa, FL
Hartley, Lynn L. ... Mayville, NY
Hartley, Martha Anderson ... Orlando, FL
Hartley, Martha M. ... Hamilton, GA
Hartley, Marvin, Jr. ... Lyons, GA
Hartley, Mary Kathleen
Santa Monica, CA
Hartley, Matthew R. ... Chicago, IL
Hartley & Mazarei ... Newport Beach, CA
Hartley, Michael J. ... Los Angeles, CA
Hartley, Michael W. ... Waxahachie, TX
Hartley, Nicholson & Hartley, P.A.
Paola, KS
Hartley, P. Richard ... Greenville, AL
Hartley, Patricia L. ... Wellington, FL
Hartley, Paula Leátrice ... Baton Rouge, LA
Hartley, Paula Leátrice ... Port Allen, LA
Hartley, Phillip L. ... Gainesville, GA
Hartley & Puls ... Decatur, GA
Hartley, R. Dean ... Wheeling, WV
Hartley, Rebecca S. ... Washington, DC
Hartley, Richard H., III ... Glastonbury, CT
Hartley, Richard O. ... Naples, FL
Hartley, Robert L., Jr. ... Indianapolis, IN
Hartley, Roger C. ... Washington, DC
Hartley, Roger P. ... Clearwater, FL
Hartley, Ronald W. ... Atlanta, GA
Hartley, Ross C. ... Baxter Springs, KS
Hartley, Rowe & Fowler, P.C.
Douglasville, GA
Hartley, Sandra K. ... Paola, KS
Hartley, Scott A. ... Waterbury, CT
Hartley, Scott E. ... San Mateo, CA
Hartley, Sharon M. ... Hartford, CT
Hartley, S. K., Jr. ... Lafayette, LA
Hartley, Stephanie F. ... Jacksonville, FL
Hartley, Stephen L. ... El Segundo, CA
Hartley, Steven L. ... Honolulu, HI
Hartley, Susan J. ... Santa Monica, CA
Hartley, Tanya Michele ... Dallas, TX
Hartley, Ted L. ... Clovis, NM
Hartley, Teddy Lowe, Ltd. ... Clovis, NM
Hartley, Teresa M. ... Newport Beach, CA
Hartley, Thomas B. ... Kenosha, WI
Twin Lakes, WI
Hartley, Thomas Jot ... Vinita, OK
Hartley, Timothy L. ... Albuquerque, NM
Hartley, Timothy Maze ... Miami, FL
Hartley, Wade Leon ... Atmore, AL
Hartley, Wall & Norman ... Orlando, FL
Hartley, William A. ... Laconia, NH
Hartline, Ann-Marie Fassl
Lake Success, NY
Hartline, C. Vernon, Jr., ... Dallas, TX
Hartline, Dacus, Dreyer & Kern, L.L.P.
Dallas, TX
Hartline, Deborah Watson ... Houston, TX
Hartline, Edward E., P.C. ... Houston, TX
Hartline, Harold E. ... Hueytown, AL
Hartline, James R. ... Pittsburgh, PA
Hartloff, Paul W., Jr. ... Santa Barbara, CA
Hartlove, Henry W. ... Timonium, MD
Hart-Mahon, Margaret ... St. Louis, MO
Hartman, Alan J. ... Cincinnati, OH
Hartman, Alan J. Co., LPA
Cincinnati, OH
Hartman, Alan S. ... Cleveland, OH
Hartman, Alene Laska ... Cherry Hill, NJ
Hartman, Allen ... Chicago, IL
Hartman, Allison L. ... Englewood, CO
Hartman, Amy ... Chicago, IL
Hartman, Amy S. ... Bingham Farms, MI
Hartman, Andrea R. ... Burbank, CA
Hartman, Andrew ... Chicago, IL
Hartman, Andrew Warren ... Woodstock, GA
Hartman, Anne Hayes ... San Francisco, CA
Hartman, Anthony J. ... Cleveland, OH
Hartman & Armstrong, Ltd. A Professional Corporation ... Reno, NV
Hartman and Associates ... Los Angeles, CA
Hartman, Attorneys, Chartered
Moorestown, NJ
Hartman, B. Judd ... Morgantown, WV
Hartman, Ball, Brody & Kinney, P.C.
Buffalo, NY
Hartman, Barry M. ... Washington, DC
Hartman, Boyd A. ... Redmond, WA
Hartman, Bradley P. ... Phoenix, AZ
Hartman, Bradley S. ... Cooper City, FL
Hartman, Brian J. ... Wilmington, DE
Hartman, Bruce ... West Point, PA
Hartman, Burton A. ... Clearwater, FL
Hartman, C. Edward, II ... Annapolis, MD
Hartman, C. Edward, III ... Annapolis, MD
Hartman, Charles C., Jr. ... Severna Park, MD
Hartman, Charles L. ... Reno, NV
Hartman, Charles R. ... Freeport, IL
Hartman, Charles R., III ... St. Louis, MO
Hartman, Christopher J. ... Reading, PA
Hartman & Concannon ... Sherman Oaks, CA
Hartman, Cornelia A. ... Houston, TX
Hartman & Cornely, P.A. ... Miami, FL
Hartman, Craig S. ... New York, NY
Hartman, Craig T. ... Anchorage, AK
Hartman & Craven LLP ... New York, NY
Hartman, Curt Carl ... Cincinnati, OH
Hartman, Cynthia ... Malden, MA
Hartman, Cynthia M. ... Fort Collins, CO
Hartman, Dale M. ... Cleveland, OH
Hartman, Daniel J. ... Buffalo, NY
Hartman, Daniel M. ... El Segundo, CA
Hartman, Daniel W. ... Tallahassee, FL
Hartman, Darrell J. ... Abbeville, LA
Hartman, David ... New York, NY
Hartman, David ... Austin, TX
Hartman, David Lloyd ... Houston, TX
Hartman, Denise ... Rochester, NY
Hartman, Denise G. ... Tulsa, OK
Hartman, Donald R. ... Washington, DC
Hartman, Donna H. ... Newark, NJ
Hartman, Douglas C. ... Miami, FL
Hartman, Duane W. ... Valparaiso, IN
Hartman & Duvall, S.C. ... Alma, WI
Hartman, Earl F. ... Lansdale, PA
Hartman, Edward J. ... Davenport, IA
Hartman and Egeli ... Annapolis, MD
Baltimore, MD
Hartman, Elizabeth A. ... Madison, WI
Hartman, Eric F., The Law Offices of
San Jose, CA
Hartman, Eric S. ... Long Beach, CA
Hartman, Eugene R. ... Gettysburg, PA
Hartman, Fagie ... New York, NY
Hartman & Foutty ... Indianapolis, IN
Hartman, Frances A. ... Wichita, KS
Hartman, Francis J. ... Moorestown, NJ
Hartman, Franklin L. ... Cleveland, OH
Hartman, Gary E. ... Gettysburg, PA
Hartman, Gary J. ... Lakewood, CO
Hartman, Gary M. ... Valparaiso, IN
Hartman, Gary P. ... Worland, WY
Hartman, Gary T. ... St. Louis, MO
Hartman, Georgia L. ... Fort Wayne, IN
Hartman, Gerald S. ... Washington, DC
Hartman & Goldberg ... Cooper City, FL
Hartman, Grant R. ... Edina, MN
Hartman, Gregory A. ... Portland, OR
Hartman, Gregory C. ... Reading, PA
Hartman, H. Gordon ... Metairie, LA
Hartman, Hartman, Howe and Allerton, P.C.
Reading, PA
Hartman, Henrietta H. ... Kingwood, WV
Hartman, Howard J. ... Freeport, IL
Hartman, Irving N. ... Sherman Oaks, CA
Hartman, J. Benedict ... Brunswick, GA
Hartman, Jack M. ... Harrisburg, PA
Hartman, James A., (P.A.) ... Orlando, FL
Hartman, James M. ... Rochester, NY
Hartman, James O. ... Walnut Creek, CA
Hartman, James W., Jr. ... Broomall, PA
Hartman, Janice C. ... Pittsburgh, PA
Hartman, Jay T. ... St. Paul, MN
Hartman, Jeffrey A. ... Newport Beach, CA
Hartman, Jeffrey L. ... Reno, NV
Hartman, Joan E. ... Department of Justice,
Civil Division, GV
Hartman, Joel L. ... Atlanta, GA
Hartman, John E. ... San Francisco, CA
Hartman, John E. ... Boston, MA
Hartman, John H. ... Binghamton, NY
Hartman, John I., Jr. ... Lancaster, PA
Hartman, John James ... Chicago, IL
Hartman, John L. ... San Francisco, CA
Hartman, John L., III ... Birmingham, AL
Hartman, John McFarland ... Fort Myers, FL
Hartman, John McFarland, P.A.
Fort Myers, FL
Hartman, John P. ... Denver, CO
Hartman, John P., & Associates ... Denver, CO
Hartman, John W. ... Lancaster, PA
Hartman & Johnston ... Greenville, SC
Hartman, Jonathan M. ... Flint, MI
Hartman, Joseph B. ... Englewood, CO
Hartman, Judith Ann ... Cincinnati, OH
Hartman, Julieanne ... Metairie, LA
Hartman & Kahn, Co., L.P.A.
Cleveland, OH
Hartman, Katherine D. ... Moorestown, NJ
Hartman, Kathi L. ... Chestnut Hill, MA
Hartman, Kay E. ... Norwood, CO
Hartman, Kendra Kekelis ... Chicago, IL
Hartman, Kerry ... Washington, DC
Hartman, Lapham & Smith, L.L.P.
Victoria, TX
Hartman, Laura S. ... Albany, NY
Hartman, Laurie A. ... Washington, DC
Hartman, Lawrence S. ... New York, NY
Hartman, Lee K. ... Las Vegas, NV
Hartman, Leonard ... Stuart, IA
Hartman, Leslie M. ... San Francisco, CA
Hartman, Lewis H. ... Long Island City, NY
Hartman, Linda M. ... Nevada City, CA
Hartman, Lisa J. ... Victoria, TX
Hartman, Lloyd C. ... San Jose, CA
Hartman, Lynn Wickham
Cedar Rapids, IA
Hartman, Malcolm T. ... San Antonio, TX
Hartman, Marilyn A. ... Bloomfield, IN
Hartman, Mark A. ... Fort Wayne, IN
Hartman, Mark A. ... Garden City, NY
Hartman, Marshall J. ... Chicago, IL
Hartman, Mary Clare ... New Orleans, LA
Hartman, Melvin C. ... New York, NY
Hartman, Merrill L. ... Dallas, TX
Hartman, Mervin J. ... Philadelphia, PA
Hartman, Michael A. ... New York, NY
Hartman, Michael Ryan ... Indianapolis, IN
Hartman, Michael W. ... Snyder, TX
Hartman, Michelle L. ... Louisville, KY
Hartman & Miller, P.C. ... Harrisburg, PA
Hartman, Miriam L. ... Purchase, NY
Hartman, Morris J. ... Plymouth, MN
Hartman, Norman A., Jr., (P.A.)
Fort Myers, FL
Hartman & Paddock ... Bloomfield, IN
Hartman, Patricia E. ... Denver, CO
Hartman, Patricia J. ... Sacramento, CA
Hartman, Peter G. ... New Orleans, LA
Hartman, Peter M. ... Atlanta, GA
Hartman, Porter E. ... Paramus, NJ
Hartman, Ralph E. ... Dallas, TX
Hartman, Randall L. ... Fayetteville, NC
Hartman, Raymond V. ... St. Charles, IL
Hartman, Rebecca J. ... Cleveland, OH
Hartman, Rhonda G. ... Pittsburgh, PA
Hartman, Richard E. ... Englewood, CO
Hartman, Richard L. ... Palm Springs, CA
Pasadena, CA
Hartman, Richard W. ... Tucson, AZ
Hartman, Richd. J. ... Indianapolis, IN
Hartman, Rima Fawal ... Seattle, WA
Hartman, Robert J. ... Oakland, CA
Hartman, Robert J. ... Minneapolis, MN
Hartman, Robt. L., Jr. ... Charleston, WV
Hartman, Rodney T. ... Billings, MT
Hartman, Roger C. ... Los Angeles, CA
Hartman, Ronald F. ... Westerville, OH
Hartman, Ronald G. ... Pittsburgh, PA
Hartman, Ronald L. ... Thousand Oaks, CA
Hartman, Roy M. ... Miami, FL
Hartman, Russell ... New York, NY
Hartman, Russell W. ... Silverdale, WA
Hartman, Sanford L. ... Bethesda, MD
Hartman, Sheldon R. ... Cleveland, OH
Hartman, Springfield & Beckham
Birmingham, AL
Hartman, Stacie R. ... Chicago, IL
Hartman, Stephan A. ... Blue Bell, PA
Hartman, Stephen A. ... Brookfield, WI
Hartman, Stephen D. ... Carson City, NV
Hartman, Steven E. ... Beverly Hills, CA
Hartman, Steven H. ... Parsippany, NJ
Hartman, Susan D. ... Detroit, MI
Hartman, Susan J. ... St. Paul, MN
Hartman, Susan L. ... Kalamazoo, MI
Hartman, Susan M. ... Pittsburgh, PA
Hartman, Tacy A. ... Salt Lake City, UT
Hartman, Terrence S.
Department of Defense,
Armed Services Board of Contract Appeals,
GV
Hartman, Thomas E. ... Milwaukee, WI
Hartman, Todd G. ... Minneapolis, MN
Hartman, Tracey Scott ... Tallahassee, FL
Hartman Underhill & Brubaker
Lancaster, PA
Hartman, Vanessa L. ... Greenville, SC
Hartman, Victor E. ... Houston, TX
Hartman, Wayne L. ... Cuero, TX
Hartman, Wayne P. ... Austin, TX
Hartman, William C. ... Naples, FL
Hartman, William J., Jr. ... Birmingham, MI
Hartman, William R. ... Sacramento, CA
Walnut Creek, CA

Hartman, William R., Jr. ....**Seal Beach, CA**
Hartman, William W. ....Surfside, FL
Hartman, William Ragan ....Binghamton, NY
Hartman & Winnicki, P.C.
Hackensack, NJ
Paramus, NJ
Hartman & Yannetti ....**Gettysburg, PA**
Hartman Blank, Colene ....**Palo Alto, CA**
Hartman-Levy, Valerie ....Atlanta, GA
Hartmann, Alice C. ....Tucson, AZ
Hartmann, Anthony A. ....**Washington, DC**
Chicago, IL
Hartmann, Calvin A. ....Houston, TX
Hartmann, Carol A. ....West Orange, NJ
Hartmann, Charles J., Jr. ....Washington, DC
Hartmann, Christopher E. ....**Roseland, NJ**
Hartmann, Clay A. ....**Dallas, TX**
Hartmann, David G. ....Fremont, NE
Hartmann, Dennis P. ....Cincinnati, OH
Hartmann, Evelyn M. ....Woodbridge, NJ
Hartmann, Forrest D. ....**Baraboo, WI**
Sauk City, WI
Hartmann, Frederick L., Jr. ....**Chicago, IL**
Hartmann, George V. ....**Stockton, CA**
Hartmann, Gregory P. ....Cincinnati, OH
Hartmann, H. Michael ....**Chicago, IL**
Hartmann, James F., Jr.
Oklahoma City, OK
Hartmann, James M. ....**Delhi, NY**
Hartmann, Jeff L. ....Oklahoma City, OK
Hartmann, Jeffrey R. ....Orange, CA
Hartmann, Jennifer Lynn ....Chicago, IL
Hartmann, Joan R. ....Philadelphia, PA
Hartmann, John A., III ....Princeton, NJ
Hartmann, John F. ....**Chicago, IL**
Hartmann, John R. ....Philadelphia, PA
Hartmann, John T. ....**Minneapolis, MN**
Hartmann, Karen L. ....San Jose, CA
Hartmann, Karl J. ....**Chicago, IL**
Hartmann, Kenneth ....**Chicago, IL**
Hartmann, Kenneth R. ....**Miami, FL**
Hartmann, Kevin J. ....Jersey City, NJ
Hartmann, Kimberly Ann ....**Dallas, TX**
Hartmann, Kurt ....Hackensack, NJ
Hartmann, Markus U. ....**Cincinnati, OH**
Hartmann, Melanie M. ....**Baton Rouge, LA**
Hartmann, Michael E. ....San Francisco, CA
Hartmann, Michael W. ....**Detroit, MI**
Hartmann, Patricia J. ....St. Paul, MN
Hartmann, Philip K. ....**Columbus, OH**
Hartmann, Richard W. ....**Philadelphia, PA**
Hartmann, Robert G. ....Columbus, OH
Hartmann, Robert J. ....Phoenix, AZ
Hartmann, Robin P. ....**Dallas, TX**
Hartmann & Robinson, LLP
Stockton, CA
Hartmann, Ron A. ....**Los Angeles, CA**
Hartmann, Ronald A. ....Los Angeles, CA
Hartmann, Sharon Lybeck, Law Offices of
Los Angeles, CA
Hartmann, Steven H. ....**Arlington, VA**
Hartmann, Steven M. ....**Chicago, IL**
Hartmann, Susan J. ....Sarasota, FL
Hartmann, Wendy A. ....Baltimore, MD
Hartmann-Harrison, Martha D. ....Richmond, VA
Hartmere, Jon S. ....Boston, MA
Hartmere, Michael ....New Haven, CT
Hartmeyer, Sarah C. ....**Tulsa, OK**
Hartmus, Diane M. ....New York, NY
Hartmus, John A., III ....Fenton, MI
Hartnagel, William J. ....New City, NY
Hart Nassen, Regina ....Department of Justice, Criminal Division, GV
Hartnell, Bryan C. ....**Redlands, CA**
Yucaipa, CA
Hartnell, Horspool & Fox, A Professional Corporation ....**Redlands, CA**
Riverside, CA
San Bernardino, CA
Yucaipa, CA
Hartnell, Pamela A. ....Fairbanks, AK
Hartness, Edward L. ....**Gainesville, GA**
Hartness, John D., Jr. ....**Atlanta, GA**
Hartness & Link, P.C. ....**Gainesville, GA**
Hartness, Matthew ....**Little Rock, AR**
Hartnett, Alexander P. ....New York, NY
Hartnett, Anne E. ....**Dover, DE**
Hartnett, Anthony S. ....Dover, NH
Hartnett, Bernard M., Jr. ....Jersey City, NJ
Hartnett, Caroline M. ....Miamisburg, OH
Hartnett, Clare ....**Cupertino, CA**
Seattle, WA
Hartnett, Dan Dennis ....San Antonio, TX
Hartnett, Daniel ....**Accomac, VA**
Hartnett, Daniel J. ....**Chicago, IL**
Hartnett, Daniel L. ....**South Sioux City, NE**
Hartnett, Daniel T. ....**Chicago, IL**
Hartnett, David P. ....**Miami, FL**
Hartnett, David S. ....Cortland, NY
Hartnett, Deborah ....**New York, NY**
Hartnett, Deborah I. ....Wilmington, DE
Hartnett, Donna Marie ....**Buffalo, NY**
Hartnett, Edward ....Newark, NJ
Hartnett, Elaine M. ....Boston, MA
Hartnett, Elizabeth A. ....Syracuse, NY
Hartnett, Everett E. ....Houston, TX
Hartnett, F. Douglas ....Washington, DC
Hartnett, Fred ....**Dallas, TX**
Hartnett, George J. ....**Philadelphia, PA**
Hartnett, Georgia Howell ....Union, NJ
Hartnett & Hartnett ....Hockessin, DE
Hartnett & Hayes, LLP ....Fullerton, CA
Hartnett, J. Michael ....Basking Ridge, NJ
Hartnett, James J., IV ....**Minneapolis, MN**
Hartnett, James J., Jr. ....**Dallas, TX**
Hartnett, James J., (P.C.) ....**Dallas, TX**
Hartnett, James P. ....Central Islip, NY
Hartnett, Jay David ....**Dallas, TX**

Hartnett, Jean D. ....Buffalo, NY
Hartnett, Jeffrey E. ....**St. Louis, MO**
Hartnett, Jennifer Anne ....Hockessin, DE
Hartnett, Jim ....**Redwood City, CA**
Hartnett, John R. ....**Alexandria, VA**
Hartnett Law Firm, The ....**Dallas, TX**
Hartnett Law Office ....Manlius, NY
Hartnett, Lawrence F. ....Hockessin, DE
Hartnett, Lisa Dieter ....Omaha, NE
Hartnett, Lisa K. ....Omaha, NE
Hartnett, M. Catherine ....Overland Park, KS
Hartnett, Mary E. ....Washington, DC
Hartnett, Mary F. ....Red Bank, NJ
Hartnett, Maurice A., III ....Dover, DE
Hartnett, Patricia A. ....**Boston, MA**
Hartnett, Patricia L. ....New York, NY
Hartnett, Patrick I. ....Chicago, IL
Hartnett, Patrick M. ....Fullerton, CA
Hartnett, Paul J., Jr. ....**Boston, MA**
Hartnett, Peter M. ....Manlius, NY
Hartnett, Randolph J. ....St. Paul, MN
Hartnett, Robert W. ....Manlius, NY
Hartnett, Ronald J. ....**Idaho Falls, ID**
Hartnett, Stephen C. ....**St. Louis, MO**
Hartnett, Susan A. ....**Boston, MA**
Hartnett, Thomas ....Canton, MI
Hartnett, Thomas E. ....**Canton, OH**
Hartnett, Thomas F. ....Albany, NY
Hartnett, Thomas P. ....Washington, DC
Great Falls, VA
Hartnett, Thomas P. ....Chicago, IL
Hartnett, Thomas R. ....**Dallas, TX**
Hartnett, Will Ford ....**Dallas, TX**
Hartnett, William E. ....Waukegan, IL
Hartnett, William M. ....**New York, NY**
Hartney, Kevin P. ....Boca Raton, FL
Hartney, Mark R. ....**Los Angeles, CA**
Hartney, Meghan M. ....**Los Angeles, CA**
Hartney, Michael T. ....**San Diego, CA**
Hart-Nibbrig, Harold C. ....Los Angeles, CA
Hart-Nibbrig, Leonard C. ....Fair Oaks, CA
Hartnick, Allan J. ....**New York, NY**
Hartnig, Richard A. ....**Atlanta, GA**
Hart-Nova, Tara J. ....**Hartford, CT**
Hartofilis, Michael John ....New York, NY
Hartog, Jack P. ....Miami, FL
Hartog, John A. ....**Orinda, CA**
Hartog, John A., Inc. ....**Orinda, CA**
Hartog, Kathleen Irish ....Orinda, CA
Hartog, Ross R. ....**Tucson, AZ**
Harton & Henry ....Atlanta, GA
Harton, Lee M. ....**Hopkinsville, KY**
Harton, Ollie M. ....**Atlanta, GA**
Harton, Patrick A. ....Atlanta, GA
Harton, Steve ....**Rock Springs, WY**
Hartounian, Michael ....**Santa Monica, CA**
Hartquist, David A. ....**Washington, DC**
Hartrampf, Carl R., III ....Atlanta, GA
Hartranft, Dennis M., Jr. ....Lancaster, PA
Hartranft, John C. ....**Columbus, OH**
Hartranft, Melissa Davis ....**Detroit, MI**
Hartrich, Phyllis A. ....St. Louis, MO
Hartrick, Bruce G. ....Troy, MI
Hartrick and Hartrick, P.C. ....Troy, MI
Hartrick, James G. ....Troy, MI
Hartrick, Janice K. ....Houston, TX
Hartrick, Kathryn M. ....**Chicago, IL**
Hartridge, Julian, Jr. ....Savannah, GA
Hartridge, Walter C. ....**Savannah, GA**
Hartrum, J. Elin ....**Portola Valley, CA**
Hartse, Russell L. ....Missoula, MT
Hartsell, Craig W. ....San Diego, CA
Hartsell, David L. ....**Atlanta, GA**
Hartsell, Fletcher L., Jr. ....**Concord, NC**
Hartsell, Hartsell & White, PA
Albemarle, NC
Concord, NC
Davidson, NC
Kannapolis, NC
Salisbury, NC
Hartsell, John Sharpe ....**Concord, NC**
Hartsell, Marsha L. ....Efland, NC
Hartsell, Stephen L. ....Bakersfield, CA
Hartsell, Steven C. ....**Fort Myers, FL**
Hartsell, Tiffany L. ....**Los Angeles, CA**
Hartsfield, Almand & Grisham
Little Rock, AR
Hartsfield, Arnett L., Jr. ....Los Angeles, CA
Hartsfield, Cynthia Ann ....Kerrville, TX
Hartsfield, Dan ....**Dallas, TX**
Hartsfield, Denise S. ....Winston-Salem, NC
Hartsfield & Gaering ....Memphis, TN
Hartsfield, J. Andrew, IV
United States Senate, Committee Legal Personnel, GV
Hartsfield, Judy A. ....Highland Park, MI
Hartsfield, Larry J. ....Little Rock, AR
Hartsfield, Marshall B. ....**Raleigh, NC**
Hartsfield, Mel Charles ....Tallahassee, FL
Hartsfield, Michael T. ....Memphis, TN
Hartsfield, Paul B. ....Albuquerque, NM
Hartsfield, Paul F., Jr. ....Tallahassee, FL
Hartsfield, Paul F., P.A. ....Tallahassee, FL
Hartsfield, Shannon B. ....**Tallahassee, FL**
Hartsfield, William E. ....Dallas, TX
Hartshorn, David B. ....New Britain, CT
Hartshorn, Donald M. ....**Peoria, IL**
Hartshorn, Edwin S., III ....Fairplay, CO
Hartshorn, L. Scott ....**Houston, TX**
Hartshorn, Laurel B. ....Saxonburg, PA
Hartshorn, Michael W. ....**Columbus, OH**
Hartshorn, Scott R. ....Oklahoma City, OK
Hartshorne, Marcia S. ....Tucson, AZ
Hartsig-Breuch, Anne T. ....Detroit, MI
Hartsock, Dick H. ....Lincoln, NE
Hartsock, John Allan ....**Rock Island, IL**
Hartsock, Phyllis E. ....Arlington, VA
Hartsock, Robert W. ....Bakersfield, CA

Hartsock, Walter D. ....Canton, OH
Hartsock, William D. ....**Laguna Niguel, CA**
Hartsoe, Brown & Mansfield, P.L.L.C.
Alexandria, VA
Fairfax, VA
Leesburg, VA
Hartsoe, Joseph R. ....Washington, DC
Hartsoe, R. Anthony ....**Winston-Salem, NC**
Hartsoe, Robert J. ....**Fairfax, VA**
Hartson, Robert W. ....Dallas, TX
Hartsook, David M. ....Brighton, MI
Hartsook, Scott ....Des Moines, IA
Hartsough, Douglas J. ....Livermore, CA
Hartsough & Kenny ....Hamilton, NJ
Hartsough, Michael T. ....Hamilton, NJ
Hartsough, Ronald H. ....San Francisco, CA
Hartsough, Tisha M. ....Columbus, OH
Hartstein, Barry A. ....**Chicago, IL**
Hartstein, Daniel P. ....Stratford, NJ
Philadelphia, PA
Hartstein, David S. ....Englewood, NJ
Hartstein, Diana R. ....**Washington, DC**
Hartstein, Elliott D. ....**Long Grove, IL**
Hartstein & Hartstein ....Englewood, NJ
Hartstein, Lawrence F. ....St. Louis, MO
Hartstein, Maria H. Mendes
Philadelphia, PA
Hartstein Poger & Sherman ....St. Louis, MO
Hartstein, Ronald D. ....New York, NY
Hartstein, Samuel ....Englewood, NJ
Hartstein, Yael ....**Los Angeles, CA**
Hartstern, Patricia C. ....**Dallas, TX**
Hartston, Amos E. ....**Los Angeles, CA**
Hartstone, Joel Martin ....Farmington, CT
Hartsuff, Todd C. ....Burlington, VT
Hartsuyker, Craig L. ....Ventura, CA
Hartt, Dudley N. ....Cazenovia, NY
Hartt, Edgar R. ....Duncansville, PA
Hartt, Grover, III ....Dallas, TX
Hartt, Grover, Jr., (P.C.) ....Dallas, TX
Hartt, Susan K. ....Santa Clara, CA
Hartt, Toby G. ....Springfield, MA
Hartung, Barbara J. ....**St. Louis, MO**
Hartung, Barbara L. ....Richmond, VA
Hartung, Barbara Reid ....**Louisville, KY**
Hartung, Dale E. ....San Antonio, TX
Hartung, David D. ....New York, NY
Hartung, Edwin A. ....**Jersey City, NJ**
Hartung, John D. ....Des Moines, IA
Hartung, John H. ....Manhattan Beach, MN
Hartung, John J. ....St. Louis, MO
Hartung, Jon F. ....**San Francisco, CA**
Hartung, Karen D. ....Louisville, KY
Hartung, Kirk M. ....**Des Moines, IA**
Omaha, NE
Hartung, Michael ....**Jackson, MS**
Hartung, Steven J. ....**Milwaukee, WI**
Hartung, Timothy Ryan ....Orlando, FL
Hartung, Timothy Ryan, P.A. ....Orlando, FL
Hartunian, Aram A. ....Chicago, IL
Hartunian, Aram A., A Professional Corporation
Chicago, IL
Hartvigsen, David B. ....**Salt Lake City, UT**
Hartweg, Darrell L. ....**Bloomington, IL**
Hartweg, Elizabeth Fegan ....**Chicago, IL**
Hartweg, Mueller, Turner & Wood, P.C.
Bloomington, IL
Hartweger, Gordon G. ....St. Louis, MO
Hartweger, Peter K. ....**Kansas City, MO**
Hartwell, Davis ....Portland, ME
Hartwell, Deborah L. ....**Philadelphia, PA**
Hartwell, Donald O. ....Tallahassee, FL
Hartwell, Jane Barry ....Portland, ME
Hartwell, Janice K. ....Palatine, IL
Hartwell, John Steven ....San Diego, CA
Hartwell, Judith Bacon ....Foxboro, MA
Hartwell, Kimberly K. ....**Washington, DC**
Hartwell, Leslie L. ....Sherman Oaks, CA
Hartwell, Mortimer H.
San Francisco, CA
Hartwell, Mortimer H., Jr. ....**Portland, OR**
Hartwell, Ray V., III ....**Washington, DC**
Richmond, VA
Hartwell, Robert M.
Manchester Center, VT
Hartwell, Roy A. ....Dallas, TX
Hartwell, Sharon M. Shiller
Sacramento, CA
Hartwell, Stephen E. ....San Diego, CA
Hartwell, Thomas M. ....South Elgin, IL
Hartwell, Wayne E. ....**Boston, MA**
Hart-White, Susan M. ....**Kenilworth, NJ**
Hartwich, Douglas R. ....**Seattle, WA**
Hartwick, Dwain D. ....**Enterprise, AL**
Hartwick, Fred M., III ....Palo Alto, CA
Hartwick, Jeffrey A. ....**Torrance, CA**
Hartwick, Jo Esta ....**Dallas, TX**
Hartwick, R. Dean ....Palos Verdes Estates, CA
Hartwick, Ronald S. ....Los Angeles, CA
Hartwig, Asa C. ....**Cullman, AL**
Hartwig, David R. ....**Salt Lake City, UT**
Hartwig, Edward Joseph
Youngstown, OH
Hartwig, Elizabeth A. ....San Diego, CA
Hartwig, Eugene L. ....**Detroit, MI**
Hartwig, George H., III ....**Macon, GA**
Hartwig, Gordon E. ....Wichita, KS
Hartwig, Gregory J. ....**Milwaukee, WI**
Hartwig, James C. ....Milwaukee, WI
Hartwig, James E. ....**Janesville, WI**
Hartwig, J. D. ....St. Joseph, MI
Hartwig, John P. ....**Bloomfield Hills, MI**
Hartwig, Judith ....**Escondido, CA**
Hartwig, Lawrence E. ....Washington, DC
Hartwig, Robert ....Des Moines, IA
Hartwig, Thomas G. ....St. Johns, MI
Hartwig, Thomas M. ....**Hollywood, FL**
Hartwyk, Christopher M. ....South Orange, NJ

Harty, Frank B. ....**Des Moines, IA**
Harty, J. Michael ....New York, NY
Harty, James Q. ....**Pittsburgh, PA**
Harty, Jeffrey D. ....**Des Moines, IA**
Omaha, NE
Harty, Kevin S. ....**Lansing, MI**
Harty and Kimble ....Greenville, MS
Harty, Mark P. ....**Boston, MA**
Harty, Martin J. ....Department of Defense, Armed Services Board of Contract Appeals, GV
Harty, Mary K. ....Rosenberg, TX
Harty, Paul W. ....Birmingham, MI
Harty, Richard B. ....Orland Park, IL
Harty, Ronan P. ....**New York, NY**
Harty, Thomas S. ....**Cherry Hill, NJ**
Philadelphia, PA
Harty, William T. ....West Medway, MA
Hartye, Frank J. ....Hollidaysburg, PA
Harty-Golder, Barbara J. ....Sarasota, FL
Hartz, Charles A., Jr. ....**Richmond, VA**
Hartz, Charles Michael ....**Miami, FL**
Hartz, Christy Garesche ....St. Louis, MO
Hartz, Douglas A. ....Wheat Ridge, CO
Hartz, Frederick J. ....LaGrange, IN
Hartz, Gayle E. ....**Albany, NY**
Hartz, Harris L ....**Washington, DC**
Skillman, NJ
Hartz, J. Ernest, Jr. ....**San Francisco, CA**
Hartz, James A. ....Abington, PA
Hartz, James P. ....Utica, NY
Hartz, Jay N. ....**Los Angeles, CA**
Hartz, Judith A. ....**Roseland, NJ**
Hartz, Max S. ....**Owensboro, KY**
Hartz, Michael O. ....**Chicago, IL**
Hartz, Morton M. ....St. Louis, MO
Hartz, Raymond A ....Miami, FL
Hartz, Richard L. ....**Morristown, NJ**
New York, NY
Hartz, Steven E. M. ....**Miami, FL**
Hartz, Steven J. ....Palmerton, PA
Hartz, Susan L. ....New York, NY
Hartz, Sylvester H. ....Teterboro, NJ
Hartz, Tracey W. ....Bolingbrook, IL
Hart-Zafra, Christopher ....**New York, NY**
Hartzel & Bush ....Doylestown, PA
Hartzel, J. Franklin ....Doylestown, PA
Hartzel, John F. ....Doylestown, PA
Hartzel, Paul W. ....**Palo Alto, CA**
Hartzel, Terry J. ....Newark, NJ
Hartzell, Anderson ....Conshohocken, PA
Hartzell, Andrew C., Jr. ....**New York, NY**
Hartzell, Andrew K. ....**Irvine, CA**
Hartzell, Clyde ....**Frankfort, IN**
Hartzell, Douglas R. ....Longmont, CO
Hartzell, Franklin M. ....**Carthage, IL**
Macomb, IL
Hartzell, George W. ....Cheraw, SC
Hartzell, Glidden, Tucker and Hartzell
Carthage, IL
Macomb, IL
Hartzell, J. Jerome ....**Raleigh, NC**
Hartzell, John M. ....**Harrisburg, PA**
Hartzell, John M., Jr. ....**Pittsburgh, PA**
Hartzell, John V. ....**Watertown, NY**
Hartzell, Keith P. ....**Columbus, OH**
Hartzell, Kevin D. ....**Omaha, NE**
Hartzell, Lynda J. ....**Portland, OR**
Hartzell, Matthew H. ....Houston, TX
Hartzell, Page Elizabeth ....**Chicago, IL**
Hartzell, Patsy Jane ....St. Joseph, MI
Hartzell, Roland M. ....Rochester, NY
Hartzell, Thomas C., Jr. ....Pittsford, NY
Hartzell, Thomas C., Sr. ....Pittsford, NY
Hartzell, Thomas F. ....**Carthage, IL**
Macomb, IL
Hartzell & Whiteman, L.L.P. ......**Raleigh, NC**
Hartzenbusch, Catharine A.
Washington, DC
Hartzer, Mark J. ....San Antonio, TX
Hartzer, Timothy James ....Albuquerque, NM
Hartzfeld, Howard A., Jr. ....Phoenix, AZ
Hartzheim, Charles J. ....**Appleton, WI**
Hartzler, Gregory A. ....**Goshen, IN**
Hartzler, J. Alex ....**Harrisburg, PA**
Hartzler, Lynda Jo ....Phoenix, AZ
Hartzler, Mark B. ....**Los Angeles, CA**
Hartzler, Nancy D. ....El Monte, CA
Hartzman, Richard M. ....Bronx, NY
Hartzog Conger & Cason, A Professional Corporation ....**Oklahoma City, OK**
Hartzog, Dan M. ....**Raleigh, NC**
Hartzog, Dee ....**Sacramento, CA**
Hartzog, H. Mark ....**Franklin, TN**
Hartzog, James R. ....Clinton, MS
Hartzog, Larry D. ....**Oklahoma City, OK**
Hartzog, Robert L., Jr. ....**Clayton, MO**
Hartzog, Silva & Davies ....**Franklin, TN**
Hartzog, Steven L. ....Denver, CO
Harum, Albert E., Jr. ....Miami, FL
Harum & Harum ....Miami, FL
Harunaga, Toshio ....San Jose, CA
Harutunian, Peter H. ....**Tampa, FL**
Harvalis, Constantine C., (Mr.) ....Chicago, IL
Harvard, Andrew C. ....**Fort Wayne, IN**
Harvard, Timothy J. ....**Fort Worth, TX**
Harvard, William D. ....**Athens, GA**
Harvat, Keith A. ....**North Platte, NE**
Harvath, Gerald J. ....Pacific, MO
Harvath, Lee W., Jr. ....**Boca Raton, FL**
Fort Lauderdale, FL
Harvatin, Theodore J. ....**Springfield, IL**
Harvel, Thomas G. ....**Peoria, IL**
Harvell, Brian Lee ....**St. Louis, MO**
Harvell, Cecil S. ....**Morehead City, NC**
Harvell, Cecil S., P.A. ....**Morehead City, NC**
Harvell, James H., III ....Newport News, VA
Harvell, John E. ....Kansas City, MO

Harwood, Charles A. ....Silver City, NM
Harwood, Charles A. ....Seattle, WA
Harwood, Craig S. ....Framingham, MA
Harwood, David B. ....Norwalk, OH
Willard, OH
Harwood, David J. ....Cincinnati, OH
Harwood, Deanna R. ....Long Beach, CA
Harwood, Dennis W. ....Newport Beach, CA
Harwood, Donald A. ....New York, NY
Harwood, Dorothy G. ....Fort Worth, TX
Harwood, Frank E., Jr. ....Glen Cove, NY
Harwood, George D. ....St. Albans, VT
Harwood, Gregory B. ....Boise, ID
Harwood, Jeremy J. ....New York, NY
Harwood, John A. ....Atlanta, GA
Harwood, John H., II ....Washington, DC
Harwood, John P. ....Kenosha, WI
Harwood, Jonathan R. ....Hawthorne, NY
Harwood, Joseph D. ....Houston, TX
Harwood, Karen E. ....Spokane, WA
Harwood, Karen J. ....Fairfax, VA
Harwood, Kathryn McC.
Birmingham, AL
Harwood, Kathryn McC. ....Tuscaloosa, AL
Harwood, Lee C. ....Houston, TX
Harwood Lloyd, LLC ....Hackensack, NJ
Jersey City, NJ
Morristown, NJ
Newark, NJ
Paterson, NJ
Ridgewood, NJ
New York, NY
Harwood, Michael C. ....New York, NY
Harwood, Mila Allen ....Silver City, NM
Harwood, Nevin R. ....Minneapolis, MN
Harwood, Pamela R. ....Detroit, MI
Harwood, Paul L. ....West Palm Beach, FL
Harwood, Peter R. ....Cleveland, OH
Harwood, R. Michael ....San Francisco, CA
Harwood, Richard S. ....Colorado Springs, CO
Harwood, Ripley B. ....Albuquerque, NM
Harwood, Robert B., Jr. ....Tuscaloosa, AL
Harwood, Robert I. ....New York, NY
Harwood, Robert M. ....Ketchum, ID
Harwood, Sally S. ....East Lansing, MI
Harwood, Stanley ....Garden City, NY
Harwood, Stephen L.
Department of Justice,
Criminal Division, GV
Harwood, Steven J. ....Norfolk, VA
Harwood, Susan B. ....Orlando, FL
Harwood, Thomas A. ....Uvalde, TX
Harwood, Thomas E. ....Trenton, TN
Harwood, Thomas M. ....Glendale, CA
Harwood, Thos. P., Jr. ....Richmond, VA
Harwood, Walter F. ....Houston, TX
Harwood, William S. ....Portland, ME
Harz, G. Michael ....Evergreen, CO
Harz, Rachelle L. ....Englewood Cliffs, NJ
Harz, Steven B. ....Secaucus, NJ
Harzem, Emma E. ....New York, NY
Harzenski, Sharon S. ....Philadelphia, PA
Harzman, Brent A. ....Chicago, IL
Hasak, Janet E. ....South San Francisco, CA
Hasak-Lowy, Taal ....San Francisco, CA
Hasan, Jannette E. ....Washington, DC
Hasan, Rashidah N. ....East Orange, NJ
Hasan, Salim A. ....Chicago, IL
Hasan, Syed A. ....Pasadena, CA
Hasani, Fred ....Menlo Park, CA
Hasani, Nancy H. ....Newport Beach, CA
Hasapidis, Annette ....New York, NY
Hasbargen, Amy J. ....Minneapolis, MN
Hasbrook, Daniel T. ....Indianapolis, IN
Hasbrook, David T. ....Bellevue, WA
Hasbrook, Denise M. ....Toledo, OH
Hasbrook, Edward D. ....Oklahoma City, OK
Hasbrook, John E. ....Portland, OR
Hasbrook, Richard C. ....Toledo, OH
Hasbrook, T. David ....Oklahoma City, OK
Hasbrook, William A. ....Indianapolis, IN
Hasbrouck, Bruce C. ....Woodbury, NJ
Hasbrouck, Catherine O'Malley
Norcross, GA
Chicago, IL
Hasbrouck, David C. ....Linwood, NJ
Hasbrouck, Gail Durham ....Oak Brook, IL
Hasbrouck, Jennifer R. ....Los Angeles, CA
Hasbrouck, Peter V. ....Atlanta, GA
Hasbrouck, Richard L. ....Guthrie Center, IA
Hasbrouck, Scott R. ....East Grand Forks, MN
Hasbrouck & Uliase ....Woodbury, NJ
Hasbun, Marcos E. ....Washington, DC
Hasbun, Michelle G. ....Miami, FL
Hascall, E. Dean ....Bellevue, NE
Hascall, Jungers, Garvey & Delaney
Bellevue, NE
Hascall, Karl B. ....Grand Rapids, MI
Hasche, Tilman ....Portland, OR
Hascheff, Pierre A. ....Reno, NV
Haschemeyer, Delbert D. ....Springfield, IL
Haschke, Lara Anne ....Houston, TX
Hasco, Thomas E. ....San Jose, CA
Hasday, Cynthia E. ....Los Angeles, CA
Hasday, Robert J. ....New York, NY
Hasdorff, Julie K. ....San Antonio, TX
Hase, David J. ....Milwaukee, WI
Hase, Don ....Arlington, TX
Hasegawa, Nancy L. ....Lincolnshire, IL
Hasegawa, Raymond K. ....Hilo, HI
Hasegawa, Raymond K., Attorney At Law, A Law Corporation ....Hilo, HI
Haselden, Alford ....Lake Wylie, SC
Haselden, Andrew E. ....Columbia, SC
Haselden, Frances L. ....Louisville, KY
Haselden, M. Terry ....Spartanburg, SC
Haselden, Owen & Boloyan ....Lake Wylie, SC
Haselden, William Murdock
Tallahassee, FL
Haseley, John ....Portsmouth, OH
Haselhoff, Annette ....New York, NY
Haselhoff, Otto, & Associates
Santa Monica, CA
Haselhoff, Otto L. ....Santa Monica, CA
Haselkamp, H. James, Jr. ....Milford, CT
Haselkorn, David L. ....Washington, DC
Haselkorn, Jason S.
West Palm Beach, FL
Haselkorn, Zev ....Charlotte, NC
Has-Ellison, M.D. ....La Mesa, CA
Ramona, CA
Haselman, Alexandria L ....Richmond, VA
Haselman, Scott A. ....Toledo, OH
Haseltine, Arthur S. ....Springfield, MO
Haseltine, Benjamin W. ....Pittsburgh, PA
Haseltine, Edwin C. ....Springfield, MO
Haseltine, John Mark ....Springfield, MO
Haselton, Britt D.L. ....Soquel, CA
Haselton & Haselton ....Soquel, CA
Haselton, Joseph G. ....Soquel, CA
Haselton, Rick T. ....Salem, OR
Haselwood, Hilda P. ....Cotati, CA
Haseman, Christine Tally ....Bloomington, IN
Haseman, Julie A. ....Alexandria, MN
Haseman, Paul B. ....Fullerton, CA
Haseman, Roger A. ....Houston, TX
Hasen, David M. ....San Francisco, CA
Hasen, Joel ....New York, NY
Hasen, Richard L. ....Los Angeles, CA
Hasenauer, Judith A. ....Westport, CT
Lauderdale-By-The-Sea, FL
Hasenauer, Mark David ....Westmont, NJ
Philadelphia, PA
Hasenauer, William E. ....Westport, CT
Hasenbalg, Craig D. ....Aurora, IL
Hasenbalg, Stacee A. ....Chicago, IL
Hasenbalg, Wayne W. ....Teaneck, NJ
Hasenbank, Russell W. ....Liberal, KS
Hasenburg, Laurie Jeannene ....Freeland, MI
Hasenflue, Oliver W. ....Cleveland, OH
Hasenfratz, Sally A. ....Oklahoma City, OK
Hasenfus, James C. ....North Dartmouth, MA
Hasenfus, Jim ....North Hollywood, CA
Hasenmiller, John D. ....Chicago, IL
Hasenstab, Neal E. ....Woburn, MA
Hasenyager, James R. ....Ogden, UT
Hasfurther, William D.
General Accounting Office,
Office of the General Counsel, GV
Hash, C. Mark ....Kalispell, MT
Hash, Charles L. ....Kalispell, MT
Hash, Edgar ....Phoenix, AZ
Hash, Joanne V. ....Lebanon, OH
Hash, Joseph C., Jr. ....Ravenswood, WV
Hash & O'Brien, PLLP ....Kalispell, MT
Hash, Paul E. ....Dallas, TX
Hash, R. D. ....Maryville, TN
Hash, Robert W. ....Indianapolis, IN
Hash, Stephen M. ....Austin, TX
Hashem, Hani W. ....Monticello, AR
Hashim, John S., Jr. ....Baltimore, MD
Hashim, Michael D., Jr. ....Pittsfield, MA
Hashim, Paul C. ....Richardson, TX
Hashim & Spinola ....Pittsfield, MA
Hashimoto, Dean M. ....Newton, MA
Hashimoto, Gail M. ....San Jose, CA
Hashimoto, Go ....New York, NY
Hashimoto, Lynn Y. ....New York, NY
Hashimoto, Roy ....Hayward, CA
Hashimoto, Steven W. ....South Pasadena, CA
Hashish, Fahnda W. ....Santa Ana, CA
Hashmall, David L. ....Minneapolis, MN
Hashmall, David M. ....New York, NY
Hashmall, Jay B. ....White Plains, NY
Hashmall, Sheer, Bank & Geist
White Plains, NY
Hasiak, Raymond J. ....Omaha, NE
Hasin, David V. ....Poughkeepsie, NY
Hasiotis, Christine ....Boston, MA
Hasiotis, Georgette Morphis ....Amherst, NY
Hasis, Thomas A., (P.A.)
Lighthouse Point, FL
Haskel, Brian A. ....New York, NY
Haskel, Jules J. ....Garden City, NY
Haskel, Michael A. ....New York, NY
Haskel, Paul B. ....New York, NY
Haskel, Peter B. ....Austin, TX
Haskel, William M. ....Madison, NJ
Haskell, Alene V. ....St. Louis, MO
Haskell, Andrew R. ....New York, NY
Haskell, Ann K. ....Toms River, NJ
Haskell, Anne S. ....New York, NY
Haskell, April ....Glastonbury, CT
Haskell, B. Kemp ....Jacksonville, FL
Haskell, Boris ....Washington, DC
Haskell, Brian R. ....Hartford, CT
Haskell, Christopher E.
Santa Barbara, CA
Haskell, Craig S. ....Raleigh, NC
Haskell, Dan L. ....Nashville, TN
Haskell, Daniel M. ....Denver, CO
Haskell, David F. ....Worcester, MA
Haskell, Dean S. ....Hilton Head Island, SC
Haskell, Donald M. ....Chicago, IL
Haskell, Edwin C., III ....Spartanburg, SC
Haskell, Floyd K. ....Washington, DC
Haskell, Frank B., III ....Upper Marlboro, MD
Haskell, George B. P. ....Painesville, OH
Haskell, George O., III ....Macon, GA
Haskell & Goodman, LLP ....Hayward, CA
Haskell, Grant P. ....Westport, CT
Haskell, H. Scott ....Amesbury, MA
Haskell, Jack R. ....Huntington, NY
Haskell, James W. ....Bemidji, MN
Haskell, Jeffrey D. ....New York, NY
Haskell, Laurel A. ....Chicago, IL
Haskell, Lawrence H. ....Spokane, WA
Haskell, Lee F. ....San Diego, CA
Haskell, Lori S. ....Seattle, WA
Haskell, Mark R. ....Washington, DC
Haskell, Mary ....Lexington, MA
Haskell, Paul G. ....Chapel Hill, NC
Haskell, Paul Timmons ....Ocean City, MD
Haskell & Perrin ....Chicago, IL
Haskell and Rice ....Upper Marlboro, MD
Haskell, Richard N. ....Fort Worth, TX
Haskell, Roger L., Law Offices of
San Diego, CA
Haskell, Russell K. ....Denver, CO
Haskell Slaughter Young & Gallion, L.L.C.
Montgomery, AL
Haskell Slaughter & Young, L.L.C.
Birmingham, AL
Haskell, Steven P. ....Santa Ana, CA
Haskell, Sue Ann ....Denver, CO
Haskell, William W. ....Hayward, CA
Haskell, William Z. ....Upper Marlboro, MD
Haskell, Wyatt Rushton ....Birmingham, AL
Haskell & Zimmerman
Upper Marlboro, MD
Haskett, Amber C. ....San Francisco, CA
Haskett, David M. ....Indianapolis, IN
Haskett, Deborah J. ....Jackson, MI
Haskett, Lida Stout ....Barstow, CA
Haskett, Martin C. ....Aransas Pass, TX
Haskett, Steven P. ....San Diego, CA
Haskew, Derek C. ....Mexican Hat, UT
Haskin, Benjamin J. ....Washington, DC
Haskin, Harley V. ....Lenexa, KS
Haskin, J. Michael ....Olathe, KS
Haskin, J. Michael, P.A. ....Olathe, KS
Haskin, Jeffrey M. ....Atlanta, GA
Haskin, John H. ....Indianapolis, IN
Haskin Lauter Cohen & LaRue
Indianapolis, IN
Haskin, Lawrence J. ....Oak Creek, WI
Haskin, Lyle B. ....Wheaton, IL
Haskin, Michelle L. ....Albany, NY
Haskin, Warren C. ....Chicago, IL
Haskin, William G., Jr. ....Baton Rouge, LA
Haskins, Angela S. ....Los Angeles, CA
Haskins, Ann ....Los Angeles, CA
Haskins & Blunt, P.A. ....Fairview, NJ
Haskins, Brenda R. ....Madison, WI
Haskins, Brodnax ....Richmond, VA
Haskins, Daniel R. ....Redding, CA
Haskins, Deane, Law Offices of
San Diego, CA
Haskins, Deborah Farrall ....Denver, CO
Haskins, Donald B. ....Greensboro, NC
Haskins, Elena L. ....San Rafael, CA
Haskins, Frederick M. ....Des Moines, IA
Haskins, Gail Ferbend ....Chicago, IL
Haskins, Gerald M. ....La Crosse, FL
Haskins, Harry W. ....Sarasota, FL
Haskins, Helen D. ....St. Louis, MO
Haskins, Howard E., Jr. ....Sacramento, CA
Haskins, James C. ....Salt Lake City, UT
Haskins, James W. ....Martinsville, VA
Stuart, VA
Haskins, Jennifer Wheeler
Fayetteville, AR
Haskins, John F., Jr. ....Norristown, PA
Haskins, Joseph J., Jr. ....Fairview, NJ
Haskins, Keith A. ....Santa Ana, CA
Haskins, Kevin ....Santa Ana, CA
Haskins, Linda E. ....Beverly Hills, CA
Haskins, Mark A. ....Sarasota, FL
Haskins, Mary E. ....Tallahassee, FL
Haskins, Mary S. ....Houston, TX
Haskins, Matthew P. ....Washington, DC
Haskins, Michelle Daum ....Independence, MO
Haskins, Nena Jo ....Rancho Santa Fe, CA
Haskins, P. Hayden, Jr. ....Orlando, FL
Haskins, Patrick D. ....Bel Air, MD
Haskins, Paul A. ....Chicago, IL
Haskins, Richard D. ....Mount Clemens, MI
Haskins, Richard E. ....Des Moines, IA
Haskins, Richard J. ....North Kansas City, MO
Haskins, Robert L. ....Portland, OR
Haskins, Robert R. ....Poughkeepsie, NY
Haskins, Robert W. ....Rocky River, OH
Haskins, S. Stewart, II ....Atlanta, GA
Haskins, Sidney ....Atlanta, GA
Haskins, Steven W. ....Bonita, CA
Haskins, Terry E. ....Greenville, SC
Haskins, Thomas F., Jr. ....Akron, OH
Haskins, Thomas G. ....Midlothian, VA
Haskins, Thomas M., III
Colorado Springs, CO
Haskins, Walter D., P.C. ....Tulsa, OK
Haskins, Yvonne B. ....Philadelphia, PA
Haskin Will, Jennifer L.
Minneapolis, MN
Hasko, John J. ....Ithaca, NY
Hasko, Judith A. ....Palo Alto, CA
Haskovec, Joseph M. ....Cresco, IA
Haskvitz, Ronald L. ....Minneapolis, MN
Hasl, Rudolph C. ....St. Louis, MO
Haslach, Timothy F. ....Portland, OR
Haslag, Ralph J. ....Rolla, MO
Haslam, Barbara C. ....Fremont, NE
Haslam, Daniel B., III ....Tucson, AZ
Haslam, Dennis V. ....Salt Lake City, UT
Haslam, Donald G. ....Ontario, CA
Haslam, Elizabeth M. ....Salt Lake City, UT
Haslam Firm, The ....Fort Worth, TX
Haslam, Geoffrey C. ....Salt Lake City, UT
Haslam, George D., Jr. ....Hugo, OK
Haslam, John L. ....Racine, WI
Haslam, Robert E. ....Fort Worth, TX
Haslam, Robert T. ....Palo Alto, CA
Haslam, Roy G. ....Salt Lake City, UT
Haslam, William D. ....Ghent, WV
Haslanger, Kathryn D. ....New York, NY
Haslebacher, Henry, II ....Charleston, WV
Haslem, James R. ....Los Angeles, CA
Santa Barbara, CA
Hasler, B. Lane ....Chicago, IL
Hasler, Fonfara and Maxwell, LLP
Fort Collins, CO
Hasler, Joseph J. ....Reedsburg, WI
Hasler, Samuel C. ....Anderson, IN
Hasler, Timothy W. ....Fort Collins, CO
Haslerud, Gary E. ....Redding, CA
Haslett, David W. ....Newark, DE
Haslett, Donald B. ....Portland, OR
Haslett, George A., Jr. ....Lake Oswego, OR
Haslett, Jon A. ....Houston, TX
Haslett, Stephen L. ....Plainwell, MI
Haslett, Stephen L., P.C. ....Plainwell, MI
Hasley, Gregory M. ....Houston, TX
Hasley, Raymond G. ....Pittsburgh, PA
Haslinger, Barbara ....Bend, OR
Haslinger, Connie J. ....Akron, OH
Haslinger, Donna L. ....Buffalo, NY
Haslinger, John E. ....Buffalo, NY
Haslinger, Nancy L. ....Ellicott City, MD
Haslinger, Robert H. ....Gaithersburg, MD
Hasluck, John J. ....New York, NY
Haslun, William I., II ....Greenwich, CT
Haslup, Charles L., III
Federal Maritime Commission,
Bureau of Enforcement, GV
Hasman, Joseph J. ....Chicago, IL
Hasnas, John ....Arlington, VA
Hasner, Louis G. ....Cherry Hill, NJ
Hasner, Mark M. ....Miami, FL
Hasner, Stephen R. ....Atlanta, GA
Hason, Michael J. ....Beverly Hills, CA
Haspel, Joseph J. ....New York, NY
Haspel, Linda ....Rockville, MD
Haspel & Meiselman, Chartered
Rockville, MD
Hasper, David J. ....Grand Rapids, MI
Haspil, Marie A. ....San Antonio, TX
Hass, Burton J. ....Malden, MA
Hass, D. Winthrop ....Milwaukee, WI
Hass, D. Winthrop, S.C. ....Milwaukee, WI
Hass, Erwin ....New York, NY
Hass, Frederick M., Jr. ....Pine City, MN
Hass, Fredrick R. ....Portland, OR
Hass, George H. ....Fort Collins, CO
Hass, James W. ....Rock Island, IL
Hass, James W., Jr. ....Atlanta, GA
Hass, Jeffrey J. ....New York, NY
Hass, Jeffrey K. ....Scarsdale, NY
Hass, Jeremy Dennis ....Santa Barbara, CA
Hass, Joan Barkhorn ....Boston, MA
Hass, Lawrence J. ....New York, NY
Hass, Merle Ruth ....Boston, MA
Hass, Michael A. ....New York, NY
Hass, Michael J. ....Santa Barbara, CA
Hass, Morris ....Bayside, NY
Hass, Paul A. ....Franklin, IN
Hass, Peter A. ....Richmond, CA
Hass, Robt. S. ....Philadelphia, PA
Hass, Russell Perry ....Tulsa, OK
Hass, William R. ....Alton, MO
Hass, William Thomas ....Thayer, MO
Hassakis, Demetri ....Mount Vernon, IL
Hassakis & Hassakis, P.C.
Mount Vernon, IL
Hassakis, Mark D. ....Mount Vernon, IL
Hassan, Allen C. ....Sacramento, CA
Hassan, Beedeah ....Charleston, WV
Hassan, Blake W. ....Gastonia, NC
Hassan, Christina E. ....Cincinnati, OH
Hassan, Farhan ....Duluth, MN
Hassan, Gwendolyn L. ....Chicago, IL
Hassan, J. Marvin ....Diamond Bar, CA
Hassan, James F. ....Brockton, MA
Hassan, James M. ....Los Angeles, CA
Hassan, James S. ....Charlotte, NC
Hassan, Jeanne M. ....Tustin, CA
Hassan, Kenneth O. ....Baltimore, MD
Hassan, Laura Gerard ....Chicago, IL
Hassan Law Firm ....San Francisco, CA
Hassan Law Firm, Chartered
Kansas City, KS
Hassan Law Office ....Welch, WV
Hassan, Margaret Wood ....Boston, MA
Hassan, Margo Amy ....New York, NY
Hassan, Michael R. ....Chicago, IL
Hassan & Reardon, P.C. ....Boston, MA
Scituate, MA
Providence, RI
Hassan, Rey ....San Francisco, CA
Hassan, Ronald D. ....Welch, WV
Hassan, Shannon ....New York, NY
Hassan, Shannon E. ....New York, NY
Hassan, Sulaimon Adebayo ....Kansas City, KS
Hassan, Susan S. ....Chicago, IL
Hassan, Syed Jamshed Nasim ....Newark, DE
Hassan, Tareq A. ....New York, NY
Hassan, William E. ....Northampton, MA
Hassan, William E. ....Fairfax, VA
Hassan, William M. ....Pittsburgh, PA
Hassan, Yasmeen ....New York, NY
Hassan, Yasmin ....New York, NY
Hassan, Zaha S. ....Portland, OR
Hassani, Alexander A. ....Towson, MD
Hassan-Salami, Fatima ....Dallas, TX
Hassapis, George P. ....Long Beach, CA
Hassard Bonnington LLP
San Francisco, CA
Hassay, Wayne ....Columbus, OH
Hassberg, Linda R. ....Buffalo, NY
Hasse, Ann Fingarette ....Oakland, CA
Hasse, Donald E. ....Cincinnati, OH

Hasse, Lizbeth ... Berkeley, CA
San Francisco, CA
Hasse, Michael R. ... New London, CT
Hasse Molesky ... Berkeley, CA
San Francisco, CA
Hassebrock, Scott A. ... Chicago, IL
Hassel, Conrad V. ... Manassas, VA
Hassel, Daniel L. ... Omaha, NE
Hassel, Gary R. ... Des Moines, IA
Hassel, Jennifer E. ... Lancaster, PA
Hassel, Karin G. ... Brick, NJ
Hassel, Lonie ... Washington, DC
Hassel, Richard A. ... Minneapolis, MN
Hasselbach, Gerard ... Laguna Beach, CA
Hasselbach, Kurt S. ... Springfield, OH
Hasselbach, W. Andrew ... Lebanon, OH
Hasselbacher, Martha J. ... Louisville, KY
Hasselbalch, Hal B. ... Lincoln, NE
Hasselberg, Eric E. ... Peoria, IL
Hasselberg, Michael R. ... Peoria, IL
Hasselberg, Rock, Bell & Kuppler
Peoria, IL
Hasselberg, Williams, Grebe & Snodgrass
Peoria, IL
Hasseler, Lawrence D. ... Carthage, NY
Hassell, Andrew M. ... Dallas, TX
Hassell, Ayala T. ... Plano, TX
Hassell, Charles D. ... Cleveland, OH
Hassell, Charles R., Jr. ... Raleigh, NC
Hassell, Christopher E. ... Washington, DC
Baltimore, MD
Rockville, MD
Fairfax, VA
Hassell, Donald F.
Nuclear Regulatory Commission,
Office of the General Counsel, GV
Hassell, Douglas E. ... Vicksburg, MS
Hassell, F. Bradley ... Daytona Beach, FL
Hassell, Jeffrey Don ... Tulsa, OK
Hassell, Karen F. ... Sacramento, CA
Hassell, Leonard R. ... Dallas, TX
Hassell, Leroy R. ... Richmond, VA
Hassell, Mary E. ... Greensboro, NC
Hassell, Michael W. ... Harrisburg, PA
Hassell, Robert A. ... Hillsborough, NC
Hassell, Sidney J., Jr. ... Washington, NC
Hassell, Silvia T. ... Houston, TX
Hassell, Thomas T., Jr. ... Richmond, VA
Hasselman, Allen J. ... Washington, DC
Hasselman, Erik V. ... Eugene, OR
Hasselman, Raymond L. ... Claremore, OK
Hasselman, Scot T. ... Washington, DC
Hasselquist, Maynard B. ... Minneapolis, MN
Hassels-Weiler, Ekkehart ... Los Angeles, CA
Hasseltine, Roy ... Florence, AL
Hasseman, Dean M. ... Tulsa, OK
Hassen, Joel ... Pleasanton, CA
Hassen, John R. ... Medford, OR
Hassen, Megan Elizabeth ... Salem, OR
Hassen, Michael J. ... Walnut Creek, CA
Hassen, Richard J. ... Riverside, CA
Hassen, S. R. ... Chicago, IL
Hassenberg, Barry ... Los Angeles, CA
Hassenfeld, H. Daniel ... Newton, MA
Hassenfeld & Lederman ... Boston, MA
Hassenfeld, Merrill I., P.C. ... Boston, MA
Hassenfelt, Stephen C. ... Greensboro, NC
Hassenplug, Michael W. ... Coffeyville, KS
Hassenplug, Richard D. ... Torrance, CA
Hassenstab, Chris M. ... Seattle, WA
Hassenstab, Donald W. ... St. Paul, MN
Hasser, James E., Jr. ... Mobile, AL
Hassett, Annemarie ... New York, NY
Hassett, Arlyne F. ... Waltham, MA
Hassett, Arthur J., III ... Brockton, MA
Hassett, Brian R. ... Cleveland, OH
Hassett & Buendo ... Springfield, MA
Hassett, Charles M.
Environmental Protection Agency,
Office of Congressional and Legislative
Affairs, GV
Hassett, Cohen, Goldstein & Port, LLP
Atlanta, GA
Hassett, Daniel B. ... Washington, DC
Hassett, David F. ... Worcester, MA
Hassett & Donnelly ... Boston, MA
Springfield, MA
Worcester, MA
Hassett, Edward P. ... Springfield, MA
Hassett, George ... Boston, MA
Hassett, George & Siegel, P.C.
Hartford, CT
Simsbury, CT
Hassett, John F. X. ... New City, NY
Hassett, John Maurice ... Baltimore, MD
Hassett, Joseph L. ... Philadelphia, PA
Hassett, Joseph M. ... Washington, DC
Hassett, Kristie S. ... Washington, DC
Hassett, Lewis E. ... Atlanta, GA
Hassett, Lynn S. ... Atlanta, GA
Hassett, Mark J. ... Chardon, OH
Hassett, Mark J., Co., L.P.A.
Chardon, OH
Hassett, Michael J. ... Iselin, NJ
Hassett, Michael T. ... Springfield, MA
Hassett, Myles P. ... Phoenix, AZ
Hassett, Myles P., P.C. ... Phoenix, AZ
Hassett, Neil A. ... Hartford, CT
Hassett, P. Scott ... Madison, WI
Hassett, Patricia ... Syracuse, NY
Hassett, Paul Michael ... Buffalo, NY
Hassett, Raymond M. ... Hartford, CT
Hassett, Robert F. ... Indianapolis, IN
Hassett, Robert W. ... Atlanta, GA
Hassett, Timothy J. ... St. Paul, MN
Hassett, Walter D. ... McLean, VA
Hassett, William J. ... Monroe, MI
Hassevoort, Karen ... Kalamazoo, MI
Hassey, Raymond A. ... Wilkes-Barre, PA
Hassi, David G. ... Pleasantville, NY
Hassid, André ... Walnut Creek, CA
Hassid, Jack ... New York, NY
Hassiepen, John P. ... Peoria, IL
Hassig, Logan M. ... New Martinsville, WV
Hassin, Donald J., Jr. ... Waukesha, WI
Hassin, Kathryn J. ... Waukesha, WI
Hassin, Michael D. ... Rockville Centre, NY
Hassine, Eli ... New York, NY
Hassing, Steven D., (P.C.)
Salt Lake City, UT
Hassing, Thomas A. ... Sunnyvale, CA
Hassing, William J. ... Minneapolis, MN
Hassinger, David S. ... Birmingham, AL
Hassinger, Douglas John ... Norcross, GA
Hassinger, Karen ... Washington, PA
Hassinger, Lambert J. ... New Orleans, LA
Hassinger, Lambert J., Jr. ... Metairie, LA
Hassinger, Patricia Cotter
Sinking Spring, PA
Hassinger, Susan M. ... Buffalo, NY
Hassinger, Timothy W. ... Metairie, LA
Hassler, Alan N. ... Grand Junction, CO
Hassler, Albert M., II ... Houston, TX
Hassler, Allison R. ... Springfield, OR
Hassler, Carl A. ... Atlanta, GA
Hassler, Christina M. ... Buffalo, NY
Hassler, Craig A. ... Vacaville, CA
Hassler, David P. ... El Paso, TX
Hassler, Gregory L. ... Greenville, NC
Hassler, Janine D. ... Stilwell, KS
Hassler, John T. ... Honolulu, HI
Hassler, Keith A. ... York, PA
Hassler, Kenneth D. ... Kansas City, MO
Hassler Law Firm, The, P.C.
Grand Junction, CO
Hassler, Mark D. ... Terre Haute, IN
Hassler and Smalling ... Byrdstown, TN
Hassler, William Gregory ... Houston, TX
Hassler, William T. ... Washington, DC
Hassman, Gaylen V. ... Waverly, IA
Hassner, Marla L. ... New York, NY
Hassold, Robert W., Jr. ... Greenville, SC
Hasson, Aron P. ... Los Angeles, CA
Hasson, Barry J. ... Bellevue, WA
Hasson, Bernard J. ... Arlington, VA
Hasson, C. Christopher ... Greensburg, PA
Pittsburgh, PA
Hasson, Harvey R. ... San Diego, CA
Hasson, James J. ... Staten Island, NY
Hasson, James K., Jr. ... Atlanta, GA
Hasson, Jeffrey I. ... Portland, OR
Hasson, John V. ... Fort Washington, PA
Hasson, Joseph K. ... Chicago, IL
Hasson, Keith S. ... Durham, NC
Hasson, Kevin J. ... Washington, DC
Hasson, Kirke M. ... Palo Alto, CA
Hasson, Marie Loepp ... Arlington, VA
Hasson, Patrick J. ... Philadelphia, PA
Hasson, Ralph H. ... Austin, TX
Hasson, Robert Bruce ... Fremont, CA
Hasson, Samuel J. ... Rosendale, NY
Hasson, Steve S. ... Torrance, CA
Hass-Perlman, Naomi A. ... Miami, FL
Hast, Allison D. ... Houston, TX
Hast, Brian Douglas ... San Francisco, CA
Hast, Julie Ann ... Martinez, CA
Hast, Patrick J. ... Northridge, CA
Hast, William T. ... York, PA
Hastedt, Robert W. ... Austin, TX
Hasten, Barry G. ... Arlington, TX
Hasten, Bradley A. ... Atlanta, GA
Hastert, Bryan M. ... Ottawa, KS
Hastert, Diane Deskins ... Honolulu, HI
Hastert, Thomas J. ... Penn Valley, CA
Hastie, C. Edward ... Lexington, KY
Hastie, Calvin K., Sr. ... Columbia, SC
Hastie, J. Drayton, III ... Columbia, SC
Hastie, John D. ... Oklahoma City, OK
Hastie, Karen A. ... Wampsville, NY
Hastie, McCutcheon and Maye, A Professional
Corporation ... Oklahoma City, OK
Hastie, Nona ... Charleston, SC
Hastie, Robert C. ... Long Beach, CA
Hastie, Thomas J., Jr. ... Newark, NJ
Hastie, William H. ... Los Angeles, CA
Hasting, Constance W. ... El Dorado Hills, CA
Hasting, H. Duane ... Forreston, IL
Freeport, IL
Lena, IL
Hasting, Howard H. ... San Antonio, TX
Hasting, Howard H., Jr. ... San Antonio, TX
Hastings, Alan D. ... Atlanta, GA
Hastings, Alcee L. ... Oakland Park, FL
Hastings & Allan ... Ridgefield, CT
Hastings, Allison R. ... Fryeburg, ME
Hastings, Ann E. ... Fryeburg, ME
Hastings, Arthur L. ... Raleigh, NC
Hastings, Brett M. ... St. Louis, MO
Hastings, Celia Farrar ... Port Huron, MI
Hastings, Charles L. ... Stockton, CA
Hastings, Charles R. ... Prescott, AZ
Hastings, Charles W. ... Hastings, NE
Hastings, Christopher G.
Grand Rapids, MI
Hastings, Christopher J.
Bloomfield Hills, MI
Hastings, Clifton Floyd ... Troy, AL
Hastings, Craig R. ... Ames, IA
Hastings, D. Jean ... Walnut Creek, CA
Hastings, D. Mark ... Knoxville, TN
Hastings, Dan ... New York, NY
Hastings, David G. ... Tempe, AZ
Hastings, David M. ... Rochester, NY
Hastings, David R., II ... Fryeburg, ME
Hastings, David R., III ... Fryeburg, ME
Hastings, Donald C. ... Loudonville, NY
Hastings, Douglas A. ... Washington, DC
Hastings, E. Eugene ... Monroe, LA
Hastings, Edwin H. ... Providence, RI
Hastings, Ellen M. ... Montgomery, AL
Hastings and Estreicher, P.A.
St. Petersburg, FL
Hastings, George C. ... Hartford, CT
Hastings, George L., Jr.
United States Court of Federal Claims,
Office of Special Masters, GV
Hastings, George S., Jr. ... Hermitage, TN
Hastings, H. Keith ... San Francisco, CA
Hastings & Hastings, P.C. ... Tempe, AZ
Hastings, Henry J. ... Grosse Pointe Farms, MI
Hastings, Honey ... Nashua, NH
Hastings, J. Christopher ... Tulsa, OK
Hastings, J. Gary ... Los Angeles, CA
Hastings, James C. ... Mankato, MN
Hastings, James H.
Rancho Palos Verdes, CA
Hastings, James R. ... Department of Justice,
Criminal Division, GV
Hastings, Jamie A. ... Yonkers, NY
Hastings, Jeffrey P. ... Westlake, OH
Hastings, Jeffrey W. ... Houston, TX
Hastings, John M., Jr. ... Syracuse, NY
Hastings, John M., (P.C.) ... Chicago, IL
Hastings, John P. ... Kansas City, MO
Hastings, John T. ... Los Angeles, CA
Hastings, Jon E. ... Nashville, TN
Hastings, Joseph L. ... Colorado Springs, CO
Hastings, Joyce E. ... Costa Mesa, CA
Hastings, J. R. ... San Anselmo, CA
Hastings, Karen M.
Department of Commerce,
Patent and Trademark Office, GV
Hastings, Karis A. ... Washington, DC
Hastings, Kerry P. ... Cincinnati, OH
Hastings, Kim M. ... Cleveland, OH
Hastings Law Office, P.A. ... Fryeburg, ME
Hastings, Lawrence V. ... Coral Gables, FL
Hastings, Lewis B. ... Phoenix, AZ
Hastings, Mark R. ... New York, NY
Hastings, Mark W. ... Fryeburg, ME
Hastings, Mary F. ... St. Paul, MN
Hastings, Michael L. ... St. Petersburg, FL
Hastings, Michael W. ... Springfield, IL
Hastings, Patricia G. ... Hermitage, TN
Hastings, Patricia L. ... Gulfport, FL
Hastings, Paul David ... Jackson, MS
Hastings, Peter G. ... Fryeburg, ME
Hastings, Peter G., II ... Portland, ME
Hastings, Philip M. ... Concord, NH
Hastings, Richard E. ... Hudson, MA
Hastings, Richard G. ... Lexington, VA
Hastings, Richard P. ... Ridgefield, CT
Hastings, Ripley E. ... Portland, ME
Boston, MA
Hastings, Robert C. ... Hampton, VA
Hastings, Robert J. ... Doylestown, PA
Hastings, Robert R., Jr. ... Cincinnati, OH
Hastings, Robert U., Jr. ... Vero Beach, FL
Hastings, Robert W. ... Pittsburgh, PA
Hastings, Robert Wm., II
Kailua-Kona, HI
Hastings, Robert Wm., II, Atty. at Law, A
Law Corp. ... Kailua-Kona, HI
Hastings, Stephanie Osler
Santa Barbara, CA
Hastings, Stephen Ross ... La Quinta, CA
Hastings, Steve T. ... Corpus Christi, TX
Hastings, Steven G. ... Chicago, IL
Hastings, Stewart ... Cleveland, OH
Hastings, Susan C. ... Cleveland, OH
Hastings, Susan G. ... Tempe, AZ
Hastings, Thomas C. ... San Jose, CA
Hastings, Thomas E. ... Indianapolis, IN
Hastings, Thomas E. ... Princeton, NJ
Hastings, Thomas W. ... Sanford, FL
Hastings, Vivien Norborne
Bonita Springs, FL
Hastings, W. Scott ... Dallas, TX
Hastings, Willard ... Santa Barbara, CA
Hastings, William C. ... Lincoln, NE
Hastings, William S. ... Dallas, TX
Hastings, Willmore C. ... Naperville, IL
Hastings, W. R., Jr. ... Searcy, AR
Hastings-Hale, Margaret P. ... Sacramento, CA
Hastoe, Nona M. ... Charleston, SC
Haston, Arch B. ... San Antonio, TX
Haston, Carroll Cleo ... Florham Park, NJ
Haston, Charles D. ... McMinnville, TN
Haston, Charles Lynn ... Sparta, TN
Haston, Craig ... Houston, TX
Haston, Fred M., III ... Birmingham, AL
Haston, Lynn ... Sparta, TN
Haston, William E.C., Sr. ... Dallas, TX
Hastreiter, Roberta L. ... Chicago, IL
Hasty, David H. ... Fayetteville, NC
Hasty, Dennis K. ... Orange, CA
Hasty, Fred ... Macon, GA
Hasty, Frederick E., III ... Miami, FL
Hasty, Jason C. ... Fairview, OK
Hasty, Jason R. ... Marietta, GA
Hasty, Jason R., P.C. ... Marietta, GA
Hasty, John H. ... Charlotte, NC
Hasty, Paul, Jr. ... Overland Park, KS
Hasty, Philip A. ... Atlanta, GA
Hasty, Robert A. ... Fort Worth, TX
Hasty, Robert A., Jr. ... Fayetteville, NC
Hasty, Robert E. ... Washington, DC
Hasty, Rodney G. ... Asheville, NC
Hasty, Victoria Merritt ... Seattle, WA
Hasty, William D., Jr. ... Birmingham, AL
Hasty, William G., Jr. ... Canton, GA
Haswell, Andrew J., Jr. ... Cincinnati, OH
Haswell, Harold R. ... Oakland, CA
Haswell, John H. ... Gainesville, FL
Haswell, Leslie S., (Ms.) ... Gainesville, FL
Haszard, James L. ... Lincoln, NE
Haszto, Stephen J. ... Carol Stream, IL
Hata, Harumi ... Los Angeles, CA
Hatab, Anthony J. ... Bronx, NY
New York, NY
Hatala, Joseph V. ... Dayton, OH
Hatala, Robert S. ... Cedar Rapids, IA
Hatamiya, Julie Y. ... Los Angeles, CA
Hatamyar, Patricia W. ... Oklahoma City, OK
Hatch, Allen & Shepherd, P.A.
Albuquerque, NM
Hatch & Associates ... Camas, WA
Hatch, Barbara R. ... St. Paul, MN
Hatch, Barry M. ... Phoenix, AZ
Hatch, Braddon B. ... Chico, CA
Hatch, Brent O. ... Salt Lake City, UT
Hatch, Brian A. ... Scottsdale, AZ
Hatch, Brian T. ... East Greenwich, RI
Hatch, Bryan S. ... Lincoln, NE
Hatch, Carl A. ... Helena, MT
Hatch, Carol J. ... Janesville, WI
Hatch, Charles G. ... Andover, MA
Hatch, Colin K. ... Columbus, OH
Hatch, Craig A. ... Lemoyne, PA
Hatch, Daniel R. ... Atlanta, GA
Hatch, David L. ... Richardson, TX
Hatch, David S. ... Montesano, WA
Hatch, David W. ... Monroe, MI
Hatch, Denison H., Jr. ... Wilmington, DE
Hatch, Denton M. ... Spanish Fork, UT
Hatch, Dorothy ... New Hartford, CT
Hatch, Douglas L. ... Arlington, VA
Hatch, Edwin I. ... Atlanta, GA
Hatch, Eiden & Pihlstrom ... Woodbury, MN
Hatch, Elaine F. ... Santa Fe, NM
Hatch, Ernest H., Jr. ... Fort Myers, FL
Hatch, Everard Enos ... Dover, NH
Hatch, Farrell M. ... Durant, OK
Hatch, Gary W. ... Atlanta, GA
Hatch, George W., III ... Tallahassee, FL
Hatch, Gerald B. ... Largo, FL
Hatch, H. James, III ... Columbus, OH
Hatch, H. van den Berg ... Kalamazoo, MI
Hatch, Hilary Joy ... Los Angeles, CA
Hatch, Howard (Wally), Jr. ... Plainview, TX
Hatch, Ira C., Jr. ... Vero Beach, FL
Hatch, Ira C., P.A. ... Vero Beach, FL
Hatch, J. Michael ... Oakland, CA
Hatch, Jack G. ... St. Charles, IL
Hatch, Jacqueline ... Flagstaff, AZ
Hatch & James, P.C. ... Salt Lake City, UT
Hatch, James R. ... Homer, LA
Hatch, Jay E., (Ms.) ... Birmingham, MI
Hatch, Jeffrey J. ... Roanoke, VA
Hatch, Jeffrey J. ... Walla Walla, WA
Hatch, John D. ... Ocala, FL
Hatch, John D., P.C. ... Ocala, FL
Hatch, Jonathan C. ... Lynnwood, WA
Hatch, Jonathan D. ... Bloomfield, CT
Hatch, Jonathan L. ... New York, NY
Hatch, Jonathan Lee ... Benson, NC
Hatch, Joseph E. ... Salt Lake City, UT
Hatch, Joseph E., P.C. ... Salt Lake City, UT
Hatch, Josiah O., III ... Denver, CO
Hatch, Kendall P. ... Salt Lake City, UT
Hatch Law Firm, The, A Professional
Corporation ... Corpus Christi, TX
Hatch, Lawrence R. ... Champaign, IL
Hatch, Leighton ... Sacramento, CA
Hatch, Leslie F. (Les) ... Lubbock, TX
Hatch, Little & Bunn, L.L.P. ... Raleigh, NC
Hatch, M. Sean ... Little Rock, AR
Hatch, Mary Ann ... Belleville, IL
Hatch, Matthew D. ... Bettendorf, IA
Hatch & McPheters, Lawyers, P.C.
Champaign, IL
Urbana, IL
Hatch, Michael A. ... Woodbury, MN
Hatch, Michael W. ... Milwaukee, WI
Hatch & Moschetti, LLC ... Denver, CO
Hatch, Murray K. ... Oakland, CA
Hatch, Nelita A. ... Houston, TX
Hatch, Orrin G. ... Salt Lake City, UT
Hatch and Parent ... Oxnard, CA
San Diego, CA
Santa Barbara, CA
South Lake Tahoe, CA
Hatch, Patti Durio ... Baton Rouge, LA
Hatch, Q. Dale ... Phoenix, AZ
Hatch, R. Noel ... Los Angeles, CA
Hatch, Ralph ... Holbrook, AZ
Hatch, Richard C. ... Cary, NC
Hatch, Richard D. ... Aransas Pass, TX
Hatch, Richard D., III ... Aransas Pass, TX
Hatch, Richard J., Jr. ... Corpus Christi, TX
Hatch, Richard J., Sr. ... Corpus Christi, TX
Hatch, Richard O. ... Department of the Army,
U.S. Army Legal Services Agency, GV
Hatch, Robert M. ... Chicago, IL
Hatch, Robert W. ... Burlington, MA
Hatch, Robert W., II ... Denver, CO
Hatch, Roberta A. ... Bridgeport, CT
Hatch, Robertson ... Hauppauge, NY
Hatch, Ronald D. ... Moses Lake, WA
Hatch & Smith ... Homer, LA
Hatch, Stanley C. ... Santa Barbara, CA
Hatch, Stanley N. ... Albuquerque, NM
Hatch, Thomas B. ... Minneapolis, MN
Hatch, Thomas F. ... Detroit, MI
Hatch, Timothy J. ... Los Angeles, CA
Hatch, Timothy P. ... Andover, MA
Hatch, Victoria E. ... Camas, WA
Hatch, Willard ... Seattle, WA
Hatch, William K. ... Tully, NY
Hatch, William L. ... Champaign, IL
Hatch, William Worth ... New York, NY
Hatchadorian, Matthew J. ... Cleveland, OH

Hatchell, Mary H. Molly .... Tyler, TX
Hatchell, Michael A. .... Tyler, TX
Hatcher, B. Paul .... Chattanooga, TN
Hatcher, Barbara A. .... Atlanta, GA
Hatcher, Bernard L. .... Boulder, CO
Denver, CO
Hatcher, Carla S. .... Dallas, TX
Hatcher, Charles L., III .... Jefferson City, MO
Hatcher, Charles M., Jr. .... Huntington, WV
Hatcher, Daniel L. .... Takoma Park, MD
Hatcher, Diller, Rice & Beebe .... Toledo, OH
Van Wert, OH
Hatcher, Drew W. .... Treasury Department,
U.S. Customs Service, GV
Hatcher, Elmer W., Jr. .... Aiken, SC
Hatcher, Emory G. .... Denver, CO
Hatcher, Eugene S. .... Macon, GA
Hatcher, Gailyn .... St. Louis, MO
Hatcher, Henry M., Jr. .... Marietta, GA
Hatcher, Irvin & Pressley .... Marietta, GA
Hatcher, J. Gregory .... Charlotte, NC
Hatcher, J. Kate .... Charlotte, NC
Hatcher, J. Madden, Jr. .... Columbus, GA
Hatcher, James .... Peoria, IL
Hatcher, James A. .... Atlanta, GA
Hatcher, Jerry B. .... Atlanta, GA
Hatcher, Jerry B., P.C. .... Atlanta, GA
Hatcher, Jim J. .... Gainesville, TX
Hatcher, John A. .... Booneville, MS
Hatcher, John A., P.A. .... Booneville, MS
Hatcher, John L. (Jack) .... Cleveland, MS
Hatcher, John Randolph .... Cincinnati, OH
Hatcher, John W., Jr. .... Fayetteville, WV
Hatcher, Johnson, Meaney & Gothard, PLLC
Chattanooga, TN
Hatcher, Judi K. .... Columbus, OH
Hatcher, Julia A. .... Washington, DC
Hatcher, Julia C. .... Galveston, TX
Hatcher, Julia K. .... Richmond, VA
Hatcher, Julia Kate Harris .... Charlotte, NC
Hatcher, Kenneth B. .... Wilmington, NC
Hatcher, Linda .... Los Angeles, CA
Hatcher, Linda J. .... Newton, NC
Hatcher, Lizzie R. .... Las Vegas, NV
Hatcher, Louis E. .... Albany, GA
Hatcher, M. Raymond .... Austin, TX
Hatcher, Mary .... Elizabethtown, KY
Hatcher, Melvin N. .... Richland, WA
Hatcher, Merrick D. .... Chicago, IL
Hatcher, Michael R. .... Washington, DC
Hatcher, Milford B., Jr. .... Atlanta, GA
Hatcher, Patrick G., (P.C.) .... Hartford, CT
Hatcher, Richard G. .... Gary, IN
Hatcher, Robert K. .... Houston, TX
Hatcher, Robert T. .... Pacific Grove, CA
Hatcher, Ronald N., Jr. .... Tucson, AZ
Hatcher & Rose .... Peoria, IL
Hatcher, Ross L., III .... Chattanooga, TN
Hatcher, Samuel F. .... Atlanta, GA
Hatcher, Sarah (Sally) .... Denver, CO
Hatcher, Scott P. .... Santa Fe, NM
Hatcher, Sharna Davis .... Highland Park, MI
Hatcher, Shelton .... Hendersonville, TN
Hatcher, Sondra Burling .... Houston, TX
Hatcher, Stephen B. .... Orlando, FL
Hatcher, Stuart M. ....
Department of State, GV
Hatcher, Stubbs, Land, Hollis & Rothschild
Phenix City, AL
Columbus, GA
Hatcher, Sullivan & Grand, P.A.
Santa Fe, NM
Hatcher, Susan Frances .... Edinburg, TX
Hatcher, Todd E. .... Atlanta, GA
Hatcher, Tony N. .... Mobile, AL
Hatcher, W. Edward .... Van Wert, OH
Hatcher, W. Thompson, III .... Atlanta, GA
Hatcher, William J. .... El Cajon, CA
Hatcher, William W., Jr. .... Santa Rosa, CA
Hatcher-Capers, Lola M. ....
United States Postal Service, GV
Hatchett, Bonita L. .... Chicago, IL
Hatchett, Charles T., Jr. .... Round Rock, TX
Hatchett, David L. .... Indianapolis, IN
Hatchett, Diana Adams .... Kensington, MD
Hatchett, Joseph W. .... Tallahassee, FL
Hatchett, Michael E. .... Washington, DC
Hatchett, Michael K. .... Houston, TX
Hatchett, Philip L. .... Hampton, VA
Hatchett, Sharon Denise .... Detroit, MI
Hatchett, William M. .... Pontiac, MI
Hatchett-Stoner, Olivia .... Pittsburgh, PA
Hatchfield, Richd. J., Jr. .... South Easton, MA
Hatchimonji, Douglas Jun .... Santa Ana, CA
Hatchion, Ann A. .... Chandler, AZ
Hatchman, Jeffrey W. .... Arcadia, CA
Hatchner, Jeffrey A. .... Warren, OH
Hateley, Donald Patrick .... Los Angeles, CA
Hateley & Hampton .... Los Angeles, CA
Hatem, Albert A. .... White Plains, NY
Hatem, David J. .... Boston, MA
Hatem, Frederick D. .... Port St. Lucie, FL
Hatem, Frederick J., Jr. .... Bel Air, MD
Hatem, James V. .... Manchester, NH
Hatem & Mahoney .... Salem, NH
North Andover, MA
Hatem, Michael D. .... Salem, NH
Hatem, Peter L. .... North Andover, MA
Hatem, Robert J. .... San Diego, CA
Hatem, Susan MacDonald .... Concord, NH
Hatem, Victor L. .... North Andover, MA
Salem, NH
Hatesohl, Kent D. .... Kansas City, MO
Hatfield, Amber L. .... Austin, TX
Hatfield, Anderson E. .... Gainesville, FL
Hatfield, B. Eugene .... Chattanooga, TN
Hatfield, Ben F., Jr. .... Indianapolis, IN
Hatfield, Brad K. .... Horseshoe Bay, TX
Hatfield, C. Kent .... Louisville, KY
Hatfield, Cecile .... Miami, FL
Hatfield, Christian A. .... Santa Fe, NM
Hatfield, Christopher D. .... Bend, OR
Hatfield, Curt .... Covington, KY
Hatfield, Cynthia A. .... Greensboro, NC
Hatfield, David G. .... Evansville, IN
Hatfield, David M. .... Newport Beach, CA
Hatfield, Dionna .... Elizabethtown, KY
Hatfield, Donald H. .... Scottsdale, AZ
Hatfield, Douglas S., Jr. .... Hillsborough, NH
Hatfield, G. David .... Knoxville, TN
Hatfield, Gary F. .... Central City, NE
Hatfield, Gene .... Belmont, CA
Hatfield, George W. .... Sacramento, CA
Hatfield, Gerald M. .... Philadelphia, PA
Hatfield, Gregory C. .... Englewood, CO
Hatfield, Gus D., Jr. .... Chattanooga, TN
Hatfield, Guy E. .... Post Falls, ID
Hatfield, G. W., Jr. .... Whitley City, KY
Hatfield, Hadrian N. .... Bethesda, MD
Hatfield, Harry M. .... Madison, WV
Hatfield, Heather Lu .... Columbus, OH
Hatfield, Jack K. .... Tulsa, OK
Hatfield, Jason M. .... Fayetteville, AR
Hatfield, Jeffrey W. .... Fayetteville, AR
Hatfield, Joan C. .... East Hampton, NY
Riverhead, NY
Hatfield, John, Jr. .... Schaumburg, IL
Hatfield, Kathleen H. .... Washington, DC
Hatfield, Kathryn Van Deusen
Newark, NJ
Hatfield & Lassiter .... Little Rock, AR
Hatfield, Marie Mieko .... Waianae, HI
Hatfield, Martin L. .... London, KY
Hatfield, McGinnis E., Jr. .... Bluefield, WV
Hatfield, Michael A., Jr. .... Milwaukee, WI
Hatfield, Michael H. .... Umatilla, FL
Hatfield, Moran & Barry, Professional
Association .... Hillsborough, NH
Hatfield, Mountcastle, Deal, Van Zandt &
Mann, L.L.P. .... Winston-Salem, NC
Hatfield, Nina R.
Department Of The Interior,
Bureau of Land Management, GV
Hatfield, Patricia L. .... West Chicago, IL
Hatfield, Patricia M. .... Durham, NC
Hatfield, Patrick J. .... Blythewood, SC
Hatfield, Paul G. .... Billings, MT
Hatfield, Richard F. .... Little Rock, AR
Hatfield, Richard W. .... Beaumont, TX
Hatfield, Scott C. .... Raleigh, NC
Hatfield, Suzan .... Santa Rosa, CA
Hatfield, Timothy G. .... Louisville, KY
Hatfield, Timothy James .... Boston, MA
Hatfield, Weston P. .... Winston-Salem, NC
Hatfield, W. F. .... Hazel Park, MI
Hatfield, William P. .... Florence, SC
Hatfield, William S. .... Morristown, NJ
Hatfield-Wise, Joyce A. .... Washington, PA
Hatges, Georgia .... Flourtown, PA
Hathaway, Amy P. .... Detroit, MI
Hathaway, Anna K. .... Houston, TX
Hathaway, Barbara Drexler .... Austin, TX
Hathaway, Benjamin H. .... Austin, TX
Hathaway, Benson L., Jr.
Salt Lake City, UT
Hathaway, Bradley F. .... Greenville, MS
Hathaway, Carolyne R. .... Washington, DC
Hathaway, Christine A. .... Dallas, TX
Hathaway, David B. .... Warwick, RI
Hathaway, David E. .... Grand Rapids, MI
Hathaway, David E. .... Cincinnati, OH
Hathaway, David F. .... Rumford, ME
Hathaway, David T. .... Los Angeles, CA
Hathaway, Diane Duty .... Cincinnati, OH
Hathaway, Dixie A. .... New York, NY
Hathaway, Donald E., Jr. .... Shreveport, LA
Hathaway, Edgar, Jr. .... Elmer, NJ
Hathaway, Fred W. .... Alexandria, VA
Hathaway, Galen .... Willits, CA
Hathaway, Gary R. .... Ulysses, KS
Hathaway, Genaro R. .... Stratham, NH
Hathaway, Geoffrey J. .... Appleton, MN
Montevideo, MN
Hathaway, George H. .... Detroit, MI
Hathaway, Gerald T. .... New York, NY
Hathaway, Gregory S. .... Portland, OR
Hathaway, Harry L. .... Los Angeles, CA
Hathaway, Homer C. .... Grants Pass, OR
Hathaway, Irene Bruce .... Detroit, MI
Hathaway, Irving R. .... Coldwater, MI
Hathaway, James D. .... Tucson, AZ
Hathaway, James E., III .... Little Rock, AR
Hathaway, Janet .... San Francisco, CA
Hathaway, Jeffrey D. .... Los Angeles, CA
Hathaway, John R. .... Ann Arbor, MI
Hathaway, John S. .... The Woodlands, TX
Hathaway, John W. .... Tillamook, OR
Hathaway, John W. .... Seattle, WA
Hathaway, John W., P.L.L.C. .... Seattle, WA
Hathaway, K. Kleigh .... Palo Alto, CA
Hathaway, Karen L. .... Los Angeles, CA
Hathaway, Kathryn Ann .... Tallahassee, FL
Hathaway, Kent S. .... Charlotte, NC
Hathaway, Kimball & Campbell, LLP
Tribune, KS
Ulysses, KS
Hathaway, Kristie P. .... Boston, MA
Hathaway, Lisa A. .... Toledo, OH
Hathaway, Manning, Jr. .... Palm Harbor, FL
Hathaway, Mark H. .... Richmond, VA
Hathaway, Mark M. .... Los Angeles, CA
Hathaway, Merrill F., Jr.
Federal Energy Regulatory Commission,
Office of the General Counsel, GV
Hathaway, Michael M. .... Detroit, MI
Hathaway, Nancy L. .... Lafayette, IN
Hathaway, Noreen Nelligan
Burtonsville, MD
Hathaway, P. Scott .... Tulsa, OK
Hathaway, Perrett, Webster, Powers &
Chrisman, A Prof. Corp. .... Ventura, CA
Hathaway, Raeburn B., Jr. .... Dover, MA
Hathaway, Richard G. .... Jacksonville, FL
Hathaway, Robert E. .... Akron, OH
Hathaway, Robert E. Lee, II .... Detroit, MI
Hathaway, Sarah L. .... Cortland, IL
Hathaway, Speight & Kunz
Cheyenne, WY
Hathaway, Stanley K. .... Cheyenne, WY
Hathaway, Susanna E. .... Los Angeles, CA
Hathaway, Thomas M. J. .... Detroit, MI
Hathaway, Todd J. .... Manchester, NH
Hathaway, William D. .... McLean, VA
Hathaway, William F.
New Smyrna Beach, FL
Hathaway, William F., P.A.
Daytona Beach, FL
New Smyrna Beach, FL
Hathaway, William J. .... Detroit, MI
Hathaway, William J. .... Erie, PA
Hathaway, William M.
Securities and Exchange Commission,
Division of Enforcement, GV
Hathcock, J. Andrew .... Austin, TX
Hathcox, VaLinda .... Sulphur Springs, TX
Hatherley, Dale J. .... Hanford, CA
Hatherley, John E., (A Professional
Corporation) .... Los Angeles, CA
Hatheway, Gordon W., Jr.
Washington, DC
Hatheway, Tamara S. .... Kansas City, MO
Hathhorn, Brent W. .... Blue Springs, MO
Hathorn & Hathorn .... Louisville, MS
Hathorn, Hugh .... Louisville, MS
Hathorn, Mary M. .... Fairlee, VT
Hathorn, Meredith L. .... New Orleans, LA
Hathorn, Stanley H. .... Louisville, MS
Hathorn, Steven A., P.C. .... Covington, GA
Hathorn, Steven A., (P.C.) .... Covington, GA
Hathorn, William E. .... Prentiss, MS
Hathout, Mona .... Los Angeles, CA
Hathout, Samer M. .... Los Angeles, CA
Hathway, Charles T. .... Bethesda, MD
Hathway, Craig W. .... El Campo, TX
Hathy, John J. .... Washington, DC
Columbia, MD
Hatic, Haas A. .... Miami, FL
Hatkoff, Bruce A. .... Los Angeles, CA
Hatkoff, Bruce A., A Law Corporation
Los Angeles, CA
Hatlen, Kari L. .... Seattle, WA
Hatler, Patricia R. .... Philadelphia, PA
Hatler, Ray A. .... Los Osos, CA
Hatley, Angela Kay .... Kansas City, MO
Hatley, Angela M. .... Fayetteville, NC
Hatley, Charles C. .... New Madrid, MO
Hatley, Gregory J. .... Great Falls, MT
Hatley, Morris L. .... Oklahoma City, OK
Hatley, Rodney J. .... San Diego, CA
Hatley, W. Joseph .... Overland Park, KS
Hatley, William D. .... Lincoln Park, MI
Hatlie, Martin J. .... Chicago, IL
Hatling, John .... Fergus Falls, MN
Hatmaker, David J. .... Harrisonburg, VA
Hatmaker, Frederick D. .... Louisville, KY
Hatmaker & Hall .... Jacksboro, TN
Hatmaker, J. Chadwick .... Knoxville, TN
Hatmaker, Michael G. .... Jacksboro, TN
Hatmaker, Susan K. .... Fresno, CA
Hatmaker, Wesley L. .... Knoxville, TN
Hatoff, Howard I. .... Philadelphia, PA
Hatrak, Bruce M. .... Chantilly, VA
Hatridge, Irvin C., Jr. .... Corpus Christi, TX
Hatridge, Stephen Andrew .... Houston, TX
Hatry, Patricia .... New York, NY
Hatt, Daniel T. .... Redlands, CA
Hatt, Donald G. .... Glenmont, NY
Hatt, Frederick K. .... Reading, PA
Hatt, Norman S. .... Syracuse, NY
Hattabaugh, Rebecca D. .... Fort Smith, AR
Hattam, Mark J. .... San Diego, CA
Hattan, M. Candice .... Lafayette, LA
Hattar, Jacqueline .... New York, NY
Hattaway, Ashley H. .... Birmingham, AL
Hattaway, Brett .... Kansas City, KS
Hattaway, James A. .... Orlando, FL
Hatteberg, Andrea D. .... Irving, TX
Hattem, Dave S. .... New York, NY
Hattem, Pamela .... Cranford, NJ
Hatten, Byron M. .... Altadena, CA
Hatten, Canterbury T. .... Eastsound, WA
Hatten, Louis G. .... Key Biscayne, FL
Hatten, Mark D. .... Fort Worth, TX
Hatten, Robert R. .... Newport News, VA
Richmond, VA
Hatten, Russell R. .... Garland, TX
Hatten, Stephen P. .... Huntington, WV
Hatten, Steven A. .... Columbus, OH
Hatten, W. Edward, Jr. .... Gulfport, MS
Hatten, William M. .... Houston, TX
Hattenbach, Benjamin .... Los Angeles, CA
Hattenbach, Gina M. .... Los Angeles, CA
Hattenbach, Jonathan A.
Arlington Heights, IL
Hattenbach, Steve .... Santa Fe, NM
Hattendorf, Janice K. .... Fort Wayne, IN
Hattendorf, L. Steven .... Santa Ana, CA
Hattenhauer, Paul M. .... Charlotte, NC
Hattenhauer, Richard R. .... Portland, OR
Hatter, Debra Gatison .... Austin, TX
Hatter, Donovan & McFaul, LLP
Mineola, NY
Riverhead, NY
Rye, NY
Hatter, Jacqueline .... Madison, WI
Hatter, James M. .... Cortez, CO
Hatter, James R. .... Mineola, NY
Hatter, John P., Jr. .... Indianapolis, IN
Hatter, Rodney R. .... Irvine, CA
Hatter, Scott Wilson .... Los Angeles, CA
Hattersley, Patricia J. .... Pasadena, CA
Hattersley, Thomas E., III .... Helena, MT
Hattervig, Karen A. .... Sioux Falls, SD
Hattery, David P. .... Seattle, WA
Hattery, John J. .... Galesburg, IL
Hattery, Patricia A. .... Galesburg, IL
Hattery, Simpson & West .... Galesburg, IL
Monmouth, IL
Roseville, IL
Hattier, Craig J. .... Covington, LA
Hattier, John B. .... New Orleans, LA
Hattier, Maurice T. .... New Orleans, LA
Hattis, Russell E. .... Highland Park, IL
Hattler, Eric R. .... Los Angeles, CA
Hattner, Louis J. .... Toledo, OH
Hatton, George D. .... Margate, FL
Hatton, Gregory M. .... Anaheim, CA
Hatton, Janice E. .... Eugene, OR
Hatton, Jerry L. .... Warren, TX
Hatton, Katherine .... Philadelphia, PA
Hatton, Kathleen G. .... Department of Justice,
Office of the Pardon Attorney, GV
Hatton, Melinda Reid .... Washington, DC
Hatton, Nikki C. .... Portland, OR
Hatton, Peter L. .... Merrillville, IN
Hatton, Robert G. .... Sacramento, CA
Hatton, Sharon A. .... White Plains, NY
Hatton, Vincent P. .... Corning, NY
Hatton, William G. .... Memphis, TN
Hatton Harrington, Lisa .... Los Angeles, CA
Hattori, Ken-Ichi .... Washington, DC
Hattrick, David L. .... Portland, OR
Hatwell, Roberta R.
Department Of Health And Human Services,
Office of Community Services, GV
Hatz, Scott R. .... Syracuse, NY
Hatza, Kimon C. .... Philadelphia, PA
Hatzakis, P. Nicole .... Akron, OH
Hatzell, C. Michael .... Louisville, KY
Hatzell & Groves .... Louisville, KY
Hatzell, James L. .... Haddonfield, NJ
Hatzell, John J., Jr. .... Philadelphia, PA
Hatzenbuehler, Mari Rose .... Chicago, IL
Hatzenbuhler, Belinda Ann .... Miami, FL
Hatzenbuhler, John D. .... Martinez, CA
Hatzer, Richard C. .... Los Angeles, CA
Hatzis, Chris M. .... New York, NY
Hatzis, Peter .... Stamford, CT
Hatzis-Schoch, Brent .... Bridgewater, NJ
Hatzmann, George R. .... New York, NY
Haub, Johnathan S. .... Portland, OR
Hauben, Ronald B. .... New York, NY
Hauben, Warren P. .... New York, NY
Haubenreich, John G. .... Atlanta, GA
Haubenstock, Arthur L. .... San Francisco, CA
Haubenstock, Mark S. .... Wayne, NJ
Hauber, Catherine M. .... Kansas City, MO
Hauber, David W. .... Kansas City, KS
Hauber, John M. .... Indianapolis, IN
Hauber, Marcy D. .... Boston, MA
Hauber, Mark C. .... Fort Pierce, FL
Hauber, Vincent P. .... Buffalo, NY
Hauberg, Kyle R. .... Bloomfield Hills, MI
Hauberg, Robert Engelbrecht, Jr.
Washington, DC
Jackson, MS
Haubert, Harry L. .... Vista, CA
Haubert, William H., II
Department of Education,
Office of the General Counsel, GV
Haubert, William J. .... Wilmington, DE
Haubiel, Charles W., II .... Columbus, OH
Haubner, J. Wesley .... Philadelphia, PA
Haubrich, Greg .... Oklahoma City, OK
Haubrich, Karen K. .... San Diego, CA
Haubrich Law Firm, The, A Professional
Corporation .... Oklahoma City, OK
Hauch, Jeanne M. .... Washington, DC
Hauch, Sandra J. .... Valley Village, CA
Hauck, Bradley W. .... Madison, WI
Hauck, Bryan G. .... Conshohocken, PA
Hauck, Cathy A. .... Greenwich, CT
Hauck, Charles L. .... Gainesville, FL
Hauck, Daniel Alan .... Miamisburg, OH
Hauck, Darren C. .... Atlanta, GA
Hauck, David L. .... Richmond, VA
Hauck, Dolly Bowman .... Washington, DC
Hauck, Earl August .... Denver, CO
Hauck, G. Hamilton .... San Francisco, CA
Hauck, Gregory J. .... Philadelphia, PA
Hauck, James M. .... Indianapolis, IN
Hauck, John G. .... Yuba City, CA
Hauck, John W. .... Cincinnati, OH
Hauck, Kathleen M. .... Brooklyn Park, MN
Hauck, L. Christian .... Hays, KS
Hauck, Louis H. .... Flushing, NY
Hauck, Mark E. .... Detroit, MI
Hauck, Michael A. .... Sioux Falls, SD
Hauck, Russell J. .... White Plains, NY
Hauck, Sheldon J., Jr. .... Bozeman, MT
Hauck, Stephen G. .... New York, NY
Hauck, Stephen L. .... Batavia, OH
Hauck, Terry C. .... Portland, OR
Hauck, William R. .... St. Louis Park, MN
Haude, Daniel R. .... Cleveland, OH
Haude, Deborah Gage .... Washington, DC
Chicago, IL
Haude, Irene R. .... Nashville, TN
Hauder, Bernie E. .... Dallas, TX
Hauder, Edward A. .... Chicago, IL
Hauder, Sharis L. .... Dallas, TX
Haueisen, Anthony J. .... Fairlawn, OH

Hauenstein, Charles J. ... **Minneapolis, MN**
Hauenstein, Denise J. ... San Diego, CA
Hauer, Albert J. ... Fond du Lac, WI
Hauer, Fargione & Love, P.A.
Minneapolis, MN
Hauer, Harvey I. ... **Bingham Farms, MI**
Hauer, Harvey I., P.C.
Bingham Farms, MI
Detroit, MI
Pontiac, MI
Hauer, J. Michael ... New Brighton, MN
Hauer, John L., (P.C.) ... **Dallas, TX**
Hauer Law Offices ... Fond du Lac, WI
Hauer, Melissa ... **Bismarck, ND**
Hauer, Nicole J. ... **Bingham Farms, MI**
Hauer, Richard J., Jr. ... **Cleveland, OH**
Hauer, Robert J., Jr. ... Minneapolis, MN
Hauer, Robin ... **East Rutherford, NJ**
Hauer, Wm. S. ... Cincinnati, OH
Haueter, Daniel B. ... San Bernardino, CA
Haueter, Eric S. ... **San Francisco, CA**
Hauf & Forsythe, P.C. ... Billings, MT
Hauf, John A. ... Billings, MT
Haufe, Stephen D. ... **Clinton, IA**
Hauff, Charles F., Jr. ... **Phoenix, AZ**
Hauff, David J. ... **Fargo, ND**
Hauff, Edmund G. ... Allentown, PA
Hauffe & Hauffe, P.C. ... Saginaw, MI
Hauffe, Irwin F., II ... Saginaw, MI
Hauffe, Kurt P. ... Saginaw, MI
Haufler Associates ... **Norwell, MA**
Haufler, Heather P. ... **Tampa, FL**
Haufler, R. Christian, Jr. ... **Norwell, MA**
Haufrect, Lynn G. ... **Houston, TX**
Hauft, Alfred B. ... Sun City Center, FL
Hauft, Kathryn N. ... Sun City Center, FL
Haug, Anne M. ... Nashua, NH
Haug, Daniel T. ... Phoenix, AZ
Haug, Edgar H. ... **New York, NY**
Haug, Eric S. ... Tallahassee, FL
Haug, James R., Jr. ... **Burlington, VT**
Haug, Janis M. ... Phoenix, AZ
Haug, John A. ... North Attleboro, MA
Haug, John Robert ... **St. Louis, MO**
Haug, Lauri Ann ... Bloomington, MN
Haug Law Office, P.C. ... **Burlington, VT**
Haug, Shain B. ... San Diego, CA
Haug, Wayne H. ... El Dorado Hills, CA
Haug, William A. ... **Minneapolis, MN**
Haug, William F. ... **Phoenix, AZ**
Haugaard, John H. ... Decatur, GA
Haugaard, Steven G. ... Sioux Falls, SD
Haugaard, William C. ... Wading River, NY
Haugabrook, Nathaniel, II ... **Valdosta, GA**
Haugan, David R. ... Mount Clemens, MI
Haugan, Robert ... Newport Beach, CA
Haugdahl, Eric J. ... Tallahassee, FL
Hauge, Carol H. ... **New York, NY**
Hauge, Cortlen R. ... **Long Beach, CA**
Hauge, David F. ... **Los Angeles, CA**
Hauge, Jennifer Chandler
Morristown, NJ
Hauge, John E. ... Montgomery, AL
Hauge, Lane M. ... Havre, MT
Hauge, Leah Elizabeth ... Minneapolis, MN
Hauge, Paul H. ... **Eagan, MN**
Hauge, Paul M. ... **Newark, NJ**
Hauge, Rhonda A. ... Wilmington, DE
Hauge, Richard A. ... Wilmington, DE
Hauge, Russell D. ... Port Orchard, WA
Hauge, Susan Lynn-Paul ... St. Cloud, MN
Hauge, Todd D. ... Custer, SD
Haugeberg, David C. ... **McMinnville, OR**
Haugeberg, Rueter, Stone, Gowell & Fredricks, P.C. ... **McMinnville, OR**
Haugen, Darin G. ... **Bangor, ME**
Haugen, Denise C. ... **Houston, TX**
Haugen, Eric O. ... **Minneapolis, MN**
Haugen, Gary J. ... **Minneapolis, MN**
Haugen, Gary M. ... Seattle, WA
Haugen, Gregory K. ... **Sioux Falls, SD**
Haugen, Halver H. ... Middletown, OH
Haugen, Henry ... Seattle, WA
Haugen, Karen A. ... Chicago, IL
Haugen, Kari ... **Los Angeles, CA**
Haugen, Kristin Lee ... Henderson, KY
Haugen Law Firm, PLLP
Minneapolis, MN
Haugen, Mark K. ... Honolulu, HI
Haugen, Orrin M. ... **Minneapolis, MN**
Haugen, Phebe S. ... Minneapolis, MN
Haugen, Robert G. ... **Minneapolis, MN**
Haugen, Walter S. ... **Newnan, GA**
Haugen, Willis G. ... **Newnan, GA**
Haugens, Edward E. ... Peoria, IL
Hauger, H. Keith ... North Huntingdon, PA
Hauger, Leslie S., Jr. ... Tulsa, OK
Haugerud, Michael O. ... Lilburn, GA
Haugh & Associates ... Wilsonville, OR
Haugh, Charles R. ... **Charlottesville, VA**
Haugh, Dennis J. ... Louisville, KY
Haugh, Edw. M., Jr. ... Milwaukee, WI
Haugh & Haugh, P.C. ... **Charlottesville, VA**
Haugh, Howard F. ... **Mankato, MN**
Haugh, John F. ... York, PA
Haugh, John J. ... Wilsonville, OR
Haugh, Lair Dayton ... **Charlottesville, VA**
Haugh, Mary Holly ... Kensington, CA
Haugh, Michael A. ... Chicago, IL
Haugh & Mullins ... Scarsdale, NY
Haugh, Robert J. ... St. Paul, MN
Haugh, Rodney E. ... Alexandria, VA
Haugh, Scott C. ... Roselle, IL
Haugh, Stephen J. ... New York, NY
Haugh, Stephen M. ... Harvard, IL
Haugh, Thomas P. ... Western Springs, IL
Haugh, Valerie A. ... **Chicago, IL**
Haugh, William E., Jr. ... **St. Paul, MN**
Haugh, William L., Jr. ... **Frederick, MD**
Haughan, Peter P. ... Indianapolis, IN
Haughee, Christopher R. ... Tallahassee, FL
Haughey, Charles S., Jr. ... **San Diego, CA**
Haughey, David O. ... **Grand Rapids, MI**
Haughey, Douglas R. ... **Tulsa, OK**
Haughey, Edmund J., III
Washington, DC
Haughey, Gerald E. ... **Moorestown, NJ**
Haughey, Hugh F. ... Staten Island, NY
Haughey, James M. ... **Billings, MT**
Haughey, Jeffrey T. ... **Kansas City, MO**
Haughey, Joseph C. ... Chicago, IL
Haughey, Patrick J., Jr. ... Blauvelt, NY
Haughey, Paul C. ... **Palo Alto, CA**
Haughey, Philpot & Laurent, P.A.
Laconia, NH
Haughey, Roger E. ... **Champaign, IL**
Haughey, Roger J., II ... **Tampa, FL**
Haughey, Sheila C. ... **Charlottesville, VA**
Haughey, Stephen N. ... **Cincinnati, OH**
Haughey, Thomas J. ... **Kenilworth, NJ**
Haughey, Thomas M. ... **Laconia, NH**
Haughn, James E., II ... McComb, OH
Haughney, Edward W. ... Carlisle, PA
Haughney, Jane ... Tampa, FL
Haughney, Patrick ... Waukesha, WI
Haughney, Patrick B. ... New York, NY
Haught, Beryl H., Jr. ... Boynton Beach, FL
Haught, Bruce A. ... **Destin, FL**
Haught, Bruce A., P.A. ... **Destin, FL**
Fort Walton Beach, FL
Panama City, FL
Haught, David A. ... **Hartford, CT**
Haught, Doug ... Sayre, OK
Haught, Ira M. ... **Harrisville, WV**
Haught, Jack Gregg ... **Columbus, OH**
Haught, John E. ... **Beaumont, TX**
Haught, Mary E. ... **Austin, TX**
Haught, R. Steven ... **Oklahoma City, OK**
Haught, Rex A. ... Fresno, CA
Haught, Sharon K. ... Wooster, OH
Haught, Susan H. ... **Oklahoma City, OK**
Haught, Timothy E. ... New Martinsville, WV
Haught, Tricia A. ... **Hartford, CT**
Haught & Wade ... **Little Rock, AR**
Haught, William Dixon ... **Little Rock, AR**
Haughton, Brian S. ... **San Francisco, CA**
Haughton, Elizabeth Anne ... Los Angeles, CA
Haughton, Herbert D. ... **Tallahassee, FL**
Haughton, John A. ... **Long Beach, CA**
Haughton, Thomas H. ... La Mirada, CA
Haughton, William B. ... Long Beach, CA
Haughwout, Carey ... **West Palm Beach, FL**
Haughwout, Robert A. ... Stockton, CA
Haugland, Charles B. ... Hawarden, IA
Alcester, SD
Haugland, Corey W. ... **El Paso, TX**
Haugland, Halbach & Halbach
Devils Lake, ND
Haugland, John C. ... Devils Lake, ND
Haugland, Richard C. ... Muskogee, OK
Haugner, Richd. A. ... Oakland, CA
Haugo, Roger E. ... Lennox, SD
Haugrud, Allen ... Fergus Falls, MN
Haugrud, K. Jack ... Department of Justice, Environment and Natural Resources Division, GV
Haugrud, Thomas R. ... St. Paul, MN
Hauhart, Robert C. ... Washington, DC
Hauhuth, Jennifer A. ... **Stamford, CT**
Hauk, A. Andrew ... Los Angeles, CA
Haukaas, H. Craig ... Ashland, WI
Hauke, Thomas A. ... Milwaukee, WI
Haukedahl, Catharine F.
Minneapolis, MN
Haukedalen, Barbara ... Sacramento, CA
Haukedalen, Danny L. ... Sacramento, CA
Haukohl, Robert T. ... Milwaukee, WI
Haukom, Larry A. ... Madison, WI
Haukom & Ritchie ... Madison, WI
Haule, Anne M. ... **Chicago, IL**
Haule, R. James ... Wasco, IL
Hauler, T. J. ... Chesterfield, VA
Haulman, Robin L. ... **Pasadena, CA**
Haulsee, Hada V. ... **Winston-Salem, NC**
Haumann, William A. ... **Princeton, NJ**
Haun, Harold L. ... Topeka, KS
Haun, Kymberly L. ... Claremont, CA
Haun, Lawrence A., Law Office of
Sonora, CA
Haun, Marvin G. ... Fremont, CA
Haun, Michael D. ... **Atlanta, GA**
Haun, Stephanie ... Miami, FL
Haun, Verna L. ... **Bolivar, MO**
Haungs, Michael J. ... **Washington, DC**
Haunschild, Christopher R.
Washington, DC
Haunson, Howell M. ... Atlanta, GA
Haunz, Foster L. ... **Louisville, KY**
Haunz & Lueke, Law Offices
Louisville, KY
Haupert, Amy E. ... **Irvine, CA**
Haupert, R. Bruce ... **Iowa City, IA**
Haupert, Robertson & Weiss
Marshalltown, IA
Haupert, Sue Ellen ... Lutz, FL
Haupt, Carol M. ... Detroit, MI
Haupt, Erika L. ... **Columbus, OH**
Haupt, Fred J. ... **Alliance, OH**
Canton, OH
Salem, OH
Haupt, James S. ... St. Louis, MO
Haupt, Jeffrey D. ... Canton, OH
Haupt, Kathryn J. ... Fond du Lac, WI
Haupt, Keith R. ... **Cincinnati, OH**
Haupt, Michael D. ... **San Francisco, CA**
Haupt, Renee A. ... **Los Angeles, CA**
Haupt, Samuel P. ... Pittsfield, MA
Haupt, Wayne L. ... Ann Arbor, MI
Hauptfuehrer, Sara E. ... **Washington, DC**
Hauptfuhrer, George J., Jr.
Philadelphia, PA
Hauptfuhrer, Sally D. ... Atlanta, GA
Hauptman, Aaron H. ... New York, NY
Hauptman, Arnold J. ... Massapequa, NY
Hauptman, Benjamin J. ... **Alexandria, VA**
Hauptman, Gordon R. ... **Omaha, NE**
Hauptman, Gregory B. ... **Washington, DC**
Hauptman, H. Ronald ... Los Angeles, CA
Hauptman, James E. ... Billings, MT
Hauptman, John L. ... Morrison, IL
Hauptman, Laurie A. ... Livingston, NJ
Hauptman, Martin D. ... **West Orange, NJ**
Hauptman, Martin R. ... Brooklyn, NY
Hauptman, Michael W.
San Francisco, CA
Hauptman, Mitchell Z. ... Lakeport, CA
Hauptman, Nancy M. ... Wheaton, IL
Hauptman, O'Brien, Wolf & Lathrop, P.C.
Omaha, NE
Hauptman & Richmond, P.A.
Morristown, NJ
West Orange, NJ
Hauptman, Vida I. ... Mayfield Village, OH
Hauptman, W. Reed ... **Toledo, OH**
Hauptman, Wesley E. ... Omaha, NE
Hauptman, William ... New York, NY
Hauptman, Yale S. ... Livingston, NJ
Hauptmann, David W. ... Harrisburg, IL
Haurin, Robert J. ... **Philadelphia, PA**
Hauritz, Tyrone D. ... Canton, OH
Haury, John C. ... Bedford, IN
Haury, Richard L., Jr. ... **Atlanta, GA**
Haury, William W., Jr.
Fort Lauderdale, FL
Haury & Woodward ... Bedford, IN
Haurykiewicz, John M. ... **Minneapolis, MN**
Haus, Alan J. ... **San Francisco, CA**
Haus, Alexander Lee ... San Bernardino, CA
Haus, Daniel J. ... **Kansas City, MO**
Haus, Julia E. ... San Diego, CA
Haus, Robert J. ... Des Moines, IA
Haus, Ronald R. ... Oneonta, NY
Haus, William ... Madison, WI
Haus, William Craig ... Apache Junction, AZ
Hausauer, Albert R. ... Bismarck, ND
Hausbeck, Joseph J. ... Depew, NY
Hausbeck, Kimberly ... Hardin, MT
Hausburg & Ellis, P.A. ... Sarasota, FL
Hausburg, Jonathan E. ... Sarasota, FL
Hauscarriague, Yvonne M.
Emeryville, CA
Hausch, Adrienne Flipse ... Mineola, NY
Hausch, James O. ... **Philadelphia, PA**
Hauschild, Gordon G. ... **Tacoma, WA**
Hauschild, Natalie J. ... St. Cloud, MN
Hauschild, Vernon F. ... Manchester, CT
Hause, Ann M. ... Denver, CO
Hause, Benton A. ... Arlington, VA
Hause, Larry D. ... **Minneapolis, MN**
Hause, Paul J. ... Columbus, OH
Hause, Richard L. ... **Garden City, NY**
Hause, Robert F. ... Grand Island, NY
Hause, Thomas L. ... **Anchorage, AK**
Hause, W. Troy ... Greeley, CO
Hause, William G. ... **Dothan, AL**
Hauselman, Martin F. ... Chicago, IL
Hauselman & Rappin ... Chicago, IL
Hauselt, Denise A. ... **Corning, NY**
Hauselt, Sharon L. ... Wellsville, NY
Hauseman, Stanley Robt. ... Chicago, IL
Hausen, Janelle ... Houston, TX
Hausen, Robert J. ... **New York, NY**
Hausen, Stanley S. ... Mineola, NY
Hausenfluck, Glenn ... **Fort Worth, TX**
Hauser, Adam I. ... **Austin, TX**
Hauser, Allison Hunnicutt
Jacksonville, FL
Hauser, Barbara R. ... Minneapolis, MN
Hauser, Brian Ross ... Phoenix, AZ
Hauser, Carolyn Sue ... Murrysville, PA
Hauser, Charles K. ... Las Vegas, NV
Hauser, Christopher G. ... **Bradford, PA**
Hauser, Crane C. ... Chicago, IL
Hauser, David J. ... Fergus Falls, MN
Hauser, Deborah ... **San Francisco, CA**
Hauser, Dennis M. ... Woodbridge, CA
Hauser, Eric A. ... **Virginia Beach, VA**
Hauser, Errol E. ... Sleepy Eye, MN
Hauser, Gloria A. ... Berkeley, CA
Hauser, Gregory F. ... **New York, NY**
Hauser, Harry R. ... **Boston, MA**
Hauser, Helen Ann ... **Miami, FL**
Hauser, Henry A. ... **Chicago, IL**
Hauser, Herbert C. ... Sarasota, FL
Hauser, J. Christian ... **Detroit, MI**
Hauser, J. Vincent ... Waterford, CT
Hauser, Jack C., Jr. ... **Jefferson City, MO**
Hauser, James A. ... Miami, FL
Hauser, James A., P.A. ... Miami, FL
Hauser, James C. ... Orlando, FL
Hauser, James C. ... **Tallahassee, FL**
Hauser, James C. ... Gurnee, IL
Hauser, James L. ... **Boston, MA**
Hauser, James M. ... **Freeport, IL**
Hauser, Jerry R. ... **San Francisco, CA**
Hauser, John A. ... Rancho Cucamonga, CA
Hauser, John A. ... **Thomasville, NC**
Hauser, John N. ... **San Francisco, CA**
Hauser, Jonathan L. ... **Norfolk, VA**
Hauser, Judith Marie ... Hillsborough, NC
Hauser, Karen A. ... **Cleveland, OH**
Hauser, Karla K. ... **Houston, TX**
Hauser, Kathleen A. ... **Kansas City, MO**
Hauser, Kimberly S. ... New Orleans, LA
Hauser, Kristen L. ... New York, NY
Hauser, Laura A. ... **Columbus, OH**
Hauser, Lawrence I. ... Orange City, FL
Orlando, FL
Hauser, Lawrence L. ... Norwalk, CT
Hauser, Lisa Tewksbury ... Phoenix, AZ
Hauser, Lisa Z. ... **West Palm Beach, FL**
Hauser, Marc D. ... **Chicago, IL**
Hauser, Mark R. ... **Southfield, MI**
Hauser, Mark Steven ... New York, NY
Hauser, Michael D. ... **Atlanta, GA**
Hauser, Michael F. ... Winona, MN
Hauser, Michele ... **New York, NY**
Hauser, Michele M. ... Beaumont, TX
Hauser & Mouzes ... Woodbridge, CA
Hauser, Noel W. ... New York, NY
Hauser, Paul J. ... New York, NY
Hauser, Peter V. ... Berwyn, PA
Hauser, Ralph A. ... Deerfield Beach, FL
Hauser, Raymond A. ... **Chicago, IL**
Chicago Heights, IL
Hauser, Regina ... **Portland, OR**
Hauser, Richard A. ... **Washington, DC**
Hauser, Richard A. ... Algoma, WI
Sister Bay, WI
Sturgeon Bay, WI
Hauser, Richard B. ... Phoenix, AZ
Hauser, Richard B. ... Willard, OH
Hauser, Richard G. ... St. Louis, MO
Hauser, Richard J. ... Orland Park, IL
Hauser, Richard J., Jr. ... **Freeport, IL**
Hauser, Rita E. ... **New York, NY**
Hauser, Robert E. ... High Point, NC
Hauser, Robert J. ... **West Palm Beach, FL**
Hauser, Robert J. ... **Waukegan, IL**
Hauser, Robert M. ... Chicago, IL
Hauser, Robert S. ... New Haven, CT
Hauser, Robert S. ... Plantation, FL
Hauser, Ronald B. ... **West Palm Beach, FL**
Hauser, Ross G. ... Cedar Rapids, IA
Hauser, Sandra D. ... **New York, NY**
Hauser, Sandra W. ... Austin, TX
Hauser and Schmid ... Sleepy Eye, MN
Hauser, Seth A. ... New York, NY
Hauser, Steven F. ... **Houston, TX**
Hauser, Steven K. ... Santa Monica, CA
Hauser, Susan E. ... Durham, NC
Hauser, Susan L. ... Rochester, NY
Hauser, Terry V. ... Miami, FL
Hauser, Terry V., P.A. ... Miami, FL
Hauser, Thomas A. ... **Baltimore, MD**
Hauser, Thomas C. ... New York, NY
Hauser, Thomas W. ... Del Mar, CA
Hauser, Timothy D. ... Department of Labor, Office of the Solicitor, GV
Hauser, Tracy C. ... United States Court Of Appeals District Of Columbia Circuit, GV
Hauser, W. Patrick ... Barbourville, KY
Hauser, W. Patrick, P.S.C. ... Barbourville, KY
Hauser, Wade R., III ... **Des Moines, IA**
Hauser, William H. ... Richmond, VA
Hauserman, Nancy R. ... Iowa City, IA
Hauserman, Sandra Smith ... Tahoe City, CA
Hausfater, Jere R. ... **Burbank, CA**
Hausfeld, David E. ... San Diego, CA
Hausfeld, Michael D. ... **Washington, DC**
Haushalter, Barbara Joan ... Bellefontaine, OH
Haushalter, Harry ... **Hamilton Square, NJ**
Haushalter, Harry ... **New Brunswick, NJ**
Princeton, NJ
Trenton, NJ
Haushalter, Jerry C.
Palos Verdes Estates, CA
Haushalter, John M ... Irvine, CA
Haushalter, William R. ... **Philadelphia, PA**
Pittsburgh, PA
Hausheer, M. Rene ... Topeka, KS
Hausherr, Ruby L. B. ... Lawrence, KS
Haushild, Sarah Elyse ... **Seattle, WA**
Hausken, Gary L. ... Department of Justice, Civil Division, GV
Hausken, Philip D. ... Chicago, IL
Hausknecht, Michael A. ... **Rochester, NY**
Hausladen, Erin M. ... New York, NY
Hauslaib, Mark C. ... Storrs, CT
Hausle, Edward P. ... Greenville, NC
Hausle, Edward P., P.A. ... Greenville, NC
Hauslein, Jackson A., Jr.
Department of the Air Force, Office of the General Counsel, GV
Hauslein, Richard E. ... Bartlett, IL
Hausler, Donald A. ... St. Paul, MN
Hausler, Ellen Elizabeth ... **New York, NY**
Hausler, Gary J. ... Marco Island, FL
Hausler, Jeanette F. ... Miami, FL
Hausler, Kurt F. ... **Raleigh, NC**
Hausler, Larry N. ... Houston, TX
Hausler, Richd. A. ... Coral Gables, FL
Hausler, Sanford ... Paramus, NJ
New York, NY
Hauslinger, Morton J. ... Chicago, IL
Hausman, Alan B. ... **McLean, VA**
Hausman, Allen W. ... Department of Justice, Civil Division, GV
Hausman, B. Mark ... **Marietta, GA**
Hausman, C. Michael ... Waukesha, WI
Hausman, Dale E. ... **Washington, DC**
Hausman, Dion F. ... Oakland, NJ
Hausman, Donald L. ... Glendale, CA
Hausman, Harry M. ... Pembroke Pines, FL
Hausman, Irwin J. ... **Hartford, CT**
Hausman, James D. ... Rochester, MN
Hausman, James T. ... **New York, NY**
Hausman, Jay S. ... Mineola, NY
New York, NY
Hausman, Jeffrey M. ... Encino, CA
Hausman, Joel E. ... **Pittsburgh, PA**

Hausman, Joseph ... Brooklyn, NY
Hausman, Kenneth G. ... San Francisco, CA
Hausman, Madelynn J. ... Chicago, IL
Hausman, Mary ... Nashville, TN
Hausman, Matthew M. ... Bridgeport, CT
Hausman, Michael J. ... Garden City, NY
Hausman, Mitchell ... New York, NY
Hausman, Richard H. ... Philadelphia, PA
Hausman, Robert M. ... Washington, DC
Hausman, Roy J. ... Clinton, NJ
Hausman, Samuel M. ... Boston, MA
Hausman & Sosa ... Encino, CA
Hausman, Thomas I. ... Cleveland, OH
Hausmann, Arthur R. ... Santa Ana, CA
Hausmann, Charles J. ... Milwaukee, WI
Hausmann, David R. ... Morristown, NJ
Hausmann, Edwin D. ... Los Angeles, CA
Hausmann, Frank G., Jr. ... Albany, OR
Hausmann, Frank W., Jr.
Grosse Pointe Farms, MI
Hausmann, Karl F. ... Everett, WA
Hausmann & McNally, S.C. ... Milwaukee, WI
Hausmann, Ronald C. ... San Francisco, CA
Hausmann, W. Dirk ... Menomonee Falls, WI
Hausman-Smith, Barbara ... Lexington, KY
Hausner, Christina L. ... Lancaster, PA
Hausner, Robert ... Bellmore, NY
Hausrath, David L. ... Covington, KY
Hausrath, Les A. ... Oakland, CA
Hauss, Karen ... Staten Island, NY
Hauss, Rudolph C. ... Eastpointe, MI
Hausser, Robert ... San Antonio, TX
Haussermann, Arthur H.
Wellesley Hills, MA
Haussermann, Oscar W., Jr. ... Boston, MA
Haussman, Theodore F., Jr.
Philadelphia, PA
Hausten, Lisa A. ... Chicago, IL
Hausthor, Brett W. ... Great Neck, NY
Hauswirth, Bradley D. ... St. Paul, MN
Hauswirth, Scott J. ... San Francisco, CA
Haut, Andrew R. ... Bakersfield, CA
Haut, Annette Ruth Ciavarella ... Cadiz, OH
Haut, Irwin H. ... New York, NY
Haut, Lawrence R. ... New York, NY
Haut, Nathan ... Santa Ana, CA
Haut, Robert A. ... Santa Monica, CA
Haut, Sharon G. ... Roslyn Heights, NY
Haut, Shellie L. ... Bay City, MI
Haut, Susan ... Big Rapids, MI
Haut, Tina Kowalsky ... New York, NY
Haut, William D. ... Elkhart, IN
Hautaluoma, Jodi L. ... San Diego, CA
Hautanen, Sandra L. ... Boston, MA
Hauth, Jane Majors ... Birmingham, AL
Hauth & Lee, LLC ... Birmingham, AL
Hauth, Robert F. ... Olympia, WA
Hautman, Joseph W. ... Minneapolis, MN
Hautman, Kenneth J. ... McLean, VA
Hautot, James J., Jr. ... Lafayette, LA
Hautzinger, James E. ... Denver, CO
Hautzinger, Richard J. ... Omaha, NE
Hauver, Elwood E. ... Hagerstown, MD
Hauver, Terence L. ... New Orleans, LA
Havach, James M. ... Cleveland, OH
Havard, Frederick
National Labor Relations Board,
Office of the General Counsel, GV
Havard, James J.
Environmental Protection Agency,
Office of the General Counsel, GV
Havard, Michael A. ... Beaumont, TX
Havas, David B. ... Layton, UT
Ogden, UT
Havas, Edward B. ... Salt Lake City, UT
Havas, John ... Hershey, PA
Havas, Tim ... Monticello, NY
Havasy, Edward S. ... Port Washington, NY
Havazelet, Revital D. ... New York, NY
Havekost, Roger N. ... San Antonio, TX
Havel, Craig S. ... West Roxbury, MA
Havel, Dennis G. ... Louisville, KY
Havel, Derek R. ... Los Angeles, CA
Havel, Paul L. ... Portland, OR
Havel, Richard W. ... Los Angeles, CA
Havelaar, Tamara S. ... Phoenix, AZ
Haveles, H. Peter, Jr. ... New York, NY
Haveles, Harry P. ... Boston, MA
Havelka, David P.
Department Of Veterans Affairs,
Board of Veterans Appeals, GV
Havelock, John E. ... Anchorage, AK
Havely, Katherine A.
Federal Trade Commission, GV
Haveman, John A. ... Minneapolis, MN
Havemann, Carol A. ... Houston, TX
Havemann, William L. ... Dayton, OH
Haven, Aaron Alan ... Portsmouth, OH
Haven, David S. ... McLean, VA
Haven, Gail Reizenstein
United States Court Of Appeals District Of
Columbia Circuit, GV
Haven, Milton M. ... Poughkeepsie, NY
Haven, Nancy C.
Commodity Futures Trading Commission,
Division of Enforcement, GV
Haven & Oddy ... Athol, MA
Haven, Peter T. ... Los Angeles, CA
Haven, Robert R. ... Athol, MA
Haven, Robert R., Jr. ... Athol, MA
Haven, Ronald R. ... Sacramento, CA
Haven, Russ ... Albany, NY
Haven, Thomas E. ... Atherton, CA
Havener, Charles R. ... Dayton, OH
Havener, Darrell L. ... Kansas City, MO
Havener, Kathleen B. ... Cleveland, OH
Havener, Lance P. ... Shreveport, LA
Havener, Paula-Jean ... New Windsor, NY

Havener, Thomas G. ... Cleveland, OH
Havenith, Karl B. ... Chicago, IL
Havens, Catherine M. ... West Hartford, CT
Havens, Charles W., III (P.C.)
Washington, DC
Havens, Cloyd E., II ... Glendora, CA
Havens, Deborah L. ... Trenton, MO
Havens, Denise K. ... Memphis, TN
Havens, Donald E. ... Upper Darby, PA
Havens and Havens ... Storm Lake, IA
Havens, Hunter S. ... Cleveland, OH
Havens, James R. ... Columbus, OH
Havens, John D. ... Canon City, CO
Havens, Keith R. ... Chevy Chase, MD
Havens & Lombard ... Flushing, NY
New York, NY
Havens, Lyle E. ... Davis, CA
Havens, Marcia André ... Churchville, NY
Havens, Mark M. ... Lewiston, ID
Havens, Megali S. D. B. ... Sacramento, CA
Havens, Nancy G. ... Plainfield, IN
Havens, Oliver H. ... Hobe Sound, FL
Havens, Paul D. ... Storm Lake, IA
Havens, Philip E. ... Storm Lake, IA
Havens, Phillip D. ... Daytona Beach, FL
Havens, Rex A. ... Bloomington, IL
Havens, Robert S. ... Marina Del Rey, CA
Havens, Suzanne L. ... Los Angeles, CA
Havens, Sylvia ... Los Angeles, CA
Havens, Terry C. ... Rockville, MD
Havens, Thomas C. ... New York, NY
Havens Willis, LLC ... Columbus, OH
Havens-Cortes, Lisa L. ... Temple, TX
Haver, Dennis T. ... Charlotte, NC
Haver, Kohel M. ... Portland, OR
Haver, Mark L. ... Defiance, OH
Haver, Ronald J. ... Pittsburgh, PA
Haverberg, Blake D. ... Honolulu, HI
Havercamp, James R. ... Davenport, IA
Havercamp, Steven J. ... Davenport, IA
Havercroft, Jeffrey Venton
Birmingham, AL
Haverfield, Craig M. ... Fort Lauderdale, FL
Haverfield, William T., II ... Fort Myers, FL
Haverkamp, Albert E. ... San Diego, CA
Haverkamp, Brinker, Rebold & Riehl Co.,
L.P.A. ... Cincinnati, OH
Haverkamp, Bryce ... Garden City, KS
Haverkamp, Gary J. ... Cincinnati, OH
Haverkamp, James A. ... Alameda, CA
Haverkamp, Janelle M. ... Gainesville, TX
Haverkamp, Jennifer A.
Executive Office Of The President,
Office of the U.S. Trade Representative, GV
Haverkamp, Michael F. ... Cincinnati, OH
Haverkamp, Ralph E. ... Sacramento, CA
Haverkamp, Robert J. ... Columbus, OH
Haverkamp, Roy J. ... Overland Park, KS
Haverkos, Harry C. ... Cincinnati, OH
Haverkos, Sue A. ... South Bend, IN
Haverlah, Edward E. ... Pleasanton, TX
Haverlah & Hart ... Pleasanton, TX
Haverly, Harry C. ... Hastings, NE
Haverly, Jon K. ... Sioux Falls, SD
Haverly, Martin ... Wilmington, DE
Havermann, Donald L. ... Washington, DC
Havern, Robert A., III ... Arlington, MA
Havers, Michael J. ... Seattle, WA
Haverson, Jeffrey G. ... Virginia Beach, VA
Haverson, Michael J. ... Philadelphia, PA
Haverson, Shelby L. ... Frazer, PA
Haverstick, Amanda D. ... New York, NY
Haverstick, Barry E. ... Lancaster, PA
Haverstick, George ... San Diego, CA
Haverstick, Jessica Whalen ... Short Hills, NJ
Haverstock, Bell & Pitman ... Murray, KY
Haverstock, Charles B. ... St. Louis, MO
Haverstock, Garrett and Roberts
St. Louis, MO
Haverstock, Gary R. ... Murray, KY
Haverstock, Henry W., Jr. ... Edina, MN
Haverstock and Owens, L.L.P.
Palo Alto, CA
Haverstock, Thomas B. ... Palo Alto, CA
Haverstrom, Lois Ann ... Seattle, WA
Haverty, Alan W. ... Menlo Park, CA
Haverty & Feeney ... Plymouth, MA
Haverty, Jane M. ... Atlanta, GA
Haverty, John W. ... Plymouth, MA
Haverty, Kevin ... Haddonfield, NJ
Haverty, Matthew C. ... Overland Park, KS
Haverty, Steven J. ... Darlington, WI
Haverty, Tim S. ... Kansas City, MO
Haves, Stanley ... Miami, FL
Haveson, Hal K. ... Princeton, NJ
Haveson, Laurence D. ... San Jose, CA
Haveson and Otis ... Princeton, NJ
Havey, Arthur W. ... Cambridge, MA
Havey, Brian R. ... Chicago, IL
Havey, C. Tyler ... Philadelphia, PA
Havey, James M. ... Toms River, NJ
Havey, Laura Katheryn ... Jacksonville, FL
Havian, Eric R. ... San Francisco, CA
Havice, J. Lancaster ... Bartow, FL
Havighorst, Arthur P., II ... Morristown, NJ
Havighurst, Alan W. ... Cleveland, OH
Havighurst, Clark C. ... Durham, NC
Havilan, Karen A. ... Burlingame, CA
Haviland, Bancroft D. ... Philadelphia, PA
Haviland, Betty ... Santa Monica, CA
Haviland, Charles R., Jr. ... Albany, NY
Haviland, Charles S. ... Westwood, KS
Haviland, Dana ... Palo Alto, CA
Haviland, Donald E., Jr. ... Philadelphia, PA
Haviland, Gail M. ... Missoula, MT
Haviland, James M. ... Charleston, WV
Haviland, James T., II ... New London, CT
Haviland, John F., Jr. ... Dayton, OH

Haviland, Kathleen Mary
San Francisco, CA
Haviland, Paul W. ... Medford, OR
Haviland, Peter L. ... Los Angeles, CA
Haviland, Richard D. ... New London, CT
Haviland, Robert W. ... Flint, MI
Haviland, Sam Z. ... Chicago, IL
Charlotte, NC
Haviland, Warren E. ... San Diego, CA
Havill, James F. ... Washington, IN
Havill, James F., Atty. at Law, Prof. Corp.
Washington, IN
Havins, Janice M. ... Houston, TX
Havins, John W. ... Houston, TX
Havins & O'Dea, P.C. ... Houston, TX
Havins, Weldon E. ... Las Vegas, NV
Havird, Pamela E. ... La Jolla, CA
Havis, Andrew Lee ... Silver Spring, MD
Haviza, Peter D. ... Winchester, IN
Havkin, Stella Anne ... Woodland Hills, CA
Havkins, Abraham E. ... New York, NY
Havlena, Thomas J. ... Los Osos, CA
Havlicek, Franklin J. ... Washington, DC
Havlicek, Glenn T. ... Park Forest, IL
Havlick, Donald G. ... Houston, TX
Havlick, Milton E., Jr. ... Tomball, TX
Havlick, Scott ... Boulder, CO
Denver, CO
Havlik, Mark D. ... Boca Raton, FL
Havlik, Michael Damien ... Omaha, NE
Havlisch, Hal B. ... Fresno, CA
Havluciyan, Mikael ... Irvine, CA
Havn, Scott S. ... Littleton, CO
Havner, Kyle Wayne ... Pine Bluff, AR
Havran, Jeffrey E. ... Scranton, PA
Havranek, Beatrice Elizabeth ... Kingston, NY
Havranek, John F. ... Fremont, NE
Havre, Henry ... Los Angeles, CA
Havrilak, Sandra L. ... Fairfax, VA
Havrilesko, Michael K. ... Rockford, IL
Havron, James C. ... Nashville, TN
Havron, James T. ... Goodlettsville, TN
Haw, Alexander M. ... Waco, TX
Haw, George E., Jr. ... Richmond, VA
Haw, John S. ... Costa Mesa, CA
Haw, Stuart M. ... St. Louis, MO
Hawaii Law Clinic ... Kailua-Kona, HI
Hawal, William ... Cleveland, OH
Hawari, Kenneth G. ... Dallas, TX
Hawash, Michael A. ... Houston, TX
Hawbaker, Donald F. ... Dallas, TX
Hawbaker, Janice M. ... Chambersburg, PA
Hawbaker, Thomas A. ... Newport Beach, CA
Hawbecker, Hale W.
Environmental Protection Agency,
Office of the General Counsel, GV
Hawbecker, Karen
Department Of The Interior,
Office of the Solicitor, GV
Hawbecker, Michael L. ... Sacramento, CA
Hawbecker-Rios, William J.
San Antonio, TX
Hawco, Kenneth B. ... New York, NY
Hawe, Kathe M. ... Seattle, WA
Hawekotte, Angela ... Pasadena, CA
Hawekotte, Kim B. ... Omaha, NE
Hawekotte, Robert S., Jr. ... Long Beach, CA
Hawekotte, Thomas J., (P.C.) ... Chicago, IL
Hawes, Albert C., Jr. ... Covington, KY
Hawes, Amanda ... San Jose, CA
Hawes, Benjamin W., Jr. ... Owensboro, KY
Hawes, Brian E. ... Campbell, CA
Hawes, C. Erik ... Minneapolis, MN
Hawes, Charles A. ... Toledo, OH
Hawes, Daniel L. ... Fairfax, VA
Hawes, Douglas W., (P.C.) ... New York, NY
Hawes, Edna E. ... Decatur, GA
Hawes, Eric Everett ... Woodland Hills, CA
Hawes, Gregg W. ... Baltimore, MD
Hawes, Hardin W. ... Springfield, IL
Hawes, James E. ... Laguna Beach, CA
Hawes, Kinne F. ... Seattle, WA
Hawes, Lesley Anne ... Los Angeles, CA
Hawes, Leslie Anne ... Boston, MA
Hawes, Michael A. ... Houston, TX
Hawes, Nina R. ... Kingsville, MD
Hawes, Peyton S., Jr. ... Atlanta, GA
Hawes, Philip ... Santa Barbara, CA
Hawes, R. Kyle ... Houston, TX
Hawes, Richard K., Jr. ... Westport, MA
Hawes, Sheila Phillips ... Omaha, NE
Hawes, Steven John ... New York, NY
Hawes, Sue ... Santa Barbara, CA
Hawes, Taylor E. C. ... Silverthorne, CO
Hawfield, W. B., Jr. ... Charlotte, NC
Hawgood, William Shepard, II
Phoenix, AZ
Hawie, Edward J. ... Atlanta, GA
Hawk & Associates, Law Offices of
Osage Beach, MO
Hawk, Barry E. (IBA) ... New York, NY
Hawk, Beverly ... Dayton, OH
Hawk, Boyce E. ... Little Rock, AR
Hawk & Bristley ... Fremont, OH
Hawk, Charles C. ... Grand Rapids, MI
Hawk, Christopher ... Hermosa Beach, CA
Hawk, Christopher M. ... Dayton, OH
Hawk, Clarence W. ... Osage Beach, MO
Hawk, David K. ... Fort Wayne, IN
Hawk, Dennis J. ... Los Angeles, CA
Hawk Firm, The ... Augusta, GA
Hawk, Galen D. ... Springfield, PA
Hawk, Haynie, Gallmeyer & Chickedantz
Fort Wayne, IN
Hawk, Howard G. ... Arab, AL
Hawk, Jacque Dulaine ... Augusta, GA
Hawk, James E., Jr. ... St. Louis, MO
Hawk, James M. ... Olympia, WA

Hawk, Janet Corey ... Lima, OH
Hawk, Johanne L. ... Portland, ME
Hawk, John T. ... St. Louis, MO
Hawk, Mary Ruth ... Sarasota, FL
Hawk & Mattingly ... St. Louis, MO
Hawk, Melvin R. ... Akron, OH
Hawk, Michael ... Dallas, TX
Hawk, Morris L. ... Cleveland, OH
Hawk, Richard E. ... San Jacinto, CA
Hawk, Robert B. ... Palo Alto, CA
Hawk, Robert D. ... Merrillville, IN
Hawk, Robert D., Jr. ... Merrillville, IN
Hawk, Robert F. ... Butler, PA
Hawk, Samuel David Tigert
Charlottesville, VA
Hawk, Tracey E. ... Seattle, WA
Hawk, Victor C. ... Augusta, GA
Hawk, Victor, P.C. ... Augusta, GA
Hawk, Wilbert, Jr. ... Dayton, OH
Hawk, Wynee E. ... Annapolis, MD
Hawk, Zelda J. ... Gainesville, FL
Hawke, Constance S. ... Solon, OH
Hawke, Daniel M. ... Washington, DC
Hawke, Katherine A. ... Boston, MA
Hawke, Lee Allen ... Trinidad, CO
Hawke, Nancie Divilbiss ... Columbia, MO
Hawke, Richard D. ... St. Paul, MN
Hawke, Roger J. ... New York, NY
Hawke, Sharon L. ... Polson, MT
Hawke, Stephanie D. ... Raleigh, NC
Hawke, Stephen D. ... Jefferson City, MO
Hawke, William T. ... Harrisburg, PA
Hawken, Kevin P. ... Chicago, IL
Hawkens, E. Roy ... Department of Justice,
Civil Division, GV
Hawker, Heather Anne ... Denver, CO
Hawker, Mary Stake ... St. Louis, MO
Hawker, Norman ... Lansing, MI
Hawker, Paula Jeanne ... Salt Lake City, UT
Hawker, Thomas L. ... Atlanta, GA
Hawkes, Anne E. ... Washington, DC
Hawkes, Christina I.K. ... Mount Olive, NJ
Hawkes, Clarence E. ... Camden, NY
Hawkes, Diane E. ... Los Angeles, CA
Hawkes, Donald G. ... Dallas, TX
Hawkes, Emmet J. ... Santa Barbara, CA
Hawkes, F. Townsend ... Tallahassee, FL
Hawkes, Gregory L. ... Tualatin, OR
Hawkes, Jane V. ... Worcester, MA
Hawkes, Jeffrey J. ... Binghamton, NY
Hawkes, John H. ... Bangor, ME
Hawkes, John W. ... Santa Rosa, CA
Hawkes, Joseph Edward ... Pomona, CA
Hawkes & Kennedy, P.A. ... Jupiter, FL
Hawkes, Kenneth G. ... Miami Beach, FL
Hawkes, Lowell N. ... Pocatello, ID
Hawkes, Mary B. ... Stratham, NH
Hawkes, Randy ... Dover, NH
Hawkes, Robert T. ... Treasury Department,
Internal Revenue Service, GV
Hawkes, Roger H. ... Seattle, WA
Hawkes, Susan ... Augusta, ME
Hawkes, Timothy J. ... Jersey City, NJ
Hawkes, William S. ... Boston, MA
Hawkes, Winslow D., III ... Jupiter, FL
Hawkesworth, J. Arthur, Jr. ... Ocala, FL
Hawkey, G. Michael ... Boston, MA
Hawkey, Harold R. ... Verona, NJ
Hawkey, Philip A. ... Kettering, OH
Hawk Gutman, Carrie ... Fort Wayne, IN
Hawkins, A. David ... Rustburg, VA
Hawkins, Alfred E. ... Daytona Beach, FL
Hawkins, Alicia M. ... Washington, DC
Hawkins, Allan ... Midland, TX
Hawkins, Allen R. ... Honolulu, HI
Hawkins, Amber M. ... Minneapolis, MN
Hawkins, Ann Ainsworth ... Houston, TX
Hawkins, Ann Marie ... Cleveland, OH
Hawkins, Armis E. ... Houston, MS
Hawkins, Ashton ... New York, NY
Hawkins, Barry C. ... Stamford, CT
Hawkins, Bernard F., Jr. ... Columbia, SC
Hawkins, Beth Rauer ... Charleston, WV
Hawkins, Bethany E. ... Bloomfield Hills, MI
Hawkins • Blick ... San Jose, CA
Hawkins & Boisvert ... Bridgton, ME
Portland, ME
Hawkins, Boyd J. ... Salt Lake City, UT
Hawkins, Brent ... Salt Lake City, UT
Hawkins, Brent A. ... Chicago, IL
Hawkins, Brian C. ... Bridgton, ME
Hawkins, Burcher & Boester, P.C.
Hampton, VA
Hawkins, Calvin D. ... Gary, IN
Hawkins, Carl S. ... Provo, UT
Hawkins, Carmen D. ... Van Nuys, CA
Hawkins, Carol A. Burkett ... Atlanta, GA
Hawkins, Carol Ann Burkett ... Maywood, IL
Hawkins, Charles A. ... Atlanta, GA
Hawkins, Charles F. ... San Jose, CA
Hawkins, Charles J., II ... Orlando, FL
Hawkins, Charles L. ... Minneapolis, MN
Hawkins, Charles W. ... Richton Park, IL
Hawkins, Christopher D. ... Concord, NH
Hawkins, Claude S., Jr. ... Fort Smith, AR
Hawkins & Co., L.P.A. ... Cleveland, OH
Hawkins, Connie Lynn ... Austin, TX
Hawkins, Corrine Monnett ... Dallas, TX
Hawkins, Cynthia L. ... Springdale, AR
Hawkins, D. Lamar ... Phoenix, AZ
Hawkins, Daniel C. ... Sterling, IL
Hawkins, Darrell Curtiss ... Batavia, OH
Hawkins, Daryl ... Herington, KS
Hawkins, Daryl G. ... Columbia, SC
Hawkins, David ... New York, NY
Hawkins, David ... Bellevue, WA
Hawkins, David A. ... Helena, MT
Hawkins, David C. ... Tallahassee, FL

Haxton, Harold K. ... Muskogee, OK
Haxton, Manford R. ... Mount Airy, NC
Haxton, Timothy L. ... Eureka, CA
Hay, Alys ... Cupertino, CA
Hay, Andrew R. ... Tacoma, WA
Hay, Brandin ... Pueblo, CO
Hay, Carol A. ... Pittsboro, NC
Hay, Cedric P. ... Hudson, FL
Hay, Charles L. ... Meridian, ID
Hay, Charles R. ... Topeka, KS
Hay & Dailey, A Professional Association
Boston, MA
Hay, Dana Handy ... Charlotte, NC
Hay, David B. ... Scottsdale, AZ
Hay, David S. ... Indianapolis, IN
Hay, David S. ... Virginia Beach, VA
Hay, Deanne Watts ... Topeka, KS
Hay, Deirdre L. ... Washington, DC
Hay, Dennis L. ... Tracy, CA
Hay, Doris Hogan ... Cleveland, OH
Hay, Edward C., Jr. ... Asheville, NC
Hay, Elizabeth L. ... Houston, TX
Hay, Frae E. ... Rock Springs, WY
Hay, Frederick B. ... House of Representatives, Committee on House Administration, GV
Hay, G. Kenneth ... New Albany, IN
Hay, Harold F. ... Flushing, NY
Hay, Howard C. ... Costa Mesa, CA
Hay, James C. ... Horseshoe Bay, TX
Hay, James D. ... Saddle River, NJ
Hay, James E. ... Warren, NJ
Hay, James I. ... Suwanee, GA
Hay, Jeffrey S. ... Charlotte, NC
Hay, Jennifer A. ... Washington, DC
Hay, Jess T. ... Dallas, TX
Hay, John (A Professional Law Corporation)
Montecito, CA
Hay, John A., Jr. ... San Angelo, TX
Hay, John, (A Professional Law Corporation)
Montecito, CA
Hay, John J. ... New York, NY
Hay, John L. ... Phoenix, AZ
Hay, John L. ... Seattle, WA
Hay, Jonathan L. ... Jacksonville, FL
Hay, Jonathan M. ... Framingham, MA
Hay, Karen H. ... Denver, CO
Hay, Karl S. ... Akron, OH
Hay, Kirkham E. ... Portland, OR
Hay, Linda J. ... Chicago, IL
Hay, Lorin D. ... Virginia Beach, VA
Hay, Malcolm ... Birmingham, MI
Hay, Margaret McColl ... Long Beach, CA
Hay, Mary E. ... Champaign, IL
Hay, Mary Michele ... Macon, GA
Hay, Michael J. ... Lawrenceville, GA
Hay, Nancy E. ... New York, NY
Hay, Nick ... Minneapolis, MN
Hay, Norman E. ... Cannelton, IN
Hay & O'Rourke, P.C. ... Lansing, MI
Hay, Pamela A. ... Cambridge, MA
Hay, Richard ... Somerset, KY
Hay, Robert N., Jr. ... New York, NY
Hay, Rodger K. ... Warren, IL
Hay, Ted B., III ... Clarksville, TN
Hay, Thomas H. ... Lansing, MI
Hay, Thomas S. ... Minneapolis, MN
Hay, Timothy D. ... Carson City, NV
Hay, Walter ... Brunswick, OH
Hay, William L. ... Mount Clemens, MI
Hay, William P., Jr. ... Farmville, VA
Hayakawa, Hideyo ... New York, NY
Hayase, Helen M. ... Los Angeles, CA
Hayase, Paul H. ... Torrance, CA
Hayashi, Alice K. ... San Francisco, CA
Hayashi, Arthur K. ... Spokane, WA
Hayashi, Carolyn E. ... Honolulu, HI
Hayashi, Derwin ... Honolulu, HI
Hayashi, Elizabeth H. ... St. Louis, MO
Hayashi, Gary T. ... Honolulu, HI
Hayashi, Joe ... San Jose, CA
Hayashi, Junie ... Honolulu, HI
Hayashi, Kazuichiro ... Los Angeles, CA
Hayashi, Leslie Ann ... Honolulu, HI
Hayashi, Roberta S. ... San Jose, CA
Hayashi, William P. ... Boulder, CO
Hayashi, Yoshimi ... Honolulu, HI
Hayashida, Joel J. ... Oakland, CA
Hayashida, John E. ... Tustin, CA
Hayball, Carolyn J. ... Houston, TX
Hayber, Richard E. ... Hartford, CT
Haycock & Associates ... Sacramento, CA
Haycock, Cynthia J. ... Pittsburgh, PA
Haycock, D. Jack ... Sacramento, CA
Haycock, Don H. ... Los Angeles, CA
Haycock & Neidinger ... Pittsburgh, PA
Haycock, Steven L. ... Department of the Navy, Office of the Judge Advocate General, GV
Haycook, Heidi Jo ... Orlando, FL
Haycook, Karina ... West Palm Beach, FL
Haycox, Rolanda Moore ... Indianapolis, IN
Haycox, Sue E. ... Fort Wayne, IN
Haycox, Terry James ... Nashville, TN
Haycraft, Don K. ... New Orleans, LA
Haydanek, Ronald E. ... Philadelphia, PA
Haydel, Augustavia J. ... Los Angeles, CA
Haydel, Douglas A. ... Stockton, CA
Haydel, Leslie Sudbury ... Cary, NC
Haydel, Shannon E. ... Metairie, LA
Haydel, Victor J., III ... San Francisco, CA
Hayden, Barbara A. ... Superior, WI
Hayden, Beverly S. ... Nashville, TN
Hayden, Bruce E. ... Phoenix, AZ
Hayden & Butler, P.S.C. ... Lexington, KY
Hayden, C. Donald
Department Of Veterans Affairs, Board of Veterans Appeals, GV
Hayden, Calvin E. ... Jacksonville, FL
Hayden, Cameron W. ... Bismarck, ND
Hayden, Carl T. ... Elmira, NY
Hayden, Carol Mills ... Memphis, TN
Hayden, Chad R. ... Henrietta, NY
Rochester, NY
Hayden, Charles ... Fairless Hills, PA
Hayden, Charles J. ... Newark, NJ
Hayden, Charles M. ... Federal Way, WA
Hayden, Charles W. ... San Jose, CA
Hayden, Christopher G. ... Houston, TX
Hayden, Clifton W. ... Bozeman, MT
Hayden, D. Wade ... San Antonio, TX
Hayden, David L. ... Fayetteville, NC
Hayden, Debra Evans ... Williamsville, NY
Hayden, Dennis D. ... Santa Ana, CA
Hayden, Dennis R. ... Baltimore, MD
Hayden, Derek L. ... Amsterdam, NY
Hayden, Diane DePriest
Department of Defense, Defense Legal Services Agency, GV
Hayden, Donald J. ... Miami, FL
Hayden, Donald S. ... Memphis, TN
Hayden, Douglas J. ... New York, NY
Hayden, Edgar H., Jr. ... Modesto, CA
Hayden, Facciolo & Millsaps
Amelia Island Plantation, FL
Fernandina Beach, FL
Jacksonville, FL
Hayden, Frances J. ... Hollywood, CA
Hayden, G. Price ... Baltimore, MD
Hayden, Gary L. ... Dearborn, MI
Hayden, George A. ... Scituate, MA
Hayden, George F. ... Westfield, NJ
Hayden, Glenn M. ... Woodland Hills, CA
Hayden, Henry E. ... Owensboro, KY
Hayden, Howard B. ... Memphis, TN
Hayden, Hugh M. ... Riverwoods, IL
Hayden, J. Howard ... Austin, TX
Hayden, J. Patrick ... Charlotte, NC
Hayden, Jack W. ... Houston, TX
Hayden, James F. ... New York, NY
Hayden, James G. ... Williamsville, NY
Hayden, James L. ... Lexington, KY
Hayden, James R. ... Hattiesburg, MS
Hayden, James T. ... Elmira, NY
Hayden, Jan Marie ... New Orleans, LA
Hayden, Jerry M. ... North Miami, FL
Hayden, Joan N. ... Parsippany, NJ
Hayden, John A., III ... Towson, MD
Hayden, John F. ... Washington, DC
Hayden, John J. ... Morristown, NJ
Hayden, John R. ... Denver, CO
Hayden, John W., Jr. ... Lacey, WA
Hayden, Jon E. ... Boston, MA
Hayden, Jonathan P. ... San Francisco, CA
Hayden, Joseph A., Jr. (P.C.)
Weehawken, NJ
Hayden & Kassel, A Law Corporation
Woodland Hills, CA
Hayden, Katharine Sweeney ... Newark, NJ
Hayden, Kathryn A. ... Monterey Park, CA
Hayden, Kelly A. ... Chicago, IL
Chicago Heights, IL
Hayden, Kenneth M. ... Versailles, MO
Hayden, Kevin T. ... Santa Ana, CA
Hayden, Kimberly K. ... Montpelier, VT
St. Johnsbury, VT
Hayden, Lauren L. Shanks ... Priest River, ID
Hayden, Lawrence E., Jr.
Jacksonville Beach, FL
Hayden, Leeon E. ... Lakewood, CO
Hayden, Leeon E., P.C. ... Lakewood, CO
Hayden, Lovell E., III ... Monroe, LA
Hayden, Margaret M. ... Newark, NJ
Hayden, Marian J. ... Frankfort, KY
Hayden, Mark ... Chicago, IL
Hayden, Mark T. ... Covington, KY
Hayden, Mary C. ... Houston, TX
Hayden, Mary St Clair ... Novi, MI
Hayden, Maynard J.V. ... Des Moines, IA
Hayden, Melva J. ... New York, NY
Hayden, Michael ... Palo Alto, CA
Hayden, Michael ... Kent, WA
Hayden, Michael A. ... Arlington, VA
Hayden, Michael J. ... Evansville, IN
Hayden and Milliken, P.A.
Cape Canaveral, FL
Miami, FL
Tampa, FL
Hayden, Moore & Ryan ... Monroe, LA
Hayden, Patricia L. ... Victoria, TX
Hayden, Patrick L. ... Norfolk, VA
Hayden, Patrick M. ... Sedro Woolley, WA
Hayden, Paul T. ... Indianapolis, IN
Hayden, Perle & Silber ... Weehawken, NJ
Hayden, Peter Ridgeway ... Fort Lee, VA
Hayden, Raymond P. ... New York, NY
Hayden, Reginald M., Jr.
Cape Canaveral, FL
Miami, FL
Tampa, FL
Hayden, Richard C. ... Mattoon, IL
Hayden, Richard J. ... Spokane, WA
Hayden, Richard J., P.S. ... Spokane, WA
Hayden, Richard T. ... Washington, DC
Hayden, Robert C. ... Los Angeles, CA
Hayden, Robert Emmet ... San Francisco, CA
Hayden, Robert J. ... Coram, NY
Hayden, Robert W. ... Oklahoma City, OK
Hayden, Roger A., II ... Bethesda, MD
Hayden, Rosemary Jennifer ... Rosedale, NY
Hayden, Scott R. ... St. Louis, MO
Hayden, Stephen A. ... Henderson, KY
Hayden, Steven T. ... San Jose, CA
Hayden, Steven Todd ... Dallas, TX
Hayden, Susan C. ... Sacramento, CA
Hayden, Suzanne J. ... Canonsburg, PA
Hayden, Ted M. ... Memphis, TN
Hayden, Thomas A.P. ... Pittsburgh, PA
Hayden, Thomas C., Jr. ... La Plata, MD
Hayden, Thomas C., Jr., P.A.
La Plata, MD
Hayden, Thomas N. ... Superior, WI
Hayden, Thomas P. ... Chicago, IL
Hayden, Todd K. ... Chicago, IL
Chicago Heights, IL
Hayden, Vanessa C. ... Harrisonville, MO
Hayden, Walter Charles, III ... Clanton, AL
Hayden, William ... Columbus, OH
Hayden, William H. ... Toledo, OR
Hayden, William K. ... Kansas City, MO
Hayden, William R. ... Phoenix, AZ
Hayden, William T. ... Cincinnati, OH
Hayden, William T., L.P.A.
Cincinnati, OH
Hayden, Xavier P. ... Philadelphia, PA
Hayden-Wood, Pamela A. ... Nashville, TN
Haydett, Gordon Andrew ... Detroit, MI
Haydock, Roger S. ... St. Paul, MN
Haydon, Ben T., Jr. ... Louisville, KY
Haydon, Brian C. ... Sacramento, CA
Haydon, Charles ... New York, NY
Haydon, David J. ... Kansas City, MO
Haydon & Dockter ... Louisville, KY
Haydon, George R., Jr. ... Kansas City, MO
Haydon, John B. ... Milwaukee, WI
Haydon, Keith L., Jr. ... Clayton, CA
Haydon, Peter S. ... East Greenwich, RI
Haydon, Steven R. ... Tucson, AZ
Haydon, Straci & Cooper ... New York, NY
Haydon, Trevor A., Jr. ... Concord, MA
Haydu, Eugene P. ... Sacramento, CA
Haydu, Gary ... Chatham, NJ
Haydu, Lori Ann ... Smyrna, GA
Hayduchok, George L. ... Moorestown, NJ
Hayduk, Andrews & Hypnar, P.C.
Detroit, MI
Pontiac, MI
Hayduk, Joseph Cole ... Denver, CO
Hayduk, Kenneth R. ... Washington, DC
Hayduk, Mark S. ... Detroit, MI
Haye, Clifford S. ... New York, NY
Haye, Edward ... New Hyde Park, NY
Haye, Julia R. ... Los Angeles, CA
Hayeck, Ernest S. ... Worcester, MA
Hayeck, Paul G.
Commodity Futures Trading Commission, Division of Enforcement, GV
Hayek, C. Peter ... Iowa City, IA
Hayek, Carolyn J. ... Federal Way, WA
Hayek, Elias J. ... Sacramento, CA
Hayek, Hayek & Brown, L.L.P.
Iowa City, IA
Hayek, Jill Christine ... Richmond, VA
Hayek, John W. ... Iowa City, IA
Hayek, Kathy L. ... Memphis, TN
Hayek, Kristi A. ... Milwaukee, WI
Hayek, Matthew J. ... Chicago, IL
Hayek, Patricia ... Hopatcong, NJ
Hayek, Thomas J. ... St. Louis, MO
Hayen, David E. ... Santa Monica, CA
Hayenga, John M. ... Salem, OR
Hayenga, Wayne A. ... Bryan, TX
Hayer, George J. ... Greenfield, MA
Hayers, Paul H. ... Electra, TX
Hayes, A. Dawn ... Tampa, FL
Hayes, A. Lee ... Albany, GA
Hayes, Abbott S., Jr. ... Gainesville, GA
Hayes, Albert J. ... Columbia, MD
Hayes, Alex B. ... Seattle, WA
Hayes, Allan M. ... Royal Oak, MI
Hayes, Amy E. ... Salt Lake City, UT
Hayes, Andrew W. ... Armonk, NY
Hayes, Angela M. ... New York, NY
Hayes, Ann Marie ... New York, NY
Hayes, Anna R. ... Raleigh, NC
Hayes, Anne M. ... Fort Lauderdale, FL
Hayes, Anne Miyako ... Sacramento, CA
Hayes, Anne S. ... Richmond, VA
Hayes, Anthony C. ... Columbia, SC
Hayes, Armstead Lester, III
Montgomery, AL
Hayes, Arthur ... Nashville, TN
Hayes, Arthur H., III ... New York, NY
Hayes, B. Douglas ... Goshen, IN
Hayes, B. Drennan ... Rock Hill, SC
Hayes, Ben J. ... St. Petersburg, FL
Hayes, Benjamin H. ... Fairmont, WV
Hayes, Bill ... Boise, ID
Hayes, Brandon L. ... Nashville, TN
Hayes, Brett L. ... Costa Mesa, CA
Hayes, Brian E. ... Springfield, MA
Hayes, Brian K. ... Madison, WI
Hayes, Brian T. ... Monticello, FL
Hayes, Brian T., P.A. ... Monticello, FL
Hayes, Bryan H. ... Louisville, KY
Hayes, Burgain G. ... Austin, TX
Hayes, Byron, Jr. ... Los Angeles, CA
Hayes, C. Kevin ... Baton Rouge, LA
Hayes, C. W. & H. M., P.A.
Dover-Foxcroft, ME
Hayes, Camilla Lynn ... Orlando, FL
Hayes, Carl E. ... San Luis Obispo, CA
Hayes, Carol Crofoot ... Atlanta, GA
Hayes, Charles A. ... Eunice, LA
Hayes, Charles J. ... Norwell, MA
Hayes, Charles R. ... San Diego, CA
Hayes, Charlotte A. ... Atlanta, GA
Hayes, Chester B. ... Clayton, MO
Hayes, Chester F. ... Mountain View, CA
Hayes, Christopher G. ... Denver, CO
Hayes, Christopher G. ... New York, NY
Philadelphia, PA
Hayes, Christopher H. ... Oak Ridge, TN
Hayes, Christopher J. ... San Francisco, CA
Hayes, Christopher J. ... St. Louis, MO
Hayes, Christopher John ... San Diego, CA
Hayes, Christopher T.
West Palm Beach, FL
Hayes, Clifford J. ... Houston, TX
Hayes, Coffey & Berry, P.C. ... Denton, TX
Hayes, Collin I. ... Dallas, TX
Hayes, Cooper, Campbell & Prest
Cadiz, OH
Steubenville, OH
Hayes, Copenhaver & Crider
New Castle, IN
Hayes, Cornelius B. (Neil)
Fort Wayne, IN
Hayes, Cornelius M., III
Corpus Christi, TX
Hayes, Craig ... Nashville, TN
Hayes, Craig P. ... Bellingham, WA
Hayes, D. Michael ... Natchitoches, LA
Hayes, Dale A. ... Las Vegas, NV
Hayes, Dale C. ... Chicago, IL
Hayes, Dale H. ... Morgan City, LA
Hayes, Daniel A., Jr. ... Andover, MA
Hayes, Daniel B. ... Los Angeles, CA
Hayes, Daniel B. ... Clayton, MO
Hayes, Daniel E. ... Bay City, TX
Hayes, Daniel F. ... New York, NY
Hayes, Daniel G. ... Manassas, VA
Hayes, Daniel J. ... Belleville, IL
Hayes, Daniel J. ... Chicago, IL
Hayes, Daniel J. ... Houston, TX
Hayes, Daniel L. ... Spokane, WA
Hayes, Daniel W. ... Columbia, SC
Hayes, Dant & Steiner ... Loogootee, IN
Washington, IN
Hayes, Darin ... Wichita, KS
Hayes, David F. ... Boston, MA
Hayes, David G. ... San Francisco, CA
Hayes, David G. ... Jackson, TN
Hayes, David J. ... Washington, DC
Hayes, David J.A., III ... Overland Park, KS
Hayes, David J. A., Jr. ... Chicago, IL
Hayes, David K. ... Baltimore, MD
Hayes, David L. ... Newport Beach, CA
Hayes, David L. ... Palo Alto, CA
Hayes, David M. ... Detroit, MI
Hayes, David M. ... Syracuse, NY
Hayes, David P. ... Washington, DC
Hayes, David R. ... Buffalo, NY
Hayes, David S. ... Denver, CO
Hayes, David T. ... Cedar Rapids, IA
Hayes, Davis & Dellenbusch, P.L.C.
Grand Rapids, MI
Hayes, D. D. ... Muskogee, OK
Hayes, Dean A. ... Columbia, SC
Hayes, Deborah K. ... Nashville, TN
Hayes, Deborah Lark ... Charlottesville, VA
Hayes, Debra A. ... Oakland, CA
Hayes, Debra Brewer ... Houston, TX
Hayes, Dennis Courtland ... Baltimore, MD
Hayes, Dennis E. ... Jacksonville, FL
Hayes, Dennis J. ... San Diego, CA
Hayes, Dennis J. ... New York, NY
Hayes, Dewey N., Jr. ... Douglas, GA
Hayes, Dewey N., Sr. ... Douglas, GA
Hayes, Diane C. ... Austin, TX
Hayes, Diane R. ... Hartford, CT
Hayes, Dion W. ... Richmond, VA
Hayes, Don M. ... Billings, MT
Hayes, Donald A. ... Valencia, CA
Hayes, Donald E., Jr. ... Norcross, GA
Hayes, Donald Eugene, Jr.
Birmingham, AL
Hayes, Donald J. ... Hartford, CT
Hayes, Donald R. ... Washington, DC
Hayes, Douglas E. ... Bluefield, WV
Hayes, Douglas R. ... Santa Barbara, CA
Hayes, Dwight George ... United States Senate, Senatorial Assistants, GV
Hayes, E. Anne ... Patchogue, NY
Hayes, Edward A. ... New York, NY
Hayes, Edward D. ... Victor, NY
Hayes, Edward J. ... Syracuse, NY
Hayes, Edward J. ... Philadelphia, PA
Hayes, Edward R. ... Des Moines, IA
Hayes, Edward R. ... Boston, MA
Hayes, Edward T. ... New Orleans, LA
Hayes, Edward W. ... New York, NY
Hayes, Edward W., P.C. ... New York, NY
Hayes, Eileen M. ... Detroit, MI
Hayes, Elisabet C. ... Burlington, MA
Hayes, Eraclides, Hall & Greene, L.L.P.
Sarasota, FL
Tampa, FL
Hayes, Eric P. ... Boston, MA
Hayes, Frank P. ... Olympia, WA
Hayes, Fred P. ... Fullerton, CA
Hayes, Frederick B. ... Tacoma, WA
Hayes, Frederick B., III ... Boston, MA
Hayes, Frederick Brevard
Beverly Hills, CA
Hayes, Fredric G. ... Lafayette, LA
Hayes, G. Calvin ... Tampa, FL
Hayes, G. Edmond ... Wichita, KS
Hayes, Gail H. ... Monterey Park, CA
Hayes, Gail L. ... Monterey Park, CA
Hayes, Gail O. ... Department of Commerce, Patent and Trademark Office, GV
Hayes, Garry L. ... Las Vegas, NV
Hayes, Garry L., A Prof. Corp., Law Offices of ... Las Vegas, NV
Hayes, Gaylon C. ... Oklahoma City, OK
Hayes, Gaylon C. & Susan B. Pinkerton, A Professional Association
Oklahoma City, OK
Hayes, Geo. L., Jr. ... Shreveport, LA
Hayes, George L., III ... St. Petersburg, FL
Hayes, George N. ... Anchorage, AK
Hayes, Gerald J. ... New York, NY
Hayes, Gerald R. ... Portland, OR

Hayes, Gerald V. ... Poughkeepsie, NY
Hayes, Gerald W., Jr. ... Dunn, NC
Hayes, Gina Clark ... Washington, DC
Hayes, Glenn S. ... Salisbury, NC
Hayes, Gordon H., Jr. ... Boston, MA
Hayes, Gordon O. ... Rapid City, SD
Hayes, Gregory A. ... Greenwich, CT
Stamford, CT
Hayes, Gregory R. ... Hickory, NC
Hayes, Gregory W. ... Chicago, IL
Hayes, Griffith H. ... Costa Mesa, CA
Hayes, Hammer, Miles, Cox & Ginzkey
Bloomington, IL
Hayes, Harkey, Smith & Cascio, L.L.P.
Monroe, LA
Hayes, Harold C. ... Parsippany, NJ
Hayes, Harold L., Jr. (P.C.) ... Hyannis, MA
Hayes, Harold Robert, III ... El Paso, TX
Hayes, Harrison Frensley ... Littleton, CO
Hayes, Harry R. ... Albany, NY
Hayes, Harry R., III, Law Office of
Albany, NY
Hayes & Hayes ... Fort Wayne, IN
Hayes and Hayes ... Oskaloosa, KS
Hayes & Hayes ... Quincy, MA
Hayes and Hayes ... Dillon, SC
Hayes & Hayes, Attorneys at Law, P.C.
Hyannis, MA
Hayes, Heather L. ... Boston, MA
Hayes and Heiber ... Beloit, WI
Hayes, Holidae H. ... United States Senate,
Committee Legal Personnel, GV
Hayes, Holly A. ... Los Angeles, CA
Hayes, Hugh D. ... Naples, FL
Hayes, Hugh J. ... Madison, WI
Hayes, Ivan E. ... West Hartford, CT
Hayes, J. Allie ... North Wilkesboro, NC
Hayes, J. Chauncey ... Sacramento, CA
Hayes, J. Kevin ... Tulsa, OK
Hayes, J. Mark, II ... Spartanburg, SC
Hayes, J. Marland ... Tuscaloosa, AL
Hayes, J. Martin ... Tallahassee, FL
Hayes, J. Michael ... Tampa, FL
Hayes, J. Michael ... Buffalo, NY
Hayes, J. Stephen ... Walpole, MA
Hayes, J. Stoddard, Jr. ... Wilmington, DE
Hayes, J. Stoddard, Jr. ... Media, PA
Philadelphia, PA
West Chester, PA
Hayes, J. Suzanne ... Sacramento, CA
Hayes, J. Todd ... Edwardsville, IL
Hayes, Jack A. ... Boulder Creek, CA
Hayes, Jack H., Jr. ... Columbus, MS
Hayes, Jacqueline Jourdain ... Burbank, CA
Hayes, James A. ... Washington, DC
Hayes, James Arthur, Jr.
Laguna Niguel, CA
Hayes, James B. ... Princeton, NJ
Hayes, James B., (P.A.) ... Boca Raton, FL
Hayes, James C., III ... Amsterdam, NY
Hayes, James E. ... Bristol, CT
Hayes, James E. ... Garden City, NY
Hayes, James F. ... Richmond, VA
Hayes, James H. ... Chicago, IL
Hayes, James H. ... Cincinnati, OH
Hayes, James J., Jr. ... Detroit, MI
Hayes, James Joseph, IV ... Midland, MI
Hayes, James L., Jr. ... Dallas, TX
Hayes, James M. ... Binghamton, NY
Hayes, James M. ... Hempstead, NY
Hayes, James P. ... Clearwater, FL
Hayes, James P. ... Nappanee, IN
Plymouth, IN
Hayes, James P. ... Iowa City, IA
Hayes, James P. ... Boston, MA
Hayes, James P. ... Chesterfield, MO
Hayes, James W., III ... North Kingstown, RI
Hayes, Janet Strevel ... Knoxville, TN
Hayes, Janice L. ... Oskaloosa, KS
Hayes, Jason William ... Lincoln, NE
Hayes, Jeanine L. ... Los Angeles, CA
Hayes, Jeffery C. ... New York, NY
Hayes, Jeffrey D. ... Santa Rosa, CA
Hayes, Jeffrey E. ... Loogootee, IN
Washington, IN
Hayes, Jeffrey S. ... Detroit, MI
Hayes, Jeffrey T. ... Columbus, OH
Hayes, Jeffry M. ... Mundelein, IL
Hayes, Jennifer ... Manchester, NH
Hayes, Jennifer Anne ... Providence, RI
Hayes, Jennifer Connors ... Emeryville, CA
Hayes, Jennifer L. ... Flushing, NY
Hayes, Jere G. ... Dallas, TX
Hayes, Jeremiah M. ... Tupper Lake, NY
Hayes, Jerome J. ... Huntington, NY
Hayes, Jerrie M. ... Minneapolis, MN
Hayes, Jerry L. ... Ravenna, OH
Hayes, Jill ... Toledo, OH
Hayes, Jill L. ... New York, NY
Hayes, Jill Suzanne ... Sacramento, CA
Hayes, Joe W. ... Amarillo, TX
Hayes, Joel R., Jr. ... Greeley, CO
Hayes, Johanna A. ... Vista, CA
Hayes, John ... Birmingham, MI
Hayes, John A. ... San Francisco, CA
Hayes, John A., Jr. ... Baltimore, MD
Hayes, John A., Jr. ... New York, NY
Hayes, John B. ... Atlanta, GA
Hayes, John B. ... Oklahoma City, OK
Hayes, John B. ... Pittsburgh, PA
Hayes, John C. ... Salem, MA
Hayes, John C., III ... York, SC
Hayes, John C., Jr. ... Washington, DC
Hayes, John C. T. ... Watkins Glen, NY
Hayes, John D. ... Denver, CO
Hayes, John D. ... Traverse City, MI
Hayes, John E. ... San Luis Obispo, CA
Hayes, John E. ... Denver, CO
Hayes, John E., III ... Denver, CO
Hayes, John F. ... Hutchinson, KS
Wichita, KS
Hayes, John F., II ... Allentown, PA
Hayes, John Finbarr ... San Francisco, CA
Hayes, John G. ... Springfield, IL
Hayes, John G., Jr. ... Richmond, VA
Hayes, John Gardner ... Los Angeles, CA
Hayes, John Gardner, A Professional Corporation ... Los Angeles, CA
Hayes, John H. ... Albany, GA
Hayes, John J. ... Chicago, IL
Hayes, John J. ... Brooklyn, NY
Hayes, John J., III ... Boston, MA
Hayes, John J., Jr. ... Boston, MA
Hayes, John Michael ... Walpole, MA
Hayes, John O. ... Moline, IL
Hayes, John P. ... Seattle, WA
Hayes, John P. ... Milwaukee, WI
Hayes, John S. ... Lehigh Valley, PA
Hayes, John T. ... Chicago, IL
Hayes, John V. ... New York, NY
Hayes, John W. ... Naperville, IL
Hayes, Joseph A. ... Houston, TX
Hayes, Joseph C. ... Scituate, MA
Hayes, Joseph M. ... Detroit, MI
Hayes, Joseph Michael ... Hartford, CT
Hayes, Joseph W. ... Coldwater, MI
Hayes, Josephine Ellen ... Cambridge, OH
Hayes, Joyce Koria ... Wilmington, DE
Hayes, Judith H. ... Miami, FL
Hayes, Justin H. ... Atlanta, GA
Hayes, Kara M. ... Genoa, NV
Hayes, Karen L. ... Monroe, LA
Hayes, Kathleen E. ... Cincinnati, OH
Hayes, Kathleen M. ... San Francisco, CA
Hayes, Keith Q. ... Kansas City, KS
Hayes, Kelly M. ... Southfield, MI
Hayes, Kenneth ... Newark, NJ
Hayes, Kenneth T. ... Grand Rapids, MI
Hayes, Kevin D. ... Harrison, MI
Hayes, Kevin M. ... Warwick, RI
Hayes, Kim ... Lubbock, TX
Hayes, Kim R. ... Crowley, LA
Hayes, Kristine L. ... Columbus, OH
Hayes, L. Mifflin ... Scotch Plains, NJ
Hayes, Lacy, Jr. ... Harrisburg, PA
Hayes, Laraine Bellini ... East Hampton, NY
Hayes, Larry ... Fort Worth, TX
Hayes, Larry D. ... Greenfield, OH
Hayes, Larry E. ... Monterey, CA
Hayes, Larry G., Jr. ... Nashville, TN
Hayes Law Firm ... Charlevoix, MI
Chelsea, MI
Detroit, MI
Grand Rapids, MI
Traverse City, MI
Hayes Law Firm, The, P.A. ... Eagan, MN
Hayes Law Offices ... Surprise, AZ
Olympia, WA
Hayes, Lawrence J. ... Boston, MA
Hayes, Lawrence J. ... Minneapolis, MN
Hayes, Lawrence J., Jr. ... Eagan, MN
Hayes, Lawrence L., Jr. ... Hillsdale, MI
Hayes, Lawrence R. ... West Chester, PA
Hayes, Le Roy H. ... Boise, ID
Hayes, Leigh Frizzell ... Fort Myers, FL
Hayes, Leo F. ... Syracuse, NY
Hayes, Leslie A. ... Philadelphia, PA
Hayes, Leslie A., Jr. ... Brookfield, WI
Hayes, Lillard Cody ... Fort Smith, AR
Hayes, Linda M. ... Palo Alto, CA
Hayes & Lindell, P.A. ... Jacksonville, FL
Hayes, Lisa A. ... Seattle, WA
Hayes, Lisa Aceves ... El Paso, TX
Hayes, Lisa D. ... New York, NY
Hayes, Lisa H. Rice ... Baltimore, MD
Hayes, Lisa R. ... Indianapolis, IN
Hayes, Lloyd W. ... New Orleans, LA
Hayes Lorenzen, PLC ... Iowa City, IA
Hayes, Louise ... Philadelphia, PA
Hayes, Louise Bryant ... Waukegan, IL
Hayes, Lu Pendleton ... Carthage, NC
Pinehurst, NC
Hayes, Lynn K. ... Olympia, WA
Hayes, M. Jonathan ... Encino, CA
Hayes, M. Katharine ... Monte Vista, CO
Hayes, M. Vinson ... New York, NY
Hayes & Magrini ... Oklahoma City, OK
Hayes, Marcus Edward, Sr. ... Asheboro, NC
Hayes, Margaret B. ... Greenville, OH
Hayes, Margaret Frailey
Department of Commerce,
National Oceanic and Atmospheric
Administration, GV
Hayes, Margaret L. ... Boston, MA
Hayes, Margaret M. ... Bristol, CT
Hayes, Margaret O. ... Rochester, NY
Hayes, Maria D. ... Houston, TX
Hayes, Mark C. ... Falls Church, VA
Hayes, Mark F. ... Northville, MI
Hayes, Mark H. ... Huntington, WV
Hayes, Mark L. ... Dyersburg, TN
Hayes, Mark Paul ... Boston, MA
Hayes, Mark Robert ... North Little Rock, AR
Hayes, Mark S. ... Birmingham, AL
Hayes, Martin F. ... Harrison, NY
Hayes, Mary D. ... Quincy, MA
Hayes, Mary E. ... Hempstead, NY
Hayes, Mary F. F., (Mrs.) ... Dillon, SC
Hayes, Mary G. ... Fort Mitchell, KY
Hayes, Maryann C. ... Chicago, IL
Hayes, Maryann V. ... Great Neck, NY
Hayes, Matthew S. ... Charleston, WV
Hayes, Megan ... Fort Collins, CO
Hayes, Melinda L. ... Los Angeles, CA
Hayes, Merrick C. ... Bloomington, IL
Hayes, Michael A., Jr. ... Poughkeepsie, NY
Hayes, Michael C. ... Oskaloosa, KS
Hayes, Michael C. ... Houston, TX
Hayes, Michael D. ... Chicago, IL
Hayes, Michael G. ... Poughkeepsie, NY
Hayes, Michael J. ... Milford, CT
Hayes, Michael J. ... Carbondale, IL
Hayes, Michael J. ... Hyannis, MA
Hayes, Michael J., Jr. ... Chicago, IL
Hayes, Michael J., Sr. ... Chicago, IL
Hayes, Michael L. ... Hamilton, MT
Hayes, Michael M. ... Milwaukee, WI
Hayes, Michael S. ... Pasco, WA
Hayes, Michael W.S. ... North Weymouth, MA
Hayes, Michael Z. ... Salt Lake City, UT
Hayes, Michele D. Miller ... Madison, WI
Hayes & Mitchell ... Oakland, CA
Hayes & Moredock ... Charleston, WV
Hayes, N. Robert, Jr. ... Latham, NY
Hayes, Nancy L. ... San Francisco, CA
Hayes, Nathan M. ... Utica, NY
Hayes, Neil B. ... Chicago, IL
Hayes, Neil J. ... Palm Beach Gardens, FL
Hayes, Norman R. ... Gaylord, MI
Hayes, Oliver W. ... Manchester, NH
Hayes, Pamela D. ... New York, NY
Hayes, Patricia ... Austin, TX
Hayes, Patrick H. ... Alamosa, CO
Hayes, Patrick J. ... New York, NY
Hayes, Patrick O. ... Houston, TX
Hayes, Patrick O'Neill ... Newport, RI
Hayes, Patrick O'Neill, Jr. ... Newport, RI
Hayes, Patrick T. ... Lebanon, NH
Hayes, Patrick W. ... Rockford, IL
Hayes, Paul J. ... Boston, MA
Hayes, Paul P., Jr. ... Quincy, MA
Hayes, Peggy Ann ... Colorado Springs, CO
Hayes, Perry S. ... Somerville, TN
Hayes, Peter S. ... Walnut Creek, CA
Hayes, Philip H. ... Evansville, IN
Hayes, Philip J. ... San Francisco, CA
Hayes, Phillip M. ... Irvine, CA
Hayes, Phillips & Maloney, P.C.
Denver, CO
Hayes, R. Michael ... Des Moines, IA
Hayes, R. Scott ... New Castle, IN
Hayes, Randa A. ... Overland Park, KS
Hayes, Randal Allan ... Ormond Beach, FL
Hayes, Randall M. ... Hartford, CT
Hayes, Randolph ... Atlanta, GA
Hayes, Ray ... Surprise, AZ
Olympia, WA
Tacoma, WA
Hayes, Raymond R. ... Tucson, AZ
Hayes, Rhonda R. ... Magee, MS
Hayes, Richard A. ... Los Angeles, CA
Hayes, Richard D. ... Springfield, MA
Hayes, Richard D. ... Denton, TX
Hayes, Richard E. ... Spokane, WA
Hayes, Richard F. ... Miami, FL
Hayes, Richard G. ... Pekin, IL
Hayes, Richard K. ... New York, NY
Hayes, Robert C. ... Stafford, VA
Hayes, Robert E. ... Sioux Falls, SD
Hayes, Robert F. ... Boston, MA
Hayes, Robert G. ... Washington, DC
Hayes, Robert Hitchcock ... San Diego, CA
Hayes, Robert L. ... Tacoma, WA
Hayes, Robert M. ... Portland, ME
Hayes, Robert R. ... Graham, NC
Hayes, Robert S. ... Oakland, CA
Hayes, Robert S. ... Kissimmee, FL
Hayes, Robert S., P.A. ... Kissimmee, FL
Hayes, Robert W. ... Atlanta, GA
Hayes, Robert W. ... Philadelphia, PA
Hayes, Robert W., Jr. ... Rock Hill, SC
Hayes, Robin Belton ... Washington, DC
Hayes, Robt. E. ... Front Royal, VA
Hayes, Roderick D. ... Moreno Valley, CA
Hayes, Rodney A. ... Oklahoma City, OK
Hayes, Roger S. ... New York, NY
Hayes, Roland H. ... Winston-Salem, NC
Hayes, Ronald C. ... Cincinnati, OH
Hayes, Ronald N. ... Houston, TX
Hayes, Rosemary H. ... Winter Park, FL
Hayes & Rothstein ... Milwaukee, WI
Hayes, Roy C. ... Charlevoix, MI
Chelsea, MI
Hayes, Roy C., III ... Charlevoix, MI
Chelsea, MI
Hayes, Rufus D. ... Baton Rouge, LA
Hayes & Salah, LLP ... San Francisco, CA
Hayes, Scott E., (P.C.) ... Dallas, TX
Hayes, Sean Erik ... New York, NY
Hayes, Shae ... San Luis Obispo, CA
Hayes, Sharon A. ... Morgantown, WV
Hayes, Sherrard L., Jr. ... Austin, TX
Hayes Simpson Greene, LLP
Newport Beach, CA
Hayes Simpson Greene LLP
San Diego, CA
Hayes, Soloway, Hennessey, Grossman & Hage, A Professional Corporation
Tucson, AZ
Manchester, NH
Hayes, Sophia F. Cadwalader
West Chester, PA
Hayes, Stacey A. ... Tucson, AZ
Hayes, Stephanie J. ... Alamo, CA
Hayes, Stephen D. ... Washington, DC
Hayes, Stephen M. ... Redwood City, CA
Hayes, Stephen P. ... Boston, MA
Hayes, Stephen T. ... Augusta, ME
Hayes, Stephen W. ... Department of the Army,
Office, Chief of Engineers/Headquarters,
U.S. Army Corps of Engineers, GV
Hayes, Stephen W. ... Milwaukee, WI
Hayes, Steven B. ... Columbus, OH
Hayes, Steven E. ... Metairie, LA
Hayes, Steven K. ... Fort Worth, TX
Hayes, Steven L. ... Los Angeles, CA
Hayes, Steven M. ... New York, NY
Hayes, Steven R. ... New York, NY
Hayes, Steven T. ... Providence, RI
Hayes, Susan D. ... Providence, RI
Hayes, Susan E. ... Boulder, CO
Hayes, Susan J. ...
Administrative Office Of The United States
Courts, GV
Hayes, Susan N. ... Worthington, OH
Hayes, Susan Scott ... Birmingham, AL
Hayes, Susanne F. ... Raleigh, NC
Hayes, Suzannah ... Columbia, SC
Hayes, Theresa McQuaid ... Georgetown, DE
Hayes, Thomas ... Woodstock, VT
Hayes, Thomas A. ... Cincinnati, OH
Hayes, Thomas B. ... Fort Myers, FL
Hayes, Thomas B. ... St. Louis, MO
Hayes, Thomas D. ... Anoka, MN
Hayes, Thomas E. ... Pittsburg, KS
Hayes, Thomas E. ... Milwaukee, WI
Hayes, Thomas F. ... Columbus, OH
Hayes, Thomas F. ... Chattanooga, TN
Hayes, Thomas M. ... Peoria, IL
Hayes, Thomas M. ... Charleston, WV
Hayes, Thomas M., III
Department of Transportation,
U. S. Coast Guard, GV
Hayes, Thomas M., III ... Monroe, LA
Hayes, Thomas P. ... Milwaukee, WI
Hayes, Thomas W. ... Chicago, IL
Hayes, Thomas W. ... Oceanside, NY
Hayes, Thos. W., Jr. ... St. Paul, MN
Hayes, Timothy A. ... Akron, OH
Hayes, Timothy E. ... St. Louis, MO
Hayes, Timothy G. ... Lutz, FL
Hayes, Timothy G. ... Richmond, VA
Hayes, Timothy M. ... Irving, TX
Hayes, Timothy P. ... Yuba City, CA
Hayes, Timothy R. ... Terre Haute, IN
Hayes, Todd C. ... Seattle, WA
Hayes, Tom E. ... Milwaukee, WI
Hayes, Valerie O. ... Ithaca, NY
Hayes, Vilia B. ... New York, NY
Hayes, Virginia F. ... Madison, WI
Hayes, Waldron S., Jr. ... Buffalo, NY
Hayes, Walter ... Fort Worth, TX
Hayes, Walter R., Jr. ... Baltimore, MD
Hayes, Warren Dennis, Sr.
Palm Beach, FL
Hayes, Webb C., III ... Washington, DC
Hayes, William A. ... Middlesboro, KY
Hayes, William A. ... Beverly Hills, MI
Hayes, William B., III ... Littleton, CO
Hayes, William D. ... Cincinnati, OH
Hayes, William G. ... Santa Barbara, CA
Hayes, William J. ... Collings Lakes, NJ
Hayes, William J. ... Houston, TX
Hayes, William J. ... Beloit, WI
Hayes, William J. C. ... Flint, MI
Hayes, William K. ... South Pasadena, CA
Hayes, William Michael ... Folsom, CA
Hayes, William P. ... New York, NY
Hayes, William Q. ... San Diego, CA
Hayes, William R. ... Houston, TX
Hayes, William S. ... Houston, TX
Hayes, William S., Jr. ... Richmond, VA
Hayes, William T. ... Boston, MA
Hayes, Williams & Turner, P.A.
Dunn, NC
Hayes-Cote, Margaret R. ... Providence, RI
Hayes-Deckebach, Jill ... Toledo, OH
Hayes-Snow, Louise Breckinridge
North Conway, NH
Hayford, Stephen L. ... Bloomington, IN
Haygood, Becky C. ... Clearwater, FL
Haygood, Charles B., Jr. ... Forsyth, GA
Haygood, Cleveland & Pierce LLP
Auburn, AL
Opelika, AL
Haygood, Curtis Gray ... Houston, TX
Haygood, Daniel C. ... Athens, GA
Haygood, Erin H. ... Smithfield, NC
Haygood, Frederick S. ... Baton Rouge, LA
Haygood, Howard ... Greenville, AL
Haygood, J. Michael
West Palm Beach, FL
Haygood, James K., Jr. ... Auburn, AL
Haygood, John T. ... San Francisco, CA
Haygood, John W. ... Metairie, LA
Haygood, Katharine H.
Federal Deposit Insurance Corporation,
Professional Liability Section, GV
Haygood, Lynch, Harris & Melton
Forsyth, GA
Monticello, GA
Haygood, Paul M. ... New Orleans, LA
Haygood, Ralph F. ... Atlanta, GA
Haygood, Richard David ... Raleigh, NC
Haygood, Sebraien M., & Associates
Cleveland, OH
Haygood, Susan Caroline
Birmingham, AL
Haygood, Tammy B. ... San Francisco, CA
Haygood, Terry ... Rome, GA
Haygood, Weldon Terry, Jr. ... Rome, GA
Hayhoe, Christopher S. ... Minneapolis, MN
Hayhoe, Richard G. ... Mason, MI
Hayhow, Van L. ... Attleboro, MA
Hayhurst, David G. ... Portland, OR
Hayhurst, L. Nelson ... Fresno, CA
Hayhurst, Paul D. ... Midland, MI
Hayhurst, Ren R ... Irvine, CA
Hayhurst, Richard A. ... Parkersburg, WV
Hayko, Eva Lynn M. ... Albany, NY
Hayko, John F. ... Guilderland, NY
Hayle, Brian W. ... San Francisco, CA

Hayles, Janice ...... **New York, NY**
Haylett, Nicholas F. ...... **New York, NY**
Hayley, Benjamin F. ...... Birmingham, AL
Haylon, Patricia ...... **Houston, TX**
Haylor, Jane T. ...... **Cleveland, OH**
Hayman, Andrea S. ...... New York, NY
Hayman, Bret S. ...... **Salt Lake City, UT**
Hayman, Bruce M. ...... Chicago, IL
Hayman, David M. ...... Appleton, WI
Hayman, Edward A. ...... Rocky River, OH
Hayman, Heather M. ...... Stamford, CT
Hayman, Jane Cameron ...... Largo, FL
Hayman, Jennie Jarrell ...... Raleigh, NC
Hayman, Jill ...... **New York, NY**
Hayman, Judith Buckley ...... Salem, MA
Hayman & Kirshenbaum ...... Chicago, IL
Hayman, Linda C. ...... **New York, NY**
Hayman, Lisa S. ...... Walnut Creek, CA
Hayman, Margaret ...... New Haven, CT
Hayman, Milton A. ...... Steubenville, OH
Hayman, Milton A., The Law Firm of
Steubenville, OH
Hayman, R. Patrick ...... Princess Anne, MD
Hayman, Randy E. ...... **St. Louis, MO**
Hayman, Russell ...... **Los Angeles, CA**
Hayman, Selma ...... Wilmington, DE
Hayman, Stephen Daniel ...... Tampa, FL
Hayman, Susanne ...... Chestertown, MD
Hayman, Thomas G. ...... Waddell, AZ
Hayman, Thomas H. ...... **Boston, MA**
Hayman, William ...... Clarendon Hills, IL
Hayman, Wilson ...... **Raleigh, NC**
Haymans, Kenton H. ...... Punta Gorda, FL
Haymans, Michael P. ...... **Punta Gorda, FL**
Haymer, Robert D. ...... **Los Angeles, CA**
Haymes, Catherine Anne ...... Los Angeles, CA
Haymes, Ellsworth ...... Marshfield, MO
Haymes, Jennifer Renee ...... Sarasota, FL
Haymes, Mitchell ...... Miami Beach, FL
Haymes, Patricia V. ...... **Richmond, VA**
Haymes, Sims & Thompson
Marshfield, MO
Haymon, Cordell H., Ltd. ...... Baton Rouge, LA
Haymon, Selma ...... Wilmington, DE
Haymond, Daniel M. ...... **Cleveland, OH**
Haymond, David ...... Hartford, CT
Haymond, Ester F. ...... Lexington, SC
Haymond, Gary L. ...... Iowa City, IA
Haymond, John, Law Firm of ...... Hartford, CT
Haymond, Philip H. ...... **Irvine, CA**
Haymond, Steven D. ...... **Columbia, SC**
Haymond, W. Bradley ...... **Palo Alto, CA**
Haymore, Douglas S., II
Salt Lake City, UT
Haymore, Greg Tyler ...... **Danville, VA**
Hayn, Linda Susan ...... Department of Justice, Federal Bureau of Investigation, GV
Hayn, Robert C. ...... **New York, NY**
Haynal, Andrew J. ...... Redlands, CA
Haynam, Douglas G. ...... **Toledo, OH**
Hayne, C. Peck, Jr. ...... **New Orleans, LA**
Hayne, Louise D. ...... **Philadelphia, PA**
Hayne, Robert A.
Federal Communications Commission, Mass Media Bureau, GV
Hayne, Stephen W. ...... Bellevue, WA
Hayner & Edwards, P.C. ...... **Bend, OR**
Hayner, H. H. ...... **Walla Walla, WA**
Hayner, James K. ...... **Walla Walla, WA**
Hayner, Jeannette C. ...... Walla Walla, WA
Hayner, John F. ...... Independence, MO
Hayner, Jon W. ...... **Bend, OR**
Hayner & Moynihan ...... Schenectady, NY
Hayner, Thomas B. ...... Schenectady, NY
Hayner, William, and Associates
Dallas, TX
Hayner, William M. ...... **Dallas, TX**
Hayner, William M., Jr ...... **Dallas, TX**
Haynes, A. Myles ...... Charlotte, NC
Haynes, Alicia K. ...... Birmingham, AL
Haynes, Allyson W. ...... **New York, NY**
Haynes, Alton C. ...... **Chicago, IL**
Joliet, IL
Haynes, Andrew Ky ...... **Kansas City, MO**
Haynes, Barbara N. ...... Nashville, TN
Haynes & Beffel LLP ...... **Half Moon Bay, CA**
Palo Alto, CA
Haynes, Bill E. ...... Olathe, KS
Haynes and Boone, LLP ...... **Washington, DC**
Austin, TX
Dallas, TX
Fort Worth, TX
Houston, TX
San Antonio, TX
Haynes, Brian F. ...... Martinez, CA
Haynes, Brian K. ...... **Syracuse, NY**
Haynes, Brian L. ...... **Owensboro, KY**
Haynes, Bryan ...... **Dallas, TX**
Haynes, Bryan M. ...... **Washington, DC**
Haynes, Burton J. ...... Washington, DC
Haynes, Charlene S. ...... **Tampa, FL**
Haynes, Charles R. ...... Hoisington, KS
Haynes, Chris ...... **El Paso, TX**
Haynes, Craig A. ...... **Dallas, TX**
Haynes, Dan A. ...... **Hartford, CT**
Haynes, Daniel J. ...... Glen Ellyn, IL
Haynes, Darrell E. ...... **Brownwood, TX**
Haynes, Darryl G. ...... **Atlanta, GA**
Haynes, David A. ...... San Francisco, CA
Haynes, David D. ...... Terre Haute, IN
Haynes, David E. ...... Harrisonburg, VA
Haynes, David J. ...... **Waynesville, NC**
Haynes, David K. ...... McKinney, TX
Haynes, David L. ...... Canton, IL
Haynes, David M. ...... **Boulder, CO**
Haynes, David N. ...... **Minneapolis, MN**
Haynes, David S. ...... Bristol, TN
Haynes, David S., P.C. ...... Bristol, TN

Haynes, Douglas B. ...... Moorpark, CA
Haynes, Douglas B., Law Office of
Moorpark, CA
Haynes, Douglas James ...... Columbus, OH
Haynes, Douglas Jay ...... Burlington, CO
Haynes, Douglas S. ...... **Louisville, KY**
Haynes, Duncan E. ...... Napa, CA
Haynes, Eileen M. ...... **Glens Falls, NY**
Haynes, Eleanor E. Beavers ...... Columbus, OH
Haynes, Elizabeth R. ...... Far Rockaway, NY
Haynes, Ford & Rowe ...... **Lewisburg, WV**
Haynes, Frances J. ...... **Phoenix, AZ**
Haynes, Francis J. ...... Vero Beach, FL
Haynes, Frank L., Jr. ...... Newark, NJ
Haynes, Fred E. ...... Washington, DC
Haynes & Freeman, P.L.C.
Goodlettsville, TN
Haynes, Gary J. ...... Lafayette, LA
Haynes, Gene ...... Claremore, OK
Haynes, Geoffrey W. ...... **San Francisco, CA**
Haynes, George Cleve ...... Seattle, WA
Haynes, George William ...... Utica, MS
Haynes, Glenda R. ...... Jackson, MS
Haynes, H. Wilson, Jr., P.C. ...... **Augusta, GA**
Haynes, Harry H. ...... Bisbee, AZ
Haynes & Haynes ...... Baldwyn, MS
Haynes & Haynes ...... Columbus, OH
Haynes & Haynes, P.C. ...... Birmingham, AL
Haynes, Helen ...... Chicago, IL
Haynes, Helen R. ...... Raleigh, NC
Haynes, Helen S. ...... **San Francisco, CA**
Haynes, Hoover ...... **Hazard, KY**
Haynes, Hull, Rieder & Ewell, P.A.
Tullahoma, TN
Haynes, J. David ...... Largo, FL
Haynes, J. Michael ...... **Knoxville, TN**
Haynes, Jacquelyn C. ...... **Chicago, IL**
Haynes, James A. ...... Hamilton, MT
Haynes, James A., Jr. ...... Norwich, NY
Haynes, James, Jr. ...... Laredo, TX
Haynes, Janet A. ...... Grand Rapids, MI
Haynes, Jas. M. ...... Knoxville, TN
Haynes, Jason Blake ...... Houston, TX
Haynes, Jean Reed ...... **New York, NY**
Haynes, Jeffrey Alan ...... Sarasota, FL
Haynes, Jeffrey K. ...... **Bloomfield Hills, MI**
Haynes, Jerry ...... **New York, NY**
Haynes, Jim Tom ...... **Washington, DC**
Haynes, Joe M. ...... Goodlettsville, TN
Haynes, Joe R. ...... **Knoxville, TN**
Haynes, Joey D. ...... **Hillsville, VA**
Haynes, John C. ...... Edwardsville, IL
Haynes, John C., Jr. ...... Tucson, AZ
Haynes, John M. ...... Arlington Heights, IL
Haynes, John R. ...... **Nashville, TN**
Haynes, John S. ...... Elyria, OH
Haynes, John, Sr. ...... Baldwyn, MS
Haynes, John W., IV ...... New Albany, MS
Haynes, Joseph B. ...... **Atlanta, GA**
Haynes, K. Gregory ...... **Louisville, KY**
Haynes, Kathleen J. ...... Harrisburg, PA
Haynes, Keith E. ...... **Baltimore, MD**
Haynes, Kenneth D. ...... Birmingham, AL
Haynes, Kimberley H. ...... **Washington, DC**
Haynes, Kristie G. ...... **Washington, DC**
Haynes, Lloyd R. ...... Little Rock, AR
Haynes, Lucy Honey ...... Nashville, TN
Haynes, M. Paul, Jr. ...... Baldwyn, MS
Haynes, Malenda S. ...... Grayson, KY
Haynes, Marcelita V. ...... Los Angeles, CA
Haynes, Margaret Campbell
Washington, DC
Haynes, Mark A. ...... **Half Moon Bay, CA**
Haynes, Mark E. ...... **Denver, CO**
Haynes, Mark M. ...... **Boulder, CO**
Haynes, Mark W. ...... Ellisville, MO
Haynes, Mary Mullin ...... New York, NY
Haynes, Matthew Edward
West Palm Beach, FL
Haynes, Meek & Summers ...... **Knoxville, TN**
Haynes, Michael N. ...... **Washington, DC**
Haynes Montgomery Dugger Hunt
Oklahoma City, OK
Haynes, Nan Lipsitz ...... **Buffalo, NY**
Haynes, Olen G. ...... **Johnson City, TN**
Knoxville, TN
Abingdon, VA
Haynes, Patricia L. ...... Ellisville, MO
Haynes, Paul R. ...... Wappingers Falls, NY
Haynes, Priscilla H. ...... Manteca, CA
Haynes, R. Anderson ...... **Columbus, NC**
Haynes, R. Anderson ...... **Tryon, NC**
Haynes, R. Michael, Law Offices of
Washington, DC
Haynes, R. Stephen ...... Oklahoma City, OK
Haynes, Randall C. ...... Nashville, TN
Haynes, Randall L. ...... Little Rock, AR
Haynes, Randall Stark
Alexander City, AL
Haynes, Richard ...... Houston, TX
Haynes, Richard, Associates, P.C.
Houston, TX
Haynes, Richard B. ...... Santa Cruz, CA
Haynes, Richard D. ...... **Dallas, TX**
Haynes, Richard E., II ...... **Laredo, TX**
Haynes, Richard T. ...... **Clawson, MI**
Plymouth, MI
Haynes, Robert B. ...... **New York, NY**
Haynes, Robert C. ...... Nashville, TN
Haynes, Robert M. ...... Colorado Springs, CO
Haynes, S. Geoffrey ...... Baltimore, MD
Haynes, Scott K. ...... **Nashville, TN**
Haynes & Sontich ...... **Youngstown, OH**
Haynes, Sophia E. ...... Prichard, AL
Haynes, Stacey D. ...... Columbia, SC
Haynes, Stan M. ...... **Baltimore, MD**
Haynes, Stephen C. ...... **McAllen, TX**
Haynes, Stephen E. ...... **Dallas, TX**

Haynes, Stephen K. ...... San Diego, CA
Haynes, Stephen L. ...... Minneapolis, MN
Haynes, Thomas B. ...... Chicago, IL
Haynes, Thomas C. ...... Linwood, NJ
Haynes, Thomas J. ...... Murfreesboro, TN
Haynes, Thomas R. ...... Omaha, NE
Haynes, Thomas V. ...... Conyers, GA
Haynes, Timothy John ...... Grand Rapids, MI
Haynes, Todd James ...... Chicago, IL
Haynes, Tressa ...... **Columbia, SC**
Haynes, Valerie W. ...... Trenton, NJ
Haynes, Vicki K. ...... **Longview, TX**
Haynes, W. Christopher W. ...... **Dallas, TX**
Haynes, W. Thomas ...... **Atlanta, GA**
Haynes, William Allen ...... **Shreveport, LA**
Haynes, William C. ...... Lancaster, PA
Haynes, William E. ...... San Francisco, CA
Haynes, William G. ...... **Topeka, KS**
Haynes, William J., II ...... **Washington, DC**
Haynes, William J., III ...... **Nashville, TN**
Haynes, William J., Jr. ...... Nashville, TN
Haynes, William S. ...... **Montgomery, AL**
Haynes, William S. ...... Bowling Green, KY
Haynes, William T., Jr. ...... **Louisville, KY**
Haynes, Winston G. ...... Marietta, GA
Haynes-Garrett, Reetha ...... **Los Angeles, CA**
Haynes-Palmquist, Karen ...... Redmond, WA
Haynes-Palmquist, Karen, P.S.
Redmond, WA
Haynie, Allen D. ...... **San Diego, CA**
Haynie, Amy J. ...... South Charleston, WV
Haynie, Barbara G. ...... **New Orleans, LA**
Haynie, Douglas R. ...... **Marietta, GA**
Haynie, Erick J. ...... **Portland, OR**
Haynie, F. Warren, Jr. ...... **Heathsville, VA**
Haynie, Gilmore S., Jr. ...... Fort Wayne, IN
Haynie, Higier, Maris & Foxman, P.C.
Dallas, TX
Haynie, Howard E. ...... Chicago, IL
Haynie, Kenneth G., Jr. ...... Evansville, IN
Haynie, Kenneth H. ...... **Des Moines, IA**
Haynie, Laurie A. ...... **Chicago, IL**
Haynie & Litchfield, P.C. ...... **Marietta, GA**
Haynie, Louis M. ...... Midvale, UT
Haynie, M. Todd, III ...... **Columbia, SC**
Haynie, Mark S. ...... Dallas, TX
Haynie, Richard J., Jr ...... San Diego, CA
Haynie, Robert M. ...... South San Francisco, CA
Haynie, Sandra Prudhomme Payne
Shreveport, LA
Haynie, Sarah H. ...... **Austin, TX**
Haynie, Stephen W. ...... Charleston, WV
Haynie, Suzanne E. ...... **McLean, VA**
Haynie, Timothy C. ...... Altus, OK
Haynie, Tony W. ...... **Tulsa, OK**
Haynie, Van E. ...... **San Diego, CA**
Haynie, William T., Jr. ...... Mobile, AL
Haynor, Charles R. ...... **Minneapolis, MN**
Haynsworth Baldwin Johnson & Greaves LLC ...... **Jacksonville, FL**
Tampa, FL
Charlotte, NC
Greensboro, NC
Raleigh, NC
Columbia, SC
Greenville, SC
Haynsworth, Harry J., IV ...... St. Paul, MN
Haynsworth, Knox L., III ...... **Greenville, SC**
Haynsworth, Knox L., Jr.
Jacksonville, FL
Tampa, FL
Charlotte, NC
Greensboro, NC
Raleigh, NC
Columbia, SC
Greenville, SC
Haynsworth, Marion, McKay & Guérard, L.L.P. ...... **Charleston, SC**
Columbia, SC
Greenville, SC
Haynsworth, Perry, Bryant, Marion & Johnstone ...... **Greenville, SC**
Haynsworth, Stuart ...... Houston, TX
Haynsworth, Suzanne Marie ...... Greenville, SC
Hayob, John L. ...... **Kansas City, MO**
Hayos, Meridith L. ...... **San Francisco, CA**
Hayostek, Thomas ...... Utica, NY
Hays, Almus T. ...... Salt Lake City, UT
Hays, Andrew W. ...... San Luis Obispo, CA
Hays, Benjamin J. ...... Winchester, KY
Hays, Bill J. ...... **Overland Park, KS**
Hays, Brent M. ...... Mount Juliet, TN
Hays, Brian I. ...... **Chicago, IL**
Hays, Charles J. ...... Eugene, OR
Hays, Christopher, Law Offices of
San Francisco, CA
Hays, Christopher W. ...... Dumas, AR
Hays, Claude A., Jr. ...... Georgetown, TX
Hays, Clyde L. ...... Amarillo, TX
Hays, Daniel P. ...... Port Washington, NY
Hays, David ...... Marion, VA
Hays, David A. ...... Tucson, AZ
Hays, David Edward ...... **Irvine, CA**
Hays, David W. ...... Acton, MA
Hays, Deborah A. ...... **Haddonfield, NJ**
Hays, Denise ...... **Austin, TX**
Hays, Denise C. ...... **Minot, ND**
Hays, Dennis ...... Beloit, WI
Hays, Dennis R. ...... Bakersfield, CA
Hays, Dolph ...... Arlington, VA
Hays, Edward D. ...... **Danville, KY**
Hays, Edward R. ...... **Lexington, KY**
Hays, Ernest F., II ...... Bluefield, WV
Hays, Eugene H. ...... Tucson, AZ
Hays, Faye Whittington ...... Jonesboro, GA
Hays, Frances P. ...... Fairfax, VA
Hays, Frances S. ...... Lafayette, LA
Hays, Frank L. ...... Denver, CO

Hays, Frank M. ...... Wooster, OH
Hays, Gary Martin ...... Atlanta, GA
Hays, Gary W. ...... **Dallas, TX**
Hays, George E. ...... San Francisco, CA
Hays, George T. ...... McKee, KY
Hays, Gerry A. ...... **Indianapolis, IN**
Hays, Gillian G. ...... **Palo Alto, CA**
Hays & Gordon ...... **Chickasha, OK**
Hays, Gregory B. ...... Milwaukee, WI
Hays, Grider ...... Ballinger, TX
Hays, Hamilton Kirk ...... Austin, TX
Hays, Harry Kenneth ...... Chattanooga, TN
Hays, Harry S. ...... Memphis, TN
Hays and Hays ...... Winchester, KY
Hays, Hays & Hays ...... Shelbyville, KY
Hays, Heather J. ...... St. Louis, MO
Hays, Howard H., Jr. ...... Riverside, CA
Hays, J. Phillip ...... **Lubbock, TX**
Hays, J. Ray ...... Houston, TX
Hays, J. Spencer ...... Bossier City, LA
Hays, Jack C. ...... Pontiac, MI
Hays, James H. ...... Phoenix, AZ
Hays, James Hite ...... Shelbyville, KY
Hays, James M., III ...... Oklahoma City, OK
Hays, James N. ...... **Fresno, CA**
Hays, James R. ...... **New York, NY**
Hays, James W. ...... **Atlanta, GA**
Hays, Jeffrey B. ...... Hamilton, MT
Hays, Jeffrey L. ...... **Champaign, IL**
Hays, John C. K.
Federal Communications Commission, Common Carrier Bureau, GV
Hays, John D. ...... Pikeville, KY
Hays, John David ...... Murfreesboro, TN
Hays, John P. ...... Las Vegas, NM
Santa Fe, NM
Hays, John R., Jr. ...... **Austin, TX**
Hays, John W. ...... **Lexington, KY**
Hays, Johnine R. ...... West Des Moines, IA
Hays, Jonathan W. ...... Greeley, CO
Hays, Joy D. ...... **Merriam, KS**
Hays, Karl E. ...... **Austin, TX**
Hays, Katherine L. ...... **Colorado Springs, CO**
Hays, Kathryn L. ...... **Houston, TX**
Hays, Keith J. ...... Indianapolis, IN
Hays, Kelly, (Mr.) ...... Stillwater, OK
Hays, Keltie L. ...... Danville, VA
Hays, Kevin K., P.C. ...... Pelham, AL
Hays, Kevin Kenneth ...... Pelham, AL
Hays, Kimberly C. ...... Utica, MI
Hays, Kirk H. ...... **Phoenix, AZ**
Hays, Kristin L. ...... **Kansas City, MO**
Hays, L. Keith, Jr. ...... Monticello, IL
Hays, Laurie E. ...... Arnett, OK
Hays Law Firm ...... **Austin, TX**
Hays, Louis B.
Department Of Health And Human Services, GV
Hays, Lowell B. ...... Houston, TX
Hays, Lynn Cooper ...... Tucson, AZ
Hays, M. Alan ...... Ithaca, NY
Hays, Margaret T. ...... Washington, DC
Hays, Marilyn Patricia ...... Ormond Beach, FL
Hays, Mark R. ...... **Minot, ND**
Hays, Martha J. ...... **Philadelphia, PA**
Hays & Martin ...... **Garland, TX**
Hays, Mary Vidal ...... **Chicago, IL**
Hays & Maysilles, P.C. ...... Atlanta, GA
Hays, McConn, Rice & Pickering
Houston, TX
Hays, Melissa Padgett ...... **Chattanooga, TN**
Hays, Michael D. ...... **Washington, DC**
Hays, Michael O. ...... Chico, CA
Hays, Michael S. ...... **Houston, TX**
Hays, Michelle L. ...... Columbus, OH
Hays, Nanci M. ...... **St. Louis, MO**
Hays, Patricia J. ...... Little Rock, AR
Hays, Patricia L. ...... Canonsburg, PA
Hays, Patrick B. ...... North Platte, NE
Hays, Patrick H. ...... North Little Rock, AR
Hays, Paul C. ...... **Portland, OR**
Hays, Penny Dianne ...... Birmingham, AL
Hays, Porter, Spanier & Curtis
Great Neck, NY
Hays & Potter, P.C. ...... **Atlanta, GA**
Hays & Randall ...... Scottsburg, IN
Hays, Randall A. ...... Lodi, CA
Hays, Richard J. ...... **Lauderhill, FL**
Hays, Richard J., P.A.
Fort Lauderdale, FL
Lauderhill, FL
Hays, Richard M. ...... Pittsburgh, PA
Hays, Richard R. ...... **Atlanta, GA**
Hays, Richard S. ...... Denver, CO
Hays, Robert C. ...... San Francisco, CA
Hays, Robert D. ...... **Columbus, OH**
Hays, Robert D., Jr. ...... **Atlanta, GA**
Hays, Robert J. ...... **Chickasha, OK**
Hays, Robert P. ...... Los Angeles, CA
Hays, Roger K. ...... Mesa, AZ
Hays, Rogers N. ...... **Pulaski, TN**
Hays, Rory C. ...... Phoenix, AZ
Hays, Ruth ...... **St. Louis, MO**
Hays, St. John, Abramson & Heilbron
New York, NY
Hays, Sam S. ...... Mountain Brook, AL
Hays, Sara L. ...... Chicago, IL
Hays, Sarah W. ...... Kansas City, MO
Hays, Shawn M. ...... San Diego, CA
Hays, Spencer B. ...... **New York, NY**
Hays, Stanley R. ...... Lakewood, CO
Hays, Steele ...... Conway, AR
Hays, Steven A. ...... Joplin, MO
Hays, Stuart J. ...... San Jose, CA
Hays, Stuart R., (P.C.) ...... Virginia Beach, VA
Hays, Susan ...... **Dallas, TX**
Hays, Susan A. ...... **Hartford, CT**
Hays, Terry Michael ...... **Shreveport, LA**

Hays, Thomas C. ... **Indianapolis, IN**
Hays, Thomas E. ... Little Rock, AR
Hays, Thomas P. ... Los Angeles, CA
Hays, Thomas R. ... **Lexington, KY**
Hays, Thomas R. ... Toledo, OH
Hays, Timothy F. ... **Chehalis, WA**
Hays, Von E. ... **Kansas City, MO**
Hays, W. Arthur, Jr. ... **Murphy, NC**
Hays, Walter V., (P.C.) ... Palo Alto, CA
Hays, Walter W. ... Colquitt, GA
Hays, Walter W., Jr. ... **Athens, GA**
Hays, Warren ... **Garland, TX**
Hays, Will, Jr. ... Crawfordsville, IN
Hays, William C., and Associates **Boston, MA**
Hays, William C., Jr. ... **Irving, TX**
Hays, William H., III ... Nantucket, MA
Hays, William H., Jr. ... Shelbyville, KY
Hays, William R., III ... **Dallas, TX**
Hays, William T. ... Mission Viejo, CA
Hays, William W. ... **Worcester, MA**
Hays, Wm. H. ... Shelbyville, KY
Hayse, David F. ... Lexington, KY
Hayse, Richard F. ... **Topeka, KS**
Hayskar, Stephen G. ... **Fort Pierce, FL**
Hayslett, J. Kevin ... Clearwater, FL
Hayslett, Richard R. ... **Dallas, TX**
Hayslett, Thomas L., III ... **Chattanooga, TN**
Haysley, Michael Thomas ... Houston, TX
Hayslip, Gordon F. ... Houston, TX
Hayslip, Michael W. ... Hamilton, OH
Hayslip, Victor L. ... **Birmingham, AL**
Haysom, Simon ... **Goshen, NY**
Haysom, Simon, LLC ... **Goshen, NY**
Hayssen, Joann K. ... Andover, MA
Haystead, Ronald M. ... Wyandotte, MI
Hayt, Hayt & Landau ... Eatontown, NJ
Hayt, Hayt & Landau ... Garden City, NY **Great Neck, NY**
Hayt, Lester J. ... Sun City, AZ
Hayt, Nancy Guller ... **New Haven, CT**
Hayt, Paul A. ... New York, NY
Hayt, Percy & Mermelstein ... New York, NY
Haytayan, Harry M., Jr. ... Hudson, NH
Haytcher, Gary L. ... East Moline, IL
Haytcher, Paul J. ... Whitehall, OH
Hayter, Dana W. ... **Palo Alto, CA**
Hayter, David B. ... New York, NY
Hayter, Don M. ... Greenville, TX
Hayter, John F. ... **Gainesville, FL**
Hayter, John O., III ... **Shreveport, LA**
Hayter, Karen M. ... Kalamazoo, MI
Hayter, Kristine K. **Colorado Springs, CO**
Hayter, Philip ... Dallas, OR
Hayter, Robert L. ... Houston, TX
Hayter, Robert P. ... Farmington, CT
Hayter, William G. ... Seal Beach, CA
Haythe, Thomas M. ... New York, NY
Haythe, Winston M. Environmental Protection Agency, Office of Enforcement and Compliance Assurance, GV
Haythorn, Joseph D. ... Costa Mesa, CA
Haythorne, Robert E. ... Geneva, IL
Hayton, Arthwell C. ... **Newport Beach, CA**
Hayton, C. Andrew ... Wheaton, IL
Hayton, Geoffrey O. ... **Victorville, CA**
Hayton Law Corporation ... **Barstow, CA** **Victorville, CA**
Hayton, Theresa E. ... Riverside, CA
Hayton, Thomas ... **Seattle, WA**
Hayum, Edward ... **New York, NY**
Hayum, George T. ... **Los Angeles, CA**
Hayutin, Arthur B. ... Denver, CO
Hayutin, David L. ... **Los Angeles, CA**
Hayutin & Hayutin ... Denver, CO
Hayutin, Irving J. ... Denver, CO
Hayutin, Marc I. ... Los Angeles, CA
Hayutin, Robin G. ... Washington, DC
Hayward, Allison R. ... Washington, DC
Hayward, Archie B., Jr. ... Fort Myers, FL
Hayward, Barbara J. ... Bay City, MI
Hayward, Blake ... **Tallahassee, FL**
Hayward, Daniel T. ... **Reno, NV**
Hayward, Edward J. ... **Minneapolis, MN**
Hayward, Erica Elizabeth **Los Angeles, CA**
Hayward, Ernest L., Law Office of Orange, CA
Hayward, Gary L. ... Des Moines, IA
Hayward, George J. ... **New York, NY**
Hayward, Guy J. ... Middletown, NY
Hayward, H. Garrett ... Poughkeepsie, NY
Hayward, Henry A. ... Hingham, MA
Hayward, John F. ... **Toledo, OH**
Hayward, John G. ... **Bloomfield Hills, MI**
Hayward, John L. ... St. Louis, MO
Hayward, John O. ... Waltham, MA
Hayward, John P. ... **Toledo, OH**
Hayward, Kathleen B. ... Knoxville, TN
Hayward, Lisa Rediger ... **Seattle, WA**
Hayward, Marvin C. ... Fort Myers, FL
Hayward, Michelle L. ... **Baltimore, MD**
Hayward, Parker & O'Leary Middletown, NY
Hayward, Raymond A. ... **Rochester, MN**
Hayward, Richard C. ... Alexandria, VA
Hayward, Robert M. ... **Phoenix, AZ**
Hayward, Samuel G. ... **Louisville, KY**
Hayward, Thomas S. ... Seattle, WA
Hayward, Thomas Z., Jr. ... **Chicago, IL**
Hayward, Tom R. ... Tallahassee, FL
Hayward, William D. ... **Addison, TX**
Haywood, Alwin M. ... New Brunswick, NJ
Haywood, Arthur L., III ... Philadelphia, PA
Haywood, Benjamin V., (P.A.) Pompano Beach, FL
Haywood, Charles R. ... **Chicago, IL**
Haywood, Cheryl Jenkins ... Brooklyn, NY
Haywood, Constance Patterson **Atlanta, GA**
Haywood, D., & Associates, P.C. Lansing, MI
Haywood, David J. ... Lansing, MI
Haywood, Denny & Miller, L.L.P. **Chapel Hill, NC** **Durham, NC**
Haywood, E. Burke ... Raleigh, NC
Haywood, Elizabeth B. ... **Washington, DC**
Haywood, Guy A. ... **Wailuku, HI**
Haywood, Harry L. ... Eldora, IA
Haywood, Herbert H. ... Department of the Navy, GV
Haywood, James S., Jr. ... Brownsville, TN
Haywood, Janis A. ... Eau Claire, WI
Haywood, John A. ... Port Isabel, TX
Haywood, John D. ... Durham, NC
Haywood, Julie ... **Philadelphia, PA**
Haywood, K. Reed ... **Philadelphia, PA**
Haywood Law Firm ... Brownsville, TN
Haywood, Margaret A. ... Washington, DC
Haywood, Mark F. ... **St. Louis, MO**
Haywood, R. Alan ... **Austin, TX**
Haywood, Rosa ... Brownsville, TN
Haywood, Ryan H. ... **Toledo, OH**
Haywood & Spencer ... Brownsville, TN
Haywood, Suneese R. ... **Dallas, TX**
Haywood, Yvonne S. House of Representatives, Office of Legislative Counsel, GV
Haywoode, M. Douglas ... New York, NY
Hayworth, Andrea E. ... **Atlanta, GA**
Hayworth & Chaney, P.A. ... Melbourne, FL
Hayworth, John C. ... **Nashville, TN**
Hayworth, Michael B ... Colstrip, MT
Hayworth, Michael S. ... Melbourne, FL
Haza, Michael D. ... Campbellsport, WI
Hazan, David L. ... **Waukegan, IL**
Hazan, Scott L. ... **New York, NY**
Hazapis, Anthony N. ... Seattle, WA
Hazarabedian, Arthur J. ... **Los Angeles, CA**
Hazard, B. Stevens ... **Jackson, MS**
Hazard, Dean W. ... **Ventura, CA**
Hazard, Elizabeth S. ... Toledo, OH
Hazard, Geoffrey C., Jr. ... Philadelphia, PA
Hazard, Holly E. ... Rockville, MD
Hazard, J. Wyatt ... **Jackson, MS**
Hazard, James L. ... **Walnut Creek, CA**
Hazard, Jeffrey B. ... Phoenix, MD
Hazard, John F., Jr. ... Freehold, NJ
Hazard, John N. ... New York, NY
Hazard, John W., Jr. ... **Washington, DC**
Hazard, Katherine W. ... Department of Justice, Environment and Natural Resources Division, GV
Hazard, Kristin A. ... **Portland, OR**
Hazard, Paul L. ... Belfast, ME
Hazard, Robert F. ... Tullahoma, TN
Hazard, Rowland K. ... East Greenwich, RI
Hazard, Stephen B. ... **Hartford, CT**
Hazard, Susan J. ... **Los Angeles, CA**
Hazard, Thomas E. J. ... **Denver, CO**
Hazard, William R. ... Evanston, IL
Hazarian, Natasha ... **El Paso, TX**
Hazday, Salomon, Jr. ... **Pleasanton, CA**
Hazel, Carolyn S. ... Houston, TX
Hazel, Claude R. ... Houston, TX
Hazel, David P. ... Yakima, WA
Hazel, Donald H. ... Sanger, CA
Hazel, Donald H., A P.C. ... Sanger, CA
Hazel, Frank T. ... Media, PA
Hazel, George A. ... Stanfordville, NY
Hazel, George E. ... Lynn, MA
Hazel, J. Patrick ... Austin, TX
Hazel, James M. ... Buffalo, NY
Hazel, Janice L. ... **Salem, OR**
Hazel, Joel P. ... **Coeur d'Alene, ID**
Hazel, John T., Jr. ... **Falls Church, VA**
Hazel, Karen F. ... **Oakland, CA**
Hazel, Kristen E. ... **Chicago, IL**
Hazel, Lea G. ... **Tifton, GA**
Hazel, Michael B. ... Caruthersville, MO
Hazel, Robert A. ... Arlington, VA
Hazel, Robert W. ... Perrysburg, OH
Hazel & Thomas, A Professional Corporation **Fairfax, VA** **Falls Church, VA** **Leesburg, VA** **Richmond, VA**
Hazel, Timothy M. ... **Pittsburgh, PA**
Hazel, William A. ... Boston, MA
Hazelbaker, Elizabeth A. ... **Columbus, OH**
Hazelbaker, Mark ... Sun Prairie, WI
Hazelbaker, Ralph Brian ... Laguna Beach, CA
Hazelett, David N. ... Colchester, VT
Hazelett, Leonard Walsine ... Akron, OH
Hazelhurst, Dawn Marie ... Bronx, NY
Hazelip, Christopher C. ... **Jacksonville, FL**
Hazell, David Tully ... **Atlanta, GA**
Hazell, Maja D. ... **New York, NY**
Hazell, Monique B. ... Houston, TX
Hazell, Roger K. ... Pago Pago, TT
Hazelrigg, Christopher A. **Springfield, MO**
Hazelrigg and Cox ... **Frankfort, KY**
Hazelrigg and Roberts, P.C. **Springfield, MO**
Hazelrigg, Steven H. ... **Fort Wayne, IN**
Hazeltine, Colin R. ... **Ship Bottom, NJ**
Hazeltine, Earl H. ... Madison, WI
Hazeltine, Glenna M. ... Philadelphia, PA
Hazeltine, Sheri L. ... Juneau, AK
Hazeltine, William A. ... **Wilmington, DE**
Hazelton, Arthur G., Jr. ... Phoenix, AZ
Hazelton, David R. ... **Washington, DC**
Hazelton, Gary M. ... Bemidji, MN
Hazelton, Jean Marie ... New York, NY
Hazelton, Laner & Batson ... Kansas City, MO
Hazelton, Lindsey Helmer ... **Syracuse, NY**
Hazelton, Penelope A. ... Seattle, WA
Hazelton, Peter M. ... Columbus, OH
Hazelton, Stephanie G. ... Kansas City, MO
Hazelton, William A. ... **Albany, NY**
Hazelwood, Charles W., Jr. ... Springfield, VA
Hazelwood, Harry, Jr. ... Newark, NJ
Hazelwood, John A. ... **Milwaukee, WI**
Hazelwood, Joshua A. ... **Hartford, CT**
Hazelwood & Kasle ... Cleveland, OH
Hazelwood, Keith W. ... **St. Charles, MO**
Hazelwood, Kimball E. ... Charlottesville, VA
Hazelwood, Mark Foster **San Francisco, CA**
Hazelwood, Michael ... Cleveland, OH
Hazelwood, Pamela Martin ... Little Rock, AR
Hazelwood, Sara M. ... New York, NY
Hazelwood & Weber, LLC **St. Charles, MO**
Hazemey, Victoria K. ... **Columbus, OH**
Hazen, Deanna E. ... **New York, NY**
Hazen, Edwin R. ... Washington, DC
Hazen, Glen E., Jr. ... Cincinnati, OH
Hazen, Herman L. ... Atlanta, GA
Hazen, James M. ... **Newark, NJ** **New York, NY**
Hazen, Jane S. ... **Denver, CO** Fairplay, CO
Hazen, Laura E. ... Camas, WA
Hazen & Madigan, PLLC ... Camas, WA
Hazen, Marielle F. ... Butler, PA
Hazen, Renee L. ... Department of Justice, Federal Bureau of Investigation, GV
Hazen, Rhonda R. ... **Madison, WI**
Hazen, Richard Johnson ... Venice, FL
Hazen, Richard Johnson, P.A. ... Venice, FL
Hazen, Robt. L. ... Tucson, AZ
Hazen, Scott P. ... **Dallas, TX**
Hazen & Terrill, P.C. ... Austin, TX
Hazen, Terry L. ... New York, NY
Hazen, Thomas L. ... Chapel Hill, NC
Hazen, Vincent L. ... Austin, TX
Hazen, William A. ... Hanford, CA
Hazen, William H. ... New York, NY
Hazenberg, Hein J. M. ... New York, NY
Hazin, Slava ... **New York, NY**
Hazlaris, Karen Hallstrom ... Harvey, LA
Hazlegrove, Wilbur L. ... **Roanoke, VA**
Hazlehurst, John L. ... **Charlotte, NC**
Hazlehurst, Robert, Jr. ... **Houston, TX**
Hazlehurst, Robert P., Jr. ... Short Hills, NJ
Hazleton, William L. ... Atlanta, GA
Hazlett, Allan A. ... **Overland Park, KS**
Hazlett, Allan A. ... **Topeka, KS**
Hazlett, Allan A. ... **Wichita, KS**
Hazlett, Carl E. ... **Tucson, AZ**
Hazlett, David G. ... **Louisville, KY**
Hazlett, Dennis S. ... Santa Fe, NM
Hazlett, Don F. ... Lawrence, KS
Hazlett, George S. ... Wheeling, WV
Hazlett, Guy ... Borger, TX
Hazlett, J. Richard ... **Charlotte, NC**
Hazlett, Katharine B. ... **Washington, DC**
Hazlett, Kevin M. ... **St. Louis, MO**
Hazlett, Mark A. ... **Honolulu, HI**
Hazlett, Melissa A. ... St. Petersburg, FL
Hazlett & Reizner, P.C. ... **Ann Arbor, MI** **Jackson, MI**
Hazlett, Sandra A. ... **Ann Arbor, MI**
Hazlett, Sandra W. ... Lawrence, KS
Hazlett, Stanton A. ... Topeka, KS
Hazlett, Susan L. ... Topeka, KS
Hazlett, Thomas Mck. ... St. Clairsville, OH Wheeling, WV
Hazlett, Timothy J. ... Louisville, KY
Hazlett & Wilkes ... **Tucson, AZ**
Hazlewood, Anne Morris ... Lubbock, TX
Hazlewood, Beverley E. Small Business Administration, Office of the General Counsel, GV
Hazlewood, David ... Lubbock, TX
Hazlewood, Fred H. ... Manitowoc, WI
Hazlewood and Hazlewood ... Lubbock, TX
Hazlewood, Jack ... **Amarillo, TX**
Hazlewood, James H. ... Scottsdale, AZ
Hazlewood, Milburn E. ... Austin, TX
Hazlewood, N. Russell ... **Wichita, KS**
Hazlewood, Yanick T. ... Department of Labor, Pension and Welfare Benefits, GV
Hazley-Williams, Viola P. ... Milwaukee, WI
Hazlitt, Arthur ... **New York, NY**
Hazlitt, Catherine A. ... **Washington, DC**
Hazlitt, Christopher M. ... **Boulder, CO**
Hazlitt, Kristin E. ... Ithaca, NY
Hazlitt, Walter C., Jr. ... **Washington, DC**
Hazlitt, William H. ... Arvada, CO
Hazouri, Cathryn L. ... **Boulder, CO**
Hazouri, Cathryn L., P.C. ... **Boulder, CO**
Hazouri, David R. ... **Miami, FL**
Hazouri, Fred A. ... West Palm Beach, FL
Hazouri, Kenneth P. ... **Orlando, FL**
Hazra, Suneeta ... **Washington, DC**
Hazzard, Andrea L. ... **New York, NY**
Hazzard, Elaine M. ... New York, NY
Hazzard, Gerald F. ... New York, NY
Hazzard, John P. ... Kansas City, MO
Hazzard, John P., IV ... Concord, NC
Hazzard, John Potter, V ... Columbia, SC
Hazzard, Lisa Swiszcz ... **Boston, MA**
Hazzard, Michael B. ... Washington, DC
Hazzard, Robert D. ... **White Plains, NY**
Hazzard, William J. ... **Naples, FL**
Hazzard, Yakub, (A Professional Corporation) ... **Los Angeles, CA**
Hazzouri, Edward J. ... Philadelphia, PA
HCM Intellectual Property Law Group, P.C. Atlanta, GA
He, Junhua Melody ... **New York, NY**
Hea, David B. ... Southfield, MI
Heaberlin, P. Franklin ... **Prestonsburg, KY**
Heaberlin, Penny R. ... **Minneapolis, MN**
Heacock, John M., Jr. ... **Huntsville, AL**
Heacock, John W. ... **Nashville, TN**
Heacock, Laurel E. ... Boise, ID
Heacock, Mark A. ... Washington, DC
Heacock, Pamela P. ... Waltham, MA
Heacock, Steven R. ... Grand Rapids, MI
Heacox, Gregory G. ... St. Paul, MN
Heacox, Hartman, Mattaini, Koshmrl, Cosgriff & Johnson, P.A. ... St. Paul, MN
Head, Albon O., Jr. ... **Fort Worth, TX**
Head, Allan B. ... Raleigh, NC
Head, Anne L. ... Augusta, ME
Head, Barbara G. ... Kansas City, MO
Head, Ben T. ... Austin, TX
Head, Brenda L. ... **Topeka, KS**
Head, Brendan P. ... **Chicago, IL**
Head, C. Andrew ... **Atlanta, GA**
Head, Christopher A. ... Buffalo, NY
Head, C. J. ... **New York, NY**
Head, Clark ... **Indio, CA**
Head, Craig L. ... Department of the Air Force, Office of the Judge Advocate General, GV
Head, Dale A. ... Phoenix, AZ
Head, Dale A. ... **Houston, TX**
Head, Daniel M. ... Port Republic, MD
Head, David C. ... **Carrollton, GA**
Head, David C. ... **Nashville, TN**
Head, Donna L. ... Chicago, IL
Head, Donna Lyn ... St. Louis, MO
Head, Donna M. ... **Manchester, NH**
Head, Dora L. ... Greensboro, NC
Head, Douglas M. ... **Minneapolis, MN**
Head, Elisa B. ... Ravenna, OH
Head, Elizabeth ... New York, NY
Head, Elizabeth J. ... **Washington, DC**
Head, Fred C. ... Athens, TX
Head, George M. ... Bloomfield Hills, MI
Head, H. Garland, III ... Woodstock, GA
Head, Hayden W., Jr. ... Corpus Christi, TX
Head, Head & Head ... **Heflin, AL** **Wedowee, AL** **Buchanan, GA** **Carrollton, GA** **Franklin, GA**
Head, Henry C. ... **Carrollton, GA**
Head, J. Frank ... **Columbiana, AL**
Head, James B. ... **Carrollton, GA**
Head, James F. ... McLean, VA
Head, James G. ... San Francisco, CA
Head, James L. ... West Chester, PA
Head, James P. ... **Washington, DC**
Head, James R. ... **Tulsa, OK**
Head, James W. ... Oakland, CA
Head, James W. ... Savannah, GA
Head, Janice S. ... Mount Olive, NC
Head, Janice S., P.A. ... Mount Olive, NC
Head, Jeffry Alan ... **Mobile, AL**
Head, Jerry L. ... Garland, TX
Head, John D. ... **Austin, TX**
Head, John F. ... Denver, CO
Head, John F., P.C. ... Denver, CO
Head, John V. ... Lincoln, NE
Head, John Vernon ... Orlando, FL
Head, Johnson & Kachigian **Fayetteville, AR** **Oklahoma City, OK** **Tulsa, OK**
Head, Jonathan Byron ... **Bay Minette, AL** **Daphne, AL** **Foley, AL**
Head, Joseph H., Jr. ... Covington, KY
Head, Keith L. ... Houston, TX
Head, Koko ... **Jacksonville, FL**
Head, Koko, P.A. ... **Jacksonville, FL** **Orange Park, FL**
Head, Kristen E. ... Kansas City, MO
Head, Louis E., Jr. ... Whittier, CA
Head, Marie Hillery ... Birmingham, AL
Head, Martin P. ... Chicago, IL
Head, Mary S. ... **Washington, DC**
Head, Michelle L. Atkins ... **Milwaukee, WI**
Head, Mike ... Athens, TX
Head, Moss & Fulton, P.A. **Orange Park, FL**
Head, Neil W. ... West Chester, PA
Head, Oliver P. ... Columbiana, AL
Head, Patrick J. ... **Chicago, IL**
Head, Randall L. ... Ironton, MO
Head, Richard J. ... Louisville, KY Simpsonville, KY
Head, Richard W. ... Manchester, NH
Head, Robert J., Jr. ... **Orange Park, FL**
Head, Seifert & Vander Weide, A Professional Association **Minneapolis, MN**
Head, Smith, Metcalf, Aguilar, Moss, Sieron & Perritt, P.A. ... Orange Park, FL
Head, Stacy S. ... **New Orleans, LA**
Head, Steven L. ... **Atlanta, GA**
Head, Suzanne ... Columbus, OH
Head, Thomas E., III ... Elba, AL
Head, Thomas W. ... Birmingham, AL
Head, Thomas & Webb, LLC **Atlanta, GA** **Decatur, GA** **Jonesboro, GA** **Lawrenceville, GA** **Marietta, GA**
Head, Wallace L. ... Chicago, IL
Head, Whitney McGee ... Bentonville, AR
Head, William C. ... **Atlanta, GA**
Head, William W., Jr. ... Gallup, NM

Headen, Frederick ... Lansing, MI
Headen, Raymond C. ... Cincinnati, OH
Cleveland, OH
Headings, Theodore H. ... Plano, TX
Headington, Rodney Ian
San Francisco, CA
Headley, C. Christopher ... Santa Monica, CA
Headley, Charles Jan ... Omaha, NE
Headley, Darah S. ... Houston, TX
Headley, David L. ... Norton, OH
Headley, Dean R. ... Tahoe City, CA
Headley, Frank M., Jr. ... Scarsdale, NY
Headley, George B. ... Brooklyn, NY
Headley, Jack W. R. ... Kansas City, MO
Headley, James G. ... Cincinnati, OH
Headley, Jennifer Ann ... Springfield, MO
Headley, Laurel L. ... Oakland, CA
Headley, Linda Ottinger ... Houston, TX
Headley, Mark J. ... New York, NY
Headley, Matthew L. ... Greencastle, IN
Headley, Russell K. ... St. Paul, MN
Headley, Tim ... Dallas, TX
Houston, TX
Headley, Trevor L. ... Brooklyn, NY
Headman, A. O., Jr. ... Salt Lake City, UT
Headrick, Amy E. ... Anchorage, AK
Headrick, Charles H. ... Stillwater, OK
Headrick, David D. ... Chicago, IL
Headrick, Everett C. ... Nashville, TN
Headrick, Linda J. ... Oakland, CA
Headrick, Richard A. ... Port Angeles, WA
Headrick, Robert L. ... Fort Lauderdale, FL
Headrick, S. Russell ... Memphis, TN
Headrick, Thomas E. ... Buffalo, NY
Heady, Barbara Jean ... Des Moines, IA
Heady, Brian David ... East St. Louis, IL
Heady, Douglas J.
Department of the Air Force,
Office of the General Counsel, GV
Heady, Eugene J. ... Atlanta, GA
Heady, Karen Woodall ... Marion, KY
Heady, Kenneth ... Oklahoma City, OK
Heady, Stephen ... Portland, OR
Heafey, Edwin A., Jr. ... Oakland, CA
Heafey, Michael F. ... Palo Alto, CA
Heafey, Richard J. ... Oakland, CA
Heafitz, Harvey B. ... Boston, MA
Heafitz & Sullivan ... Boston, MA
Heafner, Gregory A. ... Carrboro, NC
Heafner, Mary ... Houston, TX
Heafner, William H. ... Asheboro, NC
Heagen, Matthew J. ... Toms River, NJ
Heagerty, Christopher D. ... Knoxville, TN
Heagler, Douglas M. ... Jefferson City, MO
Heagney, Daniel ... St. Louis, MO
Heagney, Lawrence ... Spartanburg, SC
Heagney, Lennon & Slane LLP
Fairfield, CT
Greenwich, CT
Stamford, CT
White Plains, NY
Heagney, Philip ... St. Louis, MO
Heagney, Robert W. ... East Hartford, CT
Heagney, Thomas J. ... Greenwich, CT
Heagney, Virginia E. ... St. Louis, MO
Heagy, Warren ... Odessa, TX
Heal, Noel F. ... Palos Verdes Estates, CA
Healan, Michael D. ... Boston, MA
Heald, Anthony M. ... Delaware, OH
Heald & Associates ... Providence, RI
Heald, Daniel A., IV ... Encino, CA
Heald, Deborah D. ... Atlanta, GA
Heald, Garth R. ... West Chester, PA
Heald, Howard J. ... Atlantic City, NJ
Heald, Jennifer P. ... Hackensack, NJ
Heald, John H. ... Portland, OR
Heald, Karen S. ... Rutland, VT
Heald & Long ... Delaware, OH
Heald, Nan ... Portland, ME
Heald, Philip J ... Ironton, OH
Heald, Rachel M. ... Los Angeles, CA
Heald, Randall M.
Department of the Air Force,
Office of the General Counsel, GV
Heald, Robert C. ... Lubbock, TX
Heald, Roger W. ... Fairfax, VA
Heald, Russell W. ... Beaumont, TX
Heald, Seth G. ... Department of Justice,
Tax Division, GV
Heald, Thomas W. ... Providence, RI
Healey, Arthur H. ... New Haven, CT
Healey, Arthur T. ... Harrisburg, PA
Healey, Brendan J. ... Chicago, IL
Healey, Brian W. ... Washington, DC
Healey, Carol L. ... Emeryville, CA
San Francisco, CA
Healey, Catherine A. ... Bonifay, FL
Healey, Charles M., III ... Boston, MA
Healey, Christopher D. ... Providence, RI
Healey, Christopher J. ... San Diego, CA
Healey, Christopher P. ... Washington, DC
Healey, Colleen M. ... Denver, CO
Healey, David J. ... Houston, TX
Healey, David W. ... Quincy, MA
Healey, Davidson & Hornack ... Pittsburgh, PA
Healey, Dennis J. ... Palm Desert, CA
Healey, Deshaies & Gagliardi, PC
Amesbury, MA
Healey, Edw V., Jr. ... Cranston, RI
Healey, Edward G. ... Clifton, NJ
Healey, Elizabeth ... Columbia, MO
Healey, Frank T., Jr. ... Waterbury, CT
Healey & Healey ... Indian Wells, CA
Palm Desert, CA
Healey, James P. ... Palm Desert, CA
Healey, James R. ... Southbury, CT
Healey, James Sean ... Houston, TX
Healey, James T. ... Hartford, CT
Healey, Janis S. ... San Diego, CA
Healey, John Dennis ... Peabody, MA
Healey, John F., Jr. ... Richmond, TX
Healey, John M. ... Denver, CO
Healey, John M. ... New York, NY
Healey, John P. ... Amesbury, MA
Healey, Joseph Timothy ... Scranton, PA
Healey, Kristen ... Washington, DC
Healey, Laura Valleau ... Portland, ME
Manchester, NH
Healey, Leah C. ... Short Hills, NJ
Healey, Lisa Cangelosi ... Fairfax, VA
Healey, Marie ... New Orleans, LA
Healey, Mary Joy ... Meriden, CT
Healey, Michael J. ... Denver, CO
Healey, Michael J. ... Pittsburgh, PA
Healey, Nancy Spodick ... Charlottesville, VA
Healey, Patrick J. ... Philadelphia, PA
Healey, Patrick W. ... Lincoln, NE
Healey, Paul D. ... St. Paul, MN
Healey, Peter F., Jr. ... Washington, DC
Healey & Phelan ... Waterbury, CT
Healey, Phillip J. ... Chicago, IL
Healey, R. Michael ... Portland, OR
Healey, Richard B. ... Los Angeles, CA
Healey, Richard P. ... Hartford, CT
Healey, Robert E. ... Hartford, CT
Healey, Robert T. ... St. Louis, MO
Healey, Robert T. ... Mount Holly, NJ
Healey, Roger W. ... Cincinnati, OH
Healey, Rosemary ... Providence, RI
Healey, Russell L. ... Jacksonville, FL
Healey & Smith, A Professional Law
Corporation ... New Orleans, LA
Healey, Thomas C. ... Wilton, CT
Healey, Thomas E. ... Washington, DC
Healey, Thomas H. ... New York, NY
Healey, Thomas J., Jr. ... Atlanta, GA
Healey, Thomas L. ... Houston, TX
Healey, Tracy Muir ... Del Mar, CA
Healey & Wieland ... Lincoln, NE
Healey, William F. ... Hartford, CT
Healey, William F., Jr. ... Milford, CT
Healey, William H. ... Newark, NJ
Philadelphia, PA
Healey, William J. ... McLean, VA
Healey, William V. ... New York, NY
Healing, Robert E. ... Fairfield, CT
Healow, James P. ... Billings, MT
Healow, Terrence M. ... Butte, MT
Health Law Firm, The ... Little Rock, AR
Healy, Angela Boutwell ... Jackson, MS
Healy, Angela E. ... Fresno, CA
Healy, Ava L. ... Rockville, MD
Healy & Baillie, LLP ... Stamford, CT
New York, NY
Healy, Bernard F. ... Rockford, IL
Healy, Bernard P. ... Providence, RI
Healy, Brett L. ... Los Angeles, CA
Healy, Brian S. ... San Francisco, CA
Healy, Bridget M. ... Franklin Lakes, NJ
Healy, Christopher W. ... New York, NY
Healy, Daniel J. ... Vallejo, CA
Healy, Daniel J. ... Spring Lake Heights, NJ
Healy, Daniel J. ... New York, NY
Healy, Daniel K. ... New York, NY
Healy, Daniel Lawrence ... New Britain, CT
Healy, Danl. A., Jr. ... Chatham, MA
Healy, David P. ... Tallahassee, FL
Healy, David W. ... Palo Alto, CA
Healy, Debra Solle ... Irvine, CA
Healy, Dennis D. ... El Paso, TX
Healy, Dennis J., Jr. ... Carson City, NV
Healy, Donald J., Jr. ... Oak Brook, IL
Healy, Dwight A. ... New York, NY
Healy, Edmund J. ... Slatington, PA
Healy, Edward J. ... Wichita, KS
Healy, Edward P. ... Worcester, MA
Healy, Elise A. ... Dallas, TX
Healy, Elizabeth B. ... Kansas City, MO
Healy, Elizabeth Slatten ... New Orleans, LA
Healy, F. Dale, Jr. ... Tucson, AZ
Healy, F. James ... Albany, OR
Healy & Falk ... Belford, NJ
Healy Firm, The ... Sheridan, WY
Healy, Fiske and Woodbury ... Cambridge, MA
Healy, G. Patrick ... Tacoma, WA
Healy, Gary M. ... Omaha, NE
Healy, George E., Jr. ... Providence, RI
Healy, George R. ... Chicago, IL
Healy, George W., III ... New Orleans, LA
Healy, George W., IV ... New Orleans, LA
Healy, Gerard A. ... Los Angeles, CA
Healy, Grace M. ... Stamford, CT
Healy, Harold H., Jr. ... New York, NY
Healy and Healy, P.C. ... Wellesley Hills, MA
Healy, Henry S. ... Boston, MA
Healy, Herman D. ... New Albany, IN
Healy & Hester, P.C. ... Tyler, TX
Healy, Howard T. ... Neenah, WI
Healy, J. Casey ... Wilton, CT
Healy, J. Kevin ... New York, NY
Healy, J. Raymond ... San Francisco, CA
Healy, Jack S. ... Cincinnati, OH
Healy, James B. ... Trenton, NJ
Healy, James E. ... New York, NY
Healy, James F. ... Middle Village, NY
Healy, James G. ... Silver Spring, MD
Healy, James G. ... Wellesley Hills, MA
Healy, James M., Jr. ... Tacoma, WA
Healy, James M., Jr., Inc., P.S. ... Tacoma, WA
Healy, James P. ... Tacoma, WA
Healy, Jared Timothy ... Columbia, MD
Healy, Jeffray A. ... Cleveland, OH
Healy, Jennifer R. ... Waterbury, CT
Healy, Jeremiah F., III ... Boston, MA
Healy, Joan M. ... Winston-Salem, NC
Healy, Jody A. ... New York, NY
Healy, John A. ... New York, NY
Healy, John C. ... Chicago, IL
Healy, John D., Jr. ... St. Paul, MN
Healy, John J., III ... Jackson, MS
Healy, John L. ... Wellesley, MA
Healy, John M. ... Hartford, CT
Healy, John P. ... Columbia, MD
Healy, John P. ... Kansas City, MO
Healy, John P. ... New York, NY
Healy, John P., P.A. ... Columbia, MD
Healy, John Patrick ... San Francisco, CA
Healy, John Patrick ... Chicago, IL
Healy, Jos. L. ... Wellesley, MA
Healy, Joseph P. ... Jersey City, NJ
Healy, Joseph R. ... Albany, NY
Healy, Kathleen C. ... Renton, WA
Healy, Kathleen G. ... Cheyenne, WY
Sheridan, WY
Healy, Kevin ... Woodcliff Lake, NJ
Healy, Kevin G. ... Newark, DE
Healy, Kevin George ... Seattle, WA
Healy, Kevin J. ... New York, NY
Healy, Kevin Joseph ... San Diego, CA
Healy, Kevin Michael ... Sacramento, CA
Healy, Liam P. ... Boston, MA
Healy, Lisa H. ... Boston, MA
Healy, Loretta A. ... Hingham, MA
Healy, Lynn D. ... Newark, NJ
Healy, M. Catherine ... Hartford, CT
New Haven, CT
Healy, Margaret Glenn ... Wichita, KS
Healy, Margaret Hartley ... San Francisco, CA
Healy, Marilyn Mullen ... Tampa, FL
Healy, Martin ... Roseland, NJ
Healy, Martin ... Alexandria, VA
Healy, Martin J., Jr. & Associates
Chicago, IL
Healy, Martin R. ... Boston, MA
Healy, Martin William ... Boston, MA
Healy, Mary Ann ... Pasadena, CA
Healy, Mary E. ... Department of Justice,
Civil Rights Division, GV
Healy, Mary J. ... Cincinnati, OH
Healy, Maureen A. ... Kew Gardens, NY
Healy, Maureen R. ... New York, NY
Healy, Maurice Dixon ... Dallas, TX
Healy, Michael F. ... San Francisco, CA
Healy, Michael F. ... Washington, DC
Healy, Michael F. ... Chicago, IL
Healy, Michael J. ... Uniondale, NY
Healy, Michael P. ... Lexington, KY
Healy, Michael P. ... Holliston, MA
Healy, Michael P., (P.C.) ... Kansas City, MO
Healy, Michael T. ... Petaluma, CA
Healy, Michael T. ... Portland, ME
Healy, Michelle L. ... New York, NY
Healy, Nancy A. ... Department of Justice,
Federal Bureau of Investigation, GV
Healy, Nicholas J. ... New York, NY
Healy, Nicole M. ... Palo Alto, CA
Healy, Patricia ... Palo Alto, CA
Healy, Patricia A. ... Tarrytown, NY
Healy, Patricia A. ... Garrisonville, VA
Stafford, VA
Healy, Patrick D. ... Belford, NJ
Healy, Patrick F. ... Melbourne, FL
Healy, Patrick F. ... Palos Heights, IL
Healy, Patrick F., III ... Chicago, IL
Healy, Patrick S. ... Pittsburgh, PA
Healy, Paul E. ... Cambridge, MA
Healy, Paul F., Jr. ... Boston, MA
Healy, Paul J. ... Jacksonville, FL
Healy, Peter R. ... Overland Park, KS
Healy, Peter T. ... San Francisco, CA
Healy, Regina ... Cambridge, MA
Healy, Richard J. ... Riverside, CA
Healy, Richard L. ... Gaithersburg, MD
Healy, Richard L. ... Fargo, ND
Healy, Richard L., P.C. ... Gaithersburg, MD
Healy, Richard M. ... Lyons, NY
Healy, Richard M., III
Oklahoma City, OK
Healy, Robert H. ... Detroit, MI
Healy, Robert J. ... St. Paul, MN
Healy, Robert J., Jr. ... Clearwater, FL
Healy, Robert W. ... Washington, DC
Healy, Rosemary B.
General Accounting Office,
Office of the General Counsel, GV
Healy, Scott Patrick ... Hillsboro, OR
Healy, Sean A. ... Bronx, NY
Healy, Sean P. ... Tucson, AZ
Healy, Sean P. ... Tyler, TX
Healy, Sheryl E. ... Chicago, IL
Healy, Stephen J. ... Novato, CA
Healy, Stephen J. ... Chicago, IL
Healy, Stuart S. ... Sheridan, WY
Healy, Stuart S., III ... Sheridan, WY
Healy & Studwell Law Firm, P.C.
Tucson, AZ
Healy & Svoren ... Toccoa, GA
Healy, Terence Michael ... Washington, DC
Healy, Theresa A. ... Portland, OR
Healy, Thomas E. ... White Plains, NY
Healy, Thomas F. ... Wellesley Hills, MA
Healy, Thomas G. ... New Berlin, WI
Healy, Thomas M. ... Paramus, NJ
Healy, Thomas P., Jr. ... Glen Ellyn, IL
Healy, Thomas R. ... Arlington, VA
Healy, Thomas W. ... Rochester, MN
Healy, Tim W. ... Ogden, UT
Healy, Tim W., P.C. ... Ogden, UT
Healy, Timothy J. ... Farley, IA
Healy, Timothy J. ... Richmond, VA
Healy, Timothy P. ... Toccoa, GA
Healy, Walter F. X. ... New York, NY
Healy, William Charles ... Miami, FL
Healy, William J. ... San Diego, CA
Healy, William J. ... San Mateo, CA
Healy, William J. ... Rockville Centre, NY
Healy, William M. ... Edgartown, MA
Healy, William T. ... Tucson, AZ
Healy Glasgow, Carol J.
Fort Lauderdale, FL
Tampa, FL
West Palm Beach, FL
Heaman, Michael A. ... Citrus Heights, CA
Heamon, Theresa M. ... Elkhart, IN
Heaner, William E., Jr. ... Beaumont, TX
Heaney & Associates ... King Of Prussia, PA
Philadelphia, PA
Heaney, Brian R. ... Grand Rapids, MI
Heaney, Brion P. ... Arlington, VA
Heaney, C. E., Jr. ... Omaha, NE
Heaney, Chris J. ... South Holland, IL
Heaney, Donald L. ... Madison, WI
Heaney, Gerald W. ... Duluth, MN
Heaney & Heaney ... Bernardsville, NJ
Heaney, James C. ... Tonawanda, NY
Heaney, James R., (P.C.) ... Florham Park, NJ
Heaney, Julia ... Wilmington, DE
Heaney, Kathleen A. ... Elk River, MN
Heaney, Mark O. ... Los Angeles, CA
Heaney, Michael K. ... Bernardsville, NJ
Heaney, Robin Mary ... Rockville Centre, NY
Heaney, Susan M. ... San Francisco, CA
Heaney, Suzanne M. ... Brooklyn, NY
Heaney, Terence K. ... King Of Prussia, PA
Heaney, Thomas F., Jr. ... Asbury Park, NJ
Heaney, Timothy M. ... Minneapolis, MN
Heaney, Tricia ... Dallas, TX
Heap, David N. ... Phoenix, AZ
Heap, Edw. L. ... Bakersfield, CA
Heap, Elmer L., Jr. ... San Diego, CA
Heap, Frank K. ... Chicago, IL
Heap, Theodore H. ... Portland, OR
Heap, William G. ... Robinson, IL
Heape, Donald R., Sr. ... Placerville, CA
Heaphey, Christopher J. ... Anchorage, AK
Heaphy, Chris B. ... Bloomfield Hills, MI
Heaphy, Hayden F., Jr. ... Cheyenne, WY
Sheridan, WY
Heaphy, John M. ... Chicago, IL
Heaphy, John M. ... Detroit, MI
Heaphy, Kathleen A.
Department Of Veterans Affairs,
Office of the General Counsel, GV
Heaphy, Kathleen V. ... Long Beach, CA
Heaphy, Mark W. ... New Haven, CT
Heaphy, William J., III ... Columbus, OH
Heaps, Carlos E. ... Birmingham, AL
Heaps, Martin D. ... Redwood City, CA
Heard, Adella Malvezzi ... Memphis, TN
Heard, Arthur B. ... Cleveland, OH
Heard, Bradley E. ... Atlanta, GA
Heard, C. Stephen, Jr. ... New York, NY
Heard, Charles W. ... Concord, NH
Wolfeboro, NH
Heard, Craig T. ... New York, NY
Heard, Dan W. ... Port Lavaca, TX
Heard, Debora Denise ... Chattanooga, TN
Heard, Denman H. ... Houston, TX
Heard, Donald B. ... Pittsburgh, PA
Heard, Drew R. ... Dallas, TX
Heard, Dwight A. ... Fort Worth, TX
Heard, Frank L., Jr. ... Houston, TX
Heard, Frank Lane, III ... Washington, DC
Heard, H. Roderic ... Chicago, IL
Heard, Harry R. ... Longview, TX
Heard, J. Cliff ... Montgomery, AL
Heard, James H. ... Chicago, IL
Heard, James L., Jr. ... Yuma, AZ
Heard, Jesse S., Jr. ... West Monroe, LA
Heard, John F. ... Houston, TX
Heard, John G. ... Houston, TX
Heard, John H. ... Danville, VA
Heard, John H., P.C. ... Danville, VA
Heard, John R. ... San Antonio, TX
Heard, Joseph H. ... Raleigh, NC
Heard, Joseph M. ... Houston, TX
Heard, Joshua Taylor ... Los Angeles, CA
Heard, Keith W. ... New York, NY
Heard, Kevin D. ... Huntsville, AL
Heard, Laura D., Law Office of
San Antonio, TX
Heard Linebarger Graham Goggan Blair
Peña & Sampson, LLP ... New Orleans, LA
Philadelphia, PA
Austin, TX
Beaumont, TX
Brownsville, TX
Conroe, TX
Corpus Christi, TX
Corsicana, TX
Dallas, TX
Denton, TX
Edinburg, TX
El Paso, TX
Fort Worth, TX
Houston, TX
Laredo, TX
Longview, TX
Odessa, TX
Richmond, TX
San Antonio, TX
Sherman, TX
The Woodlands, TX
Tyler, TX
Heard, Maria Colsey ... Washington, DC
Heard & Medack, P.C. ... Houston, TX
Heard, Oliver S., Jr. ... San Antonio, TX
Heard, Paul Douglas ... Houston, TX
Heard, Render M., Jr. ... Tifton, GA
Heard, Richard A. ... Irving, TX
Heard, Richard W. ... Columbus, MT
Heard, Robert A. ... Hillsboro, OR

Heard, Robert M. ... Elberton, GA
Heard, Rosemarie B. ... Irvine, CA
Heard, Ruth E. ... New York, NY
Heard, Scott M. ... Billings, MT
Heard & Smith ... San Antonio, TX
Heard, Stephen K. ... Nashville, TN
Heard, Viddell L., Jr. ... Los Angeles, CA
Heard, W. Kenneth ... Fairhope, AL
Heard, William A., III ... Treasury Department, Internal Revenue Service, GV
Heard, William M., Jr. ... Mobile, AL
Heard & Wright, P.C. ... Fort Worth, TX
Heard, Wyatt H. ... Albuquerque, NM
Hearey, Bruce G. ... Cleveland, OH
Hearey, Dianne Foley ... Cleveland, OH
Hearey, Elizabeth B. ... Pleasanton, CA
Hearin, Jesse B., III ... Baton Rouge, LA
Hearin, Robert M., Jr. ... New Orleans, LA
Hearin & Warriner, L.L.C. ... New Orleans, LA
Hearing, Annette ... Media, PA
Hearing, Gregory A. ... Tampa, FL
Hearing, Ross E. ... La Grande, OR
Hearl, Phillip G. ... Abingdon, VA
Hearle, Matthew ... New York, NY
Hearn, Brittain & Martin, P.A. ... Conway, SC; Myrtle Beach, SC
Hearn, Charles J. ... Humble, TX
Hearn, Cherry J. ... Denver, CO
Hearn, Christian E. ... Ashland, OR
Hearn, Christine A. ... Tampa, FL
Hearn, Clayton ... Houston, TX
Hearn, Clifford B., Jr. ... Odessa, DE; Wilmington, DE
Hearn, Clifford B., Jr., P.A. ... Odessa, DE; Wilmington, DE
Hearn, Colleen K. ... Utica, NY
Hearn, Curtis R. ... New Orleans, LA
Hearn, David L. ... Carmel, IN
Hearn, David W. ... Roanoke, VA
Hearn, Edward R. ... San Jose, CA
Hearn, Edward W. ... Valparaiso, IN
Hearn, Eric D. ... Zebulon, GA
Hearn, Eric Lee ... Jacksonville, FL
Hearn, Etta Kay ... Baton Rouge, LA
Hearn, Francis J., Jr. ... New York, NY
Hearn, Frederick W. ... Glendale, CA
Hearn, George G. ... Raleigh, NC
Hearn, George H. ... New York, NY
Hearn, George J., III ... Monroe, GA
Hearn, George M., Jr. ... Conway, SC; Myrtle Beach, SC
Hearn, George W. ... Memphis, TN
Hearn, Holly M. ... Seattle, WA
Hearn, James D. ... Encino, CA
Hearn, Jeffrey A. ... Indianapolis, IN
Hearn, John J. ... Coral Springs, FL
Hearn, John J. ... Miami Shores, FL
Hearn, John J. ... Columbia, SC
Hearn, John R. ... Des Moines, IA
Hearn, Kathleen A. ... Charlestown, MA
Hearn, Kathleen K. ... Pueblo, CO
Hearn, Kaye Gorenflo ... Conway, SC
Hearn, Kenneth A. ... Los Angeles, CA
Hearn, Lynn C. ... Tampa, FL
Hearn, Mark ... Richardson, TX
Hearn, Michael A. ... Anaheim, CA
Hearn, Michael D. ... Charlotte, NC
Hearn, Nancy Peeler ... Dallas, TX
Hearn, Pamela D. ... Phoenix, AZ
Hearn, Patrick H. ... Olathe, KS
Hearn, Peter ... Philadelphia, PA
Hearn, Peter Lee, Sr. ... Conway, SC; Myrtle Beach, SC
Hearn, Peter, P.C. ... Philadelphia, PA
Hearn, Philip C. ... Jackson, MS
Hearn, R. Steven ... Warsaw, IN
Hearn, Reginald G. ... Belvedere-Tiburon, CA
Hearn, Richard A. ... Pocatello, ID
Hearn, Robert L. ... Miamisburg, OH
Hearn, Robert L. ... Greenfield, TN
Hearn, Robert R. ... Tampa, FL
Hearn, Samuel A. ... Ruxton, MD
Hearn, Sharon B. ... Indianapolis, IN
Hearn, Sharon Sklamba ... New Orleans, LA
Hearn, Stephen K., Jr. ... Ruston, LA
Hearn, Steven L. ... Sun City Center, FL; Tampa, FL
Hearn, Tarrow Leigh ... Durham, NC
Hearn, Timothy S. ... Minneapolis, MN
Hearn, William C. ... Washington, DC
Hearn, William R., Jr. ... Summerville, SC
Hearnburg, William V. ... Carrollton, GA
Hearne & Bailey, P.A. ... Ocean City, MD; Salisbury, MD; Snow Hill, MD
Hearne, D. David ... Lufkin, TX
Hearne, David A. ... Chesapeake, VA
Hearne, Douglass D. ... Austin, TX
Hearne, Douglass D., Jr. ... Austin, TX
Hearne, Eppright & Gest, A Professional Corporation ... Austin, TX
Hearne, Frank L. ... Tampa, FL
Hearne, John L. ... Jefferson City, MO
Hearne, John Q. ... Washington, DC
Hearne, Mark F. (Thor), II ... Kansas City, MO; St. Louis, MO
Hearne, Matthew Hill ... St. Louis, MO
Hearne, Nancy S. ... Princeton, NJ
Hearne, Nickolaus, Green & Beetem ... Jefferson City, MO
Hearne & Phillips, L.L.P. ... Kilgore, TX
Hearne & Pivac ... Springfield, MO
Hearne, Roy N. ... Kilgore, TX
Hearne & Spery ... Salisbury, MD
Hearne, Stephen M. ... Salisbury, MD
Hearne, Steve ... San Antonio, TX
Hearne, Steven G. ... Charlotte, NC
Hearne, Thomas H. ... Springfield, MO
Hearne, Treva J. ... Reno, NV
Hearne, Victoria E. ... Los Angeles, CA
Hearne, W. Lake ... Shreveport, LA
Hearne, William T. ... Tulsa, OK
Hearne, W. M. ... Dallas, TX
Hearnes, Warren E. ... Charleston, MO
Hearney, Michael P. ... San Francisco, CA
Hearns, Henry J. ... Miami, FL
Hearnsberger, Carla Wilson ... El Dorado, AR
Hearnsberger, Marcia R. ... Hot Springs National Park, AR
Hearon, Dennis L. ... Southfield, MI
Hearon, Duff C. ... Tucson, AZ
Hearon, Robert J., Jr. ... Austin, TX
Hearon, William C. ... Miami, FL
Hearrell, Randy ... Topeka, KS
Hearsch, David W. ... Sandusky, MI
Hearsch, Francis J., Jr. ... Mount Clemens, MI
Hearsch & Rinn ... Sandusky, MI
Hearsh, Bradford I. ... New York, NY
Hearshman, Timothy W. ... Kansas City, MO
Hearst, Alice L. ... Northampton, MA
Hearst, David W. ... Pasadena, CA
Hearst, Gayle D. ... Fresno, CA
Heartfield, J. Thad ... Beaumont, TX
Heartfield & McGinnis, L.L.P. ... Beaumont, TX
Heartquist, Richard P. ... Lowell, MA
Hearth, David A. ... San Francisco, CA
Heartney, Matthew T. ... Los Angeles, CA
Heartsill, James A., III ... Montgomery, AL
Heartwell, William L., III ... Daleville, VA
Heary & Jackson, P.C. ... Watertown, NY
Heary, James ... Watertown, NY
Heary, Nicole A. ... Buffalo, NY
Heary, Robert P. ... Buffalo, NY
Heaslet, Timothy J. ... Riverside, CA
Heaslett, David J. ... Graeagle, CA
Heasley, C. Wayne ... Charlotte, NC
Heasley, David K. ... Rockville, MD
Heasley, Howard N. ... Cleveland, OH
Heasley, Phillip L. ... Steubenville, OH
Heasley, Ross E. ... Chevy Chase, MD
Heasley, Staciellen S. ... Boston, MA
Heaslip & Heaslip ... Rockford, IL
Heaslip, Patrick L. ... Rockford, IL
Heaston, Curtis ... Chicago, IL
Heaston, Elaine Therese ... Omaha, NE
Heaston, William P. ... Irene, SD
Heasty, Monte K. ... Independence, KS
Heater, Henry E. ... San Diego, CA
Heater, John E. ... St. Louis, MO
Heath, Andrew D. ... New York, NY
Heath, Arlene N. ... San Francisco, CA
Heath, Arthur J. ... New York, NY
Heath, Bayard E. ... Miami, FL
Heath, Bayard W. ... Tallahassee, FL
Heath, Beth A. ... Shrewsbury, MA
Heath, Brannon ... New York, NY
Heath, Brenda Vaughn ... Albion, NY
Heath, C. Craig ... Portland, OR
Heath, C. Robert ... Austin, TX
Heath, Candina S. ... Dallas, TX
Heath, Charisse L. ... Forest Hills, NY
Heath, Charles D. ... Marinette, WI
Heath, Charles D. ... Onalaska, WI
Heath, Charlotte A. ... Durham, NC
Heath, Christine C. ... Austin, TX
Heath, Claude S. ... Leoti, KS
Heath, Cynthia G. ... St. Louis, MO
Heath, Daniel G. ... Fort Wayne, IN
Heath, David J. ... Berkeley, MO
Heath, David L. ... New York, NY
Heath, David P. ... Tallahassee, FL
Heath, Davis & McCalla, P.C. ... Austin, TX
Heath, Donald F., Jr. ... Oklahoma City, OK
Heath, Douglas M. ... Holley, NY
Heath, Edward D., Jr. ... Wichita, KS
Heath, Edward R., Sr. ... St. Petersburg, FL
Heath, Edward V., Jr. ... Owings Mills, MD
Heath, Edwin D., Jr. ... Richardson, TX
Heath, Elizabeth ... Spokane, WA
Heath, Elizabeth A. ... Kinston, NC
Heath, F. Richard ... Utica, OH
Heath, Frederick Wm. ... Bloomfield Hills, MI
Heath, G. Ronald ... Indianapolis, IN
Heath, Geoffrey R. ... Department Of The Interior, GV
Heath, George ... Vero Beach, FL
Heath, Gregory S. ... Dallas, TX
Heath, Harold E., Law Offices ... Holdenville, OK
Heath, Helena M. ... Albany, NY
Heath, Henry E. ... Salt Lake City, UT
Heath, Honor S. ... Hartford, CT
Heath, Jack L. ... Topeka, KS
Heath, James A., Jr. ... Department Of Health And Human Services, Office of Community Services, GV
Heath, James E. ... Springfield, OH
Heath, James J. ... Cincinnati, OH
Heath, James L. ... San Jose, CA
Heath, James V. ... Cincinnati, OH
Heath, Jason M. ... Sacramento, CA
Heath, Jennifer R. ... Charlotte, NC
Heath, Jesse B., Jr. ... Denver, CO
Heath, John A. ... Columbus, OH
Heath, John C. ... Livingston, TN
Heath, John E., Jr. ... Spokane, WA
Heath, John R. ... Nacogdoches, TX
Heath, John W. ... Los Angeles, CA
Heath, John W., Jr. ... Los Angeles, CA
Heath, Joseph A. ... Long Beach, CA
Heath, Joseph J. ... Syracuse, NY
Heath, Julie E. ... Dallas, TX
Heath, Lawrence R. ... Rhinelander, WI
Heath, Leonard C., Jr. ... Newport News, VA
Heath, M. Steven ... Athens, GA
Heath, Marc B. ... Burlington, VT
Heath, Margaret J. ... Nashville, TN
Heath, Mark E. ... Charleston, WV
Heath & Martin ... Holley, NY
Heath, Mary Ena J. ... Huntsville, AL
Heath, Maryeve ... Milwaukee, WI
Heath, Maureen A. ... San Jose, CA
Heath, Megan ... Snohomish, WA
Heath, Melissa Allen ... Atlanta, GA
Heath, Michael John ... Norfolk, VA
Heath, Michael T. ... Novato, CA
Heath, Millard C. ... Houston, TX
Heath, Milton Scott ... Austin, TX
Heath, Monica Robinson ... Syracuse, NY
Heath, Morris L. ... Fort Collins, CO
Heath, Paul E. ... Dallas, TX
Heath, Paul N. ... Wilmington, DE
Heath, R. Terry ... Indianapolis, IN
Heath, Richard E. ... Boca Raton, FL
Heath, Richard R. ... San Francisco, CA
Heath, Robert A. ... Louisville, KY
Heath, Robert A. ... Houston, TX
Heath, Robert E. ... Bozeman, MT
Heath, Robert E. ... Holley, NY
Heath, Robert F. ... Whitefish Bay, WI
Heath, Robert J. ... Milwaukee, WI
Heath, Robert L. ... Wichita, KS
Heath, Robert N., Jr. ... Pensacola, FL
Heath, Robert N., P.A. ... Pensacola, FL
Heath, Roberta Binder ... Altoona, PA
Heath, S. Rollins, Jr. ... Denver, CO
Heath, Sandra L. ... La Grange, GA
Heath, Sharon K. ... Oakland, CA
Heath, Shawn M. ... Baton Rouge, LA
Heath, Steven A. ... Tulsa, OK
Heath, Stuart M. ... Kalamazoo, MI
Heath, Susan Moore ... San Diego, CA
Heath, Symantha L. ... Livonia, MI
Heath, Symantha L. ... Livonia, MI
Heath, Taryn L. ... Canton, OH
Heath, Thomas C. ... Fort Lauderdale, FL; Tampa, FL; West Palm Beach, FL
Heath, Warne S. ... Huntsville, AL
Heath, William C. ... San Jose, CA
Heath, William P. ... Fort Walton Beach, FL
Heathco, Michael Charles ... Mangum, OK
Heathcock, Douglas E. ... Joliet, IL
Heathcock, Kathryn A. ... Stuart, FL
Heathcote • Gantner, A Professional Corporation ... Somerville, NJ
Heathcote, Nancy D. ... East Lansing, MI
Heathcote, Phillips E., Jr. ... Somerville, NJ
Heathcotte, Bruce R. ... Evansville, IN
Heather, Cornelia Loughran ... Calabasas, CA
Heather, Fred D. ... Los Angeles, CA
Heather, John G. ... Dallas, TX
Heather, Timothy P. ... Cincinnati, OH
White Oak, OH
Heather Elizabeth, Hersh ... Santa Monica, CA
Heatherly, Gail E. ... New York, NY
Heatherly, Glenn E. ... Abilene, TX
Heatherly & Myers ... Abilene, TX
Heatherman, Patricia L. ... Bend, OR
Heatherman, Paul B. ... Bend, OR
Heathman, Brooks ... Rice Lake, WI
Heathman, H. William, III ... Houston, TX
Heatley, Berry A. ... Department of Justice, Tax Division, GV
Heatly, Eugene N. ... Vernon, TX
Heatly, John B. ... Oklahoma City, OK
Heatly, Thomas J. ... Glendale, CA
Heaton, Beth M. ... Sparta, IL
Heaton, David N. ... Atlanta, GA
Heaton, David R. ... Richmond, IN
Heaton & Doescher, Ltd. ... Carson City, NV
Heaton, Fred K. ... Kanab, UT
Heaton, George R., Jr. ... Newton, MA
Heaton, Gerald ... Bellefontaine, OH
Heaton, Holly L. ... San Diego, CA
Heaton, J. Andrew ... Washington, DC
Heaton, J. Lade ... Park City, UT
Heaton, J. Michael ... Chicago, IL
Heaton, James W. ... Atlanta, GA
Heaton, Jeffrey C. ... Cherry Hill, NJ
Heaton, Joe ... Oklahoma City, OK
Heaton, John L. ... Lebanon, PA
Heaton, Jon C. ... Park City, UT; Salt Lake City, UT
Heaton, Joseph E., Jr. ... Sterling, IL
Heaton and Kellogg-Martin ... Bellefontaine, OH
Heaton, Kirsten M. ... Palo Alto, CA
Heaton, Mary Margaret ... Atlanta, GA
Heaton, Michael G. ... Sacramento, CA
Heaton, Murray P. ... Geneva, NY
Heaton, Paul F. ... Milwaukee, WI
Heaton, R. Kirk ... Ogden, UT
Heaton, Richard D. ... Sonora, KY
Heaton, Richard L. ... Newport Beach, CA
Heaton, Robert E. ... Seattle, WA
Heaton, Robert L. ... Auburn, WA
Heaton, Robert W. ... Bardstown, KY
Heaton, Robert W., Jr. ... Mountain City, GA
Heaton, Rodger A. ... Springfield, IL
Heaton, Scott J. ... Carson City, NV
Heaton, Sharon B. ... Herndon, VA
Heaton, Stephen M. ... Chicago, IL
Heaton, Stuart A. ... Reston, VA
Heaton, Wilford H. ... San Antonio, TX
Heaton, William Cliff ... Clarksdale, MS
Heaton, William F., III ... West Islip, NY
Heaton, William H. ... Las Vegas, NV
Heaton, William W. ... Memphis, TN
Heatter, Justin W. ... Falmouth, MA
Heatwole, Mark M. ... Chicago, IL
Heatzig, Bonnie R. ... West Palm Beach, FL
Heaukulani, Charles M. ... Kailua-Kona, HI
Heaven, Lewis A., Jr. ... Merriam, KS
Heavener, Mac D., III ... Casselberry, FL
Heavenrich, John D. ... Cleveland, OH
Heavens, Christopher Joseph ... Boothwyn, PA; Charleston, WV
Heavens Law Offices ... Boothwyn, PA; Charleston, WV
Heaver, Barry A. ... Tulsa, OK
Heavey, Edward ... Seattle, WA
Heavey, John C. ... Newark, NJ
Heavey, Michael W., (P.C.) ... Papillion, NE
Heavey, Richard, (P.C.) ... Brookline, MA
Heavey, Thomas J. ... Brick, NJ
Heavican, Michael G. ... Lincoln, NE
Heavilin, Albert M. ... Chagrin Falls, OH
Heaviside, Michael W. ... Alexandria, VA
Heaviside, W. Timothy ... Purchase, NY
Heavner, B. Brett ... Washington, DC
Heavner, Bruce G. ... Braymer, MO; Kansas City, MO
Heavner, Gary Lee ... New City, NY
Heavner, Handegan & Scott ... Decatur, IL
Heavner, J. Mark ... Gastonia, NC
Heavner, James R., Jr. ... Washington, DC
Heavner, Jarrett & Kimball, A Prof. Corp. ... Braymer, MO; Kansas City, MO; Cameron, MO
Heavner, Ralph O., Jr. ... Pomona, NY
Heavner, Timothy B. ... Martinsburg, WV
Heavrin, M. Christina ... Louisville, KY
Heavrin, Thomas C. ... Chicago, IL
Heban, Kevin A. ... Toledo, OH
Heban, Linda A. ... Chicago, IL
Hebard, George R., Jr. ... Hamburg, NY
Hebb, Donald B., Jr. ... Baltimore, MD
Hebb, Edwin Gordon, Jr. ... Hartford, CT
Hebb, John F. Le Baron ... Santa Monica, CA
Hebb, John S., III ... Baltimore, MD
Hebb, Robert L. ... Baltimore, MD
Hebbe, James R. ... Appleton, WI
Hebbeler, Regis J. ... Knoxville, TN
Hebbeln, Mark E. ... Atlanta, GA
Hebberger, William R. ... Kansas City, MO
Hebble, Robert M. ... New York, NY
Hebbler, George P., Jr. ... New Orleans, LA
Hebda, Bernard A. ... Pittsburgh, PA
Hebda, Paul Thomas ... Dallas, TX
Hebda, Robert E. ... Herndon, VA
Hebdon, Jack ... San Antonio, TX
Hebe, William A. ... Wellsboro, PA
Hebeisen, Keith A. ... Chicago, IL
Hebel, Chas. W., Jr. ... Louisville, KY
Hebel & Hornung, P.S.C. ... Louisville, KY
Hebel, Linda G. ... Lenoir, NC
Hebel, Michael Steven ... San Francisco, CA
Hebeler, Suzanne M. ... Burlington, VT
Hebeler, William R. ... Lynnwood, WA
Heben, Edward J., Jr. ... Cleveland, OH
Heben, Lawrence W. ... Treasury Department, GV
Hebenstreit, Michael J. ... Indianapolis, IN
Hebenstreit, Patricia A. ... Indianapolis, IN
Hebenstreit, Sandra L. ... Chicago, IL
Hebenstreit, Stephen L. ... Columbus, OH
Heber, Albert H. ... Chicago, IL
Heberer, Eugene O. ... Kirkland, WA
Heberer, William M., III ... New York, NY
Heberle, Denise M. ... Chester, PA
Heberle, Douglas M. ... Greensboro, NC
Heberle, Thomas D. ... Erie, PA
Heberley, Grayson H., III ... Princeton, NJ
Heberlig, Brian M. ... Washington, DC
Heberlig, H. Dean, Jr. ... Syracuse, NY
Heberlig, Jon L. ... Kalispell, MT
Heberling, Richard D. ... Toledo, OH
Hebert, A. Leon ... Baton Rouge, LA
Hebert, Angella R. ... Lafayette, LA; New Orleans, LA
Hebert, Ann M. ... Houston, TX
Hebert, Arthur R. ... Oakland, CA
Hebert, Barbara ... Boston, MA
Hebert, Brian P. ... Palo Alto, CA
Hebert, Carl J. ... New Orleans, LA
Hébert, Carl M. ... Reno, NV
Hebert, Carol S. ... Department of Justice, Office of Information and Privacy, GV
Hebert, Charles J. ... Metairie, LA
Hebert, Colette Flannick ... Beverly Hills, CA
Hebert, Dale L. ... Detroit, MI
Hebert, Dale M. ... Birmingham, AL
Hébert, Danial J. ... Detroit, MI; Farmington Hills, MI
Hebert, Daniel ... Springfield, MA
Hebert, Daniel L. ... Salina, KS
Hebert, David J. ... Marrero, LA
Hebert, David K. ... Forest Lake, MN
Hebert, Deborah A. ... Royal Oak, MI
Hebert, Donald F. ... Concord, NH
Hebert, Donald W. ... Opelousas, LA
Hebert, Douglas L., Jr., A Prof. Law Corp. ... Kinder, LA
Hébert, Edward, II ... New Orleans, LA
Hebert, Emile L., III ... New Orleans, LA
Hebert, Erin T. ... New Orleans, LA
Hebert, Gary G. ... New Orleans, LA
Hebert, George S. ... Houston, TX
Hebert, Gerald I. ... Lafayette, LA
Hebert, Gwendolyn S. ... New Orleans, LA
Hebert, Hamilton D. ... Tallahassee, FL

Hebert, Irby, Jr. ... Abbeville, LA
Hebert, J. Byron ... Abbeville, LA
Hebert, J. Gerald ... Alexandria, VA
Hebert, Janel Bennett ... Leominster, MA
Hebert, Jay A. ... Clearwater, FL
Hebert, Jay H. ... Dallas, TX
Hebert, John E., IV ... Chicago, IL
Hebert, John J. ... Phoenix, AZ
Hebert, Joseph P. ... Lafayette, LA
Hebert, Julius P., Jr. ... Houma, LA
Hebert, Kathryn M. ... Minneapolis, MN
Hebert, Kenneth C. ... Winter Park, FL
Hebert, L. Camille ... Columbus, OH
Hebert, Larry C. ... Lafayette, LA
Hebert Law Group ... Clearwater, FL
St. Petersburg, FL
Hebert, Lorane F. ... Washington, DC
Hebert, Lorna M. ... Quincy, MA
Hebert, Louise Bowyer ... Silver Spring, MD
Hebert, Marc C. ... Washington, DC
Hebert and Marceaux ... Houma, LA
Hebert, Marilyn S. ... Santa Fe, NM
Hebert, Mark J. ... Boston, MA
Hebert, Mary Beth ... Atlanta, GA
Hebert, Maureen H. S. ... Needham, MA
Hebert, Maurice C., Jr. ... New Orleans, LA
Hebert, Michael D. ... Lafayette, LA
Hebert, Michael L. ... Baton Rouge, LA
Hebert, Michael V. ... Farmington, CT
Hebert, Nancy Johnson ... Houston, TX
Hebert, Nicol M. ... Austin, TX
Hebert, P. Michael ... Austin, TX
Hebert, Patricia A. M. ... Agawam, MA
Hebert, Paul A. ... Mount Laurel, NJ
Hebert, Paul J. ... Lafayette, LA
Hebert, Paul M., Jr. ... Baton Rouge, LA
Hebert, Peter J. ... Ann Arbor, MI
Hebert, Peter M. ... Santa Monica, CA
Hebert, Quinn J. ... Houston, TX
Hebert, Raymond ... Palo Alto, CA
Hebert, Richard J. ... Fairfax, VA
Hebert, Robert B. ... Indianapolis, IN
Hébert, Roy C. ... Saugatuck, MI
Hebert, Schenk & Johnsen, P.C.
Phoenix, AZ
Scottsdale, AZ
Hebert and Spencer ... Baton Rouge, LA
Hébert, Stanley P. ... Oakland, CA
Hebert, Steve ... Baytown, TX
Hebert, Theresa R. ... Florham Park, NJ
Hebert, Thomas B. ... Lake Oswego, OR
Hebert, Todd ... Baton Rouge, LA
Hebert, Victor A. ... Los Angeles, CA
San Francisco, CA
Hebert, Welch & Humphreys, P.A.
Forest Lake, MN
Hebert, William F. ... Dayton, OH
Hebert, William N. ... San Francisco, CA
Hebert, William T. (Tom)
Corpus Christi, TX
Hébert, Yves A. ... Ukiah, CA
Hebert-Fajardo, Genevieve ... New York, NY
Heberton, Craig, IV ... Hoffman Estates, IL
Heberton, George H. ... Atlanta, GA
Heberton, Pamela M. ... Los Angeles, CA
Hebets, Noel ... Phoenix, AZ
Hebinck, Bernard L. ... Houston, TX
Hebinck, Marilyn Tanner ... Houston, TX
Hebisen, Ronnie V. ... Houston, TX
Hebl, Gary A. ... Sun Prairie, WI
Hebl and Hebl ... Sun Prairie, WI
Hebl, Johannah K. ... Verona, WI
Hebl, Joseph Terry ... Eau Claire, WI
Hebl, Kevin J. ... St. Paul, MN
Hebl, Thomas L. ... Sun Prairie, WI
Heblack, Alan ... New York, NY
Heblich, Frederick T., Jr.
Charlottesville, VA
Hebner, David A. ... Charlotte, NC
Hebner, Diane ... Austin, TX
Hebner, Diane, Law Office of ... Austin, TX
Hebrank, Jeffrey S. ... Edwardsville, IL
Hebron & Hebron ... Carlinville, IL
Hebron, M. E. ... Carlinville, IL
Hebron, Robert J. ... New York, NY
Hebron, William S. ... Carlinville, IL
Hebson, Tony Shayne ... Birmingham, AL
Hechavarria, Omar ... Marathon, FL
Heche, Raymond G. ... Bridgeport, CT
Heching, Harry G. ... New York, NY
Heching, Moshe ... New York, NY
Hechinger, Brian M. ... Washington, DC
Hechinger, John F. ... Chicago, IL
Hechl, Thomas P. ... Washington, DC
Hechler, Jill N. ... Orlando, FL
Hechmer, Teresa M. ... King Of Prussia, PA
Hecht, Abraham ... Forest Hills, NY
Hecht, Alan John, (A Professional Corporation) ... San Diego, CA
Hecht, Alan R. ... Miami, FL
Hecht, Alissa S. ... Federal Trade Commission, Bureau of Competition, GV
Hecht, Allan S. ... New York, NY
Hecht, Allan S., P.C. ... New York, NY
Hecht, Allen M. ... New York, NY
Hecht, Amy F. ... Garden City, NY
Hecht, Andrea Renata ... New York, NY
Hecht, Andrew V. ... Aspen, CO
Hecht, Barbara E. ... Kansas City, MO
Hecht, Barbara E., P.C.
Overland Park, KS
Kansas City, MO
Osage Beach, MO
Hecht, Barbara J. ... Miami, FL
Hecht, Beth P. ... Fort Lee, NJ
Hecht and Chapper ... Baltimore, MD
Hecht, Charles B. ... Denver, CO
Hecht, Charles J. ... New York, NY
Hecht, Craig A. ... Mount Sinai, NY
Hecht, Daniel H. ... New York, NY
Hecht, Daryl L. ... Sioux City, IA
Hecht, David P. ... Seattle, WA
Hecht, David S., Jr. ... Seattle, WA
Hecht, Donald D. ... Baltimore, MD
Hecht, Donald S. ... Jericho, NY
Hecht, Edward M. ... Chicago, IL
Hecht, Eliezer ... New York, NY
Hecht, Elizabeth M. ... White Plains, NY
Hecht, Emanuel H. ... Cleveland, OH
Hecht, Ephrem ... Brooklyn, NY
Hecht, F. Thomas ... Chicago, IL
Hecht, Gary A. ... Philadelphia, PA
Hecht, Geoffrey A. ... New Haven, CT
Hecht, Gerald ... Danbury, CT
Hecht, Gordon E. ... Livingston, NJ
Hecht, Greg K. ... Morrow, GA
Hecht & Hecht ... Brooklyn, NY
Hecht, Henry L. ... Berkeley, CA
Hecht, Herbert W., II ... Washington, DC
Hecht, Ira R. ... New York, NY
Hecht, Irene M. ... Seattle, WA
Hecht, Isaac ... Baltimore, MD
Hecht, Jacob ... Brooklyn, NY
Hecht, James C. ... Washington, DC
Hecht, James P. ... Woodstock, IL
Hecht, Jay M. ... New York, NY
Hecht, Jesse A. ... New York, NY
Hecht, Jesse B. ... New York, NY
Hecht, Judy H. ... Englewood, CO
Hecht, Julie L.
Department of Justice, GV
Hecht, Julien A. ... Baltimore, MD
Hecht, Karen Juster ... San Francisco, CA
Hecht, Kenneth ... San Francisco, CA
Hecht, Kenneth G. ... Glenview, IL
Hecht, Kenneth G., Jr. ... Oakland, CA
Hecht & Riskin ... Cheshire, CT
Hecht, Kevin J. ... Cheshire, CT
Hecht, Kevin J., P.C., Law Offices of
Cheshire, CT
Hecht, Kevin W. ... Denver, CO
Hecht, Larry H. ... Brooklyn, NY
Hecht, Leonard H. ... New York, NY
Hecht, Lisa Mendelson ... New York, NY
Hecht, Liza J. ... Bridgeport, CT
Hecht, Louis A. ... Lisle, IL
Hecht, Marc L. ... Chicago, IL
Hecht, Mervyn L. ... Los Angeles, CA
Hecht, Michael W. ... New York, NY
Hecht, Nathan L. ... Austin, TX
Hecht, Neil S. ... Boston, MA
Hecht, Norman ... Virginia Beach, VA
Hecht, Peggy ... St. Louis, MO
Hecht, Philip H. ... Washington, DC
Hecht, Rachel R.
Federal Energy Regulatory Commission, Office of the General Counsel, GV
Hecht, Raquel E. ... Eugene, OR
Hecht, Richard L. ... El Centro, CA
Hecht, Richard L. ... White Plains, NY
Hecht, Richd. H. ... New York, NY
Hecht & Riskin ... Los Angeles, CA
Hecht, Robert ... Beverly Hills, CA
Hecht, Robert D. ... Topeka, KS
Hecht, Robert F. ... Wayne, PA
Hecht, Robert G. ... Pittsburgh, PA
Hecht, Roger D. ... Cleveland, OH
Hecht, Ronald A. ... Houston, TX
Hecht, Scott C. ... Kansas City, MO
Hecht, Sean B. ... Santa Monica, CA
Hecht, Solberg, Robinson & Goldberg, LLP
San Diego, CA
Hecht, Stanley M.
Pension Benefit Guaranty Corporation, Office of the General Counsel, GV
Hecht & Steckman, P.C. ... New York, NY
Hecht, Steven ... Los Angeles, CA
Hecht, Steven A. ... Houston, TX
Hecht, Steven M. ... Roseland, NJ
Hecht, Suzanne M. ... Philadelphia, PA
Hecht, Theodore L. ... New York, NY
White Plains, NY
Hecht, Thomas, P.C. ... New York, NY
Hecht, Thomas T. ... New York, NY
Hecht, Warren S. ... Forest Hills, NY
Hecht, William A. ... White Plains, NY
Hecht, William D. ... New York, NY
Hecht, William E. ... Exton, PA
Hecht, William M. ... New York, NY
Hechter, Samuel Z. ... Minneapolis, MN
Hecht Helmer, Leslie L.
Santa Monica, CA
Hechtkopf, Alan ... Department of Justice, Tax Division, GV
Hechtman, Abigail R. ... Boston, MA
Hechtman, Barton G. ... San Jose, CA
Hechtman, Jeffrey A. ... Chicago, IL
Hechtman, Sarah B. ... New York, NY
Hecimovich, Lawrence ... Palo Alto, CA
Heck, Barbara ... Bloomington, MN
Heck, Bill ... Marion, IN
Heck, Caroline ... Miami, FL
Heck, Charles H. ... Monroe, LA
Heck, Charles H., Jr. ... Monroe, LA
Heck, Christopher J. ... Los Angeles, CA
Heck, Cynthia M. ... Dayton, OH
Heck, David A. ... San Francisco, CA
Heck, Donald D. ... Chesterfield, MO
Heck, Donald L. ... Kadoka, SD
Heck, Erma L. ... Birmingham, MI
Heck, Eugene L. ... Minneapolis, MN
Heck, F. Donald, Jr. ... Quincy, IL
Heck, Gary A. ... Minneapolis, MN
Heck, George C. ... Old Lyme, CT
Heck, Gregory J. ... St. Paul, MN
Heck, Hendrix, Wright & Sheppeard, P.A.
Topeka, KS
Heck, J. Jeffrey ... Mansfield, OH
Heck, Janet L. ... Wichita, KS
Heck, Jay Robert ... Liberty, MO
Heck, Jeff K. ... Tyler, TX
Heck, Jeff R. ... South Bend, IN
Heck, Jill R. ... Medina, OH
Heck, Judith M. ... St. Clair Shores, MI
Heck, Judith Rea ... Chicago, IL
Heck, Keith R. ... Racine, WI
Heck, Keith W. ... Chickasha, OK
Heck, Mathias H., Jr. ... Dayton, OH
Heck, Michael A. ... Troy, MI
Heck, Michael D. ... Topeka, KS
Heck, Nancy J. ... Houston, TX
Heck, Patrick G.
Treasury Department, GV
Heck, Peter J. ... Morristown, NJ
Heck, Robert ... New York, NY
Heck, Ronald D. ... Topeka, KS
Heck, Ronald D., P.A. ... Topeka, KS
Heck, Ronald H. ... Pittsburgh, PA
Heck, Samuel L. ... Chestertown, MD
Heck, Sandra F. ... Wurtsboro, NY
Heck, Steven S. ... Kansas City, MO
Heck, Todd W. ... Vineland, NJ
Heck, William C. ... New York, NY
Heck, William J. ... Granbury, TX
Heck, William R. ... Chattanooga, TN
Heckadon, David R. ... Palo Alto, CA
Heckart, Kevin E. ... Burgaw, NC
Heckart, Robert L. ... New York, NY
Heckathorn, Alexander ... Santa Rosa, CA
Heckathorn, Ben M. ... Red Oak, TX
Heckathorn, I. James ... Kalispell, MT
Heckathorn, Vera J. ... Whitefish, MT
Heckathorne, Holly E. ... Chicago, IL
Heckbert, James G. ... Steamboat Springs, CO
Heckel, Catherine M. ... Sterling, CO
Heckel, James E. ... St. Louis, MO
Heckel, John M. ... Cedar Rapids, IA
Heckel, Norris J. ... Mesa, AZ
Heckelman, David R. ... Chicago, IL
Heckemeyer, Anthony J. ... Detroit, MI
Heckemeyer, Anthony J. ... Benton, MO
Heckenbach, David W. ... Lone Tree, CO
Heckendorn, C. Henry ... Seattle, WA
Heckenkamp, Robert G. ... Springfield, IL
Heckenkamp, Simhauser, Ward & Zerkle
Springfield, IL
Heckenkemper, Wm. Brad ... Tulsa, OK
Heckenlively, John J. ... Sacramento, CA
Heckenlively, John W. ... Walnut Creek, CA
Hecker, Arnold ... North Miami Beach, FL
Hecker Brown Sherry and Johnson
Haddonfield, NJ
Bethlehem, PA
Philadelphia, PA
Hecker, Cynthia W. ... Berkeley, CA
Hecker, David A. ... Lincoln, NE
Hecker, Dustin F. ... Boston, MA
Hecker, Edwin W., Jr. ... Lawrence, KS
Hecker, Elissa D. ... New York, NY
Hecker, Eric ... Washington, DC
Hecker & Feilberg ... Seattle, WA
Hecker, Fred S. ... Westminster, MD
Hecker, Gary A. ... Los Angeles, CA
San Jose, CA
Hecker, George S. ... St. Louis, MO
Hecker, H. ... White Plains, NY
Hecker, H. Scott ... Fort Lauderdale, FL
Hecker, H. Scott, P.A., Law Offices of
Fort Lauderdale, FL
Hecker & Harriman ... Los Angeles, CA
San Jose, CA
Hecker, Holly C. ... Buffalo, NY
Hecker, Ian D. ... Manchester, NH
Hecker, James M. ... Washington, DC
Hecker, James T. ... Evergreen, CO
Hecker, Joel L. ... New York, NY
Hecker, John Z. ... Champaign, IL
Hecker, Jordan M. ... Seattle, WA
Hecker, Joseph W. ... Baton Rouge, LA
Hecker, Judith M. ... Madison, WI
Hecker, Laurence A., (P.C.) ... Toms River, NJ
Hecker, Lawrence M. ... Tucson, AZ
Hecker, Leonard D. ... White Plains, NY
Hecker, Leslie F. ... Coral Gables, FL
Hecker, Lynette D. ... Fresno, CA
Hecker, Martin J. ... Lakewood, CO
Hecker, M. J. & Associates, P.C.
Lakewood, CO
Hecker, Peter S. ... San Francisco, CA
Hecker, Phillips & Zeeb ... Tucson, AZ
Hecker, Robert J. ... White Plains, NY
Hecker, Robert J., and Associates, P.C.
White Plains, NY
Hecker, Ronald A. ... Beverly Hills, CA
Hecker, Sharon W. ... Hooksett, NH
Hecker, Stephen A. ... Baltimore, MD
Hecker, Stuart N. ... Department of Commerce, Patent and Trademark Office, GV
Hecker, Susan Barrett ... Sarasota, FL
Hecker, Thomas R. ... Bristol, PA
Langhorne, PA
Hecker, U. Joseph, III ... Silver Spring, MD
Heckerling, Dale A. ... Miami, FL
Heckerling, Jeremy A. ... New York, NY
Heckerling, Joan B. ... Far Rockaway, NY
Heckerling, Morton J. ... New York, NY
Heckerman, Arthur R. ... Cincinnati, OH
Heckeroth, Sally E. ... Atlantic City, NJ
Heckers, John H. ... Wheat Ridge, CO
Heckert, Carl W. ... Wilmington, DE
Heckert, John D. ... Clearwater, FL
Heckert, Lynne F. ... Haverford, PA
Heckert, Rowena ... Cheyenne, WY
Heckinger, John F., Jr. ... Rockford, IL
Heckler, Alan E. ... Freehold, NJ
New York, NY
Heckler, Alma A. ... Wichita, KS
Heckler, Charles K. ... Marietta, OH
Heckler, David R.
Environmental Protection Agency, Environmental Appeals Board, GV
Heckler, David W. ... Doylestown, PA
Heckler, Douglas J. ... Indianapolis, IN
Heckler, Frabizzio & Durstein
Wilmington, DE
Heckler, George B., Jr. ... Wilmington, DE
Heckler, Gerard V. ... Santa Ana, CA
Heckler, Martin G. ... Philadelphia, PA
Heckler, Russell S. ... Hatfield, PA
Heckley, Gregg G. ... Tampa, FL
Heckman, Adrienne Sauro ... Santa Ana, CA
Heckman, Annejanette K.
Department of Agriculture, Office of the General Counsel, GV
Heckman, August W. ... Secaucus, NJ
Heckman, Brett Steven ... Edwards, CO
Heckman, C. Luther ... Columbus, OH
Heckman, Carey Eugene ... Stanford, CA
Heckman, Carol E. ... Buffalo, NY
Heckman, Charles A. ... Hamden, CT
Heckman, D. Christopher ... Irving, TX
Heckman, Darrell L. ... Urbana, OH
Heckman, Donald Rex, II, (Inc.)
Sacramento, CA
Heckman, J. William, Jr. ... San Francisco, CA
Heckman, James W. ... Troy, MI
Heckman, Jerome H. ... Washington, DC
Heckman, John H. ... Greenville, SC
Heckman, Karl W. ... Cleveland, OH
Heckman, Mary Ann ... Overland Park, KS
Heckman, Michael B. ... Pine Bush, NY
Heckman, Michael D. ... Washington, DC
Heckman & O'Connor, P.C.
Edwards, CO
Vail, CO
Heckman, R. Harper ... Greensboro, NC
Heckman, Sarah Howland ... Yuba City, CA
Heckman, Scott C. ... Allentown, PA
Heckman, Sheryl ... Cupertino, CA
Heckman, Stanley D. ... New York, NY
Heckman, Stephen G. ... Blue Bell, PA
Heckman, Tamara S. ... Department of Justice, Tax Division, GV
Heckman, Thomas P. ... New York, NY
Heckmann, Amy C. ... Madison, WI
Heckmann, Brian D. ... Pasadena, CA
Heckmann, James M. ... Dubuque, IA
Heckner, Howard G. ... Ligonier, IN
Heckscher, Martin A. ... Philadelphia, PA
West Conshohocken, PA
Heckscher, Maurice ... Philadelphia, PA
Heckscher, Teillon, Terrill & Sager, A Professional Corporation
Philadelphia, PA
West Conshohocken, PA
Heckscher, Yvon Oscar ... Sebastopol, CA
Heckt, Melvin D. ... Minnetonka, MN
Hecox, Debra A. ... Lakewood, CO
Hecox, Lawrence A.
Colorado Springs, CO
Hecox, Morris B., Jr. ... Denver, CO
Hector, Alice G., (P.A.) ... Miami, FL
Hector, Brian D. ... Chicago, IL
Hector, Bruce J. ... Franklin Lakes, NJ
Hector, Gregory T. ... Austin, TX
Hector & Harke LLP ... Miami, FL
Hector, John F. ... San Diego, CA
Hector, Louis G. ... Evanston, IL
Hector, Louis J. ... Miami, FL
Hed, Maren L. ... Minneapolis, MN
Hed, Melissa Fischler ... Westwood, MA
Heda, Jack ... Fort Lauderdale, FL
Hedahl, Joan E. ... Fayetteville, NC
Hedahl & Radtke ... Fayetteville, NC
Hedal, Joseph A. ... Westwood, MA
Hedani & Choy ... San Francisco, CA
Hedani, Dean ... San Francisco, CA
Hedayat, Mazyar Malek ... Naperville, IL
Hedayati-Grob, Afsaneh ... Van Nuys, CA
Hedback, John A. ... St. Anthony, MN
Hedback, Peggy J. ... St. Anthony, MN
Hedberg, Arthur C., Jr. ... Des Moines, IA
Hedberg, Beth Barban ... New York, NY
Hedberg, Joel D. ... Eagan, MN
Hedberg, John C. ... Knoxville, TN
Hedberg, John W. ... St. Louis Park, MN
Hedberg, Mark ... Des Moines, IA
Hedberg, Mark S. ... Richmond, VA
Hedberg, Olaf W. ... Yuba City, CA
Hedberg, Owens & Vonderhaar, P.C.
Des Moines, IA
Hedberg, Peter J. ... Edina, MN
Hedberg, Steven M. ... Portland, OR
Seattle, WA
Hedberg, Tobin, Flaherty & Whalen, A Professional Corporation ... Chicago, IL
Hedberg, Victor ... Chicago, IL
Hedblom, John M. ... Chicago, IL
Hedblom, Milda K. ... Minneapolis, MN
Hedden, Andrew S. ... New York, NY
Hedden, David L. ... Dublin, OH
Hedden, Herbert A. ... Columbus, OH
Hedden, J. Michael ... Fort Worth, TX
Hedden, James H. ... Columbus, OH
Hedden, Kathryn N. ... Atlanta, GA
Hedden, Margaret M. ... Columbus, OH
Hedden, William H. ... Hillsborough, CA
Hedden, William R., Jr. ... Piscataway, NJ
Hedderman, John G. ... Westminster, CA
Heddesheimer, Don J. ... Cleveland, OH
Heddesheimer, Walter J. ... Cleveland, OH
Hedding, Ronald D. ... Encino, CA

Heddings, Raymond E.
Department of Defense,
Defense Legal Services Agency, GV
Heddon, Shari L. .... Brighton, MI
Hedeen, Arnold R. .... Seattle, WA
Hedeen, Barbara A. .... Newark, NJ
Hedeen & Caditz .... Seattle, WA
Hedeen, Clemens V., Jr. .... Sturgeon Bay, WI
Hedeen, Herbert V., Jr. .... Chicago, IL
Hedeen, Hughes, Wetering & Kness
Adrian, MN
Worthington, MN
Hedeen, Lawrence C. .... Mesa, AZ
Hedeen, Michael J. .... Rockford, IL
Hedeen, Peter A. .... Denver, CO
Hedeen, Scott K. .... Dothan, AL
Hedeen, William T. .... Adrian, MN
Worthington, MN
Hedegard, Alan Harald .... Salinas, CA
Hedeker, Dean Richard .... Deerfield, IL
Hedeker, Dean Richard, Ltd. .... Deerfield, IL
Hedelund, Alicia A. .... Yuma, AZ
Hedeman, Robert .... Towson, MD
Hedemann, Eric J. .... Houston, TX
Hedemann, G. Christian .... Irvine, CA
Hedemann, Linda S. .... Leawood, KS
Heder, Bill O. .... Provo, UT
Hederstedt, David R. .... Hutchinson, KS
Hederstedt, Laura A. .... Hutchinson, KS
Hedesh, Robert A. .... Edison, NJ
Hedgbeth, Llewellyn H. ....
Department of State, GV
Hedgbeth, Roger A. .... Salem, VA
Hedge, Brook .... Washington, DC
Hedge, Dennis A. .... Fort Myers, FL
Hedge, Robert J. .... Mobile, AL
Hedge, William E. .... La Porte, IN
Hedgebeth, Reginald D. .... Atlanta, GA
Hedgecock, Roger A. .... La Jolla, CA
Hedgecoth, John D. .... Cedar Rapids, IA
Hedgepath, Catherine M. .... Conway, SC
Hedgepath, Charles E. .... Columbia, SC
Hedgepath, Richard R. .... Nashville, TN
Hedgepeth, C. Grant .... Laurel, MS
Hedgepeth, D. Lee .... Modesto, CA
Hedgepeth, Jay H. .... Jacksonville, FL
Hedgepeth, Lisa C. .... Silver Spring, MD
Hedger, Cecil R. .... Salt Lake City, UT
Hedger, David .... Port Orchard, WA
Hedger & Hedger .... Harrisburg, PA
Hedger, Jeff .... Billings, MT
Hedger, Raymond C., Jr. .... Harrisburg, PA
Hedges, Adele O. .... Houston, TX
Hedges, Bryan R. .... Syracuse, NY
Hedges, C. Robert .... Russellville, KY
Hedges, Charles F., Jr. .... Midland, TX
Hedges, Christine M. .... Spencer, WV
Hedges, Christopher C. .... Merrillville, IN
Hedges, D. Christopher .... Charleston, WV
Hedges, Daniel K. .... Houston, TX
Hedges, David T., Jr. .... Houston, TX
Hedges, Donald H. .... Edmonds, WA
Hedges, George R. .... Los Angeles, CA
Hedges, H. Ric .... Tulsa, OK
Hedges, Hamilton S. .... Columbus, OH
Hedges, Jackson C. .... Lebanon, OH
Hedges, James K. .... Los Angeles, CA
Hedges, John A. .... Chicago, IL
Hedges, John M. .... Morgantown, WV
Hedges, Jones, Whittier & Hedges
Spencer, WV
Hedges, Katherine R. .... McLean, VA
Hedges, Kevin T. .... Houston, TX
Hedges, Leslie Joe .... Tulsa, OK
Hedges, Michael R. .... San Antonio, TX
Hedges, Michele M. .... Houston, TX
Hedges, Norman J. .... Indianapolis, IN
Hedges, Patricia T. .... Covington, LA
Hedges, Philip H. .... New York, NY
Hedges, Phyllis I. .... Los Alamos, NM
Hedges, Robert O. .... Springfield, IL
Hedges, Ronald J. .... Newark, NJ
Hedges, Russell D. .... Tullahoma, TN
Hedges, Steven D. .... Greensboro, NC
Hedges, Steven G. .... Mt. Summit, IN
Hedges, Steven R. .... Minneapolis, MN
Hedges, William E. .... Philadelphia, PA
Hedglin, C. John .... Jackson, MS
Hedglon, Mead J., III .... Bethany, OK
Hedglon, Peter F. .... Oneida, NY
Hedgpeth, Joseph C., II .... Winston-Salem, NC
Hedgpeth, Patti J. .... Dallas, TX
Hedgpeth, Tiffany R. .... Los Angeles, CA
Hedgpeth, Todd W. .... New York, NY
Hedgspeth, James E., Jr. .... Gadsden, AL
Hedian, H. Victoria .... Baltimore, MD
Hedican, Christopher R. .... Omaha, NE
Hedican, Jason M. .... Minneapolis, MN
Hedien, Colette J. .... Northbrook, IL
Hedien, Mark J. .... Columbus, OH
Hedigan, Daniel C. .... Newport Beach, CA
Hediger, Daniel D. .... Paramus, NJ
Hediger, Pamela S. .... Corvallis, OR
Hedin, Craig R. .... Mount Vernon, IL
Hedin, Douglas A. .... Minneapolis, MN
Hedin & Goldberg, P.A. .... Minneapolis, MN
Hedin, Janet Ann .... Detroit, MI
Hedin, Melinda .... Los Angeles, CA
Hedin, Randi-Jean G. .... Stamford, CT
Hedin, Todd C. .... San Rafael, CA
Hedine, Kristian Einar .... Walla Walla, WA
Hedinger, Keith G. .... Jasper, IN
Hedinger & Lawless .... Florham Park, NJ
New York, NY
Hedinger, Robert .... Florham Park, NJ
New York, NY
Hedinger, Stephen F. .... Springfield, IL

Hedland, Brennan, Heideman & Cooke, A Professional Corporation
Anchorage, AK
Bethel, AK
Hedland, John S. .... Anchorage, AK
Hedley, Mary K. .... San Francisco, CA
Hedley, Neville S. .... Chicago, IL
Hedlund, Carel T. .... Baltimore, MD
Hedlund, Carl S. .... Salem, MA
Hedlund, Earl F. .... Red Bluff, CA
Hedlund, Erica L. .... Palm Springs, CA
Hedlund, Eugenia L. .... Mankato, MN
Hedlund, Gary L. .... Klamath Falls, OR
Hedlund Hanley & John .... Chicago, IL
Hedlund, James W. .... Washington, DC
Hedlund, Jeffrey D. .... Minneapolis, MN
Hedlund, Karen J. .... Los Angeles, CA
Hedlund, Lowell A. .... Columbus, OH
Delaware, OH
Hedlund, Nancy A. .... Grand Rapids, MI
Hedlund, Paul J. .... Los Angeles, CA
Hedlund, Reuben L. .... Chicago, IL
Hedman, Bryan R. .... Sioux Falls, SD
Hedman, Donald E. (Gene)
Whitefish, MT
Hedman, Edward A. .... New York, NY
Hedman, Frederick A. ....
Department of Housing and Urban
Development, GV
Hedman, Gibson & Costigan, P.C.
New York, NY
Hedman, Hileman & Lacosta
Eureka, MT
Whitefish, MT
Hedman, Jason .... Merritt Island, FL
Hedman, Kent S. .... Cleveland, OH
Hedman, R. Annette .... Seattle, WA
Hedquist, Heather .... San Antonio, TX
Hedric, Craig D. .... Hamilton, OH
Hedrich, John C. .... Princeton, IL
Hedrich, John F. .... Chicago, IL
Hedrich, Laurie A. .... Albuquerque, NM
Hedrick, Alexandra Krueger
Jacksonville, FL
Hedrick, Andra J. .... Jackson, TN
Hedrick & Blackwell, L.L.P.
Wilmington, NC
Hedrick, Charles C. .... Augusta, ME
Hedrick, Charles V. .... Jacksonville, FL
Hedrick, Christopher R. .... Newport News, VA
Hedrick, David W., P.A. .... Orlando, FL
Hedrick, Dewberry & Regan, P.A.
Jacksonville, FL
Hedrick Eatman Gardner & Kincheloe, L.L.P. .... Charlotte, NC
Raleigh, NC
Hedrick, Edgar J., III .... Orlando, FL
Hedrick, Edward L., IV .... Taylorsville, NC
Hedrick, George R., III .... Gainesville, FL
Hedrick, Hal C., Jr. .... Cleveland, OH
Hedrick, James E. .... Dayton, OH
Hedrick, James L. .... Tyler, TX
Hedrick, James T. .... Durham, NC
Hedrick, James T., Jr. .... Charlotte, NC
Hedrick, Janet M. .... Chicago, IL
Hedrick, Jeffery M. .... Boone, NC
Hedrick, John R. .... Northbrook, IL
Hedrick, John W. .... Tallahassee, FL
Hedrick & Jordan Co., A Legal Professional Association .... Dayton, OH
Hedrick, J. W., Jr. .... Riverbank, CA
Hedrick, Kyle E. .... Chattanooga, TN
Hedrick, L. Bruce .... Atlanta, GA
Hedrick and Lane .... Washington, DC
Hedrick, Laura Lucile .... Lexington, NC
Hedrick, Mark .... El Paso, TX
Hedrick, Molly A. .... Hearne, TX
Hedrick, N. John, Jr. .... Melbourne, FL
Hedrick, P. Scott .... Wilmington, NC
Hedrick, Peggy S. .... Springfield, MO
Hedrick, R. A. (Fred) .... Raleigh, NC
Hedrick, Reesa D. .... Houston, TX
Hedrick, Rita F. .... Charleston, WV
Hedrick, Robert S. .... Sacramento, CA
Hedrick, Robert T. .... Raleigh, NC
Hedrick, Robert W. .... Fort Worth, TX
Hedrick, Thomas J. .... Glendale, CA
Hedrick, Vincent J. X., II
Wilmington, DE
Hedrick, William H. .... Albany, GA
Hedrick, William K. .... Skokie, IL
Hedspeth, David J. .... Van Buren, MO
Hedstrom, Edward E. .... Palatka, FL
Hedstrom, John E. .... Washington, DC
Hedstrom, Paul A. .... Boston, MA
Providence, RI
Hedstrom, Richard L. .... Jackson, MI
Hedstrom & Smith, L.L.P. .... Palatka, FL
Hedtke, John F. .... Duluth, MN
Hedvat, Valantina Mikail .... West Caldwell, NJ
Hee, Alfred H. H. .... Honolulu, HI
Hee, Lynelle K. .... Vista, CA
Hee, Sherman S. .... Honolulu, HI
Hee, Sherman S., Attorney at Law, A Law Corporation, Law Office of
Honolulu, HI
Hee, Stacey C. G. .... Honolulu, HI
Heeb, Donald B. .... Newark, NJ
Heeb, Jeffrey O. .... Lawrence, KS
Heeb, Louis J. .... Connersville, IN
Heeb, Robert H. .... Fort Bragg, CA
Heebe, Adrea D. .... Harvey, LA
Heebe, Bernhardt C. .... New Orleans, LA
Heebe, Frederick J. R. .... New Orleans, LA
Heebe, Frederick R. .... Harvey, LA
Heebe & Heebe .... Harvey, LA
Heebner, Baggett & Daniels
Daytona Beach, FL

Heebner, Peter B., (P.A.)
Daytona Beach, FL
Heed, James R. .... New York, NY
Heed, John T. .... Mineola, NY
Heed, Peter W. .... Keene, NH
Heed, Samuel W. .... West Chester, PA
Heedwohl, Paula .... Alhambra, CA
Heefner, Timothy A. .... Pauls Valley, OK
Heefner, William F. .... Morrisville, PA
Heeg, Casey .... Toluca Lake, CA
Heeg, Megan G. .... Dixon, IL
Heeg, Peggy A. .... Houston, TX
Heeg, Suzanne J. .... Los Angeles, CA
Heegaard, Roger W. .... Minneapolis, MN
Heege, George F., III .... St. Louis, MO
Heege, John H. .... Sioux Falls, SD
Heege, Robert C. .... Sioux Falls, SD
Heeger, D. Maurine Holland .... Sioux City, IA
Heeger, Phillip L. .... Los Angeles, CA
Heeke, B. Allen, Jr.
Altamonte Springs, FL
Heeke, Sandra L. .... Jeffersonville, IN
Heekin, Albert E., III .... Cincinnati, OH
Heekin, Denise M. .... Miami, FL
Heekin, James F., Jr. .... Orlando, FL
Heekin, James Patrick .... Bronx, NY
Heekin, John Charles .... Port Charlotte, FL
Heekin, John Charles, P.A.
Port Charlotte, FL
Heekin, Katherine R. .... Portland, OR
Heekin, Robert A. .... Jacksonville, FL
Heekin, T. Geoffrey .... Jacksonville, FL
Heekin, Thomas D. .... Cincinnati, OH
Heekin, W. Michael .... Tallahassee, FL
Heelan, Bernard F. .... Towson, MD
Heelen, J. Patrick .... Department of Commerce,
Office of the General Counsel, GV
Heeley, Steven J.W. .... Sacaton, AZ
Heels, Erik J. .... Boston, MA
Heely, Daniel G. .... Honolulu, HI
Heeman, Donald G. .... St. Paul, MN
Heemskerk, Bart W. .... Springfield, MA
Heen, Douglas B. .... Devils Lake, ND
Heen, John H. .... Lincoln, NE
Heen, Mary L. .... Richmond, VA
Heen, Walter M. .... Honolulu, HI
Heenan, Althen & Roles .... Washington, DC
Charleston, WV
Heenan Blaikie, A California Professional Corp. .... Beverly Hills, CA
Los Angeles, CA
Heenan, Cynthia .... Detroit, MI
Heenan, Douglas J. .... Platteville, WI
Heenan, Marianne .... Oroville, CA
Heenan, Michael T. .... Washington, DC
Heenan, Palmer T. .... Detroit, MI
Heenan, Palmer T., Jr. .... Southfield, MI
Heenan, Patricia A. .... Elkins Park, PA
Heenan, Patricia A. .... Philadelphia, PA
Heenan, Thomas W. .... Chicago, IL
Heene, Fred L., Jr. .... Chino, CA
Heeney, Armstrong & Heeney
Rockville, MD
Heeney, Barney J., Jr. .... Topeka, KS
Heeney, James T. .... West Caldwell, NJ
Heeney, Richard D. .... Marysville, KS
Heeney, Thomas L. .... Rockville, MD
Heeney, Thomas P., Jr. .... Warrington, PA
Heep, Jeremy .... Washington, DC
Heer & Cleveland, A Professional Corporation
Stockton, CA
Heer, Holly Hickman .... Columbus, OH
Heer, John A., II .... Cleveland, OH
Heer, John E., III .... Albuquerque, NM
Heer, Michael E. .... Stockton, CA
Heer, Naranjan S." Jack " .... Fremont, CA
Heer, Valeri J. .... Danville, CA
Heerema, M. Timothy .... Pella, IA
Heeren, Brent D. .... Toledo, IA
Heeren, Lance J. .... Cedar Rapids, IA
Heeren, Neal A. .... Bolton, MA
Heerens, Joseph R. .... Indianapolis, IN
Heerin, James E., Jr. .... Roswell, GA
Heerman, Max Christian .... Minneapolis, MN
Heerman, William R. .... Appleton, WI
Heermance, Brian P. .... Boston, MA
Heermans, High R. .... Seattle, WA
Heermans, Nancy Snyder
Pension Benefit Guaranty Corporation,
Office of the General Counsel, GV
Heers, Frank W. .... St. Paul, MN
Heerwagen, Elwood J., Jr. .... Rockaway, NJ
Heerwagen, Kurt .... Riverside, IL
Heerwagen, Peter H. .... Loudonville, NY
Heery, Frank W. .... Englewood, CO
Heesch, Harold R. .... Newton, MA
Heesch & Kelly .... Newton, MA
Heeseman, Rex .... Los Angeles, CA
Heet, Kathryn K. .... Denver, CO
Heeter, James A. .... Kansas City, MO
Heeter, Jeffrey .... Pittsburgh, PA
Heeter, John M. .... Indianapolis, IN
Heeter, Joseph L. .... Columbus, OH
Heeter, Judith S. .... Kansas City, MO
Heeter, Richard D. .... Lima, OH
Heeter, Terry R. .... Clarion, PA
Heeter, William S. .... Cleveland, OH
Heetland, Gerald C. .... Las Vegas, NV
Heettner, Barry N. .... Flushing, NY
Hefel, Kristy L. .... Dubuque, IA
Hefele, Bernd E. .... Mount Arlington, NJ
Heffan, Ira .... Boston, MA
Heffel, Spencer D. .... Phoenix, AZ
Heffelfinger, Christopher T., Jr.
San Francisco, CA
Heffelfinger, Gregory G. .... Houston, TX
Heffelfinger, Jeffrey R. .... Huntington, IN
Heffelfinger, Thomas B. .... Minneapolis, MN

Heffelman, M. Kevin .... Ashland City, TN
Hefferan, George B., III .... Chicago, IL
Hefferan, George B., Jr. .... Portland, ME
Hefferan, John R., Jr. .... Orlando, FL
Hefferan, Patricia R. .... Wasilla, AK
Hefferan, Richard P. .... Schaumburg, IL
Hefferin, Victor C. .... Portland, OR
Hefferlin, Charles H. .... Sunnyvale, CA
Heffern, Allison M. .... Cedar Rapids, IA
Heffern, H. James, Jr. .... Binghamton, NY
Heffern & Heffern .... Binghamton, NY
Heffern, Jay M. .... St. Paul, MN
Heffern, Richard C. .... Buffalo, NY
Heffernan, Barbara K. .... Washington, DC
Heffernan, Bart T. .... Fort Lauderdale, FL
Heffernan, Bart T., P.A. .... Fort Lauderdale, FL
Heffernan, Brenda A. .... Washington, DC
Heffernan, Brian F. .... Department of Justice,
Civil Rights Division, GV
Heffernan, Brian J. .... Los Angeles, CA
Heffernan, Christopher J. .... Baltimore, MD
Heffernan, Daniel C. .... New Haven, CT
Heffernan, Daniel T.S. .... Boston, MA
Heffernan, David .... Washington, DC
Heffernan, David R. .... Miami, FL
Heffernan, Donal J. .... Stillwater, MN
Heffernan, Douglas J. .... Minneapolis, MN
Heffernan, E. Michael .... West Haven, CT
Heffernan, Edward A. .... Cleveland, OH
Heffernan, Edward D. .... Washington, DC
Heffernan, Elizabeth Blossom
Washington, DC
Heffernan & Farr, L.L.P. .... Hartford, CT
Heffernan, Gerald A. .... West Haven, CT
Heffernan, Gerald T. .... Miami, FL
Heffernan & Gilson .... Providence, RI
Heffernan & Heffernan .... Canton, CT
West Hartford, CT
Heffernan & Heffernan .... West Haven, CT
Heffernan, Henry J. .... Augusta, GA
Heffernan, J. Warren .... South Weymouth, MA
Heffernan, James H. .... Salt Lake City, UT
Heffernan, James P. .... Jamaica, NY
Heffernan, James P. .... New York, NY
Heffernan, James Patrick .... Portland, OR
Heffernan, James V. .... Washington, DC
Heffernan, John B. .... Newport Beach, CA
Heffernan, John B., A Law Corp.
Newport Beach, CA
Heffernan, John Connery .... Hartford, CT
Heffernan, John J. .... Buffalo, NY
Heffernan, John M. .... Cleveland, OH
Heffernan, Joseph P., (A P.C.)
Los Angeles, CA
Heffernan, Kevin .... Portland, ME
Heffernan, Kevin N. .... Torrance, CA
Heffernan, Lawrence P. .... Boston, MA
Heffernan, Licia .... San Diego, CA
Heffernan, Linda F. .... Oak Park, IL
Heffernan, Martin J. .... Fort Collins, CO
Heffernan, Mary G. .... Alexandria, VA
Heffernan, Maureen Brown
Sioux City, IA
Heffernan, Michael J. .... Tacoma, WA
Heffernan, Michael Patrick
White Plains, NY
Heffernan, Michael S. .... Madison, WI
Heffernan, Michele M. .... Boston, MA
Heffernan, Michele O. .... Buffalo, NY
Heffernan, Nathan S. .... Madison, WI
Heffernan, Pamela G. .... Ogden, UT
Heffernan, Patricia Ann .... Washington, DC
Heffernan, Patricia Anne .... Marlboro, NJ
Heffernan, Patricia B. .... Seattle, WA
Heffernan, Patrick A. .... Chicago, IL
Heffernan, Robert D., Jr. .... Medford, OR
Heffernan & Sweet .... Buffalo, NY
Heffernan, T. Daniel .... Bellevue, WA
Heffernan, Terrence R. .... Columbus, OH
Heffernan, Thomas A. .... Cleveland, OH
Heffernan, Timothy E. .... McLean, VA
Heffernan, Walter J. .... Windham, NY
Heffernan & Wersinger .... Marlboro, NJ
Heffernan, William C. .... New York, NY
Heffernan, William J., Jr. .... Marathon, FL
Heffernan, William M. .... Providence, RI
Heffernan, William P. .... Chicago, IL
Heffernen, James J. .... Norristown, PA
Heffernen, Leslie Kennedy
King Of Prussia, PA
Hefferon, Paul .... Charlotte, NC
Hefferon, Thomas J. .... Charlotte, NC
Hefferon, Thomas M. .... Washington, DC
Hefferon, Thomas W. .... Schenectady, NY
Hefferon, Timothy W. .... Southfield, MI
Heffes, Michele .... Oakland, CA
Heffington, Donna K. .... Billings, MT
Heffington, Jack G. .... Murfreesboro, TN
Heffington, Joseph A., III .... Carrollton, TX
Heffington, Joseph R. .... Austin, TX
Hefflefinger, Matthew S. .... Peoria, IL
Heffler, Curt L. .... Philadelphia, PA
Heffler, James M. .... Rockville, MD
Heffler, Paul M. .... Jasper, AL
Heffley, J. Ronald .... Arvada, CO
Heffley, L. Kyle .... Little Rock, AR
Heffley, Marilyn .... Philadelphia, PA
Heffling, John D. .... West Palm Beach, FL
Hefflinger, David L. .... Omaha, NE
Heffner, Adam G. .... Boca Raton, FL
Heffner, Donald C. .... San Diego, CA
Heffner, Douglas J. .... Washington, DC
Heffner, Earl S., Jr. .... Bethlehem, PA
Heffner, George W. .... Pottsville, PA
Heffner, Jann Kathryn .... Columbus, OH
Heffner, John D. .... Washington, DC
Heffner, Lawrence E., Jr. .... Frederick, MD
Heffner, Mary P. .... Providence, RI

Heffner, Matthew T. .... **Houston, TX**
Heffner, Paul T. .... Louisville, KY
Heffner, R. Merle .... Huntingdon, PA
Heffron, A. Richard .... Wilmington, DE
Heffron, Frank H. .... Binghamton, NY
Heffron, Howard A. .... Washington, DC
Heffron, Jonathon K. .... **Houston, TX**
Heffron, Karen M. .... **Oceanside, CA**
Heffron, Matthew F. .... **Omaha, NE**
Heffron, Wm. G. .... Buffalo, NY
Heffter, Sarah L. .... Chardon, OH
Hefler, Elliott D. .... **New York, NY**
Hefler, Herbert H. .... Brooklyn, NY
Hefler, Karen Sue .... New York, NY
Hefler, Marcie L. .... Chicago, IL
Hefley, Joyce G. .... Londonderry, NH
Heflin, Donald L. .... Department of State, Foreign Service Officers (Overseas), GV
Heflin, H. Ray .... **Washington, DC**
Heflin, H. Thomas, Jr. .... **Florence, AL**
Heflin, H. Thomas, Jr. .... **Tuscumbia, AL**
Heflin, Howell Thomas .... **Tuscumbia, AL**
Heflin, Jack R. .... Shalimar, FL
Heflin, Janet R. Sheley .... **Alton, IL**
Heflin, John J., III .... **Memphis, TN**
Heflin, Julie W. .... Boston, MA
Heflin, Linda J. .... Lubbock, TX
Heflin, Mary L. .... Mammoth Lakes, CA
Heflin, Peter J. .... Milwaukee, WI
Heflin, Ray .... Washington, DC
Heflin, Robert P. .... Los Angeles, CA
Heflinger, James D. .... Dublin, OH
Hefner & Eberspacher .... **Mattoon, IL**
Hefner, Gerard A. .... **New York, NY**
Hefner, Hal L. .... Owasso, OK
Hefner, Jona Rae .... Oklahoma City, OK
Hefner, Kenneth .... Oklahoma City, OK
Hefner, M. Daniel .... **Chicago, IL**
Hefner, M. John, Jr. .... **Mattoon, IL**
Hefner, Randy V. .... **Adel, IA**
Hefner, Robert A. .... Saipan, TT
Hefner, Stark & Marois, LLP **Sacramento, CA**
Hefner, Thomas E. .... Greenville, RI
Heft, Adam J. .... **New York, NY**
Heft, Carolyn M. .... **New York, NY**
Heft, Frank W., Jr. .... Louisville, KY
Heft, Robert R. .... Solana Beach, CA
Heft, Staaden & Heft, S.C. .... Racine, WI
Hefte, Carrie A. .... Minneapolis, MN
Hefte, Richard C. .... St. Paul, MN
Heftel, Christopher Lee .... Nashville, TN
Hefter & Carroll .... **Chicago, IL**
Hefter, Daniel S., (P.C.) .... **Chicago, IL**
Hefter, Ellen Roberts .... New York, NY
Hefter, Eva H. .... Lawrence, NY
Hefter, Laurence R. .... **Washington, DC**
Hefter, Marcia Zipser .... **Riverhead, NY** Water Mill, NY
Hefter, Mark .... **Austin, TX**
Hefter, Michael C. .... **New York, NY**
Heftka, Robert V. .... Rochester, NY
Heftler, Pierre V. .... Detroit, MI
Heftler, Thomas E. .... **New York, NY**
Heftman, Ronald N. .... Chicago, IL
Hefton, Holly .... **Oklahoma City, OK**
Hefty, Christopher D. .... Sterling, CO
Hefty, Sarah A. .... **Chicago, IL**
Hefty, Thomas L. .... **Chicago, IL**
Hefty, Thomas R. .... Milwaukee, WI
Hefty & Wiley, P.C. .... Richmond, VA
Hefty, William H. .... Richmond, VA
Hegamin, Keisha L. .... Philadelphia, PA
Hegan, William M. .... Chicago, IL
Hegar, Dara Grisbee .... **Houston, TX**
Hegar, Glenn Allen, Jr .... Hockley, TX
Hegar, Joseph W., Jr. .... Katy, TX
Hegarty, Charles S. .... **Detroit, MI**
Hegarty, Cynthia L. .... Minneapolis, MN
Hegarty, David R. .... Boston, MA
Hegarty, Edward J. .... Orinda, CA
Hegarty, James E. .... Denver, CO
Hegarty, Jeremiah J. .... Milwaukee, WI
Hegarty, Kathleen Quirk .... Birmingham, MI
Hegarty, Mark .... Albuquerque, NM
Hegarty, Mark C. .... **Kansas City, MO**
Hegarty, Mary F. .... Park Ridge, IL
Hegarty, Maureen A. .... **Milwaukee, WI**
Hegarty, Michael E. .... Denver, CO
Hegarty, Michael K. .... Brighton, MI
Hegarty, Nancy T. .... **Boston, MA**
Hegarty, Patrick J. .... Monrovia, CA
Hegarty, Richard P. .... Lutherville, MD
Hegarty, Terrence K. .... Chicago, IL
Hegarty, Terrence K., & Associates, Ltd. Chicago, IL
Hegarty, Timothy F. .... **New York, NY**
Hegarty, Walter C. .... Williston Park, NY
Hegarty, William A. .... Ocean City, MD
Hegarty, William E. .... Greenwich, CT
Hegarty, William J. .... Andover, MA
Hegberg, Jeffrey J. .... **Parker, AZ**
Hegboum, Margaret A. .... Dallas, TX
Hegde, Satyanarayan S. .... **New York, NY**
Hege, Brent D. .... Ames, IA
Hegé & Rasmussen .... **Arcadia, CA** **Pasadena, CA**
Hegedus, Candice Lea Horn **Haverford, PA**
Hegedus, Jason S. .... **Troy, MI**
Hegedus, Jeff S. .... **Los Angeles, CA**
Hegedus, Joseph K. .... **Los Angeles, CA**
Hegedus, Joseph M. .... **Columbus, OH**
Hegedus, Laura E. .... New York, NY
Hegedus, Lisa M. .... **Chicago, IL**
Hegedus, Mark S. .... Department of Justice, Antitrust Division, GV
Hegedus, Sharon H. .... Danbury, CT

Hegel, Edward J., Jr. .... **Tustin, CA**
Hegel, Elizabeth Bettner .... Rockton, IL
Hegel, Joe L. .... Miles City, MT
Hegeler, Barton H. .... **San Diego, CA**
Hegeler, Barton H., Atty. at Law, A Prof. Corp. .... **San Diego, CA**
Hegeman, Alan .... Chatham, NY
Hegeman, Carmen B. .... El Paso, TX
Hegeman, John E. .... **Evansville, IN**
Hegeman, Louis R. .... **Chicago, IL**
Hegeman, Thomas .... Oneonta, NY
Hegemier, Jennifer Susan .... San Diego, CA
Hegen, Kathleen E. .... **Oakland, CA**
Hegenbart, Frederick J. .... **Tulsa, OK**
Heger, Andrew W. .... **Los Angeles, CA**
Heger, David R. .... Paola, KS
Heger, Ellen J. .... Bellflower, CA
Heger, Molly S. .... **Los Angeles, CA**
Heger, Thomas F. .... Madison, WI
Heger, Victoria A. .... Detroit, MI
Hegerle, Ashlie Muss .... Minneapolis, MN
Hegermiller, Kimberly L. .... Norwalk, CT
Hegg, Phillip W. .... Charlotte, NC
Hegg, Robert M. .... **Alexandria, MN**
Hegge, Carolyn A. .... **Madison, WI**
Hegge, Colleen M. .... **Cincinnati, OH**
Hegge, Kristen M. .... **Stockton, CA**
Heggemeier, Ronald R. .... Parker, CO
Heggen, I. Nelson, Law Offices of **Houston, TX**
Heggen, Karen A. .... Ballston Spa, NY
Heggen, R.L. .... San Ramon, CA Walnut Creek, CA
Heggeness, Clark .... Long Beach, CA
Heggeness & Sweet, A Prof. Corp. San Diego, CA
Heggeness, Terry .... San Diego, CA
Heggestad, Robert E. .... **Washington, DC**
Heggestad & Weiss, P.C. .... **Washington, DC**
Heggie, G. Brent .... Las Vegas, NV
Heggie, Hunter D. .... Chattanooga, TN
Heggie, Karen .... San Jose, CA
Heggie, Mark E. .... **Greenville, OH**
Heggie, Robert M. .... **St. Louis, MO**
Heggland, Roy T. .... Cincinnati, OH
Heggs, Gary S. .... St. Charles, MO
Heggy, Rodney J. .... **Oklahoma City, OK**
Heghmann, Robert A. .... Avon, CT
Hegi, Alan D. .... **Fort Worth, TX**
Hegland, Kenny .... Tucson, AZ
Hegland, Paul G. .... Treasury Department, Office of Regulations and Rulings, GV
Hegland, Roberta J. .... **Corpus Christi, TX**
Heglar, Ronald O. .... Chicago, IL
Hegle, Charlotte Marie .... Davis, CA
Hegle, Juliane K. .... Williston, VT
Hegle, Terry D. .... Bay City, MI
Hegler, Jean A. .... **Garden City, NY**
Heglin, Robert W. .... **Phoenix, AZ**
Hegner, A. A. Lee .... Denver, CO
Hegner, Richard R. .... Victorville, CA
Hegner, Robin L. .... Charlottesville, VA
Hegness, J. Timothy .... San Bernardino, CA
Hegness, Paul C., (A Professional Corporation) .... **Newport Beach, CA**
Hegre, Jonathan J. .... **Minneapolis, MN**
Hegsted, Ralph B. .... Denver, CO
Hegstrom, Gerard D. .... Scottsdale, GA
Hegtvedt, Leo C. .... Boone, IA
Hegwood, David B. Department of Agriculture, Foreign Agricultural Service, GV
Hegy, Sheila H. .... Chicago, IL
Hegyes, Dean K. .... Willoughby, OH
Hegyi, Karen R. .... Barrow, AK
Hegyi, Louis L. .... South Bend, IN
Heher, Garrett M. .... **Princeton, NJ**
Heher, Harry, Jr. .... Princeton, NJ
Heher, John Robert .... **Princeton, NJ**
Heher, R. J. .... **Palo Alto, CA**
Hehir, Diane E. .... Selah, WA
Hehir, L. Thos. .... San Francisco, CA
Hehir, Patrick J. .... **Sacramento, CA**
Hehl, Bernard Warren .... Union, NJ
Hehl & Hehl, A Professional Corporation Union, NJ
Hehl, Lambert, Jr. .... Fort Thomas, KY
Hehl, Stephen F. .... Union, NJ
Hehmeyer, Charles P. .... Philadelphia, PA
Hehn, Curtis A. .... **Philadelphia, PA**
Hehn, Karina E. .... **Cherry Hill, NJ**
Hehn, Marla R. .... Fort Collins, CO
Hehn, William A. .... Las Vegas, NV
Hehner, James W. .... Indianapolis, IN
Hehr, Albert G., Jr. .... Mayfield, OH
Hehr, Albert G., Jr. & Marjia R. Hehr Mayfield, OH
Hehr, David M. .... **Buffalo, NY**
Hehr, Marjia R. .... Mayfield, OH
Hehre, Frederick W., III Vineyard Haven, MA
Heib, Malcolm G. .... Los Angeles, CA
Heibein, Alan N. .... Menlo Park, CA
Heiber, Gary L. .... Beloit, WI
Heiberg, Eric R. .... **Minneapolis, MN**
Heiberg, James L. .... McLean, VA
Heiberg, Kathryn A. .... Westlake Village, CA
Heiberg, Robert A. .... **Minneapolis, MN**
Heichel, Eric P. .... New York, NY
Heichel, William D. .... **Mansfield, OH** **Sandusky, OH**
Heichel, William S. .... Canton, OH
Heick, Kenneth W. .... **McLean, VA**
Heicklen, Wayne B. .... **New York, NY**
Heid, Brigid E. .... Columbus, OH
Heid, Christopher .... Norris City, IL
Heid, Daniel B. .... Lakewood, WA
Heid, David W. .... **San Jose, CA**

Heid, Edward P. .... Eugene, OR
Heid, George J. .... Lafayette, IN
Heid, Harry W. .... Rancho Santa Fe, CA
Heid, Janice M. .... Pacifica, CA
Heid, Robert C. .... Fremont, OH
Heid, Sally R. .... Fremont, OH
Heid, Sheryl R. .... **Greensburg, PA** **Uniontown, PA**
Heida, John M. .... Bellevue, NE
Heidbreder, Kay Kurtz .... **Blacksburg, VA**
Heide, H. Elliott .... **Los Angeles, CA**
Heide, John H. .... **Green Bay, WI**
Heide, Kelley L. .... **Dallas, TX**
Heide, Richard T. .... Lafayette, IN
Heide Sandy Deets & Kennedy Lafayette, IN
Heideck, Robert E. .... **Philadelphia, PA**
Heidecker, Perry S. .... New Hyde Park, NY
Heidel, Cindy J. .... Gaithersburg, MD
Heidel, Lynne L. .... **San Diego, CA**
Heidel, Samberson, Newell & Cox **Lovington, NM**
Heidelbach, James T. .... **Baltimore, MD**
Heidelbaugh, Heather S. .... **Pittsburgh, PA**
Heidelberg, A. Jane .... Clarksdale, MS
Heidelberg, C. Maison .... **Jackson, MS**
Heidelberg, Evelyn F. .... **Los Angeles, CA**
Heidelberg, James H. .... **Pascagoula, MS**
Heidelberg, James M., Jr. .... San Antonio, TX
Heidelberg, R. Webster, III **Hattiesburg, MS**
Heidelberg, Tanya .... New York, NY
Heidelberg & Woodliff, P.A. **Hattiesburg, MS** **Jackson, MS**
Heidelberger, Brian L. .... **Chicago, IL**
Heidelberger, Candace S. .... Auburn, CA
Heidelberger, Elliot .... Hanover Park, IL
Heidelberger, Jonathan .... Northport, NY
Heidelberger, Louis M. .... **Philadelphia, PA**
Heidelberger, William A. .... Nevada City, CA
Heidell, Pittoni, Murphy & Bach, LLP **Stamford, CT** **New York, NY**
Heidell, Robert C. .... **New York, NY**
Heidelman, Charles E. .... Newport, KY
Heideloff, Glenn F. .... Cleveland, OH
Heideman, James L. .... **San Francisco, CA**
Heideman Law Group, The, P.C. **Washington, DC**
Heideman, Lila .... Boston, MA
Heideman, Richard D. .... **Washington, DC**
Heideman, Robert I. .... Clearwater, FL
Heideman, Roger J. .... **Lincoln, NE**
Heideman, Sara E. .... **Anchorage, AK**
Heidemann, Bret Matthew .... Golden, CO
Heidemann, Craig Richard .... **Bolivar, MO**
Heidemann, Elaine .... Auburn Hills, MI
Heidemann and Heidemann, P.C. Auburn Hills, MI Rogers City, MI
Heidemann, Karl W. .... Rogers City, MI
Heidemann, Raymond L. .... **San Diego, CA**
Heiden, Daniel R. .... Brookfield, WI
Heiden, George F. .... **Omaha, NE**
Heiden, Julie H. .... **Falls Church, VA**
Heiden, Richard Thomas .... **Clearwater, FL**
Heiden, Thomas J. .... **Grand Rapids, MI**
Heidenberg, Robert .... Closter, NJ
Heidenberger, Peter .... **Washington, DC**
Heidenfelder, Randy S. .... Lake Zurich, IL
Heidenheimer, Mark E. .... Austin, TX
Heidenreich, Diane Doster Woodland Hills, CA
Heidenreich, Douglas R. .... St. Paul, MN
Heidenreich, Gregg T. .... Milwaukee, WI
Heidenreich, Joan Victoria San Francisco, CA
Heidenreich, Joseph J. .... Odebolt, IA
Heidenreich, Kristen F. .... **Kansas City, MO**
Heidenreich, Roger K. .... **St. Louis, MO**
Heidenreich, Ute .... Norfolk, VA
Heidenry, Eve .... **Chicago, IL**
Heidepriem, Scott N. .... **Sioux Falls, SD**
Heidepriem, Widmayer, Zell & Jones Highmore, SD Miller, SD
Heider, A. Gretchen .... Lafayette, LA
Heider, Patrick F. .... St. Louis, MO
Heider, Richard A. .... Springfield, MO
Heider, Robert R. .... Elm Grove, WI
Heider, Susan M. .... St. Louis, MO
Heider, Tony K. .... Bakersfield, CA
Heider, Wallace B. .... Santa Ana, CA
Heiderscheit, John W., III .... Washington, DC
Heiderscheit, Richard T. .... La Crescent, MN
Heidewald, William M. .... Weed, CA
Heidgerd, C. D. .... **Raleigh, NC**
Heidgerd, Frederick C. .... **Boca Raton, FL**
Heidgerd, Frederick C. **Fort Lauderdale, FL**
Heidig, Elizabeth A. .... Sacramento, CA
Heidkamp, Thomas S. .... Fort Myers, FL
Heidlage, Katharine Sanderson .... Boston, MA
Heidlage, Richard C. .... **Boston, MA**
Heidlauf, Howard A. .... Sycamore, IL
Heidler, Gregory .... Waialua, HI
Heidloff, Virginia L. .... **Cleveland, OH**
Heidman, Marvin F. .... **Sioux City, IA**
Heidman, Redmond, Fredregill, Patterson, Plaza & Dykstra, L.L.P. .... **Sioux City, IA** **South Sioux City, NE** **Dakota Dunes, SD**
Heidorn, David L. .... Des Plaines, IL
Heidorn, O. Chris .... Glen Ellyn, IL
Heidorn, Robert E. .... Indianapolis, IN
Heidrich, Dean R. .... Reno, NV
Heidrich, Sharon A. .... Bloomfield Hills, MI

Heidrich, William A., III .... Cincinnati, OH
Heidrick, Charles F. .... Beaumont, TX
Heidrick, G. A., Jr. .... Columbia, MD
Heidrick, R. Clarke, Jr. .... **Austin, TX**
Heidrick, S. Andrew .... Salina, KS
Heidt, Arthur J., Jr. .... Destin, FL Farmington Hills, MI
Heidt, Frances .... **Birmingham, AL**
Heidt, Gregory L. .... Erie, PA
Heidt, James K. .... Clockville, NY
Heidt, Janice D. .... **Indianapolis, IN**
Heidt, Jeffrey L., (P.C.) .... **Boston, MA**
Heidt, Kathryn R. .... Pittsburgh, PA
Heidt, Lawrence L. .... **Salisbury, MD**
Heidt, Michael .... Hollywood, FL
Heidt, Wesley .... Daytona Beach, FL
Heidtke, Curtis L. .... Littleton, CO
Heidtke, Curtis L., P.C. .... Littleton, CO
Heiduk, Don F. .... **Santa Barbara, CA**
Heier, David S. .... Columbus, OH
Heier, Gregory S. .... Lincoln, NE
Heier & Kroeger, LLP .... Columbus, OH
Heier, Patricia E. Wilkin .... Columbus, OH
Heier, Ronald O. .... **St. Louis, MO**
Heiferman, Robert .... **White Plains, NY**
Heifets, Helen .... **Philadelphia, PA**
Heifetz, Alan W. Department of Housing and Urban Development, Office of Administrative Law Judges, GV
Heifetz, Elmer M. .... Chicago, IL
Heifetz, Gary S. .... **St. Louis, MO**
Heifetz, Kimberly R. .... Department of Justice, Bureau of Prisons, GV
Heifetz, Melissa T. .... Bronx, NY
Heifetz, Richard E. .... **Boston, MA**
Heifetz, Stephen R .... Department of Justice, Criminal Division, GV
Heiffel, Roger W. .... Brooklyn, NY
Heigaard, William S. .... Langdon, ND
Heigel, Catherine Edwards .... **Charlotte, NC**
Heigele, Christopher L. .... **Gladstone, MO**
Heiger, Neil W. .... **Boston, MA**
Heigham, James C., (P.C.) .... Boston, MA
Heigle, Kevin G. .... **Metairie, LA**
Heike, John G. .... Austin, TX
Heiken, Marilyn .... **Eugene, OR**
Heikenen, Charles E. .... Roseville, MN
Heikens, Steven G. .... Minneapolis, MN
Heikes, Graham .... Minneapolis, MN
Heikes, Michael L. .... Norfolk, VA
Heikkila, John E. .... **Marquette, MI**
Heikkinen, Arthur .... Howell, MI
Heikkinen, Donald C. .... Lansing, MI
Heikkinen Law Firm, P.C. .... Howell, MI
Heikkinen, Ralph J. .... Murphysboro, IL
Heikkinen, Richard A. .... Howell, MI
Heikkinen, Robert D. .... Marquette, MI
Heikkinen and Strisar .... Marquette, MI
Heiko & Levy, P.C. .... New York, NY
Heiko, Melvin H. .... New York, NY
Heil, Carla J. .... Philadelphia, PA
Heil, Chris .... Little Rock, AR
Heil, David R. .... Winter Park, FL
Heil, Dennis J. .... Medford, OR
Heil, Dennis J., P.C. .... Medford, OR
Heil, Francis C. .... **Dallas, TX**
Heil, Gary M. .... San Mateo, CA
Heil, James R. .... Alton, IL
Heil, Jennifer Ann .... Media, PA
Heil, John P. .... **Omaha, NE**
Heil, Joseph B. .... Philadelphia, PA
Heil, Kevin C. .... **Camden, NJ** **Westmont, NJ**
Heil, Lieselotte .... Lewisburg, WV
Heil, Lucy G. .... Mission Viejo, CA
Heil, Nicholas .... Accomac, VA
Heil, Richard F., Jr. .... **Springfield, OH**
Heil, Robert J. .... Oakland, CA
Heil, Robert M. .... Salem, OR
Heil, Scott Richard .... **Riverside, CA**
Heil, Stephen W. .... **Chicago, IL**
Heil, Summer E. .... **Chicago, IL**
Heil, Tchad Marie .... Pittsburgh, PA
Heiland, Constance R. .... Quechee, VT
Heilberg, David L. .... **Charlottesville, VA**
Heilbron, David M. .... **San Francisco, CA**
Heilbron, Louis H. .... **San Francisco, CA**
Heilbron, Patricia B. .... **Oakland, CA**
Heilbron, Richard H. .... **San Francisco, CA**
Heilbron, Richd. H. .... Overland Park, KS
Heilbroner, David R. .... New York, NY
Heilbronn, Charles .... New York, NY
Heilbronner, Edward .... **Hollywood, FL**
Heilbronner, Michael K. .... Beaverton, OR
Heilbronner, Susan L. .... Department of Justice, Civil Rights Division, GV
Heilbronner, Warren H. .... **Rochester, NY**
Heilbronner, Warren M. .... **Boston, MA**
Heilbrun, David G. .... San Francisco, CA
Heilbrun, Emily .... Eugene, OR
Heilbrun, John L. .... **Cincinnati, OH**
Heilbrun, Kim L. .... **Austin, TX**
Heilbrun, Mark R. .... **Washington, DC**
Heilbrun, Robyn O. .... Salt Lake City, UT
Heilbrunn, Bernice A. .... Houston, TX
Heilbrunn, Elise R. .... **Mountain View, CA**
Heilbrunn, Evelyn G. .... **Palo Alto, CA**
Heilbrunn, Finkelstein, Heilbrunn, Alfonso, Goldstein & Pape, A Professional Corporation .... Old Bridge, NJ
Heilbrunn, Jonathan M. .... Old Bridge, NJ
Heilbrunn, Lloyd J. Palm Beach Gardens, FL
Heilbut, Philip R. .... Fresno, CA
Heile, C. Donald .... Cincinnati, OH
Heileman, Dennis W. Charlotte Amalie, St. Thomas, VI

Heiler, James J. ... Phoenix, AZ
Heiler, Randall S. ... Roseville, CA
Heileson, Marvin D. ... Los Angeles, CA
Heilferty, Robert John
Department of Commerce, Office of the General Counsel, GV
Heilig, George B. ... Corvallis, OR
Heilig, John A. ... Norfolk, VA
Heilig, McKenry, Fraim & Lollar
Virginia Beach, VA
Norfolk, VA
Heilig, Melissa D. ... East Quogue, NY
Heilig, Richard J. ... Edina, MN
Heiligenstein & Badgley, Professional Corporation ... Belleville, IL
Heiligenstein, Bernard G. ... Carlyle, IL
Heiligenstein, Bernard G., Ltd. ... Carlyle, IL
Heiligenstein, Christian E. ... Belleville, IL
Heiligenstein, Joseph B. ... Carlyle, IL
Heiligenthal, Susan ... Austin, TX
Heiligenthaler, Paul J. ... Medina, NY
Heiligman, Joel N. ... Minneapolis, MN
St. Paul, MN
Heiligman, Martin J. ... Philadelphia, PA
Heiligman & Mogul, P.C. ... Philadelphia, PA
Heiling, Dean ... Portland, OR
Heiling, Dean, & Associates ... Portland, OR
Heilizer, Deborah Gail
Securities and Exchange Commission, Division of Enforcement, GV
Heilizer, Glenn E. ... Chicago, IL
Heilizer, Ruth I.
Federal Election Commission, Office of the General Counsel, GV
Heilman, Alfred J. ... Rochester, NY
Heilman, Ann L. ... New York, NY
Heilman, D. Randall ... Council Grove, KS
Heilman, David H. ... Council Grove, KS
Heilman, David J. ... San Francisco, CA
Heilman, Edward G. ... Minneapolis, MN
Heilman, Elizabeth A. ... Carrollton, KY
Heilman, H. H., Jr. ... Kittanning, PA
Heilman, James M. ... Roslyn, NY
Heilman, John ... Los Angeles, CA
Heilman, John R. ... Poughkeepsie, NY
Heilman, Julia M. ... White Plains, NY
Heilman, Karen L. ... Santa Monica, CA
Heilman Law Firm ... Minneapolis, MN
Heilman, Linda ... New York, NY
Heilman & McClister ... Kittanning, PA
Heilman, Michael A. ... Jackson, MS
Heilman, Michael J. ... Department of Justice, Executive Office for Immigration Review, GV
Heilman, Michael J. ... Pittsburgh, PA
Heilman, Nancy L. ... Pittsburgh, PA
Heilman, Pamela Davis ... Buffalo, NY
Heilman, Shannon M. ... Chicago, IL
Heilmann, C. E. ... El Dorado, KS
Heilmann, Charles E. ... Huntington, WV
Heilmann, David M. ... Chicago, IL
Heilmann, Ekman & Associates, Inc.
Burlington, VT
Heilmann, Michael G. ... Southfield, MI
Heilmann, Michael G., P.C.
Southfield, MI
Heilmann, Peter T. ... San Francisco, CA
Heilmann, Thomas F. ... Burlington, VT
Heilprin, J. D. ... Los Angeles, CA
Heilweil, Toby Z.
National Labor Relations Board, Office of Board Members, GV
Heily & Blase, A Prof. Law Corp.
Ventura, CA
Heim, Angela M. ... Philadelphia, PA
Heim, Anne Scholtz ... Louisville, KY
Heim, Barbara E. ... Charlotte, NC
Heim, Bret ... Iola, KS
Heim, Brian E. ... Charlotte, NC
Heim, Charles E., Jr.
Indian Harbour Beach, FL
Heim, Charles E., Jr., P.A.
Indian Harbour Beach, FL
Heim, David L. ... Omaha, NE
Heim, David Michael
North Tonawanda, NY
Heim, Diane A. ... Department of Labor, Office of the Solicitor, GV
Heim, Gary J. ... Harrisburg, PA
Heim, Herbert C. ... Toms River, NJ
Heim, Herbert H. ... East Syracuse, NY
Heim, Jack D. ... Kittanning, PA
Heim, Jack L. ... Naperville, IL
Heim, James E. ... Mexico, MO
Heim, Janet Murphy ... San Jose, CA
Heim, Joan L. ... Washington, DC
Heim, John R. ... Minnetonka Beach, MN
Heim, Jon S. ... Tiburon, CA
Heim, Judith A. ... Florham Park, NJ
Heim, Juerg A. ... Greenwich, CT
Heim, Kristen J. ... Anaheim, CA
Heim, Larry C. ... York, PA
Heim, Lori A. ... Clearwater, FL
Heim, Maggie ... Culver City, CA
Heim, McEnroe & Urciuoli
Florham Park, NJ
Heim, Michael F. ... Houston, TX
Heim, Patricia M. ... La Crosse, WI
Heim, Paul J. ... Houston, TX
Heim, Paul M. ... Minneapolis, MN
Heim, Robert C. ... Philadelphia, PA
Heim, Robert G. ... New York, NY
Heim, Ross C. ... Libertyville, IL
Heim, Ross C., P.C. ... Libertyville, IL
Heim, Sharon J. ... Brighton, MA
Heim, Sharon M. ... Buffalo, NY
Heim, Stephanie G. ... San Diego, CA
Heim, Steven J. ... Washington, DC
Heim, Tedman John ... Rochester, MN
Heim, Thomas G. ... Woodbury Heights, NJ
Heim, Thomas M. ... El Centro, CA
Heim, William V. ... Cranford, NJ
Heiman, Aba ... Woodbury, NY
Heiman, Aber, Goldlust & Baker
Wilmington, DE
Heiman, Bruce J. ... Washington, DC
Heiman, David G. ... Cleveland, OH
Heiman, Henry A. ... Wilmington, DE
Heiman, Laura A. ... New York, NY
Heiman, Lee B., Jr. ... Helena, MT
Heiman, Lee C. ... Washington, DC
Heiman, Martin A. ... Great Neck, NY
Heiman, Matthew R.A. ... Lexington, KY
Heiman, Oren ... New York, NY
Heiman, Richard J. ... Washington, DC
Heiman, Ron S. ... Seattle, WA
Heiman, Ronald T. ... Sharon, PA
Heiman, Tondra Netherton
New Orleans, LA
Heiman, William M. ... Philadelphia, PA
Heimann, Christopher M. ... Washington, DC
Heimann, Danielle ... New York, NY
Heimann, Fritz F. ... Fairfield, CT
Heimann, Gerhard M. ... Burbank, CA
Heimann, James A. ... Decatur, IN
Heimann, Mary Christine ... West Haven, CT
Heimann, Richard M. ... San Francisco, CA
Heimann, Stephen B. ... Philadelphia, PA
Heimann, Stephen R. ... Columbus, IN
Heimann, Wendy J. ... Chicago, IL
Heimann-McGhee, Robin
Washington, DC
Heimanson, Ilan ... Los Angeles, CA
Heimanson, Neil L. ... Darien, GA
Heimark, Julie J. ... Los Angeles, CA
Heimbach, Candy Barr ... Bethlehem, PA
Heimbach, David T. ... Centreville, MD
Chestertown, MD
Heimbach, Gary W. ... Tucson, AZ
Heimbach, Gary W., P.C. ... Tucson, AZ
Heimbach, Kenneth G., Jr. ... St. Paul, MN
Heimbach, Leah J. ... Fairmont, WV
Heimbach, Spitko & Heckman
Allentown, PA
Heimbach, Thomas L. ... Allentown, PA
Heimbaugh, Rebecca DiDonato ... Akron, OH
Heimbecher, Reed R. ... Denver, CO
Heimberg, Eve ... New York, NY
Heimberg, Gary A. ... Washington, DC
Heimberg & Lumer ... Boca Raton, FL
Miami, FL
Heimberg, Paul E. ... Boca Raton, FL
Heimberg, Richard L. ... Elgin, IL
Heimberg, Scott M. ... Washington, DC
Heimberg, Sidney ... Mashpee, MA
Heimberg, Steven A. ... Los Angeles, CA
Heimberger, Ann Marie
San Francisco, CA
Heimbinder, Isaac ... Houston, TX
Heimbold, Charles A., Jr. ... New York, NY
Heimbold, Michael R. ... Los Angeles, CA
Heimbrook, William D. ... Richmond, TX
Heimbuch, James T. ... Detroit, MI
Heimbuch, John F. ... Union, NJ
Heimbuch & Solimano, P.C.
Hackensack, NJ
Heimbuch, William J. ... Hackensack, NJ
Heimbuck, Lorie A. ... Rochester, NY
Heimburger, Ray A. ... Long Beach, CA
Heimdahl, Peter D. ... West Palm Beach, FL
Heimer, Dorit Schutzengel ... Westport, CT
Heimer, Owen ... New York, NY
Heimer, Robert F. ... Davenport, IA
Heimer, Theodore E. ... Riverwoods, IL
Heimerg, Brian L. ... Elgin, IL
Heimerl, Herbert J., III ... Buffalo, NY
Heimerl, Herbert J., Jr. ... Buffalo, NY
Heimerl, Kathleen M. ... Jackson, WY
Heimerl, Keenan & Longo ... Buffalo, NY
Heimerl, Melissa O. ... Buffalo, NY
Heimert, Andrew J. ... Washington, DC
Heimert, Robert L. ... Baltimore, MD
Heimes, Joseph C. ... Great Falls, MT
Heimlich, Ellen Kramer ... Hollywood, FL
Heimlich, James C. ... Westfield, NJ
Heimlich, Judith D. ... Department of Labor, Office of the Solicitor, GV
Heimlich, Mark L. ... Denver, CO
Heimlich, Michael M. ... Columbus, OH
Heimos, David M. ... St. Louis, MO
Heimos, John G. ... St. Louis, MO
Heimovics, Joseph B. ... Atlanta, GA
Heimowitz, Philip A. ... New York, NY
Heims, Howard K. ... Stuart, FL
Heims, Louis F. ... Dyersville, IA
Heimsath, Virginia Fortuna ... Dallas, TX
Heimsoth, Mark E. ... Aurora, IL
Hein, Christopher D. ... Haverford, PA
Hein, Debra J. ... Newcastle, WY
Hein, Donald M. ... Hyattsville, MD
Hein, Edward H. ... Morristown, NJ
Hein, Heather M. ... Mountain View, CA
Hein, Janice J. ... Pleasanton, CA
Hein, Jennifer A. ... Bethesda, MD
Hein, John W. ... Milwaukee, WI
Hein, Jonathan A. ... Batavia, OH
Hein, Jonathan P. ... Greenville, OH
Hein, Joseph ... Altamont, NY
Hein, Kevin P. ... Denver, CO
Hein, Laura J. ... Minneapolis, MN
Hein, Michael W. ... Miami, FL
Hein, Peter C. ... New York, NY
Hein, Raymond A. ... Crownsville, MD
Hein, Richard B. ... St. Louis, MO
Hein, Robert P. ... Atlanta, GA
Hein, Ronald J., Jr. ... Chicago, IL
Hein, Ronald R. ... Topeka, KS
Hein, Sara L. ... Hamilton, OH
Hein, Smith, Berezin, Maloof & Jacobs, L.L.C. ... Hackensack, NJ
Hein, Steven E. ... Austin, TX
Hein and Weir, Chartered ... Topeka, KS
Hein, Werner J. ... Washington, DC
Hein, William J. ... Cincinnati, OH
Heinbach, Andrea D. ... Boston, MA
Heinbach, Charles C., Jr. ... Canton, OH
Heinbaugh, Gilbert F. ... Petal, MS
Heinberg, Christine O'Connor ... Raleigh, NC
Heinberg, Jack Lance ... New York, NY
Heinberg, Jennifer Faye ... Pleasantville, NY
Heinberg, Marshall A. ... New York, NY
Heindel, Edward M. ... Cleveland, OH
Heindl, Michael B.
Hot Springs National Park, AR
Heindl, Phares M. ... Altamonte Springs, FL
Heindl, Phares M., P.A.
Altamonte Springs, FL
Heindl, Walter E. ... Philadelphia, PA
Heindselman, Melissa Beeson
Oklahoma City, OK
Heine, Andrew N. ... New York, NY
Heine, Bruce V. ... Hilliard, OH
Heine, Charles G. ... Mineola, NY
Heine, D. William, Jr. ... Los Angeles, CA
Heine, Edward J., Jr. ... New York, NY
Heine, Edwina J. ... Encino, CA
Heine, Elaine L. ... San Diego, CA
Heine and Ferguson ... Cambridge, OH
Heine, Frank E. ... Spring Lake, NJ
Heine, H. Eugene ... Punta Gorda, FL
Heine, Holliday C. ... Boston, MA
Heine, James E. ... Belmar, NJ
Heine, James L. ... Minneapolis, MN
Heine, Linda J. ... New Ulm, MN
Heine, Margaret A. M. ... Fullerton, CA
Heine, Mary J. ... Walnut Creek, CA
Heine & Murray ... Spring Lake, NJ
Heine, Spencer H. ... Chicago, IL
Heine, Stephen C. ... Cambridge, OH
Heine, Stephen J. ... Peoria, IL
Heine, Timothy J. ... New York, NY
Heine, William J. ... Mansfield, OH
Heineck, David M. ... Seattle, WA
Heinecke, Peter S. ... Palo Alto, CA
Heinecke, Philip S. ... San Anselmo, CA
Heinecke, Richard M. ... Treasury Department, Internal Revenue Service, GV
Heinecke, Walter H. ... St. Louis, MO
Heinegg, Andrew C. ... Seattle, WA
Heineke, Burke, Healy & Bodach
Chicago, IL
Heineman, Andrew D. ... New York, NY
Heineman, Ben W. ... Chicago, IL
Heineman, Benjamin W., Jr. ... Fairfield, CT
Heineman, Geoffrey W. ... New York, NY
Heineman, Jeffrey P. ... Omaha, NE
Heineman, Justin B. ... Atlanta, GA
Heineman, Kenneth R. ... St. Louis, MO
Heineman, Melvin L. ... New York, NY
Heineman, Michael J. ... Framingham, MA
Heineman, Norman A. ... Bowling Green, OH
Heineman, Richard W. ... Wibaux, MT
Heineman, Robert M. ... Newton, NJ
Heineman, Roy W. ... Plano, TX
Heineman, Steven ... Elk Grove Village, IL
Heineman, Steven P. ... New York, NY
Heineman, William A. ... Little Rock, AR
Heinemann, David L. ... Kansas City, MO
Heinemann, Edward E. ... New York, NY
Heinemann, Eric ... North Andover, MA
Heinemann, Guy L. ... New York, NY
Heinemann, Guy L., P.C. ... New York, NY
Heinemann, Jas. J. ... Houston, TX
Heinemann, John W. ... Bellingham, WA
Heinemann, Peter M. ... San Francisco, CA
Heinemann, Richard A. ... Madison, WI
Heinemann, Robert C. ... Brooklyn, NY
Heinemann, Thomas B. ... Department of State, Office of the Legal Adviser, GV
Heinemann, William H. ... San Francisco, CA
Heinemeyer, L. Chris ... San Antonio, TX
Heinen & Associates ... Oklahoma City, OK
Tulsa, OK
Heinen, Gary J. ... Oklahoma City, OK
Heinen, John J. ... Milwaukee, WI
Heinen, Mark L. ... Detroit, MI
Heinen, Nancy R. ... Cupertino, CA
Heinen, Steven G. ... Tulsa, OK
Heinen, Timothy W., Sr.
Oklahoma City, OK
Tulsa, OK
Heiner, Blake T. ... Salt Lake City, UT
Heiner, David A., Jr. ... Redmond, WA
Heiner, Donald R. ... Ridgefield Park, NJ
Heiner, Elizabeth A. ... Madison, WI
Heiner, Randall R. ... Salt Lake City, UT
Heines, M. Henry ... San Francisco, CA
Heiney, Clifford L. ... Mesa, AZ
Heiney, George G., II ... Oxford, PA
Heiney, John H. ... Fort Wayne, IN
Heinhold, Christopher
Oklahoma City, OK
Heinhold, James C. ... Cleveland, OH
Heinhold, Matthew L. ... Las Vegas, NV
Heinhold, Tracey L. ... Las Vegas, NV
Heinichen, Jeffrey K. ... Cincinnati, OH
Heinicke, Brenda K. (Buege)
Colorado Springs, CO
Heinicke, Malcolm A. ... San Francisco, CA
Heinicke, Martha A. ... Council Bluffs, IA
Heinicke, Philip C. ... Delta, CO
Heininger, Erwin C. ... Greeneville, TN
Heininger, K. Daniel ... Solon, OH
Heininger, Kenneth L. ... St. Louis, MO
Heininger, Richard A. ... Council Bluffs, IA
Omaha, NE
Heinisch, Andrew J. ... Rockford, IL
Heinisch, Frank C. ... Geneva, NE
Heinisch Law Office ... Geneva, NE
Heinish, Ned O. ... Williamsburg, VA
Heinke, Lowell L. ... Cleveland, OH
Heinke, Rex S. ... Beverly Hills, CA
Heinkel, Jeffrey L. ... San Jose, CA
Heinkel, John C. ... Marysville, OH
Heinkel, R. Lawrence ... Orlando, FL
Heinkele, Peggy Anne ... New York, NY
Heinl, James ... Auburn, NY
Heinl, Kevin J. ... Southfield, MI
Heinle, Matthew A. ... Akron, OH
Heinle, Richard A. ... Orlando, FL
Heinlein & Balcerzak ... Columbus, OH
Heinlein, David J. ... Hartford, CT
Heinlein, David J. ... Columbus, OH
Heinlein, David W. ... Boston, MA
Heinlein, Edward A. ... Redwood City, CA
Heinlen, Ronald E. ... Cincinnati, OH
Heinley & Aljets ... Carrington, ND
Heinley, R. C. ... Carrington, ND
Heinly, Benson, Killian & Kramer
Tustin, CA
Heinly, Harold E. ... Santa Ana, CA
Heinmiller, Shawna S. ... Fresno, CA
Heino, Adina B. ... New York, NY
Heino, Joseph S. ... Brookfield, WI
Heinold, Dean A. ... Newton, MA
Heinold, Douglas L. ... Marlton, NJ
Heinold, Keith D. ... Philadelphia, PA
Heinonen, Kevin S. ... Scottsdale, AZ
Heinonen, Stacey L. ... Kalamazoo, MI
Heinrich, Albert J., Jr. ... Austin, TX
Heinrich, Albert J., Jr., P.C. ... Austin, TX
Heinrich, Amy B. ... Baltimore, MD
Heinrich, Benjamin ... Bronx, NY
Heinrich, Brett D. ... Chicago, IL
Heinrich, Brian P. ... Amarillo, TX
Heinrich, Caroline A. ... Clarksburg, WV
Heinrich, Christopher E. ... Houston, TX
Heinrich, Colleen Walsh ... Syracuse, NY
Heinrich, Donald J. ... Des Moines, IA
Heinrich, Eileen D. ... La Jolla, CA
Heinrich, Eugene L. ... Fort Lauderdale, FL
Heinrich, Fred K. ... Urbana, IL
Heinrich Gordon Hargrove Weihe & James, P.A. ... Fort Lauderdale, FL
Miami, FL
Orlando, FL
West Palm Beach, FL
Heinrich & Hill ... Scottsdale, AZ
Chicago, IL
Heinrich, J. Thomas ... Honolulu, HI
Heinrich, Jay N. ... New York, NY
Heinrich, Jeffrey B. ... San Diego, CA
Heinrich, John E. ... Baton Rouge, LA
Heinrich, John E. ... Smithtown, NY
Heinrich, John H. ... Detroit, MI
Heinrich, Kerry L. ... Redlands, CA
Heinrich, Nancy Siegel ... Scottsdale, AZ
Heinrich, Patrick C. ... Charlotte, NC
Heinrich, Randall W. ... Houston, TX
Heinrich, Robert M. ... Scottsdale, AZ
Heinrich, Steven A. ... Corvallis, OR
Heinrich, Suzanne A. ... San Jose, CA
Heinrich, Thomas A. ... Seattle, WA
Heinrich, Thomas W. ... Sheboygan, WI
Heinrich, Timothy J. ... Houston, TX
Heinrich, Walter J. ... Sheboygan, WI
Heinrich, Walter R. ... Tampa, FL
Heinrichs, A. Chris ... San Antonio, TX
Heinrichs, De Gennaro & Associates
San Antonio, TX
Heinrichs, Donna B. ... Delmar, NY
Heinrichs, Jane Ganz
Securities and Exchange Commission, Office of Compliance Inspections and Examinations, GV
Heinrichs, Julia Garrett ... San Antonio, TX
Heinrichs, Steven S. ... Jeffersonville, IN
Heinritzi, Walter G. ... Lansing, MI
Heins, Edwin S., Jr. ... Bryn Mawr, PA
Heins, George V. ... Indianapolis, IN
Heins, Henry L., III ... Los Angeles, CA
Heins, Janet L. ... Mequon, WI
Heins, Karen J.
Department of Labor, GV
Heins Law Office, LLC ... Mequon, WI
Heins, M. Christine ... Murphysboro, IL
Heins, Marjorie ... Boston, MA
Heins, Marjorie E. ... New York, NY
Heins Mills & Olson, P.L.C.
Minneapolis, MN
Heins, Richard D. ... Wilmington, DE
Heins, Richard M. ... Middleton, WI
Heins, Samuel D. ... Minneapolis, MN
Heins, Sharon Szewc ... Midland, MI
Heinsma, David J. ... Atlanta, GA
Heinsohn, Loretta A. ... East Providence, RI
Heinsohn, Walter L. ... Rock Hill, SC
Heinson, Gordon P. ... Minneapolis, MN
Heinson, Timothy J. ... Albany, OR
Heinstadt, John P. ... Duxbury, MA
Heinsz, Timothy J. ... Columbia, MO
Heintel, Carl C. ... Cleveland, OH
Heintel, Robert C. ... Cleveland, OH
Heintschel, Thomas W. ... Toledo, OH
Heintz, Frank J. ... Atlanta, GA
Heintz, George W. ... Chicago, IL
Merrillville, IN
Heintz, Helen C. ... New York, NY
Heintz, J. Eric ... Ames, IA
Heintz, James M. ... Washington, DC
Heintz, Janet R. ... Oak Brook, IL
Heintz, Jeffrey A. ... Los Angeles, CA

Heintz, Jeffrey D. ... Youngstown, OH
Heintz, Jeffrey T. ... Akron, OH
Heintz, John E. ... Washington, DC
Heintz, Joshua H. ... Albany, NY
Syracuse, NY
Harrisburg, PA
Heintz, Julie A. ... Troy, MI
Heintz, Lisa B. ... Denver, CO
Heintz, Madelynn ... New York, NY
Heintz, Michael S. ... Sacramento, CA
Heintz, Patrick E. ... Traverse City, MI
Heintz, Paul Bryan ... Clinton, NY
Heintz, Paul C. ... Philadelphia, PA
Heintz, Peter ... Carmichael, CA
Heintz, Rebecca C. ... Portland, OR
Heintz, Robert A ... Gold River, CA
Heintz, Sarah E. ... Woodsville, NH
Heintz, Steven E. ... Bradenton, FL
Heintz, Steven E., P.A. ... Bradenton, FL
Heintz, Vincent G. ... Bronx, NY
Heintzelman, Jonathan R. ... Evanston, IL
Heintzelman, Peter M. ... Worcester, MA
Heintzelman, Scott W. ... Boone, NC
Heintzelman, Yvette ... Chicago, IL
Heintzman, Michael D. ... Pittsburgh, PA
Heintzman, Warren, Wise & Fornella, P.C.
Pittsburgh, PA
Heiny, Charles J. ... Fort Wayne, IN
Heiny, Claude R., II ... Department of Defense, Defense Legal Services Agency, GV
Heiny, James R. ... Manly, IA
Mason City, IA
Heiny, Jon C. ... Des Moines, IA
Heiny, Vincent J. ... Fort Wayne, IN
Heinz, Ann B. ... Chicago, IL
Heinz, Elise B. ... Arlington, VA
Heinz, Eric A. ... Philadelphia, PA
Heinz, Gerald J. ... Kenosha, WI
Heinz, Jean M. ... San Diego, CA
Heinz, Jessica F. ... Los Angeles, CA
Heinz, Joan M. ... Indianapolis, IN
Heinz, John H.
Environmental Protection Agency, Office of the General Counsel, GV
Heinz, John P. ... Chicago, IL
Heinz, Kenneth J. ... St. Louis, MO
Heinz, Kurt J. ... Chicago, IL
Heinz, Laurie D. ... Issaquah, WA
Heinz, Leonard R. ... Pittsburgh, PA
Heinz, Peter D. ... Wilmington, DE
Heinz, Rhonda Richards ... Decatur, IL
Heinz, Richard P. ... Polson, MT
Heinz, Robert G. ... Plymouth, WI
Heinz, Thomas C.
Department of Housing and Urban Development, Office of Administrative Law Judges, GV
Heinz, V. Michael ... Westminster, CO
Heinz, Von S. ... Las Vegas, NV
Heinz, William D. ... Chicago, IL
Heinze, Bernd G. ... Philadelphia, PA
Heinze, Christie Baty ... Washington, DC
Heinze, Jeffrey R. ... Grand Rapids, MI
Heinze, Mark F. ... Hackensack, NJ
Heinze, Robert W. ... Palatine, IL
Heinze, Roland H. ... Oconomowoc, WI
Heinze, Stephen Lawrence ... Chicago, IL
Heinze, William F. ... Alexandria, VA
Heinzel, James T. ... Portland, OR
Heinzelman, Kris F. ... New York, NY
Heinzen, Bernard G. ... Philadelphia, PA
Heinzen, Bernard G., Ltd. ... Philadelphia, PA
Heinzen, Steven A. ... Madison, WI
Heinzen, William M. ... New York, NY
Heinzer, Charles J. ... Norwalk, CT
Heinzer, James W. ... San Francisco, CA
Heinzerling, Barbara M. ... Akron, OH
Heinzerling, Joyce E. ... New York, NY
Heinzerling, Karl K. ... Minneapolis, MN
Heinzl, Joe Lawrence ... Tempe, AZ
Heinzman, Richard Ruel ... Montgomery, AL
Heinzmann, Jeffrey M. ... Indianapolis, IN
Heinzmann, Joseph Charles, Jr.
White Plains, NY
Heiple, Harold L. ... Norman, OK
Heiple, James D. ... Peoria, IL
Heiple, Jeremy H. ... Peoria, IL
Heiple, Jonathan J. ... Peoria, IL
Heiple Law Offices ... Peoria, IL
Heiple Law Offices, Inc. ... Norman, OK
Heiple, Rae C., II ... Peoria, IL
Heiple, Russell J. ... Johnstown, PA
Heir, Baldev ... Sacramento, CA
Heir, Cynthia L. ... Pensacola, FL
Heir, Dennis K. ... Allentown, PA
Heir, Douglas R. ... Cherry Hill, NJ
Heires, David ... New York, NY
Heiring, Paul W. ... Minneapolis, MN
Heironimus, Paul D. ... Morgantown, WV
Heirshberg, Gayle C. ... Encino, CA
Heirtzler, Paul L. ... Concord, NH
Heis, Forest S. ... Cincinnati, OH
Heis & Wenstrup Co., LPA
Cincinnati, OH
Heisa, Mark H. ... Ravenna, OH
Heisdorffer, Steven L. ... Denver, CO
Heise, Beth R. ... Fort Myers, FL
Heise, Brian L. ... Barrington, IL
Heise, Carol R. ... Evanston, IL
Heise, Catherine West ... Troy, MI
Heise, Douglas R. ... Belleville, IL
Heise, Erika M. ... New York, NY
Heise, Frederick C." Fritz "
Sacramento, CA
Heise, John I., Jr. ... Gaithersburg, MD
Heise Jorgensen & Stefanelli, P.A.
Gaithersburg, MD
Heise, Knut C. ... St. Louis, MO

Heise, Leigh Jameson ... Adrian, MI
Heise, Mark J. ... Miami, FL
Heise Markarian P.A. ... Miami, FL
Heise, Michael R. ... Indianapolis, IN
Heise, Robert H. ... Fort Myers, FL
Heise, Robt. S. ... Annapolis, MD
Heise, Roy A. ... Brockport, NY
Heise, W. Steven ... Ontario, CA
Heisel, Dendy M. ... Glenwood Springs, CO
Heisel, Eric A. ... Hagåtña, GU
Heisel, Manville M. ... Central Point, OR
Heisenberg, Christoph C. ... New York, NY
Heiser, Daniel ... Bloomington, IN
Heiser, David E. ... Wilmington, DE
Heiser, David M. ... New York, NY
Heiser, Donald E. ... Cleveland, OH
Heiser, E. John ... Wilmington, DE
Heiser, Edward J., Jr. ... Milwaukee, WI
Heiser, Edward N. ... Akron, OH
Heiser, Gary L. ... Tallahassee, FL
Heiser, Gregory Mark ... Norman, OK
Heiser, Henry O., III ... Gettysburg, PA
Heiser, James S. ... Long Beach, CA
Heiser, Janet Lessin ... Rye Brook, NY
Heiser, Jeffrey D. ... Stockton, CA
Heiser, Joel S. ... Cleveland, OH
Heiser, K. Gabriel ... Nashville, TN
Heiser, Kevin J. ... Columbia, SC
Heiser, Larry W. ... Macomb, IL
Heiser, Laura ... Department of Justice, Antitrust Division, GV
Heiser, Lawrence A. ... Wellston, OH
Heiser, Michael P. ... Ketchikan, AK
Heiser, Richard D. ... Cincinnati, OH
Heiser, Richard W. ... Penacook, NH
Heiser, Scott A. ... Corvallis, OR
Heiser, Stacey M. ... Miamisburg, OH
Heiser, T. Walter ... Ridgewood, NJ
Heiser, Theodore Woods ... Baltimore, MD
Rockville, MD
Morristown, NJ
Heiserman, J. E. ... Cedar Rapids, IA
Heiserman, Robert G. ... Aspen, CO
Denver, CO
Heiserman, Robert G., P.C. ... Aspen, CO
Denver, CO
Heisey, Dawn M. ... Fort Lauderdale, FL
Heisey, Glenn P. ... Harrisburg, PA
Heisey, James R. ... San Francisco, CA
Heisey, John K. ... Pittsburgh, PA
Heisey, Michael C. ... Fort Pierce, FL
Heisey, Philip T. ... Albuquerque, NM
Heisick, Debra J. ... Minneapolis, MN
Heising, Ellen E. ... Boston, MA
Heising, Riccarda ... Atlanta, GA
Heisinger, Buck, Morris & Rose
Carmel, CA
Monterey, CA
Heisinger, James G., Jr. ... Carmel, CA
Heisinger, Jennifer ... Denver, CO
Chicago, IL
Heiskala, Win ... La Mesa, CA
Heiskell, Christopher Neil ... Raleigh, NC
Heiskell, Edgar F., III ... Charleston, WV
Heiskell, Michael P. ... Fort Worth, TX
Heisler & Associates ... Roseville, CA
Sacramento, CA
Heisler, Barry N., II
West Palm Beach, FL
Heisler, Bradley P. ... Roseville, CA
Heisler, Bray & Beeson
Woodland Hills, CA
Heisler, Brian J. ... Houston, TX
Heisler, C. David, (P.A.) ... Essex, MD
Towson, MD
Heisler, David E. ... Scranton, PA
Heisler, David H. ... San Bernardino, CA
Heisler, David M. ... Chicago, IL
Heisler, Donald E. ... The Dalles, OR
Heisler, Edwin A. ... Portland, ME
Heisler, Frederick P. ... New Orleans, LA
Heisler, Glenn August
Panama Canal Commission, Office of the General Counsel, GV
Heisler, Irving ... New York, NY
Heisler, Jennifer L. ... Cambridge, MA
Heisler, Jeremy ... New York, NY
Heisler, John A. ... Sioux Falls, SD
Heisler, John C. ... Towson, MD
Heisler, John E., Jr. ... Liverpool, NY
Heisler, John J., Jr. ... Corpus Christi, TX
Heisler, Lance R. ... Detroit Lakes, MN
Heisler, Lara J. ... Bronx, NY
Heisler, Lawrence ... Brooklyn, NY
Heisler, Marc H. ... Evanston, IL
Heisler, Quentin G., Jr. ... Chicago, IL
Heisler, Robert E. ... Clayton, MO
Heisler, Stanley D. ... New York, NY
Heisler, Steven H. ... Baltimore, MD
Heisler, Stewart & Daniels, Inc.
Monterey, CA
Heisler, Trey H. ... Woodland Hills, CA
Heisler, William J. ... Toms River, NJ
Heisler, Williams & Lazzaro, L.L.C.
Essex, MD
Towson, MD
Heisler & Wysocki ... New Orleans, LA
Heisley, E. Stephen ... Fairfax, VA
Heisman, James D. ... Wilmington, DE
Heisman, Lewis J. ... Rochester, NY
Heisner, John R. ... San Diego, CA
Heiss, Carla L. ... New York, NY
Heiss, David E. ... Chicago, IL
Heiss, David K. ... Bloomfield Hills, MI
Heiss, Frederick P. ... Chicago, IL
Heiss, Howard E. ... New York, NY
Heiss, Marjorie A. ... Washington, DC

Heiss, Robert G.
Environmental Protection Agency, Office of Enforcement and Compliance Assurance, GV
Heiss, Robin ... Chicago, IL
Heiss, Sharon K.
Office of Personnel Management, GV
Heiss, Susan E. ... Casper, WY
Heiss, William N. ... Casper, WY
Heisse, John R., II ... San Francisco, CA
Heissenbuttel, Frederick C. ... Wayne, NJ
Heisserer, John P. ... Cape Girardeau, MO
Heist, Dale M. ... Philadelphia, PA
Heist, Harry Anthony ... Fort Myers Beach, FL
Heist, Kathleen J. ... Bryn Mawr, PA
Heist, Robert B. ... Reading, PA
Heist, Robert C. ... Chicago, IL
Heistand, Paul K. ... St. Petersburg, FL
Heistein, Martin J. ... New York, NY
Heister, Jan L. ... Tulsa, OK
Heister, Marcia E. ... Wilmington, DE
Heister, Peter B. ... Little Rock, AR
Heister, Robert J., Jr. ... Pittsburgh, PA
Heisterkamp, David V., II ... Denver, CO
Heisterkamp, Jon E. ... Council Bluffs, IA
Heisterkamp, Kenneth L. ... Rapid City, SD
Heisz, Jimmy L. ... Dallas, TX
Heisz, Kenneth L. ... Los Angeles, CA
Heisz, Laura A. ... Dallas, TX
Heit, Albert ... New York, NY
Heit, Judy A. ... Bothell, WA
Heit, Martin M. ... Rochester, NY
Heit, Max ... Sarasota, FL
Heit, Warren S. ... Palo Alto, CA
Heitczman, George A. ... Bethlehem, PA
Heiter, Judy Anthony ... Memphis, TN
Heiter, Matthew S. ... Memphis, TN
Heiter, Warren M. ... Beverly Hills, MI
Heiter, Warren M., P.C. ... Beverly Hills, MI
Heitert, Gilbert R. ... Springfield, MA
Heitger, Renée E. ... Buffalo, NY
Heith, Cory D. ... Boca Raton, FL
Heithecker, Philip H. ... Chico, CA
Heithoff, Curtis J. ... Council Bluffs, IA
Heithoff, John P. ... Council Bluffs, IA
Heithoff, Robert C. ... Council Bluffs, IA
Heiting & Irwin ... Los Angeles, CA
Riverside, CA
San Bernardino, CA
Heiting, James O. ... Riverside, CA
Heitkamp, Colleen K.
Federal Communications Commission, Common Carrier Bureau, GV
Heitkamp, John R., Jr. ... Mequon, WI
Heitke, Aaron M. ... Paynesville, MN
Heitkemper, Allard J. ... Portland, OR
Heitland, Ann Rae ... Flagstaff, AZ
Heitland, Jon E. ... Des Moines, IA
Heitland, Scott A. ... St. Louis, MO
Heitler, Bruce F. ... Denver, CO
Heitler, George ... Southbury, CT
Heitler, Perrie N. ... St. Paul, MN
Heitler, Sherry K. ... New York, NY
Heitman, Dianne M. ... Marquette, MI
Heitman, Donald H.
Commodity Futures Trading Commission, Executive Staff, GV
Heitman, Edward H. ... Lincoln, NE
Heitman, Eugene S. ... St. Louis, MO
Heitman, George C. ... Pleasant Hill, CA
Heitman, Jane Hilary ... West Simsbury, CT
Heitman, Karena L. ... Youngstown, OH
Heitman, Marvin L. ... Marquette, MI
Heitman, Nancy M. ... New Iberia, LA
Heitman, Richard J. ... La Crosse, WI
Sparta, WI
Heitmanek, Carl A. ... Fredericksburg, VA
Heitmanis, George J.A. ... Troy, MI
Heitmann, Edmund K. ... Gulfport, FL
Heitmann, John J. ... Washington, DC
Heitmann, Richard J. ... Jackson, MS
Heitner, Brian Ross ... Woodbury, NY
Heitner, Dean J. M. ... New York, NY
Heitner, Howard M. ... Los Angeles, CA
Heitner, Jody M. ... Los Angeles, CA
Heitner, Kenneth H. ... New York, NY
Heitner, Michael, (P.C.) ... New York, NY
Heitritter, Wilfred H. ... San Bernardino, CA
Heitsch, Bonnie E. ... Salem, OR
Heitsch, Lawrence D. ... Birmingham, MI
Heitsch, Lawrence D., P.C. ... Birmingham, MI
Heitz, Bruce A. ... Dallas, TX
Heitz, David T. ... San Rafael, CA
Heitz, Dennis H. ... Cincinnati, OH
Heitz, John P. ... O'Neill, NE
Heitz, Julia E. ... Jasper, IN
Heitz, Kenneth R. ... Los Angeles, CA
Heitz Law Office ... O'Neill, NE
Heitz, Mark V. ... Topeka, KS
Heitz, Michael G. ... New York, NY
Heitz, Misty L. Carr ... Clarksburg, WV
Heitz, Philip G. ... Chicago, IL
Heitz, Russell J. ... Naperville, IL
Heitz, Stephen T. ... Harrisonburg, VA
Heitz, Steven F. ... St. Louis, MO
Heitzenrater, Stacey R. ... Pittsburgh, PA
Heitzenroder, Melanie ... Minneapolis, MN
Heitzinger, Kent A. ... Winnetka, IL
Heitzler, Eileen B. ... New York, NY
Heitzman, Robert J.
General Accounting Office, Office of the General Counsel, GV
Heitzman, Thomas J. ... Trenton, NJ
Heitzman, Walter ... Des Moines, IA
Heizer, Dean C. ... Denver, CO
Heizer, Francenia B. ... Columbia, SC
Myrtle Beach, SC
Heizer, Harry T., Jr. ... Columbia, SC

Heizer, K. Janée ... Dallas, TX
Heizler, Gregory S. ... Toms River, NJ
Hejazi, Sharon ...
Department of Defense, GV
Hejinian, Paull ... New York, NY
Hejl, Ted W. ... Taylor, TX
Hejlek, Edward J. ... St. Louis, MO
Hejmanowski, Lee E. ... San Diego, CA
Hejmanowski, Paul ... Las Vegas, NV
Hejtmanek, Danton C. ... Topeka, KS
Hekimian, Frank V. ... Salem, NH
Hekker, John M. ... New City, NY
Hekking, John Louis ... Norristown, PA
Hekman, Mary A. ... Washington, DC
Hekman, Ralph K. ... Riverside, CA
Hektner, Candice E. ... Minneapolis, MN
Hektner, Mark ... Palm Beach Gardens, FL
Heland, Kenneth V. ... Washington, DC
Helander, John E., Jr. ... Northbrook, IL
Helander, Robert C. ... New York, NY
Helander, Willard R., (Mrs.) ... Libertyville, IL
Helart, Gayle L. ... Hanford, CA
Helberg, Daniel D. ... Los Angeles, CA
Helberg, Ellen J. ... Denver, CO
Helberg, Jerry M. ... Morland, KS
Helbert, Daniel L. ... San Luis Obispo, CA
Helbert, David P. ... Oklahoma City, OK
Helbert, Jan E. ... Indianapolis, IN
Helbert, Michael C., Law Offices of
Emporia, KS
Helbig, Sandra D. ... West Orange, NJ
Helbig, Thomas B. ... Scranton, PA
Helbing, Michael Scott ... Houston, TX
Helbling, James J. ... Tacoma, WA
Helbling, Jill Washburn ... Charleston, WV
Helbling, Lauren A. ... Cleveland, OH
Helbling, Marcia S. ... New York, NY
Helbock, Robert J., Jr. ... Staten Island, NY
Helbraun, David M. ... San Francisco, CA
Helbraun, Fred ... Chicago, IL
Helbush, Terry J. ... San Francisco, CA
Held, Alyssa J. ... Brooklyn, NY
Held, Amy M. ... New York, NY
Held, Ariana V. ... Dallas, TX
Held, Barbara Ann ... Bradenton, FL
Held, C. Daniel ... Towson, MD
Held, Claude C., II ... Watertown, WI
Held, David ... Los Angeles, CA
Held, Donald J. ... Buffalo, NY
Held, Edward, (P.C.) ... Brooklyn, NY
Held, Eric J. ... Washington, PA
Held, Gary K. ... Castro Valley, CA
Held, Gary M. ... Miami Beach, FL
Held, Gerald N. ... Stamford, CT
Held, Gerald S. ... Brooklyn, NY
Held, Griffin and Associates, P.A.
Little Rock, AR
Held, Guy W. ... Benton, MS
Held, Halley ... Fort Lauderdale, FL
Held, Harvey ... Milwaukee, WI
Held, Howard Y. ... Minneapolis, MN
Held, Huyler C. ... New York, NY
Held, Irving I., Jr. ... Richmond, VA
Held, Jack E. ... Birmingham, AL
Held, James G. ... Atlanta, GA
Held, Jeffrey B. ... Oxnard, CA
Held, Jeffrey M. ... Boston, MA
Held, Jeffrey S. ... New York, NY
Held, Jerry E. ... Birmingham, AL
Held, Joel ... Dallas, TX
Held, John J. ... Chicago, IL
Held, John R. ... Albany, NY
Held, Judith E. ... New York, NY
Held, Kenneth ... La Verne, CA
Held, Kenneth P. ... New York, NY
Held, Lewis I. ... Richmond, VA
Held, Linda ... Oyster Bay, NY
Held, Lindsay M. ... New York, NY
Held, Margaret Meeks ... Little Rock, AR
Held, Mark ... Austin, TX
Held, Michael A. ... New York, NY
Held, Michael S. ... Dallas, TX
Held, Paul D. ... Claremont, CA
Held, Philip D. ... Brooklyn, NY
Held, Ramon D. ... New York, NY
Held, Randee S. ... Minneapolis, MN
Held, Rhonda M. ... Rockville Centre, NY
Held, Richard N. ... Philadelphia, PA
Held, Robert S. ... Chicago, IL
Held, Ronald J. ... Winchester, MA
Held, Ronald S. ... Anniston, AL
Held, Samuel J. ... Minneapolis, MN
Held, Stephen G. ... Camp Hill, PA
Held, Susan Groves ... Chicago, IL
Held, Troy ... Yreka, CA
Held, Valerie ... St. Louis, MO
Helde, Richard A. ... Minneapolis, MN
Heldenbrand, J. Mark, Law Office of
Phoenix, AZ
Heldenbrand, Paul J. ... Arlington, VA
Heldenfels, Hugo C., Jr. ... Corpus Christi, TX
Helder, Donald L. ... Big Rapids, MI
Helder, Jake C. ... Monroe, NC
Helder, Jan P., Jr. ... Kansas City, MO
Helder, Jeffrey K. ... Holland, MI
Helder, Vernon D. ... Grand Rapids, MI
Helderman, Joshua D. ... Los Angeles, CA
Heldfond, Robert D. ... San Francisco, CA
Helding, Carol E. ... Hanford, CA
Helding, Neil A. ... Hanford, CA
Held Jr., Edwin W. ... Jacksonville, FL
Heldman, Alan W. ... Birmingham, AL
Heldman, James G. ... Cincinnati, OH
Heldman, Paul W. ... Cincinnati, OH
Heldman, Samuel H. ... Washington, DC
Heldmyer, Michelle McCain
Jacksonville, FL
Heldreth, Sylvia E. ... Cape Coral, FL

Heldrich, Gerard C., Jr. ... Chicago, IL
Heldrich, Gutman & Associates ... Chicago, IL
Heldt, Bruce A. ... Chicago, IL
Heldt, Carl A. ... Evansville, IN
Heldt, Gisèle L. ... New York, NY
Heldt, Jeffrey A. ... Bingham Farms, MI
Heldt, Nicholas W. ... San Francisco, CA
Heldt, Randall J. ... Houston, TX
Heldt, Sharon D. ... Houston, TX
Heldt, Steven H. ... Lexington, NE
Heleen, Mark L. ... Reston, VA
Heleen, Wendy Denton ... Pittsburgh, PA
Helein & Associates, P.C.
Washington, DC
McLean, VA
Helein, Charles H. ... McLean, VA
Heleman, Beth ... Washington, DC
Helenbolt, Johnny N. ... Tucson, AZ
Helene, Kathryn ... Vero Beach, FL
Helenhouse, James D. ... Chicago, IL
Heleniak, David W. ... New York, NY
Heleniak, Richard J. ... Plymouth Meeting, PA
Helenius, Christopher A.
San Luis Obispo, CA
Helewa, Juliane M. ... Middlesex, NJ
Helewa, Kevin ... Short Hills, NJ
Heley, John M. ... Quakertown, PA
Heley, Mark J. ... Minneapolis, MN
Helf, Mary C. ... Sellersville, PA
Helf, Sheila ... Department of Justice, Executive Office for Immigration Review, GV
Helf, Thomas E. ... Bethesda, MD
Helfand, Alan J. ... New York, NY
Helfand, Andrew B. ... New York, NY
Helfand, Barry H. ... Rockville, MD
Helfand, Barry, P.A. ... Rockville, MD
Helfand, David A. ... Miami, FL
Helfand & Helfand ... Newark, NJ
New York, NY
Helfand, Jerry M. ... St. Paul, MN
Helfand, Leonard T. ... Miami, FL
Helfand, Marcy C. ... Dallas, TX
Helfand, Mark J. ... Chicago, IL
Helfand, Marvin S. ... Chicago, IL
Helfand, Michael J. ... Chicago, IL
Helfand, Michael T. ... Culver City, CA
Helfand, Richard ... Kansas City, MO
Helfand, Robert ... New York, NY
Helfand, Robert D. ... New York, NY
Helfand, Robert F. ... San Diego, CA
Helfand, Tanya N. ... Dover, NJ
Helfand, Thomas R. ... Dallas, TX
Helfand, William L. ... Annapolis, MD
Helfand, William S. ... Houston, TX
Helfant, Adam S. ... Beaverton, OR
Helfant, David ... New York, NY
Helfant, David A. ... Los Angeles, CA
Helfant, Martin B. ... Petersburg, VA
Helfat, Bernard A. ... New York, NY
Helfat, Jonathan N. ... New York, NY
Helfen, Spencer J. ... Beverly Hills, CA
Helfenbein, Gerald J. ... Worcester, MA
Helfenstein, Allegra ... Eugene, OR
Helfenstein, Hugh J. ... New York, NY
Helfer, Erica Tina ... Chicago, IL
Helfer, Glenn Joe ... Englewood, CO
Helfer, Jeffrey S. ... Woodland Hills, CA
Helfer, L. Bradley ... Dover, NH
Helfer, Michael S. ... Washington, DC
Helfer, Norman C. ... Lansing, MI
Helfer, Paul F. ... New York, NY
Helferich, William H., III ... Buffalo, NY
Rochester, NY
Helfers, George E. ... St. Louis, MO
Helfers, Mark A. ... St. Louis, MO
Helfferich, Krista E. ... Beverly Hills, CA
Helfgot, Alvin J. ... Chicago, IL
Helfgot, Ira N., Law Offices of
Chicago, IL
Helfgott, Eliezer ... New York, NY
Helfgott, Gale R. ... New York, NY
Helfgott & Karas, P.C. ... New York, NY
Helfgott, Samson ... New York, NY
Helfing, Laurie ... Los Angeles, CA
Helfing, Robert F. ... Los Angeles, CA
Helfman, Arthur L. ... Hartsdale, NY
Helfman, Benjamin K. ... San Bernardino, CA
Helfman, Cindy S. ... Montclair, NJ
Helfman, Dennis J. ... Woodcliff Lake, NJ
Helfman, Gary S. ... West Palm Beach, FL
Helfman, James A. ... Baltimore, MD
Helfman, Jill Friedman ... Cleveland, OH
Helfman, Jill Friedman, Co., L.P.A.
Cleveland, OH
Helfman, Larry ... Torrance, CA
Helfman & Mehr, P.A.
West Palm Beach, FL
Helfman, Neil A. ... El Cerrito, CA
Helfman, Randy M. ... New York, NY
Helfman, Richard D. ... White Plains, NY
Helfman, Stanley M. ... San Francisco, CA
Helfman, Stephen J. ... Miami, FL
Helfman, Steven M. ... Miami, FL
Helfrey, David B. B. ... St. Louis, MO
Helfrey, Simon & Jones, P.C.
St. Louis, MO
Helfrich, Carl R. ... St. Louis, MO
Helfrich, Cornelius David ... Bel Air, MD
Helfrich, Cornelius David, P.A. ... Bel Air, MD
Helfrich, Elizabeth A. ... Salinas, CA
Helfrich, George F. ... Washington, DC
Helfrich, George P. ... Florham Park, NJ
Helfrich, George P., Jr. ... Livingston, NJ
Helfrich, Gerald J. ... Florham Park, NJ
Helfrich, Gregory P. ... Morristown, NJ
Helfrich, James C. ... Indianapolis, IN
Helfrich, James S. ... Denver, CO
Helfrich, Jan L. ... Ventura, CA
Helfrich, Jeanette ... Department of Energy, Office of the General Counsel, GV
Helfrich, Jeffrey K. ... Evansville, IN
Helfrich, John W. ... East Setauket, NY
Helfrich, Lee Ellen ... Washington, DC
Helfrich, Leonard J. ... Fort Wayne, IN
Helfrich, Loretta Marie ... Cincinnati, OH
Helfrich, Paul D. ... Whippany, NJ
Helfrich, Robert B. ... Hattiesburg, MS
Helfrich, Robert E. ... Chicago, IL
Helfrich, Thomas A. ... New York, NY
Helfrich, Timothy J. ... Ontario, OR
Helfrick, Joseph R. ... Sea Cliff, NY
Helfrick, Susan A. ... New York, NY
Helfrick, William F. ... Los Angeles, CA
Helfstein, Lewis B. ... Irvine, CA
Helge, Ralph K., & Associates
Pasadena, CA
Helgemo, Stephen L. ... Fort Myers, FL
Helgen & Helgen, P.A. ... Minneapolis, MN
Helgen, Henry M., III ... Minneapolis, MN
Helgen, Howard P. ... Minneapolis, MN
Helgen, John D. ... Minneapolis, MN
Helgesen, Andrew
Palm Beach Gardens, FL
Helgesen, Jack C. ... Ogden, UT
Helgesen, Michael P. ... St. Paul, MN
Helgesen, Paul W. ... Nyack, NY
Helgesen, Robert L. ... Santa Maria, CA
Helgesen, Stephanie M. ... Minneapolis, MN
Helgesen, Waterfall and Jones, P.C.
Ogden, UT
Helgeson, Kristi L. ... Seattle, WA
Helgeson, Richard M. ... Los Angeles, CA
Helgeson, Steven P. ... Olympia, WA
Helgeson, Thomas C. ... Wheat Ridge, CO
Helgeson, Thomas C., P.C.
Wheat Ridge, CO
Helget, Gerald E. ... Minneapolis, MN
Helget, Kasha
Federal Energy Regulatory Commission, Office of the General Counsel, GV
Helgoe, Jennifer ... Huntington, WV
Helgoe, Lisa R. ... Houston, TX
Helgren, Heidi Rae ... Midland, MI
Helgren, Michael D. ... Seattle, WA
Helgren, Penny F. ... Minneapolis, MN
Helguera, Roberto Tomas ... New York, NY
Helhoski, Maria R. ... New York, NY
Helhoski, Ronald E. ... Middletown, NY
Helhoski, Ronald E., P.C.
Middletown, NY
Helies, Bruce E. ... Red Bank, NJ
Heligman, Mark ... St. Louis, MO
Helikson, Lloyd W. ... Eugene, OR
Helikson, Wayne G. ... Eugene, OR
Helin, Rauni V. ... Fitchburg, MA
Heline, Gregory R. ... Spokane, WA
Helinger, James A., Jr. ... Clearwater, FL
Helinger, John Jay (Jack) ... St. Petersburg, FL
Helis, Stephen C. ... Chicago, IL
Helis, Steven ... Chicago, IL
Helisek, Kenneth P. ... Johnson City, NY
Helitzer, Jack B. ... Roslyn, NY
Helke, Joel E. ... Treasury Department, Internal Revenue Service, GV
Helkowski, Lawrence Scott ... Wauseon, OH
Helland, Diane M. ... Minneapolis, MN
Helland, Hans O. ... Wisconsin Dells, WI
Helland Law Offices ... Wisconsin Dells, WI
Helland, Lynn ... Detroit, MI
Helland, Mark D. ... Eau Claire, WI
Helland, Robert ... Tacoma, WA
Helland, Robert L. ... Minneapolis, MN
Helland, Steven C. ... Madison, WI
Helland, Steven C., S.C. ... Madison, WI
Helland, Steven E. ... Minneapolis, MN
Hellander, Martha E. ... Wilmette, IL
Hellauer, Diane M. ... Camden, NJ
Hellauer, Gretchen A. ... Shelton, CT
Hellauer, Marianne Schmitt
Baltimore, MD
Hellauer, Robert Eugene, Jr. ... Baltimore, MD
Hellbeck, Eckhard R. ... Washington, DC
Hellberg, Brian S. ... Minneapolis, MN
Hellberg, Jeffrey W. ... Amarillo, TX
Hellberg, Jeffrey W., Jr. ... Dallas, TX
Hellbusch, Ronald Lyle ... Denver, CO
Helldorfer, Bernard G. ... Flushing, NY
Helle, Alice Eastman ... Des Moines, IA
Helle, Steven J. ... Urbana, IL
Helle, Susan Hanes ... Fisher, IL
Helle, Todd L. ... Muskegon, MI
Hellebush, John F. ... Cincinnati, OH
Hellegers, John F. ... Jenkintown, PA
Hellegers, Paul M. ... New York, NY
Hellekson, Edward D. ... St. Paul, MN
Hellekson, Owen H., Jr. ... Honolulu, HI
Hellems, Earl Kent ... Hinton, WV
Hellen, Howard Bennett
Rancho Bernardo, CA
San Diego, CA
Hellén, Olof K. ... Anchorage, AK
Hellen, Tim Wade ... Memphis, TN
Hellenbrand, Samuel H. ... New York, NY
Hellendale, Robert ... Riverside, CT
Hellenkamp, Amy S. ... San Diego, CA
Hellenkamp, Mark ... San Diego, CA
Hellenkamp, Terry J. ... San Diego, CA
Hellenthal, David ... Spokane, WA
Hellenthal, David, P.C. ... Spokane, WA
Heller, Abr. ... Webster, MA
Heller, Adam T. ... Washington, DC
Heller, Alan A. ... New York, NY
Heller, Albert C. ... Milwaukee, WI
Heller, Alison Hallie ... Denver, CO
Heller, Allan H. ... New York, NY
Heller, Alvin H. ... Flushing, NY
Heller, Amanda L. ... Old Bridge, NJ
Heller, Amy Cohen ... Hoffman Estates, IL
Heller, Andra K. ... Chicago, IL
Heller, Anthony M. ... New York, NY
Heller, Arthur F. ... Miami, FL
Heller & Associates, P.C. ... Houston, TX
Heller, Barry M. ... Washington, DC
Heller, Belle ... Carle Place, NY
Heller, Bennett R. ... Chicago, IL
Heller, Bette ... Aurora, CO
Heller, B. J. ... Orlando, FL
Heller, Brian A. ... Dulles, VA
Heller, Brian L. ... Miami, FL
Heller, Brian S. ... Miami, FL
Heller, Bruce E. ... Seattle, WA
Heller, Byron M. ... Baltimore, MD
Heller, Carol Ruth ... Miami, FL
Heller, Catherine A. ... Portland, TX
Heller, Cheryl A. ... Rochester, NY
Heller, Christopher J., (P.A.)
Little Rock, AR
Heller, Craig M. ... Fairfield, NJ
Heller, Craig S. ... Garden City, NY
Heller, Cynthia S. ... Tempe, AZ
Heller, Dan L. ... Atlanta, GA
Heller, Dan P. ... Miami, FL
Heller, Daniel G. ... Troy, MI
Heller, Daniel Neal ... Miami, FL
Heller, Daniel T. ... Clifton, NJ
Heller & Darvas ... Seattle, WA
Heller, David E. ... Nashville, TN
Heller, David H. ... Bellaire, TX
Heller, David J. ... Englewood, CO
Heller, David M. ... Scottsdale, AZ
Heller, David M. ... Elmsford, NY
Heller, David S. ... Chicago, IL
Heller, David S. ... New York, NY
Heller, David S. ... Seattle, WA
Heller, Deborah ... San Jose, CA
Heller, Deborah Sutter ... Atlanta, GA
Heller, Diane ... New York, NY
Heller, Dona L. ... Los Angeles, CA
Heller, Donald H. ... Sacramento, CA
Heller, Donald H., A Law Corporation
Sacramento, CA
Heller, Donald R. ... Fresno, CA
Heller, Donna Nelson ... Stamford, CT
Heller, Donna R. ... Baltimore, MD
Heller, Douglas P. ... New York, NY
Heller, Draper, Hayden & Horn, L.L.C.
New Orleans, LA
Heller, Edward Harris ... New York, NY
Heller, Edward J. ... Murphysboro, IL
Heller, Edward M. ... New Orleans, LA
Heller, Edward P., III ... Scotts Valley, CA
Heller, Edward, P.C. ... Houston, TX
Heller, Edward, (P.C) ... Houston, TX
Heller & Edwards ... Beverly Hills, CA
Los Angeles, CA
Heller, Edwin, (P.C.) ... New York, NY
Heller Ehrman White & McAuliffe
Anchorage, AK
La Jolla, CA
Los Angeles, CA
Menlo Park, CA
Palo Alto, CA
San Francisco, CA
Washington, DC
New York, NY
Portland, OR
Seattle, WA
Heller, Elizabeth A. ... Los Angeles, CA
Heller, Ellen M. ... Baltimore, MD
Heller, Elliot H. ... La Jolla, CA
Heller, Ernest A. ... Olympia, WA
Heller, F. Arnold ... Philadelphia, PA
Heller, Floyd E. ... Bethlehem, PA
Heller, Francis H. ... Lawrence, KS
Heller, Frank ... Mission Viejo, CA
Heller, Frank ... New York, NY
Heller, Franklin W. ... Buffalo, NY
Heller, Fred I. ... Merrick, NY
Heller, Frederic W. ... Ann Arbor, MI
Heller & Friedman, P.A. ... Orlando, FL
Heller and Frisone, Ltd. ... Chicago, IL
Heller, Gary Mark ... New York, NY
Heller, Gerald W. ... Greenbelt, MD
Silver Spring, MD
Heller, Glen L. ... Newburgh, NY
Heller, Gregory B. ... Philadelphia, PA
Heller, Gregory John ... Chicago, IL
Heller, Gregory L. ... Rochester, IN
Heller, H. Kent ... Mattoon, IL
Heller, Hanes A. ... Englewood Cliffs, NJ
Heller, Harlan ... Mattoon, IL
Heller, Harry ... Washington, DC
Heller, Harry B. ... Uncasville, CT
Heller, Harvey J. ... Houston, TX
Heller, Harvey R. ... Southfield, MI
Heller, Heller & McCoy ... Uncasville, CT
Heller & Heller, P.C. ... St. Louis, MO
Heller, Henry ... Montgomery, AL
Heller, Holmes & Associates, P.C.
Charleston, IL
Effingham, IL
Marshall, IL
Mattoon, IL
Olney, IL
Robinson, IL
Heller, Horowitz & Feit, P.C.
New York, NY
Heller, Howard E. ... White Plains, NY
Heller, Hugh M. ... New York, NY
Heller, Huron, Chertkof, Lerner, Simon & Salzman ... Washington, DC
Heller, Irving L. ... Cleveland, OH
Heller, Irwin A. ... Richmond, VA
Heller, Irwin M. ... Boston, MA
Heller, J. Brian ... Washington, IL
Heller, J. Brian, P.C. ... Washington, IL
Heller, J. Dean ... Los Angeles, CA
Heller, J. Roderick, III ... Washington, DC
Heller, Jack I. ... Washington, DC
Heller, Jacob W. ... New York, NY
Heller, James H. ... Washington, DC
Heller, James H. ... Philadelphia, PA
Heller, James R. ... Tacoma, WA
Heller, James S. ... Williamsburg, VA
Heller, James W." Mike " ... Portland, OR
Heller, Jay A. ... Chicago, IL
Heller, Jeffrey A. ... Cranford, NJ
New York, NY
Heller, Jeffrey S. ... Houston, TX
Heller, Jeffrey T. ... East Northport, NY
Heller, Jennifer ... Philadelphia, PA
Heller, Jerold W. ... Kalama, WA
Heller, Jerome S. ... New York, NY
Heller, Joan S. ... Denver, CO
Heller, Jodi Ann ... New York, NY
Heller, John A. ... Chicago, IL
Heller, John A. ... San Antonio, TX
Heller, John G. ... San Francisco, CA
Heller, Jonathan A. ... Miami, FL
Heller, Jonathan D. ... New York, NY
Heller, Jonathan I. ... Houston, TX
Heller, Jonathan O. ... New York, NY
Heller, Joyce Zarosky ... Victoria, TX
Heller, Justin A. ... Albany, NY
Heller and Kaplan ... Miami, FL
Heller, Kapustin, Gershman & Vogel
Norristown, PA
Philadelphia, PA
Blue Bell, PA
Heller, Karen E. ... Springfield, NJ
Heller, Karen L. ... Bedford, NH
Heller, Kathryn A. ... Jonesboro, GA
Heller, Kenneth ... New York, NY
Heller, Kenneth D. ... San Diego, CA
Heller, Kim F., II ... Daytona Beach, FL
Heller, Laurie E. ... Warren, OH
Heller, Lawrence A. ... Saltville, VA
Heller, Lawrence E. ... Beverly Hills, CA
Heller, Lawrence H. ... Santa Monica, CA
Heller, Lawrence I. ... Rochester, NY
Heller, Lawrence R. ... Miami, FL
Heller, Leon Z. ... Horsham, PA
Heller, Leonard H., Jr. ... St. Paul, MN
Heller, Levin & Seksay, P.C. ... Boston, MA
Heller, Lewis L. ... New York, NY
Heller, Linda J. ... New York, NY
Heller, Lisa B. ... Salem, OR
Heller, Lisa L. ... Atlanta, GA
Heller, Lloyd J. ... White Plains, NY
Heller, Marc B. ... New York, NY
Heller, Marilyn ... United States Senate, Committee Legal Personnel, GV
Heller, Mark A. ... Washington, DC
Heller, Mark L. ... Albany, NY
Heller, Mark R. ... Austin, TX
Heller, Martha E. ... Washington, DC
Heller, Martin, P.C. ... Philadelphia, PA
Heller, Maurice L. ... Cleveland, OH
Heller, Maurice W. ... New York, NY
Heller, Melvin ... St. Louis, MO
Heller, Mervin A., Jr. ... Wyomissing, PA
Heller, Michael B. ... Clive, IA
Heller, Michael J. ... Melville, NY
Heller, Michael J. ... Roslyn Heights, NY
Heller, Michael J. ... Philadelphia, PA
Heller, Michael L. ... Monroe, MI
Heller, Michael S. ... Palm Beach, FL
Heller, Michael W. ... Peoria, IL
Heller, Michelle Marie ... Orlando, FL
Heller, Mickey Zale ... Brooklyn, NY
Heller, Milton, & Associates
Washington, DC
Heller, Morgan S. ... Philadelphia, PA
Heller, Nancy J. ... Cleveland, OH
Heller, Nancy R. ... New York, NY
Heller, Nancy S. ... Brookline, MA
Heller, Neil H. ... Great Neck, NY
Heller, Norman B. ... Carle Place, NY
Heller, Norman H. ... Melville, NY
Heller, Norman M. ... New York, NY
Heller, Norman S. ... New York, NY
Heller, Paul ... Brooklyn, NY
Heller, Paul A. ... Willimantic, CT
Heller, Paul H. ... New York, NY
Heller, Paul M. ... San Francisco, CA
Heller, Paul M. ... Chicago, IL
Heller, Paula R. ... Englewood, CO
Heller, Peter S. ... Miami, FL
Heller, Peter S. ... New York, NY
Heller, Peter S., P.A. ... Miami, FL
Heller, Philip ... Los Angeles, CA
Heller, Philip A. ... New Bedford, MA
Heller, Philip F., & Associates ... Lenox, MA
Heller, Philip F., & Associates
Stockbridge, MA
Heller, Randy J. ... New York, NY
Heller, Ray A. ... Reisterstown, MD
Heller, Rebecca M. ... New York, NY
Heller, Renee P. ... Cleveland, OH
Heller, Richard ... Boston, MA
Heller, Richard ... New York, NY
Heller, Richard A. ... Carlsbad, CA
Heller, Richard A. ... Orlando, FL
Heller, Richard B. ... New York, NY
Heller, Richard D. ... Fort Lauderdale, FL
Heller, Richard L. ... Basking Ridge, NJ
Heller, Richard M. ... Media, PA
Heller, Richard P. ... Philadelphia, PA
Heller, Richard S. ... San Diego, CA
New York, NY
Heller & Richmond ... Chicago, IL

Heller, Robert .... West Orange, NJ
Heller, Robert .... Westlake Village, CA
Heller, Robert E. .... Duluth, MN
Heller, Robert G. .... New Orleans, LA
Heller, Robert H., Jr. .... Annapolis, MD
Heller, Robert I. .... Seattle, WA
Heller, Robert J. .... Seattle, WA
Heller, Robert L. .... Youngstown, OH
Heller, Robert M. .... Beverly Hills, CA
Heller, Robert M. .... New York, NY
Heller, Robt. N. .... Delray Beach, FL
Heller, Rochelle S. .... Coral Springs, FL
Heller, Roger D. .... Cleveland, OH
Heller, Ronald G. .... Woodcliff Lake, NJ
Heller, Ronald I. .... Honolulu, HI
Heller, Rosemarie A. .... Naperville, IL
Heller & Rosenberg, P.C. .... Garden City, NY
Heller & Rosenblatt .... Washington, DC
Heller, Ruth G. .... Albany, NY
Heller, Ruth K. .... Syracuse, NY
Heller, Sally I. .... St. Louis, MO
Heller, Samuel L. .... Fort Lauderdale, FL
Heller, Samuel L., P.A. .... Fort Lauderdale, FL
Heller, Sanders D. .... Gouverneur, NY
Heller, Scott T. .... Morristown, NJ
Heller, Sherri R. .... Miami, FL
Heller, Simon .... New York, NY
Heller, Stanley J. .... Chicago, IL
Heller, Stanley L. .... Richmond, VA
Heller, Stanley S. .... Santa Monica, CA
Heller, Stephanie A. .... New York, NY
Heller, Stephen B. .... Chicago, IL
Heller, Stephen F. .... Fremont, CA
Heller, Stephen H. .... Encino, CA
Heller, Stephen H., A Professional Corporation .... Encino, CA
Heller, Steve W. .... New York, NY
Heller, Steven D. .... Philadelphia, PA
Heller, Steven M. .... Gold River, CA
Heller, Steven M.
National Transportation Safety Board, Office of Administrative Law Judges, GV
Heller, Steven P. .... Santa Monica, CA
Heller, Susan L. .... San Francisco, CA
Heller, Terry Lee .... Albuquerque, NM
Heller, Thomas .... New York, NY
Heller, Thomas G. .... Los Angeles, CA
Heller, Todd A. .... Deerfield, IL
Heller, Todd E. .... New York, NY
Heller, Ulf R." Ron " .... Oklahoma City, OK
Heller, Warren H. .... New York, NY
Heller, Warren S. .... Milford, MA
Heller, Warren S., P.C. .... Milford, MA
Heller, Wayne E. .... White Plains, NY
Heller, Wendy .... Los Angeles, CA
Heller, Wendy C .... Middleton, MA
Heller, William
Charlotte Amalie, St. Thomas, VI
Heller, William A. .... Coral Springs, FL
Heller, William A. .... Hollywood, FL
Heller, William J. .... Newark, NJ
Heller, William J. .... Milwaukee, WI
Heller, William T., IV .... Houston, TX
Heller, Z. Edward .... Blue Bell, PA
Hellerer, Cuomo & O'Connor .... Amherst, NY
Hellerer, Mark R. .... New York, NY
Hellerer, Robt. J. .... Amherst, NY
Hellerich, Charles L. .... San Diego, CA
Hellerich, Thomas E. .... Greeley, CO
Hellerman, Eric .... New York, NY
Hellerman, Jeffrey T. .... New York, NY
Hellerman, Richard K. .... Chicago, IL
Heller-Marotta, Kim M. .... Milwaukee, WI
Hellerstedt, Carl H., Jr. .... Pittsburgh, PA
Hellerstein, Alvin K. .... New York, NY
Hellerstein & Associates .... Denver, CO
Hellerstein, Cara S. .... Columbus, OH
Hellerstein, Dina R. .... Woodland Hills, CA
Hellerstein, Jerome R. .... New York, NY
Hellerstein, Joseph Z. .... New York, NY
Hellerstein and Shore, P.C. A Professional Corporation .... Denver, CO
Hellerstein, Stephen A. .... Denver, CO
Hellerstein, William E. .... New York, NY
Heller-Toig, Elly .... Pittsburgh, PA
Hellerud & Larson .... Ada, MN
Hellerud, Mark R. .... Ada, MN
Hellewell, Edward D. .... Houston, TX
Hellewell, Read R. .... Salt Lake City, UT
Hellewell, Robert John .... Washington, DC
Hellewell, Ronald M. .... Salem, OR
Hellewell, Ronald M., P.C. .... Salem, OR
Hellgren, Janne .... Cambridge, MA
Hellickson, James A. .... Clearwater, FL
Hellickson, Paul L. .... Minneapolis, MN
Hellige, Eric M. .... New York, NY
Hellige, James R. .... Chicago, IL
Hellige, Lundberg, Meis, Erickson & Frey
Sioux City, IA
South Sioux City, NE
Dakota Dunes, SD
Hellige, Michael R. .... Sioux City, IA
Helliker, Carol .... Houston, TX
Helline, Denise M. .... Louisville, KY
Helling, Brian J. .... Burlington, IA
Helling, Christopher J. .... Dallas, TX
Helling, Dorothy L. .... Montpelier, VT
Helling, Ernest N. .... Harrisburg, PA
Helling, Henry E., III .... Columbus, OH
Helling, James K. .... St. Paul, MN
Helling, Joseph T. .... Granger, IN
Helling, Katheen A. .... Latrobe, PA
Helling, Lisa L.
Department of State, GV
Helling, Pamela J. .... Brookline, MA
Helling, Steven R. .... Casper, WY
Hellinger, Andrew B. .... Miami, FL
Hellinger, Jeffery A. .... Bellevue, WA
Hellinger, Jim .... Roslyn Heights, NY
Hellinger, John R. .... Nashville, TN
Hellinger, Mark S. .... Houston, TX
Hellinger, Susan Kopecky .... Houston, TX
Hellings, Harry P., Jr. .... Covington, KY
Helliwell, Carol Henderson .... Fall River, MA
Hellman, Alan L. .... Peoria, IL
Hellman, Allen .... Goldens Bridge, NY
Hellman, Bernard A. .... Boca Raton, FL
Hellman, Bobby E. .... Lubbock, TX
Hellman, Burt S. .... Miami Beach, FL
Hellman, Charles D. .... New York, NY
Hellman, Charles S. .... New York, NY
Hellman, Cheryl L. .... Grand Rapids, MI
Hellman, Daniel Paul .... Knoxville, TN
Hellman, David N. .... Great Barrington, MA
Hellman, Dennis I. .... New York, NY
Hellman, Dolph M. .... San Francisco, CA
Hellman, George E. .... New York, NY
Hellman, Irving H. .... Hollywood, FL
Hellman, James R. .... Waterloo, IA
Hellman, Jay S. .... Garden City, NY
Hellman, Jeffrey .... Bridgeport, CT
Hellman, Jeffrey S. .... New York, NY
Hellman, Joel M. .... Chicago, IL
Hellman, Jonathan J. .... Denver, CO
Hellman, Joseph S. .... New York, NY
Hellman, Katherine Likoudis .... Woodside, NY
Hellman, Kenneth A. .... Department of Labor, Office of the Solicitor, GV
Hellman, Lawrence K. .... Oklahoma City, OK
Hellman, Lewis R. .... Detroit, MI
Hellman, Lloyd S. .... Kansas City, MO
Hellman & Maas .... Homestead, FL
Hellman, Mark D. .... Chicago, IL
Hellman, Matt D., P.A. .... Fort Lauderdale, FL
Hellman, Michael D. .... Santa Barbara, CA
Hellman, Michael P. .... Chicago, IL
Hellman & Redmond .... Towson, MD
Hellman, Richard A. .... Washington, DC
Hellman, Robert J. .... New York, NY
Hellman, Ronald B. .... Douglaston, NY
Hellman, Samuel I. .... New York, NY
Hellman & Shearn
Great Barrington, MA
Hellman, Stanley H. .... Towson, MD
Hellman, Stephen Richard .... Sayville, NY
Hellman, Theodore A. .... San Francisco, CA
Hellman, Thomas J. .... Manchester, MO
Hellmann, Brett J. .... Jefferson City, MO
Hellmann & Cook .... Terre Haute, IN
Hellmann, Deborah L. .... Wood River, IL
Hellmann, Jane A. .... Seattle, WA
Hellmann, Juda M. .... Louisville, KY
Hellmann, Lori A. .... Milford, PA
Hellmann, Mark H. .... Chicago, IL
Hellmann, Robert F. .... Terre Haute, IN
Hellmann, William E. .... Louisville, KY
Hellmer, Jerome P. .... Salina, KS
Hellmer, Victoria L. .... Denver, CO
Hellmer, Werner .... Durango, IA
Hellmers, Niles A. .... New Orleans, LA
Hellmich, Christopher .... Washington, DC
Hellmich, Heather A. .... Clayton, MO
Hellmich, William A. .... St. Louis, MO
Hellmold, Richard D. .... Natick, MA
Hellmold, Richard D., P.C. .... Natick, MA
Hellmuth, David G. .... Eden Prairie, MN
Hellmuth & Johnson, P.A.
Eden Prairie, MN
Hellmuth, Theodore H., (P.C.)
St. Louis, MO
Hellner, Mark .... Chicago, IL
Hellner-Cord, Leigh A. .... New York, NY
Hellow, John R. .... Los Angeles, CA
Hellquist, George A. .... Feeding Hills, MA
Hellreich, Steven M. .... Woodbury, NY
Hellriegel, Wolf J. .... Seattle, WA
Hellring, Heidi H. .... Maplewood, NJ
Hellring Lindeman Goldstein & Siegal LLP
Englewood, NJ
Newark, NJ
Hellring, Margaret Dee .... Englewood, NJ
Newark, NJ
Hellrung, Donald E. .... Galesville, WI
Hellrung, M. Cecilia .... Rockville, MD
Hellrung, Stephen A. .... North Wilkesboro, NC
Hellsten, Mats .... San Francisco, CA
Hellstern, Cynthia W. .... Waxahachie, TX
Hellstern, Joyce M. .... Dallas, TX
Hellstern, Richard R. .... New York, NY
Hellstrom, George W. .... Salt Lake City, UT
Hellstrom, Harlow J., Jr. .... Milwaukee, WI
Hellstrom, Per E. .... San Diego, CA
Hellum, Linda Sue .... Chino, CA
Hellums, Bonnie Crane .... Houston, TX
Hellums, Chris T. .... Birmingham, AL
Hellums, Clarence T., Jr. .... Centreville, AL
Hellums, Hartley & Johnson .... Centreville, AL
Hellums, Nathan J. .... Houston, TX
Hellweg, Douglas R. .... Golden Valley, MN
Hellweg, Mary G. .... Des Moines, IA
Hellwege, Donald J. .... Tulsa, OK
Hellwege, James W. .... Arlington, VA
Hellwig, Frank Z. .... St. Louis, MO
Hellwig, Larry H. .... St. Louis, MO
Hellwig, Raymond G. .... Alhambra, CA
Hellwig, Robb E. .... Atlanta, GA
Hellyer, David R. .... Chelan, WA
Hellyer, Donald R. .... Quincy, IL
Hellyer, George W., Jr. .... San Francisco, CA
Hellyer, William .... Crystal Lake, IL
Hellyer, William S. .... San Bernardino, CA
Helm, Alice K. .... Bethesda, MD
Helm, Amy .... Houston, TX
Helm, Ann .... Lafayette, OR
Helm, Ardee, Jr. .... Montpelier, ID
Helm & Associates .... Anchorage, AK
Helm & Associates .... Austin, TX
Helm, Beverly M. .... Palatine, IL
Helm, Boone & Donaldson
Oklahoma City, OK
Helm, Bradley B. .... Albany, NY
Helm, Catherine H. .... Los Angeles, CA
Helm, Cathryn Celeste .... Department of Labor, Office of the Solicitor, GV
Helm, Charles L. .... Oklahoma City, OK
Helm, Charles Minor .... Richardson, TX
Helm, Charles P. (IBA) .... Seattle, WA
Helm, Christopher R. .... Seattle, WA
Helm, Dale H. .... Arvada, CO
Helm, Douglas W. .... Denver, CO
Helm, Edward G. .... Department of Labor, Office of the Solicitor, GV
Helm, Elizabeth .... Dallas, TX
Helm, Elizabeth C. .... Atlanta, GA
Helm, Eric Paul .... Aliso Viejo, CA
Helm, George A., III .... Maitland, FL
Helm, Greta Louise .... Hollister, CA
Helm, Helm & Lovejoy, Inc., P.S.
Seattle, WA
Tacoma, WA
Helm & Helm, P.C. .... Roanoke, VA
Salem, VA
Helm, Hugh B.
Department Of Health And Human Services, Social Security Administration, GV
Helm, Hugh H. .... Los Angeles, CA
Helm, Jacquelyn V. .... Washington, DC
Helm, John D. .... Tempe, AZ
Helm, John H. .... Austin, TX
Helm, John R. .... Indianapolis, IN
Helm, Joseph B. .... Louisville, KY
Helm, Joseph H., Jr.
Menomonee Falls, WI
Helm, Kenneth D. .... Portland, OR
Helm, Kevin E. .... Las Vegas, NV
Helm & Kyle, Ltd. .... Tempe, AZ
Helm, Lana Lee McLario
Menomonee Falls, WI
Helm, Lucy Lee .... Seattle, WA
Helm, Mark B. .... Los Angeles, CA
Helm, Michael G. .... New Orleans, LA
Helm, Miller & Miller .... Detroit, MI
Helm, Milton M. .... Metropolis, IL
Helm, Minor L., Jr. .... Waco, TX
Helm, Murray M., Jr. .... San Diego, CA
Helm, Nancy S. .... Salem, VA
Helm, Nelson, Jr. .... Louisville, KY
Helm, Patrick O. .... Gainesville, FL
Helm, Paul C. .... Bartow, FL
Helm, Pletcher, Bowen & Saunders
Houston, TX
Helm, Purcell & Wakeman
Westlake Village, CA
Helm, Reagan C. .... Houston, TX
Helm, Richard A. .... Anchorage, AK
Helm, Richard K. .... Warsaw, IN
Helm, Robert E. .... Albany, NY
Helm, Robert G. .... San Marcos, CA
Helm, Robert H. .... Louisville, KY
Helm, Robert W. .... Washington, DC
Helm, Rolf L. .... Sterling, IL
Helm, Ronald R. .... Westlake Village, CA
Helm, Sallie H. .... Washington, DC
Helm, Sally-Jo .... Knoxville, TN
Helm, Shapiro, Anito & McCale, P.C.
Albany, NY
Helm, Stephen D. .... Sarasota, FL
Naperville, IL
Helm, Steve, & Associates .... Sarasota, FL
Naperville, IL
Helm, Steven F. .... Salem, VA
Helm, T. Kennedy, III .... Louisville, KY
Helm, T. Kennedy, Jr. .... Louisville, KY
Helm, William A. .... Harrisburg, PA
Helm, William Anthony .... Memphis, TN
Helman, Clifton E. .... Boston, MA
Helman, Ellen Y. .... Columbia, SC
Helman, Frank G. .... New York, NY
Helman, Gerald B.
Department of State, GV
Helman, Grant M. .... Louisville, KY
Helman, Herbert A. .... Baltimore, MD
Helman, Irving J., (P.C.) .... Boston, MA
Helman, Joseph S. .... Los Angeles, CA
Helman, Mark A. .... Boston, MA
Helman, Michael John .... Terre Haute, IN
Helman, Nard S. .... Miami, FL
Helman, Nard S., P.A. .... Miami, FL
Helman, Richard K. .... Roslyn Heights, NY
Helman, Robert A. .... Chicago, IL
Helman, Roger S. .... Harbor Springs, MI
Helman, S. Charles .... New York, NY
Helman, Stephen A. .... New York, NY
Helman, Stephen Jody .... Austin, TX
Helmanis, Ansis M. .... Washington, DC
Chicago, IL
New York, NY
Helmann Sullivan & White, P.C.
Hastings, NE
Helmbacher, Kevin .... San Diego, CA
Helmbacher, William R. .... Aurora, IL
Helmbold, William Ross .... Redding, CA
Helmcamp, Carrie D. .... El Paso, TX
Helme and Cole .... Ossipee, NH
Helme, George W., IV .... Wilmington, DE
Helme, Wenda T. .... Ossipee, NH
Helmen, Randall C. .... Indianapolis, IN
Helmenstine, Robert A. .... Mill Valley, CA
Helmer, Colleen M. .... Chicago, IL
Helmer, David A. .... Breckenridge, CO
Helmer, David A. .... Frisco, CO
Helmer, Dennis C., (P.S.C.) .... Florence, KY
Helmer, Gregory D. .... Venice, CA
Helmer, James B., Jr. .... Cincinnati, OH
Helmer Johnson Misiaszek & Hughes
Utica, NY
Helmer, Kassel & Stowell, A Professional Association .... Haddon Heights, NJ
Helmer, Kathy Dutton .... Morristown, NJ
Helmer, M. Christie, P.C. .... Portland, OR
Helmer, Martins & Morgan Co., L.P.A.
Cincinnati, OH
Helmer, Maureen O. .... Albany, NY
Helmer, Meredith A. .... Boston, MA
Helmer, Michael E. .... Florham Park, NJ
Helmer, Nicholas J., II .... Chicago, IL
Helmer, Pamela J. .... Redwood City, CA
Helmer, Robert A. .... St. Louis, MO
Helmer, Robert F. .... Utica, NY
Helmer, Roger M. .... Southfield, MI
Helmer, Stephen T. .... Syracuse, NY
Helmer, Steven J. .... Reston, VA
Helmer, William S. .... Albany, NY
Helmer, Yaron .... Haddon Heights, NJ
Helmerick, Jeffery L. .... Lafayette, IN
Helmerick, Smith and Fountain
Lafayette, IN
Helmers, David L. .... Lexington, KY
Helmers, Eric V. .... Nashville, TN
Helmers, John H. .... Owensboro, KY
Helmers, John H., Jr. .... Louisville, KY
Helmers, Kristin M. .... New York, NY
Helmers, Rod .... Brandon, FL
Helmers, Rod, P.A. .... Brandon, FL
Helmers, Steven J. .... Rapid City, SD
Helmholdt, Thomas D. .... Troy, MI
Helmholz, Richard .... Chicago, IL
Helmholz, Scott C. .... Springfield, IL
Helmich, Kevin M. .... Destin, FL
Helmich, Terry O. .... Springfield, IL
Helmick, Bertha G. .... Cincinnati, OH
Helmick, Cindy S. .... Parker, CO
Helmick, Dennis P. .... Seattle, WA
Helmick, Dennis S. .... Cincinnati, OH
Helmick, Jeffrey J. .... Toledo, OH
Helmick, John P., Jr. .... Jacksonville, FL
Helmick, John V. .... Parker, CO
Helmick, Karen Henry .... Toledo, OH
Helmick, Prajsner & Hoolahan .... Toledo, OH
Helmick, Richard A. .... Washington, DC
Helmick, Richard R. .... Denver, CO
Helmick, Robert H. .... Des Moines, IA
Helmig, Charles W., III .... Granville, IL
Peru, IL
Helming, Frederick G., Jr. .... Mobile, AL
Helmink, Meri-jo .... Chicago, IL
Helminski, Frank .... Rochester, MN
Helmkamp, Alan C. .... Livonia, MI
Helmke, Beams, Boyer & Wagner
Fort Wayne, IN
Helmke, Edward H. .... Princeton, NJ
Helmke, Mark S. .... San Antonio, TX
Helmke, Paul .... Fort Wayne, IN
Helmke, Walter P. .... Fort Wayne, IN
Helmke-Elmore, Janet M. .... Hartford, CT
Helmling, Margaret R., (Mrs.)
Cincinnati, OH
Helmlinger, Colleen Ferg .... Baltimore, MD
Helmlinger, J. Andrew .... Walnut Creek, CA
Boise, ID
Helmlinger, Robyn L. .... Boise, ID
New York, NY
Helmore, Alan S. .... Southfield, MI
Helmreich, Dennis Peter .... Lexington, GA
Helmreich, Loren G. .... Houston, TX
Helmreich, Louis P. .... Temecula, CA
Helmreich, Martha S. .... Pittsburgh, PA
Helmreich, Richard J. .... Columbus, OH
Helmrich, Joel M. .... Pittsburgh, PA
Helmrich, Richard D. .... Benton Harbor, MI
Helms, Andy L. .... Pasadena, TX
Helms and Associates, P.C. .... Denver, CO
Helms, Bonnie J. .... Key West, FL
Helms, Bonnie J., P.A. .... Key West, FL
Helms, Brenda Porter .... Chicago, IL
Helms, Brent Alan .... Plano, TX
Helms, Cannon, Hamel & Henderson, Professional Association .... Charlotte, NC
Concord, NC
Helms, Carol S., Law Offices of
Houston, TX
Helms, Catherine Harris .... Homerville, GA
Helms, Charles P., Jr. .... Huntsville, AL
Helms, Charles R. .... Dallas, TX
Helms, Christine Dent .... Lithia Springs, GA
Helms, Christopher A. .... Houston, TX
Helms, Conner L. .... Oklahoma City, OK
Helms, David B. .... St. Louis, MO
Helms, Dennis J. .... Princeton, NJ
Helms, Dorothy M. .... Columbia, SC
Helms, Ernest E. .... Detroit, MI
Helms, F. James .... Chicago, IL
Helms, Fred A. .... Austin, TX
Helms, H. Parks .... Charlotte, NC
Helms, Hanrahan & Myers .... Arcadia, CA
Glendale, CA
Los Angeles, CA
Pasadena, CA
Helms & Helms .... Lithia Springs, GA
Helms and Helms, P.C. .... Homerville, GA
Helms, Howard Brent
Winston-Salem, NC
Helms, Irl R. .... Santa Fe, NM
Helms, J. Jeffrey .... Homerville, GA
Helms, James Michael .... Little Rock, AR
Helms, James R. .... Bloomfield, CT
Helms, James R., Jr. .... Arcadia, CA
Helms, Jana C. .... Kalamazoo, MI
Helms, Jeffrey L. .... Charlotte, NC
Helms, John A. .... Duluth, GA
Helms, John M. .... Dallas, TX
Helms, John M. .... Houston, TX

Helms, Judith Fournie .... Chicago, IL
Helms, Julian D. .... Oklahoma City, OK
Helms, Katherine Dudley .... Columbia, SC
Helms, Kenna J. .... Palo Alto, CA
Helms, Larry R. .... Muncie, IN
Helms, Larry S. .... Winter Haven, FL
Helms Law Firm .... Little Rock, AR
Helms, Lawrence .... Chicago, IL
Helms, Linda L. .... Winston-Salem, NC
Helms, Louise A. .... Oklahoma City, OK
Helms, Marshall L., Jr. .... Lithia Springs, GA
Helms, Mary Moffatt .... Knoxville, TN
Morristown, TN
Helms, Michael E. .... Wilkesboro, NC
Helms, Michael G. .... Phoenix, AZ
Helms, Mira L. .... Austin, TX
Helms, Neal G. .... Charlotte, NC
Helms, Norman E. .... Trenton, TN
Helms, R. Kenneth, Jr. .... Monroe, NC
Helms, Ralph L. .... Kokomo, IN
Helms, Richard L. .... Nashville, TN
Helms, Roger D. .... Winter Park, FL
Helms, Susan A. .... Fort Worth, TX
Helms, Thomas E. .... Atlanta, GA
Helms, Thomas J. .... Denver, CO
Steamboat Springs, CO
Helms, Tom .... Houston, TX
Helms & Underwood .... Oklahoma City, OK
Helms, Victoria L. .... Atlanta, GA
Helms, W. Richard .... Chicago, IL
Helms, William C., III .... Charleston, SC
Helms, William Franklin, III .... Monroe, NC
Helms, Wm. W. .... St. Paul, MN
Helmsing, Frederick G. .... Mobile, AL
Helmsing, Frederick G., Jr. .... Mobile, AL
Helmsing, Gregg A. .... Delta, CO
Helmsing, Sims & Leach, P.C.
Bay Minette, AL
Fairhope, AL
Foley, AL
Gulf Shores, AL
Mobile, AL
Helmstetter, Carl H. .... Kansas City, MO
Helmueller, Mark J. .... San Rafael, CA
Helmus, Arthur H., Jr. .... San Diego, CA
Helmuth, Karen S. .... Phoenix, AZ
Helmuth, Louis W. .... San Diego, CA
Helmuth, R. J. .... Orrville, OH
Helmuth, Ronald L. .... Tarzana, CA
Helon & Manfredo .... Fresno, CA
Helon, Marvin E. .... Fresno, CA
Helon, Marvin T. .... Fresno, CA
Helou, Alexandra K. .... Treasury Department, Internal Revenue Service, GV
Helou, Elie .... Chicago, IL
Helow, Ronald J. .... Sausalito, CA
Helpa, Jon J. .... Springfield, MA
Helper, Cara D. .... Minneapolis, MN
Helper, Kim R. .... Nashville, TN
Helperin, Alex N. .... Los Angeles, CA
Helpern, Martin W. .... New York, NY
Helpern, Robert E. .... New York, NY
Helphand & Rich .... Glendale, CA
Helphand, Richard J. .... Glendale, CA
Helphrey, Eric G. .... Sacramento, CA
Helpling, Ray D. .... Archer, FL
Helppie, Jane E. .... Pittsburgh, PA
Helppie, Sally C. .... Dallas, TX
Helring, Gracelia Riden .... Arlington, VA
Helring, Gracelia Riden, P.C. .... Arlington, VA
Helsby, Wayne L. .... Orlando, FL
Helscher, David C. .... Roanoke, VA
Helsel, Benjamin G., Jr. .... Mount Gretna, PA
Helsel, Janet S. .... Wichita, KS
Helsel, Jennifer D. .... Pasadena, CA
Helsel, Jennifer Ramey .... Washington, DC
Fairfax, VA
Helsel, Kathleen L. .... Washington, DC
Helsel, Robert C. .... Wichita, KS
Helsel, Scott D. .... Washington, DC
Helsel, William G. .... Falls Church, VA
Helsell Fetterman LLP .... Seattle, WA
Helser, Gregory C. .... Pickerington, OH
Helser, Kristin A. .... West Palm Beach, FL
Helseth, Angela M. .... Minneapolis, MN
Helseth, Dennis J. .... Elbow Lake, MN
Helsing, J. Eric .... Liberty, MO
Helsinger, Howard M. .... Chicago, IL
Helsley & Clough, P.C. .... Harrisonburg, VA
Helsley, Michael S. .... Fresno, CA
Helsley, William W. .... Harrisonburg, VA
Helson, D. Richard .... East Lansing, MI
Helson Manning, PLC .... East Lansing, MI
Helsper, Richard J. .... Brookings, SD
Helsper, William H.
Department Of Health And Human Services, Social Security Administration, GV
Helstad, Orrin L. .... Madison, WI
Helsten, Bradley R. .... Salt Lake City, UT
Helsten, Charles F. .... Rockford, IL
Helsten, David L. .... Scottsdale, AZ
Helstoski, Renata A. .... Montvale, NJ
Helstowski, Robert W. .... Dallas, TX
Helstrom, W. Richard .... Fort Wayne, IN
Helt, Brenda M. .... Holmdel, NJ
Helt, Christopher .... Chicago, IL
Helt, Daniel W. .... Dana, IN
Helt, Lloyd R., Jr. .... Sykesville, MD
Helt, Michael L. .... Kansas City, MO
Helt, Nancy R. .... Wellesley Hills, MA
Helt, Peter R. .... Washington, DC
Baltimore, MD
Burtonsville, MD
Helton, Arthur C. .... New York, NY
Helton, Barry M. .... Corbin, KY
Helton, Daniel G. .... Detroit, MI
Helton, Ephraim W. .... Danville, KY
Helton, Farmer .... Pineville, KY
Helton & Helton .... Pineville, KY
Helton, J. Campbell .... Des Moines, IA
Helton, J. C. .... Pineville, KY
Helton, Jeanne E. .... Jacksonville, FL
Helton, Jeffery Wade .... Pineville, KY
Helton, Kennard K. .... Dardanelle, AR
Helton, Lynda D. .... Corpus Christi, TX
Helton, Mary Anne .... Tallahassee, FL
Helton, Michael R. .... Renton, WA
Helton & Petrie .... Danville, KY
Helton, Ralph, Associates .... Long Beach, CA
Helton, Ralph G. .... Long Beach, CA
Helton, Robert H., Jr. .... London, KY
Helton, Robert M. .... Wichita Falls, TX
Helton, Sabina A. .... Los Angeles, CA
Helton, Thomas O. .... Chattanooga, TN
Nashville, TN
Helton, William Shepard .... Cartersville, GA
Heltz, Michael K. .... Gramercy, LA
Heltzel, James G. .... Salem, OR
Heltzel, Jerry P. .... Floresville, TX
Heltzel, Paul E. .... Warren, OH
Heltzel, Timothy W. .... Portland, OR
Heltzel, Upjohn, Williams, Yandell & Roth, P.C. .... Salem, OR
Heltzer, Harold J. .... Washington, DC
Heltzer, Lester A.
National Labor Relations Board, Office of Board Members, GV
Heltzer, Michael .... Chicago, IL
Heltzer, Rebecca J. .... Minneapolis, MN
Helvenston, Edward B. .... Sanford, FL
Helvenston, Edward G. .... Orlando, FL
Helverson, Alana L. .... Chicago, IL
Helverson, Sandra .... Atlantic City, NJ
Northfield, NJ
Helvestine, William A. .... San Francisco, CA
Helveston, Fredrick W. .... San Antonio, TX
Helveston, James C. .... West Point, MS
Helveston, Mary Anne M., & Associates
Detroit, MI
Helveston, Ronald R. .... Detroit, MI
Helvey, Frank W., Jr. .... Charleston, WV
Helvey, Jeffrey T. .... Washington, DC
Helvey, Larry D. .... Cedar Rapids, IA
Helvey, Mary A. .... Palo Alto, CA
Helvey, Sandra .... Edmond, OK
Helvie, Kirk R. .... Boise, ID
Helvie, Scott P. .... Lincoln, NE
Helvie, Todd G. .... Purchase, NY
Helvin, Stephen H. .... Charlottesville, VA
Helvy, J. Paul .... Harrisburg, PA
Helweg, Joseph E., III .... Charlotte, NC
Helweg, Sally G. .... Charlotte, NC
Helweil, Mark S. .... Hackensack, NJ
New York, NY
Helweil, Robert H. .... Lake Success, NY
Helwick, Christine .... Long Beach, CA
Helwick, Robert C. .... Oakland, CA
Helwick, Timothy J. .... New York, NY
Helwig, Catherine A. .... New York, NY
Helwig, David P. .... Pittsburgh, PA
Helwig, Gilbert J. .... Pittsburgh, PA
Helwig, Griffin .... Jacksonville, FL
Helwig, Griffin, P.A. .... Jacksonville, FL
Helwig, Mark W. .... Sudbury, MA
Helwig, Nancy C. .... Cincinnati, OH
Helwig, Nina Macfadden .... Rockville, MD
Helwig, Norman R. .... Vail, CO
Helwig, Norman R., P.C. .... Vail, CO
Helwig, Patricia .... Jacksonville, FL
Helwig, Peter F. .... Lakeland, FL
Helwig, Robert S. .... New Brunswick, NJ
Helwig, Stephen J. .... Los Angeles, CA
Helwig, Ted S. .... Chicago, IL
Helwig, Todd K. .... Worcester, MA
Hely, Charles J. .... Boston, MA
Hely, James .... Mountainside, NJ
Hely, Joe .... San Antonio, TX
Hely, M. Christine .... Glendale, CA
Helyar, L. Rachel Lerman
Los Angeles, CA
Helyar, Pamela S.
Research Triangle Park, NC
Helyer, Joseph A. .... Great Falls, VA
Helz, Terrance V. .... Houston, TX
Helzberg, Richard .... San Francisco, CA
Helzberg, Richard .... San Rafael, CA
Helzel, Leo B. .... Oakland, CA
Helzer, Richard G. .... Beaverton, OR
Helzlsouer, William J. .... Dravosburg, PA
Hem, Ronald M. .... Aurora, IL
Hemaidan, Jordan J. .... Madison, WI
Hemann, John H. .... San Francisco, CA
Hemann, John L. .... Salem, OR
Hemann, Patricia A. .... Cleveland, OH
Hemar & Associates .... Los Angeles, CA
Santa Monica, CA
Hemar, Peter S. .... Santa Monica, CA
Hemar, Richard P. .... Encino, CA
Hemar & Rousso, LLP .... Encino, CA
Los Angeles, CA
Hemba, Alton W. .... Port St. Lucie, FL
Hembacher, Brian .... Los Angeles, CA
Hemberger, Joseph W. .... Kansas City, KS
Hembree, Charles R. .... Lexington, KY
Hembree, Christopher W.
Washington, DC
Hembree, Deborah Bittl .... Mobile, AL
Hembree, George Dewey, III .... Canton, MS
Jackson, MS
Hembree and Hembree .... Stilwell, OK
Hembree, J. Gregory
North Myrtle Beach, SC
Hembree, Jeffrey Charles .... Houston, TX
Hembree, Jenine Lawlor .... Stilwell, OK
Hembree, Mary K.
Department of Energy, GV
Hembree, Russell L. .... Jefferson City, MO
Hembree, Thomas D. .... Tracy City, TN
Hembree, Todd .... Stilwell, OK
Hembrow, Sarah .... Petaluma, CA
Hemby, Ronald Paul .... Ketchikan, AK
Hemelsoet, Katrien A. .... Pittsburgh, PA
Hemelt, Leo R., II .... Covington, LA
Hemelt, Mary D. .... Bel Air, MD
Hemenway, Andrew M. .... Juneau, AK
Hemenway & Barnes .... Boston, MA
Hemenway, Bonnie L. .... New York, NY
Hemenway, Christina S. .... Bloomington, IL
Hemenway, James K. .... Dayton, OH
Hemenway, John F. .... Boston, MA
Hemenway, S. Craig .... Atlanta, GA
Hemeon, Robert L. .... Laconia, NH
Hemer, Barkus & Clark .... Glendale, CA
Ontario, CA
Hemer, Michael R. .... Austin, TX
Hemer, Ralph S. .... Glendale, CA
Ontario, CA
Hemeryck, Sondra A. .... Chicago, IL
Hemeter, Elizabeth P. .... Baltimore, MD
Hemhauser, Valerie .... Fair Haven, NJ
Heming, Charles E. .... New York, NY
Heming, Martin M. .... Los Angeles, CA
Heming, William B. .... Peoria, IL
Hemingsen, Donald R. .... Stanton, MI
Hemington, Matthew B. .... Palo Alto, CA
Hemingway, Alfred H., Jr. .... New York, NY
Hemingway, Carole C. .... Spokane, WA
Hemingway, Charles W. .... Falls Church, VA
Hemingway, Colleen Elizabeth
Markleeville, CA
Hemingway, D. Scott .... Dallas, TX
Hemingway, Deja Marie .... Costa Mesa, CA
Hemingway, Gary L. .... Spokane, WA
Hemingway, George F. .... Los Angeles, CA
Hemingway, Herman W. .... Boston, MA
Hemingway, Jon F. .... Seattle, WA
Hemingway Law Office .... Webster City, IA
Hemingway, Richard B., Jr. .... Houston, TX
Hemingway, Ronald L. .... Cincinnati, OH
Hemingway, Tim D. .... Macon, GA
Hemingway, Whitley M. .... Webster City, IA
Hemingway, W. W. .... Macon, GA
Heminway, Joan M. .... Boston, MA
Hemke, Donald E. .... Tampa, FL
Hemker, F. Roger .... St. Louis, MO
Hemker, Joseph B. .... Kalamazoo, MI
Hemleben, Scott P. .... Jackson, MS
Hemley, Brandon K. .... San Francisco, CA
Hemley, M. Rogue .... Incline Village, NV
Hemley, Robert B. .... Burlington, VT
Hemm, John E. .... Piqua, OH
Hemm, Michael W. .... Troy, OH
Hemmann, Denise Fears .... Jackson, GA
Hemmann & Hemmann, P.C. .... Jackson, GA
Hemmann, Paul E. .... Jackson, GA
Hemmat, Chad P. .... Littleton, CO
Hemmat, Steven A. .... Seattle, WA
Hemmat, Steven A., P.S., The Law Office of
Seattle, WA
Hemme, Cynthia C.
Research Triangle Park, NC
Hemme, Jerry D. .... La Jolla, CA
Hemmeline, Barbara J. .... Lubbock, TX
Hemmen, Mary Ellen .... Seattle, WA
Hemmendinger, Eric .... Baltimore, MD
Hemmendinger, Lisa M. .... Washington, DC
Hemmendinger, Noel .... Washington, DC
Hemmendinger, Thomas S.
Providence, RI
Hemmer, Bernard C., Jr. .... Houston, TX
Hemmer, Camille H. .... Sacramento, CA
Hemmer, Donald M. .... Fort Mitchell, KY
Hemmer, J. Michael .... Washington, DC
Hemmer, James A. .... Milwaukee, WI
Hemmer, James P. .... Chicago, IL
Hemmer, John K. .... Indio, CA
Hemmer, Lisa
Department Of The Interior, GV
Hemmer, Paul C. .... Sheboygan, WI
Hemmer, Paul K. .... Columbus, OH
Hemmer, Spoor, Pangburn, DeFrank & Kasson, P.L.L.C. .... Fort Mitchell, KY
Cincinnati, OH
Hemmerle, Denis L. .... Mill Valley, CA
Hemmerle, Mark David .... Amelia, OH
Hemmerle, Steven P. .... Denver, CO
Hemmerling, Barry L. .... Gibbon, NE
Lincoln, NE
Hemmerling, Geraldine S.
Los Angeles, CA
Hemmersbaugh, Paul A. .... Washington, DC
Hemmert, William F. .... Dayton, OH
Hemmesch, Donald F., Jr. .... Chicago, IL
Hemmett, Gordon M., Jr. .... Fort Edward, NY
Hemmi, John U. .... San Antonio, TX
Hemming, C. Gerald .... Plymouth, MI
Hemming, Joseph H. .... Farmington Hills, MI
Hemming, Michael J. .... Diamond Bar, CA
Hemming, Polaczyk and Cronin, P.C.
Plymouth, MI
Hemming, Richard E. .... Janesville, WI
Hemming, Seth M. .... Chicago, IL
Hemming, Tony O. .... Burbank, CA
Hemminger, David G. .... Cincinnati, OH
Hemminger, Gary H. .... Glendale, CO
Hemminger, Pamela Lynn
Los Angeles, CA
Hemminger, Steven D. .... San Jose, CA
Hemmings, John B. .... Abingdon, VA
Hemmings, Richard A. .... Chicago, IL
Hemmingson, Mark L. .... Le Mars, IA
Hemmingway, Leroy H. .... Portland, OR
Hemnes, Thomas M. S. .... Boston, MA
Hemond, David L. .... Hartford, CT
Hemond, Kerry F. .... Washington, DC
Hempe, A. Henry .... Madison, WI
Hempel, Alan G. .... Bedminster, NJ
Hempel, Helen B. .... Eugene, OR
Hempel, Jasper E. .... Sacramento, CA
Hempel, Paul T. .... Wellesley, MA
Hempel, William J.
Marine On St. Croix, MN
Hempelman, B. Eric .... Fallston, MD
Hempelmann, John W. .... Seattle, WA
Hempen, Rita G. .... Fayetteville, AR
Hempey, Daniel G. .... San Bruno, CA
Hempfling, Richard .... Dayton, OH
Hemphill, Angel L. .... Lebanon, MO
Hemphill, Carrie M. .... Los Angeles, CA
Hemphill, Charles W. .... Denver, CO
Hemphill, Christopher D. .... Columbus, MS
Hemphill, Cynthia B. .... Fairfax, VA
Hemphill, Dallett .... West Chester, PA
Hemphill, Deborah Wiemers .... Houston, TX
Hemphill, D. L. .... Brownsville, TX
Hemphill, Donald J. .... Spencer, IA
Hemphill, Dwaine Reynolds .... Canton, OH
Hemphill, Elizabeth A. .... San Jose, CA
Hemphill, Emily P. .... Palm Springs, CA
Hemphill, Gary A. .... New Orleans, LA
Hemphill & Gavenus .... Newland, NC
Hemphill, Geoffrey G. .... Norfolk, VA
Hemphill, Harry G. .... Midwest City, OK
Hemphill, Heath A. .... Abilene, TX
Hemphill & Hemphill .... Brownsville, TX
Hemphill, Hemphill & Coleman, P.A.
Chester, SC
Hemphill, Holly K. .... Washington, DC
Hemphill, James A. .... Austin, TX
Hemphill, Jan E. .... Dallas, TX
Hemphill, Jean C. .... Philadelphia, PA
Hemphill, Jill M. .... Minneapolis, MN
Hemphill, John B. .... San Angelo, TX
Hemphill, John C. .... Columbus, OH
Hemphill, Joi E. .... Wooster, OH
Hemphill, Kathryn G. .... Newland, NC
Hemphill, Kenneth T. .... Montgomery, AL
Hemphill Law Office .... Spencer, IA
Hemphill, Linda G. .... Santa Fe, NM
Hemphill, M. Scott .... Allentown, PA
Hemphill, Meredith, Jr. .... Bethlehem, PA
Hemphill, Michael M.K. .... Seattle, WA
Hemphill, Patricia .... Des Moines, IA
Hemphill, Paul .... Brownsville, TX
Hemphill, R. Craig, & Associates
Jacksonville, FL
Hemphill, Richard A. .... Bellefontaine, OH
Hemphill, Robert D. .... Dallas, TX
Hemphill, Robert N. .... Winter Park, FL
Hemphill, Robert W., Jr. .... Columbia, SC
Hemphill, Ross H. .... Dallas, TX
Hemphill, Roy R. .... Greenwood, SC
Hemphill, S. Todd .... Raleigh, NC
Hemphill, Stephen R. .... Monett, MO
Hemphill, Stephen R., P.C. .... Monett, MO
Hemphill, Stuart R. .... Minneapolis, MN
Hemphill, William B. .... Philadelphia, PA
Hemphill, William R., Jr. .... Austin, TX
Hempill, John R. .... New York, NY
Hempstead, David M. .... Detroit, MI
Hempstead, George H., III .... Red Bank, NJ
Hempstead, Gerard F. .... St. Louis, MO
Hempstead, Keith D. .... Durham, NC
Hempstead, Robert B. .... Hartford, CT
Hempstead, Robert R. .... Newark, NJ
Hempstead, Walter East .... Lady Lake, FL
Hemr, Kurt Wm. .... Boston, MA
Manchester, NH
Hemric, Gary S. .... Charlotte, NC
Hemric, H. Clay, Jr. .... Burlington, NC
Hemric, Lambeth Champion & Moseley, P.A.
Burlington, NC
Hemric, Nancy G. .... Burlington, NC
Hemrich, Veronica E. .... Washington, DC
Hemrick, John J. .... West Monroe, LA
Hemry, Gene H. .... Oklahoma City, OK
Hemry, Hemry & McDoniel, P.C., The Law Offices of .... Oklahoma City, OK
Hemry, Jerome E. .... Oklahoma City, OK
Hemry, Jerry L. .... Oklahoma City, OK
Hemry, Kenneth M. .... Oklahoma City, OK
Hemry, Tom A. .... Denver, CO
Hemsath, H. Evans, Jr. .... Westfield, NJ
Hemschoot, Andrea M. .... Atlantic City, NJ
Hemschoot, Paul J., Jr. .... Englewood, CO
Hemschot, Ernest, III .... Paterson, NJ
Hemsell, Lindsey .... Louisville, KY
Hemsing, Joseph F. .... Sheboygan, WI
Hemsley, Alexander, III .... Westfield, NJ
Hemsley, Bonnie J. .... Laurel, MS
Hemsley, Michael C. .... Newtown Square, PA
Hemsley, Sidney D. .... Knoxville, TN
Hemstad, Peter N. .... International Falls, MN
Hemstad, Richard W. .... Olympia, WA
Hemstad, Ronald B. .... Minneapolis, MN
Hemstreet, Albert E., Jr. .... Angelica, NY
Hemstreet, Harold W., III .... Houston, TX
Hemstreet, James A. .... Easton, PA
Hemstreet, Nitchkey & Freidl .... Easton, PA
Hemsworth, Caryn .... New York, NY
Henager, Douglas W. .... Waco, TX
Henak, Robert R. .... Milwaukee, WI
Henard, Branch H., III .... Nashville, TN
Henatsch, Harry R. .... Omaha, NE
Henatsch, R. Joseph .... Omaha, NE
Henault, Emile J., Jr. .... Glen Burnie, MD
Henault, Martial E. .... Medford, OR
Henault & Sysko, Chartered
Glen Burnie, MD
Hench, Allen E. .... Newport, PA
Hench, Virginia Ellen .... Philadelphia, PA
Henchel, Gregory J. .... Dublin, OH

Henchey, Terence M. ....Brooklyn, NY
Henchy, John L. ....Baton Rouge, LA
Henchy, William C. ....Barnstable, MA
Orleans, MA
Henchy, William C., P.C. ....Barnstable, MA
Orleans, MA
Henck, Charles S. ....Washington, DC
Henck, John C. ....Cleveland, OH
Henck, Jonathan K. ....Chesterfield, MO
Henckel, Mark S. ....Baltimore, MD
Hencken, Robert L. ....Kalamazoo, MI
Hendee, Brett, P.A. ....Tampa, FL
Hendee, Brett T. ....Tampa, FL
Hendee, Kirby ....Madison, WI
Hendel, Caroline Grace ....New Haven, CT
Hendel & Collins, P.C. ....Springfield, MA
Hendel, David P. ....Washington, DC
Vienna, VA
Hendel, Donald S. ....New Haven, CT
Hendel, Douglas R. ....Mercer Island, WA
Hendel, Maurice W. ....Lincoln, RI
Hendel, Myron H. ....Waterford, CT
Hendel, Philip J. ....Springfield, MA
Hendel, Seymour L. ....New London, CT
Hendel, Sharon S. ....Perrysburg, OH
Hendel, Stephen ....New York, NY
Hendel, Stuart J. ....New York, NY
Hendel, Toni L. ....Costa Mesa, CA
Hendeles, Moise Edward ....Los Angeles, CA
Hender, Danielle M. ....Malden, MA
Hender, George S. ....Chicago, IL
Hender, Peter E. ....Elkins Park, PA
Henderer, Peter Lawshe ....Richmond, VA
Henderer, Thomas D. ....Wilmington, DE
Henderickson, Jack R., Jr. ....Ann Arbor, MI
Henderlong, Karla D. ....Dublin, CA
Henderman, Keith B. ....Irvine, CA
Hendershot, Elizabeth L. ....Columbus, OH
Hendershot, Karen A. ....Round Rock, TX
Hendershot, Margaret A ....Chesterland, OH
Hendershot, Neil ....Harrisburg, PA
Hendershot, Randy M. ....Auburn, KS
Hendershot, Robert N., II
Edwardsville, IL
St. Louis, MO
Hendershot, Rodger K. ....Indianapolis, IN
Hendershot, Simon (Trey) W., III
Houston, TX
Hendershot, Thomas R. ....Washington, DC
Greenbelt, MD
Hendershott, Gregory A. ....Seattle, WA
Hendershott, Herman P. ....Eugene, OR
Hendershott, Howard E., Jr.
Pepper Pike, OH
Hendershott, James A. ....Eugene, OR
Hendershott, Kurt T. ....Alameda, CA
Hendershott, Mark ....Sutherlin, OR
Hendershott, Patrick David ....Toledo, OH
Henderson, A. Faxon, Jr. ....Palm Beach, FL
Henderson, A. A. (Trey) ....Houston, TX
Henderson, A. D. ....Palestine, TX
Henderson, Alan D. ....Jacksonville, FL
Henderson, Alexander, III ....Lancaster, PA
Henderson, Alexander P. ....Stoughton, MA
Henderson, Alexander T. ....Los Angeles, CA
Henderson, Alicia Blumer ....Lincoln, NE
Henderson, Allen N. ....Salt Lake City, UT
Henderson, Alma C. ....Washington, DC
Henderson, Amy Bokinsky ....Boston, MA
Henderson, Amy Catherine ....Washington, DC
Henderson, Andrew M. ....Sacramento, CA
Henderson, Andrew R. ....Los Angeles, CA
Henderson, Ann Marie ....Staten Island, NY
Henderson, Ann W. ....Groton, CT
Henderson, Arnold R., V ....Richmond, VA
Henderson, Artie G. ....San Diego, CA
Henderson, B. Thomas ....Austin, TX
Henderson, Barbara A. ....Tacoma, WA
Henderson, Barbara L. ....Milwaukee, WI
Henderson, Baxter, Alford & Taylor, P.A.
New Bern, NC
Henderson, Ben ....Dallas, TX
Henderson, Bessie C.
Department of Housing and Urban Development,
Office of General Counsel, GV
Henderson, Bjarne R. ....Chesterton, IN
Henderson, Blair M. ....Klamath Falls, OR
Henderson & Borgeson ....Santa Barbara, CA
Henderson, Boyd A. ....Grand Rapids, MI
Henderson, Brandt & Vieth
Spartanburg, SC
Henderson & Brennan ....Bronx, NY
Carmel, NY
New City, NY
New York, NY
White Plains, NY
Henderson, Brian C. ....White Plains, NY
Henderson, Brian C. ......Oklahoma City, OK
Henderson, Brian D. ....Washington, DC
Henderson, Brian J. ....Milwaukee, WI
Henderson, Brice B. ....Washington, DC
Henderson & Bromley ....Eugene, OR
Henderson, Bruce ....Monmouth, OR
Henderson, Bruce E. ....Plano, TX
Henderson, Bruce H. ....Tuscaloosa, AL
Henderson, B. T., II ....Raleigh, NC
Henderson & Butler ....Huntsville, AL
Henderson, C. David ....Monroe City, MO
Henderson, C. Earl ....Tallahassee, FL
Henderson, C. Keith ....Manasquan, NJ
Henderson, C. Keith, & Associates, P.C.
Manasquan, NJ
Henderson, Carl R. ....The Woodlands, TX
Henderson, Carol ....Fort Lauderdale, FL
Henderson, Carol M. ....Trenton, NJ
Henderson, Casey J. ....Indianapolis, IN
Henderson, Catherine G. ....Houston, TX

Henderson, Catherine L. ....New York, NY
Henderson, Chad ....Houston, TX
Henderson, Charles E. ....East Lansing, MI
Henderson, Charles Gerald ....Lithonia, GA
Henderson, Charles I. ....Milwaukee, WI
Henderson, Charles J. ....Charlotte, NC
Henderson, Charles P. ....Denver, CO
Henderson, Cheryl L. ....Huntington, WV
Henderson, Christal D. ....Cincinnati, OH
Henderson, Christopher J.
Costa Mesa, CA
Henderson, Clay ....New Smyrna Beach, FL
Henderson, Clinton J. ....Clarkston, WA
Henderson, Covington, Messenger, Newman & Thomas Co., L.P.A. .....Youngstown, OH
Wexford, PA
Henderson, Craig D. ....Corpus Christi, TX
Henderson, Craig Lee ....San Jose, CA
Henderson, Craig P. ....Sterling, CO
Henderson, Craig P. ....Dallas, TX
Henderson, Curt B. ....McKinney, TX
Henderson, Cynthia A. VanWart ....Tampa, FL
Henderson Daily Withrow & DeVoe
Indianapolis, IN
Henderson, Dan S. ....Spartanburg, SC
Henderson, Dana A. ....New Orleans, LA
Henderson, Daniel E. ....Hampton, SC
Ridgeland, SC
Henderson, Daniel E., III
Santa Barbara, CA
Henderson, Daniel E., Jr. .....Santa Barbara, CA
Henderson, Daniel M. ....Norwood, MA
Henderson, Danny D. ....Huntsville, AL
Henderson Dantone, P.A. ....Greenville, MS
Henderson, Darryl K. ....Washington, DC
Henderson, David ....Chico, CA
Henderson, David ....New Castle, PA
Henderson, David A. ....Covington, GA
Henderson, David B. ....Cleveland, OH
Henderson, David C. ....Boston, MA
Henderson, David D. ....Lakeland, FL
Henderson, David D., P.A. ....Lakeland, FL
Henderson, David E. ....Baton Rouge, LA
Henderson, David E. ....Steubenville, OH
Henderson, David H. ....Charlotte, NC
Henderson, David L. ....Charlotte, NC
Henderson, David S. ....New Bern, NC
Henderson, David T. ....Toledo, OH
Henderson, Dawnald R. ....Old Chatham, NY
Henderson & de Bie ....Sacramento, CA
Henderson and de Courcy, P.C.
Tazewell, VA
Henderson, Deirdre R. ....New York, NY
Henderson, Dennis J. ....New York, NY
Henderson, Dennis M. ....Baltimore, MD
Henderson, Diane Haden ....Winfield, AL
Henderson, Don B. ....The Woodlands, TX
Henderson, Donald B., Jr. ....New York, NY
Henderson, Donald F. ....Hyannis, MA
Henderson, Donald F., P.C. ....Hyannis, MA
Henderson, Donald G. ....Bedford, IN
Henderson, Donald O.
Lookout Mountain, TN
Henderson, Donald R. ....Orlando, FL
Henderson, Donald W. ....Carle Place, NY
Henderson, Donna R. ....Waukegan, IL
Henderson, Dorlee ....Houston, TX
Henderson, Douglas A. ....Atlanta, GA
Henderson, Douglas B. ....Washington, DC
Henderson, E. Randall, Jr. ....Nashville, TN
Henderson, Edward C., Jr. ....Atlanta, GA
Henderson, Edward J. ....New York, NY
Henderson, Edward L. ....Ruston, LA
Henderson, Eleanor D. ....Atlanta, GA
Henderson, Elizabeth Ann ....Bakersfield, CA
Henderson, Ellen Elizabeth
Birmingham, AL
Henderson, Erskine D. ....New York, NY
Henderson, Eugene H. ....Sacramento, CA
Henderson, Eugene L. ....Indianapolis, IN
Henderson, E. W. ....Amarillo, TX
Henderson, F. Daniel ....Keene, NH
Henderson, Felicia A. ....New York, NY
Henderson, Forrest E. ....Carmel, CA
Henderson, Frances ....United States Senate,
Senatorial Assistants, GV
Henderson, Frances J. ....Washington, DC
Henderson, Frances P. ....Watsonville, CA
Henderson, Frank E. ....Pierre, SD
Henderson, Frank W. ....Tyler, TX
Henderson, Franklin, Starnes & Holt, Professional Association ....Fort Myers, FL
Naples, FL
Henderson, Frederick A. ....Ladysmith, WI
Henderson, Fredk. G., Jr. ....Greensboro, NC
Henderson, Gary D. ....Houston, TX
Henderson, George B., II ....Boston, MA
Henderson, George E. .....Department of Justice,
Community Relations Service, GV
Henderson, George E. ....Austin, TX
Henderson, George S. ....Long Beach, CA
Henderson, Gerald O., Jr.
Huntington, WV
Henderson, Gilbert N. ....Dayton, OH
Henderson, Glenn C. ....Davie, FL
Henderson, Gordon D., (P.C.)
New York, NY
Henderson, H. Robert ....Davenport, IA
Des Moines, IA
Omaha, NE
Henderson, Hal R. ....Arcadia, LA
Henderson & Hammon, L.L.P.
Houston, TX
Henderson, Hanemann & Morris, A Professional Law Corporation
Houma, LA
Henderson, Harold ....Washington, DC
Henderson, Harold L. ....Kingsport, TN

Henderson, Harold W. ....Cleveland, OH
Henderson, Harpster & Vanosdall
Ashland, OH
Henderson, Harvey ....Sumner, MS
Henderson, Harvey E., Jr. ....Honolulu, HI
Henderson, Harvey, P.A. ....Sumner, MS
Henderson, Heather M.
Environmental Protection Agency,
Program Office Attorneys, GV
Henderson & Henderson ....Chico, CA
Henderson & Henderson ....Pembroke, GA
Richmond Hill, GA
Henderson & Henderson ....Waukegan, IL
Henderson & Henderson ....Bedford, IN
Henderson, Henry L. ....Chicago, IL
Henderson, Herbert H. ....Huntington, WV
Henderson, Herbert P., II ....Lancaster, PA
Henderson, Howard R. ....Pell City, AL
Henderson, Hugh C. ....Birmingham, AL
Henderson, Hunt ....LeRoy, IL
Henderson, Ian Y. ....Louisville, KY
Henderson, Isaac E. ....Houston, TX
Henderson, J. Bruce ....Carefree, AZ
Henderson, J. Christopher ....Columbia, SC
Henderson, J. Collinsworth
Citrus Heights, CA
Henderson, J. Curtis ....Dallas, TX
Henderson, J. Harrison, III
New Orleans, LA
Henderson, J. John ....Waukegan, IL
Henderson, J. Randle ....Houston, TX
Henderson, J. Welles ....Philadelphia, PA
Henderson, Jack D. ....Denver, CO
Henderson, James A. ....Chicago, IL
Henderson, James A., Jr. ....Ithaca, NY
Henderson, James Andrew ....Denver, CO
Henderson, James B. ....Wilmette, IL
Henderson, James C. ....Miami, FL
Henderson, James C. ....Batavia, OH
Henderson, James Corley ....Sherman, TX
Henderson, James D. ....Los Angeles, CA
Henderson, James D. ....Boston, MA
Henderson, James D. ....Chattanooga, TN
Henderson, James D., Jr.
Los Angeles, CA
Henderson, James F. ....Phoenix, AZ
Henderson, James G. ....Birmingham, AL
Henderson, James H. ....Charlotte, NC
Henderson, James H., P.C. ....Charlotte, NC
Henderson, James L., III
Washington, DC
Atlanta, GA
Henderson, James M., II ....Princeton, WV
Henderson, James Matthew, Sr.
Washington, DC
Henderson, James R., IV ....Tazewell, VA
Henderson, James S. ....Newport Beach, CA
Henderson, James W., Jr.
Sacramento, CA
Henderson, Janet E. ....Chicago, IL
Henderson, Janice K. ....Carmel, IN
Henderson, Janice M. ....Sacramento, CA
Henderson, Jay H. ....Houston, TX
Henderson, Jeffrey S. ....Philadelphia, PA
Henderson, Jeffry M. ....Chicago, IL
Henderson, Jennifer J. ....Hillsdale, MI
Henderson, Jennifer L. ....Columbus, OH
Henderson, Jennifer R. ....Houston, TX
Henderson, Jill Lynn ....Danville, CA
Henderson, Joan B. ....Jeffersonville, IN
Henderson, Joann P. ....Moscow, ID
Henderson, Joe B., Jr. ....Huntsville, TX
Henderson, Joe H. ....Santa Rosa, CA
Henderson, Joel J. ....Greenville, MS
Henderson, John B., Jr. ....Cameron, TX
Henderson, John E. ....Cambridge, OH
Henderson, John F. ....New Castle, PA
Henderson, John G.
Export-Import Bank of The United States,
Office of the General Counsel, GV
Henderson, John H. ....Henderson, KY
Lexington, KY
Henderson, John H., Jr. ....Franklin, TN
Henderson, John K. ....Denver, CO
Henderson, John K., Jr. ....Wichita, KS
Henderson, John L. ....Eugene, OR
Henderson, John M., Jr. ....Springfield, MO
Henderson, John N. ....Stigler, OK
Henderson, John P. ....Auburn, CA
Henderson, John R. ....Boulder, CO
Henderson, John R. ....Chicago, IL
Henderson, John R., (P.C.) ....Dallas, TX
Henderson, John T., Jr. ....Harrisburg, PA
Henderson, John Thomas, Jr. ....Landover, MD
Henderson, John W. ....Springfield, OH
Henderson, John W., Jr. ....Austin, TX
Henderson, Jonathan K. ....Fort Worth, TX
Henderson, Joseph F. ....Minneapolis, MN
Henderson, Joseph R. ....Ventura, CA
Henderson, Joshua M. ....San Francisco, CA
Henderson, J. P. ....Elyria, OH
Henderson, Julie A. ....San Bruno, CA
Henderson, Justin L. ....West Union, WV
Henderson, Karen LeCraft
United States Court Of Appeals District Of
Columbia Circuit, GV
Henderson, Karla J. ....Cedar Rapids, IA
Henderson Keasler Law Firm
Jacksonville, FL
Henderson, Keith L. ....Palo Alto, CA
Topeka, KS
Henderson, Kelly ....Miami, FL
Henderson, Kenneth D. ....Bradenton, FL
Henderson, Kenneth D. ....Harrisburg, PA
Henderson, Kenneth D. ....Memphis, TN
Henderson, Kenneth L. ....New York, NY
Henderson, Kenny W. ....Little Rock, AR
Henderson, Keno M., Jr. ....Houston, TX

Henderson, Kevin J. ....Birmingham, AL
Henderson, Kevin L. ....Los Angeles, CA
Henderson, Kimberly ....Chico, CA
Henderson, Kimberly A. ....Troy, MI
Henderson, Kirk J. ....Pittsburgh, PA
Henderson, Kristin A. ....Seattle, WA
Henderson, Kyle W. ....Chicago, IL
Henderson, Larry B. ....Daytona Beach, FL
Henderson, Laure S. ....Los Angeles, CA
Henderson, Laurens L., Jr. ....Mesa, AZ
Henderson Law Office ....Bend, OR
Henderson, Lawrence ....Jersey City, NJ
Henderson, Lee A. ....Minneapolis, MN
Henderson, Lee W. ....Newport Beach, CA
Henderson, Leon, Jr. ....Rocky Mount, NC
Henderson, Leroy, Jr. ....Booneville, MS
Henderson, Lester D. ....Sapulpa, OK
Henderson, Lester D., P.C. ....Sapulpa, OK
Henderson & Levihn ....Milwaukee, WI
Henderson, Lewis E. ....Houston, TX
Henderson, Lewis M. ....Columbia, SC
Henderson & Lipscomb, P.A. ....Duluth, GA
Henderson, Lisa K.
Securities and Exchange Commission, GV
Henderson, Lloyd ....Atlantic City, NJ
Henderson, Loretta J. ....Cincinnati, OH
Henderson, Louis G. ....Cleveland, OH
Henderson & Lyman ....Chicago, IL
Henderson, Lynn Garrett ....New York, NY
Henderson, Lynne N. ....Palo Alto, CA
Bloomington, IN
Henderson, M. Elizabeth ....Lexington, KY
Henderson, M. Suellen ....Atlanta, GA
Henderson, Maire M. ....Santa Barbara, CA
Henderson, Malcolm G. ....Boston, MA
Henderson, Marion K. ....Buffalo, NY
Henderson, Mark Ellis ....Fayetteville, NC
Henderson, Mark G. ....Davis, CA
Henderson, Mark H. ....Stamford, CT
Henderson, Mark J. ....Long Beach, CA
Henderson, Mark M. ....Woodland Hills, CA
Henderson, Martha D. ....Mission Hills, CA
Henderson, Mary Jane Nettles
New Smyrna Beach, FL
Henderson, Mary T. ....Augusta, ME
Henderson, Matthew A. ....Spartanburg, SC
Henderson, Matthew J. ....Newark, NJ
Henderson, Matthew R. ....Chicago, IL
Henderson, Melodie W. ....St. Louis, MO
Henderson, Michael A. ....Sioux Falls, SD
Henderson, Michael E. ....Birmingham, AL
Henderson, Michael E. ....Ellicott City, MD
Henderson, Michael J. ....Oakland, CA
Henderson, Michael S. ....Costa Mesa, CA
Henderson, Michele ....Richmond Hill, GA
Henderson, Milton E. ....Nashville, TN
Henderson, Molatore & Klein
Klamath Falls, OR
Henderson, Monica Elaine ....Louisville, KY
Henderson & Morgan, LLC ....Reno, NV
Henderson, Nancy G.
Rancho Santa Fe, CA
Henderson, Nick A. ....Washington, DC
Henderson, Nina E. ....San Antonio, TX
Henderson, Nolan B. ....Glendale, CA
Henderson, Norma E. ....Boston, MA
Henderson, Oliver E. ....Seattle, WA
Henderson, Pamela Cole ....Atlanta, GA
Henderson, Patrick E. ....Atchison, KS
Henderson, Patrick J. ......Overland Park, KS
Henderson, Paul B. ....Jackson, MS
Henderson, Paul D. ....Orange, TX
Henderson, Paul F., III ....Somerset, KY
Henderson, Paul F., Jr. ....Richmond, KY
Henderson, Paul T. ....Pittsburgh, PA
Henderson, Paula M. ....Oklahoma City, OK
Henderson, Penny Rose ....Bellingham, WA
Henderson, Peter B. ....Clinton Township, MI
Henderson, Peter S. ....Indianapolis, IN
Henderson, Philip C. ....Washington, DC
Henderson, Philip E. ....Houma, LA
Henderson, Philip G. ....Bend, OR
Henderson, Philip J. ....San Mateo, CA
Henderson, Quentin, Jr. ....Duluth, GA
Henderson, R. David ....Raleigh, NC
Henderson, R. Michael ....Peoria, IL
Henderson, R. Scott ....Boston, MA
Henderson, Ralph A. ....Hamilton, OH
Henderson, Randall S. ....Pasadena, CA
Henderson, Rebecca L. ....Palm Beach, FL
Henderson, Rebecca S. ....Charlotte, NC
Henderson, Reese J., Jr. ....Jacksonville, FL
Henderson, Regina Anita
St. Petersburg, FL
Henderson, Reginald ....San Jose, CA
Henderson, Reginald R. ....Memphis, TN
Henderson, Richard ....Fargo, ND
Henderson, Richard A. ....Fort Worth, TX
Henderson, Richard A., Law Offices of
Cohasset, MA
Henderson, Richard A., P.C.
Fort Worth, TX
Henderson, Richard C. ....Fresno, CA
Los Angeles, CA
Henderson, Richard E.L. ....Pittsburgh, PA
Henderson, Richard J. ....Ukiah, CA
Henderson, Robert A. ....Kansas City, MO
Henderson, Robert E. ....Charlotte, NC
Henderson, Robert E. ....Ashland, OH
Henderson, Robert F. ....Walnut Creek, CA
Henderson, Robert F. ....Dallas, TX
Henderson, Robert H. ....Salt Lake City, UT
Henderson, Robert J. ....Port Huron, MI
Henderson, Robert J. ....Pittsburgh, PA
Henderson, Robert K. ....Klamath Falls, OR
Henderson, Robert L., Jr. ....Slidell, LA
Henderson, Robert M.
South Lake Tahoe, CA

Henderson, Robert P. ...Fort Myers, FL
Henderson, Robert W. ...Dallas, TX
Henderson, Robin A. ...Department of Energy, Office of the General Counsel, GV
Henderson & Robinson, P.A.
Palm Beach, FL
Henderson, Robt. E. ...Daphne, AL
Henderson, Roger C. ...Tucson, AZ
Henderson, Roger E. ...Anchorage, AK
Henderson, Roger Edward ...Chesterfield, SC
Pageland, SC
Henderson, Ronald A. ...Fresno, CA
Henderson, Ronald D. ...Amherst, VA
Henderson, Ronald R. ...Toledo, OH
Henderson, Ronald S. ...Batesville, IN
Henderson, Roy J. ...Austin, TX
Henderson, Russell V. ...Houston, TX
Henderson, Ryan M. ...Chicago, IL
Henderson, S. Scott ...Denver, CO
Henderson, Sally Ann ...Muncie, IN
Henderson, Samuel Judson, III
St. Petersburg, FL
Tampa, FL
Henderson, Samuel R. ...Wichita, KS
Henderson, Samuel S. ...Melbourne, FL
Henderson, Sandra L. ...Minneapolis, MN
Henderson, Scott C. ...Seattle, WA
Henderson, Scott E. ...Pittsburgh, PA
Henderson, Scott K. ...Phoenix, AZ
Henderson, Sharon Ann ...Alexandria, VA
Henderson, Sharon Roberts
Jacksonville, FL
Henderson, Sherwood C. ...Kinston, NC
Henderson, Sonya W. ...Murfreesboro, TN
Henderson, Stanley D. ...Charlottesville, VA
Henderson, Stephanie R. ...Baltimore, MD
Henderson, Stephen Hunt ...LeRoy, IL
Henderson, Stephen J. ...Olympia, WA
Henderson, Stephen J. ...Seattle, WA
Henderson, Stephen P. ...Cincinnati, OH
Henderson, Steve L. ...Vero Beach, FL
Henderson, Steven Scott ...Lakewood, CO
Henderson, Stuart C. ...Albany, NY
Henderson & Sturm ...Washington, DC
Davenport, IA
Des Moines, IA
Omaha, NE
Henderson, Susan ...Dallas, TX
Henderson, Susan A. ...Niles, IL
Henderson, Susan E. F. ...Bluefield, WV
Henderson, Susan Elizabeth ...Atlanta, GA
Henderson, Susan M. ...Department of Justice, Environment and Natural Resources Division, GV
Henderson, Susan Moebius
Oklahoma City, OK
Henderson, Susan Susel ...Cleveland, OH
Henderson, Suzanne M. ...Los Angeles, CA
Henderson, T. Gerald ...Alexandria, LA
Henderson, Tanya D. ...Dallas, TX
Henderson, Terrance F. ...Dallas, TX
Henderson, Terrill L. ...Seattle, WA
Henderson, Thelton E. ...San Francisco, CA
Henderson, Theodore Martin ...Kearney, NE
Henderson, Thomas ...Des Moines, IA
Henderson, Thomas C. ...Topeka, KS
Henderson, Thomas D. ...Memphis, TN
Henderson, Thomas H., Jr. ...Washington, DC
Henderson, Thomas J. ...Washington, DC
Henderson, Thomas K. ...Hagerstown, MD
Henderson, Thomas L. ...Columbus, OH
Henderson, Thomas L. ...Memphis, TN
Henderson, Thomas M. ...Houston, TX
Henderson, Thomas M., P.C. ...Houston, TX
Henderson, Thomas N., III ...Tampa, FL
Henderson, Thomas S., III ...Houston, TX
Henderson, Thomas W.
Newport Beach, CA
Henderson, Thomas W. ...Englewood, CO
Henderson, Thomas W. ...Pittsburgh, PA
Henderson, Tiffany M., (Mr.)
Glen Cove, NY
Henderson, Timothy J. ...Bellaire, TX
Henderson, Timothy J., (Ltd.) ...Reno, NV
Henderson, Timothy R. ...Annapolis, MD
Henderson, Timothy R. ...Oklahoma City, OK
Henderson, Tracey Leigh ...Jacksonville, FL
Henderson, Troy L., Jr. ...Memphis, TN
Henderson, Vera S. ...San Francisco, CA
Henderson, Victor Edward ...Atlanta, GA
Henderson, Victor P. ...Chicago, IL
Henderson, Vincent C., II ...Little Rock, AR
Henderson, Wade J. ...Washington, DC
Henderson, Wallace J.
House of Representatives, Congressional Assistants, GV
Henderson, Walter L. ...Green Valley, AZ
Tucson, AZ
Henderson, Walter L., P.C.
Green Valley, AZ
Tucson, AZ
Henderson, Walter T., Jr. ...Atlanta, GA
Henderson, Wayne S. ...Boston, MA
Henderson, W. D. ...San Antonio, TX
Henderson, Wetherill, O'Hey & Horsey
Norristown, PA
Henderson, Wiley P. ...Flomaton, AL
Henderson, William C.
Department of Defense, Defense Legal Services Agency, GV
Henderson, William C. ...Winter Park, FL
Henderson, William D. ...Macomb, IL
Henderson, William E., Jr.
Madisonville, KY
Henderson, William F. ...Alexandria, LA
Henderson, William L. ...Atlanta, GA
Henderson, William N. ...Albuquerque, NM
Henderson, William T. ...New York, NY
Henderson, William T. ...Beloit, WI
Henderson, William W. ...Logan, OH
Henderson, William W., Jr. ...Pensacola, FL
Henderson, Winston ...New York, NY
Henderson, Wohlgemuth & Bohl, A Professional Corporation
Los Angeles, CA
San Luis Obispo, CA
Santa Barbara, CA
Ventura, CA
Woodland Hills, CA
Henderson-Lewis, Maria L.
Philadelphia, PA
Henderzahs, Leslie Craig ...Noblesville, IN
Hendez, Ana Maria
Department of Agriculture, Food and Consumer Service, GV
Hendi, Daniel R. ...Trenton, NJ
Hendin, Jonathan ...New York, NY
Hendin, Richard B. ...San Antonio, TX
Hendin, Roy ...Chesterfield, MO
Hendison, Tara M. ...Portland, OR
Hendl, Jamie Sacks ...Washington, DC
Hendler, Clifford B. ...Washington, DC
Hendler, David A. ...North Brunswick, NJ
Hendler, Elizabeth S. ...Boston, MA
Hendler, Jason P. ...Los Angeles, CA
Hendler, Lynne Greenwald ...New York, NY
Hendler, Marcia L. ...North Brunswick, NJ
Hendler, Michael B. ...Akron, OH
Hendler, Michael G. ...Baltimore, MD
Hendler, Pablo Daniel ...New York, NY
Hendler, Richard M. ...New York, NY
Hendler, Robert B. ...North Brunswick, NJ
Hendler, Samuel I. ...Mineola, NY
Hendler, Stanley B. ...New York, NY
Hendley, Darron C. ...Montgomery, AL
Hendley & Datsko, P.C. ...Manchester, MI
Hendley, Gayle C. ...Minneapolis, MN
Hendley, H. John ...Queensbury, NY
Hendley, Kathryn ...Madison, WI
Hendley, William R. ...Santa Fe, NM
Hendlin, Richard D. ...San Diego, CA
Hendlish, Martin A. ...Pasadena, CA
Hendon, Carrie A. ...Vail, CO
Hendon, Elizabeth A. ...Chattanooga, TN
Hendon, E. T., Jr. ...Decatur, GA
Hendon, Ezra ...Oakland, CA
Hendon, George Ward ...Asheville, NC
Hendon, George Ward, Jr. ...Atlanta, GA
Hendon, Jeremy N. ...Portland, OR
Hendon, Lynn F. ...Louisville, KY
Hendon, Mack W. ...Lithonia, GA
Hendon, Robert C., Jr. ...Princeton, NJ
Hendon, Zack ...Atlanta, GA
Hendra, Kenneth R. ...Bay Shore, NY
Hendra, Susan Jayne ...San Francisco, CA
Hendren and Andrae ...Jefferson City, MO
Hendren, Ashley Hutchings
Pascagoula, MS
Hendren, David F. ...Newton, MA
Hendren, David M. ...San Diego, CA
Hendren, Ed W. ...Oroville, CA
Hendren, James R. ...Mount Laurel, NJ
Hendren, Jason B. ...Little Rock, AR
Hendren, Jennifer B. ...Little Rock, AR
Hendren, Jimm Larry ...Fayetteville, AR
Hendren, Larissa Karpovics ...San Diego, CA
Hendren Law Offices ...Oroville, CA
Hendren, Paul C. ...Champaign, IL
Hendren, Robert H. ...Indianapolis, IN
Hendren, Scott A. ...Tulsa, OK
Hendren, Sharon A. ...Moorestown, NJ
Hendren, Suann ...Albuquerque, NM
Hendrian, James A. ...Decatur, IL
Hendrian, William V. ...Sandusky, MI
Hendrich, Robin M. ...Provincetown, MA
Hendrich, Steven L. ...Fort Morgan, CO
Hendrick, Andrew M. ...Virginia Beach, VA
Hendrick, Andy E. ...Myrtle Beach, SC
Hendrick, B. Calvin, VII ...Odessa, TX
Hendrick, Bob ...Montgomery, AL
Hendrick, David R. ...Carmel, CA
Hendrick, David R. ...Atlanta, GA
Hendrick, Frank O., III ...Atlanta, GA
Hendrick, Gerald P. ...Boston, MA
Hendrick & Hendrick ...Montgomery, AL
Hendrick, Howard H. ...Oklahoma City, OK
Hendrick & Hunter, L.L.C. ...Atlanta, GA
Hendrick, James T. ...San Francisco, CA
Hendrick, James T. ...Key West, FL
Hendrick, Jerry, Jr. ...Chesterfield, VA
Hendrick, Jeulia ...Montgomery, AL
Hendrick, Kevin S. ...Detroit, MI
Hendrick, Kirk D. ...Las Vegas, NV
Hendrick Law Firm ...Winston-Salem, NC
Hendrick, Lee W. ...Houston, TX
Hendrick, Max, III ...Houston, TX
Hendrick, Phillips, Schemm & Salzman, A Professional Corporation ...Atlanta, GA
Hendrick, Robert ...Oklahoma City, OK
Hendrick, Roy W. ...Houston, TX
Hendrick, T. Paul ...Winston-Salem, NC
Hendrick, William J. ...East Rockaway, NY
Hendricks, Aime L. ...New York, NY
Hendricks, Allen J. ...Edmonds, WA
Hendricks, Anne E.
Huntingdon Valley, PA
Hendricks, Beatice E. ...Washington, DC
Hendricks, Ben. F. ...Covington, GA
Hendricks, Brad ...Little Rock, AR
Hendricks, Brad Lowber, The Law Offices of ...Little Rock, AR
Hendricks, Bruce H. ...Charleston, SC
Hendricks, Bruce J. ...Merced, CA
Hendricks, Bruce J. ...Akron, OH
Hendricks, Burton B. ...Landisville, PA
Hendricks, Catherine ...Seattle, WA
Hendricks, Charles B. ...Corsicana, TX
Dallas, TX
Hendricks, Christy Lee ...Louisville, KY
Hendricks, Curtis B., Jr.
Oklahoma City, OK
Hendricks, David G. ...Oklahoma City, OK
Hendricks, David P. ...Dallas, TX
Hendricks, David R. ...Coronado, CA
Hendricks, Douglas G. ...Sacramento, CA
Hendricks, Douglas L. ...San Francisco, CA
Hendricks, Duane C. ...Houston, TX
Hendricks, Ed ...Phoenix, AZ
Hendricks, Ed, Jr. ...Phoenix, AZ
Hendricks, Eric K. ...Billings, MT
Hendricks, Frank W. ...Vernon Hills, IL
Hendricks, George F. ...New Brunswick, NJ
Hendricks, Gregory G. ...Phoenix, AZ
Hendricks & Hendricks ...Coral Gables, FL
Hendricks & Hendricks
New Brunswick, NJ
Trenton, NJ
Woodbridge, NJ
Hendricks, Hendricks & Shakes, P.C.
Colorado Springs, CO
Hendricks, Hugh ...Crossville, TN
Hendricks, James F., Jr. ...Chicago, IL
Hendricks, James L. ...Rochester, NY
Hendricks, James P. ...Phoenix, AZ
Hendricks, Jane E. ...Miami, FL
Hendricks, Jean Martin ...San Diego, CA
Hendricks, Jeffrey M. ...Cincinnati, OH
Hendricks, Jennifer S. ...Helena, MT
Hendricks, Joe Wayne, Jr. ...Ellijay, GA
Hendricks, John C. ...Phoenix, AZ
Hendricks, John C. ...Bethesda, MD
Hendricks, John D. ...Pittsburgh, PA
Hendricks, John H. ...Superior, WI
Hendricks, John L. ...Dallas, TX
Hendricks, John Wade ...Louisville, KY
Hendricks, Julie Ann ...Northbrook, IL
Hendricks, Karen ...Albany, NY
Hendricks, Kate Sigman ...Durham, NC
Hendricks, Katherine ...Seattle, WA
Hendricks, Keith L. ...Phoenix, AZ
Hendricks, Knudson, Gee, Hayden, Torvinen & Weiby, S.C. ...Superior, WI
Hendricks, L. Lesesne, Jr. ...Easley, SC
Hendricks, Larry D. ...Topeka, KS
Hendricks, Laura Rule ...Knoxville, TN
Hendricks Law Firm ...Pine River, MN
Hendricks, Leslie Ann ...Jacksonville, FL
Hendricks & Lewis ...Seattle, WA
Hendricks, Lewis S. ...Rockwell City, IA
Hendricks, Lloyd A. ...Lincoln, NE
Hendricks, Lloyd I. ...Columbia, SC
Hendricks, Louis J., Jr. ...Cincinnati, OH
Hendricks, Mark A. ...Fort Lauderdale, FL
Hendricks, Mark Christian ...Glendale, CA
Hendricks, Mark E. ...Albuquerque, NM
Hendricks, Matthew R. ...Edmonds, WA
Hendricks, Matthew S. ...St. Louis, MO
Hendricks, Michael E.
Colorado Springs, CO
Hendricks, Myrrel C., Jr.
Treasury Department, Office of the Comptroller of the Currency, GV
Hendricks, Napoleon, Jr. ...Lithonia, GA
Hendricks, Nathan V., III ...Atlanta, GA
Hendricks, Nicole M. ...Albany, OR
Hendricks, Norman B. ...Piedmont, CA
Hendricks, Peter J. ...New Brunswick, NJ
Hendricks, Phillip F. ...Houston, TX
Hendricks, Randal A. ...Spring, TX
Hendricks, Randall E. ...Kansas City, MO
Hendricks, Rhonda Lynn ...Akron, OH
Hendricks, Richard E. ...Mansfield, OH
Hendricks, Robert A. ...Coral Gables, FL
Hendricks, Robert E. ...Bound Brook, NJ
Hendricks, Robert G. ...East Kingston, NH
Hendricks, Robert J. ...Deerfield Beach, FL
Hendricks, Robert Jon ...Los Angeles, CA
Hendricks, Robert R. ...Beach Haven, NJ
Hendricks, Robt. R. ...McKinney, TX
Hendricks, Sharon ...Menlo Park, CA
Hendricks, Sheila Jo ...Jackson, MS
Waco, TX
Hendricks, Stanley, (P.A.) ...Sarasota, FL
Hendricks, Stephen C. ...Portland, OR
Hendricks, Stephen C., P.C. ...Portland, OR
Hendricks, Steven W. ...Fort Dodge, IA
Hendricks, Stuart F. ...Richardson, TX
Hendricks, Susan L. ...New York, NY
Hendricks, Terence R. ...Costa Mesa, CA
Hendricks, Teresa M. ...Grand Rapids, MI
Hendricks, Terry D.
Colorado Springs, CO
Hendricks, Therese A. ...Boston, MA
Hendricks, Thomas A. ...Somerville, NJ
Hendricks, Thomas A. ...West Chester, PA
Hendricks, Thomas M. ...Atlanta, GA
Hendricks, Todd Allen ...Grand Rapids, MI
Hendricks, Valeria ...Tampa, FL
Hendricks & Wiersma, P.L.C.
Grand Rapids, MI
Hendricks, Wilbert E. ...Pine River, MN
Hendricks, William C., III
Washington, DC
Hendricks, William D. ...Lyons, NY
Sodus, NY
Hendricks, William L., Jr. ...Memphis, TN
Hendricks, William P. ...St. Helena Island, SC
Hendricksen, Mark W. ...Spokane, WA
Hendricksen, Toni Anne ...Trenton, NJ
Hendrickson, Albert C., Jr. ...Dover, NJ
Hendrickson, Brian W. ...Tempe, AZ
Hendrickson, Calvin W.
Oklahoma City, OK
Hendrickson, Carl, Jr. ...Cedar Rapids, IA
Hendrickson, Craig R. ...Lubbock, TX
Hendrickson, C. T. ...Raleigh, NC
Hendrickson, D. John ...Los Angeles, CA
Hendrickson, Dale R. ...Aurora, CO
Hendrickson, Daniel M. ...Bellevue, WA
Hendrickson, David B. ...Keokuk, IA
Hendrickson, David K. ...Charleston, WV
Hendrickson, Debra B. ...Indianapolis, IN
Hendrickson, Donald G. ...Boonville, IN
Hendrickson, Edwin F. ...Melville, NY
Hendrickson, Elizabeth A. ...Oakland, CA
Hendrickson, Eric D. ...Waupaca, WI
Hendrickson, Eric J. ...Sacramento, CA
Hendrickson, Everson, Noennig & Woodward, P.C. ...Billings, MT
Hendrickson & Fuller ...Mesa, AZ
Hendrickson, Gary C. ...Mesa, AZ
Hendrickson, George M. ...Sacramento, CA
Hendrickson, Gregory D. ...San Francisco, CA
Hendrickson, H. Kent ...Harlan, KY
Hendrickson, Holly ...Fort Payne, AL
Hendrickson, J. Waldo ...Boonville, IN
Hendrickson, Jay P. ...San Francisco, CA
Hendrickson, Jerome O. ...Arlington, VA
Hendrickson, John C. ...Chicago, IL
Hendrickson, John L. ...Seattle, WA
Hendrickson, John P. ...Chicago, IL
Hendrickson, John S. ...Wilmington, DE
Hendrickson, John W. ...Anchorage, AK
Fairbanks, AK
Hendrickson, John W., Jr. ...Minneapolis, MN
Hendrickson, Karen M. ...Santa Rosa, CA
Hendrickson, Kathleen D. ...Pittsburgh, PA
Hendrickson, Kathleen M. ...Dunwoody, GA
Hendrickson, Kathryn B. ...Maysville, KY
Hendrickson, Kevin H. ...Fort Pierce, FL
Hendrickson, Kevin H., P.A. ...Fort Pierce, FL
Hendrickson, Konrad ...Springfield, MO
Hendrickson, Lance C. ...Hesperia, MI
Hendrickson, Leslie J. ...Denver, CO
Hendrickson & Long ...Charleston, WV
Hendrickson, Maribeth Brickley
Los Altos Hills, CA
Hendrickson, Mark Hart ...Boonville, IN
Hendrickson, Marla B. ...Santa Ana, CA
Hendrickson, Martin C. ...Boise, ID
Hendrickson, Matthew P. ...New York, NY
Hendrickson, Michael Eric ...Arlington, VA
Hendrickson, Michael O.
Jefferson City, MO
Hendrickson, Michael P. ...Hartford, CT
Hendrickson, Michele F. ...Chicago, IL
Hendrickson, Nancy L. ...Chicago, IL
Hendrickson, Nora Cecile ...Cincinnati, OH
Hendrickson, Patrick S. ...Salt Lake City, UT
Hendrickson, R. David ...Birmingham, AL
Hendrickson, Ray ...Irvine, CA
Hendrickson, Richard E. ...Indianapolis, IN
Hendrickson, Richard L. ...Bloomington, MN
Hendrickson, Rob Ross ...Baltimore, MD
Hendrickson, Robert Allen ...Monroe, OH
Hendrickson, Robert C.
San Francisco, CA
Hendrickson, Robert E. ...Billings, MT
Hendrickson, Robert W., III
Bradenton, FL
Hendrickson, Robt. ...Youngstown, OH
Hendrickson, Ronald A. ...Moorestown, NJ
Hendrickson, Russell L.
Oklahoma City, OK
Hendrickson, Russell R. ...Reno, NV
Hendrickson, Scott A. ...Minneapolis, MN
Hendrickson, Stacey J. ...Renton, WA
Hendrickson, Steven ...Oklahoma City, OK
Hendrickson, Susan E. ...Washington, DC
Hendrickson, Susan M. ...Princeton, NJ
Hendrickson, Tamara J. ...Seattle, WA
Hendrickson, Ted R. ...Portola, CA
Hendrickson, Thomas ...Gaithersburg, MD
Hendrickson, Thomas A. ...Indianapolis, IN
Hendrickson, Todd N. ...St. Louis, MO
Hendrickson, Tracy S. ...Sacramento, CA
Hendrickson, Wm. R. ...Monroe, OH
Hendricks-Richardson, Lisa ...Newark, NJ
Hendrie, Alexander Gibson
San Antonio, TX
Hendrie, Barbara H. ...Fall River, MA
Hendrie, Daniel S. ...Fall River, MA
Hendrie, Donald A., Jr. ...Stamford, CT
Hendrie, Donald F. ...San Antonio, TX
Hendrie & Hendrie ...Fall River, MA
Hendrie, Marie Anne ...South Bend, IN
Hendrie, Richard L., Jr. ...Portland, OR
Salem, OR
Hendriksen, Douglas G.
Kennedy Space Center, FL
Hendriksen, James A. ...Treasury Department, Office of Thrift Supervision, GV
Hendriksen, Margie ...Eugene, OR
Hendrikson, Bradley D. ...Minneapolis, MN
Hendrix, Alan B. ...Denver, CO
Hendrix & Associates, LLP, Attorneys At Law
San Diego, CA
Hendrix, Billy J. ...Miami, FL
Hendrix & Brennan ...Fort Pierce, FL
Melbourne, FL
Vero Beach, FL
Hendrix & Brinich, LLP ...Bend, OR
Hendrix, C. Kennon ...Vero Beach, FL
Trenton, NJ
Hendrix, C. Thomas, Jr. ...Chicago, IL
Hendrix, Carl ...Houston, TX
Hendrix, Charles W. ...Champaign, IL
Hendrix, Cheryl K. ...Phoenix, AZ
Hendrix, Christine Miller ...O'Fallon, MO
Hendrix, Danna D. ...Flagstaff, AZ
Hendrix, Darryl E. ...San Francisco, CA

Hendrix, David M. ....Little Rock, AR
Hendrix, David S. ....Tampa, FL
Hendrix, Dennis E. ....Edinburg, TX
Hendrix, Dina M. ....Hayesville, NC
Murphy, NC
Hendrix, Douglas ....Tuscaloosa, AL
Hendrix, Eric V. ....Stamford, CT
Hendrix, Garnett E., Jr. ....Dallas, TX
Hendrix, Glenn E. ....Minneapolis, MN
Hendrix, Glenn P. ....Atlanta, GA
Hendrix, Greg ....Bend, OR
Hendrix, J. Blake ....Little Rock, AR
Hendrix, J. Roger ....Topeka, KS
Hendrix, Jack ....St. Joseph, MO
Hendrix, Jack H. ....McCook, NE
Hendrix, James L., Jr. ....Zebulon, GA
Hendrix, Jerrell T. ....Richmond Hill, GA
Hendrix, Jill Higgins ....Seattle, WA
Hendrix, Joey W. ....Shreveport, LA
Hendrix, Johanna Gaynelle ....Brooklyn, NY
Hendrix, John W. ....Savannah, GA
Hendrix, Jonathan R. ....Lexington, SC
Hendrix, Joseph A. ....Mission Viejo, CA
Hendrix, Joyce Fackler ....Ottawa, KS
Hendrix, Kelley Ann ....Charlotte, NC
Hendrix, Kimberly A. ....Philadelphia, PA
Hendrix Law Firm, The
Richmond Hill, GA
Savannah, GA
Hendrix Law Offices ....Ottawa, KS
Hendrix, Lynda L. ....Birmingham, AL
Hendrix, Lynn Parker ....Denver, CO
Hendrix, M. Brent ....Springfield, MO
Hendrix, Mark A., (P.C.) ....Dallas, TX
Hendrix, Mark Stephen ....Columbia, MO
Hendrix, Michael E. ....Murphy, NC
Hendrix, Pamela Lohr ....Athens, GA
Greensboro, GA
Hendrix, Paul L. ....Spartanburg, SC
Hendrix, R. Brian ....Washington, DC
Hendrix, R. Clay ....Las Vegas, NV
Hendrix, Richard G. ....Elverta, CA
Hendrix, Richard W. ....Atlanta, GA
Hendrix, Robert K. ....Xenia, OH
Hendrix, Roger B. ....Davidson, NC
Hendrix, Ronald L. ....Naperville, IL
Hendrix, Ronald M. ....Myrtle Beach, SC
Hendrix, Rori ....Salt Lake City, UT
Hendrix, Roy W., Jr. ....Memphis, TN
Hendrix, Samuel L. ....Washington, DC
Hendrix, Scott R. ....Tupelo, MS
Hendrix & Smith ....Zebulon, GA
Hendrix & Steigner ....Lexington, SC
Hendrix, Steven M. ....Jackson, MS
Hendrix, Thomas C. ....Chula Vista, CA
Hendrix, Thomas C. ....Ottawa, KS
Hendrix, Thomas K., Jr. ....Warrensburg, MO
Hendrix, Tracy Nevels ....Birmingham, AL
Hendrix, Walker A. ....Ottawa, KS
Hendrix, William Holland ....San Diego, CA
Hendrix, Willis H. ....Brookwood, AL
Hendrixson, Peter S. ....Minneapolis, MN
Hendry, Andy ....New York, NY
Hendry, Brent James ....Houston, TX
Hendry, Carol A. ....Atlanta, GA
Hendry, David D. ....Tampa, FL
Hendry, Diana M. ....Newark, NJ
Hendry, Gordon A. ....Indianapolis, IN
Hendry, Harry O. ....Fort Myers, FL
Hendry, James W. ....Portland, OR
Hendry, John ....LaBelle, FL
Hendry, John A. ....Glendale, CA
Hendry, John F. ....Garden Grove, CA
Hendry, John V. ....Lincoln, NE
Hendry, Joseph M., II ....Clewiston, FL
Hendry Law Firm, The, P.A.
Fort Myers, FL
Hendry, Lloyd G. ....Fort Myers, FL
Hendry, Nancy H. ....Peace Corps, Office of the General Counsel, GV
Hendry, Phillip M. ....Little Rock, AR
Hendry, Richard A. ....Watsonville, CA
Hendry, Robert R. ....Orlando, FL
Hendry, Ronald L. ....Tacoma, WA
Hendry, Stoner, Sawicki & Brown, P.A.
Kissimmee, FL
Orlando, FL
Hendry, William L. ....Okeechobee, FL
Hendrycy, Kenneth E. ....Dallas, TX
Hendryx, Bruce Douglas ....Youngstown, OH
Hendryx, Gina L. ....Oklahoma City, OK
Hendryx, Michael ....Houston, TX
Hendrzak, Bernard J. ....Kingston, PA
Hendy, Elizabeth A. ....Geneva, NY
Hendy, James D. ....Santa Rosa, CA
Hendy, Penny Unkraut ....Fort Mitchell, KY
Henebry, Brian T. ....Waterbury, CT
Henebry, Susan LoFaso ....Waterbury, CT
Henefer, E. Thomas ....Reading, PA
Henefield, Frank ....Blooming Prairie, MN
Henegan, James C. ....Lebanon, PA
Henegan, James K. ....Hoffman Estates, IL
Henegan, John C. ....Jackson, MS
Henegan, Maureen A. ....New York, NY
Henegar, Charles G. ....Portland, ME
Heneghan, Brendan T. ....New York, NY
Heneghan, F. Lal ....Washington, DC
Heneghan, James C. ....Pittsburgh, PA
Heneghan, Laura A. ....Danbury, CT
Heneghan, Martin J. ....Laguna Hills, CA
Heneghan, Michael H. ....Rocky Hill, CT
Heneghan, Patrick J. ....Chicago, IL
Heneghan, Pikor, Kennedy & Allen
Rocky Hill, CT
Heneghan, Rena W. ....Baltimore, MD
Heneghan, Rusha Tejani ....Boston, MA
Heneghan, Sean F. ....Boston, MA
Heneghan, Shannon M. ....Buffalo, NY
Heneghan, Thomas Patrick ....Madison, WI
Heneghan, Wisla C. ....Boston, MA
Henehan, David L. ....Avon, NY
Henehan, Donovan & Isaacson, Ltd.
Chicago, IL
Henehan, Margaret N. ....Boston, MA
Henehan, Thomas J. ....Chicago, IL
Henehan, Thomas P. ....Chicago, IL
Henein, Samy Saad ....San Diego, CA
Heneks, Jack R. ....Uniontown, PA
Henel, Carolyn E. ....Oakland, CA
Henel, George V. ....Buffalo, NY
Henely, Bernard D. ....Mishawaka, IN
Henely, John J. ....Chicago, IL
Henely, John J., Ltd. ....Chicago, IL
Henen, Emil Larry ....Santa Clarita, CA
Henenberg, Karen A. ....Arlington, VA
Henenway, Jay ....Princeton, MO
Henes, Christopher C. ....Dedham, MA
Henes and Donovan ....Dedham, MA
Henes & Henes ....Boston, MA
Henes, James R. ....Chicago, IL
Henes, Jas. C. ....Boston, MA
Henes, Jonathan S. ....New York, NY
Henes, Nomi C., (Mr.) ....Boston, MA
Henes, Pamela K. ....New York, NY
Henes, Richd. W. ....Paradise Valley, AZ
Henes, Samuel E. ....Cleveland, OH
Heneson, Allan ....Baltimore, MD
Heneson, Howard M. ....Baltimore, MD
Heneson, Howard M., P.A.
Baltimore, MD
Heneveld, L. Allen ....Laguna Beach, CA
Heneveld, Lloyd A. ....Grand Rapids, MI
Heney, Thos. T. ....New York, NY
Henfey, Edward M. ....Hartford, CT
Heng, Donald J., Jr. ....San Francisco, CA
Heng, Patrick M. ....Omaha, NE
Heng, Stephanie L. ....Calabasas, CA
Hengber, Gregory P. ....Coral Gables, FL
Hengehold, Steven D. ....Cincinnati, OH
Hengelbrok, James W. ....Cincinnati, OH
Hengeler Mueller Weitzel Wirtz
New York, NY
New York, NY
Hengen, Elaine S. ....El Paso, TX
Hengen & Hengen ....Biloxi, MS
Hengen, Nancy L. ....New York, NY
Hengen, Steven E. ....Concord, NH
Hengen, Wayne L. ....Biloxi, MS
Henger, Rex R. ....Dallas, TX
Hengerer, Carla J. ....Buffalo, NY
Hengerer, Edward W. ....Washington, DC
Hengerer, Linton W. ....Washington, DC
Henges, James W. ....Beaumont, TX
Henges, Victoria A. ....Kansas City, MO
Hengesbach, Daren E.
Rancho Cucamonga, CA
San Bernardino, CA
Hengesbach, Scott ....Los Angeles, CA
Hengesbach, Theodor J. ....Elkhart, IN
Henghold, Margaret V. ....Miami, FL
Hengstebeck, Bethany L. ....Chicago, IL
Hengst, Michael J. ....Houston, TX
Hengstler, Gary ....Chicago, IL
Henican, C. Ellis, Jr. ....New Orleans, LA
Henican, James & Cleveland
Metairie, LA
New Orleans, LA
Henican, Joseph P., III ....Metairie, LA
Henican, Thomas P. ....New Orleans, LA
Henick, Howard N. ....New York, NY
Henick, Julia ....Newark, NJ
Henick, Richard D. ....Los Angeles, CA
Heniff, Joseph W. ....La Grange, IL
Henifin, Arvo H. ....Savannah, GA
Henifin, Mary Sue ....Princeton, NJ
New York, NY
Henig, John A., Jr. ....Montgomery, AL
Henig, Sammy S. ....Princeton, NJ
Henigan, Michael J. ....Baltimore, MD
Henigan, Patrick T. ....Woodstown, NJ
Philadelphia, PA
Henig-Elona, Lee ....New York, NY
Henigman, Laura M. ....Kew Gardens, NY
Henigson, Robert ....Los Angeles, CA
Henika, Anthony G. ....Franklin, WI
Henin, Larry D. ....New York, NY
Henin-Clark, Catherine R. ....Orlando, FL
Henin-Clark, Catherine R., P.A.
Orlando, FL
Heninger, Burge, Vargo and Davis, LLP
Birmingham, AL
Jasper, AL
Tuscaloosa, AL
Heninger and Heninger, Professional Corporation ....Rock Island, IL
Davenport, IA
Heninger, Jeffrey L. ....McLean, VA
Heninger, John R. ....Portland, OR
Heninger, Ralph H. ....Davenport, IA
Heninger, Ralph W. ....Davenport, IA
Heninger, Stephen D. ....Birmingham, AL
Henion, Dohn R. ....Crescent City, CA
Henion Law Firm, The, LLP
Crescent City, CA
Henits, Les ....New York, NY
Henjes, Kurt ....Philadelphia, PA
Henjum, Kenneth H. J. ....Ventura, CA
Henk, Böck, Leonard & Vega, Inc.
Sacramento, CA
Henk, Leonard A. ....Bloomfield Hills, MI
Henk, Peter M. ....Houston, TX
Henk, Robert Peter ....Sacramento, CA
Henke & Associates ....Houston, TX
Henke, Bradley F. ....Seattle, WA
Henke, Bruce R. ....Columbus, OH
Henke, Charles L., Jr. ....Houston, TX
Henke, Dan ....San Francisco, CA
Henke, Danferd W. ....Seattle, WA
Henke, E. W. ....Pharr, TX
Henke, Frank E. ....Sterling Heights, MI
Henke, Frank X., III ....Tulsa, OK
Henke, James D. ....Grand Rapids, MI
Henke, James P. ....Elk Grove, CA
Henke, Jeff ....Houston, TX
Henke, John W. ....Bloomfield Hills, MI
Henke, Joseph T. ....San Francisco, CA
Henke, Kenneth M. ....Lafayette, LA
Henke, Lawrence E. ....Dallas, TX
Henke, Mark J. ....Roeland Park, KS
Henke, Michael J. ....Washington, DC
Henke, Nora A. ....New York, NY
Henke, Paul W., Jr. ....La Crosse, WI
Henke, Raymond L. ....Las Vegas, NV
Henke, Richard C. ....Lansing, MI
Henke & Richter ....Seattle, WA
Henke, Robert E. ....San Bernardino, CA
Henke, Robert J. ....Fish Creek, WI
Henke, Ronald ....Downs, KS
Henke, Ronald J. ....Lincoln, NE
Henke, Steven H. ....Carmel, IN
Henke, Theodore R. ....Madison, NJ
Henke, Therese M. ....Mequon, WI
Henke, Therese M. ....Milwaukee, WI
Henke, W. Kurt ....Clarksdale, MS
Henke-Bufkin ....Helena, AR
Clarksdale, MS
Henkel, Beth H. ....Indianapolis, IN
Henkel, C. M., III ....Corpus Christi, TX
Henkel, David S. ....New York, NY
Henkel, George B. ....Roseland, NJ
Henkel, Glenn A. ....Haddonfield, NJ
Henkel, Harold P. ....Grand Rapids, MI
Henkel, Jan W. ....Athens, GA
Henkel, Kathryn G. ....Dallas, TX
Henkel, Kurt H. ....Denver, CO
Henkel, Lee H., III ....Houston, TX
Henkel, Lee H., Jr. ....Atlanta, GA
Henkel, Lisa M. ....Omaha, NE
Henkel, Mark S. ....Stevens Point, WI
Henkel, Mary C. ....Cincinnati, OH
Henkel, Michelle M. ....Atlanta, GA
Henkel, Oliver C., Jr. ....Cleveland, OH
Henkel, Richard E. ....Cincinnati, OH
Henkel, Ronald W. ....Albuquerque, NM
Henkel, Sean C. ....Corpus Christi, TX
Henkel & Sloan, P.C. ....Albuquerque, NM
Henkel, Thomas M., Jr. ....Orlando, FL
Henkel, Timothy D. ....Miami, FL
Henkel, William G. ....Dallas, TX
Henkel-Benjamin, Jana L. ....Detroit, MI
Henkelman, Willard M. ....Scranton, PA
Henkelmann, Henry G., Jr. ....Lutherville, MD
Henkels, Maurice M., Jr. ....Efland, NC
Henkels, Tanya M. ....Dallas, TX
Henken, Arthur G. ....Carlyle, IL
Henken, H. David ....Boston, MA
Henken, Marla S. ....Boise, ID
Henkener, Ann E. ....Columbus, OH
Henkener, Roger J. ....Minster, OH
Henkenius, Richard J. ....Omaha, NE
Henker-Mattiessen, Jean ....Northlake, IL
Henkin, Alice P. ....Brooklyn, NY
Henkin, David Lane ....Honolulu, HI
Henkin, Doron A. ....Philadelphia, PA
Henkin, Douglas W. ....New York, NY
Henkin & Henkin ....Brooklyn, NY
Henkin, Howard A. ....Cleveland, OH
Henkin, Louis ....New York, NY
Henkin, Morris R. ....New York, NY
Henkin, Norman E. ....Brooklyn, NY
Henkin, Robert A. ....Youngstown, OH
Henkin, Russell D. ....Philadelphia, PA
Henkin & Seewald ....Cleveland, OH
Henkind, Hilary M. ....New York, NY
Henkind, Lewis ....White Plains, NY
Henkle, Albert L. ....Phoenix, AZ
Henkle, Robert F., Jr. ....Milwaukee, WI
Henkler, Richard L. ....Dallas, TX
Henkoff, David M. ....New York, NY
Henkoff, Hertz N. ....Boston, MA
Henkoff, Isaac ....Roseland, NJ
New York, NY
Henle, Arthur M. ....New York, NY
Henle, Patricia E. ....San Francisco, CA
Henle, Robert ....Hauppauge, NY
Henlein, Carl Arthur ....Louisville, KY
Henley, Albert Thomas ....Portola Valley, CA
Henley, Barron K. ....Dublin, OH
Henley, C. A." Chet ", Jr. ....Jackson, MS
Henley, Charles F., Jr. ....Jacksonville, FL
Henley, Charles Patton ....Jackson, MS
Henley, Craig D. ....Phoenix, AZ
Henley, Cynthia Russell ....Houston, TX
Henley, Dale W. ....Winchester, KY
Henley, Earl H. ....Athens, TN
Henley, Earle B., Jr. ....Chappaqua, NY
Henley, Edna K. ....San Francisco, CA
Henley, Garland F. ....Dallas, TX
Henley, Geoff J. ....Brownsville, TX
Henley, H. Brand, Jr. ....Hazlehurst, MS
Jackson, MS
Henley, Harris B. ....Hazlehurst, MS
Jackson, MS
Henley, J. Smith ....Harrison, AR
Henley, James L., Jr. ....Jackson, MS
Henley, James T. ....Dearborn, MI
Henley, James W. ....Hazlehurst, MS
Henley, John A. ....San Bernardino, CA
Henley, John B. ....Omaha, NE
Henley, John H. ....Jackson, MS
Henley, John I. ....Casper, WY
Henley, John J. ....San Diego, CA
Henley, Kathleen Moran ....Pasadena, CA
Henley, Keith F. ....Columbus, OH
Henley, Kenneth ....Bala Cynwyd, PA
Henley, L. Gaylene ....Oklahoma City, OK
Henley, Lee ....Dallas, GA
Henley, Lotterhos & Henley, PLLC
Hazlehurst, MS
Jackson, MS
Henley, Madeline ....Department of Justice, Civil Division, GV
Henley, Mark A. ....Williamsburg, VA
Henley, Martha N. E. ....Yukon, OK
Henley, Martha S. ....Mineola, NY
Henley, Mia Gianotti ....Memphis, TN
Henley, Ralph G. ....Lawrence, KS
Henley, Randall W. ....Boca Raton, FL
Henley, Robert A. ....Carlsbad, CA
Henley, Robert E., III ....Richmond, VA
Henley, Ross E. ....Jackson, MS
Henley, Roy H. ....Lansing, MI
Henley, Stephen L., Sr. ....Seattle, WA
Henley, Susanne K. ....Annapolis, MD
Henley, Thad Pitchford ....Picayune, MS
Henley, Thomas C. ....Colorado Springs, CO
Henley, Thomas R. ....Knoxville, TN
Henley, Tucker L. ....Richmond, VA
Henley, Victoria B. ....San Francisco, CA
Henley, Walter ....Northport, AL
Henley, William B., Jr. ....Dallas, TX
Henley, William K., (P.C.) ....Pasadena, CA
Henley, William M. ....Albany, CA
Henley, William Saunders, II
Jackson, MS
Henline, Roy B. ....Vadnais Heights, MN
Henlon, E. Venessa ....San Francisco, CA
Henmueller, Paul A. ....Chicago, IL
Henn, Catherine E. C. ....Boston, MA
Henn, Cecilia M. ....San Jose, CA
Henn, David M. ....Indianapolis, IN
Henn, Elizabeth S. ....Baltimore, MD
Henn & Etzel, Inc. ....San Francisco, CA
Henn, Eugene E. ....Indianapolis, IN
Henn, Frances J. ....New York, NY
Henn, Jo Allison ....Albany, NY
Henn, John H. ....Boston, MA
Henn, Peter J. ....Boca Raton, FL
Henn, R. Charles, Jr. ....Atlanta, GA
Henn, Robert L. ....San Francisco, CA
Henn, Robert L. ....Philadelphia, PA
Henn, Stephen K. ....East Hartford, CT
Henn, William L., Jr. ....Baltimore, MD
Henne, Fred E. ....North Little Rock, AR
Henne, Jean M. ....Winter Haven, FL
Henne, Steven P. ....Gaithersburg, MD
Henne, Terrance R. ....Pittsburgh, PA
Henneberger, Craig J. ....Uniondale, NY
Henneberger, Glenn T. ....Syosset, NY
Henneberger, John A.
Palm Beach Gardens, FL
Henneberger, Lawrence F.
Washington, DC
Henneberry, Edward P. ....Washington, DC
Henneberry, Edward P.
Gaithersburg, MD
Henneberry, Jay R. ....Los Angeles, CA
Henneberry, Joseph W. ....White Plains, NY
Henneberry, Lisa Goekjian
Washington, DC
Henneberry, Michael L. ....Princeton, IL
Henneberry, Thomas F. ....Dorchester, MA
Henneboehle, Alfred ....St. Louis, MO
Henneburg, Frank H. ....Washington, DC
Hennecke, Curt F. ....Chicago, IL
Hennecy, Guy E. ....West Palm Beach, FL
Hennefer, James A. ....San Francisco, CA
Henneforth, Jeffrey C. ....Los Angeles, CA
Hennegan, A. Owen ....Towson, MD
Hennegan, John O. ....Baltimore, MD
Henneger, Richard W. ....Madison, WI
Hennekam, Richard L.
West Palm Beach, FL
Henneke, David C. ....Enid, OK
Henneke, Edward G. ....Flint, MI
Henneke, Frederick L. ....Kerrville, TX
Henneke, McKone & Fraim, P.C. ....Flint, MI
Hennelly, Collis M. ....Rockford, IL
Hennelly, Debra Sabatini ....Basking Ridge, NJ
Hennelly, Denise D. ....Norristown, PA
Hennelly, Edmund P. ....Babylon, NY
Hennelly & Grossfeld ....Los Angeles, CA
Sacramento, CA
Hennelly, Helene F. ....St. Peters, MO
Hennelly, James J. ....St. Charles, MO
Hennelly, John E. ....Atlanta, GA
Hennelly, John J., Jr. ....Los Angeles, CA
Hennelly, Thomas ....Chicago, IL
Hennelly, Victoria J. ....Los Angeles, CA
Henneman, Andrea Lodahl
New York, NY
Henneman, Carolyn H. ....Baltimore, MD
Henneman, Edward O. ....Savannah, GA
Henneman, Edward O. ....Lexington, VA
Henneman, Jane Hays ....Champaign, IL
Henneman, Larry E., Jr. ....San Jose, CA
Henneman, Larry R. ....Minneapolis, MN
Henneman, Laurel R. ....New York, NY
Henneman, Matthew B. ....Houston, TX
Hennemann, Theresa ....Anchorage, AK
Hennemuth, Jeffrey A.
Administrative Office Of The United States Courts, GV
Hennen, Bradley J. ....Minneapolis, MN
Hennen, Claudia M. ....Westford, MA
Hennen, Dennis W. ....Monroe, LA
Hennen, Floyd A. ....Tallahassee, FL
Hennen, John E. ....St. Paul, MN
Hennen, John G. ....Olympia, WA
Hennen, Michael H. ....Albuquerque, NM
Hennen, Thomas R. ....Dallas, TX
Hennen, Thomas W. ....Seattle, WA

Hennen, William E. ....Tampa, FL
Hennenberg & Associates ....Cleveland, OH
Hennenberg, Michael C. ....Cleveland, OH
Hennenfent, George M. ....Roseville, IL
Hennenhoefer, James A. ....Vista, CA
Hennenhoefer, James A., A Professional Corporation ....Vista, CA
Hennessy, Andrew D. ....Providence, RI
Henner, Janet L. ....New York, NY
Henner, Joseph Paul ....Atlanta, GA
Henner, Lester N. ....New York, NY
Henner, M. ....Hicksville, NY
Henner, M., P.C. ....Hicksville, NY
Henner, Martin E. ....Eugene, OR
Hennerich, Paul A., III ....Eureka, MO
Hennes, David B. ....New York, NY
Hennes, Matthew E. ....Palm Springs, CA
Hennes, Paul L. ....Plantation, FL
Hennes, Peter S. ....Brick, NJ
Hennesay, A. Kenneth, Jr. ....Irvine, CA
Hennesey, John J. ....Park Ridge, NJ
Henness, Mark G. ....Las Vegas, NV
Hennessee, Heather M. ....Hickory, NC
Hennessee, Karl K. ....Houston, TX
Hennessee, Keith C. ....Houston, TX
Hennessey, Christopher P. ....Canton, MA
Hennessey, Christopher P., P.C. ....Canton, MA
Hennessey, Colleen M. ....Boston, MA
Hennessey, David J. ....Windsor, CT
Hennessey, Edward F. ....Hartford, CT
Hennessey, Edward F. ....Boston, MA
Hennessey, Edward F., IV ....Charlotte, NC
Hennessey, Edward J. ....Mastic, NY
Hennessey, Geoffrey C. ....New Orleans, LA
Hennessey, Gilbert H., III ....Boston, MA
Hennessey, Gilbert H., Jr., (Ltd.)
Chicago, IL
Hennessey & Hennessey ....Pottstown, PA
Hennessey, James J. ....Albany, NY
Hennessey, James R. ....Seattle, WA
Hennessey, James W. ....Philadelphia, PA
Hennessey, Jevera Kaye ....Greenwich, CT
Hennessey, John W. ....Corpus Christi, TX
Hennessey, Joseph A. ....Washington, DC
Hennessey, Joseph F. ....Bethesda, MD
Hennessey, Katherine Clark
Shreveport, LA
Hennessey, Kathleen M. ....Chicago, IL
Hennessey, Kevin F. ....Jefferson City, MO
Hennessey, Kevin F. ....Pottstown, PA
Hennessey, Lynne K. ....Boca Raton, FL
Hennessey, Mary C. ....Washington, DC
Hennessey, M. F. ....Butte, MT
Hennessey, Michele B. ....Mount Airy, MD
Hennessey, Molly Ann ....Columbus, OH
Hennessey, Patricia ....New York, NY
Hennessey, Patrick A. ....Irvine, CA
Hennessey, Patrick J., Jr. ....San Diego, CA
Hennessey, Richard F. ....Denver, CO
Hennessey, Robert J. ....Minneapolis, MN
Hennessey, Robert P. ....Edwardsville, IL
Hennessey, Shannon ....New York, NY
Hennessey, Sheila M. ....Wethersfield, CT
Hennessey, Stephen P. ....Bellevue, WA
Hennessey, Stuart P. ....Bellevue, WA
Hennessey, Thomas J. ....Boston, MA
Hennessey, Thomas L. ....Towson, MD
Hennessey, Thomas L., P.A. ....Towson, MD
Hennessey, Thomas M. ....Columbus, OH
Hennessey, Thos. E. ....San Antonio, TX
Hennessey, Timothy F. ....Pottstown, PA
Hennessey, Walter M. ....Butte, MT
Hennessey, Wendy Y. ....Atlanta, GA
Hennessey, William J., Jr. ....Stamford, CT
Hennessey, William John ....Bridgeport, CT
Hennessey, William M. ....Minneapolis, MN
Hennessey, William Owen
Manchester, NH
Hennessey, William T., III
West Palm Beach, FL
Hennessey, Wm. E. ....Spokane, WA
Hennessy, Bernard J. ....Chicago, IL
Hennessy & Cihak, P.C. ....Chicago, IL
Hennessy, Colleen M. ....Chicago, IL
Hennessy, Daniel K. ....Dallas, TX
Hennessy, Darcy V. ....Kansas City, MO
Hennessy, Donald J. ....Sacramento, CA
Hennessy, Donald J. ....Naperville, IL
Hennessy, Donna S. ....Chicago, IL
Hennessy, Edward J. ....Houston, TX
Hennessy, Edward L. ....Chicago, IL
Hennessy, Ellen A. ....Washington, DC
Hennessy, Erin S. ....Morristown, NJ
Hennessy, F. D., Jr. ....Lansdowne, PA
Hennessy, Francis D., Jr. ....Elkins Park, PA
Hennessy, Francis X. ....Hartford, CT
Hennessy, Gardner & Barth ....Houston, TX
Hennessy, Gerald T. ....Schenectady, NY
Hennessy, Greg W. ....Williston, ND
Hennessy, J. Kevin ....Chicago, IL
Hennessy, J. Patrick ....Shreveport, LA
Hennessy, James E. ....San Diego, CA
Hennessy, James H. ....Minneapolis, MN
Hennessy, James M. ....Phoenix, AZ
Hennessy, James R. ....New York, NY
Hennessy, John F., Jr. ....Kenilworth, IL
Hennessy, John T. ....Luray, VA
Hennessy, Joseph H. ....Philadelphia, PA
Hennessy, Kevin S. ....West Palm Beach, FL
Hennessy, Killgoar & Politi ....Boston, MA
Hennessy Law Office, P.C. ....Williston, ND
Hennessy, Margaret E. ....Salisbury, MD
Hennessy, Martha Durant
Bay Minette, AL
Daphne, AL
Foley, AL
Hennessy, Mary Ellen ....Chicago, IL
Hennessy, Mary Kim Hascher
Ann Arbor, MI
Hennessy, Matt ....Houston, TX
Hennessy, Michael J. ....Chicago, IL
Hennessy, Michael J. ....Pittsburgh, PA
Hennessy, Mickee ....New York, NY
Hennessy, Nicholas J. ....Bowling Green, OH
Hennessy, Patricia A. ....Boston, MA
Hennessy, Patrick B. ....Minneapolis, MN
Hennessy, Paul K. ....Secaucus, NJ
Hennessy, Peggy ....Portland, OR
Hennessy & Roach, P.C. ....Chicago, IL
Hennessy, Robert A. ....Chicago, IL
Hennessy, Robert C. ....Norwood, NJ
Hennessy, Robert J. ....Chicago, IL
Hennessy & Scheinfield ....Lansdowne, PA
Media, PA
Hennessy, Shirley L. ....Chesterfield, VA
Hennessy, Shirley L., J.D., P.C.
Chesterfield, VA
Richmond, VA
Hennessy, Stephen G. ....Boston, MA
Hennessy, Suzanne E. ....Sacramento, CA
Hennessy, Teresa A.
Federal Election Commission,
Office of the General Counsel, GV
Hennessy, Thomas F. ....Chesapeake, VA
Hennessy, Thomas F., III ....Belleville, IL
Hennessy, Thomas G. ....Chicago, IL
Hennessy, Thomas M. ....Annapolis, MD
Hennessy, Timothy P. ....Rochester, NY
Hennessy, W. Louis ....Washington, DC
Hennessy, William J. ....Chicago, IL
Hennessy, William J. ....Grand Marais, MN
Hennessy, William J., Jr. ....Charleston, SC
Mount Pleasant, SC
Henney, C. Allen ....New Orleans, LA
Hennesy, Sarah E. ....Alexandria, VA
Hennewinkel, Michael J. ....Plainsboro, NJ
Henney, David D. ....Pasadena, CA
Henney, Raymond W. ....Detroit, MI
Henney, Timothy C. ....Portage, WI
Hennick, Charles R. ....Towson, MD
Hennier, Andrew D. ....Kansas City, MO
Hennig, Arthur W. ....Indianapolis, IN
Hennig, Bernard A. ....Chicago, IL
Hennig, Bernard A., Sr. ....Chicago, IL
Hennig, Coleen P. ....Stockton, CA
Hennig, Gene H. ....Minneapolis, MN
Hennig, Janet L. ....Cleveland, OH
Hennig, Julian, III ....Columbia, SC
Hennig, Michael J. ....Chicago, IL
Hennig, Pamela Jean
West Palm Beach, FL
Hennig, Richard A. ....Painesville, OH
Hennig, Richard A. ....Laramie, WY
Hennig, Richard Paul ....Schaumburg, IL
Hennig, Virginia G. ....Columbia, SC
Hennigan, Brian J. ....Los Angeles, CA
Hennigan, Dan H. ....Houston, TX
Hennigan, Dennis P. ....Syracuse, NY
Hennigan, J. Michael ....Los Angeles, CA
Hennigan, James W., Jr. ....Boston, MA
Hennigan, Jerome S. ....Arlington, TX
Hennigan, Jerome S., P.C. ....Arlington, TX
Hennigan, Jo Anne B. ....Spartanburg, SC
Hennigan, John J. ....Syracuse, NY
Hennigan, John P. ....Jamaica, NY
Hennigan, Lloyd E., Jr. ....Jena, LA
Hennigan, Mercer & Bennett
Los Angeles, CA
Hennigan, Oliver William, Jr. ....Oceanport, NJ
Hennigan, Timothy M. ....Syracuse, NY
Hennigar, Mary Jo ....San Rafael, CA
Hennigar, William Grant, Jr.
Grand Island, NY
Henniger, David T. ....St. Petersburg, FL
Henniger, R. Gregory ....New York, NY
Hennigh, Mark S. ....San Francisco, CA
Hennigh, Scott E. ....San Francisco, CA
Hennighausen, Frederick H. ....Roswell, NM
Henning, Ann L ....Houston, TX
Henning, Christian F., III ....Northbrook, IL
Henning, Edward J. ....Atlanta, GA
Henning, Fred E. ....Toledo, OH
Henning, Grace W. ....Chicago, IL
Henning, Harry L. ....Naples, FL
Columbus, OH
Henning, Heidi Ebel ....Chevy Chase, MD
Henning, Jack C. ....San Francisco, CA
Henning, Jane L. ....Los Angeles, CA
Henning, Jeffrey W. ....Chicago, IL
Merrillville, IN
Henning, Joel F. ....Chicago, IL
Somerset, NJ
Henning, John A., Jr. ....Los Angeles, CA
Henning, John F. ....Franklin, NC
Henning, John F., Jr. ....San Francisco, CA
Henning, John L. ....Los Angeles, CA
Henning, John L. ....Elkins, WV
Henning, Jon M. ....Fort Lauderdale, FL
Henning & Keedy, P.L.L.C. ....Kalispell, MT
Henning, Larry A. ....Denver, CO
Henning, Lee C. ....Kalispell, MT
Henning, Margaret ....Dallas, TX
Henning, Marilyn Jadene ....Denver, CO
Henning, Mark G. ....Chicago, IL
Henning, Mary K. ....White Plains, NY
Henning, Patti Englander
Fort Lauderdale, FL
Henning, R. Denise ....Kansas City, MO
Henning, Renee S.
Federal Trade Commission,
Bureau of Competition, GV
Henning, Richard E., Jr. ....Fairfax, VA
Henning, Richard L. ....Massillon, OH
Henning, Robert D. ....Memphis, TN
Henning, Sally D. ....Massillon, OH
Henning, Sonja L. ....Los Angeles, CA
Henning, Stephanie A. ....Arlington, VA
Henning, Stephen J. ....Los Angeles, CA
Henning, Stephen L. ....Batesville, MS
Henning, Susan E. ....New Orleans, LA
Henning, Teri L. ....Bala Cynwyd, PA
Harrisburg, PA
Henning, Thomas A. ....Baltimore, MD
Henning, Thomas G. ....Lake Charles, LA
Henning, Thomas W. ....Los Angeles, CA
Henning, Tom ....Dickinson, ND
Henning, Vernon O. M. ....Hobbs, NM
Henning, W. Scott ....Harrisburg, PA
Lancaster, PA
Henning, William H. ....Galesburg, IL
Henning, William H. ....Columbia, MO
Henning, William L. ....Sulphur, LA
Henning & Yost, L.P.A. ....Massillon, OH
Henninger, Audrey J. ....Los Angeles, CA
Henninger, Carl F. J. ....Wheaton, IL
Henninger, David P. ....Los Angeles, CA
Henninger, David P. ....Towson, MD
Henninger, Francis J. ....Bel Air, MD
Henninger, John ....St. Petersburg, FL
Henninger, John C. ....New York, NY
Henninger, Joseph B., Jr. ....Charlotte, NC
Henninger, Laura L. ....Bel Air, MD
Henninger, Peter R., Jr. ....Middletown, PA
Henninger & Robinson ....Butler, PA
Henninger, Stephen Douglas ....Dallas, TX
Henninger, Ursula M. ....Winston-Salem, NC
Henninger, William John ....Boulder, CO
Hennings, David L. ....Seattle, WA
Hennings, James D. ....Portland, OR
Hennings, Laury H. ....Portland, OR
Hennings, Mark Steven ....Long Beach, CA
Hennings, Richard W. ....Tavares, FL
Hennings, Ronald J. ....Chicago, IL
Hennings, Todd E. ....Atlanta, GA
Hennings, Werner R. ....Mount Clemens, MI
Henningsen, Andrea Hackett
San Francisco, CA
Henningsen, David S. ....San Jose, CA
Henningsen, Ellen J. ....Madison, WI
Henningsen, Gail R. ....Lambertville, NJ
Henningsen, Gary A., Jr. ....Morristown, NJ
Henningsen, Gary M. ....Omaha, NE
Henningsen, George H. ....Trenton, NJ
Henningsen, Kimberley Erin
Palo Alto, CA
Henningsen, Lisa A. ....East Brunswick, NJ
Henningsen, Peter J. ....Milwaukee, WI
Henningsen, Pressley W. ....Maquoketa, IA
Henningsen, Vucurovich & Richardson, P.C.
Butte, MT
Henningsgaard, Blair J. ....Astoria, OR
Henningson, L. David ....Minneapolis, MN
Henningson & Snoxell Ltd.
Brooklyn Center, MN
Maple Grove, MN
Minneapolis, MN
Hennington, B. Judson, III
Birmingham, AL
Hennington, Lorna D. ....Los Angeles, CA
Hennion, Serene M. ....Newark, NJ
Hennis, Ann ....Corpus Christi, TX
Hennis, William McKinley, III ....Durham, NC
Hennon, Douglas W. ....Jefferson City, MO
Hennon, Reed D. ....New Castle, PA
Heno, David R. ....Metairie, LA
Houston, TX
Henoch, Bruce A. ....Bethesda, MD
Henoch, Gilbert ....Garden City, NY
Melville, NY
New York, NY
Henoch, Lisa Jean ....Kansas City, MO
Henoch, Rex Wayne ....Lenexa, KS
Henock, Arlen F. ....Stamford, CT
Henon, Paul J. ....Arlington, VA
Henratty, Scott L. ....Ocala, FL
Henretta, Cross, Ness & Dolan
Minneapolis, MN
Minnetonka, MN
Henretta, J. Thomas ....Akron, OH
Henretty, Brian" D " ....Boise, ID
Henri, Anita L. ....Washington, DC
Henri, David C. ....Los Angeles, CA
Henri, Joseph R. ....Anchorage, AK
Henri, J.P. ....Deerfield, IL
Henri, William F. ....Houston, TX
Henrich, Caroline ....Charleston, WV
Henrich, Lizabeth Huff ....Philadelphia, PA
Henrich, Matthew D. ....Lake Charles, LA
Henrich, Patricia M. ....Philadelphia, PA
Henrich, William J., Jr. ....Philadelphia, PA
Henrich, William M. ....San Diego, CA
Henrichs, Canella E. ....Chicago, IL
Henrichs, Dee A. ....Ottawa, KS
Henrichs, John D. ....Beverly Hills, CA
Henrichs, Katherine McKee ....Durham, NC
Henrichs, Ragna ....Houston, TX
Henrichs, Russell W., (P.A.) ....Dallas, TX
Henrichsen, Christen B.
Thousand Oaks, CA
Henrichsen, Christian K. G. ....Phoenix, AZ
Henrichsen, Neil L. ....Washington, DC
West Palm Beach, FL
Henrichsen, Susan ....San Diego, CA
Henrichsen and Witting ....Simi Valley, CA
Thousand Oaks, CA
Westlake Village, CA
Henrichson, E. G. ....Edinburg, TX
Henrichson, Gary L., Law Office of
Edinburg, TX
Henrichson, Preston, A Prof. Corp., Law Offices of ....Edinburg, TX
Henrichson, Preston E. ....Edinburg, TX
Henrici, Craig B. ....Wallingford, CT
Henrici, Kelly A. ....Dayton, OH
Henrick, Michael F. ....Waukegan, IL
Henrick, William R. ....Purchase, NY
Henricks, Arne T. ....Hilo, HI
Henricks, Christine Mille
Santa Monica, CA
Henricks, James A. ....El Segundo, CA
Henricks, Steven C. ....Kansas City, MO
Henricks, Susan ....Austin, TX
Henricks, Tiffany A. ....Washington, DC
Henricksen & Henricksen, Inc.
Bethany, OK
El Reno, OK
Henricksen, Jon S. ....Gladstone, OR
Henricksen, Lanita ....El Reno, OK
Henricksen, Mark ....El Reno, OK
Henrickson, Lance B. ....West Bend, WI
Henrie, Gary R. ....Salt Lake City, UT
Henrie, Homer H. ....Upland, CA
Henrie, Larry J. ....Denton, TX
Henrie & O'Boyle ....Seaford, NY
Henrie, Scott B. ....Seattle, WA
Henries, George E. ....New York, NY
Henriksen, C. Richard, Jr.
Salt Lake City, UT
Henriksen, C. Richard, Sr.
Salt Lake City, UT
Henriksen, David K. ....Chicago, IL
Henriksen, Gary A. ....Lansing, MI
Henriksen & Henriksen, P.C.
Salt Lake City, UT
Henriksen, Jack W. ....Valencia, CA
Henriksen, John C. ....Springfield, IL
Henriksen, John E. ....Georgetown, DE
Henriksen, John R. ....Gladstone, OR
Henriksen, Kay E. ....Jacksonville, IL
Henriksen, Kelly E. ....Juneau, AK
Henriksen, M. Gene ....St. Paul, MN
Henriksen, Roger D. ....Salt Lake City, UT
Henriksen, Roscoe L. ....Ventura, CA
Henrikson, Gregory R. ....Anchorage, AK
Henrikson, Harold L. ....North Hollywood, CA
Henrikson, Kirk R. ....Cleveland, OH
Henrikson, Matthew H. ....Charleston, SC
Henriod, Joseph L. ....Salt Lake City, UT
Henriod, Joseph L., P.C.
Salt Lake City, UT
Henriod, Stephen L. ....Salt Lake City, UT
Henrion, Paul B. ....Stow, MA
Henriot, James F. ....Tacoma, WA
Henrioulle, Stevan J., Law Offices of
San Mateo, CA
Henriques, Allan ....Roseville, CA
Henriques, Christina T. ....Lansing, MI
Henriques, Janalie Ann ....San Jose, CA
Henriques, Mark P. ....Charlotte, NC
Henriquez, François G., II
Overland Park, KS
Henry, A. Michael ....New York, NY
Henry, A. Wayne ....Loudon, TN
Henry, Adam C. ....New York, NY
Henry, Alaric A. ....Chattanooga, TN
Henry, Albert C. ....Las Vegas, NV
Henry, Alice Katherine ....Cleveland, OH
Henry & Allen ....Port Townsend, WA
Henry, Andrew ....Philadelphia, PA
Henry, Angela L. ....Fort Worth, TX
Henry, Anita K. ....Atlanta, GA
Henry, Ann R. ....Fayetteville, AR
Henry, Anna ....Los Angeles, CA
Henry, Anne M. ....Bettendorf, IA
Henry, Anne P. ....Kansas City, MO
Henry, Austin P. ....Pittsburgh, PA
Henry, Barbour & DeCell ....Yazoo City, MS
Henry & Beaver LLP ....Lebanon, PA
Henry, Bill ....Austin, TX
Henry, Bill E. ....Houston, TX
Henry, Blair C. ....Seattle, WA
Henry, Bradford L. ....Pontotoc, MS
Tupelo, MS
Henry, Bradley Mead ....Boston, MA
Henry, Brendan L. ....Austin, TX
Henry, Brent L. ....Washington, DC
Henry, Brian L. ....Kingsport, TN
Henry, Brian P. ....Bloomfield Hills, MI
Henry, Brian R. ....Greenville, SC
Henry, Brian T. ....Chicago, IL
Henry, Brian W. ....New York, NY
Henry, Bruce R. ....Boston, MA
Henry, Bruce W. ....Fairfax, VA
Henry, Bryan Scott ....Lauderhill, FL
Henry, Bryan Scott, P.A. ....Lauderhill, FL
Henry, Buchanan, Hudson, Suber, Carter & Kaywell, L.C. ....Punta Gorda, FL
Henry, Buchanan, Hudson, Suber & Carter, P.A. ....Tallahassee, FL
Henry, C. Brad ....Shawnee, OK
Henry, C. Kenneth ....St. Clairsville, OH
Henry, Carl N. ....Los Angeles, CA
Henry, Carolyn M. ....Buffalo, NY
Henry, Carter P. ....Quakertown, PA
Henry, Carver L. ....Houston, TX
Henry, Catherine A. ....Gloucester, MA
Henry, Celia E. ....Blue Bell, PA
Henry, Charles E. ....Lakewood, CO
Henry, Charles Gibbons ....Stockton, CA
Henry, Charles H., Jr. ....Jacksonville, NC
Henry, Charles O. ....Kankakee, IL
Henry, Charles R. ....Fairfax Station, VA
Henry, Charles T. ....Shawnee, OK
Henry, Charles T., Inc. ....Shawnee, OK
Henry, Charles V., III ....Lebanon, PA
Henry, Charles V., IV ....Santa Fe, NM
Henry, Charles W. ....Southbury, CT
Waterbury, CT
Henry, Chris W. ....Overland Park, KS
Henry, Christian G. ....Atlanta, GA
Henry, Christian M. ....Oklahoma City, OK

Henry, Christopher C. ... **Boston, MA**
Henry, C. J., Jr. ... Bay Village, OH
Henry, Claudeth J. ... Gainesville, FL
Ocala, FL
Henry, Clifford J. ... **Conway, AR**
Henry, Corcelius, Gates, Gill & Ody
Huntingdon, PA
Henry, Courtney Rae ... Little Rock, AR
Henry and Cox
Hot Springs National Park, AR
Henry, Craig L. ... Texarkana, TX
Henry, Curtis R. ... **Denver, CO**
Henry, Cynthia Lynn ... Diamond, OH
Henry, D. Craig ... Grand Blanc, MI
Henry, D. Mitchell ... **Montgomery, AL**
Henry, D. Steven ... **Dallas, TX**
Henry, Dan O. ... La Jolla, CA
Henry, Daniel J. ... Falls Church, VA
Henry, Daniel J., Jr. ... Hamburg, NY
Henry, Daniel J., P.C. ... Falls Church, VA
Henry, Daniel W. ... San Diego, CA
Henry, Darrell L. ... Annapolis, MD
Henry, David G. ... Stuttgart, AR
Henry, David G. ... **Tampa, FL**
Henry, David G. ... **Buffalo, NY**
Henry, David G. ... **Pittsburgh, PA**
Henry, David G. ... **Waco, TX**
Henry, David L. ... Tell City, IN
Henry, David L. ... Olympia, WA
Henry, David M. ... Troy, OH
Henry, David M. ... **Milwaukee, WI**
Henry, David P. ... Little Rock, AR
Henry, David P. ... Oklahoma City, OK
Henry, David W. ... **Orlando, FL**
Henry, Dawanna Williams ... New York, NY
Henry, De Lysle L. ... Alpena, MI
Henry, Dean ... Tiffin, OH
Henry, Deborah C. M. ... **St. Louis, MO**
Henry, Deborah Epstein ... **Philadelphia, PA**
Henry, Deborah J. ... Greensburg, PA
Henry, Debra Lynn ... Pittsburgh, PA
Henry, Deirdre G. ... **Cleveland, OH**
Henry, Don M. ... West Plains, MO
Henry, Donald H. ... **Little Rock, AR**
Henry, Donald W. ... **Waterbury, CT**
Henry, Donna H. ... Fairfax, VA
Henry, Douglas ... Nashville, TN
Henry, Douglas L. ... Clarkesville, GA
Henry, Douglas M. ... **Dubuque, IA**
Henry, Douglas M. ... Boston, MA
Henry, Douglas R. ... **Rockford, IL**
Henry, Duane G. ... San Francisco, CA
Henry, Edmund T., III ... **Miami, FL**
Henry, Edwin M., Jr. ... Ellicott City, MD
Henry, Edwin M., Jr., LLC, Law Offices of
Ellicott City, MD
Henry, Edwin S., Jr. ... Philadelphia, PA
Henry, E. L. ... **Baton Rouge, LA**
Henry, Elizabeth J. ... San Antonio, TX
Henry, Elizabeth Lea ... Wichita, KS
Henry, Ellen ... Jewell, IA
Henry, Eric B. ... Kensington, MD
Henry, Eveleen ... Eugene, OR
Henry, Evelyn V. ... **Braintree, MA**
Henry, Everett L. ... Lumberton, NC
Henry, F. Bryant, Jr. (P.C.) ... La Fayette, GA
Henry, Forrest A. ... Southfield, MI
Henry, Francis Aaron ... Englewood, CO
Henry, Frank H. ... **Miami, FL**
Henry, Frederic T., Jr. ... Canandaigua, NY
Henry, Frederick E. ... **Chicago, IL**
Henry & Fuller ... **Beaumont, TX**
Henry, G. Edward, II ... **Lexington, KY**
Henry, G. Steven ... **Birmingham, AL**
Henry, Gary W. ... Harrisonville, MO
Henry, Gaylord L. ... San Diego, CA
Henry, Geo. A., Jr. ... Indianapolis, IN
Henry, George L. ... Columbus, OH
Henry, George S., Law Office of
Dallas, TX
Henry, Godfrey C. ... Newark, NJ
Henry, Grady W. ... Jesup, GA
Henry, Gregory A. ... Bradford, PA
Henry, Gregory B. ... **San Jose, CA**
Henry, Gregory D. ... Reading, PA
Henry, Guido R., Jr. ... Dorset, VT
Henry, Guy E. ... Austin, TX
Henry, H. David ... **Los Angeles, CA**
Henry, H. Lynn ... West Plains, MO
Henry, Halsey & Thyer, PLC
Jonesboro, AR
Henry, Harold L. ... West Plains, MO
Henry, Harriet P. ... Windham, ME
Henry, Harry W., Jr. ... St. Louis, MO
Henry, Hatcher & Schiller, P.C.
Gainesville, TX
Henry, Helene S. ... Trenton, NJ
Henry & Henry ... **Conway, AR**
Henry & Henry ... Natchitoches, LA
Henry, Henry, Henry, Engelbrecht & Williams,
P.C. ... West Plains, MO
Henry & Henry, P.C. ... Fairfax, VA
Henry and Henry, Professional Company
Lakewood, CO
Henry, Henry & Speer, P.C. ... **Pulaski, TN**
Henry, Herbert W. ... Bay City, TX
Henry, J. Christian ... Natchitoches, LA
Henry, J. Hue ... Athens, GA
Henry, J. Hue, P.C. ... Athens, GA
Henry, J. Lawton ... **Houston, TX**
Henry, J. Walker ... **Detroit, MI**
Henry, Jack B. ... Pulaski, TN
Henry, James ... **Costa Mesa, CA**
Henry, James A. ... Seattle, WA
Henry, James C. ... Lakewood, CO
Henry, James D. ... Department of Labor,
Office of the Solicitor, GV
Henry, James E. ... Columbus, OH

Henry, James F. ... **Birmingham, AL**
Henry, James F. ... Chicago, IL
Henry, James H. ... **Tullahoma, TN**
Henry, James H., II ... **Tullahoma, TN**
Henry, James L. ... New Bedford, MA
Henry, James L., Jr. ... Chattanooga, TN
Henry, James N., Jr. ... **Dallas, TX**
Henry, James P. ... Bernardsville, NJ
Henry, James R. ... Groton, NY
Henry, James S. ... New York, NY
Henry, James W. ... Kansas City, MO
Henry, Janet J. ... **Columbus, OH**
Henry, Janis C. ... Seattle, WA
Henry, Jeanett P. ... **Washington, DC**
Henry, Jeannie C. ... Tulsa, OK
Henry, Jeffrey G. ... **Austin, TX**
Henry, Jeffrey S. ... Kansas City, MO
Henry, Jeffrey S. ... Murfreesboro, TN
Henry, Jennifer A. ... Riverhead, NY
Henry, Jennifer Pettijohn ... **Fort Worth, TX**
Henry, Jerry E. ... Fresno, CA
Kerman, CA
Henry, Jessica V. ... **Saddle Brook, NJ**
Henry, Joan C. DeMichael ... Cape Coral, FL
Henry, Joanne ... **Tacoma, WA**
Henry, John A. ... Durham, ME
Henry, John A. ... Seattle, WA
Henry, John A., & Assoc., Inc., & Assoc., Inc.,
P.S. ... Seattle, WA
Henry, John A., Jr. ... **Philadelphia, PA**
Henry, John A., Jr. ... Richmond, VA
Henry, John C. ... **Portsmouth, VA**
Henry, John C., Jr. ... **Washington, DC**
Henry, John E. ... Wheaton, IL
Henry, John E. ... Boston, MA
Henry, John F. ... Mattydale, NY
Henry, John F., Jr. ... **Chattanooga, TN**
Henry, John J. ... **Albany, NY**
Henry, John P. ... **Conway, SC**
Henry, John R. ... Cherry Valley, AR
Henry, John R. ... Pomeroy, WA
Henry, John V. ... White Plains, NY
Henry & Johnson ... Jesup, GA
Henry, Jonathan D. ... Chagrin Falls, OH
Henry & Jones, L.L.P. ... **Dallas, TX**
Henry, Joseph C. ... **Houston, TX**
Henry, Joseph Ward, Jr. ... **Pulaski, TN**
Henry, Judith B. ... **Richmond, VA**
Henry, Judy Shipler ... Salem, OR
Henry, Judy Simmons ... **Little Rock, AR**
Henry, Julia A. ... **Dallas, TX**
Henry, Karen A. ... **San Francisco, CA**
Henry, Karen H. ... Auburn, CA
Henry, Karen H., Inc., Attorneys at Law
Auburn, CA
Henry, Katherine Flynn ... **Kernersville, NC**
Henry, Katherine J. ... **Washington, DC**
Henry, Kathleen B. ... **Dallas, TX**
Henry, Kathleen Green ... Vienna, VA
Henry, Kathleen O'Connell ... **Dallas, TX**
Henry, Kathrine L.
Department Of The Interior,
Office of the Solicitor, GV
Henry, Keith R. ... **Junction City, KS**
Manhattan, KS
Henry, Kelly Sue ... **Louisville, KY**
Henry, Kenneth A. ... Chicago, IL
Henry, Kenneth Charles, Jr.
East Northport, NY
Henry, Kenneth R. ... Santa Barbara, CA
Henry, Kevin G. ... **Lexington, KY**
Henry, Kevin L. ... Tyler, TX
Henry, Kim M. ... Ellicott City, MD
Henry, Kimberly Taylor ... Denver, CO
Henry, L. Michael, Jr. ... Denver, CO
Henry, Larry D. ... **Tulsa, OK**
Henry, Laura A. ... Chicago, IL
Henry, Laura A. ... Cleveland, OH
Henry, Laura E. ... **Los Angeles, CA**
Henry, Laurence D. ... Dallas, TX
Henry Law Firm ... Jewell, IA
Henry Law Firm, P.A. ... Little Rock, AR
Henry Law Firm, The, P.C.
St. Louis, MO
Henry, Lawrence M. ... Denver, CO
Henry, Leigh Hermance ... Potomac, MD
Henry, Leslie M. ... **Houston, TX**
Henry, Levon B. ... Tohatchi, NM
Henry, Linda G. ... **Palo Alto, CA**
Henry, Lloyd A., Jr. ... Little Rock, AR
Henry, Lloyd W. ... East Troy, WI
Henry, Logoluso & Blum, Inc. ... Fresno, CA
Kerman, CA
Henry, Lois McKenna ... **Washington, DC**
Henry, Louis G., P.C. ... Portland, OR
Henry, Louis J. ... Westlake Village, CA
Henry, Lowerre, Johnson, Hess & Frederick
Austin, TX
Henry, Lucian J. ... Dearborn Heights, MI
Henry, Lucy Kimbrough ... **Gainesville, GA**
Henry, Lyndus A. ... Prairie Village, KS
Henry, M. Diane ... Cleveland, OH
Henry, Marc Patrick ... **Beaumont, TX**
Henry, Marcia G. ... San Francisco, CA
Henry, Margaret C. ... **New York, NY**
Henry, Margaret S. ... Santa Monica, CA
Henry, Marianne ... Philadelphia, PA
Henry, Marie R. ... Loch Sheldrake, NY
Henry, Marion Oliver ... Dallas, TX
Henry, Marjorie E. ... Sarasota, FL
Henry, Mark ... Jackson, MS
Henry, Mark J. ... **Washington, DC**
Henry, Mark Murphey ... **Little Rock, AR**
Henry, Mark R. ... **St. Louis, MO**
Henry, Mary E.
Department of Labor, GV
Henry, Matthew C. ... **Dallas, TX**
Henry, Matthew D. ... Pawnee, OK

Henry, Maureen ... **Phoenix, AZ**
Henry, Maureen Patricia ... Phoenix, AZ
Henry, Maurice G., Jr. ... Mount Kisco, NY
Henry, Max E. ... San Bernardino, CA
Henry, Maynard M. ... Alexandria, VA
Henry, McCord, Bean & Miller, P.L.L.C.
Manchester, TN
Tullahoma, TN
Winchester, TN
Henry, Merton G. ... **Portland, ME**
Henry, Michael ... Natchitoches, LA
Henry, Michael A. ... **Allentown, PA**
Henry, Michael A. ... Quanah, TX
Henry, Michael F. ... **Philadelphia, PA**
Henry, Michael G. ... **Washington, DC**
Henry, Michael J. ... New York, NY
Henry, Michael J. ... Bryn Mawr, PA
Henry, Michael J. ... **Fort Worth, TX**
Henry, Michael Joseph ... **Pleasanton, CA**
Henry, Michael L. ... Somerset, KY
Henry, Michael P. ... Lexington, MA
Henry, Michael P. ... **Toledo, OH**
Henry, Michael R. ... Jefferson City, MO
Henry, Michael R. ... **Columbus, OH**
Henry, Michael S. ... **Philadelphia, PA**
Henry, Milton R. ... Bloomfield Hills, MI
Henry, Miriam W. ... **New Orleans, LA**
Henry and Mooney ... Cherry Valley, AR
Henry, Morriss M. ... Fayetteville, AR
Henry, Nancy Hagan ... **Miami, FL**
Henry, Nancy L. ... **Murray Hill, NJ**
Henry Oddo Austin & Fletcher, A
Professional Corporation ... **Dallas, TX**
Henry, Pamela R. ... **Chicago, IL**
Henry, Patricia A. ... Pittsburgh, PA
Henry, Patricia C. ... Westbury, NY
Henry, Patricia J. ... Atlanta, GA
Henry, Patricia S. ... Deerfield, IL
Henry, Patrick ... Chicago, IL
Henry, Patrick E. ... **Homer, LA**
Henry, Patrick F. ... Atlanta, GA
Henry, Patrick K. ... Bridgeport, CT
Henry, Patrick L. ... Midlothian, VA
Henry, Patrick W. ... Portland, OR
Henry, Paul D. ... Eaton, OH
Henry, Paul F. ... **Metropolis, IL**
Henry, Paul Gregory ... **St. Louis, MO**
Henry, Paul J. ... Staten Island, NY
Henry, Paul J. ... Colville, WA
Henry, Paul J., Inc. ... Colville, WA
Henry, Paul M. ... **Pittsburgh, PA**
Henry, Paula F. ... **Costa Mesa, CA**
Henry, Peter E. ... **Morristown, NJ**
Henry, Peter R. ... **Asheville, NC**
Henry, Peter Y. ... San Antonio, TX
Henry, Philip C. ... **Atlanta, GA**
Henry, Q. Robert ... Rome, GA
Henry, R. Mark ... Dayton, OH
Henry, R. Paul ... Tulsa, OK
Henry, Randall C. ... Hutchinson, KS
Sterling, KS
Henry, Rebecca Ann ... Tallahassee, FL
Henry & Regan-Henry ... White Plains, NY
Henry, Reginald Keith ... Washington, DC
Henry, Rennae K. ... **Houston, TX**
Henry, Richard B. ... Honesdale, PA
Henry, Richard C. ... **Tucson, AZ**
Henry, Richard L., (L.T.D.)
Hot Springs National Park, AR
Henry, Richard M. ... Irvine, CA
Henry, Robert ... **Phoenix, AZ**
Henry, Robert C. ... **Pulaski, TN**
Henry, Robert D. ... **Orlando, FL**
Henry, Robert D. ... Newburg, ND
Henry, Robert D. ... Denver, CO
Henry, Robert E. ... Tyler, TX
Henry, Robert E., Jr., (P.C.) ... Tyler, TX
Henry, Robert H. ... Denver, CO
Henry, Robert H. ... Vernon, TX
Henry, Robert J. ... Lafayette, CA
Henry, Robert J. ... **Naperville, IL**
Henry, Robert J. ... Kansas City, KS
Henry, Robert J. ... **Reading, PA**
Henry, Robert J. ... **Seattle, WA**
Henry, Robert L. ... Toledo, OH
Henry, Robert L. ... Spokane, WA
Henry, Robert L., III ... **Little Rock, AR**
Henry, Robert M. ... **Princeton, NJ**
Henry, Robert S. ... Los Angeles, CA
Henry, Robert W. ... **Conway, AR**
Henry, Robert W. ... **St. Louis, MO**
Henry, Robert W., Jr. ... Moraga, CA
Henry, Robin A. ... **Armonk, NY**
Henry, Robyn A. ... Atlanta, GA
Henry, Rodney D. ... Quakertown, PA
Henry, Rolanne ... Madison, NJ
Henry, Ronald E. ... El Paso, TX
Henry, Ronald G. ... Bryn Mawr, PA
Henry, Ronald K. ... **Washington, DC**
Henry, Ronald T. ... Jacksonville, FL
Henry, Rosanna ... Little Rock, AR
Henry, Roxann E. ... **Washington, DC**
Henry, Russell D. ... **Valdosta, GA**
Henry, Russell R. ... Jewell, IA
Henry, Ryan ... **Brownsville, TX**
Henry, Sally McDonald ... **New York, NY**
Henry, Sam O., III ... West Monroe, LA
Henry, Sam O., IV ... West Monroe, LA
Henry, Samuel C. ... Atlanta, GA
Henry, Sara A. ... **Park City, UT**
Henry, Schaun D. ... **Harrisburg, PA**
Henry, Sharon A. ... Highlands Ranch, CO
Henry, Sharon Susanne ... Visalia, CA
Henry, Sharyn L. ... New York, NY
Henry, Stephen F. ... **San Francisco, CA**
Henry, Stephen John ... Greenville, SC
Henry, Stephen R. ... Fresno, CA
Henry, Steven C. ... Albuquerque, NM
Henry, Steven J. ... **Boston, MA**

Henry, Steven R. ... **Phoenix, AZ**
Henry, Stuart N. ... Austin, TX
Henry, Susan G. ... **Dallas, TX**
Henry, Susan Regan ... White Plains, NY
Henry, Terry M. ... Department of Justice,
Civil Division, GV
Henry, Terry M. ... **Philadelphia, PA**
Henry, Thomas A. ... **Sacramento, CA**
Henry, Thomas A., Jr. ... **La Jolla, CA**
Henry, Thomas C. ... St. Michaels, MD
Henry, Thomas Eugene, Jr. ... Stamford, CT
Henry, Thomas J. ... Fort Worth, TX
Henry, Thomas J., Law Offices of
Corpus Christi, TX
Henry, Thomas J. A. ... San Francisco, CA
Henry, Thomas M. ... Peoria, IL
Henry, Thomas Q. ... **Indianapolis, IN**
Henry, Thomas R. ... Boise, ID
Henry, Thornton M.
West Palm Beach, FL
Henry, Tidal B., Jr. ... **New York, NY**
Henry, Troy ... **Jonesboro, AR**
Henry, Ursula K. ... Farmington, MI
Henry, Varice T.
Equal Employment Opportunity
Commission,
Office of Federal Operations, GV
Henry, Veronica ... **Lake Success, NY**
Henry, Vic H. ... **Dallas, TX**
Henry, Vickie L. ... **Boston, MA**
Henry, W. Craig ... **Monroe, LA**
Henry, W. Dale, Jr. ... **Dallas, TX**
Henry, W. Eugene ... Biloxi, MS
Henry Watz Gardner Sellars & Gardner,
PLLC ... **Lexington, KY**
Henry, Wayne B. ... **Omaha, NE**
Henry, W. C. ... Port Townsend, WA
Henry, William A. ... **Washington, DC**
Henry, William A., II ... Rochester, NY
Henry, William B. ... Winamac, IN
Henry, William L. ... Brookville, PA
Henry, William O. E. ... **Lakeland, FL**
Orlando, FL
Henry, William P. ... Las Vegas, NV
Henry, William R. ... Austin, TX
Henry, William S. ... **Fort Myers, FL**
Henry, Wm. D. ... Columbus, OH
Henry-Hebert, Susan ... Baton Rouge, LA
Henry-Rummel, Donna ... Friendswood, TX
Henrys, Patricia ... **Miami, FL**
Henryson, Herbert, II ... **New York, NY**
Henry-Webb, Rhonda J. ... **St. Louis, MO**
Hens, Tanja E. ... **Washington, DC**
Hensal, James E. ... **Archbold, OH**
Hensal, Jennifer L. ... **Medina, OH**
Hensarling, Jon D. ... **Houston, TX**
Hensarling, Nolan B. ... Dallas, TX
Hensarling, Ray ... Woodville, TX
Hensas, Gregory M. ... Roslyn Heights, NY
Hensch, Janet L. ... **New York, NY**
Henscheid, James Ray ... Des Moines, IA
Henschel, Andrew S. ... Aventura, FL
Henschel, David F. ... **Harrisburg, PA**
Henschel, George L. ... Department of Labor,
Office of the Solicitor, GV
Henschel, Herbert J. ... New York, NY
Henschel, John J. ... Newark, NJ
Henschel, Virginia P. ... **Camp Hill, PA**
Henschen, Curtis Anthony ... Austin, TX
Henschen, Gina ... Atlanta, GA
Henschen, Sharon M. ... Pana, IL
Henschke, Marc N. ... **Boston, MA**
Hense, Jennifer B. ... **Prairie Village, KS**
Hense, Thaddeus J. ... Baltimore, MD
Hensel, Donald J. ... Riverside, CA
Hensel, Donald P. ... **Atlanta, GA**
Hensel, Harold N. ... Toms River, NJ
Hensel, Jack ... Kansas City, MO
Hensel, Jan E. ... **Columbus, OH**
Hensel, John M. ... Lenexa, KS
Hensel, Karen A. ... Louisville, KY
Hensel, Karin B. ... Fort Lauderdale, FL
Hensel, Luain T. ... Tallahassee, FL
Hensel, Lyn Howell ... Columbia, SC
Hensel, Paul C. ... Bath, PA
Hensel, Paul H. ... **Chicago, IL**
Hensel, R. A. ... Waterville, WA
Wenatchee, WA
Hensel, Randall J. ... Pensacola, FL
Hensel, Rene F. ... Rochester, NY
Hensel, Robert E. ... Upper Sandusky, OH
Hensel, Stephen John ... Albany, NY
Hensel, Wendy F. ... Atlanta, GA
Hensel, William H. ... Columbia, SC
Hensel-Jaroch, Susan L. ... Harrisburg, PA
Hensen, Virginia G. ... Beaverton, OR
Hensey, Allison P. ... **Portland, OR**
Hensey, Charles McK. ... Raleigh, NC
Hensgens, Catherine E. ... **Lafayette, LA**
Hensgens, Scott N. ... **Baton Rouge, LA**
Hens-Greco, Kathryn M. ... **Pittsburgh, PA**
Hens-Greco, Sam R ... **Pittsburgh, PA**
Henshall, James F., Jr. ... **Irvine, CA**
Henshall, Kathryn Suzanne ... Boulder, CO
Henshall, Patricia E. ... Topeka, KS
Henshall, Pennington & Brake
Chanute, KS
Henshall, Ronald S. ... **West Point, PA**
Henshaw, A.J., Jr. ... Sallisaw, OK
Henshaw & Brady ... Morristown, NJ
Henshaw, Charles L., Jr. (P.C.)
Columbia, SC
Henshaw, Douglas R. ... Morristown, NJ
Henshaw, Gregory Dent ... Winston-Salem, NC
Henshaw, Harry P., III ... Charleston, WV
Henshaw & Ivey ... Cape Coral, FL
Henshaw, James M. ... Youngstown, OH
Henshaw, Jarrod ... **St. Louis, MO**

Henshaw, Mark D. ... Manassas, VA
Henshaw, Michael J. ... Harrisburg, IL
Henshaw, Sigrid M., (P.A.) ... Cape Coral, FL
Henshaw, Todd Maxwell ... Tulsa, OK
Henshaw, Weld S., (P.C.) ... Boston, MA
Henshel, Annie Glass ... Beverly Hills, CA
Henshell, Jules S. ... Harrisburg, PA
Henshon, Amanda F. ... Boston, MA
Henshon, Matthew T. ... Boston, MA
Henshue, Thomas W. ... Madison, WI
Hensiak, Kathryn K. ... Milwaukee, WI
Hensick, Bert M. ... Howell, MI
Hensick, Christopher D. ... Brighton, MI
Hensick, Michael T. ... Denver, CO
Hensick, Timothy L. ... Howell, MI
Hensien, John P. ... Detroit, MI
Hensinger, Fred W. ... Lexington, KY
Hensinger, Irene deVaux ... Saginaw, MI
Henslee and Cassidy, LLP ... Dallas, TX
Henslee, Donald G. ... Austin, TX
Henslee, Fowler, Hepworth & Schwartz, L.L.P. ... Austin, TX
Dallas, TX
Edinburg, TX
Houston, TX
McAllen, TX
San Antonio, TX
Tyler, TX
Henslee, Marshall T. ... Baton Rouge, LA
Henslee, R. Kent ... Gadsden, AL
Henslee, Robertson & Strawn, L.L.C.
Anniston, AL
Gadsden, AL
Henslee, Thomas T. ... Dallas, TX
Hensleigh, Barbara J. ... Los Angeles, CA
Hensleigh, Howard E. ... Carlisle, MA
Hensler, Arthur C., Jr. ... Newark, NJ
Hensler, David J. ... Washington, DC
Hensler, Louis W., III ... Norfolk, VA
Hensler, Robert James ... Collingswood, NJ
Hensley, D. Murray ... Lubbock, TX
Hensley, Darren R. ... Denver, CO
Hensley, David C. ... Long Beach, CA
Hensley, David C. ... Los Angeles, CA
Hensley, David F. ... Chattanooga, TN
Hensley, David R. ... Chesterfield, MO
Hensley, Deborah S. ... Huntsville, AL
Hensley, Dennis C. ... New York, NY
Hensley, Devin Grayson ... Gloucester, VA
Hensley, Douglas L. ... Cincinnati, OH
Hensley, Dunn, Ross & Howard
Horse Cave, KY
Hensley, Earl Wesley, III ... Wenatchee, WA
Hensley, Edward F., Jr. ... San Antonio, TX
Hensley, Fred T. ... Clovis, NM
Hensley, Guy Wayne ... Brookwood, AL
Hensley, Harold L., Jr. ... Roswell, NM
Hensley & Hensley ... Kansas City, MO
Raymore, MO
Hensley, Howard D. ... Arlington, VA
Hensley, J. Thomas ... Danville, KY
Hensley, J. Thomas, Jr. ... Kirksville, MO
Hensley, James A. ... Huber Heights, OH
Hensley, Jeffrey D. ... Flatwoods, KY
Hensley, Jeffrey M. ... Kansas City, MO
Hensley, Jeffrey W. ... Lafayette, IN
Hensley, John B. ... Champaign, IL
Hensley, John C., Jr. ... Asheville, NC
Hensley, John F. ... Boulder, CO
Hensley, Jos. L. ... Madison, IN
Hensley, Joseph E. ... Bellaire, TX
Hensley, Joseph L. ... Springfield, MO
Hensley, Karen Lynn ... New York, NY
Hensley, Kathy L. ... Emeryville, CA
Hensley, Kelly L. ... Los Angeles, CA
Hensley & Kennedy, P.C. ... Boulder, CO
Hensley, Kenneth C. ... Raymore, MO
Hensley, Kevin M. ... Boston, MA
Hensley & King ... Round Rock, TX
Hensley, Lawrence N. ... Sacramento, CA
Hensley & Leadingham ... Flatwoods, KY
Hensley, Lynn C., (Mr.) ... Round Rock, TX
Hensley, Mark D. ... Los Angeles, CA
Hensley, Max D. ... Foster City, CA
Hensley, Megan R. ... Lakewood, OH
Hensley, Melissa M. ... Dallas, TX
Hensley, Michael Alan ... Alabaster, AL
Hensley, Michael E. ... Phoenix, AZ
Hensley, Michael J. ... Madison, IN
Hensley, Michael Robert ... Miamisburg, OH
Hensley, Muth, Garton & Hayes
Bluefield, WV
Hensley, Nancy A. ... Detroit, MI
Hensley, Nelson T. ... Houston, TX
Hensley, Noel M.B. ... Dallas, TX
Hensley, Pamela W. ... Houston, TX
Hensley, Patricia A. ... Seattle, WA
Hensley, Patricia Laura ... Los Angeles, CA
Hensley, Paula J. ... Fresno, CA
Hensley, Peter R. ... Palo Alto, CA
Hensley, Robert B. ... Horse Cave, KY
Hensley, Robert E. ... Bradenton, FL
Hensley, Robert E. ... Franklin, NC
Hensley, Robert G. ... Minneapolis, MN
Hensley, Robert W., Jr. ... Birmingham, AL
Hensley, Russell J. ... Memphis, TN
Hensley, S. Scott ... Raleigh, NC
Hensley, Sam P., Jr. ... Marietta, GA
Hensley, Schellie L., III ... Sebastopol, CA
Hensley & Smith ... Danville, KY
Hensley, Stephen L. ... Chicago, IL
Hensley, Teresa ... Raymore, MO
Hensley, Todd E. ... Springfield, MO
Hensley, Walro, Collins & Hensley
Madison, IN
Hensley, William A., III ... Wichita, KS
Hensley, William E. ... Oregon City, OR
Hensley, William Michael ... Irvine, CA
Hensley, Wm. J. ... Warrensburg, MO
Henslovitz, Elliot H. ... New York, NY
Henson, A. Benjamin ... Bloomfield Hills, MI
Henson, A. Elizabeth ... Denver, CO
Henson, Alexander T. ... Carmel Valley, CA
Henson, Almon E. ... Shawnee, OK
Henson, Arnold ... Old Greenwich, CT
Henson, Barbara A. ... Mission Viejo, CA
Henson, Bradley Winn, Sr. ... Ship Bottom, NJ
Henson, Burt M. ... Ventura, CA
Henson, Carlton M. ... Atlanta, GA
Henson, Charles (Chuck) ... Denver, CO
Henson, Charles N. ... Topeka, KS
Henson, Christopher ... Galesburg, IL
Henson, Colleen A. ... New York, NY
Henson, D. Keith ... St. Louis, MO
Henson, David S. ... Rocky Mount, NC
Henson, Deborah M. ... New Orleans, LA
Henson, Diane, Law Firm of ... Austin, TX
Henson, Diane M. ... Austin, TX
Henson, Donald W. ... Okmulgee, OK
Henson, Dorothy F. ... San Francisco, CA
Henson, Doug ... Roanoke, VA
Henson, Douglas A. ... Springfield, OH
Henson, Douglas C. ... Albuquerque, NM
Henson, E. Bryan, Jr. ... Tulsa, OK
Henson & Efron, P.A. ... Minneapolis, MN
Henson, Eric B. ... Philadelphia, PA
Henson, F. Ewin, III ... Greenwood, MS
Henson, Franklin S. ... Spartanburg, SC
Henson and Fuerst, P.A.
Rocky Mount, NC
Henson, H. Kirk, Law Office of ... Atlanta, GA
Henson & Henson ... Pasadena, CA
San Francisco, CA
Henson, Henson, Henson, Marshall & Milburn, LLP ... Shawnee, OK
Henson & Henson, L.L.P.
Greensboro, NC
Henson, Hugh E., Jr. ... Waco, TX
Henson, India Marie ... Chattanooga, TN
Henson, J. Boyd ... White Plains, NY
Henson, J. Edwin ... Cashiers, NC
Henson, J. Roger ... Shawnee, OK
Henson, Jackson W. ... Winston-Salem, NC
Henson, Jacqueline A. ... Washington, DC
Henson, James B. ... White Plains, NY
Henson, James D. ... Mansfield, OH
Henson, James E., Sr. ... Ellicott City, MD
Henson, James H. ... Mount Vernon, IL
Henson, James J. ... Columbus, OH
Henson, Jeffrey A. ... Charlotte, NC
Henson, Jill ... Clovis, NM
Henson, John P. ... Greenwood, MS
Henson, John S. ... Missoula, MT
Henson, Josiah Douglas ... Falls Church, VA
Henson, Karen Ann ... Shawnee, OK
Henson, Karen Kemper ... Boston, MA
Henson, Kenneth M. ... Sea Island, GA
Henson, Kenneth M., Jr. ... Columbus, GA
Henson, Kenneth M., Jr., P.C.
Columbus, GA
Henson, Larry D. ... Pasadena, CA
San Francisco, CA
Henson, Larry W. ... Minneapolis, MN
Henson Law Firm, LLP ... Spartanburg, SC
Henson, Leonard J. ... Boston, MA
Henson, Lucy B. ... Timonium, MD
Henson, Lucy J. ... Ferndale, WA
Henson, Margaret Marie ... Topeka, KS
Henson, Martha W. ... Marietta, GA
Henson, Monty H. ... Austin, TX
Henson, P. Douglas, II ... Roanoke, VA
Henson, Paul F. ... Santa Fe, NM
Henson & Paul, P.A. ... Brevard, NC
Cashiers, NC
Henson, Perry C. ... Greensboro, NC
Henson, Perry C., Jr. ... Greensboro, NC
Henson, Randolph C. ... Houston, TX
Henson, Ray D. ... San Francisco, CA
Henson, Rex A. ... Poplar Bluff, MO
Henson, Robert A. ... Seattle, WA
Henson, Robert F. ... Minneapolis, MN
Henson, Ronald ... Galesburg, IL
Henson, Ronald C. ... Washington, DC
Henson, Sandra Kathleen
Charleston, WV
Henson, T. Donald ... La Salle, IL
Henson, Theresa J. ... Philadelphia, PA
Henson, Thomas M. ... Westminster, CO
Henson, Thomas W. ... Rocky Mount, NC
Henson, Thomas W., Jr.
Rocky Mount, NC
Henson, Tom ... Tyler, TX
Henson, Virginia D. ... Shawnee, OK
Henson, Warren W., III ... Oklahoma City, OK
Henson, Willard H. ... Montgomery, AL
Henson, William H. ... Maysville, OK
Henson, William L. ... Sacramento, CA
Henson, William W. ... New York, NY
Hensrud, Lloyd W. ... Mekinock, ND
Henss, Donald A. ... Champaign, IL
Henss, Mark D. ... Urbana, IL
Henstridge, Robert M.
Laguna Niguel, CA
Hentchel, Theodore P., Jr. ... Battle Creek, MI
Henteleff, Thomas O. ... Washington, DC
Hentell, Marc A. ... Los Angeles, CA
Hentemann, Henry A. ... Cleveland, OH
Hentemann, Paul H. ... Willoughby, OH
Hentges, Harlan G. ... Oklahoma City, OK
Hentges, Robert C. ... Minneapolis, MN
Henthorn, B. Christopher ... Yukon, OK
Henthorn, C. Rex ... Crawfordsville, IN
Henthorn, Carl F. ... Crawfordsville, IN
Henthorn, Harris, Taylor & Weliever, P.C.
Crawfordsville, IN
Henthorn, Rick J. ... Yukon, OK
Henthorne, Christine B. ... Chillicothe, OH
Henthorne, D. Michael ... Mauldin, SC
Hentoff Law Office ... Phoenix, AZ
Hentoff, Nicholas S. ... Phoenix, AZ
Hentoff, Thomas G. ... Washington, DC
Hentrel, Michael L.
Board of Governors Of The Federal Reserve System,
Division of Consumer and Community Affairs, GV
Hentrich, John J. ... San Diego, CA
Hentrich, William T. ... Floral Park, NY
Hentschel, Craig N. ... Los Angeles, CA
Hentschel, Ernest G., II ... Charleston, WV
Hentschel, Naomi A. ... Los Angeles, CA
Hentschel, Peter C. ... Quincy, CA
Hentschell, Mark S. ... St. Louis, MO
Hentschke, Daniel S. ... Solana Beach, CA
Henty, David L. ... Los Angeles, CA
Hentz, David ... La Fayette, GA
Hentz, Kurt A. ... St. Louis, MO
Hentz, Nancy L. ... Houston, TX
Hentz, William Walter ... Dallas, TX
Hentzel, John I. ... Clarendon Hills, IL
Hentzell, Richard L. ... Denver, CO
Hentzen, James H. ... Leawood, KS
Hentzen, Michael J. ... Milwaukee, WI
Henvey, John W. ... Dallas, TX
Henward, DeBanks M., III
Paradise Valley, AZ
Henwood, Drew F. ... San Francisco, CA
Heny, Joseph S. ... San Antonio, TX
Henz, Donald J. ... Cincinnati, OH
Henze, Brian D. ... Mason City, IA
Henze, Jeffrey L. ... Oakland, CA
Henze, Lawrence Carroll ... Chicago, IL
Henze, Mark T. ... San Clemente, CA
Henze, Robt. J. ... Detroit, MI
Henze, Thomas E. ... Danville, CA
Henze, Tom ... Phoenix, AZ
Henze, William F., II ... New York, NY
Henzel, D. Ben ... Portland, OR
Henzel, Marc S. ... Philadelphia, PA
Henzell, Arthur A. ... Santa Barbara, CA
Henzes, Randall J. ... Philadelphia, PA
Henzi, Karen E. ... San Jose, CA
Henzi, Matthew I. ... Southfield, MI
Henzie, George M. ... Los Angeles, CA
Henzke, Leonard J., Jr. ... Washington, DC
Henzl, Robert R. ... Racine, WI
Henzler, Maribel ... Pittsburgh, PA
Henzy, Eric A. ... Hartford, CT
Heo, Kyun ... Seattle, WA
Heon, Alfred A. ... Milwaukee, WI
Heon, Larry L. ... Novato, CA
Heon, Lawrence M ... Santa Fe, NM
Heos, George N., Jr. ... Boston, MA
Heos, James T. ... Lansing, MI
Hepburn, Carol L. ... Seattle, WA
Hepburn, George C., III ... Houston, TX
Hepburn, James Roger ... Tuscaloosa, AL
Hepburn, Michael A. ... Washington, DC
Hepburn, Michael T. ... Chicago, IL
Hepburn, Philip R. ... Philadelphia, PA
Hepburn, Robert D. ... Terre Haute, IN
Hepburn, Rodger M. ... Portland, OR
Hepburn Willcox Hamilton & Putnam
Philadelphia, PA
Hepfer, Cheryl Lynn ... Rockville, MD
Upper Marlboro, MD
Hepfer, Cheryl Lynn
Upper Marlboro, MD
Hepfer, Richard G. ... Columbia, SC
Hepfinger, Mark L. ... Brookfield, WI
Hepfner, Donald C. ... Austintown, OH
Hepford, H. Joseph ... Harrisburg, PA
Hepler, Bruce W. ... Irvine, CA
Hepler, Carl F., Jr. ... Bensalem, PA
Langhorne, PA
Hepler, Erik W. ... New York, NY
Hepler, Gordon E. ... San Francisco, CA
Hepler, Jeanne M. ... Covington, VA
Hepler, Larry E. ... Edwardsville, IL
Hepler, Robert W. ... United States Senate,
Senatorial Assistants, GV
Hepler, Saunders, Barkes & Kolbus, LLP
Goshen, IN
Hepner, Daniel A. ... Boulder, CO
Hepner, George D., III ... Falmouth, ME
Hepner, Irv ... Los Angeles, CA
Hepner, Jane E. ... Pittsburgh, PA
Hepner, Michael D. ... Englewood, CO
Hepner, William P ... New York, NY
Hepp, Pamela E. ... Pittsburgh, PA
Hepp, W. Terry ... Chicago, IL
Heppard, Jeffrey P. ... Cherry Hill, NJ
Heppberger, Melinda P.
San Francisco, CA
Heppe, Harry J. ... Scottsdale, AZ
Heppe, Robert S., Jr. ... Worcester, MA
Heppel, Alan B. ... Los Angeles, CA
Heppell, Gary K. ... Vallejo, CA
Heppenheimer, Korpal & Toth, P.C.
South Bend, IN
Heppenheimer, Mitchell R. ... South Bend, IN
Heppenstall, Edward M. ... Denver, CO
Heppenstall, Savage, Trower & Muller, LLC
Denver, CO
Hepper, Raymond W. ... Augusta, ME
Hepperle, Winifred L. ... San Francisco, CA
Hepperly, Foster J. ... El Cajon, CA
Hepperly, Michael D. ... Wichita, KS
Heppermann, Roger A. ... Chicago, IL
Heppler, Wesley R. ... Washington, DC
Hepplewhite, David W. ... Chicago, IL
Heppner, Daniel G. ... Kingston, NY
Heppner, George C. ... San Diego, CA
H[illegible]pner, Peter E. ... Easton, MA
Hepps, Michael B. L. ... Philadelphia, PA
Hepps, Steven M. ... Brea, CA
Heppt, Joseph M. ... New York, NY
Heptig, J. Pat ... Dallas, TX
Heptig, Lawrence W. ... Ithaca, NY
Hepworth, H. Jed ... Minneapolis, MN
Hepworth, J. Charles ... Boise, ID
Hepworth, James D. ... Santa Monica, CA
Hepworth, Jeffrey J. ... Twin Falls, ID
Hepworth, Joanne Roney
Washington, DC
Hepworth, Joanne Roney ... Rockville, MD
Hepworth, John C. ... Twin Falls, ID
Hepworth, Joseph M. ... Mesa, AZ
Hepworth, Kenneth E. ... Seattle, WA
Hepworth, Lezamiz & Hohnhorst, Chartered
Boise, ID
Twin Falls, ID
Hepworth, Michael R. ... New York, NY
Hepworth, Roger D. ... Austin, TX
Hepworth, Wesley W. ... Dallas, TX
Herak, Charles D. ... Wilmington, DE
Herak, Daniel L. ... Cleveland, OH
Herald, Alice A. ... Los Angeles, CA
Herald, Bruce A. ... Exton, PA
Herald, Bruce Alan, A P.C. ... Exton, PA
Herald, Charles W. ... Pittsburgh, PA
Herald, Darrell A ... Jackson, KY
Herald, J. Patrick ... Chicago, IL
Herald, James M. ... Columbus, OH
Herald, James R. ... Portland, OR
Herald, James W., Jr. ... Whitesburg, KY
Herald, John E. ... Green Bay, WI
Herald, Keith A. ... Kenmore, NY
Herald, Lynn Ethel ... Jackson, KY
Herald, Marybeth ... Saipan, TT
Herald, Sally J. ... Fort Thomas, KY
Herald, Sara Barli ... Miami, FL
Herald, Susan ... San Francisco, CA
Herald, Thomas A. ... Arlington, TX
Heramb, Brent R. ... San Diego, CA
Heran, Charles W., Jr. ... Albany, NY
Heran, Colin J. ... Sacramento, CA
Heran, Jeanne M. ... Albany, NY
Heran, Michael A. ... White Plains, NY
Herasimchuk, Cathleen C. ... Houston, TX
Heraty, John E. ... Boston, MA
Heraty, Peter E. ... Chicago, IL
Heraty, Peter F. ... Chicago, IL
Herauf, William A. ... Dickinson, ND
Heravi, Behzad D. ... Reseda, CA
Herb, Alice H. ... Brooklyn, NY
Herb, F. Steven ... Sarasota, FL
Herb, Hans W., Law Offices of
San Francisco, CA
Herb, Hans W., Law Offices of
Santa Rosa, CA
Herb, James A. ... Boca Raton, FL
Herb, James M. ... Pittsburgh, PA
Herb, Leonard N. ... Reading, PA
Herb, Lisa M. ... Seattle, WA
Herb & Mednick, P.A. ... Boca Raton, FL
Delray Beach, FL
Fort Lauderdale, FL
West Palm Beach, FL
Herb, Peter L. ... New York, NY
Herbach, Andrew N. ... Milwaukee, WI
Herbach, Barry D. ... Grand Rapids, MI
Herbach, Etta Gail ... San Francisco, CA
Herbage, Cathleen B. ... Gold Beach, OR
Herbage, Michael G. ... Gold Beach, OR
Herbaugh, Phillip L. ... Cuyahoga Falls, OH
Herbe, Diana J. ... Tiffin, OH
Herbeck, Charles R. ... Texas City, TX
Herbenick, Bernard M. ... Miami Beach, FL
Herber, Darrell F. ... Shattuck, OK
Herber, Linda J. ... Chicago, IL
Herberg, Peter E. ... Tucson, AZ
Herberger, Robert J., Jr.
Youngstown, OH
Herberich, Frederick D. ... Boston, MA
Herbers, John A. ... Milwaukee, WI
Herbers, Lucy T. ... St. Louis, MO
Herbers, Paul V. ... Kansas City, MO
Herbert, A.J., III ... New Orleans, LA
Herbert, Antonia Rago, (Mrs.) ... Chicago, IL
Herbert, Augustus S. ... Louisville, KY
Herbert, Barry S. ... Chicago, IL
Herbert & Benson ... Akron, OH
Canton, OH
Herbert, Betty Reece ... Glasgow, KY
Herbert, Beverly S. ... Santa Barbara, CA
Herbert, Celeste H. ... Knoxville, TN
Herbert, Charles E. ... Piedmont, CA
Herbert, Clarke E. ... Marina, CA
Herbert, Daniel B. ... Los Angeles, CA
Herbert, Daniel C. ... San Diego, CA
Herbert, David B. ... Nashville, TN
Herbert, David L. ... Canton, OH
Herbert, David L. ... Dallas, TX
Herbert, Dennis P. ... Philadelphia, PA
Herbert, Dirk ... Santa Monica, CA
Herbert, Donna F. ... Thousand Oaks, CA
Herbert, Douglas C., Law Office of
Washington, DC
Herbert, Edwin L. ... Toledo, OH
Herbert, Elizabeth R. ... Topeka, KS
Herbert, Eugene T. ... Washington, DC
Herbert, Frances G. ... San Bernardino, CA
Herbert, Gary N. ... Denver, CO
Herbert, George E. ... Long Grove, IL
Herbert, George K. ... Austin, TX
Herbert, George L. ... Palo Alto, CA
Herbert, Georgia H. ... The Plains, VA
Herbert, Gordon B. ... Raleigh, NC
Herbert, Gregory F. ... St. Louis, MO
Herbert, Gregory W. ... Orlando, FL
Herbert, H. Jefferson, Jr. ... Glasgow, KY

Herbert, Harvey A. ... Brooklyn, NY
Herbert & Herbert ... Edmonton, KY
Glasgow, KY
Herbert, Ian A. ... Washington, DC
Herbert, Irving ... New York, NY
Herbert, J. Stephen ... Dayton, OH
Herbert, James D. ... Boston, MA
Herbert, John C. ... Buffalo, NY
Rochester, NY
Herbert, John C. ... Houston, TX
Herbert, John D. ... Chandler, AZ
Herbert, John D. ... Cincinnati, OH
Herbert, John F., III ... Baltimore, MD
Herbert, John G. ... Denver, CO
Herbert, John G., P.C. ... Denver, CO
Herbert, John K., III ... Boston, MA
Herbert, John S. ... New York, NY
Herbert, John W. ... Dublin, OH
Herbert, Joseph A. ... Phoenix, AZ
Herbert, Joseph E. ... Cleveland, OH
Herbert, Joseph E. ... Houston, TX
Herbert, Jule R., Jr. ... Gulf Shores, AL
Herbert, Karen Jones ... Washington, DC
Herbert, Kenneth W. ... Palisades Park, NJ
Herbert, Lenese L. ...
Department of Justice, GV
Herbert, Leon F. ... Los Altos, CA
Herbert, Leon L., II ... Altadena, CA
Herbert, Lynn A. ... Philadelphia, PA
Herbert, Marc K. ... Lancaster, CA
Herbert, Margaret L. ... Chicago, IL
Herbert, Marjorie M. ... Georgetown, TX
Herbert, Mark D. ... Jackson, MS
Herbert, Marsha Brown ... Hollywood, FL
Herbert, Michael C. ... Baton Rouge, LA
Herbert, Michael J. ... Princeton, NJ
Herbert, Michael William ... Princeton, NJ
Herbert, Nancy B. ... Treasury Department,
Internal Revenue Service, GV
Herbert, Patricia Franklin ... Paramus, NJ
Herbert, Paul D. ... Redwood City, CA
Herbert, Paul M., II ... Columbus, OH
Herbert, Peter ... New York, NY
Herbert, Raymond L. ... New York, NY
Herbert & Rees, P.A. ... Phoenix, AZ
Herbert, Richard J. ... Phoenix, AZ
Herbert, Ronald P. ... Richmond, VA
Herbert, Rosemary ... New York, NY
Herbert, Seth Earl (IBA) ... New York, NY
Herbert, Shanna A. ... McLean, VA
Herbert Smith ... New York, NY
Herbert, Stephen R. ... Stamford, CT
New York, NY
Herbert, T. Ronald ... Chicago, IL
Herbert, Thomas M. ... Punta Gorda, FL
Herbert, Thomas O. ... Palo Alto, CA
Herbert, Toni-Junell ... Alexandria, VA
Herbert, Van Ness, Cayci & Goodell, A Professional Corporation ... Princeton, NJ
Trenton, NJ
Herbert, Victor ... New York, NY
Herbert, W. David ... Riverton, WY
Herbert, Walter A., Jr. ... Upper Marlboro, MD
Herbert, William A. ... Albany, NY
Herbert, William B., IV ... Nashville, TN
Herbert, William C., III ... Ashland, VA
Herbert, William F. ... Washington, DC
Herbert, William S. ... Santa Fe, NM
Herbert, Williard A. ... Addison, TX
Herbert, Wm. Carlisle ... Chicago, IL
Herbert-Peterson, Sophia L. ... Atlanta, GA
Herbich, Sue Vo ... Honolulu, HI
Herbig, John H. ... Richmond, VA
Herbison, Gretchen ... Seattle, WA
Herbison, John E. ... Nashville, TN
Herbold, Barrie J. ... Portland, OR
Herbold, Carl F. ... Claremont, CA
Herbold, Marita Ilene ... Bethpage, NY
Herbolich, Michael J. ... Douglas, AZ
Herbolich, Michael J., A Professional Corporation ... Douglas, AZ
Herbolsheimer, Lannon, Henson, Duncan and Reagan, P.C. ... La Salle, IL
Ottawa, IL
Herbon, Ellis R. ... Milwaukee, WI
Herbon, Geoffrey M. ... Milwaukee, WI
Herbon, McLaughlin & Herbon
Milwaukee, WI
Herbort, James H., Attorney at Law, P.C.
Burnet, TX
Herbort, James H., (P.C.) ... Burnet, TX
Herbrand, Michael P. ... Grafton, WI
Herbruck, John H. ... Beaver, PA
Herbsman, Jonas Evan ... New York, NY
Herbst, Abbe Ilene ... Hackensack, NJ
New York, NY
Herbst, Adrian E. ... Washington, DC
Herbst, Andrea Birnbaum ... New City, NY
Herbst, C. Donald ... Phoenix, AZ
Herbst, Christopher C. ... Durham, NC
Herbst, David I. ... Chicago, IL
Herbst, David W. ... Palo Alto, CA
Herbst, Gary F. ... Wantagh, NY
Herbst & Greenwald, LLP ... New York, NY
Herbst, Henry Nicholas ... Norman, OK
Herbst, Hilary F. ... Indianapolis, IN
Herbst, Jay A. ... Troy, MI
Herbst, John C., III ... Cromwell, CT
Herbst, John J. ... New York, NY
Herbst, Jonathan D. ... Philadelphia, PA
Herbst, Julie A. ... Boston, MA
Herbst, Lawrence ... Newburgh, NY
Herbst, Mark C. ... Annapolis, MD
Herbst, Melinda Socol ... New York, NY
Herbst, Michael A. ... Seattle, WA
Herbst, Paul M. ... Fairfax, VA
Herbst, Peter C., Law Offices of
Torrington, CT
Herbst, Ralph L., III ... Philadelphia, PA
Herbst, Robert L. ... New York, NY
Herbst, Robert S. ... New York, NY
Herbst, Ronald S. ... Stamford, CT
New York, NY
Herbst, Scott A. ... Washington, DC
Herbst, Scott E. ... Indianapolis, IN
Herbst, Timothy J. ... Charlotte, NC
Herbst, Todd L. ... New York, NY
Herbster, Avrom J. ... Boston, MA
Herbster, George A. ... Lowell, MA
Manchester, MA
Herbstman, Janet S. ... Flossmoor, IL
Herce & Herce ... Tampa, FL
Herce, Mario N. ... Tampa, FL
Herce, Robert A. ... Tampa, FL
Herceg, Marjorie A. ... Chicago, IL
Hercenberg, Jerrold J. ... Reston, VA
Herchel, Dennis S. ... Springfield, MA
Herchenroder, Jane A. ... Flemington, NJ
Herchenroder, John A. ... Brooklyn, NY
Herchenroether, Henry C., Jr.
Pittsburgh, PA
Herchenroether, Peter Y. ... Pittsburgh, PA
Hercher, David W., P.C. ... Portland, OR
Hercl, Daniel P. ... Columbus, OH
Hercules, Larry K. ... Plano, TX
Hercules, Larry K., P.C. ... Plano, TX
Hercz, Michael G. ... Los Angeles, CA
Herczeg, Susan J. ... Philadelphia, PA
Herd, Charles F., Jr. ... Houston, TX
Herd, Charles H. ... Greensburg, KS
Herd, Daniel W. ... Austin, TX
Herd, David A. ... Columbus, OH
Herd, Elizabeth (Betsey) T. ... Tampa, FL
Herd, Harold S. ... Topeka, KS
Herd, James B. ... St. Louis, MO
Herd, James H. (Skip) ... Coldwater, KS
Herd, Michael D. ... Wichita, KS
Herd, Tevis ... Midland, TX
Herd, Thomas C. ... Newark, NJ
Herd, Thomas J. ... Colorado Springs, CO
Herd, William A., Jr. ... Elizabethtown, PA
Herde, Michael E. ... Stamford, CT
Herdeg, du Pont & Dalle Pazze, LLP
Wilmington, DE
Herdeg, John A. ... Wilmington, DE
Herdelin, Thomas M. ... Haddonfield, NJ
Herdell, Kathleen A. ... St. Helena, CA
Herder, Arthur E., Jr. ... St. Louis, MO
Herder, Diane M. ... Laingsburg, MI
Herder & Herder, P.C. ... St. Louis, MO
Herder, Lisa Ann ... St. Louis, MO
Herder, Mark Albert ... Columbus, OH
Herder, Robert Rex, Jr. ... Willow Grove, PA
Herder, Thomas J. ... Orlando, FL
Herdes, Elizabeth B.
Colorado Springs, CO
Herdes, William ... Jamaica, NY
Herdman, Christine L. ... Beverly Hills, CA
Herdman, David A. ... Battle Creek, MI
Herdman, Frank T. ... Santa Fe, NM
Herdman, G. Douglas ... Dayton, OH
Herdman, Harry T. ... Portsmouth, OH
Herdman, Paul N. ... Lebanon, OH
Herdman, Walter C. ... Frankfort, KY
Herdoiza, C. Albert ... Kansas City, KS
Herdrich, Madeline A. ... Washington, DC
Herdzik, Arthur A. ... Buffalo, NY
Herdzik, Matthew B., Jr. ... Buffalo, NY
Herdzina, John W. ... Omaha, NE
Hered, A. Ann ... Menlo Park, CA
Heredia, Barbara A. ... Riverside, CA
Heredia, Carlos D. ... San Diego, CA
Heredia, Claudio ... Eagle Pass, TX
Heredia, F. Samuel ... Oxnard, CA
Heredia, Maria C. ... San Diego, CA
Hereford, Darren L. ... Santa Monica, CA
Hereford, Earle J. ... Seattle, WA
Hereford, Earle J., P.L.L.C. ... Seattle, WA
Hereford, Harvey ... San Francisco, CA
Hereford & Hemker ... St. Louis, MO
Hereford & Hereford ... Charleston, WV
Hereford, James S., Jr. ... Fayetteville, TN
Hereford, Martha Neville ... St. Louis, MO
Hereford, Philip B. ... Charleston, WV
Hereford, Richard P. ... St. Louis, MO
Hereford, Stephen M. ... St. Louis, MO
Hereford, Susanne Öst ... Santa Clara, CA
Hereford, William E. ... Pell City, AL
Hereford, William M. ... Sarasota, FL
Hereford, William S. ... Birmingham, AL
Herendeen and Bryan, A Professional Corporation ... Salinas, CA
Herendeen, Christine L. ... Tampa, FL
Herendeen, George E. ... South Bend, IN
Herendeen, Michael L. ... East Lansing, MI
Herendeen, Michael L., P.C.
East Lansing, MI
Herendeen, Robert P. ... Salinas, CA
Herer, David I. ... Buffalo, NY
Herescu, Radu, Law Offices of
New York, NY
Heretick, Stephen E. ... Norfolk, VA
Herf, Charles W. ... Phoenix, AZ
Herfel, Gary L. ... Covington, KY
Herff, Christian G. ... San Antonio, TX
Herff, F. Peter, II ... San Antonio, TX
Herfkens, Janice M. ... Des Moines, IA
Herfort, John A. ... New York, NY
Herge, J. Curtis ... McLean, VA
Herge, Sparks & Christopher, LLP
Washington, DC
McLean, VA
Hergen, James G. ... Department of State,
Office of the Legal Adviser, GV
Hergenhan, Kenneth W., P.C. ... Portland, OR
Hergenhan, Michael A. ... Newburgh, NY
Hergenroeder, Charles W., III ... Pittsburgh, PA
Hergenroeder, Chas. W., Jr. ... Pittsburgh, PA
Hergenroether, Scott J. ... Phoenix, AZ
Tucson, AZ
Hergenrother, Thos. E. ... Chicago, IL
Herger, James C. ... Hudson Falls, NY
Hergert & Associates, P.C. ... Oregon City, OR
Hergert, Jonathan K. ... Pittsburgh, PA
Hergert, Ronald E. ... Oregon City, OR
Herget, Georgette Renata
Los Angeles, CA
Herget, James E. ... Houston, TX
Hergott, Alan S. ... Beverly Hills, CA
Hergott, Daniel W., (P.A.)
Minneapolis, MN
Hergott, Jay S. ... Northbrook, IL
Hergott, Wayne A. ... Minneapolis, MN
Herhold, Theodore T. ... Palo Alto, CA
Herhusky, Evamarie Cheung ... Carmel, CA
Herhusky, Stacey F. ... Incline Village, NV
Heria, Fernando E. ... Hialeah, FL
Heriaud, Neal ... Chicago, IL
Heriford, Joel K. ... Davenport, IA
Herigstad, Mitchell A. ... Sioux City, IA
Herigstad, Roger O. ... Minot, ND
Herin, David V. ... Corpus Christi, TX
Herin, David V., P.C. ... Corpus Christi, TX
Herin, John Raymond, Jr ... Miami, FL
Hering, Barbara A. ... Des Moines, IA
Hering, Benjamin A. ... New York, NY
Hering, Denise Harbaugh
Newport Beach, CA
Hering, G. Clark, IV ... Greensboro, NC
Hering, George C., III ... Wilmington, DE
Hering, Glenn Z. ... Chicago, IL
Hering, Grant B. ... New York, NY
Hering, Heidi B. ... McLean, VA
Hering, Jim ... Waco, TX
Hering, Laura F. ... Fairfax, VA
Hering, Louis ... Hume, VA
Hering, Louis G. ... Wilmington, DE
Hering, Michele Slochowsky ... Brooklyn, NY
Hering, Ross C. ... West Palm Beach, FL
Heringer, Carl S. ... Lawrenceville, NJ
Heringer, Michael P. ... Billings, MT
Herington, Harry H. ... Atlanta, GA
Herington, Jack E. ... Pawleys Island, SC
Herington, Leigh E. ... Aurora, OH
Herink, Daniel D. ... Brownsville, TX
Herink, Kent A. ... Des Moines, IA
Herisko, Ronald J. ... Palm Springs, CA
Heritage, Harold Christopher
San Francisco, CA
Heritage, Katherine Keeney ... Troy, MI
Heritage, William H., III ... Detroit, MI
Heritage, William H., Jr.
Grand Rapids, MI
Heritier Nance & Sheridan, P.C. ... Troy, MI
Heritier, Robert L. ... Troy, MI
Herkala, David William ... Syracuse, NY
Herkamp, Nathan D. ... Cincinnati, OH
Herke, John M. ... Hattiesburg, MS
Herkenham, James J. ... Slate Hill, NY
Herkenham, M. Dawn ... Department of Justice,
Federal Bureau of Investigation, GV
Herkenham, Thomas L. ... Albany, NY
Herkenhoff, Kathleen A. ... Los Angeles, CA
Herkert, Nancy Neidich ... Hialeah, FL
Herkins, Robert C. ... Reynoldsburg, OH
Herklotz, Johann F. ... Lexington, KY
Herlach, Mark D. ... Washington, DC
Herlache, Ralph F. ... Sturgeon Bay, WI
Herlache, Thomas L. ... Sturgeon Bay, WI
Herlan, Eric R. ... Portland, ME
Herland, Elliot A. ... Brooklyn Center, MN
Herland, Karen Swedenburg
Minneapolis, MN
Herland, Warren A. ... New York, NY
Herland, Warren C. ... Bronx, NY
Herlands, Jonathan ... New York, NY
Herlands, Krushinski & Rothenberg
Scranton, PA
Herlands, Scott A. ... Scranton, PA
Herlein, Claudia K. ... San Jose, CA
Herleth, Joyce Savio ... St. Louis, MO
Herlevich, Camilla M. ... Wilmington, NC
Herlich, Theodore Marc ... Brooklyn, NY
Herlick, Stanford D. ... Highland, CA
Herlick, Susan ... Sterling, VA
Herlihy, Barry H. ... Pasadena, CA
Herlihy, David A. ... Newton, MA
Herlihy, Edward D. ... New York, NY
Herlihy, Eileen M. ... Boston, MA
Herlihy, Ellen M. ... Boston, MA
Herlihy, George M. ... Arlington, MA
Herlihy, Glenn David ... Haverhill, MA
Herlihy, Harker & Kavanaugh
Wilmington, DE
Herlihy, Jerome O. ... Wilmington, DE
Herlihy, Joanne ... Denver, CO
Herlihy, John E. ... Fort Myers, FL
Herlihy, John E. ... Glens Falls, NY
Herlihy, John F. ... San Jose, CA
Herlihy, John F., Jr. ... Revere, MA
Herlihy, John J. C. ... Boston, MA
Herlihy, Joseph M. ... Chestnut Hill, MA
Herlihy, Kevin M. ... Haverhill, MA
Herlihy, Kimberly Weber ... Columbus, OH
Herlihy, Linda M. ... Paramus, NJ
Herlihy, Mark E. ... Washington, DC
Herlihy, Mary Ann Hoff ... Wilmington, DE
Herlihy, Sarah B. ... New York, NY
Herlihy, Scott B. ... Austin, TX
Herlihy, Scott C. ... Washington, DC
Herlihy, T Mark ... Boston, MA
Herlihy, Tara F. ... Cambridge, MA
Herlihy, Thomas, III ... Wilmington, DE
Herlihy, Thomas M. ... San Francisco, CA
Herlihy, Thomas W.
Department of Transportation,
Office of the General Counsel, GV
Herlihy, Thursby and Herlihy, LLP
Boston, MA
Herlihy, William F. ... Norwalk, CT
Herlihy, William M. ... Charleston, WV
Herlik, Anna ... Del Mar, CA
Herlin, Marilyn J. ... Walnut Creek, CA
Herling, Bertram ... Valley Stream, NY
Herling, Daniel J. ... San Diego, CA
San Francisco, CA
Herling, Jane F. ... Radnor, PA
Herling, Julius ... White Plains, NY
Herling, Marc Jay ... Newark, NJ
Herling, Michael J. ... Stamford, CT
Herling, Simon ... New York, NY
Herling-Tighe, Lynn ... Arlington Heights, IL
Herlinsky, Victor J., Jr. ... Hackensack, NJ
New York, NY
Herlitzka, Margaret Ahne ... La Crosse, WI
Herlitz-Pollak, Karen ... Dallas, TX
Herlocker, J. Dennis ... Winfield, KS
Herlocker, Lucy L. ... Wichita, KS
Herlocker, Roberts & St. Peter, L.L.C.
Winfield, KS
Herlocker, Thomas D. ... Winfield, KS
Herlofsky, Susan C. ... Minneapolis, MN
Herlong, Dennis G. ... Houston, TX
Herlong, Henry M., Jr. ... Greenville, SC
Herlong, Robert W. ... Columbia, SC
Herlong, Warren C., Jr. ... Mobile, AL
Herlong, William D. ... Greenville, SC
Herm, Jeffrey ... Denver, CO
Herm, Jeffrey, P.C. ... Denver, CO
Herm, Stephen R. ... Department of Justice,
Environment and Natural Resources
Division, GV
Hermalyn, Lawrence L. ... Chicago, IL
Herman, Adrienne D. ... Los Angeles, CA
Herman, Alan D. ... Wichita, KS
Herman, Alan F. ... Atlanta, GA
Herman, Alan I. ... Washington, DC
Herman, Alan S. ... Putnam, CT
Herman, Alison P. ... Miami, FL
Herman, Andrew Dewald
Washington, DC
Herman, Andrew M. ... Washington, DC
Herman, Ann W. ... Buffalo, NY
Herman, Anthony ... Washington, DC
Herman, Antoinette A. ... Staten Island, NY
Herman, Arthur ... Northbrook, IL
Herman, Arthur A. ... Mount Vernon, NY
Herman, Arthur P. ... San Francisco, CA
Herman, Avram C. ... Metairie, LA
Herman & Beinin ... New York, NY
Herman, Benjamin J. ... New York, NY
Herman, Bernard H. ... Hyannis, MA
Herman, Bertram ... Oyster Bay, NY
Herman, Bertram, P.C. ... Oyster Bay, NY
Herman, Bradley S. ... Minneapolis, MN
Herman, Brett P. ... Brooklyn, NY
Herman, Brian A. ... New York, NY
Herman, Brian J. ... Richmond Hill, NY
Herman, Bruce ... New York, NY
Herman, Bruce K. ... Fort Lauderdale, FL
Herman, Bruce L. ... Southfield, MI
Herman, Carl J. ... Livingston, NJ
Herman, Carolyn ... Jacksonville Beach, FL
Herman, Charles E. ... Cassopolis, MI
Herman, Charlotte A., (Mrs.) ... Ada, OK
Herman, Chas. ... New York, NY
Herman, Christopher C.
Environmental Protection Agency,
Program Office Attorneys, GV
Herman, D. Duffy ... Baltimore, MD
Herman, Daniel D. ... Irvington, NJ
Herman, Daniel Ian ... New Castle, PA
Herman, Daniel J. ... Largo, FL
Herman, Daniel S. ... Miami, FL
Herman, David A. ... Springfield, IL
Herman, David H. ... Spokane, WA
Herman, David P. ... Miami, FL
Herman, David R. ... Tallahassee, FL
Herman, David Z. ... East Meadow, NY
Herman, Dean B. ... Los Angeles, CA
Herman, Dean M. ... San Francisco, CA
Herman, Deborah Platt ... Cleveland, OH
Herman, Debra Starkman ... Miami, FL
Herman, Denise T. ... Tampa, FL
Herman, Dennis J. ... Denver, CO
Herman, Dimitry S. ... Boston, MA
Herman, Donald Charles ... Auburn, CA
Herman, Douglas D. ... Monticello, IA
Herman, DuWayne W. ... Decatur, IN
Herman, Edmund ... San Diego, CA
Herman, Edward H. ... Princeton, NJ
Herman, Edward Ian ... St. Louis, MO
Herman, Edward Jayson ... Dallas, TX
Herman, Edward N. ... Forest Hills, NY
Herman, Elizabeth A. ... Washington, DC
Herman, Elyse ... Princeton, NJ
Herman, Emil W. ... Pittsburgh, PA
Herman, Eugene F. ... Elkton, MD
Herman, Flory G. ... Buffalo, NY
Herman, Fred L. ... New Orleans, LA
Herman, Fred L., A Professional Law Corporation ... New Orleans, LA
Herman, G. Nicholas ... Chapel Hill, NC
Herman, Gary H. ... New York, NY
Herman, Gary W. ... Wapakoneta, OH
Herman, Gill & Herman, LLP
New York, NY
Herman, Glenn A. ... New York, NY
Herman, Goldstein & Forsyth, P.C.
Phoenix, AZ
Scottsdale, AZ
Herman, Gregg ... Milwaukee, WI

Herman Grubman & Moore ... Miami, FL
Herman, Guy S. ... Austin, TX
Herman, H. Paul ... Trumbull, CT
Herman, H. Robert ... Rochester, NY
Herman, Harold C. ... Woodmere, NY
Herman, Harold J., II ... Topeka, KS
Herman, Harold S. ... New York, NY
Herman, Harry ... Bronx, NY
Herman, Harvey R. ... Chicago, IL
Herman, Henry ... North Miami Beach, FL
Herman, Herbert ... Spring Valley, NY
Herman & Herman ... Metairie, LA
Herman & Herman ... High Point, NC
Herman, Herman & Jolley, P.S.
Spokane, WA
Herman, Herman, Katz & Cotlar, L.L.P.
New Orleans, LA
Herman, Howard H. ... Spokane, WA
Herman, Howard J. ... New York, NY
Herman, Howard J. ... Spring Valley, NY
Herman, Howard R. ... New York, NY
Herman & Howry, L.L.P. ... Austin, TX
Georgetown, TX
San Antonio, TX
Herman, Hyman ... Bay Shore, NY
Herman, Ira L. ... New York, NY
Herman, Irene M. ... Boston, MA
Herman, J. Jeffrey ... Camarillo, CA
Herman, J. Jeffrey ... Oxnard, CA
Herman, J. Jeffrey ... Ventura, CA
Herman, Jack J., P.C. ... Chicago, IL
Herman, James ... Cherry Hill, NJ
Herman, James B. ... Philadelphia, PA
Herman, James E. ... Santa Barbara, CA
Herman, Jamie L. ... Johnson City, TN
Herman, Janet Stone ... Palo Alto, CA
Herman, Jason P. ... Orlando, FL
Herman, Jay M. ... Mineola, NY
Herman, Jayne F. ... Lafayette, CA
Herman, Jeffery D. ... Santa Barbara, CA
Herman, Jeffrey David ... Roslyn Heights, NY
Herman, Jeffrey G. ... Waterford, PA
Herman, Jeffrey L. ... Seattle, WA
Herman, Jeffrey M. ... Miami, FL
Herman, Jeffrey M. ... Pembroke Pines, FL
Herman, Jeffry B. ... Marlton, NJ
Herman, Jerald M. ... New York, NY
Herman, Jerry R. ... San Rafael, CA
Herman, Jill A. ... Scottsdale, AZ
Herman, Jill Ann ... San Diego, CA
Herman, Joan Optican ... Kansas City, MO
Herman, John C. ... Atlanta, GA
Herman, John C. ... Hays, KS
Herman, John E. ... Minster, OH
Wapakoneta, OH
Herman, John F. ... Akron, OH
Herman, John H. ... Pittsburgh, PA
Herman, John H., (P.A.)
Minneapolis, MN
Herman, Jonathan M. ... New Orleans, LA
Herman, Jonathan M. ... New York, NY
Herman, Joseph E. ... Los Angeles, CA
Herman, Judith F. ... New York, NY
Herman, Judith R. ... Farmington Hills, MI
Herman, June R. ... Hauppauge, NY
Herman, Kathy E. ... Fort Washington, PA
Herman, Kenneth B. ... New York, NY
Herman, Kent H. ... Allentown, PA
Herman & Kessler ... Chicago, IL
Herman, Kimberly B. ... Boston, MA
Herman, Larry D. ... Laurel, MT
Herman, Laurence Robert ... New York, NY
Herman, Laurie A. ... Scottsdale, AZ
Herman Law Firm, P.C. ... Laurel, MT
Herman, Lawrence ... Columbus, OH
Herman, Lawrence R.
Consumer Product Safety Commission,
Commissioners Office, GV
Herman, Lee E. ... Houston, TX
Herman, Lee M. ... Haddonfield, NJ
Herman, Lee M., P.C. ... Haddonfield, NJ
Herman, Leigh ... Redwood City, CA
Herman, Leonard K. ... Ardsley, NY
Herman, Leonard S. ... Southfield, MI
Herman, Leonard S., P.C. ... Southfield, MI
Herman, Lewis ... New York, NY
Herman, Linda R. ... New York, NY
Herman, Lloyd A. ... Spokane, WA
Herman, Lloyd J. ... New York, NY
Herman, Louise A. ... New York, NY
Herman, Louise F. (Garrido) ... Boston, MA
Herman, Lowell G. ... Baltimore, MD
Herman, M. Gerald ... Bellevue, WA
Herman, M. Jack ... Miami, FL
Herman, Malcolm Paul ... Rockville, MD
Herman, Mario L. ... Washington, DC
Herman, Mark ... Minneapolis, MN
Herman, Mark Alan ... Cassopolis, MI
Herman, Mark D. ... New York, NY
Herman, Mark E. ... Baltimore, MD
Herman, Mark P. ... Kansas City, MO
Herman, Martin A. ... Woodbury, NJ
Herman, Marvin L. ... Chicago, IL
Herman, Matthew J. ... Aurora, IL
Herman, Maury A., (A Professional Law Corporation) ... New Orleans, LA
Herman, Melanie L. ... Washington, DC
Herman, Michael Bernard ... Montgomery, AL
Herman, Michael G. ... Los Angeles, CA
Herman, Michael R. ... Corona Del Mar, CA
Herman, Michael R. ... Parsippany, NJ
Herman, Middleton, Casey, Kitchens & Mandell, LLP ... Atlanta, GA
Herman, Milton J. ... Bridgeport, CT
Herman, Milton S. ... Goshen, NY
Herman, Miriam Z. ... Calabasas, CA
Herman, M. J. ... Pittsburgh, PA
Herman, Mona E. ... Weatogue, CT
Herman, Morton L. ... Fort Worth, TX
Herman, Nancy ... Chicago, IL
Herman, Nancy J. ... Rockville, MD
Herman, Neil E. ... New York, NY
Herman, Nicole L. ... Philadelphia, PA
Herman, Patricia K. ... Orlando, FL
Herman, Patrick E. ... El Cajon, CA
Herman, Patrick W. ... Kitty Hawk, NC
Norfolk, VA
Herman, Paul A. ... Coral Gables, FL
Herman, Paul C. ... Los Angeles, CA
Herman, Paul I. ... Carrollton, TX
Herman, Paul M. ... Palm Beach Gardens, FL
Herman, Paul R. ... Princeton, NJ
New York, NY
Herman, Paula Lacey ... Hartford, CT
Herman, Peter ... New York, NY
Herman, Peter G. ... Fort Lauderdale, FL
Herman, Peter G. ... Taholah, WA
Herman, Peter R. ... Woodbridge, NJ
Herman, Peter R. ... New York, NY
Herman, Peter S. ... New York, NY
Herman, Peter S. ... Salem, OR
Herman, Peter Windley ... New York, NY
Herman, Philip A. ... Boston, MA
Herman, Raymond C. ... Buffalo, NY
Herman, Regina A. ... Haddonfield, NJ
Herman, Rhonda Diamond ... Teaneck, NJ
Herman, Richard A. ... Farmington Hills, MI
Herman, Richard A. ... Wayne, NJ
Herman, Richard A. ... Columbus, OH
Herman, Richard B., P.C. ... New York, NY
White Plains, NY
Herman, Richard Bruce ... New York, NY
White Plains, NY
Herman, Richard Charles
Los Angeles, CA
Herman, Richard P. ... Laguna Beach, CA
Herman, Richard Sael ... Modesto, CA
Herman, Robert C. ... Carson City, NV
Herman, Robert J. ... Oxnard, CA
Herman, Robert L. ... Atlanta, GA
Herman, Robert L. ... Kinsman, OH
Herman, Robert M. ... Hollywood, FL
Herman, Robert M. ... Dallas, TX
Herman, Robert M., P.A. ... Hollywood, FL
Herman, Robert M., P.C. ... Dallas, TX
Herman, Robert Neil ... Washington, DC
Herman, Robert S. ... Palm Beach Gardens, FL
Herman, Robert S. ... Overland Park, KS
Kansas City, MO
Herman, Robin A. ... Walnut Creek, CA
Herman, Robin S. ... New York, NY
Herman, Robt. E. ... Great Neck, NY
Herman, Rodman C. ... Irvington, NJ
Herman, Roger M. ... St. Louis, MO
Herman, Roseann ... Los Angeles, CA
Herman, Ross N. ... Newark, NJ
Herman, Russ ... Department of Commerce,
Patent and Trademark Office, GV
Herman, Russ M., (A Professional Law Corporation) ... New Orleans, LA
Herman, Russell R. ... Paulding, OH
Herman, S. Sanford
Hastings-On-Hudson, NY
Herman, Samuel S. ... Bingham Farms, MI
Herman, Sarah Andrews ... Fargo, ND
Herman, Sherril A. ... New Orleans, LA
Herman, Sidney N. ... Denver, CO
Chicago, IL
Herman, Sonia F. ... Great Neck, NY
Herman, Spencer H. ... Brooklyn, NY
Herman, Stanley ... Winsted, CT
Herman, Stanley M. ... High Point, NC
Herman, Stephen A. ... Hackensack, NJ
Herman, Stephen C. ... Chicago, IL
Herman, Stephen M. ... Winnetka, IL
Herman, Stephen P. ... Curtis, NE
North Platte, NE
Herman, Steve ... New Orleans, LA
Herman, Steven ... Zephyrhills, FL
Herman, Steven A.
Environmental Protection Agency,
Office of Enforcement and Compliance
Assurance, GV
Herman, Steven H. ... San Francisco, CA
Herman, Steven J. ... Washington, DC
Herman, Steven M. ... San Francisco, CA
Herman, Stewart B. ... New York, NY
Herman, Stuart P. ... Los Angeles, CA
Herman, Susan N ... Brooklyn, NY
Herman, Susan P. ... Lewiston, ME
Herman, Suzanne ... Southfield, MI
Herman, Thomas A. ... Treasury Department,
Office of Thrift Supervision, GV
Herman, Thomas C. ... Atlanta, GA
Herman, Thomas D. ... Boston, MA
Herman, Thomas G. ... Grand Rapids, MI
Herman, Thomas M. ... Eureka, CA
Herman, Thomas R. ... Batavia, OH
Herman, Thomas W. ... Macon, GA
Herman, Timothy J. ... Austin, TX
Herman, Victoria M. ... Greensboro, NC
Herman & Wallach, Professional Corporation
Los Angeles, CA
Herman, Walter E. (Rusty) ... Humble, TX
Herman, Wendi L. ... Huntington, NY
Herman, William C. ... New York, NY
Herman, William R. ... Philadelphia, PA
Hermance, James P. ... Atlanta, GA
Herman-Giddens, Gregory
Chapel Hill, NC
Wilmington, NC
Herman-Giddens, Gregory ... Wilmington, NC
Hermanies, John H. ... Cincinnati, OH
Hermanies, Major, Castelli & Goodman
Cincinnati, OH
Herman-Katz, M. L. ... Baltimore, MD
Hermann, Andrew ... Baltimore, MD
Hermann & Bateman ... Westfield, NJ
Hermann, Brian Steven ... New York, NY
Hermann, Cahn & Schneider
Cleveland, OH
Hermann, Christopher R. ... Portland, OR
Hermann & Company, P.C. ... Portland, OR
Hermann, Cynthia G. ... Redding, CA
Hermann, Dale M. ... Portland, OR
Hermann, Darice C. ... Mequon, WI
Hermann, Diane L. ... San Francisco, CA
Hermann, Donald H. J., III ... Chicago, IL
Hermann, Fred K. ... Detroit, MI
Hermann, Gary D. ... Cleveland, OH
Hermann, Gerard P. ... Roseland, NJ
Hermann & Hermann, P.C. ... Libertyville, IL
Hermann, Howard W. ... Loudon, TN
Hermann, James J., Jr. ... Libertyville, IL
Hermann, James R. ... Orinda, CA
Hermann, James R. ... Libertyville, IL
Hermann, Jeffery D. ... Los Angeles, CA
Hermann, Jennifer M. ... Libertyville, IL
Hermann, Jerry L. ... Houma, LA
Hermann, John J. ... Flint, MI
Hermann, Karen L. ... Irvine, CA
Hermann, Kerri Stahlecker ... St. Paul, MN
Hermann, Kristin A. ... Detroit, MI
Hermann, Leonard S. ... Norwalk, CT
Hermann, Linda C. ... St. Louis, MO
Hermann, Martin J. ... Glen Head, NY
Hermann, Mary Alice ... New Orleans, LA
Hermann, Michele S.G. ... Albuquerque, NM
Hermann, Miriam W. ... New York, NY
Hermann, Paul D. ... Atlanta, GA
Hermann, Paul D., P.C. ... Atlanta, GA
Decatur, GA
Hermann, Philip J. ... Aurora, OH
Hermann, Randi Lana ... Woodbury, NY
Hermann, Raymond P. ... San Francisco, CA
Hermann, Renaé L. ... Indianapolis, IN
Hermann, Richard L. ... Washington, DC
Hermann, Richard P., II
Fort Lauderdale, FL
Hermann, Robert F. ... Westfield, NJ
Hermann, Robert H. ... New York, NY
Hermann, Robert J. ... Houston, TX
Hermann, Robert L., Jr ... Dover, NH
Manchester, NH
Hermann, Robert L., Law Offices of
Manchester, NH
Hermann, Robert W. ... Hillsboro, OR
Hermann, Robin L. ... Des Moines, IA
Hermann, Robyn J. ... Miami, FL
Hermann, Susan E. ... Cincinnati, OH
Hermann, Susan M. ... Chicago, IL
Hermann, Thomas G. ... Cleveland, OH
Hermann, William C. ... Chicago, IL
Hermanns, Karl R. ... Seattle, WA
Hermanns, Kurt P. ... Seattle, WA
Hermanowski, Joan A. ... Miami, FL
Hermans, Stephen G. ... Exeter, NH
Hermansdorfer, H. David ... Ashland, KY
Hermansen, Knud E. ... Old Town, ME
Hermansen, Kurt D. ... San Diego, CA
Hermansen, Tom ... Corpus Christi, TX
Hermanson, Barbara A. ... Wausau, WI
Hermanson, Beth J. ... Boston, MA
Hermanson, Diane M. ... Spokane, WA
Hermanson, Eric Bradford ... Boston, MA
Hermanson, Gary L. ... Detroit, MI
Hermanson, Gary L. ... Cleveland, OH
Hermanson, Harold M. ... Muskegon, MI
Hermanson, Jeffrey A. ... Boston, MA
Hermanson, Ronald E. ... Norco, CA
Hermele, Jerry N.
National Labor Relations Board,
Division of Administrative Law Judges, GV
Hermelee, Bruce G. ... Jacksonville, FL
Miami, FL
Hermelee & Sharp, L.L.C.
Jacksonville, FL
Miami, FL
Hermeling, Caroline L. ... St. Louis, MO
Hermeling, Dale E. ... Belleville, IL
St. Louis, MO
Hermenau, Ronald S. ... Princeton, NJ
Hermenze, David R. ... Westport, CT
Hermenze & Marcantonio ... Westport, CT
Hermer, Susan J. ... Deer Park, NY
Hermes, Brian ... Dallas, TX
Hermes, Brian D., Law Office of
Abington, MA
Hermes, Dwayne J. ... Dallas, TX
Hermes, Francis X. ... Somerset, NJ
Hermes, Fred ... San Francisco, CA
Hermes, Jeffrey Peter ... Boston, MA
Hermes, John N. ... Oklahoma City, OK
Hermes, Kathryn O. ... Dallas, TX
Hermes Law Firm, PSC ... Everett, WA
Hermes, Michael L. ... Green Bay, WI
Hermes, Natalie ... Mount Pleasant, MI
Hermes, Netburn, O'Connor & Spearing, P.C. ... Boston, MA
Hermes, Pamela J. ... Lafayette, IN
Hermes, Peter G. ... Boston, MA
Hermes, Peter T. ... Beverly Hills, CA
Hermes, Robert N. ... Chicago, IL
Hermes, Russel J. ... Everett, WA
Hermes, Wendy H. ... Dallas, TX
Hermesmann, Patrick J. ... Cranford, NJ
Hermeston, Robert J. ... Anderson, SC
Hermida, Angel G. ... San Juan, PR
Hermida, Elizabeth E.M. ... New York, NY
Hermida, Maria C. ... New York, NY
Hermilla, Nelson D. ... Department of Justice,
Civil Rights Division, GV
Hermistone, William J.
North Attleboro, MA
Hermiz, Aram D. ... Washington, DC
Hermiz, Laith Mansour
West Bloomfield, MI
Hermle, Lynne C. ... Menlo Park, CA
Hermo, Alfonso D. ... Whittier, CA
Hermon, Gary R. ... Lima, OH
Hermon, Gary R., Co., L.P.A., A Legal Prof. Assn. ... Lima, OH
Hermon, James F. ... Detroit, MI
Hermosa, Virginia I. ... Austin, TX
Hermosillo, Christine N. ... Los Angeles, CA
Hermosillo, Sharon F. ... San Jose, CA
Hermosillo, Teresa J. ... Hermosa Beach, CA
Herms, C. Dean, Jr. ... Houston, TX
Herms, Gerald R. ... Tampa, FL
Hermsen, James R. ... Seattle, WA
Hermsen, Michael L. ... Chicago, IL
Hermundstad, Mark A.
Grand Junction, CO
Moab, UT
Hermundstad, Sara S. ... Grand Junction, CO
Hern, Andrew J. ... Hartford, CT
Hern, Andrew James ... Glastonbury, CT
Hern, Christopher J. ... Boston, MA
Hern, Cynthia M. ... Boston, MA
Hern, David, Jr. ... Norwood, MA
Hern, J. Brooke ... Roseland, NJ
Hern, John J., Jr. ... Detroit, MI
Hern, Joseph L. ... Boston, MA
Hern, Kevin, Jr. ... Boston, MA
Hern, Micheal L. ... Glen Allen, VA
Richmond, VA
Hernacki, Raymond P. ... Laguna Beach, CA
Hernaez, Alexander ... San Francisco, CA
Hernaez, Eric M. ... South Plainfield, NJ
Hernan, Richard A., Jr. ... Warren, PA
Hernan, Robert Emmet ... New York, NY
Hernand, David M. ... Los Angeles, CA
Hernand, Stephanie Kaufman
Los Angeles, CA
Hernandez, Alan N. ... Washington, DC
Hernandez, Alberto M. ... Miami, FL
Hernandez, Alexander ... Dade City, FL
Zephyrhills, FL
Hernandez, Alfred E. ... San Antonio, TX
Hernandez, Alfredo M. ... New York, NY
Hernandez, Alicia E. ... Dallas, TX
Hernandez, Allie R. ... Miami, FL
Hernandez, Alpha ... Del Rio, TX
Hernandez, Amarilis ... Arlington, TX
Hernandez, Andrew G. ... Columbia, MO
Hernandez, Anne E. ... Santa Rosa, CA
Hernandez, Anthony ... Bridgeport, CT
Hernandez, Anthony R. ... San Diego, CA
Hernandez, Anthony W. ... Houston, TX
Hernandez, Anthony W., P.C. ... Houston, TX
Hernandez, Antonia ... Los Angeles, CA
Hernandez, Antonino G. ... Miami, FL
Hernandez, Aristides F. ... West New York, NJ
Hernandez, Arthur ... Jacksonville, FL
Hernandez, Arturo ... Silver Spring, MD
Hernandez, Arturo V. ... Miami, FL
Hernandez, Arturo V., P.A. ... Miami, FL
Hernández, B. C. ... Albuquerque, NM
Hernandez, Bernice ... Los Angeles, CA
Hernandez, Carl, III ... Bakersfield, CA
Hernandez, Carlos E., Jr. ... Harlingen, TX
McAllen, TX
Hernandez, Carlos J.
Palm Beach Gardens, FL
Hernandez, Carlos M. ... Pittsburgh, PA
Hernandez, Carmen D. ... Beltsville, MD
Hernandez, Christopher R. ... Houston, TX
Hernandez, Daniel A. ... San Jose, CA
Hernandez, Daniel H. ... El Paso, TX
Hernandez, Daniel J. ... Albuquerque, NM
Hernandez, Daniel M. ... Tampa, FL
Hernandez, Daniel M., P.A. ... Tampa, FL
Hernandez, David J. ... Brooklyn, NY
Hernandez, David, Jr. ... Pomona, CA
Hernández, David N. ... Albuquerque, NM
Hernández, David N., & Associates, P.A.
Albuquerque, NM
Hernandez, David O. ... Fresno, CA
Hernandez, Deborah Kaye ... Wichita, KS
Hernandez, Deborah S. ... Orlando, FL
Hernandez, Dennis ... Tampa, FL
Hernandez, Dennis ... Tampa, FL
Hernandez, Dennis F. ... Los Angeles, CA
Hernandez, Diane L. ... San Jose, CA
Hernandez, Don A. ... Los Angeles, CA
Hernandez, Don J. ... New Orleans, LA
Hernandez, Eduardo J. ... Miami, FL
Hernandez, Edward ... Coral Gables, FL
Hernández, Edward ... El Paso, TX
Hernández, Efren, III ... Department of Justice,
Immigration and Naturalization Service, GV
Hernandez, Elizabeth M. ... Coral Gables, FL
Hernandez, Eloy I. ... Edinburg, TX
Hernandez, Enrique A. ... Lakewood, CA
Hernandez, Enrique, Jr. ... Alhambra, CA
Hernandez, Esteban ... San Diego, CA
Hernandez, Eugenio ... Miami, FL
Hernandez, Fernando V. ... San Jose, CA
Hernandez, Frank P. ... Dallas, TX
Hernandez, Fred C. ... Irvine, CA
Hernandez, Gary A. ... San Francisco, CA
Hernandez, George B., Jr. ... San Antonio, TX
Hernandez, George C., Jr. ... Pleasanton, CA
Hernandez, George J., Jr.
Los Angeles, CA
Hernandez, Gerardo J. ... San Juan, PR
Hernandez, Gilberto ... Chicago, IL
Hernandez, Gilberto ... San Antonio, TX
Hernandez, Gladys M.
Federal Labor Relations Authority,
Federal Service Impasses Panel, GV
Hernandez, Gregorio W. (Willie) ... Dallas, TX

Hernandez, H. Manuel .... Orlando, FL
Hernandez, Hector I., Sr. .... Washington, DC
Hernandez, Henry A. .... San Francisco, CA
Hernandez, Hosey .... Miami, FL
Hernandez, Iris G. .... Miami, FL
Hernandez, Irma Virginia .... Hialeah, FL
Hernandez, Irving K. .... San Juan, PR
Hernandez, Irving K. .... San Juan, PR
Hernandez, Jacqueline C.
White Plains, NY
Hernandez, James A. .... Houston, TX
Hernandez, James Antonio .... Jacksonville, FL
Hernandez, James Z. .... Wichita, KS
Hernandez, Janet .... Washington, DC
Hernandez, Javier .... New York, NY
Hernandez, Jeffrey Vidal .... Los Angeles, CA
Hernandez, Jennifer L.
San Francisco, CA
Hernandez, Jerry .... Phoenix, AZ
Hernandez, Jess .... San Francisco, CA
Hernandez, Jesse S. .... Los Angeles, CA
Hernández, Jessica .... San Juan, PR
Hernandez, Jesus" Jesse " .... Edinburg, TX
Hernandez, Jesus M. .... El Paso, TX
Hernandez, Joe H., Jr. .... San Antonio, TX
Hernandez, John Ashby, III .... Carencro, LA
Hernandez, Jose J. .... Plano, TX
Hernandez, Jose W. .... Cherry Hill, NJ
Hernandez, Joseph D. .... Palo Alto, CA
Hernandez, Joseph M. .... Miami, FL
Hernandez, Juan B. .... Hayward, CA
Hernandez, Juanita C. .... San Antonio, TX
Hernandez, Judith S.
Palm Beach Gardens, FL
Hernandez, Judy S. .... Buffalo, NY
Hernandez, Kelly S. .... Jacksonville, FL
Hernandez, Kerry E. .... San Francisco, CA
Hernandez, Kristine .... St. Paul, MN
Hernandez, Laura A. .... Los Angeles, CA
Hernandez, Laura B. .... Virginia Beach, VA
Hernandez, Leo H. .... Santa Monica, CA
Hernandez, Leonard R. .... Elizabeth, NJ
Hernandez, Ligia I. .... Los Angeles, CA
Hernandez, Lisa .... Dallas, TX
Hernandez, Lisa Soto .... San Francisco, CA
Hernandez, Louis R. .... Chicago, IL
Hernandez, Lourdes T. .... Houston, TX
Hernandez, Luis R. .... Brownsville, TX
Hernandez, Mack Ray .... Austin, TX
Hernandez, Manuel C. .... Bandon, OR
Hernández, Marco A. .... Hillsboro, OR
Hernandez, Marcos F. .... Pasadena, CA
Hernandez, Marcos, Jr. .... San Marcos, TX
Hernández, Margarita Paláu .... Pasadena, CA
Hernandez, Marisel A. .... Chicago, IL
Hernandez, Mark A. .... Iselin, NJ
New York, NY
Hernandez, Martha-Ibis .... New York, NY
Hernandez, Mary T. .... San Francisco, CA
Hernandez, Mateo M. .... Long Beach, CA
Hernandez, Matthew .... Long Beach, CA
Hernandez, Maureen J. .... Atlanta, GA
Hernandez, Mauricio E. .... La Puente, CA
Hernandez, Michael .... San Antonio, TX
Hernandez, Michael J. .... Chicago, IL
Hernandez, Michael J. .... Newark, NJ
Hernandez, Michael M.
Santa Monica, CA
Hernandez, Michael M. .... Miami, FL
Hernandez, Michael V. .... Virginia Beach, VA
Hernandez, Michelle T.L. .... Madison, WI
Hernandez, Miguel A. .... Salinas, CA
Hernandez, Miguel Antonio, III
San Antonio, TX
Hernandez, Mike, Jr. .... San Antonio, TX
Hernandez, Moises R. .... Harlingen, TX
Hernandez, Nilda C. .... Jersey City, NJ
Hernandez, Nora M. .... Chicago, IL
Hernandez, Omar .... Boston, MA
Hernandez, Patricia A. .... Brownsville, TX
Hernandez, Patricia F. .... Cranford, NJ
Hernandez, Patricia M. .... Miami, FL
Hernandez, Patricia Y. .... Toledo, OH
Hernandez, Patrick Lynn .... Denver, CO
Hernandez, Paul Ramon .... Norfolk, VA
Hernandez, Pedro .... New York, NY
Hernandez, Pedro V., Jr. .... San Antonio, TX
Hernandez, Philip E. .... Redding, CA
Hernandez & Ramirez .... Fresno, CA
Hernandez, Raymond .... Tampa, FL
Hernández, René .... Northbrook, IL
Hernandez, Richard A. .... Columbus, OH
Hernandez, Richard F. .... El Monte, CA
South Gate, CA
West Covina, CA
Hernandez, Rita A. .... New York, NY
Hernandez, Robert L. .... Pueblo, CO
Hernandez, Robert L. .... Malden, MA
Hernandez, Roberto P. .... Miami, FL
Hernandez, Roland A. .... Pasadena, CA
Hernandez, Ronald S. .... Eatontown, NJ
Hernandez, Rory Michael
Los Angeles, CA
Hernandez, Rosana E. .... Miami, FL
Tampa, FL
Hernandez, Ruben M. .... Alamosa, CO
Hernandez, Rudy .... Jacksonville, FL
Hernandez, Rudy, P.A. .... Jacksonville, FL
Hernandez, Sarah .... Frankfort, KY
Hernandez and Schapiro .... Pomona, CA
Hernandez, Shannon M. .... Memphis, TN
Hernandez, Steven L. .... Las Cruces, NM
Hernandez & Stewart .... New Orleans, LA
Hernandez, Sunshine .... Washington, DC
Hernandez, Susan .... Bronx, NY
Hernandez, Tanya .... Jamaica, NY
Hernandez, Thais .... Miami, FL
Hernandez, Thomas .... San Antonio, TX

Hernandez, Victor .... Ponce, PR
Hernandez, Victor .... Lubbock, TX
Hernández Arroyo, Edna .... San Juan, PR
Hernandez-Arroyo, Mauricio .... Brooklyn, NY
Hernández Cardona, Luis .... San Juan, PR
Hernandez-Chapman, Cynthia M.
Washington, DC
Hernandez-Colon, Cesar A. .... Ponce, PR
Hernandez Colon, Miguel .... Mayaguez, PR
Hernandez Colon, Rafael .... Ponce, PR
Hernandez Espinosa, Cesar .... Roswell, GA
Hernandez-Francis, Pamela .... Brooklyn, NY
Hernandez-Malaby, Cristina D.
Boston, MA
Hernandez-Morales, Raul .... Coral Gables, FL
Hernández-Nieves, Benjamín .... San Juan, PR
Hernandez-Prewitt, Rufina A. .... Denver, CO
Hernandez-Reyes, Pedro .... San Juan, PR
Hernández-Ruiz, Francisco R.
San Juan, PR
Hernandez Sanchez, Jesus M. .... San Juan, PR
Hernández-Sánchez, Namyr I.
San Juan, PR
Hernandez-Toraño, Jorge L. .... Miami, FL
Hernández-Truyol, Berta Esperanza
Jamaica, NY
Hernandez-Vivoni, Luis A. .... San Juan, PR
Hernandez-Weimer, Janet F. .... Lafayette, LA
Hernando, Julio R. .... Weymouth, MA
Hernando, Mariano V. .... Honolulu, HI
Hernando, Orlando M.
Oklahoma City, OK
Hernden, Adolph L. .... San Antonio, TX
Herndon, Bobby F. .... Savannah, GA
Herndon, Boyd K. .... Dallas, TX
Herndon, Brian L. .... Winston-Salem, NC
Herndon, Charles A., Jr. .... Baltimore, MD
Herndon, Charles B.
Charlotte Amalie, St. Thomas, VI
Herndon, Charles T., III
Johnson City, TN
Herndon, Charles T., IV
Johnson City, TN
Herndon, Coleman, Brading & McKee
Johnson City, TN
Herndon, David .... Austin, TX
Herndon, David R. .... East St. Louis, IL
Herndon, David S. .... Moultrie, GA
Herndon, Deborah D. .... St. Louis, MO
Herndon, Dennis .... Tuscaloosa, AL
Herndon, Diane L. .... Washington, DC
Herndon, Donald R. .... Billings, MT
Herndon, Douglas W. .... Las Vegas, NV
Herndon, E. Wayne .... Houston, TX
Herndon, Gayle W. .... Fairfield, CT
Herndon, Gregory J. .... Wheeling, WV
Herndon, H. David .... Austin, TX
Herndon, Henry N., Jr. .... Wilmington, DE
Herndon, Howard E., Jr. .... Nashville, TN
Herndon, Howard W. .... Nashville, TN
Herndon, J. Hugh, and Associates
Midwest City, OK
Herndon, James C. .... Blackfoot, ID
Herndon, Jane Neuhauser
Indianapolis, IN
Herndon, Jerry W.
Research Triangle Park, NC
Herndon, John D. .... Birmingham, AL
Herndon, John E. .... Anadarko, OK
Herndon, John E., Jr. .... Hollywood, FL
Herndon, Laurel T. .... Wheaton, IL
Herndon, Lisa A. .... Louisville, KY
Herndon, Lisa D. .... Bartow, FL
Herndon, M. Daniel .... Frankfort, KY
Herndon, Mark A. .... Dallas, TX
Herndon, Mary C. .... Los Angeles, CA
Herndon, Matthew H. .... Boston, MA
Herndon, Michael N. .... Columbus, GA
Herndon, Milton T. .... Charleston, WV
Herndon, Morton, Herndon & Yaeger
Wheeling, WV
Herndon, Randolph K. .... Wilmington, DE
Herndon, Richard D. .... Cincinnati, OH
Herndon, Richard G. .... Wheeling, WV
Herndon, Rick D. .... Department of Agriculture,
Office of the General Counsel, GV
Herndon, Robert D. .... Oregon City, OR
Herndon, Robert E. .... Macon, GA
Herndon, Robert G. .... Overland Park, KS
Herndon, Robert G., P.A.
Overland Park, KS
Herndon, Robert H. .... Milledgeville, GA
Herndon, Stanley P. .... Ormond Beach, FL
Herndon, Stephen D. .... Wheeling, WV
Herndon, Steven K. .... Montgomery, AL
Herndon, Steven L. .... Boise, ID
Herndon, Susan P. .... Knoxville, TN
Herndon, Sweeney & Halverson, P.C.
Billings, MT
Herndon, Thomas David .... Catonsville, MD
Herndon, Thomas R. .... Savannah, GA
Herndon, W. Banks, Jr. .... Phenix City, AL
Herndon, Warren R., Jr. .... Columbia, SC
Herndon, William B. .... Marietta, GA
Herndon, William C. .... Dallas, TX
Herner, Donald A., Law Offices of
Greenwich, CT
Herner, Donald A., Law Offices of
Stamford, CT
Herner, Donald A., Law Offices of
Scarsdale, NY
Hernick, John N. .... Philadelphia, PA
Hernly, Harold G., Jr. .... Alexandria, VA
Hernly, Timothy D. .... South Bend, IN
Hernon, Martin J. .... Framingham, MA
Hernon, William J., III .... Salem, MA
Hernquist, William C., II .... San Diego, CA
Herns, Daniel G. .... San Jose, CA

Herns, H. Tica .... Dallas, TX
Herns, Louis P. .... Charleston, SC
Hernsberger, W. Stephen .... El Paso, TX
Hernstadt, Edward .... New York, NY
Hernstadt, Sharon S. .... Hartsdale, NY
Hero, Andrew W. .... Houston, TX
Hero, Byron A., Jr. .... New York, NY
Hero, George F. .... Miami, FL
Hero Law Office, P.A. .... Northfield, MN
Hero, Michael W. .... Northfield, MN
Hero, Milton J. C. .... New Orleans, LA
Hero, Sophocles A. .... Alexandria, VA
Hero, Suzanne J. .... Dallas, TX
Herochik, Priscilla Andrea .... Merrillville, IN
Herochik, William R. .... Chicago, IL
Herod, Angela J. .... Indianapolis, IN
Herod, James T. .... Dallas, TX
Heroian, Ara P. .... Worcester, MA
Herold, Andrew D. .... San Diego, CA
Herold, Arthur L. .... Washington, DC
Herold, Bruce G. .... Oakland, CA
Herold, Charles W., III .... Monroe, LA
Herold, David E. .... East Meadow, NY
Herold, Frederick G. .... Philadelphia, PA
Herold & Geneux .... Shreveport, LA
Herold, Gerald P. .... Omaha, NE
Herold and Haines, Professional Association
Morristown, NJ
Newark, NJ
Somerville, NJ
Warren, NJ
Herold, Henry L. .... Los Angeles, CA
Herold, J. Thomas .... Garland, TX
Herold, Janet .... Pasadena, CA
Herold, Joel F. .... New York, NY
Herold, John W.
Department of Housing and Urban Development,
Office of General Counsel, GV
Herold, Joseph G. .... Topeka, KS
Herold, Karl G. (IBA) .... New York, NY
Herold, Kim Marie .... Clovis, CA
Fresno, CA
Herold, Lloyd G. .... Palm Beach Gardens, FL
Herold, Richard .... Ellijay, GA
Herold, Richard H. .... Warren, NJ
Herold, Richard H., Jr. .... Phoenix, AZ
Herold, Sidney E. .... Philadelphia, PA
Herold, Susan M. .... St. Louis, MO
Herold, Theodore .... Brooklyn, NY
Herold, Thomas C. .... Seattle, WA
Heron, Carol E., & Associates, A Prof Law Corp. .... Glendale, CA
Granada Hills, CA
Tarzana, CA
Heron, Carol Ellen .... Glendale, CA
Granada Hills, CA
Heron, Catherine L. (IBA) .... Los Angeles, CA
Heron, Dawson C. .... Concord, MA
Heron, Gregory W. .... Denver, CO
Heron, John J. .... Dayton, OH
Heron, Julian B., Jr. .... Washington, DC
Heron, Melissa S. .... Huntsville, AL
Heron, Michael H. A. .... Niagara Falls, NY
Heron, Michael J. .... Oklahoma City, OK
Heron, Robert A. .... Los Angeles, CA
Heron, Robert D. .... Los Angeles, CA
Heronimus, John R. .... Denver, CO
Heronimus, Marcy M. .... Denver, CO
Heronimus, Thomas J.
Grundy Center, IA
Heroux, Christopher S., P.C., A Professional Corporation .... Tulsa, OK
Heroux, Christopher S. .... Tulsa, OK
Heroux, Clingen, Callow, Wolfe and McLean
Wheaton, IL
Heroux, Francis A. .... Wheaton, IL
Heroux, Mark Stoddard .... Denver, CO
Heroux, Robert C. .... Taunton, MA
Heroux, Robert O. .... New York, NY
Heroy, David F. .... Chicago, IL
Heroy, Donna Tuke .... Chicago, IL
Herp, Daniel J. .... San Francisco, CA
Herp, Paul A. .... San Francisco, CA
Herpe, David A. .... Chicago, IL
Herpel, Stefan B. .... Ann Arbor, MI
Herpel, Stefan B., P.C. .... Ann Arbor, MI
Herpich, Charles R., Jr. .... Houston, TX
Herpich, Scott M. .... Kansas City, MO
Herpin & deGeneres, L.L.C.
Baton Rouge, LA
Herpin, Eric J. .... Houston, TX
Herpin, James M. .... Baton Rouge, LA
Herpin, Michael J. .... Abbeville, LA
Herr, Allison L. .... Las Vegas, NV
Herr, Beth S. .... Cambridge, MA
Herr, Brett W. .... Belmont, CA
Herr, Bruce .... Santa Fe, NM
Herr, C. Ryman, Jr. .... Flemington, NJ
Herr, Charles Foltz .... Lancaster, PA
Herr, Cowles W. .... Flemington, NJ
Herr, Cynthia Greco .... Redwood City, CA
Herr, Daniel C. .... Lancaster, PA
Strasburg, PA
Herr, Daniel Lynn .... Richmond, VA
Herr, David F. .... Minneapolis, MN
Herr, Dwight L. .... Santa Cruz, CA
Herr and Fisher .... Flemington, NJ
Herr, Greer & Hoberg .... Lancaster, PA
Herr, J. Michael .... Dayton, OH
Herr, James J. .... Chatsworth, IL
Kempton, IL
Pontiac, IL
Herr, Julie Kitzes .... Department of State,
Office of the Legal Adviser, GV
Herr, Katherine E. .... Great Neck, NY
Herr, Leonard C. .... Visalia, CA

Herr & Low, P.C. .... Lancaster, PA
Strasburg, PA
Herr, Maria Teresa .... San Antonio, TX
Herr, Mark E. .... Oviedo, FL
Herr, Michael J. .... Aledo, IL
Herr, Philip C. .... Radnor, PA
Herr, Philip C., II .... Radnor, PA
Herr, Richard C. .... Westminster, CA
Herr, Richard E. .... Wishek, ND
Herr, Robert C. .... San Francisco, CA
Herr, Robert W. .... St. Paul, MN
Herr, Staci .... Apple Valley, MN
Herr, Stanley S. .... Baltimore, MD
Herr, Thomas A. .... Fort Wayne, IN
Herr, Thomas E. .... Pontiac, IL
Herr, Thomas J. .... Lafayette, IN
Herr, Timothy E. .... San Jose, CA
Herr, William H. .... Pittsburg, CA
Herran, Alex .... Chicago, IL
Herranen, Alena M. .... San Diego, CA
Herrara Lopez, Sylvia .... San Juan, PR
Herrbach, William F., Law Offices of
Michigan City, IN
Herr-Cardillo, Joy E. .... Tucson, AZ
Herrell, Christine L. .... Washington, DC
Herrell, Gregory R. .... Lebanon, VA
Herrell, Matthew B. .... Beverly Hills, CA
Herrell, Peter F. .... Eau Claire, WI
Herrell, Robert R. .... Washington, DC
Herrell, Robin L. .... Cincinnati, OH
Herrell, Roger W. .... Philadelphia, PA
Herrell, Stephen B. .... Portland, OR
Herrell, William C. .... Stockton, CA
Herreman, Jon S. .... Milwaukee, WI
Herren & Adams .... Lexington, KY
Herren, Daniel E. .... St. Louis, MO
Herren & Dare .... St. Louis, MO
Herren, Harry K. .... Louisville, KY
Herren, Jeffrey N. .... Denver, CO
Herren, K. Wood .... Birmingham, AL
Herren, Lawson, King, Hentges & Shelton, PLLC .... Oklahoma City, OK
Tulsa, OK
Herren, Mitchell L. .... Wichita, KS
Herren, Rex E. .... Cordell, OK
Herren, Richard D. .... Oklahoma City, OK
Herren, Robert H. .... Paris, KY
Herren, Thomas K. .... Lexington, KY
Herren, William C. .... Houston, TX
Herrenkohl, Amy Martin .... Huntington, WV
Herrera, Alfred R. .... Austin, TX
Herrera, Angela M. .... San Francisco, CA
Herrera, Ann J. .... Decatur, GA
Herrera, Araly .... Miami, FL
Herrera, Carlos M. .... St. Louis, MO
Herrera, Cynthia M. .... Riverside, CA
Herrera, David M. .... Fort Collins, CO
Herrera, Dennis J. .... San Francisco, CA
Herrera, Diana .... Phoenix, AZ
Herrera, Diana Silva .... Dallas, TX
Herrera, Esteban, Jr. .... Baton Rouge, LA
Herrera • Forgeron .... Battle Mountain, NV
Herrera, Frank, Jr. .... San Antonio, TX
Herrera, Frederick M.
House of Representatives,
Congressional Assistants, GV
Herrera, Georgia L. .... Racine, WI
Herrera, Hildy M. .... Miami, FL
Herrera, Jerry Daniel .... Albuquerque, NM
Herrera, Jessica Rae
Department of Justice, GV
Herrera, Jesus R. .... El Paso, TX
Herrera, John A. .... West Palm Beach, FL
Herrera, Jorge C. .... El Paso, TX
Herrera, Judith C. .... Santa Fe, NM
Herrera, Lawrence .... Dallas, TX
Herrera, Long & Pound, P.A.
Santa Fe, NM
Herrera, Louis E., Jr. .... Atlanta, GA
Herrera, Luis .... West Des Moines, IA
Herrera, M. Teresa .... Irvine, CA
Herrera, Mark E. .... Westmont, NJ
Herrera, Nicomedes Sy .... New York, NY
Herrera, Norma R. .... Laredo, TX
Herrera, Richard X. .... Phoenix, AZ
Herrera, Robert James .... Dallas, TX
Herrera, Robert N. .... Thousand Oaks, CA
Herrera, Steve .... Santa Fe, NM
Herrera, Sylvia M. .... Austin, TX
Herrera, Tanya .... San Francisco, CA
Herrera, Theodore C. .... Battle Mountain, NV
Herreras, William A. .... Grover City, CA
Herreras, William A., A Prof. Law Corp.
Grover City, CA
Herrero, Abel .... Corpus Christi, TX
Herrero, Alberto Z. .... Portsmouth, VA
Herrero, Ismael H., III .... San Juan, PR
Herrero, Ismael H., Jr. .... San Juan, PR
Herrero, José M., Chrtd. .... Washington, DC
Herrero, Maria-Milagros .... Springfield, NJ
Herrero, Reed .... Miami, FL
Herrero, Van J. .... Waukegan, IL
Herrick, Andrew H. .... Williamsburg, VA
Herrick, Ary, Cook, Cook, Cook & Cook
Cherokee, IA
Herrick & Associates .... Arcadia, CA
Azusa, CA
Baldwin Park, CA
Claremont, CA
Covina, CA
Diamond Bar, CA
El Monte, CA
Glendora, CA
La Puente, CA
La Verne, CA
Monrovia, CA
Ontario, CA
Pasadena, CA

Hersem, Thomas G. ....Clearwater, FL
Herseth, Harold B. ....Jamestown, ND
Herseth, Stephen S. ....Chicago, IL
Hersey, Christopher J. ....San Jose, CA
Hersey, Jonathan P. ....San Francisco, CA
Hersey, Rachel ....Palo Alto, CA
Hersey, Scott A. ....Hastings, MN
Hersey, Thomas F. ....Portsmouth, NH
Hersh, Adam S. ....Tallahassee, FL
Hersh, Alan S. ....San Jose, CA
Hersh, Alvin D. ....Morristown, NJ
Hersh, Barry D. ....Little Rock, AR
Hersh, Barry S. ....Dallas, TX
Hersh, Brian R. ....Miami, FL
Hersh, Bruce D. ....Nutley, NJ
Hersh, Caren S. ....Wheaton, MD
Hersh, Charles S. ....Sharon, PA
Hersh, Claude I. ....New York, NY
Hersh, David P. ....Englewood, CO
Hersh, Dennis G. ....Hartford, CT
Hersh, Ellen N. ....New York, NY
Hersh FamilyLaw Practice, A Professional Corporation ....San Francisco, CA
Hersh, Fredk. R. ....Peekskill, NY
Hersh, Gail C., Jr. ....Cincinnati, OH
Hersh, Harry D. ....Hauppauge, NY
Hersh & Hersh, A Professional Corporation San Francisco, CA
Hersh & Hersh, P.C. ....Peekskill, NY
Hersh, Jeffrey M. ....Columbus, OH
Hersh, Jennifer Dale ....Far Rockaway, NY
Hersh, Jerome J. ....Peekskill, NY
Hersh, Jerre F., Jr. ....Leawood, KS
Hersh, Jill ....San Francisco, CA
Hersh, John H. ....Peekskill, NY
Hersh, Kathy L. ....Los Angeles, CA
Hersh Law Offices ....Mequon, WI
Milwaukee, WI
Hersh, Lawrence ....New York, NY
Hersh, Leonard W. ....Los Angeles, CA
Hersh, LeRoy ....San Francisco, CA
Hersh, Louis R. ....Woodland Hills, CA
Hersh, Nancy ....San Francisco, CA
Hersh, Neal Raymond, Law Offices of Beverly Hills, CA
Hersh, Neal Raymond, Law Offices of Los Angeles, CA
Hersh, Philip ....Peekskill, NY
Hersh, Ramsey & Berman, A Professional Corporation ....Morristown, NJ
Newark, NJ
Hersh, Raymond T. ....Fort Lauderdale, FL
Hersh & Ritson ....Hartford, CT
Hersh, Robert ....Peekskill, NY
Hersh, Robert K. ....Arlington, VA
Hersh, Robert L. ....San Rafael, CA
Hersh, Robert L. ....Mequon, WI
Hersh, Robert M. ....New York, NY
Hersh and Russak, A Professional Corporation Woodland Hills, CA
Hersh, Sara E. ....Los Angeles, CA
Hersh, Susan B. ....Dallas, TX
Hersh, Susan B., P.C. ....Dallas, TX
Hersh, Vivien H. ....San Francisco, CA
Hersh, Wayne A. ....Irvine, CA
Hersha, Alex J. ....Naples, FL
Hersha, Alex, Law Offices ....Naples, FL
Hersha, Linda S. ....New York, NY
Hersha, Peter J. ....Columbus, OH
Hershberg, Allen J. ....New York, NY
Hershberg, David S. ....Armonk, NY
Hershberg, Eileen W. ....San Francisco, CA
Hershberg, Komal Jain ....Washington, DC
Hershberg, Paul J. ....Louisville, KY
Hershberger, Alan H. ....Bethlehem, PA
Hershberger, Alison M. ....San Jose, CA
Hershberger, Eric B. ....Columbus, OH
Hershberger, J. David ....Denver, CO
Hershberger, J. Ronald ....Palo Alto, CA
Hershberger, John D. ....San Diego, CA
Hershberger, John W., II ....Baltimore, MD
Hershberger, Mark L. ....Columbia, SC
Hershberger, Patterson, Jones & Roth, L.C. Wichita, KS
Hershberger, Richard B. ....Los Angeles, CA
Hershberger, William S. ....Evergreen, CO
Hershcopf, Cathy ....New York, NY
Hershcopf, Gerald T. ....New York, NY
Hershdorfer, Victor J. ....Syracuse, NY
Hershel, Michelle Lynn ....Tallahassee, FL
Hershenberg, Vera Cramer ....Cherry Hill, NJ
Hershenhorn, Howard S. ....New York, NY
Hershenhorn, Robert G. ....Palatine, IL
Hershenhorn, Robert G. ....Wilmette, IL
Hershenov, Eileen B. ....New York, NY
Hershenson, Arthur ....Monterey Park, CA
Hershenson, C. Daniel ....Norwich, VT
Hershenson, Carter, Scott & McGee, P.C. Norwich, VT
Hershenson, Gerald M. ....Doylestown, PA
Hershenson, Gerald M. ....Langhorne, PA
Hershenson, Joseph Bert San Francisco, CA
Hershenson, Richard E. ....New York, NY
Hersher, Judy H. ....Sacramento, CA
Hersher, Wayne B. ....Merrimack, NH
Hershewe, Edward J. ....Joplin, MO
Hershewe & Gulick, P.C. ....Carthage, MO
Joplin, MO
Neosho, MO
Hershey, Adrian V. ....Steubenville, OH
Hershey, Catherine C. ....Brentwood, TN
Hershey, Dale ....Pittsburgh, PA
Hershey, David E. ....Harrisburg, PA
Hershey, Emma Rae ....Nashville, TN
Hershey, James H. ....Honolulu, HI
Hershey, Jane E. ....Denver, CO
Hershey, John ....New York, NY
Hershey, Laurie S. ....Commack, NY
Hershey, Lisa L. ....Portland, OR
Hershey, Mark A. ....Philadelphia, PA
Hershey, Nathan ....Pittsburgh, PA
Hershey, Paul L. ....Arlington, VA
Hershey, Roger W. ....Kansas City, MO
Hershey, Steven P. ....Philadelphia, PA
Hershey, Stewart R. ....Stuart, FL
Hershey-Webb, David S. ....New York, NY
Hershfang, Rachel E. ....Boston, MA
Hershfield, Alan L. ....Glendale, CA
Hershfield, Edward S. ....Boston, MA
Hershfield, Leonie ....Waterbury, CT
Hershfield, Leslie D. ....Baltimore, MD
Hershfield, Rochelle D. ....San Diego, CA
Hershfield, Rochelle D., A P.C. San Diego, CA
Hershinger, Jessalyn ....Nashville, TN
Hershinson, Pamela R. ....West Hartford, CT
Hershiser, Julia A. ....Omaha, NE
Hershiser, Margaret Coyle ....Omaha, NE
Hershkoff, Helen ....New York, NY
Hershkowitz, Benjamin ....New York, NY
Hershkowitz, Daniel A. ....Oakland, CA
Hershkowitz, Ira I. ....Miami Beach, FL
Hershkowitz, Joseph M. ....New York, NY
Hershkowitz, Leonard ....Brooklyn, NY
Hershkowitz, Marcia Berger ....Mineola, NY
Hershkowitz, Max H. ....Schenectady, NY
Hershkowitz, Meryl Louise Department of Commerce, Patent and Trademark Office, GV
Hershkowitz, Ronald M. ....Morristown, NJ
Hershkowitz, Russell S. ....Longwood, FL
Hershkowitz, Sandra J. ....Walnut Creek, CA
Hershkowitz, Stephen E. Federal Election Commission, Office of the General Counsel, GV
Hershkowitz, Steven A. ....New York, NY
Hershler, James M. ....New York, NY
Hershman, Brian D. ....Santa Monica, CA
Hershman, Bryan G. ....Tacoma, WA
Hershman, Daniel A. ....Columbia, MD
Hershman, Don S. ....Chicago, IL
Hershman, Donald S. ....Boca Raton, FL
Hershman, Douglas M. ....Wilmington, DE
Hershman, Ellyn A. ....Chicago, IL
Hershman, Harold M. ....New York, NY
Hershman, Hilary Weinert ....Boston, MA
Hershman, Howard B. ....Toledo, OH
Hershman, Janet C. ....Deerfield, IL
Hershman, Jordan D. ....Boston, MA
Hershman, Kenneth N. ....New York, NY
Hershman, K. L. Clayton Los Angeles, CA
Hershman & Leicher, P.C. ....New York, NY
Hershman, Linda D. ....Hartford, CT
Hershman, Marc I. ....San Mateo, CA
Hershman, Marc J. ....Seattle, WA
Hershman, Mendes ....New York, NY
Hershman, Meryl M. ....Fairfax, VA
Hershman & Moliken, L.L.P. ....Fairfax, VA
Hershman, Morris P. ....Feasterville, PA
Hershman, Peter D. ....New Haven, CT
Hershman, Richard K. ....New York, NY
Hershman, Scott E. ....New York, NY
Hershman, Scott S. ....Dallas, TX
Hershman, Stuart ....Chicago, IL
Hershner, Gary R. ....Richmond, VA
Hershner, Hunter, Andrews, Neill & Smith, LLP ....Eugene, OR
Florence, OR
Hershner, James L. ....Eugene, OR
Hershner, John D., Jr. ....Denver, CO
Hershner, Philip A. ....Cedar Rapids, IA
Hershner, Robert F., Jr. ....Macon, GA
Hershner, Ronald L. ....York, PA
Hershoff, Jay ....Key Largo, FL
Tavernier, FL
Hershoff, Lupino, DeFoor & Gregg, P.A. Key Largo, FL
Hershoff & Lupino, LLP ....Tavernier, FL
Hershon, Leonard A. ....Bay Shore, NY
Hershorin, David M. ....Los Angeles, CA
Hershovitz, Marc B. ....Atlanta, GA
Decatur, GA
Hersh-Sinsel, Eleanor A. ....Fort Bragg, CA
Hersko, Bart S. ....Cincinnati, OH
Herskovic, Maurice ....Detroit, MI
Southfield, MI
Herskovits, David P. ....Highlands Ranch, CO
Herskovits, Robert L. ....New York, NY
Herskovitz, Mark H. ....Glendale, CA
Herskovitz, Paul J. ....Brooklyn, NY
Herskovitz, Richard S. ....Pittsburgh, PA
Herskovitz, S. Marc ....Tallahassee, FL
Herskovitz, Samuel ....Northvale, NJ
Herskovitz and Wynn ....Aliquippa, PA
Herskowitz, Elaine N. Equal Employment Opportunity Commission, Office of Legal Counsel, GV
Herskowitz, Herbert J. ....Bronx, NY
Herskowitz, Howard ....Fort Lauderdale, FL
Herskowitz, Jack L. ....Miami, FL
Herskowitz, Jack L., P.A. ....Miami, FL
Herskowitz, Jean E. ....New York, NY
Herskowitz, Jeffrey ....Cherry Hill, NJ
Herskowitz, Jon ....Miami, FL
Herskowitz, Mark E. ....Miami Beach, FL
Herskowitz, Melissa T. ....Cherry Hill, NJ
Philadelphia, PA
Herskowitz, Michael V. ....Miami, FL
Herskowitz, Sol ....Brooklyn, NY
Herskowitz, Suzan D. ....Stuart, FL
Hersman, Nancy B. ....Los Angeles, CA
Hersman, William G. ....Miami, FL
Hersom, Patricia R. ....Walnut Creek, CA
Herson, Alan R. ....Medford, OR
Herson, Michael .... Department of Defense, GV
Hersperger, John W. ....Warren, NJ
Hersperger, Stephanie Lynn Philadelphia, PA
Hersrud, Leslie R. ....Lemmon, SD
Herst, Lawrence A. ....Chicago, IL
Herst, Michael A. ....Lincolnshire, IL
Herst, Patricia Urken ....Princeton, NJ
Herst, Robert L. ....Northfield, IL
Herst, Theodore J. ....Winnetka, IL
Herst, William S. ....Northbrook, IL
Herstam, David N. ....Bakersfield, CA
Herstein, Carl W. ....Detroit, MI
Herster, Andrew L., Jr. ....Easton, PA
Herster, Newton & Murphy ....Easton, PA
Herstic, Mitchel I. ....New York, NY
Herstik, Neal ....Woodbridge, NJ
Herston, Deborah Herron ....Knoxville, TN
Herston, K.O. ....Knoxville, TN
Hert & Baker, A Professional Corporation Stillwater, OK
Hert, Robert L., Jr. ....Stillwater, OK
Hertach, Gerald E. ....Hutchinson, KS
Hertan, Gaye E. ....Los Angeles, CA
Hertel, Bryant G. ....Kansas City, MO
Hertel, Charles J. ....Oshkosh, WI
Hertel, Colleen Denny ....Winchester, MA
Hertel, David C. ....Milwaukee, WI
Hertel, Edward J., II ....Spokane, WA
Hertel, Harry R. ....Eau Claire, WI
Hertel, Richard H. ....Overland Park, KS
Hertel, Robert G., Jr. ....Chicago, IL
Hertel, Theodore B., Jr. ....Milwaukee, WI
Hertel, White, & Schilling, S.C. Eau Claire, WI
Hertel, William E. ....Brillion, WI
Chilton, WI
Hertell, Hans H. ....San Juan, PR
Herten, Burstein, Sheridan, Cevasco, Bottinelli & Litt ....New York, NY
Hackensack, NJ
Herten, Thomas J. ....Hackensack, NJ
Hertenstein, Edward C. ....Columbus, OH
Herter, Alice E. ....Santa Fe, NM
Herter, Christopher R. Bloomfield Hills, MI
Herter, Thomas, & Associates, L.C. Houston, TX
Herter, Thomas J., Jr. ....Houston, TX
Herth, H. Lawrence ....Reno, NV
Herthel, Nick J. ....Bedford, IN
Herthneck, Richard E. ....Rocky River, OH
Herting, Claireen M. ....Park Ridge, IL
Herting, E. Dyson ....Philadelphia, PA
Hertlein, Charles F., Jr. ....Cincinnati, OH
Hertlein, Donald A. ....Westerville, OH
Hertlein, Douglas L. ....Columbus, OH
Hertlein, Susan M. ....Golden, CO
Hertline, Everitt W. ....Glenview, IL
Hertog and Coster ....Seattle, WA
Hertog, John H. ....Seattle, WA
Hertoghe, Marlene E. ....Fair Oaks, CA
Hertogs, Samuel H. ....Hastings, MN
Hertogs, Scott J. ....Hastings, MN
Hertrick, Paul W. ....Medina, OH
Hertsch, Frank F. ....Bel Air, MD
Hertsch, Gessner & Snee, P.A. ....Bel Air, MD
Hertslet, Byron B. ....Baltimore, MD
Hertz, A. Burke ....Washington, VA
Hertz, Amy Janet ....San Rafael, CA
Hertz, Bradley W. ....Santa Monica, CA
Hertz, Bruce Lovett ....New York, NY
Hertz, Christy L. ....Coral Gables, FL
Hertz, Clifford I., (P.A.) West Palm Beach, FL
Hertz, David A. ....Jacksonville, FL
Hertz, David B. ....Coral Gables, FL
Hertz, David C. ....Paterson, NJ
Hertz, David N. ....New York, NY
Hertz, Denise ....Sparta, WI
Hertz, Diane C. ....New York, NY
Hertz, Elliot ....Roslyn Heights, NY
Hertz, Eric James ....Atlanta, GA
Hertz, E. W. ....Menno, SD
Hertz, Frederick C. ....Oakland, CA
Hertz, Gerald M. ....New York, NY
Hertz, Giles T. ....Florence, KY
Hertz, Harlan Stone ....Cleveland, OH
Hertz, Harvey S. ....Beverly Hills, CA
Hertz & Hertz ....Brooklyn, NY
Hertz, Howard ....Hayward, CA
Hertz, Howard ....Bloomfield Hills, MI
Hertz, Jack A. ....Chicago, IL
Hertz, Jacob ....Brooklyn, NY
Hertz, James A. ....Sioux Falls, SD
Hertz, James G. ....Chicago, IL
Hertz, Jay D. ....Albuquerque, NM
Hertz, Jeffrey A. ....Wausau, WI
Hertz, John D. ....Stamford, CT
Hertz, John D. ....Eau Claire, WI
Hertz, John F. ....Los Angeles, CA
Hertz, Kenneth B. ....Beverly Hills, CA
Hertz, Lawrence M. ....New York, NY
Hertz, Leo J. ....Armour, SD
Hertz, Linda Collins ....Miami, FL
Hertz & Link, P.C. ....Atlanta, GA
Hertz, Louise S. ....Baltimore, MD
Hertz, Marc R. ....Van Nuys, CA
Hertz, Marian S. ....New York, NY
Hertz, Martin A. ....Crofton, MD
Hertz, Martin J. ....New York, NY
Hertz, Michael F. ....Department of Justice, Civil Division, GV
Hertz, Michael J. ....Brattleboro, VT
Hertz, Michael K. ....New York, NY
Hertz, Michael T. ....Fresno, CA
Hertz, Michelle D. ....Washington, DC
Hertz, Mitchell F. ....Washington, DC
Hertz, Natalie Z. ....Harrison, NY
Hertz, Oscar ....Brooklyn, NY
Hertz, Philip R. Pension Benefit Guaranty Corporation, Office of the General Counsel, GV
Hertz, Raymond M. ....Greenbelt, MD
Hertz, Raymond M., & Associates, P.A. Washington, DC
Greenbelt, MD
Hertz, Richard S. ....Inverness, CA
Hertz, Roger J. Federal Communications Commission, Common Carrier Bureau, GV
Hertz, Ronald W. ....Stroudsburg, PA
Hertz, Schram & Saretsky, P.C. Bloomfield Hills, MI
Detroit, MI
Hertz, Seymour ....New York, NY
Hertz, Stephen G. ....Miami Beach, FL
Hertz, Stephen R. ....New York, NY
Hertz, Thomas W. ....Menno, SD
Hertz, William F., II ....Glendale, CA
Hertzberg, Alan D. ....Pittsburgh, PA
Hertzberg, Brett A. ....Mount Vernon, NY
Hertzberg, Catherine M. Priebe Milwaukee, WI
Hertzberg, David G. ....Birmingham, MI
Hertzberg, Eleanor R. ....Acton, MA
Hertzberg, Elisabeth M. ....Washington, DC
Hertzberg, Harold J. ....Beverly Hills, CA
Hertzberg, Harry ....Bronx, NY
Hertzberg, Howard R. ....Denver, CO
Hertzberg, John D. ....Southfield, MI
Hertzberg, Linda A. ....Cupertino, CA
Hertzberg, Michael ....New York, NY
Hertzberg, Michael A. ....Washington, DC
Hertzberg, Michael Lee ....New York, NY
Hertzberg and Noveck ....Bingham Farms, MI
Hertzberg, Richard J. ....Phoenix, AZ
Hertzberg, Richard L. ....Woodbridge, NJ
Hertzberg, Robert A. ....Phoenix, AZ
Hertzberg, Robert C. ....Montclair, NJ
Hertzberg, Robert D. ....Miami, FL
Hertzberg, Robert D., P.A. ....Miami, FL
Hertzberg, Robert M. ....Los Angeles, CA
Hertzberg, Robert S. ....Bloomfield Hills, MI
Hertzberg, Sandra L. ....Northbrook, IL
Hertzberg, Steven M. ....Red Bank, NJ
Hertzberg, Stuart E. ....Detroit, MI
Hertzberg, Todd F. ....Palm Harbor, FL
Hertzberg, William A. ....Chicago, IL
Hertzel, David E. ....San Diego, CA
Hertzer, J. David ....San Francisco, CA
Hertzfeld, Henry R. ....Bethesda, MD
Hertzfeld, Robert E. ....Bryn Mawr, PA
Hertzfeld, Stanley W. ....Brooklyn, NY
Hertzig, Catherine J. ....New York, NY
Hertzig, David ....Miami, FL
Hertzig, Michael S. ....Department of Labor, Office of the Solicitor, GV
Hertzke, Jon D. ....Stamford, CT
Hertzler, Megan J. ....St. Paul, MN
Hertzman, Glenda Morgan Cincinnati, OH
Hertzmark, Alan H. ....Waterbury, CT
Hertzmark & Crean, P.C. ....Waterbury, CT
Hertzo, Richard J. ....Phoenix, AZ
Hertzog, David B. ....New York, NY
Hertzog, H. Katerina ....Palo Alto, CA
Hertzog, Jeanne R. ....Lexington, SC
Hertzog, Michelle G. ....Dallas, TX
Herubin, John F. ....Mayfield Village, OH
Herum, Crabtree, Brown, Dyer, Zolezzi & Terpstra, Inc. ....Stockton, CA
Herum, Steven A. ....Stockton, CA
Hervas, Charles E. ....Itasca, IL
Hervas, Sotos, Condon & Bersani, P.C. Itasca, IL
Hervatin, Lisa T. ....Anaheim, CA
Hervatin, Lydia A. ....Los Angeles, CA
Hervert, Raymond A. ....Kearney, NE
Hervey, Barber & McKee ....New York, NY
Hervey, Delwin E. ....Dallas, TX
Hervey, Geoffrey T. ....Bethesda, MD
Hervey, Harcourt, III ....Pasadena, CA
Hervey, James Edgar, (A P.C.) San Diego, CA
Hervey, Jay R. ....Bassett, VA
Hervey, Linda F. ....Eureka, CA
Hervey, Matsoukas & Schuman New York, NY
Hervey, Matthew C. ....San Diego, CA
Hervey, Muriel G. ....Concord, MA
Hervey, Paul B. ....Canton, OH
Hervey, Richard M. ....New York, NY
Hervey, Robert A. ....Catskill, NY
Hervey, Scott M. ....Sacramento, CA
Hervey, Thomas S. ....Cadiz, OH
Hervey, Virgil W. ....New York, NY
Hervey, Wood & Hervey, LLP San Diego, CA
Hervieux-Osgood, Michele Fort Edward, NY
Herwig, Barbara L. ....Department of Justice, Civil Division, GV
Herwig, Bruce S. ....Highland, CA
Herwig, Jeffrey C. ....Baltimore, MD
Herwig, Kathryn A. ....Tulsa, OK
Herwins, M. Joe ....Revere, MA
Herwitz, Carla B., (P.C.) ....Boston, MA
Herwitz, David R. ....Cambridge, MA
Hery, Mary Jane ....Cincinnati, OH
Heryford, Craig S. ....Pittsburgh, PA
Herz, Andrew D. ....New York, NY
Herz, Andrew L. ....New York, NY
Herz, Arnold D. ....New York, NY

Herz, David Raphael ... New York, NY
Herz, Emanuel A. ... Margate, FL
Herz, Frank F. ... Philadelphia, PA
Herz, George W., II ... Farmingdale, NY
Herz, Gerald ... Washington, DC
Herz, Harry J. ... Montclair, NJ
Herz, Homer F. ... Reno, NV
Herz, Irwin M., Jr. (P.C.) ... Galveston, TX
Herz, Jane Lebovitz ... Garden City, NY
Herz, Jeffrey F. ... Great Neck, NY
Herz, Joel L., Law Offices of ... Tucson, AZ
Herz, Joseph A. ... New York, NY
Herz, Karen R. ... San Francisco, CA
Herz, Lisa S. ... New York, NY
Herz, Michael E. ... New York, NY
Herz, Richard W. ... San Jose, CA
Herz, Steven E. ... New York, NY
Herz, Stuart M. ... Garden City, NY
Herz, Thomas G. A. ... Milwaukee, WI
Herz, William D. ... Los Angeles, CA
Herzbach, Richard ... East Meadow, NY
Herzberg, Alan W., Jr. ... Milwaukee, WI
Herzberg, Aliza F. ... New York, NY
Herzberg & Associates, P.C. ... Monument, CO
Herzberg, Douglas J. ... Monument, CO
Herzberg, James R. ... Houston, TX
Herzberg, Jeffrey ... Bay Shore, NY
Herzberg, Judith K. ... Los Angeles, CA
Herzberg, Morris M. ... Satellite Beach, FL
Herzberg, Peter J. ... Morristown, NJ
New York, NY
Herzberg, Steven B. ... Freehold, NJ
Herzberg, Susan L. ... Northampton, MA
Herzberg, Sydelle S. ... New Rochelle, NY
Herzberger, Mark J. ... Cedar Rapids, IA
Herzberger, William A. ... Cleveland, OH
Herzbrun, Herman ... Torrance, CA
Herzchel, Kristin N. ... Reno, NV
Herzeca, Lois F. ... New York, NY
Herzel, Leo ... Chicago, IL
Herzer, David L. ... Lorain, OH
Herzer, David L., Jr. ... Portland, ME
Herzer, Eva ... Kensington, CA
Herzfeld, Alan ... Boise, ID
Herzfeld, Alexander R. ... Corning, NY
Herzfeld, Allen J. ... Uniondale, NY
Herzfeld, Joel I. ... Philadelphia, PA
Herzfeld, Marc J. ... Salem, OR
Herzfeld, Oliver J. ... New York, NY
Herzfeld, Paul ... Brooklyn, NY
Herzfeld, Robert ... White Plains, NY
Herzfeld, Robin N. ... Denver, CO
Herzfeld, Ronald ... Owings Mills, MD
Herzfeld & Rubin ... Newport Beach, CA
Miami, FL
Herzfeld & Rubin LLP ... Los Angeles, CA
Herzfeld & Rubin, P.C. ... New York, NY
Herzhaft, Marilyn Jacobs ... Los Angeles, CA
Herzig, Albert M., (Professional Corporation)
Beverly Hills, CA
Herzig, Andrew M. ... Washington, DC
Herzig, Barbara E. ... San Francisco, CA
Herzig & Berlese ... San Francisco, CA
Herzig, David J. ... Louisville, KY
Herzig, Pamela J. ... San Francisco, CA
Herzik, Michael L. ... Houston, TX
Herzing, Donna ... San Francisco, CA
Herzing, Philip H. ... St. Marys, OH
Herzing, William C. ... Lutherville, MD
Herzinger, Mark F. ... New York, NY
Herzl-Betz, Louise ... Elmira, NY
Herzlich, Allan E. ... Encino, CA
Herzlich, Gary E. ... New York, NY
Herzoff, Michael P. ... Southfield, MI
Herzog, Albert P. ... Farmington, MI
Herzog, Amy B. ... Milwaukee, WI
Herzog, Amy Field ... Chicago, IL
Herzog, Arnold A. ... Chagrin Falls, OH
Herzog, Barbara N. ... Easton, CT
Herzog, Barry ... New York, NY
Herzog, Barry A. ... Santa Monica, CA
Herzog & Bimbler ... New York, NY
Herzog, Bruce C. ... Houston, TX
Herzog, C. William ... Fort Collins, CO
Herzog, Crebs & McGhee, LLP
Belleville, IL
St. Louis, MO
Herzog, David ... Fremont, CA
Herzog, David K. ... Indianapolis, IN
Herzog, David L. ... Omaha, NE
Herzog, David R. ... Chicago, IL
Herzog, Debra E. ... Fort Lauderdale, FL
Herzog, Engstrom & Koplovitz, P.C.
Albany, NY
Herzog, Fisher, Grayson & Wolfe, A Law Corporation ... Beverly Hills, CA
Herzog, Frank C. ... Houston, TX
Herzog, Frederick C. ... San Francisco, CA
Herzog, Fredrick J. ... New Orleans, LA
Herzog, Gary Drew ... Los Angeles, CA
Herzog, Gordon I. ... St. Louis, MO
Herzog, Gregory S. ... Lafayette, LA
Herzog, Harry A. ... Houston, TX
The Woodlands, TX
Herzog, Harry W. ... Basking Ridge, NJ
Herzog & Herzog, P.C. ... Omaha, NE
Herzog, Howard ... New York, NY
Herzog, Ian, A Professional Corporation
Santa Monica, CA
Herzog, Israel J. ... Canton, MA
Herzog, James P. ... Beverly Hills, CA
Herzog, Jeanne ... New York, NY
Herzog, John P. ... Farmington, MI
Herzog, John R. ... Shreveport, LA
Herzog, Jonathan C. ... New York, NY
Herzog, Julianne Dunn ... Omaha, NE
Herzog, Julie A. ... Chatsworth, CA
Herzog, Julie A. ... Denver, CO
Herzog, Kanter & Hoffert, LLP
St. Louis, MO
Herzog, Karen M. ... Buffalo, NY
Herzog, Karen Schneider
New Rochelle, NY
Herzog, Laura J. ... Allentown, PA
Herzog, Leonard H. ... Anchorage, AK
Herzog, Lester B. ... Brooklyn, NY
Herzog, Malcolm O. ... Valley Stream, NY
Herzog, Mark E. ... Washington, DC
Herzog, Michael W. ... Phoenix, AZ
Herzog, Mitchell L. ... St. Louis, MO
Herzog, Morey J. ... New Hyde Park, NY
Herzog, Morey J., P.C. ... New Hyde Park, NY
Herzog and O'Connor, P.C. ... Phoenix, AZ
Herzog, Patricia ... Corona Del Mar, CA
Herzog, Peter F. ... Chicago, IL
Herzog, Peter W., III ... St. Louis, MO
Herzog, Peter W., Jr. ... St. Louis, MO
Herzog, Richard B. ... Washington, DC
Herzog, Richard B., Jr. ... Atlanta, GA
Herzog, Richard C. ... Los Angeles, CA
Herzog, Richard R. ... Palo Alto, CA
Herzog, Robert P. ... New York, NY
Herzog, Rochelle A. ... Beverly Hills, CA
Herzog, Ronald S. ... New York, NY
Herzog, Sarah C. ... Morristown, NJ
Herzog, Scott ... Princeton, NJ
Herzog, Stephen B. ... Fort Thomas, KY
Herzog, Stephen Frank ... Pocatello, ID
Herzog, Steven C. ... New York, NY
Herzog, Stuart ... Tucson, AZ
Herzog, Theodore D. ... Minneapolis, MN
Herzog, Theodore G. ... Portland, OR
Herzog, Theodore W. ... Key West, FL
Herzog, Thomas A. ... West Bloomfield, MI
Herzog, Thomas P. ... O'Neill, NE
Herzog, Thomas P. ... Waukesha, WI
Herzog, Vern E., Jr. ... Pocatello, ID
Herzog, W. Scott ... Minneapolis, MN
Herzog, Wendy A. ... Los Angeles, CA
Herzog, William E., The Law Offices of
Kankakee, IL
Herzstein, Mortimer H.
San Francisco, CA
Herzstein, Robert E. ... Washington, DC
Herzweig, Benjamin L. ... Patchogue, NY
Hesby, Philip S. ... Galion, OH
Hesch, Jerome M. ... Miami, FL
Hesch, Joel D. ... Department of Justice,
Civil Division, GV
Hesch, William E. ... Fort Mitchell, KY
Hescheles, Norma ... Glendale, CA
Hesco, Carrie R. ... Cheyenne, WY
Hescock, William H. ... North Stonington, CT
Hescox, James E. ... Universal City, CA
Heselton, George W. ... Gardiner, ME
Heselton, Joseph K., Jr.
Oklahoma City, OK
Heseman, Polly D. ... St. Louis, MO
Hesen, Ellen M. ... Louisville, KY
Hesford, A. Margaret ... Fort Lauderdale, FL
Hesford, A. Margaret, P.A.
Fort Lauderdale, FL
Hesi, David O. ... Alton, IL
Hesik, April A. ... Los Angeles, CA
Hesik, George A. ... Willowbrook, IL
Hesik, George A., & Associates, Ltd.
Willowbrook, IL
Hesik, Richard J. ... Seattle, WA
Hesketh, James F. ... Mattapoisett, MA
Hesketh, Thomas A. E. ... San Francisco, CA
Heskett & Heskett ... Bartlesville, OK
Heskett, Jack ... Bartlesville, OK
Heskett, John Franklin ... Bartlesville, OK
Heskett, Nicola R. ... Kansas City, MO
Heskin, Allan D. ... Oakland, CA
Heskin, Keersten ... Orlando, FL
Heslam, Sharlyn Carter ... Dallas, TX
Heslen, Cynthia ... Cambridge, MA
Heslep, Katherine W. ... Washington, DC
Heslep & Kearney, P.C. ... Lexington, VA
Heslep, Nacole D. ... Anchorage, AK
Heslep, Thomas T. ... Washington, DC
Heslep, W. Wayne ... Lexington, VA
Heslet, Jim H. ... Tulsa, OK
Heslin, Brian Scott ... Rockville, MD
Heslin, Holly A. ... Bridgeport, CT
Heslin, James F. ... Philadelphia, PA
Heslin, James M. ... Palo Alto, CA
Heslin, Kerrie R. ... Newark, NJ
Heslin, Lisa Page ... New Haven, CT
Heslin, Martin F. ... New York, NY
Heslin, Raymond J. ... New York, NY
Heslin, Robert E. ... Albany, NY
Heslin & Rothenberg, P.C. ... Albany, NY
Heslin, Thomas P. ... Hartford, CT
Heslinga, Garold F. ... Oskaloosa, IA
Heslinga, Harold B. ... Oskaloosa, IA
Heslinga, Heslinga & Dixon ... Oskaloosa, IA
Heslinga, Mark A. ... Dallas, OR
Heslop, John W., Jr. ... Altoona, PA
Heslop, Ronald D. ... Tacoma, WA
Heslop, Ronald D., P.S. ... Tacoma, WA
Hesmer, John R. ... Marietta, GA
Hesni, George S. ... New Orleans, LA
Hesp, Richard ... Menlo Park, CA
Hespe, David C. ... Belle Mead, NJ
Hespe, Frank ... Pacific Grove, CA
Hespel, Paul W. ... New York, NY
Hespen, James F. ... St. Louis, MO
Hespos, Gerald E. ... New York, NY
Hess, Adam R. ... Washington, DC
Hess, Aimee L. ... Dallas, TX
Hess, Alan M. ... Binghamton, NY
Hess, Amy Morris ... Knoxville, TN
Hess, Andrew C. ... Cincinnati, OH
Hess, Barbara J. ... Newport Beach, CA
Hess, Barry ... Mobile, AL
Hess, Brenda R. ... Berwick, PA
Hess, Bruce D. ... Huntingdon Valley, PA
Hess, C. Victor ... Berkeley, CA
Hess, Cameron L. ... Sacramento, CA
Hess & Carlman, LLC ... Jackson, WY
Hess, Carol L. ... Bow, NH
Hess, Carolyn June ... Baltimore, MD
Hess, Carrie L. ... Southfield, MI
Hess, Carroll E. ... Jeffersonville, IN
Hess, Catherine Ann ... Hartford, CT
Hess, Charles B. ... Atlanta, GA
Hess, Charles W., Law Office of
Wichita, KS
Hess, Charles White ... Kansas City, MO
Hess, Charley ... Columbus, OH
Hess, Christine L. ... Anchorage, AK
Hess, Christopher J. ... Pittsburgh, PA
Hess, Cletus C. ... Fort Smith, AR
Hess, Clifford S." Stan " ... Seattle, WA
Hess, Clifford W. ... Ridgewood, NY
Hess, Cynthia Clarfield ... Portland, OR
Hess, Daniel B. ... Grand Rapids, MI
Hess, Daniel J. ... Santa Ana, CA
Hess, Daniel L. ... Torrance, CA
Hess, Daniel M. ... Milwaukee, WI
Hess, Danielle A. ... Seattle, WA
Hess, David D. ... Millburn, NJ
New York, NY
Hess, David J. ... Minneapolis, MN
Hess, David M. ... Royal Oak, MI
Hess, David R. ... St. Louis, MO
Hess, David W. ... Sacramento, CA
Hess, David W. ... Manchester, NH
Hess, David Warren, Law Offices of
Sacramento, CA
Hess, Debra Shaw ... White Plains, NY
Hess, Dexter, Reinertson & Brunner, S.C.
Wausau, WI
Hess, Donald C. ... Cincinnati, OH
Hess, Donald H. ... Lancaster, PA
Hess, Douglas A. ... Dayton, OH
Hess, Douglas M. ... Detroit, MI
Hess, Douglas S. ... Lake Oswego, OR
Hess, E. Frank ... Jackson, WY
Hess, Edward D. ... Washington, DC
Hess, Elizabeth B. ... New York, NY
Hess, Elizabeth Barnes
Downers Grove, IL
Hess, Emerson G. ... Pittsburgh, PA
Hess, Eric W. ... Weehawken, NJ
Hess, Eva T. ... Harrington Park, NJ
Hess, Frank A. ... River Edge, NJ
Hess, Frederick D. ... Department of Justice,
Criminal Division, GV
Hess, Frederick J. ... Belleville, IL
Hess, G. Robinson ... Dallas, TX
Hess, Gary ... Baltimore, MD
Hess, Gary C. ... San Francisco, CA
Hess, Gary S. ... Meade, KS
Hess, Gary S. ... St. Cloud, MN
Hess, George A. ... Lewiston, ME
Hess, George F., II, (P.A.)
Fort Lauderdale, FL
Hess, Gerald E. ... Farmington, UT
Hess, Gerald W. ... Denver, CO
Hess, Geraldine Welikson ... Rockville, MD
Upper Marlboro, MD
Hess, Glen E., (P.C.) ... New York, NY
Hess, Glenn L. ... Panama City, FL
Hess, Gregory M. ... Mobile, AL
Hess, Gregory M. ... Salt Lake City, UT
Hess, H. Ober ... Philadelphia, PA
Hess, H. Robert ... Toledo, OH
Hess, H. Todd ... Weehawken, NJ
Hess, Harvey K., Jr. ... Kill Devil Hills, NC
Hess, Henry L., Jr. ... Portland, OR
Hess & Hess ... Lake Oswego, OR
Hess & Hess, A Professional Corporation
Grand Rapids, MI
Hess & Hess, P.C. ... Roscommon, MI
Hess & Hess, P.C. ... Hughesville, PA
Hess, Jacob F., Jr. ... Canton, OH
Hess, James E. ... Rochester Hills, MI
Hess, James M. ... Maitland, FL
Hess, James M. ... Rockford, IL
Hess, James P. ... Huntsville, AL
Hess, James W. ... Elk River, MN
Hess, Jane A. ... Department of Education,
Office of the General Counsel, GV
Hess, Jason C. ... Philadelphia, PA
Hess, Jeff A. ... New York, NY
Hess, Jeffery L. ... Boise, ID
Hess, Jeffrey L. ... Kansas City, MO
Hess, Jerry E. ... Fort Mill, SC
Hess, Jimmie L., Jr. ... Abingdon, VA
Hess, John C. ... Hermitage, TN
Hess, John C., P.C. ... Hermitage, TN
Hess, John E. ... Mesa, AZ
Hess, John H. ... Grand Rapids, MI
Hess, John J. ... New York, NY
Hess, John L. ... Carmel, IN
Hess, John Robert ... Lancaster, PA
Hess, Jonathan E. ... Phoenix, AZ
Hess, Joseph A. ... Washington, DC
Hess, Joseph E. ... Buena Vista, VA
Hess, Karen ... Irving, TX
Hess, Kendy M. ... Chicago, IL
Hess, Kristin A. ... Milladore, WI
Hess, Kristofer W. ... Washington, DC
Hess, L. Stephen ... Baltimore, MD
Hess, Laura J. ... Detroit, MI
Hess, Laura L. ... Fort Lauderdale, FL
Hess, Lawrence E., Jr. ... Fort Washington, PA
Hess, Lawrence J. ... St. Louis, MO
Hess, Leah ... Oakland, CA
Hess, Lee A. ... Westlake Village, CA
Hess, Lee M. ... Portland, OR
Hess, Lee M., P.C. ... Portland, OR
Hess, Les ... Orlando, FL
Hess, Lester C., Jr. ... Wheeling, WV
Hess, Linda D. ... Bishop, CA
Mammoth Lakes, CA
Hess, Lois K. ... Prospect, KY
Hess, Loren H. ... Fairborn, OH
Hess, Lynn H., (Mr.) ... Seattle, WA
Hess, Marc A. ... Lebanon, PA
Hess, Mark David ... Birmingham, AL
Hess, Mark G. ... Toledo, OH
Hess, Mark H. ... Los Angeles, CA
Hess, Martha J. ... San Antonio, TX
Hess, Martha S. ... Baton Rouge, LA
Hess, Mary Ann ... Mesa, AZ
Hess, Mary J. ... Chicago, IL
Hess, Matthew C. ... Elizabethtown, KY
Hess, Matthew L. ... Atlanta, GA
Hess & McMurtrie, P.C. ... Huntsville, AL
Hess, Melinda A. ... Los Angeles, CA
Hess, Melinda G. ... Omaha, NE
Hess, Melvin H. ... Lancaster, PA
Hess, Michael A. ... Washington, DC
Hess, Michael R. ... Jackson, MS
Hess, Michael W. ... Angola, IN
Hess, Myron J. ... Austin, TX
Hess, Newman W., III ... Naugatuck, CT
Hess, Norman J.
Department Of The Interior, GV
Hess, Norman L. ... Lake Placid, NY
Hess, Otis R., Jr. ... Cincinnati, OH
Hess, P. Gregory ... New York, NY
Hess & Parkinson ... Macon, MO
Hess, Patrick C. ... Chicago, IL
Hess, Patrick R. ... Fort Wayne, IN
Hess, Paul J., Jr. ... Columbus, OH
Hess, Paul R. ... Columbus, OH
Hess, Paul W. ... Draper, UT
Hess, Paula L. ... Hacienda Heights, CA
Hess, Peter E., The Law Office of
Wilmington, DE
Maywood, NJ
Hess, Peter L. ... Hartford, CT
Hess, Philip G. ... Crystal City, MO
Hess, Philip J. ... Los Angeles, CA
Hess, Philip M. ... St. Louis, MO
Hess, Ralph Matthew ... Prescott, AZ
Hess, Randy M. ... Campbell, CA
Hess, Raymond A. ... Spirit Lake, IA
Hess, Raymond K. ... Reading, PA
Hess, Raymond L. ... New Orleans, LA
Hess, Rebecca J. ... Columbus, OH
Hess, Richard Jay ... Chicago, IL
Hess, Richard M., Jr. ... Denver, CO
Hess, Richard V. ... Englewood, CO
Hess, Robert A. ... Roscommon, MI
Hess, Robert B. ... Chicago, IL
Hess, Robert C. ... Chillicothe, OH
Hess, Robert D., III ... New Orleans, LA
Hess, Robert E. ... Newport Beach, CA
Hess, Robert F. ... Southfield, MI
Hess, Robert G. ... Huntingdon Valley, PA
Hess, Robert J. ... New York, NY
Hess, Robert K. ... Southfield, MI
Hess, Robert L. ... Los Angeles, CA
Hess, Robert M. ... Hammond, IN
Hess, Robert P. ... Los Angeles, CA
Hess, Robert P., P.C. ... Los Angeles, CA
Hess, Robert W. ... Philadelphia, PA
Hess, Roberta A. ... Phoenix, AZ
Hess, Ronnie F. ... Allentown, PA
Hess, Russell I. ... Cedar Rapids, IA
Hess, Ruth E. ... Santa Ana, CA
Hess, Scott A. ... Centralia, WA
Hess, Scott D. ... Boise, ID
Hess, Scott L. ... Roscommon, MI
Hess, Sharon D. ... Boca Raton, FL
Hess, Sidney J., Jr. ... Chicago, IL
Hess, Stephanie C. ... Charlotte, NC
Hess, Stephen A. ... Colorado Springs, CO
Hess, Stephen B.
Environmental Protection Agency,
Office of the General Counsel, GV
Hess, Steven C. ... Detroit, MI
Hess, Steven D. ... Hughesville, PA
Hess, Steven L. ... New York, NY
Hess, Steven M. ... Reno, NV
Hess, Teresa Mayhew ... St. Louis, MO
Hess, Thaddeus J ... Nashville, TN
Hess, Theodore G. ... Department of the Navy,
Office of the Judge Advocate General, GV
Hess, Thomas ... North Jackson, OH
Hess, Thomas D. ... Hughesville, PA
Hess, Thomas J. ... Miami, FL
Hess, Thomas W. ... Columbus, OH
Hess, Victor H., Jr. ... Covington, LA
Hess, Vincent J. ... Dallas, TX
Hess, Virginia Turner ... San Jose, CA
Hess, W. Ashley ... Louisville, KY
Hess, Walter A. ... Chicago, IL
Hess, Walter D., III ... Westminster, MD
Hess, Walter, Jr. ... Rockville, MD
Hess, Wayne G. ... New York, NY
Hess, Wendy Castor ... Jenkintown, PA
Hess, Wilda D. ... White Plains, NY
Hess, William C. ... Wausau, WI
Hess, William F. ... Prairie Village, KS
Hess, William H. ... New York, NY
Hess, William J. ... Bloomington, IL
Hess, William L. ... Kansas City, MO
Hess, William R. ... Los Angeles, CA
Hess, William Thomas ... Stuart, FL
Hessberg, Albert, III ... Albany, NY
Hessberg, Lee R. ... Albany, NY
Hessburg, John Paul ... Detroit, MI
Hesse, Alfred W., Jr. ... Napa, CA

Hesse, Alice P.
Department Of Health And Human Services, Public Health Service, GV
Hesse and Butterworth ... St. Francisville, LA
Bay St. Louis, MS
Hesse, Carolyn S. ... Chicago, IL
Chicago, IL
Hesse, Cheryl L. ... Los Angeles, CA
Hesse, Daniel M. ... Jackson, WY
Hesse, David R. ... New York, NY
Hesse, Donald F. ... San Francisco, CA
Hesse, Gregory ... Dallas, TX
Hesse, Gregory G. ... Dallas, TX
Hesse, Helen E. ... Los Angeles, CA
Hesse, J. Francis ... Wichita, KS
Hesse, J. Marc ... Dallas, TX
Hesse, James A. ... St. Louis, MO
Hesse, James Christopher ... St. Louis, MO
Hesse, Joel P. ... Wichita, KS
Hesse, John W., II ... Silver Spring, MD
Hesse, Jon M. ... Livingston, MT
Hesse & Jones ... Dallas, TX
Hesse, Karl N. ... Wichita, KS
Hesse, Karl O. ... Charlotte, NC
Hesse, Katherine A. ... Quincy, MA
Hesse, Keith J. ... Orlando, FL
Hesse, Lisa A. ... Dayton, OH
Hesse, Margaret A. ... St. Louis, MO
Hesse, Margaret C. ... Treasury Department, Office of the Comptroller of the Currency, GV
Hesse, Mary Patricia ... Wichita, KS
Hesse, Matthew C. ... Wichita, KS
Hesse, Michael D. ... Dallas, TX
Hesse, Michael O. ... St. Francisville, LA
Bay St. Louis, MS
Hesse, Michael V. ... Riverside, CA
Hesse, Paul D. ... Los Angeles, CA
Hesse & Potenberg, P.L.L.C.
Bozeman, MT
Livingston, MT
Hesse, Renata B. ... Washington, DC
Hesse, Richard A. ... Concord, NH
Hesse, Robert L. ... Sarasota, FL
Hesse, Robertson C. ... Severna Park, MD
Hesse, Siegfried D. ... San Francisco, CA
Hesse, Stephen B., Jr. ... Houston, TX
Hesse, Thomas H. ... Charleston, SC
Hesse, Wendy Ann ... Annapolis, MD
Hesse, William Scott ... Topeka, KS
Hessee, Susan Y. ... Urbana, IL
Hessekiel, Jeffrey J. ... Palo Alto, CA
Hessel and Aluise, P.C. ... Washington, DC
Hessel, Arthur R. ... Washington, DC
Hessel, Chad J. ... Colorado Springs, CO
Hessel, Daniel L. ... Philadelphia, PA
Hessel, John M. ... St. Louis, MO
Hessel, Mark L. ... Wheaton, MD
Hesselbach, Bruce ... Brattleboro, VT
Hesselbacher, Robert W., Jr.
Baltimore, MD
Hesselgrave, T. Reginald ... Indianapolis, IN
Hesselholt, Claire ... Olympia, WA
Hesselink, Ann P. ... New York, NY
Hesselink, Kevin Lee ... Gaylord, MI
Hessell, Robert E. ... Solana Beach, CA
Hesseltine, David J. ... Irvine, CA
Hesseltine, W. G. ... Lafayette, CA
Hessen, Arnold D. ... Miami, FL
Hessen, J. J. L. ... New York, NY
Hessen, Neal J. ... Duluth, MN
Hessen, Schimmel & De Castro, P.A.
Miami, FL
Hessen, Stephen ... Melbourne, FL
Hessen, Stephen J. ... Kalamazoo, MI
Hessenbruch, Katherine A. ... Louisville, KY
Hessenius, Barry C. ... San Anselmo, CA
Hessenius, Richard S., (A Professional Corporation) ... Los Angeles, CA
Hessenthaler, Erika ... Pittsboro, NC
Hessenthaler, Erika, P.A., Law Office of
Pittsboro, NC
Hessenthaler, Joseph S. ... Philadelphia, PA
Hesser, David C. ... Lafayette, LA
Hesser, Dennis ... Chicago, IL
Hesser, Randall G. ... Elkhart, IN
Hessert, Stephen ... Portland, ME
Hessey & Hessey, P.A. ... Baltimore, MD
Hessey, Hurst R. ... Baltimore, MD
Hessey, Mahlon W. ... Baltimore, MD
Hess-Homeier, Ted ... Missoula, MT
Hessian & McKasy, P.A.
Minneapolis, MN
St. Paul, MN
Hessick, Terry Ford ... Baton Rouge, LA
Hessing, David F. ... Paris, TN
Hessing, Ilana G. ... Blue Bell, PA
Hessinger, Carl J. W. ... Allentown, PA
Hessinger, Edward F. ... Fort Myers, FL
Hessinger, Gregory J. ... New York, NY
Hessinger, Kathleen T. ... St. Petersburg, FL
Hessinger, Mark Edward ... Phoenix, AZ
Hession & Bekoff ... Mineola, NY
Hession, Cathi A. ... Jersey City, NJ
New York, NY
Hession, Christopher D. ... Chicago, IL
Hession, Conal L. ... Yutan, NE
Hession, Dennis C. ... San Mateo, CA
Hession, Dennis P. ... Spokane, WA
Hession, Frank W. ... Jacksonville, FL
Hession, Gregory A. ... Belchertown, MA
Hession & Guild ... Jacksonville, FL
Hession, James A. ... Livingston, NJ
Hession, Jeanne M. ... Braintree, MA
Hession, John J. ... New York, NY
Hession, John M. ... Boston, MA
Hession, Joseph F. ... Miami, FL
West Palm Beach, FL
Hession, Leo J. ... Wellesley, MA
Hession, Michael ... New York, NY
Hession, Michael A. ... Miami, FL
Hession, Thomas R. ... Mineola, NY
Hesslein, Robert W. ... Boston, MA
Hessler & Associates, Chartered
Washington, DC
Hessler, Charles A. ... Indianapolis, IN
Hessler, David J. ... Cleveland, OH
Hessler, Jane Titus ... Indianapolis, IN
Hessler, Kevin G. ... Rockville, MD
Hessler, Nathan E. ... Cleveland, OH
Hessler, Peter A. ... Cleveland, OH
Hessler, Robert J. ... Dublin, OH
Hessler, Stephen O. ... Washington, DC
Hessley, Bernard J. ... Warren, PA
Hesslin, Daniel D. ... Manistee, MI
Hessling, Robert A. ... Los Angeles, CA
Hess-Mahan, Theodore M. ... Boston, MA
Hessman, Robert L. ... Tallahassee, FL
Hessmer, F. William, IV ... Bethesda, MD
Hessney, William P., Jr. ... Troy, NY
Hesson & Associates ... Neenah, WI
Hesson, Carol A. ... Quincy, MA
Hesson, Jeffrey L. ... Neenah, WI
Hesson, Larry R. ... Plainfield, IN
Hesson, Robert C. ... Venice, FL
Hesson, Terry W. ... Breckenridge, CO
Abilene, TX
Hesson, William M., Jr. ... Towson, MD
Hest, Bruce H. ... Boca Raton, FL
Hest, Bruce H., P.A. ... Boca Raton, FL
Hest, Lionel G. ... New York, NY
Hestad, Sally A. ... Madison, WI
Hester, Ann L. ... Charlotte, NC
Hester, B. R. ... Bartlett, TN
Hester, Brooks E. ... Baton Rouge, LA
Hester, C. Scott ... Jacksonville, FL
Hester, Catherine Chen ... Baltimore, MD
Hester, Catherine S. ... Atlanta, GA
Hester, Cecille L. ... Los Angeles, CA
Hester, Charles E. ... Dallas, TX
Hester, Chuck ... Canyon, TX
Hester, Daniel W. ... Louisville, CO
Hester, David G. ... Atlanta, GA
Hester, David J. ... Ottumwa, IA
Hester, Deborah Kay ... Long Beach, MS
Hester, Delacie C. ... Montgomery, AL
Hester, Dennis J. ... Kalispell, MT
Hester, Diane ... New York, NY
Hester, Edward C. ... Rescue, CA
Hester, Elizabeth G. ... Richmond, VA
Hester, Eric J. ... Sacramento, CA
Hester, Ernest G. ... Guin, AL
Hester, Frank B. ... Lithia Springs, GA
Hester, G. McCelvey ... Fort Collins, CO
Hester, Grady, Hester, Greene & Payne
Elizabethtown, NC
Hester, Gwanita G. ... Ambler, PA
Hester, H. Clifton ... Elizabethtown, NC
Hester, Henry G. ... Phoenix, AZ
Hester & Hester ... Lithia Springs, GA
Hester & Hester ... Long Beach, MS
Hester, Hugh S. ... Reidsville, NC
Hester, J. Lawson ... Jackson, MS
Hester, J. Robert, Jr. ... Fort Worth, TX
Hester, James C. ... Pasadena, CA
Hester, James D. ... Laurel, MS
Hester, James M. ... San Diego, CA
Hester, Jerrold W. ... Norcross, GA
Saint Simons Island, GA
Hester, Jerrold W., P.C. ... Norcross, GA
Saint Simons Island, GA
Hester, John F. ... Gulfport, MS
Hester, John P. ... Pittsburgh, PA
Hester, John W. ... Santa Monica, CA
Hester, John Wm. ... Chesapeake, VA
Hester, Jon L. ... Oklahoma City, OK
Hester, Jon L., P.C., A Professional Corporation ... Oklahoma City, OK
Hester, Joseph M., Jr. ... Rocky Mount, NC
Hester, Joseph P., Jr. ... Binghamton, NY
Hester, Kathryn H. ... Jackson, MS
Hester, Lance M. ... Tacoma, WA
Hester, Larry T. ... Houston, TX
Hester, Linda Gordon ... Houston, TX
Hester, Lisa Clephas ... Louisville, KY
Hester, Mark A. ... Troy, MI
Hester, Mary C. ... New Orleans, LA
Hester, Maryellen S. ... Houston, TX
Hester, McGlasson & Cox ... Canyon, TX
Hester, Michael C. ... Long Beach, MS
Hester, Michael D. ... Knoxville, TN
Hester, Michael J. ... Ardmore, OK
Hester, Michael J., Inc. ... Ardmore, OK
Marietta, OK
Hester, Oma H., Jr. ... Hickory, NC
Hester, Orben Sidney ... El Centro, CA
Hester, Patrick J. ... Boston, MA
Hester, Rena L. ... Baton Rouge, LA
Hester, Richard M. ... Lithia Springs, GA
Hester, Robert F. ... Northport, NY
Hester, Robert H. ... Baton Rouge, LA
Hester, Robert J. ... Jacksonville, FL
Hester, Samuel D. ... Rome, NY
Utica, NY
Hester, Sean W. ... Tyler, TX
Hester, Stephen M. ... Cincinnati, OH
Hester, Steven P. ... Jacksonville, FL
Hester, Theodore M. ... Washington, DC
Hester, Thomas P. ... Chicago, IL
Hester, Thomas P., Jr. ... Department of Justice, Office of Information and Privacy, GV
Hester, Timothy C. ... Washington, DC
Hester, Tracy D. ... Houston, TX
Hester, W. Dean ... El Paso, TX
Hester, Worth H. ... Elizabethtown, NC
Hesterberg, Brett A. ... Chicago, IL
Hesterberg, Gregory X. ... Brooklyn, NY
Garden City, NY
Hesterberg & Keller ... Oradell, NJ
Brooklyn, NY
Garden City, NY
Hester III, William E. ... New Orleans, LA
Jackson, MS
Hester-Tone, Mary M. ... Park Ridge, IL
Hestle, John J. ... Clarksville, TN
Hestnes, Erik ... Fort Lee, NJ
Hestnes, Harold ... Boston, MA
Heston, Frank Joseph ... Coral Springs, FL
Heston, Frank Joseph, P.A.
Coral Springs, FL
Fort Lauderdale, FL
Heston, Halli B. ... Newport Beach, CA
Heston & Heston ... Newport Beach, CA
Heston, James R. ... Fairfax, VA
Heston, Joseph J. ... Kingston, PA
Heston, Joseph S. ... Sacramento, CA
Heston, Julia Anne ... Seattle, WA
Heston, Kristopher S. ... Chicago, IL
Heston, Laura Crowley ... Port Orchard, WA
Heston, Mary Jo ... Seattle, WA
Heston, Michael E. ... Haddonfield, NJ
Heston, Richard G. ... Newport Beach, CA
Heston, Robert L., Jr. ... Houston, TX
Hestor, Sue C. ... San Francisco, CA
Hestres-Velez, Eugene F. ... San Juan, PR
Hetchka & Bachmann, P.A. ... Clifton, NJ
Hetchka, Donald P. ... Clifton, NJ
Hetchler, Robert M. ... Clinton Township, MI
Hete, Emily M. ... Akron, OH
Hetey, Michael C. ... Las Vegas, NV
Hetfield, George F. ... Plainfield, NJ
Heth, Georgia Kay ... Peoria, IL
Heth, Jacob A. ... Portland, OR
Heth, Rhonda J. ... Los Angeles, CA
Heth, William G. ... Dickinson, ND
Hetherington, Bryan D. ... Rochester, NY
Hetherington, Carey Jordan ... Houston, TX
Hetherington, Charlotte H. ... Santa Fe, NM
Hetherington, Edwin S. ... New York, NY
Hetherington, H. Lee ... Jackson, MS
Hetherington, J. George ... Honolulu, HI
Hetherington, J. A. C. ... Charlottesville, VA
Hetherington, Jack J. ... Hilltown, PA
Hetherington, James F. ... San Francisco, CA
Hetherington, John W. ... New York, NY
Hetherington, Leon R. ... Fort Collins, CO
Hetherington, Mark L. ... Williamsburg, MI
Hetherington, Michael ... Woodside, CA
Hetherington, Robert A., III
Hackensack, NJ
Hetherington, Robert B. ... Rockville, MD
Hetherington, Thomas F., Attorney at Law, P.C.
Carefree, AZ
Hetherington, Thomas F.A. ... Houston, TX
Hetherington, Thomas G. ... Pawtucket, RI
Hetherington, W. Joseph ... Chicago, IL
Hetherington, William C., Jr. ... Norman, OK
Hetherton, Judith
Department of Housing and Urban Development, Office of the Inspector General, GV
Hetherwick, Gilbert L. ... Shreveport, LA
Hetlage, James C. ... St. Louis, MO
Hetlage, Richard A. ... St. Louis, MO
Hetlage, Robert O. ... St. Louis, MO
Hetlage, W. Laird ... St. Louis, MO
Hetland, James L., Jr. ... Minneapolis, MN
Hetland, Janice E. ... St. Louis, MO
Hetland, John R. ... Berkeley, CA
Orinda, CA
Hetland & Kneeland, A Professional Corporation ... Berkeley, CA
Orinda, CA
Hetland, Steven T. ... Minneapolis, MN
Hetler, Dennis W. ... Chicago, IL
Hetley, Geoffrey W. ... Kansas City, MO
Hetman, Joseph E. ... Chicago, IL
Hetman, Nicholas W. ... Owensboro, KY
Hetreed, Patricia E. ... Blacksburg, VA
Hetrick, Brenda Lynn ... Mobile, AL
Hetrick, Byron T. ... Jackson, MS
Hetrick, Carolyn K. ... Lancaster, PA
Hetrick, Demaris Page ... Stamford, CT
Hetrick, Elizabeth T. ... San Antonio, TX
Hetrick, John R. ... Walterboro, SC
Hetrick, Joseph K. ... Philadelphia, PA
Hetrick, Keith C. ... Tallahassee, FL
Hetrick Law Firm ... Walterboro, SC
Hetrick, Norman P. ... Harrisburg, PA
Hetrick, Patrick H. ... Oakland, CA
Hetrick, Patrick K. ... Buies Creek, NC
Hetrick, Randall Scott ... Mobile, AL
Hetsko, Jeffrey F. ... Atlanta, GA
Hetson, Jack ... Los Angeles, CA
Hett, Thomas A. ... Chicago, IL
Hettel, Joseph ... Ottawa, IL
Hettena, Marion Kimball ... San Francisco, CA
Hettenbach, Joyce ... Boise, ID
Hettenbach, Wayne D. ... Washington, DC
Hetterman, Paul C. ... St. Louis, MO
Hettick, David Charles ... San Francisco, CA
Hettig, David W. ... Palo Alto, CA
Hettig, Steven E. ... Hutchinson, MN
Olivia, MN
Renville, MN
Hettinger, Alfred K. ... Allentown, PA
Hettinger, Edwin LaVerne ... Kalamazoo, MI
Hettinger, Glen J. ... Dallas, TX
Hettinger, James L. ... Riverton, WY
Hettinger, Kyle B. ... Phoenix, AZ
Hettinger, Lee T. ... Chicago, IL
Hettinger & Leedy ... Riverton, WY
Hettinger, Michael Alan ... Kalamazoo, MI
Hettinger, Richard E. ... San Antonio, TX
Hettinger, Susan ... Olympia, WA
Hettle, Nadine C. ... Los Angeles, CA
Hettleman, Eugene ... Baltimore, MD
Hettler, Kenneth Richard
East Rockaway, NY
Hettler, Michael R. ... Corfu, NY
Kenmore, NY
Hettrick, Clyde M., III ... Los Angeles, CA
Hettrick, George H. ... Richmond, VA
Hettrick, Jane C. ... Buffalo, NY
Hetz, James T. ... Sun Valley, CA
Hetz, Joseph F. ... Chicago, IL
Hetzel, David G. ... Pittsburgh, PA
Hetzel, H. Lawrence ... Houston, TX
Hetzel, James V. ... Liberty Corner, NJ
Hetzel, John S. ... Atlanta, GA
Hetzel, Joyce A. ... Detroit, MI
Hetzel, Otto J. ... Washington, DC
Hetzel, Ryan J. ... Milwaukee, WI
Hetzel, William B., Jr. ... Boston, MA
Hetzer, John ... Milwaukee, WI
Hetzer, Nicholas W. ... Toledo, OH
Hetzer, Nicholas W., & Co., L.P.A.
Toledo, OH
Hetzler, Dale C. ... Marietta, GA
Hetzler, Mark W. ... Chicago, IL
Hetzler, Robert L. ... Bay City, MI
Hetzler, Stanley A. ... Belvidere, IL
Hetzner, Marc A. ... Indianapolis, IN
Heubach, Jacqueline ... Kingston, NY
Heubach, Randolph E. ... San Rafael, CA
Heubaum, William L. ... Dakota Dunes, SD
Heubeck, David J. ... Baltimore, MD
Heubel, Gerard J. ... New York, NY
Heubel, Richard C. ... North Bergen, NJ
Heuberger, John H. ... Chicago, IL
Heuberger, Michael A. ... Northbrook, IL
Heuberger, Steven R. ... Libertyville, IL
Heubi, Magnus F. ... Jeffersonville, IN
Heublein, Jennifer A. ... Seattle, WA
Heublein, Vincent W. ... Mission Hills, CA
Heubusch, Paul H. ... Woodstock, VA
Heuck, Kenneth, Jr. ... Cincinnati, OH
Heuck, Robert, II ... Cincinnati, OH
Heuel, Carlson & Spelhaug, P.A.
Rochester, MN
Heuel, Daniel J. ... Rochester, MN
Heuel, Terence M. ... Chicago, IL
Heuer, Byrne & Rosenbaum, S.C.
Milwaukee, WI
Heuer, Charles R. ... Cambridge, MA
Heuer, Christopher K. ... Portland, OR
Heuer, Doris K. ... Chicago, IL
Heuer, G. P. ... Rocklin, CA
Heuer, Henry T. ... Los Angeles, CA
Heuer, J. Reid ... Blacksburg, VA
Heuer, James A., Jr. ... Minneapolis, MN
Heuer, James R. ... Columbia City, IN
Heuer, Jeffrey G. ... Detroit, MI
Heuer, Jeffrey S. ... St. Louis, MO
Heuer, John A. ... Los Alamitos, CA
Heuer, John F. ... Los Angeles, CA
Heuer, John M. ... Milwaukee, WI
Heuer, Karen L. ... Eden Prairie, MN
Heuer, Moriah A. ... Albertson, NY
Heuer, Ronald K. ... Redding, CA
Heuer, Sam ... Little Rock, AR
Heuer, Thomas R. ... Sacramento, CA
Heuer, Walter J. ... Houston, TX
Heuer, William C. ... New York, NY
Heuerman, Henry N. ... Toledo, OH
Heuerman, James F. ... Morrison, IL
Heuerman, Paul K. ... Naples, FL
Heuermann, Laura Hall ... Sioux Falls, SD
Heuermann, William H. ... Sioux Falls, SD
Heuertz and Monen, P.C. ... Rogue River, OR
Heugel, John C. ... Green Bay, WI
Heugle, Robert L., Jr. ... Freehold, NJ
Heuhsen, Louanna O. ... Richmond, VA
Heuisler, Charles W. ... Haddonfield, NJ
Heuler, Victoria E. ... Tallahassee, FL
Heuman, Donna R. ... Menlo Park, CA
Heumann, H. David ... Long Beach, CA
Heumann, Linda Shannon
Newport Beach, CA
Heumann, Michael ... Los Angeles, CA
Heumann, Ronald R. ... Riverside, CA
Heun, Brian D. ... Atlantic City, NJ
Heupel, Gerald F., Jr. ... Washington, DC
Heuring, Paulette A. ... Norridge, IL
Heurlin, Brian R. ... Vancouver, WA
Heurlin, Bruce R. ... Tucson, AZ
Heurlin, John M., Law Offices of
Santa Ana, CA
Heurlin & Potter, P.S. ... Vancouver, WA
Heusdens, James ... Porterville, CA
Heusel, Cornelius R. ... New Orleans, LA
Heusel, Mark V. ... Ann Arbor, MI
Heuser, Gregory M. ... Fountain Valley, CA
Heuser, John M. ... Lebanon, VA
Heuser, Peter E. ... Palo Alto, CA
Boise, ID
Portland, OR
Heuser, Ralph S., Jr. ... Matawan, NJ
Heusinger, Joel D. ... Lincoln, NE
Heussi, Jonathan A. ... Lake Placid, NY
Heussler, Barbara Turney
Securities and Exchange Commission, Division of Investment Management, GV
Heusted, David A. ... Orlando, FL
Heustis, Evan F. ... Devils Lake, ND
Heuston, Stephen P. ... Melbourne, FL
Heutmaker, Jeffrey M. ... Seattle, WA
Heutsche, John V. ... Cleveland, OH
Heutsche, John V., Co., L.P.A.
Cleveland, OH
Medina, OH
Parma, OH

Heutsche, Victor S. ... Sharon, PA
Hevalow, Jas. R. ... Reading, PA
Hevel, Avalon Gayle ... Fayetteville, AR
Stafford, VA
Hevel, David R., Law Office of
Kennewick, WA
Hevel, David R., Law Office of ... Pasco, WA
Hevener, James J. ... Los Angeles, CA
Hevener, Mary B. ... Washington, DC
Hevener, Rosemary J. ... Charlottesville, VA
Heveri, Alex ... Tucson, AZ
Heverin, Timothy J. ... Chicago, IL
Heverly, Michelle B. ... San Jose, CA
Heverly, Robert Allen ... Albany, NY
Hevertz, Loren L. ... Rogue River, OR
Hevesy, Patrick M. ... Sierra Madre, CA
Hevey, Richard P. ... Augusta, ME
Hevia, Jesus M. ... Port Charlotte, FL
Hevia, Mariana A. ... Pasadena, CA
Hevier, Jan J., (Mr.) ... Apalachicola, FL
Hevly, Amy C. ... Seattle, WA
Hevrin, Matthew M. ... Rockford, IL
Hevron, Kenric R. ... Plano, TX
Hew, Jessica K. ... Winter Park, FL
Heward, Lynn P. ... Salt Lake City, UT
Hewatt, Clarence H. ... Riverside, CA
Hewell, Harold M. ... San Diego, CA
Hewelt Cazel, Victoria ... Madison, WI
Hewer, Joel Edward ... Washington, DC
Hewes, C. Alexander, Jr. ... Washington, DC
Hewes, Gaston H., Jr. ... Gulfport, MS
Hewes, Gelband, Lambert & Dann, P.C.
Washington, DC
Rockville, MD
Hewes, George B., III ... Orlando, FL
Hewes, George Lemuel ... Atlanta, GA
Hewes, George P., III ... Jackson, MS
Hewes, James S. ... Portland, ME
Hewes, Jonathan W. ... Albuquerque, NM
Hewes, Joseph P. ... Atlanta, GA
Hewes, Margaret C. ... Portland, ME
Hewes, Mark V. ... Portland, ME
Hewes, Nancy Becker ... Atlanta, GA
Hewes & Nye ... Alfred, ME
Portland, ME
Hewes, Philip A. ... Rosemont, IL
Hewes, Richard D. ... Portland, ME
Hewes, Richard N. ... Portland, ME
Hewetson, Bruce A. ... Bedford, IN
Hewetson, Gary A. ... Largo, FL
Hewett, Alan Bryant" Chip " ... Smithfield, NC
Hewett, Arthur E. ... Dallas, TX
Hewett, Catherine A. ... Philadelphia, PA
Hewett, David T. ... Palm Beach, FL
Hewett, Ernest J. ... Miami, FL
Hewett, George A. ... Boston, MA
Hewett, Gregory A. ... St. Louis, MO
Hewett, Herbert F. (Jack)
Oklahoma City, OK
Hewett, Jeffrey D. ... Midland, TX
Hewett, Laura Oleck ... Atlanta, GA
Hewett, Marceliers ... Little Rock, AR
Hewett, Mark ... Fort Smith, AR
Hewett, Scott W. ... Santa Rosa, CA
Hewett, Timothy Worth ... Atlanta, GA
Hewett, W. Curtis ... Council Bluffs, IA
Hewey, Melissa A. ... Portland, ME
Hewgley, Michael E. ... Memphis, TN
Hewicker, John A., II ... San Diego, CA
Hewig, William, III ... Boston, MA
Hewins, Daniel F. ... Evansville, IN
Hewins, Elvin H. ... Evansville, IN
Hewins and Hewins ... Evansville, IN
Hewins, Jo Ellen ... Corpus Christi, TX
Hewins, John M.
General Services Administration,
Office of Regional Counsel, GV
Hewins, Ward D. ... Bedford, MA
Hewit, Russell L. ... Cranford, NJ
Hewitson, Mary Guynn ... Atlanta, GA
Hewitson, Steven J. ... Atlanta, GA
Hewitt, A. Kenneth, III ... Atlanta, GA
Hewitt, Adrienne D. ... Rock Island, IL
Hewitt, Alfred W. ... Grand Rapids, MI
Hewitt, Andrea A. ... Hartford, CT
Hewitt, Antoinette P. ... Santa Ana, CA
Hewitt, Arthur E. ... Marysville, CA
Hewitt, Arthur E., Inc., A Prof. Corp.
Marysville, CA
Hewitt, Benjamin N. ... Niagara Falls, NY
Hewitt, Brian C. ... Greenwood, IN
Hewitt, C. Lee ... Fremont, CA
Hewitt, Carl H. ... New York, NY
Hewitt, Charles C. ... Hilton Head Island, SC
Hewitt, Charles T. ... Bay City, MI
Hewitt, Christopher J. ... Cleveland, OH
Hewitt, Christopher L. ... New Orleans, LA
Hewitt, Christopher M. ... Dallas, TX
Hewitt, Daniel J. ... Greensburg, PA
Hewitt, Davis, The, Law Firm, P.C.
Atlanta, GA
Hewitt, Deborah Lynn ... Garden City, NY
Hewitt, Dennis R. ... Rochelle, IL
Hewitt, Devon Elizabeth ... McLean, VA
Hewitt, Douglass G. ... Chicago, IL
Hewitt, Elizabeth ... New York, NY
Hewitt, Elizabeth C. ... Palo Alto, CA
Hewitt, Emily ... Washington, DC
Hewitt, F. Dean ... Sebring, FL
Hewitt, Floyd G., Jr. ... Biloxi, MS
Hewitt, Gregory A. ... Oak Hill, WV
Hewitt, Henry H. ... Portland, OR
Hewitt, Henry S. ... Oakland, CA
Hewitt & Hewitt, P.C. ... Dallas, TX
Hewitt, Hugh ... Irvine, CA
Hewitt, James H., III ... Cleveland, OH
Hewitt, James O. ... San Diego, CA
Hewitt, James P., III ... Niagara Falls, NY
Hewitt, James T. ... Greenville, SC
Hewitt, James W. ... Lincoln, NE
Hewitt, Jason I. ... Washington, DC
Hewitt, Jeffrey R. ... New York, NY
Hewitt, Jennifer Day ... Charleston, WV
Hewitt, Joan M. ... Niagara Falls, NY
Hewitt, John C. ... Omaha, NE
Hewitt, John R. ... New York, NY
Hewitt, John W.
Palm Beach Gardens, FL
Hewitt, Julie B. ... Kennedy, NY
Hewitt, Karen P. ... Department of Justice,
Civil Division, GV
Hewitt, Katz & Dumich ... Atlanta, GA
Hewitt, Kelly ... Washington, DC
Hewitt, Kimbally Haworth
Palm Beach Gardens, FL
Hewitt, Lancelot Basil ... New York, NY
Hewitt Law Firm ... Alvin, TX
Hewitt, Lawrence W. ... Charlotte, NC
Hewitt, Lester L. ... Houston, TX
Hewitt, Linda G. ... Kalispell, MT
Hewitt, Linda J. ... Santa Ana, CA
Hewitt, Lisa Marie ... Boston, MA
Hewitt, Lowe Arthur ... Philadelphia, PA
Hewitt, Margaret Sutherland
Winter Park, FL
Hewitt, Mark A. ... Orange, CA
Hewitt, Marsha A. ... New York, NY
Hewitt, Mary J. ... Lincoln, NE
Hewitt, Mary L. ... Omaha, NE
Hewitt & McGuire, LLP ... Irvine, CA
Hewitt, Melvin L., Jr. ... Atlanta, GA
Hewitt, Michael Conrad ... Laguna Hills, CA
Hewitt, Nancy M. ... Santa Fe, NM
Hewitt, Otto D., III ... Alvin, TX
Hewitt, Patricia ... New York, NY
Hewitt, Patricia S. ... Sacramento, CA
Hewitt, Patrick A. ... Pittsburgh, PA
Hewitt, Paul B. ... Washington, DC
Hewitt, Peter E. ... Stamford, CT
Hewitt & Prout ... Los Angeles, CA
Sacramento, CA
Hewitt, Richard G. ... New York, NY
Hewitt, Richard M. ... Westlake, TX
Hewitt, Richard M., P.C. ... Irving, TX
Westlake, TX
Hewitt, Robert G. ... Coral Gables, FL
Hewitt, Robert L. ... Oroville, CA
Hewitt, Robert S. ... West Palm Beach, FL
Hewitt, Robin C. ... Atlanta, GA
Hewitt, Robin R. Ferstl ... Cincinnati, OH
Hewitt, Rondi Rauch
Research Triangle Park, NC
Hewitt, Roy W. ... Los Angeles, CA
Hewitt, Sara E. ... New York, NY
Hewitt, Sara S. ... Dallas, TX
Hewitt, Sarah ... New York, NY
Hewitt, Sarah J. ... Chicago, IL
Hewitt, Scott K. ... Tampa, FL
Hewitt, Sheilann P. ... Philadelphia, PA
Hewitt & Smiley, P.A.
Palm Beach Gardens, FL
Hewitt, Stephanie A. ... Casper, WY
Hewitt, Stephen L., (A Professional
Corporation) ... Los Angeles, CA
Hewitt, Stephen W. ... Lake Oswego, OR
Hewitt, Susan ... Nutley, NJ
Hewitt, Susan L. ... Gulfport, MS
Hewitt, Timothy G. ... Latrobe, PA
Hewitt, Warren E.
Department of State, GV
Hewitt, William B. ... Fairlawn, OH
Hewitt, William D. ... Portland, ME
Hewitt, William Davis ... Atlanta, GA
Hewitt, William E. ... Silver Spring, MD
Hewitt, William H. ... Atlanta, GA
Hewitt, William J. ... New York, NY
Hewitt, William R. ... Warren, OH
Hewitt, William S., Jr. ... Manchester, NH
Hewitt-jones, Kathryn ... Audubon, NJ
Hewka, Nadia ... Philadelphia, PA
Hewlett, Brian Leslie ... Catlettsburg, KY
Hewlett, Clothilde V. ... San Francisco, CA
Hewlett, Collins and Allard
Wilmington, NC
Hewlett, David R. ... Austin, TX
Hewlett, Elizabeth M. ... Riverdale, MD
Hewlett, Gwendolyn Baptist ... Southaven, MS
Hewlett, Reneen E. ... Richmond, VA
Hewlett, Richard T. ... Detroit, MI
Hewlett, Robert A. ... Benson, AZ
Hewlett, Sydney B. ... Fort Worth, TX
Hewlett, William K. ... Tuscumbia, AL
Hewlette, Earl D., Jr. ... Charleston, SC
Hewlette and Hewlette ... Charleston, SC
Hewlette, Mary Peck ... Charleston, SC
Hewman, Susan H. ... Lewisburg, WV
Hewner, Thomas F. ... Buffalo, NY
Hews, Arthur N., Jr. ... Santa Ana, CA
Hewson, Harry C. ... Charlotte, NC
Hewson, James F. ... Warren, MI
Hewson, John M., III ... Atlanta, GA
Savannah, GA
Hewson, Patrick J. ... Carbondale, IL
Hewson, Stacey Lynch ... Columbia, SC
Hewson, Timothy L. ... Columbia, SC
Hewson & Van Hellemont, P.C. ... Warren, MI
Hext, Christy A. ... Houston, TX
Hext, Stephen R. ... Cincinnati, OH
Hexter, Christopher T. ... St. Louis, MO
Hexter, Rachel A. ... Newport, VT
Hey, David A. ... North Sioux City, SD
Hey, Friedrich E.F. ... New York, NY
Hey, Keith J. ... Lansing, MI
Hey, Marilyn S. (Duncan) ... Wichita, KS
Hey, Mary L. ... Boulder, CO
Hey, Randy E. ... San Jose, CA
Heyaime, Maribel ... Tampa, FL
Heyamoto, Craig R. ... Seattle, WA
Heybl, Jaye G. ... Thousand Oaks, CA
Heybl, Jill Renee ... Santa Barbara, CA
Heyboer, David R. ... Port Huron, MI
Heyboer & Floyd, P.L.L.C. ... Port Huron, MI
Heyburn, John ... Houston, TX
Heyburn, John D. ... Louisville, KY
Heyburn, John G., II ... Louisville, KY
Heyburn, Paul R. ... Beaumont, TX
Houston, TX
Heyck, Joseph G., Jr. ... Tampa, FL
Heyck, Theodore D. ... Los Angeles, CA
Heyd, Charles G. ... Cincinnati, OH
Heyd, Daniel C. ... Cincinnati, OH
Heyd, Jana L. ... Seattle, WA
Heyd, Joseph D. ... Cincinnati, OH
Heyd, Louis A., Jr. ... New Orleans, LA
Heyda, James J. ... Chicago, IL
Heydasch, Axel ... Miami, FL
Heyde, Christina R. ... Chicago, IL
Heyde, John M. ... Chicago, IL
Heyde, Lee L. ... Warsaw, IN
Heydemann, Helaine Wachs ... Chicago, IL
Heyden, Eric D. ... New York, NY
Heyden, Kania & O'Neill ... Wilmington, DE
Heyden, Michael C. ... Wilmington, DE
Heyder, Kenneth ... Pembroke Pines, FL
Heyder, Markus B. ... Washington, DC
Heydinger, Lisa C. ... Charleston, SC
Heydinger, Thomas A. ... Bellefontaine, OH
Heydinger, Thomas E. ... Norwalk, OH
Heydinger, Timothy A. ... Chinle, AZ
Heydman, William I. ... Garden City, KS
Heydon, Beverly Irene ... Columbia, MD
Heydon, Kathleen M. ... Los Angeles, CA
Heydon, Paul D. ... San Antonio, TX
Heydorn, Robert W. ... Cuyahoga Falls, OH
Heydrich, Alfred L. ... Bellingham, WA
Heydt, Donald A.
Federal Energy Regulatory Commission,
Office of the General Counsel, GV
Heydt, Marybeth ... Woodland Hills, CA
Heydt, Michael J. ... Colorado Springs, CO
Houston, TX
Heydt, Tara E. ... Los Angeles, CA
Heye, John J. ... Treasury Department,
Bureau of the Public Debt, GV
Heye, Thomas J. ... Richland, WA
Heyen, Richard D. ... Baytown, TX
Heyen, Shari L. ... Houston, TX
Heyer & Associates, P.A.
Fort Lauderdale, FL
Heyer, Barbara A. ... Fort Lauderdale, FL
Heyer, Christopher ... Cliffside Park, NJ
Heyer, G. John
Committee For Purchase From People Who
Are Blind or Severely Disabled, GV
Heyer, James W. ... Denver, CO
Heyer, John H. ... Olean, NY
Heyer, Michelle L. ... Cleveland, OH
Heyer, Morgan ... New York, NY
Heyer, Suzanne Stahl ... Emerson, NJ
Heyer, Thomas N. ... Washington, DC
Heyer-Bednar, Lori L.
Fort Lauderdale, FL
Heyerdahl, Lauris ... Minneapolis, MN
Heygood, Michael E. ... Hurst, TX
Heygood, Susan Bernal ... Dallas, TX
Heying, Brad J. ... Dubuque, IA
Heying, Elizabeth Johnson
Minneapolis, MN
Heying, John R. ... Naperville, IL
Heyink, Marian Louise ... Cleveland, OH
Heyison, Joseph A. ... Ridgewood, NJ
Heyison, J. R. ... Oil City, PA
Heyison, Michael R. ... Boston, MA
Heyke, J. Ericson, III
Board of Governors Of The Federal Reserve
System,
Office of the General Counsel, GV
Heykes, Nancy N. ... Appleton, WI
Heyl, Andrew R. ... Lenexa, KS
Heyl, Dorothy ... New York, NY
Heyl, Erica L. ... Antioch, IL
Heyl, J. A. ... Houston, TX
Heyl, Jonathan ... Greensboro, NC
Heyl, Nicholas E. ... Norwich, VT
Heyl, Richard F. ... Naperville, IL
Heyl, Royster, Voelker & Allen, Professional
Corporation ... Edwardsville, IL
Peoria, IL
Rockford, IL
Springfield, IL
Urbana, IL
Heylman, Paul M. ... Washington, DC
Heym, Robert W. ... Woodbridge, NJ
Heyman, Amy R.
Federal Energy Regulatory Commission,
Office of the General Counsel, GV
Heyman, Charles B. ... Baltimore, MD
Heyman, Daniel G. ... Scarsdale, NY
Heyman, Edith K. ... Bridgewater, NJ
Heyman, Frederic C. ... Baltimore, MD
Heyman, Ginger F. ... Los Angeles, CA
Heyman, Glenn R. ... Chicago, IL
Heyman, Gordon B. ... Baltimore, MD
Heyman, Howard S. ... Livonia, MI
Heyman, I. Austin ... Bethesda, MD
Heyman, Ian A. ... Columbus, OH
Heyman, Ira M. ... Berkeley, CA
Heyman, Isidore ... Bronx, NY
Heyman, J. Nicole ... Metairie, LA
Heyman, Jerome J. ... Plainfield, NJ
Heyman, John S. ... Arlington, VA
Heyman, Jon B. ... Florence, MA
Heyman, Joseph S. ... Toledo, OH
Heyman, Kent F. ... Fresno, CA
Heyman, Kerkorian & Magarian, LLP
Fresno, CA
Heyman, Kim V. ... New York, NY
Heyman, Kurt M. ... Wilmington, DE
Heyman, Michael G. ... Chicago, IL
Heyman, Philip J. ... New Brunswick, NJ
Heyman, Philip, P.C. ... New Brunswick, NJ
Heyman, Rachel C. ... Chicago, IL
Heyman, Ralph E. ... Dayton, OH
Heyman, Raymond S. ... Phoenix, AZ
Heyman, Richard S. ... Bronx, NY
Heyman, Robert E. ... Clearwater, FL
Heyman, Robert G. ... Albuquerque, NM
Heyman, Roger P. ... Los Angeles, CA
Heyman, Ronnie F. ... Westport, CT
Heyman, Samuel J. ... Wayne, NJ
Heyman, Scott J. ... Chicago, IL
Heyman, Sherri R. ... Baltimore, MD
Heyman, Sidney ... Rochester, NY
Heyman & Sizemore ... Atlanta, GA
Heyman, Stanley E. ... Los Angeles, CA
Heyman, Steven J. ... Chicago, IL
Heyman, Steven S. ... Albany, NY
Heyman, Thomas V. ... New York, NY
Heyman, William H. ... New York, NY
Heyman, William L. ... Thousand Oaks, CA
Heyman, William S. ... Baltimore, MD
Heyman-Magarian, Rebecca
Baltimore, MD
Heymann, Andrew ... New York, NY
Heymann, Constance A. ... New York, NY
Heymann, David J. ... Jericho, NY
Heymann, Erik G. ... Houston, TX
Heymann, George M. ... Bronx, NY
Heymann, Idrienne L. ... Chicago, IL
Highland Park, IL
Heymann, Jane A. ... Madison, WI
Heymann, John C. ... Corpus Christi, TX
Heymann, Laura A. ... Washington, DC
Heymann, Ronald S. ... Mount Freedom, NJ
Heymsfeld, David A.
House of Representatives,
Committee Legal Personnel, GV
Heyn, Kathleen McGraw ... Saginaw, MI
Heynderickx, David W. ... Salem, OR
Heyne, Barbara M. ... Atlanta, GA
Heyne, Michael A. ... Akron, OH
Heyne, Robert J. ... Chicago, IL
Heyneman, Daniel S. ... Washington, DC
Heyns, Anne L. ... Jackson, MI
Heynssens, Paul B. ... Pasadena, CA
Heyrich, Donald ... Bellevue, WA
Heyrich, Michael T. ... Newark, NJ
Heyrman, Heidi A. ... Milwaukee, WI
Heyrman, Mark J. ... Chicago, IL
Heysell, R. Ray ... Medford, OR
Heyser, Carlton E. ... Silver Spring, MD
Heysinger, Jack D. ... Kansas City, MO
Heyson, Harry H., III ... Newport News, VA
Heytow, Richard D. ... Chicago, IL
Heyward, Allan M., Jr. ... Richmond, VA
Heyward, Jeanne ... Miami, FL
Heyward, Peter E. ... Washington, DC
Heyward, Robert B. ... Raleigh, NC
Heyward, Robert J. ... New York, NY
Heyward, W. Rowland ... Atlanta, GA
Heyward, Willie Bruce ... Charleston, SC
Heywood & Cari ... Hudson, WI
Heywood, Christopher M.
Washington, DC
Heywood, Harriett T.
Department Of Veterans Affairs,
Office of Employment Discrimination
Complaints Adjudication, GV
Heywood, John D. ... Hudson, WI
Heywood, John Quentin ... Washington, DC
Heywood & Miles ... Mesa, AZ
Phoenix, AZ
Heywood, Richard G. ... St. Louis, MO
Heywood, Robert G., (P.C.) ... Oakland, CA
Heywood, Robert P. ... Keene, NY
Heywood, Roger L. ... Mesa, AZ
Heywood, Thomas A. ... Charleston, WV
Heywood, William H., III ... Toledo, OH
Hezel, George M. ... Buffalo, NY
Hezel, Sally C. ... East Aurora, NY
Hiaasen, Connie L. ... Fort Lauderdale, FL
Hialeah Legal Center ... Hialeah, FL
Miami, FL
Hiam, Peter ... Boston, MA
Hianik, Mark W. ... Chicago, IL
Hiaring, Anne ... San Francisco, CA
Hiaring, Robert D. ... Billings, MT
Hiatt, Constance M. ... San Francisco, CA
Hiatt, Cynthia M. ... Providence, RI
Hiatt, Daniel V. ... Overland Park, KS
Kansas City, MO
Hiatt, David P. ... Mount Airy, NC
Hiatt, Derrin K. ... Ponca City, OK
Hiatt, Douglass B. ... Minneapolis, MN
Hiatt, Eugene W. ... Topeka, KS
Hiatt & Hiatt ... Mount Airy, NC
Hiatt & Hoke, LLP ... Quincy, MA
Hiatt, James H. ... Fort Collins, CO
Hiatt, James T. ... Nashville, TN
Hiatt, Jeffrey E. ... Louisville, KY
Hiatt, Jerry Michael, (A Law Corporation)
Honolulu, HI
Kamuela, HI
Hiatt, Jonathan P. ... Boston, MA
Hiatt, Mahilani E.K. ... Honolulu, HI
Hiatt, Martha Azar ... Prairie Village, KS
Hiatt, Matthew T. ... Quincy, MA
Hiatt, Pamela B. ... Palo Alto, CA
Hiatt, Robert E. ... Topeka, KS
Hiatt, Robert T. ... Minneapolis, MN
Hiatt, Roger L. ... Kansas City, MO
Hiatt, Susan E. ... Houston, TX

Hiatt, V. Talmage .... Mount Airy, NC
Hiatt, Virginia R. .... Fort Lauderdale, FL
Hibbard, B. Scott .... Frankfort, IN
Hibbard, Caldwell & Schultz, A Professional Corporation .... Oregon City, OR
Portland, OR
Hibbard, Crystelle M. .... Danbury, CT
Hibbard, David W. .... Des Moines, IA
Hibbard, Edmund S. .... Laconia, NH
Portsmouth, NH
Hibbard, Edward A. .... Tacoma, WA
Hibbard, Emerson W. .... East Mansfield, MA
Hibbard, Gayla M. .... Saginaw, MI
Hibbard, George L. .... Wilsonville, OR
Hibbard, Helene W. .... Tuscaloosa, AL
Hibbard, James D. .... Portland, OR
Hibbard, James E. .... London, KY
Hibbard, John D. .... Eau Claire, WI
Hibbard, John W. .... Centerville, MA
Hibbard Law Office .... Eau Claire, WI
Hibbard, Paul R. .... Spartanburg, SC
Hibbard, Richard A. .... Newark, NJ
Hibbard, Robert L. .... Phoenix, AZ
Hibbard, Roger W., III .... Denver, CO
Hibbard, Stephen D. .... San Francisco, CA
Hibbard, William C. .... Steamboat Springs, CO
Hibbard, William C., P.C.
Steamboat Springs, CO
Hibbe, Steven H. .... Coral Gables, FL
Hibbeln, Brenda S. .... Sarasota, FL
Hibberd, Blaine H. .... Fort Lauderdale, FL
Hibberd, Blaine H., P.A.
Fort Lauderdale, FL
Hibberd, Paul V. .... Louisville, KY
Hibberd, William F. .... New York, NY
Hibbert, Carl W. .... Raleigh, NC
Hibbert, George .... Atlanta, GA
Hibbert, Melinda Checketts
Los Angeles, CA
Hibbert, Paige M. .... Gold River, CA
Hibbert, Robert G. .... Washington, DC
Hibbert, Scott M. .... Springfield, MA
Hibbett, Missy Homan .... Florence, AL
Hibbits, Roger M. .... Florissant, MO
Hibbitts, Fay .... Grundy, VA
Hibbitts, Thurman L. .... Lexington, KY
Hibbler, Bill G. .... Cheyenne, WY
Hibbler, William J. .... Chicago, IL
Hibbs, Carol Dey .... Portland, OR
Hibbs, Christina K. .... Salem, MA
Hibbs, Don .... Leesburg, FL
Hibbs, Gary David .... Riverdale, MD
Hibbs, George E. .... Atlanta, GA
Hibbs, Gretchen K. .... Bala Cynwyd, PA
Hibbs, Guy Jantzen .... Louisville, KY
Hibbs, Harry R. .... Ventura, CA
Hibbs, Harry R., Law Corporation
Ventura, CA
Hibbs, J. Robert .... Bloomington, MN
Hibbs, John S., (P.A.) .... Minneapolis, MN
Hibbs, Kathy L. .... Palo Alto, CA
Hibbs, Kelcie A. .... Fort Worth, TX
Hibbs, Kristin Lucas .... Iowa City, IA
Hibbs, Linda J. .... Philadelphia, PA
Hibbs, Loyal Robert .... Reno, NV
Hibbs, Mark J. .... Redford, MI
Hibbs, Melanie L. .... Washington, DC
Hibbs, Melissa L. .... San Diego, CA
Hibbs, Robert E. .... Seattle, WA
Hibbs, William R. .... Minneapolis, MN
Hibbs, William R., II .... Temple, TX
Hibel, Edwina S. .... Paterson, NJ
Hibel, Miriam J. .... New York, NY
Hiber, Edwin H. .... Fresno, CA
Hiber, Harvey H., Jr. .... San Diego, CA
Hibey, David M. .... Washington, DC
Hibey, James F. .... Washington, DC
Hibey, Richard A. .... Washington, DC
Hibino, Don Y. .... Portland, CT
Hiblar, Andrew F. .... Tacoma, WA
Hibler, J. Michael .... Woodland Hills, CA
Hibler, P. Otis .... San Antonio, TX
Hibner, Don T., Jr. .... Los Angeles, CA
Hibner, John Raymond .... Hempstead, NY
Hibnick, Cynthia Barnett .... Miami, FL
Hibon, Henri-Frederic .... New York, NY
Hibschman, John S. .... Reading, PA
Hibschweiler, Arlene M. .... Fredonia, NY
Hibschweiler, Robert F. .... Denver, CO
Hibsher, William .... New York, NY
Hichar, Mark N. G. .... West Greenwich, RI
Hichman, Donna J. .... Rochester, NY
Hicinbothem, John R. .... Framingham, MA
Hick, Douglas A. .... Kansas City, MO
Hick, Robert K. .... Holland, MI
Hickam, D. Scott
Hot Springs National Park, AR
Hickam, Elliott .... Spencer, IN
Hickam & Hickam .... Spencer, IN
Hickam, Kent L. .... Albany, OR
Hickam, Kent L., P.C. .... Albany, OR
Hickam, Terry L. .... Blue Springs, MO
Hickcox, Geoffrey Brent .... Durango, CO
Hickcox, Jeffrey E. .... Atlanta, GA
Hickcox, Joanne B. .... Sleepy Hollow, NY
Hickel, Gerard F. .... Pittsburgh, PA
Hickel, Gregory J. .... Columbia, IL
Hickel, Richard M. .... Polson, MT
Hickel, Robert .... St. Louis, MO
Hickel, Timothy T. .... Federal Way, WA
Hicken, Jeffrey P. .... Anoka, MN
Hicken, Michael B. .... Laguna Beach, CA
Hicken, Robert A. .... Mount Laurel, NJ
Hickernell, Craig T. .... New York, NY
Hickernell, Mark Andrew .... Newton, MA
Hickerson, David A. .... Washington, DC
Hickerson, Elizabeth J. .... Anchorage, AK
Hickerson, Glen D. .... Sapulpa, OK
Hickerson, J. Arthur .... Springfield, MA
Hickerson, Michelle A. .... Atlanta, GA
Hickerson, Patti Wade .... Houston, TX
Hickerson, Robert K. .... Anchorage, AK
Hickert, Bernard J. .... Overland Park, KS
Hickert, B.J. .... Topeka, KS
Hickes, Susan H. .... Annapolis, MD
Hickethier, David E. .... Milwaukee, WI
Hickey, Allen M. .... Wichita, KS
Hickey, Andrea A. .... Cambridge, MA
Hickey, Andrew J. .... Boston, MA
Hickey, Anne T. .... Washington, DC
Hickey, B. Thomas, Jr. .... Chattanooga, TN
Hickey, Barbara J. .... Dennis, MA
Hickey, Brandon J. .... Hartford, CT
Hickey, Brian J. .... Chicago, IL
Hickey, Brian P. .... Riverside, CA
Hickey, Brian P., Jr. .... Mineola, NY
Hickey, Bruce D. .... Boston, MA
Hickey, Bryan Francis .... Greenville, SC
Hickey, Catherine T. .... Dover, DE
Hickey, Charles D. .... St. Johnsbury, VT
Hickey, Charles E. Ned .... Farmington, CT
Hickey, Christine B. .... New York, NY
Hickey, Christine Hayes .... Indianapolis, IN
Hickey, Christopher J. .... Salisbury, NC
Hickey, Christopher S. .... Los Angeles, CA
Hickey & Cianciolo, P.C. .... Detroit, MI
Hickey, Colleen M. .... Collegeville, PA
Hickey, Cornelius J. .... Woodbury, NY
Hickey, Cynthia A. .... Chicago, IL
Hickey, Dan .... Anchorage, AK
Hickey, Daniel C. .... New York, NY
Hickey, David E. .... Mission Viejo, CA
Hickey, David H. .... Waukesha, WI
Hickey, David J. .... Boston, MA
Hickey, David M. .... Los Angeles, CA
Hickey, David T. .... Washington, DC
Hickey, Deborah .... New York, NY
Hickey, Denise M. .... San Diego, CA
Hickey, Denise P. .... Troy, MI
Hickey, Don E. .... Denton, TX
Hickey, Don E., A Professional Corporation
Denton, TX
Hickey, Driscoll, Kurfirst, Patterson & Melia, Chartered .... Chicago, IL
Hickey, Edward J., Jr. .... Washington, DC
Hickey, Edward V., III .... Washington, DC
Hickey, Elizabeth A. .... Cleveland, OH
Hickey, Elizabeth T. .... Colorado Springs, CO
Hickey, Eugene F., II .... Philadelphia, PA
Scranton, PA
Hickey, Firmin A., Jr. .... Houston, TX
Hickey, Francis J., Jr. .... Houston, TX
Hickey, Harold V. .... Miami, FL
Hickey, Howard M., Jr. .... Aiken, SC
Hickey, J. Michelle .... Los Angeles, CA
Hickey, J. Patrick, (P.C.) .... Washington, DC
Hickey, Jacqueline K. .... San Clemente, CA
Hickey, James .... Phoenix, AZ
Hickey, James .... Philadelphia, PA
Hickey, James A. .... Easton, PA
Hickey, James C. .... Louisville, KY
Hickey, James E., Jr. .... Hempstead, NY
Hickey, James G. .... West Hartford, CT
Hickey, James J. .... Chicago, IL
Hickey, James J. .... Reno, NV
Hickey, James P. .... Oakwood, OH
Hickey, James R. .... Los Angeles, CA
Hickey, James R., Jr. .... Ithaca, NY
Hickey, Jane D. .... Richmond, VA
Hickey, John A. .... Washington, DC
Hickey, John C. .... Kansas City, MO
Hickey, John E. .... Armonk, NY
Hickey, John H. (Jack) .... Miami, FL
Hickey, John K. .... Lexington, KY
Hickey, John M. .... Santa Fe, NM
Hickey, John M. .... Tulsa, OK
Hickey, John M. .... Media, PA
Hickey, John P. .... Philadelphia, PA
Hickey, John P. .... Philadelphia, PA
Hickey, John T. .... Vernon Hills, IL
Hickey, John T., Jr. (P.C.) .... Chicago, IL
Hickey & Jones, P.A.
Fort Lauderdale, FL
Miami, FL
Hickey, Joseph .... El Dorado, AR
Hickey, Joseph H. .... Bloomfield Hills, MI
Hickey, Julia Kreidler .... McLean, VA
Hickey, Kathleen A. .... Manchester, NH
Hickey, Kathleen O'Callaghan
Detroit, MI
Hickey, Kenneth F. .... Kensington, MD
Hickey, Kevin P. .... Minneapolis, MN
Hickey, Laurence L. .... Rochester, NY
Hickey, Leonard M. .... Grand Rapids, MI
Hickey, Lori F. .... Buffalo, NY
Hickey, Lynn M. .... Tinley Park, IL
Hickey, M. Christine .... Syracuse, NY
Hickey, Mackey, Evans & Walker
Cheyenne, WY
Hickey, Margaret W. .... Milwaukee, WI
Hickey, Mary S. .... Detroit, MI
Hickey, Maunsel W. .... New Orleans, LA
Hickey, Michael A. .... Boston, MA
Hickey, Michael C.
Department Of The Interior, Office of the Solicitor, GV
Hickey, Michael C., Jr. .... Edgewood, MD
Hickey, Michael E. .... Santa Ana, CA
Hickey, Michael H. .... Wichita, KS
Hickey, Michael J. .... Columbus, OH
Hickey, Michael M. .... Rapid City, SD
Hickey, Michael P. .... New Brunswick, NJ
Hickey & Moutoux .... San Mateo, CA
Hickey and Nemzin .... Chicago, IL
Hickey, Odran R. .... Philadelphia, PA
Hickey, Patricia M. .... Chevy Chase, MD
Hickey, Patrick F. .... Detroit, MI
Hickey, Paul .... Little Rock, AR
Hickey, Paul J. .... Cheyenne, WY
Hickey, Paul, P.A. .... Little Rock, AR
Hickey, Peter J. .... Albany, NY
Hickey, Peter J. .... Green Bay, WI
Hickey, Peter J., III .... Chicago, IL
Hickey, Peter R. .... Mashpee, MA
Hickey, Philip E. .... Keyport, WA
Hickey, Philip E., P.S. .... Keyport, WA
Hickey, Richard E., III .... Woodbury, NJ
Hickey, Richard J., III .... Chicago, IL
Hickey, Richard S. .... Miami, FL
Helen, GA
Hickey & Riess, L.L.C. .... New Orleans, LA
Hickey, Robert A. .... Falls Church, VA
Hickey, Robert E., Jr. .... Columbus, OH
Dayton, OH
Hickey, Robert J. .... Washington, DC
Hickey, Robert N. .... Washington, DC
Hickey, Robert O. .... Stamford, CT
Hickey, Robert P. .... Vista, CA
Hickey, Robert W. .... Riverdale, IL
Hickey, Robin Moffett .... Atlanta, GA
Hickey, Scott Walker .... Denton, TX
Hickey, Sean C. .... San Mateo, CA
Hickey, Sharon Salazar .... Los Alamos, NM
Hickey, Sheehan & Gates, P.C.
Binghamton, NY
Hickey, Shelley J. .... Seattle, WA
Hickey, Steven M. .... Detroit, MI
Hickey, Stockard Robert, III
Louisville, KY
Hickey, Susan .... El Dorado, AR
Hickey, Susan G. .... New York, NY
Hickey, Terry Daffron .... San Antonio, TX
Hickey, Theresa Ann .... Cleveland, OH
Hickey, Thomas A. .... West Palm Beach, FL
New York, NY
Hickey, Thomas A. .... Joliet, IL
Hickey, Thomas A., III .... Boston, MA
Hickey, Thomas D. .... Reston, VA
Hickey, Thomas F. .... New York, NY
Hickey, Thomas J. .... Stamford, CT
Hickey, Thomas J. .... Binghamton, NY
Hickey, Thomas J. .... White Plains, NY
Hickey, Thomas R. .... Omaha, NE
Hickey, Timothy A. .... Chicago, IL
Hickey, Timothy A. .... Cincinnati, OH
Hickey, Timothy A., Jr. .... Atlanta, GA
Hickey, Timothy S. .... Hoffman Estates, IL
Hickey, W. Douglas .... Englewood, CO
Hickey, William A. .... San Francisco, CA
Hickey, William E. .... Quincy, MA
Hickey, William F., III .... Waterbury, CT
Hickey, William J., Jr. .... Chevy Chase, MD
Hickey, William K. .... Denver, CO
Hickey, William N. .... San Antonio, TX
Hickey, William N., P.C. .... San Antonio, TX
Hickey-Niezgoda, Renee L.
Mount Pleasant, MI
Hickham, Arthur F., Jr. .... New Orleans, LA
Hickie, Jane .... Washington, DC
Austin, TX
Hickie, Michael J. .... Johnson City, TN
Hickisch, John R. .... Denver, CO
Hickle, Frederick C. .... Tucson, AZ
Hickle, William E. .... Rolla, MO
Hicklen, Dianne L. .... Chicago, IL
Hicklin, E. A. .... Wapello, IA
Hicklin, Keith W. .... Platte City, MO
Hicklin & Matthews .... Wapello, IA
Hicklin, Stephen T. .... Glendale, CA
Hickling, Douglas H. .... Oakland, CA
Hickman, Brett A. .... Salt Lake City, UT
Hickman, Brian D. .... San Jose, CA
Hickman, Carol .... Santa Monica, CA
Hickman, Charles F. .... Belleville, IL
Hickman, Charles L. .... Hannibal, MO
Hickman, Charles R. .... Palm Beach, FL
Hickman, Charles R., P.A. .... Palm Beach, FL
Hickman, Charles Russell .... Shelbyville, KY
Hickman, Cynthia Annette .... New York, NY
Hickman, David C. .... Arlington, VA
Hickman, David H. .... Washington, DC
Hickman, David W. .... Vevay, IN
Hickman, David W. .... Bellevue, WA
Hickman, Deanna E. .... Englewood, CO
Hickman, Dennis P. .... La Jolla, CA
Hickman, Donald J. .... Bedford, IN
Hickman, Donald P. .... Costa Mesa, CA
Hickman, E. Cameron .... Valdosta, GA
Hickman, Earl L. .... Atlanta, GA
Hickman, Edward C. .... Shreveport, LA
Hickman, Fran C., (P.A.) .... Little Rock, AR
Hickman, Frank A. .... Greenville, AL
Hickman, Frank Robt. .... Tulsa, OK
Hickman, Franklin J. .... Cleveland, OH
Hickman, Frederic W., (P.C.) .... Chicago, IL
Hickman, Frederick J. .... Los Angeles, CA
Hickman, Gary E. .... Fountain Valley, CA
Hickman, Gerald T. .... Phoenix, AZ
Hickman, Goza & Gore, P.A.
Batesville, MS
Clarksdale, MS
Columbus, MS
Greenville, MS
Greenwood, MS
Grenada, MS
Houston, MS
Jackson, MS
New Albany, MS
Oxford, MS
Southaven, MS
Tupelo, MS
Hickman, Gregory A. .... Dublin, OH
Hickman, Harry O. .... Englewood, CO
Hickman & Hickman .... Tulsa, OK
Hickman, Howard A. .... Austin, TX
Hickman, Howard M. .... Kirksville, MO
Hickman, J. Gary .... Atlanta, GA
Hickman, J. Scott .... Nashville, TN
Hickman, James C. .... Boulder, CO
Hickman, James K. .... St. Petersburg, FL
Tampa, FL
Hickman, Jason E. .... Akron, OH
Hickman, Jeremy J. .... Jenison, MI
Hickman, Jeremy J., Law Offices of, P.C.
Jenison, MI
Hickman, John R. .... Atlanta, GA
Hickman, John R. .... Tacoma, WA
Hickman, Jonathan R. .... Palmdale, CA
Hickman, Jonathan W. .... Newnan, GA
Hickman, Joseph L. .... Dallas, TX
Hickman, Joseph W. .... Benton, IL
Hickman, Kelly D. .... Irvine, CA
Hickman, Kenneth L. .... Shreveport, LA
Hickman, Kim I. .... Sacramento, CA
Hickman, Lawrence .... Colfax, WA
Hickman, Linda .... Harlowton, MT
Hickman, Linda L. .... Williston, ND
Hickman, Lori A .... Boise, ID
Hickman & Lowder Co., L.P.A.
Cleveland, OH
Hickman, M. Sperry .... Independence, MO
Hickman, Marcus T. .... Charlotte, NC
Hickman & Martens, P.C. .... Chandler, AZ
Hickman, Michael .... Chandler, AZ
Hickman, Michael B. .... Overland Park, KS
Hickman, Michael J. .... San Diego, CA
Hickman, Mike A. .... Maryville, TN
Hickman, Molly E. .... Portland, OR
Hickman, M. Sperry, P.C.
Independence, MO
Hickman, Paul J. .... Omaha, NE
Hickman, Paul L. .... Palo Alto, CA
Hickman, Paula Hazelrig .... Shreveport, LA
Hickman, Richard A. .... Moraga, CA
Hickman, Robert M.
North Kansas City, MO
Hickman, Ross A. .... Central Lake, MI
Hickman, S. Barrett .... Carmel, NY
Hickman, Stephen D. .... Washington, DC
Hickman Stephens Coleman & Hughes, LLP
Campbell, CA
Palo Alto, CA
Hickman, Steven R. .... Tulsa, OK
Hickman, Susan M. .... Chicago, IL
Hickman, Susanna B. .... Williamsburg, VA
Hickman, T. Scott .... Sallisaw, OK
Hickman, Thomas E. .... Westminster, MD
Hickman, Troy J. .... Seattle, WA
Hickman, Virgil W. .... Lanham, MD
Hickman & Webster, P.S. .... Colfax, WA
Hickman, Will A. .... Grenada, MS
Jackson, MS
New Albany, MS
Oxford, MS
Hickman, William B. .... Dallas, TX
Hickman, William H.
Oklahoma City, OK
Hickman, William, III .... Pikeville, KY
Hickman, William J., Law Offices of, S.C.
West Bend, WI
Hickman, William L. .... Tulsa, OK
Hickman, William R. .... Seattle, WA
Hickmann, Charles A. .... Huntington, NY
Hickmann, George S.
Cranberry Township, PA
Hickmann, Michael P. .... Madison, WI
Hickmann, W. J. .... West Bend, WI
Hickmon, Sandra A. .... Columbia, SC
Hickok, Arthur F. .... Chicago, IL
Hickok, Craig W. .... Cedar Rapids, IA
Hickok, Harold M. .... Portland, OR
Hickok, Marshall D. .... Manchester, NH
Hickok, Mary B. .... Wilmington, DE
Hickok, Michael .... Los Angeles, CA
Newport Beach, CA
Hickok, Philip H. .... Los Angeles, CA
Hickok, Robert L. .... Cherry Hill, NJ
Philadelphia, PA
Hickok, Sally K. .... Wolf Point, MT
Hickok, Stephen M. .... Minneapolis, MN
Hickok, W. Lee, III .... Charlottesville, VA
Hickox, J. Michael .... Highland, MI
Hickox, Kenneth N., Jr. .... Washington, DC
Hickox, Stacy A. .... Okemos, MI
Hicks, A. C. Reeves .... Princeton, NJ
Hicks, Adam Stone .... Gainesville, GA
Hicks, Alan S. .... Roxboro, NC
Hicks, Alan S., P.A. .... Roxboro, NC
Hicks, Albert C. .... Bay City, MI
Hicks, Alvin J. (Bud) .... Las Vegas, NV
Reno, NV
Hicks & Anderson, P.A. .... Miami, FL
Hicks, Andrea N. .... Mason, OH
Hicks, Angela Medders .... Columbus, GA
Hicks, Anne H. .... Atlanta, GA
Hicks & Associates .... Newport Beach, CA
Hicks & Associates, P.C. .... Dallas, TX
Hicks & Bailly .... Albany, NY
Hicks & Baker .... Fredericksburg, VA
Hicks, Basha V. .... Key Biscayne, FL
Hicks, Basil V., Jr. (P.A.)
North Little Rock, AR
Hicks, Ben E., Jr. .... Soquel, CA
Hicks, Benjamin P. .... Lexington, KY
Hicks, Bethany G. .... Mesa, AZ
Hicks, Bethany L. .... Richmond, VA
Hicks, Bill F. .... Mount Vernon, TX
Hicks, Billy D. .... El Paso, TX
Hicks, Billy L. .... Prescott, AZ
Hicks, Boyd, Chandler & Falconer
Anchorage, AK
Hicks, B. R. .... Springfield, VA

Hicks, Bradley O'Neal .... Leesville, LA
Hicks, Brams & Scher
West Palm Beach, FL
Hicks, Brian E. .... Indianapolis, IN
Hicks, Brian W. .... Boston, MA
Hicks, C. Flippo .... Richmond, VA
Hicks, C. Gary .... Mobile, AL
Hicks, C. Thomas, III .... Tysons Corner, VA
Hicks, Carole A. .... Statesville, NC
Hicks, Carrol Ann .... North Little Rock, AR
Hicks, Casey, Young & Barber, P.C.
Marietta, GA
Hicks, Cassandra P. .... Bethesda, MD
Hicks, Catherine Henry .... Gainesville, GA
Hicks, Cecil .... Santa Ana, CA
Hicks, Charles F. .... Atlanta, GA
Hicks, Charles George, Law Office of
Atlanta, GA
Hicks, Charles L. .... Camden, TN
Hicks, Charles L., Jr. .... Laurinburg, NC
Hicks, Charles O. .... Boston, MA
Hicks, Charles R. .... Little Rock, AR
Hicks, Cheryl L. .... Oakland, CA
Hicks, Christopher Allen .... Charlotte, NC
Hicks, Claude W., Jr. .... Macon, GA
Hicks, Colleen E. .... Wilmington, DE
Philadelphia, PA
Hicks, Cynthia A. .... Salem, OR
Hicks, Daniel .... Ocala, FL
Hicks, Daniel C. .... Hopkinsville, KY
Hicks, Daniel K. .... Greenville, SC
Hicks, Daniel, P.A. .... Ocala, FL
Hicks, Darryl L. .... Warrenton, MO
Hicks, Darryl L., P.C. .... Warrenton, MO
Hicks, David .... Oakland, CA
Hicks, David G. .... Omaha, NE
Hicks, David L. .... Houston, TX
Hicks, David N., Jr. .... Salem, OR
Hicks, Deborah Whitmore .... Eufaula, AL
Hicks, Deron R. .... Columbus, GA
Hicks, Dewitt T., Jr. .... Columbus, MS
Hicks, Donald C. .... New Bern, NC
Hicks, Donald L. .... Phoenix, AZ
Hicks, Donald R. .... Atlanta, GA
Hicks, Donald R. .... Akron, OH
Hicks, Donovan O. .... Baton Rouge, LA
Hicks, Douglas L. .... Boston, MA
Hicks, DuVal Q. .... Fredericksburg, VA
Hicks, Edward D. .... New Bedford, MA
Hicks, Edward E. .... Boston, MA
Hicks, Edward J., III .... Tulsa, OK
Hicks, Elizabeth Jane .... Jackson, MS
Hicks, Elliot G. .... Charleston, WV
Hicks, Eric O .... Baltimore, MD
Hicks, Eugene C., III .... Charlotte, NC
Hicks, Francis H. .... Mountain Home, ID
Hicks, Fred A. .... Altamont, IL
Hicks, Fred A. .... Charlotte, NC
Hicks, G. Stewart .... Santa Ana, CA
Hicks, Gary Ellis .... Manchester, NH
Hicks, Gary L. .... Lansing, MI
Hicks, George G. .... Boise, ID
Hicks, George G. .... Minneapolis, MN
Hicks, George R., III .... Fayetteville, NC
Hicks, George R., Jr. .... Cleveland, OH
Hicks, Gerald C. .... Sacramento, CA
Hicks, Gerald Lee .... Lockport, NY
Hicks, Gerald O. .... Boston, MA
Hicks, Ginger J. .... Little Rock, AR
Hicks, Graham M., P.C. .... Portland, OR
Hicks, Gregory A. .... Seattle, WA
Hicks, Gregory L. .... Boise, ID
Hicks, Gregory V. .... Warren, OH
Hicks, Guy M., III .... Nashville, TN
Hicks, H. Bryan .... Marble Falls, TX
Hicks, H. Melville, Jr. .... New York, NY
Hicks, H. Thomas .... Newport Beach, CA
Hicks, Harold J. .... Chicago, IL
Hicks, Harry J. .... Virginia Beach, VA
Hicks & Havrilak, P.C. .... Fairfax, VA
Hicks, Henry W., (P.A.) .... Tampa, FL
Hicks & Hubley .... Shreveport, LA
Hicks, I. Faison .... Charlotte, NC
Hicks, Ira E. .... New Canaan, CT
Hicks, J. Portis .... New York, NY
Hicks, J. Randolph .... Roswell, GA
Hicks, J. Ridge .... Phoenix, AZ
Hicks, J. Seth .... Dallas, TX
Hicks, J. Wiley .... Miami, FL
Hicks, Jack B. .... Greensboro, NC
Hicks, Jack B., III .... Los Angeles, CA
Hicks, Jack D. .... Lufkin, TX
Hicks, James B. .... Los Angeles, CA
Hicks, James B., III .... Eastland, TX
Hicks, James D. .... Philadelphia, PA
Hicks, James F., Jr.
Office of Personnel Management,
Merit Systems Division, GV
Hicks, James H. .... West Palm Beach, FL
Hicks, James L., Jr. .... Dallas, TX
Hicks, James M. .... Warren, MI
Hicks, James R. .... Tulsa, OK
Hicks, James T. .... River Forest, IL
Hicks, James V. .... Knoxville, IA
Hicks, James Virgil, Jr. .... United States Senate,
Senatorial Assistants, GV
Hicks, Janet Brooks .... Greensboro, NC
Hicks, Janice E. .... Chicago, IL
Hicks, Jerry .... Dallas, TX
Hicks, Jerry Lee .... Huntsville, AL
Hicks, Jim .... Santa Ana, CA
Hicks, Jimmie B., Jr. .... New Bern, NC
Hicks, Jimmie D. .... Mesa, AZ
Hicks, Joan L. .... Milwaukee, WI
Hicks, Joe H. .... Boston, MA
Hicks, John C. .... Princeton, IN
Hicks, John F. .... Tulsa, OK
Hicks, John G. .... Jeffersontown, KY
Hicks, John H. .... Fort Myers, FL
Hicks, John L. .... Clarkston, MI
Hicks, John O., III .... Calhoun, KY
Hicks, John P. .... Albany, NY
Hicks, John S. .... Chester, NY
Hicks, John S. .... Nashville, TN
Hicks, John W. .... Mount Vernon, WA
Hicks, John W., Jr. .... Dallas, TX
Hicks, Josephine H. .... Charlotte, NC
Hicks, Joshua J. .... Reno, NV
Hicks, Joyce M. .... Oakland, CA
Hicks, Karyn T. .... Boston, MA
Hicks, Kenneth A. .... New York, NY
Hicks, Kenneth A. .... Wagoner, OK
Hicks, Kevin L. .... Philadelphia, PA
Hicks, Kirkland L. .... Washington, DC
Hicks, Kristin L. .... Boston, MA
Hicks, L. Clark, Jr. .... Hattiesburg, MS
Hicks, L. James .... Flint, MI
Hicks, L. Westcott, Jr. .... Los Angeles, CA
Hicks, Larry R. .... Reno, NV
Hicks, Larry W. .... El Paso, TX
Hicks, Laurinda L. .... Washington, DC
Hicks, Lawrence E. .... Old Greenwich, CT
Hicks, Lawrence W. .... Pittsburgh, PA
Hicks, Leo Barron .... Madison, WI
Hicks, Leon .... Jonesboro, GA
Hicks, Lisa B. .... Fort Lauderdale, FL
Hicks, Lloyd L. .... Visalia, CA
Hicks, Loren D. .... Salem, OR
Hicks, Louise Day .... Boston, MA
Hicks & Lucky .... Las Cruces, NM
El Paso, TX
Hicks, Lucy C. .... Birmingham, AL
Hicks, Lynne .... Mocksville, NC
Hicks, Lynne L. .... Denver, CO
Hicks, M. Brent .... Metairie, LA
Hicks, M. Lawrence, Jr. .... Dallas, TX
Hicks, M. Maxine .... Atlanta, GA
Hicks, Margit M. .... Fayetteville, NC
Hicks, Marion L. .... Fort Worth, TX
Hicks, Mark .... Miami, FL
Hicks, Mark C., Jr. .... Jonesborough, TN
Hicks, Mark S. .... San Jose, CA
Hicks, Mark S. .... Dublin, VA
Hicks, Mark W. .... Richmond, VA
Hicks, Marsha Theiss .... Fort Lauderdale, FL
Hicks, Martin P. .... New Brunswick, NJ
Hicks, Marvis L. .... Milwaukee, WI
Hicks & Massey .... Dublin, GA
Winder, GA
Hicks, Matthew M. .... Boise, ID
Hicks, Matthew R. .... Los Angeles, CA
Hicks, McDonald, Allen & Noecker, L.L.P.
Greensboro, NC
Hicks, Michael D. .... Lubbock, TX
Hicks, Michael H. .... Vancouver, WA
Hicks, Michael J. .... Brookfield, WI
Hicks, Michael M. .... Washington, DC
Baltimore, MD
Rockville, MD
Hicks, Michael W. .... Cupertino, CA
Hicks, Michelle E. .... Houston, TX
Hicks, Nathan A., Jr. .... Charleston, WV
Hicks, Nelson K. .... Oxford, NC
Hicks, Pamela .... Glendale, CA
Hicks, Patricia A. .... Tacoma, WA
Hicks, Patricia Lynne .... Phoenix, AZ
Hicks, Patrick H. .... Las Vegas, NV
Reno, NV
Hicks, Paul D. .... Honolulu, HI
Hicks, Paul DeF., Jr. .... New York, NY
Hicks, Paul L. .... Morgantown, WV
Hicks, Paul W. .... Dallas, TX
Hicks, Peggy L. .... Minneapolis, MN
Hicks, Perry L. .... Bisbee, AZ
Hicks, Preston B. .... Waynesboro, VA
Hicks, Preston L. .... Foley, AL
Hicks, R. Eldridge .... Anchorage, AK
Hicks, R. Javoyne .... Atlanta, GA
Hicks, R. Thomas .... Atlanta, GA
Hicks, Ralph H. .... Atlanta, GA
Hicks, Ralph L. .... Cashiers, NC
Hicks, Ralph W. .... St. Joseph, MO
Hicks, Randall B. .... Riverside, CA
Hicks, Randolph S. .... Redwood City, CA
Hicks, Reiko J. .... Ontario, CA
Hicks, Renardo Lee .... Louisville, KY
Hicks, Renea .... Austin, TX
Hicks, Richard A. .... Honolulu, HI
Hicks, Richard E. .... Roswell, GA
Hicks, Richard H., Jr. .... Greensboro, NC
Hicks, Richard J. .... Santa Rosa, CA
Hicks, Rick .... Los Angeles, CA
Hicks, Robert .... San Diego, CA
Hicks, Robert .... Orem, UT
Hicks, Robert A. .... Indianapolis, IN
Hicks, Robert B. .... Tampa, FL
Hicks, Robert D. .... Royal Oak, MI
Hicks, Robert D. .... Gloucester, VA
Hicks, Robert E. .... Atlanta, GA
Hicks, Robert G. .... Springfield, NJ
Hicks, Robert W. .... San Diego, CA
Hicks, Ronald L. .... Spotsylvania, VA
Hicks, Ronald L., Jr. .... Pittsburgh, PA
Hicks, Ross H. .... Clarksville, TN
Hicks, Ruben G. .... Whitley City, KY
Hicks, Russell B. .... Bakersfield, CA
Hicks, Ryan R.C. .... Houston, TX
Hicks, S. Baylor .... Walnut Creek, CA
Hicks, S. Maurice, Jr., (P.C.)
Shreveport, LA
Hicks, S. Richard .... Seattle, WA
Hicks, Samuel D. .... Marietta, GA
Hicks, Schmidlin & Bancroft, P.C. .... Flint, MI
Hicks & Schreiber, P.A. .... Miami, FL
Hicks, Sharon A. .... Champaign, IL
Hicks, Stephanie Marshall .... Seattle, WA
Hicks, Stephen .... Harrison, NY
Hicks, Stephen C. .... Boston, MA
Hicks, Steve E. .... Baton Rouge, LA
Hicks, Steven R., The Law Office of, Inc.
Cincinnati, OH
Hicks, Susan Massie .... Fairfax, VA
Hicks, Sylvia S. .... Vienna, VA
Hicks, T. Lawrence .... Florence, KY
Hicks, T. Todd .... Oklahoma City, OK
Hicks, Taylor M., Jr. .... Houston, TX
Hicks, Thomas L., Jr. .... Richmond, VA
Hicks Thomas & Lilienstern, LLP
Amarillo, TX
Dallas, TX
Houston, TX
Hicks, Thomas S. .... Wilmington, NC
Hicks, Timothy C. .... Englewood, CO
Hicks, Timothy G. .... Muskegon, MI
Hicks, Todd C. .... Chardon, OH
Hicks, Vicki J. .... Department of Agriculture,
Farm Service Agency, GV
Hicks, W. Daniel, Jr. .... Atlanta, GA
Hicks & Walt .... Las Vegas, NV
Reno, NV
Hicks, William A. .... Abilene, TX
Hicks, William A., III .... Phoenix, AZ
Tucson, AZ
Hicks, William C. .... Boston, MA
Hicks, William C. .... Minneapolis, MN
Hicks, William C. .... Springfield, OH
Hicks, William Christopher .... Cincinnati, OH
Hicks, William E. .... Dublin, GA
Hicks, William F. .... Sacramento, CA
Hicks, Zoe M. .... Atlanta, GA
Hicks, Zoe M., P.C. .... Atlanta, GA
Hickson, David L. .... San Diego, CA
Hickson, H. Michael .... Salisbury, MD
Hickson, Lenel, Jr.
Commodity Futures Trading Commission,
Division of Enforcement, GV
Hickson, Nina R. .... Duluth, GA
Hickson, Robert C., Jr. .... Mt. Gilead, OH
Hickson, Suzy I. .... Harrison, NY
Hickton, David J. .... Pittsburgh, PA
Hickton, Dawne S. .... Niles, OH
Hicky, Philip, (Ltd.) .... Forrest City, AR
Hicky, Preston G. .... Forrest City, AR
Hicok, Benjamin L. .... Cadillac, MI
Hida, Heidi M. .... Milwaukee, WI
Hidalgo, Boris A. .... Houston, TX
Hidalgo, Bryan .... Los Angeles, CA
Hidalgo, Jaime P. .... Anchorage, AK
Hidalgo, Lawrence L., Jr. .... Lansing, MI
Hidalgo, Manuel .... Los Angeles, CA
Hidalgo, Michael X. .... Grand Rapids, MI
Hidalgo, Paul Gregory .... Dallas, TX
Hidalgo, Richard Paul .... Irvine, CA
Hidalgo, Rolando .... Los Angeles, CA
Hidalgo, Tracy Kern .... New Orleans, LA
Hidalgo, William B. .... New Orleans, LA
Hidani, Donald R. .... Honolulu, HI
Hiday, Lisa A. .... Indianapolis, IN
Hiday & Ricke, P.A. .... Jacksonville, FL
Orlando, FL
Hiday, Robert D. .... Jacksonville, FL
Hidde, Curt W. .... Indianapolis, IN
Hidde, Kandi K. .... Indianapolis, IN
Hidde, Orval L. .... Watertown, WI
Hidden, Holli D. (Colburn) .... Atlanta, GA
Hiddleson, Christopher .... Los Angeles, CA
Hiddleston, Clark A. .... Visalia, CA
Hiden, David Vincent .... San Diego, CA
Hiden, Robert B., Jr. .... New York, NY
Hiden Rott and Oertle .... San Diego, CA
Hider & Associates, P.C. .... Dallas, TX
Hider, Frank C. (Chip) .... Dallas, TX
Hider, Judith L. .... Dallas, TX
Hider, Michael S. .... Merced, CA
Hider, Patricia A. .... Cincinnati, OH
Hidey, Coyle & Monteleone
Cumberland, MD
Oakland, MD
Keyser, WV
Hidey, W. Stevens .... Cumberland, MD
Hidley, Ondrea Dae .... Irving, TX
Hidnert, Scott J. .... Miami Shores, FL
Hiduke, Eric A. .... Austin, TX
Hidy, Joseph D. .... Naples, FL
Columbia, SC
Hidy, Kathleen McGarvey .... Cincinnati, OH
Hieatt, Jay A. .... San Luis Obispo, CA
Hieatt, Jennifer Fraley .... Cincinnati, OH
Hieatt, Steven W. .... Cincinnati, OH
Hieb, Dixie K. .... Sioux Falls, SD
Hieb, E. Allen, Jr. .... Jacksonville, FL
Hieber, Cheryl Millhouse .... Concord, NH
Hieber, Christina J. .... Washington, DC
Hieber, Darrel J. .... Los Angeles, CA
Hieber, Glen .... Hillsboro, OR
Hieber, John R. .... North Riverside, IL
Hieber, John R., Ltd. .... North Riverside, IL
Hieber, Raymond C. .... Xenia, OH
Hieber, Sherry M. .... Manchester, NH
Hiebert, David L. .... Wichita, KS
Hiebert, Leslie A. .... Anchorage, AK
Hiebert, Peter N. .... Washington, DC
Hiebert, Timothy H. .... Boston, MA
Hiebler, James R. .... New Hyde Park, NY
Hiebsch, Kenneth H. .... Wichita, KS
Hieda, George I. .... Honolulu, HI
Hiedeman, Mark L. .... Pocatello, ID
Hiefield, Mark A. .... Portland, OR
Hiefield, Preston C., Jr. .... Portland, OR
Hiegel, Richard J. .... New York, NY
Hieken, Charles .... Boston, MA
Hielscher, William J. .... Northfield, IL
Hiemer, Linda J. .... Anchorage, AK
Hiemstra, Anne H. .... Detroit, MI
Hiemstra, Charles J. .... Grand Rapids, MI
Hiendlmayr, Thomas R. .... St. Paul, MN
Hieneman, Bruce D. .... Honolulu, HI
Hieneman, Jonathan G. .... Campbellsville, KY
Hieneman, Ramona C.
Campbellsville, KY
Hiener, Michael A. .... Madison, OH
Hienton, Diane D. .... Phoenix, AZ
Hienton Fry, P.C. .... Phoenix, AZ
Hienton, James R. .... Phoenix, AZ
Hienton, Joseph P. .... Phoenix, AZ
Hienz, William M., III .... Minneapolis, MN
Hiepler & Hiepler, Law Offices of
Oxnard, CA
Hiepler, Mark O. .... Oxnard, CA
Hiepler, Michelle R. .... Oxnard, CA
Hier, Marshall D. .... St. Louis, MO
Hier, Teresa .... Winston-Salem, NC
Hierholzer, Virginia A. .... Baltimore, MD
Hiering, Dupignac & Stanzione, A
Professional Corporation
Toms River, NJ
Hiering, William T. .... Toms River, NJ
Hierl, Michael A. .... Chicago, IL
Hierl, Thomas J. .... New York, NY
Hieronymi, Brent E. .... Huntsville, AL
Hieronymus, John O. .... Department of Justice,
Drug Enforcement Administration, GV
Hiers, B. Monroe .... Bamberg, SC
Hiers, David W. .... Pensacola, FL
Hiers, James B., Jr. .... Atlanta, GA
Hiers, L. Danner .... Winter Park, FL
Hiers, Richard H. .... Gainesville, FL
Hiers, Thomas S. .... Boston, MA
Hiers, William N., Jr. .... Atlanta, GA
Hiersche, G. Rudy, Jr. .... Oklahoma City, OK
Hiersche, Jerry L. .... Addison, TX
Hiersche, Martens, Hayward, Drakeley & Urbach, P.C. .... Addison, TX
Hierseman, Jerome A. .... Milwaukee, WI
Hiersteiner, Richard .... Boston, MA
Hiersteiner, Walter .... Kansas City, MO
Hiesrodt, Brian L. .... Lansing, MI
Hiestand, Fred J., A Professional Corporation
Sacramento, CA
Hiestand, Fred J., A Professional Corporation
Sacramento, CA
Hiestand, Harley K. .... Wellesley, MA
Hiestand, Herbert H., Jr. .... Encino, CA
Hiestand, Jean C., (Mr.) .... Bloomington, IL
Hiestand, Kristen Davidson .... Dublin, OH
Hiestand, Michael C. .... Washington, DC
Hiestand, N. Lynn .... Chicago, IL
Hiestand, O. S., Jr. .... Bethesda, MD
Hiestand, Sarah A. .... Fort Wayne, IN
Hiestand, Sarah A. .... Nashville, TN
Hiestand, Sheila P. .... Lexington, KY
Hiestand, Terry K., Law Offices of
Chesterton, IN
Hiester, Thomas L. .... Daly City, CA
Hietala, Eric A. .... Burlingame, CA
Hietbrink, Paul D. .... Des Moines, IA
Pella, IA
Hietpas, Quentin J. .... St. Paul, MN
Hiffa, Joseph Michael .... Boston, MA
Higa, Clifford K., (Atty. At Law, A Law Corp.) .... Honolulu, HI
Higa, Davis D. .... Honolulu, HI
Honolulu, HI
Higa, Dennis S. .... Santa Clara, CA
Higa, Dexter T. .... Honolulu, HI
Higa, Emlyn .... Honolulu, HI
Higa, Kase .... Wailuku, HI
Higa, Lisa Shea .... Palo Alto, CA
Higa, Patricia A. .... San Francisco, CA
Higa, Ray Masao .... Honolulu, HI
Higa, Robert J. .... Los Angeles, CA
Higaki, Paul F., Jr. .... Oakland, CA
Higashi, Lynn H. .... Kailua-Kona, HI
Higashi, Thomas Y. .... Keizer, OR
Higbe, Clifton M. H. .... Sacramento, CA
Higbee, Avece M. .... Las Vegas, NV
Higbee, Charan M. .... Walnut Creek, CA
Higbee, Charlotte M. .... Bradenton, FL
Higbee, David A. .... Frederick, MD
Higbee, G. William .... Topsham, ME
Higbee, Geo. M. .... Bradenton, FL
Higbee, Heather L. .... Orlando, FL
Higbee, Jensen & MacFarlane, P.C.
Page, AZ
Cedar City, UT
Kanab, UT
Panguitch, UT
St. George, UT
Higbee, Paul N., Jr. .... Morrow, GA
Higbee, R. Alan .... Tampa, FL
Higbee, Ronald P. .... Jacksonville, FL
Higbee, Scott A. .... Minneapolis, MN
Higbee, Thomas M. .... Cedar City, UT
Higbie, Alanson .... Colorado Springs, CO
Higbie, Marcy, (P.C.) .... Houston, TX
Higbie, Richard A. .... Newport Beach, CA
Higbie, Roger C. .... New York, NY
Higbie, Wesley R., Law Offices of
San Francisco, CA
Higby, Annette Marie .... Randolph, VT
Higby, Clifford C. .... Panama City, FL
Higdon, David B. .... Macon, GA
Higdon, Frederick A. .... Lebanon, KY
Higdon, Gerald (Jerry) .... Houston, TX
Higdon, Hardy & Zuflacht, L.L.P.
San Antonio, TX
Higdon, Jack W. .... Houston, TX
Higdon, James N. .... San Antonio, TX
Higdon, James Raymond .... Anniston, AL
Higdon, James S. .... Greenbelt, MD
Higdon, Jason James-Logan .... Joplin, MO
Higdon, Jeffrey F. .... Lutherville, MD

Higdon, Mark B. ... Jackson, MS
Higdon, Patrick M. ... Bloomfield Hills, MI
Higdon, Paul A. ... Midland, TX
Higdon, Philip R. ... Tucson, AZ
Higdon, Polly S. ... Portland, OR
Higdon, Robert E. ... Washington, DC
Higdon, Robert J., Jr. ... Charlotte, NC
Higdon, Stephen V. ... Monroe, NC
Higer, Dale G. ... Boise, ID
Higer, Gary ... Valley Village, CA
Higer, Michael J. ... Miami, FL
Higer, Nathan W. ... Burley, ID
Higer, Richard P. ... New York, NY
Higer, Samuel ... Stoneham, MA
Higerd, Jeffrey J. ... Cleveland, OH
Higey, Todd M. ... Birmingham, AL
Higgason, James D., Jr. ... Houston, TX
Higgason, John M., Jr. ... Chattanooga, TN
Higgason, Kelly Noel ... Houston, TX
Higgason, Maxie E., Jr. ... Corbin, KY
Higgerson, Richard G. ... Carbondale, IL
Higginbotham & Bowman, PLC
Orange, VA
Higginbotham, C. Dean ... Princeton, IN
Higginbotham, Cary Lynn ... Houston, TX
Higginbotham, Deanna S. ... Dothan, AL
Higginbotham, Don, (P.C.) ... Georgetown, TX
Higginbotham, Douglas C. ... Jacksonville, FL
Higginbotham, Elizabeth L. ... Austin, TX
Higginbotham, Ernest R., (P.C.)
Dallas, TX
Higginbotham, George M. ... Bessemer, AL
Higginbotham, H. Irene ... Tampa, FL
Higginbotham, J. Lanham, III ... Dallas, TX
Higginbotham, J. Michael
San Francisco, CA
Higginbotham, James E. ... Jackson, MS
Higginbotham, Jeffrey ... Quantico, VA
Higginbotham, John D. ... Riverside, CA
Higginbotham, John E. ... Florence, AL
Higginbotham, John T. ... New York, NY
Higginbotham, Kathryn D. ... Knoxville, TN
Higginbotham, Michael W. ... Memphis, TN
Higginbotham, N. Brent ... Fairfax, VA
Higginbotham, Patricia G.
Washington, DC
Higginbotham, Patrick E. ... Dallas, TX
Higginbotham, Phyllis Shelton ... Altavista, VA
Higginbotham, R. E. ... Tulsa, OK
Higginbotham, Robert J. ... San Francisco, CA
Higginbotham, Robert T., Jr. ... Jackson, MS
Higginbotham, Ronald M. ... Roswell, NM
Higginbotham, Rufus T., Jr. ... Dallas, TX
Higginbotham, Samuel P., II ... Orange, VA
Higginbotham, Susan D. ... Sanford, NC
Higginbotham, Toni Manning
Baton Rouge, LA
Higginbotham, Whitten & McCutcheon
Florence, AL
Muscle Shoals, AL
Higginbotham, Wm. Earl
Jacksonville, FL
Higginbotham-Brooks, Renee
Fort Worth, TX
Higginbotham-Hassan, Wendi
New York, NY
Higginbottom, David B. ... Frostproof, FL
Higginbottom, Samuel L., Jr.
Federal Energy Regulatory Commission,
Office of the General Counsel, GV
Higgins, Alexander J. ... Seattle, WA
Higgins, Alicia S. ... Columbia, SC
Higgins, Andrew J. ... Jefferson City, MO
Higgins, Andrew Jackson
Jefferson City, MO
Lake Ozark, MO
Higgins, Andrew M. ... Boston, MA
Higgins, Ann-Michele G. ... Philadelphia, PA
Higgins, Anthony R. ... Livingston, NJ
Higgins, Anthony Sherwood
Washington, DC
Higgins, Barbara A. ... Los Angeles, CA
Higgins, Barbara J. ... Los Angeles, CA
Higgins, Bardon ... Duluth, MN
Higgins, Bart F. ... Chicago, IL
Higgins, Bernard F. ... Potomac, MD
Higgins, Bernard F., P.A. ... Potomac, MD
Higgins, Beth McFadin ... Mt. Vernon, IN
Higgins, Biddle, Chester and Trew
Athens, TN
Higgins, Brian S. ... New York, NY
Higgins, Brian Scott ... Washington, DC
Higgins, Brian T. ... West Paterson, NJ
Higgins, Brian W. ... Washington, DC
Higgins, Brigid M. ... Las Vegas, NV
Higgins, Byron H. ... Urbana, IL
Higgins, C. Daniel ... Stroudsburg, PA
Higgins, Cara A. ... East Brunswick, NJ
Higgins, Carlos ... Austin, TX
Higgins, Catherine E. ... Springfield, MA
Higgins, Cavanagh & Cooney
Providence, RI
Higgins, Cecelia E. ... Department of Labor,
Office of Secretary, GV
Higgins, Celeste Siblesz ... Miami, FL
Higgins, Charles B. ... Bloomfield, CT
Higgins, Charles L. ... Solana Beach, CA
Higgins, Charles N., Jr. ... Concord, OH
Higgins, Cheryl V. ... Charlottesville, VA
Higgins, Chris W. ... Seattle, WA
Higgins, C. K., Jr. ... Greenfield, MO
Higgins, Claudia R.
Federal Trade Commission,
Bureau of Competition, GV
Higgins, Clifford B. ... Macon, GA
Higgins, Colin O. ... Berwyn, IL
Higgins, Craig K. ... St. Louis, MO
Higgins, Daniel B. ... San Francisco, CA
Higgins, Daniel C. ... Raleigh, NC
Higgins, Daryl A. ... Gretna, LA
Higgins, David B. ... Denver, CO
Higgins, David D. ... Wellesley, MA
Higgins, David K. ... Charleston, WV
Higgins, David L. ... Kansas City, KS
Higgins, David S. ... Needham, MA
Higgins, Dean J. ... Saratoga Springs, NY
Higgins, Denise M. ... Chicago, IL
Higgins, Dennis O. ... Sacramento, CA
Higgins & Dubner ... Atlanta, GA
Higgins, Earl J. ... New Orleans, LA
Higgins, Edward J. ... Detroit, MI
Higgins, Edward J. ... New York, NY
Higgins, Edwin C., III ... Putnam, CT
Higgins, Eric M. ... Stamford, CT
Higgins, Erin K. ... Boston, MA
Higgins, Eugene V. ... Providence, RI
Higgins, Felicia H. ... New Orleans, LA
Higgins and Fournier ... Spokane, WA
Higgins, Francis J. ... Chicago, IL
Higgins, Frankstone, Graves & Morris, P.A.
Cary, NC
Chapel Hill, NC
Higgins, G. Michael ... Fort Wayne, IN
Higgins, G. Peter ... North Tonawanda, NY
Higgins, Gabrielle E. ... Palo Alto, CA
Higgins, Georganne R. ... Columbus, OH
Higgins, George ... Oakland, CA
Higgins, George B., Jr. ... Plano, TX
Higgins, George J., Jr. ... New Orleans, LA
Higgins, George L., III ... Pineville, LA
Higgins, George V. ... Milton, MA
Higgins, Gerry M. ... Bozeman, MT
Higgins, H. Henry ... Spokane, WA
Higgins & Halligan ... Media, PA
Higgins, Harris-Sherman & Rohr
Palm Desert, CA
Higgins & Higgins ... San Francisco, CA
Higgins, Higgins & Higgins ... Manhasset, NY
Higgins & Himmelberg ... Nashville, TN
Higgins, Hugh B. ... Cleburne, TX
Higgins, J. Donald ... Manhasset, NY
Higgins, J. Donald, Jr. ... Manhasset, NY
Higgins, J. Eric ... Plano, TX
Higgins, J. Gregory ... Stoneham, MA
Higgins, James A. ... Cincinnati, OH
Higgins, James A. ... Wausau, WI
Higgins, James C., Jr. ... Philadelphia, PA
Higgins, James E. ... Wilmette, IL
Higgins, James E. ... Concord, NH
Manchester, NH
Higgins, James E. ... Binghamton, NY
Higgins, James E., Jr. ... Hopkinsville, KY
Higgins, James F., Jr. ... Denver, CO
Higgins, James J. ... New York, NY
Higgins, James J., Jr. ... Morristown, NJ
Higgins, James K. ... Wilmington, DE
Higgins, James M., Jr. ... Manchester, CT
Higgins, James R., Jr. ... Louisville, KY
Higgins, James S. ... Nashville, TN
Higgins, James Stuart ... Stuart, FL
Higgins, James T. ... Cumberland, RI
Higgins, Jas. C. ... Beckley, WV
Higgins, Jay W. ... Bloomfield Hills, MI
Higgins, Jeffery D. ... Tavares, FL
Higgins, Jeffrey A. ... Chelmsford, MA
Higgins, Jeffrey J. ... Lakewood, CO
Higgins, Jeffrey P. ... Menlo Park, CA
Higgins, Jenny L. ... Columbus, OH
Higgins, John B. ... St. Charles, IL
Higgins, John B. ... New York, NY
Higgins, John E. ... Latham, NY
Higgins, John E., Jr.
National Labor Relations Board,
Office of Solicitor, GV
Higgins, John F., IV ... Houston, TX
Higgins, John J. ... Malibu, CA
Higgins, John J. ... Palm Desert, CA
Higgins, John J. ... Jacksonville, FL
Higgins, John J. ... Silver Spring, MD
Higgins, John J. ... Omaha, NE
Higgins, John J. ... Trenton, NJ
Higgins, John M. ... Indianapolis, IN
Higgins, John P. ... St. Petersburg, FL
Higgins, John P. ... Waltham, MA
Higgins, John P. ... Midland, MI
Higgins, John P. ... Mantoloking, NJ
Higgins, John P. ... New York, NY
Higgins, John P. ... Charlotte, NC
Higgins, John P. ... Milwaukee, WI
Higgins, John R., Jr. ... Grand Island, NE
Higgins, John S. ... Cleveland, OH
Higgins, John Stuart ... Visalia, CA
Higgins, John T. ... Hopewell Junction, NY
Higgins, John T., Jr. ... Greensboro, NC
Higgins, John W. ... Albuquerque, NM
Higgins, Joseph A., Jr. ... Montvale, NJ
Higgins, Joseph J. ... Chicago, IL
Higgins, Joseph L. ... West Chester, PA
Higgins, Joseph M. ... West Islip, NY
Higgins, June Elizabeth ... Spring, TX
Higgins, Karen Nielsen ... Los Angeles, CA
Higgins, Karen R. ... Montvale, NJ
Higgins, Keith F. ... Boston, MA
Higgins, Keith L. ... Riverside, CA
Higgins, Keith T. ... San Francisco, CA
Higgins, Kelsen & O'Hara ... Syracuse, NY
Higgins, Kenneth D. ... Athens, TN
Higgins, Kenneth E. ... Minneapolis, MN
Higgins, Kerry E. ... Red Bank, NJ
Higgins, Kevin G. ... Reno, NV
Higgins, Kight L. ... Fort Worth, TX
Higgins, L. Ashley ... Helena, AR
Higgins, L. Ashley, P.A. ... Helena, AR
Higgins, Laura L. Hanlon ... Boston, MA
Higgins, Laurence E. ... Louisville, KY
Higgins, Lauretta J. ... Chicago, IL
Higgins, Lawrence M. ... Edina, MN
Higgins, Lawrence P. ... Washington, DC
Higgins, Lee E. ... Buena Park, CA
Higgins, Leonard H. ... Charleston, WV
Higgins, Lisa N. ... Atlanta, GA
Higgins, Lise-Kirsten Scholer ... Trenton, NJ
Higgins, Louis H. ... Lake Placid, NY
Higgins, Lynn E. ... Oakland, CA
Higgins, Malcolm B., II ... Virginia Beach, VA
Higgins, Maria Tilaro ... Boston, MA
Higgins, Mark A. ... Eloy, AZ
Higgins, Mark F. ... Great Falls, MT
Higgins, Mark P. ... Franklin, MA
Higgins, Mark R. ... Miami, FL
Higgins, Mark T. ... Seattle, WA
Higgins, Mary B. ... Washington, DC
Higgins, Mary P. ... Chicago, IL
Higgins, Mary P. ... Philadelphia, PA
Higgins, Maryann E. ... Allentown, PA
Higgins, Matthew S. ... Omaha, NE
Higgins, Maureen P. ... Chicago, IL
Higgins, McGovern & Smith, L.L.C.
Washington, DC
Higgins, Melanie ... Statesboro, GA
Higgins, Melissa Ann ... Monterey Park, CA
Higgins, Melvin T. ... Kingston, NY
Higgins, Mescall & Lee ... Albuquerque, NM
Higgins, Mia ... New York, NY
Higgins, Michael A. ... Warwick, RI
Higgins, Michael F. ... Newark, OH
Higgins, Michael F. ... Seattle, WA
Higgins, Michael J. ... San Francisco, CA
Higgins, Michael J. ... Chicago, IL
Higgins, Michael J. ... Wheaton, IL
Higgins, Michael J. ... Omaha, NE
Higgins, Michael J. ... New York, NY
Higgins, Michael J. ... Horsham, PA
Higgins, Michael P. ... Vancouver, WA
Higgins, Michael P., P.C. ... Lapeer, MI
Higgins, Michael W. ... Atlanta, GA
Higgins, Mindy B. ... Mars, PA
Higgins, Molly ... San Antonio, TX
Higgins, Nancy M. ... San Diego, CA
Higgins, Neil C. ... Boston, MA
Higgins, Neil E. ... New York, NY
Higgins, Nicholas ... Fenton, MO
Higgins, Norbert A. ... Binghamton, NY
Higgins, O. Warren ... Media, PA
Higgins, Pamela Robinson
Montgomery, AL
Higgins, Patricia A. ... New York, NY
Higgins, Patricia M. ... Naperville, IL
Higgins, Patrick Bryan ... Maywood, NJ
Higgins, Patrick H. ... Hockessin, DE
Higgins, Patrick J. ... Delmar, NY
Higgins, Patrick J., Jr. ... Granger, IN
Higgins, Patrick M. ... Beaufort, SC
Higgins, Paul B. ... DeSoto, TX
Higgins, Paul J. ... New York, NY
Higgins, Paul M. ... Washington, DC
Upper Marlboro, MD
Higgins, Pauline Edwards ... Houston, TX
Higgins, Peter B. ... Salem, OR
Higgins, Peter F. ... Chicago, IL
Chicago, IL
Des Plaines, IL
Higgins, Ralph P. ... Rocky River, OH
Higgins, Ralph P., Jr. ... Cleveland, OH
Higgins, Raymond B. ... El Dorado, AR
Higgins, Raymond F., III
Fort Walton Beach, FL
Panama City, FL
Pensacola, FL
Higgins, Regina E. ... Elmhurst, NY
Port Washington, NY
Higgins, Richard Arthur ... San Diego, CA
Higgins, Richard E. ... Fairfield, CT
Higgins, Richard J. ... Department of State,
Foreign Service Officers (Overseas), GV
Higgins, Richard J. ... Framingham, MA
Higgins, Rick D. ... Salt Lake City, UT
Higgins, Robert E. ... Framingham, MA
Higgins, Robert F. ... Orlando, FL
Higgins, Robert F., Jr. ... Macon, GA
Higgins, Robert G. ... Chicago, IL
Higgins, Robert G. ... McMinnville, OR
Higgins, Robert J. ... Washington, DC
Higgins, Robert J. ... Department of Justice,
Tax Division, GV
Higgins, Robert M. ... Boston, MA
Higgins, Robert M. ... Cleveland, OH
Higgins, Roberts, Beyerl & Coan, P.C.
Albany, NY
Schenectady, NY
Higgins, Robin K. ... Westport, CT
Higgins, Robt. M. ... Oak Park, IL
Higgins, Roger D. ... Dallas, TX
Higgins, Roger J. ... Chicago, IL
Higgins, Roger W. ... Falls Church, VA
Higgins, Ronald C. ... Gadsden, AL
Higgins, Ronald J. ... Los Angeles, CA
Higgins, Ryan K. ... New York, NY
Higgins, Sara Wyche ... Charlotte, NC
Higgins, Sarah Swanson ... Knoxville, TN
Higgins, Sean K. ... Irvine, CA
Higgins, Sean M. ... Houston, TX
Higgins, Sean T. ... Las Vegas, NV
Higgins, Sean T. ... New York, NY
Higgins, Sean W. ... Springfield, NJ
New York, NY
Higgins, Sharon A. ... Colorado Springs, CO
Higgins, Shelley J. ... Juneau, AK
Higgins & Slattery ... Providence, RI
Higgins, Starrs & Macdonell
Farmington Hills, MI
Higgins, Stephen B. ... St. Louis, MO
Higgins, Stephen R. ... Denver, CO
Higgins, Steven A. ... Montgomery, AL
Higgins, Susan L. ... Ann Arbor, MI
Higgins, T. Scott ... Tucson, AZ
Higgins, Tara ... San Rafael, CA
Higgins, Tara A. ... New York, NY
Higgins, Tara Mary ... Department of Justice,
Antitrust Division, GV
Higgins, Terence M. ... Manhasset, NY
Higgins, Terrence J. ... Providence, RI
Higgins, Terrence P. ... Buffalo, NY
Higgins, Thomas ... Peoria, IL
Higgins, Thomas A. ... Nashville, TN
Higgins, Thomas C. ... Chicago, IL
Higgins, Thomas D., III ... Chapel Hill, NC
Higgins, Thomas E. ... Glastonbury, CT
Higgins, Thomas M. ... Burlington, VT
Higgins, Thomas M., III
Kansas City, MO
Higgins, Thomas P. ... Los Angeles, CA
Higgins, Thomas P. ... New York, NY
Higgins, Thomas P. ... New York, NY
Higgins, Thomas S. ... Newark, NJ
Higgins, Thomas W., Jr. ... Syracuse, NY
Higgins, Tim M. ... Spokane, WA
Higgins, Timothy J. ... Collingswood, NJ
Higgins, Timothy J. ... Albany, NY
Higgins, Timothy P. ... Manhasset, NY
Higgins, Tracy E. ... New York, NY
Higgins & Trippett ... New York, NY
Higgins, Trish ... Sacramento, CA
Higgins, Val M. ... Minneapolis, MN
Higgins, Valerie J. ... San Francisco, CA
Higgins & Walker ... Ringwood, NJ
Higgins, Warren J. ... Los Angeles, CA
Higgins, Wayne Phillip ... Los Angeles, CA
Higgins, William E. ... Nashville, TN
Higgins, William F. ... Springfield, MA
Higgins, William H. ... Charlotte, NC
Higgins, William J. ... Columbus, OH
Higgins, William K., Jr. ... Jasper, AL
Higgins, William M., Jr. ... Concord, MA
Higgins, William O. ... Columbia, SC
Higgins, William P. ... Omaha, NE
Higgins, William P., Jr. ... Shrewsbury, NJ
Higgins, William P., (P.A.) ... Wichita, KS
Higgins, William P., Sr. ... Ringwood, NJ
Higgins, William R. ... Claremore, OK
Higgins, William S. ... Sacramento, CA
Higgins, William T., V ... La Grange, TX
Higgins, Willis E. ... Palo Alto, CA
Higgins, Wm. ... San Francisco, CA
Higgins, Zachariah A. ... San Francisco, CA
Higgins-Goodell, Tristan E. ... San Diego, CA
Higginson, Carla J. ... Friday Harbor, WA
Higginson, Charles ... Department of State,
Foreign Service Officers (Overseas), GV
Higginson, Don ... San Diego, CA
Higginson Law Offices, A Professional Service Corporation ... Friday Harbor, WA
Higginson, Robert K. ... Dyer, IN
Higginson, Terence ... Lynbrook, NY
Higginson, Thomas L., Jr.
Washington, DC
Higginson, Timothy B. ... Chicago, IL
Higgs, A. James, Jr. ... Frankfort, KY
Higgs, Andrea Kelli ... Armonk, NY
Higgs, Arthur E. ... Sun City Center, FL
Higgs, Craig D. ... San Diego, CA
Higgs, David C. ... Minneapolis, MN
Higgs, David L. ... Peoria, IL
Higgs, David W. ... Englewood, CO
Higgs, Deane P. ... Somerset, KY
Higgs & Emerson ... Huntsville, AL
Higgs, F. Norman ... Bay City, MI
Higgs, Fletcher & Mack LLP
San Diego, CA
Higgs, George F. ... Memphis, TN
Higgs, J. Zach, Jr. ... Huntsville, AL
Higgs, John H. ... New York, NY
Higgs, Joseph W., Jr. ... Houston, TX
Higgs, Judith A. ... Sioux City, IA
Higgs Law Offices ... Bay City, MI
Higgs, Lynne A. ... San Francisco, CA
Higgs, Milton E. ... Bay City, MI
Higgs, Robert B. ... Houston, TX
Higgs, Sharon ... Stockton, CA
Higgs, Steven L. ... Roanoke, VA
Higgs, W. Otis, Jr. ... Memphis, TN
Higgs, W. Victor ... Wilmington, DE
Higgs, William L., Law Offices of
Mountaintop, PA
Wilkes-Barre, PA
Higgs-Caldwell, Jacqueline P.
United States Information Agency,
Office of the General Counsel, GV
High, Anne S. ... Palo Alto, CA
High, C. Allen ... Nashville, TN
High, Charles A., Jr. ... Nashville, TN
High, Charles C., Jr. ... El Paso, TX
High, Daniel J. ... Saipan, TT
High, David E. ... Nashville, TN
High, David R. ... Oklahoma City, OK
High, David R. ... Pittsburgh, PA
High, Diane Ayres ... Frankfort, KY
High, Don N. ... McKinney, TX
High, Elizabeth C. ... Raleigh, NC
High, Elizabeth T. ... Portland, ME
High, George B. ... Department of State,
Director General—Foreign Service, GV
High, Gilbert P., Jr. ... Norristown, PA
High, Harriett B. ... Edmond, OK
High, Hilary Coggins ... Tampa, FL
High, Jess F. ... Paradise, CA
High, John Alan ... Whiteville, NC
High, Kelly R. ... Tampa, FL
High, Kenneth M., Jr. ... Oxnard, CA
High, L. Sneed ... Fayetteville, NC
High, Lance W. ... Washington, DC

High, Larry A. ... Alden, IA
Iowa Falls, IA
High, Lee E. ... Reading, PA
High, Les ... San Diego, CA
High, Louis W. ... Spring Hill, FL
High, Mark R. ... Detroit, MI
High, Mary Katherine Y. ... Tacoma, WA
High, Michael E. ... Portland, ME
High, Michael K. ... Lincoln, NE
High, Patricia Leigh ... Oklahoma City, OK
High, Robert King, Jr. ... Tallahassee, FL
High, Stack, Lazenby, Palahach & Feiler
Coral Gables, FL
Melbourne, FL
Miami, FL
High, Suzanne I. ... Lisle, IL
High, Swartz, Roberts & Seidel, LLP
Norristown, PA
High, Thomas B., P.A. ... Twin Falls, ID
High, W. Hackney, Jr. ... Edenton, NC
High, William F. ... Overland Park, KS
Higham, Daniel ... Baltimore, MD
Higham, Douglas F. ... Laguna Niguel, CA
Higham, Frank C., Jr. ... Lafayette, CA
Higham, Frederick A., Jr.
St. Petersburg, FL
Higham, Harold V. ... Tallman, NY
Higham, James G. ... Washington, DC
Higham, John R. ... Boston, MA
Higham, Kathy K. ... Honolulu, HI
Higham, McConnell & Dunning LLP
Laguna Niguel, CA
Higham, Robert W. ... Akron, OH
Higham, Terry Lee ... Los Angeles, CA
Highberger, Dennis J. ... Lawrence, KS
Highberger, William F. ... Los Angeles, CA
Highcove, W. Dean ... Baltimore, MD
Highet, David W. ... Franklin Lakes, NJ
Highet, Keith ... Washington, DC
Highfield, Duke R. ... Charleston, SC
Highfield, James H. ... New Castle, KY
Highfield, Michael D. ... Ann Arbor, MI
Highfield, Robert E. ... Indianapolis, IN
Highfield, Susan J. ... Wilmington, DE
Highgas, William, Jr. ... Woburn, MA
Highland, Cecil B., Jr. ... Clarksburg, WV
Highland, Gary J. ... Newport Beach, CA
Highland, John N. ... Southfield, MI
Highland Law Corporation
Newport Beach, CA
Highland, Michael G. ... Bonner Springs, KS
Highland, William D. ... Ithaca, NY
Highland & Zanetti ... Southfield, MI
Highlander, Christie G. ... Belleville, IL
Highlander, Reid S. ... St. Louis, MO
Highlander, Steven L. ... Austin, TX
Highman, Bruce J. ... San Francisco, CA
Highman, David R. ... Irvine, CA
Highman, Eric M. ... Cleveland, OH
Highman, Fuller, Brown & Corrado, LLP
Irvine, CA
Highman, Highman & Ball, Law Offices of
San Francisco, CA
Highman, Louis A. ... San Francisco, CA
Highmark, Louis A., Jr.
West Hartford, CT
High-McAuley, Susan R. ... Nashville, TN
Highnote, Gregory T. ... San Diego, CA
Highsaw, Mahoney & Clarke, P.C.
Washington, DC
Highsaw, Robert ... Midwest City, OK
Highsmith, Anne Marie ... Jacksonville, FL
Highsmith, David J. ... Hagåtña, GU
Highsmith, Eric Paul ... Irvine, CA
Highsmith, Eugene ... Brunswick, GA
Highsmith & Highsmith ... Baxley, GA
Highsmith, James A. ... Fairfield, CA
Highsmith, J. C., Jr. ... Gainesville, GA
Highsmith, John H. ... Fort Worth, TX
Highsmith, Mose L. ... Waynesville, NC
Highsmith, Newell L. ... Department of State, Office of the Legal Adviser, GV
Highsmith, Norwood H. ... Dalton, GA
Highsmith, Robert E. ... Key West, FL
Highsmith, Robert M. ... Tishomingo, OK
Highsmith, Robert S. ... Baxley, GA
Highsmith, Robert S., Jr. ... Atlanta, GA
Highsmith, Shelby ... Miami, FL
Highsmith, Teresa L. ... Alameda, CA
Highstreet, Marcelle C. ... New Orleans, LA
Hight, B. Boyd ... Los Angeles, CA
Hight, Bob T. ... Torrance, CA
Hight, Brenda Neel ... Dallas, TX
Hight, Charles E. ... Harrisonville, MO
Hight, Clint ... Greenfield, IA
Hight, Clint, P.C. ... Greenfield, IA
Hight, C. T." Rusty " ... Liberty, TX
Hight, David H. ... Oakbrook Terrace, IL
Hight, Faulkner & Ross ... Henderson, NC
Hight Green & Yalowitz ... Seattle, WA
Hight, Henry W., Jr. ... Henderson, NC
Hight and Hight, A Professional Corporation
Dallas, TX
Hight, James S. ... Cincinnati, OH
Hight, Robert S. ... Henderson, NC
Hight, Steven E. ... Louisburg, NC
Hight, Steven E., P.A. ... Louisburg, NC
Hight, Thomas B. ... Bloomfield, NJ
Hight, Thomas H., Jr. ... Dallas, TX
Hight, Thomas H., Sr. ... Dallas, TX
Hight, Tony H., (P.C.) ... Union City, GA
Hight, William P. ... Seattle, WA
Hightman, Carrie Jankauer ... Chicago, IL
Hightower, A. Rick ... Austin, TX
Hightower, Alexandra M. ... Raleigh, NC
Hightower, Alison M. ... San Francisco, CA
Hightower, Anne ... Oakland, CA
Hightower, Anthony
Department of Education, Office for Civil Rights, GV
Hightower, Dale R. ... Miami, FL
Hightower, Daniel L. ... Ocala, FL
Hightower, Daniel L., P.A. ... Ocala, FL
Hightower, David E. ... Bloomington, IL
Hightower, Dennis J. ... Orlando, FL
Hightower and Doane ... Orlando, FL
Hightower, Doris A. ... Englewood Cliffs, NJ
Hightower, E. Avery, P.A. ... Wadesboro, NC
Hightower, Edwin E., Jr. ... Miami, FL
Hightower, Edwin L. ... Baton Rouge, LA
Hightower, Eric D. ... West Palm Beach, FL
Hightower, George W. ... Los Angeles, CA
Hightower, Hillary M.
Bowling Green, KY
Hightower, J. Vince ... Tulsa, OK
Hightower, Jack E. ... Austin, TX
Hightower, James A., Jr. ... Mobile, AL
Hightower, James W. ... Dallas, TX
Hightower, Janet R. ... Pittsburgh, PA
Hightower, Jeffrey W., Jr. ... Dallas, TX
Hightower, John J. ... Houston, TX
Hightower, Judith L. ... Department of Defense, Defense Legal Services Agency, GV
Hightower, Judith M. ... Seattle, WA
Hightower, Judson R. ... Department of Energy, Office of the General Counsel, GV
Hightower, Karen L. ... Salem, OR
Hightower, Lemmie O. ... Shreveport, LA
Hightower, M. Monty ... Lawton, OK
Hightower, Margaret Day ... Clearwater, FL
Hightower, Meredith C. ... Los Angeles, CA
Hightower, Paul R. ... Little Rock, AR
Hightower, R. Nathan ... Clearwater, FL
Hightower, Richard F., P.C. ... Houston, TX
Hightower, Rick W. ... Dallas, TX
Hightower, Robert S. ... Tallahassee, FL
Hightower & Rudd, P.A.
Fort Lauderdale, FL
Fort Myers, FL
Key West, FL
Miami, FL
Palm Beach, FL
West Palm Beach, FL
Hightower, Sharon L. ... San Jose, CA
Hightower, Stephen Philip ... New York, NY
Hightower, Thomas E. ... Irving, TX
Hightower, Thomas R., Jr. ... Lafayette, LA
Hightower, Thomas R., Jr., A Professional Law Corporation ... Lafayette, LA
Hightower, Timothy R. ... Houston, TX
Hightower, Wanda Morris ... Washington, DC
Hightower, Wesley M. ... Fort Worth, TX
Hightower, William G. ... Troy, AL
Higie, Jonathan G. ... Washington, PA
Higier, Gerald M. ... Coral Gables, FL
Higier, Thomas I. ... Dallas, TX
Higinbotham, George R. ... Fairmont, WV
Higinbotham & Higinbotham ... Fairmont, WV
Higinbotham, Jacquelyn J. ... Fort Morgan, CO
Higinbotham, James E., Jr. ... Uniontown, PA
Higinbotham, John C. ... Fairmont, WV
Higinbotham, Larry K., Jr. ... Pueblo, CO
Higinbothom, Kristal Louvera
Bel Air, MD
Higle, Charles K. ... Hawks, MI
Higley & Barfield, P.A.
Altamonte Springs, FL
Orlando, FL
Higley, David A. ... Altamonte Springs, FL
Higley, David O. ... San Francisco, CA
Higley, Donald S., II ... Greenville, NC
New Bern, NC
Higley, John K. ... Menomonie, WI
Higley, Laura C. ... Houston, TX
Higley, Norman W. ... Denver, CO
Higley, Roberta C. ... Canton, OH
Higley, Russell B. ... Cambridge, MA
Higley, William E., II ... Monroe, MI
Higley, William E., II ... Toledo, OH
Higman, Leslie Ross ... Memphis, TN
Higman, Victoria A. ... Rosslyn, VA
Higney, David C. ... Chattanooga, TN
Higson, Daniel A. ... Ventura, CA
Higson, John J. ... Cherry Hill, NJ
Philadelphia, PA
Higuchi, Edward James ... Los Angeles, CA
Higuchi & Higuchi ... Los Angeles, CA
Higuchi, Michelle D. ... Portland, OR
Higuchi, Peter T. ... Los Angeles, CA
Higuchi, Wiley H. ... Los Angeles, CA
Higuera, Albert A. ... Evanston, IL
Higuera, Joseph G. ... Tustin, CA
Higuera, Lori A. ... Phoenix, AZ
Higuera, Marie ... Seattle, WA
Higuel, Charisse S. ... Brooklyn, NY
Higuel, F. Eugene ... New York, NY
Hijii, Lori L. Y. ... Honolulu, HI
Hijjawi, Amy A. ... Chicago, IL
Hikel, Gordon ... Carrollton, TX
Hiken, Louis N. ... San Francisco, CA
Hiken Lapens, Cynthia E. ... Chicago, IL
Hikida, Marcy L. ... Bothell, WA
Hikida, Richard H. ... Los Angeles, CA
Hikoyeda, Allan T. ... San Jose, CA
Hila, John A. ... Avenel, NJ
Hilado, Alfred J. ... Orlando, FL
Hilaire, Elmina M. ... Westbury, NY
Hilal, Mark J. ... Petoskey, MI
Hiland, Douglas E. ... Indianapolis, IN
Hiland, Edward L. ... Nashville, TN
Hiland & Mathes ... Nashville, TN
Hiland, Tammy L. ... Reynoldsburg, OH
Hilario, Lisa Ann ... Santa Rosa, CA
Hilary, Jerold W. ... Portland, OR
Hilary, Jerold W. ... Tigard, OR
Hilary, Joyce ... Holmdel, NJ
Hilb, Carrie B. ... Chicago, IL
Hilbelink, Rose J. ... Lutz, FL
Hilber, Albert C. ... Newark, NJ
Hilberg, Frank C. ... New Castle, DE
Hilberg, Frank C., Jr. ... Wilmington, DE
Hilberg, Scott B. ... San Diego, CA
Hilberman, Joe W. ... Los Angeles, CA
Hilberman, Rebecca B. ... Washington, DC
Hilbers, L. F. ... Birmingham, AL
Hilbert, Anne M. ... Palo Alto, CA
Hilbert, Christopher ... New York, NY
Hilbert, Douglas R. ... Oklahoma City, OK
Hilbert, James R., Jr. ... Clearwater, FL
St. Petersburg, FL
Hilbert, John S. ... Buffalo, NY
Hilbert, John W., II ... Toledo, OH
Hilbert, John W., III ... Washington, DC
Hilbert, Lawler & Power ... Chicago, IL
Hilbert, Otis F. ... Minneapolis, MN
Hilbert, Otto K. ... Colorado Springs, CO
Hilbert, Otto K., II ... Denver, CO
Hilbert, Paul J. ... Houston, TX
Hilbert, Perry A. ... Greenbelt, MD
Hilbert, Peter L., Jr., (P.C.)
New Orleans, LA
Hilbert, Robert N. ... Chicago, IL
Hilberth, Kurt S. ... Hollywood, FL
Hilberth, Thomas R. ... Clifton, NJ
Hilbig, Steven C. ... San Antonio, TX
Hilboldt, James S., Jr. ... New York, NY
Hilboldt, Jas. S. ... Kalamazoo, MI
Hilborn, Andrea G. ... Philadelphia, PA
Hilborn, Craig E. ... Birmingham, MI
Hilborn, George A. ... Birmingham, MI
Hilborn, Harold B. ... Chicago, IL
Hilborn & Hilborn, P.C. ... Birmingham, MI
Hilborn, Michael G. ... Chicago, IL
Hilborne, Hawkin & Co. ... Orange, CA
Hilborne, Rebecca H. ... Tulsa, OK
Hilborne, Thomas G., Jr. ... Tulsa, OK
Hilborne & Weidman, A Professional Corporation ... Tulsa, OK
Hilbrecht & Associates, Chartered
Las Vegas, NV
Hilbrecht, Norman Ty ... Las Vegas, NV
Hilbrich, Cunningham & Schwerd
Highland, IN
Portage, IN
Hilbrich, John F. ... Highland, IN
Portage, IN
Hilbun, Ben F., Jr. ... Starkville, MS
Hilbun, Samuel A. ... Dublin, GA
Hilburg, Lore ... Woodland Hills, CA
Hilburger, Albert W. ... Fairfield, CT
Hilburn, Barbara A. ... Houston, TX
Hilburn, Calhoon, Harper, Pruniski & Calhoun, Ltd. ... Little Rock, AR
North Little Rock, AR
Hilburn, Carol Sabel ... Dallas, TX
Hilburn, Cary A. ... Dallas, TX
Hilburn, David A. ... Bossier City, LA
Hilburn, Elizabeth Brown ... Alexandria, LA
Hilburn, James L. ... Baton Rouge, LA
Hilburn, James V. ... Dublin, GA
Hilburn, Katherine B. ... Gainesville, FL
Hilburn, L. Breland ... Jackson, MS
Hilburn, O. Nathaniel, Jr. ... Memphis, TN
Hilburn, Patricia Gwynett ... Greenville, NC
Hilburn, Paula A. ... Atlanta, GA
Hilburn, Regina L. ... Columbus, OH
Hilburn, Sam ... Little Rock, AR
North Little Rock, AR
Hilburn, Shores & Sherer, L.L.P.
Houston, TX
Hilburn, Thomas L. ... Walnut Ridge, AR
Hilbush, Kathryn L. ... Media, PA
Hilby, Gerald M. ... Manhattan Beach, CA
Hilcoff, Stephan L., (P.C.) ... New Haven, CT
Hild, Guy M. ... Cincinnati, OH
Hild, Kimberly R. ... Philadelphia, PA
Hild, Robert Alex ... Knoxville, TN
Hildabrand, Karl R. ... Harrisburg, PA
Hildahl, George E. ... Bonita, CA
Hildalgo, Nilda López ... San Juan, PR
Hilde, Janet A. ... Quincy, CA
Hilde, Jean M. ... Seattle, WA
Hildebeidel, Kevin R. ... Fairfax, VA
Hildebran-Bachofen, Deborah L.
Raleigh, NC
Hildebrand, Brien F. ... Beaverton, OR
Hildebrand, Carl J. ... Casper, WY
Hildebrand, Carol ... Denver, CO
Hildebrand, Charles D. ... Green Valley, AZ
Hildebrand, Charles F. ... Hartford, CT
Hildebrand, Christa ... New York, NY
Hildebrand, Christopher S. ... Phoenix, AZ
Hildebrand, Dale ... Mt. Gilead, OH
Hildebrand, Daniel G. ... Chicago, IL
Hildebrand, Daniel W. ... Madison, WI
Hildebrand, Deana Marie ... Fort Myers, FL
Hildebrand, Donald D. ... Nashville, TN
Hildebrand, Eric W. ... Brooklyn, NY
Hildebrand, H. Joseph ... Oshkosh, WI
Hildebrand, Henry E., III ... Nashville, TN
Hildebrand, James A. ... Foster City, CA
Hildebrand, James C. ... Pasadena, CA
Hildebrand, John Allen ... Marietta, GA
Hildebrand, John P. ... Fairview Park, OH
Hildebrand, Julianne Caylor ... Austin, TX
Hildebrand, Kirsten L. ... Milwaukee, WI
Hildebrand, Martha L. ... Seattle, WA
Hildebrand, Mary J. ... Roseland, NJ
Hildebrand, Max B. ... Corunna, MI
Hildebrand, McLeod & Nelson, Inc.
Oakland, CA
Hildebrand, Merle H. ... New Castle, PA
Hildebrand, Micheel J. ... Sedona, AZ
Hildebrand, Sam K. ... Austin, TX
Hildebrand, Stanley W. ... Chattanooga, TN
Hildebrand, Thomas C., Jr.
Charleston, SC
Hildebrand, Thomas E., Jr. ... Granite City, IL
Hildebrand, Vicky R. ... Tulsa, OK
Hildebrand & Wick ... Mt. Gilead, OH
Hildebrand, William B. ... Westmont, NJ
Hildebrand, William B. ... White Plains, NY
Hildebrand, William, Jr. ... Maplewood, NJ
Hildebrand, Williams & Farrell
Fairview Park, OH
Hildebrandt, Ann ... Detroit, MI
Hildebrandt, Charles ... Washington, DC
Hildebrandt, Christian E.
Birmingham, MI
Hildebrandt, Christopher Todd
Pittsburgh, PA
Hildebrandt, Corbin P. ... Albuquerque, NM
Hildebrandt, David A. ... Washington, DC
Hildebrandt, Duane M. ... Lansing, MI
Hildebrandt, George F. ... Syracuse, NY
Hildebrandt, James E. ... New York, NY
Hildebrandt, Joseph P. ... Madison, WI
Hildebrandt, Karen C. ... Jersey City, NJ
Hildebrandt, Lee H., Jr. ... Cincinnati, OH
Hildebrandt, Stephanie C. ... New Orleans, LA
Hildebrandt, Stephen Austin
Potomac, MD
Hildebrandt, Thomas J. ... Cleveland, OH
Hildebrant, D. Renée ... Chickasha, OK
Oklahoma City, OK
Hildebrant, Jeffrey P. ... Washington, DC
Hildebrant, Kristin E. ... Columbus, OH
Hilden, Joseph F. ... Rockford, IL
Hilden, Julie C. ... Washington, DC
Hilden, Ronald L. ... Dickinson, ND
Hildenbrand, Christian G. ... New York, NY
Hildenbrand, Janice G. ... Southfield, MI
Hildenbrand, Leon M. ... Solvay, NY
Hildenbrand, Norma L. ... Pittsburgh, PA
Hildenbrand, Steven G. ... Baltimore, MD
Hilder, Elizabeth R.
Federal Trade Commission, Bureau of Competition, GV
Hilder, Frazer C.
Department of Transportation, Research and Special Programs Administration, GV
Hilder, Frazer F. ... Sarasota, FL
Hilder, Philip H. ... Houston, TX
Hilder, Philip H., & Associates, P.C.
Houston, TX
Hilder, Robert K. ... Salt Lake City, UT
Hilderbran, Gregory S. ... Charlotte, NC
Hilderbrand, Marcley J. ... Franklin, NY
Hilderbrandt, Randall D. ... Rochester, NY
Hilderley, Susan H. ... Los Angeles, CA
Hildes, Lawrence A. ... Berkeley, CA
Hilding Kipnis Lyon & Kelly
San Diego, CA
Hilding, Paul A. ... San Diego, CA
Hildner, Phillips B., II ... Fenton, MI
Hildner, Thomas V. ... Newark, NJ
Hildre, Donald F. ... San Diego, CA
Hildreth, Emmett F., Jr. ... Atmore, AL
Hildreth, Gary R. ... Pittsburgh, PA
Hildreth, Horace A., Jr. ... Portland, ME
Hildreth, Kent W. ... San Diego, CA
Hildreth, Linda A. ... Washington, DC
Hildreth, Mark D. ... Sarasota, FL
Hildreth, Martin A. ... Rancho Cucamonga, CA
Hildreth, Morris D. ... Coffeyville, KS
Hildreth, Phyllis D. K. ... Baltimore, MD
Hildreth, Richard ... Washington, DC
Arlington, VA
Hildreth, Richard G. ... Eugene, OR
Hildreth, Ronald B. ... New York, NY
Hildreth, Russell B. ... Sacramento, CA
Hildreth, Thomas W. ... Nashua, NH
Hildreth, Tiffany Gurkin ... Dallas, TX
Hildreth, William M. ... Burlington, IA
Hile, Christiane ... Camarillo, CA
Hile, Donald L. ... Newport Beach, CA
Hile, James S. ... Houston, TX
Hile, Michael W. ... Indianapolis, IN
Hile, Norman C. ... Sacramento, CA
Hile, Richard C. ... Austin, TX
Hile, Steven J. ... Albuquerque, NM
Hileman, Byron P., Jr. ... Winter Haven, FL
Hileman, Charles C., III ... Philadelphia, PA
Hileman, Charles E., Jr. ... Collinsville, IL
Hileman, Daniel W. ... Kalispell, MT
Hileman, Elizabeth L. ... Bethesda, MD
Hileman, Franklin L. ... Miami, FL
Hileman, L. Diana ... Boynton Beach, FL
Hileman, Mark Palmer ... Burlington, MA
Hileman, Nicole A. ... St. Louis, MO
Hileman, Peter M. ... Allentown, PA
Doylestown, PA
Stroudsburg, PA
Hileman, Richard G., Jr.
Cedar Rapids, IA
Hileman, William E., Jr. ... Eureka, MT
Hilen, Christopher A. ... San Francisco, CA
Hilen, Delney N. ... Seattle, WA
Hilen, Sterling L. ... Santa Rosa, CA
Hiler, Bonnie J. ... Brea, CA
Hiler, Bruce A. ... Washington, DC
Hiler, Gail K. ... Larchmont, NY
Hiler, James F. X. ... New York, NY
Hiler, Robert J. ... Kansas City, MO
Hiles, Bradley S. ... St. Louis, MO
Hiles, Gordon ... Atlanta, GA
Hiles, Patricia A. K. ... Santa Barbara, CA
Hiles, Paul D. ... Walnut Creek, CA
Hiles, Rowen & Klonoski, P.C. ... Atlanta, GA
Hiles, Russel D. ... Beverly Hills, CA

Hiley, Raymond D. ... **Pittsfield, MA**
Hilf, Allison ... New York, NY
Hilf, Michael G. ... New York, NY
Hilfer, Kyle-Beth ... **New York, NY**
Hilfer, Richard J. ... **Seattle, WA**
Hilferty, Dwan S. ... New Orleans, LA
Hilfiger, Roger ... Muskogee, OK
Hilfiker, Alan F. ... **Fort Myers, FL**
Naples, FL
Hilfiker, H. Max ... Malden, MO
Hilfiker-Ladd, Inga ... Malden, MO
Hilfinger, Steven H. ... **Detroit, MI**
Hilford, Bill ... Midland, TX
Hilford, Daniel A. ... San Luis Obispo, CA
Hilgard, Adaline ... San Francisco, CA
Hilgeman, John P. ... Dayton, OH
Hilgeman, John R. ... Riverhead, NY
Hilgeman, Mary ... **New York, NY**
Hilgemann, David A. ... Salem, OR
Hilgendorf, Edward C. ... South Bend, IN
Hilgendorf & Gottlieb ... Arlington Heights, IL
Hilgendorf & Hilgendorf ... South Bend, IN
Hilgendorf, John A. ... **Birmingham, MI**
Hilgendorf, Robert N. ... Santa Fe, NM
Hilgendorf, Sean Patrick ... South Bend, IN
Hilgendorff, David N. ... Mattituck, NY
Hilgendorff, Hugo A., III
Florham Park, NJ
Morristown, NJ
Hilgendorff, Hugo A., IV ... **Parsippany, NJ**
Hilgendorff, Peter B. ... **Florham Park, NJ**
Morristown, NJ
Hilgendorff, Peter B., Jr. ... Sparta, NJ
Hilgendorff, Robert F. ... Fairfield, CT
Hilger, Fred ... Vista, CA
Hilger, Jeff Garcia ... **Los Angeles, CA**
Hilger, Stephen A. ... **Grand Rapids, MI**
Hilgers, David W. ... **Austin, TX**
Hilgers, Gerri J. ... New Brighton, MN
Hilgers, Gregory M. ... Broomfield, CO
Hilgers, Mike ... Arvada, CO
Hilgers, Shauna L. ... Arvada, CO
Hilgers, Stephen A. ... McPherson, KS
Hilgers & Watkins, A Professional Corporation ... **Austin, TX**
Bastrop, TX
Burnet, TX
Dripping Springs, TX
Georgetown, TX
Lockhart, TX
Round Rock, TX
San Marcos, TX
Hilgers, William B. ... **Austin, TX**
Hilicki, Michael S. ... **Chicago, IL**
Hilicus-Pellegrino, Valerie J. ... Seattle, WA
Hilinski, Chester C. ... **Philadelphia, PA**
Hilke, Wallace G. ... **Minneapolis, MN**
Hilker, Anne K. ... **New York, NY**
Hilker, Samuel R. ... Dayton, OH
Hilker, Stephen E. ... Palatka, FL
Hilker, Stephen E., P.A. ... Palatka, FL
Hilkert, David W. ... **Akron, OH**
Hilkert, Douglas L. ... **Clearwater, FL**
Hilkert, Douglas L., P.A. ... **Clearwater, FL**
Hilkert, Jennifer R. ... **Cleveland, OH**
Hilkert, Mark ... **Akron, OH**
Hilkey, Sigrid R. ... Palm Springs, CA
Hilko, Paul A. ... **Pittsburgh, PA**
Hilkowitz, Steve B. ... Philadelphia, PA
Hill, A. Edward ... **Binghamton, NY**
Hill, A. Karen ... Washington, DC
Hill, Alan D. ... Englewood, OH
Hill, Alan G. ... **Louisville, CO**
Hill, Albert K. ... Buffalo, NY
Hill, Alden V. ... **Fort Collins, CO**
Hill, Alexander D. ... Seattle, WA
Hill, Alfred ... New York, NY
Hill, Alfred J. ... **Woodbridge, NJ**
Hill, Alison M. ... Palo Alto, CA
Hill, Allan D. ... San Francisco, CA
Hill, Allen Edward ... **Atlanta, GA**
Hill, Alyce E. ... **High Point, NC**
Hill, Amanda (Amy) K. ... **Tampa, FL**
Hill, André Robert ... Walnut Creek, CA
Hill, Andrew J., III ... **Athens, GA**
Hill, Andrew J., Jr. ... Lavonia, GA
Hill, Angela J. ... Madera, CA
Hill, Ann L. ... San Diego, CA
Hill, Anne Marie ... **Boston, MA**
Hill, Anne Pendergrass ... Portland, OR
Hill, Anthony J. ... Pasadena, CA
Hill, Antonia K. ... San Francisco, CA
Hill, Antonia R. ... Philadelphia, PA
Hill, Arden L. ... Elizabethton, TN
Hill, Arthur F., Jr. ... Chicago, IL
Hill, Arthur L., IV
Research Triangle Park, NC
Hill, Arthur S. ... Littleton, MA
Hill, Arthur W. ... Brooklyn, NY
Hill & Associates ... **Morgantown, WV**
Hill, B. Harvey, Jr. ... **Atlanta, GA**
Hill, Barbara J. ... Washington, DC
Hill, Barbara J. ... Weston, MA
Hill, Barbara Joy ... Hauppauge, NY
Hill & Barlow, A Professional Corporation
Boston, MA
Hill, Barry M. ... **Wheeling, WV**
Hill, Barry R. ... Syracuse, NY
Hill & Bartlett, A Professional Corporation
Austin, TX
Hill, Beam-Ward & Kruse, LLC
Overland Park, KS
Kansas City, MO
Hill, Beatty, Butcher & Gallagher
Fort Worth, TX
Hill, Belinda J. ... Houston, TX
Hill, Ben L., III ... Jasper, TN
Hill, Benjamin H., III ... **Tampa, FL**
Hill, Benjamin H., IV ... **Tampa, FL**
Hill, Betts & Nash LLP ... **Washington, DC**
Newark, NJ
New York, NY
Hill, Beverly Jones ... Gainesville, FL
Hill & Beyer, A Professional Law Corporation ... **Abbeville, LA**
Crowley, LA
Lafayette, LA
New Iberia, LA
Opelousas, LA
Hill, Bill J. ... Midland, TX
Hill, Billy, & Associates ... Schaumburg, IL
Strongsville, OH
Dallas, TX
Hill, Billy B., Jr. ... Schaumburg, IL
Strongsville, OH
Dallas, TX
Hill, Blaise L. ... Alexandria, LA
Hill and Bleiberg ... **Atlanta, GA**
Hill, Bobbye C. ... Wheeler, TX
Hill, Boren, Drew & Martindale
Jackson, TN
Hill, Boyd L. ... **Los Angeles, CA**
Hill, Brad R. ... Fresno, CA
Hill, Bradley D. ... Denver, CO
Hill, Bradley J. ... Arroyo Grande, CA
Hill, Brent ... **Carrollton, TX**
Hill, Brett M. ... **Fort Collins, CO**
Hill, Brian ... Miami, FL
Hill, Brian A. ... Folsom, CA
Hill, Brian A. ... **Washington, DC**
Hill, Brian D. ... **Orlando, FL**
Hill, Brian E. ... Santa Barbara, CA
Hill, Brian R. ... **Santa Ana, CA**
Hill, Brockton D. ... Baldwin Park, CA
Hill, Bruce C. ... Woodland Hills, CA
Hill, Bruce C. ... **Baltimore, MD**
Hill, Bruce H. C. ... **San Antonio, TX**
Hill, Bryan ... **Atlanta, GA**
Hill, Bryan W. ... Bedford, TX
Hill, Bryce A. ... Tulsa, OK
Hill, C. Dennis ... Essex Junction, VT
Montpelier, VT
Hill, C. Dickinson ... **Los Angeles, CA**
Hill, C. Michael ... **Lafayette, LA**
Hill & Calk, P.C. ... **Longview, TX**
Hill, Cameron S. ... **Chattanooga, TN**
Hill, Camille A. ... Santa Ana, CA
Hill, Camille Wolnik ... **Syracuse, NY**
Hill, Candace Groot ... Louisville, KY
Hill, Carey L. ... **Orlando, FL**
Hill, Carl D. ... Sacramento, CA
Hill, Carl D. ... Pittsburgh, PA
Hill, Carol L. ... Manassas, VA
Hill, Carolyn Ann ... **Melville, NY**
Hill, Carolyn DuPree ... Clearwater, FL
Hill, Carolyn Gregg ... **Oklahoma City, OK**
Hill & Cartozian, A Professional Corporation
Folsom, CA
Hill, Cassandra L. ... **Houston, TX**
Hill, Caton N., Jr. ... Philippi, WV
Hill, Cecil J. ... **Brevard, NC**
Hill, Celeste A. ... **Chicago, IL**
Hill & Chaplin ... Ravenel, SC
Hill, Charles B., II ... Kingston, TN
Hill, Charles D. ... Delhi, NY
Hill, Charles E. ... Irvine, CA
Hill, Charles E. ... Washington, DC
Hill, Charles E. ... Wichita, KS
Hill, Charles E. ... **Columbia, SC**
Hill, Charles L. ... Norman, OK
Hill, Charles M., III ... Medley, FL
Hill, Charles W. ... Albany, GA
Hill, Charles W. ... **Memphis, TN**
Hill, Cheryl L. ... **Marquette, MI**
Hill, Cheryl R. Brown ... **Philadelphia, PA**
Hill, Christie A. ... McLean, VA
Hill, Christina ... **Dearborn, MI**
Hill, Christina L. ... Los Angeles, CA
Hill, Christopher ... Madison, CT
Hill, Christopher D. ... Tempe, AZ
Hill, Christopher R. ... Chicago, IL
Hill, Christopher S. ... Porterville, CA
Hill, Christopher T. ... **Orlando, FL**
Hill, Christopher T. ... Portland, OR
Hill, Cindy Ellen, Law Office of
Middlebury, VT
Hill, Cindy Lee ... Sacramento, CA
Hill, Claire A. ... Arlington, VA
Hill, Claire V. ... Fayetteville, NC
Hill, Claralyn Martin ... Provo, UT
Hill, Clark Dickinson ... **Los Angeles, CA**
Hill, Clyde ... Yates Center, KS
Hill, Clyde Vernon, Jr. ... Grenada, MS
Hill, Constance A. ... Cincinnati, OH
Hill, Craig R. ... Tulsa, OK
Hill, Curtis T., Jr. ... Elkhart, IN
Hill, Cynthia J. ... Austin, TX
Hill, Cynthia L. ... **Fort Worth, TX**
Hill, Cynthia L. ... Houston, TX
Hill, Cynthia P. ... **Corpus Christi, TX**
Hill, D. David ... **Chicago, IL**
Hill, D. Frank, III ... Shepherdstown, WV
Hill, D. Garrison ... **Greenville, SC**
Hill, Daina H. ... New York, NY
Hill, Daniel A. ... Salem, OR
Hill, Daniel B. ... **Durham, NC**
Hill, Daniel D. ... Austin, TX
Hill, Daniel J. ... Hermiston, OR
Hill, Darla ... **Houston, TX**
Hill, Darrell C. ... St. Paul, MN
Hill, Darrell R. ... **Lehigh Acres, FL**
Hill, David ... Newport, TN
Hill, David ... **Henderson, TX**
Hill, David A. ... Eugene, OR
Hill, David A. ... Sioux Falls, SD
Hill, David A. ... **Arlington, VA**
Hill, David A., Jr. ... **Hartford, CT**
Hill, David C. ... Brainerd, MN
Hill, David C. ... Dallas, TX
Hill, David E. ... **Tucson, AZ**
Hill, David E. ... Ocala, FL
Hill, David G. ... **Boulder, CO**
Hill, David G. ... **Hartford, CT**
Hill, David G. ... Oxford, MS
Hill, David G. ... **Cleveland, OH**
Hill, David H. ... Arlington, VA
Hill, David J. ... **Washington, DC**
Hill, David J. ... **Chattanooga, TN**
Hill, David J. ... Nashville, TN
Hill, David K. ... Barrington, IL
Hill, David K. ... Eugene, OR
Hill, David K. ... **Milwaukee, WI**
Hill, David L. ... **Washington, DC**
Hill, David L. ... Bloomington, IL
Hill, David L. ... Philadelphia, PA
Hill, David L. ... **Knoxville, TN**
Hill, David L. ... Hurricane, WV
Hill, David M. ... **Summit, NJ**
New York, NY
Hill, David P. ... **Orlando, FL**
Hill, David R. ... **Washington, DC**
Hill, David R. ... Department of Defense, Defense Legal Services Agency, GV
Hill, David R. ... **Chicago, IL**
Hill, David W. ... **Washington, DC**
Hill, David W. ... **Memphis, TN**
Hill, Dayne W. ... **Paramus, NJ**
Hill, D.B. ... **Darien, CT**
Hill, Dean B. ... Alexandria, VA
Hill, Dean G. ... Washington, DC
Hill, Deanna D. ... Austin, TX
Hill, Deborah Fish ... **Chicago, IL**
Hill, Debra A. ... **Phoenix, AZ**
Hill, Deirdre Hughes ... Los Angeles, CA
Hill, Denise A. ... Omaha, NE
Hill, Denise Adams ... **Chevy Chase, MD**
Hill, Denise Matthess ... Madison, AL
Hill, Dennis D. ... **Los Angeles, CA**
Hill, Dennis H. ... **Rapid City, SD**
Hill, Devon Wm. ... **Washington, DC**
Hill, Devoron K. ... Galt, CA
Hill, Diane E. ... **Lakeland, FL**
Hill, Dianne L. ... Monroe, LA
Hill, Donal M. ... San Diego, CA
Hill, Donald Cavin ... **Reno, NV**
Hill, Donald E. ... **Wichita, KS**
Hill, Donald E. ... **Dallas, TX**
Hill, Donald Kenneth ... Houston, TX
Hill, Donald M., Jr. ... **Charlotte, NC**
Hill, Donald P. ... Jackson, MS
Hill, Donald W. ... Warren, OH
Hill, Donald W. ... Dallas, TX
Hill, Donna L. ... Lido Beach, NY
Hill, Donna M. ... **Philadelphia, PA**
Hill, Dorothy ... **New York, NY**
Hill, Douglas A. ... **Marietta, GA**
Hill, Douglas J. ... **Indianapolis, IN**
Hill, Douglas P. ... Meredith, NH
Hill, Douglas Roman ... **Reno, NV**
Hill, Ducloux, Carnes & Clark
Austin, TX
Hill, E. Ashton, III ... Mobile, AL
Hill, E. Brent ... **Nashville, TN**
Hill, E. Franklin, Jr. ... Fort Wayne, IN
Hill, Earl C. ... San Antonio, TX
Hill, Earl C., Jr. ... Department of Defense, Defense Legal Services Agency, GV
Hill, Earl M. ... **Reno, NV**
Hill, Earl W. ... Britt, IA
Hill, Edward A. ... **Tampa, FL**
Hill, Edward C., Jr. ... Tallahassee, FL
Hill, Edward E. ... Renton, WA
Hill, Edward H. ... **Amarillo, TX**
Hill, Edward J. ... Tallahassee, FL
Hill, Edward J. ... **Portland, OR**
Hill, Edward R., Jr. ... **Boston, MA**
Hill, Edward S. ... **Hartford, CT**
Hill, Edwards, Edwards & Adkison, L.L.C.
Carbondale, CO
Hill, Edwin V., Jr. ... Mayfield Heights, OH
Hill, Elaine E. ... **Palm Springs, CA**
Hill, Elaine M. ... Miami, FL
Hill, Eleanor J. ... **Washington, DC**
Hill, Elizabeth ... Leawood, KS
Hill, Elizabeth ... **Dallas, TX**
Hill, Elizabeth A. ... Lexington, KY
Hill, Elizabeth A. ... Brooklyn, NY
Hill, Elizabeth Holden ... Minneapolis, MN
Hill, Ellis, Hill and Shea ... Sherman, TX
Hill, Elton D.
Board of Governors Of The Federal Reserve System, Division of Banking Supervision and Regulation, GV
Hill, Eric S.
Commodity Futures Trading Commission, Division of Enforcement, GV
Hill, Ethel M.B. ... Baltimore, MD
Hill, Eva H. ... **Baltimore, MD**
Columbia, MD
Hill, Evans, Duncan, Jordan & Davis
Greensboro, NC
High Point, NC
Hill, Evelyn I. ... Mountainburg, AR
Hill, Evelyn I., P.A. ... Mountainburg, AR
Hill, Evelyn W. ... Raleigh, NC
Hill, Farrer & Burrill LLP
Los Angeles, CA
Hill, Fiona F. ... Oak Ridge, TN
Hill & Fischer, P.C. ... Syracuse, NY
Hill, Floyd S. ... Fresno, CA
Hill, Foley, Stone & Miles
Havre de Grace, MD
Towson, MD
Hill, Forest D. ... Long Beach, CA
Hill, Frank ... **Chicago, IL**
Arlington, TX
Hill, Frank B. ... Muscatine, IA
Hill, Frank D. ... **Oklahoma City, OK**
Hill, Frank F. ... San Antonio, TX
Hill, Frank L. ... **Austin, TX**
Hill, Frank T., The Law Office of
Lakewood, CO
Hill, Frank Y., Jr. ... Boerne, TX
Hill, Frederick L. R. ... Boynton Beach, FL
Hill, Frederick W. ... **Los Angeles, CA**
Hill, Frederick Wells ... Pittsburgh, PA
Hill, Fulwider, McDowell, Funk & Matthews, Professional Corporation
Indianapolis, IN
Hill, G. Bruce ... **Orlando, FL**
Hill, G. Edison ... Asheville, NC
Hill, G. Richard ... **Salt Lake City, UT**
Hill, G. Richard ... **Seattle, WA**
Hill, G. Russell ... **El Paso, TX**
Hill, Gadi G. ... **New York, NY**
Yorktown Heights, NY
Hill, Gary ... **Atlanta, GA**
Hill, Gary D. ... Oregon City, OR
Hill, Gary J. ... **Santa Barbara, CA**
Hill, Gary J. ... **El Paso, TX**
Hill, Gary J., P.C. ... **Santa Barbara, CA**
Hill, Gary L. ... Roseburg, OR
Hill, Gary L. ... Provo, UT
Hill, Gavin E. ... **Dallas, TX**
Hill, George E. ... Storrs, CT
Hill, George E. ... Washington, DC
Hill, George J., Jr. ... Dunwoody, GA
Hill, George M. ... Phoenix, AZ
Hill, George T. ... **Mount Olive, NJ**
Hill, George W. ... Parkersburg, WV
Hill, Gerald N. ... Sonoma, CA
Hill, Gerald P. ... Bartow, FL
Hill Gilstrap, A Professional Corporation
Arlington, TX
Dallas, TX
Fort Worth, TX
Hill Gilstrap Adams & Graham
Austin, TX
Hill Gilstrap & Balson, A Professional Corporation ... **Chicago, IL**
Hill Gilstrap Perkins & Warner, A Professional Corporation
Little Rock, AR
Hill, Glowacki, Jaeger, Reiley, Zimmer & Hughes ... **Madison, WI**
Hill, Greg T. ... **Torrance, CA**
Hill, Gregg ... **Hillsboro, TX**
Hill, Gregory B. ... Hartford, KY
Hill, Gregory C. ... **Houston, TX**
Hill, Gregory M. ... Princeton, NJ
Hill, Gregory Q. ... **Decatur, IL**
Hill, Gregory S. ... Leawood, KS
Hill, Gregory S. ... Philadelphia, PA
Hill, Guy ... Stuart, FL
Hill, Guy H. ... **Flint, MI**
Hill, Guy H. ... Trenton, NJ
Hill, H. Allen, Jr. ... **Austin, TX**
Hill, H. Daniel, III ... North East, PA
Hill, H. Edgar ... Louisville, KY
Hill, H. Roberson, Law Offices Of
Anchorage, AK
Hill, Harold N., Jr. ... Atlanta, GA
Hill, Harriet Jo ... Dallas, TX
Hill, Harry G. ... **Garden City, NY**
Hill, Harry R., Jr. ... **Trenton, NJ**
Hill, Harry V. ... **Madison, WI**
Hill, Hassel, Jr. ... Glendale, CA
Hill, Hazel C. ... Woodstock, IL
Hill, Henderson ... **Charlotte, NC**
Hill, Henry ... **Point Richmond, CA**
Hill, Henry ... **San Francisco, CA**
Hill, Henry A., Jr. ... **Princeton, NJ**
Hill, Herbert ... Aurora, IL
Hill, Herbert D. ... Evanston, IL
Hill, Herbert M. ... Orlando, FL
Hill, Herbert M., P.A. ... Orlando, FL
Hill, Herbert W. ... San Antonio, TX
Hill & Hill ... Bloomsburg, PA
Hill & Hill ... **Houston, TX**
Hill & Hill ... **Longview, TX**
Hill & Hill, A Professional Corporation
Fort Collins, CO
Hill, Hill, Carter, Franco, Cole & Black, P.C.
Greenville, AL
Hayneville, AL
Luverne, AL
Montgomery, AL
Prattville, AL
Troy, AL
Tuskegee, AL
Union Springs, AL
Wetumpka, AL
Hill, Hill & Grundman ... Madison, CT
Hill & Hill, P.C. ... Mobile, AL
Hill, Hollister (Holly) Anne ... **Atlanta, GA**
Hill, Horace E. ... Daytona Beach, FL
Hill & Hovis ... High Point, NC
Hill, Hoyt W. ... **Opelika, AL**
Hill, Hugh Ezra ... **Durant, OK**
Hill, Hugh Ezra, P.C., Law Offices of
Durant, OK
Hill, Hugh F., III ... Bethesda, MD
Hill, Hugo E. ... Compton, CA
Hill and Hunn, LLP ... **Fort Worth, TX**
Hill, Ira R. ... Pittsburgh, PA
Hill, Irene L. ... Washington, DC
Hill, J. Brian ... Gladstone, MO
Hill, J. Carey ... Ellijay, GA
Hill, J. Douglas ... Matthews, NC
Hill, J. Drewry ... **Heathsville, VA**
Hill, J. Jason ... **San Diego, CA**

Hill, J. Jeptha ... Mobile, AL
Hill, J. Kermit ... Sherman, TX
Hill, J. Marcus ... Houston, TX
Hill, J. Reginald ... Nashville, TN
Hill, J. Stanley ... Hutchinson, KS
Hill, J. Suzanne ... Bakersfield, CA
Hill, Jack ... San Francisco, CA
Hill, Jackie L. ... Virginia Beach, VA
Hill, Jackie L., Jr. ... Oklahoma City, OK
Hill, James A., Jr. ... Salem, OR
Hill, James C. ... Fernandina Beach, FL
Hill, James D. ... Cambridge, MA
Hill, James D. ... Cincinnati, OH
Hill, James E., Jr. ... Leeds, AL
Hill, James E., Jr. ... Whiteville, NC
Hill, James F. ... Seguin, TX
Hill, James Gregory ... New York, NY
Hill, James H. ... Madison, TN
Hill, James J. ... Chicago, IL
Hill, James J., III ... Chattanooga, TN
Hill, James J., Jr. ... New York, NY
Hill, James K. ... Circleville, OH
Hill, James M. ... Beavercreek, OH
Dayton, OH
Hill, James M. ... Cleveland, OH
Hill, James M., Jr. ... Austin, TX
San Antonio, TX
Hill, James P. ... San Diego, CA
Hill, James P. ... United States Senate, Senatorial Assistants, GV
Hill, James R. ... Durham, NC
Hill, James S., P.C. ... Bismarck, ND
Hill, James Scott ... Princeton, NJ
Hill, James T. ... Trenton, NJ
Hill, James T. ... Durham, NC
Hill, James V. ... Robinson, IL
Hill, James W. ... Phoenix, AZ
Hill, James W. ... Newport Beach, CA
Hill, James W. ... Denver, CO
Hill, James W. ... Racine, WI
Hill, James W., Ltd. ... Phoenix, AZ
Hill, James Wells, III ... Elizabethtown, NC
Hill, Janet E. ... Athens, GA
Decatur, GA
Hill, Janet K. ... Littleton, CO
Hill, Janet L. ... Tacoma, WA
Hill, Janet R. ... Lima, OH
Hill, Janile S. ... Chicago, IL
Hill, Jay ... Anna Maria, FL
Hill, Jay D. ... Albuquerque, NM
Hill, Jean A. ... New Orleans, LA
Hill, Jean P. ... New York, NY
Hill, Jefferson B.
Executive Office Of The President, Office of Management and Budget, GV
Hill, Jeffrey A. ... New York, NY
Hill, Jeffrey B. ... Kansas City, MO
Hill, Jeffrey H. ... Valencia, CA
Hill, Jeffrey L. ... Aurora, CO
Hill, Jeffrey L. ... Albany, NY
Hill, Jeffrey L. ... Nashville, TN
Hill, Jeffrey L., P.C., Law Offices of
Aurora, CO
Hill, Jeffrey R. ... Palm Bay, FL
Hill, Jeffrey R. ... Austin, TX
Hill, Jeffrey V. ... Portland, OR
Hill, Jeffrey W. ... San Diego, CA
Hill, Jeffrey W. ... New London, CT
Hill, Jennifer L. ... Minneapolis, MN
Hill, Jep, Law Offices of ... Austin, TX
Hill, Jeptha P. ... Austin, TX
Hill, Jerald L. ... Kansas City, MO
Hill, Jerilyn Bowie ... St. Louis, MO
Hill, Jerome D. ... Detroit, MI
Hill, Jerome, IV ... Austin, TX
Hill, Jerri ... Denver, CO
Hill, Jerry C. ... Washington, DC
Hill, Jerry G. ... Houston, TX
Hill, Jerry W. ... Longview, TX
Hill, Jesse David ... St. Louis, MO
Hill, Jesse Landis ... Aptos, CA
Hill, Jesse W. ... Atlanta, GA
Hill, Jimmy L. ... Harrisonburg, VA
Staunton, VA
Winchester, VA
Hill, Joan G. ... Charleston, WV
Hill, John A. ... Columbia, SC
Hill, John, & Associates A Prof. Corp.
Glendale, CA
Irvine, CA
Los Angeles, CA
San Bernardino, CA
Torrance, CA
Ventura, CA
Hill, John D. ... Sherman, TX
Hill, John E. ... Atlanta, GA
Hill, John E., Law Offices of ... Oakland, CA
San Francisco, CA
Hill, John F. ... Akron, OH
Hill, John G. ... Fort Worth, TX
Hill, John G., Jr. ... Houston, TX
Hill, John G., Jr. ... Milwaukee, WI
Hill, John G., Jr., P.C. ... Houston, TX
Hill, John Graham ... Houston, TX
Hill, John H. ... Pittsburgh, PA
Hill, John H., III ... Tacoma, WA
Hill, John I. ... Waynesboro, VA
Hill, John J., Jr. ... Jersey City, NJ
Hill, John L. ... Annapolis, MD
Hill, John L., Jr. ... Houston, TX
Hill, John M. ... Dallas, TX
Hill, John M. ... Charleston, WV
Hill, John R. ... Chicago, IL
Hill, John R. ... Minneapolis, MN
Hill, John R. ... Allentown, PA
Hill, John R., Jr. ... Gunnison, CO
Hill, John S. ... Columbus, MS
Tupelo, MS

Hill, John S. ... Fallon, NV
Hill, John S. ... Portland, OR
Hill, John T. ... Roseville, CA
Hill, John Torkel ... Sacramento, CA
Hill, John W. ... Torrance, CA
Hill, John W. ... Worthington, OH
Hill, John W. ... Portland, OR
Hill, John W., Jr. ... Worthington, OH
Hill, Johnson & Schmutz, L.C. ... Provo, UT
Hill, Jon Hurd ... Corinth, MS
Hill, Jonathan ... Chicago, IL
Hill, Jonathan B. ... Washington, DC
Hill, Jonathan Bruce ... Houston, TX
Hill, Jonathan E. ... Morristown, NJ
Hill, Jonel C. ... Pasadena, CA
Hill, Jon-Jamison ... Los Angeles, CA
Hill, Joseph A. ... Madison, CT
Hill, Joseph C. ... New York, NY
Hill, Joseph D. ... Kingston, NY
Hill, Joseph H. ... Oak Brook, IL
Hill, Joseph M. ... Lebanon, PA
Hill, Joseph M. ... Houston, TX
Hill, Joseph W. ... Hyattsville, MD
Upper Marlboro, MD
Hill, J. T. ... Jackson, MS
Hill, Judith C. Moss ... Tyler, TX
Hill, Judith D. ... Las Vegas, NV
Hill, Julia A. ... Salinas, CA
Hill, Julie K. ... Fresno, CA
Hill, Karl N., Jr. ... Greensboro, NC
Hill, Kate ... Santa Rosa, CA
Hill, Katharine G., Law Office of
Maryville, TN
Hill, Katherine W. ... Camden, SC
Hill, Kathryn E. ... Covington, LA
Hill, Kathryn J. ... Vero Beach, FL
Hill, Kaye A. ... Sterling Heights, MI
Hill, Keith E. ... San Francisco, CA
Hill, Keith T. ... Altamonte Springs, FL
Hill, Keith T. ... Gulfport, MS
Hill, Kelley B. ... Fort Worth, TX
Hill, Kelly K. ... Little Rock, AR
Hill, Kendall W. ... Bedford, TX
Hill, Kenneth A. ... Dallas, TX
Hill, Kenneth C. ... Fort Worth, TX
Hill, Kenneth E. ... Marshall, TX
Hill, Kenneth M. ... Wisconsin Rapids, WI
Hill, Kenneth S. ... Baton Rouge, LA
Hill, Kenton L. ... Chicago, IL
Hill, Kevin D. ... Ada, OH
Hill, Kevin E. ... Oklahoma City, OK
Hill, Kevin M. ... Hiawatha, KS
Hill, Kevin M. ... New York, NY
Hill, Kevin Tyler ... Tampa, FL
Hill, Kimberly A. ... Hollywood, FL
Hill & Knight ... Tulsa, OK
Hill, Kristen D. ... Hammond, IN
Hill, Kristie ... Indianapolis, IN
Hill, L. Elizabeth ... Irving, TX
Hill, Lance ... Doylestown, PA
Hill, Larry ... Pensacola, FL
Hill, Larry B. ... La Fayette, GA
Hill, Larry L. ... Redding, CA
Hill, Laurie Goodine ... Dallas, TX
Hill, Laurie L. ... Miami, FL
Hill Law Firm, The, Ltd. ... Chicago, IL
Hill Law Office ... Circleville, OH
Hill, Lawrence H. ... Albuquerque, NM
Hill, Lawrence M. ... New York, NY
Hill, Lawrence R. ... Littleton, CO
Hill, Leah Aileen ... New York, NY
Hill, Leah C. ... Des Moines, IA
Hill, Lee O. ... Charleston, WV
Hill, Lena S. ... Charleston, WV
Hill, Leo B. ... Orange Park, FL
Hill, Leo H. ... Greenville, SC
Hill, Leonard ... Boise, ID
Hill, LeRoy ... Belle Fourche, SD
Hill, Lester R. ... Melville, NY
Hill, Lewis H., III ... Tampa, FL
Hill, Linda G. ... Washington, DC
Hill, Linda M. ... St. Augustine, FL
Hill, Lisa Jo ... Gardendale, AL
Hill, Lloyd H. ... Milton, MA
Hill, Lonnie C. ... Lewisburg, PA
Hill, Lori H. ... Overland Park, KS
Hill, Louise L. ... Wilmington, DE
Hill, Luther L., Jr. ... Des Moines, IA
Hill, Lynda Motes ... Chattanooga, TN
Hill, Lynn Fisher ... Pittsburgh, PA
Hill, M. Joseph ... Glen Carbon, IL
Hill, M. King, III ... Towson, MD
Hill, M. King, Jr. ... Baltimore, MD
Hill, Marcus E. ... Durham, NC
Hill, Margaret A. ... Washington, DC
Hill, Margaret R. ... Berkeley, CA
Hill, Marguerite Coyne
Santa Fe Springs, CA
Hill, Marguerite J. ... Guntersville, AL
Hill, Marguerite J. ... Boston, MA
Hill, Marianne B. ... Albuquerque, NM
Hill, Marie E. ... Easton, MD
Hill, Mark C. ... Fort Worth, TX
Hill, Mark E. ... Vero Beach, FL
Hill, Mark J. ... Tavares, FL
Hill, Mark J., & Associates, P.C.
Moorestown, NJ
Philadelphia, PA
Hill, Mark L. ... Des Moines, IA
Hill, Mark S. ... Glendale, CA
Hill, Marlon Andrew ... Miami, FL
Hill, Marny Joell ... Oklahoma City, OK
Hill, Marshall C. ... Detroit, MI
Hill, Marta K. ... Houston, TX
Hill, Martha ... Little Rock, AR
Hill, Martin D. ... Dixon, IL
Hill, Mary Ammons ... San Francisco, CA
Hill, Mary Jane ... Sandusky, OH

Hill, Mary Liatti ... Indianapolis, IN
Hill, Mary Lou ... Raleigh, NC
Greenville, SC
Hill, Matthew E. ... Cape Girardeau, MO
Hill, Maureen A. ... Chicago, IL
Hill & McCready ... Buffalo, NY
Hill & McDonough ... Washington, DC
Hill, Megan Day ... Albuquerque, NM
Hill, Melinda J. ... Powell, OH
Hill, Melisande ... New York, NY
Hill, Melissa ... Los Angeles, CA
Hill, Melissa ... Raleigh, NC
Hill, Melissa C. ... Austin, TX
Hill, Melvin B., Jr. ... Athens, GA
Hill, Melvin L. ... Roanoke, VA
Hill, Michael C. ... Gulfport, MS
Hill, Michael D. ... Raleigh, NC
Hill, Michael E. ... Boston, MA
Hill, Michael Finbar ... Orange, CA
Hill, Michael H. ... Portland, ME
Hill, Michael J. ... Eureka, CA
Hill, Michael L. ... El Paso, TX
Hill, Michael L., Inc., P.C. ... El Paso, TX
Hill, Michael O. ... Washington, DC
Hill, Michael R. ... Milan, TN
Hill, Michael R. ... Nashville, TN
Hill, Michael W. ... New Orleans, LA
Hill, Mitchel A. ... New York, NY
Hill, Mitzi L. ... Atlanta, GA
Hill, Monroe T., Jr. ... Atlanta, GA
Hill, Morris G. ... San Diego, CA
Hill, Myron G., Jr. ... Washington, DC
Hill, Myron T., Jr. ... Greenville, NC
Hill, N. Eugene ... Sacramento, CA
Hill, Nadell ... Brighton, MA
Hill, Nancy C. ... Charleston, WV
Hill, Nancy P. ... New York, NY
Hill, Natasha B. ... Massena, NY
Hill, Nora J. ... Leesburg, FL
Hill, Norman E. ... Sacramento, CA
Hill, Odis R. ... Longview, TX
Hill, Oliver W. ... Richmond, VA
Hill, Owen D. ... Dallas, TX
Hill, P.C., Samuel Tyler, Law Offices of
Fort Lauderdale, FL
Hill, P. Jeffrey ... Bloomsburg, PA
Hill, Pamela A. ... Boston, MA
Hill, Pamela Gronauer ... Atlanta, GA
Hill & Parker, A Professional Corporation
Houston, TX
Hill, Patricia, & Associates ... Houston, TX
Hill, Patricia J. ... Boston, MA
Hill, Patricia J. ... Woodbury, NY
Hill, Patricia Jeanne ... Jacksonville, FL
Hill, Patricia Tolle ... Morgantown, WV
Hill, Paul ... Corpus Christi, TX
Hill, Paul C. ... Portsmouth, RI
Hill, Paul D. ... Atlanta, GA
Hill, Paul F. ... Tallahassee, FL
Hill, Paul F. ... Omaha, NE
Hill, Paul J. ... Newport, KY
Hill, Peter A. ... Southern Pines, NC
Hill, Peter G. ... Minneapolis, MN
Hill, Peter N. ... Orlando, FL
Hill, Peter R. ... Alpharetta, GA
Hill, Peter W. ... Oneonta, NY
Hill, Peterson, Carper, Bee & Deitzler, P.L.L.C. ... Charleston, WV
Hill, Philip ... Lansing, IL
Hill, Philip B. ... New Martinsville, WV
Hill, Philip, P.C. ... Lansing, IL
Hill, Philip S. ... Scarsdale, NY
Hill and Ponton, Professional Association
Orlando, FL
Hill, Preston W. ... Los Gatos, CA
Hill, R. Braxton, III ... Norfolk, VA
Hill, R. Braxton, IV ... Richmond, VA
Hill, R. Corey ... Phoenix, AZ
Hill, R. Edison ... Charleston, WV
Hill, R. Terrence (Terry) ... Kalispell, MT
Hill, R. Tony ... High Point, NC
Hill, Rachel W. ... Fresno, CA
Hill & Rainey ... Dinwiddie, VA
Petersburg, VA
Hill, Ralph A. ... Batavia, OH
Hill, Ralph B., III ... Hammonton, NJ
Hill, Ralph E. ... Lexington, KY
Hill, Ralph G. ... Philadelphia, PA
Hill, Randal W. ... Corpus Christi, TX
Hill, Randall K. ... Arlington, TX
Hill, Randle W., Jr. ... Gallatin, TN
Hill, Randolph J. ... Boise, ID
Hill, Randolph J. ... Raleigh, NC
Hill, Randolph L.
Environmental Protection Agency, Office of the General Counsel, GV
Hill, Randy L. ... Arkadelphia, AR
Hill, Ranlyn Tilley ... Los Angeles, CA
Hill, Raymond C. ... Laurens, SC
Hill, Raymond M., & Associates
Houston, TX
Hill, Rebecca ... Salt Lake City, UT
Hill, Rebecca T. ... San Francisco, CA
Hill, Rebekah Tyrell ... San Diego, CA
Hill, Reginald J. ... Chicago, IL
Hill, Reis, Adams, Hall & Schieffelin, P.A.
Orlando, FL
Hill, Renee Corley ... Bronx, NY
Hill, Renée F. ... Durham, NC
Hill, Reuben B. ... Indianapolis, IN
Hill, Rhonda K. ... Christiansted, St. Croix, VI
Hill, Richard A., Jr. ... New York, NY
Hill, Richard B. ... Bethesda, MD
Hill, Richard C. ... Columbus, OH
Hill, Richard E. ... Washington, DC
Hill, Richard E. ... Bedford, TX
Hill, Richard F. ... Berkeley, CA
Hill, Richard G. ... Reno, NV

Hill, Richard H., II ... Atlanta, GA
Hill, Richard H., Jr. ... Atlanta, GA
Hill, Richard J. ... Santa Ana, CA
Hill, Richard L. ... South Bend, IN
Hill, Richard L. ... Raleigh, NC
Hill, Richard L. ... Provo, UT
Hill, Richard M. ... Binghamton, NY
Hill, Richard N. ... San Francisco, CA
Hill, Richard P. ... San Francisco, CA
Hill, Richard Pilcher ... Brownsville, TX
McAllen, TX
Hill, Richard W. ... Louisville, KY
Hill, Richard W. ... Boxford, MA
Hill, Richard W. ... Newark, NJ
Hill Rivkins & Hayden LLP
Jersey City, NJ
New York, NY
Houston, TX
Hill & Robbins, P.C. ... Denver, CO
Hill, Robert A. ... Rockville, MD
Hill, Robert A. ... Minneapolis, MN
Hill, Robert, & Associates, Ltd.
Minneapolis, MN
Hill, Robert B. ... San Bernardino, CA
Hill, Robert B. ... Atlanta, GA
Hill, Robert B. ... Dinwiddie, VA
Petersburg, VA
Hill, Robert C. ... San Francisco, CA
Hill, Robert C., Jr. ... Fort Myers, FL
Hill, Robert Charles ... Washington, DC
Hill, Robert D. ... Atlanta, GA
Hill, Robert D., (P.C.)
Colorado Springs, CO
Hill, Robert E. ... Baton Rouge, LA
Hill, Robert E. ... Socorro, NM
Hill, Robert E. ... Pendleton, OR
Hill, Robert F. ... Denver, CO
Hill, Robert J. ... Washington, DC
Hill, Robert J. ... Washington, DC
Hill, Robert J. ... Camden, NJ
Hill, Robert J. ... Dallas, TX
Hill, Robert J. ... Fairfax, VA
Hill, Robert K. ... Susanville, CA
Hill, Robert Karl ... Wilmington, DE
Hill, Robert L. ... West Hartford, CT
Hill, Robert L. ... New York, NY
Hill, Robert M. ... Boston, MA
Hill, Robert M. ... Richmond, MO
Hill, Robert M., Jr. ... Florence, AL
Hill, Robert N. ... Hampton, SC
Hill, Robert P. ... Salt Lake City, UT
Hill, Robert S. ... Benton, IL
Hill, Robert S., III ... Montgomery, AL
Hill, Robert S., Jr. ... Montgomery, AL
Hill, Robert W. ... Springfield, MO
Hill, Robert W. ... University Heights, OH
Hill, Robt. S. ... Ottawa, KS
Hill, Robyn M. ... Trenton, NJ
Hill, Roderick D. ... Oakland, CA
Hill, Rodney C. ... Santa Barbara, CA
Hill, Ronald C. ... Denver, CO
Hill, Ronald Michael ... Chicago, IL
Hill, Ronald T. ... Memphis, TN
Hill, Ronald W. ... Department of Agriculture, Office of the General Counsel, GV
Hill, Rosemary Williams ... Boston, MA
Hill, Roy G. ... Deming, NM
Hill, Roy L. ... Elmsford, NY
Hill, Roy W. ... Fairfield, TX
Hill, Russell B. ... San Francisco, CA
Hill, Russell B. ... Helena, MT
Hill, Russell H. ... Dallas, TX
Hill, Russell J. ... Des Moines, IA
Hill, Rustan J. ... Cincinnati, OH
Hill, Ryan R. ... Longview, TX
Hill, S. Allan ... Greenville, SC
Hill, S. Gordon ... Tampa, FL
Hill, Sam ... Oklahoma City, OK
Hill, Sam C. ... Crawford, CO
Hill, Samuel D. ... Towson, MD
Hill, Samuel M. ... Birmingham, AL
Hill, Samuel Tyler ... Fort Lauderdale, FL
Hill, Sandra Jaribu ... Greenville, MS
Hill, Scot A. ... Kansas City, MO
Hill, Scott F. ... Evansville, IN
Hill, Scott J. ... St. Louis, MO
Hill, Sean Dennis ... Buffalo, NY
Hill, Sean J. ... New York, NY
Hill, Sharon Ann ... Portland, OR
Hill, Sharon Robison ... Huntsville, AL
Hill, Sherwood P. ... Indianapolis, IN
Hill, Sidney Woodson ... Kansas City, MO
Hill, Simon J. ... Chicago, IL
Hill & Simpson, A Professional Corporation
Chicago, IL
Arlington, VA
Hill, Sister Elizabeth A. ... Brooklyn, NY
Hill, Sonia E. ... Atlanta, GA
Hill, Stacy L. ... Gilbert, AZ
Hill, Stanford P. ... Minneapolis, MN
Hill, Stanley L. ... Chicago, IL
Hill, Stephanie J. ... Minneapolis, MN
Hill, Stephen A. ... Cleveland, OH
Hill, Stephen A. ... East Palestine, OH
Hill, Stephen B. ... Portland, OR
Hill, Stephen D. ... Paola, KS
Hill, Stephen J. ... Salt Lake City, UT
Hill, Stephen L., Jr. ... Liberty, MO
Hill, Stephen S. ... Washington, DC
Hill, Stephen V. ... Garland, TX
Hill, Steve G. ... Atlanta, GA
Hill, Steven ... Las Vegas, NV
Hill, Steven Allen ... Reynoldsburg, OH
Hill, Steven F. ... Washington, DC
Hill, Steven F. ... Vancouver, WA
Hill, Steven L. ... Port Huron, MI
Hill, Steven M. ... San Diego, CA
Hill, Susan C. ... Austin, TX

Hill, Susan J. .... Oakbrook Terrace, IL
Hill, Susan M. .... Bloomsburg, PA
Hill, Suzanne M. Barto .... Orlando, FL
Hill, T. Bowen, III .... Montgomery, AL
Hill, T. Robert .... Jackson, TN
Hill, Tanya Adrienne
Environmental Protection Agency, Office of the General Counsel, GV
Hill, Teresa J. .... Corbin, KY
Hill, Terrence M. .... Evanston, IL
Hill, Terrie Lee .... Granville, OH
Hill, Terry L. .... Nashville, TN
Hill, Thelma M. .... Raleigh, NC
Hill, Thomas A. .... Highland, IL
Hill, Thomas A. .... Youngstown, OH
Hill, Thomas C. .... Carbondale, CO
Hill, Thomas C. .... Moline, IL
Hill, Thomas C. .... Cincinnati, OH
Hill, Thomas C., Jr. .... St. Paul, MN
Hill, Thomas C., (P.C.) .... Washington, DC
Hill, Thomas E. .... Los Angeles, CA
Hill, Thomas E. .... Chicago, IL
Hill, Thomas E. .... Dallas, TX
Hill, Thomas H. .... Fairfield, CT
Hill, Thomas H. .... Upper Saddle River, NJ
Hill, Thomas H. .... Austin, TX
Hill, Thomas K. .... Portland, OR
Hill, Thomas L. .... Yuba City, CA
Hill, Thomas R. .... Chicago, IL
Hill, Thomas R. .... Overland Park, KS
Kansas City, MO
Hill, Thomas W. .... Columbus, OH
Hill, Thomas W., Jr. .... West Palm Beach, FL
Hill, Thurman, Jr. .... Springfield, VA
Hill, Timothy A. .... Riverside, CA
Hill, Timothy B. .... Parsippany, NJ
Hill, Timothy H. .... Seattle, WA
Hill, Timothy J. .... Cedar Rapids, IA
Hill, Timothy J. .... Houston, TX
Hill, Timothy L. .... St. Louis, MO
Hill, Timothy L., Professional Corporation
St. Louis, MO
Hill, Timothy P. .... Fargo, ND
Hill, Tina L. .... Jackson, MS
Hill, Tom E. .... Fort Worth, TX
Hill, Tommy E., (P.A.) .... Birmingham, AL
Hill, Tonya S. .... Tampa, FL
Hill, Tracy .... Valrico, FL
Hill, Tracy D. .... Portland, ME
Hill, Trenton J. .... Los Angeles, CA
Hill, Tucker & Marsh .... Richmond, VA
Hill, Ullman & Erwin .... New York, NY
Scarsdale, NY
Hill, Unsworth, Barra & Bowles
Essex Junction, VT
Montpelier, VT
Hill, Valarie A. .... Milwaukee, WI
Hill, Vance K. .... Bismarck, ND
Hill, Vern W.
Federal Maritime Commission, Bureau of Enforcement, GV
Hill, Veronica R. .... Washington, DC
Hill, Vic Brown .... Marietta, GA
Hill, Victor G., Jr. .... Oklahoma City, OK
Hill, Vincent .... Atlanta, GA
Hill, Virgil B. .... Clarkson Valley, MO
Hill, Vonciel Jones .... Dallas, TX
Hill, W. Bernard .... Memphis, TN
Hill, W. Bradford, Jr. .... Houston, TX
Hill, W. James, III, (P.L.C.)
Shreveport, LA
Hill, W. Michael .... Tulsa, OK
Hill, W. Wright, Jr. .... Jackson, MS
Hill Walker .... Palm Springs, CA
Hill Wallack .... Princeton, NJ
Trenton, NJ
Hill, Walter B., Jr. .... Costa Mesa, CA
Hill, Walter I. .... Newton, NJ
Hill, Walter L. .... Boulder, CO
Hill, Walton F. .... Harrington Park, NJ
Hill, Ward & Henderson, A Professional Association .... Bradenton, FL
Clearwater, FL
St. Petersburg, FL
Tampa, FL
Hill, Warren P. .... Chicago, IL
Hill, Wayne A., Jr. .... Rochester, NY
Hill, Wayne T. .... Houston, TX
Hill, Weldon J., II .... Baton Rouge, LA
Hill, Wendy Y. .... New York, NY
Hill, Willard W., Jr. .... New Orleans, LA
Hill, William A. .... Porterville, CA
Hill, William A.
National Labor Relations Board, Office of Board Members, GV
Hill, William A. .... Fargo, ND
Hill, William A. .... Austin, TX
Hill, William A., Jr. .... Fort Smith, AR
Hill, William. B. .... Pittsford, NY
Hill, William B., Jr. .... Atlanta, GA
Hill, William C. .... Montpelier, VT
Hill, William D. .... Willingboro, NJ
Hill, William E. .... New Haven, CT
Hill, William H., III .... Roanoke, VA
Hill, William H., Jr. .... Ponte Vedra Beach, FL
Hill, William I., II .... Montgomery, AL
Hill, William Inge, Jr. .... Montgomery, AL
Hill, William J. .... Lakewood, NJ
Hill, William J. .... Oklahoma City, OK
Hill, William K., (P.A.) .... Miami, FL
Hill, William Kim .... Bloomsburg, PA
Hill, William L. .... Greensboro, NC
Hill, William L., II .... Wilmington, NC
Hill, William M. .... Boston, MA
Hill, William M. .... Ravenel, SC
Hill, William M. .... Austin, TX
Hill, William M. .... Conroe, TX
Hill, William M., Jr. .... Warren, PA
Hill, William R. .... Oakland, CA
Hill, William Smith, Jr. .... Severna Park, MD
Hill, William T. (Bill), Jr. .... Dallas, TX
Hill, William Timothy .... Nashville, TN
Hill, William U. .... Cheyenne, WY
Hill, Wilmer B. .... Portland, OR
Hill, W. J. .... Berkeley, CA
Hill, Wm. J. .... Kansas City, MO
Hill, Wm. Ralph, Jr. .... La Fayette, GA
Hill, Womble & Phillips, P.A.
Elizabethtown, NC
Hill, Wyatt & Bannister, L.L.P.
Greenville, SC
Hill, Yerger, III .... Smithville, TX
Hill & Young .... Florence, AL
Hill, Yvonne Utley .... Kingston, TN
Hill, Zana Reinshagen .... San Antonio, TX
Hill, Zane M., Jr.
United States Postal Service, Postal Inspection Service, GV
Hilla, Christine M. .... New York, NY
Hillaert, Diane Shields .... South Bend, IN
Hillaert, Diane Shields, P.C. .... South Bend, IN
Hillan, Lisa L. .... San Diego, CA
Hillard, Deborah A. .... Columbia, SC
Hillard, Jimmie W. .... Plymouth, NC
Hillard, Lila Anderson .... Kentfield, CA
Hillard, Major M., Jr. .... Chesapeake, VA
Hillard, Martin Jon .... Grand Rapids, MI
Hillary, G. Patrick .... Grand Rapids, MI
Hillary, Richard E., II .... Grand Rapids, MI
Hillary, Rosetta .... Department of Education, Office for Civil Rights, GV
Hillas, Elaine Malin .... Portland, OR
Hillas, James M. .... Portland, OR
Hillas, James R., Jr. .... Long Valley, NJ
Hillberg, Loren E. .... Mountain View, CA
Hillberg, Marylou E. .... Santa Rosa, CA
Hillberg, Ronald W. .... Turlock, CA
Hillberg, Ronald W. .... Turlock, CA
Hilldrup, James W. .... Fredericksburg, VA
Hille, David G. .... New York, NY
Hille, Henry M. .... Bath, NY
Hille, Robert B. .... Hackensack, NJ
Hille, Robert F. .... Niagara Falls, NY
Hille, Robert J. .... St. Louis, MO
Hilleary, Anne S. .... San Jose, CA
Hilleary, Donald S. .... St. Louis, MO
Hilleary, Donald S., P.C. .... St. Louis, MO
Hilleary, Harry L. .... St. Louis, MO
Hilleary, Shawna R. .... Hollywood, CA
Hilleboe, Charles R. .... Clearwater, FL
Hilleboe, Charles R., P.A. .... Clearwater, FL
Hilleboe, Douglas L. .... Department of Justice, Antitrust Division, GV
Hillebrand, Albert J. .... Irvine, CA
Hillebrand, Gail K. .... San Francisco, CA
Hillebrand, H. Stephen .... Sarasota, FL
Hillebrand, Jane L. .... Livermore, CA
Hillebrand, Joseph R. .... Belleville, IL
Hillebrand, Joseph R. .... Toledo, OH
Hillebrand, Robert J. .... Belleville, IL
Hillebrecht, John M. .... New York, NY
Hill-Edgar, Keyes .... New York, NY
Hillegas, Joseph M. .... Phoenix, AZ
Hillegas, Kathleen A. .... Kingwood, TX
Hillegass, Helen G.
Federal Communications Commission, Office of Communications Business Opportunities, GV
Hillegass, Michael .... Lancaster, PA
Hillegonds, Timothy .... Grand Rapids, MI
Hillemann, Carl B., III .... St. Louis, MO
Hillemann, Steven B. .... St. Charles, MO
Hillen, Jens H. .... Menlo Park, CA
Hillen, W. Reed, III .... Tupelo, MS
Hillenbrand, Carl M. .... San Diego, CA
Hillenbrand, Catherine E. C. .... Seattle, WA
Hillenbrand, Gerald .... New York, NY
Hillenbrand, Hyman .... Miami, FL
Hillenbrand, Joan H. .... Morristown, NJ
Hillenbrand, Laura M. .... Richmond, VA
Hillenbrand, Mark A. .... Minneapolis, MN
Hillencamp & Alvarez, P.A. .... Key West, FL
Miami, FL
Hillencamp, Ibis J. .... Miami, FL
Hiller, Adam .... Baltimore, MD
Hiller, Albert H. .... Houston, TX
Hiller, Aleece M. .... Asheville, NC
Hiller, Arthur A. .... Bridgeport, CT
Hiller, B. Kendall .... Florence, SC
Hiller and Barnett .... Ann Arbor, MI
Hiller, Benjamin .... Boston, MA
Hiller, Carol B. .... Manhasset, NY
Hiller, Charles W. .... Toledo, OH
Hiller, Cherie A. .... Florham Park, NJ
Hiller, David D. .... Chicago, IL
Hiller, David L. .... Denver, CO
Hiller, David P. .... Cleveland, OH
Dublin, OH
Hiller, Deborah L. .... Boise, ID
Hiller, Deborah Lewis .... Cleveland, OH
Hiller, Edward J. .... Owings Mills, MD
Hiller, Elise L. .... Albany, NY
Hiller, Gary S. .... Los Angeles, CA
Hiller, George L. .... Richmond, VA
Hiller, George M. .... Atlanta, GA
Hiller, Georgia A. .... Naples, FL
Hiller, Georgia A., P.A. .... Naples, FL
Hiller, Gladys Kay .... New York, NY
Hiller, Herbert M. .... Milwaukee, WI
Hiller, J. James .... Ann Arbor, MI
Hiller, Jack A. .... Valparaiso, IN
Hiller, James A. .... Southfield, MI
Hiller, James A. .... Milwaukee, WI
Hiller, James L. .... Portland, OR
Hiller, Jeffrey A. .... San Antonio, TX
Hiller, Jeffrey S. .... Winston-Salem, NC
Hiller, Jennifer .... Cherry Hill, NJ
Hiller, John L. .... Mineola, NY
Hiller, Joseph, (P.C.) .... Houston, TX
Hiller, Kayla Korkow .... Janesville, WI
Hiller, Kelly Lane .... Boston, MA
Hiller, Kenneth R. .... Buffalo, NY
Hiller, Laurie B. .... Los Angeles, CA
Hiller, Marc David .... Albany, NY
Hiller, Mark A. .... Irvine, CA
Hiller, Michael D., (Inc.) .... Encino, CA
Hiller, Michael S. .... New York, NY
Hiller, Neil H. .... Phoenix, AZ
Hiller, Randall S. .... Greenville, SC
Hiller, Randall S., P.A. .... Greenville, SC
Hiller, Richard E. .... Shreveport, LA
Hiller, Richard J. .... New York, NY
Hiller, Robert L. .... Estes Park, CO
Hiller, Robert L., P.C. .... Estes Park, CO
Hiller, Robert S. .... Cincinnati, OH
Hiller, Roberta Lynn .... New York, NY
Hiller, Roy S. .... New York, NY
Hiller, Russell L. .... Shillington, PA
Hiller, Simon R. .... Hollywood, CA
Hiller, Stacey .... New York, NY
Hiller, Steven .... Ann Arbor, MI
Hiller, Steven E. .... New York, NY
Hiller, Terrance A., Jr. .... Troy, MI
Hiller, Theodore F., Jr. .... Princeton, NJ
Hiller, Thomas R. .... Boston, MA
Hiller, William E. .... New York, NY
Hilleren, Billy Wright .... Covington, LA
Hilleren, David A. .... Covington, LA
Hilleren & Hilleren, L.L.P.
Covington, LA
New Orleans, LA
Hillerich, Gary R. .... Louisville, KY
Hillerich, Ronald P. .... Louisville, KY
Hillerman, Eric A. .... Amarillo, TX
Hillerman, Gerald D. .... Tecumseh, OK
Hillerman, Holly Marie .... Enid, OK
Hillerson, Robert P. .... Silver Spring, MD
Hillery, David W. .... Indianapolis, IN
Hillery, James A. .... Woodland Hills, CA
Hillery, John M. .... Chicago, IL
Hillery, Judith A. .... Poughkeepsie, NY
Hillery, Martin T. .... New York, NY
Hilles, Frederick W. .... Brooklyn, NY
Hillestad, Charles, Law Offices of
Astoria, OR
Hillestad, Charles, Law Offices of
Cannon Beach, OR
Hillestad, Charles, Law Offices of
Portland, OR
Hill-Everett, Linda V. .... Atlanta, GA
Hilley, Benjamin W. .... Bigfork, MT
Hilley, Joseph H. .... Birmingham, AL
Mobile, AL
Hilley, Lara S. .... Sacramento, CA
Hilley, Ronald L. .... Tucker, GA
Hilley, Sheila Ann .... Albany, NY
Hilley, V. Donald .... Palm Beach Gardens, FL
Hilley, V. Donald, P.A.
Palm Beach Gardens, FL
Hilley, Van G. .... San Antonio, TX
Hill-Files, McLaurin .... Chicago, IL
Hillgen, Jennifer M.F. .... Stratford, CT
Hillger, Gene P. .... San Diego, CA
Hillger, Wendy L. .... San Francisco, CA
Hillgren, Nancy C. .... Irvine, CA
Hill-Gunter, Shawn .... Anniston, AL
Hill-Harvey, Karimu F. .... East Orange, NJ
Hillhouse, Andrew F., Jr. .... La Jolla, CA
Hillhouse, Randy .... Lawrenceburg, TN
Hillhouse, Richard A. .... Cottonwood, AZ
Hillhouse, Thomas R. .... Cincinnati, OH
Hillhouse, William A., II .... Denver, CO
Hilliard, Andrea Riddle .... Arlington, VA
Hilliard, Anthony A. .... Pine Bluff, AR
Hilliard, C. Robert .... Pensacola, FL
Hilliard, Carl B., Jr. .... San Diego, CA
Hilliard, Carol Rogers .... Cleveland, OH
Middleburg Heights, OH
Hilliard, Carol Rogers .... Rocky River, OH
Hilliard, Christopher L. .... Houston, TX
Hilliard, Clayton P. .... Lafayette, LA
Hilliard, Craig S. .... Princeton, NJ
Hilliard, Curtis R. .... Malvern, PA
Hilliard, D. Mark .... Norcross, GA
Hilliard, David Craig .... Chicago, IL
Hilliard, David E. .... Washington, DC
Hilliard, Delmar Shelley
Corpus Christi, TX
Hilliard, Earl F., Jr. .... Los Angeles, CA
Hilliard, Elaine C. .... Cleveland, OH
Hilliard, Frank P. .... Louisville, KY
Hilliard, Henning .... Louisville, KY
Hilliard, Hylas A. .... Columbus, OH
Hilliard, James P. .... Chicago, IL
Hilliard, James R. .... Dallas, TX
Hilliard, James T. .... Walpole, MA
Hilliard, Jeffrey D. .... Union, MO
Hilliard, Jennifer L. .... Washington, DC
Hilliard, Kenneth J. .... Carmichael, CA
Hilliard, Kevin P. .... Short Hills, NJ
Hilliard, Kristi L. .... Kearney, NE
Hilliard, Linda B. .... Princeton, NJ
Hilliard, M. Hakim .... Atlanta, GA
Hilliard, Mark D. .... Tinley Park, IL
Hilliard, Maurice H., Jr. .... Roswell, GA
Hilliard, Michael W. .... Dallas, TX
Hilliard & Muñoz .... Corpus Christi, TX
Hilliard, Richard R. .... Overland Park, KS
Hilliard, Robert C., P.C.
Corpus Christi, TX
Hilliard, Russell F. .... Concord, NH
Hilliard, Ruth Harris .... Phoenix, AZ
Hilliard, Stephen P .... Encinitas, CA
Hilliard, Terrance A., P.C.
Commodity Futures Trading Commission, Division of Enforcement, GV
Hilliard, Thomas P. .... Washington, DC
Hilliard, Troy A. .... Milwaukee, WI
Hilliard, Warren S. .... Buffalo, NY
Hilliard, Wayne .... Portland, OR
Hilliard, William R., Jr. .... Lexington, KY
Hilliard, William T. .... Bedminster, NJ
Hilliard, Zenola M. .... Pine Bluff, AR
Hillier, Andrea L. .... Chicago, IL
Hillier & Associates, P.A. .... Boca Raton, FL
Hillier, David Martin .... Los Angeles, CA
Hillier, David R. .... Asheville, NC
Hillier, Dennis W. .... Boca Raton, FL
Hillier, Donald T. .... Shelburne Falls, MA
Hillier, Eric R. .... Pleasanton, CA
Hillier, Frederic F. .... Minneapolis, MN
Hillier, Jeffrey S. .... New York, NY
Hillier, Kenneth R. .... Los Angeles, CA
San Francisco, CA
Hillier, Margaret .... Oakland, CA
Hillier & Scheibmeir, P.S. .... Chehalis, WA
Hillier, Thomas S. .... Portland, OR
Hillier, Thomas W., II .... Seattle, WA
Hillier, Todd R. .... Bozeman, MT
Hillier, William T. .... Chehalis, WA
Hillig, Elizabeth A. .... Boston, MA
Hilligan, Marion M. .... Lansing, MI
Hilligan, Thomas J. .... Red Bluff, CA
Hilligoss, Thomas J., Jr. .... Kokomo, IN
Hilliker, Donald B. .... Chicago, IL
Hilliker, Todd D. .... St. Louis, MO
Hillin, Hunter Thomas .... Dallas, TX
Hillin & Owen, L.L.P. .... Dallas, TX
Hillin, Wayne K. .... Houston, TX
Hillings, David M. .... Santa Monica, CA
Hillis, Anne .... Binghamton, NY
Hillis Clark Martin & Peterson, A Professional Service Corporation
Seattle, WA
Hillis, David .... Hayward, CA
Hillis, Edmund M. .... Wilmington, DE
Hillis, Elwood H. .... Kokomo, IN
Hillis, G. Wayne, Jr. .... Atlanta, GA
Hillis & Hillis .... Logansport, IN
Hillis, Howard F. .... Wilmington, DE
Hillis, James F. .... Roachdale, IN
Hillis, Jeffrey William .... Boston, MA
Hillis, Jerome L. .... Seattle, WA
Hillis, John R. .... Logansport, IN
Hillis, John T. .... Binghamton, NY
Hillis, Mark B. .... St. Louis, MO
Hillis, Michael S. .... New Haven, CT
Hillis, Paul H., Jr. .... Salem, IL
Hillis, R. Tom .... Tulsa, OK
Hillis, Robert M. .... Fremont, NE
Hillis, Robert W. .... Binghamton, NY
Hillis, Ruth A. .... Nashville, TN
Hillis, Sanders N. .... Indianapolis, IN
Hillis, Scott T. .... Zanesville, OH
Hillison, Robert E. .... Lake Forest, IL
Hillison, Robert K. .... Fresno, CA
Hillje, Barbara Brown .... Langhorne, PA
Hill-Kennedy, Scott P. .... Big Rapids, MI
Hill-Little, Holly .... Alexandria, VA
Hillman, Adria S. .... New York, NY
Hillman, Albert J. .... San Francisco, CA
Hillman, Allan P. .... Baltimore, MD
Hillman, Andrew S. .... Boca Raton, FL
Hillman, Arthur B. .... Atlanta, GA
Hillman, Arthur J. .... Bethesda, MD
Hillman, Arthur L., Jr. .... San Mateo, CA
Hillman, Barbara J. .... Chicago, IL
Hillman, Bertha M. .... Thibodaux, LA
Hillman, Brenda G. .... Los Angeles, CA
Hillman, Bret D. .... Tulare, CA
Hillman, Brooke K. .... Chicago, IL
Hillman Brown & Darrow, P.A.
Annapolis, MD
Hillman, Charles H. .... Mobile, AL
Hillman, Daniel A. .... Atlanta, GA
Hillman, David A. .... New York, NY
Hillman, David C. .... Portland, ME
Hillman, David M. .... New York, NY
Hillman, Donald C. .... Boston, MA
Hillman, Donald S. .... New York, NY
Hillman, Edward L. .... Long Beach, NY
Hillman, Elena Kondos
San Francisco, CA
Hillman, Eugene L. .... Omaha, NE
Hillman, Forman, Nelsen Childers, Lingo & McCormack .... Omaha, NE
Hillman, George A. .... Indianapolis, IN
Hillman & Gouras, L.L.P. .... Tukwila, WA
Hillman, Harry D. .... Cincinnati, OH
Hillman, Jack A. .... Kensington, MD
Hillman, James L. .... Oakland, CA
Hillman, James P. .... Fremont, CA
Hillman, Jean M. .... Cleveland, OH
Hillman, Jerry Dean .... Birmingham, AL
Hillman, Jill Anne .... Los Angeles, CA
Hillman & Jones .... Fairfield, CA
Hillman, Jordan J. .... Evanston, IL
Hillman, Joseph, Jr. .... Belmar, NJ
Hillman, Kimberly R. .... Richmond, VA
Hillman, Lawrence S. .... Meriden, CT
Hillman, Lisa M. W. .... Washington, DC
Hillman, M. Kendall .... Fairfield, CA
Hillman, Marcy .... New York, NY
Hillman, Mark J. .... Tukwila, WA
Hillman, Marvin .... New Hempstead, NY
Hillman, Milton H. .... Pasadena, CA
Hillman, Nathan .... Boca Raton, FL
Hillman, Noel L. .... Newark, NJ
Hillman, Paul M. .... Las Vegas, NV
Hillman, Peggy A. .... Indianapolis, IN
Hillman, Peter N. .... New York, NY

Hillman, Reed V. ... Sturbridge, MA
Hillman, Regina L. ... San Diego, CA
Hillman, Richard D. ... Syracuse, NY
Hillman, Richard L. ... East Lansing, MI
Hillman, Robert A. ... Ithaca, NY
Hillman, Robert D. ... Boston, MA
Hillman, Robert E. ... Boston, MA
Hillman, Robert H. ... Rockville, MD
Hillman, Robert L. ... Raleigh, NC
Hillman, Robert S. ... Baltimore, MD
Hillman, Roger L. ... Seattle, WA
Hillman, Shane D. ... Salt Lake City, UT
Hillman, Sherra L. ... Waynesboro, MS
Hillman, Stephen J. ... Los Angeles, CA
Hillman, Stephen M. ... Stoughton, MA
Hillman, Steven E. ... Dublin, OH
Hillman, Stuart S. ... Beverly Hills, CA
Hillman, Timothy S. ... Gardner, MA
Hillman, William C. ... Boston, MA
Hillman, William H., Jr. ... Grand Rapids, MI
Hillman, Windy A. ... Birmingham, AL
Hillmann, Michael J. ... Closter, NJ
Hillmann, William D. ... Edgewood, KY
Hillman-Waller, Louis M. ... Coral Gables, FL
Hillmer, Felicity M. ... Toledo, OH
Hillmer, Siegfried O. ... Los Angeles, CA
Hillmyer, Barry R. ... Fort Myers, FL
Hillmyer, Barry R., P.A. ... Fort Myers, FL
Hillowe, Bruce V. ... Mineola, NY
Hillowe, Bruce V. ... New York, NY
Hills, Carla Anderson ... Washington, DC
Hills, Cheryl C. ... San Francisco, CA
Hills, Christina D. ... Monroe, MI
Hills, Christopher M. ... Monroe, MI
Hills, Cornell D. ... Arlington, VA
Hills, David R. ... Lenexa, KS
Hills, David W. ... Cincinnati, OH
Hills, Henry Monroe, III ... Charleston, WV
Hills & Hicks, S.C. ... Brookfield, WI
Hills, James D. ... Kalamazoo, MI
Hills, James L. ... Myrtle Beach, SC
Hills, James L. ... North Myrtle Beach, SC
Hills, Jeffrey T. ... Tulsa, OK
Hills, Joseph E. ... Springfield, MO
Hills, Laura H. ...
Overseas Private Investment Corporation, GV
Hills, Lee ... Miami, FL
Hills, Mark E. ... Grand Rapids, MI
Hills, Megan E. ... Washington, DC
Hills, Richard A., Jr. ... Atlanta, GA
Hills, Richard M. ... San Francisco, CA
Hills, Richard T. ... Atlanta, GA
Hills, Rick E. ... Brookfield, WI
Hills, Roderick M. ... Washington, DC
Hills, Sharon K. ... Apple Valley, MN
Hills & Stern ... Washington, DC
Hills, Thomas J. ... Roswell, GA
Hills, Thorburn W. ... Methuen, MA
Hills, Wendy J. ... Overland Park, KS
Hillsberg, Donald S. ... Fort Lauderdale, FL
Hillsberg, Geoffrey ... Media, PA
Hillsberg, Jon G. ... Philadelphia, PA
Hillsberg, Richard W. ... Buffalo Grove, IL
Hillsberg, Sanford J. ... Los Angeles, CA
Hillsberg, Sharp, Corbacio & Vitiello
Syracuse, NY
Hillshafer, Robert D. ... Sherman Oaks, CA
Hillsinger and Costanzo, Professional Corporation ... Los Angeles, CA
Orange, CA
Hillsinger, George R. ... Los Angeles, CA
Orange, CA
Hillsman, Donald Andrew ... Decatur, GA
Hillsman, Frances F. ... Tulsa, OK
Hillsman, John R. ... San Francisco, CA
Hillsman, Marvin C., Jr. ... Elkton, VA
Hillsman, Thomas C. ... Dallas, TX
Hillsman, W. Mark
Cruz Bay, St. John, VI
Charlotte Amalie, St. Thomas, VI
Hillson, Randall A. ... Minneapolis, MN
Hillstrom, Bruce G. ... Chicago, IL
Hillstrom, Donald A. ... Minneapolis, MN
Hillstrom, Floyd A. ... Sarasota, FL
Hillstrom, George D. ... Chicago, IL
Hillstrom & Hillstrom ... Chicago, IL
Hillstrom, Robert A. ... Minneapolis, MN
Hillstrom, Scott David ... Bloomington, MN
Hillstrom, Scott L. ... Chicago, IL
Hill-Whilton, R. Scott ... Boston, MA
Hillwig, Craig W. ... Philadelphia, PA
Hilly, James D. ... Philadelphia, PA
Hilly, Maryellen ... Mamaroneck, NY
Hillyard Anderson & Olsen ... Logan, UT
Hillyard, Clare ... Chicago, IL
Hillyard, Lyle W. ... Logan, UT
Hillyard, Mary Kirk ... San Francisco, CA
Hillyard, Neil A. ... Englewood, CO
Hillyard, Steven D., (P.C.)
Newport Beach, CA
Hillyard, Susan B. ... Delta, CO
Hillyer, Bradley L. ... Uhrichsville, OH
Hillyer, Haywood H., III ... New Orleans, LA
Hillyer, Haywood H., III ... New Orleans, LA
Hillyer, Haywood H., Jr., (P.C.)
New Orleans, LA
Hillyer, Hudson ... Uhrichsville, OH
Hillyer & Irwin, A Professional Corporation
San Diego, CA
Hillyer, Kevin Pauley ... Los Angeles, CA
Hillyer, Rebecca Lee ... Salem, OR
Hill-Yonis, Jeannette M. ... Los Angeles, CA
Hilmen, Dale A. ... San Diego, CA
Hilmen, Richard T., Jr. (A P.C.)
San Diego, CA
Hilmer, Charles A. ... Three Oaks, MI
Hilmer, Tracy L. ... Washington, DC

Hilmes, John D. (Jack) ... Des Moines, IA
Hilmes, Sharon A. ... Indianapolis, IN
Hilmoe, Karen ... Sioux Falls, SD
Hilmy, S. Stephen ... Corpus Christi, TX
Hilner, Howard K. ... Pittsburgh, PA
Hilovsky, Richard T. ... San Jose, CA
Hilow, Henry Joseph ... Cleveland, OH
Hilowitz, Lynne S. ... Garden City, NY
Hilowitz, Lynne S. ... New City, NY
Hilpert, Edward T., Jr. ... Seattle, WA
Hilpert, Robert J. ... Croton-On-Hudson, NY
Hils, David F. ... University Heights, OH
Hils, M. Gabrielle ... Cincinnati, OH
Hils, Mary Elizabeth ... Cincinnati, OH
Hilsabeck, Michael D. ... Tulsa, OK
Hilsbos, John T. ... Falls Church, VA
Hilscher & Hilscher ... Hannacroix, NY
Hilscher, J. Theodore ... Hannacroix, NY
Hilscher, Nancy R. ... Hannacroix, NY
Hilsee, Steven C. ... Lake Buena Vista, FL
Hilsen, Linda Teal ... Sherman Oaks, CA
Hilsen, Mark Norman ... Kent, WA
Hilsen, Scott P. ... Atlanta, GA
Hilsenbeck, Paula M. ... Austin, TX
Hilsenrath, Eugene ... New York, NY
Hilser, John E. ... Philadelphia, PA
Hilsheimer, Lawrence A. ... Columbus, OH
Hilsher, Donna M. ... Kingwood, TX
Hilsher, V. J." Jay ", Jr. ... Houston, TX
Hilsinger, Patricia D. ... Philadelphia, PA
Hilsman, Ashby G. ... Philadelphia, PA
Hilsman, Deborah E. ... Seattle, WA
Hilsman, John E. ... Silver Spring, MD
Hilson, Arthur T. ... Woodbridge, NJ
Hilson, Daniel G. ... Columbus, OH
Hilson, John Francis ... Los Angeles, CA
Hilson, Robert P. ... Hingham, MA
Hilson, William C., Jr. ... Sacramento, CA
Hilst, Ronald P. ... Rochester, NY
Hilst, Yvonne M. ... Chicago, IL
Hilstad, Paul A. ... New York, NY
Hilston, Thomas A. ... Akron, OH
Hilt, Angela Christine ... San Francisco, CA
Hilt, John F. ... Grove City, OH
Hilt, Matthew L. ... Atlanta, GA
Hiltabrand, Lori Poppe ... Springfield, IL
Hiltachk, Thomas W. ... Sacramento, CA
Hiltebrand, Stephen M. ... Voorhees, NJ
Hiltgen & Brewer, P.C.
Oklahoma City, OK
Hiltgen, Cary E. ... Oklahoma City, OK
Hilton, Alexander E. ... Newport Beach, CA
Hilton, Andrew C., Jr. ... Buffalo, NY
Hilton, Ariel C., (Miss) ... Playa Del Rey, CA
Hilton & Bishop, A Professional Corporation
Falmouth, MA
Hilton, Bruce F. ... St. Louis, MO
Hilton, Bryan P. ... Atlanta, GA
Hilton, Catherine M. ... Atlanta, GA
Hilton, Charles F. ... Harrisonburg, VA
Hilton, Claude M. ... Alexandria, VA
Hilton, Constance M. ... Cambridge, MA
Hilton, Cory ... Las Vegas, NV
Hilton, David Austin ... Boston, MA
Hilton, David D. ... Kennewick, WA
Hilton, David L. ... Fairfax, VA
Hilton & Davidge, L.L.P. ... Denton, TX
Hilton, Douglas ... San Luis Obispo, CA
Hilton, Douglas, A Law Corp.
San Luis Obispo, CA
Hilton, Elyse ... New York, NY
Hilton, Ernest W. ... Madison, ME
Hilton, Francis W., Jr. ... Rockville, MD
Hilton, Frank H., Jr. ... Portland, OR
Hilton, Frederic H. ... Falmouth, MA
Hilton, Gillespie & Kiesewetter, L.L.C.
St. Louis, MO
Hilton, Glenn Russell ... Norfolk, VA
Hilton, H. Eric ... Atlanta, GA
Hilton, Helen J. ... Department of Defense, Defense Legal Services Agency, GV
Hilton, Hilton, Kolk, Penson & Roesch
Panama City, FL
Tallahassee, FL
Hilton, Holly P. ... Stafford, VA
Hilton, Homer, Jr. ... Marquette, MI
Hilton, Hope ... Readfield, ME
Hilton, James M., (P.S.) ... Seattle, WA
Hilton, James R. ... New Brunswick, NJ
Hilton, John C. ... Hartford, CT
Hilton, John E. ... St. Louis, MO
Hilton, Joseph ... New York, NY
Hilton, Julie K. ... Panama City, FL
Hilton, Kenneth H. ... Princeton, NJ
Hilton, Kenneth S. ... New York, NY
Hilton, L. Charles, Jr. ... Panama City, FL
Tallahassee, FL
Hilton, Laura A. ... Fort Worth, TX
Hilton, Lawrence D. ... Martinez, CA
Hilton, Lawrence F. ... Santa Barbara, CA
Hilton, Lawrence J. ... Newport Beach, CA
Hilton, Leigh ... Denton, TX
Hilton, Lydia Mitchell ... Atlanta, GA
Hilton, Lyle F. ... Wyomissing Hills, PA
Hilton, Matthew M. F. ... Springville, UT
Hilton, P. Gregory ... Greenbelt, MD
Hilton, Paul ... Boulder, CO
Denver, CO
Hilton, Paul ... Denver, CO
Hilton Penson & Padgett ... Tallahassee, FL
Hilton, R. Donn ... Salt Lake City, UT
Hilton, Ralph W., II ... Sacramento, CA
Hilton, Robert E. ... Pittsburgh, PA
Hilton, Robert E. ... Dallas, TX
Hilton, Robert G. ... Department of Justice, Civil Division, GV
Hilton, Robert K., III ... Utica, NY
Hilton, Robert W., Jr. ... Cincinnati, OH

Hilton, Seth D. ... Walnut Creek, CA
Hilton, Stanley G. ... San Francisco, CA
Hilton, Steven M. ... Washington, DC
Hilton, Susan M. ... Los Angeles, CA
Hilton, William E. ... Boston, MA
Hilton, William M. ... New York, NY
Hilton-Phillips, Tija Rose ... Camp Hill, PA
Hilts, Earl T. ... Clifton Park, NY
Hilts, Jonathan M. ... Dearborn, MI
Hiltunen, Charles T., III ... Indianapolis, IN
Hiltunen, Don R. ... Hancock, MI
Hiltunen, Scott E. ... Los Angeles, CA
Hilty, Amanda S. ... Houston, TX
Hilty, Eric L. ... Denver, CO
Hilty, George E. ... Honolulu, HI
Hiltz, L. Thomas ... Covington, KY
Hiltz, Peter F. ... Detroit, MI
Hiltz, Walter G. ... Canton, MA
Hiltz, Wiedemann, Allton & Koch Co., LPA
Norwalk, OH
Hiltzik, Abraham A. ... New York, NY
Hiltzik, George J. ... New York, NY
Hilvert, Joanna Giorgio ... Boston, MA
Hilvert, Margaret A. ... Cincinnati, OH
Hilyard, Chad S. ... Denver, CO
Hilyard, Joseph M. ... Holyoke, MA
Hilyard, Mary J. ... Van Nuys, CA
Hilyard, M. J., & Associates ... Van Nuys, CA
Hilyard, Sutton G., Jr. ... Orlando, FL
Hilyer, Elizabeth Barnes ... Clanton, AL
Hilyer, Ken R. ... Tifton, GA
Hilyerd, William A. ... Frankfort, KY
Hilzer, John J. ... Portland, OR
Himber, Debra M. ... Forked River, NJ
Himber & Stork ... Forked River, NJ
Hime, Clinton T., Jr. ... Houston, TX
Himebauch, Gregory L. ... Milwaukee, WI
Himebaugh, Kevin R. ... Detroit, MI
Himebaugh, Teri B. ... Schwenksville, PA
Himel, Jeffrey J. ... Houma, LA
Himel, Lloyd R. ... Lutcher, LA
Himel, René H., Jr. ... New Orleans, LA
Himel, Shelley J. ... Oklahoma City, OK
Himel, Yoshinori H. T. ... Sacramento, CA
Himelblau, Robert Enrique ... Stockton, CA
Himelein, Larry M., III ... Little Valley, NY
Himelein, Levant M., Jr. ... Gowanda, NY
Himeles, Martin S., Jr. ... Baltimore, MD
Himelewski, Valerie J. ... New York, NY
Himelfarb, Allison J. ... Chicago, IL
Himelfarb, David ... Santa Monica, CA
Himelfarb, Jane ... New York, NY
Himelfarb, Phyllis-Jo
Securities and Exchange Commission, Division of Corporation Finance, GV
Himelfarb, Regina Cooper
Fort Worth, TX
Himelfarb, Richard J. ... Baltimore, MD
Himelfarb, Stephen R. ... Bethesda, MD
Himelhoch, Alan F. ... Flint, MI
Himelhoch, Jeffrey J. ... Flint, MI
Himelhoch, Richard C. ... Chicago, IL
Himelman, Daniel J. ... Red Bank, NJ
Himelman, David ... Woodbridge, NJ
Himelman, William ... Red Bank, NJ
Himelrick, Richard G. ... Phoenix, AZ
Himelson, David Leon ... Santa Ana, CA
Himelspach, Daniel C. ... Denver, CO
Himelstein, Ben ... Moorhead, MS
Himelstein, Julieanne ... Washington, DC
Himelstein, Mandel E. ... Coronado, CA
Himelstein, Mark ... Berkeley, CA
Himelstein, Steven I. ... New York, NY
Himeno, Sharon R. ... Honolulu, HI
Himes, A. Lynn ... Chicago, IL
Chicago Heights, IL
Himes, Anne L. ... Brevard, NC
Himes, Carol Lieb ... Brooklyn, NY
Himes, H. Paul, Jr. ... Denver, CO
Himes, Harris D. ... Hamilton, MT
Himes, Harry C. J. ... Philadelphia, PA
Himes, J. Fraser ... Orlando, FL
Tampa, FL
Himes, James E. ... Huntingdon, PA
Himes, Jay L. ... New York, NY
Himes, John R. ... Terre Haute, IN
Himes, Lance D. ... Cincinnati, OH
Himes, Laurence T., Jr. ... York, PA
Himes, Michael ... Seattle, WA
Himes, Patricia Ledvina ... Tulsa, OK
Himes, Richard ... New York, NY
Himes, Rita K. ... San Francisco, CA
Himes, Robert H. ... Santa Ana, CA
Himes, Roger P. ... Lakewood, CO
Himes, Scott M. ... New York, NY
Himes, Suzanne M. ... Ocala, FL
Himes, Suzanne M., P.A. ... Ocala, FL
Himes, Terry J. ... Pittsburgh, PA
Himes, Timothy G., Sr. ... Omaha, NE
Himfar, Evan M. ... San Diego, CA
Himle, Robert D. ... Anoka, MN
Himler, Thomas A., Jr. ... Latrobe, PA
Himley-Grandi, Dawn A. ... Chicago, IL
Himlie, David D. ... Edina, MN
Himmel, Albert F. ... Cleveland, OH
Himmel, Amy Ellen ... Pittsburgh, PA
Himmel, Andrew D. ... New York, NY
Himmel, Brian T. ... Pittsburgh, PA
Himmel, Ellen J. ... Seattle, WA
Himmel, Florence K. ... Lansdale, PA
Himmel, Gary L. ... Akron, OH
Himmel, Geo. F. ... Braintree, MA
Himmel, Ira K., Law Offices of
Baltimore, MD
Himmel, Michael B. ... Woodbridge, NJ
Himmel, Michael S. ... New York, NY
Himmel, Renée ... Manhasset, NY
Himmel, Robert M. ... Radford, VA

Himmelberg, Daniel E. ... Columbia, MO
Himmelberg, Don M. ... Nashville, TN
Himmelberg, John M. ... Washington, DC
Himmelberger, David J. ... Wellesley, MA
Himmelberger, John G., Jr. ... Atlantic City, NJ
Himmelberger, Lance ... Rio Rancho, NM
Himmelberger, Robert L. ... Phoenix, AZ
Himmelfarb, Bernard ... Louisville, KY
Himmelfarb, Cynthia ... Brentwood, TN
Himmelfarb, Edward ... Department of Justice, Civil Division, GV
Himmelfarb, Henry ... Vernon, CA
Himmelfarb, Martin ... Boston, MA
Himmelfarb, Morris D. ... Kew Gardens, NY
Himmelfarb, Norman D.
White Plains, NY
Himmelheber, Dan M. ... San Mateo, CA
Himmelhoch, Judith E. ... Pittsburgh, PA
Himmelhoch, Sarah D.
Department of Justice, Environment and Natural Resources Division, GV
Himmelman, David A. ... Oakland, CA
Himmelman, Harold ... Washington, DC
Himmelmann, John W. ... Denver, CO
Himmelreich, Bruce E. ... Houston, TX
Himmelreich, Charles I. ... Harrison City, PA
Himmelreich, David M. ... Nashville, TN
Himmelrich, Ned T. ... Baltimore, MD
Himmelrich, Sue L. ... Santa Monica, CA
Himmelsbach, Leo F. ... San Jose, CA
Himmelspach, Rebecca L. ... Milwaukee, WI
Himmelspach, Thomas R. ... Canton, OH
Himmelstein, Alan G. ... Tarrytown, NY
Himmelstein, Barry R. ... San Francisco, CA
Himmelstein, Cheryl ... Tucson, AZ
Himmelstein, John ... Newton, MA
Himmelstein, Mark S. ... Irvine, CA
Himmelstein & McConnell ... New York, NY
Himmelstein, Samuel J. ... New York, NY
Himmelwright, Amy J. ... Auburn, AL
Himmer, Jennifer Foye
Vineyard Haven, MA
Himmer, Susan E. ... Atlanta, GA
Himmler, Kathleen Ann ... Oklahoma City, OK
Himonas, Deno G. ... Salt Lake City, UT
Himonidis, Nicholas G. ... New York, NY
Himrich, Jeffrey L. ... Des Moines, IA
Himrod, Robert M. ... Los Angeles, CA
Himrod, Thomas E. ... Los Angeles, CA
Himschoot, Robert A. ... Dillingham, AK
Himsel, Jane Ann ... Indianapolis, IN
Himsel, Scott D. ... Indianapolis, IN
Himstedt, D. J. ... Denver, CO
Himstreet, Jeffrey Otis ... Washington, DC
Himsworth, James J., Jr. ... Norristown, PA
Himsworth, Mark F. ... Lansdale, PA
Hinaman, Alan R. ... Houston, TX
Hincapie, Devon D. ... Boston, MA
Hinch, Diane B. ... Corona Del Mar, CA
Hinch, Wesley N. ... Houston, TX
Hinchcliff, John Moss ... Ithaca, NY
Hinchcliffe, Everett S. ... Los Angeles, CA
Walnut Creek, CA
Hinchcliffe, John J. ... Phoenix, AZ
Hinchey & Cummings ... Norwich, CT
Hinchey, Edward T. ... Boston, MA
Hinchey, James J., Jr. ... Charleston, SC
Hinchey, John W. ... Atlanta, GA
Hinchey, Joseph M. ... Stonington, CT
Hinchey, Lloyd E. ... Norwich, CT
Hinchey, Michael T. ... Westwood, MA
Hinchey, Robert E. ... Dover, NH
Hinchey, Sara ... Boston, MA
Hinchey, Thomas M. ... Philadelphia, PA
Hinchion, Michael ... Nashville, TN
Hinchliff, James ... Chicago, IL
Hinchliffe, Lisa F. ... Los Angeles, CA
Hinchman, James F.
General Accounting Office, Office of the Comptroller General, GV
Hinchman, Lillian M. ... Phoenix, AZ
Hinchman, Robert ... Department of Justice, Office of Policy Development, GV
Hinchman, William R. ... Philadelphia, PA
Hinch-Perkins, Toni Ann ... New York, NY
Hinchy, J. William ... San Diego, CA
Hinchy, Witte, Wood, Anderson & Hodges, A Law Corporation ... Rancho Bernardo, CA
San Diego, CA
Hinck, Elizabeth Cardle
Minneapolis, MN
Hinck, Gary E. ... Lawrence, KS
Hinckle, Michael H. ... Washington, DC
Hinckley, Allen & Snyder LLP
Boston, MA
Providence, RI
Hinckley, Franklin G. ... Brewer, ME
Hinckley, George R., Jr. ... New York, NY
Hinckley, Gerard J. ... Walnut Creek, CA
Hinckley, Harry G., Jr. ... Fort Lauderdale, FL
Hinckley, James C. ... Maitland, FL
Hinckley, James C., P.A. ... Maitland, FL
Orlando, FL
Hinckley, Robert C. ... San Jose, CA
Hinckley, Sandra F. ... Clearwater, FL
Hinckley, Stuart W. ... Salt Lake City, UT
Hinckley, William S. ... Omaha, NE
Hincks, Benjamin L. ... Boston, MA
Hincks, John W. ... Hartford, CT
Hincks, Patrick M. ... Oak Brook, IL
Hincks, Richard K. ... Salt Lake City, UT
Hind, Gary M. ... Albany, NY
Hind, Hobart M., Jr. ... Tampa, FL
Hind, M. Christie ... Los Angeles, CA
Hind, Ronald W. ... St. Louis, MO
Hindahl, Phillip K. ... Winslow, IN
Hinde, Daniel E. ... Houston, TX

Hinde, Georgia ... New York, NY
Hinde, John G. ... Rice Lake, WI
Hindelang, Robert L.
Grosse Pointe Farms, MI
Hindelang, Robert L., P.C.
Grosse Pointe Farms, MI
Hindels, James H.
Charlotte Amalie, St. Thomas, VI
Hinden, Barry H. ... Los Angeles, CA
Hinden, David R. ... Los Angeles, CA
Hinden, Frederick A. ... Sacramento, CA
Hinden, Grueskin & Aguirre
Los Angeles, CA
Hinden, Jon A. ... Pembroke Pines, FL
Hinden, Richard A. ... Oak Brook, IL
Hindenlang, Walter J. ... El Segundo, CA
Hindera, Cheryl Young ... Lubbock, TX
Hinderaker, Allen W. ... Minneapolis, MN
Hinderaker, Irving A. ... Watertown, SD
Hinderaker, John C. ... Tucson, AZ
Hinderaker, John H. ... Minneapolis, MN
Hinderaker, Paul I. ... Watertown, SD
Hinderaker & Rauh PLC ... Tucson, AZ
Hinderaker, Ted H. ... Tucson, AZ
Hinderberger, Philip R. ... San Francisco, CA
Hinderer, H. William, III ... Fenton, MO
Hinderer, Paul ... Kent, WA
Hinderks, Mark D. ... Leawood, KS
Hinderliter, Harry E., III ... Las Vegas, NV
Hinderliter, J. Dean ... Dallas, TX
Hinderliter, Jay D. ... Washington, DC
Hinders, Andrew J. ... Celina, OH
Hinders, Edward B. ... San Antonio, TX
Hinders & Hinders ... Celina, OH
Hinders, John J. ... Celina, OH
Hinders, Rodney J. ... New Bremen, OH
Hinderstein, Carro L. ... Houston, TX
Hindert, Daniel W. ... Salt Lake City, UT
Hindert, Edward M. ... Kalamazoo, MI
Hindert, Patrick J. ... Cincinnati, OH
Hindes, Thomas Joseph ... Westerville, OH
Hindes, Van G. ... Fremont, MI
Hindi, Fadia R. ... Roseland, NJ
Hindin & Abel, LLP ... Los Angeles, CA
Hindin, Barbara A. ... Washington, DC
Hindin, Bettina D. ... New York, NY
Hindin, David A.
Environmental Protection Agency,
Office of Enforcement and Compliance
Assurance, GV
Hindin, Karen L. ... Los Angeles, CA
Hindin, Malcolm E. ... Boston, MA
Hindin, Mark D.
Department Of Veterans Affairs,
Board of Veterans Appeals, GV
Hindin, Perry J. ... Washington, DC
Hindin, Robert M. ... Los Angeles, CA
Hindin, Ronald ... Glencoe, IL
Hindin, Ronald, Ltd. ... Glencoe, IL
Hindin, Seymour ... Port Jefferson, NY
Hinding, John E. ... Washington, DC
Hindle, Marilyn C. ... Ventura, CA
Hindle, Robert W. ... New Orleans, LA
Hindley, Dixon D. ... Salt Lake City, UT
Hindley, Elina Beim ... Denver, CO
Hindley, Mark E. ... Salt Lake City, UT
Hindley, R. Craig ... Portland, OR
Hindley, Reginald R. ... Santa Rosa, CA
Hindley, Sharon R. ... Sacramento, CA
Hindley, Susie Inskeep
Salt Lake City, UT
Hindley, Vanessa A. ... Los Angeles, CA
Hindlian, Richard J. ... Boston, MA
Hindman, Darwin A., III ... Nashville, TN
Hindman, Darwin A., Jr. ... Columbia, MO
Hindman, Dean R. ... Springfield, MA
Hindman, Dennis M. ... Bellingham, WA
Hindman, Donald deForest
Elk Grove Village, IL
Hindman, Goldstein & Harder, P.C.
Columbia, MO
Hindman, John B. ... Dover, DE
Hindman, John Ward ... Pittsburgh, PA
Hindman, Kathryn M. ... Portland, OR
Hindman, Kenneth A. ... Atlanta, GA
Hindman, Kimberly Handlan ... Somerset, PA
Hindman, Larrie C. ... Kansas City, MO
Hindman, Matthew K. ... San Francisco, CA
Hindman, Richard A. ... Washington, DC
Hindman, Richard R. ... Golden, CO
Hindman, Robert ... Tyler, TX
Hindman, Robert J. ... Riverhead, NY
Hindman, Robert R. ... Boston, MA
Hindman, Scott A. ... Sioux City, IA
Hindman, Thomas J. ... Wheat Ridge, CO
Hindman, Tommy K. ... Knoxville, TN
Hindmand, Rick L. ... Chicago, IL
Hindmarch, Thomas M. ... Wilmington, DE
Bridgewater, NJ
Hindmarsh, Jack ... San Luis Obispo, CA
Hindmon, James O., Jr. ... Marietta, GA
Hindo, Shareen M. ... Pontiac, MI
Hindoien, Jeffrey M. ... Helena, MT
Hindriks, Inge ... New York, NY
Hinds, Alice (Ande) ... Dallas, TX
Hinds, Alison C. ... New York, NY
Hinds, Amanda M. ... St. Petersburg, FL
Tampa, FL
Hinds, Anna F. ... Knoxville, TN
Hinds, Anne ... Tucson, AZ
Hinds, Caroline Wells ... Mobile, AL
Hinds, Charlotte G. ... Bastrop, TX
Hinds, Clay B. ... Dallas, TX
Hinds, Collin Mcdermitt ... Tulsa, OK
Hinds, Cowan, Strange & Geer
Georgetown, SC
Myrtle Beach, SC
Hinds, Desmond J., Jr. ... Santa Monica, CA

Hinds, Donna P. ... Houston, TX
Hinds, Douglas L. ... Georgetown, SC
Hinds, Douglas W. ... St. Paul, MN
Hinds, E. Burke, III ... Minneapolis, MN
Hinds, Eldon L. ... Houston, TX
Hinds, Elizabeth A. ... Birmingham, AL
Greensboro, NC
Hinds, Elizabeth J. ... Morris, MN
Hinds, Elliot D. ... Los Angeles, CA
Hinds, Gordon D. ... Colorado Springs, CO
Hinds, Ian G. ... Department of Justice,
Immigration and Naturalization Service, GV
Hinds, Jackson C., Jr. ... Houston, TX
Hinds, James Andrew, Jr.
Los Angeles, CA
Hinds, James M. ... Tulsa, OK
Hinds, Jeffrey L. ... Clearwater, FL
St. Petersburg, FL
Hinds, Jill ... San Rafael, CA
Hinds, Joseph J. ... Las Vegas, NV
Hinds, Lawrence H. ... Logansport, IN
Hinds, Lennox S. ... New York, NY
Hinds, Leo M. ... Bakersfield, CA
Hinds, Leslie M. ... Bronx, NY
Hinds, Leslie M., P.C. ... Bronx, NY
Hinds, Linda A. ... Houston, TX
Hinds, M. Edwin, Jr. ... Myrtle Beach, SC
Hinds, Melanie Markovic ... Naperville, IL
Hinds, Richard D. ... Washington, DC
Hinds, Richard deC. ... Washington, DC
Hinds, Robert T., III
Greenwood Village, CO
Hinds, Robert T., Jr.
Greenwood Village, CO
Hinds, Robert T., Jr. and Associates, P.C.
Denver, CO
Greenwood Village, CO
Hinds, Russell E. ... Columbus, GA
Hinds, Stephanie M. ... San Francisco, CA
Hinds, Sylvia Ometa ... New York, NY
Hinds, Tamara ... San Francisco, CA
Hinds, Thomas M. ... Hillsboro, OR
Hinds, Vance W. ... Dallas, TX
Hinds, Warren R. ... Atlanta, GA
Hinds, Warren R., P.C. ... Atlanta, GA
Hinds, William L., Jr. ... Birmingham, AL
Hinds, William R. ... Arlington, VA
Hindt, Noel C. ... Ames, IA
Hindus, Michael S. ... San Francisco, CA
Hindy, George V. ... Brooklyn, NY
Hindy, Gregory J. ... Newark, NJ
Hine, Allen D. ... Sacramento, CA
Hine, Christopher W. ... Bakersfield, CA
Hine, Cynthia B. ... Franklin, TN
Hine, Edward, Jr. ... Rome, GA
Hine, Henry B. ... St. Louis, MO
Franklin, TN
Hine, Jeffrey P. ... Cape Girardeau, MO
Hine, John C. ... Goldsboro, NC
Hine, Kelly D. ... Dallas, TX
Hine Law Firm, The ... St. Louis, MO
Franklin, TN
Hine & Niedrach, P.C. ... Rome, GA
Hine, Sarah Anne ... New York, NY
Hine, Steve C. ... Miami, FL
Hine, Theresa L.
Department of Commerce, GV
Hine, William J. ... New York, NY
Hine, Zeena Young ... Stamford, CT
Hinebaugh, Jeffrey P. ... Cincinnati, OH
Hinegardner, Laura A. ... Covington, KY
Hinek, Jos. ... Elmont, NY
Hineline, Curt Roy ... Seattle, WA
Hineline, William R. ... Grand Rapids, MI
Hinely, Susan D. ... East Setauket, NY
Hineman, Charles M. ... Austin, TX
Hineman, Phillip D., Jr. ... Tempe, AZ
Hineman, Phillip D., Jr., P.C., Law Office of
Tempe, AZ
Hineman, Thomas G. ... Dallas, TX
Hiner, Alisha K. ... Wilmington, DE
Hiner, E. Lindsay ... Atlanta, GA
Hiner, Edwin A. ... Phoenix, AZ
Hiner, J. Randall ... New Bern, NC
Hiner, John R., Jr. ... Newark, DE
Hiner & Keesler ... Atlanta, GA
Hiner, Leslie Davis ... Indianapolis, IN
Hiner, Lucian W. ... Richmond, VA
Hiner, Thomas Y. ... Richmond, VA
Hinerfeld, Matthew B. ... Chicago, IL
Hinerfeld, Robert E. ... Los Angeles, CA
Hinerman & Associates, PLLC
Weirton, WV
Hinerman, Dana M. ... Haddon Heights, NJ
Hinerman, Heather A. ... Weirton, WV
Hinerman, Philip L. ... Philadelphia, PA
Hinerman, Raymond A. ... Weirton, WV
Hines, Ahlquist & Creitz, P.A. ... Erie, KS
Hines & Allen ... Ithaca, NY
Hines, Ashley ... Greenville, MS
Hines, Barbara Gasper ... Muncie, IN
Hines, Barry A. ... Louisville, KY
Hines, Barry O. ... Springfield, IL
Hines, Billy H. ... New Orleans, LA
Hines, Bonnie A. ... New Bern, NC
Raleigh, NC
Hines, Burton A., Jr. ... Cadillac, MI
Hines, Burton A., Sr. ... Cadillac, MI
Hines, Carol M. ... Chicago, IL
Hines, Caryn L. ... Department of Commerce,
Patent and Trademark Office, GV
Hines, Charles C., Law Offices of
Carbondale, IL
Hines, Charles D. ... Venice, FL
Hines, Christine E. ... West Palm Beach, FL
Hines, Cynthia A. ... Framingham, MA
Hines, Dane L. ... Provo, UT
Hines, Darryl A. ... Lilburn, GA

Hines, David H. ... San Francisco, CA
Hines, Dean Edward ... Beavercreek, OH
Hines, Deborah K. ... Washington, DC
Hines & Dentes ... Ithaca, NY
Hines, Donald A. ... Lansing, MI
Hines, Donna J. ... Framingham, MA
Hines, Doris Johnson ... Washington, DC
Hines, Dorothy L. ... Palo Alto, CA
Hines, Douglas E. ... Harrisburg, IL
Hines, Douglas E., P.C., Law Offices of
Harrisburg, IL
Hines, Earl S. ... Beaumont, TX
Hines, Edward F., Jr. (P.C.) ... Boston, MA
Hines, Edward M. W. ... New York, NY
Hines, Edward T. ... Brewton, AL
Hines, Ellen K. ... Atlanta, GA
Hines, Eric W. ... Lufkin, TX
Hines, Erin Bolan ... Chicago, IL
Hines, Ester Tomicic ... New York, NY
Hines, Eugene E. ... Washington, DC
Hines Firm, The ... Atlanta, GA
Hines, Frank M. ... Elk Grove Village, IL
Hines, Frederick ... Chesterfield, MO
Hines, Frederick Oscar ... Spencer, WV
Hines, G. Robert ... Cincinnati, OH
Hines, Geraldine S. ... Boston, MA
Hines, Glen Ray, Jr. ... San Diego, CA
Hines, Harold D. ... Oklahoma City, OK
Hines, Heather F. ... Chicago, IL
Hines & Henderson ... Long Beach, CA
Hines & Hines ... Cadillac, MI
Hines, J. Michael ... Washington, DC
Hines, J. Thomas ... Treasury Department,
Internal Revenue Service, GV
Hines, J. Thomas, Jr. ... Mobile, AL
Hines, James J. ... Arlington, VA
Hines, James P. ... Sun City Center, FL
Tampa, FL
Hines, James P., Jr. ... Sun City Center, FL
Tampa, FL
Hines, Jan Allen ... Annapolis, MD
Hines, Jeffrey A. ... Plano, TX
Hines, Jeffrey C. ... Baltimore, MD
Hines, Jeffrey J. ... Washington, DC
Fairfax, VA
Hines, Jennifer ... Denver, CO
Hines, Jim ... Cordell, OK
Hines, John G. ... Providence, RI
Hines, John J. ... Waterloo, IA
Hines, John L., Jr. ... Chicago, IL
Hines, John M. ... Farmville, NC
Hines, John P. ... Atlanta, GA
Hines, John R., III ... Waxahachie, TX
Hines, Jonathan H. ... New York, NY
Hines, Joseph E., Jr. ... Spartanburg, SC
Hines, Judith K. ... Department of Justice,
Executive Office for Immigration Review,
GV
Hines, Judith M. ... Elmhurst, IL
Hines, Judson T., Jr. ... Seattle, WA
Hines, Julius H. ... Charleston, SC
Hines, Karene-Sean E. ... Jamaica Plain, MA
Hines, Kim A. ... West Palm Beach, FL
Hines, Kimberly J. ... Newark, NJ
Hines, Kingsley B. ... Rosemead, CA
Hines, Kirsten C. ... Belleville, IL
Hines, L. Cecily ... Minneapolis, MN
Hines, Larry L. ... Oxnard, CA
Hines, Laura Jean ... Washington, DC
Hines, Lauren G. ... Winnetka, IL
Hines Law Firm, The, L.L.C.
Columbia, MO
Hines, Leelane E. ... Los Altos, CA
Hines, Linda J. ... St. Louis Park, MN
Hines, Lynne Wallin ... West Des Moines, IA
Hines, Marc S. ... Long Beach, CA
Hines, Marshall A. ... Fort Worth, TX
Hines, Mary H. ... Atlanta, GA
Hines, Michael J. ... Spokane, WA
Hines, Michael S. ... Ashland, WI
Hines, Michael T. ... Davenport, IA
Hines, N. William, Jr. ... Iowa City, IA
Hines Norman & Associates, P.L.
Sun City Center, FL
Tampa, FL
Hines, Norman P., Jr. ... Dallas, TX
Hines, P. Harris ... Atlanta, GA
Hines, Patrick Jay ... Arlington, VA
Hines & Patz, Inc. ... Providence, RI
Hines, Paul B. ... Bingham Farms, MI
Hines, Paul J. ... Boston, MA
Hines, Paul K. ... Stuart, FL
Hines, Paul W. ... Southfield, MI
Hines, Paula M. ... Grand Rapids, MI
Hines, R. Ken ... Wichita Falls, TX
Hines, Raymond W.
Research Triangle Park, NC
Hines, Richard A. ... New York, NY
Hines, Richard D. ... Spokane, WA
Hines, Richard K., V ... Atlanta, GA
Hines, Richard L. ... Erie, KS
Hines, Richard S. ... Columbus, OH
Hines, Robert B. ... Millersburg, OH
Hines, Robert Bolin, II ... Jonesville, VA
Hines, Robert G. ... Naples, FL
Hines, Robert H., (P.C.) ... Columbia, MO
Hines, Robert J. ... Paducah, KY
Hines, Robert J. ... Ithaca, NY
Hines, Robert, Jr. ... Paducah, KY
Hines, Robert L. ... San Francisco, CA
Hines, Robert L. ... Syracuse, IN
Hines, Robert, (P.C.) ... Columbia, MO
Hines, Rodney Alan ... Birmingham, AL
Hines, Roger D. ... Ocean Springs, MS
Hines, Sarah Hardin ... New York, NY
Hines, Stanford A. ... Savannah, GA
Hines, Stephen A. ... El Paso, TX
Hines, Stephen J. ... Boston, MA

Hines, Susan Hamrick ... Sarasota, FL
Hines, Suzanne ... Chicago, IL
Hines, Terence J. ... Brooklyn, NY
Hines & Thomas ... San Francisco, CA
Hines, Thomas J. ... Philadelphia, PA
Hines, Thomas M. ... Santa Monica, CA
Hines, Travis N. ... Trinity, TX
Hines, Virginia A. ... Salinas, CA
Hines, W. Christian, III ... Birmingham, AL
Hines, Walter V. ... Springfield, OH
Hines, William A. ... San Francisco, CA
Hines, William H. ... New Orleans, LA
Hines, William J. ... Washington, DC
Hines, William J. ... Boise, ID
Hines, William J. ... Columbia, SC
Hines, William R. ... Canton, OH
Hines, William T. ... Seattle, WA
Hines Bass, Ramona ... Philadelphia, PA
Hinesley, Harold A. ... Warrenton, GA
Hinesley, Rex A. ... San Bernardino, CA
Hinesley, William F., III ... Savannah, GA
Hinesley, William W. ... Dothan, AL
Hiney, Don D. ... San Diego, CA
Hiney & Trestick ... San Diego, CA
Hing, Bill O. ... San Francisco, CA
Hing, Conrad Anthony Lee ... New York, NY
Hing, Dari S. ... Phoenix, AZ
Hing, Glenn F. ... Philadelphia, PA
Hing, Gregory Ong ... Scottsdale, AZ
Hing, Kevin L. ... Los Angeles, CA
Hing, Lawrence S. ... Palo Alto, CA
Hing, Robert Ong ... Scottsdale, AZ
Hing, Stuart ... Oakland, CA
Hing, Valarie A. ... New York, NY
Hinga, Margaret Gilligan ... Allentown, PA
Hingeley, James ... Lynchburg, VA
Hinger, Susan Mc Cain ... San Antonio, TX
Hingerton, Patricia M. ... Hauppauge, NY
Hingle, Charles W. ... Billings, MT
Hingle, Michael E. ... San Jose, CA
Hingle, Norwood N., Jr. ... New Orleans, LA
Hingle, Waldon Michael ... Slidell, LA
Hingson, John Henry, III ... Oregon City, OR
Hingson, John Henry, III, P.C.
Oregon City, OR
Hingst, Steven M. ... Orange, CA
Hingston, Andrew L. ... St. Helena, CA
Hingston, Mark K. ... Treasury Department,
Office of the General Counsel, GV
Hingston, Robert A. ... Miami, FL
Hinig, Richard W. ... New Philadelphia, OH
Hiniker, James J., Jr. ... Stillwater, MN
Hiniker, Kevin J. ... St. Paul, MN
Hiniker, Lisa A. ... St. Paul, MN
Hiniker, Richard C. ... White Bear Lake, MN
Hink, Frederick P. ... Washington, DC
Hink, John A. ... Phoenix, AZ
Hink, Ralph M. ... Cleveland, OH
Hink, Valerie C. ... Tucson, AZ
Hink, Vincent F., Jr. ... Media, PA
Hink, William N. ... Minneapolis, MN
Hinkebein, B. Greg ... Jackson, MS
Hinkebein, Robert J. ... St. Louis, MO
Hinkel, Gregory E. ... Phoenix, AZ
Hinkel, J. William ... Towson, MD
Hinkel, Jay C. ... Topeka, KS
Hinkel, John E., Jr. ... Lexington, KY
Hinkel, Kevin M. ... Cleveland, OH
Hinkel, Mark J. ... Lexington, KY
Hinkelman, Lloyd ... Sacramento, CA
Hinkemeyer, Jonathan E. ... Chicago, IL
Hinkes, William E. ... Newton, NJ
Hinkfuss, Christopher R. ... Green Bay, WI
Hinkfuss, Sickel, Petitjean & Hinkfuss
Green Bay, WI
Hinkfuss, Timothy A. ... Fairfield, CT
Hinkfuss, William ... Green Bay, WI
Hinkhouse, Joseph A. ... Chicago, IL
Hinkle, Anthony W. ... Pittsburgh, PA
Hinkle & Associates, P.C. ... Atlanta, GA
Lawrenceville, GA
Hinkle, Barry E. ... Oakland, CA
Hinkle, Bernard David ... Jackson, GA
Hinkle, Buckner, Jr. ... Lexington, KY
Hinkle, Catherine D. ... Raleigh, NC
Hinkle, Catherine Sweeney ... Nevada, MO
Hinkle, Charles F. ... Portland, OR
Hinkle, Christina G. ... Chapel Hill, NC
Hinkle, Cox, Eaton, Coffield & Hensley,
L.L.P. ... Albuquerque, NM
Roswell, NM
Santa Fe, NM
Amarillo, TX
Austin, TX
Midland, TX
Hinkle, Donald E. ... Indianapolis, IN
Hinkle, Donald M. ... Tallahassee, FL
Hinkle, Edward H. ... San Diego, CA
Hinkle Elkouri, Law Firm L.L.C.
Wichita, KS
Hinkle & Gibbs ... Danville, IN
Indianapolis, IN
Hinkle & Guilfoyle ... Abilene, KS
Hinkle, Harlan H. ... Danville, IN
Hinkle, Herbert D. ... Lawrenceville, NJ
Hinkle, Jachimowicz & Pointer
San Jose, CA
Hinkle, James A. ... Lawrenceville, GA
Hinkle, James L. ... Roswell, NM
Hinkle, James R. ... Laguna Hills, CA
Hinkle, Jamison H. ... Raleigh, NC
Hinkle, John H. ... San Jose, CA
Hinkle, K. Daniel ... Sugar Land, TX
Hinkle, Kevin J. ... Danville, IN
Hinkle, Lawrence C. ... Los Angeles, CA
Hinkle, Lisa English ... Lexington, KY
Hinkle, Margaret R. ... Boston, MA
Hinkle, Marianne C. ... Dedham, MA

Hinkle, Matthew L. ... **Carmel, IN**
Hinkle, Max M. ... Abilene, KS
Hinkle, Michael W. ... **Oklahoma City, OK**
Hinkle, Patrick J. ... **South Bend, IN**
Hinkle, Racster & Lopez, Professional Corporation ... **Portland, IN**
Hinkle, Robert L. ... Tallahassee, FL
Hinkle, Ronald G. ... Olathe, KS
Hinkle, Samuel D., IV ... **Lexington, KY**
Louisville, KY
Hinkle & Smith ... Tulsa, OK
Hinkle, Stephen M. ... Oceanside, CA
Hinkle, Steven D. ... Cleveland, OH
Hinkle, Thomas L. ... **Ventura, CA**
Hinkle, Timothy H. ... **Lincoln, NE**
Hinkle, Timothy J. ... **Boston, MA**
Hinkle, Ward B. ... **Buffalo, NY**
Hinkle, Wayne W. ... **Portland, IN**
Hinkle, William H. ... Tulsa, OK
Hinkle, William W. ... **Portland, IN**
Hinkle, Winton M. ... **Wichita, KS**
Hinkley, Clare M. ... Colebrook, NH
Hinkley, Gerald M. ... **San Francisco, CA**
Hinkley & Giunta ... Dallas, TX
Midland, TX
Odessa, TX
Hinkley, Jeffrey ... **Midland, TX**
Hinkley, Joseph D. S. ... **Boston, MA**
Hinkley, Mark C. ... Lakeside, CA
Hinkly, Paul R. ... Fresno, CA
Hinko, Michael ... Tarpon Springs, FL
Hinkson, Yvonne Elizabeth
Department of Justice,
Bureau of Prisons, GV
Hinkston, Mark R. ... **Racine, WI**
Hinkston, Ulanda Rippy ... Hayward, CA
Hinley, Lacy W. ... Rincon, GA
Hinlicky, Timothy J. ... **Moorestown, NJ**
Hinman & Carmichael LLP
San Francisco, CA
Hinman, Clyde E. ... Raymore, MO
Hinman, Cynthia McKee ... Chicago, IL
Hinman, Dawn R. ... **Las Vegas, NV**
Hinman, Diane S. ... **Buffalo, NY**
Hinman, Frank M. ... **San Francisco, CA**
Hinman, Gary L. ... Newport Beach, CA
Hinman, George Burke ... **San Diego, CA**
Hinman, Harvey D. ... **San Francisco, CA**
Hinman, Howard & Kattell, LLP
Binghamton, NY
New York, NY
Norwich, NY
Oneonta, NY
Hinman, James S. ... Rochester, NY
Hinman, John A. ... **San Francisco, CA**
Hinman, Kevin M. ... **Bloomfield Hills, MI**
Detroit, MI
Hinman, Louis F., III ... Philadelphia, PA
Hinman, M. Karlynn ... Salt Lake City, UT
Hinman, Margaret B. ... Idaho Falls, ID
Hinman, Marion v. G. ... West New York, NJ
Hinman, Michael H. ... Idaho Falls, ID
Hinman, Michael J. ... Bismarck, ND
Hinman, Ralph M. ... **Dalton, GA**
Hinman, Richard C. ... San Francisco, CA
Hinman, Straub, Pigors & Manning, P.C.
Washington, DC
Albany, NY
Hinman, William H. ... **Menlo Park, CA**
San Francisco, CA
Hinn, Helen Kelly ... Wilmington, NC
Hinnant, A. Ray ... Columbia, SC
Hinnant, Christopher M. ... **Wilmington, NC**
Hinnant, Ernest B. ... Florence, SC
Hinnant, George R. ... **Richmond, VA**
Richmond, VA
Hinnant, Lee L. ... Coral Gables, FL
Hinnant, Lori Privette
Winston-Salem, NC
Hinnant, Patrice A. ... Greensboro, NC
Hinnant, Walter R. ... **Winston-Salem, NC**
Hinnebusch, Rosie ... Bradenton Beach, FL
Hinnegan, Ambrose J. ... Winston-Salem, NC
Hinnen, Nancy Patterson ... **Portland, OR**
Hinnen, Robert A. ... Portland, OR
Hinnen, Todd M. ... **Seattle, WA**
Hinnenkamp, Lawrence F. ... Lancaster, PA
Hinnenthal, Robert D. ... **New Ulm, MN**
Hinners, Charles C. ... Madison, WI
Hinners, Debra L. ... Tampa, FL
Hino, Akira ... Wahiawa, HI
Hino, Jayanne A. ... **Seattle, WA**
Hino, Michael S. ... **Berwyn, PA**
Hino, Roxanne M. ... Cape Coral, FL
Hinojosa, A. Robert ... Houston, TX
Hinojosa, Beatriz A. ... Dallas, TX
Hinojosa, Federico G., Jr. ... Edinburg, TX
Hinojosa, J. L." Larry " ... Houston, TX
Hinojosa, Joe R. ... **San Antonio, TX**
Hinojosa, Khougaz & Wallet
Los Angeles, CA
Hinojosa, Lynard C. ... **Los Angeles, CA**
Hinojosa, Nora E. ... **San Antonio, TX**
Hinojosa, Ricardo H. ... McAllen, TX
Hinoki, George ... San Jose, CA
Hinote, Thomas W. ... **Tuscaloosa, AL**
Hinrichs, C. Randall ... Central Islip, NY
Hinrichs, Cynthia Carol ... Atlanta, GA
Hinrichs, Fred T. ... New Orleans, LA
Hinrichs, John F. ... Stafford, TX
Hinrichs, Joyce D. ... Eureka, CA
Hinrichs, Laura ... Westminster, CA
Hinrichs, Liane K. ... New Orleans, LA
Hinrichs, Lloyd D. ... Dumfries, VA
Hinrichs, Lynn Ann ... **St. Louis, MO**
Hinrichs, Padma G. ... **Louisville, KY**
Hinrichs, Pamela J. ... **Bellevue, WA**
Hinrichs, Patricia Davis ... Coos Bay, OR
Hinrichs, Robert M. ... Geyserville, CA
Hinrichs, Timothy C. ... **Bethalto, IL**
Hinrichs, William H., Jr. ... Williamsburg, VA
Hinrichsen, Claudia A. ... **Garden City, NY**
Hinrichsen, Julieanne L. ... Sacramento, CA
Hinrichsen, Patrick L. ... **Sacramento, CA**
Hinsch, Claudia ... **Washington, DC**
Hinsch, Matthew E. ... **San Francisco, CA**
Hinsch, Randall A. ... **Phoenix, AZ**
Hinsdale, Beth ... **Roseland, NJ**
Hinsdale, Jane Z. ... San Francisco, CA
Hinsdale, Wayne E. ... Yuba City, CA
Hinsey, Joseph, IV ... **New York, NY**
Hinsey, N. Bruce, Jr. ... San Antonio, TX
Hinshaw, Alice J. ... **Helena, MT**
Hinshaw, Bradford J. ... Saratoga, CA
Hinshaw, Caroline K. ... **San Francisco, CA**
Hinshaw, Charlene M. ... Colfax, CA
Hinshaw & Culbertson ... **Phoenix, AZ**
San Francisco, CA
Fort Lauderdale, FL
Jacksonville, FL
Miami, FL
Tampa, FL
Belleville, IL
Champaign, IL
Chicago, IL
Crystal Lake, IL
Joliet, IL
Lisle, IL
Peoria, IL
Rockford, IL
Springfield, IL
Waukegan, IL
Munster, IN
Minneapolis, MN
St. Louis, MO
Appleton, WI
Brookfield, WI
Milwaukee, WI
Hinshaw, Curtis T., III ... **Longview, TX**
Hinshaw, Curtis T., III ... **Marshall, TX**
Hinshaw, Cynthia F. ... Raleigh, NC
Hinshaw, David C. ... Los Angeles, CA
Hinshaw, David L. ... **Houston, TX**
Hinshaw, Debra L. ... **Indianapolis, IN**
Hinshaw, Ed ... Panhandle, TX
Hinshaw, Edward A. ... Saratoga, CA
Hinshaw, Garl Edward (Eddie), Jr.
Charlotte, NC
Hinshaw, George A., (P.C.) ... Aurora, CO
Hinshaw, George W. ... Marshalltown, IA
Hinshaw, Greg L. ... **Raleigh, NC**
Hinshaw, James M. ... **Indianapolis, IN**
Hinshaw, Janice W. ... **Dallas, TX**
Hinshaw, Linda Cary ... **St. Louis, MO**
Hinshaw, Paul O. ... **Marquette, MI**
Hinshaw, Robert D. ... Winston-Salem, NC
Hinshaw, Robt. G. ... Sacramento, CA
Hinshaw, S'Lee Arthur, II ... Kansas City, MO
Hinshaw, Thomas M. ... Santa Barbara, CA
Hinshaw, Thomas V. ... Oakland, CA
Hinshaw, Winkler, Draa, Marsh & Still
Saratoga, CA
Hinshelwood, Bruce ... Orlando, FL
Hinshelwood, Mary Ann ... Christiansburg, VA
Hinsley, Christopher M. ... **St. Louis, MO**
Hinsley, Claude W. ... Pleasanton, CA
Hinsley, Jay C. ... Omaha, NE
Hinsley, Kelley ... **Morristown, TN**
Hinson, Alexander L. ... **Quincy, FL**
Hinson, Bobby D. ... **Charlotte, NC**
Hinson, Carl C., P.A. ... Tampa, FL
Hinson, Carl Coy ... Tampa, FL
Hinson, Christine Sampson
Huntsville, AL
Hinson, Dale B. ... **Washington, DC**
Hinson, Diane S. ... **Washington, DC**
Hinson, Edgar A. ... Tampa, FL
Hinson, Edward T., Jr. ... **Charlotte, NC**
Hinson, Eric W. ... Chapel Hill, NC
Hinson, Eric W., P.A. ... Chapel Hill, NC
Hinson, G. D. ... Graham, TX
Hinson, H. Douglas ... **Atlanta, GA**
Hinson, Herbert H. ... Panama City, FL
Hinson, Howard, Jr. ... Prescott, AZ
Hinson, Jerry T. ... Atlanta, GA
Hinson, Kelli M. ... **Dallas, TX**
Hinson, Lance W. ... Mount Pleasant, TX
Hinson, Leesa A. ... **Nashville, TN**
Hinson, Lynn James ... **Orlando, FL**
Hinson, Michael H. ... **Flagstaff, AZ**
Hinson, Michelle Hall ... Houston, TX
Hinson, Reid G. ... **Wilmington, NC**
Hinson, Richard L. ... **Florence, SC**
Hinson, Robert L. ... **St. Louis, MO**
Hinson, Robin L. ... **Charlotte, NC**
Hinson, Roxanne M. ... **Macon, GA**
Hinson, Russell C. ... Chattanooga, TN
Hinson, Thomas H. ... **Macon, GA**
Hinson, Thomas Lee ... Collierville, TN
Hinson, Walter B. ... Portland, OR
Hinson, Walter L. ... **Wilson, NC**
Hinson, Walter L., P.A. ... **Wilson, NC**
Hinson, Wayne E. ... Houston, TX
Hinsvark, Kenneth D. ... Palm Springs, CA
Hinterlong, James E. ... Grand Ridge, IL
Hintermeister, Anne O. ... New York, NY
Hintermeister, Jeffrey P. ... **Louisville, KY**
Hintermeister, John L. ... **Muscatine, IA**
Hintermeister, Knoernschild & Eichelberger
Muscatine, IA
Hintlian, Edward ... Boston, MA
Hinton, A. Jack ... **Atlanta, GA**
Hinton & Alfert, A Professional Corporation
Walnut Creek, CA
Hinton, Andrew J. ... Brooklyn, NY
Hinton, Andrew Paul ... Arlington, VA
Hinton, Barbara C. ... Martinez, CA
Hinton, Brent N. ... Corinth, MS
Hinton, Bynum E., Jr. ... Rockville, MD
Hinton, Carol D. ... **Greenville, SC**
Hinton, Catherine J. ... **Boston, MA**
Hinton, Charlene Louise ... Richmond, VA
Hinton, Charles D. ... St. Petersburg, FL
Hinton, Charles L., III ... Raleigh, NC
Hinton, Charles M., Jr. ... Garland, TX
Hinton & Cochran ... **Santa Rosa, CA**
Hinton, Donald E., Jr. ... **Hattiesburg, MS**
Hinton, Eric F. ... **Washington, DC**
Hinton, Floyd ... Portland, OR
Hinton, Frederick J. ... Richmond, VA
Hinton, Gregory T. ... Fairmont, WV
Hinton, Harry R. (Hank) ... Madisonville, KY
Hinton and Hewett ... Smithfield, NC
Hinton, J. Forrest ... **Birmingham, AL**
Hinton, J. Timothy, Jr. ... **Kingston, PA**
Hinton, Jack B., Jr. ... **Montgomery, AL**
Hinton, Jacki D. ... Indianapolis, IN
Hinton, James B. ... **Santa Rosa, CA**
Hinton, James R. ... Akron, OH
Hinton, James R., Co., L.P.A. ... Akron, OH
Hinton, Jas. M., Jr. ... Augusta, GA
Hinton, Jennifer Nock ... **Cleveland, OH**
Hinton, John B. ... Boise, ID
Hinton, John, III ... Department of Justice,
Tax Division, GV
Hinton, John, IV ... **Atlanta, GA**
Hinton, Joy Henry ... **New York, NY**
Hinton, Kristi L. ... **Springfield, MO**
Hinton, Larry E. ... Bowie, MD
Hinton, Larry F. ... **Bowling Green, KY**
Hinton, Leone, (Mrs.) ... Memphis, TN
Hinton, Loretta M. ... Memphis, TN
Hinton, Mark E. ... North Hills, CA
Hinton, Melissa C. ... **Sioux Falls, SD**
Hinton, Michael J. ... **Stamford, CT**
Hinton, Michael J. ... **Houston, TX**
Hinton, Myra L. ... Port Richey, FL
Hinton, Patrick L. ... Truckee, CA
Hinton, Paula W. ... **Houston, TX**
Hinton, Peter J. ... **Walnut Creek, CA**
Hinton, Phil R. ... Corinth, MS
Hinton & Powell ... **Atlanta, GA**
Hinton, Richard L. ... Flemingsburg, KY
Hinton, Robert, & Associates, P.C.
Dallas, TX
Hinton, Robert C. ... **New Haven, CT**
Hinton, Robert C., Jr. ... **Dallas, TX**
Hinton, Robert F., The Law Offices of
Los Angeles, CA
Hinton, Robert Granville ... **Lenoir City, TN**
Hinton, Robert M. ... Belmont, CA
Hinton, Shirley A. B. ... **Washington, DC**
Hinton, Susanna L. K. ... **Dallas, TX**
Hinton Sussman Bailey & Davidson
Houston, TX
Hinton, Violet K. ... Battle Creek, MI
Hinton, W. Kenneth ... Smithfield, NC
Hinton, Walter H., II ... **Greenville, SC**
Hinton, William W. ... San Mateo, CA
Hinton-Braaten, Kathleen
Newport Beach, CA
Hintz, Alfred R. ... Garden City, NY
Hintz, Donna Kathleen ... Kingston, NY
Hintz, Eric H. ... **Sacramento, CA**
Hintz, Gail Margaret ... Stony Brook, NY
Hintz, Hamilton L., Jr. ... Sacramento, CA
Hintz, Heather L. ... **Oklahoma City, OK**
Hintz, James G. ... Tallahassee, FL
Hintz, John E. ... Milwaukee, WI
Hintz, John M. ... **New York, NY**
Hintz, John P. ... **Lansing, MI**
Hintz, Patricia A. ... **Milwaukee, WI**
Hintz, Steven ... Ventura, CA
Hintz & Welch ... **Sacramento, CA**
Hintz, Werner E. ... Chicago, IL
Hintz, Werner E., & Associates ... Chicago, IL
Hintze, Harold A. ... Salt Lake City, UT
Hintze, Herbert O., Jr. ... Somers, NY
Hintze, H. J. ... Salt Lake City, UT
Hintze, John D. ... **Des Moines, IA**
Hintze, Michael D. ... **Phoenix, AZ**
Hintze, Michael D. ... **Redmond, WA**
Hintze, Michael D., & Associates, Ltd.
Phoenix, AZ
Hintze, Russell P. ... **Orlando, FL**
Hintze, William L. ... Seattle, WA
Hintze, William R. ... **San Antonio, TX**
Hintze & Wright ... Anchorage, AK
Seattle, WA
Hintzen, Erich H. ... **Troy, MI**
Hintzke, Edward S. ... Winnetka, IL
Hintzman, Steven A. ... Madison, WI
Hinueber, Mark A. ... Fort Smith, AR
Hinz, Edward A., Jr.
Rancho Palos Verdes, CA
Hinz, Harold W. ... Putnam Valley, NY
Hinz, Harry O. ... Triangle, VA
Hinz, Leon C. ... Minden City, MI
Hinz, Michele Gentry ... Seattle, WA
Hinz, Richard J. ... Phoenix, AZ
Hinz, Robert E. ... Galt, CA
Hinz, Stephanie L. ... **Cedar Rapids, IA**
Hinz, Susan ... Redding, CA
Hinz, William A. ... Los Angeles, CA
Hinze, Bruce Hunter ... **Redwood City, CA**
Hinze, Chrysten S. ... Greeley, CO
Hinze, Russell J. ... Cedar Falls, IA
Hinze, Stephani M. ... Minneapolis, MN
Hinze, Stephen C. ... **San Diego, CA**
Hinzey, Gregory W. ... St. Clairsville, OH
Hinzpeter, Denise M. ... New York, NY
Hiotaky, Julie A. ... Berkley, MI
Hiotis, Stephen C. ... **St. Louis, MO**
Hiott-Levine, Natalie M. ... **New York, NY**
Hipes, Jeanne Bynum ... **Norcross, GA**
Hipes, John D. ... **Norcross, GA**
Hipes & Norton, P.C. ... **Atlanta, GA**
Norcross, GA
Hipkens, Henry L. ... **Nashville, TN**
Hipler, Harry M. ... Dania, FL
Hipolit, James E. ... Lancaster, PA
Hipolit, Richard J.
Department Of Veterans Affairs,
Office of the General Counsel, GV
Hipolito, Alan J. ... Portland, OR
Hipp, Augustus J. ... Mendota Heights, MN
Hipp, Cheryl A. ... **Cleveland, OH**
Hipp, David C. ... New Philadelphia, OH
Hipp, David W. ... **Detroit, MI**
Hipp, Douglas G. ... Allison Park, PA
Hipp, Earl Clayton, Jr. ... Clemson, SC
Hipp, Edward B. ... Raleigh, NC
Hipp, Janie Simms ... Siloam Springs, AR
Hipp, John F. ... Bloomfield, NJ
Hipp, Karen Bruning ... Greenville, SC
Hipp, Kathryn M. ... Minneapolis, MN
Hipp, Kenneth B. ... **Honolulu, HI**
Hipp, Kent Lee ... **Orlando, FL**
Hipp, Logan A., Jr. ... San Antonio, TX
Hipp, Michele A. ... **Orlando, FL**
Hipp, P. Seale ... La Grange, GA
Hipp, Richard A. ... Houston, TX
Hipp, Richard A., P.C. ... Houston, TX
Hipp, Rodney V. ... **Overland Park, KS**
Kansas City, MO
Hipp, Spencer H. ... **Fresno, CA**
Hipp, Steve L. ... Wichita, KS
Hipp, Thomas U. ... **Wheaton, IL**
Hippard, Grayson M. ... Katy, TX
Hippard, James J., Jr. ... Houston, TX
Hippard, James J., Jr., Law Offices of
Houston, TX
Hippard, James J., Sr. ... Houston, TX
Hippe, James H. ... Richmond, VA
Hippe, Robert O. ... Gering, NE
Hippe, Russell H., Jr. ... **Nashville, TN**
Hippee, Charles W. ... Cedar Rapids, IA
Hippee, William H., Jr. ... **Minneapolis, MN**
Hippen, Sherrilyn A. ... **Baltimore, MD**
Hippenmeyer, Reilly & Moodie, S.C.
Mukwonago, WI
Waukesha, WI
Hippensteel-Hines, Lee A. ... Auburn, IN
Hipperson, Brian G. ... Spokane, WA
Hippert, Roger H. ... New Ulm, MN
Hippert, Thomas G. ... Tucson, AZ
Hippick, J. Michael ... Albany, NY
Hipple, Barbara Croft ... Atlanta, GA
Hipple, Michael D. ... Department of Defense,
Defense Legal Services Agency, GV
Hippler, Robert T. ... Aurora, CO
Hippler, Steven J. ... **Boise, ID**
Hippler, Thomas A. ... **Boston, MA**
Hippman, Howard B. ... Madison, WI
Hippo, C. Wayne, Jr. ... **Hollidaysburg, PA**
Hipps, Jonathan L. ... Monroe, NC
Hipps, Michael L. ... Columbus, GA
Hippsley, Heather A.
Federal Trade Commission,
Bureau of Consumer Protection, GV
Hipsh, Harlene Janet ... Kansas City, MO
Hipsh, Louise C. ... Kansas City, MO
Hipshman, Barry ... **New York, NY**
Hipskind, Alexander N. ... Roselle, IL
Hipskind, Joseph F., Jr. ... **St. Louis, MO**
Hipsman, Mitchell A.
Bay Harbor Islands, FL
Hipsman, Stacey H. S. ... Fort Lauderdale, FL
Hipwell, Arthur P. ... Louisville, KY
Hira, Archana ... Chicago, IL
Hirabayashi, Glen T.
United States Tax Court, GV
Hirabayashi, Mark J. ... Los Angeles, CA
Hirahara, S. Judy ... **Los Angeles, CA**
Hirai, Brian T. ... **Honolulu, HI**
Hirai, Colleen K. ... Honolulu, HI
Hirai, Craig K. ... **Honolulu, HI**
Hirai, Douglas T. ... **New York, NY**
Hirai, Lum & Tomita ... Honolulu, HI
Hirai, Richard H. ... Honolulu, HI
Hirai, Rina ... Oakland, CA
Hiraide, Mark T. ... **Torrance, CA**
Hiraide, Toshiro ... Torrance, CA
Hirakami, Sarah R. ... **Honolulu, HI**
Hiraldo-Sanchez, Herman ... **San Juan, PR**
Hiramatsu, Beverly Lynne K.
Honolulu, HI
Hiramoto, Joni T. ... San Francisco, CA
Hirani, Meenakshi A ... Winter Park, FL
Hirano, Kathryn Gale ... Los Angeles, CA
Hirano, Robert F. ... Honolulu, HI
Hirano, Ronald M. ... Los Angeles, CA
Hiraoka, Keith K. ... **Honolulu, HI**
Hirasuna, Robert Y. ... **Austin, TX**
Hirata, Hilda H. ... **Detroit, MI**
Hirata, Hilda H., P.C. ... **Detroit, MI**
Hirata, Irene K.
Department of Justice, GV
Hirata, Karen Jeffries ... Carlsbad, CA
Hirata, Lynne T. ... **San Francisco, CA**
Hirata, Masanori ... Los Angeles, CA
Hirata, Norman N. ... Santa Monica, CA
Hirata, William L. ... **Charlotte, NC**
Hirby, H. Oscar ... **Little Rock, AR**
Hird, David B. ... **Washington, DC**
Hird, Eldon R. ... Blanchardville, WI
Hird, Frederick S., Jr. ... **Washington, DC**
Hird, Gary M. ... Albert Lea, MN
Hird, T. Michael ... **San Diego, CA**
Hird, Thomas D. ... **Tulsa, OK**
Hire, Charles H. ... **Columbus, OH**
Hire, John S. ... **Mansfield, OH**

Hires, Jack M. ... Valparaiso, IN
Hires, W. Jefferson ... Jesup, GA
Hirji, Munira ... New York, NY
Hirka, Sara C. ... Hamilton, OH
Hirlinger, Charles L. ... Oklahoma City, OK
Hirn, Marvin J. ... Louisville, KY
Hirn, Michael Marvin ... Louisville, KY
Hirniak, Roman B. ... Princeton, NJ
Hirohama, Janis R. ... Los Angeles, CA
Hirons, Allen R. ... Marietta, GA
Hirose, Kathleen N. ... Los Angeles, CA
Hirose, Paul O. ... Santa Monica, CA
Hirose, William Y. ... San Francisco, CA
Hirose, Yuki A. ... New York, NY
Hiroshima, Jacobs, Roth and Lewis, A Law Corporation ... Sacramento, CA
Hiroshima, Philip ... Sacramento, CA
Hirota, Maile M. ... Honolulu, HI
Hirota, Ryan K., (A Prof. Law Corp.) Long Beach, CA
Hirotsu, Sandra L. ... Glendale, CA
Hirrel, Michael J. ... Department of Justice, Antitrust Division, GV
Hirrel, Richard J. ... Pasadena, CA
Hirsberg, David M. ... Savannah, GA
Hirsberg, D. H. ... Nashville, TN
Hirsch, Adams, Krekel, Putnam & Cahill Burlington, IA
Hirsch, A. E., Jr. ... Warren, NJ
Hirsch, Alan Seth ... Raleigh, NC
Hirsch, Albert ... Dallas, TX
Hirsch, Alison R. ... New York, NY
Hirsch, Allen I. ... Atlanta, GA
Hirsch, Amy E. ... St. Louis, MO
Hirsch, Amy Ellen ... Philadelphia, PA
Hirsch, Amy Susanne ... Miami, FL
Hirsch, Andrea E. ... Washington, DC
Hirsch, Andrea G. ... New York, NY
Hirsch, Andrea S. ... White Plains, NY
Hirsch, Andrew J. ... Palo Alto, CA
Hirsch, Andrew S. ... New York, NY
Hirsch, Arnold N. ... Apache Junction, AZ
Hirsch, Arnold W. ... Donora, PA
Hirsch, Arthur I. ... New York, NY
Hirsch, Aubrey B., Jr. ... New Orleans, LA
Hirsch, Austin L. ... Chicago, IL
Hirsch, Barbara B. ... Chicago, IL
Hirsch, Barry ... New York, NY
Hirsch, Barry I. ... Washington, DC
Hirsch, Barry L. ... Los Angeles, CA
Hirsch, Bernard ... North Miami Beach, FL
Hirsch, Brandon H. ... Washington, DC
Hirsch, Brian E. ... New York, NY
Hirsch, Brian M. ... Reston, VA
Hirsch, Bruce L. ... Columbus, OH
Hirsch, Burton M. ... Columbus, OH
Hirsch & Caplan Public Interest Law Firm Philadelphia, PA
Hirsch, Carl ... Newton, MA
Hirsch, Carl P., Jr. ... Chillicothe, OH
Hirsch, Cathy Brice ... Towson, MD
Hirsch, Charles A. ... Cranston, RI
Hirsch, Charles L. ... Garland, TX
Hirsch, Charles S. ... Baltimore, MD
Hirsch, Clifford ... Walnut Creek, CA
Hirsch, Clifford, A Professional Law Corporation ... Walnut Creek, CA
Hirsch, Corrine ... Cambridge, MA
Hirsch, Cynthia L. ... Dallas, TX
Hirsch, Daniel ... New York, NY
Hirsch, Daniel C. ... Washington, DC
Hirsch, Daniel I. ... New York, NY
Hirsch, Daniel M. ... New York, NY
Hirsch, Daniel O. Securities and Exchange Commission, Office of the General Counsel, GV
Hirsch, Davi L. ... Highland Park, IL
Hirsch, David A. ... Burlington, IA
Hirsch, David A. ... Fairfax, VA
Hirsch, David B. ... Seattle, WA
Hirsch, David H. ... Lompoc, CA
Hirsch, David J. ... Chicago, IL
Hirsch, David J. ... Towson, MD
Hirsch, David J. ... Mount Laurel, NJ
Hirsch, David J. ... Pittsburgh, PA
Hirsch, David L. ... Columbus, GA
Hirsch, David L., P.C. ... Columbus, GA
Hirsch, David M. ... Redding, CA
Hirsch, Debra T. ... Hackensack, NJ
Hirsch, Dennis D. ... Columbus, OH
Hirsch, Dennis R. ... New York, NY
Hirsch, Donald J. ... Chicago, IL
Hirsch, Douglas K. ... Rockville, MD
Hirsch, Douglas R. ... New York, NY
Hirsch, E. Kent ... Springdale, AR
Hirsch, E. Lynne ... Haddonfield, NJ
Hirsch, Edward D. ... Atlanta, GA
Hirsch, Elizabeth L. ... Santa Clara, CA
Hirsch, Emil ... Washington, DC
Hirsch, Ephraim J. ... Los Angeles, CA
Hirsch, Eric A. ... New York, NY
Hirsch, Eugene Jay ... Southfield, MI
Hirsch, Frank A., Jr. ... Charlotte, NC
Hirsch, Fred M. ... New York, NY
Hirsch, Frederic H. ... New York, NY
Hirsch, Gary D. ... New York, NY
Hirsch, Gayle Farb ... Pomona, NY
Hirsch, Geoffrey M. ... Memphis, TN
Hirsch, George ... New York, NY
Hirsch, George R. ... Florham Park, NJ New York, NY
Hirsch, Gerald B. ... Tucson, AZ
Hirsch, Gerald S. ... Bakersfield, CA
Hirsch, Gillian A. ... Latham, NY
Hirsch, Gladys E. ... Bethesda, MD
Hirsch, Gordon S. ... Skokie, IL
Hirsch, Gregg P. ... New York, NY
Hirsch, Guliet D. ... Flemington, NJ
Hirsch, H. Thomas ... Odessa, TX
Hirsch, H. Thomas, P.C. ... Odessa, TX
Hirsch, Hal M. ... Waldwick, NJ New York, NY
White Plains, NY
Hirsch, Hannah W. ... San Francisco, CA
Hirsch, Harry ... Fairfield, CT
Hirsch, Harry D. ... Bloomfield Hills, MI
Hirsch, Harry M. ... Richmond, VA
Hirsch, Henry L. ... Burlington, IA
Hirsch, Herbert ... New York, NY
Hirsch and Hofman ... Battle Creek, MI
Hirsch, Howard E. ... Los Angeles, CA
Hirsch, Howard J. ... Orange, CA
Hirsch, Howard S. ... Atlanta, GA
Hirsch, I. Jerome ... Phoenix, AZ
Hirsch, Ian J. ... Hackensack, NJ
Hirsch, Irving B. ... New York, NY
Hirsch, Irving H., (P.C.) ... Salinas, CA
Hirsch, Iva S. ... Phoenix, AZ
Hirsch, Ivan A. ... Fairfield, CT
Hirsch, J. Michael ... Minneapolis, MN
Hirsch, Jack H. ... Phoenix, AZ
Hirsch, James B. ... New York, NY
Hirsch, James E. ... Montpelier, VT
Hirsch, Janice L. Holtorf Lake Oswego, OR
Hirsch, Jason Ross ... Southfield, MI
Hirsch, Jay D. ... Houston, TX
Hirsch, Jay F. ... Atlanta, GA Columbus, GA
Hirsch, Jeffrey Allan ... Fort Lauderdale, FL
Hirsch, Jeffrey H. ... New York, NY
Hirsch, Jeffrey L. ... Crystal Lake, IL
Hirsch, Jeffrey L. ... Boston, MA
Hirsch, Jeffrey M. ... Houston, TX
Hirsch, Jerome C. ... Southfield, MI
Hirsch, Jerome S. ... New York, NY
Hirsch, Jessica E. ... New York, NY
Hirsch, Jocelyn A. ... Chicago, IL
Hirsch, Joel G. ... Los Angeles, CA
Hirsch, John B. ... Chicago, IL
Hirsch, John E. ... Department of Defense, GV
Hirsch, John E., Jr. ... Alexandria, VA
Hirsch, John J. ... Baltimore, MD
Hirsch, Jonathan C. ... Southfield, MI
Hirsch, Joram ... Bridgeport, CT
Hirsch, Joseph A. ... Bala Cynwyd, PA
Hirsch, Joseph I. ... Palo Alto, CA
Hirsch & Joyce ... Buffalo, NY
Hirsch, Judith M. ... Clearwater, FL
Hirsch & Kallman, P.C. ... Garden City, NY
Hirsch, Karen Weiss ... New York, NY
Hirsch, Karl F. ... Oklahoma City, OK
Hirsch, Kenneth L. ... Pittsburgh, PA
Hirsch, Kevan F. ... Norristown, PA
Hirsch, Kevin B. ... Bingham Farms, MI
Hirsch, Larry J. ... Westerly, RI
Hirsch, Lauren E. S. ... Troy, MI
Hirsch Law Office, P.C. ... Phoenix, AZ Scottsdale, AZ
Hirsch, Lawrence ... New Canaan, CT
Ridgefield, CT
Hirsch, Lawrence D. ... Phoenix, AZ
Hirsch, Lawrence Elliott ... Philadelphia, PA
Hirsch, Lee J. ... New York, NY
Hirsch, Leonard A. ... Dallas, TX
Hirsch, Linda ... New York, NY
Hirsch, Linda J. ... Pasadena, CA
Hirsch, Lonny ... Jersey City, NJ
Hirsch, Lori F. ... Whitehouse Station, NJ
Hirsch, Marcia P. ... Jamaica, NY
Hirsch, Marjorie A. ... Houston, TX
Hirsch, Mark ... Albuquerque, NM
Hirsch, Mark L. ... Fremont, CA
Hirsch, Mark S. ... Great Neck, NY New York, NY
Hirsch, Marla Durben ... Bethesda, MD
Hirsch, Martin ... Mount Vernon, NY
Hirsch, Martin J. ... Chicago, IL
Hirsch, Marvin ... Mineola, NY
Hirsch, Matthew I. ... New Brunswick, NJ
Wayne, PA
Hirsch, Matthew S. ... Stamford, CT New York, NY
Hirsch, Melissa ... Odessa, TX
Hirsch, Melvin L. ... Sarasota, FL
Hirsch, Merrill M. ... San Jose, CA
Hirsch, Meyer M. ... Hallandale Beach, FL
Hirsch, Michael A. ... Houston, TX
Hirsch, Michael A., Law Offices of, P.C. Houston, TX
Hirsch, Michael B. Federal Emergency Management Agency, Office of the General Counsel, GV
Hirsch, Michael D. ... Los Angeles, CA
Hirsch, Milton ... Columbus, GA
Hirsch, Milton C. ... Miami, FL
Hirsch, Mitchell H. ... Hempstead, NY
Hirsch, Morris W. ... San Francisco, CA
Hirsch, Nancy L. ... Chicago, IL
Hirsch, Neal W. ... Parsippany, NJ
Hirsch, Norman M. ... Chicago, IL
Hirsch, Partin, Grogan & Grogan, P.C. Columbus, GA
Hirsch, Patricia K. Environmental Protection Agency, Office of the General Counsel, GV
Hirsch, Paul J. ... Buffalo, NY
Hirsch, Perry L. ... Los Angeles, CA
Hirsch, Peter W. ... Battle Creek, MI
Hirsch, Peter W. ... Philadelphia, PA
Hirsch, Philip J. ... New York, NY
Hirsch & Pratt, LLP ... Oakley, KS Oberlin, KS
Hirsch, Raymond R. ... St. Louis, MO
Hirsch, Rebecca L. ... Washington, DC
Hirsch, Reginald A. ... Houston, TX
Hirsch, Renard A., Sr. ... Nashville, TN
Hirsch, Richard A. ... San Rafael, CA
Hirsch, Richard A. ... Tampa, FL
Hirsch, Richard G. ... Santa Monica, CA
Hirsch, Richard M. ... Los Angeles, CA
Hirsch, Richard M. ... Chicago, IL
Hirsch, Richard T. ... Atlanta, GA
Hirsch, Robert A. ... Washington, DC
Hirsch, Robert B. ... Washington, DC
Hirsch, Robert E. ... Riverhead, NY
Hirsch, Robert H. ... Chicago, IL
Hirsch, Robert J., (P.C.) ... Rochester, NY
Hirsch, Robert K. ... Framingham, MA
Hirsch, Robert M. ... San Francisco, CA
Hirsch, Ross H. ... Los Angeles, CA
Hirsch, Samuel ... New York, NY
Hirsch, Sandra C. ... New York, NY
Hirsch, Sarah Anne ... Rapid City, SD
Hirsch, Scott R. ... Hempstead, NY
Hirsch & Sheline ... Cincinnati, OH
Hirsch, Singer & Laatsch ... Akron, OH
Hirsch, Sondra Modell ... New York, NY
Hirsch, Stan B. ... Indianapolis, IN
Hirsch, Stanhope & Co., L.P.A. Chillicothe, OH
Hirsch, Stanley ... Garden City, NY
Hirsch, Stephen C. ... Chicago, IL
Hirsch, Steven A. ... Phoenix, AZ
Hirsch, Steven A. ... San Francisco, CA
Hirsch, Steven A. ... Chicago, IL
Hirsch, Steven F. United States Postal Service, Law Department, GV
Hirsch, Steven H. ... Irvine, CA
Hirsch, Steven J. ... Warwick, RI
Hirsch, Steven W. ... Oberlin, KS
Hirsch, Stewart M. ... Canton, MA
Hirsch, Stuart C. ... New York, NY
Hirsch, Stuart D. ... San Diego, CA
Hirsch, Susan L. ... Mill Valley, CA
Hirsch, Susan Lee ... Twinsburg, OH
Hirsch, Terry L. ... St. Petersburg, FL
Hirsch, Theodore M. ... Department of State, Office of the Legal Adviser, GV
Hirsch, Theresa connors ... Kansas City, MO
Hirsch, Thomas J. ... Kalamazoo, MI
Hirsch, Thomas J. ... Ocean Township, NJ
Hirsch, Tracy G. ... Miami, FL
Hirsch & Tubiolo ... Rochester, NY
Hirsch, V. Christopher ... Springfield, NJ
Hirsch, Valerie G. Smith ... Falls Church, VA
Hirsch, Velma B. ... Pittsburgh, PA
Hirsch & Westheimer, P.C. ... Houston, TX
Hirsch, William A. ... Kansas City, MO
Hirsch, William B. ... San Francisco, CA
Hirsch, William C. ... Cincinnati, OH
Hirsch, William J. ... Wayne, PA
Hirsch, William R. ... St. Louis, MO
Hirsch, William R., P.C. ... St. Louis, MO
Hirsch, William Reece ... San Francisco, CA
Hirsch & Wolf, P.C. ... Phoenix, AZ
Hirschauer, Gretchen A. ... Cleveland, OH
Hirschauer & Hirschauer, A Professional Association ... Logansport, IN
Hirschauer, Jay T. ... Logansport, IN
Hirschauer, Tom F. ... Logansport, IN
Hirschbach, George L. ... Sioux City, IA
Hirschberg, Cynthia J. ... New York, NY
Hirschberg, D. Jeffrey ... Washington, DC
Hirschberg, David ... Uniondale, NY
Hirschberg, David J. ... Randolph, MA
Hirschberg, Edwin ... New York, NY
Hirschberg & Friedman ... Calabasas, CA
Los Angeles, CA
Hirschberg, Gert K. ... Los Angeles, CA
Hirschberg, Larry L. ... Farnhamville, IA
Hirschberg, Leslie D. ... Calabasas, CA
Los Angeles, CA
Hirschberg, Mark L. ... Long Beach, CA
Hirschberg, Michael ... New York, NY
Hirschberg, Michel ... Los Angeles, CA
Hirschberg, Stuart M., Jr. ... Groton, CT
Hirschberg, Timothy D. ... Glendale, CA
Hirschberg, William E. ... New York, NY
Hirschberger, Gloria A. ... Johnstown, PA
Hirschberger, Ted L. ... Los Angeles, CA
Hirschboeck, David W. ... Chicago, IL
Hirschel, Joel ... New York, NY
Hirschel, Rebecca L. ... Spokane, WA
Hirschel, Ronald M. ... Gaithersburg, MD
Potomac, MD
Hirschel, Savitz, Parker & Hollman, P.A. Gaithersburg, MD
Potomac, MD
Hirschen, Jerrold I. ... New York, NY
Hirschen & Singer ... New York, NY
Hirschen, Thomas M. ... Schenectady, NY
Hirschenbein, Richard A. ... Norridge, IL
Hirschey, David B. ... Chicago, IL
Hirschey, Steven A. ... Lakewood, CO
Hirschfeld, Adam B. ... Winston-Salem, NC
Hirschfeld, Alan H. ... New York, NY
Hirschfeld, Audrey R. ... New York, NY
Hirschfeld, Clyde E. ... Newport Beach, CA
Hirschfeld, Fred G. ... Celina, OH
Hirschfeld, Jill A. ... Denver, CO
Hirschfeld, John C. ... Champaign, IL
Hirschfeld, Laura L. ... Nashville, TN
Hirschfeld, Laura W. ... New York, NY
Hirschfeld, Marcy D. ... New York, NY
Hirschfeld, Mark D. ... St. Louis, MO
Hirschfeld, Mary S. ... Scottsdale, AZ
Hirschfeld, Michael ... New York, NY
Hirschfeld, Michael A. ... Cincinnati, OH
Hirschfeld, Michael L. ... New York, NY
Hirschfeld and Mielke ... Celina, OH
Hirschfeld, Neal W. ... Fort Lauderdale, FL
Hirschfeld, Neil B. ... New York, NY
Hirschfeld, Phyllis K. ... Denver, CO
Hirschfeld, Sidney ... Mineola, NY
Hirschfeld, Stephen J. ... San Francisco, CA
Hirschfeld, William ... Garden City, NY
Hirschfelder, Beth L. ... Washington, DC
Hirschfield, Frederic L. ... Petaluma, CA
Hirschfield, James D. ... Litchfield, CT
Hirschfield, Jeffrey L. ... Stockton, CA
Hirschfield, Joseph B. ... White Plains, NY
Hirschfield, Marc E. ... New York, NY
Hirschfield, Martha ... Department of Justice, Civil Division, GV
Hirschfield, Paul R. ... Pittsburgh, PA
Hirschhaut, Suanne P. ... Chicago, IL
Hirschhorn, Alan K. ... Garden City, NY
Hirschhorn, Andrew J. ... Roslyn Heights, NY
Hirschhorn, Arthur J. ... Philadelphia, PA
Hirschhorn, Austin ... Troy, MI
Hirschhorn, Austin, P.C. ... Troy, MI
Hirschhorn, David B. ... New York, NY
Hirschhorn, David Meir ... Longmeadow, MA
Hirschhorn, Edward A. ... Bel Air, MD
Hirschhorn, Eric L. ... Washington, DC
Hirschhorn, Herbert H. ... New York, NY
Hirschhorn, James M. ... Newark, NJ New York, NY
Hirschhorn, Joel ... Coral Gables, FL
Hirschhorn, Joel, P.A. ... Coral Gables, FL Miami, FL
Hirschhorn, Leonard J. ... Montebello, NY
Hirschhorn, Madeleine S. ... Garden City, NY
Hirschhorn, Mark P. ... New York, NY
Hirschhorn, Philip L. ... New York, NY
Hirschhorn, Robert B. ... Lewisville, TX
Hirschhorn, Roy A. ... Treasury Department, Internal Revenue Service, GV
Hirschhorn, Steven J. ... New York, NY
Hirschi, David P. ... West Bountiful, UT
Hirschi, Helen ... Marietta, OH
Hirschi, J. Rand ... Salt Lake City, UT
Hirschi, Jean Ann ... Palm Desert, CA
Hirschi, Kenneth D. ... Washington, DC
Hirschklau, Morton ... Fair Lawn, NJ
Hirschkop & Associates, P.C. Alexandria, VA Fairfax, VA
Hirschkop, Philip J. ... Alexandria, VA
Hirschkorn, Jerry Y. ... Morristown, NJ
Hirschl, Peter D. ... Hartford, CT
Hirschler, Arthur A. ... New York, NY
Hirschler, Fleischer, Weinberg, Cox & Allen A Professional Corporation Fredericksburg, VA Richmond, VA
Hirschman, Elizabeth Hurst ... Carmel, IN
Hirschman, Jason T. ... Los Angeles, CA
Hirschman, Jodi Ellen ... Bronx, NY
Hirschman, John F. ... Chicago, IL
Hirschman, Karen L. ... Dallas, TX
Hirschman, Kenneth E. San Francisco, CA
Hirschman, Robert ... Encino, CA
Hirschman, Robert ... Los Angeles, CA
Hirschman, Sherman J. West Bloomfield, MI
Hirschman, Stuart Z. ... New York, NY
Hirschmann, Allen E. ... Arlington, VA
Hirschmann, Ralph F., Law Offices of Los Angeles, CA
Hirschmann, Ross A. ... Los Angeles, CA
Hirschmann, Thomas R. ... Huntington, NY
Hirschmiller, Howard J. ... Buffalo, NY
Hirschoff, Jon T. ... New Haven, CT
Hirschoff, Mary-Michelle Upson Bethany, CT
Hirschorn, Elyse G. ... New York, NY
Hirschorn, Mark G. ... Buffalo, NY
Hirschson, Linda B. ... New York, NY
Hirschsprung, Abraham J. ... New York, NY
Hirschtick, Michael J. ... Chicago, IL
Hirschtick, Steven R. ... Los Angeles, CA
Hirschtritt, Joel S. ... New York, NY
Hirschtritt, Richard ... Chicago, IL
Hirschtritt, Shelly Matthew ... Chicago, IL
Hirschy, John A. ... Portland, OR
Hirsen, Mary W. ... Lake Forest, IL
Hirsen, Sarah S. ... Evanston, IL
Hirsh, A. David ... New York, NY
Hirsh, Adam D. ... Department of Justice, Antitrust Division, GV
Hirsh, Bernard ... Dallas, TX
Hirsh, Bjorgaard & Rogers, P.L.C. Tucson, AZ
Hirsh, Bobbe ... Chicago, IL
Hirsh, Bruce R. Executive Office Of The President, Office of the U.S. Trade Representative, GV
Hirsh, David A. ... Washington, DC
Hirsh, David B. ... Philadelphia, PA
Hirsh, Dwight C. ... Newport Beach, CA
Hirsh, Dwight C. ... Newport Beach, CA
Hirsh, Ernest H. ... Cincinnati, OH
Hirsh, Esther Z. ... Berkeley, CA
Hirsh, Fred J. ... New York, NY
Hirsh, Frumeth Brenda ... Flint, MI
Hirsh, Gilbert ... Denver, CO
Hirsh, Harold L. ... Washington, DC
Hirsh, Irving M. ... Plainfield, NJ
Hirsh, James G. ... Minneapolis, MN
Hirsh, Jeffrey S. ... Miami, FL
Hirsh, Judith G. ... Harrisburg, PA
Hirsh, Kenneth J. ... Durham, NC
Hirsh, Lawrence S. ... New York, NY
Hirsh, Lester H. ... Lynbrook, NY
Hirsh, Merril Jay ... Washington, DC
Hirsh, Paul J. ... Parsippany, NJ
Hirsh, Richard L. ... Hinsdale, IL

Hirsh, Robert J. .... Tucson, AZ
Hirsh, Robert M. .... New York, NY
Hirsh, Robert M. .... New York, NY
Hirsh, Robert W., & Associates
Beverly Hills, CA
Hirsh, Solomon I. .... Chicago, IL
Hirsh, Steven J. .... Chicago, IL
Hirsh, Theodore W. .... Baltimore, MD
Hirsh, William D. .... San Jose, CA
Hirshberg, Amy Lederman .... Tucson, AZ
Hirshberg, David Gordon .... Nashville, TN
Hirshberg, Glen H. .... Livonia, MI
Hirshberg, Gustine & Straka, LLP
Pittsburgh, PA
Hirshberg, Kimberly M.
Plymouth Meeting, PA
Hirshberg, Neil J. .... Farmington Hills, MI
Hirshberg, Philip M. .... Boston, MA
Hirshberg, Robert L. .... Washington, DC
Hirshberg, Spencer D. .... Pittsburgh, PA
Hirshen, Annick T. .... San Francisco, CA
Hirshfeld, David W. .... New York, NY
Hirshfeld, Neal L. .... Nyack, NY
Hirshfield, Ruth G. .... New York, NY
Hirshfield, Adam E. .... New York, NY
Hirshfield, Joel A. .... White Plains, NY
Hirshfield, Matthew S. .... New York, NY
Hirshfield, Peter B. .... New York, NY
Hirshfield, Stuart .... New York, NY
Hirshfield, Thomas .... Los Angeles, CA
Hirshland, David L. .... Hollywood, CA
Hirshland, Michael J. .... United States Senate, Committee Legal Personnel, GV
Hirshland, Samuel L. .... Philadelphia, PA
Hirshman, Alise B. .... New York, NY
Hirshman, Ellen Hobbs .... Cleveland, OH
Hirshman, Harold C. .... Chicago, IL
Hirshman, Jesse A. .... Pittsburgh, PA
Hirshman, Karl J. .... Boston, MA
Hirshman, Linda R. .... Chicago, IL
Hirshman, Melvin .... Crownsville, MD
Hirshman, Michele .... New York, NY
Hirshman, Neil S. .... Chicago, IL
Hirshon, David M. .... Portland, ME
Hirshon, Jack T. .... San Jose, CA
Hirshon, Robert E. .... Portland, ME
Hirshon, Sheldon I. .... New York, NY
Hirshorn, Donald P. .... Albany, NY
Hirshorn, M. Bruce .... Vienna, VA
Hirshorn, Richard E. .... Voorhees, NJ
Hirshowitz, Melvin S. .... New York, NY
Hirsig, Peter J. .... Sacramento, CA
Hirsman, Kathleen Roche .... Chicago, IL
Hirson, David .... Newport Beach, CA
New York, NY
Hirson, Kevin M. .... New York, NY
Hirson Wexler Perl & Stark, A Professional Corporation .... Phoenix, AZ
Los Angeles, CA
Newport Beach, CA
San Diego, CA
Las Vegas, NV
New York, NY
Hirst, Albert E. .... Redlands, CA
Hirst & Applegate, A Professional Corporation .... Cheyenne, WY
Hirst & Baughman .... Redlands, CA
Hirst, Christopher Lee .... Seattle, WA
Hirst, Frank L. .... La Mesa, CA
Hirst, Gary T. .... San Antonio, TX
Hirst, Holly .... Chicago, IL
Hirst, Marti V. .... Jersey City, NJ
Hirst, Peter G. .... Washington, DC
Hirst, Ronald Vance .... Chicago, IL
Hirst, William A. .... Pleasanton, CA
Hirt, David S. .... Kent, OH
Hirt & Hirt .... Kent, OH
Hirt, Janet R. .... Nashville, TN
Hirt, Jeffrey A. .... Houston, TX
Hirt, Juliette L. .... San Francisco, CA
Hirt, Lisa J. .... Kent, OH
Hirt, MacArthur & Ruggirello, P.C.
Mount Clemens, MI
Hirt, Matthew E.
Federal Labor Relations Authority, Authority Member Staff, GV
Hirt, Priscilla V. .... Troy, MI
Hirt, Stanley .... Mount Clemens, MI
Hirt, Theodore C. .... Department of Justice, Civil Division, GV
Hirte, John D. .... St. Paul, MN
Hirter, Amy L. .... Denver, CO
Hirth, Alan N. .... Cleveland, OH
Hirth, Leon B. .... New York, NY
Hirth, Michelle J. .... San Francisco, CA
Hirth, Robert W. .... New York, NY
Hirtle, Robert L. .... Hartford, CT
Hirtreiter, Richard P. .... St. Petersburg, FL
Hirtriter, Kellye H. .... Houston, TX
Hirtz, Kenneth C. .... Richmond, VA
Hirtz, Ted .... Houston, TX
Hirtzel, Gregory S. .... Lancaster, PA
Hirzel, Jeff L. .... Guthrie, OK
Hirzel, Jeff L., Inc. .... Guthrie, OK
Hirzel, Patrick S. .... Battle Creek, MI
Hisaka, Steven Katsumi .... Honolulu, HI
Hisaka Stone Goto Yoshida Cosgrove & Ching .... Honolulu, HI
Hisatomi, Carol Katsuko Ouye
Sacramento, CA
Hiscock & Barclay, LLP .... Albany, NY
Buffalo, NY
Islandia, NY
Syracuse, NY
Hiscock, Dana W. .... New York, NY
Hiscock, David F. .... Seattle, WA
Hiscock, David K. .... Seattle, WA
Hiscock, Matthew G. .... Akron, OH
Hiscock, William C. .... Coronado, CA
Hiscocks, Patrick D. .... Oxnard, CA
Hiscocks, Richard I. .... San Francisco, CA
Hiscott, Gilbert E. .... Toms River, NJ
Hiscott, John A. .... Milford, PA
Hiscott, John A. .... Stroudsburg, PA
Hiscott, Thomas O.
West Conshohocken, PA
Hiscox, David B. .... Kingston, PA
Hiscox, Frank S. .... San Jose, CA
Hiscox, Harry R. .... Kingston, PA
Hiscox & Musto .... Kingston, PA
Wilkes-Barre, PA
Hise, Daniel G. .... Jackson, MS
Hise, James C. .... Washington, DC
Hise, Lisa M. .... Tucson, AZ
Hise, Lloyd, Jr. .... Spruce Pine, NC
Hise, Lloyd, Jr., P.A. .... Spruce Pine, NC
Hise, Stephen D. .... Decatur, GA
Hise, William P. .... Minneapolis, MN
Hiser, Benjamin E. .... Piqua, OH
Hiser, Deborah C. .... Austin, TX
Hiser, Eric L. .... Phoenix, AZ
Hiser, Helen F. .... Washington, DC
Hiser, Matthew F. .... Detroit, MI
Hiser, Miriam, Law Offices of
San Francisco, CA
Hiser, Susan Hartmus
Bingham Farms, MI
Hiser, Ted S. .... Cleveland, OH
Hiser, William L., P.C. .... Laramie, WY
Rawlins, WY
Hiser, Wray C. .... Indianapolis, IN
Hisert, George A. .... San Francisco, CA
Hisey, Allan J. .... Albuquerque, NM
Hisey & Cadigan, LLP .... Albuquerque, NM
Hisey, D. Michael .... Ardmore, OK
Hisey, Randy S. .... South Sioux City, NE
Hishon Firm, The, LLC .... Atlanta, GA
Hishon, Lori M. .... Boston, MA
Hishon, Robert H. .... Atlanta, GA
Hishta, Kevin P. .... Atlanta, GA
Hisiger, Gary C. .... Garden City, NY
Hisiger, James I. .... New York, NY
Hisim, Ahmet .... Baltimore, MD
Hisiro, Carl S. .... Harrisburg, PA
Hiskes, John A. .... Orland Park, IL
Hiskey, David D. .... Placentia, CA
Hiskey, Timothy Grant .... Washington, DC
Hiskey, Carolyn Gilmer .... Charlotte, NC
Hislip, Daniel W. .... Florham Park, NJ
Hislop, Carney and Troupe .... Boston, MA
Hislop, David C. .... Florham Park, NJ
Hislop, Jack B. .... Bakersfield, CA
Hislop, John D., III .... Boston, MA
Hislop, John J. .... Wayne, NJ
Hislop, Michael D. .... Alexandria, LA
Hislop, Reginald M., Jr. .... West Allis, WI
Hisrich, Thomas H. .... Dover, OH
Hiss, Bernard F. .... South Bend, IN
Hiss, Ryan A. .... Raleigh, NC
Hiss, Stephanie Lindsey .... Richmond, VA
Hissam Greider, Christine P. .... Naples, FL
Hissong, Anthony L. .... Columbus, OH
Hissong, David C. .... Detroit, MI
Hissong, Joseph G. .... New York, NY
Hissong, Marcia L. .... Plymouth, MI
Hissong, Rebecca L. .... New York, NY
Hissong, Stacy L. .... Lansing, MI
Histed, Bradley J. .... Columbus, OH
Histen, Harry J. .... Riverside, CA
Hitaffer, James V. .... Laurel, MD
Hitaffer, Thedford I. .... Toledo, OH
Hitch, Dwight Hobart .... Nicholasville, KY
Hitch, Horace .... Minneapolis, MN
Hitch, Jason W. .... Guymon, OK
Hitch, Leon F. .... Santa Monica, CA
Hitch, Robert M., III .... Savannah, GA
Hitch, Thomas M. .... East Lansing, MI
Hitchan, Gregory D. .... San Francisco, CA
Hitchcock, Bion E. .... Bartlesville, OK
Hitchcock, Bowman, Schachter & Beverly, A Professional Corporation .... Torrance, CA
Hitchcock, Christopher B. .... New York, NY
Hitchcock, Claude Edward
Baltimore, MD
Hitchcock, Clayburn Christopher
Bisbee, AZ
Hitchcock, Consuelo J. .... Washington, DC
Hitchcock, Cornish F. .... Washington, DC
Hitchcock & Cunningham, P.A.
Fort Lauderdale, FL
Hitchcock, Daniel E. .... Oregon City, OR
Hitchcock, David L. .... Dallas, TX
Hitchcock, Donald A. .... Memphis, TN
Hitchcock, Edward J. .... St. Paul, MN
Hitchcock, Frederick L. .... Chattanooga, TN
Hitchcock, Greg K. .... Portland, OR
Hitchcock, Harold K. .... Shreve, OH
Hitchcock, Hicks and Conlogue
Bisbee, AZ
Douglas, AZ
Hitchcock, J. Franklin .... Sparta, GA
Hitchcock, James E. .... Defiance, OH
Hitchcock, John Franklin .... Smiths, AL
Hitchcock, John W. .... McMinnville, OR
Hitchcock, Judy L. .... San Francisco, CA
Hitchcock, Mark L. .... Edmond, OK
Hitchcock, Mindy L. .... Southfield, MI
Hitchcock, Paul R. .... Jacksonville, FL
Hitchcock, Peter T. .... Houston, TX
Hitchcock & Potts .... Charleston, SC
Summerville, SC
Hitchcock, Raebern B., Sr. .... St. Paul, MN
Hitchcock, Randy M. .... Lowell, MA
Hitchcock, R. H. Bo .... Fort Lauderdale, FL
Hitchcock, Richard E. .... Bakersfield, CA
Hitchcock, Robin L. .... Charleston, SC
Summerville, SC
Hitchcock, Russell W. .... Tampa, FL
Hitchcock, Sara L. .... Albany, GA
Hitchcock, Stephen Jay .... Detroit, MI
Hitchcock, Steven D. .... Washington, DC
Hitchcock, Teresa K. .... Irving, TX
Hitchcock, Vernon T. .... Santa Rosa, CA
Hitchcock, Walter P. .... San Mateo, CA
Hitchcock, Wendy S. .... Lake Oswego, OR
Hitchcock, William D. .... Anchorage, AK
Hitchen, Kenneth E. .... St. Marys, OH
Hitchens, Christopher E. .... Rockville, MD
Hitchens, Donna J. .... San Francisco, CA
Hitchens, Glenn E. .... Dover, DE
Hitchens, J. Robert .... Lewes, DE
Hitchens, James W. .... St. Petersburg, FL
Hitchens, Linda S. .... Long Beach, CA
Hitchens, Lyle R. .... Daytona Beach, FL
Hitchens, Paul W. .... St. Petersburg, FL
Hitchens, Paul W., P.A. .... St. Petersburg, FL
Hitchens, William R., Jr. .... Wilmington, DE
Hitchery, Mary M. .... Dallas, TX
Hitching, H. James .... Chattanooga, TN
Hitchings, Andrew M. .... Sacramento, CA
Hitchings, Barry P. .... San Antonio, TX
Hitchings, Joseph L. .... Lemoyne, PA
Hitchings, Pollock & Bernard
San Antonio, TX
Hitchings, Timothy L. .... Bear, DE
Hitchins, Kevin R. .... Marshalltown, IA
Hitchman, Terry D. .... Mansfield, OH
Hitchner, Carl H. .... San Francisco, CA
Hitchner, Elam M., III .... Philadelphia, PA
Hite, C. E. .... Hartville, OH
Hite, Collin J. .... Richmond, VA
Hite, Daniel Durand .... Nashville, TN
Hite, David L. .... Newark, OH
Hite, Douglas N. .... Plymouth, IN
Hite, Frederic C. .... Worcester, MA
Hite and Heath .... Utica, OH
Hite, Hollis M. .... Buffalo, NY
Hite, J. Eppa, III .... Palo Alto, CA
Hite, James N. .... Williamsville, NY
Hite, John E. .... Woodbury, MN
Hite, John William, III .... New Orleans, LA
Hite, Kelly Sweeney .... Alexandria, VA
Hite, Kendall L. .... Santa Ana, CA
Hite, Kenneth G. .... Greenville, NC
Hite, Loraine Lombardi .... Arundel, ME
Hite, M. Catherine .... Miami, FL
Hite, Margery .... Everett, WA
Hite, Matthew Edelen .... Lexington, KY
Hite, Nora J. .... Long Beach, CA
Hite & Pruitt .... Abbeville, SC
Hite, Randall L. .... Santa Ana, CA
Hite, Richard C. .... Wichita, KS
Hite, Robert G. .... Honolulu, HI
Hite, Robert S. .... Albany, NY
Hite, Ronald G. .... Jamestown, NY
Hite, Teresa Moss .... Memphis, TN
Hite, Thomas E., Jr. .... Abbeville, SC
Hites, Earle F. .... Merrillville, IN
Portage, IN
Hitesman, Darcy L. .... Minneapolis, MN
Hitman, Mark K. .... Sacramento, CA
Hitov, Steven A. .... Lakeland, FL
Hitpas, Patrick J. .... Carlyle, IL
Hitselberger, Carol A. .... Chicago, IL
Hitselberger, Joseph G. .... Arlington, VA
Hitson, Brent D. .... Birmingham, AL
Hitson, C. Peter .... Pittsburgh, PA
Hitson, Gillian L. .... Pittsburgh, PA
Hitson, Kenneth A., Jr. .... Montgomery, AL
Hitt, Alvin .... Savannah, GA
Hitt, Brian M. .... Charlotte, NC
Hitt, Charles L. .... Dallas, TX
Hitt, Curtis Wayne .... Paragould, AR
Hitt, Cynthia K. .... Baltimore, MD
Hitt, Danny L., Jr. .... Portland, OR
Hitt, David H. .... Dallas, TX
Hitt, Dwayne D. .... Fort Worth, TX
Hitt, F. Richard .... St. Petersburg Beach, FL
Hitt, Fred A. .... Cheshire, CT
Hitt, Fredric M. .... Sanford, FL
Hitt, Gregory P. .... Austin, TX
Hitt, Heather .... Fort Worth, TX
Hitt, Hiller & Monfils, LLP .... Portland, OR
Hitt, Jeffrey B. .... Dallas, TX
Hitt, Jeffrey W. .... Houston, TX
Hitt, John C., Jr. .... Chicago, IL
Hitt, John J. .... Boston, MA
Hitt, John Rockwell .... Boston, MA
Hitt, Laura M. .... Birmingham, AL
Hitt, Leo N. .... Pittsburgh, PA
Hitt, Mark Donald .... Chicago, IL
Hitt, Michael D. .... Tacoma, WA
Hitt, Michael G. .... Madison, WI
Hitt, Michele .... Los Angeles, CA
Hitt, Patrick C. .... Green Bay, WI
Hitt & Patterson .... Houston, TX
Hitt, Richard D. .... Jackson, MI
Hitt, Sachner & Miele .... Cheshire, CT
Hitt, Sandra Lee .... Los Angeles, CA
Hitt, Shelley Sharp .... Englewood, CO
Hitt, Stephanie A. .... Oakbrook Terrace, IL
Hitt, Susan Z. .... Columbia, SC
Hitt, W. Chas. .... Greenwood, VA
Hitt, William Howell .... San Diego, CA
Hittelman, Paul M. .... Beverly Hills, CA
Hittelman, Steven G. .... Orange, CA
Hittelman, Tara Beaudoin .... Houston, TX
Hitter, Joseph I. .... Dayton, OH
Hittig, H. Christopher .... San Francisco, CA
Hittinger, Carl W. .... Philadelphia, PA
Hittinger, J. Brian .... Merrillville, IN
Hittinger, Richelle D. .... Bala Cynwyd, PA
Hittinger, Stewart T. .... Indianapolis, IN
Hittle, David W. .... Salem, OR
Hittle, Jack G. .... Noblesville, IN
Hittle, Kathleen J. .... Naperville, IL
Hittle, L. Bradley
Executive Office Of The President, Office of National Drug Control Policy, GV
Hittle, Larry G. .... Portland, OR
Hittle, Max W., Jr. .... Indianapolis, IN
Hittle, Richard M. .... Chicago, IL
Hittleman, Michael J. .... Fort Lauderdale, FL
Hittler, William D. .... Minneapolis, MN
Hittner, Arthur D., (P.C.) .... Boston, MA
Hittner, Barry G. .... Providence, RI
Hittner, Bernard J. .... Costa Mesa, CA
Hittner, David .... Houston, TX
Hittner, Peter F. .... Birnamwood, WI
Schofield, WI
Hitz, Lori A. .... Dallas, TX
Hitz, William .... Annapolis, MD
Hitzeman, Donald W.
San Bernardino, CA
Hitzeman, James W. .... Chicago, IL
Hitzeman, Steven D. .... Milwaukee, WI
Hitzemann, Diane D. .... Pottsville, PA
Hitzig, Susan .... New York, NY
Hitzler, S. Ted .... Fond du Lac, WI
Hiu, Natalie S. .... Honolulu, HI
Hiura, Stephen K. .... Los Angeles, CA
Hively, Brian D. .... Kennett, MO
Malden, MO
Hively, Herbert L., II .... Charleston, WV
Hurricane, WV
Hively and Ketz .... Batesville, AR
Hively, Richard W. .... Kirkland, WA
Hively, T. J. .... Batesville, AR
Hives, Harry G. .... New York, NY
Hivner, James M. .... Florence, AL
Hivnor, James Otis .... New York, NY
Hix, Andrea N. .... Denver, CO
Hix, Andrew J. .... Boerne, TX
Hix, Billy Joe .... La Habra, CA
Hix, Donna Stanaland .... Columbus, GA
Hix, E. Jane .... Philadelphia, PA
Hix, Ernest T. .... Dayton, OH
Hix Gray & Nave, PLLC .... Nashville, TN
Hix, Kathy .... Longmont, CO
Hix, Marshall L. .... Nashville, TN
Hix, Phyllis M. .... Phoenix, AZ
Kernville, CA
Hix, R. Steve .... Little Rock, AR
Hix, Richard P. .... Tulsa, OK
Hix, Thomas N. .... Hendersonville, NC
Hix, Timothy .... Los Angeles, CA
Hix, Vickie Lynn .... Santa Ana, CA
Hix, William J. .... Gatesville, TX
Hix, Wm. B. .... San Diego, CA
Hixenbaugh, Gregg A. .... Elkhart, IN
Mishawaka, IN
Hixon, Edward Cary .... Montgomery, AL
Hixon, Eric C. .... Houston, TX
Hixon, James A. .... Norfolk, VA
Hixon, Samuel W., III .... Richmond, VA
Hixon, Sara Armstrong .... Houston, TX
Hixon, Stephen L. .... San Antonio, TX
Hixon, Todd C. .... Tucson, AZ
Hixon, Todd R. .... Dallas, TX
Hixon-Brown, Ida .... Atlanta, GA
Hixon-Holley, Lynne .... Naples, FL
Hixon-Holley, Lynne, P.A. .... Naples, FL
Hixson, Barry W. .... Roswell, GA
Hixson, Boyd G. .... Allentown, PA
Hixson and Cleveland Law Office
Paris, AR
Hixson, David F. .... Schaumburg, IL
Hixson, Everett L., Jr. .... Chattanooga, TN
Hixson, George G. .... Chattanooga, TN
Hixson, J. Russell .... Des Moines, IA
Hixson, John A. .... Arlington, TX
Hixson, Justin K. .... New York, NY
Hixson, Kenneth B. .... Pomona, CA
Hixson, Kenneth S. .... Tontitown, AR
Hixson Law Office .... Bowling Green, KY
Hixson, Marshall R. .... Lexington, KY
Hixson, Raymond H., Jr. .... Palo Alto, CA
Hixson, R. H." Buddy " .... Paris, AR
Hixson, Richard A. .... Tallahassee, FL
Hixson, Richard D. .... Zanesville, OH
Hixson, Stephen L. .... Bowling Green, KY
Hixson, Thomas .... San Francisco, CA
Hixson, Wendell M. .... Yukon, OK
Hiyama, Dean Ilarvo .... Fresno, CA
Hiyane, Brian Y. .... Honolulu, HI
Hiza, Paula E. .... Chicago, IL
Hizami, Cynthia Siegal
Santa Monica, CA
Hizami, David E. .... Los Angeles, CA
Hizer, Alan F. .... Winamac, IN
Hizer Law Office .... Winamac, IN
Hiznay, Juliet Dawn .... Arlington, VA
Richmond, VA
Hjelle, Robert T. .... Sherman Oaks, CA
Hjellum, Debbie V. .... Littleton, CO
Hjelm, Carla E. .... Harrington Park, NJ
Hjelm, Lars-Erik A. .... Washington, DC
Hjelm, Scott Douglas .... Tulsa, OK
Hjelm, Steven Erik .... Tulsa, OK
Hjelmaas, Joel S. .... Des Moines, IA
Hjelmeset, Fred Sture .... San Francisco, CA
Hjelmfelt, David C. .... Englewood, CO
Hjelmstad, Jerald A. .... Bismarck, ND
Hjelmstad, Teri R. .... Littleton, CO
Hjelmstad, William D. .... Casper, WY
Hjelte, Marshall C. .... Seattle, WA
Hjerpe, Macrina G. .... Treasury Department, Office of Thrift Supervision, GV
Hjerpe and Pryer .... Eureka, CA
Hjerpe, Thomas B. .... Eureka, CA
Hjort, Barry L. .... Denver, CO

Hjort, Deborah A. ....Saco, ME
Hjort, Gary J. ....Minneapolis, MN
Hjort, Ivan E. ....Greenwood Village, CO
Hjort, Rhonda T. ....San Francisco, CA
Hjorth, Beverly E. ....Boston, MA
Hjortsberg, Lara L. ....Baltimore, MD
Hjortsberg, Matthew G. ....Baltimore, MD
Hladik, Barbara Harrington ....Philadelphia, PA
Hladik, Dennis W. ....Enid, OK
Hladio, Andrew M. ....Ambridge, PA
Hladkyj, Yaropolk R. ....Colorado Springs, CO
Hlady, Robert L. ....Albuquerque, NM
Hlafcsak, Judith J. ....Pittsburgh, PA
Hlapatsos, George, Jr. ....White Plains, NY
Hlatky, Sandra DeSarno
Ocean Township, NJ
Hlava, John Jeffrey ....Chicago, IL
Hlava, Kate T. ....Oak Park, IL
Hlavac, Dana P. ....Colorado Springs, CO
Hlavac, Dana P., P.C. ....Colorado Springs, CO
Hlavac, George C. ....Allentown, PA
Hlavac, William K. ....Stevens Point, WI
Hlavacek, Valerie G. ....Chevy Chase, MD
Hlavacka, Anne M. ....Milwaukee, WI
Hlavaty, Joel R. ....Cleveland, OH
Hlavaty, Marie D. ....Greenwich, CT
Hlavaty, Michael C. ....Moline, IL
Hlavenka, Frank S., Jr. ....Woodbridge, NJ
Hlavenka and Weisberg ....Woodbridge, NJ
Hlavin, Brian C. ....Chicago, IL
Hlavin, Joseph R., Jr. ....St. Charles, IL
Hlavinka, Charles J. ....Texarkana, TX
Hlavinka, J. Jonathan ....Houston, TX
Hlavinka, Jade L., P.C. ....Houston, TX
Hlavinka, Jade Lynn ....Houston, TX
Hlavinka & Lowman, L.L.P. ....Houston, TX
Hlavinka, Paul T. ....Houston, TX
Hlavinka, Victor F. ....Houston, TX
Texarkana, TX
Hlavka, John R. ....Cleveland, OH
Hlawatsch, Alfred G. ....National City, CA
Hlawatsch, Thomas R. ....West Trenton, NJ
Hlawaty, Roland ....New York, NY
Hlebasko, Rebecca V. ....San Francisco, CA
Hlesciak, Jeffrey P. ....Fort Washington, PA
Hletko, Paul M. ....Chicago, IL
Hlinka, Craig L. ....Munster, IN
Hluchan, Deborah M. ....Cherry Hill, NJ
Hluchan, Richard M. ....Voorhees, NJ
Hluchaniuk, Michael J. ....Bay City, MI
Hluchyj, Nicholas J.
Department of Housing and Urban Development,
Office of General Counsel, GV
Hludzik, George R. ....Hazleton, PA
Hlustik, Huizenga, Williams & VanDer Woude, Ltd. ....Chicago, IL
Hlustik, Jack R. ....Chicago, IL
Hlywa, Terrence ....Fullerton, CA
Hmiel, Frederick J. ....Albany, NY
Hnasko, Thomas M. ....Santa Fe, NM
Hnat, Frederick B. ....Armonk, NY
Hnat, James G., II ....New York, NY
Hnat, Joann M. ....Salem, MA
Hnat, John A. ....Cleveland, OH
Hnateyko, Timothy K. ....Roseland, NJ
Hnath, David M. ....Stratford, CT
Hnath, Gary M. ....Washington, DC
Hnath, Michael D. ....Butler, PA
Hnatowski, Thomas C.
Administrative Office Of The United States Courts, GV
Hnatt, Kelly M. ....New York, NY
Hnilo, James M. ....Chicago, IL
Hnot, Walter R., Jr. ....Phillipsburg, NJ
Hnylka, Joseph M. ....Solana Beach, CA
Ho, Audrey ....Los Angeles, CA
Ho, Betty ....Palo Alto, CA
Ho, Bryan Y. Y., Law Office of
Honolulu, HI
Ho, Cathleen ....Costa Mesa, CA
Ho, Chadwick A. ....Los Angeles, CA
Ho, Cheryl Lee ....Portland, OR
Ho, Christopher V. ....San Francisco, CA
Ho, Deborah Ye-Shen
Department of Justice, Civil Division, GV
Ho, Diane L. ....Wailuku, HI
Ho, Edith May ....San Francisco, CA
Ho, Edward C. ....Los Angeles, CA
Ho, Elizabeth W. ....Washington, DC
Ho, Eric ....Tustin, CA
Ho, Garrett S. ....New York, NY
Ho, Geoffrey T.C. ....Madison, NJ
Ho, George J. ....San Francisco, CA
Ho, Gordon C. C. ....Kaneohe, HI
Ho, Gordon K. ....Palo Alto, CA
Ho, Gregory P. ....New York, NY
Ho, Heidi K. ....Boston, MA
Ho, Heidi M. ....Honolulu, HI
Ho, Helen Kwok-Wai ....Bethesda, MD
Ho, Herbert H. ....Ada, MI
Ho, Jane ....Washington, DC
Rockville, MD
Ho, Jeanette H. ....Pittsburgh, PA
Ho, Jessie S. ....San Francisco, CA
Ho, John Si ....New York, NY
Ho, Katherine M. ....Washington, DC
Ho, Laura L. ....Oakland, CA
Ho, Libby N. ....Denver, CO
Ho, Li-Chung Daniel ....Chicago, IL
Ho, Mae Y. ....San Francisco, CA
Ho, Martin B. ....Minneapolis, MN
Ho & Moss ....Boston, MA
Ho, Néstor F. ....Austin, TX
Ho, Peter Peck-Koh ....Carmel, IN
Ho, Pik Kwan ....Dallas, TX
Ho, Queena C. ....Los Angeles, CA
Ho, Raymond J. ....Washington, DC

Ho, Robert J. ....Arlington, TX
Ho, Samantha ....Wichita, KS
Ho, Steven L. F. ....Honolulu, HI
Ho, Tamara ....West Covina, CA
Ho, Thomas T. M. ....Honolulu, HI
Ho, Tonny K. ....New York, NY
Ho, Valerie ....Los Angeles, CA
Ho, Victoria M. ....Naples, FL
Ho, Wendy ....Houston, TX
Ho, Widdy S. ....Boston, MA
Hoad, Robert A. ....San Diego, CA
Hoad, Robert A., A Professional Law Corporation ....San Diego, CA
Hoade, Jane Richter ....Miami, FL
Hoadley, Diane L. ....St. Louis, MO
Hoadley, Guy P. ....Detroit, MI
Hoadley, Philip M., Jr. ....Escondido, CA
Hoadley, Thomas A. ....Palm Beach, FL
Hoag, Arthur L. ....New York, NY
Hoag, Charles Edwin, Jr. ....Claverack, NY
Hoag, Donald W. ....Evanston, IL
Hoag, Hallack W. ....Los Angeles, CA
Hoag, Harold ....Spring Lake, MI
Hoag, Jack C. ....Janesville, WI
Hoag, James W. ....Everett, WA
Hoag, Joan ....Cleveland, OH
Hoag, John A ....Miami, FL
Hoag, John C. ....Glendale, CA
Hoag, John E. ....Eugene, OR
Hoag, John T. ....Fort Myers, FL
Hoag, John W., III ....Greenville, SC
Hoag, M. Jean ....Phoenix, AZ
Hoag, Margaret A. ....Newton, MA
Hoag, Mary Moore ....Raleigh, NC
Hoag & Overholt ....Los Angeles, CA
Hoag, Perry W. ....Chicago, IL
Hoag, Robert P. ....Pittsburgh, PA
Hoag, Rush M., II ....Eugene, OR
Hoag & Sullivan ....Marshfield, MA
Hoag, Wesley F. ....Dublin, OH
Hoag, William A. ....Summerfield, FL
Hoagland, Alexander C., Jr.
New York, NY
Hoagland, Diane ....New Brunswick, NJ
Hoagland, Donald W. ....Denver, CO
Hoagland, Edward, Jr. ....New Brunswick, NJ
Hoagland, Fitzgerald, Smith & Pranaitis
Alton, IL
Edwardsville, IL
St. Louis, MO
Hoagland, Gary J. ....New Brunswick, NJ
Hoagland, Grant T. ....Downey, CA
Hoagland, Henry W. ....Boston, MA
Hoagland, Jennifer Lynn
Philadelphia, PA
Hoagland, John J. ....New Brunswick, NJ
Hoagland, John R.
Federal Trade Commission,
Bureau of Competition, GV
Hoagland, Joseph J. ....Leavenworth, KS
Hoagland, Karl K., Jr. ....Alton, IL
Hoagland, Longo, Moran, Dunst & Doukas
New Brunswick, NJ
Hoagland, Mary T. ....Denver, CO
Hoagland, Nancy Theresa Tessaro
Perry Park, KY
Hoagland, Peter ....Washington, DC
Hoagland, Richard J. ....New York, NY
Hoagland, Robert L. ....San Antonio, TX
Hoagland, Samuel A. ....Boise, ID
Hoagland, William H. ....Alton, IL
Hoaglund, Cyrus V., Jr. ....Wausau, WI
Hoaglund, Eric Daniel ....Birmingham, AL
Hoaglund, Eric W. ....Milwaukee, WI
Hoaglund, John B. ....Santa Monica, CA
Hoaglund, John R., Jr. ....Pewaukee, WI
Hoaglund, John R., Jr., S.C.
Pewaukee, WI
Hoaglund, Robert H., II ....Boston, MA
Hoaglund, Susan M. ....Milwaukee, WI
Hoague, Kathleen G. ....Miami, FL
Hoahng, Sue Ann ....New York, NY
Hoak, Frank W. ....Chatham, NJ
Hoak, James M., Jr. ....Dallas, TX
Hoak, Jonathan S. ....Dayton, OH
Hoalst, Laura McCarthy ....Anaheim, CA
Hoang, Anthony P. ....Department of Justice,
Environment and Natural Resources Division, GV
Hoang, Christine Linh-Chau
Palo Alto, CA
Hoang, Douglas H. ....Los Angeles, CA
Hoang, John T. ....Washington, DC
Hoang, Kim-Thoa T. ....San Diego, CA
Hoang, Lan ....Newark, NJ
Hoang, Minh T. ....Los Angeles, CA
Hoang, Nguyen-Hong Kelly
Costa Mesa, CA
Hoang, Phuong-Quan ....Irvine, CA
Hoang, Son Thai ....Granada Hills, CA
Hoar, Jere R. ....Oxford, MS
Hoar, John ....San Francisco, CA
Hoar, John S. ....Sumter, SC
Hoar, Samuel ....Boston, MA
Hoar, Samuel, Jr. ....Burlington, VT
Hoar, Sean B. ....Eugene, OR
Hoar, Steven S. ....Evansville, IN
Hoar, William O.
Commodity Futures Trading Commission,
Division of Enforcement, GV
Hoard, E. David
Department of the Air Force,
Office of the General Counsel, GV
Hoard, Edward F. ....Boston, MA
Hoard, Heidi M. ....Minnetonka, MN
Hoard, John C. ....Indianapolis, IN
Hoard, John C. ....Casper, WY
Hoard, Steven L. ....Amarillo, TX

Hoard, Vivian D. ....Atlanta, GA
Hoard, W. E. ....Beloit, WI
Sharon, WI
Hoare, Christopher J. ....Philadelphia, PA
Hoare, Frank G. ....New York, NY
Hoare, George P., Jr. ....New York, NY
Hoare, James J. ....Farmington Hills, MI
Hoare, John J. ....Stoneham, MA
Hoare, John J., P.C. ....Stoneham, MA
Hoare and Lyda ....Farmington Hills, MI
Hoarfrost, Daniel G. ....Beaverton, OR
Hoarty, Thomas F., Jr. ....Omaha, NE
Hoats, Joseph M. ....Los Angeles, CA
Hoback, Charles V. ....Salem, VA
Hoback, Jeffrey J. ....Portage, IN
Hoback, William A. ....Louisville, KY
Hoback, William G. ....Oakland, CA
Hobaica, Peter M. ....Utica, NY
Hoballah, Wafa Jawad ....Los Angeles, CA
Hoban, Barrett J. ....Newton, MA
Hoban, Edward L. ....Westwood, MA
Hoban, George S. ....Chicago, IL
Hoban, James P. ....Worcester, MA
Hoban, Jeffrey ....Dallas, TX
Hoban, Peter D. ....Medford, MA
Hoban, Robert G. ....Chicago, IL
Hoban, Robert P., III ....Chicago, IL
Hoban, Stephen P. ....Mineola, NY
Hoban, Thomas M. ....Cleveland, OH
Hoban, Timothy J. ....Irvine, CA
Hoban, Timothy P. ....Tavares, FL
Hobart, Alisa Rebecca ....Reading, PA
Hobart, Ann R. ....Phoenix, AZ
Hobart, C. Dana ....Los Angeles, CA
Hobart, Catherine M. ....Atlanta, GA
Hobart, G. Dana, (P.C.)
Marina Del Rey, CA
Hobart, Garret A., IV ....South Royalton, VT
Hobart, J. Donald, Jr. ....Raleigh, NC
Hobart, James D. ....Chicago, IL
Hobart, Jean A. ....Irvine, CA
Hobart, Jean A. ....Los Angeles, CA
Hobart, Keith K. ....Worthington, OH
Hobart, Michael M. ....Sioux City, IA
Hobart, Rachel C. ....Siasconset, MA
Hobart, Susan L. ....New York, NY
Hobart, Thomas D. ....Iowa City, IA
Hobaugh, Gary L. ....Tulsa, OK
Hobaugh, Ike A. ....Tulsa, OK
Hobaugh, Robert J., Jr. ....Reading, PA
Hobbes, Carol G. ....Washington, DC
Hobbes, John W. ....Riverhead, NY
Hobbes, Laurence P. ....Fairfax, VA
Hobbes, Thomas B. ....Washington, DC
Hobbes & Tonetti ....Riverhead, NY
Hobbet, Richard Duane ....Washington, DC
Hobbib, Patricia L. ....Philadelphia, PA
Hobbie, David B. ....Boston, MA
Hobbie, Edward J. ....Cranford, NJ
Hobbie, Gregg M. ....Eatontown, NJ
Hobbie, Mary Kyle
Department of Agriculture,
Office of the General Counsel, GV
Hobbie, Melissa A. ....Richmond, VA
Hobbie, Michael R. ....Middletown, NJ
Hobbie, Norman M. ....Middletown, NJ
Toms River, NJ
Hobbins, Barry J. ....Saco, ME
Hobbins, Gardner, Gardner & Murphy, LLC
Saco, ME
Hobbins, Kathleen L. ....Chicago, IL
Hobbins, Robert L. ....Minneapolis, MN
Hobbs & Adondakis, L.C.
Salt Lake City, UT
Hobbs, Ann S. ....Washington, DC
Hobbs, Barry R. ....Dallas, TX
Hobbs, Barry R., A Professional Corporation
Dallas, TX
Hobbs, Ben B. ....Tipton, IN
Hobbs, Bonnie L. ....Los Angeles, CA
Hobbs, Carl W. ....Houston, TX
Hobbs, Carol S. ....Atlanta, GA
Hobbs, Caswell O., III ....Washington, DC
Hobbs, Charles A. ....Washington, DC
Hobbs, Charles M. ....Fort Morgan, CO
Hobbs, Charles R., II ....St. Louis, MO
Hobbs, Chester H, IV ....Towson, MD
Hobbs, Daniel H. ....Madison, IN
Hobbs, Darryl P. ....Vienna, VA
Hobbs, Deborah S. ....Department of Labor,
Pension and Welfare Benefits, GV
Hobbs, Dianne ....Boston, MA
Hobbs, Douglas C. ....Wichita, KS
Hobbs, Eric E. ....Milwaukee, WI
Hobbs, Evan S. ....Albuquerque, NM
Hobbs, F. Beard ....La Mesa, CA
Hobbs, Franklin D., III ....Los Angeles, CA
Hobbs, Frederick H. ....Pottsville, PA
Hobbs, Garnett, Naramore & Strause, P.A.
Hot Springs National Park, AR
Hobbs, Gary C. .... Glens Falls, NY
Saratoga Springs, NY
Hobbs, Gayle B. ....Owensboro, KY
Hobbs, George D. ....Malvern, PA
Hobbs, Gregory J., Jr. ....Denver, CO
Hobbs, H. Steven ....Lewisburg, OH
Miamisburg, OH
Hobbs & Hain, P.C. ....Centreville, AL
Marion, AL
Selma, AL
Hobbs, Harold H. ....Blakely, GA
Hobbs, Harriet J. ....Provincetown, MA
Hobbs, Harry M. ....Tampa, FL
Hobbs, Harry M., P.A. ....Tampa, FL
Hobbs, Helen K. ....Clearwater, FL
Hobbs, Henry G. ....Minden, LA
Hobbs, Henry G., Jr. ....Austin, TX
Hobbs, Howard C.M. ....Washington, DC

Hobbs, J. Timothy ....Washington, DC
Hobbs, Jacqueline S. ....Cincinnati, OH
Hobbs, James A. ....West Monroe, LA
Hobbs, James D. ....San Francisco, CA
Hobbs, James D., Jr. ....Richmond, VA
Hobbs, James R. ....Kansas City, MO
Hobbs, Jeremy W. ....Chicago, IL
Hobbs, Jodeen Marie ....Philadelphia, PA
Hobbs, Joe Brian ....Allen, TX
Hobbs, Joe W. ....Jackson, MS
Hobbs, John A. ....Floral Park, NY
Hobbs, John S. ....Phoenix, AZ
Hobbs, Jonathan P. ....Sacramento, CA
Hobbs, Joseph M. ....Florham Park, NJ
Hobbs, Karin Stone ....Salt Lake City, UT
Hobbs, Kathlyn Corbett ....Cary, NC
Hobbs, Kendall E. ....San Rafael, CA
Hobbs, Kenneth ....Seattle, WA
Hobbs, Kenneth L. ....Edwards, CA
Hobbs, Kenneth ....Knoxville, TN
Hobbs, Kevin ....Des Moines, IA
Hobbs, Kevin F. ....New City, NY
Hobbs, Lanita K. ....New York, NY
Hobbs, Larry F. ....Denver, CO
Hobbs, Larry F., P.C. ....Denver, CO
Hobbs, Laurie B. (Laura) ....Austin, TX
Hobbs, Lincoln W. ....Salt Lake City, UT
Hobbs, Linda G. Noda ....San Diego, CA
Hobbs, Lonnie ....Odessa, TX
Hobbs, Lynne M. ....Los Angeles, CA
Hobbs, Marion R. ....Brewster, MA
Hobbs, Marmaduke A. ....Salem, IN
Hobbs, Max E. ....Fort Wayne, IN
Hobbs, Micah L. ....Kansas City, MO
Hobbs, Michael D., Jr. ....Atlanta, GA
Hobbs, Michael E. ....Atlanta, GA
Hobbs, Michael E. ....Alexandria, VA
Hobbs, Michael W. ....Ashland, KY
Hobbs, Nancy S. ....New York, NY
Hobbs, Neil ....Fond du Lac, WI
Hobbs, Patrick Esmond ....Newark, NJ
Hobbs, Paul C. ....Ashland, KY
Hobbs, Penny ....Austin, TX
Hobbs, Phillip Kirk ....San Francisco, CA
Hobbs & Pottenger ....Tipton, IN
Hobbs, R. Dee ....Chattanooga, TN
Hobbs, R. Lucas ....Abingdon, VA
Hobbs, Rachel E. ....Los Angeles, CA
Hobbs, Ralph N. ....Selma, AL
Hobbs, Randall E. ....Exton, PA
Hobbs, Richard A. ....Crete, IL
Hobbs, Richard A., P.C. ....Crete, IL
Hobbs, Richard W.
Hot Springs National Park, AR
Hobbs, Richd. L. ....Towson, MD
Hobbs, Robert ....Fort Worth, TX
Hobbs, Robert B., Jr. ....Nags Head, NC
Hobbs, Robert G. ....Richmond, VA
Hobbs, Robert J. ....Boston, MA
Hobbs, Robert S. ....Tampa, FL
Hobbs, Royce A. ....Perry, OK
Hobbs, Royce A. ....Stillwater, OK
Hobbs, S. Bolling ....Lynchburg, VA
Hobbs, Sandra L. ....Minneapolis, MN
Hobbs, Sharon Denise .... Austin, TX
San Antonio, TX
Hobbs, Sharon G. ....St. Cloud, MN
Hobbs, Steven A. ....New York, NY
Hobbs, Straus, Dean & Walker, LLP
Washington, DC
Norman, OK
Portland, OR
Hobbs, Truman M., Jr. ....Montgomery, AL
Hobbs, Veronica ....Fremont, OH
Hobbs, Vincent E. ....El Toro, CA
Hobbs, Walter O. ....Tampa, FL
Hobbs, William A. ....Colorado Springs, CO
Hobbs, William C. ....Los Angeles, CA
Hobbs, William E. ....Oklahoma City, OK
Hobbs, William P. ....Lafayette, CA
Hobby, Clarke Goode
New Port Richey, FL
Hobby, David T. ....Fitzgerald, GA
Hobby, Grey & Reeves
New Port Richey, FL
Tampa, FL
Hobby, H. Clyde .... New Port Richey, FL
New Port Richey, FL
Hobby, H. Clyde, P.A. ....New Port Richey, FL
Hobby, John B. ....New York, NY
Hobby, R.J. ....Dallas, TX
Hobby, Scott M. ....Atlanta, GA
Hobby, Wensley ....Reidsville, GA
Hobby, William M., III ....Orlando, FL
Hobby, William M., III ....Winter Park, FL
Hobday, George F., Jr. ....Washington, DC
Hobday, John D. ....Columbus, OH
Hobday, Margaret C. ....Minneapolis, MN
Hobday & Piper ....Columbus, OH
Hobdey, Cecil D. ....Gooding, ID
Hobdey, Craig ....Gooding, ID
Hobdey & Hobdey ....Gooding, ID
Hobe, Frederick B. ....Fort Atkinson, WI
Hobel, Lawrence A. ....San Francisco, CA
Hobel, Michael S. ....Los Angeles, CA
Hobelman, Carl D., (P.C.)
Washington, DC
Hoben, Danford L. ....Estes Park, CO
Hoben, Thomas J. ....Minneapolis, MN
Hoberg, Allen C. ....Bismarck, ND
Hoberg, Finger, Brown, Cox & Molligan, A Professional Corporation
San Francisco, CA
Hoberg, Gordon O. ....Wishek, ND
Hoberg, Jay J. ....Lancaster, PA
Hoberg, John W. ....Columbus, OH
Hoberg, Kristen E. ....Oakland, CA
Hoberg, Mary N. ....Bismarck, ND

Hoberg, Robert S. ... Joliet, IL
Hoberg, Timothy E. ... Cincinnati, OH
Hoberman, Anna L. ... Hartford, CT
Hoberman, Daniel ... Hackensack, NJ
Parsippany, NJ
Hoberman, Eric Scott ... New York, NY
Hoberman, Harvey ... Hartford, CT
Boston, MA
Hoberman, Henry S. ... New York, NY
Hoberman, Jennifer Mae
North Miami Beach, FL
Hoberman, Lori S. ... New York, NY
Hoberman, Matthew J. ... Hartford, CT
Hoberman, Michael A. ... Encino, CA
Hoberman, Owen O. ... Brooklyn, NY
Hoberman, Resch, DiPiazza & Driscoll, P.C.
Hackensack, NJ
Parsippany, NJ
Hoberman, Stuart A. ... Woodbridge, NJ
Hoberman, Sussman & Herman, P.C.
Brooklyn, NY
Hoberman, Thomas H. ... Beverly Hills, CA
Hoberock, Christopher ... Nevada, MO
Hobert, Ben W. ... Kansas City, MO
Hobert, J. Michael ... Berryville, VA
Hobert, Kerr & Perka, P.C. ... Berryville, VA
Hobert, Kimberly K. ... St. Paul, MN
Hobert, Mark" Marcus "V. ... East Moline, IL
Hoberty, Charles L. ... Indianapolis, IN
Hobfoll, Jerrold V. ... Skokie, IL
Hobgood, Byron L. ... Madisonville, KY
Hobgood, Charles H. ... Raleigh, NC
Hobgood, Hamilton ... Louisburg, NC
Hobgood, Harry L. ... Greensboro, NC
Hobgood, Henry Herbert ... Monroe, LA
Hobgood, J. Robert ... Houston, TX
Hobgood, Leigh A. ... Charlotte, NC
Hobgood, Mari Perez ... Marietta, GA
Hobgood, Robert H. ... Louisburg, NC
Hobgood, Ronald A. ... Tampa, FL
Hobgood, T. Tucker ... Atlanta, GA
Hobgood, William P. ... Chicago, IL
Hobika, Andrew J. ... Marcy, NY
Utica, NY
Hobika, Joseph H. ... Marcy, NY
Utica, NY
Hobika, Joseph Habib, Jr. ... Marcy, NY
Utica, NY
Hobika, Luke J. ... Utica, NY
Hobin, Karen Bautista ... Redwood City, CA
Hobin, Katharine A. ... San Francisco, CA
Hobin, Patrick S. ... Houston, TX
Hobin, Raymond M. ... Durham, NC
Hobin, Richard D. ... Antioch, CA
Hobish, Richard S. ... White Plains, NY
Hobkirk, Linda K. ... Philadelphia, PA
Hoblet, Vaughn A. ... Ann Arbor, MI
Findlay, OH
Port Clinton, OH
Toledo, OH
Hoblin, Philip J., Jr. ... New York, NY
Hoblit, R. Clay ... Corpus Christi, TX
Hoblitzell, John R. ... Charleston, WV
Hoblock, Michael J., Jr. ... Albany, NY
Hoblock, Susan A. ... Albany, NY
Hoblock, William J. ... Albany, NY
Hoblock, William M. ... Albany, NY
Hobock, Barbara ... Humboldt, TN
Hobson, Alice W. ... Frankfort, KY
Hobson, Arnold, Jr. ... Honolulu, HI
Hobson, Barbara A. ... Battle Creek, MI
Hobson, Bernard E. ... Richmond, TX
Hobson & Bowman ... Frankfort, KY
Hobson, Cady & Cady ... Hampton, IA
Hobson, Carol P. M. ... Washington, DC
Hobson, Charles L. ... Sacramento, CA
Hobson, Charles M., III ... San Francisco, CA
Hobson, Constance Claire ... Metairie, LA
Hobson, Constance J. ... Detroit, MI
Hobson & Coutu, Ltd. ... Warwick, RI
Hobson, David G. ... Kent, WA
Hobson, David H. ... Clinton, NC
Hobson, David L. ... Springfield, OH
Hobson, David N., Jr. ... Aloha, OR
Hobson, David N., Sr. ... Aloha, OR
Portland, OR
Hobson, Derrick A. ... Houston, TX
Hobson, Edwin L., Jr. ... Burlington, VT
Hobson, Edwin L., P.C. ... Burlington, VT
Hobson, Eric ... Indianapolis, IN
Hobson, Everett K. ... Washington, DC
Hobson, Garron M. ... Sandy, UT
Hobson, Gordon ... Columbus, OH
Hobson, Harry L. ... Denver, CO
Hobson, Henry W., Jr. ... Cincinnati, OH
Hobson, Herschel L. ... Beaumont, TX
Hobson, Herschel L., Law Offices of
Beaumont, TX
Hobson & Hobson, P.C. ... Aloha, OR
Portland, OR
Hobson, James R. ... Washington, DC
Hobson, Jason A. ... San Francisco, CA
Hobson, John A. ... Portland, ME
Hobson, John H. ... Santa Monica, CA
Hobson, Josef V. ... Fort Smith, AR
Hobson, K. Alexander ... Green Valley, AZ
Tucson, AZ
Hobson, Kathleen Friel ... New Orleans, LA
Hobson, Kenneth H. ... Carrollton, IL
Hobson, Kevin J. ... Sutter Creek, CA
Hobson, L. Robert ... Raleigh, NC
Hobson, Leila Safi ... El Paso, TX
Hobson, Lisa ... Encino, CA
Hobson, Mark D. ... Miami, FL
Hobson, Mary L. ... Fresno, CA
Hobson, Mary S. ... Boise, ID
Hobson, Maureen A. ... Warwick, RI
Hobson, Melissa B. ... Brownsburg, IN
Hobson, Montie ... Forrest City, AR
Hobson, Neal D., (P.C.) ... New Orleans, LA
Hobson, Paula A. ... Los Angeles, CA
Hobson, Peter James ... Tampa, FL
Hobson, Richard R. G. ... McLean, VA
Hobson & Ringler ... Tempe, AZ
Hobson, Robert L. ... San Francisco, CA
Hobson, Roderique S. ... Lubbock, TX
Hobson, Sandra K. ... Dayton, OH
Hobson, Sherri Walker ... San Diego, CA
Hobson, Steven L. ... Kansas City, MO
Hobson, Steven R., II ... Akron, OH
Hobson, Susan M. ... Fort Wayne, IN
Hobson, Traci L. ... Asheboro, NC
Hobson, William H. ... St. Louis, MO
Hobson, William Patrick ... Charlotte, NC
Hobson, William R. ... Tempe, AZ
Hobson, William T., Law Offices of
San Diego, CA
Hobson-Phillips, Patricia L.
Department of Housing and Urban Development, GV
Hobson-Williams, Tanya ... New York, NY
Hobt, Stephen D. ... Cleveland, OH
Hoburg, Paul D. ... Department of Defense, Defense Legal Services Agency, GV
Hoch, A. Elaine ... Omaha, NE
Hoch, Alan D. ... Boston, MA
Hoch, Allison B. ... New York, NY
Hoch, Andrea Lynn ... Sacramento, CA
Hoch, Benjamin ... New York, NY
Hoch, Brian J. ... Toledo, OH
Hoch, Brian R. ... White Plains, NY
Hoch, Carol A. ... Seattle, WA
Hoch, Carol W. ... Houston, TX
Hoch, Diane E. ... Gainesville, FL
Hoch, Donna Albani ... Glen Mills, PA
Hoch, Funke & Kelch ... Auburn, NE
Nebraska City, NE
Hoch, Gary W. ... Minneapolis, MN
Hoch, Guy A. ... Chicago, IL
Hoch, Karl J., Jr. ... Hawthorne, CA
Hoch, Kenneth D. ... Harrisburg, PA
Hoch, Kenneth H. ... Chicago, IL
Hoch, Laurence A. ... Albany, NY
Hoch, Laurence J. ... Boston, MA
Hoch, Lewis J. ... Philadelphia, PA
Hoch, Lori Kaczynski ... Milwaukee, WI
Hoch & McHugh ... Boston, MA
Hoch, Ramon R. ... Arlington, VA
Hoch, Rand ... West Palm Beach, FL
Hoch, Richard H. ... Nebraska City, NE
Hoch, Roland F. ... Tucson, AZ
Hoch, Steven L., (A Professional Corporation) ... Santa Monica, CA
Hoch, Theodore K. ... Bath, ME
Hoch, Timothy M. ... Oklahoma City, OK
Dallas, TX
Fort Worth, TX
Hoch, William H. ... Oklahoma City, OK
Hoch, William M. ... Bronx, NY
Hoch, Wyatt A. ... Wichita, KS
Hochadel, Joseph M. ... Portland, ME
Hochanadel, Donald L. ... Overland Park, KS
Hochbaum, Charles S. ... Garden City, NY
Hochbaum, Seth H. ... Wakefield, MA
Hochbein, Joseph J. ... Cincinnati, OH
Hochberg, Allen ... Spring Valley, NY
Hochberg, Alvin S. ... Boston, MA
Hochberg, Andrew M. ... Pittsfield, MA
Hochberg, Andrew M., P.C.
Great Barrington, MA
Pittsfield, MA
Hochberg, Andrew S. ... Niles, IL
Hochberg, Andrew S. ... Newton, MA
Hochberg, Ann P. ... Charlestown, MA
Hochberg & Associates, P.C. ... Dallas, TX
Hochberg, Bayard Z. ... Baltimore, MD
Hochberg, Brenda J. ... Cambridge, MA
Hochberg, Burton S. ... Chicago, IL
Hochberg, Cheryl D. ... Hollywood, FL
Hochberg, Chiarello & Costello
Baltimore, MD
Hochberg, D. Peter ... Cleveland, OH
Hochberg, Donna S. ... Northbrook, IL
Hochberg, D. Peter, Co., L.P.A.
Cleveland, OH
Hochberg, Edwin H. ... New York, NY
Hochberg, Faith S. ... Newark, NJ
Hochberg, Jane E. ... Boise, ID
Hochberg, Jeffrey D. ... New York, NY
Hochberg, Jennifer E. ... New York, NY
Hochberg, Jerome A. ... Washington, DC
Hochberg, Jory M.
Board of Governors Of The Federal Reserve System, Office of the General Counsel, GV
Hochberg, Joshua R. ... Department of Justice, Criminal Division, GV
Hochberg, Karen Elisa ... Brooklyn, NY
Hochberg, Kevin J. ... Chicago, IL
Hochberg, Krieger, Danzig & Garubo
Roseland, NJ
Hochberg, Larry J. ... Niles, IL
Hochberg, Lawrence P. ... Dallas, TX
Hochberg, Lester ... New York, NY
Hochberg, Lloyd James, Jr. ... Honolulu, HI
Hochberg, Michael D. ... Boston, MA
Hochberg, Norman ... Baltimore, MD
Hochberg, Norman, P.A. ... Baltimore, MD
Hochberg, Philip R. ... Washington, DC
Hochberg, R. Mark ... Huntington, NY
Hochberg, Ralph R. ... New York, NY
Hochberg, Robert A. ... Hartford, CT
Hochberg, Sam ... Portland, OR
Hochberg, Sheldon E. ... Washington, DC
Hochberg, Stanley J. ... Brooklyn, NY
Hochberg, Stephanie P. ... Wilmington, DE
Hochberg, Stephen ... New York, NY
Hochberg, Steven M. ... New York, NY
Hochberg, Steven R. ... New York, NY
Hochberg, Steven Y. ... New York, NY
Hochberg, Susan Jill ... New York, NY
Hochberg, William D. ... Edmonds, WA
Hochberg, Zelda C. ... New York, NY
Hochberger, Donald E. ... Ketchum, OK
Hochberger, Michael ... Flushing, NY
Hochberger, Ruth S. ... New York, NY
Hochderffer, Kris ... Austin, TX
Hochenberg, William S. ... New York, NY
Hocherman, Henry M. ... Mount Kisco, NY
Hocherman, Henry W. ... Elizabeth, NJ
Hochfelder, John M. ... White Plains, NY
Hochfelder, John M., The Law Firm of
White Plains, NY
Hochfelder, Scott Z. ... Chicago, IL
Hochfelsen, Jay J. ... Plainview, NY
Hochfelsen, Jeffrey S. ... Boca Raton, FL
Hochfield, Marilyn A. ... Buffalo, NY
Hochhauser, Barry M. ... New York, NY
Hochhauser, Sheila P. ... Manhattan, KS
Hochhauser, Stephen ... Scarsdale, NY
Hochhausler, John M. ... Los Angeles, CA
Hochheiser, Alan C. ... Cleveland, OH
Hochheiser, Daniel Adam ... New York, NY
Hochheiser, Lawrence ... New York, NY
Hochheiser, Leonard ... New York, NY
Hochholzer, Franklin D.
Rehoboth Beach, DE
Hochkammer, Karl A. ... Southfield, MI
Hochkammer, William O. ... Detroit, MI
Hochler, Don L. ... Roslyn Heights, NY
Hochman, Alan R. ... Miami, FL
Hochman, Alan R., P.A. ... Miami, FL
Hochman, Bruce B. ... Portland, ME
Hochman, Bruce I. ... Beverly Hills, CA
Hochman, Charles B. ... New York, NY
Hochman, Clifford S. ... Mansfield, MA
Hochman, David B. ... Cleveland, OH
Hochman, David J. ... Chicago, IL
Hochman, David S. ... Los Angeles, CA
Hochman, Debra G. ... Sherman Oaks, CA
Hochman, Edward S. ... New York, NY
Hochman, Elliot F.
Palm Beach Gardens, FL
Hochman, Fredrica ... New York, NY
Hochman and Goldin ... Miami, FL
Hochman, Harry D. ... Los Angeles, CA
Hochman, Howard J. ... Miami, FL
Hochman, James A. ... Chicago, IL
Hochman, James B. ... Dayton, OH
Hochman, Jarrod M. ... Revere, MA
Hochman, Jeffrey J. ... Fort Lauderdale, FL
Hochman, Jeffrey L. ... Fort Lauderdale, FL
Hochman, Jeffrey S. ... New York, NY
Hochman, Jerrald J. ... Cherry Hill, NJ
Hochman, Jonathan L. ... New York, NY
Hochman, Joseph I. ... Seattle, WA
Hochman, Kenneth A. ... Sunrise, FL
Hochman, Kenneth G. ... Cleveland, OH
Hochman, Lauren J. ... New York, NY
Hochman, Lawrence D. ... Livonia, MI
Hochman, Lori A. ... Universal City, CA
Hochman, Marci Levin ... Trenton, NJ
Hochman, Marilyn J. ... Oviedo, FL
Hochman, Mark S. ... Wall Township, NJ
Hochman, Martin M. ... Jericho, NY
Hochman, Martin P. ... Los Angeles, CA
Hochman, Michael C. ... Washington, DC
Hochman, Michael H. ... Jersey City, NJ
Hochman, Nancy E. ... Portland, OR
Hochman, Nathan Joseph
Beverly Hills, CA
Hochman & Nugent, P.C. ... Mansfield, MA
Hochman, Peter R. ... San Jose, CA
Hochman, Ralph ... Bronx, NY
Hochman, Richard Craig ... New York, NY
Hochman & Roach Co., L.P.A.
Dayton, OH
Enon, OH
Springfield, OH
Hochman, Rodger L. ... Miami, FL
Hochman, Russell C. ... Stamford, CT
Hochman, Salkin, Rettig, Toscher & Perez, A Professional Corporation
Beverly Hills, CA
Los Angeles, CA
Hochman, Scott Gregg ... Miami, FL
Hochman, Stanley ... Longboat Key, FL
Hochman, Stephen A. ... New York, NY
Hochman, Talia ... New York, NY
Hochman, William S. ... San Rafael, CA
Hochnadel, Ronald D. ... Seattle, WA
Hochner, David H. ... Costa Mesa, CA
Hochron, R. Manuel ... Binghamton, NY
Hochron, Stuart M., M.D. ... Woodbridge, NJ
Hochroth, Stanley ... Boca Raton, FL
Hochstadt, Jordan ... Denver, CO
Hochstadt, Straw, Strauss & Silverman, P.C.
Denver, CO
Hochstatter, McCarthy & Rivas, S.C.
Milwaukee, WI
Hochstatter, Thomas C. ... Milwaukee, WI
Hochstein, Ilene M. ... Millbrae, CA
Hochstein, Leora
Federal Communications Commission, Wireless Telecommunications Bureau, GV
Hochstein, Robert ... New York, NY
Hochster, Albert R. ... New York, NY
Hochstetler, Bruce ... Daytona Beach, FL
Hochstetler, Douglass C. ... Chicago, IL
Hochstetler, William S. ... Cedar Rapids, IA
Hochstetter, Sandra L. ... Little Rock, AR
Hochstim, Theodore S. ... Dallas, TX
Hochsztein, Fred B. ... Aventura, FL
Hochsztein, Howard ... Plantation, FL
Hochsztein, Howard, P.A. ... Plantation, FL
Hochsztein, Jerald A. ... St. Louis, MO
Hochul, Denise Catherine ... Buffalo, NY
Hochul, William J., Jr. ... Hamburg, NY
Hochuli, Daniel J. ... Tucson, AZ
Hochuli, Daniel J., P.C., and Associates
Tucson, AZ
Hochuli, Edward G. ... Phoenix, AZ
Hochuli, Peter W. ... Tucson, AZ
Hochwald, Susan Kirp ... Nantucket, MA
Hochwalt, Michael A. ... Dayton, OH
Hochwarth, Robert F. ... Baltimore, MD
Hock, A. Brooks ... Richmond, VA
Hock, Alan S. ... Garden City, NY
Hock, Barry L. ... Newton, MA
Hock, Frederick Wyeth ... Livingston, NJ
Hock, Gregory J. ... Colorado Springs, CO
Hock, Jennifer A. ... Glastonbury, CT
Hock, Jered L. ... Harrisburg, PA
Hock, Jerome ... Bowling Green, OH
Hock, Karen Elizabeth Stadele ... Salem, OR
Hock, Kirby C. ... San Rafael, CA
Hock, Ronald G., The Law Office of
Orlando, FL
Hock, Steven L. ... San Francisco, CA
Hock, Tammy Jo ... Alexandria, VA
Hock, Vincent M. ... Baltimore, MD
Hock, W. Fletcher, Jr. ... Hackensack, NJ
Hockabout, Tom D ... Madison, NE
Hockaday, Daniel M. ... Burnsville, NC
Hockaday, Donald E., III ... Houston, TX
Hockaday, Heather N. ... Burnsville, NC
Hockaday & Hockaday, P.A. ... Burnsville, NC
Hockaday, Irvine O., Jr. ... Kansas City, MO
Hockaday, Michael Leon
Virginia Beach, VA
Hockberger, John J., Jr. ... Boise, ID
Hockel, Thomas K. ... San Francisco, CA
Hockema, David H. ... Edinburg, TX
Hockema, Tippit & Escobedo, L.L.P.
Edinburg, TX
Hockemeier, Farrell D. ... Richmond, MO
Hockemeyer, Greggory William
Columbia City, IN
Hocken, Natalie L. ... Portland, OR
Hockenberg, Harlan (Bud)
Des Moines, IA
Hockenberg, Louis R. ... Des Moines, IA
Hockenberry, John F. ... Washington, DC
Hockenbury, Jay Donald ... Wilmington, NC
Hockenbury, John C. ... Washington, DC
Hockenjos, Kathryn A. ... Bridgewater, NJ
Hockensmith, Dana ... St. Louis, MO
Hockensmith, Frank M. ... Grand Junction, CO
Hockensmith, George Jeremy ... Keene, NH
Hockensmith, Robert R. ... Fort Wayne, IN
Hockensmith Sherby Tatlow & Zoole, P.C.
St. Louis, MO
Hocker, Donald B. ... Laurens, SC
Hocker, George B. ... Lexington, KY
Hocker, George H., Jr. ... Baltimore, MD
Hocker, James S., Sr. ... Estes Park, CO
Hocker, Jeron E. ... Austin, TX
Fort Worth, TX
Houston, TX
Hocker, Keith J. ... Oklahoma City, OK
Hocker, Lon ... St. Louis, MO
Hocker, Morrow & Mathews ... Spring, TX
Hocker, R. Kelly ... Tempe, AZ
Hocker, Robert N. ... San Diego, CA
Hocker, Wesley H. ... Spring, TX
Hockersmith, Michael D. ... Montrose, CO
Ouray, CO
Hockert, Lorance ... New York, NY
Hockert Pressman & Flohr ... New York, NY
Hockett, Christopher B.
San Francisco, CA
Hockett, Harlan M. ... Des Moines, IA
Hockett, Jennifer M. ... El Reno, OK
Hockett, Joel M. ... Riverhead, NY
Hockett, Marshall York ... San Diego, CA
Hockett, Marshall York, A Professional Law Corporation ... San Diego, CA
Hockett, Sharon Lee ... Roseburg, OR
Hockett, Tobey C. ... Sarasota, FL
Hockett, Verden L., Jr. ... Roseburg, OR
Hockey, Laurel Ann ... Washington, DC
Hockey, Martin F., Jr.
Department of Justice, Civil Division, GV
Hockfield, Barry J. ... Cherry Hill, NJ
Hockfield, Hasner, Weiss & Rosenberg, P.A.
Cherry Hill, NJ
Hockfield, Steven A. ... Charlotte, NC
Hocking, David M. ... St. Louis, MO
Hocking, Greg Michael ... Charlotte, MI
Hocking, John R. ... Plymouth, MI
Hocking, Joseph J. ... River Edge, NJ
Hocking, Melanie E. ... Wintersville, OH
Hocking, Wendy A.
United States Postal Service, Law Department, GV
Hocking-Cortez, Brigitte ... Dallas, TX
Hockley, Michael D. ... Kansas City, MO
Hockley, Sandra D. ... Longmont, CO
Hockley-Cann, Denise C. ... Chicago, IL
Hockman, Allison Doliner ... Miami, FL
Hockman, Donald D. ... Winter Park, FL
Hockman, Louis ... Collingswood, NJ
Blue Bell, PA
Philadelphia, PA
Hockman, Louis, P.C. ... Collingswood, NJ
Blue Bell, PA
Philadelphia, PA
Hockman, Mark D. ... Fayetteville, NC
Hockman, Mark D., P.A., The Law Offices of
Fayetteville, NC
Hockman, Peter M. ... Miami, FL
Hockman, Richard E. ... New York, NY

Hockman, Thomas P. ......Winter Park, FL
Hockstad, Karen S. ......Columbus, OH
Hockstein, Diane L. ......Philadelphia, PA
Hockstein, Gerald L. ......Baltimore, MD
Hockstein, Linda J. ......Bayonne, NJ
Hocky, Eric M. ......Philadelphia, PA
Hoctor, James J. ......Orlando, FL
Hocum, Monica C. ......Waukesha, WI
Hocutt, Robert B. ......Atlanta, GA
Hodach, Albertina E. ......Milwaukee, WI
Hodach, Stephanie Markos
Ocean Township, NJ
Hodak, Corinne C. ......Jacksonville, FL
Hodan, Doster & Ganzer, S.C.
Milwaukee, WI
Hodan, Joseph Jerome ......Depew, NY
Hodan, Patrick J. ......Milwaukee, WI
Hodan, Theodore J. ......Milwaukee, WI
Hodapp, James D. ......Northbrook, IL
Hodapp, Jos. F. ......Boston, MA
Hodapp, Lawrence M.
Federal Trade Commission, Bureau of Consumer Protection, GV
Hodapp, Lisa N. ......Tamarac, FL
Hodapp, Michael T. ......Woodland Hills, CA
Hodapp, Paul F. ......Denver, CO
Hodapp, Robert E. ......Coral Springs, FL
Hodapp, Ruey F., Jr. ......Dayton, OH
Hodara, Fred S. ......New York, NY
Hodari, Ajili ......Columbus, OH
Hodas, Thomas ......West Palm Beach, FL
Hodaszy, Steven Z. ......New York, NY
Hodavance, Robert S. ......Philadelphia, PA
Hodde, A. W., Jr. ......Brenham, TX
Hodde & Lacina ......Brenham, TX
Hodder, Broady R. ......Palo Alto, CA
Las Vegas, NV
Hodder, Douglas G. ......San Francisco, CA
Hodder, Janet B. ......Modesto, CA
Hodder, Kenneth G. ......Atlanta, GA
Hodder, Lucy C. ......Concord, NH
Hoddinott, Alfred H., Jr. ......Ridgefield, CT
Stamford, CT
Hodek, Fred A. ......Tempe, AZ
Hodel, Matthew A. ......Costa Mesa, CA
Hodel, Thomas G. ......Lakewood, CO
Hodell, Douglas M. ......Sacramento, CA
Hodes, Alan S. ......Palo Alto, CA
Hodes, Andrew S. ......Great Neck, NY
Hodes & Braun, P.A. ......Short Hills, NJ
Hodes, Cynthia R. ......Los Angeles, CA
Hodes, Daniel M. ......Newport Beach, CA
Hodes, Debra Ann ......White Plains, NY
Hodes, Gail S. ......Santa Rosa, CA
Hodes, Garrett M. ......Independence, MO
Hodes, Irvine ......San Rafael, CA
Hodes, Irving L. ......Short Hills, NJ
Hodes, Jay L. ......Manchester, NH
Hodes, Joel C. ......Westport, CT
Hodes, Joel L. ......Albany, NY
Hodes, Jonathan R. ......Los Angeles, CA
Hodes, Karen Lynn ......New York, NY
Hodes, Keating & Pilon ......Chicago, IL
Hodes and Lochton ......Santa Rosa, CA
Hodes, Matthew L. ......Miami, FL
Hodes, Michael C. ......Bethesda, MD
Towson, MD
Hodes, Michael G. ......Chicago, IL
Hodes, Neil M. ......Bala Cynwyd, PA
Hodes, Paul W. ......Concord, NH
Hodes, Robert B. ......New York, NY
Hodes, Robert D. ......Short Hills, NJ
Hodes, Robert M. ......Topanga, CA
Hodes, Rochelle ......Treasury Department, Internal Revenue Service, GV
Hodes, Sanford J. ......Newark, NJ
Hodes, Scott ......Chicago, IL
Hodes, Scott A. ......Department of Justice, Federal Bureau of Investigation, GV
Hodes, Scott D. ......Chicago, IL
Hodes, Sheldon ......Chicago, IL
Hodes, Sidney S. ......Hollywood, FL
Hodes, Ulman, Pessin & Katz, P.A.
Washington, DC
Baltimore, MD
Bethesda, MD
Columbia, MD
Havre de Grace, MD
Towson, MD
Hodes, W. William ......Indianapolis, IN
Hodesblatt, Alan ......Newark, DE
Hodesblatt, Robert P. ......Pearl River, NY
Hodess, Ronald E. ......Troy, MI
Hodes-Urbont, Lisa E. ......Brooklyn, NY
Hodgden, Bryce ......Woodward, OK
Hodgden, Cody B. ......Woodward, OK
Hodgden, Hallren, Smithton & Hodgden, P.L.L.C. ......Woodward, OK
Hodgdon, Ann Perrine
Nuclear Regulatory Commission, Office of the General Counsel, GV
Hodgdon, J. Russell ......Norwell, MA
Hodgdon, Mark P ......Concord, NH
Hodgdon, Sally ......Hartford, CT
Hodgdon, Samuel K. ......Bingham Farms, MI
Hodgdon, T. Todd
Federal Mine Safety and Health Review Commission, Office of the Administrative Law Judges, GV
Hodgdon, Terry L. ......Portland, ME
Hodgdon, Thaddeus B. ......Raleigh, NC
Hodgdon, Timothy F. ......New York, NY
Hodge, Albert Z. ......Gaithersburg, MD
Hodge, Albert Z., P.C. ......Gaithersburg, MD
Hodge, Arthur D. ......Los Angeles, CA
Hodge, B. Michael ......Dulles, VA
Hodge, Barry Cameron ......Virginia Beach, VA
Hodge, Barry R. ......Fall River, MA

Hodge, Bradley H. ......Knoxville, TN
Hodge, Brian Ray ......Pasadena, CA
Hodge, Brian W. ......Louisville, KY
Hodge, Bruce W. ......Harlingen, TX
Hodge, Byron W. ......Del Rio, TX
Hodge, Charles J. ......Spartanburg, SC
Hodge, Charles S. P. ......Department of Labor, Office of the Solicitor, GV
Hodge, Christopher M. ......Jacksonville, FL
Hodge, Craig E. ......Department of the Army, Army Materiel Command, GV
Hodge, David ......Boca Raton, FL
Hodge, David E. ......Greenville, SC
Hodge, David J. ......Mill Valley, CA
Hodge, David J. ......San Francisco, CA
Hodge, David M. ......Springfield, MA
Hodge, Dennis A. ......Ellicott City, MD
Hodge, Derek M.
Christiansted, St. Croix, VI
Hodge, Derek M., P.C., Law Offices of
Christiansted, St. Croix, VI
Hodge, Dewain W. ......Springdale, AR
Hodge, Diana K. ......Portland, OR
Hodge & Dwyer ......Springfield, IL
Hodge, E. Clifton, Jr. ......Jackson, MS
Hodge, Edward D. ......Mexico, MO
Hodge, Elizabeth Fisher ......Ocala, FL
Hodge & Francois
Charlotte Amalie, St. Thomas, VI
Hodge, Frederick W., Jr. ......Nashville, TN
Hodge, G. Marcus ......Athens, GA
Hodge, Garrick J. ......Deerfield, IL
Hodge, Gerald K. ......Aurora, IL
Hodge, Glenn M. ......Harrisonburg, VA
Hodge, Gregory E. ......Oakland, CA
Hodge, Gwendolyn D. ......Little Rock, AR
Hodge, Heather R. ......Schaumburg, IL
Hodge, Henry P., Jr. ......Wichita Falls, TX
Hodge, Howard B. ......Covington, KY
Hodge, James Blythe ......San Francisco, CA
Hodge, James G., Sr. ......Louisville, KY
Hodge, James & Hernandez, L.L.P.
Brownsville, TX
Edinburg, TX
Harlingen, TX
McAllen, TX
Rio Grande City, TX
Hodge, James M. ......West Des Moines, IA
Hodge, James T. ......Lexington, KY
Hodge, Jamie Leigh ......Bloomington, MN
Hodge, Janet Gray ......Danville, KY
Hodge, Jay E., Jr. ......Cheraw, SC
Hodge, Jeffrey T. ......Houston, TX
Hodge, John Adams ......Charleston, SC
Columbia, SC
Greenville, SC
Hodge, John E., Jr. ......Charlotte, NC
Hodge, John L. ......Boston, MA
Hodge, John S. ......Shreveport, LA
Hodge, John W. ......New Castle, PA
Hodge, Karen E. ......Chicago, IL
Hodge, Katherine ......Prospect, KY
Hodge, Katherine D. ......Springfield, IL
Hodge, Kay H. ......Boston, MA
Hodge & Kelley ......Louisville, KY
Hodge, Kelly S. ......Junction City, KS
Hodge, Leigh Anne ......Birmingham, AL
Hodge, Linda Joyce ......Thousand Oaks, CA
Hodge, Maria Tankenson, (P.C.)
Charlotte Amalie, St. Thomas, VI
Hodge, Mark Wade ......Little Rock, AR
Hodge, Mark Wilson ......Little Rock, AR
Hodge, Michael J. ......Lansing, MI
Hodge, Michael P. ......Austin, TX
Hodge, Michael V. ......Washington, DC
Hodge, Nicholas S. ......Boston, MA
Hodge, Pamela Morgan ......Cincinnati, OH
Hodge, Randall P. ......Oklahoma City, OK
Hodge, Rhys S.
Charlotte Amalie, St. Thomas, VI
Hodge, Richard A. ......Oakland, CA
Hodge, Richard E. ......Santa Monica, CA
Hodge, Richard E., LLP ......Los Angeles, CA
Santa Monica, CA
Hodge, Richard L. ......Albany, GA
Hodge, Robert B. ......Boise, ID
Hodge, Robert K. ......Smyrna, GA
Hodge, Robert L. ......Houston, TX
Hodge, Ronald S. ......Boise, ID
Hodge, Ross A. ......Reno, NV
Hodge, Ryan ......Wichita, KS
Hodge, Samuel D., Jr. ......Philadelphia, PA
Hodge, Sean P. ......Cincinnati, OH
Hodge, Sharon Asbill ......Columbia, SC
Hodge, Sheldon D. S. ......Sacramento, CA
Hodge, Stanley W. ......San Bernardino, CA
Hodge, Stedmann
Charlotte Amalie, St. Thomas, VI
Hodge, Stephan L. ......Indianapolis, IN
Hodge, Stephen T. ......Los Angeles, CA
Hodge, Steven J. ......Dubuque, IA
Hodge, T. Paul ......Fort Lauderdale, FL
Hodge, Thomas Arthur ......Atlanta, GA
Hodge, Thomas J. ......Lexington, KY
Hodge, Thomas S. ......Seattle, WA
Hodge, Timothy A. ......Glendale, CA
Ventura, CA
Hodge, Timothy A., Jr. ......Baltimore, MD
Hodge, Timothy L. ......San Luis Obispo, CA
Hodge, Verne A.
Charlotte Amalie, St. Thomas, VI
Hodge, Victor A. ......Dayton, OH
Hodge, Victor L. ......Edmond, OK
Hodge, Victor L., & Associates
Edmond, OK
Hodge, William C. ......Portland, OR
Hodge, William H. ......De Queen, AR
Hodge, Wilson E. ......Garland, TX

Hodgeman, Mark ......Philadelphia, PA
Hodgeman, Roger Benjamin ......Scarsdale, NY
Hodgen, Philip D. W. ......Beverly Hills, CA
Hodgen, Philip D. W., A Professional Corporation ......Beverly Hills, CA
Los Angeles, CA
Hodgens, Donald J. ......Charlotte, NC
Hodgens, James J. ......Stroud, OK
Hodgens, John M., Jr.
Department of Justice, Tax Division, GV
Hodges, A. Clifton ......Glendale, CA
Hodges, A. Earl ......Houston, TX
Hodges, Alice F. ......Savannah, GA
Hodges, Allyson C. ......Denver, CO
Hodges, Andrew F. ......Atlanta, GA
Hodges, Andrew Jackson, IV
Baton Rouge, LA
Hodges, Ann C. ......Washington, DC
Hodges, Anthony L. ......Houston, TX
Hodges, Ashley M. ......Kennesaw, GA
Hodges, Avrutis & Pretschner, P.A.
Sarasota, FL
Hodges, Barbara I.
Department of Justice, GV
Hodges, Bryan T. ......Eugene, OR
Hodges, C. Wes, II ......Wilmington, NC
Hodges, C. A. ......Memphis, TN
Hodges, Campbell & Stanley
Wytheville, VA
Hodges, Carl H. ......Jonesboro, GA
Hodges, Carl H., and Associates, P.C.
Jonesboro, GA
Hodges & Carle, P.A. ......Zephyrhills, FL
Hodges, Carlton W. ......Portland, OR
Hodges, Carolyn M. ......Union City, GA
Hodges & Carry, P.A. ......Fort Lauderdale, FL
Hodges, Charles E., II ......Atlanta, GA
Hodges, Charles E., Jr. ......Portland, OR
Hodges, Charles E., Jr., P.C. ......Portland, OR
Hodges, Charles R. ......Dallas, TX
Hodges, Charles R., P.C. ......Dallas, TX
Hodges, Christi Lewis ......Atlanta, GA
Hodges, Clinton M. ......Woodland Hills, CA
Hodges, David A. ......Little Rock, AR
Hodges, David A., Jr. ......Little Rock, AR
Hodges, David E. ......Birmingham, AL
Hodges, David L. ......Waco, TX
Hodges, David W. ......Houston, TX
Hodges & Davis, P.C. ......Crown Point, IN
Hammond, IN
Merrillville, IN
Portage, IN
Valparaiso, IN
Hodges, Dean Lee ......Birmingham, AL
Hodges, Debra Lynn ......Milwaukee, WI
Hodges, Denyse Graham ......Westbury, NY
Hodges, Donna J. ......Jackson, MS
Hodges, Doughty and Carson, PLLC
Knoxville, TN
Hodges, E. Peyton ......Orlando, FL
Hodges, Edward F., Jr ......Danville, VA
Hodges, Elaine ......Northbrook, IL
Hodges, Eleanor H. ......Houston, TX
Hodges, Elizabeth B. ......Atlanta, GA
Hodges, Elizabeth L. ......Houston, TX
Hodges, Elizabeth T. ......Charlotte, NC
Hodges, Erroll Anne Y. ......Greenville, SC
Hodges, Erwin, Hedrick & Coleman, LLP
Albany, GA
Hodges, Fleming ......Dyersburg, TN
Hodges, Fred H., Jr. ......Macon, GA
Hodges, Gary J. ......Clarksville, TN
Hodges, Geoffrey Todd ......Tampa, FL
Hodges, George A., (Ltd.) ......Chicago, IL
Hodges, George R. ......Charlotte, NC
Hodges, George S. ......Albany, NY
White Plains, NY
Hodges, Glen A. ......Austin, TX
Hodges, Grace Elizabeth Taylor
Charlotte, NC
Hodges, Gregory H.
Charlotte Amalie, St. Thomas, VI
Hodges, H. Raiford, Jr. ......Decatur, GA
Hodges, H. William, III ......Baldwin, NY
Hodges & Haynes ......Bowling Green, KY
Hodges, Helen J. ......San Diego, CA
Hodges, Henry ......Little Rock, AR
Hodges, Henry, P.A. ......Little Rock, AR
Hodges & Hodges ......Little Rock, AR
Lonoke, AR
Hodges, Hoy P. ......Bowling Green, KY
Hodges, Hugh M., Jr. ......Dallas, TX
Hodges, I. Gregory ......Savannah, GA
Hodges, Jack D. ......Johnson City, TN
Hodges, Jack William ......San Francisco, CA
Hodges, James C. ......Tulsa, OK
Hodges, James D., Jr. ......Cedar Rapids, IA
Hodges, James H. ......Lancaster, SC
Hodges, James M. ......Signal Hill, CA
Hodges, James P. ......McLean, VA
Hodges, James R. ......Abingdon, VA
Hodges, James W. ......San Diego, CA
Hodges, Jana Park ......Hermosa Beach, CA
Hodges, Jay ......Fairbanks, AK
Hodges, Jennifer L. ......Miami, FL
Hodges, John ......Royal Oak, MI
Hodges, John A. ......Washington, DC
Hodges, John C. ......Alpharetta, GA
Hodges, John Christian ......White Stone, VA
Hodges, John F. ......Arroyo Grande, CA
Hodges, John G. ......Tampa, FL
Hodges, John M." Jack " ......Sarasota, FL
Hodges, John S. ......East Weymouth, MA
Hodges, Joseph G., Jr. ......Denver, CO
Hodges, Joseph W., Jr. ......Morrow, GA
Stockbridge, GA
Hodges, Joseph W., Jr. ......Silver City, NM
Hodges, Jot, Jr. ......Missouri City, TX

Hodges, Kaneaster, Jr. ......Newport, AR
Hodges, Karen B. ......Lubbock, TX
Hodges, Kenneth A. ......Russellville, AR
Hodges, Kenneth B., III ......Albany, GA
Hodges, Kenneth R. ......Newport Beach, CA
Hodges, Kevin M. ......Washington, DC
Hodges Law Firm ......Memphis, TN
Hodges, Leland A. ......Fort Worth, TX
Hodges, Leslie Charles ......Dearborn, MI
Hodges & Leverett, L.L.C. ......Elberton, GA
Hodges, Lincoln A. R. ......Memphis, TN
Hodges, Loizzi, Eisenhammer, Rodick & Kohn
Arlington Heights, IL
Hodges, Lucian B. ......Mobile, AL
Hodges, Mark C. ......Houston, TX
Hodges, Mark E. ......Bellevue, WA
Hodges, Mark E., P.S. ......Bellevue, WA
Hodges, Michael W. ......Ballwin, MO
Hodges, Michelle ......Irvine, CA
Hodges, Mick ......Twin Falls, ID
Hodges, Norman ......Silver City, NM
Hodges, P. Jay ......Tulsa, OK
Hodges, Paul E. ......Knoxville, TN
Hodges, Paul V. ......Lakewood, CO
Hodges, Perry W., Jr. ......Fort Lauderdale, FL
Hodges, R. Mark ......Jackson, MS
Hodges, Ralph B. ......Oklahoma City, OK
Hodges, Ralph C. ......Jacksonville, FL
Hodges, R.E., Jr. ......Marietta, GA
Hodges, Rex A. ......Oklahoma City, OK
Hodges, Richard K. ......Scranton, PA
Hodges, Richard M. ......Denver, CO
Hodges, Richard T. ......Hollywood, FL
Hodges, Robert E. ......Nebo, NC
Hodges, Robert G. ......Detroit, MI
Hodges, Robert H. ......Baton Rouge, LA
Hodges, Robert H., Jr.
United States Court of Federal Claims, GV
Hodges, Robert L. ......Scottsboro, AL
Hodges, Robert L. ......Richmond, VA
Hodges, Robert R. ......Hermosa Beach, CA
Hodges, Robert W. ......Danville, CA
Hodges, Robert W. ......Los Angeles, CA
Hodges, Robert W. ......Ocala, FL
Hodges, Ronald S. ......Irvine, CA
Hodges, S. Terry ......Atlanta, GA
Hodges, Sam D., III ......Nashville, TN
Hodges, Sherrie R. ......West Jefferson, NC
Hodges, Sheryl L. ......Northbrook, IL
Hodges, Stephen M. ......Abingdon, VA
Hodges, Sue J. ......San Diego, CA
Hodges, Susan S. ......Mount Laurel, NJ
Hodges, Susan T.
Environmental Protection Agency, Program Office Attorneys, GV
Hodges, Suzanne B. ......Tucson, AZ
Hodges, Ted A. ......Houston, TX
Hodges, Therese Linden
Arlington Heights, IL
Hodges, Thomas E. ......Benson, NC
Hodges, Thomas G. ......Wytheville, VA
Hodges, Thomas L., III ......Elberton, GA
Hodges, Thomas T. ......Greenville, SC
Hodges, Warner ......Memphis, TN
Hodges, Warner, III ......Memphis, TN
Hodges, Warren C. ......Winston-Salem, NC
Hodges, Warren O., Jr. ......Los Angeles, CA
Hodges, William H. ......Virginia Beach, VA
Hodges, William V., III ......Aspen, CO
Hodges, William W. ......Columbia, SC
Hodges, Wm. Terrell ......Jacksonville, FL
Hodgesmith, Martha J. ......Topeka, KS
Hodgin, Julie Gregory ......Roanoke, VA
Hodgin, Scott Allen ......Statesboro, GA
Hodgins, Amalija J. ......Austin, TX
Hodgins, Daniel S. ......Oklahoma City, OK
Hodgins, David B. ......Houston, TX
Hodgins, Halleck H. ......Seattle, WA
Hodgins, Mary Rafferty ......Atlanta, GA
Hodgins, Michael A. ......Augusta, ME
Hodgins, Robert A. ......Pearl River, NY
Hodgkin, Andrew M. ......Providence, RI
Hodgkin, Kathryn E. ......Loma Linda, CA
Hodgkins, Elizabeth Marguerite
Anaheim, CA
Hodgkins, Gerald W. ......Washington, DC
Hodgkins, J. Scott ......Los Angeles, CA
Hodgkins, James F. ......Oakland, CA
Hodgkins, Michael G. ......Lake Charles, LA
Hodgkins, Michael G., L.L.C.
Lake Charles, LA
Hodgkins, William E. ......Baton Rouge, LA
Hodgkinson, Donald M. ......Chicago, IL
Hodgkinson, Frank W. ......White Plains, NY
Hodgkinson, Martha J. ......Portland, OR
Hodgkinson, Randall L. ......Kingman, AZ
Hodgkiss, Anita S. ......Department of Justice, Civil Rights Division, GV
Hodgkiss, Brian P. ......Stevens Point, WI
Hodgkiss, Judy ......Paris, TX
Hodgman, Blair ......Cleveland, OH
Hodgman, David R. ......Chicago, IL
Hodgman, Donald R. ......New York, NY
Hodgman, Robert S., and Associates
Greensboro, NC
Hodgman, William D. ......Detroit, MI
Troy, MI
Hodgman, William W. ......Los Angeles, CA
Hodgson, Allen L. ......Salt Lake City, UT
Hodgson, Anita M. ......Indianapolis, IN
Hodgson, Arthur C. ......Lyons, KS
Hodgson, Beverly J. ......Waterbury, CT
Hodgson, C. Clark, Jr. ......Philadelphia, PA
Hodgson, Cheryl L. ......Los Angeles, CA
Hodgson, Christopher M. ......Bridgeport, CT
Hodgson, Curtis D. ......Carrollton, TX
Hodgson, Daniel B. ......Atlanta, GA
Hodgson, Debra ......Denver, CO

Hodgson, Douglas B. ... **Des Moines, IA**
Hodgson, Earl E., Jr. ... San Antonio, TX
Hodgson, Jada D.L. ... Parker, KS
Hodgson, John E. ... **Worcester, MA**
Hodgson, Jonathan A. ... **Annapolis, MD**
Hodgson & Kahler ... **Lyons, KS**
Hodgson, Kia Fadel ... Bountiful, UT
Hodgson, Kimberly C. ... **Mobile, AL**
Hodgson, Lara J. ... **San Jose, CA**
Hodgson Legal Resources ... Parker, KS
Hodgson, Margaret U. ... Atlanta, GA
Hodgson, Mélida N.
Executive Office Of The President, Office of the U.S. Trade Representative, GV
Hodgson, Morgan D. ... **Washington, DC**
Hodgson, Paul R. ... **Tulsa, OK**
Hodgson, Richard B. ... Afton, VA
Hodgson, Richard J. ... Norristown, PA
Hodgson, Robert J., III ... Elmira, NY
Hodgson, Ronald L. ... Clay Center, KS
Hodgson, Russ, Andrews, Woods & Goodyear, LLP ... **Boca Raton, FL**
Newark, NJ
Albany, NY
Buffalo, NY
Gloversville, NY
New York, NY
Hodgson, Sandra L. ... Portland, OR
Hodgson, Shirley I.C. ... **Sacramento, CA**
Hodgson, Stephen S. ... **Houston, TX**
Hodgson and Straight, A Professional Corporation ... Sacramento, CA
Hodgson, Timothy E. ... Sacramento, CA
Hodian, Laurie M. ... Trenton, NJ
Hodik, John J., Jr. ... San Diego, CA
Hodin, Alan J. ... Miami, FL
Hodin, Alan J., P.A. ... Miami, FL
Hodin, Daniel P. ... **Bethesda, MD**
Hodinar, Michael ... Hillsdale, NJ
Hodkin, Adam J. ... **Fort Lauderdale, FL**
Hodkin, Fredric ... Fort Lauderdale, FL
Hodkin, Michele J. ... **Boca Raton, FL**
Hodkin, Peter M. ... Fort Lauderdale, FL
Hodkin, Peter M., P.A. ... Fort Lauderdale, FL
Hodkinson, Mark P. ... **Minneapolis, MN**
Hodkowski, William A. ... **San Jose, CA**
Hodne, Nathan A. ... Dakota Dunes, SD
Hodnett, David R. ... **Atlanta, GA**
Hodnett, Frederick A., Jr. ... Richmond, VA
Hodnett, Michael K. ... Gastonia, NC
Hodnett, Paul J. ... Boston, MA
Hodnett, Ray ... Van Buren, AR
Hodnett-Brooks, Sarah ... Rolling Fork, MS
Hodnett-Brooks, Sarah, P.A.
Rolling Fork, MS
Hodnette, Robert E., Jr. ... Mobile, AL
Hodny Currie Lawyers ... **Grafton, ND**
Park River, ND
Hodny, Jake C. ... **Grafton, ND**
Hodoian, Lynne R. ... Cambridge, MA
Hodor, Judith ... **Miami, FL**
Hodor, Judith, P.A. ... **Miami, FL**
Hodos, Herbert H. ... Greenfield, MA
Hodosh, Frederick R. ... West Chester, PA
Hodosh & Lyon ... Warwick, RI
Hodosh, Marvin R. ... Warwick, RI
Hodosh, Spinella & Angelone
Providence, RI
Hodosy, Kenneth G. ... Amherst, NY
Hodous, Barbara S. ... **Los Angeles, CA**
Hodous, David F. ... Rocky River, OH
Hodous, Robert P. ... **Charlottesville, VA**
Hodowal, John R. ... Indianapolis, IN
Hodrick, Nakeitha S. ... Fort Lauderdale, FL
Hodsdon, Beth C. ... Charlottesville, VA
Hodsdon, Charles W., II ... Bangor, ME
Hodsdon, Nicholas ... **Miami, FL**
Hodsdon, Read & Shepard
Kennebunk, ME
Portland, ME
Hodsdon, Richard D. ... Stillwater, MN
Hodsdon, Stephen Y. ... **Kennebunk, ME**
Hodskins, Edward ... **Owensboro, KY**
Hodson, Charles B. ... Chapel Hill, NC
Hodson, Christopher R. ... Pasadena, CA
Hodson, Donald D. ... Beckley, WV
Hodson, Eugene F. ... Sheboygan, WI
Hodson, Evan S. ... Temple, TX
Hodson, Evelyn J. ... **Sacramento, CA**
Hodson, Fred W., Jr. ... Houston, TX
Hodson, Gerald K. ... New Castle, IN
Hodson, James T. ... **Lafayette, IN**
Hodson, Jerry B., P.C. ... **Portland, OR**
Hodson, John D. ... **Vacaville, CA**
Hodson, John D. ... Rochester, NY
Hodson, Jones & Pennock, Ltd.
Centralia, IL
Hodson, Kendra S. Meinert
Los Angeles, CA
Hodson, Kenneth A. ... **Phoenix, AZ**
Hodson, Kenneth J. ... Washington, DC
Hodson, M. Diane ... St. Petersburg, FL
Hodson & Mullin ... **Vacaville, CA**
Hodson, Richard G. ... Denver, CO
Hodson, Richard H. ... Garden City, KS
Hodson, Robert E. ... Washington, DC
Hodson, Samuel ... **Indianapolis, IN**
Hodson, Thane R. ... **Denver, CO**
Hodson, Thomas F. X. ... **Hartford, CT**
Hodson, Thomas S. ... Athens, OH
Hodson, Thomas Z. ... Champaign, IL
Hodson, Treaver K. ... **Sacramento, CA**
Hodson, Wayne C. ... Huntsville, MO
Hodulik, David S. ... Moorestown, NJ
Hodulik, Matthew J. ... **Newark, NJ**
Hodum, Charles E. ... Walnut, MS
Collierville, TN
Hodum, Robert Ethan, Jr. ... Knoxville, TN
La Follette, TN
Norton, VA
Hodur, Myreon M. ... **Los Angeles, CA**
Hodynsky, Walter ... Hudson, WI
Hodys, Deborah Anne ... Great Neck, NY
Hodys, Paul N. ... New York, NY
Hodza, Richard ... South Salem, NY
Hodzic, Zani I. ... Carnegie, PA
Hoe, Allen K. ... Honolulu, HI
Hoe, E. Sanderson ... **Washington, DC**
Hoe, Richard L. ... Norwalk, CT
Hoebeke, Daniel G. ... Schererville, IN
Hoebel, Elisabeth A. ... Chicago, IL
Hoebelheinrich, Lisa E. ... Kansas City, MO
Hoeber, Paul R. ... **San Francisco, CA**
Hoeberling, Jas. C. ... Beverly Hills, MI
Hoebich, James P. ... New Brunswick, NJ
Hoecherl, Heather ... **Los Angeles, CA**
San Francisco, CA
Hoeck, Kathryn Bessmer ... **Orlando, FL**
Hoecker, Eric Rowland
West Palm Beach, FL
Hoecker, Gary W. ... Pasadena, CA
Hoecker, James J.
Federal Energy Regulatory Commission, Office of the Commissioners, GV
Hoecker, Lawrence E. ... **Horseshoe Bay, TX**
Hoecker, Robert L. ... Denver, CO
Hoecker, Thomas R. ... **Phoenix, AZ**
Hoecker, Wayne H. ... **Kansas City, MO**
Hoecklin, Barbara E. ... **New York, NY**
Hoedebeck, Charles L. ... Irving, TX
Hoedebeck, Charles L., P.C. ... Irving, TX
Hoedeman, Alfred L. ... Minneapolis, MN
Hoedeman & Christy, P.A.
Minneapolis, MN
Hoefer, Anthony D. ... Sumter, SC
Hoefer, Bruce R., Jr. (P.C.)
New Orleans, LA
Hoefer, Craig J. ... **St. Louis, MO**
Hoefer, David A. ... Kansas City, MO
Hoefer, Frederick A., II ... **Florence, SC**
Hoefer, Gladys ... Wichita, KS
Hoefer, J. Anthony ... Omaha, NE
Hoefer, John E. ... Odessa, FL
Hoefer, John M. S. ... **Columbia, SC**
Hoefer, Kathryn C. ... Bronx, NY
Hoefer, Mary K. ... Iowa City, IA
Hoefer, William K. ... Bronx, NY
Hoeferkamp, Michael ... **Albuquerque, NM**
Hoefert, John W. ... Alton, IL
Hoefert, John W., Jr. ... Alton, IL
Hoefert, Joseph E. ... Alton, IL
Hoefert & Perica, P.C. ... Alton, IL
Hoeffel, Funkhouser, Hanna & Fisher
Napoleon, OH
Hoeffel, Joseph M., III ... Norristown, PA
Hoeffel, Paul E. ... **Bucyrus, OH**
Hoeffel, Sue E. ... Columbus, OH
Hoefferle, Joseph, Jr. ... **New York, NY**
Hoefferle, Robert J. ... Ridgewood, NY
Hoeffgen, Sean Marcel ... **Las Vegas, NV**
Hoeffler, John ... **Chicago, IL**
Hoefflin, Reynold C. ... Beavercreek, OH
Hoefflin, Richard M. ... **Encino, CA**
Hoeffner, Bilek & Eidman, L.L.P.
Houston, TX
Hoeffner, Christine T. ... **Sherman Oaks, CA**
Hoeffner, James V. ... **Austin, TX**
Hoeffner, Patrick J. ... **New York, NY**
Hoeffner, Timothy E. ... **New York, NY**
Hoeffner, W. Todd ... Houston, TX
Hoefges, R. Michael ... San Antonio, TX
Hoefinghoff, Lee ... Fort Mitchell, KY
Hoefker, Paul A. ... **Houston, TX**
Hoefle, Daniel C. ... **Portsmouth, NH**
Hoefle, H. Fred ... Cincinnati, OH
Hoefle, Paul R. ... **Waukesha, WI**
Hoefle, Phoenix & Gormley, Professional Association ... **Portsmouth, NH**
Hoefle, W. O. ... St. Louis, MO
Hoeflich, Adam L. ... **Denver, CO**
Chicago, IL
Hoeflich, Denise G. ... Waukegan, IL
Hoefling, John W. ... **Mineola, NY**
Riverhead, NY
Hoefling, Richard G. ... Charlotte, NC
Hoefling, Richard G. ... Falls Church, VA
Hoefling, Richard K.
Nuclear Regulatory Commission, Office of the General Counsel, GV
Hoefling, Virginia A. ... Boston, MA
Hoefling, Wade A. ... **Houston, TX**
Hoefs, Richard A. ... Houston, TX
Hoeft, Arnold E. ... Issaquah, WA
Hoeft, Brad M. ... Port Washington, WI
Hoeft, Christine M. ... **Alexandria, VA**
Hoeft, Donald L. ... Minneapolis, MN
Hoeft, James D. ... **Minneapolis, MN**
Hoeft, John T. ... Dallas, TX
Hoeft, Peter N. ... Green Bay, WI
Hoeft, Steven H. ... **Chicago, IL**
Hoeft, Timothy E. ... Holdrege, NE
Hoeg, A. Everett, III ... **Falls Church, VA**
Hoeg, Catherine W. ... **Houston, TX**
Hoeg, Edward J. ... Fort Lauderdale, FL
Hoeg, Gregory J. ... Princeton, NJ
Hoeg, Larry S. ... Fishers, IN
Hoeg, Matthew L. ... **Houston, TX**
Hoeg, Patricia M. ... Hopewell Junction, NY
Hoeg, Silvia M. ... **Orlando, FL**
Hoegen, Francis J. ... **Wilkes-Barre, PA**
Hoegen, Hoegen & Kelley L.L.P.
Scranton, PA
Wilkes-Barre, PA
Hoegen, Peter J. ... **Wilkes-Barre, PA**
Hoeger, Donald L. ... Independence, IA
Hoeger & McClintock ... Independence, IA
Hoegh, Leo A. ... Colorado Springs, CO
Hoegh, Richard B. ... Los Angeles, CA
Hoegle, Robert L. ... **Washington, DC**
Hoeglund, Christina Ruth ... Minneapolis, MN
Hoegstedt, Kingsley T. ... Carmel, CA
Hoeh, Jeffrey D. ... **New York, NY**
Hoeh, Thomas L. ... Perryville, MO
Hoehl, John R. ... Miami, FL
Hoehler, Raymond J. ... **Pittsburgh, PA**
Hoehler, William J. ... **San Francisco, CA**
Hoehn, Charles, III ... Point Richmond, CA
Hoehn, Elmer L. ... Jeffersonville, IN
Hoehn, Marla A. ... **Palo Alto, CA**
Hoehn, Peter C. ... Plainsboro, NJ
Hoehn, Richard N., (P.C.) ... **Boston, MA**
Hoehn, Robert E. ... **Nashville, TN**
Hoehne, Jeffry M. ... Cincinnati, OH
Hoehne, Thomas V. ... Peoria, IL
Hoehnen, Janet M. ... **Milwaukee, WI**
Hoehner, Adrianne L. ... **South Bend, IN**
Hoehner, Daniel J. ... **Oklahoma City, OK**
Hoehner, Holly Johnsen ... **New York, NY**
Hoehner, John F. ... St. Louis, MO
Hoehn-Saric, Alexander D. ... **New York, NY**
Hoek, Danny Arthur ... **Palm Springs, CA**
Hoekel, Boyd S. ... **Houston, TX**
Hoekel, Marshall R. ... **St. Louis, MO**
Hoekel, Tari Lessard ... **Houston, TX**
Hoekema, Susan B. ... **Grand Rapids, MI**
Hoekendijk, Jens E. ... **Redwood City, CA**
Hoekenga, Daniel J. ... Southfield, MI
Hoekman, Will J. ... Des Moines, IA
Hoeksema, Douglas A. ... Maitland, FL
Hoeksema, Kristin E. ... Chicago, IL
Hoeksema, Steven C. ... Des Moines, IA
Hoeksema, Terry L. ... Grand Rapids, MI
Hoeksma, Gerben ... **Los Angeles, CA**
Hoekstra, Cynthia Koos ... Philadelphia, PA
Hoekstra, David J. ... St. Paul, MN
Hoekstra, Jaclyn A. ... **Los Angeles, CA**
Hoekstra, Joel P. ... Grand Rapids, MI
Hoekstra, John A. ... Bloomington, IL
Hoekstra, Kathlyn B.
Federal Deposit Insurance Corporation, Liquidation Branch, GV
Hoekstra, Leslie J. ... **San Jose, CA**
Hoekstra, Michael T. ... Wayzata, MN
Hoekstra, Thomas S. ... **Dallas, TX**
Hoekstra, Victoria M. ... Orinda, CA
Hoel and Associates, P.C. ... Douglasville, GA
Hoel, Carlton H. ... Dallas, TX
Hoel, Charlotte R. ... Douglasville, GA
Hoel, Cristopher Charles ... **Pittsburgh, PA**
Hoel, David E. ... Madison, WI
Hoel, David K. ... Tulsa, OK
Hoel, David K., P.C. ... Tulsa, OK
Hoel, Donald K. ... Kansas City, MO
Hoel, J. Richard, Jr. ... Downers Grove, IL
Hoel, John E. ... **Washington, DC**
Hoel, Jonathan C. ... **Atlanta, GA**
Hoel, Kari S. ... Madison, WI
Hoel, Mary ... Cornell, WI
Hoel, Raymond L. ... Cornell, WI
Hoel, Richard A. ... **Minneapolis, MN**
St. Paul, MN
Hoeland, Jas. W. ... Jacksonville, FL
Hoeler, Thomas M. ... **Tampa, FL**
Hoelle, Maria Isabel ... **Miami, FL**
Hoellen, John J. ... Chicago, IL
Hoellen & Lukes ... Chicago, IL
Hoellen, Robert B. ... Chicago, IL
Hoeller, Mary J. ... Indianapolis, IN
Hoeller, Susie L. ... **Dallas, TX**
Hoellering, Michael F. ... **New York, NY**
Hoellrich, Gene R. ... Versailles, OH
Hoellwarth, Larry A. ... **Chicago, IL**
Hoelmer, David R. ... Mankato, MN
Hoelschen, Paul E., Jr. ... **Sacramento, CA**
Hoelscher, Brian G. ... **Minneapolis, MN**
Hoelscher, Ellen M. ... Columbia, MO
Hoelscher, Lipsey & Elmore, P.C.
Bryan, TX
College Station, TX
Hoelscher, Michael R. ... **College Station, TX**
Hoelscher, Richard C. ... Hereford, TX
Hoelscher, Robert J. ... Philadelphia, PA
Hoelscher, William C. ... Richmond, IN
Hoelter, Michael L. ... Memphis, TN
Hoelter, Timothy K. ... Milwaukee, WI
Hoelting, Cheryl A. ... Arcadia, CA
Hoelz, Joseph G. ... San Diego, CA
Hoelzel, Cynthia Lynn ... Glendale, CA
Hoelzel, Jeffery K. ... **Chicago, IL**
Hoelzer, Kelly Culp ... **Baltimore, MD**
Hoelzl, Diane M. ... **St. Louis, MO**
Hoelzle, Achim W. ... **San Francisco, CA**
Hoemann, Cynthia L. ... Clayton, MO
Hoemeke, Robert B. ... **St. Louis, MO**
Hoen, Cynthia N. ... **Morristown, NJ**
Hoen, J.F. ... **Hampton, VA**
Hoene & Krause, P.A. ... **St. Paul, MN**
Hoene, Mary Joan ... New York, NY
Hoene, Robert C. ... **St. Paul, MN**
Hoener, James A. ... **Jacksonville, FL**
Hoener, Kurt C. ... St. Louis, MO
Hoener, Sonya Harrell ... **Jacksonville, FL**
Hoenicke, Jeanne E. ... **Washington, DC**
Hoenig, D. Bernard ... Cedarhurst, NY
Hoenig, James K. ... Honolulu, HI
Hoenig, Karl Blake ... Oklahoma City, OK
Hoenig, Kathryn L. ... New York, NY
Hoenig, Lawrence L. ... **San Francisco, CA**
Hoenig, Mark ... **New York, NY**
Hoenig, Michael ... **New York, NY**
Hoenig, Peter ... **New York, NY**
Hoenig, Ronald J. ... Orland Park, IL
Hoeniger, Berthold H. ... Bridgewater, CT
New York, NY
Hoeniger, Berthold H., P.C. ... Bridgewater, CT
New York, NY
Hoenigman, Richard A. ... **Cleveland, OH**
Hoening, Tracie Diane ... Bartow, FL
Hoenings, Marie Ann ... **Garden City, NY**
Hoenisch, Sandra J. ... Wausau, WI
Hoens, Helen E. ... Roseland, NJ
Hoeper, Peter J. ... Waupun, WI
Hoepker, Todd M. ... **Orlando, FL**
Hoepker, Todd M., P.A. ... **Orlando, FL**
Hoeppner, Carl O. ... Plymouth, WI
Hoeppner, Delmar R. ... **Valparaiso, IN**
Hoeppner Wagner & Evans LLP
Crown Point, IN
Hammond, IN
Merrillville, IN
Valparaiso, IN
Hoeppner-Crawford, Shirley J. ... Ramsey, NJ
Hoeppner-Freitas, Jacqueline Ann
Oakland, CA
Hoequist, Charles E. ... **Orlando, FL**
Hoerbert, Russel D. ... Decatur, IL
Hoerchner, Eric A. ... **Long Beach, CA**
Hoerger, Maureen S. ... Hauppauge, NY
Hoerger, Robert G. ... Palo Alto, CA
Hoerger, Susan K. ... **Palo Alto, CA**
Hoerig, Joseph P. ... **Mansfield, OH**
Hoering, Thomas Francis ... Garden City, NY
Hoerman, Tor A. ... **Chicago, IL**
Hoerner, Barbara Anstey ... **Phoenix, AZ**
Hoerner, Daniel J. ... **New Orleans, LA**
Hoerner, Dennis R., Jr. ... **St. Louis, MO**
Hoerner, Garrett Patrick ... Belleville, IL
Hoerner, J. William ... **Ada, MI**
Hoerner, Kevin T. ... Belleville, IL
Hoerner, Mark W. ... Baltimore, MD
Hoerner, Meghan Jane ... **Philadelphia, PA**
Hoerner, Robert J. ... Cleveland, OH
Hoerner, William F. ... Whittier, CA
Hoernig, Brenda M. ... Honolulu, HI
Hoernig, Deborah D. ... Eugene, OR
Hoernig, Glenn A.
Department Of Health And Human Services, GV
Hoernle, Bettina C. ... **Kansas City, MO**
Hoerr, John Peter, IV ... Brockton, MA
Hoerrner, Karen M. ... Newark, NJ
Hoerrner, Mark D. ... **Newark, NJ**
Hoerst, Frank J. ... Woodstown, NJ
Hoersten, Craig A. ... **Dallas, TX**
Hoerster, John K. ... **Seattle, WA**
Hoerster, Pamela S. ... Houston, TX
Hoerster, Pamela S., P.C. ... Houston, TX
Hoerster, Richard ... Fredericksburg, TX
Hoerster, Richard L. ... Fredericksburg, TX
Hoersting, Stephen M. ... **Dublin, OH**
Hoertel, Edward ... Rolla, MO
Hoertel, William W. ... Rolla, MO
Hoerter, Jeffrey ... Bronx, NY
Hoerth, Joseph G. ... Stamford, CT
Hoes, Donald A. ... Wilmington, DE
Hoesch and Dekker ... Zeeland, MI
Hoesch, Kenneth W. ... Zeeland, MI
Hoesch, Timothy A. ... Zeeland, MI
Hoeschen, Andrea F. ... **Milwaukee, WI**
Hoeschler, John G. ... Minneapolis, MN
Hoeschler, John G., P.A. ... Minneapolis, MN
Hoese, Lawrence R. ... Alexandria, VA
Hoese, William E. ... **Philadelphia, PA**
Hoese, William L. ... Hoffman Estates, IL
Hoesly, Bruce J. ... Madison, WI
Hoestenbach, John L., Jr. ... Odessa, TX
Hoetger, Craig M. ... **Chicago, IL**
Hoeth, Thea ... Albany, NY
Hoeting, Donald ... Springfield, VA
Hoevel, John J. ... Chicago, IL
Hoevel, Talbot, & Associates, P.C.
Chicago, IL
Hoevel, Talbot C. ... Chicago, IL
Hoeveler, William M. ... Miami, FL
Hoevet, Ronald H. ... **Portland, OR**
Hoevet, Snyder & Boise, P.C.
Portland, OR
Hoewing, Karen L. ... Richland, WA
Hoexter, Laura E. ... **Bellevue, WA**
Hoey, Barbara E. ... **New York, NY**
Hoey, Barton F. ... San Rafael, CA
Hoey, Benjamin J. ... Buffalo, NY
Hoey, Beverly M., The Law Offices of
Pleasanton, CA
Hoey, Charles G. ... **Atlanta, GA**
Hoey, Cheryl A. ... Santa Rosa, CA
Hoey, Christian J. ... **Plymouth Meeting, PA**
Hoey, Christine M. ... **Pawtucket, RI**
Hoey, Christopher J. ... **New York, NY**
Hoey, Colleen A. ... **Miami, FL**
Hoey, David J. ... Medford, MA
Hoey, David M. ... Maitland, FL
Hoey, James D., III ... San Diego, CA
Hoey, James M. ... **Chicago, IL**
Hoey, Joseph P. ... Mineola, NY
Hoey, King, Toker & Epstein
New York, NY
Hoey, Marjorie M. ... **New York, NY**
Hoey, Patrick T. ... New York, NY
Hoey, Thomas M., Jr. ... New York, NY
Hoey, William E. ... Tequesta, FL
Hoey, William L. ... Grosse Pointe Park, MI
Hoey, William M. ... Woodbury, CT
Hoeynck, Robert E., Jr. ... Fort Lauderdale, FL
Hof, George M. ... Minneapolis, MN
Hof, Monica L. ... New Orleans, LA
Hof, Philip M. ... **Easton, PA**
Hof, Ronald J. ... **New Orleans, LA**
Hofacker, Velda K. ... Columbus, OH
Hofaker, Paula D. ... Hill City, KS

Hofbauer, Lawrence J. .... **Springfield, OH**
Hofbauer, Thomas C. .... **Chicago, IL**
Hofberg, Adam E. .... Los Angeles, CA
Hofberg, Steven H. .... **Rockville, MD**
Hofberg, Steven H., P.C. .... **Rockville, MD**
Hofeld, Albert F., (Ltd.) .... Chicago, IL
Hofeld, Anthony R. .... **Chicago, IL**
Hofeld, B. Curtis .... Riverside, CA
Hofeld, Frederick R. .... Los Angeles, CA
Hofeld and Schaffner, A Prtnshp. incl. A Prof. Corp. .... Chicago, IL
Hofele, David M. .... Savannah, GA
Hofelich, James A. .... **Cleveland, OH**
Hofelich & King .... **Cleveland, OH**
Hofeling, J. Keven .... Salt Lake City, UT
Hofen, Renee A. .... **St. Louis, MO**
Hofer, Alan K. .... Fort Wayne, IN
Hofer, Dennis J. .... Ashland, OR
Hofer, James M. .... Lansing, MI
Hofer, Julie E. .... **Oakland, CA**
Hofer, Kathy Jean .... **Dearborn, MI**
Hofer, Keith R. .... Akron, OH
Hofer, Marianna .... Redondo Beach, CA
Hofer, Mark A. .... **Boston, MA**
Hofer, Michael F. .... Indianapolis, IN
Hofer, Patrick F. .... **Washington, DC**
Hofer, Ralph C. .... **Los Angeles, CA**
Hofer, Robert D. .... **Pierre, SD**
Hofer, Ronald L. .... **Troy, MI**
Hofer, Ronald R. .... Waukesha, WI
Hofer, Roy E. .... **Chicago, IL**
Hofer, Scott D. .... **Kansas City, MO**
Hofer, Stephen R. .... **Santa Monica, CA**
Hofer, Steven C. .... **Midland, TX**
Hofer, Steven R. .... Indianapolis, IN
Hofer, Stewart L. .... Freeman, SD
Hofer, Susan L. .... **Bloomfield Hills, MI**
Hofer, Terry L. .... **Rapid City, SD**
Hoferer, Paul R. .... Fort Worth, TX
Hofert, Daniel C. .... Chicago, IL
Hofert, Edward C. .... Chicago, IL
Hofert, James M. .... **Chicago, IL**
Hoff, Alan J. .... **Baltimore, MD**
Hoff, Alan S. .... Appleton, WI
Hoff, Allison L. .... **Detroit, MI**
Hoff, Barry & Kuderer, P.A. .... Eden Prairie, MN
Hoff, Bonnie Lee .... Marquette, MI
Hoff, Bradley W. .... **Seattle, WA**
Hoff, Carolyn .... **Los Angeles, CA**
Hoff, Charles S. .... Rancho Palos Verdes, CA
Hoff, Charles Y. .... **Atlanta, GA**
Hoff, Christopher P. .... Environmental Protection Agency, Office of Congressional and Legislative Affairs, GV
Hoff, Curtis, Pacht, Cassidy & Frame, P.C. .... Portland, ME
Burlington, VT
Rutland, VT
Hoff, D. Warren, Jr. .... St. Louis, MO
Hoff, Daniel J. .... Appleton, WI
Hoff, David D. .... **Seattle, WA**
Hoff, David H. .... Urbana, IL
Hoff, Deborah K. .... Waynesboro, PA
Hoff, Don J. .... **Greeley, CO**
Hoff, E. Michael .... Bloomington, IN
Hoff, Ellen Harris .... **Phoenix, AZ**
Hoff, Frederick T., Jr. .... **Gulfport, MS**
Hoff, Gary D. .... Van Nuys, CA
Hoff, Gary L. .... **Boston, MA**
Hoff, George C. .... Eden Prairie, MN
Hoff, George L. .... Akron, OH
Hoff, Gerald T. .... Manchester, MO
Hoff, Gerhardt M. .... Atlanta, GA
Hoff, Howard M. .... Summit, IL
Hoff, J. Williams .... Bellevue, WA
Hoff, James E. .... Dowagiac, MI
Hoff, John H. .... Waukesha, WI
Hoff, John Scott .... Chicago, IL
Hoff, John Scott, P.C. .... Chicago, IL
Hoff, Jonathan M. .... **New York, NY**
Hoff, Katherine Kemmeries .... Scottsdale, AZ
Hoff, Kay Seeber .... **West Palm Beach, FL**
Hoff, Kenneth M. H. .... **Los Angeles, CA**
Hoff, Lawrence C., Jr. .... Houston, TX
Hoff, Linda S. .... Brooklyn, NY
Hoff, Louis A. .... Cincinnati, OH
Hoff, Martha W. .... Washington, DC
Hoff, Mary K. .... St. Louis, MO
Hoff, Michael R. .... Los Angeles, CA
Hoff, Michael R. .... Newton, MA
Hoff, Nancy K. .... Phoenix, AZ
Hoff, Neil .... **Tacoma, WA**
Hoff, Patricia M. .... United States Senate, Committee Legal Personnel, GV
Hoff, Paul .... Sacramento, CA
Hoff, Paul M. .... **Napa, CA**
Hoff, Paul S. .... **Washington, DC**
Hoff, Peter A. .... Breckenridge, MN
Hoff, Philip H. .... **Burlington, VT**
Hoff, Richard J., Jr. .... **Philadelphia, PA**
Hoff, Robert T. .... Chicago, IL
Hoff, Robin J. .... Los Angeles, CA
Hoff, Timothy .... Tuscaloosa, AL
Hoff, Valerie M. Knecht .... Bellevue, WA
Hoff, Victor V. .... **Seattle, WA**
Hoff, William J. .... Washington, DC
Hoff, Wm. Bruce, Jr. .... **Chicago, IL**
Hoffa, Robert A. .... **Bensalem, PA**
Hoffa, Thomas E. .... Chicago, IL
Hoffar, Julian F. .... **McLean, VA**
Hoffar, Taylor .... Seymour, IN
Hoffart, Michele Raia .... Cleveland, OH
Hoffberg, Anilkumar J. .... **Baltimore, MD**
Hoffberg, David E. .... New York, NY
Hoffberg, David L. .... **Rochester, NY**
Hoffberg, Robert J. .... Windsor, CT
Hoffberg, Steven M. .... Ventura, CA
Hoffberg, Steven M. .... **New York, NY**
White Plains, NY
Hoffberger, LeRoy E. .... **Baltimore, MD**
Hoffbuhr, Tamara .... **Denver, CO**
Hoffe, R. Bruce .... **Richmond, CA**
Hoffecker, Frederick H. .... Lansing, MI
Hoffecker, Heidi R. .... **Chattanooga, TN**
Hoffee, Alicia A. .... Sacramento, CA
Hoffee, Carl O. .... **Springfield, IL**
Hoffee-Hunt, Susan .... **Springfield, IL**
Hoffeins, Arthur M. .... Dearborn, MI
Hoffelder, Susan A. .... **Niles, MI**
Hoffelt, Richard H. .... **Sacramento, CA**
Hoffen & Hoffen, A P.C. .... Los Angeles, CA
Hoffen, John F., Jr. .... Baltimore, MD
Hoffen, Lillian P. .... Los Angeles, CA
Hoffenberg, Alan D. .... Chicago, IL
Hoffenberg, Betty S. .... Pacific Palisades, CA
Hoffenberg, Howard L. .... Los Angeles, CA
Hoffenberg, Lynne S. .... **Washington, DC**
Hoffenberg, Mark R. .... Treasury Department, Departmental Offices, GV
Hoffer, Brian L. .... Nappanee, IN
Hoffer, Bruce A. .... Beaumont, TX
Hoffer, C. Allan .... New Albany, IN
Hoffer, Caroline M. .... **Lancaster, PA**
Hoffer, Christopher J. .... Anoka, MN
Hoffer, Daniel P. .... **Los Angeles, CA**
Hoffer, David P. .... Seattle, WA
Hoffer, F. S., Jr. .... West Hartford, CT
Hoffer, George E. .... Carlisle, PA
Hoffer, Gerald F. .... West Sayville, NY
Hoffer, Harold .... La Mesa, CA
Hoffer, Jay L. .... Tampa, FL
Hoffer, Jeremiah Anthony, II .... Toledo, OH
Hoffer, Jerry .... Cleveland, TN
Hoffer, Joan M. .... General Services Administration, Office of Regional Counsel, GV
Hoffer, Marcia W. .... Santa Monica, CA
Hoffer, Mark D. .... Corona, NY
Hoffer, Peri .... Merrick, NY
Hoffer, Philip .... New York, NY
Hoffer, Robert J. .... **Boston, MA**
Hoffer, Robert M. .... **Covington, KY**
Hoffer, Rose L. .... New York, NY
Hoffer, Steven M. .... Corte Madera, CA
Hoffer, Stewart .... **Houston, TX**
Hofferbert, Louis .... Knoxville, TN
Hoffer-Landsman, Donna H. .... Bronx, NY
Hofferman, Jeffrey D. .... **Cherry Hill, NJ**
Philadelphia, PA
Hoffert & Associates, P.C. .... **Southfield, MI**
Hoffert, Dennis K. .... St. Louis, MO
Hoffert, Huckabee & Weiler, P.C.
Birdsboro, PA
Reading, PA
Shillington, PA
Hoffert, J. Stanley .... Wausau, WI
Hoffert, John A., Jr. .... Birdsboro, PA
Reading, PA
Shillington, PA
Hoffert, John R. .... **Lincoln, NE**
Hoffert, Myles B. .... **Southfield, MI**
Hoffey, Matthew W. .... Hudson, IA
Hoffhaus, Charles E. .... **Kansas City, MO**
Hoffheimer, Daniel J. .... **Cincinnati, OH**
Hoffheimer & Downey, P.C.
Washington, DC
Hoffheimer, Harry M. .... Cincinnati, OH
Hoffheimer, Jon .... **Cincinnati, OH**
Hoffheimer, Lawrence S. .... Washington, DC
Hoffheimer, Michael H. .... University, MS
Hoffing, I. Mark .... San Diego, CA
Hoffinger, Adam S. .... **Washington, DC**
Hoffinger, Fran .... **New York, NY**
Hoffinger Friedland Dobrish & Stern, P.C.
New York, NY
Hoffinger, Jack S. .... **New York, NY**
Hoffinger, Julie M. H. .... Portland, OR
Hoffinger, Susan D. .... New York, NY
Hoffius, Dirk .... **Grand Rapids, MI**
Hoffius, Leonard M. .... **Grand Rapids, MI**
Hoffius, R. Stuart .... **Grand Rapids, MI**
Hoffiz, Benjamin T., Jr. .... Troy, MI
Hoffkins, Kevin L. .... **Stamford, CT**
Hoffland, Eric L. .... **San Diego, CA**
Hofflich, Richard A. .... New York, NY
Hofflund, Paul .... San Diego, CA
Hoffman, A. Drew .... **Albuquerque, NM**
Hoffman, Aaron E. .... **Chicago, IL**
Hoffman, Abraham .... Wilmington, DE
Hoffman, Abraham .... Brooklyn, NY
Hoffman, Adonis E. .... Washington, DC
Hoffman, Aggie R. .... **Los Angeles, CA**
Hoffman, Alan B. .... **St. Louis, MO**
Hoffman, Alan C. .... Chicago, IL
Hoffman, Alan C., & Associates .... Chicago, IL
Hoffman, Alan F. .... Lansing, MI
Hoffman, Alan J. .... **Wilmington, DE**
Philadelphia, PA
Hoffman, Alan M. .... **New York, NY**
Hoffman, Alan R. .... **Boston, MA**
Hoffman, Alan S. .... Buffalo, NY
Hoffman, Alan S. .... **New York, NY**
Hoffman, Albert .... Denver, CO
Hoffman, Alfred J. .... Kansas City, MO
Hoffman, Alice J. .... New York, NY
Hoffman, Alison Nancy .... West Hartford, CT
Hoffman, Allan C., Jr. .... Jenkintown, PA
Hoffman, Allan L. .... West Palm Beach, FL
Hoffman, Allan M. .... **Philadelphia, PA**
Hoffman, Allan S. .... Washington, DC
Hoffman, Allen J. .... Vail, CO
Hoffman, Allison .... New York, NY
Hoffman, Andrew D. .... Allentown, PA
Hoffman, Andrew P. .... **New York, NY**
Hoffman, Ann Fleisher .... Avenel, NJ
Hoffman, Anna Marie .... Downers Grove, IL
Hoffman, Anne .... **Boston, MA**
Hoffman, Annemarie .... Canonsburg, PA
Hoffman, Anthony Michael .... **Mobile, AL**
Hoffman, Arnold J. .... **Palm Beach, FL**
Hoffman, Arnold J. .... **West Palm Beach, FL**
Hoffman & Arshack, P.C. .... **New York, NY**
Hoffman, Arthur E. .... Kirkwood, MO
Hoffman, Arthur K. .... **Harrisburg, PA**
Hoffman, Austin J., II .... Syracuse, NY
Hoffman, B. Carole .... **New York, NY**
Hoffman, Barbara (IBA) .... New York, NY
Hoffman, Barbara .... **New York, NY**
Hoffman, Barbara M. .... Newark, NJ
Hoffman, Barnett E. .... New Brunswick, NJ
Hoffman, Barry A. L. .... El Segundo, CA
Hoffman, Barry G. .... Boca Raton, FL
Hoffman, Barry M. .... Scotch Plains, NJ
Hoffman, Barry M. .... **New York, NY**
Hoffman, Barry P. .... **Livonia, MI**
Hoffman, Bernard H. .... **Red Bank, NJ**
Hoffman, Bert C., Jr. .... Fresno, CA
Hoffman, Beryl W. .... Bloomfield Hills, MI
Hoffman, Beth L. .... Buffalo, NY
Hoffman, Bita L. .... San Diego, CA
Hoffman, Bradley E. .... Columbus, OH
Hoffman, Brenda Lee .... Treasury Department, Bureau of the Public Debt, GV
Hoffman, Brent L. .... Philadelphia, PA
Hoffman, Brian L. .... **Los Angeles, CA**
Hoffman, Brian M. .... **Palo Alto, CA**
Hoffman, Bruce A. .... Los Angeles, CA
Hoffman, Bruce A. .... **Cincinnati, OH**
Hoffman, Bruce Edward .... Gainesville, FL
Hoffman, Bruce F. .... **Northbrook, IL**
Hoffman, Bruce H. .... **Sterling Heights, MI**
Hoffman, Bruce R. .... Beaufort, SC
Hoffman, Burt M. .... **Stamford, CT**
Hoffman, Burton L. .... Chicago, IL
Hoffman, Burton S. .... Treasury Department, Internal Revenue Service, GV
Hoffman, C. Roger .... **Florham Park, NJ**
Hoffman, Carl .... Buffalo, NY
Hoffman, Carl H. .... **Miami, FL**
Hoffman, Carol L. .... Berkeley, CA
Hoffman, Carol M. .... **Garden City, NY**
Hoffman, Carrie B. .... **Dallas, TX**
Hoffman, Cary S. .... **New York, NY**
Hoffman, Catherine .... Houston, TX
Hoffman, Catherine E. .... New York, NY
Hoffman, Catherine F. .... **Miami, FL**
Hoffman, Cathy .... **Washington, DC**
Hoffman, Chad Tyler .... Houston, TX
Hoffman, Charlene A. .... South Portland, ME
Hoffman, Charles A. .... **Minneapolis, MN**
Hoffman, Charles B. .... Duluth, MN
Hoffman, Charles C. .... Gainesville, FL
Hoffman, Charles F. .... Berea, KY
Hoffman, Charles G. .... Cheboygan, MI
Hoffman, Charles J. .... Pebble Beach, CA
Hoffman, Charles L., Jr. .... **Pensacola, FL**
Hoffman, Charles P., Jr. .... Ann Arbor, MI
Hoffman, Charles R. .... **Phoenix, AZ**
Hoffman, Charlotte A. .... **Huntington, WV**
Hoffman, Christian M. .... **Boston, MA**
Hoffman, Christopher .... **Somers, NY**
Hoffman, Christopher C.
Newport Beach, CA
Hoffman, Christy .... Washington, DC
Hoffman, Clelia Patrizio .... Pittsburgh, PA
Hoffman, Clifford G., (P.C.) .... **Atlanta, GA**
Hoffman, Comfort, Galloway & Offutt, LLP
Baltimore, MD
Westminster, MD
Hoffman, Connie .... Philadelphia, PA
Hoffman, Corey E. .... Miami, FL
Hoffman, Craig P. .... Jacksonville, FL
Hoffman, Curtis B. .... **Provo, UT**
Hoffman, Curtis R. .... Martinez, CA
Hoffman, Cynthia Corbett
Fredericksburg, VA
Hoffman, D. Bruce .... **Miami, FL**
Hoffman, Dan G. .... Houston, TX
Hoffman, Dana H. .... **New York, NY**
Hoffman, Dana P. .... **Orlando, FL**
Hoffman, Daniel .... New York, NY
Hoffman, Daniel C. .... **Valdosta, GA**
Hoffman, Daniel C. .... Vineland, NJ
Hoffman, Daniel C. .... Memphis, TN
Hoffman, Daniel C., The Law Firm of
Memphis, TN
Hoffman, Daniel E. .... **Glendale, CA**
Hoffman, Daniel J. .... The Woodlands, TX
Hoffman, Daniel N. .... Santa Clara, CA
Hoffman, Daniel S. .... **Denver, CO**
Hoffman, David .... Los Angeles, CA
Hoffman, David .... Wichita, KS
Hoffman, David .... Cresskill, NJ
Hoffman, David .... New Brunswick, NJ
Hoffman, David .... Pittsburgh, PA
Hoffman, David A. .... **Atlanta, GA**
Hoffman, David A. .... Northbrook, IL
Hoffman, David A. .... **Kansas City, KS**
Overland Park, KS
Hoffman, David A. .... **Boston, MA**
Hoffman, David B. .... Northbrook, IL
Hoffman, David C. .... Rock Island, IL
Hoffman, David D. .... **Monticello, AR**
Hoffman, David D. .... Caro, MI
Saginaw, MI
Hoffman, David D., P.C. .... Caro, MI
Saginaw, MI
Hoffman, David G. .... Fairfax, VA
Hoffman, David I. .... **Telluride, CO**
Hoffman, David L. .... **Novato, CA**
Hoffman, David L. .... **Santa Monica, CA**
Hoffman, David M. .... Springfield, NJ
Hoffman, David M. .... New York, NY
Hoffman, David N. .... **New York, NY**
Hoffman, David S. .... Tucson, AZ
Hoffman, David S. .... Campbell, CA
Hoffman, Deborah .... Miami, FL
Hoffman, Deborah F. .... Columbus, OH
Hoffman, Debra B. .... **Chicago, IL**
Hoffman, Dewey .... Philadelphia, PA
Hoffman, Dianna Z. .... Davis, CA
Hoffman, Dianne L. .... Lake City, MI
Hoffman, DiMuzio & Hoffman
Franklinville, NJ
Woodbury, NJ
Hoffman, Dolly .... **New York, NY**
Hoffman, Donald A. .... **New Orleans, LA**
Hoffman, Donald E. .... Hampstead, MD
Hoffman, Donald F. .... **Hays, KS**
Hoffman, Donald M. .... **Glendale, CA**
Hoffman, Donald R. .... Topeka, KS
Hoffman, Doreen L. .... **Birmingham, MI**
Hoffman, Douglas .... Chicago, IL
Hoffman, Douglas A. .... **Bloomington, IN**
Fort Wayne, IN
Hoffman, Douglas E. .... Sioux Falls, SD
Hoffman, Douglas F. .... **Fort Lauderdale, FL**
Hoffman, Douglas J. .... Washington, DC
Hoffman, Douglas R. .... Auburn, CA
Hoffman, Douglas R. .... **Chicago, IL**
Hoffman, Douglas W. .... Severna Park, MD
Hoffman Drewry Hancock & Simmons
Indianapolis, IN
Hoffman, E. Eric .... San Jose, CA
Hoffman, E. Leslie, III .... **Washington, DC**
Hoffman, E. Lynn .... **Baltimore, MD**
Hoffman, E. Michael .... Aspen, CO
Hoffman & Edelson .... **Doylestown, PA**
Hoffman, Edward A. .... Los Angeles, CA
Hoffman, Edward A. .... Trenton, NJ
Hoffman, Edward A., Law Offices of
Los Angeles, CA
Hoffman, Edward F. .... Lincoln, NE
Hoffman, Edward J. .... **Philadelphia, PA**
Hoffman, Edward L. .... Toledo, OH
Hoffman, Edwin L. .... Duluth, GA
Hoffman, Edwin W. .... **Boca Raton, FL**
Hoffman, Eileen .... **New York, NY**
Hoffman, Eileen B. .... Federal Mediation and Conciliation Service, GV
Hoffman, Eileen L. .... Ligonier, PA
Hoffman, Elliot L. .... **New York, NY**
Hoffman, Elliot P. .... **New York, NY**
Hoffman, Elmo R. .... **Orlando, FL**
Orlando, FL
Hoffman, Emily Long .... Harrisburg, PA
Hoffman, Eric .... Newark, DE
Hoffman, Eric G. .... **San Antonio, TX**
Hoffman, Eric J. .... **Newport Beach, CA**
Hoffman, Eric R. .... **Cleveland, OH**
Hoffman, Erik T. .... **Washington, DC**
Hoffman, Everett C. .... Louisville, KY
Hoffman, F. Herbert, Jr. .... Columbus, OH
Hoffman, Finney & Sandel
San Francisco, CA
Hoffman Firm, The .... Washington, DC
Hoffman Firm, The, P.S.C. .... Elsmere, KY
Hoffman, Flora Houn .... **Santa Clara, CA**
Hoffman, Florice .... Pasadena, CA
Hoffman, Floyd G. .... Aurora, IL
Hoffman & Fowler, LLP .... **Atlanta, GA**
Hoffman, Fran L. .... **Wayne, PA**
Hoffman, Francis M. .... New York, NY
Hoffman, Frank A. .... **Indianapolis, IN**
Hoffman, Frank E. .... Bloomington, IL
Pekin, IL
Hoffman, Frank H. .... Houston, TX
Hoffman, Frank P. .... **Plainsboro, NJ**
Hoffman, Frederick C. .... Palo Alto, CA
Hoffman, Frederick E. .... **Southampton, NY**
Hoffman, Frederick G. .... **Peoria, IL**
Hoffman, Frederick W., IV
Highland Park, MI
Hoffman, Fredric A. .... **Miami, FL**
Hoffman, G. Scott .... **Atlanta, GA**
Hoffman, G. A., (Miss) .... San Diego, CA
Hoffman, Gail Joy .... Milwaukee, WI
Hoffman, Gary .... Pittsburgh, PA
Hoffman, Gary C. .... Roseville, CA
Hoffman, Gary C. .... Lake City, MI
Hoffman, Gary H. .... Cleveland, OH
Hoffman, Gary K. .... **Kansas City, MO**
Hoffman, Gary L. .... **Orange, CA**
Hoffman, Gary L. .... **Omaha, NE**
Hoffman, Gary M. .... **Washington, DC**
Hoffman, Gary P. .... Lakewood, CO
Hoffman, Gary R. .... Harrisburg, PA
Hoffman, Geo. B., Jr. .... Indianapolis, IN
Hoffman, Geoffrey A. .... Ann Arbor, MI
Hoffman, George H. .... Pittsburgh, PA
Hoffman, George, III .... Franklin, IN
Hoffman, George M. .... **Chicago, IL**
Hoffman, George R. .... Baltimore, MD
Hoffman, Gerald L. .... Henderson, KY
Hoffman, G. F., II .... Leon, IA
Hoffman, G. F., III .... Leon, IA
Hoffman, Gilbert A. .... Baltimore, MD
Hoffman, Gilbert M. .... Syracuse, NY
Hoffman, Grace L. .... **Martins Ferry, OH**
St. Clairsville, OH
Hoffman, Gregory H. .... **New York, NY**
Hoffman, Gregory R. .... **Ellsworth, KS**
Hoffman, H. Bradford .... **Springfield, MA**
Hoffman, H. Tim .... Oakland, CA
Hoffman, Hank D. .... West Hartford, CT
Hoffman, Harlan H. .... Lawrenceburg, IN
Hoffman, Harold .... Fair Lawn, NJ
Hoffman, Harold .... **Dallas, TX**

Hoffman, Harold L. .... **Los Angeles, CA**
Roseland, NJ
New York, NY
Hoffman, Harold M. .... **Englewood, NJ**
New York, NY
Hoffman, Harold M. .... **New York, NY**
Hoffman, Harry A. .... Stow, OH
Hoffman, Hart & Wagner .... **Portland, OR**
Redmond, OR
Kirkland, WA
Hoffman, Harvey J. .... Lansing, MI
Hoffman, Harvey W. .... Santa Rosa, CA
Hoffman, Heidi K. .... **Freehold, NJ**
Hoffman, Herbert B. .... San Diego, CA
Hoffman, Herbert E. .... San Diego, CA
Hoffman, Herbert E. .... Sarasota, FL
Hoffman, Herbert E. .... **Philadelphia, PA**
Hoffman, Herbert K. .... Clayton, MO
Hoffman, Herman .... White Plains, NY
Hoffman & Hertzig, P.A.
Coral Gables, FL
Miami, FL
Hoffman, Hillary E. .... Albuquerque, NM
Hoffman and Hoffman .... Sacramento, CA
Hoffman & Hoffman .... **Boston, MA**
Hoffman & Hoffman, P.A.
Fort Lauderdale, FL
Key West, FL
Miami, FL
Naples, FL
Hoffman, Holley A. .... San Diego, CA
Hoffman, Howard J.
Environmental Protection Agency, Office of the General Counsel, GV
Hoffman, Howard M., Law Offices of
Sacramento, CA
Hoffman, Hughes, McWhorter & Wener, P.C.
Memphis, TN
Hoffman, I. Leonard .... **Bensalem, PA**
Hoffman, Ian D. .... Department of Justice, Antitrust Division, GV
Hoffman, Ilisa Widom .... **Miami, FL**
Hoffman, Irene Anne
Department of Transportation, U. S. Coast Guard, GV
Hoffman, Irving .... Palm Springs, CA
Hoffman, Israel .... New York, NY
Hoffman, J. Daniel .... **Portland, ME**
Hoffman, J. Frederick .... **Lafayette, IN**
Hoffman, Jack D. .... **Portland, OR**
Hoffman, Jack L. .... **Grand Rapids, MI**
Hoffman, Jack L. .... **Portland, OR**
Hoffman, Jack W. .... Ballston Lake, NY
Hoffman, James .... **Schaumburg, IL**
Hoffman, James A. .... **San Antonio, TX**
Hoffman, James Allen .... **Raleigh, NC**
Hoffman, James B. .... New York, NY
Hoffman, James C. .... Cupertino, CA
Hoffman, James D. .... Davenport, IA
Hoffman, James D., P.C. .... Davenport, IA
Hoffman, James E., III .... Brookfield, OH
Hoffman, James F. .... Chicago, IL
Hoffman, James Garland, Jr. .... Chicago, IL
Hoffman, James M. .... Schaumburg, IL
Hoffman, James M. .... **Rockville, MD**
Hoffman, James P., Law Offices of
Keokuk, IA
Hoffman, James W. .... Eugene, OR
Hoffman, James W., P.C. .... Eugene, OR
Hoffman, Jane B. .... **Nashville, TN**
Hoffman, Janet Goelz .... **Chicago, IL**
Hoffman, Janet L. .... **New York, NY**
Hoffman, Janet Lee .... **Portland, OR**
Hoffman, Janet S. .... Beverly Hills, CA
Los Angeles, CA
Hoffman, Janice L. .... Baltimore, MD
Hoffman, Janine M. .... Philadelphia, PA
Hoffman, Jason Foster .... **Washington, DC**
Hoffman, Jason K. .... Tifton, GA
Hoffman, Jason P. .... Topeka, KS
Hoffman, Jay C. .... Belleville, IL
Hoffman, Jay R. .... Chicago, IL
Hoffman, Jeannette A. .... Keyport, NJ
Hoffman, Jeffrey .... Carrboro, NC
Hoffman, Jeffrey C. .... **New York, NY**
Hoffman, Jeffrey Lee .... Houston, TX
Hoffman, Jeffrey S. .... Los Angeles, CA
Hoffman, Jeffrey S. .... **Naples, FL**
Hoffman, Jeffry S. .... **New York, NY**
Hoffman, Jennifer R. .... **St. Louis, MO**
Hoffman, Jeremy M. .... **Salt Lake City, UT**
Hoffman, Jerold Bruce .... **Doylestown, PA**
Hoffman, Jerome A. .... **Philadelphia, PA**
Hoffman, Jerome W. .... **Tallahassee, FL**
Hoffman, Jerry S. .... **Albany, NY**
Hoffman, Jill James .... **San Francisco, CA**
Hoffman, Jilliane P. .... Miami, FL
Hoffman, Jo Ann .... Fort Lauderdale, FL
Hoffman, Jodi Fatland .... Tacoma, WA
Hoffman, Jodi S. .... **East Meadow, NY**
Hoffman, Joel B. .... Long Beach, CA
Hoffman, Joel E. .... **Washington, DC**
Hoffman, Joel I. .... **Rockville, MD**
Hoffman, Joel L. .... Southfield, MI
Hoffman, Joel S. .... New York, NY
Hoffman, John A. .... Bloomington, MN
Hoffman, John A. .... **Woodbridge, NJ**
Hoffman, John B. .... Department of the Army, U.S. Army Legal Services Agency, GV
Hoffman, John C. .... **Baraboo, WI**
Hoffman, John Charles .... Elk River, MN
Hoffman, John D. .... **San Francisco, CA**
Hoffman, John D. .... **Miami, FL**
Naples, FL
Hoffman, John D. .... **Charleston, WV**
Hoffman, John E. .... Fort Wayne, IN
Hoffman, John E., Jr. .... **Columbus, OH**
Hoffman, John F. .... **Fort Wayne, IN**
Hoffman, John F. .... **Kenilworth, NJ**
Hoffman, John G. .... Woodstown, NJ
Hoffman, John J. .... Department of Justice, Civil Division, GV
Hoffman, John J. .... Walpole, MA
Hoffman, John L. .... New York, NY
Hoffman, John R. .... Elburn, IL
Hoffman, John R. .... Minneapolis, MN
Hoffman, John R. .... **Kansas City, MO**
Hoffman, John R., Jr. .... Canton, OH
Hoffman, John R., Sr. .... North Canton, OH
Hoffman, John Stanley .... **Henderson, KY**
Lexington, KY
Hoffman, John W. .... **Edwardsville, IL**
Hoffman, John W. .... West Des Moines, IA
Hoffman, John W. .... **Reno, NV**
Hoffman, John W., IV .... **St. Louis, MO**
Hoffman, Johnnie W., Jr. .... **Houston, TX**
Hoffman, Jonathan M. .... **Anchorage, AK**
Portland, OR
Hoffman, Jonathan M. .... **Mineola, NY**
Hoffman, Joseph .... **Larkspur, CA**
Hoffman, Joseph A. .... Sacramento, CA
Hoffman, Joseph A. .... **Dallas, TX**
Hoffman, Joseph B. .... **Washington, DC**
Hoffman, Joseph C. .... South Amboy, NJ
Hoffman, Joseph C. .... **Cleveland, OH**
Hoffman, Joseph J., Jr., (P.C.) .... Woodbury, NJ
Hoffman, Joseph M. .... **Versailles, KY**
Hoffman, Joseph M. .... Newton, NJ
Hoffman, Joseph V. .... Cincinnati, OH
Hoffman, Joyce N. .... Des Moines, IA
Hoffman, Juanita C. .... Fullerton, CA
Hoffman, Judith Ann .... Columbus, OH
Hoffman, Judy K. .... Omaha, NE
Hoffman, Julie K. .... **Washington, DC**
Hoffman, Julius J. .... **Jackson, MI**
Hoffman, Julius J., P.C. .... **Jackson, MI**
Hoffman, June Galkoski .... **Miami, FL**
Hoffman, Junius .... Tucson, AZ
Hoffman, Karen A. .... **Columbus, OH**
Hoffman, Karen M. .... **New York, NY**
Hoffman, Katherine Lynn .... St. Louis, MO
Hoffman, Kathryn .... **Bellevue, WA**
Hoffman, Keith D. .... Abilene, KS
Hoffman, Keith M. .... **Tampa, FL**
Hoffman Kelley, L.L.P. .... **Austin, TX**
Dallas, TX
Hoffman, Kelly Freeland .... McAllen, TX
Hoffman, Kenneth A. .... **Tallahassee, FL**
Hoffman, Kenneth B. .... **Boston, MA**
Hoffman, Kenneth C. .... **Miami, FL**
Hoffman, Kenneth D. .... **San Francisco, CA**
Hoffman, Kenneth F. .... **Tallahassee, FL**
Hoffman, Kenneth R. .... **Washington, DC**
Baltimore, MD
Hoffman, Kenneth S. .... Albany, NY
Hoffman, Kenneth T. .... Boston, MA
Hoffman, Kenneth V. .... Vancouver, WA
Hoffman, Kenneth V., P.S. .... Vancouver, WA
Hoffman, Kerri M. .... New York, NY
Hoffman, Kevin E. .... **Ocean Township, NJ**
Hoffman, Kevin M. .... Burnsville, MN
Hoffman, Kevin T. .... **Greenwich, CT**
Hoffman, Kirkman J. .... San Jose, CA
Hoffman, Kirsten .... **Boston, MA**
Hoffman, Kris .... Beverly Hills, CA
Hoffman, Kristin A. .... Sarasota, FL
Hoffman, Kristin C. .... Paradise Valley, AZ
Hoffman, Kyle W. .... **San Diego, CA**
Hoffman, L. Bruce .... Bensalem, PA
Hoffman, L. Dennis, Jr. .... **Cleveland, OH**
Hoffman, L. Joseph .... Coral Gables, FL
Hoffman, Lange .... Houston, TX
Hoffman, Larin & Agnetti, P.A.
Fort Lauderdale, FL
Miami, FL
North Miami Beach, FL
Hoffman, Larry C. .... Clearwater, FL
Hoffman, Larry C. .... **Overland Park, KS**
Hoffman, Larry J. .... **Miami, FL**
Hoffman, Laura L. .... **Washington, DC**
Hoffman, Lauren S. .... Kansas City, MO
Hoffman, Laurence J. .... **Washington, DC**
Hoffman, Laurence K. .... Bridgeport, CT
Hoffman Law Firm .... Leon, IA
Hoffman Law Offices .... **Tahoe City, CA**
Hoffman Law Offices .... Walpole, MA
Hoffman, Lawrence A. .... New York, NY
Hoffman, Lawrence E. .... Miami, FL
Hoffman, Lawrence E. .... Olympia, WA
Hoffman, Lawrence L. .... **Tahoe City, CA**
Hoffman, Lee A., Jr. .... **White Plains, NY**
Hoffman, Lee D. .... **Hartford, CT**
Hoffman, Leigh A. .... **Albany, NY**
Hoffman, Leo J., (P.C.) .... **Dallas, TX**
Hoffman, Leo L. .... **Garden City, NY**
Hoffman, Leon .... Baltimore, MD
Hoffman, Leonard .... Morris, IL
Hoffman, Leonard E., III .... **Dallas, TX**
Hoffman, Leonard E., Jr. .... Dallas, TX
Hoffman, Leora K. .... Washington, DC
Hoffman, Leslie R. .... **Washington, DC**
Hoffman, Leslie Weber .... **Fairfax, VA**
Hoffman, Lewis .... Eugene, OR
Hoffman, Linda A. .... **New Orleans, LA**
Hoffman, Linda M. .... **Washington, DC**
Hoffman, Lisa D. .... **Los Angeles, CA**
Hoffman, Lisa Kristine .... Pikesville, MD
Hoffman, Lloyd E. .... **Dallas, TX**
Hoffman, Lori J. .... **New York, NY**
Hoffman, Louis I. .... Dayton, OH
Hoffman, Louis J. .... Scottsdale, AZ
Hoffman, Louis J., P.C. .... Scottsdale, AZ
Hoffman, Louis L. .... Princeton, MN
Hoffman, Luhman & Busch .... **Lafayette, IN**
Hoffman, Lynda Lucille .... North Platte, NE
Hoffman & Lyons, P.C. .... **Rockville, MD**
Hoffman, M. Gayle .... Elsmere, KY
Hoffman, Manuel S. .... Skokie, IL
Hoffman, Marc E. .... Baltimore, MD
Hoffman, Marc H. .... Boca Raton, FL
Hoffman, Marc H., P.A. .... Boca Raton, FL
Hoffman, Margaret Knodell .... Austin, TX
Hoffman, Maria Greta .... Elsmere, KY
Hoffman, Marianne .... **Stamford, CT**
Hoffman, Marilyn L. .... Los Angeles, CA
Hoffman, Marjorie .... Treasury Department, Internal Revenue Service, GV
Hoffman, Mark .... Short Hills, NJ
Hoffman, Mark A. .... Harleysville, PA
Hoffman, Mark A., Associates, P.C.
Harleysville, PA
Hoffman, Mark David .... Dillon, MT
Hoffman, Mark E. .... **Birmingham, AL**
Hoffman, Mark E., P.C. .... **Birmingham, AL**
Hoffman, Mark F. .... **Seattle, WA**
Hoffman, Mark L. .... Shaker Heights, OH
Hoffman, Mark S. .... Los Angeles, CA
Hoffman, Mark S. .... Walpole, MA
Hoffman, Mark W. .... New Orleans, LA
Hoffman, Marta J. .... **Detroit, MI**
Hoffman, Martin J. .... Philomath, OR
Hoffman, Martin L. .... Fort Lauderdale, FL
Miami, FL
North Miami Beach, FL
Hoffman, Martin P. .... **Arlington, VA**
Hoffman, Martin W. .... West Hartford, CT
Hoffman, Mary F. .... **Albuquerque, NM**
Hoffman, Mathew B. .... **Roseland, NJ**
Hoffman, Mathew E. .... **New York, NY**
Hoffman, Matthew .... Houston, TX
Hoffman, Matthew E. .... **Fresno, CA**
Hoffman, Matthew M. .... **Washington, DC**
Hoffman, Maurice J. .... Southlake, TX
Hoffman, Max R., Jr. .... **Okemos, MI**
Hoffman, Melanie B. .... Buffalo Grove, IL
Hoffman, Melvin .... Brooklyn, NY
Hoffman, Melvin H. .... Ottawa, IL
Hoffman, Melvin S. .... **Boston, MA**
Hoffman, Melvyn L. .... La Crosse, WI
Hoffman, Merle Faye .... Houston, TX
Hoffman, Merryl .... New York, NY
Hoffman, Michael .... **San Francisco, CA**
Hoffman, Michael A. .... **Southfield, MI**
Hoffman, Michael D. .... **Portland, OR**
Kirkland, WA
Hoffman, Michael F. .... Albany, NY
Hoffman, Michael G. .... Lancaster, TX
Hoffman, Michael H. .... **Miami, FL**
Hoffman, Michael J. .... Southgate, KY
Hoffman, Michael K. .... **New York, NY**
Hoffman, Michael P. .... Department of Energy, Office of the General Counsel, GV
Hoffman, Michael R. .... Los Angeles, CA
Hoffman, Michael R. .... Mandan, ND
Hoffman, Michael Robert
Los Angeles, CA
Hoffman, Michael S. .... Jacksonville, FL
Hoffman, Michael S., P.A. .... Jacksonville, FL
Hoffman, Michael V. .... San Jose, CA
Hoffman, Michele D. .... Joplin, MO
Hoffman, Mikel J. .... Babylon, NY
Hoffman, Mitchell J. .... **New Orleans, LA**
Hoffman, Mitchell L. .... Waukegan, IL
Hoffman, Mitchell Scott .... Newton, MA
Hoffman, Morris B. .... Denver, CO
Hoffman, Mueller & Creedon, P.C.
Ottawa, IL
Hoffman, Nancie Hudell
South Barrington, IL
Hoffman, Nancy .... San Jose, CA
Hoffman, Nancy A. .... **Lafayette, CA**
Hoffman, Nancy E. .... Albany, NY
Hoffman, Nancy M. .... Chicago, IL
Hoffman, NancyRuth .... **Los Angeles, CA**
Hoffman, Nathalie R., & Associates
Los Angeles, CA
Hoffman, Nathalie R., & Associates
Santa Monica, CA
Hoffman, Nathan P. .... Tyler, TX
Hoffman, Nathan V. .... Culver City, CA
Hoffman, Nathaniel A. .... **Milwaukee, WI**
Hoffman, Neil .... Feasterville, PA
Hoffman, Neil W. .... Atlanta, GA
Hoffman, Nicholas M.W. .... **New York, NY**
Hoffman, Norman J. .... **Los Angeles, CA**
Hoffman, Norman J., Inc., A Professional Corporation .... **Encino, CA**
Los Angeles, CA
Hoffman, P. Lawrence .... Cayce, SC
Hoffman, Patricia A. .... Wood Dale, IL
Hoffman, Patrick A. .... **Albuquerque, NM**
Hoffman, Paul .... **New York, NY**
Hoffman, Paul A. .... **Los Angeles, CA**
Hoffman, Paul A. .... **Plano, TX**
Hoffman, Paul A., P.C. .... **Plano, TX**
Hoffman, Paul G. .... St. Cloud, MN
Hoffman, Paul G. .... **Milwaukee, WI**
Hoffman, Paul Gordon .... **Los Angeles, CA**
Hoffman, Paul, Jr. .... **Lakewood, WA**
Hoffman, Paul K. .... The Dalles, OR
Hoffman, Paul L. .... Santa Monica, CA
Hoffman, Paul M. .... **Juneau, AK**
Hoffman, Paul M. .... **Norcross, GA**
Hoffman, Paul, (P.C.)
Charlotte Amalie, St. Thomas, VI
Hoffman, Paul R. .... **Chicago, IL**
Hoffman, Paul S. .... Beverly Hills, CA
Hoffman, Paul S. .... **Croton-On-Hudson, NY**
Hoffman, Paul S., P.C.
Croton-On-Hudson, NY
Hoffman, Paul W. .... Lexington, KY
Hoffman, Paul W. .... Sewickley, PA
Hoffman, Paula P. .... Camarillo, CA
Hoffman, Perry Jay .... **Chicago, IL**
Hoffman, Peter A. .... **Boston, MA**
Hoffman, Peter B. .... West Hartford, CT
Hoffman, Peter B. .... Hamilton, GA
Hoffman, Peter B. .... **St. Louis, MO**
Hoffman, Peter C. .... Monrovia, CA
Hoffman, Peter J. .... **Philadelphia, PA**
Hoffman, Peter M. .... **Great Neck, NY**
Hoffman, Peter T. .... Lincoln, NE
Hoffman, Philip R. .... **New York, NY**
Hoffman, Philip T., Jr. .... Pensacola, FL
Hoffman, Pittman & Associates
La Crosse, WI
Hoffman Pollok & Pickholz LLP
New York, NY
Hoffman, R. Douglas .... Trenton, NJ
Hoffman, R. Neal .... **Westminster, MD**
Hoffman, R. Thomas .... Skokie, IL
Hoffman, Ralph O. .... Chatham, NY
Hoffman, Rand .... New York, NY
Hoffman, Randi S. .... Philadelphia, PA
Hoffman, Raymond G., Jr.
New Orleans, LA
Hoffman, Rence H. .... Sacramento, CA
Hoffman, Richard A. .... Tulsa, OK
Hoffman, Richard B. .... Washington, DC
Hoffman, Richard B. .... **Chicago, IL**
Hoffman, Richard C. .... **New York, NY**
Hoffman, Richard D. .... Beverly Hills, CA
Hoffman, Richard D. .... **San Francisco, CA**
Hoffman, Richard G. .... Walpole, MA
Hoffman, Richard H. .... **Chicago, IL**
Hoffman, Richard H. .... St. Paul, MN
Hoffman, Richard J. .... Weehawken, NJ
Hoffman, Richard L. .... Mesa, AZ
Hoffman, Richard L. .... Boston, MA
Hoffman, Richard Lawrence
Woodstock, NY
Hoffman, Richard M. .... **Chicago, IL**
Hoffman, Richard M. .... **New York, NY**
Hoffman, Richard S. .... Washington, DC
Hoffman, Richard S. .... **Washington, DC**
Hoffman, Richard S., Law Office of
Brownsville, TX
Hoffman, Richard S., (P.C.) .... Woodbury, NJ
Hoffman, Richard W. .... Miami, FL
Hoffman, Richard W., Law Office of
Newtown, PA
Hoffman, Rick L. .... Yakima, WA
Hoffman, Robert .... Carmichael, CA
Hoffman, Robert A. .... **Champaign, IL**
Hoffman, Robert A. .... **Towson, MD**
Hoffman, Robert A. .... **Haddonfield, NJ**
Hoffman, Robert A. .... White Plains, NY
Hoffman, Robert A. .... Charleston, WV
Hoffman, Robert B. .... **Phoenix, AZ**
Hoffman, Robert B. .... **Harrisburg, PA**
Hoffman, Robert C. .... Elsmere, KY
Hoffman, Robert D. .... **Los Angeles, CA**
Hoffman, Robert D., Jr. .... **New Orleans, LA**
Hoffman, Robert E. .... Prairie Village, KS
Hoffman, Robert J. .... Sarasota, FL
Hoffman, Robert J. .... **Indianapolis, IN**
Hoffman, Robert J. .... **Kansas City, MO**
Hoffman, Robert L. .... Charlevoix, MI
Hoffman, Robert L. .... **Minneapolis, MN**
Hoffman, Robert M. .... Miami, FL
Hoffman, Robert M. .... Columbus, OH
Hoffman, Robert M. .... **Dallas, TX**
Hoffman, Robert P. .... Sacramento, CA
Hoffman, Robert S. .... **Houston, TX**
Hoffman, Robert W. .... Petaluma, CA
Hoffman, Robert W. .... **St. Louis, MO**
Hoffman, Robert W. .... Schenectady, NY
Hoffman & Robin .... Los Angeles, CA
Hoffman, Robt. J. .... **Boston, MA**
Hoffman, Rodger I. .... **Honolulu, HI**
Hoffman, Rodney G. .... **Boston, MA**
Hoffman, Rodney J. .... **Kansas City, MO**
Hoffman, Roger W. .... Milwaukee, WI
Hoffman, Ronald E. .... Rumford, ME
Hoffman, Ronald F. .... San Diego, CA
Hoffman, Ronald N. .... Los Angeles, CA
Hoffman, Ronne .... **New York, NY**
Hoffman, Roy A. .... Orange, CA
Hoffman, Rubin .... Boca Raton, FL
Hoffman, Rudolph A. .... Burlingame, CA
Hoffman, Ruth .... Treasury Department, Internal Revenue Service, GV
Hoffman, S. David .... Highland Park, IL
Hoffman, Sabban & Watenmaker, A Professional Corporation
Los Angeles, CA
Hoffman, Samuel F. .... **San Diego, CA**
Hoffman, Samuel R. .... Walpole, MA
Hoffman & Schreiber, A Professional Corporation .... **Red Bank, NJ**
Hoffman, Scott D. .... New York, NY
Hoffman, Scott L. .... **Richwood, OH**
Hoffman, Scott V. .... Rosemont, IL
Hoffman, Sharon Corey
Department of Justice, Executive Office for Immigration Review, GV
Hoffman, Sheffield & Sauseda .... Amarillo, TX
Hoffman, Sheldon H. .... Hollywood, FL
Hoffman, Shepard A. .... Baltimore, MD
Hoffman, Sheree L. .... Memphis, TN
Hoffman, Sheri L. .... Sacramento, CA
Hoffman, Sherri J. .... Los Angeles, CA
Hoffman, Sherry V. .... Newark, DE
Hoffman, Sidney .... Pittsburgh, PA
Hoffman, Siegel, Seydel, Bienvenu & Centola, A Professional Law Corporation
New Orleans, LA
Hoffman, Stanley .... **Washington, DC**
Hoffman, Stephanie A. M. .... Chicago, IL
Hoffman, Stephen C. .... **Rapid City, SD**
Hoffman, Stephen D. .... **Phoenix, AZ**

Hoffman, Stephen D. ... New York, NY
Hoffman, Stephen E. ... San Diego, CA
Hoffman, Stephen L. ... Chicago, IL
Hoffman, Stephen L., & Associates, A Prof. Corp. ... Chicago, IL
Hoffman, Stephen M. ... Lakewood, NJ
Hoffman, Stephen Vincent
Fort Lauderdale, FL
Hoffman, Steven C. ... Peoria, IL
Hoffman, Steven D. ... Cupertino, CA
Hoffman, Steven E. ... Allentown, PA
Hoffman, Steven J. ... Downey, CA
Hoffman, Steven J. ... Washington, DC
Hoffman, Steven K. ... Washington, DC
Hoffman, Steven L. ... Boston, MA
Hoffman, Steven M. ... Worcester, MA
Hoffman, Steven R. ... New York, NY
Hoffman, Stuart C. ... Boca Raton, FL
Hoffman, Stuart K. ... Miami, FL
Hoffman & Suenram ... Dillon, MT
Hoffman, Susan D. ... Detroit, MI
Hoffman, Susan Katz ... Philadelphia, PA
Hoffman, Susan L. ... Los Angeles, CA
Hoffman, Susan Landers ... Providence, RI
Hoffman, Susan M. ... Washington, DC
Hoffman, Terry L. ... Oklahoma City, OK
Hoffman, Test, Guinan & Collier, A Professional Corporation ... Reno, NV
Hoffman, T. G., Jr. ... Fairfax, VA
Hoffman, Theodore ... St. Louis, MO
Hoffman, Theresa E. ... Waterloo, IA
Hoffman, Thomas ... New York, NY
Hoffman, Thomas A. ... Upland, CA
Hoffman, Thomas A. ... Grand Rapids, MI
Hoffman, Thomas C., II ... Erie, PA
Hoffman, Thomas D. ... Kenilworth, NJ
Hoffman, Thomas E. ... Chicago, IL
Hoffman, Thomas E. ... Minneapolis, MN
Hoffman, Thomas G. ... Northbrook, IL
Hoffman, Thomas G. ... Bay Shore, NY
Hoffman, Thomas J. ... Batavia, IL
Hoffman, Thomas J. ... Le Mars, IA
Hoffman, Thomas K. ... Crown Point, IN
Hoffman, Thomas L. ... Pottstown, PA
Hoffman, Thomas M. ... Dallas, TX
Hoffman, Thomas Oliver ... Monrovia, CA
Hoffman, Thomas, P.C., Law Offices of
New York, NY
Hoffman, Thomas R. ... Reston, VA
Hoffman, Tila Fleming ... Albuquerque, NM
Hoffman, Tila Fleming, P.C.
Albuquerque, NM
Hoffman, Tim ... Amarillo, TX
Hoffman, Timothy D. ... Dayton, OH
Hoffman, Timothy V. ... Chicago, IL
Hoffman, Timothy W. ... Santa Rosa, CA
Hoffman, Timothy Walter ... Decatur, GA
Hoffman, Tracy ... Riverhead, NY
Hoffman, Valerie J. ... Chicago, IL
Hoffman, Victoria J. ... Wilmington, DE
Hoffman, Victoria J. ... Atlanta, GA
Hoffman, Victoria J., P.C., Law Offices of
Atlanta, GA
Hoffman, W. Andrew, III ... Cleveland, OH
Hoffman, Wachtell, Koster & Maier
New York, NY
White Plains, NY
Hoffman and Walker Co., L.P.A.
Brookfield, OH
Hoffman & Wallach, Attorneys, P.C.
St. Louis, MO
Hoffman, Warnick & D'Alessandro LLC
Albany, NY
Hoffman, Warren A. ... Houston, TX
Hoffman, Warren S. ... Mineola, NY
Hoffman, Wartell & Pazner ... Detroit, MI
Southfield, MI
Hoffman, Wasson & Gitler, P.C.
Washington, DC
Arlington, VA
Hoffman, Wesley W. ... Menominee, MI
Hoffman, William B. ... Treasury Department, Office of Foreign Assets Control, GV
Hoffman, William B. ... Canton, OH
Hoffman, William B., (P.S.C.)
Jeffersonville, IN
Louisville, KY
Hoffman, William C. ... Brooklyn, NY
Hoffman, William D. ... Miami, FL
Naples, FL
Hoffman, William D. ... Springfield, OH
Hoffman, William H. ... Palo Alto, CA
Hoffman, William H., Jr. ... Houston, TX
Hoffman, William J. ... San Diego, CA
Hoffman, William J. ... New York, NY
Hoffman, William K. ... Englewood, CO
Hoffman, William Lewis ... Princeton, NJ
Hoffman, William M. ... Pittsburgh, PA
Hoffman, William M., Jr.
Silver Spring, MD
Hoffman, William P. ... Los Altos, CA
Hoffman, William P., Jr.
San Francisco, CA
Hoffman, William R. ... Exton, PA
Hoffman, William T., III ... Denver, CO
Hoffman-Hill, Barbara K. ... Dallas, TX
Hoffmann, Abraham M. ... Trumbull, CT
Hoffmann, Andrew S. ... New York, NY
Hoffmann, Arnold J. ... Mount Laurel, NJ
Hoffmann, Arthur E., Jr. ... New York, NY
Hoffmann & Baron, LLP ... Parsippany, NJ
Mineola, NY
Syosset, NY
Hoffmann, Betty ... Richardson, TX
Hoffmann, Brian ... New York, NY
Hoffmann, Carl K. ... Atlantic Beach, FL
Hoffmann, Charles E., III ... New York, NY
Hoffmann, Charles R. ... Syosset, NY
Hoffmann, Christian J., III ... Phoenix, AZ
Hoffmann, Christopher M. ... Somers, NY
Hoffmann, Corey Y. ... Denver, CO
Hoffmann, David Henry ... Batavia, OH
Hoffmann, David S. ... Cleveland, OH
Hoffmann, Deborah S. R. ... Milwaukee, WI
Hoffmann & Dineff, Ltd. ... Chicago, IL
Hoffmann, Donald ... East St. Louis, IL
Hoffmann, Douglas R. ... Westbury, NY
Hoffmann, Edmund J., Jr. ... Cortland, NY
Hoffmann, Eleanor A. ... New York, NY
Hoffmann, Elinor R. ... New York, NY
Hoffmann, Elizabeth A. ... Madison, WI
Hoffmann, Eric ... Chicago, IL
Hoffmann, Erich H. ... Portland, OR
Hoffmann, Frederick B. ... Springfield, IL
Hoffmann, Gary R. ... Cincinnati, OH
Hoffmann, Gary R. Co., LPA
Cincinnati, OH
Hoffmann, Georges A. ... Atlanta, GA
Hoffmann, Gregory D. ... St. Louis, MO
Hoffmann, Gregory F. ... St. Louis, MO
Hoffmann, Herman C., Jr.
New Orleans, LA
Hoffmann, Howard J. ... West New York, NJ
Hoffmann, Howard M. ... Chicago, IL
Hoffmann, Hubert, Hoffmann & Greenough
Syracuse, NY
Hoffmann, J. Bruce ... Coral Gables, FL
Hoffmann, James E. ... Encino, CA
Hoffmann, James M. ... St. Louis, MO
Hoffmann, James R., Jr. ... Annapolis, MD
Hoffmann, James T. ... Cleveland, OH
Hoffmann, James W. E. ... Los Angeles, CA
Hoffmann, Jeanne A. ... Richland, MI
Hoffmann, Jeanne M. ... Chicago, IL
Hoffmann, Jeffrey R. ... Elkins Park, PA
Hoffmann, John J. ... Dayton, OH
Hoffmann, John P. ... San Jose, CA
Hoffmann, John P. ... Waupaca, WI
Hoffmann, Jon K. ... Des Moines, IA
Hoffmann, Joseph L. ... Washington, DC
Hoffmann, Joseph M. ... Newton, NJ
Hoffmann, Kenneth A. ... Jericho, NY
Hoffmann, Kent R. ... Port Washington, WI
Hoffmann, Kimberly F. ... Southfield, MI
Hoffmann, Leslie A. ... McLean, VA
Hoffmann, Linda ... Wadsworth, OH
Hoffmann, Linda L. ... Des Moines, IA
Hoffmann, Lorraine C. ... Fort Lauderdale, FL
Hoffmann, Malcolm A. ... New York, NY
Hoffmann, Malcolm A., Law Firm of
New York, NY
Hoffmann, Margaret A. O'Connor
Portland, OR
Hoffmann, Mark S. ... Jacksonville, FL
Hoffmann, Martha A. ... Mission Viejo, CA
Hoffmann, Martin ... Washington, DC
Hoffmann, Maureen W. ... Brown Deer, WI
Hoffmann & McConkey, P.L.C., Law Offices of ... Des Moines, IA
Hoffmann, Michael J. ... San Francisco, CA
Hoffmann, Michael R. ... Des Moines, IA
Hoffmann, Nancy Little
Fort Lauderdale, FL
Hoffmann, Nancy Little, P.A.
Fort Lauderdale, FL
Hoffmann, Patricia D. ... Carlsbad, CA
Hoffmann, Paul M. ... Kansas City, MO
Hoffmann, Paul R. ... Binghamton, NY
Hoffmann, Richard ... Hauppauge, NY
Hoffmann, Richard S. ... Bensalem, PA
Hoffmann, Richard W. ... Des Moines, IA
Hoffmann, Richard W. ... Troy, MI
Hoffmann, Robert G. ... Philadelphia, PA
Hoffmann, Robin L. ... Newport, RI
Hoffmann, Steven W. ... San Antonio, TX
Hoffmann, Susan J. ... Lexington, KY
Hoffmann, Sydney J. ... Washington, DC
Alexandria, VA
Hoffmann, Terrance J. ... Syracuse, NY
Hoffmann, Theodore D. ... Garden City, NY
Hoffmann, Thomas J. ... Chicago, IL
Hoffmann, W.H., Attorney at Law
Eastland, TX
Hoffmann, Walter F. ... Wayne, NJ
Hoffmann, Warren J. ... Lexington, KY
Hoffmann, Wilfred E. ... Syracuse, NY
Hoffmann, William E., Jr. ... Atlanta, GA
Hoffmann, William H., Jr. ... Eastland, TX
Hoffmann, William J. ... Chicago, IL
Hoffmeier Zamora, Nancy
Los Angeles, CA
Hoffmeister, Bruce F. ... Washington, DC
Hoffmeister, David M. ... Palo Alto, CA
Hoffmeister, Edward J. ... Scarsdale, NY
Hoffmeister, Jacqueline T. ... Atlanta, GA
Hoffmeister, John Kenneth ... Knoxville, TN
Hoffmeister, Mark Joseph
Overland Park, KS
Hoffmeister, Nicole M. ... Stamford, CT
Hoffmeyer, Dan ... Mesquite, TX
Hoffmeyer, Duane E. ... Sioux City, IA
Hoffmeyer & Grass, Inc. ... Mesquite, TX
Hoffmeyer, Kevin T. ... Chicago, IL
Hoffmeyer & Semmelman ... York, PA
Hoffmeyer, W. James ... Florence, SC
Hoffmeyer, William F. ... York, PA
Hoffmire, Philip W. ... San Francisco, CA
Hoffnagle, James J. ... Chicago, IL
Hoffnagle, Susan B. ... Bloomfield, CT
Hoffner, David S. ... New York, NY
Hoffner, Edward H. ... Stroudsburg, PA
Hoffner, Stephen M. ... Plano, TX
Hoffner, Steven A. ... New York, NY
Hoffner, Tara J. ... Wilmington, DE
Hoffner, Thomas A. ... Madison, WI
Hoffnung & Brochin, P.C.
New Haven, CT
Hoffnung, Daniel N. ... New Haven, CT
Hoffnung, Joseph ... Oceanside, NY
Hofford, Mary ... Palm Beach Gardens, FL
Hoff-Patrinos, Kathryn E.
Washington, DC
Hoffpauir, Angela N. ... Crowley, LA
Hoffpauir, G. Todd ... Cincinnati, OH
Hoffpauir, Norma Briscoe ... Wheaton, MD
Hoffpauir, Saja J. ... Knoxville, TN
Hoffpauir, Sandra Parker ... Huntsville, AL
Hoffsis, Stephen B. ... Cincinnati, OH
Hoffstein, Fred L. ... North Weymouth, MA
Hoffstot, Henry P., Jr. ... Pittsburgh, PA
Hofgard, Kurt C. ... Boulder, CO
Hofgard, Linda Diane Blank ... Boulder, CO
Hofheimer, Charles R.
Virginia Beach, VA
Hofheimer, Charles R., P.C., The Law Office of ... Virginia Beach, VA
Hofheimer Gartlir & Gross, LLP
Roseland, NJ
New York, NY
Hofheimer, Harry ... Columbus, OH
Hofheimer, Norma J. ... Richmond, VA
Hofheimer Nusbaum, P.C. ... Norfolk, VA
Hofheinz, Fred ... Houston, TX
Hofheinz, Fred, Law Offices of, P.C.
Houston, TX
Hofheinz, Monica M. ... Fort Lauderdale, FL
Hofheinz, Walter Wm. ... Dallas, TX
Hofing, Sidney L. ... Trenton, NJ
Hofker, Raymond G. ... Houston, TX
Hofkin, Leah A. ... Washington, DC
Hofkin, Susan E. ... New York, NY
Hofler, Hayes, & Associates, P.A.
Durham, NC
Hofler, R. Hayes ... Durham, NC
Hofling, Phillip A. ... Montpelier, VT
Hofman, Fred J. ... Fargo, ND
Williston, ND
Hofman, Harold W., Jr. ... Pomona, CA
Hofman, John H. ... Battle Creek, MI
Hofman, Joseph H. ... Los Angeles, CA
Hofman, Kenneth G. ... Grand Rapids, MI
Hofman, Kevin D. ... Minneapolis, MN
Hofmann, Arthur Gerard ... Dallas, TX
Hofmann, Arthur R, Jr. ... Boston, MA
Hofmann, Bernard J. ... Rock Island, IL
Hofmann, Burt S. ... Moraga, CA
Hofmann, Christine A.
Hilton Head Island, SC
Hofmann, Clifford J. ... Tucson, AZ
Hofmann, Clifford J., Jr. ... Pueblo, CO
Hofmann, Daniel T. ... Woodstock, IL
Hofmann, David J. ... San Jose, CA
Hofmann, Douglas A. ... Seattle, WA
Hofmann, Elke A. ... Philadelphia, PA
Hofmann, George B. ... Albany, NY
Hofmann, Herbert H., II ... Tampa, FL
Hofmann, John H. ... San Angelo, TX
Hofmann, John R. ... Louisville, KY
Hofmann, John Richard, Jr.
San Francisco, CA
Hofmann, Joseph P. ... Lancaster, PA
Wayne, PA
Hofmann, Kyle Reid ... Boston, MA
Hofmann, Lawrence T. ... Minneapolis, MN
Hofmann, Leroy W. ... Phoenix, AZ
Hofmann, Lucinda A. ... Miami, FL
Hofmann, Mary Pat ... Des Moines, IA
Hofmann, Melinda E. ... New York, NY
Hofmann, Michael J. ... Denver, CO
Hofmann, Milissa K. ... Davenport, IA
Hofmann, Nicholas H. ... Dallas, TX
Hofmann, Otto F., Jr. ... Harrisburg, PA
Hofmann, Paul G. ... Tucson, AZ
Hofmann, Paul T. ... San Francisco, CA
Newark, NJ
New York, NY
Hofmann, Robert A. ... Brick Town, NJ
Hofmann, Robert A. ... New Brunswick, NJ
Hofmann, Robert C. ... Danville, IL
Hofmann, Robt. ... Miami, FL
Hofmann, Salcito & Stevens ... Phoenix, AZ
Hofmann, Tina F. ... Washington, DC
Hofmann, William E. ... Chicago, IL
Hofmann, William W. ... Petoskey, MI
Hofmann, Yuri ... San Diego, CA
Hofmann-Geye, Dana Linn
Bloomington, MN
Hofmann-Mullett, Sarah ... Mount Vernon, IL
Hofmayer, Michael D. ... Berkeley, CA
Hofmeister, Brian W. ... Lawrenceville, NJ
Hofmeister, C. Larry, Jr. ... Baltimore, MD
Hofmeister, Cyril T. ... Sebastopol, CA
Hofmeister, Dan J., Jr. ... Chicago, IL
Hofmeister, Edith M. ... San Francisco, CA
Hofmeister, Kent S. ... Dallas, TX
Hofmeister, Paul D. ... Dearborn Heights, MI
Hofmeister, Paul E. ... Scottsbluff, NE
Hofmeister, Theresa S. ... Pasadena, CA
Hofmeyer, Hurley & Hanson, P.C.
Fayette, IA
Hofmeyer, John W., III ... Oelwein, IA
Hofmeyer, John W. D. ... Fayette, IA
Hofreiter, Larry W. ... Vista, CA
Hofrichter, Alex ... Miami, FL
Hofrichter, Alex, P.A. ... Miami, FL
Hofrichter, John T. ... Washington, PA
Hofrichter, Lawrence S. ... New York, NY
Hofrichter, Michael J. ... Tucker, GA
Hofstad, Chris E. ... Minneapolis, MN
Hofstad, Kevin A. ... Pine City, MN
Hofstad & Lewis ... Petersburg, AK
Hofstad, Susan K. ... Petersburg, AK
Hofstadter, David A. ... Rancho Mirage, CA
Hofstadter, Louis J. ... Hamilton, OH
Hofstadter, Sarah K. ... Novato, CA
Hofstead, Jas. W. ... Nashville, TN
Hofstedt, H. Roland ... Seattle, WA
Hofstein, Carole H. ... New York, NY
Hofstein, David N. ... Philadelphia, PA
Hofstein, Gertrude ... Little Neck, NY
Hofstein & Widman, P.C. ... Philadelphia, PA
Hofstetter, Bruce ... Poughkeepsie, NY
Hofstetter, Christian S. ... Nashville, TN
Hofstetter, Dana Lieberman ... Boise, ID
Hofstetter, Daniel F. ... Glenview, IL
Hofstetter, Edwin T. ... Chardon, OH
Hofstetter & Hofstetter ... Nashville, TN
Hofstetter, James C. ... Nashville, TN
Hofstetter, James W., Jr. ... Nashville, TN
Hofstetter, Kathleen W. ... Toms River, NJ
Hofstetter, Marilynn K. ... Ferndale, CA
Hofstetter, O. B., Jr. ... Nashville, TN
Hofstetter, Oscar B., III ... Nashville, TN
Hofstetter, Patricia J. ... Whittier, CA
Hofstetter, Richard ... New York, NY
Hofstetter, Richard R. ... Greenwood, IN
Hofstetter, Thomas F. ... Baltimore, MD
Hofstetter, Thomas L. ... Morristown, NJ
Hofstetter, William C. ... Chardon, OH
Hofstetter, William S. ... Nashville, TN
Hofstra, Patricia S. ... Chicago, IL
Hofstra, Peter T. ... Seminole, FL
Hofstrom, Peter A. ... Boulder, CO
Hoft, John W., Jr. ... Tampa, FL
Hoft, Thomas W. ... Cincinnati, OH
Hofvendahl, Russell L. ... Campbell, CA
Hogaboam, Don L. ... Tacoma, WA
Hogaboom, Kathleen M. ... Los Angeles, CA
Hogan, Alan P. ... San Jose, CA
Hogan, Albert L., III ... Chicago, IL
Hogan, Alma Tina ... San Francisco, CA
Hogan, Andrew J. ... Cincinnati, OH
Hogan, Anne M. ... Albuquerque, NM
Hogan, Austin ... Philadelphia, PA
Hogan, Barbara A. ... Lancaster, NH
Hogan, Barry P. ... Moorhead, MN
Hogan, Baynes & Haworth
Los Angeles, CA
Hogan, Beth A. ... Old Lyme, CT
Hogan, Betty Marie ... Puyallup, WA
Hogan, Booker T., Jr. ... Brenham, TX
Hogan, Brian C. ... Orlando, FL
Hogan, Brian D. ... Chicago, IL
Hogan, Brian J. ... Irvine, CA
Hogan, Brian M. ... Boston, MA
Hogan, Bridget C. ... Decatur, IL
Hogan, Bruce W. ... Santa Barbara, CA
Hogan, Carla E. ... Albany, NY
New York, NY
Hogan, Carol C. ... Chicago, IL
Hogan, Carol M. ... Lansing, MI
Hogan, Caroline A. ... Milwaukee, WI
Hogan, Carolyn M. ... Farmington, CT
Hogan, Charles Marshall ... Cincinnati, OH
Hogan, Cheryl Potvin ... Albany, NY
Hogan, Christine A. ... Bismarck, ND
Hogan, Christopher ... Columbus, OH
Hogan, Christopher B. ... Philadelphia, PA
Hogan, Christopher J. ... Oakland, CA
Hogan, Cleo G. ... Clarksville, TN
Hogan, Corey J., and Associates
Amherst, NY
Hogan, Cynthia Claire ... United States Senate, Committee Legal Personnel, GV
Hogan, Cynthia Elkins ... Encino, CA
Hogan, Daniel F. ... Orlando, FL
Hogan, Daniel James ... Glens Falls, NY
Hogan, Daniel K. ... Wilmington, DE
Hogan, Daniel P. ... Chicago, IL
Hogan, David E. ... Metairie, LA
Hogan, Deborah A. ... Denver, CO
Hogan, Deborah Rzasnicki ... Chicago, IL
Hogan, Denise J. ... West Orange, NJ
Hogan, Dennis A. ... Columbus, OH
Hogan, Dennis D. ... Ames, IA
Hogan, Dennis J. ... Carbondale, IL
Hogan, Dennis P., III ... Omaha, NE
Hogan & Dobis ... Easton, PA
Hogan, Donald P. ... Newton, NJ
Hogan Dubose & Townsend, L.L.P.
Houston, TX
Hogan, E. Desmond ... Washington, DC
Hogan, Edward A. ... Morristown, NJ
New York, NY
Hogan, Edward A. ... Cincinnati, OH
Hogan, Edward C. ... Cherry Hill, NJ
Hogan, Edward M. ... Chicago, IL
Hogan, Edward M. ... Somerville, NJ
Hogan, Edward T. ... East Providence, RI
Hogan, Elizabeth A. ... Beverly, MA
Hogan, Elizabeth Wood ... Little Rock, AR
Hogan, Elwood, Jr. ... Clearwater, FL
Hogan, Erin C. ... Department of the Air Force, Office of the Judge Advocate General, GV
Hogan, Ervin B. ... Medford, OR
Hogan, F. Gerard ... Lockport, NY
Hogan & Fisher, P.L.C. ... Des Moines, IA
Hogan, Frances X. ... Boston, MA
Hogan, Francis P. ... Honolulu, HI
Hogan, Frank W. ... Stamford, CT
Hogan, Frank W. ... Indianapolis, IN
Hogan, Frank W., Jr. ... Cranford, NJ
Hogan, Fred H. ... Belleville, MI
Hogan, Frederic G. ... Chicago, IL
Hogan, Garland ... Fort Lauderdale, FL
Hogan, Gerald F. ... Bethesda, MD
Hogan, Gerald W. ... Minneapolis, MN
Hogan, Gerard V. ... Department of Justice, Civil Rights Division, GV
Hogan, Glenn P. ... Ann Arbor, MI
Hogan, Greer & Shapiro ... Miami, FL

Hogan Guiney ... San Diego, CA
Hogan, Guy Miller, II ... Goodlettsville, TN
Hogan, Harry J. ... Bethesda, MD
Hogan & Hartson L.L.P. ... Los Angeles, CA
Newport Beach, CA
Broomfield, CO
Colorado Springs, CO
Denver, CO
Washington, DC
Baltimore, MD
Rockville, MD
New York, NY
McLean, VA
Hogan, Henry J., III ... Acton, MA
Hogan & Hogan ... Locust Valley, NY
Hogan & Hogan ... Saratoga Springs, NY
Hogan & Hogan ... East Providence, RI
Providence, RI
Wakefield, RI
Hogan and Hogan ... Knoxville, TN
Hogan, Howard G. ... Knoxville, TN
Hogan, Howard T. ... Locust Valley, NY
Hogan, Howard Thomas, Jr.
Fort Lauderdale, FL
Locust Valley, NY
Hogan, J. Gerard ... Fort Myers, FL
Hogan, J. Michael ... Salinas, CA
Hogan, James A. ... Cleveland, OH
Hogan, James B. ... Indianapolis, IN
Hogan, James C. ... Easton, PA
Hogan, James D., Jr., P.C. ... Marietta, GA
Hogan, James E. ... Los Angeles, CA
Hogan, James F. ... Treasury Department, Internal Revenue Service, GV
Hogan, James Jay ... Miami, FL
Hogan, James P. ... Celina, OH
Hogan, Jane C. ... St. Louis, MO
Hogan, Janet L. ... Knoxville, TN
Hogan, Janice Marchiafava
Washington, DC
Hogan, Jean Magee ... Tupelo, MS
Hogan, Jeffrey D. ... Waterbury, CT
Hogan, Jennifer Bruch ... Houston, TX
Hogan, Jerry E. ... Hagåtña, GU
Hogan, Jerry Leonard ... Easton, PA
Hogan, Jimmy A. ... Wichita Falls, TX
Hogan, Joanne M.
Environmental Protection Agency, Office of the General Counsel, GV
Hogan, John B. ... Binghamton, NY
Hogan, John E. ... House of Representatives, Committee on District of Columbia, GV
Hogan, John E. ... Woodbridge, NJ
Hogan, John J. ... Brewster, NY
Hogan, John J. ... Providence, RI
Hogan, John J. ... Rhinelander, WI
Hogan, John J., Jr. ... New York, NY
Hogan, John M. ... Miami, FL
Hogan, John M. ... New York, NY
Hogan, John M., III ... Saratoga Springs, NY
Hogan, John M., Jr. ... Saratoga Springs, NY
Hogan, John Michael ... Wayne, PA
Hogan, John P. ... Morristown, NJ
Hogan, John W. ... Parsippany, NJ
Hogan, John W., Jr. ... New Haven, CT
Hogan, Joris M. ... New York, NY
Hogan, Joseph C., III ... Boston, MA
Hogan, Joseph H. ... Brighton, MA
Hogan, Judith R. ... Boston, MA
Hogan, Judy L. ... Geneva, IL
Wheaton, IL
Hogan, Judy L., P.C. ... Geneva, IL
Wheaton, IL
Hogan, Karen ... Austin, TX
Hogan, Katherine A. ... New York, NY
Hogan, Kathleen A. ... Denver, CO
Greenwich, CT
Westport, CT
Hogan, Kathleen B. ... Boston, MA
Hogan, Kathleen B. ... Albany, NY
Hogan, Kathryn H. ... Louisville, KY
Hogan, Kathryn Kane ... San Jose, CA
Hogan, Kellie E. ... Emporia, KS
Hogan, Kelly M. ... Ogallala, NE
Hogan, Kevin M. ... Buffalo, NY
Hogan, Kristine D. ... Casper, WY
Hogan, Larry S. ... Richmond, VA
Hogan, Laura E. ... Los Angeles, CA
Hogan Law Firm, The ... Brooksville, FL
Hogan Law Firm, The, P.C.
Moorhead, MN
Fargo, ND
Hogan, Lawrence A. ... Hendersonville, NC
Hogan, Lawrence J. ... Lawrenceville, GA
Hogan, Leah Pavetti ... Stamford, CT
Hogan, Leigh P. ... Marblehead, MA
Hogan, Lesley S. ... West Palm Beach, FL
Hogan, Lila Tritico ... Hammond, LA
Hogan, Linda ... St. Louis, MO
Hogan, Lisa ... Denver, CO
Hogan, Lisa B. ... Atlanta, GA
Hogan, Margaret L. ... East Providence, RI
Wakefield, RI
Hogan, Marian Bethanie ... Elizabethtown, KY
Hogan, Marian L. ... Annapolis, MD
Baltimore, MD
Hogan, Mariana J. ... Bronx, NY
Hogan, Marie F. ... San Mateo, CA
Hogan & Marken ... Oakland, CA
Hogan, Marren & McCahill, Ltd.
Chicago, IL
Hogan, Martha Burroughs ... Pasadena, CA
Hogan, Marvan Jordan ... Redding, CA
Hogan, Mary Beth ... New York, NY
Hogan, Mary Christine ... Lafayette, CA
Hogan, Mary Eller ... Los Angeles, CA
Hogan, Mary Kathryn ... Savannah, GA
Hogan, Mary Kay ... Denver, CO
Hogan, Mason ... Wilmington, NC
Hogan, Matthew F. ... Harrison, NY
Hogan, Matthew J. ... Denver, CO
Hogan, Matthew J. ... Boston, MA
Hogan, Matthew S. ... Saratoga Springs, NY
Hogan, Maureen P. ... Boston, MA
Hogan, Maurice R., Jr. ... Los Angeles, CA
Hogan, Maurya ... Altadena, CA
Hogan & McGann ... Ocean Grove, NJ
Hogan, Michael G. ... Costa Mesa, CA
Hogan, Michael J. ... Fresno, CA
Hogan, Michael J. ... Chicago, IL
Hogan, Michael J. ... Burlington, NJ
Hogan, Michael J. ... New York, NY
Hogan, Michael J. ... Rockville Centre, NY
Hogan, Michael J. ... Milwaukee, WI
Hogan, Michael M. ... San Diego, CA
Hogan, Michael R. ... Eugene, OR
Hogan, Michael T. ... Aberdeen, SD
Hogan, Michael Todd ... Louisa, KY
Hogan, Michael W. ... Springfield, IL
Hogan, Michael W. ... McAlester, OK
Hogan, Moira A. ... Campbell, CA
Hogan, Nancy Adele ... New York, NY
Hogan, Norma E. ... Albany, NY
Hogan, Palace & Scully ... Hackensack, NJ
Hogan, Patricia B. ... Cincinnati, OH
Hogan, Patricia J. ... Chicago, IL
Hogan, Patricia L. ... New York, NY
Hogan, Patrick J. ... San Francisco, CA
Hogan, Patrick James ... Fishers, IN
Hogan, Patrick R. ... Lansing, MI
Hogan, Paul D. ... Wichita, KS
Hogan, Paul D., Jr. ... Knoxville, TN
Hogan, Paul M. ... Los Angeles, CA
Hogan, Paul M. ... San Jose, CA
Hogan, Peter J. ... Syracuse, NY
Hogan, Philip J. ... Lake Forest, IL
Hogan, R. Benjamin, III ... Birmingham, AL
Hogan, Rebecca M. ... Dallas, TX
Hogan, Richard A. ... Rocky Hill, CT
Hogan, Richard A. ... Seattle, WA
Hogan, Richard J., Jr. ... Niagara Falls, NY
Hogan, Richard P., Jr. ... Houston, TX
Hogan, Richard P., Sr. (P.C.) ... Houston, TX
Hogan, Richard W. ... Ocean Grove, NJ
Hogan, Richard W. ... Richmond, VA
Hogan, Rick D. ... Little Rock, AR
Hogan & Rini, P.C. ... New Haven, CT
Hogan, Robert ... Chicago, IL
Hogan, Robert B. ... Cincinnati, OH
Hogan, Robert C. ... Warwick, RI
Hogan, Robert E. ... Springfield, MO
Hogan, Robert G. ... Honolulu, HI
Hogan, Robert J. ... Department of Commerce, National Oceanic and Atmospheric Administration, GV
Hogan, Robert J. ... Houston, TX
Hogan, Robert K. ... Cincinnati, OH
Hogan, Robert L. ... Hendersonville, NC
Hogan, Robert L. ... Huntington, WV
Hogan, Robert N., II ... Jupiter, FL
Hogan, Robert P. ... Madisonville, LA
Hogan, Robert S. ... Temple, TX
Hogan, Robert V. ... Glenview, IL
Hogan, Robert W. ... San Jose, CA
Hogan, Roberta R. ... Bloomington, IL
Hogan, Robyne M. ... West Milford, NJ
Hogan, Sara J. ... Allentown, PA
Hogan & Sarzynski, L.L.P.
Binghamton, NY
Hogan, Scott H. ... Grand Rapids, MI
Hogan, Sean J. ... Fort Bragg, CA
Hogan, Smith & Alspaugh, P.C.
Birmingham, AL
Hogan, Stephen ... New York, NY
Hogan, Stephen P. ... Albany, NY
Hogan, Steven L. ... Beverly Hills, CA
Hogan & Sumner, Inc. ... Warwick, RI
Hogan, Susan L. ... Kansas City, MO
Hogan, Susan Murray ... San Francisco, CA
Hogan, Susan S. ... Orchard Park, NY
Hogan, Ted ... Lubbock, TX
Hogan, Teresa A. ... Medford, OR
Hogan, Theresa ... Easton, PA
Hogan, Thomas ... Fayetteville, NY
Hogan, Thomas A. ... Hackensack, NJ
Hogan, Thomas D. ... Kearny, NJ
Hogan, Thomas D. ... Richmond, VA
Hogan, Thomas F. ... Litchfield, CT
Hogan, Thomas F.
United States District Court For The District Of Columbia, GV
Hogan, Thomas J. ... Providence, RI
Hogan, Thomas L. ... Chicago, IL
Hogan, Thomas M. ... Chicago, IL
Hogan, Thomas M. ... Fairfax, VA
Hogan, Thomas M. ... Redmond, WA
Hogan, Thomas P. ... Alamo, CA
Hogan, Thomas P. ... Grand Rapids, MI
Hogan, Thomas P. ... Providence, RI
Hogan, Thomas P., Jr. ... West Chester, PA
Hogan, Thomas R., Law Offices of
Redwood City, CA
Hogan, Thomas R., Law Offices of
San Jose, CA
Hogan, Thomas R., Law Offices of
San Mateo, CA
Hogan, Thomas S., Jr. ... Brooksville, FL
Hogan, Timothy A. ... Los Angeles, CA
Hogan, Timothy C. ... Des Moines, IA
Hogan, Timothy E. ... St. Louis, MO
Hogan, Timothy J. ... Los Angeles, CA
Hogan, Timothy J. ... Honolulu, HI
Hogan, Timothy J. ... Houston, TX
Hogan, Timothy J. ... Seattle, WA
Hogan, Timothy K. ... Baltimore, MD
Hogan, Timothy S. ... Cincinnati, OH
Hogan & Veith ... Wilmington, DE
Hogan, Walter J. ... San Bernardino, CA
Hogan, Wayne ... Jacksonville, FL
Hogan, William C. ... San Francisco, CA
Hogan, William D. ... Cherry Hill, NJ
Hogan, William E. ... New York, NY
Hogan, William Hughes ... Burbank, CA
Hogan, William J. ... Galveston, TX
Hogan, William James ... Springfield, IL
Hogan, William K. ... San Rafael, CA
Hogan, William P. ... St. Louis, MO
Hogan, William P. ... Easton, PA
Hogan, William R. P. ... New York, NY
Hogan, William T., III ... Boston, MA
Hogan, Wm. M., Jr. ... Boston, MA
Hogan, Wyatt L. ... Houston, TX
Hogancamp, Michael W. ... Bardwell, KY
Hogans, Carolyn T. ... Fairfax, VA
Hogans, Daniel Lee ... Washington, DC
Hoganson, Heather Faith Cline
Sacramento, CA
Hoganson, Jon J. ... Minneapolis, MN
St. Paul, MN
Hogben, Virginia Lynn ... Philadelphia, PA
Hoge, Alyce B. ... Houston, TX
Hoge, Andrew E. ... Anchorage, AK
Hoge, Anne E. ... Washington, DC
Hoge, Arthur F., III ... Oklahoma City, OK
Hoge, Charles T. ... San Diego, CA
Hoge, Christopher G. ... Washington, DC
Hoge, Fenton, Jones & Appel, Inc.
Pleasanton, CA
San Jose, CA
Hoge, Gail Scott ... Tallahassee, FL
Hoge and Lekisch, A Professional Corporation ... Anchorage, AK
Hoge, Michael W. ... Seattle, WA
Hoge, Nettie Y. ... San Francisco, CA
Hoge, Richard C. ... Longmont, CO
Hoge, Richard C. ... Washington, DC
Hoge, Sara Skantz ... Minneapolis, MN
Hoge, Steven S. ... St. Louis Park, MN
Hoge, Stewart B. ... Dallas, TX
Hoge, William L., III ... Louisville, KY
Hogeboom, C. Patrick, III
Department of Justice, Tax Division, GV
Hogeboom, Charles E.
Department Of Veterans Affairs, Board of Veterans Appeals, GV
Hogeboom, Robert Wood
Los Angeles, CA
Hogel, Maureen L. ... Pittsburgh, PA
Hogeland, Andrew S. ... Pittsfield, MA
Hogeland, Anne W. ... Pittsfield, MA
Hogeland, Webster ... Bedford, VA
Hogeland, William H., Jr. ... New York, NY
Hogeland-Hannah, Hallie D. ... Irvine, CA
Hogeman, Hubert H., III ... Atlanta, GA
Hogeman, Jane D. ... Greenwich, CT
Hogen, Philip N. ... Washington, DC
Hogenauer, Clare L. ... New York, NY
Hogenauer, Julie K. ... San Antonio, TX
Hogen-Kind, Vanya S. ... Minneapolis, MN
Hogenmiller, Jerry R. ... Pittsburgh, PA
Hogenmuller, John N. ... Tallahassee, FL
Hogenson, Edward B. ... Orange, CA
Hogerty, John J., II ... Neenah, WI
Hogerty, Morgan O'Regan ... Neenah, WI
Hogewood, A. Lee, III ... Raleigh, NC
Hogewood, Ashley L., Jr. ... Charlotte, NC
Hogewood, Mark M. ... Birmingham, AL
Hogfoss, Robert E. ... Atlanta, GA
Hogg, Allen, Norton & Blue, Professional Association ... Miami, FL
Hogg, Bert C. ... Ruston, LA
Hogg, Cathy Senzel ... Laurel Hollow, NY
Hogg, Christopher G. ... New York, NY
Hogg, David A. ... Cadillac, MI
Hogg, David K. ... Dothan, AL
Hogg, F. Byrd ... Whitesburg, KY
Hogg, Gary L. ... Kearney, NE
Hogg, George, Jr. ... Detroit, MI
Hogg, George M. ... Olive Hill, KY
Hogg, James F. ... St. Paul, MN
Hogg, James S. ... Cleveland, OH
Hogg, Jerry D. ... Charleston, WV
Hogg, Jesse S. ... Miami, FL
Miami Beach, FL
West Palm Beach, FL
Hogg, John L. ... Monterey Park, CA
Hogg, Jon Mark ... San Angelo, TX
Hogg, Kathleen A. ... Shaker Heights, OH
Hogg, Kevin D. ... Cincinnati, OH
Hogg, Kristi Womack ... Olive Hill, KY
Hogg, Melanie J. ... Raleigh, NC
Hogg, Michael H., (P.L.C.) ... Metairie, LA
Hogg, P. Hiram ... Louisville, KY
Hogg, Rhonda L. ... Simi Valley, CA
Hogg, Robert M. ... Cedar Rapids, IA
Hogg, Ronald R. ... Ellicott City, MD
Hogg, Ryce & Hudson ... Miami, FL
Miami Beach, FL
West Palm Beach, FL
Hogg, Stephen L. ... Pikeville, KY
Hogg, William N. ... Cleveland, OH
Mentor, OH
Hoggan, Craig A. ... Salt Lake City, UT
Hoggan, Judith A. ... Germantown, MD
Hoggan, Judith A., P.C., The Law Offices of
Germantown, MD
Hoggan, L. Brent ... Logan, UT
Hoggan, Michael D. ... Las Vegas, NV
Hoggard, Denise Reid ... Little Rock, AR
Hoggard, Jay E. ... El Dorado, AR
Hoggard, Lewis W. ... Windsor, NC
Hoggard, Rick B. ... Salt Lake City, UT
Hoggard, William C. ... Santa Ana, CA
Hoggarth, Robert L. ... Alexandria, VA
Hoggatt, Ralph C. ... Deadwood, SD
Hoggatt, Victoria Johnson ... Oxford, MS
Hoggatt, Wallace R. ... Bisbee, AZ
Hogge, Elijah M. ... Frankfort, KY
Hogge, Jeffery A. ... Sacramento, CA
Hogge, Jerry W., III ... Falls Church, VA
Hogge, Mark L. ... Washington, DC
Hogge, Raymond L., Jr. ... Norfolk, VA
Hogger and Sheeler ... Closter, NJ
Hoggren, Birgitta S. ... Deerfield, IL
Hoghaug, Karen Orr ... Daytona Beach, FL
Hoghaug, Robert G. ... Denver, CO
Hoghooghi-Esfahani, Babak
Washington, DC
Hogie & Hogie ... Santa Ana, CA
Hogie, Stephen W. ... Santa Ana, CA
Hogie, William A. ... Santa Ana, CA
Hogin, Bradley R. ... Orange, CA
Hogin, Christi ... Malibu, CA
Hogin, Robert D. ... Cupertino, CA
Hoglan, Theodore R. ... Marshalltown, IA
Hogle, Chris R. ... Salt Lake City, UT
Hogle, Doreen M. ... Lexington, MA
Hogle, James E., Jr. ... Ravenna, OH
Hogle, Merry Ann ... Denver, CO
Hogle, Yvonne Rodriguez
Salt Lake City, UT
Hoglin, Warren D. ... Minneapolis, MN
Hoglund, Chwialkowski & Greeman, P.L.L.P. ... St. Paul, MN
Hoglund, Elizabeth A. ... Portland, ME
Hoglund, John A. ... Olympia, WA
Hoglund, John A., P.S. ... Olympia, WA
Hoglund, Robert J. ... St. Paul, MN
Hoglund, Sandra K. ... Sioux Falls, SD
Hogoboom, John D. ... Roseland, NJ
Hogoboom, Roger D. ... Denver, CO
Hogoboom, William P. ... Los Angeles, CA
Hogon, O. Lang, Jr. ... Sumter, SC
Ho-González, William ... Department of Justice, Office of Attorney Personnel Management, GV
Hogren, Charles V. ... Chicago, IL
Hogreve, Bradley W. ... Sarasota, FL
Hogreve, Lisa L. ... Melbourne, FL
Hogreve & Shults ... Sarasota, FL
Hogrogian, John ... New York, NY
Hogroian, Steven ... Cruz Bay, St. John, VI
Hogroian, Vahan ... Lawrenceville, NJ
Hogsett, Joseph H. ... Indianapolis, IN
Hogsett, Joseph P. ... Oklahoma City, OK
Hogsett, Matthew J. ... Westminster, CO
Hogsette, Sarah M. (IBA) ... Atlanta, GA
Hogshead, Charles R. ... Tulsa, OK
Hogshead, Nancy ... Jacksonville, FL
Hogshire, Edward L. ... Charlottesville, VA
Hogstad, Christopher J. ... Spokane, WA
Hogsten, Michael J. ... Fort Lauderdale, FL
Hogston, Chad E. ... Wilmington, NC
Hogtanian, A. Gina ... Los Angeles, CA
Hogue, Amy D. ... Los Angeles, CA
Hogue, Bryan K. ... Columbus, OH
Hogue, Curtis E., Law Office of
Fayetteville, AR
Hogue, Cyrus D., III ... Hillsborough, NC
Hogue, Cyrus D., Jr. ... Wilmington, NC
Hogue, Cyrus D. III, P.A. ... Hillsborough, NC
Hogue, Dale Curtis, Sr. ... Arlington, VA
Hogue, Darrell L. ... Oklahoma City, OK
Hogue, David J. ... Minot, ND
Hogue & Dunlap, LLP ... Hailey, ID
Ketchum, ID
Hogue, Forrest J. ... Fairborn, OH
Hogue, Forrest J., Co., L.P.A. ... Fairborn, OH
Hogue, Hill, Jones, Nash and Lynch, L.L.P.
Wilmington, NC
Hogue, Jack Porter ... San Antonio, TX
Hogue, J. H., Jr. ... Yazoo City, MS
Hogue, J. O. ... Flandreau, SD
Hogue, Joel R. ... Amarillo, TX
Hogue, Jon Geoffrey ... Pittsburgh, PA
Hogue, L. Eades ... New Orleans, LA
Hogue, L. Lynn, Mr. ... Atlanta, GA
Hogue & Langhammer ... Los Angeles, CA
Pasadena, CA
Hogue & Lannis ... Pittsburgh, PA
Hogue, Laura D. ... Macon, GA
Hogue, Lisha D. ... Tampa, FL
Hogue, Mary M. ... Wausau, WI
Hogue, Mary M., Law Office, LLC
Wausau, WI
Hogue, Michael W. ... Columbia, SC
Hogue, Michael W. ... Friendswood, TX
Hogue, Monty C. ... Spring, TX
Hogue, Monty Gene ... Denver, CO
Hogue, Nichole Michelle ... Camden, AR
Hogue, Norman K. ... Dallas, TX
Hogue, P. Mason, Jr. ... Columbia, SC
Hogue, Paul J.
Hot Springs National Park, AR
Hogue, Phyllis C. ... Tampa, FL
Hogue, Rebecca J. ... Los Angeles, CA
Hogue, Robert A. ... Charleston, WV
Hogue, Robert G. ... Dallas, TX
Hogue, Robert G., P.C. ... Dallas, TX
Hogue, Terry G. ... Hailey, ID
Ketchum, ID
Hogue, Thomas D. ... Pasadena, CA
Hogue, Tina M. ... Rapid City, SD
Hogue Katz, Melissa ... Fairfax, VA
Hogue-Mauro, Kelli ... Birmingham, AL
Hoguet, Albert W. ... Portland, OR
Hoguet, Laura B. ... New York, NY
Hoguet Newman & Regal, LLP
New York, NY
Hogwood, Stephen F. ... Washington, DC
Hogwood, Terry E. ... Houston, TX
Hogya, Joseph J., Jr. ... Perth Amboy, NJ

Hogzett, Donald D. .... Oakland, IA
Hoh, Tony C. .... **San Francisco, CA**
Hoham, Julia M. .... Valparaiso, IN
Hohauser, Herman J. .... Alexandria, VA
Hohauser Law Firm .... Novi, MI
Rochester, MI
Troy, MI
Hohauser, Michael S. .... Novi, MI
Rochester, MI
Troy, MI
Hohauser, William Alan .... **New York, NY**
Hohbach, Harold C. .... **Palo Alto, CA**
Hohe, Sara M. .... Rockford, IL
Hohein, George D.
Department of Commerce, Patent and Trademark Office, GV
Hohenadel, Bernadette M. .... **Lancaster, PA**
Hohenadel, John C. .... Elizabethtown, PA
Lancaster, PA
Hohenadel, John P. .... **Lancaster, PA**
Hohenadel, Michael J. .... Elizabethtown, PA
Lancaster, PA
Hohenberger, Christopher E. .... Walbridge, OH
Hohenberger, Raymond W. .... Orrville, OH
Hohenberger, Robert .... Houston, TX
Hohenberger, Sarah .... Philadelphia, PA
Hohenberger, Wayne P. .... **Mansfield, OH**
Hohenberger, William C. .... Jarrettsville, MD
Hohener, Conrad F., III .... Santa Ana, CA
Hohenfeldt, Ralph G. .... **Brookfield, WI**
Hohengarten, William A. .... **Washington, DC**
Hohenlohe, Nora R. .... Washington, DC
Hohenlohe, Philip A.
United States Court Of Appeals District Of Columbia Circuit, GV
Hohensee, Eugene L. .... **Denver, CO**
Hohenshell, Ann E. Heiny .... Minneapolis, MN
Hohenshell, Jeffrey J. .... **St. Paul, MN**
Hohenstein, Anne Kennedy .... Albany, NY
Hohenstein, Gail A. .... Green Bay, WI
Hohenstein, James H. .... **New York, NY**
Hohenstein, Joseph C. .... Philadelphia, PA
Hohenstein, Richard .... Dallas, TX
Hohenstein, Richard C. .... **Flint, MI**
Hohenstein, Thomas P. .... **St. Louis, MO**
Hohenthal, Gary W. .... Vernon, CT
Hohenthaner, Jon T. .... **New York, NY**
Hohenthaner, Thomas G.
Washington, DC
Hohenwarter, Joseph E. .... Ventura, CA
Hohl, Doren E. .... **Los Angeles, CA**
Hohl, E. David .... New York, NY
Hohl, Ruth Ann .... Columbus, OH
Hohl, Thomas J. .... Marlborough, MA
Hohlbein, Holly M. .... Bellevue, WA
Hohler, Barbara A. .... Darien, CT
Hohler, Daniel C. .... **Boston, MA**
Hohler, Heidi .... Woodland Hills, CA
Hohler, Kathleen .... **Cleveland, OH**
Hohlt, House & DeMoss .... Nashville, IL
Hohlt, John R. .... **Houston, TX**
Hohlt, Lawrence J. .... **New York, NY**
Hohlt, Mark William .... Salem, OR
Hohlt, Wilbert J. .... Nashville, IL
Hohman, A. J., Jr. .... San Antonio, TX
Hohman, David M. .... **Omaha, NE**
Hohman, Georges & Gehring, L.L.P.
San Antonio, TX
Hohman, Harry .... **Alexandria, MN**
Appleton, MN
Hohman, John A., Jr. .... Monroe, MI
Hohman, Matthew M. .... **Fort Wayne, IN**
Hohman, Russell J. .... **Ada, MI**
Hohmann, Boukis & Curtis Co., L.P.A.
Cleveland, OH
Hohmann, Guy M. .... **Austin, TX**
Hohmann, Heather A .... **Dallas, TX**
Hohmann, Joseph G. .... Chicago, IL
Hohmann & Taube, L.L.P. .... **Austin, TX**
Hohmann, William T. .... **Cleveland, OH**
Hohn, Christopher M. .... **St. Louis, MO**
Hohn and Dulberg .... Norwalk, CT
Hohn, Edward L. .... **Daingerfield, TX**
Hohn, Harry G., Jr. .... New York, NY
Hohn, John .... San Marcos, TX
Hohn, Linda C. .... Bala Cynwyd, PA
Hohn, Michael .... Cincinnati, OH
Hohn, Richard G. .... New York, NY
Hohn, Richard K. .... **Philadelphia, PA**
Hohn & Scheüerle .... **Philadelphia, PA**
Hohnbaum, Cory .... **Charlotte, NC**
Hohnbaum, James L. .... **Phoenix, AZ**
Hohner, Hallie G. .... Chicago, IL
Hohnhorst, John C. .... **Twin Falls, ID**
Hohnke, Michelle K. .... Nashville, TN
Hohns, Christopher C. .... Grass Valley, CA
Hohnsbeen, George H., II .... Palo Alto, CA
Hohnsbeen, Roger Blake .... **Oakland, CA**
Hoi, Thomas C. .... **New York, NY**
Hoiby, Eugene S. .... Livonia, MI
Hoiby, Glenn W. .... North Hollywood, CA
Hoiby, Randall C. .... **Los Angeles, CA**
Hoida, Joseph A. .... Green Bay, WI
Hoidal, Ernest A. .... **Boise, ID**
Hoidal & Hannah, P.L.C. .... **Phoenix, AZ**
Hoidal, Thomas M. .... **Phoenix, AZ**
Hoiland, David Jon .... **Minneapolis, MN**
Hoiland, Karen K. .... **Denver, CO**
Hoiles Dasinger & Hollon, P.C.
Robertsdale, AL
Hoiles, David G., Jr. .... **Los Angeles, CA**
Hoiles, Sharon R. .... Robertsdale, AL
Hoilman, Marta .... Department of Justice, Environment and Natural Resources Division, GV
Hoin, Stacey Weinsheimer .... Stamford, CT
Hoines, David A. .... Fort Lauderdale, FL
Hoines, Nathan J. .... **Great Falls, MT**
Hoing, Debra H. .... Washington, DC
Hoing, Scott .... **Houston, TX**
Hoinkes, H. Dieter
Department of Commerce, Patent and Trademark Office, GV
Hoinkes, Mary Elizabeth
Department of State, Office of the Legal Adviser, GV
Hoiriis, David S. .... Billerica, MA
Hois, Laura L. .... **Oak Brook, IL**
Hoisington, Carrie Palmer
Oklahoma City, OK
Hoisington, H. Steven .... **Ogden, UT**
Hoisington, Joan E. .... Bellingham, WA
Hoisington, Miles E. .... Westport, MA
Hoisington, Ralph E. .... Charleston, SC
Hoisington, Robert D.
Oklahoma City, OK
Hoisington, William L. .... San Francisco, CA
Hoistad, Dean A. .... **Missoula, MT**
Hoitink, William C. .... Marietta, GA
Hoium, Elizabeth J. .... Minneapolis, MN
Hoium, Vernon S. .... Minneapolis, MN
Hojan, Candice M. .... St. Paul, MN
Hojem, Douglas E. .... **Pendleton, OR**
Hojnacki, Cynthia L. .... Wilton, CT
Hojnacki, Kathleen A. .... Cleveland, OH
Hojnowski, Claudia Rich .... Newington, CT
Hokanson, Charles W. .... **Los Angeles, CA**
Hokanson, Frederick R. .... Tacoma, WA
Hokanson, Jeffrey A. .... Indianapolis, IN
Hokanson, Jon E. .... **Los Angeles, CA**
Hokanson, Lynn E. .... Houston, TX
Hokanson, Martin M. .... Houston, TX
Hokanson, Mary A. .... **Bellevue, WA**
Hokanson, Maynard .... Indianapolis, IN
Hokanson, Russell V. .... **Seattle, WA**
Hoke, Anne E. .... **Baltimore, MD**
Hoke, Carroll Clausing .... Wichita, KS
Hoke, Charles E., II .... Wichita, KS
Hoke, Chris G. .... Raleigh, NC
Hoke & Clausing .... Wichita, KS
Hoke, Danny L. .... Sugar Land, TX
Hoke, Frank A. .... Aquilla, TX
Hoke, G. Scott .... Anoka, MN
Hoke, G. Scott, P.A. .... Anoka, MN
Hoke, Harold R. .... Charlotte, NC
Hoke, Heather L. .... Vancouver, WA
Hoke, Jack .... Springfield, MO
Hoke, James E. .... Harrisonville, MO
Hoke, James E., P.C. .... Harrisonville, MO
Hoke, John L. .... Rawlins, WY
Hoke, Julia Renfrow
Research Triangle Park, NC
Hoke, Martin D. .... Schererville, IN
Hoke, Matthew M. .... Cleveland, OH
Hoke & Miller .... Springfield, MO
Hoke, Patricia A. .... **Carbondale, IL**
Hoke, Richard L. .... Honolulu, HI
Hoke, Robert L. .... Newport Beach, CA
Hoke, Robert W., II .... **St. Paul, MN**
Hoke, Robin Smith .... **North Chicago, IL**
Hoke, S. Candice .... Cleveland, OH
Hoke, Sheila D. .... Quincy, MA
Hoke, Stephen .... Roseville, MN
Hokemeyer, Paul L. .... Los Angeles, CA
Hokenson, Earl P. .... San Rafael, CA
Hokenson, H. John .... Basking Ridge, NJ
Hokenson, Michael E.
Department of the Army, U.S. Army Legal Services Agency, GV
Hokinson, Thomas C. .... Los Angeles, CA
Hokit, David T. .... **Kent, WA**
Hokky, Naomi .... Cleveland, OH
Hokokian, Paul Suren .... Fresno, CA
Hokstad, Gerald W. .... Encinitas, CA
Holaday, Arnold W. .... **Los Angeles, CA**
Holaday, Beverly .... **Lansing, MI**
Holaday, John G. .... **Jackson, MS**
Holaday, Keith .... Irwindale, CA
Holaday, Krislyn M. .... Oconomowoc, WI
Holaday, Rodney A. .... **Columbus, OH**
Holaday, Ted J. .... Indianapolis, IN
Holady, Mark J. .... Beaverton, OR
Holahan, Carol J. .... Concord, NH
Holahan, Dennis .... Santa Monica, CA
Holahan, Edward J., Jr. .... **Fairfield, CT**
Holahan, Frank .... **Hackensack, NJ**
New York, NY
Holahan, Gumpper & Dowling
Bridgeport, CT
Fairfield, CT
Holahan, J. Patrick, II & Associates
Kennett Square, PA
Holahan, James .... Rochester, NY
Holahan, John M. .... New Orleans, LA
Holahan, John M., Jr. .... Metairie, LA
Holahan, Malloy, Maybaugh, Monnich & Delie .... **Detroit, MI**
East Tawas, MI
Mount Clemens, MI
Pontiac, MI
Troy, MI
Holahan, Maureen .... East Tawas, MI
Holahan, Richard D., Jr. .... New York, NY
Holahan, Sharon M. .... Short Hills, NJ
Holahan, Shawn L. .... **New Orleans, LA**
Holajter, Leonard M. .... **Highland, IN**
Holan, Raymond J. .... Stafford, TX
Holand, Donald C. .... Fargo, ND
Holand Law Office .... Fargo, ND
Holand, Roy A. .... La Moure, ND
Holappa, Susan D. .... **Minneapolis, MN**
Holbein, Bruce E. .... **Boston, MA**
Holbein, James R. .... **Washington, DC**
Holben, Donald R. .... **San Diego, CA**
Holben, Janice LaRue .... Kittanning, PA
Holber, Ida .... Carmel, CA
Holber, Robert H. .... Media, PA
Holber, Stuart M. .... **Haverhill, MA**
Holberg and Holberg, P.C. .... **Mobile, AL**
Holberg, Michael Ralph .... **Mobile, AL**
Holberg, Ralph G., III .... **Mobile, AL**
Holberg, Roger D.
Federal Communications Commission, Mass Media Bureau, GV
Holbert, J. Howard .... Elizabethtown, KY
Holbert, Kenneth F. ....
Department of Housing and Urban Development, GV
Holbert, Richard N. .... Little Rock, AR
Holbert, Stephanie Tyner .... Little Rock, AR
Holberton, John C. .... **Los Angeles, CA**
Holborn, Carl D. .... **Milwaukee, WI**
Holbreich, Curt .... **San Francisco, CA**
Holbreich, Stephen .... Syosset, NY
Holbreich, Toby .... **Newark, NJ**
Holbritter, Margaret F. .... Delmar, NY
Holbrock, Hugh D. .... Hamilton, OH
Holbrock, Jonson, Evans & Olivas, Law Firm
Hamilton, OH
Holbrook, Akel, Cold, Stiefel & Ray, P.A.
Jacksonville, FL
Holbrook, Alan A. .... Forestville, CA
Holbrook, Alfred S., Jr. .... Atlanta, GA
Holbrook, Allen W. .... **Owensboro, KY**
Holbrook & Associates, Ltd.
Covington, KY
Cincinnati, OH
Holbrook, Brad C. .... Monterey, CA
Holbrook, Bradley D. .... **Kearney, NE**
Holbrook, Brian M. .... **Los Angeles, CA**
Holbrook, C. Ray, Jr. .... Galveston, TX
Holbrook, Charles R., III .... **Ashland, KY**
Holbrook, Connie Cannon
Salt Lake City, UT
Holbrook, Cris M. .... Sacramento, CA
Holbrook, Cynthia K. .... San Francisco, CA
Holbrook, Cynthia M. .... **Santa Monica, CA**
Holbrook, Cyrus A. .... Raleigh, NC
Holbrook, Dan W. .... **Knoxville, TN**
Holbrook, David L. .... **Orlando, FL**
Holbrook, David L. .... Lawrenceville, GA
Holbrook, Dean .... **New York, NY**
Holbrook, Deborah A. .... Juneau, AK
Holbrook, Donald B. .... **Salt Lake City, UT**
Holbrook, Donald C. .... Austin, TX
Holbrook, Donald E., Jr. .... Lansing, MI
Holbrook, Douglas H. .... Salt Lake City, UT
Holbrook, Douglas R. .... Newport, OR
Holbrook, E. Bradford, III .... New York, NY
Holbrook, E. Scott, Jr. .... **Covina, CA**
Holbrook, Francine D. .... Miami, FL
Holbrook, Francis S., II .... **Newport, RI**
Holbrook, Frank A. .... Harker Heights, TX
Holbrook, Frank L. .... **Jackson, MS**
Holbrook, Frederic P., Jr. .... Bellevue, WA
Holbrook, Frederick J. .... Spencerport, NY
Holbrook, George H. .... **Hoosick Falls, NY**
Holbrook, George L. .... El Centro, CA
Holbrook, Gregory M. .... Salt Lake City, UT
Holbrook, H. Leon .... **Jacksonville, FL**
Holbrook, H. Leon, III .... **Jacksonville, FL**
Holbrook, H. Michael .... Hinsdale, IL
Holbrook, Heaven & Osborn, P.A.
Kansas City, KS
Merriam, KS
Olathe, KS
Kansas City, MO
Holbrook, J. Kevin .... Paintsville, KY
Holbrook, J. Mark .... **Austin, TX**
Holbrook, James R. .... **Salt Lake City, UT**
Holbrook, Janet Smith .... **Ashland, KY**
Charleston, WV
Huntington, WV
Holbrook & Jezek .... Harker Heights, TX
Holbrook, Jimmy D., Jr. .... **Knoxville, TN**
Holbrook, John .... New York, NY
Holbrook, John D. .... Willmar, MN
Holbrook, John Patrick .... Hornell, NY
Holbrook, John S., Jr. .... **Madison, WI**
Holbrook & Johnston .... **Cambridge, NY**
Hoosick Falls, NY
Troy, NY
Holbrook, L. Win .... **Oklahoma City, OK**
Holbrook, Lanae .... **Washington, DC**
Holbrook, Lanny R. .... Covington, KY
Cincinnati, OH
Holbrook, Laura M. .... **Roanoke, VA**
Holbrook Law Firm .... **Orlando, FL**
Holbrook, Marco S. .... Fruita, CO
Holbrook, Margaret A. .... Englewood, NJ
Holbrook, Martin E. .... Congers, NY
Holbrook, Mary .... Albany, CA
Holbrook, Megan .... Sebastopol, CA
Holbrook, Michael E., P.C. .... **Atlanta, GA**
Holbrook, Michael J. .... Columbus, OH
Holbrook, Morton J., III
Department of State, Foreign Service Officers (Overseas), GV
Holbrook, Morton J., Jr. .... **Owensboro, KY**
Holbrook & Murphy .... **Boston, MA**
Holbrook, Nancy J. .... Hermosa Beach, CA
Holbrook, Neil E. .... Goshen, IN
Holbrook, Nina G. .... **Morristown, NJ**
Holbrook, Patricia A. .... Irvine, CA
Holbrook, Paul K. .... Buffalo, NY
Holbrook, Paula J. .... Lexington, KY
Holbrook, Peter D. .... **Irvine, CA**
Holbrook & Peterson, PLLC
Knoxville, TN
Holbrook & Pitt .... **Ashland, KY**
Holbrook, Reid F. .... **Kansas City, KS**
Holbrook, Richard B., Jr.
Washington, DC
Holbrook, Richard E. .... **Salinas, CA**
Holbrook, Robin Rowe .... Riverside, CA
Holbrook, Seth S. .... **Boston, MA**
Holbrook, Timothy .... **Washington, DC**
Holbrook, Todd S. .... **Portland, ME**
Holbrook & Toffoli .... **Oklahoma City, OK**
Holbrook, William F. .... **Los Angeles, CA**
Holbrook, William H. .... Sheboygan, WI
Holbrook, William K. .... **Birmingham, AL**
Holbrow, Frederick W. .... Hanover, MA
Holbrow, Willmore F., III
Los Angeles, CA
Holburn, Andrea E. .... **Seattle, WA**
Holby, Wegard D. .... Upper Black Eddy, PA
Holby, William A. .... **Atlanta, GA**
Holchin, James W. .... **Los Angeles, CA**
Holck, Kelly L. .... Superior, WI
Holck, Laura E. .... Vista, CA
Holcomb, Alfred G. .... **San Antonio, TX**
Holcomb, Andrew C. .... Milpitas, CA
Holcomb, Barbara Levine .... Chicago, IL
Holcomb, Bonnie .... Los Angeles, CA
Holcomb, C. Lawrence .... Silver Spring, MD
Holcomb, Carol J. .... **Chapel Hill, NC**
Holcomb, Carrie A. .... **Kansas City, MO**
Holcomb, Charles M. .... Titusville, FL
Holcomb, Charles R. .... Rusk, TX
Holcomb, D. Clay .... **Amarillo, TX**
Dallas, TX
Houston, TX
Holcomb, David J. .... Walnut Creek, CA
Holcomb and DeCort, P.A. .... **Tampa, FL**
Holcomb, Dina E. .... Albuquerque, NM
Holcomb, Donald W. .... **Austin, TX**
Holcomb Dunbar, A Professional Association
Batesville, MS
Charleston, MS
Clarksdale, MS
Hernando, MS
Holly Springs, MS
Marks, MS
New Albany, MS
Oxford, MS
Pontotoc, MS
Senatobia, MS
Southaven, MS
Tunica, MS
Holcomb, Frank H. .... Houston, TX
Holcomb, Frank H., P.C. .... Houston, TX
Holcomb, Franklin .... Houston, TX
Holcomb, Gregory F.
Saint Simons Island, GA
Holcomb, Harkins & Olmstead .... Buffalo, OK
Laverne, OK
Holcomb, Helen .... **Boston, MA**
Holcomb, Herbert A. .... **Rogersville, TN**
Holcomb & Holcomb .... Chicago, IL
Holcomb & Hyde .... Hamilton, OH
Holcomb, J. Byron .... Bainbridge Island, WA
Holcomb, J. Marshall .... Charleston, WV
Holcomb, James A. .... **Merrillville, IN**
Holcomb, James M. .... **Des Moines, IA**
Holcomb, James R. .... **Lansing, MI**
Holcomb, James T. .... Trenton, MO
Holcomb, Janet Shoenhard .... Corvallis, OR
Holcomb, Jean McCulley .... Seattle, WA
Holcomb, Jeffrey G. .... Hamilton, OH
Holcomb, Jennifer H. .... **Portland, OR**
Holcomb, Jerry L. .... **Joplin, MO**
Holcomb, John E. .... Akron, OH
Holcomb, John F. .... Hamilton, OH
Holcomb, John K. .... Colorado Springs, CO
Holcomb, John L. .... **Tampa, FL**
Holcomb, John M. .... Hamilton, OH
Holcomb, John W. .... **Newport Beach, CA**
Holcomb, Johnnie R. .... Little Rock, AR
Holcomb, K. Alan .... **Phoenix, AZ**
Holcomb, Karen S. .... Rockford, MI
Holcomb, Kent Martin .... North Royalton, OH
Holcomb, Kevin .... **Austin, TX**
Holcomb, Lee Angela .... **Chattanooga, TN**
Holcomb, Lori S. .... Tallahassee, FL
Holcomb, Lyle Donald, Jr. .... Tallahassee, FL
Holcomb, M. Marcus .... Buffalo, OK
Laverne, OK
Holcomb, Mark E. .... **Tallahassee, FL**
Holcomb, Mark E. .... **Tacoma, WA**
Holcomb, Mary Catherine .... **Charlotte, NC**
Holcomb, Mary Catherine, P.A.
Charlotte, NC
Holcomb, M. C. .... Galena, MO
Holcomb, Noah L., Jr. .... East Chicago, IN
Holcomb, R. Bruce .... **Washington, DC**
Holcomb, Raymond W., III
Franklin Lakes, NJ
Holcomb, Reed C. .... San Luis Obispo, CA
Holcomb, Richard D. .... United States Senate, Committee Legal Personnel, GV
Holcomb, Rick J. .... Charlotte, NC
Holcomb, Roger M. .... Irving, TX
Holcomb, Ryan Scott .... **Houston, TX**
Holcomb, S. Richard .... Chattanooga, TN
Holcomb, Scott A. .... **Phoenix, AZ**
Holcomb, Shannon Charles .... **Enid, OK**
Holcomb, Tanya D. .... **Mount Olive, NJ**
Holcomb, Thomas C. .... **Atlanta, GA**
Holcomb, Todd .... San Francisco, CA
Holcomb, Tom .... Olympia, WA
Holcomb, Victor W. .... **Tampa, FL**
Holcomb, W. Robert .... San Bernardino, CA
Holcomb, Warren L. .... **Milford, CT**
Holcomb, Weldon G. .... Tyler, TX
Holcomb, William A., Jr. .... Houston, TX
Holcomb, William T. .... Chicago, IL
Holcomb, William W. .... **Los Angeles, CA**
Holcomb & Wright, L.L.C.
Silver Spring, MD
Holcombe, Andrew T. .... Chico, CA

Holcombe, Bomar, Gunn and Bradford, P.A.
Gaffney, SC
Greenville, SC
Spartanburg, SC
Union, SC
Holcombe, David G. ... Cincinnati, OH
Holcombe, Decatur J. ... Houston, TX
Holcombe, Donna R. ... Mary Esther, FL
Holcombe, Glenn D. ... North Bend, OR
Holcombe, Janet Stern ... Ardmore, PA
Holcombe, John H. ... Tucson, AZ
Holcombe, Jon K. ... Alexandria Bay, NY
Clayton, NY
Holcombe, Joseph B.
San Juan Capistrano, CA
Holcombe, Judith K. ... Boise, ID
Holcombe, Marshall M. ... Naples, FL
Holcombe, Nick G. ... New York, NY
Holcombe, P. Scott ... Rochester, NY
Holcombe, Pamela M. M.
Fort Lauderdale, FL
Holcombe, Paul A., Jr.
Research Triangle Park, NC
Holcombe, Paul Amos, III
Murfreesboro, TN
Holcombe, Robert S. ... Costa Mesa, CA
Holcombe, Steven L. ... Stillwater, OK
Holcombe, Thomas H. ... Texarkana, TX
Holcombe, Tina L. ... Macon, MS
Holcombe, Walter M. ... Pecos, TX
Holcombe, Wayne ... Pittsburgh, PA
Holcomb-Keller, Betty Jeanne, (Mrs.)
Lincoln, NE
Holczer, Benjamin Z. ... New York, NY
Holdahl, Scott A. ... Minneapolis, MN
Holdaway, Ernest M. ... Richmond, VA
Holdaway, Jeffrey A. ... Washington, DC
Atlanta, GA
Holdaway, Richard E. ... Chino, CA
Holdaway, Ronald M. ...
United States Court Of Veterans Appeals, GV
Holdcroft, James P., Jr. ... New York, NY
Holdefer, Timothy Sean ... Birmingham, AL
Holden, Ann Barrett ... Orleans, MA
Holden, Bill ... Sacramento, CA
Holden, Blythe A. ... Los Angeles, CA
Holden Brothers, P.C. ... New York, NY
White Plains, NY
Holden, Bruce G. ... Irvine, CA
Holden, C. Byron ... Charlotte, NC
Holden, Carol Kischel ... Aurora, CO
Holden, Catharine C. ... San Francisco, CA
Holden, Charles L., Jr. ... Gainesville, FL
Holden, Charles St. George
San Francisco, CA
Holden, Craig E. ... Los Angeles, CA
Holden, Craig L. ... Fryeburg, ME
Holden, Daniel W. ... Orange, CA
Holden, David G. ... Springfield, MO
Holden, David W. ... Tulsa, OK
Holden, Douglas S., (P.C.) ... Golden, CO
Holden, Edna Mae ... Enid, OK
Holden, Edwin H., III
Federal Energy Regulatory Commission, Office of the General Counsel, GV
Holden, Eric A. ... New Orleans, LA
Holden & Fergus ... Orange, CA
Holden, Francis E., Jr. ... Hialeah, FL
Holden, Francis E., Jr., P.A. ... Hialeah, FL
Holden, Frederick D., Jr.
San Francisco, CA
Holden, G. Graham, A Professional Corporation ... Atlanta, GA
Holden, Gail K. ... Spokane, WA
Holden & Garcia ... New Orleans, LA
Holden, George Graham ... Atlanta, GA
Holden, Glendening & McKenna, P.C.
Tulsa, OK
Holden, Gwynne L. ... Bel Air, MD
Holden & Hahn ... Sheboygan, WI
Holden, Helen R. ... Phoenix, AZ
Holden, Helen R., P.C. ... Phoenix, AZ
Holden & Holden ... Shirley, MA
Holden, Howard W.
West Palm Beach, FL
Holden, James B. ... Denver, CO
Holden, James D. ... San Francisco, CA
Holden, James F. ... Hilton Head Island, SC
Holden, James H., Jr.
Federal Trade Commission, Bureau of Competition, GV
Holden, James, Jr. ... White Plains, NY
Holden, James P. ... Washington, DC
Holden, James T. ... Pittsburgh, PA
Holden, James T., Jr. ... Richfield, OH
Holden, Jane ... Mineola, NY
Holden, Jennifer Ann ... Santa Ana, CA
Holden, Jerry J. ... Phoenix, AZ
Holden, John A. ... Bloomington, MN
Holden, John B., Jr., (P.C.) ... Dallas, TX
Holden, John C. ... Minneapolis, MN
Holden, John C. ... Dayton, OH
Holden, John C. ... Bartlesville, OK
Holden, John F., Jr. ... White Plains, NY
Holden, John G. ... Portland, OR
Holden, John K. ... Homewood, IL
Holden, John R. ... Sheboygan, WI
Holden, John T. ... White Plains, NY
Holden, Joseph M. ... Akron, OH
Holden, Juanita E. ... Philadelphia, PA
Holden, Julie B. ... Philadelphia, PA
Holden, Justin S. ... Providence, RI
Holden, Karen S. ... New York, NY
Holden, Kathryn L. ... Hamilton, OH
Holden, Keith B. ... New York, NY
Holden, Kenneth P. ... Syracuse, NY
Holden, Kevin D. ... Richmond, VA

Holden, Kevin L. ... St. Cloud, M[illegible]
Holden, Kidwell, Hahn & Crapo, P.L.L.C.
Idaho Falls, ID
Holden, Lawrence T., Jr. ... Lincoln, MA
Holden, Leta R. ... Denver, CO
Holden, Lisa A. ... Department of Justice, Environment and Natural Resources Division, GV
Holden, Lon T. ... Great Falls, MT
Holden, M. Lance ... Winter Haven, FL
Holden, Margaret Ellis ... Springfield, MO
Holden, Mark A. ... Baton Rouge, LA
Holden, Mark G. ... St. Louis, MO
Holden, Mark V. ... Wichita, KS
Holden, Mary Gayle ... Washington, DC
Holden, Matthew J. ... Harrisburg, PA
Holden, Michael B. ... Fort Lauderdale, FL
Holden, Michael J. ... Phoenix, AZ
Holden, Michael J. ... New York, NY
Holden & O'Brien, Inc. ... Providence, RI
Holden, Oliver, Jr. ... San Antonio, TX
Holden & Oreskovich ... Spokane, WA
Holden Padjen and Laufer LLC
Denver, CO
Holden, Patricia ... Voorhees, NJ
Holden, Patricia S. ... Port Washington, NY
Holden, Patrick F. ... Salt Lake City, UT
Holden, Peter V. ... Bennington, VT
Holden, Rappenecker, Eubank and Mills, P.A. ... Gainesville, FL
Holden, Richard D. ... Cedar Rapids, IA
Holden, Robert E. ... New Orleans, LA
Holden, Robert J. ... Long Branch, NJ
Holden, Robt. U. ... Shirley, MA
Holden, Ronald R. ... Annapolis, MD
Holden, Ross J. ... New York, NY
Holden, S. Craig ... Baltimore, MD
Holden, Scott A. ... Phoenix, AZ
Holden & Steggall ... Cedar Rapids, IA
Holden, Stephen, III ... White Plains, NY
Holden, Stephen J. ... Shawano, WI
Holden, Stephen M. ... Cherry Hill, NJ
Holden, Stephen R. ... Sacramento, CA
Holden, Stephen W. ... Dexter, MO
Jefferson City, MO
Holden, Steven E. ... Tulsa, OK
Holden, Steven M. ... Oklahoma City, OK
Holden, Stewart M. ... Santa Barbara, CA
Holden, Susan M. ... Minneapolis, MN
Holden, Thomas ... Walnut Creek, CA
Holden, Thomas P. ... Schaumburg, IL
Holden, Virgil Leornard ... Norman, OK
Holden, Virginia H. ... Chicago, IL
Holden & Welker ... New York, NY
Holden, William H., Jr. ... Falls Church, VA
Holden, Zachery J. ... Kansas City, MO
Holdenried, John R. ... Omaha, NE
Holden-Smith, Barbara J. ... Ithaca, NY
Holder, Angela Roddey ... New Haven, CT
Holder, Aubrey ... New York, NY
Holder, C. Wayne, & Associates
Freeport, TX
Holder, Campbell M. ... New York, NY
Holder, Carolyn S. ... Lafayette, IN
Holder, Daisy M. ... Birmingham, AL
Holder, Dan W. ... Bloomington, IL
Holder, David Lawrence ... Alexandria, VA
Holder Davis and Smith ... Lafayette, IN
Holder, Eric H., Jr. ... Department of Justice, Office of the Deputy Attorney General, GV
Holder, Eugene L. ... Yucaipa, CA
Holder, E. V., Jr. ... Vanceburg, KY
Holder, Floyd D., Jr., Law Firm of
Lubbock, TX
Holder, Franklin D. ... Fort Smith, AR
Holder, Gary ... Birmingham, AL
Holder, Glenn J. ... Fresno, CA
Holder, Gregory P. ... Tampa, FL
Holder & Holder ... Angleton, TX
Holder, Holly I. ... Denver, CO
Holder, Holly I., P.C. ... Castle Rock, CO
Denver, CO
Holder, J. David ... Tallahassee, FL
Holder, James T. ... Clearwater, FL
Holder, Janice M. ... Memphis, TN
Holder, John M. ... Vanceburg, KY
Holder, Jon F. ... Portland, ME
Holder, Kathy Paulette ... Louisville, KY
Holder, Kenneth C. ... Kew Gardens, NY
Holder, Lewis C. ... Horseshoe Bay, TX
Holder, Linda L. ... Granite City, IL
Holder, Lofton P. ... New York, NY
Holder & Lykins, P.S.C. ... Vanceburg, KY
Holder, Lynne L. ... Houston, TX
Holder, Marc W. ... Angleton, TX
Holder, Moore, Lawrence & Langley
Fayette, AL
Holder, Phillip A. ... Austin, TX
Holder, Randall J. ... Tulsa, OK
Holder, Robert L. ... Columbus, OH
Holder, Stephanie G. ... Spokane, WA
Holder, Terri Tipton ... Angleton, TX
Holder, Thomas L. ... Atlanta, GA
College Park, GA
Holder, Timothy D. ... Brooklyn Heights, OH
Holder, Wayne A. ... New York, NY
Holder, W. F. (Bubba), II ... Gulfport, MS
Holder, William D., Jr. ... Key Biscayne, FL
Holder, William L. ... Seattle, WA
Holder, William P., Jr. ... Fairlawn, OH
Holder, William W. ... Phoenix, AZ
Holderead, Jerome T. ... Marion, IN
Holderle, Karl E., III ... St. Louis, MO
Holderman & Associates ... Cleveland, OH
Holderman, Gretchen A. ... Cleveland, OH
Holderman, James F. ... Chicago, IL
Holderman, Mark V. ... Columbus, OH
Holderman, Paula Hudson ... Chicago, IL

[illegible], Richard A. ... Washington, DC
[illegible] Bradley, Elizabeth ... Columbia, SC
[illegible]ess, A. Sidney, Jr. ... Houston, TX
Hol[illegible]ess, Howard, III
San Francisco, CA
Holderness, Kevin J. ... Boise, ID
Holderness Law Firm, The ... Auburn, CA
Folsom, CA
Jackson, CA
Placerville, CA
Sacramento, CA
Holderness, Richard A.
San Francisco, CA
Holderness, Robert G. ... Folsom, CA
Holderness, Thomas P. ... Charlotte, NC
Holdford, William H. ... Wilson, NC
Holdgrafer, Michael E. ... Tulsa, OK
Holdgreiwe, Daniel C. ... Washington, DC
Holding, Cheryl A. ... Mercer Island, WA
Holding, Christopher T. ... Boston, MA
Holding, Dana Ziegler
Fort Lauderdale, FL
Holding, Graham D., Jr. ... Charlotte, NC
Holding, Megan C. ... Boston, MA
Holditch, C. John ... Birmingham, AL
Holdman, Robert K. ... Bronx, NY
Holdman, Travis L. ... Markle, IN
Holdmann, Lee F. ... Annapolis, MD
Bethesda, MD
Frederick, MD
La Plata, MD
Leonardtown, MD
Holdmann, Lee F., Chartered
Washington, DC
Annapolis, MD
Bethesda, MD
Frederick, MD
La Plata, MD
Leonardtown, MD
Holdorf, Paul S. ... Summit, NJ
Holdorff, Allison M. ... Pacific Palisades, CA
Holdredge, John A. ... Santa Rosa, CA
Holdrege, Elizabeth A. ... Atlanta, GA
Holdreith, Jake M. ... Minneapolis, MN
Holdren, W. Douglas ... Horsham, PA
Holdridge, Christopher ... Westmoreland, VA
Holdridge, Guy ... Gonzales, LA
Holdridge, John ... New Orleans, LA
Holdridge, William E. ... Peoria, IL
Holdsman, Gabriel H. ... Mount Laurel, NJ
Philadelphia, PA
Holdsman, Kenneth B. ... Philadelphia, PA
Holdstock, Charles ... Oklahoma City, OK
Holdsworth, Curtis P. ... Irvine, CA
Holdsworth, David J. ... Sandy, UT
Holdsworth, David K. ... Liberty, MO
Holdsworth, Janine L. ... Lowell, MA
Holdsworth, K. Jay ... Salt Lake City, UT
Holdsworth, Lynn D. ... Boston, MA
Holdsworth, Mark A. ... New York, NY
Holdsworth, Michael L. ... Phoenix, AZ
Holdsworth, Patricia P.
Owings Mills, MD
Holdsworth, Robert J., Jr. ... Ithaca, NY
Holdway, David C., III ... San Diego, CA
Holdway, Robert G. ... Boston, MA
Holdwick, Daniel J. ... Marquette, MI
Holdych, Thomas J. ... Tacoma, WA
Hole, Brian K. ... Fort Lauderdale, FL
Hole, Geoffrey H. ... Portland, ME
Hole, James C. ... Bellevue, WA
Hole, Lewis L. ... Harrison, MI
Hole, Richard D. ... Syracuse, NY
Hole, Richard E., II ... Greenville, OH
Hole, Robert R. ... Martinez, CA
Hole, Ronald G., Law Offices of
McAllen, TX
Hole, Sonja M. ... Asheboro, NC
Holec, David A. ... Lumberton, NC
Holecek, Christopher A. ... Cleveland, OH
Holecek, Tanja M. ... Cleveland, OH
Hole-Curry, Leah ... Olympia, WA
Holefca, Deborah G. ... Bloomfield Hills, MI
Holeman, Brian F. ... Washington, DC
Holeman, Clarence D. ... Wichita, KS
Holeman, Daniel E., P.C. ... Tulsa, OK
Holeman, Jacob J. ... Portland, OR
Holeman, Joseph A. ... Tacoma, WA
Holeman, William D. ... Memphis, TN
Holen, Lee, Law Office ... Anchorage, AK
Holen, Marvin L. ... Los Angeles, CA
Holenski, Mark A. ... Buffalo, NY
Holers, Jeffrey F. ... Winter Springs, FL
Holert, Ronald F. ... Tarzana, CA
Holesinger, Russell J. ... Fulton, IL
Morrison, IL
Holeski, Walter L. ... Lyndhurst, OH
Holett, Steven G. ... Monarch Beach, CA
Holevas, John J. ... Rockford, IL
Holewinski, Ann ... Denver, CO
Holewinski, Debra ... Green Bay, WI
Holewinski, Kevin P. ... Pittsburgh, PA
Holfeld & Becker ... Dover, DE
Wilmington, DE
Holfeld, Stephen J. ... Wilmington, DE
Holfester, Michael K. ... Garden City, NY
Holford, Alden D. (Doug) ... Houston, TX
Holford, Gary A. ... Tustin, CA
Holford, Maureen P. ... Fresno, CA
Holford, Neal S. ... Dallas, TX
Holgate, Denyce ... Jericho, NY
Holgate, Trent D. ... Logan, UT
Holgate, Willard G. ... Altoona, WI
Holgerson, John L. ... New Bedford, MA
Holguin, Claudia Roberta ... Los Angeles, CA
Holguin, Henry A. ... Los Angeles, CA
Holguin, John R. ... Silver City, NM
Holguín, Salvador O. ... Cerritos, CA

Holguin, Steven R. ... Los Angeles, CA
Holguin, Vida M. ... Manhattan Beach, CA
Holian, Thomas P.
Department of Transportation, Federal Highway Administration, GV
Holian, Victoria A. ... Boston, MA
Holiber, James M. ... Bayonne, NJ
Holiber, Judith A. ... San Francisco, CA
Holicky, Bruce J. ... Aurora, CO
Holiday, Ann L. ... Los Angeles, CA
Holiday, Cecily C.
Federal Communications Commission, International Bureau, GV
Holiday, Debra A. ... San Jose, CA
Holiday, Edith E. ... Washington, DC
Holiday, James E. ... New Palestine, IN
Holiday, Kathleen ... Eagan, MN
Holiday Law Firm P.C. ... Stoughton, MA
Wellesley Hills, MA
Holiday, Michael ... Stoughton, MA
Holiday, Newton S., III ... Nashville, TN
Holidy, Dale M." Rett " ... Beaumont, TX
Houston, TX
Holien, Sandra J. ... Marshalltown, IA
Holifield, Bishop C. ... Tallahassee, FL
Holifield, Dennis J. ... Ocean Springs, MS
Holifield, George W., Jr. ... Seattle, WA
Holifield, James A. (Al) ... Knoxville, TN
Holifield, Johnathan M. ... Cincinnati, OH
Holifield, Marilyn J. ... Miami, FL
Holifield, T. Joe ... Paragould, AR
Holifield, Teresa R. ... Flint, MI
Holifield, Thomas J. ... Laurel, MS
Holifield, W. Major ... Laurel, MS
Holihan Diaz ... Maitland, FL
Orlando, FL
Holihan, Gary M. ... Chicago, IL
Holihan, Gavin P. ... Allentown, PA
Holihan, Margaret ... New York, NY
Holihan, Michael W. O. ... Maitland, FL
Holihen, Terrence R. ... Orlando, FL
Holik, Susan Z. ... Washington, DC
Holiman, Harvey H. ... Freeport, TX
Holiman, M. Christine ... Lebanon, MO
Holiman, Richard E. ... Little Rock, AR
Holiman, Susan C. ... Department of Justice, Drug Enforcement Administration, GV
Holincheck, Michael A.
Department Of Veterans Affairs, Board of Veterans Appeals, GV
Holinder, Sara Judith ... New York, NY
Holiner, Emil W. ... San Antonio, TX
Holingue, David R., Ltd. ... Chicago, IL
Holinka, John G. ... Buffalo, NY
Holinsky, Ronald A.
Securities and Exchange Commission, GV
Holinstat, Steven H. ... New York, NY
Holiona, Hope Malia ... Department of Justice, Executive Office for Immigration Review, GV
Holisky, Jerald ... Chicago, IL
Holitik, Diane Schratz ... Memphis, TN
Holitzke, Pat H. ... Flint, TX
Holjes, Crystal S. ... Pompano Beach, FL
Holk, Eric N. ... Carmel, CA
Holkeboer, Dirk J. ... Orland Park, IL
Holkeboer, Van E. ... Chicago, IL
Holker, Kenneth M. ... Monticello, MN
Holko, Joseph A. ... Allentown, PA
Holko, Mark E. ... Columbus, OH
Holl, Albert E., Jr. ... Media, PA
Holl, Alfred O. ... Oklahoma City, OK
Holl, David J. ... Horsham, PA
Holl, Jeffrey P. ... San Francisco, CA
Holl, Jorn A. ... New York, NY
Holl, Kevin J. ... San Francisco, CA
Holl, Philip K. ... Los Angeles, CA
Holl, Robert E. ... Philadelphia, PA
Hollaar, Audrey M. ... Salt Lake City, UT
Hollabaugh, Jacalyn A. ... Houston, TX
Hollabaugh, James M. ... Fremont, CA
Hollabaugh, Lela M. ... Nashville, TN
Hollabaugh, Lewis B. ... Nashville, TN
Hollabaugh, Raymond A. ... Stamford, TX
Holladay, C. Randolph ... New York, NY
Holladay, David A. ... Lexington, KY
Holladay, Don G. ... Oklahoma City, OK
Holladay, Durand A. ... Charlotte, NC
Holladay, Harry R. ... New Orleans, LA
Holladay, H. E. ... Pell City, AL
Holladay, Hugh E. ... Pell City, AL
Holladay, Jayson C. ... Pocatello, ID
Holladay, John Ross ... Mobile, AL
Holladay, Kimberly D. ... Atlanta, GA
Holladay, Louis P. ... Wilmington, DE
Holladay, Marcus B. ... Washington, DC
Holladay, N. Victoria ... Memphis, TN
Holladay, Philip E., Jr. ... Atlanta, GA
Holladay, Richard F., Jr. ... Virginia Beach, VA
Holladay, Richard F., P.C.
Virginia Beach, VA
Holladay, Robert Lawson ... Drew, MS
Holladay, S. David ... Baton Rouge, LA
Holladay, W. Paul, Jr. ... Houston, TX
Hollaender, Kim ... Philadelphia, PA
Hollahan, Michael J. ... Pittsfield, IL
Hollan, Albert E. ... Houston, TX
Hollan, Robert J. ... Rapid City, SD
Hollan, Rosemary L. ... San Antonio, TX
Holland, A. Randolph, Jr. ... Falls Church, VA
Holland, Alan R. ... Falls Church, VA
Holland, Alexander J. ... Greenwich, CT
Holland, Alfred E. ... Sacramento, CA
Holland, Alfred J. ... Paragould, AR
Holland, Alice ... Fort Worth, TX
Holland, Alicia M. ... Irvine, CA
Holland, Andrew R. ... New York, NY
Holland, Ann Madigan ... Beaumont, TX

Holland & Associates ... Houston, TX
Holland, Audrey H. ... Huntington Beach, CA
Holland, Barbara J. ... Haverford, PA
Holland, Barbara L. ... Seattle, WA
Holland, Baxter F. ... New York, NY
Holland, Bill D. ... West Monroe, LA
Holland, Billie D., Law Offices of, A Professional Law Corporation
West Monroe, LA
Holland & Bonzagni, P.C.
Longmeadow, MA
Springfield, MA
Holland, Brantseg & Ash ... Sisseton, SD
Holland, Brendan ... Washington, DC
Holland, Brennan T. ... San Antonio, TX
Holland, Brian ... Butte, MT
Holland, Brian ... Houston, TX
Holland, Brian G. ... Morrisville, NC
Holland, Brian K. ... Denver, CO
Holland, Brian P. ... Bushnell, IL
Holland, Bruce ... Providence, RI
Holland, Bryce L., Jr. ... Seattle, WA
Holland, C. Joseph ... Iowa City, IA
Holland, C. Thomas ... Crestview, FL
Holland, C. Warren ... Indianapolis, IN
Holland, Carol F. ... San Antonio, TX
Holland, Carol V. ... Oakland, CA
Holland, Catherine J.
Newport Beach, CA
Holland, Cecil F., Jr. ... New York, NY
Holland, Celeste R. ... Jacksonville, FL
Holland, Charles D. ... Palo Alto, CA
Holland, Charles M. ... Landover, MD
Holland, Charles P. ... San Diego, CA
Holland, Charlotte A. ... Atlanta, GA
Holland, Charlton G., III ... Oakland, CA
Holland, Cheryl A. ... Los Angeles, CA
Holland, Christopher A.
Albuquerque, NM
Holland, Christopher A. ... Nashville, TN
Holland, Christopher M. ... Houston, TX
Holland, Christopher T.
San Francisco, CA
Holland, Claire M. ... Boston, MA
Holland, Clarence H. ... Jackson, MS
Holland, Clarke B. ... San Francisco, CA
Holland, Clinton W. ... La Habra, CA
Holland, Clinton W., Inc., A Prof. Law. Corp.
La Habra, CA
Holland, Clyde Paul ... Nashville, TN
Holland, Craig D. ... New York, NY
Holland, Curtis M. ... Overland Park, KS
Holland, Dalton ... Harper, KS
Holland, Daniel E., Jr. ... Rocky Hill, CT
Holland, Daniel G. ... Boston, MA
Holland, Daniel M. ... Eugene, OR
Holland, Daniel R. ... Concord, MA
Holland, Darrell W. ... North Canton, OH
Holland, David E. ... Fresno, CA
Holland, David E. ... Erie, PA
Holland, David F. ... Des Plaines, IL
Holland, David L., (P.C.) ... Butte, MT
Holland, David P. ... Tulsa, OK
Holland, David R. ... Cleveland, OH
Holland, David S. ... Alexandria, VA
Holland, David S. ... Virginia Beach, VA
Holland, David W. ... Williamsburg, VA
Holland, David Wes ... San Antonio, TX
Holland & Delaney ... Falmouth, MA
Holland, Dempster K. ... St. Louis, MO
Holland, Dennis K. ... Chicago, IL
Holland, Diane G. ... Melville, NY
Holland, Dick R. ... Midland, TX
Holland, Don R. ... Sacramento, CA
Holland, Donald H. ... Camden, SC
Holland, Donald J., (P.C.) ... Malone, NY
Holland, Donald R. ... St. Louis, MO
Holland, Donald S. ... Longmeadow, MA
Springfield, MA
Holland & Donnelly ... Monrovia, CA
Holland, Donovan, Beckett, Hermans & Davison, Professional Association
Exeter, NH
Holland, Douglas C. ... Lawrenceburg, IN
Rising Sun, IN
Holland, Edward M. ... Arlington, VA
Holland, Edward M. ... Falls Church, VA
Holland, Edward W., Jr. ... Palo Alto, CA
Holland, E. J., Jr. ... Kansas City, MO
Holland, Elizabeth J. ... New York, NY
Holland, Elva M. ... Washington, DC
Holland & Endres ... Tyler, TX
Holland, Eric D. ... North Little Rock, AR
St. Louis, MO
Holland, Fern ... Tulsa, OK
Holland, Frances Chasan ... West Orange, NJ
Holland, Frances Schmid ... Dallas, TX
Holland, Francis G. ... Nashua, NH
Holland, Frank L. ... Newark, NJ
Holland, Franklin B. ... Philadelphia, PA
Holland, Fred A. ... Williamsport, PA
Holland, G. Edison, Jr. ... Savannah, GA
Holland, G. Lance ... San Marcos, TX
Holland, Gary C. ... Daytona Beach, FL
Holland, Gary Lindsey ... Daytona Beach, FL
Holland, George ... Oakland, CA
Holland, George D. ... Sacramento, CA
Holland, George M. ... Wayne, NJ
Holland, George T. ... Tyler, TX
Holland, George V. ... Milford, MA
Holland, George W. ... Russell, KS
Holland, Gilbert Harrison ... Houston, TX
Holland, Greg ... Los Angeles, CA
Holland, Gregory D. ... Jacksonville, FL
Holland, Gregory F. ... Richmond, VA
Holland, Gregory G. ... Greensboro, NC
Holland, Gregory L. ... Reseda, CA
Holland, Gretchen D. ... Columbia, SC
Holland, Gwenn Dorb ... At[illegible]
Holland, H. Brian ... Bo[illegible]A
Holland, H. Russel ... Ancho[illegible], AK
Holland, Haman W. ... Wilmington, NC
Holland & Hart ... Cheyenne, WY
Jackson, WY
Holland & Hart LLP ... Aspen, CO
Boulder, CO
Colorado Springs, CO
Denver, CO
Greenwood Village, CO
Boise, ID
Billings, MT
Salt Lake City, UT
Holland, Heidi S. ... Spokane, WA
Holland, Hilde ... New York, NY
Holland and Holland ... St. Petersburg, FL
Holland & Holland ... Ashburn, GA
Holland and Holland ... Bushnell, IL
Holland and Holland ... Cairo, IL
Mound City, IL
Holland & Holland ... Indianapolis, IN
Holland & Holland, A Professional Corporation
West Orange, NJ
Holland & Holland, (Associated)
Chicago, IL
Holland and Holland Law Offices
Knoxville, TN
San Antonio, TX
Holland, J. Allen, Jr. ... Boston, MA
Holland, J. Jeffrey ... Somersworth, NH
Holland, J. Kent ... Salt Lake City, UT
Holland, J. Kent, Jr. ... Washington, DC
Vienna, VA
Holland, J. Mark ... Newport Beach, CA
Holland, J. Terry ... Knoxville, TN
Holland, J. Walker, (P.C.)
Fort Worth, TX
Holland, J. William ... Chicago, IL
Holland, Jack H. ... Athens, TX
Holland, Jack K. ... Atlanta, GA
Holland, James C. ... Ventura, CA
Holland, James C. ... Kansas City, MO
Holland, James C., Jr. (P.C.) ... Houston, TX
Holland, James D. ... Jackson, MS
Holland, James Erwin ... Horn Lake, MS
Holland, James G. ... Indianapolis, IN
Holland, James P. ... Charleston, WV
Holland, James R., II ... Birmingham, AL
Jacksonville, FL
Atlanta, GA
Holland, James R., II ... Kansas City, MO
Holland, James W. ... Columbus, IN
Holland, Janet M. ... Novato, CA
Holland, Jay P. ... Greenbelt, MD
Holland, Jay Putnam ... La Quinta, CA
Holland, Jennifer L. ... Anchorage, AK
Holland, Jerry H. ... Carthage, TX
Holland, John ... Denton, TX
Holland, John A. ... Sacramento, CA
Holland, John D. ... Wilmington, CA
Holland, John G. ... Fort Smith, AR
Holland, John G. ... Washington, DC
Holland, John G. ... Cairo, IL
Holland, John G., Jr. ... Cairo, IL
Holland, John G., Jr. ... New York, NY
Holland, John Howard ... Ashburn, GA
Holland, John J. Cosmo ... Harrisburg, PA
Holland, John M. ... Bedford, TX
Holland, John R. ... Denver, CO
Holland, John R. ... Warren, MI
Holland, John R. ... Pittsburgh, PA
Holland, John R., P.C. ... Denver, CO
Holland, John S. ... Manchester, NH
Holland, John W., Jr. ... Falmouth, MA
Holland, Johns & Schwartz, L.L.P.
Fort Worth, TX
Holland, Jon E. ... Atlanta, GA
Holland, Jon Michael ... Fredericksburg, VA
Holland, Joseph ... White Plains, NY
Holland, Joseph L. ... Bethesda, MD
Holland, Joseph T. ... San Diego, CA
Holland, Joseph W. ... Boise, ID
Holland, Julie F. ... Ames, IA
Holland, Julie M. ... Mount Laurel, NJ
Philadelphia, PA
Holland, Kaplan & Pagliuca, P.C.
Denver, CO
Holland, Karen P. ... New Orleans, LA
Holland, Kathryn E. ... Vancouver, WA
Holland Kaufmann & Bartels, LLC
Greenwich, CT
Stamford, CT
Holland, Kenneth A. ... Bakersfield, CA
Holland, Kenneth D. ... Monrovia, CA
Holland, Kenneth L. ... Gaffney, SC
Holland, Kenneth L., P.A. ... Gaffney, SC
Holland & Knight LLP
San Francisco, CA
Washington, DC
Bradenton, FL
Fort Lauderdale, FL
Jacksonville, FL
Lakeland, FL
Melbourne, FL
Miami, FL
Orlando, FL
St. Petersburg, FL
Tallahassee, FL
Tampa, FL
West Palm Beach, FL
Atlanta, GA
Boston, MA
Falls Church, VA
Holland, Kristin L. ... Los Angeles, CA
Holland, Lamoine ... San Antonio, TX
Holland, Laurel Anne ... Austin, TX
Holland, Lauren S. ... Eugene, OR
Holland Law Office, The ... Albuquerque, NM
Holland Law Offices ... Fairfield, CA
Holland, Lawrence R. ... Boston, MA
Holland, Leonard ... New York, NY
Holland, Leonard R. ... Dayton, IA
Holland, Lesley D. ... Stockton, CA
Holland, Leslie Lindley ... Canadian, TX
Holland, Lori W. ... Jackson, MS
Holland, Louis F. ... Reno, NV
Holland, Lyman F., Jr. ... Mobile, AL
Holland, Marcella A. ... Baltimore, MD
Holland, Marcy F. ... Denver, CO
Holland, Margaret A. ... Trenton, NJ
Holland, Margaret E., (P.C.)
Fort Worth, TX
Holland, Margaret M. ... Boston, MA
Holland, Mark ... New York, NY
Holland, Mark ... San Antonio, TX
Holland, Mark B. ... Danville, VA
Holland, Mark H. ... Denver, CO
Holland, Mark, P.C. ... San Antonio, TX
Holland, Martha Carol ... Nashville, TN
Holland, Martha J. ... Houston, TX
Holland, Martin K. ... Albuquerque, NM
Holland, Martin O. ... Chicago, IL
Holland, Marvin A. ... Brooklyn, NY
Holland, Marvin S. ... Pawtucket, RI
Holland, Mary S. ... New York, NY
Holland, Max K. ... Sylva, NC
Holland, Michael ... Salem, OR
Holland, Michael H. ... Chicago, IL
Holland, Michael J. ... New York, NY
Holland, Michael L. ... Houston, TX
Holland, Michael P. ... Boston, MA
Holland, Michael S. ... Russell, KS
Holland, Michael S., II ... Russell, KS
Holland, Michael W. ... Indianapolis, IN
Holland, Michael W. ... Minneapolis, MN
Holland, Michael W. ... Williston Park, NY
Holland, Michael W. ... Beloit, WI
Holland, Michelle D. ... Denver, CO
Holland, Mike ... Seattle, WA
Holland, Mona ... New York, NY
Holland, Nancy E. ... Burbank, CA
Holland, Nathaniel L., Jr. ... Mullica Hill, NJ
Holland, Nigel B. ... Columbia, SC
Holland, Noel R. ... Midland Park, NJ
Holland, Pamela ... Washington, DC
Holland, Patricia ... Chicago, IL
Holland, Patricia A. ... Chicago, IL
Holland, Patricia L. ... Raleigh, NC
Holland, Paul G., Jr. ... Stamford, CT
Holland, Peter A. ... Annapolis, MD
Holland, Peter A., P.A. ... Annapolis, MD
Stevensville, MD
Holland, Peter M. ... Hartford, CT
Holland, Poole, Holland & Sanderson, P.A.
Clinton, NC
Holland, R. Morgan ... San Diego, CA
Holland, Ralph L. ... Tupelo, MS
Holland, Randall A. ... Orange, CA
Holland, Randy J. ... Georgetown, DE
Holland, Ray ... Ashburn, GA
Holland, Ray, Upchurch & Hillen, P.A.
Aberdeen, MS
Oxford, MS
Tupelo, MS
Holland, Raymond C., Jr. ... Tiverton, RI
Holland, Raymond R. ... San Francisco, CA
Holland, Raymond W. ... Las Vegas, NV
Holland, Richard M. ... Williamsville, NY
Holland, Rick ... Louisville, KY
Holland, Robert A. ... Los Angeles, CA
Holland, Robert B. ... Huntington Beach, CA
Holland, Robert B., III ... Dallas, TX
Holland, Robert E. ... Boston, MA
Holland, Robert H. ... Bethlehem, PA
Holland, Robert J. ... Butte, MT
Holland, Robert J. ... Columbus, OH
Holland, Robert L. ... Monroe, NC
Holland, Robert L. ... West Union, WV
Holland, Robert L., Jr. ... West Union, WV
Holland, Robert L., P.A. ... Monroe, NC
Holland, Robert M. ... Ormond Beach, FL
Holland, Robert M. ... Spartanburg, SC
Holland, Robert M., Jr. ... Nashville, TN
Holland, Robert S. ... Honolulu, HI
Holland, Robert S. ... Knoxville, TN
Holland, Robert T. ... New York, NY
Holland, Robert V., Jr. ... Houston, TX
Holland, Robert W. ... Miami, FL
Holland, Robert W. ... Austin, TX
Holland, Robin E. McCann
Mercer Island, WA
Holland & Robinson ... Honolulu, HI
Holland, Roger William ... Urbana, IL
Holland, Ronald J., II ... San Francisco, CA
Holland, Ronald W. ... Fairfield, CA
Holland, Roscoe" Ross "M., Jr.
Clinton, NC
Holland, S. Aaron ... Fort Worth, TX
Holland, Samara S. ... Naples, FL
Holland, Samuel C. ... Beaver, PA
Holland & Scott ... Denver, CO
Holland, Shannon M. ... Knoxville, TN
Holland, Shaylee N. ... Woodland Hills, CA
Holland, Sheri E. ... Red Bank, NJ
New York, NY
Holland, Stephen E. ... Bushnell, IL
Holland, Steven A. ... Bartlesville, OK
Holland, Steven B. ... Chicago, IL
Holland, Steven J. ... Minneapolis, MN
Holland, Steven N. ... Palo Alto, CA
Holland, Steven W. ... Evanston, WY
Holland, Susan L. ... San Rafael, CA
Holland, Susan M. ... Tucson, AZ
Holland, Suzanne J., (P.C.)
Los Angeles, CA
Holland, Suzanne K. ... Akron, OH
Holland & Sweat ... Daytona Beach, FL
Holland, Sweet & Barr ... Wood River, IL
Holland, Terry ... McRae, GA
Holland, Thalia J. ... Boston, MA
Holland, Thomas J. ... Adams, MA
Holland, Thomas More ... Hainesport, NJ
Philadelphia, PA
Holland, Thomas R. ... Boston, MA
Holland, Thomas W. ... Wood River, IL
Holland, Timothy J. ... Wilkes-Barre, PA
Holland, Tom L. ... Tulsa, OK
Holland, Tommy T. ... Atlanta, GA
Holland, Tracy Jolles ... San Francisco, CA
Holland, Troy D. ... Mendota, IL
Holland, Troy W. ... St. Petersburg, FL
Holland, Tucker & Oliveros ... Miami, FL
Holland, Verda A. ... Phoenix, AZ
Holland, W. Langston ... St. Petersburg, FL
Holland, W. A., Jr. ... Smithfield, NC
Holland, Wallace G. ... Charleston, SC
Holland, Walter Sam ... Miami, FL
Holland, Wendell F. ... Philadelphia, PA
Holland, William C. ... Denver, CO
Holland, William E. ... Valdosta, GA
Holland, William E. ... New York, NY
Holland, William G. ... Gastonia, NC
Holland, William K. ... St. Louis, MO
Holland, William M. ... Lake Park, FL
Holland, William M. ... Rusk, TX
Holland, William M., Jr. ... Tampa, FL
Holland, Woodrow A. ... Houston, TX
Holland, Zera J. ... Olympia, WA
Holland-Chatman, Jan A. ... Washington, DC
Hollander, Adam K. ... Chicago, IL
Hollander, Alan S. ... Wilkes-Barre, PA
Hollander, Allison B. ... New York, NY
Hollander, Andrew J. ... New York, NY
Hollander, Barry I. ... Fairfax, VA
Hollander, Barry M. ... St. Louis, MO
Hollander, Bart Q ... Trenton, NJ
Hollander & Bartelstone ... Miami, FL
Hollander, Bernard M.
Department of Justice,
Antitrust Division, GV
Hollander, Brian Wade ... Chicago, IL
Hollander, C. Jay ... Point Richmond, CA
Hollander, Carl R. ... New York, NY
Hollander and Company, L.L.C.
New York, NY
Hollander, David A. ... Los Angeles, CA
Hollander, David B. ... Plano, TX
Hollander, David H., Jr. ... Baltimore, MD
Hollander, David J. ... San Diego, CA
Hollander, David J. ... Portland, OR
Hollander, Ellen Lipton ... Baltimore, MD
Hollander, Eugene C. ... Indianapolis, IN
Hollander, Eugene K., Law Offices of, The
Chicago, IL
Hollander, Evan C. ... New York, NY
Hollander, Fredda ... Boston, MA
Hollander, Gary P. ... Chicago, IL
Hollander, Geoffrey S. ... New York, NY
Hollander, George M. ... Chicago, IL
Hollander, Harry ... New York, NY
Hollander, Howard ... New York, NY
Hollander, Howard D. ... Chicago, IL
Hollander, Howard J. ... Miami, FL
Hollander & Irion ... San Francisco, CA
Hollander, Jacob ... New York, NY
Hollander, James F. ... Dallas, TX
Hollander, James R. ... San Francisco, CA
Hollander, Jay ... New York, NY
Hollander, Jay M. ... Woodbridge, NJ
Hollander, Jeanie Fiskin ... Glendale, CA
Hollander, Jeffrey B. ... Grand Blanc, MI
Hollander, Jeffry ... New York, NY
Hollander, Joseph H. ... Kalamazoo, MI
Hollander, Larry B. ... Clifton, NJ
Garden City, NY
New York, NY
Hollander, Lauren M. ... New York, NY
Hollander Law Firm, P.L.C.
Washington, DC
Fairfax, VA
Hollander, Lee ... Naples, FL
Hollander, Marlene S. ... New York, NY
Hollander, Mitchell D. ... New York, NY
Hollander, Nancy ... Albuquerque, NM
Hollander, Paul S. ... Fort Lee, NJ
Hollander, Rachel L. ... New York, NY
Hollander, Reed J. ... Raleigh, NC
Hollander, Rhonda ... Hollywood, FL
Hollander, Rhonda G. ... Boston, MA
Hollander, Richard A. ... Richmond, VA
Hollander, Richard J. ... Naples, FL
Hollander, Robert S. ... Farmington Hills, MI
Hollander, Ronald A. ... New York, NY
Hollander, Ross A. ... Wichita, KS
Hollander, Russell S. ... New York, NY
Hollander, Sam ... New York, NY
Hollander, Sanford Lloyd ... Newton, NJ
Hollander, Sheila B. ... Oakland, CA
Hollander, Strauss & Mastropietro, L.L.P.
Clifton, NJ
Newark, NJ
Albany, NY
Brooklyn, NY
Garden City, NY
New York, NY
White Plains, NY
Hollander, Stuart J. ... Suttons Bay, MI
Hollander, Susan E. ... San Francisco, CA
Hollander, Thomas ... Pittsburgh, PA
Hollander, Toby H. ... Lewiston, ME
Hollander & Tocco, PLC ... Suttons Bay, MI
Hollander, Walter J. ... Hollywood, FL
Hollander, William H. ... Louisville, KY

Hollins-Davidson, Virginia ......Richmond, CA
Hollinshead, Barbara A. ......Pittsburgh, PA
Hollinshead, E. D., Jr. ......Pittsburgh, PA
Hollinshead, Linda B. ......Philadelphia, PA
Hollinshead, Warren H. ......Pittsburgh, PA
Hollis, André D. ......House of Representatives, Congressional Assistants, GV
Hollis, Bernadette M. ......Glens Falls, NY
Hollis, Brandon J. ......Seattle, WA
Hollis, Castles R. ......Atlanta, GA
Hollis, Charles F., III ......Cincinnati, OH
Hollis, Charles Franklin, III ......Atlanta, GA
Hollis, Charles H. ......New Orleans, LA
Hollis, Cheryl A. ......Doylestown, OH
Hollis, Debra ......Montgomery, AL
Hollis, Debra L.
Department Of Health And Human Services, Office of the General Counsel, GV
Hollis, Debra, P.C. ......Montgomery, AL
Hollis, Duncan B. ......Department of State, Office of the Legal Adviser, GV
Hollis, Edward E., III ......Indianapolis, IN
Hollis, Everett L. ......Chicago, IL
Hollis, Gideon ......New York, NY
Hollis, Graham S. P., (Inc.) ......San Diego, CA
Hollis, Henry A. ......Davenport, IA
Hollis, Howell, III ......Atlanta, GA
Hollis, James G. ......Rockville, MD
Hollis, James M. ......Little Rock, AR
Hollis, James N. ......San Antonio, TX
Hollis, Jeffrey K. ......Birmingham, AL
Hollis, John L. ......Albuquerque, NM
Hollis, John L., P.A. ......Albuquerque, NM
Hollis, John M. ......Virginia Beach, VA
Hollis, John W. ......Newbury Park, CA
Hollis and Johnson ......Chicago, IL
Hollis, Keith J. ......Santa Ana, CA
Hollis, L. Andrew, Jr. ......Birmingham, AL
Hollis, Laurence R. ......Wichita, KS
Hollis, Laurie E. ......Crosby, TX
Hollis, Leathers & Leathers ......Fayette, AL
Hollis, Leathers & Leathers, P.C.
Winfield, AL
Hollis, Lee J. ......Prairie Village, KS
Hollis, Lee M. ......Birmingham, AL
Hollis, Leigh Anna ......Chattanooga, TN
Hollis, Lori R. ......Chicago, IL
Hollis & Mauerman ......Santa Ana, CA
Hollis & Montgomery ......Portland, OR
Hollis, Morgan A. ......Nashua, NH
Hollis, Murry C., Jr. ......Winfield, AL
Hollis, Nicholas P. ......Lowell, MA
Hollis, Orlando John ......Eugene, OR
Hollis, P. Daniel, III ......Mount Kisco, NY
Hollis, Pamela S. ......Chicago, IL
Hollis, Paula J. ......Dallas, TX
Hollis, Paula Sanders, Inc. ......Dallas, TX
Hollis, Phillip G. ......Camden, TN
Hollis, Richard A. ......Springfield, IL
Hollis, Richard Ray ......Des Moines, IA
Hollis, Robert ......Inverness, IL
Hollis, Robert M. ......Department of Justice, Civil Division, GV
Hollis, Robert R. ......Portland, OR
Hollis, Samuel B., Jr. ......Morgan, GA
Hollis, Scott Burnham ......Greenwood, MS
Hollis, Sheila Slocum ......Washington, DC
Hollis, Stacie M. ......New Orleans, LA
Hollis, Steven A., (P.C.) ......Dallas, TX
Hollis, Steven E. ......Houston, TX
Hollis, W. Joseph, Jr. ......Chattanooga, TN
Hollis-Ross, Shari D. ......San Francisco, CA
Hollister & Brace, A Professional Corporation ......Santa Barbara, CA
Hollister, C. L. ......Bellingham, WA
Hollister, Gail D. ......New York, NY
Hollister, George C., Law Offices of
Sacramento, CA
Hollister, J. James, III
Santa Barbara, CA
Hollister, Jeffrey L. ......Marietta, OH
Hollister, John A. ......Hammond, LA
Hollister, John C. ......Atlanta, GA
Hollister, Jonathan D. ......Honolulu, HI
Hollister, Leiby, Hanna & Rasnick
Akron, OH
Hollister, Lindsay ......New York, NY
Hollister, P. Keyburn ......Pittsfield, MA
Hollister, Raymond L. ......Moline, IL
Hollister, Robert B. ......Findlay, OH
Hollister, Terry R. ......Akron, OH
Hollister, Timothy S. ......Hartford, CT
Holliway, William E. ......Towson, MD
Hollman, Amy K. ......Boston, MA
Hollman, Charles D. ......Westminster, MD
Hollman, Dennis W. ......Milwaukee, WI
Hollman, Donald L. ......Friendship, WI
Hollman, Gary A. ......Milwaukee, WI
Hollman, Harold L. ......Chamberlain, SD
Hollman & Hollman ......Chamberlain, SD
Hollman, Hughes, Finch & Maguire, Chartered ......Baltimore, MD
Westminster, MD
Hollman, James E. ......Saipan, TT
Hollman, James W. ......Porterville, CA
Hollman, K. Hollyn ......Nashville, TN
Hollman, Lawrence D. ......Washington, DC
Hollman, Lewis J. ......Pacoima, CA
Hollman, Mary E. ......West Bloomfield, MI
Hollman, Michael C. ......Gaithersburg, MD
Hollman, Philip S. ......Concord, NH
Hollman & Pollex, LLP ......Friendship, WI
Hollman, Steven P. ......Washington, DC
Hollmann, Daniel J. ......Odessa, TX
Hollmann, Douglas Clark ......Annapolis, MD
Hollmann, Larry D. ......Chamberlain, SD
Hollmann, Leslie ......New York, NY
Hollmann, Lyon, Patterson & Durell, Inc.
Odessa, TX
Hollmann and Nussbaum, LLC
Annapolis, MD
Hollmann, Robert ......Odessa, TX
Hollmuller, Russell E. ......Mineola, NY
Hollnagel, Daryl L. ......Charlotte, NC
Hollo, Elana R. ......Philadelphia, PA
Hollo, Judith A. ......Denver, CO
Hollo, Leslie S. ......Madison, CT
Hollobaugh-Dugan, Ellen ......Santa Ana, CA
Hollodick, George E. ......Winston-Salem, NC
Holloman, Charles R., Jr. ......Ocala, FL
Holloman, Charles R., P.A. ......Ocala, FL
Holloman, David C. ......Arcadia, FL
Holloman, Frank C. ......Hernando, MS
Holloman, Frank C., Jr. ......Memphis, TN
Holloman, James H., Jr.
Oklahoma City, OK
Holloman, John H., III ......Jackson, MS
Holloman, Lynn O. ......Oklahoma City, OK
Holloman, Scotty ......Hobbs, NM
Holloman, Sharron D. ......Raleigh, NC
Hollombe, Jos. B. ......Los Angeles, CA
Hollomon, Chester D. ......Jackson, MS
Hollomon, Duncan ......Alexandria, VA
Hollomon, Joe M. ......Jackson, MS
Hollomon, Lisa A. ......Seattle, WA
Hollomon, Michael P., Jr. ......Encino, CA
Hollomon, Stephen J. ......Bellevue, WA
Hollomon, Stephen N. ......Warner Robins, GA
Hollon, Alva A., Jr. ......Jacksonville, FL
Miami, FL
Hollon, Dan S. ......Fairfax, VA
Hollon, Frank T. ......Robertsdale, AL
Hollon, Gordon L. ......Boerne, TX
Hollon, Gregory J. ......Seattle, WA
Hollon, H. Rick ......Douglas, WY
Hollon, Hollon & Collins ......Hazard, KY
Hollon, John O. ......Jacksonville, FL
Hollon, Leon L. ......Hazard, KY
Hollon, Thomas K. ......Beattyville, KY
Hollonquest, Barbara J. ......Evansville, IN
Hollopeter, Charles ......Pasadena, CA
Holloran, Francis A., Jr. ......Media, PA
Holloran, James P. ......St. Louis, MO
Holloran, John C. ......Harrisonburg, VA
Holloran Law Firm, The, P.C.
St. Louis, MO
Holloran, Matthew C. ......Washington, DC
Holloran, Michael J.
Steamboat Springs, CO
Holloran, Patti A. ......Boston, MA
Holloran & Stickler, LLC
Steamboat Springs, CO
Holloran, Thomas E. ......Minneapolis, MN
Hollos, Cynthia ......Los Angeles, CA
Hollow, John L. ......Helena, MT
Hollow, Richard L. ......Knoxville, TN
Holloway, Alan G. ......Oklahoma City, OK
Holloway and Associates, P.C.
Eatonton, GA
Holloway, Aubrey Jefferson, Jr.
Birmingham, AL
Holloway, Bill R. ......McGehee, AR
Holloway, Bruce D. ......Oakland, CA
Holloway, Calvin E., Sr. ......Hagåtña, GU
Holloway, Carl L., Jr. ......Columbia, SC
Holloway, Charles H. ......Clearwater, FL
Holloway, Charles R., III ......Portland, OR
Holloway, Cynthia A. ......Tampa, FL
Holloway, Dan L. ......Oklahoma City, OK
Holloway, Dana C. ......Knoxville, TN
Holloway, Denny L. ......Dothan, AL
Holloway, Dobson, Bachman & Jennings, A Professional Corporation
Oklahoma City, OK
Tulsa, OK
Holloway, Donald P. ......Akron, OH
Holloway, Douglas A. ......San Francisco, CA
Holloway, Edward, Jr. ......New York, NY
Holloway Elliott & Moxley, LLP
Montgomery, AL
Holloway, Eugene C., III ......Bridgewater, NJ
Holloway, Francis J. ......Albany, NY
Holloway, G. Duane ......Yorktown, VA
Holloway, George ......Culver City, CA
Holloway, Gordon A. ......Houston, TX
Holloway, Gregory A. ......Houston, TX
Holloway, J. Christopher ......Stockton, CA
Holloway, J. Gregory ......Dallas, TX
Holloway, J. Michael ......Baltimore, MD
Holloway, James C. ......Greensboro, NC
Holloway, James E. ......Greenville, NC
Holloway, James E. ......Canton, OH
Holloway, James P. ......Washington, DC
Holloway, James T. ......Tampa, FL
Holloway, Jan C. ......Baton Rouge, LA
Holloway, Jean F. ......Minneapolis, MN
Holloway, Jennifer S. ......Chicago, IL
Holloway, Jesse A., Jr. ......Abilene, TX
Holloway, John E. ......Norfolk, VA
Holloway, John H. ......Los Angeles, CA
Holloway, John H. ......Houston, TX
Holloway, John M., III ......Richmond, VA
Holloway, John M., Jr. ......Montgomery, AL
Holloway, John P. ......Boulder, CO
Holloway, John P., Jr.
Steamboat Springs, CO
Holloway, Joseph W. ......Liberty, IL
Holloway, Julia H. ......Boston, MA
Holloway, Julie M. ......Palo Alto, CA
Holloway, K. Jack ......Tulsa, OK
Holloway, K. Paul ......Plainview, TX
Holloway, Lorenzo
Federal Election Commission, Office of the General Counsel, GV
Holloway, Lorinda G.
Oklahoma City, OK
Holloway, Lynn S.
Environmental Protection Agency, Office of Enforcement and Compliance Assurance, GV
Holloway, Mallory G. ......Amarillo, TX
Holloway, Margaret W. ......Chapel Hill, NC
Holloway, Mark A. ......Indianapolis, IN
Holloway, Mark C. ......Winston-Salem, NC
Holloway, Mary Jo ......Brenham, TX
Holloway, Maurice D. ......Greenville, SC
Holloway, Michael S. ......Dallas, TX
Holloway & Monaghan ......Tulsa, OK
Holloway, Nell H. ......Houston, TX
Holloway Odegard & Sweeney, P.C.
Phoenix, AZ
Prescott, AZ
Tucson, AZ
Holloway, Oscar, Jr. ......Rochester, NY
Holloway, Oscar M., II ......Washington, DC
Holloway, Pat S. ......Austin, TX
Holloway, Paul W. ......Phoenix, AZ
Holloway, Paul W. ......Rochester, NY
Holloway, Philip A. ......Tifton, GA
Holloway, Philip R. ......Kansas City, MO
Holloway, R. Kurtz ......Pottstown, PA
Holloway, Richard G. ......Atlanta, GA
Holloway, Richard Q. ......Chicago, IL
Holloway, Rick ......Houston, TX
Holloway, Robert L., Jr. ......Danvers, MA
Holloway, Robert Lee, Jr. ......Columbia, TN
Holloway, Ronald A. ......Breckenridge, TX
Holloway, Ronald C. ......Portland, OR
Holloway, Ronald Kent ......Detroit, MI
Holloway & Rowley, P.C. ......Houston, TX
Holloway, Roy C. ......Burley, ID
Holloway, Russell B. ......Oklahoma City, OK
Holloway, S. Sue ......Minneapolis, MN
Holloway, Sally ......San Diego, CA
Holloway, Stanley ......Burley, ID
Holloway, Steven G. ......Toluca Lake, CA
Holloway, Steven L. ......Elk City, OK
Holloway, Strickland, Jr. ......Eatonton, GA
Holloway, Terry W. ......Louisville, KY
Holloway, Thomas A. ......Beaufort, SC
Holloway, Thomas N. ......Fort Lauderdale, FL
Holloway, Timothy M. ......Detroit, MI
Holloway, Walter C., IV ......Dallas, TX
Holloway, Wanda Greathouse ......Irving, TX
Holloway, Wendell ......Madisonville, KY
Holloway, William B., Jr. ......Dallas, TX
Holloway, William J., Jr.
Oklahoma City, OK
Holloway, William J., (P.C.) ......Chicago, IL
Holloway, William W. ......Austin, TX
Holloway-Garcia, Ruth G. ......Dublin, CA
Hollowed, John J., Sr. ......Olympia, WA
Hollowell & Albertson, P.A. ......Fremont, NC
Goldsboro, NC
Hollowell, Bernard B. ......Bayboro, NC
Hollowell, Bernard B., Jr. ......Bayboro, NC
Hollowell, Billie G. (Bill) ......Grand Saline, TX
Hollowell, Donald L. ......Atlanta, GA
Hollowell, Edward E. ......Raleigh, NC
Hollowell, Eileen W. ......Tucson, AZ
Hollowell, George F., Jr., (P.A.)
Greenville, MS
Hollowell & Hollowell ......Bayboro, NC
Hollowell, Jean P. ......Fremont, NC
Hollowell, Linwood Branton, Jr.
Gastonia, NC
Hollowell, Melvin J., Jr. ......Detroit, MI
Hollowell, Peacock & Meyer, P.A.
Raleigh, NC
Hollowell, Steven Earl ......Bayboro, NC
Hollowell, T. Douglas ......New York, NY
Hollowell, Thomas P. ......Charlotte, NC
Hollowell, Wallace C., III ......Raleigh, NC
Hollowell, William E. ......Medford, OR
Hollowick, Bruce ......Houston, TX
Hollowood, Edward F. ......Grand Prairie, TX
Hollows, Gregory G. ......Sacramento, CA
Hollows, William H. ......New Bern, NC
Hollowwa, J. Kerwin ......Albuquerque, NM
Hollrah, David ......Houston, TX
Hollrah, James M. ......San Antonio, TX
Hollrah, Russell A. ......Washington, DC
Hollstein, Barbara R., P.C. ......East Lansing, MI
Hollstein, Edmund W. ......Rushville, NE
Hollstein, John A. ......Morrison, CO
Hollstein Keating Cattell Johnson & Goldstein, P.C. ......Wilmington, DE
Voorhees, NJ
Philadelphia, PA
Hollstein, Richard W. ......Philadelphia, PA
Hollums, John R. ......Floydada, TX
Hollweg, Robert W. ......Jericho, NY
Hollworth, Dawn E. ......New York, NY
Holly, Albert J. ......Spring, TX
Holly, Barbara Patrice ......Folsom, CA
Holly, Carter P. ......Stockton, CA
Holly, Charles E. ......Boston, MA
Holly, Christopher C. ......Topeka, KS
Holly, Daniel D., (P.C.) ......Tempe, AZ
Holly, David E. ......St. Louis, MO
Holly, David M. ......Greenwood, MS
Holly, Donald E. ......St. Cloud, MN
Holly, Douglas W. ......Phoenix, AZ
Holly, Gregory J. ......St. Paul, MN
Holly, Hazel Jenette ......Detroit, MI
Holly, James M. ......Augusta, GA
Aiken, SC
Holly, John J. ......Santa Clara, CA
Holly, Kathleen P. ......Somerville, NJ
Holly, Lacy E., III ......Wilmington, DE
Holly, Mark H. ......Boston, MA
Holly, Martin D. ......Los Angeles, CA
Holly, Norman D. ......Omaha, NE
Holly, Pamela Christine ......New York, NY
Holly, Powell W., Jr. ......Simsbury, CT
Holly, Richard E. ......Ventura, CA
Holly, Wayne D. ......New York, NY
Hollyday, James D. ......Philadelphia, PA
Hollyer, A. Rene ......New York, NY
Hollyer Brady Smith Troxell Barrett Rockett Hines & Mone LLP ......New York, NY
Hollyer, Richard V. ......Newton, NJ
Hollyfield, J. Scott ......Austin, TX
Hollyfield, John S. ......Houston, TX
Hollyfield, Jon Scott ......Austin, TX
Holly-Fox, Barbara L. ......Neenah, WI
Holly-Hicks, Chandra LaCarol
Little Rock, AR
Hollywood, Bernard L., Jr. ......Chicago, IL
Hollywood, Harrison R. ......San Diego, CA
Hollywood, Joseph Cletus ......Easton, PA
Holm, Alison L. ......Providence, RI
Holm, Anita K. ......Philadelphia, PA
Holm, Bambace & Cotton, LLP
Houston, TX
Holm, Bradley D. ......Phoenix, AZ
Holm, Carl W. ......Redwood City, CA
Holm, Carol J. ......Dayton, OH
Holm, Carol Jacobi ......Dayton, OH
Holm, Charles B. ......Houston, TX
Holm, Chris L. ......New York, NY
Holm, Donald S., III ......Memphis, TN
Holm, Esther P. ......Costa Mesa, CA
Holm, Fred ......Pine City, MN
Holm, H. Daniel, Jr. ......Waterloo, IA
Holm, Jeannette C. ......San Diego, CA
Holm, Joel G. ......Houston, TX
Holm, John E. ......Denver, CO
Holm, Karen L. ......Burbank, CA
Holm, Kenneth B. ......Omaha, NE
Holm, Kenneth E. ......Kansas City, KS
Holm, Klas S. D. ......New York, NY
Holm, Kristi G. ......Sioux Falls, SD
Holm, Laura M. ......Fort Lauderdale, FL
Holm, Mallory Gayle ......Jacksonville, FL
Holm, Margaret Cunniff ......Olympia, WA
Holm, Margaret Manton ......Santa Ana, CA
Holm, Mary L. ......Redmond, WA
Holm, Mary Shafer ......Bucyrus, OH
Holm, Mogren, Glessner & Roti, P.S.
Renton, WA
Holm & O'Hara LLP ......New York, NY
Holm, Peter L. ......Denver, CO
Holm, Phillip H. ......Kenwood, CA
Holm, Richard T. ......St. Paul, MN
Holm, Richard V. ......Beloit, WI
Holm, Roger G. ......Minneapolis, MN
Holm, Stevan A. ......Ames, IA
Holm, Thomas N. ......Santa Clara, CA
Holm, Timothy C. ......Albuquerque, NM
Holm, W. Michael ......Alexandria, VA
Holm, William D. ......Phoenix, AZ
Holm, William P. ......New York, NY
Holm, William R. ......Roseburg, OR
Holma, Karin L. ......Honolulu, HI
Holma, Paul J. ......Portland, OR
Holma, Sherri Gautney ......Hillsboro, OR
Holman, Abigail M. ......Portland, ME
Holman, Allan W., Jr. ......New Bloomfield, PA
Holman, Barbara N. ......Western Springs, IL
Holman, Brian L. ......Los Angeles, CA
Holman, Bud G. ......New York, NY
Holman, Burke ......Houston, TX
Holman Cahill, PLLC ......Seattle, WA
Holman, Cary B. ......Orlando, FL
Holman, Charles F., III
Department of Justice, Civil Rights Division, GV
Holman, Charles R., Jr. ......Atlanta, GA
Holman, Craig A. ......Washington, DC
Holman, D. Miles ......Sandy, UT
Holman, David ......Sheboygan, WI
Holman, David C. ......Eden Prairie, MN
Holman, David S. ......Burnsville, MN
Holman, David W. ......Chicago, IL
Holman, David W. ......Houston, TX
Holman, Diane R. ......Cathedral City, CA
Holman, Dixon W. ......Fort Worth, TX
Holman, Dolores S. ......Milwaukee, WI
Holman, Donald R. ......Portland, OR
Holman, E. Thomison ......Asheville, NC
Holman, Edsel Ford ......Nashville, TN
Holman, Frank W. ......Seattle, WA
Holman, F.W., Jr. ......Arlington, VA
Holman, Gary ......Melville, NY
Holman, Gary J. ......Berryville, AR
Holman, Gary R. ......Hastings, MI
Holman, Gerry B. ......Salt Lake City, UT
Holman, H. Donald ......Fayetteville, TN
Holman, H. Kent ......Sacramento, CA
Holman Hansen & Colville, P.C.
Prairie Village, KS
Kansas City, MO
Holman, Heidi L. ......Redmond, WA
Holman & Holman ......New Bloomfield, PA
Holman & Holman ......Fayetteville, TN
Holman, H. T. ......Fayetteville, TN
Holman, J. Alan ......Austin, TX
Holman, J. Blanding, IV ......Chapel Hill, NC
Holman, J. Hawley ......Texarkana, TX
Holman, James C. ......Baltimore, MD
Holman, James D. ......Idaho Falls, ID
Holman, James J. ......Philadelphia, PA
Holman, James L., & Associates
Tacoma, WA
Holman, James Michael ......Clarksville, AR
Holman, Jeannette Kay ......Salem, OR
Holman, Jennifer S. ......Sacramento, CA
Holman, John Clarke ......Washington, DC
Holman, John F. ......Plano, TX

Holman, John H., Jr. ... Dallas, TX
Holman, John P. ... McLean, VA
Holman, Jonathan H. ... Brooklyn, NY
Holman, Joseph F. ... Farmington, ME
Holman, Joseph P. ... Delray Beach, FL
Holman, Joseph Y. ... Prairie Village, KS
Holman, Keith W. ... Washington, DC
Holman, Kingsley D. ... Bloomington, MN
Holman, Kirk A. ... Peoria, IL
Holman, Kristina S. ... Las Vegas, NV
Holman & Langdon, L.L.P.
Texarkana, AR
Texarkana, TX
Holman, Larry C. ... Park City, UT
Holman Law Firm, The, P.C.
Houston, TX
Holman, Leslie A. ... Burlington, VT
Holman, Lewis A. ... Yarmouth, ME
Holman, Marvin ... Sheboygan, WI
Holman, Maureen ... Fargo, ND
Holman, Michael John ... Napa, CA
Holman, Michael S. ... Columbus, OH
Holman, Michael W. ... Ketchikan, AK
Holman, Monica T.
Corporation for National and Community Service,
Office of Americorps, GV
Holman, Nancy Ann ... Seattle, WA
Holman & O'Grady ... San Francisco, CA
Holman, Phillip J. ... Detroit, MI
Holman, R. Craig ... Seattle, WA
Holman, Ralph M. ... Salem, OR
Holman, Randy B. ... Los Angeles, CA
Holman, Rebekah ... Los Angeles, CA
Holman, Richard A. ... New York, NY
Holman, Robert P. ... Orlando, FL
Holman, Robert W. ... Pinellas Park, FL
Holman Robertson Eldridge, A Professional Corporation ... Dallas, TX
Holman, Robin C. ... New Bloomfield, PA
Holman, Robyn M. ... Louisville, KY
Holman, Ronald D., II ... Cleveland, OH
Holman, Ronald O. ... Dallas, TX
Holman & Rosenberg ... Roslyn Heights, NY
Holman, S. Christian (Christy)
San Francisco, CA
Holman, Sandra J. ... Springfield, IL
Holman, Sarah Kroos ... Vancouver, WA
Holman, Scott ... Holyoke, MA
Holman & Shumaker ... Yarmouth, ME
Holman, Stephen J. ... Silverdale, WA
Holman, Stephen P. ... Washington, DC
Holman, Stephen T. ... Panama City, FL
Pensacola, FL
Holman, Stephen T., P.A. ... Panama City, FL
Pensacola, FL
Holman & Stern, Chartered
Washington, DC
Holman, Thomas A. ... New York, NY
Holman, Thomas C. ... San Francisco, CA
Holman, Thomas I., Jr. ... Nashville, TN
Holman, Tiffany Ann ... Minneapolis, MN
Holman, Timothy J. ... Philadelphia, PA
Holman Walker & Hutchings, LC
Sandy, UT
Holman, William D. ... San Diego, CA
Holman, William K. ... Peoria, IL
Holman, William M. ... Bellevue, WA
Holman, Wm. Steele, II ... Mobile, AL
Holmans, Charles F., III ... Dallas, TX
Holmberg, Alan ... Oxnard, CA
Holmberg, Anna K. ... Ithaca, NY
Holmberg, Brian D. ... Los Angeles, CA
Holmberg, C. Soren ... Port Salerno, FL
Holmberg, Carolyn M. ... Arlington, TX
Holmberg, Christine A. ... Henderson, NV
Holmberg, Edward R. ... Waukegan, IL
Holmberg, Eric B. ... Washington, DC
Holmberg, Galbraith, Holmberg, Galbraith, Van Houten & Miller ... Ithaca, NY
Holmberg, James J., III ... San Diego, CA
Holmberg, James M. ... Kansas City, KS
Holmberg, Jas. J. ... Columbus, NE
Holmberg, Julie Tatsugi ... Los Angeles, CA
Holmberg, Kent R. ... Ely, MN
Holmberg, Laura H. ... Ithaca, NY
Holmbo, Todd A. ... New York, NY
Holme, John C., Jr. ... Rutland, VT
Holme, Justus M., Jr., P.C. ... Fairfax, VA
Holme, Richard P. ... Denver, CO
Holme Roberts & Owen LLP
Boulder, CO
Colorado Springs, CO
Denver, CO
Salt Lake City, UT
Holmen & Carpenter ... St. Cloud, MN
Holmen, Eugene E. ... Baltimore, MD
Holmen, Gary L. ... Los Angeles, CA
Holmen, Jeffrey A. ... Minneapolis, MN
Holmen, Katherine A. Brown
St. Paul, MN
Holmen, Neil E. ... Chicago, IL
Holmen, Phyllis Jane ... Atlanta, GA
Holmen, Ralph W. ... Chicago, IL
Holmen, Robert R. ... Long Beach, CA
Holmen, Robert W. ... St. Cloud, MN
Holmer, Alan F. ... Washington, DC
Holmer, C. Anders ... Truckee, CA
Holmer, Ray T., Jr. ... Fall River Mills, CA
Holmes, A. Rutherfoord ... Owings Mills, MD
Holmes, Alan T. ... Orange, CA
Holmes, Albritton & Ward, L.L.P.
Longview, TX
Holmes, Alexa A. ... New York, NY
Holmes, Alfred P., Jr. ... Mobile, AL
Holmes, Alfred S. ... New York, NY
Holmes, Alicia T. ... Kansas City, MO
Holmes, Alison A.M. ... Durham, NC
Holmes, Allan R. ... Charleston, SC
Holmes, Andrew S. ... Stamford, CT
Holmes, Ann M. ... Seattle, WA
Holmes & Associates, Ltd.
Minneapolis, MN
Holmes, Audrey Dale ... Sandston, VA
Holmes, Barbara D. ... Nashville, TN
Holmes, Barbara E. ... Pittsburgh, PA
Holmes, Bernard T. ... Virginia Beach, VA
Holmes, Berndt C. ... Grand Junction, CO
Holmes, Bradly J. ... Denver, CO
Holmes, Brenda Ozaki ... Atlanta, GA
Holmes, Brent D. ... Mattoon, IL
Holmes, Bret P. ... Charlotte, NC
Holmes, Brian R. ... Wethersfield, CT
Holmes, Broox G. ... Mobile, AL
Holmes, Broox G., Jr. ... Mobile, AL
Holmes, C. Lawrence ... Cherry Hill, NJ
Philadelphia, PA
Holmes, Cameron H. ... Phoenix, AZ
Holmes, Carl C. ... Santa Ana, CA
Holmes, Carl E. ... Gaithersburg, MD
Holmes, Carol ... Troy, MI
Holmes, Catherine DeBono
Los Angeles, CA
Holmes, Chandra L. ... Lawton, OK
Holmes, Charles E. ... New Orleans, LA
Holmes, Charles V. ... Memphis, TN
Holmes, Chip, Jr. ... Charlotte, NC
Holmes, Christopher McG. ... Charleston, SC
Holmes, Christopher W. ... Dallas, TX
Holmes, Christy M. ... Cincinnati, OH
Holmes, Cindee Dale ... Birmingham, AL
Holmes, Claire E. ... Englewood, CO
Holmes, Clarence H. ... Cleveland, OH
Holmes, Clifton L." Scrappy "
Longview, TX
Holmes, Craig T. ... Atlanta, GA
Holmes, Curtis C., II ... Anaheim, CA
Holmes, Cynthia S. ... St. Louis, MO
Holmes, Dallas, (P.C.) ... Riverside, CA
Holmes, Daniel Edward ... Hughesville, PA
Holmes, Daniel P. ... Boston, MA
Holmes, David A. ... Port Charlotte, FL
Holmes, David B. ... Department of Justice,
Executive Office for Immigration Review, GV
Holmes, David E. ... Los Angeles, CA
San Luis Obispo, CA
Holmes, David E., Legal Offices of
San Luis Obispo, CA
Holmes, David F. ... Slocomb, AL
Holmes, David F. ... Hutchinson, KS
Holmes, David G. ... Brundidge, AL
Holmes, David K. ... Wichita, KS
Holmes, David L. ... Kalamazoo, MI
Holmes, David M. ... Chicago, IL
Holmes, David P.
Central Intelligence Agency,
Office of the Executive Director, GV
Holmes, David R. ... Bremen, IN
Plymouth, IN
Holmes, David W. ... Greenville, SC
Holmes, David W. ... Grapevine, TX
Holmes, Debbi R. ... Huron, SD
Holmes, Deborah Anne ... Hopewell, VA
Holmes, Deborah M. ... Glendale, CA
Holmes, Denise ... Lawrenceville, GA
Holmes, Dennis R. ... Sioux Falls, SD
Holmes, Donald C., Jr. ... Easton, MD
Holmes, Donald E. ... Palatka, FL
Holmes, Donald F., Jr. ... Washington, DC
Holmes, Donna L. ... New York, NY
Holmes, Doreen Randi ... Washington, DC
Holmes, Douglas J. ... Ogden, UT
Holmes, Douglas M. ... Chapel Hill, NC
Holmes, Douglas R. ... Santa Fe Springs, CA
Holmes, Douglas R. ... Metairie, LA
Holmes, Dunbar ... Lincoln, MA
Holmes, Duris L. ... New Orleans, LA
Holmes, Edgar R. ... Atlantic City, NJ
Holmes & Edmonds, A Professional Corporation ... Virginia Beach, VA
Holmes, Edward S. ... Pittsboro, NC
Holmes, Edwin T. ... Rockport, MA
Holmes, Elizabeth E.Z. ... Concord, MA
Holmes, Elizabeth W. ... Eagle Butte, SD
Holmes & Ells, PLLC ... Hampton, NH
Holmes, Elmore, III ... Memphis, TN
Holmes, Emily ... La Jolla, CA
Holmes, Ervin R. ... Salt Lake City, UT
Holmes, Eugene M. ... Arlington, VA
Holmes Firm, The, A Professional Corporation ... Dallas, TX
Holmes, Frederick T. ... Truckee, CA
Holmes, G. David ... Hendersonville, TN
Holmes, Gale H. ... Des Moines, IA
Holmes, Gary ... Los Angeles, CA
Holmes, Gary W. ... Hampton, NH
Holmes, George H. ... Scottsdale, AZ
Holmes, George L., Jr. ... Fairfield, CT
Holmes, Georgia L. ... Mankato, MN
Holmes, Gerald A. ... Santa Rosa, CA
Holmes, Gerry E. ... Cedartown, GA
Holmes, Gilbert A. ... Newark, NJ
Holmes, Greg ... Frankfort, KY
Holmes, Gregory A. ... Manchester, NH
Holmes, H. Alexander ... Raleigh, NC
Holmes, H. Jack ... Jackson, TN
Holmes, H. Sidney, III ... New York, NY
Holmes, H. Thomas ... Los Angeles, CA
Holmes, Hardin ... Denver, CO
Holmes, Harry, Jr. ... Houston, TX
Holmes, Hayes & Walter, L.L.P.
Bremen, IN
Elkhart, IN
Nappanee, IN
Plymouth, IN
Holmes, Helene M. ... Brooklyn, NY
Holmes, Henry W., (P.C.)
Beverly Hills, CA
Holmes, Herbert A., Jr. ... Glendale, CA
Holmes and Holmes ... Cedar Rapids, IA
Holmes & Holmes ... Kinder, LA
Holmes & Holmes ... Yazoo City, MS
Holmes, Horace B. ... Boulder, CO
Holmes, Houston E., Jr. ... Dallas, TX
Holmes, Howard M. ... Philadelphia, PA
Holmes, Hugh K. ... Pasadena, MD
Holmes, Ingrid H. ... Commerce City, CO
Holmes, Irene Saal ... San Francisco, CA
Holmes, J. Calloway, Jr. ... Cedartown, GA
Holmes, J. Kevin ... Charleston, SC
Holmes, J. Leon ... Little Rock, AR
Holmes, J. Scott ... Charlotte, NC
Holmes, Jack F. ... Indianapolis, IN
Holmes, Jack P. ... Fullerton, CA
Holmes, Jack Spain ... Raleigh, NC
Holmes, Jacqueline M. ... Washington, DC
Holmes, Jacqueline S.
Federal Energy Regulatory Commission,
Office of the General Counsel, GV
Holmes, James A. ... New Orleans, LA
Holmes, James A. ... Dallas, TX
Holmes, James Andrew ... Henderson, TX
Holmes, James C. ... Cedar Rapids, IA
Holmes, James E. ... Tampa, FL
Holmes, James E. ... Atlanta, GA
Holmes, James F. ... New Orleans, LA
Holmes, James Garrott, III ... Yazoo City, MS
Holmes, James H." Blackie ", III
Dallas, TX
Holmes, James J. S. ... Los Angeles, CA
Holmes, James S. ... Minneapolis, MN
Holmes, James T. ... Cedar Rapids, IA
Holmes, James T. ... Princeton, NJ
Holmes, James W. ... Kingsport, TN
Holmes, Jay T. ... Rochester, NY
Holmes, J. E., III ... Riverside, CA
Holmes, Jean Anderson ... Germantown, TN
Holmes, Jeanne L. ... Brockton, MA
Holmes, Jeffery D. ... Santa Monica, CA
Holmes, Jeffrey E. ... Birmingham, AL
Holmes, Jeffrey K. ... Englewood, CO
Holmes & Jeffrey, L.L.P. ... Beaumont, TX
Holmes, Jeffrey M. ... Bartow, FL
Holmes, Jeffrey M., Professional Association
Bartow, FL
Holmes, Jennifer C. ... Washington, DC
Holmes, Jerry E. ... Treasury Department,
Internal Revenue Service, GV
Holmes, Jerry (Gerald), Jr. ... Nederland, TX
Holmes, Jessica R. ... Department of State,
Office of the Legal Adviser, GV
Holmes, Jill Barton ... Bow, NH
Holmes, Joe ... Pine Bluff, AR
Holmes, John A. ... Seattle, WA
Holmes, John Allen ... Mansfield, OH
Holmes, John C. ... Los Angeles, CA
Holmes, John C. ... Department of Labor,
Office of Secretary, GV
Holmes, John D., Jr. ... Houston, TX
Holmes, John E. ... Washington, DC
Holmes, John H. ... Portland, OR
Holmes, John H., Jr. ... Southfield, MI
Holmes, John Joseph ... Brooklyn, NY
Holmes, John L. ... Torrance, CA
Holmes, John M. ... Kolonia, TT
Holmes, John R. ... Battle Creek, MI
Holmes, John R., III ... Seattle, WA
Holmes, John Sharp ... Yazoo City, MS
Holmes, John Sharp, Jr. ... Yazoo City, MS
Holmes, John T. ... San Diego, CA
Holmes, John T. ... Metairie, LA
Holmes, John V. A. ... Orlando, FL
Holmes, Joseph D., Jr. ... Seattle, WA
Holmes, Joseph M. ... Las Cruces, NM
Holmes, Joseph M., P.A. ... Las Cruces, NM
Holmes, Joseph O. ... New York, NY
Holmes, Joseph W. ... Westford, MA
Holmes, Juanita E. ... Seattle, WA
Holmes, Judith H. ... Denver, CO
Holmes, Judith L. ... Amherst, MA
Holmes, Julie Melander ... Golden Valley, MN
Holmes, Justin K. ... Syosset, NY
Holmes, Karen A. ... San Diego, CA
Holmes, Karen A. ... Albany, NY
Holmes, Karen M. ... Akron, OH
Holmes, Katherine M. ... Minneapolis, MN
Holmes, Kathleen E. ... Lancaster, PA
Holmes, Kathleen J. L. ... Alexandria, VA
Holmes, Keith Cordell ... Diamond Bar, CA
Holmes, Keith T. ... Los Angeles, CA
Holmes, Kenneth E. ... Ponca City, OK
Holmes, Kenneth H. ... Cary, NC
Holmes, Kesha M. ... Hallandale Beach, FL
Holmes, Kurt A. ... Wichita, KS
Holmes, Kurt S. ... Mineola, NY
Holmes, Laura Denson ... Baton Rouge, LA
Holmes, Laurie A. ... Washington, DC
Holmes Law Firm ... Greenville, SC
Holmes Law Firm, The ... Cedartown, GA
Holmes Law Firm, The ... Alamogordo, NM
Holmes, Lee B. ... McLean, VA
Holmes, Lee M., & Associates
Oklahoma City, OK
Holmes, Leslie ... San Jose, CA
Holmes, Linda A. ... Westminster, MD
Holmes, Linda F. ... Bowling Green, OH
Holmes, Linda Lynn Walls ... Memphis, TN
Holmes, Linda S. ... Dayton, OH
Holmes, Lindsey A. ... Chico, CA
Holmes, Lisa A. ... Coeur d'Alene, ID
Holmes, Lorraine C. ... Fort Pierce, FL
Holmes, Lyman L. ... Machias, ME
Holmes, Marilyn J.
Administrative Office Of The United States Courts, GV
Holmes, Marilynn J. ... Frankfort, KY
Holmes, Marjorie Randolph ... Hayward, CA
Holmes, Mark ... Washington, DC
Holmes, Mark D. ... Irvine, CA
Holmes, Mark L. ... Oklahoma City, OK
Holmes, Mark R. ... Greenville, SC
Holmes, Mark van Dyke ... Washington, DC
Holmes, Martin Douglas ... Nashville, TN
Holmes, Martin J. ... Toledo, OH
Holmes, Martin J., Jr. ... Toledo, OH
Holmes, Mary H. ... Kinder, LA
Holmes, Mary L. Grier, (P.C.)
New Orleans, LA
Holmes, Matthew A. ... Englewood, CO
Holmes, Max ... Stamford, CT
Holmes & McLaurin ... Pittsboro, NC
Holmes, Melinda K. ... Washington, DC
Holmes, Melvin C. ... Cary, IL
Holmes, M. H., Jr. ... Trenton, TN
Holmes, Michael A. ... Detroit, MI
Holmes, Michael B. ... Kinder, LA
Holmes, Michael C. ... Houston, TX
Holmes, Michael G. ... Lake Oswego, OR
Holmes, Michael J. ... San Diego, CA
Holmes, Michael M. ... Seattle, WA
Holmes, Michael P. ... San Jose, CA
Holmes, Michael S. ... Troy, MI
Holmes, Michael S., Law Office of
Houston, TX
Holmes, Mike ... Odessa, TX
Holmes, Milton D. ... Rocky River, OH
Holmes, Miriam R. ... Washington, DC
Holmes, Nicholas H., Jr. ... Chillicothe, OH
Holmes, Nicholas K. ... Manchester, NH
Holmes, Niles W. ... Dallas, TX
Holmes, Norman L. ... Washington, DC
Holmes, Odell S., Jr. ... El Paso, TX
Holmes, Oliver L. ... San Francisco, CA
Holmes, Oliver Wendell, III
Baton Rouge, LA
Holmes, Owen M., IV ... Newberry, SC
Holmes, P. King ... Columbia, SC
Holmes, Pamela J. ... Whittier, CA
Holmes, Patricia B. ... Chicago, IL
Holmes, Patricia Hunt ... Houston, TX
Holmes, Paul B. ... Chicago, IL
Holmes, Paul J. ... Beaumont, TX
Holmes, Paul K., III ... Fort Smith, AR
Holmes, Paul K., Jr. ... Newport, AR
Holmes, Paul R. ... Rochester, NY
Holmes, Paul W. ... Fremont, CA
Holmes, Peter D. ... Detroit, MI
Holmes, Peter L. ... El Segundo, CA
Holmes, Peter S., P.C. ... Seattle, WA
Holmes, Philip ... Oklahoma City, OK
Holmes, Philip B., Jr. ... Manchester, NH
Holmes, Philip J. ... Boston, MA
Holmes, Phillip A. ... Hillsborough, NC
Holmes & Pickens, P.A. ... Palatka, FL
Holmes, Priscilla ... Washington, DC
Holmes & Quigley ... Tipton, IN
Holmes, Ralph A., Jr. ... Falls Church, VA
Holmes, Ralph F. ... Manchester, NH
Holmes, Randall D. ... Burlington, VT
Holmes, Randall T. ... Owasso, OK
Holmes, Regena L. ... Lexington, KY
Holmes, Rene C. ... Salem, OR
Holmes, Renée ... Cincinnati, OH
Holmes, Rhonda C. ... Washington, DC
Holmes, Rhonda J. ... San Diego, CA
Holmes, Rich, Sigler & Riddick, P.C., Law Offices of ... Jackson, TN
Holmes, Richard A. ... Pittsburgh, PA
Holmes, Richard A. ... Austin, TX
Holmes, Richard E.
Huntington Beach, CA
Holmes, Richard E. ... Ventura, CA
Holmes, Richard E., Jr.
Grand Rapids, MI
Holmes, Richard Kent ... Tulsa, OK
Holmes, Richard M. ... Covington, IN
Holmes, Richard W. ... Topeka, KS
Holmes & Rickles ... Portland, OR
Holmes, Robb P. ... Tucson, AZ
Holmes, Robert A. ... Denver, CO
Holmes, Robert A., Jr. ... Mount Pleasant, MI
Holmes, Robert C. ... Perth Amboy, NJ
Holmes, Robert C. ... New York, NY
Holmes, Robert D. ... Columbus, OH
Holmes, Robert E. ... Culver City, CA
Holmes, Robert E. ... Powell, OH
Holmes, Robert E., Jr. ... Dallas, TX
Holmes, Robert H. ... Little Rock, AR
Russellville, AR
Holmes, Robert H., II ... Dallas, TX
Holmes, Robert H., II ... Dallas, TX
Holmes, Robert H., II, L.P. ... Dallas, TX
Holmes, Robert K. ... Glendale, CA
Holmes, Robert P. ... Arlington, VA
Holmes, Robert P., IV ... Raleigh, NC
Holmes, Robert W., Jr. ... Boston, MA
Holmes, Roger F. ... Anchorage, AK
Holmes, Roger W. ... Springfield, IL
Holmes, Roger W. ... Boston, MA
Holmes, Ronald E. ... Albuquerque, NM
Holmes, Ronald E. ... Houston, TX
Holmes, Ronald L. ... Manteca, CA
Holmes, Ronald L. ... Dallas, TX
Holmes, Rosenberg & Doherty, P.C.
Arlington, VA
Holmes, Roxanne L. ... San Francisco, CA
Holmes, Russell W. ... Tupelo, MS
Holmes, Samuel L. ... Lafayette, CA
Holmes, Sarah F. ... Boston, MA

Holmes, Schwartz & Gordon
Washington, DC
Easton, MD
Rockville, MD
Garden City, NY
Holmes, Scott C. .... Boston, MA
Holmes, Scott D. .... Columbus, OH
Holmes, Shannon A. .... Troy, MI
Holmes, Sherie Shortridge .... Atlanta, GA
Holmes, Sherman W. .... Portland, OR
Holmes, Stacy J. .... Madison, NJ
Holmes, Stacy L. .... Washington, DC
Holmes, Stephanie A. .... New York, NY
Holmes, Stephen .... Menlo Park, CA
Holmes, Stephen H. .... Nevada, IA
Holmes, Stephen J. .... Baltimore, MD
Holmes, Stephen J. .... Providence, RI
Holmes, Stephen P. .... Denver, CO
Holmes, Stephen S. .... Honolulu, HI
Holmes, Stephen S. .... Cincinnati, OH
Holmes, Stephen W. .... New York, NY
Holmes, Steven D. .... Fort Myers, FL
Holmes, Steven DeWitt, P.A.
Fort Myers, FL
Holmes, Steven T. .... Dallas, TX
Holmes, Stuart A. .... Claremont, CA
Holmes, Sunanda Kumari .... Bethesda, MD
Holmes, Susan L. .... Amsterdam, NY
Holmes, Susan N. .... Camarillo, CA
Holmes, Sven Erik .... Tulsa, OK
Holmes, T. Elaine .... Tampa, FL
Holmes, T. Michael .... Grand Junction, CO
Holmes, T. Wesley .... Dallas, TX
Holmes, Terry A. .... New York, NY
Holmes, Terry S. .... Toledo, OH
Holmes, Theodore A. .... Delmar, NY
Holmes, Theresa L. .... Lexington, KY
Holmes, Thomas J. .... Pocatello, ID
Holmes, Thomas M. .... Scranton, PA
Holmes, Thomas T. .... Cleveland, OH
Holmes & Thomson, L.L.P.
Charleston, SC
Columbia, SC
Holmes, Todd A. .... Alamogordo, NM
Holmes, Ursula Y. .... Nashville, TN
Holmes, Vera M. .... Wilmington, DE
Holmes, W. Bradley .... Sacramento, CA
Holmes, Walter C., III .... Dallas, TX
Holmes, Warren Lane .... Jackson, MS
Holmes, Wayne F. .... Nantucket, MA
Holmes, Wayne S. .... Indianapolis, IN
Holmes Weddle & Barcott, A Professional Corporation .... Anchorage, AK
Seattle, WA
Holmes, Wendell A. .... Waterloo, IA
Holmes, Wendell H. .... Baton Rouge, LA
Holmes, Wendell S. .... Atlanta, GA
Holmes, Whitney A. .... Denver, CO
Holmes, William A. .... Menlo Park, CA
Holmes, William C. .... Chicago, IL
Holmes, William D. M.
Department of Justice, Tax Division, GV
Holmes, William H. .... Portland, OR
Holmes, William J. .... Virginia Beach, VA
Holmes, William J. O. .... San Mateo, CA
Holmes, William K. .... Grand Rapids, MI
Holmes, William M. .... Bend, OR
Holmes, William R. (Bill) .... Norman, OK
Holmes, William T. .... Fairmont, WV
Holmes, Woods & Garza .... Dallas, TX
Houston, TX
McKinney, TX
Holmes, Zoe Ann Kerbey .... Merriam, KS
Holmes a Court, DiVonne M. Jarecki
New York, NY
Holmes-Bowie, Cristal .... Mount Holly, NJ
Holmes-Gaar, Elizabeth G. .... Portland, OR
Holmgreen, John C., Jr.
Corpus Christi, TX
Holmgren, Deborah A. .... Las Vegas, NV
Holmgren, Janet Clark .... Rockford, IL
Holmgren, R. Bruce .... Des Plaines, IL
Holmgren, Randall J. .... Salt Lake City, UT
Holmgren, Sally .... St. Paul, MN
Holm Jensen, Paula .... Portland, OR
Holmlund, Mary L. .... St. Paul, MN
Holmoe, Marlin A. .... San Jose, CA
Holmquest, Donald L. .... Nashville, TN
Holmquest, Thomas K. .... Oak Park, IL
Holmquist, Arthur S. .... Holden, MA
Holmquist, C. John, Jr. .... Detroit, MI
Farmington Hills, MI
Holmquist, David K. .... Youngstown, OH
Holmquist, David R. .... Beverly Hills, CA
Holmquist, James L. .... Lincoln, NE
Holmquist, Michael G. .... Charlotte, NC
Holmquist, Paul R. .... Columbus, OH
Holmquist, Richard H. .... Seattle, WA
Holmquist, Roy W. .... Starbuck, MN
Holms, Richard L., Jr. .... Fairfield, CT
Holms, William R. .... Corpus Christi, TX
Holms, William R., P.C., Law Office of
Corpus Christi, TX
Holmsen, Robert M. .... Hackensack, NJ
Holmstead, Jeffrey R. .... Washington, DC
Holmsten, Fred H. .... Shreveport, LA
Holmstrand, Jeffrey A. .... Wheeling, WV
Holmstrom, Angela L. .... Chetek, WI
Holmstrom, Gregory L. .... Granite Falls, MN
Holmstrom, Jeffrey R. .... Dowagiac, MI
Holmstrom, John, III .... Loves Park, IL
Holmstrom, John, Jr. .... Rockford, IL
Holmstrom & Kennedy, P.C.
Rockford, IL
Holmstrom & Kvam .... Granite Falls, MN
Holmstrom, Mark D. .... Kansas City, MO
Holmstrom, Richard J. .... New York, NY
Holmstrom, Richard P. .... Duluth, MN

Holmstrup, Mark A.
Department of Transportation, Office of the General Counsel, GV
Holness, Andrew A. .... Tamarac, FL
Holness, Gina Dines .... Cambridge, MA
Holness, Janice P. .... Newark, NJ
Holness, Vielka V. .... New York, NY
Holniker, Kenneth .... Sykesville, MD
Holo, Robert E. .... New York, NY
Holo, Sanford .... Los Angeles, CA
Holober, Nadia V. .... Millbrae, CA
Holobinko, John E. .... Middletown, NJ
Holoboski, H. Craig .... Anaheim, CA
Holochuck, Joseph .... Minersville, PA
Holod, Douglas T. .... Minneapolis, MN
Holodak, Edward F. .... Fort Lauderdale, FL
Holodnak, Robert B. .... Columbus, OH
Holody, Karen J. .... Austin, TX
Holohan, Brian .... Phoenix, AZ
Holohan, Elizabeth R. .... Seattle, WA
Holohan, Mary T. .... Shrewsbury, MA
Holohan, Michael H., Jr. .... Mineola, NY
Holohan, Richard .... New York, NY
Holohan, William A. .... Phoenix, AZ
Holohan Zanon, PLC .... Phoenix, AZ
Holomon, Karla Risdon .... Houston, TX
Holotka, Joseph S. .... East Islip, NY
Holoubek, Jerome F. .... Bronx, NY
Holowacz, Elizabeth F. .... New York, NY
Holoway, Michael E. .... Covington, LA
Holoway, Michael E., A Professional Law Corporation .... Covington, LA
Holowinski, Elizabeth M.
Washington, DC
Holowka, Nick O. .... Lapeer, MI
Holownia, John E. .... Central Islip, NY
Holozubiec, Francis M. .... New York, NY
Holper, James A. .... Anaheim, CA
Holper, John C. .... Minneapolis, MN
St. Paul, MN
Holper, Richard D. .... Phoenix, AZ
Minneapolis, MN
Holper, Welsh & Joanis, Ltd.
Minneapolis, MN
Holper, Welsh & Mitchell, Ltd.
Phoenix, AZ
Minneapolis, MN
Holquin, Donna .... Houston, TX
Holroyd, Donald D. .... Phoenix, AZ
Holroyd, Frank J., Jr. .... Sarasota, FL
Holroyd, Fred F. .... Charleston, WV
Holroyd, Laura A. .... New York, NY
Holroyd, Mary-Jacq .... Arlington, VA
Holroyd, Rick .... Charleston, WV
Holroyd, Robert E. .... Princeton, WV
Holroyd, Yost & Evans .... Charleston, WV
Hols, David R. .... Minneapolis, MN
Holsapple, Dennis L. .... Omaha, NE
Holsapple, Henry T. .... Winston-Salem, NC
Holsapple, Lynaia M. .... Kansas City, KS
Holsberry, W. David .... Las Vegas, NV
Holscher, Emma Stallings .... Greenville, NC
Holscher, Franz F. .... Washington, NC
Holscher, Frederick Norman
Washington, NC
Holscher, Louis M. .... San Jose, CA
Holscher, Marilyn R. .... Munster, IN
Holscher, Mark C. .... Los Angeles, CA
Holscher, Patrick T. .... Casper, WY
Holscher, Richard H. .... Milwaukee, WI
Holschuh, John D. .... Columbus, OH
Holschuh, John D., Jr. .... Cincinnati, OH
Holschuh, Laurel A. .... Minneapolis, MN
Holschuh, Wendy G. .... Cincinnati, OH
Holsenback, J. Daniel .... La Jolla, CA
Holsenbeck, G. Penn .... New York, NY
Holsey, Joyce Edline .... Tucson, AZ
Holshouser, Eric J. .... Jacksonville, FL
Holshouser, James E., Jr. .... Pinehurst, NC
Raleigh, NC
Holshouser, John L., Jr. .... Salisbury, NC
Holshouser, Ted P. .... Oklahoma City, OK
Holshouser, Theodore Paul
Oklahoma City, OK
Holsing, Christopher P. .... North Reading, MA
Holsinger, Alan .... Indiana, PA
Holsinger, Candice D. .... Pittsburgh, PA
Holsinger, John Paul .... Pittsburgh, PA
Holsinger, John R. .... Montvale, NJ
Holsinger, Russelle L. .... Morris, IL
Holsinger, Steven J. .... Hershey, PA
Holsinger, Thomas M. .... Modesto, CA
Holsinger & Westover .... Morris, IL
Holsinger, William H., Law Offices of
Burlingame, CA
Holsman & Bedell .... San Francisco, CA
Holsman, William K. .... San Francisco, CA
Holsonback, John P. .... Tampa, FL
Holst, Brian J. .... Longmont, CO
Holst, Clifford W. .... Anchorage, AK
Holst, Dale L. .... Colorado Springs, CO
Holst, Elmer .... Falls Church, VA
Holst & Hartshorn .... Falls Church, VA
Holst, Henry L. .... Honolulu, HI
Holst, Jack A. .... Colorado Springs, CO
Holst, Jack A., P.C. .... Colorado Springs, CO
Holst, James E. .... Oakland, CA
Holst, John G., Jr. .... Fort Myers, FL
Holst, John H. .... Grand Rapids, MI
Holst, Jon D. .... Denver, CO
Holst, Richard C. .... Wyoming, MI
Holst, Vogel, Erdmann & Vogel
Red Wing, MN
Holst, William G. .... Commack, NY
Holste, Carla G. .... Jefferson City, MO
Holstead, David N. .... Topeka, KS
Holstead, George B. .... Ruston, LA
Holstead, John B. .... Houston, TX

Holstedt, John R. .... Sacramento, CA
Holstedt and Kinnison Law Offices, P.C.
Sheridan, WY
Holstedt, R. Brooke .... Salem, OR
Holstedt, Robert E. .... Sheridan, WY
Holstein, Darrel J. .... New York, NY
Holstein, David A. .... Syracuse, NY
Holstein, E. Timothy .... St. Louis, MO
Holstein, Howard M. .... Washington, DC
Holstein, Jack L. .... East Brunswick, NJ
Holstein, John C. .... Jefferson City, MO
Holstein, Linda L. .... Minneapolis, MN
Holstein, Lisa .... New York, NY
Holstein, Mark .... Chicago, IL
Holstein, Philip L. .... Lutherville, MD
Holstein, Richard L. .... Buffalo, NY
Holstein, Robert A. .... Chicago, IL
Holstein, Robert M., Jr. .... Riverside, CA
Holstein, Taylor & Unitt .... Riverside, CA
Holsten, Andrea Lundgren .... St. Paul, MN
Holsten, Jennifer L. .... Media, PA
Holsten Law Office, P.A. .... Stillwater, MN
Holsten, Roy W. .... Stillwater, MN
Holsten, Stephen E. .... Washington, DC
Holsten, William F., II .... Media, PA
Holster, Charles E., III .... Mineola, NY
Holster, Patti S. .... San Antonio, TX
Holston, Amy S. .... Albuquerque, NM
Holston, Brenda W. .... Philadelphia, PA
Holston, Dixon M. .... Los Angeles, CA
Holston, J. Wesley .... Miami, FL
Holston, James M. .... Philadelphia, PA
Holston, John S., Jr. .... Woodbury, NJ
Holston, MacDonald and Uzdavinis, A Professional Corporation .... Woodbury, NJ
Holston, Michael J. .... Philadelphia, PA
Holston, Patrick J. .... Camden, NJ
Westmont, NJ
Holston, Richard H. .... Mobile, AL
Holston, Robert G. .... Woodbury, NJ
Holston, Timothy L. .... Columbus, OH
Holston, Van .... Minneapolis, MN
Holston, William O., Jr. (P.C.) .... Dallas, TX
Holstrom, David .... Sonora, CA
Holstrom, Dayn A. .... Corona, CA
Holstrom, Jack A. .... Helena, MT
Holstrom, Robert W. P. .... San Francisco, CA
Holsworth & Associates .... Pittsburgh, PA
Holsworth, Charles L. .... Pittsburgh, PA
Holsworth, Mark E. .... Houston, TX
Holt, Amanda C. .... Boston, MA
Holt, Anthony E. .... Portland, ME
Holt, Arthur Lee .... Lutherville, MD
Holt, B. Jane Chandler .... Topeka, KS
Holt & Babington, P.C. .... Las Cruces, NM
Holt, Bradley D. .... Manchester, NH
Holt, Brett D. .... Sacramento, CA
Holt, C. Corley .... Charlotte, NC
Holt, C. Mark .... Raleigh, NC
Holt, Carl T. .... Wilton, CT
Holt, Carolyn M. .... Tampa, FL
Holt, Cathy M. .... Phoenix, AZ
Holt, Charles .... Rockwall, TX
Holt, Charles, Jr. .... Rockwall, TX
Holt, Charles M. .... Memphis, TN
Holt, Charles W., Jr. .... Lawrenceburg, TN
Holt, Christopher .... Berkeley, CA
Holt, Christopher B. .... New York, NY
Holt, Christopher G. .... Jackson, MS
Holt, Clark M. .... Reidsville, NC
Holt, Clyde, III .... Raleigh, NC
Holt, Colette, & Associates
Kansas City, MO
Holt, Connie A. .... Auburn, CA
Holt, Cooper & Upshaw .... Birmingham, AL
Holt, D. Michael .... College Station, TX
Holt, Darry E. .... Framingham, MA
Holt, Darry Robert .... Concord, MA
Holt, David C. .... Irvine, CA
Holt, David E. .... Pampa, TX
Holt, David E., III .... Arlington, VA
Holt, David T. .... Kansas City, MO
Holt, Diana L. .... Atlanta, GA
Holt, Don, Jr., Law Offices of
Ventura, CA
Holt, Donald E. .... Florence, AL
Holt, Donald H. .... Beachwood, OH
Holt, Donna Keene .... Knoxville, TN
Holt, Douglas W. .... Burlingame, CA
Holt, Duncan W., Jr. .... Dallas, TX
Holt, E. Berry, III .... Nashville, TN
Holt, Edmund W. .... Pensacola, FL
Holt, Elyn C. .... Irvine, CA
Holt, Emily Potter .... Winchester, KY
Holt, Erick R. .... New York, NY
Holt, Eugene L. .... New York, NY
Holt, Eugene L. .... New York, NY
Holt, F. Thomas, III .... Fayetteville, NC
Holt, Farley G. .... York, PA
Holt, Fleck & Free .... Noblesville, IN
Holt, Frank T. .... Thomasville, GA
Holt, F. W. Chip, Jr. .... Austin, TX
Holt, George E. .... Las Vegas, NV
Holt, George W. .... Sacramento, CA
Holt, Glenn A. .... Santa Ana, CA
Holt, Gregory Oggie .... Fairfax, VA
Holt, Gregory W. .... Warner Robins, GA
Holt, H. Barry .... Phoenix, AZ
Holt, Harriette L. .... Wailuku, HI
Holt, Heather L. .... Grants Pass, OR
Holt and Hirsch .... Dallas, TX
Holt, Howard .... New York, NY
Holt, Hugh Leslie .... Pleasanton, CA
Holt, J. David .... Bloomfield, IN
Holt, J. Mike .... Dallas, TX
Holt, J. Nicklas .... Knoxville, TN
Holt, J. Stephen .... Little Rock, AR
Holt, Jack .... Pineville, LA

Holt, Jack D. .... San Bernardino, CA
Holt, Jack Erskine, III .... Orlando, FL
Holt, James D. .... Department of Agriculture, Office of the General Counsel, GV
Holt, James D. .... Wichita, KS
Holt, James H. .... Washington, DC
Holt, James H. .... Denison, TX
Holt, James L., Jr. .... Memphis, TN
Holt, Janet Lee .... Stafford, VA
Holt, Janet Pitterle .... Washington, DC
Holt, Jason .... East Orange, NJ
Holt, Jason .... Providence, RI
Holt, Jay A. .... New York, NY
Holt, Jenifer C. .... Scottsboro, AL
Holt, Jennifer E. .... Bethesda, MD
Holt, Jennifer Ilene .... Denver, CO
Holt, Jeremy .... Orlando, FL
Holt, Jill L. .... Fairfax, VA
Holt, Jill M. .... Los Angeles, CA
Holt, Joan M. .... St. Louis, MO
Holt, Joe D. .... Columbia, MO
Fulton, MO
Holts Summit, MO
Holt, Joel H. .... Christiansted, St. Croix, VI
Holt, John Aaron .... Nashville, TN
Holt, John B. .... Florence, AL
Holt, John B.
United States Court Of Appeals For The Armed Forces, GV
Holt, John D. .... Valdosta, GA
Holt, John Fox .... Dallas, TX
Holt, John M. .... Indianapolis, IN
Holt, John M. .... Kansas City, MO
Holt, John N. .... Birmingham, AL
Holt, John S. .... Aurora, CO
Holt, John T. .... Thomasville, GA
Holt, John T. .... Loris, SC
Holt, John W. .... Salt Lake City, UT
Holt, Jon D. .... Dayton, OH
Holt, Jordan Oliver S. (Josh) .... Dallas, TX
Holt, Joseph A. .... Chicago, IL
Holt, Judd B. .... Denton, TX
Holt, Judith D. .... Birmingham, AL
Holt, Julianne M. .... Tampa, FL
Holt, Karen E. .... Charlottesville, VA
Holt, Karen M. .... Kaunakakai, HI
Holt, Katherine R. .... Madison, NJ
Holt, Kathleen Ann .... Merrimack, NH
Holt, Kenneth H. .... Houston, TX
Holt, Kerri A. .... Newark, NJ
Holt, Kevin W. .... Roanoke, VA
Holt, Kimberly P. .... Chesapeake, VA
Holt, Larry G. .... Bryan, TX
Holt, Larry G. .... College Station, TX
Holt, Laura K. .... Boston, MA
Holt, Lawrence J. .... Selden, NY
Holt, L. C., Jr. .... Allentown, PA
Holt, Leigh Ann
General Services Administration, Office of Regional Counsel, GV
Holt, Leonard Thomas .... Watertown, MA
Holt, Lester F. .... Amery, WI
Holt, Lewis A. .... Elizabethton, TN
Holt, Lisa D. .... Kansas City, MO
Holt, Longest, Wall & Blaetz, P.L.L.C.
Burlington, NC
Holt, Lowell C. .... Gilmer, TX
Holt, Marcia Chadwick .... Denver, CO
Holt, Marion G. .... Nacogdoches, TX
Holt, Marjorie S. .... Baltimore, MD
Holt, Marvin A. .... Minneapolis, MN
Holt, Mary Gray .... Department of Commerce, National Oceanic and Atmospheric Administration, GV
Holt, Matthew P. .... Las Cruces, NM
Holt, Mays & Brady .... Columbia, MO
Fulton, MO
Holts Summit, MO
Holt, McPherson, Jr. .... Boise, ID
Holt, Michael B. .... Hoboken, NJ
New York, NY
Holt, Michael D. .... Iowa Falls, IA
Holt, Michael D. .... Greensboro, NC
Holt, Michael E. .... Rochelle Park, NJ
Holt, Michael J. .... Springfield, IL
Holt, Michael J. .... Apple Valley, MN
Holt, Michael S. .... Hartsville, SC
Holt, Montessa D. .... Riverside, CA
Holt, Mussleman & Holt .... Florence, AL
Holt, Nancy H. .... Chicago, IL
Holt, Nathan M. .... Longview, TX
Holt, Neil H. .... Lansing, MI
Holt Ney Zatcoff & Wasserman, LLP
Atlanta, GA
Marietta, GA
Holt, Oscar, III .... Corona, NY
Holt, Patricia Hurst .... Los Angeles, CA
Holt, Patrick A. .... Seeley Lake, MT
Holt, Patti L. .... Durham, NC
Holt, Philetus H., IV .... New Haven, CT
Holt, R Jared .... Las Vegas, NV
Holt, Ralph .... Memphis, TN
Holt, Ralph E. .... Florence, AL
Holt, Rebecca L. .... Los Angeles, CA
Holt, Reginald L. .... Washington, DC
Holt, Renata B. .... New York, NY
Holt, Richard D. .... West Palm Beach, FL
Holt, R.M. .... Issaquah, WA
Holt, Robert B., Jr. .... Farmington Hills, MI
Holt, Robert Blaine .... Denver, CO
Holt, Robert E. .... Baltimore, MD
Holt, Robert G. .... Salt Lake City, UT
Holt, Robert G., (P.C.) .... Atlanta, GA
Holt, Robert H. .... Anchorage, KY
Holt, Robert T. .... Collegeville, PA
Holt, Robert W. .... Englewood, CO
Holt, Robert W. .... Lake Forest, IL
Holt, Roger J. .... Beverly Hills, CA

Holt, Ronald L. .... **Kansas City, MO**
Holt & Russell .... Christiansted, St. Croix, VI
Holt, Scott .... Layton, UT
Holt, Scott A. .... **Wilmington, DE**
Holt, Sheila B. .... **St. Paul, MN**
Holt, Shirley W. .... Philadelphia, PA
Holt, Stephen D. .... Milwaukee, WI
Holt, Steven A. .... **Noblesville, IN**
Holt, Steven A. .... **Livingston, NJ**
Holt, Stuart Joshua .... Chicago, IL
Holt, Susanna K. .... Austin, TX
Holt, Tammy M. .... **El Paso, TX**
Holt, Tatum & Fischer .... Nacogdoches, TX
Holt, Thaddeus .... Point Clear, AL
Washington, DC
Holt, Theodore J. .... **Gold River, CA**
Holt, Thomas F., Jr. .... **Boston, MA**
Holt, Thomas L. .... **Chicago, IL**
Holt, Thomas R. .... **Chapel Hill, NC**
Holt, Timothy W. .... Phoenix, AZ
Holt, Vic E. .... Tulsa, OK
Holt, W. Clary .... **Burlington, NC**
Holt, W. Paul, Jr. .... **Sylva, NC**
Holt, W. Paul, Jr., P.A. .... **Sylva, NC**
Holt & Watt .... **Eden, NC**
Reidsville, NC
Holt, Willard S., III .... Southfield, MI
Holt, William D. .... Toledo, OH
Holt, William E. .... **Tacoma, WA**
Holt, William Gary .... **Little Rock, AR**
Holt, William H. .... **Cleveland, OH**
Falls Church, VA
Holt, William J. .... Lancaster, OH
Holt, William M. .... Tampa, FL
Holt, William R., Jr. .... Sevierville, TN
Holt, Wythe W., Jr. .... Tuscaloosa, AL
Holt York McDarris, LLP .... **Cary, NC**
Raleigh, NC
Research Triangle Park, NC
Holtam, Sheryl Dugger .... Nashville, TN
Holtan, Bruce D. .... Salem, OR
Holtan, Harvey A. .... Lakefield, MN
Holtan, Mark H. .... Munster, IN
Holtan, Ramer B., Jr. .... **Seattle, WA**
Holtaway, John A. .... Chicago, IL
Holtby, Nancy T. .... **Rochester, NY**
Holt-Charles, Teri .... **Chicago, IL**
Holt-Duecaster, Jane .... Fort Worth, TX
Holte, H. Scott .... Everett, WA
Holte, Robert W. .... Stanley, ND
Holte, Yvonne M. .... Chicago, IL
Holten, Cort C. .... **Minneapolis, MN**
St. Paul, MN
Holten, John S. .... **Minneapolis, MN**
Holter, Amos A. .... **Frederick, MD**
Holter, Dwight J. .... Rochester, NY
Holter, Kathleen Lisa .... **Minneapolis, MN**
Holter, Reid A. .... Victor, NY
Holter, Robert M. .... Great Falls, MT
Holter, Terrance C. .... Bemidji, MN
Holter, Thomas H. .... **Nashville, TN**
Holtermann, David T. .... Carol Stream, IL
Holtey, Jud .... Ashland, OR
Holth, Fredrik D. .... **New London, CT**
Holth, Kollman, Fairlie & Golembeski
Hartford, CT
New London, CT
Holtham, William J. .... Salem, NH
Holthaus, Craig F. .... **Baton Rouge, LA**
Holthaus, Roger R. .... **Omaha, NE**
Holthaus, Tracy L. .... **Cincinnati, OH**
Holthausen, Peter D. .... Raleigh, NC
Holthoff, Timothy Neal .... Little Rock, AR
Holthouse, Philip J. .... Newport Beach, CA
Holthus, Brian E. .... **Las Vegas, NV**
Holthus, Douglas P. .... Columbus, OH
Holthus, Gary N. .... Gainesville, FL
Holthus, Larry W. .... Pagosa Springs, CO
Holthus, Thomas J. .... La Jolla, CA
Holtkamp, Alan L. .... Jefferson City, MO
Holtkamp, Alvin G. .... **St. Louis, MO**
Holtkamp, James A. .... **Salt Lake City, UT**
Holtkamp, Liese, Beckemeier & Childress, P.C. .... **St. Louis, MO**
Holtkamp, Lynne .... Durham, NC
Holtkamp, Lynne M. .... **Greensboro, NC**
Holtman, Charles B. .... **Minneapolis, MN**
Holtman, Donald R. .... **Hartford, CT**
Holtman, Jason P. .... **Seattle, WA**
Holtman, Reina J. .... Pittsburg, KS
Holtman, Ronald E. .... **Wooster, OH**
Holtman, Stephen J. .... **Cedar Rapids, IA**
Holtmann, Harold L. .... Tulsa, OK
Holtmann, John A. .... **Kansas City, MO**
Holtmann, John J. .... Vancouver, WA
Holtmann, Michael A. .... **Miami, FL**
Holtmeier, Denis G. .... Cincinnati, OH
Holtmeier, Jay Jeffrey .... **New York, NY**
Holtom, Gregory L. .... Pacific Grove, CA
Holtom, Kimbrely Anne .... Seattle, WA
Holton, A. Linwood, Jr. .... **Richmond, VA**
Holton, Anne B. .... Richmond, VA
Holton, Anne Baudino .... **Denver, CO**
Holton, Charles R. .... **Durham, NC**
Holton, David Michael
North Charleston, SC
Holton, Deborah Denise .... **Tallahassee, FL**
Holton, Elie L. .... Douglas, GA
Holton, Frank P., Jr. .... Lexington, NC
Holton & Holton .... Lexington, NC
Holton Howard & Goodman, P.C.
Nashville, TN
Holton, I. J. .... Austin, MN
Holton, James W. .... Madeira Beach, FL
Holton, Jas. T. .... Evanston, IL
Holton, John M., Jr. .... New London, NH
Holton Law Office .... **Helena, MT**
Holton, Leonard J. .... Tallahassee, FL
Holton, Mark B. .... **New York, NY**
Holton, Martin L., III
Winston-Salem, NC
Holton, Melissa Anemojanis
Department of Justice,
Tax Division, GV
Holton, Nancy .... Denver, CO
Holton, Peter S. .... **West Palm Beach, FL**
Holton, Raymond O., Jr.
Fort Lauderdale, FL
Holton, Richard D. .... **Nashville, TN**
Holton, Robert E. .... **New York, NY**
Holton, Stephen C. .... Lexington, NC
Holton, Thomas .... Newark, NJ
Holton, Thomas A. .... **Dayton, OH**
Holton, Thomas John .... **Boston, MA**
Holton, Walter C., Jr. .... Winston-Salem, NC
Holton, Wendy .... **Helena, MT**
Holton, William L. .... San Francisco, CA
Holton, William R., Jr. .... Oklahoma City, OK
Holtorf, Bradley D. .... **Fremont, NE**
Holtorf, Kovarik, Ellison & Mathis, P.C.
Alliance, NE
Bridgeport, NE
Gering, NE
Scottsbluff, NE
Holtrey, Travis L. .... **Owensboro, KY**
Holtrust, Gezina .... New York, NY
Holtry, Kelly A. .... **Phoenix, AZ**
Holtsberg, C. Edw., Jr. .... Evanston, IL
Holtsberg, Philip A., (P.A.)
Watkinsville, GA
Holtschneider, Mark T. .... Baltimore, MD
Holtschulte, Jeffery M. .... Columbus, OH
Holtsclaw Law Firm, The, L.L.C.
Kansas City, MO
Holtsclaw, Rick D. .... **Kansas City, MO**
Holtsford, Alex L., Jr. .... **Montgomery, AL**
Holtshouser, Steven E. .... St. Louis, MO
Holtsinger, Clay A. .... **Tampa, FL**
Holtz, Albert L. .... **Bloomfield Hills, MI**
Holtz, Albert L., Law Offices of, P.C.
Bloomfield Hills, MI
Holtz, Amy K. .... Penn Valley, PA
Holtz, Barbara L. .... Upper Marlboro, MD
Holtz, Charlene L. .... Chicago, IL
Holtz, Claire J. .... Stoughton, WI
Holtz, Craig A. .... Glendale, CA
Holtz, D. Charles .... Mobile, AL
Holtz, David C. .... Los Angeles, CA
Holtz, Dawn Michele .... Philadelphia, PA
Holtz, Debra A. .... St. Paul, MN
Holtz, Dennis A. .... **Philadelphia, PA**
Holtz, Dixie L. .... Sherman Oaks, CA
Holtz, Douglas .... New York, NY
Holtz & Foret, LLC .... **Washington, DC**
Bethesda, MD
Chevy Chase, MD
Rockville, MD
Upper Marlboro, MD
Holtz, Geoffrey T. .... San Francisco, CA
Holtz, Gerald I. .... **Chevy Chase, MD**
Holtz Gilman Grunebaum .... **Boston, MA**
Holtz, Gregory T. .... Cleveland, OH
Holtz, H. Edward .... Washington, DC
Holtz, Harry L. .... Lillydale, MN
Holtz, Herbert L. .... **Boston, MA**
Holtz, James F. .... **San Diego, CA**
Holtz, John A. .... Laramie, WY
Holtz, John B. .... Los Angeles, CA
Holtz, Judith A. .... Bloomfield Hills, MI
Holtz, Larry R. .... La Plata, MD
Holtz, Leonard .... New York, NY
Holtz, Lloyd K. .... Tulsa, OK
Holtz, Mark A. .... Chagrin Falls, OH
Holtz, Michael D. .... **Los Angeles, CA**
Holtz, Norman .... **Boston, MA**
Holtz, Randall M. .... Baraboo, WI
Holtz, Rebecca J.
Department of Housing and Urban
Development,
Office of General Counsel, GV
Holtz, Richard R. .... Bellflower, CA
Holtz, Richard R., and Associates, Law Offices of .... Bellflower, CA
Holtz, Richard W. .... **Boston, MA**
Holtz, Robert E. .... Mequon, WI
Holtz, Robert J. .... Philadelphia, PA
Holtz, Robert W. .... Beatrice, NE
Holtz, Sara .... Granite Bay, CA
Holtz, Steven M. .... **New York, NY**
Holtz, Theodore S. .... Garfield Heights, OH
Holtz, William E. .... Boston, MA
Holtzapfel, Richard E. .... **Charleston, WV**
Holtzapple, Robert C. .... **San Francisco, CA**
Holtzclaw, Brian L. .... **Seattle, WA**
Holtzclaw, Shawn R. .... **Atlanta, GA**
Holtze, Robert C. .... St. Louis Park, MN
Holtzen, Timothy C. .... Phoenix, AZ
Holtzendorf, Howard C. .... Arcadia, FL
Holtzendorff, Frances D. .... Little Rock, AR
Holtzer, David .... **New York, NY**
Holtzer, Gary T. .... **New York, NY**
Holtzer, James A. .... York, PA
Holtzer, Mark M. .... **New York, NY**
Holtzhouser, Jay R. .... **Robinson, IL**
Holtzinger, John E., Jr. .... Washington, DC
Holtzlander, Stephanie Franco
Indianapolis, IN
Holtzman, Alexander .... New York, NY
Holtzman, Arthur M. .... **Chicago, IL**
Holtzman, Barbara L. .... Tucson, AZ
Holtzman, Barney M. .... **Phoenix, AZ**
Tucson, AZ
Holtzman, David C. .... St. Ann, MO
Holtzman, Diana I. .... New York, NY
Holtzman, Edw. G. .... St. Louis, MO
Holtzman, Elizabeth .... **New York, NY**
Holtzman, Ellen B. .... **Nanuet, NY**
Holtzman, Ellen B. .... **New City, NY**
Holtzman, Eric H. .... **Hauppauge, NY**
Holtzman, Gail Golman .... **Tampa, FL**
Holtzman, Gerald T. .... **Houston, TX**
Holtzman, H. Steven .... **St. Petersburg, FL**
Holtzman, Harriet .... New York, NY
Holtzman, Harvey Alan .... Denver, CO
Holtzman, Howard L. .... Los Angeles, CA
Holtzman, Jan M. .... Cincinnati, OH
Holtzman, Jeffrey W. .... Santa Rosa, CA
Holtzman, Jill .... Washington, DC
Holtzman, John .... Washington, IL
Holtzman, Jonathan V. .... San Francisco, CA
Holtzman, Joseph S. .... Chicago, IL
Holtzman, Joyce Ann .... Miami, FL
Holtzman, Krinzman, Equels & Furia
Miami, FL
Orlando, FL
Tallahassee, FL
Holtzman, Louis L. .... Coral Gables, FL
Holtzman, Michael .... Atascadero, CA
Holtzman, Paul V. .... **Boston, MA**
Holtzman, Robert A. .... **Los Angeles, CA**
Holtzman, Robert B. .... Phoenix, AZ
Holtzman, Robert N. .... **New York, NY**
Holtzman, Sarge R. .... Mill Valley, CA
Holtzman, Scott R. .... **Burbank, CA**
Holtzman, Shannon Skelton
New Orleans, LA
Holtzman, Stephen D. .... **Linwood, NJ**
Holtzman, Sylvan (Sonny) .... **Miami, FL**
Holtzmann, Edward M. .... New York, NY
Holtzmann, Howard M. .... **New York, NY**
Holtzmuller, Paul E. .... Eaton, OH
Holtzschue, Karl B. .... **New York, NY**
Holtzworth, James W. .... **Gloversville, NY**
Holub, Cynthia A. .... **Houston, TX**
Holub, David W. .... **Hammond, IN**
Holub, Edward W. .... **Denver, CO**
Holub, Fred P. .... Bay City, TX
Holub, Hugh A. .... Phoenix, AZ
Tucson, AZ
Holub, Hugh A., P.L.C. .... Phoenix, AZ
Tucson, AZ
Holub, Jerome L. .... Akron, OH
Holub, Kathy J. .... New York, NY
Holub, Michael J. .... Newton, NJ
Holub, Ronald E. .... **Dallas, TX**
Holub, Ronald E., P.C. .... **Dallas, TX**
Holuba, Robert J. .... Kearny, NJ
Holubar, Jennifer Tara Geter
Washington, DC
Holubec, Ulana .... **Ithaca, NY**
Holubeck, Philip A. .... Livonia, MI
Holum, Everett A. .... Tacoma, WA
Holum, Gary A. .... Minot, ND
Holum, John D. .... Department of State,
Office of the Secretary, GV
Holum, Thomas E. .... Chicago, IL
Holveck, John K., Jr. .... Des Moines, IA
Holverson, Michael P. .... **Chicago, IL**
Holvick, Valerie A. .... Palo Alto, CA
Holvik, Julie A.
United States Postal Service,
Mid-Atlantic Office, GV
Holvino, Roberto .... San Juan, PR
Holwadel, D. Russell .... **New Orleans, LA**
Holwager, Byers and Caughey, A Professional Association .... Beech Grove, IN
Holwager, William J. .... Beech Grove, IN
Holway, Donal F. .... New York, NY
Holway, James R. .... Washington, DC
Holweger, Marie Polizzi .... **Los Angeles, CA**
Holwell, Richard J. .... **New York, NY**
Holwerda, Jack B. .... Grand Rapids, MI
Holwerda, Steven J. .... Newton, IA
Holwey, Michelle M. .... **Birmingham, MI**
Columbus, OH
Holwig, William M. .... Livonia, MI
Holwitt, Scott P. .... **St. Louis, MO**
Holy, John S. .... Weston, WV
Holy, Lori J. .... **Washington, DC**
Holy, Michael C. .... **Chicago, IL**
Holy, Richard F. .... Minneapolis, MN
Holya, John Robert .... Phoenix, AZ
Holyfield, James, Jr. .... Denver, CO
Holyfield, Sharmista N. .... **Torrance, CA**
Holyoak, Kerry Dale .... Fredonia, KS
Holyoak, William D. .... **Salt Lake City, UT**
Holyoke, Thomas T. .... **Scottsbluff, NE**
Holz, Arthur F. .... San Diego, CA
Holz, Dennis E. .... Oceanside, CA
Holz, Harry G. .... **Milwaukee, WI**
Holz, Joy M. .... New York, NY
Holz, Marvin .... Milwaukee, WI
Holz, Maureen L. .... Tallahassee, FL
Holz, Michael H. .... Dayton, OH
Holz, Otto C. .... **San Francisco, CA**
Holz, Rana .... **Fort Myers, FL**
Holz, Richard W. .... **Columbus, OH**
Holz, Robert F., Jr. .... **Des Moines, IA**
Holz, Robert J. .... **Irving, TX**
Holz, Scott J.
Board of Governors Of The Federal Reserve
System,
Office of the General Counsel, GV
Holz, Shannon G. .... Des Moines, IA
Holz, Stephen D. .... Los Angeles, CA
Holz, Suzanne C. .... **Brick, NJ**
Holzapfel, Eric C. .... **Cincinnati, OH**
Holzapfel, George S. .... **Seattle, WA**
Holzapfel, James W. .... Toms River, NJ
Holzapfel, John E. .... Columbus, OH
Holzapfel, Leonard F. .... Jackson, OH
Holzapfel, Marc F. .... **New York, NY**
Holzapfel, Richard D. .... **Sandusky, OH**
Holzapfel, Robert S. .... Willows, CA
Holzapfel, William R. .... Newark, NJ
Holzbach, David M. .... Danbury, CT
Holzbach, James T. .... Cleveland, OH
Holzback, Stephanie M. .... **New York, NY**
Holzberg, Bryan J. .... Melville, NY
Holzberg, David E. .... New York, NY
Holzberg, Edward P. .... Peabody, MA
Holzberg, Ernest .... New York, NY
Holzberg, Glenn J. .... Miami, FL
Holzberg, Kenneth E. .... **Framingham, MA**
Holzberg, Maria M. .... Middletown, CT
Holzberg, Rachel S. .... San Francisco, CA
Holzberg, Robert L. .... Waterbury, CT
Holzberg, Suzanne B. .... New York, NY
Holzberger, Cheryl L. .... North Providence, RI
Holzborn, M. Travis .... **Monroeville, AL**
Holzderber, David J. .... Florence, KY
Holzem, Peter J. .... Chama, NM
Holzem, Scott W. .... Fort Myers, FL
Holzenthal, Karen T. .... **New Orleans, LA**
Holzer, Corey Daniel .... **Atlanta, GA**
Holzer, Henry Mark .... Santa Fe, NM
Holzer, J. Carroll .... **Towson, MD**
Holzer, Kurt D. .... **Boise, ID**
Holzer & Lee .... **Towson, MD**
Holzer, Nathaniel Peter
Corpus Christi, TX
Holzer, Peter .... Los Angeles, CA
Holzer, Richard J. .... Dayton, OH
Holzer, Richard J., Jr. .... **Denver, CO**
Holzer, Sidney .... Huntington, NY
Holzer, Stephen T. .... **Los Angeles, CA**
Holzer, Steven L. .... Indianapolis, IN
Holzer, Stuart J. .... New York, NY
Holzer, Walter S. .... **Cleveland, OH**
Holzfaster, Byron E. .... **Dayton, OH**
Holzfaster, Cecil, McKnight & Mues, A Legal Professional Association
Dayton, OH
Holzgraefe, John R. .... **Dallas, TX**
Holzgrafe, Roger E. .... **Peoria, IL**
Holzhall, Marianne Craigmile
Chicago, IL
Holzhall, Vincent I. .... **Chicago, IL**
Holzhauer, Gregory L. .... **Winter Park, FL**
Holzhauer, James D. .... **Chicago, IL**
Holzhauer, Mark Joseph .... **St. Joseph, MO**
Holzhauer, Marsha Diane .... Breese, IL
Holzhauer, William J. .... Syracuse, NY
Holzhaus, Dominic T. .... Los Angeles, CA
Holzheimer, Edward T. .... Cleveland, OH
Holzheimer, Richard D., Jr. .... **McLean, VA**
Holzhuter, John W. .... **Janesville, WI**
Holzinger, James J. .... Bethlehem, PA
Holzinger, Jan K. .... **Houston, TX**
Holzinger, Richard G. .... New York, NY
Holzka, Denise Anne .... **Philadelphia, PA**
Holzknecht, Michael D., P.C.
Kansas City, MO
Holzle, Catherine M.
Nuclear Regulatory Commission,
Office of the General Counsel, GV
Holzman & Baron .... **Baltimore, MD**
Holzman, Beth F. .... Sacramento, CA
Holzman, Charles J. .... Southfield, MI
Holzman, Daniel M. .... **Hollywood, CA**
Holzman, Daniel S. .... **New York, NY**
Holzman, Deborah A. .... **Roseland, NJ**
Holzman, Donald J. .... **Buffalo, NY**
Holzman, Ellen D. .... **Chicago, IL**
Holzman, Erwin A. .... Farmington Hills, MI
Holzman, Henry .... **Baltimore, MD**
Holzman and Holzman .... Southfield, MI
Holzman & Holzman .... Cincinnati, OH
Holzman, James A. .... Harrisburg, PA
Holzman, James L. .... **Wilmington, DE**
Holzman, Joan K. .... Buffalo, NY
Holzman, Lara A. .... **New York, NY**
Holzman, Lawrence .... **New York, NY**
Holzman, Lawrence J. .... Vancouver, WA
Holzman, Lawrence R. .... Rockville, MD
Holzman, Michael Glenn .... Chicago, IL
Holzman, Robert S. .... Cincinnati, OH
Holzman, Ruth N. .... **Los Angeles, CA**
Holzman, Sheridan V. .... Southfield, MI
Holzman, Susan Medinets .... **Roseland, NJ**
Holzman, Thomas L.
Federal Deposit Insurance Corporation,
Trial Litigation Section, GV
Holzman, Wallace Ross, Jr. .... Cincinnati, OH
Holzman, William M. .... **Chicago, IL**
Holzmann, Barbara .... Milwaukee, WI
Holzmann, Dean J., Jr. .... Rocky Point, NY
Holzmann, Rochelle C.
San Francisco, CA
Holznecht, Charles A. .... Janesville, WI
Holzrichter, Linda M. .... Aurora, IL
Holzwarth, Elsie G. .... Chicago, IL
Holzwarth, Lori L. .... Fort Smith, AR
Holzwarth, Lori Reinhart .... Springfield, MO
Holzwarth, Roberta L. .... **Rockford, IL**
Holzwarth, William C. .... Anaheim, CA
Holzworth, David .... Washington, DC
Holzworth, Michael P. .... Des Moines, IA
Hom, Andrea M. .... **Irvine, CA**
Hom, Anthony J. .... New York, NY
Philadelphia, PA
Hom, Curtis D. W. .... **Redmond, WA**
Hom, Cynthia L. .... La Jolla, CA
Hom, David A. .... **Atlanta, GA**
Hom, Ernest F. .... Bethesda, MD
Hom, Eugene R. .... Detroit, MI
Hom, Frances M. .... Washington, DC
Hom, George S. S. .... Honolulu, HI
Hom, Harold L. .... **Cleveland, OH**
Hom, Howard .... Los Angeles, CA
Hom, Judith S.H. .... **San Jose, CA**
Hom, Lawrence .... San Francisco, CA

Hom, Martha L. ... Fairlawn, OH
Hom, Mon Bill, (A Professional Law Corporation) ... Los Angeles, CA
Hom, Paul F. ... San Diego, CA
Hom, Peter D. ... San Jose, CA
Hom, Phillip ... New York, NY
Hom, Robin S. ... San Leandro, CA
Hom, Russell L., Law Offices of
Sacramento, CA
Hom, Sandy ... New York, NY
Hom, Sharon K. ... Berkeley, CA
Hom, Steven R.
Nuclear Regulatory Commission, Office of the General Counsel, GV
Hom, Tony C. ... New York, NY
Hom, Wendy ... Stamford, CT
Hom, Wilton A. ... Farmington Hills, MI
Homa, James A. ... Fairfield, CT
Homa, Joseph M. ... Piscataway, NJ
Homa, Leonard S. ... Edgewater, MD
Homady, Theresa C. ... Ebensburg, PA
Homampour, Arash ... Beverly Hills, CA
New York, NY
Homan, Arthur Wilbourn ... Palo Alto, CA
Homan, Cynthia A. ... Chicago, IL
Homan, David C. ... East Lansing, MI
Homan, Frederick C. ... Westborough, MA
Homan, Jean P. ... Tacoma, WA
Homan, John C. ... Albuquerque, NM
Homan, Judith L. ... Laconia, NH
Homan, Kimberly ... Boston, MA
Homan, Laura A. ... Los Angeles, CA
Homan, Molly E. ... Denver, CO
Homan & Mulligan, P.C. ... Carneys Point, NJ
Homan and Pearce ... Clyde, OH
Homan, Robert L. ... Lincoln, NE
Homan, Robert W. ... Manhattan Beach, CA
Homan, Ronald Charles ... Riverside, CA
Homan, Ruth E. ... Cincinnati, OH
Homan, Warren W. ... Carneys Point, NJ
Homann, Kurt R. ... Crawfordsville, IN
Homann, Matthew W. ... Highland, IL
Homans, James A. P. ... Boston, MA
Homans, Joseph A. ... Dawsonville, GA
Gainesville, GA
Homans, Michael D. ... Philadelphia, PA
Homans, William P. ... Boston, MA
Homans, William V. ... New York, NY
Homant, Danielle ... Boston, MA
Homayoun, Aresh ... Washington, DC
Homayun, Edna ... Los Angeles, CA
Hombach, Stephen C. ... Columbus, OH
Homberg, Thomas R. ... Milwaukee, WI
Homburg, John R. ... Charleston, WV
Homburg, Randal D. ... Oklahoma City, OK
Homburger, Thomas C. ... Chicago, IL
Homchick, Robert G. ... Seattle, WA
Homchick, Sheila A. ... Brush Prairie, WA
Home, Greg ... Bellevue, WA
Home, Greg, Inc., P.S. ... Bellevue, WA
Home, Maureen M. ... Los Angeles, CA
Home, W. Stuart, II ... Fresno, CA
Home, W. Stuart, III ... Sacramento, CA
Homec, Martin ... El Sobrante, CA
Homeier, Edward L. ... Dearborn, MI
Homelson, Rochelle ... Hartford, CT
Homen, Mark A. ... Hayward, CA
Homen, Norman J., Jr. ... Garden Grove, CA
Homer, Barry W. ... San Francisco, CA
Homer Bonner & Delgado, P.A.
Fort Lauderdale, FL
Miami, FL
Homer, Charles A. ... Idaho Falls, ID
Homer, Christine Y. ... New York, NY
Homer, David R. ... Albany, NY
Homer, Donald M. ... Boca Raton, FL
Homer, Elizabeth Lohah ... Albuquerque, NM
Homer, Gregg ... Los Angeles, CA
Homer, Gregg, P.C. ... Los Angeles, CA
Homer, Gregory W. ... Washington, DC
Homer, Ilyse Wrubel ... Miami, FL
Homer, Jeffrey B. ... Davie, FL
Homer, Jennifer D. ... Chicago, IL
Homer, Jeremy W. ... Dover, DE
Homer, Kenneth David ... Mansfield, OH
Homer, Kevin B. ... Idaho Falls, ID
Homer, Lauren B. ... St. Louis, MO
Homer, Leonard C. ... Baltimore, MD
Homer, Lewis H., III ... Sanford, FL
Homer, Melanie ... Kansas City, MO
Homer, Michael W. ... Salt Lake City, UT
Homer, Paul, (P.C.) ... Chicago, IL
Homer, Peter W. ... Miami, FL
Homer, Richard S. ... Chicago, IL
Homer, Ronald C. ... Boston, MA
Homer, Stephen C. ... Oakland, CA
Homer, Thomas J. ... Ottawa, IL
Homer, William J., III ... New York, NY
Homerin, Dennis R. ... Chicago, IL
Homes, Justin H. ... New Orleans, LA
Homes, Robert O., Jr. ... Gulfport, MS
Homesley, Clifton W. ... Mooresville, NC
Homesley, Jones, Gaines, Homesley & Dudley ... Mooresville, NC
Statesville, NC
Homesley, Troy C., Jr. ... Mooresville, NC
Statesville, NC
Homeyer, Michael L. ... Houston, TX
Homeyer, Yvonne M. ... St. Louis, MO
Homich, James L. ... Mobile, AL
Homick, Daniel J. ... Raleigh, NC
Homick, Paul ... Latrobe, PA
Homick, Victoria M. ... Raleigh, NC
Hominick, Ronald N. ... Honolulu, HI
Homire, James L., Jr. ... St. Louis, MO
Homire, Richard C. ... St. Louis, MO
Homire and Wilkes, P.C. ... St. Louis, MO
Homisak, Theresa ... Edison, NJ

Homko, Judith A. ... Fort Lauderdale, FL
Homm, George H. ... Burlington, CO
Homma, Michiharu ... Indianapolis, IN
Homme, Marc S. ... Palm Desert, CA
Homme, Marc S., A Professional Law Corporation ... Palm Desert, CA
Homme, O. Jason ... Seattle, WA
Hommel, John G. ... Hinsdale, IL
Hommel, Robert J. ... Scottsdale, AZ
Hommel, Theodore E., Jr.
Garden City, NY
Hommel, Thomas E. ... New York, NY
Hommel, William S., Jr. ... Tyler, TX
Hommer, J. Scott, III ... McLean, VA
Hommert, Douglas D. ... St. Louis, MO
Homnack, Peter A. ... Ambridge, PA
Homola, Benjamin C. ... Elburn, IL
Homola, Harry F. ... Chicago, IL
Homola, James R. ... Fresno, CA
Homolak, Diane I. ... Strongsville, OH
Homolak, Gloria Rowland ... Cleveland, OH
Homolak, Gloria Rowland ... Parma, OH
Homolak, John R. ... Cleveland, OH
Homolka, C. Dean, II ... Wichita, KS
Homolka, Daniel M. ... Minneapolis, MN
Homonoff, Howard B. ... Fort Lee, NJ
Homonoff, Marvin H. ... Providence, RI
Hompesch & Associates, A Professional Corporation ... Anchorage, AK
Fairbanks, AK
Hompesch, Richard W., II ... Fairbanks, AK
Homrighausen, Paul E.
San Francisco, CA
Homsey, Cooper, Hill, & Associates
Oklahoma City, OK
Homsey, Gary B. ... Oklahoma City, OK
Homsey, Kenneth M. ... Lawrence, MA
Homsey, Michael S. ... Oklahoma City, OK
Homsey, Michael S." Mickey ", & Associates, P.C. ... Oklahoma City, OK
Homsey, Philip R., II ... Glendale, CA
Homsey, Walter, Jr. ... Cedar Rapids, IA
Homsher, David G. ... Lancaster, PA
Homsy, David M. ... Los Angeles, CA
Homsy, Dimitri ... Milton, MA
Homsy, Joseph G. ... Chicago, IL
Homsy, Paul C. ... New York, NY
Homyak, Mark J. ... Pittsburgh, PA
Homyak, Michael R. ... Denver, CO
Homyk, Donald Lee ... Chicago, IL
Homza, Brian A. ... Shreveport, LA
Hon, Charles O., III ... Chattanooga, TN
Hon, Daniel, A Professional Law Corporation
Santa Clarita, CA
Hon, William Lee ... Livingston, TX
Honabach, Dennis R. ... South Royalton, VT
Honabach, Elmer W. ... Falls Church, VA
Honaker, Elizabeth J. ... Billings, MT
Honaker, Hampton & Newman, LC
Rock Springs, WY
Honaker, Jas. M. ... Frankfort, KY
Honaker, Jay J. ... Van Nuys, CA
Honaker, Richard H. ... Rock Springs, WY
Honaker, William H. ... Bloomfield Hills, MI
Honaman, Peter K. ... Lancaster, PA
Honan, John J. ... Buffalo, NY
Honan, Maryanne E.
Palos Verdes Peninsula, CA
Honan, Stephen M. ... Nyack, NY
Honan, William J., III ... New York, NY
Honan, William M. ... Atlantic City, NJ
Honara, Charles J. ... Rego Park, NY
Honart, Charles M. ... Wayne, PA
Honarvar, Hermine E. ... Laguna Hills, CA
Honath, Sandra K., The Law Office of
Montrose, CO
Honchariw, Nicholas J.
Belvedere-Tiburon, CA
Honchell, Donald S. ... Chicago, IL
Honda, Hester ... Orange, CA
Honda, Mark T., Law Offices of
Wailuku, HI
Hondagneu, Michel R. ... Menlo Park, CA
Hondorp, William J. ... Grand Rapids, MI
Hondros, John G. ... Columbus, OH
Hondros, Lisa C. ... Minneapolis, MN
Hone, Andrew M. ... Boston, MA
Hone, Cheryl ... Kew Gardens, NY
Hone, Elizabeth A.
Federal Trade Commission, Bureau of Consumer Protection, GV
Hone, Eric D. ... Boise, ID
Hone, Francis J. ... New York, NY
Hone, Graham R. ... New York, NY
Hone, Jay R. ... Albuquerque, NM
Philadelphia, PA
Hone, John Llewellyn ... Washington, DC
Silver Spring, MD
Hone, John S. ... Farmington Hills, MI
Hone, John S., P.C. ... Detroit, MI
Farmington Hills, MI
Hone Law Firm, The, P.C.
Albuquerque, NM
Hone, Michael C. ... San Francisco, CA
Hone, Robert E. ... Fort Lauderdale, FL
Hone, Robert E. ... Wheaton, IL
Hone, Thomas E. ... New York, NY
Hone, William J. ... New York, NY
Honea, F. Franklin, II ... Dallas, TX
Honea, Gary L. ... Magnolia, MS
Honea, Robert M. ... Fort Smith, AR
Honea, Sterling ... Los Angeles, CA
Honeck, Richard D. ... Akron, OH
Honecker, Benjamin R. ... Wheeling, WV
Honecker & Bippus Law Offices
Wheeling, WV
Honecker, Kathryn A. ... Rockford, IL
Honecker, Lee C. ... Basking Ridge, NJ

Honecker, Rodman E. ... Iselin, NJ
New York, NY
Honegan-Pounder, Sandra ... New York, NY
Honegger, Andrew A. ... Boston, MA
Honegger, Michael J. ... Hanna City, IL
Honegger, Scott C. ... Lafayette, CA
Honegger, Sue M. ... Kansas City, MO
Honemann, Daniel H. ... Baltimore, MD
Honen, Richard E. ... Albany, NY
Honen & Wood, P.C. ... Albany, NY
Honenberger, Christopher J. ... Orange, VA
Honenberger, Sarah Collins ... Orange, VA
Honer, James A. ... Grass Valley, CA
Honer, Joseph C., Jr. ... Media, PA
Honer, Sherri L. ... Tustin, CA
Honerlaw & Honerlaw Co., L.P.A.
Cincinnati, OH
Honerlaw, Joseph ... Cincinnati, OH
Honerlaw, Michael J. ... Cincinnati, OH
Honess, Mary E. ... Minneapolis, MN
Honesty, Edward F. ... Oak Brook, IL
Honet, Lauren D. ... Bloomfield Hills, MI
Honeth, Naomi ... Portland, ME
Honetschlager, Beth A. ... Minneapolis, MN
Honett, Steven H. L. ... Plano, TX
Honey, Charles L." Chuck " ... Prescott, AR
Honey, Charles M. ... Prescott, AR
Honey, Daniel Walker ... Milwaukee, WI
Honey, Edgar Thomas ... New York, NY
Honey & Honey, P.A. ... Prescott, AR
Honey, Jennifer ... Manhattan Beach, CA
Honey, Jennifer M., P.C., Law Office of
Manhattan Beach, CA
Honey, John K., Jr. ... Richmond, VA
Honey, Roger G. ... Los Angeles, CA
Honey, Suanne I., Law Offices of
Orange, CA
Honey, William C. ... Montgomery, AL
Honeycheck, Linda J. ... Nutley, NJ
Honeychurch, Denis A. ... Fairfield, CA
Honeychurch and Finkas ... Fairfield, CA
Honeycutt, Alan B. ... Los Angeles, CA
Honeycutt, D. Blayne
Denham Springs, LA
Honeycutt, Hetrick & Carter, LLP
Mobile, AL
Honeycutt, J. David ... Houston, TX
Honeycutt, J. Marvin ... Van Buren, AR
Honeycutt, James M. ... Lexington, NC
Honeycutt, J.D., III ... Tuscaloosa, AL
Honeycutt, Joan K. ... Laguna Niguel, CA
Honeycutt, John B., Jr. ... Charlotte, NC
Honeycutt, Karen ... New York, NY
Honeycutt, Kenneth W. ... Monroe, NC
Honeycutt, Pamela B. ... Jonesboro, AR
Honeycutt, Steve M., Jr. ... Lawrenceville, GA
Honeycutt, Timothy M. ... Cypress, TX
Honeycutt, Walter Herbert ... Mobile, AL
Honeyman, Jason M. ... Boston, MA
Honeyman, John D. ... Troy, MI
Honeyman, Marshall ... Alexandria, VA
Honeyman, Marshall S.
Department of Commerce, Patent and Trademark Office, GV
Honeyman, Richard L. ... Wichita, KS
Honeyman, Robert W. ... Norristown, PA
Honeyman, Sandra M. ... Boston, MA
Honeymar, Michael G., Jr. ... New York, NY
Honeysuckle, Janan E. Kemp
Little Rock, AR
Honeywell, Charlene Edwards ... Tampa, FL
Honeywell, Dan H. ... Orlando, FL
Honeywell, Elizabeth A. ... Norman, OK
Honeywell, Elizabeth C. ... Baltimore, MD
Honeywell, James W. ... New Berlin, NY
Honeywell, Jeffrey D. ... Albany, NY
Honeywell, Mark G. ... Seattle, WA
Honeywell, Robert T. ... Houston, TX
Honeywell, Valen H. ... Tacoma, WA
Hong, Anna J. ... New York, NY
Hong, Arlene S. ... New York, NY
Hong, Carol Lee ... Honolulu, HI
Hong & Chang ... Los Angeles, CA
Hong, Christina G. ... San Francisco, CA
Hong, Christine E. ... Cambridge, MA
Hong, David A. ... San Francisco, CA
Hong, Deborah Wansun ... Philadelphia, PA
Hong, Edward ... New York, NY
Hong, Elizabeth ... Los Angeles, CA
Hong, Frederick W. ... Pasadena, CA
Hong, George S. W. ... Honolulu, HI
Hong, Grace ... Chicago, IL
Hong, Haeji ... Los Angeles, CA
Hong & Hong, LLP ... Las Vegas, NV
Hong, Iwai, Hulbert & Kawano
Honolulu, HI
Hong, Janet ... Cedar Rapids, IA
Hong, Jeanne E. ... Mountain View, CA
Hong, Jennifer L. ... Washington, DC
Hong, Ji Hoon ... New York, NY
Hong, John Y. ... Las Vegas, NV
Hong, Joon P. ... New York, NY
Hong, Joseph Y. ... Las Vegas, NV
Hong, Ki P. ... Washington, DC
Hong, Kimberly J. ... Pittsburgh, PA
Hong & Kwock ... Honolulu, HI
Hong, Laura Kingsley ... Cleveland, OH
Hong, Lea O. ... Honolulu, HI
Hong, Malcolm E. ... Aiea, HI
Hong, Matthew Christopher
Los Angeles, CA
Hong, Michael D. ... Honolulu, HI
Hong, Michele H. ... New York, NY
Hong, Nina L. ... Palo Alto, CA
Hong, Nowland C. ... Los Angeles, CA
Hong, Patricia E. ... Washington, DC
Hong, Paul S. ... New York, NY
Hong, Peder B. ... Red Wing, MN

Hong, Peter S. ... Beverly Hills, CA
Hong, Richard L. ... San Francisco, CA
Hong, Ryan S. ... Los Angeles, CA
Hong, Sebong ... Los Angeles, CA
Hong, Sharon C. ... Palisades Park, NJ
Hong, Simon Song-Jin ... Los Angeles, CA
Hong, Song Yook ... New York, NY
Hong, Sonya C. ... San Francisco, CA
Hong, Soo Ah ... Costa Mesa, CA
Hong, Stanley W. ... Honolulu, HI
Hong, Stephanie J. ... Walnut Creek, CA
Hong, Sung A. ... Livingston, NJ
Hong, Susan F. ... Los Angeles, CA
Hong, Tany S. ... Honolulu, HI
Hong, Ted H. S. ... Hilo, HI
Hong, Thomas H. ... Atlanta, GA
Hong, Walton D. Y., Law Offices of
Lihue, HI
Hong, Yeu S. ... Los Angeles, CA
Hongladarom, Jon G. ... Seattle, WA
Hongo, Jeff T. ... St. Louis, MO
Honhart, Mark E. ... Frisco, CO
Honhorst, Nancy J. ... Olympia, WA
Honi, Raghubeer S. ... New York, NY
Honick, Eric ... New York, NY
Honick, Gary ... Baltimore, MD
Honicky, David A. ... Cleveland, OH
Honig, Barbara ... Los Angeles, CA
Honig and Barnes ... Haverhill, MA
Honig, Daniel A. ... Washington, DC
Honig, David A. ... San Francisco, CA
Honig, Deborah B. ... San Francisco, CA
Honig, Douglas S. ... Santa Ana, CA
Honig, Edward H. ... Carle Place, NY
Honig, Eric ... Marina Del Rey, CA
Honig, Glen A. ... Tucson, AZ
Honig, Gregory D. ... Phoenix, AZ
Honig, Helaine ... Seattle, WA
Honig & Honig ... Waldwick, NJ
Honig, Isadore A. ... Silver Spring, MD
Honig, Jennifer ... Boston, MA
Honig, Joan B. ... Framingham, MA
Honig, Jonathan D. ... New York, NY
Honig, Keith C. ... Los Angeles, CA
Honig, Kelly Bennett ... Pasadena, CA
Honig, Leslie A. ... New York, NY
Honig, Lisa ... Oakland, CA
Honig, Marvin I. ... Albany, NY
Honig, Melvyn ... Los Angeles, CA
Honig, Michelle S. ... New York, NY
Honig, Milton L. ... Edgewater, NJ
Honig, Murray ... Voorhees, NJ
Honig, Richard B. ... Englewood, NJ
Newark, NJ
Honig, Richard E. ... Hamburg, NJ
Honig, Robert L. ... New York, NY
Honig, Robyn Frye ... Haverhill, MA
Honig, Roger S. ... Scottsdale, AZ
Honig, Ron I. ... Boston, MA
Honig, Ronald D. ... Dallas, TX
Honig, Ross A. ... New York, NY
Honig, Seymour L. ... Tampa, FL
Honig, Sheldon ... Huntington, NY
Honig, Stephen M. ... Boston, MA
Honig, Steven M. ... Waldwick, NJ
Honig, William J. ... Norristown, PA
Honigberg, Carol C. ... Falls Church, VA
Honigberg, Martin P. ... Concord, NH
Honigberg, Paul M. ... Department of Justice, Civil Division, GV
Honigberg, Renee D. ... Chicago, IL
Honigfeld, Jared D. ... Somerset, NJ
Honigfeld, Marc J. ... Hackensack, NJ
Honig-Gold, Debra B. ... New York, NY
Honigman, Barry K. ... Melville, NY
Honigman, Daniel M. ... Southfield, MI
Honigman, David M. ... Lansing, MI
Honigman, Donald S. ... Walnut Creek, CA
Honigman & Donner ... Melville, NY
Honigman, Lori J. ... Washington, DC
Honigman Miller Schwartz and Cohn
Detroit, MI
Lansing, MI
Honigman, Robert D. ... Birmingham, MI
Honigman, Robert G. ... Treasury Department, Internal Revenue Service, GV
Honigman, Steven S. ... Washington, DC
Honigmann, Peter H., Jr. ... Phoenix, AZ
Honigman-Singer, Kay ... Birmingham, MI
Honik, Ruben ... Philadelphia, PA
Honikel, Kevin Charles ... Washington, DC
Honish, Kalieh R. ... Montebello, CA
Honjas, Elainie ... San Jose, CA
Honkanen, Rodney A. ... St. Paul, MN
Honken, Dale S. ... Sibley, IA
Honken Law Office ... Sibley, IA
Honkisz, James E. ... Atlanta, GA
Honkonen, Elizabeth B. ... Menlo Park, CA
Honn, Carver E. ... Riverside, CA
Honn, Darin D. ... Portland, OR
Honn, Dorothy L. ... Riverside, CA
Honn, Richard A. ... Los Angeles, CA
Honn, Richard C. ... Tulsa, OK
Honn & Secof LLP ... Los Angeles, CA
Honnaka, Sharlene A. ... Los Angeles, CA
Honnold, Bradley B. ... Charlotte, NC
Honnold, Bradley D. ... Kansas City, MO
Honnold, Douglas L. ... Bozeman, MT
Honnold, Edward E. ... Washington, DC
Honnold, John O., Jr. ... Philadelphia, PA
Honohan, Epley, Braddock & Brenneman
Hills, IA
Iowa City, IA
Kalona, IA
Lone Tree, IA
North Liberty, IA
Honohan, Jay H. ... Hills, IA
Iowa City, IA

Hooper, R. Ray ....Houston, TX
Hooper, Rachel B. ....San Francisco, CA
Hooper, Ralph E. ....Valley City, ND
Hooper, Randal W. ....Oakland, CA
Hooper, Richard K. ....New York, NY
Hooper, Robert Niles ....Jackson, MS
Hooper, Rose Mons ....Detroit, MI
Hooper, Ruth J. ....Portland, OR
Hooper, Samuel E. ....Houston, TX
Hooper, Scott A., P.C. ....Houston, TX
Hooper, Sharel VanSandt
Chattanooga, TN
Hooper, Shawn K. ....St. Paul, MN
Hooper, Stephen E. ....Fort Myers, FL
Hooper, Stephen R. ....Salinas, CA
Hooper, Suzanne Sawochka ....Palo Alto, CA
Hooper, Thomas G. ....Greensboro, NC
Hooper, Thomas K. ....Portland, OR
Hooper, Timothy J., III ....La Plata, MD
Hooper, William D., Jr. ....Towson, MD
Hooper, William, Jr. ....University, MS
Hooper, William T. ....Conroe, TX
Hooper, Winfred, Jr. ....Fort Worth, TX
Hoopes & Adams, PLC ....Mesa, AZ
Phoenix, AZ
Hoopes, Albert H. ....Bloomington, IL
Hoopes, D. Fredrick ....Idaho Falls, ID
Hoopes, Dallett ....Litchfield, CT
Hoopes, Darlington, Jr. ....Reading, PA
Hoopes, David S. ....Wethersfield, CT
Hoopes, Edward ....Pittsburgh, PA
Hoopes, Gayle ....Kansas City, KS
Hoopes, James P. ....Douglaston, NY
Hoopes, J.C. (Jack), Jr. ....St. Anthony, ID
Hoopes, John R. ....Mesa, AZ
Hoopes, Kenneth S. ....North Muskegon, MI
Hoopes, Lauren Mattleman ....Lawrence, KS
Hoopes, Maria L. ....North Muskegon, MI
Hoopes, Marilyn K. ....Sutter Creek, CA
Hoopes, Mary Anne ....Department of Justice, Office of Professional Responsibility, GV
Hoopes, Pamela S. ....Minneapolis, MN
Hoopes, Robbin S. ....Cincinnati, OH
Hoopes, Robert P. ....Doylestown, PA
Hoopes, Spencer W. ....San Francisco, CA
Hoopes, Terence J. ....Department of Labor, Pension and Welfare Benefits, GV
Hoopes, Thomas M. ....Boston, MA
Hoopes, Todd ....Marysville, OH
Hoopingarner, John M.
New Philadelphia, OH
Hoopingarner, Kirk A. ....Chicago, IL
Hoopis, Harry J. ....Warwick, RI
Hoopis & Hoopis ....Warwick, RI
Hoopis, Jennifer S. ....Warwick, RI
Hoopman, Ray I. ....Douglas, WY
Hoops, Daniel Jon, (P.C.) ....Dallas, TX
Hoops, Daniel S. ....Detroit, MI
Hoops, Frederick H., III ....Detroit, MI
Hoops, Frederick K. ....Farmington Hills, MI
Hoops, Hoops & Hoops, P.L.C.
Farmington Hills, MI
Hoops & Levy, L.L.P. ....Houston, TX
San Antonio, TX
Hoops, Timothy G. ....Seal Beach, CA
Hoops, William D. ....Houston, TX
San Antonio, TX
Hoorneman, Evan R. ....South Harwich, MA
Hoornstra, Charles D. ....Madison, WI
Hoornstra, Dennis W. ....Wheaton, IL
Hoort, Catherine Davies ....Portland, MI
Hoort, Edward J. ....Flint, MI
Hoort, Eric C. ....Spokane, WA
Hoort, Steven T. ....Boston, MA
Hoos, E. Lou ....Grand Rapids, MI
Hoos, John O. ....Lincolnshire, IL
Hoose, David P. ....Springfield, MA
Hoose, Mark L. ....Edmond, OK
Hoose, Richard A. ....Wickliffe, OH
Hooser, Eugene A. ....Oceanside, CA
Hooser, Gregory D. ....Austin, TX
Hooser, Harvey C., Jr. ....Big Spring, TX
Hooshmand, Mark ....Palo Alto, CA
Hoot, Molly Elizabeth ....San Diego, CA
Hoot, W. E. Scott ....New York, NY
Hooten, Carol A. ....Eagan, MN
Hooten, Jennifer A. ....Jacksonville, FL
Hooten, John R. ....Kinston, NC
Hooten, Nancy E. ....San Francisco, CA
Hooten, Roy W. ....Silver Spring, MD
Hooten-Soele, Sherry E. ....San Antonio, TX
Hooth, William L. ....Detroit, MI
Hootman, Gregory W. ....Sarasota, FL
Hootman, Timothy A. ....Houston, TX
Hooton, Mark A. ....Chattanooga, TN
Hooton, Michael E. ....Pittsburgh, PA
Hooton, Thomas L. ....Dallas, TX
Hoots, D. L. ....Klamath Falls, OR
Hoots, Douglas L., CPCU ....Lexington, KY
Hoots, James M. ....Bartlett, TN
Hoots, John Henry ....Winston-Salem, NC
Hootsell, Sessions Ault, III
New Orleans, LA
Hootsmans, Alice M.S. ....Hartford, CT
Hooven, Julie Osswald ....Chicago, IL
Hooven, Nan R. ....San Francisco, CA
Hoover, Albert K. ....Dublin, OH
Hoover, Alicia Rae ....Baton Rouge, LA
Hoover, Allen E. ....Chicago, IL
Hoover, Allen J. ....Chicago, IL
Hoover, Andrew, & Attorneys ....Pulaski, TN
Springhill, TN
Hoover, Ann L. ....Topeka, KS
Hoover, Arthur W. ....Alton, NH
Rochester, NH
Hoover, Bax & Slovacek, L.L.P.
Houston, TX
Hoover, Bradley W. ....Sugar Land, TX
Hoover, Bruce W. ....Buffalo, NY
Hoover, C. Mark ....Lansing, MI
Hoover, Catherine James ....Akron, OH
Hoover, Catherine Roubal ....Olympia, WA
Hoover, Charles R. ....Phoenix, AZ
Hoover, Christopher N. ....Plano, TX
Hoover, Christopher N., P.C., Law Offices of
Dallas, TX
Denton, TX
Fort Worth, TX
Plano, TX
Hoover, Craig A. ....Washington, DC
Hoover, Craig M. ....Washington, DC
Hoover, Cynthia J. ....Fort Lauderdale, FL
Hoover, David A. ....Kenmore, NY
North Tonawanda, NY
Hoover, David K. ....Milwaukee, WI
Hoover, David S. ....Denver, CO
Hoover, Dean S. ....Cuyahoga Falls, OH
Dallas, TX
Hoover, Dennis J. ....Baltimore, MD
Hoover, Donald E. ....Mansfield, OH
Hoover, Donnie ....Charlotte, NC
Hoover, Douglas E. ....Worthington, OH
Hoover, Dwayne A. ....Fort Worth, TX
Hoover, E. Ralph ....Indianapolis, IN
Hoover, Earl E. ....Pagosa Springs, CO
Hoover, Earl L. ....Libertyville, IL
Hoover, Eliza Williams ....Dayton, VA
Hoover, Eric N. ....San Francisco, CA
Hoover, Evans & Turner, P.C.
Birmingham, AL
Hoover, Frank A. ....Bakersfield, CA
Hoover, Frank R. ....Spokane, WA
Hoover, Franklin ....Flagstaff, AZ
Hoover, Garin C. ....Cleveland, OH
Hoover, Gary ....San Diego, CA
Hoover, George W, II ....Los Angeles, CA
Hoover, Gilbert C., IV ....New York, NY
Hoover, Gregory A. ....Texarkana, TX
Hoover, Gregory G., Sr. ....Goshen, NY
Hoover, Gregory G., Sr., P.C. ....Goshen, NY
Hoover, Gretchen P. ....San Diego, CA
Hoover, Henry A. ....South Bend, IN
Hoover, Herbert C. ....Tampa, FL
Hoover, Heydorn & Herrnstein Co., L.P.A.
Cuyahoga Falls, OH
Hoover, Hilary E. ....New York, NY
Hoover & Hoover ....Covington, KY
Hoover, Howard S. ....Houston, TX
Hoover, James ....Birmingham, AL
Hoover, James B. ....Harrisonburg, VA
Hoover, James C. ....Atlanta, GA
Hoover, James L. ....New York, NY
Hoover, James L. ....Galion, OH
Hoover, Jeffrey H. ....Jamestown, KY
Hoover, Jessica M. ....Emeryville, CA
Hoover, John B. ....Washington, DC
Hoover, John David ....Indianapolis, IN
Hoover, John K. ....Portland, OR
Hoover, Joseph S., Jr. ....Washington, DC
Hoover, Judith Jennings ....Marion, IA
Hoover, Kathryn Ann ....Richmond, CA
Hoover, Kenley K. ....Rockville, MD
Hoover, Kevin A. ....Indianapolis, IN
Hoover, Kim R. ....Cuyahoga Falls, OH
Hoover, Kimberly Hill ....Washington, DC
Hoover, Larry B. ....Nashville, TN
Hoover, Lawrence H., Jr.
Harrisonburg, VA
Hoover Legal Associates, A Professional Corporation ....Dallas, TX
Hoover, Lesa Noblitt ....Washington, DC
Hoover, Linda J. ....San Diego, CA
Hoover, Lois M. ....Kansas City, KS
Hoover, Lonnie R. ....Franklin, TN
Hoover, Luann L. ....Columbus, OH
Hoover, Lucy A. ....Jacksonville, FL
Hoover, Lydia ....Baltimore, MD
Hoover, Lynn C. ....Kansas City, MO
Hoover, Lynn M. ....Toledo, OH
Hoover, M. Andrew ....Pulaski, TN
Springhill, TN
Hoover, M. Kathryn ....Albuquerque, NM
Hoover, Marianne K. ....Charleston, WV
Hoover, Marilyn K. ....Tulsa, OK
Hoover, Mark J. ....Boston, MA
Hoover, Mark L. ....Abilene, TX
Hoover, Marlene L. ....Manhattan Beach, CA
Hoover, Marsha K. ....Chicago, IL
Hoover, Martin W., Jr. ....Chattanooga, TN
Hoover, Mary Anne ....San Francisco, CA
Hoover, Mary U. ....New York, NY
Hoover, Melody ....Covington, KY
Hoover, Michael A. ....Atlanta, GA
Hoover, Michael C. ....Seattle, WA
Hoover, Michael E. ....Pittsburgh, PA
Hoover, Michael J. ....Minneapolis, MN
Hoover, Michael J. ....Alexandria, VA
Hoover, Michael R. ....Oklahoma City, OK
Hoover, Michael W. ....Wausau, WI
Hoover, Mike J. ....Chicago, IL
Hoover, Orval R. ....Cuyahoga Falls, OH
Hoover Partners ....Washington, DC
Hoover, Patrick J. ....Rockville, MD
Hoover, Paul D. ....Texarkana, TX
Hoover, Paul T., Jr. ....Memphis, TN
Hoover, Paul W., Jr. ....Little Rock, AR
Hoover, Penrod, Davenport & Crist
Harrisonburg, VA
Hoover, Phillip D. ....Piqua, OH
Hoover, Phillip E. ....Chattanooga, TN
Hoover, R. Dennis ....Michigan City, IN
Hoover, R.S., & Associates ....Chicago, IL
Lake Forest, IL
Hoover, R. Sam ....Chicago, IL
Hoover, R. Tracy ....Portsmouth, OH
Hoover, Rebecca L. ....Wilmette, IL
Hoover, Reynold N. ....Jacksonville, FL
Hoover, Robert ....Covington, KY
Hoover, Robert D. ....Baton Rouge, LA
Hoover, Robert D. ....Fort Worth, TX
Hoover, Robert D., P.L.C., Law Offices of
Baton Rouge, LA
Hoover, Robert H. ....Newark, OH
Hoover, Robert L. ....San Jose, CA
Hoover, Robert S. ....Chicago, IL
Hoover, Robert T. ....Fort Wayne, IN
Hoover, Roger K. ....Bethesda, MD
Hoover, Ronald C. ....Portland, OR
Hoover, Russell J. ....Chicago, IL
Hoover, Sara Francis ....Los Angeles, CA
Hoover, Sarah J. ....Los Angeles, CA
Hoover, Schermerhorn, Edwards, Pinaire & Rombold, Chartered ....Junction City, KS
Hoover, Scott A. ....Paducah, KY
Hoover, Sidney Odom ....Birmingham, AL
Hoover, Steven G. ....Long Beach, CA
Hoover, Stuart G. ....Dubuque, IA
Hoover, Theresa L. ....Westlake Village, CA
Hoover, Thomas B. ....New Kent, VA
Hoover, Thomas J. ....Bigfork, MT
Hoover, Thomas O. ....Lexington, MA
Hoover, Timothy W. ....Columbus, OH
Hoover, Valoria C. ....Akron, OH
Hoover, W. Jerry ....Houston, TX
Hoover, William A., Jr. ....Murphy, NC
Hoover, William D. ....Lemoore, CA
Hoover, William E., Jr. ....Exton, PA
Hoover, William H., Jr. ....Houston, TX
Hoover & Williams, P.A. ....Charlotte, NC
Hoovestal, Palmer Arthur ....Helena, MT
Hoovestol, Calvin J. ....Bismarck, ND
Hoovler, David Marion ....Bronx, NY
Hooy & Hooy, A Professional Law Corporation ....Concord, CA
Hooy, Robert J. ....Concord, CA
Hooy, William J. ....Concord, CA
Hopcroft, Ann Victoria ....Penn Valley, CA
Hope, A. Bice ....Gainesville, FL
Hope, Allen C.
Department of Housing and Urban Development, Office of General Counsel, GV
Hope, Anthony J. ....Washington, DC
Hope, Camille ....Macon, GA
Hope & Causey, P.C. ....Bryan, TX
Conroe, TX
Houston, TX
Huntsville, TX
Liberty, TX
Hope, Charles Allan ....Boston, MA
Hope, David S. ....Philadelphia, PA
Hope, Frederick H. ....Palm Beach, FL
Hope, Frederick H., P.A. ....Palm Beach, FL
Hope, Garland ....Pauls Valley, OK
Hope, Henry W. ....Houston, TX
Hope, Inez D. ....Los Angeles, CA
Hope, J. Wade ....Montgomery, AL
Hope, James A. ....Dickinson, ND
Hope, James Joseph ....Tavares, FL
Hope, John C., Jr. ....Reno, NV
Hope, John E. ....Los Angeles, CA
Hope, Jon ....Savannah, GA
Hope, Judith Richards ....Washington, DC
Hope, Karin Marie
House of Representatives, Congressional Assistants, GV
Hope, Keith E. ....Miami, FL
Tallahassee, FL
Hope, Keith, P.A. ....Tallahassee, FL
Hope, Kenneth R. ....Littleton, CO
Hope, Kenneth R., Professional Corporation
Littleton, CO
Hope, Leonard J. ....Atlanta, GA
Hope, Michael R. ....Denver, CO
Hope, Mills, Bolin, Collins & Ramsey
Garden City, KS
Hope, Norman D. ....Dallas, TX
Hope, Richard F. ....Basking Ridge, NJ
Hope, Robert M., Jr. ....Mobile, AL
Hope, Roger Charles ....Cambria, CA
Hope, Ronald A. ....Little Rock, AR
Hope, Roseanne M. ....Minneapolis, MN
Hope, Ruben W., Jr. ....Conroe, TX
Hope, Stephanie B. ....Atlanta, GA
Hope, Stephen D. ....Charlotte, NC
Hope, Tamia L. ....Los Angeles, CA
Hope, Theodore S., Jr. ....New York, NY
Hopeman, Jon M. ....Minneapolis, MN
Hopeman, M. Jennifer ....Boston, MA
Hopen, Anton J. ....Clearwater, FL
Hopen, Daniel P. ....Sunnyvale, CA
Hopen, Richard M. ....Fort Lauderdale, FL
Hopen, Richard M., P.A.
Fort Lauderdale, FL
Hopen, Stuart Neil ....Hollywood, FL
Hopenfeld, Bruce Robert ....Milpitas, CA
Hopenfeld, James E. ....Palo Alto, CA
Hopengarten, Fredric J. ....Lincoln, MA
Hopewell, Craig S. ....Cincinnati, OH
Hopewell, Dwight F. ....Richmond, VA
Hopewell, James B. ....Riverdale, MD
Hopewell, James L. ....Grand Rapids, MI
Hopewell, John C., III ....Baton Rouge, LA
Hopewell, Michael S. ....Florence, SC
Hopewell, Paul Steven ....Minneapolis, MN
Hopf, James F. ....Greenville, NC
Hopf, James F., Law Offices of
Greenville, NC
Hopf, Nancy A. ....Denver, CO
Hopf, Wm. V. ....Wheaton, IL
Hopfenbeck, Ann E. ....Denver, CO
Hopfenbeck, George M., Jr. ....Denver, CO
Hopfenberg, David H. ....Providence, RI
Hopfensperger, Terese A. ....Chicago, IL
Hopfer, Jason L. ....House of Representatives, Committee Legal Personnel, GV
Hopfer, Louis Kenneth ....Santa Rosa, CA
Hopfinger, Jane B. ....Pittsford, NY
Rochester, NY
Hopfl, Charles E. ....New York, NY
Hopfl, Karen M. ....Washington, DC
Hopgood, Calimafde, Kalil & Judlowe LLP
New York, NY
Hopgood, J. Christopher ....Henderson, KY
Hopgood, Linda M. ....Lexington, KY
Hopgood, Myka L. ....Louisville, KY
Hopgood, Richard M. ....Lexington, KY
Hopgood, Roy C. ....New York, NY
Hopgood, Tom K. ....Bismarck, ND
Hopgood-Jovet, Alfredo M. ....San Juan, PR
Hopke, Debra J. ....Rockville Centre, NY
Hopke, Fred ....Woodbridge, NJ
Hopkin, William R., Jr. ....Haddonfield, NJ
Hopkins, Alben N. ....Gulfport, MS
Jackson, MS
Hopkins, Alben Norris, Jr. ....Gulfport, MS
Hopkins, Albert E. ....Pasadena, CA
Hopkins, Albert R., Jr. ....Washington, DC
Hopkins, Alexander G. ....Chicago, IL
Hopkins, Alfred I. ....Miami, FL
Hopkins, Alfred J. ....Scarsdale, NY
Hopkins, Alton H. ....Atlanta, GA
Hopkins, Alva J., III ....Folkston, GA
Hopkins, Ann ....Oakland, CA
Hopkins, Anthony Marc ....Lancaster, PA
Hopkins, Arthur C., Jr. ....Clifton, NJ
Hopkins, Benjamin W. ....Des Moines, IA
Hopkins, Billy G. ....Carlisle, KY
Hopkins, Breck G. ....Little Rock, AR
Hopkins, Brenda L. ....Washington, DC
Hopkins, Brian P. ....New York, NY
Hopkins, Brian R. ....Charleston, WV
Hopkins, Bruce G. ....Cincinnati, OH
Hopkins, Bruce R. ....Kansas City, MO
Hopkins, Bryan E. ....Sunrise, FL
Hopkins, C. Mark ....Irvine, CA
Hopkins, C. Mark ....Irvine, CA
Hopkins, C. Thomas ....Santa Barbara, CA
Hopkins, C. Timothy ....Idaho Falls, ID
Hopkins, Cameron A. ....Pasadena, CA
Hopkins, Caridad Diego ....Cherry Hill, NJ
Philadelphia, PA
Hopkins & Carley, A Law Corporation
San Jose, CA
Hopkins, Carlos L. ....Richmond, VA
Hopkins, Carol L. ....Towson, MD
Hopkins, Catherine E. ....Chicago, IL
Hopkins, Charles A. ....Oklahoma City, OK
Hopkins, Charles I., Jr. ....Washington, DC
Hopkins, Charles P., II ....Shrewsbury, NJ
Hopkins, Christine K. ....Plantation, FL
Hopkins, Christine K., P.A. ....Plantation, FL
Hopkins, Christopher B.
West Palm Beach, FL
Hopkins, Christopher M. ....Anniston, AL
Hopkins, Clack D., III ....Mount Pleasant, SC
Hopkins, Craig L. ....Dallas, TX
Hopkins, Crawley, Bagwell & Upshaw, P.L.L.C. ....Gulfport, MS
Jackson, MS
Hopkins, Curran & Smith, PLLC
Southfield, MI
Hopkins, Curt Y. ....Loveland, OH
Hopkins, D. Douglas ....New York, NY
Hopkins, Daniel R. ....Oklahoma City, OK
Hopkins, David A. ....Great Falls, MT
Hopkins, David B. ....San Diego, CA
Hopkins, David B. ....Albany, NY
Hopkins, David H. ....Chicago, IL
Hopkins, David J. ....Du Bois, PA
Hopkins, David William ....Hagåtña, GU
Hopkins, Debra A. ....Butler, MO
Hopkins, Dennis C. ....New York, NY
Hopkins, Donald G. ....Tulsa, OK
Hopkins, Donald J. ....Denver, CO
Hopkins, Donald R. ....Oakland, CA
Hopkins, Edward J., (P.A.)
West Palm Beach, FL
Hopkins, Edward R., III ....Smithtown, NY
Hopkins, Elizabeth ....Department of Labor, Office of the Solicitor, GV
Hopkins, Elizabeth A. ....Red Bank, NJ
Hopkins, Eric W. ....Doylestown, PA
Hopkins, Esther ....Los Angeles, CA
Hopkins, Esther A. H. ....Framingham, MA
Hopkins, F. Thomas, III ....Sarasota, FL
Hopkins, Flo ....Juliette, GA
Hopkins, Forhan & Girard, P.L.L.C.
Bloomfield Hills, MI
Hopkins, Fortescue W. ....New Castle, VA
Hopkins, Franklin H. ....Worcester, MA
Hopkins, Fred ....Issaquah, WA
Hopkins, Gains E., Jr.
Department of Housing and Urban Development, Office of General Counsel, GV
Hopkins, Garrett P. ....Garden City, NY
Hopkins, Gary L. ....Greenville, TX
Hopkins, Genevieve Dwaihy
Bloomfield Hills, MI
Hopkins, George ....Malvern, AR
Hopkins, George ....Denton, TX
Hopkins, George A. ....Kokomo, IN
Hopkins, George C. ....Washington, DC
Hopkins, George M. M. ....Atlanta, GA
Hopkins, Gerald E. ....Houston, TX
Hopkins, Gerald P. ....San Francisco, CA
Hopkins & Gibbs ....Tulsa, OK
Hopkins, Grace B. ....Austin, TX
Hopkins, Gregory M. ....Little Rock, AR
Hopkins, Gregory V. ....Aurora, CO
Hopkins & Gresham, P.C. ....Atlanta, GA

Hopkins, Grover Prevatte ... Tarboro, NC
Hopkins, Guy E., & Associates ... Conroe, TX
Hopkins, H. Kate ... Dallas, TX
Hopkins, H. Lowell ... Atlanta, GA
Hopkins, Harriet S. ... Durham, NC
Hopkins, Harry ... Fort Worth, TX
Hopkins, Harry L. ... Birmingham, AL
Hopkins, Henry C. ... Santa Ana, CA
Hopkins, Henry H. ... Baltimore, MD
Hopkins & Higgins ... Lake Placid, NY
Hopkins & Hopkins ... Doylestown, PA
Hopkins & Huebner, P.C. ... Davenport, IA
Des Moines, IA
Hopkins, J. David ... Denver, CO
Hopkins, J. David ... Atlanta, GA
Hopkins, J. Edward ... Pensacola, FL
Hopkins, Jacques V. ... Providence, RI
Hopkins, James C., III ... Syracuse, NY
Hopkins, James E. ... Marion, IL
Hopkins, James E. ... Sulphur, LA
Hopkins, James H. ... Seattle, WA
Hopkins, James J. ... Atlanta, GA
Carrollton, GA
Hopkins, James M. ... Fort Lauderdale, FL
Hopkins, James R. ... Boston, MA
Hopkins, James T. ... Everett, WA
Hopkins, James T. ... Seattle, WA
Hopkins, Jane Francis ... San Jose, CA
Hopkins, Jas. D. ... White Plains, NY
Hopkins, J. B., (P.A.) ... Pensacola, FL
Hopkins, Jeffrey A. ... Charlotte, NC
Hopkins, Jeffrey D. ... Houston, TX
Hopkins, Jelsing, Tri & West ... Everett, WA
Hopkins, Jennifer P. ... Manchester, NH
Hopkins, Jo Anne ... Wrentham, MA
Hopkins, Joan Munn ... Kearney, NE
Hopkins, John ... Frankfort, KY
Hopkins, John B. ... Barnstable, MA
Hopkins, John D. ... Greensboro, NC
Hopkins, John F. ... San Jose, CA
Hopkins, John F., Jr. ... Cambridge, MA
Hopkins, John J. ... Granite City, IL
Hopkins, John J. ... Basking Ridge, NJ
Hopkins, John J. ... Newark, NJ
Hopkins, John J. ... Dallas, TX
Hopkins, John L. ... Belle Haven, VA
Hopkins, John L., Jr. ... Southfield, MI
Hopkins, John Lee ... Rocky Mount, VA
Hopkins, John O. ... Boca Raton, FL
Hopkins, John Paul ... Conroe, TX
Hopkins, John R. ... Harrisburg, PA
Hopkins, John R., Jr. ... Poplar Bluff, MO
Hopkins, John S., III ... Cleveland, OH
Hopkins, John W. ... San Francisco, CA
Hopkins, Joseph E. ... Newark, NJ
Hopkins, Joseph T. ... Commack, NY
Hopkins, Joseph W. ... Philadelphia, PA
Hopkins, Joyce Kettren ... Los Gatos, CA
Hopkins, Juanita S. ... Odenton, MD
Hopkins, Julia B. ... McDaniel, MD
Hopkins, Julian H. ... Lincoln, NE
Hopkins, Karen S. ... Columbia, SC
Hopkins, Karl V. ... Houston, TX
Hopkins, Kathleen Joan ... Seattle, WA
Hopkins, Kathleen M. ... Tarrytown, NY
Hopkins, Kathryn D. ... Mineola, NY
Hopkins, Kenneth M. ... Willows, CA
Hopkins, Kenneth R. ... Laurel, MD
Hopkins, L. Bryan ... St. Louis, MO
Hopkins, Larry L. ... Boulder, CO
Hopkins Law Firm, A Professional Association ... Little Rock, AR
Hopkins Law Office, P.C. ... Plymouth, NH
Hopkins, Leonard, Jr. ... Troy, MI
Hopkins, Linda M. ... Petaluma, CA
Hopkins, Linda Weeden ... Doylestown, PA
Hopkins, Lisa ... Mesa, AZ
Hopkins, Lisa A. ... Charleston, WV
Hopkins, Loyd Byron ... Frederick, MD
Hopkins, Loyd Byron, P.C. ... Frederick, MD
Hopkins, Lucinda ... Manchester, NH
Hopkins, Margaret Lynch ... Fort Worth, TX
Hopkins, Mariam T. ... Little Rock, AR
Hopkins, Mark D. ... Austin, TX
Hopkins, Mark E. ... Newark, NJ
Hopkins, Mark L. ... Long Valley, NJ
Hopkins, Martha W. ... Grand Island, NE
Hopkins, Maximilian J.B. ... San Rafael, CA
Hopkins, Michael A. ... Washington, DC
Hopkins, Michael B. ... New York, NY
Hopkins, Michael B. ... Dallas, TX
Hopkins, Michael D. ... Houston, TX
Hopkins, Michael T. ... Milwaukee, WI
Hopkins, Nancy ... McLean, VA
Hopkins, Nancy C. ... Towson, MD
Hopkins, Pamela Lynn ... Fremont, NE
Hopkins, Patrick J. ... Des Moines, IA
Hopkins, Paul M. ... New York, NY
Hopkins, Paula ... Vinalhaven, ME
Hopkins, Paula ... Pittsburgh, PA
Hopkins, Percy I., Jr. ... Tequesta, FL
Hopkins, Peter A., Jr. ... Lake Placid, NY
Hopkins, Peter J. ... Washington, DC
Hopkins, Peter J. ... Chittenango, NY
Hopkins, Philip W. ... Aurora, CO
Hopkins, Randall A. ... Ashland, OR
Hopkins, Randolph B., (P.A.) ... Little Rock, AR
Hopkins, Raymond E. ... Denver, CO
Hopkins, Regina M. ... Americus, GA
Hopkins, Richard A. ... Decatur, IL
Hopkins, Richard B., II ... Los Angeles, CA
Hopkins, Richard C., Jr. ... Denver, CO
Hopkins, Richard W. ... Cape May Court House, NJ
Hopkins, Robert B. ... Baltimore, MD
Hopkins, Robert B. ... Portland, OR
Hopkins, Robin H. ... Dallas, TX
Hopkins Roden Crockett Hansen & Hoopes, PLLC ... Washington, DC
Boise, ID
Idaho Falls, ID
Hopkins, Ronald K. ... Jefferson, GA
Hopkins, Ronald W. ... Los Angeles, CA
Hopkins, Russell A. ... Cleveland, OH
Hopkins, Ruth M. ... Pasadena, CA
Hopkins, Saml. ... Baltimore, MD
Hopkins, Samp Craig, Jr. ... Albemarle, NC
Hopkins, Samuel B. ... Baltimore, MD
Hopkins, Sean W. ... Buffalo, NY
Hopkins, Sharon Lee ... Augusta, GA
Hopkins, Shelley A. ... Missoula, MT
Hopkins, Sheryl L. ... Dallas, TX
Hopkins, Stacy M. ... Los Angeles, CA
Hopkins, Stacy Sluser ... Redwood City, CA
Hopkins, Stephanie A. ... San Francisco, CA
Hopkins, Stephen A. ... Boston, MA
Hopkins, Stephen A. ... New York, NY
Hopkins, Stephen Ford ... Santa Maria, CA
Hopkins, Stephen J. ... Bloomfield Hills, MI
Hopkins, Stephen L. ... Minneapolis, MN
Hopkins, Stephen L. ... Livingston, NJ
Hopkins, Stephen M. ... Phoenix, AZ
Hopkins, Stephen P. ... Denver, CO
Hopkins, Stephen T. ... San Diego, CA
Hopkins, Steven M. ... Greenville, SC
Hopkins, Steven W. ... Newport Beach, CA
Hopkins & Sutter ... Washington, DC
Chicago, IL
Troy, MI
Hopkins, Tammy ... Washington, DC
Hopkins, Tangela ... Tampa, FL
Hopkins & Taylor, LLP ... Atlanta, GA
Carrollton, GA
Hopkins, Terrence A. ... Des Moines, IA
Hopkins, Theodore J., Jr. ... Charleston, SC
Columbia, SC
Greenville, SC
Hopkins, Theodore S. ... Pittsburgh, PA
Hopkins & Thomas ... Atlanta, GA
Hopkins, Thomas A. ... New York, NY
Hopkins, Timothy H. ... San Jose, CA
Hopkins, Timothy J. ... Uniondale, NY
Hopkins, Virginia Emerson ... Anniston, AL
Hopkins, W. Wylie, Jr. ... Bel Air, MD
Hopkins, Wallace, (P.C.) ... Omaha, NE
Hopkins, William B. ... Roanoke, VA
Hopkins, William B., Jr. ... Roanoke, VA
Hopkins, William (" Bill ") ... Marble Hill, MO
Hopkins, William C. ... Alexandria, VA
Hopkins, William C., II ... Kansas City, MO
Hopkins, William D. ... Washington, DC
Hopkins, William E. ... Austin, TX
Hopkins, William E., Jr. ... Columbia, SC
Hopkins, William H. ... Plymouth, NH
Hopkins, William P., Jr. ... Santa Ana, CA
Hopkins, William S. ... Alexandria, VA
Hopkins, William T., Jr. ... Fort Wayne, IN
Hopkins, Ziyad S. ... Boston, MA
Hopkins, Zoe P. ... Stamford, CT
Hopkins-Fisher, Jane G. ... Springfield, MA
Hopkins Garrett, Nancy Jo ... Boise, ID
Hopkins-Klima, Susanne M. ... Arlington, VA
Hopkins-Luder, John M. ... Los Angeles, CA
Hopkinson, Brian L. ... Park Ridge, IL
Hopkinson, H. Richard ... Worland, WY
Hopkinson, Ingrid B. ... Philadelphia, PA
Hopkinson, James A. ... Portland, ME
Hopkinson, James R. ... Chicago, IL
Hopkinson, Keith G. ... Austin, TX
Hopkinson, R. Ronald ... New York, NY
Hopkinson, Reginald F. ... Hawthorne, NJ
Hopkinson, Rodney K. ... Portland, OR
Hopkinson, Vernon L. ... Salt Lake City, UT
Hopko, Dorothy J. ... Carmel, IN
Hopko, Kathleen M. ... Stratford, CT
Hopmann, David E. ... San Francisco, CA
Hopmann, Ernest O., III ... Houston, TX
Hopp, Alexander ... Sheboygan, WI
Hopp, Amy M. ... Pontiac, MI
Hopp, Andrew D. ... Montvale, NJ
Hopp, Anthony G. ... Chicago, IL
Hopp and Associates, P.C. ... Longmont, CO
Hopp & Associates, P.L.L.C., The Law Offices of ... Washington, DC
Hopp, Blaine, Jr. ... Yakima, WA
Hopp, Daniel F. ... Benton Harbor, MI
Hopp, Edgar C. ... Elmwood Park, IL
Hopp, Gregory D. ... Chicago, IL
Hopp, Harold W. ... Indian Wells, CA
Hopp, Kevin R. ... Omaha, NE
Hopp, Powell, Raftery & Bauer ... Sheboygan, WI
Hopp, R. Richard ... Washington, DC
Hopp, Rachel M. ... Washington, DC
Hopp, Richard A. ... Seattle, WA
Hopp, Richard W. ... Decatur, IL
Hopp, Robert John ... Englewood, CO
Hopp, Steven J. ... Seattle, WA
Hopp, Walter J. ... Longmont, CO
Hopp, William M. ... Placida, FL
Hoppas, Gerald W. ... Houston, TX
Hoppe, Albert D. ... Houston, TX
Hoppe, Barbara ... Columbia, MO
Hoppe, Bill ... Miami, FL
Hoppe, Carrie A. ... Omaha, NE
Hoppe, Charles C., Jr. ... Des Plaines, IL
Hoppe, Craig A. ... Las Vegas, NV
Hoppe, David B. ... New York, NY
Hoppe, David E. ... Laconia, NH
Hoppe, David G. ... Klamath Falls, OR
Hoppe, Deborah Comfort ... New York, NY
Hoppe, Donald N. ... Wheaton, IL
Hoppe, Frank I. ... San Francisco, CA
Hoppe, Gary ... New York, NY
Hoppe, Harold G. ... Honolulu, HI
Hoppe, Henry B., Jr. ... Metairie, LA
Hoppe, Henry, III ... Slidell, LA
Hoppe, Herbert J., Jr. ... Cleveland, OH
Hoppe, James H. ... Lincoln, NE
Hoppe, Jean B. ... St. Paul, MN
Hoppe, John C. ... Chicago, IL
Hoppe, Jon A. ... Rockville, MD
Hoppe, Jonn D. ... Lakeland, FL
Lake Wales, FL
Winter Haven, FL
Hoppe, K Allan ... Ferguson, MO
Hoppe, Kyle Bryce ... Salem, OR
Hoppe, L. Theodore, Jr. ... Media, PA
Hoppe, Lisa A. ... Tampa, FL
Hoppe, Mark H. ... Winston-Salem, NC
Hoppe, Monica K. ... San Francisco, CA
Hoppe, P. Dyke ... Edmond, OK
Hoppe, Richard A. ... Waterbury, CT
Hoppe, Robert D. ... Fresno, CA
Hoppe & Stokes, P.A. ... Miami, FL
Hoppe, T. Gavin ... New Orleans, LA
Hoppe, Theodore W. ... Fresno, CA
Monterey, CA
Hoppe, Ward Fred ... Lincoln, NE
Hoppe, Wayne G. ... Chicago, IL
Hoppe, William J. ... Richmond, VA
Hoppel, Mayer & Coleman ... Washington, DC
Hoppel, Robert G., Jr. ... Washington, DC
Hoppell, Casey Wm. ... San Diego, CA
Hoppen, William ... New York, NY
Hoppenstand, Gregory B. ... Miami Beach, FL
Hoppenstein, David ... Waco, TX
Hoppenstein, Norman J. ... Dallas, TX
Hopper, Adrianne ... Garden City, NY
Hopper, Alysia C. ... Oshkosh, WI
Hopper, Arthur M. ... Watertown, SD
Hopper, Brett L. ... Scottsdale, AZ
Hopper, Brian C. ... Oakland, CA
Hopper, Bruce E. ... Worcester, MA
Hopper, Calvin A. ... Jackson, MS
Hopper, Cameron F. ... Greenwich, CT
Hopper, Charles D. ... Las Vegas, NV
Hopper, Clifford E. ... Tulsa, OK
Hopper, Craig ... Austin, TX
Hopper, Curtis F. ... Savannah, TN
Hopper, David D. ... Richmond, VA
Hopper, David T. ... Oklahoma City, OK
Hopper, David W. ... Greenwich, CT
Hopper, David W. ... Anderson, IN
Hopper, Deana K. ... San Diego, CA
Hopper, Donald A. ... Garden City, NY
New York, NY
Hopper, Edward B., II ... Indianapolis, IN
Hopper, Edward L. ... Huntsville, AL
Hopper, Elizabeth W. ... New York, NY
Hopper, Galliher & Tucker, P.C. ... Indianapolis, IN
Hopper, Geoffrey H. ... Riverside, CA
Hopper, George ... Cincinnati, OH
Hopper, George W. ... Indianapolis, IN
Hopper, Herbert H. ... Wichita, KS
Hopper & Hicks, L.L.P. ... Oxford, NC
Hopper & Holmes ... Santa Fe Springs, CA
Hopper, J. Brent ... Chicago Heights, IL
Hopper, J. Steven ... Newport Beach, CA
Hopper, James A. ... Savannah, TN
Hopper, James L. ... Anchorage, AK
Hopper, James R. ... Santa Fe Springs, CA
Hopper, James W. ... Richmond, VA
Hopper, Jane A. ... Cardiff-By-The-Sea, CA
Hopper, Janice M. ... Charlottesville, VA
Hopper, Jeffrey A. ... Indianapolis, IN
Hopper, John W. ... Birmingham, AL
Hopper, Joseph A. ... Moon Township, PA
Hopper, Julia L. ... Jackson, TN
Hopper, Kent R. ... Jefferson City, MO
Hopper, Kevin J. ... Cincinnati, OH
Hopper, Kevin Patrick ... Raleigh, NC
Hopper & Krause
Greenwich, CT
Old Greenwich, CT
Stamford, CT
Hopper, Lelia Baum ... Richmond, VA
Hopper, Lewis B. ... Barbourville, KY
Hopper, Lynn C. ... Austin, TX
Hopper, M. Allen ... Sacramento, CA
Hopper, M. Reed ... Sacramento, CA
Hopper, Mark A. ... Ann Arbor, MI
Hopper, Mary McFall ... Philadelphia, PA
Hopper & Mathews, L.L.P. ... Raleigh, NC
Hopper, Myles ... St. Louis, MO
Hopper, Orlin Woodie ... Tulsa, OK
Hopper, Pamella A. ... Houston, TX
Hopper, Paul E. ... Horseshoe Bend, AR
Hopper, Penelope S. ... Kansas City, MO
Hopper & Plunk, PLLC ... Savannah, TN
Hopper, Richard E., Jr. ... Boulder, CO
Hopper, Richard M. ... Denver, CO
Hopper, Robert E. ... Houston, TX
Hopper, Robert R. ... Minneapolis, MN
Hopper, Roger G. ... Saluda, VA
Hopper, S. David ... Watonga, OK
Hopper, Sara E. ... Minneapolis, MN
Hopper, Sharon Keith ... St. Peters, PA
Hopper, Tracey C. ... Charlottesville, VA
Hopper, Travis Wade ... Galveston, TX
Hopper, Virginia K. ... Birmingham, AL
Hopper, Walter E. ... New York, NY
Hopper, William A., Jr. ... Canal Winchester, OH
Hopper, William L. ... Oxford, NC
Hoppers, John Wm. ... Columbus, OH
Hoppes, Andrew P. ... Philadelphia, PA
Hoppes, Ronald L. ... Lafayette, IN
Hoppess, Karl C., & Assocs., P.C. ... Houston, TX
Hoppess, Karl C., P.C. ... Houston, TX
Hoppin, Charles S. ... New York, NY
Hoppin, Charles T. ... Golden, CO
Hoppin & Hoppin, Inc. ... Woodland, CA
Hoppin, Lawrence W. ... Woodland, CA
Hoppin, Richard P. ... Woodland, CA
Hopping, Edwin N. ... Cincinnati, OH
Hopping, George B. ... Petoskey, MI
Hopping Green Sams & Smith, Professional Association ... Tallahassee, FL
Hopping, John W., IV ... Dallas, TX
Hopping, Wade L. ... Tallahassee, FL
Hopping, William Glenn ... Dallas, TX
Hopple, E. James ... Columbus, OH
Hopple, Richard M. ... Cincinnati, OH
Hopple, Roy E., Jr. ... Columbus, OH
Hoppman, Robert E. ... San Francisco, CA
Hoppmann, Karin B. ... Department of Justice, Criminal Division, GV
Hoppmeyer, Calvin C. ... New Orleans, LA
Hoppner, Lloyd ... Fairbanks, AK
Hoppner & Paskvan, P.C. ... Fairbanks, AK
Hoppner, William R. ... Lincoln, NE
Hoppock, Joseph S. ... Keene, NH
Hoppock, Nancy Siuda ... Kansas City, MO
Hoppock, Theodore H. ... Federal Trade Commission, Bureau of Consumer Protection, GV
Hopps, James K. ... Fort Worth, TX
Hopps, Lisa R. ... Cleveland, OH
Hopson, Bruce E. ... St. Louis, MO
Hopson, Christopher Paul ... Lafayette, IN
Hopson, Darrel L. ... Jonesboro, GA
Hopson, Derek D. ... Clarksdale, MS
Hopson, Douglas ... Chicago, IL
Hopson, Edward A. ... Ontario, CA
Hopson, Edwin S. ... Louisville, KY
Hopson, E. E., Jr. ... McGehee, AR
Hopson and Habenicht, Ltd. ... Chester, VA
Richmond, VA
Hopson, Harvey A., Jr. ... Cleveland, OH
Hopson, James F. ... Seguin, TX
Hopson, John ... South Gate, CA
Hopson, Lionel D. ... Denver, CO
Hopson, Mark D. ... Washington, DC
Hopson & Parris ... Cadiz, KY
Oak Grove, KY
Hopson, R. Craig ... Chester, VA
Hopson, R. Keith ... Austin, TX
Hopson, Raymond Leo ... Greenville, TX
Hopson, Richard E. ... Kingsport, TN
Hopson, Robert M. ... Houston, TX
Hopson, Sharilyn J. ... Huntington Beach, CA
Hopson, Stirling J. ... Fullerton, CA
Hopson, Thornton ... Dearborn, MI
Hopson, Todd A. ... Ocala, FL
Hopson, W. Briggs, III ... Vicksburg, MS
Hopson, W. Howell, III ... Cadiz, KY
Oak Grove, KY
Hopson, William Wimberly ... Atlanta, GA
Hopson, Wm. Stevenson, IV ... Charlottesville, VA
Hopstetter, David P. ... Naples, FL
Hopstetter, Robert A ... Lebanon, PA
Hopt, Larry W. ... Seattle, WA
Hoptowit, Dennis R. ... Chico, CA
Hopwood, Beth Clare ... Redwood City, CA
Hopwood, David J. ... Norwood, MA
Hopwood, Donald D. ... Kodiak, AK
Hopwood, Howard H., III ... Milwaukee, WI
Hopwood, John L. ... Houston, TX
Hopwood, Martin M., Jr. ... Tuckahoe, NY
Hopwood, Randal B. ... Palo Alto, CA
Hor, Spenser Y. ... New York, NY
Hora, L. Robert ... Houston, TX
Hora, Peggy F. ... Hayward, CA
Horace, Donald S. ... Atlanta, GA
Horace, Stephen J. ... St. Louis, MO
Horace-Braxton, Toni J. ... Tuskegee, AL
Horacek, Chris A. ... Wilber, NE
Horacek, Frank J. ... Wilbraham, MA
Horacek, Joseph, III, (P.C.) ... Los Angeles, CA
Horack, Benj. S. ... Charlotte, NC
Horack, Bruce M. ... Rock Island, IL
Horack, Talley, Pharr & Lowndes, A Professional Association ... Charlotte, NC
Horahan, Edward B., III ... Washington, DC
Horak, Anthony J. ... Bethesda, MD
Horak, Bernard F. ... Great Neck, NY
Horak, Heidi ... St. Petersburg, FL
Horak, John M. ... Hartford, CT
Horak, Mark F. ... Baltimore, MD
Horak, Shelley A. ... Sioux City, IA
Horak, Shelley A., Law Firm ... Sioux City, IA
Horak, Stanley F. ... Vancouver, WA
Horak, Steven D. ... Overland Park, KS
Horak, Thomas E. ... Berwyn, PA
Horan, Anne Puidk ... Terrell, TX
Horan, Annette ... Tampa, FL
Horan, Austin J., Law Office ... Tucson, AZ
Horan, Barbara E. ... Denver, CO
Horan, Ben F. ... Water Valley, MS
Horan, Bernard Duffy ... Charleston, WV
Horan, Brian R. ... Pasadena, CA
Horan, Brien P. ... Hartford, CT
Horan, Cecilia Anne ... Chicago, IL
Horan, David A. ... Manchester, NH
Horan, David C. ... Buffalo, NY
Horan, David F. ... White Plains, NY
Horan, David Paul ... Key West, FL
Horan, David W. ... Chicago, IL
Horan, Diana H. ... Worcester, MA
Horan, Douglas S. ... Boston, MA
Horan, Edward W. ... Key West, FL

Horan, Elizabeth A. ... **Syosset, NY**
Horan, Gerald M. ... Treasury Department, Internal Revenue Service, GV
Horan, Glenn M. ... Newport Beach, CA
Horan and Horan ... **Key West, FL**
Horan & Horan ... **New York, NY**
White Plains, NY
Horan, James F. ... Troy, NY
Horan, James J. ... West Orange, NJ
Horan, James P. ... **Worcester, MA**
Horan, Janet K. ... Chicago, IL
Horan, John A. ... Vero Beach, FL
Horan, John C. ... Burbank, CA
Horan, John D. ... **Hackensack, NJ**
Horan, John E. ... **Millburn, NJ**
New York, NY
Horan, John G. ... **Washington, DC**
Horan, John J. ... Syracuse, NE
Horan, John J. ... Sea Girt, NJ
Horan, John L. ... **Lincoln, NE**
Horan, John P. ... **Orlando, FL**
Horan, John R. ... **New York, NY**
Horan, Karan M. ... Middletown, OH
Horan, Kathleen C. ... **Albuquerque, NM**
Horan, Kevin R. ... Dayton, OH
Horan, Kevin W. ... Chicago, IL
Horan, Laurence P. ... **Monterey, CA**
Horan, Lawrence J., III ... Richardson, TX
Horan, Leonard P. ... New York, NY
Horan, Lloyd, Karachale, Dyer, Schwartz, Law & Cook, Incorporated ... **Carmel, CA**
Monterey, CA
Salinas, CA
Horan, Marilyn J. ... Butler, PA
Horan, Matthew ... **Fort Smith, AR**
Horan, Matthew B. ... **Orlando, FL**
Horan, Maura Hughes ... **Hartford, CT**
Horan, Mern ... Washington, DC
Horan, Michael A. ... Irvine, CA
Horan, Michael F. ... **Pawtucket, RI**
Horan, Michael P. ... Washington, DC
Horan, Michael P. ... **Tampa, FL**
Horan, Michael T. ... **San Francisco, CA**
Horan, Michele Costanza
White Plains, NY
Horan, Monica ... **Pawtucket, RI**
Horan, Patrick K. ... St. Louis Park, MN
Woodbury, MN
Horan, R. Kevin ... Pawtucket, RI
Horan, Richard T., Jr. ... **McLean, VA**
Horan, Robert ... **New York, NY**
Horan, Robert F., III ... **Fairfax, VA**
Horan, Robert F., Jr. ... Fairfax, VA
Horan, Robert J. ... St. Louis, MO
Horan, Ronald L. ... Highlands, NJ
Horan, Sheila Kathleen ... **Wheaton, IL**
Horan, Stephen E. ... **Sacramento, CA**
Horan, Thomas J. ... **Albuquerque, NM**
Horan, Thomas Lawrence
Federal Communications Commission, Cable Services Bureau, GV
Horan, Thomas M. ... Cedar Rapids, IA
Horan, Timothy, Jr. ... **Houston, TX**
Horan, Timothy Jude ... Houston, TX
Horan, Vincent G. ... Manlius, NY
Horan, William C. ... Costa Mesa, CA
Horan, William J. ... Woodbury, NY
Horan, William K. ... New York, NY
Horan, William Patrick, Jr. ... Hartford, CT
Horany, Jimmy P. ... Wichita Falls, TX
Horany, John K. ... **Dallas, TX**
Horany, John K., P.C. ... **Dallas, TX**
Horas, John M. ... **St. Louis, MO**
Horas Radice & Dean, LLC
St. Louis, MO
Horbaczewski, Henry Z. ... **Newton, MA**
Horbaly, Jan
United States Court Of Appeals For The Federal Circuit, GV
Horbaly, Robert S. ... **Cleveland, OH**
Horbaly, Will G. ... Cleveland, OH
Horbatiuk, Kevin ... New York, NY
Horberg, Andrew L. ... Burnham, IL
Horberg, Kurt J. ... **Cambridge, IL**
Horblit, Jeffrey P. ... **Summit, NJ**
New York, NY
Horchani, Lina ... **Washington, DC**
Horcher, Paul V. ... Diamond Bar, CA
Horchler, Kathleen M.
Bloomfield Hills, MI
Hord, Charles E., III ... **New York, NY**
Hord, James C. ... Charlotte, NC
Hord, Joy M. ... **Charlotte, NC**
Hord, Mark E. ... Dallas, TX
Hord, Michael F. ... **Dallas, TX**
Hord, Michael F., Jr. ... **Houston, TX**
Hord, Robert C., Jr. ... **Charlotte, NC**
Hord, Terry L. ... Kenton, OH
Horde, G. Wilson ... Oak Ridge, TN
Horde, G. Wilson, III ... **Atlanta, GA**
Hordell, Michael A. ... **Washington, DC**
Horder, Richard A. ... **Atlanta, GA**
Hordern, James L., Jr. ... **Houston, TX**
Hordes, Donald B. ... **Cincinnati, OH**
Hording, Kyle ... Los Angeles, CA
Hordon, Cheryl E. ... New York, NY
Hordon, Sheila F. ... **Princeton, NJ**
Horecky & Associates, Law Offices of
Hagåtña, GU
Horecky, D. J. ... Jackson, MS
Horecky, Frederick J. ... Hagåtña, GU
Horejs, Edward R., Jr. ... Cleveland, OH
Horejsi, Peter J. ... Minneapolis, MN
Horeled, John J. ... Crystal Lake, IL
Horelick, Douglas E. ... **Miami, FL**
Horelick, Mary G. ... Newington, CT
Horelly, Anne J. ... Glendale, CA
Horen, & Associates, P.C. ... Denver, CO
Horen, Robert P. ... Denver, CO
Horenberger, M. Jill ... Mays Landing, NJ
Horenstein, Joan Dymond ... Miami, FL
Horenstein, John D ... **New York, NY**
Horenstein, Jonathan P. ... Dearborn, MI
Horenstein, Josepher & Gewanter, P.C.
New York, NY
Horenstein, Kenneth P. ... **New York, NY**
Horenstein, Neal G. ... Phoenix, AZ
Horenstein, Neal G., P.A. ... Phoenix, AZ
Horenstein, Nicholson & Blumenthal, A Legal Professional Association ... Dayton, OH
Horenstein, Peter ... New York, NY
Horenstein, Raymond ... Southfield, MI
Horenstein, Scott J. ... **Vancouver, WA**
Horenstein, Scott, The, Law Firm
Portland, OR
Vancouver, WA
Horenstein, Sol ... Babylon, NY
Horenstein, Stephen W. ... **Vancouver, WA**
Horenstein, Steven B. ... Dayton, OH
Horesh, Tom ... Los Angeles, CA
Horetski, Gayle A. ... Juneau, AK
Horewitz and Cordaro ... Connellsville, PA
Horewitz, Gary Mark ... Connellsville, PA
Horewitz, Murray I. ... Connellsville, PA
Horey, Edward M. ... Olean, NY
Horey, Joseph E. ... **Saipan, TT**
Horgan, Christopher J. ... **New York, NY**
Horgan, Daniel E. ... **Secaucus, NJ**
Trenton, NJ
Horgan, Daniel J. ... New London, CT
Horgan, Danl. J., Jr. ... Lynn, MA
Horgan, Dermot ... **Chicago, IL**
Horgan, Everett F. ... Brewster, MA
Horgan, Gary M. ... **Los Angeles, CA**
Horgan, J. Kevin ... **Washington, DC**
Horgan, J. Matthew ... **Pittsburgh, PA**
Horgan, James J. ... **Boston, MA**
Horgan, Janet L. ... **St. Louis, MO**
Horgan, John C. ... Bensenville, IL
Horgan, John J. ... **St. Louis, MO**
Horgan, John L. ... Jerome, ID
Horgan, John L., Jr. ... Hyattsville, MD
Horgan, John P. ... San Francisco, CA
Horgan, John P., III ... Sacramento, CA
Horgan, Mark M. ... Department of the Navy, Office of the Judge Advocate General, GV
Horgan, Michael F. ... Bronxville, NY
Horgan, Michael F., Jr. ... Bronxville, NY
Horgan, Michael O. ... Washington, GA
Horgan, Michael O., P.C. ... Washington, GA
Horgan, Nancy E. ... Vashon, WA
Horgan, Paul C. ... Los Angeles, CA
Horgan, Paul F. ... St. Louis, MO
Horgan, Richard J. ... St. Cloud, MN
Horgan, Roger D. ... **Pittsburgh, PA**
Horgan, Ronald W. ... Houston, TX
Horgan, Rosen, Beckham & Coren, L.L.P.
Los Angeles, CA
Pasadena, CA
Woodland Hills, CA
Horgan, Thomas C. ... Boston, MA
Horgan, Thomas M. ... Beaverton, OR
Horgen, Cindy L. ... Minneapolis, MN
Horger, Barnwell & Reid, L.L.P.
Orangeburg, SC
Horger, Dave, Jr. ... Hurst, TX
Hörger, Hörger, Lanier & Knight, L.L.P.
Orangeburg, SC
Summerville, SC
Horger, Kellyann Elizabeth
Philadelphia, PA
Hörger, Michael P. ... **Orangeburg, SC**
Summerville, SC
Horger, Paul D. ... **Scranton, PA**
Horger, Robert R. ... **Orangeburg, SC**
Hori, Fraser ... Boston, MA
Hori, Susan K. ... **Irvine, CA**
Horiates, George G. ... Pennsauken, NJ
Horie, Tadashi ... **Chicago, IL**
Horie, Walter K. ... Honolulu, HI
Horigan, Horigan & Lombardo, P.C.
Amsterdam, NY
Saratoga Springs, NY
Horigan, Richard T. ... **Amsterdam, NY**
Saratoga Springs, NY
Horigan, Timothy ... **Amsterdam, NY**
Saratoga Springs, NY
Horii, Dwayne M. ... **Los Angeles, CA**
Horikawa, Harvey M. ... **Torrance, CA**
Horikawa, Joyce M. ... Department of Justice, Bureau of Prisons, GV
Horikawa, Paul L. ... Wailuku, HI
Horikawa, Saori ... **New York, NY**
Horikoshi, Neil H. ... White Plains, NY
Horin, William A. ... **Washington, DC**
Horine, Marvin K. ... Wabash, IN
Horine, Robt. G. ... Columbia, SC
Horinek, Peggy S. ... **Oklahoma City, OK**
Horing, Saul ... New York, NY
Horing Welikson & Rosen, P.C.
Forest Hills, NY
New York, NY
Horiskey, James P. ... Cheyenne, WY
Horiszny, Heather Ann ... Denver, CO
Horiszny, John T. ... Saginaw, MI
Horiszny, Laurene H. ... Chicago, IL
Horiuchi, Anne T. ... **Honolulu, HI**
Horiuchi, Mimi K. ... Honolulu, HI
Horjus, Kenneth M. ... **Grand Rapids, MI**
Horka & Horberg, P.C. ... Burnham, IL
Horka, R. F. ... Kountze, TX
Horkan, Derek J. ... **Reedsburg, WI**
Wonewoc, WI
Horkan, Frank D. ... Moultrie, GA
Horkan, George A., Jr. ... Moultrie, GA
Horkan, George A., Jr. ... Upperville, VA
Horkan, J. Timothy
North Palm Beach, FL
Horkan, Thomas A., Jr. ... Tallahassee, FL
Horkan, William H. ... Fairfax, VA
Horkay, Joan Butler ... Cleveland, OH
Horkey, W. R. ... Tulsa, OK
Horkin, Margaret R. ... Corpus Christi, TX
Horkitz, Peter D. ... Washington, DC
Horkovich, Robert M. ... **New York, NY**
Horky, Alan R. ... **Pensacola, FL**
Horky, Kenneth A. ... **Fort Lauderdale, FL**
Horky, Kenneth L. ... Lake Worth, FL
Horlacher, H. Matthew
Salt Lake City, UT
Horland, James A. ... Miami, FL
Horlander, Joseph C. ... Noblesville, IN
Horlbeck, John M. ... Charleston, SC
Horlbeck, William G. ... **Denver, CO**
Horlbeck, William G., P.C. ... **Denver, CO**
Horlen, Holt & Hollas, PLLC
College Station, TX
Horlen, Joe P. ... College Station, TX
Horlick, Chester W. ... Youngstown, OH
Horlick, Gary N. ... **Washington, DC**
Horlick, Lisa L. ... **Los Angeles, CA**
Horlick, Michael D. ... **Venice, FL**
Horlick, Michael D., P.A. ... **Venice, FL**
Horlings, Mark ... Koror, TT
Horlock, Laura C. ... Decatur, GA
Horlock, William W., Jr. ... **Atlanta, GA**
Hormachea, Nancy ... Oakland, CA
Horman, George T. ... **Frederick, MD**
Horman, Russell T. ... Frederick, MD
Hormann, Dale K. ... Salem, OR
Hormann, Karl ... Cambridge, MA
Hormberg, William J. ... St. Louis, MO
Hormel, Clairmont E. ... Ephrata, WA
Hormel, Peter ... Tucson, AZ
Hormel, Richard A. ... Culver City, CA
Hormell, Oliver N. ... Tyrone, PA
Hormozi, Mitra ... **New York, NY**
Hormuth, Kevin Francis ... **St. Louis, MO**
Horn, Alan B. ... Uniondale, NY
Horn, Albert J. ... **Burlingame, CA**
Horn, Alec H. ... **Houston, TX**
Horn, Allwin E., III ... Birmingham, AL
Horn, Allwin E., IV ... Birmingham, AL
Horn, Alycia ... Philadelphia, PA
Horn, Amanda Lacey ... Lake Oswego, OR
Horn, Andrew W. ... **Miami, FL**
Horn, Andrew W., Professional Association
Miami, FL
Horn, Ariane M. ... **New York, NY**
Horn, Arthur S. ... **Nutley, NJ**
Horn, Arthur S., P.A. ... **Nutley, NJ**
Horn, Aylward & Bandy, LLC
Kansas City, KS
Kansas City, MO
Horn, Barbara N. ... Oakland, CA
Horn & Bennett, P.A. ... **Baltimore, MD**
Towson, MD
Horn, Bernard P. ... Washington, DC
Horn, Bonnie P. ... Columbia, SC
Horn, Brenda S. ... **Chicago, IL**
Indianapolis, IN
Horn, Bryan W. ... **Richmond, VA**
Horn, Byron J. ... **Cleveland, OH**
Horn, C. Steven ... **New York, NY**
Horn, C. A. ... Shelby, NC
Horn, Carl, III ... Charlotte, NC
Horn, Carl L. ... Standish, MI
Horn, Carla Brown ... Washington, PA
Horn, Carolyn Hafner ... New York, NY
Horn, Carolyn J. ... **New York, NY**
Horn, Charles F. ... Kettering, OH
Horn, Charles H. ... **San Francisco, CA**
Horn, Charles J. ... Kettering, OH
Horn, Charles L. ... **Minneapolis, MN**
Horn, Charles M. ... **Washington, DC**
Horn, Christine M. ... Boynton Beach, FL
Horn, Christopher ... Chagrin Falls, OH
Horn, Christopher B. ... **Chicago, IL**
Horn, Craig W. ... **Saginaw, MI**
Horn, Cynthia M. ... Philadelphia, PA
Horn, Dale W. ... San Diego, CA
Horn, Dan K. ... Irving, TX
Horn, Dara M. ... Detroit, MI
Horn, David B. ... **New York, NY**
Horn, David C. ... **Cincinnati, OH**
Horn, Debora L. ... **Jackson, MS**
Horn, Debra J. ... **Cleveland, OH**
Horn, Dennis L. ... **Madison, MS**
Horn, Dennis M. ... **Washington, DC**
Horn, Diane L. ... Williamsport, PA
Horn, Don L. ... **Miami, FL**
Horn, Donald H.
Department of Transportation, Office of the General Counsel, GV
Horn, Donald H. ... Chickasha, OK
Horn, Donald H., P.C. ... Chickasha, OK
Horn, Douglas M. ... **Boca Raton, FL**
Horn, Douglas R. ... Independence, MO
Horn, Earl G. ... Phoenix, AZ
Horn, Ellen M. ... Springfield, NJ
Horn, Eric L. ... **New York, NY**
Horn, Erica L. ... **Lexington, KY**
Louisville, KY
Horn, Ethan A. ... Irvine, CA
Horn, Eugene J. ... Jersey City, NJ
Horn, Frances L. ... **Washington, DC**
Horn, Francoise A. Hartley ... Gainesville, FL
Horn, Frederick C. ... **Lansdale, PA**
Horn, Frederick L. ... Philadelphia, PA
Horn, Frederick M., (P.C.) ... New York, NY
Horn, Garfield H. ... **New York, NY**
Horn, Gary A. ... Forest Hills, NY
Horn, Geoffrey M. ... **New York, NY**
Horn, George E. ... **South Bend, IN**
Horn, Gerald B. ... **New York, NY**
Horn, Gerson S. ... **Santa Monica, CA**
Horn, Gregory A. ... Richmond, IN
Horn, H. Chester, Jr. ... Los Angeles, CA
Horn, Henry Z. ... New Bedford, MA
Horn, Herbert ... Atlantic City, NJ
Horn, Howard C. ... Pasadena, CA
Horn, Howard Ira ... Garden City, NY
Horn, J. Bradley ... **Vienna, VA**
Horn, J. Russell ... Austin, TX
Horn, Jack A. ... **New York, NY**
Horn, Jack H. ... Inez, KY
Horn, James C. ... St. Helens, OR
Horn, James T. ... Chicago, IL
Horn, Jan M. ... **Houston, TX**
Horn, Jeff J., Jr. ... **Alexandria, LA**
Horn, Jeffrey A. ... New York, NY
Horn, Jeffrey D. ... Williamstown, NJ
Horn, Jennifer B. ... **Floydada, TX**
Horn, Jennifer B. ... **Lubbock, TX**
Horn, Jennifer M. ... Baltimore, MD
Horn, Jerold I. ... **Peoria, IL**
Horn, Jesse J. ... Oklahoma City, OK
Horn, Jesse J., Inc. ... Oklahoma City, OK
Horn, Joanne L. ... Wilmington, DE
Horn, Joel H. ... Northfield, NJ
Horn, John A. ... Madison, WI
Horn, John E. ... Tinley Park, IL
Horn, John G. ... Buffalo, NY
Horn, John H. ... Eugene, OR
Horn, John J. ... Milwaukee, WI
Horn, John R. ... Santa Clara, CA
Horn & Johnson ... Oakland, CA
Horn, Jon S. ... Phoenix, AZ
Horn, Jonathan F. ... **New York, NY**
Horn, Joseph ... New York, NY
Horn, Joshua ... **Philadelphia, PA**
Horn, Karen G. ... San Diego, CA
Horn, Keith D., Jr. ... Pittsburgh, PA
Horn, Keith L. ... New York, NY
Horn, Kenneth E. ... New York, NY
Horn, Kevin J.
Securities and Exchange Commission, GV
Horn & Kim, P.C. ... **New York, NY**
Horn, Kirk A. ... **Indianapolis, IN**
Horn, Kristin Daniels ... **Birmingham, AL**
Horn, Kristin M. ... Kansas City, MO
Horn Law Firm, The, P.C.
Independence, MO
Horn, Lawrence R. ... Mill Valley, CA
Horn, Lawrence S. ... **Newark, NJ**
New York, NY
Horn, Leah" Toni " ... Austin, TX
Horn, Leonard C. ... Atlantic City, NJ
Horn, Linda C. ... New York, NY
Horn, Linda J. ... Brooklyn, NY
Horn, Lizabeth F. ... **Chicago, IL**
Horn, Marcia ... Phoenix, AZ
Horn, Margaret A. ... Wilmington, DE
Horn, Marian Blank
United States Court of Federal Claims, GV
Horn, Mark ... North Miami, FL
Horn, Mark ... West Palm Beach, FL
Horn, Mark R.A. ... **New Bern, NC**
Horn, Martin E. ... Birmingham, AL
Horn, Martin J. ... **Creedmoor, NC**
Durham, NC
Greensboro, NC
Raleigh, NC
Horn, Martin R. ... Los Angeles, CA
Horn, Mary ... **Washington, DC**
Horn, Matthew A. ... Honolulu, HI
Horn, Maurita Elaine ... **Washington, DC**
Horn, Meredith Kersey ... Washington, DC
Horn, Michael A. ... **Burbank, CA**
Horn, Michael D. ... Brooklyn, NY
Horn, Michael D. ... Cleveland, OH
Horn, Michael E. ... Dallas, TX
Horn, Michael M. ... **Newark, NJ**
Horn, Michael R. ... **Marshalltown, IA**
Horn, Michele Annette
Department of Justice, GV
Horn, Michele Renee ... Fulton, MS
Horn, Neil A. ... Harrisonburg, VA
Horn & Payne, PLLC ... **Madison, MS**
Horn, Philip Charles ... Carpentersville, IL
Horn, Polly ... **Los Angeles, CA**
Horn, R. Steven ... Tulsa, OK
Horn, Richard D. ... **Washington, DC**
Horn, Richard H. ... York, PA
Horn, Richard L. ... **Chicago, IL**
Horn, Richard M. ... San Diego, CA
Horn, Richard P. ... Pittsburgh, PA
Horn, Richard W. ... Cincinnati, OH
Horn & Rife ... Kettering, OH
Horn, Robert A. ... **Kansas City, MO**
Horn, Robert A. ... New York, NY
Horn, Robert H. ... **Los Angeles, CA**
Horn, Robert H. ... Sacramento, CA
Horn, Robert J., Jr. ... Hollis, NH
Horn, Robert L. ... Bradenton, FL
Horn, Robert Seemann ... Durham, CT
Horn, Robin B. ... Newark, NJ
Horn, Robt. W. ... Valders, WI
Horn, Ronald F. ... **Albuquerque, NM**
Horn, Russell J. ... Austin, TX
Horn, S. Hayes, Jr. ... Stafford, TX
Horn, Sam ... Wheaton, MD
Horn, Sanford L. ... Pasadena, CA
Horn, Sarah C. ... Oakland, CA
Horn, Scott T. ... **New York, NY**
Horn, Sharon Y. ... Treasury Department, Internal Revenue Service, GV
Horn Shechtman & Hirsch, P.C.
Jersey City, NJ
Horn, Shelby P. ... Pittsburg, KS
Horn, Stanley J. ... Chicago, IL
Horn, Stephanie D. ... Cincinnati, OH

Horn, Stephen ... Washington, DC
Randolph, MA
Horn, Stephen M. ... Charleston, WV
Horn, Stephen P. ... Kansas City, MO
Horn, Steven Gary ... Jersey City, NJ
Horn, Steven M. ... Atlantic City, NJ
Horn, Susan A. ... Los Angeles, CA
Horn, Susan R. ... Syracuse, NY
Horn, Susan W. ... Chicago, IL
Horn, Sydney I. ... Lake Charles, LA
Horn, Sydney I., A.P.L.C. ... Lake Charles, LA
Horn, Tammy L. ... Kansas City, MO
Horn, Thomas E. ... San Francisco, CA
Horn, Thomas R. ... San Pedro, CA
Horn, Todd J. ... Baltimore, MD
Horn, Valerie F. ... Beverly Hills, CA
Horn, Vicky C. ... Lexington, KY
Horn, Vincent J., Jr. ... Littleton, CO
Horn, Warren ... New Orleans, LA
Horn, William A. ... Grand Rapids, MI
Horn, William C. ... The Plains, VA
Horn, William D. ... Downers Grove, IL
Horn, William P. ... Washington, DC
Horn, Wm. Lee ... Nashville, TN
Hornacek, Thomas K.
Hoffman Estates, IL
Hornack, Joseph S. ... Pittsburgh, PA
Hornaday, James C. ... Homer, AK
Hornaday, Kathy L. ... Owensboro, KY
Hornaday, Scott D. ... Owensboro, KY
Hornak, Kimberly K. ... Salt Lake City, UT
Hornak, Maria A. ... Costa Mesa, CA
Hornak, Mark Raymond ... Pittsburgh, PA
Hornak, Michael T. ... Costa Mesa, CA
Hornak, Thomas J. ... Philadelphia, PA
Hornbach, Bernard J. ... San Francisco, CA
Hornbach, Kim Charles ... Naples, FL
Hornbach, Oskar M. ... Lansing, MI
Hornbacher, Bradley D. ... Coral Gables, FL
Hornback, Katherine J. ... Lexington, KY
Hornback, William A. ... Bakersfield, CA
Hornbaker, Lee ... Junction City, KS
Hornbaker, Richard R. ... Princeton, IL
Hornbaker, Robert D. ... Los Angeles, CA
Hornbaker, Steven ... Junction City, KS
Hornbeck, Daniel L. ... Overland Park, KS
Hornbeck, David A. ... Reno, NV
Hornbeck, David B. ... Columbus, OH
Hornbeck, John W. ... Beverly Hills, CA
Hornbeck, John W.
National Labor Relations Board,
Office of the General Counsel, GV
Hornbeck, Marion A. ... Green Valley, AZ
Hornbeck, Richard L. ... Brunswick, ME
Hornbeck, Sean K. ... Washington, DC
Hornbeck, William J., II ... St. Petersburg, FL
Hornbeck, William J., II, P.A., Law Offices of
St. Petersburg, FL
Hornbeck-Prezelski, Lisa ... Bristol, PA
Doylestown, PA
Hornbeek, Krahl & Vitali
Oklahoma City, OK
Hornbeek, Richard E. ... Oklahoma City, OK
Hornberger, Charles M. ... San Antonio, TX
Hornberger, Ghazarians & Brewer
Los Angeles, CA
Hornberger, Jacob G. ... Fairfax, VA
Hornberger, Lee ... Cincinnati, OH
Hornberger, Nicholas W. ... Los Angeles, CA
Hornberger, Robert E. ... Bentonville, AR
Fort Smith, AR
Little Rock, AR
Hornberger, Ronald ... San Antonio, TX
Hornberger, William H. ... Dallas, TX
Hornblower, Donald S. ... Lewiston, ME
Hornblower, Jonathan M.
Corpus Christi, TX
Hornblower, Manning, Ward & Bernardino, Professional Corporation
Los Angeles, CA
Hornblower, Manning & Ward, Professional Corporation ... Corpus Christi, TX
Hornblower, Marshall ... Washington, DC
Hornbostel, John F., Jr. ... Sharon, PA
Hornbostel, John P. ... New York, NY
Hornbostel, Peter A. ... Washington, DC
New York, NY
Hornbostel, William J.
Colorado Springs, CO
Hornbrook, John H. ... Canton, OH
Hornbrook, Michael J. ... Chicago, IL
Hornbuckle, Bruce Darby ... Marietta, GA
Hornbuckle, Stephen S. ... Houston, TX
Hornbuckle, Thomas S. ... Houston, TX
Hornbuckle, Thomas S., & Associates, P.C.
Houston, TX
Hornbuckle, William E. ... San Antonio, TX
Hornburg, Diggs, Backhaus & Simon, P.C.
Olean, NY
Hornburg, Earl H. ... Olean, NY
Hornburg, Kirk D. ... Detroit, MI
Hornburg, Philip T. ... Visalia, CA
Hornby, D. Brock ... Portland, ME
Hornby, Mary T. ... Boston, MA
Hornby, Robert K. ... Flemington, NJ
Hornby, Scott G. ... Wyandotte, MI
Horne, Alexandra J. ... San Jose, CA
Horne, Allan W. ... Little Rock, AR
Horne, Alvin A. ... Saipan, TT
Horne, Andrea L. ... Chicago, IL
Horne, Andrew J. ... Louisville, KY
Horne, Arlynn B. ... Idaho Falls, ID
Horne, Arthur J., Jr. ... Largo, MD
Horne, B. Davis, Jr. ... Raleigh, NC
Horne, Bistrow & Dulberg, P.C.
Phoenix, AZ
Horne, Brian ... Newport Beach, CA
Horne, Brockman
Department Of Health And Human Services,
Social Security Administration, GV
Horne, Charles F., IV ... Buffalo, NY
Horne, Charles G. ... Platteville, WI
Horne, Chastiti N. ... Houston, TX
Horne, Chevis F., Jr. ... Denver, CO
Horne & Childs ... White Plains, NY
Horne, Clarence R., Jr. ... Conyers, GA
Horne, Damian Trajan ... Gloucester, VA
Horne, Daniel C. ... San Francisco, CA
Horne, David A. ... Alexandria, VA
Horne, David B. ... Fayetteville, AR
Horne, David J. ... Cincinnati, OH
Horne, David L. ... Virginia Beach, VA
Horne, David P. ... Boston, MA
Horne, Denise A. ... Oak Brook, IL
Horne, Earl W., Jr. ... Sugar Land, TX
Horne, Edward W. ... East Hampton, NY
Horne, Eric L. ... Pittsburgh, PA
Horne, Foy S., Jr. ... Athens, GA
Horne, Foy S., Jr., P.C. ... Athens, GA
Horne, Franklin S., Jr. ... Macon, GA
Horne, Frederick J.
Federal Trade Commission,
Bureau of Competition, GV
Horne, Gay Dawn, (Miss) ... Jackson, MS
Horne, Glenn L. ... White Plains, NY
Horne, H. Forest, Jr. ... Raleigh, NC
Wilmington, NC
Horne, Hillery E. ... Centreville, MS
Horne, Hoke I., II ... Norton, VA
Horne, Hollingsworth & Parker, A Professional Association ... Little Rock, AR
Horne & Horne, A Prtnrshp. incl. A Prof. Corp.
Albuquerque, NM
Horne, Hugh R. ... Albuquerque, NM
Horne, James E. ... Seattle, WA
Horne, James F. ... St. Louis, MO
Horne, James M. ... State College, PA
Horne, James R. ... Paradise, CA
Horne, Jennifer Elizabeth
Redwood City, CA
Horne, Jennifer M. ... Sacramento, CA
Horne, Jenny Anderson ... Spartanburg, SC
Horne, Joe L. ... New Orleans, LA
Horne, Joe L., A Professional Law Corporation
New Orleans, LA
Horne, Joedaniel ... Austin, TX
Horne, John D. ... Memphis, TN
Horne, John G., II ... Frankfort, KY
Horne, John H. ... Atlanta, GA
Greenville, SC
Horne, John H., Jr. ... Laurinburg, NC
Horne, John S. ... Putnam, CT
Horne, Kathleen ... Savannah, GA
Horne, Kathleen B. ... Herndon, VA
Horne, Kay ... Sacramento, CA
Horne, Kevin M. ... Lexington, KY
Horne, Kevin P. ... New Orleans, LA
Horne, Leon R. ... Arlington, VA
Horne, Mallory E. ... Tallahassee, FL
Horne, Mark J. ... Jacksonville, FL
Horne, Mark J. ... Chicago, IL
Horne, Mark J., P.A. ... Jacksonville, FL
Horne, Melissa M. ... Providence, RI
Horne, Michael S. ... Washington, DC
Horne, Nathan ... Austin, TX
Horne, Neil P. ... New York, NY
Horne, Nettie Ann ... Gaithersburg, MD
Horne, O. Wendell, III ... Atlanta, GA
Macon, GA
Horne, O. Wendell, Jr. ... Cordele, GA
Horne, Patricia S. ... Raleigh, NC
Horne, Patrick T. ... Richmond, VA
Horne, Philip S. ... San Francisco, CA
Horne, Richard D. ... Bay Minette, AL
Horne, Richard D. ... Mobile, AL
Horne, Richard J. ... New York, NY
Horne, Richard P., Jr. ... Mount Pleasant, SC
Horne, Robert A. ... New York, NY
Horne, Roger M. ... Phoenix, AZ
Horne, Samuel T. ... Waterville, ME
Horne, Scott ... La Crosse, WI
Horne, Scott J. ... Washington, DC
Horne, Sharon K. ... Springfield, MA
Horne, Sheila Ryan ... Norfolk, VA
Horne & Shiver ... Macon, GA
Horne, Stephen F., II ... Greenville, NC
Horne, Stephen F., II, P.A. ... Greenville, NC
Horne, Susan Smith ... Versailles, KY
Horne, Suzanne U. ... Jacksonville, FL
Horne, Terrell T. ... Sumter, SC
Horne, Terry D. ... Charlotte, NC
Horne, Thomas C. ... Phoenix, AZ
Horne, Thomas D. ... Leesburg, VA
Horne, Thomas J., (P.C.) ... Albuquerque, NM
Horne, Thomas M. ... Chattanooga, TN
Horne, Tom Lee, Jr. ... Franklin, LA
Morgan City, LA
Horne, Tommy A. ... Meridian, MS
Horne, Toni Ann ... Naples, FL
Horne, Vicki Kuftic ... Pittsburgh, PA
Horne, Walter H. ... Cypress, TX
Horne, Wayne T. ... Grundy, VA
Horne & West, P.C. ... Gloucester, VA
Horne, William A. ... Boston, MA
Horne, William M., Jr. ... New York, NY
Horne, William S. ... Easton, MD
Horneber, Alice Schumacher
South Sioux City, NE
Horneber Law Offices ... Sioux City, IA
South Sioux City, NE
Wakefield, NE
Dakota Dunes, SD
Horneber, William F.
South Sioux City, NE
Wakefield, NE
Horneck, John E. ... Denver, CO
Hornecker, Cowling, Hassen & Heysell, L.L.P. ... Medford, OR
Hornecker, Gregory T. ... Medford, OR
Hornecker, Mitchell E. ... Portland, OR
Horneff, Elizabeth ... Philadelphia, PA
Horneffer, Steven G. ... Longwood, FL
Horneman, H. Carl ... Louisville, KY
Horner, Beth A. ... St. Petersburg, FL
Horner, Burtis W. ... Newark, NJ
New York, NY
Horner, Cecelia Philipps ... Richmond, VA
Horner, Chad ... Kent, WA
Horner, Charles ... Seattle, WA
Horner, Charles D. ... Kansas City, MO
Horner, Cheryl D. ... Las Vegas, NV
Horner, Clare A. ... Pittsburgh, PA
Horner, Clifford R. ... Walnut Creek, CA
Horner, Clifford R. ... Walnut Creek, CA
Horner, Denise J. ... Des Moines, IA
Horner, Dennis L. ... Kansas City, KS
Horner, Derrick L. ... New York, NY
Horner & Duckers, Chartered
Kansas City, KS
Horner, Edwin P. ... Waco, TX
Horner, Gail W. ... Germantown, TN
Horner, Gary C. ... Johnstown, PA
Horner, George R. ... Vermillion, SD
Horner, Henry C. ... Worcester, MA
Horner, Jack B. ... Lancaster, PA
Horner, James A., Jr.
Steamboat Springs, CO
Horner, James E. ... Cincinnati, OH
Horner, James F., Jr. ... Memphis, TN
Horner, Jeffrey John ... Houston, TX
Horner, Jeffrey W. ... Oakland, CA
Horner, Jimmie W. ... Dresden, TN
Horner, John L. ... Great Bend, KS
Horner, Kathy D. ... Houston, TX
Horner, Kurt F. ... Vandalia, OH
Horner, Linda P. ... Long Beach, CA
Horner, Martin ... New York, NY
Horner, Michael L. ... San Jose, CA
Horner, Michael W. ... Westmont, NJ
Horner, Nanette L. ... Atlantic City, NJ
Horner, Nathan P., Jr. ... New Orleans, LA
Horner, Patricia ... Toledo, OH
Horner, Patrick A. ... Fulton, MO
Horner, Peter J. ... Sioux Falls, SD
Horner, Philip W. ... Folsom, CA
Horner, Randy ... Charleston, SC
Horner, Robert B. ... Beverly Hills, CA
Horner, Robert D. ... Midlothian, VA
Horner, Robert W., III ... Naperville, IL
Horner, Robin R. ... Honolulu, HI
Horner, Roger A. ... Brentwood, TN
Horner, Ronald D. ... Phoenix, AZ
Horner, Russell G., Jr.
Oklahoma City, OK
Horner, Sharon N. ... Richmond, VA
Horner, Stephen B. ... Prairie Village, KS
Horner, Stephen P., Law Office of
Norwalk, CT
Horner, Stuart J., Jr. ... Greensburg, PA
Horner, Susan L. ... San Diego, CA
Horner, Susan Morath ... Boulder, CO
Horner, Terry D. ... Newburgh, NY
Horner, Thomas E. ... Wilkesboro, NC
Horner, Timothy L. ... Grand Rapids, MI
Horner, Timothy M. ... Ithaca, NY
Horner, Warren M. ... Minneapolis, MN
Horner, Wayne J. ... Bismarck, ND
Horner, William C. ... Salem, NJ
Horner, William J., Jr. ... Titusville, FL
Horner, William L. ... Salem, NJ
Horner, William M. ... Dallas, OR
Horner, William R. ... New York, NY
Hornewer, Charles A. ... Chicago, IL
Hornewer, John R. ... Wood Dale, IL
Horney, Kenneth A. ... Cincinnati, OH
Horngrad, Douglas ... San Francisco, CA
Horngren, Scott W. ... Portland, OR
Hornick, Blake ... New York, NY
Hornick, Damian C. ... Overland Park, KS
Hornick, Harriet L. ... Philadelphia, PA
Hornick, John F. ... Washington, DC
Hornick, Robert N. ... New York, NY
Hornickel, Daniel P. ... Mount Holly, NJ
Hornickel, John H. ... St. Paul, MN
Hornidge, Ann-Ellen Marcus ... Boston, MA
Hornig, Christopher W. ... Washington, DC
Hornig, Constance R. ... Los Angeles, CA
Hornig, David R. ... New York, NY
Hornig, Steven A. ... Minneapolis, MN
Hornig, Thomas S. ... Janesville, WI
Horn III, Raymond J. ... Schaumburg, IL
Hornik, Alex S. ... Miami Beach, FL
Hornik, David H. ... Nashville, TN
Hornik, David M. ... San Francisco, CA
Hornik, Esther L. ... Philadelphia, PA
Hornik, Jonathan L. ... New York, NY
Hornik, Joseph J. ... New York, NY
Hornik, Philip ... Portland, OR
Hornik, Robert ... Milwaukee, WI
Hornilla, Arlene L. ... St. Paul, MN
Horning, Duane S. ... San Diego, CA
Horning, Edward F., III ... Louisville, KY
Horning, Fred A. ... Portland, OR
Horning, Gerald R. ... Cleveland, OH
Horning, Johnson, Grove, Hulett & Thompson, A Professional Corporation
Oklahoma City, OK
Horning, Kathryn D. ... San Diego, CA
Horning, Kurt D. ... New York, NY
Horning, Mark F. ... Washington, DC
Horning, Patrick J. ... Brookfield, WI
Horning, Philip F. ... Oklahoma City, OK
Horning, Richard A. ... Salem, OH
Horning, Richard Allan ... Palo Alto, CA
Horning, Robin S. ... Washington, DC
Horning, Timothy F. ... Rockford, IL
Hornish, Mary Adele ... Livingston, NJ
Hornish, Thomas E. ... San Diego, CA
Hornisher, Michael ... Tucson, AZ
Hornkohl, Jason L. ... Knoxville, TN
Hornney, Regan M. ... Portland, ME
Hornor, Boyd E. (John), III ... Fair Oaks, CA
Hornor, John ... Fair Oaks, CA
Hornor, Mark ... San Francisco, CA
Hornreich, Michael A. ... Orlando, FL
Hornreich, Samuel ... Roseburg, OR
Hornsby, Anne Sikes ... Birmingham, AL
Hornsby, Avis Karen ... Atlanta, GA
Hornsby, Brad W. ... Murfreesboro, TN
Hornsby, Brandon ... Atlanta, GA
Hornsby, Clare Sekul ... Biloxi, MS
Hornsby, Clay ... Alexander City, AL
Hornsby, Cyrus E., III ... Miami, FL
Hornsby, David Thomas ... Walnut Creek, CA
Hornsby, Douglas L. ... Newport News, VA
Virginia Beach, VA
Hornsby, Ernest C. ... Montgomery, AL
Hornsby, Ernest H. ... Dothan, AL
Hornsby, Joey ... Dothan, AL
Hornsby, J. W., Jr. ... Newport News, VA
Hornsby, Karen Hurt ... Murfreesboro, TN
Hornsby, Kenneth L. ... Donalsonville, GA
Hornsby, Lawrence H. ... Winter Park, FL
Hornsby & Littman, P.A. ... Winter Park, FL
Hornsby, Mark L. ... Shreveport, LA
Hornsby, Ralph W., Jr. ... Huntsville, AL
Hornsby, Ralph W., Sr. ... Huntsville, AL
Hornsby, Robt. S., Sr. ... Williamsburg, VA
Hornsby Sacher Zelman Paul & Beiley, P.A.
Miami, FL
Hornsby, Thomas E. ... Dixon, IL
Hornsby, Troy A. ... Texarkana, TX
Hornsby, Watson & Meginniss
Athens, AL
Decatur, AL
Guntersville, AL
Huntsville, AL
Scottsboro, AL
Hornsby, William E., Jr. ... Chicago, IL
Hornschemeier, Patrick ... Georgetown, OH
Hornsey, James M. ... Fayetteville, AR
Hornstein, Alan D. ... Baltimore, MD
Hornstein, Barry M. ... Phoenix, AZ
Hornstein, Bruce H. ... Miami Beach, FL
Hornstein, Charlotte, (Miss) ... Chicago, IL
Hornstein, Diane G. ... Bridgeport, CT
Hornstein, Donald N. ... Norfolk, VA
Hornstein, Ellen R.
Department of Agriculture,
Office of the General Counsel, GV
Hornstein, Gail R. ... Phoenix, AZ
Hornstein, Gertrude H. ... Tucson, AZ
Hornstein, Howard B. ... New York, NY
Hornstein, J. Leonard ... Bayonne, NJ
Hornstein, Jacob D. ... Baltimore, MD
Hornstein, James E. ... Los Angeles, CA
Hornstein, James T. ... Providence, RI
Hornstein, Jeffrey H. ... Chicago, IL
Hornstein, Joel Mark ... New York, NY
Hornstein, Michael D. ... Washington, DC
Hornstein, Nancy ... New York, NY
Hornstein, Palumbo & Keith ... New York, NY
Hornstein, Robert D. ... St. Gabriel, LA
Hornstein, Roger A. ... Washington, DC
Hornstein, Samuel B. ... Doylestown, PA
Hornstein, Samuel B., P.C.
Doylestown, PA
Hornstein & Sproul, LLP ... San Rafael, CA
Hornstein, Steven J. ... New York, NY
Hornstein, Val Dawson ... San Rafael, CA
Hornthal, L. Phillip, III
Elizabeth City, NC
Hornthal, L. P., Jr. ... Elizabeth City, NC
Hornthal, Riley, Ellis & Maland, L.L.P.
Elizabeth City, NC
Kill Devil Hills, NC
Manteo, NC
Nags Head, NC
Hornung, David J. ... Newport Beach, CA
Hornung, Ernest O. ... Detroit, MI
Hornung, Gerald K. ... Woodstock, VT
Hornung, Michael F. ... Fort Myers, FL
Hornung, Michael F., P.A.
Fort Myers, FL
Hornung, Richard V. ... Louisville, KY
Hornung, Robert J. ... Wichita, KS
Hornyak, Joseph P. ... Washington, DC
Hornyak, Juleann ... Springfield, IL
Hornyak, Stephen J. ... Gretna, LA
Hornyak, Stephen J., A Professional Corporation ... Gretna, LA
Horodeck, Richard A. ... New York, NY
Horodyski, Joseph B., III
Garden Grove, CA
Horoho, Kenneth J., Jr. ... Pittsburgh, PA
Horohoe, Earl T. ... Kenmore, NY
Horohoe, Kathleen E. ... Derby, NY
Horoschak, Donna R. ... Wausau, WI
Horoschak, Mark J. ... Charlotte, NC
Horoszko, Nichlaus P. ... Carnegie, PA
Horoupian, Grace Y. ... Los Angeles, CA
Horoupian, Mark S. ... Los Angeles, CA
Horovitz, Arnold M. ... Pittsburgh, PA
Horovitz, Paul S. ... Boston, MA
Horovitz, Peter A. ... Honolulu, HI
Horowitt, Darryl J. ... Fresno, CA
Horowitz, Abe ... Columbus, OH
Horowitz, Alan C. ... Williamstown, NJ
Horowitz, Alan I. ... Washington, DC
Horowitz, Alfred J. ... Fort Lauderdale, FL

Horowitz, Alfred J., P.A.
Fort Lauderdale, FL
Horowitz, Allan .... Bergenfield, NJ
Horowitz, Allan H.
Department of Transportation, Federal Aviation Administration, GV
Horowitz, Amy J. .... Hartford, CT
Horowitz, Andrea D. .... Garden City, NY
Port Washington, NY
Horowitz, Andrew D. .... Atlanta, GA
Horowitz, Arthur A.
Federal Labor Relations Authority, Office of the Administrative Law Judges, GV
Horowitz, Barry D. .... Hartford, CT
Horowitz, Barry W. .... New Brunswick, NJ
New York, NY
Horowitz, Benedict .... Needham, MA
Horowitz, Bertram H. .... Philadelphia, PA
Horowitz, Bruce A. .... San Jose, CA
Horowitz, Burton R. .... South Orange, NJ
Horowitz, Charles A. .... New York, NY
Horowitz, Corey M. .... New York, NY
Horowitz, Craig A. .... Los Angeles, CA
Horowitz, Craig M. .... New York, NY
Horowitz, Daniel A. .... Oakland, CA
Horowitz, Daniel S. .... New York, NY
Horowitz, David A. .... Hartford, CT
Horowitz, David E.
Federal Communications Commission, Office of the General Counsel, GV
Horowitz, David H. .... New York, NY
Horowitz, David J. .... Rockville, MD
Horowitz, David N. .... Phoenix, AZ
Horowitz, David N. .... Boynton Beach, FL
Islip, NY
Horowitz, David P. .... New York, NY
Horowitz, David, (P.C.) .... New York, NY
Horowitz, Donald A. .... St. Louis, MO
Horowitz, Donald J .... Seattle, WA
Horowitz, Donald L. .... Durham, NC
Horowitz, Donald, Law Offices of
Hackensack, NJ
Horowitz, Edward J. .... Los Angeles, CA
Horowitz, Edward J., A Professional Corporation .... Los Angeles, CA
Horowitz, Edward S. .... Greenbelt, MD
Horowitz, Eliot C.
Department of Housing and Urban Development, GV
Horowitz, Elizabeth M. .... Monterey Park, CA
Horowitz, Elsa M. .... Los Angeles, CA
Horowitz, Eric S. .... New York, NY
Horowitz, Erica D. .... Boston, MA
Horowitz, Eugene G. .... Washington, DC
Horowitz, Florence D. .... Brooklyn, NY
Horowitz, Foran & Sonntag, P.A.
Greenbelt, MD
Horowitz, Fredric R. .... Santa Monica, CA
Horowitz, Gary I. .... Washington, DC
Horowitz, Gary I. .... New York, NY
Horowitz, Gary Jon .... North Brunswick, NJ
Horowitz, Gary N. .... New York, NY
Horowitz, Gedale B. .... New York, NY
Horowitz, Gregg Martin .... Sarasota, FL
Horowitz, Gregory Aaron .... New York, NY
Horowitz, Gregory H. .... Newark, NJ
Horowitz, Harold W. .... Los Angeles, CA
Horowitz, Harvey J. .... New York, NY
Horowitz, Herbert D. .... Wheaton, MD
Horowitz, Herbert M. .... New York, NY
Horowitz, Howard B. .... Washington, DC
Horowitz, I. Ronald .... New York, NY
Horowitz, Ira M. .... New York, NY
Horowitz, Irwin A. .... Secaucus, NJ
Horowitz, Jacob .... New York, NY
Horowitz, James M. .... Universal City, CA
Horowitz, Jason .... New York, NY
Horowitz, Jay L. .... New Bedford, MA
Horowitz, Jay S. .... Denver, CO
Horowitz, Jay S. .... Gaithersburg, MD
Horowitz, Jay S., P.C. .... Gaithersburg, MD
Horowitz, Jeff .... Baltimore, MD
Horowitz, Jeffrey H .... Greenbelt, MD
Horowitz, Jeffrey I. .... Houston, TX
Horowitz, Jeffrey L.
National Labor Relations Board, Office of the General Counsel, GV
Horowitz, Jeffrey M. .... White Plains, NY
Horowitz, Jeffrey R. .... Fairfield, NJ
Horowitz, Jennifer L. .... New York, NY
Horowitz, Jerald .... New York, NY
Horowitz, Jerome .... Ogden, UT
Horowitz, Jessica Inez .... New City, NY
Horowitz, Joel A. .... New York, NY
Horowitz, Joel E. .... Cherry Hill, NJ
Philadelphia, PA
Horowitz, John .... New York, NY
Horowitz, Jonathan D. .... New York, NY
Horowitz, Jonathan D. .... Houston, TX
Horowitz, Joseph A. .... Perth Amboy, NJ
Horowitz, Joseph L. .... New York, NY
Horowitz, Joshua M. .... San Ramon, CA
Horowitz, Judith Leah .... Philadelphia, PA
Horowitz, Julie K. .... New York, NY
Horowitz, Karen G. .... New York, NY
Horowitz, Kenneth H. .... San Mateo, CA
Horowitz, Kenneth P. .... New York, NY
Horowitz, Kenneth S. .... Uniondale, NY
Horowitz, Larry Eric .... New York, NY
Horowitz, Lawrence Ivan
Yorktown Heights, NY
Horowitz, Lawrence S. .... Bedford Hills, NY
Horowitz, Leon .... Union City, NJ
Horowitz, Leonard I. .... New York, NY
Horowitz, Leslie R. .... Los Angeles, CA
Horowitz, Lewis M. .... Portland, OR

Horowitz, Linda
Administrative Office Of The United States Courts, GV
Horowitz, Lisa B. .... Washington, DC
Horowitz, Lisa D. .... Portland, OR
Horowitz, Lori Ellen .... Westbury, NY
Horowitz, Louise S. .... New York, NY
Horowitz, Marcie R. .... Indianapolis, IN
Horowitz, Mark A. .... Fort Myers, FL
Horowitz, Mark David .... Boca Raton, FL
Horowitz, Mark J. .... New York, NY
Horowitz, Marshall P. .... Los Angeles, CA
Horowitz, Martin M. .... Oakland, CA
Horowitz, Marvin I. .... Farmington Hills, MI
Horowitz, Matthew M. .... Hartford, CT
Horowitz, Melanie .... Margate, FL
Horowitz, Mencher, Klosowski & Nestler, P.C. .... Garden City, NY
Mineola, NY
Riverhead, NY
Horowitz, Michael E. .... New York, NY
Horowitz, Michael J. .... Washington, DC
Horowitz, Michael J.
Environmental Protection Agency, Office of the General Counsel, GV
Horowitz, Michael K. .... Fort Pierce, FL
Horowitz, Michael M. .... New York, NY
Horowitz, Michelle J. .... New York, NY
Horowitz, Milton .... Flushing, NY
Horowitz, Milton A. .... New York, NY
Horowitz, Mitchell I. .... Tampa, FL
Horowitz, Mort M. .... New York, NY
Horowitz, N. Edward .... Charleston, SC
Horowitz, Nathan .... Carmel, NY
White Plains, NY
Horowitz, Pamela S. .... Washington, DC
Horowitz, Paul A. .... New York, NY
Horowitz, Paul I. .... Mount Vernon, NY
Horowitz, Paul, (Ltd.) .... Chicago, IL
Horowitz, Phil .... San Francisco, CA
Horowitz, Philip D. .... New York, NY
Horowitz, Philip M. .... Washington, DC
Horowitz, Philip R. .... Miami, FL
Horowitz, Rachel J. .... Trenton, NJ
Horowitz, Raymond J. .... New York, NY
Horowitz, Richard .... New York, NY
Horowitz, Richard F. .... New York, NY
Horowitz, Richard I. .... Kew Gardens, NY
Horowitz, Richard M. .... Bronx, NY
Mount Vernon, NY
Horowitz, Richard M. .... New York, NY
Horowitz, Robert .... Great Neck, NY
Horowitz, Robert .... Madison, WI
Horowitz, Robert A. .... Stamford, CT
Horowitz, Robert B. G. .... New York, NY
Horowitz, Robert D. .... Canton, OH
Horowitz, Robert E. .... Peoria, AZ
Horowitz, Robert H. .... New Haven, CT
New York, NY
Horowitz, Robert M. .... Denver, CO
Horowitz, Robert M. .... Washington, DC
Horowitz, Robert S. .... Atlanta, GA
Horowitz, Robert S. .... Annandale, VA
Horowitz, Ron Joseph .... Mineola, NY
Horowitz, Ronald .... Red Bank, NJ
Horowitz & Rubinoff .... Oakland, CA
Horowitz, Sanford I. .... Sonoma, CA
Horowitz, Saul .... Monsey, NY
Horowitz, Saul .... West Hempstead, NY
Horowitz, Seth R. .... New York, NY
Horowitz, Sharri H. .... Chevy Chase, MD
Horowitz, Sherry L. .... Bala Cynwyd, PA
Horowitz, Stan G. .... New York, NY
Horowitz, Steve C. .... Charlotte, NC
Horowitz, Steven .... New York, NY
Horowitz, Steven .... New York, NY
Horowitz, Steven A. .... Garden City, NY
Horowitz, Steven A. .... New York, NY
Horowitz, Steven B. .... South Orange, NJ
Horowitz, Steven B. .... New York, NY
Horowitz, Steven G. .... New York, NY
Horowitz, Steven S. .... Mineola, NY
New York, NY
White Plains, NY
Horowitz, Susan J. .... Parsippany, NJ
Horowitz, Susan L. .... St. Louis, MO
Horowitz, Tami .... Los Angeles, CA
Horowitz & Tannenbaum, P.C.
Great Neck, NY
Horowitz, Tina A. .... Philadelphia, PA
Horowitz, Victor J. .... Piscataway, NJ
Horowitz & Wake .... Denver, CO
Horowitz and Weinstein .... Chicago, IL
Horowitz, William N. .... Fort Myers, FL
Horowitz, Zachary I. .... Universal City, CA
Horr, Chas. C. .... Portsmouth, OH
Horr, David J. .... Miami, FL
Horr, Linfors and Skipp, P.A.
Fort Lauderdale, FL
Miami, FL
Horr, William H. .... Portsmouth, OH
Horrall, Curtis L. .... Drummond, OK
Horrall, Patricia A.
Department of Commerce, Patent and Trademark Office, GV
Horras, Linda K. .... Chicago, IL
Horrell, Jack E. .... Cincinnati, OH
Horrell, Karen Holley .... Cincinnati, OH
Horrell, Mary F. .... Covington, LA
Horrell, Robert W. .... Lake Worth, FL
Horrell, Walter J. .... Covington, LA
Horres, E. Stratton, Jr. .... Dallas, TX
Horri, Peyman .... Dallas, TX
Horrigan, Christine S. .... Hartford, CT
Horrigan, Courtney C.T. .... Pittsburgh, PA
Horrigan, Daniel M. .... Washington, DC
Horrigan, Dean A. .... Toledo, OH
Horrigan, George R., Jr. .... Bakersfield, CA

Horrigan & Goehrs, L.L.P. .... Houston, TX
Horrigan, John J. .... Akron, OH
Horrigan, Joseph M.
Department Of Veterans Affairs, Board of Veterans Appeals, GV
Horrigan, Joseph S. .... Houston, TX
Horrigan, Mark S. .... Boston, MA
Horrigan, Maurice R., Jr. .... Quincy, MA
Horrigan, Michelle G. .... Worcester, MA
Horrigan, Molly A. .... Chicago, IL
Horrigan, Molly A. .... Chicago, IL
Horrocks, Dawn E. .... Los Angeles, CA
Horrocks, Michael Blaine
Coeur d'Alene, ID
Horrom, Michael H. .... Department of Defense, Defense Legal Services Agency, GV
Horrom, Nancy J. .... Laurel, MD
Horrow, Avigal .... Los Angeles, CA
Horrow, C. Richard .... Philadelphia, PA
Horrow, C. Richard, P.C. .... Philadelphia, PA
Horrow, Harry R. .... San Francisco, CA
Horrow, Michael B. .... Claremont, CA
Horrow, Richard B.
Palm Beach Gardens, FL
Horrox, Donald E. .... Oldsmar, FL
Horrox & Glugover, P.A.
Daytona Beach, FL
Horrox, Joseph Michael
Daytona Beach, FL
Horsburgh, Beverly .... Miami, FL
Horsch, Christopher J. .... Chicago, IL
Horsch, Richard A. .... New York, NY
Horseman, Elmer L., Jr. .... Kansas City, MO
Horseman, Karen S. .... Indianapolis, IN
Horsey, Andrew T. .... Dover, DE
Horsey, D. Francis .... Las Vegas, NV
Horsey, Henry R. .... Dover, DE
Horsey, William F., Jr. .... Los Altos, CA
Santa Rosa, CA
Horshok, James S. .... Houston, TX
Horshok, James S., P.C. .... Houston, TX
Horsky, Charles A. .... Washington, DC
Horsky, E. Roger .... Leavenworth, KS
Horsky, Eugene G. .... Claymont, DE
Horsley, Allen C. B. .... Boston, MA
Horsley, Diane Baccus .... Indialantic, FL
Horsley, Elizabeth Mason .... Richmond, VA
Horsley, G. William .... Springfield, IL
Horsley, Guy W., Jr. .... Richmond, VA
Horsley & Horsley .... Richmond, VA
Horsley, J. Garrett .... Richmond, VA
Horsley, Jack E. .... Mattoon, IL
Horsley, James R. (Ronnie) .... Tyler, TX
Horsley, John O'Hara
Federal Trade Commission, Bureau of Competition, GV
Horsley, John W. .... Salt Lake City, UT
Horsley, Matthew E. .... Palo Alto, CA
Horsley, Richard F. .... Birmingham, AL
Horsley, Waller H. .... Richmond, VA
Horsley, William F. .... Opelika, AL
Horsley, William F. .... Greensboro, NC
Horsley, William F., P.A. .... Greensboro, NC
Horsman, Darryl G. .... Minneapolis, MN
Horsman, Simon M. J. .... Torrance, CA
Horsman-Wiitala, Elizabeth A. .... Helena, MT
Horsnail, Joanna K. .... Chicago, IL
Horsnell, Christian A. .... Nashville, TN
Horspool, J. David .... Redlands, CA
Yucaipa, CA
Horst, Brent Owen .... Nashville, TN
Horst, Carl H. .... San Diego, CA
Horst, Charlene R. .... Kutztown, PA
Horst, Colin D. .... Palo Alto, CA
Horst, Donald J. .... Golden, CO
Horst, Gary W. .... Madison, WI
Horst, Heidi Ann .... Tacoma, WA
Horst, J. Robert .... Cleveland, OH
Horst, Jeffrey D. .... Atlanta, GA
Horst, John R., P.A. .... Caney, KS
Horst, Robert T. .... Philadelphia, PA
Horst, Theodore L. .... Columbus, OH
Horsted, Darrel Cameron
San Francisco, CA
Horstemeyer, Scott A. .... Atlanta, GA
Horsting, Timothy M. .... Coral Springs, FL
Horstkamp, Julie A. .... Sarasota, FL
Horstkamp, Tracy Bryan .... Stafford, VA
Horstman, Allen .... Albion, MI
Horstman, Andrew W. .... Minneapolis, MN
Horstman, Gregory C. .... Woodland Hills, CA
Horstman, Henry J. .... Schenectady, NY
Horstman, James K. .... Chicago, IL
Horstman, Marne J. .... Seattle, WA
Horstman, Michael G., Jr. .... Chicago, IL
Horstman, Patrice M. .... Flagstaff, AZ
Horstman, Paul L. .... Dayton, OH
Horstman, Richard L. .... Findlay, OH
Horstmann, Henry J. .... Philadelphia, PA
Horstmann, Herbert E. .... Lodi, CA
Horstmann, John F. .... Philadelphia, PA
Horstmann, Paul H. .... San Francisco, CA
Horstmann, Peter C. .... Boston, MA
Horstmann, Randall G. .... Des Moines, IA
Horstmeyer, Eric S.
Charlotte Amalie, St. Thomas, VI
Horstmeyer, Todd S. .... Lexington, KY
Horstock, Itai .... New York, NY
Horswill, Joseph L. .... Tulare, CA
Hort, Michael D. .... New York, NY
Hort, Peter Lawrence .... New York, NY
Horta, Alfredo .... Orlando, FL
Horta, Ronald J. .... Providence, RI
Horte, Alton L., Jr. .... Hingham, MA
Horten, Michael R. .... Atlanta, GA
Hortenstine, Matthew R. .... Effingham, IL
Horter, Josef A. .... Charleston, WV
Horter, Patricia Buck .... Philadelphia, PA

Horth-Neubert, Stacy R. .... New York, NY
Hortin, Chadly D. .... Salt Lake City, UT
Hortin, Coutts & Auld .... Ann Arbor, MI
Hortin, David W. .... Ann Arbor, MI
Horting, Erin Leigh .... Harrisburg, PA
Hortman, Norman Gene, Jr. .... Laurel, MS
Horton, A. Benjamin .... Silver Spring, MD
Horton, Albert L., Jr. .... Sun City, CA
Horton, Amy .... Peace Corps, Office of the General Counsel, GV
Horton, Andrew M. .... Portland, ME
Horton, Arletha Ruth .... Buena Park, CA
Horton, Audrey Shumaker .... Asheville, NC
Horton, B. Russell .... Austin, TX
Horton, Barbara A. .... New York, NY
Horton Barbaro & Reilly .... Santa Ana, CA
Horton, Bobby J. .... Houston, TX
Horton, Brett Earle .... Cleveland, OH
Horton, Bruce .... Douglas, WY
Horton, C. Manly, Jr. .... New Orleans, LA
Horton, Carl B. .... Plainville, CT
Horton, Carl P. .... Oakton, VA
Horton, Carl P., P.C. .... Oakton, VA
Horton, Carl T. .... Washington, DC
Horton, Charles P. .... Altus, OK
Horton, Christiaan D. .... Springfield, MO
Horton, Corwin R. .... Kentfield, CA
Horton, Craig A. .... Houston, TX
Horton & Crutchfield, P.A.
Snow Hill, NC
Horton, Cynthia L. .... Tucker, GA
Horton, Dana Weber .... Pittsburgh, PA
Horton, Darciann G. .... San Diego, CA
Horton, David .... Carson City, NV
Horton, David L. .... Birmingham, AL
Horton, David P. .... Silverdale, WA
Horton, Debbie K. .... Cleveland, OH
Horton, Deirdre R. .... Rockville, MD
Horton, Dennis L. .... Clermont, FL
Horton, Dixie E. .... Arlington, VA
Horton, Don G., P.C. .... Dallas, TX
Horton, Donald E., Jr. .... Rocky Mount, NC
Horton, Donald G. .... Coushatta, LA
Horton, Donald J. .... Houston, TX
Horton, Drawdy, Ward & Black, P.A.
Greenville, SC
Horton, E. Lee .... Los Angeles, CA
Horton, E. Milton .... Dallas, TX
Horton, Earle C. .... Washington, DC
Cleveland, OH
Horton, Edward Stockton .... Boston, MA
Horton, Elizabeth .... Los Angeles, CA
Horton, Elizabeth .... Winston-Salem, NC
Horton, Felton G. .... Shreveport, LA
Horton, Fenn C., III .... San Jose, CA
Horton, Frank .... Washington, DC
Horton, Frank C. .... Jackson, MS
Horton, Fred E., Jr. .... Garden City, NY
Horton, Gary A. .... Batavia, NY
Horton, Geoffrey C. .... Treasury Department, Internal Revenue Service, GV
Horton, George R. .... New York, NY
Horton, Gregory .... Charleston, SC
Horton, H. Hollis, III .... Beaumont, TX
Horton, Hamilton C., Jr.
Winston-Salem, NC
Horton, Harlan L. .... Farmville, VA
Horton, Harlan L., P.C. .... Farmville, VA
Horton, Harland B., Jr. .... Akron, OH
Horton, Heather L. .... Shreveport, LA
Horton, Helen E. .... Arlington, VA
Horton, Horace W. .... Portland, ME
Horton & Horton, P.A. .... Asheville, NC
Horton, I. Joseph .... Snow Hill, NC
Horton, J. Bauer .... Beaumont, TX
Horton, J. Robert .... New York, NY
Horton, J. Wiley .... Tallahassee, FL
Horton, J. Wright .... Greenville, SC
Horton, Jack I. .... Sacramento, CA
Horton, Jack K. .... Los Angeles, CA
Horton, Jack R. .... Dallas, TX
Horton, Jacklyn Becker .... San Diego, CA
Horton, James D. .... Vancouver, WA
Horton, James H. .... Denton, TX
Horton, James R. .... Denver, CO
Horton, James R. .... Signal Mountain, TN
Horton, James R. .... Dimmitt, TX
Horton, Janet Little .... Houston, TX
Horton, Jas. C. .... Glen Ellyn, IL
Horton, Jay Cordell, (A Professional Corporation) .... Santa Ana, CA
Horton, J.D. .... Los Angeles, CA
Horton, Jeanne M. .... Barrington, IL
Horton, Jennifer Lynn .... Little Rock, AR
Horton, Joel D. .... Boise, ID
Horton, John D., II .... Louisville, KY
Horton, John J. .... Oakland, CA
Horton, John T. .... Nashville, TN
Horton, John Thomas .... Rockville, MD
Horton, John Wiley .... Tallahassee, FL
Horton, Judith Anne .... Conroe, TX
Horton, Judith Anne, P.C. .... Conroe, TX
Horton, June C. .... Beverly Hills, CA
Horton, Kara Leigh .... St. Louis, MO
Horton, Kenneth E. .... Salt Lake City, UT
Horton, Kenneth L. .... Boston, MA
Horton, Kenneth T., Jr. .... Atlanta, GA
Horton, Knox, Carter & Foote
Brawley, CA
El Centro, CA
Horton, Kurt A. .... Denver, CO
Horton, Larry Bruce .... Charlottesville, VA
Horton, Laura L. .... Los Angeles, CA
Horton, Laura M. .... Miami, FL
Horton, Laura M. .... Munhall, PA
Horton Law Office, S.C. .... Madison, WI
Horton, Lawrence R. .... Tarzana, CA
Horton, Lewis S. .... Charleston, SC

Horton, Lewis S. ... Mount Pleasant, SC
Horton, Lincoln V. ... Los Angeles, CA
Horton, Luther W. ... Riverside, CA
San Diego, CA
Horton, Lyle R. ... Palm Springs, CA
Horton, Maddox & Anderson, PLLC
Chattanooga, TN
Horton, Mallory H. ... Miami, FL
Horton, Marvin V. ... Tarboro, NC
Horton, Mary M. Vincent ... Warren, IL
Horton, Michael J. ... Oakland, CA
Horton, Michael W. ... Nyssa, OR
Ontario, OR
Horton, Michel Yves ... Los Angeles, CA
Horton, N. Thomas, II ... Fort Wayne, IN
Horton, Neil F. ... Oakland, CA
Horton, Norman H., Jr. ... Tallahassee, FL
Horton, Odell, Jr. ... Memphis, TN
Horton, Patricia A. ... Northridge, CA
Horton, Patricia K. ... Memphis, TN
Horton, Paul ... San Diego, CA
Horton, Paul B. ... Dallas, TX
Horton, Perry J. ... Lilburn, GA
Horton, Philip W. ... Washington, DC
Horton, Quinton F. ... McMinnville, TN
Horton, Ralph A. ... Rochester, NY
Horton, Raymond D. ... New York, NY
Horton, Richard L. ... Dulles, VA
Horton, Richard W. ... Reno, NV
Horton, Riley E., Jr. ... Montclair, NJ
Horton, Robert ... Austin, TX
Horton, Robert E. ... Seneca Falls, NY
Horton, Robert W. ... Nashville, TN
Horton, Roberta Lazarus
Washington, DC
Horton, Ronald W. ... San Diego, CA
Horton, Ross G. ... Nokesville, VA
Horton & Ryan, A Professional Corporation
Riverside, CA
San Diego, CA
Horton, Sally E. ... Nashua, NH
Horton, Scott ... New York, NY
Horton, Scott A. ... Los Angeles, CA
Horton, Shelby E., Jr. ... Asheville, NC
Horton, Sherman D., Jr. ... Concord, NH
Horton, Shields & Cormier, P.C.
Hartford, CT
Horton, Sloan & Gerber, PLLC
Winston-Salem, NC
Horton, Starr W. ... St. Augustine, FL
Horton, Stephen B. ... New York, NY
Horton, Stephen L. ... Bloomington, IL
Horton, Steven T. ... Oklahoma City, OK
Horton, Steven W. ... Honolulu, HI
Horton, Susan Morgan ... Austin, TX
Horton, Theresa A. ... Greenville, SC
Horton, Theresa A., P.A. ... Greenville, SC
Horton, Thomas F. ... Menlo Park, CA
Hyannis, MA
Horton, Thomas H. ... Marietta, GA
Horton, Thomas Jeffrey
Department of Justice,
Antitrust Division, GV
Horton, Thomas Maitland ... Dallas, TX
Horton, Thomas Maitland, P.C. ... Dallas, TX
Horton, Thomas R. ... Fort Pierce, FL
Horton, Timothy S. ... Columbus, OH
Horton, Victoria G. ... Sacramento, CA
Horton, Virginia Byrnes ... Littleton, CO
Horton, W. Michael ... Fort Wayne, IN
Horton, Walter Lee, Jr. ... Raleigh, NC
Horton, Wesley W. ... Hartford, CT
Horton, Whiteley & Cooper
Newport Beach, CA
Oakland, CA
Horton, William B., II ... New York, NY
Horton, William E. ... San Francisco, CA
Horton, William H. ... Detroit, MI
Horton, William H. ... Newark, NJ
Horton, William H. ... Chattanooga, TN
Horton, William H., Jr. ... New York, NY
Horton, William L. ... Tucker, GA
Horton, William L., Jr. ... Washington, DC
Horton, William P. ... Eugene, OR
Horton, William Patrick ... Portland, OR
Horton, William W. ... Birmingham, AL
Horton, William W. ... Atlanta, GA
Horton, Wm. Pharis ... Madison, WI
Horton-Billard, Cecilia M. ... Bakersfield, CA
Horton-Billard, Theodore P., Jr.
Los Angeles, CA
Horton-Brown, L. Kathleen
Pensacola, FL
Horttor, Bretton J. ... St. Paul, MN
Horttor, Donald J ... Topeka, KS
Horty, John ... Pittsburgh, PA
Horty, Springer & Mattern, P.C.
Pittsburgh, PA
Horun, Andrew M. ... Edison, NJ
Horvack, John R., Jr. ... Waterbury, CT
Horvat, Henry M. ... Pittsburgh, PA
Horvat, Robert J., Jr. ... Portland, OR
Horvat, Stephen P. ... Salt Lake City, UT
Horvat, Stephen P., Jr. ... Chicago, IL
Horvat, Z. Stephen ... Bethesda, MD
Horvath, Alfred J. ... Vienna, VA
Horvath, Andrew L. ... Johnstown, PA
Horvath, Anthony W. ... Wentzville, MO
Horvath, August T. ... New York, NY
Horvath, C. Calvin, Jr. ... Orlando, FL
Horvath, Cary A. ... Blue Island, IL
Horvath, Daniel R. ... Pensacola, FL
Horvath, Darren T. ... Atlanta, GA
Horvath, David E.
Palm Beach Gardens, FL
Horvath, David F. ... Hollywood, FL
Horvath, David J. ... Brecksville, OH
Horvath, David Louis ... Stroudsburg, PA
Horvath, Diane E. ... Richmond, VA
Horvath, Donald Joseph ... Coarsegold, CA
Horvath, Donald S. ... Chicago, IL
Horvath, Fawn M. ... New York, NY
Horvath, Frank J. ... Littleton, CO
Horvath, Frank J. ... Elyria, OH
Horvath, Frank J., P.C. ... Littleton, CO
Horvath, George ... Medina, OH
Horvath, James F. ... New Brunswick, NJ
Horvath, Jane C. ... Vienna, VA
Horvath, Jeffrey T. ... New York, NY
Horvath, Joan E. ... Cleveland, OH
Horvath, John F. ... Chicago, IL
Horvath, Jordan A. ... New York, NY
Horvath, Joseph J. ... Malvern, PA
Horvath, Julius" Jay "G. ... Wichita, KS
Horvath, Katherine F. ... Cincinnati, OH
Horvath & Kraus, P.C. ... Vienna, VA
Horvath, Laurence ... New York, NY
White Plains, NY
Horvath, Leonard M. ... Manchester, CT
Horvath & Lieber, P.C. ... Chicago, IL
Horvath, Patrick John ... New York, NY
Horvath, Paul E. ... Des Moines, IA
Horvath, Peter ... Lisbon, OH
Horvath, Richard F. ... Cleveland, OH
Horvath, Robert David, Jr. ... Sterling, VA
Horvath, Stephen A. ... Fairfax, VA
Horvath, Theodore J. ... Shaker Heights, OH
Horvath, Thomas L. ... Columbus, OH
Horvath, Thomas L. ... La Crosse, WI
Horvath, Valerie C. ... Indianapolis, IN
Horvatt, Catherine C., (Mrs.)
Baltimore, MD
Horvay, Christopher J. ... Chicago, IL
Horvei, Gubbe & Baehman, P.A.
Roseville, MN
Horvei, John J. ... New Brighton, MN
Horvick & Green ... New Hope, MN
Horvick, Paul D. ... New Hope, MN
Horvitz, Alissa A. ... Washington, DC
Horvitz, Allen N. ... Baltimore, MD
Horvitz, Anne Accardo ... Grand Rapids, MI
Horvitz & Brilhante, L.L.P.
Fall River, MA
Horvitz & Caisse ... New London, CT
Norwich, CT
Putnam, CT
Horvitz, David S. ... Pittsburgh, PA
Horvitz, David W. ... Fort Lauderdale, FL
Horvitz, Ellis J., (A P.C.) ... Los Angeles, CA
Horvitz, Ephraim F., Law Offices of
Fall River, MA
Horvitz, Eric F. ... Fairfax, VA
Horvitz, James H. ... South Gate, CA
Horvitz, Jerome S. ... Houston, TX
Horvitz, Laurie B. ... Bethesda, MD
Horvitz & Levy, LLP ... Encino, CA
Los Angeles, CA
Horvitz, Martha E. ... Columbus, OH
Horvitz, Michael J. ... Cleveland, OH
Horvitz, Paul S. ... Fall River, MA
Horvitz, Philip E. ... Philadelphia, PA
Horvitz, Richard A. ... Cleveland, OH
Horvitz, Ronald B. ... Gloucester, MA
Horvitz, Selwyn A. ... Philadelphia, PA
Horvitz, Sheila S. ... Norwich, CT
Horvitz, Sidney E. ... Los Angeles, CA
Horvitz, Steven Jay ... Washington, DC
Horwart, Christine ... Bentonville, AR
Horwatt, Michael, & Associates, P.C.
Washington, DC
Fairfax, VA
McLean, VA
Horwatt, Michael S. ... McLean, VA
Horwich, Allan ... Chicago, IL
Horwich, Carolyn Ann ... New York, NY
Horwich, Esther J. ... Boston, MA
Horwich, Francine ... Coral Gables, FL
Horwich, Harold S. ... Hartford, CT
Horwich, Madelon Jane ... Tallahassee, FL
Horwich, Mitchell A. ... Coral Gables, FL
Horwich, Richard J. ... Coral Gables, FL
Horwich, Terri Finesmith ... Chicago, IL
Horwich, Willard D. ... Beverly Hills, CA
Horwich, William E. ... Oakland, CA
Horwich & Zager, P.A. ... Coral Gables, FL
Horwick, Daniel M. ... La Mesa, CA
Horwick, Shawn R. ... Fort Lauderdale, FL
Horwin, Leonard, Law Offices of
Beverly Hills, CA
Horwitch, Daniel B. ... East Hartford, CT
Horwitch, David S. ... Chicago, IL
Horwitch, Robert M. ... Chicago, IL
Horwitch, Robin R. ... Leominster, MA
Horwith, Jeffrey L. ... Los Angeles, CA
Horwitt, Jed ... Bridgeport, CT
Horwitz, Abby K. ... St. Louis, MO
Horwitz, Alan G. ... Baltimore, MD
Horwitz, Allan M. ... Coatesville, PA
Horwitz, Andrew ... Brooklyn, NY
Horwitz, Andrew J. ... Chicago, IL
Horwitz, Arthur H. ... Richmond, VA
Horwitz, Barbara L. ... Hamilton, OH
Horwitz & Beam ... Irvine, CA
Newport Beach, CA
Horwitz, Bernard ... Newark, NJ
Horwitz, Carol H.
Department Of Health And Human Services,
Office of Community Services, GV
Horwitz, Cathy E. ... Skokie, IL
Horwitz, Charles ... Brooklyn, NY
Horwitz, Clifford W. ... Chicago, IL
Horwitz, Clint H. ... Fresno, CA
Horwitz, Daniel J. ... New York, NY
Horwitz, David L. ... Camp Hill, PA
Horwitz, David M. ... Los Angeles, CA
Horwitz, David N. ... San Diego, CA
Horwitz, Dean M. ... Milwaukee, WI
Horwitz, Deborah S. ... Boston, MA
Horwitz, Donald L. ... Chicago, IL
Horwitz, Donald P. ... Chicago, IL
Horwitz, Elizabeth A. ... Cincinnati, OH
Horwitz, Ellis A. ... New York, NY
Horwitz, Errol I. ... Woodland Hills, CA
Horwitz, Ethan ... New York, NY
Horwitz, Eve T. ... Boston, MA
Horwitz & Frankel ... Tonawanda, NY
Horwitz & Fussell, A Prof. Assn., Law
Offices of ... Orlando, FL
Horwitz, Gary B. ... El Segundo, CA
Horwitz, Gary M. ... Billerica, MA
Horwitz, Hal ... Santa Barbara, CA
Horwitz, Harry A. ... Cherry Hill, NJ
Horwitz, Horwitz & Associates, Ltd.
Chicago, IL
Horwitz, Howard L. ... Los Angeles, CA
Horwitz, James D. ... Bridgeport, CT
Horwitz, James D. ... Glens Falls, NY
Horwitz, Jeffrey A. ... New York, NY
Horwitz, Jeffrey W. ... Chicago, IL
Horwitz, John B. ... Orange, CA
Horwitz, John H. ... Los Angeles, CA
Horwitz, Jonathan A. ... Dayton, OH
Horwitz, Jonathan A. ... Dayton, OH
Horwitz, Jonathan A., Co., L.P.A.
Dayton, OH
Horwitz, Jos. ... Beachwood, OH
Horwitz, Joseph H. ... Wheaton, IL
Horwitz, Joshua M. ... Washington, DC
Horwitz, Julian V. ... El Paso, TX
Horwitz, Kenneth ... New York, NY
Horwitz, Kenneth M. ... Dallas, TX
Horwitz, Lanny A. ... Jupiter, FL
Horwitz Law Group ... New York, NY
Horwitz, Lawrence W. ... Irvine, CA
Horwitz, Lester ... New York, NY
Horwitz, Lewis ... Miami, FL
Horwitz, Lisa Loeffler ... Calabasas, CA
Horwitz, Lynn D. ... New York, NY
Horwitz, Marc A. ... Chicago, IL
Horwitz, Mario ... Santa Monica, CA
Horwitz, Mark J. ... Chicago, IL
Horwitz, Mark L. ... Orlando, FL
Horwitz, Martin ... New York, NY
Horwitz, Martin J. ... Florence, KY
Cincinnati, OH
Horwitz, Martin L. ... Beverly Hills, CA
Horwitz, Martin S. ... Cleveland, OH
Horwitz & Maruzo, P.C. ... Norwich, CT
Horwitz, Marvin M. ... Norwich, CT
Horwitz, Marvin Q. ... Farmington, MI
Horwitz, Marvin Q., P.C. ... Farmington, MI
Horwitz, Mayer ... Philadelphia, PA
Horwitz, Melvin ... Manchester, CT
Horwitz, Merle G. ... West Chester, PA
Horwitz, Merle H. ... Los Angeles, CA
Horwitz, Michael S. ... New York, NY
Horwitz, Mike R. ... Woodland Hills, CA
Horwitz, Miriam R. ... Milwaukee, WI
Horwitz, Mitchell W. ... Chicago, IL
Horwitz, Morris L. ... Tonawanda, NY
Horwitz, Morton J. ... Cambridge, MA
Horwitz, Murray S. ... Department of Justice,
Tax Division, GV
Horwitz, Neil M. ... New York, NY
Horwitz, Paul S.
Environmental Protection Agency,
Program Office Attorneys, GV
Horwitz, Philip H. ... Bridgewater, CT
Horwitz, Reid B. ... Department of Justice,
Antitrust Division, GV
Horwitz, Richard L. ... Wilmington, DE
Horwitz, Robert M. ... Detroit, MI
Horwitz, Robert S. ... Santa Ana, CA
Horwitz, Robert S. ... Boca Raton, FL
Horwitz, Roger D. ... Los Angeles, CA
Horwitz, Roger D., A Professional Corporation
Los Angeles, CA
Horwitz, Ronald M. ... Phoenix, AZ
Horwitz, Sara L. ... Riverwoods, IL
Horwitz, Seymour ... Richmond, VA
Horwitz, Sid A. ... Phoenix, AZ
Horwitz, Sidney W. ... St. Louis, MO
Horwitz, Stephen B. ... Chicago, IL
Horwitz, Stuart M. ... Akron, OH
Horwitz, Susan Byrne ... Los Gatos, CA
Horwitz, Susan F. ... Boston, MA
Horwitz, Susan J. ... New York, NY
Horwitz, Susan R. ... Cleveland, OH
Horwitz, Sylvia
Environmental Protection Agency,
Office of the General Counsel, GV
Horwitz, Valerie J. ... Oakland, CA
Horwitz, Valerie L. ... Denver, CO
Horwitz, Wendi A. ... Los Angeles, CA
Horwitz, William R. ... Newark, NJ
Horwitz, Wilma S. ... Orinda, CA
Horwood, Frederick C. ... New York, NY
Horwood, James N. ... Washington, DC
Horwood Marcus & Berk, Chartered
Chicago, IL
Horwood, Richard M. ... Chicago, IL
Horz, Laurie Sayevich ... Melville, NY
Hosack, Charles R. ... Corsicana, TX
Hosack, Charles W. ... Coeur d'Alene, ID
Hosack, Coleen Daugherty ... Marietta, GA
Hosack, John L. ... Los Angeles, CA
Hosack, Karen A. ... Indianapolis, IN
Hosack, Mary Stephenson ... Louisburg, KS
Hosafros, F. Jean ... Washington, IL
Hosain, Tulasi ... Larkspur, CA
Hosaka, Diane E. ... Honolulu, HI
Hosang, Michael T. ... Columbus, OH
Hosay, Robert H. ... Tallahassee, FL
Hosbach, Marguerette N. ... New York, NY
Hosbein, Gary G. ... St. Joseph, MI
Hosch, Burton B., Jr. ... Natchez, MS
Hosch, Charles M. ... Dallas, TX
Hosch, Chester J. ... Atlanta, GA
Hosch, Elizabeth Hawkins ... Dallas, TX
Hosch, Heyward C., III ... Birmingham, AL
Hosch, Robert H., Jr. ... Orlando, FL
Hosch, Stephen J. ... Olympia, WA
Hoschander, Avrohom A. ... Baltimore, MD
Hoscheit, Dale H. ... Washington, DC
Hoscheit, John J. ... St. Charles, IL
Hoscheit & McGuirk, P.C. ... St. Charles, IL
Hoschner, Robert H. ... Corunna, MI
Hose, John C. ... Metairie, LA
Hose, Ralph L. ... Ardmore, PA
Hose, W. Russell ... Fresno, CA
Hosea, Kimberly Clark ... Versailles, KY
Hosea, Stephen C. ... Annapolis, MD
Greenbelt, MD
Hoseck, Camron D. ... Pierre, SD
Hosein, Hanson Riad ... New York, NY
Hoseit & Koelewyn ... Sacramento, CA
South Lake Tahoe, CA
Hoseit, Max H. ... Sacramento, CA
South Lake Tahoe, CA
Hoselton, George ... Gladstone, OR
Hoseman, Daniel ... Chicago, IL
Hoseman, Joan E. ... Chicago, IL
Hoseman, Linda Lemel ... Chicago, IL
Hosemann, C. Delbert, Jr. ... Jackson, MS
Hosemann, Constance M. ... Oakland, CA
Hosemann, H. Gerald ... Vicksburg, MS
Hosen, Sheldon D. ... New Haven, CT
Hosenball, S. Neil ... Arlington, VA
Hosenpud, David Glenn ... Portland, OR
Hoseth, Suzanne G. ... Ionia, MI
Hoseus, Edwin L., Jr. ... Milford, OH
Hosey, Lawrence P. ... Richmond, VA
Hosey, Peter E. ... San Antonio, TX
Hosey, Philip E. ... Galveston, TX
Hosey, R. Fred ... Dallas, TX
Hosey, Richard A. ... Cuyahoga Falls, OH
Hosey, Richard K. ... San Diego, CA
Hosey, Tiffany A. ... Washington, DC
Baltimore, MD
Rockville, MD
Vienna, VA
Hosford, Barbara L. ... Omaha, NE
Hosford & Creasey, P.C. ... Dallas, TX
Hosford, Donald C., Jr. ... Omaha, NE
Hosford, Elizabeth M.
Department of Justice, Civil Division, GV
Hosford, Geoffrey W. ... Fayetteville, NC
Hosford, Henry C., Jr. ... El Paso, TX
Hosford, Irene L. ... Dallas, TX
Hosford, Matthew L. ... Troy, NY
Hosford, Robert B. ... Kansas City, MO
Hosford, Stephen C. ... Tustin, CA
Hosford, Stephen C., Inc. ... Tustin, CA
Hosford, Stephen E. ... Las Cruces, NM
Hoshall, Carol L. ... Washington, DC
Hoshaw, William D. ... San Diego, CA
Hoshibata, John T. ... Honolulu, HI
Hoshida & Bento ... Honolulu, HI
Hoshida, Sandra Y. ... Honolulu, HI
Hoshide, Kyle Y. ... Santa Monica, CA
Hoshino, Paul K. ... Honolulu, HI
Hoshiyama, Gary ... San Francisco, CA
Hoshizaki, Eric S. ... Carson City, NV
Hoshor, Peter B. ... Dayton, OH
Hoshor & Tosi, Inc., L.P.A. ... Hebron, OH
Hosick, Robt. H. ... Kalamazoo, MI
Hosie, Spencer ... San Francisco, CA
Hosier, Gerald D. ... Las Vegas, NV
Hosilyk, David A. ... Redwood City, CA
Hosinski, David A. ... South Bend, IN
Hosinski, John S. ... South Bend, IN
Hosinski, Peter M. ... New York, NY
Hosinski, William A. ... South Bend, IN
Hosken, Glenn R. ... Tallahassee, FL
Hosken, Mark D. ... Rochester, NY
Hoskin, Charles J. ... Las Vegas, NV
Hoskin, Charles P. ... Pensacola, FL
Hoskin, Farina, Aldrich & Kampf,
Professional Corporation
Grand Junction, CO
Hoskin, Graham & Wilde ... Las Vegas, NV
Hoskin, Gregory K. ... Grand Junction, CO
Hoskin, Lisa K. ... Atlanta, GA
Hosking, Jeffrey D ... Oakland, CA
Hosking, Richard W. ... Pittsburgh, PA
Hosking, Tina D. ... Cincinnati, OH
Hosking, Valentina K. ... Brooklyn, NY
Hosking, Wayne Frederick, Jr.
Washington, DC
Hosking-Linch, Suzanne ... Westerville, OH
Hoskins, Anne E. ... Newark, NJ
New York, NY
Hoskins, Anne E. H. ... Marion, IA
Hoskins, Bonnie ... Lexington, KY
Hoskins, Charles Daniel ... Greenville, SC
Hoskins, Cheryl D. ... Columbus, OH
Hoskins, Clayton C. ... Columbus, OH
Hoskins, Craig R. ... Evanston, IL
Hoskins, D. Irene ... Frankfort, KY
Hoskins, David A. ... San Francisco, CA
Hoskins, David Clark ... Parker, CO
Hoskins, David L. ... Louisville, KY
Hoskins, David L. ... Lake Charles, LA
Hoskins, David S. ... Corbin, KY
Hoskins, Donald C. ... Marion, IA
Hoskins, E. David ... Baltimore, MD
Towson, MD
Hoskins, Edwin Paul ... Sidney, NY
Hoskins, Glenn A. ... Lexington, KY
Hoskins, Harry D., III ... New Orleans, LA
Hoskins, Jack D. ... Los Angeles, CA
Hoskins, Jacqueline A. ... Virginia Beach, VA

Hoskins, James C., II .... Houston, TX
Hoskins, Jeffrey J. .... Hillsboro, OH
Hoskins, Jones H. .... Brookhaven, MS
Hoskins, Joseph C. .... Wilmington, OH
Hoskins, Julie Christine .... Greeley, CO
Hoskins, Kalnins, McNamara & Day
Lancaster, WI
Hoskins, Kathleen L. .... Phoenix, AZ
Hoskins, Kathleen L., P.C. .... Phoenix, AZ
Hoskins, Kathryn J. .... Sioux Falls, SD
Hoskins, Kathryn Kelley .... Baltimore, MD
Hoskins, Keith C. .... Phoenix, AZ
Hoskins, Lance R. .... Billings, MT
Hoskins, Larry W. .... Southfield, MI
Hoskins, Lorine A. .... Fountain Valley, CA
Hoskins, Mark H. .... San Diego, CA
Hoskins, Mark H., Jr. .... Lancaster, WI
Hoskins, Maryann G. .... Metairie, LA
Hoskins, Max E. .... Lawton, OK
Hoskins, Nancy I. .... New Haven, CT
Hoskins, Paul D. .... Sacramento, CA
Hoskins, Philip J. .... Los Angeles, CA
Hoskins, Phillip J. .... Columbia, MO
Hoskins, Ralph W. .... Corbin, KY
Hoskins, Renee G. .... Louisville, KY
Hoskins, Richard J. .... Chicago, IL
Hoskins, Robert E. .... Greenville, SC
Hoskins, Robert E. .... Galveston, TX
Hoskins, Robert H. .... Cincinnati, OH
Hoskins, Robert L., III (P.A.)
Clearwater, FL
Hoskins, Ronald G. .... Kansas City, MO
Hoskins, Ronald G., Jr. .... Kansas City, MO
Hoskins, Royce E. .... Roswell, NM
Hoskins, Sonya D. .... Dallas, TX
Hoskins, Stephen P. .... Fort Pierce, FL
Hoskins, Steven A. .... Mason, OH
Hoskins, Steven Barrett .... Newark, NJ
Hoskins, Terri L. .... Chicago, IL
Hoskins, W. Conrad .... Dayton, WA
Hoskins, William A., III .... Frankfort, KY
Lexington, KY
Hoskins, William H. .... Orinda, CA
Hoskins, William K. .... Kansas City, MO
Hoskins-Hart, Teresa L. .... Little Rock, AR
Hoskinson, James R., Jr. .... Los Angeles, CA
Hoskinson, Richard K.
Chambersburg, PA
Hoskinson & Wenger .... Chambersburg, PA
Hosko, Ronald T. .... Chicago, IL
Hoskyn, Robert W. .... Atlanta, GA
Hosler, Paula E. .... Overland Park, KS
Hosler, Richard M. .... Kerrville, TX
Hosler, Rick V. .... Phoenix, AZ
Hosler, William E., III .... Birmingham, MI
Hoslet, Charles B. .... Madison, WI
Hoslet, Gary E. .... Bingham Farms, MI
Hoslett, Al Warren .... Stockton, CA
Hosley, Frank David .... Maitland, FL
Hosley, Richard E. .... Sarasota, FL
Hosmer, Alicia W. .... Fairfax, VA
Hosmer, Alison .... Sarasota, FL
Hosmer, Charles F. .... Louisville, KY
Hosmer, David E. .... Irvine, CA
Hosmer, David M. .... Yankton, SD
Hosmer, Donald M. .... Indianapolis, IN
Hosmer, E. Chandler, III
Philadelphia, PA
Hosmer, E. Joseph .... Springfield, MO
Hosmer, Gregory C. .... Philadelphia, PA
Hosmer, James T. .... Arlington, VA
Hosmer, John R., Jr. .... Charlotte, NC
Hosmer & Kettering .... Yankton, SD
Hosmer, Larry F. .... Yankton, SD
Hosmer, Lawrence S. .... Dallas, TX
Hosmer, Patricia F. .... Charlotte, NC
Hosmer, William Craig .... Springfield, MO
Hosoda, Lyle S. .... Honolulu, HI
Hosp, Edward A. .... Birmingham, AL
Hosp, F. Phillip .... Pasadena, CA
Hosp, Gilbert & Associates, A Law Corporation .... Los Angeles, CA
Monterey, CA
Pasadena, CA
Hosp, Martha M. .... Riverdale, IL
Hosp, R. David .... Boston, MA
Hosperdales, Rhonda
Christiansted, St. Croix, VI
Hospodar, Joseph David .... Atlanta, GA
Hoss, Frank A., Jr. .... Manassas, VA
Hoss, Henry D. .... Oklahoma City, OK
Hoss, Peter T. .... Monterey, CA
Salinas, CA
Hoss, Richard T. .... Shelton, WA
Hoss, Sammye .... Kansas City, MO
Hoss, Winifred Thomson .... Bakersfield, CA
Hossack, Christopher D.C. .... Mesa, AZ
Hossack, Christopher D.C., P.C., Law Offices of .... Mesa, AZ
Phoenix, AZ
Hossain, L. Lamis .... Atlanta, GA
Hossein Bor, M. .... Washington, DC
Hosseini, Roya .... Palo Alto, CA
Hossenlopp, John J.A. .... New York, NY
Hossler, David J. .... Yuma, AZ
Hossler, Jerome H. .... Canton, OH
Hossner, W. Lynn .... St. Anthony, ID
Hossofsky, Katherine A.
Treasury Department, Internal Revenue Service, GV
Hossrich, John .... New York, NY
Host, Bonnie J. .... New York, NY
Host, David L. .... Dalton, GA
Host & Keane .... Brookfield, WI
Host, Thea M. .... Brookfield, WI
Hosta, Verne L. .... Middleburg, VA

Hostage, Barbara A.
Environmental Protection Agency, Program Office Attorneys, GV
Hostage, Christopher A. .... Washington, DC
Hostak, Henzl & Bichler, S.C.
Milwaukee, WI
Racine, WI
Hostak, Kenneth F. .... Racine, WI
Hoste, Douglas W. .... Mount Clemens, MI
Hosten, Kathy Ann .... Northville, MI
Hosteny, John M. .... Springfield, IL
Hosteny, Joseph N., III .... Chicago, IL
Hoster, Craig W. .... Tulsa, OK
Hoster, Jeffrey M. .... Chicago, IL
Hoster, Scott .... Joliet, IL
Hosterman, J. Michael .... Pleasanton, CA
Hosterman, John W. .... Ashville, OH
Circleville, OH
Hosterman, Mark A. .... Blue Bell, PA
Hosterman, O. Charles .... Columbus, OH
Hostetler, Bonnie J. .... Columbus, NE
Hostetler, Brian J. .... Bridgeton, MO
Hostetler, Charles A. .... Raeford, NC
Hostetler, Charles M. .... Fenton, MI
Hostetler, Daniel J. .... Wooster, OH
Hostetler, Darrin A. .... San Diego, CA
Hostetler, David L. .... Coshocton, OH
Hostetler, David R. .... Chapel Hill, NC
Hostetler, Eric G. .... Department of Justice, Environment and Natural Resources Division, GV
Hostetler, Gary Lynn .... Indianapolis, IN
Hostetler, H. Franklin, III .... Gardena, CA
Hostetler, H. Stephen .... Long Beach, CA
Hostetler, James M., Jr. .... Pittsburgh, PA
Hostetler, James S. .... Washington, DC
Hostetler & Kowalik, P.C.
Indianapolis, IN
Hostetler, Mark S. .... St. Louis, MO
Hostetler & McNeill .... Raeford, NC
Hostetler, Michelle V. .... Wichita, KS
Hostetler, Pamela E.
Equal Employment Opportunity Commission, Office of Federal Operations, GV
Hostetler, Richard A. .... Denver, CO
Hostetler, Sally Ann .... Fairfax, VA
Hostetler, Steven L. .... Elkhart, IN
Mishawaka, IN
Hostetler, Thomas K. .... Decatur, IL
Hostetler, Thomas M. .... San Francisco, CA
Hostetler & Vargas LLP .... Gardena, CA
Los Angeles, CA
Hostetler, Zona F. .... Washington, DC
Hostetter, Alan J. .... Dallas, TX
Hostetter, Charles E. .... Brownsburg, IN
Hostetter, D. Rahn .... Enterprise, OR
Hostetter, David L. .... Harrisburg, PA
Hostetter, Dwight W. .... Cleveland, OH
Hostetter, Heather Quinn .... Annapolis, MD
Hostetter, J. Ross .... Dallas, TX
Hostetter, James W. .... Newark, OH
Hostetter, Mark David .... New York, NY
Hostetter, Michael D. .... Atlanta, GA
Hostetter & O'Hara .... Brownsburg, IN
Hostetter, Sarah L. .... Lakewood, CO
Hostetter, Theodore L. .... Charleston, SC
Hostetter, Theodore L., P.A. .... Charleston, SC
Hostettler, R. Aaron .... London, KY
Hostina, Michael P. .... Fairbanks, AK
Hostler, D. David .... Somers, NY
Hostler, Stanley M. .... Huntington, WV
Hostnik, Charles R. .... Tacoma, WA
Hostnik, Rosanne .... Detroit, MI
Hosto, Bryan E. .... Little Rock, AR
Hosto & Buchan, P.L.L.C. .... Little Rock, AR
Hosty, Patrick J. .... Chicago, IL
Hosty, Thomas C. .... Overland Park, KS
Hosty, Thomas W. .... Oklahoma City, OK
Hostyk, Aaron
National Aeronautics And Space Administration, Office of the General Counsel, GV
Hotaling, Elizabeth I. .... Hartford, CT
Hotaling, Gregory W. .... New York, NY
Hotaling, Marybeth .... Brooklyn, NY
Hotaling, Michael E. .... Hartford, CT
Hotard, Calvin J., Jr. .... Gretna, LA
Hotard, Keith C., Jr. .... New Orleans, LA
Hotard, T. Gabriel, Jr. .... Baldwin, GA
Hotard, Tera Sims .... La Place, LA
Hotch, Marilyn L. .... Owls Head, ME
Hotchkin, Lee T. .... Reno, NV
Hotchkin, Richard E. .... Beloit, WI
Hotchkiss, Andra R. .... Boston, MA
Hotchkiss, Anita .... Morristown, NJ
New York, NY
Hotchkiss, Bruce .... San Francisco, CA
Hotchkiss, Charles A. .... Wichita Falls, TX
Hotchkiss, Darrell A. .... Lebanon, NH
Hotchkiss, David L. .... Meadville, PA
Hotchkiss, Edward S. .... Minneapolis, MN
Hotchkiss, Glenn B. .... Phoenix, AZ
Hotchkiss, Herbert G. .... Cleveland, OH
Hotchkiss, Katherine R. .... Watsonville, CA
Hotchkiss, Kirsten Anne .... Parsippany, NJ
Hotchkiss, Lynnette .... New York, NY
Hotchkiss, Martin .... Dallas, TX
Hotchkiss, Mary A. .... Seattle, WA
Hotchkiss, Nancy .... Sacramento, CA
Hotchkiss, Peter A. .... Sunrise, FL
Hotchkiss, Ray C. .... Dallas, TX
Hotchkiss, Robert B. .... Bloomfield Hills, MI
Hotchkiss, Robert P. .... Mountain City, TN
Hotchkiss, S. David .... Los Angeles, CA
Hotchkiss, Sharon M. .... Los Angeles, CA
Hotchkiss, Todd B. .... Albuquerque, NM
Hotelling, Harold .... Southfield, MI

Hotes, David W. .... Washington, DC
Hotes, William J. .... Washington, DC
Hoth, Christine Rothe .... Denver, CO
Hoth, Steven C. .... Denver, CO
Hoth, Steven S., Law Offices
Burlington, IA
Hotham, Jeffrey A. .... Phoenix, AZ
Hotham, Judith E. .... Dover, NH
Hotine, Susan J. .... Washington, DC
Hotis, Dimitra .... Phoenix, AZ
Hotsenpiller, Dan W. .... Montrose, CO
Hotsinpiller, Jami B. .... Albuquerque, NM
Santa Fe, NM
Hott, Amy Elizabeth .... Ellicott City, MD
Hott, Donald C. .... Keyser, WV
Hott, Douglas R. .... New York, NY
Hott, Joel O. .... Lansing, MI
Hott, Lawrence R. .... Haydenville, MA
Hott & Margolis .... Jersey City, NJ
Hott, Richard D. .... New York, NY
Hott, Timothy R. .... Jersey City, NJ
Hotte, John F. .... Fort Lauderdale, FL
Hottel, Deborah Ann .... Columbia, SC
Hottell, Dennis M., & Associates
Fairfax, VA
Hottenroth, E. Richard .... Galion, OH
Hottenroth, Garverick & Tilson Co., L.P.A.
Galion, OH
Hottenroth, Theresa M. .... Madison, WI
Hottensmith, Mark H. .... Columbus, OH
Hottinger, Darryl C. .... Los Angeles, CA
Hottinger, George C. .... Minneapolis, MN
Hottinger, John C. .... St. Peter, MN
Hottle, Douglas M. .... Pittsburgh, PA
Hottman, E. Todd .... Olathe, KS
Hottmann, David G. .... Sioux Falls, SD
Hotto, William R. .... Fairview Heights, IL
Hotvedt, Gary R. .... Charlotte, TN
Hotvedt, Richard C. .... Washington, DC
Hoty-Bliss, Diane .... Cleveland, OH
Hotz & Associates, P.C. .... Atlanta, GA
Tucker, GA
Hotz, Edward D. .... Omaha, NE
Hotz, Gary A. .... Westlake, OH
Hotz, John H. .... Garden City, KS
Hotz, Joseph A. .... Salinas, CA
Hotz, Mark B. .... Brooklandville, MD
Hotz, Mark J. .... Pontiac, MI
Hotz, Todd E. .... San Antonio, TX
Hotz, Walter H. .... Tucker, GA
Hotz & Weaver .... Omaha, NE
Hotz, William A. .... Knoxville, TN
Hotze, Rachel L. .... Memphis, TN
Hou, Fong Joe .... Cranford, NJ
Hou, Howard S. .... Los Angeles, CA
Hou, Hsin-Pin Ashley
Small Business Administration, Office of the General Counsel, GV
Hou, John .... San Francisco, CA
Hou, Junwei Wayne .... Bethesda, MD
Hou, William C. .... Washington, DC
Houar, John L. .... Cedar Rapids, IA
Houchen, Vernon H. .... Decatur, IL
Houchens, John H. .... St. Paul, MN
Houchens, Matthew C. .... Chicago, IL
Houchin, John T. .... Miami, FL
Houchin, Karen L. .... Floydada, TX
Houchin, Larry K. .... Albany, OR
Houchins, John O. .... Houston, TX
Houchins, Michael James .... Spencer, IA
Houchins, R. Corbin, Law Offices of
Seattle, WA
Houck, Annette M. .... Columbus, OH
Houck & Balisok .... Glendale, CA
Los Angeles, CA
Houck, Bowen D. .... Richland Center, WI
Houck, C. Weston .... Florence, SC
Houck, Cara M. .... Chicago, IL
Houck, Carol S. .... Ventura, CA
Houck, Cynthia D. .... Vernon, CT
Houck, Danielle M. .... Napa, CA
Houck, David C. .... Plano, TX
Houck, David J. .... Indianapolis, IN
Houck, Deward J. .... Lakeside, CA
Houck, G. Todd .... Mullens, WV
Houck, George .... Scranton, PA
Houck & Gingrich .... Belleville, PA
Lewistown, PA
Houck, Harold A. .... Topeka, KS
Houck, James M. .... Greencastle, IN
Houck, James W. .... Department of the Navy, Office of the Judge Advocate General, GV
Houck, John B. .... Los Angeles, CA
Houck, Katheryn Ann .... Saginaw, MI
Houck, Kathryn Anne .... Visalia, CA
Houck, Kent C. .... Richland Center, WI
Houck, Leighton S. .... Lynchburg, VA
Houck, Lenore A. .... Blue Hill, ME
Houck, Malcolm H. .... Woburn, MA
Houck, Mark R. .... Miami, FL
Port Canaveral, FL
Houck & McCarron .... Upper Marlboro, MD
Houck, Nathan L. .... New York, NY
Oriskany, NY
Houck, Oliver A. .... New Orleans, LA
Houck, Paul R. .... Gettysburg, SD
Houck, Richard C. .... Bath, NY
Houck, Rima K. .... San Anselmo, CA
Houck, Robert G. .... New York, NY
Houck, Robt. D. .... Gettysburg, SD
Houck, Rudolph S. .... New York, NY
Houck, S. Bradley .... Atlanta, GA
Houck, Terence Patrick .... Doylestown, PA
Houck, Thomas K. .... Milwaukee, WI
Houck, Tracy Ann .... Fredericksburg, VA
Houck, Victoria E. .... Washington, DC
Houde, Ardeth L., (Mrs.) .... Rochester, NY
Houde, Cheryl A. .... San Bernardino, CA

Houde, Elizabeth R. .... Hartford, CT
Houde, Matthew S. .... Hartford, CT
Houde, Steven M. .... Wellesley Hills, MA
Houdek, Bruce C. .... Kansas City, MO
Houdek, Bruce C., P.C. .... Kansas City, MO
Houdek, Dennis W. .... New York, NY
Houdek, Frank G. .... Carbondale, IL
Houder, D. Charles .... Philadelphia, PA
Houdlett, Ronald R. .... New York, NY
Houdyschell, Jendonnae Lycan
Huntington, WV
Houdyshell, Lisa Anne .... St. Louis, MO
Houdyshell, Ronald G. .... Austin, TX
Houfek, Dennis F. .... Dallas, TX
Houfek, James T. .... Dublin, OH
Houff, Bowen C. .... Winston-Salem, NC
Houff, Edward F. .... Baltimore, MD
Houff, W. Dale .... Harrisonburg, VA
Luray, VA
Hougabrook, Nathaniel, II .... Cordele, GA
Hougan, Evelyn M. .... Corona Del Mar, CA
Houge, Benjamin S. .... Minneapolis, MN
Hougen, Donna M. .... Scottsdale, AZ
Hougen, Eric J. .... Washington, DC
Hougen, H. Montgomery .... Reston, VA
Houger, L. William .... Bellevue, WA
Houger & Walt, A Professional Service Corporation .... Bellevue, WA
Hough, A. Randolph .... Columbia, SC
Hough, Andrew R. .... Washington, DC
Hough, Blaque Wynn .... Zeeland, MI
Hough, Bonnie Rose .... Novato, CA
Hough, Brian C. .... Appleton, WI
Hough, C. Michael .... Homer, AK
Hough, Clayton Lee .... Washington, DC
Hough, Daniel L. .... Winchester, CA
Hough, David B. .... Winston-Salem, NC
Hough, David J. .... Minneapolis, MN
Hough, Duane-David .... New York, NY
Hough, E. Mitchell .... Ozark, MO
Hough, F. Eugene .... Tulsa, OK
Hough, George B., Jr. .... Stuart, FL
Hough, George B., Jr., P.A. .... Stuart, FL
Hough, Gerald B. .... Glenville, WV
Hough, Gina A. .... Washington, DC
Hough, Hough & Hughes, P.A.
Fort Smith, AR
Hough, Jacqueline D. .... Irvine, CA
Hough, James E. .... New York, NY
Hough, James E. .... Madison, WI
Hough, James L. .... Merrillville, IN
Hough, Jessica A. .... Washington, DC
Hough, John G. .... Mesa, AZ
Hough, John Harrison .... Palm Beach, FL
Hough, John W. .... Chicago, IL
Hough, John W. .... Olympia, WA
Hough, Joseph Mark .... Cary, NC
Hough, Lannie D., Jr. .... Tallahassee, FL
Hough Law Offices .... Mesa, AZ
Hough, Mark M. .... Seattle, WA
Hough, Mary Patricia .... San Francisco, CA
Hough, Mary Urban .... Omaha, NE
Hough, Melinda M. .... Houston, TX
Hough, Michael H. .... Mesa, AZ
Hough, Nicole R. .... San Diego, CA
Hough, Patrick H. .... El Segundo, CA
Hough & Rabil .... Winston-Salem, NC
Hough, Robert E., Jr. .... Fort Smith, AR
Hough, Robert P. .... Austin, TX
Hough, Robin McDaniel .... Baltimore, MD
Hough, Shannon L. .... Department of Justice, Tax Division, GV
Hough, Stephen G. .... Fort Smith, AR
Hough, Stephen J. .... Olney, IL
Hough, Steven H. .... Westminster, CA
Hough, Suzanne B. .... Villanova, PA
Hough, Therese Martin .... Morristown, NJ
Hough, Thomas E. .... Cypress, TX
Hough, Thomas H. M. .... Pittsburgh, PA
Hough, Thomas J., Jr. .... Marietta, GA
Hough, Thomas J., Jr., P.C. .... Marietta, GA
Hough, Timothy R. .... Philadelphia, PA
Hough, Wayne C. .... Mount Airy, MD
Hough, William T. .... Basking Ridge, NJ
Hougham, Martin T. .... San Antonio, TX
Houghland, David M. .... Mesa, AZ
Houghtaling, Anne Valeska .... Wheaton, IL
Houghtaling, Chris A. .... Whitehall, MI
Houghtaling, John W., II .... Metairie, LA
Houghtaling, Julie A. .... Buffalo, NY
Houghtaling, Linda L. .... Miami, FL
Houghtaling, Walter N. .... Denver, CO
Houghtling, Lance E. .... Tulsa, OK
Houghton, Amy Barry .... Denver, CO
Houghton, Andrew T. .... New York, NY
Houghton & Antilla .... Negaunee, MI
Houghton, Bruce L. .... Negaunee, MI
Houghton, Charles .... Stoneham, MA
Houghton, Charles T.
Colorado Springs, CO
Houghton, Craig A. .... Fresno, CA
Houghton, Cynthia D. .... Encinitas, CA
Houghton, Darcy K. .... Reno, NV
Houghton, David S. .... Omaha, NE
Houghton, Denise H. .... Philadelphia, PA
Houghton, Donald E. .... Springfield, MA
Houghton, Elaine M. .... Tacoma, WA
Houghton, Eric A. .... Dunedin, FL
Houghton, Frederick C. .... Universal City, CA
Houghton, Gary J. .... Warren, MI
Houghton, Heidi .... Chicago, IL
Houghton, J. Drew .... Oklahoma City, OK
Houghton, Jack E., Jr. .... Pittsfield, MA
Houghton, James D. .... Iowa City, IA
Houghton, James F. .... Boston, MA
Houghton, James P. .... Albuquerque, NM
Houghton, John J. .... Pontiac, MI
Houghton, John W. .... Indianapolis, IN

Houghton, Katherine G. ... Paramus, NJ
Houghton, Kendall L. ... Washington, DC
Houghton, Kerry J. ... New York, NY
Houghton, Kimberly J. ... Washington, DC
Houghton, Kimberly J. ... Hampton, NH
Houghton, M. Brooks ... Chico, CA
Houghton, Margaret M. ... Tucson, AZ
Houghton, Mark ... Wilmington, DE
Houghton, Mary M. ... Pittsburgh, PA
Houghton, Michael ... Wilmington, DE
Houghton, Ralph H., Jr. ... Birmingham, MI
Houghton, Richard C. ... Indian Wells, CA
Houghton, Robert D. ... Cedar Rapids, IA
Houghton, Rodney N. ... Boca Raton, FL
Newark, NJ
Houghton, Stephen M. ... Pittsburgh, PA
Wheeling, WV
Houghton, Thomas D. ... Prospect Park, PA
Houghton, Thomas Woodward
Houston, TX
Houghton, Tryntje I. ... Boston, MA
Houghton, Vivian A. ... Wilmington, DE
Hougland, Gerald L. ... Olathe, KS
Hougland, Whayne M. ... Lexington, KY
Hougland, William G. ... Houston, TX
Hougum, Alan L. ... Wausau, WI
Houha, Evellen ... Orlando, FL
Houha, Leonard J. ... Oak Park, IL
Houin, Connie Hoopingarner ... Detroit, MI
Houk, Brent G. ... Richmond, VA
Houk, D. Charles ... Atlanta, GA
Houk, D. Reed ... Nashville, TN
Houk, Diane L. ... Department of Justice, Civil Rights Division, GV
Houk, Gareth W., Jr. ... Visalia, CA
Houk, Hasty & Church ... Fairview, OK
Houk & Hicks, A Professional Corporation
Visalia, CA
Houk, Jane A. ... Miami, FL
Houk, Joe C. ... Fairview, OK
Houk, John Talbott ... Falls Church, VA
Houk, Julie M. ... Berkeley, CA
Houk, Karen M. ... Indianapolis, IN
Houk, Larry K., (P.A.) ... St. Paul, MN
Houk, Loren H. ... Wichita, KS
Houk, Loren H., P.A. ... Wichita, KS
Houk, Melanie McCall
Newport Beach, CA
Houk, Paul J. ... Louisville, KY
Houk, Peter D. ... Mason, MI
Houk, Phillip E. ... Fort Wayne, IN
Houk, Rose A. ... Lansing, MI
Houke, Robert E. ... Santa Fe, NM
Houlahan, Jill M. ... San Diego, CA
Hould, Stephen A. ... Neptune Beach, FL
Houlden, Michael S. ... Boston, MA
Houlding, Andrew L. ... Bridgeport, CT
Houldsworth, Edwin C.
Federal Deposit Insurance Corporation, Corporate Affairs Section, GV
Houle, Antoine F., P.C. ... Port Huron, MI
Houle, Antoinette G. ... Horton, KS
Houlé, Gregory ... Los Angeles, CA
Houle, Heather M. ... Boston, MA
Houlé & Houlé ... Los Angeles, CA
Houle, James A. ... Portland, ME
Houle, Jeffrey R. ... Tysons Corner, VA
Houle, Joseph E. ... Southfield, MI
Houle, Kristyn J. ... Detroit, MI
Houle, Linda M. ... Flagstaff, AZ
Houle, Mark D. ... Newport Beach, CA
Houle, Mary J. ... New York, NY
Houle, Patricia C. ... West Chicago, IL
Houle, Philip P.
Federal Deposit Insurance Corporation, Compliance and Enforcement Section, GV
Houle, Renee Marie ... New London, CT
Houlé, Richard ... Los Angeles, CA
Houle, Robert E. ... Bakersfield, CA
Houle, William Albert ... Placerville, CA
Houlehan, Donald A. ... Denver, CO
Houlehan, Edward J. ... Kansas City, MO
Houlehan and Waterman ... Kansas City, MO
Houlette, Christopher C. ... Rapid City, SD
Houlette, Jacqueline M. ... Houston, TX
Houlf, Daniel M. ... Dearborn, MI
Houlihan, A. Patricia ... Des Moines, IA
Houlihan, Charles D., Jr. ... Simsbury, CT
Houlihan, Christopher M. ... New York, NY
Houlihan, Daniel E. ... Zelienople, PA
Houlihan, Daniel J. ... Scranton, PA
Houlihan, Daniel L. ... Chicago, IL
Houlihan, David P. ... Washington, DC
Houlihan, F. Robert ... Brookline, MA
Houlihan, Gerald J. ... Miami, FL
Houlihan, John A. ... Boston, MA
Houlihan, John C. ... Minocqua, WI
Houlihan, John E. ... Minneapolis, MN
Houlihan, John J., Jr. ... Hartford, CT
Houlihan, John P. ... Wheaton, IL
Houlihan, John P. ... Council Bluffs, IA
Houlihan, John P. ... Princess Anne, MD
Salisbury, MD
Houlihan, John P., P.A. ... Salisbury, MD
Houlihan, Joseph T. ... Newport, RI
Houlihan, Joseph T., Jr. ... Newport, RI
Houlihan, Katharine B. ... Washington, DC
Houlihan, Kevin M. ... Washington, DC
Houlihan & Managhan ... Newport, RI
Houlihan, Maureen M. ... North Chicago, IL
Houlihan, Michael J. ... Traverse City, MI
Houlihan & Partners ... Miami, FL
Houlihan, Patrick J. ... La Crosse, WI
Houlihan, Richard ... Miami, FL
Houlihan, Richard P. ... Worcester, MA
Houlihan, Robert F. ... Lexington, KY
Houlihan, Robert F., Jr. ... Lexington, KY
Houlihan, Stephen P. ... Boston, MA
Houlihan, Terry J. ... San Francisco, CA
Houlihan, Thomas R ... Akron, OH
Houliston, Deborah Battle ... Dayton, OH
Houliston, Michael L. ... Annandale, VA
Houliston, Michael L., P.C. ... Annandale, VA
Houllis, Michael A. ... Tarpon Springs, FL
Houlon and Berman, LLC
New Carrollton, MD
Rockville, MD
Houlon, Victor A. ... New Carrollton, MD
Rockville, MD
Houman, Robert W. ... Decatur, GA
Hounchell, Charles A. ... Tampa, FL
Hounchell, Charles A., P.A. ... Tampa, FL
Hounsell, M. Cindy ... Washington, DC
Houp, Kenneth E., Jr. ... Austin, TX
Houpe, David V. ... Department of Defense, Armed Services Board of Contract Appeals, GV
Houpt, Barbara Ann ... Deerfield, IL
Houpt, Corinne A. ... Chapel Hill, NC
Houpt, James E. ... Sacramento, CA
Houpt, Jefferson V. ... Glenwood Springs, CO
Houpt, Richard V. ... Chicago, IL
Oak Brook, IL
Houpt, Robert C. ... Paoli, PA
Houpt, Timothy C. ... Salt Lake City, UT
Houpt, William P. ... Santa Monica, CA
Houpt, Wolffe & Huganir, Ltd. ... Paoli, PA
Hourahan, Sandra ... Philadelphia, PA
Houran, Steven M. ... Concord, NH
Ho-Urano, Teresa ... Los Angeles, CA
Hourcade, Pierre (IBA) **... Los Angeles, CA**
Hourcle, Laurent R. ... Washington, DC
Houren, Jay R. ... Houston, TX
Hourican, Timothy G. ... New York, NY
Hourican, William R. ... Allentown, PA
Philadelphia, PA
Hourigan, Brian F. ... Lompoc, CA
Santa Barbara, CA
Hourigan, Francis J., III
Palos Verdes Peninsula, CA
Hourigan, Jacqueline L. ... Detroit, MI
Hourigan, Kluger & Quinn, A Professional Corporation ... Allentown, PA
Scranton, PA
Wilkes-Barre, PA
Hourigan, Michael K. ... Baltimore, MD
Hourigan, Yvette ... Lexington, KY
Hourihan, Brian T. ... Boston, MA
Hourihan, Daniel J. ... Boston, MA
Hourihan, Daniel J. ... Foxboro, MA
Hourihan, Daniel J., P.C. ... Boston, MA
Hourihan, Edward, Jr. ... Rochester, NY
Hourihan, James A. ... Washington, DC
Hourihan, John D. ... Walnut Creek, CA
Hourihan, Joseph A. ... West Hartford, CT
Hourihan, Neil A. ... Salem, MA
Hourihan, Paul F. ... Chicago, IL
Hourihan, Paul T. ... Washington, DC
Hourihane, John N. ... Chicago, IL
Hourihane, John N., Jr. ... Chicago, IL
Hourin, James J. ... Diamondhead, MS
Houry, Edward ... Department of Agriculture, Board of Contract Appeals, GV
Housch, John C. ... Summerville, GA
Housch, Paul T. ... Nashville, TN
House, Andrew Ray ... Corpus Christi, TX
House, Ann B. ... Fort Worth, TX
House, Arthur G. ... Washington, DC
House, Bill ... Cedar Vale, KS
House, Brian C. ... London, KY
House, Brian M. ... Ringgold, GA
Chattanooga, TN
House, Briane M. ... Indianapolis, IN
House, Bryan B. ... Washington, DC
House, C. Gilbert ... Austin, TX
San Antonio, TX
House, Calvin R. ... Pasadena, CA
House, Cecil R. ... Roseland, NJ
House, Charles L. ... Kansas City, MO
House, Clinton C. ... Caro, MI
House, Dale W. ... Anchorage, AK
House, David C. ... Columbus, OH
House & Davidson ... Richmond, VA
House, Deborah M. ... Washington, DC
House, Don R. ... Winston-Salem, NC
House, Donald R. ... Phoenix, AZ
House, Doris J. ... Joplin, MO
House, Ellen M. ... Midland, TX
House, Emmitt C. ... Chicago, IL
House, Gary ... Sedan, KS
House, Geo. C. ... Indianapolis, IN
House, George W. ... Greensboro, NC
Raleigh, NC
House, Glenn W., Jr. ... Grand Rapids, MI
House, Holly A. ... San Francisco, CA
House & House ... San Antonio, TX
House & Ingersoll, PLLC
Winston-Salem, NC
House, J. David ... Blountstown, FL
Marianna, FL
House, J. Gordon, Jr. ... Mobile, AL
House, Jacqueline A.
Department of the Air Force, Office of the General Counsel, GV
House, James B. ... Austin, TX
San Antonio, TX
House, James Byron ... Nashville, IL
House, James G., III ... Mobile, AL
House, James L. ... Humble, TX
House, James M. ... Amarillo, TX
House, Jeffrey G. ... San Antonio, TX
House, Jennifer Annan ... Danville, CA
House, Jennifer L. ... Houston, TX
House, John H. ... Topeka, KS
House, John Howell ... Dallas, TX
House, John L. ... Los Angeles, CA
House, John L. ... Manhattan Beach, CA
House, Joseph R. ... Washington, DC
House, Juliette A. ... Pensacola, FL
House, June P. ... Nashville, TN
House, Kay B. ... Winston-Salem, NC
House, Kingsmill & Riess, L.L.C.
New Orleans, LA
Houston, TX
House, Korey J. ... Los Angeles, CA
House, Larry B. ... Huntsville, AL
House, Lawrence P. ... Los Angeles, CA
House, Linda L. ... Cleveland, OH
House, Luther P., Jr. ... Atlanta, GA
House, Mark E. ... Birmingham, AL
House, Mary M. ... Stockbridge, GA
House, Meredith A. ... Richmond, VA
House, Michael D. ... Phoenix, AZ
House, Michael P. ... Washington, DC
House, Michelle S. ... St. Louis, MO
House, Mitchel P., Jr. ... Macon, GA
House & Morgan ... Mobile, AL
House, Nicole Lomangino ... Atlanta, GA
House, Oscar Gayle ... Manchester, KY
House, P. Douglas ... Mercer Island, WA
House, Perry & Kavanaugh, L.L.C.
Huntsville, AL
House, R. A., Jr. ... Kittanning, PA
House, Rachael K. ... Cincinnati, OH
House, Randolph E. ... Milwaukee, WI
House, Robert B. ... Jackson, MS
House, Robert J. ... Medford, NY
House, Robert L. ... Salinas, CA
House, Robert N. ... Cleveland, OH
House, Robert O. ... Macon, GA
House, Robert O., P.C. ... Macon, GA
House, Ronald L. ... Columbus, OH
House, Ronald R. ... San Diego, CA
House, Sara S. ... Greensboro, NC
House, Sharon Cornelius ... Oneida, WI
House, Stanley C. ... Augusta, GA
House, Stanley C. ... Martinez, GA
House, Stanley J. ... San Jose, CA
House, Stella B. ... Manchester, KY
House, Stella B., P.S.C. ... Manchester, KY
House, Stephen E. ... Toledo, OH
House, Stephen J. ... Wichita, KS
House, Stuart N. ... Pompano Beach, FL
House, Susan T., (P.C.) ... Pasadena, CA
House, Ted C. ... St. Charles, MO
House, Thomas J. ... Decatur, AL
House, Thomas P. ... Watsonville, CA
House, W. Richard, Jr. ... New Orleans, LA
Houston, TX
House, Wanda ... Soquel, CA
House, W. B." Bennie ", Jr. ... Houston, TX
House, William C. ... New York, NY
House, William M. ... Gainesville, GA
House, William Mike ... Washington, DC
House, Wm. M., Jr. ... Palestine, TX
Househal, Dona E. ... Rockville, MD
Houseal, John I., Jr. ... Memphis, TN
Houseal, Sean Douglas
North Charleston, SC
Houseal, Timothy Jay ... Wilmington, DE
Houseal, William ... St. Joseph, MI
House-Harvath, Ellen M. ... Lansing, MI
Householder, David A. ... Los Angeles, CA
Householder, David K. ... Cleveland, OH
Householder, Gina M. ... Hagerstown, MD
Householder, Joseph A. ... El Segundo, CA
Householder, Steven L. ... Indianapolis, IN
Householter, J. Gregory ... Kankakee, IL
Houseknecht, Pamela M. ... Mission Viejo, CA
Housel, Jerry W. ... Cody, WY
Housel, John O. ... Cody, WY
Housel, Robert V. ... Cleveland, OH
Housel, Robert V., Co., L.P.A.
Cleveland, OH
Housel, Theodore F. ... Northfield, NJ
Houseman, Alan W. ... Washington, DC
Houseman, Edward E. ... Reading, PA
Houseman and Feind, LLP ... Grafton, WI
Houseman, Ralph E. ... Grafton, WI
Houseman, Scott D. ... Salem, MA
Housen, Susan W. ... Atlanta, GA
Houser, Ann ... Chicago, IL
Houser, Barbara J. ... Dallas, TX
Houser, Barney M. ... Orangeburg, SC
Houser & Berkland ... Belmond, IA
Houser, Bradley D. ... Miami, FL
Houser, Bradley W. ... Raleigh, NC
Houser, Carolee G. ... San Francisco, CA
Houser, Cheryl ... Cupertino, CA
Houser, David M. ... Stoughton, WI
Houser, Douglas G. ... Portland, OR
Houser, Eric D. ... Irvine, CA
Houser, Franklin D. ... San Antonio, TX
Houser, Gordon W. ... Austin, TX
Houser, H. Neil ... Louisville, KY
Houser, Harold L. ... Aurora, CO
Houser, Herbert A. ... Port Hueneme, CA
Houser, James E. ... Belmond, IA
Houser, Janet P. ... Philadelphia, PA
Houser, John B. (Ben) ... Mt. Orab, OH
Houser, John E. ... Thomasville, GA
Houser, John G. ... Tuckahoe, NY
Houser, Joseph M. ... Youngstown, OH
Houser, K. Ross ... Greensburg, PA
Houser, Kaye K. ... Birmingham, AL
Houser, Kimberly A. ... Chicago, IL
Houser, Kirk D. ... Pittsburgh, PA
Houser, Kristin ... Seattle, WA
Houser, Mark S. ... Dallas, TX
Houser, Martha R. ... Denver, CO
Houser, Mary Beth ... Youngstown, OH
Houser, Michael E. ... Belmond, IA
Houser, Norwin D. ... Jefferson City, MO
Houser, Paul W. ... Renton, WA
Houser, Paul W. (Bud), Jr. ... Renton, WA
Houser, Philip ... Austin, TX
Houser, Ralph L. ... Reston, VA
Houser, Renee J. ... Columbus, OH
Houser, Robert C., Jr. ... Phoenix, AZ
Houser, Robert F., (P.C.) ... Boston, MA
Houser, Ronald E. ... Athens, GA
Houser, Stephen D., Law Offices of
Jupiter, FL
Houser, Susana Elizabeth
Fort Lauderdale, FL
Houser, Terry L. ... Atlanta, GA
Houser, Tessie V. ... Grass Valley, CA
Houser, Thomas J. ... Des Moines, IA
Houser, Thomas W. ... Bethlehem, PA
Houser, Timothy C. ... Knoxville, TN
Houser, Virginia Zock ... St. Petersburg, FL
Tampa, FL
Houser, Wade A. ... Denver, CO
Houser, Wayne K., Jr. ... Knoxville, TN
Houser, William C. ... McMinnville, OR
Houser, William D. ... Dallas, TX
Houser, William Spencer ... Dalton, PA
Houseweart, George W. ... Allentown, PA
Housewirth, Gregory L. ... Dallas, TX
Housey, Donald J. ... Eastpointe, MI
Housey, Donald J., P.C. ... Eastpointe, MI
Housey, Janice W. ... Washington, DC
Housey, Paul J. ... New York, NY
Housh, Ronald G. ... Seattle, WA
Housh, Tedrick A., III ... Kansas City, MO
Housholder, Doris H. ... Daytona Beach, FL
Housholder, Larry A. ... Beaver Falls, PA
Housholder, Quentin L. ... Nashville, TN
Houska, Josef D. ... Oxnard, CA
Santa Barbara, CA
Houska, Scot J. ... Grand Junction, CO
Houske, Robert H. ... Kansas City, MO
Houske & Rollins, P.C. ... Kansas City, MO
Houslanger, Todd E. ... Huntington, NY
Housley, Allan D. ... Washington, DC
Housley, Casey O. ... Kansas City, MO
Housley, Darlene M. ... Arlington, VA
Housley, James F. ... Salt Lake City, UT
Housley, John W. ... Springfield, MO
Housley Kantarian & Bronstein, P.C.
Washington, DC
Housley, R. Mark ... Topeka, KS
Housley, Robert V. ... Boston, MA
Housley, Roger O. ... Norman, OK
Housley, William Wayne, Jr. ... Tupelo, MS
Housman, Craig ... Paducah, KY
Housman, David G. ... Albuquerque, NM
Housman, Frances S. ... Dover, NJ
Housman, Linda ... New City, NY
Housman, Marlon G., Law Office of
Sebastopol, CA
Housman, Robert A. ... Beverly Hills, CA
Housman, Ronald S. ... Glendale, CA
Housman, Simon A. ... Rancho Mirage, CA
Housman, Walden Glover, Jr. ... Athens, GA
Housman, Wendy M. ... Los Angeles, CA
Housouer, Ben ... Upland, CA
Houssels, J. K., Jr. ... Las Vegas, NV
Houssiere, Charles R., III ... Houston, TX
Houssiere, Durant & Houssiere, LLP
Houston, TX
Houssiere, Linda D. ... Houston, TX
Houst, Henry E., Jr. ... Boise, ID
Houst Law Office ... Boise, ID
Houston, Alma Faye ... Akron, OH
Houston, Andrew C. ... New York, NY
Houston, Ann Holland ... Louisville, KY
Houston, Bart A. ... Fort Lauderdale, FL
Houston, Bradley L. ... Austin, TX
Houston, Brent Dillon ... Arkadelphia, AR
Houston, Brent W. ... Denver, CO
Houston, Bruce R.
United States Postal Service, Judicial Officer, GV
Houston, Chandra G. ... Minneapolis, MN
Houston, Charles E., Jr. ... San Diego, CA
Houston, Charles O., III, P.C.
St. Clair Shores, MI
Houston, Charles T. ... Ste. Genevieve, MO
Houston, Christopher E. ... Boston, MA
Houston, Cinamon S. ... Dayton, OH
Houston, Clarence H., Jr.
Jacksonville, FL
Houston, Daniel R. ... Cincinnati, OH
Houston, David A. ... Memphis, TN
Houston, David E. ... Cleburne, TX
Houston, David J. ... Lansing, MI
Houston, David R. ... Reno, NV
Houston, David S. ... Anchorage, AK
Houston, David S. ... McLean, VA
Houston, David W., III ... Aberdeen, MS
Houston, Deane B. ... San Diego, CA
Houston, Diane ... Albuquerque, NM
Houston & Donaghue ... Atlanta, GA
Houston, Donald F. ... Bridgeport, CT
Houston, Douglas ... Omaha, NE
Houston, Drenaye L. ... Department of Justice, Environment and Natural Resources Division, GV
Houston, Farley G. ... Dallas, TX
Houston, Francis ... Blackshear, GA
Houston, Gary B. ... Paducah, KY
Houston, Gladys M. ... Oakland, CA
Houston, Glen L. ... Hobbs, NM
Houston Harbaugh, A Professional Corporation ... Greensburg, PA
Pittsburgh, PA
Houston, Harris & Denkewalter, L.L.C.
Urbana, OH
Houston, Heather ... Seattle, WA
Houston & Henderson, A P.C.
Anchorage, AK

Houston, Henry W. ....Urbana, OH
Houston & Houston ....Anchorage, AK
Houston & Houston ....Albuquerque, NM
Houston & Howard ....Washington, DC
Houston, Ira Sam ....Denton, TX
Houston, J. Brooke ....Atlanta, GA
Houston, J. Edward ....Fort Lauderdale, FL
Houston, J. Gorman, Jr. ....Montgomery, AL
Houston, J. Grant ....Lexington, MA
Houston, J. Robert ....Geneseo, NY
Houston, J. Steven ....Marathon, TX
Houston, J. Steven, Law Offices of
Marathon, TX
Houston, James M. ....Pittsburgh, PA
Houston, Jamie G., III ....Jackson, MS
Houston, Janet L. ....Cincinnati, OH
Houston, Jeffrey A. ....McPherson, KS
Houston, Jeni Rhoads ....San Antonio, TX
Houston, John A. ....San Diego, CA
Houston, John A. ....Bartlesville, OK
Houston, John C. ....Bingham Farms, MI
Houston, John D., II ....Pittsburgh, PA
Houston, John R. ....Minneapolis, MN
Houston, John T. ....Topeka, KS
Houston, Johnny D., Jr. ....Chattanooga, TN
Houston, Jolie ....San Jose, CA
Houston, Joseph G. ....Washington, DC
Houston, Joseph G. ....Hackettstown, NJ
Houston, Joseph W., II ....Las Vegas, NV
Houston, Julia A. ....Atlanta, GA
Houston, Julian T. ....Boston, MA
Houston, Karen M. ....San Francisco, CA
Houston, Katherine J. ....Ukiah, CA
Houston, Kay ....Richardson, TX
Houston, Kimberly ....Atlanta, GA
Houston Law Firm, P.A. ....Jonesboro, AR
Houston, Lee ....Anchorage, AK
Houston, Lee C. ....Anchorage, AK
Houston, Leslie G. ....Albuquerque, NM
Houston, Malcolm W. ....Kensington, MD
Houston, Marek & Griffin, L.L.P.
Port Lavaca, TX
Victoria, TX
Houston, Margaret F. ....Pittsburgh, PA
Houston, Mary Ruth ....Orlando, FL
Houston, Matthew David
Mount Olive, NJ
Houston, Matthew M. ....New York, NY
Houston, Melvin ....Houston, TX
Houston, Nancy J. ....Morgantown, WV
Houston, Neil D. ....Sacramento, CA
Houston, Noyl ....Jonesboro, AR
Houston and Osborn, P.C. ....Pawnee, OK
Stillwater, OK
Houston, Palmer and Ligos
Hackettstown, NJ
Houston, Paris T. ....Vienna, VA
Houston, Patricia A. ....Santa Ana, CA
Houston, Patrick J. ....Long Beach, CA
Houston, Paul A. ....Anchorage, AK
Houston, Paul David ....Henderson, TX
Houston, Paul E. ....Albuquerque, NM
Houston, Phillip C. ....West Palm Beach, FL
Houston, Phillip C., P.A.
West Palm Beach, FL
Houston, Randall V. ....Montgomery, AL
Houston, Randolph B., Jr. ....Austin, TX
Houston, Rex ....Henderson, TX
Houston, Richard A. ....Corpus Christi, TX
Houston, Richard Andrew, III
Metairie, LA
Houston, Richard C., Jr. ....Midland, TX
Houston, R. K. ....Bay Springs, MS
Houston, R. L. ....Brandon, MS
Houston, Robert B. ....Spokane, WA
Houston, Robert L., III ....Scottsburg, IN
Houston, Robert P. ....Port Lavaca, TX
Victoria, TX
Houston, Russell, III ....Grifton, NC
Houston, Samuel A. ....Houston, TX
Houston, Samuel Sykes, Jr. ....Austin, TX
Houston, Scott H. ....Phoenix, AZ
Houston & Shahady, P.A.
Fort Lauderdale, FL
Houston, Sondra Fogley ....Tulsa, OK
Houston, Stacey S. ....Wetumpka, AL
Houston, Steven L. ....Los Angeles, CA
Houston, Stuart E. ....Washington, DC
Houston, Thomas M. ....Omaha, NE
Houston and Thompson, P.C. ....Scottsburg, IN
Houston, Tom K. ....Los Angeles, CA
Houston, W. Michael ....Dallas, TX
Houston, William A. ....Pittsburgh, PA
Houston, William B. ....Houston, TX
Houston, William K., Jr.
Walnut Creek, CA
Houston, William McC. ....Pittsburgh, PA
Houston, Winfrey D. ....Stillwater, OK
Houston-Reeve, David M. ....Seattle, WA
Housum, Virginia Anne ......Minneapolis, MN
Housworth, Evan H. ....Decatur, GA
Hout, Barbara J. ....Santa Barbara, CA
Hout, Gregory J. ....San Diego, CA
Hout, Phillip D. ....Newport, AR
Hout, Rebecca Morse ....Altamont, NY
Houtchens, Barnard ....Greeley, CO
Houtchens, Daniel & Greenfield, LLC
Greeley, CO
Houtchens, John B. ....Greeley, CO
Houtchens, Kathryn ....New York, NY
Houtchens, Kim R. ....Greeley, CO
Houtchens, Richard K. ....Corpus Christi, TX
Houtchens, Thomas A. ....Greeley, CO
Houtman, Richard D. ....Highland Park, MI
Houts, John W. ....San Diego, CA
Houts, Joseph K. ....St. Joseph, MO
Houts, Marshall W. ....Corona Del Mar, CA
Houts, Randolph C. ....San Diego, CA

Houtsma, Cornelius J., Jr. ....Markham, IL
Houtsma, Peter C. ....Denver, CO
Houtz, H. Monroe ....Tunkhannock, PA
Houtz, John A. ....Forsyth, MT
Houtz, Lester C. ....Denver, CO
Chicago, IL
Houtz, Linda K. ....Lafayette, IN
Houtz, Michael K. ....Tampa, FL
Houtz, Michael V. ....Ogden, UT
Houwman, Robin Jacobson ....Sioux Falls, SD
Houy, Margaret L. ....Boston, MA
Houze, Stephen A. ....Portland, OR
Hovan, John J. ....Tunkhannock, PA
Hovancik, Damian M. ....Albany, NY
Hovanec, George A., Jr. ....Alexandria, VA
Hovanec, George J., III ....Woodbridge, NJ
Hovanec, John A. ....Lake Station, IN
Hovanesian, Ara ....Pasadena, CA
Hovanesian, Archibald, Jr. ....Pensacola, FL
Hovaniec, Jennifer A. ....Wheaton, IL
Hovannisian, Armen K. ....Sherman Oaks, CA
Hovannisian, Garo K. ....Santa Monica, CA
Hovarth, George P. ....Pawtucket, RI
Hovastak, Michael W.
Oklahoma City, OK
Hovater, William R. ....Tuscumbia, AL
Hovatter, Edward J. ....Moorestown, NJ
Hovatter, Eric M. ....Costa Mesa, CA
Hovda, Louis ....Green Bay, WI
Hovda, Theodore J. ....Garner, IA
Hovde, F. Boyd ....Indianapolis, IN
Hovde, Frederick R. ....Indianapolis, IN
Hovde Law Firm ....Indianapolis, IN
Hovde, Michael D., Jr. ....Bloomingdale, IL
Hovde, Michael D., Jr. ....Bloomingdale, IL
Hovden, Del D. ....Whittier, CA
Hovden, Jeffrey A. ....New York, NY
Hovden, Lisa Chorness ....Long Beach, CA
Hovdesven, Arne ....Wilmington, NC
Hovdesven, Eric R. ....Atlanta, GA
Hove, Aaron G. ....Topeka, KS
Hove, Arnie A. ....Circle, MT
Hove, John N. ....Tulsa, OK
Hove, Ralph C. ....Seattle, WA
Hove, Randall A. ....Philadelphia, PA
Hove, Richard E. ....Hayward, CA
Hovel, John F. ....Milwaukee, WI
Hovel, Roy B. ....Sun Prairie, WI
Hovell, William P. ....Spring Valley, CA
Hoveman, Virginia A. ....Syracuse, NY
Hoven, David L. ....Pacific, MO
Hoven, J. Daniel ....Helena, MT
Hovendick, James V. ....Montgomery, TX
Hovendon, John C. ....Tryon, NC
Hovenkamp, Mark A. ....Houston, TX
Hover, Charles S., III ....Phoenix, AZ
Hover, Dan N. ....Denver, CO
Hover, Dan N., P.C. ....Denver, CO
Hover, John C. ....Phoenix, AZ
Hover, John C., P.C. ....Phoenix, AZ
Hover, Marilyn C. ....San Jose, CA
Hover, Wade H. ....Los Gatos, CA
Hover, Wade H., P.C. ....Los Gatos, CA
Hover, William J. ....South Haven, MI
Hovermale, Kenneth W., Jr. ....Portland, ME
Hovermill, Joseph W. ....Baltimore, MD
Hovermill, Virginia S. ....Baltimore, MD
Hoversen, William E., Jr. ....Chicago, IL
Hoversland, Ken W. ....Scobey, MT
Hoversland, Ken W., P.C. ....Scobey, MT
Hover-Smoot, Julia G. ....Los Gatos, CA
Hover-Smoot, Scott R. ....Milpitas, CA
Hoverson, Michael K. ....Minneapolis, MN
Hoverson, Ronald A. ....Oklahoma City, OK
Hoversten, David V. ....Austin, MN
Hoversten, Johnson, Beckmann, Wellmann & Hovey, LLP ....Austin, MN
Hoversten, Kermit F. ....Austin, MN
Hoversten, William L. ....Waseca, MN
Hovet, Kenneth J. ....Ventura, CA
Hovey, George D. ....Hickory, NC
Hovey, Gregg B. ....San Diego, CA
Hovey, James D. ....Grand Forks, ND
Hovey, John D. ....New Rockford, ND
Hovey, Justin D. ....San Francisco, CA
Hovey & Kirby, A Professional Corporation
San Diego, CA
Hovey & Koenig LLP ....Boston, MA
Plymouth, MA
Hovey Law Offices, P.C.
New Rockford, ND
Hovey, M. Leslie ....San Diego, CA
Hovey, Robert D., (P.C.)
Kansas City, MO
Hovey, Robert J. ....Bellevue, NE
Hovey, Robert J., Law Offices Of, P.C.
Bellevue, NE
Hovey, Steven J. ....Austin, MN
Hovey, Susan J. ....Cincinnati, OH
Hovey, Tara S. ....Harrison, MI
Hovey, William V. ....Boston, MA
Plymouth, MA
Hovey, Williams, Timmons & Collins
Kansas City, MO
Hoving, Christopher H. ....Silver Spring, MD
Hovious, Nat J. ....Vicksburg, MS
Hovious, Robert Gregg ....Louisville, KY
Hovis and Associates ....Annandale, VA
Hovis, Barry D. ....San Francisco, CA
Hovis & Boyette, P.A. ....Clermont, FL
Hovis, David J. ....Minneapolis, MN
Hovis, G. Neil ....San Luis Obispo, CA
Hovis, George E. ....Clermont, FL
Hovis, James B. ....Yakima, WA
Hovis, James W. ....Charlotte, NC
Hovis, Nancy E. ....Seattle, WA
Hovis, Raymond L. ....York, PA
Hovis, Richard D. ....High Point, NC

Hovis, Robert H., III ....Annandale, VA
Hovis, Smith, Stewart, Lipscomb & Cross, LLP
San Francisco, CA
Hovis, Steven M. ....York, PA
Hovis, W. Ryan, (P.A.) ....Rock Hill, SC
Hovland, Carl M. ....Torrance, CA
Hovland, Daniel L. ....Bismarck, ND
Hovland, Debra L. ....Wayzata, MN
Hovland, James B. ....Minneapolis, MN
Hovland, Marie Elizabeth ....Sioux Falls, SD
Hovland, Robert J. ....Rugby, ND
Hovland, Valerie Bruce ....Perrysburg, OH
Hovnatanian, Levon G. ....Houston, TX
Hovorka, Martha ....Cicero, IL
Hovren, James D. ....Boise, ID
Hovsepian, Nora ....Sherman Oaks, CA
Hovsepian, Steven Edward ....Tampa, FL
How, Mark H. ....Dallas, TX
Howald, Brandon G. ....Palo Alto, CA
Howald, J. Kent ....Steelville, MO
Howald, John W. ....Hillsboro, MO
Howald, Kevon V. ....Dallas, TX
Howald, Michael ....Los Angeles, CA
Howald, Robin Bronzaft ......Los Angeles, CA
Howald, Walter G. ....Newport Beach, CA
Howald, Walter G., Incorporated
Newport Beach, CA
Howaniec, James P. ....Lewiston, ME
Howanski, Kristine Kappeler ....Towson, MD
Howansky, I. Paul ....Mineola, NY
Riverhead, NY
Howard, A. Ryland, III ....San Antonio, TX
Howard, A. E. Dick ....Charlottesville, VA
Howard, Alan B. ....New York, NY
Howard, Alan J. ....St. Louis, MO
Howard, Albert O., Jr. ....Phenix City, AL
Howard & Aldridge ....Huntsville, AL
Howard, Alex T., Jr. ....Mobile, AL
Howard, Alicia B. ....Georgetown, DE
Howard, Alvahteen E. S., (Mrs.)
New York, NY
Howard, Alvin F., (A L.C.)
Marina Del Rey, CA
Howard, Amos H., Jr. ....Lubbock, TX
Howard, Amy Kohler ....Allentown, PA
Howard, Amy R. ....Charlotte, NC
Howard, Andrew B. ....Hudson, NY
Howard, Ann Gill ....United States Senate, Committee Legal Personnel, GV
Howard, Ann M. ....Southfield, MI
Howard, Anne Kelley ....Bethesda, MD
Howard, Antoria D. ....Hartford, CT
Howard, April R. ....Evanston, IL
Howard, Arthur ....Bloomfield Hills, MI
Howard, Arthur R. ....Lubbock, TX
Howard, Arthur W. ....Louisville, KY
Howard, Arthur W., Jr. ....Louisville, KY
Howard & Associates, P.A.
Fort Lauderdale, FL
Tallahassee, FL
Howard & Associates, P.C.
Newport Beach, CA
Howard, Austin A. ....Bloomfield Hills, MI
Howard, Barbara J. ....Cincinnati, OH
Howard, Barry L. ....Pontiac, MI
Howard, Barry L. ....Nashville, TN
Howard, Bernadine Sterzinger ......St. Paul, MN
Howard, Bernard L. ....Phoenix, AZ
Howard, Bethany K. V. ....Jacksonville, FL
Howard, Betty Taylor ....Seattle, WA
Howard, Beverly J. ....Montgomery, AL
Howard, Bill J. ....Midland, TX
Howard, Blair D. ....Warrenton, VA
Howard & Bodnar Co., L.P.A.
Cincinnati, OH
Howard & Bowie ....Damariscotta, ME
Howard, Bowling J., Jr. ....Aberdeen, MD
Howard, Brad A. ....Santa Ana, CA
Howard, Bradley D. ....Chicago, IL
Howard, Bradley W. ....Amarillo, TX
Howard, Brawner & Stone ....Miami, FL
Howard, Brenner & Nass, P.C.
Westmont, NJ
Philadelphia, PA
Howard, Brent C. ....Tyler, TX
Howard, Brent T. ....Tiffin, OH
Howard, Bruce C. ....Chicago, IL
Howard, Bruce P. ....Los Angeles, CA
Howard, Bryan ....Nashville, TN
Howard, Butler & Melfa, P.A. ....Towson, MD
Howard, Byron K. ....Corbin, KY
Howard, C. Elaine ....Houston, TX
Howard, C. Stephen ....Los Angeles, CA
Howard, C. Vernon ....Madison, WI
Howard, Calvin M. ....Birmingham, AL
Howard, Candiss L. ....Atlanta, GA
Howard, Carl Richard ....New York, NY
Howard, Carl V. ....New York, NY
Howard, Carrie K. ....Louisville, KY
Howard, Carswell & Bennett, P.C.
Baxley, GA
Jesup, GA
Nahunta, GA
Howard, Carter ....Chicago, IL
Howard, Catherine ....Edinburg, TX
Howard, Catherine Rayala
Washington, DC
Howard, Cathie Watts ....Richmond, VA
Howard, Cecil W., Jr. ....Los Angeles, CA
Howard, Charles B. ....Charles Town, WV
Howard, Charles C. ....Dublin, OH
Howard, Charles D. ....Hinesville, GA
Howard, Charles E. ....Greenville, SC
Howard, Charles F. ....Fayetteville, NC
Howard, Charles K., Jr. ....Atlanta, GA
Howard, Charles L. ....Hartford, CT
Howard, Charles L. ....Philadelphia, PA
Howard, Charles L., III ....Birmingham, AL

Howard, Charles O. ....Edina, MN
Howard, Charles S. ....Fayetteville, AR
Howard, Charles Scott ....Portland, OR
Howard, Charlton T. ....Dundalk, MD
Howard, Charlton T., III ....Beaufort, SC
Howard, Cherie Hill ....Brooklyn, NY
Howard, Cheryl Johnson ....Pensacola, FL
Howard, Cheryl Johnson, P.A., Law Offices of
Pensacola, FL
Howard, Cheryl L. ....New York, NY
Howard, Cheryl Lynne ....Greenbelt, MD
Howard, Cheryl R. ....New York, NY
Howard, Chris C., Jr. ....Douglasville, GA
Howard, Christine E. ....Atlanta, GA
Howard, Christine N. ....Minneapolis, MN
Howard, Christopher E. ....Portland, ME
Howard, Christopher Holm ....Seattle, WA
Howard, Christopher L. ....Nashville, TN
Howard, Christopher M. ....Cranford, NJ
Howard, Clark E. ....New York, NY
Howard, Clark & Mercer, LLC
Atlanta, GA
Douglasville, GA
Howard, Clayton N. ....Damariscotta, ME
Howard, Clyde W., III ....Nacogdoches, TX
Howard, Colin C. ....Spokane, WA
Howard, Connie L. ....Minneapolis, MN
Howard, Craig S. ....Anchorage, AK
Howard, Cynthia A. ....Sioux Falls, SD
Howard, Cynthia Theresa ....New Canaan, CT
Howard, D. Christopher
Winston-Salem, NC
Howard, D. Douglas ....New Orleans, LA
Howard, D. Douglas, Jr. ....New Orleans, LA
Howard, D. Gregory ....Washington, DC
Annapolis, MD
Owings Mills, MD
Howard, Daggett H. ....Vienna, VA
Howard, D'Ambra ....Overland Park, KS
Howard, Darrin ....Haddonfield, NJ
Howard, Darryl W. ....Dallas, TX
Howard, David ....London, KY
Howard, David A. ....Boca Raton, FL
Howard, David A. ....Chicago, IL
Howard, David A. ....Bennington, VT
Howard, David A. ....Bennington, VT
Howard, David C. ....St. Louis, MO
Howard, David C. ....Flushing, NY
Howard, David K. ....Florence, AL
Howard, David Lloyd
Town and Country, MO
Howard, David M. ....Philadelphia, PA
Howard, David M. ....Spring, TX
Howard, David W. ....Kansas City, MO
Howard, Davis & Bunt, P.C. ....Tyler, TX
Howard, Davis J. ....Elizabeth, NJ
Howard, Deborah ....New York, NY
Howard, Deborah A. ....Dale, IN
Howard, Deborah J. ....St. Petersburg, FL
Howard, Deborah Singer ....Baltimore, MD
Howard & Delaney ....Marietta, GA
Howard, Denise M. ....Kansas City, MO
Howard, Denne ....Rancho Mirage, CA
Howard, Derek A. ....Austin, TX
Howard, Derek G. ....Greenbrae, CA
Howard, Derrick ....Philadelphia, PA
Howard, Diane B. ....Sacramento, CA
Howard, Diane C. ....Cape Girardeau, MO
Howard, Dickee M. ....Towson, MD
Howard, Don A. ....Huntsville, AL
Howard, Donald E. ....Shaker Heights, OH
Howard, Donald J. ....Worcester, MA
Howard, Donald John ....Fairfax, VA
Howard, Donald L. ....Oklahoma City, OK
Howard, Donna B. ....Southfield, MI
Howard, Dorothy Y. ....North Little Rock, AR
Howard, Douglas A. ....New York, NY
Howard, Douglas C. ....Benson, AZ
Howard, Douglas D. ....Columbus, MT
Howard, Dunn, Howard & Howard
Wetumpka, AL
Howard, Edward Cader ....Raleigh, NC
Howard, Edward J. ....Princeton, NJ
Howard, Edward O. ....New Rochelle, NY
Howard, Edward P. ....Santa Monica, CA
Howard, Edwin H. ....Fitchburg, MA
Howard, Edwin J. ....Beverly Hills, CA
Howard, Elizabeth ....Houston, TX
Howard, Elizabeth A. ....Menlo Park, CA
Howard, Elizabeth A. ....Dallas, TX
Howard, Elizabeth G. ....Columbia, SC
Howard, Elizabeth R. ....Gadsden, AL
Howard, Elizabeth R. ....Phoenixville, PA
Howard, Ellen ....North Charleston, SC
Howard Ellsworth Ipsen & Perry, PLLC
Boise, ID
Howard, Emanuel ....Newton, MA
Howard, Eric A. ....Boston, MA
Howard, Eric C. ....Georgetown, DE
Howard, Erick C. ....Chicago, IL
Howard, Ernest E., III ....New Orleans, LA
Howard, Ernest J. ....Greenville, SC
Howard, Eugene J. ....Miami Beach, FL
Howard, Eve N. ....Washington, DC
Howard, Evelyn G. ....Media, PA
Howard, Francis A. ....Holbrook, MA
Howard and Francis, LLP
Fort Collins, CO
Howard, Frank ....Marysville, OH
Howard, Frank A. ....North Massapequa, NY
Howard, Frank A., Jr. ....Miami, FL
Howard, Frank D. ....Seattle, WA
Howard, Frank E., Jr. ....Oakland, CA
Howard, Frank M. ....Chicago, IL
Howard, Frank N., Jr. ....Crawfordsville, IN
Howard, Frank T. ....Elkton, MD
Howard, Fred D. ....Provo, UT
Howard, Fred G., Jr. ....New York, NY

Howard, Frederic K. ....New York, NY
Howard, Friedman & Gebbie
San Bernardino, CA
Howard, G. Houston, II ....Wetumpka, AL
Howard, G. Robert ....Townsend, GA
Howard & Gaffney Co., L.P.A. ....Akron, OH
Howard, Garland W. ....Owensboro, KY
Howard, Garry L. ....Wichita, KS
Howard, Gary D. ....San Antonio, TX
Howard, Gary F., (P.C.) ....Phoenix, AZ
Howard, Gary Lane ....Birmingham, AL
Howard, Gene C. ....Tulsa, OK
Howard, Geoffrey M. ....San Francisco, CA
Howard, George D. ....San Diego, CA
Howard, George H., P.C. ....Norwood, MA
Howard, George, Jr. ....Little Rock, AR
Howard, George P. ....Wetumpka, AL
Howard, George S., Jr. ....San Diego, CA
Howard, George W., III ....Westmont, NJ
Philadelphia, PA
Howard, Gil ....Marietta, GA
Howard, Gina Schaar
Federal Trade Commission,
Bureau of Consumer Protection, GV
Howard, Glen S. ....Washington, DC
Howard, Glenn A. ....Silver Spring, MD
Howard, Graeme K., Jr. ....Philadelphia, PA
Howard, Green & McDarris, L.L.P.
Cary, NC
Raleigh, NC
Research Triangle Park, NC
Howard, Gregory C. ....Boston, MA
Howard, Gregory L., Jr. ....Huntington, WV
Howard, Gregory R. ....Minneapolis, MN
Howard, G. W., III ....Mount Vernon, IL
Howard, H. Cabanne ....Portland, ME
Howard, H. Edgar ....Gadsden, AL
Howard, H. James, II ....Houston, TX
Howard, Hampton W. ....Keene, NH
Howard, Harold K. ....Austin, TX
Howard, Harolyn R. ....Pikeville, KY
Howard, Harry C. ....Atlanta, GA
Howard, Harry H. ....New Orleans, LA
Howard, Harry R. ....Parsippany, NJ
Howard, Harry R., P.A. ....Parsippany, NJ
Howard, Harvey A. ....Beverly Hills, CA
Howard, Heather ....Seattle, WA
Howard, Heather H. ....Department of Justice,
Antitrust Division, GV
Howard, Heather H. ....St. Petersburg, FL
Howard & Helmers, PLC ....Louisville, KY
Howard, Henry W. ....San Francisco, CA
Howard & Howard ....Edmond, OK
El Reno, OK
Howard & Howard Attorneys, P.C.
Peoria, IL
Ann Arbor, MI
Bloomfield Hills, MI
Detroit, MI
Grand Rapids, MI
Kalamazoo, MI
Lansing, MI
Howard, Howard, Francis & Reid, L.L.P.
Greenville, SC
Howard & Howard, P.C. ....Norfolk, VA
Virginia Beach, VA
Howard, Howell H., III
Department of State, GV
Howard, Hubert H. ....Jesup, GA
Howard, Hugh D. ....Morton Grove, IL
Howard, Irene C. ....Jackson, MS
Howard, J. Carlton, Jr. ....Fairfax, VA
Howard, J. Marcus ....Atlanta, GA
Howard, J. Myrick ....Raleigh, NC
Howard, J. Robert ....Hemphill, TX
Howard, J. Scott ....Tyler, TX
Howard, Jackie M. ....Roseville, CA
Howard, Jackson ....Provo, UT
Howard, James ....Washington, DC
Howard, James A. ....Tarzana, CA
Howard, James A., II ....Virginia Beach, VA
Howard, James Blake ....Grand Rapids, MI
Howard, James C. ....Atlanta, GA
Howard, James C., Jr. ....Atlanta, GA
Howard, James E. ....Washington, DC
Howard, James E. ....Stone Mountain, GA
Howard, James E. ....Lexington, KY
Howard, James E. ....Boston, MA
Howard, James E., LLC ....Boston, MA
Howard, James G. ....Elm Grove, WI
Howard, James H. ....Manchester, CT
Howard, James I. ....Horse Cave, KY
Howard, James J. ....Baltimore, MD
Howard, James M. ....Phoenix, AZ
Howard, James R. ....Atlanta, GA
Howard, James R. ....Syracuse, IN
Howard, James T. ....Lakeside, MT
Howard, James W. ....Phoenix, AZ
Howard, James W., Jr. ....Las Vegas, NV
Howard, Janine N. ....Wilmington, DE
Howard, Jason A. ....San Diego, CA
Howard, Jasper A. ....Washington, DC
Howard, Jay ....Kansas City, MO
Howard, Jay Monroe ....White Plains, NY
Howard, Jean G. ....Miami, FL
Howard, Jeanne C.DeHayes
West Palm Beach, FL
Howard, Jeffrey A. ....Dallas, TX
Howard, Jeffrey C. ....Winston-Salem, NC
Howard, Jeffrey G. ....Mount Vernon, IL
Howard, Jeffrey H. ....Washington, DC
Howard, Jeffrey L. ....Southfield, MI
Howard, Jeffrey M. ....Belvedere-Tiburon, CA
Howard, Jeffrey M. ....Newport Beach, CA
Howard, Jeffrey M. ....Chicago, IL
Howard, Jeffrey R., (P.C.) ....Boston, MA
Manchester, NH
Howard, Jeffrey S. ....Austin, TX

Howard, Jo Ann Jay ....Austin, TX
Howard, Jo Ann Jay, P.C. ....Austin, TX
Howard, Joel A. ....Amarillo, TX
Howard, Joel M., III ....Albany, NY
Howard, John A. ....San Bernardino, CA
Howard, John A. ....Atlanta, GA
Howard, John A. ....White Plains, NY
Howard, John A. ....Elyria, OH
Howard, John Addison ....Baltimore, MD
Howard, John B. ....Towson, MD
Howard, John B. ....Northampton, MA
Howard, John B., Jr. ....Baltimore, MD
Howard, John C. ....Portland, ME
Howard, John C. ....Kalamazoo, MI
Howard, John C. ....Edmond, OK
El Reno, OK
Howard, John Cooper ....Clarendon, TX
Howard, John D. ....
Administrative Office Of The United States
Courts, GV
Howard, John F. ....Sebring, FL
Howard, John Gregory ....Hamilton, OH
Howard, John H. ....Ventura, CA
Howard, John J. ....San Diego, CA
Howard, John J. ....Columbus, GA
Howard, John J. ....New York, NY
Howard, John Jurey, III ....Memphis, TN
Howard, John L. ....Lake Forest, IL
Howard, John M. ....Washington, DC
Howard, John M., Jr. ....Danville, IN
Howard, John M., Jr. ....Harlingen, TX
Howard, John P. ....Jacksonville, FL
Howard, John P. ....Boise, ID
Howard, John, P.A. ....Jacksonville, FL
Howard, John R. ....Houston, TX
Howard, John Robert ....New Rochelle, NY
Howard, John Scott ....Austin, TX
Howard, John V. ....Hurst, TX
Howard, John V., Jr. ....Denver, CO
Howard, John V., P.C., Law Office of
Fort Worth, TX
Hurst, TX
Howard, John W. ....Peoria, IL
Howard, John W. ....Tulsa, OK
Howard, John W., III ....Greenville, SC
Howard, John W., III, P.A. ....Greenville, SC
Howard, Johnny M. ....Washington, DC
Howard, Jolie M. ....Austin, TX
Howard, Joseph B. ....Corbin, KY
Howard, Joseph C. ....Baltimore, MD
Howard, Joseph C., Jr.
Redwood City, CA
Howard, Joseph D. ....Indianapolis, IN
Howard, Joseph E. ....Treasury Department,
Office of Regulations and Rulings, GV
Howard, Joseph G. ....Chicago, IL
Howard, Joseph G., P.C., Law Offices of
Chicago, IL
Howard, Joseph T. ....Tulsa, OK
Howard, Judith E. ....Minot, ND
Howard, Judith Hall ....McLean, VA
Howard, Judith S. ....McLean, VA
Howard, Judith S., P.C., Law Offices of
Fairfax, VA
McLean, VA
Howard, Julia Saunders ....Knoxville, TN
Howard, Julie McGhee ....Atlanta, GA
Howard, Julie W. ....Dover, NH
Howard, Juliet Pearl ....Brooklyn, NY
Howard, J.W. ....San Diego, CA
Howard, Karen K. ....Kansas City, MO
Howard, Karen M. ....Los Angeles, CA
Howard, Karen Wilson ....Chicago, IL
Howard, Katherine Kelly ....Baltimore, MD
Howard, Kathleen A. ....San Francisco, CA
Howard, Kathleen M. ....Kahului, HI
Howard, Kathryn M. ....Eden Prairie, MN
Howard, Kay L. ....Perrysburg, OH
Howard, Keith ....Walnut Creek, CA
Howard, Keith ....Omaha, NE
Howard, Keith A. ....Wetumpka, AL
Howard, Keith L. ....Lafayette, CA
Howard, Keith W. ....Wenatchee, WA
Howard, Kelley C. ....Tampa, FL
Howard, Ken M. ....Elizabethtown, KY
Howard, Kenneth A. ....Dunwoody, GA
Howard, Kenneth B. ....Raleigh, NC
Howard, Kenneth B., Jr. ....Coeur d'Alene, ID
Howard, Kenneth C., Jr. ....Washington, DC
Howard, Kenneth H. ....Lancaster, PA
New Holland, PA
Howard, Kenneth R. ....Reno, NV
Howard, Kenyon Bales ....Boise, ID
Howard, Kevin Anthony
Salt Lake City, UT
Howard, Kevin L. ....Louisville, KY
Howard, Killis T. ....Lynchburg, VA
Howard, Kim R. ....New York, NY
Howard, Kimberly E. ....Indianapolis, IN
Howard & Kobelan ....Austin, TX
Howard, Kohn, Sprague & FitzGerald
Glastonbury, CT
Hartford, CT
Manchester, CT
Howard, Kristin Klausen ....Atlanta, GA
Howard, Kristine M. ....Winston-Salem, NC
Howard, L. Joseph ....Springfield, IL
Howard, L. Richard ....Tulsa, OK
Howard, Laddie Tyrone ....Columbia, SC
Howard, Larry K. ....Atlanta, GA
Howard, Laudumiey & Mann
New Orleans, LA
Howard, Laura T. ....San Francisco, CA
Howard, Lauran Frances ....Troy, MI
Howard, Lauren R. ....Washington, DC
Howard, Laurence E. ....Grand Rapids, MI
Howard, Laurence W., III
Jacksonville, FL

Howard Law Firm, P.C. ....Minot, ND
Howard Law Firm, The, P.C. ....Atlanta, GA
Howard Law Office ....Atlantic, IA
Howard Law Office, The ....Cambridge, OH
Howard, Lawr. ....Tucson, AZ
Howard, Lawson & Wood ....Danville, IN
Howard, Lee J. ....Starkville, MS
Howard, Lee M. ....Chicago, IL
Howard, Leggans, Piercy & Howard
Mount Vernon, IL
Howard, Leland R., II ....Louisville, KY
Howard, Leo ....New York, NY
Howard, Lewis & Petersen, P.C.
Provo, UT
Howard, Lewis S. ....Knoxville, TN
Howard, Lewis S., Jr. ....Knoxville, TN
Howard, Lewis S., Jr., P.C. ....Knoxville, TN
Howard, Libbye C. ....Houston, TX
Howard, Lin S. ....Nashville, TN
Howard, Lindsay P. ....Pittsburgh, PA
Howard, Lowell B. ....Columbus, OH
Howard, Lowell B., Jr. ....Marysville, OH
Howard, Lucia Fakonas ....Phoenix, AZ
Howard, Lytle, Petersen and Mah
Daly City, CA
Foster City, CA
Howard, M. Katherine ....Pueblo, CO
Howard, Malcolm J. ....Greenville, NC
Howard, Malia L. ....Fort Worth, TX
Howard, Marcia Morales
Jacksonville, FL
Howard & Marcus ....Hyattsville, MD
Howard, Marcy Pevaroff ....Calabasas, CA
Howard, Margaret ....Nashville, TN
Howard, Margie E. ....Anaheim, CA
Howard, Marilyn H. ....Melbourne, FL
Howard, Marjorie C. ....Chicago, IL
Howard, Mark D. ....Peoria, IL
Howard, Mark E. ....Manchester, NH
Howard, Mark G. ....Canton, MA
Howard, Mark S. ....Tampa, FL
Howard, Mark S. ....Waynesboro, MS
Howard, Mark S. ....San Antonio, TX
Howard, Mark W. ....Covington, KY
Howard, Martin B. ....Los Angeles, CA
Howard, Marty R. ....Milwaukee, WI
Howard, Marven E. ....Costa Mesa, CA
Howard, Mary Ellen Niles
Northampton, MA
Howard, Mary Lou ....Grand Rapids, MI
Howard, Mary M. ....Camarillo, CA
Howard, MarySusan ....St. Paul, MN
Howard, Matthew F. ....Eldon, MO
Howard, Matthew J. ....Marietta, GA
Howard, Matthew L. ....Ukiah, CA
Howard, Max ....Anderson, IN
Howard, Maxine Dale ....Ardsley, NY
Howard and McMillan ....Middletown, CT
Howard, Merton A. ....San Francisco, CA
Howard, Michael ....Los Angeles, CA
Howard, Michael A. ....Noblesville, IN
Howard, Michael A. ....Rochester, NY
Howard, Michael C. ....Hudson, NY
Howard, Michael D. ....San Francisco, CA
Howard, Michael H. ....Woodbury, NY
Howard, Michael L. ....Burlington, MA
Howard, Michael L. ....North Canton, OH
Howard, Michael S. ....Tampa, FL
Howard, Michele ....Nashville, TN
Howard, Michelle ....San Francisco, CA
Howard, Milton M. ....Bloomfield Hills, MI
Howard, Molly M. ....Savannah, GA
Howard, Molly N. ....High Point, NC
Lexington, NC
Howard & Morrone ....San Jose, CA
Howard, Moss, Loveder, Strickroth & Walker, LLP ....Riverside, CA
San Diego, CA
Santa Ana, CA
Howard & Motta ....Cranford, NJ
Howard, Myra E.
Federal Trade Commission,
Bureau of Consumer Protection, GV
Howard, Nancy E. ....Los Angeles, CA
Howard, Nancy H. ....Baltimore, MD
Howard, Nathan S. ....New York, NY
Howard, Neal J. ....Wilmington, DE
Howard, Nigel L. ....New York, NY
Howard, Norman C. ....San Jose, CA
Howard, Oliver S. ....Tulsa, OK
Howard & Owens, P.A. ....Coeur d'Alene, ID
Howard, P. Tim ....Fort Lauderdale, FL
Tallahassee, FL
Howard, Pal G. ....Benton, KY
Howard, Pamela ....New York, NY
Howard, Pamela Fitzsimons
San Antonio, TX
Howard, Patrice S. ....Eatonton, GA
Howard, Patricia J. ....New York, NY
Howard, Patrick J. ....Cambridge, OH
Howard, Paul L., Jr. ....Atlanta, GA
Howard, Peggy Ann ....Dallas, TX
Howard, Peggy Sue ....Charlotte, NC
Howard, Penny L. ....Guthrie, OK
Howard, Peter J. ....Atlanta, GA
Howard, Peter J., P.C. ....Atlanta, GA
Howard, Peter L. ....Santa Barbara, CA
Howard, Peter M. ....Chicago, IL
Howard, Peter M. ....Fairfax, VA
Howard, Philip E. ....San Francisco, CA
Chicago, IL
Howard, Philip K. ....New York, NY
Howard, Phillip H. ....Burbank, CA
Howard, Phillip J. ....Treasury Department,
Internal Revenue Service, GV
Howard, Phillips & Andersen, P.C.
Salt Lake City, UT
Howard, Pierre ....Atlanta, GA

Howard, Preston B. ....Las Vegas, NV
Howard, R. Craig ....Reno, NV
Howard, R. Michael
Cape Girardeau, MO
Howard, R. Price ....Weatherford, TX
Howard, R. Scott ....Pittsburgh, PA
Howard, Randall K., (P.C.) ....Houston, TX
Howard, Raymond W. ....Houston, TX
Howard, Rice, Nemerovski, Canady, Falk & Rabkin, A Professional Corporation
Newport Beach, CA
Palo Alto, CA
San Francisco, CA
Howard, Richard A. ....Spring Hill, FL
Howard, Richard A. ....Boston, MA
Howard, Richard C. ....Muskogee, OK
Howard, Richard C., Jr. ....Perkasie, PA
Howard, Richard D. ....Redondo Beach, CA
Howard, Richard D. ....Dallas, TX
Howard, Richard F. ....Boston, MA
Howard, Richard G. ....Chatsworth, CA
Howard, Richard G. ....Atlantic, IA
Howard, Richard J. ....Kalamazoo, MI
Howard, Richard L. ....Walnut Creek, CA
Howard, Richard M. ....Jericho, NY
Howard, Richard Staunton, Jr. ....Vail, CO
Howard, Rick A. ....Montgomery, AL
Howard & Ridge ....Knoxville, TN
Howard, Robert ....Floral Park, NY
Howard, Robert A. ....Indianapolis, IN
Howard, Robert A. ....Anoka, MN
Howard, Robert C. ....St. Petersburg, FL
Howard, Robert C. ....Chicago, IL
Howard, Robert C., Jr. ....Scottsdale, AZ
Howard, Robert D. ....New York, NY
Howard, Robert E. ....Fort Lauderdale, FL
Howard, Robert E. ....Fort Lauderdale, FL
Howard, Robert E. ....Raleigh, NC
Howard, Robert E. ....Tulsa, OK
Howard, Robert K. ....Riverhead, NY
Howard, Robert L. ....Mount Prospect, IL
Howard, Robert L. ....Wichita, KS
Howard, Robert L. ....New York, NY
Howard, Robert L. ....Cambridge, WI
Howard, Robert, Law Office
Henniker, NH
Weare, NH
Howard, Robert M. ....San Diego, CA
Howard, Robert M. ....Denver, CO
Howard, Robert P., Jr. ....Washington, DC
Howard, Robert R., III ....Henniker, NH
Howard, Robert W. ....Hilton Head Island, SC
Howard, Robin Lustig ....Albuquerque, NM
Howard, Rod J. ....Palo Alto, CA
Howard, Rodney C. ....Chicago, IL
Howard, Roger D. ....Atlanta, GA
Howard, Roger H. ....Los Angeles, CA
Howard, Roland V., Sr. ....Merced, CA
Howard Rome Martin & Ridley LLP
Redwood City, CA
Howard, Ronald C. ....Oak Park, IL
Howard, Ronna D. ....Boston, MA
Howard & Rouse ....Phoenix, AZ
Tucson, AZ
Howard, Roy S. ....Broomfield, CO
Howard, S. Gregory ....Fowler, IN
Howard, Sallie Meade ....Frankfort, KY
Howard, Sally A. ....Lawrence, KS
Howard, Samuel A. ....Brevard, NC
Howard, Sandra L. ....Baltimore, MD
Howard, Sandra P. ....Traverse City, MI
Howard, Scarlett A. ....Edmond, OK
El Reno, OK
Howard, Schildknecht and Howard
Louisville, KY
Howard & Scott ....Atlanta, GA
Howard, Scott B. ....New York, NY
Howard, Scott H. ....Glendale, CA
Howard, Scott W. ....Traverse City, MI
Howard, Sean P. ....Merced, CA
Howard, Seymour ....New York, NY
Howard, Seymour S. ....Jericho, NY
Howard, Sharon Bowles ....Edmonton, KY
Howard, Sharon Effatt ....Atlanta, GA
Howard, Sharon S. ....Bellevue, WA
Howard, Sherry L. ....Chicago Heights, IL
Howard, Sheryl M. ....New Orleans, LA
Howard, Smith & Levin LLP
New York, NY
Howard, Solochek & Weber, S.C.
Milwaukee, WI
Howard, Stacie A. ....Sherman Oaks, CA
Howard, Stacy Marie ....Roseville, CA
Howard, Stallings, From & Hutson, P.A.
Cary, NC
New Bern, NC
Raleigh, NC
Research Triangle Park, NC
Howard, Stephen C. ....Orange, TX
Howard, Stephen E. ....Fort Collins, CO
Howard, Stephen G. ....Boston, MA
Howard, Stephen L. ....Providence, RI
Howard, Stephen M. ....Columbus, OH
Howard, Stephen W. ....Longview, TX
Howard, Steven C. ....Houston, TX
Howard, Steven D. ....Los Angeles, CA
Howard, Steven G. ....Newport, AR
Howard, Steven H. ....Omaha, NE
Howard, Steven P. ....Irvine, CA
Howard, Steven P. ....Plentywood, MT
Howard, Steven P. ....Staten Island, NY
Howard, Steven R. ....New York, NY
Howard, Stewart L. ....Mobile, AL
Howard & Stone ....Dundalk, MD
Howard, Susan ....Princeton, NJ
Howard, Susan A. ....Lansing, MI
Howard, Susan Carolyn ....Memphis, TN
Howard, Susan E. ....Toledo, OH

Howard, Susan Hering .... Tiffin, OH
Howard, Susan W. .... Los Altos, CA
Howard, Suzanne S. .... Jacksonville, FL
Howard, Tarek .... Fargo, ND
Howard, Ted R. .... Columbus, OH
Howard, Theodore A. .... Washington, DC
Howard, Theodore R., (A Professional Corporation) .... Santa Ana, CA
Howard, Theron E. .... Le Roy, NY
Howard, Thomas A. .... Southfield, MI
Howard, Thomas C. .... Phoenix, AZ
Howard, Thomas I. .... Edisto Island, SC
Walterboro, SC
Howard, Thomas J. .... Phoenix, AZ
Howard, Thomas L. .... Washington, DC
Howard, Thomas L. .... Jupiter, FL
Howard, Thomas L. .... Clarkston, MI
Howard, Thomas L., P.A. .... Jupiter, FL
Howard, Thomas P. .... Boston, MA
Howard, Thomas P. .... Racine, WI
Howard, Thomas R. .... Minneapolis, MN
Howard, Thomas S. .... Hackensack, NJ
New York, NY
Howard, Timothy J.
Palm Beach Gardens, FL
Howard, Timothy J. .... Peoria, IL
Howard, Timothy J. .... Cleveland, OH
Howard, Timothy J. .... Houston, TX
Howard, Timothy K. .... Minneapolis, MN
Howard, Timothy W. .... Clinton, NC
Howard, Timson & Stack .... Norwood, MA
Howard, Tracey Brice .... Las Vegas, NV
Howard, Tracy .... Miami, FL
Howard, Tracy L. .... Houston, TX
Howard, Vernice Britt .... Murfreesboro, NC
Howard, Victor C. .... Liberty, MO
Howard, Vincent K. .... Wausau, WI
Howard, Virgil .... Corpus Christi, TX
Howard, Virginia C. .... Tucson, AZ
Howard, W. Cliff .... Atlanta, GA
Howard, W. Edward, Jr. .... Lexington, SC
Howard, W. Ray .... Houston, TX
Howard, Wade T. .... Houston, TX
Howard & Walker .... Anderson, IN
Howard & Waller .... Lubbock, TX
Howard, Walter John, Jr. .... Garland, TX
Howard, Walter Kenneth, Jr. .... San Jose, CA
Howard, Wayne N. .... Phoenix, AZ
Howard, Wesley B., Jr. .... Denver, CO
Howard & Whatley, P.C. .... Savannah, GA
Howard and Widdows, P.C. .... Tulsa, OK
Howard, William .... Middletown, CT
Howard, William B. .... Houston, TX
Howard, William D. .... Grand Rapids, MI
Howard, William E. .... Akron, OH
Howard, William E. .... Port Townsend, WA
Howard, William F. .... Baltimore, MD
Howard, William F. .... Nashville, TN
Howard, William F., III .... Springfield, MA
Howard, William G. .... Olathe, KS
Howard, William H. .... Philadelphia, PA
Howard, William H., III
New Orleans, LA
Howard, William H. F. .... Piedmont, CA
Howard, William J. .... Phoenix, AZ
Howard, William J. .... Rockford, IL
Howard, William J. .... Hyattsville, MD
Howard, William J., Incorporated
Santa Ana, CA
Howard, William L. .... Jonesboro, AR
Howard, William L. .... Malvern, PA
Howard, William L. .... Charleston, SC
Howard, William M. .... Phoenix, AZ
Howard, William McNova, Jr.
Pine Bluff, AR
Howard, William N. .... Chicago, IL
Howard, William P. .... Enka, NC
Howard, William R., Jr. .... Oklahoma City, OK
Howard, William S. .... Lexington, KY
Howard, Winston S. .... Denver, CO
Howard, Wm. R. .... Lancaster, PA
Howard-Algarin, John A. .... Baltimore, MD
Howard-Duhon, Shannon
New Orleans, LA
Howard-Hand, Evelyn N. .... Austin, TX
Howard-Hodesh, Janine .... Cincinnati, OH
Howard-Martin, Jane .... Pittsburgh, PA
Howard-Smith, Richard H.
Charlottesville, VA
Howarter, Alan R. .... Ottawa, IL
Howarter, Wendy S. .... Oregon, IL
Howarth, Alan J. .... Sandy, UT
Howarth, Cooley R., Jr. .... Dayton, OH
Howarth, Don .... Los Angeles, CA
Howarth, James C. .... Detroit, MI
Howarth, James C., P.C. .... Detroit, MI
Howarth, Joan .... San Francisco, CA
Howarth, John S. .... Philadelphia, PA
Howarth, Kim A. .... Elkhorn, WI
Howarth Law Offices, S.C. .... Elkhorn, WI
Howarth, Liese Gallagher .... Haydenville, MA
Howarth, Marthy Brown .... Pittsburgh, PA
Howarth, Read S. .... Trenton, NJ
Howarth, Richard A., Jr. .... Elkhorn, WI
Howarth, Robert F. .... Columbus, OH
Howarth, Robert L. .... Hampden, MA
Howarth, Rodney L. .... Newark, OH
Howarth & Smith .... Los Angeles, CA
Howarth, Steven P. .... Fremont, CA
Howat, Andrew J. .... Hartford, CT
Howat, Bruce B., Jr. .... Chicago, IL
Howat, G. Gregory .... Toledo, OH
Howatt, Kimberly Diane .... San Diego, CA
Howatt, William J., Jr. .... San Diego, CA
Howayeck, Gary P. .... Fall River, MA
Howayeck, Renee .... Fall River, MA
Howbert, Edgar C. .... Detroit, MI
Howbert, Irving .... Colorado Springs, CO

Howd, Hadleigh H. .... Fort Lauderdale, FL
Howd, Jay B. .... Carbondale, IL
Howd, Lavieri & Finch, LLP
Winsted, CT
Howd & Ludorf .... Hartford, CT
Howden, Charles J. .... Madison, WI
Howden, Jonathan R. .... San Francisco, CA
Howdeshell, Christopher M.
Hattiesburg, MS
How-Downing, Lindsey
San Francisco, CA
Howdyshell, Donald E. .... Barberton, OH
Howdyshell, Walter J., (Co. L.P.A.)
New Lexington, OH
Howe, A. Berry .... Fort Thomas, KY
Howe & Addington LLP .... New York, NY
Howe, Alan R. .... Newark, NJ
Howe, Amy L. .... Washington, DC
Howe, Amy Schipper .... Boise, ID
Howe, Anderson & Steyer, P.C.
Washington, DC
Howe, Andrea Hilton .... Washington, DC
Howe, Andrew N. .... Reading, PA
Howe, Anne Berry .... New York, NY
Howe, Arthur G. .... Charleston, SC
Howe, Arthur J. .... Chicago, IL
Howe, Arvil R. .... South Bend, IN
Howe, Barbara .... Buffalo, NY
Howe, Barbara Kerr .... Towson, MD
Howe, Bonnie .... Denver, CO
Howe, Bradley B. .... Spencer, IA
Howe, Brian C. .... St. Louis, MO
Howe, Brian R. .... Newark, NJ
Howe, Brian V. .... St. Clair Shores, MI
Howe, Bruce R. .... Dickinson, ND
Howe, Carl E., Jr.
Department Of Veterans Affairs, Office of the General Counsel, GV
Howe, Carmi L. .... Dickinson, ND
Howe, Chester M. .... Winchester, MA
Howe, Christopher E. .... Fort Worth, TX
Howe, Christopher H. .... Fair Haven, VT
Howe, Clare M. .... Boston, MA
Howe, Claude H., III .... Clinton, SC
Howe, Clyde F. .... Raytown, MO
Howe, Craig H. .... Salt Lake City, UT
Howe, Cranston H. .... Fair Haven, VT
Howe, Cunningham & Lowe, P.L.C.
Des Moines, IA
Howe, Cynthia Graham
Myrtle Beach, SC
Howe, Cynthia J. .... Sudbury, MA
Howe, David .... Elmont, NY
Howe, David D. .... New York, NY
Howe, David E. .... Peoria, IL
Howe, David M. .... Concord, NH
Howe, David S. .... Syracuse, NY
Howe, Donald B., Jr. .... Douglasville, GA
Howe, Donald H. .... Charleston, SC
Howe, Drayton F., Jr. .... Emeryville, CA
San Francisco, CA
Howe, Earnest .... Fresno, CA
Howe, Edith C. .... Boston, MA
Howe, Edwin A., II .... Denver, CO
Howe, Edwin A., Jr. .... New York, NY
Howe, Edwin A., P.C., The Law Firm of
Denver, CO
Howe, Eunice S. .... Belmont, MA
Howe, F. Curtis .... Madison, NC
Howe, Faith S. .... Lawrence, KS
Howe, Frank E., III .... Shrewsbury, MA
Howe, Fred T. .... Kingston, PA
Howe, Garry Frank .... Houston, TX
Howe, Gary L. .... Monclova, OH
Howe, Gary R. .... Salt Lake City, UT
Howe, Gedney M., III .... Charleston, SC
Howe, Gedney M., III, P.A.
Charleston, SC
Howe, Gordon A., II .... Rochester, NY
Howe, Gregory A. .... Thousand Oaks, CA
Howe, Gregory J. .... Portland, OR
Howe, Gregory P. .... Newport, VT
Howe, Grover R. .... Ventura, CA
Howe, H. Evan .... Manhattan, KS
Howe, Hardy, Galloway & Maus, P.C.
Dickinson, ND
Howe, Harry L. .... Scottsdale, AZ
Howe, Harry L., P.C. .... Scottsdale, AZ
Howe, Helen M. .... Baltimore, MD
Howe, Henry H. .... Grand Forks, ND
Howe, Henry S. .... Gallup, NM
Howe, Howard .... Indianapolis, IN
Howe & Howe .... Fair Haven, VT
Howe & Hutton, Ltd. .... Washington, DC
Chicago, IL
Howe, Jack D. .... Gresham, OR
Howe, Jack G. .... Waxahachie, TX
Howe, James C. .... Portland, OR
Howe, James P. .... Crystal Lake, IL
Howe, Janice W. .... Boston, MA
Howe, Jas. Murray .... Boston, MA
Howe, Jay E. .... Greenfield, IA
Howe, Jeffrey G. .... Boise, ID
Howe, Jennifer J. .... Chicago, IL
Howe, Jerald S., Jr. .... Washington, DC
Howe, Jeremy W. .... Newport, RI
Howe, Jody L. .... Salt Lake City, UT
Howe, Joel Andrew .... Macon, GA
Howe, John E. .... Jefferson City, MO
Howe, John R. .... Tallahassee, FL
Howe, John T. .... Grand Junction, CO
Howe, John William .... Douglasville, GA
Howe, Jonathan T. .... Washington, DC
Chicago, IL
Howe, Joseph D. .... Phoenix, AZ
Howe, Joseph G., III .... Washington, DC
Howe, Karen L. .... Cortland, NY
Howe, Karl J. .... Marietta, GA

Howe, Karl J., P.C. .... Marietta, GA
Howe, Kenneth A. .... Cincinnati, OH
Howe, Kevin F. .... Des Moines, IA
Howe, Kevin P. .... Minneapolis, MN
Howe, Larry M. .... Syracuse, NY
Howe, Lawrence .... Winnetka, IL
Howe, Leslie M. .... Austin, TX
Howe, Linda N. .... Bridgeport, CT
Howe, Lise Courtney M.
Department of Energy, Office of the General Counsel, GV
Howe, Louise Nicholson .... Washington, DC
Howe, Marcia L. .... Farmington Hills, MI
Howe, Mark P. .... Washington, DC
Howe, Mark P. .... Green Bay, WI
Howe, Mark R. .... Santa Ana, CA
Howe, Marlynn P. .... Newport Beach, CA
Howe, Martha E. .... Lowell, MA
Howe, Marvin L. .... Glendive, MT
Howe, Mary Elizabeth ....
Treasury Department, GV
Howe, Michael D. .... Omak, WA
Howe, Michael P. .... Kansas City, MO
Howe, Miriam A. .... Treasury Department, Internal Revenue Service, GV
Howe, Nelson H., II .... St. Louis, MO
Howe, Noel C. .... Kirkland, WA
Howe & Olesen .... Greenfield, IA
Howe, Osmond C., Jr., (P.A.) .... Miami, FL
Howe, Patricia Bowman .... St. Louis, MO
Howe, Patrick M. .... San Diego, CA
Howe, Philip M. .... Quincy, MA
Howe, Ralph W., III .... Plainfield, VT
Howe, Randall M. .... Phoenix, AZ
Howe, Reginald H. .... Belmont, MA
Howe, Richard C. .... Salt Lake City, UT
Howe, Richard D. .... Des Moines, IA
Howe, Richard, Jr.
Federal Energy Regulatory Commission, Office of the General Counsel, GV
Howe, Richard K. .... Stonington, ME
Howe, Richard M. .... Marietta, GA
Howe, Richard M. .... Springfield, MA
Howe, Richard P. .... Lowell, MA
Howe, Richard R. .... Canton, MO
Howe, Richard R. .... New York, NY
Howe, Rita B. .... Shelburne, VT
Howe, Robert G. .... Charleston, SC
Howe, Robert L. .... Brooklyn, NY
Howe, Robert R. .... Beaverton, OR
Howe, Robinson & Watkins, LLP
Miami, FL
Howe, Ruth Baehr .... Springfield, MA
Howe, Ruth-Arlene W. .... Newton, MA
Howe, Scott W. .... Orange, CA
Howe & Seaworth .... Grand Forks, ND
Howe, Shannon M. .... Atlanta, GA
Howe, Sheryl L. .... Denver, CO
Howe, Shippen .... Washington, DC
Howe, Stephanie .... Houston, TX
Howe, Stephen G. .... Rockville, MD
Howe, Stephen W. .... Boston, MA
Howe, Steven G. .... San Diego, CA
Howe, Steven Greg .... Hartford, CT
Howe, Susan G. .... Portland, OR
Howe & Tanner .... Salt Lake City, UT
Howe, Theodore W. .... Cincinnati, OH
Howe, Thomas M. .... Ashland, KY
Howe, Thomas P. .... Olivette, MO
Howe, Thomas P. .... Portland, OR
Howe, Thomas R. .... Shakopee, MN
Howe, Thomas R. .... Blue Bell, PA
Howe, Thomas W. .... Universal City, TX
Howe, Valerie L. .... Princeton, NJ
Howe, Victoria M. .... Washington, DC
Howe, Waring S., Jr. .... Charleston, SC
Howe, Waters & Carpenter, P.A.
Hendersonville, NC
Howe, William B. W. .... Hendersonville, NC
Howe, William D. .... Cincinnati, OH
Howe, William E. .... Sweetwater, TN
Howe, William H. .... Washington, DC
Howe, William J., III .... Portland, OR
Howe, Wilson C. .... Suwanee, GA
Howe & Wyndham, L.L.P.
Charleston, SC
Howe-Fernandez, Karen .... Bloomington, IN
Howe-Gebers, Gwen K.
Bowling Green, OH
Howell, A. Del .... Birmingham, AL
Howell, A. Peter .... Honolulu, HI
Howell, A. Peter, A Law Corporation
Honolulu, HI
Howell, Alfred G. .... Honesdale, PA
Howell, Alfred J. .... Honesdale, PA
Howell, Andrew L. .... Atlanta, GA
Howell, Armand J. .... Calabasas, CA
Simi Valley, CA
Howell, Arthur .... Atlanta, GA
Howell, Arthur, III .... Atlanta, GA
Howell, Bart L. .... McAlester, OK
Howell, Baxter C. .... Albany, GA
Howell, Belinda Manning .... Austin, TX
Houston, TX
Howell, Ben Burke .... Philadelphia, PA
Howell, Beryl A. .... United States Senate, Committee Legal Personnel, GV
Howell, Bobby L. .... Texarkana, TX
Howell, Brett A. .... Kalamazoo, MI
Howell, Brian E. .... Waco, TX
Howell, Brian G. .... Hammonton, NJ
Howell, Brian G., P.C. .... Hammonton, NJ
Howell & Britt .... Texarkana, TX
Howell, Bruce F. .... Dallas, TX
Howell, Byron L. .... Otis, CO
Howell, C. David .... Park Ridge, IL
Howell, Carl, Jr. .... Hodgenville, KY
Howell, Carl, Jr., P.S.C. .... Hodgenville, KY

Howell, Chanley T. .... Jacksonville, FL
Howell, Charles Ben .... Dallas, TX
Howell, Charles Cook, III
Jacksonville, FL
Howell, Charles T.
House of Representatives, Committee on House Administration, GV
Howell, Christopher S. .... Washington, DC
Howell, Clewell, Jr. .... Towson, MD
Howell, Clifton L., Jr. .... Winter Haven, FL
Howell, Courtney .... Louisville, KY
Howell, Courtney R. .... Louisville, KY
Howell, D. Clayton .... Atlanta, GA
Howell, Danny M. .... McLean, VA
Howell, Daugherty & Brown .... Norfolk, VA
Howell, David F. .... Midwest City, OK
Howell, David R. .... Jacksonville, FL
Howell, David W. .... Dallas, TX
Howell, Debby L. .... Costa Mesa, CA
Howell, Deneen C. .... Washington, DC
Howell, Denise M. .... Los Angeles, CA
Howell, Dennis L. .... Burnsville, NC
Howell, Dennis L., P.A. .... Burnsville, NC
Howell, Dennis P. .... Monterey, CA
Howell, Diana R. .... Kansas City, MO
Howell, Dixon R. .... San Jose, CA
Howell, Donald D. .... Knoxville, TN
Howell, Donald L. .... Houston, TX
Howell, Donald W. .... Atlantic Beach, FL
Howell, Donna Wolff .... Atlanta, GA
Howell, Dorman, Anderson, Berg & Smyer, L.L.P. .... Fort Worth, TX
Howell, Dorothy J. .... South Royalton, VT
Howell, Douglas W., III .... Bryan, TX
Howell, Douglas W., Jr. .... Bryan, TX
Howell, Edward J. .... Sherman Oaks, CA
Howell, Edward S. .... Houston, TX
Howell, Eileen J. .... Riverside, CA
Howell, Eric B. .... Irvine, CA
Howell, Evan Park, III .... New Orleans, LA
Howell & Fisher, PLLC .... Nashville, TN
Howell, F. J., Jr. .... Little Rock, AR
Howell, Gary M. .... Houston, TX
Howell, Gary W. .... Chicago, IL
Howell, Gary W. .... Lapeer, MI
Howell, Geoffrey A. .... Boston, MA
Howell, George B., III .... Tampa, FL
Howell, George C. .... Ashland, KY
Howell, George C., III .... Richmond, VA
Howell, George H. .... Prattville, AL
Howell, George L. .... Atlanta, GA
Howell, Georgena .... Columbus, OH
Howell, Gibson and Hughes, P.A.
Beaufort, SC
Charleston, SC
Howell, Gordon K. .... Chatom, AL
Mobile, AL
Howell & Greer .... Birmingham, AL
Howell, Griffin E., III .... Griffin, GA
Howell & Haferkamp, L.C.
St. Louis, MO
Howell, Harold .... Prattville, AL
Howell, Hubert W. .... Fayetteville, GA
Howell, J. Mark .... Fort Worth, TX
Howell, Jack H. .... Columbus, OH
Howell & Jackson, PLLC .... Nashville, TN
Howell, James A. .... Los Angeles, CA
Howell, James C. .... Saginaw, MI
Howell, James C. .... Norfolk, VA
Howell, James D. .... Matthews, NC
Howell, James F. .... Midwest City, OK
Howell, James F., & Associates
Midwest City, OK
Howell, James Fleet .... Shreveport, LA
Howell, James G. .... Covington, LA
Howell, James P. .... Tucson, AZ
Howell, James R. .... Wichita, KS
Howell, James S.S., Law Offices of
Atlanta, GA
Howell, Jamie W., Jr. .... Southaven, MS
Howell, Jane H. .... Honolulu, HI
Howell, Jason Glenn .... Chattanooga, TN
Howell, Jay C. .... Jacksonville Beach, FL
Howell, Jay D., Jr. .... Houston, TX
Howell, Jeffrey J. .... Reading, PA
Howell, Jennifer R. .... Punta Gorda, FL
Howell, J. F." Jack ", III .... Amarillo, TX
Howell, Joel W., III .... Jackson, MS
Howell, John A. .... Washington, DC
Howell, John B. .... Sheboygan Falls, WI
Howell, John C. .... Morristown, NJ
Howell, John C. .... San Antonio, TX
Howell, John E. .... Washington, DC
Howell, John E. .... Meridian, MS
Howell, John E. .... Dallas, TX
Howell, John G., III .... Fairfield, CT
Howell, John M. .... St. Louis, MO
Howell, John M. .... Cincinnati, OH
Howell, John M. .... Salem, OR
Howell, John Moffitt .... Jacksonville, FL
Howell, John P. .... Covington, GA
Howell, John P. .... Dallas, TX
Howell, John R. .... Pasadena, CA
Howell, John R. .... Hattiesburg, MS
Howell, John W. .... Orlando, FL
Howell, Johnston & Langford .... Mobile, AL
Howell, Joseph A. .... La Jolla, CA
Howell, Joseph A., Jr. .... Singer Island, FL
Howell, Joseph Robert, Jr.
Salt Lake City, UT
Howell, Joseph T. .... Wendell, NC
Howell, Joshua M. .... Marion, IN
Howell, Joyce A. .... Philadelphia, PA
Howell, Julie C .... Huntsville, TX
Howell, Julius A. .... Winston-Salem, NC
Howell, Kathryn R. .... Chicago, IL
Howell, Kenneth C. .... Jacksonville Beach, FL
Howell, Kenneth C. .... Boise, ID

Howell, Kenneth C. ... Detroit, MI
Howell, Kenneth W. ... San Antonio, TX
Howell, Kevin M. ... Poulsbo, WA
Howell & Krause ... Honesdale, PA
Howell, Kristen ... St. Louis, MO
Howell, Ladson F. ... Beaufort, SC
Howell, Laura ... Treasury Department, Internal Revenue Service, GV
Howell, Laura K. ... Raleigh, NC
Howell, Laurie ... Alameda, CA
Howell, Leanne Saloom ... New Orleans, LA
Howell, Lee, III ... Jackson, MS
Howell, Leigh M. ... San Jose, CA
Howell, Lembhard G. ... Seattle, WA
Howell, Lembhard G., P.S., Law Offices of ... Seattle, WA
Howell, Leonard ... Midland, TX
Howell, Leslie M. ... Atlanta, GA
Howell, Linda A. ... Department Of Veterans Affairs, Board of Veterans Appeals, GV
Howell, Linda S. ... Grand Haven, MI
Holland, MI
Howell, Lori Armbrust ... Eliot, ME
Howell, Louis P. ... Spartanburg, SC
Howell, Lynn Ann ... Burton, MI
Howell, M. Melanie ... Oroville, CA
Howell, Mabel Grey ... Pasadena, TX
Howell, Maria F. ... Baltimore, MD
Howell, Mark S. ... San Francisco, CA
Howell, Mary E. ... New Orleans, LA
Howell, Matthew L. ... Mesa, AZ
Howell, Matthew R. ... Salt Lake City, UT
Howell, Max ... Little Rock, AR
Howell, Maxwell A., Jr. ... Rockville, MD
Howell, Michael B. ... Boise, ID
Howell, Michael G. ... Raleigh, NC
Howell, Michael R. ... Sparta, IL
Howell Moore & Gough, L.L.P. ... Santa Barbara, CA
Howell, Nancy ... Birmingham, AL
Howell & O'Neal ... Jacksonville, FL
Howell, Pamela J. ... Boulder, CO
Howell, Patrick B. ... Milwaukee, WI
Howell, Patrick C. ... Orlando, FL
Howell, Paul A., Jr. ... Atlanta, GA
Howell, Paul B. ... Gulfport, MS
Howell, Paul E. ... Celina, OH
Howell, Paul R. ... Costa Mesa, CA
Howell, P. B., Jr., (P.A.) ... Leesburg, FL
Howell, R. Boatner ... Centreville, MS
Howell, R. Nachael ... Fort Worth, TX
Howell, R. Thomas, Jr. ... Chicago, IL
Howell, Ralph Wyatt, Jr. ... Hamilton, AL
Howell, Reese S. ... Salt Lake City, UT
Howell, Richard K. ... Costa Mesa, CA
Howell, Richard L. ... Dallas, TX
Howell, Richard L., P.C., The Law Offices of ... Dallas, TX
Howell, Richard M. ... Greenville, OH
Howell, Richard T., Jr. ... Houston, TX
Howell, Robert C. ... Austin, TX
Howell, Robert D. ... Atlanta, GA
Howell, Robert I. ... Austin, TX
Howell, Robert Lyndon ... Fairfax, VA
Howell, Robert Preston ... Charleston, WV
Howell, Roberta F. ... Madison, WI
Howell, Ronald, P.A. ... Longwood, FL
Howell, Ronald R. ... Longwood, FL
Howell, Ronald W. ... Burnsville, NC
Howell, Ronald W., P.A. ... Asheville, NC
Burnsville, NC
Howell, Ronnie Allen ... Memphis, TN
Howell, Roy A., III ... Charleston, SC
Howell, Roy C. ... Washington, DC
Howell, Russell D. ... Houston, TX
Howell, S. Janice ... Department of the Army, Office, Chief of Engineers/Headquarters, U.S. Army Corps of Engineers, GV
Howell, S. Kent ... Oxford, MS
Howell, Sabina I. ... Harrisburg, PA
Howell, Samuel W., IV ... Charleston, SC
Howell, Sarto & Howell ... Prattville, AL
Howell, Shaun Barbara Ann ... Bountiful, UT
Howell, Shepherd L. ... Cartersville, GA
Howell, Sheryl L. ... Palo Alto, CA
Howell, Shirley Darby ... Montgomery, AL
Howell, Sidney P. ... Salem, SC
Howell, Stephen C. ... Fort Worth, TX
Howell, Stephen J. ... Ames, IA
Howell, Stephen Q. ... San Francisco, CA
Howell, Steven G. ... Detroit, MI
Howell, Steven J. ... Oroville, CA
Howell, Sue ... Greensboro, NC
Howell, Susan E. ... Forest, MS
Howell, Synder ... Marion, IL
Howell, T. Anthony ... Stamford, CT
Howell & Talkington, L.L.C. ... Montgomery, AL
Howell, Taylor & Duggan ... Leesburg, FL
Tavares, FL
Howell, Terry R. ... Atlanta, GA
Howell, Thomas G. ... Department of Commerce, Patent and Trademark Office, GV
Howell, Thomas J. ... Dallas, TX
Howell, Thomas M. ... Fort Myers, FL
Howell, Thomas Pitchlynn, IV ... Oklahoma City, OK
Howell, Thomas R. ... Washington, DC
Howell & Thornhill ... Winter Haven, FL
Howell, Tim E. ... Little Rock, AR
Howell, Timothy D. ... Fort Worth, TX
Howell, T. O., Jr. ... Mobile, AL
Howell, Todd R. ... Los Angeles, CA
Santa Maria, CA
Howell, Torrence L. ... Covina, CA
Howell, Tracy T. ... Albuquerque, NM
Howell, Trent A. ... Albuquerque, NM
Howell, Trent L. ... Water Valley, MS
Howell, Trevor W. ... Nashville, TN
Howell, Trice & Hope, P.A. ... Conway, AR
Little Rock, AR
Howell, Velveta Golightly ... Denver, CO
Howell, Virginia H. ... St. Louis, MO
Howell, W. Craig ... Omaha, NE
Howell, W. Kerry ... Macon, GA
Howell, Warren E. ... Pasadena, CA
Howell, Watson M., Jr. ... Austin, TX
Howell, Watson M., Jr., P.C. ... Austin, TX
Howell, Wayne ... Westfield, NJ
Howell, Weldon U., Jr. ... Santa Barbara, CA
Howell, Wesley G., Jr. ... Los Angeles, CA
New York, NY
Howell, William Ashley, III ... Birmingham, AL
Howell, William B. ... Ridgeland, MS
Howell, William B., Ltd. ... Ridgeland, MS
Howell, William D. ... Dover, TN
Howell, William E. ... Wakefield, MA
Howell, William H. ... Manvel, TX
Howell, William J. ... San Diego, CA
Howell, William J. ... Fredericksburg, VA
Howell, William J., Jr. ... Miami, FL
Howell, William L. ... Mobile, AL
Howell, William L., P.A. ... Mobile, AL
Howell, William M. ... Jacksonville, FL
Howell, William R. ... Indianapolis, IN
Howell, William R. ... New York, NY
Howell, William S. ... Thousand Oaks, CA
Howell, William S., Jr. ... Destin, FL
Howell, William T. ... Walterboro, SC
Howell-Baxter, Kathryn ... New York, NY
Howell III, Earl S. ... Chattanooga, TN
Howell-Maillet, Janet K. ... Bishop, CA
Howells, Dana D. ... Los Angeles, CA
Howells, George A. ... Sarasota, FL
Sandusky, OH
Howells, Louise A. ... Houston, TX
Howen, Stephen D. ... Dallas, TX
Howenstein, Christian B. ... Columbus, OH
Hower, Dennis R. ... Minnetonka, MN
Hower, Henry ... Tampa, FL
Hower, John A. ... Englewood, CO
Hower, Mary V. ... St. Joseph, MO
Hower, Thomas R. ... Trenton, NJ
Hower, Ward E. ... Cascade, ID
Howerton, Donald P. ... Tulsa, OK
Howerton, E. Kay ... Muskogee, OK
Howerton, Herman H. ... San Francisco, CA
Howerton & Howerton ... Greensboro, NC
Howerton, Hugh James ... Houston, TX
Howerton, J. William ... Paducah, KY
Howerton & Jantz ... Garnett, KS
Howerton, Joy ... Smithfield, NC
Howerton, Kent C. ... Federal Trade Commission, Bureau of Consumer Protection, GV
Howerton, Lynn ... McAllen, TX
Howerton, Michael C. ... Muskogee, OK
Howerton, Robert H. ... Marion, IL
Howerton, Vernon C., Jr. ... Dallas, TX
Howerton, Z. H., Jr. ... Greensboro, NC
Howery, W. Michael ... Salt Lake City, UT
Howes & Anderson, P.C. ... Des Moines, IA
Howes, Bradford Ted ... New York, NY
Howes, Brian T. ... Kansas City, MO
Howes, Constance A. ... Providence, RI
Howes, David A. ... Pittsburgh, PA
Howes, Davis C. ... New Bedford, MA
Howes, Dwight A. ... Pittsburgh, PA
Howes, G. Paul ... San Diego, CA
Howes, Harrison S. ... Columbia, SC
Howes, James D. ... Louisville, KY
Howes, John R. ... Fort Lauderdale, FL
Howes, John R., A Professional Association ... Fort Lauderdale, FL
Howes, Kelley Abbott ... Denver, CO
Howes Law Firm, P.C. ... Cedar Rapids, IA
Howes, Loretta M. ... West Hatfield, MA
Howes, Margaret M. K. ... Chapel Hill, NC
Howes, Mark W. ... Marietta, GA
Howes, Oliver P., Jr. ... New York, NY
Howes, Philip E. ... Canton, OH
Howes, Ralph F. ... La Porte, IN
Howes, Richard J. ... Des Moines, IA
Howes, Robert C. ... Statesville, NC
Howes, Shirley E. ... North Canton, OH
Howes, Steven E. ... Cedar Rapids, IA
Howes, Timothy J. ... Springfield, MA
Howes, William G., III ... Hyannis, MA
Howeth, Allan ... Fort Worth, TX
Howeth, Jefferson E. ... Dallas, TX
Howeth, Jerry W. ... Austin, TX
Howett, John C., Jr. ... Harrisburg, PA
Howett, Kissinger & Miles, P.C. ... Harrisburg, PA
Howett, Timothy M. ... Sherman Oaks, CA
Howey, Cynthia J. ... Seattle, WA
Howey, John K. ... Woodhaven, MI
Howey-Fox, Wanda ... Yankton, SD
Howg, Lyle C., Jr. ... Richfield, MN
Howick & Associates ... Oklahoma City, OK
Howick, Jodi L. ... Salt Lake City, UT
Howick, Karen L. ... Oklahoma City, OK
Howick, Susan L. ... Atlanta, GA
Howicz, James J. ... Lake Forest, IL
Howicz, Jim ... Riverwoods, IL
Howie, Andrew B. ... Des Moines, IA
Howie, Brian A. ... Washington, DC
Howie, Bruce G. ... St. Petersburg, FL
Howie, Clinton D. ... Baton Rouge, LA
Howie, Donald L. W. ... Patchogue, NY
Howie, Homer Lee ... Jackson, MS
Howie, Irene E. ... Annandale, VA
Howie, James E., Jr. ... Oak Park, IL
Howie, John R. ... Dallas, TX
Howie, Julie N. ... Chicago, IL
Howie, Katherine L. ... Hattiesburg, MS
Howie, Long, La Force & Smith ... Burlingame, CA
El Cerrito, CA
San Francisco, CA
San Jose, CA
San Mateo, CA
Walnut Creek, CA
Howie, Margaret-Ann F. ... Towson, MD
Howie, Mary M. ... Salem, NH
Howie, Robert G. ... Burlingame, CA
San Francisco, CA
San Jose, CA
Howie, Robert M. ... Seattle, WA
Howie, S. Mitchell ... Huntsville, AL
Howie, Scott D. ... Irvine, CA
Howie, Scott Langford ... Chicago, IL
Howie & Sweeney, L.L.P. ... Dallas, TX
Howie, Tami J. ... Washington, DC
Baltimore, MD
Howie, Teresa A. ... Washington, DC
Howie, Thomas E. ... Flint, MI
Howie, Timothy E. ... Lanham, MD
Howington, Joseph W. ... Claremont, CA
Howington, Richard B. ... Winston-Salem, NC
Howison, Gregory M. ... Dallas, TX
Howison & Handley, L.L.P. ... Dallas, TX
Howison, Robert C., Jr. ... Raleigh, NC
Howison, William C. ... Pasadena, CA
Howison, William H. ... Portland, ME
Howitson, Mark S. ... San Jose, CA
Howitt, Ann A. ... Los Angeles, CA
Howitt, David M. ... Beaverton, OR
Howitt, Deborah F. ... Boston, MA
Howitt, Deborah Fran ... Albany, NY
Howitt, Harvey M. ... Detroit, MI
Howitt, Idelle Anne ... New York, NY
Howitt, John P. ... New York, NY
Howitt, Stanley ... Anchorage, AK
Howitt, Walter W. ... East Aurora, NY
Howkins, John H. ... Atlanta, GA
Howland, Amy DeLaplace ... Phoenix, AZ
Howland, Bixler W. ... Louisville, KY
Howland, Bixler W., P.S.C. ... Louisville, KY
Howland, Brian G. ... Jenkintown, PA
Howland, Charles B., Jr. ... Philadelphia, PA
Howland, Charles S. ... Cardington, OH
Mt. Gilead, OH
Howland, Christian G. ... Bakersfield, CA
Howland, David C. ... Atlanta, GA
Howland, David R., Law Offices of ... Coral Gables, FL
Howland, David R., Law Offices of ... Miami, FL
Howland, Eric J. ... Greenville, NC
Howland, Gary M. ... Marysville, KS
Howland, Glenn C. ... Montpelier, VT
Howland, Hess, Guinan & Torpey ... Huntingdon Valley, PA
Howland, Hollis ... Mt. Gilead, OH
Howland, Jeffrey C. ... Winston-Salem, NC
Howland, John E. ... Tulsa, OK
Howland, John P. ... Claremont, CA
Newport Beach, CA
Howland, John R. ... Huntingdon Valley, PA
Howland, Kimberly N. ... Jackson, MS
Howland, Kinnaird ... Providence, RI
Howland, Lori ... Mesa, AZ
Howland, Lori L. ... Birmingham, AL
Howland, Michael ... Des Moines, IA
Howland, Neil ... Saugus, MA
Howland, Nicole ... Columbia, PA
Howland, Patricia L. ... New York, NY
Howland, Richard M. ... Amherst, MA
Howland, Richard M., The Legal Infirmary ... Amherst, MA
Howland, Robert Holmes ... Trenton, NJ
Howland, Roger W. ... Fort Thomas, KY
Howland, Ronald L. ... Oklahoma City, OK
Howland, Wilfred G. ... Sun City Center, FL
Howland, William L. ... Lincoln, NE
Howland, William Lee ... Portsmouth, OH
Howland-Butler, Ann ... Oklahoma City, OK
Howle, C. Wayne ... Carson City, NV
Howle, Jack D., Jr. ... Sumter, SC
Howle, Jeffrey A. ... Gastonia, NC
Howle, Lisa Pinkos ... Grosse Pointe Woods, MI
Howle, Newton I., Jr. ... Darlington, SC
Howlett & Associates, Ltd. ... Elmhurst, IL
Howlett, Bobby L., Jr. ... Norfolk, VA
Howlett, David B. ... Department of the Army, U.S. Army Legal Services Agency, GV
Howlett, Fred J. ... Warren, NJ
Howlett, H.L." Hank " ... San Diego, CA
Howlett, James L. ... Bloomfield Hills, MI
Howlett, Jane F. ... Bristol, RI
Howlett, John E. ... Elmhurst, IL
Howlett, Melanie J. ... Stamford, CT
Howlett, Michael J., Jr. ... Chicago, IL
Howlett, Oscar D. ... Portland, OR
Howlett, Rupert F. ... Montclair, NJ
Howlett, Timothy H. ... Detroit, MI
Howley, Corinne L. ... Department Of Health And Human Services, Food & Drug Administration, GV
Howley, David A. ... Boston, MA
Howley, Edward J. ... West Hartford, CT
Howley & Howley-Westwater ... Quincy, MA
Howley, J. Waide ... Old Saybrook, CT
Howley, James M. ... Scranton, PA
Howley, John ... Poughkeepsie, NY
Howley, John J. ... Rockaway Park, NY
Howley, John J. P. ... New York, NY
Howley, Kevin J. ... Milwaukee, WI
Howley, Loren B. ... Charleston, WV
Howley, Michael J. ... Plattsburgh, NY
Howley, Patrick J. ... Washington, DC
Howley, Robert John ... Quincy, MA
Howley, Sean M. ... Portland, OR
Howley, Susan Smith ... Rockville, MD
Howley, Thomas A. ... Houston, TX
Howley and Venezia ... Charleston, WV
Howley-Westwater, Julie ... Quincy, MA
Howorth, Andrew K. ... New Albany, MS
Oxford, MS
Howorth, Charles L., Jr. ... Nashville, TN
Howorth, Claire A. ... Woburn, MA
Howorth, David B. ... Portland, OR
Howorth, H. Philip ... Nashua, NH
Howorth, Laura Stewart ... University, MS
Howrani, Faris A. ... Lansing, MI
Howren, Donald R. ... Richmond, VA
Howrey, Edward F. ... Washington, DC
Howrey & Simon ... Los Angeles, CA
Menlo Park, CA
Washington, DC
Howry, Melvin A. ... Woodland Hills, CA
Howry, Randy R. ... Austin, TX
Howry, Scott D. ... Bakersfield, CA
Howryla, Gloria M. ... Las Vegas, NV
Howsare, Daniel Lee ... Bedford, PA
Howse, G. Craig ... Brooklyn Center, MN
Howse, Kristin L. ... Aspen, CO
Howser & Brown, A Professional Corporation ... Newport Beach, CA
Howser, Fred A. ... Newport Beach, CA
Howser, Hugh C. ... Nashville, TN
Howser, Hugh C., Jr. ... Nashville, TN
Howser, Newman & Besley, L.L.C. ... Columbia, SC
Howser, R. Davis ... Columbia, SC
Howser, Richard G. ... Chicago, IL
Howser, Thomas C. ... Ashland, OR
Howser, Thomas C., P.C. ... Ashland, OR
Howsley, Richard T. ... Vancouver, WA
Howsmon, Susan E. ... West Palm Beach, FL
Howson, Arthur L., Jr. ... Greenville, SC
Howson, Christine E. ... Irvine, CA
Howson, Debra A. ... Palm Coast, FL
Howson & Howson ... Philadelphia, PA
Spring House, PA
Howson, Hubert F. ... Hartford, CT
Howson, John A. ... Chappaqua, NY
Howson, Walter Y. ... Devon, PA
Howton, David T. ... Chicago, IL
Howze, Ethel O. Reatha ... Decatur, AL
Howze, J. Wesley, Jr. ... Melbourne, FL
Howze, Karen Aileen ... Silver Spring, MD
Howze, Karen Aileen, P.C. ... Silver Spring, MD
Howze, Patricia J. ... San Francisco, CA
Howzell, Terence J. ... San Francisco, CA
Hoxie, Herbert E. ... Racine, WI
Hoxie, Joel P. ... Phoenix, AZ
Hoxie, John K. ... San Diego, CA
Hoxie, Kerry ... San Diego, CA
Hoxie, Timothy G. ... San Francisco, CA
Hoxsie, G. Gordon, Jr. ... Salt Lake City, UT
Hoxsie, Kenneth A. ... Boston, MA
Hoy, Carleton R. ... Sioux Falls, SD
Hoy, Colleen M. ... San Francisco, CA
Hoy, David E. ... Oak Park, IL
Hoy, David E. ... Alexandria, VA
Hoy, David R. ... Reno, NV
Hoy, Debbra L. ... Roca, NE
Hoy, Donald A. ... Ankeny, IA
Hoy, Douglas Richard ... Burlington, NC
Hoy, Edmund C. ... Pasadena, CA
Hoy, Edmund C., A Prof Corp., Law Offices of ... Pasadena, CA
Hoy, Gilbert R., Jr. ... Chestnut Hill, MA
Hoy, Gordon W. ... Durand, MI
Hoy & Hoy ... Sioux Falls, SD
Hoy, James L. ... Sioux Falls, SD
Hoy, Jane M. ... Stone Harbor, NJ
Hoy, Jason J. ... Indianapolis, IN
Hoy, John J. ... West Palm Beach, FL
Hoy, Judson ... Cincinnati, OH
Hoy, Justin E. ... New York, NY
Hoy, Kelly Montgomery ... Cleveland, OH
Hoy, Kristina M. ... Chicago, IL
Hoy, Matthew H. ... Lawrence, KS
Hoy, Michael D. ... Reno, NV
Hoy, Michael J. ... Oak Brook, IL
Hoy, Michelle L. ... Rancho Cucamonga, CA
Hoy, Pamela E. ... Pittsburgh, PA
Hoy, Peter J. ... Milton, MA
Hoy, Robert G. ... West Fargo, ND
Hoy, Robert H., Jr. ... El Paso, TX
Hoy, Robert L. ... Milton, MA
Hoy, Robert V. ... Lewiston, ME
Hoy, Scott G. ... Sioux Falls, SD
Hoy, Scott, Trial Lawyers, P.C. ... Sioux Falls, SD
Hoy, Susan ... Atlanta, GA
Hoy, Suzanne H. ... Columbus, OH
Hoy, Thomas A. ... Louisville, KY
Hoy, Timothy A. ... Harrisburg, PA
Hoy, Valentine S., VIII ... San Diego, CA
Hoy, William A. ... Amarillo, TX
Hoy, William A., IV ... Chicago, IL
Hoy, William T. ... Laguna Niguel, CA
Hoya, Thomas W. ... Environmental Protection Agency, Office of Administrative Law Judges, GV
Hoybach, Frederick W. ... Fairfax, VA
Hoychick, John B. ... Rayville, LA
Hoychick, John, Jr. ... Rayville, LA
Hoychick, M. Terrance, (A Professional Law Corporation) ... Eunice, LA

Hoye, Brian M. .... Los Angeles, CA
Hoye, Daniel B. .... San Francisco, CA
Hoye & Hoye .... Gloversville, NY
Hoye, John R., Jr. .... Uniontown, PA
Hoye, Maria Pilar .... Los Angeles, CA
Hoye, Polly .... Gloversville, NY
Hoye, Theodore E., Jr. .... Gloversville, NY
Hoyer, David Andrew .... Charleston, WV
Hoyer, Gary L. .... Fort Madison, IA
Hoyer, Gary, Law Firm, P.L.C.
Fort Madison, IA
Hoyer, Hoyer, Smith & Miesner
Charleston, WV
Hoyer, Judy Schropp .... St. Petersburg, FL
Tampa, FL
Hoyer, Kevin L. .... Akron, CO
Hoyer, Mark A. .... Greensburg, PA
Pittsburgh, PA
Hoyer, Ralph W. .... Charleston, WV
Hoyer, Richard A. .... San Francisco, CA
Hoyer, Steny Hamilton .... Mitchellville, MD
Hoyer, Stephen Patrick .... Charleston, WV
Hoyer, W. Christian .... St. Petersburg, FL
Tampa, FL
Hoyerman, Richard S. .... Sister Bay, WI
Sturgeon Bay, WI
Hoyert, Robert S. .... Lanham, MD
Hoyert & Yoho, Chartered .... Lanham, MD
Hoying, Fred H. .... Madison, IN
Hoyl, Basil L., Jr. .... Bedford, TX
Hoyl, Ron J. .... Dallas, TX
Hoyland, Robert M. .... Baton Rouge, LA
Hoyle, Alison D. .... Philadelphia, PA
Hoyle, Barry L. .... Erwin, NC
Hoyle, Brian T. .... Longview, TX
Hoyle, Catherine N. .... Chicago, IL
Hoyle, Clifford D. .... Ansonia, CT
Hoyle, D. Robert .... Bradenton, FL
Hoyle, Heather A. .... Walnut Creek, CA
Hoyle, Jeffrey P. .... King Of Prussia, PA
Media, PA
Hoyle, John C. .... Department of Justice,
Civil Division, GV
Hoyle, Kenneth R. .... Sanford, NC
Hoyle, Larry Glenn .... Gastonia, NC
Hoyle, Lawrence G. .... Canton, MA
Hoyle, Lawrence T., Jr. .... Philadelphia, PA
Hoyle, Michael Lwayne .... De Valls Bluff, AR
Hoyle, Morris & Kerr LLP
Philadelphia, PA
Hoyle, Peggy A. .... Washington, DC
Hoyle, Robin L. .... Orlando, FL
Hoyle, William R. .... Greensboro, NC
Hoyle, William S. .... Rocky Mount, NC
Hoyle, William V. .... Newport News, VA
Hoyle, William V., Jr. .... Newport News, VA
Hoyle, William V., Jr., P.C. .... Hampton, VA
Newport News, VA
Norfolk, VA
Hoyle-Payne, Connie F. .... Rock Hill, SC
Hoyler, Robert C. .... Cohasset, MA
Hoylman, Barbara Nestor .... Columbus, OH
Hoylman, Brad M. .... New York, NY
Hoyman, John F. .... Greeley, CO
Hoyman, John R. .... Indianola, IA
Hoyman, William, Jr. .... Pennsville, NJ
Hoyme, Christopher E. .... Omaha, NE
Hoynacki, Jan J. .... New York, NY
Hoyne, Andrew T. .... St. Louis, MO
Hoyne, Scott W. .... Chicago, IL
Hoyne, Stephen D. .... St. Louis, MO
Hoynes, Louis L., Jr. .... Madison, NJ
Hoyng, Charles F. .... San Francisco, CA
Hoyns, John K. .... New York, NY
Hoyos, Gustavo Andres .... New York, NY
Hoyos, Maria T. .... Miami, FL
Hoysa, Walter A. .... Chula Vista, CA
Hoyt, Anastasia Swiatek .... Los Angeles, CA
Rancho Cucamonga, CA
Hoyt, Angela Rae .... Houston, TX
Hoyt, Anne R. .... Hartford, CT
Moosup, CT
Hoyt & Blewett .... Great Falls, MT
Hoyt, Bradley M. .... Atlanta, GA
Hoyt, Brendan L., Jr. .... Reading, MA
Hoyt, Brooks P. .... Tampa, FL
Hoyt, Bruce A. .... Babylon, NY
Hoyt, Carolyn S. .... Bloomington, IL
Hoyt, Chadwick A. .... Chicago, IL
Hoyt, Charles E. .... Fairfax, VA
Hoyt, Charlotte W. .... Walden, NY
Hoyt, Daniel R. .... Chicago, IL
Hoyt, David A. .... Carroll, IA
Grand Junction, IA
Jefferson, IA
Hoyt, David E. .... Newton, MA
Hoyt, David J. .... New York, NY
Hoyt, Donald B. .... York, PA
Hoyt, Douglas R. .... New Rochelle, NY
Hoyt, Drew W. .... Boston, MA
Hoyt, Elizabeth E. .... Menlo Park, CA
Hoyt, Elizabeth Jane .... St. Louis, MO
Hoyt, Eugene R. .... Houston, TX
Hoyt, Everett E. .... Rapid City, SD
Hoyt, F. Timothy, Jr. .... Minnetonka, MN
Hoyt, Forrest T. .... Scottsdale, AZ
Hoyt, Francis C., Jr. .... West Des Moines, IA
Hoyt, Frederick J. .... Oklahoma City, OK
Hoyt, Garth G. .... Wayne, PA
Hoyt, George L. .... Alma, GA
Hoyt, H. Lawrence .... Boulder, CO
Hoyt, Harger W. .... Conyers, GA
Hoyt, Harger W., P.C. .... Conyers, GA
Hoyt, Harry E. .... Swarthmore, PA
Hoyt, Heather A. .... Philadelphia, PA
Hoyt, Helen F. .... Washington, DC
Hoyt, Henry M. .... Morristown, NJ
Hoyt, Irvin N. .... Pierre, SD

Hoyt, Jacqueline D. .... Tucson, AZ
Hoyt, James Grier .... Washington, DC
Hoyt, Joanna M. .... Woodbridge, CT
Hoyt, Joanne McGilvra .... Hillsboro, OR
Hoyt, John C. .... Great Falls, MT
Hoyt, John O. .... Humble, TX
Hoyt, John S., III .... Morristown, NJ
Hoyt, Jonathan .... Westbrook, CT
Hoyt, Julius Larkin .... Wallkill, NY
Hoyt, Keith A. .... Golden, CO
Hoyt, Kelly Dawn .... Broadalbin, NY
Hoyt, Kenneth M. .... Houston, TX
Hoyt, Kevin J. .... San Diego, CA
Hoyt, Kim E. .... Salem, OR
Hoyt, L. Douglas .... Denver, CO
Hoyt, L. Phillips .... New York, NY
Hoyt, Lawrence K. .... Middletown, OH
Hoyt, MacLeod, Callan, Sproles & Slade
Rome, GA
Hoyt, Marcia H. .... Oakland, CA
Hoyt, Marcia Swigart .... Columbus, OH
Hoyt, Margaret E. .... Davis, CA
Hoyt, Mark C. .... Salem, OR
Hoyt, Matthew R. .... Albuquerque, NM
Hoyt, Merlyn H. .... Ely, NV
Hoyt, Merrill C. .... Chicago, IL
Hoyt, Mont P. .... Dallas, TX
Houston, TX
Hoyt, N. Landon, IV .... Crystal Lake, IL
Hoyt, Nancy V. .... Minneapolis, MN
Hoyt, Norris .... Norwich, VT
Hoyt, R. Terry .... Minocqua, WI
Hoyt, R. Val .... Englewood, CO
Hoyt, Ralph B. .... Lafayette, CA
Hoyt, Richard W. .... Walden, NY
Hoyt, Robert F. .... Washington, DC
Hoyt, Robert G. .... Annapolis, MD
Hoyt, Robert P. .... Cumming, GA
Hoyt, Robert Q. .... Tucson, AZ
Hoyt, Robert Q., P.C. .... Tucson, AZ
Hoyt, Scott R. .... Dallas, TX
Hoyt, Seth R., Jr. .... Stockton, CA
Hoyt, Shawn S. .... Boston, MA
Hoyt, Ted W. .... Lafayette, LA
Hoyt, Theodora W. Joven .... Brooklyn, NY
Hoyt, Thomas H. .... Eugene, OR
Hoyt, Tyler E. .... Marietta, GA
Hoyt, V. Richard .... Atlanta, GA
Hoyt, Wade C., III .... Rome, GA
Hoyt & Waller, P.C. .... Chicago, IL
Wheaton, IL
Hoyt, Wesley E. .... Lufkin, TX
Hoyt, Wesley W. .... Englewood, CO
Hoyt, Willard W. .... Columbus, OH
Hoyt, William K., Jr. .... Miami, FL
Hoyt, Wilson G. .... Brooklyn, NY
Hoyte, Alfred F. .... Falls Church, VA
Hoyte, Jahna Y. (Jay)
Fort Lauderdale, FL
Hoyte-Hayes, Joan E.
National Labor Relations Board,
Office of the General Counsel, GV
Hoyum, Charles D. .... Minneapolis, MN
Hoza, George Gregory .... Bradenton, FL
Hoza, Lydia A. .... Shelby, NC
Hozalski, Donna M. .... Philadelphia, PA
Hozduk, Thomas F. .... Santa Ana, CA
Woodland Hills, CA
Hozempa, Gary J.
Equal Employment Opportunity
Commission,
Office of Legal Counsel, GV
Hozier, Brooks T. .... Phoenix, AZ
Hozore, Judith S. .... New York, NY
Hozubin, Rebecca J. .... Anchorage, AK
Hrab, Michael J. .... Syracuse, NY
Hrabak, William H., Jr. .... Summit, IL
Hrabal, J. Michael .... Fort Worth, TX
Hrabcak, Michael .... Columbus, OH
Hrabchak & Gebo, P.C. .... Watertown, NY
Hrabik, Joseph A. .... Pittsburgh, PA
Hrach, James A. .... Columbus, OH
Hracho and Landis .... Reading, PA
Hracho, Lawrence J. .... Reading, PA
Hrachovy, Amanda K. .... Houston, TX
Hradil, Jennifer A. .... Newark, NJ
Hrajnoha, James A. .... Chicago, IL
Hranitzky, Dennis H. .... New York, NY
Hranitzky, Rachel R. .... Addison, TX
Hray, Alexander, Jr. .... Spartanburg, SC
Hrbacek, Dean A. .... Sugar Land, TX
Hrbacek, Patrick A. .... Minneapolis, MN
Hrdlicka, Albert F. .... Saugerties, NY
Hrdlicka, Charles R. .... Detroit, MI
Hrdlicka, George A. .... Houston, TX
Hrdlicka, Richard F. .... New York, NY
Hrdlicka, Steven R., & Associates
Fresno, CA
Hrdy, Alice S. .... Federal Trade Commission,
Bureau of Consumer Protection, GV
Hrdy, Veronica L. .... New York, NY
Hrebec, John E. .... Chicago, IL
Hrebec, Matt G. .... Lansing, MI
Hrebek, Robert J. .... Sea Girt, NJ
Hrebiniak, Gregory S.
Department of Justice, Tax Division, GV
Hrehorovich, Anne M. .... Baltimore, MD
Hrenchir, Patrick R. .... Topeka, KS
Hrenya, Mark M. .... Denver, CO
Hribar, Joyce Ann .... Euclid, OH
Hribar, Paul J. .... Euclid, OH
Hribar, Robert J. .... Mount Clemens, MI
Hribernick, Paul R. .... Portland, OR
Hric, Michael .... Sarasota, FL
Hricik, David C. .... Houston, TX
Hricik, James M.
Department Of Veterans Affairs,
Veterans Benefits Administration, GV

Hricko, Andrew R. .... Locust Grove, VA
Hrin, Jeanette M. .... Houston, TX
Hrin, Michael .... Amarillo, TX
Hrindac, William G.
Federal Deposit Insurance Corporation,
Division of Bank Supervision, GV
Hriszko, Robert W. .... Hinsdale, IL
Hritsco, William A. .... Dillon, MT
Hritz, George F. .... New York, NY
Hritz, James E. .... Metairie, LA
Hritz, John G. .... Middletown, OH
Hrko, John S. .... Pineville, WV
Hrna, Brian K. .... Red Bank, NJ
Houston, TX
Hrna, Daniel Joseph .... Houston, TX
Hrncir, John A. .... San Antonio, TX
Hrnjak, Marilyn Eve .... Hammond, IN
Hrobowski, Tamika B. .... Little Rock, AR
Hroch & Horacek .... Wilber, NE
Hroch, Joseph J. .... Houston, TX
Hroch, Michael M. .... Wilber, NE
Hroma, Catherine L. .... Long Beach, CA
Hromadka, Donald J. .... Los Angeles, CA
Santa Barbara, CA
Hromadka, Donald J., A Prof. Corp., Law
Offices of .... Los Angeles, CA
Hromadnik, Jerome A., Jr. .... Baltimore, MD
Hromy, John G. .... Horsham, PA
Hron, John W., Jr. .... Ponca City, OK
Hron, Michael G. .... Chicago, IL
Hroncich, Ann .... Brooklyn, NY
Hronek, Frank E. .... Scottsdale, AZ
Hronek, Thomas R. .... Ames, IA
Hrones and Garrity .... Boston, MA
Concord, MA
Londonderry, NH
Hrones, Stephen B. .... Boston, MA
Concord, NH
Hronis, William .... Allentown, PA
Hronsky, Rosalie J. .... New York, NY
Hrouda, Thomas G. .... Santa Ana, CA
Hrozenchik, Mark W. .... Washington, DC
Hroziencik, Michael .... Redwood City, CA
Hrubetz, Matthew F. .... Des Moines, IA
Hrubiec, Robert T. .... West Chester, PA
Hrubovcak, John M. .... Harrisburg, PA
Hruby, Francis J. .... St. Louis, MO
Hruby, Frank S. .... Lackawanna, NY
Hruby, Michael J. .... Phoenix, AZ
Hruby, Patricia J. .... Scottsdale, AZ
Hruby, Ralph R. .... Wheaton, IL
Hruby, Timothy J. .... Washington, DC
Hruby-Mills, Elizabeth A.
Salt Lake City, UT
Hrusa, Thomas H. .... Darien, CT
Hruska, Alan J. .... New York, NY
Hruska, Dan .... Bellville, TX
Hruska, Gary M. .... Dayton, OH
Hruska, Laura C. .... New York, NY
Hruska, Robert A. .... Marion, IA
Hruska-Claeys, Lucinda L.
Minneapolis, MN
Hrusoff, Ronald R. .... San Diego, CA
Hrvol, Joseph J. .... Council Bluffs, IA
Hrvol, Joseph J., (P.C.) .... Council Bluffs, IA
Hrycak, Michael Paul .... Westfield, NJ
Hrycay, Allen J. .... Portland, ME
Hryck, David M. .... New York, NY
Hrycyn, Christina M. .... New York, NY
Hrydziusko, Wayne .... Tallahassee, FL
Hryekewicz, James W. .... Dallas, TX
Hryhorchuk, Danny .... Morristown, TN
Hrymack, Joseph M. .... Brick, NJ
Hryshko, Maurice .... Maplewood, NJ
Hryszko, Walter J. .... Houston, TX
Hsi, Jeffrey D. .... Chicago, IL
Hsi, Petrina S. .... Palo Alto, CA
Hsia, David C. .... San Jose, CA
Hsia, David C.
Department Of Health And Human Services,
Agency for Health Care Policy & Research,
GV
Hsia, David W. .... New York, NY
Hsia, James Cheng-Tai .... Vienna, VA
Hsia, Martin E. .... Honolulu, HI
Hsia, Richard C. .... Garden City, NY
Hsia, Roger .... New York, NY
Hsiang, Jean N. .... Cupertino, CA
Hsiang, William L. .... City of Industry, CA
Hsiao, Douglas H. .... Washington, DC
Hsiao, Lisa K. .... Washington, DC
Hsiao, Monica .... New York, NY
Hsiao, Peter .... Los Angeles, CA
Hsiao, Stanley T. .... Seattle, WA
Hsieh, Amy .... San Francisco, CA
Hsieh, An-Ping .... Maynard, MA
Hsieh, Christine J. .... Houston, TX
Hsieh, Eileen
Agency for International Development,
Office of the General Counsel, GV
Hsieh, Lawrence S. .... New York, NY
Hsieh, Mae H. .... New York, NY
Hsieh, Marina C. .... Berkeley, CA
Hsieh, Nancy C. .... Los Angeles, CA
Hsieh, Nathaniel K. .... Department of the Navy,
Office of the Judge Advocate General, GV
Hsieh, Nelson S. .... Walnut Creek, CA
Hsieh, Peter .... Palo Alto, CA
Hsieh, Richard W.
La Canada Flintridge, CA
Hsieh, Richard W., P.C.
La Canada Flintridge, CA
Hsieh, Shing J. .... Boston, MA
Hsieh, Stewart .... Los Angeles, CA
Malibu, CA
Hsieh, Timothy M. .... Washington, DC
Hsieh, Vincent I. S. .... New York, NY
Hsin, Y. Ernest .... Washington, DC

Hsing, Benjamin C. .... New York, NY
Hsing, Helen Hong-hen
General Accounting Office,
Office of Congressional Relations, GV
Hsiung, Ann .... New York, NY
Hsu, Amber Wong .... Bethesda, MD
Hsu, Angela .... Atlanta, GA
Hsu, Belle H. .... Los Angeles, CA
Hsu, Christine P. .... Washington, DC
Hsu, David A. .... Palo Alto, CA
Hsu, Diana Juliet .... Chicago, IL
Hsu, Diane Law .... Washington, DC
Hsu, Emilie .... New York, NY
Hsu, Gregory T. K. .... New York, NY
Hsu, Hway-Ling .... San Jose, CA
Hsu, Jack C. .... Chicago, IL
Hsu, James C. .... New York, NY
Hsu, Judy S. .... Minneapolis, MN
Hsu, Julie L. .... Palo Alto, CA
Hsu, Lee .... San Francisco, CA
Hsu, Linda Wendell .... San Francisco, CA
Hsu, Mark K. .... New York, NY
Hsu, Richard C. .... Menlo Park, CA
Hsu, Rick R. .... Reno, NV
Hsu, Roger Y. K. .... Wickliffe, OH
Hsu, Shi-Ling .... Washington, DC
Hsu, Victor .... Los Angeles, CA
Hsu, Wei-Fu .... Los Angeles, CA
Hsu, Wesley L. .... Los Angeles, CA
Hsu, William C. .... Los Angeles, CA
Hsu, Yee Ling Vivienne .... Lincoln, MA
Hsuan, Abraham B. .... New York, NY
Hsue, James S. .... San Francisco, CA
Santa Clara, CA
Hsueh, Richard T. .... Irvine, CA
Hsueh, Robert W. .... Dallas, TX
Htoo, Susan S. .... Poughkeepsie, NY
Hu, Amy Y. .... Irvine, CA
Hu, Ben B. .... Baton Rouge, LA
Hu, Christopher K. .... New York, NY
Hu, Dan C. .... Houston, TX
Hu, Daniel D. .... Houston, TX
Hu, Frederic M.C. .... Honolulu, HI
Hu, Harold K. C. .... Honolulu, HI
Hu, Howard M. S. .... Honolulu, HI
Hu, Joseph S. Y. .... Honolulu, HI
Hu, Kathryn R. .... Baltimore, MD
Hu, Patrick H. .... Washington, DC
Hu, Paula Ping .... Treasury Department,
Internal Revenue Service, GV
Hu, Wei .... Atlanta, GA
Hu, Wenchi .... New York, NY
Hu, Xiaohui Leo .... Silver Spring, MD
Hu, Yitai .... Washington, DC
Hua, Jennifer H. .... Chicago, IL
Huaco, Marcia Brown .... Santa Fe, NM
Huahn, Traci L. .... Sacramento, CA
Huang, Albert Y. .... Los Angeles, CA
Huang, Allen Y. .... New York, NY
Huang, Amy S. .... New York, NY
Huang, Amy T.
Environmental Protection Agency,
Office of the General Counsel, GV
Huang, Andrew S. .... San Francisco, CA
Huang, Andy Y. .... Artesia, CA
Huang, Anny .... New York, NY
Huang, Audrey I-Wei .... Boston, MA
Huang, Chelun .... Honolulu, HI
Huang, Chung .... San Francisco, CA
Huang, Cynthia J. .... Indianapolis, IN
Huang, David C. .... Washington, DC
Huang, David E. .... Westborough, MA
Huang, David M. .... Cerritos, CA
Huang, David T. .... Newport Beach, CA
Huang, Eric .... New York, NY
Huang, Eugene .... Morristown, NJ
Huang, Felicia .... Denver, CO
Huang, Fiona W. .... San Francisco, CA
Huang, Frank F. .... Boston, MA
Huang, Franklin P. .... San Francisco, CA
Huang, Gail C. .... Los Angeles, CA
Huang, George C. .... Chicago, IL
Huang, Hans H. .... Charlotte, NC
Huang, Irene J. .... McLean, VA
Huang, Jade H.J. .... New York, NY
Huang, James Y. .... New York, NY
Huang, Jerry C. J. .... Los Angeles, CA
Huang, Jixiang (Jennifer) .... Tucson, AZ
Huang, John Zhengdong .... Chicago, IL
Huang, Joyce S. .... New York, NY
Huang, Joyce Yan Tzu .... New York, NY
Huang, Julie .... Los Angeles, CA
Huang, Julie S. .... Houston, TX
Huang, Justin Tze-Chieh
Philadelphia, PA
Huang, Kelleen K. .... Atlanta, GA
Huang, Mark M. .... New York, NY
Huang, Mark S. .... Los Angeles, CA
Huang, Michael K.
Rancho Cucamonga, CA
Huang, Ming-Hsiu (Mark) .... New York, NY
Huang & Mitchell, A Professional Law
Corporation .... Los Angeles, CA
Huang, Patrick K. .... Los Angeles, CA
Huang, Paul C. .... Rockville, MD
Huang, Peggy .... Menlo Park, CA
Huang, Peter Juen-Wen .... Baltimore, MD
Huang, Roy .... Chicago, IL
Huang, Sharon T. .... New York, NY
Huang, Stuart T. F. .... Washington, DC
Huang, Thomas Weishing .... Boston, MA
Huang, Vivian Wenhuey Chen .... Boston, MA
Huang, Warren .... Houston, TX
Huang, Wendy W. .... Torrance, CA
Huang, Wynn R. .... Princeton, NJ
Huang, York Y. .... El Cerrito, CA
Huard, David Leo .... Los Angeles, CA
Huard, Denise E. .... Fort Lauderdale, FL

Huard, Guy M. ..... Hammond, LA
Huard, Paul R. ..... Washington, DC
Huard, Robert F. ..... Needham, MA
Huarte, Anne M. ..... Hermosa Beach, CA
Hubacek, Lisa A. ..... College Station, TX
Hubach, Francis P., Jr. ..... Dallas, TX
Hubach, Jenny D. ..... Reno, NV
Hubach, Joseph F. ..... Dallas, TX
Hubachek, F. B., Jr. ..... Chicago, IL
Hubacher, Arthur S. ..... Washington, DC
Hubacher, Edward D. ..... Alexandria, VA
Hubacher, Mary L. ..... Milwaukee, WI
Hubal, Mark A. ..... Binghamton, NY
Hubalik, Timothy M. ..... Elmhurst, IL
Hubanks, John F. ..... Walnut Creek, CA
Hubanks, Tanya A. ..... Cincinnati, OH
Hubard, Harrison, Jr. ..... Richmond, VA
Hubard, Tazewell T., III ..... Norfolk, VA
Hubb, David Alan ..... Palo Alto, CA
Hubbard, Alexander F. ..... Monterey, CA
Hubbard, Allan C. ..... Washington, DC
Hubbard, Allan P. ..... Madison, WI
Hubbard, Allen S., Jr. ..... New York, NY
Hubbard, Allison B. ..... Mountain View, CA
Hubbard, Amy E. ..... Bedford, MA
Hubbard, Angela R. ..... Charlotte, NC
Hubbard, Ann ..... Chapel Hill, NC
Hubbard & Associates ..... Dallas, TX
Hubbard, Barton A. ..... Columbus, OH
Hubbard, Benjamin A., III
Chesapeake, VA
Hubbard, B. H. B., III ..... Irvington, VA
Hubbard & Biederman, L.L.P. ..... Dallas, TX
Hubbard, Breeden & Terry
Heathsville, VA
Irvington, VA
Kilmarnock, VA
Saluda, VA
White Stone, VA
Hubbard, Brian J. ..... Dallas, TX
Hubbard, Bruce A. ..... Denver, CO
Hubbard, Bruce A. ..... New York, NY
Hubbard, Bruce A. ..... Sturgis, SD
Hubbard, Bruce E. ..... Newark, DE
Hubbard, C. Dale ..... Highland Park, MI
Hubbard, C. Garman ..... White Plains, NY
Hubbard, Candace J. ..... Modesto, CA
Hubbard, Carl B. ..... Sullivan's Island, SC
Hubbard, Carol P. ..... Oklahoma City, OK
Hubbard, Carolyn M. ..... Dallas, TX
Hubbard, Carolyn R. ..... Ventura, CA
Hubbard, Cates & Long ..... Roxboro, NC
Hubbard, Charles A. ..... Needham, MA
Hubbard, Charles E. ..... Roxboro, NC
Hubbard, Charles S. ..... Sacramento, CA
Hubbard, Charlotte F. ..... Dunedin, FL
Hubbard, Christine Donelan ..... Boston, MA
Hubbard, Christine W. ..... Annapolis, MD
Hubbard, Clinton D. ..... San Diego, CA
Hubbard, Clinton L. ..... Tustin, CA
Hubbard, D. Seeley ..... Stamford, CT
New York, NY
Hubbard, Daniel M. ..... Denver, CO
Hubbard, David J. ..... New York, NY
Hubbard, David N. ..... New Preston, CT
Hubbard, David P. ..... San Diego, CA
Hubbard, David R. ..... Bloomfield, CT
Hubbard, Deborah Delores ..... Philadelphia, PA
Hubbard, Dirk L. ..... Overland Park, KS
Hubbard, Donald C., Jr. ..... Washington, DC
Hubbard, Donald G. ..... Monterey, CA
Hubbard, Donald K. ..... Batavia, IL
Hubbard, Edward A. ..... Manhasset, NY
Hubbard, Edward G. ..... Columbus, OH
Hubbard, Edward H. ..... Tuscaloosa, AL
Hubbard, Edward L. ..... Newport News, VA
Hubbard, Edward S. ..... Houston, TX
Hubbard, Elizabeth J.C. ..... Eugene, OR
Hubbard, Elizabeth Louise ..... Chicago, IL
Hubbard, Elizabeth Lynn ..... Seattle, WA
Hubbard, Eric R. ..... New York, NY
Hubbard, Ernest T., Sr. ..... Colusa, CA
Hubbard, Eugene P. ..... Syracuse, NY
Hubbard, Evelyn ..... Sylvania, GA
Hubbard, Faith M. ..... Tulsa, OK
Hubbard, Ford, Jr. ..... Houston, TX
Hubbard, Fox, Thomas, White & Bengtson, P.C. ..... Lansing, MI
Hubbard, Fred L. ..... Danville, IL
Hubbard, G. Wendell, Jr. ..... Sherman, TX
Hubbard, G. William, II ..... Chicago, IL
Hubbard, Geo. T. ..... Kingsville, TX
Hubbard, George M., III ..... Savannah, GA
Hubbard, George M., P.C.
Richmond Hill, GA
Rincon, GA
Savannah, GA
Hubbard, Gerald J. ..... East Aurora, NY
Hubbard, Gordon K. ..... Ventura, CA
Hubbard, Grant L. ..... Apache Junction, AZ
Hubbard, Grant R. ..... Fort Wayne, IN
Hubbard, Grant R., P.C. ..... Fort Wayne, IN
Hubbard, Harold Macoubrey ..... Norcross, GA
Hubbard, Heidi K. ..... Washington, DC
Hubbard, Herbert H. ..... Baltimore, MD
Hubbard, Howard H. ..... Bridgewater, NJ
Hubbard & Hubbard LLP ..... Monterey, CA
Hubbard, Hubbard, O'Brien & Hall
Chicago, IL
Hubbard, J. Lister ..... Montgomery, AL
Hubbard, James A. ..... Isom, KY
Hubbard, James C. ..... Worthington, OH
Hubbard, James C. ..... Fond du Lac, WI
Hubbard, James R. ..... West Palm Beach, FL
Hubbard, James R. ..... Olathe, KS
Hubbard, James R. ..... Texarkana, TX
Hubbard, James S. ..... Anniston, AL
Hubbard, Jeffrey B. ..... Virginia Beach, VA
Hubbard, Jeffrey P. ..... Phoenix, AZ
Hubbard, Jeffrey P. ..... Jackson, MS
Hubbard, Jeffrey T. ..... Dallas, TX
Hubbard, John A. ..... Farmington Hills, MI
Hubbard, John Dana ..... Bedford, MA
Hubbard, John Douglas ..... Bardstown, KY
Hubbard, John E. ..... Omaha, NE
Hubbard, John G. ..... Dunedin, FL
Hubbard, John L. ..... Stamford, NY
Hubbard & Johnson, P.C. ..... Denver, CO
Hubbard, Joseph D. ..... Anniston, AL
Hubbard, Julian J. ..... San Mateo, CA
Hubbard, K. Dean, Jr. ..... New York, NY
Hubbard, Karen Laine ..... Dallas, TX
Hubbard, Kenneth ..... Wheaton, IL
Hubbard, Kenneth D. ..... Denver, CO
Hubbard, Kenneth W. ..... New York, NY
Hubbard, Kevin L. ..... Chesapeake, VA
Hubbard, Kim R. ..... Newport Beach, CA
Hubbard, Kurtz, Taylor, L.L.P.
Kansas City, MO
Hubbard, Kyle T. ..... Louisville, KY
Hubbard, Laura A. ..... Tucson, AZ
Hubbard Law Office, P.C. ..... Waitsburg, WA
Hubbard, Lewis J., Jr. ..... Austin, TX
Hubbard, Lorenzo K. ..... White Hall, IL
Hubbard, Lynn ..... Woodland Hills, CA
Hubbard, Lynn, III ..... Chico, CA
Hubbard, M. Gilbert ..... Clinton, NY
Hubbard, Marc A. ..... Dallas, TX
Hubbard, Marion J., (Miss) ..... New York, NY
Hubbard, Mark A. ..... Platte City, MO
Hubbard, Mark E. ..... Southfield, MI
Hubbard, Mary Campbell
New Orleans, LA
Hubbard, Mary Frances ..... Richmond, VA
Hubbard, Matt R. ..... Kansas City, MO
Hubbard, Melissa D. ..... Denver, CO
Hubbard, Michael B. ..... Washington, DC
Hubbard, Michael L. ..... Cheyenne, WY
Hubbard, Michael V. ..... Waitsburg, WA
Hubbard, Michael W. ..... Raleigh, NC
Hubbard, Michael W. ..... Dallas, TX
Hubbard, Michelle R. ..... New Canaan, CT
Hubbard, Neal ..... Elyria, OH
Hubbard, Nerman Dobynes
Washington, DC
Hubbard & O'Connor, Ltd. ..... Chicago, IL
Hubbard, Otis L. ..... Los Angeles, CA
Hubbard, Patricia A. ..... Phoenix, AZ
Hubbard, Patricia L. ..... Chicago, IL
Hubbard, Patricia L. ..... Dallas, TX
Hubbard, Patrick G. ..... Kingwood, TX
Hubbard, Patrick L. ..... Washington, DC
Hubbard, Paul H. ..... Waco, TX
Hubbard, Paul M. ..... Fargo, ND
Hubbard, Peter L. ..... Syracuse, NY
Hubbard, Philip G., Jr. ..... Seattle, WA
Hubbard & Quinn ..... Amherst, NH
Hubbard, R. Carl ..... Georgetown, SC
Hubbard, Ralph S., III ..... New Orleans, LA
Hubbard, Randall E. ..... Denver, CO
Hubbard, Read S.T. ..... New York, NY
Hubbard & Rehard, P.C. ..... Platte City, MO
Hubbard, Richard A. ..... Norwell, MA
Hubbard, Richard C., III ..... Cleveland, OH
Hubbard, Richard L. ..... Washington, DC
Hubbard, Richard R. ..... Whitinsville, MA
Hubbard, Richard W. ..... Wilmington, DE
Hubbard, Robert C. ..... New York, NY
Hubbard, Robert J., Jr. ..... Phoenix, AZ
Hubbard, Robert L. ..... New York, NY
Hubbard, Robert R. ..... Stamford, CT
Hubbard, Robyn G. ..... Omaha, NE
Hubbard, Rodney L. ..... Dallas, TX
Hubbard, Russelle Louis ..... Pinson, AL
Hubbard, Sandra Hinojosa
Louisville, KY
Hubbard, Scott D. ..... Grand Rapids, MI
Hubbard, Sheila A. Caviel ..... Boston, MA
Hubbard, Smith, McIlwain, Brakefield & Browder, P.C. ..... Eutaw, AL
Montgomery, AL
Tuscaloosa, AL
Hubbard, Stephen F. ..... Defiance, OH
Hubbard, Stephen L., (P.C.) ..... Dallas, TX
Hubbard, Steven W. ..... Fort Myers, FL
Hubbard, Stimpson B. ..... Boston, MA
Hubbard, Susan C. ..... Topsfield, MA
Hubbard, Susan L. ..... Dearborn, MI
Hubbard, Thomas J. ..... New York, NY
Hubbard, Tim ..... Pittsboro, NC
Hubbard, Unger & Urquhart
Fairfield, CA
Vacaville, CA
Hubbard, Vaughn ..... Waitsburg, WA
Hubbard, Vincent K. ..... New York, NY
Hubbard, Wade A. ..... Pierre, SD
Hubbard, William B. ..... Nashville, TN
Hubbard, William C. ..... Columbia, SC
Hubbard, William L. ..... Kansas City, MO
Hubbard, William L. ..... Harlingen, TX
Hubbard, William N. ..... New York, NY
Hubbard-Hopkins, Monie
San Luis Obispo, CA
Hubbard-Palmer, Elaine L. ..... Houston, TX
Hubbart, Kevin J. ..... Fort Myers, FL
Hubbart, Phillip A. ..... Miami, FL
Hubbarth, Michael P. ..... Chicago, IL
Hubbel, Carter C., Jr. ..... Rockville, MD
Hubbel, Angela Marie ..... Nashville, TN
Hubbell, Billy J., Law Office of
Crossett, AR
Hubbell, Cindy A. ..... Sparta, TN
Hubbell, Daniel A. ..... Traverse City, MI
Hubbell, Donn A. ..... Cadillac, MI
Hubbell, Ernest ..... Kansas City, MO
Hubbell, Fred C. ..... Lebanon, OH
Hubbell, Frederick R. ..... Kalamazoo, MI
Hubbell, Frederick S. ..... Des Moines, IA
Hubbell & Hubbell, P.C. ..... Traverse City, MI
Hubbell, James W. ..... Denver, CO
Hubbell, Jonathan ..... Irvine, CA
Hubbell, Joseph T. ..... Traverse City, MI
Hubbell, Marlene A. ..... Clovis, CA
Hubbell, Michael R. ..... Baton Rouge, LA
Hubbell, Paul A. ..... Traverse City, MI
Hubbell, Phyllis L. ..... Berkeley, CA
Hubbell, Richard C. ..... Los Angeles, CA
Hubbell, Robert B. ..... Los Angeles, CA
Hubbell, S. Ross ..... Merrillville, IN
Hubbell, Saundra Jones ..... Valley Center, CA
Hubbell, Sawyer, Peak, O'Neal & Napier
Kansas City, MO
Hubbell, Scott C. ..... Franklin, MA
Hubbell, Stuart D. ..... Traverse City, MI
Hubbert, Christopher J. ..... Cleveland, OH
Hubbert, E. A., Jr. ..... Sacramento, CA
Hubbert, James D. ..... Farmington Hills, MI
Hubbert, James L. ..... Brooklyn, NY
Hubbert, John J., III ..... Philadelphia, PA
Hubbert, Jonathon F. ..... Birmingham, AL
Hubbert Law Firm, The ..... Sacramento, CA
Hubbert, Richard S. ..... Lubbock, TX
Hubble, G. Craig ..... Fort Worth, TX
Hubble, James A. ..... Stanford, MT
Hubble, John L. ..... Dallas, TX
Hubble, Lester J. ..... St. Louis, MO
Hubble, Linda Chindberg ..... Dallas, TX
Hubble, Mark A. ..... Minneapolis, MN
Hubble, William A. ..... Grand Rapids, MI
Hubbs, Donald H. ..... Pacific Palisades, CA
Hubbs, Earl W. ..... Alton, IL
Hubbs, Fred L., Jr. ..... Atlanta, GA
Hubbs, Robert C. ..... San Francisco, CA
Hubbs, Steven R. ..... San Bernardino, CA
Hubbuch, John A. ..... Chicago, IL
Hubby, Albert G., III ..... Arlington, TX
Hubby, Frank W., 3rd ..... Niantic, CT
Hubchen, Stephen K. ..... Houston, TX
Hubel, Dennis J. ..... Portland, OR
Hubel, Gordon K. ..... Los Angeles, CA
Hubel, Ronald P. ..... Las Vegas, NV
Hubelbank, Stephanie Laura ..... New York, NY
Hubell, Richard A. ..... New York, NY
Huben, Brian D. ..... Los Angeles, CA
Huben, Christina E. ..... Greenwich, CT
Huben, Kevin M. ..... Trumbull, CT
Hubenak, Hollis A. ..... Houston, TX
Hubenak, L. Jeffrey ..... Austin, TX
Hubenak, Priscilla M. ..... Austin, TX
Hubener, Louis F. ..... Tallahassee, FL
Hubeny, John R., & Associates
Westmont, IL
Hubeny, Lola Jan ..... Stateline, NV
Huber, Alyssa ..... Hopkinton, MA
Huber, Ann A. ..... Randolph, NJ
Huber, Anne M. ..... Chicago, IL
Huber, Arlene B. ..... Medina, OH
Huber, Bernhard J. ..... Eggertsville, NY
Huber, Birgit A. ..... Los Angeles, CA
Huber, Book, Cortese, Happe & Brown, P.L.C. ..... Des Moines, IA
Huber, Brent W. ..... Indianapolis, IN
Huber, Brian C. ..... Wenatchee, WA
Huber, Bryan Wm. ..... Chaska, MN
Huber, C. Ben ..... Denver, CO
Huber, Charles C. ..... Seattle, WA
Huber, Charles H. ..... St. Ann, MO
Huber, Charles J. ..... Portland, OR
Huber, Charles N. ..... Chicago, IL
Huber, Charles R. ..... La Porte, TX
Huber, Christopher J. ..... Washington, DC
Huber, Craig A. ..... Torrance, CA
Huber, Craig J. ..... Haddonfield, NJ
Huber, Cynthia S. ..... Department of Justice, Environment and Natural Resources Division, GV
Huber, Daniel C. ..... Neenah, WI
Huber, David ..... Louisville, KY
Huber, David L. ..... New York, NY
Huber, David P. ..... Chicago, IL
Huber, David Talbert ..... Seattle, WA
Huber, Dennis M. ..... Hillsboro, IL
Huber, Donald K. ..... Hartford, CT
Huber, E. Burke, Jr. ..... San Antonio, TX
Huber, Elizabeth A. ..... Washington, DC
Crofton, MD
Huber, Evans ..... Wellesley, MA
Huber, Ezra ..... Westbury, NY
Huber, Fred D., Jr. ..... Hartland, WI
Huber, Fredrick E. ..... Kankakee, IL
Huber, George A. ..... Pittsburgh, PA
Huber, George H. ..... Vandalia, IL
Huber, George L., Jr. ..... Baltimore, MD
Huber, Gerald Patrick ..... Hillsboro, IL
Huber, Gerd B. ..... Laguna Niguel, CA
Huber, Giselle K. ..... Cincinnati, OH
Huber, Gordon J. ..... Robbinsdale, MN
Huber, Gregory A. ..... Medina, OH
Huber, Gregory M. ..... San Antonio, TX
Huber, Gregory P. ..... Fort Pierce, FL
Huber, Gregory W. ..... Phoenix, AZ
Huber, Gunnar D. ..... Hollywood, FL
Huber, H. Peter ..... St. Louis, MO
Huber, Helga E. ..... Chicago, IL
Huber, J. David ..... Tell City, IN
Huber, J. Kendall ..... Memphis, TN
Huber, J. Neil, Jr. ..... St. Louis, MO
Huber, James A. ..... Williamsville, NY
Huber, James C. ..... Des Moines, IA
Huber, James O. ..... Milwaukee, WI
Huber, James R. ..... Tulsa, OK
Huber, James T. ..... Allentown, PA
Huber, Jamie Leeson ..... Boca Raton, FL
Huber, Janine N. ..... Binghamton, NY
Huber, Jason E. ..... Charleston, WV
Huber, Jay Patrick ..... Durham, NC
Huber, Jeannine ..... St. Louis, MO
Huber, Jeffrey A. ..... McLean, VA
Huber, Jennifer J. ..... Vero Beach, FL
Huber, Jennifer L. ..... Atlanta, GA
Huber, Jennifer S. ..... Washington, DC
Huber, John B. ..... Beavercreek, OH
Huber, John E. ..... Lancaster, PA
Huber, John F. ..... Marmora, NJ
Huber, John J. ..... Washington, DC
Huber, John L. ..... Atlanta, GA
Huber, John P. ..... Smithtown, NY
Huber, Joseph H. ..... San Jose, CA
Huber, Joseph M. ..... Pittsburgh, PA
Huber, Joseph V. ..... Greensburg, PA
Huber, Karen A. ..... Bangor, ME
Huber, Karen S. ..... Renton, WA
Huber, Karen V. ..... Little Rock, AR
Huber, Karl ..... Newark, NJ
Huber, Kenneth B. ..... Minneapolis, MN
Huber, Kevin D. ..... Casper, WY
Huber, Laura A. ..... Boston, MA
Huber Lawrence & Abell
Washington, DC
New York, NY
Huber, Lee M. ..... Houston, TX
Huber, Louis A., III ..... Kansas City, MO
Huber, M. Cathleen ..... Appleton, WI
Huber, Marie Oh ..... Palo Alto, CA
Huber, Mary Elizabeth ..... Cleveland, OH
Huber, Matthew Barton ..... Dayton, OH
Huber, Michael ..... Haddonfield, NJ
Huber, Michael D. ..... Chicago, IL
Huber, Michael E. ..... Sandy, UT
Huber, Michael E. ..... Casper, WY
Huber, Michael R. ..... Lansing, MI
Huber, Michael W. ..... Pittsburgh, PA
Huber, Nina V. ..... Boston, MA
Huber, Paul J. ..... Durand, IL
Huber, Paul R. ..... Irvine, CA
Huber, Peter M. ..... Norfolk, VA
Huber, Peter W. ..... Washington, DC
Huber, Ralph P. ..... New York, NY
Huber, Raymond S. ..... Clintonville, WI
Huber, Richard L. ..... Grand Island, NE
Huber, Richard M. ..... Jonesboro, GA
Huber, Richard R. ..... Milan, OH
Huber, Robert D. ..... San Francisco, CA
Huber, Robert, Esquire ..... Philadelphia, PA
Huber, Robert G. ..... Lansing, MI
Huber, Robert J. ..... Minneapolis, MN
Huber, Robert K. ..... Roscommon, MI
Huber, Robert L., Jr. ..... Aurora, IL
Huber, Robert M. ..... Washington, DC
Huber, Robert Odell ..... Simi Valley, CA
Huber, Robert V. ..... Wilmington, DE
Huber, Roger L. ..... Bangor, ME
Huber, Ronald M. ..... Charlottesville, VA
Huber Samuelson APC ..... San Jose, CA
Huber, Scott E. ..... Fenton, MO
Huber, Shawn C. ..... Camden, NJ
Westmont, NJ
Huber, Sheila M. ..... Olympia, WA
Huber, Sigmund E. ..... Cincinnati, OH
Huber, Stephen K. ..... Houston, TX
Huber & Takasugi ..... Simi Valley, CA
Huber, Terrance P. ..... Los Angeles, CA
Huber, Terrance P., A Professional Corporation
Los Angeles, CA
Huber, Thomas K. ..... Wichita, KS
Huber, Thomas M. ..... Chicago, IL
Huber, Thomas M. ..... Pittsburgh, PA
Huber, Thomas P. ..... Honolulu, HI
Huber, Thomas W. ..... Seattle, WA
Huber, Timothy H. ..... Sacramento, CA
Huber, Timothy James ..... Lebanon, PA
Huber, Timothy T. ..... Palo Alto, CA
Huber and Waldron ..... Allentown, PA
Huber, William E. ..... St. Marys, OH
Huber, William W. ..... Washington, DC
Huber, Wm. Dennis ..... Lancaster, NY
Huber, Wm. H. ..... Toms River, NJ
Huberfeld, Harold ..... Hopewell Junction, NY
Huberfeld, Nicole ..... Woodbridge, NJ
Huber-Happy, Jeanne ..... Newport News, VA
Huber-Happy Law Group, The
Newport News, VA
Huberman, Christina E. ..... Santa Monica, CA
Huberman, David A. ..... Washington, DC
Huberman & Gentile ..... Youngstown, OH
Huberman, Gisela ..... Washington, DC
Huberman, Hartley C. ..... Brooklyn, NY
Huberman, Mark A. ..... Youngstown, OH
Huberman, Michael Stuart ..... Richmond, VA
Huberman, Richard L.
Occupational Safety and Health Review Commission, Office of the Chairman, GV
Huberman, Seth L. ..... Beverly Hills, CA
Hubert, Andrew C. ..... Riverside, CA
Hubert, Carl R. ..... Houston, TX
Hubert, Craig J. ..... Trenton, NJ
Hubert, Cynthia K. ..... Houston, TX
Hubert, Dan L. ..... San Diego, CA
Hubert, David L. ..... San Jose, CA
Hubert, David M. ..... Danielson, CT
Hubert, David P. ..... Waconia, MN
Watertown, MN
Hubert, Donald, & Associates ..... Chicago, IL
Hubert, Edwin G. ..... Tucson, AZ
Hubert, Frank J. ..... Rockville Centre, NY
Hubert, Frank W. R., Jr. ..... Houston, TX
Hubert, Garry J. D. ..... San Francisco, CA
Hubert, Herbert W. ..... Syracuse, NY
Hubert & Hernandez, P.A.
Las Cruces, NM
Hubert, H. J. ..... Syracuse, NY

Hubert, James B. ... Oak Brook, IL
Hubert, Joseph A. ... Fort Lauderdale, FL
Hubert, Judith L. ... San Bernardino, CA
Hubert, Lawrence L. ... Woodbury, NJ
Hubert, Martin A. ... Austin, TX
Hubert, Norman G. ... Waterford, MI
Hubert, Peter R. ... San Jose, CA
Hubert, Pierre ... Austin, TX
Hubert, Randall J. ... Wichita, KS
Hubert, Randy Karafin ... Haddonfield, NJ
Philadelphia, PA
Hubert, Richard N. ... Atlanta, GA
Hubert, Shalina M. ... Chicago, IL
Hubert, Sherry L. ... Rochester, MN
Hubert, Stephen A. ... Las Cruces, NM
Hubert, Steven L. ... Brooklyn, NY
Hubert, Steven R. ... San Jose, CA
Hubert, Thaddeus J., III
New Brunswick, NJ
Hubert, Thomas P. ... New Orleans, LA
Hubert, Timothy J. ... Evansville, IN
Hubert, Vanessa H. ... Riverside, CA
Hubert, Yasutake & Hoh, A Professional Corporation ... San Francisco, CA
Huberty, James J. ... Chicago, IL
Huberty, Joseph P. ... Guilderland, NY
Huberty, Patricia L. ... San Bernardino, CA
Huberty, Theresa ... Sacramento, CA
Hubertz, Elizabeth J. ... Birmingham, AL
Hubicki, Joseph S. ... Jericho, NY
Hubing, Marion Rita ... Philadelphia, PA
Hubka, Harlan D. ... Beatrice, NE
Hubka, Harold C. ... Daytona Beach, FL
Daytona Beach, FL
Maitland, FL
Hubka, Jeffrey B. ... Beatrice, NE
Hubka, Ronald J. ... Chicago, IL
Hubka, Verne R. ... San Diego, CA
Hublar, Robert T. ... New Albany, IN
Hubler, Charles D. ... Eaton, OH
Hubler, Charles D., L.P.A. ... Eaton, OH
Hubler, Diane M. ... Rhinelander, WI
Hubler, James T. ... Portland, OR
Hubler, Karen F. ... Denver, CO
Hubler, Katherine Gorman ... Peoria, IL
Hubler, Kenneth T. ... Marion, IL
Hubler, Lloyd E., III ... Columbus, OH
Hubler, Mary E. ... Rice Lake, WI
Hubley, Helen W. ... Shreveport, LA
Hubley, Michael S. ... Shreveport, LA
Hubley, Norman A. ... Boston, MA
Hubley, Ralph I., III ... Lincolnshire, IL
Hubly, Julie R. ... Hammond, IN
Hübner, Christian A. ... Austin, TX
Hubner, Michael E. ... Riverdale, NJ
Hubner, Michael S. ... New York, NY
Hubner, Shelley K. ... San Francisco, CA
Hubona, Kenneth U. ... Tampa, FL
Hubsch, Allen W., Jr. ... Los Angeles, CA
Hubsch, Daniel F. ... Jacksonville, FL
Hubscher, Bernard ... New York, NY
Hubscher, Sofia C. ... New York, NY
Hubschman, Arthur M. ... New York, NY
Hubschman, George H.
Charlotte Amalie, St. Thomas, VI
Hubschman, Henry A. ... Cincinnati, OH
Hubschman, Richard A., Jr.
Palisades Park, NJ
Hubschman & Roman, A Professional Corporation ... Palisades Park, NJ
Hubsher, Muriel ... Brooklyn, NY
Hucek, Jeffrey M. ... Oak Brook, IL
Huch, Peter M. ... Minneapolis, MN
Huchel, David ... Newport Beach, CA
Huchenski, Jackie M. ... New York, NY
Huchital, Ellen Beth ... Houston, TX
Huchting, Joanna C. ... Los Angeles, CA
Huchting, Stephen H. ... Los Angeles, CA
Huchton, Hadley A. ... El Paso, TX
Huck, Bouma, Martin, Jones & Bradshaw, P.C.
Wheaton, IL
Huck, Christopher W. ... Hartford, CT
Huck, James M., Jr. ... Wheaton, IL
Huck, James W. ... St. Louis, MO
Huck, John B. ... Chicago, IL
Huck, Kasey L. ... Dallas, TX
Huck, Kevin J. ... Wheaton, IL
Huck, L. Francis ... New York, NY
Huck, Martin T.
United States Tax Court, GV
Huck, Paul C. ... Miami, FL
Huck, Paul C., Jr. ... Miami, FL
Huck, Paul D. ... St. Louis, MO
Huck, Paul G. ... New York, NY
Huck, Richard F., III ... St. Louis, MO
Huck, Robert J. ... Omaha, NE
Huck, Thomas B. ... East Tawas, MI
Huck, Thomas B., P.C. ... East Tawas, MI
Tawas City, MI
Huckaba, Frank J. ... Mountain Home, AR
Huckaba Law Firm, A Professional Association ... Mountain Home, AR
Huckabay, C. Caldwell H. ... Chattanooga, TN
Huckabay, Charles A. ... Southfield, MI
Huckabay, D. Michael, Jr.
Little Rock, AR
Huckabay, George B. ... Bethesda, MD
Huckabay, John R. ... Sacramento, CA
Huckabay, Mike ... Little Rock, AR
Huckabay, Munson, Rowlett & Tilley, P.A.
Little Rock, AR
Huckabee, Brett A. ... Reading, PA
Huckabee, Brian W. ... Tulsa, OK
Huckabee, Darita DeLoach ... Tulsa, OK
Huckabee, Dean ... Houston, TX
Huckabee, Gregory M. ... Jonesboro, GA
Huckabee, Harlow M. ... Arlington, VA
Huckabee and Huckabee, Inc. ... Tulsa, OK
Huckabee, Hugh ... Fort Worth, TX
Huckabee, Lori M. M. ... Orlando, FL
Huckabee, Mary Ellen ... Atlanta, GA
Huckabee, P. Sanders ... Cabot, AR
Huckabone, Darrell A. ... Buffalo, NY
Huckabone, Joan M. ... Newport Beach, CA
Huckaby, Christian S.
Oklahoma City, OK
Huckaby, Curtis L. ... Lake City, AR
Huckaby, Elizabeth Young ... Little Rock, AR
Huckaby, Fleming, Frailey, Chaffin, Cordell, Greenwood & Perryman, L.L.P.
Chickasha, OK
Oklahoma City, OK
Huckaby, Gary C. ... Huntsville, AL
Huckaby, Hannah D. ... Austin, TX
Huckaby, James C., Jr. ... Birmingham, AL
Huckaby, Karl W., Jr. ... Milwaukee, WI
Huckaby, Lauren R. ... San Antonio, TX
Huckaby, Melody Renae ... Pryor, OK
Huckaby, Michelle ... McLean, VA
Huckaby, Robert L. ... Oklahoma City, OK
Huckaby, Robert P. ... Marina Del Rey, CA
Huckaby, Thomas O'Dell, Jr.
Fort Collins, CO
Huckaby, Tom ... Wichita Falls, TX
Huckeba, John B. ... Alvin, TX
Huckeby, Richard M. ... Pinellas Park, FL
Huckel, Wayne P. ... Charlotte, NC
Huckenpahler, Robert H. ... Costa Mesa, CA
Huckenpoehler, John S. ... Baltimore, MD
Hucker, Brian S. ... Chicago, IL
Hucker, Robert E. ... Jacksonville, FL
Huckerby, Nicole J. ... Princeton, NJ
Huckert, John W. ... Washington, DC
Huckestein, Theodore F., Jr. ... Pittsburgh, PA
Huckin, William P., Jr. ... Tulsa, OK
Huckins, Donald E. ... Yuba City, CA
Huckins, R. Gordon ... San Diego, CA
Huckins, William J. ... Honolulu, HI
Huckins, William W. ... San Francisco, CA
Huckleberry, Carolyn ... Fort Worth, TX
Huckleberry, Robert J. ... Newport, OR
Hucks, Carol A. ... Cherry Hill, NJ
Hucksam, John R., Jr. ... Boston, MA
Huckstep, Charles L., II ... Dallas, TX
Huckstep, Lee ... Houston, TX
Huckstep, M. Ann ... Birmingham, AL
Hudacek, Daniel A. ... Long Valley, NJ
Hudacek, Michael J. ... Plymouth, PA
Hudachek, Diane S. ... Newtown, PA
Hudachek, Diane S., Law Offices of, P.C.
Newtown, PA
Hudacko, Andrew R. ... Cleveland, OH
Hudacsek, John J., Jr. ... Beaver Falls, PA
Hudacsek & Lewis ... Beaver Falls, PA
Hudak, Andrea D. ... Doylestown, PA
Hudak, Charles A. ... Atlanta, GA
Hudak, Clara J. ... Columbus, OH
Hudak, Clara J., Co., L.P.A. ... Columbus, OH
Hudak, Daniel J. ... Akron, OH
Hudak, David J. ... Akron, OH
Hudak, Dennis S. ... Bethlehem, PA
Hudak, Elizabeth D. ... Carmel, NY
Hudak, Elizabeth J. ... Kansas City, MO
Hudak, Frank R. ... Collinsville, IL
Hudak, James A. ... Cleveland, OH
Hudak, John G. ... Roseland, NJ
Hudak, Jon A. ... Orinda, CA
Hudak, Mark D. ... New Orleans, LA
Hudak, Michael C. ... Hialeah, FL
Hudak, Michael J. ... Richmond, VA
Hudak, Richard D. ... Walnut Creek, CA
Hudak, Stephen ... Detroit, MI
Hudak, Timothy Q. ... Pittsburgh, PA
Hudak, William J., Jr. ... Saugus, MA
Hudanich, John ... Johnson City, NY
Hudanish, David Michael ... New York, NY
Hudders, Andrew D. ... New York, NY
Hudders, John R. ... Allentown, PA
Huddle, David F. ... Lake Charles, LA
Huddle, John M. ... Roanoke, VA
Huddle, Lewis A., Jr. ... Roland, AR
Huddle, Lindsey M. ... Burlington, VT
Huddle, Mark A. ... Chicago, IL
Huddle, Robert L. ... Stillwater, OK
Huddle, Roger A. ... Wapello, IA
Huddle, Wm. Gehrett ... Columbus, OH
Huddles & Jones, P.C. ... Washington, DC
Baltimore, MD
Columbia, MD
Huddles, William M. ... Columbia, MD
Huddleson, Charles R. ... Fort Collins, CO
Huddleson, Edwin E., III
Washington, DC
Huddleson & Lane Co., L.P.A.
Cincinnati, OH
Huddleson, Mary Catherine ... Boston, MA
Huddleson, William A. ... Cincinnati, OH
Huddleston, Andrea ... Lawrenceburg, TN
Huddleston, Benjamin Cockrill
Nashville, TN
Huddleston, Bolen, Beatty, Porter & Copen
Ashland, KY
Charleston, WV
Huntington, WV
Huddleston, Brannon ... Nashville, TN
Huddleston, C. Lawrence ... Columbus, OH
Huddleston, Charles T. ... Atlanta, GA
Huddleston, David M. ... Portsmouth, OH
Huddleston, Dona J. ... Newport Beach, CA
Huddleston, Earl ... Columbia, KY
Huddleston, Ed ... Fort Worth, TX
Huddleston, Gary W. ... Houston, TX
Huddleston, George, III ... Birmingham, AL
Huddleston, H. Martin ... Atlanta, GA
Huddleston, Harold K.
Elizabethtown, KY
Huddleston, Harry J. ... Sheffield, AL
Huddleston & Huddleston ... Warsaw, KY
Huddleston, James P. ... Petoskey, MI
Huddleston, Joe M. ... Anchorage, AK
Huddleston, John Alex ... San Antonio, TX
Huddleston, John P. ... Concord, CA
Huddleston, Jon D. ... Leesburg, VA
Huddleston, Jonathan E. ... Windsor, NC
Huddleston, Joseph R. ... Bowling Green, KY
Huddleston, LeAnna Carr ... Birmingham, AL
Huddleston, Lee ... Bowling Green, KY
Huddleston & Loy ... Columbia, KY
Huddleston, Mark D. ... Medford, OR
Huddleston, Mary P. ... Melbourne, FL
Huddleston, Megan A. ... Hartford, CT
Huddleston, Michael C. ... DeLand, FL
Huddleston, Michael W. ... Phoenix, AZ
Huddleston, Michael W. ... Dallas, TX
Huddleston, Pamela L. ... Gulfport, MS
Huddleston, Pat, II ... Marietta, GA
Huddleston, Philip I. ... Bowling Green, KY
Huddleston, Pike, Hayes & Henderson
Oklahoma City, OK
Huddleston & Reed ... Bowling Green, KY
Huddleston, Rhonda W. ... Warsaw, KY
Huddleston, Robert A., Law Offices of
Walnut Creek, CA
Huddleston, Roxanna ... Los Angeles, CA
Huddleston, Sheila A. ... Hartford, CT
Huddleston, Stephen Lee ... Franklin, IN
Huddleston, Stephen Lee ... Indianapolis, IN
Huddleston, Stephen P. ... Warsaw, KY
Huddleston, Tamara L. ... Chandler, AZ
Huddleston and Van Zant, P.S.C.
Elizabethtown, KY
Huddlestone, Cameron D. ... Champaign, IL
Huddlestun, James E. ... Palm Harbor, FL
Huddy, Mark H. ... Lewis Center, OH
Hudec, David A. ... East Troy, WI
Hudec, Gerald J. ... San Diego, CA
Hudec, James G. ... Columbia, MD
Hudec Law Offices, S.C. ... East Troy, WI
Elkhorn, WI
Lake Geneva, WI
Hudec, Mary Dolan ... Chicago, IL
Hudec, Pamela A. ... Cleveland, OH
Hudec, Patrick J. ... East Troy, WI
Hudek, James R. ... Kansas City, MO
Hudek, Paul R. ... Dallas, TX
Hudelson, Michael J. ... Addison, IL
Hudenko, Benjamin J. ... Detroit, MI
Hudes, Erving ... Orange, CA
Hudes, Karen ... Washington, DC
Hudetz, Joseph B. ... Naperville, IL
Hudgens, A. Neil ... Mobile, AL
Hudgens, David E. ... Mobile, AL
Hudgens, James L. ... Santa Barbara, CA
Hudgens, James W. ... Spartanburg, SC
Hudgens, Joe B. ... Alhambra, CA
Hudgens, Jon K. ... Longview, TX
Hudgens, Joseph W. ... Newberry, SC
Hudgens, Margaret A. ... Grenada, MS
Hudgens, Ronald C. ... Palo Alto, CA
Maynard, MA
Hudgeons, Megan J. ... Austin, TX
Hudgin, Barry F. ... Toledo, OH
Hudgins, A. Fraser, III ... Fairfax, VA
Hudgins, Ann S. ... Washington, DC
Alexandria, VA
Hudgins & Associates, L.L.C. ... Denver, CO
Hudgins, C. Reid, III ... Kalamazoo, MI
Hudgins, Dave M. ... Athens, GA
Hudgins, David D. ... Washington, DC
Alexandria, VA
Norfolk, VA
Hudgins, David R. ... Dallas, TX
Hudgins, Donald M. ... Houston, TX
Hudgins, Edward H. ... Atlanta, GA
Hudgins & Ege, P.C. ... Virginia Beach, VA
Hudgins, Gary A. ... Dothan, AL
Hudgins, Geoffrey C. ... Austin, TX
Hudgins, Hudgins & Warrick, A Professional Corporation ... Houston, TX
Hudgins, James F. ... Houston, TX
Hudgins, Jessica T. ... Dallas, TX
Hudgins, John M., IV, (P.C.) ... Atlanta, GA
Hudgins, L. Paul ... Atlanta, GA
Hudgins Law Firm ... Washington, DC
Baltimore, MD
Alexandria, VA
Arlington, VA
Fairfax, VA
Leesburg, VA
Norfolk, VA
Hudgins, Marcia A. ... Boston, MA
Hudgins, Mary Ellen ... Seattle, WA
Hudgins, Michael D. ... San Diego, CA
Hudgins, Michael D. ... Houston, TX
Hudgins, Nancy E. ... San Francisco, CA
Hudgins, Nancy E., Law Offices of
San Francisco, CA
Hudgins, Paul S. ... Bluefield, WV
Hudgins, R. Stanley ... Virginia Beach, VA
Hudgins, Richard S. ... Tucson, AZ
Hudgins, Richard W. ... Newport News, VA
Hudgins, Robert W. ... Searcy, AR
Hudgins, Stephen A. ... Newport News, VA
Hudgins, Steven F. ... Houston, TX
Hudgins, Thomas F. ... Naples, FL
Hudgins, W. Edward, Jr. ... Virginia Beach, VA
Hudgins, William S., Jr. ... Roanoke, VA
Hudgins, William T., III ... Denver, CO
Hudgins, Willie L., Jr.
Department of Justice, Antitrust Division, GV
Hudiak, David M. ... Upper Darby, PA
Hudig, Marguerite ... Houston, TX
Hudis, Jonathan ... Arlington, VA
Hudkins, Arthur L. ... Springfield, MO
Hudman, Douglas R. ... Fort Worth, TX
Hudman, Wade C. ... Odessa, TX
Hudnall, Cohn & Abrams, P.C.
Atlanta, GA
Norcross, GA
Hudnall, H. Gilman ... Atlanta, GA
Hudnall, Lonnie M. ... Miami, FL
Hudnall, Mark D. ... Summersville, WV
Hudnall, Matthew N. ... Dallas, TX
Hudnall, Michael H. ... Stanford, CA
Hudnall, Robert D. ... Dallas, TX
Hudnall, Shannon M. ... New York, NY
Hudnall, Thomas R. ... Dallas, TX
Hudnell, Faith T. ... New York, NY
Hudnell III, Lewis E. ... New York, NY
Hudner, H. Kennedy ... Hartford, CT
Hudner, Philip ... San Francisco, CA
Hudnet, Wm. M. ... Baltimore, MD
Hudnut, James H. ... Bloomfield Hills, MI
Hudnut, Stewart S. ... Glenview, IL
Hudnutt, Dean ... Richmond, VA
Hudoba, Stephen M. ... Tampa, FL
Hudock, A. Ted ... Punxsutawney, PA
Hudock, Bruce P. ... Stamford, CT
Hudock, Daniel C. ... Pittsburgh, PA
Hudock, David A. ... Pittsburgh, PA
Hudock, Joseph A. ... Greensburg, PA
Hudock, Joseph A. ... Pittsburgh, PA
Hudock, Leslie Wager ... Tampa, FL
Hudock, Michael J., III ... Pittsburgh, PA
Hudock, Michael T. ... Mifflinburg, PA
Hudock, Philip F. ... Vienna, VA
Hudock, Robert P. ... Vienna, VA
Hudock, Sawyer & Azarcon, P.C.
Vienna, VA
Hudock, William L. ... Glen Burnie, MD
Hudolin, Kimberly K. ... Detroit, MI
Hudon, Edward G. ... Brunswick, ME
Hudon, Paul A. ... West Hartford, CT
Hudson & Alden, LLP
Oklahoma City, OK
Hudson, Ann Beane ... Forrest City, AR
Hudson & Associates ... Sarasota, FL
Hudson & Associates, P.C. ... Atlanta, GA
Hudson, Barbara J. ... Rockville, MD
Hudson, Barbara Shapiro
Department of Commerce, Patent and Trademark Office, GV
Hudson, Barry A. ... Wheat Ridge, CO
Hudson, Benjamin G., Jr. ... Macon, GA
Hudson, Benjamin, Jr. ... St. Louis, MO
Hudson, Blake ... Fort Scott, KS
Hudson & Bondurant, P.C. ... West Point, VA
Hudson, Boyd D. ... Pasadena, CA
Hudson, Brandon T. ... San Antonio, TX
Hudson, Bruce G. ... Lansing, MI
Hudson, Bruce L., Law Office of
Dover, DE
Georgetown, DE
Hudson, Bruce L., Law Office of
Wilmington, DE
Hudson, C. Anne ... El Cajon, CA
Hudson, C. Gilbert, Jr. ... Emporia, VA
Hudson, Camelinda V. ... Athens, TN
Hudson, Cathleen Ann ... Baltimore, MD
Hudson, Charles A. ... Racine, WI
Hudson, Charles F. ... Portland, OR
Hudson, Cheryl L. ... Washington, DC
Hudson, Chris C. ... Dallas, TX
Hudson, Christine A. ... San Jose, CA
Hudson, Christopher A. ... Charlotte, NC
Hudson, Christopher C. ... Scottsville, VA
Hudson, Clarence L. ... Troy, MI
Hudson, Clark R. ... San Diego, CA
Hudson, Clyde M. ... Rockwall, TX
Hudson Cook, LLP ... Washington, DC
Baltimore, MD
Crofton, MD
Hudson, Craig S. ... Philadelphia, PA
Hudson, Creyke, Koehler & Tacke
Alexandria, VA
Hudson, D. Bradley ... Seattle, WA
Hudson, Dale A. ... Irvine, CA
Hudson, Daniel Hurd ... Purvis, MS
Hudson, Daryl J., III, Law Offices of
Washington, DC
Hudson, David E. ... Augusta, GA
Aiken, SC
Hudson, David M. ... Miami, FL
Hudson, David M. ... Minneapolis, MN
Hudson, David S. ... White Marsh, VA
Hudson, Dennis L. ... Hoffman Estates, IL
Hudson, Diana M. ... Houston, TX
Hudson, Dirk L. ... Los Angeles, CA
Hudson, Donald ... Fayetteville, NC
Hudson, Donald C. ... St. Charles, IL
Hudson, Dorothy A. ... Vero Beach, FL
Hudson & Dougherty ... Bristol, TN
Hudson, Douglas W. ... Woodland, CA
Hudson, Edw. R., Jr. ... Fort Worth, TX
Hudson, Edward G. ... Tacoma, WA
Hudson, Edward J. ... Boston, MA
Hudson, Edward L. ... Nashville, TN
Hudson, Edward P. ... Atlanta, GA
Hudson, Edwin R. ... Tallahassee, FL
Hudson, Elbert T. ... Los Angeles, CA
Hudson, Eliot R. ... San Francisco, CA
Hudson, Emanuel K. ... Irvine, CA
Hudson, Eric E. ... Burlington, VT
Hudson, Eric V. ... New York, NY
Hudson, Eugene L. ... San Jose, CA
Hudson & Felzer, P.C. ... Marlton, NJ
Hudson, Fletcher L. ... Memphis, TN
Hudson, Frances Elizabeth
Myrtle Beach, SC
Hudson, Franklin N. ... Houston, TX
Hudson, Fred, Jr. ... Center, TX

Hudson, Frederick G. ....Paradise Valley, AZ
Hudson, Frederick M. ....Elkhart, IA
Hudson and Galloway, A Professional Corporation ....Pooler, GA
Hudson, Gary L., Jr. ....Phoenix, AZ
Hudson, Gary N. ....London, KY
Hudson, Gene ....Hamilton, OH
Hudson & Gentry, L.L.C. ....Shallotte, NC
Conway, SC
Myrtle Beach, SC
Hudson, Geoffrey R. ....Portola Valley, CA
Hudson, George (Dewey), Jr.
Kenansville, NC
Hudson, Gerald A. ....Detroit, MI
Hudson, Gerald M. ....Tuscaloosa, AL
Hudson, Gregory E. ....Providence, RI
Hudson, Gretchen K. ....Irvine, CA
Hudson, H. Eugene ....Myrtle Beach, SC
Hudson, H. Webb, Jr. ....Luray, VA
Hudson, Hal S. ....Houston, TX
Hudson, Harold J., Jr. ....Key Largo, FL
Hudson, Harry E. ....Stockton, CA
Hudson, Heather E. ....San Francisco, CA
Hudson, Heather E. ....Kalamazoo, MI
Hudson, Heidi Dammers
Farmington Hills, MI
Hudson, Helen Clare
Department Of Health And Human Services, GV
Hudson, Henry A. ....Watertown, NY
Hudson, Henry A., Jr. ....Greensburg, PA
Hudson, Henry C. ....Mt. Vernon, IN
Hudson, Henry E. ....Fairfax, VA
Hudson, Hope L. ....Palo Alto, CA
Hudson, Howard V., Jr.
Winston-Salem, NC
Hudson, Howard W., Jr. ....Georgetown, DE
Hudson, H.W. ....Atlanta, GA
Hudson, Ike A. ....Newnan, GA
Hudson, Isham B., Jr. ....Raleigh, NC
Hudson, J. Clifford ....Oklahoma City, OK
Hudson, J. Dwight ....Shallotte, NC
Conway, SC
Myrtle Beach, SC
Hudson, J. Greg ....Austin, TX
Hudson, J. Steven ....Deerfield Beach, FL
Hudson, J. William ....Chantilly, VA
Hudson, Jack L. ....Colorado Springs, CO
Hudson, James C. ....Pocahontas, IA
Pomeroy, IA
Hudson, James C. ....Frankfort, KY
Hudson, James D.
Federal Deposit Insurance Corporation, Liquidation Branch, GV
Hudson, James D. ....Douglas, GA
Hudson, James D., P.C. ....Douglas, GA
Hudson, James E. ....Athens, GA
Hudson, James E., III ....Houston, TX
Houston, TX
San Antonio, TX
Hudson, James H., III ....West Point, VA
Hudson, James L., Jr. ....Highland Park, MI
Hudson, James M. ....Roswell, NM
Hudson, James T., Jr. (Professional Corporation) ....Los Angeles, CA
Hudson, James W. ....Pocahontas, IA
Hudson, Jas. H. ....Austin, TX
Hudson, Jean Ann ....Tulsa, OK
Hudson, Jean Barrett ....Charlottesville, VA
Hudson, Jeffrey L. ....Troy, MI
Hudson, Jeffrey Reid ....Los Angeles, CA
Hudson, Jill M. ....Phoenix, AZ
Hudson, Joel B. ....Fort Worth, TX
Hudson, John ....Evanston, IL
Hudson, John ....Oklahoma City, OK
Hudson, John A. ....Eugene, OR
Hudson, John D. ....Irvine, CA
Hudson, John D. ....Des Moines, IA
Hudson, John E. ....Torrington, CT
Hudson, John N. ....Natchez, MS
Hudson, John R. ....Fayetteville, AR
Hudson, John R., Jr. ....Pisgah Forest, NC
Hudson, John T. ....Salisbury, NC
Hudson, Jones, Jaywork & Fisher
Dover, DE
Georgetown, DE
Rehoboth Beach, DE
Hudson, Joseph B., Jr. ....Los Angeles, CA
Hudson, Joseph B., Jr. ....Culpeper, VA
Hudson, Joseph D. ....Lexington, KY
Hudson, Joseph W. ....Jasper, AL
Hudson, Judith L. ....Detroit, MI
Hudson, Judith M. ....Chicago, IL
Hudson, Karen Wagner ....Murfreesboro, TN
Hudson, Kathleen ....Miami, FL
Hudson, Kathleen E. ....Washington, DC
Hudson, Kathleen R. ....Ruskin, FL
Hudson, Kenna M. ....Roseland, NJ
Hudson, Kevin H. ....Atlanta, GA
Hudson and Kilby ....Essex, CT
Hudson & King ....Decatur, GA
Hudson, Kirk M. ....Alexandria, VA
Hudson & Kooiman ....Monrovia, CA
Hudson, Kurt L. ....Chicago, IL
Hudson, Lauri A. ....Marlton, NJ
Hudson, Laurie B. ....Little Rock, AR
Hudson Law Firm ....Pocahontas, IA
Pomeroy, IA
Hudson, Leigh C. ....Fort Scott, KS
Hudson, Lisa R. ....San Antonio, TX
Hudson, Lise L. ....Boca Raton, FL
Delray Beach, FL
Palm Beach Gardens, FL
Hudson, Lise L. ....West Palm Beach, FL
Hudson, Lydie Arthos ....Madison, WI
Hudson, M. Ashton ....Atlanta, GA
Hudson, M. Leah ....Washington, DC
Hudson, Mabeth W. ....Towson, MD
Hudson, Marcus ....Chapel Hill, NC
Hudson, Marilyn L. ....Knoxville, TN
Hudson, Mark A. ....Nashville, TN
Hudson, Mark W. ....San Francisco, CA
Hudson, Martin, Ferrante & Street
Monterey, CA
Hudson, Mary Jo ....Columbus, OH
Hudson, Mary L. ....San Francisco, CA
Hudson, Mary-Nona ....San Jose, CA
Hudson, Matthew L. ....Petaluma, CA
Hudson, Maureen ....Santa Clara, CA
Hudson, Michael A. ....Renton, WA
Hudson, Michael B. ....San Jose, CA
Hudson, Michael C. ....Durham, NC
Hudson, Michael E. ....Washington, DC
Hudson, Michele Haft ....Miami, FL
Hudson, Michelle M.
Merit Systems Protection Board, Washington, D.C. Regional Office, GV
Hudson, Molly M. ....Forsyth, GA
Hudson, Montgomery and Kalivoda
Athens, GA
Hudson & Mullies, L.L.C. ....Fort Scott, KS
Hudson, Murray ....Miami, FL
Miami Beach, FL
West Palm Beach, FL
Hudson, Nobie E. ....Hanceville, AL
Hudson, Nora M. ....Detroit, MI
Hudson, Ozell, Jr. ....Boston, MA
Hudson, Patricia A. ....Lakewood, CO
Hudson, Patrick A. ....Dallas, TX
Hudson, Paul B. ....San Francisco, CA
Hudson, Paul B. ....Washington, DC
Hudson, Paul C. ....Los Angeles, CA
Hudson, Paul F. ....Springfield, VT
Hudson, Paul L., Jr. ....Atlanta, GA
Hudson, Paul S. ....Albany, NY
Hudson, Paul S., P.C., Law Offices of
Albany, NY
Hudson, Perry W. ....Norman, OK
Hudson and Peterson ....Brevard, NC
Hudson, Phillip M., III ....Miami, FL
Hudson, Potts & Bernstein ....Monroe, LA
Hudson, Quinton T. ....Atlanta, GA
Hudson, R. Kent, Law Offices of
Natchez, MS
Hudson, R. Read ....Springdale, AR
Hudson, R. Seth ....Philadelphia, PA
Hudson, Rebecca Wilson ....Tampa, FL
Hudson, Rene Reilly ....Jacksonville, NC
Hudson, Richard A. ....Charleston, WV
Parkersburg, WV
Hudson, Richard B., & Associates
Escondido, CA
Hudson, Richard J. ....Hastings, MI
Hudson, Richard Lee ....Chattanooga, TN
Hudson, Richard T. ....Chattanooga, TN
Hudson, R. J., II ....Des Moines, IA
Hudson, Robert A. ....Detroit, MI
Hudson, Robert Aaron, II ....Yukon, OK
Hudson, Robert B. ....San Jose, CA
Hudson, Robert C. ....Culpeper, VA
Hudson, Robert D. ....Covington, KY
Cincinnati, OH
Hudson, Robert F., Jr. ....Miami, FL
Hudson, Robert L. ....Guthrie, OK
Hudson, Robert L. ....Nashville, TN
Hudson, Robert W. ....Miami, FL
Hudson, Robyn Anne ....Tavares, FL
Hudson, Rockney W. ....Chicago, IL
Hudson, Roger J. ....Des Moines, IA
Hudson, Roger L. ....Anchorage, AK
Hudson, Roger W. ....Murfreesboro, TN
Hudson, Ronald N. ....Tuscumbia, AL
Hudson, Ronald R. ....Oklahoma City, OK
Hudson, Ruth J. ....Cleveland, OH
Hudson, Sally A. ....Chicago, IL
Hudson, Samuel W., III ....Dallas, TX
Hudson, Sanchia ....Houston, TX
Hudson, Scott ....Dallas, TX
Hudson, Scott N. ....New York, NY
Hudson, Shijuana Biancaá ....Birmingham, AL
Hudson, Stanley D. ....Dallas, TX
Hudson, Stephen E. ....Atlanta, GA
Hudson, Steven Daniel ....Trenton, MO
Hudson, Stewart C. ....Harker Heights, TX
Hudson, Ted R. ....Department Of The Interior, Bureau of Land Management, GV
Hudson, Thomas B. ....Washington, DC
Crofton, MD
Hudson, Thomas B., Jr. ....Austin, TX
Hudson, Thomas G. ....De Witt, AR
Hudson, Thomas H. ....Washington, DC
Hudson, Thomas L. ....Phoenix, AZ
Hudson, Thomas L. ....Grove City, OH
Hudson, Thomas N. ....Roseville, CA
Hudson, Thomas R. ....Ontario, CA
Hudson, Thomas R. ....Jackson, MS
Hudson, Thomas R., A Prof. Law Corp., Law Offices of ....Ontario, CA
Hudson, Thomas S. ....Sarasota, FL
Hudson, Tighe F. ....Los Angeles, CA
Hudson, Timothy C. ....Columbus, MS
Hudson, Timothy W. ....Bristol, TN
Hudson, Tracy C. ....Manassas, VA
Hudson, Victor T. ....Mobile, AL
Hudson, Vinette Morris, Law Offices of
Orlando, FL
Hudson, W. Banks, III ....Danville, KY
Hudson, W. Banks, III ....Danville, KY
Hudson, W. Bryan ....Louisville, KY
Hudson, W. Campbell, III ....Essex, CT
Hudson, W. Thomas ....Richmond, VA
Hudson & Watts, L.L.P. ....Mobile, AL
Hudson, Wendy Wiedemann ....St. Louis, MO
Hudson, Wilbur N., III ....Phoenix, AZ
Hudson, William A., II ....Fort Worth, TX
Hudson, William C. ....Pocomoke City, MD
Hudson, William C. ....Aitkin, MN
Hudson, William C., Jr. ....Los Angeles, CA
Hudson, William D. ....Gadsden, AL
Hudson, William E. ....Greensburg, KY
Hudson, William J., Jr. ....Fort Myers, FL
Hudson, William J., P.A. ....Fort Myers, FL
Hudson, William L. ....San Francisco, CA
Hudson, William M., III ....Lafayette, LA
Hudson, William Newt ....Tarpon Springs, FL
Hudson, William R. ....Philadelphia, PA
Hudson, William S. ....Dover, DE
Hudson, William T. ....Pooler, GA
Hudson, William T., Jr. ....Decatur, GA
Hudson, Yana S. ....Washington, DC
Hudson Youngblood ....Seattle, WA
Hudson-Winfield, Gilda ....Chicago, IL
Hudspeth, Amy Rene ....Boston, MA
Hudspeth, Brent S. ....Decatur, GA
Hudspeth, C. M. ....Houston, TX
Hudspeth, Donald W. ....Phoenix, AZ
Hudspeth, Donald W., A Prof. Corp., The Law Offices of ....Phoenix, AZ
Hudspeth, George L. ....Jacksonville, FL
Hudspeth, Glen C. ....Texarkana, TX
Hudspeth, Harry L. ....El Paso, TX
Hudspeth, Harvey Gresham ....Itta Bena, MS
Hudspeth, John A., Jr. ....Carlyle, IL
Hudspeth, Matthew J. ....Okemah, OK
Hudspeth, N. Lawrence, III
Yadkinville, NC
Hudspeth, Reginald A. ....Norcross, GA
Hudspeth, Robert S. ....Fort Mill, SC
Hudspeth, Stephen M. ....New York, NY
Hudspeth, Thomas S. ....Los Angeles, CA
Hudspeth, William J., Jr. ....Austin, TX
Hudzietz, John, II ....Clearwater, FL
Hudzik, James B. ....Pittsburgh, PA
Hudzik, John C. ....Mineral Ridge, OH
Hudzik, Richard F. ....Downers Grove, IL
Hudzin, Walter J. ....Jersey City, NJ
Hudzinski, Michael E. ....Cleveland, OH
Hue, Donald C. ....Sun Prairie, WI
Hue, Frank ....Roseville, CA
Hue, William Felice ....Jefferson, WI
Hueber, Carl E. ....Spokane, WA
Hueber, Susan Jan ....Fort Worth, TX
Huebner, Adele L. ....Grosse Pointe Farms, MI
Huebner, Allen G. ....Chicago, IL
Huebner, Bert L. ....Bay City, TX
Huebner, Charles E. ....Houston, TX
Huebner, Christine A. ....New York, NY
Huebner, David ....Los Angeles, CA
Huebner, Fredrick D. ....Seattle, WA
Huebner, Gary W. ....New London, CT
Huebner, Harold C., Jr. ....Oak Park, IL
Huebner, Janine ....McLean, VA
Huebner, Karl E. ....Edgerton, WI
Huebner, Kelley Beckes, (Mrs.) ....Shoals, IN
Huebner, Kurt B. ....San Francisco, CA
Huebner, Larry B. ....Kansas City, MO
Huebner, Marshall S. ....New York, NY
Huebner, Robert A. ....Berkeley Heights, NJ
Huebner, Robert E. ....Fort Lauderdale, FL
Huebner, Robert E., Professional Association
Fort Lauderdale, FL
Huebner, Ted R. ....Los Angeles, CA
Huebner, William L. ....Bloomfield Hills, MI
Huebsch, Jeffrey B. ....Oakbrook Terrace, IL
Huebsch, Mark J. ....Newport Beach, CA
Huebsch, Maurice O. ....Monterey Park, CA
Huebsch, Neal D. ....Eustis, FL
Huebsch, Robert P. ....Chicago, IL
Huebsch, Ronald A. ....Buffalo, NY
Huebsch, William L. ....St. Paul, MN
Huebschman, Martin J., Jr.
Salt Lake City, UT
Huebschman, Matthew ....Roanoke, VA
Huebschmann, Jeffrey A. ....Boston, MA
Hueckel, Donna L. ....Los Angeles, CA
Huecker, Michael P. ....Baltimore, MD
Huefner, Carl F. ....Salt Lake City, UT
Huefner, Dixie Snow ....Salt Lake City, UT
Huefner, Steven F. ....United States Senate, Office of Senate Legal Counsel, GV
Huefner, William F. ....Minneapolis, MN
Huegel, H. Donald ....Sacramento, CA
Huegel, L. James ....Pittsburgh, PA
Huegel, Peter A. V. ....Newport News, VA
Huegel, Russell J. ....River Edge, NJ
Huegel, Tamara K. ....Chicago, IL
Huegel, Teresa Christine ....Baldwinsville, NY
Huegli, James D. ....Portland, OR
Huegli & Jones, P.C. ....Portland, OR
Huegli, Richard F., Jr. ....Port Huron, MI
Huelat & Gardner ....Michigan City, IN
South Bend, IN
Huelat, Jerry E. ....Michigan City, IN
Huelbig, Larry L. ....Houston, TX
Huelsberg, Henry J., III ....Norfolk, VA
Huelsenbeck, Peter W. ....Santa Ana, CA
Huelskamp, Robert D.
Ste. Genevieve, MO
Huelskamp, Terrence L. ....Wichita, KS
Huelsman, Brian D. ....Dayton, OH
Huelsman, Joanne B. ....Waukesha, WI
Huelsman, Kristopher M. ....Columbus, OH
Huelsman, Lisa A. ....Toledo, OH
Huelsmann, Martin J. ....Highland Heights, KY
Huelson, Lloyd Donald, Jr ....Olathe, KS
Huelster, Pamela A. ....New York, NY
Huemmer, Thomas J. ....Lorain, OH
Huemoeller, Bryce D. ....Prior Lake, MN
Huemoeller, James L. ....Denver, CO
Huempfner, Lee D. ....Racine, WI
Huenergardt, Darrel J. ....Kimball, NE
Huenergardt & Neilan ....Kimball, NE
Huenink, Jennifer E. ....Portland, OR
Huenke, Theodore E. ....Melville, NY
Huennekens, Deborah Legome ....Danville, CA
Huennekens, Kevin R. ....Richmond, VA
Huerta, Alberto R. ....Corpus Christi, TX
Huerta & Associates ....San Diego, CA
Huerta, Hastings & Allison, L.L.P.
Corpus Christi, TX
Huerta, John E. ....Los Angeles, CA
Huerta, John E. ....Washington, DC
Huerta, Lawrence A. ....San Diego, CA
Huerta, Marcelino J., III ....Tampa, FL
Huerta, Marcelino J., III, P.A. ....Tampa, FL
Huerta, Michael A. R. ....Bloomington, IN
Huerta, Miguel A. ....Austin, TX
Huerta, Nancy E. ....Richmond, VA
Huerta, Sharon A. ....San Diego, CA
Huertas-Jourda, Tatiana ....Portland, OR
Huerter, Joseph P. ....Topeka, KS
Huerter, M. Jane ....Omaha, NE
Huerter-Morgan, Holly A. ....Omaha, NE
Hueschen, Gordon W. ....Kalamazoo, MI
Hueschen, Gordon W., Law Firm of
Kalamazoo, MI
Huesemann, Raymond T. ....Osceola, MO
Hueser-Stubbs, Courtney Anne
Kansas City, MO
Hueske, Jodie Williams ....Prineville, OR
Hueske, Neal A. ....Bend, OR
Portland, OR
Huesman, Jennifer Lilore ....Baltimore, MD
Huesman Jones & Miles ....Baltimore, MD
Towson, MD
Huesman, Joseph I. ....Towson, MD
Huesman, Susan M. ....Towson, MD
Huesmann, Nicole J. ....Miami, FL
Miami, FL
Huesmann, Nicole J., P.A. ....Miami, FL
Hueso, Felipe D. ....San Diego, CA
Huessy, Hans G. ....Rutland, VT
Huestis, Carolyn M. ....Los Angeles, CA
Huestis, Lisa ....New York, NY
Huestis, Samuel M. ....Ventura, CA
Hueston, Hueston, Sheehan & Cooney
Elizabeth, NJ
Hueston, John C. ....Newport Beach, CA
Hueston, McNulty & Mueller, A Professional Corporation ....Atlantic City, NJ
Elizabeth, NJ
Florham Park, NJ
Hackensack, NJ
Jersey City, NJ
Morristown, NJ
Newark, NJ
Toms River, NJ
Hueston, Robert G. ....Denver, CO
Hueston, Robert J. ....Florham Park, NJ
Toms River, NJ
Hueston, Robert T. ....Elizabeth, NJ
Hueston, Suzanne N. ....Harrisburg, PA
Huet, David R. ....Stamford, CT
Huether, Alvin L. ....Tumwater, WA
Huether, Gregory J. ....Rochester, NY
Huetsch, Jay M. ....Columbia, IL
Huettel, Gina D. ....Pleasanton, CA
Huettel, Richard C. ....Chicago, IL
Huetteman, Raymond T., Jr.
Ann Arbor, MI
Huetteman, William F. ....Detroit, MI
Huetter, Glenn A., Jr. ....Pittsburgh, PA
Huettner, Frank E. ....Cadott, WI
Huettner, Henry A. ....Atlanta, GA
Huettner, Richard A. ....New York, NY
Huettner, Susan A. ....Falmouth, MA
Hyannis, MA
Huevler, Raymond A. ....Greenfield, WI
Huey, Benjamin M., II ....Milan, TN
Huey, Charles M. ....San Antonio, TX
Huey, Clint ....Warren, AR
Huey, David W. ....Bismarck, ND
Huey, Erik B. ....Washington, DC
Atlanta, GA
Huey, Frances C. ....Sacramento, CA
Huey, Guilday & Tucker, P.A.
Tallahassee, FL
Huey, J. Michael ....Tallahassee, FL
Huey, Jeanne M. ....Dallas, TX
Huey, John W. ....Kansas City, MO
Huey, Joseph M. ....Phoenix, AZ
Huey, Kelly L. ....Oakland, CA
Huey & Leon ....Mobile, AL
Huey, Mary Ann, Law Offices of
Dallas, TX
Huey, Mary Carroll ....Stamford, CT
Huey, Michael G. ....Mobile, AL
Huey, Nora A.
General Services Administration, Office of the General Counsel, GV
Huey, Paul L. ....Tampa, FL
Huey, Robert H. ....Washington, DC
Huey, Robert M. ....Austin, TX
Huey, Vanessa A. ....Brea, CA
Huey, William R., Jr. ....Indianapolis, IN
Huey-Burns, Paul
Securities and Exchange Commission, Division of Enforcement, GV
Huez, Kenneth L. ....Sacramento, CA
Huez, Marlys Fredrickson ....Sacramento, CA
Hufbauer, Gary C. ....Chevy Chase, MD
Huff, A. Newton ....Philadelphia, PA
Huff, Barbara Kay ....Lawrence, KS
Huff, Barbara S. ....Fresno, CA
Huff, Bart ....Chicago, IL
Huff, Bernard ....Indianapolis, IN
Huff, Bob ....Lubbock, TX
Huff, Bradley E. ....Springfield, IL
Huff, Bryant ....Lawrenceville, GA
Huff, C. Wayne ....Dallas, TX
Huff, Carrie Kiger ....Chicago, IL
Huff, Carrie Lee ....Dallas, TX

Huff & Cauthen, LLC ... **Columbia, SC**
Irmo, SC
Huff, Charles E. ... **Las Vegas, NV**
Reno, NV
Huff, Chris M. ... Cumming, GA
Huff, Cindy M. ... Tacoma, WA
Huff, Curtis W. ... **Houston, TX**
Huff, Daniel J. ... **Atlanta, GA**
Huff, David ... Riverside, CA
Huff, David J. ... Birmingham, MI
Huff, David L. ... **Lexington, KY**
Huff, David M. ... **Los Angeles, CA**
Huff, David O. ... **Nashville, TN**
Huff, Debra K. ... Athens, OH
Huff, Diane M. ... **Chicago, IL**
Huff, Donald N. ... **Washington, DC**
Huff, Donald S. ... **Marshall, MO**
Huff, E. Gail ... Houston, TX
Huff, Elizabeth Ann ... **Harlan, KY**
Huff, Emmett Sterling ... Houston, TX
Huff, Ernest R. (Ros), Jr. ... **Irmo, SC**
Huff, Frederick, Law Offices of
Denver, CO
Huff & Gaines Ltd. ... **Chicago, IL**
Huff, Gary D. ... **Seattle, WA**
Huff, Gayle G. ... **Harlan, KY**
Huff, George B., Jr.
Administrative Office Of The United States Courts, GV
Huff, George R. ... Othello, WA
Huff, George S. ... **Marshall, MO**
Huff, Glen A. ... **Virginia Beach, VA**
Huff, Glen D. ... **Oklahoma City, OK**
Huff, Harley ... Lubbock, TX
Huff, Henry B. ... Louisville, KY
Huff and Huff ... **Marshall, MO**
Huff, J. Brian ... **Birmingham, AL**
Huff, J. Schuyler ... **Cranbury, NJ**
Huff, J. Warren ... Charlestown, MA
Huff, Jack ... Midland, TX
Huff, James B. ... **Aiken, SC**
Huff, James B. ... **North Augusta, SC**
Huff, James G., Jr. ... Raleigh, NC
Huff, James R., II ... Altoona, PA
Huff, Jay S. ... Muscatine, IA
Huff, Jean Smiertka ... **New York, NY**
Huff, Jewett E. ... Amarillo, TX
Huff, John Chafer ... **Chicago, IL**
Huff, John L. ... **Chicago, IL**
Huff, John M. ... **Grand Rapids, MI**
Huff, John M. ... Kansas City, MO
Huff, Joseph B. ... Marshall, NC
Huff, Joseph H. ... **Augusta, GA**
Huff, Julia A. ... **St. Paul, MN**
Huff, Kay Elizabeth ... Santa Rosa, CA
Huff & Kennedy ... Chicago, IL
Huff, Kevin B. ... **Washington, DC**
Huff, Kevin D. ... Jackson, MS
Huff Law Offices ... **Harlan, KY**
Huff, Margaret D. ... **Scotia, NY**
Huff, Margaret M. ... **Indianapolis, IN**
Huff, Margaret M. ... Nashville, TN
Huff, Marilyn L. ... San Diego, CA
Huff, Marsha E. ... **Milwaukee, WI**
Huff, Max E. ... Oneida, TN
Huff, Melinda S. ... **Dallas, TX**
Huff, Michael N. ... Philadelphia, PA
Huff, Michael S. ... Marietta, GA
Huff, Michael S., & Associates, P.C.
Marietta, GA
Huff, Michelle C., Law Office of
Cherokee Village, AR
Huff, Moran & Orron ... **Cranbury, NJ**
Monroe Township, NJ
Huff & Nelson ... Louisville, KY
Huff, P. Samuel ... **Marietta, GA**
Huff, Pamela B. ... San Antonio, TX
Huff, Parks F. ... **Marietta, GA**
Huff, Paul J., Jr. ... **Chicago, IL**
Huff, Poole & Mahoney, A Professional Corporation ... **Chesterfield, VA**
Lynchburg, VA
Virginia Beach, VA
Huff, R. Randall ... **Los Angeles, CA**
Huff, R. Robert ... **Tulsa, OK**
Huff, R. Stuart, (P.A.) ... **Tallahassee, FL**
Huff, Ralph R. ... Plymouth, IN
Huff, Raymond L. ... Peoria, IL
Huff, Richard D. ... **Houston, TX**
Huff, Richard L. ... Department of Justice, Office of Information and Privacy, GV
Huff, Richard L. ... Berrien Springs, MI
Huff, Robert J. ... Watkinsville, GA
Huff, Robert M. ... Charlottesville, VA
Huff, Rodrick D. ... Sarasota, FL
Huff, Roger M. ... Chicago, IL
Huff, Roy B., Jr. ... **Peachtree City, GA**
Huff, Stephen E. ... **Marshall, NC**
Huff, Stephen F. ... **New York, NY**
Huff, Steven D. ... Fresno, CA
Huff, Steven D. ... **Milwaukee, WI**
Huff, Steven K. ... **Des Moines, IA**
Huff, Steven S. ... **Omaha, NE**
Huff, Stewart A. ... **Sioux City, IA**
Huff, Thomas E. ... Aiken, SC
Huff, Thomas T. ... **Kalamazoo, MI**
Huff, Timothy R. ... St. Charles, MO
Huff, Valerie S. ... **Dallas, TX**
Huff, William A. ... Chicago, IL
Huff, William H., III ... **Irving, TX**
Huff, William S. ... **Denver, CO**
Huff, William Stacy ... **Harlan, KY**
Huff, Winter R., (Ms.) ... **Somerset, KY**
Huff, Woods and Hamby ... **Marietta, GA**
Huffaker & Conway, A Professional Corporation ... **Albuquerque, NM**
Santa Fe, NM
Huffaker, Dale C. ... Victorville, CA

Huffaker, David Alan ... **Pasadena, CA**
Huffaker & Furlow P.L.L.C.
Lubbock, TX
Tahoka, TX
Huffaker, Gerald ... **Tahoka, TX**
Huffaker, Green & Huffaker ... **Tahoka, TX**
Huffaker, Gregory D., Jr.
Albuquerque, NM
Santa Fe, NM
Huffaker, Jeffrey D. ... Pittsburg, CA
Huffaker, John ... **Amarillo, TX**
Huffaker, John B. ... **Washington, DC**
Berwyn, PA
Philadelphia, PA
Huffaker, Joseph M. ... **Nashville, TN**
Huffaker, Robert A. ... **Montgomery, AL**
Huffaker, Stephen L. ... Las Vegas, NV
Huffaker, Thomas K. ...
Department of State, GV
Huffaker, W. Calloway ... **Tahoka, TX**
Huffard, Susan P. ... **New York, NY**
Huffenus, Daniel S. ... **Charlotte, NC**
Huffer, Duane ... Warsaw, IN
Huffer and Huffer Co., L.P.A.
Circleville, OH
Huffer, James R. ... Delphi, IN
Huffer Law Office ... Story City, IA
Huffer, Michael K. ... **Omaha, NE**
Huffer, Robert H. ... **Circleville, OH**
Huffer, Robert L. ... Story City, IA
Huffer, Roy H., Jr. ... **Circleville, OH**
Huffer, Steven K. ... **Indianapolis, IN**
Huffer & Weathers, P.C. ... **Indianapolis, IN**
Huffhines, Robert W., Jr., Law Office of
Kelso, WA
Huffine, David E. ... **Wilmington, NC**
Huffine, David E., P.A. ... **Wilmington, NC**
Huffine, Ellen C. ... **West Covina, CA**
Huffine, Loretta B. ... Aurora, CO
Huffine, Virginia Shirley Cosby
Baltimore, MD
Huffines, James P., Jr. ... Lewisville, NC
Huffington, Jean E. ... Seattle, WA
Huffman, A. Kate ... **Phoenix, AZ**
Huffman, Alisa D. ... Raleigh, NC
Huffman, Allen C. ... Arlington, VA
Huffman & Associates, P.C.
Chadds Ford, PA
Huffman, B. Scott ... Arlington, TX
Huffman, Barbara L. ... Rockford, IL
Huffman, Barry L. ... Leawood, KS
Huffman, Bart W. ... **San Antonio, TX**
Huffman, Bill ... Princeton, WV
Huffman, Bradford W. ... Newport News, VA
Huffman, Brock ... San Antonio, TX
Huffman, Bruce C. ... New Smyrna Beach, FL
Fremont, OH
Huffman, Bruce E. ... Reno, NV
Huffman, Byron Keith, Jr.
Washington, DC
Huffman, Byron L. ... **Landover, MD**
Huffman, Byron L., P.C. ... **Washington, DC**
Landover, MD
Huffman, C. Wayne ... Austin, TX
Huffman, Carol L. ... Monroe, NC
Huffman, Charles A. ... Newport News, VA
Huffman, Charles S., Jr. ... Westlake, OH
Huffman, Cheryl Rylander ... **New York, NY**
Huffman, Clifford R. ... Santa Barbara, CA
Huffman, Dale E. ... **Englewood, CO**
Huffman, Damon R. ... Flushing, MI
Huffman, Darlene A. ... San Rafael, CA
Huffman, David L. ... Chadds Ford, PA
Huffman, David M. ... San Diego, CA
Huffman, David R. ... Graham, NC
Huffman, Dennis L. ... Tampa, FL
Huffman, Diane Rausch
Bowling Green, OH
Huffman, Donald J. ... Cleveland, OH
Huffman, Donald R. ... Bentonville, AR
Huffman, Donald R. ... Wadesboro, NC
Huffman, Donald W., & Associates, P.C.
Roanoke, VA
Huffman, Donald Wise ... Roanoke, VA
Huffman, Douglas W. ... **Findlay, OH**
Huffman, Dwight J. ... Pompey, NY
Huffman, Earl R. ... Cincinnati, OH
Huffman, Elizabeth M. ... Gahanna, OH
Huffman, Fordham E. ... **Columbus, OH**
Huffman, Gerald J., Jr. ... **New Orleans, LA**
Huffman, Gregory A. ... **Muncie, IN**
Huffman, Gregory A. ... **St. Louis, MO**
Huffman, Gregory D. ... Hickory, NC
Huffman, Gregory S. C. ... **Dallas, TX**
Huffman, H. Dale ... Omaha, NE
Huffman, Harry V. ... Indianapolis, IN
Huffman & Huffman ... Newport News, VA
Huffman, J. Andrew ... **Wilmington, DE**
Huffman, James D. ... St. Helens, OR
Huffman, James L. ... Orange, CA
Huffman, James L. ... Portland, OR
Huffman, Jared W. ... **San Rafael, CA**
Huffman, Jarrett L. ... Pasadena, TX
Huffman, Jennifer I. ... **New York, NY**
Huffman, Jeremy K. ... **Washington, DC**
Huffman, John C. ... **Lima, OH**
Huffman, John L. ... **Toledo, OH**
Huffman, John P. ... Treasury Department, Internal Revenue Service, GV
Huffman, John W. ... **Carbondale, IL**
Huffman, Julie A. ... Ventura, CA
Huffman, Kathryn Maher ... Troy, OH
West Milton, OH
Huffman, Kathy ... Houston, TX
Huffman, Keith P. ... Bluffton, IN
Huffman, Kent ... Palm Beach, FL
Huffman, Kevin ... **Washington, DC**

Huffman, Landis, Weaks & Wist Co., L.P.A.
Tipp City, OH
Troy, OH
West Milton, OH
Huffman, Laura ... Pleasant Hill, CA
Huffman, Laurence M.
Oklahoma City, OK
Huffman, Lawrence A. ... **Lima, OH**
Huffman, Lawrence S. ... **Lima, OH**
Huffman, Lee W. ... Santa Fe, NM
Huffman, Lyle R. ... Phoenix, AZ
Huffman, Mark F. ... Dallas, TX
Huffman, Mark Gordon ... **Wellesley, MA**
Huffman, Mark R. ... **San Francisco, CA**
Huffman, Mary Katherine ... Troy, OH
Huffman, Matthew C. ... **Lima, OH**
Huffman, Med Z. ... Columbus Grove, OH
Huffman, Michael J. ... **Saginaw, MI**
Huffman, Michael J., P.C. ... **Saginaw, MI**
Huffman, Michael S. ... Independence, MO
Huffman, Nina R. ... **New York, NY**
Huffman, Odell H. ... Princeton, WV
Huffman, Peggy W. ... Fort Worth, TX
Huffman, Philip S. ... Hartville, MO
Huffman, Rex H. ... **Bowling Green, OH**
Rossford, OH
Huffman, Richard D. ... San Diego, CA
Huffman, Richard E. ... **Rapid City, SD**
Huffman, Richard L. ... **New York, NY**
Huffman, Richard L., Jr. ... **Salisbury, NC**
Huffman, Richard R. ... **Anchorage, AK**
Huffman, Richard W. ... **Minneapolis, MN**
Huffman, Robert A., Jr. ... **Tulsa, OK**
Huffman, Robert J. ... Troy, OH
West Milton, OH
Huffman, Robert J., Jr. ... Troy, OH
West Milton, OH
Huffman, Robert K. ... **Washington, DC**
Huffman, Robert L. ... Monroe, NC
Huffman, Rosemary Adams ... Indianapolis, IN
Huffman, Roxie A. ... Orange, TX
Huffman, Rubin ... Brooklyn, NY
Huffman, Samuel L. ... Troy, OH
Huffman, Sharon Jackson
Wilmington, NC
Huffman, Stephen D. ... Alexandria, LA
Huffman, Stephen D., A P.L.C.
Alexandria, LA
Huffman, Terry D. ... Norfolk, VA
Huffman, Thad S. ... **Washington, DC**
Huffman & Thomas ... Cleveland, OH
Huffman, Thomas A. ... Hillsboro, OR
Huffman Thomas & Rounds ... Tulsa, OK
Huffman, Timothy E. ... **Charleston, WV**
Huffman, Usem, Saboe, Crawford & Greenberg, P.A. ... **Minneapolis, MN**
Huffman, Vickie L. ... Roanoke, VA
Huffman, W. George ... Hickory, NC
Huffman, Walter B. ... Department of the Army, Office of the Judge Advocate General, GV
Huffman, William C. ... Westlake, OH
Huffman, William H. ... Tulsa, OK
Huffman, William H., III
Securities and Exchange Commission, GV
Huffman, William M. ... Marshall, TX
Huffman, William M., P.C. ... Marshall, TX
Huffman, William R. ... Troy, MI
Huffman, Yale ... Denver, CO
Huffman, Zenger & Rich, P.C.
Hillsboro, OR
Huffmire, Madelyn M.
Mansfield Center, CT
Hufford, Brian D. ... San Leandro, CA
Hufford, C. Benson ... **Flagstaff, AZ**
Hufford, Catherine A. ... Chicago, IL
Hufford, Chas T., Jr. ... Hillsborough, CA
Hufford, D. Brian ... **New York, NY**
Hufford, Horstman, Mongini, Parnell & McCarthy, P.C. ... **Flagstaff, AZ**
Hufford, J. Stephen ... Atlanta, GA
Hufford, Judith L. ... Colorado Springs, CO
Hufford, Marc G. ... Rio Rancho, NM
Hufford, Wade H. ... Oakland, CA
Hufford, Wendy Lynn ... **Stamford, CT**
Huffsmith, Richard L. ... Wilkes-Barre, PA
Huffsteter, Raymond ... Phoenix, AZ
Huffstetler, David L. ... Raleigh, NC
Huffstetler, L. R., Jr., Law Offices of
Brooksville, FL
Huffstetler, Michael R. ... **Washington, DC**
Huffstetler, Noah H., III ... **Raleigh, NC**
Huffstetler, Palmer E. ... Cherryville, NC
Huffstetler, Palmer E., Jr. ... Cherryville, NC
Huffstetler, Rachel Healey ... **Charlotte, NC**
Huffstickler, Patrick L. ... **San Antonio, TX**
Huffstutler, J. Terry, Jr. ... Guntersville, AL
Huffstutler, Joe D. ... Tyler, TX
Huffstutler, John Haven ... Charlotte, NC
Huffstutler, Miles M. ... Birmingham, AL
Huffstutter, Dan E. ... Nashville, TN
Hufft, Ashley E. ... **Atlanta, GA**
Hufft, David M. ... **Belle Chasse, LA**
Hufft, Michael D. ... Mission, KS
Kansas City, MO
Hufft, Patrick H. ... **New Orleans, LA**
Hufft, Ronald C. ... Walnut Creek, CA
Hufham, Barbara F. ... New York, NY
Hufjay, Robert A. ... Mount Vernon, NY
Hufnagel, John E. ... **Scarsdale, NY**
Hufnagel & Lake ... Winthrop, ME
Hufnagel, Lynne M. ... **Denver, CO**
Hufnagel, Wendy ... Heber City, UT
Hufnagel, William F. ... Winthrop, ME
Hufstader, Dennis L. ... Columbus, OH
Hufstader, Donald K. ... Santa Ana, CA
Hufstader, Richard W. ... Petaluma, CA
Hufstedler, Seth M. ... **Los Angeles, CA**
Hufstedler, Shirley M. ... **Los Angeles, CA**

Huft, John F. ... Beulah, MI
Huft, Michael J. ... **Chicago, IL**
Huftalen, Arnold H. ... Concord, NH
Hufziger, Paul T. ... **Stamford, CT**
Hug, Charles M. ... Bronxville, NY
Hug, Charles R. ... **Chicago, IL**
Indianapolis, IN
Hug, Christopher J. ... **Hartford, CT**
Hug, Christopher N. ... **Boston, MA**
Hug, Gerald I. ... Fairfax, CA
Hug, Gretchen Dean ... Palo Alto, CA
Hug, Jack P. ... **San Francisco, CA**
Hug, John T., Jr., (P.C.) ... Brooklyn, NY
Hug, Michael A. ... Elizabeth, CO
Hug, Procter J. ... **Reno, NV**
Hug, Procter, Jr. ... Reno, NV
Hug, William J. ... **West Trenton, NJ**
Huganir, Frederick I. ... Carlisle, PA
Huganir, William S. ... Paoli, PA
Huganir, Wm. L. ... Norristown, PA
Hugar, Terrence A. ... Denver, CO
Hugdahl, Heidi ... **Denver, CO**
Huge, Harry ... **Washington, DC**
Huge, Ted H. ... **Charleston, SC**
Huge, Todd A. ... **San Francisco, CA**
Hugel, Paul Scott ... **New York, NY**
Hugelmeyer, John D. ... Newark, NJ
Hugener, Janice Rourke ... **Los Angeles, CA**
Hugenschmidt, James J. ... Asheville, NC
Huger, Bernard C. ... **St. Louis, MO**
Huger, Daniel E., Jr. ... Charleston, SC
Huget, J. Michael ... **Ann Arbor, MI**
Huget, John C. ... Clinton, MI
Huget, John C., P.C. ... Clinton, MI
Huget, Kirby G. ... **Hartford, CT**
Hugg, Frank B. ... San Francisco, CA
Hugg, Jonathan W. ... **Philadelphia, PA**
Hugg, Joseph A. ... **Boston, MA**
Hugg, Patrick R. ... New Orleans, LA
Huggard, James T. ... **Boston, MA**
Worcester, MA
Huggard, John P. ... Raleigh, NC
Huggard, Stephen G. ...
Department of Justice, GV
Huggard, Victor A., Jr. ... Albany, NY
Huggenberger, Steven ... Lincoln, NE
Huggett, Chas. A. ... Pound Ridge, NY
Huggett, Laura W. ... **Atlanta, GA**
Huggett Law Firm, The ... **Miami, FL**
Huggett, Thomas Benjamin (Ben)
Philadelphia, PA
Huggett, William ... **Miami, FL**
Huggin, David M. ... **New York, NY**
Huggins, Allen E. ... Kings Park, NY
Huggins & Allen, P.C. ... **Augusta, GA**
Huggins, Arthur E. ... Southaven, MS
Huggins, Bret H. ... Holbrook, AZ
Huggins, Bruce W. ... **Lumberton, NC**
Huggins, C. Thomas ... **Augusta, GA**
Huggins, Charles T., Jr. ... **Augusta, GA**
Huggins, Clyde G., Jr. ... Oxford, MS
Huggins, David M. ... **Mobile, AL**
Huggins, David R. ... **Memphis, TN**
Huggins, Elizabeth A. ... Springdale, AR
Huggins, Eugene ... Bennettsville, SC
Huggins, Frederick G. ... Louisville, KY
Huggins & Huggins ... Springdale, AR
Huggins, James S. ... **Marietta, OH**
Huggins, Janet L. Oakley
Federal Energy Regulatory Commission, Office of the General Counsel, GV
Huggins, Joel O. ... Springdale, AR
Huggins, John C. ... **New Haven, CT**
Huggins, John M. ... **New York, NY**
Huggins, John S. ... Irmo, SC
Huggins, Laura H. ... **Columbia, SC**
Huggins, Lisa ... **Birmingham, AL**
Huggins, Matthew ... **Washington, DC**
Huggins, Matthew P. ... **Chattanooga, TN**
Huggins, Michael L. ... Lafayette, LA
Huggins, Nicole A. ... Denver, CO
Huggins, Norella V. ... **St. Louis, MO**
Huggins, Norman W. ... Milton, MA
Huggins, Palma K. ... Conway, SC
Huggins, Pounds & Davis, L.L.P.
Lumberton, NC
Huggins, Randall D. ... **Tulsa, OK**
Huggins, Robin C., Law Office of
Mission Viejo, CA
Huggins, Roger N. ... **West Chester, PA**
Huggins, Rollin C., Jr. ... **Chicago, IL**
Huggins, Ross R. ... Sacramento, CA
Huggins, Sandra G. ... Hamden, CT
Huggins, Sara L. Collins ... Louisville, KY
Huggins, Scott Chandler ... **Macon, GA**
Huggins, William O., III ... Durango, CO
Huggins, Wm. G. ... Columbus, OH
Huggins-Cook, Salley K. ... Dillon, SC
Huggler, David H. ... **Berwyn, PA**
Huggler, James W. ... Tyler, TX
Huggler, Lyndall J. ... **Pittsburgh, PA**
Huggs, Gerald E. ... Shreveport, LA
Hughart, Charlotte A. ... Irving, TX
Hughel, George K. ... Anderson, IN
Hughes, A. Blair ... **Chicago, IL**
Hughes, A. John, Jr. ... **Fort Myers, FL**
Hughes, A. Scott ... Birmingham, AL
Hughes, Alan B. ... **Seattle, WA**
Hughes, Alan B., P.S. ... **Seattle, WA**
Hughes, Alan D. ... Hutchinson, KS
Hughes, Alfred E. ... Dubuque, IA
Hughes, Alice H. ... New Hope, PA
Newtown, PA
Hughes, Allyson ... New Port Richey, FL
Hughes, Allyson, P.A. ... New Port Richey, FL
Hughes, Alvin E. ... New Orleans, LA
Hughes, Amy M. ... **San Marcos, TX**
Hughes, Andrew ... Alamosa, CO

Hughes, Andrew S. ....Melbourne, FL
Hughes, Andy K. ....Macon, MS
Hughes, Angela L. ....Department of Justice, Antitrust Division, GV
Hughes, Anne R. ....Port Allen, LA
Hughes, Anne R., APLC
Baton Rouge, LA
Port Allen, LA
Hughes, Arlene A. ....Rochester, NY
Hughes, Arthur W., III ....Boston, MA
Hughes, Artus & Goodwin
Oklahoma City, OK
Hughes & Asack ....Rockport, TX
Hughes & Associates ....St. George, UT
Hughes & Bailey, LLP ....Atlanta, GA
Decatur, GA
Tucker, GA
Hughes, Barbara F. C. ....Milton, MA
Hughes, Barbara S. ....Madison, WI
Hughes, Barry E. ....Daytona Beach, FL
Hughes, Benjamin T. ....Charleston, WV
Hughes, Benny H. ....Beaumont, TX
Hughes, Beth Jackson ....Montgomery, AL
Hughes, Bette A. ....Point Pleasant, NJ
Hughes, Bill R. ....Prescott, AZ
Hughes, Brett A. ....Memphis, TN
Hughes, Brett G. ....Tulsa, OK
Hughes, Brian D. ....Washington, DC
Hughes, Bruce A. ....Salem, MA
Hughes, Bruce R. ....Kentfield, CA
Hughes, Bryan J. ....Malone, NY
Hughes, C. Dennis ....Birmingham, AL
Hughes, Caralisa P. ....San Jose, CA
Hughes, Carl D. ....Oklahoma City, OK
Hughes, Carmina Szunyog ....Baltimore, MD
Hughes, Carole A. ....San Francisco, CA
Hughes, Carolyn Cozad ....Chicago, IL
Hughes, Carson M. ....Jackson, MS
Hughes & Carver, P.C. ....Albuquerque, NM
Hughes, Catherine C. ....Conway, AR
Hughes, Catherine L. ....Sacramento, CA
Hughes, Catherine M. ....Florence, AZ
Hughes, Catherine S. ....Nashville, TN
Hughes, Catherine Veihmeyer
McLean, VA
Hughes, Charles B. ....Springfield, VA
Hughes, Charles B., III ....New York, NY
Hughes, Charles C. ....Decatur, IL
Hughes, Charles E. ....Jackson, MS
Hughes, Charles E. ....Houston, TX
Hughes, Charles J. ....Peoria, IL
Hughes, Charles J. ....San Angelo, TX
Hughes, Charles L. ....Birmingham, AL
Hughes, Charles M. ....Encino, CA
Hughes, Charles M. ....Bogalusa, LA
Mandeville, LA
Hughes, Charles M. ....Framingham, MA
Hughes, Charles M., Jr. ....Bogalusa, LA
Mandeville, LA
Hughes, Charles S. ....Chicago, IL
Hughes, Chauney F. ....Brunswick, TN
Hughes, Cheryl Risley ....Washington, DC
Hughes, Chris ....Fitzgerald, GA
Hughes, Christian D. ....Shelton, CT
Hughes, Christine ....Cambridge, MA
Hughes, Christopher A. ....New York, NY
Hughes, Christopher B. ....Madison, WI
Hughes, Christopher H. ....Jackson, MS
Hughes, Christopher J. ....Montgomery, AL
Hughes, Christopher J. ....Cornwall, NY
Hughes, Cindy R. ....Orange, CA
Hughes, Clayton J. ....Hopewell Junction, NY
Hughes, Clifford B. ....Hesperia, CA
Hughes, Clifton E. ....Pueblo, CO
Hughes Clikeman & Associates, P.C.
Denver, CO
Hughes, Coit I., III ....Phoenix, AZ
Hughes, Coit I., Jr. ....Phoenix, AZ
Hughes & Coleman ....Bowling Green, KY
Hughes, Constance L. ....Salt Lake City, UT
Hughes & Costello ....St. Paul, MN
Hughes, Craig E. ....Salt Lake City, UT
Hughes, Craig M. ....San Francisco, CA
Hughes, Craig Stuart ....Paramus, NJ
Hughes, D. Bryan ....Henderson, TX
Hughes, Dale D. ....Lake Hill, NY
Hughes, Dan S., (P.C.)
Colorado Springs, CO
Hughes, Daniel C. ....Lafayette, LA
Hughes, Daniel C., PLC ....Lafayette, LA
Hughes, Daniel F. ....Grants Pass, OR
Hughes, Daniel J. ....Cleveland, OH
Hughes, Daniel T. ....New York, NY
Hughes, David ....St. Louis, MO
Hughes, David A. ....Newport Beach, CA
Hughes, David A. ....Atlanta, GA
Hughes, David A. ....Chicago, IL
Hughes, David A. ....Alexandria, LA
Hughes, David Alan ....Birmingham, AL
Hughes, David B. ....Indianapolis, IN
Hughes, David Bowen ....Montgomery, AL
Hughes, David C., Jr. ....Albuquerque, NM
Hughes, David Evan ....Golden, CO
Hughes, David J. ....New Brunswick, NJ
Hughes, David J. ....Wauwatosa, WI
Hughes, David K. ....Santa Barbara, CA
Hughes, David L. ....Costa Mesa, CA
Hughes, David L.
Department Of The Interior, Office of Hearings & Appeals, GV
Hughes, David L. ....Hillsdale, NJ
Hughes, David M. ....Cascade, IA
Hughes, David M. ....El Paso, TX
Hughes, David R. ....Department of Energy, Office of the General Counsel, GV
Hughes, David R. ....Tucker, GA
Hughes, David R. ....Newark, IL
Hughes, David R. ....Lawrence, PA
Hughes, David W. ....Walnut Creek, CA
Hughes, David W. ....Prairie Village, KS
Hughes, Deborah A. ....Harrisburg, PA
Hughes, Deborah J. ....Cedar Rapids, IA
Hughes, Deborah L. ....Topeka, KS
Hughes, Dennis M. ....Princeton, NJ
Hughes, Desmond ....Buffalo, NY
Hughes, Diana L. ....Elmira, NY
Hughes, Diane L. ....Cleveland, OH
Hughes, Donald A., Jr. ....Columbus, OH
Hughes, Donald P. ....Elgin, IL
Hughes, Donald W. ....Columbus, OH
Hughes, Donna Marie ....New York, NY
Hughes, Donnie Clay, Jr. ....Birmingham, AL
Hughes, Dorian J. ....Arlington, VA
Hughes, Douglas E. ....Carmen, OK
Hughes, Douglas M. ....Muskegon, MI
Hughes, D. P. ....Fort Lauderdale, FL
Hughes, Duane L. ....New York, NY
Hughes, E. Aurora ....Riverside, CA
Hughes, E. Cutter, Jr. ....Huntsville, AL
Hughes, Ed. W. ....Phoenix, AZ
Hughes, Edward J. ....Boston, MA
Hughes, Edward J. ....Norristown, PA
Hughes, Edward J., Jr. ....New York, NY
Hughes, Edward L. ....McLean, VA
Hughes, Edward M. ....Savannah, GA
Hughes, Edward M.
Hilton Head Island, SC
Hughes, Edward R. ....New York, NY
Hughes, Edward W. ....Scottsdale, AZ
Hughes, Edwin H., III ....Niceville, FL
Hughes, Edwin J. ....Madison, WI
Hughes, Edwin R. ....Dallas, TX
Hughes, Elaine M. ....Boston, MA
Hughes, Elizabeth ....Washington, DC
Hughes, Elizabeth A. ....Lansing, MI
Hughes, Elizabeth A. ....Okemos, MI
Hughes, Elizabeth Buenger ....Deansboro, NY
Hughes, Elizabeth R. ....Baltimore, MD
Hughes, Elizabeth S. ....Lexington, KY
Hughes, Ellen Schmitz ....Madison, WI
Hughes, Eric G. ....Arkadelphia, AR
Hughes, Eric J. ....Morristown, NJ
Hughes, Ernest W. ....Carmichael, CA
Hughes, Everett N. ....Brooklyn, NY
Hughes, F. Gerald ....Worcester, MA
Hughes, F. Jefferson ....Department of Justice, Civil Division, GV
Hughes, F. Marion ....Greenville, SC
Hughes, F. Warren ....Burnsville, NC
Hughes, Farrell W. ....Burnsville, NC
Hughes and Finnerty, P.C. ....Bayonne, NJ
Hughes, Francis J. ....San Jose, CA
Hughes, Francis J. ....Milwaukee, WI
Hughes, Frank J., Jr. ....Mount Holly, NJ
Hughes, Fred J. ....St. Cloud, MN
Hughes, Fred J. ....New Providence, NJ
Hughes, Frederick G. ....Joplin, MO
Hughes, G. Charles ....Moundsville, WV
Hughes, G. Charles, L.C. ....Moundsville, WV
Hughes, Gary A. ....Atlanta, GA
Hughes, Gary A. ....Palmyra, NY
Hughes, Gary E. ....Washington, DC
Hughes, George E. ....Centerport, NY
Hughes, George J. ....Washington, DC
Hughes, George W. ....Raleigh, NC
Hughes, Gerald A. ....Trenton, NJ
Hughes, Gerald T. ....Chestnut Hill, MA
Hughes, Gerard J. ....Baton Rouge, LA
Hughes, Gianni M. ....Kansas City, MO
Hughes, Gordon R., Jr. ....Aurora, IL
Hughes, Graham ....New York, NY
Hughes, Gregg B. ....Downey, CA
Hughes, Gregory D. ....Atlanta, GA
Hughes, Gregory F. ....Casselberry, FL
Hughes, Gregory J. ....Roseville, CA
Hughes, Gregory T. ....Ludlow, KY
Hughes, Guy E. ....Lexington, KY
Hughes, H. David ....Austin, TX
Hughes, Harold B. ....Clare, MI
Hughes, Harold J. ....Albany, NY
Hughes, Harold J. ....Salt Lake City, UT
Hughes, Harold O. ....San Mateo, CA
Hughes, Harry D. ....Odenton, MD
Hughes, Harry M.
Department of the Air Force, Office of the Judge Advocate General, GV
Hughes, Harry R. ....Baltimore, MD
Hughes, Heather M. ....Houston, TX
Hughes, Heidi ....Tallahassee, FL
Hughes & Hendrix, A Professional Corporation
Trenton, NJ
Hughes, Henry E. ....Lexington, KY
Hughes, Hill & Tenney, L.L.C.
Decatur, IL
Hughes, Hobart B. ....Salisbury, MD
Hughes & Hobby, P.C. ....Fitzgerald, GA
Hughes, Howard M. ....Jupiter, FL
Hughes Hubbard & Reed LLP
Los Angeles, CA
Washington, DC
Miami, FL
New York, NY
Hughes, Hugh D. ....New Haven, CT
Hughes & Hughes ....Washington, DC
Hughes & Hughes, P.A. ....Searcy, AR
Hughes & Hughes, P.C. ....San Angelo, TX
Hughes, Hunter R., III ....Atlanta, GA
Hughes, Imogene E. ....Philadelphia, PA
Hughes, Irene Vera ....Los Angeles, CA
Hughes, J. Andrew ....Tupelo, MS
Hughes, J. Barry ....Westminster, MD
Hughes, J. Bruce ....Houston, TX
Hughes, J. David ....Washington, DC
Hughes, J. David ....Alexandria, VA
Hughes, J. Joseph ....Tallahassee, FL
Hughes, J. Marshall ....Bowling Green, KY
Hughes, J. Michael ....Encino, CA
Hughes, J. Michael ....Jacksonville, FL
Hughes, J. Russell, Jr. ....Lincoln, MI
Hughes, J. Trevor ....Portland, ME
Hughes, J. Vance ....Washington, DC
Atlanta, GA
Hughes, Jack W. ....Mountain View, CA
Hughes, Jacqueline A. Alicia ....Chicago, IL
Hughes, James A. ....San Francisco, CA
Hughes, James A. ....Houston, TX
Hughes, James A. ....St. Albans, VT
Hughes, James A., Jr. ....Washington, DC
Hughes, James A., Jr. ....Clinton, NY
Hughes, James B., Jr. ....Atlanta, GA
Hughes, James C. ....Los Angeles, CA
Hughes, James C. ....Gainesville, GA
Hughes, James D. ....Orange, CA
Hughes, James D. ....Portland, OR
Hughes, James D. ....Carlisle, PA
Hughes, James Donald ....Birmingham, AL
Hughes, James E. ....Indianapolis, IN
Hughes, James E. ....Syracuse, NY
Hughes, James E. ....Columbus, OH
Hughes, James E. ....Longview, TX
Hughes, James E., Jr. ....New York, NY
Hughes, James Elliott ....Stony Brook, NY
Hughes, James F. ....Clifton Park, NY
Hughes, James H. ....Fayetteville, NY
Hughes, James H. ....Durham, NC
Hughes, James H. ....Bartlesville, OK
Hughes, James J. ....Columbus, OH
Hughes, James J., III ....Columbus, OH
Hughes, James L. ....Atlanta, GA
Hughes, James L. ....Ann Arbor, MI
Detroit, MI
Hughes, James M. ....Fairfield, CT
Hughes, James M. ....Hingham, MA
Hughes, James M. ....Fort Lee, NJ
Hughes, James M. ....Columbus, OH
Hughes, James M. ....Charleston, SC
Hughes, James M. ....San Antonio, TX
Hughes, James P., Jr. ....Wilmington, DE
Hughes, James R. ....Washington, DC
Hughes, James Robert ....Panama City, FL
Hughes, James W. ....Dallas, TX
Hughes, James W. ....Texarkana, TX
Hughes, Jan Louise ....Decatur, GA
Hughes, Jas. E. ....Lenox, IA
Hughes, Jay W., Jr. ....Columbia, MD
Hughes, Jefferson D., III ....Walker, LA
Hughes, Jeffery S. ....Menomonee Falls, WI
Hughes, Jeffrey J. ....Santa Monica, CA
Hughes, Jeffrey P. ....New York, NY
Hughes, Jeffrey R. ....Grand Rapids, MI
Hughes, Jeffrey Shawn ....Torrance, CA
Hughes, Jennifer J. ....New York, NY
Hughes, Jennifer K. ....Pittsburgh, PA
Hughes, Jeromy D. ....Houston, TX
Hughes, Jerry S. ....Cambridge, ID
Hughes, Jerry S. ....Dallas, TX
Hughes, Jessica Lynn ....Minneapolis, MN
Hughes, Jim D. ....Rockport, TX
Hughes, Joan E. ....Sebring, FL
Hughes, John A. ....San Francisco, CA
Hughes, John B. ....New Haven, CT
Hughes, John C. ....Anchorage, AK
Hughes, John C. ....Phoenix, AZ
Hughes, John C. ....San Diego, CA
Hughes, John C. ....Minneapolis, MN
Hughes, John D. ....Mishawaka, IN
Hughes, John D. ....Mishawaka, IN
Hughes, John D. ....Salt Lick, KY
Hughes, John D. ....Boston, MA
Hughes, John D. ....Granbury, TX
Hughes, John D. ....Houston, TX
Hughes, John E. ....Merrillville, IN
Hughes, John E. ....Manchester, NH
Hughes, John Edward, III
Fort Lauderdale, FL
Hughes, John Edward, III ....Jackson, MS
Hughes, John F. ....San Francisco, CA
Hughes, John F. ....Purchase, NY
Hughes, John H. ....Lafayette, LA
Hughes, John J. ....Bayonne, NJ
Hughes, John J. ....Trenton, NJ
Hughes, John J., Jr. ....New York, NY
Hughes, John J., Jr. ....Sleepy Hollow, NY
Hughes, John K. ....Washington, DC
Hughes, John K. ....Chicago, IL
Hughes, John L. ....Milwaukee, WI
Hughes, John M. ....Chicago, IL
Hughes, John M. ....St. Paul, MN
Hughes, John M. ....St. Louis, MO
Hughes, John N. ....Des Moines, IA
Hughes, John N. ....Frankfort, KY
Hughes, John R. ....Sioux Falls, SD
Hughes, John R., Jr. ....Lebanon, NH
Hughes, John S. ....Chesterfield, MO
Hughes, John S., IV ....Raleigh, NC
Hughes, John T. ....Sturgis, SD
Hughes, John W. ....Lake Forest, IL
Hughes, John W. ....New York, NY
Hughes, John W. ....Fort Worth, TX
Hughes, Jon C. ....Philadelphia, PA
Hughes, Jonathan P. ....New York, NY
Hughes, Jonathan W. ....San Francisco, CA
Hughes, Joseph A. ....Tupelo, MS
Hughes, Joseph D. ....Paragould, AR
Hughes, Joseph D. ....Bakersfield, CA
Hughes, Joseph D. ....Pittsburgh, PA
Hughes, Joseph D. ....Austin, TX
Hughes, Joseph D., & Associates, P.A.
Paragould, AR
Hughes, Joseph G. ....Perth Amboy, NJ
Hughes, Joseph P. ....Geneva, AL
Hughes, Joseph Simeon ....Berrien Springs, MI
Hughes, Joyce A. ....Chicago, IL
Hughes, Joyce B. ....Los Angeles, CA
Hughes, J. P." Jay ", Jr. ....Oxford, MS
Hughes, Juanita G. ....Detroit, MI
Hughes, Julian E. ....Benton Harbor, MI
Hughes, Julie ....San Angelo, TX
Hughes, Julie K. ....Chicago, IL
Hughes, Justin ....Belvedere-Tiburon, CA
Hughes, Justin ....Department of Commerce, Patent and Trademark Office, GV
Hughes, Kalkbrenner & Adshead, LLP
Norristown, PA
Hughes, Karen G. ....Tyler, TX
Hughes, Karen J. ....Little Rock, AR
Hughes, Karen J. ....New York, NY
Hughes, Kathleen A.
Environmental Protection Agency, Office of Enforcement and Compliance Assurance, GV
Hughes, Kathleen A. ....Minneapolis, MN
Hughes, Kathryn A. ....Alamogordo, NM
Hughes, Kayci Bair ....Tulsa, OK
Hughes, Keith F. ....St. Cloud, MN
Hughes, Keith L. ....Boston, MA
Hughes, Kellner, Sullivan & Alke
Helena, MT
Hughes, Kenneth D. ....Houston, TX
Hughes, Kenneth R. ....Carbondale, IL
Hughes, Kenneth Robert ....Rochester, NY
Hughes, Kent H. ....Washington, DC
Hughes, Kerry A. ....Miami, FL
Hughes, Kevin ....Honolulu, HI
Hughes, Kevin ....Armonk, NY
Hughes, Kevin D. ....Los Angeles, CA
Hughes, Kevin D. ....Pittsburgh, PA
Hughes, Kevin J. ....Walnut Creek, CA
Hughes, Kevin J. ....St. Cloud, MN
Hughes, Kevin J. ....Philadelphia, PA
Hughes, Kevin P. ....New York, NY
Hughes, Kevin T. ....Garden City, NY
Hughes, Kieran P. ....Springfield, NJ
Hughes, Kimberly A. ....Tacoma, WA
Hughes, Kristen Grim ....McLean, VA
Hughes, Kristin Ashurst ....Oakland, CA
Hughes, Kurt M. ....Burlington, VT
Hughes, L. Anderson, Jr. ....Richmond, VA
Hughes, L. Wearen ....Nashville, TN
Hughes & Lane, Professional Association
Jacksonville, FL
Hughes, Larry D. ....Sunnyvale, CA
Hughes, Laurence B. ....Worthington, MN
Hughes, Laurie ....Nashville, TN
Hughes Law Firm, P.C.
Hilton Head Island, SC
Hughes Law Offices ....Sioux Falls, SD
Hughes, Lawrence D.
Department of Agriculture, Office of the General Counsel, GV
Hughes, Lawrence F. ....Jamaica, NY
Hughes, Lee J. ....Vineland, NJ
Hughes, Lennie L. ....Elizabeth City, NC
Hughes, Leonard V., Jr. ....Memphis, TN
Hughes, Letcher & Williamson, PSC
Owingsville, KY
Hughes, Lin ....Austin, TX
Hughes, Linda A. ....Utica, NY
Hughes, Linda P ....San Diego, CA
Hughes, Linda Renate ....Tampa, FL
Hughes, Lindsey H. ....Portland, OR
Hughes, Lisa Bobbie Schreiber
Department of State, Foreign Service Officers (Overseas), GV
Hughes, Lisa M. ....Orange, CA
Hughes, Lisa Marie ....Falls Church, VA
Hughes, Lisa Stewart ....New York, NY
Hughes, Lon V. ....New York, NY
Hughes, Lori P. ....Atlanta, GA
Hughes & Luce, L.L.P. ....Austin, TX
Dallas, TX
Houston, TX
Hughes, Lyman G. ....Dallas, TX
Hughes, Lynn N. ....Houston, TX
Hughes, M. Daniel ....Fort Lauderdale, FL
Hughes, M. Richard ....Birmingham, AL
Hughes, Malcolm C. ....Margaretville, NY
Hughes, Maria W. ....Charleston, WV
Hughes, Mark A. ....Reno, NV
Hughes, Mark B. ....Houston, TX
Hughes, Mark F., Jr. ....Little Silver, NJ
Hughes, Mark J.A. ....Phoenix, AZ
Hughes, Mark L. ....Sundance, WY
Hughes, Martin J., III ....Columbus, OH
Hughes, Mary Ann Schneider ....Santa Fe, NM
Hughes, Mary D. ....Downers Grove, IL
Hughes, Mary D. ....Brooklyn, NY
Hughes, Mary K. ....Anchorage, AK
Hughes, Mary L. ....Charleston, SC
Hughes, Mary M. ....Silver Spring, MD
Hughes, Mary Rose ....Washington, DC
Hughes, Mathews & Didier, P.A.
St. Cloud, MN
Hughes, Mathewson, Carns & Slattery
Oshkosh, WI
Hughes, Matthew B.E. ....Houston, TX
Hughes, Matthew J. ....Chicago, IL
Hughes, Matthew W. ....Cincinnati, OH
Hughes, Maura L. ....Cleveland, OH
Hughes & Maxey ....Birmingham, AL
Hughes, McCorry, Cardoza, Herrmann & Grammatico ....Garden City, NY
Hughes, M. Daniel, P.A.
Fort Lauderdale, FL
Hughes, Melissa Larkin ....Cheyenne, WY
Hughes, Melvin R., Jr. ....Richmond, VA
Hughes, Michael B. ....Galveston, TX
Hughes, Michael C. ....Phoenix, AZ
Hughes, Michael D. ....Dunedin, FL
Hughes, Michael D. ....Pittsburgh, PA
Hughes, Michael D. ....St. George, UT
Hughes, Michael E. ....St. Louis, MO

Hughes, Michael E. .... Philadelphia, PA
Hughes, Michael F. .... White Plains, NY
Hughes, Michael F. .... Bellingham, WA
Hughes, Michael H. .... Department of Justice, Office of Information and Privacy, GV
Hughes, Michael J. .... Alamo, CA
Hughes, Michael J. .... Santa Clara, CA
Hughes, Michael J. .... Chicago, IL
Hughes, Michael J. .... Pontiac, MI
Hughes, Michael J. .... Helena, MT
Hughes, Michael J. .... Newark, NJ
Hughes, Michael J., The Intell. Prop. Law Office of .... Santa Clara, CA
Hughes, Michael L. .... St. Francisville, LA
Hughes, Michael M. .... Cleveland, OH
Hughes, Michael S. .... Los Angeles, CA
Hughes, Michael T. .... Hopkins, MN
Hughes, Michael T. .... New York, NY
Hughes, Michelle A. .... Virginia Beach, VA
Hughes, Miles W. .... Tallahassee, FL
Hughes, Miranda L. .... Des Moines, IA
Hughes, M. M., Jr. .... San Antonio, TX
Hughes, N. Lynne .... Atlantic City, NJ
Hughes, Nancy .... Pearl River, NY
Hughes, Nancy C. .... Birmingham, AL
Hughes, Nancy Mayer .... Lancaster, PA
Hughes, Naomi Y. .... Walnut Creek, CA
Hughes, Nathalie L. .... Miami, FL
Hughes, Nathaniel B., III .... Memphis, TN
Hughes, Nicholls & O'Hara .... Dunmore, PA
Hughes, Nicole .... Washington, DC
Greenbelt, MD
Hughes & Nunn .... San Diego, CA
Hughes, Owen C. B. .... Boulder, CO
Hughes, Owen T. .... West Orange, NJ
Hughes, Patricia .... Schaumburg, IL
Hughes, Patricia L. .... Kansas City, MO
Hughes, Patricia L. .... Liberty, MO
Hughes, Patricia M. .... Boston, MA
Hughes, Patrick B. .... Wichita, KS
Hughes, Patrick J. .... Chicago, IL
Hughes, Patrick J. .... Princeton, NJ
Hughes, Patrick J. .... Roseland, NJ
Hughes, Patrick J., Jr. .... Springfield, IL
Hughes, Patrick L. .... Houston, TX
Hughes, Patrick P. .... Anniston, AL
Hughes, Patrick R. .... Covington, KY
Hughes, Paul A. .... Hartford, CT
Hughes, Paul C. .... New York, NY
Hughes, Paul G. .... Stamford, CT
Hughes, Paul Gordon .... Broomall, PA
Hughes, Paul M. .... Detroit, MI
Hughes, Paul S. .... Bogalusa, LA
Mandeville, LA
Hughes, Paul S. .... Newton, MA
Hughes, Paula .... Owingsville, KY
Hughes, Peggy Bellanca .... Burbank, CA
Hughes, Peggy C. .... Seattle, WA
Hughes, Peggy W. .... Tallahassee, FL
Hughes, Perry S. .... Los Angeles, CA
Hughes, Peter .... Englewood, CO
Hughes, Peter C. .... Philadelphia, PA
Hughes, Peter J. .... San Diego, CA
Hughes, Peter J., A Professional Corporation San Diego, CA
Hughes, Peter L., III .... Flemington, NJ
Hughes, Peter M. .... San Diego, CA
Hughes, Peter O. .... Morristown, NJ
Hughes, Philip D. .... Meridian, MS
Hughes, Philip E., Jr. .... Blue Bell, PA
Hughes, Philippa Pham Bates
Charlottesville, VA
Hughes, Phillip Francis Luke
Myrtle Beach, SC
Hughes, Phillip M. .... Uvalde, TX
Hughes, Phyllis R. .... Phoenix, AZ
Hughes, Priscilla C. .... New York, NY
Hughes, R. Courtney .... Carbondale, IL
Hughes, R. Dale .... Atlanta, GA
Hughes, R. Murray .... Greenville, SC
Hughes, R. Murray .... Pickens, SC
Hughes, R. Paul, III .... Fort Smith, AR
Hughes, Ralph E. .... San Diego, CA
Hughes, Ralph E. .... Clarkston, GA
Hughes, Randall L. .... Atlanta, GA
Hughes, Randell .... Wilson, NC
Hughes & Rardon, P.A. .... Tampa, FL
Hughes, Rathwell & Nizialek, L.L.P.
Houston, TX
Hughes, Ray .... Deming, NM
Hughes, Raymond H. .... Wilton, CT
Hughes, Rebecca .... San Jose, CA
Hughes, Rebecca R. .... Carlisle, PA
Hughes, Rebekah Tinsley .... Matthews, NC
Hughes, Rena G. .... Las Vegas, NV
Hughes, Rhonda M.
United States International Trade Commission, Office of the General Counsel, GV
Hughes, Richard D. .... Denver, CO
Hughes, Richard D. .... Muncie, IN
Hughes, Richard D. .... Port Arthur, TX
Hughes, Richard G. .... St. Louis, MO
Hughes, Richard H. .... Tyler, TX
Hughes, Richard J., Law Office of
Seattle, WA
Hughes, Richard K. .... Syracuse, NY
Hughes, Richard L. .... Fairfield, CA
Hughes, Richard L. .... Denver, CO
Hughes, Richard L. .... Otisville, MI
Hughes, Richard L. .... St. Louis, MO
Hughes, Richard Morris, III .... Kingston, PA
Hughes, Richard O. .... New York, NY
Hughes, Richard O., Jr. .... Birmingham, AL
Hughes, Richard T. .... Houston, TX
Hughes, Richard W. .... Clare, MI
Hughes, Richard W. .... Santa Fe, NM
Hughes, Rob .... San Antonio, TX
Hughes, Robert A. .... Louisville, KY
Hughes, Robert B. .... Bellingham, WA
Hughes, Robert C. .... Cold Spring Harbor, NY
Hughes, Robert D. .... Chicago, IL
Hughes, Robert D., P.C. .... Chicago, IL
Hughes, Robert F. .... Gibsonia, PA
Hughes, Robert G. .... Exton, PA
Hughes, Robert H., Jr. .... Dallas, TX
Hughes, Robert L. .... Oakland, CA
Hughes, Robert L. .... Richmond, VA
Hughes, Robert L., Jr. .... Boston, MA
Hughes, Robert M. .... Wichita, KS
Hughes, Robert M., III .... Norfolk, VA
Hughes, Robert S. .... Greenport, NY
Hughes, Robert T. .... Tampa, FL
Hughes, Robert T. .... New Orleans, LA
Hughes, Robert W., Jr. .... Atlanta, GA
Hughes, Robert Wiley .... Richmond, VA
Hughes, Rodney G. .... Berkeley, CA
Hughes, Roger M. .... Oakland, CA
Hughes, Roger M. .... San Francisco, CA
Hughes, Roger W. .... Harlingen, TX
Hughes, Roland D. .... Everett, MA
Hughes, Ronald A. .... Westlake Village, CA
Hughes, Rosemary .... Bedminster, NJ
Hughes, Roy C., Jr. .... Dallas, TX
Hughes, Roy F. .... Honolulu, HI
Hughes, Ruth A. .... Spring, TX
Hughes, Ruth Calhoun .... Mountaintop, PA
Hughes and Sallee .... Indianapolis, IN
Hughes, Sally A. .... Department of the Navy, Office of the Judge Advocate General, GV
Hughes, Sandra L. .... Crofton, MD
Alexandria, VA
Hughes & Schacht, P.S. .... Bellevue, WA
Bellingham, WA
Hughes, Scott A. .... Bellevue, WA
Hughes, Scott D. .... Laguna Niguel, CA
Hughes, Scott H. .... Lansing, MI
Hughes, Shalas J. .... North Plains, OR
Hughes, Shantelle Denise
Washington, DC
Hughes, Sharon Coverly, Law Offices of
Los Angeles, CA
Hughes, Shauna M. .... Henderson, NV
Hughes, Simon H. .... Houston, TX
Hughes, Sisk & Glancy, P.A.
Wilmington, DE
Hughes, Stacey Johnson
Bowling Green, KY
Hughes, Staples .... Durham, NC
Hughes, Stefan R. .... Bowling Green, KY
Hughes, Stephen E. .... Washington, DC
Hughes, Stephen G. .... Santa Fe, NM
Hughes, Stephen J. .... Towson, MD
Hughes, Stephen J. .... Dallas, TX
Hughes, Stephen L. .... Milan, TN
Hughes, Stephen M. .... Buffalo, NY
Hughes, Stephen P. .... Beaufort, SC
Hughes, Steven H. .... Hillsboro, OR
Hughes, Steven H., P.C. .... Hillsboro, OR
Hughes, Steven J. .... Little Rock, AR
Hughes, Steven J. .... St. Louis, MO
Hughes, Steven L. .... El Paso, TX
Hughes, Steven W. .... Spokane, WA
Hughes & Stewart, P.C. .... Malone, NY
Hughes & Strumor, Ltd. Co.
Albuquerque, NM
Santa Fe, NM
Hughes, Susan B. .... Baltimore, MD
Hughes, Susan M. .... Chicago, IL
Hughes & Taosaka, Attorneys At Law, A Law Corporation .... Honolulu, HI
Hughes, Teresa Burridge
Treasury Department, Internal Revenue Service, GV
Hughes, Teresa L. Cloud .... Searcy, AR
Hughes, Terrence O. .... Santa Monica, CA
Hughes, Theodore E. .... Lansing, MI
Hughes, Thomas A. .... Detroit, MI
Hughes, Thomas C. .... Seattle, WA
Hughes, Thomas C., III .... Sacramento, CA
Hughes, Thomas D., IV .... Alexandria, VA
Hughes, Thomas Donald .... New York, NY
Hughes, Thomas E. .... Oshkosh, WI
Hughes, Thomas F. .... Philadelphia, PA
Hughes, Thomas G. .... Wilmington, DE
Hughes, Thomas H. .... Louisville, KY
Hughes, Thomas J. .... Lansing, MI
Hughes, Thomas J., II .... Tampa, FL
Hughes, Thomas J., Jr. .... Bronxville, NY
Hughes, Thomas L. .... New York, NY
Hughes, Thomas M. .... Washington, DC
Hughes, Thomas M. .... Minneapolis, MN
Hughes, Thomas M., III .... Searcy, AR
Hughes, Thomas P. .... Utica, NY
Hughes, Thomas R. .... St. Paul, MN
Hughes, Thomas S. .... El Paso, TX
Hughes, Thomas W. .... Dallas, TX
Hughes, Thoreen, Relph & Hanson, P.A.
St. Cloud, MN
Hughes Thorsness Powell Huddleston & Bauman LLC .... Anchorage, AK
Hughes, Thos. W. .... Dallas, TX
Hughes, Timothy A. .... Birmingham, AL
Hughes, Timothy J. .... Los Angeles, CA
Hughes, Timothy M. .... Sarasota, FL
Hughes, Timothy M. .... Chicago, IL
Hughes, Timothy M. .... New York, NY
Hughes, Timothy M. .... Milwaukee, WI
Hughes, Timothy Mark .... Boston, MA
Hughes, Timothy R. .... Washington, DC
Hughes, Timothy R. .... Falls Church, VA
Hughes, Timothy T. .... Miami, FL
Hughes, Tina A. .... Oklahoma City, OK
Hughes, Tina N. .... Cheyenne, WY
Hughes, Tisa K. .... Boston, MA
Hughes, Todd Christopher .... Augusta, GA
Hughes, Todd E. .... Montgomery, AL
Hughes, Todd M. .... Department of Justice, Civil Division, GV
Hughes, Tommy D. .... Albuquerque, NM
Hughes, Tommy L. .... South Gate, CA
Hughes, Tracy E. .... Santa Ana, CA
Hughes & Trannel, P.C. .... Dubuque, IA
Hughes, Troy E. .... Charleston, WV
Hughes, Valerie L. .... Seattle, WA
Hughes, Valertina G. .... Birmingham, AL
Hughes, Van Aaron .... Denver, CO
Hughes, Van V. .... Coronado, CA
Hughes, Vanette Hinch .... Chattanooga, TN
Hughes, Verlin .... Department of Justice, Civil Rights Division, GV
Hughes, Vester T., Jr. .... Dallas, TX
Hughes, Virginia E. .... Roseland, NJ
Hughes, W. Boyd .... Dunmore, PA
Hughes, W. Gregory .... Mobile, AL
Hughes, Walter T., Jr. .... Longboat Key, FL
Hughes, Watters & Askanase, L.L.P.
Houston, TX
Hughes, Wayne Alan .... San Diego, CA
Hughes, Wendy Marshall
Redondo Beach, CA
Hughes & Wesp .... Buffalo, NY
Hughes and Whitaker .... New York, NY
Hughes and White .... Atlanta, GA
Hughes, Wilbert (Will) .... Harlingen, TX
Hughes, Wilford H.
Charlotte Amalie, St. Thomas, VI
Hughes, William .... Baltimore, MD
Hughes, William D., (A Professional Corporation) .... San Diego, CA
Hughes, William E. .... Tulsa, OK
Hughes, William E., III .... Milwaukee, WI
Hughes, William F. .... Washington, DC
Hughes, William G. .... Bozman, MD
Hughes, William H. .... San Jose, CA
Hughes, William H., III .... Tallahassee, FL
Hughes, William H., Jr. .... Atlanta, GA
Hughes, William J. .... Vernon, CA
Hughes, William J. .... Conyers, GA
Hughes, William J. .... Noblesville, IN
Hughes, William L. .... Palo Alto, CA
Hughes, William L., Jr. .... San Francisco, CA
Hughes, William L., Jr. .... Fort Worth, TX
Hughes, William Lloyd
San Francisco, CA
Hughes, William R. .... San Rafael, CA
Hughes, William R. .... Somerset, PA
Hughes, William R. .... Houston, TX
Hughes, William R., Jr.
Council Bluffs, IA
Hughes, William T. .... Graham, NC
Hughes, William V. .... Muncie, IN
Hughes, William W. .... Greeley, CO
Hughes, Wm. R. .... Baltimore, MD
Hughes, W. R., Jr. .... Los Alamos, NM
Hughes & Zehntbauer, L.L.P. .... Portland, OR
Hughes-Coons, Cynthia .... Kansas City, MO
Hughesian, James H. .... Detroit, MI
Hughet, William N. .... Washington, DC
Hughey, Andrew C. .... Wilberforce, OH
Hughey, Bob W. .... El Reno, OK
Hughey, Christopher
Federal Maritime Commission, Office of the General Counsel, GV
Hughey, Derek S. .... Nashville, TN
Hughey, Flick & Catania .... Media, PA
Hughey, Gaylord T., Jr. .... Tyler, TX
Hughey, Harris R. .... Bedford, TX
Hughey, J. Harmond .... San Francisco, CA
Hughey, James F., III .... Birmingham, AL
Hughey, James F., Jr. .... Birmingham, AL
Hughey, Joe A. .... Marshall, TX
Hughey, Joel J. .... Atlanta, GA
Hughey, John R. .... Oklahoma City, OK
Hughey, Kevin A. .... San Francisco, CA
Hughey, Kristine F. .... Media, PA
Hughey, Maggie L. .... Trenton, NJ
Hughey and Parker .... El Reno, OK
Hughey, Richard Kohlman
Pollock Pines, CA
Hughey, Richard L. .... Media, PA
Hughey, Richard M. .... Kalamazoo, MI
Hughey, Richard M., Jr. .... Kalamazoo, MI
Hughey, Roger D. .... Wichita, KS
Hughey, Thos. W. .... Columbus, GA
Hughitt, Elizabeth A.
Department of Commerce, Office of the General Counsel, GV
Hughlett, Harold T. .... Falls Church, VA
Hughlett, Tamela R. .... Oklahoma City, OK
Hughmanick, D. D. .... Burlingame, CA
San Jose, CA
Hughs, John Cook .... Mountain Home, ID
Hughson, Amy Meltzer .... Stamford, CT
Hughston, Doryce S. .... Phoenix, AZ
Hughston, James D. .... Muscle Shoals, AL
Hughston, James D., P.C.
Muscle Shoals, AL
Hughston, Thomas L., Jr. .... Greenwood, SC
Hughto, Karen L. .... Department of Defense, Defense Legal Services Agency, GV
Hughto, Sean D. .... Federal Trade Commission, Offices of Commissioners, GV
Hugi, Frederick A. .... Eugene, OR
Hugi, Robert F. .... Chicago, IL
Hugie, Eldon R. .... Bakersfield, CA
Hugie, Steven E. .... Salt Lake City, UT
Hugill, Elbert A., Jr. .... San Diego, CA
Hugill, Olivia I. .... New York, NY
Hugins, Jana Bain .... Miami, FL
Hugler, Edward C.
Department of Labor, GV
Hugley, David Glen .... Austin, TX
Huglin, Mark L. .... Portland, OR
Hugly, Harry W. .... Midland, TX
Hugney-Shope, Barbara J. .... Clearfield, PA
Hugo, Christopher R. .... Woodland, CA
Hugo, David A. .... Sacramento, CA
Hugo, Edward R. .... San Francisco, CA
Hugo, Heidi Kohn .... San Francisco, CA
Hugo, John T. .... Boston, MA
Hugo, Michael P. .... Raleigh, NC
Hugo, Michael R. .... Boston, MA
Hugo & Pollack, A Prof. Corp., Law Offices of .... Boston, MA
Hugo, Richard G. .... Milwaukee, WI
Hugon, Bruce A. .... Indianapolis, IN
Hugon, Nancy Brown .... Conroe, TX
Hugo-Vidal, Ross Alexander .... Portland, ME
Hugstad, Vicki J. .... Los Angeles, CA
Huguelet, David E. .... Milwaukee, WI
Huguely, J. Rand .... Dallas, TX
Huguenard, James A. .... Houston, TX
Huguenin, A. Eugene, Jr. .... Burlingame, CA
Huguenin, Annis & Lewis .... Martinez, GA
Huguenin, David L. .... Martinez, GA
Huguenin, Edward R. .... Orange, CA
Huguenor, Thomas M. .... San Diego, CA
Huguenot, Michael Zazen .... Bronx, NY
Huguet, Maurice E., Jr. .... Martinez, CA
Hugunin, Guy J. .... Gretna, NE
Huh, Elizabeth K. .... Plymouth, MN
Huh, Joon-Yeung .... New York, NY
Huhn, Henry F. .... Orlando, FL
Huhn, Jeffrey J. .... Corpus Christi, TX
Huhn, Michelle Rene .... Austin, TX
Huhn, Nan R. .... Washington, DC
Huhn, Richard M. .... Columbus, OH
Huhn, Stephen T. .... White Plains, NY
Huhn, William D. .... New York, NY
Huhn, Wilson Ray .... Cleveland, OH
Huhne, Emily R. .... Orlando, FL
Huhnke, Michelle M. .... Washington, DC
Huhs, John I. .... New York, NY
Huhs, Roy E., Jr. .... Bellevue, WA
Huhta, Adam Spencer .... Minneapolis, MN
Huhtanen, Richard E. .... Eugene, OR
Hui, Arthur P. .... Brooklyn, NY
Hui, Helen Y. H. .... San Francisco, CA
Hui, John C. .... New York, NY
Hui, Karen Y. .... St. Louis, MO
Hui, Lawrence D. .... New York, NY
Hui, Paula Martin .... Sacramento, CA
Hui, Susan Fountain .... Fayetteville, AR
Hui, Timothy K. .... Dallas, TX
Hui, Yu .... Washington, DC
Huibonhoa, Joy Anne .... New York, NY
Huibonhoa, Katherine C.
San Francisco, CA
Huibregtse, Bruce D. .... Madison, WI
Huibregtse, Robert R. .... Orange City, IA
Huidekoper, Catherine K. .... Charlotte, NC
Huie, Dennis C. .... Sacramento, CA
Huie, Fernambucq and Stewart, LLP
Birmingham, AL
Huie, Joseph H. .... Knoxville, TN
Huie, Marsha Cope .... San Antonio, TX
Huie, Patricia A. .... Clearwater, FL
Huie, Paul D. .... Palo Alto, CA
Huie, Peter M. .... Los Angeles, CA
Huie, Robert B. .... Birmingham, AL
Huie, Stacey Swatek .... San Francisco, CA
Huie, W. Grady .... Sarasota, FL
Huie, W. Stell .... Atlanta, GA
Huie, William LaFont .... Austin, TX
Huie, Wm. O. .... Austin, TX
Huiet, Ben T., Jr. .... Atlanta, GA
Huige, John D. .... Detroit, MI
Huigens, Kyron J. .... New York, NY
Huijgen-Stepanovich, Diane .... Palo Alto, CA
Huinker, A. Theodore .... Dubuque, IA
Huiras, Autumn L. .... Minneapolis, MN
Huiras, Farrell & Antoine
Port Washington, WI
Huiras, Ralph J. .... Port Washington, WI
Huiras, Scott M. .... Appleton, WI
Huiras, Willis E. .... Indianapolis, IN
Huis, Randolph J. .... Philadelphia, PA
Huish, Karl N. .... Mesa, AZ
Huish, Karl N., P.C. .... Mesa, AZ
Huisinga, Wesley B. .... Cedar Rapids, IA
Huisjen, John H. .... Fort Collins, CO
Huisjen, John H., P.C. .... Fort Collins, CO
Huismann, James E. .... Waukesha, WI
Huitfeldt, Erik T. .... Rochester, NY
Huitink, Michael D. .... Milwaukee, WI
Huitink, Terry L. .... Orange City, IA
Huitt, Earl M., Jr. .... Bay City, TX
Huitt, Jimmie L., Jr. .... Richmond, VA
Huizar, Jose L. .... Los Angeles, CA
Huizenga, Elmer E. .... St. Louis, MO
Huizenga, H. Scott .... Miami, FL
Huizenga, Karen M. .... Davenport, IA
Huizenga, Peter H. .... Oak Brook, IL
Huizenga, Scott A. .... Grand Rapids, MI
Huizenga, Timothy .... Chicago, IL
Huizinga, Anne-Marie .... Seattle, WA
Huizinga, James Alan .... Washington, DC
Huizinga, Jennifer L. .... Sugar Land, TX
Hujar, Thomas F. .... Bainbridge Island, WA
Hujsa, Howard M. .... Naples, FL
Hukel, Tonya K. .... Gatesville, TX
Hukill, Craig W. .... Department of Labor, Office of the Solicitor, GV
Hukill, David De Hass .... Carlisle, PA
Hukill, Kregg .... Plainview, TX
Hukill, Sheree Lee .... Skiatook, OK
Hulac, Edw. V. .... Omaha, NE
Hulac, Michelle A. .... Canoga Park, CA
Hulbert, Bradley J. .... Chicago, IL
Hulbert, Carl A. .... Salt Lake City, UT

Hulbert, Catherine J.
Bloomfield Hills, MI
Hulbert, Charles E. ... Stafford, TX
Hulbert, David F. ... Lake Stevens, WA
Hulbert, David P. ... Perry, GA
Hulbert, David P., Jr. ... Perry, GA
Hulbert, Deborah A. ... New York, NY
Hulbert, Donna P. ... Manhattan Beach, CA
Hulbert, Gregory M. ... Manhattan Beach, CA
Hulbert, Henry L. ... Oneonta, NY
Hulbert, James R. ... Grand Rapids, MI
Hulbert, James W. ... Chicago, IL
Hulbert, Jonathan H. ... Boston, MA
Hulbert, Mark C. ... Los Angeles, CA
Hulbert, Neil F. ... Honolulu, HI
Hulbert, Ralph E. ... Columbia, SC
Hulbert, Richard W. ... New York, NY
Hulbert, Robert B., Jr. ... Snow Hill, NC
Hulbert, Serena Noel ... Delavan, WI
Hulbert, Sharon L. ... Indianapolis, IN
Hulbert-Batiste, Lesia M. ... Chicago, IL
Hulburt, Barbara Lane ... Mechanicsville, VA
Hulburt, Louis A. ... Charlton City, MA
Hulburt, Peter K. ... State College, PA
Hulburt, R. Christian, (P.C.)
San Diego, CA
Hulce, Mary Ellen ... Geneva, IL
Hulchiy, Nicholas P. ... Lafayette, CA
Huldin, Elizabeth I. ... Maumee, OH
Huleatt, Jayme A. ... Washington, DC
Hulen, Charles Michael ... Littleton, CO
Hulen, C. M., Jr. ... Moberly, MO
Hulen, Mike ... Littleton, CO
Hulen, Wm. Ronald ... Bellevue, WA
Hulett, Carrie S. ... Oklahoma City, OK
Hulett, Eric J. ... Beckley, WV
Hulett, Jimmy D." Skip ", Jr.
San Antonio, TX
Hulett, Kirk B. ... San Diego, CA
Hulett, Mary ... Los Angeles, CA
Hulett, Robert S. ... Indianapolis, IN
Hulett, Timothy J. ... Indianapolis, IN
Hulett, William E. ... Dallas, TX
Hulette & Arnett ... Morganfield, KY
Hulette, Sidney H. ... Morganfield, KY
Hulewicz, Michael L. ... Port Huron, MI
Huley, Beverly McDowell ... Richmond, VA
Hulina, Amy L. ... Washington, DC
Huling, Elijah, Jr. ... Syracuse, NY
Huling, Geoffrey Paul ... Philadelphia, PA
Huling, Valerie M. ... Albuquerque, NM
Hulings, Mark J. ... Corpus Christi, TX
Hulit, Felicia ... Philadelphia, PA
Hulka, Travis B. ... Tulsa, OK
Dallas, TX
Hulkower, M. Walter ... Sherman Oaks, CA
Hulkower, Mark J. ... Washington, DC
Hull, A. Eugene, Jr. ... King Of Prussia, PA
Hull, A. Lewis ... Hammond, IL
Hull, Alan K. ... Boise, ID
Hull, Alexandra ... Akron, OH
Hull, Allan ... Cleveland, OH
Hull, Andrew R. ... Palo Alto, CA
Hull, Andrew W. ... Indianapolis, IN
Hull, Anne M. ... Wichita, KS
Hull & Associates, P.C. ... Houston, TX
Hull, B. Jeanine ... Fairfax, VA
Hull, Brandon P. ... Aurora, CO
Hull, Branstetter & Simpson, Chartered
Wallace, ID
Hull, Bruce M. ... Seattle, WA
Hull, C. D. ... Middleburg Heights, OH
Hull, Christine A. ... Los Angeles, CA
Hull, Christopher Scott ... Seattle, WA
Hull, Daniel L. ... Fargo, ND
Hull, Daniel T., Jr. ... Birmingham, AL
Hull, David E. ... Portland, OR
Hull, David J. ... Tallahassee, FL
Hull, David M. ... Chicago, IL
Hull, David N. ... Napa, CA
Hull, David N., Law Office of ... Helena, MT
Hull, David R. ... Appleton, WI
Hull, Diana H. ... Miami, FL
Hull, Diane L. ... Vienna, VA
Hull, Donald E. ... San Juan, PR
Hull, Donald R. ... Miami, FL
Hull, Donald W. ... Hood River, OR
Hull, Douglas J. ... Toms River, NJ
Hull, E. Patrick ... Kingsport, TN
Hull, Edith H. ... Georgetown, DE
Hull, Edwin J. ... Pittsburgh, PA
Hull, Edwin J., III ... Chicago, IL
Hull, Floyd V., Jr. ... Fort Lauderdale, FL
Hull, Frank M. ... Atlanta, GA
Hull, Gary D. ... Hagåtña, GU
Hull, Geoffrey P. ... Murfreesboro, TN
Hull, Gerald W., Jr. ... Florham Park, NJ
Hull, Gordon M. ... Columbus, NE
Hull, Gregory D. ... Palo Alto, CA
Hull, Gregory E. ... Hamilton, OH
Hull, Grover A. ... Cleveland, OH
Hull, Guy W., II ... Garland, TX
Hull, Harriet Morley ... Afton, VA
Hull, Harry E., Jr. ... Sacramento, CA
Hull, Harry R., Jr. ... Pass Christian, MS
Hull, Henry H. ... St. Augustine, FL
Hull, Hewes T. ... Birmingham, AL
Hull and Hull ... Cleveland, OH
Hull, J. Milfred ... Stuart, FL
Hull, J. Tyler ... Seattle, WA
Hull, Jack D. ... Los Angeles, CA
Hull, Jack E. ... Elko, NV
Hull, James N. ... Houston, TX
Hull, John Daniel, IV ... Washington, DC
Pittsburgh, PA
Hull, John F. ... St. Paul, MN
Hull, John H. ... St. Louis, MO
Hull, John M. ... Chattanooga, TN

Hull, John P. ... Baltimore, MD
Hull, John T.
Nuclear Regulatory Commission,
Office of the General Counsel, GV
Hull, Jonathan ... Cleveland, OH
Hull, Jonathan C. ... Damariscotta, ME
Hull, Jonathan H. ... New Braunfels, TX
Hull, Joseph L., A Professional Corporation
Tulsa, OK
Hull, Joseph L., III ... Tulsa, OK
Hull, Joseph L., Jr. ... Tulsa, OK
Hull, Joseph W. ... Grove City, OH
Hull, Julius H. ... Woodridge, IL
Hull, Karen B. ... Columbus, OH
Hull, Karen R. ... Boston, MA
Hull, Karen S. ... San Francisco, CA
Hull, Kimball E.C. ... Boston, MA
Hull, LaVail ... Big Rapids, MI
Hull Law Offices ... Salineville, OH
Hull, Lewis W. ... St. Petersburg, FL
Hull, Lisa D. ... Sherman, TX
Hull, Lloyd N. ... Greenwich, CT
Hull, Lyman W. ... Seattle, WA
Hull, Margaret Warren ... Orlando, FL
Hull, Mary A. ... Kansas City, MO
Hull, Maurice S. S. ... High Point, NC
Hull McGuire P.C. ... Washington, DC
Pittsburgh, PA
Hull, Michael B. ... Mission Viejo, CA
Hull, Michael H. ... Irving, TX
Hull, Michael R. ... Chicago, IL
Hull, Michael R. ... Chanute, KS
Hull, Michael S. ... Austin, TX
Hull, N. E. H. ... Camden, NJ
Hull, Norman L. ... Orlando, FL
Hull, Norman Linder, P.A. ... Orlando, FL
Sanford, FL
Hull, Oliver ... Melville, NY
Hull, Owens L., Jr. ... Platte City, MO
Hull, Pamela K. ... Santa Barbara, CA
Hull, Paul Gerald, Jr. ... Chicago, IL
Hull, Paul R. ... Clearwater, FL
Hull, Peter W. ... Hartford, CT
Hull, Philip G. ... Palm Beach, FL
New York, NY
Hull, Ralph T. ... Houston, TX
Hull, Rebecca A. ... San Francisco, CA
Hull, Richard A. ... Marietta, GA
Hull, Richard A. ... Buffalo, NY
Hull, Richard A., III ... Biddeford, ME
Hull, Richard E.
Department of Commerce, GV
Hull, Richard J. ... Arvada, CO
Hull, Richard J. ... Livingston, NJ
Hull, Richard M. ... Dallas, TX
Hull, Richard S. ... Laguna Niguel, CA
Hull, Rick ... Arvada, CO
Hull, Rick L. ... Salineville, OH
Hull, Robbi B. ... Austin, TX
Hull, Robert G. ... Sedona, AZ
Hull, Robert H. ... Santa Ana, CA
Hull, Robert H., Jr. ... Charlotte, NC
Hull, Robert Joe ... Houston, TX
Hull, Robert Kingsley ... Penn Yan, NY
Hull, Robert Martin ... Hillsboro, OR
Hull, Roger A. ... Torrance, CA
Hull, Ronald G. ... Rochester, NY
Hull, Ronald R. ... Wichita, KS
Hull, Sander Marcus ... Milwaukie, OR
Hull, Sarah S. ... Norfolk, VA
Hull & Simonton, Co., L.P.A. ... Akron, OH
Hull, Stephanie A. ... Linthicum, MD
Hull, Stephen ... Salt Lake City, UT
Hull, Steven H. ... Portland, OR
Hull, Susan McMurray ... Dallas, TX
Hull, T. Clark ... Danbury, CT
Hull, Terrence ... Jersey City, NJ
Hull, Terry L. ... San Antonio, TX
Hull, Tevis W. ... Sandpoint, ID
Hull, Thomas G. ... Greeneville, TN
Hull, Thomas J. ... Binghamton, NY
Hull, Thomas M. ... Grants Pass, OR
Hull, Thomas M. ... Tullahoma, TN
Hull, Towill, Norman, Barrett & Salley, A Professional Corporation ... Atlanta, GA
Augusta, GA
Aiken, SC
Hull, T. P., Jr. ... Houston, TX
Hull, Vincent E., Jr. ... Freehold, NJ
Hull, W. Allen ... Round Rock, TX
Hull, W. Gary ... Tempe, AZ
Hull, Ward D. ... Loganville, GA
Hull, Webber & Reis, LLP
Bennington, VT
Rutland, VT
Hull, William D. ... Minneapolis, MN
Hull, Wood A. ... Omaha, NE
Hull & Zimmerman, P.C. ... Arvada, CO
Hulla, Patrick F. ... Wichita, KS
Hullender, David M. ... Kings Mountain, NC
Hullender, William A. ... Chattanooga, TN
Huller, Kelly G. ... Philadelphia, PA
Huller, Mark J. ... Fairfield, OH
Huller, Stanley R. ... Dallas, TX
Hullett, G. Randal ... McKinney, TX
Hulley, Patricia A. ... Rochester, NY
Hulley, Patricia C. ... San Francisco, CA
Hulley, Roger M. ... New Paltz, NY
Hullinger, Danny D. ... Los Angeles, CA
Hullinghorst, Gene ... Lansing, MI
Hull-Johnson, Edith Helene ... Landover, MD
Hullman, Mark A. ... Traverse City, MI
Hullum, Billy D. ... Fort Worth, TX
Hullverson & Hullverson, L.L.C.
St. Louis, MO
Hullverson, James E. ... St. Louis, MO
Hullverson, James E., Jr. ... St. Louis, MO
Hullverson, John E. ... St. Louis, MO

Hullverson Law Firm, The ... St. Louis, MO
Hullverson, Thomas C. ... St. Louis, MO
Hulme, Antonia L. ... Jupiter, FL
Hulme, Daniel S. ... New York, NY
Hulme, James H. ... Washington, DC
Hulme, James Norton
Westhampton Beach, NY
Hulme, James W. ... North Salem, NY
Hulme, Loyal C. ... Salt Lake City, UT
Hulme, Michael E., Jr. ... Northbrook, IL
Hulme, Randall K. ... Washington, DC
Hulme, Richard D. ... Wellesley, MA
Hulme, Roy A. ... Cleveland, OH
Hulme, Stephen E. ... Dallas, TX
Hulmes, Donald W. ... Fort Lauderdale, FL
Hulmes, Lori A. ... Houston, TX
Hulnick, Leslie F. ... Wichita, KS
Hulnick, Leslie F., P.A. ... Wichita, KS
Hulnick, Pamela A. ... Teaneck, NJ
Hulscher, Gerald L. ... Puyallup, WA
Hulse, B. Geoffrey ... Goldsboro, NC
Hulse, Brian D. ... Seattle, WA
Hulse, Carole D. ... United States Senate,
Committee Legal Personnel, GV
Hulse, Dale E. ... Salt Lake City, UT
Hulse, Gary R. ... Phoenix, AZ
Hulse, George H. ... Burlington, NJ
Hulse & Germano ... Burlington, NJ
Hulse, Gregory A. ... Adel, IA
Hulse, H. Bruce, Jr. ... Goldsboro, NC
Hulse, Janis L. ... Santa Ana, CA
Hulse, Jeffrey B. ... Hauppauge, NY
Hulse, John I., IV ... New Orleans, LA
Hulse, John K., Jr. ... Moorestown, NJ
Hulse, Jonathan V. ... Minneapolis, MN
Hulse, Lacey, Hardacre, Austin & Shine, P.C.
Anderson, IN
Hulse, Leslie A. ... New York, NY
Hulse, Lori M. ... Brooklyn, NY
Hulse, Minard E., Jr. ... Chicago, IL
Hulse, Robert F., Jr. ... Fremont, CA
Hulse, Robert S. ... Orlando, FL
Hulse, Sharon K. ... Beverly Hills, CA
Hulse, Stan O. ... Irving, TX
Hulse, Thomas L. ... Anderson, IN
Hulse, V. David ... Cedar Falls, IA
Hulse, W. Brian ... Salt Lake City, UT
Hulse & Wanek, A Professional Law Corporation ... Covington, LA
Metairie, LA
New Orleans, LA
Hulse, Wendel T. ... Grand Prairie, TX
Hulse, William (" Butch ") F., IV
San Antonio, TX
Hulse, William F. ... Charlotte, NC
Hulse, William L. ... Santa Monica, CA
Hulse, William L., A Professional Corporation
Santa Monica, CA
Hulseberg, Daniel J. ... North Chicago, IL
Hulsebosch, Lisa Montanaro
East Lansing, MI
Hulser, Frederick E. ... San Juan, PR
Hulser, Raymond N. ... Department of Justice,
Criminal Division, GV
Hulsey, Angela T. ... Washington, DC
Hulsey, Benjamin H. ... St. Louis, MO
Hulsey, Julius M. ... Gainesville, GA
Hulsey, Mark ... Jacksonville, FL
Hulsey, Mark, III ... Jacksonville, FL
Hulsey, Oliver & Mahar, LLP
Gainesville, GA
Hulsey, Paul H. ... Charleston, SC
Hulsey, Robert J. ... Alpharetta, GA
Roswell, GA
Hulsey, Roger D. ... Stockton, CA
Hulsey, Roger D., A Prof. Law Corp.
Stockton, CA
Hulsey, Royce G. ... San Francisco, CA
Hulsey, Tracy Lynn ... Greenville, SC
Hulsey, V. Michele ... Louisville, KY
Hulsey, William N., III ... Austin, TX
Hulsh, Andrew ... Miami, FL
Hulshizer, Robin M. ... Chicago, IL
Hulshoff, Ric D. ... Los Angeles, CA
Hulsizer, Russell H. ... Summit, NJ
Hulslander, Kevin E. ... Syracuse, NY
Hulslander, Victor L. ... Gainesville, FL
Hulsman, Steven J. ... Phoenix, AZ
Hulst, Jary J. ... Mountain View, CA
Hulst, Thomas R. Vander ... Grandville, MI
Hulston, John K. ... Springfield, MO
Hulston, Jones, Gammon & Marsh
Springfield, MO
Hulstrand, Brian D. ... Willmar, MN
Hulstrand, George E. ... Willmar, MN
Hulswit, David E., Jr. ... Grand Rapids, MI
Hulsy & Hulsy ... Bakersfield, CA
Hulsy & Hulsy ... Santa Ana, CA
Hulsy, James R. ... Bakersfield, CA
Hulsy, William M. ... Santa Ana, CA
Hulsy, William S. ... Santa Ana, CA
Hult, Ann-Gail Bregianes ... New York, NY
Hult Garlin Driscoll & Murray, LLC
Boulder, CO
Denver, CO
Hult, James M., (P.C.) ... Boulder, CO
Hult, John K. ... Palo Alto, CA
Hult, Keith C. ... Chicago, IL
Hult, Kimberly M. ... Boulder, CO
Hult, Matthew ... Menlo Park, CA
Hult, Robert J. ... Bloomington, IL
Hult, Stephanie Smith ... Boulder, CO
Hultay, Dennis M. ... Bloomfield, NJ
Hultberg, Steven P. ... Portland, OR
Hulten, Thomas A. ... Everett, WA
Hulteng, Richard J. ... Salem, OR
Hulteng, Robert G. ... San Francisco, CA
Hultgren, Andrew D. ... St. Cloud, MN

Hultgren, Betteann Fitt ... Safety Harbor, FL
Hultgren, David R. ... Monmouth, IL
Hultgren, Inger ... Washington, DC
New York, NY
Hultgren, James J. ... Dallas, TX
Hultgren, Jerry R. ... Fresno, CA
Hultgren, Jon R. ... Phoenix, AZ
Hultgren, Julian E. ... San Francisco, CA
Hultgren, Randall M. ... Carol Stream, IL
Hultgren, Richd. E. ... Red Bluff, CA
Hultgren, William C. ... Dearborn, MI
Hultgrenn, Dan F. ... Pasco, WA
Hulthen, Amy McKee ... Akron, OH
Hulthen, Martin R. ... Akron, OH
Hultin, Jerry MacArthur ... Columbus, OH
Hultin, Pamela N. ... Cleveland, OH
Hultin, Paul F. ... Denver, CO
Hulting, Frederick B., Jr. ... Sacramento, CA
Hulting, Patricia Mullen ... Des Moines, IA
Hultink, Albertus ... Ada, MI
Hultman, Alan C. ... Downers Grove, IL
Hultman, Carl T. ... Tacoma, WA
Hultman, Eric R. ... Seattle, WA
Hultman, George H. ... Calabasas, CA
Hultman, Jeffrey J. ... Northridge, CA
Hultman, John H. ... Rockville Centre, NY
Hultman, John R. ... Redlands, CA
Hultman and Johnson, P.C.
Downers Grove, IL
Hultman, Kenneth W. ... San Francisco, CA
Hultman, Lorraine Maass
Fort Myers, FL
Sarasota, FL
Tampa, FL
Hulton, Jeffrey A. ... Mc Connellsburg, PA
Hulton, Patrick T. ... Hartford, CT
Hultquist, Christopher E. ... Providence, RI
Hultquist, Gary L. ... San Francisco, CA
Hultquist, James T. ... Chicago, IL
Hultquist, Larry ... Sacramento, CA
Hultquist, Michael D. ... Chicago, IL
Hultquist, Robert C. ... Downers Grove, IL
Hultquist, Roger W. ... Fort Wayne, IN
Hultquist, Steven J. ... Chapel Hill, NC
Hultquist, Wiedel, Hudzik & Russ
Downers Grove, IL
Hults & Helder ... Big Rapids, MI
Hults, Michael D. ... Big Rapids, MI
Hults, Pauline Jayne ... Indianapolis, IN
Hultstrand, Charles ... Mesa, AZ
Hultstrand, Charles, P.C. ... Mesa, AZ
Hultzen, Robert L. ... Santa Cruz, CA
Hulvey, Craig W. ... Arlington, VA
Hulwi, James J., Jr. ... Mankato, MN
Hum, Betty L. ... Chandler, AZ
Hum, Craig William ... Los Angeles, CA
Hum, Gary S. ... San Francisco, CA
Hum, Grace ... San Francisco, CA
Hum, Robert W., II ... Columbiana, OH
Human, Daniel L. ... St. Louis, MO
Human, David R. ... St. Louis, MO
Human, F. William, Jr. ... St. Louis, MO
Human, Jeffrey A. ... Buffalo, NY
Human, Kenneth R. ... Bay St. Louis, MS
Human, Randy E. ... Columbus, OH
Human, W. Gene, Jr. ... Houston, TX
Humanic, John W. ... Southfield, MI
Humann, James W. ... Naples, FL
Tampa, FL
Humann, John F. ... Buffalo, NY
Humann, Kirstin L. ... Nashville, TN
Humann, Walter J. ... Dallas, TX
Humbach, Gregory D. ... Wichita Falls, TX
Humbach, John A. ... White Plains, NY
Humbach, Thomas E. ... Hamilton, OH
Humber, Christopher E. ... Chicago, IL
Humber, Erik A. ... Point Reyes Station, CA
Humber, John D. ... Tuscaloosa, AL
Humber, Rivers H. ... Clarksdale, MS
Humberd, David S., (P.C.) ... Cleveland, TN
Humberstone, Bruce E. ... Salt Lake City, UT
Humberstone, Michelle ... Portland, OR
Humbert, C. Mark ... Walnut Creek, CA
Humbert, Daniel W. ... New York, NY
Humbert, Ernest C. ... Waterloo, NY
Humbert, Mark A. ... Cincinnati, OH
Humbert, Richard B. ... Corona Del Mar, CA
Humbert, Ted A. ... Cleveland, OH
Humbert, Thomas C., Jr. ... New York, NY
Humbert, Vernon H. ... Cincinnati, OH
Humbert, William H. ... Mebane, NC
Humbert, X. Paul ... Newark, NJ
Humble, Barbara ... New York, NY
Humble, Charles D. ... Lincoln, NE
Humble, Charles G. ... Oklahoma City, OK
Humble, Don G. ... Cameron, TX
Humble, George A. ... Groesbeck, TX
Humble and Humble, L.L.P. ... Cameron, TX
Humble, J. Randolph ... Knoxville, TN
Humble, Mark M. ... Cameron, TX
Humble, Monty ... Dallas, TX
Humble, Scott Brian ... Phoenix, AZ
Humble, Scott F. ... Jamestown, NY
Humble, Sharon N. ... San Antonio, TX
Humbracht, H. Frederick, Jr.
Nashville, TN
Humburg, Reinhard ... New York, NY
Hume, Anthony ... Dallas, TX
Hume & Associates ... Stamford, CT
Hume, Bradley R. ... Louisville, KY
Hume, Cameron R. ... Department of State,
Foreign Service Officers (Overseas), GV
Hume, Carlton L. ... Hartford, CT
Hume, Charles Lea ... Miami, FL
Hume, Christopher G., III ... Mobile, AL
Hume, Claus J. ... Denver, CO
Hume, Clayton R. ... Louisville, KY
Hume, Daniel ... New York, NY

Hume, David G. ... New York, NY
Hume, David G. ... Austin, TX
Hume, Duncan B. ... Stamford, CT
Hume, E. C., Jr. ... Louisville, KY
Hume, Edward A. ... Woodside, CA
Hume, Edward C. ... Enid, OK
Hume, Edward S. ... Syracuse, NY
Hume, Ernest E., Jr. ... Elyria, OH
Hume, Forest ... Richmond, KY
Hume, Gaye L. ... Department of Justice, Civil Rights Division, GV
Hume, Gene D. ... West Sacramento, CA
Hume, Hamish P.M. ... Washington, DC
Hume, Harold N., Jr. ... Fort Myers, FL
Hume, James Clay ... Albuquerque, NM
Hume, James E. ... Petersburg, VA
Hume, John ... Coral Springs, FL
Hume, John M. ... Marysville, PA
Hume, John P. ... Washington, DC
Hume, John T., III ... Indianapolis, IN
Hume, John T., Jr. ... Indianapolis, IN
Hume, Johnetta D.
Department Of Veterans Affairs, Office of Employment Discrimination Complaints Adjudication, GV
Hume & Johnson, P.A. ... Coral Springs, FL
Pompano Beach, FL
Hume, Leslie D. ... Austin, TX
Hume, Linda S. ... Seattle, WA
Hume, Martin S. ... Youngstown, OH
Hume & Moger ... West Sacramento, CA
Hume, Patrick H. ... Washington, DC
Hume, Robert H., Jr. ... Anchorage, AK
Hume, Robert P. ... Orleans, MA
Hume, Robert T. ... Washington, DC
Hume Smith Geddes Green & Simmons
Indianapolis, IN
Hume, Sophie Hager ... Seattle, WA
Hume, Stephen L. ... London, OH
Hume, Stephen N. ... New Milford, CT
Hume, William F. ... Port Chester, NY
Hume, William G. ... Prospect, KY
Humenik, Daniel M. ... St. Cloud, MN
Humenik, Mark F. ... Cleveland, OH
Humenuk, William A. ... Philadelphia, PA
Humer, Kenneth G. ... Jackson, MS
Humes, Botzow, Wagner & Miller
Darien, CT
New York, NY
Humes, Douglas P. ... Kennett Square, PA
Humes, Gary E. ... Washington, DC
Humes, Jack H., Jr. ... Edwardsville, IL
Humes, James C. ... Philadelphia, PA
Humes, James E., II ... Columbus, GA
Humes, James M. ... San Francisco, CA
Humes, John W., Jr. ... Jacksonville, FL
Humes, Melvin ... Birmingham, AL
Humes, Richard M.
Securities and Exchange Commission, Office of the General Counsel, GV
Humes, Stephen J. ... Bridgeport, CT
Humes, Traci Duvall ... Washington, DC
Humes & Wagner ... Locust Valley, NY
Humick, Thomas C. C. ... Morristown, NJ
Humiston, Carol Ann ... Los Angeles, CA
Humiston, David M. ... Los Angeles, CA
Humiston, Susan M. ... Minneapolis, MN
Humke, Brian J. ... Ames, IA
Des Moines, IA
Humke, Herbert C. ... Sheboygan, WI
Humke, Herbert C., III ... Sheboygan, WI
Humke, Steven K. ... Indianapolis, IN
Humleker Law Office ... Neenah, WI
Humleker, Peter D., III ... Neenah, WI
Humm, S. Randall ... Department of Justice, Environment and Natural Resources Division, GV
Humm, Timothy S. ... St. Louis, MO
Hummel, Amy Louise ... Brookline, MA
Hummel, Bradley ... Columbus, OH
Hummel, Brian G. ... Glendale, CA
Hummel, C. Cleveland ... Bloomsburg, PA
Hummel, Carl A. ... Kansas City, MO
Hummel, Carla ... Fort Lee, NJ
Hummel, Carole M. ... Smithton, IL
Hummel, Chad S. ... Los Angeles, CA
Hummel, Christian F. ... Troy, NY
Hummel, Cleveland C. ... Bloomsburg, PA
Hummel & Coan ... Louisville, KY
Hummel, David Wayne, Jr ... Wheeling, WV
Hummel, Denise L. ... Mill Valley, CA
Boulder, CO
Hummel, Dennis J. ... Louisville, KY
Hummel, Don ... Scottsdale, AZ
Hummel & Fletcher, Chtd. ... Boise, ID
Hummel, Fred D. ... Brockway, PA
Punxsutawney, PA
Hummel, Gregory W. ... Chicago, IL
Hummel, Holly Jane ... Portland, OR
Hummel, Jack L. ... Littleton, CO
Hummel, James E. ... Rancho Cucamonga, CA
Hummel, Jaqueline M. ... Springfield, MA
Hummel, Jeffrey C. ... Bristol, CT
Hummel, Jeffrey D. ... Rochester, NY
Hummel, Jeffrey M. ... Washington, DC
Hummel, Jill Rubin ... St. Louis, MO
Hummel, Jill Rubin ... St. Louis, MO
Hummel, John C. ... Boise, ID
Hummel, John F. ... Fairfax, VA
Hummel, John J. ... St. Louis, MO
Hummel, John J. ... Bend, OR
Hummel, John W. ... Central City, NE
Hummel, Jon F. ... Lansing, MI
Hummel, Jonathan A., Jr. ... Denver, CO
Hummel, Joseph Patrick ... Louisville, KY
Hummel, K. Sue ... Citrus Heights, CA
Hummel, Keith R. ... New York, NY
Hummel Law Offices ... Columbia, SC
Hummel & Lewis ... Bloomsburg, PA
Hummel, Lynn J. ... Detroit Lakes, MN
Hummel, Moira Kristof ... Pasadena, CA
Hummel, Paul M. ... Chicago, IL
Hummel, Philip L., IV ... Orange, CA
Hummel, Ralph A. ... Huntington, NY
Hummel, Randy A. ... Sunbury, PA
Hummel, Richard A. ... Clearfield, UT
Hummel, Ronald Steven ... St. Louis, MO
Hummel, Sinclair, Evans, Hunt & Heisler, P.A.
Detroit Lakes, MN
Hummel, Terry V. ... Columbus, OH
Hummel, Thomas J. ... Columbia, SC
Hummel, Timothy B. ... Oklahoma City, OK
Hummel, Timothy D. ... Pasadena, CA
Hummel, Valerie L. ... Miami, FL
Hummel, Zachary A. ... St. Louis, MO
Hummell, Chester H. ... Canal Winchester, OH
Hummell, Michael H. ... Corpus Christi, TX
Hummell, William D. ... New York, NY
Hummer, Donal, Jr. ... Toledo, OH
Hummer, J. Franklin ... Topeka, KS
Hummer, J. Thomas ... Sacramento, CA
Hummer, John C. ... Pasadena, CA
Hummer, John L. ... Laguna Niguel, CA
Hummer, Laurence L. ... Los Angeles, CA
Hummer Legal Services Corporation, L.P.A.
Toledo, OH
Hummer, Maria D., (P.C.)
Los Angeles, CA
Hummer, Mark A. ... Columbus, OH
Hummer, Michelle J. ... Baltimore, MD
Hummer, Paul M. ... Philadelphia, PA
Hummer, Philip L. ... New York, NY
Hummer, Robert P., Jr. ... Largo, FL
Hummer, Wayne G., Jr. ... Lancaster, PA
Hummers, Edward W., Jr.
Washington, DC
Hummers, Herbert J. ... New York, NY
Hummert, Michael A. ... Dallas, TX
Humpal, Donna M. ... Davenport, IA
Humpal, LeRoy C. ... San Rafael, CA
Humpert, Samuel J. ... Colorado Springs, CO
Humpert, William A. ... Fort Mitchell, KY
Humpherys, Keith S. ... Chico, CA
Humpherys, L. Rich ... Salt Lake City, UT
Humphress, Stephen B. ... Lebanon, KY
Humphreville, John D. ... Naples, FL
Humphrey, Albert B. ... Great Barrington, MA
Humphrey, Alison C. ... Minneapolis, MN
Humphrey, Andrew G. ... Minneapolis, MN
Humphrey & Associates, P.C. ... Denver, CO
Humphrey, Barbara C. ... New York, NY
Humphrey, Bernard L. ... Detroit, MI
Humphrey, Brian C. ... St. Louis, MO
Humphrey, Brian E. ... Chattanooga, TN
Humphrey, Bruce B. ... Jacksonville, FL
Humphrey, Charles G. ... Williamsville, NY
Humphrey, Charles M., III ... Okmulgee, OK
Humphrey, Christopher M. ... Raleigh, NC
Humphrey, Christopher S. ... Canton, OH
Humphrey, Claudia N. ... Stamford, CT
Humphrey, Currun C. ... Harvest, AL
Humphrey, Currun C., P.C. ... Harvest, AL
Humphrey, Dianne ... Glendale, CA
Humphrey, Don W., Jr. ... Salem, OH
Humphrey, Donald James ... Boulder, CO
Humphrey, Dudley ... Winston-Salem, NC
Humphrey, Farrington & McClain, P.C.
Independence, MO
Kansas City, MO
Humphrey, G. Scott ... Greenville, SC
Humphrey, George ... Houston, TX
Humphrey, George Dudley, III
Greenville, NC
Humphrey, George M., II ... Chicago, IL
Humphrey, Geralyn G. ... Roseland, NJ
Humphrey, Gordon L., Jr. ... Little Rock, AR
Humphrey, Gregory J. ... Fort Madison, IA
Humphrey, Griffith L. ... San Francisco, CA
Humphrey, Guy R. ... Columbus, OH
Humphrey and Haas, P.C. ... Des Moines, IA
Humphrey, Hannon, Moriarity & Schoener
Detroit, MI
Holland, MI
Troy, MI
Humphrey, Herman L. ... Louisville, KY
Humphrey, Hubert ... Greensboro, NC
Humphrey, Hubert H., III ... St. Paul, MN
Humphrey, Isabel M. ... Scottsdale, AZ
Humphrey, J. Scott ... Chicago, IL
Humphrey, James A. ... Palatine, IL
Humphrey, James A. ... Great Falls, MT
Humphrey, James D. ... Lawrenceburg, IN
Humphrey, James D., II ... New York, NY
Humphrey, James M., IV ... Kansas City, MO
Humphrey, James T. ... Fort Myers, FL
Humphrey, James W., Jr. ... Kansas City, MO
Humphrey, Janet E. ... Irvine, CA
Humphrey, Jere L. ... Plymouth, IN
Humphrey, John J. ... Washington, DC
Humphrey, John M. ... Williamsport, PA
Humphrey, John R. ... Kansas City, MO
Humphrey & Jones ... Amarillo, TX
Humphrey, Joseph H. ... Duncan, OK
Humphrey, Kathryn J. ... Detroit, MI
Humphrey, Kenneth S. ... Malibu, CA
Humphrey & Knott, P.A. ... Cape Coral, FL
Fort Myers, FL
Naples, FL
Punta Gorda, FL
Sanibel, FL
Humphrey, Kyle J. ... Bakersfield, CA
Humphrey, Kyler L. ... St. Louis, MO
Humphrey, Laurie F. ... Cleveland, OH
Humphrey, Lawrence D. ... Norwell, MA
Humphrey, Lawrence T. ... Atlanta, GA
Humphrey, Leslie Anne ... Kansas City, KS
Humphrey, Lewis Peyton
Charlottesville, VA
Humphrey, Maclyn A. ... Raleigh, NC
Humphrey, Margot Smiley
Washington, DC
Humphrey, Mark A. ... Orlando, FL
Humphrey, Mark A. ... Des Moines, IA
Humphrey, Mark Anthony ... Collinsville, IL
Humphrey, Mark E. ... Wichita, KS
Humphrey, Mark R. ... Portland, OR
Humphrey, Marshall, III ... Tucson, AZ
Humphrey, Mary E. ... El Prado, NM
Humphrey, Mary Jane ... Evansville, IN
Humphrey, Matthew S. ... Boulder, CO
Humphrey, Michael C. ... Cleveland, OH
Humphrey, Michael J. ... Cleveland, OH
Humphrey, Michael R. ... Kansas City, MO
Humphrey, Michelle M. ... Los Angeles, CA
Humphrey, Monica L. ... Kokomo, IN
Humphrey, Norman, Jr.
Independence, MO
Humphrey, O.J. (Buz), III ... Seattle, WA
Humphrey & Parker, LLC
Williamsville, NY
Humphrey, Patricia L. ... Chatham, IL
Humphrey, Paul N. ... Rochester, NY
Humphrey, Paul W. ... Madison, WI
Humphrey, Rachel A. ... Atlanta, GA
Humphrey, Ralph L. ... Ashtabula, OH
Humphrey, Randy L. ... St. Johns, MI
Humphrey, Rebecca L. ... Erie, PA
Humphrey, Richard F. ... Hayward, CA
Humphrey, Richard S. ... Newport, RI
Providence, RI
Humphrey, Richard S. ... Tiverton, RI
Humphrey, Robert F. ... Le Roy, NY
Humphrey, Robert H. ... Tiverton, RI
Humphrey, Robert J. ... Troy, MI
Humphrey, Robert M. ... Cleveland, OH
Humphrey, Robin A. ... Ankeny, IA
Humphrey, Robin Rochelle ... Baldwin, NY
Humphrey, Russell A. ... Nashville, TN
Humphrey, Scott J. ... Birmingham, AL
Humphrey, Stephen L. ... Washington, DC
Humphrey, Steven R. ... Hartford, CT
Stamford, CT
Humphrey, Theodore ... Youngstown, OH
Humphrey, Thomas B. ... Boise, ID
Humphrey, Thomas B., Jr. ... Yuma, AZ
Humphrey, Thomas E. ... Sanford, ME
Humphrey, Thomas P. ... Washington, DC
Humphrey, Thomas W. ... Cincinnati, OH
Humphrey, Timothy J. ... San Francisco, CA
Humphrey, Timothy J., Sr.
Albuquerque, NM
Humphrey, William C. ... Annapolis, MD
Humphrey, William R. ... Denver, CO
Humphrey, William Warren, III
Kansas City, MO
Humphrey III, William W.
Kansas City, MO
Humphreys, Amy R. ... Charleston, WV
Humphreys, Andrew W. ... Hempstead, NY
Humphreys, Angela L. ... Seattle, WA
Humphreys, Ann B. ... Norfolk, VA
Humphreys, Ben L. ... Girard, KS
Humphreys, B. J. ... Saginaw, MI
Humphreys, Bruce L. ... North Bergen, NJ
Humphreys, Burrell I. ... Parsippany, NJ
Humphreys, Cecil C., Jr. ... Memphis, TN
Humphreys, Charles J. ... Cohasset, MA
Humphreys, Christian D. ... San Diego, CA
Humphreys, Daphne M. ... Los Angeles, CA
Humphreys, David C., Jr. ... Charleston, SC
Humphreys, David Craig ... Joplin, MO
Humphreys, David J. ... Pittsburgh, PA
Humphreys, David J. ... Reston, VA
Humphreys, Donald H. ... Great Bend, KS
Humphreys, Donald L. ... San Francisco, CA
Humphreys, Douglas K. ... San Diego, CA
Humphreys Dunlap Wellford Acuff & Stanton, A Professional Corporation
Memphis, TN
Humphreys, Earl Locklar ... Houston, TX
Humphreys, Edwin E. ... Birmingham, AL
Humphreys, Elizabeth ... Stockton, CA
Humphreys, Ernest D. ... Providence, RI
Humphreys, Gene Lynn ... Louisville, KY
Humphreys, Harrie M.
Jacksonville Beach, FL
Humphreys, Hugh C. ... Wampsville, NY
Humphreys, Ivan H. ... Palo Alto, CA
Humphreys, J. Fraser, III ... Memphis, TN
Humphreys, J. Fraser, Jr. ... Memphis, TN
Humphreys, Jahn E. ... Seabrook, TX
Humphreys, James A., Jr.
Newport Beach, CA
Humphreys, James E. ... Passaic, NJ
Humphreys, James F. ... Charleston, WV
Humphreys, James F., & Associates, L.C.
Charleston, WV
Huntington, WV
Humphreys, James N. L.
Johnson City, TN
Kingsport, TN
Humphreys, Janet L. ... Miami, FL
Humphreys, Jennifer ... Portland, ME
Humphreys, Jerry R. ... Nashville, TN
Humphreys, Jodie Louanne Rosell ... Azle, TX
Humphreys, John D. L. ... Saginaw, MI
Humphreys, John M. ... Denver, CO
Humphreys, Jordan M. ... Columbia, MO
Humphreys, Joseph O. ... Amelia, VA
Humphreys, Julie Payne ... Orange, CA
Humphreys, Karen M. ... Wichita, KS
Humphreys, Kevin E. ... Columbus, OH
Humphreys, Kevin L. ... Ridgeland, MS
Humphreys, Lloyd Charles ... Garland, TX
Humphreys, Lynn M. ... San Francisco, CA
Humphreys, Mark S. ... Grand Prairie, TX
Humphreys, Michael A. ... New York, NY
Humphreys, Noel D. ... Newark, NJ
New York, NY
Humphreys, Owen R. ... Forest Lake, MN
Humphreys, Peter S. ... New York, NY
Humphreys, Philip D. ... Berkeley, CA
Humphreys, R. Hunter ... Memphis, TN
Humphreys, R. Max ... Jefferson City, MO
Humphreys, Richard H., Jr. ... Portland, OR
Humphreys, Robert B. ... Los Angeles, CA
Humphreys, Robert E., Jr. ... Owensboro, KY
Humphreys, Robert J. ... Virginia Beach, VA
Humphreys, Robert R. ... United States Senate, Committee Legal Personnel, GV
Humphreys, Robert W. ... San Jose, CA
Humphreys, Stephen F. ... Atlanta, GA
Humphreys, Steven A. ... Prineville, OR
Humphreys, Steven L. ... Washington, DC
Humphreys, Tanya D. ... Tulsa, OK
Humphreys, Thomas A. ... New York, NY
Humphreys, Thomas Lee, II ... Tacoma, WA
Humphreys, Victoria V. ... Virginia Beach, VA
Humphreys, Warren P. ... Schaumburg, IL
Humphreys, William C., Jr. ... Atlanta, GA
Humphries, Alan R. ... Pine Bluff, AR
Humphries, Bert W., Jr. ... Upland, CA
Humphries, Clay Dean ... Fort Worth, TX
Humphries, Cynthia C. ... Washington, DC
Humphries, Cynthia L. ... Cooper, TX
Humphries, Derrick A. ... Washington, DC
Humphries, Derrick A., P.C.
Washington, DC
Humphries, Edward Francis
Staten Island, NY
Humphries, Erin H. ... Anaheim Hills, CA
Humphries, Gregory P. ... Santa Monica, CA
Humphries, Guy B. ... Denver, CO
Humphries, Guy E., Jr. ... Alexandria, LA
Humphries, Homer H., Jr.
Jacksonville, FL
Humphries & Humphries ... Alexandria, LA
Humphries, J. Bob ... Tampa, FL
Humphries, J. Gregory ... Orlando, FL
Humphries, J. Robert ... Washington, DC
Humphries, James N. ... Detroit, MI
Humphries, J.D., III, (P.C.) ... Atlanta, GA
Humphries, John W., Jr. ... Newburyport, MA
Humphries, Kenneth W. ... Hopkinsville, KY
Humphries, Kim Sheftall ... Chevy Chase, MD
Humphries, L. Lee ... Long Beach, CA
Humphries, Laura B. ... Washington, DC
Humphries & Lewis ... Pine Bluff, AR
Humphries, Lynne B. ... Houston, TX
Humphries, M. Clayton, Jr.
West Point, GA
Humphries, Mary Nicholas ... Baltimore, MD
Humphries, Nathaniel A. ... Washington, DC
Humphries, Neil E. ... Spokane, WA
Humphries & Oberdier, P.A.
Jacksonville, FL
Humphries, Patterson & Lewis
Spokane, WA
Humphries, Ralph, (P.A.)
Jacksonville, FL
Humphries, Robert H. ... Treasury Department, U.S. Customs Service, GV
Humphries, Scott A. ... Houston, TX
Humphries, Stacy Kleiner ... Houston, TX
Humphries, Steven L. ... Birmingham, AL
Humphries, William F., III ... Tampa, FL
Humphries, William H., III ... Pittsburgh, PA
Humphries, Wm. N., Jr. ... Chesterfield, VA
Humphry, Steven K. ... Fresno, CA
Humphrys, Dawn A. ... Akron, OH
Humrickhouse, Stephani Wilson
Raleigh, NC
Humsey, Joseph R. ... St. Paul, MN
Humsjo, Stephen A. ... East Islip, NY
Humway, Christina M.
Department of Justice, Civil Division, GV
Hunacek, Mark ... Ames, IA
Huneiker, Kurt ... New York, NY
Huncke, John G. ... Beverly Hills, CA
Hunckler, Tracy K. ... Sacramento, CA
Hunczak, Paul G. ... Newton, NJ
Hund, Carrie Lynne ... St. Paul, MN
Hund, Edward J., Jr. ... Wichita, KS
Hund, Jim ... Lubbock, TX
Hund, Michael L. ... Harrisburg, PA
Hundere, Nan Porett ... San Antonio, TX
Hundertmark, Brian J. ... Chevy Chase, MD
Hundertmark, J. Randolph
Williston Park, NY
Hundertmark, Jay L. ... Northfield, NJ
Hundertmark, Robert J. ... Woburn, MA
Hunderup, Ted M. ... Humboldt, TN
Hundhausen, Arthur A. ... Denver, CO
Hundley, Adam Roy ... Boston, MA
Hundley, C. Clay, Jr. ... Tompkinsville, KY
Hundley, Chanta G. ... Tallahassee, FL
Hundley, Charles W. ... Richmond, VA
Hundley, Charlton C. ... Tompkinsville, KY
Hundley, Claude E., III ... Huntsville, AL
Hundley, Franklin M. ... Boston, MA
Hundley, George R. ... Salisbury, NC
Hundley, Henry R. ... Costa Mesa, CA
Hundley, James D. ... Richmond, VA
Hundley, James R. ... High Point, NC
Hundley, James T. ... Ocean Grove, NJ
Hundley, James W. ... Fairfax, VA
Hundley, John D. ... Panama City, FL
Hundley, John F. ... Washington, DC
Alexandria, VA
Hundley, John T. ... Chicago, IL
Hundley, Joyce B. ... Department of Justice, Antitrust Division, GV

Hundley, Kelly Michael ... **Atlanta, GA**
Hundley, Laura S. ... **Boulder, CO**
Denver, CO
Hundley & Parry, P.C. ... Ocean Grove, NJ
Hundley, Patrick E. ... Boerne, TX
Hundley, Paul B. ... **Los Angeles, CA**
Hundley, Richard L. ... Hartselle, AL
Hundley, Richard W. ... Santa Clara, CA
Hundley, Ron L. ... Dallas, TX
Hundley, Thomas C. ... **Louisville, KY**
Hundley, Wayland E. ... Madison, NC
Hundley, Wayne E. ... Topeka, KS
Hundley, William G. ... **Washington, DC**
Hundman, Douglas J. ... Bloomington, IL
Hundman, James E. ... **Wheaton, IL**
Hundman, William T. ... **Bloomington, IL**
Hunegs, Richard Gene ... **Minneapolis, MN**
Hunegs, Steven M. ... **Minneapolis, MN**
Hunegs, Stone, Koenig, LeNeave & Kvas, P.A. ... **Minneapolis, MN**
Huneke, Edward W. ... Seattle, WA
Huneke, John ... Spokane, WA
Huneke, Nancy A. ... Oakland, CA
Huneke, William L. ... Toms River, NJ
Huner, Jana Marie ... Southfield, MI
Huneycutt, Alice R. ... **Tampa, FL**
Huneycutt, D. J. ... **Newport News, VA**
Huneycutt, John Mark ... Fayetteville, AR
Huneycutt, Stephanie ... Williamsburg, VA
Hung, David S. ... Schaumburg, IL
Hung, Francis Curtis, Jr. ... Los Angeles, CA
Hung, Jennifer C. ... Beverly Hills, CA
Hung, Maan-Huei (Ms.), Law Offices of
Los Angeles, CA
Hung, Samuel M. ... Irvine, CA
Hung, Syou Yun Susan ... Pelham, NY
Hung, Yea-Tung ... Vienna, VA
Hung, Yuen-Siang ... Claremont, CA
Hungar, Thomas G. ... **Washington, DC**
Hungate, Dan P. ... **Seattle, WA**
Hungate, Mark E. ... **St. Petersburg, FL**
Hungate, Richard ... **Los Angeles, CA**
Hungate, William L. ... St. Louis, MO
Hunger, Frank W. ... **Washington, DC**
Hunger, Scott A. ... Rocklin, CA
Hungerford, Charles M. ... **Palo Alto, CA**
Hungerford, Diane L. ... Kalamazoo, MI
Hungerford, Eric S. ... Dayton, OH
Hungerford, James E. ... Shelton, WA
Hungerford, James M. ... Cleveland, OH
Hungerford, John D. ... Bryans Road, MD
Hungerford, John D., P.A.
Bryans Road, MD
Hungerford, Lisa M. ... **Dallas, TX**
Hungerford, Mark S. ... St. Louis, MO
Hungerford, Nancy ... Oregon City, OR
Hungerford, Rex S., Jr. ... Los Angeles, CA
Hungerford, Robert L., Jr. ... Phoenix, AZ
Hungerford, Sean K. ... **Fresno, CA**
Hungerford, Thomas Richard
Indian River, MI
Hungerman, Andrew J., IV
Washington, DC
Hungness, Michael B. ... San Diego, CA
Hung-Tucker, Asa ... Universal City, CA
Hunigman, Richard J. ... Philadelphia, PA
Hunka, John K. ... Norristown, PA
Hunkapiller, James Robert ... Orlando, FL
Hunke, Carlton J. ... **Fargo, ND**
Hunke, Maurice R. ... Dickinson, ND
Hunkele, Edward G. ... Pittsburgh, PA
Hunken, Alan J. ... Chicago, IL
Hunker, Frederick ... Columbus, OH
Hunker, George H., Jr. ... **Roswell, NM**
Hunker, Paul B., Jr. ... **St. Louis, MO**
Hunker-Fedric, P.A. ... **Roswell, NM**
Hunkin, Eni F., Jr. ... Pago Pago, TT
Hunkins, Blaine B. ... Columbus, OH
Hunkins, Brian W. ... Cherry Hill, NJ
Hunkins, Melinda W. ... San Jose, CA
Hunkins, Raymond B. ... **Wheatland, WY**
Hunkler, Dolores G. ... Austin, TX
Hunkler, Jennifer A. ... **Washington, DC**
Hunko, Roger A. ... Silverdale, WA
Hunley, Charlton D. ... **New Orleans, LA**
Hunley, H. Martin, Jr. ... **New Orleans, LA**
Hunley, Paul E. ... Frankfort, KY
Hunn, Alan R. ... Irving, TX
Hunn, Eric S. ... **Pocatello, ID**
Hunn, J. Thomas ... Gastonia, NC
Hunn, Melvin A. ... **Fort Worth, TX**
Hunn, Nicole M. ... **New York, NY**
Hunn, Paul William ... **Austin, TX**
Hunn, Richard L. ... **Houston, TX**
Hunn, Robert N. ... **Philadelphia, PA**
Hunn, Serena C. ... **New York, NY**
Hunn, Stanford S. ... **Elkins Park, PA**
Hunn, Trina R. ... **New York, NY**
Hunnefeld, Angelika ... **Miami, FL**
Hunnefeld, Henry J. ... Coral Gables, FL
Hunnes, Jeffery A. ... **Billings, MT**
Hunnewell, Arnold W. ... **Boston, MA**
Hunnewell, Arnold W., Jr. ... **Boston, MA**
Hunnicutt & Appelman, P.C. ... **Denver, CO**
Hunnicutt, Buford Douglas ... Macon, GA
Hunnicutt, Charles A. ... **Washington, DC**
Hunnicutt, Charles L. ... Greenville, SC
Hunnicutt, David J. ... St. Helens, OR
Hunnicutt, J. Stephen ... **Dallas, TX**
Hunnicutt, James T. ... La Grange, GA
Hunnicutt, John F. ... St. Helens, OR
Hunnicutt, John F. & David J. Hunnicutt
St. Helens, OR
Hunnicutt, Joseph F. ... Norton, VA
Hunnicutt, Karen Lynn ... **Phoenix, AZ**
Hunnicutt Law Firm, The ... **Dallas, TX**
Hunnicutt, Richard W., III
San Antonio, TX
Hunnicutt, Wilfred E. ... Dallas, TX
Hunnicutt, William J. ... **Des Moines, IA**
Hunnicutt, William L. ... **Denver, CO**
Hunnicutt-Hauser, Allison ... Jacksonville, FL
Hunniecutt, Robert L. ... Daly City, CA
Hunnius, Patrick O. ... Los Angeles, CA
Hunold, Cynthia Cook ... Jacksonville, FL
Hunold, Karen Ann ... Department of Justice, Civil Division, GV
Hunolt, James A. ... Department of Justice, Civil Division, GV
Hunoval, Edward R. ... South Orange, NJ
Hunsader, Gregory R. ... Janesville, WI
Hunsader, Joseph E. ... **Washington, DC**
Hunsader & Schulz, S.C. ... Janesville, WI
Hunsaker, Barry, Jr. ... Houston, TX
Hunsaker, Charles R. ... Marietta, OH
Hunsaker, Christopher J. ... Port Tobacco, MD
Hunsaker, Craig E. ... **San Diego, CA**
Hunsaker, David M. ... **Sterling, VA**
Hunsaker, Hy Dillman
Department Of The Interior, Office of Hearings & Appeals, GV
Hunsaker, I. Franklin, III ... **Portland, OR**
Hunsaker, James M. ... **Castle Rock, CO**
Hunsaker, Keith A., Jr. ... Phoenix, AZ
Hunsaker, Kevin ... **San Jose, CA**
Hunsaker, Pamela B. ... **Salt Lake City, UT**
Hunsaker, Quinn D. ... Brigham City, UT
Hunsaker, Ralph E. ... **Phoenix, AZ**
Hunsaker, Richard K. ... **Rockford, IL**
Hunsaker, Scott ... **Houston, TX**
Hunsaker, William J. ... Wheat Ridge, CO
Hunsberger, Daniel P. ... Monroe, CT
Hunsberger, David R. ... Berkeley, CA
Hunsberger, Donald A. ... Orange, CA
Hunsberger, Joseph L. ... **Melville, NY**
Hunsberger, Kurt O. ... **Reno, NV**
Hunseder, Michael J. ... **Washington, DC**
Hunsicker, J. Bruce ... **Akron, OH**
Hunsicker, J. Freedley, Jr.
Philadelphia, PA
Hunsicker, Karen K. ... Washington, DC
Hunsicker, Oscar A., Jr. ... **Akron, OH**
Hunsicker, Roger A. ... Stockbridge, GA
Hunsicker, Scott A. ... Baltimore, MD
Hunsicker, Sheila O'Malley ... St. Louis, MO
Hunsicker, Steven R. ... **Washington, DC**
Hunsinger, Jeffrey B. ... **Boston, MA**
Hunsinger, Michael D. ... Seattle, WA
Hunsinger, Paul O. ... Columbus, OH
Hunsinger, Suzanne E. ... San Jose, CA
Hunsinger, Terry L. ... Olathe, KS
Hunstein, Carol W. A. ... Atlanta, GA
Hunstein, Ralph J. ... Monroe, GA
Hunston, Jane S. ... **Jupiter, FL**
Hunston, W. Jay, Jr.
West Palm Beach, FL
Hunsucker, Gregory M. ... **Tupelo, MS**
Hunsucker, J. Thomas ... **Los Angeles, CA**
Hunsucker, John E. ... Oklahoma City, OK
Hunsucker, John E., LLC
Oklahoma City, OK
Hunsucker, Keith E. ... Atlanta, GA
Hunsucker, Philip C. ... **Lafayette, CA**
Hunsucker, Richard G. ... Rockville, MD
Hunt & Adams, A Professional Corporation
Santa Ana, CA
Hunt, Alan Reeve ... **Philadelphia, PA**
Hunt, Alan T. ... South Harwich, MA
Hunt, Alvin D. ... Lake Charles, LA
Hunt, Amy J. ... Duluth, MN
Hunt, Amy K. ... **Dallas, TX**
Hunt, Angela A. ... **Dallas, TX**
Hunt, Arthur L. ... De Ridder, LA
Hunt & Associates ... **Paso Robles, CA**
San Luis Obispo, CA
Hunt & Associates, P.C. ... Chicago, IL
Hunt & Associates, P.C. ... **Portland, OR**
Hunt & Ayres ... **Philadelphia, PA**
Hunt, Barbara E. ... Boston, MA
Hunt, Barbara E., A Professional Corporation
Boston, MA
Hunt, Barbara R. ... Dallas, TX
Hunt, Bert W. ... Denver, CO
Hunt, Beverly J. ... **Stamford, CT**
Hunt, Billy H. ... Punta Gorda, FL
Hunt, Bradford E. ... Alton, IL
Hunt, Brady R. ... Midwest City, OK
Hunt, Brenda L. ... **Seattle, WA**
Hunt, Brian J. ... **Chicago, IL**
Hunt, Brian T. ... Indianapolis, IN
Hunt, Brooks H. ... Department of Commerce, Patent and Trademark Office, GV
Hunt, Bruce E. ... **Springfield, MO**
Hunt, Carolyn A. ... Beverly Hills, CA
Hunt, Carroll E. ... Dayton, OH
Hunt, Cathy Cubbon
Research Triangle Park, NC
Hunt, Cecil ... Department of Commerce, Office of the General Counsel, GV
Hunt, Cecil J., II ... New York, NY
Hunt, Chadwick G. ... Savannah, TN
Hunt, Charles J., Jr. ... **Victorville, CA**
Hunt, Charles L. ... Olivia, MN
Hunt, Charles M. (Mickey) ... Dallas, TX
Hunt, Charles N. ... Metamora, OH
Sylvania, OH
Hunt, Charles R. ... Dawson, GA
Hunt, Charlie A., Jr. ... **Spruce Pine, NC**
Hunt, Chirstopher ... **Boston, MA**
Hunt, Christian H. ... Atlanta, GA
Hunt, Christina L. ... Yakima, WA
Hunt, Christopher A.D. ... Boston, MA
Hunt, Christopher B. ... **Minneapolis, MN**
Hunt, Christopher J. ... **San Francisco, CA**
Hunt, Christopher Michael
Oklahoma City, OK
Hunt, Christopher R. ... Tallahassee, FL
Hunt, Cindy B. ... Conway, SC
Hunt, Clifford B. ... Honolulu, HI
Hunt, Clifton T. ... Charlotte, NC
Hunt, Clifton T., P.A. ... Charlotte, NC
Hunt, Cook, Riggs, Mehr & Miller, P.A.
Boca Raton, FL
Hunt, Craig A. ... St. Louis, MO
Hunt, Craig M. ... **San Francisco, CA**
Hunt, Craig R. ... Rantoul, IL
Hunt, D. Andrew ... **Lake Wales, FL**
Hunt, D. Lynne ... Independence, MO
Hunt, Dale C. ... **San Diego, CA**
Hunt, Dale E. ... Muncie, IN
Hunt, Daniel E. ... **Jefferson City, MO**
Lake Ozark, MO
Hunt, Daniel E., Law Office of ... Easley, SC
Hunt, Daniel G. ... Colma, CA
Hunt, Daniel W. ... Emeryville, CA
Hunt, Darryl W. ... **Birmingham, AL**
Hunt, David A. ... Peoria, IL
Hunt, David D., II ... Oklahoma City, OK
Hunt, David E. ... **Brunswick, ME**
Camden, ME
Kennebunk, ME
Hunt, David E. ... **Portland, ME**
Hunt, David E. ... **York, ME**
Hunt, David E. ... Flint, MI
Hunt, David Ford ... Dallas, TX
Hunt, David L. ... Sacramento, CA
Hunt, David L.
Federal Communications Commission, Common Carrier Bureau, GV
Hunt, David M. ... **Birmingham, AL**
Hunt, David M. ... Rochester, MN
Hunt, David R. ... **Paso Robles, CA**
San Luis Obispo, CA
Hunt, David R. ... **Clarksdale, MS**
Hunt, David S. ... Phoenix, AZ
Hunt, David W. ... **Washington, DC**
Hunt, Dean D. ... **Houston, TX**
Hunt, Dean K. ... **Lexington, KY**
Hunt, Deborah D. ... **Dayton, OH**
Hunt, Dennis ... Kansas City, MO
Hunt, Derek W. ... Santa Ana, CA
Hunt, Dewey A., Jr. ... Dallas, TX
Hunt, Diana J. ... **Los Angeles, CA**
Hunt, Diego G. ... **Englewood, CO**
Hunt & Doherty ... South Harwich, MA
Hunt, Donald B. ... Raleigh, NC
Hunt, Donald L. ... **Los Angeles, CA**
Hunt, Donald M. ... **Lubbock, TX**
Hunt, Donna M. ... **Cambridge, MA**
Hunt, Douglas B. ... Charleston, WV
Hunt, Douglas B., L.C. ... Charleston, WV
Hunt, Douglas Jesse ... Stone Ridge, NY
Hunt, Douglass ... Chapel Hill, NC
Hunt, E. Leigh ... Wilmington, DE
Hunt, Edward E., III
Department of the Air Force, Office of the Judge Advocate General, GV
Hunt, Edward J. ... **Milwaukee, WI**
Hunt, Edward W. ... Fresno, CA
Hunt, Eileen M. ... Riverside, CA
Hunt, E. L. Roy ... Gainesville, FL
Hunt, Elizabeth ... Alhambra, CA
Hunt, Elizabeth P. ... **Portland, ME**
Hunt, Ellen M. ... Chicago, IL
Hunt, Eric R. ... Royal Oak, MI
Hunt, Ernest C., Jr. ... Lake Charles, LA
Hunt, Ernest L., Jr. ... **San Diego, CA**
Hunt, Eugene, P.A. ... Pine Bluff, AR
Hunt, Evelyn M. ... San Mateo, CA
Hunt & Faherty ... Lambertville, NJ
Hunt, Francis E., Jr. ... Syracuse, NY
Hunt, Franklin G. ... New York, NY
Hunt, Fred B., Jr. ... **Shelbyville, TN**
Hunt, Gary C. ... Ellsworth, ME
Hunt, Gary M. ... Norman, OK
Hunt, Gary P. ... **Greensburg, PA**
Pittsburgh, PA
Hunt, George A. ... **Salt Lake City, UT**
Hunt, George E. ... Graham, NC
Hunt, George W. ... San Diego, CA
Hunt, Gerald D. ... Florence, KY
Hunt, Gerald W. ... **Yuma, AZ**
Hunt, Gordon, (A Professional Corporation)
Pasadena, CA
Hunt, Gordon E. ... Phoenix, AZ
Hunt, Grady L. ... Pembroke, NC
Hunt, Greg Allen ... Eugene, OR
Hunt, Gregory A. ... **Durham, NC**
Hunt, Gregory K. ... Brooklyn, NY
Hunt, Gwendolyn E. ... Dallas, TX
Hunt, H. Thomas, III ... **Cherry Hill, NJ**
Hunt, Hassler & Lorenz ... **Brazil, IN**
Clinton, IN
Greencastle, IN
Sullivan, IN
Terre Haute, IN
Hunt, Heather F. ... Bridgeport, CT
Hunt, Heather H. ... Department of Justice, Criminal Division, GV
Hunt, Heather M. ... **Chippewa Falls, WI**
Hunt & Henriques ... San Jose, CA
Hunt, Herbert C., Jr. ... Columbus, OH
Hunt, Herman E. ... Columbus, OH
Hunt, Hollis S. ... Draper, UT
Hunt, Horace S., III ... Clearwater, FL
Hunt & Hossler ... **Yuma, AZ**
Hunt, Howard ... Odessa, TX
Hunt, Isaac C., Jr.
Securities and Exchange Commission, Executive Staff, GV
Hunt, J. Conway ... Bethesda, MD
Hunt, J. Kevin ... Oregon City, OR
Hunt, J. Robin ... Bainbridge Island, WA
Hunt, Jacquelyn ... St. Louis, MO
Hunt, Jake ... Oklahoma City, OK
Hunt, James A. ... Santa Barbara, CA
Hunt, James A. ... Batavia, OH
Hunt, James A. ... Spokane, WA
Hunt, James B. ... **Moline, IL**
Hunt, James B., Jr. ... Raleigh, NC
Hunt, James C. ... **Portland, ME**
Hunt, James E. ... Sandpoint, ID
Hunt, James Edgar ... Niagara Falls, NY
Hunt, James F. ... **Troy, MI**
Hunt, James F., Jr. ... Columbus, OH
Hunt, James G. ... **Stamford, CT**
Hunt, James G. ... Helena, MT
Hunt, James G. ... **New York, NY**
Hunt, James I. ... Lima, OH
Hunt, James L. ... Tuscumbia, AL
Hunt, James L. ... **San Francisco, CA**
Hunt, James L. ... Raleigh, NC
Hunt, James L. ... Eugene, OR
Hunt, James M. ... Oakland, CA
Hunt, James M. ... **Lombard, IL**
Hunt, James M. ... Traverse City, MI
Hunt, James R. ... Houston, TX
Hunt, James W. ... **Los Angeles, CA**
Hunt, James William ... Dallas, TX
Hunt, Jan ... Los Angeles, CA
Hunt, Janet B. ... **Philadelphia, PA**
Hunt, Janet E. ... New York, NY
Hunt, Jeffery Wayne ... Carrollton, GA
Hunt, Jeffrey A. ... Sacramento, CA
Hunt, Jeffrey B. ... **St. Louis, MO**
Hunt, Jeffrey J. ... **Salt Lake City, UT**
Hunt, Jeffrey P. ... Brevard, NC
Hunt, Jennifer A. ... Morristown, NJ
Hunt, Jennifer Gremmel ... Dallas, TX
Hunt, Jennifer H. ... **Denver, CO**
Hunt, Jerry D. ... Lebanon, TN
Hunt, Jimmy ... Lake City, FL
Hunt, Joan ... Cameron, LA
Hunt, Joanna Leigh ... Berkeley, CA
Hunt, John ... **Boston, MA**
Hunt, John A. ... **Las Vegas, NV**
Hunt, John B. ... Leavenworth, KS
Hunt, John C. ... Augusta, ME
Hunt, John E. ... East Lansing, MI
Hunt, John Earl ... Prestonsburg, KY
Hunt, John F. ... **New York, NY**
Hunt, John F. ... **Baytown, TX**
Hunt, John Frazier ... **Philadelphia, PA**
Hunt, John J. ... Trumbull, CT
Hunt, John R. ... **Atlanta, GA**
Hunt, John R. ... Plentywood, MT
Hunt, John W. ... Las Vegas, NV
Hunt, John W. ... Tulsa, OK
Hunt, Jolyn E. McKune ... **Houston, TX**
Hunt, Jonathan B. ... Greenfield, MA
Hunt, Jonathan J. ... Savannah, GA
Hunt, Joseph D. ... **Tampa, FL**
Hunt, Joseph F. ... **Boston, MA**
Hunt, Joseph H. ... **Atlanta, GA**
Hunt, Joseph R. ... Shelby, MT
Hunt, JuanCarlos M. ... **Cleveland, OH**
Hunt, Judy K. ... Orlando, FL
Hunt, Karen L. ... Anchorage, AK
Hunt, Karen M. ... Sedalia, MO
Hunt, Karen S. ... Cleveland, OH
Hunt, Kathleen A. ... **Los Angeles, CA**
Hunt, Kathleen A. ... Laramie, WY
Hunt, Kathleen Dillon ... **San Francisco, CA**
Hunt, Kathleen Dillon, Law Offices of
San Francisco, CA
Hunt, Kay N. ... **Minneapolis, MN**
Hunt, Keith L. ... Chicago, IL
Hunt & Kelly ... Pine Bluff, AR
Hunt, Kelly J. ... **Dallas, TX**
Hunt, Kelly K. ... Southfield, MI
Hunt, Kenneth A. ... **Albuquerque, NM**
Hunt, Kenneth Alan, Jr. ... Piedmont, AL
Hunt, Kenneth C. ... **Milwaukee, WI**
Hunt, Kenneth L. ... **Tulsa, OK**
Hunt, Kevan T. ... Menlo Park, CA
Hunt, Kevin T. ... **Syracuse, NY**
Hunt, Kimball Haines ... **Hartford, CT**
Hunt, Korbey G. ... Seattle, WA
Hunt, Kristy K. ... Phoenix, AZ
Hunt, L. Alvin ... **Charleston, WV**
Hunt, L. Rush, III ... Madisonville, KY
Hunt, Laura ... Oak Brook, IL
Hunt, Laura D. Blish ... **Norfolk, VA**
Hunt, Laurason T. ... Bellevue, WA
Hunt, Laurie J. ... Hartford, CT
Hunt Law Firm, A Professional Law Corporation ... Lake Charles, LA
Hunt Law Group, The ... **Milwaukee, WI**
Hunt Law Offices ... **Sacramento, CA**
Hunt, Lawrence B. ... **Portland, OR**
Hunt, Lawrence H., Jr. ... **Chicago, IL**
Hunt & Lees, L.C. ... **Charleston, WV**
Hunt Leibert Chester & Jacobson, P.C.
Hartford, CT
Hunt, Leslie R. ... Clinton, TN
Hunt, Lev ... **Corpus Christi, TX**
Hunt, Lewis E., Jr. ... Oklahoma City, OK
Hunt, Linda C. ... Detroit Lakes, MN
Hunt, Lisa A. ... **Washington, DC**
Hunt, M. Roberts ... Falmouth, ME
Hunt, Margaret McDermott ... Brevard, NC
Hunt, Mark A. ... Charleston, WV
Hunt, Mark B. ... Mattoon, IL
Hunt, Mark E. ... **San Diego, CA**
Nashville, TN
Hunt, Marsha A. ... Syracuse, NY
Hunt, Marshall C., Jr. ... Cincinnati, OH
Hunt, Marshall T. ... Newport Beach, CA
Hunt, Martin J. ... **Houston, TX**
Hunt, Michael D. ... **Baton Rouge, LA**
Hunt, Michael E. ... Bloomington, IN
Hunt, Michael Emmett ... Bingham Farms, MI

Hunt, Michael P. ... Albany, NY
Hunt, Michael R. ... Viera, FL
Hunt, Michael S. ... San Jose, CA
Hunt, Millican, DeVictor & O'Brien
Sylvania, OH
Hunt, Moritz & Johnson ... Lima, OH
Hunt, Nadine M. ... Philadelphia, PA
Hunt, Nancy B.
National Labor Relations Board, Office of Board Members, GV
Hunt, Nancy Merrill ... Atlanta, GA
Hunt Narayan, LLP ... San Francisco, CA
Hunt, Neal ... Oklahoma City, OK
Hunt, Nelson ... Chehalis, WA
Hunt, Nina L. ... Atlanta, GA
Hunt, Ortmann, Blasco, Palffy & Rossell, Inc. ... Los Angeles, CA
Newport Beach, CA
Pasadena, CA
Hunt, P. Kathlyne ... Rockledge, FL
Hunt, Pamela Trimble ... Washington, DC
Hunt, Patricia F. ... Quincy, MA
Hunt, Patrick E. ... Island Falls, ME
Hunt, Patrick M. ... Fort Lauderdale, FL
Hunt, Paul A. M. ... Quincy, MA
Hunt, Paul B. ... South Bend, IN
Hunt, Paul D. ... Washington, DC
Hunt, Paul D. ... Cincinnati, OH
Hunt, Paul J. ... Washington, DC
Hunt, Peter C. ... Danbury, CT
Hunt, Peter J. ... New York, NY
Hunt, Philip G. ... Mobile, AL
Hunt, Philip C. ... Portland, ME
Hunt, Philip W. ... Brewster, MA
Hunt, R. Todd ... Cleveland, OH
Hunt, Randall C. ... Canton, OH
Salem, OH
Hunt, Reecer, Tobias & Davis, P.C.
Albuquerque, NM
Hunt, Richard C. ... Portland, OR
Hunt, Richard G. ... Los Angeles, CA
Hunt, Richard H. ... Coral Gables, FL
Hunt, Richard H., & Associates, P.A.
Coral Gables, FL
Miami, FL
Hunt, Richard J. ... Billings, MT
Hunt, Richard M. ... Dayton, OH
Hunt, Richard M. ... Dallas, TX
Hunt, Richard V. ... Watertown, NY
Hunt, Richard W. ... Marlton, NJ
Hunt, Robert C. ... Akron, OH
Hunt, Robert C. ... Houston, TX
Hunt, Robert C., Jr. ... Hartford, CT
Hunt, Robert D. ... Springfield, VT
Hunt, Robert E. ... Peoria, IL
Hunt, Robert E. ... Alexandria, VA
Hunt, Robert F. ... Terre Haute, IN
Hunt, Robert G. ... Henderson, KY
Hunt, Robert J. ... Boca Raton, FL
Hunt, Robert K. ... Louisville, KY
Hunt, Robert L. ... La Junta, CO
Orem, UT
Hunt, Robert W. ... Sacramento, CA
Hunt, Robin Kert ... Denver, CO
Hunt, Roger ... Las Vegas, NV
Hunt, Roger B. ... Boston, MA
Hunt, Roger D. ... Colorado Springs, CO
Hunt, Roger W. ... Brandon, SD
Hunt, Ronald F. ... New Bern, NC
Hunt & Ross, A Professional Association
Clarksdale, MS
Hunt, Ross F., Jr. ... Alexandria, VA
Hunt, Roy D., Law Office of ... Beeville, TX
Hunt, Russell D., Jr. ... Waco, TX
Hunt, Russell David ... Austin, TX
Georgetown, TX
Hunt, Russell David ... Round Rock, TX
Waco, TX
Hunt, Russell David ... Round Rock, TX
Hunt, Russell L. ... Searcy, AR
Hunt, Ryan J. ... Macomb, IL
Hunt, Sallie H. ... Charleston, WV
Hunt, Samuel P., III ... Framingham, MA
Hunt, Sarah ... McLean, VA
Hunt, Sarah G. ... Boston, MA
Hunt, Sarah J. ... Cambridge, MA
Hunt, Sarah S. ... Montgomery, AL
Hunt & Scaramella, P.C. ... Cherry Hill, NJ
Hunt, Scott ... St. Louis, MO
Hunt, Scott N. ... Portland, OR
Hunt, Sean Antone ... Nashville, TN
Hunt, Shannon A. ... Bloomfield Hills, MI
Lansing, MI
Hunt, Shannon M. ... Beverly Hills, CA
Hunt, Sharlene A. ... Middletown, NJ
Hunt, Sharon L. ... Woodridge, IL
Hunt, Sidney C. ... Westwood, KS
Hunt, Skilken & Wehner ... Dayton, OH
Hunt, Spencer C. ... Boston, MA
Hunt, Stephen C. ... Naples, FL
Hunt, Stephen R. ... Cincinnati, OH
Hunt, Steven B. ... Portland, OR
Hunt, Steven D. ... Los Angeles, CA
Hunt, Stuart E. ... Washington, DC
Hunt Suedhoff, LLP ... Fort Wayne, IN
South Bend, IN
Hunt, Susan ... Berkeley, CA
Hunt, Susan L. ... Greensboro, NC
Hunt, Susan M. ... Kansas City, MO
Hunt, Susan Scott ... Springtown, PA
Hunt, Sylvia Fortney ... Treasury Department, Internal Revenue Service, GV
Hunt, Tandy L. ... Roswell, NM
Hunt, Tann H. ... Tallahassee, FL
Hunt, Tanner T., Jr. ... Beaumont, TX
Hunt, Terrance C. ... Portland, OR
Hunt, Terrell E. ... Houston, TX
Hunt, Thomas B. ... Troy, NY

Hunt, Thomas C. ... Bensenville, IL
Hunt, Thomas E., III ... Paris, TX
Hunt, Thomas F., Jr. ... Minneapolis, MN
Hunt, Thomas J. ... Boston, MA
Hunt, Thomas L. ... Duluth, MN
Hunt, Thomas M. ... Sacramento, CA
Hunt, Thomas M., Jr. ... Sacramento, CA
Hunt, Thomas P. ... West Palm Beach, FL
Hunt, Thomas R. ... Marion, IN
Hunt, Thomas R. ... New Bedford, MA
Hunt, Thomas R., Jr. ... Wilmington, DE
Hunt, Thomas R., Sr. ... Wilmington, DE
Hunt, Timothy A. ... Tampa, FL
Hunt, Todd Christopher ... Los Angeles, CA
Hunt, Tristam W. ... Independence, MO
Hunt, V. William ... Columbus, IN
Hunt, Vernon W., Jr. ... Santa Ana, CA
Hunt, Vicki Jean ... Washington, DC
Hunt, Victor Donald ... Jackson, MS
Hunt, Walter F. ... Sylvania, OH
Hunt, Wendell B. ... Birmingham, AL
Houston, TX
Hunt & White ... Graham, NC
Hunt, William A. ... Newport News, VA
Hunt, William A., Jr. ... Virginia Beach, VA
Hunt, William E. ... Cincinnati, OH
Hunt, William E., Sr. ... Helena, MT
Hunt, William H. ... Cleveland, OH
Hunt, William J. ... Cambridge, MA
Providence, RI
Hunt, William J. ... Hackensack, NJ
Hunt, William P., III ... Louisville, CO
Hunt, William S. ... Honolulu, HI
Hunt, William T. ... Double Springs, AL
Hunt, William T. ... Pharr, TX
Hunt, William W., III ... Nashville, TN
Hunt, Willis B., Jr. ... Atlanta, GA
Hunt, Wilson F. ... Clayton, MO
Hunte, Adrian C. ... Mohegan Lake, NY
Hunte, Dale Angela ... New York, NY
Hunter, A. Troy ... Kirkland, WA
Hunter, Alan F. ... San Jose, CA
Hunter, Alexander M. ... New York, NY
Hunter, Alexander M., Jr. ... Boulder, CO
Hunter, Alexander W., Jr. ... Bronx, NY
Hunter, Allan O. ... Washington, DC
Hunter, Alvin D. ... Oakland, CA
Hunter, Amanda ... Mobile, AL
Hunter, Anabella Q. ... Long Beach, CA
Hunter, Andrew R. ... Los Angeles, CA
Hunter, Ann Herron ... New York, NY
Hunter, Anne Elizabeth ... Goshen, NY
Hunter, Anne L. ... Los Angeles, CA
Hunter, Antoinette ... Austin, TX
Hunter & Associates ... New York, NY
Hunter, B. Scott ... Miami, FL
Hunter, Barry D. ... Lexington, KY
Hunter, Barry W. ... Norfolk, VA
Hunter, Betty Elrod ... Oklahoma City, OK
Hunter, Blazier, O'Dowd & Moreno, A Professional Law Corporation
Lake Charles, LA
Hunter, Bristol E. ... Clawson, MI
Hunter, Brooke Anne C. ... Richmond, VA
Hunter & Brooks ... Orlando, FL
Hunter & Brown ... Salt Lake City, UT
Hunter, Bruce A. ... Cincinnati, OH
Hunter, Bruce E. ... Gaithersburg, MD
Hunter, B. S. ... Blooming Grove, NY
Hunter, Burton D. ... Kenilworth, NJ
Hunter, Bynum M. ... Greensboro, NC
Hunter, C. Gail ... Boulder, CO
Hunter, C. Howard ... Tampa, FL
Hunter, C. Mac, P.A. ... Erwin, NC
Hunter, C. Wayne
Department of Housing and Urban Development, GV
Hunter & Cameron ... Fort Worth, TX
Hunter, Candess J. ... Scottsdale, AZ
Hunter, Carol ... Sacramento, CA
Hunter, Carol J. ... Spokane, WA
Hunter, Carol S. ... Lafayette, LA
Hunter, Carroll R. ... Laconia, NH
Hunter, Catherine C. ... Charlotte, NC
Hunter, Catherine L. ... Greenville, SC
Hunter, Charles Eugene ... Everett, WA
Hunter, Charles R., Jr. ... Bennettsville, SC
Hunter, Charles W. ... Indianapolis, IN
Hunter, Charlotte I. ... Ocala, FL
Hunter, Charlotte I., P.A. ... Inverness, FL
Ocala, FL
Hunter, Charlton Lee, Law Offices of
Miami, FL
Hunter, Cheryl Plaxico
Oklahoma City, OK
Hunter, Christopher B. ... Godfrey, IL
Hunter, Christopher C., Law Offices of, The
Southfield, MI
Hunter, Christopher H. ... Cleveland, OH
Hunter, Christopher J. ... Walnut Creek, CA
Hunter, Christopher J. ... Boston, MA
Hunter, Christopher P. ... Garden City, NY
Hunter, Christopher C., Law Offices of, The
Pontiac, MI
Hunter, Clare P. ... New Orleans, LA
Hunter, Clark Mangum ... Pasadena, CA
Hunter, Claudia A. ... Boston, MA
Hunter, Clayton ... Wichita, KS
Hunter Colianni Cole & Bennett
Christiansted, St. Croix, VI
Charlotte Amalie, St. Thomas, VI
Hunter, Craig C. ... Los Angeles, CA
Hunter, Curtis B. ... Tallahassee, FL
Hunter, Cynthia L. ... Bellaire, TX
Hunter, Daniel F. ... New York, NY
Hunter, Daniel J. ... Columbus, OH
Hunter, Daniel M. ... Winter Park, FL
Hunter, Daniel R. ... Washington, DC

Hunter, Dannye L. ... Brandon, MS
Hunter, Darren J. ... Chicago, IL
Hunter, David C. ... Yorba Linda, CA
Hunter, David H. ... Department of Justice, Civil Rights Division, GV
Hunter, David L., Jr. ... Erie, PA
Hunter, David M. ... New Orleans, LA
Hunter, David M. ... Akron, OH
Hunter, David M. ... Loudonville, OH
Hunter, David R. ... Marietta, GA
Hunter, David T. ... Seattle, WA
Hunter, Dennis J. ... Orlando, FL
Hunter, Dennis M. ... Vancouver, WA
Hunter, Don Curtis ... Lee, MA
Hunter, Don R. ... Kent, WA
Hunter, Donald F. ... Minneapolis, MN
Hunter, Donna Joy ... Miami, FL
Hunter, Douglas Allen ... Monterey, CA
Hunter, Dustin K. ... El Paso, TX
Hunter, E. Allen ... Caribou, ME
Hunter, E. Collins, II ... Kansas City, MO
Hunter, E. Marshall ... Tyler, TX
Hunter, Edw. J. ... Tampa, FL
Hunter, Edward ... Trenton, NJ
Hunter, Edward A., Jr.
Salt Lake City, UT
Hunter, Edward J. ... Parsippany, NJ
Hunter, Edward J., P.A. ... Tampa, FL
Hunter, Edward O. ... Los Angeles, CA
Hunter, Edwin F., Jr. ... Lake Charles, LA
Hunter, Edwin K., (P.C.)
Lake Charles, LA
Houston, TX
Hunter, Edwin P. ... Buffalo, NY
Hunter, Edwin Rhodes, Jr. ... Des Moines, IA
Hunter, Elizabeth ... Dallas, TX
Hunter, Ellen E. ... Irvine, CA
Hunter, Elmo B. ... Kansas City, MO
Hunter, E. T." Dick " ... Hollywood, FL
Hunter, Eugenia C. ... Carbondale, IL
Hunter, F. Doré ... Boston, MA
Hunter, Forrest W. ... Atlanta, GA
Hunter, Foster & Phillips, P.A.
Greenville, SC
Hunter, Francis R., Jr. ... Columbia, MD
Hunter, Francis R., Jr., P.A. ... Columbia, MD
Hunter, Frank A. ... Charlotte, NC
Hunter, Frank R., Jr. ... Sarasota, FL
Hunter, Fraser L., Jr. ... New York, NY
Hunter, Fred ... Dallas, TX
Hunter, Fred R. ... Anaheim, CA
Hunter, Fred R., III ... Allegan, MI
Hunter, G. Martin ... Charlotte, NC
Hunter, G. Patrick, III ... Charlotte, NC
Hunter, G. Patrick, Jr. ... Charlotte, NC
Hunter, Garland D. ... Eugene, OR
Hunter, Garry E. ... Athens, OH
Hunter, Garry E., Law Offices, Inc, L.P.A.
Athens, OH
Hunter, Gary H. ... Philadelphia, PA
Hunter, Gary K., Jr. ... Tallahassee, FL
Hunter, George ... St. Petersburg, FL
Hunter, George T. ... Seattle, WA
Hunter, Gerald M. ... Oglesby, IL
Hunter, Gerald W. ... Sallisaw, OK
Hunter, Gina Pearson ... Birmingham, AL
Hunter, Gregory Lane ... St. Helena, CA
Hunter, H. Douglas ... Opelousas, LA
Hunter, Hal E., III ... New Madrid, MO
Hunter, Hal E., Jr. ... New Madrid, MO
Hunter, Hal Edward ... New Madrid, MO
Hunter & Handel, P.C. ... Austin, TX
Corpus Christi, TX
Hunter, Harold H. ... Dallas, TX
Hunter, Harold J. ... Carlsbad, CA
Hunter, Harold J., Jr. ... Los Angeles, CA
Hunter, Harry H. ... Sylvania, GA
Hunter and Hartnett ... Syracuse, NY
Hunter, Heidi A. ... Monterey, CA
Hunter, Henley A. ... Alexandria, LA
Hunter, Henry C. ... Tallahassee, FL
Hunter, H. M. ... Lucedale, MS
Hunter, Hugh T. ... Sylvania, GA
Hunter & Hunter ... Boulder, CO
Hunter & Hunter ... Sylvania, GA
Hunter & Hunter ... New Madrid, MO
Hunter & Hunter ... Alliance, OH
Hunter & Hunter, P.A. ... Hollywood, FL
Hunter, Ian Charles ... Malden, MA
Hunter, J. Burton, III ... Buckhannon, WV
Hunter, J. Jeffrey ... St. Paul, MN
Hunter, J. Michael ... Bartow, FL
Hunter, J. Philip ... Elmira, NY
Hunter, J. Randal ... New Bern, NC
Hunter, J. Reid ... Atlanta, GA
Hunter, J. Scott ... Salt Lake City, UT
Hunter, J. Steven ... Charleston, WV
Hunter, Jack ... Flushing, NY
Hunter, Jack D. ... Fort Wayne, IN
Hunter, Jack D., II ... McAllen, TX
Hunter, Jack E. ... Corpus Christi, TX
Hunter, Jack, P.C. ... Flushing, NY
Hunter, Jack W., Jr. ... Cocoa Beach, FL
Hunter, Jack W., Jr. P.A. ... Cocoa Beach, FL
Hunter, James A., Jr. ... Philadelphia, PA
Hunter, James D. ... Tucson, AZ
Hunter, James E. ... Phoenix, AZ
Hunter, James G., III ... Lynchburg, VA
Hunter, James G., Jr. ... Chicago, IL
Hunter, James H. ... Metairie, LA
Hunter, James H., Jr. ... Brownsville, TX
Hunter, James K., III ... Columbus, OH
Hunter, James K. T. ... Los Angeles, CA
Hunter, James M. ... Gallatin, TN
Hunter, James Mac ... Atlanta, GA
Hunter, James Monroe, Jr. ... Summit, NJ
Hunter, James Ray, Jr. ... Jacksonville, FL
Hunter, Jamie G. ... Makawao, HI

Hunter, Jan M. ... Atlanta, GA
Hunter, Janice K. Johnson ... Riverdale, MD
Hunter, Jason E. ... Marengo, IL
Hunter, Jayne Conway ... Charlotte, NC
Hunter, Jayne M. ... Fort Smith, AR
Hunter, Jeffrey ... Morristown, NJ
Hunter, Jeffrey G. ... Montgomery, AL
Hunter, Jeffrey L. ... Denver, CO
Hunter, Jeffrey W. ... Wilmington, DE
Hunter, Jennifer A. ... Scottsdale, AZ
Hunter, Jerry ... Camden, AR
Hunter, Jerry L. ... Washington, DC
Hunter, Jerry M. ... St. Louis, MO
Hunter, Jesse W., Jr. ... Los Angeles, CA
Hunter, Jill F. ... New York, NY
Hunter, Jocelyn J. ... Atlanta, GA
Hunter, John C. ... Asheville, NC
Hunter, John D. ... Des Moines, IA
Hunter, John G. ... Savannah, GA
Hunter, John G. ... Grayling, MI
Hunter, John G. ... Upper Sandusky, OH
Hunter, John J. ... Ventura, CA
Hunter, John J. ... Toledo, OH
Woodville, OH
Hunter, John J. ... Philadelphia, PA
Hunter, John J., Jr. ... Toledo, OH
Hunter, John L.
Securities and Exchange Commission, Division of Enforcement, GV
Hunter, John L. ... Pascagoula, MS
Hunter, John Logan ... Pasadena, CA
Hunter, John M. ... Mobile, AL
Hunter, John M., Jr. ... Aiken, SC
Hunter, John R. ... Fort Worth, TX
Hunter, John S. ... New Orleans, LA
Hunter, John T. ... Manlius, NY
Hunter, John V., III ... Raleigh, NC
Hunter, John V., IV ... Oxford, MS
Hunter, Johnston, Elam & Benjamin, PLLC
Greensboro, NC
Hunter, Jon Thomas ... Honolulu, HI
Hunter, Jonathan A. ... New Orleans, LA
Hunter, Joseph ... Alvin, TX
Hunter, Joseph M. ... Seattle, WA
Hunter, Judith L. ... Akron, OH
Hunter, Judith T. ... Madison, WI
Hunter, Julius H., Jr. ... Phenix City, AL
Hunter, Justin H. ... Frankfort, IN
Hunter, Karen A. ... Chicago, IL
Hunter, Karen C. ... New York, NY
Hunter, Karen R. ... Washington, DC
Hunter, Karl V. ... McKinney, TX
Hunter, Katherine A. ... Indianapolis, IN
Hunter, Katherine Mauldin ... Atlanta, GA
Hunter, Kathleen A. ... Boston, MA
Hunter, Kathryn L. ... Stamford, CT
Hunter, Kathryn L. ... Pittsburgh, PA
Hunter, Keith A. ... Kingston, PA
Hunter, Keith B. ... Louisville, KY
Hunter, Keith G. ... Santa Monica, CA
Hunter, Kevin G. ... Phoenix, AZ
Hunter, Kim M. ... Oakland, CA
Hunter & Kramer, A Professional Corporation ... McKinney, TX
Hunter, Larry C. ... Boise, ID
Hunter, Larry C. ... Vidor, TX
Hunter, Laura B. ... Irvine, CA
Hunter, Laura Shuffett ... Frankfort, KY
Hunter, Laurie A. ... Englewood, CO
Hunter, Lawrence M., Jr. ... Greenville, SC
Hunter, Lee Ford ... Salt Lake City, UT
Hunter & Levine, The Law Offices of
Buckhannon, WV
Hunter, Lewis & Brannon, LLP
Savannah, GA
Hunter, Lisa S. ... Garden City, NY
Hunter, Lise G. ... Brooklyn, NY
Hunter, Luke ... Chicago, IL
Hunter, M. Katherine ... Miami, FL
Hunter, M. Reed ... Los Angeles, CA
Hunter, Maclean, Exley & Dunn, P.C.
Atlanta, GA
Savannah, GA
Hunter & Marchman, P.A. ... Orlando, FL
Winter Park, FL
Hunter, Margaret Adams ... Detroit, MI
Hunter, Marilynn L. ... Indianapolis, IN
Hunter, Marjorie deCou ... Atlanta, GA
Hunter, Mark C. ... Metropolis, IL
Hunter, Mark R. ... Huntsville, AL
Hunter, Mark S. ... Houston, TX
Hunter, Mark W. ... Omaha, NE
Hunter, Mark W. ... Shawano, WI
Hunter, Marsha ... Boston, MA
Hunter, Marsha L. ... Dallas, TX
Hunter, Martha L. ... Pittsburgh, PA
Hunter, Mary Scott ... Tuscaloosa, AL
Hunter, Maureen A. ... Ottawa, IL
Hunter, Michael B. ... Kansas City, MO
Hunter, Michael B. ... St. Louis, MO
Hunter, Michael B. ... Fort Worth, TX
Hunter, Michael B. ... San Antonio, TX
Hunter, Michael J. ... Columbus, OH
Hunter, Michael S. ... Charlotte, NC
Hunter, Michael T. ... Eldora, IA
Hunter, Michele D. ... New York, NY
Hunter, Miles M. ... New York, NY
Hunter, Milton S., III ... Randolph, NJ
Hunter, Morgan ... Austin, TX
Hunter & Murray ... Carbondale, IL
Hunter, Nan D. ... Brooklyn, NY
Hunter, Nancy A. ... Carmel Valley, CA
Hunter, Nancy S. ... West Palm Beach, FL
Hunter, Nancy Scheurwater ... Chicago, IL
Hunter, Naren Malcolm ... Santa Monica, CA
Hunter, Nathaniel C. ... Pittsburgh, PA
Hunter, Ninah J. ... La Mesa, CA
Hunter, Norma B. ... Los Angeles, CA

Hunter, Norman Michael .... Detroit, MI
Hunter & Oelke .... Dalhart, TX
Hunter, Oliver R. .... Albany, GA
Hunter, Pamela A. .... Houston, TX
Hunter, Patricia A. .... Los Angeles, CA
Hunter, Patrick M. .... Casper, WY
Hunter, Patti L. .... Seattle, WA
Hunter, Paul E., Jr. .... Yuma, AZ
Hunter, Paul S. .... Milwaukee, WI
Hunter, Paula Marie .... Oak Park, IL
Hunter, Peter A. .... Acton, MA
Hunter, Peter J., Jr. .... Roanoke, VA
Hunter, Philip G. .... Alexandria, LA
Hunter, R. Ian .... Troy, MI
Hunter, R. William .... Chicago, IL
Hunter, Rachel Lea .... Erie, PA
Hunter, Randolph W. .... Greenville, SC
Hunter, Randolph W., P.A. .... Greenville, SC
Hunter, Randolph White .... Baton Rouge, LA
Hunter, Raymond M., (P.C.) .... Phoenix, AZ
Hunter, Reagan E. .... Tyler, TX
Hunter, Richard A. .... San Jose, CA
Hunter, Richard C. .... Brookline, MA
Hunter, Richard F. .... Malone, NY
Hunter, Richard H.
Christiansted, St. Croix, VI
Hunter, Richard J. .... Hot Springs, SD
Hunter, Richard M. .... New York, NY
Hunter, Richard N. .... Waukesha, WI
Hunter, Richard P. .... Philadelphia, PA
Hunter, Richard S. .... Jackson, OH
Hunter, Richard S., Jr. .... Raleigh, NC
Hunter Richey Di Benedetto & Brewer, LLP
Sacramento, CA
Hunter, Rilla & Graziano .... Lee, MA
Hunter, Robert .... Chicago, IL
Hunter, Robert B. .... Phoenix, AZ
Hunter, Robert B. .... Denver, CO
Hunter, Robert B. .... Great Neck, NY
Hunter, Robert B., II .... Pleasant Hill, CA
Hunter, Robert C. .... Des Moines, IA
Hunter, Robert C. .... Kansas City, MO
Hunter, Robert C. .... Raleigh, NC
Hunter, Robert D. .... Birmingham, AL
Hunter, Robert D. .... Concord, MA
Hunter, Robert G. .... Medford, OR
Hunter, Robert J. .... Atlanta, GA
Hunter, Robert L. .... Santa Monica, CA
Hunter, Robert L., Jr. .... Missoula, MT
Hunter, Robert M. .... Madison, WI
Hunter, Robert N., Jr. .... Greensboro, NC
Hunter, Robert R., Jr. .... Alliance, OH
Hunter, Robert R., Sr. .... Alliance, OH
Hunter, Robert S. .... Quincy, IL
Hunter, Robert V. .... Syracuse, NY
Hunter, Robert W., III .... Augusta, GA
Hunter, Robt. S., Jr. .... New Castle, IN
Hunter, Roger D. .... Charleston, WV
Hunter, Ronald A. .... Omaha, NE
Hunter, Ronald E. .... Minneapolis, MN
Hunter, Ronald W. .... Omaha, NE
Hunter, Russell M. .... Ravenswood, WV
Hunter, S. Barcus .... Fort Worth, TX
Hunter, S. Kyle .... Wynne, AR
Hunter, S. Kyle, P.A. .... Wynne, AR
Hunter & Samaha .... Baton Rouge, LA
Hunter, Samuel J. .... Omaha, NE
Hunter, Sandra K. .... Cleveland, OH
Hunter, Sara R. .... Cleveland Heights, OH
Hunter, Sarah E. .... Birmingham, MI
Hunter, Sarah L. .... Seattle, WA
Hunter & Schank Co., L.P.A. .... Toledo, OH
Woodville, OH
Hunter, Scott .... Jonesboro, AR
Hunter, Scott A. .... Los Angeles, CA
Hunter, Scott A. .... Kansas City, MO
Hunter, Scott D. .... Youngstown, OH
Hunter, Scott G. .... Caribou, ME
Hunter, Scott R. .... Simi Valley, CA
Hunter, Scott R. .... North Haven, CT
Hunter, Shane H. .... Boston, MA
Hunter, Shawn .... Houston, TX
Hunter, Shepton F. .... Lafayette, LA
Hunter, Sheri R. .... Austin, TX
Hunter, Smith, Carnahan & Shoub
Columbus, OH
Hunter, Smith & Davis, LLP
Greeneville, TN
Johnson City, TN
Kingsport, TN
Abingdon, VA
Bristol, VA
Gate City, VA
Hunter, Solomon, Jr. .... Philadelphia, PA
Hunter, Sommers & Bartelt, LLP
Waukesha, WI
Hunter, Stephanie Yancey .... Columbus, GA
Hunter, Stephen B. .... Somerville, NJ
Hunter, Stephen C. .... Dayton, OH
Hunter, Stephen Craig .... Sacramento, CA
Hunter, Stephen R. .... Goshen, NY
Hunter, Steven Kent .... Miami, FL
Hunter, Steven T. .... Davenport, IA
Hunter, Stewart M. .... Oklahoma City, OK
Hunter, Susan E. .... Portland, ME
Hunter, Susan M. .... Indianapolis, IN
Hunter, T. Keith .... Hercules, CA
Hunter, T. Parkin .... Columbia, SC
Hunter, Tanya L. .... Los Angeles, CA
Hunter, Terence J. .... Boulder, CO
Hunter, Teresa A. .... Laredo, TX
Hunter, Theodora L. .... New York, NY
Hunter, Thomas A. .... Houston, TX
Hunter, Thomas D. .... Cincinnati, OH
Columbus, OH
Hunter, Thomas E. .... Clarkston, MI
Hunter, Thomas F., Jr. .... Beverly Hills, CA
Hunter, Thomas J. .... Belleville, IL
Hunter, Thomas M. .... Savannah, GA
Hunter, Thomas O. .... Gloucester, MA
Hunter, Thomas R. .... Charlottesville, VA
Hunter, Timothy W. .... Philadelphia, PA
Hunter, Todd A. .... Austin, TX
Corpus Christi, TX
Hunter, Tom .... San Francisco, CA
Hunter, Trane M. .... Santa Monica, CA
Hunter, W. Raymond .... Gulfport, MS
Hunter, Wallace A. .... Baton Rouge, LA
Hunter, Walter C. .... Providence, RI
Hunter, Walter M., Jr. .... Alexandria, LA
Hunter, Walter O., Jr. .... Shreveport, LA
Hunter, Walter S. .... San Mateo, CA
Hunter, William .... Dalhart, TX
Hunter, William A. .... Boston, MA
Hunter, William A. .... Cavendish, VT
Hunter, William C. .... Healdsburg, CA
Hunter, William C. .... Merced, CA
Hunter, William D. .... San Francisco, CA
Hunter, William D.
Executive Office Of The President,
Office of the U.S. Trade Representative, GV
Hunter, William D. .... Morgan City, LA
Hunter, William D. .... Detroit, MI
Hunter, William F. .... Nantucket, MA
Hunter, William F., Jr. .... Hollywood, FL
Hunter, William H. .... Chicago, IL
Hunter, William Jay, Jr. .... Louisville, KY
Hunter, William M. .... Panama City, FL
Hunter, William P., III .... Sylva, NC
Hunter, William S. .... Sacramento, CA
Hunter, William T., Jr. .... Easton, MD
Hunter, Willis C. .... Camden, AR
Hunter, Wm. A. .... Dallas, TX
Hunter, Wm. Michael .... Marianna, FL
Hunter, Wm. Michael .... Panama City, FL
Hunter Johnson, Debra .... Dallas, TX
Hunter-Olney, Janet Clack .... Clearwater, FL
Hunterton & Associates .... Las Vegas, NV
Hunterton, C. Stanley .... Las Vegas, NV
Hunter-Wilson, Jo-Renee .... Detroit, MI
Huntine, Michael S. .... Indianapolis, IN
Hunting, Bruce D. .... Okemos, MI
Hunting, Mark P. .... Grand Rapids, MI
Hunting, Roger Bryant .... Richmond, VA
Hunting, Stephen R. .... Charlotte, NC
Hunting, W. Fred, Jr. .... Grand Rapids, MI
Huntingdon, Kenneth O., Jr. .... Fairborn, OH
Huntington, Allyson M. .... Wellesley, MA
Huntington, Clayton B. .... Lake Forest, CA
Huntington, Curtis E. .... Ann Arbor, MI
Huntington, Daniel Edward .... Spokane, WA
Huntington, David S. .... New York, NY
Huntington, Edward B. .... San Diego, CA
Huntington, Franklin C., IV .... Boston, MA
Huntington & Haviland, A Professional
Corporation .... San Diego, CA
Huntington Hodge Franklin & Valenza, A
Professional Corporation .... Abington, PA
Philadelphia, PA
Huntington, Jay F. .... Hartford, CT
Huntington, John S. .... Christiansburg, VA
Huntington, John T.
Oakbrook Terrace, IL
Huntington, Jonathan B.
Dover-Foxcroft, ME
Huntington, Laurence E. .... Dearborn, MI
Huntington, Lee Ann .... San Francisco, CA
Huntington, Marjorie A. .... San Diego, CA
Huntington, Mary Ann K.
Washington, DC
Huntington, Mary Hyer .... Las Vegas, NV
Huntington, Matthew H.
White River Junction, VT
Huntington, Patrick J. .... Boston, MA
Huntington, R. Danny .... Alexandria, VA
Huntington, Robert A. .... Oak Park, IL
Huntington, Robert H. .... Portland, OR
Huntington, Russell R. .... Westwood, NJ
Huntington, Stephen N. .... Philadelphia, PA
Huntington, Susan R. .... Simsbury, CT
Huntington, T. Andrew .... Oakland, CA
Huntington, Thomas S. .... Oceanside, CA
Hunt-Jester, Valerie .... Front Royal, VA
Huntley, Ann V. .... San Jose, CA
Huntley & Associates .... Wilmington, DE
Huntley, Christopher F. .... Boise, ID
Huntley, Dale .... Erie, PA
Huntley, Daphne W. .... Akron, OH
Huntley, David M. .... Pittsburgh, PA
Huntley, David S. .... Dallas, TX
Huntley, Dennis L. .... Traverse City, MI
Huntley, Diane K. .... Riverside, CA
Huntley, Donald W. .... Wilmington, DE
Huntley, Edward W. .... Springfield, IL
Huntley, Felice F. .... Breckenridge, CO
Huntley, Gerald T. .... Ridgecrest, CA
Huntley & Giganti .... Springfield, IL
Huntley, Janet Taylor .... Detroit, MI
Huntley, Jeffrey .... Breckenridge, CO
Huntley, Jeffrey L. .... Columbus, OH
Huntley, John .... Baker, MT
Huntley, John D., Jr. .... Baltimore, MD
Huntley, John E. .... Columbus, OH
Huntley, John F. .... Hastings, MI
Huntley, John S. .... Chicago, IL
Huntley, Jordan, & Associates, P.C.
Mobile, AL
Huntley, Larke L., Jr. .... Grand Rapids, MN
Huntley, Park, Thomas, Burkett, Olsen &
Williams, LLP .... Boise, ID
Huntley, Robert C., Jr. .... Boise, ID
Huntley, Robert E. R. .... Richmond, VA
Huntley, Russell G. N. .... Wayne, NJ
Huntley, Wendi R. .... Columbus, OH
Huntley, Willie J., Jr. .... Mobile, AL
Huntley-Robertson, Kathleen
Roseland, NJ
Hunton, Eppa .... Richmond, VA
Hunton & Williams .... Washington, DC
Miami, FL
Atlanta, GA
New York, NY
Charlotte, NC
Raleigh, NC
Knoxville, TN
Fairfax, VA
McLean, VA
Norfolk, VA
Richmond, VA
Huntoon, Barbara Dale .... Philadelphia, PA
Huntoon, David A. .... Torrington, CT
Huntoon, David A., LLC, Law Offices of
Torrington, CT
Huntoon, David L. .... Ann Arbor, MI
Huntoon, H. Karl .... Moline, IL
Huntoon, Martin T. .... Los Angeles, CA
Huntoon & Nowinski, Ltd. .... Moline, IL
Huntoon, Robert P. .... San Diego, CA
Huntrods, R. Ann .... St. Paul, MN
Huntsberger, Jeffrey R. .... Cleveland, OH
Huntsberger, Thomas A. .... Springfield, OR
Huntsberger, Thomas A., P.C.
Springfield, OR
Huntsinger, Lester R. .... Salem, OR
Huntsinger, Randall .... Austin, TX
Huntsman, Ann Atsuko .... Los Angeles, CA
Huntsman, Clair L. .... Ottawa, OH
Huntsman, David M. .... Los Angeles, CA
Huntsman, Gary R. .... Las Vegas, NV
Huntsman Law Offices .... Las Vegas, NV
Huntsman, Lawrence D. .... Washington, DC
Fairfax, VA
Huntsman, Peter R. .... Hartford, CT
Huntsman, Rulon J. .... Las Vegas, NV
Huntwork, James R. .... Phoenix, AZ
Huntwork, Patience T. .... Phoenix, AZ
Huntzinger, Donald B. .... Grand Junction, CO
Huntzinger, Keith Richard .... Weirton, WV
Hunvald, Edward H., Jr. .... Columbia, MO
Hunyadi, Stephen L. .... Richmond, IN
Hunzeker & Lyon, P.C. .... Alexandria, VA
Annandale, VA
Arlington, VA
Fredericksburg, VA
Lake Ridge, VA
McLean, VA
Oakton, VA
Reston, VA
Hunzeker, Mark A. .... Lincoln, NE
Hunzeker, Matthew J. .... McLean, VA
Hunziker, Christine A. .... Ames, IA
Hunziker, Gregory A. .... Peoria, IL
Hunziker, Jones, Champion & Romer, P.A.
Paterson, NJ
Wayne, NJ
West Milford, NJ
Hunziker, Robert M. .... Purchase, NY
Hunziker, Robin Morris .... Findlay, OH
Hunziker, Thomas J. .... Minneapolis, MN
Hunziker, Walter J., Jr. .... Wayne, NJ
Huo, Sunny S. .... San Francisco, CA
Huon, Meanith .... Chicago, IL
Huong, Angello Lin .... King Of Prussia, PA
Huot, David O. .... Laconia, NH
Huot, Paul R. .... Hackensack, NJ
Huotari, Kristin M. .... Madison, WI
Huotari, Michael E. .... Denver, CO
Huott, Brian J. .... West Palm Beach, FL
Huovinen, H. Alan .... Danville, CA
Hupe, Robert M. .... Torrance, CA
Hupert, Daniel .... New York, NY
Hupert, Jeffrey D. .... Chicago, IL
Hupert Richards & Wood .... Chicago, IL
Hupertz, Lawrence R. .... Cleveland, OH
Hupf, Paul M. .... Daly City, CA
Hupfeld, Kelly J. .... Chicago, IL
Hupfer, A. Michael .... Johnston, IA
Hupfer, Justin D. .... Des Moines, IA
Hupfer, Kyle J. .... Indianapolis, IN
Hupfer, Sandra L. .... Green Bay, WI
Hupp, Alfred R., Jr. .... Kansas City, MO
Hupp, David W. .... Louisville, KY
Hupp, Dennis L. .... Woodstock, VA
Hupp, Diane H. .... Cleveland, OH
Hupp, George C. .... Ottawa, IL
Hupp, George C., Jr. .... Ottawa, IL
Hupp, Harry L. .... Los Angeles, CA
Hupp, Jason H. .... Bridgewater, NJ
Hupp, John W. .... Chicago, IL
Hupp, Lanuti, Irion & Martin, P.C.
Ottawa, IL
Hupp, Lin-Marie .... Seattle, WA
Hupp, M. Theresa C. .... Kansas City, MO
Hupp, Michael M. .... Omaha, NE
Hupp, R. Craig .... Detroit, MI
Hupp, Randall Alan .... Louisville, KY
Hupp, Robert B. .... Aurora, IL
Hupp, Stephanie R. .... Lincoln, NE
Hupp, Steven J. .... Cleveland, OH
Huppe, Michael J. .... Washington, DC
Hupper, John R. .... New York, NY
Hupper, John Roscoe, Jr. .... New York, NY
Huppert, Alla E. .... Jersey City, NJ
Huppert, Andrew D. .... Great Falls, MT
Huppert, Arnold, Jr. .... Livingston, MT
Huppert, Charles B. .... Indianapolis, IN
Huppert & Hurabiell .... San Francisco, CA
Huppert, Lynda F. .... Indianapolis, IN
Huppert, Michael D. .... Des Moines, IA
Huppert, Michael S. .... Washington, DC
Huppert, Peter A. .... San Francisco, CA
Huppert & Swindlehurst, P.C.
Livingston, MT
Huppertz, Matthew H. .... Waukesha, WI
Huppin, C. Eugene .... Spokane, WA
Huppin Ewing Anderson & Paul, P.S.
Coeur d'Alene, ID
Spokane, WA
Huppin, Joel D. .... Spokane, WA
Hupprich, William R. .... Anchorage, AK
Huppuch, Thomas W. .... Maynard, MA
Huprich & Associates, P.C. .... Tucker, GA
Huprich, David L. .... Cincinnati, OH
Huprich, Don C. .... Tucker, GA
Hupy and Hupy, P.C. .... Menominee, MI
Hupy, Michael F. .... Milwaukee, WI
Hupy, Michael F., & Associates, S.C.
Milwaukee, WI
Hupy, Wilfred J. .... Menominee, MI
Hupy, William A. .... Menominee, MI
Hur, Robert C. .... Gaithersburg, MD
Hur, Robert C., P.C. .... Gaithersburg, MD
Hura, Douglas J. .... York, PA
Hura, Mark S. .... Seven Hills, OH
Hurabiell, John P., Sr. .... San Francisco, CA
Hurabiell, Marie .... San Francisco, CA
Hurand, Robert M. .... East Lansing, MI
Huray, Scott D. .... Atlanta, GA
Hurbis, Charles J. .... Ann Arbor, MI
Hurchanik, Richard L. .... Hamilton, OH
Hurd, Albert L. .... San Jose, CA
Hurd, Calvin F., Jr. .... Cleveland, OH
Hurd, Charles H. .... Honolulu, HI
Hurd, Charles W. .... Houston, TX
Hurd, Christy Stone .... Kansas City, MO
Hurd, David N. .... Utica, NY
Hurd, Douglas H. .... Trenton, NJ
Hurd, Dwight I. .... Columbus, OH
Hurd & Ferkler .... Laurel, MD
Hurd, George N., Jr. .... Boston, MA
Hurd, Hollis T. .... Pittsburgh, PA
Hurd, Horvath & Dinkin, P.A.
Palm Beach Gardens, FL
Hurd, James A., Jr.
Charlotte Amalie, St. Thomas, VI
Hurd, James F., Jr. .... Fairfax, VA
Manassas, VA
Hurd, Janis A. .... Woburn, MA
Hurd, Jeffrey G. .... Rapid City, SD
Hurd, Jeffrey J. .... New York, NY
Hurd, John C. .... Lincoln, NE
Hurd, John K. .... Cincinnati, OH
Hurd, John R. .... San Antonio, TX
Hurd & Luria .... Honolulu, HI
Hurd, Marc S. .... Riverside, CA
Hurd, Matthew A. .... Chicago, IL
Hurd, Matthew G. .... New York, NY
Hurd, Michael B. .... Kansas City, MO
Hurd, Michael T. .... Deltaville, VA
Hurd, Patrick C. .... Tucson, AZ
Hurd, Patrick J. .... Washington, DC
Hurd, Paul G. .... Portland, OR
Hurd, Peter G. .... Plaistow, NH
Hurd, Rhynette Northcross .... Memphis, TN
Hurd, Richard D. .... Sioux Falls, SD
Hurd, Richard W. .... Merriam, KS
Hurd, Robert H. .... Meredith, NH
Hurd, Robert J. .... Chicago, IL
Hurd, Roger C. .... Palm Beach Gardens, FL
Hurd, Rusten C. .... Orlando, FL
Hurd, S. Mark .... Wilmington, DE
Hurd, Sandra N. .... Syracuse, NY
Hurd, Steven D. .... New York, NY
Hurd, Susan E. .... Atlanta, GA
Hurd, Thomas R. .... Evesham, NJ
Philadelphia, PA
Hurd, William H. .... Richmond, VA
Hurdle, Janet Lynn .... Irvine, CA
Hurdle, Melody L. .... Birmingham, AL
Hurdle, Paul C., III .... Charlotte, NC
Hurdle, Sidney L. .... Holly Springs, MS
Hurdle, Steven L. .... Knoxville, TN
Hurdlow, Paul E. .... Austin, TX
Hurel, Marc .... New York, NY
Huresky, Michele Coleman
Florham Park, NJ
Hurevitz, Linda B. .... Glendale, CA
Hurewitz, Alison J. .... Washington, DC
Hurewitz, Barry J. .... Washington, DC
Hurewitz, Lane Steven .... Washington, DC
Hurewitz, Phalen G. .... Beverly Hills, CA
Hurewitz, Steven Zachary .... Hackensack, NJ
Hurey, Michael .... Los Angeles, CA
Hurford, Jennifer H. .... Boston, MA
Hurford, Mark T. .... Wilmington, DE
Hurford, Richard L. .... Taylor, MI
Hurich, Dwight F. .... Gillette, WY
Hurka, Thomas F. .... Indianapolis, IN
Hurlbert, Carla T. .... Richmond, VA
Hurlbert, Richard L., Jr. .... Richmond, VA
Hurlbert, Robert P. .... Bloomfield Hills, MI
Hurlbett, Robert E. .... Santa Barbara, CA
Hurlburt, Allan L. .... Sharon Springs, KS
Hurlburt, David A. .... Lafayette, LA
Hurlburt, Lawrence A. .... Saginaw, MI
Hurlburt, Privat & Monrose, A Professional
Law Corporation .... Lafayette, LA
Hurlburt, Richard .... San Francisco, CA
Hurlburt, Tsiros, Allweil & Perez, P.C.
Saginaw, MI
Hurlbut, Ann Marie .... San Jose, CA
Hurlbut, Bruce P. .... Little Rock, AR
Hurlbut, Chris L. .... Cleveland, OH
Hurlbut, Fred J. .... San Clemente, CA
Hurlbut, Jennifer Ann .... Boston, MA
Hurlbut, John B., Jr. .... Costa Mesa, CA
Hurlbut, John F. .... Chicago, IL
Hurlbut, Robert E., Jr. .... Atlanta, GA
Hurlbut, Roger L. .... Arlington, TX
Hurlbut, Stephen B. .... Washington, DC
Vienna, VA

Hurlbut, Terrill C. ... Stamford, CT
Hurlbut, Clevenger, Long, Rauber & Nelson ... Visalia, CA
Hurlbutt, Daniel C., Jr. ... Twin Falls, ID
Hurlbutt, Edmund C. ... Visalia, CA
Hurlbutt, Guy G. ... Boise, ID
Hurlbutt, James E. ... Northfield, IL
Hurlbutt, James P. ... Visalia, CA
Hurlbutt, Robert G. ... Oswego, NY
Hurley, A. Peyton ... Memphis, TN
Hurley, Andrew J. ... North Hollywood, CA
Hurley, Andrew L. ... Carson, CA
Hurley, Ann C. ... Department of Justice, Environment and Natural Resources Division, GV
Hurley, Anne M. ... Albany, NY
Hurley, Anne Marie ... Charlton, MA
Hurley, Benjamin G., Jr. ... West Jefferson, NC
Hurley, Betsy Glaser ... Lockport, NY
Hurley, Brandon T. ... Fort Worth, TX
Hurley, Brian E. ... Cincinnati, OH
Hurley, Brian J. ... Valparaiso, IN
Hurley, Brian M. ... Boston, MA
Hurley, Brigid K. ... Boston, MA
Hurley, Burish & Milliken, S.C. ... Madison, WI
Hurley, Charles D. ... Fayette, IA
Hurley, Charles P. ... Department of Justice, Tax Division, GV
Hurley, Chas. E. ... Yreka, CA
Hurley, Christian P. ... Sacramento, CA
Hurley, Christopher J. ... Buffalo, NY
Hurley, Christopher J. ... Kirkland, WA
Hurley, Christopher T. ... Chicago, IL
Hurley, Cornelius K., Jr. ... Boston, MA
Hurley, Cynthia A. ... Des Moines, IA
Hurley, D. Michael ... New London, CT
Hurley, D. Scott ... Knoxville, TN
Hurley, Dan M. ... Lubbock, TX
Hurley, Daniel C., Jr. ... Department of Commerce, GV
Hurley, Daniel J. ... Columbus, OH
Hurley, Daniel M. ... Short Hills, NJ
Hurley, Daniel T. K. ... West Palm Beach, FL
Hurley, Daniel W. ... Lubbock, TX
Hurley, David R. ... Houston, TX
Hurley, Delores R. ... Quincy, IL
Hurley, Denis R. ... Hauppauge, NY
Hurley, Denis R., Jr. ... Albany, NY
Hurley, Dennis J. ... Albany, NY
Hurley, Dennis R. ... South Sioux City, NE
Hurley, Dierdre M. ... Atlanta, GA
Hurley, Donald O. ... Ventura, CA
Hurley, Donnell L. ... Atlanta, GA
Hurley, Drew M. ... Somerville, NJ
Hurley, Edmund P. ... Lowell, MA
Hurley, Edward C., III ... Chicago, IL
Hurley, Edward F. ... Summerville, GA
Hurley, Eileen M. ... Florence, SC
Hurley, Elizabeth Anne ... Washington, DC
Hurley, Elizabeth C. ... South Bend, IN
Hurley, Ellen R. ... South Pasadena, CA
Hurley, Emmet D., Jr. ... Borrego Springs, CA
Hurley, Erin K. ... New York, NY
Hurley, Erin T. ... San Francisco, CA
Hurley, Fox, Selig & Kelleher ... New City, NY; Stony Point, NY
Hurley, Francis P. ... Des Moines, IA
Hurley, Geoffrey K. ... New York, NY
Hurley, George E., Jr. ... Chula Vista, CA; **La Jolla, CA**
Hurley, Grady S. ... New Orleans, LA
Hurley, Gregory F. ... Newport Beach, CA
Hurley, Gregory S. ... Fayetteville, WV
Hurley, Grier ... Jefferson, NC
Hurley, Henry H. ... Seattle, WA
Hurley, Howard E., Jr. ... Department of the Navy, GV
Hurley & Howard, P.C. ... Boston, MA
Hurley, Jack F., Jr. ... Harrisburg, PA
Hurley, Jack S., Jr. ... Bluefield, VA
Hurley, Jack S., Jr., P.C. ... Bluefield, VA
Hurley, James B., Jr. ... Jackson, MS
Hurley, James D. ... Burbank, CA
Hurley, James E. ... Palm Beach, FL
Hurley, James E., Jr. ... New York, NY
Hurley, James G., Jr. ... Norfolk, VA
Hurley, James H., Jr. ... Santa Barbara, CA
Hurley, James M. ... Bedford, MA
Hurley, James M. ... Cincinnati, OH
Hurley, James N. ... Miami, FL
Hurley, James P. ... New Brunswick, NJ
Hurley, James P. ... Rapid City, SD
Hurley, James P. ... Yakima, WA
Hurley, James T. ... St. Paul, MN
Hurley, James V. ... Bend, OR
Hurley, Jeanne M. ... White Plains, NY
Hurley, Jennifer D. ... Utica, NY
Hurley, Jennifer L. ... New York, NY
Hurley, Joanne F. ... Chicago, IL
Hurley, Joanne F., Ltd. ... Chicago, IL
Hurley, John A. ... Santa Ana, CA
Hurley, John E. ... Westhampton Beach, NY
Hurley, John F., Jr. ... Worcester, MA
Hurley, John J. ... Buffalo, NY
Hurley, John J., Jr. ... Painesville, OH
Hurley, John L. ... Buffalo, NY
Hurley, John M. ... Waco, TX
Hurley, John Matthew Brooks ... Fort Lauderdale, FL
Hurley, John P. ... Kansas City, MO
Hurley, John, P.A. ... Fort Lauderdale, FL
Hurley, John R. ... Naples, FL
Hurley, John R. ... New York, NY
Hurley, John R. ... Rochester, NY
Hurley, Joseph A. ... Wilmington, DE
Hurley, Joseph A., P.A. ... Dover, DE; Georgetown, DE; Wilmington, DE
Hurley, Joseph C. ... Burlington, MA
Hurley, Joseph E. ... Department of Justice, Environment and Natural Resources Division, GV
Hurley, Joseph G. ... North Hollywood, CA
Hurley, Joseph J. ... Framingham, MA
Hurley, Joseph P. ... Braintree, MA
Hurley, Joseph P., III ... Dedham, MA
Hurley, Joseph P., Jr. ... Wilmington, DE
Hurley, Kahla R. ... Oklahoma City, OK
Hurley, Kay Allen ... Oklahoma City, OK
Hurley, Keith N. ... Richmond, VA
Hurley, Kenneth M. ... Westminster, CA
Hurley, L. Mark ... Milford, CT
Hurley & Laird, A Professional Corporation ... Visalia, CA
Hurley, Lawrence J. ... Morris Plains, NJ
Hurley, Lisa Jones ... Winter Park, FL
Hurley, Lisa M. ... Tallahassee, FL
Hurley, Lynch & Re, P.C. ... Bend, OR
Hurley, Margaret J. ... Worcester, MA
Hurley, Marijane ... Manlius, NY
Hurley, Marion M. ... Pasadena, CA
Hurley, Marshall R. ... Greensboro, NC
Hurley, Mary Joan ... Rockville, MD
Hurley, Matthew C. ... Boston, MA
Hurley, Matthew H. ... Sunnyvale, CA
Hurley, Maureen ... New York, NY
Hurley, Maureen D. O'Connor ... Scituate, MA
Hurley, Maureen O'Connell ... Buffalo, NY
Hurley, Maureen Z. ... Washington, DC
Hurley and McCrea ... Somerville, NJ
Hurley, Megan M. ... New York, NY
Hurley, Meyer & Melcher, LLC ... Atlanta, GA
Hurley, Michael ... San Jose, CA
Hurley, Michael C. ... Raleigh, NC
Hurley, Michael E. ... Phoenix, AZ
Hurley, Michael F. ... Minneapolis, MN
Hurley, Michael F. ... New York, NY
Hurley, Michael J. ... Washington, DC
Hurley, Michael J. ... Bedminster, NJ
Hurley, Michael J. ... New York, NY
Hurley, Michael P. ... Painesville, OH
Hurley, Michel V. ... Atlanta, GA
Hurley, Miles P. ... Atlanta, GA
Hurley, Mitchell P. ... New York, NY
Hurley, Morgan ... Ridgewood, NJ
Hurley, Nancy A. ... Dorchester, MA
Hurley, Natalie A. ... Memphis, TN
Hurley, Noel Langston ... Atlanta, GA
Hurley, Nora L. ... Cleveland, OH
Hurley, Patrick ... San Antonio, TX
Hurley, Patrick B. ... Wheaton, IL
Hurley, Patrick E. ... Tallahassee, FL
Hurley, Patrick J. ... Wichita, KS
Hurley, Patrick J. ... Dallas, TX
Hurley, Patrick W. ... Albuquerque, NM
Hurley, Paul A. ... White Plains, NY
Hurley, Paul V. ... Buffalo, NY
Hurley, Paula J. ... Manchester, NH
Hurley, R. Bruce ... Houston, TX
Hurley, Rebecca ... Dallas, TX
Hurley, Regina M. ... Boston, MA
Hurley, Rex A. ... Orlando, FL
Hurley, Richard E. ... Scotia, NY
Hurley, Richard K., Jr. ... Somerville, NJ
Hurley, Robert B. ... Melville, NY
Hurley, Robert E. ... Phoenix, AZ
Hurley, Robert E. ... Chicago, IL
Hurley, Robert F. ... Indio, CA
Hurley, Robert J. ... New York, NY
Hurley, Robert P. ... Bloomfield Hills, MI
Hurley, Robert W. ... San Jose, CA
Hurley, Roger L., (Co., L.P.A.) ... Greenville, OH
Hurley, Rogner, Miller, Cox & Waranch, P.A. ... Fort Pierce, FL; **Orlando, FL**
Hurley, Ronald J. ... Santa Clara, CA
Hurley, Rupert B., Jr. ... Duncan, SC
Hurley, Russell F. ... Visalia, CA
Hurley & Sowder ... Lubbock, TX
Hurley, Stephen P. ... Madison, WI
Hurley, Steven L. ... Xenia, OH
Hurley, Steven Paul ... Groton, CT
Hurley, Sydney J., IV ... Dallas, TX
Hurley, T. Michael, Jr. ... Atlanta, GA
Hurley, Tara A. ... Department of Justice, Civil Division, GV
Hurley, Terry L. ... Kansas City, MO
Hurley, Thomas F. ... Philadelphia, PA
Hurley, Thomas J. ... Haddonfield, NJ
Hurley, Thomas J. ... Buffalo, NY
Hurley, Thomas J. ... Cincinnati, OH
Hurley, Thomas J., Jr. ... Colorado Springs, CO
Hurley, Timothy J. ... Cincinnati, OH
Hurley, Timothy P. ... New Orleans, LA
Hurley, Tina L. ... Plantation, FL
Hurley, Toevs, Styles, Hamblin & Panter, P.A. ... Albuquerque, NM
Hurley, Troy C. ... Belton, TX
Hurley & Vasios, A Professional Corporation ... Elizabeth, NJ; Morristown, NJ; Newark, NJ; Paterson, NJ; Short Hills, NJ
Hurley, Vincent P., Law Offices of ... Aptos, CA; **Salinas, CA**
Hurley, Vincent P., Law Offices of ... Santa Cruz, CA
Hurley, Walter J. ... Boston, MA
Hurley, Wells & Costley ... Louisville, KY
Hurley, William B. ... Summerville, GA
Hurley, William C. ... Dearborn, MI
Hurley, William F. ... Geneva, IL
Hurley, William J. ... Portsmouth, NH
Hurley, William J., III ... Chicago, IL
Hurley, William K. ... San Jose, CA
Hurley, William N. ... Lowell, MA
Hurley, William P. ... Boston, MA
Hurley, William P. ... New York, NY
Hurley, William P., Jr. ... Louisville, KY
Hurley-Bruce, Linda L. ... Santa Monica, CA
Hurley-Bruno, Mary ... Marshfield, MA
Hurley-Leslie, Craig A. ... Syracuse, NY
Hurlie-Dunn, Coleen ... Bridgeport, CT
Hurlimann, Mary Ann ... San Carlos, CA
Hurlock, Jacqueline F. ... Newark, NJ
Hurlock, James B. ... New York, NY
Hurlock, Matthew H. ... New York, NY
Hurlock, Pamela Ann ... Houston, TX
Hurlock, William Louis ... Newark, NJ
Hurlocker, Andrea B. ... Richmond, VA
Hurlocker, Eric W. ... Richmond, VA
Hurlstone-Peggs, José ... Wichita, KS
Hurly, Kathleen M. ... San Francisco, CA
Hurly, Robert ... Glasgow, MT
Hurm, Stephen Decatur ... Ocala, FL
Hurme, Sally Balch ... Washington, DC
Hurmence, Roberta (Robin) Weaver ... Fayetteville, NC
Hurn, Bert C. ... Neosho, MO
Hurn, Marcus ... Concord, NH
Hurn, Matthew M. ... Des Moines, IA
Hurndon & Gaffney, A Law Corporation ... New Orleans, LA
Hurndon, Joseph H. ... New Orleans, LA
Hurne, Gordon J. ... Pueblo, CO
Hurney, John W. ... Los Angeles, CA
Hurney, Julia O'Halloran ... Charleston, WV
Hurney, Robert L. ... Kissimmee, FL
Hurney, Thomas J., Jr. ... Charleston, WV
Hurney, William J. ... Tacoma, WA
Hurns, Robert J. ... Des Plaines, IL
Hurnyak, Christina K. ... Pittsburgh, PA
Huron, Douglas B. ... Washington, DC
Huron, Jeffrey G. ... Los Angeles, CA
Huron, Zieve & Kierstead ... Ontario, CA; Portland, OR; **Los Angeles, CA**
Hurowitz, Charles Jonathan ... New York, NY
Hurowitz, Marvin ... Singer Island, FL
Hurowitz, Merle ... Chicago, IL
Hurowitz, Neil ... Bala Cynwyd, PA; Philadelphia, PA
Hurowitz, Stuart M. ... Nashua, NH
Hurr, Charles M. ... New York, NY
Hurr, Wanda L. ... Milwaukee, WI
Hurrell, Dianne Lenert ... Aurora, IL
Hurrell, Thomas C. ... Los Angeles, CA
Hurren, Kathleen A. ... San Antonio, TX
Hurricane, Jean H. ... Emeryville, CA
Hurrington, R. Kenneth ... Federal Deposit Insurance Corporation, GV
Hurse, Lonathan ... Chicago, IL
Hursh, Curtis L. ... Kansas City, MO
Hursh, Dennis G. ... Harrisburg, PA
Hursh, Frank W. ... Mission, KS
Hursh, Gary E. ... Carmichael, CA
Hursh & Hursh, P.C. ... Harrisburg, PA
Hursh, Jack E. ... Carmichael, CA
Hursh, John G. ... Palo Alto, CA
Hursh, John R. ... Riverton, WY
Hursh, Lynn W. ... Olathe, KS; Kansas City, MO
Hursh, Randal W. ... Los Angeles, CA
Hursh, Yvonne Machelle ... Harrisburg, PA
Hurson, D. Joseph ... Seattle, WA
Hurson, James E. ... Ellensburg, WA
Hurson, John A. ... Rockville, MD
Hurst, Alan S. ... Boca Raton, FL
Hurst, Andrew L. ... Washington, DC
Hurst, Annette L. ... San Francisco, CA
Hurst, Ashley R. ... Atlanta, GA
Hurst, Barbara ... Providence, RI
Hurst, Brian ... Chicago, IL
Hurst, Brian J. ... Dallas, TX
Hurst Brothman & Yusick ... Angola, NY; Evans, NY
Hurst, Bruce H. ... Seattle, WA
Hurst, C. David ... Santa Rosa, CA
Hurst, C. Douglas ... Denver, CO
Hurst, Carol Galat ... Charlotte Amalie, St. Thomas, VI
Hurst, Charles W. ... Irvine, CA
Hurst, Christine G. ... Phillipsburg, NJ
Hurst, Christopher J. ... Jacksonville, FL
Hurst, Christopher M. ... Wichita, KS
Hurst, Clint L. ... Miami, FL
Hurst, Corinne Tatum ... Opelika, AL
Hurst, Dan R. ... Tyler, TX
Hurst, Daniel J. ... Appleton, WI
Hurst, David B. ... Houston, TX
Hurst, David M. ... Abilene, TX
Hurst, David Thomas ... San Luis Obispo, CA
Hurst, Dennis Michael ... Clarklake, MI
Hurst, E. Rich ... Woodland Hills, CA
Hurst, Edwin S. ... Tulsa, OK
Hurst, Elizabeth A., (P.C.) ... Dallas, TX
Hurst, Emily J. ... Birmingham, AL
Hurst, Eric R. ... Tallahassee, FL
Hurst, Ernest C. ... Houston, TX
Hurst, Everett J. ... Amarillo, TX
Hurst, Floyd H. ... Angola, NY
Hurst, Fred A. ... Calabasas, CA
Hurst, Frederick A. ... Springfield, MA
Hurst, Gary R. ... Atlanta, GA
Hurst, George G. ... San Diego, CA
Hurst, Gerald P. ... Charlotte, NC
Hurst, Grant A. ... Plano, TX
Hurst, Guy L. ... Piedmont, OK
Hurst, Harold ... Newton, MA
Hurst, Harold Clayburn ... Kiowa, CO
Hurst, Harry S., Jr. ... Jonesboro, AR
Hurst, Herbert D. ... Memphis, TN
Hurst, J. Michael ... Cincinnati, OH
Hurst, J. Stephen ... La Follette, TN
Hurst, J.W., P.C. ... Austin, TX
Hurst, James F. ... Chicago, IL
Hurst, James H. ... Longview, TX
Hurst, James M. ... Arlington, TX; **Dallas, TX**
Hurst, James M., P.C. ... Arlington, TX
Hurst, James R. ... La Grange, IL
Hurst, Jay W. ... Austin, TX
Hurst, Jeffrey S. ... Los Angeles, CA
Hurst, Jennifer ... Fort Lauderdale, FL
Hurst, Jennifer K. ... Waco, TX
Hurst, Joe Jack ... Jackson, MS
Hurst, John L. ... Caldwell, ID
Hurst, John P. ... Mayfield Village, OH
Hurst, Joseph B., Jr. (P.A.) ... Little Rock, AR
Hurst, Larry M. ... Pearland, TX
Hurst Law Firm ... Hot Springs National Park, AR
Hurst, Lawrence J. ... St. Louis, MO
Hurst, Linda D. ... San Luis Obispo, CA
Hurst, Linda R. ... Tallahassee, FL
Hurst, Lionel A. ... New York, NY
Hurst, Lisa W. ... Dallas, TX
Hurst, Lloyd L. ... San Francisco, CA
Hurst, Lynn O. ... Seattle, WA
Hurst, M. Dwight ... Albuquerque, NM
Hurst, Margaret A. ... Westbury, NY
Hurst, Margaret Benny ... Phoenix, AZ
Hurst, Marjorie J. ... Springfield, MA
Hurst, Mark A. ... Sacramento, CA
Hurst, Mary E. (Betty) ... Austin, TX
Hurst & McNeil ... Davis, OK; Sulphur, OK
Hurst, Melissa Ann ... Reston, VA
Hurst, Melissa B. ... Washington, DC
Hurst, Michael D. ... Winston-Salem, NC
Hurst, Michael K. ... Dallas, TX
Hurst, Michael L. ... Dallas, TX
Hurst, Michael P. ... San Francisco, CA
Hurst, Monte K. ... Dallas, TX
Hurst, O. Gene ... Clark, NJ
Hurst, O. Mason, II ... Fort Lauderdale, FL
Hurst, Patricia A. ... Providence, RI
Hurst, Patricia C. ... Columbia, SC
Hurst, Patricia L. ... Department of Justice, Environment and Natural Resources Division, GV
Hurst, Paul A. ... Jackson, MS
Hurst, Paul R. ... Washington, DC
Hurst, Phil S. ... Sulphur, OK
Hurst, Q. Byrum, Jr. ... Hot Springs National Park, AR
Hurst, Richard E. ... Treasury Department, Bureau of Alcohol, Tobacco and Firearms, GV
Hurst, Richard S. ... Detroit, MI
Hurst, Robert M. ... Fairfax, VA
Hurst, Robert W. ... Atlanta, GA
Hurst, Ronald D. ... Dallas, TX
Hurst, Ronald E. ... Cherry Hill, NJ; Philadelphia, PA
Hurst, Royce Orleans ... Fullerton, CA
Hurst, Rufus B. ... Columbus, OH
Hurst, Sara Williams ... Sheridan, WY
Hurst, Stephen A. ... Topeka, KS
Hurst, Stephen D. ... Minneapolis, MN
Hurst, Stephen E. ... Encinitas, CA
Hurst, Steve ... Austin, TX
Hurst, Steve, P.C. ... Austin, TX
Hurst, Susan A. ... Atlanta, GA
Hurst, Terresa ... Memphis, TN
Hurst, Terry E. ... Newport, TN
Hurst, Thomas C. ... San Antonio, TX
Hurst, Thomas J.B. ... Louisville, KY
Hurst, Thomas L. ... Miami, FL
Hurst, Thomas R. ... Gainesville, FL
Hurst, Tiffani D. ... Springfield, MA
Hurst, Tracey A. ... Chicago, IL
Hurst & Vanderburg, L.L.P. ... Austin, TX
Hurst, Walter E. ... Los Angeles, CA
Hurst, Walter K. ... Sacramento, CA
Hurst, Wesley D. ... Los Angeles, CA
Hurst, Wiley G. ... Yakima, WA
Hurst, Willard ... Madison, WI
Hurst, William A. ... Albany, NY
Hurst, William B. ... Flagstaff, AZ
Hurst, William M. ... Los Angeles, CA
Hurst, William R. ... Dunwoody, GA
Hurst, William S. ... Highland Park, MI
Hurst, William W. ... Indianapolis, IN
Hurstell, Stephen F. ... New Orleans, LA
Hurst Newell, Shayne ... Houston, TX
Hurston, Joseph W. ... Hattiesburg, MS
Hurt, Adrienne D. ... Board of Governors Of The Federal Reserve System, Division of Consumer and Community Affairs, GV
Hurt, Arthur C., Jr. ... Los Angeles, CA
Hurt, Blanche O. ... Chicago, IL
Hurt, Carolyn ... Dallas, TX
Hurt, Charles C. ... Orlando, FL
Hurt, Charles D., Jr. ... Atlanta, GA
Hurt, Charles E. ... Charleston, WV
Hurt, Charles N., Jr. ... St. Johnsbury, VT
Hurt, Darryl A. ... Lucedale, MS
Hurt, Darryl A., Jr. ... Lucedale, MS

Hurt, David S. ... Department of the Army, U.S. Army Legal Services Agency, GV
Hurt, Douglas L. ... Visalia, CA
Hurt, Edd S., Jr ... Clarksville, TN
Hurt, Edward H., Jr. ... Orlando, FL
Hurt, Edward H., Jr., P.A. ... Orlando, FL
Hurt, Eugene S. ... Brownsville, TX
Hurt & Gallant ... Hooper, NE
Hurt, Gary B. ... Aurora, IL
Hurt, Harold T. ... Murray, KY
Hurt, H. E., Jr. ... Hooper, NE
Scribner, NE
Hurt and Hurt, Ltd., A Professional Law Corporation ... Lucedale, MS
Hurt, J. Brian ... Orlando, FL
Hurt, James P., Jr., (P.A.) ... Sykesville, MD
Hurt, James W. ... Cordele, GA
Hurt, Jeffrey B. ... Wichita, KS
Hurt, Jeffrey W. ... Dallas, TX
Hurt, Jennings L., III ... Orlando, FL
Hurt, John P. ... Barberton, OH
Hurt, John Roger ... Oklahoma City, OK
Hurt and Jones ... Murray, KY
Hurt, Joseph Richard ... Jackson, MS
Hurt, Marc A. ... Olathe, KS
Hurt, Marcia ... Cleveland, OH
Hurt, Marcus E. ... San Francisco, CA
Hurt, Mark A. ... Kokomo, IN
Hurt, Martha R. ... Philadelphia, PA
Hurt, Michael C. ... Menomonee Falls, WI
Hurt, Patricia A. ... Montclair, NJ
Hurt, Patton & Peay, P.L.C.
Clarksville, TN
Hurt, Paula B. ... Olathe, KS
Hurt, Randolph D. ... Crockett, TX
Hurt, Richard T. ... Orlando, FL
Hurt, Sam F., Jr. ... Midland, TX
Hurt, Steve D. ... Burkesville, KY
Hurt, Steve L. ... Plainview, TX
Hurt, Susan ... Charlottesville, VA
Hurt, Tracy L. ... Palo Alto, CA
Hurt, Valerie E. ... Washington, DC
Hurt, William C., Jr. ... Lexington, KY
Hurt, William Rollins ... Houston, TX
Hurtado, Daniel J. ... Chicago, IL
Hurtado, Jorge Enrique ... Fort Lauderdale, FL
Hurtado, Kimberly A. ... Brookfield, WI
Hurtado, S.C. ... Brookfield, WI
Hurtak, Donna Catoe ... Miami, FL
Hurtak, Jerome J. ... North Miami, FL
Hurteau, Daniel J. ... Albany, NY
Hurteau, Mary Alice ... Albany, NY
Hurtekant, Thomas R. ... Dallas, TX
Hurter, Michael A. ... Lexington, KY
Hurtgen, P. Nicholas ... Madison, WI
Hurtgen, Peter J.
National Labor Relations Board, Board Members, GV
Hurth, Charles A., Jr. ... Boulder, CO
Hurth, Yeager & Sisk ... Boulder, CO
Hurtig, Adam S. ... Fort Lauderdale, FL
Hurtig, Becky C. ... Wichita, KS
Hurtig, Robt. L. ... Portland, OR
Hurtt, Diane Rae ... West Lafayette, IN
Hurtt, John M. ... Exeter, PA
Hurtt, John M. ... Scranton, PA
Wilkes-Barre, PA
Hurtt, Laurie J. ... Boston, MA
Hurtt, Michael D. ... Dalton, GA
Hurtt, Stewart M. ... Laurel, MD
Hurtt, W. Keith ... New Orleans, LA
Hurtt, William C. ... Pittsburgh, PA
Hurtubise, Elizabeth R. ... Red Bank, NJ
Hurtuk & Daroff Co., L.P.A.
Cleveland, OH
Hurtuk, Edward A. ... Cleveland, OH
Hurvich, Fred A Rico ... San Rafael, CA
Hurvitz, Aaron M. ... Milwaukee, WI
Hurvitz, Alan M. ... Detroit, MI
Hurvitz, Gary S. ... Rockville, MD
Hurvitz, Henry B. ... Hartford, CT
Hurvitz, Henry B. ... West Hartford, CT
Hurvitz, John A. ... Washington, DC
Hurvitz, Laurie Farnham ... Washington, DC
Hurvitz, Marc L. ... Atlantic City, NJ
Hurvitz, Ralph ... Seattle, WA
Hurvitz, Ralph A. ... Palo Alto, CA
Hurvitz, Steven S. ... State College, PA
Hurvitz, Yardenna ... Beverly Hills, CA
Hurwich, Evelyn M. ... Washington, DC
Hurwich, Robert A. ... Rye, NY
Hurwich, Saul ... Chicago, IL
Hurwit, Jeffrey M. ... Boston, MA
Hurwitz & Abramson ... Washington, DC
Bethesda, MD
Hurwitz, Adam M. ... New York, NY
Hurwitz, Andrew D. ... Phoenix, AZ
Hurwitz, Andrew P. ... New York, NY
Hurwitz, Ann ... Dallas, TX
Hurwitz, Arthur H. ... Jacksonville, FL
Hurwitz, Barrett A. ... New Bedford, MA
Hurwitz, Barry N. ... Boston, MA
Hurwitz, Bernard R. ... Rochester, NY
Hurwitz, Bruce ... Fort Lauderdale, FL
Hurwitz, David I. ... Los Angeles, CA
Hurwitz, David L. ... New York, NY
Hurwitz, David N. ... New York, NY
Hurwitz, Diana M. ... Fairview Heights, IL
Hurwitz, Elliot L. ... New York, NY
Hurwitz, Ely ... Washington, DC
Hurwitz & Fine, P.C. ... Albion, NY
Buffalo, NY
Niagara Falls, NY
Hurwitz, Gary A. ... Cherry Hill, NJ
Media, PA
Hurwitz, Gerald J. ... New York, NY
Hurwitz, Gerald S. ... Department of Justice, Executive Office for Immigration Review, GV
Hurwitz, Harold ... New Bedford, MA
Hurwitz & Humphreys, A Prof. Law Corp., Law Offices of ... Orange, CA
Hurwitz & Hurwitz ... Orange, CA
Hurwitz and Hurwitz ... New Bedford, MA
Hurwitz & Hurwitz, P.C. ... New City, NY
Hurwitz, Irving L. ... Newark, NJ
Hurwitz, Isaac D. ... Brooklyn, NY
Hurwitz, Ivan J. ... New York, NY
Hurwitz, James D.
Federal Trade Commission, Office of the General Counsel, GV
Hurwitz, Jeffrey A. ... San Francisco, CA
Hurwitz, Jeffrey E. ... Tampa, FL
Hurwitz, Jeffrey N. ... Philadelphia, PA
Hurwitz, Jeffrey S. ... Princeton, NJ
Hurwitz, Jerald P. ... Harrisburg, PA
Hurwitz, Jill P. ... New York, NY
Hurwitz, Jocelyn B. ... Bridgeport, CT
Hurwitz, Joel M. ... Chicago, IL
Hurwitz, Jonathan H. ... New York, NY
Hurwitz, Joseph D. ... Hartford, CT
Hurwitz, Julie H. ... Detroit, MI
Hurwitz, Julie H., P.C. ... Detroit, MI
Hurwitz, Karen S. ... Houston, TX
Hurwitz, Karp, Wallach & Gantz, P.C.
Dearborn Heights, MI
Hurwitz, Kenneth D. ... New York, NY
Hurwitz, Kenneth G. ... Washington, DC
Baltimore, MD
Hurwitz, Kerry Stelzer ... Newton, MA
Hurwitz, Lauren M. ... Troy, MI
Hurwitz, Lawrence Terry ... New York, NY
Hurwitz, Leah W. ... San Diego, CA
Hurwitz, Lewis A. ... Milford, CT
Hurwitz, Lon F. ... Orange, CA
Hurwitz, Louis N. ... Baltimore, MD
Hurwitz, Louis R. ... Sioux Falls, SD
Hurwitz, Marc S. ... Los Angeles, CA
Hurwitz, Mark D. ... Los Angeles, CA
Hurwitz, Mark E. ... Orange, CA
Hurwitz, Mark S. ... Buffalo, NY
Hurwitz, Martin ... New City, NY
Hurwitz, Melvin M. ... Brooklyn, NY
Hurwitz, Melvyn L. ... Buffalo, NY
Hurwitz, Michael ... New York, NY
Hurwitz, Michael A. ... San Jose, CA
Hurwitz, Michael H.
Securities and Exchange Commission, Division of Corporation Finance, GV
Hurwitz, Miles A. ... Dearborn Heights, MI
Hurwitz, Neal J. ... New York, NY
Hurwitz, Norman E. ... New Haven, CT
Hurwitz, Peter A. ... New City, NY
Hurwitz, Phillip R. ... Rochester, NY
Hurwitz, Ralph B. ... Boca Raton, FL
Hurwitz, Randy J. ... Scottsdale, AZ
Hurwitz, Raymond ... Cleveland, OH
Hurwitz, Rhonda Ann ... Rockville, MD
Hurwitz, Robert M. ... Park Ridge, NJ
Hurwitz, Robert S. ... Chicago, IL
Hurwitz, Robert W. ... Providence, RI
Hurwitz, Roger T. ... Kansas City, MO
Hurwitz & Sagarin, P.C. ... Milford, CT
Hurwitz, Samuel A. ... Flint, MI
Hurwitz, Samuel M. ... New Haven, CT
Hurwitz, Seymour I. ... New York, NY
Hurwitz, Sheldon ... Buffalo, NY
Hurwitz, Sheralee S. ... Lansing, MI
Hurwitz, Sol L. ... Altamonte Springs, FL
Hurwitz, Stephen A. ... Boston, MA
Hurwitz, Steven ... Tampa, FL
Hurwitz, Steven M. ... New York, NY
Hurwitz, Steven S. ... Marshall, CA
Hurwitz, Susan B. ... Treasury Department, Internal Revenue Service, GV
Hurwitz, Thomas R. ... St. Louis Park, MN
Hurwitz & Vail ... New York, NY
Hurwitz, Warren J. ... Chestnut Hill, MA
Hury, Charles W. ... Edinburg, TX
Huryn, Christopher M. ... Canton, OH
Huryn, Kathleen D. ... Palo Alto, CA
Huryn, Marianna O. ... Los Angeles, CA
Huryn, Natalia A. ... Pasadena, CA
Hus, Mark ... New York, NY
Husa, Christopher J. ... Woodland Hills, CA
Husaby, Scott G. ... Minneapolis, MN
Husain, Karim Patrick ... Philadelphia, PA
Husain, Nomi K. ... Houston, TX
Husak, Judith M.Z. ... Charlotte, NC
Husami, Mateen I. ... North Chicago, IL
Husar, Cornelius J. ... Herndon, VA
Husar, Linda S. ... Los Angeles, CA
Husarchik, Cynthia A. ... Southfield, MI
Husaynu & Plezia, P.C. ... Southfield, MI
Husaynu, Ryan A. ... Southfield, MI
Husband, B. Paul ... Burbank, CA
Husband, Eileen K. ... Detroit, MI
Husband, Howard O. ... San Antonio, TX
Husband, John M. ... Denver, CO
Husband, Phillip L. ... Alexandria, VA
Husband, Richard A. ... Connellsville, PA
Husband, Richard M. ... Manchester, NH
Husband, Robert E. ... Gulfport, MS
Husband, Thomas F. ... Paradise Valley, AZ
Husband, Warren H. ... Tallahassee, FL
Husbands, Carl Anderson ... Brooklyn, NY
Husbands, James C. ... Panama City, FL
Husbands, James W. ... Minneapolis, MN
Husbands, Patricia K. ... San Antonio, TX
Husby, David M. ... Sioux Falls, SD
Husby, Eric O. ... Detroit, MI
Husby, Kenneth C. ... Salinas, CA
Husby, Michael S. ... Duluth, MN
Husby, Robert L., Jr. ... Gainesville, GA
Husby, Robert L., Jr., P.C.
Gainesville, GA
Husby, Stephen K. ... Seattle, WA
Husch & Eppenberger, LLC ... Peoria, IL
Overland Park, KS
Wichita, KS
Jefferson City, MO
Kansas City, MO
St. Louis, MO
Springfield, MO
Husch, Gerald T. ... Boise, ID
Huschen & Huschen ... Roanoke, IL
Huschen, John B. ... Roanoke, IL
Huscher, David V. ... Redding, CA
Huscher, Paul E. ... Des Moines, IA
Huscher, Paul R. ... Des Moines, IA
Husdon, Ronald D. ... Los Angeles, CA
Huse, Charles P., Jr. ... Belmont, MA
Huse, F. Peter ... Omaha, NE
Huse, Mark J. ... Hyannis, MA
Huse, Stacey A. ... Louisville, KY
Huseby, Brodin & McManus, Ltd.
Duluth, MN
Huseby, H. William ... Denver, CO
Huseby, Robert C. ... Duluth, MN
Huseby, Robert N., Sr. ... Providence, RI
Huselid, Sevrin J. ... Globe, AZ
Huselton, Gary D. ... Dallas, TX
Huseman, Brian ... Tulsa, OK
Huseman, Eugene L. ... Lompoc, CA
Huseman, James C. ... Lompoc, CA
Huseman, Kathryn M. ... Englewood, CO
Huseman, Van ... Corpus Christi, TX
Husemoen, Odine H. ... Longview, WA
Husen, Richard L. ... Levelland, TX
Huser, Carmella A. ... Milwaukee, WI
Huser, Huser & Lively ... Wewoka, OK
Huser, Mary T. ... Palo Alto, CA
Huser, Paul ... Schulenburg, TX
Huser, Richard A. ... Indianapolis, IN
Huser, Stanley, Jr. ... Holdenville, OK
Huser, Thomas A. ... New York, NY
Huser, Troy V. ... Manhattan, KS
Huser, William D. ... Wewoka, OK
Hush, Howard H., Jr. ... Chicago, IL
Hushagen, James M. ... Tacoma, WA
Hushon, Jeremy Ambler ... Washington, DC
Hushon, John D. ... Washington, DC
Husian, Zain E. ... New York, NY
Husic, Yvonne M. ... Harrisburg, PA
Husick, Gail Clayton ... Palo Alto, CA
Husick, Gloria J. ... Dublin, CA
Husick, Lawrence A. ... Media, PA
Husid, Douglas M. ... Boston, MA
Husin, Bernice S ... Flushing, NY
Husing, Sylvia Lee ... San Bernardino, CA
Husisian, Gregory ... Washington, DC
Husisian, Jeffrey ... Binghamton, NY
Husk, John T. ... Vienna, VA
Huske, I. Manning ... Charlotte, NC
Huskey, Christina ... Arcata, CA
Huskey, Dow T. ... Dothan, AL
Huskey, J. David, Jr. ... Fort Lauderdale, FL
Huskey, Michael Conrad ... Bensenville, IL
Huskey, S. Renee ... Atlanta, GA
Huskey, Steven C. ... Los Angeles, CA
Huskey, T. Philip ... Ridgeland, MS
Huskey, Timothy M. ... Kansas City, MO
Huskey, W. Vandy ... Spartanburg, SC
Huskin, John T., Jr. ... Oakland, CA
Huskins, Amelia Hughes ... Atlanta, GA
Huskins, Carl T. ... Chattanooga, TN
Huskins, Donald W. ... Eatonton, GA
Huskins & Huskins ... Eatonton, GA
Huskins, J. Frank ... Raleigh, NC
Huskins, John ... Orlando, FL
Huskins, Louis A., (P.C.) ... Los Angeles, CA
Huskins, Sylvia S. ... Eatonton, GA
Huskison, Berkley N. ... Columbus, MS
Husman, David L. ... Chicago, IL
Husman, Stephen A. ... Columbia, SC
Husmann, John D. ... St. Louis, MO
Husmann, Michael E. ... Milwaukee, WI
Husmann, Reinert W. ... Union City, IN
Husmann & Stemmer ... Union City, IN
Husney, Elliott R., (P.C.) ... Denver, CO
Husney, Evan J. ... Albany, NY
Husock, Bernard ... South Euclid, OH
Huson, Christina C. ... St. Paul, MN
Huson, Herbert C. ... St. Clair Shores, MI
Huson, Lisa M. ... Charleston, IL
Huson, Roland T. ... Charleston, WV
Huspeni, Doris O. ... St. Paul, MN
Huss, A. J., Jr. ... St. Paul, MN
Huss, Allan M. ... Auburn Hills, MI
Huss, Christopher M. ... Tacoma, WA
Huss, Dan E. ... Oxford, OH
Huss, David J. ... Rapid City, SD
Huss, Edward H. ... Philadelphia, PA
Huss, Gary L. ... Fresno, CA
Huss, George W. ... Miles City, MT
Huss, John B. ... Grayling, MI
Huss, Jon B. ... Casper, WY
Huss, Joseph J. ... Pembroke Pines, FL
Huss, Joseph J. ... Lemoyne, PA
Huss, Karen L. Gleason ... Carlsbad, CA
Huss, Louis David ... Miami, FL
Huss, Louis David, P.A. ... Miami, FL
Huss, Michael E. ... Omaha, NE
Huss, R. Bradford ... San Francisco, CA
Huss, Rebecca Jean ... Valparaiso, IN
Huss, W. F." Bill " ... Carson City, NV
Huss, William W. ... Los Angeles, CA
Hussa, John A. ... Brooklyn, NY
Hussain, Farah ... New York, NY
Hussain, Farheen ... Dallas, TX
Hussain, Homira Riaz ... Lake Success, NY
Hussain, Khurram ... Chicago, IL
Hussain, Mahrukh S. ... Chicago, IL
Hussain, Sabeena ... Bloomfield, CT
Hussain, Tasneem ... Washington, DC
Hussar, Jeffrey F. ... Whitehall, PA
Hussar, Robert A. ... Albany, NY
Hussar, Ted W. ... Annandale, VA
Hussein, Samir H. ... New York, NY
Husseini, Richard Allen ... Houston, TX
Hussell, John F., IV ... Charleston, WV
Hussell, Monika ... Charleston, WV
Husser, John D. ... Rochester, NY
Husser, John S. ... Cedartown, GA
Husserl, Kenneth W. ... Bellmore, NY
Hussey, Alison Charney ... LaBelle, FL
Hussey, Brian M. ... Mineola, NY
Hussey, Bruce L. ... Missoula, MT
Hussey, Charles E., II ... Chicago, IL
Hussey, Colleen P. ... Providence, RI
Hussey, Curtis R. ... Provo, UT
Hussey, D. Brennan ... Shreveport, LA
Hussey, Daniel J. ... Edison, NJ
Hussey, Daniel S. ... Las Vegas, NV
Hussey, D. Brennan, A P.L.C.
Shreveport, LA
Hussey, Edward J. ... Merrillville, IN
Hussey & Hussey ... Mars Hill, ME
Hussey, J. Michael ... Fort Myers, FL
Hussey, James E. ... Chicago, IL
Hussey, Jeffrey R. ... Maitland, FL
Hussey, Jeffrey W. ... Hartford, CT
Hussey, John B. ... Shreveport, LA
Hussey, John D. ... Los Angeles, CA
Hussey, Margaret L. ... Tyler, TX
Hussey, Nathaniel T. ... Hallowell, ME
Hussey, Patrick F. ... Everett, WA
Hussey, R. Gaynell ... Gastonia, NC
Hussey, Ramona ... Belchertown, MA
Hussey, Richard F. ... Fort Lauderdale, FL
Hussey, Richard F., P.A.
Fort Lauderdale, FL
Hussey, Robert R., Co., L.P.A.
North Olmsted, OH
Hussey, Robert R., II ... North Olmsted, OH
Hussey, September L. ... St. Petersburg, FL
Hussey, Stetson H., Jr. ... Mars Hill, ME
Hussey, Ward M. ... Alexandria, VA
Hussey, William C., II ... Philadelphia, PA
Hussey, William D. ... Treasury Department, Internal Revenue Service, GV
Hussey, William R. ... Lantana, FL
Hussin, Christopher J. ... Denver, CO
Hussle, Robert C. ... Atlanta, GA
Hussmann, William G., Jr. ... Evansville, IN
Hussock, Janice A. ... New York, NY
Hust, Bridget A. ... Minneapolis, MN
Hust, Bruce K. ... Cincinnati, OH
Hust, John W. ... Cincinnati, OH
Hust, Robert L. ... Marysville, OH
Hust, Wilbor J., Jr. ... Tuscaloosa, AL
Hustace, Cedric ... Evansville, IN
Hustace, Frank W., Jr. ... Honolulu, HI
Hustad, Cynthia K. ... San Francisco, CA
Hustad, John C. F. ... Dayton, OH
Hustava, John Henry ... Collinsville, IL
Husted, Frances J. ... Huntington, WV
Hustead Law Firm, The, A Professional Corporation ... Denver, CO
Hustead, Patrick Q. ... Denver, CO
Hustead, Robert M. ... Homestead, FL
Husted, Aleta H. ... Missoula, MT
Husted, Cliff ... Houston, TX
Husted, Eldon L. ... Mesa, AZ
Husted, Gerald E. ... Columbus, OH
Husted, Leslie ... Lubbock, TX
Husted, Ralph W. ... Indianapolis, IN
Husted, Richard W. ... Dundee, IL
Husted, Rose Ann ... Lansing, MI
Husted, Stanley N., II ... Springfield, OH
Hustein, Joseph E. ... San Jose, CA
Huster, F. Thomas ... San Francisco, CA
Huster, John K. ... San Francisco, CA
Huster & Schneider ... San Francisco, CA
Hustis, Jonathan K. ... Dallas, TX
Hustoles, Carol L. J. ... Kalamazoo, MI
Hustoles, Thomas P. ... Kalamazoo, MI
Huston, Andrea C. ... Oakland, CA
Huston, Andrea K. ... Akron, OH
Huston & Angus ... Washington, DC
Arlington, VA
Huston, Barry S. ... New York, NY
Huston & Bertram ... Lee's Summit, MO
Huston, Brett A. ... Tucson, AZ
Huston, Brett A., P.C. ... Tucson, AZ
Huston, Brett O. ... Boulder, CO
Huston, Catherine E. ... Columbus, OH
Huston, Charles D. ... Austin, TX
Huston, Charles M. ... Akron, OH
Huston, Charles R. ... Kokomo, IN
Huston & Clark, Law Office, P.C.
Broken Bow, NE
Huston & Clifford ... Lisbon Falls, ME
Huston, Daniel H. ... London, OH
Huston, David C. ... Grand Island, NE
Huston, David W. ... Las Vegas, NV
Reno, NV
Huston, DeVerille A. ... Chicago, IL
Huston, F. Craig ... Coventry, RI
Huston, G. Winton ... Lee's Summit, MO
Huston, Gary W. ... Pensacola, FL
Huston, Gerald W. ... Chicago, IL
Huston, Graham C. ... Arlington, VA
Huston, Gretchen D. ... St. Louis, MO
Huston, H. Curran ... Houston, TX
Huston, H. Tracy ... Crestwood, MO
Huston & Higgins ... Grand Island, NE
Huston & Huston, PLC ... Des Moines, IA
Huston, J. Michael ... Lisbon Falls, ME
Huston, J. Randolph ... Los Angeles, CA

Huston, James H. ... Milwaukie, OR
Huston, James L. ... Milwaukee, WI
Huston, James W. ... San Diego, CA
Huston, Janet Galloway ... Des Moines, IA
Huston, Joanne L. ... Madison, WI
Huston, John A. ... Milford, NJ
Huston, John C. ... Seattle, WA
Huston, John H. ... Chicago, IL
Huston, John R. ... Sanbornville, NH
Huston, Jon ... Randolph, NJ
Huston, Joseph H., Jr. ... Wayne, PA
Huston, Julia ... Boston, MA
Huston, Kenneth D. ... San Diego, CA
Huston, Kimberly M. ... Detroit, MI
Huston, Larry L. ... Cincinnati, OH
Huston, M. Lynn ... Covina, CA
Huston, Margery A. ... Corpus Christi, TX
Huston, Marilyn M. ... Houston, TX
Huston, Mark William ... Orange, CA
Huston, Michael B. ... Portland, OR
Huston, Michael J. ... Indianapolis, IN
Huston, Michael L. ... Des Moines, IA
Huston, Nancy L. ... Houston, TX
Huston, Penn C. ... Houston, TX
Huston, Peter ... San Francisco, CA
Huston, Phillip M., Jr. ... New York, NY
Huston, Richard R. ... Indianapolis, IN
Huston, Richd. H. ... Indianapolis, IN
Huston, Robert E. ... Lincoln, NE
Huston, Robert J., III ... Newport Beach, CA
Huston, Robert K. ... Aurora, OH
Huston, Robert T. ... Portland, OR
Huston, Robert W. ... Costa Mesa, CA
Los Angeles, CA
Huston & Schuller, P.C. ... New York, NY
Huston, Steven C. ... Chicago, IL
Huston, Tedd C. ... Broken Bow, NE
Huston, Thomas C. ... Lincoln, NE
Huston, Tom Charles ... Indianapolis, IN
Huston, William T. ... Los Angeles, CA
Huston-Kinworthy, Carlene ... Lima, OH
Hustwick, David E. ... San Diego, CA
Husum, Carol A. ... Kalamazoo, MI
Husum, Howard F. ... New York, NY
Huszagh, Elenie K. ... Chicago, IL
Huszagh, Fritz K. ... Chicago, IL
Huszagh, Richard S. ... Chicago, IL
Huszagh, Victor Lee ... Tallahassee, FL
Huszar, Arlene C. ... Gainesville, FL
Huszar, Thomas G. ... New York, NY
Hut, A. Stephen, Jr. ... Washington, DC
Hutaff, Richard R. ... Monroe, NC
Hutchen, Bridget W. ... Lake Forest, IL
Hutchen, Bridget W. ... Waukegan, IL
Hutchen, Todd ... Bethesda, MD
Hutchens, Charley ... Lafayette, LA
Hutchens, Curtis ... Gainesville, FL
Hutchens, H. Terry ... Fayetteville, NC
Hutchens, Harry P. ... Conroe, TX
Hutchens & Hutchens, P.C. ... Richmond, VA
Hutchens, J. Brett ... Sarasota, FL
Hutchens, James A. ... San Diego, CA
Hutchens, James R. ... Sarasota, FL
Hutchens, John G., Jr. ... Matthews, NC
Hutchens, John N. ... Vale, OR
Hutchens, Michael D. ... Minneapolis, MN
Hutchens & Montgomery ... Lafayette, LA
Hutchens, Patricia Y. ... Morgantown, WV
Hutchens, Randall A. ... Murray, KY
Hutchens, Rita M. D. ... Duluth, MN
Hutchens, Robert A. ... Orlando, FL
Greencastle, IN
Hutchens, Robt. S. ... Champaign, IL
Hutchens, Suzette Lynn ... Richmond, VA
Hutchens, Teresa J. ... Bend, OR
Hutchens, Timothy C. ... Washington, DC
Hutchens, William P. ... Okemos, MI
Hutchens, William V. ... Indianapolis, IN
Hutchens, Willis F. ... Richmond, VA
Hutcheon, Peter D. ... Somerville, NJ
Hutcher, Andrew M. ... New York, NY
Hutcher, Larry ... New York, NY
Hutcherson, Floyd E. ... Rockwood, TN
Hutcherson, James P. ... Columbia, SC
Hutcherson, James W. ... Brooklyn, NY
Hutcherson, Joseph L., II ... Monroe, NC
Hutcherson & Rhodes, Ltd. ... Chatham, VA
Rocky Mount, VA
Stuart, VA
Hutcherson, Ronald W. ... Reno, NV
Hutcherson, William H., Jr.
Cincinnati, OH
Hutches, Clarence F., II ... Kerrville, TX
Hutcheson, Anna Northington
Tuscaloosa, AL
Hutcheson, Bellenden Rand ... Boston, MA
Hutcheson, Courtney H. ... Houston, TX
Hutcheson, Douglas A.
Fort Walton Beach, FL
Hutcheson, Drewry B., Jr. ... Alexandria, VA
Hutcheson, Geoffrey C. ... Modesto, CA
Hutcheson & Hull, P.C. ... Loganville, GA
Hutcheson, J. Kennedy ... Jacksonville, FL
Hutcheson, J. Kennedy, P.A.
Jacksonville, FL
Hutcheson, Jennifer M.
San Francisco, CA
Hutcheson, Jim B. ... Austin, TX
Hutcheson, John Palmer ... Houston, TX
Hutcheson, John T.
Department Of Veterans Affairs, Board of Veterans Appeals, GV
Hutcheson, Jon S. ... Houston, MO
Hutcheson, Joseph C., II ... Boston, MA
Hutcheson, Kevin S. ... Redwood City, CA
Hutcheson, Laura McNeill
Washington, DC
Hutcheson, Mark A. ... Seattle, WA
Hutcheson, Mark S. ... Austin, TX
Hutcheson, Milton H., Jr. ... Loganville, GA
Hutcheson, Nancy L. ... Troy, MI
Hutcheson, Norma Brown
United States Postal Service, Mid-Atlantic Office, GV
Hutcheson, Philip F. ... Birmingham, AL
Hutcheson, Pinchak, Powers & Disheroon
Chattanooga, TN
Hutcheson, R. Michael ... Daytona Beach, FL
Hutcheson, Robert W. ... Xenia, OH
Hutcheson, Shannon H. ... Austin, TX
Hutcheson, Stephen T. ... Dallas, TX
Hutcheson, Sterling ... San Diego, CA
Hutcheson, Terry G. ... Fort Payne, AL
Hutcheson, Thomas A. ... Sandersville, GA
Hutcheson, Thomas A. ... Charleston, SC
Hutcheson, Thomas T. ... Houston, TX
Hutcheson, William G. ... Toledo, OH
Hutcheson and Wynne, P.C.
Sandersville, GA
Hutchings, Adrienne C. ... Irvine, CA
Hutchings, Barsamian & Levy, P.C.
Boston, MA
Wellesley, MA
Hutchings, Ellen Ashley A.
Ocean Springs, MS
Hutchings, Jeffrey D. ... Washington, DC
Hutchings, John A. ... Denver, CO
Hutchings, John R., IV ... Maysville, KY
Hutchings, Lawrence W.
Walnut Creek, CA
Hutchings, Mary P. ... Cleveland, OH
Hutchings, Michael L. ... Sandy, UT
Hutchings, Philip J. ... Rochester, NY
Hutchings, Stephen H. ... Anchorage, AK
Hutchings, Virginia A. ... Yorba Linda, CA
Hutchings, W. Michael ... Seattle, WA
Hutchins, A. Mark ... Oakland, CA
Hutchins, A. Robert ... Springfield, OH
Hutchins, Amy S. ... Los Angeles, CA
Hutchins & Associates, LLC ... Denver, CO
Hutchins, Bradley A. ... Atlanta, GA
Hutchins, Brian R. ... Carson City, NV
Hutchins, Calvin W. ... Jefferson, OH
Hutchins, Christina M. ... Portland, OR
Hutchins, Constantine, Jr. ... Needham, MA
Hutchins, Creighton S. ... Seattle, WA
Hutchins, Cynthia Hayes ... Wheaton, IL
Hutchins, Cynthia Hayes, P.C., The Law Office of ... Wheaton, IL
Hutchins, Cynthia M. ... Pittsburgh, PA
Hutchins, David F. ... Lafayette, LA
Hutchins, Deborah Dean ... Princeton, WV
Hutchins, Edward J., Jr. ... Baltimore, MD
Hutchins, Elizabeth Dennis ... Columbia, CT
Hutchins, Elizabeth Holland
Birmingham, AL
Hutchins, Eugene P. ... Trenton, NJ
Hutchins, Frank L. ... Manchester Center, VT
Hutchins, Fred S., Jr. ... Winston-Salem, NC
Hutchins, Gregory D. ... Asheville, NC
Hutchins, Harley ... Chicago, IL
Hutchins, Holly ... Irvine, CA
Hutchins, J. Todd ... Washington, DC
Hutchins, James E. ... Mathews, VA
Hutchins, Jeffrey D. ... Boston, MA
Hutchins, Jeremy Todd ... Washington, DC
Hutchins, John C. ... Boston, MA
Hutchins, John M. ... Denver, CO
Hutchins, John P. ... Atlanta, GA
Hutchins, John R. ... Washington, DC
Hutchins, Karen K. ... Little Rock, AR
Hutchins, Kristin E. ... San Francisco, CA
Hutchins, Laurie ... Winston-Salem, NC
Hutchins Law Firm, P.A. ... Plymouth, NC
Hutchins, Lemuel C. ... Tyler, TX
Hutchins, Lynn ... San Francisco, CA
Hutchins, Michael E. ... Atlanta, GA
Hutchins, Michael Paul ... Irvine, CA
Hutchins, Miriam B. ... Baltimore, MD
Hutchins, Peter ... Cortland, NY
Hutchins, Peter E. ... Manchester, NH
Hutchins, R. Clayton ... Grand Prairie, TX
Hutchins, Richard G. ... Coldwater, MI
Hutchins, Rob J. ... Orlando, FL
Hutchins, Robert B. ... Glendale, CA
Hutchins, Robert B. ... Oakland, CA
Hutchins, Robert G. ... Tacoma, WA
Hutchins, Robert Wendel ... Plymouth, NC
Hutchins, Ronald Dean ... Flint, MI
Hutchins, Shelby V. ... Delaware, OH
Hutchins, Steven R. ... Denver, CO
Hutchins, Terry R. ... Pembroke, NC
Hutchins, Theodore S. ... Paducah, KY
Hutchins, Thomas ... Laredo, TX
Hutchins, Thomas J. ... Ventura, CA
Hutchins, Van A. ... McAllen, TX
Hutchins, W. James ... Columbus, OH
Hutchins, Waldo, III ... Locust Valley, NY
Hutchins, Wesley D. ... Salt Lake City, UT
Hutchins, Wheeler & Dittmar, A Professional Corporation ... Boston, MA
Hutchins, William A. ... Department of Justice, Environment and Natural Resources Division, GV
Hutchins, William M. ... Richmond, VA
Hutchins, William T., Jr. ... Bardstown, KY
Hutchins, William T., Jr. ... Durham, NC
Hutchinson, Adam A. ... Mission Viejo, CA
Hutchinson, Alan D. ... Chicago, IL
Hutchinson, A'Lan S. ... Puyallup, WA
Hutchinson, Alvan S., Jr. ... Oyster Bay, NY
Hutchinson, Anderson, Cox, Coons & DuPriest, P.C. ... Eugene, OR
Hutchinson, Asa ... Fort Smith, AR
Hutchinson, B. Clyde, III ... Oakland, CA
Hutchinson, Barbara B.
New Carrollton, MD
Hutchinson Black and Cook, LLC
Boulder, CO
Hutchinson, Campbell C., (P.C.)
New Orleans, LA
Hutchinson, Clifton T. ... Dallas, TX
Hutchinson, Cynthia S. ... Elmira, NY
Hutchinson, Daniel P. ... Los Angeles, CA
Hutchinson, Darrell A. ... Powell, OH
Hutchinson, David C. ... St. Paul, MN
Hutchinson, David H. ... Milwaukee, WI
Hutchinson, David J. ... Ann Arbor, MI
Hutchinson, David P. ... Denver, CO
Hutchinson, David P. ... Boston, MA
Hutchinson, David V.
Department of Justice, Civil Division, GV
Hutchinson, Dennett L. ... Denver, CO
Hutchinson, Donald J. ... Detroit, MI
Hutchinson, Donald K. ... Portland, OR
Hutchinson, Douglas A
San Francisco, CA
Hutchinson, Durward L. ... Monroe, MI
Hutchinson, Ernest H., III
Mount Laurel, NJ
Philadelphia, PA
Hutchinson, Forney, Jr. ... Roxboro, NC
Hutchinson, Forrest ... Duluth, MN
Fargo, ND
Hutchinson, Franklin G. ... Springfield, VA
Hutchinson, George E. ... Montgomery, AL
Hutchinson, George E. ... Washington, DC
Hutchinson, George F. ... Lawrenceville, GA
Hutchinson, Gov ... Los Angeles, CA
Hutchinson, Gregory F. ... Winchester, VA
Hutchinson, Harvey A., III ... Birmingham, AL
Hutchinson, Heidi D. ... Pullman, WA
Hutchinson, Henry H. ... Montgomery, AL
Hutchinson, J. Edwin ... College Park, MD
Hutchinson, Jack T. ... Dunwoody, GA
Hutchinson, James A. ... Washington, DC
Hutchinson, James H., III ... Bellaire, TX
Hutchinson, James Neal, Jr.
Coral Gables, FL
Hutchinson, James S. ... Washington, DC
Hutchinson, John C. ... Holland, MI
Hutchinson, John D. ... Coldwater, MI
Hutchinson, John G. ... New York, NY
Hutchinson, John L. ... Warrenville, IL
Hutchinson, John R ... Marshfield, WI
Hutchinson, Joseph F., Jr. ... Cleveland, OH
Hutchinson, Joseph W., III ... Butler, AL
Hutchinson, Katherine A. ... Wichita, KS
Hutchinson, Larry M. ... McKinney, TX
Hutchinson, Laura A. ... Chicago, IL
Hutchinson, Leland E. ... Chicago, IL
Hutchinson, Leland P. ... Hightstown, NJ
Hutchinson, Leland W., Jr. ... Chicago, IL
Hutchinson, Louise ... Harrisburg, PA
Hutchinson, M. Suzanne Hayes
Calhoun, GA
Hutchinson, Marc K.
North Kansas City, MO
Hutchinson, Marilyn B. ... Lincoln, NE
Hutchinson, Mark A. ... Berwyn, PA
Hutchinson, Mark R. ... Lexington, KY
Owensboro, KY
Hutchinson, Michael C. ... Stillwater, MN
Hutchinson, Michael J. ... Detroit, MI
Hutchinson, Michael J. ... Midland, MI
Hutchinson, Michael L. ... Denver, CO
Hutchinson, Michelle Anne ... Rochester, NY
Hutchinson & Paradoski, P.C.
Detroit, MI
Hutchinson, Patti (Powell) ... Rolla, MO
Hutchinson, Paula K. ... Houston, TX
Hutchinson, Peter J. ... St. Maries, ID
Hutchinson, Philip A., Jr. ... Troy, MI
Hutchinson, Phillip H.
West Palm Beach, FL
Hutchinson, Reed ... Huron, SD
Hutchinson, Richard Lewis ... Oyster Bay, NY
Hutchinson, Robert A. ... West Liberty, KY
Hutchinson, Robert B. ... Beverly Hills, CA
Hutchinson, Robert L. ... Orlando, FL
Hutchinson, Robert, Law Firm
Aurora, CO
Denver, CO
Englewood, CO
Highlands Ranch, CO
Hutchinson, Robert W. ... Denver, CO
Englewood, CO
Hutchinson, Rodney E. ... Jupiter, FL
Hutchinson, Ron R. ... Arlington, VA
Hutchinson, Sam E.
Department of Housing and Urban Development, Office of General Counsel, GV
Hutchinson, Sandra J. ... Glens Falls, NY
Hutchinson, Scott M. ... Portland, OR
Hutchinson, Shauneen Cruise
Wilmington, DE
Hutchinson, Simone E. Handler
Roseland, NJ
Hutchinson, Stafford ... Dallas, TX
Hutchinson, Stephen A. ... Eugene, OR
Hutchinson, Stephen F.
Salt Lake City, UT
Hutchinson, Steven G. ... Topeka, KS
Hutchinson, Susan E. ... Corpus Christi, TX
Hutchinson, Susan Fayette ... Woodstock, IL
Hutchinson, Susan L. ... Katy, TX
Hutchinson, T. Henry ... Boulder, CO
Hutchinson, Thomas D. ... Milwaukee, WI
Hutchinson, Thomas F. ... Minneapolis, MN
Hutchinson, Thomas H. ... Los Angeles, CA
Hutchinson, Thomas J. ... Ventura, CA
Hutchinson, Thomas L. ... New Orleans, LA
Hutchinson, Thomas N. ... Indianapolis, IN
Hutchinson, Timothy C. ... Butler, AL
Hutchinson, Todd H. ... Vancouver, WA
Hutchinson, Tony M. ... Bristol, VA
Norton, VA
Hutchinson, Trudy ... Cleveland, OH
Hutchinson, Vicki H. ... Danbury, CT
Hutchinson, William B., Jr.
Merchantville, NJ
Hutchinson, William C. ... Needham, MA
Hutchinson, William J. ... Wilmington, DE
Bridgewater, NJ
Hutchison, A. Colleen ... Houston, TX
Hutchison, Anders and Hickey
Tinley Park, IL
Hutchison, Ann E. ... Vail, CO
Hutchison & Benson, S.C. ... Brookfield, WI
Hutchison, Bert ... Madison, WI
Hutchison, Brian A. ... Frederick, MD
Hutchison, Brian D. ... Indianapolis, IN
Hutchison & Charlap ... Corning, NY
Hutchison, D. Bradley ... Paris, TX
Hutchison, Dan C. ... Tulsa, OK
Hutchison, Danny Clifford ... Tulsa, OK
Hutchison, David C. ... Vancouver, WA
Hutchison, Donna M. ... Elmira, NY
Hutchison, E. Ray ... Dallas, TX
Hutchison, Edward A., Jr.
Panama City, FL
Hutchison, Eliza B. ... Washington, DC
Kansas City, MO
Hutchison, Frances E., P.C. ... Dallas, TX
Hutchison, Fred D. ... Raleigh, NC
Hutchison, Fred J. ... Albany, NY
Hutchison, Ginabeth B. ... Atlanta, GA
Hutchison, Gordon B. ... Phoenix, AZ
Hutchison, Gregg H. ... Lawrenceville, NJ
Hutchison, H. Gray, Jr. ... Raleigh, NC
Hutchison, Hammond, Walsh, Herndon & Goss, A Professional Corporation
Oregon City, OR
Portland, OR
West Linn, OR
Hutchison, Harry G. ... Mineral Point, WI
Hutchison, Hugh J. ... Philadelphia, PA
Hutchison, James Wellington ... Chicago, IL
Hutchison, Janet B. ... Phoenix, AZ
Hutchison, Jean L. ... Findlay, OH
Hutchison, Jennifer R. ... Jamestown, KY
Hutchison, John A., III ... Houston, TX
Hutchison, John Blair ... Ogden, UT
Hutchison, John C. ... West Linn, OR
Hutchison, John L. ... Spearman, TX
Hutchison, John L., Attorney at Law, P.C.
Spearman, TX
Hutchison, John W. ... Lafayette, LA
Hutchison, Kenneth D. ... Naples, FL
Hutchison, Larry M. ... McKinney, TX
Hutchison, Lawrence J. ... New York, NY
Hutchison, Lois E. ... Lake Orion, MI
Hutchison, Mamele & Coover, P.A.
Sanford, FL
Hutchison, Marc K. ... Kansas City, MO
Hutchison, Mark A. ... Las Vegas, NV
Hutchison, Mark H. ... Sanford, FL
Hutchison, Mark P. ... Corning, NY
Hutchison & Mason PLLC ... Raleigh, NC
Hutchison, Michael E. ... Knoxville, TN
Hutchison, Neider, Ward & King
Salt Lake City, UT
Hutchison, Phillip T. ... Seattle, WA
Hutchison, Ray, Jr. ... Columbia, KY
Hutchison, Richard C.
Fort Lauderdale, FL
Hutchison, Richard C. ... Salt Lake City, UT
Hutchison, Richard L. ... Tinley Park, IL
Hutchison, Richard Peter ... Kansas City, MO
Hutchison, Robert A. ... Des Moines, IA
Hutchison, Robert C. ... Jackson, MS
Hutchison, Robert H., Jr. ... Columbia, KY
Hutchison, Robert N. ... Chicago, IL
Hutchison, Robin M. ... Waverly, NY
Hutchison, Samuel R. ... Phoenix, AZ
Hutchison, Samuel Robert, P.A.
Phoenix, AZ
Hutchison, Scott J. ... Brookfield, WI
Hutchison & Steffen ... Las Vegas, NV
Hutchison & Stephenson, L.L.P.
Dallas, TX
Hutchison, Stewart C. ... Joliet, IL
Hutchison, Stuart N., III ... Pittsburgh, PA
Hutchison, Susan E. ... Fort Worth, TX
Hutchison, Susan R. ... Albany, NY
Hutchison, Theodore M. ... Des Moines, IA
Hutchison, Thomas F. ... Chesterfield, MO
Hutchison, Warren D. ... Boston, MA
Hutchison, William D. ... Helena, MT
Hutchison, William L. ... Dallas, TX
Hutchison, William P., Jr. ... Portland, OR
Hutensky, Steven D. ... New York, NY
Huter, Jeffrey B. ... Indianapolis, IN
Huter, Lawrence D. ... Lafayette, LA
Hutfilz, Edgar E., II ... Palm Harbor, FL
Huth, Deborah A. ... Emporia, KS
Huth & Grinnell, LLC ... Stamford, CT
Huth, Henry H. ... Ponca City, OK
Huth, Jeffrey A. ... Cleveland, OH
Huth, Lester C., (Co., L.P.A.) ... Tiffin, OH
Huth, Lynett and Scudi ... Detroit, MI
Huth, Patsy D. ... Los Angeles, CA
Huth, Paul H. ... Detroit, MI
Huth, Robert A., Jr. ... Boca Raton, FL
Fort Lauderdale, FL
Huth, Thomas C. ... Newark, NJ
Huth, William E. ... Stamford, CT
Huther, Christopher S. ... Washington, DC
Huthnance, Guy T. ... Tuscaloosa, AL
Huthnance, John R. ... Birmingham, AL

Huthwaite, W. Ernest C. ... Pontiac, MI
Hutkin, Allen K. ... San Luis Obispo, CA
Hutkin, Maria ... San Luis Obispo, CA
Hutlas, Alice A. ... Shreveport, LA
Hutmacher, Matthew A. ... Quincy, IL
Hutmacher, Rapp & Ortbal, P.C. ... Quincy, IL
Hutner, Florence A. ... New York, NY
Hutner, Joseph L. ... New York, NY
Hutner, Susan Klavens ... Treasury Department, Office of Foreign Assets Control, GV
Hutnick, Melroy B. ... Belleville, IL
Hutnick, Paulette F. ... Overland Park, KS
Kansas City, MO
Hutnyan, Diane Cafferata ... Palo Alto, CA
Hutsell, Randall A. ... Massillon, OH
Hutsler, Kearney D., III ... Birmingham, AL
Hutson, Benne C. ... Charlotte, NC
Hutson, Bennett A. ... Gainesville, FL
Hutson, Brenda Kaye ... Detroit, MI
Hutson, Cara D. ... Victorville, CA
Hutson, Denise Lowry ... Gainesville, FL
Hutson, D. L. ... La Follette, TN
Hutson, Don ... Lebanon, MO
Hutson, Douglas W. ... Athens, TN
Hutson & Elrod ... Decatur, AL
Hutson, Geoffrey ... Houston, TX
Hutson, Harrison D. ... Washington, DC
Hutson Hughes & Powell, P.A.
Durham, NC
Hutson, Jack W. ... Fort Myers, FL
Hutson, Jed. W. ... Newburgh, IN
Hutson, Jeffrey W. ... Columbus, OH
Hutson, J. J. ... Seattle, WA
Hutson, John N., Jr. ... Raleigh, NC
Hutson, John S. ... Vancouver, WA
Hutson, Karen ... New York, NY
Hutson, Keith E. ... Monticello, IL
Hutson, Kristin E. ... Oak Brook, IL
Hutson, L. A., Jr. ... Charlotte, NC
Hutson, Mark A. ... Columbiana, OH
Hutson, Mary Lou ... Charlotte, NC
Hutson, Mel S. ... Atlanta, GA
Hutson, Melvin R. ... Washington, DC
Hutson, Michael J. ... El Paso, TX
Hutson, Michael W. ... Troy, MI
Hutson, Paul K. ... Santa Ana, CA
Hutson, Preston D. ... Beaumont, TX
Hutson, R. Christion ... Paducah, KY
Hutson, Richard M., II ... Durham, NC
Hutson, Robert ... Decatur, AL
Hutson, Robert ... Los Angeles, CA
Hutson, Rutledge Q. ... Decatur, GA
Arlington, VA
Hutson, Sawyer, Chapman & Reilly
Auburn Hills, MI
Detroit, MI
Troy, MI
Hutson, Shelley V. ... Houston, TX
Hutson, Susan A. ... Houston, TX
Hutson, William F. ... Westfield Center, OH
Hutson-Dunn, D. Camille ... Houston, TX
Hutson-Wiley, Diane M. ... Vienna, VA
Hutt, Abraham V ... Denver, CO
Hutt, Abraham V, P.C. ... Denver, CO
Hutt, David M. ... Woodbridge, NJ
Hutt, J. Clifford ... Montrose, VA
Hutt, John C. ... Los Angeles, CA
Hutt, Laurence J. ... Los Angeles, CA
Hutt, Martin Jay ... Bethesda, MD
Hutt, Peter B., II ... Washington, DC
Hutt, Peter Barton ... Washington, DC
Hutt & Robertson, Ltd. ... Montrose, VA
Hutt, Sherry ... Phoenix, AZ
Hutt, Stewart M. ... Woodbridge, NJ
Hutta, Jane ... New York, NY
Huttar, Adolph H. ... Syracuse, NY
Huttar, Elizabeth J. ... Baltimore, MD
Huttash, Hallie L., (Mrs.) ... Austin, TX
Huttash, Robert A. ... Austin, TX
Huttemann, Joseph C., II ... Philadelphia, PA
Huttemann, Kathleen N. ... Boston, MA
Huttenbach, William P." Pat "
Houston, TX
Huttenburg, Jeffrey L.
Wisconsin Rapids, WI
Huttenhower, James A. ... Chicago, IL
Hutter, Alfons G. ... Anderson, SC
Hutter, Allen M. ... Washington, DC
Hutter, Bradley L. ... Madison, WI
Hutter, Christopher R. ... Washington, DC
Hutter, Jacqueline M. ... Atlanta, GA
Hutter, James R. ... Los Angeles, CA
Hutter, Michael J., Jr. ... Albany, NY
Hutter, Michael N. ... Orlando, FL
Hutter, Nancy H. ... Philadelphia, PA
Hutter, Paul J.
Department Of Veterans Affairs, VA Regional Counsel Office, Washington, D.C., GV
Hutter, Randolph L. ... Department of Justice, Tax Division, GV
Hutter, Robert ... Rochester, NY
Hutter, Robert G. ... Wellsville, NY
Hutterer & Krenn ... Minneapolis, MN
Hutterer, Vincent K. ... Minneapolis, MN
Hutterli, Conrad G. ... Beaverton, OR
Huttie, LesLee ... Kansas City, MO
Hutting, Augustus W. ... Detroit, MI
Huttl, John R. ... Medford, OR
Huttle, Frank, III ... Hackensack, NJ
Huttler, Shlomo" Steven " ... New York, NY
Huttler, Stephen B., (P.C.)
Washington, DC
Huttman, Laurence C.
West Palm Beach, FL
Huttner, Bruce S. ... Albany, NY
Huttner, Constance S. ... New York, NY
Huttner, Edward I. ... Denver, CO
Huttner, Lee Michael ... New York, NY
Huttner, Leland S. ... Englewood, CO
Huttner, Richard B. ... Denver, CO
Huttner, Richard D. ... Brooklyn, NY
Hutto, Bill R. ... Panama City, FL
Hutto and Bodiford ... Panama City, FL
Hutto, C. Bradley ... Orangeburg, SC
Hutto, Cynthia Bankhead ... Charleston, SC
Hutto, Elizabeth Bangston ... Columbia, SC
Hutto, F. Chase, III ... Washington, DC
Hutto, H. Marie ... Winston-Salem, NC
Hutto, Ingrid ... Washington, DC
Hutto, James A., Jr. ... Columbia, SC
Hutto, John W. ... Hattiesburg, MS
Hutto, J. S. ... Brunswick, GA
Hutto, Louis H., III ... Bluffton, SC
Hilton Head Island, SC
Hutto & Palmatary, P.A. ... Brunswick, GA
Hutto, Randolph L. M. ... Atlanta, GA
Hutto, Robert Edward ... Carpinteria, CA
Hutto, Ronald E. ... Orangeburg, SC
Hutto, S. Keith ... Columbia, SC
Hutto, Scott W. ... Columbia, SC
Hutto, Wade ... Llano, TX
Huttoe, Arthur E., (P.A.) ... Miami, FL
Hutton, Albert L., III ... Boston, MA
Hutton, Albert Lee, Jr. ... Boston, MA
Hutton, Andrew W. ... San Diego, CA
Hutton, Andrew W. ... Wichita, KS
Hutton, Anne ... Wayne, NJ
Hutton, Anne P. ... Abingdon, VA
Hutton, Arthur H. ... Forest Hills, NY
Hutton, Arthur J. ... Tucson, AZ
Hutton, Brett M. ... New York, NY
Hutton, Brian D. ... Portland, OR
Hutton, Bruce A. ... Willoughby, OH
Hutton, Christopher W. ... Hampton, VA
Hutton, Clark H., III ... New York, NY
Hutton, David J. ... Minneapolis, MN
Hutton, David J. ... Abingdon, VA
Hutton, David W. ... Pulaski, TN
Hutton, E. Jeremy
Office of Personnel Management, Office of the Inspector General, GV
Hutton, E. William ... Houston, TX
Hutton, Edgar L., Jr. ... Memphis, TN
Hutton, Elizabeth S. ... Santa Rosa, CA
Hutton, Freese and Einspahr, P.C.
Norfolk, NE
Hutton, G. Thompson, Law Office of
New York, NY
Hutton, Gail ... Huntington Beach, CA
Hutton, Gary W. ... San Antonio, TX
Hutton, Gerald J. ... Pittsburgh, PA
Hutton, Greta T. ... Glendale, CA
Hutton, Harry J. ... Boston, MA
Hutton, Herbert J. ... Philadelphia, PA
Hutton & Hutton ... Wichita, KS
Hutton, Jack Withrow ... Fort Lauderdale, FL
Hutton, James J. ... Indianapolis, IN
Hutton, James L. ... Blacksburg, VA
Hutton, James L., Jr. ... Kansas City, MO
Hutton, James P. ... Yakima, WA
Hutton, Jared R. B. ... Santa Monica, CA
Hutton, Jeffrey D. ... Philadelphia, PA
Hutton, John B., III ... Miami, FL
Hutton, John G., Jr. ... Waitsfield, VT
Hutton, John H. ... Topeka, KS
Hutton, John W. ... King City, CA
Hutton, John Whetstone ... Bethesda, MD
Hutton, Kathryn A. ... Nashville, TN
Hutton & Kennedy ... Minneapolis, MN
Hutton, Laury, Young & Lietz
Danville, IL
Hutton, Lawrence A. ... Colton, CA
Hutton, Lee J. ... Cleveland, OH
Hutton, Linette Bailey ... Salt Lake City, UT
Hutton, Lynn D., Jr. ... Norfolk, NE
Hutton, Lynn D., Jr., P.C. ... Norfolk, NE
Hutton, M. Ames ... Dallas, TX
Hutton, M. Prudence ... Wichita, KS
Hutton, Marilyn S. ... Albuquerque, NM
Hutton, Mark B. ... Wichita, KS
Hutton, Mary Christine ... Lansing, MI
Hutton, Mary Ellyn LaBach ... Cincinnati, OH
Hutton, Michael R. ... Seattle, WA
Hutton, Michelle A. ... Metairie, LA
Hutton, Paul S. ... Lexington, MA
Hutton, Paul Scott ... Boston, MA
Hutton, Peter W. ... Barnstable, MA
Yarmouth Port, MA
Hutton, Richard A. ... Glendale, CA
Hutton, Robert Louis ... Memphis, TN
Hutton, Roy F. ... New York, NY
Hutton, Shelley Portney ... Orchard Lake, MI
Hutton & Solomon LLP ... New York, NY
Hutton, Steven D. ... Sarasota, FL
Hutton, Suzanne A. ... Baltimore, MD
Hutton, Terrence ... Chicago, IL
Hutton, Thomas A. ... Harrisburg, PA
Hutton, Thomas C. ... Cincinnati, OH
Hutton, Thomas J. ... Washington, DC
Hutton, Thomas P. ... Washington, DC
Hutton, T. L., Jr. ... Abingdon, VA
Hutton, Todd J. ... Papillion, NE
Hutton, Todd W. ... Dallas, TX
Hutton, W. Randall ... San Antonio, TX
Hutton, W. Thomas ... Memphis, TN
Hutton, Warren A. ... Hickory, NC
Hutton, William L. ... St. Louis, MO
Hutton, William T. ... San Francisco, CA
Hutton, William W., II ... Kansas City, KS
Hutton & Withrow ... Fort Lauderdale, FL
Hutts, Melissa K. ... Dallas, TX
Hutul, Pamela J. ... Chicago, IL
Hutyera, Andrew ... Cadiz, OH
Hutz, R. Eric ... Wilmington, DE
Hutz, Rudolf E. ... Wilmington, DE
Hutzel, Rachel A. ... Dayton, OH
Hutzell, J. Scott ... Houston, TX
Hutzelman, Martha L. ... Alexandria, VA
Hutzelman, Stephen H. ... Erie, PA
Hutzler, Barbara ... San Antonio, TX
Hutzler, Laurie H. ... Santa Monica, CA
Huusko, Gary L. ... Eagan, MN
Huusko, Laurie Paulsen ... St. Paul, MN
Huva, Susie L. ... Oregon City, OR
Huval, Jacques N. ... Lafayette, LA
Huval, Thomas H. ... Lafayette, LA
New Orleans, LA
Huvard, Bruce K. ... Northbrook, IL
Huvelle, Ellen Segal ... Washington, DC
Huvelle, Jeffrey G. ... Washington, DC
Huver, Richard A. ... San Diego, CA
Huvos, Philip A. ... Boston, MA
Huwaldt, Mary ... Paoli, PA
Huwe, Gregory P. ... St. Paul, MN
Huwel, George A., IV ... Franklin Square, NY
Hux, Alan M. ... Indianapolis, IN
Hux, Douglas R. ... Eden, NC
Hux, George A. ... Enfield, NC
Hux & Hux ... Sikeston, MO
Hux, James M. ... Sikeston, MO
Hux, Livermon & Armstrong, L.L.P.
Enfield, NC
Halifax, NC
Roanoke Rapids, NC
Hux, Paul D. ... Richmond, VA
Huxoll, Gaye L. ... Miami, FL
Huxster, Peter K. ... Malibu, CA
Huyck, James H., III ... Herkimer, NY
Huyck, Philip M. ... New York, NY
Huyck, Ronald K. ... Grand Rapids, MI
Huyck, Steven Michael ... Flossmoor, IL
Huyck, William Thomas ... Chicago, IL
Huycke, Patrick G. ... Medford, OR
Huyett, Daniel B. ... Reading, PA
Huyett, Daniel H., 3rd ... Reading, PA
Huyett, Ellen Magnuson ... Birdsboro, PA
Huyett, Kanette L. ... Martinsburg, WV
Huyett, Scott L. ... Reading, PA
Huyett, Timothy J. ... Lincoln, IL
Huynh, Francette H. ... Milpitas, CA
Huynh, Hong N.
Department Of The Interior, Office of the Solicitor, GV
Huynh, Kelly My ... Santa Ana, CA
Huynh, My T. ... Los Angeles, CA
Huynh, Nathalie ... Reno, NV
Huynh, Tung ... Boston, MA
Huynh Nguyen, Ann ... Department of Justice, Executive Office for Immigration Review, GV
HuYoung, Michael ... Chesterfield, VA
Huysentruyt, Kurt D. ... San Francisco, CA
Huysman, Michel ... Miami, FL
Huzinec, Patrick A. ... Houston, TX
Huzior-Balzan, Regina T. ... Ozone Park, NY
Hval, Nina ... New York, NY
Hval, Steven B. ... Portland, OR
Hvalsoe, Lynn E. ... Mercer Island, WA
Hvalsoe, Susan Komori ... Olympia, WA
Hvass, Charles T. ... Minneapolis, MN
Hvass, Charles T., Jr. ... Minneapolis, MN
Hvass, Weisman & King, Chartered
Minneapolis, MN
Hveem, Michael William ... Greenwich, CT
Hvidsten, William E. ... Sacramento, CA
Hvistendahl, David J. ... Northfield, MN
Hvistendahl & Moersch, P.A.
Northfield, MN
Hvizdos, Cynthia E. ... Columbus, OH
Hvizdos, David P. ... McMurray, PA
Hvizdos, Emily C. ... Colorado Springs, CO
Hvizdos, John D. ... Columbus, OH
Hvolbøll, Eric P. ... Santa Barbara, CA
Hvolboll, Lionel K. ... San Bruno, CA
Hvozdovic, Bernard P., Jr.
North Brunswick, NJ
Hwa, Catherine L. ... Chicago, IL
Hwa, E. David ... Los Angeles, CA
Hwa, James ... New York, NY
Hwalek, Donna L. ... Tampa, FL
Hwang, Amy ... Montclair, NJ
Hwang, Andrew B. ... Monterey Park, CA
Hwang & Associates, P.C.
Haddonfield, NJ
Blue Bell, PA
Media, PA
Philadelphia, PA
Hwang, Audrey ... Seattle, WA
Hwang, Bonita B. ... Chicago, IL
Hwang, Catherine C. ... Los Angeles, CA
Hwang, Charles C. ... Washington, DC
Hwang, Chi-Yuan ... Flushing, NY
Hwang, Christina ... San Diego, CA
Hwang, Christine ... San Francisco, CA
Hwang, Daniel ... New York, NY
Hwang, David H. ... New York, NY
Hwang, Dennis J. ... Honolulu, HI
Hwang, Elizabeth K. ... Walnut Creek, CA
Hwang, Gordon ... New York, NY
Hwang, Hojoon ... San Francisco, CA
Hwang, Ivy ... New York, NY
Hwang, Jane J. ... Chicago, IL
Hwang, John C. ... Department of Commerce, Patent and Trademark Office, GV
Hwang, Joseph R. ... Alameda, CA
Hwang, Juri ... Stanford, CA
Hwang, Keith J. ... Washington, DC
Hwang, Kelley K. ... New York, NY
Hwang, Lee D. ... Los Angeles, CA
Hwang, Marian C. ... Baltimore, MD
Hwang, Phillip ... San Jose, CA
Hwang, Ray Lee ... Rockville, MD
Hwang, Robert C. ... Dallas, TX
Hwang, Robert C., P.C. ... Dallas, TX
Hwang, Roland ... Lansing, MI
Hwang, Sam Y. ... Philadelphia, PA
Hwang, Sharon A. ... Chicago, IL
Hwang, Shou Shan ... Floral Park, NY
Hwang, Soo Won ... New York, NY
Hwang, Steve Sonsik ... Houston, TX
Hwang, Su W. ... Palo Alto, CA
Hwang, Susie Lee ... Boston, MA
Hwang, Victor W. ... Los Angeles, CA
Hwang, William C. ... Roseland, NJ
Hwass, Edward R. ... Punta Gorda, FL
Hwu, Peter S. ... San Francisco, CA
Hwu, Roxana ... Palo Alto, CA
Hwung, Ping F. ... Redwood City, CA
Hyacinthe, Sylvere M. ... Mineola, NY
New York, NY
White Plains, NY
Hyams, Harold ... Tucson, AZ
Hyams, Harold, & Associates, P.C.
Tucson, AZ
Hyams, Jean K. ... San Francisco, CA
Hyams, Jerrold E. ... New York, NY
Hyams, Jonathan D. ... Detroit, MI
Hyams, Michael T. ... Newport Beach, CA
Hyams, Milton Mark ... San Rafael, CA
Hyams, Paul J. ... Latham, NY
Hyams, Robert S. ... Department of State, Foreign Service Officers (Overseas), GV
Hyams, Ross A. ... Princeton, NJ
Hyans, Hollis L. ... New York, NY
Hyat, Adrienne
Securities and Exchange Commission, Division of Enforcement, GV
Hyatt, Alan J. ... Annapolis, MD
Hyatt, Alfred Darrell ... Henderson, TX
Hyatt, Allen B. ... Minneapolis, MN
Hyatt, Amy J. ... San Francisco, CA
Hyatt, Andrea ... Philadelphia, PA
Hyatt, Andrea ... Dallas, TX
Hyatt, Armand M. ... Lawrence, MA
Hyatt, Arthur S. ... St. Louis, MO
Hyatt, C. Wayne ... Gallatin, TN
Hyatt, Catherine B.
General Services Administration, Board of Contract Appeals, GV
Hyatt, Chris Foote ... Anchorage, AK
Hyatt, Clifford C. ... Los Angeles, CA
Hyatt, Crabtree & Moore, P.C.
Dallas, TX
Hyatt, Daniel R ... La Junta, CO
Hyatt, Dennis M. ... Buffalo, NY
Rochester, NY
Hyatt, Donald L., II ... Metairie, LA
Hyatt, Donna K. ... Sacramento, CA
Hyatt, Elizabeth J. ... Denver, CO
Hyatt & Flynn ... Lawrence, MA
Salem, NH
Hyatt, Garry ... Huntingdon Valley, PA
Hyatt, Hudson ... Cleveland, OH
Hyatt & Hyatt ... Chapin, SC
Hyatt & Hyatt, P.C. ... Atlanta, GA
Decatur, GA
Hyatt, J. Marlene ... Waynesville, NC
Hyatt, J. Michael ... Santa Fe, NM
Hyatt, Jack I. ... Baltimore, MD
Hyatt, Jack N. ... Denver, CO
Hyatt, James A. ... Germantown, MD
Hyatt, James C. ... Chapin, SC
Hyatt, James V. ... Boston, MA
Hyatt, John ... Austin, TX
Hyatt, John E. ... Chicago, IL
Hyatt, John M. ... Decatur, GA
Hyatt, Judith A. ... Newton, MA
Hyatt, June Lorraine ... Des Moines, IA
Hyatt, Karla R. ... Nashville, TN
Hyatt, Kevin ... Sacramento, CA
Hyatt, Kristi Franklin ... Midland, TX
Hyatt, Mark N. ... St. Louis, MO
Hyatt, Marvin A., Jr. ... Rock Hill, SC
Hyatt, Meredith R., Jr. ... Santa Rosa, CA
Hyatt, Peters & Weber ... Annapolis, MD
Baltimore, MD
Hyatt, R. Grant ... Kingsport, TN
Hyatt, Randi Klein ... Baltimore, MD
Hyatt, Richard J. ... Seattle, WA
Hyatt, Richard V., Law Office of
Carlsbad, CA
Hyatt, Richard V., Law Office of
Vista, CA
Hyatt, Robert F., III ... Houston, TX
Hyatt, Robert S. ... Jefferson City, MO
Hyatt, Rodney N. ... Huntsville, AL
Hyatt, Ronald I. ... Vienna, VA
Hyatt, Ronald I., P.C. ... Vienna, VA
Hyatt & Rosenbaum, P.A. ... Indianapolis, IN
Hyatt, Sheila K. ... Denver, CO
Hyatt, Sherry V. ... New York, NY
Hyatt, Stephen J. ... Indianapolis, IN
Hyatt, Steven W. ... Miami, FL
Hyatt & Stubblefield, P.C. ... Atlanta, GA
Hyatt, Susan E. ... Fayetteville, NC
Hyatt, Susan M. ... Cleveland, OH
Hyatt, Terry P. ... Dallas, TX
Hyatt, Thomas K. ... Washington, DC
Hyatt, Thomas S. ... Bridgeton, MO
Hyatt, Todd A. ... Baltimore, MD
Hyatt, Townsend ... Portland, OR
Hyatt, W. Roland, Jr. ... Fair Oaks, CA
Hyatt, Wayne S. ... Atlanta, GA
Hyatt, Wilbur A. ... Lawrence, MA
Hyatt, William D. ... Cullowhee, NC
Hyatt, William H., Jr. ... Morristown, NJ
Hyatt, William S. ... San Francisco, CA
Hyatte, Diane ... Naperville, IL
Hyatte, Michael
Securities and Exchange Commission, Division of Corporation Finance, GV

Hyatte, Thomas P. .... Chicago, IL
Hybel, Paul A. .... **Chicago, IL**
Hyberg, Enid L. .... **Atlantic City, NJ**
Pleasantville, NJ
Hyberg, Lars S. .... **Northfield, NJ**
Hyberger, Reginald G. .... Cleveland, TN
Hybertsen, Paul S. .... Portland, OR
Hybertson, Brion L. .... **Minneapolis, MN**
Hybl, Laurie Martin .... **Chicago, IL**
Hybl, William J. .... Colorado Springs, CO
Hyche, J. Tod .... **Greenville, SC**
Hyche, Jeffery N. .... Tuscaloosa, AL
Hyche, Keith A. .... Newton, NJ
Hyche, Vicki J. .... Treasury Department,
Internal Revenue Service, GV
Hyche, Wilburn .... Brandon, MS
Hydak, Janis Wende .... Austin, TX
Hyde, A. Marie .... Charlottesville, VA
Hyde, Alan K. .... **Phoenix, AZ**
Hyde, Alan L. .... Cleveland, OH
Hyde, Alice J. .... Des Moines, IA
Hyde & Allred, LLP .... **Aberdeen, SD**
Hyde, Andrea .... **Garden City, NY**
Hyde, C. Edwin .... Murphy, NC
Hyde, Carol Ann .... **Albany, NY**
Hyde, Charles R., Jr. .... Richmond, IN
Hyde, Christopher W. .... Morristown, NJ
Hyde, Connie B. .... **Denver, CO**
Hyde, Cornelius J., III .... Baton Rouge, LA
Hyde, C. W. (Bill) .... Aberdeen, SD
Hyde, Cynthia J. .... Springfield, MO
Hyde, Dana J. .... **Washington, DC**
Hyde, Daniel A. .... **Houston, TX**
Hyde, Daniel V. .... **Los Angeles, CA**
Hyde, David A. .... Olney, IL
Hyde, David R. .... **New York, NY**
Hyde, David T., Jr. .... Evergreen, AL
Hyde, David W. .... Boise, ID
Hyde & Del Beccaro .... Walnut Creek, CA
Hyde, Dolores M. .... Fort Lauderdale, FL
Hyde, Douglas G. .... South Burlington, VT
Hyde, Frederick W., Jr. .... Seattle, WA
Hyde, Gary D., Jr.
United States Postal Service,
Postal Inspection Service, GV
Hyde, Gordon B. .... New Orleans, LA
Hyde, Gordon I. .... Henderson, NV
Hyde, Gregory D. .... **Birmingham, AL**
Hyde, Heather .... San Jose, CA
Hyde, Henry, III .... **Dayton, OH**
Hyde, Henry J. .... Chicago, IL
Hyde, Herbert K., Jr. .... Oklahoma City, OK
Hyde, Herbert L. .... Asheville, NC
Hyde, Herbert L., P.A. .... Asheville, NC
Hyde, Hoover & Lindsay .... Murphy, NC
Hyde, Howard L. .... **Washington, DC**
Hyde, James C. .... **San Jose, CA**
Hyde, James C. .... **Andover, MA**
Hyde, James Dudley .... **Oklahoma City, OK**
Hyde, James W., IV .... **Utica, NY**
Hyde, Jeffrey L. .... **Stamford, CT**
Hyde, Jerry D. .... Mayville, NY
Hyde, Jill Rosen .... Needham, MA
Hyde, Joe T. .... **Dallas, TX**
Hyde, John A. .... Hammond, IN
Hyde, John F. .... Rehoboth Beach, DE
Hyde, John G. .... Midland, TX
Hyde, John Keith .... **Beaumont, TX**
Hyde, John R. .... Hartford, CT
Hyde, Jon A. .... San Antonio, TX
Hyde, Kent .... **Aberdeen, SD**
Hyde, Kent O. .... **Springfield, MO**
Hyde, Kevin E. .... **Jacksonville, FL**
Tallahassee, FL
Tampa, FL
West Palm Beach, FL
Hyde, Laurance M., Jr. .... Reno, NV
Hyde, Laurel L. .... **Irvine, CA**
Hyde, Laurel Lee .... **San Diego, CA**
Hyde Law Corporation, The
San Francisco, CA
Hyde, Lawrence E. .... Dover, MA
Hyde, Lisa .... Dallas, TX
Hyde, Maclay R. .... **Minneapolis, MN**
Hyde, Martha L. .... Denver, CO
Hyde, Michael Q. .... **Washington, DC**
Hyde, Michael T. .... **Westwood, KS**
Hyde, Miller, Owen & Trost, A Professional Corporation .... **Sacramento, CA**
Hyde, Myra B. .... Washington, DC
Hyde, Nathan R., Law Office Of .... Sandy, UT
Hyde, Noel S. .... **Salt Lake City, UT**
Hyde, Patrick A. .... Silver Spring, MD
Hyde, Patrick C., (P.C.) .... Denver, CO
Hyde, Patrick M., (P.C.) .... Walnut Creek, CA
Hyde, Peter W. .... **Kansas City, MO**
Hyde, Reginald D.
Department of State, GV
Hyde, Richard A. .... Hoffman Estates, IL
Hyde, Richard A. .... Hamilton, OH
Hyde, Richard H. .... **Sacramento, CA**
Hyde, Robbie Alexander .... Opelika, AL
Hyde, Robert A. .... **Somerville, NJ**
Hyde, Robert C. .... **Salt Lake City, UT**
Hyde, Robert D. .... **Memphis, TN**
Hyde, Robert E. .... **Knoxville, TN**
Hyde, Robert R. .... Oriental, NC
Hyde, Robert T., Jr. .... **Jacksonville, FL**
Hyde, Robert W., Jr.
Whitehouse Station, NJ
Hyde, Roger Q. .... Sterling Heights, MI
Hyde, Roger Q., P.C. .... Sterling Heights, MI
Hyde, Sally M. .... Edmonds, WA
Hyde, Schoen, Miller & Stewart, A Professional Law Corporation .... Baton Rouge, LA
Hyde, Sheila Meck .... Silver Creek, NY
Hyde, Sheral A. .... **Mission Viejo, CA**
Hyde, Stacy D. .... **New Orleans, LA**
Hyde, Stephen J. .... Aberdeen, WA
Hyde, Terrill A. .... **Washington, DC**
Hyde, Thomas F. .... **San Francisco, CA**
Hyde, Thomas Newcomb .... Tampa, FL
Hyde, Thomas R. .... **Buffalo, NY**
Hyde, Tracey J. .... **Panama City, FL**
Hyde, Tracy T. .... **Raleigh, NC**
Hyde, Tristram T., IV .... Heathsville, VA
Hyde, Troy K. .... Potosi, MO
Hyde, Vernon D. .... **Oklahoma City, OK**
Hyde, W. Brent .... **Raleigh, NC**
Hyde, W. Thomas .... Skowhegan, ME
Hyde and Waters .... San Diego, CA
Hyde, Wendy J. .... Minneapolis, MN
Hyde, Wetherell, Bray, Haff & French, A Professional Company .... Boise, ID
Hyde, William A. .... St. Louis, MO
Hyde, William H. .... Albuquerque, NM
Hyde, William L. .... **Tallahassee, FL**
Hyde, William Pitt .... Upland, CA
Hyde, William R. .... Penrose, CO
Hyde, William R. .... Salt Lake City, UT
Hyde, William S. .... Arlington, VA
Hyde, Wm. H. .... Baltimore, MD
Hyde-DeLattre, Kelly .... **Orlando, FL**
Hydeman, Lee M. .... Washington, DC
Hyden, Cary K. .... **Costa Mesa, CA**
Hyden, James W. .... **Little Rock, AR**
Pine Bluff, AR
Hyden, Joe Bailey .... **Dallas, TX**
Hyden, Larry G. .... **Corpus Christi, TX**
Hyden, Miron & Foster, PLLC
Conway, AR
Hot Springs National Park, AR
Hot Springs Village, AR
Little Rock, AR
Pine Bluff, AR
Hyden, Timothy M. .... San Ramon, CA
Hyder, Charles F. .... Phoenix, AZ
Hyder, Elton M., III .... Fort Worth, TX
Hyder, Elton M., Jr. .... Fort Worth, TX
Hyder, Fred J. .... Phoenix, AZ
Hyder, Gregg T. .... Columbia, MO
Hyder, Henry K., III .... Methuen, MA
Hyder & Hyder .... Fort Worth, TX
Hyder, Jack W., Jr. .... **Bristol, TN**
Hyder, James D., Jr. .... **Augusta, GA**
Hyder, James D., Jr., P.C. .... **Augusta, GA**
Hyder, Jeanne M. .... Augusta, GA
Hyder, Mark .... South Lancaster, MA
Hyder, Oris D. .... Johnson City, TN
Hyder, Scott W. .... **Phoenix, AZ**
Hyder, Stephen Talbert .... **Knoxville, TN**
Hyder, Syed I. .... Richmond, VA
Hyder, Wade F. .... Santa Rosa, CA
Hyder, William F. .... Phoenix, AZ
Hyderally, Ty .... **Roseland, NJ**
Hydes, David B., P.C. .... Canyon City, OR
Hydinger, David J. .... Los Angeles, CA
Hydrick, A. J., Jr. .... Orangeburg, SC
Hydrick, Augustus S. .... Richmond, VA
Hydrick, Augustus S., Jr. .... Richmond, VA
Hydrick, Jeffrey S. .... **Washington, DC**
Hydrick, John H., Jr. .... West Columbia, SC
Hydrick Law Offices .... Richmond, VA
Hydrusko, Michelle S. .... **Newark, NJ**
Hyduk, Mary Elizabeth .... Phoenix, AZ
Hyer, Andrea McDermott .... New York, NY
Hyer, Charles H. .... Kansas City, MO
Hyer, J. Walter, III .... Redmond, WA
Hyer, Kathryn Burrer .... Chicago, IL
Hyer, Leigh A. .... **Washington, DC**
Hyer, Michael H. .... San Ramon, CA
Hyer, Paul F. .... Los Angeles, CA
Hyer, Suzanne E. .... New York, NY
Hyer, Wm. H. .... San Bernardino, CA
Hyer-Huntington, Mary .... Las Vegas, NV
Hyers, Courtney George .... **Richmond, VA**
Hyers, Kemper K. .... **Richmond, VA**
Hyett, Michael A. .... **Atlantic City, NJ**
Hyink, Benjamin P. .... **Chicago, IL**
Hyink & Scannicchio, Chtd. .... **Chicago, IL**
Hyjek, Mark A. .... **Fairfield, CA**
Fair Oaks, CA
Napa, CA
Hykan, Robert A. .... **Denver, CO**
Hykan, Wayne H. .... **Denver, CO**
Hykel, John J. .... Philadelphia, PA
Hykel, Judith R. .... Philadelphia, PA
Hykel, Rose M. .... King Of Prussia, PA
Hykes, John E. .... Columbus, OH
Hylan, Bernard W. .... New York, NY
Hyland, Anita M. .... **New York, NY**
Hyland, Anne-Marie M. .... **Boston, MA**
Hyland, Carmen C. .... Alexandria, VA
Hyland, Carol A. .... Chicago, IL
Hyland, Charles J. .... Laguna Beach, CA
Hyland, Charles J. .... **Kansas City, MO**
Hyland, Christine M. .... Carmel, CA
Hyland, Clement L. .... **Orlando, FL**
Hyland, D. Christopher .... Greenville, NC
Hyland, David F. .... **Murray Hill, NJ**
Hyland, Edward David .... Brooklyn, NY
Hyland, G. Arthur, Jr. .... **Hyannis, MA**
Hyland, H. N. .... Washington, KS
Hyland and Hyland Co., L.P.A.
Cleveland, OH
Hyland and Hyland, P.A. .... Washington, KS
Hyland, J. Patrick .... Washington, KS
Hyland, James F. .... East Brunswick, NJ
Hyland, James J. .... Lafayette, CA
Hyland, James M. .... **New Haven, CT**
Hyland, Jerry E. .... **Indianapolis, IN**
Hyland, John .... San Francisco, CA
Hyland, John A. .... New York, NY
Hyland, John D. .... Madison, WI
Hyland, John F. .... **San Francisco, CA**
Hyland, John F., Jr. .... Department of Justice,
Criminal Division, GV
Hyland, John J. .... **New York, NY**
Hyland, John J., IV .... **Fontana, CA**
Hyland, John J., IV .... **San Bernardino, CA**
Hyland, John Patrick .... Neptune, NJ
Hyland, John T. .... Denver, CO
Hyland, John T., P.C. .... Denver, CO
Hyland, Kenneth C. .... Rochester, NY
Hyland, Kevin Thomas .... **New York, NY**
Hyland Law Firm, The, P.C. .... Houston, TX
Hyland, Leo J. .... Cleveland, OH
Hyland, Mariann .... Salem, OR
Hyland, Mark J. .... **New York, NY**
Hyland, Mark K. .... **San Francisco, CA**
Hyland, Marti Nell .... **Washington, DC**
Hyland, Patricia A. .... Princeton, NJ
Hyland, Richard .... Camden, NJ
Hyland, Richard S. .... **Cherry Hill, NJ**
Hyland, Richard W. .... Lafayette, CA
Hyland, Robert E. .... Farmington, CT
Hyland, Robert G. .... Cincinnati, OH
Hyland, Stephen J. .... Houston, TX
Hyland, Thomas P. .... Des Moines, IA
Hyland, Thomas W. .... **New York, NY**
Hyland, Timothy B. .... **Fairfax, VA**
Hyland, Timothy R. .... **Phoenix, AZ**
Hyland, William .... New York, NY
Hyland, William F. .... **Morristown, NJ**
Trenton, NJ
Hyland, William F., Jr. .... **Moorestown, NJ**
Hyland, William G., Jr. .... Palm Harbor, FL
Hyland, William H., Jr. .... Washington, DC
Hyland, William J., Jr.
Palm Beach Gardens, FL
Hyldburg, Carl A. .... Asheville, NC
Hylden, Eric L. D. .... **Duluth, MN**
Hylden, Thomas .... **Washington, DC**
Hyle, Francis M. .... Cincinnati, OH
Hyle, Joann .... **Philadelphia, PA**
Hyle, John S. .... **Ocean City, MD**
Hyle, John S., P.C. .... **Ocean City, MD**
Snow Hill, MD
Hyle & Mecklenborg, Co., L.P.A.
Cincinnati, OH
Hylemon, Jennifer A. .... **Cambridge, MA**
Hylen, William K. .... Phoenix, AZ
Hyler, George B., Jr. .... Asheville, NC
Hyler & Lopez, P.A. .... Asheville, NC
Hyles, Stephen .... Columbus, GA
Hylind, Kenneth G. .... Bethesda, MD
Hylla, David A. .... East Alton, IL
Hylton, Alison Wells .... **Hazard, KY**
Hylton, Daniel N.
Department of Agriculture,
Office of the General Counsel, GV
Hylton, Deborah J.
Research Triangle Park, NC
Hylton, Eric Michael .... Indianapolis, IN
Hylton, G. Hartwell .... **New York, NY**
Hylton & Gonzales .... **Baltimore, MD**
Hylton & Hylton, P.C. .... Detroit, MI
Hylton, Kenneth N., Jr. .... Detroit, MI
Hylton, Kenneth N., Sr. .... Detroit, MI
Hylton, Maria O'Brien .... Chicago, IL
Hylton, Michelle L. .... **Washington, DC**
Hylton, Myles T. .... **Roanoke, VA**
Hylton, Patrick C. .... Washington, DC
Hylton, R. Stacy .... Marietta, GA
Hylton, Walter H., III
Department of the Army,
Office, Chief of Engineers/Headquarters,
U.S. Army Corps of Engineers, GV
Hylton, William A., Jr. .... **Baltimore, MD**
Hylton, William W., III .... Little Rock, AR
Hyman, Abby Linett .... San Bernardino, CA
Hyman, Alan B. .... **New York, NY**
Hyman, Allen .... Studio City, CA
Hyman, Amy .... Tamarac, FL
Hyman, Andrew .... Louisville, KY
Hyman, Andrew D.
Department Of Health And Human Services,
GV
Hyman, Andrew M. .... Port Washington, NY
Hyman, Andrew S. .... **Washington, DC**
Hyman, Andrew W. .... **Encino, CA**
Hyman, Andrew W. .... **Los Angeles, CA**
Hyman, Barry S. .... **Chicago, IL**
Hyman, Bernard .... **East Meadow, NY**
Hyman, Betty .... Miami, FL
Hyman, Bruce E.
Department Of Veterans Affairs,
Board of Veterans Appeals, GV
Hyman, Bruce W. .... **San Francisco, CA**
Hyman, Cantor & Klau, P.C. .... Hartford, CT
Hyman, Carolyn C. .... **Gadsden, AL**
Hyman & Carter .... **Knoxville, TN**
Powell, TN
Hyman, Charles .... Maplewood, NJ
New York, NY
Hyman, Charles M. .... Elyria, OH
Hyman, Cynthia J. .... Denver, CO
Hyman, Cyril .... Brooklyn, NY
Hyman, D. Jay .... Gaithersburg, MD
Hyman, Daniel D. .... Howell, NJ
Hyman, David .... **Washington, DC**
Hyman, David A. .... San Francisco, CA
Hyman, David A. .... Oakwood, OH
Paulding, OH
Hyman, David J. .... **Tulsa, OK**
Hyman, David L. .... **Montclair, NJ**
Hyman, David M. .... **Newark, NJ**
Hyman, David M. .... **Burlington, VT**
Hyman, Donna J. .... **New York, NY**
Hyman, Douglas A. .... **Birmingham, MI**
Hyman, Douglas W. .... **Chicago, IL**
Hyman, E. Marc .... **New York, NY**
Hyman, Earl M. .... **Torrance, CA**
Hyman, Elaine K. .... Montclair, NJ
Hyman, Elizabeth A. .... **Washington, DC**
Hyman, Engel, Wiener & Bergstein
Allentown, PA
Hyman, Eric S. .... **Los Angeles, CA**
Hyman, Eugene M. .... San Jose, CA
Hyman, Franklin C. .... Garden City, NY
Hyman, Franklin C., P.C. .... Garden City, NY
Hyman, Frederick D. .... **New York, NY**
Hyman, Gary M. .... **Baltimore, MD**
Hyman, Gerald F.
Agency for International Development, GV
Hyman & Gilbert .... **Larchmont, NY**
Hyman, Harvey A. .... **San Francisco, CA**
Hyman, Harvey E. .... Paulding, OH
Hyman, Harvey S. .... Miami, FL
Hyman, Herbert G. .... New Haven, CT
Hyman, Howard M. .... Cherry Hill, NJ
Elkins Park, PA
Philadelphia, PA
Hyman & Hyman .... Paulding, OH
Hyman, J. Leonard .... **Birmingham, MI**
Hyman, Jacob D. .... Buffalo, NY
Hyman, James F. .... Newport, RI
Hyman, Jeffrey A. .... **Denver, CO**
Hyman, Jeffrey A. .... **Detroit, MI**
Hyman, Jeffrey M. .... **North Brunswick, NJ**
Hyman, Jeffrey N. .... **Emeryville, CA**
Hyman, Jeffrey S. .... New York, NY
Hyman, Jerome E. .... **New York, NY**
Hyman, Jerry A. .... Hockessin, DE
Hyman, Jonathan S. .... **Fort Worth, TX**
Hyman, Jonathan T. .... **Cleveland, OH**
Hyman, Joseph D. .... Great Neck, NY
Hyman, Joshua S. .... Chicago, IL
Hyman & Kaplan, P.A.
Fort Lauderdale, FL
Miami, FL
Hyman, Laurence J. .... **San Francisco, CA**
Hyman Law Firm .... Baton Rouge, LA
Hyman Law Firm, The .... **Conway, SC**
Florence, SC
Hyman, Lawrence H. .... Chicago, IL
Hyman, Leslie S. .... **San Antonio, TX**
Hyman, Lester S. .... **Washington, DC**
Hyman Lippitt, P.C. .... **Birmingham, MI**
Detroit, MI
Hyman, Lisa J. .... **White Plains, NY**
Hyman, Lori C. .... Department of Justice,
Civil Division, GV
Hyman, M. Allan .... **East Meadow, NY**
Hyman, Marshal E. .... Birmingham, MI
Hyman, Marshal E., & Associates, P.C.
Birmingham, MI
Hyman, Martin S. .... **New York, NY**
Hyman, Marvin J. .... **New York, NY**
Hyman, Merle D. .... Boston, MA
Hyman, Michael B. .... **Chicago, IL**
Hyman, Michael I. .... New York, NY
Hyman, Michael Joseph .... Aurora, CO
Hyman, Michael L. .... **Miami, FL**
Hyman, Michael L. .... Baton Rouge, LA
Hyman, Midge M. .... **New York, NY**
Hyman, Milton B., (P.C.)
Los Angeles, CA
Hyman, Miriam O. .... **New York, NY**
Hyman, Mitchel S. .... Treasury Department,
Internal Revenue Service, GV
Hyman, Morris .... Fremont, CA
Hyman, Morris H. .... New Orleans, LA
Hyman, Morton P. .... New York, NY
Hyman, Morton P., Law Offices of
New York, NY
Hyman, M. R., Jr. .... Charleston, SC
Hyman, Myron A. .... New York, NY
Hyman, Natasha Lynn .... **Los Angeles, CA**
Hyman, Neal K. .... Reno, NV
Hyman, Norman .... **Detroit, MI**
Hyman, Paul B. .... **New York, NY**
Hyman, Paul G., Jr. .... Fort Lauderdale, FL
Hyman, Paul M. .... **Washington, DC**
Hyman, Phelps & McNamara, P.C.
Irvine, CA
Washington, DC
Hyman, Randy E. .... Atlanta, GA
Hyman, Robert A. .... Pleasantville, NY
Hyman, Robert A., P.C. .... Pleasantville, NY
Hyman, Robert E. .... **Richmond, VA**
Hyman, Robert G. .... Stafford, VA
Hyman, Robert M. .... Baltimore, MD
Hyman, Roger D. .... **Knoxville, TN**
Hyman, Ronald .... Highland Park, NJ
Hyman, Scott Ari .... Northampton, MA
New York, NY
Hyman, Scott J. .... **Irvine, CA**
San Francisco, CA
Hyman, Shari Corinne .... New York, NY
Hyman, Sharon .... New York, NY
Hyman, Sherry Lefkowitz .... Jupiter, FL
Hyman, Stanley .... **West Palm Beach, FL**
Hyman, Stanley M. .... Bronx, NY
Hyman, Steven A. .... Philadelphia, PA
Hyman, Steven J. .... Orange Park, FL
Hyman, Steven J. .... **New York, NY**
Hyman, Stuart I. .... **Orlando, FL**
Hyman, Stuart I., P.A. .... **Orlando, FL**
Hyman, Sue-Helen .... Tampa, FL
Hyman, Susan D. .... **San Francisco, CA**
Hyman, Sydney .... Fort Lee, NJ
Hyman, Terry S. .... Harrisburg, PA
Hyman, Thomas B., Jr. .... **Atlanta, GA**
Hyman, Thomas H. .... Cordele, GA
Hyman, Thomas S. .... New Haven, CT
Hyman, Toby H. .... Miami, FL
Hyman, Toby R. .... United States Senate,
Office of Senate Chief Counsel for
Employment, GV
Hyman, Todd .... **New York, NY**

Icenogle, Norton & Seter, A Professional Corporation .... **Greenwood Village, CO**
Icenogle, Richard .... **Wailuku, HI**
Icenogle, T. Edward
Greenwood Village, CO
Icenogle, W. James .... Camdenton, MO
Icenogle, William .... Camdenton, MO
Ichel, Albert L. .... Edison, NJ
Ichel, Albert L., P.A. .... Edison, NJ
Ichel, David W. .... **New York, NY**
Ichel, Gregory A. .... Morristown, NJ
Ichida, Wesley W. .... **Honolulu, HI**
Ichiho, Akemi .... Los Angeles, CA
Ichikawa, Dennis P. .... Seattle, WA
Ichikawa, Garry T. .... Fairfield, CA
Ichikawa, Robert K., (Atty. At Law, A Law Corp.) .... **Honolulu, HI**
Ichinaga, Daniel J. .... **Seattle, WA**
Ichinaga, Jon Morris .... Los Angeles, CA
Ichinose, Susan M. .... **Honolulu, HI**
Ichiye, Keiko .... **Dallas, TX**
Ichniowski, Stephen P.
Equal Employment Opportunity Commission,
Office of Federal Operations, GV
Ichter, Cary .... **Atlanta, GA**
Icken, Laura L. .... **Washington, DC**
Ickes, Comfrey Scott .... Monroeville, PA
Ickes, Harold .... **Washington, DC**
Mineola, NY
Ickes, L. Scott .... Fremont, OH
Ickes, Patrick J. .... **Omaha, NE**
Ickes, R. Dennis .... **Salt Lake City, UT**
Ickes, R. Dennis, Professional Corporation
Salt Lake City, UT
Icklan, James R. .... Toms River, NJ
Icklan, Joan F. .... Roseland, NJ
Ickler, Kory J. .... **New Orleans, LA**
Ickler, Nancy L. .... **South Bend, IN**
Ickowicz, Terry A. .... Los Angeles, CA
Ickowitz, Allan H. .... **Los Angeles, CA**
Icobelli, Raymond G. .... Tappan, NY
Icove, Edward A. .... Cleveland, OH
Icove, Keith S. .... White Plains, NY
Icove, Meryl S.
Federal Communications Commission,
Cable Services Bureau, GV
Icsman, Donald C. .... Sandusky, OH
Icsman, Robert D. .... Akron, OH
Iczkovitz, Leslie K. .... Richardson, TX
Idalski, Annette A. .... **Atlanta, GA**
Idar, Edward, Jr. .... San Antonio, TX
Iddings, Jeffrey S. .... **Greensboro, NC**
Iddins, Ron S. .... Columbus, GA
Ide, Carol Koehler .... Department of Justice,
Tax Division, GV
Ide, Clark F. .... **Fountain Valley, CA**
Ide, Haigney & Rado, LLP .... New York, NY
Ide, Henry C. .... **Avon, CT**
Ide, J. Christopher .... Alexandria, VA
Ide, Matthew James .... **Seattle, WA**
Ide, Nathan D. .... **Visalia, CA**
Ide, R. William .... **St. Louis, MO**
Ide, Robert A. .... Holdrege, NE
Ide, Vivien Cienfuegos .... Glendale, CA
Idehen, Francis .... **New York, NY**
Idelberg, Mark A. .... Englewood, CO
Idelchik, Inna .... **New York, NY**
Idell, Berman & Seitel, A Law Association
San Francisco, CA
Idell, Edward .... **Los Angeles, CA**
Idell, John T. .... **Plymouth Meeting, PA**
Idell, Richard J. .... **San Francisco, CA**
Idelson, Janine H. .... Boston, MA
Idelson, Sarah E. .... **Boston, MA**
Idema & Keyser, P.C. .... **Grand Rapids, MI**
Idema, Philip M. .... **Grand Rapids, MI**
Ideman, James M. .... Los Angeles, CA
Iden, Alexander R. .... Winchester, VA
Iden, Bruce F. .... **Miami, FL**
Iden, Charles R. .... **Akron, OH**
Iden, Mika M. .... Carlsbad, CA
Iden, Mitchell S. .... **New York, NY**
Iden, Randall E. .... Philadelphia, PA
Iden, Stephen Douglas .... Ottawa, IL
Ideus, Darla S. .... **Lincoln, NE**
Idiart, Michael G. .... Fresno, CA
Iding, Allan E. .... **Milwaukee, WI**
Idinopulos, Lea Spector .... Columbus, OH
Idleman, Doralee .... **Little Rock, AR**
Idol, David H. .... **High Point, NC**
Idol, Robert A. .... **Durham, NC**
Idol, Walter S. .... Irving, TX
Idouchi, John K. .... New York, NY
Idrissi, Rima N. .... Larchmont, NY
Idzik, Daniel R. .... New York, NY
Idzik, Martin F. .... **Fredonia, NY**
Jamestown, NY
Ieleja, Linda T. .... **Chicago, IL**
Iemma, Anthony J. .... Elkhart, IN
Iemma and Hughes .... Elkhart, IN
Iennaco, Francis V. .... **Orlando, FL**
Ieraci, Vincent .... **Mineola, NY**
Ierardi, Ernest J. .... **Washington, DC**
Rochester, NY
Ierardi, Joan P. .... Far Rockaway, NY
Ierardi, Pasquale R. .... Haddam, CT
Ierulli, Frank M. .... Eugene, OR
Iervolino, Frank G. .... Belle Mead, NJ
Ieyoub, Christopher P. .... **Lake Charles, LA**
Ieyoub, Richard P. .... Lake Charles, LA
Iezman, Stanley Leonard .... Glendale, CA
Iezza, Nick I. .... Westlake Village, CA
Iezza, Sylvia L. .... San Fernando, CA
Iezzi, Jacinta M. .... Melbourne, FL
Iezzi, Patsy A., Jr. .... Greensburg, PA
Iezzi, Patsy A., Jr., P.C. .... Greensburg, PA
Ifcher, Joel B. .... New York, NY

Ifeduba, Stephen E. .... **Columbus, OH**
Ifert, J. Richard .... Punxsutawney, PA
Ifft, Kristin L. .... **Pittsburgh, PA**
Ifft, Richard A. .... **Washington, DC**
Ifill, Michelle C. .... Rye Brook, NY
Ifill, Sherrilyn A. .... Baltimore, MD
Ifrah, A. Jeff .... **Washington, DC**
Ifshin & Friedman, P.L.L.C.
Washington, DC
Igarashi, John Y. .... **Irvine, CA**
Igasaki, Paul M. .... Chicago, IL
Igdaloff, David A. .... Boca Raton, FL
Ige, Douglas H. .... Wailuku, HI
Ige, Gary S. .... Honolulu, HI
Igel, Marlene J. .... **Chicago, IL**
Igel, Peter A. .... **Cleveland, OH**
Igel, Rachel A. .... **Minneapolis, MN**
Igelmund, Joseph R. .... San Francisco, CA
Iger, Denise .... Newport Beach, CA
Iger, Linda B. .... **Pleasantville, NY**
Iger, Robert S. .... **Irvine, CA**
Iggens, Sharon K. .... Menomonee Falls, WI
Ighani, Nosratollah .... Silver Spring, MD
Igielski, Christopher T. .... Federal Way, WA
Igl, Gerald H. .... Seattle, WA
Iglar, Richard F. .... Morristown, NJ
Iglecias, Alex .... Santa Monica, CA
Iglehart, Francis N., Jr. .... Towson, MD
Iglehart, Richard B. .... Sacramento, CA
Igleheart, Harford W. .... Charleston, SC
Igleheart, Harford W. Attorney At Law, L.L.C.
Charleston, SC
Igleheart, Ted L. .... Shelbyville, KY
Igler, A. George .... **Tallahassee, FL**
Winter Park, FL
Igler & Dougherty, P.A. .... **Orlando, FL**
Tallahassee, FL
Tampa, FL
Winter Park, FL
Iglesia, Jose R. .... Miami, FL
Iglesias, Alvaro J. .... Houston, TX
Iglesias, Alvaro L. .... North Bergen, NJ
Iglesias, Danilo J. .... **Fort Lauderdale, FL**
Iglesias, Gisela .... **Honolulu, HI**
Iglesias, Joanna Elisa .... **Miami, FL**
Iglesias, Lisa G. .... Fort Lauderdale, FL
Iglesias, Mario A. .... **Miami, FL**
Iglesias, Michael A. .... Reno, NV
Iglesias, Michael A., Chtd., A Professional Corporation .... Reno, NV
Iglesias, Raymond, III .... **New York, NY**
Iglesias, Silvia .... **Tampa, FL**
Igliozzi, David V. .... Cranston, RI
Iglitzin, Dmitri .... **Seattle, WA**
Iglow & Bachrach .... Los Angeles, CA
Iglow, Lawrence I. .... Los Angeles, CA
Iglow, Robert A. .... Los Angeles, CA
Ignacio, Benjamin R.C. .... **Honolulu, HI**
Ignacio, David G., Jr. .... Woodside, NY
Ignagni, Elizabeth Ann
Farmington Hills, MI
Ignal, Howard Evan .... **Bridgeport, CT**
Ignall, David J.
Securities and Exchange Commission,
Division of Enforcement, GV
Ignasher, Ann-Marie L. .... Smithfield, RI
Ignatin, Gary R. .... Culver City, CA
Ignatius, Amy L. .... Concord, NH
Ignatius, Linda M. .... Santa Ana, CA
Ignatoff, Mitchell E. .... **Elizabeth, NJ**
Ignatoff, Mitchell E. .... **Middlesex, NJ**
Ignatoff, Mitchell E. .... **New Brunswick, NJ**
Somerville, NJ
Ignatowski, Gary James .... **Baltimore, MD**
Ignatowski, James R. .... **Southfield, MI**
Ignatowski, John J. .... **Southfield, MI**
Ignatuck, William M., Jr. .... Tampa, FL
Ignatuk, J. Ronald .... **Newport Beach, CA**
Ignatz-Hoover, Gail, Co., L.P.A. .... Elyria, OH
Ignatz-Hoover, Gail M. .... Elyria, OH
Ignell, David E. .... Cardiff-By-The-Sea, CA
Ignelzi, Philip A. .... **Pittsburgh, PA**
Ignozzi, Kenneth J. .... **Dayton, OH**
Igo, C. Merle .... Columbus, OH
Igo, Louis D .... Huntington Beach, CA
Igo, Richard B. .... Columbus, OH
Igoa, Joseph A. .... Fresno, CA
Igoe, Alison Marie .... Department of Justice,
Civil Division, GV
Igoe, Daniel J. .... Columbus, OH
Igoe, James J. .... San Francisco, CA
Igoe, John G. .... **Palm Beach, FL**
Igoe, Jonathan W. .... **St. Louis, MO**
Igoe, Michael H. .... **Columbus, OH**
Igoe, Michael L., Jr. .... **Chicago, IL**
Igoe, Patricia J. .... **Providence, RI**
Igoe, Patrick Joseph .... Gaithersburg, MD
Igoe, Paul G. .... Newton, MA
Igoe, Sheila M.
Environmental Protection Agency,
Office of the General Counsel, GV
Igoe, Tammy W. .... Charlotte, NC
Igoe, Thomas J., Jr. .... **New York, NY**
Igoe, Vincent F., Jr. .... **Liberty, MO**
Igou, A. Richard .... Fort Payne, AL
Igou, Jeffrey M. .... **St. Louis, MO**
Igou, Richard James .... Chapel Hill, NC
Igou & Smith .... **Orlando, FL**
Igou, Steven Wood .... **Orlando, FL**
Iguchi, Paul M. .... **Honolulu, HI**
Iguina & Polish .... San Juan, PR
Iguina de la Rosa, José A. .... Ponce, PR
Iguina Oharriz, Carlos R. .... San Juan, PR
Ihara, Craig I. .... Reno, NV
Ihde, Regan P. .... Buffalo, NY
Ihfe & Associates, P.C. .... San Antonio, TX
Ihfe, Richard H. .... San Antonio, TX
Ihlan, Amy J. .... **Minneapolis, MN**

Ihle, Ronald M. .... **Dallas, TX**
Ihle, Tim E. .... Riverwoods, IL
Ihlenfeld & Ihlenfeld .... Wheeling, WV
Ihlenfeld, William J. .... Wheeling, WV
Ihlenfeldt, Dale E. .... Milwaukee, WI
Ihlo, Jennifer E. .... Department of Justice,
Tax Division, GV
Ihm, Stephen L. .... **Northbrook, IL**
Ihnat, Patricia A. .... Phoenix, AZ
Ihne, Robert W. .... **Livingston, NJ**
Ihne, Ruth A. .... **New York, NY**
Ihnen, Jeffrey L. .... **Washington, DC**
Ihnot, James R., P.S. .... Kirkland, WA
Ihns, Darrell F. .... Phoenix, AZ
Ihrie, Robert D. .... **St. Clair Shores, MI**
Ihrie, Scarfone & O'Brien
St. Clair Shores, MI
Ihrig, Frederick G. .... Englewood, CO
Ihrig, Jonathan C., & Associates
Blackwell, OK
Ihrig, Mark Andrew .... Bristow, OK
Ihrig, Mark E. .... Burlington, KY
Ihrig, Richard M. .... **Minneapolis, MN**
Ihrig, Scott N. .... **Minneapolis, MN**
Ihrig, Stephen D. .... Lansing, MI
Ihrig, William Kent .... **Tampa, FL**
Ihringer, Dunkerly & Yoseph
Vancouver, WA
Ihringer, Gayle A. .... Vancouver, WA
Ihrke, James H. .... **Chicago, IL**
Ihrke, Robert C., (A Professional Corporation) .... **Irvine, CA**
Ihrke, William Heath .... **Costa Mesa, CA**
Ii, Jeffrey R. .... **Palo Alto, CA**
Iiams, Jill Allison .... Kansas City, MO
Iiams, Sarah E. .... Lake Charles, LA
New Orleans, LA
Iida, Geoffrey Y. .... **Newport Beach, CA**
Iida, Kristine E. .... Chicago, IL
Iijima, Ann L. .... Minneapolis, MN
Iijima, Chris K. .... Springfield, MA
Iino, John Masao .... **Los Angeles, CA**
New York, NY
Iizuka, Maria A. .... Sacramento, CA
Ijams, Michael B. .... **Modesto, CA**
Ikard, Frank N., Jr. .... **Austin, TX**
Ikard & Golden, P.C. .... **Austin, TX**
Ikard, James A. .... Oklahoma City, OK
Ikard, Robert W. .... Las Cruces, NM
Ikard, William F. .... **Austin, TX**
Ikari, Carolyn A. .... Hartford, CT
Ikari, Ken .... **Los Angeles, CA**
Ikari, Sharra Lee .... **Denver, CO**
Ikazaki, Herbert T. .... Honolulu, HI
Ikbal, Farruk .... Arden, NC
Ikeda, Cynthia Y. .... **New York, NY**
Ikeda, Dale .... **Fresno, CA**
Ikeda, Gary L. .... Seattle, WA
Ikeda, George A. .... **New York, NY**
Ikeda, Roy H. .... **San Francisco, CA**
Ikeda, Tatsuya .... **Montville, NJ**
Ikeda, Thomas M. .... Seattle, WA
Ikeda, Walter H. .... Honolulu, HI
Ikeda, Wesley H. .... **Honolulu, HI**
Ikefugi, Bruce A. .... Buffalo, NY
Ikegami, Cheryl A. .... **Phoenix, AZ**
Ikegawa, Jima .... Yorba Linda, CA
Ikehara, Archie T. .... **Honolulu, HI**
Ikehara, Patrick .... **Pasadena, CA**
Ikei, Clayton C. .... Honolulu, HI
Ikei, Clayton C., A Law Corporation
Honolulu, HI
Ikejiri, Kris H. .... Arlington, VA
Ikejiri, Ronald Kunio .... Burke, VA
Ikeler, Kim E. .... **Denver, CO**
Ikelman, Douglas C. .... Atlanta, GA
Ikemire, Elizabeth A., Law Office of
Sacramento, CA
Ikenaga, Rogers M. .... Honolulu, HI
Ikenberry, D. Kevin .... **Tulsa, OK**
Ikenson, Frederick L. .... **Washington, DC**
Ikenson, Frederick L., P.C.
Washington, DC
Ikerd, Dawn M. .... Maitland, FL
Iketani, Diana N. .... **Los Angeles, CA**
Ikeya, Margaret Chu .... **Palo Alto, CA**
Ikezawa, Wendy H. .... Department of Justice,
Executive Office for Immigration Review,
GV
Iklé, Richard A. .... Jersey City, NJ
Ikola, Raymond J. .... Santa Ana, CA
Ikonen, Gregory J. .... **Menlo Park, CA**
Ikuta, Sandra Segal .... **Los Angeles, CA**
San Francisco, CA
Ilagan, Mark L. .... San Diego, CA
Ilagan, Michael D. .... **Chicago, IL**
Ilan, Ella M. .... New York, NY
Ilan, Esther Kinneret .... **New York, NY**
Ilan, Ruth .... New York, NY
Ilangwa, Ashley .... **San Francisco, CA**
Ilardi, Anthony, Jr. .... **Bloomfield Hills, MI**
Ilardi, Constance G. .... **Morristown, NJ**
Ilardi, Gregg A. .... **Hackensack, NJ**
Ilardi, Terry J. .... Yorktown Heights, NY
Ilardo, Anthony C. .... Hamburg, NY
Ilardo, Edwin R. .... Hamburg, NY
Ilaria, Alfonso F. .... Howell, NJ
Ilaria, Ralph R. .... Brooklyn, NY
Ilasz, Livius M. .... New York, NY
Ilberg, Stephanie M. .... Barre, VT
Ilchert, George .... New York, NY
Ildstad, Lee .... Edina, MN
Ile, Michael L. .... Chicago, IL
Ilecki, William .... Tonawanda, NY
Ilenda, Christopher T. .... Denver, CO
Ilenstine, Jennifer M. .... **Seattle, WA**
Iler, Alexander B. .... Shrewsbury, NJ
Iler, Anthony T. .... **Los Angeles, CA**

Iler, Arthur W. .... Wilmington, DE
Iler, Clifton M. .... **Atlanta, GA**
Iler, Daniel J. .... Washington, PA
Iler, David R. .... **Houston, TX**
Iler, Don C. .... Cleveland, OH
Iler, Don C., Co., L.P.A. .... Cleveland, OH
Iler, Iris J. .... **Yonkers, NY**
Iler, Kirby J. .... Cody, WY
Iler, Nancy C. .... Cleveland, OH
Iler, Richard W. .... **Louisville, KY**
Iler, W. Gordon .... Owensboro, KY
Iles, James D. .... Everett, WA
Iles, Kenneth W. .... **Overland Park, KS**
Iles, Kenneth W. .... **Kansas City, MO**
Iles, R. Scott .... **De Ridder, LA**
Lafayette, LA
Lake Charles, LA
Iles, Terry A. .... Topeka, KS
Ilg, Carl H. .... Chino Hills, CA
Ilg, Carl H. .... **Newport Beach, CA**
Ilg, Gavin C. .... Lubbock, TX
Ilg, Reynold A., Jr. .... Lowell, MA
Ilg, Shawn M. .... Omaha, NE
Superior, NE
Ilgenfritz, Heide H. .... **New York, NY**
Ilgenfritz, Scott C. .... **Clearwater, FL**
Tampa, FL
Ilhardt, Lora S. .... Chicago, IL
Ilibassi, John A. .... Glen Oaks, NY
Ilic, Zorica .... West Des Moines, IA
Ilich, Rhoda Lorraine .... Bellmore, NY
Iliev, Mikhail I. .... **New York, NY**
Iliff & Associates, P.A. .... **Edina, MN**
Iliff, Charles E., Jr. .... **Baltimore, MD**
Iliff, Christopher C. .... Overland Park, KS
Iliff, Cynthia G. .... **San Diego, CA**
Iliff, John W. .... **Omaha, NE**
Iliff & Meredith, P.C. .... **Baltimore, MD**
Iliff, Thomas L. .... Edina, MN
Iliff, Todd R. .... **Edina, MN**
Ilitch-Lites, Denise D. .... **Detroit, MI**
Ilkhanoff, Bernard .... Baltimore, MD
Ilkka, Richard C. .... Stillwater, MN
Ilkowitz, Linda S. .... **New York, NY**
Ilkson, Atilla Steven .... New York, NY
Illa, Stephan R. .... Seattle, WA
Illa, Stephan R., Inc., P.S., Law Offices of
Seattle, WA
Iller, Brian J. .... **Kennewick, WA**
Illes, Bruce H. .... Cleveland, OH
Illgen, Richard F. .... Anchorage, AK
Illgen, Rudy V. .... Minneapolis, MN
Illges, Ralph W. .... **Columbus, GA**
Illies, Heather L. .... **Scottsdale, AZ**
Illig, Alan .... **Rochester, NY**
Illig, Andrea .... Marydel, MD
Illig, Dale, (P.C.) .... Georgetown, TX
Illig, Robert C. .... **New York, NY**
Illingworth, Stephen R. .... Hastings, NE
Illions, David M. .... Los Angeles, CA
Illk, Deane F. .... Inver Grove Heights, MN
Illmensee, Thomas A. .... Garden City, NY
Illmer, Richard A. .... **Dallas, TX**
Illner, Michael D. .... Elyria, OH
Illouz, Yael .... Los Angeles, CA
Illovsky, Eugene G. .... **Walnut Creek, CA**
Illoway, Eleanor Morris .... **Philadelphia, PA**
Illsley, Gladys E. .... Baltimore, MD
Illsley, Roger J. .... Santa Rosa, CA
Illston, Susan Y. .... San Francisco, CA
Ilsley, John P. .... Sheridan, WY
Ilstrup, Thomas G. .... Toledo, OH
Ilten, Mark O. .... **Stevens Point, WI**
Iltz, Kenneth E. .... **Portland, OR**
Ilvedson, Duane H. .... **Fargo, ND**
Ilyin & Barrese .... **San Francisco, CA**
Ilyin, Dimitri K. .... **San Francisco, CA**
Im, Hyun S. .... Santa Monica, CA
Im, Jae W. .... **Roseland, NJ**
Im, Kyong-Su .... Honolulu, HI
Im, Richard .... **Princeton, NJ**
New York, NY
Im, Sonny" Seung Woo "
New Port Richey, FL
Im, Soo H. .... **New York, NY**
Im, Tae J. .... **Irvine, CA**
Im, Yongjin .... **New York, NY**
Imahara, Kathryn K. .... Los Angeles, CA
Imai, Bruce .... **San Francisco, CA**
Imai, David Y. .... Aptos, CA
Imai, Keiichiro .... Calabasas, CA
Imai, Tadlock & Keeney, LLP
San Francisco, CA
Imai, Yasuhiko .... **New York, NY**
Imam, Maryam .... Palo Alto, CA
Imami, Shaheen I. .... **Farmington Hills, MI**
Imami, Shaheen I., PLLC
Farmington Hills, MI
Imamshah, Nicole M. .... **Atlanta, GA**
Imamura, Diane F. .... **Honolulu, HI**
Imanaka, Mitchell A. .... **Honolulu, HI**
Imasogie, Osagie O. (IBA) .... **Chadds Ford, PA**
Imata, Michelle C. .... **Honolulu, HI**
Imatani, Edward .... **Lakewood, CO**
Imaye, Scott M. .... **Honolulu, HI**
Imbacuan, Michael H. .... **New York, NY**
Imbalzano, Maria P. .... **Princeton, NJ**
Imbasciani, Joseph, Esq. .... Melville, NY
Imber, Annabelle Clinton .... Little Rock, AR
Imber, Bernard M. .... Lexington Park, MD
Imber, Daniel S. .... **Los Angeles, CA**
Imber, Michael H. .... **West Palm Beach, FL**
Imber, Robert C., Law Office of, Prof. Corp.
San Francisco, CA
Imber, Robert Charles .... San Francisco, CA
Imber, Steven L. .... **Overland Park, KS**
Imberg, Alexander P. .... **San Francisco, CA**
Imberman, Jacob .... **New York, NY**

Imbernino, Karen L. ....**Costa Mesa, CA**
Imbert, Monique Vinet ....Elizabeth, NJ
Imberto Faria, Corinne A. ....**New York, NY**
Imbesi, Patricia Q. ....Philadelphia, PA
Imbierowicz, Angela ....Hinsdale, IL
Imblum, Gary J. ....**Harrisburg, PA**
Imbornone, Angela C. ....**New Orleans, LA**
Imbornone, Charles J. ....New Orleans, LA
Imbornone, Francis V. ....**New York, NY**
Imbornone, Salvatore, Jr. ....Florham Park, NJ
Imbornoni, Brian ....**Phoenix, AZ**
Imbra, Richard J. ....**San Diego, CA**
Imbrecht, Charles R. ....Pasadena, CA
Imbrescia, Philip S. ....Everett, MA
Imbriaco, James ....**New York, NY**
Imbriaco, Joseph E. ....**Summit, NJ**
Imbriani, Joseph G. ....**Boston, MA**
Imbriani, Mark D. ....Somerville, NJ
Imbrie, Charity J. ....Pittsburgh, PA
Imbriglia, Stephen J. ....**Philadelphia, PA**
Imbrogno, Cynthia ....Spokane, WA
Imbrogno, Richard ....**New York, NY**
Imbroscio, Michael X. ....**Washington, DC**
Imbrunone, Thomas L. ....Royal Oak, MI
Imburg, Gary A. ....Riverside, CA
Imburg, Stephen V. ....**Modesto, CA**
Imburgio, Susan M. ....New York, NY
Imel, John M. ....**Tulsa, OK**
Imel, Judith A. ....Sacramento, CA
Imeri, Jeff ....**New York, NY**
Imerman, Laurence R. ....Bingham Farms, MI
Imerman, Lisa R. ....Waterford, MI
Imerman, Stanley C. ....**Los Angeles, CA**
Imerman Schey, Miriam
Bloomfield Hills, MI
Imes, Andrew C. ....Williston, ND
Imes, Elizabeth H. ....Atlanta, GA
Imes, Kathleen E. Key ....Williston, ND
Imes, Linda ....**New York, NY**
Imes, Roger L. ....**La Crosse, WI**
Imesch, John ....Troy, MI
Imfeld, Bert C. ....Hamilton, OH
Imfeld, Louis A. ....Williamsburg, VA
Imfeld, Michael D. ....**Woodland Hills, CA**
Imgrund, William H. ....Westfield, NJ
Imhof, Heidi E. ....**Tampa, FL**
Imhof, Heidi Elizabeth ....Tacoma, WA
Imhof, John F., Jr. ....**New York, NY**
Imhof, John V. ....Cambridge, NY
Imhof, Patrick L. ....Tallahassee, FL
Imhof, Peter T. ....Oakland, CA
Imhof, Roger J. ....**Springfield, NJ**
Imhoff, Don, Jr. ....**Middletown, OH**
Imhoff, Earl J., Jr. ....**Los Angeles, CA**
Imhoff, Elizabeth R. ....**Denver, CO**
Imhoff, Gregory S. ....Dallas, TX
Imhoff, Herbert F., Jr. ....Oakbrook Terrace, IL
Imhoff, John W., Jr. ....Norwalk, CT
Imhoff, Joseph M., Jr. ....Boise, ID
Imhoff, Joshua A. ....**Dallas, TX**
Imhoff, Mary Sheila ....Glen Rock, NJ
Imhoff, Steffan ....Del Mar, CA
Imhoff, Stephen P. ....**Louisville, KY**
Imhoff, Sylvia H. ....**Austin, TX**
Imhoff, Vincent Michael ....Chicago, IL
Imholte, Ralph D. ....Minneapolis, MN
Imholz, Elizabeth M. ....San Francisco, CA
Imholz, Kathleen ....White Plains, NY
Imhoof, Christina Tatjana ....San Diego, CA
Imig, Robert A., Jr. ....**Deerfield, IL**
Imig, William G. ....Denver, CO
Imke, Charles W. ....Alto, NM
Imke, Charles W., A Professional Corporation
Alto, NM
Imlay, Alexander R. ....San Rafael, CA
Imlay, Christopher D. ....Washington, DC
Imlay, Gerard G. ....Atlanta, GA
Imler, Kyle L. ....Tacoma, WA
Imm, Stephen E. ....**Cincinnati, OH**
Immel, Howard M. ....**Iola, KS**
Immel, Immel & Works, P.A. ....**Iola, KS**
Immel, James M. ....**Iola, KS**
Immel, J. J. Scott ....San Jose, CA
Immel, John J. ....Lawrence, KS
Immel, Melissa A. ....**Los Angeles, CA**
Immel, Otto W. ....**Philadelphia, PA**
Immel, Thomas J. ....Alton, IL
Immel, Vincent C. ....St. Louis, MO
Immell, Michael W. ....**Costa Mesa, CA**
Immell, Todd M. ....Cincinnati, OH
Immelt, Stephen J. ....**Baltimore, MD**
Immen, David W. ....Concord, NH
Immer, John G. ....**New York, NY**
Immergut, Karin J. ....Portland, OR
Immergut, Mel M. ....**New York, NY**
Immerman Daniel and Fontaine
Greenfield, MA
Northampton, MA
Springfield, MA
Immerman, Elaine ....**New York, NY**
Immerman, Harvey A. ....Montgomery, OH
Immerman, Isidore S. ....New York, NY
Immerman, L. Andrew ....**Atlanta, GA**
Immerman, Mark D. ....Greenfield, MA
Northampton, MA
Springfield, MA
Immerman, Paul A. ....**New York, NY**
Immerman, Sharon Gwin ....**Las Vegas, NV**
Immerman, Stanley A. ....Baldwin, NY
Immerman, William J. ....**Los Angeles, CA**
Immigrant Law Center ....Chicago, IL
Immigration Law Center ....**Whittier, CA**
Immigration Law Offices ....Miami, FL
Pompano Beach, FL
Immler, G. Matthew ....Easton, MD
Immormino, Mark ....Cleveland, OH
Imms, Michael T. ....**West Chester, PA**
Imms, Stephen P., Jr. ....Harleysville, PA

Imobersteg, Anne D. ....San Jose, CA
Imobersteg, Gail A. ....Sacramento, CA
Imossi, Richard T. ....**Livingston, NJ**
Impagliazzo, Joseph M. ....Providence, RI
Impara, Joseph V. ....Garden City, NY
Impara, Joseph V., Jr. ....Garden City, NY
Imparato, Andrew J.
Equal Employment Opportunity Commission, Office of the Commissioners, GV
Imparato, Jill A. ....Philadelphia, PA
Imparato, Maria A. ....Boston, MA
Imparato, William A. ....Phoenix, AZ
Impastato, Arthur A. ....**Washington, DC**
Impastato, David J. ....**Los Angeles, CA**
Impastato, Joseph N. ....Eastpointe, MI
Impastato, Melanie K. ....**Springfield, IL**
Impellizzeri, Amy K. ....**Newark, NJ**
Impellizzeri, Frances A. ....**Dallas, TX**
Imperati, Samuel J. ....Portland, OR
Imperato, Cynthia Gelmine
Fort Lauderdale, FL
Imperato, Gabriel L., (P.A.)
Fort Lauderdale, FL
Imperato, Joseph J. ....Miami, FL
Imperato, Ralph E. ....Dayton, OH
Imperatore, Brant David
New Orleans, LA
Imperatore, Edward F. G. ....Brooklyn, NY
Imperatore, Edward G. ....**Hackensack, NJ**
New York, NY
Imperatrice & Amarant
Newtown Square, PA
Imperatrice, Rocco P., III
Newtown Square, PA
Imperial, George T. ....Montclair, NJ
Imperial, Robert K. ....**Columbus, GA**
Imperial, Zazzaro & Calabro, P.A.
Montclair, NJ
Imperiale, Thomas A. ....Baltimore, MD
Impert, John E. ....Seattle, WA
Impey, W. Richard ....Chicago, IL
Impicciche, Joseph R. ....**Indianapolis, IN**
Imprevento, Michael F. ....**Norfolk, VA**
Imre, Christina J. ....**Los Angeles, CA**
Imrich, Ian J. ....Los Angeles, CA
Imse, Peter F. ....**Concord, NH**
Imudia, Martins I. ....New Orleans, LA
Imus, Lisa Michael ....Tampa, FL
Imus, Neil W. ....**Washington, DC**
Imwalle, Randall J. ....Columbus, OH
Imwalle, William M. ....**Carrollton, TX**
Imwinkelried, Edward J. ....Davis, CA
Inaba, Gail M. ....**New York, NY**
Inaba, Mark L. ....Los Angeles, CA
Inabinet, Cary T. ....**Phoenix, AZ**
Inabinet, George L. ....Barnwell, SC
Inabinet, Macre S. ....**Phoenix, AZ**
Inabinett, David E. ....**Lexington, NC**
Inabnet, J. Ashley ....**New Orleans, LA**
Inabnett, Amanda M. ....**Dallas, TX**
Inabnett, Carrick B. ....Monroe, LA
Inabnett, Carrick R. ....**Monroe, LA**
Inabnett, Chris ....**Dallas, TX**
Inabnett, Joe M. ....New Orleans, LA
Houston, TX
Inabnit, Brent E. ....**South Bend, IN**
Inacio, Antonio ....Newark, NJ
Inadomi, Elizabeth Ann ......Mountain View, CA
Inadomi, Minoru ....Santa Ana, CA
Inafuku, Alison L. ....**New York, NY**
Inagaki, Caron M. ....Honolulu, HI
Inagaki, Lorrie K. ....Sacramento, CA
Inama, Christopher R., Law Office of
Redwood City, CA
Inama-Torvinen, Barbara A. ....Elko, NV
Inamine, Brian S. ....**Los Angeles, CA**
Inbar, Jill Ilan Berger ....**Washington, DC**
Inbar, Tomer J. ....**Washington, DC**
Inbau, Fred E. ....Chicago, IL
Inboden, Marc B. ....Canton, OH
Inboden, Stephen ....Trumann, AR
Inbody, Brian T. ....**Tulsa, OK**
Inbody, Diane E. ....**Riverhead, NY**
Inbody, Everett O. ....Wahoo, NE
Inbody, Mark E. ....**Redwood City, CA**
Ince, George R., Jr. ....**New York, NY**
Ince, James K. ....**Fort Worth, TX**
Ince, Karen Williams ....Anchorage, AK
Ince, Mary Ann Rapp ....Baltimore, MD
Ince, Peter James ....Madison, WI
Ince, William K. ....**Washington, DC**
Incerto, Michael Scott ....**Austin, TX**
Inclima, Charles P. ....Rochester, NY
Incollingo, Robert J. ....Haddonfield, NJ
Incontro, Thomas G. ....**Omaha, NE**
Incorvaia & Associates, A Professional Corporation ....**San Diego, CA**
Incorvaia, Joel L. ....**San Diego, CA**
Incorvaia, Joseph M. ....White Plains, NY
Incorvaia, Santo T. ....Cleveland, OH
Incorvaia Mroz, Denise ....**Washington, DC**
Incorvati, Robert A. ....Akron, OH
Indahl, Pamela Joan Larson
Department of State, GV
Indall, Jon J. ....**Santa Fe, NM**
Inde, Vilis R. ....Minneapolis, MN
Indech, Barbara E. ....Postal Rate Commission, Office of the General Counsel, GV
Indeck, Andrew L. ....**Bedminster, NJ**
Indeglia, Gilbert V. ....Providence, RI
Indeglia, Marc A. ....**Newport Beach, CA**
Indek, Ben A. ....**New York, NY**
Indelicarto, Thomas C. ....**Pittsburgh, PA**
Indelicato, Charlene M. ....New Rochelle, NY
Indelicato, Cherie ....**Albany, NY**
Indelicato, Joseph, Jr., ...**Houston, TX**
Indelicato, Joseph, Jr., P.C. ....**Houston, TX**

Indelicato, Mario ....**New York, NY**
Indelicato, Mark S. ....**New York, NY**
Inden, Arthur ....**Wilmington, DE**
Indenbaum, Michael A. ....**Detroit, MI**
Inderbitzen, Martin W. ....Pleasanton, CA
Inderbitzin, Michael ....**New York, NY**
Inderbitzin, Sarah L.
Department Of The Interior, Office of the Solicitor, GV
Inderlied, H. F., Jr. ....Chardon, OH
Inderlied, Julie A. ....**Scottsdale, AZ**
Indermark, Kristen Jones ....**Atlanta, GA**
Inderwish, John H. ....**Aurora, CO**
Lincoln, NE
Indest, George F., III ....**Orlando, FL**
Indest, Maurice G. ....New Orleans, LA
Indiano, David C. ....**San Juan, PR**
Indiano, E. Victor ....**Indianapolis, IN**
Indiano, Williams & Weinstein-Bacal
San Juan, PR
Indick, Jos. H. ....Elizabeth, NJ
Indick, Murray A. ....Washington, DC
Indictor, Penny S. ....**Camden, NJ**
Philadelphia, PA
Indie, Michael T. ....Kailua, HI
Indig, Paul ....**New York, NY**
Indig-Smith, Jessica Ann
Hastings-On-Hudson, NY
Indik, Martin K. ....**Princeton, NJ**
Philadelphia, PA
Indik & McNamara ....**Denville, NJ**
Princeton, NJ
Philadelphia, PA
Indiviglio, Frank J. ....East Meadow, NY
Indivino, Deborah A. ....Spencerport, NY
Indoe, William F. ....**New York, NY**
Indomenico, Sal ....Chicago, IL
Indorf, David C. ....Dallas, TX
Indorf, Ronald P. ....Dover, NH
Indovina, Thomas M. ....Santa Monica, CA
Indran, Ron ....San Jose, CA
Indritz Law Offices, Ltd. ....Minneapolis, MN
Mound, MN
Indritz, Richard ....Minneapolis, MN
Mound, MN
Indritz, Tova ....Albuquerque, NM
Indursky, Arthur I. ....**New York, NY**
Indursky, Harry ....Lauderhill, FL
Indyg, Charles J. ....Vineland, NJ
Indyk, Eugene S. ....**Iselin, NJ**
Indyke, Craig M. ....**Albany, NY**
Indyke, Darren K. ....New York, NY
Indyke, Jay Randall ....**New York, NY**
Indzonka, Allen J. ....Newburgh, NY
Indzonka, Erik F. ....Goshen, NY
Ineich, Paul J., II ....New Orleans, LA
Inemer, Timothy P. ....Camden, NJ
Inendino, James V. ....**Chicago, IL**
Ines, Victor D. ....**Tampa, FL**
Infald, Louis ....Paterson, NJ
Infante, Edward A. ....San Jose, CA
Infante, Frederick A. ....Chatham, NJ
Infante, Kathryn ....**San Jose, CA**
Infante, Marie Catherine
Washington, DC
Infante, Mark A. ....West Orange, NJ
Infante, Renée ....**Cincinnati, OH**
Infante, Stephen A. ....**New York, NY**
Infante, Thomas E. ....Youngstown, OH
Infante-Garcia, Ofelia ....Las Cruces, NM
Infanti, Anthony C. ....**New York, NY**
Infantino and Berman ....**Orlando, FL**
Winter Park, FL
Infantino, Fred J. ....Rochester, NY
Infantino, Jerald A. ....San Jose, CA
Infantino, Michael B. ....Albany, NY
Infantino, Philip J., III ....**Chesapeake, VA**
Infantino, Susan M. ....**Menlo Park, CA**
Infantino, Thomas V. ....**Winter Park, FL**
Infarinato, Joan T. ....New Hope, PA
Infarinato, Robert M. ....Collegeville, PA
Infausto, Felix ....Loudonville, NY
Infeld, William S. ....Westbury, NY
Infelise, Frank ....Swampscott, MA
Infelise, Robert D. ....**San Francisco, CA**
Inferrera, John M. ....Los Angeles, CA
Infield, Todd A. ....Fennimore, WI
Infinger, Anne S. ....**Atlanta, GA**
Infinger, Glenn T. ....**Atlanta, GA**
Infinger, Marvin D. ....**Charleston, SC**
Infinger, Paul H. ....**Beaufort, SC**
Infinger, Peggy M. ....Charleston, SC
Infinger, Russell T. ....**Greenville, SC**
Inforzato, Valerie Fogel ....**Vancouver, WA**
Infosino, Alfred M. ....Delray Beach, FL
Infosino, John M. ....Westlake, OH
Infranco, Joseph P. ....Commack, NY
Infurna, Thomas J. ....**White Plains, NY**
Infusino, Thomas P. ....Sacramento, CA
Ing, Dennis A. ....Honolulu, HI
Ing, Earl T. W. ....Honolulu, HI
United States Tax Court, GV
Ing, Edwin T.C. ....**Washington, DC**
Ing, Gloria M. ....**Rosemead, CA**
Ing, Ige & Horikawa ....Wailuku, HI
Ing, J. Douglas, (Atty. At Law, A Law Corp.)
Honolulu, HI
Ing, John Jacob ....Honolulu, HI
Ing, John Jacob, A Law Corporation
Honolulu, HI
Ing, Lawrence N. C. ....Wailuku, HI
Ing & Lebb ....Honolulu, HI
Ing, Louise K. Y. ....**Honolulu, HI**
Ing, M. Gordon ....**Detroit, MI**
Ing, Phillis J. ....Sonoma, CA
Ing, Phyllis J. ....Boca Raton, FL
Ing, Richard A. ....**Honolulu, HI**
Ing, Richard B. W. ....Honolulu, HI

Inga, Lynette ....Fairport, NY
Ingaldson Maassen, P.C. ....**Anchorage, AK**
Ingaldson, William H. ....**Anchorage, AK**
Ingall, Seth M. ....Washington, DC
Ingalls & Blackman ....**Van Nuys, CA**
Woodland Hills, CA
Ingalls, David G. ....Spartanburg, SC
Ingalls, Donald R., (A Professional Corporation) ....**Woodland Hills, CA**
Ingalls, Dorothy M. ....**Washington, DC**
Ingalls, Everett P., III ....**Portland, ME**
Ingalls, George L. ....**Binghamton, NY**
Ingalls, George S., Jr. ....Baltimore, MD
Ingalls, George S., P.A. ....Baltimore, MD
Ingalls, James W. ....Coeur d'Alene, ID
Ingalls, John S. ....Boston, MA
Ingalls, Kenneth F. ....Auburn, WA
Ingalls, Lance Jeffrey ....Denver, CO
Ingalls, Lisa M. ....**Minnetonka, MN**
Ingalls, Melissa D. ....**Los Angeles, CA**
Ingalls, P. David ....**Medford, OR**
Ingalls, Richard W., Jr.
Grosse Pointe Woods, MI
Ingalls, Ronald E. ....**Austin, TX**
Ingalls, William G. ....Bellevue, WA
Ingalsbe, Lynn R. ....Abilene, TX
Ingalsbe, Raymond G.
Palm Beach Gardens, FL
Ingalsbe, Raymond G., P.A.
Palm Beach Gardens, FL
Ingalsbe, Ward W., III ....**Kingston, NY**
Ingalsbe, Ward W., Jr. ....Kingston, NY
Ingalsbe, William J., (P.C.)
Santa Ana, CA
Ingarra, Joseph M. ....Kingston, NY
Ingato, Robert J. ....Parsippany, NJ
Ingber, Abby L. ....**New York, NY**
Ingber, Adam F. ....**New York, NY**
Ingber & Aronson, P.A. ....**Minneapolis, MN**
Ingber, Charles ....Elmhurst, NY
Ingber, Charles J. ....Portland, OR
Ingber, Clifford J. ....Greenwich, CT
Ingber, Corey A. ....Woodland Hills, CA
Ingber, Craig ....**Westport, CT**
New York, NY
Ingber & Ingber ....Greenwich, CT
Ingber & Ingber ....**Goshen, NY**
Monticello, NY
Ingber, Jack S. ....**Monticello, NY**
Ingber, Jeffrey F. ....**New York, NY**
Ingber, Jerome ....**Minneapolis, MN**
Ingber, Joe ....Los Angeles, CA
Ingber, Jonathan S. ....Hollywood, FL
Ingber, Joseph S. ....New York, NY
Ingber, Karol H. ....**Orange, CA**
Ingber, Kathy Kresch ....**Washington, DC**
Ingber, Keith G. ....**Monticello, NY**
Ingber, Kenneth ....Los Angeles, CA
Ingber, Kenneth ....**Boston, MA**
Ingber, Larry H. ....**Garden City, NY**
Ingber, Laura R. ....Department of Justice, Federal Bureau of Investigation, GV
Ingber, Mark J. ....**Secaucus, NJ**
Ingber, Marvin C. ....**Minneapolis, MN**
St. Paul, MN
Ingber, Matthew D. ....**New York, NY**
Ingber, Norman ....New York, NY
Ingber, Paul M. ....Southfield, MI
Ingber, Sidney ....**New York, NY**
Ingber, Stanley ....Des Moines, IA
Ingber, Victoria M. ....Greenwich, CT
Ingber, Warren J. ....**New York, NY**
Ingberg, Mary Ann ....**Washington, DC**
Vienna, VA
Inge, Herndon, III ....Mobile, AL
Inge, Herndon, Jr. ....**Mobile, AL**
Inge, John R. ....**Washington, DC**
Inge, McMillan & Coley ....**Mobile, AL**
Inge, Robert L. ....Salisbury, NC
Inge, Samuel W. ....**Fairhope, AL**
Inge, Samuel W. ....**Mobile, AL**
Inge, Twitty & Duffy ....**Mobile, AL**
Inge, Vernon E., Jr. ....**Richmond, VA**
Inge, Wayne D. ....Roanoke, VA
Inge, Wm. B., Jr. ....Mobile, AL
Inge, Zebulon M. P., Jr. ....**Mobile, AL**
Ingebrand, George B., Jr.
Minneapolis, MN
Ingebretsen, Harold B. ....Denver, CO
Ingebretsen, James C.
Rancho Palos Verdes, CA
Ingebretsen, S. Kirk ....**Denver, CO**
Ingebretson, Charles L. ....**Washington, DC**
Ingebritsen, Jeffrey C. ....Monroe, WI
Ingebritsen, Samuel A. ....Menlo Park, CA
Ingebritson and Associates
Minneapolis, MN
Ingebritson, Russell A. ....**Minneapolis, MN**
Ingegneri, Richard F. ....Fort Lee, NJ
Ingellis, Patricia ....Old Saybrook, CT
Ingels, Edgar D. ....Jackson, MS
Ingels, Lorraine Snead ....**Cedar Rapids, IA**
Ingelstrom, John B. ....**Pocatello, ID**
Ingemansen, Dean B. ....Seattle, WA
Ingemie, Ronald B. ....Fitchburg, MA
Ingemunson, Dallas C. ....Yorkville, IL
Ingeneri, Philip L. ....Bangor, ME
Ingenito, Gennaro ....Mill Valley, CA
Inger, Robert J. ....Houston, TX
Inger, Roger A. ....Winchester, VA
Ingerman, Brett ....**Baltimore, MD**
Ingerman, Bruce E. ....**Baltimore, MD**
Columbia, MD
Cumberland, MD
Frederick, MD
Hagerstown, MD
Salisbury, MD

Ingerman & Horwitz, L.L.P.
Baltimore, MD
Columbia, MD
Cumberland, MD
Frederick, MD
Hagerstown, MD
Salisbury, MD
Ingerman, Jeffrey H. ....New York, NY
Ingerman, Joanne Sherman
New York, NY
Ingerman, Peter K. ....New York, NY
Ingerman, Randi Sue ....Stoughton, MA
Ingerman Smith, L.L.P. ....Northport, NY
Ingerman, Steven L. ....New York, NY
Ingersoll, Christina Lynn ....Overland Park, KS
Ingersoll, Cynthia L. ....Washington, DC
Ingersoll, David ....Modesto, CA
Ingersoll, Donald M. ....Olympia, WA
Ingersoll, Douglas L. ....Concord, NH
Ingersoll, Frank B., Jr. ....Burlingame, CA
Ingersoll & Ingersoll ....Olympia, WA
Ingersoll, Jared ....Mechanicsburg, PA
Ingersoll, Josy W. ....Wilmington, DE
Ingersoll, Laura A. ....Department of Justice, Criminal Division, GV
Ingersoll, Marc W. ....Winston-Salem, NC
Ingersoll, Richard K. ....Honolulu, HI
Ingersoll, Robert M. ....Cleveland, OH
Ingersoll, Shaun A. ....Raleigh, NC
Ingersoll, Stephen B. ....New Orleans, LA
Ingersoll, Timothy E. ....Rochester, NY
Ingersoll, William D. ....Springfield, IL
Ingham, Bruce A. ....Clinton, IA
Ingham, Colin E. ....Delhi, NY
Ingham, Cranford A. ....Bloomington, IL
Ingham, Kevin M. ....Atlanta, GA
Ingham, Linda Cobb ....Jacksonville, FL
Ingham, Marc C. ....Wilmington, NC
Ingham, Michael F. ....Farmingdale, NY
Ingham, Richard G. ....Oklahoma City, OK
Ingham, Ronald G. ....Atlanta, GA
Chattanooga, TN
Ingham, Samuel D., III ....Beverly Hills, CA
Ingham, Samuel D., III ....Los Angeles, CA
Inghram & Inghram ....Quincy, IL
Inghram, James R. ....Quincy, IL
Inghram, John T., IV ....Quincy, IL
Ingle, Allen C. ....Farmington Hills, MI
Ingle, Chester ....Thermopolis, WY
Ingle, Gordon D. ....Corydon, IN
Ingle, J. Derek ....Tulsa, OK
Ingle, Jay E. ....Lexington, KY
Ingle, John, Associates, PLLC ....Boone, NC
Hickory, NC
Lenoir, NC
Lincolnton, NC
Morganton, NC
Statesville, NC
Taylorsville, NC
Ingle, John D. ....Hickory, NC
Ingle, John E.
Federal Communications Commission, Office of the General Counsel, GV
Ingle, John M. ....San Jose, CA
Ingle, John P., III ....Tallahassee, FL
Ingle, Karen ....La Fayette, GA
Ingle, Margaret R. ....Lubbock, TX
Ingle, Nancy Jean ....Lawrence, KS
Ingle, Nicole A. F. ....Hartford, CT
Ingle, Robert H., III ....Baltimore, MD
Ingle, Stacy Armstrong ....Memphis, TN
Ingle, Tracey A.L. ....Boston, MA
Ingleby, Steven L. ....Salt Lake City, UT
Ingledue, Tom C., (A Law Corporation)
Honolulu, HI
Inglefield, David L.
Federal Trade Commission, Bureau of Competition, GV
Inglehart, George G., Jr. ....Watertown, NY
Ingler, Michael A. ....Long Beach, CA
Ingles, Breckenridge ....Gloucester, VA
Ingles, David C. ....New York, NY
Ingles, McClanahan ....Gloucester, VA
Ingles, Richard O.
Department Of Health And Human Services, Social Security Administration, GV
Ingles, Richard P. ....Syracuse, NY
Inglesby, Falligant, Horne, Courington & Nash, A Professional Corporation
Savannah, GA
Inglesby, Gerald A. ....Elkton, MD
Inglesby, Paul D. ....Bala Cynwyd, PA
Inglesby, Sam P., Jr. ....Savannah, GA
Inglese, Joseph H. ....Hillsborough, CA
Inglese, Samuel C. ....Metuchen, NJ
Milltown, NJ
Inglesino, John P. ....Roseland, NJ
Ingleson, Harry, II ....Cheboygan, MI
Ingley, Mary Ellen ....Tallahassee, FL
Inglima, Robert J., Jr. (P.A.)
Woodcliff Lake, NJ
Inglima, Robert J., (P.A.) ....Paramus, NJ
Inglima, Thomas Corbett ....Norfolk, VA
Inglin, Sonja A. ....Los Angeles, CA
Inglis, Alan L. ....Rancho Cucamonga, CA
Inglis, Alan L. ....Dallas, TX
Inglis, Barbara S. ....Encino, CA
Inglis, Charles K. ....St. Petersburg, FL
Inglis, David S. ....Cleveland, OH
Inglis, Eric A. ....Morristown, NJ
Inglis, Ernest A., Jr. ....Hartford, CT
Inglis, Hazel ....New Bedford, MA
Inglis, Ian B. ....Austin, TX
Inglis, John S. ....Tampa, FL
Inglis, Lawrence D. ....Gurnee, IL
Inglis, Ledbetter & Gower
Los Angeles, CA
Inglis, Michael K. ....Los Angeles, CA

Inglis, Patricia Marcus ....Cleveland, OH
Inglis, Patrick J. ....Boise, ID
Inglis, Richard J. ....Boston, MA
Inglis, Richard, Jr. ....Westwood, MA
Inglis, Richard K. ....Fort Lauderdale, FL
Inglis, Robert D. ....Greenville, SC
Inglis, Shannon Elizabeth ....Renton, WA
Inglis, Sherman & Associates ....Encino, CA
Inglish, Edwin C., Jr. ....Dallas, TX
Inglish, G. Robert, Jr. ....Okmulgee, OK
Inglish & Inglish, Professional Corporation
Okmulgee, OK
Inglish, John W. ....California, MO
Jefferson City, MO
Lake Ozark, MO
Inglish & Monaco, P.C. ....California, MO
Jefferson City, MO
Lake Ozark, MO
Ingman, Winston C. ....Mercer Island, WA
Ingogha, Eugene ....New York, NY
Ingoglia, Donald D. ....Sacramento, CA
Ingoglia, Glenn J. ....New York, NY
Ingoglia, Lawrence S. ....Water Mill, NY
Ingoglia, Marskey, Kearney, Lobner & Bull, A Prof. Corp. ....Sacramento, CA
Ingoglia, Teresa M. ....Bedford, PA
Ingold, Christopher L. ....Denver, CO
Ingold, David A. ....Treasury Department, Financial Management Service, GV
Ingold, David P. ....Stafford, VA
Ingold, Douglas A. ....Garberville, CA
Ingold, James V. ....Fairfax, VA
Ingold, John S. ....Midland, MI
Ingold, Marianne Roman ....Alexandria, VA
Ingold, Robert G. ....Bolivar, MO
Ingold, Susanne E. ....Phoenix, AZ
Ingoldsby, Thomas M. ....Washington, DC
Ingolia, Diane E. ....Redwood City, CA
Ingolia, Joseph N.
Department of Transportation, U. S. Coast Guard, GV
Ingolia, Richard K. ....Metairie, LA
Ingraffia, Courtney E. ....Washington, DC
Ingraffia, Salvatore A. ....Lodi, NJ
Ingraham, Andrew C., Jr.
East Hampton, NY
Ingraham, Arnold A. ....Medina, OH
Ingraham, C. Walker ....Atlanta, GA
Ingraham, Carl F. ....Birmingham, MI
Ingraham, Charles O. ....Binghamton, NY
Ingraham, Craig S. ....St. Louis, MO
Ingraham, Debra M. ....Charlotte, NC
Ingraham, Donald G. ....Oakland, CA
Ingraham, Donald S. ....Schenectady, NY
Ingraham, F. Lloyd ....Ronan, MT
Ingraham, Frank C. ....Nashville, TN
Ingraham, Frederic B. ....New York, NY
Ingraham, Greg L. ....Ronan, MT
Ingraham, Irad S. ....Norwich, NY
Ingraham, James F. ....Denver, CO
Ingraham, James H. ....Kansas City, MO
Ingraham, Jeffrey R. ....Celina, OH
Ingraham, John F. ....Kansas City, MO
Ingraham, John W. ....Tulsa, OK
Ingraham, L. Lee ....Enid, OK
Ingraham Law Office ....Ronan, MT
Ingraham, Lesa Marie ....Chicago, IL
Ingraham, Mark A. ....Miami, FL
Ingraham, Mark W., Jr. ....Rockport, ME
Ingraham, Mary Sue ....Scottsdale, AZ
Ingraham, Millard F. ....Santa Barbara, CA
Ingraham, Philip G. ....Pontiac, MI
Ingraham, R. Jay ....Kansas City, MO
Ingraham, Roger R. ....Medina, OH
Ingraham, Sandra Jo ....McLoud, OK
Ingraham, Stephen A. ....Milwaukee, WI
Ingraham, Stevens L. ....Rochester, NY
Ingraham, Timothy A. ....Tucson, AZ
Ingraham, William A., Jr. ....Miami, FL
Ingraham, William A., Jr., P.A.
Miami, FL
Ingram, Alan W. ....St. Paul, MN
Ingram, Allen R. ....Lafayette, LA
Ingram, Andrea J. ....San Francisco, CA
San Jose, CA
Ingram, Andrew E., Jr. ....Rahway, NJ
Ingram, Angie Hubbard ....Montgomery, AL
Ingram, April A. ....Nashville, TN
Ingram, Arthur C. ....Toledo, OH
Ingram & Associates, P.L.L.C.
Hattiesburg, MS
Jackson, MS
Ingram, Barbara J. ....Bradenton, FL
Ingram, Barbara L. ....Pleasant Hill, CA
Ingram, Bernard E. ....Oceanside, CA
Ingram, Bobby F. ....Hiram, GA
Ingram, Bradford B. ....Peoria, IL
Ingram, Brian Keith ....Austin, TX
Ingram, Bruce L. ....Columbus, OH
Ingram, Carl B. ....Majuro, TT
Ingram, Carolyn Burnette ....Kenansville, NC
Ingram, Carroll H. ....Hattiesburg, MS
Jackson, MS
Ingram, Charles M. ....Kenansville, NC
Ingram, Cheryl A. ....Philadelphia, PA
Ingram, Cheryl D. ....Chicago, IL
Ingram, Christopher B.
San Francisco, CA
Ingram, Claud A., Jr. ....Eugene, OR
Ingram, Craig ....Oakland, MD
Ingram, Dale L. ....Kansas City, MO
Ingram, Damani K. ....Columbia, MO
Ingram, David L. ....Springport, MI
Ingram, David Michael ....Gold River, CA
Ingram, David T. ....Shawnee, OK
Ingram, Dennis R. ....Grants Pass, OR
Ingram, Denny O. ....Austin, TX
Ingram, Derrick E. ....Lexington, MA

Ingram, Dick G., (P.C.) ....Austin, TX
Ingram, Douglas Stephen ....Irvine, CA
Ingram, E. Michael ....Atlanta, GA
Ingram, Edsam M. ....Austin, TX
Ingram, Ernest M. ....Aberdeen, WA
Ingram, Forrest L. ....Chicago, IL
Ingram, Forrest L., P.C. ....Chicago, IL
Ingram, Frank J. ....Wilmington, MA
Ingram, G. Conley ....Marietta, GA
Ingram, G. Stephen ....Red Bank, NJ
Ingram, Gary L. ....Dallas, TX
Fort Worth, TX
Ingram, Georgia V. ....Fullerton, CA
Ingram, Gerald B. ....Philadelphia, PA
Ingram, Germaine ....Philadelphia, PA
Ingram, Harry R. ....Amarillo, TX
Ingram, Harvey L. ....Cincinnati, OH
Ingram, Henry M. ....Pittsburgh, PA
Ingram & Ingram ....Kenansville, NC
Ingram, J. Charles ....Orlando, FL
Ingram, J. Edward ....Knoxville, TN
Ingram, J. Fredric ....Birmingham, AL
Ingram, Jack T. ....Commerce, TX
Ingram, James F. ....Danville, VA
Ingram, James M. ....San Jose, CA
Ingram, James W., (P.C.) ....Austin, TX
Ingram, Jeffrey C. ....Penn Valley, CA
Ingram, Jennifer M. ....Los Angeles, CA
Ingram, Jerry Dana ....Gardendale, AL
Ingram, Joe K. ....Roanoke, VA
Ingram, Joel W. ....Hattiesburg, MS
Ingram, John D. ....Chicago, IL
Ingram, John G. ....New York, NY
Ingram, John J., Jr. ....Austin, TX
Ingram, John M. ....Washington, DC
Ingram, John N. ....Atlanta, GA
Ingram, John Randolph, II ....Cary, NC
Ingram, Jolanda E. ....Eureka, CA
Ingram, Jon E., Jr. ....Augusta, GA
Ingram, Jonathan A. ....Spartanburg, SC
Ingram, Karen Cannatti ....Santa Barbara, CA
Ingram, Kathleen M. ....Columbus, OH
Ingram, Kenneth F. ....Ashland, AL
Ingram, Kenneth J. ....Washington, DC
Ingram, Kenneth, Jr. ....Alexander City, AL
Ingram, Kenneth, Jr. & Associates, P.C.
Alexander City, AL
Ingram, Kevin R. ....Belton, MO
Ingram, Kim D. ....Tuscaloosa, AL
Ingram, Kristin M. ....Portland, OR
Ingram, LaTrena Davis ....Memphis, TN
Ingram Law Firm, The ....Potsdam, NY
Ingram Law Office ....Burley, ID
Ingram, Lawrence P. ....Tampa, FL
Ingram, Linda L. ....Abilene, TX
Ingram, Lindsey W., III ....Lexington, KY
Ingram, Lindsey W., Jr. ....Lexington, KY
Ingram, L. N., III ....Naples, FL
Ingram, Mark A. ....Irwindale, CA
Ingram, Mark A. ....Burley, ID
Ingram, Mark D. ....Youngstown, OH
Ingram, Mark E. ....Columbia, SC
Ingram, Michael E. ....Tallahassee, FL
Ingram, Michael M. ....Boca Grande, FL
Tampa, FL
Ingram, Michael S. ....Monroe, LA
Ingram, Michele A.
Springfield Gardens, NY
Ingram, Miller S., Jr. ....Cheraw, SC
Ingram, Monica ....Austin, TX
Ingram, Nadia E. ....Coral Gables, FL
Ingram, Nancy E. ....Richmond, VA
Ingram, Niki T. ....Philadelphia, PA
Ingram, Patricia ....Owings Mills, MD
Ingram, Phyllis A. ....Nyack, NY
Ingram, R. Carl ....Tulsa, OK
Ingram, Richard A., Jr. ....Augusta, GA
Ingram, Richard J. ....Santa Rosa, CA
Ingram, Robert A. ....Middletown, OH
Ingram, Robert Allen, Jr. ....Hickory, NC
Ingram, Robert B. ....San Rafael, CA
Santa Ana, CA
Ingram, Robert D. ....Marietta, GA
Ingram, Robert J. ....Blacksburg, VA
Pulaski, VA
Ingram, Robert P. ....Denver, CO
Ingram, Roderick R. ....Virginia Beach, VA
Ingram, S. Patrick ....Charlottesville, VA
Ingram, Samuel M. ....Montgomery, AL
Ingram, Samuel W., Jr. ....New York, NY
Ingram, Sarah Hall ....Treasury Department, Internal Revenue Service, GV
Ingram, Sheldon Lewis ....Norton, VA
Ingram, Sherrin Ross ....Chicago, IL
Ingram, Sherry A. ....Washington, DC
Ingram, Sidney P. ....Houma, LA
Ingram, Stan T. ....Jackson, MS
Ingram, Stephen D. ....Albuquerque, NM
Ingram, Stephen J. ....Cordele, GA
Ingram, Susan ....New York, NY
Ingram, Susan, P.C. ....New York, NY
Ingram, T. Glenn ....Dallas, TX
Ingram, Temple B., Jr. ....El Paso, TX
Ingram, T. F. ....Lenoir City, TN
Ingram, Thomas ....Jacksonville, FL
Ingram, Thomas A., Jr. ....Sherman Oaks, CA
Ingram, Thomas E., Jr. ....Cheraw, SC
Ingram, Thomas L. ....Montrose, CO
Ingram, Thomas P. ....Midland, TX
Ingram, Timothy H. ....Manhattan Beach, CA
Ingram, Timothy M. ....Clearwater, FL
Ingram, Timothy P. ....Annapolis, MD
Ingram, Tom C., Jr. ....Dallas, TX
Ingram, V. Lee ....Kalamazoo, MI
Ingram, Verlin A. ....Wichita, KS
Ingram, Verner M., Jr. ....Potsdam, NY
Ingram, W. Nicholas ....Santa Monica, CA
Ingram, W. Ronald ....San Francisco, CA

Ingram, Wayne ....Flemington, NJ
Ingram, William A. ....San Jose, CA
Ingram, William P. ....Washington, DC
Ingram, William Ray ....Memphis, TN
Ingram, William T. ....Roswell, GA
Ingram & Witko ....Toledo, OH
Ingram, Yolanda D. ....Kansas City, MO
Ingram Yuzek Gainen Carroll & Bertolotti, LLP ....New York, NY
Ingram, Zelasko & Goodwin, LLP
Aberdeen, WA
Montesano, WA
South Bend, WA
Ingram-Leonard, Rebecca, Law Office of
Miami, FL
Ingrao, Anthony P. ....Baltimore, MD
Ingrao, Joseph A. ....Commack, NY
Ingrao, Lynn A. ....Commack, NY
Ingrao, Terrance J. ....Mineola, NY
Ingrassia, Angelo ....Goshen, NY
Ingrassia, Christopher Robert ....Nanuet, NY
Ingrassia, David N. ....Phoenix, AZ
Ingrassia, Deborah R. ....New Paltz, NY
Ingrassia, Jean ....Des Moines, IA
Ingrassia, John ....Newburgh, NY
Ingrassia, John R. ....Washington, DC
Ingrassia, Katherine ....Summit, NJ
Ingrassia, Paul J. ....Rye, NY
Ingrassia, Thomas S. ....Los Angeles, CA
San Diego, CA
Santa Ana, CA
Ingrassia, Vincent B. ....Boynton Beach, FL
Ingrid, Eagly ....Los Angeles, CA
Ingrisano, Joseph A. ....Washington, DC
Ingriselli, Frank C. ....White Plains, NY
Ingro, John F. ....San Bernardino, CA
Ingros, John M. ....Punxsutawney, PA
Ingrum, Andrew A. ....Austin, TX
Ingrum, Donald W. ....Branson, MO
Ingrum, Robert G. ....Gallatin, TN
Ingrum, Wilson, Griffin & Akers LLC
Branson, MO
Ingulli, Elaine D. ....Philadelphia, PA
Ingvaldson, Eric W. ....Minneapolis, MN
Ingvoldstad, David R. ....Melville, NY
Ingwalson, Carl F., Jr. ....San Diego, CA
Ingwersen, Richard C. ....Atlanta, GA
Inhof, Diana April ....Treasury Department, Internal Revenue Service, GV
Inhofe, Douglas L. ....Tulsa, OK
Inhofe & Jorgenson, A Professional Corporation ....Tulsa, OK
Inhofe, Perry D., Jr. ....South Padre Island, TX
Inhofe, Tara A. ....Tulsa, OK
Inigo, Alvaro A. ....Charlottesville, VA
Iniguez, Guadalupe ....Phoenix, AZ
Iniguez, Hermilio ....Phoenix, AZ
Injeian, Gregory G. ....Bowling Green, KY
Injejikian, Ara S. ....Van Nuys, CA
Injejikian, Avo G. ....Los Angeles, CA
Injeyan, Maral ....Glendale, CA
Injijian, Susie ....Oakland, CA
Injury & Consumer Law Center, Inc., A Professional Law Corporation
Santa Ana, CA
Ink, Stephen D. ....San Jose, CA
Inkelaar, Thomas T., II ....Wichita, KS
Inkellis, Barbara G. ....Bethesda, MD
Inkellis, Steven A. ....Washington, DC
Inker, Jennifer E. ....Boston, MA
Inker, Lauren Ruth ....Boston, MA
Inker, Monroe L. ....Boston, MA
Inker, Murray ....Hollywood, FL
Inkley, John J., Jr. ....St. Louis, MO
Inks, Allen W. ....Toledo, OH
Inkster, Elizabeth M. ....New Haven, CT
Inlander, David W. ....Chicago, IL
Inlander, Richard P. ....San Francisco, CA
Inlow, Laura E. ....Los Angeles, CA
Inlow, Michael D. ....Webster, TX
Inlow, Neely S. ....Lynchburg, VA
Inman, Arthur J. ....Peoria, IL
Inman & Associates, P.C. ....Beverly Hills, CA
Inman, Charles E. ....Hudson, NY
Inman, Christopher ....Troutdale, OR
Inman, Daniel (Trey) ....Atlanta, GA
Inman Deming LLP ....Washington, DC
Kalamazoo, MI
Inman, Dennis H. ....Greeneville, TN
Inman, Diana Hamner ....Charlotte, NC
Inman, Douglas B. ....Newport Beach, CA
Inman, Doyle B. ....Whitley City, KY
Inman and Fernandez, P.A.
Jacksonville, FL
Inman Flynn & Biesterfeld, P.C.
Denver, CO
Inman, George C., Jr. ....Seattle, WA
Inman, Gerri Anne ....Tulsa, OK
Inman, Harry A. ....Washington, DC
Honolulu, HI
Inman, Hugh M. ....Atlanta, GA
Inman, Iris Nell ....Conway, SC
Inman, Jack C. ....Maitland, FL
Inman, James E. ....Akron, OH
Inman, Kathaleen A. ....Vero Beach, FL
Inman, Kenneth C. ....Conway, SC
Inman, Kenneth Randall ....Somerville, TN
Inman, Leslie L. ....New Orleans, LA
Inman, Lisa D. ....Raleigh, NC
Inman, Lucy Noble ....Beverly Hills, CA
Inman, Lynne C. ....Chicago, IL
Inman, Mary A. ....San Francisco, CA
Inman, Maurice C., Jr. ....Beverly Hills, CA
Inman, Michael ....Chicago, IL
Inman, Michael A. ....Virginia Beach, VA
Inman, Nelwyn W. ....Knoxville, TN
Inman, Nick C. ....Dallas, TX
Inman, Norman H. ....Houston, TX

Inman, Paul D. ... New York, NY
Inman, Robert D. ... Denver, CO
Inman, Roger A. ... Ventura, CA
Inman, Rudolph J., Jr. ... Jacksonville, FL
Inman, Stacey M. ... Louisville, KY
Inman, Stacy Jo Lorraine ... Bakersfield, CA
Inman, Stephen G. ... Fayetteville, NC
Inman & Strickler, PLC ... Virginia Beach, VA
Inman, Tim ... Burnet, TX
Inman, Valantino R. ... Sacramento, CA
Inman, Wayne C. ... Detroit, MI
Inman, William ... Rockville, MD
Inman, William J. ... Washington, DC
Rockville, MD
Inman-Campbell, Gail ... Harrison, AR
Inmon, Shelli R. ... Dallas, TX
Innabi, Abdalla J. ... Los Angeles, CA
Innamorati, Joesph E. ... New York, NY
Innamorati, Joseph E. ... New York, NY
Innamorato, Arthur J., Jr. ... Pittsburgh, PA
Innamorato, Don A. ... Princeton, NJ
Innarelli, Albert V. ... Springfield, MA
Innelli, John F. ... Philadelphia, PA
Innelli and Molder ... Philadelphia, PA
Inneo, Susan A. ... Binghamton, NY
Innes, Gerald A. ... Elyria, OH
Innes, James B. ... Fort Lauderdale, FL
Innes, Kenneth F., III
United States Postal Service, Postal Inspection Service, GV
Innes, Laura E. ... San Francisco, CA
Innes, Linda S. ... Washington, DC
Cleveland, OH
Innes, Michael D. ... Boston, MA
Innes, Paul ... Hamilton, NJ
Innes, R. Perry ... Ann Arbor, MI
Innes, Robert K. ... San Francisco, CA
Innes, Roger G. ... Ellsworth, ME
Innes, Ronald D. ... Wichita, KS
Innes, Scott F. ... Bedford, NH
Innis & Barker Co., L.P.A. ... Columbus, OH
Innis, David F. ... San Francisco, CA
Innis, E. Eugene ... Chicago, IL
Innis, Mary E. ... Chicago, IL
Innis, Richard J. ... Boston, MA
Innis, Richard L. ... Columbus, OH
Inniss, Marie S. ... Detroit, MI
Innis-Thompson, Janice ... Purchase, NY
Innocenti, Trevor J. ... Columbus, OH
Lancaster, OH
Innocenzi, Louis D. ... Lawrenceville, NJ
Inoff, Darren Scott ... Houston, TX
Inokon, Charles M. ... Washington, DC
Inomata, Renee ... Boston, MA
Inosencio, Bruce Allen, Jr. ... Jackson, MI
Inoue, K. Anne ... Torrance, CA
Inoue, Toby ... New York, NY
Inouye, Cid H. ... Honolulu, HI
Inouye, Daniel H. ... New York, NY
Inouye, Daniel K. ... Honolulu, HI
Inouye, Daro G. ... San Francisco, CA
Inouye, Douglas H. ... Honolulu, HI
Inouye, Lance M. ... Honolulu, HI
Inouye, Lawrence G. ... Los Angeles, CA
Inouye, Margaret C. ... Seattle, WA
Inouye, Michael S. ... Newport Beach, CA
Inouye, Michelle M. ... Los Angeles, CA
Inouye & Ogden ... Torrance, CA
New York, NY
Inouye, Ralph S. ... Honolulu, HI
Inouye, Robert W. ... Yakima, WA
Inouye, Ronald N. ... New York, NY
Inouye, Sharon S. ... Santa Clara, CA
Inouye, Warren S. ... Irvine, CA
Insabella, John ... Tulsa, OK
Insabella, Philip ... Basking Ridge, NJ
Insalaco, Michelene ... San Francisco, CA
Insalaco, Richard C. ... New York, NY
Insalata, S. John ... Chicago, IL
Insana, Sam ... Phoenix, AZ
Insani Law Firm, The ... Rockwall, TX
Insani, Robert C. ... Rockwall, TX
Insardi, Janet M. ... Melville, NY
Mineola, NY
Insco, Michael A. ... St. Joseph, MO
Inscoe, Laura D. ... Richmond, VA
Inscoe, Linda M. ... San Francisco, CA
Inscore, Larry L. ... Mansfield, OH
Inscore, Michael L. ... Mansfield, OH
Inscore, Rinehardt, Whitney & Enderle Co., L.P.A. ... Mansfield, OH
Insel, A. Perry ... Beverly Hills, CA
Insel, Michael S. ... New York, NY
Insel, Neil Zvi ... Baltimore, MD
Insel, Steven J. ... Los Angeles, CA
Inselbuch, Elihu ... New York, NY
Inselmann, Robert K., Jr. ... Houston, TX
Inserni, Frank D. ... San Juan, PR
Inserni, Robert M. ... Corpus Christi, TX
Inserra, Daniel L. ... Jackson, MS
Inserra, Donna ... Bethesda, MD
Inserra, Elizabeth Bilotta ... New York, NY
Inserra, Francis C. ... Treasury Department, Internal Revenue Service, GV
Inserra, John P. ... Omaha, NE
Inserra, Joseph P. ... Omaha, NE
Inserra Law Offices ... Council Bluffs, IA
Omaha, NE
Insignares, Luis E. ... Cape Coral, FL
Fort Myers, FL
Lehigh Acres, FL
Insinga, Cheryl ... Binghamton, NY
Insinger, R. John ... Boise, ID
Insinna, Paul W. ... White Plains, NY
Inskeep, Carl D. ... Austin, TX
Inskeep, Don R. ... Riverside, CA
Inskeep, James W. ... Newport Beach, CA
Inskeep, Kenneth H. ... Indianapolis, IN
Inskeep, Kenneth H. ... Hubbard, OH
Inskeep, Leroy G. ... Chicago, IL
Inskip, Gregory A. ... Wilmington, DE
Inslee, Best, Doezie & Ryder, P.S.
Bellevue, WA
Seattle, WA
Inslee, Evan E. ... Bellevue, WA
Inslee, Jay R. ... Tacoma, WA
Insler, Amy L. ... Brooklyn, NY
Insler, Barbara Shayne Hirsch
New Orleans, LA
Insler, Bernard ... New Haven, CT
Insler, Lewis B. ... White Plains, NY
Insler, Michael S. ... Fort Lauderdale, FL
Insley, Brynda Rodriguez ... Atlanta, GA
Insley, David W. ... Columbus, OH
Insley, Edward J. ... Hackensack, NJ
Long Beach, NY
Insley, Edward J., P.A. ... Hackensack, NJ
Long Beach, NY
Insley, Gordon ... New York, NY
Insley, James S. ... Yorktown, VA
Insley and Race, LLC ... Atlanta, GA
Insley, Richard H. ... Hackensack, NJ
Insley, Richard W. ... St. Joseph, MI
Insley, Steven J. ... Paterson, NJ
Insley, Thomas I. ... Lake Elmo, MN
Insley, Wade H., III ... Salisbury, MD
Insogna, Anthony M. ... New York, NY
Insogna, Richard A. ... Amsterdam, NY
Insolia, Robert S. ... New York, NY
Insolio, Diana L. ... New Haven, CT
Insul, Alan M. ... Encino, CA
Insul, Donald A. ... Cleveland, OH
Intagliata, Patricia Shordt ... Toledo, OH
Intagliata, Sal D. ... Wichita, KS
Intagliata, Salvatore D. ... Wichita, KS
Intellectual Property Law Group
San Jose, CA
San Marino, CA
Intellectual Property/Technology Law
Chapel Hill, NC
Intemann, William H., Jr.
Lake Pleasant, NY
Interdonato, Andrew P. ... Temple Hills, MD
Interdonato, Anthony P. ... Potomac, MD
Interdonato, Anthony P., J.D., LLC
Potomac, MD
Interdonato, Julie A. ... New York, NY
Interdonato, Paul F. ... Potomac, MD
Interian, Alberto ... Miami, FL
Interlandi, James J. ... Chicago, IL
Interlichia, Joseph G. ... Rochester, NY
International Business Law Firm, P.C., The
Washington, DC
Arlington, VA
International Law Associates, L.L.P.
Great Falls, VA
International Law Collaborative
Cambridge, MA
International Legal Group, P.C.
Houston, TX
International Professional Services (IPS), Law Offices of ... San Francisco, CA
Internicola, Charles ... New York, NY
Interrante, Ashley E. ... Dallas, TX
Interrante, John G. ... Department of Justice, Civil Division, GV
Intihar, Stephen ... Columbus, OH
Intili, Ann Marie ... Cleveland, OH
Intili, Thomas J. ... Dayton, OH
Intintoli, Anthony J., Jr. ... Vallejo, CA
Intlekofer, Paul S. ... Bethesda, MD
Intner, Robert J. ... San Francisco, CA
Intner, Scott K. ... Baltimore, MD
Intoccia, Gary J. ... Florham Park, NJ
New York, NY
Intoccia, Gregory F. ... Washington, DC
Intoccia, Vincent P., III ... Birmingham, AL
Intrater, Karen A.
United States Postal Service, Law Department, GV
Intrater, Neil D. ... Silver Spring, MD
Intrator, Margo L. ... New York, NY
Intravaia, Barbara A. ... Salem, MA
Intravatola, Jeffrey S.
New Brunswick, NJ
Intravia, John J ... Fort Lauderdale, FL
Intravia, Joseph ... East Hartford, CT
Intravia, Sebastian A. ... East Hartford, CT
Intriago, Charles A. ... Miami, FL
Intrieri, Mark G. ... San Francisco, CA
San Jose, CA
Intriligator, Marc S. ... New York, NY
Introcaso, Anthony L. ... Manchester, NH
Introcaso, Julie A. ... Manchester, NH
Intschert, Cindy Foote ... Watertown, NY
Intzekostas, Erica A. ... Philadelphia, PA
Inveen, Laura C. ... Clyde Hill, WA
Inveiss, Andris E. ... San Diego, CA
Inveiss, Roberts E. ... Indianapolis, IN
Invergo, Anne ... Buffalo Grove, IL
Invernizzi, Frederick W. ... Baltimore, MD
Invicta Law Group PLLC ... Seattle, WA
Inwald, Chester ... New York, NY
Inwald, Jacob ... New York, NY
Inwald, Joseph M. ... Bloomfield Hills, MI
Inwood, John D. ... Hartford, CT
Inz, Jennifer M. ... Minneapolis, MN
Inz, Richard A. ... New York, NY
Inzeo, Jennifer Z. ... Madison, WI
Inzeo, Nicholas M., II
Equal Employment Opportunity Commission, Office of Legal Counsel, GV
Inzer, Haney, Johnson & McWhorter, P.A.
Gadsden, AL
Inzer, James C., III ... Gadsden, AL
Inzer, James C., Jr. ... Gadsden, AL
Inzerillo, Richard J. ... Smithtown, NY
Inzerillo, Richard J., P.C. ... Smithtown, NY
Inzetta, Mark S. ... Dublin, OH
Ioakimedes, Michael G. ... Vallejo, CA
Ioanes, Joyce ... Jamestown, RI
Ioannides, Margaret ... Jacksonville, FL
Ioannou, Angeline N. ... Cheshire, CT
Ioannou & Associates ... New York, NY
Ioannou, John M. ... New York, NY
Ioannou, Michael J. ... San Jose, CA
Ioannou, Michael J. ... Boca Raton, FL
Ioannou, Peter C. ... Morristown, NJ
Ioanou, Johnny A. ... Southfield, MI
Ioas, Chas. M. ... Alexandria, VA
Iobst, Frederick William ... Wilmington, DE
Iocco, Denise L. ... New York, NY
Iocolano, George R. ... Auburn, NY
Iocovozzi, Mary M. ... Herkimer, NY
Iodice, Frank P. ... Hartford, CT
Iodice, Pamela M. ... Annapolis, MD
Ioffredo, Glen J. ... Orlando, FL
Iola, Mark H. ... Tulsa, OK
Dallas, TX
Iola, Randall L. ... Tulsa, OK
Iola, Randall L., P.L.L.C., Law Offices of
Tulsa, OK
Iole, John E. ... Pittsburgh, PA
Ioli, Felicia ... Farmington Hills, MI
Ionescu, Istrate, II ... Stratford, CT
Ionetz, Misterovich & Paul ... Eastpointe, MI
Ionetz, Ronald G. ... Eastpointe, MI
Ionno, John M. ... Canton, OH
Ionta, Robert W. ... Gallup, NM
Ioppolo, Donna Krier ... Chicago, IL
Ioppolo, Frank J. ... North Babylon, NY
Ioppolo, Frank S. ... Lake Buena Vista, FL
Ioppolo, Frank S., Jr. ... Orlando, FL
Iorfido, Gary A. ... Hunt Valley, MD
Iori, Massimo E. ... Greenwich, CT
Iori, Ralph J., Jr. ... Scranton, PA
Iorii, Regina A. ... Wilmington, DE
Iorillo, Mario A., (P.C.) ... Los Angeles, CA
Iorio, Eileen Conway ... Pittsburgh, PA
Iorio, Fillipe S. ... Grand Rapids, MI
Iorio, Gary F. ... Oceanside, NY
Iorio, Richard ... Wichita, KS
Iorio, Theodore M. ... Grand Rapids, MI
Iorio-Power, Sandra G. ... Chicago, IL
Iossa, Rocco F. ... Newark, NJ
Iossa, Susan W. ... Philadelphia, PA
Iovacchini, Eric V. ... Asheville, NC
Iovenko, Michael ... New York, NY
Iovieno, Philip J. ... Albany, NY
New York, NY
Iovine, Luke P., III ... New York, NY
Iovinelli, Edward G., Jr. ... Scotia, NY
Iovino, Anthony F. ... Mineola, NY
Iovino, Charlyn Adlis ... Fairfax, VA
Iovino, Shelli L. ... Milford, PA
Iozzi, Vincent J. ... Philadelphia, PA
Iozzio, Frank J. ... Fair Lawn, NJ
Ip, Kamcheung T. ... New York, NY
Ipaktchi, Cyrus Kourosh ... San Mateo, CA
Iparraguirre, Roland H. ... Salem, OR
Ipavec, Charles F. ... Cleveland, OH
Ipe, J. Bruce ... Wilton, CT
Ipema, Bradley J. ... Treasury Department, Financial Management Service, GV
IPO Corporate Law Group
San Francisco, CA
Ipolito, Dorothy A. ... Upper Marlboro, MD
Ippel, Mary L. ... St. Paul, MN
Ippoliti, Marc D. ... Media, PA
Ippoliti, Michael R. ... Wilmington, DE
Ippolito, Alphonse ... New Haven, CT
Ippolito, Carl M. ... Pennington, NJ
Ippolito, Frank P. ... Lancaster, PA
Ippolito, Henry R. ... Rochester, NY
Ippolito, Jim R., Jr. ... Montgomery, AL
Ippolito, Joseph P. ... Medford, MA
Ippolito, Joseph T. ... New York, NY
Ippolito, Joseph V. ... Liberty Corner, NJ
Ippolito, Kenneth P. ... New York, NY
Ippolito, Loretta A. ... New York, NY
Ippolito, Marcia McGair ... Providence, RI
Ippolito, Mario J. ... Stamford, CT
Ippolito, Nancy Hahn ... Birmingham, AL
Ippolito, Nancy Underwood ... Dallas, TX
Ippolito, Peter J. ... San Diego, CA
Ippolito, Richard N. ... Buffalo, NY
Ippolito, Russell J. ... Tarrytown, NY
Ippolito, Russell T., Jr. ... Buffalo, NY
Ippolito, Ugo F. ... Atlanta, GA
Ipsaro, John R. ... Cincinnati, OH
Ipsen, Henry W. ... Denver, CO
Ipsen, Loren C. ... Boise, ID
Ipson, Steven E. ... Los Angeles, CA
Ipswitch, Candis Tyson, (Inc.)
Pasadena, CA
Iqbal, Walid ... New York, NY
Irace, Steven A. ... Garden City, NY
Iracki, Joseph F. ... Kingston, PA
Iraj, Cameron D. ... New York, NY
Irak, Joseph S. ... Merrillville, IN
Irani, Alice Davis ... Ann Arbor, MI
Irani, Jamshid S. ... New York, NY
Irani, Phillip M. ... Pittsburgh, PA
Irani, Rita Mankovich ... Dallas, TX
Houston, TX
Iraola, Roberto ... Washington, DC
Iraolagoitia, Amaya ... San Juan, PR
Irby, Curtis M. ... Wichita, KS
Irby & Heard, P.C. ... Fairhope, AL
Irby, Holt ... Garland, TX
Irby, James S. ... Seattle, WA
Irby, Jeanette A. ... Warrenton, VA
Irby, Jeanne K. ... Seattle, WA
Irby, Jeffrey S. ... Warrenton, VA
Irby, Jo A ... Detroit, MI
Irby, John Charles ... Casselton, ND
Irby, John H. ... Atlanta, GA
Irby, John R. ... Bakersfield, CA
Irby, Paul ... Tustin, CA
Irby, Peyton S., Jr. ... Jackson, MS
Irby, Richard M., III ... Washington, DC
Irby, Russell L. ... Eufaula, AL
Irby, Russell L., III ... Birmingham, AL
Irby, Sam W. ... Fairhope, AL
Irby, Terry M. ... Baton Rouge, LA
Irby, Todd Darrow ... Newport Beach, CA
Ircink, J.D. ... Oklahoma City, OK
Iredale, Eugene G. ... San Diego, CA
Iredale, Nancy L., (P.C.) ... Los Angeles, CA
Irel, Monica L. ... Miami, FL
Irelan & Associates ... Houston, TX
Irelan, Bradford Wald ... Houston, TX
Irelan, William T. ... Washington, DC
Ireland, Andrea (Andy) L.
Mountain View, CA
Ireland, Bruce L. ... Spokane, WA
Ireland, Carroll & Kelley, P.C. ... Tyler, TX
Ireland, Curt ... Rapid City, SD
Ireland, D. Jeffrey ... Dayton, OH
Ireland, Elizabeth L. ... Salisbury, MD
Ireland, Emory ... Milwaukee, WI
Ireland, Faith Enyeart ... Seattle, WA
Ireland, Gary E. ... New York, NY
Ireland, Glenn E. ... Birmingham, AL
Ireland, H. B., P.C. ... Dallas, TX
Ireland, H. Kelly ... Tyler, TX
Ireland, H. B., Jr. ... Dallas, TX
Ireland, H. C." Trey ", III
Birmingham, AL
Ireland, James F., III ... Washington, DC
Ireland, Joel T. ... Tucson, AZ
Ireland, Judy S. ... San Francisco, CA
Ireland, Kevin T. ... Seattle, WA
Ireland, Lawrence P. ... Topeka, KS
Ireland, Leonard E., Jr. ... Gainesville, FL
Ireland, M. Kevin ... Salina, KS
Ireland, Matthew C. ... Boston, MA
Ireland, Michael C. ... Aspen, CO
Ireland, Michael C., P.C. ... Aspen, CO
Ireland, Michael J. ... Thousand Oaks, CA
Ireland, Michael R. ... Terre Haute, IN
Ireland, Micheal A. ... Holton, KS
Ireland, Oliver I.
Board of Governors Of The Federal Reserve System, Office of the General Counsel, GV
Ireland, Pamela T. ... Fairfield, CT
Ireland, R. Eric ... Wichita, KS
Ireland, R. Timothy ... San Diego, CA
Ireland, Roderick L. ... Boston, MA
Ireland, Selby Allen ... Jackson, MS
Ireland, Sharon S. ... Pompano Beach, FL
Ireland, Stapleton, Pryor & Pascoe, P.C.
Denver, CO
Ireland, Thomas J. ... Baltimore, MD
Ireland, Timothy G. ... Akron, OH
Ireland, Timothy J. ... Richmond, VA
Ireland, Victor C. ... Newport Beach, CA
Ireland, William E. ... Santa Monica, CA
Irell, Eugene ... Rancho Mirage, CA
Irell, Lawrence E. ... Los Angeles, CA
Irell & Manella LLP ... Los Angeles, CA
Newport Beach, CA
Irenas, Joseph E. ... Camden, NJ
Irene, Juan E., Law Office of ... Buffalo, NY
Irenic, Michael A., Jr. ... New Brunswick, NJ
Ireson, Lansford O., Jr. ... Houston, TX
Ireson, Margot M. ... Houston, TX
Ireson & Weizel, P.C. ... Houston, TX
Ireton, C. Andrew, Jr. ... Columbus, OH
Ireton, Louis A. ... Cincinnati, OH
Ireton, Thomas F. ... Columbia, MD
Irey, Annabelle V. ... Buffalo, NY
Irey, Clark R., II ... Kansas City, MO
Irey, David J. ... Stockton, CA
Irey, James W. ... Los Angeles, CA
Irey, Stephanie S. ... Pasadena, CA
Irfan, Kareem M. ... Palatine, IL
Irgang, Scott L. ... New York, NY
Irgens, Ted L. ... Minneapolis, MN
Iriarte-Abdo, Maria ... Los Angeles, CA
Irick, Joan Fullam ... Indianapolis, IN
Irick, Laura J. ... Topeka, KS
Irick, Mark K. ... Dallas, OR
Irigoin, Katherine M. ... Sidney, MT
Irigonegaray, Pedro L. ... Topeka, KS
Iriguchi, Kathleen Ann ... Folsom, CA
Iriki, Steven L. ... San Francisco, CA
Irion, Frederick W. ... Champaign, IL
Irion, James E. ... Memphis, TN
Irion, James R., III ... Austin, TX
Irion, J. E. ... Memphis, TN
Irion, Jeffrey C. ... Gun Barrel City, TX
Irion, Joan K. ... La Jolla, CA
Irion, John S., Jr ... Lafayette, LA
Irion, Susan J. ... Hoffman Estates, IL
Irion, Terrence L. ... Austin, TX
Irion, William H. ... Smithtown, NY
Irish & Associates ... Oklahoma City, OK
Irish, Bruce D. ... West Frankfort, IL
Irish, Craig T. ... Phoenix, AZ
Irish, Douglas L. ... Phoenix, AZ
Irish, Ellen Eder ... Mount Vernon, IL
Irish, Herbert A. ... Washington, DC
Irish, James H. ... New York, NY
Irish, James L., III ... Dallas, TX
Irish, Jennifer E. ... Oklahoma City, OK
Irish, Jonathan M. ... Lubbock, TX
Irish, Robert L. ... Wheaton, IL
Irish, Roy M. ... Des Moines, IA
Irish, Ruthann Wendel ... Schaumburg, IL

Irizarry, Angelina .... Denver, CO
Irizarry, Anselmo Irizarry .... Ponce, PR
Irizarry, Armando .... New York, NY
Irizarry, Diana M. .... Rochester, NY
Irizarry, Francisco A. .... Miamisburg, OH
Irizarry, Frank .... New York, NY
Irizarry, George, Jr. .... Brooklyn, NY
Irizarry, McCall & Squarrell, P.C.
Denver, CO
Irizarry, Sigfredo A. .... San Juan, PR
Irizarry, Yolanda .... New York, NY
Irizarry-Díaz, Carmen .... Washington, DC
Irizarry-Rivera, Aníbal .... San Juan, PR
Irizarry-Rosso, Carmen V. .... San Juan, PR
Irizarry-Silvestrini, Rosalie .... San Juan, PR
Irizarry-Yunque, Carlos J. .... San Juan, PR
Irla, Barbara .... East Providence, RI
Irlbeck, Dennis H. .... Princeton, NJ
Irle, Judith L. .... Chicago, IL
Irmas, Sydney M. .... Los Angeles, CA
Irmen, J. Douglas .... Kansas City, MO
Irmen, James H. .... Toledo, OH
Irmer, Cynthia G. .... Falls Church, VA
Irminger, Douglas R. .... Upper Marlboro, MD
Irmscher, David P. .... Fort Wayne, IN
Irmscher, Scott W. .... Pittsburgh, PA
Irmscher, Susan .... Chicago, IL
Irom, Joseph M. .... Bronx, NY
Irom, Larry H. .... New York, NY
Irom, Wittels & Freund, P.C. .... Bronx, NY
Ironman, David G. .... Staten Island, NY
Irons, Ann Marie R. .... Quincy, MA
Irons, Ben G., II .... Greenville, NC
Irons, David R. .... North Kingsville, OH
Irons, Donald B. .... Blacksburg, VA
Irons, Ernest W. .... Skokie, IL
Irons & Glass .... Seattle, WA
Irons, Janet A. .... Seattle, WA
Irons, John H., Jr. .... Los Angeles, CA
Irons, Jonathan .... New York, NY
Irons, Paulette R. .... New Orleans, LA
Irons, Peter H. .... La Jolla, CA
Irons, Philip E. .... Lincoln, RI
Irons, Robert A. .... Union, WV
Irons, Spencer E. .... Flossmoor, IL
Irons, Tammy L. .... Florence, AL
Irons, Thomas J. .... Dallas, TX
Irons, William C. .... Memphis, TN
Ironson, Burton J. .... Elizabeth, NJ
Ironson, David H. .... Denville, NJ
Iroz, John M. .... Winnemucca, NV
Irpino, Mark A. .... Palatine, IL
Irpino & Miller .... Palatine, IL
Irrgang, Jennifer A. .... Philadelphia, PA
Irsfeld, Hannah C. .... Las Vegas, NV
Irsfeld, Irsfeld & Younger LLP
Glendale, CA
Los Angeles, CA
Ventura, CA
Irsfeld, James B., Jr. .... Glendale, CA
Irsfeld, Nicholas A. .... Fort Worth, TX
Irsfeld, Peter J., (P.C.) .... Glendale, CA
Irtz, Frederick G., II .... Lexington, KY
Irvin, A. McArthur .... Atlanta, GA
Irvin, A. Vann .... Durham, NC
Irvin, Alan J. .... Indianapolis, IN
Irvin, Ben L. .... Washington, DC
Irvin, Benny L. .... Marietta, GA
Irvin, Carol .... Chesterland, OH
Irvin, Cheryl E. .... Houston, TX
Irvin, Christopher J. .... Pacific Palisades, CA
Irvin & Clark .... Houston, TX
Irvin, D. Brent .... Nicholasville, KY
Irvin, David A. .... Winston-Salem, NC
Irvin, David R. .... Nicholasville, KY
Irvin, Donald E. .... Mount Vernon, IL
Irvin, Douglas M. .... Silver Spring, MD
Irvin, H. Stuart, Jr. .... Washington, DC
Irvin, Howard S. .... Concord, NC
Irvin, J. Edgar .... Eureka, NV
Irvin, J. Roger .... Butler, MO
Irvin, James K., (P.C.) .... New Orleans, LA
Irvin, James T. .... Toccoa, GA
Irvin, James T., III .... Columbia, SC
Irvin, James T., Jr. .... Beaufort, SC
Irvin, Jayne E. Whitehead .... Columbia, MO
Irvin, J. C. .... Shenandoah, IA
Irvin, Jefferson J. .... San Antonio, TX
Irvin, Jill .... New York, NY
Irvin, John G., Jr. .... Lexington, KY
Irvin, John J. .... Dallas, TX
Irvin, John S. .... Salem, OR
Irvin, Kathleen E. .... Dallas, TX
Irvin, Kenneth W. .... Washington, DC
Irvin Law Offices .... Boulder, CO
Irvin, Lester R. .... Rancho La Costa, CA
Irvin, Linda-Marie .... Boston, MA
Irvin, Mark M. .... Thomaston, GA
Irvin, Michael D. .... Goodland, KS
Irvin, Michael P. .... Houston, TX
Irvin, Patricia L. .... Washington, DC
Irvin, Paul B. .... Oviedo, FL
Winter Park, FL
Irvin, R. Lee .... Shreveport, LA
Irvin, Richard D. .... Boulder, CO
Irvin, Richd. W. .... Akron, OH
Irvin, Robert A. .... Atlanta, GA
Irvin, Robert D. .... Denver, CO
Irvin, Robert G. .... Los Angeles, CA
Irvin, Robert J. .... Coral Gables, FL
Irvin, Ruth K. .... Boulder, CO
Irvin, Stanford & Kessler, LLP
Atlanta, GA
Irvin, Stanley R. .... Marion, IL
Irvin, Susan K. .... Charlotte, NC
Irvin, Tiana Hinnant .... Durham, NC
Irvin, W. Arch, Jr. .... Pittsburgh, PA
Irvin, Walter L. .... Dallas, TX
Irvin, Wayne M. .... Dallas, TX
Irvin, William B. .... Granada Hills, CA
Irvin, William C. .... Cocoa Beach, FL
Irvin, William J. .... Fredericksburg, VA
Richmond, VA
Irvin, Wilmot B. .... Columbia, SC
Irvin, Wm Robert .... Washington, DC
Irvine, Bruce A. .... Media, PA
Irvine & Cooper .... Palo Alto, CA
Irvine, David H., II .... Dysart, IA
Irvine, David J., Jr. .... Williamston, NC
Irvine, David R. .... Salt Lake City, UT
Irvine, David R., A Professional Corporation
Salt Lake City, UT
Irvine, Dianne M. .... Cambridge, MA
Irvine, Douglas R. .... Los Angeles, CA
Irvine, Francis S. .... Oklahoma City, OK
Irvine, George R., III .... Bay Minette, AL
Daphne, AL
Foley, AL
Irvine, Ian M. .... San Francisco, CA
Irvine, J. Nelson .... Chattanooga, TN
Irvine, James D. .... Plymouth, MI
Irvine, John A. .... Houston, TX
Irvine, Joseph R. .... Columbus, OH
Irvine, Julie L. .... Sioux Falls, SD
Irvine, Katie A. .... Chicago, IL
Irvine, Kenneth F., Jr. .... Knoxville, TN
Irvine, Mark R. .... Los Angeles, CA
Irvine, Michael H. .... Cedar Rapids, IA
Irvine, Michael S. .... Buena Vista, VA
Irvine, Mori .... Washington, DC
Irvine, P. Bernard .... Manhattan, KS
Irvine, Patricia A. .... Perham, MN
Irvine, Patricia K. .... Seguin, TX
Irvine, Patricia K., P.C. .... Seguin, TX
Irvine, Perry A., (P.C.) .... Palo Alto, CA
Irvine, Peter M. .... Perham, MN
Irvine, Ramstad, Briggs, Karkela & Ziegler, P.A. .... Detroit Lakes, MN
Perham, MN
Irvine, Randy C. .... El Dorado Hills, CA
Irvine, Richard L. .... Department of Justice, Antitrust Division, GV
Irvine & Robbins .... Cedar Rapids, IA
Irvine, Robert J., III .... Chicago, IL
Irvine, Ronald A. .... Cottage Grove, OR
Irvine, Ronald A., P.C. .... Cottage Grove, OR
Irvine, R. W. .... Detroit Lakes, MN
Irvine, Sol L. .... New York, NY
Irvine, Stephanie B. .... Williamston, NC
Irvine, Stephen R. .... Marshalltown, IA
Irvine, Thomas B. .... Des Moines, IA
Irvine, Thomas K. .... Phoenix, AZ
Irvine, Timothy K. .... Austin, TX
Irvine Van Riper, P.A. .... Phoenix, AZ
Irvine, William H. .... Santa Barbara, CA
Irving, Alfred S., Jr. .... Department of Justice, Civil Division, GV
Irving, Andrew .... New York, NY
Irving, Andrew M. .... Treasury Department, Internal Revenue Service, GV
Irving, Brenza R. .... Monroe, LA
Irving, Brett .... Pittsfield, IL
Irving, Charles J. .... New London, CT
Irving, Christopher Lyle
Port Washington, NY
Irving, Daniel R. .... Red Bluff, CA
Irving, David L. .... Glasgow, MT
Irving, Dubicki & Camassar
New London, CT
Irving, Euclid A. .... New York, NY
Irving, Gary J. .... St. Joseph, MI
Irving, Gary L. .... Dedham, MA
Irving, George G. .... New York, NY
Irving, Ginny .... Berkeley, CA
Irving & Irving, P.C. .... Pittsfield, IL
Irving, J. Bruce .... Miami, FL
Irving, J. Lawrence .... San Diego, CA
Irving, James V. .... Springfield, VA
Irving, Jane E. (Basserman)
Millersburg, OH
Irving, Janelle .... Salem, OR
Irving, Janice .... Baton Rouge, LA
Irving, Jeanine M. .... Leesburg, VA
Irving, Jeanne E. .... Los Angeles, CA
Irving, Jeffrey A. .... Great Neck, NY
Irving, John F. X. .... Morristown, NJ
Irving, John R. .... Montrose, CO
Irving, John S., Jr. .... Washington, DC
Irving, Karen Whitmer .... Lexington, KY
Irving & Lynch .... New York, NY
Irving, Macculloch M. .... New York, NY
Irving, Margaret A. .... Washington, DC
Irving, Michael W. .... Los Angeles, CA
Irving, Nancy S. .... Olympia, WA
Irving, Paul D. .... Los Angeles, CA
Irving, Paul D. .... Rochester, NY
Irving, Paul H. .... Los Angeles, CA
Irving, Paul R. .... Phoenix, AZ
Irving, Rebecca A. .... Machias, ME
Irving, Richard C. .... Washington, DC
Irving, Richard H., III .... Montgomery, AL
Irving, Stephen A. .... Knoxville, TN
Irving, Stephen Eric .... Washington, DC
Irving, Stephen M. .... Baton Rouge, LA
Irving, Stephen W. .... Atlanta, GA
Irving, Stephen W., P.C. .... Atlanta, GA
Irving, Suzanne J. .... New York, NY
Irving, Thomas L. .... Washington, DC
Irving, Timothy P. .... Irvine, CA
San Diego, CA
Irving, William H. .... Dearborn, MI
Irvings, Augusta F. .... New York, NY
Irvings, Mark .... Brookline, MA
Irvings, Ruth J. .... Wauwatosa, WI
Irwin, Andrew D. .... Washington, DC
Irwin, Ann B. .... Rochester, NY
Irwin, Barbara Jane .... Chicago, IL
Irwin, Barry D. .... Dallas, TX
Irwin, Barry F. .... Chicago, IL
Irwin, Barry Gordon .... Athens, GA
Irwin, Bart G. .... Port Angeles, WA
Irwin, Betty J. .... Mendocino, CA
Irwin & Boesen, P.C. .... Denver, CO
Irwin, Bradley R. .... Denver, CO
Irwin, Campbell & Tannenwald, P.C.
Washington, DC
Irwin, Catherine E. S. .... San Bernardino, CA
Irwin, Charles A. .... Bisbee, AZ
Irwin, Charles J. .... Trenton, NJ
Irwin, Claude K. .... Pullman, WA
Irwin, Craig D. .... New Haven, CT
Irwin, Dale K. .... Kansas City, MO
Irwin, Dana Dahl .... Dallas, TX
Irwin, David A. .... Washington, DC
Irwin, David B. .... Conyers, GA
Irwin, David B. .... Baltimore, MD
Irwin, David K. .... Williamsport, PA
Irwin, David M. .... New York, NY
Irwin, Debra .... Austin, TX
Irwin, Dennis F. .... Albany, NY
Irwin, Donald P. .... Richmond, VA
Irwin, Douglas J. .... Wichita, KS
Irwin, Douglas R. .... San Diego, CA
Irwin, Douglas S. .... Beverly Hills, CA
Irwin, E. David .... New York, NY
Irwin, Edward D. .... Aspen, CO
Irwin, Felix M., III .... Bel Air, MD
Irwin, Gary .... Minneapolis, MN
Irwin, Gary J. .... Crown Point, IN
Irwin, Geoffrey S. .... Washington, DC
Chicago, IL
Irwin, George H., IV .... Emeryville, CA
Irwin Green & Dexter, L.L.P.
Baltimore, MD
Irwin, Gregory J. .... Hackensack, NJ
Irwin, H. Allyn .... Jacksonville, FL
Irwin, Harold S., III .... Carlisle, PA
Irwin, Helen .... Los Angeles, CA
Irwin, Herbert W. .... Pompton Plains, NJ
Irwin, J. Kaye .... Springfield, MO
Irwin, J. Lawrence .... Auburn, ME
Irwin, James .... Lower Burrell, PA
Irwin, James A. .... Los Angeles, CA
Irwin, James B. .... New Orleans, LA
Irwin, James L. .... Austin, TX
Irwin, James R. .... Meadville, PA
Irwin, James R. .... Seattle, WA
Irwin, James S. .... Hamilton, OH
Irwin, Jay R. .... Yuma, AZ
Irwin, Jeanne .... Portland, ME
Irwin, John A. .... Milton, MA
Irwin, John A., Jr. .... Milton, MA
Irwin, John E., Jr .... Los Angeles, CA
Irwin, John G. .... Telluride, CO
Irwin, John K. .... Sylvan Lake, MI
Irwin, John K., P.C. .... Sylvan Lake, MI
Irwin, John P., III .... New York, NY
Irwin, John R. .... Cleveland, OH
Irwin, John S. .... Amarillo, TX
Irwin & Johnson .... Carrollton, TX
Irwin, Jon .... Coeur d'Alene, ID
Irwin, Jonathan E. .... Chicago, IL
Irwin, Jordan R. .... Cherry Hill, NJ
Irwin, Karl H. .... Upper Arlington, OH
Irwin, Kathleen S. .... Madison, WI
Irwin, Kevin E. .... Cincinnati, OH
Irwin, Laura Schleich .... Pittsburgh, PA
Irwin, Lauren Simon .... Concord, NH
Irwin, Lewin, Cohn & Lewin, P.C.
New York, NY
Irwin, Lori K. .... Philadelphia, PA
Irwin, Lynn Snyderman .... Pittsburgh, PA
Irwin, Martha W. .... Phoenix, AZ
Irwin, McKnight & Hughes .... Carlisle, PA
Irwin, Michael E. .... Heber Springs, AR
Irwin, Michael J. .... Los Angeles, CA
Irwin, Michael K. .... Indianapolis, IN
Irwin, Michael T. .... Westerville, OH
Irwin, Micheal Lawrence .... Orlando, FL
Irwin, Myklebust, Savage & Brown, P.S.
Clarkston, WA
Pullman, WA
Irwin, Pat .... Oklahoma City, OK
Irwin, Paul S. .... Arlington, TX
Irwin, Paul S. .... Irving, TX
Irwin, Peter A. .... New York, NY
Irwin, Philip D. .... Los Angeles, CA
Irwin, Philip D. .... Nashville, TN
Irwin & Post, P.A. .... Newark, NJ
Irwin, R. Chris .... Atlanta, GA
Irwin, R. Dean .... Downers Grove, IL
Irwin, R. Dean, III .... Houston, TX
Irwin, R. Dean, Ltd. .... Downers Grove, IL
Irwin, R. Neil .... Phoenix, AZ
Irwin, R. Robert .... Englewood, CO
Irwin, Richard H. .... Riverside, CA
Irwin, Robert E. .... Russellville, AR
Irwin, Robert P. .... San Diego, CA
Irwin, Robert Thomas, II .... Tulsa, OK
Irwin, Roger B. .... Carlisle, PA
Irwin, Ross C. .... Pomona, CA
Irwin, Sandra McMahan .... Pasadena, CA
Irwin, Scott D. .... Cleveland, OH
Irwin, Stephanie Lottinger
New Orleans, LA
Irwin, Stephen .... New York, NY
Irwin, Stephen B. .... New York, NY
Irwin, Steven D. .... Pittsburgh, PA
Irwin, Steven J. .... Gulfport, MS
Irwin, Steven R. .... West Orange, NJ
Irwin, Susan E. .... Phoenix, AZ
Irwin, Susan J. .... Boston, MA
Irwin, Susan Rae .... Bellevue, WA
Irwin, Susan Wachtel
General Accounting Office, Office of the General Counsel, GV
Irwin, Teresa L. Boron .... Sacramento, CA
Irwin, Theodore H., Jr. .... Portland, ME
Irwin, Thomas F. .... Manchester, NH
Irwin, Thomas J. .... Princeton, NJ
Irwin, Thomas L. .... Verona, NJ
Irwin, Thomas M. .... Hastings, MN
Irwin, Timothy E. .... Knoxville, TN
Irwin, William A.
Department Of The Interior, Office of Hearings & Appeals, GV
Irwin, William D. .... St. James City, FL
Irwin, William P. .... Fresno, CA
Irwin, William R. .... San Francisco, CA
Irwin, William W., Jr. .... Baton Rouge, LA
Irwin, Wm. B., Jr. .... Galena Park, TX
Irwin, Woodrow N. .... Los Angeles, CA
Iryami, Dara .... New York, NY
Irza, Helen S. .... San Diego, CA
Isaac, Allen H. .... New York, NY
Isaac, Andrew L. .... Eureka, CA
Isaac, Anne A. .... Greensboro, NC
Isaac, Brant, Ledman & Teetor
Columbus, OH
Isaac, Brian J. .... New York, NY
Isaac, Charles D. .... Glastonbury, CT
Isaac, Christopher P. .... Washington, DC
Isaac, David A. .... New York, NY
Isaac, Dennis P. .... San Francisco, CA
Isaac, Donald .... Fort Myers, FL
Isaac, Eldad Philip .... Trenton, NJ
Isaac, Elliot S. .... Phoenix, AZ
Isaac, Evelyn K. .... White Plains, NY
Isaac, Frank K. .... Westlake, OH
Isaac, Fred C. .... Jacksonville, FL
Isaac, Frederick M. .... Columbus, OH
Isaac, Gary A. .... Chicago, IL
Isaac, Geoffrey L. .... Chicago, IL
Isaac, Godfrey .... Los Angeles, CA
Isaac, Gregory A. .... Prestonsburg, KY
Isaac, Holly Hambrick .... Little Rock, AR
Isaac, John L. .... Boulder, CO
Isaac, Kathleen Mahon
San Francisco, CA
Isaac, Lance E. .... Bismarck, ND
Isaac, Leonard M. .... Waterbury, CT
Isaac, Paul K. .... West Seneca, NY
Isaac, Philip D. .... Hagåtña, GU
Isaac, Ramsen .... Lincolnwood, IL
Isaac, Richard B. .... Westminster, MD
Isaac, Robert M. .... Colorado Springs, CO
Isaac, Robert P., Jr. .... Salamanca, NY
Isaac, Roger G. .... Flint, MI
Isaac, Ronald G. .... Federal Trade Commission, Bureau of Consumer Protection, GV
Isaac, Ronald G. .... Indianapolis, IN
Isaac, Ruth Ellen .... Atlanta, GA
Isaac, Sheila R. .... Lexington, KY
Isaac, Teresa Ann .... Lexington, KY
Isaac, Thomas R. .... Des Moines, IA
Isaac, Thomas W. .... Fresno, CA
Isaac, Tina K. .... Inver Grove Heights, MN
Isaacks, Bruce .... Carrollton, TX
Isaacks, Lewis L., Jr. .... Plano, TX
Isaacman, Alan L. .... Beverly Hills, CA
Isaacman, David .... Elizabeth, NJ
Isaacman, Geoffrey .... Minneapolis, MN
Isaacman, Kaufman & Painter
Beverly Hills, CA
Los Angeles, CA
Isaacman, Seymour .... Elizabeth, NJ
Isaacs, Alley & Harvey, L.L.P.
Columbia, SC
Lexington, SC
Isaacs, Anna H. .... Frankfort, KY
Isaacs, Asher .... Los Angeles, CA
Isaacs, Audrey J. .... New York, NY
Isaacs, Barak .... Van Nuys, CA
Isaacs, Bernard M. .... New York, NY
Isaacs, Bruce Alan .... Beverly Hills, CA
Isaacs, Burton E. .... Southfield, MI
Isaacs & Clouse .... Los Angeles, CA
Santa Monica, CA
Isaacs, Craig A. .... New York, NY
Isaacs, Cynthia A. .... Seattle, WA
Isaacs, Daniel M. .... New York, NY
Isaacs, Darryl L. .... Louisville, KY
Isaacs, Davida H. .... Washington, DC
Isaacs, Dean Alan .... Chicago, IL
Isaacs, Denise Rappaport .... Boca Raton, FL
Isaacs, Dorothy M. .... Fairfax, VA
Isaacs, Dwayne C. .... Indianapolis, IN
Isaacs, Elissa L. .... Chicago, IL
Isaacs & Evans, LLP .... New York, NY
Isaacs, Fred M. .... Portland, OR
Isaacs, Garvin A. .... Oklahoma City, OK
Isaacs, Garvin A., Inc.
Oklahoma City, OK
Isaacs, Gary A. .... West Palm Beach, FL
Isaacs, Glen H. .... San Francisco, CA
Isaacs, Gregory P. .... Knoxville, TN
Isaacs, H. Carl, Jr. .... Birmingham, AL
Isaacs, Hanan M. .... Princeton, NJ
Isaacs, Harvey A. .... New York, NY
Isaacs and Isaacs, P.S.C. .... Louisville, KY
Isaacs, Jack D. .... San Francisco, CA
Isaacs, James B., Jr. .... Santa Monica, CA
Isaacs, Jason B. .... San Diego, CA
Isaacs, Jed P. .... New York, NY
Isaacs, Jeffrey .... San Diego, CA
Isaacs, Jeffrey B. .... Los Angeles, CA
Isaacs, Jeffrey S. .... Newark, NJ
Isaacs, Joan R. .... Beverly Hills, CA
Isaacs, Jonathan Dean .... Rockville, MD
Isaacs, Joseph M. .... Brooklyn, NY
Isaacs, Kandi Kay .... Fort Worth, TX

Isaacs, Lawrence ... Tarrytown, NY
Isaacs, Leigh R. ... New York, NY
Isaacs, Leonard B. ... Valley Stream, NY
Isaacs, Lori D. ... Chicago, IL
Isaacs, Marc J. ... New York, NY
Isaacs, Marc J., P.C. ... New York, NY
Isaacs, Michael A. ... San Francisco, CA
San Jose, CA
Isaacs, Michael B. ... East Greenwich, RI
Isaacs, Michael J. ... Wilmington, DE
Isaacs, Michael L. ... Westport, CT
Isaacs, Michael S. ... Westwood, NJ
Isaacs, Patricia A. ... El Cajon, CA
Isaacs, Paul F. ... Frankfort, KY
Isaacs, Randi S. ... New York, NY
Isaacs, Rayson & Ramsey ... Knoxville, TN
Isaacs, Robert C. ... West Lebanon, NH
Isaacs, Ronald L ... Carbondale, IL
Isaacs, Rosalie ... Downers Grove, IL
Isaacs, Sabrina B. ... New York, NY
Isaacs, Samuel E., II ... Lexington, KY
Isaacs, Sheldon N. ... Louisville, KY
Isaacs, Stephanie A. ... St. Petersburg, FL
Isaacs, Stephen A., Law Office
Richmond, VA
Isaacs, Steve E. ... Chicago, IL
Isaacs, Steven A. ... New York, NY
Isaacs, W. Joseph ... Columbia, SC
Isaacs-McLeod, Molly A. ... Southfield, MI
Isaacsohn, Louis J. ... Philadelphia, PA
Isaacson, Allen ... Washington, DC
Isaacson, Allen I., (P.C.) ... New York, NY
Isaacson, Andrew L. ... Silver Spring, MD
Isaacson, Barry W. ... Chicago, IL
Isaacson, Cathy Wright ... New York, NY
Isaacson, Darrell J. ... Mason City, IA
Isaacson, David ... New City, NY
New York, NY
Isaacson, David C. ... Washington, DC
Isaacson, Donald G. ... Phoenix, AZ
Isaacson, Eric A. ... San Diego, CA
Isaacson, Erin B. ... Rosemont, IL
Isaacson, George S. ... Lewiston, ME
Isaacson, Henry ... New York, NY
Isaacson, Henry H. ... Greensboro, NC
Isaacson, Herbert G. ... Farmington, CT
Isaacson, Irving ... Lewiston, ME
Isaacson, Irving M. ... Des Moines, IA
Isaacson & Isaacson ... Los Angeles, CA
Isaacson & Isaacson ... Greensboro, NC
High Point, NC
Isaacson, Jack S. ... New York, NY
Isaacson, James M. ... Cadott, WI
Isaacson, Jeffrey ... New York, NY
Isaacson, Jeffrey J. ... Taunton, MA
Isaacson, Jeffrey Mark ... North Riverside, IL
Isaacson, Joel R. ... Los Angeles, CA
Isaacson, John C. ... Princeton, IL
Isaacson, Keli B.C. ... Baltimore, MD
Isaacson, Kenneth J. ... West Orange, NJ
Isaacson, Laurence Bryan ... New York, NY
Isaacson, Leonard A. ... New York, NY
Isaacson, Lon B. ... Los Angeles, CA
Isaacson, Marc L. ... Greensboro, NC
Isaacson, Marc R. ... Pasadena, CA
Isaacson, Mark J. ... Minneapolis, MN
Isaacson, Maureen B. ... Los Angeles, CA
Isaacson, Nancy ... Chatham, NJ
Isaacson, Paul N. ... Salt Lake City, UT
Isaacson, Philip M. ... Lewiston, ME
Isaacson & Raymond, P.A. ... Lewiston, ME
Isaacson, Richard I. ... Beverly Hills, CA
Isaacson, Richard R. ... Pittsburgh, PA
Isaacson, Rodger J. ... Klamath Falls, OR
Isaacson, Rosenbaum, Woods & Levy, P.C.
Denver, CO
Isaacson, Samuel B. ... Chicago, IL
Isaacson, Sandy N. ... Chicago, IL
Isaacson, Schiowitz, Korson & Solny, LLP
New York, NY
Isaacson, Scott Emery ... Salt Lake City, UT
Isaacson, Seymour Z. ... Randallstown, MD
Isaacson, Steven B. ... Chicago, IL
Isaacson, Steven C. ... St. Cloud, MN
Isaacson, Steven H. ... Florham Park, NJ
Isaacson, Tara L. ... Salt Lake City, UT
Isaacson, Thomas A. ... Washington, DC
Isaacson, Thomas A. ... Washington, DC
Isaacson, Thomas Lynn ... Gallup, NM
Isaacson, Toby ... Clearwater, FL
Isaacson, Toby, P.A., Law Office of
Clearwater, FL
Isaacson, Troy L. ... San Diego, CA
Isaacson, Walter H. ... Milton, WI
Isaacson, William A. ... Washington, DC
Armonk, NY
Isaacson, William H. ... Phoenix, AZ
Tucson, AZ
Isaacson, William J. ... Chicago, IL
Isaak, Charles J. ... St. Louis, MO
Isaak, Charles N. ... Beaverton, OR
Isaak, G. Eugene ... Tucson, AZ
Isaak, Malka ... Tampa, FL
Isaak, Malka, P.A., Law Offices of
Tampa, FL
Isaak, Marcia ... Baltimore, MD
Isabel, Alexander B. ... Fonda, NY
Isabel, David L. ... Morristown, NJ
Isabella, Carlene M. ... Virginia Beach, VA
Isabella, Duane A. ... Baltimore, MD
Isabella, Joseph V. ... Belleville, NJ
Isabella, Mary Margaret ... Pittsburgh, PA
Isackson, Carol ... San Diego, CA
Isackson, Neering & Quinn, P.C.
Bay City, MI
Isackson, Ralph J. ... Bay City, MI
Isackson, Robert M. ... New York, NY
Isacoff, Adrienne L. ... West Orange, NJ
Isacoff, Mitchell A. ... Doylestown, PA
Isacoff, Richard I. ... Pittsfield, MA
Isacoff, Richard I., P.C. ... Pittsfield, MA
Isacson, John P., Jr. ... Washington, DC
Isacson, Linda M. ... Department of Commerce,
Patent and Trademark Office, GV
Isadore, Harold W. ... Baton Rouge, LA
Isaeff, Marianne D. ... San Bernardino, CA
Isaeff, Randall S. ... San Bernardino, CA
Isaeff, William E. ... Sparks, NV
Isaf, Daniel Martin ... Beverly, MA
Isaf, Fred T. ... Atlanta, GA
Isaf, Louis T. ... Atlanta, GA
Isaf, Mark R. ... Paris, IL
Isaf, Vaughan & Kerr, P.C. ... Atlanta, GA
Marietta, GA
Isaia, Russell E. ... Boston, MA
Isakoff, Andrew H. ... Cleveland, OH
Isakoff, Janice A. ... Cleveland, OH
Isakoff, Louis A. ... Virginia Beach, VA
Isakoff, Peter D. ... Washington, DC
Isakow, Norma-May ... Denver, CO
Isaksen, Robert D. ... Middleton, WI
Isakson, Carole Clark ... Minneapolis, MN
Isakson, Charles R. ... Bismarck, ND
Isales, Lydia ... Philadelphia, PA
Isaly, Charles W. ... Cincinnati, OH
Isaminger, Amy S. ... San Antonio, TX
Isanuk, Barry D. ... Aberdeen, NJ
Isasi, José A., II ... Chicago, IL
Isaza, Catherine A. ... Greenville, SC
Isaza, John J. ... Irvine, CA
Isban, Mary G. ... Phoenix, AZ
Isbell, Allan L. ... Walnut Creek, CA
Isbell, Bonney & Associates, P.C.
Muskogee, OK
Oklahoma City, OK
Isbell, Cecily A. ... Hartford, CT
Isbell, David B. ... Washington, DC
Isbell, David W. ... Colorado Springs, CO
Isbell, Ernest E. ... Sweetwater, TN
Isbell, Gregory D. ... Chicago, IL
Isbell, James N. ... Houston, TX
Isbell, Joe H. ... New Braunfels, TX
Isbell, John A. ... Dallas, TX
Isbell, Jonathan ... Edwardsville, IL
Isbell, Michael T. ... New York, NY
Isbell, Robert H. ... Avon Lake, OH
Isbell, Sheila Dianne ... Gadsden, AL
Isbell, Will D. ... San Diego, CA
Isbell, William C. ... Muskogee, OK
Oklahoma City, OK
Isberg, Arthur L. ... Norwood, MA
Isbester, A. James ... San Francisco, CA
Isbill, Charlotte Shuford ... Lowell, NC
Isbister, John B. ... Baltimore, MD
Isbrandtsen, Carl W. ... Virginia Beach, VA
Isbrandtsen, Carl W., P.C.
Virginia Beach, VA
Isby, Michael ... New York, NY
Iscaro, Robert ... New York, NY
Ischie, Wilbur N. ... Painesville, OH
Ischy, David E. ... Kingwood, TX
Iscoe, Craig ... Department of Justice,
Office of the Deputy Attorney General, GV
Iscoe, Gary Thomas ... Boynton Beach, FL
Isdale-Ryan, Margaret Holly ... New York, NY
Ise, A. Richard ... Philadelphia, PA
Ise, Ashley Anne Roberts ... St. Petersburg, FL
Ise, William H. ... Dodge Center, MN
Isele, Cheryl A. ... San Francisco, CA
Isele, Michele A. ... Washington, DC
Iseley, Christopher J. ... Jacksonville, FL
Iseley, Robert Craig ... Sacramento, CA
Iseley, Robert F., Jr. ... Jacksonville, FL
Iselin, Benjamin B. ... New York, NY
Iselin, Harold N. ... Albany, NY
Iselin, Josephine Lea ... New York, NY
Iseman, Charles J.
Federal Communications Commission,
Office of Engineering & Technology, GV
Iseman, Cunningham, Riester & Hyde, LLP
Albany, NY
Canandaigua, NY
Schenectady, NY
Troy, NY
Iseman, Harvey ... Philadelphia, PA
Iseman, James M., Jr.
Winston-Salem, NC
Iseman, John J. ... Sterling Heights, MI
Iseman, Robert Hall ... Albany, NY
Iseman, William J. ... Santa Clara, CA
Isen and Grant, Incorporated
Los Angeles, CA
Isen, John M. ... Los Angeles, CA
Isen, Julian C. ... Los Angeles, CA
Isen, Kenneth A. ... Bethesda, MD
Isen, Lance G. ... San Bernardino, CA
Isen, Richard S. ... Treasury Department,
Bureau of Alcohol, Tobacco and Firearms, GV
Isenbarger, Phil L. ... Indianapolis, IN
Isenberg, Adam H. ... Philadelphia, PA
Isenberg, Andrew B. ... Buffalo, NY
Isenberg, Bruce K. ... Chappaqua, NY
Isenberg, Charles R. ... Louisville, KY
Isenberg, Clifford Scott ... Washington, DC
Isenberg, Craig ... Washington, DC
Isenberg, Daniel ... Los Angeles, CA
Isenberg, David ... Los Angeles, CA
Isenberg, Douglas M. ... Atlanta, GA
Isenberg, Harriet C. ... Atlanta, GA
Isenberg & Hewitt, P.C. ... Atlanta, GA
Isenberg, James E. ... Louisville, KY
Isenberg, Jeffrey P. ... Eden Prairie, MN
Isenberg, Jennifer L. ... San Francisco, CA
Isenberg, Jerry A.
Securities and Exchange Commission,
Division of Enforcement, GV
Isenberg, Jody L. ... San Bernardino, CA
Isenberg, Joel S. ... Birmingham, AL
Isenberg, Kenneth T. ... San Antonio, TX
Isenberg, Lawrence M. ... Woodland Hills, CA
Isenberg, Lawrence T. ... Pompton Lakes, NJ
Isenberg, Marc D. ... Houston, TX
Isenberg, Marc N., (P.A.) ... Maywood, NJ
Isenberg, Michael A. ... Boston, MA
Isenberg, Michael L. ... Raleigh, NC
Isenberg, Michael R. ... Southport, NC
Isenberg, Nancy S. ... Tallahassee, FL
Isenberg, Phillip L. ... Sacramento, CA
Isenberg, Randall Blair ... Dallas, TX
Isenberg & Riskind ... Houston, TX
Isenberg, Robin ... Alexandria, VA
Isenberg, Steven L. ... New York, NY
Isenberg, Thomas L., Jr. ... Harrisburg, PA
Isenberg, William S. ... Fort Lauderdale, FL
Isenbergh, Joseph ... Chicago, IL
Isenburg, Dennis L. ... San Francisco, CA
Isenhart, Heidi W. ... Winter Park, FL
Isenhour, Sharon A. ... San Leandro, CA
Isenhour, Thomas K. ... Elizabeth, NJ
Isenhour, William O., Jr. ... Olathe, KS
Isenhower, C. Randall ... Newton, NC
Isenhower, Daniel ... Austin, TX
Isenhower, David L. ... Newton, NC
Isenhower, Wood & Cilley, P.A.
Newton, NC
Isenman, Barry ... Paoli, PA
Isenman, Etta Landau ... Bethesda, MD
Isenman, Michael K. ... Washington, DC
Isensee, Earl H. A., Jr. ... Edina, MN
Isensee, Lynne C. ... New York, NY
Isensee, Robt. H. ... Clear Lake, IA
Isenstein, Tania B. ... New York, NY
Iser, Lawrence Y. ... Los Angeles, CA
Iseringhausen, Ferdinand J., Jr.
Lafayette, LA
Iserman, Iserman & Gathman
Cold Spring Harbor, NY
Iserman, James J. ... El Paso, TX
Iserman, Jordan Marshall
Cold Spring Harbor, NY
Isern, Jane M. ... Great Bend, KS
Isern, Kevin A. ... Amarillo, TX
Isern, Martin ... Ellinwood, KS
Iserson, Andrew Martin ... Rochester, NY
Isert-Kott, Ilene M. ... San Francisco, CA
Isgard, Richard E. ... New York, NY
Isgett, Christopher C. ... Columbia, SC
Isgrigg, John W. ... Pontiac, MI
Isgrigg, Laura L. ... Newbury Park, CA
Isgrigg, Robert G., Jr. ... Pontiac, MI
Isgro, Connie L. ... Portland, OR
Isgro, Francesco ... Department of Justice,
Civil Division, GV
Isgur, Marvin ... Houston, TX
Isgur, Michael Stuart ... Middletown, NY
Ish, Mark L. ... Santa Fe, NM
Ishado, Lester J. ... Hilo, HI
Ishak, April Caso ... Wilmington, DE
Ishak, Paul W. ... Bel Air, MD
Havre de Grace, MD
Isham, Don ... Seattle, WA
Isham, Duane L. ... Akron, OH
Isham, Paul C. ... Huntsville, TX
Isham, Richard B. ... Visalia, CA
Isham, Robert T., Jr. ... Chicago, IL
Isham, Rodney Shay ... Stephenville, TX
Ishaq, Rebecca T. ... Bakersfield, CA
Ishbia & Gagleard, P.C. ... Birmingham, MI
Ishbia, Jeffrey A. ... Birmingham, MI
Ishee, David M. ... Pascagoula, MS
Ishee, Dixie White ... Memphis, TN
Ishee, James J. ... Fairfax, VA
Ishee, Lee Herold ... Lafayette, LA
Ishee, Roger E. ... Lafayette, LA
Isherwood, Boyd K. ... Wichita, KS
Isherwood, Gary R. ... Plover, WI
Isherwood, Howard ... Allenhurst, NJ
Isherwood & Isherwood, P.C.
Christiansted, St. Croix, VI
Isherwood, James F. ... Newark, NJ
Isherwood, James H.
Christiansted, St. Croix, VI
Isherwood, James H., III
Christiansted, St. Croix, VI
Isherwood, John Scott ... Walnut Creek, CA
Isherwood, Raymond T. ... Clearwater, FL
Isherwood, Thomas ... Wall Township, NJ
Ishibashi, Jon M. ... San Ramon, CA
Ishibashi, Peter ... Rock Island, IL
Ishida, Lincoln J. ... Honolulu, HI
Ishida, Lyle Minoru ... Honolulu, HI
Ishida, Ronna Mae ... Hercules, CA
Ishihara, John ... Honolulu, HI
Ishihara, Margaret A. ... Mattapoisett, MA
Ishii, Elizabeth Ann ... Honolulu, HI
Ishii, Robert T. ... Palo Alto, CA
Ishii-Regan, Suzanne K. ... Anchorage, AK
Ishikawa, Brendon T. ... Davis, CA
Ishikawa, Brian K. ... Mesa, AZ
Ishikawa, Jesse S. ... Milwaukee, WI
Ishikawa, Jin ... Fresno, CA
Ishikawa, Mark D. ... Phoenix, AZ
Ishikawa, Renee R. ... Wailuku, HI
Ishikawa, Richard M. ... Los Angeles, CA
Ishikawa, Richard M. ... Seattle, WA
Ishikawa, Robert ... Fresno, CA
Ishimaru, Mikio ... Sunnyvale, CA
Ishimaru, Stuart J. ... Department of Justice,
Civil Rights Division, GV
Ishimatsu, Bruce L. ... Santa Monica, CA
Ishimatsu, Kyle Machara
Pacific Palisades, CA
Ishimoto, James H. ... San Antonio, TX
Ishizuka, Yuki ... Bellevue, WA
Ishmael, Fox & Rasansky, L.L.P. ... Dallas, TX
Ishmael, James D., Jr. ... Lexington, KY
Ishmael, R. Edward, Jr. ... Dallas, TX
Ishmael, Randall W. ... Jonesboro, AR
Ishofsky, Harvey J. ... Great Neck, NY
Ishola, Hakeem ... Salt Lake City, UT
Ishon, Jane Jordan ... Hampton, VA
Isicoff, Eric D. ... Miami, FL
Isicoff, Laurel M. ... Miami, FL
Isicoff & Ragatz, P.A. ... Miami, FL
Isicrate, Paul V. ... Blackwood, NJ
Isikoff, Anita ... Washington, DC
Isidor, John M. ... Cincinnati, OH
Isidro, Gil A. ... New York, NY
Isidro, Jose G., Jr. ... Flushing, NY
Isikow, Michael S. ... New York, NY
Ising, Judith G. ... Pittsboro, NC
Ising, Paul D.
Department Of Veterans Affairs,
Veterans Benefits Administration, GV
Isiogu, Orjiakor N. ... Lansing, MI
Isip, Michael Julius ... Sacramento, CA
Iskalis, Thomas C. ... Racine, WI
Iskanian, Talar ... New York, NY
Isken, Donald Nelson ... Wilmington, DE
Isken, Gerard L. ... Magnolia, TX
Isken, Gerard, P.C. ... Magnolia, TX
Isken, J. Eric ... Rosemead, CA
Iskenderian, Alex ... Vail, CO
Iski, David Thomas ... Tulsa, OK
Iskin, Constance M. ... Cleveland, OH
Iskiwitch, Joel S. ... St. Louis, MO
Isko, Irving D. ... Morristown, NJ
Isko, Jennifer Coen ... New York, NY
Isko, Norman S. ... Manchester, CT
Isko, Steven R. ... Boca Raton, FL
Wichita, KS
Iskowich, Charles H. ... De Kalb, IL
Iskowich, David Harris ... Chicago, IL
Iskra, Allan J. ... Parsippany, NJ
Iskra, Eric W. ... Charleston, WV
Iskra, Sharon F. ... Charleston, WV
Iskrant, John D. ... Philadelphia, PA
Iskyan, Tami A. ... Los Angeles, CA
Isla, Roger A. ... Steubenville, OH
Isla, Ruby M. ... Washington, DC
Islam, Shahan ... Roseland, NJ
Islami, Jahan S. ... Miami, FL
Island, Elizabeth M. ... Mars, PA
Island, E. R. ... Santa Monica, CA
Islas, Judith S. B. ... Los Angeles, CA
Islas, Luis E. ... El Paso, TX
Isler, Charles S., III ... Panama City, FL
Panama City Beach, FL
Isler, Curtiss L. ... Los Angeles, CA
Isler, Edward Lee ... Vienna, VA
Isler, Frank A. ... Riverhead, NY
Isler, Lloyd I. ... Paradise Valley, AZ
Isler, Mai Lan ... Newport News, VA
Isler, Robert A. ... Long Island City, NY
Isler & Sombathy, P.A. ... Panama City, FL
Panama City Beach, FL
Isles, Adam Revere ... Washington, DC
Isles, Scott A. ... Midland, MI
Isley, A. Mark ... Denver, CO
Isley, Cheryl Kaufman ... Charlotte, NC
Isley, Dale E. ... Denver, CO
Isley, Dale E., P.C. ... Denver, CO
Isley, Elwood C., Jr. ... Chesapeake, VA
Isley, Hugh G., Jr. ... Fort Lauderdale, FL
Isley, Kenneth D. ... Indianapolis, IN
Isley, Laura Boyce ... Raleigh, NC
Isley, Paul A. ... Detroit, MI
Isley, Philip R. ... Raleigh, NC
Islieb, Frederick Scott ... Norcross, GA
Islinger, David ... Morristown, NJ
Islip, Philip N. ... Dallas, TX
Islip, Robert W. ... Marysville, CA
Islon, Harold ... West Palm Beach, FL
Isma, Antoine ... North Miami Beach, FL
Ismail, Kamil ... Baltimore, MD
Ismail, Sherille
Federal Communications Commission,
International Bureau, GV
Ismail, Tarek ... Chicago, IL
Ismailer, David ... New York, NY
Isman, Stewart J. ... Commack, NY
Ismay, Peter Chamberlain ... McLean, VA
Ismert, Stephen J. ... Denver, CO
Ismond, R. L. ... Naperville, IL
Isnard, Linda S. ... Racine, WI
Isobe, Ann S. ... Honolulu, HI
Isokait, William A. ... Kensington, MD
Isokawa, Ned N. ... San Francisco, CA
Isola, Anita T. ... Brooklyn, NY
Isola, David R. ... Lodi, CA
Isola, Hugh L., (Inc.) ... San Jose, CA
Isola, Mark V. ... San Jose, CA
Isola, Paula ... Boston, MA
Isola, Peter L. ... San Francisco, CA
Isolda, Richard Alan ... Riverside, NJ
Isoldi, Ted ... Mercer, PA
Isom, A. Woodson, Jr. ... Tampa, FL
Isom, A. Woodson, Jr., P.A. ... Tampa, FL
Isom, Brandy Kearney
Oklahoma City, OK
Isom, Charles E. ... Anniston, AL
Isom, Chervis ... Birmingham, AL
Isom, Claudia Rickert ... Tampa, FL
Isom, Dallas W. ... Salem, OR
Isom, David K., Law Offices
Salt Lake City, UT
Isom, J.O. ... Marion, AL

Isom, Jackson & Bailey, P.C.
Anniston, AL
Isom, J. O. ... Hamilton, AL
Isom, John Gober ... Marietta, GA
Isom, John H. ... Harrisburg, PA
Isom, LaMonte H. ... Redondo Beach, CA
Isom, Mary ... Vail, CO
Isom, Patrick F. ... Lansing, MI
Isom, Phillip, IV ... New York, NY
Isom, Sandra C. ... Memphis, TN
Ison, Cynthia Ann ... Alhambra, CA
Ison, David A. ... Powell, OH
Ison, Elizabeth R. ... Sacramento, CA
Ison, Eric L. ... Louisville, KY
Ison Law Offices ... San Jose, CA
Ison, Mary K. ... San Jose, CA
Ison, Neil ... San Jose, CA
Ison, Randy K. ... Oklahoma City, OK
Ison, Richard G. ... Columbus, OH
Ison, Robert E. ... Hopkinsville, KY
Ison, Timothy M. ... Los Angeles, CA
Ison, Todd M. ... Sacramento, CA
Ison, William H. ... Jonesboro, GA
Isonhood, James H. ... Brandon, MS
Ispahani, Laleh ... New York, NY
Isphording, Brian C. ... Birmingham, AL
Isphording, Roger O. ... Venice, FL
Isphording, White & Roden, P.A.
Venice, FL
Isquith, Fred Taylor ... West Palm Beach, FL
New York, NY
Israel, Alan ... New York, NY
Israel, Albert S. ... Long Beach, CA
Israel, Allen D. ... Seattle, WA
Israel, Arthur J. ... New York, NY
Israel, Ashley J. ... Bingham Farms, MI
Israel, Audrey C. ... Los Angeles, CA
Israel, Barbara H. ... Bridgewater, NJ
Israel & Benezra ... Los Angeles, CA
Israel, Benjamin Lee ... Washington, DC
Israel, Brian D. ... Department of Justice, Environment and Natural Resources Division, GV
Israel, Carl B. ... Boston, MA
Israel, Carolyn J. ... Washington, DC
Baltimore, MD
Rockville, MD
Israel, Chana S. ... New York, NY
Israel, Daniel M. ... Bloomfield Hills, MI
Israel, David ... Metairie, LA
Israel, David B. ... Miami, FL
Israel, David M. ... New York, NY
Israel, Deborah J. ... Washington, DC
Israel, Deborah J. ... Chicago, IL
Israel, Donald P. ... Lansing, MI
Israel, Donald, (P.C.) ... Great Neck, NY
Israel, Elliott B. ... Chicago, IL
Israel, Eric A. ... New York, NY
Israel, Eric M. ... Chicago, IL
Israel, Eric P., (A Professional Corporation)
Los Angeles, CA
Israel, Evan S. ... New York, NY
Israel, Frank Glenn ... Dallas, TX
Israel & Friedberg, LLP ... Los Angeles, CA
Israel, Gary ... New York, NY
Israel, Gary M. ... Tucson, AZ
Israel, Gary S. ... West Palm Beach, FL
Israel, Gertrude H. ... White Plains, NY
Israel, Glenn ... Portland, ME
Israel, Harold D. ... Chicago, IL
Israel, Herbert G. ... Roswell, GA
Israel, Herbert J. ... New York, NY
Israel, Howard F. ... Oklahoma City, OK
Israel, Howard F., A Professional Corporation
Oklahoma City, OK
Israel & Israel ... Hollywood, FL
Israel, James F. ... Pittsburgh, PA
Israel, Jasmine ... Fairfax, VA
Israel, Jay G. ... Oklahoma City, OK
Israel, Jay G., A Professional Corporation
Oklahoma City, OK
Israel, Jeff A. ... Atlanta, GA
Israel, Jerold H. ... Ann Arbor, MI
Israel, John R., Jr. ... Birmingham, AL
Israel, John Vance ... Baltimore, MD
Israel, Jonathan L. ... New York, NY
Israel, Jules R. ... Miami Beach, FL
Israel & Kaplan, LLP ... Brooklyn, NY
Israel, Kenneth T. ... Marietta, GA
Israel, Kimberly Held ... Jacksonville, FL
Israel, Kyle A. ... Phoenix, AZ
Israel, Laurie ... Brookline, MA
Israel, Laurie M. ... Kew Gardens, NY
Israel, Mardon R. ... Great Neck, NY
Israel, Marilyn R. ... Hollywood, FL
Israel, Mark R. ... Los Angeles, CA
Israel, Mervyn R. ... Los Angeles, CA
Israel, Michael J. ... Buffalo, NY
Israel, Michael M. ... Ventura, CA
Israel, Nancy D. ... Wellesley, MA
Israel, Peggy M. ... Manhattan, KS
Israel, Perry E. ... Sacramento, CA
Israel, Peter O. ... Beverly Hills, CA
Israel, R. Ted ... Pocatello, ID
Israel, Rachel ... New York, NY
Israel, Richard E. ... Annapolis, MD
Israel, Richard J. ... Providence, RI
Israel, Richard S. ... Atlantic City, NJ
Israel, Robert L., (P.S.) ... Seattle, WA
Israel, Robert S. ... Saratoga Springs, NY
Israel, Ronald L. ... New York, NY
Israel, Sam P. ... New York, NY
Israel, Samuel ... Los Angeles, CA
Israel, Samuel H. ... Philadelphia, PA
Israel, Samuel L. ... Columbia, MD
Israel, Sara Fairbanks ... Little Rock, AR
Israel, Scott M. ... Milwaukee, WI
Israel, Seymour ... Southport, CT
Israel, Sharon A. ... Houston, TX
Israel, Sheryl R. ... Washington, DC
Israel, Sigmund ... Brooklyn, NY
Israel, Stanley ... Brooklyn, NY
Israel, Stanley E. ... Hollywood, FL
Israel, Stephen ... Pittsburgh, PA
Israel, Stuart M. ... Southfield, MI
Israel, Stuart M. ... Great Neck, NY
Israel, Susan Elisabeth ... New York, NY
Israel, Susan M. ... Redlands, CA
Columbus, OH
Israel, Tiffany J. ... Santa Ana, CA
Israel, Timothy P. ... Sayre, OK
Israel, Waldo W. ... Yuma, AZ
Israel, Wm. G. ... Thousand Oaks, CA
Israel, Wood & Puntil, P.C.
Pittsburgh, PA
Israelashvili, Diana ... New York, NY
Israel-Cowin, Rachel A. ... Boston, MA
Israeli, Millet ... New York, NY
Israelit, Ronald H. ... Philadelphia, PA
Israelite, David Z. ... Long Beach, NY
Israeloff, Sim ... Dallas, TX
Israelow, Edward A. ... Edison, NJ
Israels & Brink, A Professional Law Corporation ... Modesto, CA
Walnut Creek, CA
Israels, Michael J. ... Secaucus, NJ
New York, NY
Israels, Philip D. ... Santa Monica, CA
Sherman Oaks, CA
Israels, Sidney A. ... Modesto, CA
Walnut Creek, CA
Israels, Valli ... Stockton, CA
Israelsen, D. Brent ... Provo, UT
Israelsen, Ned A. ... San Diego, CA
Israelsen, R. Burns ... Salt Lake City, UT
Israelson, Max R. ... Baltimore, MD
Israelson, Paul J. ... Plainview, NY
Israelson, Salsbury, Clements & Bekman, L.L.C. ... Baltimore, MD
Israelstam, Alfred W. ... Buffalo Grove, IL
Israelstam, Alfred W., P.C.
Buffalo Grove, IL
Israelton, Harvey S. ... New York, NY
Israely, Martina Nicholls ... Weston, CT
Isralowitz, Jason P. ... New York, NY
Isralsky, Jeffrey
Department Of Health And Human Services, Office of Community Services, GV
Israni, Nanik R. ... Jamaica, NY
Isrin, Jeanne White
General Accounting Office, Office of the General Counsel, GV
Isroff, Brian D. ... Cleveland, OH
Isroff, Ronald H. ... Cleveland, OH
Issacs, Steve E. ... New York, NY
Issadore, Bruce A. ... Norwell, MA
Issadore & Miller ... West Collingswood, NJ
Issadore, Murray S. ... West Collingswood, NJ
Issagholian, Rita H. ... Los Angeles, CA
Isseks, Robert N. ... Middletown, NY
Isselbacher, Jody F. ... Newton, MA
Isselhard, Susan D. ... Portland, OR
Isselhard, Terrell J. ... Chicago, IL
Isselmann, John E., Jr. ... Portland, OR
Issenberg, Adam ... Department of Justice, Civil Division, GV
Issenhuth, Thomas M. ... Madison, SD
Issenman, David J. ... Jersey City, NJ
Issenman, Tina-May ... Santa Cruz, CA
Issenmann, John K. ... Cincinnati, OH
Isser, Deborah H. ... New York, NY
Isser, Stefanie B. ... New York, NY
Isser, Gary M. ... New York, NY
Isser, Steven D. ... New York, NY
Isserlis, Joan ... San Francisco, CA
Isserlis, Kenneth L. ... Spokane, WA
Isserlis, Milton L. ... Provincetown, MA
Isserlis, Nancy L. ... Bethpage, NY
Isserman, Joan L. ... Wheat Ridge, CO
Isshiki, Taro ... Palo Alto, CA
Washington, DC
Issinghoff, Stanley A. ... Wichita, KS
Issler, Harry ... New York, NY
Issler, Harry, PLLC ... New York, NY
Issler, Paul S. ... Los Angeles, CA
Issokson, Alan G. ... Dedham, MA
Issokson, Gerald ... New Orleans, LA
Istafanous, Nabil W. ... Washington, DC
Istanboulian, Flora ... Fresno, CA
Istas, James E. ... Eden Prairie, MN
Istivan, Ronald D. ... Montclair, NJ
Istook, Ernest J., Jr. ... Oklahoma City, OK
Istrabadi, Feisal Amin ... Merrillville, IN
Istre, F. John, III ... Waco, TX
Istre, Richard M. ... Lafayette, LA
Istvan, Jeffrey S. ... Philadelphia, PA
Istvan, Rudyard L. ... Winnetka, IL
Iszard, Alexis S. C. ... Washington, DC
Isztwan, Alexis Dillett ... Philadelphia, PA
Isztwan, Andrew G. ... Princeton, NJ
Ita, Timothy A. ... Cleveland, OH
Italiaander, Scott ... Atlanta, GA
Italiano, Mary J. ... Worcester, MA
Italiano, Philip G. ... Haddonfield, NJ
Italiano, Theresa M. ... Cherry Hill, NJ
Philadelphia, PA
Itchhaporia, Nita ... San Jose, CA
Iten, Carol Marie ... Denver, CO
Iten, Jonathan D. ... Columbus, OH
Ithurburn, Bertrand F. ... Yuba City, CA
Ithurburn, Fred ... Yuba City, CA
Itin, Jim ... Galveston, TX
League City, TX
Itkin, David ... Washington, DC
Itkin, Gerald H. ... Portland, OR
Itkin, Judith H. ... New York, NY
Itkin, Mark A. ... Beverly Hills, CA
Itkin, Perry S. ... Fort Lauderdale, FL
Itkin, Perry S., Lawyer, P.A.
Fort Lauderdale, FL
Itkin, Robbin L. ... Los Angeles, CA
Itkin, Robert J. ... Scottsdale, AZ
Itkin, Sharon L. ... New York, NY
Itkoff, David F. ... Penns Park, PA
Itkoff, David F., & Associates, A Prof. Corp.
Penns Park, PA
Itkoff, Valerie ... Miami, FL
Itkowitz & Harwood ... New York, NY
Itkowitz, Jay B. ... New York, NY
Itlaner, Sherman A. ... Santa Rosa, CA
Itnyre, Nancy Gerarda ... Detroit, MI
Ito, Akira ... Chicago, IL
Ito, Alvin T. ... Honolulu, HI
Ito, Charlotte K. ... San Francisco, CA
Ito, Chiaki ... Carolina Beach, NC
Ito, Ernest A. ... Honolulu, HI
Ito, Isao ... Honolulu, HI
Ito & Johnson ... San Francisco, CA
Ito, Kenji ... Alhambra, CA
Ito, Lance Allan ... Los Angeles, CA
Ito, Marie D'Aguanno
Securities and Exchange Commission, Division of Market Regulation, GV
Ito, Mark F. ... Honolulu, HI
Ito, Michael T. ... Walnut Creek, CA
Ito, Pete K. ... Department of State, Foreign Service Officers (Overseas), GV
Ito, Peter W. ... San Diego, CA
Ito, Robert T. ... Hilo, HI
Ito, Roger T. ... Los Angeles, CA
Ito, Ronald W. ... Los Angeles, CA
Ito, Takashi ... Akron, OH
Ito, Valerie A. U. ... Honolulu, HI
Ito, Yoshihide ... Washington, DC
Itoi, Anna ... Palo Alto, CA
Itoku, Amy A. ... Rolling Meadows, IL
Itomura, Darlene Y. Fujimoto
Honolulu, HI
Iton, Brian D. ... Westbury, NY
Itrato, Kenneth A. ... Boston, MA
Itri, Mark J. ... Costa Mesa, CA
Itri, Robert J. ... Phoenix, AZ
Itschner, Dale H. ... Flagstaff, AZ
Itskowitch, Stanley ... New York, NY
Itskowitz, Herman ... New York, NY
Itteilag, Michael V. ... Oakland, CA
Ittenbach, John F. ... Indianapolis, IN
Ittersagen, Scott D. ... Englewood, FL
Port Charlotte, FL
Ittig, Gary M. ... San Francisco, CA
Ittig, Gerard W. ... Washington, DC
Ittig, Judith B. ... Washington, DC
Ittig, Robert G. ... Redwood City, CA
Ittleman, Cynthia A. ... Boston, MA
Ittleman, Leona R. ... Springfield, MA
Ittner, Lori A. ... Grand Rapids, MI
Ittner, Robert A. ... New York, NY
Itts, Tracey L. ... Las Vegas, NV
Iturralde, Edward ... Miami, FL
Iturregui, Juan Carlos ... Washington, DC
Itzkoff, Donald M. ... Washington, DC
Itzkoff, Mark L. ... Washington, DC
Itzkoff, Norman Jay ... Riverdale, NY
Itzkowitz, Eric A. ... New Haven, CT
Itzkowitz, Jack R. ... St. Louis, MO
Itzkowitz, Jay ... Beverly Hills, CA
Itzkowitz, Jeffrey H. ... Roseland, NJ
Itzkowitz, Karen L. ... Basking Ridge, NJ
Itzkowitz, Mark Floyd ... Boston, MA
Itzkowitz, Marvin L.
Nuclear Regulatory Commission, Office of the General Counsel, GV
Itzkowitz, Theodore D. ... New York, NY
Itzler, Ellen R. ... Boca Raton, FL
Itzler, Ronald S. ... New York, NY
Iuculano, Russel P. ... Washington, DC
Iulianelli, Lisa M. ... La Mesa, CA
Iuliani, Anthony J. ... Newark, NJ
Iuliano and Concannon ... Watertown, MA
Iuliano, Linda C. ... Providence, RI
Iuliano, Michael P. ... New York, NY
Iuliano, Philip S. ... Watertown, MA
Iuliano, Robert W. ... Cambridge, MA
Iuliano, Veronica Marie ... New York, NY
Iuliano, Vincent J. ... San Diego, CA
Iulo, Kenneth D. ... Passaic, NJ
Iungerich, Russell ... Los Angeles, CA
Iungerich, Russell, A Professional Law Corporation ... Los Angeles, CA
Iunker & Champagne, P.S. ... Spokane, WA
Iunker, William B. ... Spokane, WA
Iuppa, Barney, Jr. ... Colorado Springs, CO
Iurillo, Camille J. ... St. Petersburg, FL
Iurino, John N. ... Tucson, AZ
Iurlano, August A. ... Pittsburgh, PA
Iurlano, John P. ... Allison Park, PA
Iurlano, Paul A. ... Pittsburgh, PA
Iushewitz, Diane E. ... New York, NY
Iuso, Angela A. ... Roseland, NJ
Iuteri, Edward R. ... New York, NY
Ivan, Jennifer R. ... Round Rock, TX
Ivan, John E. ... Merriam, KS
Ivan, John M. ... Richmond, VA
Ivan, Michael J. ... Tucson, AZ
Ivan, Michael J., Jr. ... Jacksonville, FL
Ivan, Neal S. ... Torrance, CA
Ivanchak, Terry F. ... Warren, OH
Ivancic, Gregory T. ... Buffalo, NY
Ivancich, Lisa E. ... Oakland, CA
Ivancovich, Anthony J. ... Washington, DC
Ivandick, Mark J. ... Clarksville, TN
Ivanhoe, Robert J. ... New York, NY
Ivanick, Carol W. Trencher
New York, NY
Ivanick, Peter A. ... New York, NY
Ivanjack & Lambirth ... Los Angeles, CA
Ivanjack, Larry G., (P.C.)
Los Angeles, CA
Ivanko, Kathleen ... Fairfield, CT
Ivanoski, Leonard A. ... Philadelphia, PA
Ivanov, Arne W. ... Anchorage, AK
Ivanov, Bridget H. ... San Francisco, CA
Ivanovic, Diana R. ... Philadelphia, PA
Ivans, Richard B. ... Miami, FL
Ivans, Steven D. ... Short Hills, NJ
Ivansek, Donald F. ... Chicago, IL
Ivanson, Gary S. ... Tiverton, RI
Ivanson, Gary S., Ltd. ... Tiverton, RI
Ivanyi, Shannon M. ... Phoenix, AZ
Ivanyi, Thomas P. ... New York, NY
Ivarinen, Nancy ... Mount Vernon, WA
Ivarsson, Carl G., Jr. ... Fayetteville, NC
Ivary, Eric H. ... Oakland, CA
Ivashkiv, Sophia marta
Department of Justice, Federal Bureau of Investigation, GV
Ivashuk, Jeffrey N. ... Fort Lauderdale, FL
Ivashuk, Jeffrey N., P.A.
Fort Lauderdale, FL
Ivaska, Paul R. ... Boston, MA
Ivener & Holt LLP ... Los Angeles, CA
Ivener, Mark A. ... Los Angeles, CA
Ivens, Gary L. ... Federal Trade Commission, Bureau of Consumer Protection, GV
Ivens, J. Michael ... Knoxville, TN
Ivers, Brian C. ... Davenport, IA
Ivers, Cornelius J. ... Meriden, CT
Ivers, David L. ... Little Rock, AR
Ivers, Donald L. ...
United States Court Of Veterans Appeals, GV
Ivers, James F., III ... Bryn Mawr, PA
Ivers, John D., Jr. ... Meriden, CT
Ivers, Larry E. ... Eagle Grove, IA
Renwick, IA
Ivers, Melissa L. ... Washington, DC
Ivers, Paul ... Brooklyn, NY
Ivers, Richard A. ... Pembroke Pines, FL
Ivers, William ... Indianapolis, IN
Ivers, William F., Jr. ... New Castle, KY
Iversen, Christian E. ... Paso Robles, CA
Iversen, Christine J. ... Chicago, IL
Iversen, Einer C. ... Waseca, MN
Iversen, Eric P. ... New York, NY
Iversen, Gary D. ... Waterloo, IA
Iversen, Judd C. ... San Francisco, CA
Iversen Law Firm ... Waseca, MN
Iversen, Paul W. ... St. Paul, MN
Iversen, Roland E. ... Auburn, CA
Iversen, Rolf E. ... Waseca, MN
Iversen, Sharon Moody ... Richmond, CA
Iversen, Yvonne A. ... Lebanon, OH
Iverson, Amman & Wood ... Monroe, LA
Iverson, A. T., Jr. ... Detroit, MI
Iverson, B. Gerald ... Monroe, LA
Iverson, Clark M. ... Fridley, MN
Iverson, Craig E. ... Portland, OR
Iverson, Dale Ann ... Grand Rapids, MI
Iverson, David W.
Charlotte Amalie, St. Thomas, VI
Iverson, E. Rodney ... Arkansas City, KS
Iverson, Eric H. ... Memphis, TN
Iverson, Erik H. ... Seattle, WA
Iverson, Gregory L. ... Everett, WA
Iverson & Iverson, P.A.
Arkansas City, KS
Iverson, John E. ... Seattle, WA
Iverson, John I. ... Bethlehem, PA
Iverson, Jon C. ... Seattle, WA
Iverson, Jon K. ... Minneapolis, MN
Iverson, Katherine Ellen Welbaum
St. Cloud, MN
Iverson, Kelly Hughes ... Baltimore, MD
Iverson, Kenneth A. ... St. Paul, MN
Iverson, L. Peter ... Indianapolis, IN
Iverson, Marc Brian ... St. Cloud, MN
Iverson, Mark E. ... San Francisco, CA
Iverson, Mark R. ... Spokane, WA
Iverson, Marlinee Constance-Clark
Memphis, TN
Iverson, Marvin A. ... Des Moines, IA
Iverson, Matthew J. ... Chicago, IL
Iverson, Michelle Lynn ... Corpus Christi, TX
Iverson, Neal J. ... Dayton, TX
Iverson, Norman M. ... Arkansas City, KS
Iverson, Norman M., Jr.
Arkansas City, KS
Iverson, Rachel E. ... Los Angeles, CA
Iverson, Rachel K. ... Cumming, GA
Iverson, Roland K., Jr. ... Marysville, CA
Iverson, William D. ... Washington, DC
Iverson, Yoakum, Papiano & Hatch
Los Angeles, CA
Ives, A. Bradley ... Charlotte, NC
Ives, Andrew Michael
North Miami Beach, FL
Ives, Bruce S. ... Palo Alto, CA
Ives, Daniel D. ... Camden, AR
Ives, David A. ... Woodland Park, CO
Ives, Garrison ... New York, NY
Ives, George S. ... Sarasota, FL
Ives, H. Bryan, III ... Charlotte, NC
Ives, Helen T. ... New York, NY
Ives, Howard ... New York, NY
Ives and Ives ... Delphi, IN
Ives, J. Mackey ... McLean, VA
Ives, Joseph T., Jr. ... Delphi, IN
Ives, Karen Lee ... Minneapolis, MN
Ives, Kathleen T. ... New York, NY
Ives, Kirwan & Dibble, A Prfessional Corporation ... Irvine, CA
Los Angeles, CA
Riverside, CA

San Diego, CA
Ives, Kristin Hay .... **Columbus, OH**
Ives, Patricia Salazar .... **Santa Fe, NM**
Ives, Peter N. .... Santa Fe, NM
Ives, Rhonda B. .... Lansing, MI
Ives, Robert N., Jr. .... **Irvine, CA**
Ives, Robert S. .... Van Nuys, CA
Ives, Robert T. .... Delphi, IN
Ives, Scott S. .... **Sterling, VA**
Vienna, VA
Ives, Sherri Hall .... Frisco, CO
Ives, Stephen B., Jr. .... Washington, DC
Ives, William C. .... **Chicago, IL**
Ivester, David M. .... **San Francisco, CA**
Ivester, Hermann .... **Little Rock, AR**
Ivester, Ivester & Ivester .... **Sayre, OK**
Ivester, J. Eric .... **Chicago, IL**
Ivester, J. Fred .... Marietta, GA
Ivester, Jack W. .... **Sayre, OK**
Ivester, John Ed T. .... **Sayre, OK**
Ivester, Mary J. .... Wichita, KS
Ivester, Robert L. .... **McAlester, OK**
Ivey, A. Lynn, III .... Richmond, VA
Ivey, Alison G. .... **Seattle, WA**
Ivey & Associates, P.A. .... **Augusta, GA**
Ivey, Barnum & O'Mara, LLC
Greenwich, CT
Norwalk, CT
Stamford, CT
Ivey, Carole Jean .... Washington, DC
Ivey, Catherine M., (P.A.) .... Cape Coral, FL
Ivey, Charles M., III .... **Greensboro, NC**
Ivey, Christopher D. .... **Newport Beach, CA**
Ivey, Christy Wilkins .... Brentwood, TN
Nashville, TN
Ivey, David M. .... **Atlanta, GA**
Ivey, Elizabeth A. .... Wailuku, HI
Ivey, Floyd E. .... **Kennewick, WA**
Ivey, Garve W., Jr. .... **Jasper, AL**
Ivey, Gary C. .... **Charlotte, NC**
Ivey, Gerald F. .... **Washington, DC**
Ivey, Gila .... Jamaica, NY
Ivey, Ivan Joe .... **Wilson, NC**
Ivey, J. Carlton .... Jonesboro, GA
Ivey, J. Michael .... **Parsons, TN**
Ivey, Jack Todd .... **Houston, TX**
Ivey, James D. .... Oakland, CA
Ivey, Janna L. .... Houston, TX
Ivey, J.K. .... **Dallas, TX**
Ivey, Jon David .... **Houston, TX**
Ivey & Kadlec, L.L.P. .... **Houston, TX**
Ivey, Lance C. .... **West Palm Beach, FL**
Ivey, McClellan, Gatton & Talcott, L.L.P.
Greensboro, NC
Ivey, O. Torbitt, Jr. .... **Augusta, GA**
Ivey, Parish & Johns .... Huntingdon, TN
Ivey, R. Henry .... South Fulton, TN
Ivey & Ragsdale .... **Jasper, AL**
Ivey, Raymond L. .... Huntingdon, TN
Ivey, Raymond M. .... **Gainesville, FL**
Ivey, Reef C., II .... **Raleigh, NC**
Ivey, Robert F. .... Norwalk, CT
Ivey, Robert L. .... **Los Angeles, CA**
Ivey, Robert L. .... **Houston, TX**
Ivey, Tamela W. .... **Tallahassee, FL**
Ivey, Thomas J. .... **Los Angeles, CA**
Ivey, Timothy C. .... Akron, OH
Canton, OH
Ivey, Weldon E. .... Bonifay, FL
Ivey, William G., II .... Reese, MI
Ivey, William T. .... Merced, CA
Ivey, William W. .... Asheboro, NC
Ivey & Williams, Co., L.P.A. .... Akron, OH
Canton, OH
Ivie, Alfred J., Jr. .... Dade City, FL
Ivie, Charles C. .... **Los Angeles, CA**
Ivie, McNeill & Wyatt, A Professional Law Corporation .... **Los Angeles, CA**
Ivie, Patricia E. .... Montgomery, AL
Ivie, R. Phil .... **Provo, UT**
Ivie, Rickey .... **Los Angeles, CA**
Ivie, Robert S. .... Bellevue, WA
Ivie, Stephen L. .... Ashburn, GA
Ivie & Young .... **Cedar City, UT**
Provo, UT
St. George, UT
Ivill, William J., III .... Pittsburgh, PA
Ivill, Wm. J., Jr. .... Pittsburgh, PA
Ivins, Benjamin F. P., II .... **Washington, DC**
Ivins, James M. .... **Phenix City, AL**
Ivins, James R. .... Sandy, UT
Ivins, John C., Jr. .... **Richmond, VA**
Ivins, John E. .... South Euclid, OH
Ivins, L. Reid .... Orem, UT
Ivins, Lisa A. .... **Wilmington, DE**
Ivins, Phillips & Barker, Chartered
Washington, DC
Ivins, Steven D. .... Washington, DC
Ivits, Christopher J. .... Dallas, TX
Ivker, Naomi C. .... Gretna, LA
Ivler, James J. .... Manalapan, NJ
Ivnik, Geoffrey D. .... Miamisburg, OH
Ivone, Devine & Jensen, LLP
Lake Success, NY
Mineola, NY
Riverhead, NY
Ivone, Michael T. .... **Lake Success, NY**
Ivory, Michael Leo .... Pittsburgh, PA
Ivory, Thomas H. .... Philadelphia, PA
Ivory-Moore, Ruth M. .... **Fairfax, VA**
Ivry, Rebecca A. .... Concord, NH
Ivry, William H. .... Santa Fe, NM
Ivsan, John V. .... **Toledo, OH**
Ivy, Canetta I. .... Bentonville, AR
Ivy, Charles H. .... **Atlanta, GA**
Ivy, Dan .... Fayetteville, AR
Ivy, Deborah K. .... Anchorage, AK
Ivy, Ellen Rubright .... **Denver, CO**
Ivy, Fred E., Jr. .... **Memphis, TN**
Ivy, James Harley .... Waurika, OK
Ivy, Jimmy D. .... Dallas, TX
Ivy, Jonathan R. .... Marina Del Rey, CA
Ivy, Joseph W., Jr. .... Prairie Village, KS
Ivy, Laryn Elizabeth .... **Chicago, IL**
Ivy, Michelle Bushey .... North Miami, FL
Ivy, Paul Thomas .... Plano, TX
Ivy, R. Lee .... **Portland, ME**
Ivy, Red .... Chickasha, OK
Ivy, Rena .... Brooklyn, NY
Ivy, Sarah K. .... **Reading, PA**
Ivy, Scott J. .... **Los Angeles, CA**
Ivy, Timothy H. .... **Jackson, TN**
Ivy, Vance E. .... **Amarillo, TX**
Ivy, Victor L. .... **Jackson, TN**
Ivy, William O., Jr. .... Chicago, IL
Iwafuchi, Brandi K. .... **Beverly Hills, CA**
Iwahiro, Michael K. .... **Sacramento, CA**
Iwai, Donald K. .... Honolulu, HI
Iwai & Morris, Attorneys at Law, A Law Corporation .... **Honolulu, HI**
Iwai, Wilfred K. .... **Honolulu, HI**
Iwakoshi, Kenneth A. .... Riverside, CA
Iwama, Frank A. .... Atherton, CA
Iwamoto, Jani .... Oakland, CA
Iwamoto, Raymond S. .... **Honolulu, HI**
Iwamura, Steven T. .... Honolulu, HI
Iwan Cray Huber Horstman & VanAusdal LLC .... **Chicago, IL**
Clarendon Hills, IL
Wheaton, IL
Iwan, Lori E. .... **Chicago, IL**
Iwan, Michael .... **Minneapolis, MN**
Iwanaga, Michiro .... **Honolulu, HI**
Iwanaga, Yuji .... **Los Angeles, CA**
Iwanejko, Gerald J., Jr .... Pittsburgh, PA
Iwanicki, Don B. .... Batavia, NY
Iwanicki, John P. .... **Boston, MA**
Iwanyshyn, Deborah L. .... Allison Park, PA
Iwanyshyn, Roman .... **Pittsburgh, PA**
Iwasaki, Bruce Gen .... Los Angeles, CA
Iwasaki, Lannie Yoko .... Denver, CO
Iwasaki, Robert Y. .... **Los Angeles, CA**
Iwasaki & Sheffield, A Professional Association .... **Los Angeles, CA**
Iwase, Randall Y. .... **Honolulu, HI**
Iwashita, Andrew S. .... Hilo, HI
Iwashita, Andrew S., A Law Corporation
Hilo, HI
Iwashko, Nina A. .... **Denver, CO**
Iwasko, Harry G., Jr. .... Lansing, MI
Iwasko, James F. .... Santa Maria, CA
Iwata, Jere D. .... Tulsa, OK
Iwataki, Dale M. .... Chicago, IL
Iwata-Yamashita, Ellyn T. .... Santa Ana, CA
Iweanoge, John O. .... **Washington, DC**
Iwen, John F. .... Great Falls, MT
Iwerebon, Felix E. .... Chicago, IL
Iwicki, Matthew L. .... **Roanoke, VA**
Iwinski, David, Jr. .... Pittsburgh, PA
Iwinski, Kenneth A. .... Wisconsin Rapids, WI
Iwler, Jerome .... Mayfield Village, OH
Iwrey, Howard B. .... **Detroit, MI**
Ix, John M., Jr. .... Morristown, NJ
Ix, Thomas O. .... **Philadelphia, PA**
Iyeki, Marc H. .... New York, NY
Iyer, Deepa V. .... Indianapolis, IN
Iyer, Rajita M. .... **Jackson, MS**
Izadian, Ebbi .... Los Angeles, CA
Izakowitz, David Z. .... **Charlottesville, VA**
Izakowitz, Pamela H. .... Tallahassee, FL
Izant, Bertram C. .... San Francisco, CA
Izant, Bertram C., A Prof. Corp.
San Francisco, CA
Izard, Clyman E., Jr. .... Little Rock, AR
Izard, Craig R. .... Birmingham, AL
Izard, Robert Andrews, Jr. .... **Hartford, CT**
Izbiky, Julian M. .... Englewood, CO
Izek, David .... Minneapolis, MN
Izen, Afton Jane .... Bellaire, TX
Izen, Irwin S. .... Smithtown, NY
Izen, Stephanie H. .... **Los Angeles, CA**
Izen, Tina L. .... Sacramento, CA
Izenman, Jeffrey D. .... Chicago, IL
Izenson, Daniel E. .... **Cincinnati, OH**
Izenson, Fred M. .... Dayton, OH
Izenson, Fuchsman & Brinkman
Dayton, OH
Izenson, Mark Steven .... Atlanta, GA
Izenstark, Susan R. .... **Los Angeles, CA**
Izes, Judith Stutman .... Norristown, PA
Izett, Barbara .... **New York, NY**
Izfar, Syed N. .... Houston, TX
Izhak, Ben-Meir .... Harrison, NY
Izhakoff, David E. .... **New York, NY**
Izhakoff, Joseph H. .... Miami, FL
Izmirian, Robert E. .... **San Francisco, CA**
Izor, David E. .... Germantown, OH
Izor, Paul H. .... Campbell, CA
Izower, Aron .... **New York, NY**
Izquierdo, Alexis .... Hialeah, FL
Izsak, Michael H. .... **St. Louis, MO**
Izsak, Rory D. .... Chula Vista, CA
Izsak-Niimura, Eva .... **New York, NY**
Izu, Yvonne Y. .... **Honolulu, HI**
Izuel, Leeanna .... **Los Angeles, CA**
Izumi, Francis M. .... Honolulu, HI
Izumi, Francis M., A Law Corp.
Honolulu, HI
Izumi, Lance Takeo .... Sacramento, CA
Izydore, Julian J. .... Leonardtown, MD
Izyk, Edward J. .... Oswego, NY
Izzard, Thomas W. .... Fort Lee, NJ
Izzi, Louis P. .... Melrose, MA
Izzi, Richard .... Birmingham, AL
Izzi, Stephen A. .... **Providence, RI**
Izzillo, Joseph A[illegible] .... **Stamford, CT**
Izzo, Alec Anthony .... Miami, FL
Izzo, Barbara A. .... **Palo Alto, CA**
Izzo, Carl P., Jr. .... Greensburg, PA
Izzo, Daniel A. .... Chicago, IL
Izzo, David A. .... Chicago, IL
Izzo, Dianne L. .... **Newport, RI**
Izzo, John M. .... **Chicago, IL**
Chicago Heights, IL
Izzo, John Thomas .... **Round Rock, TX**
Izzo, Margaret Scott .... **Washington, DC**
Izzo & McLaughlin, L.L.C.
Southington, CT
Izzo, Michael A. .... Holly, MI
Izzo, Michael J., Jr. .... Westmont, NJ
Philadelphia, PA
Izzo, Paul A. .... **Boston, MA**
Izzo, Paul G. .... **Richmond, VA**
Izzo, Richard A. .... Denver, CO
Izzo, Robert A. .... Southington, CT
Izzo, Ronald A., Jr. .... **Providence, RI**
Izzo, Todd A. .... **Washington, DC**

Jaafar, Randa A. .... **New York, NY**
Jaap, Joseph B. .... **Cincinnati, OH**
Jaaskelainen, James G. .... Ahmeek, MI
Jaasma, Keith D. .... **Houston, TX**
Jabaay, Myra Nell .... Grand Rapids, MI
Jabaley, Charles E. .... Cleveland, TN
Jabaley, G. Gerard .... **Knoxville, TN**
Jabar, George M., II .... Waterville, ME
Jabar, John P. .... Waterville, ME
Jabar, Joseph M., Sr. .... Waterville, ME
Jabara, Abdeen M. .... Washington, DC
Jabara, Lloyd W. .... Miami, FL
Jabara, Ronald W. .... Miami, FL
Jabas, F. H. .... Menominee, MI
Jabber, Eva L. .... Los Angeles, CA
Jabbour, R. Jerome .... Morristown, NJ
Jabbour, Stephen J. .... Victoria, TX
Jabbour, Suzanne J. .... **Winston-Salem, NC**
Jabenis, Jon Lance .... Omaha, NE
Jaber, Edward J. .... Alameda, CA
Jaber, J. Daniel .... Grand Junction, CO
Jaber, Joyce S. .... San Francisco, CA
Jaber, Makram .... Washington, DC
Jaber, Paul N. .... **Danbury, CT**
Jaber, Susan J. .... **San Francisco, CA**
Jabin & Jabin .... Rancho Mirage, CA
Jabin, Lelia H. .... Rancho Mirage, CA
Jabin, Marvin .... Rancho Mirage, CA
Jabin, Norman E. .... Grand Rapids, MI
Jabin, Timothy P. .... **Cincinnati, OH**
Jabkowski, Susan .... **Los Angeles, CA**
Jablinski, David S. .... **Dayton, OH**
Jablinski, Eugene A. .... **Dayton, OH**
Jablinski, Folino, Roberts & Martin, A Legal Professional Association .... **Dayton, OH**
Jablon, Arnold .... Timonium, MD
Jablon, Barry P. .... Los Angeles, CA
Jablon, Brian S. .... **Ellicott City, MD**
Severna Park, MD
Jablon, Cara S. .... **Washington, DC**
Jablon, Clark A. .... **Philadelphia, PA**
Jablon, David .... New York, NY
Jablon, Robert A. .... **Washington, DC**
Jablon, Saul .... Hunt Valley, MD
Jablon, Scott W. .... Tacoma, WA
Jablon, Steven .... Kissimmee, FL
Jablonover, Lisa L. .... **Baltimore, MD**
Jablonow, Jill .... Los Angeles, CA
Jablonowski, Katherine Ann .... Dundee, IL
Jablons, Jane E. .... **New York, NY**
Jablonski, Carol A. .... **Plano, TX**
Jablonski, Dawn Kristen .... Albany, NY
Jablonski, Edward C. .... **Islip, NY**
Jablonski, Frank W. .... Kearny, NJ
Jablonski, Heather L. .... **Wheaton, IL**
Jablonski, Isabelle J. .... **Burbank, CA**
Jablonski, James A. .... **Denver, CO**
Jablonski, James J., (Ltd.) .... Orland Park, IL
Jablonski, John J. .... Buffalo, NY
Jablonski, Jon S. .... **Nashville, TN**
Jablonski, Julie Ann .... Boston, MA
Jablonski, Mary J. .... Garden City, NY
Jablonski, Michael A. .... Flint, MI
Jablonski, Michael K. .... **Marietta, GA**
Jablonski, Paul D. .... Farmington Hills, MI
Jablonski, Raymond L. .... Janesville, WI
Jablonski, Richard W. .... Cleveland, OH
Jablonski, Robert .... **Austin, TX**
Jablonski, Robert C. .... Cleveland, OH
Jablonski, Sandra McLean
Department of Education, Office of the General Counsel, GV
Jablonski, Stuart Raymond .... Glen Cove, NY
Jablonski, Zygmunt .... **Atlanta, GA**
Jablow, Benjamin A. .... **Boca Raton, FL**
Jabour, Clare T. .... Providence, RI
Jabour, George R. .... Chestnut Hill, MA
Jabour, John Wayne .... Vicksburg, MS
Jabour, Paul V. .... Providence, RI
Jabour, Robin A. .... **Lancaster, PA**
Jabro, John A. .... Tavernier, FL
Jabs, LeAnne K. .... **Portland, OR**
Jaburek, Donald W., Jr. .... Chicago, IL
Jaburg, Gary J. .... **Phoenix, AZ**
Jaburg & Wilk, P.C. .... **Phoenix, AZ**
Jaburian, Shant .... **Los Angeles, CA**
Jacaman, Charles .... **Houston, TX**
Jaccard, Walter B. .... Bellevue, WA
Jaccoma, Barbara Ann .... Nutley, NJ
Brooklyn, NY
Jacek, Joseph W., Jr. .... Rochester, NY
Jacewicz, John Steven .... Hartford, CT
Jach, Anthony P. .... **Dallas, TX**
Jach, Virginia A. V. .... Oak Lawn, IL
Jachens, John W. .... Sacramento, CA
Jachera, Jill E. .... **Princeton, NJ**
Jachimczyk, Joseph A. .... Houston, TX
Jachimczyk, Michael C. .... **Stamford, CT**
Jachimiak, Mark J.
Greenwood Village, CO
Jachimiec, Chester J. .... Houston, TX
Jachimowicz, Albie B. .... **San Jose, CA**
Jachimowicz, Lucien J. .... Hartford, CT
Jachimowski, Phyllis A. .... Chicago, IL
Jachna, Mary Ann .... Summerfield, FL
Sebree, KY
Jachnycky, Lubomyr M. .... Minneapolis, MN
Jachowicz, Robert P. .... **Framingham, MA**
Jachzel, Vanessa .... **Roseland, NJ**
Jacinto, Ramiro .... Los Angeles, CA
Jacinto, Richard J. .... Sacramento, CA
Jack, Alan R. .... Oregon City, OR
Jack, Arnold L. .... Columbus, OH
Jack, Arnold L., Co., L.P.A. .... Columbus, OH
Jack, Billy C. .... Columbia, TN
Jack, Claude .... Santa Fe, NM
Jack, Claudia S. .... Columbia, TN
Jack, Connie Williams .... Owings Mills, MD
Jack, Darold J. .... Oelwein, IA
Jack, David C. .... Decatur, IL
Jack, David C. .... Akron, OH
Wadsworth, OH
Jack, David J. .... Cannon Beach, OR
Jack, Donald T., Jr. .... **Little Rock, AR**
Jack, Everett W., Jr. .... **Portland, OR**
Jack, Frances Baker .... Portland, OR
Jack, Frederick S. .... Tekamah, NE
Jack, Gary A. .... Fairmont, WV
Jack, Howard A. .... Albany, NY
Jack, J. Michael .... **Los Angeles, CA**
Jack & Jack .... Athens, GA
Jack & Jack .... Columbia, TN
Jack, James A. .... Reading, MA
Jack, Janis Graham .... Corpus Christi, TX
Jack, Jeffry L. .... **Parsons, KS**
Jack, Jesse W. .... San Jose, CA
Jack, John R. .... Blue Springs, MO
Jack & Keegan .... San Jose, CA
Jack, Kenneth H. .... **Wichita, KS**
Jack, Kevin .... **Chicago, IL**
Jack Kintzele & Associates, P.C.
Denver, CO
Jack, Laura M. .... Athens, GA
Jack, Lewis N., Jr. .... **Miami, FL**
Jack, Louis B. .... Laguna Niguel, CA
Jack, Lyon & Jones, P.A. .... **Conway, AR**
Little Rock, AR
Nashville, TN
Jack, Mary G. .... Fort Myers, FL
Jack, Michael J. .... **Baltimore, MD**
Jack, Otto A., Jr. .... Steubenville, OH
Jack, Philip C., Jr. .... Newton, MA
Jack, Rand .... **Bellingham, WA**
Jack, Richard H. .... Athens, GA
Jack, Robert B. .... **Palo Alto, CA**
Jack, Robert E. .... Cameron, TX
Jack, Robert J. .... **Orlando, FL**
Jack, Robert J., P.A. .... **Orlando, FL**
Jack, Robert W. .... Arlington, TX
Jack, Steven W. .... Denver, CO
Jack, Thomas Lee .... Long Beach, CA
Jack, Travis R. .... Los Angeles, CA
Jack, W. Andrew .... **Washington, DC**
Jack, Wellborn, Jr. .... Shreveport, LA
Jack, William F. .... Minneapolis, MN
Jack, William W., Jr. .... **Grand Rapids, MI**
Jacka, Barton L. .... **San Diego, CA**
Jackal, Thomas M. .... Valley Forge, PA
Jackaway, Harry N. .... New Britain, CT
Jacke, H. Clay .... Los Angeles, CA
Jackel, Dana L. .... **Marietta, GA**
Jackel, Jonathan C. .... San Jose, CA
Jackel, Jonathan E. .... **Washington, DC**
Jackel, Jonathan E. .... Gaithersburg, MD
Jackel, Martin S. .... Savannah, GA
Jackel, Max .... New York, NY
Jackel, Monte A. .... Treasury Department, Internal Revenue Service, GV
Jackel, Rainey, Marsh & Busch, L.L.C.
Marietta, GA
Jackelen, Michael D. .... **Milwaukee, WI**
Jackere, Alan L. .... Tulsa, OK
Jackerson, Richard H. .... Bradenton, FL
Jackier, Gould, Bean, Upfal & Eizelman, P.C. .... **Bloomfield Hills, MI**
Detroit, MI
Jackier, Lawrence S. .... **Bloomfield Hills, MI**
Jackier, Robert H. .... Rochester Hills, MI
Jackl & Katzen, LLP .... **Walnut Creek, CA**
Jackl, Ronni .... Walnut Creek, CA
Jackl, V. James .... **Walnut Creek, CA**
Jackle, Sally A. .... Minturn, CO
Vail, CO
Chicago, IL
Jackle, Timothy L. .... **Medford, OR**
Jackley & Flint .... Sturgis, SD
Jackley, Marty J. .... **Rapid City, SD**
Jackley, Michael A. .... Sturgis, SD
Jackley, Michael D. .... **Greenbelt, MD**
Jacklin, Beverly L. .... Rochester, NY
Jacklin, Eve M. .... Foster City, CA
Jacklin, Nancy .... **New York, NY**
Jacklin, Pamela L. .... **Portland, OR**
Jackman, Arthur E. .... Sarasota, FL
Jackman, Brad M. .... Doylestown, PA
Jackman, Cheryl S. .... **Boca Raton, FL**
Jackman, David H. .... London, OH
Jackman & Dixon .... Doylestown, PA
Jackman, Edward F. .... **West Paterson, NJ**
Jackman, Francis X. .... Dorchester, MA
Jackman, Frederick A. .... Orem, UT
Jackman, George L. .... Tamarac, FL
Jackman, J. Warren .... **Tulsa, OK**

Jackman, James A. ... Santa Ana, CA
Jackman, Jonathan ... Calabasas, CA
Jackman, Mark I. ... Santa Ana, CA
Jackman, Michael C. ... Minneapolis, MN
Jackman, Michael N. ... San Diego, CA
Jackman, Mitchell A. ... Santa Cruz, CA
Jackman, Norman ... Cambridge, MA
Jackman, Patrick A. ... Washington, DC
Jackman, Paul R. ... Harper Woods, MI
Jackman, Peter A. ... Washington, DC
Jackman, Philip A. ... Galena, IL
Jackman, Robert J. ... New York, NY
Jackman & Roth, P.A. ... Cambridge, MA
Jackman, Russell H. ... Tiburon, CA
Jackman, Scott A. ... Wausau, WI
Jackman, Steven B. ... New York, NY
Jackman, Steven H. ... Huntsville, AL
Jackman, Titus ... Kent, OH
Jackman, Wade P. ... Birmingham, MI
Jackman-Brown, Pam Badoria ... Brooklyn, NY
Jacknewitz, Dennis J. ... Belleville, IL
Jacknick, Laura J. ... Fairbanks, AK
Jacknin, Jay R. ... West Palm Beach, FL
Jacknowitz, Melvyn S. ... New York, NY
Jacko, Jerry S. ... St. Louis, MO
Jacko, John J., III ... Philadelphia, PA
Jackofsky, Michael W. ... Encinitas, CA
Jackomino, Jeffrey T. ... Rhinelander, WI
Jackovic, Joseph M. ... Pittsburgh, PA
Jackoway, James R. ... Los Angeles, CA
Jackoway, Robin ... Los Angeles, CA
Jackowiak, Lawrence V. ... Chicago, IL
Jackowitz, Anne Rickard ... Boston, MA
Jackowitz, Sydney L. ... Orlando, FL
Jackowski, Joseph P. ... Tacoma, WA
Jackowski, Julia L. ... Ankeny, IA
Jackowski, Mark V. ... New York, NY
Jackowski, Sarah Daly ... Washington, DC
Bethesda, MD
Jackowski, Thomas J. ... Des Moines, IA
Jacks, Adams & Westerfield, P.A.
Aberdeen, MS
Batesville, MS
Clarksdale, MS
Cleveland, MS
Greenville, MS
Greenwood, MS
Grenada, MS
Hernando, MS
Oxford, MS
Jacks, Amy E. ... Pasadena, CA
Jacks, Bradley W. ... Los Angeles, CA
Jacks, Dan M. ... Dallas, TX
Jacks, Gerald H. ... Cleveland, MS
Jacks, James T. ... Dallas, TX
Jacks, John D. ... Austin, TX
Jacks, Kenneth M. ... East Haven, CT
Jacks, Margaret Stevens ... Baltimore, MD
Jacks, Maston T. ... Raleigh, NC
Jacks, Ronald A. ... Chicago, IL
Jacks, Tommy ... Austin, TX
Houston, TX
Jacks, Ulysses ... Boston, MA
Jacks, Warren J., Jr. ... Springfield, MA
Jacksack, Susan M. ... Riverwoods, IL
Jackson, A. Leo ... Orlando, FL
Jackson, A. Pierre ... Farmville, VA
Jackson, A. Scott ... Greensboro, NC
Jackson, Aaron L. ... Austin, TX
Jackson, Aaron S. ... Gold River, CA
Jackson & Abdalah, A Professional Corporation ... Cupertino, CA
Jackson, Adrian D. ... Department Of Veterans Affairs, Board of Veterans Appeals, GV
Jackson, Alan ... East Orange, NJ
Jackson, Alan R. ... Tyler, TX
Jackson, Alan W. ... Newnan, GA
Jackson, Alex W. ... Montgomery, AL
Jackson, Alfred E. ... Ventura, CA
Jackson, Alfred, Jr. ... Bay Shore, NY
Jackson, Alice Kennedy ... Atlanta, GA
Jackson, Alison W. ... New York, NY
Jackson, Allen E. ... Federal Maritime Commission, Other Offices of the Commission, GV
Jackson, Allen E. ... St. Louis, MO
Jackson, Allen L. ... Richmond, VA
Jackson, Allen R. ... San Francisco, CA
Jackson, Allison G. ... Eureka, CA
Jackson, Alma Fitzgerald ... Spartanburg, SC
Jackson, Amos E. ... North Palm Beach, FL
Jackson, Amy Berman ... Washington, DC
Jackson, Amy L. ... San Diego, CA
Jackson, Andre L. ... Chicago, IL
Jackson, Andrea ... Clayton, MO
Jackson, Andrew ... Middlebury, VT
Jackson, Andrew B. ... Sebring, FL
Jackson, Angela Diggs ... Oak Park, MI
Jackson, Angela L. ... Ann Arbor, MI
Jackson, Angelina D.D.B. ... Montgomery, AL
Jackson, Ann Shannon ... Atlanta, GA
Jackson, Anne Marie ... Washington, DC
Jackson, Annette ... Rockmart, GA
Jackson, Annette M. ... Kansas City, KS
Jackson, Anthony A. ... Chattanooga, TN
Jackson, Anthony D. ... Philadelphia, PA
Jackson, Anthony E. ... Philadelphia, PA
Jackson, Anthony L. ... Oklahoma City, OK
Jackson, Antoinette M. ... Houston, TX
Jackson, April L. ... Baltimore, MD
Jackson, Arthur D. ... New York, NY
Jackson, Arthur D., Jr. ... Seattle, WA
Jackson, Arthur E. ... Princeton, NJ
Jackson, Arthur E., Jr. ... Lockport, NY
Jackson, Arthur Gregg ... Philadelphia, PA
Jackson, Arthur L. ... Cincinnati, OH
Jackson, Arthur L. ... Houston, TX
Jackson & Associates ... Bella Vista, AR
Springdale, AR
Jackson & Associates ... Milwaukee, WI
Jackson and Associates, P.C. ... Troy, MI
Jackson & Associates, P.C. ... Oklahoma City, OK
Jackson, Auzville, Jr. ... Richmond, VA
Jackson, B. Lynn ... Kansas City, MO
Jackson, Barbara A. ... Raleigh, NC
Jackson, Barbara Parker ... Houston, TX
Jackson & Barkett, A Professional Association ... Vero Beach, FL
Jackson, Barry W., Law Office of ... Fairbanks, AK
Jackson, Bartlett A., (A Professional Corporation) ... San Francisco, CA
Jackson, Belinda Bartley ... Charleston, WV
Jackson, Benjamin Brown ... Oklahoma City, OK
Jackson, Benjamin S. ... Indianapolis, IN
Jackson & Benson ... Kirksville, MO
Jackson, Bernard Hampton ... New York, NY
Jackson, Beth Anne ... Houston, TX
Jackson, Bethany ... Baltimore, MD
Jackson, Betsy Grabel ... Tulsa, OK
Jackson, Billy R. ... Jupiter, FL
Jackson, Billy W. ... Cullman, AL
Jackson, Blaine A. ... Bella Vista, AR
Springdale, AR
Jackson, Blair Thomas ... Orlando, FL
Jackson, Blaise J. ... San Diego, CA
Jackson, Bonnie J. ... Orlando, FL
Jackson & Bowers ... Fairfield, CA
Jackson, Bradley A. ... Tulsa, OK
Jackson, Bradley A. ... Houston, TX
Jackson, Bradley D. ... Madison, WI
Jackson, Brandon D. ... Mobile, AL
Jackson, Brenda L. ... Canon City, CO
Jackson, Brant, Jr. ... Atlanta, GA
Jackson, Brian A. ... Kansas City, MO
Jackson, Brian F. ... Harrisburg, PA
Jackson, Brian Gregory ... Austin, TX
Jackson, Brian K. ... Richmond, VA
Jackson, Brian Keith ... Minneapolis, MN
Jackson, Brian L. ... Houston, TX
Jackson, Brian P. ... Albany, OR
Jackson, Brown & Efting ... Sunnyvale, CA
Jackson, Bruce A. ... New York, NY
Jackson, Bruce C., Jr. ... Kansas City, MO
Jackson, Bruce D. ... Trumbull, CT
Jackson, Bruce G., (A Law Corporation) ... Honolulu, HI
Jackson, Bruce H. ... San Francisco, CA
Jackson, Bruce H., Jr. ... Wilmington, NC
Jackson, Bryan C. ... Los Angeles, CA
Jackson & Buckley, P.C. ... Princeton, NJ
Jackson, C. Bennett, Jr. ... Irvine, CA
Jackson, C. Michael (Mike), P.A. ... Fort Myers, FL
Jackson, C. Michael (Mike) ... Fort Myers, FL
Jackson, C. Phillip ... Glendale, CA
Jackson, C. Scott ... Franklin, TN
Jackson, Calvin M. ... Fort Worth, TX
Jackson & Campbell, P.C.
Washington, DC
Baltimore, MD
Rockville, MD
Vienna, VA
Jackson, Campbell Y. ... Burlington, NJ
Jackson, Candy L. ... Pocatello, ID
Jackson, Carl, III ... Southfield, MI
Jackson, Carl, III, P.C. ... Detroit, MI
Southfield, MI
Jackson, Carl James ... Baton Rouge, LA
Jackson, Carla Layne ... Dallas, TX
Jackson, Carla Suesberry ... Houston, TX
Jackson, Carmen Nicole ... Upper Marlboro, MD
Jackson, Carol D. ... Hammond, IN
Jackson, Carol E. ... St. Louis, MO
Jackson, Carol Johnson ... Bedford, TX
Jackson, Caroline V. ... Fresno, CA
Jackson, Carolyn C. ... Pleasanton, CA
Jackson, Catherine A. ... Oakland, CA
San Francisco, CA
Jackson, Cathie R. B. ... Ashburn, VA
Jackson, Cavanagh and Stivale
Media, PA
Philadelphia, PA
Jackson, Cavanagh and Stivale P.C.
Springfield, PA
Jackson, Cecil C., Jr. ... Asheville, NC
Jackson, Cecily L. ... Washington, DC
Jackson, Celia M. ... San Francisco, CA
Jackson, Celia M. ... Milwaukee, WI
Jackson, Chara Fisher ... Atlanta, GA
Jackson, Charla D. ... Department of Justice, Civil Rights Division, GV
Jackson, Charles B. ... Friday Harbor, WA
Jackson, Charles C. ... Chicago, IL
Jackson, Charles E., Jr. ... Atlanta, GA
Jackson, Charles H., III ... San Antonio, TX
Jackson, Charles M. ... Department of Labor, Office of the Solicitor, GV
Jackson, Charles M. ... Augusta, ME
Jackson, Charles M. ... Oklahoma City, OK
Jackson, Charles P., III ... Nashville, TN
Jackson, Charles S. ... Berryville, AR
Jackson, Chas. W. ... Chilo, OH
Jackson, Chatwin M., Jr. ... Kosciusko, MS
Jackson, Cheryl ... Bloomington, IL
Jackson, Cheryl L. ... Lawrence, KS
Jackson, Christine P. ... New York, NY
Jackson, Christopher M. ... Fairfield, CA
Jackson, Christy ... Birmingham, AL
Jackson, Cindy D. ... Fort Lee, NJ
Jackson, Claudine Germain ... Fort Worth, TX
Jackson, Clay A. ... Napa, CA
Jackson, Cliff ... Hot Springs National Park, AR
Jackson, Cliff, P.C. ... Hot Springs National Park, AR
Jackson, Clinton A. ... Washington, DC
Jackson, Clyde J., Jr. ... Corpus Christi, TX
Jackson, Constance G. ... Claremont, NH
Jackson & Consumano ... New York, NY
Jackson, Cook, Caracappa & Bloom, P.C. ... Fairless Hills, PA
Jackson, Craig L. ... Houston, TX
Jackson, Cris R. ... New Orleans, LA
Jackson & Curtin, Co., LPA ... Columbus, OH
Jackson, Cynthia C. ... Jacksonville, FL
Jackson, Cynthia J. ... Palm Beach Gardens, FL
Jackson, Cynthia L. ... Palo Alto, CA
Jackson, D. LeAnne ... Dallas, TX
Jackson, Dale J. ... Atlanta, GA
Jackson, Dan R. ... Hartford, KY
Jackson, Dan S. ... Administrative Office Of The United States Courts, GV
Jackson, Daniel G., III ... Kansas City, MO
Jackson, Daniel James ... Boston, MA
Jackson, Daniel L. ... Phoenix, AZ
Jackson, Daniel R. ... Baytown, TX
Jackson, Daniel W. ... Hartford, CT
Jackson, Danna Rae ... Great Falls, MT
Jackson, Darnell ... Lansing, MI
Jackson, Darrel ... Phoenix, AZ
Jackson, Darrell D. ... Fairfax, VA
Jackson, Darren ... Zebulon, NC
Jackson, Darryl ... New Orleans, LA
Jackson, Darryl W. ... Washington, DC
Jackson, Dartaganan L. ... Buffalo, NY
Jackson, David A. ... Burbank, CA
Jackson, David A. ... Boston, MA
Jackson, David A. ... Hackensack, NJ
Jackson, David B. ... Fairfax, VA
Reston, VA
Jackson, David C. ... Richmond, VA
Jackson, David D. ... Dallas, TX
Jackson, David E. ... Austin, TX
Jackson, David H. ... Prairie Village, KS
Jackson, David L. ... Helena, MT
Jackson, David L. ... Kerrville, TX
Jackson, David L. ... Moundsville, WV
Jackson, David O. ... Bridgeport, CT
Jackson, David S. ... Columbus, OH
Jackson, David W. ... Spokane, WA
Jackson, David William ... Dallas, TX
Jackson, Dean S. ... Calvert City, KY
Jackson, Deania M. ... New Orleans, LA
Jackson, Deborah A. ... Bronx, NY
Jackson, Deborah S. ... Honolulu, HI
Jackson, Debra O. ... Florence, SC
Jackson, Debra O'Neal ... Prairie Village, KS
Jackson, DeMarco & Peckenpaugh, A Law Corporation ... Irvine, CA
Westlake Village, CA
Jackson, Denise ... Cleveland, OH
Jackson, Denise E. ... Boulder, CO
Jackson, Denise E. ... Washington, DC
Jackson, Denise L. ... Washington, DC
Jackson, Denise R. ... Chicago, IL
Jackson, Dennis C. ... Broadview Heights, OH
Jackson, Dennis M. ... Denver, CO
Jackson, Derek ... Los Angeles, CA
Jackson, Derek Joseph ... Albany, NY
Jackson, Derry O. ... Knoxville, TN
Jackson, Diana Allen ... Santa Barbara, CA
Jackson, Dillon E. ... Seattle, WA
Jackson, Dimetria A. ... San Francisco, CA
Jackson, Don ... Houston, TX
Jackson, Don L. ... Knoxville, TN
Jackson, Don S. ... Whitefish, MT
Jackson, Donald A. ... Fresno, CA
Jackson, Donald D. ... Houston, TX
Jackson, Donald E. ... Amarillo, TX
Jackson, Donald H., Jr. ... Boston, MA
Jackson, Donald H., Jr. ... Hanover, MA
Jackson, Donald L. ... Arlington, VA
Jackson, Donald M., II ... Quincy, MA
Jackson, Donald Maurice ... Montgomery, AL
Jackson, Donald R. ... Peoria, IL
Jackson, Donald W. ... Houston, TX
Jackson, Donald W. ... Houston, TX
Jackson, Donna J. ... Oklahoma City, OK
Jackson, Doreen M. ... Washington, DC
Jackson, Dorothy T. ... Baltimore, MD
Jackson, Douglas E. ... Alexandria, VA
Jackson, Douglas H. ... Chicago, IL
Jackson, Douglas L. ... Enid, OK
Jackson, Douglas R. ... Columbus, OH
Jackson, Douglas T. ... New York, NY
Jackson, Durman Zolly ... Chicago, IL
Jackson, Dwight D. ... Landover, MD
Jackson, Dylan E. ... Great Falls, MT
Seattle, WA
Jackson, Earl Fletcher ... Little Rock, AR
Jackson, Earl, Jr. ... Battle Ground, WA
Jackson, Earsa R. ... Dallas, TX
Jackson, Eben J. ... Wausau, WI
Jackson, Edith Allen ... El Cerrito, CA
Jackson, Edward ... Washington, DC
Jackson, Edward ... Beattyville, KY
Jackson, Edward M. ... Rockledge, FL
Jackson, Edward M. ... Rock Hill, SC
Jackson, Edward P. ... Jacksonville, FL
Jackson, Edward R. ... Jasper, AL
Jackson, Ed[illegible] ... Chicago, IL
Jackson, E[illegible] ... Philadelphia, PA
Jackson, [illegible] ... Honolulu, HI
Kualapuu, HI
Jackson, Elmer C., Jr. ... Kansas City, KS
Jackson, Elmer J. ... Omaha, NE
Jackson and Elwood ... Nutley, NJ
Jackson, Eric M. ... Mesa, AZ
Payson, AZ
Jackson, Eric S. ... Washington, DC
Jackson, Ericka M. ... Southfield, MI
Jackson, Erik L. ... Los Angeles, CA
Jackson, Erika Nicole ... Atlanta, GA
Jackson, Ernie E. ... General Accounting Office, Office of the General Counsel, GV
Jackson, Eugene E. ... Springfield, VA
Jackson, Eugene W. ... Bangor, ME
Jackson, Ewell H." Jack ", IV ... Houston, TX
Jackson, F. Matthew ... Albany, NY
Jackson, F. Scott ... Irvine, CA
Jackson & Fenwick ... Kosciusko, MS
Jackson & Fitzgerald ... Roxboro, NC
Jackson, Flora M. ... Miami, FL
Jackson, Francis E., Jr., Law Offices of ... Charlotte Amalie, St. Thomas, VI
Jackson, Francis M. ... Portland, ME
Jackson, Frank ... Austin, TX
Jackson, Frank ... Dallas, TX
Jackson, Frank A. ... Wheeling, WV
Jackson, Frank B. ... Hendersonville, NC
Jackson, Frank W. ... Detroit, MI
Jackson, Frank Y. ... Lancaster, CA
Jackson, Franklin D. ... General Accounting Office, Office of the General Counsel, GV
Jackson, Fred S. ... Topeka, KS
Jackson, G. Brian S. ... Nashville, TN
Jackson, G. Gene ... Baltimore, OH
Jackson, G. Michael ... Los Angeles, CA
Jackson, G. Terry ... Savannah, GA
Jackson, G. Todd ... Tucson, AZ
Jackson, Gabriel A. ... San Francisco, CA
Jackson, Gabrielle M. ... Los Angeles, CA
Jackson, Garth R. ... Plymouth, MI
Jackson, Gary ... Los Angeles, CA
Jackson, Gary A. ... Fredericksburg, VA
Jackson, Gary D. ... Lindale, TX
Jackson, Gary E. ... Federal Deposit Insurance Corporation, Liquidation Branch, GV
Jackson, Gary E. ... Atlanta, GA
Jackson, Gary H. ... Hattiesburg, MS
Jackson, Gary L. ... Sidney, MT
Jackson, Gary L. ... Tulsa, OK
Jackson, Gary M. ... Yorktown, VA
Jackson, Gary M., (P.C.) ... Denver, CO
Jackson, Gary W. ... Charlotte, NC
Raleigh, NC
Jackson, Gayle A. ... Northbrook, IL
Jackson, George H., III ... Danielson, CT
Jackson, George T. ... Houston, TX
Jackson, George Thomas ... Clayton, AL
Jackson, George W. ... Roxboro, NC
Jackson, Gerald L. ... Tulsa, OK
Jackson, Gerald M. ... Shaker Heights, OH
Jackson, Gerard J. ... Cherry Hill, NJ
Jackson, Germaine T. ... Thibodaux, LA
Jackson & Glass, S.C. ... Dodgeville, WI
Jackson, Glenn A. ... Detroit, MI
Jackson, Glenn B. ... Orange, CA
Jackson, Glenn I. ... Hollister, CA
Jackson, Glenn K. ... North Hollywood, CA
Jackson, Glenn K., A Prof. Law Corp. ... North Hollywood, CA
Jackson, Gloria A. ... Lindale, TX
Jackson & Godbey ... Honolulu, HI
Jackson, Gordon D. ... Woodland Park, CO
Jackson, Gordon E. ... Memphis, TN
Jackson, Gordon M., Jr. ... San Diego, CA
Jackson, Gordon S. ... Alexandria, VA
Jackson, Graden P. ... Denver, CO
Jackson, Greer P., Jr. ... Richmond, VA
Jackson, Gregory A. ... Helena, MT
Jackson, Gregory C. ... Palo Alto, CA
Jackson, Gregory S. ... Fort Worth, TX
Jackson, Gregory W. ... North Mankato, MN
Jackson, Grover G. ... Atlanta, GA
Jackson, Guy C., III ... Anahuac, TX
Jackson, Guy W. ... Oklahoma City, OK
Jackson, H. Bruce ... Atlanta, GA
Jackson, H. Girard ... Wayne, NJ
Jackson, H. Herbert ... Sacramento, CA
Jackson, Hall & Associates ... Oklahoma City, OK
Jackson, Hank ... West Palm Beach, FL
Jackson, Hannah-Beth ... Santa Barbara, CA
Ventura, CA
Jackson, Harold B., Jr. ... Milwaukee, WI
Jackson, Harold L. ... Tustin, CA
Jackson, Harold S. ... Iuka, MS
Jackson Harris Burlingame & Hubert, LLC ... Danielson, CT
Jackson, Harry C. ... Columbus, GA
Jackson, Harvey R. ... Lake Havasu City, AZ
Jackson, Harvey S., Jr. ... Jasper, AL
Jackson, Heather ... Chicago, IL
Jackson, Hedy S. ... Duncan, OK
Jackson, Helena Everett ... Duluth, MN
Jackson & Hemer, L.L.P. ... Austin, TX
Jackson, Herbert L. ... Alexandria, VA
Jackson & Hertogs ... San Francisco, CA
Jackson, Howard B. ... Atlanta, GA
Jackson, Howell Y. ... Sacramento, CA
Jackson, Hugh F. ... Sunnyvale, CA
Jackson, Hunter ... Dallas, TX
Jackson, Irene ... Dallas, TX
Jackson, Irene ... Irving, TX
Jackson, J. Andrew ... Washington, DC
Jackson, J. Andrew ... Seattle, WA
Jackson, J. Brantley ... Spokane, WA
Jackson, J. Brian ... Charlottesville, VA

Jackson, J. Christopher **Fort Lauderdale, FL**
Jackson, J. David ... **Minneapolis, MN**
Jackson, J. Derrick ... **Columbia, SC**
Jackson, J. Douglas ... Denver, CO
Jackson, J. Ronald, Law Offices of **Paducah, KY**
Jackson, J. Scott ... **Dallas, TX**
Jackson, J. Theodore ... **Montgomery, AL**
Jackson, J. Thomas ... Crown Point, IN
Jackson, J. Walton ... **Mobile, AL**
Jackson, Jack A. ... Tyler, TX
Jackson, Jack P. ... **New York, NY**
Jackson & Jackson ... Los Angeles, CA
Jackson & Jackson ... East Moline, IL
Jackson & Jackson ... **Hendersonville, NC**
Jackson & Jackson ... Columbia, SC
Jackson & Jackson, Attorneys at Law, P.C. **San Antonio, TX**
Jackson and Jackson, PLLC **Hattiesburg, MS** **Jackson, MS**
Jackson, Jacqueline Department Of The Interior, Office of the Solicitor, GV
Jackson, Jacqueline L. ... Treasury Department, Bureau of the Public Debt, GV
Jackson & Jaggers ... **Paducah, KY**
Jackson, Jaima Marie ... Santa Fe, NM
Jackson, Jaime D. ... **Lancaster, PA**
Jackson, James A. ... Aptos, CA
Jackson, James A. ... Fort Bragg, CA
Jackson, James A. ... Indian Wells, CA
Jackson, James A. ... **Providence, RI**
Jackson, James B. ... Kansas City, MO
Jackson, James B., Jr. ... **Orangeburg, SC**
Jackson, James D. ... Detroit, MI
Jackson, James E. ... Cupertino, CA
Jackson, James F. ... Golden, CO
Jackson, James F. ... West Palm Beach, FL
Jackson, James H. ... Ypsilanti, MI
Jackson, James J. ... Culver City, CA
Jackson, James J. ... **Las Vegas, NV**
Jackson, James K. ... **Washington, DC**
Jackson, James K. ... Fairfax, VA
Jackson, James L. ... Atlantic City, NJ
Jackson, James L. ... **Houston, TX**
Jackson, James L., Jr. ... **Fort Worth, TX**
Jackson, James M. ... **Los Angeles, CA**
Jackson, James P. ... Walnut Creek, CA
Jackson, James R. ... Anchorage, AK
Jackson, James R. ... **Bryant, AR**
Jackson, James R. ... Birmingham, MI
Jackson, James T. ... Mission Viejo, CA
Jackson, James T. ... **Decatur, IL**
Jackson, James W. ... **Fort Wayne, IN**
Jackson, James W. ... **Boston, MA**
Jackson, James W. ... Painesville, OH
Jackson, Jami M. ... **Charlotte, NC**
Jackson, Jane C. ... **Winston-Salem, NC**
Jackson, Jane E. Federal Communications Commission, Common Carrier Bureau, GV
Jackson, Janet Crawford ... Los Angeles, CA
Jackson, Janet E. ... Columbus, OH
Jackson, Janet K. ... Atlanta, GA
Jackson, Janet Mills ... **Seymour, IN**
Jackson, Janice E. ... Portland, OR
Jackson, Janice T. ... Jackson, MS
Jackson, Jay ... Fairfax, CA
Jackson, Jay M. ... Dallas, TX
Jackson, Jay, P.C. ... Fairfax, CA
Jackson, Jay R. ... Salem, OR
Jackson, Jay S. ... Nacogdoches, TX
Jackson, Jay W. ... **Hartford, CT** **West Hartford, CT**
Jackson, Jayne Gosnell ... Mount Pleasant, SC
Jackson, Jean H. United States International Trade Commission, Office of the General Counsel, GV
Jackson, Jeanne Cabezas ... Media, PA
Jackson, Jeff D. ... **Tampa, FL**
Jackson, Jeff D., P.A. ... **Tampa, FL**
Jackson, Jeffery A. ... Pittsburgh, PA
Jackson, Jeffrey ... Jackson, MS
Jackson, Jeffrey B. ... **Seymour, IN**
Jackson, Jeffrey G. ... New York, NY
Jackson, Jeffrey L. ... San Diego, CA
Jackson, Jeffrey L. ... **Harlingen, TX**
Jackson, Jeffrey W. ... Bloomington, IL
Jackson, Jennifer ... **San Francisco, CA**
Jackson, Jennifer Ann ... **Santa Monica, CA**
Jackson, Jennifer Conron ... **Baltimore, MD**
Jackson, Jennifer G. ... **Dallas, TX**
Jackson, Jennifer O. ... Hendersonville, NC
Jackson, Jerald B. ... Houston, TX
Jackson, Jerald E. ... **Decatur, IL**
Jackson, Jerome D. ... **Washington, DC** Alexandria, VA
Jackson, Jerome M. ... El Segundo, CA
Jackson, Jerry B. ... Hurst, TX
Jackson, Jerry D. ... New Orleans, LA
Jackson, Jerry L. ... **Washington, DC**
Jackson, Jerry W. ... **Haleyville, AL**
Jackson, Jerry W. ... Mc Comb, MS
Jackson & Jessup, P.C. ... **Washington, DC** **Arlington, VA**
Jackson, Jill V. ... **San Francisco, CA**
Jackson, Jim ... Little Rock, AR
Jackson, Jo Bess ... Dallas, TX
Jackson, Joan T. ... San Diego, CA
Jackson, JoAnne Spears ... **Springfield, MO**
Jackson, Joe David ... **Atlanta, GA**
Jackson, Joe L. ... Arnett, OK
Jackson, Joe M. ... Spring, TX
Jackson, Joel ... Great Bend, KS
Jackson, Joey ... New York, NY
Jackson, John ... Corsicana, TX
Jackson, John B., III ... Bremerton, WA
Jackson, John B., III, Inc., P.S. Bremerton, WA
Jackson, John D. ... Ottawa, OH
Jackson, John D. ... **Dallas, TX**
Jackson, John D. ... Chantilly, VA
Jackson, John E., A Law Corporation New Orleans, LA
Jackson, John E., III ... **Kansas City, MO**
Jackson, John E., Jr. ... New Orleans, LA
Jackson, John Ezell ... Lake Charles, LA
Jackson, John F. ... Sunnyvale, CA
Jackson, John G. ... **Falls Church, VA**
Jackson, John Gerard ... **Chattanooga, TN**
Jackson, John H. ... Chicago, IL
Jackson, John H. ... Ann Arbor, MI
Jackson, John H. ... **Fayetteville, NC**
Jackson, John H. ... Burlington, VT
Jackson, John Hanson ... Madisonville, LA
Jackson, John Henry, IV ... Cambridge, MA
Jackson, John Hollis, Jr. ... **Clanton, AL**
Jackson, John J. ... Hannibal, MO
Jackson, John J., III ... Metairie, LA
Jackson, John J., III ... **Brick, NJ**
Jackson, John L. ... Austin, TX
Jackson, John M. ... Minneapolis, MN
Jackson, John Martin ... **Dallas, TX**
Jackson, John Michael ... Dallas, TX
Jackson, John P. ... Corydon, IN
Jackson, John R. ... Chicago, IL
Jackson, John R. ... Grand Rapids, MI
Jackson, John S. ... Minneapolis, MN
Jackson, John T. ... San Jose, CA
Jackson, John V., II ... **Cleveland, OH**
Jackson, John W. ... **Sacramento, CA**
Jackson, John W. ... Arlington, VA
Jackson, John Zen ... **Liberty Corner, NJ**
Jackson, Johnnie M., Jr. ... **Norwalk, CT**
Jackson, Jon Mitchell ... Irvine, CA San Jose, CA
Jackson, Jon Scott ... Harker Heights, TX
Jackson, Jone Lemos ... Fort Bragg, CA
Jackson, Joseph Dale ... Round Rock, TX
Jackson, Joseph E. ... Detroit, MI
Jackson, Joseph E. ... Carthage, TX
Jackson, Joseph E. ... Cedar City, UT
Jackson, Joseph F. ... **Vienna, VA**
Jackson, Joseph J. ... Metropolis, IL
Jackson, Joseph P., Jr. ... Royal Oak, MI
Jackson, Joseph R. ... East Wenatchee, WA
Jackson, Judith ... Washington, DC
Jackson, Judith A. ... Houston, TX
Jackson, Julie H. ... Marietta, GA
Jackson, Julie M. ... **Washington, DC**
Jackson, Jullane J. ... Milwaukee, WI
Jackson, June ... Hempstead, TX
Jackson, June A. ... **Seattle, WA**
Jackson, K. Stephen ... Birmingham, AL
Jackson, Karen ... **Cleveland, OH**
Jackson, Karoline E. ... **Chicago, IL**
Jackson, Katharine P. ... Englewood, CO
Jackson, Kathryn A. ... Framingham, MA
Jackson, Kathryn A. ... **Buffalo, NY**
Jackson, Kathryn Altizer ... Natick, MA
Jackson, Kathryn E. ... Salem, OR
Jackson, Kathy King ... Pascagoula, MS
Jackson, Kaye D. ... Atlantic City, NJ
Jackson, Keith ... **Los Angeles, CA**
Jackson, Keith N. ... **Minneapolis, MN**
Jackson & Kelly ... **Denver, CO** **Washington, DC** Frankfort, KY **Lexington, KY** **Charleston, WV** Charles Town, WV Clarksburg, WV **Fairmont, WV** **Martinsburg, WV** **Morgantown, WV** **New Martinsville, WV** **Parkersburg, WV** **Wheeling, WV**
Jackson, Kelly L. ... Overland Park, KS
Jackson, Kelly L. ... Carson City, NV
Jackson, Kenneth A. ... Lexington, KY
Jackson, Kenneth M. ... Nashville, TN
Jackson, Kent S. ... **Overland Park, KS**
Jackson, Kerry Ann Painton Oklahoma City, OK
Jackson & Kessie ... **Canadian, TX**
Jackson, Ketanji Brown Supreme Court Of The United States, GV
Jackson, Kevin B. ... Andrews, TX
Jackson, Kevin R. ... **Fort Lauderdale, FL**
Jackson, Kevin T. ... Washington, DC
Jackson, Kim Monroe ... **Atlanta, GA**
Jackson, Kimberly A. ... **Washington, DC**
Jackson, Kimberly A. ... **Kailua-Kona, HI**
Jackson, Kimberly L. ... **Sacramento, CA**
Jackson, Kristen M. ... **Orlando, FL**
Jackson, K. Stephen, P.C. ... Birmingham, AL
Jackson, Kurt M. ... **Great Falls, MT**
Jackson, Kweller, McKinney & Badger **Nashville, TN**
Jackson, L. Anne ... Southaven, MS
Jackson, L. Tipton ... Tucson, AZ
Jackson, Lance A. ... **Virginia Beach, VA**
Jackson, Larry A. ... **Bellevue, WA**
Jackson, Larry D. ... Philadelphia, PA
Jackson, Larry K. ... Tampa, FL
Jackson, Larry R. ... **Indianapolis, IN**
Jackson, Laura L. ... **Blue Bell, PA**
Jackson, Laurence D. ... **Los Angeles, CA**
Jackson, Lavonda ... Detroit, MI
Jackson Law Company, The Shaker Heights, OH
Jackson Law Corporation ... Tustin, CA
Jackson Law Office ... Fort Bragg, CA
Jackson Law Office ... **Cedar Rapids, IA**
Jackson Law Office ... **Nashville, TN**
Jackson Law Offices, P.C. ... **Lindale, TX**
Jackson Law Offices, P.C., The Augusta, GA
Jackson Law Offices, P.S. East Wenatchee, WA
Jackson Law Offices, The, P.C. ... **Aiken, SC**
Jackson, Lawanda Ann ... New York, NY
Jackson, Lawrence D. ... **Camden, NJ** **Philadelphia, PA**
Jackson, Lawrence W. ... **Dallas, TX**
Jackson, Lawton R. ... Miami, FL
Jackson, Leah Witcher ... Waco, TX
Jackson, Lee David ... **Palo Alto, CA**
Jackson, Lee W. ... **Washington, DC**
Jackson, Leighton M. ... Brooklyn, NY
Jackson, Leila M. ... **Miami, FL**
Jackson, Lenwood A. ... Atlanta, GA
Jackson, Leo A. ... Cleveland, OH
Jackson, Leo P. ... **Philadelphia, PA**
Jackson, Leon D. ... Baton Rouge, LA
Jackson, LeRay G. ... Delta, UT
Jackson, Leslie D. ... Upper Marlboro, MD
Jackson & Lewis ... Los Angeles, CA
Jackson, Lewis, Schnitzler & Krupman **Los Angeles, CA** **Sacramento, CA** **San Francisco, CA** **Hartford, CT** **Stamford, CT** **Washington, DC** **Miami, FL** **Orlando, FL** **Atlanta, GA** **Chicago, IL** **Boston, MA** **Minneapolis, MN** **Morristown, NJ** **New York, NY** **White Plains, NY** **Woodbury, NY** **Pittsburgh, PA** **Greenville, SC** **Dallas, TX** **Seattle, WA**
Jackson, Linda K. ... **Houston, TX**
Jackson, Linda M. ... **McLean, VA**
Jackson, Linda Z. ... Columbia, SC
Jackson, Lisa E. ... Arlington, VA
Jackson, Lisa L. ... **Greenbelt, MD**
Jackson, Lloyd G. ... Des Moines, IA
Jackson, Lloyd G., II ... Hamlin, WV
Jackson, Lois C. ... St. Louis, MO
Jackson, Lon R. ... Troy, MI
Jackson, Lorenzo, Jr. ... **Coral Gables, FL**
Jackson, Lori A. ... **Philadelphia, PA**
Jackson, Lori Betler ... Clarksburg, WV
Jackson, Lori L. ... Rockville, MD
Jackson, Louise A. ... **Toledo, OH**
Jackson, Lynn E. ... Indianapolis, IN
Jackson, Lynn Robertson ... Clayton, AL
Jackson, Lynne D. ... Danbury, CT
Jackson, M. Kay ... **Augusta, GA**
Jackson, M. Keith ... Los Angeles, CA
Jackson, Maija B. ... Baltimore, MD
Jackson, Marcia Nelson ... **Dallas, TX**
Jackson, Margaret DuRant ... Manning, SC
Jackson, Mari Beth G. ... Dakota City, NE
Jackson, Marian E. ... **Dallas, TX**
Jackson, Marie N. ... Warren, NJ
Jackson, Marjorie L. ... New Orleans, LA
Jackson, Mark A. ... Coeur d'Alene, ID
Jackson, Mark A. ... East Moline, IL
Jackson, Mark A. ... **Adrian, MI**
Jackson, Mark B. ... San Diego, CA
Jackson, Mark D. ... **Washington, DC**
Jackson, Mark E. ... **Decatur, IL**
Jackson, Mark G. ... **Seattle, WA**
Jackson, Mark R. ... **Hartford, CT**
Jackson, Marsha A. ... Plainfield, NJ
Jackson, Marshell R. ... Birmingham, AL
Jackson, Martin E. ... Houston, TX
Jackson, Martin T. ... Los Angeles, CA
Jackson, Marty T., (P.A.) ... **Olathe, KS**
Jackson, Marvin P., Jr. ... Florence, SC
Jackson, Mary Alice G. ... Anadarko, OK
Jackson, Mary Ann ... **Memphis, TN**
Jackson, Mary Dahlberg ... Lake Forest, IL
Jackson, Mary Dougherty **Baton Rouge, LA**
Jackson, Mary Kay ... El Cajon, CA
Jackson & Mason, P.A. ... **Jacksonville, FL**
Jackson & Mathison ... Santa Barbara, CA
Jackson, Matthew E. ... **Tarzana, CA**
Jackson, Maynard Holbrook, Jr. (P.C.) Atlanta, GA
Jackson & McPherson, L.L.C. **New Orleans, LA**
Jackson, Melissa ... **Milwaukee, WI**
Jackson, Melissa Carow ... Brooklyn, NY
Jackson, Melissa J. ... **Lansing, MI**
Jackson, Melissa M. ... Fort Wayne, IN
Jackson, Melissa M. ... **Bellevue, WA**
Jackson, Meredith S. ... **Los Angeles, CA**
Jackson, Merryl S. ... New York, NY
Jackson, Michael E. ... **Cleveland, OH**
Jackson, Michael H. ... Denver, CO
Jackson, Michael L. ... **Birmingham, AL**
Jackson, Michael L. ... Baton Rouge, LA
Jackson, Michael L. ... **Jackson, MO**
Jackson, Michael L. ... Jefferson City, MO
Jackson, Michael L. ... **Buffalo, NY**
Jackson, Michael M. ... Topeka, KS
Jackson, Michael P. ... Columbus, OH
Jackson, Michael Richard ... **Orlando, FL**
Jackson, Michael S. ... **New York, NY** New York, NY **Philadelphia, PA** West Chester, PA
Jackson, Michael T. ... **Little Rock, AR**
Jackson, Micheal S. ... **Montgomery, AL**
Jackson, Michele C. ... **San Francisco, CA**
Jackson, Michelle Moore ... **Chicago, IL**
Jackson, Millard I., Jr. ... Philadelphia, PA
Jackson, Mills & Carter, P.A. **Wilmington, NC**
Jackson, Mitchell & Jackson Baton Rouge, LA
Jackson, Mittlesteadt & Miller Redwood City, CA
Jackson, Monet T. ... Fort Washington, MD
Jackson, Monica M. ... Miami, FL
Jackson, Murdo, Grant & McFarland, P.C. **Helena, MT**
Jackson, Murray ... Los Angeles, CA
Jackson, Myrick, Chambers & Byrne, L.L.C. **Mobile, AL**
Jackson, Myron E. ... University Heights, OH
Jackson, Nancy H. ... Decatur, GA
Jackson & Nash ... Greenwich, CT **New York, NY**
Jackson, Natasha D. ... Pelham, AL
Jackson, Natasha Waldrop ... Gadsden, AL
Jackson, Nathaniel H. ... New York, NY
Jackson, Neal A. ... Washington, DC
Jackson, Neil W. ... Portland, OR
Jackson, Nelson E. ... Little Rock, AR
Jackson & Newell ... **Double Springs, AL** **Haleyville, AL** **Hamilton, AL**
Jackson, Nicholas M. ... Mount Clemens, MI
Jackson, Nicola ... **Chicago, IL**
Jackson, Nicole A. ... **Chicago, IL**
Jackson, Norman B. ... Knoxville, TN
Jackson, Norris D. ... Jena, LA
Jackson, Norvell F., Jr. ... Bellingham, WA
Jackson, O. Scott ... Lake Oswego, OR
Jackson, O'Keefe and Phelan **Bethlehem, CT** **Hartford, CT** **West Hartford, CT**
Jackson, Otha M. ... Cleveland, OH
Jackson, Page S. ... Tallahassee, FL
Jackson, Paige Stallings Roton **Opelika, AL**
Jackson, Pamela A. ... Jasper, TX
Jackson, Pamela B. ... Atlanta, GA
Jackson, Pamela C. ... Vacaville, CA
Jackson, Patricia A. ... **New York, NY**
Jackson, Patricia L. ... Dallas, TX
Jackson, Patricia Louise ... Atlanta, GA
Jackson, Patricia Nolan ... Metairie, LA
Jackson, Patrick D. ... La Porte, TX
Jackson, Patrick L. ... Pensacola, FL
Jackson, Patrick R. ... Bossier City, LA
Jackson, Patrick R., A Professional Law Corporation ... Bossier City, LA
Jackson, Paul ... Berryville, AR
Jackson, Paul D. ... Seattle, WA
Jackson, Paul E. ... San Antonio, TX
Jackson, Paul J. ... Nutley, NJ
Jackson, Paul L. ... **Akron, OH**
Jackson, Paul R. ... **Muskegon, MI**
Jackson, Peter A. ... **Detroit, MI**
Jackson, Peter K. ... Battle Ground, WA
Jackson, Phil H. ... Rancho Mirage, CA
Jackson, Philip D. ... Freeport, NY
Jackson, Phillip ... Atlanta, GA
Jackson, Phillip L. ... **New York, NY**
Jackson, Phillip T. ... **Hendersonville, NC**
Jackson, Price A., Jr. ... Zionsville, IN
Jackson, Prince Albert, III ... Savannah, GA
Jackson, Priscilla Ruesink ... Adrian, MI
Jackson, R. Brooke ... Golden, CO
Jackson, R. Michael ... Lakewood, CO
Jackson, R. Scott, Jr. ... **Nashville, TN**
Jackson, R.T." Terry ", P.C. Colorado Springs, CO
Jackson, R. Terry ... Colorado Springs, CO
Jackson, Rachel Elaina ... **Richmond, VA**
Jackson, Rachel K. ... **Oklahoma City, OK**
Jackson, Rader ... **New Orleans, LA**
Jackson, Rahkel Bouchet ... Nashville, TN
Jackson, Ralph F. ... Portsmouth, VA
Jackson, Ralph N. ... **Dublin, GA**
Jackson, Randall C. ... **San Antonio, TX**
Jackson, Randall R. ... St. Joseph, MO
Jackson, Randolph ... Brooklyn, NY
Jackson, Randolph C. ... **Fort Smith, AR**
Jackson, Randy S., Jr. ... **Covington, KY**
Jackson, Ray D. ... Woodward, OK
Jackson, Raymond A. ... Redding, CA
Jackson, Raymond A. ... Palm Bay, FL
Jackson, Raymond A. ... Norfolk, VA
Jackson, Raymond C., III ... **Lafayette, LA**
Jackson, Raymond L., Jr. ... Montgomery, AL
Jackson, Raymond S., Jr. ... **New York, NY**
Jackson, Rebecca L. ... **Washington, DC**
Jackson, Rebecca L. ... Kansas City, MO
Jackson, Rebecca R. ... **St. Louis, MO**
Jackson and Reed ... Cheshire, CT
Jackson, Reed ... Fairfield, TX
Jackson, Regina A. ... **Bowling Green, KY**
Jackson, Reginald L. ... Des Moines, IA
Jackson, Reginald S., Jr. ... **Toledo, OH**
Jackson, Reginald W. ... **Columbus, OH**
Jackson, Renee L. ... **Minneapolis, MN**
Jackson, Rex S. ... Milpitas, CA
Jackson, Rhakel Bouchet ... Nashville, TN
Jackson & Rhodes, P.C. ... **Dothan, AL**
Jackson, Ricardo C. ... Philadelphia, PA
Jackson & Rice ... **Helena, MT**
Jackson, Richard A. ... **San Diego, CA**

Jackson, Richard A. ....San Francisco, CA
Jackson, Richard B. ....Miami, FL
Jackson, Richard D. ....Redondo Beach, CA
Jackson, Richard Eli ....Elkton, MD
Jackson, Richard H. ....Crystal Lake, IL
Jackson, Richard K. ....Philadelphia, PA
Jackson, Richard L. ....Birmingham, AL
Jackson, Richard M., Jr. ....Cleveland, OH
Jackson, Richard P. ....Huntsville, AL
Jackson, Richard R., Jr. ....Owings Mills, MD
Jackson, Rich'd L. ....Birmingham, AL
Jackson, Rick ....Kirksville, MO
Jackson, Robbi J. ....Denver, CO
Lakewood, CO
Jackson, Robert ....Vero Beach, FL
Jackson, Robert A. ....Danbury, CT
Jackson, Robert A. ....Oklahoma City, OK
Jackson, Robert B. ....New York, NY
Jackson, Robert B. ....Dallas, TX
Jackson, Robert Bradley ....Orlando, FL
Jackson, Robert C. ....Panama City, FL
Jackson, Robert D. ....Peoria, IL
Jackson, Robert E. ....Staten Island, NY
Jackson, Robert F. ....Chicago, IL
Jackson, Robert G. ....Daly City, CA
Jackson, Robert G. ....Baton Rouge, LA
Jackson, Robert G., Jr. ....Mobile, AL
Jackson, Robert H. ....Washington, DC
Jackson, Robert H. ....Cleveland, OH
Jackson, Robert J. ....Irvine, CA
Jackson, Robert J. ....Salem, OR
Jackson, Robert J. ....Dodgeville, WI
Jackson, Robert James ....Springfield, PA
Jackson, Robert K. ....Little Rock, AR
Jackson, Robert L. ....Nampa, ID
Jackson, Robert L. ....Columbia, SC
Jackson, Robert L. ....Nashville, TN
Jackson, Robert L., III ....Chicago, IL
Jackson, Robert L., Jr. ....Kansas City, MO
Jackson, Robert L., Jr. ....Milwaukee, WI
Jackson, Robert Lewis, (P.C.)
St. Louis, MO
Jackson, Robert M. ....Washington, DC
Jackson, Robert M. ....Atlanta, GA
Jackson, Robert M. ....Detroit, MI
Jackson, Robert M. ....Jasper, TX
Jackson, Robert Moore ....Atlanta, GA
Jackson, Robert O. ....Birmingham, AL
Jackson, Robert R. ....New York, NY
Jackson, Robert T., Jr. ....Hattiesburg, MS
Jackson, Robert T., Sr. ....Hattiesburg, MS
Jackson, Robert Todd ....Nashville, TN
Jackson, Robert W. ....Fallbrook, CA
Jackson, Robert W. ....Charlottesville, VA
Jackson, Robert W., Jr. ....Cypress, TX
Jackson, Robin Jones ....Miami, FL
Jackson, Robtert C., Jr. ....Corsicana, TX
Jackson, Rochelle H. ....Chicago, IL
Jackson, Rockney L. ....Yakima, WA
Jackson, Roger A. ....Denver, CO
Jackson, Roger C. ....Houston, TX
Jackson, Ronald A. ....New York, NY
Jackson, Ronald D. ....Portland, OR
Jackson, Ronald E. ....Columbiana, AL
Jackson, Ronald L. ....Carmel, IN
Jackson, Ronald L. ....El Paso, TX
Jackson, Rosemary B. ....San Antonio, TX
Jackson, Roy D., Jr. ....El Paso, TX
Jackson, Roy V. ....Wilmington, DE
Jackson, Ruth B. ....Newport, KY
Jackson, S. Edward ....Dothan, AL
Jackson, S. Farrell ....Lancaster, OH
Jackson, Sally Finck ....Arcadia, CA
Jackson, Sally G. ....Charles Town, WV
Martinsburg, WV
Jackson, Samuel E.
Department of the Navy, GV
Jackson, Samuel G., Jr. ....Los Angeles, CA
Jackson, Samuel Omar, Jr.
Baltimore, MD
Jackson, Samuel W., Jr. ....Birmingham, AL
Jackson, Sandra E. ....Little Rock, AR
Jackson, Sandra L. ....Dallas, TX
Jackson, Sandra R. ....Kansas City, MO
Jackson, Sarah Bruce ....Birmingham, AL
Jackson and Schiavone ....Savannah, GA
Jackson, Schuyler ....Montpelier, VT
Jackson, Scott M. ....Yakima, WA
Jackson, Scott R. ....Oklahoma City, OK
Jackson, Sean A. ....Baton Rouge, LA
Jackson, Shanon R. ....Atlanta, GA
Jackson, Sharon E. ....Los Angeles, CA
Jackson, Sharon Fonsworth ....Dallas, TX
Jackson, Shaun Bryan ....Buffalo, NY
Jackson, Shawn R. ....Rohnert Park, CA
Jackson, Shelley R. ....Boston, MA
Jackson, Shelli Ganson ....Houston, TX
Jackson, Sherry L. ....Texarkana, TX
Jackson, Sheryl ....Gettysburg, PA
Jackson, Shields, Yeiser & Cantrell
Memphis, TN
Jackson, Sidney W., III ....Mobile, AL
Jackson & Sjoberg, LLP, Law Offices of
Austin, TX
Jackson, Stacey E. ....Crofton, MD
Jackson, Stanley G. ....Augusta, GA
Aiken, SC
Jackson, Stanley L. ....Detroit, MI
Jackson, Stephanie D. ....Houston, TX
Jackson, Stephanie M.
Department of Justice, Civil Division, GV
Jackson, Stephen ....New York, NY
Jackson, Stephen B. ....Cedar Rapids, IA
Jackson, Stephen B. ....Gaithersburg, MD
Jackson, Stephen B. ....Hattiesburg, MS
Jackson, Stephen B., Jr.
Cedar Rapids, IA
Jackson, Stephen C. ....Birmingham, AL
Jackson, Stephen C. ....New York, NY
Jackson, Stephen D.
Department of Transportation,
U. S. Coast Guard, GV
Jackson, Stephen D. ....Huntingdon, TN
Jackson, Stephen D. ....Conroe, TX
Jackson, Stephen E. ....Phoenix, AZ
Jackson, Stephen R. ....Norfolk, VA
Jackson, Steve M. ....Eau Claire, WI
Jackson, Steven Andrew ....Asheville, NC
Jackson, Steven B. ....Lebanon, MO
Jackson, Steven C. ....Paducah, KY
Jackson, Steven F. ....Jamaica, NY
Jackson, Steven F. ....McLean, VA
Jackson, Steven Farrell ....Lancaster, OH
Jackson, Steven L. ....Atlanta, GA
Jackson, Steven L. ....Fort Wayne, IN
Jackson, Steven L. ....Canton, OH
Jackson, Stuart A. ....New York, NY
Jackson, Stuart P. ....Watertown, NY
Jackson, Susan A., Law Office of
Boston, MA
Jackson, Susan B. ....Santa Ana, CA
Jackson, Susan J. ....Los Angeles, CA
Jackson, Susan K. ....Stamford, CT
Jackson, Susan S. ....Pittsburgh, PA
Jackson, Susan Serad ....Charlotte, NC
Jackson and Sutherland, P.C. ....Quincy, MA
Jackson, Suzanne H. ....Washington, DC
Jackson, T. Frank ....Memphis, TN
Jackson, T. Haller, III ....Shreveport, LA
Jackson, T. Haller, Jr. ....Shreveport, LA
Jackson, T. Jerry ....Atlanta, GA
Jackson, T. Michael ....Oklahoma City, OK
Jackson, Tara L. ....Phoenix, AZ
Jackson Taylor & Martino, P.C.
Bay Minette, AL
Mobile, AL
Biloxi, MS
Pascagoula, MS
Jackson, Teri ....San Francisco, CA
Jackson, Terrence A. ....Tucson, AZ
Jackson, Terrence G.
Department of Agriculture,
Office of the General Counsel, GV
Jackson, Terrence M. ....Las Vegas, NV
Jackson, Terry D. ....Atlanta, GA
Jackson, Terry D., P.C. ....Atlanta, GA
Jackson, Theodore ....North Hollywood, CA
Jackson, Theodore A. ....East Moline, IL
Jackson, Theodore R. ....Scarsdale, NY
Jackson, Theodore Warren
El Segundo, CA
Jackson, Thomas ....Port Townsend, WA
Jackson, Thomas A. ....Wheaton, IL
Jackson, Thomas A., & Associates
Cincinnati, OH
Jackson, Thomas B., III ....Columbia, SC
Jackson, Thomas C. ....Dover, DE
Jackson, Thomas C. ....Washington, DC
Jackson, Thomas E. ....Indianapolis, IN
Jackson, Thomas E. ....Detroit, MI
Jackson, Thomas F., Jr. ....Murfreesboro, TN
Jackson, Thomas Francis, III
Memphis, TN
Jackson, Thomas G. ....New York, NY
Jackson, Thomas G. ....Paoli, PA
Jackson, Thomas H. ....Washington, DC
Jackson, Thomas K. ....Norwalk, CT
Jackson, Thomas L. ....San Diego, CA
Jackson, Thomas L. ....Springfield, IL
Jackson, Thomas M. ....Cheshire, CT
Jackson, Thomas M. ....Macon, GA
Jackson, Thomas M. ....Aurora, IL
Jackson, Thomas M., Jr. ....Hillsville, VA
Jackson, Thomas M., Jr.
Independence, VA
Wytheville, VA
Jackson, Thomas P.
United States District Court For The District
Of Columbia, GV
Jackson, Thomas R. ....Dallas, TX
Jackson, Thomas W. ....Aurora, CO
Jackson, Thomas W. ....New York, NY
Jackson & Thompson, P.C. ....Portsmouth, VA
Jackson, Timothy L. ....Houston, TX
Jackson, T. K., III ....Mobile, AL
Jackson, Todd ....Oakland, CA
Jackson, Todd G. ....Cleveland, OH
Jackson, Toni L. ....Carpinteria, CA
Jackson, Tracie J. ....Belle Chasse, LA
Jackson, Tracy L. ....Houston, TX
Jackson, Travis M. ....Redwood City, CA
Jackson & Tyler, L.L.P. ....Atlanta, GA
Jackson, Valerie A. ....Woodbridge, NJ
Jackson, Van D. ....Atlanta, GA
Jackson, Vanessa Agee ....Tullahoma, TN
Jackson, Vicki C. ....Washington, DC
Jackson, W. Charles ....Milwaukee, WI
Jackson, W. Edwin ....York, PA
Jackson, W. Henry ....Worcester, MA
Jackson, W. Kevin ....Salt Lake City, UT
Jackson, W. Newton, 3rd ....Salisbury, MD
Jackson & Wade, L.L.C.
Overland Park, KS
Kansas City, MO
St. Louis, MO
Jackson, Wagner D., Jr.
Department of Justice, Civil Division, GV
Jackson Walker L.L.P. ....Austin, TX
Dallas, TX
Fort Worth, TX
Houston, TX
Richardson, TX
San Angelo, TX
San Antonio, TX
Jackson & Wallace ....Los Angeles, CA
San Francisco, CA
Jackson, Wallace ....Madison, MN
Jackson, Warner L. ....Bedford Heights, OH
Jackson White Gardner Weech & Walker, P.C. ....Chandler, AZ
Mesa, AZ
Payson, AZ
Phoenix, AZ
Tempe, AZ
Jackson, William A. ....Birmingham, AL
Jackson, William A. ....Orange, CA
Jackson, William A. ....Treasury Department,
Internal Revenue Service, GV
Jackson, William A. ....New Port Richey, FL
Jackson, William C. ....Rockford, IL
Jackson, William C. ....Tulsa, OK
Jackson, William D. ....Quincy, MA
Jackson, William D. ....Dallas, TX
Jackson, William E. ....New York, NY
Jackson, William E. ....Alexandria, VA
Jackson, William G. ....St. Johns, MI
Jackson, William H. ....Anniston, AL
Jackson, William H. ....Louisa, KY
Jackson, William Howard, III
Los Angeles, CA
Jackson, William J. ....Baltimore, MD
Jackson, William J. ....Canadian, TX
Jackson, William J. ....Houston, TX
Jackson, William J. ....Houston, TX
Jackson, William K. ....Bethesda, MD
Jackson, William L. ....Baker City, OR
Jackson, William L. ....Charlottesville, VA
Jackson, William M. ....Dothan, AL
Jackson, William M. ....New York, NY
Jackson, William P., Jr. ....Arlington, VA
Jackson, William R., Jr. ....Chicago, IL
Jackson, William S. ....Montrose, CO
Jackson, William S. ....Houston, TX
Jackson, William Stuart ....Little Rock, AR
Jackson, William T. ....Tallahassee, FL
Jackson & Williams ....Cullman, AL
Jackson, Willis, Jr. ....Knoxville, TN
Jackson & Wilson ....Irvine, CA
San Jose, CA
Jackson, Wilson & Douglas ....Lockport, NY
Jackson, Wm. T. ....Wyncote, PA
Jackson & Wyble, L.L.C. ....Baton Rouge, LA
Jackson, Yashmyn C. ....Chicago, IL
Jackson, Yazinski & McLaughlin, P.C.
Claremont, NH
Jackson, Yemi Fleming ....Seattle, WA
Jackson, Yolanda Cash
Fort Lauderdale, FL
Jackson, Yolanda M. ....San Francisco, CA
Jackson, Z. B. ....San Francisco, CA
Jackson-Davis, Calvin Orlando
Glendale, CA
Jackson-Davis, Kelly A. ....Wakefield, MA
Jackson-DeGarcia, Jacqueline
Harrisburg, PA
Jackson-Forbes, Johnlander ....Columbus, OH
Jackson-Gillison, Helen L. ....Weirton, WV
Jackson-Holmes, Flora M ....Miami, FL
Jackson-Mays, Amy E. ....Lancaster, PA
Jackson McLean, Dianne
San Francisco, CA
Jackson-Polk, Joan C. ....Omaha, NE
Jackson-Rigg, Michelle ....Maysville, KY
Jackson-Sanders, Charlann ....Lakeland, FL
Jackstadt, Eric D. ....Granite City, IL
Jackstadt, Kris T. ....Albany, NY
Jackstadt, Robert L. ....Edwardsville, IL
St. Louis, MO
Jackvony, Anthony T. ....Providence, RI
Jackvony, Bernard A. ....Providence, RI
Jackvony, Louis V., Jr. ....Lincoln, RI
Jackwig, Lee Margaret ....Des Moines, IA
Jackwood, Renee J. ....Orrville, OH
Jaco, Lyston G., Jr. ....Laguna Hills, CA
Jaco, W. Geary ....Kansas City, MO
Jacob, Ann Wear ....St. Petersburg, FL
Jacob, Anthony J. ....Chicago, IL
Jacob, Arnold M. ....Bloomfield Hills, MI
Jacob, Arthur F. ....Reisterstown, MD
Jacob, Arthur, Law Offices of
Hackensack, NJ
Jacob & Associates ....Solon, OH
Jacob, Audrey Sullivan ....Palo Alto, CA
Jacob, B. William, Jr. ....Kansas City, MO
Jacob, Barbara Ann ....Brick, NJ
Jacob, Bernard E. ....Hempstead, NY
Jacob, Bert H. ....Kansas City, MO
Jacob, Beth D. ....New York, NY
Jacob, Bill N. ....Boston, MA
Jacob, Bradford Clark ....Norfolk, VA
Jacob, Bradley P. ....Beaver Falls, PA
Jacob, Bruce R. ....St. Petersburg, FL
Jacob, Charles R., III ....New York, NY
Jacob, Clyde H., III ....New Orleans, LA
Jacob, Cynthia M. ....Somerset, NJ
Jacob, David J. ....Bloomfield Hills, MI
Jacob, Dean L. ....Marion, OH
Jacob, Diana M. ....Chicago, IL
Jacob, Edwin J., (P.C.) ....New York, NY
Jacob, Ferrigno & Jesperson ....Millville, NJ
Jacob, Fred ....Washington, DC
Jacob, Fred B.
National Labor Relations Board,
Office of the General Counsel, GV
Jacob, Frederick A. ....Millville, NJ
Jacob, George D., Jr. ....Houston, TX
Jacob, Gustave F. ....De Smet, SD
Jacob, Harry J., III ....Solon, OH
Jacob, Hedges & Allan, LLP
Los Angeles, CA
Jacob, J. Michael ....Huntington Beach, CA
Jacob, Joann ....Tonka Bay, MN
Jacob, John B., Jr. ....Alexandria, VA
Jacob, John R. ....Washington, DC
Jacob, Joseph ....Cape Coral, FL
Jacob, Joseph M. ....Dulles, VA
Jacob, Kathleen L. ....Gunnison, CO
Jacob, Kenneth S. ....Washington, DC
Jacob Law Associates, P.A. ....Pittsburgh, PA
Jacob, Lynn F. ....Richmond, VA
Jacob, Mark A. ....Houston, TX
Jacob, Mark S. ....St. Marys, PA
Jacob, Martha N. ....Houston, TX
Jacob, Marvin E. ....New York, NY
Jacob, Mathai ....Miami, FL
Jacob, Matthew M. ....Washington, DC
Jacob, Matthew M. ....Pittsburgh, PA
Jacob, Medinger & Finnegan, LLP
New York, NY
Jacob, Michael L. ....Seattle, WA
Jacob, Michael M. ....Southfield, MI
Jacob, N. Wescott ....Onancock, VA
Jacob, Nancy S.
Federal Labor Relations Authority,
Authority Member Staff, GV
Jacob, Nancy Vasileff ....Cincinnati, OH
Jacob, Phoebe A. ....Troy, MI
Jacob, Richard K. ....Louisville, KY
Shaker Heights, OH
Jacob, Richard P. ....Pittsburgh, PA
Jacob, Robert D. ....Maple Grove, MN
Jacob, Robin A. ....Dallas, TX
Jacob, Rodney James ....Saipan, TT
Jacob, Seymour M. ....Cleveland, OH
Jacob, Shalom ....New York, NY
Jacob, Steven R. ....Boynton Beach, FL
Jacob, Steven R., P.A. ....Boynton Beach, FL
Jacob, Ted K. ....Pittsburgh, PA
Jacob, Tessa K. ....Kansas City, MO
Jacob, Thomas B. ....Palo Alto, CA
Jacob, Thomas B. ....Stuart, FL
Jacob, Thomas N. ....Bloomington, IL
Jacob, Timothy J. ....Youngstown, OH
Jacob, Valerie Ford ....New York, NY
Jacob, Walter C. ....Sterling, VA
Jacob, Walter C., P.C. ....Sterling, VA
Jacob, Walter P. ....Washington, DC
Jacob, Warren C. ....Los Angeles, CA
Jacob & Weingarten
North Palm Beach, FL
Detroit, MI
Troy, MI
Jacob, William B. ....Meridian, MS
Jacob, Wm. L., Jr. ....Pittsburgh, PA
Jacobberger, Anne D. ....Pleasanton, CA
Jacobberger, Fred R. ....St. Paul, MN
Jacobberger, Jeffrey M. ....Los Angeles, CA
Jacobberger, Micallef & Assocs., P.A.
St. Paul, MN
Jacobellis, Michael ....Beaumont, TX
Jasper, TX
Jacobellis, Thomas Joseph ....Carmel, NY
Jacober, Bridget A. ....Santa Fe, NM
Jacober, John ....Lebanon, NJ
Jacober, Matthew A. ....Belleville, IL
Jacobi, Allan Kirk ....San Francisco, CA
Jacobi, Allen L. ....Miami, FL
Jacobi, Allen S., Jr. ....West Trenton, NJ
Jacobi, Barbara Melior ....Denver, CO
Jacobi, Benjamin R. ....North Miami, FL
Jacobi, D'Alessandro, Jacobi & Sieghardt, P.C.
Staten Island, NY
Jacobi, Daniel E. ....Des Moines, IA
Jacobi, David M. ....Seattle, WA
Jacobi, Elizabeth D. ....Cedar Rapids, IA
Jacobi, F. Lee ....Eureka Springs, AR
Jacobi, George R. ....Somerville, NJ
Jacobi, Herbert M. ....New York, NY
Jacobi, James J. ....Rhinelander, WI
Jacobi, James N. ....Alexandria, VA
Jacobi, Jerome F. ....Jeffersonville, IN
Jacobi, John A. ....Houston, TX
Jacobi, John F. D., III ....Attleboro, MA
Jacobi, John J. ....Washington, NC
Jacobi, John V. ....Newark, NJ
Jacobi, Joseph J. ....Indianapolis, IN
Jacobi, Judith Ann ....Tucson, AZ
Jacobi, K. Edward ....Asbury Park, NJ
Jacobi, Kappel & Case, P.C. ....Milford, CT
New Haven, CT
Jacobi, Lawrence Richard, Jr. ....Austin, TX
Jacobi, Mordecai J. ....Staten Island, NY
Jacobi, Paul ....Milford, CT
Jacobi, Paula K. ....Chicago, IL
Jacobi, Robert B. ....Washington, DC
Jacobi, Ronald N. ....Culver City, CA
Jacobi, Steven P. ....San Jose, CA
Jacobi, Susan M. ....New York, NY
Jacobi, Tara Louise ....New York, NY
Jacobi, Timothy M. ....New Albany, IN
Jacobie, Roy E. ....Dallas, TX
Jacobie, Roy E., Jr. ....Nacogdoches, TX
Jacobo-Jones, Kimberly ....Miami, FL
Jacoboni, Danielle ....Phoenix, AZ
Jacobovitz, Jeffrey S. ....Washington, DC
Jacobovitz, Victor ....Los Angeles, CA
Jacobowitz, Garfinkel & Lesman
New York, NY
Jacobowitz, Gerald N. ....Walden, NY
Jacobowitz, Grabelle, Defino, McGoughran & Latimer ....Oakhurst, NJ
Jacobowitz and Gubits, L.L.P.
Goshen, NY
Middletown, NY
Newburgh, NY
Walden, NY
Washingtonville, NY
Jacobowitz, Harold S. ....New York, NY
Jacobowitz, Harry A. ....Palmerton, PA
Jacobowitz, Henry ....Sedona, AZ
Jacobowitz, Herbert M. ....Thousand Oaks, CA
Jacobowitz, Ira Aaron ....Oakland, CA

Jacobowitz, Jan L. ... Miami, FL
Jacobowitz, Les ... New York, NY
Jacobowitz, Lisa A. ... Beverly, MA
Jacobowitz, Marc E. ... Los Angeles, CA
Jacobowitz, Marcia A. ... Walden, NY
Jacobowitz, Melvin J. ... Miami, FL
Jacobowitz, Michael ... San Leandro, CA
Jacobowitz & Ostroff, P.A. ... Miami, FL
Jacobowitz & Paz ... Walden, NY
Jacobowitz, Philip E. ... Oakhurst, NJ
Jacobowitz, Robert ... Boca Raton, FL
Jacobowitz, Sander M. ... Princeton, NJ
Jacobowitz, Stacy L. ... Miami, FL
Jacobowitz, Stacy L., P.A. ... Miami, FL
Jacobowski, Daniel G. ... St. Paul, MN
Jacobs, Abod & Caruso, A Prof. Corp.
Falls Church, VA
Jacobs, Abod & Caruso A Professional Corporation ... Rockville, MD
Jacobs, Adam H. ... Omaha, NE
Jacobs, Adam W. ... Cambridge, MA
Jacobs, Adele R. ... Fairfield, CT
Jacobs, Alan ... La Jolla, CA
Jacobs, Alan ... Delray Beach, FL
Jacobs, Alan ... Chicago, IL
Jacobs, Alan S. ... New York, NY
Jacobs, Albert L., Jr. ... New York, NY
Jacobs, Alice F. ... Buffalo, NY
Jacobs, Allan ... Ojai, CA
Jacobs, Allan R. ... Clifton, NJ
Jacobs, Allen F. ... Buffalo Grove, IL
Jacobs, Amy Osran ... Beverly Hills, CA
Jacobs, Andrea B. ... Boston, MA
Jacobs, Andrea R. ... Coral Springs, FL
Jacobs, Andrea R., P.A.
Coral Springs, FL
Fort Lauderdale, FL
Jacobs, Andrew ... Woodland Hills, CA
Jacobs, Andrew C. ... East Greenbush, NY
Jacobs, Andrew, Jr. ... Indianapolis, IN
Jacobs, Andrew M. ... Chicago, IL
Jacobs, Andrew R. ... Lexington, KY
Jacobs, Andrew R. ... Newark, NJ
New York, NY
Jacobs, Ann C. ... Houston, TX
Jacobs, Ann Sanford ... Kenosha, WI
Jacobs, Anna
Securities and Exchange Commission, Division of Investment Management, GV
Jacobs, Anne F. ... West Palm Beach, FL
Jacobs, Annie Lee ... Charlottesville, VA
Jacobs, Anthony J. ... Hurley, NM
Jacobs, Anthony N. ... Joplin, MO
Jacobs, Arlie ... Pembroke, NC
Jacobs, Arnold S. ... New York, NY
Jacobs, Arthur B. ... Monterey, CA
Jacobs, Arthur I. ... Fernandina Beach, FL
Jacobs, Arthur J. ... New York, NY
Jacobs, Arthur P., (P.C.) ... New York, NY
Jacobs Associates ... San Francisco, CA
Jacobs & Associates ... Ventura, CA
Jacobs and Associates ... Newark, NJ
New York, NY
Jacobs & Associates, Ltd. ... Chicago, IL
Jacobs, Audrey F. ... Richmond, VA
Jacobs, A.W. Victoria ... Denver, CO
Jacobs, Barbara Ann ... Clearwater, FL
Jacobs, Barbara J. ... New York, NY
Jacobs, Barbara J. Sax ... Memphis, TN
Jacobs & Barbone, P.A. ... Atlantic City, NJ
Camden, NJ
Jacobs & Barney ... Easton, MD
Jacobs, Barry ... Meriden, CT
Jacobs, Barry ... New York, NY
Jacobs, Barry J. ... Mission Viejo, CA
Jacobs, Becky L. ... Houston, TX
Jacobs and Bell, A Professional Association
Hackensack, NJ
Tenafly, NJ
Jacobs, Benjamin R. ... Washington, DC
Jacobs, Betty C. ... Wilmette, IL
Jacobs, Betty Jane ... New York, NY
Jacobs, Blair M. ... Alexandria, VA
Jacobs, Bradley L. ... San Diego, CA
Jacobs, Bradley L. ... Greensboro, NC
Jacobs & Brady P.C.
Christiansted, St. Croix, VI
Jacobs, Brenda A. ... Washington, DC
Jacobs, Brian D. ... Cleveland, OH
Jacobs, Brian J. ... Los Angeles, CA
Jacobs, Bruce D. ... New Haven, CT
Jacobs, Bruce D. ... Washington, DC
Jacobs, Bruce F. ... Cambridge, MA
Jacobs, Bruce M. ... Gilroy, CA
Jacobs, Bruce M. ... Los Angeles, CA
Jacobs, Bruce M. ... Charleston, WV
Jacobs, Burns, Sugarman, Orlove & Stanton
Chicago, IL
Jacobs, Burton A. ... Highland Beach, FL
Jacobs, Calvin R. ... New York, NY
Jacobs, Carl P. ... Los Angeles, CA
Jacobs, Carmen A., Jr. ... Alexandria, VA
Jacobs, Carolyn ... Baltimore, MD
Jacobs, Caryn L. ... Chicago, IL
Jacobs, Catherine A. ... Lansing, MI
Jacobs, Catherine H. ... Biloxi, MS
Jackson, MS
Jacobs, Catherine H. ... Ocean Springs, MS
Jacobs, Charles C., Jr. ... Cleveland, MS
Jacobs, Charles F. ... Baltimore, MD
Jacobs, Charles H. ... Denver, CO
Jacobs, Charles H. ... Dubuque, IA
Jacobs, Charles M. ... Chicago, IL
Jacobs, Charles P. ... Buffalo, NY
Jacobs Chase Frick Kleinkopf & Kelley, LLC ... Denver, CO
Jacobs, Christie J. ... Treasury Department, Internal Revenue Service, GV

Jacobs, Christina M. ... Pacific Palisades, CA
Jacobs, Christine Ogan ... San Jose, CA
Jacobs, Christopher ... La Grange, IL
Jacobs, Christopher A.
Santa Barbara, CA
Jacobs, Christopher B. ... Cleveland, OH
Jacobs, Christopher G. ... Sacramento, CA
Jacobs and Cohen ... Brooklyn, NY
Jacobs, Constance Lee Floyd
Greensboro, NC
Jacobs, Cory G. ... Philadelphia, PA
Jacobs, Craig H. ... Jefferson City, MO
Jacobs & Crumplar, P.A.
Georgetown, DE
Wilmington, DE
Jacobs & Curtis ... Toledo, OH
Jacobs, Curtis M. ... Louisville, KY
Jacobs, C. W. Daimon ... Tulsa, OK
Jacobs, Cynthia A. ... Miami, FL
Jacobs, Dale ... Wilsonville, OR
Jacobs, Dale Gardner ... Lakeland, FL
Jacobs, Dale Gardner, P.A. ... Lakeland, FL
Jacobs, Daniel S. ... Department of Justice, Environment and Natural Resources Division, GV
Jacobs, Darleen M. ... New Orleans, LA
Jacobs, Darleen M., A Professional Law Corporation ... New Orleans, LA
Jacobs, Darrel D. ... Kalamazoo, MI
Jacobs, Darryl J. ... North Miami Beach, FL
Jacobs, Darryl P. ... Chicago, IL
Jacobs, Dave ... Newkirk, OK
Jacobs, David ... Los Angeles, CA
Jacobs, David ... Chicago, IL
Jacobs, David ... New York, NY
Jacobs, David A. ... New York, NY
Jacobs, David A. ... Eugene, OR
Jacobs, David Arnold ... Alexandria, VA
Jacobs, David H. ... Washington, DC
Jacobs, David K. ... Miami, FL
Jacobs, David M. ... Minneapolis, MN
Jacobs, David P. ... Mount Holly, NJ
Jacobs, David S. ... Brooklyn, NY
Jacobs, Deborah J. ... New York, NY
Jacobs, Debra R. ... Fort Lauderdale, FL
Jacobs, deBrauwere & Dehn LLP
New York, NY
Jacobs & Dembert, P.A. ... Baltimore, MD
Jacobs, Dennis G. ... New York, NY
Jacobs, Dennis W. ... Birmingham, AL
Jacobs, Diana Nickerson ... Pittsburgh, PA
Jacobs, Diane E. ... Irvine, CA
Jacobs, Donald A. ... Hartford, CT
Jacobs, Donald F. ... Orlando, FL
Jacobs, Donald L. ... Vancouver, WA
Jacobs, Donald M. ... Goldsboro, NC
Jacobs, Donald P. ... Short Hills, NJ
Jacobs, Donald R. ... Downey, CA
Jacobs, Donald W. ... Hackensack, NJ
Jacobs, Donna ... Riverside, CA
Jacobs, Donna Brown ... Jackson, MS
Jacobs, Donna L. ... Annapolis, MD
Jacobs, Dorothy S., (P.C.)
New Orleans, LA
Jacobs, Douglas Bram ... Chico, CA
Jacobs, Douglas J. ... Miami, FL
Jacobs, Douglas J. ... Milford, PA
Jacobs, Earle E., III ... Trenton, NJ
Jacobs, Edmund F. ... Puyallup, WA
Jacobs, Edward C. ... Antioch, IL
Jacobs, Edward Haskins
Christiansted, St. Croix, VI
Jacobs, Edward L. ... Fort Thomas, KY
Jacobs, Edward W. ... Schaumburg, IL
Jacobs, Edwin H. ... Sun City Center, FL
Jacobs, Edwin J., Jr. ... Atlantic City, NJ
Jacobs and Ehler, L.L.C. ... Marshall, MO
Jacobs, Eileen D. ... Clearwater, FL
Jacobs, Elissa P. ... Seattle, WA
Jacobs, Elizabeth
Securities and Exchange Commission, Office of International Affairs, GV
Jacobs, Elizabeth C. ... Lexington, KY
Jacobs, Elizabeth G. ... Baltimore, MD
Jacobs, Elizabeth L. ... Detroit, MI
Jacobs, Elizabeth Lackey ... Chapel Hill, NC
Jacobs, Ellis R. ... Philadelphia, PA
Jacobs, Emil ... Des Plaines, IL
Jacobs and Engle, P.C. ... Jackson, MI
Jacobs, Eric M. ... Exton, PA
Jacobs, Eric P. ... San Francisco, CA
Jacobs, Eric R. ... New York, NY
Jacobs, Erik ... New York, NY
Jacobs, Erik K. ... Rockford, IL
Jacobs, Eugene ... Chicago, IL
Jacobs, Eugene B. ... Provo, UT
Jacobs, Eugene W. ... Dunellen, NJ
Jacobs, Fern V. ... Beaumont, TX
Jacobs & Forward ... Lafayette, NY
Syracuse, NY
Jacobs, Fran M. ... New York, NY
Jacobs, Francine I. ... Columbus, OH
Jacobs, Frank ... Lake City, IA
Jacobs, Frank D. ... Toledo, OH
Jacobs, Frank G. ... Carrollton, TX
Jacobs, Fred M., M.D. ... Livingston, NJ
Jacobs, Fred W., Jr. ... San Diego, CA
Jacobs, Freddy ... Brooklyn, NY
Jacobs, Frederick J. ... New York, NY
Jacobs, Frederick L. ... White Plains, NY
Jacobs, Frederick R. ... St. Paul, MN
Jacobs, Fredric C. ... Easton, PA
Jacobs, Frieda P. ... Highland Park, IL
Jacobs, G. Patrick ... Charleston, WV
Jacobs, Gail Turner
Merit Systems Protection Board, Office of Appeals Counsel, GV
Jacobs, Garrett M. ... Charleston, WV

Jacobs, Gary M. ... Washington, DC
Jacobs, Gary N. ... Los Angeles, CA
Jacobs, Gary P. ... Ventura, CA
Jacobs, Gary S. ... Los Angeles, CA
Jacobs, Gayle H. ... Los Angeles, CA
Jacobs, George A. ... Jeffersonville, IN
Jacobs, George F., Jr. ... Madison, WI
Jacobs, George J. C., III
Department of Justice, Tax Division, GV
Jacobs, George M. ... Albany, NY
Jacobs, Gerald M. ... New York, NY
Jacobs, Gerald S. ... Eastchester, NY
Jacobs, Gina M. ... Jackson, MS
Jacobs, Ginger E. ... New York, NY
Jacobs Goldman LLC ... Bridgeport, CT
Fairfield, CT
Hartford, CT
New Canaan, CT
New Haven, CT
Newtown, CT
Norwalk, CT
Stamford, CT
New York, NY
Jacobs & Gregory ... Riverside, CA
Jacobs, Gregory A. ... Atlanta, GA
Jacobs, Gregory J. ... Santa Rosa, CA
Jacobs, Gregory R. ... Dallas, TX
Jacobs, Gretchen E. ... Department of Justice, Civil Division, GV
Jacobs, Grudberg, Belt & Dow, P.C.
New Haven, CT
Jacobs, Gwen G. ... Tampa, FL
Jacobs, H. Paul ... Franklin, MI
Jacobs, H. Vincent ... Sacramento, CA
Jacobs, Hara K. ... New York, NY
Jacobs, Harold ... Philadelphia, PA
Jacobs, Harold L. ... Fort Lee, NJ
Jacobs, Harold W. ... Columbia, SC
Jacobs, Harris F. ... Cincinnati, OH
Jacobs, Harris and Jon Co., L.P.A.
Cincinnati, OH
Jacobs, Harry L. ... Merced, CA
Jacobs, Harry S. ... Chicago, IL
Jacobs, Harry W. ... Washington, DC
Jacobs, Harry W. ... New York, NY
Jacobs, Harvey A. ... Rockville, MD
Jacobs, Harvey L. ... Brooklyn, NY
Jacobs, Harvey S. ... Brooklyn, NY
Jacobs & Holt, P.C. ... Nashville, TN
Jacobs, Howard A. ... New Haven, CT
Jacobs, Howard L. ... Los Angeles, CA
Westlake Village, CA
Jacobs, Howard L. ... New York, NY
Jacobs, Howard S. ... New York, NY
Jacobs, Hugh Garret ... Kendrick, ID
Jacobs, Hyman ... Jamaica, NY
Jacobs, I. M. ... Oak Park, MI
Jacobs, India P. ... Atlantic City, NJ
Jacobs, Ira A. ... East Hartford, CT
Jacobs, Irene Prosky ... New Haven, CT
Jacobs, Irvin ... Baltimore, MD
Jacobs, J. David ... Washington, DC
Jacobs, J. Gregory ... Tampa, FL
Jacobs, J. Michael ... Nashville, TN
Jacobs, J. Patrick ... Santa Monica, CA
Jacobs, J. Thomas ... Madison, WI
Jacobs, J. Timothy ... Puyallup, WA
Jacobs, J. Zalman ... New York, NY
Jacobs, Jack B. ... Wilmington, DE
Jacobs, Jack R. ... Arlington, TX
Jacobs, Jack T. ... Ironwood, MI
Jacobs & Jacobs ... New Haven, CT
Jacobs & Jacobs ... Baltimore, MD
Jacobs & Jacobs ... Stamford, NY
Jacobs & Jacobs ... Orlando, FL
Puyallup, WA
Jacobs, Jacobs & Farber ... Rockville, MD
Jacobs & Jacobs, P.C. ... Meriden, CT
Jacobs, Jacobs & Rosenberg
Los Angeles, CA
Santa Monica, CA
Jacobs, Jacobs & Shannon, Professional Corporation ... New Haven, CT
Jacobs, James David ... New York, NY
Jacobs, James E. ... Palm Coast, FL
Jacobs, James K. ... Westborough, MA
Jacobs, James K. ... Cleveland, OH
Jacobs, James L. ... Mountain View, CA
Jacobs, James M. ... New Orleans, LA
Jacobs, James M., Jr. ... Somerset, PA
Jacobs, James P. ... St. Clair Shores, MI
Jacobs, James S. ... Chicago, IL
Jacobs, James S. ... Baltimore, MD
Jacobs, Jane B. ... New York, NY
Jacobs, Jane B. ... Philadelphia, PA
Jacobs, Jay W. ... San Francisco, CA
Jacobs, Jeffrey A. ... Miami, FL
Jacobs, Jeffrey A. ... Rochester, NY
Jacobs, Jeffrey A. ... Columbia, SC
Jacobs, Jeffrey C. ... Portland, OR
Jacobs, Jeffrey D. ... Chicago, IL
Jacobs, Jeffrey D. ... Austin, TX
Jacobs, Jeffrey I. ... Miami, FL
Jacobs, Jeffrey J. ... Monroeville, PA
Jacobs, Jeffrey L. ... New York, NY
Jacobs, Jeffrey P. ... Atlanta, GA
Jacobs, Jeffrey W. ... Washington, DC
Jacobs, Jeffrey W. ... Bloomington, MN
Jacobs, Jennifer A. ... Bloomington, IL
Jacobs, Jennifer R. ... Los Angeles, CA
Jacobs, Jennifer W. ... Houston, TX
Jacobs, Jerald A. ... Washington, DC
Jacobs, Jerilyn L. ... Los Angeles, CA
Jacobs, Jerold L. ... Washington, DC
Jacobs, Jill Eichenbaum ... Miami, FL
Jacobs, Jill M. ... Denver, CO
Jacobs, Jimmy ... Montgomery, AL
Jacobs, Jo Annette ... Marshall, MO

Jacobs, Joan M. ... Bethesda, MD
Jacobs, Joanna M. ... Philadelphia, PA
Jacobs, Jodi L. ... New Orleans, LA
Jacobs, Joey ... San Gregorio, CA
Jacobs, John C. ... Buffalo, NY
Jacobs, John C., Jr. ... Brenham, TX
Jacobs, John D ... Los Angeles, CA
Jacobs, John E. ... Southfield, MI
Jacobs, John F. ... Chicago, IL
Jacobs, John G. ... Chicago, IL
Jacobs, John H. ... Little Rock, AR
Jacobs, John Martin ... Philadelphia, PA
Jacobs, John P. ... Southfield, MI
Jacobs, John R. ... New York, NY
Jacobs, John R. ... Sewanee, TN
Jacobs, Jon B. ... Department of Justice, Antitrust Division, GV
Jacobs, Jon D.
Environmental Protection Agency, Office of Enforcement and Compliance Assurance, GV
Jacobs, Jon H. ... Cincinnati, OH
Jacobs, Jon M. ... Boston, MA
Jacobs, Jonathan E. ... New York, NY
Jacobs, Jonathan M. ... Washington, DC
Jacobs, Joni Suzan ... San Francisco, CA
Jacobs, Jonnie ... Piedmont, CA
Jacobs, Joseph ... Amsterdam, NY
Jacobs, Joseph C. ... Margate, FL
Linthicum, MD
Jacobs, Joseph J. ... Englewood, NJ
Jacobs, Joseph M. ... Atlantic City, NJ
Jacobs, Joseph M. ... Livingston, NJ
Jacobs, Joseph M. ... Princeton, NJ
Jacobs, Joseph W. ... Tallahassee, FL
Jacobs, Joshua ... St. Louis, MO
Jacobs, Judi L. ... Los Angeles, CA
Jacobs, Judith I. ... Boston, MA
Jacobs, Julian H. ... San Diego, CA
Jacobs, Julian I.
United States Tax Court, GV
Jacobs, Julie A. ... New Orleans, LA
Jacobs, Julie L. ... New York, NY
Jacobs, Julie M. ... Washington, DC
Jacobs, Julius B. ... Carteret, NJ
Jacobs, Justin M., Jr. ... Palo Alto, CA
Jacobs, Kai E. ... Miami, FL
Jacobs, Karen J. ... New York, NY
Jacobs, Karen L. ... Chicago, IL
Jacobs, Karl M. ... Fowler, IN
Jacobs, Kathleen Marie ... Riverside, CA
Jacobs, Kathy S. ... Asheville, NC
Jacobs, Katy Kerr ... Santa Barbara, CA
Jacobs, Kenneth B. ... Jacksonville, FL
Jacobs, Kenneth J. ... Forest Lake, MN
Jacobs, Kenneth L. ... Midland, MI
Jacobs, Kenneth R. ... New York, NY
Jacobs, Kenneth S. ... Sebastopol, CA
Jacobs, Kenneth S. ... Villa Park, IL
Waupaca, WI
Jacobs, Kevin P. ... Miami, FL
Jacobs, Kevin P. ... Bloomington, IL
Jacobs, Kleinman, Seibel and McNally, A Prtnshp. incl. a Legal Prof. Assn
Cincinnati, OH
Jacobs, Kristin A. ... San Jose, CA
Jacobs, Kurt H. ... Washington, DC
Jacobs, Larry E. ... Houston, TX
Jacobs, Larry S. ... New Orleans, LA
Jacobs, Laura Basem ... Bethesda, MD
Jacobs, Laura L. ... Tampa, FL
Jacobs, Laura L. ... Winter Park, FL
Jacobs, Laurie A. ... Swampscott, MA
Jacobs, Laurie Faith ... Berkeley, CA
Jacobs, Lawrence ... Los Angeles, CA
Jacobs, Lawrence A. ... Sarasota, FL
Jacobs, Lawrence A. ... New York, NY
Jacobs, Lawrence A., P.A. ... Sarasota, FL
Jacobs, Lawrence Evan ... New York, NY
Jacobs, Lawrence F. ... Westfield, NJ
Jacobs, Lawrence H. ... Hackensack, NJ
Jacobs, Lawrence S. ... Rockville, MD
Falls Church, VA
Jacobs, Leedia Gordeev ... Dana Point, CA
Jacobs, Leigh Marshall ... Newport Beach, CA
Jacobs, Leon G. ... Orlando, FL
Jacobs, Leonard ... Manchester, CT
Jacobs, Lesley ... New York, NY
Jacobs, Leslie Gielow ... Sacramento, CA
Jacobs, Leslie W. (IBA) ... Cleveland, OH
Jacobs, Lewis ... Rockville, MD
Jacobs, Linda ... New York, NY
Jacobs, Linda T. ... Philadelphia, PA
Jacobs, Lisa ... Glendale, CA
Jacobs, Lisa L. ... New York, NY
Jacobs, Lisa R. ... Philadelphia, PA
Jacobs, Lisa S. Ho ... Honolulu, HI
Jacobs, Lisalyn R. ... Department of Justice, Office of Policy Development, GV
Jacobs, Lisbeth M. ... Southfield, MI
Jacobs, Lois C. Moonitz ... Los Angeles, CA
Jacobs, Lorenzo W., Jr. ... Washington, DC
Jacobs, Louis P. ... New York, NY
Jacobs, Louise D. ... Arlington, VA
Jacobs, Louise M. ... Des Moines, IA
Jacobs, Lowell L. ... New York, NY
Jacobs, Lyn ... Department of Justice, Environment and Natural Resources Division, GV
Jacobs, Lynn B. ... Islandia, NY
Jacobs, M. Bradley ... Boston, MA
Jacobs, Manuel, Kain & Bernberg
New Orleans, LA
Jacobs, Marc A. ... Hoboken, NJ
New York, NY
Jacobs, Marc M. ... Chicago, IL
Jacobs, Marc Paul ... Los Angeles, CA
Jacobs, Marc R. ... Los Angeles, CA

Jacobs, Marc R. ..... **Chicago, IL**
Jacobs, Marc S. ..... **Philadelphia, PA**
Jacobs, Marc S. ..... **Laredo, TX**
Jacobs, Margaret A. ..... **New York, NY**
Jacobs, Margaret A. ..... New York, NY
Jacobs, Margaret A. ..... Norwich, VT
Jacobs, Margaret L.
Federal Deposit Insurance Corporation, Liquidation Branch, GV
Jacobs, Marilyn L. ..... **Sacramento, CA**
Jacobs, Marjorie Stern ..... **Philadelphia, PA**
Jacobs, Mark A. ..... Department of Defense, Defense Legal Services Agency, GV
Jacobs, Mark A. ..... Miami, FL
Jacobs, Mark B. ..... **San Francisco, CA**
Jacobs, Mark C. ..... Sacramento, CA
Jacobs, Mark D. ..... **Detroit, MI**
Jacobs, Mark E. ..... **Dallas, TX**
Jacobs, Mark E., P.C. ..... **Dallas, TX**
Jacobs, Mark I. ..... Palm Beach, FL
Jacobs, Mark J. ..... Chicago, IL
Jacobs, Mark N. ..... **New York, NY**
Jacobs, Mark R. (IBA) ..... **Norwalk, CT**
Jacobs, Mark R. ..... **Cleveland, OH**
Jacobs, Mark S. ..... **Troy, MI**
Jacobs, Mark S. ..... Cherry Hill, NJ
Jacobs, Marshall A. ..... **New York, NY**
Jacobs, Martha J. ..... Chevy Chase, MD
Jacobs, Martin ..... **Washington, DC**
Jacobs, Martin ..... Boston, MA
Jacobs, Martin E., (Inc.) ..... Los Angeles, CA
Jacobs, Marty G. ..... **Owensboro, KY**
Jacobs, Marvin A. ..... San Francisco, CA
Jacobs, Marvin E. ..... Ventura, CA
Jacobs, Marvin K. ..... Toledo, OH
Jacobs, Marvin K., Co., L.P.A. ..... Toledo, OH
Jacobs, Mary Ann ..... Cincinnati, OH
Jacobs, Mary Lee ..... Medford, MA
Jacobs, Matthew H. ..... Rochester, NH
Jacobs, Matthew J. ..... San Francisco, CA
Jacobs, Matthew L. ..... **Washington, DC**
Jacobs, Maurice ..... **Chicago, IL**
Jacobs, McClintock & Scanlon
Bennington, VT
Jacobs, McDonald, Silc & Fauerbach, P.C.
Ironwood, MI
Ashland, WI
Jacobs, Melanie B. ..... **Boston, MA**
Jacobs, Melissa ..... **Phoenix, AZ**
Jacobs, Melissa Jill ..... **Miami, FL**
Jacobs, Melvin A. ..... **Newark, NJ**
Jacobs, Micah R. ..... **Palo Alto, CA**
Jacobs, Michael A. ..... **San Francisco, CA**
Jacobs, Michael A. ..... Santa Ana, CA
Jacobs, Michael A.
Federal Labor Relations Authority, Authority Member Staff, GV
Jacobs, Michael A. ..... **Boston, MA**
Jacobs, Michael A. ..... Stamford, NY
Jacobs, Michael A. ..... **Dayton, OH**
Jacobs, Michael A. ..... Brookfield, WI
Jacobs, Michael A., Law Offices of
Houston, TX
Jacobs, Michael David ..... Chicago, IL
Jacobs, Michael E. ..... **Portland, OR**
Jacobs, Michael Eric ..... **Hamilton, OH**
Jacobs, Michael H. ..... **Washington, DC**
Jacobs, Michael J.
Federal Communications Commission, Mass Media Bureau, GV
Jacobs, Michael J. ..... Chicago, IL
Jacobs, Michael J. ..... **Easton, MD**
Jacobs, Michael P. ..... **Sioux City, IA**
Jacobs, Michael P. ..... **Mankato, MN**
Jacobs, Michael P. ..... **Lynnwood, WA**
Jacobs, Michael S. ..... Buffalo Grove, IL
Jacobs, Michael W. ..... **San Diego, CA**
Jacobs, Michelle K. ..... New York, NY
Jacobs, Michelle Lynn ..... Bronx, NY
Jacobs, Milena S. ..... **New Brunswick, NJ**
Jacobs, Milton ..... San Francisco, CA
Jacobs, Mimi Johnson ..... Oakland, CA
Jacobs, Mitchell A. ..... Los Angeles, CA
Jacobs, Mitchell B. ..... Cranford, NJ
Jacobs, Mitchell D. ..... Clayton, MO
Jacobs, Mitchell Wayne ..... **Los Angeles, CA**
Jacobs, Monica M. ..... **Austin, TX**
Jacobs, Monty S. ..... Hyattsville, MD
Jacobs & Morace ..... New York, NY
Jacobs, Morton ..... West Bloomfield, MI
Jacobs, Myles L. ..... **Joliet, IL**
Jacobs, Nan Cohan ..... **Modesto, CA**
Jacobs, Neal A. ..... Cherry Hill, NJ
Philadelphia, PA
Jacobs, Neal A., P.C. ..... Cherry Hill, NJ
Philadelphia, PA
Jacobs, Neal D. ..... Los Angeles, CA
Jacobs, Neil H. ..... **Boston, MA**
Jacobs, Neil I. ..... **Gaithersburg, MD**
Jacobs, Neil I. ..... **New York, NY**
Jacobs, Neilson S. ..... **Shreveport, LA**
Jacobs, Nicholas J. ..... **Ironwood, MI**
Jacobs, Norene D. ..... **Des Moines, IA**
Jacobs, Norman A. ..... Columbus, OH
Jacobs, Norman E.
Department Of Veterans Affairs, Office of Human Resources Management, GV
Jacobs, Norman I. ..... **Boston, MA**
Jacobs, Pamela L. ..... Millburn, NJ
Jacobs, Pamela Ravin ..... Scarsdale, NY
Jacobs, Paul ..... Boca Raton, FL
Jacobs, Paul ..... Baltimore, MD
Jacobs, Paul ..... **New York, NY**
Jacobs, Paul A. ..... **Denver, CO**
Jacobs, Paul E. ..... **San Jose, CA**
Jacobs, Paul L. ..... **Chicago, IL**
Jacobs, Paul N. ..... Newport Beach, CA
Jacobs, Paul S., P.A. ..... Hialeah, FL
Jacobs, Paul W., II ..... **Richmond, VA**
Jacobs, Paula K. ..... Dallas, TX
Jacobs, Penny Kfare ..... Orlando, FL
Jacobs Persinger & Parker
New York, NY
Jacobs, Peter C. ..... East Hartford, CT
Jacobs, Peter H. ..... **Portland, ME**
Jacobs, Peter M. ..... Las Vegas, NV
Jacobs, R. David ..... Los Angeles, CA
Jacobs, Ralph A. ..... **Philadelphia, PA**
Jacobs, Randall B. ..... Los Angeles, CA
Jacobs, Randall M. ..... Washington, IL
Jacobs, Randall S. D. ..... New York, NY
Jacobs, Randolph ..... Missoula, MT
Jacobs, Randolph, Jr. ..... **Billings, MT**
Jacobs, Raphael G. ..... **Tenafly, NJ**
Jacobs, Renée E. ..... **Los Angeles, CA**
Jacobs, Reuven ..... New York, NY
Jacobs, Rex W. ..... **Long Beach, CA**
Los Angeles, CA
Jacobs, Richard ..... **Redmond, WA**
Jacobs, Richard B. ..... Towson, MD
Jacobs, Richard B. ..... **Boston, MA**
Jacobs, Richard C. ..... **San Francisco, CA**
Jacobs, Richard E. ..... **Dayton, OH**
Jacobs, Richard F. ..... **Austin, TX**
Jacobs, Richard J. ..... **Alamosa, CO**
Jacobs, Richard J. ..... Bethlehem, PA
Jacobs, Richard L. ..... Folsom, CA
Jacobs, Richard L. ..... **New Haven, CT**
Jacobs, Richard O. ..... **St. Petersburg, FL**
Jacobs, Richard P. ..... **St. Louis, MO**
Jacobs, Richard P. ..... Albuquerque, NM
Jacobs, Richard S. ..... **Boston, MA**
Jacobs, Rita S. ..... Lansing, MI
Jacobs, R. M." Mac " ..... Lake Forest, CA
Jacobs, Robert ..... **Culver City, CA**
Jacobs, Robert ..... **Wilmington, DE**
Jacobs, Robert A. ..... **Birmingham, MI**
Jacobs, Robert A. ..... New York, NY
Jacobs, Robert A. ..... **New York, NY**
Jacobs, Robert A. ..... **New York, NY**
Jacobs, Robert A. ..... **New York, NY**
Jacobs, Robert B., Law Office of
Pleasanton, CA
Jacobs, Robert C. ..... **Philadelphia, PA**
Jacobs, Robert D. ..... **Washington, DC**
Jacobs, Robert D. ..... **St. Louis, MO**
Jacobs, Robert D. ..... Richmond, VA
Jacobs, Robert E. ..... Cincinnati, OH
Jacobs, Robert F. ..... San Jose, CA
Jacobs, Robert F. ..... **New York, NY**
Jacobs, Robert J. ..... **Jacksonville, FL**
Jacobs, Robert L. ..... Bernardsville, NJ
Jacobs, Robert Lee ..... Carlisle, PA
Jacobs, Robert M. ..... **Hackensack, NJ**
Jacobs, Robert N. ..... Los Angeles, CA
Jacobs, Robert P. ..... **Washington, DC**
Jacobs, Robert R., II ..... Fort Myers, FL
Jacobs, Robert S. ..... Chicago, IL
Jacobs, Robert Stephen ..... New York, NY
Jacobs, Robin L. ..... **Los Angeles, CA**
Jacobs, Robin R. ..... Los Angeles, CA
Jacobs, Robin S. ..... Chestnut Hill, MA
Jacobs, Robt. G. ..... San Mateo, CA
Jacobs, Rodney L. ..... Buffalo Grove, IL
Jacobs, Roger B. ..... Metairie, LA
Jacobs, Roger B. ..... **Newark, NJ**
New York, NY
Jacobs, Roger F. ..... Notre Dame, IN
Jacobs, Rolland B. ..... Fort Dodge, IA
Jacobs, Rolly W. ..... Camden, SC
Jacobs, Ron ..... New York, NY
Jacobs, Ronald ..... **Manchester, CT**
Jacobs, Ronald B. ..... Denver, CO
Jacobs, Ronald D., (P.C.) ..... **Rockville, MD**
Jacobs, Ronald H. ..... **Denver, CO**
Jacobs, Ronald H., A Professional Corporation ..... **Denver, CO**
Jacobs, Ronald J. ..... Tulsa, OK
Jacobs, Ronald L. ..... Lansing, MI
Jacobs, Ronald M. ..... **Boston, MA**
Jacobs, Ronald S. ..... **Milwaukee, WI**
Jacobs, Roy A. ..... **New York, NY**
Jacobs, Roy L. ..... **New York, NY**
Jacobs, Russell ..... Miami, FL
Jacobs & Russell, LLC ..... **Alamosa, CO**
Jacobs, Sahbra Smook ..... East Windsor, NJ
Jacobs, Samuel L. ..... **Indianapolis, IN**
Jacobs, Samuel M. ..... Seattle, WA
Jacobs, Sanford Gregg ..... Fort Lauderdale, FL
Jacobs, Sara ..... **Hackensack, NJ**
Jacobs, Scott H. ..... **Los Angeles, CA**
Jacobs, Scott H. ..... **New York, NY**
Jacobs, Scott P. ..... **Los Angeles, CA**
Jacobs, Scott R. ..... **Dallas, TX**
Jacobs, Seth A. ..... **San Francisco, CA**
Jacobs, Sharon Gregory ..... Richmond, VA
Jacobs, Sharon O. ..... **Nashville, TN**
Jacobs, Shaun Dabby ..... **Los Angeles, CA**
Jacobs, Sheldon N. ..... **Baltimore, MD**
Jacobs, Sherry R. ..... New York, NY
Jacobs, Shirley D., Law Offices of
Fremont, CA
Pleasanton, CA
Jacobs, Shirley D., Law Offices of
Hayward, CA
Walnut Creek, CA
Jacobs, Sidney N. ..... Woodbury, NY
Jacobs, Sills & Coblentz
San Francisco, CA
Jacobs & Simms ..... New York, NY
Jacobs and Slawsky, P.A. ..... **Atlanta, GA**
Jacobs, Spotswood, Casper & Murphy
San Francisco, CA
Jacobs, Stanley A. ..... **New Haven, CT**
Jacobs, Stanley G., Jr. ..... **New York, NY**
Jacobs, Stanley J. ..... New Orleans, LA
Jacobs, Stanley K. ..... **Los Angeles, CA**
Jacobs, Stanley R. ..... Rockville, MD
Jacobs, Stephen ..... **New York, NY**
Jacobs, Stephen A. ..... **San Diego, CA**
Jacobs, Stephen C. ..... New York, NY
Jacobs, Stephen C. ..... **Houston, TX**
Jacobs, Stephen D. ..... **Meriden, CT**
Jacobs, Stephen E., (P.C.) ..... **New York, NY**
Jacobs, Stephen I. ..... Washington, DC
Jacobs, Stephen James ..... **Orlando, FL**
Jacobs, Stephen L. ..... St. Paul, MN
Jacobs, Stephen T. ..... San Francisco, CA
Jacobs, Stephen T. ..... **Milwaukee, WI**
Jacobs, Steven D. ..... **New Haven, CT**
Jacobs, Steven H. ..... **Davenport, IA**
Jacobs, Steven I. ..... New York, NY
Jacobs, Steven L. ..... Castro Valley, CA
Jacobs, Steven M. ..... **Boston, MA**
Jacobs, Steven R. ..... Indianapolis, IN
Jacobs, Steven R. ..... **San Antonio, TX**
Jacobs, Stevens J. ..... Bay City, MI
Jacobs, Sue C. ..... **New York, NY**
Jacobs, Susan ..... Lincoln, NE
Jacobs, Susan A. ..... Houston, TX
Jacobs, Susan Beth ..... **Atlanta, GA**
Jacobs, Susan Beth ..... New York, NY
Jacobs, Susan Laura ..... New Haven, CT
Jacobs, Susan Lynne ..... Attleboro, MA
Jacobs, Suzan Jon ..... **Miami, FL**
Jacobs, Tamara, (P.C.) ..... **Barnesville, GA**
Jacobs, Teresa R. ..... Montgomery, AL
Jacobs, Terri R. Z. ..... **Houston, TX**
Jacobs, Terry D. ..... Hindman, KY
Jacobs, Thomas A. ..... Phoenix, AZ
Jacobs, Thomas D. ..... **Hartford, CT**
Jacobs, Thomas E. ..... Puyallup, WA
Jacobs, Thomas G. ..... Winston-Salem, NC
Jacobs, Thomas H. ..... **Bennington, VT**
Jacobs, Thomas L. ..... Cleveland, OH
Jacobs, Thomas L. ..... Mansfield, OH
Jacobs, Timothy R. ..... **San Francisco, CA**
Jacobs, Todd C. ..... **Chicago, IL**
Jacobs, Tonya A. ..... **Houston, TX**
Jacobs, Victoria McLynn ..... **Sacramento, CA**
Jacobs, W. Michael ..... Washington, DC
Jacobs, W. Sherwyn ..... Georgetown, SC
Jacobs, Walker, Rice & Basche, P.C.
Hartford, CT
Manchester, CT
Jacobs, Wallace T. ..... San Antonio, TX
Jacobs, Walter D. ..... Chicago, IL
Jacobs, Warren G. ..... Miami, FL
Jacobs, Wayne L. ..... **Cincinnati, OH**
Jacobs, Wendall E., Jr. ..... Jackson, MI
Jacobs, Wendy A. ..... **Atlanta, GA**
Jacobs, Wendy B. ..... **Boston, MA**
Jacobs, Wess M. ..... Fort Myers, FL
Jacobs, Wilbur C. ..... Toledo, OH
Jacobs, William B. ..... Riverdale, NY
Jacobs, William C. ..... Lexington, KY
Jacobs, William E. ..... San Diego, CA
Jacobs, William E., A Professional Law Corp.
San Diego, CA
Jacobs, William F., Jr. ..... Coraopolis, PA
Jacobs, William G. E. ..... Cleveland, OH
Jacobs, William H. ..... Sanibel, FL
Jacobs, William J. ..... Dubuque, IA
Jacobs, William L. ..... Parkersburg, WV
Jacobs, William N. ..... **Miami, FL**
Jacobs, William R. ..... **Cincinnati, OH**
Jacobs, William R., II ..... Des Plaines, IL
Jacobs, William S. ..... Norcross, GA
Jacobs, William W. ..... **Cleveland, OH**
Jacobs, Willis & Wilkins, L.L.P.
San Antonio, TX
Jacobs, Yvonne A. ..... New York, NY
Jacobs-Carnahan, Eve ..... Montpelier, VT
Jacobsen, Alfred L. ..... Bedford, NY
Jacobsen, Allison Aranson ..... **Dallas, TX**
Jacobsen, Andrea C. ..... Carlisle, PA
Jacobsen, Andrew R. ..... Lincoln, NE
Jacobsen, Barry H. ..... **Parsippany, NJ**
Jacobsen, Bernice H. ..... Washington, DC
Jacobsen, Bernt A. ..... **Beaverton, OR**
Jacobsen, Bradley R. ..... **Washington, DC**
Jacobsen, Brian S. ..... **Sacramento, CA**
Jacobsen, Brien Shea ..... Seattle, WA
Jacobsen, Bryan P. ..... **Los Angeles, CA**
Jacobsen, Chris Steven ..... Los Angeles, CA
Jacobsen, Craig J. ..... San Francisco, CA
Jacobsen, Craig T. ..... **Salt Lake City, UT**
Jacobsen, Dennis J. ..... Waterloo, IL
Jacobsen, Donald G. ..... Bartow, FL
Jacobsen, Douglas C. ..... Stockton, CA
Jacobsen, Eric R. ..... Huron, SD
Jacobsen, Erik Peter ..... Bedford, NY
Jacobsen, Fred B. ..... **Chicago, IL**
Jacobsen, Gary L. ..... **San Diego, CA**
Jacobsen, Glade A. ..... New York, NY
Jacobsen, J. Sidney ..... Rancho Santa Fe, CA
Jacobsen, Jack E. ..... **Dallas, TX**
Jacobsen, James C. ..... **Albuquerque, NM**
Jacobsen, James P., The Law Offices of
Seattle, WA
Jacobsen, J. E. ..... Cedar Falls, IA
Jacobsen, Jeffrey H. ..... **Kearney, NE**
Jacobsen, Jeffrey W. C. ..... Boston, MA
Jacobsen, Jennifer ..... Washington, DC
Jacobsen, Jennifer M. ..... **Sacramento, CA**
Jacobsen, John D. ..... Burke, SD
Jacobsen, John J., Jr. ..... **Chicago, IL**
Jacobsen, John McClellan
Oklahoma City, OK
Jacobsen, Joni S. ..... **Chicago, IL**
Jacobsen, Jordan E. ..... **Anchorage, AK**
Jacobsen, Karen L. ..... **Sacramento, CA**
Jacobsen, Karl P. ..... **Columbia, SC**
Jacobsen, Kenneth A. ..... **Media, PA**
Jacobsen, Kenneth T. ..... Coeur d'Alene, ID
Jacobsen, Kristian J. ..... **Walnut Creek, CA**
Jacobsen Law Office ..... Cedar Falls, IA
Jacobsen, Lewis F., (A Professional Corporation) ..... **Riverside, CA**
Jacobsen, Lisa Marie ..... **Beverly Hills, CA**
Jacobsen, Margaret A. ..... Baltimore, MD
Jacobsen, Mark P. ..... Treasury Department, Office of the Comptroller of the Currency, GV
Jacobsen, Mark W ..... Portland, OR
Jacobsen, Marybeth ..... **Beverly Hills, CA**
Jacobsen & McElroy ..... **Sacramento, CA**
Jacobsen, Michael K. ..... Newton, IA
Jacobsen, Michele A. ..... **New York, NY**
Jacobsen and Milkes ..... Carlisle, PA
Jacobsen, Orr, Nelson, Wright, Harder & Lindstrom, P.C. ..... **Kearney, NE**
Jacobsen, Philip H. ..... San Diego, CA
Jacobsen, Raymond A., Jr.
Washington, DC
Jacobsen, Sidney ..... Rancho Santa Fe, CA
Jacobsen, Steven R. ..... Oakland, CA
Jacobsen, Terri ..... **Washington, DC**
Jacobsen, Thomas P. ..... Chicago, IL
Jacobsen, Todd William
Huntington Beach, CA
Jacobsen, Van P. ..... **Rochester, MN**
Jacobsen, Wayne ..... **Newport Beach, CA**
Jacobsen, William D. ..... **Great Falls, MT**
Jacobsen, William V., Jr. ..... **Chicago, IL**
Jacobsma, Laila Havre ..... **Norwalk, CA**
Jacobsma, Michael J. ..... **Orange City, IA**
Jacobsma, Rena Janet ..... Sayre, OK
Jacobs-Meadway, Roberta
Philadelphia, PA
Jacobs-Messer, Liana ..... **Missoula, MT**
Jacobsmeyer, R. W., Law Offices of
Clayton, MO
Jacobsmeyer, Richard M.
Walnut Creek, CA
Jacobsmeyer, R. W. ..... Clayton, MO
Jacobsohn, Bruce J. ..... Charlotte, NC
Jacobsohn, David B. ..... **Washington, DC**
Jacobsohn, Robin E. ..... **Washington, DC**
Jacobson, A. Ben ..... Davis, CA
Jacobson, Aaron ..... Cleveland, OH
Jacobson, Adolph D. ..... San Antonio, TX
Jacobson, Alan D. ..... **Los Angeles, CA**
Jacobson, Alexander ..... West Hempstead, NY
Jacobson, Allan J. ..... Langhorne, PA
Jacobson, Allen C. ..... State College, PA
Jacobson, Andrew ..... Staten Island, NY
Jacobson, Andrew A. ..... **Chicago, IL**
Jacobson, Andrew C. ..... Newark, NJ
New York, NY
Jacobson, Andrew K. ..... **Oakland, CA**
Jacobson, Andrew M. ..... **San Francisco, CA**
Jacobson, Andrew N. ..... **Minneapolis, MN**
Jacobson, Arent J. ..... Chicago, IL
Jacobson, Aric D. ..... Albany, CA
Jacobson, Arthur E.
Department of Transportation, Federal Aviation Administration, GV
Jacobson, Arthur J. ..... **New York, NY**
Jacobson, Arvid V. ..... **Junction City, KS**
Jacobson, Barbara M. ..... **Sacramento, CA**
Jacobson, Barry S. ..... Brooklyn, NY
Jacobson & Beavers ..... **Greensboro, NC**
Jacobson, Bernard ..... **Miami, FL**
Jacobson, Bradley A. ..... **Boston, MA**
Jacobson, Bram ..... Phoenix, AZ
Jacobson, Brandvik & Anderson, Ltd.
Chicago, IL
Jacobson & Brecher, LLC
Mountainside, NJ
Jacobson, Bristol, Garrett & Swartz
Waukon, IA
Jacobson, Bruce B. ..... Milwaukee, WI
Jacobson, Buffalo, Schoessler & Magnuson, Ltd. ..... **Minneapolis, MN**
Jacobson, Burton C. ..... Beverly Hills, CA
Jacobson, Byron R. ..... **Phoenix, AZ**
Jacobson, Carl H. ..... **Charleston, SC**
Jacobson, Carol G. ..... Newark, NJ
Jacobson, Catherine A. ..... Chicago, IL
Jacobson, Charles E., III ..... Largo, FL
Jacobson, Chas. L. ..... Conrad, MT
Jacobson, Christine K. ..... **Indianapolis, IN**
Jacobson, Clarence A. ..... Washington, DC
Jacobson, Cohen & Cohen, P.A.
Fort Lauderdale, FL
Jacobson & Colfin, P.C. ..... Washington, DC
New York, NY
Jacobson, Craig A. ..... Beverly Hills, CA
Jacobson, Craig A. ..... **Portland, OR**
Jacobson, Craig L. ..... **Billerica, MA**
Jacobson, Dana D. ..... San Antonio, TX
Jacobson, Daniel ..... Miami, FL
Jacobson, Daniel A. ..... **Fort Lauderdale, FL**
Jacobson, Daniel C. ..... Seattle, WA
Jacobson, Daniel E. ..... Fort Lauderdale, FL
Jacobson, Daniel E. ..... Tacoma, WA
Jacobson, David A. ..... **Omaha, NE**
Jacobson, David C. ..... **Chicago, IL**
Jacobson, David C. ..... **New York, NY**
Jacobson, David E. ..... **Washington, DC**
Jacobson, David Harris ..... New York, NY
Jacobson, David L. ..... **Baltimore, MD**
Jacobson, David M. ..... Northbrook, IL
Jacobson, David M. ..... **Portland, OR**
Jacobson, David S. ..... Stamford, CT
Jacobson, David S. ..... Pepper Pike, OH
Jacobson, Deborah ..... Cincinnati, OH
Jacobson, Debra A. ..... Rochester, MN
Jacobson, Denis ..... **Greensboro, NC**
Jacobson, Dennis J. ..... **Lakewood, CO**

Jacobson, Derek B. ... **San Francisco, CA**
Jacobson, Don D. ... **Denver, CO**
Jacobson, Donald A. ... **Minneapolis, MN**
Jacobson, Donald N. ... Boca Raton, FL
Jacobson, Dorothy Schoch ... Billerica, MA
Jacobson, Douglas A. ... Gladwin, MI
Jacobson, Douglas N. ... **Washington, DC**
Jacobson, Douglas R. ... Minneapolis, MN
Jacobson & Dudgeon ... Lakewood, CO
Jacobson, Edward ... **Phoenix, AZ**
Jacobson, Edward A. ... **Lakeland, FL**
Jacobson, Edward A. ... **Ida Grove, IA**
Jacobson, Edwin ... East Islip, NY
Jacobson, Eino M. ... Phoenix, AZ
Jacobson, Eliyahu David ... **New York, NY**
Jacobson, Ellen J. ... Dallas, TX
Jacobson, Elliott B. ... White Plains, NY
Jacobson, Eric ... Los Angeles, CA
Jacobson, Erica K. ... St. Paul, MN
Jacobson, Erica P. ... New York, NY
Jacobson, Ethan A. ... Lakewood, CO
Jacobson, Fruman ... **Chicago, IL**
Jacobson, Gail E. ... Glenelg, MD
Jacobson, Gary E. ... **Bellevue, WA**
Jacobson, Gary G. ... Englewood, CO
Jacobson, Gary S. ... **Mountainside, NJ**
Jacobson, Gary S. ... **New York, NY**
Jacobson, Gilbert H. ... New York, NY
Jacobson, Glenn A. ... Livingston, NJ
New York, NY
Jacobson and Goldberg, LLP
Garden City, NY
Jacobson, Guy ... New York, NY
Jacobson, Hansen, Najarian & McQuillan
Hanford, CA
Madera, CA
Merced, CA
Stockton, CA
Visalia, CA
Bakersfield, CA
Fresno, CA
Modesto, CA
Jacobson, Harold S. ... New York, NY
Jacobson, Harvey B., Jr. ... **Washington, DC**
Jacobson, Henry I. ... Jenkintown, PA
Jacobson, Herbert ... Poughkeepsie, NY
Jacobson, Herbert L. ... Princeton, NJ
Jacobson, Howard A. ... New York, NY
Jacobson, Howard B. ... **Washington, DC**
Jacobson, Hugh H. ... **Roseland, NJ**
Jacobson, Irvin J. ... Chicago, IL
Jacobson, Irving ... New York, NY
Jacobson, Ivy Lynn ... **New York, NY**
Jacobson, J. David ... **Edmond, OK**
Jacobson, J. Douglas ... United States Senate,
Senatorial Assistants, GV
Jacobson, J. Joseph ... **New York, NY**
Jacobson, J. Paul ... **Milwaukee, WI**
Jacobson, J. Scott ... **Atlanta, GA**
Jacobson, Jack ... Santa Cruz, CA
Jacobson, Jack L. ... **New York, NY**
Jacobson, Jack M. ... **Modesto, CA**
Jacobson & Jacobson ... **Junction City, KS**
Jacobson & Jacobson ... New City, NY
Jacobson, Jacqueline S. ... **Chicago, IL**
Jacobson, James A. ... **Denver, CO**
Jacobson, James A. ... **Portland, OR**
Jacobson, James Cary ... **Plantation, FL**
Jacobson, James D. ... Chicago, IL
Jacobson, James L. ... **Dayton, OH**
Jacobson, James M. ... **Washington, DC**
Jacobson, James M. ... New York, NY
Jacobson, Jay C. ... **Phoenix, AZ**
Jacobson, Jay J. ... **New York, NY**
Jacobson, Jeannine Cline ... **Boca Raton, FL**
Jacobson, Jeffrey A.
General Accounting Office,
Office of the General Counsel, GV
Jacobson, Jeffrey A. ... Shrewsbury, PA
Jacobson, Jeffrey E. ... Washington, DC
New York, NY
Jacobson, Jeffrey S. ... **New York, NY**
Jacobson, Jennifer E. ... **Marietta, GA**
Jacobson, Jerold D. ... **New York, NY**
Jacobson, Jerome J. ... Chicago, IL
Jacobson, Jerome J. ... Mayville, NY
Jacobson, Jerry A. ... Los Angeles, CA
Jacobson, Jerry A. ... **Medford, OR**
Jacobson, Jill A. ... Norwalk, CT
Jacobson, Jill D. ... **Oakland, CA**
Jacobson, Joanne G. ... **Washington, DC**
Jacobson, Jocelyn L. ... New York, NY
Jacobson, Joe D. ... **St. Louis, MO**
Jacobson, Joel A. ... Baltimore, MD
Jacobson, Joel L. ... Jericho, NY
Jacobson, Joel N. ... **Somerville, NJ**
Jacobson, John E. ... **Minneapolis, MN**
Jacobson, John J. ... **Glendale, CA**
Jacobson, John J. ... **Hartford, CT**
Jacobson, John L. ... Toledo, OH
Jacobson, John L. ... Baker City, OR
Jacobson, John L., P.C. ... Baker City, OR
Jacobson, John P. ... Owatonna, MN
Jacobson, John R. ... **Nashville, TN**
Jacobson & Johnson ... St. Paul, MN
Jacobson, Jon A. ... **West Palm Beach, FL**
Jacobson, Jon E. ... Indianapolis, IN
Jacobson, Jon L. ... Eugene, OR
Jacobson, Jonah ... New City, NY
Jacobson, Jonathan M. ... **New York, NY**
Jacobson, Joseph ... Dallas, TX
Jacobson, Joseph David ... Sacramento, CA
Jacobson, Josh ... **Minneapolis, MN**
Jacobson, Josh, P.A., The Law Office of
Minneapolis, MN
Jacobson, Judith Ann ... **New York, NY**
Jacobson, Judith S. ... Boston, MA
Jacobson, Julie V. ... **Burbank, CA**
Jacobson, June ... New York, NY
Jacobson, Justin D. ... **Plantation, FL**
Jacobson, Kari Katzman ... **Tampa, FL**
Jacobson, Kasen H. ... Washington, DC
Jacobson, Kenneth ... Pleasant Hill, CA
Jacobson, Kenneth H. ... Monterey, CA
Jacobson, Kenneth M. ... **Chicago, IL**
Jacobson, Kenneth R. ... **Greensboro, NC**
Jacobson, Kimberley A. ... **Houston, TX**
Jacobson & Laasch ... **Edmond, OK**
Jacobson, LaMont K. ... Wausau, WI
Jacobson, Laurence E. ... New York, NY
Jacobson Law Firm, P.C. ... **Ida Grove, IA**
Jacobson Law Group
Fort Lauderdale, FL
Plantation, FL
Jacobson, Lawrence A. ... San Mateo, CA
Jacobson, Lawrence H. ... **Chicago, IL**
Jacobson, Lawrence H., (A P.C.)
Beverly Hills, CA
Jacobson, Lawrence M. ... **Los Angeles, CA**
Jacobson, Lawrence P. ... Denver, CO
Jacobson, L. B. ... Yakutat, AK
Jacobson, Lee M. ... **Fresno, CA**
Jacobson, Lee Richard ... Towson, MD
Jacobson, Leon I. ... **New York, NY**
Jacobson, Leonard G. ... Southfield, MI
Jacobson, Leonard H. ... Skokie, IL
Jacobson, Leonard S. ... Baltimore, MD
Jacobson, Leonard S., P.A. ... Baltimore, MD
Jacobson, Leslie A. ... **New York, NY**
Jacobson, Leslie D. ... Harrisburg, PA
Jacobson & Levenstein ... East Rockaway, NY
Jacobson, Linda ... Department of State,
Office of the Legal Adviser, GV
Jacobson, Lloyd S. ... Milwaukee, WI
Jacobson, M. Thomas ... San Francisco, CA
Jacobson, Malcolm B. ... **Harrisburg, PA**
King Of Prussia, PA
Jacobson, Malcolm L. ... Ellicott City, MD
Jacobson, Marc ... White Plains, NY
Jacobson, Marc ... Norfolk, VA
Jacobson, Marcia Grace ... Tucson, AZ
Jacobson, Marcia J.(Sam) ... Salem, OR
Jacobson, Margaret ... Pacifica, CA
Jacobson, Margaret J. ... Manchester, CT
Jacobson, Marian S. ... **Chicago, IL**
Jacobson, Marilyn L. ... Topeka, KS
Jacobson, Mark A. ... **Minneapolis, MN**
Jacobson, Mark E. ... **Minneapolis, MN**
Jacobson, Mark L. ... **Boca Raton, FL**
Jacobson, Mark L., P.A. ... **Boca Raton, FL**
Fort Lauderdale, FL
Jacobson, Mark T. ... Birmingham, MI
Jacobson • Markham, L.L.P.
Sacramento, CA
Jacobson, Marshall S. ... **Hazleton, PA**
Wilkes-Barre, PA
Jacobson, Martin ... East Brunswick, NJ
Jacobson, Martin C. ... Helena, MT
Jacobson, Martin D. ... **New York, NY**
Jacobson, Marvin ... St. Paul, MN
Jacobson, Mary C. ... Trenton, NJ
Jacobson, Matthew D. ... **Wheaton, IL**
Jacobson, Matthew L. ... **Palo Alto, CA**
Jacobson & McInnis, L.L.P. ... **Houston, TX**
Jacobson, Melanie C. ... West Palm Beach, FL
Jacobson, Mermelstein & Squire, LLP
New York, NY
Jacobson, Meyer ... Houston, TX
Jacobson, Michael ... **Atlantic City, NJ**
Jacobson, Michael A. ... **Chicago, IL**
Jacobson, Michael A. ... **Seattle, WA**
Jacobson, Michael F. ... **Bloomfield Hills, MI**
Jacobson, Michael R. ... **San Jose, CA**
Jacobson, Michele L. ... **New York, NY**
Jacobson, Miles R. ... **Garden City, NY**
Jacobson, Milton C. ... Chicago, IL
Jacobson, Milton L. ... **Norwich, CT**
Jacobson, Miriam N. ... Collingswood, NJ
Collingswood, NJ
Philadelphia, PA
Jacobson, Molly F. ... **San Francisco, CA**
Jacobson, Morris ... Forest Hills, NY
Jacobson, Murray Norman ... New City, NY
Jacobson & Myerberg, S.C. ... Madison, WI
Jacobson & Myerberg, P.A. ... Towson, MD
Jacobson, Myles D. ... Springfield, MA
Jacobson, Myron G. ... East Rockaway, NY
Jacobson, Nancy Alyse ... **Roseland, NJ**
New York, NY
Jacobson, Nancy Carola ... Orlando, FL
Jacobson, Nancy S. ... **Chicago, IL**
Jacobson, Neal R. ... **New York, NY**
Jacobson, Nels ... **Nashville, TN**
Jacobson, Norman E., (P.A.) ... Sarasota, FL
Jacobson, Patricia A. ... New York, NY
Jacobson, Patricia F. ... Cleveland, OH
Jacobson, Paul C. ... **Richmond, VA**
Jacobson, Paul E. ... **Richmond, VA**
Jacobson, Paul F. ... Westport, CT
Jacobson, Paul H. ... Columbus, OH
Jacobson, Paul W. ... Bismarck, ND
Jacobson, Peter A. ... **Rochester, NY**
Jacobson, Philip C. ... **Baltimore, MD**
Jacobson, Philip K. ... Minneapolis, MN
Jacobson, Price, Holman & Stern, PLLC
Washington, DC
Jacobson, R. Scott ... **Elkhorn, WI**
Jacobson, Rachel ... Department of Justice,
Environment and Natural Resources
Division, GV
Jacobson, Rachel C. ... **New York, NY**
Jacobson, Ralph ... Pinehurst, NC
Jacobson, Ralph E. ... Highland Park, IL
Jacobson, Ralph L. ... **Orinda, CA**
Jacobson, Reid S. ... **Waukegan, IL**
Jacobson, Reuben B. ... **San Francisco, CA**
Jacobson, Richard ... New York, NY
Jacobson, Richard A. ... **Tampa, FL**
Jacobson, Richard A. ... **Chicago, IL**
Jacobson, Richard B. ... Madison, WI
Jacobson, Richard C. ... **Hartford, CT**
Jacobson, Richard J. ... **Chicago, IL**
Jacobson, Richard L. ... **Washington, DC**
Jacobson, Richard M. ... **Sacramento, CA**
Jacobson, Richard M. ... Park Ridge, IL
Jacobson, Richard P. ... Boston, MA
Jacobson, Richard P. ... **New York, NY**
Jacobson, Robert D. ... Lumberton, NC
Jacobson, Robert E. ... Phoenix, AZ
Jacobson, Robert E. ... **Champaign, IL**
Jacobson, Robert E. ... Baltimore, MD
Jacobson, Robert J. ... St. Paul, MN
Jacobson, Robert J. ... Garretson, SD
Jacobson, Robert L. ... Rochester, NY
Jacobson, Robert S. ... Palm Harbor, FL
Jacobson, Robin ... **Washington, DC**
Jacobson, Ronald H. ... **Chicago, IL**
Jacobson, Ronald (Jake) ... Los Angeles, CA
Jacobson, Ronald L. ... **Palo Alto, CA**
Jacobson, Ronald M. ... Dixon, IL
Jacobson, Roni A. ... **New York, NY**
Jacobson, Ross D. ... **Seattle, WA**
Jacobson, Roy A., Jr. ... **Salt Lake City, UT**
Jackson, WY
Jacobson, Russell D. ... San Jose, CA
Jacobson, Russell D. ... Kansas City, MO
Jacobson, Russell M., Jr. ... Tulsa, OK
Jacobson, Ruthe G. ... Los Angeles, CA
Jacobson, Samuel S. ... **Jacksonville, FL**
Jacobson, Sandra A. ... **Irvine, CA**
Jacobson, Sandra Barbara ... Bryan, TX
Jacobson, Sandra W. ... **New York, NY**
Jacobson, Saul D. ... Washington, DC
Jacobson & Schwartz ... **Brooklyn, NY**
Jamaica, NY
Mineola, NY
New York, NY
Riverhead, NY
Rockville Centre, NY
Jacobson, Scott ... **New York, NY**
Jacobson, Scott B. ... Chicago, IL
Jacobson, Scott D. ... **Roseland, NJ**
Jacobson, Seth E. ... **Chicago, IL**
Jacobson, Sharon T. ... **Piscataway, NJ**
Jacobson, Simon ... White Plains, NY
Jacobson & Sorkin, Ltd. ... Chicago, IL
Jacobson, Stanley A. ... Bingham Farms, MI
Jacobson, Stanley P. ... St. Paul, MN
Jacobson, Stephen H. ... **New York, NY**
Jacobson, Stephen J. ... **Doylestown, PA**
Jacobson, Stephen W. ... Kiawah Island, SC
Jacobson, Steven ... Trenton, NJ
Jacobson, Steven A. ... **New Orleans, LA**
Jacobson, Steven B. ... **Honolulu, HI**
Jacobson, Steven J. ... Fort Lauderdale, FL
Jacobson, Steven M. ... New York, NY
Jacobson, Steven W. ... **Bethesda, MD**
Jacobson, Stewart A. ... Richmond, TX
Jacobson, Stewart L. ... Hollywood, FL
Jacobson, Sue A. ... **Sarasota, FL**
Jacobson, Susan B. ... Brookline, MA
Jacobson, Susan B. ... **New York, NY**
Jacobson, Susan C. ... **Junction City, KS**
Jacobson, Susan J. ... North Chicago, IL
Jacobson, Susan L. ... **Minneapolis, MN**
Jacobson, Susannah ... **Westport, CT**
New York, NY
Jacobson, Tamara Kluger ... New Orleans, LA
Jacobson, Terry L. ... **Corsicana, TX**
Dallas, TX
Jacobson, Terry, P.C., Law Offices of
Corsicana, TX
Jacobson, Thierolf & Dickey, P.C.
Medford, OR
Jacobson, Thomas A. ... **Alexandria, MN**
Jacobson, Thomas Hughes ... Oakland, CA
Jacobson, Thomas M. ... **Milwaukee, WI**
Jacobson, Thomas M., S.C.
Milwaukee, WI
Jacobson, Thomas N. ... **Riverside, CA**
San Bernardino, CA
Jacobson, Thomas R. ... Hudson, WI
Jacobson, Thomas W. ... **Rochester, MN**
Jacobson & Thompson, P.C.
Springfield, MA
Jacobson, Timothy A. ... Cincinnati, OH
Jacobson, Timothy S. ... **La Crosse, WI**
Jacobson, Walter B. ... Hobe Sound, FL
Jacobson, White, Diamond & Bordy, LLP
Beverly Hills, CA
Los Angeles, CA
Jacobson, William A. ... **Providence, RI**
Jacobson, William B. ... **Washington, DC**
Jacobson, William L. ... El Monte, CA
Jacobson, William N. ... Torrance, CA
Jacobson, William O. ... Brea, CA
Jacobson, William P., (P.A.)
West Palm Beach, FL
Jacobson, William S. ... **Cleveland, OH**
Jacobson Kelleher, Valerie ... Summit, NJ
Jacobs-Schwartz, Loretta ... Phoenix, AZ
Jacobs-Seward, Gail A. ... Muskogee, OK
Jacobstein, David M. ... Rochester, NY
Jacobstein, J. Myron ... Stanford, CA
Jacobstein, Pamela G. ... Hudson, OH
Jacobstein, S. Raymond
Farmington Hills, MI
Jacobstein, Stephen M. ... **Rochester, NY**
Jacobster, Michael ... **New York, NY**
Jacobs Thomas, Joan ... **Rocky River, OH**
Jacobs Wice, Alison ... **Atlanta, GA**
Jacobus, Alan P. ... **Chicago, IL**
Jacobus & Associates ... Tulsa, OK
Jacobus, Bruce W. ... Melbourne, FL
Jacobus, Bruce W., Jr. ... **Melbourne, FL**
Jacobus, D. Wm., Jr. ... Tulsa, OK
Jacobus, Frederic A. ... Visalia, CA
Jacobus, James C. ... **Newark, NJ**
Jacobus, Jay M. ... Orinda, CA
Jacobus, Jay William ... **Walnut Creek, CA**
Jacobus, John H. ... New York, NY
Jacobus, John L. ... **Washington, DC**
Jacobus, John O. ... **Fairfax, VA**
Jacobus, Kenneth P. ... **Anchorage, AK**
Jacobus, Kenneth P., P.C. ... **Anchorage, AK**
Jacobus, Michael A. ... **Toms River, NJ**
Jacobus, Philip F. ... Kane, PA
Jacobus, Phillip R. ... Grand Rapids, MI
Jacobus, Reeve G., Jr. ... **Jackson, MS**
Jacobus, Sandra L. ... **New York, NY**
Jacobus, Shari A. ... **St. Paul, MN**
Jacobus, Wendy Anne ... Miami, FL
Jacobvitz, Leonard A. ... Albuquerque, NM
Jacobvitz, Robert H. ... **Albuquerque, NM**
Jacobvitz, Thuma & Walker, A Professional Corporation ... **Albuquerque, NM**
Jacobwitz, Beth J. ... **New York, NY**
Jacoby, Aaron ... Brooklyn, NY
Jacoby, Aaron H. ... Beverly Hills, CA
Jacoby & Brimo ... Satellite Beach, FL
Jacoby & Capogrosso ... Beverly Hills, CA
Jacoby, Conrad J. ... **Washington, DC**
Jacoby, Craig D. ... **San Francisco, CA**
Jacoby, David ... **Cherry Hill, NJ**
Northfield, NJ
Jacoby, David E. ... **New York, NY**
Jacoby, David G. ... **New York, NY**
Jacoby, David H. ... Palm Bay, FL
Jacoby, David R. ... Flushing, NY
Jacoby, Diane Gilbert ... Harvey, IL
Jacoby Donner, P.C. ... **Philadelphia, PA**
Jacoby, Douglas M. ... Stamford, CT
Jacoby, Edward A. ... Armonk, NY
Jacoby, Evan S. ... Olympia, WA
Jacoby, F. Warren ... **Philadelphia, PA**
Jacoby, George W. ... Pittsburgh, PA
Jacoby, Gregory A. ... **Tacoma, WA**
Jacoby, Herbert P. ... **New York, NY**
Jacoby, Irving B. ... **Linwood, NJ**
Jacoby, James E. ... Palm Beach Gardens, FL
Jacoby, Jeffrey E. ... St. Louis, MO
Jacoby, John ... **Chicago, IL**
Jacoby, John P. ... **Chicago, IL**
Jacoby, Keith A. ... **Los Angeles, CA**
Jacoby, Kenneth N. ... Satellite Beach, FL
Jacoby, Leonard D. ... San Francisco, CA
Jacoby, M. Elaine ... **Princeton, NJ**
Jacoby, Mark A. ... **New York, NY**
Jacoby, Melvyn L. ... Medford, NY
Jacoby & Meyers ... Tucson, AZ
Sacramento, CA
San Francisco, CA
Clifton, NJ
Jersey City, NJ
Newark, NJ
Bronx, NY
Brooklyn, NY
Levittown, NY
Melville, NY
New York, NY
Rego Park, NY
Staten Island, NY
White Plains, NY
Philadelphia, PA
Jacoby, Nicolle Lipper ... **New York, NY**
Jacoby, Paul B. ... Bethesda, MD
Jacoby, Peter H. ... Basking Ridge, NJ
Jacoby, Richard A. ... West Chester, PA
Jacoby, Richard G., Jr. ... Reading, PA
Jacoby, Richard K. ... Lompoc, CA
Jacoby, Sharon A. ... **New York, NY**
Jacoby, Stephen M. ... New York, NY
Jacoby, Steven M. ... College Park, MD
Jacoby, Valerie A. ... Boston, MA
Jacoby, William S. ... Albany, NY
Jacoby, William U. ... Columbus, OH
Jacokes, Paul D. ... **McLean, VA**
Jacokes, Paul H. ... Mount Clemens, MI
Jacomb, Katherine A. ... Redwood City, CA
Jacomini, Clement H. ... Wilmington, CA
Jacomo, Nicole E. ... **Coral Gables, FL**
Jacon, Robert M. ... **East Greenbush, NY**
Jaconetta, Joseph P., Law Offices of
Glastonbury, CT
Jaconette, James I. ... **San Diego, CA**
Jaconetty, Thomas A. ... Chicago, IL
Jacoppi, Kenneth A. ... **East Setauket, NY**
Jacot, Julie A. ... Flint, MI
Jacover, Jerold A. ... **Chicago, IL**
Jacoves, Ira ... Los Angeles, CA
Jacovetty, Gerald G., Jr. ... Wheeling, WV
Jacovetty, Gerald G., Jr., L.C.
Wheeling, WV
Jacovini, Joseph H. ... **Philadelphia, PA**
Jacovino, Amedeo C. ... **Florham Park, NJ**
Jacoway, Jill R. ... Fayetteville, AR
Jacoway Law Firm, Ltd. ... Fayetteville, AR
Jacoway, Steven M. ... **Chattanooga, TN**
Jacowitz, Burton J. ... **West Trenton, NJ**
Jacowleff, Nicholas P. ... **New York, NY**
Jacox, Meckstroth & Jenkins ... **Dayton, OH**
Jacox, William R. ... Dayton, OH
Jacoy, Catherine Ellen ... Bellevue, WA
Jacquard, Lillian M. ... Providence, RI
Jacquart, Donald ... Milwaukee, WI
Jacquart & Lowe, S.C. ... Milwaukee, WI
Jacquart, Ronald E. ... Milwaukee, WI
Jacque, Onnie Barnes ... Detroit, MI
Jacquemetton, Jean N. ... Dallas, TX
Jacquemot, Susan ... **New York, NY**
Jacqueney, Stephanie A. ... **New York, NY**
Jacques, Andree R. ... Alexandria, LA

Jacques, Aurelie R. ... Springfield, VT
Jacques, Bernard E. ... Hartford, CT
Jacques, Brent R. ... Catharpin, VA
Jacques, Charles J., III ... Natrona Heights, PA
Jacques, Charles J., Jr. ... Natrona Heights, PA
Jacques, Charles T. ... Joliet, IL
Jacques, Denis A. ... San Francisco, CA
Jacques, Doris S. ... Concord, NH
Jacques, Emile W. ... Greenwich, CT
Jacques, Garry ... Gaithersburg, MD
Jacques, George C. ... Phoenix, AZ
Jacques, J. Normand ... Concord, NH
Jacques and Jacques ... Concord, NH
Jacques & Jacques, P.C.
Natrona Heights, PA
Jacques, John C. ... Green Bay, WI
Jacques, Joseph H. ... Hagerstown, MD
Jacques, Keith R. ... Saco, ME
Jacques, Keith R. ... Albany, NY
Jacques, Kenneth W. ... New Orleans, LA
Jacques, Kimberly T. ... Denver, CO
Jacques, Laurie N. ... Columbus, OH
Jacques, Mary Jane ... Natrona Heights, PA
Jacques, Mary-Elizabeth ... Stamford, CT
Jacques, Murray & Moger, P.C.
Greenwich, CT
Jacques, Nigel E. ... Los Angeles, CA
Jacques, Peter M. ... Westfield, NJ
Jacques, Raoul T. ... Phoenix, AZ
Jacques, Robert A. ... Rockville, MD
Jacques, Robert A. ... Tacoma, WA
Jacques, Robert T., Jr. ... Lake Charles, LA
Jacques, Sandra L. ... Philadelphia, PA
Jacques, Stephen L. ... Cheshire, CT
Jacques, Tammy Strange ... Washington, DC
Jacquet, Timothy J. ... New Orleans, LA
Jacquette, James M.
Fort Washington, PA
Jacquez, Lynnette Conway
Washington, DC
Jacquez, Melinda K. ... Flagstaff, AZ
Jacquinot, M. Mark ... Jamaica, NY
Jacquinot, Thomas ... Kansas City, MO
Jacquot, Darryl L. ... Anchorage, AK
Jacquot, David ... Coeur d'Alene, ID
Jacquot, David, JD, LLM (Tax), P.A.
Coeur d'Alene, ID
Jacquot, Linda ... Huntsville, TX
Jacquot, Sandra L. ... Topeka, KS
Jacunski, George G. ... Gainesville, FL
Jacus, John R. ... Denver, CO
Jacuzzi, Kaye A. ... Denver, CO
Jacuzzi, Marc L. ... Boulder, CO
Denver, CO
Jaczko, J. Christopher ... San Diego, CA
Jaczynski, Emil ... Fort Lauderdale, FL
Jadach, Christina L. ... Boston, MA
Jadallah, Maha S. ... Washington, DC
Jadd, Henry W. ... Buffalo, NY
Jadd & Jadd ... Buffalo, NY
Jadd, Robert I. ... Buffalo, NY
Jade, Aaron J ... West Bloomfield, MI
Jadhav, Rajnikant D. ... Dobbs Ferry, NY
Jadhon, John A. ... New York, NY
Jadidian, Lisa ... New York, NY
Jadoch, Christopher J. ... Buffalo, NY
Jadron, Michael Scot ... Lemont, IL
Jadwin, Jay E. ... Columbus, OH
Jadwin, Pamela J. ... Washington, DC
Jadwin, Ted R. ... Chicago, IL
Jaech, Jeffrey A. ... Fresno, CA
Jaech, Jonathan ... Union City, CA
Jaeck, William C. ... Venice, FL
Jaeckel, Carl E. ... Lawrenceville, NJ
Linwood, NJ
Jaeckel, Howard F. ... New York, NY
Jaeckel, Jeffrey A. ... Washington, DC
Jaeckh, Linda K. ... Radison, NY
Jaeckle, Brian N. ... San Antonio, TX
Jaeckle Fleischmann & Mugel, LLP
Buffalo, NY
Niagara Falls, NY
Rochester, NY
Jaeckle, Gerald W. ... Janesville, WI
Jaeckle, Ned R. ... Boulder, CO
Jaeger, Andrew D. ... New York, NY
Jaeger & Block ... Mineola, NY
Jaeger, Bruno G. ... Cincinnati, OH
Jaeger, Charles E. ... Dayton, OH
Jaeger, Charles R. ... San Francisco, CA
Jaeger, Edward A., Jr. ... Philadelphia, PA
Jaeger, Frederick S., Jr. ... Daytona Beach, FL
Jaeger, Gregory ... North Brunswick, NJ
Jaeger, Gregory T. ... Washington, DC
Jaeger, Howard R. ... Glendale, NY
Jaeger, Hugh D. ... Minneapolis, MN
Jaeger, Hugh D., P.A. ... Minneapolis, MN
Jaeger, J. Patrick ... Geneva, IL
Jaeger, James A. ... Madison, WI
Jaeger, Joerg F. ... Orlando, FL
Jaeger, Karl W. ... Los Angeles, CA
Jaeger, Kathleen D. ... Washington, DC
Jaeger, Kimberly Suzanne ... St. Paul, MN
Jaeger, Lauraine Gold ... Berkeley, CA
Jaeger, Lisa M. ... Washington, DC
Jaeger, Mark S. ... Kenosha, WI
Jaeger, Michael A. ... Bellevue, WA
Jaeger, Nicole E. ... San Francisco, CA
Jaeger, Oscar ... Brooklyn, NY
Jaeger, Otto C. ... White Plains, NY
Jaeger, Philip L. ... Chillicothe, IL
Peoria, IL
Jaeger, Philip W. ... Washington, DC
Jaeger, Ralph R. ... Tallahassee, FL
Jaeger, Richard L. ... San Francisco, CA
Jaeger, Steven M. ... Mineola, NY
Jaeger, Susan R. ... Canoga Park, CA
Jaeger, Tanya M. ... New York, NY
Jaeger & Teras ... Washington, DC
Jaeger, Tim Gerard ... Detroit, MI
Jaeger, Timothy J. ... Springfield, NJ
Jaeger, Wendy L. ... West Chester, PA
Jaeger, William L. ... San Francisco, CA
Jaegers, Robert S. ... West Palm Beach, FL
Jaekel, William C. ... Ridgewood, NJ
Jaekels, Christopher J. ... Milwaukee, WI
Jaekels, Jeffrey F. ... Green Bay, WI
Jaekels, John C. ... Green Bay, WI
Jaekle, Robert G. ... Stratford, CT
Jaenicke, Carol G. ... Los Angeles, CA
Jaenicke, J. Larson ... Los Angeles, CA
Jaenicke, Paul C. ... Seattle, WA
Jaenike, Chris E. ... San Francisco, CA
Jaenike, Karen E. ... San Francisco, CA
Jaenike, Kurt V., & Associates
Walnut Creek, CA
Jaensch, P. Christopher ... Cape Coral, FL
Sarasota, FL
Jaensch, Peter J. ... Sarasota, FL
Jaensch, Peter J., P.A., Immigration Law Firm ... Cape Coral, FL
Sarasota, FL
Jaensch, Tracey Karen ... Tampa, FL
Jaeschke, Wayne C., Jr. ... Washington, DC
Jaessing, Paul R. ... Brookfield, WI
Waukesha, WI
Jafarnia, Kamal ... Houston, TX
Jafarnia, Kamal, P.C. ... Houston, TX
Jafery, Farruq Zaffar ... Cleveland, OH
Jaff, Jennifer C. ... Hartford, CT
Jaffa, David W. ... New York, NY
Jaffa, Helene Rosenthal ... Brooklyn, NY
Jaffa, Jonathan M. ... Southfield, MI
Jaffa, Michael I. ... Charlotte, NC
Jaffa, Sol A. ... Charlotte, NC
Jaffari, Katayun I. ... Philadelphia, PA
Jaffe, A. Miriam ... Boston, MA
Jaffe, Aaron ... Chicago, IL
Jaffe, Alan H. ... New Canaan, CT
Jaffe, Alan S. ... New York, NY
Jaffe, Alice J. ... New York, NY
Jaffe, Allan ... Philadelphia, PA
Jaffe, Alvin N. ... Chicago, IL
Jaffe, Amanda Berlowe ... Morristown, NJ
Jaffe, Anne ... New York, NY
Jaffe, Arnold S. ... Carpinteria, CA
Jaffe, Arvin J., (P.A.) ... Boca Raton, FL
Jaffe and Asher ... McCoy, CO
Hawthorne, NJ
New York, NY
Jaffe, B. Edward ... New York, NY
Jaffe, Barbara ... New York, NY
Jaffe, Bernard L. ... Miami, FL
Jaffe, Bernard M. ... Secaucus, NJ
Jaffe, Bernard, (P.C.) ... New York, NY
Jaffe, Bernard R. ... Miami, FL
Jaffe, Beth M. ... Bayonne, NJ
Jaffe, Brett ... Columbus, OH
Jaffe, Brett D. ... New York, NY
Jaffe, Brian H. ... New York, NY
Jaffe Burton & DiGiorgio ... Birmingham, AL
Jaffe, Burton J. ... Metuchen, NJ
Jaffe, Carolyn Widmer ... New York, NY
Jaffe, Chaim Judah ... Syracuse, NY
Jaffe and Clemens ... Beverly Hills, CA
Los Angeles, CA
Jaffe, Cody ... White Plains, NY
Jaffe, Dan L. ... Columbus, OH
Jaffe, Daniel A. ... Cleveland, OH
Jaffe, Daniel J., (A Professional Corporation)
Beverly Hills, CA
Jaffe, Daniel M. ... Washington, DC
Jaffe, Daniel M. ... Philadelphia, PA
Jaffe, Daniel Martin ... Seattle, WA
Jaffe, Daniel P. ... St. Louis, MO
Jaffe, Daniel T. ... Orlando, FL
Jaffe, David ... Santa Rosa, CA
Jaffe, David ... New York, NY
Jaffe, David A. ... Pittsburgh, PA
Jaffe, David B. ... Auburn Hills, MI
Jaffe, David Benjamin ... Washington, DC
Jaffe, David I. ... Beachwood, OH
Jaffe, David K. ... Hartford, CT
Jaffe, David M. ... Kankakee, IL
Jaffe, David M. ... Charlestown, MA
Jaffe, David M. ... Minneapolis, MN
Jaffe, David S. ... Washington, DC
Jaffe, Deborah A. R. ... Seattle, WA
Jaffe, Donald N. ... Cleveland, OH
Jaffe, Donald S. ... Rosemont, IL
Jaffe, Donna C. ... Prescott, AZ
Jaffe, Doris N. ... Inglewood, CA
Jaffe, Douglas ... McCoy, CO
Jaffe, Edward ... New York, NY
Jaffe, Edward A. ... Honolulu, HI
Jaffe, Elizabeth A. ... New York, NY
Jaffe, Elizabeth M. ... Atlanta, GA
Jaffe, Eric M. ... New York, NY
Jaffe, Erik S. ... Washington, DC
Jaffe, Eve ... Los Angeles, CA
Jaffe, F. Filmore ... Los Angeles, CA
Jaffe, Frank W. ... Chicago, IL
Jaffe, Friedman, Schuman, Sciolla, Nemeroff & Applebaum, P.C. ... Princeton, NJ
Elkins Park, PA
Philadelphia, PA
Jaffe, Gail ... Los Angeles, CA
Jaffe, Gary ... Princeton, NJ
Elkins Park, PA
Jaffe, Geraldine ... Costa Mesa, CA
Jaffe, Harold M. ... Oakland, CA
Jaffe, Harris S. ... New York, NY
Jaffe, Harry L. ... Elizabeth, NJ
Jaffe, Helene D. ... New York, NY
Jaffe, Herbert ... Huntington, NY
Jaffe, Holli Beckerman
Pension Benefit Guaranty Corporation, Office of the General Counsel, GV
Jaffe and Hough ... Philadelphia, PA
Jaffe, Howard ... Philadelphia, PA
Jaffe, Howard A. ... Bronx, NY
Jaffe, Howard M. ... Los Angeles, CA
Jaffe, Howard S. ... New York, NY
Jaffe, Howard Todd ... Hollywood, FL
Jaffe, Ira F. ... Potomac, MD
Jaffe, Ira J. ... Detroit, MI
Southfield, MI
Jaffe, Irving ... Fort Lauderdale, FL
Jaffe, Jack L. ... Madison Heights, MI
Jaffe & Jaffe ... New Canaan, CT
Jaffe, James L. ... San Francisco, CA
Jaffe, Jane N. ... New York, NY
Jaffe, Jay ... Beverly Hills, CA
Jaffe, Jay ... Indianapolis, IN
Jaffe, Jay A. ... Westfield, NJ
Jaffe, Jeffrey R. ... New York, NY
Jaffe, Joan F. ... Philadelphia, PA
Jaffe, Jonathan D. ... San Diego, CA
Jaffe, Joseph ... Stamford, CT
Jaffe, Joseph A. ... Pittsburgh, PA
Jaffe, Joshua M. ... New York, NY
Jaffe, Judianne ... Beverly Hills, CA
Jaffe, Kenneth G. ... Washington, DC
Jaffe, Ky B., (Mrs.) ... Columbus, OH
Jaffe, Laurence R. ... Landover, MD
Jaffe, Laurie D. ... Chicago, IL
Jaffe, Lawrence E. ... Hasbrouck Heights, NJ
Jaffe, Lawrence M. ... New York, NY
Jaffe, Louis ... New York, NY
Jaffe, Luisa G. ... Santa Ana, CA
Jaffe, Marc D. ... New York, NY
Jaffe, Marc H. ... Rosemont, PA
Jaffe, Marcus C. M. ... Lexington, MA
Jaffe, Mark ... Philadelphia, PA
Jaffe, Mark ... Seattle, WA
Jaffe, Mark D. ... Wayne, NJ
Jaffe, Mark E. ... New York, NY
Jaffe, Mark M. ... New York, NY
Jaffe, Mark S. ... Albuquerque, NM
Jaffe, Martin A. ... San Francisco, CA
Jaffe, Martin B. ... Rye Brook, NY
Jaffe, Martin I. ... Fort Lauderdale, FL
Jaffe, Martin J. ... Orlando, FL
Jaffe, Martin S. ... Chicago, IL
Jaffe, Matthew E. ... Rockville, MD
Jaffe, Matthew P. ... Washington, DC
Jaffe, Matthew S. ... Washington, DC
Jaffe, Melodie Brosious ... Orlando, FL
Jaffe, Michael ... New York, NY
Jaffe, Michael ... New York, NY
Jaffe, Michael A. ... Southfield, MI
Jaffe, Michael A. ... Cleveland, OH
Jaffe, Michael B. ... New York, NY
Jaffe, Michael Evan ... Washington, DC
Jaffe, Michael J. ... Oak Park, MI
Jaffe, Michael N. ... Austin, TX
Jaffe, Miriam B. ... Los Angeles, CA
Jaffe, Mitchell S., (P.C.) ... New Haven, CT
Jaffe, Nancy Oddi ... Evanston, IL
Jaffe, Norman D. ... Butler, PA
Jaffe, Norman D., P.C. ... Butler, PA
Jaffe, Paul D. ... White Plains, NY
Jaffe, Paul L. ... Philadelphia, PA
Jaffe, Peter A. ... McCoy, CO
New York, NY
Jaffe, Peter E. ... Washington, DC
Jaffe, Phyllis S. ... New York, NY
White Plains, NY
Jaffe, Raitt, Heuer & Weiss, Professional Corporation ... Detroit, MI
Southfield, MI
Jaffe, Randall ... Homewood, IL
Jaffe, Richard ... Chicago, IL
Jaffe, Richard A. ...
Administrative Office Of The United States Courts, GV
Jaffe, Richard A. ... Philadelphia, PA
Jaffe, Richard A., Law Offices of
Houston, TX
Jaffe, Richard P. ... Philadelphia, PA
Jaffe, Richard S. ... Birmingham, AL
Jaffe, Robert A. ... Washington, DC
Jaffe, Robert D. ... Los Angeles, CA
Jaffe, Robert E. ... Boston, MA
Jaffe, Robert F. ... Vero Beach, FL
Jaffe, Robert H. ... Springfield, NJ
Jaffe, Robert H., & Associates, P.A.
Springfield, NJ
Jaffe, Robert M. ... New York, NY
Jaffe, Robert S. ... Louisville, KY
Jaffe, Robert S. ... Seattle, WA
Jaffe, Roger V. ... Sacramento, CA
Jaffe, Russell L. ... New Orleans, LA
Jaffe, Samuel G. ... Chicago, IL
Jaffe, Sanford M. ... Newark, NJ
Jaffe, Sari B. ... New Canaan, CT
Jaffe, Saul ... Los Angeles, CA
Jaffe, Scott R. ... New York, NY
Jaffe, Segal & Ross ... New York, NY
Jaffe, Seth D. ... Boston, MA
Jaffe, Seth R. ... San Francisco, CA
Jaffe, Seymour ... Staten Island, NY
Jaffe & Shapiro ... Kankakee, IL
Jaffe, Sharon E. ... New Haven, CT
Jaffe, Sheldon E. ... Woodbridge, NJ
Jaffe, Sheldon H. ... San Francisco, CA
Jaffe, Sheldon M. ... Los Angeles, CA
Jaffe, Sherman F. ... Chicago, IL
Jaffe, Sol ... Manhasset, NY
Jaffe, Stephen R. ... San Francisco, CA
Jaffe, Steven A. ... Tucson, AZ
Jaffe, Steven M. ... Manhattan Beach, CA
Jaffe, Steven R. ... Miami, FL
Jaffe, Strickland, Beasley & Drennan, P.C.
Birmingham, AL
Jaffe, Susan ... Gaithersburg, MD
Jaffe, Susan Michele ... New York, NY
Jaffe, Theodore ... Washington, DC
Jaffe, Thomas E. ... Seattle, WA
Jaffe, Trutanich, Scatena & Blum, A Professional Law Corporation
San Francisco, CA
San Pedro, CA
Jaffe, William ... New York, NY
Jaffee, Arnold M. ... Miami, FL
Jaffee, Arthur J. ... Pomona, CA
Jaffee, B. Jennifer ... Bronx, NY
Jaffee, Bennett C. ... Hampton, NH
Jaffee, Carl D. ... New York, NY
Jaffee, Charles L. ... Deerfield Beach, FL
Jaffee, Charles L., P.A. ... Boca Raton, FL
Deerfield Beach, FL
Jaffee, Cyrus G. ... Sylvania, OH
Jaffee, David M. ... Minneapolis, MN
Jaffee, Irving ... West Bloomfield, MI
Jaffee, Jacobs, & Tucker ... Toledo, OH
Jaffee, Jerome ... Jenkintown, PA
Jaffee, Jonathan W. ... San Diego, CA
Jaffee, Kenneth M. ... White City, OR
Jaffee, Neil H. ... Washington, DC
Jaffee, Susan E. ... New York, NY
Jaffee, Thomas J. ... Toledo, OH
Jaffer, David H. ... San Francisco, CA
San Jose, CA
Jaffer, John S. ... Sarasota, FL
Jaffery, Sheldon R. ... Cleveland, OH
Jaffess, Judith S. ... Newark, NJ
Jaffey, Stephen E. ... Pittsford, NY
Jaffin, Charles L. ... New York, NY
Jaffin, Conrad & Finkelstein ... New York, NY
Jaffin, George M. ... New York, NY
Jaffin, L. Donald ... Maspeth, NY
Jaffke, Cheyanna L. ... Fullerton, CA
Jaffke, Thomas A. ... Frankenmuth, MI
Saginaw, MI
Jaffray, Ernst A. ... Monarch Beach, CA
Jaffree, Ishmael ... Mobile, AL
Jaffrey, Allyn, (Ms.) ... Santa Ana, CA
Jaffry, Edward S. ... Tallahassee, FL
Jaffurs, Alexander J. ... Pittsburgh, PA
Jaffy, Marc J. ... Columbus, OH
Jaffy, Stewart, & Associates Co., L.P.A.
Columbus, OH
Jaffy, Stewart R. ... Columbus, OH
Jafri & Jafri, P.C. ... Great Neck, NY
Jafri, Lubna ... New York, NY
Jafri, Mohammed H. ... Great Neck, NY
Jafri, Reaz H. ... Great Neck, NY
Jafroodi, Darren ... Orlando, FL
Jagde, Christine ... New York, NY
Jagdmann, Joseph V. ... Richmond, VA
Jagdmann, Judith Williams ... Richmond, VA
Jagel, Christopher D. ... Rochester, NY
Jagel, Peter H. ... Naperville, IL
Jagels, Edward R. ... Bakersfield, CA
Jagelski, Bruno J. ... Ontario, OR
Jageman, Donald L. ... Martinez, CA
Jageman, Donald L., A Prof. Corp., Law Offices of ... Martinez, CA
Jagen, Richard A. ... Roseland, NJ
Jagendorf, Melanie Joy ... New York, NY
Jager, Christian D. ... New York, NY
Jager, Edward Gerard ... Boston, MA
Jager, Gregory S. ... Cedar Rapids, IA
Jager, Jacob H. ... Rancho Cucamonga, CA
Jager, Jerome L. ... Seattle, WA
Jager, Marilyn Muir ... Los Angeles, CA
Jager, Melvin F. ... Chicago, IL
Jager, Ron E. ... New York, NY
Jager, Smith & Stetler, A Professional Corporation ... Boston, MA
Jager, Steven J. ... Seattle, WA
Jager, Tammy S. ... Ontario, CA
Jagger, Bruce A. ... Glendale, CA
Jagger, Edwin B. ... St. Petersburg, FL
Jagger, James C. ... Eugene, OR
Jagger, James C., P.C. ... Eugene, OR
Jagger, Julia Bennett ... Atlanta, GA
Jagger, Melissa ... Colorado Springs, CO
Jagger, Robert E. ... St. Petersburg, FL
Jagger, Robert P. ... Pueblo, CO
Jagger, Thomas E. ... Pueblo, CO
Jaggers, Gerald H. ... Arvada, CO
Jaggers, Patrick C. ... Houston, TX
Jaggers, Serieta G. ... Paducah, KY
Jaggi, Lewis R. ... Dallas, TX
Jaggi, Sandeep ... Milpitas, CA
Jagid, Jeffrey M. ... New York, NY
Jagiela, John S. ... Washington, DC
Jagiella, Diana M. ... Peoria, IL
Jagiello, Barbara A., Barbara A.
San Francisco, CA
Jagielski, Raymond L. ... Chicago, IL
Jagla, Frances M. ... North Chicago, IL
Jaglom, Andre R. ... New York, NY
Jagmin, Dianne G. ... Honolulu, HI
Jagmin, Walter J. ... Dallas, TX
Jagoda, Andrew L. ... New York, NY
Jagoda, Deborah S. K. ... New York, NY
Jagoda, James J. ... Chicago, IL
Jagolinzer, Neil B. ... West Palm Beach, FL
Jagow, Charles H. ... New York, NY
Jagow, Jeanne Yendrek ... Littleton, CO
Jagow, Wayne A. ... Burnsville, MN
Jagtiani, Ajay A. ... Falls Church, VA
Jagusiak, Andrew C.
United States Postal Service, Postal Inspection Service, GV
Jahde, Alan R. ... Denver, CO
Jahn, Alfred H. ... Greenport, NY
Jahn, Andrea M. ... Omaha, NE

Jahn, Cynthia J. ....Trenton, NJ
Jahn, David D. ....Vancouver, WA
Jahn, Ellen M. ....Monterey, CA
Jahn, Eric R. ....Pittsburgh, PA
Jahn, F. Lorraine ....Tampa, FL
Jahn, Francis J. ....Champaign, IL
Jahn, Frederick J. ....Dellroy, OH
Jahn, Gary ....Chilton, WI
Jahn, George N. ....Winter Park, FL
Jahn, Gregory D. ....Omaha, NE
Jahn, Gregory P. ....Saginaw, MI
Jahn, Harold E. ....Mission, KS
Jahn, James H. ....Hanford, CA
Jahn, Judson Robert ....Seneca, SC
Jahn, Kirstin M., Law Offices of
Boulder, CO
Reno, NV
Jahn, Lawrence E. ....Ames, IA
Jahn, LeRoy M., (Mrs.) ....San Antonio, TX
Jahn, Martin D. ....Florence, KY
Jahn, Nina Hammon ....Denver, CO
Jahn, Paul E. ....San Francisco, CA
Jahn, Richard P., Jr. ....Chattanooga, TN
Jahn, Shawna M. ....Chicago, IL
Jahn, Stephen Michael ....Chicago, IL
Jahn, Susan R. ....Austin, TX
Jahn, W. Ray ....Little Rock, AR
San Antonio, TX
Jahn, William R., Jr. ....Burlington, IA
Jahner, Michael S. ....Albuquerque, NM
Jahnke, Carl J., Jr. ....North Plainfield, NJ
Jahnke, Frederick A. ....Milwaukie, OR
Jahnke, Herbert C., Jr. ....Houston, TX
Jahnke, Loring E. ....Hagåtña, GU
Jahnke, Mark J. ....Cincinnati, OH
Jahnke, Mark M. ....Beloit, WI
Jahnke, Mary L. ....St. Paul, MN
Jahnke, Michael W. ....New York, NY
Jahnke, Monte D. ....Detroit, MI
East Lansing, MI
Jahnke, Robert C., Jr ....Austin, TX
Jahnke, Shirley L. ....Grand Forks, ND
Jahnke, Susan Brye ....Seattle, WA
Jahnke, Tamara E. ....Grove, OK
Vinita, OK
Jahns, Brenda W. ....El Macero, CA
Jahns, Jeffrey ....Chicago, IL
Jahns, Kristina M. ....Washington, DC
Jahns, Richard H., Jr. ....Fort Lauderdale, FL
Jahns, Tammy Liska ....Ripon, WI
Jahnsen, Daniel S. ....Shrewsbury, NJ
Jahos, Broege & Shaheen ....Little Silver, NJ
Red Bank, NJ
Jahos, Evan William ....Little Silver, NJ
Jahr, Jeffrey L. ....Westland, MI
Jahr, Karen Keating ....Redding, CA
Jahr, Steven E. ....Redding, CA
Jahre, Jayne ....New York, NY
Jahrling, John C. ....Chicago, IL
Jahrling, Robert V., III (P.C.) ....Boston, MA
Jahrmarkt, Michael H. ....New York, NY
Jahss, Neil Scot ....Los Angeles, CA
Jai, Wei ....Boston, MA
Jaicks, Ronald K.
Office Of Special Counsel, GV
Jaicomo, Ronald J. ....South Bend, IN
Jaïdi, Myriam ....Seattle, WA
Jaigobind, Christine Delfino
Virginia Beach, VA
Jaikes, Eric A. ....Dartmouth, MA
New Bedford, MA
Jaile, Pedro A. ....Boston, MA
Jaime, Christopher D. ....Reno, NV
Jaime, Matthew C. ....Sacramento, CA
Jaime, Reinaldo ....Guayama, PR
Jaime, Sylvester R. ....Houston, TX
Jaimes, Brent J. ....St. Louis, MO
Jaimet, Michael G. ....Indianapolis, IN
Jain, Abhi-Shék ....Washington, DC
Jain, Anita ....Los Angeles, CA
Jain, Asheesh J. ....Washington, DC
Jain, Ashok K. ....Chicago, IL
Jain, Christopher T. ....Irvine, CA
Jain, Kavita ....Los Angeles, CA
Jain, Kristin H. ....Birmingham, AL
Dallas, TX
Jain, Lalit K. ....New York, NY
Jain, Madhulika ....Minneapolis, MN
Jain, Mishrilal L. ....Washington, DC
Jain, Nada ....New York, NY
Jain, Peeyush ....Menlo Park, CA
Jain, Rekha ....Rochester, NY
Jain, Renuka Vinchurkar ....Houston, TX
Jain, Roger G. ....Houston, TX
Jain, Roger G., P.C. ....Houston, TX
Jain, Samir ....Washington, DC
Jain, Stasha ....Chicago, IL
Jain, Veena K.
Securities and Exchange Commission,
Division of Investment Management, GV
Jainchill, Michael C. ....Hartford, CT
Jaipaul, Sonia Chand ....Philadelphia, PA
Jaipershad, Raj ....New York, NY
Jairrels, William H. ....Mayfield Heights, OH
Jaiswal, Gopaljee ....New York, NY
Jaiven, Mitchell L. ....Kingston, NY
Jajeh, Edward Butrus ....San Jose, CA
Jajonie-Daman, Eman H. ....Oak Park, MI
Jakab, Peter ....New York, NY
Jakabcin, Ann G. ....Rockville, MD
Falls Church, VA
Jakabcin, Kathryn M.
Boynton Beach, FL
Jakaboski, Theodore P. ....Houston, TX
Jakaboski, Theodore P., P.C. ....Houston, TX
Jakabovics, Sylvain R., (Mr.)
New York, NY
Jakaitis, Gary J. ....Schenectady, NY

Jakala, Stanley H. ....Berwyn, IL
Jakalski, Wayne P. ....Chicago, IL
Jakeman, Cynthia L. ....Tallahassee, FL
Jakes, Frank R. ....Clearwater, FL
Naples, FL
Tampa, FL
Jakes, John Michael ....Washington, DC
Jakes, Peter H. ....New York, NY
Jakes, Samuel, Jr. ....Atlanta, GA
Jakes, William B., III ....Nashville, TN
Jakeway, Craig E. ....Grand Blanc, MI
Jakeway, Edwin W. ....Grand Blanc, MI
Jakeway, Jakeway & Jakeway, P.C.
Flint, MI
Grand Blanc, MI
Jakeway, Morgan H. ....Grand Blanc, MI
Jakiel, Kristin J. ....Cleveland, OH
Jakimcius, Irene P. ....Deerfield, IL
Jakimedes, Nancy ....Dedham, MA
Jakimier, Mary Y. ....Dallas, TX
Jakimo, Alan L. ....New York, NY
Jakle, John B., Law Offices of
Santa Monica, CA
Jaklitsch, Michele Dane ....Annapolis, MD
Jaklitsch, Richard L. ....Annapolis, MD
Upper Marlboro, MD
Jakob, Gary L. ....Mount Laurel, NJ
Jakob, Henry A. ....Houston, TX
Jakob, Lisa A. ....New York, NY
Jakob, Steven M. ....Albuquerque, NM
Jakobek, John C., Jr. ....Easthampton, MA
Jakobi, David M. ....Bryn Mawr, PA
Jakoboski, Bethann ....Lancaster, PA
Jakobowski, Frank M. ....Philadelphia, PA
Jakobowski, Frank M., P.C.
Philadelphia, PA
Jakobowski, W. James ....Philadelphia, PA
Jakobowski, W. James, P.C.
Philadelphia, PA
Jakobsche, George J. ....Wakefield, MA
Jakobsen, James W. ....Stamford, CT
Jakobson, Galina ....Las Vegas, NV
Jakobson, Markus E. ....Boca Raton, FL
Jakoby, Arthur G. ....New York, NY
Jakofsky, Wm. ....Chicago, IL
Jakopin, David A. ....Palo Alto, CA
Jakosa, Charles ....Department of Justice,
Environment and Natural Resources
Division, GV
Jakovic, Ellen M. ....Washington, DC
Jakovic, Jay Harold ....Albany, NY
Jakovich, Derek J. ....Austin, TX
Jaksa, Michael A. ....International Falls, MN
Jakub, Lawrence M. ....Denver, CO
Jakub, Louis E., Jr. ....New York, NY
Jakuback, John F. ....Baton Rouge, LA
Jakubaitis, Janis M. ....Cleveland, OH
Jakubaitis, Jayne L. ....Cleveland, OH
Jakubanis, Paula Marie ....Durango, CO
Jakubco, P. Jerome ....Chicago, IL
Jakubczyk, John J. ....Phoenix, AZ
Jakubczyk, Lisa A. ....Bronx, NY
Jakubczyk and Saverino, P.C. ....Phoenix, AZ
Jakubeck, Robert J. ....St. Louis, MO
Jakubek, John T. ....Campbell, OH
Jakubek, Joseph T. ....Portland, OR
Jakubiak, Jeffrey M. ....Washington, DC
Jakubiak, John R. ....Milwaukee, WI
Jakubiak, Mark W. ....East Lansing, MI
Jakubiak, Thomas F. ....Harrisburg, PA
Jakubik, Gregory W. ....Detroit, MI
Jakubik, Jerome W. ....Chicago, IL
Jakubik, Mark E. ....Wayne, PA
Jakubowics, Craig E.R. ....Washington, DC
Jakubowicz, Barbara P. ....New York, NY
Jakubowicz, Gregory P. ....West Seneca, NY
Jakubowicz, Janet P. ....Louisville, KY
Jakubowicz, Jeffrey A. ....New York, NY
Jakubowicz, Robert F. ....Pittsfield, MA
Jakubowitz, Hersh ....Flushing, NY
Jakubowski, Donald S. ....Los Angeles, CA
Jakubowski, Edward W. ....St. James, NY
Jakubowski, James D. ....Troy, MI
Jakubowski, John F. ....Flushing, MI
Jakubowski, John R. ....Abington, PA
Philadelphia, PA
Jakubowski, Larry R. ....Milwaukee, WI
Jakubowski, Paul ....Boston, MA
Jakubowski, Robertson & Goldsmith, LLP
St. James, NY
Jakubowski, Ruth A. ....Timonium, MD
Jakubowski, Steven ....Boynton Beach, FL
Jakubowski, Steven R. ....Chicago, IL
Jakubowski, Susan Bradley
Grand Rapids, MI
Jakubowski, Teresa L. ....Washington, DC
Jakubowski, Walter A., Jr. ....Warren, MI
Jakubs, Linda ....Chicago, IL
Jakuc, Thomas W. ....Warren, MI
Jalaba, Anthony R. ....Taylor, MI
Jalazo, Aimée P. ....New York, NY
Jalbert, Gregory J. ....Seattle, WA
Jalbert, Gregory J., P.S. ....Seattle, WA
Jalbert, Michael J. ....Akron, OH
Jalbert, Michael L. ....Webster, MA
Jalbuena, Arnel B. ....Los Angeles, CA
Jalelian, Cerise ....Danvers, MA
Jalenak, James B. ....Memphis, TN
Jalenak, Jay M., Jr. ....Baton Rouge, LA
Jalette, Henry L. ....Rockville, MD
Jalil, James P. ....San Diego, CA
New York, NY
Jalinous, Farhad ....Washington, DC
Jalinous, Shahrzad Heyat ....Washington, DC
Jalkanen, Arthur W. ....Southfield, MI
Jalkanen, Leif E. ....Detroit, MI
Jalkut, Thomas P. ....Boston, MA
Jalkut, William D. ....Worcester, MA

Jalli, Quinn Michael ....Sacramento, CA
Jallins, Richard David ....El Cajon, CA
Jallo, Jerome R. ....Amery, WI
Jaloudi, Hala A. ....Fort Lee, NJ
Jaloudi & Lee ....Fort Lee, NJ
Pearl River, NY
Jalovec, Richard S. ....Chicago, IL
Jalovec, Richard S., & Associates, Ltd.
Chicago, IL
Jalovi, Robert A. ....Spokane, WA
Jalowayski, Scott A. ....New York, NY
JaLufka, Sheila I. ....San Marcos, TX
Jamail, Dahr ....Houston, TX
Jamail, George Michael ....Beaumont, TX
Jamail, Joseph D. ....Houston, TX
Jamail & Kolius ....Houston, TX
Jamail, S. Shawn ....Austin, TX
Jamain, Marilyn T. ....Philadelphia, PA
Jaman, Burton B. ....Glencoe, IL
Jamar, Jessie E. ....Darien, CT
Jamar, R. Bryan ....Santa Rosa, CA
Jamar, Steven D. ....Washington, DC
Jamarik, Pamela A. ....Greenville, SC
Jamason, Ellen E. ....San Diego, CA
Jambe, Suzanne M. ....Cleveland, OH
Jambeck, Jay T. ....Delray Beach, FL
Jambois, Robert ....Kenosha, WI
Jambois, Steven K. ....Chicago, IL
Jambor, Daniel F. ....Blaine, MN
Jambor, Richard Z. ....Cleveland, OH
Jambor, Robert V. ....Chicago, IL
Jamborsky, Richard J. ....Fairfax, VA
Jame, Harvey M. ....Syosset, NY
Jamerson, Robert L., Jr., (P.A.)
Miami, FL
Jamerson Sutton Surlas & Mullin LLP
Coral Gables, FL
Miami, FL
James, A. Clayton, Jr. ....Franklinton, LA
James, A. Wade, (P.A.) ....St. Petersburg, FL
James, Aimée T. ....Springfield, PA
James, Alan G.
Department of State, GV
James, Alan M. ....Lebanon, PA
James, Alan S. ....Braintree, MA
James, Albert L., III ....Darlington, SC
James, Albert L., Jr. ....Darlington, SC
James, Alesa M. ....Dearborn, MI
James, Alisa W. ....Panama City, FL
James, Alvin C., Jr. ....Portland, OR
James, Alvin K. ....Houston, TX
James, Andrew D ....Chicago, IL
James, Angela Payne ....Atlanta, GA
James, Anita Lynn ....Howell, NJ
James, Ann N. ....Houston, TX
James, Anthony B. ....Harlingen, TX
James, Anthony V. ....Irving, TX
James, Arnetta D. ....Raleigh, NC
James & Associates ....Jackson, MS
James & Assocs. ....Yankton, SD
James, Barbara La Verne ....Wichita, KS
James, Barbara M. ....Newark, DE
James, Barbara R. Heck ....Rochester, NY
James, Barrett L. L. ....Omaha, NE
James, Bart ....Louisville, KY
James, Bart C. ....Tulsa, OK
James, Benjamin D., Jr. ....San Francisco, CA
James, Bernard F. ....Cleveland, OH
James, Biagioli & Lourenco, P.C.
Independence, MO
James, Bill ....St. Petersburg, FL
Tampa, FL
James, Bill ....Yukon, OK
James, Bob D. ....Tulsa, OK
James, Brent ....Chattanooga, TN
James, Bruce A. ....Denver, CO
James, Bruce H.
Pension Benefit Guaranty Corporation,
Office of the General Counsel, GV
James, Bruce L. ....Charlotte, NC
James, Bruce L. ....San Antonio, TX
James, Brynley, III ....San Antonio, TX
James, C. Kenneth, Jr. ....Santa Rosa, CA
James, Calvin C. ....Oakland, CA
James, Carl G. ....Youngstown, OH
James, Carmen R. ....Mineola, NY
James, Carol Ann ....New York, NY
James & Carter, PLC ....Little Rock, AR
James, Charles A. ....Washington, DC
James, Charles A. ....Chesterfield, MO
James, Charles E., Jr. ....Phoenix, AZ
James, Charles F., II ....Department of Labor,
Office of the Solicitor, GV
James, Charles Henry ....Wildwood, NJ
James, Charlie ....St. Charles, MO
James, Christine P. ....Atlanta, GA
James, Christopher ....Portland, OR
James, Christopher P. ....Manassas, VA
Oakton, VA
James, Christopher P. ....Fairfax, VA
James & Cipoletti, LLP
Colorado Springs, CO
James, Clarence L. ....Washington, DC
James & Clark, LLP ....Ephrata, PA
James, Claudia M. ....Reston, VA
James, Claudine R. ....Houston, TX
James, Clayton C. ....Louisville, CO
James, Clifford ....New York, NY
James, Collie F., IV ....Costa Mesa, CA
James, Craig T. ....DeLand, FL
James, Curtis A. ....Brookfield, IL
James, Dana ....Los Angeles, CA
James, Daniel D. ....Ketchum, ID
James, Daniel H. ....West Palm Beach, FL
James, Daniel J. ....Cincinnati, OH
James, Daniel R. ....Keyser, WV
James, Daniel R. ....Keyser, WV
James, Daniel W. ....London, KY

James, Dante J. ....Denver, CO
James, Darin C. ....Charleston, WV
James, Dark & Brill ....Kalamazoo, MI
James, Daryl K. ....Boulder, CO
James, David ....North Quincy, MA
James, David ....Memphis, TN
James, David C. ....Brooklyn, NY
James, David E. ....Wilson, NC
James, David F. ....Winnetka, IL
James, David F. ....Tulsa, OK
James, David L. ....Texarkana, TX
James, David R. ....Atlanta, GA
James, David W., Jr. ....Department of Defense,
Armed Services Board of Contract Appeals,
GV
James, Dawn Marie ....Griffin, GA
James, Debra A. ....New York, NY
James, Debra Egli ....Salina, KS
James, Debra G. ....Galveston, TX
James, Debra Lynn ....Beverly Hills, CA
James, Deirdre A. ....Treasury Department,
Internal Revenue Service, GV
James, Dell ....Dallas, TX
James, Denecke, Urrutia, Marmaduke &
Lawson, P.C. ....Portland, OR
James, Dennis D. ....Grants Pass, OR
James, Dennis, Jr. ....Washington, DC
James, Dennis L. ....Little Rock, AR
James, Dennis P. ....Anchorage, AK
James, Diane M. Busch ....North Bend, OH
James, Dierdre ....New York, NY
James, Dinita L. ....Tampa, FL
James, Don ....Miami, FL
James, Donald E. ....Honolulu, HI
James, Donald E. ....Fort Wayne, IN
James, Donald E. ....Kalamazoo, MI
James, Donald E. ....Dallas, TX
James, Donald K. ....Alexandria, VA
James, Donald L. ....St. Louis, MO
James, Donald R., Jr ....Birmingham, AL
James, Donald W. ....Atlanta, GA
James, Doug ....Billings, MT
James, Drayton N. ....Birmingham, AL
James, Driggs, Walch, Santoro, Kearney,
Johnson & Thompson ....Las Vegas, NV
James, Duncan M. ....Ukiah, CA
James, Dwight W. ....Des Moines, IA
James, E. Carleton ....Tulsa, OK
James, E. William ....Memphis, TN
James, Edgar N. ....Washington, DC
James, Edmund G., Jr. ....Westerville, OH
James, Edward Monroe, Sr. ....Charlotte, NC
James, Edwin A. ....Boston, MA
James, Elaine Johnson
West Palm Beach, FL
James, Ellen S. ....Martinez, CA
James, Emmala C. ....Sarasota, FL
James, Emory F., III ....Mission Woods, KS
James, Eric A. ....Honolulu, HI
Kapolei, HI
James, Eric M. ....Charleston, WV
James, Erica Lesley ....Newton, MA
James, F. Jefferson ....Portsmouth, VA
James, Faith Stovall ....Dallas, TX
James, Fob, III, P.C. ....Birmingham, AL
James, Forrest H." Fob ", III
Birmingham, AL
James, Forrest T. ....Portland, OR
James, Francine ....New York, NY
James, Francis J. ....Los Angeles, CA
James, Francis M. (Sonny), III
Andalusia, AL
James, Frank Dennis ....Detroit, MI
James, Frank P. ....Washington, DC
James, Frank R. ....Louisville, KY
James, Frank S., III ....Birmingham, AL
James, Frank W. ....Wynnewood, OK
James and Franklin LLP ....New York, NY
James, Fred C. ....San Diego, CA
James, Frederick ....Los Angeles, CA
James, Frederick J. ....Oakland, CA
James, Frederick W. ....Des Moines, IA
James, G. Edgar ....Kansas City, MO
Springfield, MO
James, G. Edward ....Carrollton, KY
James, Gail T. ....Marlboro, NJ
James, Gary J. ....Oklahoma City, OK
James, Gary L. ....Hershey, PA
James, George C. ....Sumter, SC
James, George C., Jr. ....Sumter, SC
James, George E. ....Beaver Falls, PA
James, Gerald S. ....Fort Pierce, FL
James, Gerald W. ....Little Rock, AR
James, Gilmore & Hodgens, P.A.
Stroud, OK
James, Glen A. ....Sulphur, LA
James, Glenn Carl ....San Juan, PR
James, Gloria R. ....Seattle, WA
James, Goldman & Haugland, P.C. A
Professional Corporation ....El Paso, TX
James, Gordon, III ....Fort Lauderdale, FL
James, Gordon L. ....Monroe, LA
James, Grady W., Jr. ....Conroe, TX
James, Gray, Bronson & Swanberg, P.C.
Great Falls, MT
James, Greg ....Oklahoma City, OK
James, Gregory K. ....Greenville, NC
James, Gregory L. ....Bishop, CA
James, Gregory R., Jr. ....Chicago, IL
James, Grover R., Jr. ....East Aurora, NY
James, Gus J., II ....Norfolk, VA
James, Gustafson & Thompson, Ltd.
Naperville, IL
James, Guy R. ....Denver, CO
James, H. Nathan ....San Francisco, CA
James, H. Wynne, III ....Nashville, TN
James, Harold ....New York, NY
James, Harry ....Oklahoma City, OK

James, Henry F., Jr. ... South Barrington, IL
James, Henry, Jr. ... Charlotte, NC
James, Herbert L. ... Philadelphia, PA
James, Hilary A. ... Chicago, IL
James, Hite, Avery, Clark & Robinson, LLP
Greenville, NC
James & Hoffman, P.C. ... Washington, DC
James, Howard P. ... Brisbane, CA
James, Hoyer, Newcomer, Forizs & Smiljanich, P.A. ... St. Petersburg, FL
Tampa, FL
James, Irving A. ... New York, NY
James, J. Christopher ... Los Angeles, CA
James, J. David ... Greensboro, NC
James, J. Michael ... Paw Paw, MI
James, Jack J. ... Anaheim, CA
James, Jack P., III ... Lakeland, FL
James, Jack V. ... Sacramento, CA
James, Jacqueline M. ... New York, NY
James & James ... Andalusia, AL
James, James B. ... San Diego, CA
James, James B. ... St. Louis, MO
Springfield, MO
James, James C., III ... Aurora, IL
James, James D. ... Canton, OH
James, James & Manning, P.C. ... Dyer, IN
James, Janeane M., The Law Office of
Philadelphia, PA
James, Janet E. ... Charleston, WV
James, Janie E. ... Dallas, TX
James, Jay A. ... Los Angeles, CA
James, Jeffrey A. ... LaGrange, IN
James, Jeffrey A. ... Bellevue, WA
James, Jeffrey Adam ... Kingman, AZ
James, Jeffrey N. ... Akron, OH
James, Jennifer DuFault ... Philadelphia, PA
James, Jerome ... Norfolk, VA
James, Jerry G. ... Conway, AR
James, Jessie, Jr. ... Burke, VA
James, Jim, Law Office of ... Bryan, TX
James, Jim W., III ... Bryan, TX
James, Jimmie D. ... Independence, MO
James, Jimmy R. ... Houston, TX
James, Joey K. ... Florence, AL
James, John A., Jr. ... Andover, MA
James, John A., Jr. ... Waco, TX
James, John D. ... Naperville, IL
James, John E. ... Los Angeles, CA
James, John E. ... Wilmington, DE
James, John E. ... Macon, GA
James, John E., III ... Sumter, SC
James, John J. ... Fremont, MI
James, John Jay, II ... Darlington, SC
James, John L. ... Atlanta, GA
James, John L. ... Marietta, GA
James, John M. ... Minneapolis, MN
James, John N. ... Alameda, CA
James, John P. ... Minneapolis, MN
James, John P. ... Manalapan, NJ
New York, NY
James, Johnnie A. ... Los Angeles, CA
James, Jon Charles ... San Francisco, CA
James, Jon D. ... Oklahoma City, OK
James, Jonathan B. ... Millburn, NJ
James, Jonathan Carroll ... Harrisburg, PA
James, Jonathan J. ... Elkins Park, PA
James, Jonathan M. ... Phoenix, AZ
James, Joseph ... Beaumont, TX
James, Joseph P. ... Newport, AR
James, Joyce ... Minneapolis, MN
James, Judith L. ... Tampa, FL
James, Judith M. ... Denver, CO
James, Kay Kiner ... Gainesville, FL
James, Keith ... Bloomfield Hills, MI
James, Keith A. ... West Palm Beach, FL
James, Kenneth ... Cleveland, OH
James, Kenneth E. ... San Diego, CA
James, Kevin ... Oakland, CA
James, Kevin L. ... Los Angeles, CA
James, Kim ... Los Altos, CA
James, Kimberly ... Detroit, MI
James, Kimberly E. ... Atlanta, GA
James, Kirk L. ... San Antonio, TX
James, Kristin R. ... Chicago, IL
James, Kristin R. ... New York, NY
James, Kurt A. ... Boston, MA
James, Kurt F. ... St. Louis, MO
James, Kurt L. ... Topeka, KS
James, L. Foster ... Ballston Spa, NY
James, Lance D. ... Philadelphia, PA
James, Larry H. ... Columbus, OH
James, Larry P. ... Sacramento, CA
James, Laurence B. ... Denver, CO
James Law Firm ... Little Rock, AR
James Law Firm, The, P.C.
Des Moines, IA
James Law Offices ... San Juan, PR
James, Lawrence P. ... New York, NY
James, L. C. ... Jackson, MS
James, Lena M. ... Winston-Salem, NC
James, Leo S. ... Clarkston, MI
James, Lina Elizabeth ... Charlotte, NC
James, Linda S. ... Andalusia, AL
James, Lola M. ... Pittsburgh, PA
James, Louis D. ... Larned, KS
James, Lyndall G. ... Cleveland, OH
James, M. Tracy ... Englewood, CO
James, Marcie ... Oklahoma City, OK
James, Margaret E. (Betsy)
San Francisco, CA
James, Margo L. ... Agoura Hills, CA
James, Marion E. ... Creston, IA
James, Marissa G. ... Dallas, TX
James, Mark A. ... Las Vegas, NV
James, Mark B. ... Menlo Park, CA
James, Mark E. ... Des Plaines, IL
James, Mark F. ... South Bend, IN
James, Mark F. ... Salt Lake City, UT

James, Mark L. ... Ephrata, PA
James, Mark R. ... Pontiac, MI
James, Martha J. ... Walnut Creek, CA
James, Mary Ann ... Austin, TX
James, Mary B. ... Atlanta, GA
James, Mary Galloway ... Chicago, IL
James, Mary Lynne ... Craig, CO
James, Mary Mertens ... Salem, OR
James, Mary-Dulany ... Towson, MD
James, Matthew H. ... Reading, PA
James, McElroy & Diehl, P.A.
Charlotte, NC
James, Melanie M. ... Hertford, NC
James, Melody Lynn ... Columbia, SC
James, Merritt E. ... Lincoln, NE
James, Michael A. ... Los Angeles, CA
James, Michael A. ... Philadelphia, PA
James, Michael A. ... Philadelphia, PA
James, Michael A. ... Dallas, TX
James, Michael C. ... Oklahoma City, OK
James, Michael E. ... Chicago, IL
James, Michael H. ... Flint, MI
James, Michael H. ... Chesterfield, MO
James, Michael H., (Ms.) ... Portland, OR
James, Michael L. ... Fort Wayne, IN
James, Michael L. ... Louisville, KY
James, Michael T. ... Ottawa, IL
James, Michelle D. ... Newark, NJ
James, Mickey ... Oklahoma City, OK
James, Mihalik, Buehner & Leipold, P.C.
Bloomsburg, PA
Wilkes-Barre, PA
James, Millert, Houdek, Tyrl & Maloney
Kansas City, MO
James, Milton ... San Francisco, CA
James, Mirelle ... St. Petersburg, FL
James, Mojirade ... New York, NY
James, Mollie T. ... Charlotte, NC
James, Molly F. ... McLean, VA
James, Monica Best ... Riverdale, MD
James, Monte F. ... Austin, TX
James, Myron B. ... Corona, CA
James, Nancy Eva ... Laurel, MD
James, Nancy G. ... Los Angeles, CA
James, Nathaniel T. ... Raleigh, NC
James, Norman D. ... Phoenix, AZ
James, Norman D. ... Hermosa Beach, CA
James, Norman D. ... Los Angeles, CA
James, Oliver B. ... San Diego, CA
James, Omar F. ... Aptos, CA
James, Pamela S. ... Augusta, GA
James, Patricia Ann ... Little Rock, AR
James, Patricia Coleman
San Francisco, CA
James, Patricia Irene ... San Diego, CA
James, Patricia S. ... Cleveland, OH
James, Patricia T. ... Aiken, SC
James, Patrick R., (P.A.) ... Little Rock, AR
James, Paul A. ... Charleston, SC
James, Paul F. ... Wenatchee, WA
James, Paul G., Jr. ... Des Moines, IA
James, Paul J. ... Little Rock, AR
James, Paul M. ... Boston, MA
James, Paul M., III ... Winston-Salem, NC
James, Paul M., Jr ... Montgomery, AL
James, Paul Raymond
Fort Lauderdale, FL
James, Paul S. ... Clovis, CA
James, Paula ... Austin, TX
James, Peter Beaumont ... Vancouver, WA
James, Peter Richards ... Greenfield, MA
James, Peter W. ... Long Beach, CA
Los Angeles, CA
James, Philip E. ... Metairie, LA
James, Philip E., Jr. ... Metairie, LA
James, Philippa C. ... Oklahoma City, OK
James, Potts and Wulfers, Inc. ... Tulsa, OK
James, Quincy A. ... Pasadena, TX
James, Rae Ellen ... Department of Labor,
Office of the Solicitor, GV
James, Randall B. ... Montgomery, AL
James, Randall B., P.C. ... Montgomery, AL
James, Randolph M. ... Winston-Salem, NC
James, Randolph M., P.C.
Winston-Salem, NC
James, Randy W. ... Overland Park, KS
James, Raymond K. ... Washington, DC
James, Reid C. ... Gastonia, NC
James, Renee L. ... Syracuse, NY
James, Richard ... Stroud, OK
James, Richard A. ... Loma Linda, CA
James, Richard A. ... New York, NY
James, Richard A. ... Media, PA
James, Richard D. ... Jay, OK
Miami, OK
James, Richard D. ... Stroudsburg, PA
James, Richard F. ... Dyer, IN
James, Richard G. ... Southgate, MI
James, Richard H. ... Lawrenceville, GA
James, Richard H. ... Baltimore, MD
James, Richard L. ... Paris, IL
James, Richard P. ... Syracuse, NY
James, Richard P. ... Toledo, OH
James, Richard R. ... Amherst, VA
James, Richard S. ... Williamston, NC
James, Richard W. ... Pittsburgh, PA
James, R. L. ... Peoria, IL
James, Robert A. ... San Francisco, CA
James, Robert C. ... Pittsburgh, PA
James, Robert D. ... Tulsa, OK
James, Robert E. ... Overland Park, KS
James, Robert E. ... Oak Ridge, TN
James, Robert E., II ... Atlanta, GA
James, Robert F. ... Great Falls, MT
James, Robert G. ... Indianapolis, IN
James, Robert G. ... Monroe, LA
James, Robert G., Jr. ... Indianapolis, IN
James, Robert G., P.C. ... Indianapolis, IN

James, Robert H. ... San Francisco, CA
James, Robert H., (P.C.) ... Fallbrook, CA
James, Robert J. ... Douglasville, GA
James, Robert L. ... Vista, CA
James, Robert L. ... Washington, DC
James, Robert M. ... Muskogee, OK
James, Robert N. ... Alliance, OH
James, Robert T. ... Little Rock, AR
James, Robert T. ... Colorado Springs, CO
James, Robert W. ... Carmichael, CA
James, Robert W. ... Bay Springs, MS
James, Robert W. ... Houston, TX
James, Robin ... Los Angeles, CA
James, Robt. C. ... Oconomowoc, WI
James, Roger A., Jr. ... Asheville, NC
James, Roger Barrett ... San Jose, CA
James, Ronald E. ... Fort Wayne, IN
James, Ronald J. ... Cleveland, OH
James, Ronald M. ... Jacksonville, OR
James, Russell N., III ... Moberly, MO
James, Ryan ... Washington, PA
James, Sally Ann ... Chicago, IL
James, Sally Anne ... Hillsborough, CA
James, Sandra ... Miami, FL
James, Seymour W., Jr. ... Brooklyn, NY
James, Shaun M. ... Omaha, NE
James, Sheila Jo ... Oregon, IL
James, Sherry H. ... Winter Park, FL
James, Shirley M. ... Lincoln, NE
James, Smith, Durkin & Connelly, LLP
Harrisburg, PA
Hershey, PA
James, Stacey E. ... San Diego, CA
James, Stephen A. ... Columbus, OH
James, Stephen E., P.A. ... Clinton, AR
James, Stephen G. ... New York, NY
James, Stephen M. ... Miami, FL
James, Steven A. ... Mount Pleasant, SC
James, Steven C. ... El Paso, TX
James, Stewart W. ... Hughson, CA
James, Stuart Fawcett ... Chattanooga, TN
James, Susan G. ... Montgomery, AL
James, Susan Golden ... Atlanta, GA
James, Susan Tetrick ... Bloomsburg, PA
James, Sylvester" Sly ", Jr.
Kansas City, MO
James, Sylvia F. ... Washington, DC
James, Ta-Tanisha D. ... New York, NY
James, Teresa ... Elyria, OH
James, Teresa J. ... Wichita, KS
James, Terri ... Los Angeles, CA
James, Thomas A., Jr. ... Bloomsburg, PA
James, Thomas C., III ... Macon, GA
James, Thomas C., Jr. ... Marietta, GA
James, Thomas E. ... Montgomery, AL
James, Thomas E. ... Lockhart, TX
James, Thomas H. ... Forreston, IL
James, Thomas L. ... Washington, DC
James, Thomas M. ... Colorado Springs, CO
James, Thomas M. ... Charlottesville, VA
James, Thomas P. ... Chicago, IL
James, Thomas P. ... New Orleans, LA
James, Thomas R. ... Memphis, TN
James, Thomas S., Jr. ... Seattle, WA
James, Thomas W. ... Chicago, IL
James, Timothy C. ... Toledo, OH
James, Timothy L. ... Yankton, SD
James, Timothy W. ... Ottumwa, IA
James, Todd A. ... Santa Cruz, CA
James, Tom ... Dallas, TX
James, Tonya S. ... Newton, MA
James, Trisha Zeller ... Louisville, KY
James, Veronica Curvy ... Atlanta, GA
James, W. Craig ... Boise, ID
James, W. Ervin, II ... Pasadena, CA
James, W. Stanley ... Huntington, WV
James, Walter D., III ... Dallas, TX
James, Walter Kendrick ... Montgomery, AL
James, Wayne Anthony ... Oakland, CA
James, Wellman & White
Roanoke Rapids, NC
James, Wiley F., III ... El Paso, TX
James, William B. ... Greenville, SC
James, William B. ... Greenville, SC
James, William D. ... Richmond, VA
James, William E. ... Whiting, NJ
James, William E. ... Chattanooga, TN
James, William F. ... St. Louis, MO
James, William G. ... Willsboro, NY
James, William G., II ... New York, NY
James, William J. ... Los Angeles, CA
James, William O." Bill ", Jr.
Little Rock, AR
James, Wm. Gregory ... Oklahoma City, OK
James, Wm. J. ... Sault Ste. Marie, MI
James & Woods ... Wenatchee, WA
James, Xavier D. ... New York, NY
James, Zimmerman, Paul & Huddleston, LLP ... Daytona Beach, FL
DeLand, FL
Deltona, FL
James-Lauder, Heather ... Washington, DC
James-Lee, Kristin H. ... Cheyenne, WY
James-Moore, Beatrice L. ... Chicago, IL
Jameson, Ann H. ... Washington, DC
Jameson Babbitt Stites & Lombard, P.L.L.C.
Seattle, WA
Jameson, Bruce E. ... Wilmington, DE
Jameson, C. Robert ... Santa Ana, CA
Jameson, Carol A. ... New York, NY
Jameson, Charles W. ... Adrian, MI
Jameson, Christopher P. ... Dallas, TX
Jameson & Cooper ... Wellesley, MA
Jameson, Craig E. ... Columbia, MD
Jameson, D. Matthew, III ... Pittsburgh, PA
Jameson, David, P.C. ... Galveston, TX
Jameson, Deborah J. ... Seattle, WA

Jameson, Dianna Ferguson
Newport News, VA
Jameson and Dunagan, P.C. ... Dallas, TX
Jameson, Dustin N. ... Bakersfield, CA
Jameson, Elizabeth Jean-Marie
Lafayette, CA
Jameson, Frank W. S. ... San Marino, CA
Jameson, Gene L. ... Dallas, TX
Jameson, Helen ... Chicago, IL
Jameson, Henry C. ... Seattle, WA
Jameson, Howard ... Martinez, CA
Jameson, James J. ... Lynnwood, WA
Jameson & Jameson ... Troy, MI
Jameson, John B. ... Los Angeles, CA
Jameson, John M. ... Los Angeles, CA
Jameson, Joseph P. ... Marco Island, FL
Jameson, Kelly ... Houston, TX
Jameson, Kenneth D. ... Cincinnati, OH
Jameson, Kristin A. ... Minneapolis, MN
Jameson, Kristin L. ... Los Angeles, CA
Jameson, Louis N. ... Atlanta, GA
Jameson, M. Alison ...
United States Court Of Appeals For The
Armed Forces, GV
Jameson, Mary E. ... Greenbrae, CA
Jameson, Michael F. ... Nashville, TN
Jameson, Owen ... San Francisco, CA
Jameson, Paul W. ... Washington, DC
Jameson, Paula A. ... Washington, DC
Jameson, Peter K. ... Houston, TX
Jameson, Peter T. ... Troy, MI
Jameson, Philip G., (P.C.) ... Troy, MI
Jameson, Richard A. ... Anchorage, AK
Jameson, Robt. T., Jr. ... Ocala, FL
Jameson, Susan ... Honolulu, HI
Jameson, W. George ... McLean, VA
Jameson, William E. ... Boston, MA
Jameson, William G. ... Kalamazoo, MI
Jameson, William S. ... Glendale, CA
Jameson, William S. ... Dallas, TX
Jameson, William S., Jr. ... Phoenix, AZ
James-Riechert, Trelawney
San Francisco, CA
James-Roberts, Brenda ... Wilmington, DE
Jamesson, Athena ... Coudersport, PA
Jamgochian, Hagop H. ... Bloomfield, CT
Jamgochian, Michael ... Alexandria, VA
Jamgochyan, Jilber S. ... West Hills, CA
Jamgotchian, Betty A. ... Pasadena, CA
Jamgotchian, John J. ... Woodland Hills, CA
Jamiel, Morphis A. ... Warren, RI
Jamieson, Adele M. ... Oak Brook, IL
Jamieson, Ballard, Jr. ... Washington, DC
Jamieson, Brewster H. ... Anchorage, AK
Jamieson, Charles D. ... West Palm Beach, FL
Jamieson, D. Donald ... Philadelphia, PA
Jamieson, D. Kirk ... San Francisco, CA
Jamieson, Daniel J. ... Cleveland, OH
Jamieson, Daniel K. ... Kalamazoo, MI
Jamieson, David L., Jr. ... Coupeville, WA
Jamieson, David M. ... Modesto, CA
Jamieson, David Reams ... Pittsburgh, PA
Jamieson, David S. ... Covington, TN
Jamieson, Deborah A. ... Tempe, AZ
Jamieson, E. Dale ... Cordova, TN
Jamieson, Elizabeth A. ... Grand Rapids, MI
Jamieson, Gregory A. ... Denver, CO
Jamieson, J. Scott ... Columbus, OH
Jamieson, James P. ... Gainesville, FL
Jamieson, James P., Law Offices of
Gainesville, FL
Jamieson, Jay, Law Offices of
Bakersfield, CA
Jamieson, Jean Marie ... Greenwich, CT
Jamieson, Jeff ... St. Louis, MO
Jamieson, John, Jr. ... Philadelphia, PA
Jamieson, Krystyna L. ... Bakersfield, CA
Jamieson, Laurie S. ... Billerica, MA
Jamieson, Lee ... Boston, MA
Jamieson, Linda C. ... New York, NY
Jamieson, Lisa H. ... Fort Worth, TX
Jamieson, Mark H. ... Orlando, FL
Jamieson, Michael L. ... Tampa, FL
Jamieson, Moira R. ... Avon, CO
Jamieson, Moore, Peskin & Spicer, A Professional Corporation
Morristown, NJ
Princeton, NJ
Jamieson, Neil D., Jr. ... Saco, ME
Jamieson, Paul W. ... Washington, DC
Jamieson, R. Scott ... Reno, NV
Jamieson, Raymond D. ... Milwaukee, WI
Jamieson, Ronald B. ... Bethesda, MD
Jamieson, Stephen A. ... Playa Del Rey, CA
Jamieson, Stephen G. ... Medford, OR
Jamieson, Susan C. ... Decatur, GA
Jamieson, Thomas Crawford, Jr.
Princeton, NJ
Jamieson, W. Ray ... Memphis, TN
Jamieson, W. Ray, P.C. ... Memphis, TN
Jamieson, William G. ... Southfield, MI
Jamieson, William J., Jr.
Department of State,
Foreign Service Officers (Overseas), GV
Jamil, Deyar M. ... San Francisco, CA
Jamin, Ebell, Schmitt & Mason, A Professional Corporation ... Kodiak, AK
Seattle, WA
Jamin, Matthew D. ... Kodiak, AK
Jamin, Noah Ned ... Palm Springs, CA
Jamindar, Swati P. ... Brooklyn, NY
Jamiolkowski, Alexander J. ... Pittsburgh, PA
Jamison, Aileen M. ... New York, NY
Jamison, Allan K. ... Corpus Christi, TX
Jamison, Andrew D. ... Massillon, OH
Jamison, Ann M. ... Dallas, TX
Jamison, Birdie Hairston ... Richmond, VA
Jamison, Bruce L. ... Houston, TX

Jamison, Bryan ... St. Paul, MN
Jamison, Charles J. ... Solana Beach, CA
Jamison, Charles W. ... Santa Barbara, CA
Jamison, Chris M. ... Media, PA
Jamison, Daniel O. ... Fresno, CA
Jamison, Daniel O., A Prof. Corp., Law Offices of ... Fresno, CA
Jamison, David W., Jr. ... New Haven, CT
Jamison, Francis W. ... Denver, CO
Jamison, Frank L., Jr. ... Orange, CA
Jamison, G. Byron, II ... Dallas, TX
Jamison, I. I. ... Philadelphia, PA
Jamison, Jamey W. ... Englewood, CO
Jamison & Jamison ... St. Paul, MN
Jamison & Jamison ... Colts Neck, NJ
Long Branch, NJ
Jamison, Janet ... St. Paul, MN
Jamison, Janice Marie
Federal Communications Commission, Common Carrier Bureau, GV
Jamison, Jayme ... Newport Beach, CA
Jamison, John A. ... Fredericksburg, VA
Jamison, John O. ... Oakhurst, CA
Jamison, Judith J. ... Philadelphia, PA
Jamison & Kent ... Santa Barbara, CA
Jamison, Kevin L. ... Kansas City, MO
Jamison, Leon N. ... Pine Bluff, AR
Jamison, Mark D. ... Santa Barbara, CA
Jamison, Martha Hill ... Houston, TX
Jamison, Max K. ... Glendale, CA
Jamison, Michael Steven ... Quincy, CA
Jamison, Michael T. ... St. Louis, MO
Jamison, Mona F. ... Helena, MT
Jamison, Monroe ... Abingdon, VA
Jamison, Nancy Stone ... Phoenix, AZ
Jamison, Neal M. ... Brook Park, OH
Jamison, Oliver M. ... Fresno, CA
Jamison, P. Kent ... Dallas, TX
Jamison, Patricia K.
Department Of The Interior, Office of the Solicitor, GV
Jamison, Paul T. ... Colts Neck, NJ
Long Branch, NJ
Jamison, Peter O., III ... Wilmington, DE
Jamison & Philipp, Law Office of ... Lafayette, LA
Jamison, Robert E. ... New Castle, PA
Jamison, Robert E., Jr. ... Tulsa, OK
Jamison, Russell S. ... New York, NY
Jamison, Scott F. ... Colts Neck, NJ
Long Branch, NJ
Jamison, Scott R. ... Washington, DC
Jamison, Seltzer, Harper, Leslie & Marino
New Castle, PA
Jamison, Seth J. ... Cherry Hill, NJ
Feasterville, PA
Jamison, Shaun G. ... St. Louis Park, MN
Jamison, Shaun G., P.A. ... St. Louis Park, MN
Jamison, Shirley Bowman ... Boones Mill, VA
Jamison, Su Linda ... Kansas City, KS
Overland Park, KS
Jamison, Susan K. ... San Francisco, CA
Jamison, Theodore R., III ... Chicago, IL
Jamison, Thomas H. ... Monterey, CA
Jamison, Tracy B. ... Cincinnati, OH
Jamison, W. Richard ... Durham, NC
Jamison, Walter K., III ... Lafayette, LA
Jamison, William Charles L., II
Manassas, VA
Jamison, William H. ... Colts Neck, NJ
Long Branch, NJ
Jamison, William L. ... Berkeley, CA
Jamnback, John Hugo ... Washington, DC
Jamnik, Joel J. ... Eagan, MN
Jamnik, Thomas ... Bloomfield Hills, MI
Jamo, James S. ... Lansing, MI
Jamo, Robert J. ... Menominee, MI
Jamouneau, W. Jeffry ... Harrisburg, PA
Jampel, Alexander R. ... Honolulu, HI
Jamplis, Robin P. ... Palo Alto, CA
Jampol, Alan R. ... Beverly Hills, CA
Jampol, David R. ... Hauppauge, NY
Jampol, Steven M. ... Alpharetta, GA
Jampolsky, Karen V. ... Burbank, CA
Jamra, Grace A. ... Los Angeles, CA
Jamra, Jamille G. ... Toledo, OH
Jamroz, Judith Hurst ... Laguna Hills, CA
Jamroz, Steven T. ... Rutherford, NJ
Jamrozik, Steven J. ... Wood Dale, IL
Jamtgaard, Laurel ... Palo Alto, CA
Jan, Allen ... San Diego, CA
Jan, Gloria C. ... Los Angeles, CA
Jan & Jan ... San Diego, CA
Jan, Janet ... Huntington Beach, CA
Jan, Kendrick ... San Diego, CA
Janacek, Douglas J. ... Newark, NJ
Janack, Laurie Edwards ... Laramie, WY
Janah, Ashok K. ... San Francisco, CA
Janak, J. Christopher ... Indianapolis, IN
Janangelo, Peter John, Jr. ... Hawthorne, NY
Janard, Valerie E. ... Anchorage, AK
Janas, David M. ... Washington, DC
Janas, Thomas W. ... Elyria, OH
Janasie, John J. ... Trenton, NJ
Janaskie, Paul E. ... Washington, DC
Janaszek, Barbara J. ... Milwaukee, WI
Janata, Jerrold F. ... New City, NY
Janati, Lisa E. ... Topeka, KS
Janatka, Joseph J. ... Chicago, IL
Janavitz, Carl Max ... Pittsburgh, PA
Janavs, Dzintra I. ... Los Angeles, CA
Janc, Joseph E. ... Scranton, PA
Jancarole, Frank B. ... Phoenix, AZ
Jancevski, Colleen M. O'Connell
Williamsville, NY
Jancewicz, Stefania Petito ... Kissimmee, FL
Jancha, Paul S. ... St. Joseph, MI
Janci, David F. ... Chicago, IL
Janci, Richard M. ... Chicago, IL
Jancko-Baken, Ellen ... White Plains, NY
Janckson-Curtis, Ana J.
Federal Communications Commission, Common Carrier Bureau, GV
Janco, David J. ... Brooklyn Heights, OH
Jancourtz, Isabella ... Weston, MA
Jancovic, Bruce M. ... Park Ridge, IL
Jancovich, Karen L. ... Chicago, IL
Jancura, Diana Delmar ... Cleveland, OH
Janczewski, Janet L. ... Bridgeport, CT
Janda, Elizabeth F. ... Southfield, MI
Janda, Michael L. ... Dallas, TX
Janda, Robert J. ... St. Edward, NE
Jander, Klaus H. ... New York, NY
Jandera, John E. ... Topeka, KS
Jandial, Shailini George ... Boston, MA
Jandoli, Leslie J. ... Haddonfield, NJ
Jandrasits, James W. ... Allentown, PA
Jandt, Elizabeth C. ... Seguin, TX
Jandt & Jandt ... Seguin, TX
Jandt, John J. ... Seguin, TX
Jandt, Richard L. ... Leawood, KS
Jandura, Jeffrey M. ... El Cajon, CA
Jané, Carlos E. ... Lexington, NC
Janec, Susan J.
Department Of Veterans Affairs, Board of Veterans Appeals, GV
Janecek, Edward, III ... Missoula, MT
Janecek, Frank J., Jr. ... San Diego, CA
Janecek, Jane Wells ... Houston, TX
Janecek, Jay Thomas ... Spokane, WA
Janecek, John P.
Department of the Air Force, Office of the General Counsel, GV
Janecek, Jon J. ... Newport Beach, CA
Janecek, Paula ... Houston, TX
Janecek, Sarah ... St. Paul, MN
Janecky, J. F. (Jack) ... Birmingham, AL
Mobile, AL
Pensacola, FL
Janecky Newell, P.C. ... Birmingham, AL
Mobile, AL
Pensacola, FL
Janeczko, Mark T. ... Wood Ridge, NJ
Janega, Katherine S. ... Chicago, IL
Janega, Robert L. ... Chicago, IL
Janek, Bruce Francis ... Needham Heights, MA
Janel, Steven D. ... Philadelphia, PA
Janelle, Christopher D. ... Martinsburg, WV
Janelle, Jennifer D. ... Hartford, CT
Janello, Kenneth A. ... Bridgeport, CT
Janello, Martin P. ... Phoenix, AZ
Janenda, Joel E. ... Manchester, CT
Janensch, Ernst Paul ... Phoenix, AZ
Janer, Thomas ... Bartlesville, OK
Janer-Martínez, Francisco J.
San Juan, PR
Janer Mendia, Manuel ... San Juan, PR
Janes, Anne E. ... Surfside Beach, SC
Janes, Backus & Janes, P.C.
Mount Pleasant, MI
Janes, Bertram D. ... Auburn, CA
Janes, Brandon C. ... Austin, TX
Janes, Carol Sue ... Seattle, WA
Janes, Charles L. ... Boston, MA
Janes, Charles L. ... Columbus, OH
Janes, Charles R. (Bob) ... Columbus, OH
Janes, Clinton S., Jr. ... Corning, NY
Janes, David R. ... Fairmont, WV
Janes, David W. ... Woodland, CA
Janes, Dennis Franklin ... Louisville, KY
Janes, Eric R. ... Mount Pleasant, MI
Janes, Frank A. ... Minneapolis, MN
Janes, Gregory H. ... Beachwood, NJ
Janes, J. Paul ... Grand Rapids, MI
Janes, J. Paul, P.C. ... Mount Pleasant, MI
Janes, Janice Judge ... Batesville, IN
Janes, Jean K. ... Minneapolis, MN
Janes, John R. ... Goode, VA
Janes, Julian C. ... Minneapolis, MN
Janes, Karen S. ... Santa Fe, NM
Janes, Kathleen Miller ... Berkeley, CA
Janes, Kathryn Anne ... Houston, TX
Janes, M. Dale ... Boston, MA
Janes, Michael R. ... Mount Clemens, MI
Janes, Norman K. ... Middletown, CT
Janes, Robert J. ... Dayton, OH
Janes, Robert L. ... St. Charles, IL
Janes, Robert M. ... Albuquerque, NM
Janes, Ronald B. ... Columbus, OH
Janes, Ronald C. ... Ventura, CA
Janes, T. Andrew ... Cincinnati, OH
Janes, Terrance J. ... Hopkinsville, KY
Janes, Thomas R. ... Oakland, MD
Janes, W. Garth ... Springfield, MA
Janes, William ... Michigan City, IN
Janet, David M. ... Reston, VA
Janet, Howard Alan, (P.C.)
Baltimore, MD
Janet, Willoughby & Gershon, LLC
Baltimore, MD
Janetatos, Jack P. ... Lynchburg, VA
Janetos, Spiro P. ... Rochester, NY
Janeway, Lynn Marie ... Englewood, CO
Janeway, Roger W. ... Los Angeles, CA
Janey, Neal M. ... Baltimore, MD
Jang, Alan J. ... Berkeley, CA
Jang, Gloria Lee ... Orinda, CA
Jang, Harvey ... Los Angeles, CA
Jang, Jeannette L. ... Washington, DC
Jang, Sudeok ... Palo Alto, CA
Jangaard, Norman O. ... San Diego, CA
Jangard, Gavin C. ... Las Vegas, NV
Janger, Bruce ... Los Angeles, CA
Janger, Edward J. ... Washington, DC
Janger, Jerome ... Beverly Hills, CA
Janger, Richard K. ... Chicago, IL
Janhevich, Paul, (P.C.) ... Livonia, MI
Janhunen, Curtis M. ... Aberdeen, WA
Jani, Jerome J. ... Washington, DC
Jani, Riddhi ... St. Paul, MN
Janiak, John M. ... New Bedford, MA
Janiak, Peter A. ... San Jose, CA
Janian, Armen ... Beverly Hills, CA
Janian, Paulette ... Selma, CA
Janice, Christina M. ... Beachwood, OH
Janice, Stanley J., Jr. ... Detroit, MI
Janich, Daniel N. ... Chicago, IL
Janicik, John A. ... Chicago, IL
Janick, Herbert F., III ... Weehawken, NJ
Janick, Michelle L. ... Philadelphia, PA
Janicke, Paul M. ... Houston, TX
Janicki, Beth Anne ... Chicago, IL
Janicki, Catherine ... Seattle, WA
Janicki, Mark M. ... Lewisville, TX
Janicki, Robert L. ... Salt Lake City, UT
Janics, Kathleen A. ... Costa Mesa, CA
Janiczek, Lee J. ... Philadelphia, PA
Janidlo, Thom F. ... Anchorage, AK
Janies, Andrew B. ... Bloomfield Hills, MI
Janiga, Alan ... Houston, TX
Janiga, Frank H. ... Warren, MI
Janigian, Bruce J. ... Sacramento, CA
Janigian, Nicole ... Los Angeles, CA
Janik, Anthony P. ... Chicago, IL
Janik, David J. ... Denver, CO
Janik & Forbes ... Cleveland, OH
Janik, Frank A., III ... Elyria, OH
Janik, Frank J. ... Amherst, OH
Janik, Jeffrey L. ... Milwaukee, WI
Janik, Kenneth Allan ... Columbia, SC
Janik, Laurene K. ... Chicago, IL
Janik, Michael T. ... Washington, DC
Janik, Paul J. ... Houston, TX
Janik, Stephen T. ... Portland, OR
Janik, Steven G. ... Cleveland, OH
Janin, Blaine Covington ... San Francisco, CA
Janin, Morgan & Brenner, A Prof. Corp.
Benicia, CA
San Francisco, CA
Janin, Sandra Krevitsky ... Bronx, NY
Janine, Marisa ... San Diego, CA
Janis, Brian G., (P.C.) ... Brownsville, TX
Janis, Christine A. ... Cheshire, CT
Janis, Dean T. ... San Diego, CA
Janis, Edward M. ... Cleveland, OH
Janis, Edward M., Co., L.P.A.
Cleveland, OH
Janis, Gary M. ... Baltimore, MD
Janis, Gerald T. ... Waukesha, WI
Janis, John J. ... Boise, ID
Janis, Leslie R. ... Rockville, MD
Janis, Madeline P. ... Los Angeles, CA
Janis, Mark Weston ... Hartford, CT
Janis, N. Richard ... Washington, DC
Janis, Patrick J. ... Dayton, OH
Janis, Paul H. ... New York, NY
Janis, Ronald H. ... Morristown, NJ
New York, NY
Janis, Russell A. ... Amherst, MA
Janis, Schuelke & Wechsler
Washington, DC
Janisch, Daniel K. ... Oakland, CA
Janisch, Karen A. ... Minneapolis, MN
Janisch, Richard A. ... Los Angeles, CA
Janisch, Thomas E. ... Wenatchee, WA
Janiszewski, Steven Carl ... Denver, CO
Janiszewski, Thomas A. ... Houston, TX
Janitzky, K. R. ... Cedar Rapids, IA
Janiuk, Anthony J. ... Milford, MA
Jan Janin, Michael S. ... Erie, PA
Janka, John C. ... Chicago, IL
Janka, John P. ... Washington, DC
Janka, Patricia J. ... Appleton, WI
Janke, Albert E., Jr. ... Philadelphia, PA
Janke, Bruce C. ... Los Gatos, CA
Janke, Christopher E. ... New Orleans, LA
Janke, Garth ... Portland, OR
Janke, James F. ... Houston, TX
Janke, Laura C. ... New York, NY
Janke, Ronald R. ... Cleveland, OH
Jankell, Peter J. ... Chesapeake, VA
Jankell, Richard ... New York, NY
Jankins, Michael L. ... Des Moines, IA
Janklow, A. Russell ... Sioux Falls, SD
Janklow, Donald E. ... Greeley, CO
Janklow, Morton L. ... New York, NY
Janklow Newborn & Ashley ... New York, NY
Janklow, William J. ... Pierre, SD
Janko, Michael M. ... Schaumburg, IL
Jankoff & Gabe, P.C. ... New York, NY
Rockville Centre, NY
Jankoff, John H. ... New York, NY
Rockville Centre, NY
Jankoski, Michael Edward ... New York, NY
Jankovic, Marko ... Arlington, VA
Jankovic, Martha A. ... Trumbull, CT
Jankovic, Tanya E. ... Washington, DC
Jankovich, Jeffrey P. ... Arlington, VA
Jankovich, Michael G. ... Seattle, WA
Jankovitz, Jack J. ... Valley Forge, PA
Jankovsky, Charles S. ... Fairfield, CT
Jankower, Mervine L. ... Lafayette, LA
Jankower, Steven M. ... Lafayette, LA
Jankowicz, James A. ... Decatur, IL
Jankowitz, Barnet ... Brooklyn, NY
Jankowitz, David Eric ... Boca Raton, FL
Jankowitz, Mark ... New York, NY
Jankowitz, Stewart ... Redding, CA
Jankowski, Dallas P. ... Cusseta, GA
Jankowski, David F. ... Denver, CO
Jankowski, Deborah Tobie ... Amherst, MA
Jankowski, Diane ... Cleveland, OH
Jankowski, Gretchen L. ... Pittsburgh, PA
Jankowski, James Christopher
Washington, DC
Jankowski, James W. ... Hempstead, NY
Jankowski, Jeffrey M. ... South Bend, IN
Jankowski, Jo Anne ... Minneapolis, MN
Jankowski, John F., Jr. ... Plantation, FL
Jankowski, Joseph J. ... Woodbridge, NJ
Jankowski, Joseph J., Jr. ... Dayton, OH
Jankowski, Mark A. ... Baltimore, MD
Jankowski, Michael A. ... Woodland Hills, CA
Jankowski, Michael D. ... Milwaukee, WI
Jankowski, Richard ... Boise, ID
Jankowski, Shari M. ... Manchester, NH
Jankowski, T. Michael ... Washington, DC
Jankowski, Theodore S. ... Milwaukee, WI
Jankowsky, Joel, (P.C.) ... Washington, DC
Janks, Gregory M. ... Detroit, MI
Janku, Christopher C. ... Jefferson City, MO
Jankura, David M. ... Chicago, IL
Jankura, David M. & Assoc., Ltd.
Chicago, IL
Jann, David M. ... Chaska, MN
Jann, Irwin G. ... Northbrook, IL
Jann, Irwin G., & Associates, P.C.
Northbrook, IL
Jann, Norma Finley ... Chicago, IL
Jannace, Charles J., III ... Salisbury, MD
New York, NY
Jannace, Steven D. ... East Meadow, NY
Jannace, Susan H. ... Melville, NY
Jannace, William ... New York, NY
Jannaco, Patricia L ... New York, NY
Jannarone, Cheryl Catherine ... Matawan, NJ
Janneck, Walter F. ... Paterson, NJ
Jannen, Kenneth R. ... Fort Lauderdale, FL
Janner, Leonard P. ... Los Angeles, CA
Jannerbo, E. Mattias ... Chattanooga, TN
Jannes, Christopher P. ... Des Moines, IA
Jannett, Resa J. ... Southfield, MI
Jannetta, James M. ... Sault Ste. Marie, MI
Jannetta, Joseph E. ... Southfield, MI
Jannetta, Nadia M. ... Philadelphia, PA
Jannetta, Stephen A. ... Philadelphia, PA
Jannette, Ellen Bartman
Bloomfield Hills, MI
Janney, Anthony H. ... Cedar Rapids, IA
Janney, C. Dale ... Crownsville, MD
Janney, Christopher G. ... Washington, DC
Janney, Donald W. ... Atlanta, GA
Janney, Douglas B., III ... Nashville, TN
Janney, Eric M. ... Groton, CT
Janney, Holly C. ... Jamestown, RI
Janney & Janney ... Luray, VA
Janney, Larry K. ... Houston, TX
Janney, Oliver J. ... Sarasota, FL
Janney, Philip B. ... Vancouver, WA
Janney, Richard N. ... Chicago, IL
Janney, Robert S. ... Luray, VA
Janney, Roby G. ... Luray, VA
Janney, Stuart S., III ... Baltimore, MD
Janney, Susan ... North Wilkesboro, NC
Janney, Tonya L. ... Jacksonville, FL
Janney, William F. ... Baton Rouge, LA
Janning, Charles W. ... New Carlisle, OH
Janning, Nancy M. ... Cincinnati, OH
Jannol, Henry N. ... Los Angeles, CA
Jannol, Henry N., A Professional Corporation ... Los Angeles, CA
Jannol, Martin B., (A Prof. Corp.)
Los Angeles, CA
Jannol, Neal B. ... Los Angeles, CA
Jannon, Edward L. ... Flushing, NY
Jannone, Justin J. ... Manhasset, NY
Jannotta, Santina M. ... Treasury Department, Internal Revenue Service, GV
Jannusch, Janet L. ... Peoria, IL
Jannuzzi, Lawrence R.
San Francisco, CA
Jannuzzi, Michael J. ... Huntington, NY
Jannuzzo, Jeffrey A. ... New York, NY
Janocsko, George M. ... Pittsburgh, PA
Janoff, Adam D. ... Boston, MA
Janoff, Charles J. ... New York, NY
Janoff, Diane E. ... New York, NY
Janoff, Gerald S. ... New York, NY
Janoff, Jeffrey D. ... San Jose, CA
Janoff, Karpel & Cowan ... Carson, CA
Janoff, Paul Neil ... Lynbrook, NY
Janoff, Peter L. ... New York, NY
Janoff, Walter D. ... Carson, CA
Janofsky, Arnold ... Parsippany, NJ
Janofsky, Eric B. ... San Jose, CA
Janofsky, Jack D. ... Los Angeles, CA
Janofsky, Jacqueline A.
Palos Verdes Estates, CA
Janofsky, John S. ... Santa Monica, CA
Janofsky, Julie C. ... Baltimore, MD
Janofsky, Leonard S. ... Los Angeles, CA
Janofsky, Louis E. ... West Caldwell, NJ
Janopaul, Mona M. ... Arlington, VA
Janos, Ellen L. ... Boston, MA
Janos, John C. ... Philadelphia, PA
Janos, Mark L., Law Office of
Newburyport, MA
Janos, Peter D. ... Akron, OH
Janosik, John T. ... Pasadena, CA
Janoske, Catherine V. ... Clarksville, MD
Janoski, Debra H. ... St. Louis, MO
Janoski, Frank B. ... St. Louis, MO
Janoski, Jeffrey F. ... Plymouth Meeting, PA
Janoski, Marjorie ... Philadelphia, PA
Janoski, Robert A. ... Chicago, IL
Janoski, Stephen G. ... Washington, DC
Janossy, Maria ... Pasadena, CA
Janousek, Donald R. ... Webster Groves, MO
Janousek, Jay C. ... Seattle, WA
Janousek, Joseph O. ... Washington, DC
Janoush, Thomas B. ... Cleveland, MS

Janov, Gwenellen P. ......Albuquerque, NM
Janov, Jack A. ......Los Angeles, CA
Janov, Rick E. ......Indianapolis, IN
Janove, Jathan W. ......Salt Lake City, UT
Janove, Steven M. ......Cherry Hill, NJ
Philadelphia, PA
Janover, Robert H. ......Bloomfield Hills, MI
Janover, Thomas T. ......New York, NY
Janovetz, James M. ......Peoria, IL
Janovitz, Barbara Bellin ......Cleveland, OH
Janovsky, Liane A. ......Fort Worth, TX
Janovsky, Peter ......New York, NY
Janovsky, Rebecca ......Chicago, IL
Janow, David J. ......New York, NY
Janow, Hugh ......Pearl River, NY
Janow, Lawrence ......Amherst, VA
Janow, Merit E. ......New York, NY
Janow & Meyer, LLC ......Pearl River, NY
Janower, Todd L. ......Chicago, IL
Janowich, John W. ......Bel Air, MD
Janowitz, Brenda M. ......New York, NY
Janowitz, James A. ......New York, NY
Janowitz, Kathy Palestrant ......Washington, DC
Janowitz, Marc S. ......San Francisco, CA
Janowitz, Norman ......Mineola, NY
Janowitz, Robert J. ......Kansas City, MO
Janowitz, Warren Robert ......Miami, FL
Janowski, John F. ......Baldwin, NY
Janowski, Ziporah ......New York, NY
Janowsky, Lewis P. ......Newport Beach, CA
Janquitto, Andrew ......Towson, MD
Jans, Fred C., Jr. ......Wilmington, NC
Jans, Mary Kay ......Wayzata, MN
Jans, Peggy L. ......Peoria, IL
Jans, Richard C. ......Tavares, FL
Jans, Richard C., P.A. ......Tavares, FL
Jans, Ronald F. ......Santa Ana, CA
Jansa, Mark C. ......Portland, OR
Jansak, John W. ......Towson, MD
Jansen, Allan W. ......Irvine, CA
Jansen, Brad L. ......Chicago, IL
Jansen, Brenda ......Denver, CO
Jansen Bucco DeBona & Coviello
Boonton, NJ
Jansen, Cathleen Cassisa ......Detroit, MI
Jansen, Donald O. ......Houston, TX
Jansen, Faith ......Walnut Creek, CA
Jansen, Gary T. ......Chicago, IL
Jansen, George F. ......San Francisco, CA
Jansen, Gerald J. ......Santa Ana, CA
Jansen, Gregg ......Omaha, NE
Jansen, Gregory M. ......Milwaukee, WI
Jansen, Herbert J. ......Houston, TX
Jansen, James P. ......Antigo, WI
Jansen, James R. ......Madison, WI
Jansen, James S. ......Omaha, NE
Jansen, Jeffrey A. ......Houston, TX
Jansen, Jenneane L. ......Minneapolis, MN
Jansen, John P. ......Boonton, NJ
Jansen, Joseph A., Jr. ......New York, NY
Jansen, Ken ......Twentynine Palms, CA
Jansen, Lambertus ......Oswego, NY
Jansen & Leenerts ......San Diego, CA
Jansen, Leonard F. ......Spokane, WA
Jansen, Mark T. ......San Francisco, CA
Jansen, Mark T. ......St. Paul, MN
Jansen, Michael ......Sewickley, PA
Jansen, Michael E. ......Woodland Hills, CA
Jansen, Michael W. ......Redding, CA
Jansen, Neil P. ......Grand Rapids, MI
Jansen, Paul T. ......Dearborn Heights, MI
Jansen, R. Timothy ......Tallahassee, FL
Jansen, R. Timothy, P.A. ......Tallahassee, FL
Jansen, Richard G. ......New York, NY
Jansen, Robert F. ......Oshkosh, WI
Jansen, Roxanne S. ......Fayetteville, NC
Jansen, Susan D. ......Dayton, OH
Jansen, Todd A. ......Denver, CO
Jansen, Vernol R., Jr. ......Gulf Shores, AL
Jansen, Wendy A. ......Mount Clemens, MI
Jansen, William A. ......Madison, WI
Jansen, William L. ......San Francisco, CA
Jansen, William R. ......Southfield, MI
Jansenson, Dina R. ......New York, NY
Janser, Marc D. ......Chicago, IL
Jansing, James M. ......Cincinnati, OH
Jansing, John G. ......Dayton, OH
Jansing, Mary E. ......Castroville, CA
Janske, T. C. ......Hot Springs National Park, AR
Janski, Kathleen M. ......Denver, CO
Jansma, Steven D. ......San Antonio, TX
Jansma, Sunny J. ......San Antonio, TX
Janson, Charles E. ......Stamford, CT
Janson, Cheryl A. ......Atlanta, GA
Janson, Eric W. ......Lebanon, NH
Janson, Francis G. ......Langhorne, PA
Janson, Greg F. ......Las Vegas, NV
Janson, JoAnne G. ......Pacific Palisades, CA
Janson, Julia Smoot ......Cincinnati, OH
Janson & Koppenheffer ......Lebanon, NH
Janson, Kurt R. ......Montpelier, VT
Janson, Lars E. ......Alexandria, VA
Janson, Roger A. ......Boston, MA
Janson, Saul C. ......Venice, CA
Janson, Thomas A. ......St. Cloud, MN
Janson, Thomas C., Jr. ......White Plains, NY
Jansonius, John V. ......Dallas, TX
Jansons, Teryl A. ......Agawam, MA
Janss, Jennifer L. ......Washington, DC
Janssen, Aaron J. ......Appleton, WI
Janssen, Carmen ......West Des Moines, IA
Janssen, Carol D. ......San Luis Obispo, CA
Janssen, Charles A. ......Lansing, MI
Janssen, Clayton R. ......Eureka, CA
Janssen, Dallas J. ......Des Moines, IA
Janssen, Daniel M. ......Milwaukee, WI
Janssen, Darla (Dee) ......Tucson, AZ
Janssen, Dennis M. ......Leesburg, FL
Janssen, Don R. ......Lincoln, NE
Janssen, Gary Dale ......Houston, TX
Janssen, Henry H. ......Philadelphia, PA
Janssen, Howard A. ......Oakland, CA
Janssen, Jay H. ......Peoria, IL
Janssen, Jean T. ......Houston, TX
Janssen, Jerry F. ......Appleton, WI
Janssen, Joseph W., III ......Miami, FL
Janssen, Judith M. ......Fairfax, VA
Janssen, Kathryn R. ......Los Angeles, CA
Janssen, Laurence F. ......Los Angeles, CA
Janssen, Lizanne M. ......Collinsville, CT
Janssen, Malloy, Needham, Morrison & Reinholtsen, LLP ......Eureka, CA
Janssen, Mark B. ......San Marcos, TX
Janssen, Randolph M. ......San Antonio, TX
Janssen, Robert J. ......De Pere, WI
Janssen, Rodney L. ......Des Moines, IA
Janssen, Rodney L., Law Firm, P.C.
Des Moines, IA
Janssen, Sandra J. ......Milwaukee, WI
Janssen, Steven ......Boulder, CO
Janssen, Steven L., P.C. ......Boulder, CO
Janssen, Susan K. ......Winterset, IA
Janssen, Thomas J. ......Appleton, WI
Janssen, Thomas L. ......Minonk, IL
Janssen, Werner, Jr. ......New York, NY
Janssen, William Michael
Philadelphia, PA
Jansson, Peter N. ......Racine, WI
Jansson, Ron S. ......Barnstable, MA
Jansson, Ron S. ......Hyannis, MA
Jansson, Shupe, Bridge & Munger, Ltd.
Racine, WI
Jansz, Michael C. ......Ottawa, IL
Janszen, August T. ......Cincinnati, OH
Jánszky, Andrew B. ......New York, NY
Jantos, James s. ......Bellevue, WA
Jantsch, Daniel P. ......Phoenix, AZ
Jantz, Bradley D. ......Newton, KS
Jantz, Frederick M. ......Garnett, KS
Jantz, Paul H. ......Baton Rouge, LA
Jantz, Russell P. ......Trabuco Canyon, CA
Jantz, Sue Ann ......Newton, KS
Jantzen, Christopher M. ......Boston, MA
Jantzen, Edward R. ......Los Angeles, CA
Jantzen, Jonathan L. ......Sells, AZ
Jantzen, Karen A. ......Irvine, CA
January, Derick C. ......White Plains, NY
January, Jason ......Dallas, TX
January, Jonathan Mark ......Reston, VA
January, William H. ......Houston, TX
January-Bevers, Deborah J. ......Dickinson, TX
Janulevicus, Sally Ann ......Boston, MA
Janulis, Diane M. ......Easton, MD
Janulis, William P.
Commodity Futures Trading Commission, Division of Enforcement, GV
Janura, Arthur L., Jr. ......Rolling Meadows, IL
Janus, Ann Marie ......Philadelphia, PA
Janus, Charles J. ......Temple Hills, MD
Janus, Eric S. ......St. Paul, MN
Janus, Laurie L. ......Richmond, VA
Janus, Lincoln V. ......Chicago, IL
Janus, Mark James ......Chicago, IL
Janus, Murray J. ......Richmond, VA
Janus, Peter A. ......Hartford, CT
Janus & Rubard ......Temple Hills, MD
Januschewski, Mark ......Boynton Beach, FL
Januszewski, David G. ......New York, NY
Januszewski, Edward ......New Britain, CT
Januszewski, Kenneth J. ......Phoenix, AZ
Januszewski, McQuillan and DeNigris
Hartford, CT
New Britain, CT
Januszkiewicz, Cecilia ......Baltimore, MD
Januszkiewicz, Joseph ......State College, PA
Januta, Donatas ......Oakland, CA
Janutis, Rachel M. ......Chicago, IL
Januzzi, George ......New York, NY
Januzzi, Karl J. ......Harrisburg, PA
Januzzi, Thomas A. ......Lorain, OH
Janvey, Gordon, Herlands, Randolph, Rosenberg & Cox, L.L.P. ......New York, NY
Janvey, Ralph ......Dallas, TX
Janvey, Richard I. ......New York, NY
Janvier, William P. ......Raleigh, NC
Janz, James F. ......Milwaukee, WI
Janz, James R. ......Palo Alto, CA
Janzen, Bradley R. ......Minneapolis, MN
Janzen, Eric D. ......McAlester, OK
Janzen, Herbert A. ......Houston, TX
Janzen, Lisa Kaye ......Foley, MN
Janzen, Peter S. ......St. Paul, MN
Janzen, Sandra L. ......Phoenix, AZ
Janzen, Thomas M. ......Los Angeles, CA
Janzer, Jerome M. ......Milwaukee, WI
Janzik, Laura W. ......Phoenix, AZ
Janzik, Robert M. ......Portland, OR
Japha, Daniel S. ......Denver, CO
Japha, David C., Law Offices of
Denver, CO
Japha, Ronald D. ......Bridgeport, CT
Japinga, Kimberly L. ......New York, NY
Japlon, Howard E. ......Palatine, IL
Japlon, Mary Gilhooly ......Chicago, IL
Japour, Daniel A. ......Jacksonville, FL
Japp, Chris Hokan ......Silver Spring, MD
Jaqua, David P. ......Memphis, TN
Jaqua, Frederick W. ......New York, NY
Jaqua, John C. ......New York, NY
Jaqua, John E. ......Eugene, OR
Jaqua, Martin W. ......Portland, OR
Jaqua, Preston ......Redding, CA
Jaqua & Wheatley, P.C. ......Eugene, OR
Jaquay, Robert B. ......Cleveland, OH
Jaques Admiralty Law Firm, The
Detroit, MI
Jaques, Bruce D., Jr. ......Escondido, CA
San Diego, CA
Jaques, Dane B. ......Washington, DC
Jaques, Douglas A. ......Los Angeles, CA
Jaques, Frank H. ......Ada, OK
Jaques, Jerry J. ......Hood River, OR
Jaques, Michael T. ......Jackson, MS
Jaques, Sharp & Sherrerd ......Hood River, OR
Jaques, Timothy E. ......Kansas City, MO
Jaquess, James Fletcher ......Norcross, GA
Jaquett, Hance C. ......Ocean City, NJ
Jaquette, Daryl C. ......Jacksonville, FL
Jaquette, Peter B. ......Carson City, NV
Jaquez, Martin J. ......San Diego, CA
Jaquillard, S. Joy ......Portland, OR
Jaquint, Daniel C. ......Alpharetta, GA
Jaquint, David J. ......Hayward, CA
Jaquish, Marshall K. ......Roseville, CA
Jaquiss, M. Shawn ......Gresham, OR
Jaquith, Buddy ......Santa Maria, CA
Jaquith, Gary S. ......Orange, CA
Jaquith, Grant C. ......Syracuse, NY
Jaquith, Rosemarie Perez ......Syracuse, NY
Jaramillo, Amiel A. ......Sacramento, CA
Jaramillo, Andrew J. ......Irvine, CA
Jaramillo, Arturo L. ......Santa Fe, NM
Jaramillo, C. Mario ......Riverside, CA
Jaramillo, David J. ......Albuquerque, NM
Jaramillo, Jennifer K. ......Los Angeles, CA
Jaramillo, Jerry ......Tampa, FL
Jaramillo, Jo Ann S. ......Roswell, NM
Jaramillo, Julio C. ......Miami, FL
Jaramillo, Richard C. ......Dallas, TX
Jaramillo, Richard C., & Associates, P.C.
Dallas, TX
Jaramillo, Stacey L. ......Irvine, CA
Jaramillo, Yvonne M. ......San Francisco, CA
Jaras, William P. ......Cleveland, OH
Jarashow, Judith A. ......Newton, MA
Jarashow, Richard L. ......New York, NY
Jarashow, Ronald H. ......Washington, DC
Annapolis, MD
Owings Mills, MD
Jarasitis, Allen J. ......Boston, MA
Jarasunas, Auris" A.J. " ......Los Angeles, CA
Jaray, Kenneth A. ......Colorado Springs, CO
Jaray, Kenneth A., P.C.
Colorado Springs, CO
Jarblum, William ......Los Angeles, CA
Jarboe, Arnold J. ......Sterling Heights, MI
Jarboe, Carl F. ......Detroit, MI
Jarboe, Christopher J. ......Norwalk, CT
Jarboe, Hilmer U. ......Irvine, CA
Jarboe, J. Michael ......Pittsburgh, PA
Jarboe, John B. ......Tulsa, OK
Jarboe, John C. ......El Cajon, CA
Jarboe, Mark A. ......Minneapolis, MN
Jarboe, Michael S., (P.C.) ......Sacramento, CA
Jarboe, Paul T. ......Traverse City, MI
Jarboe, Richard A. ......Walnut Ridge, AR
Jarboe & Stoermer, A Professional Corporation ......Tulsa, OK
Jarboe, Vernon L. ......Topeka, KS
Jarbola, Andrew J., III ......Scranton, PA
Jarcho, Arthur S., (P.C.) ......White Plains, NY
Jarcho, Daniel G. ......Washington, DC
Jarcho, Harold G. ......Silver Spring, MD
Jarcho, Jane E. ......Chicago, IL
Jarchow, Bruce L.
Steamboat Springs, CO
Jarchow, Gary H. ......Wichita, KS
Jarchow, Melvin H. ......Ferryville, WI
Jarchow, Stephen P. ......Foster City, CA
Jarden, Brenda Joyce ......Houston, TX
Jardim, Kimberly J. ......Philadelphia, PA
Jardim, Thomas C. ......Newark, NJ
Jardin, Craig D. ......Columbia, SC
Jardin, James C. ......San Francisco, CA
Jardin, Manuel C. ......Pleasanton, CA
Jardin, Suzanne C. ......Norton, MA
Jardine, Alice Jarvis ......Phoenix, AZ
Jardine, Alisa R. ......Los Angeles, CA
Jardine, Baker, Hickman & Houston, P.L.L.C. ......Phoenix, AZ
Jardine, Bradley R. ......Phoenix, AZ
Jardine, Bret T. ......Clearwater, FL
Jardine, Charles M. ......La Grange, IL
Jardine, Daniel G. ......Madison, WI
Jardine, Donald M. ......St. Paul, MN
Jardine, James A. ......St. Paul, MN
Jardine, James S. ......Salt Lake City, UT
Jardine, Jeanne L. ......La Grange, IL
Jardine, John H. ......Red Lodge, MT
Jardine, Julie ......San Francisco, CA
Jardine, Kerry N. ......Englewood, CO
Sterling, CO
Jardine, Laurie C. ......Dallas, TX
Jardine, Leo A. ......Salt Lake City, UT
Jardine, Logan & O'Brien, P.L.L.P.
Owatonna, MN
St. Paul, MN
Jardine, Matthew J. ......Washington, PA
Jardine, Michelle M.
Commodity Futures Trading Commission, Division of Enforcement, GV
Jardine, Nathan N. ......Salt Lake City, UT
Jardine, Orrin S., Jr. ......Apple Valley, MN
Jardine & Pagano, A Professional Corporation ......Springfield, NJ
Jardine, Richard ......New York, NY
Jardine, Stephenson, Blewett and Weaver, P.C. ......Great Falls, MT
Havre, MT
Helena, MT
Lewistown, MT
Jardine, Susan Atwood ......Chicago, IL
Jardine, Thomas V. ......Springfield, NJ
Jardine, William S. ......Lisle, IL
Jardini, André E. ......Glendale, CA
Jardini, Nancy J. ......Department of Justice, Criminal Division, GV
Jardis, Terrill S. ......Escanaba, MI
Jardot, Leo C. ......Washington, DC
Jareaux, Kelli J. ......Washington, DC
Jarecke, David A. ......Lincoln, NE
Jarecke, George W. ......Wilmington, DE
Jarecki, Christian E. ......Roseland, NJ
Jarecki-Black, Judy ......Greenville, SC
Jareczek, Cathleen Milos ......Chicago, IL
Jared, Cynthia ......Chicago, IL
Jared, Debbie Lindsey ......Elba, AL
Jared, Eugene ......Cookeville, TN
Jared & Jared ......Elba, AL
Jared, Jerry A. ......Cookeville, TN
Jared, John Michael, Sr. ......Elba, AL
Jared, Julie C. ......Dallas, TX
Jared, Robert P. ......Davenport, IA
Jarem, Helen S. ......Mayfield Village, OH
Jarema, Robert A. ......Frankenmuth, MI
Saginaw, MI
Jarema, Taras P. ......Clawson, MI
Plymouth, MI
Jaress & Leong, Attorneys at Law, A Law Corporation ......Honolulu, HI
Jaress, R. Patrick ......Honolulu, HI
Jaress, Timothy ......San Francisco, CA
Jaret, Frederica A. ......New York, NY
Jaret & Jaret ......Irvine, CA
San Francisco, CA
Jaret, Phillip A. ......Irvine, CA
San Francisco, CA
Jaret, Robert S. ......Irvine, CA
San Francisco, CA
Jarett, Andrew R. ......Northfield, IL
Jarett, Linda W. ......
Department Of Health And Human Services, GV
Jarett & Weiner ......Northfield, IL
Jargiello, David M. ......Menlo Park, CA
Jarik, Charles L. ......Chicago, IL
Jarin, Kenneth M. ......Philadelphia, PA
Jarjour, Samuel W. ......Fort Wayne, IN
Jark, Heidi B. ......Valparaiso, IN
Jarkesy, Jill A. ......Boca Raton, FL
Jarkovsky, Isaac ......New York, NY
Jarkow, Jeff H. ......Boca Raton, FL
Jarkow, Jeffrey H. ......Miami, FL
Jarlenski, Daniel G., Jr. ......Omaha, NE
Jarman, Bruce E. ......Salem, OR
Jarman, Douglas L. ......Hillsboro, IL
Jarman, G. William ......Baton Rouge, LA
Jarman, Gregg W. ......Tinley Park, IL
Jarman, Kathy E. ......Decatur, GA
Jarman, Kimberly A. ......Lawrence, MA
Jarman, Michael G. ......Harrisburg, PA
Jarman, Michael R. ......Anaheim, CA
Jarman, Ronald J. ......Pocatello, ID
Jarman, Rufus E., Jr. ......Washington, DC
New York, NY
Jarman, Timothy T. ......Sioux City, IA
Jarmel, Dean L. ......New York, NY
Jarmel, Ottilie L. ......New York, NY
Jarmie, Mark D. ......Albuquerque, NM
Jarmon, Gary M. ......Norman, OK
Jarmon, Monique Melisan Adele Foard
Silver Spring, MD
Jarmul, Holly D. ......New York, NY
Jarmulnek, Fern J.
Federal Communications Commission, International Bureau, GV
Jarmusch, Robert T. ......Cleveland, OH
Jarnagin, Carroll E. ......Fort Worth, TX
Jarnagin, Nelson ......Brunswick, GA
Jarnagin, Veronica L. ......Indianapolis, IN
Jarner, David Paul ......Los Lunas, NM
Jarner Law Offices ......Los Lunas, NM
Jarner, Mark D. ......Los Lunas, NM
Jarnholm, Arne R. ......Wilmington, DE
Jarnicki, Harold ......Lebanon, OH
Jarnigan, Jami ......Oklahoma City, OK
Jarnis, Jane Lamkin ......St. Cloud, MN
Jaro, Michael J. ......Minneapolis, MN
Jaron, Helene S. ......Philadelphia, PA
Jaron, Martin J., Jr. ......Washington, DC
Jaron, Michael G. ......Oak Park, MI
Jaron, Michael G., P.C. ......Oak Park, MI
Jaros, Arthur G., Jr. ......Oak Brook, IL
Jaros, John A., Jr. ......Kennett Square, PA
Jaros, Joseph J., Jr. ......Chicago, IL
Jaros, Joseph Thomas ......Chicago, IL
Jaros, Lawrence ......Cleveland, OH
Jaros, Murray M. ......Schenectady, NY
Jaros, Robert E. ......Denver, CO
Jaros, Robert E. ......Southfield, MI
Jaros, Robert G. ......Lisle, IL
Jaros, Ronald L. ......Hamburg, NY
Jaros, Stanley T. ......Cleveland, OH
Jaros, Susan Stevens ......Cleveland, OH
Jaros, Thomas G. ......Chicago, IL
Jaros, Tittle & O'Toole, Limited
Chicago, IL
Jarosak, John J. ......Boston, MA
Jaroscak, Maureen ......Santa Fe Springs, CA
Jarosik, Gary R. ......Chicago, IL
Jarosinski, George S. ......Baltimore, MD
Jaroslaw, David ......New York, NY
Jaroslaw, Ilene Weininger ......Brooklyn, NY
Jaroslawicz, Aron S. ......New York, NY
Jaroslawicz, David ......New York, NY
Jaroslawicz, Isaac M. ......Miami, FL
Jarosz, Michael S. ......Houston, TX
Jarosz, Peter M. ......Phoenix, AZ
Jarosz, Richard J. ......Dearborn Heights, MI
Jarosz, William Wasyl ......New York, NY
Jaroszek, Billie J. ......Phoenix, AZ
San Diego, CA

Jaroszek, Roth & Kennedy, A Law Corporation ... Phoenix, AZ
San Diego, CA
Jaroszynski, Sally A. ... Jamestown, NY
Jarot, Edward J., Jr. ... Joliet, IL
Jarowski, Stephen A. ... Westbury, NY
Jarowyj, Alexander B. ... Detroit, MI
Jarpe, Geoffrey P. ... Minneapolis, MN
Jarquin, Joanne B. ... Washington, DC
Jarr, Lisa Anne ... Morgantown, WV
Jarrard, J. Lee, Jr. ... Round Rock, TX
Jarrard, J. Michael ... Bethesda, MD
Jarrard, Ken E. ... Atlanta, GA
Jarrard, R. Thomas ... Gainesville, GA
Jarrard & Richard ... Washington, DC
Bethesda, MD
Jarrard, Stephen D. ... Elgin, TX
Jarratt, Jeffery A. ... Memphis, TN
Jarratt, Richard D. ... St. Petersburg, FL
Jarreau, J. Steven ... Metairie, LA
Jarred, Katherine A.
Farmington Hills, MI
Jarred, Robert A. ... Lafayette, LA
Jarrel & Jarrel ... Tyler, TX
Jarrel, Willis ... Tyler, TX
Jarrel, Willis, Jr. ... Tyler, TX
Jarrell, Brenda H. ... Boston, MA
Jarrell, Charles D. ... Los Angeles, CA
Jarrell, Charles M. ... Opelousas, LA
Jarrell, Chas. R. ... High Point, NC
Jarrell, Douglas M. ... Charlotte, NC
Jarrell, Elsie ... High Point, NC
Jarrell, Eric Earl ... New Orleans, LA
Jarrell, Eugene F., III ... Media, PA
Jarrell & Everngam ... Denton, MD
Jarrell, F. Fincher ... Charlotte, NC
Jarrell, Glenn M. ... Carrollton, GA
Jarrell, Hicks, Sasser & McCarthy, P.C.
Fredericksburg, VA
Spotsylvania, VA
Jarrell, James A. ... Charleston, WV
Jarrell, James E., III ... Spotsylvania, VA
Jarrell, James E., Jr. ... Spotsylvania, VA
Jarrell, James L. ... Houston, TX
Jarrell, John W., Jr. ... Washington, DC
Jarrell, Larry C. ... Troy, AL
Jarrell, Linwood O., Jr. ... Baltimore, MD
Jarrell, Phillip W. ... Gulfport, MS
Jarrell, Reginald D. ... Rock Island, IL
Jarrell, Robert E. ... Denton, MD
Jarrell, Stacey L. ... Pittsburgh, PA
Jarrell, Thomas G. ... Louisville, KY
Jarrell-Cole, Margaret ... Gainesville, FL
Jarret, Amanda Peralta ... Bartow, FL
Jarret, Anthony L. ... Woonsocket, RI
Jarret, Aram P., Jr. ... North Smithfield, RI
Jarret, Arielle H. ... New York, NY
Jarret, Joseph Gregory ... Bartow, FL
Jarrett, Anne H. ... Atlanta, GA
Jarrett, Arthur B. ... Philadelphia, PA
Jarrett, Barbara M. ... Phoenix, AZ
Jarrett, Beth D. ... Miami, FL
Jarrett, C. Douglas ... Washington, DC
Jarrett, C. Hamilton, III ... Charlotte, NC
Raleigh, NC
Columbia, SC
Jarrett & Campisano ... Louisville, KY
Jarrett, Charles B., Jr. ... Pittsburgh, PA
Jarrett, Charles E. ... Cleveland, OH
Jarrett, Clifford R. ... Charlotte, NC
Jarrett, Clifford Wayne ... Dothan, AL
Jarrett, Danny W. ... Albuquerque, NM
Jarrett, David R. ... Houston, TX
Jarrett, Donald D. ... Olathe, KS
Jarrett, Elaine R. ... St. Louis, MO
Jarrett, Ernest J. ... Kingstree, SC
Jarrett, Ernest L. ... Detroit, MI
Jarrett, Evy M. ... Holland, OH
Jarrett, Gerald W. ... White Plains, NY
Jarrett, Glenn A. ... Burlington, VT
Jarrett, Henry K., III ... Louisville, KY
Jarrett, Howard Marshall, Jr.
Department of Justice, Office of Professional Responsibility, GV
Jarrett, Jack ... Little Rock, AR
Jarrett, James C. ... Braymer, MO
Kansas City, MO
Jarrett, James F. ... Effingham, IL
Jarrett, John L. ... Olympia, WA
Jarrett, Joseph W. ... Bermuda Dunes, CA
Jarrett, Larry E. ... Dallas, TX
Jarrett, Linda E. ... New York, NY
Jarrett, Lisa K. ... San Antonio, TX
Jarrett, Mark J. ... San Francisco, CA
Jarrett, Mary W. ... Jacksonville, FL
Jarrett, Michael E. ... Tyler, TX
Jarrett, R. Keith ... New Orleans, LA
Jarrett, Richard A. ... Jonesboro, AR
Jarrett, Rita M. ... Westlake, OH
Jarrett, Robert M., Jr. ... Willcox, AZ
Jarrett, Roy E. ... Cypress, CA
Jarrett, Russell L. ... Detroit, MI
Jarrett, Sarah D. ... Phoenix, AZ
Jarrett, Stephanie Baker ... Cleveland, OH
Jarrett, Steven R. ... Overland Park, KS
Jarrett, Terry M. ... Jefferson City, MO
Jarrett, Tommy W. ... Goldsboro, NC
Jarrett, Valerie Bowman ... Chicago, IL
Jarrett, William C.H. ... Honolulu, HI
Jarrette, Marlea F. ... Santa Barbara, CA
Jarrick, Michael A. ... Chicago, IL
Jarrico, Bill ... Springfield, IL
Jarriel, Judith E. ... Lakeland, FL
Jarriel, Thomas F. ... Macon, GA
Jarrin, Alexander M. ... Rock Island, IL
Jarrin, Alfredo Xavier ... El Segundo, CA
Jarrow, James R. ... Kansas City, MO
Jarstad, Mark A. ... Wabasha, MN

Jarsulic, Marc ... Federal Trade Commission, Bureau of Competition, GV
Jartz, John G. ... Chicago, IL
Jarus, Debra Bodenstein ... Cleveland, OH
Jarushewsky, Jayson ... New York, NY
Jarussi & Bishop ... Billings, MT
Jarussi, Gene R. ... Billings, MT
Jaruzelski, Janina A.
Agency for International Development, Legal Advisers-Overseas, GV
Jarve, Mati, (Mr.) ... Cherry Hill, NJ
Jarvela, Dennis L. ... Maumee, OH
Jarvey, John A. ... Cedar Rapids, IA
Jarvi, Jeffrey J. ... Anchorage, AK
Jarvi, Kenneth O. ... Anchorage, AK
Jarvi, Kenneth O., A Professional Corporation ... Anchorage, AK
Jarvi, Kenneth T. ... Denver, CO
Jarvi, Theodore C. ... Tempe, AZ
Jarvie, Mary P. ... Erie, PA
Jarvinen, Claire M. ... Amherst, NH
Jarvinen, Matthew L. ... Denver, CO
Järvinen, Sara ... Minneapolis, MN
Jarvinen, Toivo J. ... Lantana, FL
Jarvis, Alan J. ... Coatesville, PA
Jarvis, Alfred R. ... North Haven, CT
Jarvis, Ann Duncan ... Nashville, TN
Jarvis, Annette W. ... Salt Lake City, UT
Jarvis, Averill Rand ... Jenkintown, PA
Jarvis, Barbara ... Albuquerque, NM
Jarvis, Barbara A. ... Ashland, OR
Jarvis, Ben E. ... Tyler, TX
Jarvis, Billy Britt ... Spearman, TX
Jarvis & Blanton ... Bonham, TX
Sherman, TX
Jarvis, Carlotta P. ... New York, NY
Jarvis, Charles ... Santa Barbara, CA
Jarvis, Charles W. ... Fairfax, VA
Jarvis, Christopher A. ... Seattle, WA
Jarvis, Constance Canfield ... Portland, OR
Jarvis, David E. ... Milwaukee, WI
Jarvis, David L. ... Fort Worth, TX
Jarvis, Diana A. ... New York, NY
Jarvis, Don L. ... Sherman, TX
Jarvis, Don L., Jr. ... Sherman, TX
Jarvis, Eric David ... Los Angeles, CA
Jarvis, F. Wayne, Jr. ... Washington, DC
Jarvis, G. Derek ... Santa Ana, CA
Jarvis, Gail Stone ... Knoxville, TN
Jarvis, Geoffrey C. ... Philadelphia, PA
Jarvis, Glenn, Law Office of ... McAllen, TX
Jarvis, H. Dennis, Jr. ... Knoxville, TN
Sevierville, TN
Jarvis, H. Keith ... Denver, CO
Jarvis, Hartloff, Simon & Schmidt, L.L.P.
Santa Barbara, CA
Jarvis, Henry M. ... Richmond, VA
Jarvis, H.M." Chip " ... Sherman, TX
Jarvis, Howard E. ... Knoxville, TN
Jarvis, J. Cecil ... Clarksburg, WV
Jarvis, James H., II ... Knoxville, TN
Jarvis, James L. ... Georgetown, TX
Jarvis, James S. ... Chicago, IL
Jarvis, James S. ... Olympia, WA
Jarvis, James W. (IBA) ... **Coral Gables, FL**
Jarvis, Jane Elizabeth ... Jackson, TN
Jarvis, Jarrett S. ... Phoenix, AZ
Jarvis, J. E., Jr. ... Valdosta, GA
Jarvis, Jeff ... Harvard, MA
Jarvis, Judith A. ... Fort Lauderdale, FL
Jarvis, Judith A., P.C. ... Fort Lauderdale, FL
Jarvis, Julietta ... Troup, TX
Jarvis and Kaplan ... Burlington, VT
Jarvis, Keith L. ... Massillon, OH
Jarvis, Kingsley A. ... Norristown, PA
Jarvis, Lane K., Jr. ... Corpus Christi, TX
Jarvis, Laurence M. ... Kansas City, KS
Jarvis, Lawrence M. ... Chicago, IL
Jarvis, Lisa F. ... Charlotte, NC
Jarvis, Longaker, Koonce & Dashiell, A Law Corporation ... Sacramento, CA
Jarvis, Lynn F. ... Bend, OR
Jarvis, Mary C. ... Visalia, CA
Jarvis, Michael E. ... Florham Park, NJ
Jarvis, Michael S. ... Ukiah, CA
Jarvis, Nancy A. ... San Francisco, CA
Jarvis, Ora-Anne E. ... Norwalk, CT
Jarvis, Pamela ... New York, NY
Jarvis, Paul D. ... Burlington, VT
Jarvis, Paul G. ... Buffalo, WY
Jarvis, Percy A., Jr. ... Summit, NJ
Jarvis, Peter D. ... Seattle, WA
Jarvis, Peter R. ... Portland, OR
Jarvis, Ralph W. ... Minneapolis, MN
Jarvis, Raymond R., III ... Snow Hill, MD
Jarvis, Richard A. ... Covington, KY
Jarvis & Richards, P.A. ... Coral Gables, FL
Jarvis, Rick W. ... San Leandro, CA
Stockton, CA
Jarvis, Robert J. ... Loudonville, NY
Jarvis, Robert L., Jr. ... Live Oak, FL
Jarvis, Robert M. ... Fort Lauderdale, FL
Jarvis, Robert P. ... Mesa, AZ
Jarvis, Robert W. ... Sacramento, CA
Jarvis, Robt. Y. ... Bartlett, TN
Jarvis, Rodney Q. ... Phoenix, AZ
Jarvis, Ronald Blair ... Philadelphia, PA
Jarvis, Ronald J. ... Washington, DC
Jarvis, Sandra G. ... Tulsa, OK
Jarvis, Scott C. ... New York, NY
Jarvis, Sharon Patricia ... Sacramento, CA
Jarvis, Steven D. ... Lapeer, MI
Jarvis, Thomas L. ... Washington, DC
Jarvis, Valencia L. ... Troy, MI
Jarvis, Wayne, (Ltd.) ... Chicago, IL
Jarvis, William E. ... Chatham, VA
Jarvis, William F. ... New York, NY
Jarvis, William Stevens ... Palo Alto, CA

Jarz, Theodore J. ... Joliet, IL
Jarzabek, Joseph E. ... Sandpoint, ID
Jarzembek, Joseph T. ... Buffalo, NY
Jarzembek, Jerry J. ... Fort Worth, TX
Jarzyna, Andrew ... Chicago, IL
Jarzyna-Price, Darlene M. ... Chicago, IL
Jarzyniecki, Thomas J., Jr.
Indianapolis, IN
Jarzynka, Jerard M. ... Jackson, MI
Jas, Francois H. ... Cambridge, MA
Jasaitis, James E. ... Newark, NJ
Jasaitis, Jennifer C. ... Portland, OR
Jasaitis, Joseph C. ... Newark, NJ
Jasanoff, Sheila Sen ... Cambridge, MA
Jasen & Jasen, P.C. ... Buffalo, NY
Jasen, Mark M. ... Buffalo, NY
Jasen, Matthew J. ... Buffalo, NY
Jasen, Natalie S. ... Jamaica, NY
Jasen, Peter M. ... Buffalo, NY
Jasen, Raymond D. ... New York, NY
Jaser, George J. ... Milford, CT
Jasey, John A. ... New York, NY
Jasey, Neil N. ... Newark, NJ
Jasiak, Dawn L. ... New York, NY
Jasilli, John A. ... New York, NY
Jasinski, Carol A. ... San Francisco, CA
Jasinski, Catherine D. ... Traverse City, MI
Jasinski, David F. ... Newark, NJ
Philadelphia, PA
Jasinski, Douglas M. ... Washington, DC
Jasinski, George J. ... Palos Heights, IL
Jasinski, James J.
Department of Justice, GV
Jasinski, Jerome J. ... Albany, NY
Jasinski, Kenneth M. ... Albany, NY
Jasinski, M. Diane ... New York, NY
Jasinski and Paranac, A Professional Corporation ... Atlantic City, NJ
Newark, NJ
Philadelphia, PA
Jasinski, Paul C. ... Jackson Heights, NY
Jasinski, Sandra L. ... Lansing, MI
Jasionowski, James S. ... Chicago, IL
Jaske, John B. ... Arlington, VA
Jaski, Gerald B. ... Tallahassee, FL
Jaski, Thomas P. ... Carolina Beach, NC
Jaskiel, Solomon J. ... New York, NY
Jaskiewicz, Christopher M.
New York, NY
Jaskiewicz, Edmund M. ... Washington, DC
Jaskiewicz, Leonard A. ... Washington, DC
Jaskiewicz, Stanley Peter ... Moorestown, NJ
Philadelphia, PA
Jaskiewicz, Stanley W., Jr. ... Charleston, SC
Jaskiewicz, Stanley W., Jr., P.C.
Charleston, SC
Jaskol, Lisa R. ... Los Angeles, CA
Jaskol, Stacey J. ... Haddonfield, NJ
Jaskola, William A. ... New York, NY
Jaskolski, Michael A. ... Milwaukee, WI
Jaskolski, Ronald J. ... Milwaukee, WI
Jaskolski, Ronald J., S.C. ... Milwaukee, WI
Jaskoski, Anne W. ... Woodland Hills, CA
Jaskot & Evertz ... Hackensack, NJ
Jaskot, John J. ... Washington, DC
Jaskot, John J. ... Silver Spring, MD
Jaskot, Lawrence J. ... Hackensack, NJ
Jaskot, Paul J. ... Philadelphia, PA
Jaskowiak, F. Joseph ... Merrillville, IN
Jaskowiak, Robert B. ... Minneapolis, MN
Jaskula, Michael ... Chicago, IL
Jaskulski, Alfred A. ... Costa Mesa, CA
Jaskulski, Louisa M. ... San Francisco, CA
Jaskulski, Robert L. ... Milwaukee, WI
Jaslow, Craig A. ... Miami, FL
Jaslow, Howard M. ... New York, NY
Jasman, Frank E. ... Hialeah, FL
Jasmer, Faye A. ... Grand Forks, ND
Jasmer, Frederick D. ... Southfield, MI
Jasmin, Ernest A. ... Louisville, KY
Jasmin, Grant ... Sunnyvale, CA
Jasmine, Janis L. ... Santa Rosa, CA
Jasmine, Madeline ... Edgard, LA
Jasmund, Elizabeth D. ... Orlando, FL
Jasne, Hugh G. ... White Plains, NY
Jasne & Morell, L.L.P. ... White Plains, NY
Jaso, Eric H. ... Newark, NJ
Jaso, Kim Lorraine ... Pasadena, CA
Jason, Amanda T. ... Miami, FL
Jason, Edward C. ... Syracuse, NY
Jason & Fischer ... Boston, MA
Jason, Jay F. ... Spring Valley, NY
Jason, Judith N. ... Beverly Hills, CA
Jason, Kelly S. ... Boston, MA
Jason, Linda G. ... Boston, MA
Jason, Marc J. ... New York, NY
Jason, Marilyn S. ... New York, NY
Jason, Mark N. ... Chicago, IL
Jason, Meredith L.
National Labor Relations Board, Office of the General Counsel, GV
Jason & Nesson, L.L.P. ... New City, NY
Spring Valley, NY
Jason, Patricia M. ... Detroit, MI
Jason, Paul S. ... Scarsdale, NY
Jason, Peter ... Philadelphia, PA
Jason, Peter D. ... Lansing, MI
Jason, Raymond J. ... Marquette, MI
Jason, Robert M. ... Los Angeles, CA
Jason, Sherry B. ... Topanga, CA
Jason, Walter J. ... Rolling Hills Estates, CA
Jasons, Catherine N. ... Philadelphia, PA
Jaspan, Arthur W. ... Garden City, NY
Jaspan, Joseph ... Garden City, NY
Jaspan, Michael D. ... New York, NY
Jaspan, Michele K. ... New York, NY

Jaspan Schlesinger Hoffman LLP
Garden City, NY
Mineola, NY
Jaspan, Stanley S. ... Milwaukee, WI
Jaspen, Daniel M. ... Iron Mountain, MI
Jaspen, Gail D. ... Richmond, VA
Jaspen, Robert W. ... Richmond, VA
Jasper, Bruce R. ... Newport, NH
Jasper, Catherine R. ... Newport Beach, CA
Jasper, David ... Denver, CO
Jasper, Dennis D. ... Bettendorf, IA
Jasper, Elizabeth Slater ... Denver, CO
Jasper, Harvey M. ... New York, NY
Jasper, James H. ... Cleveland, TX
Jasper, James H., P.C. ... Cleveland, TX
Jasper, Jason ... Atlanta, GA
Jasper & Jasper ... New York, NY
Jasper & Jasper, A Professional Corporation
Newport Beach, CA
Jasper, Jill L. ... San Leandro, CA
Jasper, John A. ... Department Of The Interior, Office of the Solicitor, GV
Jasper, John G. ... Santa Fe, NM
Jasper, Jonathan Neal ... Anoka, MN
Jasper, Jos. J. ... Birmingham, AL
Jasper, Mabel M. ... Cleveland, OH
Jasper, Margaret C. ... South Salem, NY
Jasper, Matthew A. ... Parker, AZ
Jasper, Michael J. ... Chicago, IL
Jasper, Norval W. ... Tucson, AZ
Jasper, Patricia K. ... Santa Barbara, CA
Jasper, Patricia Marie ... Los Angeles, CA
Jasper, Paul G. ... Indianapolis, IN
Jasper, Seymour ... New York, NY
Jasper, Stuart P. ... Newport Beach, CA
Jasper, Warren A. ... Nashville, TN
Jaspers, Elizabeth Slater ... Denver, CO
Jaspers, Jerome W. ... Shakopee, MN
Jasperse, Joel R. ... Gallup, NM
Jasperson, Richard L. ... St. Paul, MN
Jasperson, Richard L., P.A. ... St. Paul, MN
Jaspovice, Martin L. ... Hayward, CA
Jasprica, Judy Rae ... Tacoma, WA
Jassak, Michael J. ... Lake Geneva, WI
Racine, WI
Jasse, André C. (IBA) ... **Boston, MA**
Jassen, Sheryl D. ... New York, NY
Jassin, Lloyd J. ... New York, NY
Jasso, Janine B. ... Los Angeles, CA
Jasso, Juan ... Dallas, TX
Jasso, Paul J., Jr. ... St. Louis, MO
Jasso, Rolando M. ... Eagle Pass, TX
Jassy, Everett L. ... New York, NY
Jassy, Jean-Paul ... Los Angeles, CA
Jassy, Lionel S. ... New York, NY
Jast, Raymond J. ... Chicago, IL
Jastak, Steffany Hergert ... Oregon City, OR
Jastram, Harold D. ... Minneapolis, MN
Jastrebski, Alycia K. ... Birmingham, AL
Jastroch & LaBarge, S.C. ... Waukesha, WI
Jastroch, Leonard A. ... Waukesha, WI
Jastrow, Robert E. ... Mesa, AZ
Jastrzebski, Alan F. ... Southfield, MI
Jasuta, John G. ... Austin, TX
Jaszczuk, Mark A. ... Chicago, IL
Jaszewski, Edward E. ... Sacramento, CA
Jaszewski, Samuel F. ... Tucson, AZ
Jatana, Nicky ... Los Angeles, CA
Jatlow, David C. ... Washington, DC
Jatlow, Howard S. ... Washington, DC
Jatoi, Imdad ... Fort Worth, TX
Jaubert, Lisa Shelton ... New Orleans, LA
Jauch, Richard M. ... Littleton, CO
Jauch, Roger P. ... Portland, OR
Jaudes, Mark A. ... Dallas, TX
Jaudes, Phyllis A. ... San Francisco, CA
Jaudes, Richard E. ... St. Louis, MO
Jaudes, William E. ... St. Louis, MO
Jaudon, Joseph C., Jr. ... Denver, CO
Jaudzemis, Kathleen A. ... Omaha, NE
Jaudzemis, Thomas S. ... Lincoln, NE
Jauert, Douglas S. ... Minster, OH
Wapakoneta, OH
Jauffret, Jerome M.F. ... Los Angeles, CA
Jaunal, Garry W. ... Chicago, IL
Jaunarajs, Visvaldis ... Denver, CO
Parker, CO
Jaunese, David C. ... Fremont, MI
Jaunich, R. Prescott ... Burlingame, CA
San Jose, CA
Jauregui, Arturo ... Chicago, IL
Jauregui, Jacqueline M. ... Oakland, CA
Jauregui, Jesse M. ... Los Angeles, CA
Jauregui, Paul L. ... Boise, ID
Jauregui, Phillip L., Jr. ... Montgomery, AL
Jauregui, Ron J. ... Rowland Heights, CA
Jauregui, Russell M. ... Riverside, CA
Jauregui, Valerie Rose ... Escondido, CA
Jauron, Robert E. ... Manchester, NH
Jaussi, Clair J. ... Provo, UT
Jauvtis, Robert L. ... New York, NY
Java, Joel J., Jr. ... Buffalo, NY
Javan, Robert B. ... Sacramento, CA
Javaras, George B., (P.C.) ... Chicago, IL
Javardian, Gregory ... Camden, NJ
Javarone, Albin V. ... New York, NY
Javdan, David A. ... New York, NY
Javelera, Lambert M. ... Pasadena, CA
Javerbaum, Kenneth S. ... Springfield, NJ
Javerbaum Wurgaft Hicks & Zarin, A Professional Corporation ... Springfield, NJ
Javeri, Vaishali R.
Securities and Exchange Commission, Office of Compliance Inspections and Examinations, GV
Javid, Arman ... San Francisco, CA
Javier, Carolyn S. ... Los Angeles, CA
Javier, Maurice M. ... Glendale, CA

Javier, Ramon E. ....New York, NY
Javins, L. Lee, II ....Charleston, WV
Javior, Gerald J. ....Palos Hills, IL
Javit, Felice ....New York, NY
Javitch, Block, Eisen & Rathbone P.L.L.
Cincinnati, OH
Cleveland, OH
Javitch, Daniel ....New York, NY
Javitch, Victor M. ....Cleveland, OH
Javits, Darlene C. ....Farmingdale, NY
Javits, David B. ....Miami, FL
Javits, Eric M. ....New York, NY
Javits, Joshua M. ....Washington, DC
Javitt, Gail H. ....Washington, DC
Javitz, Jayson Tory ....San Francisco, CA
Javor, R. ....Sacramento, CA
Javore, Gary W. ....San Antonio, TX
Javoronok, Michael J. ....Gering, NE
Javoronok, Michael J., Law Firm
Gering, NE
Jawdat, Zaidun ....Gaithersburg, MD
Jawetz, Steven M. ....Washington, DC
Jawgiel, Michael B. ....Waukegan, IL
Jawharjian, Hagop ....Johnston, RI
Jawin, Michele R. ....New York, NY
Jawitz, Alan ....New Rochelle, NY
Jawitz & Jawitz ....New Rochelle, NY
Jawitz, Julian ....Ringwood, NJ
Jawitz, Larry E. ....Guilford, CT
Jawitz, Lynn M. ....Wantagh, NY
Jawitz, Marvin J. ....New Rochelle, NY
Jaworowski, Susan Ekimoto ....Honolulu, HI
Jaworski, Daniel M. ....Flint, MI
Jaworski, David Paul ....Boston, MA
Jaworski, David V. ....Cheektowaga, NY
Jaworski, Edmund W. ....San Diego, CA
Jaworski, Francis S. ....Detroit, MI
Jaworski, James E. ....Paramus, NJ
Jaworski, Jon Alan ....Houston, TX
Jaworski, Joseph P. ....Houston, TX
Jaworski, Joseph P., P.C. ....Houston, TX
Jaworski, Joseph S. ....Texas City, TX
Jaworski, Leonard J. (Jack) ....St. Louis, MO
Jaworski, Norbert G. ....Lansing, MI
Jaworski, Richard F. ....New York, NY
Jaworski, Robert M. ....Princeton, NJ
Jaworski, Ronald P. ....West Palm Beach, FL
Jaworski, Rudolf A. ....Danvers, MA
Jaworski, Rudolph A., P.C. ....Danvers, MA
Jaworski, Thomas M. ....Gainesville, FL
Jaworski, William F., Jr. ....Dover, DE
Jaworsky, John M. ....El Dorado, KS
Jaworsky, Stephen ....Oklahoma City, OK
Jaxa-Debicki, Andrew A. ....Washington, DC
Jay, Beth J. ....San Francisco, CA
Jay, Clayton, Jr. ....Fitzgerald, GA
Jay, D. Frederick, Jr. ....La Jolla, CA
Jay, Dana M. ....Topanga, CA
Jay, Daniel J. ....Centerville, IA
Jay, David ....Newark, NJ
Jay, David E. ....Canton, OH
Jay, David Gerald ....Buffalo, NY
Jay, Edgar N. ....Glen Cove, NY
Jay, Edward W., Jr. ....Milton, MA
Jay, Gary K. ....Shawnee, OK
Jay, Gary M. ....Salina, OK
Jay, Gilbert Y. ....San Francisco, CA
Jay, Gregory D., (P.C.) ....Buford, GA
Jay, Harvey L., III ....Jacksonville, FL
Jay, James L. ....Houston, TX
Jay, James V., IV ....Fort Worth, TX
Jay, Jana V. ....Naples, FL
Jay, Jeremy M. ....Washington, DC
Jay, Jerry ....Newfield, NY
Jay, Jessica E. ....Denver, CO
Jay, J. L. ....El Paso, TX
Jay, John B. ....Norcross, GA
Jay, John E. ....Edina, MN
Jay, John I. ....Waynesville, NC
Jay, John Joseph ....Yakima, WA
Jay, John W. ....Oakland, CA
Jay, John William ....Irvine, CA
Jay, Jonathan D. ....St. Paul, MN
Jay, Jonathan S. ....Washington, DC
Jay, Joseph W., Jr. ....Fremont, CA
Jay, Laurence Freeman ....Los Angeles, CA
Jay, Leslie P. ....San Francisco, CA
Jay, Mark H. ....Iselin, NJ
Jay, Michael A. ....Kew Gardens, NY
Jay, Michael S. ....West Caldwell, NJ
Jay, Philip M. ....Fresno, CA
Jay, Scott R. ....Miami Beach, FL
Jay, Sherrell & Smith, P.C. ....Fitzgerald, GA
Jay, Shirley ....Smithtown, NY
Jay, Stephen M. ....Van Nuys, CA
Jay, Stewart M. ....Seattle, WA
Jay, Stuart P. ....Louisville, KY
Jay, Susan Carole ....Los Angeles, CA
Jay, Theodore C. ....Larchmont, NY
Jay, Vicki ....Miami, FL
Jay, W. Walton ....Groton, CT
Jayachandran, Prashanth ....Syracuse, NY
Jayapal, Susheela ....Beaverton, OR
Jayaraman, Karimbumkara ....Memphis, TN
Jayashekaramurthy, Mary S.
Philadelphia, PA
Jayatilka, Shireen ....Washington, DC
Jaybush, Brian G. ....Seattle, WA
Jaycox, Thomas D. ....New York, NY
Jaye, Grace A. ....Tallahassee, FL
Jaye, John C. ....Chicago, IL
Jaye, Robert P.
Department Of Health And Human Services,
Office of the General Counsel, GV
Jaye, Steven A. ....Carlsbad, CA
Jaye, Vinson Wilson ....Wetumpka, AL
Jaye, William T. ....Carle Place, NY
Jaymes, William R. ....Palm Desert, CA

Jayne A. Hartley, P.C. ....Oak Brook, IL
Jayne, Benjamin W. ....Bloomfield Hills, MI
Jayne, David G. ....San Antonio, TX
Jayne, Donald R. ....San Francisco, CA
Jayne, H. Martin ....Kirksville, MO
Jayne, Louise ....Portland, OR
Jayne, Roxanne E. ....Princeton, NJ
Jayne, Steven C. ....Des Moines, IA
Jayne, Thomas R. ....St. Louis, MO
Jaynes, Barry S. ....Sunnyvale, CA
Jaynes, Blair D. ....Boise, ID
Jaynes, David A. ....West Palm Beach, FL
Jaynes, Donald O. ....Bloomington, IL
Jaynes, John C. ....Lansing, MI
Jaynes, Joseph Patrick ....Little Rock, AR
Jaynes, Lawrence C. ....Hoffman Estates, IL
Jaynes, Michael A ....Jackson, TN
Jaynes, Ralph H. ....Fayette, MO
Jaynes, Richard A. ....Department of the Army,
U.S. Army Legal Services Agency, GV
Jaynes, Ronald C. ....Denver, CO
Jaynes, William H., Jr. ....Seattle, WA
Jaynes, William O., Jr. ....New Orleans, LA
Jayo, Juan M. ....San Francisco, CA
Jayson, Christopher P. ....Tampa, FL
Jayson, Harold E. ....West Orange, NJ
Jayson, J.M., & Associates ....Buffalo, NY
Jayson, Jeffrey K. ....Tarzana, CA
Jayson, Jeffrey M. ....Buffalo, NY
Jayson, Lisa A. ....St. Petersburg, FL
Jayson, Melinda G. ....Dallas, TX
Jayson, Melinda G., P.C. ....Dallas, TX
Jayson, Ronald P. ....Decatur, GA
Jayson, Timothy J. ....Minneapolis, MN
Jaywork, John Terence ....Dover, DE
Jazayeri, Pete ....Los Angeles, CA
Jazayerli, Rana ....Washington, DC
Jazinski-Makin, Kerry ....Indianapolis, IN
Jazlowiecki, Edward A. ....Bristol, CT
Jazwinski, Gene L. ....Pittsburgh, PA
Jazwinski, Michael S. ....Roanoke, AL
Jazzo, Frank R. ....Washington, DC
Arlington, VA
JD Associates, PLC ....Phoenix, AZ
Je, Julia Y. ....Los Angeles, CA
Jeakle, Edwin B. ....Dearborn, MI
Jeakle, W. Glen, II ....Detroit, MI
Jean, Arthur H., Jr. ....Los Angeles, CA
Jean, Denis J. ....Lake Success, NY
Jean, Edwin C.
Securities and Exchange Commission,
Division of Corporation Finance, GV
New York, NY
Jean, Joseph D. ....New York, NY
Jean, Katherine E. ....Raleigh, NC
Jean, Kenneth N. ....Ponca City, OK
Jean, Lorri L. ....Los Angeles, CA
Jean, Mitchell B. ....Laconia, NH
Jean, Paul-Johan ....Boston, MA
Jean, Rodney M. ....Las Vegas, NV
Jean-Baptiste, Carl S., Jr. ....Lutherville, MD
Jeanblanc, James K. ....Washington, DC
Jean-Charles, Lewis Y. ....New York, NY
Jean-Claude, Carine ....New York, NY
Jean-Claude, Enid D. ....New York, NY
Jeandheur, Carole A. ....Department of Justice,
Civil Division, GV
Jeandrevin & Huber ....Medina, OH
Jeandrevin, John T. ....Medina, OH
Jeanes, C. Wesley ....Richardson, TX
Jeanes, Lyle H., II ....Paris, TX
Jeanes, Lyle H., II, P.C. ....Paris, TX
Jeanetta, Kathleen A. ....Kansas City, MO
Jeanetta, Kelly A. ....Minneapolis, MN
Jeanette, Henry C. ....Kenilworth, NJ
Jeanfreau, Charles H. ....New York, NY
Jeang, Wei Wei ....Dallas, TX
Jeangerard, Robert E. ....San Carlos, CA
Jean-Jerome, Menez ....Brooklyn, NY
Jeanmarie, Andrea M. ....Marrero, LA
Jeanné , Tierre Angé ....New York, NY
Jeannero, Jane M. ....Stratham, NH
Jeannette, Frank E. ....Mount Clemens, MI
Jeannette, Michael W. ....Winston-Salem, NC
Jeanney, William C. ....Reno, NV
Jeans, David S. ....El Paso, TX
Jeans, Franklyn D. ....Reno, NV
Jeans, Sheryle L. ....Kansas City, MO
Jeans, Susan E. ....El Paso, TX
Jeanson, A. Roger ....San Francisco, CA
Jeansonne, John A., Jr. ....Lafayette, LA
Jeansonne, Mark A. ....Hessmer, LA
Jeansonne, Mark A., & Carol J. Aymond, Jr.
Hessmer, LA
Jeansonne, Mark J. ....Metairie, LA
Jeansonne, Michael D. ....Alexandria, LA
Jeansonne, Michelle E. ....Atlanta, GA
Jeansonne & Remondet, L.L.C.
Lafayette, LA
New Orleans, LA
Shreveport, LA
Jeansonne, Vernon Joseph ....Lake Arthur, LA
Jeantet & Associes ....New York, NY
New York, NY
Jeavons, Norman S. ....Cleveland, OH
JeBailey, Joseph J. ....Orlando, FL
Jebaily, George D. ....Florence, SC
Jebaily, Glass and Meacham, P.A.
Darlington, SC
Florence, SC
Jebaily, Ronald J. ....Florence, SC
Jebbia, Gayle Branaugh ....Ontario, OR
Jebejian, Sarkis ....New York, NY
Jebens, Susan Cecelia ....Indianapolis, IN
Jebo, Jerry K. ....Radford, VA
Jebo & Turk ....Radford, VA
Jebousek, Nyla Lynn ....Eugene, OR
Jech, Jennifer A. ....Los Angeles, CA

Jeck, Daniel ....Philadelphia, PA
Jeck, Harris & Jones, LLP ....Jupiter, FL
Jeck, Philippe C. ....Jupiter, FL
Jeck, Rachael K. ....Boston, MA
Jeckle, William Andrew ....Spokane, WA
Jecmen, Judith A. ....Houston, TX
Jeddeloh, Norman P. ....Chicago, IL
Jedeikin, Green, Meadows & Schneider
San Francisco, CA
Jedeikin, Joseph, (Professional Corporation)
San Francisco, CA
Jedinak, Thomas J. ....Columbus, OH
Jedlicka, Amy ....New York, NY
Jedlicka, John J. ....Omaha, NE
Jedlicka, Joseph F., III ....St. Louis, MO
Jedlicki, Rodney Edward ....Louisville, KY
Jednorski, Charles A. ....Towson, MD
Jednorski, Paul M. ....Towson, MD
Jedrey, Christopher M., (P.C.)
Boston, MA
Jedrzejek, David P. ....Palo Alto, CA
Jee, Krista M. ....Brea, CA
Jeep, Markham M. ....Waukegan, IL
Jeep & Peavey ....Waukegan, IL
Jeeter, Larry D. ....Ellicott City, MD
Jeeves, Scott R. ....St. Petersburg, FL
Tampa, FL
Jefchak, Karen G. ....Los Angeles, CA
Jefcoat, Samuel H. ....Newberry, SC
Jeffares, Floy H. ....Denver, CO
Jeffas, Gary M. ....Kearny, NJ
Jeffco, Stephen T. ....Portsmouth, NH
Jeffcoat, Carol B. ....Kansas City, MO
Jeffcoat, Jay W. ....El Centro, CA
San Diego, CA
Jeffcoat, Michael R. ....Lexington, SC
Jeffcoat, Michael R., Attorney at Law, LLC
Columbia, SC
Lexington, SC
Jeffcoat, Otis Allen, III ....Calabash, NC
Myrtle Beach, SC
North Myrtle Beach, SC
Jeffcoat, Pike & Nappier, LLC
Calabash, NC
Myrtle Beach, SC
North Myrtle Beach, SC
Jeffcoat, Scott D. ....United States Senate,
Committee Legal Personnel, GV
Jeffcoat-Sacco, Illona A. ....Bismarck, ND
Jeffe, James S. ....Chesterfield, MO
Jeffer, Bruce P., (P.C.) ....Los Angeles, CA
Jeffer, Cioffi & Cicalese, P.A.
Tequesta, FL
Jeffer, Herman M. ....Tequesta, FL
Hawthorne, NJ
Jeffer, Hopkinson & Vogel
Hackensack, NJ
Hawthorne, NJ
Paterson, NJ
Jeffer, Mangels, Butler & Marmaro LLP
Los Angeles, CA
San Francisco, CA
Jeffer, Peter A. ....Midland Park, NJ
Jeffer, Peter A., P.A. ....Midland Park, NJ
Jefferies, Alice Snow ....Chapin, SC
Jefferies, Charlotte S. ....Pittsburgh, PA
Jefferies, David E. ....Cincinnati, OH
Jefferies, Deborah Mayo ....Durham, NC
Jefferies, Edwin L., Jr. ....Westwood, NJ
Jefferies, Jack P. ....Palisades, NY
Jefferies, John J. ....West Bloomfield, MI
Jefferies, John Randall ....Phoenix, AZ
Jefferies, Kim ....Portland, OR
Jefferies, Michael S. ....St. Louis, MO
Jefferies, Renae ....Topeka, KS
Jefferies, Robert A., Jr. ....Carthage, MO
Jefferies, Scott M. ....Florence, AZ
Jefferies, T. Wade ....Austin, TX
Jefferies, Trevor R. ....Houston, TX
Jefferis, Nancy R. ....Myrtle Beach, SC
Jefferis, Paul B. ....Barnesville, OH
Jefferis, Robert F., Sr. ....Dayton, OH
Jefferis, Albert B. ....Morristown, NJ
Jefferis, Anna D. ....Baltimore, MD
Jeffers & Associates, Professional Corporation ....Fairfield, CT
Jeffers & Banack, Incorporated
Austin, TX
San Antonio, TX
Jeffers, Benjamin W. ....Detroit, MI
Jeffers, Dale F. ....Albany, NY
Jeffers, Daniel T. ....Independence, MO
Jeffers, Danielson, Sonn & Aylward, P.S.
Ephrata, WA
Moses Lake, WA
Wenatchee, WA
Jeffers, Darrell E. ....Albany, NY
Jeffers, Diane M. ....Boston, MA
Jeffers, F. Patrick ....Cohoes, NY
Jeffers, Fahari ....San Diego, CA
Jeffers, Frank E., III ....Wheaton, IL
Jeffers, Fulton P. ....Salisbury, MD
Jeffers, Fulton P., P.A. ....Salisbury, MD
Jeffers, Garfield R. ....Moses Lake, WA
Wenatchee, WA
Jeffers, Harold G. ....Oneida, TN
Jeffers, Hayward G., Jr. ....Baton Rouge, LA
Jeffers, Jack ....New York, NY
Jeffers, James D. ....San Jose, CA
Jeffers, James L. ....Miami, FL
Jeffers, Jerome L. ....Elkhart, IN
Jeffers, John R. ....Calumet City, IL
Jeffers, John W. ....Cleveland, OH
Jeffers, Judith D. ....Seattle, WA
Jeffers, Karen A. ....Fairfield, CT
Jeffers, Kevin ....New Albany, OH
Jeffers, Mark T. ....Overland Park, KS
Jeffers, Mary E. ....Denver, CO

Jeffers, Mary K. ....Brea, CA
Jeffers, Michael B. ....Irvine, CA
Jeffers, Michael D. ....Columbus, OH
Jeffers, Michael L. ....Baltimore, MD
Jeffers, Nicole B. ....Washington, DC
Jeffers, Robert M. ....Washington, DC
Jeffers, Ronald T. ....Houston, TX
Jeffers, Roy R. ....Dallas, TX
Jeffers, Shaff & Falk, LLP ....Irvine, CA
Newport Beach, CA
Jeffers, Steven P. ....Longmont, CO
Jeffers, Susannah Lee ....Beverly Hills, CA
Jeffers, Thomas J., Jr. ....Montrose, CA
Jeffers, Thomas J., Jr., Professional Corporation
Montrose, CA
Jeffers, Valarie M. ....Albany, NY
Jeffers, Veronica M. ....Los Angeles, CA
Jeffers, William A. ....Sunnyvale, CA
Jeffers, William A., Jr. ....San Antonio, TX
Jeffers Meyers, Sally ....Everett, WA
Jefferson, Andrew L., Jr. ....Houston, TX
Jefferson, Andrew McK. ....New Castle, DE
Jefferson, Bernard S. ....Inglewood, CA
Jefferson, Bradford L. ....Fort Pierce, FL
Jefferson, Brian Lee ....Portland, OR
Jefferson, Bruce A. ....Indianapolis, IN
Jefferson, Bryan K. ....New Orleans, LA
Jefferson, Carl S., III ....Chicago, IL
Jefferson, Cecelia Dianne ....Jacksonville, FL
Jefferson, Charles M. ....San Antonio, TX
Jefferson, Charmaine ....New York, NY
Jefferson, Christian G. ....Greenville, SC
Jefferson, D. Lawrence ....Surprise, AZ
Jefferson, Deadra L. ....Charleston, SC
Jefferson, Dwayne C. ....New Orleans, LA
Jefferson, Dwight E. ....Houston, TX
Jefferson, F. James ....Green Forest, AR
Jefferson, George W. ....Lexington, SC
Jefferson, Heather A. ....Plymouth, MI
Jefferson, Heather D. ....Wilmington, DE
Jefferson, James M., Jr. ....Fruita, CO
Jefferson, Jamila E. ....Washington, DC
Jefferson, Janice R. ....Elizabethtown, KY
Jefferson, Jeffrey D. ....Kenai, AK
Jefferson, Jerome S. ....Suffern, NY
Jefferson, John R. ....Austin, TX
Jefferson, John W. ....Sacramento, CA
Jefferson, Karyn D. ....New York, NY
Jefferson, Kathleen W. ....Canal Fulton, OH
Jefferson, Lamont A. ....San Antonio, TX
Jefferson Law Firm, The, PLC
McLean, VA
Jefferson Law Offices ....Surprise, AZ
Jefferson, Lisa G. ....York, SC
Jefferson, Marc T. ....Denver, CO
Jefferson, Mark E. ....Atlanta, GA
Jefferson & Mims ....Houston, TX
Jefferson, Mina Jones ....Cincinnati, OH
Jefferson, Richard G. ....Flemington, NJ
Jefferson, Richard P. ....Chestnut Hill, MA
Jefferson, Rufus O. ....Tallahassee, FL
Jefferson, Samuel L., Jr. ....Washington, DC
Jefferson, Scott M. ....Minneapolis, MN
Jefferson, Sherri L. ....Seattle, WA
Jefferson, Stephen A. ....Monroe, LA
Jefferson, Theressa ....Portland, OR
Jefferson, Thomas K. ....Huntsville, AL
Jefferson, Thomas S. ....Prospect Heights, IL
Jefferson, Thomasine ....Detroit, MI
Jefferson, Timothy ....Washington, DC
Jefferson, Timothy S. ....Champaign, IL
Jefferson, Touraine ....Dorchester, MA
Jefferson, Tricia G. ....Washington, DC
Jefferson, Wade H., IV ....Lexington, KY
Jefferson, Wallace B. ....San Antonio, TX
Jefferson, Walter, (P.C.) ....Houston, TX
Jefferson, William E. ....Elroy, WI
Jefferson, William J. ....New Orleans, LA
Jefferson, William J., III
Department Of Veterans Affairs,
Board of Veterans Appeals, GV
Jefferson-Moore, Ruby ....Madison, WI
Jefferson-Webb, Lettricea L. ....Lexington, KY
Jeffery, Carole K. ....Denver, CO
Jeffery, Donald C. ....Portland, OR
Jeffery, Donald D. ....Washington, DC
Jeffery, Donald Ethan ....Boston, MA
Jeffery, G. Randolph ....Monroe, GA
Jeffery Group, The, P.L.L.C. ....Seattle, WA
Jeffery, James R. ....Toledo, OH
Jeffery, Janine K. ....Los Angeles, CA
Jeffery, Jerry H. ....Maitland, FL
Jeffery, Kevin ....Portland, OR
Jeffery, Margaret T. ....Bar Harbor, ME
Jeffery, Mary ....Philadelphia, PA
Jeffery, Michael Ives ....Barrow, AK
Jeffery, Mona J. ....Orange, CA
Jeffery, Richard K., Jr. ....Peabody, MA
Jeffery, Robert J. ....North East, PA
Jeffery, Shann R. M. ....Denver, CO
Jeffery, Stephen G. ....St. Louis, MO
Jeffery, Teresa W. ....St. Louis, MO
Jeffery, William D. ....Flagstaff, AZ
Jeffery, William F., Jr. ....Boston, MA
Jeffery, William G. ....Seattle, WA
Jeffirs, Kent A. ....Crown Point, IN
Jefford, Christopher L. ....Boston, MA
Jefford, June ....Albuquerque, NM
Jeffords, Edward A. ....Austin, TX
Jeffords, Evander G. ....Florence, SC
Jeffords, George M. ....Jamaica, NY
Jeffords, James M. ....Washington, DC
Cuttingsville, VT
Jeffords, John M. ....Virginia Beach, VA
Jeffress, Christopher W. ....Denver, CO
Jeffress, Dorothy Ames ....Washington, DC
Jeffress, Stacy A. ....Lawrence, KS
Jeffress, Walton M., Jr. ....Fairfax, VA

Jeffress, William H., Jr. ... **Washington, DC**
Jeffrey, Adrienne ... **San Diego, CA**
Jeffrey, Alexander M., Jr. ... **New York, NY**
Jeffrey, Bernard ... Glen Cove, NY
Jeffrey, Brian A. ... **Evergreen, CO**
Jeffrey, Carl James ... Carlsbad, CA
Jeffrey, David Kenneth James
Washington, DC
Jeffrey, David L. ... Freeport, IL
Jeffrey, Deborah D.A. ... Holyoke, MA
Jeffrey, Deborah J. ... **Washington, DC**
Jeffrey, Donald E., III ... Richmond, VA
Jeffrey, Douglas C., III ... Vernon, TX
Jeffrey, Douglas J. ... **Miami, FL**
Jeffrey & Dreher, L.L.P. ... **San Diego, CA**
Jeffrey, Eric C. ... **Washington, DC**
Jeffrey, Gary A. ... **Oakland, CA**
Jeffrey, George B. ... Indianapolis, IN
Jeffrey, George M. ... San Francisco, CA
Jeffrey, Hahn, Hemmerling & Zimmerman, P.C. ... Gibbon, NE
Lincoln, NE
York, NE
Jeffrey & Heinemann ... San Francisco, CA
Jeffrey, James T., Jr. ... **Arlington, TX**
Jeffrey & Jeffrey ... Freeport, IL
Jeffrey, John D. ... East Grand Forks, MN
Jeffrey, John O. ... Bethesda, MD
Jeffrey, John W. ... **San Diego, CA**
Jeffrey, Lois E. ... **Orange, CA**
Jeffrey, M. Sheila ... **Ann Arbor, MI**
Jeffrey & Mack, P.C. ... **Evergreen, CO**
Jeffrey, Mark R. ... Savannah, GA
Jeffrey, Michael L. ... **Lincoln, NE**
York, NE
Jeffrey, Michelle L. ... **Cincinnati, OH**
Jeffrey, Pamela ... New York, NY
Jeffrey, Peter ... Fairfield, CT
Jeffrey, R. Asahel ... Groveland, CA
Jeffrey, Ray B. ... **Beaumont, TX**
Houston, TX
Jeffrey, Robert G. ... **Providence, RI**
Jeffrey, Robert Lloyd ... Lincoln, NE
Jeffrey, Robert N. ... Sheridan, AR
Jeffrey, Robert W. ... Stuart, FL
Jeffrey, Sheri ... **Los Angeles, CA**
Jeffrey, Terry D. ... **Chicago, IL**
Jeffrey, Thomas W. ... Miami, FL
Jeffrey, Timothy A. ... Dallas, TX
Jeffrey, Will ... **Albuquerque, NM**
Jeffrey & Worsham ... Vernon, TX
Jeffreys, Gary M. ... Deming, NM
Jeffreys, George P. ... Lowell, MA
Jeffreys, Herndon P., Jr. ... **Richmond, VA**
Jeffreys, Jo-Anne H. ... Hoboken, NJ
Jeffries Advocates Law Offices
Costa Mesa, CA
Jeffries, Anthony B. ... **Albuquerque, NM**
Jeffries, Bradford ... **San Francisco, CA**
Jeffries, Bryan L. ... **Columbus, OH**
Jeffries, C. Cole, Jr. ... **Brandon, FL**
Jeffries, Countess Pease ... **Costa Mesa, CA**
Jeffries, D. Wayne ... **Los Angeles, CA**
Jeffries, Dan F. ... Los Angeles, CA
Jeffries, Darrin C. ... **Phoenix, AZ**
Jeffries, David M. ... **Tampa, FL**
Jeffries, E. James H. ... Poway, CA
Jeffries, Eric Scott ... **Albuquerque, NM**
Jeffries, Gary A. ... Pittsburgh, PA
Jeffries, George J. ... Corona Del Mar, CA
Jeffries, H. Gary ... Pasadena, CA
Jeffries, Hakeem S. ... **New York, NY**
Jeffries, James D. ... Madison, WI
Jeffries, James D., Jr. ... **Mobile, AL**
Jeffries, James H., III ... Greensboro, NC
Jeffries, James H., IV ... **Greensboro, NC**
Jeffries, Jeff H. ... **Des Moines, IA**
Jeffries, John A. ... **Chicago, IL**
Jeffries, John C., Jr. ... Charlottesville, VA
Jeffries, John L. ... Laurel, MS
Jeffries, John T. ... **Charlotte, NC**
Jeffries, Johnston ... Albuquerque, NM
Jeffries, June M. ... Silver Spring, MD
Jeffries, Kathleen C. ... **Pasadena, CA**
Jeffries, Keith A. ... New Castle, KY
Jeffries, Kelly D. ... Portland, OR
Jeffries, Kube, Forrest & Monteleone Co., L.P.A. ... **Cleveland, OH**
Jeffries, Laurance T. ... Chicago, IL
Jeffries, Leah J. ... **Rapid City, SD**
Jeffries, Leslie Allen ... Norcross, GA
Jeffries, M. Hill ... **Atlanta, GA**
Jeffries, McChesney Hill ... Atlanta, GA
Jeffries, Michael ... **Fort Pierce, FL**
Jeffries, Neil A. ... **Palo Alto, CA**
Jeffries, Olson, Flom & Bullis, P.A.
Moorhead, MN
Bismarck, ND
Fargo, ND
Grand Forks, ND
Jamestown, ND
Wahpeton, ND
Jeffries, Richard N. ... **Moorhead, MN**
Fargo, ND
Jeffries, Richard P. ... **Omaha, NE**
Jeffries, Richard P. ... **Omaha, NE**
Jeffries, Rick L. ... Grain Valley, MO
Independence, MO
Jeffries, Rick L., P.C. ... Grain Valley, MO
Independence, MO
Jeffries, Robert B. ... Virginia Beach, VA
Jeffries, Ross E., Jr. ... Charlotte, NC
Jeffries & Rugge, P.C. ... **Albuquerque, NM**
Jeffries, Sarah ... **New York, NY**
Jeffries, Scott T. ... **Plymouth Meeting, PA**
Jeffries, Seymour B. ... Woodmere, NY
Jeffries, Stephen J. ... **Washington, DC**
Jeffries, Susan L. ... Alameda, CA
Jeffries, Walter S. ... Northfield, NJ
Jeffries, William L., Jr. ... Richmond, VA
Jeffries Jones, Jane ... **Charlotte, NC**
Jeffry, James P. ... **New York, NY**
Jeffry, Thomas E., Jr. ... **Los Angeles, CA**
Jeffry, William A. ... **Denver, CO**
Jeffs, A. Dean ... **Provo, UT**
Jeffs, David D. ... **Provo, UT**
Jeffs, James H. ... Midland, MI
Jeffs & Jeffs, P.C. ... **Provo, UT**
Jeffs, M. Dayle ... **Provo, UT**
Jeffs, Robert L. ... **Provo, UT**
Jeffs, William M. ... **Provo, UT**
Jeffus, Allen W. ... Chula Vista, CA
Jeffus, James T. ... Houston, TX
Jeffus, William V. ... Tyler, TX
Jefsen, John I. ... Thousand Oaks, CA
Jegasothy, S. Manoj ... **Pittsburgh, PA**
Jegen, David L. ... Boston, MA
Jegen, Lawrence A., III ... Indianapolis, IN
Jegen, William E. ... Glen Ellyn, IL
Jegen, William E., P.C. ... Glen Ellyn, IL
Jeges, Paul H. ... **Pittsburgh, PA**
Jeglikowski, Charles W.
Thousand Oaks, CA
Jeglin, Marvin H. ... Hemet, CA
Jehl, Cameron C. ... **Memphis, TN**
Jehl, John P. ... Haddonfield, NJ
Jehl, Laura E. ... **Dulles, VA**
Jehle, J. W., P.C. ... Southfield, MI
Jehle, John W. ... Southfield, MI
Jehle, Patricia A. ... New York, NY
Jehle, Philip F. ... Washington, DC
Jehring, Robert B. ... Naples, FL
Jehu, John P. ... Albany, NY
Jejna, Orest A. ... Phoenix, AZ
Jeka, Eugene J. ... Tulsa, OK
Jeka, James F. ... Fairlee, VT
Jeka, Mary R. ... United States Senate,
Senatorial Assistants, GV
Jekanowski, Harry J., Jr. ... Northampton, MA
Jekanowski, Leonard C. ... Northampton, MA
Jekanowski & O'Neil ... Northampton, MA
Jekel, Frederick J. ... **Charleston, SC**
Jekel & Howard, L.L.P. ... **Phoenix, AZ**
Scottsdale, AZ
Jekel, Louis G. ... **Scottsdale, AZ**
Jeknavorian, Garbis C. ... Fresno, CA
Jekofsky, Milton ... Washington, DC
Jelderks, John A. ... Portland, OR
Jelen, Scott ... Columbus, OH
Jelen, Susan Elizabeth ... San Francisco, CA
Jelencic, Sarah O. ... **Milwaukee, WI**
Jelenko, Martin M. ... Los Angeles, CA
Jelensky, Scott T. ... **Orange, CA**
Jelich, John W., III ... Chesapeake, VA
Jelin, Beth Maloney ... Encino, CA
Jelin, Frederick T. ... Encino, CA
Jelin, Sarah Jane ... Clark, NJ
Jelin, Sheldon C. ... Philadelphia, PA
Jelinch, Frank A. ... **Cupertino, CA**
Jelinch & Rendler, A Professional Corporation ... **Cupertino, CA**
San Jose, CA
Jelinek & Associates ... Berkeley, CA
Jelinek, Christopher P.
West Bloomfield, MI
Jelinek, Donald A. ... Berkeley, CA
Jelinek, Edward H. ... Omaha, NE
Jelinek, Frank R. ... **Arlington, TX**
Jelinek, Frank R., Inc. ... **Arlington, TX**
Jelinek, Gloria J. ... Troy, MI
Jelinek, Jerome E. ... Traverse City, MI
Jelinek, William ... New York, NY
Jelinske, Thad W. ... **Milwaukee, WI**
Jelinski, Dana L. ... **McLean, VA**
Jelkin, Elizabeth A. ... Westerville, OH
Jelkin, John L. ... Hildreth, NE
Jelks, Allen N., Jr. ... **Panama City, FL**
Jelks, Sandra A. ... **Baton Rouge, LA**
Jellema, Calvin P. ... **Atlanta, GA**
Jellen, Edward D. ... Oakland, CA
Jellen, Patricia W. ... Eastchester, NY
Jellenik, Stephen R. ... Smithtown, NY
Jelley, Philip M., (Inc.) ... **Oakland, CA**
Jelley, S. Robert ... **New Haven, CT**
Jellico, John P. ... Cocoa Beach, FL
Jelliff, Thomas B. ... Grand Forks, ND
Jelliffe, Charles R. ... **Harrisburg, IL**
Jelliffe, Ferrell, Morris, Doerge & Foster
Carmi, IL
Elizabethtown, IL
Golconda, IL
Harrisburg, IL
Marion, IL
McLeansboro, IL
Shawneetown, IL
Vienna, IL
Jelliffe, Martin R. ... **Jackson, MS**
Jellig, Russell W. ... Vista, CA
Jelline, Mitchell ... New York, NY
Jellinek, Charles B. ... **St. Louis, MO**
Jellinek, Clara G. ... Fairfax Station, VA
Jellinek, Miles A. ... **Philadelphia, PA**
Jellinger, Richard T. ... Anoka, MN
Jellinghaus, Norman K. ... **Waterbury, CT**
Jellins & Jellins ... Redwood City, CA
Jellins, Madison C. ... Redwood City, CA
Jellins, Nicholas P. ... Redwood City, CA
Jellison, Barry S. ... San Francisco, CA
Jellison, James M. ... **Phoenix, AZ**
Jellison, M. Dean ... Kalispell, MT
Jelly, George H. ... Bradenton, FL
Jelmini, Dean A. ... Playa Del Rey, CA
Jelnicky, Sandra A. ... Brentwood, NY
Jelovich, Taryn M. ... Carlsbad, CA
Jelovsek, Sandra B. ... Johnson City, TN
Jelsema, Jack R. ... Wyoming, MI
Jelsing, Larry A. ... Everett, WA
Jelsma, Franklin K. ... **Louisville, KY**
Jelsma, Phillip L. ... **San Diego, CA**
Jelte, M. Joy ... Salt Lake City, UT
Jemail, John M. ... Loveland, OH
Jemal, Alexander J., Jr. ... Mount Clemens, MI
Jemal, Joshua Michael ... Holtsville, NY
Jemela, Donald J. ... New Braunfels, TX
Jemison, Danny Gerald ... **Atlanta, GA**
Jemison, Maurice L. ... **Deerfield Beach, FL**
Jemison, Mays R. ... **Montgomery, AL**
Jemison & Mendelsohn, P.C.
Montgomery, AL
Jemison, Regina D. ... Detroit, MI
Jemison, Rex A. ... **Las Vegas, NV**
Jemison, Richard K. ... Brea, CA
Jemison, Steve ... **Cincinnati, OH**
Jemmott, William Elton
San Francisco, CA
Jen, Allynnore M. ... **Baltimore, MD**
Jen, Katherine F. ... **San Francisco, CA**
Jenab, Deena B. ... **Kansas City, MO**
Jenal, James Paul ... **Los Angeles, CA**
Jencks Law Group, The
San Luis Obispo, CA
Jencks, Michael R. ... San Luis Obispo, CA
Jendrek, John P. ... Baltimore, MD
Jendrek, Mark ... **Knoxville, TN**
Jendrek, Mark, P.C. ... **Knoxville, TN**
Jendron, Robert C., Jr. ... Columbia, SC
Jendryk, Chester F. J. ... Chicago, IL
Jendryk, James S. ... **Chicago, IL**
Jendrzejek, David P. ... **Minneapolis, MN**
Jendrzey, Carol E. ... **Houston, TX**
Jenei, Colin M. ... Doylestown, PA
Jenen, Paul R. ... Wheeling, IL
Jenerette, Noah H., Jr. ... **Jacksonville, FL**
Jenero, Kenneth A. ... **Chicago, IL**
Jenett, Bruce W. ... **Palo Alto, CA**
Jenevein, Robert Crofford ... Dallas, TX
Jeney, Carol A. ... Scotch Plains, NJ
Jeney, Robert J., Jr. ... Scotch Plains, NJ
Jenicek, Monica ... Anchorage, AK
Jenings, Byron T. ... Cincinnati, OH
Jenis, Richard ... New York, NY
Jenison, Craig A. ... Jenison, MI
Jenison, Robert J. ... Harrisburg, PA
Jenk & Goen ... Dyersville, IA
Jenk, Thomas H. ... Dyersville, IA
Jenke, Mary R. ... **Albuquerque, NM**
Jenke-Huber, Erika ... **Huntsville, AL**
Jenkel, John F. ... **Seattle, WA**
Jenkens & Gilchrist, A Professional Corporation ... **Los Angeles, CA**
Washington, DC
Austin, TX
Dallas, TX
Houston, TX
San Antonio, TX
Chicago, IL
Jenkin, Joan Alison ... Daly City, CA
Jenkins, A. Felton, Jr. ... Atlanta, GA
Jenkins, Alan R. ... **Atlanta, GA**
Jenkins, Alfred ... Los Angeles, CA
Jenkins, Amy Yager ... **Charleston, SC**
Jenkins, Angela L.
United States Postal Service,
Law Department, GV
Jenkins, Angela M. ... **Grand Rapids, MI**
Jenkins, Anita H. ... Midland, MI
Jenkins, Anthony D. ... **Kansas City, MO**
Jenkins, Arthur L., Jr. ... Norristown, PA
Jenkins, Aubrey C. ... **Knoxville, TN**
Jenkins & Awalt ... Towson, MD
Jenkins, B. Stewart ... Chattanooga, TN
Jenkins, Barbara S. ... Charlottesville, VA
Jenkins, Barry D. ... Arlington, TX
Jenkins, Bentley P. ... Vista, CA
Jenkins Block & Associates, P.C.
Baltimore, MD
Cambridge, MD
Hagerstown, MD
Richmond, VA
Jenkins & Brady ... **Bakersfield, CA**
Jenkins, Brenda S., (P.C.) ... Pearland, TX
Jenkins, Brian G. ... Richmond, VA
Jenkins, Brian R. ... **Wailuku, HI**
Jenkins, Bridget G. ... **Torrington, CT**
Jenkins, Bruce ... Columbus, OH
Jenkins, Bruce C. ... St. George, UT
Jenkins, Bruce S. ... Salt Lake City, UT
Jenkins, C. Fred ... Tennant, NJ
Jenkins, Caren ... **San Francisco, CA**
Jenkins, Carl A. ... Gaithersburg, MD
Jenkins, Carl E., (P.A.) ... Fort Lauderdale, FL
Jenkins, Carroll R. ... Troy, NY
Jenkins & Carter ... **Reno, NV**
Jenkins, Catherine S. ... Baltimore, MD
Jenkins, Cathy A. ... Wilmington, DE
Jenkins, Charles D. ... **San Francisco, CA**
Jenkins, Charles E., II ... Norfolk, VA
Jenkins, Charles G., Jr. ... Jasper, TN
Jenkins, Charles G., Sr. ... Jasper, TN
Jenkins, Charles L., Jr.
Department of Commerce,
Patent and Trademark Office, GV
Jenkins, Chastain & Smith, Law Firm of
Birmingham, AL
Jenkins, Chauntis T. ... **New Orleans, LA**
Jenkins, Cheryl L. ... Atlanta, GA
Jenkins, Christian ... Arlington, TX
Jenkins, Christian A. ... **Cincinnati, OH**
Jenkins, Christian, P.C. ... Arlington, TX
Jenkins, Christopher A. ... Austin, TX
Jenkins, Christopher R. ... **Lexington, KY**
Jenkins, Claire E. ... **Alexandria, VA**
Jenkins, Clarence G. ... Idaho Falls, ID
Jenkins, Clarence N., Jr. ... **Richmond, VA**
Jenkins, Claude W. ... De Witt, AR
Jenkins, Clay B. ... **Sheridan, WY**
Jenkins, Clay Lewis ... Waxahachie, TX
Jenkins & Clayman ... Haddon Heights, NJ
Jenkins, Corey H. ... Las Vegas, NV
Jenkins, Craig A. ... **Pittsburgh, PA**
Jenkins, Craig N. ... Tallmadge, OH
Jenkins, Cynthia S. ... Haddon Heights, NJ
Jenkins, Daniel J. ... Department of Commerce,
Patent and Trademark Office, GV
Jenkins, David ... **Boston, MA**
Jenkins, David A. ... **Wilmington, DE**
Jenkins, David A. ... Warren, NJ
Jenkins, David A. ... Burlington, VT
Jenkins, David C. ... **Pittsburgh, PA**
Jenkins, David L. ... **Des Moines, IA**
Jenkins, David L. ... Viroqua, WI
Jenkins, David M. ... **Chicago, IL**
Jenkins, David M., II ... Washington, DC
Jenkins, David R. ... **Fresno, CA**
Jenkins, David R. ... Littleton, CO
Jenkins, David S. T. ... Media, PA
Jenkins, David W. ... Chicago, IL
Jenkins & Deats, P.C. ... Austin, TX
Jenkins, Deborah A. ... **San Francisco, CA**
Jenkins, Deborah C. ... Dallas, TX
Jenkins, Debra Ann ... Valdosta, GA
Jenkins, Dee-Ann Kay ... Woodland Hills, CA
Jenkins, Dennis L. ... **Boston, MA**
Jenkins, Diane Hays ... **Dallas, TX**
Jenkins, Donald ... Lake Charles, LA
Jenkins, Donald M. ... Akron, OH
Jenkins, Donald W. ... Chicago, IL
Jenkins, Donn K. ... **Silver Spring, MD**
Jenkins, Donna Jo ... New Albany, IN
Jenkins, Dorna D. ... Atlanta, GA
Jenkins, Douglas C. ... Lisbon, OH
Jenkins, Douglas K. ... **Philadelphia, PA**
Jenkins, Dwight T. ... West Palm Beach, FL
Jenkins, E. Kenneth ... **Boston, MA**
Jenkins, E. Kenneth, III ... Boise, ID
Jenkins, Edgar J. ... Washington, DC
Jenkins, Edgar L. ... Jasper, GA
Jenkins, Edward J. ... Nashville, TN
Jenkins, Edward L. ... San Antonio, TX
Jenkins, Edwin L. ... Portland, OR
Jenkins, Elaine ... Charleston, SC
Jenkins, Elizabeth Ann ... Tampa, FL
Jenkins, Elizabeth C. ... **Dallas, TX**
Jenkins, Ellen D. ... **Chicago, IL**
Jenkins, Ellen M. ... Rochester, NY
Jenkins, Elmer ... Benton, IL
Jenkins, Emily P. ... **Tampa, FL**
Jenkins, Erika ... **New York, NY**
Jenkins, Ernest P. ... St. Petersburg, FL
Jenkins, Ernestine L. ... **New York, NY**
Jenkins, Eugene A., Jr. ... United States Senate,
Senatorial Assistants, GV
Jenkins, Eugene G. ... Goldsboro, NC
Kinston, NC
Jenkins, Evan H. ... Charleston, WV
Jenkins, Evan J. ... **Pittsburgh, PA**
Jenkins, Everett W., Jr. ... Richmond, CA
Jenkins, F. Gaither ... Winston-Salem, NC
Jenkins, Faber D., Jr. ... Sherwood, AR
Jenkins, Federico (IBA) ... **Miami, FL**
Jenkins Fenstermaker, PLLC
Ashland, KY
Charleston, WV
Huntington, WV
Jenkins, Frank E., III ... **Cartersville, GA**
Jenkins, Frank H., Jr. ... **Olathe, KS**
Jenkins, Frank P. ... La Plata, MD
Jenkins, Frank W. ... Ambler, PA
Jenkins, Franklin J. ... Goochland, VA
Jenkins, Gail C. ... **Beaumont, TX**
Jenkins, Gary E. ... Quincy, MA
Jenkins, Gayle L. ... **Los Angeles, CA**
Jenkins, George L. ... **Columbus, OH**
Jenkins, George L., Jr. ... Kinston, NC
Jenkins, George William, III ... Memphis, TN
Jenkins, Gerald L. ... **Chicago, IL**
Jenkins, Gerald R. ... Garfield, AR
Jenkins, Goodman & Neuman
San Francisco, CA
Jenkins, Gordon W. ... Idaho Falls, ID
Jenkins, Gordon W. ... Winston-Salem, NC
Jenkins, Gregory K. ... **Lexington, KY**
Jenkins, Gregory L. ... Troy, MI
Jenkins, Gregory P. ... Taylor, MI
Jenkins, Grove & Martin ... **Beaumont, TX**
Jenkins, Harold B. ... Department of Education,
Office of the General Counsel, GV
Jenkins, Harry L., III ... Jenkintown, PA
Jenkins, Hayes A. ... Akron, OH
Jenkins, Helen Bishop ... Houston, TX
Jenkins, Herbert, Jr. ... Birmingham, AL
Jenkins, Homer B. ... Sells, AZ
Jenkins, Howard ... Knoxville, TN
Jenkins, Hugh C. ... Butler, MO
Jenkins, Hyde R., II ... Natchez, MS
Jenkins, Irvin K. ... Arlington, VA
Jenkins, J. Calvin, Jr. ... Towson, MD
Jenkins, J. Craig ... **Bakersfield, CA**
Jenkins, J. James, Jr. ... **Nashville, TN**
Jenkins, J. Kathryn ... **Carmel, IN**
Jenkins, J. Kevin ... Wailuku, HI
Jenkins, James A. ... Cleveland, OH
Jenkins, James C. ... **Logan, UT**
Jenkins, James D. ... Mesa, AZ
Jenkins, James D. ... Albia, IA
Jenkins, James J. ... **Tuscaloosa, AL**
Jenkins, James K. ... **Atlanta, GA**
Jenkins, James L. ... Richmond, VA
Jenkins, James M. ... Kansas City, MO
Jenkins, James M. ... **Rochester, NY**
Jenkins, James Patrick ... Tulsa, OK
Jenkins, James R. ... Fairhope, AL

Jenkins, James R. ....Little Rock, AR
Jenkins, James R. ....Midland, MI
Jenkins, James R. ....Waxahachie, TX
Jenkins, James T. ....La Mirada, CA
Jenkins, Janet ....Sandpoint, ID
Jenkins, Janet A. ....La Crosse, WI
Jenkins, Janice Anita ....Berkeley, CA
Jenkins, Janice K. ....Atlanta, GA
Jenkins, Jay L. ....Santa Monica, CA
Jenkins, Jay T. ....Eagan, MN
Jenkins, Jeffrey E. ....Haddon Heights, NJ
Jenkins & Jenkins ....Columbia, SC
Jenkins & Jenkins ....Jasper, TN
Jenkins & Jenkins Attorneys, PLLC
Knoxville, TN
Jenkins & Jenkins, P.A. ....La Plata, MD
Jenkins & Jenkins, P.C. ....Jenkintown, PA
Jenkins & Jenkins, P.C. ....Waxahachie, TX
Jenkins, Jerri L. ....Aurora, CO
Jenkins, Jerry R. ....Indianapolis, IN
Jenkins, Jimmie F. ....Sugar Land, TX
Jenkins, Joan F. ....Houston, TX
Jenkins, Joanne Martin ....Memphis, TN
Jenkins, Joanne Rumsey ....Philadelphia, PA
Jenkins, Joel S., Jr. ....Fayetteville, NC
Jenkins, John A. ....Columbus, OH
Jenkins, John B. ....Danville, IL
Jenkins, John C. ....Indianapolis, IN
Jenkins, John E. ....New York, NY
Jenkins, John E., Jr. ....Huntington, WV
Jenkins, John J. ....Cleveland, OH
Jenkins, John L. ....Philadelphia, PA
Jenkins, John N. ....Brandon, FL
Jenkins, John R., III ....Dallas, TX
Jenkins, John R., (P.A.) ....Tallahassee, FL
Jenkins, John S. ....Washington, DC
Jenkins, John Smith, Jr.
Department of the Navy,
Office of the Judge Advocate General, GV
Jenkins, John Stephen ....Athens, GA
Jenkins, John Stephen ....Elberton, GA
Jenkins, John T. ....Armonk, NY
Jenkins, Jon K. ....Mason, MI
Jenkins, Jon M. ....San Luis Obispo, CA
Jenkins, Jon Mark ....Carlstadt, NJ
New York, NY
Jenkins, Jonathan M. ....Los Angeles, CA
Jenkins, Joryn ....Tampa, FL
Jenkins, Joseph M, Jr. ....Greenville, SC
Jenkins, Joseph R. ....Shrewsbury, MA
Jenkins, Joseph S. ....Los Angeles, CA
Jenkins, Joyce L. ....Denver, CO
Jenkins, Judy Parker ....Washington, DC
Jenkins, Julie A. ....Boston, MA
Jenkins, Julie L. ....Birmingham, AL
Jenkins & Kaiser, P.A. ....St. Petersburg, FL
Jenkins, Katherine J. ....Fairbanks, AK
Jenkins, Kathryn A. ....Cheyenne, WY
Jenkins, Kay Cargill ....El Paso, TX
Jenkins & Keating ....Grosse Pointe Farms, MI
Jenkins, Kelly A. ....Helena, MT
Jenkins, Ken ....Burleson, TX
Jenkins, Kevin G. ....Ringwood, NJ
Jenkins, Kevin P. ....Department of Justice,
Tax Division, GV
Jenkins, Kimberly ....Kansas City, MO
Jenkins, Kimberly Smith ....Greenville, NC
Jenkins, Kimble L. ....Memphis, TN
Jenkins, Kirk Christopher
San Francisco, CA
Jenkins & Kling, P.C. ....St. Louis, MO
Jenkins, Knox V., Jr. ....Smithfield, NC
Jenkins, Kristin Marie ....Fort Worth, TX
Jenkins, Larry Stuart ....Salt Lake City, UT
Jenkins Law Firm ....Helena, MT
Jenkins Law Firm ....Beaufort, SC
Hilton Head Island, SC
Jenkins Law Office ....Sheridan, WY
Jenkins, Leroy T., Jr. ....Washington, DC
Jenkins, Lewis A. ....Albany, NY
Jenkins, Lincoln C., III ....Columbia, SC
Jenkins, Linda Ann ....North Conway, NH
Jenkins, Linda F. ....Dallas, TX
Jenkins, Lisa Gillespie ....Plainsboro, NJ
Jenkins, Lisa L. ....Philadelphia, MS
Jenkins, Lon A. ....Salt Lake City, UT
Jenkins, Lori A. ....Salem, OR
Jenkins, Lori L. ....McLean, VA
Jenkins, Louis P. ....La Plata, MD
Jenkins, Louis P., Jr. ....La Plata, MD
Jenkins, Lucy B. ....Salt Lake City, UT
Jenkins, M. Dean ....Ocean City, MD
Jenkins, M. James ....Pensacola, FL
Jenkins, M. Norris ....Nashville, TN
Jenkins, Malcolm W. ....Springfield, MA
Jenkins, Manotti Lemorris
Indianapolis, IN
Jenkins, Marc A. ....New York, NY
Jenkins, Mark L. ....Waynesville, NC
Jenkins, Marten R. ....Pittsburgh, PA
Jenkins, Martha ....Kansas City, MO
Jenkins, Martin R. ....Manchester, NH
Jenkins, Mary Ann ....Dallas, TX
Jenkins, Mary Barnes ....New York, NY
Jenkins, Mary Kathleen ....Columbus, OH
Jenkins, Marylee ....New York, NY
Jenkins, Matthew Dimmock
Richmond, VA
Jenkins, Matthew R. ....Dayton, OH
Jenkins, Maurice G. ....Detroit, MI
Jenkins, Max ....Radford, VA
Jenkins, Max B. ....Department of the Navy,
Office of the Judge Advocate General, GV
Jenkins, Melanie A. ....New York, NY
Jenkins, Melvin L. ....Kansas City, MO
Jenkins, Merle R. ....Grosse Pointe Farms, MI
Jenkins, Merrill E. ....Los Angeles, CA
Jenkins, Michael ....Los Angeles, CA
Jenkins, Michael ....Rockford, IL
Jenkins, Michael A. ....Garden Grove, CA
Jenkins, Michael D. ....Issaquah, WA
Jenkins, Michael G. ....Portland, OR
Jenkins, Michele A. ....Chicago, IL
Jenkins, M. James, P.A. ....Pensacola, FL
Jenkins & Mulligan ....San Francisco, CA
Jenkins, Myron L. ....Los Angeles, CA
Jenkins, N. Baxter ....Mercer Island, WA
Jenkins, N. Donald, Jr., (P.A.) ....Alma, AR
Jenkins, Nancy L. ....Houston, TX
Jenkins, Nathan M. ....Reno, NV
Jenkins & Nelson, P.C. ....Atlanta, GA
Calhoun, GA
Canton, GA
Cartersville, GA
Cedartown, GA
Dallas, GA
Marietta, GA
Rome, GA
Jenkins, Norman Alexander, III
New York, NY
Jenkins, Olivia H. ....Montgomery, AL
Jenkins, Ondraus ....Los Angeles, CA
Jenkins & O'Neil ....Lake Elsinore, CA
Jenkins & Parron ....Arlington, TX
Jenkins, Patricia H. ....Monterey Park, CA
Jenkins, Patricia H. ....Media, PA
Jenkins, Patricia Harris ....Wilmington, DE
Jenkins, Patrick ....Charlotte, NC
Jenkins, Paul F. ....Cherry Hill, NJ
Jenkins, Paul R. ....Pittsburgh, PA
Jenkins, Peter Taber ....Placitas, NM
Jenkins Pisacano Robinson & Bailey
Lexington, KY
Jenkins, R. Lee ....Memphis, TN
Jenkins, R. Scott ....New Orleans, LA
Jenkins, R. Scott, (P.C.) ....Pasadena, CA
Jenkins, R. Stuart ....Media, PA
Jenkins, R. William ....Gallipolis, OH
Jenkins, R. Willson ....Florence, AL
Jenkins, Ralph C. ....Canton, GA
Jenkins, Ray ....Baltimore, MD
Jenkins, Ray H. ....Knoxville, TN
Jenkins, Ray Hal ....Estill Springs, TN
Jenkins, Ray L. ....Knoxville, TN
Jenkins, Raymond S. ....Harlingen, TX
Jenkins, Rebecca ....Lake Worth, FL
Jenkins, Rhonda K. ....St. Louis, MO
Jenkins, Richard C. ....Dallas, TX
Jenkins, Richard E. ....Lake Elsinore, CA
Jenkins, Richard E. ....Durham, NC
Jenkins, Richard G. ....San Antonio, TX
Jenkins, Richard S. ....Johnston, IA
Jenkins, Richard W. ....Hermitage, TN
Jenkins, Ricky L. ....Sparta, TN
Jenkins, Rivers T., III ....Charleston, SC
Jenkins, Rivers T., Jr. ....Charleston, SC
Jenkins, Robert ....Alexandria, VA
Jenkins, Robert A. ....Peachtree City, GA
Jenkins, Robert A. ....Frankfort, KY
Jenkins, Robert C. ....Long Beach, CA
Jenkins, Robert C. ....Sycamore, IL
Jenkins, Robert C. ....Ahoskie, NC
Rocky Mount, NC
Jenkins, Robert C. ....Jay, OK
Jenkins, Robert C. ....Stevens Point, WI
Jenkins, Robert D. ....Dalton, GA
Jenkins, Robert D., Jr. ....Houston, TX
Jenkins, Robert Dewey ....Gastonia, NC
Jenkins, Robert E., Jr. ....Bastrop, TX
Jenkins, Robert J. ....Chicago, IL
Jenkins, Robert J. ....Livonia, MI
Jenkins, Robert K., Jr. ....Washington, DC
Jenkins, Robert L. ....Dublin, GA
Savannah, GA
Jenkins, Robert M., III ....Washington, DC
Jenkins, Robert Max ....Radford, VA
Jenkins, Robert N., Sr. ....Greenville, SC
Jenkins, Robert O. ....Raleigh, NC
Jenkins, Robert R. ....Baltimore, MD
Cambridge, MD
Jenkins, Robert W. ....Gatlinburg, TN
Jenkins, Rodman ....Reston, VA
Jenkins, Ronald A. ....Arvada, CO
Jenkins, Ronald E. ....St. Louis, MO
Jenkins, Ronald W. ....Johnson City, TN
Jenkins, Russell I. ....Uniontown, PA
Jenkins, Sabrina W. ....Department of Justice,
Civil Rights Division, GV
Jenkins, Sam L., Jr. ....Shreveport, LA
Jenkins, Sam L., Jr., A.P.L.C.
Shreveport, LA
Jenkins, Sandra L. ....Chicago, IL
Jenkins, Sarah Nancy ....Media, PA
Jenkins, Scott H. ....Austin, TX
Jenkins, Scott J. ....Trenton, NJ
Jenkins, Scott R. ....Salt Lake City, UT
Jenkins, Sherry Lynn ....Overland Park, KS
Jenkins, Siergiej & Smith ....Ambler, PA
Jenkins, Sonja A. ....Tupelo, MS
Jenkins, Stephen ....New York, NY
Jenkins, Stephen A. ....Kansas City, MO
Jenkins, Stephen E. ....Encino, CA
Jenkins, Stephen E. ....Wilmington, DE
Jenkins, Stephen L. ....Atlanta, GA
Marietta, GA
Jenkins, Stephen L. ....Marion, OH
Jenkins, Steve ....Atlanta, GA
Jenkins, Steven R. ....Dallas, TX
Jenkins, Stewart D. ....San Luis Obispo, CA
Jenkins & Stewart, P.L. ....Tampa, FL
Jenkins & Stittleburg ....La Farge, WI
Viroqua, WI
Jenkins, Sue Ebenhoeh ....Lansing, MI
Jenkins, Susan B. ....Raleigh, NC
Jenkins, Susan M. ....Washington, DC
Jenkins, Susan Raleigh ....Washington, DC
Jenkins, T. Brent ....Ormond Beach, FL
Jenkins, T. Perry ....Tarboro, NC
Jenkins, Theresa R. ....Montgomery, AL
Jenkins, Theresa Y. ....Washington, DC
Jenkins, Thomas A. ....San Francisco, CA
Jenkins, Thomas H., III ....Washington, DC
Jenkins, Thomas J. ....Washington, DC
Jenkins, Thomas J. ....Omaha, NE
Jenkins, Thomas J. ....Franklinville, NJ
Woodbury, NJ
Jenkins, Thomas K. ....Marion, OH
Jenkins, Thomas M. ....San Francisco, CA
Jenkins, Thomas M. ....Chicago, IL
Jenkins, Thomas R.
Fort Walton Beach, FL
Panama City, FL
Pensacola, FL
Jenkins, Thomas W. ....Chicago, IL
Jenkins, Timothy W. ....Washington, DC
Jenkins, Vicki L. ....Columbus, OH
Jenkins, Vonn J. ....Reno, NV
Jenkins, W. Anthony ....Detroit, MI
Jenkins, W. Lewis, Jr. ....Dyersburg, TN
Jenkins, W. Owen ....Essex Junction, VT
Jenkins, W. Owen, P.C. ....Burlington, VT
Essex Junction, VT
Jenkins, Wadyce F. ....Statesboro, GA
Jenkins, Wallace A., Jr. ....Charlotte, NC
Jenkins, Walter Blaine, II
Oklahoma City, OK
Jenkins, Walter S. ....Philadelphia, PA
Jenkins, Wanda L. ....Fayetteville, NC
Jenkins, Warwick H. ....Waxahachie, TX
Jenkins & Watkins, P.C. ....Dallas, TX
Jenkins, Wayne A. ....Columbus, OH
Jenkins, William A. ....Sacramento, CA
Jenkins, William C.
Merit Systems Protection Board,
Washington, D.C. Regional Office, GV
Jenkins, William D. ....Fort Myers, FL
Jenkins, William G., Jr.
Hilton Head Island, SC
Jenkins, William J. ....Pasadena, CA
Jenkins, William N. ....Jacksonville, FL
Jenkins, William P. ....Ontario, CA
Jenkins, William R. ....Snow Hill, NC
Jenkins, William R., & Associates
Atlanta, GA
Jenkins, William R., Jr. ....Fort Worth, TX
Jenkins, William Scott ....Phoenix, AZ
Jenkins & Wilson, P.A. ....Durham, NC
Research Triangle Park, NC
Jenkins, Wm. R. ....Owensboro, KY
Jenkins-Chapman, Kimberly
Department of Energy,
Office of Hearings and Appeals, GV
Jenkins Hadden, Julie A. ....Boston, MA
Jenkins-Jones, Meldon D. ....Newark, NJ
Jenkins-Jones, Meldon D., P.C. ....Newark, NJ
Jenkinson, Daryl W. ....Millbrae, CA
Jenkinson, Gerald T. ....Woodland Hills, CA
Jenkinson, Gordon B. ....Kingstree, SC
Jenkinson & Jenkinson, P.A.
Kingstree, SC
Jenkinson, Mark ....Martinsburg, WV
Jenkinson, Michèle R. ....New York, NY
Jenkinson, W. E., III ....Kingstree, SC
Jenko, Christopher W. ....Atlanta, GA
Jenko, Jerome J. ....Minneapolis, MN
Jenks, Barton R. ....Sacramento, CA
Jenks, Betsy Deets ....Norfolk, VA
Jenks, Carl M. ....Cleveland, OH
Jenks, Daniel Ashley ....New York, NY
Jenks, David S. ....Washington, DC
Jenks, Debra Anne ....Jupiter, FL
Jenks, Edward P. ....Mineola, NY
Jenks, Ernest M. ....Portland, OR
Jenks, Glenn B. ....Scottsdale, AZ
Jenks, James K., III ....Lyons, IL
Jenks, John F. ....Missoula, MT
Jenks, Katherine Bryan ....Cleveland, OH
Jenks, M. Todd ....San Francisco, CA
Jenks, Michael R., (P.A.) ....Miami, FL
Jenks, Phillip A. ....Boston, MA
Jenks, Richard B. ....Southfield, MI
Jenks, Richard S. ....Baraboo, WI
Jenks, Surdyk & Cowdrey Co., L.P.A.
Dayton, OH
Lebanon, OH
Troy, OH
Jenks, Terry James ....Oklahoma City, OK
Jenks, Thad K. ....Houston, TX
Jenks, Thomas E. ....Dayton, OH
Jenks, Thomas M. ....Jacksonville, FL
Jenks, Tracy McGee ....Albuquerque, NM
Jenks, William J. ....Toledo, OH
Jennaro, William A. ....Milwaukee, WI
Jenne, Kenneth C., II ....Fort Lauderdale, FL
Jenne, Kirk ....Lancaster, PA
Jenne, Lee W. ....Hollywood, FL
Jenne, Michael E. ....Cleveland, TN
Jenne, Roger E. ....Cleveland, TN
Jenne, Scott & Jenne ....Athens, TN
Benton, TN
Cleveland, TN
Decatur, TN
Jennemann, Karen S. ....Orlando, FL
Jenner & Auxier ....Madison, IN
Jenner & Block ....Washington, DC
Chicago, IL
Lake Forest, IL
Jenner, Fred T. ....Oakland, CA
Jenner, J. Kirkham ....Grants Pass, OR
Jenner, James R. ....Berkeley, CA
Jenner, Jesse J. ....New York, NY
Jenner, Kenneth W. ....Oakland, CA
Jenner, Nancy A. ....Visalia, CA
Jenner, Pamela Creel ....Biloxi, MS
Jenner, Richard E. ....Chicago, IL
Jenner, Robert K. ....Washington, DC
Rockville, MD
Jenner, William Edward ....Madison, IN
Jennerich, Robert W. ....Rutherford, NJ
Jennerjahn, Mary Louise ....New York, NY
Jennes, Ernest W. ....Annapolis, MD
Jenness, Christine Ann ....Walpole, MA
Jenness, Evan A. ....Marina Del Rey, CA
Jenness, Janet S. ....Richmond, VA
Jenness, John S., Jr. ....South Paris, ME
Jenness, Julia L. ....Sacramento, CA
Jenness, Mark J. ....Reno, NV
Jenness, William D., III ....Lansing, MI
Jennett, Bruce D. ....Sacramento, CA
Jennett, David P. ....Storm Lake, IA
Jennett, Gilbert C. ....Houston, TX
Jennett, Laura V. ....Houston, TX
Jennett, William D. ....Los Angeles, CA
Jennette, Larry F., Jr. ....Atlanta, GA
Jennette, N. Stevenson, III
Grand Rapids, MI
Jennette, Scott R. ....Rochester, NY
Jennetten, Peter R. ....Peoria, IL
Jennetten, Robert H. ....Peoria, IL
Jennewein, Allison Sanford ....Tampa, FL
Jennewein, Jack A. ....Cincinnati, OH
Jennewein, Jonathan P. ....Tampa, FL
Jenney, Francis E. ....Waltham, MA
Jenney, Frederick E. ....Washington, DC
Jenney, John B., Jr. ....Dedham, MA
Jenney, Paul J. ....Arlington, MA
Jenney, Sandra L. ....Flagstaff, AZ
Jenney, W. F. ....Denison, TX
Jenni, Michelle C. ....Sacramento, CA
Jennings, Adrienne T. ....Santa Ana, CA
Jennings, Alfred J., Jr. ....Bridgeport, CT
Jennings, Alston ....Little Rock, AR
Jennings, Alston, Jr. ....Little Rock, AR
Jennings, Amy Remington ....Oak Brook, IL
Jennings, Andrew C. ....Seattle, WA
Jennings, Anita L. ....Vestal, NY
Jennings, Ann M. ....Torrance, CA
Jennings, Archie
Charlotte Amalie, St. Thomas, VI
Jennings, Archie, P.C.
Charlotte Amalie, St. Thomas, VI
Jennings, Barnard F. ....Fairfax, VA
Jennings, Bill F. ....Magnolia, AR
Jennings, Brian A. ....Kansas City, MO
Jennings, Bryan R. ....Adel, IA
Jennings, C. Alston, Jr. ....Little Rock, AR
Jennings, Carol J.
Federal Trade Commission,
Bureau of Consumer Protection, GV
Jennings, Cary L. ....Fort Worth, TX
Jennings, Charles E. ....Louisville, KY
Jennings, Charles H. ....Lodi, NY
Jennings, Charles T. ....Indianapolis, IN
Jennings, Charles W. ....West Branch, MI
Jennings, Charles W. ....Union, NJ
Jennings, Christopher W.
New Orleans, LA
Jennings, Clark Richard ....Lakeland, FL
Jennings, Colin R. ....Cleveland, OH
Jennings, Craig P. ....St. Joseph, MI
Jennings, Curtis A. ....Phoenix, AZ
Jennings, Daniel L.
Consumer Product Safety Commission,
Office of the General Counsel, GV
Jennings, Daniel M. ....Marietta, GA
Jennings, David ....Seattle, WA
Jennings, David B. ....St. Louis, MO
Jennings, David C. ....Knoxville, TN
Jennings, David G. ....Columbus, OH
Jennings, David G. ....Charleston, SC
Jennings, David R. ....Houston, TX
Jennings, David S. ....Las Vegas, NV
Reno, NV
Jennings, David V., Jr. ....Milwaukee, WI
Jennings, Dawn L. ....Harrisburg, PA
Jennings, Dean S. ....St. Joseph, MI
Jennings, Dean T. ....Council Bluffs, IA
Jennings, Deborah E. ....Washington, DC
Baltimore, MD
Jennings, Deborah O. ....Midlothian, VA
Jennings, Debra L. ....Omaha, NE
Jennings, Debra V. ....Houston, TX
Jennings, Dennis W. ....Kansas City, MO
Jennings, DeWan & Anderson, P.A.
North Branch, MN
Jennings, Diane I. ....Chicago, IL
Jennings, Donald G., (P.C.) ....Manistee, MI
Jennings, Donna M. ....Woodbridge, NJ
Jennings, Donnell G. ....Columbia, SC
Jennings, Douglas F. ....East Hartford, CT
Augusta, ME
Jennings, Douglas, Jr. ....Bennettsville, SC
Jennings & Drakulich ....San Diego, CA
Jennings, E. Judson ....Newark, NJ
Jennings, Edw. L. ....Nashville, TN
Jennings, Edward ....Taylorsville, NC
Winston-Salem, NC
Jennings, Edward J. ....Fort Lauderdale, FL
Jennings, Eileen K. ....Mount Pleasant, MI
Jennings, E. L., Jr. ....Irvine, CA
Jennings and Ellias, P.C. ....West Branch, MI
Jennings, Floyd C., Jr. ....Lynchburg, VA
Jennings, Floyd L. ....Houston, TX
Jennings, Flynn M. ....New Orleans, LA
Jennings, G. Penfield ....Dunedin, FL
Jennings, G. Penfield, P.A. ....Dunedin, FL
Jennings, Gena M. ....De Witt, AR
Jennings, George J., Jr. ....Tulia, TX
Jennings, George M. ....New Bern, NC
Jennings, George M. ....Okmulgee, OK
Jennings, George M. ....Salem, OR
Jennings, Gerald J. ....Albany, NY

Jennings, Gerald M., Jr. ..... Fallbrook, CA
Jennings, Glenn A., Jr ..... Marysville, CA
Jennings, Gordon B. ..... San Diego, CA
Jennings, Graham T. ..... Amelia, VA
Midlothian, VA
Jennings and Grant, P.C. ..... Manistee, MI
Jennings, Gray ..... Houston, TX
Jennings, Gregory A. ..... Henderson, KY
Jennings, Gregory A. ..... Chetek, WI
Jennings, Grover C. ..... Marion, VA
Jennings, Guy P. ..... Department of Justice,
Tax Division, GV
Jennings, Hanna B. ..... Cleveland, OH
Jennings, Harold M. ..... Bloomington, IL
Jennings & Harris ..... Bennettsville, SC
Jennings, Harry J. ..... Merrillville, IN
Jennings, Haug & Cunningham, L.L.P.
Phoenix, AZ
Jennings, J. Douglass, Jr. ..... San Diego, CA
Jennings, J. Robert ..... Alexandria, KY
Jennings, Jacknewitz & Schrader
Belleville, IL
Jennings, Jackson Y. ..... Philadelphia, PA
Jennings, Jacob H. ..... Bishopville, SC
Jennings, Jacquelynne M.
San Francisco, CA
Jennings, James A. ..... Philadelphia, PA
Jennings, James A., III
Oklahoma City, OK
Jennings, James Albert ..... Dallas, TX
Jennings, James C. ..... Washington, DC
Jennings, James J. ..... Chicago, IL
Jennings, James J. ..... Uniondale, NY
Jennings, James L. ..... Coal City, IN
Jennings, James R. ..... Gresham, OR
Jennings, James T. ..... Roswell, NM
Jennings, James W. ..... Philadelphia, PA
Jennings, James W., Jr. ..... Roanoke, VA
Jennings, Jane M. ..... Lawrenceburg, TN
Jennings, Jay T. ..... Salem, OR
Jennings, Jeffrey D. ..... Oxnard, CA
Jennings and Jennings ..... Amelia, VA
Midlothian, VA
Jennings, Jennings & Macdonald, P.C.
West Branch, MI
Jennings & Jennings, P.A. ..... Bishopville, SC
Jennings, Joan E. ..... Leesburg, VA
Jennings, John C. ..... Scottsdale, AZ
Jennings, John E. ..... Little Rock, AR
Jennings, John E. ..... Norristown, PA
Jennings, John F. ..... Short Hills, NJ
Jennings, John M. ..... Chicago, IL
Jennings, John M. ..... St. Louis, MO
Jennings, John Mark ..... Santa Ana, CA
Jennings, John P., Jr. ..... Kansas City, MO
Jennings, John W., Jr. ..... Gadsden, AL
Jennings, Jonathan S. ..... Chicago, IL
Jennings, Jonathan S. ..... Florence, KY
Jennings & Jones, L.C. ..... Roswell, NM
Jennings, Joseph F. ..... Newport Beach, CA
Jennings, Joseph F. ..... Miami, FL
Jennings, K. Michael ..... Tacoma, WA
Jennings, Karen ..... Palo Alto, CA
Jennings, Karen L. ..... Anchorage, AK
Jennings, Katherine Y. ..... New York, NY
Jennings, Kathleen L. ..... Washington, DC
Jennings, Kathleen M. ..... Wilmington, DE
Jennings, Kelly S. ..... Washington, DC
Jennings, Kim D. ..... Stockton, CA
Jennings, Kyle L. ..... Houston, TX
Jennings, L. Douglas ..... Columbus, OH
Jennings, Larry M. ..... Minneapolis, MN
Jennings, Larry M., P.A. ..... Minneapolis, MN
Jennings, Larry R. ..... Harrisburg, AR
Jennings, Laura S. ..... Department of Defense,
Defense Legal Services Agency, GV
Jennings, Lauren ..... Boston, MA
Jennings, Lee T. ..... Chicago, IL
Jennings, Leo J. ..... Washington, DC
Jennings, Linda D. ..... Richmond, VA
Jennings, Linda J. ..... Toledo, OH
Jennings, Luke David ..... Salem, VA
Jennings, M. Charles ..... Dallas, TX
Jennings, Mana L. ..... Denver, CO
Jennings, Marc J. ..... Santa Ana, CA
Jennings, Margaret A. ..... San Antonio, TX
Jennings, Marianne M. ..... Tempe, AZ
Jennings, Mark ..... North Branch, MN
Jennings, Mark B. ..... Tulsa, OK
Jennings, Mark C. ..... Duluth, MN
Jennings, Mark J. ..... Chicago, IL
Jennings, Mark S. ..... Treasury Department,
Internal Revenue Service, GV
Jennings, Mark Samuel ..... Honesdale, PA
Jennings, Martha ..... Washington, DC
Jennings, Martin J. ..... Fanwood, NJ
Jennings, Martin J., Jr. ..... West Trenton, NJ
Jennings, Mary E. ..... Guilderland, NY
Jennings, Mary L.
Merit Systems Protection Board,
Office of the General Counsel, GV
Jennings, Maureen Blackburn
New Orleans, LA
Jennings, Max H. ..... Greenville, TX
Jennings, Michael ..... Lake Success, NY
Jennings, Michael A. ..... Jacksonville, FL
Jennings, Michael B. ..... New York, NY
Jennings, Michael L. ..... Baltimore, MD
Jennings, Michael O. ..... Springfield, MA
Jennings, Michael S. ..... Chattanooga, TN
Jennings, Ned R. ..... Great Falls, MT
Jennings, Neill A., Jr. ..... Greensboro, NC
Jennings, Neill A., Jr., P.A. ..... Greensboro, NC
Jennings, Nelle P. ..... New York, NY
Jennings, Nichole Marie ..... Detroit, MI
Jennings, Norma J. ..... New York, NY
Jennings, Novick, Smalley & Davis, P.C.
Bloomington, IL
Peoria, IL
Jennings, Patricia A. ..... Huntington, WV
Jennings, Patrick J. ..... Chicago, IL
Jennings, Patrick J. ..... Hackensack, NJ
River Edge, NJ
Jennings, Paul E. ..... Nashville, TN
Jennings, Paul G. ..... Nashville, TN
Jennings, Paul R. ..... Minneapolis, MN
Jennings, R. Craig ..... Falls Church, VA
Jennings, R. Jan ..... Nashville, TN
Jennings, R. Keith ..... Lawton, OK
Jennings & Ramer ..... Nashville, TN
Jennings, Reachel A. ..... Kansas City, MO
Jennings, Regina Pena ..... Huntsville, AL
Jennings, Rhonda R. ..... Charleston, SC
Jennings, Richard A. ..... Lubbock, TX
Jennings, Richard C. ..... Denver, CO
Jennings, Richard C. E. ..... Savannah, GA
Jennings, Robert B. ..... Gainesville, FL
Jennings, Robert B., Jr. ..... Baton Rouge, LA
Jennings, Robert D. ..... Bishopville, SC
Jennings, Robert L. ..... Fort Lauderdale, FL
Jennings, Robert L. ..... Belleville, IL
Jennings, Robert L., Jr. ..... Johnstown, PA
Pittsburgh, PA
Jennings, Robert R., Jr. ..... Miami, FL
Jennings, Robert W., Jr. ..... Cincinnati, OH
Jennings, Robyn E. ..... South Barrington, IL
Jennings, Rodney W., Jr. ..... Syracuse, NY
Jennings, Roger W. ..... Alamo, CA
Jennings, Rupert J., III
Department of the Army,
Office, Chief of Engineers/Headquarters,
U.S. Army Corps of Engineers, GV
Jennings, Sandra A. ..... Treasury Department,
Office of Regulations and Rulings, GV
Jennings, Scott ..... Rochester, NY
Jennings, Sheila G. ..... New York, NY
Jennings & Sparwath, LLP ..... Marietta, GA
Jennings, Stephanie C. ..... Baltimore, MD
Jennings, Stephanie M. ..... Nashville, TN
Jennings, Stephen ..... Honesdale, PA
Jennings, Stephen L. ..... Crossville, TN
Jennings, Strouss & Salmon, P.L.C.
Phoenix, AZ
Jennings, Susan Jane Stedman ..... Dallas, TX
Jennings Taylor Wheeler & Bouwkamp, P.C.
Indianapolis, IN
Jennings, Teresa L. ..... Washington, DC
Jennings, Teri K. ..... Everett, WA
Jennings, Terry L.D. ..... Houston, TX
Jennings, Theodore C. ..... Chicago, IL
Jennings, Thomas A. ..... Bloomington, IL
Jennings, Thomas E. ..... Houston, TX
Jennings, Thomas J. ..... Fairless Hills, PA
Jennings, Thomas Parks ..... Falls Church, VA
Jennings, Thomas W. ..... Philadelphia, PA
Jennings, Tipton D., IV ..... Washington, DC
Jennings, Tracey L. ..... Bowie, TX
Jennings & Valancy, P.A.
Fort Lauderdale, FL
Jennings, Vincent J. ..... Red Bank, NJ
Jennings, W. Croft, Jr. ..... Columbia, SC
Jennings, Walter S. ..... New York, NY
Jennings, Warren A. ..... De Witt, AR
Jennings, Wayne E. ..... Bozeman, MT
Jennings, Wilbur W. ..... Las Vegas, NV
Jennings, William A. ..... San Jose, CA
Jennings, William A. ..... Roanoke, VA
Jennings, William Andrew ..... Lenoir, NC
Jennings, William Bryan ..... Irving, TX
Jennings, William D., III ..... Augusta, GA
Jennings, William G., III ..... Miami, FL
Jennings, William H., II ..... Collinsville, IL
Jennings, William Kemper
Fort Walton Beach, FL
Jennings, William Kemper, P.A., Law Offices of ..... De Funiak Springs, FL
Fort Walton Beach, FL
Jennings, William L. ..... Decatur, GA
Jennings, William L., P.A. ..... Decatur, GA
Jennings, William Morgan ..... Longview, TX
Jennings, William P. ..... West Branch, MI
Jennings, William P., Jr. ..... West Branch, MI
Jennings, William T. ..... Richmond, KY
Jennings, Yvonne M. ..... Troy, MI
Jennings-Drummond, Janelle
Kansas City, MO
Jennings-Flynn, Karen ..... Boston, MA
Jennis, Abby L. ..... New York, NY
Jennis, David S. ..... Tampa, FL
Jennis, Wendy
Administrative Office Of The United States
Courts, GV
Jennison, Jennifer L. ..... Modesto, CA
Jennison, John C., III ..... United States Senate,
Senatorial Assistants, GV
Jennison, John Nolan ..... Arlington, VA
Jennison, Judith B. ..... Menlo Park, CA
Jennison, Kathryn M. ..... Wilton Manors, FL
Jennison, Michael B.
Department of Transportation,
Federal Aviation Administration, GV
Jennison, Patrick E., (A P.C.)
Bakersfield, CA
Jennison, Susan F. ..... New Brunswick, NJ
New York, NY
Jennrich, Terry ..... Cleveland, OH
Jenny, Brian Paul ..... Washington, DC
Jenny, Frank W. ..... Pasco, WA
Jenny, John ..... Buffalo, NY
Jenny, Kristin L. ..... Oakland, CA
Jenny, Leslie Moore ..... Cleveland, OH
Jenny, Linda K. ..... Minneapolis, MN
Jenny, Ruth A. ..... Grand Forks, ND
Jenny, Scott E. ..... Pittsburg, CA
Jenour, Simon ..... Dallas, TX
Jenrette, Isaac ..... Atlanta, GA
Jens, Jeffrey L., (A Professional Corporation)
Redding, CA
Jensch, Charles C. ..... Minneapolis, MN
Jense, Sara A. ..... Salt Lake City, UT
Jensen, A. D. ..... Reno, NV
Jensen, Alan C. ..... Jacksonville Beach, FL
Jensen, Alan F. ..... Laurel, MD
Jensen, Alan N. ..... Denver, CO
Jensen, Alice J. ..... East Grand Forks, MN
Jensen, Alice Liu ..... San Francisco, CA
Jensen, Allen R. ..... Washington, DC
Jensen, Amanda J. ..... Dallas, TX
Jensen, Amy J. ..... Denver, CO
Jensen, Anne L. ..... Lexington, KY
Jensen, Anton D. ..... Newport Beach, CA
Jensen & Associates ..... Indianapolis, IN
Jensen Baird Gardner & Henry
Kennebunk, ME
Portland, ME
Jensen, Barry J. ..... Santa Ana, CA
Jensen, Berne K. ..... Boise, ID
Jensen, Bonni S. ..... West Palm Beach, FL
Jensen, Boyd F. ..... Murray, UT
Jensen, Boyd F., II ..... Riverside, CA
Santa Ana, CA
Jensen, Brenda Mallick ..... Clarks Summit, PA
Jensen, Brian L. ..... Houston, TX
Jensen, Bruce A. ..... Yuma, AZ
Jensen, Bruce H. ..... Salt Lake City, UT
Jensen & Bunnell ..... Price, UT
Jensen & Burr-Jones ..... Burley, ID
Jensen, C., & Jensen, P.A. ..... Denton, MD
Jensen, Cameron Sharick ..... Wasilla, AK
Jensen, Carl Christian
Rancho Cucamonga, CA
Jensen, Carl M. ..... Cincinnati, OH
Jensen, Carl M., Jr. ..... Lake Forest, IL
Jensen, Carolyn Stevens
Salt Lake City, UT
Jensen, Cary M. ..... Rochester, NY
Jensen, Charles F. ..... Kansas City, MO
Jensen, Charles R. ..... Woodland, CA
Jensen, Charles T. ..... Santa Rosa, CA
Jensen, Christian J. ..... Denton, MD
Jensen, Christian R. ..... Santa Ana, CA
Jensen, Christina A. ..... Burlington, VT
Jensen, Christine ..... Eugene, OR
Jensen, Christopher G. ..... Riverside, CA
Jensen, Christopher H. ..... Washington, DC
Jensen, Christopher L. ..... Amarillo, TX
Jensen, Christopher T. ..... New York, NY
Jensen, Christopher W. ..... Prescott, AZ
Jensen, Christopher W. ..... Union, MO
Jensen, Clinton D. ..... Salt Lake City, UT
Jensen, Corliss V. ..... Medford, WI
Jensen, Craig J. ..... Wood River, IL
Jensen, Curtis M. ..... St. George, UT
Jensen, Curtis S. ..... Rapid City, SD
Jensen, Cynthia L. ..... Northbrook, IL
Jensen, D. Lowell ..... Oakland, CA
Jensen, Dale ..... Fort Worth, TX
Jensen, Dallin W. ..... Salt Lake City, UT
Jensen, Daniel A. ..... Salt Lake City, UT
Jensen, Daniel G. ..... Burnsville, MN
Jensen, Darrell A. ..... Minneapolis, MN
Jensen, David B. ..... Chicago, IL
Jensen, David B. ..... Seattle, WA
Tacoma, WA
Jensen, David C. ..... Hammond, IN
Jensen, David John ..... Brookline, MA
Jensen, David L. ..... Los Angeles, CA
Jensen, David L. ..... Anoka, MN
Jensen, David L. ..... Eugene, OR
Jensen, David M. ..... Memphis, TN
Jensen, David S. ..... Boise, ID
Jensen, David W. ..... Department of Justice,
Federal Bureau of Investigation, GV
Jensen, Debra A. ..... Philadelphia, PA
Jensen, Dennis ..... Deerfield, IL
Jensen, Derek W. ..... Bothell, WA
Jensen, Diane L. ..... Fort Myers, FL
Jensen, Dick L. ..... Des Moines, IA
Jensen, Don A. ..... Westwood, KS
Jensen, Donald E. ..... Topeka, KS
Jensen, Donald F. ..... Boise, ID
Jensen, Donald L. ..... Cody, WY
Jensen, Donald W. ..... Santa Rosa, CA
Jensen, Donald W. ..... Clarks Summit, PA
Jensen, Dorothy Hunt ..... Kansas City, MO
Jensen, Douglas B. ..... Fresno, CA
Jensen, Douglas R. ..... New York, NY
Jensen, Dovre C., Jr. ..... Atlanta, GA
Jensen Draudt LLP ..... Portland, OR
Jensen, Duffin, Carman, Dibb & Jackson
Salt Lake City, UT
Jensen, E. Beth ..... Riverwoods, IL
Jensen, E. Neil
Nuclear Regulatory Commission,
Office of the General Counsel, GV
Jensen, Edison A. ..... Santa Cruz, CA
Jensen, Elizabeth Ann ..... Tacoma, WA
Jensen, Elizabeth L. ..... Peoria, IL
Jensen, Eric ..... Wasilla, AK
Jensen, Eric ..... Arlington, VA
Jensen, Eric C. ..... Palo Alto, CA
Jensen, Eric F. ..... White Plains, NY
Jensen, Eric G. ..... Springfield, MO
Jensen, Eric M. ..... Louisville, KY
Jensen, Eric P. ..... Durham, NC
Jensen, Eric S. ..... Richmond, VA
Jensen, Erik B. ..... Philadelphia, PA
Jensen, Erik G. ..... St. Paul, MN
Jensen, Erik M. ..... Cleveland, OH
Jensen, Erik S. ..... San Diego, CA
Jensen, Ernest A. ..... Conover, WI
Jensen, Eugene F., Jr. ..... Linwood, NJ
Jensen, Fadeley & Elmore, P.C. ..... Eugene, OR
Jensen, Floyd Andrew ..... Salt Lake City, UT
Jensen, Floyd E. ..... St. Francis, KS
Jensen, Frances Kleiner ..... San Marino, CA
Jensen, Frank H. ..... Van Nuys, CA
Jensen, Franklin V. ..... Lawton, OK
Jensen, Frederik W. ..... Madison, WI
Jensen, Frode, III ..... Stamford, CT
Jensen, G. Scott ..... Ogden, UT
Jensen, Gail A. ..... El Dorado, KS
Jensen, Gail K.
Federal Deposit Insurance Corporation,
Liquidation Branch, GV
Jensen, Garretson, Verrett & Morford
Anchorage, AK
Jensen, Garth B. ..... Denver, CO
Jensen, Gary D. ..... Rapid City, SD
Jensen, Gary K. ..... Eugene, OR
Jensen, Gary K., P.C. ..... Eugene, OR
Jensen, Georg ..... Cheyenne, WY
Jensen, George ..... Fort Lauderdale, FL
Jensen, Gerald Doyle ..... Kansas City, MO
Jensen, Gilbert A. ..... Oakland, CA
Jensen, Gilbert D. ..... Irvine, CA
Jensen, Gilbert, Smith & Borrello, P.C.
Midland, MI
Saginaw, MI
Jensen, Ginger A. ..... Encino, CA
Jensen & Gordon ..... Hutchinson, MN
Jensen, Gordon L. ..... Brooklyn Park, MN
Jensen & Granich, P.A. ..... Wayland, MA
Jensen, Gregg Scott ..... Moorhead, MN
Jensen, Gregory E. ..... Dallas, TX
Jensen, Gregory G. ..... Ord, NE
Taylor, NE
Jensen, Gregory L. ..... Las Vegas, NV
Jensen, Gregory S. ..... San Mateo, CA
Jensen, Gretchen R. ..... Clive, IA
Jensen, Harold L. ..... Champaign, IL
Jensen, Hassani & Focas, P.A. ..... Towson, MD
Jensen, Helen M. ..... Chicago, IL
Jensen, Herbert A. ..... Indianapolis, IN
Jensen, Herbert C. ..... Sacramento, CA
Jensen, Hicken & Scott, P.A. ..... Anoka, MN
Jensen, Holly R. ..... Charleston, SC
Jensen, Howard F. ..... Seattle, WA
Jensen, Ingrid A. ..... Grand Rapids, MI
Jensen & Irwin ..... Yuma, AZ
Jensen, J. Alan ..... Portland, OR
Jensen, J. Christopher ..... New York, NY
Jensen, J. Erik P. ..... Newtown Square, PA
Jensen, J. Kenneth ..... La Jolla, CA
Jensen, J. Wilmar ..... Modesto, CA
Newman, CA
Oakdale, CA
Jensen, Jack A. ..... Breckenridge, CO
Jensen, Jacqueline M., Inc. ..... Irvine, CA
Laguna Hills, CA
Newport Beach, CA
Jensen, Jacqueline M. ..... Irvine, CA
Jensen, James B., Jr. ..... Lansing, MI
Jensen, James B., Jr. ..... St. Cloud, MN
Jensen, James C. ..... Morristown, NJ
Jensen, James F. ..... Palo Alto, CA
Jensen, James G. ..... North Aurora, IL
Jensen, James T. ..... Salt Lake City, UT
Jensen, James W. ..... Cedar City, UT
Jensen, Jan ..... Los Angeles, CA
Jensen, Janice C. ..... Sacramento, CA
Jensen, Janice Hodge ..... Reno, NV
Jensen, Jann ..... Clear Lake, SD
Jensen, Jay E. ..... Salt Lake City, UT
Jensen, Jay W. ..... Kansas City, MO
Jensen, Jeffrey D. ..... Portland, OR
Jensen, Jeffrey J. ..... Salt Lake City, UT
Jensen, Jeffrey V. ..... Irvine, CA
Jensen, Jenine M. ..... Denver, CO
Jensen, Jennifer A. ..... Glens Falls, NY
Jensen, Jennifer L. ..... Washington, DC
Jensen, Jennifer S. ..... North Platte, NE
Jensen, Jennifer S. ..... Powell, WY
Jensen, Jenny E. ..... Atlanta, GA
Jensen & Jensen ..... Wasilla, AK
Jensen & Jensen ..... Modesto, CA
Newman, CA
Oakdale, CA
Sacramento, CA
Jensen & Jensen ..... New York, NY
Jensen & Jensen ..... Clarks Summit, PA
Jensen, Jerard J. ..... Madison, WI
Jensen, Jerrold S. ..... Salt Lake City, UT
Jensen, Jerry L. ..... Anita, IA
Jensen, Jessica M. ..... Olympia, WA
Jensen, Jill Gossin ..... Lincoln, NE
Jensen, Jimmie J., Jr. ..... Bridgeport, NE
Jensen, Jodene ..... Minneapolis, MN
Jensen, Joel H. ..... Minneapolis, MN
Jensen, Joel K. ..... Covington, KY
Jensen, John E. ..... Washington, DC
Jensen, John E. ..... Wheaton, IL
Jensen, John Eric ..... Overland Park, KS
Jensen, John L. ..... Austin, TX
Jensen, John P. ..... Tacoma, WA
Jensen, John Taylor ..... Las Vegas, NV
Jensen, John Taylor, Chartered
Las Vegas, NV
Jensen, John W. ..... Durham, NC
Jensen, John W. ..... Salem, OR
Jensen, Jon A. ..... Escondido, CA
Jensen, Jon E. ..... Newport Beach, CA
Jensen, Jon J. ..... Grand Forks, ND
Jensen, Jonathan K. ..... Farmington, UT
Jensen, Joseph J. ..... South Bend, IN
Jensen, Judy A. ..... Modesto, CA
Jensen, Julian D. ..... Salt Lake City, UT
Jensen, Julianne ..... San Francisco, CA
Jensen, Julie A. ..... Toledo, OH
Jensen, Julie M. ..... Portage, MI

Jensen, June E. ....Wayland, MA
Jensen, Karen A. Murphy ....Denton, MD
Jensen, Kathleen D. ....Great Falls, MT
Jensen, Kathleen H. ....Chicago, IL
Jensen, Kathleen N. ....Des Plaines, IL
Jensen, Keith A. ....Granite City, IL
Jensen & Kelley, P.A. ....Phoenix, AZ
Jensen, Kenneth D. ....Anchorage, AK
Jensen, Kenneth E. ....Chicago, IL
Jensen, Kent D. ....Burley, ID
Jensen, Kirsten J. ....Palo Alto, CA
Jensen, Kit A. ....Hillsboro, OR
Jensen, Kit A. ....Portland, OR
Jensen, Kris R. ....Seattle, WA
Jensen, Kristen A. ....San Francisco, CA
Jensen, Kristin A. ....Albuquerque, NM
Jensen, Lana F. ....Vineyard, UT
Jensen, Lance Priest ....Santa Ana, CA
Jensen, Larry N. ....Litchfield, MN
Jensen Law Firm, P.C. ....Prescott, AZ
Jensen Law Office ....San Francisco, CA
Jensen Law Office, The ....Granite City, IL
Jensen, Lawrence C. ....San Francisco, CA
Jensen, Lawrence J. ....Provo, UT
Jensen, Lawrence R. ....San Jose, CA
Jensen, Leon E. ....Appleton, WI
Jensen, Leonard S. ....Orange, CA
Jensen, Leslie F. ....Chatsworth, CA
Jensen, Leslie W. ....Ashland, OR
Jensen & Lewis ....Salt Lake City, UT
Jensen, Linda Collins ....Mobile, AL
Jensen, Linda S. ....Minneapolis, MN
Jensen & Magan, P.C. ....Houston, TX
Jensen, Marci A. ....Woodland, CA
Jensen, Marcia ....San Jose, CA
Jensen, Maria D. ....Vernon Hills, IL
Jensen, Marianne M. N. ....New York, NY
Jensen, Marie Sellitto ....Evergreen, CO
Jensen, Mark R. ....Modesto, CA
Newman, CA
Oakdale, CA
Jensen, Mark T. ....Towson, MD
Jensen, Mary Brandt ....University, MS
Jensen, Mary Jo A. ....St. Paul, MN
Jensen & Massa ....Winner, SD
Jensen, Matthew S. ....Kansas City, MO
Jensen, Maxwell O. ....Sacramento, CA
Jensen, Melvin L. ....Santa Ana, CA
Jensen, Michael H. ....Omaha, NE
Jensen, Michael J. ....Anchorage, AK
Jensen, Michael L. ....San Diego, CA
Jensen, Michael Paul ....Onawa, IA
Jensen, Michael R. ....Waukegan, IL
Jensen, Michael R. ....Price, UT
Jensen, Miles P. ....Logan, UT
Tremonton, UT
Jensen, Mitchell R. ....Salt Lake City, UT
Jensen, Nancy J. ....Richmond, VA
Jensen, Nathan O. ....Portland, OR
Jensen, Neal G. ....Great Falls, MT
Jensen, Neil J. ....Hutchinson, MN
Jensen, Nikki M. ....Jackson, MS
Jensen, Nola M. ....Albert City, IA
Storm Lake, IA
Jensen, Norma W. ....Hemingford, NE
Jensen, Pamela Kirkland ....Geneva, IL
Jensen, Patricia ....Havre, MT
Jensen, Patricia R. ....Kansas City, MO
Jensen, Patrick H. ....Portland, OR
Jensen, Patti Jo ....East Grand Forks, MN
Jensen, Paul E. ....Grand Rapids, MI
Jensen, Paul E. ....Winner, SD
Jensen, Paul, Law Offices of
Coleman, TX
Jensen, Paul S. ....Nantucket, MA
Jensen, Paul S. ....Grapeview, WA
Jensen, Paul S., P.C. ....Nantucket, MA
Jensen, Paul T. ....San Jose, CA
Jensen, Paul T. ....Galena, IL
Dubuque, IA
Jensen, Paul T., P.C. ....San Jose, CA
Jensen, Peter C. ....Saginaw, MI
Jensen, Peter E. ....Boston, MA
Newburyport, MA
Hampton Falls, NH
Jensen, Peter H. ....Laurel Springs, NJ
Jensen, Peter J. ....Sacramento, CA
Jensen, Peter T. ....New York, NY
Jensen, Philip F. ....Galena, IL
Dubuque, IA
Jensen, Philip K. ....San Francisco, CA
Jensen, Preben ....New York, NY
Jensen & Puntigam, P.S. ....Seattle, WA
Jensen, Raymond A. ....Lincoln, NE
Jensen, Raymond E. ....Portland, ME
Jensen, Renee E. ....Las Vegas, NV
Jensen, Richard C.
United States Postal Service, Law Department, GV
Jensen, Richard C. ....Lake Success, NY
Jensen, Richard C., Jr. ....New York, NY
Jensen, Richard D. ....Gulf Shores, AL
Jensen, Richard G. ....Minneapolis, MN
Jensen, Richard H. ....Needham, MA
Jensen, Richard H. ....Oshkosh, NE
Jensen, Richard J. ....Tacoma, WA
Jensen, Richard J., P.S. & Associates
Tacoma, WA
Jensen, Richard W. ....Stoneham, MA
Jensen, Rick E. ....Fresno, CA
Jensen, Robert A. ....Phoenix, AZ
Jensen, Robert A. ....Seattle, WA
Jensen, Robert E. ....Oakland, CA
Jensen, Robert E. ....Washington, DC
Jensen, Robert G. ....Denver, CO
Jensen, Robert John ....Thousand Oaks, CA
Jensen, Robert L. ....Brookfield, WI
Jensen, Robert M. ....St. George, UT
Jensen, Robert N. ....Washington, DC
Jensen, Robert R. ....Reno, NV
Jensen, Robert T. ....Los Angeles, CA
Jensen, Robert V. ....Lacey, WA
Jensen, Robert W. ....Miami, FL
Jensen, Roberta J. ....Tucson, AZ
Jensen, Robin A. ....Kansas City, MO
Jensen, Rodney H. ....Bloomington, MN
Jensen, Roger A. ....St. Paul, MN
Jensen, Ronald C. ....Omaha, NE
Jensen, Ronald H. ....White Plains, NY
Jensen, Rory D. ....Walnut Creek, CA
Jensen, Roxanne ....Denver, CO
Jensen, Russell J. ....St. Paul, MN
Jensen, Russell J., P.A. ....St. Paul, MN
Jensen, Russell K. ....Sacramento, CA
Jensen, Schelly K. ....Thousand Oaks, CA
Jensen, Scott D. ....Wichita, KS
Jensen, Scott D. ....Grand Forks, ND
Jensen, Scott E. ....Chicago, IL
Jensen, Scott J. ....Wilmington, DE
Jensen, Scott L. ....Portland, OR
Jensen, Sherman H. ....Prescott, AZ
Jensen, Soren S. ....Omaha, NE
Jensen, Stan R. ....Houston, TX
Jensen, Sten A. ....Washington, DC
Jensen, Stephen C. ....Newport Beach, CA
Jensen, Stephen C. ....St. Paul, MN
Jensen, Steve D. ....Seattle, WA
Jensen, Steven A. ....Greenfield, IA
Jensen, Steven A. ....Paola, KS
Jensen, Steven D. ....Washington, DC
Jensen, Steven Lawrence ....Golden, CO
Jensen, Steven R. ....Sioux City, IA
Jensen & Stockman ....Minneapolis, MN
Jensen & Stuart ....Grand Rapids, MI
Jensen, Susan S. ....Springfield, MO
Jensen Swanson & Sondrall, P.A.
Brooklyn Center, MN
Brooklyn Park, MN
Maple Grove, MN
New Hope, MN
Jensen, Sylvia L. ....Portland, OR
Jensen, Tamila C. ....Granada Hills, CA
Jensen, Tara L. ....Ava, MO
Jensen, Terence C. ....Benton, AR
Jensen, Teresa K. ....Laramie, WY
Jensen, Terry L. ....Sandpoint, ID
Jensen, Thomas A. ....Indianapolis, IN
Jensen, Thomas C. ....Washington, DC
Jensen, Thomas D. ....Minneapolis, MN
Jensen, Thomas E. ....Escondido, CA
Jensen, Thomas F. ....Oakland, CA
Jensen, Thomas H. ....St. Paul, MN
Jensen, Thomas J. ....Bloomfield Hills, MI
Jensen, Thomas L. ....London, KY
Jensen • Thompson ....Woodland, CA
Jensen, Timothy P. ....New Haven, CT
Jensen, Timothy T.A. ....Salem, OR
Jensen, Todd J. ....Phoenix, AZ
Jensen, Travis N. ....New York, NY
Jensen, Valerie M. ....St. Paul, MN
Jensen, Verlyn N., Law Offices of
Irvine, CA
Jensen, Victoria M. W. ....Dallas, TX
Jensen, W. Glenn ....Orlando, FL
Jensen, Wade D. ....Mystic, CT
Jensen, Walker A. ....Encinitas, CA
Jensen, Warren R. ....San Luis Obispo, CA
Jensen, Wayne M. ....Elgin, IL
Jensen, Wilbur C. ....Towson, MD
Jensen, William B. ....Kansas City, MO
Jensen, William B. ....Albany, NY
Jensen, William C., (P.C.) ....Denver, CO
Jensen, William E. ....Vallejo, CA
Jensen, William F., III ....United States Senate, Office of the Legislative Counsel, GV
Jensen, William M. ....Houston, TX
Jensen, William N. ....Helena, MT
Jensen, William O., Jr. ....Baltimore, MD
Jensen, Willis J. ....Carefree, AZ
Jensen, Winston H. ....Salt Lake City, UT
Jensen and Zumbado ....Boston, MA
Newburyport, MA
Hampton Falls, NH
Jensen-Conklin, Susan A.
House of Representatives, Committee Legal Personnel, GV
Jenski, Raymond A. ....Corvallis, OR
Jenson, Carol A. ....Austin, TX
Jenson, Chrystina Dee ....Ventura, CA
Jenson, Dennis D. ....Coolidge, AZ
Jenson, Eugene T. ....Anahuac, TX
Jenson, Gary W. ....Austin, TX
Jenson, Harris M. ....Metairie, LA
Jenson, Janet I. ....Salt Lake City, UT
Jenson, Karen Campbell
Salt Lake City, UT
Jenson, Linda ....Los Angeles, CA
Jenson, M. Katherine ....Costa Mesa, CA
Jenson, Margaret I. ....Lima, OH
Jenson, Mark J. ....Princeton, NJ
Jenson, Pamela J. ....White Plains, NY
Jenson, Paul T. ....Chicago, IL
Jenson, Paula R.
Securities and Exchange Commission, Division of Market Regulation, GV
Jenson, Robin D. ....Oklahoma City, OK
Jenson, Russell ....Orem, UT
Jenson, Susan Mole ....Jacksonville, FL
Jenson, William G.
Department of Agriculture, Office of the Judicial Officer, GV
Jenssen, Leif H. ....El Cerrito, CA
Jenstrom, Eino E. ....Arlington, VA
Jensvold, Jon D.
Securities and Exchange Commission, Office of the Inspector General, GV
Jenswold & Hanson ....Madison, WI
Jenswold, John F. ....Madison, WI
Jent, Larry ....Bozeman, MT
Jentes, William R., (P.C.) ....Chicago, IL
Jentis, Barbara S. ....Moonachie, NJ
Jentis, Stuart M. ....East Brunswick, NJ
Jentry-Green, Anne ....Chicago, IL
Jentsch, Erwin W. ....Mount Prospect, IL
Jentz, Gaylord A. ....Austin, TX
Jentzen, Judith L. ....Suffield, CT
Jentzen, Steven M. ....Ypsilanti, MI
Jentzen, Steven M., P.C. ....Ann Arbor, MI
Ypsilanti, MI
Jenz, James E. ....Chicago, IL
Jenzen, Thomas M. ....Fremont, CA
Jeon, Deborah A. ....Centreville, MD
Jeon, Jeff J. ....Los Angeles, CA
Jeon, Jun-Young E. ....Pasadena, CA
Jeon, Matthew J. ....New York, NY
Jeong, Rodney K. ....San Francisco, CA
Jeong, Rosa S.
Department of Commerce, GV
Jepertinger, John C. ....Florence, SC
Jepeway & Jepeway ....Miami, FL
Jepeway, Louis M., Jr. ....Miami, FL
Jeppe, Gerald L. ....Cleveland, OH
Jepperson, Thomas C. ....Salt Lake City, UT
Jeppesen, Alan K. ....Tooele, UT
Jeppesen, Betty L. ....Santa Barbara, CA
Jeppesen, Eric V. ....Bellevue, WA
Jeppesen Gray Sakai, P.S. ....Bellevue, WA
Jeppesen, John C. ....St. Paul, MN
Jeppsen, John C. ....Las Vegas, NV
Jeppson, H. Roy ....Los Angeles, CA
Oxnard, CA
Jeppson, H. Roy, A Professional Corporation
Los Angeles, CA
Oxnard, CA
Ventura, CA
Westwood, CA
Jeppson, John, III ....New York, NY
Jepsen, Carl F. ....Portland, OR
Jepsen, George C. ....Stamford, CT
Jepsen, Robin K. ....Carmel, CA
Jepsen, Tori M. ....Chicago, IL
Jepsen, William E. ....Minneapolis, MN
Jepsky, Andrew S. ....Franklin, MA
Jepsky & Sack ....Franklin, MA
Jepson, Craig S. ....Seattle, WA
Jepson, Dwight E. ....Topeka, KS
Jepson, Edward C., Jr. ....Chicago, IL
Jepson, John K. ....Farmington, CT
Jerabek, John M. ....Minneapolis, MN
Jerabek, John S. ....Ellsworth, ME
Jerabek, Peter A. ....Bloomfield Hills, MI
Jerak, John W. ....Oak Brook, IL
Jeram, Thomas W. ....Albany, NY
Jerardi, Peter J., Jr. ....Dayton, OH
Jerbic, Bradford R. ....Las Vegas, NV
Jerde, Dennis D. ....Des Moines, IA
Jerde, Jeffrey R. ....Burnsville, MN
Jerde, Michael J. ....Kansas City, MO
Jerdee, Chad T. ....Chicago, IL
Minneapolis, MN
Jerdee, Peter R. ....New York, NY
Jerden, Marcus G. ....Tucson, AZ
Jerdon, Wendy Fors ....Los Angeles, CA
Jerdonek, Elizabeth A. ....Cleveland, OH
Jereb, Brian J. ....Cleveland, OH
Jereb, Theodore B. ....Houston, TX
Jereck, Carolyn M. ....Detroit, MI
Jereck, John M. ....Battle Creek, MI
Jerejian, Edward A. ....Orange, NJ
Jeremiah, Albert, Jr. ....Kailua, HI
Jeremiah, Barbara S. ....Pittsburgh, PA
Jeremiah, Jeremiah S., Jr. ....Providence, RI
Jeremiah, Velma ....Portland, OR
Jeremiah, William S., II ....Westfield, NJ
Jeren, John A., Jr. ....Youngstown, OH
Jerge, Edward C. ....New Canaan, CT
Jerge-Lesniak, Lisa A. ....Dallas, TX
Jergensen, Keith ....Salt Lake City, UT
Jerger, Joseph L. ....Mansfield, OH
Jergesen, Allan D. ....San Francisco, CA
Jergins, Michael ....Round Rock, TX
Jericho, Eugene, (P.C.) ....Dallas, TX
Jerison, Jonathan D. ....Washington, DC
Jerkins, Joseph J. ....Kalamazoo, MI
Jerles, Jeanette E. ....Los Angeles, CA
Jerles, William R., Jr. ....Perry, GA
Jerlstrom, Bernard J. ....Cleveland, OH
Jermain, Dunnagan & Owens, P.C.
Anchorage, AK
Jermain, William K. ....Anchorage, AK
Jerman, Chas. R. (Dick) ....Alamo, TN
Jerman, Harold L. ....Phoenix, AZ
Jerman, Janis C. ....Hartford, CT
Jerman, Tom A. ....Washington, DC
Jermann, Edmond L., Jr. ....Toledo, OH
Jermon, Janis C. ....Windsor, CT
Jermyn, Alyssa R. ....Newton, MA
Jernberg, Dale L. ....Washington, DC
Greenbelt, MD
Jernberg, Dale L. ....Washington, DC
Annapolis, MD
Jernberg, Donald V. ....Chicago, IL
Jernegan, Jeffrey L. ....Seattle, WA
Jernigan, Arthur F., Jr. ....Jackson, MS
Jernigan, Christopher G. ....Portland, ME
Jernigan, Clifford E. ....Sunnyvale, CA
Jernigan, David H. ....Greenville, KY
Jernigan, Finith E. ....Crestview, FL
Jernigan, George O., Jr. ....Little Rock, AR
Jernigan, Harry W., III
Virginia Beach, VA
Jernigan, Harry W., P.C.
Virginia Beach, VA
Jernigan, J. Allen ....Raleigh, NC
Jernigan, Jack W., III ....New Orleans, LA
Jernigan, Jay L. ....Hattiesburg, MS
Jernigan, Jerry W. ....Charlotte, NC
Jernigan, Jerry W., P.A. ....Charlotte, NC
Jernigan, Joe W. ....Amarillo, TX
Jernigan, John L. ....Raleigh, NC
Jernigan, John L., III ....Brewton, AL
Jernigan, John T. ....Little Rock, AR
Jernigan Law Firm, The, A Professional Law Corporation ....Raleigh, NC
Jernigan, Leonard T., Jr. ....Raleigh, NC
Jernigan, Lisa ....Birmingham, AL
Jernigan, Mark D. ....Houghton Lake, MI
Jernigan, Milton D., II ....Annapolis, MD
Greenbelt, MD
Jernigan, Miriam K. ....Cary, NC
Jernigan, Paula K. ....Albany, GA
Jernigan, Robert M. ....Oklahoma City, OK
Jernigan, Rodney C., Jr. ....Florence, SC
Jernigan, Stacey Cowand ....Dallas, TX
Jernigan, W. Henry, Jr. ....Charleston, WV
Jernigan, Wayne ....Buena Vista, GA
Jernigan & Weiner ....New Orleans, LA
Jernigan, William J., Jr. ....Little Rock, AR
Jernow, Allison L. ....Department of State, Office of the Legal Adviser, GV
Jernstedt, Ann Townes ....Boston, MA
Jernstedt, Kenneth E. ....Portland, OR
Jerome & Austin, P.C. ....Detroit, MI
Northville, MI
Jerome, David E. ....Northville, MI
Jerome, David J. ....St. Louis, MO
Jerome, Domenic D. ....Media, PA
Jerome, Dominic A. ....Phoenix, AZ
Jerome, Emily Newton ....Eugene, OR
Jerome, Eva L. ....New York, NY
Jerome, Gibson, Stewart, Friedman, Stevenson and Engle, P.C. ....Phoenix, AZ
Jerome, Joseph B. ....Cleveland, OH
Jerome, Joseph B., and Associates
Cleveland, OH
Jerome, Louis R ....Staten Island, NY
Jerome, M. Rob, Jr. ....Eugene, OR
Jerome, Monica J. ....East Providence, RI
Jerome, Richard B. ....Department of Justice, Office of the Associate Attorney General, GV
Jerome, Robt. J. ....Newark, NJ
Jerome, Roy ....Menlo Park, CA
Jerome, Stephen D. ....Fort Lauderdale, FL
Jerome, Steven D. ....Phoenix, AZ
Jerome, William B. ....Malden, MA
Jerome, William F. ....New York, NY
Jerome, William L. ....Fort Worth, TX
Jerome, William Travers
Cruz Bay, St. John, VI
Jeronimides, H. Rosemary
Washington, DC
Jeronimus, Michael H. ....Englewood, CO
Jeroslow, Louise T. ....Miami, FL
Jeroslow, Steven Louis ....Fort Worth, TX
Jerram, Christopher D. ....Omaha, NE
Jerram, Jennifer Wolfe ....Omaha, NE
Jerrehian, Aram K., Jr. ....Bryn Mawr, PA
Jerrehian, Ellen ....Philadelphia, PA
Jerrett, Jack E. ....Allentown, PA
Jerrick, Ronald M. ....Chicago, IL
Jerris, Bruce L. ....Southfield, MI
Jerrold, Laurence ....Massapequa, NY
Jerry, Harold A." Chip ", III
Princeton, NJ
Jerry, Harold A., Jr. ....Albany, NY
Jerry, J. Michael ....Green Bay, WI
Jerry, Jacquelyn Ladd ....Albany, NY
Jerry & Jerry LLP ....Princeton, NJ
Jerry, Joseph W. ....Syracuse, NY
Jerry, Marilyn Murphy ....Princeton, NJ
Jerry, Thomas W. ....St. Louis, MO
Jersak, Maureen McGhee ....Springfield, MO
Jerse, Edward S. ....Columbus, OH
Jerse, Joseph John ....Cleveland, OH
Jerse, Shannon Fogarty ....Cleveland, OH
Jersevic, Roland J. ....Saginaw, MI
Jersey, Russell J. ....Chicago, IL
Jersild, James L. ....Wilmington, DE
Jersild, Thomas N. ....Chicago, IL
Jersin, Wayne N. ....Dallas, TX
Jerskey, James F. X. ....St. Paul, MN
Jerskey, Ralph M. ....Carlsbad, CA
Jerstad, Tina M. ....Des Moines, IA
Jeruchimowitz, Howard K. ....Chicago, IL
Jerue, James L. ....Chicago, IL
Jerue & Perkins ....Chicago, IL
Jerum, Edward M. ....La Jolla, CA
Jervey, Warren L. ....New York, NY
Jervis, Bruce M. ....Portland, ME
Jervis, Ellen D. ....Kansas City, MO
Jervis, Gerard A. ....Kailua, HI
Jervis, Herbert H. ....King Of Prussia, PA
Jervis, Herman ....New York, NY
Jervis, Jennifer L. ....Chicago, IL
Jervis, Kristin L. ....Newport Beach, CA
Jervis, Oliver W. ....Naperville, IL
Jervis, Robert Bruce ....Durham, NC
Jerz, James W. ....Wheaton, IL
Jerz, Lawrence R. ....White Plains, NY
Jerzy, Sandra L. ....Chicago, IL
Jerzy, Uve R. ....Chicago, IL
Jesaitis, Timothy J. ....St. Petersburg, FL
Jescavage, Camille H. ....Enola, PA
Plymouth, PA
Jeschke, Eric B. ....Syracuse, NY
Jesella, Edward P., Jr. ....Lewiston, NY
Jeselnik, Anthony F. ....Pittsburgh, PA
Jeselsohn, Paul B. ....New York, NY
Jesensky, Alex, Jr. ....Lorain, OH
Jeserich, Gerald N. ....Kansas City, KS
Jeseule, Vincent ....Westfield, NJ

Jesic, Michael V. ... West Covina, CA
Jesina, Carl L. ... Alexandria, VA
Jesinger, Robert E. ... San Jose, CA
Jesiolowski, Karen K. ... Morris, IL
Jesion, Paula J. ... Pittsburgh, PA
Jesk, Robin P. ... Oak Forest, IL
Jeske, Arnold C. ... Priddy, TX
Jeske, Dean M. ... Chicago, IL
Jeske, Howard L. ... Auburn, CA
Jeske, Jacqueline L. ... Seattle, WA
Jeske, James A., II ... Grand Haven, MI
Jeske, John D. ... Chicago, IL
Jeske, John D. and Assoc., Law Offices of, Ltd. Chicago, IL
Jeske, Kendra J. ... Middleburg Heights, OH
Jeske, Larry L. ... Gillett, WI
Jeske, Marc R. ... East Chicago, IN
Jeske, Paul T. ... Tampa, FL
Jeske, Staci S. ... Seattle, WA
Jeskie, Sandra ... Philadelphia, PA
Jesko, Herman ... Amarillo, TX
Jesmonth, Richard E. ... Pensacola, FL
Jesmore, Kenneth L. ... Sausalito, CA
Jespersen, Jonathan S. ... Helendale, CA
Jespersen, Kevin R. ... Short Hills, NJ
Jespersen, Robert R. ... Melbourne, FL
Jesperson, Gordon O. ... Norfolk, VA
Jesperson, JoAnna ... Washington, DC
Jesperson, John E. ... Bridgeton, NJ
Jess, Elva L. ... Southport, NC
Jess, Frank J. ... New Brunswick, NJ
Jess, James ... Palm Springs, CA
Jess, Mark A. ... Kansas City, MO
Jess, Paul D. ... Tallahassee, FL
Jessamy, Ronald C. ... Washington, DC
Jessar, Kevin L. National Archives And Records Administration, General Counsel Staff, GV
Jesse, Darrell A. ... Dakota Dunes, SD
Jesse, Franklin C., Jr. ... Minneapolis, MN
Jesse, James K. ... Buchanan, MI
Jesse, Jeanette M. ... Buchanan, MI
Jesse & Jesse ... Buchanan, MI
Jesse, Joel Lee-Eric ... Houston, TX
Jesse Law Firm, The, P.L.C. Little Rock, AR
Jesse, Mark Alan ... Little Rock, AR
Jesse, Michael S. ... Foley, MN
Jesse, Norman G. ... Des Moines, IA
Jesse, Paul D. ... Columbus, OH
Jesse, Vernon J. ... Madison, WI
Jessee, C. James, Jr. ... Marietta, GA
Jessee, C. James, Jr., P.C. ... Marietta, GA
Jessee, Charlie R. ... Abingdon, VA
Jessee, Evans B. ... Roanoke, VA
Jessee, Glenn J. Securities and Exchange Commission, Division of Market Regulation, GV
Jessee & Jessee ... Johnson City, TN
Jessee, John E. ... Abingdon, VA
Jessee, John T. ... Roanoke, VA
Jessee, Lori L. ... Morristown, TN
Jessee, Mark T., Law Offices of Thousand Oaks, CA
Jessee, Martha D. ... Yuba City, CA
Jessee & Read, P.C. ... Abingdon, VA
Jessee, Richard C. ... Morristown, TN
Jessee, Robert J. ... Johnson City, TN
Jessee, Roy M. ... Norton, VA
Jessee, Thomas C. ... Johnson City, TN
Jessel, Peggy ... Boulder, CO
Jessell, James R. ... Fort Myers, FL
Jessell, James R., Jr. ... Fort Myers, FL
Jessell, Karri Michelle West Palm Beach, FL
Jessell, Timothy J. ... Tysons Corner, VA
Jessen, Bryce R. ... Springfield, OR
Jessen, Douglas V. ... Evansville, IN
Jessen, Edward W. ... San Francisco, CA
Jessen, Jon E. ... Stamford, CT
Jessen, Linda S. ... Tallahassee, FL
Jessen, Lloyd K. ... Des Moines, IA
Jessen, Paul C. ... Omaha, NE
Jessen, Polly B. ... Denver, CO Washington, DC
Jessen, Richard T. ... St. Cloud, MN
Jessep, John D. ... Danbury, CT
Jesser, Frederick A., III ... Fayetteville, WV
Jesser & Harrington ... Fayetteville, WV
Jesserer, Henry L., III ... Rochester, NY
Jessey, Karen C. ... Providence, RI
Jessiman, Stacey R. ... New York, NY
Jesson, Bradley D. ... Fort Smith, AR
Jesson, Paula A. ... San Francisco, CA
Jesson, William F., Jr. ... Medford, MA
Jessop, Christopher G. Salt Lake City, UT
Jessop & Company, P.C. ... Denver, CO
Jessop, Douglas W. ... Denver, CO
Jessop, Jeanette Wanless ... Milwaukee, WI
Jessum, Kim R. ... Philadelphia, PA
Jessup, Clifton R., Jr. ... Dallas, TX
Jessup, Debra Ragin ... Winston-Salem, NC
Jessup, Dianna W. ... Cary, NC
Jessup, Grady ... Charlotte, NC
Jessup, James R. ... Marquette, MI
Jessup, James R., P.C. ... Marquette, MI
Jessup, John B. ... New York, NY
Jessup, Mary ... Commerce, CA
Jessup, Miles D. ... New York, NY
Jessup, Philip C., Jr. ... Washington, DC
Jessup & Probst ... Winston-Salem, NC
Jessup, Richard A. ... Seattle, WA
Jessup, Richard, Jr. ... Providence, RI
Jessup, Robert L. ... Indianapolis, IN
Jessup, Robert M., Jr. ... Chapel Hill, NC
Jessup, Ron L. ... Mount Airy, NC
Jessup, Sidney P. ... Manteo, NC
Jessup, Stephen M. ... Kokomo, IN
Jessup, W. Edgar, Jr. ... Beverly Hills, CA
Jessup, Warren T. ... Thousand Oaks, CA
Jessup, William Eugene ... Chattanooga, TN
Jesswein, Margie L. ... Tustin, CA
Jest, Joseph V. ... Washington, DC
Jester, C. G., Jr. ... Atlanta, GA
Jester, Christopher M. ... Jonesboro, AR
Jester, Clay T. ... Dover, DE
Jester, David ... Gulf Breeze, FL New Orleans, LA
Jester, David A. ... Indianapolis, IN
Jester, Elizabeth Tacy ... Washington, DC
Jester, Gary L., (P.C.) ... Florence, AL
Jester, Helen R. ... New York, NY
Jester, Jack D. ... Los Angeles, CA
Jester, Jay S. ... Denver, CO
Jester, Jeffrey C. ... Richardson, TX
Jester & Jenkins ... Florence, AL Tuscumbia, AL
Jester, Jerry L. ... Merritt Island, FL
Jester & Jester ... Lynchburg, VA
Jester, Jonathan P. ... Richmond, VA
Jester, Mary Cynthia Atchley Washington, DC
Jester, Melanie J. ... Oklahoma City, OK
Jester, Michael H. ... San Diego, CA
Jester, Michelle R. ... Minneapolis, MN
Jester, Pamela J. ... Berkeley, CA
Jester, Robert O. ... Kansas City, MO
Jester, Royston, IV ... Lynchburg, VA
Jester, Tom D., Jr. ... Denton, TX
Jester, W. David ... Gulf Breeze, FL
Jestin, Katya T P ... Brooklyn, NY
Jestings, William H. ... Providence, RI
Jestrab, Frank F. ... Chevy Chase, MD
Jesudasson, Benjamin John Los Angeles, CA
Jesuele, Robert R. ... Los Angeles, CA
Jesuele, Vincent ... Westfield, NJ
Jesup, Benjamin C. Department Of The Interior, Office of the Solicitor, GV
Jetelina, Judy K. ... San Antonio, TX
Jeter, Amy C. ... San Francisco, CA
Jeter, Ashley Higgins ... Dallas, TX
Jeter, Carolyn F. ... Knoxville, TN
Jeter, David H. ... Blue Springs, MO
Jeter, Edwin Russell ... Columbia, SC
Jeter, Gary M. ... Alexandria, VA
Jeter, J. Atwood ... Dallas, TX
Jeter, J. Roland ... Irving, TX
Jeter, J. Roland, P.C. ... Fort Worth, TX Irving, TX
Jeter, James C. ... Charleston, WV
Jeter, James Robert ... Shreveport, LA
Jeter, John I. ... Santa Clara, CA
Jeter, Joi LaVerne ... Richmond, VA
Jeter, Joseph W. ... Hays, KS
Jeter, Justin L. ... Dallas, TX
Jeter, Katherine Leslie Brash Shreveport, LA
Jeter, Kevin D. ... Los Angeles, CA
Jeter, Laura C. Macdonald ... Shawnee, OK
Jeter Law Firm, LLP ... Hays, KS
Jeter, Norman W. ... Hays, KS
Jeter, Paul H. ... Hackensack, NJ
Jeter, Rains & Byrn, L.C. Blue Springs, MO
Jeter, Robert McLean, Jr. ... Shreveport, LA
Jeter, Sheldon Leigh ... Chicago, IL
Jeter, Thomas G. ... Denver, CO
Jeter, William H., Jr. ... Jacksonville, FL
Jeter, William M. ... Memphis, TN
Jeter, William W. ... Hays, KS
Jeter & Williams, P.A. ... Columbia, SC
Jetha, Aly A. ... San Francisco, CA
Jethmalani, Anil ... New York, NY
Jetkiewicz, Valerie A. ... Latham, NY
Jetmore, Jenevieve R. ... Sedalia, MO
Jetmundsen, Norman, Jr. Birmingham, AL
Jett, A. Clark ... Guymon, OK
Jett, Adam G., Jr. ... Douglasville, GA
Jett, Daniel P. ... Pasadena, CA
Jett, Dwight M., Jr. ... Decatur, AL
Jett, E. Stephen ... Chattanooga, TN
Jett, Elaine ... Nashville, TN
Jett, Ernest C., Jr. ... Carthage, MO
Jett, Frances Q. ... Los Angeles, CA
Jett, J. Craig ... Dallas, TX
Jett, Lois M. ... Conroe, TX
Jett, Medina K. ... Hartford, CT
Jett, Norma A. T. ... Bamberg, SC
Jett, Philip N. ... Nashville, TN
Jett, R. Arthur, Jr. ... Norfolk, VA
Jett, R. Samuel, Jr. ... Baltimore, MD
Jett, R. Samuel, P.A. ... Baltimore, MD
Jett, Regina H. ... Redwood City, CA
Jett, Rick L. ... Chicago, IL
Jett, Robert A. ... Austin, TX
Jett, Robert S., III ... Cedar Rapids, IA
Jett, Robert T. ... Portland, OR
Jett, Sharon ... Dallas, TX
Jett, Stephen H. ... Cincinnati, OH
Jett, Wayne ... Pasadena, CA
Jette, Ernest A. ... Nashua, NH
Jetter, Harold ... New York, NY
Jetter, John M, IV ... Scottsdale, AZ
Jetter, Neil R. ... Fort Myers, FL
Jetter, Sherry L. ... New York, NY
Jetton, C. Loring, Jr. ... Washington, DC
Jetton, Ernest A. ... Memphis, TN
Jetton, Girard R., Jr. ... Findlay, OH
Jetton, Marion L. ... Department of Justice, Antitrust Division, GV
Jetton, Mary Paty Lynn ... Nashville, TN
Jetton, William D. ... Guntersville, AL
Jetton, William W. ... Charlotte, NC
Jeub, Herman M. ... Minneapolis, MN
Jeun, Paul B. ... New York, NY
Jeunette, Edward R., Jr. ... Baltimore, MD
Jeung, Richard ... San Francisco, CA
Jeutter, Gerald A." Jeb ", Jr. ... Raleigh, NC
Jevic, Joseph G., III ... Houma, LA
Jevicky, John E. ... Cincinnati, OH
Jevinsky, Max ... Kansas City, MO
Jevne, Franz P., III ... Indio, CA
Jevnikar, David W. ... Chardon, OH
Jevons, Jack Owen ... Boulder, CO
Jew, A. Debbie ... Honolulu, HI
Jew, Charles H. ... Redwood City, CA
Jew, Edward ... San Francisco, CA
Jew, Kenneth Anthony ... Los Angeles, CA
Jew, Michael D. ... Garden City, NY
Jew, Millie Yin ... Foster City, CA
Jew, Quana C. ... Washington, DC
Jewart, Michael E. ... Millersburg, OH
Jewel, Andrew L. ... Washington, DC
Jewel, Anne F. ... Columbus, OH
Jewel, Christine M. ... Philomath, OR
Jewel, Gary L. ... Memphis, TN
Jewel, Howard H. ... Oakland, CA
Jewel & Rich ... Memphis, TN
Jeweler, Bernard P. ... Washington, DC
Jeweler, Richard S. ... San Rafael, CA
Jeweler, Robin ... Library of Congress, Congressional Research Service, GV
Jewell, Allen L. ... Bellingham, WA
Jewell, Angela J. ... Albuquerque, NM
Jewell & Associates ... San Francisco, CA
Jewell, Barbara Duval ... Danville, CA
Jewell, Barry J. ... Little Rock, AR
Jewell and Boutin ... Portland, ME
Jewell, Carol A. ... Houma, LA
Jewell, Colin H. ... Encino, CA
Jewell, Collins & DeLay ... Norfolk, NE
Jewell, Crump & Angermeier Columbus, IN Seymour, IN
Jewell, D. Randall ... Barbourville, KY
Jewell, Daniel D. ... Norfolk, NE
Jewell, Daniel Willard ... Arlington, VA
Jewell, David R. ... New York, NY
Jewell, Douglas ... Denver, CO
Jewell, D. Randall & Associates Barbourville, KY
Jewell, Eric P. ... New York, NY
Jewell, Frank R. ... Austin, TX Dallas, TX
Jewell, Franklin P. ... Louisville, KY
Jewell, Fred A. ... Worthington, IN
Jewell, Gary Martin ... Houston, TX
Jewell, George B. ... Carmel, IN
Jewell, George H. ... Houston, TX
Jewell, Glenn A. ... Kansas City, MO
Jewell, Jefferson R. ... Boise, ID
Jewell, Jeffrey J. ... Erie, PA
Jewell & Jewell ... New Roads, LA
Jewell & Jewell ... St. Clair Shores, MI
Jewell, John F. ... St. Petersburg, FL
Jewell, John J. ... Evansville, IN
Jewell, John L. ... Stillwater, MN
Jewell, John M. ... Little Rock, AR
Jewell, John Wayne ... New Roads, LA
Jewell, Joseph P., Jr. ... New Roads, LA
Jewell, Julie T. ... Lafayette, LA
Jewell, Karen ... Houston, TX
Jewell, Karen Donohoe ... Leesburg, VA
Jewell, Keith C. ... Lake Success, NY
Jewell, Keith R. ... Fort Smith, AR
Jewell, Kenneth R. ... Lancaster, PA
Jewell, Kevin D. ... Houston, TX
Jewell, Kevin P. ... San Francisco, CA
Jewell & Lemke ... Louisville, KY
Jewell, Margaret C. ... Dallas, TX
Jewell, Mary E. ... Omaha, NE
Jewell, Matthew G. ... Kailua-Kona, HI
Jewell, Matthew J. ... Atlanta, GA
Jewell, Melinda Plass ... Memphis, TN
Jewell, Monte L. ... Missoula, MT
Jewell & Moser, A Professional Association Hot Springs National Park, AR Hot Springs Village, AR Little Rock, AR
Jewell, Norine C. ... Augusta, ME
Jewell, Paula L. ... Washington, DC
Jewell, Phyllis A. ... San Francisco, CA
Jewell, Ralph L. ... Columbus, IN
Jewell, Robert R. ... Ridgefield, CT
Jewell, Robert V. ... Houston, TX
Jewell, Ronald R. ... New York, NY
Jewell, Stephanie Francis ... Portland, OR
Jewell, Stephen Philibert ... New Roads, LA
Jewell, Stephen W. ... Logan, UT
Jewell, Susan B. ... Prospect Heights, IL
Jewell, Theodore A. ... Miami, FL
Jewell, Thomas F. ... Portland, ME
Jewell, Tommy E. ... Albuquerque, NM
Jewell, W. Horace ... Little Rock, AR
Jewell, William R. ... Grand Rapids, MI
Jewell, William R. ... St. Clair Shores, MI
Jewels, Frances M. ... Westford, MA
Jewels, Mary A. ... Uniondale, NY
Jewett, Bruce E. ... Columbus, OH
Jewett, C. Lawrence ... Atlanta, GA
Jewett, Carol H. ... Houston, TX
Jewett, Charles W. ... Norwich, CT
Jewett, Cindy A. ... Agoura Hills, CA
Jewett, Cynthia ... Monterey, CA
Jewett, Cynthia L. ... Tempe, AZ
Jewett, Dean F. ... Saco, ME
Jewett, Douglas N. ... Seattle, WA
Jewett, Dunham F. ... Houston, TX
Jewett, Edward L. ... New York, NY
Jewett, Elizabeth Croft ... Orlando, FL
Jewett, Freeborn G., Jr. ... Washington, DC
Jewett, G. David ... Springfield, OR
Jewett, Harold W., III ... Concord, CA
Jewett, Harvey C. ... Aberdeen, SD
Jewett, Henry W., II ... Orlando, FL
Jewett, Hugh I. ... Aurora, CO
Jewett, James M. ... Columbus, OH
Jewett, Jennifer ... Los Angeles, CA
Jewett, Jeremiah J., III ... Richmond, VA
Jewett, Jonathan ... New York, NY
Jewett, Katrina ... Chattanooga, TN
Jewett, Michael ... Medford, OR
Jewett, Reed P. ... Springfield, OH
Jewett, Richard K., Jr. Department Of The Interior, Office of Hearings & Appeals, GV
Jewett, Robert T. ... Cortland, NY
Jewett, Robert W. ... Basking Ridge, NJ
Jewett, Stephen F. ... Denver, CO
Jewett, Susan ... Washington, DC
Jewett, Thomas J. ... Okemos, MI
Jewett, Valerie G. ... Houston, TX
Jewett, Vernon N., Jr. ... Lake Elsinore, CA
Jewett, Willem W. ... Middlebury, VT
Jewett-Owen, Elizabeth J. ... Rochester, NY
Jewik, Patrick R. ... San Francisco, CA
Jewitt, David G. ... Philadelphia, PA
Jewitt, John R., Jr. ... Cleveland, OH
Jews, Melvin J. ... Bel Air, MD
Jex, Elizabeth A. Federal Trade Commission, Bureau of Competition, GV
Jex, Kay Parker ... New Canaan, CT
Jex, Thomas D. ... Los Angeles, CA
Jeydel, Richard K. ... Somerset, NJ
New York, NY
Jeynes, G. Fred ... Honolulu, HI
Jez, G. Sean ... Houston, TX
Jezek, Fancy H. ... Harker Heights, TX
Jezer, Aviva ... Boston, MA
Jezic, Andrew V. ... Annapolis, MD
Jezic, Nina L. ... Richmond, VA
Jezouit, Debra J. ... Washington, DC
JG, P.C Business & Corporate Law Dublin, CA Livermore, CA Pleasanton, CA
Jha, Arun ... Denver, CO
Jha, Pran ... Chicago, IL
Jha, Viraj D. ... Emeryville, CA
Jhabvala, Farrokh ... Miami, FL
Jhones, Ana Maria ... Fort Lauderdale, FL
Ji, Sang I. ... New York, NY
Ji, Xueqing (Linda) ... St. Louis, MO
Jiang, Brian B. ... San Diego, CA
Jiang, Cindy P.H. ... New York, NY
Jiang, Earl L. ... Fremont, CA
Jiang, Howard H. ... New York, NY
Jiang, Xiangyuan (Yen) ... St. Louis, MO
Jiannetti, Michael A. ... Mayfield Heights, OH
Jibilian, Gerald A. ... Madison, NJ
Jibilian, William ... Atlanta, GA
Jicka, Mark D. ... Jackson, MS
Jiganti, Jeanine Marie ... Northbrook, IL
Jiganti, John J. ... Chicago, IL
Jiganti, Mel R. ... Chicago, IL
Jiganti, Mel R. ... Chicago, IL
Jiganti, Mia P. ... Chicago, IL
Jigarjian, Robert A. ... San Francisco, CA
Jih, Victor ... Los Angeles, CA
Jike, Ryan R. ... Los Angeles, CA
Jilek, Michael F., Sr. ... Toledo, OH
Jilek, Robert M. ... Cedar Rapids, IA
Jiles, Gary D. ... Conway, AR Little Rock, AR
Jilka, Gregory F. ... Sebastopol, CA
Jilka, Michael T. ... Overland Park, KS
Jillions, Ronni S. ... Alexandria, VA
Jillisky, Donald R. ... Marysville, OH
Jillisky, Nancy L. ... Marysville, OH
Jillson, Andrew E. ... Dallas, TX
Jillson, Bedford & Hoppen ... New York, NY
Jillson, Kenneth R., Jr. ... Carson City, NV Stateline, NV
Jilnicki, John C. ... East Hampton, NY
Jilot, LuAnn Regina Ott ... Denver, CO
Jiloty, Joseph P. ... Rutland, VT
Jim, Aimee R. ... Greensburg, PA
Jim On & Beerman ... Honolulu, HI
Jim, Richard L. ... Latrobe, PA
Jimbo, Thomas M. ... Los Angeles, CA
Jimenez, Adolfo E. ... Miami, FL
Jimenez, Aimee C. ... Department of Justice, Environment and Natural Resources Division, GV
Jimenez, Alan Jay ... Denver, CO
Jimenez, Alejandro ... Los Angeles, CA
Jimenez, Augustine, III ... Phoenix, AZ
Jimenez, Baldemar A. ... San Antonio, TX
Jimenez, Carla ... Ruskin, FL
Jimenez, Carlos E. ... San Juan, PR
Jimenez, Carol S. ... Los Alamitos, CA
Jimenez, Charlene A. ... San Francisco, CA
Jimenez, Constance E. ... San Jose, CA
Jimenez, David G. ... Los Alamitos, CA
Jimenez, David R. ... Hartford, CT
Jimenez, Diana T. ... Monterey, CA
Jiménez, Emilio ... New York, NY
Jimenez, Frank R. ... Tallahassee, FL
Jimenez, Freddy A. ... Washington, DC
Jiménez, Gabriel F. ... Durham, NC Raleigh, NC
Jiménez, Graffam & Lausell San Juan, PR
Jimenez, Heidi V. ... Washington, DC
Jimenez, James M. ... Santa Monica, CA
Jimenez, Jeffrie R. ... Los Angeles, CA

Jimenez, John ....Carlsbad, CA
Jimenez, Jorge R. ....San Juan, PR
Jimenez, Jorge R., Law Offices
San Juan, PR
Jimenez, Juan Fernando ....Deerfield, IL
Jimenez, Kathy A. ....Miami, FL
Jimenez, Linda D. ....San Antonio, TX
Jimenez, Linda Johnson ....Waukesha, WI
Jiménez, Lori D. ....Boston, MA
Jimenez, Lorraine ....Guaynabo, PR
Jimenez, Magda M. ....New York, NY
Jiménez, Marcos D. ....Miami, FL
Jimenez, Martha I. ....San Francisco, CA
Jimenez, Michael ....Cambridge, MA
Jimenez, Monica M. ....Santa Ana, CA
Jiménez, Nicolás ....San Juan, PR
Jimenez, Octavio ....San Juan, PR
Jimenez, Orlando-Gerard ....San Francisco, CA
Jimenez, Oscar G. ....San Francisco, CA
Jimenez, Pamela M.
Securities and Exchange Commission,
Division of Enforcement, GV
Jiménez, Pedro A. ....Miami, FL
Jimenez, Pedro A. ....San Juan, PR
Jimenez, Philip ....Washington, DC
Jimenez, Renee ....Salt Lake City, UT
Jimenez, Roy Joseph ....Downey, CA
Jimenez, Roy R. ....San Antonio, TX
Jimenez, Ryan E. ....Lihue, HI
Jimenez & Small ....Los Alamitos, CA
Jimenez, Steven John ....Sacramento, CA
Jimenez, T. Mickell ....Salt Lake City, UT
Jimenez, Victor E. ....Orange, CA
Jiménez del Valle, José R. ....San Juan, PR
Jiménez-Ekman, David ....Chicago, IL
Jiménez Hernández, Ernesto R.
New York, NY
Jiménez-Juarbe, Héctor ....San Juan, PR
Jiménez-Meléndez, María S.
San Juan, PR
Jimenez-Melendez, Pablo F.
San Juan, PR
Jiménez-Meléndez, Teresa ....San Juan, PR
Jimenez-Orosa, Georgina
West Palm Beach, FL
Jimenez-Santiago, Alberto O. ....San Juan, PR
Jiménez Santoni, Salvador ....San Juan, PR
Jimerson, Bruce D. ....Valley Center, CA
Jimerson, Herman L. ....St. Louis, MO
Jimerson, Jay C. ....Oklahoma City, OK
Jimerson, Micheal E. ....Henderson, TX
Jimison, Holly Hendrix ....Greensboro, NC
Jimison, John W. ....Berkeley, CA
Washington, DC
Jimmerson Hansen, A Professional
Corporation ....Las Vegas, NV
Jimmerson, J. Michael ....Highland Park, IL
Jimmerson, James J. ....Las Vegas, NV
Jimmerson, Joseph A. ....Huntsville, AL
Jim On, Shelton G. W. ....Honolulu, HI
Jin, Laural S. ....Chicago, IL
Jin, Les ....United States Information Agency,
Office of the General Counsel, GV
Jin, Phyllis A. ....Uniontown, PA
Jin, Victoria Ying ....Los Angeles, CA
Jindia, Ajay K. ....Atlanta, GA
Jindra, Christy R. ....Atlanta, GA
Peachtree City, GA
Jindracek, Thomas R. ....Paterson, NJ
Jindrich, Edward S. ....Lakewood, CO
Jines, Michael L. ....Houston, TX
Jing, Xiao-Hong ....New York, NY
Jingoli, John M., Jr. ....Trenton, NJ
Jinkens, Jeffrey R. ....Columbus, OH
Jinkerson, Guyton N. ....San Jose, CA
Jinkins, David B. ....St. Louis, MO
Jinkins, Mark A. ....Algoma, WI
Sister Bay, WI
Sturgeon Bay, WI
Jinks, Jackson, Daniel & Crow, L.L.C.
Clayton, AL
Union Springs, AL
Jinks, James A. ....Woodland Hills, CA
Jinks, James R. ....Sacramento, CA
Jinks, Lynn W., III ....Union Springs, AL
Jinks, Lynn W., Jr. ....Union Springs, AL
Jinks, Thomas M. ....Troy, MI
Jinnah, Al. H. ....Redondo Beach, CA
Jinnah and Jinnah ....Redondo Beach, CA
Jinnah, Leila E. ....Redondo Beach, CA
Jinnett, Jeff ....New York, NY
Jio, David E. ....San Jose, CA
Jiongco, E. Charles ....Chicago, IL
Jira, Louis C. ....Baltimore, MD
Jirak, Jerry R. ....Winterhaven, CA
Jirak, Thomas J. ....Westminster, CO
Jiran, Edward ....Department of Energy,
Office of the General Counsel, GV
Jiran, Gabriel J. ....Columbus, OH
Jiranek, Andrew L. ....Baltimore, MD
Jiranek & Harasti, LLC ....Baltimore, MD
Jirauch, Charles W. ....Phoenix, AZ
Jircik, J. Jan ....Houston, TX
Jircik, J. Jan, P.C. ....Houston, TX
Jircik, Robt. A. ....Houston, TX
Jircik, Yvette Cornelius ....Houston, TX
Jirgil, Thomas P. ....Los Angeles, CA
Jirles, Jeffrey H. ....Clearwater, FL
Jirotka, George M. ....Clearwater, FL
Jirovec, Milena ....Costa Mesa, CA
Jischke, Mary A. ....Chicago, IL
Jishi, Reem F. ....New York, NY
Jitlal, Lara S. ....Dallas, TX
Jitner, Tina ....Santa Rosa, CA
Jitner, Walter ....Los Angeles, CA
Jiudice, Joseph ....Poughkeepsie, NY
Jiuliante, Jess S., Jr. ....Erie, PA

Jivens-McRae, Grace H.
Department Of Veterans Affairs,
Board of Veterans Appeals, GV
Jivery, Bernard E. ....Vista, CA
Jividen, Patricia ....Frederick, MD
Jizmejian, Carol A. ....Bloomfield Hills, MI
Jo, Chang Bum ....New York, NY
Jo, Grace E. ....Los Angeles, CA
Jo, Y. Soo ....Atlanta, GA
Joachim, Cynthia S. ....Biloxi, MS
Joachim, Edward B. ....Mineola, NY
Joachim, Flanzig, Frommer, Beasley &
Madigan ....Mineola, NY
Joachim, George J. ....Algonac, MI
Joachim, Lindsay ....Granada Hills, CA
Joachim, Mark Brent ....New York, NY
Joachim, Michael I. ....Boston, MA
Joachim, Robert S. ....Flushing, NY
Joachim, Scott B. ....San Diego, CA
Joachim, W. Lawrence ....New York, NY
Joachim, William B., Jr. ....Bethlehem, PA
Joachim, William D. ....New Brunswick, NJ
Joachims, Bert E. ....Portland, OR
Joanis, David E. ....Monona, WI
Joanis, K. A. ....Kenosha, WI
Joanis Law Group, The ....Minneapolis, MN
Joanis, Robert E. ....La Crosse, WI
Joanis, William J. ....Minneapolis, MN
Joannes, James T. ....Green Bay, WI
Joannes, John A. ....Los Angeles, CA
Joannes, John A., A Professional
Corporation ....Los Angeles, CA
Joannes, Nathalie ....St. Louis, MO
Joannides, George E. ....Washington, DC
Joannides, Stephanie E. ....Anchorage, AK
Joannou, John S. ....Portsmouth, VA
Joannou Knowles & Clark ....Portsmouth, VA
Joanos, James E. ....Tallahassee, FL
Joanow, Michael A. ....Hermitage, PA
Joanow, Olga J. ....Tampa, FL
Joao, Raymond A. ....Mineola, NY
Joaquin, Alan J. ....Washington, DC
Joaquin, Arcadio A., Jr. ....Chicago, IL
Joaquin, Gina R. ....Fort Worth, TX
Joaquin, Jennifer M. ....Emeryville, CA
San Francisco, CA
Joaquin, Michael S. ....Honolulu, HI
Joaquin, Pamela Schmidt ....Worcester, MA
Joaquin, Thomas E. ....Boston, MA
Joas, William C. ....Edina, MN
Job, Mary Hannorah ....East Lansing, MI
Jobe, Brian C. ....Dallas, TX
Jobe, Bruce F. ....Lumberton, NC
Jobe, Bruce F., P.A., Law Offices of
Lumberton, NC
Jobe, Catherine C. ....Houston, TX
Jobe, Everette D. ....Austin, TX
Jobe, Marjorie Wilcox ....El Paso, TX
Jobe, Melissa Ann ....Kingman, AZ
Jobe, Meredith ....Glendale, CA
Jobe, Raymond V. ....Dallas, TX
Jobe, Sharon Cannon ....Dallas, TX
Jobe, Stephen J. ....Department of Justice,
Federal Bureau of Investigation, GV
Jobe & Stoterau ....Glendale, CA
Jobe, Tony B. ....Madisonville, LA
Jobe, Tony B., P.C., Law Offices of
Madisonville, LA
New Orleans, LA
Jobe, William T. ....Oakton, VA
Jobes, Merrilee A. ....Fort Lauderdale, FL
Jobes, Theodore H. ....Philadelphia, PA
Jobeun, Larry A. ....Omaha, NE
Jobin, Christine J. ....Denver, CO
Jobin, Eugene A. ....Chicago, IL
Jobin & Flynn ....Chicago, IL
Jobin Law Firm, The, P.C. ....Denver, CO
Jobin-Davis, Camille S. ....Albany, NY
Joblin, Warren P. ....Weston, CT
Joblove, Leonard S. ....Brooklyn, NY
Joblove, Michael D. ....Miami, FL
Joblove, Richard P. ....Miami, FL
Jobse, Bruce D. ....Boston, MA
Jobsis, Anna M. ....Houston, TX
Jobson, Bruce ....Pleasanton, CA
Jobson, Franz C. ....Washington, DC
Jobson, Walter C. ....Louisville, KY
Jocelyn, Richard L. E. ....Boston, MA
Providence, RI
Jocelyn, Robert A. ....San Rafael, CA
Jocha-Ervin, Joanne ....Dayton, OH
Jochens, Amberley Gibbs ....Norfolk, VA
Jochens, Ann E. ....College Station, TX
Jochens, Nancy S. ....Kansas City, MO
Jochens, William G. ....St. Louis, MO
Jochim, Tim ....Columbus, OH
Jochims, Jeffrey T. ....Pittsburgh, PA
Jochman, Joseph J., Jr. ....Milwaukee, WI
Jochnowitz, Daniel M. ....New York, NY
Jochnowitz, Leona Deborah ....Albany, NY
Jochum, F. Eric ....Willoughby Hills, OH
Jochum, Patricia L. ....Palatine, IL
Jochum, Richard A. ....Dakota Dunes, SD
Jock, Paul F., II (P.C.) ....Chicago, IL
New York, NY
Jock, Shelly S. ....Dallas, TX
Jocke, Ralph E. ....Medina, OH
Jockers, Alan N. ....Miami, FL
Jockers, Kenneth A. ....Brooklyn, NY
Jockimo, Karen A.D. ....White Plains, NY
Jockisch, Wesley C.
Department of the Army,
Office, Chief of Engineers/Headquarters,
U.S. Army Corps of Engineers, GV
Jocks, Robert L. ....San Bernardino, CA
Jockusch, Carl G. ....San Antonio, TX
Jocoy, Sallie Rich ....Macon, GA
Jocz, Bruce R. ....Houston, TX

Jodha, Gary T. M. ....Princeton Junction, NJ
Jodi, Anderson ....Tampa, FL
Jodis, Denis F. ....Hudson, MI
Jodis, Kristina M. ....Irvine, CA
Jodka, Eric C. ....Indianapolis, IN
Jodlbauer, Julius A. ....Elkton, MD
Jodon, G. Mark ....Houston, TX
Jodrey, Donald S.
Department Of The Interior, GV
Jodrey, H. Lawrence ....Rockport, MA
Jody, Nina ....New York, NY
Jodzio, Frank M. ....San Diego, CA
Joe, Christopher M. ....Dallas, TX
Joe, David R. ....Irving, TX
Joe, Don W. ....Fort Worth, TX
Joe, Edwin L. ....San Francisco, CA
Joe, Eric Anthony ....Pasadena, CA
Joe, Gregory M. ....Oakland, CA
Joe, Harry J. ....Dallas, TX
Joe, Herbert ....Dallas, TX
Joe, Isaac, Jr. ....Baltimore, MD
Joe, Jeannie Q. ....Nashville, TN
Austin, TX
Joe, Jimmie L. ....Los Angeles, CA
Joe, L. Leianne ....Walnut Creek, CA
Joe, Melissa ....Newport Beach, CA
Joe, Spencer A. ....Sacramento, CA
Joehl, Virginia Butterfield ....Rockville, MD
Joehnck, Robert N. ....Lincoln, CA
Joehnk, Susan R. ....La Jolla, CA
Joel, Alexander W. ....Washington, DC
Joel Brooks & Associates, P.C.
Westbury, NY
Joel, David J. ....Martinsburg, WV
Joel, Donald G. ....Laguna Beach, CA
Joel, Edward T. ....New York, NY
Joel & Joel ....Oradell, NJ
Joel, Kenneth L. ....Harrisburg, PA
Joel, Kimberly A. ....Parsippany, NJ
Joel, Lawrence A. ....Oradell, NJ
Joel, Richard A. ....Oradell, NJ
Joel, Richard A., Jr. ....Oradell, NJ
Joel, William L. ....Jacksonville, FL
Joelson, Gordon A. ....Coos Bay, OR
Joelson, Kenneth ....New York, NY
Joelson, Mark R., Law Office
Washington, DC
Joelson, Peter William ....Farmington Hills, MI
Joelson, Philip R. ....Toledo, OH
Joelson & Rochkind ....New York, NY
Joens, Samuel W. ....Napa, CA
Joens, Timothy L. ....Irvine, CA
Joens, Timothy L., & Assoc., A Prof. Corp.
Irvine, CA
Joerg, Claude A. ....Lockport, NY
Joerg, David A. ....Preston, MN
Joerg, Nancy E. ....St. Charles, IL
Joergensen, John P. ....Philadelphia, PA
Joerger, Lindsey & Lindsey ....Rosenberg, TX
Joerger, Michael G. ....Costa Mesa, CA
Joerger, Nancy Bergeson
Colorado Springs, CO
Joeris, David L. ....Denver, CO
Joerling, Dale R. ....St. Louis, MO
Joern, Charles E., Jr. ....Chicago, IL
Joerres, MaryAnn ....Dallas, TX
Joers, David L. ....Dallas, TX
Joerz, Norton C. ....Chicago, IL
Joest, David R. ....Henderson, KY
Joest, Garrett L., III ....Atlantic City, NJ
Joesten, Nan E. ....San Francisco, CA
Jofery, Joann M. ....Sharon, PA
Joffe, Abraham ....Oakland, CA
Joffe, B. David ....Nashville, TN
Joffe, Carl Herbert ....Diamondhead, MS
Joffe, Carol A. ....Washington, DC
Joffe, David J. ....Miami, FL
Joffe, Dimitry ....New York, NY
Joffe, Douglas S. ....Denver, CO
Joffe, Edward M. ....Miami, FL
Atlanta, GA
Joffe, Elizabeth A. ....Portland, OR
Joffe, Elliott N. ....Baltimore, MD
Joffe, George F. ....Dix Hills, NY
Joffe, Howard H. ....Cherry Hill, NJ
Joffe, Jo Curie ....Chicago, IL
Joffe, Margaret M. ....New Orleans, LA
Joffe, Paul L. ....Washington, DC
Joffe, Richard T. ....New York, NY
Joffe, Robert D. ....New York, NY
Joffe, Scherry LeSieur ....Gulfport, MS
Joffe, Selwyn H. ....Atlanta, GA
Joffe, Serge ....Austin, TX
Joffe, Stanley M. ....West Conshohocken, PA
Joffe, Steven J. ....Los Angeles, CA
Joffe, Steven J. ....East Rutherford, NJ
Joffe, Susan H. ....Mineola, NY
New York, NY
Joffrion, Brian P. ....Shreveport, LA
Joffrion, Christopher B. ....Shreveport, LA
Joffrion, Clayton J., Jr. ....New Orleans, LA
Joffrion, Julie Dyan ....Beaumont, TX
Joffrion, Peter S. ....Huntsville, AL
Joffrion, Todd M. ....Houma, LA
Joggerst, Elizabeth K. ....Binghamton, NY
Joggerst, Scott D. ....St. Louis, MO
Jogodnik, Benjamin D. ....Philadelphia, PA
Joh, Erik Edward ....Boynton Beach, FL
Joh, Erik Edward, P.A.
Boynton Beach, FL
Delray Beach, FL
Joh, John A., III ....Atlanta, GA
Johal, Demetra G. ....Sacramento, CA
Johal, Jack S. ....Sacramento, CA
Johan, Andrea H. ....Columbus, OH
Johanek, Mary Ann Sabol ....Cleveland, OH
Johaningmeyer, Judy ....McKinney, TX

Johann, Pamela Tabari
San Francisco, CA
Johann, Susan K. ....Larkspur, CA
Johann, Thomas E. ....San Francisco, CA
Johannes, Ann K. ....Lansing, MI
Johannes, Donald R. ....Highland, IL
Johannes, Ernest G. ....Milwaukee, WI
Johannes, Jay Elgin ....Austin, TX
Johannes & Marron, P.C. ....Highland, IL
Johannes, Randall D. ....Denver, CO
Johannes, Robert J. ....Milwaukee, WI
Johannes, Ryan J. ....Houston, TX
Johannes & Stoffa ....Austin, TX
Johannesen, Amy J. ....New York, NY
Johannesen, Barbara Ruscetta ....Hinsdale, IL
Johannesen, Ingard O. ....Metairie, LA
Johannesen, Michael B. ....Naperville, IL
Johannesen, Richard ....Brooklyn, NY
Johannessen & Associates, P.S.
Seattle, WA
Johannessen, Eric G. ....Memphis, TN
Johannessen, Kim Maree ....Seattle, WA
Johannessen, Kristen ....Sarasota, FL
Johanning, Paul ....Oklahoma City, OK
Johanns, Michael O. ....Lincoln, NE
Johannsen, Brent A. ....Lansing, MI
Johannsen, Carston C. ....Lenexa, KS
Johannsen, James P. ....Columbus, OH
Johannsen, Kyle J. ....Port Clinton, OH
Johannsen, Marc A. ....Minneapolis, MN
Johannsen, Peter G. ....Boston, MA
Johannsen, Shawna L. ....Dallas, TX
Johannsen, Tonya Powers ....Dallas, TX
Johannson, Kenneth ....Crookston, MN
Johannson, Rust, Fagerlund & Unkenholz,
P.A. ....Crookston, MN
Johansen, Bruce D. ....Clinton, IA
Johansen, Carl A. ....Kirkland, WA
Johansen, Chris A. ....Anchorage, AK
Johansen, Conrad ....Salt Lake City, UT
Johansen, Craig V. ....Valencia, CA
Johansen, David G. ....Seattle, WA
Johansen, David M. ....New York, NY
Johansen, Deborah Kish ....Orlando, FL
Johansen, Eric R. ....Salem, OR
Johansen, Erling T. ....Anchorage, AK
Johansen, Gary L. ....Westport, CT
Johansen, Gary L. ....Sioux City, IA
Johansen, Gregory J. ....Orlando, FL
Johansen, James H. ....Albuquerque, NM
Johansen, Jane J. ....Washington, DC
Johansen & Johansen ....Sioux City, IA
Johansen, Kay M. ....Cedar Rapids, IA
Johansen, Kenneth ....New Port Richey, FL
Johansen, Kenneth, P.A.
New Port Richey, FL
Johansen, Kirk ....Bend, OR
Portland, OR
Johansen, Kurt D. ....Muskegon, MI
Johansen Law Firm ....Hampton, IA
Johansen Law Firm ....Winnebago, MN
Johansen, Mark L. ....Dallas, TX
Johansen, Michael C. ....Morristown, NJ
New York, NY
Johansen, Michael V. ....Annapolis, MD
Baltimore, MD
Johansen, Patricia A. ....Boston, MA
Johansen, Randy D. ....Hampton, IA
Johansen, Raymond B. ....Sioux City, IA
Johansen, Rebecca L. ....Selma, AL
Johansen, Richard B. ....Pittsfield, MA
Johansen, Robin B. ....Sacramento, CA
San Francisco, CA
Johansen, Scott N. ....Castle Dale, UT
Johansen, Wilford W. ....Atlanta, GA
Johansmeier, Kristy Christen
Pass Christian, MS
Johanson, Alfred E. ....Belle Mead, NJ
Johanson, Allison Bonner ....Houston, TX
Johanson Berenson, LLP ....Napa, CA
Washington, DC
McLean, VA
Johanson, Carolyn J. ....Denver, CO
Johanson, Charles E. ....Fairfield, IA
Johanson, Charles R., III
Birmingham, AL
Johanson, D. Michael ....Albuquerque, NM
Johanson, David O. ....Boston, MA
Johanson, David R. ....Napa, CA
Johanson, David S. ....Washington, DC
Johanson, Derek W. ....Atlanta, GA
Johanson, Douglas L. ....Winnebago, MN
Johanson, Erick T. ....Sherman Oaks, CA
Johanson & Fairless, L.L.P. ....Sugar Land, TX
Johanson, Howard C. ....Providence, RI
Johanson, John Michael ....Sugar Land, TX
Johanson, John W. ....Las Vegas, NV
Johanson, Julise M. ....Sacramento, CA
Johanson, Kenneth R. ....Summit, NJ
Johanson, Kent A. ....Naples, FL
Johanson, Kevin K. ....Salt Lake City, UT
Johanson, Koons & Constantino, LLP
Auburn, CA
Johanson, Lynn H. ....Washington, DC
Johanson, Ralph N., Jr. ....Fairfax, VA
Johanson & Robinson ....Sacramento, CA
Johanson, Shay E. ....Houston, TX
Johanson, Stanley M. ....Houston, TX
Johanson, Stephen H. ....Sacramento, CA
Johanson, Steven L. ....Forest City, IA
Johanson, Sven A. ....Boston, MA
Johanson, Tami Freedman
Rochester Hills, MI
Johanson, Theodore L., (P.C.)
Auburn, CA
Johanson, Thomas J. ....Philadelphia, PA
Johanssen, John R. ....Englewood, CO

Johansson, Jan G., Law Offices of
New York, NY
Johasky, Jeffrey W. ... Lower Burrell, PA
Johiro, Cynthia M. ... Honolulu, HI
Johl, Justin J. ... Overland Park, KS
Johlie, Christopher A. ... Chicago, IL
John, Anne N. ... Uniontown, PA
John, Christopher L. ... Boston, MA
John, Colin H., Jr. ... Southfield, MI
John, Craig L. ... Bloomfield Hills, MI
John, Douglas F. ... Washington, DC
John, E. Allen, Jr. ... Seattle, WA
John, Edmund K. ... Media, PA
John, Eric Joseph ... Atlanta, GA
John, Ernest F. ... San Antonio, TX
John, Frederick E. ... Los Angeles, CA
John, Frederick L., II ... Kittanning, PA
John, George M. ... Lexington Park, MD
John, Gerald V. ... Frazer, PA
John & Hengerer ... Washington, DC
John, Hollie B. ... Doylestown, PA
John, Hunter E. ... Seattle, WA
John, Ian G. ... New York, NY
John, Jaison C. ... Houston, TX
John & John ... Uniontown, PA
John, John T. ... Seattle, WA
John, Joseph R., Sr. ... Raleigh, NC
John, Kathy Lanita ... Department of Justice, Executive Office for Immigration Review, GV
John, Kenneth M. ... Lowell, MA
John, Leslie E. ... Philadelphia, PA
John, Louis J. ... Wheeling, WV
John, Luwana Rae ... Lawton, OK
John, Michael L. ... Canton, OH
John, Paula N. ... Philadelphia, PA
John, Peter C. ... Chicago, IL
John, Philip J., Jr. ... Houston, TX
John, Piper E. ... Oklahoma City, OK
John, R. Michael ... Southfield, MI
John, Ralph C. ... Kittanning, PA
John, Ramona F. ... Houston, TX
John, Richard M. ... Shreveport, LA
John, Richard T. ... Ithaca, NY
John, Robert ... Fairbanks, AK
John, Robert ... Evansville, IN
John, Robert M. ... Hatboro, PA
John, Sidney C. ... Toledo, OH
John, Simon B. ... Uniontown, PA
John, Stephanie G. ... New Orleans, LA
John, Steven H. ... North Myrtle Beach, SC
John, Susan V. ... Rochester, NY
John, Thomas A. ... Indianapolis, IN
John, Victor B. ... Columbia, SC
John, Wendy M. ... Department of Agriculture, Office of the General Counsel, GV
Johnakin, Jesse Sydnor ... Bennettsville, SC
Johnas, Lora J. ... Waukegan, IL
Johnathan, Kenneth L., Jr. ... Neptune, NJ
Johncox, Allen M. ... Tustin, CA
Johndroe, Mary Colchin ... Fort Worth, TX
Johndroe, S. G., III ... Fort Worth, TX
Johnedis, Daniel J. ... Woburn, MA
Johnes, Debra A. ... Sarasota, FL
Johni, Scott T. ... Tampa, FL
Johnnene, Roberta F. ... Boston, MA
Johnnidis, John E. ... Parsippany, NJ
Johnnie, Gina Anne ... Salem, OR
Johnroe, Drew ... Steamboat Springs, CO
Johnroe, Drew, P.C. ... Steamboat Springs, CO
Johns, A. Frank ... Greensboro, NC
Johns, Alan G. ... Conyers, GA
Johns, Alan L. ... Columbus, OH
Johns, Alan R. ... Las Vegas, NV
Johns, Alexis D.
Federal Communications Commission, Compliance and Information Bureau, GV
Johns, Ann Lacy ... Nashville, TN
Johns, Arthur J. ... Chula Vista, CA
Johns, Arthur L. ... Wellesley, MA
Johns, Belinda J. ... San Francisco, CA
Johns, Brent E. ... Ogden, UT
Johns, Bruce D. ... Daytona Beach, FL
Johns, C. Michael ... Bisbee, AZ
Johns, Carol C. ... Wolf Point, MT
Johns, Celeste K. ... Springfield, MO
Johns, Charles E., Jr. ... Brewton, AL
Johns, Charles F. ... Clarksburg, WV
Johns, Charles W. ... Philadelphia, PA
Johns, Charlie H., Jr. ... Annandale, VA
Johns & Christensen, A Professional Corporation ... San Rafael, CA
Johns, Christopher ... San Rafael, CA
Johns, Christopher K. ... Houston, TX
Johns, Christopher V. ... Phoenix, AZ
Johns, Clifford A., Jr. ... Mc Keesport, PA
Johns, Craig E. ... Nanuet, NY
Johns, Craig S. J. ... San Francisco, CA
Johns, D. Malcolm, Jr. ... New Orleans, LA
Johns, Daniel D. ... Kalispell, MT
Johns, Daniel L. ... Peoria, IL
Johns, Daniel V. ... Philadelphia, PA
Johns, David A. ... Cincinnati, OH
Johns, David J. ... Newark, DE
Johns, David K. ... Denver, CO
Johns, Deborah H. ... Fort Worth, TX
Johns, Del E. ... San Lorenzo, CA
Johns, Donald P. ... Madison, WI
Johns, Douglas A. ... Pittsfield, MA
Johns, Doyle T., Jr. ... Pueblo, CO
Johns, Everett L. ... New City, NY
Johns, Flaherty & Rice, S.C.
La Crosse, WI
Sparta, WI
Johns, Fleur Elizabeth ... New York, NY
Johns, Gail ... Houston, TX
Johns, George B. ... Spring Grove, PA
Johns, George T., (P.C.) ... Fort Worth, TX
Johns, Harold M. ... Elkton, KY
Johns, Horace E. ... Murfreesboro, TN
Johns, Ira ... Encino, CA
Johns, Irene Chiavaroli ... Allentown, PA
Johns, James C. ... Clinton, MO
Johns, James S. ... Montgomery, OH
Johns, Jane M. ... Nashville, TN
Johns, Janice L. ... Evansville, IN
Johns, Jeanne Deimling ... Toledo, OH
Johns, Jennifer A. ... Atlanta, GA
Johns, Jerry M. ... Altamonte Springs, FL
Johns, Jodi J. ... Minneapolis, MN
Johns, John S. ... Rockville, MD
Johns, Joseph O. ... San Bernardino, CA
Johns, Karen B. ... Birmingham, AL
Johns, Kenneth A. ... San Diego, CA
Johns, Kenneth E., Jr. ... Dallas, TX
Johns, Kent W. ... Beaumont, TX
Johns, Kimberly A. ... New York, NY
Johns, Kos N. ... Bethesda, MD
Johns, Krista R. ... University, MS
Johns, Larry C. ... Las Vegas, NV
Johns, Leslie C. ... Fort Worth, TX
Johns & Lilleston ... Clinton, MO
Johns, Lisa Anderson ... Houston, TX
Johns, Lynn ... West Palm Beach, FL
Johns, Madalyn E. ... Silver Spring, MD
Johns, Malcolm ... New Orleans, LA
Johns, Margaret Z. ... Oakland, CA
Johns, Marilyn S. ... Pittsburgh, PA
Johns, Marsha W. ... Huntingdon, TN
Johns, Michael A. ... Phoenix, AZ
Johns, Michael D. ... Cincinnati, OH
Johns, Michael R. ... Little Rock, AR
Johns, Michelle C. ... Dallas, TX
Johns, Milton C. ... Manassas, VA
Johns, N. Whitney ... Brentwood, TN
Johns, Paul J. ... Denver, CO
Johns, Phillip A. ... Gaithersburg, MD
Johns, Richard B. ... Schaumburg, IL
Johns, Richard S. E. ... San Francisco, CA
Johns, Richard W. ... Denver, CO
Johns, Robert D. ... Palm Beach, FL
Johns, Robert D. ... Seattle, WA
Johns, Robert D., Jr. ... La Crosse, WI
Johns, Robert L. ... Wheeling, WV
Johns, Robert Phillips ... Denver, CO
Johns, Roger J., Jr. ... Lafayette, LA
Johns, Sherri S. ... Clarksburg, WV
Johns, Stephen M. ... Austin, TX
Johns, Susan T. ... Syracuse, NY
Johns, Theodore M. ... Jacksonville, FL
Johns, Thomas L. ... New York, NY
Johns, Timothy J. ... Harwood Heights, IL
Johns, Timothy R. ... Deadwood, SD
Johns, Varner Jay, III ... Eugene, OR
Johns, W. Scott, III ... Devon, PA
Johns, Warren L. ... Brookeville, MD
Johns, William E. ... San Diego, CA
Johns, William F. ... Albany, CA
Johnsen, Bart J. ... Salt Lake City, UT
Johnsen, Bradley L. ... Palo Alto, CA
Johnsen, Brian R. ... Humboldt, IA
Johnsen, Carolyn J. ... Phoenix, AZ
Johnsen, Dawn E. ... Department of Justice, Office of Legal Counsel, GV
Johnsen, Diane M. ... Phoenix, AZ
Johnsen, Donald Peder ... Phoenix, AZ
Johnsen, Elizabeth C. ... San Francisco, CA
Johnsen, Eric Martin ... Columbia, SC
Johnsen, Gregg Eric ... Redmond, WA
Johnsen, Gregory J. ... Coral Gables, FL
Johnsen, Hans E. ... Seattle, WA
Johnsen, Harry L., III ... Bellingham, WA
Johnsen, Jeffrey D. ... Camarillo, CA
Johnsen, Jennifer E. ... Greenville, SC
Johnsen, Jonathan G. ... Buffalo, NY
Johnsen, Kenneth A. ... Des Moines, IA
Johnsen, Kenneth C. ... Orem, UT
Johnsen, Kirk D. ... Dayton, OH
Johnsen, Lawrence P. ... Whitsett, NC
Johnsen, Lisa L. ... Seattle, WA
Johnsen, Manfredi & Thorpe, A Professional Corporation ... Los Angeles, CA
Johnsen, Mark R. ... Seattle, WA
Johnsen, Mark Sterling ... Auburn, WA
Johnsen & Nye, P.L.C. ... Phoenix, AZ
Johnsen, Peter H. ... McLean, VA
Johnsen, R. Christian ... Washington, DC
Johnsen, Robert E., Jr. ... Oak Park, IL
Johnsen, Robert U., Jr. ... Wilmington, NC
Johnsen, Roger A. ... Philadelphia, PA
Johnsen, Roy D. ... Tulsa, OK
Johnsen, Theodore G. ... Los Angeles, CA
Johnsen, Walter C. ... Fresno, CA
Johnsen, Wayne D. ... Washington, DC
Johnsey, C. Gray ... Kinston, NC
Johnsey, Walter F. ... Birmingham, AL
Johns-Harris, LaVon M. ... Chicago, IL
Johnson, A. Clarke ... Tacoma, WA
Johnson, A. Dean ... Tallahassee, FL
Johnson, A. Harrison, Jr., Law Office of
Nashville, TN
Johnson, A. Kyle ... Seattle, WA
Johnson, A. Robert ... Gates Mills, OH
Johnson, A. Rodman ... The Woodlands, TX
Johnson, A. Scott ... Oklahoma City, OK
Johnson, A. Thomas ... Louisville, KY
Johnson, A. Victoria
Department of Housing and Urban Development, Office of General Counsel, GV
Johnson, Aaron C. ... Kansas City, MO
Johnson, Aaron P. ... Fresno, CA
Johnson, Adam L. ... Irvine, CA
Johnson, Adkins & Williams ... Corvallis, OR
Johnson, Adrian L. ... Clinton, CT
Johnson, Adrienne ... Coraopolis, PA
Johnson, Aicha Marie ... Chicago, IL
Johnson, Aileen ... Baton Rouge, LA
Johnson, Al ... Wartburg, TN
Johnson, Al W., Law Offices of
St. Louis, MO
Johnson, Alan ... Malta, MT
Johnson, Alan Anthony ... Deerfield, IL
Johnson, Alan B. ... Cheyenne, WY
Johnson, Alan D. ... Nashville, TN
Johnson, Alan E. ... Durango, CO
Johnson, Alan G. ... St. Louis, MO
Johnson, Alan R. ... New York, NY
Johnson, Alan S. ... West Palm Beach, FL
Johnson, Alan V. ... Topeka, KS
Johnson, Albert G. ... Cannon Falls, MN
Johnson, Albert Louis ... Phenix City, AL
Johnson, Albert Sidney ... Atlanta, GA
Johnson, Albert" Tim ", Jr. ... Seattle, WA
Johnson, Albert W., III ... Harrisburg, PA
Johnson, Alberta C. ... Minneapolis, MN
Johnson, Alberta D. ... Houston, TX
Johnson, Aldana ... Malden, MA
Johnson, Alden C. ... Hamburg, NY
Johnson, Alex ... New York, NY
Johnson, Alexander B. ... New York, NY
Johnson, Alexander C., Jr. ... Portland, OR
Johnson, Alexis H. ... Show Low, AZ
Johnson, Alfred E. ... Fort Myers, FL
Johnson, Alfred G. ... San Francisco, CA
Johnson, Alfred R., Jr. ... Boston, MA
Johnson, Alicia C. ... Russellville, KY
Johnson, Alicia D. ... Department of Justice, Bureau of Prisons, GV
Johnson, Alisa A. ... Washington, DC
Johnson, Alisa B. ... Houston, TX
Johnson, Alise M. ... Miami, FL
Johnson, Allan ... Akron, OH
Johnson, Allan R. ... Virginia Beach, VA
Johnson, Allen ... Austin, TX
Johnson, Allen C. ... Minneapolis, MN
Johnson, Allen C. ... Cheyenne, WY
Johnson, Allen Curtis ... Omaha, NE
Johnson, Allen D. ... Walnut Creek, CA
Johnson, Allen, Jones & Dornblaser
Tulsa, OK
Johnson, Allen L. ... Kansas City, MO
Johnson, Allen L. ... Eugene, OR
Johnson, Allen W. ... Augusta, GA
Johnson, Allison A. ... Minneapolis, MN
Johnson, Almeta A. ... Cleveland, OH
Johnson, Alton P., II ... Carrollton, GA
Johnson, Alvin D. ... Pickens, SC
Johnson, Amber Jade F. ... Winter Park, FL
Johnson, Amie L. ... Charleston, WV
Johnson, Amy ... Austin, TX
Johnson, Amy E. ... Chicago, IL
Johnson, Amy Hines ... Jacksonville, FL
Johnson, Amy K. ... Farmington, CT
Johnson, Amy K. ... Charlotte, NC
Johnson, Amy L. ... Los Angeles, CA
Johnson, Anderson & Zellmer, P.L.L.P.
Mankato, MN
Johnson, Andrea M. ... Houston, TX
Johnson, Andrea M., P.C. ... Houston, TX
Johnson, Andrea P. McCoy ... Jersey City, NJ
Johnson, Andrew ... Columbia, SC
Johnson, Andrew D. ... Roseburg, OR
Johnson, Andrew F. ... Atlanta, GA
Johnson, Andrew L., Jr. ... Cleveland, OH
Johnson, Andrew M. ... Albany, NY
Johnson, Andrew P. ... Paterson, NJ
Johnson, Andrew P. ... Carrizo Springs, TX
Johnson, Andrew P., III ... Houston, TX
Johnson, Andrew R., IV
Lake Charles, LA
Johnson, Andrew Reed ... Denver, CO
Johnson, Andrew R.K. ... Minneapolis, MN
Johnson, Andrewe W. ... Lewistown, IL
Johnson, Angela D. ... Houston, TX
Johnson, Angela F. ... Spartanburg, SC
Johnson, Angelique Kathleen ... Pasadena, CA
Johnson and Angelo ... Cleveland, OH
Columbus, OH
Johnson, Anita ... Pikeville, KY
Johnson, Anita C. ... Accomac, VA
Johnson, Anita Senese ... Chicago, IL
Johnson, Ann F. ... Newport, RI
Johnson, Ann M. ... Philadelphia, PA
Johnson, Ann M. ... Edmonds, WA
Johnson, Ann Marie ... Wilmington, DE
Johnson, Ann R. ... Wappingers Falls, NY
Johnson, Ann W. ... Eau Claire, WI
Johnson, Anne Grasso ... Harrisburg, PA
Johnson, Anne L. ... Baltimore, MD
Johnson, Anne L. ... Minneapolis, MN
Johnson, Anne M. ... Atlanta, GA
Johnson, Anne McGowan ... Dallas, TX
Johnson, Anne S. ... Wayzata, MN
Johnson, Anne S. ... Chambersburg, PA
Johnson, Anne S. ... San Antonio, TX
Johnson, Anne T. ... Minneapolis, MN
Johnson, Annette B. ... New York, NY
Johnson, Anselmo, Murdoch, Burke & George, P.A. ... Fort Lauderdale, FL
West Palm Beach, FL
Johnson, Antar Christopher ... Philadelphia, PA
Johnson, Anthony A.
Colorado Springs, CO
Johnson, Anthony B. ... Centreville, AL
Johnson, Anthony C. ... Seattle, WA
Johnson, Anthony H. ... Orlando, FL
Johnson, Antoinette D. ... Atlanta, GA
Johnson, Antone F. ... Palo Alto, CA
Johnson, Antonia K. ... Coshocton, OH
Johnson, April Shafer ... Burlington, VT
Johnson, Archie Ann
Federal Deposit Insurance Corporation, Liquidation Branch, GV
Johnson, Ariane Schallwig
Indianapolis, IN
Johnson, Arlis W. ... Hoquiam, WA
Johnson, Arne R. ... Portsmouth, RI
Johnson, Arnold C. ... Washington, DC
Johnson, Arnold E. ... Warwick, RI
Johnson, Arnold J. ... Houston, TX
Johnson, Arnold Melvin ... Los Angeles, CA
Johnson, Arthur C. ... Eugene, OR
Johnson, Arthur E. ... Indianapolis, IN
Johnson, Arthur G., Jr. ... Wichita, KS
Johnson, Arthur H. ... Gainesville, FL
Johnson, Arthur H. ... Fort Dodge, IA
Johnson, Arthur L., Jr. ... San Jose, CA
Johnson, Arthur M. ... Phoenix, AZ
Johnson, Arvid C. ... Oak Lawn, IL
Johnson, Ashley Westmoreland ... Waco, TX
Johnson and Associates ... Los Angeles, CA
Johnson & Associates ... Los Angeles, CA
Johnson & Associates ... Newport Beach, CA
Johnson & Associates ... Temecula, CA
Johnson and Associates ... Torrance, CA
Johnson and Associates ... Walnut Creek, CA
Johnson & Associates ... Arlington, VA
Johnson & Associates, P.C. ... Washington, DC
Johnson & Associates, P.C. ... Chicago, IL
Johnson & Associates, P.C.
Grand Forks, ND
Johnson, Austin B., Jr. ... Caldwell, NJ
Johnson, Avery L. ... Department of Justice, Civil Rights Division, GV
Johnson, Axel J., IV
Whitehouse Station, NJ
Johnson, Ayers & Matthews ... Roanoke, VA
Johnson, B. Ardell ... San Jose, CA
Johnson, B. Bruce ... Dallas, TX
Johnson, B. Edwin ... Clearwater, FL
Johnson, B. Gerald ... Seattle, WA
Johnson, B. Henderson, Jr. ... Aiken, SC
Johnson, B. Ruth, Law Office of
Jackson, MS
Johnson & Baggett, An Association of Attorneys ... Memphis, TN
Johnson & Bannon, P.L.L.P. ... Willmar, MN
Johnson, Barbara ... Chicago, IL
Johnson, Barbara A.
Department of Labor, GV
Johnson, Barbara Ackerman ... Burlington, NC
Johnson, Barbara Ann ... Cherry Hill, NJ
Johnson, Barbara D. ... Vancouver, WA
Johnson, Barbara E. ... Los Angeles, CA
Johnson, Barbara E. ... Pittsburgh, PA
Johnson, Barbara J.
Department of State, GV
Johnson, Barbara J. ... Bellevue, WA
Johnson, Barbara Jean ... Pasadena, CA
Johnson, Barbara K. ... Santa Ana, CA
Johnson, Barbara L. ... Houston, TX
Johnson, Barbara M. ... Boston, MA
Johnson, Barbara R. ... Inglewood, CA
Johnson, Barbara V. ... Albuquerque, NM
Johnson, Barrett G. ... Tallahassee, FL
Johnson, Barry ... Dallas, TX
Johnson, Barry A. ... San Francisco, CA
Johnson, Barry D. ... Dallas, TX
Johnson, Barry E. ... Los Angeles, CA
Johnson, Barry G. ... Fort Worth, TX
Johnson, Barry L. ... Oklahoma City, OK
Johnson, Barry L. ... Beaufort, SC
Hilton Head Island, SC
Johnson, Barry L., P.A. ... Beaufort, SC
Hilton Head Island, SC
Johnson, Barry M. ... McLean, VA
Johnson, Barry M. ... Seattle, WA
Johnson, Barry N. ... Salt Lake City, UT
Johnson, Barry W. ... Oklahoma City, OK
Johnson, Barry W., P.C. ... Oklahoma City, OK
Johnson & Baughan, P.A. ... Melbourne, FL
Orlando, FL
Rockledge, FL
Charlotte Amalie, St. Thomas, VI
Johnson, Beaman & Todd, P.C.
Marion, IN
Johnson, Becky A. ... Portland, OR
Johnson, Belinda J. ... Dallas, TX
Johnson & Bell, Ltd. ... Chicago, IL
Waukegan, IL
Wheaton, IL
Highland, IN
Johnson, Ben E. ... San Diego, CA
Johnson, Ben F., III ... Atlanta, GA
Johnson, Benjamin A. ... San Mateo, CA
Johnson, Benjamin A. ... Rock Hill, SC
Johnson, Benjamin F., IV ... Atlanta, GA
Johnson, Benjamin J. ... Atlanta, GA
Johnson, Benjamin L., Jr.
Donaldsonville, LA
Johnson, Berens & Wilson ... Fairmont, MN
Johnson, Berkeley D., Jr.
New Canaan, CT
Johnson, Bernard E. ... St. Paul, MN
Johnson, Bernard G., III ... Houston, TX
Johnson, Bernard S. ... Shreveport, LA
Johnson, Bertil F. ... Tacoma, WA
Johnson, Bertyl V., Jr. ... Nantucket, MA
Johnson, Beth Exum ... New Orleans, LA
Johnson, Beverly A. ... Irvine, CA
Johnson, Beverly G. Grant ... Tacoma, WA
Johnson, Beverly J. ... Alameda, CA
Johnson, Beverly M. ... South Orange, NJ
Johnson, Bill ... Nicholasville, KY
Johnson, Bill R. ... St. Paul, MN
Johnson, Billie L. ... Edwardsville, IL
Johnson, Billy Bruce, Jr. ... Houston, TX
Johnson, Bjarne ... Great Falls, MT
Johnson, Bjornlie & Merritt
Los Angeles, CA
Johnson, Blaine B., Jr. ... Jackson, MI

Johnson, Blaine B., Jr., P.C. ....Jackson, MI
Johnson, Blair M. ....Winter Garden, FL
Johnson, Blair M., P.A. ....Winter Garden, FL
Johnson & Blake, P.A. ....Tempe, AZ
Johnson, Blakely, Pope, Bokor, Ruppel & Burns, P.A. ....Clearwater, FL
Dade City, FL
Holiday, FL
Hudson, FL
Land O'Lakes, FL
Naples, FL
New Port Richey, FL
St. Petersburg, FL
Tampa, FL
Johnson Bobo, PLLC ....Clarksdale, MS
Johnson, Bonde Erik ....Groton, CT
Johnson, Bonnie L. ....Cincinnati, OH
Johnson, Bonnie Louise ....Burlington, MA
Johnson, Bonnie S. ....Overland Park, KS
Johnson & Bowen ....El Paso, TX
Johnson, Boyd M. ....Austin, TX
Johnson, Boyd T. ....Florence, AZ
Johnson & Boyle ....San Francisco, CA
Johnson, Brad C. ....Washington, DC
Johnson, Brad L. ....Denver, CO
Johnson, Bradford A. ....East Hartford, CT
Johnson, Bradford F. ....Richmond, VA
Johnson, Bradford H. ....Springfield, VA
Johnson, Bradley Clar ....Seattle, WA
Johnson, Bradley D. ....Bellevue, WA
Johnson, Bradley H. ....Charlotte, NC
Johnson, Bradley J. ....Decatur, IL
Johnson, Bradley R. ....Jacksonville, FL
Johnson, Bradley R. ....Tampa, FL
Johnson, Bradley R. ....Minneapolis, MN
Johnson, Bradley T. ....Washington, DC
Johnson, Bradley W. ....Fort Collins, CO
Johnson, Bradley W. ....Chicago, IL
Johnson, Bradly W. ....Olathe, KS
Johnson, Brady R. ....Seattle, WA
Johnson, Brandon A. ....Grove, OK
Johnson, Brandon G. ....Philadelphia, PA
Johnson, Brandt R. ....Edinburg, TX
Johnson, Brenda B. ....Hattiesburg, MS
Johnson, Brenda E. ....New York, NY
Johnson, Brenda M. ....Cleveland, OH
Johnson, Brendan Hinton ....Oakland, CA
Johnson, Brent ....Anchorage, AK
Johnson, Brent ....Dallas, TX
Johnson, Brent E. ....Salt Lake City, UT
Johnson, Brent M. ....Oklahoma City, OK
Johnson, Brent M. ....Salt Lake City, UT
Johnson, Brent P. ....Englewood, CO
Johnson, Brent R. ....Hudson, WI
Johnson, Brent T. ....Denver, CO
Johnson, Brent W. ....Maryville, TN
Johnson, Brett Lindsey ....Rock Springs, WY
Johnson, Brett P. ....Salt Lake City, UT
Johnson, Brian A. ....Washington, DC
Johnson, Brian A. ....Chicago, IL
Johnson, Brian C ....Salt Lake City, UT
Johnson, Brian D. ....Austin, MN
Johnson, Brian D. ....Cleveland, OH
Johnson, Brian E. ....Seminole, FL
Johnson, Brian E., P.A. ....Seminole, FL
Johnson, Brian K. ....Westfield, NJ
Johnson, Brian L. ....Traverse City, MI
Johnson, Brian L. ....Seattle, WA
Johnson, Brian M. ....Lexington, KY
Johnson, Brian N. ....Minneapolis, MN
Johnson, Brian P. ....Houston, TX
Johnson, Brian S. ....Jacksonville, FL
Johnson, Brian Scott ....Austin, TX
Johnson, Brian T. ....Cleveland, OH
Johnson, Bridget Griffin ....Dallas, TX
Johnson, Brown W. ....Florence, SC
Johnson, Bruce ....Canon City, CO
Johnson, Bruce A.
Department Of The Interior, Office of Hearings & Appeals, GV
Johnson, Bruce A. ....Minneapolis, MN
Johnson, Bruce A. ....Dripping Springs, TX
Johnson, Bruce A., Jr. ....Washington, DC
Johnson, Bruce B. ....Denver, CO
Johnson, Bruce B., Jr. ....Fresno, CA
Johnson, Bruce C. ....Silver Spring, MD
Johnson, Bruce C. ....New York, NY
Johnson, Bruce C. ....Yanceyville, NC
Johnson, Bruce D. ....Jacksonville, FL
Johnson, Bruce D. ....Fargo, ND
Johnson, Bruce E.
Department of Commerce, GV
Johnson, Bruce E. ....Des Moines, IA
Johnson, Bruce E. ....Columbus, OH
Johnson, Bruce E. H. ....Seattle, WA
Johnson, Bruce Elwood
San Francisco, CA
Johnson, Bruce F. ....Palm Springs, CA
Johnson, Bruce H. ....Oklahoma City, OK
Johnson, Bruce M. ....Clearwater, FL
Johnson, Bruce N. ....Aurora, IL
Johnson, Bruce N. ....Center City, MN
Johnson, Bruce P. ....Oakland, CA
Johnson, Bruce P. ....Atlanta, GA
Johnson, Bruce R. ....Louisville, CO
Johnson, Bruce R. ....Portland, ME
Johnson, Bruce R. S. ....Minneapolis, MN
Johnson, Bruce S. ....Minneapolis, MN
Johnson, Bruce S. ....Columbia, SC
Johnson, Bryan B. ....Columbus, OH
Johnson, Bryce B. ....Oklahoma City, OK
Johnson, Bryce M. ....Austin, TX
Johnson, Bryn R. ....Phoenix, AZ
Johnson, Bunce & Noble, P.C. ....Peoria, IL
Johnson, Burke B. ....Atlanta, GA
Johnson, Burton A. ....Sandy Spring, MD
Johnson, Burton J. ....Oklahoma City, OK
Johnson, Butch L. ....Salt Lake City, UT
Johnson, Byron ....Rochester, NY
Johnson, Byron J. ....Buena Park, CA
Johnson, Byron J. ....Boise, ID
Johnson, Byron M. ....Gering, NE
Johnson, C. Andrew ....North Mankato, MN
Johnson, C. Bedford ....New York, NY
Johnson, C. Brad ....Costa Mesa, CA
Johnson, C. Brendan ....Chicago, IL
Johnson, C. Chad ....New York, NY
Johnson, C. Clayton ....Portsmouth, OH
Johnson, C. Donald, Jr.
Executive Office Of The President, Office of the U.S. Trade Representative, GV
Johnson, C. George ....Lansing, MI
Johnson, C. Gordon, Jr.
New Orleans, LA
Johnson, C. Harlan ....Pasco, WA
Johnson, C. Howard ....Columbus, OH
Johnson, C. Judith ....Burlingame, CA
Johnson, C. Michael ....Atlanta, GA
Johnson, C. Michael ....Eastman, GA
Johnson, C. Neal ....Pasadena, CA
Johnson, C. Neil ....Edwardsville, VA
Johnson, C. Nevada, Jr. ....Medina, OH
Johnson, C. Randal ....Birmingham, AL
Johnson, C. Reginald ....Philadelphia, PA
Johnson, C. Richard ....Chicago, IL
Johnson, C. Scott ....Jasper, AL
Johnson, C. Terry ....Dayton, OH
Johnson, C. William ....Omaha, NE
Johnson, C. Winfield, III
Myrtle Beach, SC
Johnson, C. A. (Gus), II ....Mankato, MN
Johnson, Caldwell & McCoy
Lafayette, AL
Lanett, AL
West Point, GA
Johnson, Caliph ....Houston, TX
Johnson, Calvin ....New Orleans, LA
Johnson, Calvin H. ....Austin, TX
Johnson, Calvin L. ....Tallahassee, FL
Johnson, Calvin P. ....Mankato, MN
Johnson, Calvin T., Jr. ....Columbus, OH
Johnson, Camick & Keil Co., L.P.A.
Toledo, OH
Johnson, Camille ....Dallas, TX
Johnson, Camille Neddo
Salt Lake City, UT
Johnson, Candace D. ....Mobile, AL
Johnson, Candace Merifield ....Tulsa, OK
Johnson, Cara E. ....Albany, NY
Johnson, Carey H. ....Fresno, CA
Johnson, Carl B. ....San Francisco, CA
Johnson, Carl E. ....Chicago, IL
Johnson, Carl E. ....South Hamilton, MA
Johnson, Carl E., Jr. ....Birmingham, AL
Johnson, Carl E., Jr. ....Charlotte, NC
Johnson, Carl H., Jr. ....Grand Rapids, MI
Johnson, Carl I. ....Bloomfield, NJ
Johnson, Carl L. ....Gainesville, FL
Johnson, Carl L. ....St. Paul, MN
Johnson, Carl O. ....Ceres, CA
Johnson, Carl R., III ....Quincy, MA
Johnson, Carl R., III, P.C. ....Quincy, MA
Johnson, Carl T. ....El Paso, TX
Johnson, Carl T., A Prof. Corp., Law Offices of ....El Paso, TX
Johnson, Carla J. ....Sherman Oaks, CA
Johnson, Carla Register ....Atlanta, GA
Johnson, Carlene Booth ....Dillwyn, VA
Johnson, Carlton M., Jr. ....Roswell, GA
Johnson, Carmen S. ....Miami, FL
Johnson, Carol ....Hartford, CT
Johnson, Carol ....Skokie, IL
Johnson, Carol ....Dallas, TX
Johnson, Carol A. ....Anchorage, AK
Johnson, Carol A. ....Chicago, IL
Johnson, Carol Ann ....Washington, DC
Johnson, Carol Cox
Federal Energy Regulatory Commission, Office of the General Counsel, GV
Johnson, Carol Cozzi ....Chicago, IL
Johnson, Carol E. ....Grand Forks, ND
Johnson, Carol L. ....Chicago, IL
Johnson, Carol L. ....Everett, WA
Johnson, Carol M. ....Springfield, MA
Johnson, Carol S. ....San Francisco, CA
Johnson, Carol Schanno ....Washington, DC
Johnson, Carol W. ....Hopkinsville, KY
Johnson, Carolyn J. ....Kansas City, MO
Johnson, Carolyn M. ....Houston, TX
Johnson, Carolyn P. ....Lawrence, KS
Johnson, Carolyn S. ....Boulder, CO
Johnson, Carolynn M. ....Minneapolis, MN
Johnson, Carrie E. ....Los Angeles, CA
Johnson, Carroll ....Knoxville, IA
Johnson, Carroll C., III ....Memphis, TN
Johnson, Carroll C., Law Offices of
Memphis, TN
Johnson, Carroll F. ....Peoria, IL
Johnson, Carroll & Griffith, Professional Corporation ....Evansville, IN
Johnson, Cary A. ....Houston, TX
Johnson, Cary B. ....Minneapolis, MN
Johnson, Cassandra Tsintolas
Department of the Army, Army Materiel Command, GV
Johnson, Casterton & Grundhoefer, P.A.
Center City, MN
Johnson, Catherine B. ....Augusta, ME
Johnson, Catherine D. ....Richmond, VA
Johnson, Catherine G. ....Red Wing, MN
Johnson, Catherine Hope ....St. Louis, MO
Johnson, Catherine Keib ....Syracuse, NY
Johnson, Catherine W. ....Oakland, CA
Johnson, Catherine-Sylvia C. ....Hampton, VA
Johnson, Cathy A. Smith ....Kingwood, TX
Johnson, Cebula & Rygh
Los Angeles, CA
Santa Ana, CA
Long Beach, CA
Johnson, Cecil W. ....Portsmouth, VA
Johnson, Cecilia ....Asheville, NC
Johnson, Chad A. ....Eden Prairie, MN
Johnson, Chad A. ....Dallas, TX
Johnson, Chad S. ....Washington, DC
Johnson, Channing D. ....Los Angeles, CA
Johnson, Charlene Haught
San Francisco, CA
Johnson, Charles A. ....Roseville, MN
Johnson, Charles A. ....Jersey City, NJ
New York, NY
Johnson, Charles A. ....Dayton, OH
Johnson, Charles A. ....Oklahoma City, OK
Johnson, Charles A., Jr. ....Seattle, WA
Johnson, Charles B. ....New Orleans, LA
Johnson, Charles C. ....Madison Lake, MN
Johnson, Charles D. ....Leesburg, FL
Johnson, Charles D. ....Gurnee, IL
Johnson, Charles D. ....McPherson, KS
Johnson, Charles D. ....Carrizo Springs, TX
Johnson, Charles D. ....Houston, TX
Johnson, Charles E. ....Evanston, IL
Johnson, Charles E. ....Charlotte, NC
Johnson, Charles E., III ....Alpharetta, GA
Johnson, Charles F. ....Universal City, CA
Johnson, Charles F. ....Thomasville, GA
Johnson, Charles F. ....Osage Beach, MO
Johnson, Charles F. ....Dallas, TX
Johnson, Charles F., III ....Bradenton, FL
Johnson, Charles F., III ....Jackson, MS
Johnson, Charles G. ....El Centro, CA
Palm Springs, CA
San Diego, CA
Johnson, Charles G. ....Rochester, NY
Johnson, Charles G. ....Clarksburg, WV
Johnson, Charles H. ....Miami, FL
Johnson, Charles H. ....New Brighton, MN
Johnson, Charles H. ....Philadelphia, PA
Johnson, Charles J., III ....Boston, MA
Johnson, Charles J., Jr. ....New York, NY
Johnson, Charles K. ....Pittsburgh, PA
Johnson, Charles L. ....Downey, CA
Johnson, Charles L. ....San Francisco, CA
Johnson, Charles L. ....Barnstable, MA
Johnson, Charles M. ....Charleston, WV
Johnson, Charles R. ....Phoenix, AZ
Johnson, Charles R. ....Lemoore, CA
Johnson, Charles R. ....Great Falls, MT
Johnson, Charles R. ....Dallas, TX
Johnson, Charles R. ....Olympia, WA
Johnson, Charles Rick ....Gregory, SD
Sioux Falls, SD
Johnson, Charles S. ....St. Louis, MO
Johnson, Charles S. ....Houston, TX
Johnson, Charles S. ....San Antonio, TX
Johnson, Charles S., III ....Atlanta, GA
Johnson, Charles Snowdon ....Westport, CT
Johnson, Charles T. ....Taftsville, VT
Johnson, Charles T., Jr. ....Warrenton, NC
Johnson, Charles V. ....Seattle, WA
Johnson, Charles W. ....Littleton, CO
Johnson, Charles W. ....Mount Prospect, IL
Johnson, Charles W. ....Petoskey, MI
Johnson, Charles W. ....Minneapolis, MN
Johnson, Charles W., III
House of Representatives, Office of Parliamentarian, GV
Johnson, Charles W., IV ....Washington, DC
Johnson, Charles William ....Las Vegas, NV
Johnson, Charlie R. ....Sevierville, TN
Johnson, Charlotte H. ....Detroit, MI
Johnson, Charna ....Phoenix, AZ
Johnson, Chas. T. ....Belmont, MA
Johnson, Cheryl A. ....Milwaukee, WI
Johnson, Cheryl Ann ....Austin, TX
Johnson, Cheryl Barnes ....Los Angeles, CA
Johnson, Cheryl L. ....Westport, CT
Johnson, Cheryl L. ....Dallas, TX
Johnson, Cheryl Lee ....Los Angeles, CA
Johnson, Cheryl Lynn
House of Representatives, Committee Legal Personnel, GV
Johnson, Chester N. ....Bloomfield, CT
Johnson, Chris ....Houston, TX
Johnson, Chris P. ....Monterey, CA
Johnson, Chris T. ....Phoenix, AZ
Johnson, Chris T., P.C. ....Phoenix, AZ
Johnson, Christi Cameron
Minneapolis, MN
Johnson, Christian ....Cherry Hill, NJ
Johnson, Christian A. ....Chicago, IL
Johnson, Christian K. ....Ouray, CO
Johnson, Christian Peter ....Newark, NJ
New York, NY
Johnson, Christian Scott
Chattanooga, TN
Johnson, Christina L. ....Los Angeles, CA
Johnson, Christina L. ....Los Angeles, CA
Johnson, Christina Nieto ....Live Oak, FL
Johnson, Christine ....Schenectady, NY
Johnson, Christine A. ....Mariposa, CA
Johnson, Christine Anne ....Sebring, FL
Johnson, Christine E. ....Anchorage, AK
Johnson, Christine M. ....Los Angeles, CA
Johnson, Christophe A. ....Kansas City, MO
Johnson, Christopher A. ....Hastings, NE
Johnson, Christopher A. ....Cleveland, OH
Johnson, Christopher A. ....McLean, VA
Johnson, Christopher B. ....Pasadena, CA
Johnson, Christopher D. ....Phoenix, AZ
Johnson, Christopher D.
Minneapolis, MN
Johnson, Christopher F. ....Dayton, OH
Johnson, Christopher G. ....Rochester, NY
Johnson, Christopher H. ....Washington, DC
Johnson, Christopher J.
Farmington Hills, MI
Johnson, Christopher J. ....Elk River, MN
Johnson, Christopher J. ....Milwaukee, WI
Johnson, Christopher M. ....Irvine, CA
Johnson, Christopher M. .....Washington, DC
Johnson, Christopher M. ....Atlanta, GA
Johnson, Christopher N. ....Miami, FL
Johnson, Christopher P. ....New York, NY
Johnson, Christopher Paul ....Norton, VA
Johnson, Christopher R. ....Pensacola, FL
Johnson, Christopher R. ....Baltimore, MD
Johnson, Christopher, Javore & Cochran, Inc. ....San Antonio, TX
Johnson, Christopher W. ....Chicago, IL
Johnson, Cindy M. ....Chicago, IL
Johnson, Cindy M. ....Joliet, IL
Johnson, Claiborne H. ....Jacksonville, TX
Johnson, Claire D. ....Los Angeles, CA
Johnson, Clare M. ....New York, NY
Johnson, Clarence ....Cleveland, OH
Johnson, Clarence Q. ....Syracuse, NY
Johnson, Clarence R., Jr. ....Covington, GA
Johnson, Clarence T., Jr. ....Merritt Island, FL
Johnson, Clark C. ....Chicago, IL
Johnson, Clark E., III ....Guntersville, AL
Johnson, Clark E., Jr. ....Albertville, AL
Johnson, Claude W. ....Augusta, GA
Johnson, Claudia C. ....Philadelphia, PA
Johnson, Clay M. ....Sulphur Springs, TX
Johnson, Clayton R. ....Minneapolis, MN
Johnson, Clayton (Swede) ....Boulder, CO
Johnson, Clayton V. ....Detroit, MI
Johnson, Clayton V., P.C. ....Detroit, MI
Johnson, Cletus J. ....Green Bay, WI
Johnson & Cleverley ....Newton, IA
Johnson, Clifford A. ....Dover, NJ
Johnson, Clifford J. ....Taos, NM
Johnson, Clifford L. ....Warren, MI
Johnson, Clifford P. ....Memphis, TN
Johnson, Clifton E. ....Indianapolis, IN
Johnson, Clifton E. ....Charlotte, NC
Johnson, Clifton, Larson & Corson, P.C.
Eugene, OR
Johnson, Clifton M. ....Department of State, Office of the Legal Adviser, GV
Johnson, Clifton Wade ....Scottsboro, AL
Johnson, Clint P. ....Lakewood, WA
Johnson, Clinton A. ....Oakland, CA
Johnson, Clinton L. ....Chester, PA
Johnson, Cloise E., Jr. ....Kingfisher, OK
Johnson, Clyde E., Jr. ....San Antonio, TX
Johnson, Clyde F., Law Office of
Prestonsburg, KY
Johnson, Clyde J. B., III ....San Antonio, TX
Johnson, Clyde J. B., Jr. ....Bulverde, TX
Johnson, Coby R. ....Boston, MA
Johnson & Cohen, LLP ....Pearl River, NY
White Plains, NY
Johnson, Colin ....Dresden, TN
Johnson, Colin D. ....North Branford, CT
Johnson and Colmar ....Chicago, IL
Johnson, Colrena K. ....Tustin, CA
Johnson, Colton P. ....Albany, TX
Johnson & Condon, P.A.
Minneapolis, MN
Johnson, Connie E. ....Atlanta, GA
Johnson, Conrad ....New York, NY
Johnson, Conrad A. ....Pittsburgh, PA
Johnson, Constance E. ....San Francisco, CA
Johnson, Constance L. ....Houma, LA
Johnson, Cordell ....Helena, MT
Johnson, Corwin W. ....Austin, TX
Johnson, Cory A. ....Chicago, IL
Johnson, Coy ....Sulphur Springs, TX
Johnson, Coy R. ....Cumming, GA
Johnson, Craig A. ....Peoria, IL
Johnson, Craig B. ....River Edge, NJ
Johnson, Craig D. ....Broomfield, CO
Johnson, Craig E. ....Bakersfield, CA
Johnson, Craig E. ....White Plains, NY
Johnson, Craig E. ....Fargo, ND
Johnson, Craig H. ....Encinitas, CA
Los Altos, CA
Salt Lake City, UT
Johnson, Craig H. ....Buffalo, NY
Johnson, Craig Louis ....Louisville, KY
Johnson, Craig M. ....New York, NY
Johnson, Craig N. ....Denver, CO
Johnson, Craig R. ....Madison, WI
Johnson, Craig S. ....Coral Springs, FL
Johnson, Craig S. ....Jefferson City, MO
Johnson, Craig W. ....Menlo Park, CA
Johnson, Craig W. ....Austin, MN
Johnson, Cram, Harder & Wells
Eugene, OR
Johnson & Crane ....Auburn, WA
Johnson, Crēola ....Iowa City, IA
Johnson, Cris Edward ....White Plains, NY
Johnson, Crisanta A. ....Pasadena, CA
Johnson, Crista R. ....High Ridge, MO
Johnson, Curney & Fields, P.C.
San Antonio, TX
Johnson, Curt M. ....Lanett, AL
Johnson, Curtis A. ....Newark, NJ
Johnson, Curtis D. ....Memphis, TN
Johnson, Curtis G. ....Port Angeles, WA
Johnson, Curtis Lee ....Antioch, CA
Johnson, Cynthia Carney ....Rye Brook, NY
Johnson, Cynthia E. ....Boston, MA
Johnson, Cynthia L. ....Pittsburgh, PA
Johnson, Cynthia L.M. ....Detroit, MI
Johnson, Cynthia M. ....Miami, FL
Johnson, Cynthia M. ....St. Paul, MN
Johnson, Cynthia Noles ....Dalton, GA
Johnson, Cynthia P.
United States International Trade

Commission,
Office of the General Counsel, GV
Johnson, Cyrus A. ... Sacramento, CA
Johnson, Cyrus M., Jr. ... Charlotte, NC
Johnson, D. Boyd ... Atlanta, GA
Johnson, D. Keith ... Florence, KY
Johnson, D. Kyle ... Montgomery, AL
Johnson, D. Lee ... Toledo, OH
Johnson, D. Sam ... Nampa, ID
Johnson, D. Thomas ... Lubbock, TX
Johnson, Dalana W. ... Tallahassee, FL
Johnson, Dale A., (P.A.)
St. Petersburg, FL
Johnson, Dale B. ... Syracuse, NY
Johnson, Dale C. ... Springfield, OR
Johnson, Dale E. ... Boulder, CO
Johnson, Dale E. ... Birmingham, MI
Johnson, Dale H. ... Lubbock, TX
Johnson, Dale P. ... Clinton, NC
Johnson, Dale R. ... Concord, MA
Johnson, Dale R. ... San Antonio, TX
Johnson, Dan B. ... Spokane, WA
Johnson, Dana C. ... Los Angeles, CA
Johnson, D'Ana E. ... Washington, DC
Johnson, Daniel B. ... Bethesda, MD
Johnson, Daniel B. ... Minneapolis, MN
Stillwater, MN
Johnson, Daniel B. ... Springfield, MO
Johnson, Daniel C. ... Orlando, FL
Johnson, Daniel E. ... Washington, DC
Johnson, Daniel G. ... Stamford, CT
Johnson, Daniel J. ... Minnetonka, MN
Johnson, Daniel, Jr. ... Palo Alto, CA
Johnson, Daniel L. ... Chicago, IL
Johnson, Daniel L. ... Omaha, NE
Johnson, Daniel L., Jr. ... Charlotte, NC
Johnson, Daniel P. ... Wilmington, DE
Johnson, Daniel P. ... Pittsburgh, PA
Johnson, Daniel P. ... Sioux Falls, SD
Johnson, Daniel R. ... Wilton, CT
Johnson, Daniel R. ... Brookfield, WI
Johnson, Daniel T. ... Palm Springs, CA
Johnson, Daniel W. ... Whispering Pines, NC
Johnson, Daniel W. ... Yakima, WA
Johnson, Daniel W., (A Professional
Corporation) ... Woodland Hills, CA
Johnson, Danielle Z. ... Fort Collins, CO
Johnson, Danny D. ... New Philadelphia, OH
Johnson, Danya L. ... Edwardsville, IL
Johnson, Darci A. ... Los Angeles, CA
Johnson, Daren T. ... Los Angeles, CA
San Diego, CA
San Francisco, CA
Santa Ana, CA
Johnson, Darlene C. ... San Diego, CA
Johnson, Darlene J. ... Seattle, WA
Johnson, Darlene R. ... Houston, TX
Johnson, Darnisa C. Evans
West Memphis, AR
Johnson, Darrel E. ... Olathe, KS
Johnson, Darrell B. ... Minneapolis, MN
Johnson, Darrell Lee ... Los Angeles, CA
Johnson, Darrell T., Jr. ... Hardeeville, SC
Johnson, Darrell V. ... Park City, UT
Johnson, Darrell W. ... Fort Smith, AR
Johnson, Darryl Brent, Jr. ... Walker, LA
Johnson, Darryl E. ... Roseburg, OR
Johnson, Darryl E., P.C. ... Roseburg, OR
Johnson, Darwin E. ... Kansas City, MO
Johnson, Darwin F. ... Morgantown, WV
Johnson, Dave T. ... Lafayette, LA
Johnson, David A. ... Chicago, IL
Johnson, David A. ... Knoxville, IA
Johnson, David A. ... Fridley, MN
Johnson, David A. ... Tulsa, OK
Johnson, David Allen ... Hartford, CT
Johnson, David Arthur ... Honolulu, HI
Johnson, David B. ... Jackson, CA
Sacramento, CA
Johnson, David B.
Department Of The Interior,
Office of the Solicitor, GV
Johnson, David B. ... Chicago, IL
Johnson, David B. ... Eaton Rapids, MI
Johnson, David B. ... Albany, NY
Johnson, David C. ... Beverly Hills, CA
Johnson, David C. ... Carbondale, IL
Johnson, David C. ... International Falls, MN
Johnson, David C. ... St. Louis, MO
Santa Fe, NM
Johnson, David Charles ... Las Vegas, NV
Johnson, David Cromwell ... Birmingham, AL
Johnson, David D. ... Las Vegas, NV
Johnson, David D. ... Charleston, WV
Johnson, David D., III ... Charleston, WV
Johnson, David E. ... Somers, CT
Johnson, David E. ... Covington, KY
Johnson, David E. ... Boston, MA
Johnson, David E. ... Pittsburgh, PA
Johnson, David E. ... Richmond, VA
Johnson, David E., Jr. ... Trenton, NJ
Johnson, David F. ... Waco, TX
Johnson, David G. ... Brighton, MI
Johnson, David G. ... St. Paul, MN
Johnson, David G. ... Las Vegas, NV
Johnson, David George ... Prior Lake, MN
Johnson, David George, P.A., Law Office
Prior Lake, MN
Johnson, David H. ... Fort Collins, CO
Johnson, David H. ... New Haven, CT
Johnson, David H. ... Savannah, GA
Johnson, David H. ... Minneapolis, MN
Johnson, David H. ... Kansas City, MO
Johnson, David H. ... Albuquerque, NM
Johnson, David H. ... New York, NY
Johnson, David H. ... Houston, TX
Johnson, David J. ... Memphis, TN
Johnson, David J. ... Richmond, VA
Johnson, David J., Jr. ... Los Angeles, CA
Johnson, David K. ... Los Angeles, CA
Johnson, David K. ... Bloomfield, IN
Johnson, David L. ... San Luis Obispo, CA
Johnson, David L. ... United States Senate,
Committee Legal Personnel, GV
Johnson, David L. ... Westminster, MD
Johnson, David L. ... Billings, MT
Johnson, David L. ... Newton, NJ
Johnson, David L. ... Charlotte, NC
Johnson, David L. ... Fargo, ND
Johnson, David L. ... Columbus, OH
Johnson, David L. ... Columbus, OH
Johnson, David L. ... Johnston, RI
Johnson, David L. ... Nashville, TN
Johnson, David Lawther ... Indianapolis, IN
Johnson, David M. ... Colorado Springs, CO
Johnson, David M. ... Denver, CO
Johnson, David M. ... Washington, DC
Johnson, David M. ... Duluth, MN
Johnson, David N. ... Wichita, KS
Johnson, David N. ... Kansas City, MO
Johnson, David P. ... Sarasota, FL
Johnson, David P. ... Worcester, MA
Johnson, David P. ... Portland, OR
Johnson, David R. ... Irvine, CA
Johnson, David R. ... Washington, DC
Johnson, David R. ... Washington, DC
Johnson, David R. ... Washington, DC
Johnson, David R. ... Springfield, IL
Johnson, David R. ... Clarion, IA
Johnson, David R. ... Okemos, MI
Johnson, David R. ... Pittsburgh, PA
Johnson, David R. ... Richmond, VA
Johnson, David R. ... Port Orchard, WA
Johnson, David S. ... Tampa, FL
Johnson, David S. ... Minneapolis, MN
Johnson, David S. ... Seattle, WA
Johnson, David Stafford ... Denver, CO
Johnson, David V. ... Marietta, GA
Johnson, David V. ... Port Angeles, WA
Johnson, David W. ... Palo Alto, CA
Johnson, David W. ... Minneapolis, MN
Johnson, David W. ... Minneapolis, MN
Johnson, David W. ... Tupper Lake, NY
Johnson, David W. ... Houston, TX
Johnson, David W. ... Salt Lake City, UT
Johnson, David W. ... Charleston, WV
Johnson, David Wayne, Jr.
Los Angeles, CA
Johnson & Davis ... Covington, GA
Johnson, Dawn E. ... Santa Ana, CA
Johnson, Dawn Morville ... St. Louis, MO
Johnson, Dawn Roe ... Kansas City, MO
Johnson, Dean E. ... San Mateo, CA
Johnson, Dean J. ... Beaumont, TX
Johnson, Dean K. ... Minneapolis, MN
Johnson, Dean R. ... San Francisco, CA
Johnson, Deane A. ... Plainsboro, NJ
Johnson, Deann D. ... Vinita, OK
Johnson, Deanna Bell ... Nashville, TN
Johnson, Debbie Watts ... Dayton, OH
Johnson, Deborah A. ... Ann Arbor, MI
Johnson, Deborah Drayna ... Madison, WI
Johnson, Deborah H. ... Orlando, FL
Johnson, Deborah L. ... St. Paul, MN
Johnson, Deborah R. ... Tucker, GA
Johnson, Debra S. ... Orlando, FL
Johnson, Debra S., P.A. ... Orlando, FL
Johnson, Deidre ... Sacramento, CA
Johnson, Deirdre G. ... Washington, DC
Johnson, Delbert W. ... Olympia, WA
Johnson, Delia W. ... Houston, TX
Johnson, Delinda R. ... Amarillo, TX
Johnson, Delos R., Jr. ... Franklinton, LA
Johnson, Denise ... Tulsa, OK
Johnson, Denise A. ... Chicago, IL
Johnson, Denise L. ... Des Moines, IA
Johnson, Denise M. ... Columbus, OH
Johnson, Dennis A. ... Indianapolis, IN
Johnson, Dennis B. ... White Bear Lake, MN
Johnson, Dennis Edward
Watford City, ND
Johnson, Dennis F.
Federal Trade Commission,
Bureau of Competition, GV
Johnson, Dennis J., Law Offices of
South Burlington, VT
Johnson, Dennis L. ... Duluth, GA
Johnson, Dennis L. ... Nampa, ID
Johnson, Dennis L. ... Minneapolis, MN
Johnson, Dennis P. ... Lakeland, FL
Lake Wales, FL
Winter Haven, FL
Johnson, Dennis P. W. ... Chicago, IL
Johnson, Dennis R. ... Washington, DC
Johnson, Dennis R. ... Minneapolis, MN
Johnson, Dennis Ray ... Memphis, TN
Johnson, Dennis W. ... Des Moines, IA
Johnson, Derek C. ... Eugene, OR
Johnson, Derek G. ... Irvine, CA
Johnson, Derek M. ... Hartford, CT
Johnson, Derek Quinn ... New York, NY
Johnson, Deron L. ... Prestonsburg, KY
Johnson, Derren S. ... Baton Rouge, LA
Johnson, Derwood ... Waco, TX
Johnson, Desiree Calas ... Miami, FL
Johnson, Dexter ... Chicago, IL
Johnson, Dexter A. ... Salem, OR
Johnson, Diana C. ... Richmond, TX
Johnson, Diana L. ... Point Pleasant, WV
Johnson, Diane Kjaer ... Iowa City, IA
Johnson, Diane T. ... Dallas, TX
Johnson, Dianne S. ... St. Louis, MO
Johnson, Dina Cannariato ... Rockville, MD
Johnson, Dina R. ... Roseland, NJ
Johnson, Dirk D. ... Lubbock, TX
Johnson, Dixie Lynn ... Washington, DC
Johnson, Dolores J. ... Metropolis, IL
Johnson, Dominique S. ... Greenbelt, MD
Johnson, Don
Federal Communications Commission,
Wireless Telecommunications Bureau, GV
Johnson, Don ... Coleman, TX
Johnson, Don A. ... Albert Lea, MN
Kiester, MN
Johnson, Don E. ... Pinckneyville, IL
Johnson, Don H. ... West Monroe, LA
Johnson, Don I. ... La Canada Flintridge, CA
Johnson, Don O. ... Cookeville, TN
Johnson, Don W. ... Fayetteville, GA
Johnson, Donald C. ... Department of State,
Foreign Service Officers (Overseas), GV
Johnson, Donald C. ... Lafayette, IN
Johnson, Donald D. ... Golf, IL
Johnson, Donald E. ... Birmingham, AL
Johnson, Donald E. ... Chicago, IL
Johnson, Donald E. ... Eugene, OR
Johnson, Donald E., Jr. ... Fort Collins, CO
Johnson, Donald F. ... Cambridge, MD
Johnson, Donald G., Jr. ... San Diego, CA
Johnson, Donald J. ... Van Wert, OH
Johnson, Donald L. ... Chicago, IL
Johnson, Donald L. ... Newport, KY
Johnson, Donald L. ... Baton Rouge, LA
Johnson, Donald L. ... Grand Rapids, MI
Johnson, Donald O. ... Washington, DC
Johnson, Donald P. ... Los Angeles, CA
Johnson, Donald R. ... Baton Rouge, LA
Johnson, Donald R. ... Massapequa, NY
Johnson, Donald R. ... Ardmore, PA
Johnson, Donald R. ... Roanoke, VA
Johnson, Donn E. ... La Grange, IL
Johnson, Donna B. ... Roswell, GA
Johnson, Donna J. ... Northbrook, IL
Johnson, Donna J. ... Springvale, ME
Johnson, Donna Wyatt ... Macclenny, FL
Johnson, Doreen C. ... Columbus, OH
Johnson, Doris T. ... Palmyra, MO
Johnson, Dorothy A. ... San Diego, CA
Johnson, Dorothy Bertram ... Chicago, IL
Johnson, Dorothy S. ... Tallahassee, FL
Johnson, Douglas A. ... Lisle, IL
Johnson, Douglas A. ... Beverly, MA
Johnson, Douglas B. ... Lincoln, NE
Johnson, Douglas C. ... Groton, CT
Johnson, Douglas C. ... Buffalo, NY
Johnson, Douglas D. ... Wichita, KS
Johnson, Douglas F. ... Omaha, NE
Johnson, Douglas F. ... Westmont, NJ
Johnson, Douglas G. ... Anchorage, AK
Johnson, Douglas H. ... Stillwater, MN
Johnson, Douglas L. ... Sacramento, CA
Johnson, Douglas M. ... St. Paul, MN
Johnson, Douglas M. ... Souderton, PA
Johnson, Douglas M. ... Eau Claire, WI
Johnson, Douglas Michie ... Miami, FL
Johnson, Douglas O. ... Eau Claire, WI
Johnson, Douglas P. ... Fort Lauderdale, FL
Johnson, Douglas P. ... Bemidji, MN
Johnson, Douglas Q. ... Evansville, WI
Johnson, Douglas R. ... Chicago, IL
Johnson, Douglas R. ... San Antonio, TX
Johnson, Douglas T. ... Chattanooga, TN
Johnson, Douglas V. ... Anchorage, AK
Johnson, Douglas V. ... Eden Prairie, MN
Johnson, Douglas W. ... Chicago, IL
Johnson, Douglas W. ... Southfield, MI
Johnson, Douglas W. ... Albany, OR
Johnson, Dowe & Brown, LLC
Windsor, CT
Johnson, Doyle B. ... San Francisco, CA
Johnson, Drake B. ... Fort Collins, CO
Johnson, Drew C. ... Aberdeen, SD
Johnson, Drew L. ... Eugene, OR
Johnson, Drew M. ... Sacramento, CA
Johnson, Duane C., Jr. ... Medina, NY
Johnson, Duffie, Stewart & Weidner
Lemoyne, PA
Johnson, Dustan E. ... Albany, OR
Johnson, Dustan E., P.C. ... Albany, OR
Johnson, Dwight A. ... Hartford, CT
Johnson, Dwinette E.
West Palm Beach, FL
Johnson, Dyer & Everett ... Yorba Linda, CA
Johnson, E. Andrew ... Tulsa, OK
Johnson, E. Bruce ... Fort Lauderdale, FL
Johnson, E. Christopher, Jr. ... Detroit, MI
Johnson, E. David ... Punta Gorda, FL
Johnson, E. Edward ... Topeka, KS
Johnson, E. Glen ... Fort Worth, TX
Johnson, E. Jewelle ... Atlanta, GA
Johnson, E. Louis ... Owensboro, KY
Johnson, E. Michael ... Washington, DC
Johnson, E. Perry ... St. Louis, MO
Johnson, E. Preston, Jr. ... Baxley, GA
Johnson, E. Richard ... Peoria, IL
Johnson, E. Scott ... Baltimore, MD
Johnson, E. Shannon ... Keizer, OR
Johnson, Earl D. ... Oakland, CA
Johnson, Earl F. ... Dyersburg, TN
Johnson, Earl H. ... Denver, CO
Johnson, Earl, Jr. ... Los Angeles, CA
Johnson, Earl L. ... Scottsdale, AZ
Johnson, Earl L., Jr. ... Arlington, VA
Johnson, Earl M., Jr. ... Jacksonville, FL
Johnson, Earl V. ... Andalusia, AL
Johnson, Earle B. ... Bloomington, IL
Johnson, Eartha J. ... Houston, TX
Johnson, Ector R., III ... Little Rock, AR
Johnson, Ed ... San Antonio, TX
Johnson, Eddie C. ... Chicago, IL
Johnson, Edgar C., Jr. ... Laguna Hills, CA
Johnson, Edgar Leo ... Ocala, FL
Johnson, Edmond D. ... Wilmington, DE
Johnson, Edw. A. ... Barberton, OH
Johnson, Edward A. ... Chicago, IL
Johnson, Edward B. ... West Memphis, AR
Johnson, Edward B. ... Portland, OR
Johnson, Edward C.
Grosse Pointe Farms, MI
Johnson, Edward C. A. ... Alamo, CA
Johnson, Edward D.
La Canada Flintridge, CA
Johnson, Edward E. ... Des Moines, IA
Johnson, Edward F., Jr. ... Richmond, VA
Johnson, Edward G. ... Spokane, WA
Johnson, Edward H. ... Atlanta, GA
Johnson, Edward J. ... Middlesex, NJ
Johnson, Edward J., Jr., (P.A.)
Middlesex, NJ
Johnson, Edward L. ... Houston, TX
Johnson, Edward M. ... Patchogue, NY
Johnson, Edward McFarland
Birmingham, AL
Johnson, Edward R. ... Fairfax, VA
Johnson, Edward S. ... Colorado Springs, CO
Johnson, Edward S. ... New Orleans, LA
Johnson, Edward S. ... Leonardtown, MD
Johnson, Edward S. ... Belton, TX
Johnson, Edward S., Jr. ... Atlanta, GA
Johnson, Edward W. ... Evansville, IN
Johnson & Edwards LLP
Sacramento, CA
San Diego, CA
Johnson, Edwin A. ... San Diego, CA
Johnson, Edwin Lynn ... Fayetteville, NC
Johnson, Edwin W. ... Evansville, IN
Johnson, Edwin W., II ... Columbia, SC
Johnson Eiesland Huffman & Clayborne
Law Firm, LLP ... Rapid City, SD
Johnson, Eileen M. ... Fort Washington, PA
Johnson, Eileen Morgan ... Vienna, VA
Johnson, Einar Wm. ... Torrance, CA
Johnson, Elaine M. Kiefer ... Santa Maria, CA
Johnson, Elaine N. ... Portland, OR
Johnson, Elaine N., P.C. ... Portland, OR
Johnson, Elaine T. ... Boulder, CO
Johnson, Elbert S. ... Blytheville, AR
Johnson, Eldon L. ... Wayne, MI
Johnson, Eldon M. ... San Francisco, CA
Johnson, Elena Puig ... Los Angeles, CA
Johnson, Elias G.
Federal Communications Commission,
Wireless Telecommunications Bureau, GV
Johnson, Elizabeth A. ... Atlanta, GA
Johnson, Elizabeth Ann ... Frankfort, KY
Johnson, Elizabeth Belsom ... Tampa, FL
Johnson, Elizabeth Finn ... Atlanta, GA
Johnson, Elizabeth Fuller ... Birmingham, AL
Johnson, Elizabeth I. ... Anchorage, AK
Johnson, Elizabeth K. ... Boston, MA
Johnson, Elizabeth M. ... Chicago, IL
Johnson, Elizabeth M. ... New York, NY
Johnson, Elizabeth Marie ... Berkeley, CA
Johnson, Elizabeth Pringle ... Houston, TX
Johnson, Elizabeth Pryor ... Miami, FL
Johnson, Elizabeth W. ... Sacramento, CA
Johnson, Elizabeth Zaner ... Clifton, TX
Johnson, Ellana ... Reston, VA
Johnson, Ellen K. ... Malibu, CA
Johnson, Elliott W. ... Mount Vernon, WA
Johnson, Elliott W., A Prof. Serv. Corp., Law
Firm of ... Mount Vernon, WA
Johnson, Ellsworth H. ... Cincinnati, OH
Johnson, Ellsworth T. ... Gloucester, MA
Johnson, Elmer W., (P.C.) ... Chicago, IL
Johnson, Elton L., Jr. ... Tahlequah, OK
Johnson, Elwyn L. ... Modesto, CA
Johnson, Emily B. ... San Francisco, CA
Johnson, Emily F. ... New York, NY
Johnson, Emily Perry ... Raleigh, NC
Johnson, Emmett P. ... Baxley, GA
Johnson, Emmett P., & E. Preston Johnson,
Jr., P.C. ... Baxley, GA
Johnson, Erb, Bice, Kramer, Good &
Mulholland, P.C. ... Fort Dodge, IA
Gowrie, IA
Johnson, Eric ... Houston, TX
Johnson, Eric A. ... St. Paul, MN
Johnson, Eric A. ... Stillwater, MN
Johnson, Eric A. ... Columbus, OH
Johnson, Eric A. ... Burlington, VT
Johnson, Eric Arthur ... Seattle, WA
Johnson, Eric B. ... Seattle, WA
Johnson, Eric C. ... Canfield, OH
Johnson, Eric D. ... Indianapolis, IN
Johnson, Eric D. ... Bethesda, MD
Johnson, Eric D. ... Wilmington, NC
Johnson, Eric E. ... Costa Mesa, CA
Johnson, Eric E. ... Denver, CO
Johnson, Eric G. ... Minden, LA
Johnson, Eric G. ... Syracuse, NY
Johnson, Eric G. ... Hudson, WI
Johnson, Eric Heath ... Birmingham, AL
Johnson, Eric K. ... Topeka, KS
Johnson, Eric K. ... Salt Lake City, UT
Johnson, Eric L. ... Oklahoma City, OK
Johnson, Eric M. ... Elgin, IL
Johnson, Eric M. ... Rockville, MD
Johnson, Eric R. ... Indianapolis, IN
Johnson, Eric R. ... Bloomington, MN
Johnson, Eric R. ... New York, NY
Johnson, Eric S. ... Littleton, MA
Johnson, Eric S. ... New York, NY
Johnson, Eric T. ... Atlanta, GA
Johnson, Eric T. ... Salt Lake City, UT
Johnson, Eric T., P.C. ... Atlanta, GA
Johnson, Eric W. ... Hartford, CT
Johnson, Eric W. ... Waterloo, IA
Johnson, Erik C. ... Atlanta, GA
Johnson, Erik M. ... Minneapolis, MN
Johnson, Erik R. ... Carson City, NV
Johnson, Erik R. ... Fargo, ND

Johnson, Erik Smalley ... Caldwell, ID
Johnson, Erika B. ... Boston, MA
Johnson, Erika L. ... Kalispell, MT
Johnson, Erin ... Cortez, CO
Johnson, Erma L. ... Wilmington, NC
Johnson, Ernest E., (P.C.) ... Los Angeles, CA
Johnson, Ernest G. ... Oklahoma City, OK
Johnson, Ernest H. ... Monmouth, ME
Johnson, Ernest L. ... Kansas City, KS
Johnson, Ernest R. ... Newport Beach, CA
Johnson, Ervin W. ... Darlington, WI
Johnson, Erwin K. ... Kentwood, MI
Johnson, Estes ... Shreveport, LA
Johnson, Esther Jane ... Seattle, WA
Johnson, Ethan Whitcomb ... Miami, FL
Johnson, Ethel J. ... Houston, TX
Johnson, Eugene A. ... Red Bank, NJ
Johnson, Eugene E., Jr. ... Chicago, IL
Johnson, Eugene H. ... Ocala, FL
Johnson, Eugene L., (P.A.)
Minneapolis, MN
Johnson, Eugene N. ... Waukesha, WI
Johnson, Eugenie R. ... Chicago, IL
Johnson, Eunice P. ... Grand Island, NY
Johnson, Evan H. ... Decatur, IL
Johnson, Evan W. ... Rockville, MD
Johnson, Evelyn ... Brunswick, GA
Johnson, Everett C., Jr. ... Washington, DC
Johnson, F. Bradford ... Indianapolis, IN
Johnson, F. Edward ... Naples, FL
Johnson, F. McKay ... Provo, UT
Johnson, F. Mitchell, Jr. ... Charleston, SC
Johnson, Faith Anne ... Wichita, KS
Johnson, Ferdie ... Charleston, SC
Johnson, Ferguson & Pipkin ... Houston, TX
Johnson, Finkel, DeLuca & Kennedy, A Professional Corporation ... Houston, TX
Johnson, Fletcher M., Jr. ... Bluffton, SC
Johnson, Flodman, Guenzel, Eske & Widger
Lincoln, NE
Johnson and Flora ... Seattle, WA
Johnson, Florence M. ... Memphis, TN
Johnson, Forrest A. ... Lincoln, NE
Johnson, Forrest A., Jr. ... Natchez, MS
Johnson, Forrest B. ... Atlanta, GA
Johnson, Fort, Meissner & Joseph
Sacramento, CA
Johnson, Foster J., Jr. ... New Orleans, LA
Johnson, Francis R. ... Spring Hill, FL
Johnson, Frank A. ... Fairfield, CT
Johnson, Frank E. ... Norwood, CO
Johnson, Frank, Frederick and Walsh
Urbana, IL
Johnson, Frank H. ... Grand Rapids, MI
Johnson, Frank Hayes ... Spokane, WA
Johnson, Frank J. ... Somerville, NJ
Johnson, Frank J., Jr. ... San Diego, CA
Johnson, Frank L. ... Racine, WI
Johnson, Frank M., Jr. ... Montgomery, AL
Johnson, Frank R. ... Denver, CO
Johnson, Frank R. ... Daytona Beach, FL
Johnson, Frank T., Jr. ... Fort Collins, CO
Johnson, Franklin D. ... Salt Lake City, UT
Johnson, Franklin M., Jr. ... Riverdale, MD
Johnson, Fred ... Mattoon, IL
Johnson, Fred A. ... Wichita, KS
Johnson, Fred A. ... Cathlamet, WA
Johnson, Fred M. ... Tallahassee, FL
Johnson, Fred M., Jr. ... Waco, TX
Johnson, Fred W., Jr. ... Oswego, KS
Parsons, KS
Johnson, Fred W., Jr. ... Jackson, MS
Johnson, Frederick A. ... Atlanta, GA
Johnson, Frederick A. ... Peoria, IL
Johnson, Frederick A. ... Cape Elizabeth, ME
Johnson, Frederick B. ... Marysville, OH
Johnson, Frederick D. ... Peoria, IL
Johnson, Frederick J., Jr. ... North Port, FL
Johnson, Frederick Lee ... Mount Airy, NC
Johnson, Frederick N. ... Calumet, MI
Houghton, MI
Johnson, Frederick T. ... Houston, TX
Johnson, Frederick W. ... Atlanta, GA
Johnson, Fredrick G. ... Dobson, NC
Johnson & Freeman, P.A. ... Atlanta, GA
Covington, GA
Johnson, G. Donald ... Atlanta, GA
Johnson, G. Douglas ... New York, NY
Johnson, G. Martin ... Bloomington, MN
Johnson, G. Martin, Ltd. ... Bloomington, MN
Johnson, G. Randi ... Riverhead, NY
Johnson, G. Richard ... Johnson City, TN
Johnson, G. Robert ... Minneapolis, MN
Johnson, G. Thomas ... Muskegon, MI
Johnson, G. Weldon ... Indianapolis, IN
Johnson, Gage Emery ... Novato, CA
Johnson, Gail Kimberly
Department of Justice, Civil Division, GV
Johnson, Gail Laxalt ... Englewood, CO
Johnson, Gallagher, Burgio & Martin
Caldwell, NJ
Johnson, Garold E. ... Tacoma, WA
Johnson, Garrett B. ... Chicago, IL
Johnson, Garry W. ... Fort Lauderdale, FL
Johnson, Gary ... Albany, NY
Johnson, Gary C. ... Denver, CO
Johnson, Gary C. ... Rock Island, IL
Johnson, Gary C. ... Lexington, KY
Pikeville, KY
Johnson, Gary C. ... Cleveland, OH
Columbus, OH
Johnson, Gary C. ... Houston, TX
Johnson, Gary C. ... Houston, TX
Johnson, Gary C., P.S.C. ... Hazard, KY
Lexington, KY
Pikeville, KY
Richmond, KY
Johnson, Gary D. ... Fort Wayne, IN

Johnson, Gary E. ... Sioux City, IA
Johnson, Gary G. ... Bloomington, IL
Johnson, Gary H., II ... Columbia, SC
Johnson, Gary L. ... Columbus, GA
Johnson, Gary L. ... Bexley, OH
Johnson, Gary L. ... Dallas, TX
Johnson, Gary L. ... Salt Lake City, UT
Johnson, Gary L. ... Summersville, WV
Johnson, Gary M. ... Visalia, CA
Johnson, Gary M. ... Minneapolis, MN
Johnson, Gary P. ... Denver, CO
Johnson, Gary R. ... North Hollywood, CA
Johnson, Gary R. ... Walnut Creek, CA
Johnson, Gary R. ... Minneapolis, MN
Johnson, Gary R. ... Xenia, OH
Johnson, Gary R. ... Salt Lake City, UT
Johnson, Gary R. ... Madison, WI
Johnson, Gary T. ... Newnan, GA
Johnson, Gary T. ... Chicago, IL
Johnson, Gary V. ... Aurora, IL
Johnson, Gary W. ... Staten Island, NY
Johnson, Gary W. ... Cleveland, OH
Johnson, Gary W., (P.A.) ... Orlando, FL
Johnson, Gaukroger, Drewelow, Crossland & Woolett, P.S. ... Cashmere, WA
Chelan, WA
Waterville, WA
Wenatchee, WA
Johnson, Gaver & Leach, LLP
Monterey, CA
Johnson, G. B. ... Fayetteville, NC
Johnson, Gene P., Ltd. ... Fargo, ND
Johnson, Gene R. ... Marion, IN
Johnson, Geoffrey G. ... Chicago, IL
Johnson, Geoffrey McC. ... Tallahassee, FL
Saddle River, NJ
New York, NY
Johnson, Geoffrey R. ... Philadelphia, PA
Johnson, George A. ... Boulder, CO
Johnson, George Dean, Jr. ... Spartanburg, SC
Johnson, George E. ... Washington, DC
Johnson, George E.Q. ... Chicago, IL
Johnson, George F. ... Tucson, AZ
Johnson, George G.
Securities and Exchange Commission, Office of Compliance Inspections and Examinations, GV
Johnson, George G., Jr. ... Denver, CO
Johnson, George H. ... Cincinnati, OH
Johnson, George M. ... Springfield, MO
Johnson, George O. ... Sioux Falls, SD
Johnson, George R.
Rolling Hills Estates, CA
Johnson, George R. ... Treasury Department, Internal Revenue Service, GV
Johnson, George R. A. ... Minneapolis, MN
Johnson, George W. ... Downers Grove, IL
Johnson, George W. ... Muskegon, MI
Johnson, George W. ... Dover, NJ
Johnson, George W., Chartered
Las Vegas, NV
Johnson, George W., III ... Brooklyn, NY
Johnson, George Wallace ... Las Vegas, NV
Johnson, Gerald D. ... Rapid City, SD
Johnson, Gerald E., Law Offices of
Swansea, MA
Johnson, Gerald H. ... Cape Girardeau, MO
Johnson, Gerald M., III ... Houston, TX
Johnson, Gerald M., III ... Kingwood, TX
Johnson, Gerald M., Jr. ... Shreveport, LA
Johnson, Gerald S. ... San Francisco, CA
Johnson, Gerald T. ... Wailuku, HI
Johnson, Geraldine M. ... Cincinnati, OH
Johnson, Gerard A. ... Port Angeles, WA
Johnson, Geri Anne ... Eureka, CA
Johnson, Gilbert P. ... Pound Ridge, NY
Johnson, Gillard B., III ... Lexington, KY
Johnson & Gilman ... Rockville, VA
Johnson, Gina M. ... Dallas, TX
Johnson, Giselle S. ... Fairborn, OH
Johnson, Glen H. ... Rapid City, SD
Johnson, Glen W. ... Detroit, MI
Johnson, Glenda Hatchett ... Atlanta, GA
Johnson, Glendon E. ... Washington, DC
Johnson, Glendon E., Jr. ... Washington, DC
Johnson, Glenn Charles ... Phoenix, AZ
Johnson, Glenn E. ... Atlanta, GA
Johnson, Glenn E. ... Austin, TX
Johnson, Glenn H. ... Houston, TX
Johnson, Glenn L. ... Cedar Rapids, IA
Johnson, Glenn M. ... Washington, DC
Johnson, Gloria ... Brooklyn, NY
Johnson, Gloria L. ... Atlanta, GA
Johnson, Gloria L. Sunny
Huntington Beach, CA
Johnson, Gloria Michelotti ... Barrington, IL
Johnson, Golden E. ... Newark, NJ
Johnson, Gordon C.
Department Of Health And Human Services, Food & Drug Administration, GV
Johnson, Gordon J. ... New York, NY
Johnson, Gordon R. ... Austin, TX
Johnson, Gordon V. ... Minneapolis, MN
Johnson, Gordon W. ... Houston, TX
Johnson, Graddy W. ... Frankfort, KY
Johnson & Graeser, P.C. ... Sidney, IA
Johnson, Graffe, Keay & Moniz
Seattle, WA
Tacoma, WA
Johnson, Grant A. ... Minneapolis, MN
Johnson, Grant E. ... Utica, NY
Johnson, Grant L. ... Oak Brook, IL
Johnson, Grant M. ... Wenatchee, WA
Johnson, Gray & MacAbee ... Franklin, IN
Johnson, Grayson S. ... Rockville, VA
Johnson, Green, Miller & Gibson, P.A.
Milton, FL
Johnson, Greg A. ... Port Orange, FL

Johnson, Greg L. ... Sacramento, CA
Johnson, Greg L. ... New Orleans, LA
Johnson, Gregg A. ... Tampa, FL
Johnson, Gregg A. ... St. Paul, MN
Johnson, Gregg D. ... Portland, OR
Johnson, Gregg Tyler ... Albany, NY
Johnson, Gregory A. ... Birmingham, AL
Johnson, Gregory A. ... Fort Madison, IA
Johnson, Gregory B. ... Waco, TX
Johnson, Gregory G. ... Kansas City, MO
Johnson, Gregory G. ... Milwaukee, WI
Johnson, Gregory J. ... St. Paul, MN
Johnson, Gregory J. ... New York, NY
Johnson, Gregory K. ... Springfield, MO
Johnson, Gregory L. ... Los Angeles, CA
Johnson, Gregory L. ... Colorado Springs, CO
Johnson, Gregory L. ... Des Plaines, IL
Johnson, Gregory L. ... Morris Plains, NJ
Johnson, Gregory L. ... Ardmore, OK
Johnson, Gregory M. ... Wilmington, DE
Johnson, Gregory M. ... Charlottesville, VA
Johnson, Gregory P. ... Silver Spring, MD
Johnson, Gregory P. ... Billings, MT
Johnson, Gregory S. ... Metairie, LA
Johnson, Gregory S. ... Spokane, WA
Johnson, Gregory Verne ... Denver, CO
Johnson, Gregory W. ... Denver, CO
Johnson, Gregory W. ... Jacksonville, FL
Johnson, Grusin, Kee & Surprise, P.C.
Memphis, TN
Johnson, Gunnar B. ... Duluth, MN
Johnson, Gurney A. ... Catlettsburg, KY
Johnson, Guy V. ... Wilmington, DE
Johnson, Guy W. ... Dallas, TX
Johnson, Gwendolyn A. ... Detroit, MI
Johnson, H. Alan ... Alpine, CA
Johnson, H. Alexander ... Norfolk, VA
Johnson, H. Allen ... Lawton, OK
Johnson, H. Alston, III ... Baton Rouge, LA
Johnson, H. Arvid ... Carbondale, CO
Johnson, H. Dan ... Lake Wylie, SC
Johnson, H. Dee, Jr. ... Dallas, TX
Johnson, H. Eugene ... Tampa, FL
Johnson, H. Gregory ... Jackson, MS
Johnson, H. Lance ... Washington, DC
Johnson, H. Michael ... Carrollton, TX
Johnson, H. Scott, Jr ... Washington, DC
Johnson, H. Stan ... Las Vegas, NV
Johnson, H. Victor ... Olympia, WA
Johnson, H. Victor, P.S., Inc. ... Olympia, WA
Johnson, H. Wendell ... Traverse City, MI
Johnson, Hanan and Heron, P.C.
Oklahoma City, OK
Johnson, Hannibal B. ... Tulsa, OK
Johnson, Hans W. ... Denver, CO
Johnson, Harding, Jr. ... New York, NY
Johnson, Harlan ... Lamar, CO
Johnson, Harold A., Jr. ... Cheboygan, MI
Johnson, Harold D. ... Seattle, WA
Johnson, Harold E.
Department of Energy, GV
Johnson, Harold F. ... Jackson, TN
Johnson, Harold G. ... St. Ann, MO
Johnson, Harold G. ... Isle of Palms, SC
Johnson, Harold J. ... White Plains, NY
Johnson, Harold L. ... Springfield, VA
Johnson, Harold L., Jr. ... Washington, DC
Johnson, Harold V. ... Chicago, IL
Johnson, Harold W. ... Des Moines, IA
Johnson, Harriet McB. ... Charleston, SC
Johnson, Harry A., III ... Memphis, TN
Johnson, Harry B. ... Oakland, CA
Johnson, Harry E. ... Dixon, IL
Johnson, Harry I., III ... Los Angeles, CA
Johnson, Harry L. ... Valley Center, CA
Johnson, Harry M., III ... Richmond, VA
Johnson, Harry M., Jr. ... Richmond, VA
Johnson, Harry S. ... Baltimore, MD
Johnson, Harvey C. ... Camden, NJ
Johnson, Harvey C., P.C. ... Camden, NJ
Johnson, Harvey D. ... Kirkwood, MO
Johnson, Harvey George, Jr
Pasadena, CA
Johnson, Haynes N. ... Roxbury, CT
Johnson, Heather M. ... New York, NY
Johnson, Heber E.
La Canada Flintridge, CA
Johnson, Heidepriem, Miner, Marlow & Janklow, LLP ... Sioux Falls, SD
Yankton, SD
Johnson, Heidi E. ... Portland, ME
Johnson, Heidi M. ... Elm Grove, WI
Johnson, Helen A. ... Bronx, NY
Johnson, Helen D. ... New York, NY
Johnson, Helen Scott ... Lafayette, LA
Johnson & Helmuth ... Orrville, OH
Johnson, Henry Clyde ... Bloomfield Hills, MI
Johnson, Henry F. ... San Antonio, TX
Johnson, Henry P. ... Escondido, CA
Johnson, Henry Paul ... Naples, FL
Johnson, Henry S. ... Harlan, KY
Johnson, Henry W. ... Coral Springs, FL
Johnson, Herbert A. ... Columbia, SC
Johnson, Herbert J., Jr. ... Erie, PA
Johnson, Herbert T. ... Monroe, WI
Johnson, Herbert W. ... Sister Bay, WI
Sturgeon Bay, WI
Johnson, Herbert W., Jr. ... Indianapolis, IN
Johnson, Hester, Walter & Breckenridge, L.L.P. ... Ottumwa, IA
Johnson, Hilary E. ... Sioux City, IA
Johnson, Hilary K. ... Abingdon, VA
Johnson, Hillary Earnest ... Broomfield, CO
Johnson, Hjalma E. ... Dade City, FL
Johnson, Hobart C. ... Pikeville, KY
Johnson, Hollis B. ... Carrollton, GA
Johnson, Horace A. ... Lemoyne, PA

Johnson, Horace J., Jr. ... Atlanta, GA
Covington, GA
Johnson & Houlihan, S.C. ... Minocqua, WI
Rhinelander, WI
Johnson, Howard C. ... McFarland, WI
Johnson, Howard D. ... White Plains, NY
Johnson, Howard F. ... Lindstrom, MN
Johnson, Howard G. ... Los Angeles, CA
Johnson, Howard P. ... Salt Lake City, UT
Johnson, Howard R. ... Atlanta, GA
Johnson, Hubert Dee ... Dallas, TX
Johnson, Hugh ... Beverly Hills, CA
Johnson, Humphrey H. N.
South Freeport, ME
Johnson, Hurl W., III ... Modesto, CA
Johnson, Ila W. ... Cleveland, OH
Johnson, Ilene Davidson ... Denver, CO
Johnson, Inge Prytz ... Birmingham, AL
Johnson, Ingrid D. ... Princeton, NJ
Johnson, Inza E. ... Cincinnati, OH
Johnson, Irving G. ... Denver, CO
Johnson, I. S. Leevy ... Columbia, SC
Johnson, Ivan D. ... Tacoma, WA
Johnson, Iver R. ... McHenry, IL
Johnson, Iver R., & Associates, Ltd.
McHenry, IL
Johnson, J. Alan ... Pittsburgh, PA
Johnson, J. Albert ... Boston, MA
Johnson, J. Alexander ... Baxley, GA
Johnson, J. Alexander, P.C. ... Baxley, GA
Johnson, J. Alfred ... Marietta, GA
Johnson, J. Andrew ... Martinsville, VA
Johnson, J. Bart ... Denver, CO
Johnson, J. Brian ... Allentown, PA
Johnson, J. Clayton ... Baton Rouge, LA
Johnson, J. Clayton ... Kansas City, MO
Johnson, J. Craig ... Temecula, CA
Johnson, J. Dean ... Grover Beach, CA
Johnson, J. Eric ... Johnson City, TN
Johnson, J. James ... Atlanta, GA
Johnson, J. Jane ... Eden Prairie, MN
Johnson, J. Kenneth ... Pontiac, IL
Johnson, J. Kimbrough ... Memphis, TN
Johnson, J. Kyle ... Houston, TX
Johnson, J. Lee ... St. Louis, MO
Johnson, J. Lee, III ... Fort Worth, TX
Johnson, J. Leland ... Millbrae, CA
Johnson, J. Logan ... Oklahoma City, OK
Johnson, J. Lynn ... Las Vegas, NV
Johnson, J. Mark ... Trenton, TN
Johnson, J. Michael ... Baton Rouge, LA
Johnson, J. Michael ... New Orleans, LA
Houston, TX
Johnson, J. Michael ... Philadelphia, PA
Johnson, J. Paul ... Stamford, CT
Johnson, J. Philip ... Fargo, ND
Johnson, J. Ramsey ... Washington, DC
Johnson, J. Richard ... Cedar Rapids, IA
Johnson, J. Richard, Jr. ... Tulsa, OK
Johnson, J. Richardson ... Kalamazoo, MI
Johnson, J. Riley, Jr. ... Norfolk, VA
Johnson, J. Riley, Jr., P.C. ... Norfolk, VA
Johnson, J. Robert ... Westminster, MD
Johnson, J. Rodney ... Richmond, VA
Johnson, J. Rolfe ... Houston, TX
Johnson, J. Rolfe, P.C. ... Houston, TX
Johnson, J. Sam, Jr. ... Greensboro, NC
Johnson, J. Stacie ... Los Angeles, CA
Johnson, J. Terry ... Oklahoma City, OK
Johnson, J. Thomas ... Vernon, CT
Johnson, J. Tullos ... Columbus, OH
Johnson, J.W. (Don), P.C. ... Houston, TX
Johnson, J. Walker ... Washington, DC
Johnson, J. Warren ... Irwindale, CA
Johnson, J. William ... Hicksville, NY
Johnson, J. William ... Maryville, TN
Johnson, Jack G. ... Seattle, WA
Johnson, Jack Gray ... Collinsville, TX
Johnson, Jack J. ... Summit, NJ
Johnson, Jack L. ... New York, NY
Johnson, Jack L. ... Columbus, OH
Johnson, Jack L. ... Perrysburg, OH
Johnson, Jack O. ... Lakeland, FL
Johnson, Jacqueline ... Greeley, CO
Johnson, Jacqueline A. ... Santa Ana, CA
Johnson, Jacqueline A. ... Cleveland, OH
Johnson, Jacqueline C. ... Dallas, TX
Johnson, Jacquelyn G. ... St. Louis, MO
Johnson, Jake ... Houston, TX
Johnson, James ... Rochester, NY
Johnson, James A. ... Paradise, CA
Johnson, James A. ... Denver, CO
Johnson, James A. ... Valparaiso, IN
Johnson, James A. ... Baltimore, MD
Johnson, James A. ... Rhinelander, WI
Johnson, James A., Jr.
General Services Administration, Board of Contract Appeals, GV
Johnson, James A., Jr. ... Litchfield, NH
Johnson, James A., Jr. ... Memphis, TN
Johnson, James Allen ... Mobile, AL
Johnson, James B. ... Grand Rapids, MI
Johnson, James B. ... Springfield, MO
Johnson, James B. ... Somerville, NJ
Johnson, James B. ... Memphis, TN
Johnson, James B. ... Nashville, TN
Johnson, James Bennett ... Lafayette Hill, PA
Johnson, James C. ... Mountain Home, AR
Johnson, James C. ... Visalia, CA
Johnson, James C. ... Bristol, CT
Johnson, James C. ... Abilene, KS
Johnson, James C. ... Greenwood, SC
Johnson, James C. ... Seattle, WA
Johnson, James C., Jr. ... Concord, NC
Johnson, James D. ... Mission Viejo, CA
Johnson, James D. ... Denver, CO
Johnson, James D. ... Atlanta, GA
Johnson, James D. ... Atlanta, GA

Johnson, James D. ....Evansville, IN
Johnson, James D. ....Paintsville, KY
Johnson, James D. ....Hattiesburg, MS
Johnson, James D. ....Butte, MT
Johnson, James D. ....New York, NY
Johnson, James D. ....Tulsa, OK
Johnson, James D. ....San Angelo, TX
Johnson, James D., Jr. ....Ponchatoula, LA
Johnson, James D., Jr. ....Hagerstown, MD
Johnson, James E. ....Evergreen Park, IL
Johnson, James E. ....Brooklyn, NY
Johnson, James E. ....Dallas, TX
Johnson, James E., II ....Seminole, FL
Johnson, James E., Jr. ....Charlotte, NC
Johnson, James F. ....San Francisco, CA
Johnson, James F. ....Roanoke, VA
Johnson, James F., 4th ....New York, NY
Johnson, James G., Jr. ....Jesup, GA
Johnson, James G., Jr. ....New York, NY
Johnson, James G., (P.C.)
Los Angeles, CA
Johnson, James Griffin ....Baton Rouge, LA
Johnson, James H. ....Cannon Falls, MN
Johnson, James H. ....Houston, TX
Johnson, James H., III ....Durham, NC
Johnson, James H., Jr. ....Atlanta, GA
Johnson, James I. ....Muscatine, IA
Johnson, James J. ....Tinley Park, IL
Johnson, James J. ....Cincinnati, OH
Johnson, James J. ....Dallas, TX
Johnson, James J. S. ....Dallas, TX
Johnson, James K. ....Dallas, TX
Johnson, James L. ....Denver, CO
Johnson, James L. ....West Des Moines, IA
Johnson, James L. ....Mission, KS
Johnson, James L. ....Cincinnati, OH
Johnson, James L. ....Philadelphia, PA
Johnson, James L., Jr. ....Washington, DC
Johnson & James LLP ....Aptos, CA
Johnson, James M. ....Chicago, IL
Johnson, James M. ....Bossier City, LA
Johnson, James M. ....Minden, LA
Johnson, James M. ....Dunn, NC
Johnson, James M. ....Cleveland, OH
Johnson, James M. ....Charlottesville, VA
Johnson, James M. ....Olympia, WA
Johnson, James Noble ....Austin, TX
Johnson, James P. ....Westlake Village, CA
Johnson, James P. ....Colorado Springs, CO
Johnson, James P. ....Fort Collins, CO
Johnson, James P. ....Peoria, IL
Johnson, James P. ....Minneapolis, MN
Johnson, James P. ....State College, PA
Johnson, James R. ....Santa Rosa, CA
Johnson, James R. ....Atlanta, GA
Johnson, James R. ....Owosso, MI
Johnson, James R. ....Tulsa, OK
Johnson, James R. ....Hudson, WI
Johnson, James R., III ....Senatobia, MS
Johnson, James T. ....San Francisco, CA
Johnson, James T. ....Buffalo, NY
Johnson, James T. ....Raleigh, NC
Johnson, James T. ....Seattle, WA
Johnson, James T., III ....Birmingham, AL
Johnson, James U. ....Hollywood, FL
Johnson, James W. ....Phoenix, AZ
Johnson, James W. ....Decatur, IL
Johnson, James W. ....Kalispell, MT
Johnson, James W. ....New York, NY
Johnson, James W. ....Philadelphia, PA
Johnson, James W. ....McAllen, TX
Johnson, James W. ....Herndon, VA
Johnson, James W., III ....Middlebury, IN
Johnson, James W., Jr. ....Washington, DC
Johnson, James W., Jr. ....Laurens, SC
Johnson, James W., P.C. ....McAllen, TX
Johnson, Jamey B. ....Baltimore, MD
Johnson, Jamie L. ....Los Angeles, CA
Johnson, Jane McCue ....Columbia, SC
Johnson, Jane Noreen ....St. Paul, MN
Johnson, Janet A. ....White Plains, NY
Johnson, Janet E. ....Jacksonville, FL
Johnson, Janet L. ....Treasury Department, Office of Regulations and Rulings, GV
Johnson, Janet M. ....Chicago, IL
Johnson, Janice B. ....Fargo, ND
Johnson, Janice E. ....Mountain View, CA
Johnson, Janice Hackney ....Gainesville, FL
Johnson, Janie L. ....Longview, TX
Johnson, Janine L. ....United States Senate, Office of the Legislative Counsel, GV
Johnson, Janis W. ....Columbia, SC
Johnson, Jared A. ....Denver, CO
Johnson, Jared W. ....Washington, DC
Johnson, Jaroslawa Zelinsky ....Chicago, IL
Johnson, Jarret L. ....Los Angeles, CA
Johnson, Jason W. ....Lansing, MI
Johnson, Jason W. ....Springfield, MO
Johnson, Jay A. ....Wenatchee, WA
Johnson, Jay B. ....Dallas, TX
Johnson, Jay C. ....Dallas, TX
Johnson, Jay L. ....Minneapolis, MN
Johnson, Jay M. ....Scottsdale, AZ
Johnson, Jay M. ....Ventura, CA
Johnson, Jay S. ....Department of Commerce, National Oceanic and Atmospheric Administration, GV
Johnson, Jaye Pershing ....New York, NY
Johnson, J. B., Jr. ....London, KY
Johnson, J. D. ....Houston, TX
Johnson, J. E., III ....Lexington, KY
Johnson, Jean ....Seattle, WA
Johnson, Jean E., Jr. ....Marietta, GA
Johnson, Jean E., Jr., P.C. ....Marietta, GA
Johnson, Jean H. ....Redwood City, CA
Johnson, Jean M. ....Jacksonville, FL
Johnson, Jeanette A.A. ....Meriden, CT
Johnson, Jeanne F. ....Alpharetta, GA
Johnson, Jeanne K. ....Des Moines, IA
Johnson, Jebb R. ....Santa Ana Heights, CA
Johnson, Jeff E. ....San Diego, CA
Johnson, Jeffery ....Centerville, MA
Johnson, Jeffery A. ....South Bend, IN
Johnson, Jeffery W. ....Los Angeles, CA
Johnson, Jeffrey ....New York, NY
Johnson, Jeffrey A. ....Sioux City, IA
Johnson, Jeffrey A. ....Portland, OR
Johnson, Jeffrey C. ....Seattle, WA
Johnson, Jeffrey D. ....Albuquerque, NM
Johnson, Jeffrey J. ....Fort Collins, CO
Johnson, Jeffrey J. ....Raleigh, NC
Johnson, Jeffrey M. ....Washington, DC
Johnson, Jeffrey M. ....Muscatine, IA
Johnson, Jeffrey P. ....New York, NY
Johnson, Jeffrey P. ....Montpelier, VT
St. Johnsbury, VT
Johnson, Jeffrey Paul ....Westwood, KS
Johnson, Jeffrey R. ....Washington, DC
Johnson, Jeffrey R. ....Minneapolis, MN
Johnson, Jeffrey R. ....Seattle, WA
Johnson, Jeffrey S. ....Minneapolis, MN
Johnson, Jeffrey Starks ....Hammond, LA
Johnson, Jeffrey T. ....Denver, CO
Johnson, Jeffrey W. ....San Francisco, CA
Johnson, Jeffrey W. ....Fort Lauderdale, FL
Johnson, Jennifer ....Greensboro, NC
Johnson, Jennifer A. ....Phoenix, AZ
Johnson, Jennifer A. ....Milwaukee, WI
Johnson, Jennifer Anne ....Washington, DC
Johnson, Jennifer B. ....San Francisco, CA
Johnson, Jennifer B. ....Edwardsville, IL
Johnson, Jennifer Buttross ....Dallas, TX
Johnson, Jennifer Conrad ....Salem, VA
Johnson, Jennifer E. ....New York, NY
Johnson, Jennifer J.
Board of Governors Of The Federal Reserve System, Office of the Secretary, GV
Johnson, Jennifer J. ....Portland, OR
Johnson, Jennifer Jerit ....Chicago, IL
Johnson, Jennifer Kohler ....New York, NY
Johnson, Jennifer L. ....Evansville, IN
Johnson, Jennifer L. ....New York, NY
Johnson, Jennifer L. ....New York, NY
Johnson, Jennifer M. ....Knoxville, TN
Johnson, Jennifer R. ....Newport Beach, CA
Johnson, Jennifer Segars ....Nashville, TN
Johnson, Jennifer W. ....Atlanta, GA
Johnson, Jenny L. ....Chicago, IL
Johnson, Jerald S. ....Bloomington, MN
Johnson, Jerome ....Piermont, NY
Johnson, Jerome A. ....San Pedro, CA
Johnson, Jerome C. ....Milwaukee, WI
Johnson, Jerome W. ....Amarillo, TX
Johnson, Jerri L. ....Los Angeles, CA
Johnson, Jerry A. ....Clinton, IL
Johnson, Jerry A. ....Lake Charles, LA
Johnson, Jerry D. ....Dallas, TX
Johnson, Jerry E. ....Compton, CA
Johnson, Jerry G. ....St. Joseph, MI
Johnson, Jerry L. ....Bloomfield Hills, MI
Johnson, Jerry L. ....Downingtown, PA
Johnson, Jerry L. ....Leesburg, VA
Johnson, Jerry M. ....Lima, OH
Johnson, Jess D. ....Lincoln, NE
Johnson, Jesse H., Jr. ....Dundee, OR
Johnson, Jesse J., Jr. ....Suffolk, VA
Johnson, J. G. ....Oelwein, IA
Johnson, Jill D. ....Chicago, IL
Johnson, Jill L. ....Los Angeles, CA
Johnson, Jill M. ....Kingston, NY
Johnson, Jill V. ....Las Cruces, NM
Johnson, Jim ....Bentonville, AR
Johnson, Jimmy Brown ....Chattanooga, TN
Knoxville, TN
Johnson, Joan A. ....Pacific Palisades, CA
Johnson, Joan A. ....Philadelphia, PA
Johnson, Joan Vance
Department of Transportation, Federal Aviation Administration, GV
Johnson, JoAnn ....Oxnard, CA
Johnson, Joanna L. ....Billings, MT
Johnson, Joanne E. ....Baltimore, MD
Johnson, Joanne E. ....New York, NY
Johnson, Jodi ....New York, NY
Johnson, Jodi L. ....Minneapolis, MN
Johnson, Jodie L. ....Kalispell, MT
Johnson, Jody L. ....Pasadena, CA
Johnson, Jody L. ....Dallas, TX
Johnson, Joe Brent ....Fort Worth, TX
Johnson, Joe J., Jr. ....Fort Worth, TX
Johnson, Joe, Jr. ....Dallas, TX
Johnson, Joe N. ....Waco, TX
Johnson, Joe R., II ....Springfield, TN
Johnson, Joe W. ....Fulton, KY
Johnson, Joel D. ....Fort Smith, AR
Johnson, Joel D. ....Moorhead, MN
Johnson, Joel T. ....Davis, CA
Johnson, Joel Thomas ....Houston, TX
Johnson, John ....Chico, CA
Johnson, John A. ....Louisville, KY
Johnson, John A. ....Jackson, MS
Johnson, John A. ....Arlington, VA
Johnson, John Arnold ....Grand Haven, MI
Johnson, John Arthur ....Boston, MA
Johnson, John B. ....Boston, MA
Johnson, John B., III ....Jesup, GA
Johnson, John B., Jr. ....Tulsa, OK
Johnson, John C. ....Hillsboro, KS
Johnson, John Chadwick ....Roanoke, VA
Johnson, John D. ....Minden, LA
Johnson, John E. ....Santa Rosa, CA
Johnson, John E. ....Tampa, FL
Johnson, John E. ....Quincy, MA
Johnson, John E. ....Orrville, OH
Johnson, John E. ....York, PA
Johnson, John E., Jr. ....Orrville, OH
Johnson, John Edgar, III ....Gulfport, MS
Johnson, John F. ....Harrisonburg, LA
Johnson, John F., Jr. ....Bushnell, FL
Johnson, John G. ....Oklahoma City, OK
Johnson, John Grayson ....Chicago, IL
Johnson, John Griffith, Jr.
Washington, DC
Johnson, John H., Jr. ....Atlanta, GA
Johnson, John Hunter ....Dallas, TX
Johnson, John I. ....Olivette, MO
Johnson, John J. ....Fresno, CA
Johnson, John J. ....Winston-Salem, NC
Johnson, John J., Jr. ....St. Louis, MO
Johnson, John K. ....Rockford, AL
Johnson, John L. ....Jacksonville, FL
Johnson, John L. ....Kansas City, MO
Johnson, John L. ....Corpus Christi, TX
Johnson, John L. (P.A.) ....Little Rock, AR
Johnson, John M. ....Birmingham, AL
Johnson, John M.
Department Of Health And Human Services, GV
Johnson, John M. ....Bloomfield, NJ
Johnson, John M. ....Mount Olive, NJ
Johnson, John P. ....Birmingham, MI
Johnson, John P., II ....Columbus, OH
Johnson, John R. ....Atlanta, GA
Johnson, John S. ....Birmingham, AL
Johnson, John S. ....Stamford, CT
Johnson, John T. ....New York, NY
Johnson, John T. ....Houston, TX
Johnson, John T., Jr. ....Knoxville, TN
Johnson, John W. ....Talbotton, GA
Johnson, John W. ....Wichita, KS
Johnson, John W. ....Eunice, LA
Johnson, John W. ....Beaumont, TX
Johnson, John W. ....Poulsbo, WA
Johnson, John W., III ....Chattanooga, TN
Johnson, John W., Jr. ....Lanett, AL
Johnson, Johnnie L., Jr.
Equal Employment Opportunity Commission, Office of the General Counsel, GV
Johnson, Johnny B. ....Houston, TX
Johnson & Johnson ....San Diego, CA
Johnson & Johnson ....Fort Collins, CO
Johnson and Johnson ....Daytona Beach, FL
Johnson & Johnson ....Belleville, IL
Johnson & Johnson ....Metropolis, IL
Johnson & Johnson ....Minden, LA
Johnson & Johnson ....Jackson, MI
Johnson and Johnson ....Anoka, MN
Johnson & Johnson ....High Ridge, MO
Johnson & Johnson ....Dover, NJ
Johnson & Johnson ....Warsaw, NC
Johnson & Johnson ....Canfield, OH
Youngstown, OH
Johnson & Johnson ....Pawtucket, RI
Johnson & Johnson ....Greenwood, SC
Johnson and Johnson ....Austin, TX
Johnson & Johnson ....Beaumont, TX
Johnson & Johnson ....Carrizo Springs, TX
Johnson & Johnson ....Waukesha, WI
Johnson, Johnson, Barrios & Yacoubian, A Professional Law Corporation
New Orleans, LA
Johnson & Johnson, Law Offices
Las Vegas, NV
Johnson & Johnson, Ltd. ....Orland Park, IL
Johnson and Johnson, P.A. ....Jacksonville, FL
Johnson and Johnson, P.A. ....Lillington, NC
Johnson and Johnson, P.C. ....Boulder, CO
Johnson & Johnson, P.C.
Bloomfield Hills, MI
Johnson & Johnson, P.C. ....St. Ann, MO
Johnson & Johnson, P.C. ....Abingdon, VA
Johnson & Johnson & Phillips
Paintsville, KY
Johnson & Johnson, P.L.C.
Beverly Hills, CA
Johnson & Johnson, P.L.C. ....Newport, KY
Johnson, Johnson & Tanz ....Piermont, NY
Suffern, NY
Johnson, Johnson, Whittle & Snelgrove, P.A.
Aiken, SC
Johnson, Joia M. ....Atlanta, GA
Johnson, Jon ....Tampa, FL
Johnson, Jon E. ....Rockledge, FL
Johnson, Jon Erling ....Boulder, CO
Johnson, Jon H. ....Sidney, IA
Johnson, Jon J. ....Minneapolis, MN
Johnson, Jon L. ....Houston, TX
Johnson, Jonathan E. ....Los Angeles, CA
Johnson, Jonathan E., III ....Los Angeles, CA
Johnson, Jonathan J. ....Gambier, OH
Johnson, Jonathan T. ....Tallahassee, FL
Johnson, Jonathan Wesley ....Atlanta, GA
Johnson, Jones, Snelling, Gilbert & Davis, P.C.
Chicago, IL
Johnson, Joni Andignac ....Metairie, LA
Johnson, Jordan, Nipper & Monk, A Professional Corporation ....Dallas, TX
Johnson, Joseph B. ....Duluth, MN
Johnson, Joseph C. ....Northbrook, IL
Johnson, Joseph C. ....Houston, TX
Johnson, Joseph C., P.C. ....Northbrook, IL
Johnson, Joseph D. ....Anchorage, AK
Johnson, Joseph D. ....Topeka, KS
Johnson, Joseph E. ....Delray Beach, FL
Johnson, Joseph E. ....Raleigh, NC
Johnson, Joseph E., P.A.
Delray Beach, FL
Johnson, Joseph F. ....Cincinnati, OH
Johnson, Joseph H., Jr. ....Birmingham, AL
Johnson, Joseph L. ....Baltimore, MD
Towson, MD
Johnson, Joseph L. ....Springfield, MO
Johnson, Joseph L., III ....Boston, MA
Johnson, Joseph M., II ....Decatur, IN
Johnson, Joseph P., Jr. ....Abingdon, VA
Johnson, Joseph R. ....West Palm Beach, FL
Johnson, Joseph R. ....Frankfort, KY
Johnson, Joseph R., Jr. ....Waycross, GA
Johnson, Joseph R., Jr. & Associates
Lynchburg, VA
Johnson, Joseph T. ....New York, NY
Johnson, Josephine L. ....Washington, PA
Johnson, Joy A. ....Washington, DC
Johnson, Joyce A. ....Clinton, MA
Johnson, Joyce A. ....Defiance, MO
Johnson, Joyce E. ....Milford, CT
Johnson, Joyce Weaver ....Anchorage, AK
Johnson, J. R., Jr. ....Frankfort, KY
Johnson, J. R. L., Jr. ....Rockland, DE
Johnson, Jude J., Jr. ....New Orleans, LA
Johnson, Judith ....Fox Island, WA
Johnson, Judith A.
Department Of Health And Human Services, Office for Civil Rights, GV
Johnson, Judith A. ....Boston, MA
Johnson, Judith H. ....Salisbury, NC
Johnson, Judith J. ....Jackson, MS
Johnson, Judith Kay ....Dallas, TX
Johnson, Judith M. ....Houston, TX
Johnson, Judy A. ....Washington, DC
Johnson, Judy D. ....Ocala, FL
Johnson, Judy J. ....Irvine, CA
Johnson, Judy M. ....Houston, TX
Johnson, Judy, True, Guarnieri, LLP
Frankfort, KY
Johnson, Julia K. ....Boston, MA
Johnson, Julia L. ....Tallahassee, FL
Johnson, Julia R. ....Universal City, CA
Johnson, Julian ....Waukegan, IL
Johnson, Julian W. ....Richmond, VA
Johnson, Juliana L. ....St. Petersburg, FL
Johnson, Juliann ....Kansas City, KS
Johnson, Julie A. ....Los Angeles, CA
Johnson, Julie A. ....Louisville, KY
Johnson, Julie Ann ....Denver, CO
Johnson, Julie E. ....Dallas, TX
Johnson, June Adams ....Lowell, MA
Johnson, June LaRan ....Fort Lauderdale, FL
Johnson, Justice G., Jr. ....Toledo, OH
Johnson, Justin C. ....St. Petersburg, FL
Johnson, Justin F. ....Fairfield, NJ
Johnson, Justin L. ....Atlanta, GA
Johnson, Justin M. ....Pittsburgh, PA
Johnson, J. W. ....Sonora, TX
Johnson, J. W. (Don) ....Houston, TX
Johnson, K. Bridget ....New York, NY
Johnson, K. Paul ....Savannah, GA
Johnson, Kamalen K. ....Paxton, IL
Johnson, Kandice ....Columbia, MO
Johnson, Kane & Penna ....Atlanta, GA
Johnson, Karen ....San Jose, CA
Johnson, Karen A. ....Riverside, CA
Johnson, Karen A. ....Boston, MA
Johnson, Karen A. ....Custer, SD
Johnson, Karen E. Silverman
San Francisco, CA
Johnson, Karen Gren ....Dallas, TX
Johnson, Karen I. ....Kansas City, MO
Johnson, Karen Imus ....Minneapolis, MN
Johnson, Karen J. ....Vancouver, WA
Johnson, Karen L. ....Dover, DE
Johnson, Karen L. ....Katonah, NY
Johnson, Karen Lee ....San Antonio, TX
Johnson, Karen Litscher ....Chicago, IL
Johnson, Karen M. ....Orange, CA
Johnson, Karen R. ....Baltimore, MD
Johnson, Karen R. ....Austin, TX
Johnson, Karen S. ....Meadville, PA
Johnson, Karen Suzanne ....Walnut Creek, CA
Johnson, Karen V.
Federal Election Commission, Offices of the Commissioners, GV
Johnson, Kari J. ....New Ulm, MN
Johnson, Kari Russwurm ....Raleigh, NC
Johnson, Karl E. ....Albuquerque, NM
Johnson, Karl G. ....Olathe, KS
Johnson, Karl G., Jr. ....Austin, TX
Johnson, Karl L. ....Fort Myers, FL
Johnson, Karmen ....Fort Worth, TX
Johnson, Karon V. ....Hagåtña, GU
Johnson, Karyn S. ....Seattle, WA
Johnson, Kate ....Springfield, MA
Johnson, Katharyne Clark
McDonough, GA
Johnson, Katherine Beins ....Tallahassee, FL
Johnson, Katherine H. ....Birmingham, AL
Johnson, Kathleen A. ....Chicago, IL
Johnson, Kathleen B., (P.A.)
Boca Raton, FL
Johnson, Kathleen C. ....Santa Barbara, CA
Johnson, Kathleen Dinneen ....Alexandria, VA
Johnson, Kathleen E. ....Roseburg, OR
Johnson, Kathleen F. ....Glen Allen, VA
Johnson, Kathleen G. ....Dumont, NJ
Johnson, Kathleen Kelly ....Vienna, VA
Johnson, Kathleen M. ....Garden City, NY
Johnson, Kathleen P. ....Kenmore, NY
Johnson, Kathryn A. ....San Francisco, CA
Johnson, Kathryn A. ....Lakewood, CO
Johnson, Kathryn L. ....Tallahassee, FL
Johnson, Kathryn L. ....Chicago, IL
Johnson, Kathryn Michelle Sourie
Rogers, AR
Johnson, Kathryn Troy ....La Porte, IN
Johnson, Kathy Anita ....Bridgeport, CT
Johnson, Kathy J. ....Harrisonburg, LA
Johnson, Kathy Lubay ....Phoenix, AZ
Johnson, Kay E. ....Kansas City, MO
Johnson, Kay I. ....Bloomfield Hills, MI
Johnson, Kay Lawfer ....Watseka, IL

Johnson, K. C. (Casey) ....Houston, TX
Johnson, K. D. ....Idyllwild, CA
Johnson, Keen W. ....Mount Sterling, KY
Johnson, Keir R. ....St. Cloud, MN
Johnson, Keith ....Conway, AR
Johnson, Keith A. ....Claremont, CA
Johnson, Keith C. ....Marysville, CA
Johnson, Keith D. ....Minneapolis, MN
Johnson, Keith E. ....Woodbury, NJ
Johnson, Keith H. ....Jacksonville, FL
Johnson, Keith H. ....Raleigh, NC
Johnson, Keith K. ....Cincinnati, OH
Johnson, Keith L. ....Terre Haute, IN
Johnson, Keith L. ....Madison, WI
Johnson, Keith P. ....Butte, MT
Johnson, Keith W. ....Cincinnati, OH
Johnson, Kellene M. ....San Francisco, CA
Johnson, Kelley ....Princeton, NJ
Johnson, Kelly ....Newland, NC
Johnson, Kelly Jay ....Wichita, KS
Johnson, Kelly Overstreet, (P.A.)
Tallahassee, FL
Johnson, Kelly, P.A. ....Newland, NC
Johnson, Kelly S., Law Offices of
Newport Beach, CA
Johnson, Kennedy, Dahl & Willis
Wichita, KS
Johnson, Kenneth ....Wichita Falls, TX
Johnson, Kenneth A. ....Calabasas, CA
Johnson, Kenneth A. ....New Haven, CT
Johnson, Kenneth A. ....Boston, MA
Johnson, Kenneth A. ....Wayzata, MN
Johnson, Kenneth B. ....Jackson, MI
Johnson, Kenneth B. ....Lansing, MI
Johnson, Kenneth B., Jr. ....Jackson, MI
Johnson, Kenneth C. ....Columbus, OH
Johnson, Kenneth D. ....Laguna Hills, CA
Johnson, Kenneth D. ......Department of Justice,
Civil Rights Division, GV
Johnson, Kenneth D. ....Walden, NY
Johnson, Kenneth D., P.C. ....Walden, NY
Johnson, Kenneth E. ....Los Angeles, CA
Johnson, Kenneth E. ....Piedmont, CA
Johnson, Kenneth E. ....Huntington, TX
Johnson, Kenneth F. ....Oakland, CA
Johnson, Kenneth G. ....San Francisco, CA
Johnson, Kenneth G. ....Houston, TX
Johnson, Kenneth G. ....Chehalis, WA
Johnson, Kenneth H. ....Indianapolis, IN
Johnson, Kenneth H. ....Houston, TX
Johnson, Kenneth J. ....Denver, CO
Johnson, Kenneth L. ....Palo Alto, CA
Johnson, Kenneth L. ....Baltimore, MD
Johnson, Kenneth L. ....New York, NY
Johnson, Kenneth L. ....Edmonds, WA
Johnson, Kenneth L. ....Waukesha, WI
Johnson, Kenneth M. ....Greensboro, NC
Johnson, Kenneth N. ....Juneau, WI
Johnson, Kenneth P. ....Wood Dale, IL
Johnson, Kenneth P. ....Vestal, NY
Johnson, Kenneth R. ....Naples, FL
Johnson, Kenneth R. ....Minneapolis, MN
Johnson, Kenneth R. ....Ada, OK
Johnson, Kenneth S. ....Dodge City, KS
Johnson, Kenneth T., Jr. ....San Francisco, CA
Johnson, Kenneth W. ....Gaithersburg, MD
Johnson, Kenneth W. ....Springfield, MO
Johnson, Kenneth W. ....Rockwood, PA
Johnson, Kent D. ....Portland, OR
Johnson, Kent M. ....Dallas, TX
Johnson, Kent R. ....Carlisle, MA
Johnson, Kent S. ....Oklahoma City, OK
Johnson, Kerby A. ....San Antonio, TX
Johnson, Kerri A. ....San Jose, CA
Johnson, Kerry A. ....New York, NY
Johnson, Kevin A. ....San Mateo, CA
Johnson, Kevin A. ....Houston, TX
Johnson, Kevin C. ....Cincinnati, OH
Johnson, Kevin D. ....Tampa, FL
Johnson, Kevin D. ....Minneapolis, MN
Johnson, Kevin E. ....Pekin, IL
Johnson, Kevin E. ....Minneapolis, MN
Johnson, Kevin J. ....Minneapolis, MN
Johnson, Kevin K., (A Professional Law
Corporation) ....San Diego, CA
Johnson, Kevin L. ....Birmingham, AL
Johnson, Kevin L. ....Las Vegas, NV
Johnson, Kevin M. ....Philadelphia, PA
Johnson, Kevin P.B. ....Palo Alto, CA
Johnson, Kevin W. ....Denver, CO
Johnson, Kiehner ....Columbus, OH
Johnson, Kile W. ....Lincoln, NE
Johnson, Killen, Thibodeau & Seiler, A
Professional Association ....Duluth, MN
Johnson & Kim, LLC ....Anchorage, AK
Johnson, Kim R. ....Buffalo, MN
Johnson, Kim Y. ....Baltimore, MD
Johnson, Kimberly A. ....Tallahassee, FL
Johnson, Kimberly A. ....Albany, NY
Johnson, Kimberly A. ....Bismarck, ND
Johnson, Kimberly L. ....Denver, CO
Johnson, Kimberly Leach ....Naples, FL
Johnson & Kinzel ....McPherson, KS
Johnson, Kirk C. ....Reno, NV
Johnson, Kirk D. ....Texarkana, AR
Johnson, Kirk Douglas ....Las Vegas, NV
Johnson, Kirk E. ....Ada, OK
Johnson, Kirk M. ....Glendora, CA
Johnson & Klein ....Houston, TX
Johnson, Kloos & Sherton, P.C. ....Salem, OR
Johnson, Knut S. ....San Diego, CA
Johnson, Koni L. ....Chicago, IL
Johnson, Kraig N. ....Orlando, FL
Johnson, Kranz and McDaniel
Darlington, WI
Johnson, Krister D. ....St. Cloud, MN
Johnson, Kristi J. ....Seattle, WA
Johnson, Kristi K. ....Des Moines, IA

Johnson, Kristin L. ....Alameda, CA
Johnson, Kristin L. ....Atlanta, GA
Johnson, Kristin L. ....Minneapolis, MN
Johnson, Kristin M. ....San Diego, CA
Johnson, Kristina E. ....Boston, MA
Johnson, Kristina M. ....Jackson, MS
Johnson, Kristine H. ....Falls Church, VA
Johnson, Kurt A. ....Las Vegas, NV
St. George, UT
Johnson, Kurt D. ....New Ulm, MN
Johnson, Kurt E. ....Westwood, NJ
Johnson, Kurt R. ....Inver Grove Heights, MN
Johnson, Kurt W. ....Hartford, CT
Johnson, Kyle C. ....Dulles, VA
Johnson, Kyle W. ....Dallas, TX
Johnson, Kyson ....Bedford, TX
Johnson, Kyson M., P.C. ....Bedford, TX
Johnson, L. Charles ....Pocatello, ID
Johnson, L. Charles, III ....Pocatello, ID
Johnson, L. Craig ....Manchester, TN
Johnson, L. Daniel ....Memphis, TN
Memphis, TN
Johnson, L. Dean, (P.C.) ....Huntsville, AL
Johnson, L. Farnum, Jr.
Falls Church, VA
Johnson, L. Scott, Jr. ....Montgomery, AL
Johnson, Lacy Claude ....New York, NY
Johnson, Lacy M. ....Indianapolis, IN
Johnson, LaDonna Sargent ....Greenwood, SC
Johnson, Lael F. ....Chicago, IL
Johnson, Lafayette N.
Federal Emergency Management Agency,
Office of the General Counsel, GV
Johnson, Lamar C. ....Grove Hill, AL
Johnson & Lambeth ....Wilmington, NC
Johnson, Lance B. ....Cleveland, OH
Johnson, Lance G. ....Washington, DC
Johnson, Lance J. ....Lakeville, MN
Johnson, Lance J. ....Bruning, NE
Hebron, NE
Johnson & Lane ....Knoxville, IA
Johnson & Langworthy
Staten Island, NY
Johnson, Lant A. ....Honolulu, HI
Johnson, Lara Christine ....Eugene, OR
Johnson, Lara M. ....Orlando, FL
Johnson, LaRay Anseth ....Williston, ND
Johnson, Larrabee M. ....New York, NY
Johnson, Larry ....Shreveport, LA
Johnson, Larry ....New York, NY
Johnson, Larry C. ....St. Paul, MN
Johnson, Larry C. ....Fremont, NE
Johnson, Larry E. ....Albuquerque, NM
Johnson, Larry Edwin ....Springfield, VA
Johnson, Larry G. ....Denver, CO
Johnson, Larry K. ....Woodstock, IL
Johnson, Larry L. ....Chicago, IL
Johnson, Larry L. ....Louisville, KY
Johnson, Larry L. ....Jackson, MS
Johnson, Larry L. ....Orange, NJ
Johnson, Larry (Lawrence H.) ....Hobbs, NM
Johnson, Larry N. ....Seattle, WA
Johnson, Larry W. ....Atlanta, GA
Johnson, Larry W. ....Iowa Falls, IA
Johnson, Larry W. ....Minneapolis, MN
Johnson, Larry W. ....Lawton, OK
Johnson, Larry W. ....Dallas, TX
Johnson, Lars S. ....Chicago, IL
Johnson, Larson, Peterson & Meyer
Buffalo, MN
Johnson, Laura C. ....Batavia, OH
Johnson, Laura C. ....Charleston, SC
Johnson, Laura Eckert ....Olympia, WA
Johnson, Laura J. ....Springfield, MO
Johnson, Laura K. ....Atlanta, GA
Johnson, Laura L. ....Baltimore, MD
Johnson, Laura Sellers
West Palm Beach, FL
Johnson, Laura Todd ....Phoenix, AZ
Johnson, Laurence F. ....Sterling, IL
Johnson, Laurence F. ....Wheaton, MD
Johnson, Laurence M. ....Boston, MA
Johnson, Laurie Miyamoto
Redondo Beach, CA
Johnson, LaVerne M. ....Corvallis, OR
Johnson Law Firm ....Elizabethtown, NC
Johnson Law Firm ....Sulphur Springs, TX
Johnson Law Firm, A Professional
Corporation ....Little Rock, AR
Johnson Law Firm, P.A. ....Virginia, MN
Johnson Law Firm, P.A. ....Columbia, SC
Johnson Law Firm, The ....Denver, CO
Johnson Law Firm, The ....Fayetteville, GA
Johnson Law Firm, The, P.A.
Santa Fe, NM
Johnson Law Group ....Spokane, WA
Johnson Law Group, The ....Seattle, WA
Johnson Law Office Ltd., A Professional
Corporation ....Bloomington, IL
Johnson Law Offices ....Sister Bay, WI
Sturgeon Bay, WI
Johnson Law, P.C. ....Chatsworth, GA
Cohutta, GA
Dalton, GA
Ringgold, GA
Summerville, GA
Johnson Lawhead Buth & Pope, Professional
Corporation ....Indianapolis, IN
Johnson, Lawrence A. G. ....Tulsa, OK
Johnson, Lawrence C. ....Warren, NJ
Johnson, Lawrence D. ....Orlando, FL
Johnson, Lawrence D. ....Winter Park, FL
Johnson, Lawrence D. ....Hamilton, MT
Johnson, Lawrence E. ....Champaign, IL
Johnson, Lawrence E., and Associates, P.C.,
Law Offices of ....Champaign, IL
Johnson, Lawrence J. ....Detroit, MI
Johnson, Lawrence J. ....Dallas, TX

Johnson, Lawrence P. ....Redding, CA
Johnson, Lawrence P. ....Huron, OH
Johnson & Lawrence, P.C. ....Northwood, ND
Johnson, Lawrence R. ....Minneapolis, MN
Johnson, Lawrence W., Jr. ....Columbia, SC
Johnson, Lea Stromire ....Charlotte, NC
Johnson, Leahy & Mengeling, Ltd.
Woodstock, IL
Johnson, Leandra G. ....Lake City, FL
Johnson, Leanne ....Beaumont, TX
Johnson, LeDouglas G. ....Dallas, TX
Johnson, Lee ....Boston, MA
Johnson, Lee ....Beaumont, TX
Johnson, Lee A. ....Caldwell, KS
Johnson, Lee Allen ....Tempe, AZ
Johnson, Lee Allen, P.C. ....Phoenix, AZ
Tempe, AZ
Johnson, Lee Best ....Fayetteville, NC
Johnson, Lee Carol ....Washington, DC
Johnson, Lee E. ....Seattle, WA
Johnson, Lee Heinrick ....Denver, CO
Johnson, Lee N. ....Hopkins, MN
Johnson, Lee N., Law Offices of
Wethersfield, CT
Johnson, Lee R. ....Ogden, IA
Johnson, Lee R. ....St. Louis Park, MN
Johnson, Lee R. ....Houston, TX
Johnson, Lee S., Jr. ....Gainesville, FL
Johnson, Leif M. ....Billings, MT
Johnson, Leigh Gross ....Ashland, KY
Johnson, Lela D. ....Chicago, IL
Johnson, Leland T. ....Olympia, WA
Johnson, Leon ....Grenada, MS
Johnson, Leonard H. ....Dade City, FL
Johnson, Leonard J. ....Kansas City, MO
Johnson, Leonard M. ....Punta Gorda, FL
Johnson, Leonard M., P.A. ....Punta Gorda, FL
Johnson, LeRoi Callwall ....Buffalo, NY
Johnson, Leroy R., (P.C.) ....Atlanta, GA
Johnson, Lesa Lux ....Indianapolis, IN
Johnson, Leslie A. ....Ventura, CA
Johnson, Leslie A. ....Walnut Creek, CA
Johnson, Leslie A. ....Anacortes, WA
Johnson, Leslie A. Lewis ....Harrisburg, PA
Johnson, Leslie Coleman ......Walnut Creek, CA
Johnson, Leslie E., II ....Lompoc, CA
Johnson, Leslie G. ....Logan, OH
Johnson, Leslie H. ....Corte Madera, CA
Johnson, Leslie H. ....Center Sandwich, NH
Johnson, Leslie L. ....Delavan, WI
Johnson, Leslie Marie ....Oroville, CA
Johnson, Leslie R. ....Houston, TX
Johnson, Leslie S. ....Columbus, OH
Johnson, Leslie S. ....Portland, OR
Johnson, Leslie T. ....Chicago, IL
Johnson, Leslie V. ....Yakima, WA
Johnson, Lester B., III ....Savannah, GA
Johnson, Lester B., III, P.C. ....Savannah, GA
Johnson, Lester C. ....Ramona, CA
Johnson, Lewis H. ....Medina, WA
Johnson, Lewis M. ....Washington, DC
Johnson, Lilli Ann ....Sterling City, TX
Johnson, Lillian O. ....Phoenix, AZ
Johnson, Linda A. ....Elgin, IL
Johnson, Linda C. ....Los Angeles, CA
Johnson, Linda D. ....Department of Energy,
Office of the General Counsel, GV
Johnson, Linda E. ....Washington, DC
Johnson, Linda E. ....Carson City, NV
Johnson, Linda E. ....Cinnaminson, NJ
Johnson, Linda E., & Associates, P.C.
Washington, DC
Johnson, Linda F. ....San Diego, CA
Johnson, Linda F. ....Cincinnati, OH
Johnson, Linda K. ....Hammond, LA
Johnson, Linda Kristina ....Ottawa, IL
Johnson, Linda L. ....Boone, NC
Johnson, Linda L. ....Petersburg, VA
Johnson, Linda Langsdorf
Vancouver, WA
Johnson, Linda S. ....Manchester, NH
Johnson, Linda Sue
Department of Commerce,
National Oceanic and Atmospheric
Administration, GV
Johnson, Linda Urbanik ....Chicago, IL
Johnson, Lindahl O., Jr. ....Omaha, NE
Johnson & Lindberg, P.A.
Minneapolis, MN
Johnson, Lindsay ....Boston, MA
Johnson, Lindsay C. Foster
Jenkintown, PA
Johnson, Lindsay, P.C. ....Boston, MA
Johnson & Link, P.C. ....Ouray, CO
Johnson, Linnea M. ....Sacramento, CA
Johnson, Linnea R. ....Miami, FL
Johnson, Lira A. ....Detroit, MI
Johnson, Lisa A. ....Chicago, IL
Johnson, Lisa A. ....Duncan, OK
Johnson, Lisa Debrosse ....Boston, MA
Johnson, Lisa Hammond ....Cleveland, OH
Johnson, Lisa Lee ....Lexington, KY
Johnson, Lisa Michele ....Birmingham, AL
Johnson, Lisette M. ....Albany, NY
Johnson & Livingston ....Naples, FL
Winter Park, FL
Johnson, Livingstone J.
Whitehouse Station, NJ
Johnson, Lloyd G. ....Detroit, MI
Johnson, Lloyd T. ....Schaumburg, IL
Johnson, Lola L. ....Cleveland, OH
Johnson, Lolanda R. ....Flint, MI
Johnson, Lon M., Jr. ....Pikeville, KY
Johnson, Lonnie D. ....Bloomington, IN
Johnson, Lonnie L. ....Houston, TX
Johnson, Lora L. ....Dothan, AL
Johnson, Loran A. ....Orlando, FL
Johnson, Lori M. ....Buffalo, NY

Johnson, Lori-Ann ....Atlanta, GA
Johnson, Lorien Smith ....Tampa, FL
Johnson, Lorraine B. ....Culver City, CA
Johnson, Lorraine B. ....San Francisco, CA
Johnson, Lorraine Cimino ....Santa Clara, CA
Johnson, Lorraine M.
Department Of Veterans Affairs,
Office of the General Counsel, GV
Johnson, Louis P. ....Metropolis, IL
Johnson, Louise A. ....Park Ridge, NJ
Johnson, Louise Janis ....Longview, TX
Johnson, Lourdes Domingo
Fort Lauderdale, FL
Johnson, Lowell R. ....Coppell, TX
Johnson, Lucius C. ....Tampa, FL
Johnson, Lucy M. ....Dallas, TX
Johnson, Lundy L. ....Raleigh, NC
Johnson, Lynda M. ....Little Rock, AR
Johnson, Lynn ....Tacoma, WA
Johnson, Lynn A. ....Denver, CO
Johnson, Lynn A. ....Slayton, MN
Johnson, Lynn H. ....Washington, DC
Johnson, Lynn M. ....Glendale, CA
Johnson, Lynn M. ....Fort Worth, TX
Johnson, Lynn R. ....Kansas City, KS
Overland Park, KS
Kansas City, MO
Johnson, Lynn S. ....Houston, TX
Johnson, Lynne A. ....New York, NY
Johnson, Lynne B. ....Houston, TX
Johnson, Lynne E. ....Baltimore, MD
Johnson, M. Bernadine
Montague Township, NJ
Johnson, M. Brenk ....Dallas, TX
Johnson, M. Brett ....Dallas, TX
Johnson, M. David ....Denver, CO
Johnson, M. Davis ....New York, NY
Johnson, M. Diane ....Canton, OH
Johnson, M. Dwayne ....Baton Rouge, LA
Johnson, M. John ....Hixson, TN
Johnson, M. Perry, Jr.
United States Postal Service,
Office of the Deputy General Counsel, GV
Johnson, M. Scott ....Washington, DC
Johnson, M. Theresa ....Reading, PA
Johnson & Mach ....Turlock, CA
Johnson, Macklin K. ....Hallettsville, TX
Johnson & Madigan P.L.L.P.
Minneapolis, MN
Johnson, Malcolm ....New York, NY
Johnson, Mallory L. ....Stuart, FL
Johnson, Marc D. ....Tampa, FL
Johnson, Marcia K. ....Chicago, IL
Johnson, Marcia Walker ....Cleveland, OH
Johnson, Marcus C. ....Houston, TX
Johnson, Marcus L. ....Charlotte, NC
Johnson, Marcy Walker ....Columbia, SC
Johnson, Margaret E. ....Washington, DC
Johnson, Margaret K. ....St. Cloud, MN
Johnson, Margaret M. Joyce
Great Falls, MT
Johnson, Margaret N.
Cleveland Heights, OH
Johnson, Margaret R. ....Plano, TX
Johnson, Margaret T. ....Presque Isle, ME
Johnson, Margaret Voigt ....Presque Isle, WI
Johnson, Marian Parker ....Atlanta, GA
Johnson, Marianne Smith ....San Diego, CA
Johnson, Marie A. ....Kalamazoo, MI
Johnson, Marie C. Bellamy ....Chicago, IL
Johnson, Marie-Flore V. ......Minneapolis, MN
Johnson, Marilyn Grant ....Orland Park, IL
Johnson, Marion Arlene ....Atlanta, GA
Johnson, Marion J. ....Los Angeles, CA
Johnson, Marjorie M. ....Crestline, CA
Johnson, Marjorie R. ....Pinole, CA
Johnson, Mark A. ....Phoenix, AZ
Johnson, Mark A. ....San Francisco, CA
Johnson, Mark A. ....Miami, FL
Johnson, Mark A. ....Norfolk, NE
Johnson, Mark A. ....Columbus, OH
Johnson, Mark A. ....Portland, OR
Johnson, Mark A. ....White House, TN
Johnson, Mark A. ....Seattle, WA
Johnson, Mark A. ....Milwaukee, WI
Johnson, Mark A., (P.C.) ....Marietta, GA
Johnson, Mark B. ....San Francisco, CA
Johnson, Mark B. ....Andover, MA
Johnson, Mark D. ....Los Angeles, CA
Johnson, Mark D. ....Oakland, CA
Johnson, Mark D. ....Brunswick, GA
Johnson, Mark D. ....Bloomington, IL
Johnson, Mark D. ....Chicago, IL
Johnson, Mark D. ....New Albany, IN
Johnson, Mark D. ....Andover, MA
Johnson, Mark Dean ....Dallas, TX
Johnson, Mark E. ....Santa Maria, CA
Johnson, Mark E. ....Kansas City, MO
Johnson, Mark Edwin ....Seattle, WA
Johnson, Mark G. ....Dallas, TX
Johnson, Mark H. ....Monterey, CA
Johnson, Mark H. ....Savannah, GA
Johnson, Mark J. ....Minneapolis, MN
Johnson, Mark L. ....Chicago, IL
Johnson, Mark L. ....Boston, MA
Johnson, Mark P. ....Kansas City, MO
Johnson, Mark R. ....Hardy, AR
Johnson, Mark R. ....Farmington Hills, MI
Johnson, Mark R. ....Wayzata, MN
Johnson, Mark Rodman ....Charlotte, NC
Johnson, Mark S.
General Services Administration,
Office of Regional Counsel, GV
Johnson, Mark S. ....Cape Girardeau, MO
Johnson, Mark Stewart ....Tupelo, MS
Johnson, Mark T. ....Los Angeles, CA
Johnson, Mark T. ....San Francisco, CA

Johnson, Mark T. ... Minneapolis, MN
St. Paul, MN
Johnson, Mark W. ... Washington, DC
Johnson, Marlena A. ... Chicago, IL
Johnson, Marna J. ... Minneapolis, MN
Johnson, Marsha L. ... St. Louis, MO
Johnson, Marshall A. ... Benicia, CA
Johnson, Marshall E. ... Plymouth, MA
Johnson, Marshall Peyton ... Bethesda, MD
Johnson Martens Christie Andrews & Skinner, P.S. ... Seattle, WA
Johnson, Martha D. ... Columbus, OH
Johnson, Martin ... Pawtucket, RI
Johnson, Martin D. ... Omaha, NE
Johnson, Martin R. ... Richmond, VA
Johnson, Martin T. ... Pearl River, NY
White Plains, NY
Johnson, Martin W. ... San Francisco, CA
Johnson, Martin W. ... Benton, KY
Johnson, Marvin ... Phoenix, AZ
Johnson, Marvin E. ... Silver Spring, MD
Johnson, Marvin J. ... Cheyenne, WY
Johnson, Marvin, P.C. ... Phoenix, AZ
Johnson, Mary A. ... Chelan, WA
Johnson, Mary Alice ... Bloomfield, IN
Johnson, Mary Ann ... Bismarck, ND
Johnson, Mary Barb ... Lake Forest, IL
Johnson, Mary C. ... Atlanta, GA
Johnson, Mary Ebel, P.C.
Oregon City, OR
Johnson, Mary I. ... Virginia, MN
Johnson, Mary Jane ... Norwell, MA
Johnson, Mary Jo ... Boston, MA
Johnson, Mary Kathryn ... Winston-Salem, NC
Johnson, Mary L. ... Washington, DC
Johnson, Mary L. ...
National Mediation Board, GV
Johnson, Mary Louise ... New York, NY
Johnson, Mary Louise ... Philadelphia, PA
Johnson, Mary Louise, P.C.
Philadelphia, PA
Johnson, Mary S. ... New Orleans, LA
Johnson, Mary W. ... Oregon City, OR
Johnson, Mary White ... Spokane, WA
Johnson, Matte & Hobgood LLP
Atlanta, GA
Johnson, Matthew B. ... Faribault, MN
Johnson, Matthew C. ... Encinitas, CA
Johnson, Matthew E. ... Chicago, IL
Johnson, Matthew E. ... Minneapolis, MN
Johnson, Matthew E. ... Waco, TX
Johnson, Matthew G. ... Yakima, WA
Johnson, Matthew J. ... Omaha, NE
Johnson, Matthew Kinard ... Greenville, SC
Johnson, Matthew L. ... Chicago, IL
Johnson, Matthew L. ... Las Vegas, NV
Johnson, Matthew M. ... Los Angeles, CA
Johnson, Matthew M. ... Orlando, FL
Johnson, Matthew M. ... Minneapolis, MN
Johnson, Matthew Martin ... Newton, IA
Johnson, Matthew R. ... Manchester, NH
Johnson, Matthew S. ... Eugene, OR
Johnson, Matthew W. ... Los Angeles, CA
Johnson, Matthew W. ... Houston, TX
Johnson, Maureen G. ... Los Angeles, CA
Johnson, Maurice R. ... Washington, DC
Omaha, NE
Johnson, Max B. ... Walnut, CA
Johnson, Maye R., Jr. ... Greenville, SC
Johnson, Maynard R. ... Cincinnati, OH
Johnson & McElroy, L.L.P. ... Dallas, TX
Johnson McNally ... Grand Haven, MI
Johnson & McPherson, P.L.C.
Detroit, MI
Grosse Pointe Farms, MI
Johnson, Megan B. ... Pasadena, MD
Johnson, Melanye K. ... Bloomfield Hills, MI
Johnson, Melinda A. ... Long Beach, CA
Johnson, Melinda Mathison ... Ventura, CA
Johnson, Melinda O. ... Pascagoula, MS
Johnson, Melissa A. ... Nashville, TN
Johnson, Melissa C. ... Mountain View, CA
Johnson, Melissa D. ... Seattle, WA
Johnson, Melissa Ellen ... Destin, FL
Pensacola, FL
Johnson, Melvin E. ... Hartford, CT
Johnson, Melvin E. ... Seattle, WA
Johnson, Mercer, Hearn & Vinegar, PLLC
Raleigh, NC
Research Triangle Park, NC
Johnson, Meredith L. ... Houston, TX
Johnson, Merle A. ... Sioux Falls, SD
Johnson, Merle G. ... Port Allegany, PA
Johnson, Merrill N. ... Naples, FL
Winter Park, FL
Johnson, Merritt A. ... Cheney, WA
Johnson, Michael A. ... Washington, DC
Johnson, Michael A. ... Chicago, IL
Johnson, Michael A. ... Chicago, IL
Johnson, Michael A. ... Mount Pleasant, PA
Johnson, Michael A., Jr. ... Concord, NC
Johnson, Michael Anne ... Cleveland, OH
Johnson, Michael B. ... Little Rock, AR
Johnson, Michael B. ... Dallas, TX
Johnson, Michael Bradley ... Las Vegas, NV
Johnson, Michael Brian ... Chicago, IL
Johnson, Michael C. ... Phoenix, AZ
Johnson, Michael C. ... Los Angeles, CA
Johnson, Michael C. ... New Philadelphia, OH
Johnson, Michael C., P.C. ... Phoenix, AZ
Johnson, Michael D. ... Little Rock, AR
Johnson, Michael D. ... Chicago, IL
Johnson, Michael D. ... Blue Earth, MN
Minnesota Lake, MN
Wells, MN
Johnson, Michael E. ... Encino, CA
Johnson, Michael E. ... Atlanta, GA
Johnson, Michael E. ... New York, NY
Johnson, Michael Fleet ... Pikeville, KY
Johnson, Michael G. ... Chicago, IL
Johnson, Michael H. ... Fort Lauderdale, FL
Johnson, Michael H. ... Nashville, TN
Johnson, Michael J. ... Charlottesville, VA
Johnson, Michael K. ... Minneapolis, MN
Johnson, Michael K. ... Stateline, NV
Johnson, Michael Kenneth
San Francisco, CA
Johnson, Michael L. ... Rancho Cordova, CA
Johnson, Michael L. ... Chicago, IL
Johnson, Michael L. ... Springfield, MO
Johnson, Michael L. ... Grand Island, NE
Superior, NE
Johnson, Michael L. ... Aiken, SC
Johnson, Michael M. ... Los Angeles, CA
Johnson, Michael O. ... Winston-Salem, NC
Johnson, Michael P. ... Huntsville, AL
Oakland, CA
Johnson, Michael Patrick ... Quincy, MA
Johnson, Michael R. ... Denver, CO
Johnson, Michael R. ... Boise, ID
Johnson, Michael R. ... Lincoln, NE
Johnson, Michael R. ... Manchester, NH
Johnson, Michael R. ... Dallas, TX
Johnson, Michael R. ... Houston, TX
Johnson, Michael R. ... Salt Lake City, UT
Johnson, Michael R. ... Tacoma, WA
Johnson, Michael S. ... Salt Lake City, UT
Johnson, Michael T. ... New Orleans, LA
Johnson, Michael T. ... Houston, TX
Johnson, Michael T., & Associates
Alexandria, LA
Johnson, Michael Th. F. ... Concord, NH
Johnson, Michael V. ... Salem, OR
Johnson, Michael Vincent ... Victorville, CA
Johnson, Michael W. ... Department of Justice,
Civil Rights Division, GV
Johnson, Michael W. ... Ocala, FL
Johnson, Micheal Anthony ... Houston, TX
Johnson, Michele ... Costa Mesa, CA
Johnson, Michele G. ... Bismarck, ND
Johnson, Michele P. ... Port Washington, NY
Johnson, Micheline A. ... Atlanta, GA
Johnson, Micheline Kelly
Chattanooga, TN
Johnson, Michelle ... Beckley, WV
Johnson, Michelle L. ... San Francisco, CA
Johnson, Michelle L. ... Portland, OR
Johnson, Michelle R. ... Washington, DC
Johnson, Michelle T. ... Kansas City, MO
Johnson, Michelle W. ... Atlanta, GA
Johnson, Michone T. ... Washington, DC
Johnson, Mickey L. ... Pelham, AL
Johnson, Mildred L. ... Omaha, NE
Johnson, Millard A. ... Houston, TX
Johnson, Miller & Richardson, P.S.
Port Angeles, WA
Johnson, Miriam H. ...
Department of Labor, GV
Johnson, Mitchell D. ... Rapid City, SD
Johnson, Mitchell W. ... New Hope, MN
Johnson, Mitzi Conar ... Memphis, TN
Johnson, Moller R. ... Ravenna, NE
Johnson, Monica J. ... Laurel, MD
Johnson, Monika Lorice ... Memphis, TN
Johnson, Monique R. ... Lakeland, FL
Johnson, Monte E. ... Durham, NC
Johnson, Montgomery & Maguire
Cape Girardeau, MO
Johnson, Morgan H. ... Houston, TX
Johnson & Morland, P.C. ... Norfolk, NE
Johnson & Morris ... Andalusia, AL
Johnson and Morris ... Silver Bay, MN
Johnson, Morris T. ... Los Angeles, CA
Johnson, Moses W., IV ... San Bernardino, CA
Johnson & Mount ... Naples, FL
Johnson, Mullan & Brundage, P.C.
Rochester, NY
Johnson, Muriel L. ... Riverside, CA
Johnson, Myron A. ... Richmond, CA
Johnson, N. Pike, Jr. ... Phoenix, AZ
Johnson, N. Scott ... Tulsa, OK
Johnson, Nancy A. ... Sun City, CA
Johnson, Nancy B. ... Janesville, WI
Johnson, Nancy C. ... Des Moines, IA
Johnson, Nancy Clarice ... Arvada, CO
Johnson, Nancy E. ... Columbia, SC
Johnson, Nancy J. ... San Jose, CA
Johnson, Nancy Jeanne ... Manchester, CT
Johnson, Nancy L. ... Atlanta, GA
Johnson, Nancy L. ... Westmont, IL
Johnson, Nancy Orlene ... Phoenix, AZ
Johnson, Nancy S. ... Danville, IL
Johnson, Nathan ... Moulton, AL
Johnson, Nathan M. ... Dallas, TX
Johnson, Nathan W. ... Birmingham, AL
Johnson, Neal C. ... Glenview, IL
Johnson, Neal G. ... Monroe, LA
Johnson, Neal L., Jr. ... Monroe, LA
Johnson, Neal S. ... Lexington, VA
Roanoke, VA
Johnson, Neale T. ... Greensboro, NC
Johnson, Ned W. ... Houston, TX
Johnson, Neil ... Driggs, ID
Johnson, Neil E. ... Kensington, MD
Johnson, Neil E. ... Osakis, MN
Johnson, Neil L. ... Kansas City, MO
Johnson, Nelli ... Cleveland, OH
Johnson, Nels M. ... Buffalo, NY
Johnson, Nelson C. ... Atlantic City, NJ
Hammonton, NJ
Johnson, Nelson C., P.C. ... Hammonton, NJ
Johnson, Nelson D. ... Wayne, NJ
Johnson, Nely L. ... Portland, OR
Johnson, Neville L. ... Los Angeles, CA
Johnson, Newton A. ... Fairmont, MN
Johnson, Nibert J. ... Kingwood, TX
Johnson, Nicholas ... Louisville, KY
Johnson, Nicholas J. ... New York, NY
Johnson, Nicholas W. ... Charleston, WV
Johnson, Nicole C. ... New York, NY
Johnson, Nile K. ... Blair, NE
Johnson, Nils P. ... Canfield, OH
Johnson, Nils P., Jr. ... Canfield, OH
Johnson & Nimmo ... Ada, OK
Johnson & Nixon ... San Jose, CA
Johnson, Noel C. ... San Francisco, CA
Johnson, Noel Thomas ... Washington, DC
Johnson, Nora Abatelli ... Thornwood, NY
Johnson, Nord L. ... DeLand, FL
Johnson, Nord L., P.A. ... DeLand, FL
Johnson, Noreen C. ... Schenectady, NY
Johnson, Norma Holloway ...
United States District Court For The District
Of Columbia, GV
Johnson, Norma S. ... Stratford, CT
Johnson, Norman Dart ... Littleton, CO
Johnson, Norman Elwood, Jr.
Baltimore, MD
Johnson, Norman G. ... Atlanta, GA
Johnson, Norman J. ... Watkinsville, GA
Johnson, Norman S.
Securities and Exchange Commission,
Executive Staff, GV
Johnson, O. Thomas, Jr. ... Washington, DC
Johnson, Oakley Leland ... St. Petersburg, FL
Johnson, Octavia R. ... Department of Justice,
Federal Bureau of Investigation, GV
Johnson & Oliver, A Legal Professional Association ... Portsmouth, OH
Johnson, Oliver M., II
Whitehouse Station, NJ
Johnson Olson, Chartered ... Pocatello, ID
Johnson, Orlan M.
Securities and Exchange Commission,
Division of Investment Management, GV
Johnson, Orland K., Jr. ... Milwaukee, WI
Johnson, Orlano K. ... Salt Lake City, UT
Johnson, Orrin W. ... Harlingen, TX
Johnson, Orson L. (Pete) ... Birmingham, AL
Johnson, Oscar E. ... Forsyth, MT
Johnson, Otis, Jr. ... Jackson, MS
Johnson, Owen Allen ... Seattle, WA
Johnson, Owen M., Jr., (P.C.)
Washington, DC
Johnson, P. Lee ... Santa Ana, CA
Johnson, Paige Weeks ... Aiken, SC
Johnson, Pamela ... Richmond, VA
Johnson, Pamela Ann ... Denver, CO
Johnson, Pamela E. ... Dallas, TX
Johnson, Pamela G. ... Houston, TX
Johnson, Pamela J ... Red Bank, NJ
Johnson, Pamela Joenell ... Richmond, VA
Johnson, Pamela L. Hall ... Montpelier, VT
Johnson, Pamela McDade ... Towson, MD
Johnson, Pamela P.
Federal Labor Relations Authority,
Office of the Solicitor, GV
Johnson, Pamela Pope ... Dallas, TX
Johnson, Pamela R. ... Ellicott City, MD
Johnson, Pamela R. ... Charlottesville, VA
Johnson, Pamela S. ... Washington, DC
Johnson, Pamela T. ... Richardson, TX
Johnson, Pamela Tonn ... Phoenix, AZ
Johnson & Pardini ... San Francisco, CA
Johnson, Parker & Hess, P.A.
Westminster, MD
Johnson & Parsons, P.A. ... Clinton, NC
Johnson, Patricia ... Tarpon Springs, FL
Johnson, Patricia A. ... Los Angeles, CA
Johnson, Patricia Ann ... Alexandria, VA
Johnson, Patricia B. ... Weatogue, CT
Johnson, Patricia C. ... San Diego, CA
Johnson, Patricia L. ... Tampa, FL
Johnson, Patricia L. ... Anadarko, OK
Johnson, Patricia L. ... Spokane, WA
Johnson, Patricia Lynn ... Truckee, CA
Johnson, Patricia R. ... Eden Prairie, MN
Johnson, Patricia W. ... Albany, NY
Johnson, Patrick ... Nashville, TN
Johnson, Patrick A. ... Houston, TX
Johnson, Patrick J. ... New York, NY
Johnson, Patrick J. ... Toledo, OH
Johnson, Patrick, Jr. ... New Orleans, LA
Johnson, Patrick, Jr. ... Memphis, TN
Johnson, Patrick M.W. ... Austin, TX
Johnson, Patrick (Pete) H., Jr.
Clarksdale, MS
Johnson, Patrick V. ... Minneapolis, MN
Johnson, Patrick W. ... Lakewood, CO
Johnson, Paul ... New York, NY
Johnson, Paul A. ... Lodi, WI
Madison, WI
Poynette, WI
Johnson, Paul B. ... San Diego, CA
Johnson, Paul B. ... San Francisco, CA
Johnson, Paul B. ... Tampa, FL
Johnson, Paul B. ... Hattiesburg, MS
Johnson, Paul B. ... Orem, UT
Johnson, Paul C. ... Cherry Hill, NJ
Johnson, Paul D. ... Fargo, ND
Johnson, Paul D. ... Denton, TX
Johnson, Paul Duval ... Tampa, FL
Johnson, Paul G. ... Miami, FL
Johnson, Paul G. ... Huntsville, TX
Johnson, Paul H. ... Los Angeles, CA
Orange, CA
Johnson, Paul H. ... Tulsa, OK
Johnson, Paul H., III ... Fort Worth, TX
Johnson, Paul H., Jr. ... Southfield, MI
Johnson, Paul J. (IBA) **... Arlington, TX**
Johnson, Paul K. ... Chicago, IL
Johnson, Paul M. ... Salt Lake City, UT
Johnson, Paul O. ... Arden Hills, MN
Johnson, Paul O. ... Golden Valley, MN
Johnson, Paul R. ... Oakland, CA
Johnson, Paul R. ... Portland, ME
Johnson, Paul R. ... Alexandria, MN
Johnson, Paul R. ... Charlottesville, VA
Johnson, Paul S., Jr. ... Roanoke, VA
Johnson, Paul T. ... Ellicott City, MD
Johnson, Paul W. ... Tuscaloosa, AL
Johnson, Paul W. ... Edwardsville, IL
Johnson, Paul W. ... Boston, MA
Johnson, Paul W. ... New Castle, PA
Johnson, Paula A. ... Houston, TX
Johnson, Paula D. ... Stillwater, OK
Johnson, Paula M. ... Whitefish, MT
Johnson, Paula M. ... Lubbock, TX
Johnson, Paula R. ... Minneapolis, MN
Johnson, Paulette Locke ... Fayetteville, AR
Johnson, Pauline G.
Agency for International Development,
Legal Advisers-Overseas, GV
Johnson & Pavuk ... Washington, DC
Johnson, Peddrick & Stanaland, P.L.L.C.
Greensboro, NC
Johnson, Peggy J. ... Little Rock, AR
Johnson, Perry E., Jr. ... Kansas City, MO
Johnson, Peter ... Tucson, AZ
Johnson, Peter A. ... Boston, MA
Johnson, Peter C. ... St. Louis, MO
Johnson, Peter C. ... New York, NY
Johnson, Peter D. ... Augusta, GA
Johnson, Peter D. ... Smithtown, NY
Johnson, Peter J. ... Walnut Creek, CA
Johnson, Peter J. ... St. Joseph, MI
Johnson, Peter J. ... Spokane, WA
Johnson, Peter James ... New York, NY
Johnson, Peter James, Jr. ... New York, NY
Johnson, Peter K. ... Northfield, IL
Johnson, Peter, Law Offices of
Houston, TX
Johnson, Peter M. ... Denver, CO
Johnson, Peter M. ... Salt Lake City, UT
Johnson, Peter R. ... Concord, MA
Johnson, Peter R. ... Westfield, MA
Johnson, Peter S. ... Boston, MA
Johnson, Peter W. ... Wayzata, MN
Johnson, Peter William ... Towson, MD
Johnson, Petra H. ... Wichita, KS
Johnson, Philip A. ... Covington, GA
Johnson, Philip C. ... Binghamton, NY
Johnson, Philip E. ... Denver, CO
Johnson, Philip E. ... Temperance, MI
Johnson, Philip J. ... Columbus, GA
Johnson, Philip L. ... Long Beach, CA
Johnson, Philip L. ... Sturgeon Bay, WI
Johnson, Philip M. ... Taftsville, VT
Johnson, Philip McBride ... Washington, DC
Johnson, Philip S. ... Philadelphia, PA
Johnson, Philip W. ... Amarillo, TX
Johnson, Philip W. ... Berkeley, CA
Johnson, Phillip E. ... Augusta, ME
Johnson, Phillip J. ... Chicago, IL
Johnson, Phillip R. ... Wenatchee, WA
Johnson, Phillip W. ... Long Beach, CA
Johnson, Phyllis C. ... Anchorage, AK
Johnson, Phyllis Hall ... Fayetteville, AR
Johnson, P. K., IV ... Belleville, IL
Johnson, P. K., V ... Belleville, IL
Johnson, Pope D., III ... Columbia, SC
Johnson, Poulson, Coons & Slater
Los Angeles, CA
Johnson, Preston W. ... Long Beach, CA
Johnson, Price L. ... Dallas, TX
Johnson, Prioleau & Kenison, LLC
Atlanta, GA
Johnson, Priscilla S. ... Pittsburgh, PA
Johnson, Prudence Fink ... Union, MO
Johnson, Quentin ... Leesburg, FL
Johnson, Quentin T. ... Minneapolis, MN
Johnson, R. Arlen ... Milford, MA
Johnson, R. Brandon ... Lewisburg, WV
Johnson, R. Brian ... Charleston, SC
Johnson, R. Charles ... Petaluma, CA
Johnson, R. Craig ... Salt Lake City, UT
Johnson, R. Denise ... Jacksonville, FL
Johnson, R. Edgar ... Caldwell, KS
Johnson, R. Erick, II ... Portland, OR
Johnson, R. Eugene ... Evansville, IN
Johnson, R. Gilman ... Fox Lake, IL
Johnson, R. Hayes, Jr. ... Jackson, MS
Johnson, R. Keith ... Charlotte, NC
Johnson, R. Keith, P.A. ... Charlotte, NC
Johnson, R. Kinard, Jr. ... Greenville, SC
Johnson, R. Neil ... Daytona Beach, FL
Johnson, R. Randall ... Phoenix, AZ
Johnson, R. Scott ... Long Beach, CA
Johnson, R. Scott ... Chicago, IL
Johnson, R. Steven ... Terre Haute, IN
Johnson, R. Steven ... Newton, IA
Johnson, R. Tenney ... Washington, DC
Johnson, R. Todd ... Washington, DC
Johnson, R. Verle ... New York, NY
Johnson, R. Wayne ... Kingston, NY
Johnson, R. Wes ... San Antonio, TX
Johnson, Rachel E. ... Minnetonka, MN
Johnson, Rachel H. ... Albuquerque, NM
Johnson, Rachelle L. K. ... Montezuma, IA
Johnson, Radcliffe & Petrov, L.L.P.
Houston, TX
Johnson, Rady A., II ... New York, NY
Johnson, Ralph Bennion ... Murray, UT
Johnson, Ralph D. ... Englewood, CO
Johnson, Ralph H. ... Washington, DC
Johnson, Ralph O. ... Pahokee, FL
Johnson, Ralph W. ... Seattle, WA
Johnson, Ralph W., III ... Stamford, CT
Johnson, Ramona ... Philadelphia, PA
Johnson, Rand D. ... Brooklyn, NY
Johnson, Randall B. ... Fall River, MA
Johnson, Randall C. ... Fort Worth, TX

Johnson, Randall C., Jr. ...Seattle, WA
Johnson, Randall E. ...
Joint Committees And Commissions, GV
Johnson, Randall G. ...Richmond, VA
Johnson, Randall H.
Westlake Village, CA
Johnson, Randall K. ...Newport Beach, CA
Johnson, Randall L. ...Chicago, IL
Johnson, Randall L. ...Marion, IN
Johnson, Randall Lee ...Arlington, VA
Johnson, Randall W. ...Atlanta, GA
Johnson, Randall W. ...Dallas, TX
Johnson, Randle E. ...Elgin, IL
Johnson, Randy H. ...Long Beach, CA
Johnson, Randy K. ...Elgin, IL
Johnson, Randy K. ...Salt Lake City, UT
Johnson, Rasmussen & Robinson, P.L.C.
Mesa, AZ
Johnson, Raud E. ...Fairfield, CT
Johnson, Ray A. ...Washington, DC
Johnson, Rayborn C., Jr. ...Montgomery, TX
Johnson, Raymond ...Montgomery, AL
Johnson, Raymond ...Des Moines, IA
Johnson, Raymond C. ...Lakewood, CO
Johnson, Raymond E. ...Rockford, IL
Johnson, Raymond E. ...St. Paul, MN
Johnson, Raymond L. ...Los Angeles, CA
Johnson, Raymond L., Jr. ...Birmingham, AL
Johnson, Raymond Paul, The Law Offices of
Los Angeles, CA
Johnson, Raymond R.
Sulphur Springs, TX
Johnson, Rebecca J. ...Marion, KY
Johnson, Rebecca J. ...Newtown, PA
Johnson, Rebecca Nichols ...Roswell, NM
Johnson, Reed H. ...St. Petersburg, FL
Johnson, Reed R. ...Phoenix, AZ
Johnson, Rees C. ...Portland, OR
Johnson, Reginald C. ...New Orleans, LA
Johnson, Reginald H. ...Fayetteville, GA
Johnson, Reginald J. ...Mount Vernon, NY
Johnson, Reginald S. ...Bloomfield Hills, MI
Johnson, Rena ...Philadelphia, PA
Johnson, René M. ...New York, NY
Johnson, Renee L. ...Mequon, WI
Johnson and Reppart, PLLC ...Grove, OK
Johnson, Repunzelle Rachelle
Washington, DC
Johnson, Reverdy ...Sarasota, FL
Johnson, Reverdy ...Santa Fe, NM
Johnson, Rex E. ...Wheatland, WY
Johnson, Rhonda B. ...San Francisco, CA
Johnson, Richard ...Dallas, TX
Johnson, Richard A. ...Payson, AZ
Johnson, Richard A. ...Boulder, CO
Johnson, Richard A. ...Bridgeport, CT
Johnson, Richard A. ...Washington, DC
Johnson, Richard A. ...Lincoln, NE
Johnson, Richard A. ...Sioux Falls, SD
Johnson, Richard A. ...Nashville, TN
Johnson, Richard A., Jr. ...Boston, MA
Johnson, Richard B. ...Tempe, AZ
Johnson, Richard B. ...Hayward, CA
Johnson, Richard B. ...Palmer, MA
Johnson, Richard B. ...Everett, WA
Johnson, Richard B., P.S. ...Everett, WA
Johnson, Richard C. ...San Francisco, CA
Johnson, Richard C. ...Washington, DC
Johnson, Richard C. ...Lisle, IL
Johnson, Richard C. ...Foxboro, MA
Johnson, Richard C. ...Edina, MN
Johnson, Richard C. ...Albany, NY
Johnson, Richard C. ...Houston, TX
Johnson, Richard D. ...Whitney, TX
Johnson, Richard E. ...Phoenix, AZ
Johnson, Richard E. ...Stockton, CA
Johnson, Richard E. ...United States Senate,
Committee Legal Personnel, GV
Johnson, Richard E. ...Atlanta, GA
Johnson, Richard E. ...Philadelphia, PA
Johnson, Richard E. ...Waupaca, WI
Johnson, Richard F. ...Chicago, IL
Johnson, Richard G. ...Newport, KY
Johnson, Richard G. ...Cleveland, OH
Johnson, Richard G., Co., L.P.A.
Cleveland, OH
Johnson, Richard G., Jr.
Salt Lake City, UT
Johnson, Richard Gray ...Waupaca, WI
Johnson, Richard H. ...Boston, MA
Johnson, Richard H. ...Cincinnati, OH
Johnson, Richard H., II
Salt Lake City, UT
Johnson, Richard J. ...Minneapolis, MN
Johnson, Richard K. ...Chicago, IL
Johnson, Richard Kenneth ...High Ridge, MO
Johnson, Richard L. ...Oakland, CA
Johnson, Richard L. ...Denver, CO
Johnson, Richard L. ...Atlantis, FL
Johnson, Richard L. ...Hagåtña, GU
Johnson, Richard L. ...Indianapolis, IN
Johnson, Richard L. ...Des Moines, IA
Johnson, Richard L. ...Toledo, OH
Johnson, Richard L., P.C. ...Denver, CO
Johnson, Richard M. ...Los Angeles, CA
Johnson, Richard M. ...Vienna, VA
Johnson, Richard M., Jr. ...Van Nuys, CA
Johnson, Richard M., Jr. ...Chicago, IL
Johnson, Richard N. ...Vancouver, WA
Johnson, Richard N., P.C. ...Vancouver, WA
Johnson, Richard P.
General Accounting Office,
Office of the General Counsel, GV
Johnson, Richard P. ...Lexington, KY
Johnson, Richard P. ...Teaneck, NJ
Johnson, Richard P. ...Memphis, TN
Johnson, Richard P. ...Dallas, TX
Johnson, Richard R. ...Los Angeles, CA
Johnson, Richard R. ...Sacramento, CA
Johnson, Richard R. ...Kansas City, MO
Johnson, Richard R. ...Dallas, TX
Johnson, Richard R. ...Yakima, WA
Johnson, Richard S. ...Rocky Hill, CT
Johnson, Richard S. ...Fort Walton Beach, FL
Johnson, Richard S. ...Farmington, MN
Johnson, Richard S. ...Las Vegas, NV
Johnson, Richard S. ...Dallas, TX
Johnson, Richard S. ...San Antonio, TX
Johnson, Richard T. ...Shrewsbury, NJ
Johnson, Richard W. ...Stockton, CA
Johnson, Richard W. ...Hammond, IN
Johnson, Richard W. ...Grand Marais, MN
Johnson, Richard W. ...Minneapolis, MN
Johnson, Richard W. ...Omaha, NE
Johnson, Richard W. ...Philadelphia, PA
Johnson, Richard Wesley ...Walnut Creek, CA
Johnson, Richd. C. ...Woburn, MA
Johnson, Richd. E. ...Fort Worth, TX
Johnson, Rick A. ...Valley Falls, KS
Johnson, Rick A. ...Mayfield, KY
Johnson, Rifenbark & Wylie
Los Angeles, CA
Johnson, Risë Janette ...Los Angeles, CA
Johnson & Rishwain LLP
Los Angeles, CA
Johnson, Rita B. ...Independence, MO
Johnson, Rita K. ...Mill Valley, CA
Johnson, Rita K. ...San Francisco, CA
Johnson, Riva T. ...Dallas, TX
Johnson, Rivers D., Jr. ...Warsaw, NC
Johnson, Robert ...Chicago, IL
Johnson, Robert A. ...Phoenix, AZ
Johnson, Robert A. ...Irvine, CA
Johnson, Robert A. ...Elberton, GA
Johnson, Robert A. ...Minneapolis, MN
Johnson, Robert A. ...Centerville, MO
Johnson, Robert A. ...Albuquerque, NM
Johnson, Robert A. ...New York, NY
Johnson, Robert A. ...Cleveland, OH
Johnson, Robert A. ...Pittsburgh, PA
Johnson, Robert A. ...Salt Lake City, UT
Johnson, Robert A. ...McLean, VA
Johnson, Robert B. ...Lexington, KY
Johnson, Robert B. ...Dallas, OR
Johnson, Robert C. ...Chicago, IL
Johnson, Robert C. ...Kalamazoo, MI
Johnson, Robert C. ...Kansas City, MO
Johnson, Robert C. ...St. Louis, MO
Johnson, Robert C. ...Rochester, NY
Johnson, Robert C. ...North Olmsted, OH
Johnson, Robert C. ...Dallas, TX
Johnson, Robert C., Jr. ...Boston, MA
Johnson, Robert C., Jr. ...Dallas, TX
Johnson, Robert D. ...San Diego, CA
Johnson, Robert D. ...St. Paul, MN
Johnson, Robert D. ...Las Vegas, NV
Johnson, Robert Dale ...Roswell, GA
Johnson, Robert E. ...Stockton, CA
Johnson, Robert E. ...Tarzana, CA
Johnson, Robert E. ...Denver, CO
Johnson, Robert E. ...Indianapolis, IN
Johnson, Robert E. ...Omaha, NE
Johnson, Robert E. ...Aiken, SC
Johnson, Robert E. ...Austin, TX
Johnson, Robert E. ...Olympia, WA
Johnson, Robert E., II ...Hugoton, KS
Johnson, Robert E., Jr.
East Hartford, CT
Providence, RI
Johnson, Robert E., Jr. ...Atlanta, GA
Johnson, Robert E., Jr. ...Omaha, NE
Johnson, Robert E., Jr. ...Austin, TX
Johnson, Robert E., (P.A.) ...Tampa, FL
Johnson, Robert Earl ...Chicago, IL
Johnson, Robert F. ...North St. Paul, MN
Johnson, Robert F. ...Washington, NC
Johnson, Robert F. ...Milwaukee, WI
Johnson, Robert F., III ...Austin, TX
Johnson, Robert G. ...Birmingham, AL
Johnson, Robert G. ...Mankato, MN
Johnson, Robert G. ...St. Louis, MO
Johnson, Robert G. ...Salt Lake City, UT
Johnson, Robert G., Jr. ...Laguna Niguel, CA
Johnson, Robert H. ...Sacramento, CA
Johnson, Robert H. ...Middletown, OH
Johnson, Robert H. ...Rock Springs, WY
Johnson, Robert J. ...Grand Rapids, MI
Johnson, Robert J. ...Cleveland, OH
Johnson, Robert J. ...Allentown, PA
Johnson, Robert J. ...Reading, PA
Johnson, Robert J., II ...Kentwood, LA
Johnson, Robert J., Jr. ...Hackensack, NJ
Johnson, Robert James ...Prescott, AZ
Johnson, Robert K. ...Aptos, CA
Johnson, Robert K. ...Lancaster, CA
Johnson, Robert K. ...Indianapolis, IN
Johnson, Robert K., (A Professional
Corporation) ...Los Angeles, CA
Johnson, Robert Koop ...Naples, FL
Johnson, Robert Koop, P.A. ...Naples, FL
Johnson, Robert L. ...Lake Hughes, CA
Johnson, Robert L. ...San Diego, CA
Las Vegas, NV
Johnson, Robert L. ...San Francisco, CA
Johnson, Robert L. ...West Palm Beach, FL
Johnson, Robert L. ...St. Louis, MO
Johnson, Robert L. ...Lewistown, MT
Johnson, Robert L. ...Warren, OH
Johnson, Robert L. ...Washington, PA
Johnson, Robert L. ...Gainesboro, TN
Johnson, Robert L., III ...Houston, TX
Johnson, Robert L., Jr. ...Quincy, MA
Johnson, Robert Leland ...Denver, CO
Johnson, Robert Lowell ...Newark, CA
Johnson, Robert M. ...Anchorage, AK
Johnson, Robert M. ...Belvedere-Tiburon, CA
Johnson, Robert M. ...Los Angeles, CA
Johnson, Robert M. ...Los Angeles, CA
Johnson, Robert M. ...Sarasota, FL
Johnson, Robert M. ...Las Vegas, NV
Johnson, Robert M. ...New York, NY
Johnson, Robert M. ...Oklahoma City, OK
Johnson, Robert M. ...Memphis, TN
Johnson, Robert M. ...Falls Church, VA
Johnson, Robert M. A. ...Anoka, MN
Johnson, Robert N. ...Atlanta, GA
Johnson, Robert N. ...Richmond, VA
Johnson, Robert N., III ...Fort Madison, IA
Johnson, Robert P. ...Chico, CA
Johnson, Robert P. ...Great Neck, NY
Johnson, Robert P. ...Cincinnati, OH
Johnson, Robert R. ...Long Beach, CA
Johnson, Robert R. ...West Palm Beach, FL
Johnson, Robert R. ...Houston, TX
Johnson, Robert S. ...Topeka, KS
Johnson, Robert S. ...Reno, NV
Johnson, Robert S. ...Middlesex, NJ
Johnson, Robert S. ...Fort Worth, TX
Johnson, Robert S. ...Houston, TX
Johnson, Robert S. T. ...Ellicott City, MD
Johnson, Robert T. ...Phoenix, AZ
Johnson, Robert T. ...San Diego, CA
Johnson, Robert T., Jr. ...Chicago, IL
Johnson, Robert Timothy ...Madison, TN
Johnson, Robert V. ...Corona Del Mar, CA
Johnson, Robert V. ...Chicago, IL
Johnson, Robert V. ...Minneapolis, MN
Johnson, Robert V. ...Center Harbor, NH
Johnson, Robert V., II ...Center Harbor, NH
Concord, NH
Johnson, Robert W. ...Colorado Springs, CO
Johnson, Robert W. ...Indianapolis, IN
Johnson, Robert W. ...Shreveport, LA
Johnson, Robert W. ...Anoka, MN
Johnson, Robert W. ...St. Paul, MN
Johnson, Robert W. ...Statesville, NC
Johnson, Robert W. ...The Woodlands, TX
Johnson, Robert W.
Christiansted, St. Croix, VI
Johnson, Robert W. ...Shelton, WA
Johnson, Robert W., Jr.
Corpus Christi, TX
Johnson, Robert W., P.A. ...St. Paul, MN
Johnson, Robert White ...Wilmington, NC
Johnson, Robert Winthrop
Birmingham, AL
Washington, DC
Johnson, Robert Wm., III
Slingerlands, NY
Troy, NY
Johnson, Roberta Bishop ...Urbana, IL
Johnson, Roberta R. ...Wichita, KS
Johnson, Robin M. ...Columbia, SC
Johnson, Robin S. ...Raleigh, NC
Johnson, Robt. H. ...San Francisco, CA
Johnson, Robt. N. ...Chicago, IL
Johnson, Robyn Euler ...Troy, KS
Johnson, Robyn K. ...Los Angeles, CA
Johnson & Roche ...Washington, DC
McLean, VA
Johnson & Rodenburg ...Fargo, ND
Johnson, Roderick L. ...Corvallis, OR
Johnson, Rodger K. ...Lancaster, OH
Johnson, Rodman C. ...Austin, TX
Johnson, Rodney ...Stanford, CA
Johnson, Rodney A. ...San Diego, CA
Johnson, Rodney A. ...North Bend, NE
Johnson, Rodney A. ...Dallas, TX
Johnson, Rodney D. ...Lexington, MA
Johnson, Rodney G. ...Phoenix, AZ
Johnson, Rodney G., Ltd. ...Phoenix, AZ
Johnson, Rodney K. ...Northbrook, IL
Johnson, Rodney M. ...Pensacola, FL
Johnson, Rodney N. ...San Rafael, CA
Johnson, Rodney W.
Agency for International Development,
Other Offices of A.I.D., GV
Johnson, Roger A. ...Golden Valley, MN
Johnson, Roger A. ...Minneapolis, MN
Johnson, Roger A. ...Joplin, MO
Johnson, Roger C. ...Washington, DC
Johnson, Roger D. ...Colorado Springs, CO
Johnson, Roger D. ...Denver, CO
Johnson, Roger F. ...Glendale, CO
Johnson, Roger G. ...Ventura, CA
Johnson, Roger K. ...Omaha, NE
Johnson, Roger M. ...Canton, GA
Johnson, Roger W. ...Seattle, WA
Johnson, Rogers & Clifton, LLP
Birmingham, AL
Washington, DC
Johnson, Roland A. ...Roseburg, OR
Johnson, Roland K. ...Fort Worth, TX
Johnson, Roland W. ...Wallowa, OR
Johnson, Ron B. ...Waxahachie, TX
Johnson, Ronald A. ...New Orleans, LA
Johnson, Ronald B. ...Wheeling, WV
Johnson, Ronald C. ...Lake Wales, FL
Johnson, Ronald D. ...Long Beach, CA
Johnson, Ronald E. ...Middletown, CT
Johnson, Ronald E. ...Louisville, KY
Johnson, Ronald E. ...Liberty, MO
Johnson, Ronald E. ...Suffern, NY
Johnson, Ronald E. ...Carlisle, PA
Johnson, Ronald E. ...Galveston, TX
Johnson, Ronald F. ...Atlanta, GA
Johnson, Ronald F. ...St. Cloud, MN
Johnson, Ronald H. ...Iowa City, IA
Johnson, Ronald J. ...San Antonio, TX
Johnson, Ronald K. ...Ludington, MI
Johnson, Ronald L. ...San Diego, CA
Johnson, Ronald M. ...Washington, DC
Johnson, Ronald M. ...Portland, OR
Johnson, Ronald M. ...Austin, TX
Johnson, Ronald M., Jr ...Phoenix, AZ
Johnson, Ronald N. ...Daytona Beach, FL
Flagler Beach, FL
Johnson, Ronald O. ...Oak Lawn, IL
Johnson, Ronald P. ...Greensboro, NC
Johnson, Ronald R. ...Baton Rouge, LA
Johnson, Ronald R. ...Lemmon, SD
Johnson, Ronald W. ...Indian Wells, CA
Johnson, Ronald W. ...Palm Springs, CA
Johnson, Ronald W. ...Pensacola, FL
Johnson, Ronald W. ...Portland, OR
Johnson, Ronald W. ...Dallas, TX
Johnson, Ronald W., P.A. ...Pensacola, FL
Johnson, Rosalie E. ...San Francisco, CA
Johnson, Rosann K. ...Phoenix, AZ
Johnson, Rosati, Galica, LaBarge, Aseltyne &
Field, P.C. ...Bay City, MI
Farmington Hills, MI
Johnson, Rosati, Galica, LaBarge, Aseltyne &
Field, P.C. ...Lansing, MI
St. Clair Shores, MI
Johnson, Rosemary C. B. ...Omaha, NE
Johnson, Ross W. ...Phoenix, AZ
Johnson, Roy E. ...Sioux City, IA
Johnson, Roy L. ...Marion, IL
Johnson, Roy M., III ...Hayden, AL
Johnson, Roy M., Jr. ...Birmingham, AL
Johnson, Roy R. ...Bluffton, IN
Johnson, Roy W. ...Bloomfield Hills, MI
Johnson, Ruddy, McConaty & Sargent, A
Professional Corporation ...Glendale, CO
Johnson, Rufus W. ...Mason, TX
Johnson, Russell ...Loudon, TN
Johnson, Russell A. ...Franklin, IN
Johnson, Russell B.
Christiansted, St. Croix, VI
Johnson, Russell K. ...Eddyville, KY
Johnson, Russell L. ...Los Angeles, CA
Johnson, Russell L. ...San Jose, CA
Johnson, Russell L. ...St. Petersburg, FL
Johnson, Russell N. ...Chicago, IL
Johnson, Russell R., III ...Richmond, VA
Johnson, Russell S. ...San Antonio, TX
Johnson, Russell T. ...San Antonio, TX
Johnson, Ruth A. ...Indianapolis, IN
Johnson, Ruth Brammer ...Denver, CO
Johnson, Ruth Clare ...Thermopolis, WY
Johnson Rutz & Tassie ...Port Angeles, WA
Johnson, S. Anne ...San Francisco, CA
Johnson, S. Austin ...Provo, UT
Johnson, S. Greg ...Decatur, IL
Johnson, S. Howes ...Paintsville, KY
Johnson, S. Jennifer
Equal Employment Opportunity
Commission,
Office of Legal Counsel, GV
Johnson, S. Joel ...Hattiesburg, MS
Johnson, S. Joel ...Jackson, MS
Johnson, S. Lee ...Detroit, MI
Johnson, S. Mark ...Bountiful, UT
Johnson, Sabrina L. ...Biloxi, MS
Johnson, Safronia A. ...Los Angeles, CA
Johnson, Sage Brannon ...Abingdon, VA
Johnson, Sally A. ...Minneapolis, MN
Johnson, Sam ...Austin, TX
Johnson, Sam D. ...Austin, TX
Johnson, Sam H. ...Lawton, OK
Johnson, Samuel H. ...Raleigh, NC
Johnson, Samuel P., III ...Petersburg, VA
Johnson, Samuel S. ...Wahpeton, ND
Johnson, Samuel V. ...Fort Myers, FL
Johnson, Samuel W. ...Rocky Mount, NC
Johnson, Sanders & Morgan
Mountain Home, AR
Johnson, Sandra ...Nashville, TN
Johnson, Sandra H ...St. Louis, MO
Johnson, Sandra L. ...Birmingham, AL
Johnson, Sandra L. ...Redding, CA
Johnson, Sandra L. ...Lillington, NC
Johnson, Sandra W. ...Jacksonville, FL
Johnson, Sandra W., P.A.
Jacksonville, FL
Johnson, Sara E. ...Chicago, IL
Johnson, Sara J. (Sally) ...Missoula, MT
Johnson, Sara K. ...West Des Moines, IA
Johnson, Sarah A. ...Chicago, IL
Johnson, Sarah A. ...Myrtle Beach, SC
Johnson, Sarah C. ...Richmond, VA
Johnson, Sarah K. ...Chicago, IL
Johnson, Sarah M. ...Winston-Salem, NC
Johnson, Sautebin & Inderberg
Neillsville, WI
Johnson, Schachter & Collins, A Professional
Corporation ...Sacramento, CA
Johnson, Scott ...Pecos, TX
Johnson, Scott A. ...Scottsdale, AZ
Johnson, Scott A. ...San Diego, CA
Johnson, Scott A. ...Richmond, VA
Johnson, Scott A.C. ...Philadelphia, MS
Johnson, Scott Alan ...Minneapolis, MN
Johnson, Scott A. W. ...Seattle, WA
Johnson, Scott B. ...San Francisco, CA
Johnson, Scott D. ...Baton Rouge, LA
Johnson, Scott D. ...Albuquerque, NM
Johnson, Scott F. ...Concord, NH
Johnson, Scott G. ...Costa Mesa, CA
Johnson, Scott J. ...Orlando, FL
Johnson, Scott K. ...Walnut Creek, CA
Johnson, Scott L. ...Redwood City, CA
Johnson, Scott L. ...Watsonville, CA
Johnson, Scott Martin ...Orange, CA
Johnson, Scott N. ...Garner, NC
Johnson, Scott R. ...Greenwich, CT
Johnson, Scott T. ...Albany, NY
Johnson, Scott W. ...Colorado Springs, CO
Johnson, Scott W. ...Minneapolis, MN
Johnson, Scott W. ...Kennewick, WA

Johnson, Scruggs & Barfield
Nashville, TN
Johnson, Sean D. .... **Phoenix, AZ**
Johnson, Seibert & Bigham .... **Benton, IL**
Chester, IL
Du Quoin, IL
Nashville, IL
Pinckneyville, IL
Johnson, Seymore H., Jr. .... Philadelphia, PA
Johnson, Shane T. .... Cheyenne, WY
Johnson, Shanese I. .... **Philadelphia, PA**
Johnson, Shannon L. .... Los Angeles, CA
Johnson, Shannon Upton .... **Lexington, KY**
Johnson, Sharah Glass .... Durham, NC
Johnson, Shari L. .... **St. Paul, MN**
Johnson, Sharon Lee .... **Miami, FL**
Johnson, Shauna N. .... **Houston, TX**
Johnson, Sheila Diane Timmons .... Dallas, TX
Johnson, Sheila K. .... Beverly Hills, CA
Johnson, Sheila M. .... Birmingham, MI
Johnson, Shelli Wright .... Valparaiso, IN
Johnson, Shelly May .... Clearwater, FL
Johnson, Shephard S., Jr. .... Boston, MA
New Bedford, MA
Johnson, Sheri Lynn .... Ithaca, NY
Johnson, Sheridan Bracken .... **Atlanta, GA**
Johnson, Sherman D. .... Atlanta, GA
Johnson, Sherri L. .... **Sarasota, FL**
Johnson, Sherrill L. .... Chatsworth, CA
Johnson & Sherton, P.C. .... **Eugene, OR**
Johnson, Sheryl
Department of Housing and Urban Development,
Office of General Counsel, GV
Johnson, Sheryl A. .... **Denver, CO**
Johnson, Sheryl B. .... **Houston, TX**
Johnson, Shirley Merchant .... Atlanta, GA
Johnson, Shirley Z. .... **Washington, DC**
Johnson, Shubha K. .... Washington, DC
Johnson, Sidney E. .... Houston, TX
Johnson, Sidney G., II .... San Rafael, CA
Johnson, Simmerman & Broughton, L.C.
Clarksburg, WV
Johnson & Skewes, Law Offices of
Fort Madison, IA
Johnson, Smith, Hibbard & Wildman Law Firm, L.L.P. .... **Spartanburg, SC**
Johnson Smith Pence & Heath LLP
Indianapolis, IN
Johnson, Solomon E. .... Honolulu, HI
Johnson, Sonja .... Washington, DC
Johnson, Sonja Jean .... San Francisco, CA
Johnson, Sonya D. .... **New York, NY**
Johnson and Spencer .... Broken Bow, NE
Johnson & Spurr .... Seattle, WA
Johnson, Stacie M. .... **Kansas City, MO**
Johnson, Stacy L. .... Chicago, IL
Johnson, Stan C. .... Madison, WI
Johnson, Stanley .... San Francisco, CA
Johnson, Stanley A. .... Oakland, CA
Johnson, Stanley F. .... Boulder, CO
Johnson, Stanley M. .... **New York, NY**
Johnson, Stanwood C. .... San Diego, CA
Johnson, Stefan .... Portland, OR
Johnson, Steffen N. .... **Chicago, IL**
Johnson, Stephan J.
Rancho Cucamonga, CA
Johnson, Stephani Railsback .... **Dallas, TX**
Johnson, Stephanie .... United States Senate,
Committee Legal Personnel, GV
Johnson, Stephanie A. .... Brooklyn, NY
Johnson, Stephanie Armstead-Davis
Washington, DC
Johnson, Stephanie Emelle
Playa Del Rey, CA
Johnson, Stephanie Joyce .... Spokane, WA
Johnson, Stephanie R. .... Department of Justice,
Environment and Natural Resources
Division, GV
Johnson, Stephanie S. .... Lewistown, IL
Johnson, Stephen .... Marion, IN
Johnson, Stephen .... New York, NY
Johnson, Stephen A. .... Augusta, ME
Johnson, Stephen A. .... Winston-Salem, NC
Johnson, Stephen B. .... **Telluride, CO**
Johnson, Stephen B. .... **Seattle, WA**
Johnson, Stephen C. .... **Los Angeles, CA**
Johnson, Stephen C. .... **San Francisco, CA**
Johnson, Stephen C. .... **Dallas, TX**
Johnson, Stephen Chester .... Wayne, MI
Johnson, Stephen D. .... **Los Angeles, CA**
Johnson, Stephen D. .... Tustin, CA
Johnson, Stephen D. .... **Washington, DC**
Johnson, Stephen D. .... Anoka, MN
Johnson, Stephen E. .... **El Segundo, CA**
Johnson, Stephen G. .... Marlin, TX
Johnson, Stephen H. .... Columbus, OH
Johnson, Stephen J. .... Houma, LA
Johnson, Stephen J. .... San Antonio, TX
Johnson, Stephen J. .... **Woodstock, VT**
Johnson, Stephen J., Jr.
Altamonte Springs, FL
Johnson, Stephen K. .... Gainesville, FL
Johnson, Stephen K., P.A. .... Gainesville, FL
Johnson, Stephen L. .... **Syracuse, NY**
Johnson, Stephen L. .... **Lubbock, TX**
Johnson, Stephen L. .... **Richmond, VA**
Johnson, Stephen L. .... Seattle, WA
Johnson, Stephen Lane .... **Houston, TX**
Johnson, Stephen M. .... Denver, CO
Johnson, Stephen M. .... Fairfield, CT
Johnson, Stephen P. .... Mobile, AL
Johnson, Stephen P. .... San Francisco, CA
Johnson, Stephen P. .... Gaithersburg, MD
Johnson, Stephen P. .... Sister Bay, WI
Sturgeon Bay, WI
Johnson, Stephen Patrick .... **Miami, FL**
Johnson, Stephen P. H. .... **New York, NY**

Johnson, Stephen R. .... **Bartlesville, OK**
Johnson, Stephen R. .... **Oklahoma City, OK**
Johnson, Stephen S. .... Louisville, KY
Johnson, Stephen S. .... Marquette, MI
Johnson, Stephen T. .... **Denver, CO**
Johnson, Stephen W. .... **Santa Ana, CA**
Johnson, Stephen W. .... **Leesburg, FL**
Johnson, Stephen W. .... Newton, KS
Johnson, Stephen W. .... Sauquoit, NY
Johnson, Stephen W. .... **Pittsburgh, PA**
Johnson, Stephen W. .... **Dallas, TX**
Johnson, Stephen Woodward
San Luis Obispo, CA
Johnson, Stephon E. .... Detroit, MI
Johnson, Sterling, Jr. .... Brooklyn, NY
Johnson, Steve .... **Calabasas, CA**
Johnson, Steve .... Beaumont, TX
Johnson, Steve R. .... Jacksonville, FL
Johnson, Steven .... **Great Falls, MT**
Johnson, Steven A. .... Denver, CO
Johnson, Steven A. .... Boston, MA
Johnson, Steven A. .... **Fargo, ND**
Johnson, Steven A., & Associates
Crown Point, IN
Hammond, IN
Johnson, Steven A., & Associates
Merrillville, IN
Johnson, Steven A., & Associates
Valparaiso, IN
Johnson, Steven B. .... Hillsboro, OR
Johnson, Steven Boyd .... **Knoxville, TN**
Johnson, Steven C. .... Gresham, OR
Johnson, Steven D. .... **Muskegon, MI**
Johnson, Steven D. .... **Omaha, NE**
Johnson, Steven D. .... **Haddonfield, NJ**
Philadelphia, PA
Johnson, Steven D. .... **New York, NY**
Johnson, Steven E. .... Great Bend, KS
Johnson, Steven G. .... Midvale, UT
Johnson, Steven J. .... Miami Shores, FL
Johnson, Steven J. .... **Minneapolis, MN**
Johnson, Steven James .... **Palo Alto, CA**
Johnson, Steven James
Oklahoma City, OK
Johnson, Steven K. .... Pasadena, CA
Johnson, Steven K. .... **Topeka, KS**
Johnson, Steven K. .... Northfield, NJ
Johnson, Steven K., P.C. .... Northfield, NJ
Johnson, Steven M. .... Orlando, FL
Johnson, Steven M. .... **Prairie Village, KS**
Johnson, Steven M. .... **Sioux Falls, SD**
Yankton, SD
Johnson, Steven P. .... Phoenix, AZ
Johnson, Steven P. .... Sarasota, FL
Johnson, Steven R. .... **Washington, DC**
Johnson, Steven R. .... **Chicago, IL**
Johnson, Steven R. .... Hoquiam, WA
Johnson, Steven Todd .... **Seattle, WA**
Johnson, Steven V. .... Salem, OR
Johnson, Steven W. .... **Orlando, FL**
Johnson, Steven W., P.A. .... **Orlando, FL**
Johnson & Stremel .... Neosho, MO
Johnson, Stricklin & Waller .... Decatur, IL
Johnson, Stuart .... **Los Angeles, CA**
Johnson, Stuart C. .... **New Haven, CT**
Johnson, Stuart C. .... **Atlanta, GA**
Johnson, Stuart Fisk .... Washington, DC
Johnson, Stuart H. .... **Charlotte, NC**
Johnson, Stuart R. .... Boston, MA
Johnson, Stuart Yates .... **Birmingham, AL**
Johnson, Sudenga, Latham, Peglow & O'Hare, P.L.C. .... **Marshalltown, IA**
Johnson, Sue Ellen .... Marlton, NJ
Johnson, Suewan M. .... **Houston, TX**
Johnson & Sundeen .... **Killdeer, ND**
Medora, ND
New Town, ND
Watford City, ND
Johnson, Susan E. .... **Boston, MA**
Johnson, Susan Holland .... **Las Vegas, NV**
Johnson, Susan K. .... White House, TN
Johnson, Susan Kelly .... Portage, IN
Johnson, Susan M. .... **New York, NY**
Johnson, Susan M. .... **Seattle, WA**
Johnson, Susan Mullins .... Paintsville, KY
Johnson, Susan O'Neal .... East Peoria, IL
Johnson, Susan Palmer .... Johnstown, NY
Johnson, Suzanne .... New York, NY
Johnson, Suzanne Crosswell .... Tacoma, WA
Johnson, Suzanne D. .... Warren, NJ
Johnson, Suzanne L. .... Topsham, ME
Johnson, Suzanne Lehman .... Houston, TX
Johnson, Suzanne M. .... Bloomfield Hills, MI
Johnson, Suzanne M. .... **St. Cloud, MN**
Johnson, Suzette E. .... Mankato, MN
Johnson, S.V. Stuart .... Los Angeles, CA
Johnson & Swanson, P.C.
The Woodlands, TX
Johnson & Swenson .... Tulsa, OK
Johnson & Sylvan, P.C. .... **Dallas, TX**
Johnson, T. Sol .... **Milton, FL**
Johnson, Tamara Harris ...... **Birmingham, AL**
Johnson, Tandra S. .... **Fort Wayne, IN**
Johnson, Tanner, Cooke, Younce & Moseley
Greensboro, NC
Johnson & Taylor .... **Pontiac, IL**
Johnson, Taylor F. .... **Pontiac, IL**
Johnson, Ted A. .... Detroit, MI
Johnson, Ted R. .... **Frankfort, IN**
Johnson & Tekosky .... **Los Angeles, CA**
Johnson, Teresa A. .... Austin, TX
Johnson, Teresa D. .... Rochester, NY
Johnson, Teresa H. .... Minneapolis, MN
Johnson, Teresa L. .... **San Francisco, CA**
Johnson, Teresa P. .... Louisville, KY
Johnson, Terrence M. .... Barrington, IL
Johnson, Terrence M. .... Elmhurst, IL
Johnson, Terri Len .... **Columbus, OH**

Johnson, Terri Lynne .... Fort Scott, KS
Johnson, Terri S. .... Orlando, FL
Tavares, FL
Johnson, Terry E. .... **Milwaukee, WI**
Johnson, Terry G. .... Minneapolis, MN
Johnson, Terry J. .... Lake Charles, LA
Johnson, Terry L. .... **El Paso, TX**
Johnson, Terry Lee .... Twin Falls, ID
Johnson, Terry T. .... **Palo Alto, CA**
Johnson, Thad C. .... **Minneapolis, MN**
Johnson, Thaddeus Michael
Sacramento, CA
Johnson, Thane .... **Cut Bank, MT**
Johnson, Theodore .... Atlanta, GA
Johnson, Theodore L., III
Springfield, MO
Johnson, Theodore N. .... **Elkhorn, WI**
Johnson, Theodore O. .... Alpena, MI
Johnson, Theodore R. .... **Peoria, IL**
Johnson, Theodore R. .... Hobbs, NM
Johnson, Theresa Jo .... Salem, OR
Johnson, Theresa W. .... **Richmond, VA**
Johnson, Thomas .... Bryan, TX
Johnson, Thomas A. .... Modesto, CA
Johnson, Thomas A. .... Department of State,
Office of the Legal Adviser, GV
Johnson, Thomas A. .... Neosho, MO
Johnson, Thomas B. .... Knoxville, TN
Johnson, Thomas C. .... Miami, FL
Johnson, Thomas D. .... **Des Moines, IA**
Johnson, Thomas E. .... Tucson, AZ
Johnson, Thomas E. .... Pensacola, FL
Johnson, Thomas E. .... **Chicago, IL**
Johnson, Thomas E. .... Chicago, IL
Johnson, Thomas E. .... Sullivan, IN
Johnson, Thomas E. .... Minneapolis, MN
Johnson, Thomas E. .... **Omaha, NE**
Johnson, Thomas F. .... Ukiah, CA
Johnson, Thomas F. .... Philadelphia, PA
Johnson, Thomas F., Jr. .... Salisbury, MD
Johnson, Thomas G. .... **Willmar, MN**
Johnson, Thomas G. .... Madison, NJ
Johnson, Thomas G. .... **Indiana, PA**
Johnson, Thomas G. .... Seattle, WA
Johnson, Thomas G., Jr. .... Missouri City, TX
Johnson, Thomas G., Jr. .... **Norfolk, VA**
Johnson, Thomas H., Sr.
West Palm Beach, FL
Johnson, Thomas Hatcher, Jr.
Greenville, NC
Johnson, Thomas J. .... **Albany, NY**
Johnson, Thomas J. .... **Sioux Falls, SD**
Johnson, Thomas J. .... Oshkosh, WI
Johnson, Thomas J., III .... Tampa, FL
Johnson, Thomas J., P.C. .... **Canton, SD**
Sioux Falls, SD
Johnson, Thomas Kimbrough
Orlando, FL
Johnson, Thomas L. .... Carol Stream, IL
Johnson, Thomas L. .... **Minneapolis, MN**
Johnson, Thomas L. .... St. Paul, MN
Johnson, Thomas L. .... **Albuquerque, NM**
Johnson, Thomas L. .... Amarillo, TX
Johnson, Thomas L., Jr. .... **Richmond, VA**
Johnson, Thomas M. .... Osceola, MO
Johnson, Thomas Michael .... Tavares, FL
Johnson, Thomas P. .... **Denver, CO**
Johnson, Thomas Phillips .... **Pittsburgh, PA**
Johnson, Thomas Q. .... **Helena, MT**
Johnson, Thomas R. .... New York, NY
Johnson, Thomas R. .... **Pittsburgh, PA**
Johnson, Thomas S. .... **Rockford, IL**
Johnson, Thomas T. .... **Costa Mesa, CA**
Los Angeles, CA
Johnson, Thomas T. .... Los Angeles, CA
Johnson, Thomas W. .... New London, WI
Johnson, Thomas W., Jr.
Newport Beach, CA
Johnson, Thora A. .... **Baltimore, MD**
Johnson Thornbrugh & Halleran, L.L.C.
Olathe, KS
Johnson, Tiffany Thompson ...... **Houston, TX**
Johnson, Tige C. .... Grand Rapids, MI
Johnson, Tim .... San Antonio, TX
Johnson, Timothy A. .... **Minneapolis, MN**
Johnson, Timothy A., Jr. .... **Clearwater, FL**
Johnson, Timothy D. .... **Cleveland, OH**
Johnson, Timothy D. .... **El Paso, TX**
Johnson, Timothy E. .... Bristow, OK
Johnson, Timothy G. .... **Atlanta, GA**
Johnson, Timothy P. .... Yorba Linda, CA
Johnson, Timothy P. .... Rochester, NY
Johnson, Timothy R. .... Rancho Cordova, CA
Johnson, Timothy R. .... Edmeston, NY
Johnson, Timothy R. .... Memphis, TN
Johnson, Timothy S. .... Willmar, MN
Johnson, Timothy S. .... Pittsburgh, PA
Johnson, Timothy V. .... Urbana, IL
Johnson, Timothy W. .... **Atlanta, GA**
Johnson, Timothy W. .... Sycamore, IL
Johnson, Toal & Battiste, P.A.
Columbia, SC
Johnson, Todd .... **Miami, FL**
Johnson, Todd .... **Cohutta, GA**
Johnson, Todd A. .... **Grand Haven, MI**
Johnson, Todd A. .... Willmar, MN
Johnson, Todd A. .... **Springfield, MO**
Johnson, Todd C. .... **Jacksonville, FL**
Johnson, Todd H. .... **Minneapolis, MN**
Johnson, Todd J. .... Aiken, SC
Johnson, Todd Michael .... **Scottsdale, AZ**
Johnson, Tom E. .... Midland, TX
Johnson, Tom G. .... Oakland, CA
Johnson, Tom J., Jr. .... Tampa, FL
Johnson, Tom L. .... Cleveland, OH
Johnson, Tom R. .... Phoenix, AZ
Johnson & Tomlin .... **Miami, FL**
Johnson, Tommy J. .... Shreveport, LA

Johnson, Tonya Gail .... Sulligent, AL
Johnson, Tonya Hunter ...... Dover-Foxcroft, ME
Johnson, Tracey .... Morgan Hill, CA
Johnson, Tracey M. .... Cincinnati, OH
Johnson, Tracie Y. .... **Atlanta, GA**
Johnson, Tracy Cruz .... **New York, NY**
Johnson, Tracy D. .... **Irvine, CA**
Johnson, Tracy J. .... **Monmouth, IL**
Johnson, Tracy L.
United States District Court For The District
Of Columbia, GV
Johnson, Tracy Scott .... **Cleveland, OH**
Johnson, Travis C. .... **El Paso, TX**
Johnson, Travis D. .... Houston, TX
Johnson, Treazure R. .... **Boston, MA**
Johnson, Trent A. .... **Englewood, CO**
Johnson, Trenton H. .... **Denver, CO**
Johnson, Tyler M. .... **Seattle, WA**
Johnson Urban & Range Co., L.P.A.
New Philadelphia, OH
Johnson, V. Duncan .... **Providence, RI**
Johnson, Valerie Alston .... **Raleigh, NC**
Johnson, Valerie Walsh .... **Memphis, TN**
Johnson, Valner L. .... **Las Vegas, NV**
Johnson, Van H. .... Elizabeth City, NC
Johnson & Van Vliet, L.L.P. ...... **St. Paul, MN**
Johnson, Vard R. .... Omaha, NE
Johnson, Vaughn & Heiskell
Fort Worth, TX
Johnson, Verlin K. .... Redding, CA
Johnson, Vernard L. .... Kokomo, IN
Johnson, Verne C. .... Minneapolis, MN
Johnson, Vernon .... Turlock, CA
Johnson, Vernon A. .... Roseville, MN
Johnson, Vernon E. .... Orange, CA
Johnson, Vernon (Ven) R. .... **Southfield, MI**
Johnson, Vernon W., III .... **Washington, DC**
Vienna, VA
Johnson, Veronica .... O'Fallon, MO
Johnson, Vicki C. .... Santa Barbara, CA
Johnson, Vicki Lynnette .... Mesquite, TX
Johnson, Victor C. .... **Minneapolis, MN**
Johnson, Victor Calvin .... New Orleans, LA
Johnson, Victor S., III .... Nashville, TN
Johnson, Victor S., Jr. .... Nashville, TN
Johnson, Victoria .... New Orleans, LA
Johnson, Victoria .... **Cleveland, OH**
Johnson, Vincent B. .... Washington, DC
Johnson, Vincent E. .... Montezuma, IA
Johnson, Vincent E. .... **Louisville, KY**
Johnson, Vincent E. .... Minneapolis, MN
Johnson, Vincent L. .... **Emeryville, CA**
Johnson, Vincent L. .... Brooklyn, NY
Johnson, Vincent L. .... Philadelphia, PA
Johnson, Vincent R. .... San Antonio, TX
Johnson, Virgil K. .... **Omaha, NE**
Johnson, Virginia A. .... Santa Monica, CA
Johnson, Virginia Ann .... **Atlanta, GA**
McLean, VA
Johnson, Virginia Easley, (P.A.)
Miami, FL
Johnson, Virginia G. .... Lincoln, NE
Johnson, Virginia Hurt
House of Representatives,
Committee Legal Personnel, GV
Johnson, Virginia S. .... La Mesa, CA
Johnson, Voris E., Jr. .... **Atlanta, GA**
Johnson, Vreeland G. .... Andalusia, AL
Johnson, Vreeland G., P.C. .... Andalusia, AL
Johnson, W. Benjamin .... **Birmingham, AL**
Johnson, W. Bjarne .... **Great Falls, MT**
Johnson, W. Bowie .... Annandale, VA
Johnson, W. David, Jr. .... **Mobile, AL**
Johnson, W. Glen .... **Richardson, TX**
Johnson, W. Glenn .... **Tustin, CA**
Johnson, W. Glenn .... **Lillington, NC**
Johnson, W. Henry .... Neosho, MO
Johnson, W. Kelly .... Cincinnati, OH
Johnson, W. Lee .... Ennis, TX
Johnson, W. Leslie, Jr. .... Elizabethtown, NC
Johnson, W. Macy .... **New York, NY**
Johnson, W. Michael .... **Los Angeles, CA**
Johnson, W. Morgan .... Sacramento, CA
Johnson, W. Roderick, Sr.
Diamondhead, MS
Johnson, W. Roger .... **Tacoma, WA**
Johnson, W. Roscoe, III .... **Gadsden, AL**
Johnson, W. Roy .... Roseville, MN
Johnson, W. Scott .... **Richmond, VA**
Johnson, W. Stanfield .... **Washington, DC**
Johnson, W. Steven .... **Columbia, SC**
Johnson, W. Todd .... **Atlanta, GA**
Johnson, W. Welborn .... Columbus, MS
Johnson, W. A. .... Paintsville, KY
Johnson, W. A. .... **Lillington, NC**
Johnson, Wade Allen .... **Metairie, LA**
Johnson, Wade F., Jr. .... Orlando, FL
Johnson, Wade F., Jr., P.A. .... Orlando, FL
Johnson, Walker P., Jr. .... Macon, GA
Johnson, Walkley E., Jr. .... Exmore, VA
Johnson, Wallace A. .... Portland, OR
Johnson, Wallace H. .... Cody, WY
Johnson, Walter B. .... Knoxville, TN
Johnson, Walter B., II .... **Knoxville, TN**
Johnson, Walter E. .... **Atlanta, GA**
Johnson, Walter F. .... **Ottumwa, IA**
Johnson, Walter F., III .... Shreveport, LA
Johnson, Walter F., Jr. .... Columbus, GA
Johnson, Walter G., Jr. .... Meriden, CT
Johnson, Walter H. .... Des Moines, IA
Johnson, Walter J. .... **Melville, NY**
Johnson, Walter O. .... Oklahoma City, OK
Johnson, Walter R. .... Fortville, IN
Johnson, Walter S. .... Buffalo, MN
Johnson, Walter T. .... **San Francisco, CA**
Johnson, Walter T. .... **Jackson, MS**
Johnson, Walter T. .... Dallas, TX
Johnson, Walter T., Jr. .... Raleigh, NC

Johnson, Walter W., Jr. .... Silver Spring, MD
Johnson, Walton B. .... Louisville, KY
Johnson, Wanda .... Fairmont, MN
Johnson, Wanda G. .... Forsyth, GA
Johnson, Wanda M. .... Landover, MD
Johnson & Ward .... Atlanta, GA
Johnson, Ward K., III .... Grand Forks, ND
Johnson & Warner, P.L.C. .... Lexington, VA
Roanoke, VA
Johnson, Warren C. .... Lincoln, NE
Johnson, Warren D., Jr. .... Grand Forks, ND
Johnson, Warren G. .... Deadwood, SD
Johnson, Warren H. .... Naples, FL
Johnson, Warren" Jerry ".......... South Hadley, MA
Johnson, Warren P. .... Windsor, CT
Johnson, Watts C. .... Princeton, IL
Johnson, Wayne A., II .... Tyler, TX
Johnson, Wayne D. .... Houston, TX
Johnson, Wayne E. .... Los Angeles, CA
Johnson, Wayne E. .... Columbus, OH
Johnson, Wayne E. S. .... Winter Park, FL
Johnson, Wayne G. .... Silver Bay, MN
Johnson, Wayne G. .... Erie, PA
Johnson, Wayne G., Jr. .... Erie, PA
Johnson, Wayne K. .... Washington, DC
Johnson, Wayne L. .... Orland Park, IL
Johnson, Wayne R. .... Los Angeles, CA
Los Angeles, CA
Johnson, Wayne R. .... Joliet, IL
Johnson, Wayne T., Jr. .... Phenix City, AL
Johnson & Webbert, L.L.P. .... Augusta, ME
Johnson, Weirich & Pietrangelo
Memphis, TN
Johnson, Weldon N. .... St. Louis, MO
Johnson, Weldon R. .... Columbia, SC
Johnson, Wendell G. .... Scandia, MN
Johnson, Wendi .... Louisville, KY
Johnson, Wendy C. .... Bloomfield Hills, MI
Johnson, Wesley C. .... Dallas, TX
Johnson, Wesley C, L.L.P., Law Offices of
Dallas, TX
Johnson, Wesley E. .... Tulsa, OK
Johnson, Wesley S. .... Kelso, WA
Johnson, Wesley S. .... Longview, WA
Johnson, Weyman T., Jr. .... Atlanta, GA
Johnson, W. H., III
Research Triangle Park, NC
Johnson, Whitman B., III .... Jackson, MS
Johnson, Whitney .... Albuquerque, NM
Johnson, Whitney R. .... St. Cloud, MN
Johnson, Wilbur E. .... Charleston, SC
Johnson, Wilbur R. .... Redwood City, CA
Johnson, Wilbur S. .... Geneseo, IL
Johnson, Wiley, Jr. .... Memphis, TN
Johnson, Will D. .... Los Angeles, CA
Johnson, Willard A. .... Toledo, OH
Johnson, Willard K. .... Austin, TX
Johnson, William .... Miami, FL
Johnson, William .... Dallas, TX
Johnson, William A. .... Pinole, CA
Johnson, William A. .... Lake Park, FL
Johnson, William A. .... Faribault, MN
Johnson, William A. .... Oklahoma City, OK
Johnson, William A. .... Washington, PA
Johnson, William A. .... Madison, WI
Johnson, William Allen .... Window Rock, AZ
Johnson, William B. .... Jesup, GA
Johnson, William B. .... Portage, MI
Johnson, William Bruce .... New York, NY
Johnson, William C. .... Oakland, CA
Johnson, William C. .... Morristown, NJ
Johnson, William C. .... Suffolk, VA
Johnson, William C., Jr. .... Daytona Beach, FL
Johnson, William D. .... Los Angeles, CA
Johnson, William D. .... Stockton, CA
Johnson, William D. .... Clearwater, FL
Johnson, William D. .... Raleigh, NC
Johnson, William E. .... Hamburg, AR
Johnson, William E. .... Placentia, CA
Johnson, William E. .... Santa Monica, CA
Johnson, William E.
West Palm Beach, FL
Johnson, William E. .... Frankfort, KY
Johnson, William E. .... St. Louis, MO
Johnson, William E. .... Columbus, OH
Johnson, William E. .... Morgantown, WV
Johnson, William E., III .... Dallas, TX
Johnson, William E., III, P.C., Law Office of
Dallas, TX
Johnson, William E., Jr. .... Birmingham, AL
Johnson, William E., Jr. .... Houston, TX
Johnson, William F.
Environmental Protection Agency,
Program Office Attorneys, GV
Johnson, William F., Jr. .... Riverdale, NJ
Johnson, William G. .... Sacramento, CA
Johnson, William G. .... Versailles, MO
Johnson, William G. .... Morristown, NJ
Johnson, William H.
Federal Communications Commission,
Cable Services Bureau, GV
Johnson, William H. .... Manning, SC
Johnson, William H. .... Norfolk, VA
Johnson, William H., III .... San Antonio, TX
Johnson, William H., Jr. .... Decatur, MS
Johnson, William Henry .... Atlanta, GA
Johnson, William J. .... Tallahassee, FL
Johnson, William J. .... Clinton, MS
Johnson, William J. .... Bound Brook, NJ
Johnson, William J. .... Northwood, ND
Johnson, William J., Jr. .... Fort Lauderdale, FL
Johnson, William Jacob .... Aiea, HI
Johnson, William L. .... Solana Beach, CA
Johnson, William L. .... Thousand Oaks, CA
Johnson, William L. .... Detroit, MI
Johnson, William L., P.C., Law Offices of
Detroit, MI
Johnson, William M. .... Frankfort, KY

Johnson, William M. .... Port Jefferson, NY
Johnson, William P. .... Denver, CO
Johnson, William P. .... Carrollton, GA
Johnson, William P. .... Buffalo, NY
Johnson, William Paul .... Roswell, NM
Johnson, William R. .... Los Angeles, CA
Johnson, William R. .... Atlanta, GA
Johnson, William R. .... Marietta, GA
Johnson, William R. .... Pikeville, KY
Johnson, William R. .... Minneapolis, MN
Johnson, William R. .... Omaha, NE
Johnson, William R. .... Hanover, NH
Johnson, William T. .... Columbus, OH
Johnson, William T. .... Beaumont, TX
Johnson, William T. .... Houston, TX
Johnson, William T., Jr., & Associates
Conway, SC
Johnson, William Tipton, Jr. .... Tuscumbia, AL
Johnson, William V. .... Chicago, IL
Johnson and Williams .... Lemmon, SD
Johnson, Willis H., Sr. .... Jackson, MS
Johnson, Willoughby C. .... Ojai, CA
Johnson, Wilton J., III .... Jackson, MS
Johnson, Winslow W., (Mrs.)
Cincinnati, OH
Johnson, Winthrop D. .... Boulder, CO
Denver, CO
Johnson, Winthrop Edward
Montgomery, AL
Johnson, Wm. R. .... Brooklyn, NY
Johnson, Wm. Randell, Law Offices of
Dallas, TX
Johnson & Wolffarth, L.L.P. .... Dallas, TX
Johnson & Wood, P.A. .... Wayzata, MN
Johnson, Word & Simmons
Carrollton, GA
Johnson & Wortley, A Professional Corporation
Dallas, TX
Houston, TX
Johnson & Wurzer, P.C. .... Houston, TX
Johnson, Wyatt .... Pensacola, FL
Johnson, Wyatt B. .... Boise, ID
Johnson & Wyngaarden, P.C. .... Okemos, MI
Johnson & Yang, P. C. .... Washington, DC
Rockville, MD
Silver Spring, MD
Wheaton, MD
Johnson, Yolanda M. .... Providence, RI
Johnson, York .... Springfield, MO
Johnson, Young & Ault, P.L.L.C.
Leesburg, VA
Johnson, Yvonne M. .... Madison, WI
Johnson, Zane B. .... Auburn, WA
Johnson, Zora E. .... Detroit, MI
Johnson-Aldrich, Leslie .... Fargo, ND
Johnsonbaugh, Bruce H.
San Francisco, CA
Johnson-Beatty, Holly F. .... Vallejo, CA
Johnson-Boyce, Christina M. .... Tampa, FL
Johnson-Champ, Debra .... Long Beach, CA
Johnson-Clark, Laura G. .... Bronx, NY
Johnson-Drenth, Susan E. .... Moorhead, MN
Fargo, ND
Johnson-Firth, Lisa T. .... Boston, MA
Johnson-Granat, Judy L. .... Lockport, NY
Johnson-Hannah, Lisa M. .... Detroit, MI
Johnson-Hodge, Kip V. .... Brownsville, TX
Johnson-Hoffman, Nicole Alixandra
Minneapolis, MN
Johnson-Koch, LeAnn M.
Washington, DC
Johnson-Lee, Barbara R. .... Buffalo, NY
Johnson-Massie, Dionysia
San Francisco, CA
Johnson-McKewan, Karen
San Francisco, CA
Johnson-Muic, Paula S. .... Pittsburgh, PA
Johnson-Norman, Karen V. .... Baltimore, MD
Johnson-Palmer, Belinda L. .... New York, NY
Johnson-Parker, Jonnie H. .... Inglewood, CA
Johnson-Parker, Jonnie H., Inc.
Inglewood, CA
Johnson-Pertet, Margaret .... New York, NY
Johnson-Pujo, Leslie .... Washington, DC
Johnson-Velez, Susan E. .... Tampa, FL
Johnsrud, Barry Alan .... Tacoma, WA
Johnsrud, Brian L. .... Palo Alto, CA
Johnsrud, Eric P. .... Winona, MN
Johnsson, Liana J. Swann .... Ventura, CA
Johnston, A. Eric .... Birmingham, AL
Johnston, A. Sidney .... Tallahassee, FL
Johnston, A. Sidney .... Boston, MA
Johnston, Aaron, Jr. .... Dallas, TX
Johnston, Adrian Joseph .... Tamuning, GU
Johnston, Alan Cope .... Palo Alto, CA
Johnston, Alan R. .... Chicago, IL
Johnston, Alan R., (A Professional
Corporation) .... Costa Mesa, CA
San Diego, CA
San Francisco, CA
Johnston, Albert D. .... Carthage, MO
Johnston, Albert M. .... Severna Park, MD
Johnston, Alexander .... Oakland, CA
Johnston, Alfred J. .... Philadelphia, PA
Johnston, Alice Sacks .... Pittsburgh, PA
Johnston, Allison & Hord, P.A.
Charlotte, NC
Raleigh, NC
Johnston, Amy M. .... Mount Clemens, MI
Johnston, Andrew J. .... Spartanburg, SC
Johnston, Andrew J., P.A.
Spartanburg, SC
Johnston, Andrew James
Pompano Beach, FL
Johnston, Andrew M. .... Wilmington, DE
Johnston, Ann E. .... San Francisco, CA
Johnston, Ann E., Law Offices of
Boston, MA

Johnston, Ann K. .... Novato, CA
Johnston, Ann L. .... Cary, NC
Johnston, Anne Whittenburg, (Mrs.)
San Antonio, TX
Johnston, Anne Whittenburg, A Professional
Corporation .... San Antonio, TX
Johnston, Aronson & Diamond, A
Professional Corporation
Harrisburg, PA
Johnston, Arthur C., Jr. .... Jacksonville, FL
Johnston, Arthur S., III .... Jackson, MS
Johnston & Associates .... Chickasha, OK
Johnston, Ballweg & Tuley, L.C.
Overland Park, KS
Johnston, Barbara Christie
Jacksonville, FL
Johnston, Barbara I. .... Las Vegas, NV
Johnston, Barbara L. .... Rockville, MD
Johnston, Barbara L. .... Hillsboro, OR
Johnston, Barry M. .... Morristown, NJ
Johnston, Bartlett .... Huntsville, AL
Johnston Barton Proctor & Powell LLP
Birmingham, AL
Johnston, Benjamin A. .... Schaumburg, IL
Johnston, Beth S. .... Willmar, MN
Johnston, Brad M. .... New York, NY
Johnston, Bradley J. .... Phoenix, AZ
Johnston, Bradley K. .... Cincinnati, OH
Johnston, Brian M. .... Kansas City, MO
Johnston, Bruce .... Ventura, CA
Johnston, Bruce S. .... Metairie, LA
Johnston, Burrell D. .... Austin, TX
Johnston, C. David .... Atlanta, GA
Johnston, Carl R. .... Norcross, GA
Johnston, Carol .... Trenton, NJ
Johnston, Carol A. .... Los Angeles, CA
Johnston, Carol N.
Bainbridge Island, WA
Johnston, Carolyn Clark .... Sylva, NC
Johnston, Carter F. .... San Diego, CA
Johnston, Charles F., Jr. .... Wadsworth, OH
Johnston, Charles L. .... New York, NY
Johnston, Charles M., Jr.
Jacksonville, FL
Johnston, Charles Richard, Jr.
Washington, DC
Johnston, Charles S. .... East Longmeadow, MA
Johnston, Charles W. .... Harrisburg, PA
Johnston, Cheryle R. .... Houston, TX
Johnston, Chester A., Jr. .... Oakmont, PA
Johnston, Christine York .... El Paso, TX
Johnston, Christopher Colin
New Orleans, LA
Johnston, Christopher R. .... Chicago, IL
Johnston, Christopher R. .... El Paso, TX
Johnston, Clay M. .... Baton Rouge, LA
Johnston, Clinton P. .... New York, NY
Johnston & Conwell, L.L.C.
Birmingham, AL
Johnston and Coots .... Troy, AL
Johnston, Cordell A. .... Concord, NH
Johnston, Cormac J. .... Wichita, KS
Johnston, Coyt Randal .... Dallas, TX
Johnston, Craig .... Lubbock, TX
Johnston, Craig D. .... Manassas, VA
Johnston, Craig E. .... Columbus, OH
Johnston, Craig R. .... Santa Rosa, CA
Johnston, Curtis C. .... Reading, PA
Johnston, D. Brandon .... Carmel, IN
Johnston, D. Craig .... Oklahoma City, OK
Johnston, Dan L. .... New York, NY
Johnston, Dan S. .... Palo Alto, CA
Johnston, Daniel P. .... Chicago, IL
Johnston, Daniel R. .... Winston-Salem, NC
Johnston, Daniel S. .... Buffalo, NY
Johnston, Danielle M. .... Redmond, WA
Johnston, Darryl H. W. .... Honolulu, HI
Johnston, Darryl W. .... Brooksville, FL
Johnston, David A. .... Jefferson City, MO
Johnston, David A., Jr. .... Columbus, OH
Johnston, David B. .... Kirkland, WA
Johnston, David C. .... Modesto, CA
Johnston, David C. .... Paonia, CO
Johnston, David C., Jr.
Oklahoma City, OK
Johnston, David E. .... Charlotte, NC
Johnston, David G. .... Greensboro, NC
Johnston, David H. .... Austin, TX
Johnston, David R. .... Flint, MI
Johnston, David W. .... Minneapolis, MN
Johnston, David W. .... Manchester, NH
Johnston, Deborah A. .... Greenbelt, MD
Johnston, Dennis A. .... St. Clair Shores, MI
Johnston, Derek C. .... Atlanta, GA
Johnston, Di Ann B. .... Dallas, TX
Johnston, Dianna B.
Equal Employment Opportunity
Commission,
Office of Legal Counsel, GV
Johnston, Dick .... Stuttgart, AR
Johnston & Dodd, P.L.C. .... Phoenix, AZ
Johnston, Donald A. .... Lawrence, KS
Johnston, Donald A., III .... Grand Rapids, MI
Johnston, Donald F., Jr. .... Fairfield, CT
Johnston, Donald L. .... Sherman, TX
Johnston, Donna L. .... Woodbury, NJ
Johnston, Douglas A. .... Durham, NC
Johnston, Douglas C. .... Syracuse, NY
Johnston, Douglas E. .... Fort Wayne, IN
Johnston, Douglas E. .... Muscatine, IA
Johnston, Douglas S., Jr. .... Nashville, TN
Johnston, E. Ashton .... Washington, DC
Johnston, E. Brownell, Jr. .... Huntington, NY
Johnston, E. Covington .... Gainesville, FL
Johnston, E. Covington, Jr. .... Franklin, TN
Johnston, Edward A. .... Towson, MD
Johnston, Edward E. .... Edwardsville, IL
Johnston, Edward H., Jr. .... Laurinburg, NC

Johnston, Edward J. .... Cape May, NJ
Johnston, Edward M. .... Vista, CA
Johnston, Edwin C. .... Logan, OH
Johnston, Elaine L. .... Washington, DC
Johnston, Elizabeth B. .... Winchester, VA
Johnston, Ellis M., II .... Greenville, SC
Johnston, Elmer E., Jr. .... Everett, WA
Johnston, Emily G. .... Charleston, SC
Johnston, Eric O. .... Vinita, OK
Johnston, Ervin G. .... Overland Park, KS
Johnston, Esther M. .... Utica, NY
Johnston, Eugene .... Greensboro, NC
Johnston, F. Claiborne, Jr. .... Richmond, VA
Johnston, Faber L., Jr. .... Saratoga, CA
Johnston, Felix A., Jr. .... Monticello, FL
Johnston, Frances .... Menlo Park, CA
Johnston, Frances Cook .... Pittsburgh, PA
Johnston, Frank B. .... Ames, IA
Johnston, Frank E. .... San Francisco, CA
Johnston, Frank J., Jr. .... East Islip, NY
Johnston, Franklin B. .... Washington, NC
Johnston, Frederick P., Sr. .... Park Ridge, IL
Johnston, G. David .... Dothan, AL
Johnston, G. Michael .... Sacramento, CA
Johnston, Gail E. .... New York, NY
Johnston, George Butler
Mission Viejo, CA
Johnston, George W. .... Nutley, NJ
Johnston, George W., III .... Winchester, VA
Johnston, George W., (P.C.)
Baltimore, MD
Johnston, Gerald .... Santa Ana, CA
Johnston, Gerald P. .... Washington, DC
Johnston, Gilbert E., Jr. .... Birmingham, AL
Johnston, Gina M. .... Stockton, CA
Johnston, Gordon B. .... Tallahassee, FL
Johnston, Gordon S. .... Pittsburgh, PA
Johnston, Gordon W. .... Columbus, OH
Johnston, Gregory A. .... Muscatine, IA
Johnston, Gregory E. .... Minneapolis, MN
Johnston, Gregory M. .... Ridgeland, MS
Johnston, Guy W. .... Fresno, CA
Johnston, H. Dan .... Houston, TX
Johnston, H. Jeffrey .... Boca Raton, FL
Johnston, H Kenneth, II .... Broomfield, CO
Johnston, H Kenneth, II, P.C.
Broomfield, CO
Johnston, H. Morrison, Jr. .... Charlotte, NC
Johnston, Hammond & Burnett
Jacksonville, FL
St. Augustine, FL
Johnston, Harold R, II .... Indianapolis, IN
Johnston, Harris, Gerde & Jelks, P.A.
Panama City, FL
Johnston, Harry A., II
West Palm Beach, FL
Johnston, Helen, (Miss) .... Barker, TX
Johnston, Henry R., III .... Pittsburgh, PA
Johnston, Hicks, Guiter & Griffith
Knoxville, IA
Johnston, Hinesley, Flowers & Clenney, P.C.,
A Professional Corporation .... Dothan, AL
Panama City, FL
Johnston & Hladik .... Enid, OK
Johnston, Holroyd & Associates
Beckley, WV
Bluefield, WV
Princeton, WV
Johnston, Horton, Roberts & Hand LLP
Oakland, CA
Johnston, Howard H. .... Atlanta, GA
Johnston, Hoyt .... Palestine, TX
Johnston, H. R. .... Douglas, WY
Johnston, Hugh N., Jr.
Department of Justice, GV
Johnston, Hugh W. .... Gastonia, NC
Johnston, Iain D. .... Chicago, IL
Johnston, J. Bennett, Jr. .... Shreveport, LA
Johnston, J. Bradley .... Austin, TX
Dallas, TX
Johnston, J. Brooke, Jr. .... Birmingham, AL
New York, NY
Johnston, J. Lane .... Statesboro, GA
Johnston, J. Lawrence .... Tallahassee, FL
Johnston, J. Lawson .... Pittsburgh, PA
Johnston, J. Lindsay .... Philadelphia, PA
Johnston, J. Mark .... Orlando, FL
Johnston, J. Phillips L. .... Thomasville, NC
Johnston, J. Reed, Jr. .... Greensboro, NC
Johnston, J. Reese, Jr. .... Birmingham, AL
Johnston, J. Richard .... Oakland, CA
Johnston, J. Steven .... Troy, MI
Johnston, Jack B. .... Vandalia, IL
Johnston, Jacqueline J. .... Fort Smith, AR
Johnston, James A., Jr. .... Dallas, TX
Johnston, James Bryan .... Tyler, TX
Johnston, James C. .... Mobile, AL
Johnston, James C., Jr. .... Southfield, MI
Johnston, James Covington .... Fort Myers, FL
Johnston, James D.E. .... Birmingham, AL
Johnston, James E. .... Troy, AL
Johnston, James E. .... Wooster, OH
Johnston, James F. .... Orlando, FL
Johnston, James H. .... Washington, DC
Johnston, James H. .... Minneapolis, MN
Johnston, James J .... Denver, CO
Johnston, James J. .... Durham, NC
Johnston, James L. .... Anchorage, AK
Johnston, James L. .... New York, NY
Johnston, James O. .... Los Angeles, CA
Johnston, James P. .... Chicago, IL
Johnston, James P. .... Wichita, KS
Johnston, James R. .... Seattle, WA
Johnston, James T., Jr. .... Atlanta, GA
Johnston, James T., Jr., P.C. .... Atlanta, GA
Johnston, James W. .... Riverside, CA
Johnston, James W. .... Department of Justice,
Justice Management Division, GV

Johnston, James W. ..... Seattle, WA
Johnston, Janice Metros ..... McHenry, IL
Johnston, Janice S. ..... New York, NY
Johnston, Jay J. ..... Libertyville, IL
Johnston, Jeffery B. ..... Toledo, OH
Johnston, Jeffrey G. ..... Santa Fe Springs, CA
Johnston, Jeffrey M. ..... Midland, TX
Johnston, Jeffrey S. ..... Park Ridge, IL
Johnston, Jeffrey S. ..... Houston, TX
Johnston, Jenna R. ..... Oklahoma City, OK
Johnston, Jennifer J. ..... Los Angeles, CA
Johnston, Jennifer L. ..... Erie, PA
Johnston, Jerry T. ..... Brandon, MS
Johnston, Jesse
Department Of Veterans Affairs,
Board of Veterans Appeals, GV
Johnston, Jill N. ..... Bloomfield Hills, MI
Johnston, Jillian B. ..... Boston, MA
Johnston, Jim D. ..... Seattle, WA
Johnston, Jim L. ..... Tucson, AZ
Johnston, Joan M. ..... Pembroke Pines, FL
Johnston, JoAnn ..... Houston, TX
Johnston, Joanne C. ..... Poughkeepsie, NY
Johnston, Joanne S. Bennett ..... Englewood, FL
Johnston, Joel B. ..... Pittsburgh, PA
Johnston, John C. ..... Birmingham, AL
Johnston, John C. ..... Jefferson, NC
Johnston, John C., III ..... Wooster, OH
Johnston, John D., Jr. ..... Asheville, NC
Johnston, John E. ..... Greenville, SC
Johnston, John F. ..... Wilmington, DE
Johnston, John F., 2nd ..... New York, NY
Johnston, John H. ..... Burke, VA
Johnston, John J. ..... Belleville, IL
Johnston, John M. ..... Palm Beach, FL
Johnston, John M. ..... San Antonio, TX
Johnston, John Michael ..... Oklahoma City, OK
Johnston, John P. ..... Freehold, NJ
Johnston, John R. ..... Wabash, IN
Johnston, John S. ..... Kansas City, MO
Johnston, John Samuel, Jr. ..... Rustburg, VA
Johnston, John T. ..... Butte, MT
Johnston, John W. ..... Charlotte, NC
Johnston and Johnston ..... Jefferson, NC
Johnston & Johnston ..... Bloomsburg, PA
Wilkes-Barre, PA
Johnston & Johnston ..... Palestine, TX
Johnston, Johnston & Moore ..... Huntsville, AL
Johnston, Jos W. ..... Mineral City, OH
Johnston, Joseph C. ..... Cedar Rapids, IA
Iowa City, IA
Waterloo, IA
Johnston, Joseph C., Jr. ..... East Providence, RI
Johnston, Joseph E.
Rancho Cucamonga, CA
Johnston, Joseph E., Jr. ..... Brooksville, FL
Johnston, Joseph F. ..... Birmingham, AL
Johnston, Joseph F. ..... Boston, MA
Johnston, Joseph F., Jr. ..... Washington, DC
Johnston, Joseph H. ..... Nashville, TN
Johnston, Joseph H., III ..... Memphis, TN
Johnston, Joseph S. ..... Mobile, AL
Johnston, Joyce C. ..... Sacramento, CA
Johnston, Judy L. ..... Plano, TX
Johnston, Julia D. ..... Dearborn, MI
Johnston, Julie A. ..... Dallas, TX
Johnston, June F. ..... New York, NY
Johnston, Karen E. ..... Hempstead, NY
Johnston, Karen L. ..... Denver, CO
Johnston, Karen M. ..... Falls Church, VA
Johnston, Karen S. ..... Minneapolis, MN
Johnston, Kathleen A. ..... Chicago, IL
Johnston, Kathryn ..... Roseburg, OR
Johnston, Kathryn B. ..... Manchester, NH
Johnston, Kathryn L. ..... Beaver, PA
Johnston, Kathryn L. ..... Dallas, TX
Johnston, Keith E. ..... Philadelphia, PA
Johnston, Keith I. ..... Monona, WI
Johnston, Kelly W. ..... Wichita, KS
Johnston, Kenneth C. ..... Dallas, TX
Johnston, Kenneth R. ..... Chickasha, OK
Johnston, Kevin R. ..... Bay Shore, NY
Johnston, Kim ..... Sacramento, CA
Johnston, L. Paul, Jr. ..... Allentown, PA
Johnston, Laura J. ..... Fairfax, VA
Johnston, Lauretta E. ..... Philadelphia, PA
Johnston, Laurie L. ..... Seattle, WA
Johnston, Laurie M. ..... Ithaca, NY
Johnston Law Office ..... Alexandria, MN
Johnston Law Offices, The, P.A.
Wichita, KS
Johnston, Lawrence A.
House of Representatives,
Office of Legislative Counsel, GV
Johnston, Lawrence V. ..... Melbourne, FL
Johnston, Lee Frederick ..... Denver, CO
Johnston, Lehman & Guenin, P.C.
Wabash, IN
Johnston, LeRoy, III ..... Columbus, OH
Johnston, Levy S. ..... Mountlake Terrace, WA
Johnston, Linda Osgood ..... Brea, CA
Johnston, Lisa Grimes ..... Wheeling, WV
Johnston, Logan T., III ..... Phoenix, AZ
Johnston, Lorene G. ..... Jackson, OH
McArthur, OH
Johnston, Lorene G. ..... Wellston, OH
Johnston, Lowell ..... New York, NY
Johnston, Luther C. ..... Palestine, TX
Johnston, Lyman T. ..... San Jose, CA
Johnston, M. Diana ..... Trenton, NJ
Johnston, M. Elaine ..... New York, NY
Johnston, M. Kelley ..... Richmond, VA
Johnston, M. Ray ..... Kilmarnock, VA
Johnston, Madeline I. ..... Palo Alto, CA
Johnston, Marc ..... Department of Energy,
Office of the General Counsel, GV
Johnston, Margaret E. ..... Grayslake, IL
Johnston, Margaret G. ..... Raleigh, NC
Johnston, Margaret Mary ..... Stockton, CA
Johnston, Marian M. ..... Sacramento, CA
Johnston, Marianne ..... Malvern, PA
Johnston, Marilyn K. ..... San Francisco, CA
Johnston, Mark B. ..... St. Louis, MO
Johnston, Mark E. ..... Fort Wayne, IN
Johnston, Mark E. ..... Selinsgrove, PA
Johnston, Mark G. ..... Washington, DC
Johnston, Mark J. ..... Los Angeles, CA
Jamaica Plain, MA
Johnston, Martha E. ..... Philadelphia, PA
Johnston, Mary Beth
Research Triangle Park, NC
Johnston, Mary Blaine ..... Makawao, HI
Johnston, Mary Blaine ..... Wailuku, HI
Johnston, Mary E. ..... Nashville, TN
Johnston, Mary Miller ..... Wilmington, DE
Johnston, Mary T. ..... Wellesley, MA
Johnston, Matthew Charles
Hackettstown, NJ
Morristown, NJ
Trenton, NJ
Johnston, Matthew F. ..... Bethesda, MD
Arlington, VA
Leesburg, VA
Johnston, McMains & Walker, A Professional
Association ..... Seminole, OK
Johnston, Michael F. ..... New York, NY
Johnston, Michael G. ..... Durham, NC
Johnston, Michael J. ..... Cambridge, MA
Johnston, Michael K. ..... Medicine Lodge, KS
Pratt, KS
Johnston, Michael W. ..... Atlanta, GA
Johnston, Michael W. ..... Fort Worth, TX
Johnston, Mike ..... Houston, TX
Johnston, Miles W. ..... Lincoln, NE
Johnston & Minton, L.L.P.
Fort Worth, TX
Johnston, Murray L., Jr.
San Antonio, TX
Johnston, Neal ..... New York, NY
Johnston, Neil C. ..... Mobile, AL
Johnston, Norman B. ..... Oklahoma City, OK
Johnston, O. B., III ..... Grove, OK
Vinita, OK
Johnston, Olivia O. ..... West Springfield, MA
Johnston, Pamela A. ..... Dearborn, MI
Johnston, Pamela L. ..... Los Angeles, CA
Johnston, Parker C. ..... Wetumpka, AL
Johnston, Patrick J. ..... Wilmington, DE
Johnston, Patrick L. ..... Pasadena, CA
Johnston, Paul A., Jr. ..... Columbus, GA
Johnston, Paul L. ..... Medinah, IL
Johnston, Paul M. ..... Dallas, TX
Johnston, Paul R. ..... Glenmont, NY
Johnston, Paula R. ..... Minneapolis, MN
Johnston & Peck ..... Plattsburgh, NY
Johnston, Percy W. ..... Mobile, AL
Johnston, Perry C. ..... Minneapolis, MN
Johnston, Peter R. ..... Dearborn, MI
Johnston, Peter S. ..... Lawrence, KS
Johnston, Philip C. ..... Columbus, OH
Johnston, P. M. ..... Aliceville, AL
Johnston, Potterfield & Nathanson, P.C.
Cedar Rapids, IA
Iowa City, IA
Waterloo, IA
Johnston, R. Bruce ..... Bainbridge Island, WA
Johnston, R. Harvey, III
Bowling Green, KY
Johnston, R. Keith ..... Kansas City, MO
Johnston, R. Scott ..... New York, NY
Johnston, R. William ..... Pasadena, CA
Johnston, Ralph J. ..... Wilkes-Barre, PA
Johnston, Ralph J., Jr. ..... Wilkes-Barre, PA
Johnston, Randall B. ..... Columbia, MO
Johnston, Randolph M. ..... Chicago, IL
Johnston, Ray A. ..... Wilburton, OK
Johnston, Reana ..... Greenville, SC
Johnston, Regis A. ..... Camp Springs, MD
Johnston, Richard A. ..... Boston, MA
Johnston, Richard A., Jr. ..... Fort Myers, FL
Johnston, Richard Blake ..... Chicago, IL
Johnston, Richard E. ..... Oakland, CA
Johnston, Richard E. ..... Boston, MA
Johnston, Richard F. ..... Manchester, NH
Johnston, Richard H. ..... Atlanta, GA
Johnston, Richard L. ..... Dallas, TX
Johnston, Richard N. ..... Lewisville, TX
Johnston, Robert A. ..... Cincinnati, OH
Johnston, Robert B. ..... Bloomfield Hills, MI
Johnston, Robert C. ..... Princeton, NJ
Johnston, Robert C. ..... Troy, OH
West Milton, OH
Johnston, Robert Carlton ..... Columbia, MD
Johnston, Robert D., Jr. ..... Mobile, AL
Johnston, Robert E. ..... Washington, DC
Johnston, Robert E. ..... Overland Park, KS
Johnston, Robert E. ..... Lancaster, OH
Thornville, OH
Johnston, Robert G. ..... Chicago, IL
Johnston, Robert G. ..... Cleveland, MS
Johnston, Robert G., III ..... Columbus, GA
Johnston, Robert Graeme ..... Carson City, NV
Johnston, Robert H. ..... Bronx, NY
Johnston, Robert Hugh, III ..... Tulsa, OK
Dallas, TX
Johnston, Robert I. ..... Greensburg, PA
Johnston, Robert J. ..... Las Vegas, NV
Johnston, Robert J. ..... Murrells Inlet, SC
Johnston, Robert J. ..... Carrollton, TX
Johnston, Robert L. ..... Williamsville, NY
Johnston, Robert L. ..... Greensboro, NC
Johnston, Robert M. ..... New Orleans, LA
Johnston, Robert Olin ..... Washington, DC
Johnston, Robert P. ..... Charlotte, NC
Johnston, Robert R. ..... New Orleans, LA
Johnston, Robert S. ..... Mount Clemens, MI
Johnston, Robt. D. ..... Brewton, AL
Johnston, Rodger J. ..... Long Prairie, MN
Johnston, Roger L. ..... Enid, OK
Johnston, Ronald Allen ..... Portland, OR
Johnston, Ronald L., (P.C.)
Los Angeles, CA
Johnston & Root, P.C. ..... Portland, OR
Johnston, Ross M. ..... Miami, FL
Johnston, Roy E. ..... San Antonio, TX
Johnston, Sandra E. ..... Tacoma, WA
Johnston & Sasser, P.A. ..... Brooksville, FL
Spring Hill, FL
Johnston, Scot J. ..... Seattle, WA
Johnston, Scott D ..... St. Paul, MN
Johnston, Scott L. ..... Houston, TX
Johnston, Scott R. ..... New York, NY
Johnston, Scott T. ..... Alexandria, MN
Johnston, Scott W. ..... Minneapolis, MN
Johnston, Sean A.
South San Francisco, CA
Johnston & Sellers, LLP ..... New York, NY
Johnston, Sharon A. ..... Greensboro, NC
Johnston, Sharon M.
Department Of Veterans Affairs,
Office of the General Counsel, GV
Johnston, Sharon O'Donnell
Greensboro, NC
Johnston, Shepherd D. ..... Delray Beach, FL
Johnston, Sidney ..... Maynard, MA
Johnston, Sonya A. ..... New York, NY
Johnston, Spencer K. ..... Phoenix, AZ
Johnston, Stanley C. ..... Kansas City, MO
Johnston, Stanley M. ..... Salem, IL
Johnston, Stanley P. ..... Oklahoma City, OK
Johnston, Stephen ..... Dallas, TX
Johnston, Stephen ..... Seattle, WA
Johnston, Stephen A. ..... Plattsburgh, NY
Johnston, Steven G. ..... Washington, DC
Johnston, Steven Louis ..... Chicago, IL
Johnston, Stuart A. ..... Fort Wayne, IN
Johnston, Stuart Brooks, Jr. ..... Dallas, TX
Johnston, Stuart G., III ..... Dallas, TX
Johnston, Susan A. ..... Boston, MA
Johnston, Susan Power ..... New York, NY
Johnston, Susan V. (Gina) ..... Greenville, SC
Johnston, Suzanne ..... Fishkill, NY
Scarsdale, NY
Johnston, T. Scott ..... Ann Arbor, MI
Findlay, OH
Toledo, OH
Johnston, Terry E. ..... Valparaiso, IN
Johnston, Terry J. ..... Tipp City, OH
Johnston, Thomas B. ..... Washington, DC
Johnston, Thomas and Billington, LLP
Pompano Beach, FL
Johnston, Thomas C. ..... Bangor, ME
Johnston, Thomas D. ..... Washington, DC
Johnston, Thomas D. ..... Surf City, NC
Johnston, Thomas E. ..... Wheeling, WV
Johnston, Thomas F. ..... Memphis, TN
Johnston, Thomas M. ..... Minneapolis, MN
Johnston, Thomas R. ..... Springfield, MO
Johnston, Thomas S. ..... Jefferson, NC
Johnston, Thomas V. ..... Los Angeles, CA
Johnston, Thomas W. ..... Chicago, IL
Johnston, Thomas W., P.A.
Pompano Beach, FL
Johnston & Thornton, P.C. ..... Shreveport, LA
Johnston, Timothy W. ..... Naperville, IL
Johnston • Tobey, P.C. ..... Dallas, TX
Johnston, Todd D. ..... Princeton, NJ
Johnston, Todd R. ..... Eugene, OR
Johnston, Tonya Olsen ..... Kansas City, MO
Johnston, Trippe & Brown ..... Birmingham, AL
Johnston & Turbitt ..... Burke, VA
Johnston, Vivian G., III ..... Mobile, AL
Johnston, Vivian G., Jr. ..... Mobile, AL
Johnston, W. Thomas ..... Peoria, IL
Johnston, Wendell E. ..... Augusta, GA
Johnston, Wes ..... Chickasha, OK
Johnston, Wesley Alton ..... Cleveland, OH
Johnston & Westerfield, P.C
Washington, DC
Johnston, Wilkin & Williams ..... Augusta, GA
Johnston, Wilkins & Druhan, L.L.P.
Mobile, AL
Johnston, William A. ..... Winchester, VA
Johnston, William C. ..... Hoosick Falls, NY
Johnston, William D. ..... Wilmington, DE
Johnston, William D. ..... Darlington, WI
Johnston, William G., III ..... Griffin, GA
Johnston, William H. ..... Huntsville, AL
Johnston, William H., Jr. ..... Huntsville, AL
Johnston, William J. ..... Columbus, OH
Johnston, William J. ..... Bellingham, WA
Johnston, William R. ..... San Mateo, CA
Johnston, William R. ..... New York, NY
Johnston, William W. ..... Columbus, OH
Johnston, Wilson ..... Nacogdoches, TX
Johnston, Woody & Neal, Inc., Inc., P.S.
Mountlake Terrace, WA
Johnstone, Adams, Bailey, Gordon and
Harris, L.L.C. ..... Bay Minette, AL
Mobile, AL
Johnstone, Amy R. ..... Houston, TX
Johnstone, Andrea K. ..... Concord, NH
Johnstone, Andrew M. ..... Chicago, IL
Johnstone, Bruce R. ..... Redding, CA
Johnstone, Cecil Alice ..... Powell, WY
Johnstone, Charles M., II
Charleston, WV
Johnstone, Crane A. ..... Fort Lauderdale, FL
Johnstone, Debbi M. ..... Houston, TX
Johnstone, Deborah ..... Burleson, TX
Johnstone, Douglas I. ..... Mobile, AL
Johnstone, Edward H. ..... Paducah, KY
Johnstone, F. Inge ..... Mobile, AL
Johnstone, Frank A. ..... Kingsport, TN
Johnstone, Grant C. ..... Houston, TX
Johnstone, I. Blakeley, III ..... Westfield, NJ
New York, NY
Johnstone, James M. ..... Washington, DC
Johnstone, James V. ..... Fort Lauderdale, FL
Johnstone, Jeffrey M. ..... Rochester, NY
Johnstone, Judith A. ..... Lancaster, PA
Johnstone, Karl S. ..... Anchorage, AK
Johnstone, Kathryn I. ..... Los Angeles, CA
Johnstone, Keith ..... Spokane, WA
Johnstone, Kristen K. ..... Roanoke, VA
Johnstone, Larry A. ..... Edmonds, WA
Johnstone, Martin E. ..... Louisville, KY
Johnstone, Mary Howard ..... Milwaukee, WI
Johnstone, Patricia S. ..... Gloucester, MA
Johnstone, Peter H. ..... Albuquerque, NM
Johnstone, Peter H., P.C.
Albuquerque, NM
Johnstone, Philip M. ..... New London, CT
Johnstone, Quintin ..... New York, NY
Johnstone, Robert H. ..... Hobbs, NM
Johnstone, Robert H., Jr. ..... Cincinnati, OH
Johnstone, Robert M. ..... McMinnville, OR
Johnstone, Robert M., P.C.
McMinnville, OR
Portland, OR
Johnstone, Robert P. ..... Indianapolis, IN
Johnstone, Russell R. ..... Akron, OH
Johnstone, Sarah Jennings ..... Greenville, SC
Johnstone, Skok, Loughlin & Lane, A
Professional Corporation ..... Westfield, NJ
New York, NY
Johnstone, Thomas K., Jr. ..... Greenville, SC
Johnstone, Todd A. ..... Boise, ID
Johnstone, William A. ..... Minneapolis, MN
Johnstone, William S., Jr., (P.C.)
Pasadena, CA
Johnstone, William T.
United States Postal Service,
Law Department, GV
Johnstone-Brown, Cathy ..... Page, AZ
Johntz, John H., Jr. ..... Overland Park, KS
Johrendt, Cook & Eberhart, A Legal
Professional Association ..... Bexley, OH
Columbus, OH
Johrendt, Michael J. ..... Columbus, OH
Johs, Frederick C. ..... Melville, NY
Johst, David P. ..... Wilmington, MA
Johstono, Donald L., Jr. ..... Lawrenceville, GA
Joike, Rebecca Ann ..... Rockford, IL
Joike, Trevor B. ..... Chicago, IL
Joiner, Author R., I ..... Baton Rouge, LA
Joiner, Barbara A. ..... New York, NY
Joiner, Billy B. ..... Dallas, TX
Joiner, Carol M. ..... Clarksville, TN
Joiner, Charles E. ..... West Monroe, LA
Joiner, Charles R. ..... West Monroe, LA
Joiner, Charles W. ..... Ann Arbor, MI
Joiner, Devina S. ..... Parsippany, NJ
Joiner, Elizabeth Brassell ..... Birmingham, AL
Joiner, Gary S. ..... Boulder, CO
Joiner, Horace Greely, Jr. ..... Dalton, GA
Joiner, J. Alfred ..... Corvallis, OR
Joiner, J. Robert ..... Atlanta, GA
Joiner, James E., P.C. ..... Atlanta, GA
Joiner, James T. ..... Winter Haven, FL
Joiner, Joanne E. ..... Jefferson City, MO
Joiner, Joe M. ..... Sherman, TX
Joiner, John E. ..... Washington, DC
Joiner, John P. ..... Fayetteville, GA
Joiner & Joiner, A Prof. Law Corp.
West Monroe, LA
Joiner, Joseph D. ..... Oakland, CA
Joiner, Lisa Zeiler ..... Washington, DC
Joiner, Marie Antoinette ..... Clarksville, TN
Joiner, Pat ..... Austin, TX
Joiner, Ralph R., Jr. ..... Atlanta, GA
Joiner, Richard M. ..... Madisonville, KY
Joiner, S. Dennis, P.C. ..... Brandon, MS
Joiner, Sandra Burzillo ..... South Natick, MA
Joiner, Sona Jean ..... Portland, OR
Joiner, Stephanie K. ..... Los Angeles, CA
Joiner, Stephen N. ..... Little Rock, AR
Joiner & Turner, P.A. ..... Winter Haven, FL
Joiner, Zenora Williams ..... Jackson, MS
Joines, James H. ..... Galax, VA
Joines, James Robert ..... Palm Beach, FL
Joines, Timothy B. ..... North Wilkesboro, NC
Joint, William B. ..... Bath, NY
Joist, Bettina L. ..... St. Louis, MO
Jokay, Alex ..... Fort Wayne, IN
Jokela, Cynthia A. ..... Minneapolis, MN
Jokelson, David E. ..... Philadelphia, PA
Jokelson, Debra Kahn ..... Philadelphia, PA
Jokelson, Derek E. ..... Philadelphia, PA
Jokelson, Neil E. ..... New York, NY
Philadelphia, PA
Jokelson, Neil E., & Associates, P.C.
Philadelphia, PA
Joki, Mary J. ..... Eagan, MN
Jokisch, Rhonda K. ..... Chicago, IL
Jokl, John M. ..... Middle Village, NY
Jokl, Robert L., Jr. ..... Syracuse, NY
Joklik, Paul Richard ..... New York, NY
Milwaukee, WI
Joks, Det H., (P.A.) ..... Miami, FL
Jolas, Thomas E. ..... Mason City, IA
Jolas, Thomas E., P.C. ..... Mason City, IA
Jolas, Van M. ..... Dallas, TX
Joley, Charles L. ..... Belleville, IL
Joley, Lisa Annette ..... St. Louis, MO
Joliat, Michael T. ..... Flint, MI
Joliat, Michael T., P.C. ..... Flint, MI
Jolicoeur, Valerie D. ..... Spokane, WA
Joliet, Amy H. ..... Indianapolis, IN
Joliet, Christopher ..... Hagerstown, MD
Joliet, Leo J. ..... Cleveland, OH
Jolin, Becky L. ..... Austin, TX

Jolin, Michael P. ..... Chicago, IL
Joling, Robert J. ..... Kenosha, WI
Jolink, Gray Byron ..... Austin, TX
Jolis, Paul O. ..... Washington, DC
Jolish, Barak D. ..... San Francisco, CA
Jolish, Taly Leshem ..... San Francisco, CA
Jolivet, Caroleen French
Colorado Springs, CO
Jolivette, David J. ..... Chicago, IL
Jolivette & Templer, P.C. ..... Chicago, IL
Jollay, R. Dean, Jr. ..... Massillon, OH
Jollay & Stewart, Attorneys, P.A.
Winter Haven, FL
Jollensten, Suzanne E. ..... Albuquerque, NM
Jolles, Abbe ..... Washington, DC
Jolles, Bernard ..... Portland, OR
Jolles, Bernstein & Garone, P.C.
Portland, OR
Jolles, Ira H. ..... Morristown, NJ
Jolles, Isaac S. ..... Augusta, GA
Jolles, Joel M. ..... New Haven, CT
Jolles, Ronald E. ..... Silver Spring, MD
Jolles & Slaby, P.C. ..... Augusta, GA
Jolley, Denise Hopkins ..... Washington, DC
Jolley, Elizabeth M. ..... Saginaw, MI
Jolley, Frederick O. ..... Denver, CO
Jolley, Grady B. ..... Hondo, TX
Jolley, H. Vernon ..... Allendale, NJ
Jolley, J. Kent ..... Rexburg, ID
Jolley, J. Steve ..... Spokane, WA
Jolley, Jay H. ..... Provo, UT
Salt Lake City, UT
Jolley, Jennifer L. ..... Seattle, WA
Jolley, John D. ..... Saginaw, MI
Jolley, John J., Jr. ..... Omaha, NE
Jolley, John M. ..... Alexandria, VA
Jolley, M. Thomas ..... Salt Lake City, UT
Jolley, Mary Griffo ..... Daytona Beach, FL
Jolley, Maxie G., II ..... Spartanburg, SC
Jolley, R. Gardner ..... Las Vegas, NV
Jolley, Rebecca G. ..... Cedartown, GA
Jolley, Renita M. ..... New York, NY
Jolley, Rhonda G. ..... San Antonio, TX
Jolley, Richard B. ..... Seattle, WA
Jolley, Robert L., Jr. ..... Knoxville, TN
Jolley, Urga, Wirth & Woodbury
Boulder City, NV
Las Vegas, NV
Jolley, Val R. ..... Farmington, NM
Jolley, Walsh, Hurley, Raisher, Schaeffer & Roher, P.C. ..... Kansas City, MO
Jolley, William A. ..... Kansas City, MO
Jolley, William C., Jr. ..... Kansas City, MO
Jolliff, Cliff. L. ..... Gainesville, GA
Jolliffe, Donald R. ..... Detroit, MI
Jolliffe, Jay R. ..... Livonia, MI
Jolliffe, John D. ..... Canton, OH
Jolliffe, William C. ..... Colorado Springs, CO
Jolls, Christine ..... Cambridge, MA
Jolly, A. Shedrick, III ..... Spartanburg, SC
Jolly, Anne-Marie ..... Bronx, NY
Jolly, Arezou C. ..... Jacksonville, FL
Jolly & Blau, P.S.C. ..... Cold Spring, KY
Jolly, Brad S. ..... Parker, AZ
Jolly, Bruce O., Jr. ..... Washington, DC
Jolly, Bruce W. ..... Fort Lauderdale, FL
Jolly, Cameron M. ..... Costa Mesa, CA
Jolly, C. G. ..... Omaha, NE
Jolly, Charles N. ..... Chattanooga, TN
Jolly, Clayton L., III ..... Augusta, GA
Jolly, David A. ..... West Jefferson, NC
Jolly, David B. ..... Columbus, MS
Jolly, E. Grady ..... Jackson, MS
Jolly, Edward B. ..... Tallahassee, FL
Jolly, Elizabeth B. ..... Columbus, MS
Jolly, James D., Jr. ..... Anderson, SC
Jolly, Jerry A. ..... Tabor City, NC
Jolly, John D. ..... Russellville, AL
Jolly, John R., Jr. ..... Raleigh, NC
Jolly, John Russel ..... Jacksonville, FL
Jolly, John W., Jr. ..... Tallahassee, FL
Jolly, Linda E. ..... New York, NY
Jolly, Lynda S. ..... Bartlesville, OK
Jolly, Margaret E. ..... Newport, RI
Jolly, Michael B. ..... Houston, TX
Jolly, Norman, Jr. ..... Houston, TX
Jolly, P. Scott ..... Baton Rouge, LA
Jolly, Peterson & Waters, P.A.
Tallahassee, FL
Jolly, Place, Fralin & Prillaman, P.C.
Roanoke, VA
Salem, VA
Jolly, Raymond A., Jr. ..... Charlotte, NC
Jolly, Robert P. ..... San Francisco, CA
Jolly, Sheryl Barksdale ..... Augusta, GA
Jolly, Terence K. ..... Troy, MI
Jolly, Thomas A. ..... Dallas, TX
Jolly, Thomas R., (P.C.) ..... Washington, DC
Jolly, Warren H. ..... Moncks Corner, SC
Jolly, W. H. (Hank), Jr. ..... Columbus, MS
Jolly, Wilbur M. ..... Louisburg, NC
Jolly, William E. ..... San Antonio, TX
Jolly, Williamson & Williamson
Louisburg, NC
Jollymore, Nicholas J. ..... New York, NY
Jolovitz, Lester T. ..... Waterville, ME
Jolstad, Joann Marie ..... Columbus, OH
Joly, Matthew C. ..... Vernon Hills, IL
Jomantas, Paul ..... Toledo, OH
Jomp, Felicita C. ..... San Juan, PR
Jonah, Pamela M. ..... Weymouth, MA
Jonak, Jennifer L. ..... San Francisco, CA
Jonak, Michael W. ..... Brainerd, MN
Jonakait, Randolph N ..... New York, NY
Jonas, Aaron ..... Houston, TX
Jonas, Alan L. ..... Evanston, IL
Jonas, Amy M. ..... Palm Beach Gardens, FL

Jonas, Barry ..... Department of Justice, Tax Division, GV
Jonas, Bruce ..... Tampa, FL
Jonas, Charles A. ..... San Francisco, CA
Jonas, Daniel M. ..... Canton, OH
Jonas, Daniel S. ..... Utica, NY
Jonas, Donald E. ..... Columbia, SC
Jonas, Emily S. ..... New York, NY
Jonas, Eric A., Sr. ..... Charlotte, NC
Jonas, Evelyn ..... Brooklyn, NY
Jonas, Fred ..... Carlsbad, CA
Jonas, Gail E. ..... Healdsburg, CA
Jonas, Harvey A., Jr. ..... Lincolnton, NC
Jonas, Jeffrey L. ..... Boston, MA
Jonas, John ..... Elkhart, IN
Jonas, John F. ..... Washington, DC
Jonas, Joyce M. ..... Bronx, NY
Jonas, Kent ..... San Francisco, CA
Jonas & LaSorte ..... West Palm Beach, FL
Jonas Law Firm, The, P.L.L.C.
Denver, NC
Lincolnton, NC
Jonas, Lisa A. ..... New York, NY
Jonas, Lori ..... Department of Justice, Environment and Natural Resources Division, GV
Jonas, Louis ..... Berkeley, CA
Jonas, Marc ..... Utica, NY
Jonas, Marc D. ..... Lansdale, PA
Jonas, Marla ..... New York, NY
Jonas & Matthews ..... San Francisco, CA
Jonas, Michael C. ..... San Jose, CA
Jonas, Michael D. ..... San Francisco, CA
Jonas, Michael D. ..... Aberdeen, MS
Jonas, Michael N. ..... West Palm Beach, FL
Jonas, Milton ..... Garden City, NY
Jonas, R. William, Jr. ..... South Bend, IN
Jonas, Richard E. ..... Lincolnton, NC
Jonas, Ruth Waltuch, Law Offices of
Norwalk, CT
Jonas, Stephen A. ..... Boston, MA
Jonas, Susan A. ..... Holland, MI
Jonas, Thomas J. ..... Platteville, WI
Jonas, Valerie ..... Miami Beach, FL
Jonas, W. James, III ..... Washington, DC
Austin, TX
San Antonio, TX
Jonas, Weiyen M. ..... Boston, MA
Jonas and Wiggins ..... Columbia, SC
Jonasen, Jeffery Q. ..... Orlando, FL
Jonason, William A. ..... Rochester, MN
Jonassen, Frederick B. ..... Fort Wayne, IN
Jonassen, William S. ..... Largo, FL
Jonassen, William S., P.A. ..... Clearwater, FL
Largo, FL
Jonasson, W. Bradford, Jr. ..... Oregon City, OR
Jonasz, Jonathan ..... Miami Beach, FL
Jonaus, Laura J. ..... North Chicago, IL
Jonckheer, Willem F. ..... San Francisco, CA
Joncus, Stephen J. ..... Houston, TX
Jondle, Robert J. ..... Omaha, NE
Joned, Alima ..... Washington, DC
Jonelis, William M. ..... Munster, IN
Jones, A. Bruce ..... Denver, CO
Jones, A. Gary ..... Dothan, AL
Jones, A. Morgan ..... Truckee, CA
Jones, A. Quinn, III ..... Washington, DC
Jones, A. Timothy ..... Atlanta, GA
Jones, Aaron D. ..... Springfield, MO
Jones, A. B. ..... Quitman, GA
Jones, Abigail Lee ..... Englewood, CO
Jones, Abraham Penn ..... Raleigh, NC
Jones, A. D., Jr. ..... Bristol, TN
Jones & Adams ..... Kennesaw, GA
Jones and Adams, LLP ..... Coushatta, LA
Jones & Adams, P.A. ..... Miami, FL
Jones, A. H. ..... Robinson, IL
Jones, Aidan D. ..... Washington, DC
Jones, A. J. ..... Bogalusa, LA
Jones, Alan Benton ..... Dallas, TX
Jones, Alan E. ..... Waukegan, IL
Jones, Alan M. ..... Newport Beach, CA
Jones, Albert E. ..... Marietta, GA
Jones, Albert W. ..... Los Angeles, CA
Jones & Alexander, A Professional Law Corporation ..... Cameron, LA
Jones, Alexander G. ..... Princess Anne, MD
Jones, Alexander W., Jr. ..... Birmingham, AL
Jones, Alfred C., III ..... New York, NY
Jones, Alfred, Jr. ..... State College, PA
Jones, Alfred R. ..... Seminole, FL
Jones, Alicia ..... Independence, CA
Jones, Alicia A. ..... Detroit, MI
Jones, Alicia Coogle ..... Port St. Joe, FL
Jones, Alison Brown ..... Newark, NJ
Jones, Alison E. ..... Henderson, MN
Jones, Alison M. ..... Olympia, WA
Jones, Allan E. ..... Sarasota, FL
Jones, Allan Sidney ..... Birmingham, AL
Jones, Allen C. ..... Troy, AL
Jones, Allen C. ..... Memphis, TN
Jones, Allen & Fuquay, L.L.P. ..... Dallas, TX
Jones, Allen, Jr. ..... Washington, DC
Bethesda, MD
Jones, Allen P. ..... Shreveport, LA
Jones, Allison A. ..... Shreveport, LA
Jones, Allison L. ..... Poway, CA
Jones, Allston L. ..... Palo Alto, CA
Jones, Alma Salter ..... Shreveport, LA
Jones, Alvin C. ..... Tampa, FL
Jones, Alvin F. ..... Roswell, NM
Jones, Amanda ..... Jackson, MS
Jones, Amy B. ..... New York, NY
Jones, Amy Hart ..... Norfolk, VA
Jones, Amy Schmidt ..... Milwaukee, WI
Jones, Anastasia G. ..... Jackson, MS
Jones, Anderson D. ..... Roswell, NM
Jones, Andrea A. ..... Los Angeles, CA

Jones, Andrea Brucoli ..... Atlanta, GA
Jones, Andrea Cantrell ..... Atlanta, GA
Jones, Andrew ..... Los Angeles, CA
Jones, Andrew A. ..... Milwaukee, WI
Jones, Andrew David ..... New Bern, NC
Jones, Andrew M. ..... Mobile, AL
Jones, Andrew M., Jr. ..... Greenville, SC
Jones, Andrew Milam ..... Kansas City, MO
Jones, Andrew P. ..... St. Albans, NY
Jones, Andrew R ..... Portland, OR
Jones, Andrew S. ..... Fort Worth, TX
Jones, Andrew T. ..... Irving, TX
Jones, Andrew W. ..... Marietta, GA
Jones, Angela J. ..... Milton, FL
Jones, Angelyn A. ..... Wagoner, OK
Jones, Anissa M. ..... Canfield, OH
Jones, Ann C. ..... Concord, MA
Jones, Ann I. ..... Los Angeles, CA
Jones, Ann Lacroix ..... Fairfax, VA
Jones, Ann Simpson ..... Fredericksburg, VA
Jones, Ann Witherspoon ..... Birmingham, AL
Jones, Anna Belle, (Mrs.) ..... Mercer, PA
Jones, Annabel M. ..... Tulsa, OK
Jones, Anne Gué ..... Orangeburg, SC
Jones, Anne M. ..... Southfield, MI
Jones, Anne P. ..... Washington, DC
Jones, Annette ..... Waco, TX
Jones, Anthony Hunter ..... New York, NY
Jones, Anthony O. ..... Phoenix, AZ
Jones, Antoinette ..... Montgomery, AL
Jones, April Denise ..... San Jose, CA
Jones, Archer L., II ..... Newport News, VA
Smithfield, VA
Jones, Archie C., Jr. ..... Birmingham, AL
Jones, Aretha ..... Washington, DC
Jones, Arnold C. ..... Frankfort, KY
Jones, Arnold O., II ..... Goldsboro, NC
Jones, Arnold W., Jr. ..... Dallas, TX
Jones, Arthur A. ..... Springfield, IL
Jones, Arthur H., Jr. ..... Haddonfield, NJ
Jones, Arthur T. ..... Glendale, CA
Monterey, CA
Jones, Arthur W. ..... San Diego, CA
Jones, Ashby Lawton ..... Lexington, SC
Jones & Askew, L.L.P. ..... Atlanta, GA
Jones & Associates ..... Atlanta, GA
Jones Associates ..... Providence, RI
Jones & Associates, Law Offices of
West Point, MS
Jones & Associates, Ltd., Law Offices of
Chicago, IL
Jones & Associates, P.C. ..... Baltimore, MD
Jones & Associates, P.C. ..... Dallas, TX
Jones and Associates, P.C. ..... Sugar Land, TX
Jones, Athiel S. ..... Orange Park, FL
Jones, Aubrey E. ..... Weston, MA
Jones, Aubrey L., Jr. ..... Athens, TX
Jones, Audrey B. ..... Los Angeles, CA
Jones, B. Todd ..... Ann Arbor, MI
Jones & Bahret, Co., L.P.A. ..... Holland, OH
Jones, Bambi A. ..... Damariscotta, ME
Jones, Barbara A. ..... Anchorage, AK
Jones, Barbara A. ..... Indianapolis, IN
Jones, Barbara Alice ..... Westlake Village, CA
Jones, Barbara E. ..... New York, NY
Jones, Barbara Fancher ..... Orlando, FL
Jones, Barbara G. ..... Philadelphia, PA
Jones, Barbara J. R. ..... San Francisco, CA
Jones, Barbara L. ..... Richfield, MN
Jones, Barbara L. ..... Berea, OH
Jones, Barbara S. ..... New York, NY
Jones, Barbara Willett ..... Frankfort, KY
Jones, Barrie L. ..... Fernandina Beach, FL
Jones, Barry E. ..... Weslaco, TX
Jones, Barry J. ..... Glens Falls, NY
Jones, Barry K. ..... Jackson, MS
Jones, Barry W. ..... Tahoe City, CA
Jones, Barton T. ..... New York, NY
Jones, Baxter P. ..... Atlanta, GA
Jones & Beardsley ..... Bakersfield, CA
Jones, Beauchamp ..... Meridian, MS
Jones, Bell, Abbott, Fleming & Fitzgerald, L.L.P. ..... Los Angeles, CA
Jones, Benjamin ..... Monroe, LA
Jones, Benjamin A. ..... Portland, ME
Jones, Benjamin H., II ..... Columbus, OH
Jones, Bennee B. ..... Dallas, TX
Jones, Benner, III ..... Fayetteville, NC
Jones, Bennie L., Jr. ..... West Point, MS
Jones, Benny ..... Beckley, WV
Jones, Berlin C. ..... Pine Bluff, AR
Jones, Bernard C., Jr. ..... Jackson, MS
Jones, Bernard E. ..... Houston, TX
Jones, Bert M. ..... Tulsa, OK
Jones, Beryl R. ..... Brooklyn, NY
Jones, Beth Finley ..... Los Angeles, CA
Jones, Beth Tyner
Research Triangle Park, NC
Jones, Betsy J. ..... Charlotte, NC
Jones, Bette Jo ..... Connersville, IN
Jones, Betty J. ..... Walnut Creek, CA
Jones, Beverly E. ..... Washington, DC
Jones, Beverly Hood ..... Little Rock, AR
Jones, Beverly J. ..... Charlotte, NC
Jones, Beverly K. ..... Tarkio, MO
Jones, Bill ..... Houston, TX
Jones, Bill R. ..... Livingston, TX
Jones, Billy N. ..... Hinesville, GA
Jones, Blair Sheridan ..... Waterville, ME
Jones & Blaney ..... Oklahoma City, OK
Jones, Blechman, Woltz & Kelly, P.C.
Hampton, VA
Newport News, VA
Williamsburg, VA
Jones & Blouch L.L.P. ..... Washington, DC
Jones, Bobbie, (Mrs.) ..... Nashville, TN
Jones, Bobby ..... Metter, GA

Jones, Bohumila Podvalová
Fort Worth, TX
Jones, Bonnie B. ..... Philadelphia, PA
Jones, Bonnie L. ..... Hampton, VA
Jones, Bonnie McGuire ..... Clifton Park, NY
Jones, Bonnie S. ..... New York, NY
Jones Bothwell & Dion LLP
San Francisco, CA
Jones, Bowron & Selden, A Professional Corporation ..... Birmingham, AL
Jones, Boykin, Stacy & Associates
Savannah, GA
Jones, Brad C. ..... Charlottesville, VA
Jones, Brad L. ..... Burlington, KS
Jones, Bradley B. ..... Seattle, WA
Jones, Bradley B. ..... Tacoma, WA
Jones, Bradley M. ..... Minneapolis, MN
Jones, Bradley P. ..... Brandon, MS
Jones, Bradley R. ..... South Jordan, UT
Jones, Bradley T. ..... Seattle, WA
Jones, Bradley W.
Nuclear Regulatory Commission, Commission, GV
Jones & Bragg, P.C. ..... Grandview, MO
Oak Grove, MO
Jones, Brent A. ..... Ojai, CA
Jones, Brent Allen ..... Tampa, FL
Jones, Brent H. ..... Arlington, TX
Jones, Brian A. ..... Brooklyn, NY
Jones, Brian C. ..... Fairfax, VA
Jones, Brian D. ..... Britt, IA
Jones, Brian D. ..... Sylvania, OH
Jones, Brian E. ..... Minneapolis, MN
Jones, Brian Hamrick ..... Richmond, VA
Jones, Brian M. ..... Orlando, FL
Jones, Brian R. ..... Portland, OR
Jones, Brian R. ..... Roanoke, VA
Jones, Brian S. ..... Dayton, OH
Jones, Brian W. ..... San Francisco, CA
Jones, Brian W. ..... Miller, SD
Jones, Brian W. ..... Salt Lake City, UT
Jones, Bridgett E. ..... San Jose, CA
Jones, Brigham P. ..... Redding, CA
Jones, Brock, Jr. ..... Ozona, TX
Jones, Brockway J. ..... Tuscaloosa, AL
Jones, Brooks M. ..... Chagrin Falls, OH
Jones, Brower & Callery ..... Lewiston, ID
Jones, Bruce ..... Minneapolis, MN
Jones, Bruce A. ..... San Jose, CA
Jones, Bruce A. ..... Phillipsburg, NJ
Jones, Bruce C. ..... Boise, ID
Jones, Bruce D., Jr. ..... Eastville, VA
Jones, Bruce E. ..... Everett, WA
Jones, Bruce G. ..... Westlake Village, CA
Jones, Bruce G. ..... Indianapolis, IN
Jones, Bruce P. ..... Cleveland, OH
Jones & Bruce, P.A. ..... Crisfield, MD
Princess Anne, MD
Jones, Bruce T. ..... Salt Lake City, UT
Jones, Bryan ..... Half Moon Bay, CA
Jones, Burnell L., Jr. ..... Houston, TX
Jones, Burton V. ..... Canton, OH
Jones, Burwell J. ..... Sarasota, FL
Jones & Butler ..... Stanwood, WA
Jones, Byington & Durham ..... Rome, GA
Jones, Byron Lee ..... Englewood, CO
Jones, C. Barton ..... Pittsburgh, PA
Jones, C. Breck ..... Sacramento, CA
Jones, C. Bruce ..... Tulsa, OK
Jones, C. Craig ..... Borger, TX
Jones, C. Daniel ..... Houston, TX
Jones, C. Eugene ..... Sarasota, FL
Jones, C. Havird, Jr. ..... Columbia, SC
Jones, C. Hunter
Securities and Exchange Commission, Division of Investment Management, GV
Jones, C. Paul ..... St. Paul, MN
Jones, C. Randall, Jr., (P.A.)
Pass Christian, MS
Jones, C. Richard ..... Kinsman, OH
Jones, C. Robert ..... Tulsa, OK
Jones, C. Roland, Jr. ..... Spartanburg, SC
Jones, C. Shawn ..... Atlanta, GA
Jones, Cal ..... San Bernardino, CA
Jones, Calvin A. ..... Princeton, NJ
Jones, Calvin C. ..... McLean, VA
Jones, Calvin R. ..... Anchorage, AK
Jones, Cameo F. ..... San Francisco, CA
Jones, Cameron ..... Beverly Hills, CA
Jones, Camilla Towers ..... Memphis, TN
Jones, Candace M. ..... Cleveland, OH
Jones, Cannon & Freeman, P.C.
Arlington, TX
Jones & Cardozo, P.A. ..... Sarasota, FL
Jones, Carl M. ..... Austin, TX
Jones, Carl W. ..... Bartlesville, OK
Jones, Carla A. ..... Miami, FL
Jones, Carla Rae ..... Las Vegas, NV
Jones, Carleton S. ..... Fairfax, VA
Jones & Carlson ..... Norfolk, VA
Jones, Carlton H., III ..... Fairburn, GA
Jones, Carlton, III ..... Baton Rouge, LA
Jones, Carol ..... Trenton, NJ
Jones, Carol A. ..... Chicago, IL
Jones, Carol Ann ..... Jacksonville, NC
Jones, Carol J. ..... Glendale, CA
Jones, Carol L. ..... San Jose, CA
Jones, Carol Wind ..... Jacksonville, FL
Jones, Caroline ..... Austin, TX
Jones, Carolita V. ..... Department of Labor, Office of Secretary, GV
Jones, Carolyn B. ..... Fort Wayne, IN
Jones, Carolyn Christine ..... New York, NY
Jones, Carolyn D. ..... Department of Justice, Immigration and Naturalization Service, GV
Jones, Carolyn E. ..... Anchorage, AK
Jones, Carolyn J. ..... Chicago, IL
Jones, Carolynn W. ..... Palo Alto, CA

Jones, Frances E. .... Shreveport, LA
Jones, Francis G., Jr. .... Atlanta, GA
Jones, Francis J., Jr. .... Newark, DE
Jones, Francis R. .... Upper Marlboro, MD
Jones, Francis R. .... Point Pleasant, NJ
Jones, Frank C. .... Atlanta, GA
Jones, Frank C., III .... Tupelo, MS
Jones, Frank G. .... Houston, TX
Jones, Frank H. .... Rome, GA
Jones, Frank L. .... Tallahassee, FL
Jones, Frank L., Jr. .... West Yarmouth, MA
Jones, Frank & Linden, P.C.
Colorado Springs, CO
Jones, Frank N. .... Boston, MA
Jones, Frank P., Jr. .... Washington, DC
Jones, Frank S., Jr. .... Baltimore, MD
Jones, Frank W. .... Secaucus, NJ
Jones, Franklin C. .... Rochester, NH
Jones, Franklin H., III .... New Orleans, LA
Jones, Franklin, Jr. .... Marshall, TX
Jones, Franklin P. .... Fresno, CA
Jones, Fred A. .... Burlingame, CA
Jones, Fred A., Jr. .... Athens, TX
Jones, Fred E. .... Lebanon, OH
Jones, Fred E., Jr. .... Memphis, TN
Jones, Fred Howell .... Franklin, NC
Jones, Fred L. .... Indianapolis, IN
Jones, Fred M." Mickey ". .... Odessa, TX
Jones, Fred M." Mickey ", P.C. .... Odessa, TX
Jones, Fred R. .... Plymouth, IN
Jones, Fred Riley .... San Antonio, TX
Jones, Frederick C. .... Elyria, OH
Jones, Frederick D. .... Marietta, GA
Jones, Frederick F. .... Santa Barbara, CA
Jones, Frederick K. .... Florence, SC
Jones, Frederick M. .... Phoenix, AZ
Jones, Frederick W. .... Winter Park, FL
Jones, Funk & Payne .... Zanesville, OH
Jones Fussell, L.L.P. .... Covington, LA
Jones, G. Andrew .... Los Angeles, CA
Jones, G. Bradford .... Los Angeles, CA
Jones, G. Douglas .... Birmingham, AL
Jones, G. Frank .... Wilmington, NC
Jones, G. Jerome .... Galveston, TX
Jones, G. Kevin .... Salt Lake City, UT
Jones, G. Raye .... Charlottesville, VA
Jones, G. Richard .... Belleville, IL
Jones, G. Scott .... Centralia, IL
Jones, G. Scott .... Winston-Salem, NC
Jones, G. Steven .... Gridley, CA
Jones, G. A., Jr. .... Hampstead, NC
Jones, Gail G. .... Jacksonville, AL
Jones, Galligan, Key & Lozano, L.L.P.
Weslaco, TX
Jones, Garlandine .... Cleveland, OH
Jones, Garon K. .... Yakima, WA
Jones, Garrett M. .... Orlando, FL
Jones, Garry L. .... Santa Ana, CA
Jones, Garry W. .... Lewiston, ID
Jones, Garth L. .... Hoquiam, WA
Jones, Gary .... Oklahoma City, OK
Jones, Gary A. .... Santa Clara, CA
Jones, Gary A. .... Boston, MA
Jones, Gary A. .... Iselin, NJ
Jones, Gary B. .... Meridian, MS
Jones, Gary D. .... Waterbury, CT
Jones, Gary G. .... Salem, OR
Jones, Gary K. .... Wichita, KS
Jones, Gary K. .... Jackson, MS
Jones, Gary L. .... Scottsdale, AZ
Jones, Gary L. .... Columbus, OH
Jones, Gary L., Co,. L.P.A.
Cincinnati, OH
Cleveland, OH
Columbus, OH
Jones, Gary N. .... Glendale, AZ
Jones, Gary N. .... Cedar Falls, IA
Jones, Gary R. .... Gainesville, FL
Miami, FL
Jones, Gary R. .... Baltimore, MD
Jones, Gary R., P.A. .... Gainesville, FL
Jones, Gary T. .... Mount Vernon, WA
Jones, Gayla I. .... Oklahoma City, OK
Jones, Gaynelle Griffin .... Houston, TX
Jones, Gene A. .... Howard, OH
Jones, Gene A., Jr. .... Raleigh, NC
Jones, Gene M. .... La Porte, IN
Jones, Gene M. Zona .... Beaumont, TX
Jones, Geo. H., Jr. .... Montgomery, AL
Jones, Geoffrey L. .... Jupiter, FL
Jones, George .... New York, NY
Jones, George A. .... Detroit, MI
Jones, George A. .... Chatham, VA
Jones, George C. .... Morristown, NJ
Jones, George C. .... Houston, TX
Jones, George D., P.C. .... Abilene, TX
Jones, George E. .... Birmingham, AL
Jones, George Edward, III .... Selma, AL
Jones, George F. .... Baltimore, MD
Jones, George G. .... Cambridge, MA
Jones, George H. .... New Orleans, LA
Jones, George L. .... Vero Beach, FL
Jones, George M. .... Long Beach, CA
Jones, George M. .... Columbia, SC
Jones, George P., III .... Albuquerque, NM
Jones, George R. .... Germantown, MD
Jones, George R. A. .... Washington, DC
Jones, George S. .... Washington, DC
Jones, George W., Jr. .... Washington, DC
Jones, Gerald L. .... Cambridge, OH
Jones, Gerald L. .... Katy, TX
Jones, Gerald W. .... Camp Springs, MD
Jones, Gerald W. .... Enterprise, MS
Jones, Gerald W., II .... Cape Girardeau, MO
Jones, Gerald W., Jr. .... Sanford, FL
Jones, Gerard E. .... Greenwich, CT
New York, NY

Jones, Gilbert F., (Law Corporation)
Chico, CA
Jones & Gillaspia, L.L.P. .... Houston, TX
Jones, Givens, Gotcher & Bogan, A Professional Corporation .... Tulsa, OK
Jones, Gladstone N., III .... New Orleans, LA
Jones Gledhill Hess Andrews Fuhrman Bradbury & Eiden, P.A. .... Boise, ID
Nampa, ID
Jones, Glendell, Jr. .... Jonesboro, AR
Jones, Glenn M. .... Oklahoma City, OK
Jones & Glenn, P.L.C. .... Roanoke, VA
Jones, Glenn R. .... Newark, NJ
Jones, Glenn R. .... Medina, OH
Jones, Glenn W. .... Little Rock, AR
Jones, Glower W. .... Atlanta, GA
Jones, G. N., Jr. .... Waynesboro, MS
Jones & González, P.C. .... Bruni, TX
Laredo, TX
Jones, Gordon A. .... Department of Justice, Civil Division, GV
Jones, Gordon G. .... Fullerton, CA
Jones, Gordon, II .... Atlanta, GA
Jones, Gordon L. .... Austin, TX
Jones, Gordon M., III .... Boston, MA
Jones, Gorman R., Jr. .... Tuscumbia, AL
Jones, Graham O. .... Hackensack, NJ
Jones, Graham S., II .... Poughkeepsie, NY
Jones & Granger .... Houston, TX
Jones, Grant .... Corpus Christi, TX
Jones & Greer, LLP .... Atlanta, GA
Jones, Greg F. .... Robertsdale, AL
Jones, Greg W. .... Ventura, CA
Jones, Gregg, Creehan & Gerace, LLP
Pittsburgh, PA
Jones, Gregg H. .... Houston, TX
Jones, Gregory A. .... Glendale, CA
Jones, Gregory A. .... Priest River, ID
Jones, Gregory A. .... Boston, MA
Jones, Gregory B. .... Monroe, MI
Jones, Gregory C. .... Chicago, IL
Jones, Gregory D. .... Fayetteville, AR
Jones, Gregory D. .... Ocala, FL
Tampa, FL
Jones, Gregory D. H. .... Manchester, NH
Jones, Gregory E. .... San Francisco, CA
Jones, Gregory E. .... Sioux City, IA
Jones, Gregory G. .... Tampa, FL
Jones, Gregory G. .... Fort Worth, TX
Irving, TX
Jones, Gregory G., A Prof. Association, Law Offices .... Tampa, FL
Jones, Gregory J. .... Timonium, MD
Jones, Gregory K. .... Los Angeles, CA
Jones, Gregory L. .... Alexandria, LA
Jones, Gregory L. .... Wilmington, NC
Jones, Gregory L., P.A. .... Wilmington, NC
Jones, Gregory M. .... Department of Justice, Office of Legislative Affairs, GV
Jones, Gregory N. .... Houston, TX
Jones, Gregory N. .... Salt Lake City, UT
Jones, Gregory R. .... Mobile, AL
Jones, Gregory S. .... Torrington, CT
Jones, Gregory S. .... Orem, UT
Jones, Gregory T. .... Little Rock, AR
Jones, Gregory W. .... Houston, TX
Jones, Gretchen L. .... Portland, ME
Jones, Grey W. .... Columbus, OH
Jones, Grier Pat .... Dallas, TX
Jones, Griffith H. .... Montclair, NJ
Jones, Guilford L., III .... Burnet, TX
Jones, Guy E. .... Texarkana, TX
Jones, Gwen D. .... Cookeville, TN
Jones, H. Alan .... Linthicum, MD
Jones, H. Ben, Jr. .... Warrenton, VA
Jones, H. Douglas .... Covington, KY
Jones, H. Gilbert .... Costa Mesa, CA
Jones, H. Scott .... Baltimore, MD
Jones, H. Susan .... Oak Brook, IL
Jones Hall, A Professional Law Corporation
San Francisco, CA
Jones, Hamill D." Skip ", Jr.
Richmond, VA
Jones, Hancy, III .... Louisville, KY
Jones, Hansel Anthony .... Jackson, MS
Jones, Harlan E. .... Salem, OR
Jones, Harley H. .... Winston-Salem, NC
Jones, Harold D. .... New York, NY
Jones, Harold D., Jr. .... Washington, DC
Jones, Harold Dean .... Dallas, TX
Jones, Harold E. .... Bronx, NY
Jones, Harold W. .... Indianapolis, IN
Jones & Harper .... Fayetteville, AR
Fort Smith, AR
Jones, Harriett J. .... San Antonio, TX
Jones, Harrison H. .... Louisville, KY
Jones, Harry A., P.A. .... Titusville, FL
Jones, Harry C., III .... Washington, DC
New York, NY
Jones, Harry E. .... Department of Justice, Justice Management Division, GV
Jones, Harry L. .... Houston, TX
Jones, Harry R., Jr. .... Houston, TX
Jones, Harry S. .... Houston, TX
Jones, Harry T., Jr. .... Washington, DC
Jones, Harvey C., II .... Baltimore, MD
Jones, Harvey N. .... Hastings, MN
Jones, Haskins W. .... Birmingham, AL
Jones, H. E. .... Wichita, KS
Jones, Heather Heiskell .... Charleston, WV
Jones & Hegyes Co., L.P.A.
Willoughby, OH
Jones, Helen Hart .... Chicago, IL
Jones, Helen L. .... Dayton, OH
Jones & Hendrix, P.A. .... Spartanburg, SC
Jones, Henry F. .... Garden City, NY
Jones, Henry H. .... Washington, DC
Jones, Henry L., Jr. .... Little Rock, AR

Jones, Henry Thomas, IV .... Little Rock, AR
Jones, Henry W., III .... Austin, TX
Jones, Henry W., Jr. .... Raleigh, NC
Jones, Herbert C., Jr. .... Rockville, MD
Jones, Herbert D., Jr. .... Oak Park, IL
Jones, Herbert M. .... Las Vegas, NV
Jones, Herbert P. .... Baltimore, MD
Jones, Herman .... Austin, TX
Jones, Herschel B. .... Columbia, KY
Jones, Hersy, Jr. .... Shreveport, LA
Jones, Hewson & Woolard .... Charlotte, NC
Jones, Hilburn & Claxton .... Dublin, GA
Jones Hirsch Connors & Bull P.C.
Los Angeles, CA
Stamford, CT
Newark, NJ
Mineola, NY
New York, NY
White Plains, NY
Jones Hoffman & Admire .... Franklin, IN
Jones, Hoffmann & Huber
Des Moines, IA
Jones, Homer A., Jr. .... Bristol, VA
Jones, Howard E. .... Dunsmuir, CA
Jones, Howard N. .... Salt Lake City, UT
Jones, Howard W. .... Westport, CT
Jones, Howard W. .... Calhoun, GA
Jones, Hubert B. .... Dyersburg, TN
Jones and Huff .... Plymouth, IN
Jones, Hugh A. .... Sunbury, PA
Jones, Hugh J.M., III, P.C. .... Lynchburg, VA
Jones, Hugh J. M., III .... Lynchburg, VA
Jones, Hugh M., Jr. .... Naples, NY
Jones, Hugh R. .... Honolulu, HI
Jones, Hugh R. .... New Hartford, NY
Jones, Hugh R., Jr. .... Boston, MA
Jones, Huw R. .... West Haven, CT
Jones, H. W. (Sonny) .... Meridian, MS
Jones, Ida Mae .... Fresno, CA
Jones, Intili & Jones .... Dayton, OH
Jones, Ira L., II .... Houston, TX
Jones, Ira W. .... Salem, OR
Jones, Iris, & Associates, P.C. .... Austin, TX
Jones, Iris J. .... Austin, TX
Jones, Isham Russell .... Jefferson City, MO
Jones, Isobel Ann .... San Francisco, CA
Jones, Ivy Li .... Los Angeles, CA
Jones, J. Allen, (P.C.) .... Sacramento, CA
Jones, J. Barrett .... Charlottesville, VA
Jones, J. Barry .... Guntersville, AL
Jones, J. Brent .... Sarasota, FL
Jones, J. Charles .... Charlotte, NC
Jones, J. Don .... Atlanta, GA
Jones, J. Donelson .... Panama City, FL
Jones, J. Eric .... Muskogee, OK
Jones, J. Fletcher .... Andalusia, AL
Jones, J. Forrest .... Newark, NJ
Jones, J. Franklin, Jr. .... Fort Collins, CO
Jones, J. Fred .... Atlanta, GA
Jones, J. Grant .... Abilene, TX
Jones, J. Gregory .... Cincinnati, OH
Jones, J. Keith .... Charlotte, NC
Jones, J. Kenneth .... Eugene, OR
Jones, J. Kevin .... New Bern, NC
Jones, J. Mark .... Columbia, SC
Jones, J. Marshall, Jr. .... Shreveport, LA
Jones, J. Michael .... Dumas, AR
Jones, J. Michael .... Geneseo, NY
Jones, J. Mitchell .... Madison, WI
Jones, J. Patrick .... Huntington, WV
Jones, J. Phelps .... Irving, TX
Jones, J. Philip .... Memphis, TN
Jones, J. Philip .... Houston, TX
Jones, J. Phillip .... Nashville, TN
Jones, J. Rabun, Jr. .... Greenville, MS
Jones, J. Randall .... Las Vegas, NV
Jones, J. Richard .... Hartsville, SC
Jones, J. Rick .... Frankfort, KY
Jones, J. Ronald, Jr. .... Charlotte, NC
Charleston, SC
Jones, J. Sumner .... Washington, DC
Jones, J. Thomas .... Knoxville, TN
Jones, J. Todd .... Little Rock, AR
Jones, J. Turner .... Columbia, MO
Jones, J. Wesley .... Austin, TX
Jones, J. Woodfin .... Austin, TX
Jones, Jack D. .... Tulsa, OK
Jones, Jack D. .... Knoxville, TN
Jones, Jack G., Jr. .... Lexington, KY
Jones, Jack R. .... Modesto, CA
Jones, Jack R., III .... Southaven, MS
Jones, Jack W., Jr. .... Temple, TX
Jones, Jackson I. .... Louisville, KY
Jones, Jackson M. .... Little Rock, AR
Jones, Jackson & Moll, PLC
Fayetteville, AR
Fort Smith, AR
Jones, Jacqueline .... Chicago, IL
Jones, Jacqueline A.
House of Representatives, Office of Legislative Counsel, GV
Jones, Jacqueline B. .... Syracuse, NY
Jones, Jacqueline J. .... Charlotte, NC
Jones, Jacquelyn E. .... Atlanta, GA
Jones, Jade Anton .... Baltimore, MD
Jones Jain, L.L.P. .... Washington, DC
Jones, Jake, III .... Oklahoma City, OK
Jones, James A. .... Washington, DC
Jones, James A. .... Dallas, TX
Jones, James A., III .... New York, NY
Jones, James C. .... Neenah, WI
Jones, James C., II .... New York, NY
Jones, James C., II .... Martinsburg, WV
Jones, James C., III .... Waycross, GA
Jones, James C., Jr. .... San Jose, CA
San Mateo, CA
Jones, James D. .... Conroe, TX
Jones, James E. .... Toledo, OH

Jones, James E. .... Houston, TX
Jones, James E., Jr. .... Madison, WI
Jones, James G. .... Los Angeles, CA
Jones, James H., Jr. .... Everett, WA
Jones, James J., Jr. .... Lafayette, CA
Jones, James K., Jr. .... Laredo, TX
Jones, James L. .... Jackson, MS
Jones, James L. .... Billings, MT
Jones, James M. .... Pittsburgh, PA
Jones, James M., Jr. .... Fayetteville, GA
Jones, James M., Jr. .... Lewisburg, TN
Jones, James P. .... Boston, MA
Jones, James P. .... Brielle, NJ
Jones, James P. .... Abingdon, VA
Jones, James R. .... Palo Alto, CA
Jones, James R. .... Washington, DC
Jones, James R., Jr. .... Brooksville, FL
Jones, James R., Jr. .... Nashville, TN
Jones, James Reese .... Brenham, TX
Jones, James S. .... Poland, OH
Jones, James T. .... Sacramento, CA
Jones, James Thomas .... Groton, CT
Jones, James Todd .... Buena Vista, VA
Jones, James T. R. .... Louisville, KY
Jones, James V. .... Napa, CA
Jones, James W. .... Washington, DC
Jones, James W. .... Boston, MA
Jones, James Webb .... Chesapeake, VA
Jones, Jana A. .... Decatur, TX
Jones, Jane Baxter .... Mount Vernon, MO
Jones, Janet Boeth .... San Francisco, CA
Jones, Janet K. .... Silver Spring, MD
Jones, Janet L. .... Austin, TX
Jones, Janette Krutzfeldt .... Miles City, MT
Jones, Janine L. .... Washington, DC
Jones, Jas. D. .... Chatham, VA
Jones, Jas. K. .... Tulsa, OK
Jones, Jas. P. .... Dayton, OH
Jones, Jason Z. .... Miami, FL
Jones, Jay D. .... Duncan, OK
Jones, Jean Engstrom .... St. Louis, MO
Jones, Jean M. .... Akron, OH
Jones, Jean Marie .... Washington, DC
Jones, Jean Paul .... Alamosa, CO
Jones, Jeannine Padula .... White Plains, NY
Jones, Jeff Douglas .... Denver, CO
Jones, Jeff L. .... Fort Worth, TX
Jones, Jeff M. .... Houston, TX
Jones, Jeffery D. .... Austin, TX
Jones, Jeffery P. .... West Palm Beach, FL
Jones, Jeffery R. .... Farmington Hills, MI
Jones, Jeffery R., P.C., Law Office of
Farmington Hills, MI
Jones, Jeffrey .... Memphis, TN
Jones, Jeffrey A. .... Coeur d'Alene, ID
Jones, Jeffrey A. .... Chicago, IL
Orland Park, IL
Jones, Jeffrey A. .... Kenner, LA
Jones, Jeffrey B. .... Lubbock, TX
Jones, Jeffrey Bernard .... Orlando, FL
Jones, Jeffrey Brian .... Baltimore, MD
Jones, Jeffrey C. .... Seattle, WA
Jones, Jeffrey D. .... Tallahassee, FL
Jones, Jeffrey D. .... Concord, NC
Jones, Jeffrey E. .... Santa Fe, NM
Jones, Jeffrey F. .... Boston, MA
Jones, Jeffrey G. .... Cookeville, TN
Knoxville, TN
Jones, Jeffrey J. .... Columbus, OH
Jones, Jeffrey J. .... Milwaukee, WI
Jones, Jeffrey L. .... Dandridge, TN
Jones, Jeffrey M. .... Cameron Park, CA
Sacramento, CA
Jones, Jeffrey M. .... Salem, OR
Jones, Jeffrey M. .... Salt Lake City, UT
Jones, Jeffrey M., P.C., Law Office of
Sacramento, CA
Jones, Jeffrey P. .... Palo Alto, CA
Jones, Jeffrey P. .... Atlanta, GA
Jones, Jeffrey R. .... New York, NY
Jones, Jeffrey S. .... Greenville, SC
Jones, Jeffrey T. .... Charleston, WV
Jones, Jeffrey T. .... Wausau, WI
Jones, Jeffrey W. .... Topeka, KS
Jones, Jeffrey W. .... Danville, KY
Jones, Jeffrey W. .... Ellsworth, ME
Jones, Jeffrey W. .... Scarborough, ME
Jones, Jeffrey W. .... San Antonio, TX
Jones, Jeffrey W., Law Office of
San Antonio, TX
Jones, Jeffry R. .... Sacramento, CA
Jones, Jenifer L. .... Dallas, TX
Jones, Jeniver Jas. .... Gassaway, WV
Jones, Jennifer A. .... Charlotte, NC
Jones, Jennifer Elaine .... Danville, IN
Jones, Jennifer L. .... Birmingham, AL
Jones, Jennifer L. .... Santa Rosa, CA
Jones, Jennifer L. .... Wichita, KS
Jones, Jennifer L. .... Jamaica, NY
Jones, Jennifer L. .... New York, NY
Jones, Jennifer L. .... Rochester, NY
Jones, Jennings B., Jr. .... Cameron, LA
Jones, Jerald E. .... Clarksburg, WV
Jones, Jerald N. .... Shreveport, LA
Jones, Jeri L. .... Tulsa, OK
Jones, Jerilyn Satterfield .... San Diego, CA
Jones, Jerome E. .... Wichita, KS
Jones, Jerome P., Jr.
Department of Transportation, Federal Aviation Administration, GV
Jones, Jerrauld C. .... Norfolk, VA
Jones, Jerry D. .... Fresno, CA
Jones, Jerry D. .... Chicago, IL
Jones, Jerry D. .... Oklahoma City, OK
Jones, Jerry Frank .... Austin, TX
Jones, Jerry Frank, P.C. .... Austin, TX
Bastrop, TX
Jones, Jerry G. .... Cameron, LA

Jones, Jerry L. .... Cheyenne, WY
Jones, Jerry N., (P.C.) .... Denver, CO
Jones, Jerry P. .... Dallas, TX
Jones, Jerry S. .... Johnson City, TN
Jones, Jerry W. .... Indianapolis, IN
Jones, Jerry W. .... Carrollton, TX
Jones, Jesse C. .... Miami, FL
Jones, Jessica Sanders .... Richmond, VA
Jones, Jetta N. .... Chicago, IL
Jones, Jim .... Sallisaw, OK
Jones, Jim .... Miller, SD
Jones, Jim, & Associates .... Boise, ID
Jones, Jim C. .... Evergreen, CO
Jones, Jimmie B. .... Brawley, CA
Jones, J. K. .... Houston, TX
Jones, Joann Gallagher .... Atlanta, GA
Jones, Joaquin Ann .... Mason City, IA
Jones, Jocelyn Baker .... Boston, MA
Jones, Jodee Favre .... Belleville, IL
Jones, Jodie .... San Francisco, CA
Jones, John A. .... Clementon, NJ
Jones, John A. .... Corpus Christi, TX
Jones, John Alan .... Raleigh, NC
Jones, John Alan .... Miamisburg, OH
Jones, John Arthur .... Tampa, FL
Jones, John B. .... Sioux Falls, SD
Jones, John B., Jr. .... Washington, DC
Jones, John B., Jr. .... Charlottesville, VA
Jones, John Ben .... Lanett, AL
Jones, John C. .... Atlanta, GA
Jones, John C. .... Oakdale, LA
Jones, John C. .... Grand Rapids, MI
Jones, John C. .... Kansas City, MO
Jones, John Colin .... Chicago, IL
Jones, John D. .... Las Vegas, NV
Jones, John D., III .... San Francisco, CA
Jones, John David .... Phenix City, AL
Jones, John David .... Atlanta, GA
Jones, John E. .... Binghamton, NY
Jones, John E., III .... Pottsville, PA
Reading, PA
Jones, John Edward .... Casselberry, FL
Mount Dora, FL
Jones, John Edward, P.A. .... Casselberry, FL
Mount Dora, FL
Jones, John F. .... Cuyahoga Falls, OH
Jones, John F., II .... Newton, KS
Jones, John Fletcher, Jr. .... Andalusia, AL
Jones, John Frederick .... Denver, CO
Jones, John Griffin .... Jackson, MS
Jones, John H. .... Gainesville, FL
Jones, John H., Jr. .... Wausau, WI
Jones, John Harris .... Pine Bluff, AR
Jones, John J. .... Atlanta, GA
Jones, John J. .... Hightstown, NJ
Jones, John J. J. .... Hauppauge, NY
Jones, John M. .... Rancho Cucamonga, CA
Jones, John M. .... Jacksonville, FL
Jones, John M." Jack " .... Olympia, WA
Jones, John Marshall .... Memphis, TN
Jones, John Martin, Jr. .... Baltimore, MD
Jones, John P. .... Denver, CO
Jones, John P. .... Richmond, VA
Jones, John Paul .... Cartersville, GA
Jones, John Paul .... Memphis, TN
Jones, John Paul, II .... Monticello, KY
Jones, John Paul, Jr. .... Satellite Beach, FL
Jones, John Paul, Jr. .... Indianapolis, IN
Jones, John R. .... Westland, MI
Jones, John R. .... El Paso, TX
Jones, John R. .... Houston, TX
Jones, John R., Jr. .... Atlanta, GA
Jones, John R., Jr. .... Seattle, WA
Jones, John R., P.C. .... Houston, TX
Jones, John S. .... Dublin, OH
Jones, John Sills .... Naples, FL
Jones, John T. .... Billings, MT
Jones, John T., Jr. .... Phoenix, AZ
Jones, John T., Jr. .... Austin, TX
Jones, John V. .... Houston, TX
Jones, John W.
Securities and Exchange Commission,
Division of Corporation Finance, GV
Jones, John W. .... Sterling, IL
Jones, John W. .... Bridgeton, NJ
Jones, John W. .... Gallatin, TN
Jones, John W., Jr. .... Philadelphia, PA
Jones, John Wilson .... Houston, TX
Jones, John Wright .... Savannah, GA
Jones, John Z.
Department Of Veterans Affairs,
Board of Veterans Appeals, GV
Jones, Johnnie A., III .... Albuquerque, NM
Jones, Johnnie A., Jr. .... Baton Rouge, LA
Jones, Jollene M. .... New Orleans, LA
Jones, Jon E., Law Office of
Cookeville, TN
Jones, Jon Stephen .... Lyndon, KS
Jones, Jonathan E. .... Greenville, NC
Jones, Jonathan E. .... Pittsburgh, PA
Jones, Jonathan H. .... Lawrence, KS
Jones, Jonathan L. .... Hickory, NC
Jones, Jonathan P. .... South San Francisco, CA
Jones, Jonathon W. .... Fresno, CA
Jones & Jones .... Brawley, CA
Jones and Jones .... Glendale, CA
Monterey, CA
Jones and Jones .... Naples, FL
Jones & Jones .... Albany, GA
Jones & Jones .... Boise, ID
Jones & Jones .... Chicago, IL
Orland Park, IL
Jones and Jones .... Topeka, KS
Jones and Jones .... Hackensack, NJ
Jones & Jones .... Garden City, NY
Mineola, NY
Jones & Jones .... Richmond, VA
Jones & Jones, Inc., A Professional Corporation .... Marshall, TX
Jones, Jones & Jones, P.A. .... Gulfport, MS
Jones and Jones Law Offices, P.C. .... Paris, IL
Jones, Jones & Lushbaugh, PLC
Fayetteville, AR
Jones & Jones, P.C. .... Newport News, VA
Smithfield, VA
Jones and Jones, P.L.L.C. .... Dunn, NC
Jones, Jones, Vines & Hunkins
Wheatland, WY
Jones, Joni J. .... Salt Lake City, UT
Jones, Jordan Trent .... Palo Alto, CA
Jones, Joseph .... Decatur, GA
Jones, Joseph B. .... Boise, ID
Jones, Joseph C. .... Miami, FL
Jones, Joseph E. .... Omaha, NE
Jones, Joseph H. .... Pottsville, PA
Jones, Joseph H., Jr. .... Pottsville, PA
Jones, Joseph Henry, Jr. .... Ellicott City, MD
Jones, Joseph, Jr. .... Atlanta, GA
Jones, Joseph, Jr., P.C. .... Atlanta, GA
Jones, Joseph M. .... Los Angeles, CA
Jones, Joseph P., Jr. .... Mobile, AL
Jones, Joseph W., Jr. .... Greenville, GA
Jones, Josetta I. .... Department of Commerce,
Patent and Trademark Office, GV
Jones, Joy Anita .... Vista, CA
Jones, Joyce H. .... San Francisco, CA
Jones, Judith A. .... Birmingham, AL
Jones, Judith A. .... Calistoga, CA
Jones, Judith A. .... Hiawatha, KS
Jones, Judith H. .... Hartford, CT
Jones, Judith K. .... Lexington, KY
Jones, Judith M. .... Wilmington, DE
Jones, Judson D. .... Minneapolis, MN
Jones, Julia Elizabeth .... Dallas, TX
Jones, Julie .... Myrtle Creek, OR
Jones, Julie .... Janesville, WI
Jones, Julie A. .... San Diego, CA
Jones, Julie A. .... Walnut Creek, CA
Jones, Julie C. .... Boston, MA
Jones, Julie Haggerty .... Boston, MA
Jones, Julie L. .... Pensacola, FL
Jones, Julie N. .... Nashville, TN
Jones, Julie R. .... St. Louis, MO
Jones, Juliet Wehr .... Seattle, WA
Jones, J. W. .... Shreveport, LA
Jones, K. Nicholle .... Oklahoma City, OK
Jones, Ka'imi Lani .... St. Petersburg, FL
Jones, Kalin .... Atlanta, GA
Jones, Kaplin S., P.C. .... Grand Rapids, MI
Jones, Kara L. .... Carbondale, IL
Jones, Karen Berg .... Abilene, TX
Jones, Karen E. .... Portland, OR
Jones, Karen F. .... Seattle, WA
Jones, Karen L. .... Greenbrae, CA
Jones, Karen Leslie .... Bel Air, MD
Jones, Karen Lynn .... Tampa, FL
Jones, Karen R. .... Boston, MA
Jones, Karen Samuels .... Denver, CO
Jones, Karl D. .... Vinita, OK
Jones, Katharine Vanost .... Evansville, IN
Jones, Katherine A. .... Minneapolis, MN
Jones, Katherine A. .... Charleston, WV
Jones, Katherine Cobb .... Terre Haute, IN
Jones, Katherine E. .... New York, NY
Jones, Katherine Gaertner
St. Augustine, FL
Jones, Katherine Howe .... Norfolk, VA
Jones, Katherine Mason .... Washington, DC
Jones, Kathleen B. .... San Francisco, CA
Jones, Kathleen H. .... Charleston, WV
Jones, Kathryn A. .... New York, NY
Jones, Kathryn C. .... Kenosha, WI
Jones, Kathy Dunston .... Mobile, AL
Jones, Kaufman & Ackerman LLP
Los Angeles, CA
Jones, Kay Bender .... San Rafael, CA
Jones, Kay R. .... Burley, ID
Jones, Kay R. .... San Antonio, TX
Jones, Keith A. .... San Diego, CA
Jones, Keith A. .... Houston, TX
Jones, Keith A. .... Charleston, WV
Jones, Keith Allen .... Tulsa, OK
Jones, Keith C. .... Portland, ME
Jones, Keith D. .... Baton Rouge, LA
Jones, Keith J. .... Philadelphia, PA
Jones, Keith N. .... Portland, OR
Jones, Keith O. .... Eau Claire, WI
Jones, Keith P. .... Princeton, NJ
Jones, Keith R. .... Amarillo, TX
Jones, Keith S. .... Huntsville, AL
Jones & Keller, A Professional Corporation
Denver, CO
Jones, Kelly G. .... Chicago, IL
Jones, Kelly Margaret .... Rocky Mount, NC
Jones, Keltie Elizabeth .... Davis, CA
Jones, Kelvin D., III .... Nashville, TN
Jones, Ken P. .... Salt Lake City, UT
Jones, Kendall B. .... Fort Smith, AR
Jones, Kendor P. .... Denver, CO
Jones, Kenneth .... Little Rock, AR
Jones, Kenneth A. .... Wilmington, DE
Jones, Kenneth A. .... Fort Myers, FL
Jones, Kenneth B., Jr. .... South St. Paul, MN
Jones, Kenneth C. .... Orange, CA
Jones, Kenneth C. .... San Diego, CA
Jones, Kenneth C. .... Olathe, KS
Jones, Kenneth C. .... St. Louis, MO
Jones, Kenneth D. .... Wilkes-Barre, PA
Jones, Kenneth D., Jr. .... Mansfield, OH
Jones, Kenneth E. .... Detroit, MI
Farmington Hills, MI
Jones, Kenneth E. .... Grandview, MO
Oak Grove, MO
Jones, Kenneth F. .... Houston, TX
Jones, Kenneth G. .... Walnut Creek, CA
Jones, Kenneth I. .... San Francisco, CA
Jones, Kenneth I., Jr.
Oklahoma City, OK
Jones, Kenneth L. .... Chicago, IL
Jones, Kenneth L. .... Gulfport, MS
Jones, Kenneth L. .... Greensboro, NC
Jones, Kenneth M. .... Los Angeles, CA
Jones, Kenneth M. .... Plantation, FL
Jones, Kenneth N. .... Austin, TX
Jones, Kenneth P. .... Memphis, TN
Jones, Kenneth R. .... Georgiana, AL
Jones, Kenneth R., Jr. .... Nashville, TN
Jones, Kenneth W. .... San Francisco, CA
Jones, Kenneth W., Jr. .... Lafayette, LA
Jones, Kennis T. .... Sherman Oaks, CA
Jones, Kent C. .... Milwaukee, WI
Jones, Kent Davis .... Charlotte, NC
Jones, Kent L. .... Department of Justice,
Office of the Solicitor General, GV
Jones, Kenton D. .... Prescott, AZ
Jones, Kenyette C. .... San Francisco, CA
Jones, Kerr & Buck .... Sacramento, CA
Jones, Kerry Lynne .... Indianapolis, IN
Jones, Kevin A. .... Mineola, NY
Jones, Kevin C. .... Austin, MN
Jones, Kevin C. .... Pittsburgh, PA
Jones, Kevin Darrow .... Washington, DC
Jones, Kevin K. .... Orlando, FL
Jones, Kevin L. .... Salt Lake City, UT
Jones, Kevin P. .... Boston, MA
Jones, Kevin P. .... Cincinnati, OH
Jones, Kevin R. .... Department of Justice,
Office of Policy Development, GV
Jones, Kevin Richard .... St. Louis, MO
Jones, Kevin S. .... Missoula, MT
Jones, Kevin S. .... Fredericksburg, VA
Jones, Kevin W. .... Richmond, VA
Jones, Key, Melvin & Patton, P.A.
Franklin, NC
Highlands, NC
Jones, Kierith Anne .... New York, NY
Jones, Kim Cooper .... Chalmette, LA
Jones, Kimberley A. .... Pittsburgh, PA
Jones, Kimberly A. .... Baltimore, MD
Jones, Kimberly A. .... Kansas City, MO
Jones, Kimberly D. .... Library of Congress,
Congressional Research Service, GV
Jones, Kimberly G. .... Greenville, MS
Jones, Kimya I.
Office of Personnel Management,
Merit Systems Division, GV
Jones, Kindanne C. .... Oklahoma City, OK
Jones, King & Downs, P.C. .... Bristol, TN
Bristol, VA
Jones, Kirk Whitaker .... Great Barrington, MA
Jones, Knovack G. .... Hialeah, FL
Jones, Knox .... McAllen, TX
Jones, Korum, Waltrip & Jones
St. Louis, MO
Jones, K. P. .... Fort Lauderdale, FL
Jones, Kurt L. .... Farmington Hills, MI
Jones, Kurt N. .... Indianapolis, IN
Jones Kurth & Andrews, P.C.
San Antonio, TX
Victoria, TX
Jones, Kyle A. .... Indianapolis, IN
Jones, Kyle C. .... Salt Lake City, UT
Jones, Kyle M. .... Austin, TX
Jones, Kyle M. H. .... Detroit, MI
Jones, Kyle W. .... Salt Lake City, UT
Jones, L. Charles .... Yuma, AZ
Jones, L. Earl .... Albany, GA
Jones, L. Kelly .... Arlington, TX
Jones, L. Mitchell .... Mapleton, UT
Jones, L. Ray .... Medina, OH
Jones, Laird R. .... Savannah, GA
Jones, Lamar .... Kinston, NC
Jones, Lamar, P.A. .... Kinston, NC
Jones, Lamont .... Los Angeles, CA
Jones, Lamont .... Pocatello, ID
Jones, Lana Kay .... Library of Congress,
Office of the General Counsel, GV
Jones, Lance T. .... Springfield, IL
Jones, Lark W. .... North Augusta, SC
Jones, Larry B. .... Paris, IL
Jones, Larry C. .... Charlotte, NC
Jones, Larry E. .... Dallas, TX
Jones, Larry E. .... Logan, UT
Jones, Larry Elliot .... West Grove, PA
Jones, Larry J. .... Fairfax, VA
Jones, Larry M. .... Springfield, IL
Jones, Larry P. .... Duluth, GA
Jones, Larry W. .... Missoula, MT
Jones, Laura Davis .... Wilmington, DE
Jones, Laura F. .... Houston, TX
Jones, Laura H. .... Washington, DC
Jones, Laura Jeanne .... Fairview Heights, IL
Jones, Laura Semonche .... Atlanta, GA
Jones, Lauren E. .... Providence, RI
Jones, Lauren W. .... Houston, TX
Jones, Laurence B. .... New York, NY
Jones, Laurence C., Jr. .... Norwalk, CT
Jones, Laurie K. .... Los Angeles, CA
Jones, Laurie Walker
Oklahoma City, OK
Jones, Lavelle Z. .... Plainfield, NJ
Jones, Lavon L. .... Beaumont, TX
Jones Law Firm .... Cameron, LA
Jones Law Firm .... Jackson, MS
Jones Law Firm, The, P.C.
Albuquerque, NM
Jones Law Office .... Bristow, OK
Jones, Lawrence A. .... Sacramento, CA
Jones, Lawrence C. .... Santa Monica, CA
Jones, Lawrence F. .... Athens, GA
Jones, Lawrence H. .... San Francisco, CA
Jones, Lawrence L. .... Gulf Shores, AL
Jones, Lawrence L., III .... Louisville, KY
Jones, Lawrence Lea .... Gulf Shores, AL
Jones, Lawrence R. .... Toms River, NJ
Jones, Lawrence R., Jr. .... Dallas, TX
Jones, Lawrence S. .... Atlantic, IA
Jones, Lawrence T. .... Garden City, NY
Jones, LeDetra Crigler .... Wichita, KS
Jones, Lee Ann T. .... San Antonio, TX
Jones, Lee Dameron .... Memphis, TN
Jones, LeeAnn .... Atlanta, GA
Jones, Leigh A. Lockridge .... Atlanta, GA
Jones, Leland B. .... Aurora, NE
Jones, Leland H., III .... Greenwood, MS
Jones, Leland M. .... Phoenix, AZ
Jones & Lemon .... Geneva, IL
Jones, Lendsey .... New York, NY
Jones, Lendy Leggett .... Dallas, TX
Jones, Leo C., III .... Panama City, FL
Jones, Leo Paul .... Los Angeles, CA
Jones, Leon H. .... Punta Gorda, FL
Tampa, FL
Jones, Leon S. .... Atlanta, GA
Jones, Leonade D. .... Washington, DC
Jones, Leonard W. .... Brooklyn, NY
Jones, Les .... Memphis, TN
Jones, Leslie Ann .... Chicago, IL
Jones, Leslie E. .... New York, NY
Jones, Leslie R. .... Brea, CA
Jones, Leslie R. .... Atlanta, GA
Jones, Leslie T., Jr. .... Phoenix, AZ
Jones, Leslie Terry .... Las Vegas, NV
Reno, NV
Jones, Leslye E. .... Chicago, IL
Jones, Lester L. .... Los Angeles, CA
Jones, Lewis A. .... Austin, TX
Jones, Lewis B. .... Atlanta, GA
Jones, Lewis D. .... Fayetteville, AR
Jones, Lewis D. .... Fort Thomas, KY
Jones, Lewis N. .... Atlanta, GA
Jones, Ligon L. .... Hopewell, VA
Jones, Lincoln H. .... Lexington, KY
Jones, Linda B. .... Boise, ID
Jones, Linda H. .... Baltimore, MD
Jones, Linda H. .... Asheville, NC
Jones, Linda M. .... Salt Lake City, UT
Jones, Linda R. .... San Francisco, CA
Jones, Lindley H. .... Los Angeles, CA
Jones, Lindsey F. .... New York, NY
Jones, Lindy D. .... Dallas, TX
Jones, Linley .... Atlanta, GA
Jones, Linwood L. .... Raleigh, NC
Jones, Linzey D. .... Chicago, IL
Jones, Linzey D., Jr. .... Chicago, IL
Jones, Lisa A. .... Salt Lake City, UT
Jones, Lisa E. .... Department of Justice,
Environment and Natural Resources
Division, GV
Jones, Lisa G. .... Louisville, KY
Jones, Lisa Henley .... Houston, TX
Jones, Lisa Michelle .... Washington, DC
Jones, Lisbeth A. .... Vineyard Haven, MA
Jones, Lloyd R. .... Salt Lake City, UT
Jones, Loel Anne .... Santa Ana, CA
Jones, Longmire & Sindle
Hendersonville, TN
Jones, Lorelle M. .... Greenville, NC
Jones, Loren D. .... Chicago, IL
Jones, Lori B. .... Tucson, AZ
Jones, Lori Elizabeth .... Roanoke, VA
Jones, Lori Lapin .... New York, NY
Jones, Lori Polin .... Department of Agriculture,
Office of the General Counsel, GV
Jones, Lori W. .... St. Louis, MO
Jones, Loring S., III .... Birmingham, AL
Jones, Lorri W. .... Washington, DC
Jones, Lou H. .... Dallas, TX
Jones, Louis M. .... New Orleans, LA
Jones, Louis R. .... Brownfield, TX
Jones, Louis R. .... Milwaukee, WI
Jones, Louise A. D. .... West Palm Beach, FL
Jones, Loyd N. .... Tyler, TX
Jones, Lucian C. .... New York, NY
Jones, Luther .... Dallas, TX
Jones, Luther E. .... El Paso, TX
Jones, Luther E., Jr. .... Corpus Christi, TX
Jones, L.W. (Bill), III .... Haskell, TX
Jones, Lydia A. .... Phoenix, AZ
Jones, Lyman L., Jr. .... New Orleans, LA
Jones, Lynda F. .... Nashville, TN
Jones, Lynne E. .... West Palm Beach, FL
Jones, Lynne K. .... Reno, NV
Jones, Lynne Thompson .... Escondido, CA
Jones, M. Geoffrey G. .... Everett, WA
Jones, M. Kevin .... Tallahassee, FL
Jones, M. Randall .... Houston, TX
Jones, M. Samuel, III .... Little Rock, AR
Jones, M. Scott .... Houston, TX
Jones, Mack T. .... Phoenix, AZ
Jones, Madden & Grosso .... Stuart, FL
Jones, Madison R., Law Offices of
Houston, TX
Jones & Magary .... Dallas, TX
Jones, Mahoney, Brayton & Soll
Claremont, CA
Los Angeles, CA
Pomona, CA
San Bernardino, CA
Jones & Makau .... Brooklyn, NY
Jones, Malachi B., Jr. .... Washington, DC
Jones, Mandy .... Washington, DC
Jones, Marc A. .... Los Angeles, CA
Jones, Marcia G. .... Washington, DC
Jones, Marcus A., III .... Birmingham, AL
Jones, Margaret Anne .... Manhattan Beach, CA
Jones, Margaret B. .... Downers Grove, IL
Jones, Margaret F. .... Washington, DC
Jones, Margaret Sullivan .... Anchorage, AK
Jones, Margot Webster .... Denver, CO
Jones, Maria Baguer .... Boston, MA

Jones, Maria O'Toole ... Washington, DC
Jones, Maria T. ... New York, NY
Jones, Marianne E. ... Seattle, WA
Jones, Marie J. ... Atlantic City, NJ
Jones, Marie Millie ... Pittsburgh, PA
Jones, Marilyn ... Federal Communications Commission, Common Carrier Bureau, GV
Jones, Mark ... Los Angeles, CA
Jones, Mark A. ... Sacramento, CA
Jones, Mark A. ... Chicago, IL
Jones, Mark A. ... Burlington, NC
Jones, Mark A. ... San Antonio, TX
Jones, Mark A. ... Sugar Land, TX
Jones, Mark Alan ... Bakersfield, CA
Jones, Mark Alexander ... West Palm Beach, FL
Jones, Mark C. ... Flint, MI
Jones, Mark E. ... Kansas City, MO
Jones, Mark E., Jr. ... Chicago, IL
Jones, Mark E., Law Offices ... Batesville, IN
Jones, Mark H. ... Key West, FL
Jones, Mark J. ... Loogootee, IN
Jones, Mark K. ... Winsted, CT
Jones, Mark L. ... Fort Worth, TX
Jones, Mark M. ... Washington, DC
Jones, Mark M. ... Las Vegas, NV
Jones, Mark S. ... Walnut Creek, CA
Jones, Mark S. ... Kansas City, MO
Jones, Marla D. ... Fort Worth, TX
Jones, Marlen & Silvermintz ... Belleville, IL
Jones, Marlene Butcher ... South Pasadena, CA
Jones, Marquis D., Jr. ... Newark, NJ
Jones, Marshall R. ... Treasury Department, Internal Revenue Service, GV
Jones, Martha A. ... San Diego, CA
Jones, Martin J. ... St. Petersburg, FL
Jones, Martin J. ... New York, NY
Jones, Martin T. ... Seattle, WA
Jones, Marvin ... Dallas, TX
Jones, Marvin C. ... Walterboro, SC
Jones, Marvin W. ... Amarillo, TX
Jones, Mary A. ... New Haven, CT
Jones, Mary A. ... West Chester, PA
Jones, Mary Ellen ... Orlando, FL
Jones, Mary G. ... Washington, DC
Jones, Mary K. ... Santa Monica, CA
Jones, Mary Lou ... Dallas, TX
Jones, Mary N. Whigham ... Department of Transportation, Federal Aviation Administration, GV
Jones, Mary S. ... Washington, DC
Jones, Mary Taormina ... Nashville, TN
Jones, Mary Ulmer ... Atlanta, GA
Jones, Mary Virginia ... Brunswick, GA
Jones, Marzy ... Costa Mesa, CA
Jones & Matson ... Pasadena, CA
Jones, Matt ... Lafayette, LA
Jones, Matthew C. ... Philadelphia, PA
Jones, Matthew D. ... Boston, MA
Jones, Matthew Hunter ... New Albany, IN
Jones, Matthew J. ... Washington, DC
Jones, Matthew J. ... Saratoga Springs, NY
Jones, Matthew Joseph ... Carle Place, NY
Jones, Matthew L. ... Miami, FL
Jones, Matthew L. ... Stuart, FL
Jones, Matthew Lee ... Weslaco, TX
Jones, Matthew P. ... Peoria, IL
Jones, Matthew S. ... San Antonio, TX
Jones, Matthew T. ... Fort Lauderdale, FL
Jones, Maureen ... New Port Richey, FL
Jones, Maureen S. ... Boston, MA
Jones, Maurice Antonia ... Treasury Department, Community Development Financial Institutions, GV
Jones, Maurice D. ... Milwaukee, WI
Jones, Max K., Jr. ... New Orleans, LA
Jones, Maxine M. ... Houston, TX
Jones, McGlasson & Benckart, P.C. ... Bloomington, IN
Jones, Meg L. ... Louisville, KY
Jones, Melanie Grant ... Castro Valley, CA
Jones, Melanie Newkome ... Baton Rouge, LA
Jones, Melanie S. ... New York, NY
Jones, Melissa Ann ... Columbia, SC
Jones, Melody A. ... Cincinnati, OH
Jones, Melonie Davis ... Kansas City, MO
Jones, Melvin H. ... Atlanta, GA
Jones, Meredith B. ... New York, NY
Jones, Merrill G., II ... Greenville, NC; New Bern, NC
Jones, Michael ... Pensacola, FL
Jones, Michael A. ... Niceville, FL
Jones, Michael A. ... Kennesaw, GA
Jones, Michael A. ... Springfield, MO
Jones, Michael A. ... Wilmington, NC
Jones, Michael A., P.A. ... Niceville, FL
Jones, Michael Alan ... Akron, OH
Jones, Michael B. ... Anaheim, CA
Jones, Michael B. ... Buffalo, NY
Jones, Michael B. ... Aliquippa, PA
Jones, Michael Barrett ... Dallas, TX
Jones, Michael C. ... Phoenix, AZ
Jones, Michael C. ... Paulding, OH
Jones, Michael D. ... Washington, DC
Jones, Michael D. ... Winter Springs, FL
Jones, Michael D. ... Omaha, NE
Jones, Michael D. ... Cherry Hill, NJ; Philadelphia, PA
Jones, Michael D. ... Corvallis, OR
Jones, Michael D. ... Portland, OR
Jones, Michael D. ... Charleston, SC
Jones, Michael D. ... Houston, TX
Jones, Michael E. ... Luverne, AL
Jones, Michael E. ... San Diego, CA
Jones, Michael E. ... Salem, NH
Jones, Michael E. ... Hackensack, NJ
Jones, Michael E. ... New York, NY
Jones, Michael E. ... Tyler, TX
Jones, Michael F. ... Texarkana, TX
Jones, Michael F., P.C. ... Salt Lake City, UT
Jones, Michael Floyd ... Little Rock, AR
Jones, Michael G. ... Sacramento, CA
Jones, Michael G. ... Washington, DC
Jones, Michael G. ... Wichita, KS
Jones, Michael G., (P.C.) ... Boston, MA; Manchester, NH
Jones, Michael Garrison ... Leavenworth, KS
Jones, Michael J. ... Los Gatos, CA
Jones, Michael J. ... Greenwich, CT
Jones, Michael J. ... Parsippany, NJ
Jones, Michael J. ... Oconomowoc, WI
Jones, Michael K. ... Sherman Oaks, CA
Jones, Michael K. ... Philadelphia, PA
Jones, Michael L. ... Redding, CA
Jones, Michael L. ... Wichita, KS
Jones, Michael L. ... Dallas, TX
Jones, Michael L. ... Houston, TX
Jones, Michael L., Jr. ... Andalusia, AL
Jones, Michael M. ... Goldsboro, NC
Jones, Michael R. ... Mountainburg, AR
Jones, Michael R. ... Boise, ID
Jones, Michael R. ... Centralia, IL
Jones, Michael R. ... Springfield, TN
Jones, Michael S. ... Des Moines, IA
Jones, Michael S. ... Kansas City, MO
Jones, Michael S. ... Cincinnati, OH
Jones, Michael S. ... Toledo, OH
Jones, Michael T. ... Florence, AL
Jones, Michael T. ... Milwaukee, WI
Jones, Michael W. ... Sacramento, CA
Jones, Michael W. ... Denver, CO
Jones, Michael W. ... Boca Raton, FL
Jones, Michael W. ... Fort Lauderdale, FL
Jones, Michael W. ... Gainesville, FL
Jones, Michael W. ... Topeka, KS
Jones, Michael W. ... Huntingdon Valley, PA
Jones, Michael W. ... Dallas, TX
Jones, Michael W., P.A. ... Gainesville, FL
Jones, Michael Wall ... Winter Park, FL
Jones, Michaelyn ... Irvine, CA
Jones, Michelle A. ... Washington, DC
Jones, Michelle A. ... Pottsville, PA
Jones, Michelle E. ... Washington, DC
Jones, Michelle Morris ... Winchester, VA
Jones, Michelle Underwood ... Denton, TX
Jones, Michelle Y. ... Nashville, TN
Jones, Mickey K. ... Oklahoma City, OK
Jones, Mikel D. ... West Palm Beach, FL
Jones, Milton ... Columbus, GA
Jones, Milton D. ... Clearwater, FL
Jones, Milton R. ... Timonium, MD
Jones, Milton T. ... Portland, OR
Jones, Milton Van ... Los Angeles, CA
Jones, Miranda B. ... Baltimore, MD
Jones, Miriam Hellen ... Washington, DC
Jones, Mitchell & Burch, L.L.C. ... Shreveport, LA
Jones, Mitchell E. ... Chicago, IL
Jones, Mohamedu Fahnbulleh ... Washington, DC
Jones, Molly Cassaro ... Louisville, KY
Jones, Montgomery B. ... St. Louis, MO
Jones, Morgan L., Jr. ... Lockport, NY
Jones, Morgan R. ... Philadelphia, PA
Jones, Morgan T., III ... Sacramento, CA
Jones, Morris B. ... Compton, CA
Jones, Morrison & Womack, P.C. ... Atlanta, GA
Jones & Muise, L.L.P. ... Duluth, GA
Jones, Nancy E. ... Troy, NY
Jones, Nancy Hanania ... Tulsa, OK
Jones, Nancy K. ... West Des Moines, IA
Jones, Nancy K. ... Minneapolis, MN
Jones, Nancy L. ... Library of Congress, Congressional Research Service, GV
Jones, Nancy M. ... San Diego, CA
Jones, Nancy Platt ... New York, NY
Jones, Nancy R. ... San Diego, CA
Jones, Nancy S. ... Tuscaloosa, AL
Jones, Nancy S. ... Nashville, TN
Jones, Nancye Rogers ... DeLand, FL
Jones, Napoleon A., Jr. ... San Diego, CA
Jones, Nathan E. ... San Diego, CA
Jones, Nathan F. ... New York, NY
Jones, Nathan W. ... Salt Lake City, UT
Jones, Nathaniel ... New York, NY
Jones, Nathaniel E., Jr. ... Baltimore, MD
Jones, Nathaniel R. ... Cincinnati, OH
Jones, Neal T." Buddy " ... Austin, TX
Jones, Neil C. ... Greenville, SC
Jones, Nell H. ... Norcross, GA
Jones, Nelson, Ford & Screeton ... Santa Ana, CA; Sherman Oaks, CA
Jones, Nelson L. ... Greenwood, SC
Jones, Nelson M., III ... Houston, TX
Jones, Newton J. ... Dallas, TX
Jones, Newton T. ... Seattle, WA
Jones, Nicholas W. ... Delaware, OH
Jones, Nicholas W., Co., L.P.A. ... Delaware, OH
Jones, Nicole S. ... New York, NY
Jones, Nik ... Tulsa, OK
Jones, Nikola Lyn ... Portland, OR
Jones and Nix ... Jackson, MS
Jones, Nolan W ... Lakewood, CO
Jones, Nora A. ... Rochester, NY
Jones, Nora E. ... Columbus, OH
Jones, Norman Lyle, III ... Minneapolis, MN; St. Paul, MN
Jones, Norman P. ... Springfield, IL
Jones, Norman R. ... Houston, TX
Jones, Norman W. ... Washington, DC
Jones, Norpell, List, Miller & Howarth ... Newark, OH
Jones, Norwood E., Jr. ... Coats, NC
Jones, O. Steven ... Baltimore, MD
Jones Obenchain, LLP ... South Bend, IN
Jones, Odom, Spruiell, Davis & Politz, L.L.P. ... Shreveport, LA
Jones, O. F., III, Law Office of ... Victoria, TX
Jones, Olin W. ... San Diego, CA
Jones, Oliver A., (A Law Corp.) ... Oakland, CA
Jones, Oren O. ... Anderson, SC
Jones, Orlo D. ... Walnut Creek, CA
Jones, Orton A. ... Spencer, WV
Jones, Orval Edwin ... Oklahoma City, OK
Jones, Oscar E. ... Batesville, AR
Jones, Oscar E. ... Des Moines, IA
Jones, Osteen, Jones & Arnold ... Atlanta, GA; Hinesville, GA; Savannah, GA
Jones, Othello G., Jr. ... Washington, DC
Jones, Otis L. ... Dunwoody, GA
Jones, Ottesen, Feickert & Derango ... Belleville, IL
Jones, Owen D. ... Tempe, AZ
Jones, P. Amber ... Harrisburg, PA
Jones, P. Andrew ... Greeley, CO
Jones, P. Charles ... Madison, WI
Jones, P. Zeb ... Jackson, MS
Jones, Pamela J. ... Indianapolis, IN
Jones, Pamela M. ... Atlanta, GA
Jones, Pamela R. ... Shreveport, LA
Jones, Pamela S. ... Baltimore, MD
Jones, Pamela Simmons ... Dresden, TN
Jones, Patricia A. ... Indianapolis, IN
Jones, Patricia Gollhardt ... Brookfield, WI
Jones, Patricia Haule ... Houston, TX
Jones, Patricia L. ... Austin, TX
Jones, Patricia P. ... Orlando, FL
Jones, Patrick A. ... Huntsville, AL
Jones, Patrick B., III ... Dothan, AL
Jones, Patrick E. ... Metairie, LA
Jones, Patrick G. ... Atlanta, GA
Jones, Patrick H. ... Honolulu, HI
Jones, Patrick L. ... Columbia, MD
Jones, Patrick R. ... Boston, MA
Jones, Patrick T. ... Boston, MA
Jones, Patrick W. ... New York, NY
Jones, Patterson & Tucker, Professional Corporation ... Columbus, IN
Jones, Paul A. ... Research Triangle Park, NC
Jones, Paul B. ... Kotzebue, AK
Jones, Paul B. ... Minneapolis, MN
Jones, Paul Barry ... Columbia, KY
Jones, Paul D. ... Dallas, TX
Jones, Paul David ... Memphis, TN
Jones, Paul Edward ... Pikeville, KY
Jones, Paul F. ... Buffalo, NY
Jones, Paul F. ... Fort Worth, TX
Jones, Paul J. ... Milwaukee, WI
Jones, Paul J., Jr. ... Easton, MD
Jones, Paul L. ... Kinston, NC
Jones, Paul M. ... Annandale, NJ
Jones, Paul T. ... Fort Worth, TX
Jones, Paul T., Jr. ... Providence, RI
Jones, Paul W. ... Clarinda, IA
Jones, Paula A. ... Austin, TX
Jones, Paula F. ... New York, NY
Jones, Paula S. ... San Rafael, CA
Jones, Peggy A. ... Holly Springs, MS
Jones, Peggy Foley ... Cleveland, OH
Jones, Penfield, Barden & Finegold, A Professional Corporation ... San Diego, CA
Jones, Penny D. ... Dallas, TX
Jones, Penny L. ... Hermitage, PA
Jones, Peter A. ... Syracuse, NY
Jones, Peter B. ... Georgetown, DE
Jones, Peter B. ... Troy, NY
Jones, Peter Best ... Newport Beach, CA
Jones, Peter C. ... Miami, FL
Jones, Peter F. ... Denver, CO
Jones, Peter J. ... Manassas, VA
Jones, Peter Lawson ... Cleveland, OH
Jones, Philemina McNeill ... Department of Justice, Executive Office for Immigration Review, GV
Jones, Philip A. ... Chicago, IL
Jones, Philip C. ... Falls Church, VA
Jones, Philip Clark ... Washington, DC
Jones, Philip G. ... Orem, UT
Jones, Philip K., Jr. ... New Orleans, LA
Jones, Philip N. ... Portland, OR
Jones, Philip T. ... East Weymouth, MA
Jones, Philip Tenley ... McLean, VA
Jones, Phillip B. C. ... Seattle, WA
Jones, Phillip Byron ... Nashville, TN
Jones, Phillip J. ... Port Charlotte, FL
Jones, Phillip M. ... Troy, OH
Jones, Phillip R. ... Dallas, TX
Jones, Phillip Ray ... Dallas, TX
Jones, Phillip W. ... Hillsville, VA
Jones, Phyllis Gene ... St. Paul Park, MN
Jones, Proctor P. ... San Francisco, CA
Jones, Quentin Michael ... Albuquerque, NM
Jones, R. Brandon ... Dover, DE; Rehoboth Beach, DE
Jones, R. Bruce, Jr. ... Lake Worth, FL
Jones, R. David ... Cleburne, TX
Jones, R. Douglas ... Towson, MD
Jones, R. Mark ... Cleveland, OH
Jones, R. Michael ... San Diego, CA
Jones, R. Michael ... Raleigh, NC
Jones, R. Turner ... Greensboro, NC
Jones, Raleigh E. ... Madison, WI
Jones, Ralph A. ... Omaha, NE
Jones, Ralph Cole ... Dallas, TX
Jones, Ralph H., Jr. ... Pocatello, ID
Jones, Ralph L. ... Roanoke, VA
Jones, Ralph M. ... Palm City, FL
Jones, Ralph O. ... Detroit, MI
Jones, Ralph V. ... Avon, NC
Jones, Randal R. ... Seattle, WA
Jones, Randall A. ... Research Triangle Park, NC
Jones, Randall B. ... Seattle, WA
Jones, Randall Lee ... Houston, TX
Jones, Randel A. ... Olympia, WA
Jones, Randle G. ... Fort Worth, TX
Jones, Randolph B. ... Nashville, TN
Jones, Randolph B., Jr. ... Americus, GA
Jones, Randolph F. ... Seattle, WA
Jones, Randolph L., Jr. ... Tulsa, OK
Jones, Randy K. ... San Diego, CA
Jones, Randy S. ... Denver, CO
Jones, Ransom P., III ... Pascagoula, MS
Jones, Ransom P., III, P.A. ... Pascagoula, MS
Jones & Rath ... St. Louis, MO
Jones, Ray D., Jr. ... Kansas City, MO
Jones, Ray E. ... Columbia, SC
Jones, Ray L. ... Oklahoma City, OK
Jones, Ray L., Jr. ... Cordell, OK
Jones, Ray Yeatts ... Newport News, VA
Jones, Raymon G., (P.L.C.) ... New Orleans, LA
Jones, Raymond Dean ... Denver, CO
Jones, Raymond E., Jr. ... Glendale, WI
Jones, R. B. ... Birmingham, AL
Jones, Rebecca A. ... Magnolia, AR
Jones, Rebecca Carnow ... Jacksonville, IL
Jones, Rebecca Gay ... Weslaco, TX
Jones, Rebecca P. ... San Diego, CA
Jones, Rebecca Sue ... Los Gatos, CA
Jones, Reese C. ... Santa Fe, NM
Jones, Regina A. ... Mount Laurel, NJ; Philadelphia, PA
Jones, Regina B. ... Houston, TX
Jones, Reginald E. ... United States Senate, Committee Legal Personnel, GV
Jones, Reginald N. ... Richmond, VA
Jones, Rendle A. ... Camden, ME
Jones, Renée M. ... Boston, MA
Jones, Reuben E. ... Oakland, CA
Jones, Rex K. ... Hattiesburg, MS
Jones, Rex L., III, (Inc.) ... La Jolla, CA
Jones, Rhon E. ... Montgomery, AL
Jones, Rhonda J. Ellis ... Frisco, TX
Jones, Rhonda Yvette ... San Francisco, CA
Jones, Rian W. ... San Diego, CA
Jones, Richard A. ... Oakland, CA
Jones, Richard A. ... San Jose, CA
Jones, Richard A. ... Santa Ana, CA
Jones, Richard A. ... Woodland Hills, CA
Jones, Richard A. ... Atlanta, GA
Jones, Richard A. ... Nashville, TN
Jones, Richard A. ... Seattle, WA
Jones, Richard A., Jr. ... Greenville, SC
Jones, Richard A., (P.C.) ... Troy, MI
Jones, Richard B. ... Newburyport, MA
Jones, Richard B. ... Port Orchard, WA
Jones, Richard C. ... San Francisco, CA
Jones, Richard C. ... Chicago, IL
Jones, Richard C. ... Sumter, SC
Jones, Richard D. ... Brea, CA
Jones, Richard D. ... Overland Park, KS
Jones, Richard D. ... Tulsa, OK
Jones, Richard D. ... Philadelphia, PA
Jones, Richard D. ... Charleston, WV
Jones, Richard E. ... Topeka, KS
Jones, Richard E. ... Raleigh, NC
Jones, Richard F. ... Olympia, WA
Jones, Richard H. ... Washington, DC
Jones, Richard H. ... New York, NY
Jones, Richard Hastings ... Owings Mills, MD
Jones, Richard I. G. ... Wilmington, DE; Kennett Square, PA
Jones, Richard I.G., Jr. ... Wilmington, DE
Jones, Richard J. ... Rosebud, TX
Jones, Richard J., III ... St. Petersburg, FL
Jones, Richard K. ... Jacksonville, FL
Jones, Richard L. ... Birmingham, AL
Jones, Richard L. ... Department of Commerce, Patent and Trademark Office, GV
Jones, Richard L. ... Jackson, MS
Jones, Richard L. ... Petersburg, VA
Jones, Richard L. ... Neenah, WI
Jones, Richard M. ... Los Angeles, CA
Jones, Richard M. ... Denver, CO
Jones, Richard M. ... Naples, FL
Jones, Richard M. ... Merrifield, MN
Jones, Richard M. ... Omaha, NE
Jones, Richard M. ... Columbus, OH
Jones, Richard McCulloch, Jr. ... Aspen, CO
Jones, Richard McCulloch, Jr., P.C. ... Aspen, CO
Jones, Richard O. ... Melbourne, FL
Jones, Richard O., P.A. ... Melbourne, FL
Jones, Richard R. ... Orange City, FL
Jones, Richard R. ... Bel Air, MD
Jones, Richard S., Jr. ... Franklin, NC
Jones, Richard T. ... Gainesville, FL; Ocala, FL
Jones, Richard T. ... Woodstock, IL
Jones, Richard T. ... Austin, TX
Jones, Richard V. ... Florham Park, NJ
Jones, Richard W. ... Atlanta, GA
Jones, Richard W. ... Murray, KY
Jones, Richard W. ... Ogden, UT
Jones, Rickey ... Chicago, IL
Jones, Ricky E. ... Warner Robins, GA
Jones, Rikki L ... Jefferson City, MO
Jones, R. K. Kennon ... Pompano Beach, FL
Jones, Robb M. ... Chevy Chase, MD

Jones, Robert A. ... Lafayette, CA
Walnut Creek, CA
Jones, Robert A. ... Rushville, IL
Jones, Robert A. ... Lebanon, NH
Jones, Robert A. ... Newark, NJ
Jones, Robert A. ... Wayne, NJ
West Milford, NJ
Jones, Robert A., Jr. ... Birmingham, AL
Jones, Robert A., (P.C.) ... Houston, TX
Jones, Robert Alton ... Houston, TX
Jones, Robert B. ... Chicago, IL
Jones, Robert B. ... Omaha, NE
Jones, Robert B. ... Pryor, OK
Jones, Robert B., Jr. ... Raleigh, NC
Jones, Robert C. ... Washington, DC
Jones, Robert C. ... Washington, DC
Jones, Robert C. ... St. Louis, MO
Jones, Robert C ... Salem, OR
Jones, Robert C. ... Pittsburgh, PA
Jones, Robert C. ... San Antonio, TX
Jones, Robert C. ... Milwaukee, WI
Jones, Robert C., Jr. ... Charlotte, NC
Jones, Robert Clive ... Las Vegas, NV
Jones, Robert D. ... Santa Ana, CA
Jones, Robert D. ... Colorado Springs, CO
Jones, Robert D. ... Royal Palm Beach, FL
Jones, Robert D. ... Jonesboro, GA
Jones, Robert D. ... Shelbyville, IN
Jones, Robert D. ... Meridian, MS
Jones, Robert D. ... Austin, TX
Jones, Robert D. ... Chesapeake, VA
Jones, Robert D. ... Milwaukee, WI
Jones, Robert Delano ... Bloomington, IN
Jones, Robert E. ... Atlanta, GA
Jones, Robert E. ... Downers Grove, IL
Jones, Robert E. ... Wheaton, IL
Jones, Robert E. ... Brookhaven, MS
Jones, Robert E. ... Yazoo City, MS
Jones, Robert E. ... St. Louis, MO
Jones, Robert E. ... Las Vegas, NV
Jones, Robert E. ... Cortland, NY
Jones, Robert E. ... Tulsa, OK
Jones, Robert E. ... Portland, OR
Jones, Robert E. ... Houston, TX
Jones, Robert E. (Bob), II ... Lubbock, TX
Jones, Robert E., III ... Florence, AL
Jones, Robert E., III ... Washington, DC
Jones, Robert E., Jr. ... Scottsboro, AL
Jones, Robert E., Jr. ... Phoenix, AZ
Jones, Robert Edward ... Wheaton, IL
Jones, Robert E. P.
Department Of Veterans Affairs,
Board of Veterans Appeals, GV
Jones, Robert Eugene, (P.C.) ... Allen Park, MI
Jones, Robert G. ... Edwardsville, IL
Jones, Robert G. ... Olathe, KS
Jones, Robert G. ... Boston, MA
Jones, Robert G. ... St. Louis, MO
Jones, Robert G. ... Virginia Beach, VA
Jones, Robert H. ... Dunn, NC
Jones, Robert H. ... Shawnee, OK
Jones, Robert H. ... Allen, TX
Jones, Robert H. ... Houston, TX
Jones, Robert I. ... New York, NY
Jones, Robert J. ... Washington, DC
Jones, Robert J. ... St. Petersburg, FL
Jones, Robert J. ... Philadelphia, PA
Jones, Robert John ... Miami, FL
Jones, Robert K. ... Phoenix, AZ
Jones, Robert K. ... Colorado Springs, CO
Jones, Robert K. ... Littleton, CO
Jones, Robert L. ... Palo Alto, CA
Jones, Robert L.
Federal Trade Commission,
Bureau of Competition, GV
Jones, Robert L. ... Atlanta, GA
Jones, Robert L. ... Plymouth, MI
Jones, Robert L. ... Springfield, PA
Jones, Robert L. ... Sioux Falls, SD
Jones, Robert L. ... Columbia, TN
Jones, Robert L. ... Lubbock, TX
Jones, Robert L., III ... Fort Smith, AR
Jones, Robert L., III ... Winchester, VA
Jones, Robert L., Jr. ... Fort Smith, AR
Jones, Robert L., Jr. ... Chicago, IL
Jones, Robert L., Jr. ... Newark, NJ
Jones, Robert L., Jr., (Inc.) ... Fresno, CA
Jones, Robert Lee ... Little Rock, AR
Jones, Robert M. ... Santa Barbara, CA
Jones, Robert M. ... Stuart, FL
Jones, Robert M. ... Canton, MS
Jackson, MS
Jones, Robert M. ... Rock Hill, SC
Jones, Robert M. ... Dallas, TX
Jones, Robert M. ... Cavour, WI
Jones, Robert M., Jr. ... Atascadero, CA
Jones, Robert Metcalf ... San Francisco, CA
Jones, Robert P. ... Portland, OR
Jones, Robert Q., Jr. ... Atlanta, GA
Jones, Robert R. ... Binghamton, NY
Jones, Robert R. ... Athens, OH
Jones, Robert S. ... Jonesboro, AR
Jones, Robert S. ... Lawrenceville, GA
Jones, Robert S. ... Salina, KS
Jones, Robert S. ... Frankfort, KY
Jones, Robert S. ... Sandwich, MA
Jones, Robert V., Jr. ... Atlanta, GA
Jones, Robert Valliant ... Elkton, MD
Jones, Robert Victor ... Buffalo, MN
Minneapolis, MN
Jones, Robert W. ... Tulsa, OK
Jones, Robert W. ... Dallas, TX
Jones, Robert W., III
Apache Junction, AZ
Gold Canyon, AZ
Jones, Robert W., III ... Mesa, AZ
Jones, Robert W., Jr. ... Newport News, VA
Smithfield, VA
Jones, Robert Wesley ... Dayton, OH
Jones, Roberta Lee ... San Francisco, CA
Jones, Robertson C. ... Phoenix, AZ
Jones, Robin L. ... Lafayette, LA
Jones, Robt. E. ... North Bend, OR
Jones, Robt. H. ... Peoria, IL
Jones, Rod ... Orlando, FL
Jones, Rod M. ... Salem, OR
Jones, Roderick D. ... Walnut Creek, CA
Jones, Rodney C. ... Atlanta, GA
Jones, Roger C. ... Columbia, MD
Jones, Roger G. ... Nashville, TN
Jones, Roger J. ... Chicago, IL
Jones, Roger L. ... Montpelier, ID
Jones, Roger S. ... Fort Worth, TX
Jones, Roger V. ... Florham Park, NJ
New York, NY
Jones, Roger W. ... Seattle, WA
Jones, Roger W., Jr. ... Seattle, WA
Jones, Rogers & Navarro
San Antonio, TX
Jones, Roland Gary ... New York, NY
Jones, Roland S., Jr. ... Raleigh, NC
Jones, Rolland G. ... Brookings, SD
Jones, Ron R. ... Enid, OK
Jones, Ronald C., Jr. ... Lansing, MI
Jones, Ronald D. ... Benton, AR
Jones, Ronald D. ... New York, NY
Jones, Ronald E. ... West Palm Beach, FL
Jones, Ronald E., P.A.
West Palm Beach, FL
Jones, Ronald F. ... Yuma, AZ
Jones, Ronald P. ... Hanford, CA
Jones, Ronald R. ... Chicago, IL
Jones, Ronald S. ... Winter Park, CO
Jones, Ronald Scott ... Pittsburgh, PA
Jones, Ronald T. ... Hillsborough, NJ
Jones, Ronni G., Ms. ... Madison, WI
Jones, Rory R. ... Boise, ID
Jones, Rosalyn E. ... Los Angeles, CA
Jones, Roscoe R. ... Texarkana, TX
Jones, Rose M. ... Raleigh, NC
Jones, Rosemarie F. ... Palo Alto, CA
Jones, Rosemary B. ... Goshen, CT
Jones, Rosemary Sage ... Tyler, TX
Jones, Rosemary U., (Mrs.)
Coral Gables, FL
Jones, Ross B. ... Santa Rosa, CA
Jones, Ross Holiday ... Beaumont, TX
Jones, Ross L. ... Coleman, TX
Jones, Roxanne D. ... Santa Rosa, CA
Jones, Roxie J. ... Department of Commerce,
Office of the General Counsel, GV
Jones, Roy M. ... Atlanta, GA
Jones, Roy Stapleton, Jr. ... Washington, DC
Jones, Royce K. ... Los Angeles, CA
Jones, Royden E., Jr. ... Pontiac, MI
Jones, Rudolph ... Columbus, GA
Jones, Russel C. ... Owensboro, KY
Jones, Russel W. ... Costa Mesa, CA
Jones, Russell A., Jr. ... Nashville, TN
Jones, Russell C. ... Sugar Land, TX
Jones, Russell D. ... Rancho Palos Verdes, CA
Jones, Russell D. ... Kansas City, MO
Jones, Russell E. ... Tucson, AZ
Jones, Russell G. ... Lawton, OK
Jones, Russell K. ... Spokane, WA
Jones, Russell L. ... New Orleans, LA
Jones, Russell S. ... Kansas City, MO
Jones, Russell S., III ... Denver, CO
Jones, Russell S., Jr. ... Kansas City, MO
Jones, Russell W. ... Toledo, OH
Jones, Russotto & Walker, P.C.
Virginia Beach, VA
Jones, S. Gregory ... Phoenix, AZ
Jones, S. Meigs, III ... Westwood, KS
Jones, Sam ... Chattanooga, TN
Jones, Sam L., Jr. ... Corpus Christi, TX
Jones, Samuel ... Memphis, TN
Jones, Samuel C. ... Mount Vernon, MO
Jones, Samuel M., III ... Jericho, NY
Jones, Samuel R. ... Waco, TX
Jones, Samuel Shepard, Jr. ... Washington, DC
Jones, Samuel V. ... Dallas, TX
Jones, Sandra L. ... Los Angeles, CA
Jones, Sandra L. ... Minneapolis, MN
Jones, Sandra Schreur ... Minneapolis, MN
Jones, Sandra Y. ... Chicago, IL
Jones, Sanford J. ... Atlanta, GA
Jones, Sara C.
Joint Committees And Commissions, GV
Jones, Sara H. ... St. Paul, MN
Jones, Sarah Elizabeth ... Washington, DC
Jones, Sarah T. ... New York, NY
Jones, Saunders P., IV ... Stone Mountain, GA
Jones & Scheich ... Toledo, OH
Jones, Scheider & Patterson, Professional
Association ... Bluffton, SC
Charleston, SC
Hilton Head Island, SC
Jones, Schneider & Bartlett
Columbia, MO
Jones, Schonette ... Department of Justice,
Antitrust Division, GV
Jones, Scott G. ... New Orleans, LA
Jones, Scott K. ... Dayton, OH
Jones, Scott L. ... Los Angeles, CA
Jones, Scott M. ... New Haven, CT
Jones, Scott P. ... San Antonio, TX
Jones, Scott S. ... Boston, MA
Jones, Scott V. ... Du Bois, PA
Jones, Scranton ... Fort Worth, TX
Jones, Sean F. ... Dania, FL
Jones, Sean M. ... Charlotte, NC
Jones, Seth & Shuler, LLP ... Sumter, SC
Jones, Shana C. ... Washington, DC
Jones, Shanna D. ... Austin, TX
Jones, Shannon Ball ... San Francisco, CA
Jones, Shannon C. ... New York, NY
Jones, Shannon, Jr. ... Dallas, TX
Jones, Shannon R. ... Puyallup, WA
Jones, Sharon E. ... North Chicago, IL
Jones, Sharon Foster ... Atlanta, GA
Jones, Sharon M. ... Ventura, CA
Jones, Sharon R. ... Atlanta, GA
Jones, Sharon R. ... McDonough, GA
Jones, Sharon S. ... Miami, FL
Jones, Sharon Sue ... Champaign, IL
Jones, Shavon L. ... Philadelphia, PA
Jones, Shawn P. ... St. Clair, MI
Jones, Sheila A. ... Jackson, MS
Jones, Sheila D. ... Denver, CO
Washington, DC
Jones, Sheila D. ... Nashville, TN
Jones, Sheila Worley ... Sacramento, CA
Jones, Sheldon A. ... Boston, MA
Jones, Shelley Baber ... Cincinnati, OH
Jones, Shelley M. ... Harrisburg, PA
Jones, Shelton ... Houston, TX
Jones, Shelton & Malone, P.C.
Norfolk, VA
Jones, Sherryl A. ... Port Townsend, WA
Jones, Sherwood A. ... Richmond, VA
Jones, Sheryl Lynn ... Swarthmore, PA
Jones, Shirley A. ... General Accounting Office,
Office of the General Counsel, GV
Jones, Shirley B. ... Baltimore, MD
Jones, Shirley Norwood ... Jackson, MS
Jones, Sidney A., III ... Chicago, IL
Jones, Sidney Pope, Jr. ... Newnan, GA
Jones, Sidney W. ... Rancho Cucamonga, CA
Jones, Sidney W. ... Edmond, OK
Jones, Simone Pereira ... Arlington, VA
Jones, Skelton & Hochuli ... Phoenix, AZ
Jones Skivington and Kelley ... Geneseo, NY
Livonia, NY
Scottsville, NY
Jones & Smith ... Liberty, MS
Jones & Smith ... Mount Vernon, WA
Jones and Smith, P.C. ... Metter, GA
Jones, Snead, Wertheim, Wentworth &
Jaramillo, P.A. ... Albuquerque, NM
Santa Fe, NM
Jones and Soulis ... Cartersville, GA
Jones, Spitz, Moorhead, Baird & Albergotti,
P.A. ... Anderson, SC
Jones & Sport ... Luverne, AL
Jones, Stanley A. ... Kaufman, TX
Jones, Stanley C. ... Klamath Falls, OR
Jones, Stanley D. ... Washington, DC
Jones, Stanley J., Jr. ... Albany, NY
Jones, Stanley R. ... Irvine, CA
Jones, Stanley R. ... Hallowell, ME
Jones, Stanley S., Jr. ... Atlanta, GA
Jones, Stanley T., Jr. ... San Diego, CA
Jones, Stephanie A. ... Los Angeles, CA
Jones, Stephanie A. ... Chester, NJ
Jones, Stephanie C. ... Clinton, OK
Jones, Stephanie D. ... Chicago, IL
Jones, Stephanie Tubbs ... Cleveland, OH
Jones, Stephen ... Enid, OK
Jones, Stephen A. ... Denver, CO
Jones, Stephen A. ... Washington, DC
Jones, Stephen A. ... Honolulu, HI
Jones, Stephen B. ... Brewster, MA
Jones, Stephen C. ... Claremont, CA
Jones, Stephen C. ... Washington, DC
Jones, Stephen C. ... St. Louis, MO
Jones, Stephen C. ... St. Louis, MO
Jones, Stephen C. ... Green Bay, WI
Jones, Stephen D. ... Woodland Hills, CA
Jones, Stephen D. ... Columbus, OH
Jones, Stephen E. ... Washington, DC
Jones, Stephen H., Jr. ... Asheville, NC
Jones, Stephen J. ... Wichita, KS
Jones, Stephen J. ... Scarsdale, NY
Jones, Stephen J. ... Allentown, PA
Jones, Stephen L. ... Los Angeles, CA
Jones, Stephen M. ... Austin, TX
Jones, Stephen P. ... Los Angeles, CA
Jones, Stephen R. ... Department of Labor,
Office of the Solicitor, GV
Jones, Stephen W. ... Conway, AR
Little Rock, AR
Jones, Stephen W. ... San Francisco, CA
Jones, Stephen W. ... Bloomfield Hills, MI
Jones & Stephens ... Roseville, CA
Jones, Stevan M. ... Jacksonville, FL
Jones, Steve CarMichael ... Athens, GA
Jones, Steven A. ... Long Beach, CA
Jones, Steven C. ... Las Vegas, NV
Jones, Steven G. ... Decatur, IL
Jones, Steven G. ... Seattle, WA
Jones, Steven H. ... Kingsport, TN
Jones, Steven L. ... Anchorage, AK
Jones, Steven L. ... Miami Shores, FL
Jones, Steven L. ... Indianapolis, IN
Jones, Steven L. ... Spokane, WA
Jones, Steven P. ... Portland, OR
Jones, Steven R. ... Morrisville, NY
Jones, Stewart W. ... Toledo, OH
Jones, Strohm, Crain & Guthrie
Media, PA
Swarthmore, PA
Jones, Stuart A. ... Dallas, TX
Jones, Stuart C. ... Cedar City, UT
Jones, Stuart D. ... Portland, OR
Jones, Stuart E. ... San Francisco, CA
Jones, Stuart H. ... Atlanta, GA
Jones, Stuart L. ... Hartford, CT
Jones, Stuart M. ... Grand Junction, CO
Jones, Susan A. ... Denver, CO
Jones, Susan Beverly ... Lexington, KY
Jones, Susan C. V. ... Los Angeles, CA
Jones, Susan Delanty ... Seattle, WA
Jones, Susan Elizabeth ... St. Louis, MO
Jones, Susan G.
Hot Springs National Park, AR
Jones, Susan H. ... Tulsa, OK
Jones, Susan K. ... Attica, NY
Jones, Susan M. ... Tiffin, OH
Jones, Susan R ... Washington, DC
Jones, Susan Shands ... Jackson, MS
Jones, Susan Smith ... Atlanta, GA
Jones, Susanne B. ... Indianapolis, IN
Jones, Suzan Felten ... Indianapolis, IN
Jones, Suzanne Cate ... Los Angeles, CA
Jones, Suzanne DellaValla ... Evesham, NJ
Philadelphia, PA
Jones, Suzanne Dwyer ... Lowell, MA
Jones, Suzanne M. ... Covington, LA
Jones, Sylvia R. ... Atlanta, GA
Jones, T. Craig ... Fayetteville, AR
Jones, T. Douglass, III ... Wilson, NC
Jones, T. Gregory ... Salisbury, NC
Jones, T. Michael ... Columbus, GA
Jones, T. Scott ... Knoxville, TN
Jones, T. Warren ... Erie, PA
Jones, Tadiana W. ... Salt Lake City, UT
Jones, Talmadge R. ... Sacramento, CA
Jones, Tamara Lynne ... Naples, FL
Jones, Tamara R. ... Dallas, TX
Jones, Tammie Marie ... Youngstown, OH
Jones, Tammy J. ... Houston, TX
Jones, Tava Seifert ... Oklahoma City, OK
Jones, Taylor, Jr. ... Dayton, OH
Jones, Taylor W. ... Atlanta, GA
Jones, Ted I. ... Memphis, TN
Jones, Tenley M. ... Washington, DC
Jones, Teresa D. ... Sarasota, FL
Jones, Teresa D. ... Dayton, OH
Jones, Teresa Dyann ... Memphis, TN
Jones, Terrance A. ... Orange Park, FL
Jones, Terrence D. ... Washington, DC
Jones, Terrence S. ... Boise, ID
Jones, Terri Ann ... Baltimore, MD
Jones, Terry D. ... Houston, TX
Jones, Terry L. ... St. Louis, MO
Jones, Terry R. ... Denver, CO
Jones, Terry W. ... Elizabeth City, NC
Jones, Tête, Nolen, Hanchey, Fonti &
Belfour, L.L.P. ... Lake Charles, LA
Jones, Thelma H. ... Arlington, VA
Jones, Thelma Holoway ... Sugar Land, TX
Jones, Theodore Lawrence ... Washington, DC
Jones, Theodore M. ... Dallas, TX
Jones, Theodore (Ted) L.
Baton Rouge, LA
Jones, Theodore W. ... Cleveland, OH
Jones, Theresa A. ... Orange, CA
Jones, Theresa L. ... Geneseo, IL
Jones, Theresa S. ... Birmingham, AL
Jones, Thermon W. ... Decatur, GA
Jones, Thermon W., P.C. ... Decatur, GA
Jones, Thomas ... Washington, DC
Jones, Thomas ... Eupora, MS
Jones, Thomas A. ... Willmar, MN
Jones, Thomas A., III ... Birmingham, AL
Jones, Thomas ap R. ... Selma, AL
Jones, Thomas C. ... Kansas City, MO
Jones, Thomas C. ... Dallas, TX
Jones, Thomas D. ...
Department of Labor, GV
Jones, Thomas D. ...
Department Of Veterans Affairs, GV
Jones, Thomas D. ... San Antonio, TX
Jones, Thomas D., III ... Princeton, NJ
Jones, Thomas E. ... Auburn, AL
Jones, Thomas E. ... Belleville, IL
Jones, Thomas E. ... Albuquerque, NM
Jones, Thomas E., Jr. ... Atlanta, GA
Jones, Thomas F. ... St. Louis, MO
Jones, Thomas F., & Associates
Atlanta, GA
Jones, Thomas H. ... Pasadena, CA
Jones, Thomas J. ... Tallahassee, FL
Jones, Thomas J. ... South Orange, NJ
Jones, Thomas J., III ... Boise, ID
Jones, Thomas J., Jr. ... Kansas City, MO
Jones, Thomas J., Jr. ... Scranton, PA
Jones, Thomas J., Sr. ... Scranton, PA
Jones, Thomas K. ... Hartford, CT
Jones, Thomas K. ... Overland Park, KS
Jones, Thomas L. ... Tuscaloosa, AL
Jones, Thomas L. ... Washington, DC
Jones, Thomas L. ... Seneca Falls, NY
Jones, Thomas L., III ... Bangor, ME
Jones, Thomas L., Jr. ... Murfreesboro, NC
Jones, Thomas Lee ... Pittsburgh, PA
Jones, Thomas M. ... Newport Beach, CA
Jones, Thomas M. ... Chicago, IL
Jones, Thomas M. ... Lawrenceburg, KY
Jones, Thomas M. ... Seattle, WA
Jones, Thomas N. ... Albuquerque, NM
Jones, Thomas N. ... Franklin, TN
Jones, Thomas Overton ... Richmond, VA
Jones, Thomas P. ... Little Rock, AR
Orlando, FL
Jones, Thomas R. ... Walnut Creek, CA
Jones, Thomas R. ... Bowie, MD
Jones, Thomas R. ... Meridian, MS
Jones, Thomas R. ... Milwaukee, WI
Waukesha, WI
Jones, Thomas R. ... Milwaukee, WI
Jones, Thomas R., Jr. ... Tuscaloosa, AL
Jones, Thomas Rawles, Jr. ... Alexandria, VA
Jones, Thomas S. ... Irvine, CA
Jones, Thomas Scott ... Oklahoma City, OK
Jones, Thomas W. ... Sylva, NC
Jones, Thomas W., Jr. ... Washington, DC
Jones, Thomas W., Jr. ... Cincinnati, OH
Jones, Tiffany A. ... Madison, GA
Jones, Timothy ... Fresno, CA
Jones, Timothy ... Fort Myers, FL

Jones, Timothy Edward ... Miami, FL
Jones, Timothy H. ... Philadelphia, MS
Jones, Timothy J. ... Augusta, GA
Jones, Timothy J. ... Portland, OR
Jones, Timothy M. ... Fairfield, CA
Jones, Timothy M. ... Raleigh, NC
Jones, Timothy S. ... Phoenix, AZ
Jones, Timothy V. ... Cincinnati, OH
Jones, Timothy W. ... Chesterfield, MO
Jones, Timothy W. ... Sevierville, TN
Jones, Tina Cutlip
Research Triangle Park, NC
Jones, Tira ... Austin, TX
Jones, Todd A. ... Walnut Creek, CA
Jones, Todd Allen ... Raleigh, NC
Jones, Todd E. ... Atlanta, GA
Jones, Todd G. ... Kansas City, MO
Jones, Todd V. ... Tucson, AZ
Jones, Tom G. ... Franklin, IN
Jones, Tonia P., (P.A.) ... Little Rock, AR
Jones, Tony C. ... Chicago, IL
Jones, Tony M. ... Rock Hill, SC
Jones, Tracey L. ... Raleigh, NC
Jones, Tracey M. ... Houston, TX
Jones, Traci L. ... Washington, DC
Jones, Tracy F. ... Macon, GA
Jones, Travis B. ... Pierre, SD
Jones, Travis Dale ... Lubbock, TX
Jones, Trina ... Durham, NC
Jones, Trish ... Atlanta, GA
Jones & Trousdale ... Florence, AL
Tuscumbia, AL
Jones, Troyan, Pappas & Perkins, A Legal Professional Association ... Columbus, OH
Powell, OH
Jones, Tullar & Cooper, P.C.
Washington, DC
Arlington, VA
Jones, Tyree P. ... San Francisco, CA
Jones, Urrea C., Jr. ... Pasadena, CA
Jones, U. V. ... Lubbock, TX
Jones, Valerie Braswell ... Wilton, CT
Jones, Vanessa J. ... Hattiesburg, MS
Jones Vargas ... Las Vegas, NV
Reno, NV
Jones, Verlin L., Jr. ... Cordele, GA
Jones, Verlin L., Jr. ... Vienna, GA
Jones, Verna M. ... Columbus, OH
Jones, Veronica P. ... Baltimore, MD
Jones, Veronica Rhenae' ... Baton Rouge, LA
Jones, Veronica S. ... Marietta, GA
Jones, Vickie Hardy ... Memphis, TN
Jones, Vickie S. ... Fairfax, VA
Jones, Victor P. ... Lansing, MI
Jones, Viron K. ... Brooklyn, NY
Jones, Vreeland O., (Inc.) ... Fresno, CA
Jones, W. Cecil ... Philadelphia, PA
Jones, W. Clyde, III ... Geneva, IL
Jones, W. Douglas ... Tulsa, OK
Jones, W. Farley ... Troy, NY
Jones, W. Gregg ... Walnut Creek, CA
Jones, W. Hugh, Jr. ... Ahoskie, NC
Rocky Mount, NC
Jones, W. Kent ... Huntingdon, TN
Jones, W. Montgomery ... Glendale, CA
Monterey, CA
Jones, W. Philip ... Avon, CT
Jones, W. Randall ... Louisville, KY
Jones, W. Ray ... Roseville, CA
Jones, W. Roger, Jr. ... Jackson, MS
Jones, W. Russ ... Houston, TX
Jones, W. Russ, P.C. ... Houston, TX
Jones, W. Scott ... Asheville, NC
Jones, W. Seaborn ... Atlanta, GA
Jones, W. Steven ... Long Beach, CA
Jones, W. Talmage ... Wilmington, NC
Jones, W. Terence ... Boston, MA
Jones, W. Wilson ... Little Rock, AR
Jones & Wade ... North Palm Beach, FL
Jones, Wade H., III ... Spartanburg, SC
Jones, Waldo, Holbrook & McDonough, A Professional Corporation
Washington, DC
St. George, UT
Salt Lake City, UT
Jones & Waldrop ... Birmingham, AL
Jones, Walker W. (Bill), III ... Jackson, MS
Jones, Walker, Waechter, Poitevent, Carrère & Denègre, L.L.P. ... Washington, DC
Baton Rouge, LA
Lafayette, LA
New Orleans, LA
Jones & Walla, P.A. ... Elkton, MD
Jones & Wallace, LLP ... Evansville, IN
Jones & Walling, P.C. ... Atlanta, GA
Jones, Walter A. ... Decatur, GA
Jones, Walter C., IV
Palm Beach Gardens, FL
Jones, Walter C., IV, P.A.
Palm Beach Gardens, FL
Jones, Walter H., Jr. ... Mooresville, NC
Jones, Walter Henry, III ... Hackensack, NJ
Jones, Walter, Jr. ... Chicago, IL
Jones, Walter L. ... Greensboro, NC
Jones, Walter M. ... Louisville, KY
Jones, Walter M., III ... Hagerstown, MD
Martinsburg, WV
Jones, Walter Michael ... Bristow, OK
Jones, Walter P., III ... Richmond, VA
Jones, Walter Rayford ... Gulfport, MS
Jones, Walter Robert, III ... Jackson, MS
Jones, Walter W., Jr. ... Canandaigua, NY
Jones & Wanchak, L.L.C. ... Avon, CT
Jones, Wanda E. ... Highland, IN
Jones, Ward D. ... Honolulu, HI
Jones, Ward L. ... Singer Island, FL
Jones, Ward R. ... Houston, TX
Jones, Warren E. ... Nichols Hills, OK

Jones, Warren Eugene ... Boise, ID
Jones, Warren G. ... Wichita, KS
Jones, Warren H. ... Leesburg, VA
Jones, Warren K. ... Santa Fe, NM
Jones & Warren, P.A. ... Scarborough, ME
Jones, Warren S., Jr. ... Mount Holly, NJ
Jones, Waters, Bennett, Hessel & Cross, LLC
Colorado Springs, CO
Jones, Wayne A. ... Plano, TX
Jones, Wayne F. ... Montgomery, AL
Jones, Wayne L. ... Santa Ana, CA
Jones, Wayne M. ... Akron, OH
Jones, Wayne P. ... Lisbon, ND
Jones, Wayne P., P.C. ... Lisbon, ND
Jones, Wayne S. ... Paris, IL
Jones, Webb M. ... Houston, TX
Jones and Welch, P.A. ... Pensacola, FL
Jones & Weller, P.A. ... Hill City, KS
Jones, Wendell L. ... Lexington, KY
Jones, Wendell R. ... Bowling Green, OH
Jones, Wendell R. ... Midvale, UT
Jones, Wendi D. ... Sun Valley, CA
Jones, Wendy F. ... Albuquerque, NM
Jones, Wendy S. ... Torrance, CA
Jones, Wensley, Wirth & Azarian
Alton, NH
Dover, NH
Portsmouth, NH
Rochester, NH
Jones and White ... Oklahoma City, OK
Jones, Will C., IV ... San Antonio, TX
Jones, Willard F. ... Sacramento, CA
Jones, Willard, II ... Allentown, PA
Jones, William A. ... Santa Monica, CA
Jones, William A. ... Torrance, CA
Jones, William A. ... Philadelphia, PA
Jones, William A., Jr. ... Ruston, LA
Jones, William B. ... Washington, DC
Jones, William B. ... Jackson, GA
Jones, William B. ... Pascagoula, MS
Jones, William B. ... St. Louis, MO
Jones, William B. ... Tulsa, OK
Jones, William B., II ... Short Hills, NJ
Jones, William Baxter ... Ridgeland, MS
Jones, William Bryan ... Owensboro, KY
Jones, William C. ... Pensacola, FL
Jones, William C. ... St. Louis, MO
Jones, William D. ... Richmond, VA
Jones, William D., III ... Birmingham, AL
Jones, William E. ... Columbus, OH
Jones, William E. ... Houston, TX
Jones, William Evan ... Missoula, MT
Jones, William F. ... Annapolis, MD
Jones, William F. ... Park Rapids, MN
Jones, William F. ... Hattiesburg, MS
Jones, William F. ... Richmond, VA
Jones, William G. ... Charlotte, NC
Jones, William H. ... Chicago, IL
Jones, William H. ... Petal, MS
Jones, William H. ... Columbus, OH
Jones, William H., II ... Department of Justice, Antitrust Division, GV
Jones, William H., Jr. ... Ashland, KY
Jones, William I.
Federal Deposit Insurance Corporation, GV
Jones, William J.
United States Postal Service, Law Department, GV
Jones, William J. ... Lewiston, ID
Jones, William J. ... Libertyville, IL
Jones, William J. ... Waynesville, NC
Jones, William J., Jr. ... Chicago, IL
Jones, William J., Jr. ... Covington, LA
Jones, William K. ... New York, NY
Jones, William L. ... Eagle, CO
Jones, William Lloyd ... Irving, TX
Jones, William M. (Bill) ... Dallas, TX
Jones, William P. ... Chicago, IL
Jones, William P. ... Hendersonville, TN
Jones, William Paul ... Lincoln, NE
Jones, William R. ... Burlingame, CA
Jones, William R. ... Danbury, CT
Jones, William R. ... Newport, KY
Jones, William R. ... Coushatta, LA
Jones, William R. ... Las Vegas, NV
Jones, William R. ... Wheatland, WY
Jones, William R., III ... Miami, FL
Jones, William R., Jr. ... Phoenix, AZ
Jones, William R., Jr. ... Sherman, CT
Jones, William S.
Federal Deposit Insurance Corporation, GV
Jones, William Sherlo ... New York, NY
Jones, William T. ... Albany, GA
Jones, William T. ... Atlanta, GA
Jones, William T. ... Scranton, PA
Jones, William Timothy ... Jackson, MS
Jones, William" Trey ", III ... Jackson, MS
Jones, William W. ... Farmington, CT
Jones, William W. ... Rolling Meadows, IL
Jones, William W., Jr.
Hilton Head Island, SC
Jones, Willie J., Jr. ... Dunbar, WV
Jones, Willis B. ... Billings, MT
Jones, Willis B., II ... Columbus, MT
Jones, Willis P., Jr. ... Holland, OH
Jones, Wilson ... Tulsa, OK
Jones, Wilson G. ... Dallas, TX
Jones, Wilson, P.C. ... Tulsa, OK
Jones, Winfield P. ... New York, NY
Jones, Winston K. ... Cambridge, MA
Jones, Wm. A. ... Pittsburgh, PA
Jones, Wm. Jarell ... Statesboro, GA
Jones, Wm. Jarell, P.C. ... Atlanta, GA
Statesboro, GA
Jones, Wm. L. ... Eagle, CO
Jones, Wm. T. ... Greenwood, SC
Jones & Wolfe ... Fort Lauderdale, FL
Jones, Woodrow A., Jr. ... Louisville, KY

Jones, Woodrow W. ... Rutherfordton, NC
Jones & Wyatt ... Enid, OK
Jones, Yale I. ... San Francisco, CA
Jones, Yolanda P. ... Villanova, PA
Jones & Young, L.L.P. ... Sweetwater, TX
Jones-Baskaran, Amy M. ... Washington, DC
Jones-Bateman, John B. ... Baltimore, MD
Jones-Channer, Colleen J. ... New York, NY
Jonesco, Jane R. ... Oberlin, OH
Jones-Cofield, Marilee ... Long Beach, CA
Jonescu, Michael D. ... Orange, CA
Jones-Davis, Bettye A. ... Fort Wayne, IN
Jonesi, Gary
Environmental Protection Agency, Office of Enforcement and Compliance Assurance, GV
Jones-Lee, Anita ... New York, NY
Jones-McConnell, P.C. ... Mercer, PA
Jones-Mesler, Lisa A. ... Boise, ID
Jones-Moon, Bonita ... Potomac, MD
Jones-Obeng, Eunice ... Reidsville, NC
Joneson, Jennifer L. ... Pago Pago, TT
Jones-Peace, Jacqueline ... New York, NY
Jones-Peretto, Lenore A.
Research Triangle Park, NC
Jones-Richardson, Vedia ... Durham, NC
Jones-Sandler, Kristen ... Chevy Chase, MD
Jones-Smith, Kimberly Jonita ... Durham, NC
Jones-Sullivan, Jeanne ... Washington, DC
Jones-Wenger, Winifred H. ... Philipsburg, PA
Joneth, Robert A. ... Raleigh, NC
Jong, Alan E. ... Sacramento, CA
Jong, James C. ... New York, NY
Jong, Joseph M. ... Red Bank, NJ
Houston, TX
Jong, Ron S. ... Boulder, CO
Jongbloed, Peter S. ... New Haven, CT
Jongebloed, James T. ... Houston, TX
Jongeward, John H., Jr. ... Yuma, AZ
Jongeward, William Albert
White Plains, NY
Jongleux, Lynn Brundage ... Indianapolis, IN
Joniec, Diana M. ... Clementon, NJ
Jonietz, John E. ... Houston, TX
Jonikas, Joseph B. ... Boulder, CO
Jonjak, Paul L. ... Spooner, WI
Jonkel, Joan M. ... Missoula, MT
Jonker, Donald P. ... Chicago, IL
Jonker, Jeffrey David ... Palo Alto, CA
Jonker, Peter E. ... San Diego, CA
Jonker, Robert J. ... Grand Rapids, MI
Jonker, Steven K. ... San Diego, CA
Jonkers, Ronald N.
Overseas Private Investment Corporation, GV
Jonnalagadda, Srinivasa R.
New York, NY
Jonscher, Gemia McDearmon ... Chicago, IL
Jonscher, George V. ... Wilmette, IL
Jonsen, Eric R. ... Westminster, CO
Jonson, Bernice ... Seattle, WA
Jonson, Carl A. ... Seattle, WA
Jonson, Daryl D. ... Richland, WA
Jonson, David Nevin ... Columbia, SC
Jonson, George D. ... Cincinnati, OH
Jonson, George N. ... Hamilton, OH
Jonson, Hurley & Olson ... Seattle, WA
Jonson & Jonson, P.S. ... Seattle, WA
Jonson, Kenneth I. ... Washington, DC
Jonson, Michael A. ... Seattle, WA
Jonson, Nicholas D. ... Golden, CO
Jonson, Richard E. ... Seattle, WA
Jonsson, Geir T. ... Seattle, WA
Jonsson, Gregory N. ... Westport, MA
Jonsson, Jon M. ... Seattle, WA
Jonsson, Michael ... Sacramento, CA
Jonsson, Scott A. ... Portland, OR
Jontiff, Jeannie M. ... Miami, FL
Jontiff, Scott J. ... Miami Beach, FL
Jontos & Lotty ... Fairfield, CT
Jontz, Alan G. ... Minneapolis, MN
Jontz, Alan G., and Associates, P.A.
Minneapolis, MN
Jontz, Dennis E. ... Albuquerque, NM
Jontz, Jeffry R. ... Orlando, FL
Jontz, Jennifer Cook ... Cleveland, OH
Jonusaitis, Andy V. ... Chicago, IL
Joo, Anna Y. ... Los Angeles, CA
Joo, Jinho ... Menlo Park, CA
Joondeph, Jerome J. ... Akron, OH
Joondeph, Jerome J., Jr. ... Columbus, OH
Joondeph, Robert C. ... Portland, OR
Joondeph, Shaffer & Bittel, LLP
Akron, OH
Joor, William E., III ... Houston, TX
Joos, Edward J., Jr. ... Philadelphia, PA
Joos, William J. ... Jacksonville, FL
Joos, William J., P.A. ... Jacksonville, FL
Joost, Elaine Economides
Department of Transportation, Research and Special Programs Administration, GV
Joost, Robert H.
Department of Transportation, Office of the General Counsel, GV
Joost and Torres ... Larkspur, CA
Joost, William E., Jr. ... Larkspur, CA
Joost, William J. ... Eagle River, WI
Joosten, Jan J.H. (IBA) ... New York, NY
Joosten, Richard L., Jr. ... Dallas, TX
Joosten, Stephen D. ... Oklahoma City, OK
Joplin, Charles A. ... Lubbock, TX
Joplin, James E. ... Lubbock, TX
Joplin, Joe M. ... McKinney, TX
Joplin, Mike, (P.C.) ... Dallas, TX
Joplin, Stephen J. ... San Diego, CA
Joplin, Susan L. ... Cleveland, OH
Jopling, James Kerby ... San Antonio, TX

Jopling, John D. ... Gainesville, FL
Jopling, Wallace M. ... Gainesville, FL
Jopp, Harold D., Jr. ... Baltimore, MD
Joppa, Glenn L. ... Trevose, PA
Joppa, Teresa L. ... Moorhead, MN
Joppich, Richard J. ... Ann Arbor, MI
Joppich, Steven P. ... Farmington Hills, MI
Joralemon, Christopher M.
New York, NY
Joran, A. David ... New York, NY
Jorandby, Richard L. ... West Palm Beach, FL
Joranko, David B. ... Chicago, IL
Jorda, Karl F. ... Concord, NH
Jordaan, Ashley Warren
Colorado Springs, CO
Jordaan, Hendrik F.
Colorado Springs, CO
Jordaan, Jakes ... Dallas, TX
Jordaan & Pennington ... Dallas, TX
Jordahl, Kimberly S. ... Minneapolis, MN
Jordak, John A., Jr. ... Atlanta, GA
Jordan, A. Bob ... Oklahoma City, OK
Jordan, A. Gayle ... Norfolk, VA
Jordan, Adalberto ... Miami, FL
Jordan, Albert L. ... Birmingham, AL
Jordan, Alexander J., Jr. ... Boston, MA
Jordan, Alice M. ... Fairfield, IL
Jordan, Alison M. ... Charlotte, NC
Jordan, Althea Lee ... Palo Alto, CA
Jordan, Amy L. ... Seattle, WA
Jordan, Amy R. ... Jacksonville, NC
Jordan, Amy Rogers ... Charleston, SC
Jordan, Andrew C. ... Novato, CA
Jordan, Andrew S. ... Santa Monica, CA
Jordan, Angela T. ... Loris, SC
Jordan, Anne H. ... Portland, ME
Jordan, Anne S. ... Pleasanton, CA
Jordan, Anthony T., Jr. ... Bayville, NY
Jordan, April Ann ... Dayton, OH
Jordan, Arcie Izquierdo ... Austin, TX
Jordan, Barbara E. ... Atlanta, GA
Jordan, Barbara K. ... San Francisco, CA
Jordan, Baynetta M. ... Lubbock, TX
Jordan, Beth S. ... San Francisco, CA
Jordan, Blake T. ... Denver, CO
Jordan, Bobbiretta E.
Charlotte Amalie, St. Thomas, VI
Jordan & Bodner ... Atlanta, GA
Jordan, Brenda M. ... Manhattan, KS
Jordan, Brenna B. ... Woonsocket, RI
Jordan, Brent J. ... San Francisco, CA
Jordan, Brian J. ... Phoenix, AZ
Jordan, Brian J. ... Flushing, MI
Jordan, Brian K. ... Charleston, SC
Jordan & Bristol ... Brunswick, GA
Hinesville, GA
Saint Simons Island, GA
Jordan, Bruce A. ... Fort Lauderdale, FL
Jordan, Bruce A. ... Bangor, ME
Jordan, Bruce E. ... San Antonio, TX
Jordan, Bruce M. ... Glens Falls, NY
Jordan, C. Lance ... Sacramento, CA
Jordan Caplan & Etter ... Portland, OR
Jordan, Caroline ... Dallas, TX
Jordan, Carolyn Comparet
Los Angeles, CA
Jordan, Carolyn D. ... United States Senate, Committee Legal Personnel, GV
Jordan, Carolyn S. ... Jackson, CA
Jordan, Carolyn V. ... Atlanta, GA
Jordan, Casey E. ... Syracuse, NY
Jordan, Castle W. ... Vero Beach, FL
Jordan, Catherine A. ... New York, NY
Jordan, Cecil E. ... Albuquerque, NM
Jordan, Cecilia ... Hayward, CA
Jordan, Cedestra L.
Department of Transportation, GV
Jordan & Chappell ... Ottawa, KS
Jordan, Charles ... Seattle, WA
Jordan, Charles A. ... Los Angeles, CA
Jordan, Charles B. ... Colorado Springs, CO
Jordan, Charles B., Jr. ... Myrtle Beach, SC
Jordan, Charles C. ... Dallas, TX
Jordan, Charles M., (P.C.) ... Houston, TX
Jordan, Cheryl ... Palo Alto, CA
Jordan, Cheryl M. ... Spring Valley, NY
Jordan, Chester L., II ... Alexandria, VA
Jordan, Chester Scott ... Concord, NH
Jordan, Christian F.P.
Department of Transportation, Federal Aviation Administration, GV
Jordan, Christopher G. ... Dallas, TX
Jordan, Clark L. ... Salmon, ID
Jordan, Clifford E. ... Solvang, CA
Jordan, Colleen N. ... Worcester, MA
Jordan, Constance M. ... Kansas City, MO
Jordan, Cox & Reznicek, L.L.P. ... Dallas, TX
Jordan Coyne & Savits, L.L.P.
Washington, DC
Baltimore, MD
Rockville, MD
Fairfax, VA
Leesburg, VA
Jordan, Craig S. ... San Bernardino, CA
Jordan, D. Bradley ... Seneca, SC
Jordan, D. Charles ... Eau Claire, WI
Jordan, D. James ... Macon, GA
Jordan, Dan H. ... Nashville, TN
Jordan, Daniel B. ... Washington, DC
Jordan, Daniel C. ... Chicago, IL
Jordan, Daniel C. ... Richmond, VA
Jordan, Daniel D. ... Boston, MA
Jordan, Daniel G. ... Los Angeles, CA
Newport Beach, CA
Jordan, Daniel G. ... Chicago, IL
Jordan, Daniel P., III ... Jackson, MS
Jordan, Daniel R.E. ... Jefferson City, MO
Jordan, Daniel W. ... Austin, TX

Jordan, William S., III ... Akron, OH
Jordan, William T., Jr. ... Dyersburg, TN
Jordan, William Welch ... Greensboro, NC
Jordan, Winnie M. ... Dallas, TX
Jordan, Wm. H., Jr. ... United States Senate,
Committee Legal Personnel, GV
Jordan-Curtis, Willie ... Tucson, AZ
Jordan-Davis, Madelyn
San Francisco, CA
Jordanger, Dan J. ... Richmond, VA
Jordan-Holmes, Clark ... Tampa, FL
Jordan-Huffman, David L. ... St. Paul, MN
Jordanich, Edward J. ... New York, NY
Jordan-Musa, Enrique A. ... Caguas, PR
Jordano, Joseph A. ... Omaha, NE
Jordano, Mary Ann ... Harrisburg, PA
Jordan-Price, Kelley ... Boston, MA
Providence, RI
Jordan-Walker, Deneice ... Chicago, IL
Jorde, Thomas M. ... Berkeley, CA
Jorden & Bischoff, P.L.C. ... Phoenix, AZ
Jorden Burt Boros Cicchetti Berenson &
Johnson LLP ... Washington, DC
Miami, FL
Jorden, Danielle ... Tallahassee, FL
Jorden, Douglas A. ... Phoenix, AZ
Jorden, James F. ... Washington, DC
Miami, FL
Jorden, Kathryn L. ... Washington, DC
Jorden, R. Thomas, Jr. ... Lafayette, LA
Jorden, Robert T. ... Lafayette, LA
Jorden, Stephen J. ... Washington, DC
Jorden and White ... Meadville, PA
Jorden, William T. ... Meadville, PA
Jordening, Steven D. ... Nevada, IA
Jordison, Diana Moore ... Kansas City, MO
Jordon, Albert D. ... New York, NY
Jordon, Carl F. ... Redlands, CA
Jordon, D. Robert ... Wheaton, MD
Jordon, Jacquelyn A. ... Morgantown, WV
Jordon, Jane B. Lund ... Westport, CT
Jordon, Leslie M. ... Los Angeles, CA
Jordon, Tracy ... Palm Desert, CA
Jordon, Wayne A. ... Alamogordo, NM
Jordt, Jeffery P. ... Lake Barrington, IL
Jorge, Aisha T. ... Pittsburgh, PA
Jorge, David A. ... New Bedford, MA
Jorge, Jo Ann M. ... Winchester, MA
Jorge, Linda E. ... Tampa, FL
Jorge, Paul A. ... Dallas, TX
Jorgensen, Aimée E. ... Los Altos, CA
Jorgensen, Allen C. ... Banning, CA
Redlands, CA
Jorgensen, Ann ... San Francisco, CA
Jorgensen, Ann Brackley ... Wheaton, IL
Jorgensen, Anne B. ... Longmont, CO
Jorgensen, Arlene A. ... Washington, DC
Jorgensen, Arthur W., III ... Madison, WI
Jorgensen, Arthur W., Jr. ... Madison, WI
Jorgensen & Barnes ... Edison, NJ
Woodbridge, NJ
Jorgensen, Brian ... Dallas, TX
Jorgensen, Bruce L. ... Saipan, TT
Jorgensen, Bruce L. ... Logan, UT
Tremonton, UT
Jorgensen, Caryn Geraghty ... Seattle, WA
Jorgensen, Casey L. ... Seattle, WA
Jorgensen, Cheryl F. ... Columbus, OH
Jorgensen, Christian J. ... Homewood, IL
Jorgensen, Christopher L. ... Marengo, IA
Jorgensen, Craig A. ... Tampa, FL
Jorgensen, Craig R. ... Pocatello, ID
Jorgensen, D. Michael ... Salina, UT
Jorgensen, David M. ... Wailuku, HI
Jorgensen, David W. ... Kearney, NE
Jorgensen, Donald K. ... Los Alamitos, CA
Jorgensen, Donald L. ... Bismarck, ND
Linton, ND
Jorgensen, E. Bruce ... Las Vegas, NV
Jorgensen, Edward ... Remsenburg, NY
Jorgensen, Edward D. ... Council Bluffs, IA
Jorgensen, Eric B. ... Atlanta, GA
Jorgensen, Eric P. ... Juneau, AK
Jorgensen, Eric Todd ... Los Angeles, CA
Jorgensen, Eric W. ... Sonoma, CA
Jorgensen, Erik ... San Francisco, CA
Jorgensen, Gerald L. ... Longmont, CO
Jorgensen, Gerald R. ... Fairfax, VA
Jorgensen, Hanne Merete ... Columbus, OH
Jorgensen, Herbert W. ... Gaithersburg, MD
Jorgensen, Ivor N.C. ... Eagan, MN
Jorgensen, J. Christopher ... Las Vegas, NV
Jorgensen, James A. ... St. Paul, MN
Jorgensen, James A. ... Houston, TX
Jorgensen, James D. ... Phoenix, AZ
Jorgensen, James L. ... Valparaiso, IN
Jorgensen, James Niels ... Raleigh, NC
Jorgensen, James R. ... Peoria, IL
Jorgensen, Jay T.
Supreme Court Of The United States, GV
Jorgensen, Jeanne M. ... Irvine, CA
Jorgensen, Jeffrey G. ... San Luis Obispo, CA
Jorgensen, John A. ... Woodbridge, NJ
Jorgensen, John F. ... Wichita, KS
Jorgensen, John M.
Palm Beach Gardens, FL
Jorgensen, Judy ... Salt Lake City, UT
Jorgensen, Julie A. ... Minneapolis, MN
Jorgensen, Karli Kristine ... Issaquah, WA
Jorgensen, Katherine Will
Newport Beach, CA
Jorgensen, Kenneth L. ... St. Paul, MN
Jorgensen, Langdon J. ... Denver, CO
Jorgensen Law Office, S.C. ... Madison, WI
Jorgensen, Mark G. ... St. Paul, MN
Jorgensen, Mary Beth ... Evanston, IL
Jorgensen, Mary Lou ... Sioux Falls, SD
Jorgensen, Melanie L. ... Gate City, VA
Jorgensen, Michael W. ... Dallas, TX
Jorgensen, Mike E. ... Jacksonville, FL
Jorgensen, Norman Eric ... San Jose, CA
Jorgensen, Paul C. ... Silver Spring, MD
Jorgensen, Paul Victor ... Middletown, MD
Jorgensen, Pepin & Smith, P.C.
Longmont, CO
Jorgensen, Peter A. ... Vero Beach, FL
Jorgensen, Ralph G. ... Tabor City, NC
Jorgensen, Randall D. ... Pueblo, CO
Jorgensen, Rian D. ... Menlo Park, CA
Jorgensen, Richard A. ... Orange, CA
Jorgensen, Sarah O. ... Washington, DC
Jorgensen, Sharon Perkner ... Tampa, FL
Jorgensen, Steve ... Viborg, SD
Jorgensen, Stuart S. ... Westminster, CO
Jorgensen, Suzanne M. ... Brick, NJ
Jorgensen, Thomas A. ... Cleveland, OH
Jorgensen, Thomas C. ... Long Beach, CA
Jorgensen, Thomas P. ... West Des Moines, IA
Jorgensen, Walter, Jr. ... Farmington Hills, MI
Jorgensen, Yvonne V. ... Walnut Creek, CA
Jorgenson, Anthony Joseph ... Tulsa, OK
Jorgenson, Duane M. ... Darlington, WI
Jorgenson, Edward ... Dallas, TX
Jorgenson, Eric C. ... Fort Morgan, CO
Jorgenson, Frederick R. ... Charlotte, NC
Jorgenson, J. David ... Tulsa, OK
Jorgenson, J. Harry
Board of Governors Of The Federal Reserve
System,
Office of Inspector General, GV
Jorgenson, James R. ... Miami, FL
Jorgenson, Jandra Susanne ... Tulsa, OK
Jorgenson, Janet ... St. Louis, MO
Jorgenson, John D. ... Menlo Park, CA
Jorgenson, Kathleen M. ... Los Angeles, CA
Jorgenson, Larry G. ... Warren, MN
Jorgenson, Larry L. ... Dubois, WY
Jackson, WY
Jorgenson Law Offices ... Dubois, WY
Jackson, WY
Jorgenson, Leif G. ... Department of Labor,
Office of the Solicitor, GV
Jorgenson, Linda M. ... Cambridge, MA
Jorgenson, Lisa K. ... Carrollton, TX
Jorgenson, Mary Ann ... Cleveland, OH
Jorgenson, Michael L.
Thief River Falls, MN
Jorgenson, Neil T. ... Portland, OR
Vancouver, WA
Jorgenson, Richard A. ... Spokane, WA
Jorgenson, Siegel, McClure & Flegel, LLP
Menlo Park, CA
Jorgenson, William H. ... Staten Island, NY
Jorissen, James M. ... Minneapolis, MN
Jorissen, Paul A. ... Chicago, IL
Jorjani, Daniel H. ... Washington, DC
Jorjani, David B. ... Williamsburg, KY
Jorjani, Parisa ... San Francisco, CA
Jorling, James M. ... Washington, DC
Jorns, Janice J. ... Pratt, KS
Jorquera, Sarah V. ... New York, NY
Jorrie, Kathy A. ... Los Angeles, CA
Jorrin, Hector M. ... Stockton, CA
Jors, Jennifer A. ... Chicago, IL
Jorstad, David W. H. ... Minneapolis, MN
Jorstad, Diane Yohnka ... Morris, IL
Jorstad, Eric E. ... Minneapolis, MN
Jorstad, Kristofer ... Los Angeles, CA
Jorstad, Steven A. ... Wanamingo, MN
Jortberg, Laura K. ... Chicago, IL
Jortner, Wayne R. ... New York, NY
Jory, Donald R. ... Jennings, LA
Jory, Jay V. ... Fresno, CA
Jory, Peterson, Watkins & Smith
Fresno, CA
Jory & Smith, L.C. ... Elkins, WV
Jory, Stephen G. ... Elkins, WV
Jorzak, Richard H. ... Chicago, IL
Joscelyn, Alan L. ... Helena, MT
Joscelyn, Kent B. ... Ann Arbor, MI
Joscelyn, McNair and Jeffrey, P.C.
Ann Arbor, MI
Joscelyn, Miriam A. ... Richmond, CA
José, Bagué A. ... San Juan, PR
Jose, David Elliott ... Indianapolis, IN
Jose, Donald E. ... West Chester, PA
Jose, Frank A. ... Silver Spring, MD
Jose, Harold ... Atlanta, GA
Jose, Henry, Brantley & Keltner, L.L.P.
Fort Worth, TX
Jose, John S. ... Fort Worth, TX
Jose & Wiedis ... West Chester, PA
Josef, Andrew S. ... Boston, MA
Josef, Franklin A. ... Fayetteville, NY
Josef and Marmor ... Fayetteville, NY
Joseff, Mark F. ... Newport Beach, CA
Joseffer, Alice Accola ... Buffalo, NY
Joseffer, Daryl ... Washington, DC
Josefiak, Mary M. ... Denver, CO
Josefiak, Thomas J. ... Alexandria, VA
Josefsberg, Henry J. ... Long Beach, CA
Josefsberg, John C. ... Phoenix, AZ
Josefsberg, Robert C. ... Miami, FL
Josefson, Jennifer A. ... Houston, TX
Josefson, Lois E. ... Fergus Falls, MN
Josefson, Mary L. ... Golden Valley, MN
Josel, Alan J. ... Norristown, PA
Josel, John D. ... Stamford, CT
Josel, Kevin Howard ... New York, NY
Josel, Stephen C. ... Philadelphia, PA
Josel, Wayne M. ... New York, NY
Joseloff, Gerald A. ... Wethersfield, CT
Joseloff & Joseloff ... Wethersfield, CT
Joselow, Robert B. ... Washington, DC
Joselson, Emily J. ... Middlebury, VT
Joselson, Henry C. ... New York, NY
Joselson, Tracy Jennifer ... Baltimore, MD
Joselyn, William A., Sr.
Bloomfield Hills, MI
Josem, Ernest L. ... Norwalk, CT
Josem, Milton B. ... Norwalk, CT
Josem, William T. ... Philadelphia, PA
Josenhans, Paul J. ... Columbus, OH
Joseph, Alan ... Wichita, KS
Joseph, Alan A. ... Los Angeles, CA
Joseph, Alan H. ... Glendale, NY
Joseph, Alan L. ... Goshen, NY
Joseph, Alexandra Bradley ... Glendale, CA
Joseph, Alfred S., III ... Louisville, KY
Joseph, Allan A. ... Miami, FL
Joseph, Allan J. ... San Francisco, CA
Joseph, Allen T. ... Washington, DC
Joseph, Amy ... San Francisco, CA
Joseph, Andrew B. ... Florham Park, NJ
Joseph, Anne G. ... Jacksonville, FL
Joseph, Anne M. ... San Antonio, TX
Joseph, Anthony A. ... Birmingham, AL
Joseph, Anthony C. ... San Diego, CA
Joseph, Anthony L.
Federal Trade Commission,
Bureau of Competition, GV
Joseph, Antoine L.
Frederiksted, St. Croix, VI
Joseph, Arnold C. ... Atlanta, GA
Joseph, Arthur ... Oceanside, NY
Joseph, Arthur S. ... New York, NY
Joseph & Associates, P.C. ... Lansing, MI
Okemos, MI
Joseph, Barbara A. ... Philadelphia, PA
Joseph, Bernard A. ... Washington, DC
Joseph, Beth S. ... Jenkintown, PA
Joseph, Beth Storper ... Miami, FL
Joseph, Brett R. ... Seattle, WA
Joseph, Bruce G. ... Washington, DC
Joseph, Burton ... Chicago, IL
Chicago Heights, IL
Joseph, Burton S. ... Westbury, NY
Joseph, Caran L. ... Chicago, IL
Joseph, Carol M. ... Fort Lee, NJ
New York, NY
Joseph, Cassondra E. ... New York, NY
Joseph, Cathey L. ... Phoenix, AZ
Joseph, Celia M. ... Philadelphia, PA
Joseph, Charles Alan ... Wichita, KS
Joseph, Charles E., The Law Office of
New York, NY
Joseph, Charles Ian ... Baltimore, MD
Joseph, Charles S. ... Jacksonville, FL
Joseph, Cheney C. ... Baton Rouge, LA
Joseph, Christine Alfieri ... Edison, NJ
Joseph, Christy D. ... Irvine, CA
Joseph, Corcoran & Telgenhof
Charlevoix, MI
Joseph, Daniel ... Washington, DC
Joseph, Daniel ... New Kensington, PA
Joseph, David H. ... Philadelphia, PA
Joseph, David L. ... East Lansing, MI
Joseph, David R. ... Philadelphia, PA
Joseph, Donald K. ... Philadelphia, PA
Joseph, Donald R. ... South San Francisco, CA
Joseph, Donna R. ... North Miami, FL
Joseph, Duane E., (P.A.)
Minneapolis, MN
Joseph E. Cheeley, III, P.C. ... Duluth, GA
Joseph, E. George ... Irvine, CA
Joseph, Edward B. ... Philadelphia, PA
Joseph, Edward P. ... Chevy Chase, MD
Joseph, Eleanor A. ... Atlanta, GA
Joseph, Ellen M. ... Manchester, NH
Joseph, Ellen R. ... New York, NY
Joseph, Elliott P. ... New Hyde Park, NY
Joseph, Emile, Jr. ... Lafayette, LA
Joseph, Ernest M. ... Flint, MI
Joseph, F. Michael ... Springfield, MA
Joseph & Feldman ... Fort Lee, NJ
New York, NY
Joseph, Francie E. ... Parsippany, NJ
Joseph, Francis J. ... Butte, MT
Joseph, Frank E., Jr. ... Cleveland, OH
Joseph, Frederick M. ... New York, NY
Joseph, G. Christopher ... Monroe, MI
Joseph, G. Paul ... Myrtle Beach, SC
Joseph, Gary F. ... Jacksonville, FL
Joseph, Georgann ... Evanston, IL
Joseph, George ... Erie, PA
Joseph, George A. ... Chicago, IL
Joseph, George J. ... Charleston, WV
Joseph, George M. ... Portland, OR
Joseph, George Wm., Jr. ... Lakewood, OH
Joseph, Gerson M. ... Miami, FL
Joseph, Gloria J.
National Labor Relations Board,
Office of the General Counsel, GV
Joseph, Greenwald and Laake, P.A.
Greenbelt, MD
Upper Marlboro, MD
Joseph, Gregory P. ... Washington, DC
New York, NY
Joseph, H. Marc ... Phoenix, AZ
Joseph, Heidi R. ... Short Hills, NJ
Joseph, Howard ... Chicago, IL
Joseph, Howard L. ... Los Angeles, CA
Joseph, Irving B. ... Sacramento, CA
Joseph, Irwin H. ... Santa Cruz, CA
Joseph, Jack ... Chicago, IL
Joseph, James G. ... Cleveland, OH
Joseph, James H. ... Pittsburgh, PA
Joseph, James Helton ... Pittsburgh, PA
Joseph, James J., (A Professional
Corporation) ... Los Angeles, CA
Joseph, James N. ... Syosset, NY
Joseph, James P. ... Washington, DC
Joseph, Jane ... Houston, TX
Joseph, Jane E. ... Newport Beach, CA
Minneapolis, MN
Joseph, Jason W. ... Chicago, IL
Joseph, Jeffrey A. ... San Diego, CA
Joseph, Jeffrey A. ... Canfield, OH
Joseph, Jeffrey D. ... Denver, CO
Joseph, Jeffrey F. ... White Plains, NY
Joseph, Jeffrey H. ... Washington, DC
Joseph, Jeffrey W. ... Sanford, FL
Joseph, Jennifer J. ... Columbus, OH
Joseph, Jerome M. ... Denver, CO
Joseph, Jesse D. ... Nashville, TN
Joseph, Joe A. ... Birmingham, AL
Joseph, John A., III ... Tonawanda, NY
Joseph, John J. ... Columbus, OH
Joseph, John M. ... Austin, TX
Joseph, John P. ... Miami, FL
Joseph, Jon A. ... Las Vegas, NV
Joseph, Jon A. ... Eugene, OR
Joseph, Jonathan D. ... San Francisco, CA
Joseph, Jonathan M. ... Richmond, VA
Joseph & Joseph ... Los Angeles, CA
Joseph & Joseph ... Columbus, OH
Delaware, OH
Joseph, Joseph M. ... Hermitage, PA
Joseph, Joseph T., Jr. ... Cleveland, OH
Joseph, Judith ... Fort Lee, NJ
New York, NY
Joseph, Justin G. ... Tarpon Springs, FL
Joseph, Karleen ... Baton Rouge, LA
Joseph, Kathryn Theresa ... Cleveland, OH
Joseph, Kelley A. ... Fort Lauderdale, FL
Joseph, Kenneth D. ... Pittsburgh, PA
Joseph, Kevin C. ... Boston, MA
Joseph, Kirby Gamblin ... Denver, CO
Joseph, Kirlyn H. ... Kew Gardens, NY
Joseph, L. Anthony, Jr. ... New York, NY
Joseph Law Firm, P.C. ... Denver, CO
Joseph Law Offices, P.C. ... Pittsburgh, PA
Joseph, Lawrence ... Jamaica, NY
Joseph, Lawrence J. ... Washington, DC
Joseph, Lawrence M. ... Morristown, NJ
Joseph, Lee N. ... Houston, TX
Joseph, Leonard ... New York, NY
Joseph, Leslie A. ... Boston, MA
Joseph, Lester M. ... Department of Justice,
Criminal Division, GV
Joseph, Linda D. ... New York, NY
Joseph, Linda H. ... Buffalo, NY
Joseph, Lori Ann ... Sacramento, CA
Joseph, Louis S. ... Houston, TX
Joseph, Marc ... Fort Lee, NJ
New York, NY
Joseph, Marc D.
South San Francisco, CA
Joseph, Marc R. H. ... Kansas City, MO
Joseph, Marc S. ... Fort Lauderdale, FL
Joseph, Marc S. ... Chicago, IL
Joseph, Marc W. ... Dallas, TX
Joseph & Marees, P.A. ... Jacksonville, FL
Joseph, Maria L. ... Berkeley, CA
Joseph, Marie L. ... Roswell, GA
Joseph, Mario A. ... New York, NY
Joseph, Mark C. ... Pittsburgh, PA
Joseph, Mark E. ... Van Nuys, CA
Joseph, Marla A. ... Philadelphia, PA
Joseph, Mary Terrell ... Baton Rouge, LA
Joseph, Matthew A., Law Offices of
Menlo Park, CA
Joseph, Matthew Harris ... Washington, DC
Joseph, Matthew P. ... New York, NY
Joseph, Maurice ... Washington, DC
Joseph, McDermott & Reiner, P.C.
Washington, DC
Joseph, Melanie Ann ... Columbia, SC
Joseph, Melbourne E., Jr. ... Las Vegas, NV
Joseph, Michael ... Washington, DC
Joseph, Michael A.
Christiansted, St. Croix, VI
Joseph, Michael B. ... Wilmington, DE
Joseph, Michael D. ... Los Angeles, CA
Joseph, Michael E. ... Oklahoma City, OK
Joseph, Michael I. ... Rockville, MD
Joseph, Michael P. ... New York, NY
Joseph, Michael S. ... Gresham, OR
Joseph, Monu J. ... Irvine, CA
Joseph & Moore, P.C. ... Austin, TX
Joseph, Myron L. ... Milwaukee, WI
Joseph, Nan M. ... Fairfax, VA
Leesburg, VA
Joseph, Neil D. ... Tarzana, CA
Joseph, Pamela Davis ... Wilmington, DE
Joseph, Pamela N. ... Boston, MA
Joseph, Patricia A. ... Topeka, KS
Joseph, Paul R. ... Fort Lauderdale, FL
Joseph, Paul T. ... Okemos, MI
Joseph and Perrin, P.C. ... Eugene, OR
Joseph, Peter A. ... Far Rockaway, NY
Joseph, Philip C. ... Austin, TX
Joseph, Phillip E. ... Portland, OR
Joseph, Pius ... Glendale, CA
Joseph, R. Anthony ... Atlanta, GA
Joseph, R. David ... Greensboro, NC
Joseph, Raymond, & Associates
East Lansing, MI
Joseph, Raymond, & Associates
Lansing, MI
Mason, MI
Joseph, Raymond B. ... Jacksonville, FL
Joseph, Regina M. ... Toledo, OH
Joseph, Regina Waynes ... East Orange, NJ
Joseph, Richard D. ... Chicago, IL
Joseph, Richard E. ... Charlevoix, MI
Joseph, Richard J. ... Atlanta, GA
Joseph, Richard M. ... Peoria, IL
Joseph, Richard N. ... Los Angeles, CA
Joseph, Richard P. ... Pittsburgh, PA
Joseph, Richard S. ... Cincinnati, OH

Joseph, Robert E. ....Portland, OR
Joseph, Robert G. ....Washington, DC
Joseph, Robert J. ....Chicago, IL
Joseph, Robert L. J. ....Yorba Linda, CA
Joseph, Robert R. ....Atlanta, GA
Joseph, Robert S. ....Mount Laurel, NJ
Joseph, Robert T. ....Chicago, IL
Joseph, Roger P. ....Boston, MA
Joseph, Ronald E. ....New York, NY
Joseph, Ronald L. ....Flint, MI
Joseph, Roseann B. ....Easton, PA
Joseph, Scott A. ....Wellesley, MA
Joseph, Serge ....Brooklyn, NY
Joseph, Seth P. ....Miami, FL
Joseph, Seymour ....Denver, CO
Joseph, Shannon R. ....Greensboro, NC
Joseph, Sheri Taplitz ....Belvedere-Tiburon, CA
Joseph & Stalonas ....New York, NY
Joseph, Stanford R. ....Mount Kisco, NY
Joseph, Stephanie R. ....New York, NY
Joseph, Stephen E. ....New Brunswick, NJ
Joseph, Stephen H. ....Mount Laurel, NJ
Joseph, Stephen M. ....Miami, FL
Joseph, Stephen M. ....Wichita, KS
Joseph, Steven J. ....La Grande, OR
Joseph, Steven J., P.C. ....La Grande, OR
Joseph, Steven W. ....Cleveland, OH
Joseph, Susan B. ....New York, NY
Joseph, Susan E. ....Washington, DC
Joseph, Susan M. ....Succasunna, NJ
Joseph, Tammy L. ....McLean, VA
Joseph & Terracciano ....Syosset, NY
Joseph, Terry B. ....Houston, TX
Joseph, Thomas E.
Commodity Futures Trading Commission,
Division of Trading and Markets, GV
Joseph, Todd M. ....Buffalo, NY
Joseph, Tom ....San Antonio, TX
Joseph, Tom, P.C. ....San Antonio, TX
Joseph, Warren M. ....Treasury Department,
Internal Revenue Service, GV
Joseph, Willan Franklin ....Philadelphia, PA
Joseph, William D. ....Zanesville, OH
Joseph, William G. ....Pittsburgh, PA
Joseph, William M. ....Atlanta, GA
Joseph, William R. ....Cleveland, OH
Joseph, William R., Jr.
San Francisco, CA
Joseph, Wolf, Endean & Stahle, P.C.
Saginaw, MI
Joseph, Yves-Georgs ....Santa Ana, CA
Joseph, Zvi ....New York, NY
Josepher & Batteese, P.A. ....Tampa, FL
Josepher, Myron J. ....New York, NY
Josepher, Richard A. ....Fort Lauderdale, FL
Josepher, Ronald H. ....Tampa, FL
Josephic, David J. ....Cincinnati, OH
Josephic, Matthew David ....Atlanta, GA
Josephs, Babette ....Philadelphia, PA
Josephs, Barry D. ....Needham, MA
Josephs, Bonnie P. ....New York, NY
Josephs, David R. ....Providence, RI
Josephs, Ernest H., Jr. ....Wilson, NC
Josephs, Gary S. ....Stony Brook, NY
Josephs, J. Herbert ....Toms River, NJ
Josephs, Jack & Gaebe, P.A. ....Miami, FL
Josephs, John P., Jr. ....Richmond, VA
Josephs, Judith ....Lynn, MA
Josephs, Laura B.
Securities and Exchange Commission,
Division of Enforcement, GV
Josephs, Laurie R. ....Greenwich, CT
Josephs, Lori S. ....New York, NY
Josephs, Marilyn K. ....Pittsburgh, PA
Josephs, Mark L. ....Department of Justice,
Civil Division, GV
Josephs, Mark T. ....Dallas, TX
Josephs, Michael ....New York, NY
Josephs, Michael I. ....Merrick, NY
Josephs, Michael R. ....Miami, FL
Josephs, Sheri L. ....Brooklyn, NY
Josephs, Steven H. ....Los Angeles, CA
Josephs, William V., Jr. ....Loris, SC
Josephsohn, Ralph S. ....Thornton, CO
Josephson, Andrea K. ....Scarsdale, NY
Josephson, Andrew L. ....Anchorage, AK
Josephson, Anne L. ....Boston, MA
Josephson, April ....Santa Ana, CA
Josephson & Associates, P.C.
Anchorage, AK
Josephson, Barry S. ....Los Angeles, CA
Josephson, Celia M. ....East Hampton, NY
Josephson, Daryl C. ....Palo Alto, CA
Josephson, Donald A. ....Farmington, CT
Josephson, Donna L. ....Pacific Palisades, CA
Josephson, Edwin I. ....Chicago, IL
Josephson, Eliott ....Chicago, IL
Josephson & Fink ....Ann Arbor, MI
Josephson, Jessica J. ....New York, NY
Josephson, Joan Kane ....Lawrenceville, NJ
Josephson, Joe P. ....Anchorage, AK
Josephson, Kenneth ....Seattle, WA
Josephson, Laurence P. ....Torrance, CA
Josephson, Lawrence B. ....Chicago, IL
Josephson, Lovell & Dringman
Big Timber, MT
Josephson, Mark Lee ....Chicago, IL
Josephson, Marvin ....New York, NY
Josephson, Maury B. ....New York, NY
Josephson, Nancy A. ....New York, NY
Josephson, Norton ....Daytona Beach, FL
Josephson, Paul P. ....Newark, NJ
Josephson, Peter S. ....New York, NY
Josephson, Philip ....Coral Gables, FL
Josephson, R. Mark ....Big Timber, MT
Josephson, Richard C. ....Portland, OR
Josephson, Richard L. ....Houston, TX
Josephson, Richard W. ....Big Timber, MT
Josephson, Robert M. ....Louisville, KY
Josephson, Roy H. ....Bronx, NY
Josephson, Scott ....Chicago, IL
Josephson, Stephanie N. ....Houston, TX
Josephson, Stephen G. ....Ann Arbor, MI
Josephson, Warren ....Basking Ridge, NJ
Josephson, William ....New York, NY
Josephs-Walborsly, Aileen N.
West Palm Beach, FL
Joset, Jennelle London ....Superior, WI
Josey, J. Diane ....Atlanta, GA
Josey, J. René ....Florence, SC
Josey, Robert F. ....Austin, TX
Joshi, Jui M. ....Pittsburgh, PA
Joshi & Larkin, P.C. ....Skokie, IL
Joshi, Maneesha S. ....Atlantic City, NJ
Pleasantville, NJ
Joshi, Michael ....Fairfax, VA
Joshi, Nandan M. ....Washington, DC
Joshi, Nikhil N. ....Fort Myers, FL
Sarasota, FL
Tampa, FL
Joshi, Premkumar K. ....Skokie, IL
Joshi, Safal K. ....New York, NY
Joshowitz, James H. ....Pittsburgh, PA
Josiah, Selika B. ....Millburn, NJ
New York, NY
Josias, Goren, Cherof, Doody & Ezrol, P.A.
Fort Lauderdale, FL
Josias, Steven L. ....Fort Lauderdale, FL
Joslin, Clark A. ....Cambridge, MN
Joslin & Derderian ....Beverly, MA
Joslin, Fletcher B. ....Montpelier, VT
Joslin, Fletcher Brian (Ted)
Montpelier, VT
Joslin, James C. ....Chicago, IL
Joslin, John E. ....Kansas City, MO
Joslin, Lana E. ....Uniondale, NY
Joslin, Lisa Ferro ....Albany, NY
Joslin, Margaret M. ....Atlanta, GA
Joslin, Norman E. ....Niagara Falls, NY
Joslin, Peter B. ....Montpelier, VT
Joslin, Peter Baird, Jr. ....Albany, NY
Joslin, Richard A., Jr.
Bloomfield Hills, MI
Joslin, Rodney D. ....Chicago, IL
Joslin, Roger ....Bloomington, IL
Joslin & Sedberry ....Raleigh, NC
Joslin, William ....Raleigh, NC
Joslove, Scott Kevin ....Dallas, TX
Joslyn, Brian B., (P.A.)
West Palm Beach, FL
Joslyn, Charles M. ....Choteau, MT
Joslyn, D. Richard ....Gurnee, IL
Joslyn, David L. ....Chicago, IL
Joslyn, Janice H. ....Edina, MN
Joslyn Keydel & Wallace, LLP
Detroit, MI
Joslyn, Nanette ....Richmond, CA
Joslyn, Patrick R. ....Caro, MI
Joslyn, Richard B. ....Pasadena, CA
Joslyn, Robert B. ....St. Clair Shores, MI
Joslyn, Robert B., P.C. ....Detroit, MI
St. Clair Shores, MI
Josovitz, Robert M. ....Fairfield, CT
Jospin, Deborah R.
Corporation for National and Community
Service,
Office of Americorps, GV
Jospin, Walter E. (IBA) **....Atlanta, GA**
Joss, Eric H. ....Los Angeles, CA
Joss, Judy H. ....Anaheim, CA
Joss, Marisa ....New York, NY
Joss, William B. ....Louisville, CO
Josselsohn, Bennett E. ....New York, NY
Josselson, Barry H. ....Orange, CA
Josselson, Potter & Roberts ....Portland, OR
Josselson, Richard M. ....Haddonfield, NJ
Josselyn, Kenneth L. ....New York, NY
Jossem, Jared H. ....Honolulu, HI
Jossem & Toyofuku ....Honolulu, HI
Jossen, Robert J. ....New York, NY
Jossen, Sanford ....Los Angeles, CA
Jossen, Sanford ....Manhattan Beach, CA
Josserand, Carrie Elizabeth ....Olathe, KS
Josserand, Jon ....Lawrence, KS
Josserand, Michael W. ....Denver, CO
Josslin, Richard D. K. ....Bellevue, WA
Jost, Anthony R. ....Indianapolis, IN
Jost, Barbara S. ....Washington, DC
New York, NY
Jost, Henry L., Jr. ....Kansas City, MO
Jost, John C. ....Washington, DC
Jost, Kenneth ....Washington, DC
Jost, Kenneth L. ....Department of Justice,
Civil Division, GV
Jost, Lawrence J. ....Milwaukee, WI
Jost, Lewis W. ....Houston, TX
Jost, Perry W. ....Florham Park, NJ
Jost, Peter Hafner ....Washington, DC
Jost, Richard A. ....Lakewood, CO
Jost, Richard F. ....Las Vegas, NV
Jost, Ruth Stoltzfus ....Columbus, OH
Jost, Timothy S. ....Columbus, OH
Jostad Associates, P.C. ....Fort Collins, CO
Jostad, David R. ....Salem, OR
Jostad, John A. ....Fort Collins, CO
Josten, Carol S. ....Milwaukee, WI
Josten, Robert E. ....Des Moines, IA
Josten, Roy J. ....Racine, WI
Jostmeier, Beata I. ....New York, NY
Jostock, Eric H. ....Chicago, IL
Jostock, Henry J. ....Chicago, IL
Jostock, Henry J., P.C. ....Chicago, IL
Joswick, David D., (P.C.) ....Detroit, MI
Joswick, Theresa C. ....Bloomfield Hills, MI
Jotch, Dwayne F. ....Palm Harbor, FL
Jouannet, Francis L., Jr. ....Cleveland, OH
Jouard, Stephen J. ....Fort Collins, CO
Jouben, Jon Aaron ....Clearwater, FL
Joubert, John T. ....Baton Rouge, LA
Jena, LA
Joubert, Lanette Smith ....Corpus Christi, TX
Joublanc, Mary Beth ....Phoenix, AZ
Jouette, Barbara Lindsay ....Dallas, TX
Jouflas, G. Greg ....Grand Junction, CO
Jough, Katherine ....St. Louis, MO
Joughin, Leslie E., III ....Tampa, FL
Jouhet, Sandra Vozza ....Clinton Township, MI
Joung, Meerie M. ....Boston, MA
Joung, Minnie P. ....Boston, MA
Jouppi, John R. ....Holland, MI
Jouras, Jas. P. ....Kansas City, MO
Jouras, Peter A., Jr., Law Offices of
Overland Park, KS
Jourdain, Peter A. ....Holyoke, MA
Jourdain, William F. ....Dalton, GA
Jourdan, Carolyn ....United States Senate,
Committee Legal Personnel, GV
Jourdan, J. Phillip ....Pontiac, MI
Jourdan, James M. ....Southfield, MI
Jourdan, Jeanne M. ....South Bend, IN
Jourdan, Jeanne M. ....St. Louis, MO
Jourdan, Paul J. ....Brooklyn, NY
Jourdane, Maurice ....San Diego, CA
Jourdin, Willis W., Jr. ....Washington, DC
Jouret, Stefan L. ....Washington, DC
Jouret, Tandy V. ....Dallas, TX
Journell, Thomas W. ....Grove City, OH
Journey, Drexel D. ....Washington, DC
Journey, James K. ....Clinton, MO
Journey, Kelso ....Clinton, MO
Journey, Phillip B. ....Wichita, KS
Journick, Francis X., Jr. ....Woodbridge, NJ
Jourolmon, Leon ....Elberton, GA
Jovan, William J. ....Chicago, IL
Jovanovic, Cindy J. ....Downers Grove, IL
Jovanovic, Teresia B. ....Rochester, NY
Jovanovich, Jody A. ....Bremerton, WA
Jovanovich, Nick ....Fort Lauderdale, FL
Jovanovich, Stefan ....Orinda, CA
Jovanovich, Thomas G. ....St. Cloud, MN
Jove, David ....Miami Beach, FL
Jove, Ivan Pasarell ....San Juan, PR
Jove, Julius A. ....White Plains, NY
Joven, Robert W. ....Irving, TX
Jovick, Robert L. ....Livingston, MT
Jowanna, Matthew J. ....Tampa, FL
Jowdy & Church, P.C. ....Norwood, MA
Jowdy, James J., Jr. ....Danbury, CT
Jowdy, Jeffrey J. ....Danbury, CT
Jowdy, John ....Danbury, CT
Jowdy & Jowdy ....Danbury, CT
Jowdy, Raymond F. ....Norwood, MA
Jowers, Gerald D. ....Columbia, SC
Jowers, Kirk L. ....Washington, DC
Jowers, Robert D. ....Houston, TX
Jowers, Stacy A. ....Baton Rouge, LA
Jowett, Juliet Lawson ....Ocean Springs, MS
Joworisak, Donald T. ....Metuchen, NJ
Joy & Associates, A Professional Corporation
Irvine, CA
Joy, Bernard F. ....Milford, CT
Joy, Bryan K. ....Burlington, KS
Joy, Christopher J. ....Walnut Creek, CA
Joy, Daniel ....Sarasota, FL
Joy, David D., Jr. ....Treasury Department,
Office of the General Counsel, GV
Joy, David R. ....Washington, DC
Joy, Edward P. ....San Francisco, CA
Joy, Elizabeth Renee ....Orlando, FL
Joy, E. V. E. ....St. Petersburg, FL
Joy, Fredk. van B. ....New York, NY
Joy, George E. ....San Antonio, TX
Joy, Harry J. ....Hinsdale, IL
Joy, J. Michael ....Lee's Summit, MO
Joy, Jeffrey C. ....Irvine, CA
Joy, Jo Ann ....Phoenix, AZ
Joy, Jo Ann, P.C. ....Phoenix, AZ
Joy, John P. ....Miami, FL
Joy & Jones ....Burlington, KS
Joy, Joseph R., III ....Lafayette, LA
Joy, Latrelle Bright ....Lubbock, TX
Joy, Louise M. ....Austin, TX
Joy, Margaret P. ....Pittsburgh, PA
Joy, Mark ....Chicago, IL
Joy, Mark ....Brooklyn, NY
Joy, Mark M. ....Hillsboro, IL
Joy, Maurice E. ....Fresno, CA
Joy, Michele F. ....Washington, DC
Joy, Peter A. ....Cleveland, OH
Joy, Poffenberger & Poffenberger ....Perry, IA
Joy, Richard M. ....Champaign, IL
Joy, Robert P. ....Boston, MA
Joy, S. Gregory ....Atlanta, GA
Joy, Steven B. ....Cedar Rapids, IA
Mechanicsville, IA
Mt. Vernon, IA
Joy, Terrence R. ....Minneapolis, MN
Joy, Thomas J. ....Los Angeles, CA
Joy, Thomas J. ....Medford, MA
Joy, Walter W. ....Aurora, IL
Joy, William C. ....Atlanta, GA
Joy, William F., Jr. ....Boston, MA
Joy, William H. ....Perry, IA
Joya, Alejandro Paulino ....Miami, FL
Joyal, Edmond R., Jr. ....Pittsburgh, PA
Joyal, Richard J. ....Manchester, NH
Joyce, Aelish M. ....San Francisco, CA
Joyce, Albert J., III
Panama Canal Commission,
Office of the General Counsel, GV
Joyce, Alexander M. ....Bourne, MA
Joyce, Ann C. ....Colorado Springs, CO
Joyce, Anne ....Department of State,
Office of the Legal Adviser, GV
Joyce, Arlene ....El Cerrito, CA
Joyce, Arthur E. ....Fairfield, CT
Joyce, Austin M. ....Worcester, MA
Joyce, Bernard F., (P.C.) ....New York, NY
Joyce & Bittner ....Pittsburgh, PA
Joyce, Bob H. ....Bakersfield, CA
Joyce, Brenda J. ....Buffalo, NY
Joyce, Brian A. ....Boston, MA
Joyce, Brian R. ....Allentown, PA
Joyce, Carlton E. ....Savannah, GA
Joyce, Catherine M. ....Arlington, VA
Joyce, Catherine Wozniak ....Chicago, IL
Joyce, Charles T. ....Philadelphia, PA
Joyce, Christopher J. ....Hackensack, NJ
Joyce, Christopher P. ....Chicago, IL
Joyce, Craig D. ....Denver, CO
Joyce, D. Kevin ....Hillsborough, NC
Joyce, Dana K. ....Jefferson City, MO
Joyce, Daniel G. ....Blacksburg, VA
Joyce, Daniel J. ....Minneapolis, MN
Joyce, Daniel P. ....Buffalo, NY
Joyce, David E. ....New York, NY
Joyce, David K. ....Kenner, LA
Joyce, David L. ....Boston, MA
Joyce, David P. ....Martinsville, VA
Joyce, David Patrick ....Chardon, OH
Joyce, Deborah L. Dye ....Columbus, OH
Joyce, Debra A. ....Boston, MA
Joyce, Deirdre J. ....Burlington, VT
Joyce, Dennis R. ....Wilkesboro, NC
Joyce, Dennis R. ....Pittsburgh, PA
Joyce, Diane Scobie ....Raleigh, NC
Joyce, Douglas M. ....Haddonfield, NJ
Joyce, Dumas, David & Hanstein
Farmington, ME
Mexico, ME
Joyce, Edward J. ....Boston, MA
Joyce, Edward J., Jr. ....Boston, MA
Joyce, Edward M. ....New York, NY
Joyce, Edward M., Jr. ....Boston, MA
Joyce, Edward T. ....Chicago, IL
Joyce, Edward T., & Associates, P.C.
Chicago, IL
Joyce, Eileen C. ....Pittsburgh, PA
Joyce, Eileen M. ....Cleveland, OH
Joyce, Elizabeth A. ....Boston, MA
Joyce, Elizabeth W. ....Coral Gables, FL
Joyce, Elizabeth W. ....White Stone, VA
Joyce, Erin E. ....Dallas, TX
Joyce, Erin M. ....Los Angeles, CA
Joyce, Eugene L. ....Oak Ridge, TN
Joyce, Frederick M. ....Washington, DC
Joyce, Georgia L. ....Chicago, IL
Joyce, Gerald P., III ....Washington, DC
Joyce, Gerard F., Jr. ....New York, NY
Joyce, H. Sherman ....United States Senate,
Committee Legal Personnel, GV
Joyce, J. Michael ....Pittsfield, MA
Joyce, J. Patrick ....Los Angeles, CA
Joyce, J. Patrick, Jr. ....Springfield, IL
Joyce, James ....New York, NY
Joyce, James C., Jr. ....Roanoke, VA
Joyce, James D. ....Carson, CA
Joyce, James E., Jr. ....Needham, MA
Joyce, James J., Jr. ....Worcester, MA
Joyce, James M. ....Deerfield, IL
Joyce, James M. ....Worcester, MA
Joyce, James M. ....Grand Rapids, MI
Joyce, James M. ....Buffalo, NY
Joyce, James R. ....Madison, CT
Joyce, James V. ....Menlo Park, CA
Joyce, Janet M. ....New York, NY
Joyce, J. C. ....Tulsa, OK
Joyce, Jeffrey J. ....Dallas, TX
Joyce, Jeffrey L. ....Houston, TX
Joyce, Jeffrey R. ....Atlanta, GA
Joyce, Jena Kirsch ....San Diego, CA
Joyce, JoAnne Smith ....Deerfield, IL
Joyce, John Brian ....Pittsburgh, PA
Joyce, John C. ....Bethesda, MD
Joyce, John C. ....Tulsa, OK
Joyce, John E. ....Menomonie, WI
Joyce, John F. ....Mount Carroll, IL
Joyce, John F. ....New York, NY
Joyce, John J. ....Columbia, MD
Joyce, John J., Jr. ....Worcester, MA
Joyce, John M. ....Orlando, FL
Joyce, John P. ....Pittsburgh, PA
Joyce, John R. ....Fresno, CA
Joyce, John R. ....Monterey, CA
Joyce, John R. ....Northfield, IL
Joyce, John R. ....Monroe, LA
Joyce, John W. ....Atlanta, GA
Joyce, Jonathan R. ....Washington, DC
Joyce, Joseph B. ....Des Moines, IA
Joyce, Joseph J. ....Purchase, NY
Joyce, Joseph J. ....Salt Lake City, UT
Joyce, Joseph M. ....Eden Prairie, MN
Joyce & Joyce ....Boston, MA
Joyce & Joyce ....Pittsburgh, PA
Joyce, Kathleen Marie ....Washington, DC
Joyce, Kenneth F. ....Buffalo, NY
Joyce, Kenneth J. ....Fort Lauderdale, FL
Joyce, Kenneth L. ....Overland Park, KS
Joyce, Kevin E. ....Washington, DC
Joyce, Kevin E. ....Toledo, OH
Joyce, Kevin Joseph ....Schaumburg, IL
Joyce, Kevin M. ....Mexico, ME
Joyce, Kim Brennan ....Melville, NY
Joyce, Laurie A. ....San Francisco, CA
Joyce Law Firm, The, L.L.C.
Kansas City, MO
Joyce, Leonard S. ....Washington, DC
Joyce, Linda M. ....Etna, NH
Joyce, Lisa C. ....Mount Kisco, NY
Joyce, Margaret H. ....Euclid, OH
Joyce, Marian ....Livingston, NJ
Joyce, Martin J. ....Longmont, CO

Joyce, Martin R. .... **New York, NY**
Joyce, Mary Patricia .... Chicago, IL
Joyce, Mary Sheila .... Orchard Park, NY
Joyce, Maryann .... Altoona, PA
Joyce, Melissa J. .... Washington, DC
Joyce, Melissa Jo .... Department of Labor, Office of Secretary, GV
Joyce, Meredith, Flitcroft & Normand **Oak Ridge, TN**
Joyce, Michael D. .... Boston, MA
Joyce, Michael E. .... Haddonfield, NJ
Joyce, Michael J. .... Denver, CO
Joyce, Michael P. .... **Kansas City, MO**
Joyce, Michael T. .... Erie, PA
Joyce, Morton Harrison .... Martinsville, VA
Joyce, Patricia A. .... Sterling, IL
Joyce, Patricia M. .... **Metairie, LA**
Joyce, Patricia M. .... East Greenwich, RI
Joyce, Patricia Steimle .... Jefferson City, MO
Joyce, Patrick .... New York, NY
Joyce, Patrick E. .... Farmington, ME
Mexico, ME
Joyce, Patrick J. .... **Omaha, NE**
Joyce, Patrick J. .... Sherburne, NY
Joyce, Patrick M.
Securities and Exchange Commission, Division of Enforcement, GV
Joyce, Paul .... Chicago, IL
Joyce, Paul A., Jr. .... Edina, MN
Joyce, Paul G. .... **Falls Church, VA**
Joyce, Paul M. .... Yuma, AZ
Joyce, Paul M. .... Brockton, MA
Joyce and Pollard .... **Tulsa, OK**
Joyce, R. Michael .... **Irvine, CA**
Joyce, Randall Steven .... **Bakersfield, CA**
Joyce, Randolph K. .... Simi Valley, CA
Joyce & Reyes .... **St. Petersburg, FL**
Tampa, FL
Joyce, Richard F. .... Miami, FL
Joyce, Richard F. .... **Plymouth, IN**
Joyce, Richard F., III .... Miami, FL
Joyce, Richard J. .... Pittsburgh, PA
Joyce, Rita Ferko .... Pittsburgh, PA
Joyce, Robert H. .... **Chicago, IL**
Joyce, Robert J. .... San Diego, CA
Joyce, Robert J. .... **Tulsa, OK**
Joyce, Robert L. .... **New York, NY**
Joyce, Robert N., Jr. .... Lexington, VA
Joyce, Robert P. .... Chapel Hill, NC
Joyce, Robert P., Jr. .... **Newton, MA**
Joyce, Robert T. .... **Tampa, FL**
Joyce, Robert W. .... Newton, MA
Joyce, Robin Mitchell .... **Nashville, TN**
Joyce, Rodney L. .... **Washington, DC**
Joyce, Sally O. .... **Northbrook, IL**
Joyce, Sandra .... Milwaukee, WI
Joyce, Sarah E. .... **Chicago, IL**
Joyce, Sean P. .... **Portland, ME**
Joyce, Sharon K. .... Fairfield, CA
Joyce, Sharon M. .... Newark, NJ
Joyce, Stephanie A. .... **Washington, DC**
Joyce, Stephen M. .... Sherman Oaks, CA
Joyce, Susan A. .... **New York, NY**
Joyce, Thomas A. .... Hartford, CT
Joyce, Thomas B. .... Dallas, TX
Joyce, Thomas F. .... **Chicago, IL**
Joyce, Thomas F. .... Butte, MT
Joyce, Thomas J. .... Hartford, CT
Joyce, Thomas J. .... Chicago, IL
Joyce, Thomas J., III .... Woodbury, NJ
Philadelphia, PA
Joyce, Thomas M. .... Chicago, IL
Joyce, Thomas M. .... Boston, MA
Joyce, Thomas P. .... Chicago, IL
Joyce, Thomas W. .... **Macon, GA**
Joyce, Thomas W. E .... Southampton, NY
Joyce, Thomas W. E., III .... Newark, NJ
Joyce, Thomas W. E., Jr. .... Southampton, NY
Joyce, Timothy C. .... Minneapolis, MN
Joyce, Timothy E. .... Aurora, CO
Joyce, Timothy H. .... Hudson, MA
Joyce, Timothy J. .... **White Plains, NY**
Joyce, Timothy M. .... **Warrenton, MO**
Joyce, Virginia M. .... Wilton, CT
Joyce, Walter E., Jr. .... New York, NY
Joyce, William D., III .... **Jersey City, NJ**
New York, NY
Joyce, William F. .... **Seattle, WA**
Joyce, William J. .... Wichita, KS
Joyce, William J. .... **New Orleans, LA**
Joyce, William J. .... Sharon, PA
Joyce, William M. .... Rye, NY
Joyce, William R. .... **Minneapolis, MN**
Joyce, William R. .... Brooklyn, NY
Joyce, William R., Jr. .... Washington, DC
Joyce, William T. .... Menlo Park, CA
Joyce, Willie M. .... Atlantic City, NJ
Joyce-Romani, Sheila D. .... **Chicago, IL**
Joye, Gary M. .... **Los Angeles, CA**
Joye, John M. .... Crestline, CA
Joye, Larry W. .... **Kansas City, MO**
Joye Law Firm, L.L.P. .... North Charleston, SC
Joye, Mark C. .... North Charleston, SC
Joye, Mark C. .... **Houston, TX**
Joye, Reese I., Jr. .... North Charleston, SC
Joye, Richard Scott .... Beaufort, SC
Joyer, Paulette .... Minneapolis, MN
Joyner, Arthenia L. .... **Tampa, FL**
Joyner, Barbra R. .... Orlando, FL
Joyner, Barry H. .... Department of Labor, Office of the Solicitor, GV
Joyner, Bill .... Concord, NH
Joyner, Bob .... Norman, OK
Joyner & Burnette, P.C. .... Decatur, GA
Joyner, C. David .... Blackshear, GA
Joyner, C. Ray .... Rocky Mount, NC
Joyner, Carver C. .... Chesapeake, VA
Joyner, Charles T. .... **Indianapolis, IN**

Joyner, Conrad F., Jr. .... San Luis Rey, CA
Joyner, D. Whitten .... Cleveland, TN
Joyner, Dawson L. .... Boulder, CO
Joyner, Dexter D. .... Pasadena, TX
Joyner, Elizabeth A. .... **Tulsa, OK**
Joyner, F. Kimball, Jr. .... **Fairfax, VA**
Joyner, F. William .... **Springfield, MO**
Joyner & Fewson, P.C. .... Boulder, CO
Joyner, G. William, III .... **Charlotte, NC**
Raleigh, NC
Joyner, Gary K. .... **Raleigh, NC**
Joyner, Gordon L. .... Atlanta, GA
Joyner, H. Wayne .... Tahoe City, CA
Joyner, Helen K. .... **Southfield, MI**
Joyner, Irving L. .... Durham, NC
Joyner, J. Curtis .... Philadelphia, PA
Joyner, J. Gregory .... Clarksville, IN
Louisville, KY
Joyner, J. Mitchell .... Anchorage, AK
Joyner, Jacqueline J. .... Charleston, SC
Joyner, James W. .... **Jacksonville, NC**
Joyner, Jane Clare
Department Of Veterans Affairs, Office of the General Counsel, GV
Joyner, Jay A. .... Minneapolis, MN
Joyner, Jay A., Ltd. .... Minneapolis, MN
Joyner, Jeffrey K. .... **Beverly Hills, CA**
Joyner, Jim H., Jr. .... **Burlington, NC**
Joyner, John C. .... Decatur, GA
Joyner, John C., Jr. .... Asheville, NC
Joyner, Joseph D., Jr. .... **Raleigh, NC**
Joyner, Kevin S. .... **Raleigh, NC**
Joyner, Lee A., Jr. .... Weatherford, TX
Joyner, Matthew R. .... **Middlebury, CT**
Joyner, Michael E. .... Columbus, GA
Joyner, Reginald T. .... Taylorsville, NC
Joyner, Robert E.
Department Of Health And Human Services, Social Security Administration, GV
Joyner, Robert P. .... Richmond, VA
Joyner, Robert W. .... **San Antonio, TX**
Joyner, Roger Scott .... **Palo Alto, CA**
Joyner, Sam A. .... Tulsa, OK
Joyner, Ulysses P., Jr. .... Orange, VA
Joyner, Veronica D. .... St. Louis, MO
Joyner, Wade R. .... **Chicago, IL**
Joyner, Walton K. .... **Raleigh, NC**
Joyner, William H. .... Roswell, GA
Joynes, Lisa A. .... **Albuquerque, NM**
Santa Fe, NM
Joynes, Louis N., II .... Virginia Beach, VA
Joynes & Marcari, P.C. .... Virginia Beach, VA
Joynes, Stanley K., III .... **Richmond, VA**
Joynt, F. William, III .... Albany, NY
Joynt, Jack A. .... Louisville, KY
Joynt, Joseph Q. .... Tahoe City, CA
Joynt, Michael P. .... **Des Moines, IA**
Joynt, Richard G. .... **Richmond, VA**
Joynt, Stephen M. .... Evergreen, CO
Joynt, Stephen M., P.C. .... Evergreen, CO
Joynton, Stanley F. .... San Angelo, TX
Jozaitis, Laura J. .... **Chicago, IL**
Jozefacki, Linda M. .... Milwaukee, WI
Jozefek, Jane M. .... Syosset, NY
Jozefiak, Stanley W. .... Chicago, IL
Jozus, Ivar A. .... **Middletown, CT**
Jozus, Milardo & Thomasson
Middletown, CT
Jozwiak, John R. .... Chicago, IL
Jozwiak, Steven J. .... Cherry Hill, NJ
Jozwiak-Boylan, Darlene .... Milwaukee, WI
Jozwick, John T. .... Paradise Valley, AZ
Jozwicki, Edward M. .... New York, NY
Jreisat, Wijdan .... **Cincinnati, OH**
Juall, David J. .... Chalfont, PA
Juan, Leslie O. .... **New York, NY**
Juan, Peter D. .... Greenwich, CT
Juan, William L. .... **Corning, NY**
Juanico, Mark T. .... Miami, FL
Juanós i Timoneda, Jesús
Salt Lake City, UT
Juantorena, Felix R. .... New York, NY
Juantorena, Jorge U. .... **New York, NY**
Juan-Urrutia, María T. .... **San Juan, PR**
Juarbe, Carmen Rosa .... **San Juan, PR**
Juarbe Jimenez, Luis F. .... **San Juan, PR**
Juarez, Angel N. .... Los Angeles, CA
Juarez, Anna L. .... Deming, NM
El Paso, TX
Juarez, Bennie R. .... Dallas, TX
Juarez, Christian R. .... Los Angeles, CA
Juarez, Daniel .... Los Angeles, CA
Juarez, David R. .... Brighton, CO
Juarez, Eduardo J. .... Washington, DC
Juarez, George A. .... **Torrance, CA**
Juarez, George A. .... Laredo, TX
Juárez, José .... El Paso, TX
Juarez, Jose Roberto, Jr. .... San Antonio, TX
Juarez, Paul .... Austin, TX
Juarez, Philip .... Austin, TX
Juarez, Richard J. .... **Chicago, IL**
Juarez, Roderick .... Albuquerque, NM
Juarez, Roland M. .... **Dallas, TX**
Juba, George E. .... Portland, OR
Juba, Gregory M. .... Linden, NJ
Juban, Christopher C. .... **Houston, TX**
Juban, Joseph E. .... **Baton Rouge, LA**
Jubanowsky, David L. .... **Newton, NJ**
Jubanyik, Kimberly A. .... **Philadelphia, PA**
Jubanyik, Richard J. .... **Cherry Hill, NJ**
Jubas, Gary .... Ebensburg, PA
Jubas, Marvin .... **Los Angeles, CA**
Jubb, David R. .... Portland, OR
Jubb, Sarah C. .... **Sardis, MS**
Jubber, Gary E. .... **Salt Lake City, UT**
Jubelirer, Carothers, Krier & Halpern
Altoona, PA
Hollidaysburg, PA

Jubelirer, Eliot S. .... **San Francisco, CA**
Jubelirer, James L. .... State College, PA
Jubelirer, Pass and Intrieri, P.C.
Pittsburgh, PA
Jubelirer, Philippa L. .... Oakland, CA
Jubelirer, Robert C. .... **Altoona, PA**
Jubelt, Mark L. .... **Los Angeles, CA**
Jubien, Sidney Mannheim .... Sacramento, CA
Jubin, Gregg S. .... **Washington, DC**
Jubin, Thomas B. .... **Cheyenne, WY**
Jubinsky, Andrew G. .... **Dallas, TX**
Jubinsky, James A. .... **Stamford, CT**
Jubinsky, John .... Honolulu, HI
Jubinville, Robert L. .... Milton, MA
Jubran, Samyah G .... Knoxville, TN
Juby, Jeffrey J. .... **Toledo, OH**
Juceam, Robert E. .... **Washington, DC**
New York, NY
Juchatz, Wayne W. .... **Providence, RI**
Juchau, Blaine, Law Offices of .... Davis, CA
Juckett, Christian L. .... **Louisville, KY**
Louisville, KY
Juckett, Ellen B. .... King Of Prussia, PA
Juckett, Russ .... **Everett, WA**
Juckniess, Frederick R. .... **Minneapolis, MN**
Jud, Austen D. .... Lenoir, NC
Juda, Gary H. .... Hollywood, FL
Juda, Mark A. .... Schenectady, NY
Juda, Nancy M. .... **Washington, DC**
Juda, Richard S., Jr. .... Buffalo, NY
Juda, Scott .... **Los Angeles, CA**
Judah, Armand I. .... Louisville, KY
Judah, Janeen S. .... Houston, TX
Judah, Peter J. .... Hot Springs, VA
Judas, Christine L. .... San Francisco, CA
Judas, Suzanne Meyer .... **Jacksonville, FL**
Juday, Jerome H. .... **Anchorage, AK**
Judd, Amy L. .... **St. Joseph, MI**
Judd, Ardon B., Jr. .... Washington, DC
Judd, Bruce M. .... **Las Vegas, NV**
Judd, C. DeMont, Jr. .... Ogden, UT
Judd, Darin T. .... **San Francisco, CA**
Judd, David E. .... Dallas, TX
Judd, David J. .... Davis, CA
Judd, Dawn L. .... **Palo Alto, CA**
Judd, Dennis L. .... Vernal, UT
Judd, Dennis L., P.C. .... Vernal, UT
Judd, Emilie D. .... Los Angeles, CA
Judd, Evan V. .... Los Gatos, CA
Judd, Gary V. .... **Novato, CA**
Judd, George P. .... Princeton, NJ
Judd, H. Marshall .... Cookeville, TN
Judd, Harlan E. (Lanny), Jr.
Burkesville, KY
Judd, Harold T. .... Concord, NH
Judd, Hugh W. .... **Redmond, WA**
Judd, Jacqueline J. .... **Annapolis, MD**
Judd, James F. .... Coeur d'Alene, ID
Judd, James S. .... Woodcliff Lake, NJ
Judd, Jeffrey M. .... **San Francisco, CA**
Judd, Jeffrey M. .... New York, NY
Judd, Jeffrey S. .... Fresno, CA
Judd, Joel S. .... **Denver, CO**
Judd, Jonathan A. .... **New York, NY**
Judd, Judith D. .... **Denver, CO**
Judd, Kenneth L. .... Schaumburg, IL
Judd, Kenneth M. .... Portland, OR
Judd, Kenni F. .... Palm Beach, FL
Judd, Kenni F., P.A. .... Palm Beach, FL
Judd, Laurie M. .... **Peoria, IL**
Judd Law Office, P.A. .... Post Falls, ID
Judd, Lawrence K. .... Fort Lauderdale, FL
Judd, Lee T. .... **Englewood, CO**
Judd, Linda .... Post Falls, ID
Judd, Lisa F. .... Indianapolis, IN
Judd, Meaghan .... Garden City, NY
Judd & Moss, P.C. .... Ronkonkoma, NY
Judd, M. V. Peter .... Seattle, WA
Judd, M.V. Peter, P.S. .... Seattle, WA
Judd, Phillip D., P.C. .... Ogden, UT
Judd, R. Roth .... Madison, WI
Judd, Richard A. .... **San Francisco, CA**
Judd, Richard D. .... **Denver, CO**
Judd, Richard D., P.C. .... **Denver, CO**
Judd, Robert A. .... **Minneapolis, MN**
Judd, Robert B. .... **Fort Lauderdale, FL**
Judd, Robert L. .... **Benton Harbor, MI**
Judd, Robert M. .... Dallas, TX
Judd & Sailer, P.L.L.C. .... **Redmond, WA**
Seattle, WA
Judd, Sam R. .... San Diego, CA
Judd, Stephanie .... Ronkonkoma, NY
Judd, Stephen H. .... Sidney, NY
Judd, Steven H. .... Sarasota, FL
Judd, T. Conrad .... Encinitas, CA
Judd, Thomas A. .... **Minneapolis, MN**
Judd, Thomas R. .... Phoenix, AZ
Judd, Ulrich & Dean, P.A. .... Sarasota, FL
Judd, William H., Jr. .... New Britain, CT
Judds, Jay B. .... **Grand Island, NE**
Jude & Coco, P.A. .... **Hattiesburg, MS**
Jude, Cox & Tardy .... Newport, ME
Jude, John S. .... Racine, WI
Jude, Rebecca K. .... **Hattiesburg, MS**
Jude, Thaddeus V. (Tad) .... Fridley, MN
Judell, Harold B. .... **New Orleans, LA**
Judell, Lynn E. .... **New York, NY**
Judelle, Elise F. .... **Tallahassee, FL**
Judelsohn, David Kent
Federal Communications Commission, Wireless Telecommunications Bureau, GV
Judelson, Bruce I. .... **New Haven, CT**
Judelson, Charles A. .... Middletown, NY
Judelson, Steven M. .... Mount Vernon, NY
Juden, Alexander C. .... **Houston, TX**
Judge, Alan P. .... **Huntsville, AL**
Judge, Amanda .... Vallejo, CA
Judge, Amanda I. .... **Danville, CA**

Judge, Amy B. .... **Indianapolis, IN**
Judge, Anoop (Ann) .... **Hayward, CA**
Judge, Brendan .... **Roseland, NJ**
Judge, Brian .... Crofton, MD
Judge & Brim, P.C. .... **Austin, TX**
Judge, Catherine T. .... Boston, MA
Judge, Cathleen C. .... **Philadelphia, PA**
Judge, Charles M. .... Livingston, NJ
Judge, Christopher E. .... **Richmond, CA**
Judge, Christopher E. .... **Fairfield, CA**
Oakland, CA
Vallejo, CA
Judge, Connie Margaree
Department of Commerce, Patent and Trademark Office, GV
Judge, Daniel .... San Francisco, CA
Judge & Duffy .... **Glens Falls, NY**
Judge, Frank T., III .... **Middlebury, CT**
Judge, Geoffrey Graham .... Newark, OH
Judge, George A. .... Weston, CT
Judge, H. Wayne .... **Glens Falls, NY**
Judge, James A. .... Irvine, CA
Judge, James & Dutton, Ltd. .... Park Ridge, IL
Judge, James F. .... Orange, CA
Judge, James R. .... Wailuku, HI
Judge, Janet P. .... **Portland, ME**
Judge, Jay S. .... Park Ridge, IL
Judge, Joan E. .... Austin, TX
Judge, Joanne M. .... **Reading, PA**
Judge, John .... **Austin, TX**
Judge, John C. .... Moscow, ID
Judge, John D. .... Norton, OH
Judge, John P. .... **Cherry Hill, NJ**
Philadelphia, PA
Judge, Joseph C. .... **Davenport, IA**
Judge, Joseph E., Jr. .... Oceanside, CA
Judge, Judith W. .... Ann Arbor, MI
Judge, Kevin J. .... Worcester, MA
Judge, Margaret Amoroso .... Philadelphia, PA
Judge, Mark W. .... Boston, MA
Judge, Martin P. .... Holyoke, MA
Judge, Marty M. .... **Princeton, NJ**
Judge & McCormick, S.C. .... Oconto, WI
Judge, Michael E. .... Sylvania, OH
Judge, Michael M. .... Clinton, IA
Judge, Michael P. .... Los Angeles, CA
Judge, Michael T. .... Oconto, WI
Judge, Patricia A. .... **West Palm Beach, FL**
Judge, Patrick, Jr. .... **Haddonfield, NJ**
Judge, Raju S. .... **Palo Alto, CA**
Judge, Richard J., Jr. .... **Houston, TX**
Judge, Robert Edward .... Scarsdale, NY
Judge, Robert P. .... San Gabriel, CA
Judge, Robert S. .... Arlington, MA
Judge, Sean E. .... **Santa Monica, CA**
Judge, Shana Marie .... Albuquerque, NM
Judge, Stephen J. .... Concord, NH
Judge, Thomas C. .... Chicago, IL
Judge, Thomas J. .... **Washington, DC**
Judge, W. Patrick .... **St. Paul, MN**
Judge, Walter E., Jr. .... **Burlington, VT**
Judge and Warren, P.A.
Daytona Beach, FL
Judge, William C. .... **San Francisco, CA**
Judge, William J. .... River Forest, IL
Judge, William M. .... Milwaukee, WI
Judice & Adley, A Professional Law Corporation .... **Lafayette, LA**
Judice, Anne Keaty .... Lafayette, LA
Judice, C. Raymond .... Austin, TX
Judice, Gregory Van .... Lake Charles, LA
Judice, Kenneth R. .... Houston, TX
Judice, Kenneth R., Attorney, P.C.
Houston, TX
Judice, Marc W. .... **Lafayette, LA**
Judice, Margaret E. .... **Franklin, LA**
Judice, Ronald J. .... **Lafayette, LA**
Judice, Steven C. .... **Baton Rouge, LA**
Judin, Carl H., Jr. .... Kerrville, TX
Judin, Carl Henry, III .... **Dallas, TX**
Judin, C.H." Hank ", III .... **Dallas, TX**
Judin, Jennifer .... **Dallas, TX**
Judin, Jerry M. .... Staten Island, NY
Judis, Brian J. .... Toledo, OH
Judiscak, Kevin M. .... **Phoenix, AZ**
Judisch, Clara M. .... Bradenton, FL
Judish, Julia Eden .... **Washington, DC**
Judish, Nathan P. .... **Washington, DC**
Judkins, Greg D. .... San Diego, CA
Judkins & Hayes .... Greenfield, OH
Judkins, James C. .... **Fairfax, VA**
Judkins, James P. .... **Tallahassee, FL**
Judkins, Joe R. .... **Wartburg, TN**
Judkins, Julia B. .... **Fairfax, VA**
Judkins, Louise A. .... Sacramento, CA
Judkins, Richard D. .... **Palo Alto, CA**
Judkins, Robert J. .... Greenfield, OH
Judkins, William B. .... **Richmond, VA**
Judlowe, Stephen B., (P.C.)
New York, NY
Judlowitz, David .... Westbury, NY
Judnick, Jesse L. .... Martinez, CA
Judson, Bruce D. .... New York, NY
Judson, C. James .... **Seattle, WA**
Judson, Charles B. .... **Traverse City, MI**
Judson, Craig L. .... **Walnut Creek, CA**
Judson, David B. .... Sacramento, CA
Judson, David H. .... **Dallas, TX**
Judson, Douglas A. .... Arlington Heights, IL
Judson, Gerald R. .... **Santa Monica, CA**
Judson, Henry H., III .... Seattle, WA
Judson, K. Leonard .... **Phoenix, AZ**
Judson, Kenneth G. .... **Pittsburgh, PA**
Judson, Lilia G. .... Indianapolis, IN
Judson, Linda S. .... **Pittsburgh, PA**
Judson, Mark M. .... Lake Charles, LA
Judson, Nancy L. .... New York, NY
Judson, Philip L. .... **Austin, TX**

Juntunen, Michael E. ....Grand Forks, ND
Juo, James ....Los Angeles, CA
Jupena, James R. ....Altamonte Springs, FL
Jupin, Seth M. ....Cleveland, OH
Jupiter, Clare ....New Orleans, LA
Jupiter, Jay A.
Federal Deposit Insurance Corporation, GV
Jupiter, Robert M. ....Bayside, NY
Jupiter, Steven ....Baton Rouge, LA
Jura, Michele Kay ....San Antonio, TX
Juracek, Jerry D. ....Baltimore, MD
Juracka, Jay F. ....Schenectady, NY
Jurado, Ray G. ....Los Angeles, CA
Jurado, Rebecca ....Fullerton, CA
Jurakhan, Nirmala ....New York, NY
Juran, Belinda M. ....Boston, MA
Juran, Kevin A. ....New York, NY
Juran, Lawrence B. ....West Palm Beach, FL
Juran, Maureen Herr ....Denver, CO
Juran, M. L. ....New Orleans, LA
Juran, Peter J. ....Winston-Salem, NC
Jurand, Robert B. ....Naples, FL
Juranek, Frank J. ....Niles, IL
Juraniec, Joseph M. ....Boston, MA
Juras, Kristen Gustafson ....Great Falls, MT
Jurasek, Robert J. ....Anchorage, AK
Juravich, J. Christopher ....Sugar Land, TX
Jurca, David F. ....Seattle, WA
Jurca, Jeffrey J. ....Columbus, OH
Jurca, Melanie Campbell ....Columbus, OH
Jurch, George R., III ....Salisbury, NC
Jurcyk, John David ....Lenexa, KS
Jurcyk, John J., Jr. ....Kansas City, KS
Jurczak, Richard J. ....Avon, CT
Jurczenko, Alexander ....Cleveland, OH
Jurczyk, Richard A. ....Rolling Meadows, IL
Jurdem, Scott ....Denver, CO
Jurden, Jan R. ....Wilmington, DE
Jurden, Leonard W. ....Kansas City, MO
Jurdy, F. Dale ....Spokane, WA
Jure, Curt W. ....Redlands, CA
Jurecko, Kevin D. ....Gainesville, FL
Jurecky, George T. ....Fort Lee, NJ
Jurecky, Stephen G. ....El Paso, TX
Jureidini, Nazario J. ....Las Vegas, NV
Jureit, Ross C. ....Naples, FL
Jureit, William F. ....St. Augustine, FL
Jurek, Julie A. ....San Diego, CA
Jurek, Kenneth J. ....Chicago, IL
Jurek, Lynne ....Houston, TX
Jureller, John E., Jr. ....New York, NY
Jureller, Paul D. ....Albany, NY
Juren, Harold P. ....Norfolk, VA
Jurenka, David P. ....Hartford, CT
Juretic, Scott T. ....San Luis Obispo, CA
Jurewicz, Richard M. ....Philadelphia, PA
Jurgeleit, Peter B. ....Chicago, IL
Jurgemeyer, Donald W. ....Columbus, IN
Jurgemeyer, D. W., P.C. ....Columbus, IN
Jurgens, Dale H. ....Dallas, TX
Jurgens, George B., III ....New Orleans, LA
Jurgens, J.A., P.A. ....Longwood, FL
Orlando, FL
Jurgens, J.A. ....Longwood, FL
Tampa, FL
Jurgens, James R. ....Santa Fe, NM
Jurgens, James S. ....East Longmeadow, MA
Jurgens, John H. ....New York, NY
Jurgens, Julien F. ....New Orleans, LA
Jurgens, Larry C. ....Chicago, IL
Jurgens, Roland J. ....Oak Lawn, IL
Jurgensen, Dale E. ....Ellsworth, WI
Jurgensen, Marlene Pose ....Costa Mesa, CA
Jurgensen, Thomas E. ....San Diego, CA
Jurgensmeyer, Randy R. ....Dallas, TX
Jurges, Richard ....New York, NY
Jurgeson, Ronald L. ....Lee's Summit, MO
Jurgovan, Jon M. ....Atlanta, GA
Jurgovan, Richard J. ....Chicago, IL
Juric, Catherine ....Chicago, IL
Juric, Zelimira ....Columbus, OH
Jurich, John A. ....Bakersfield, CA
Jurich, Lance N. ....Los Angeles, CA
Jurina, Raymond P., Jr. ....LaGrangeville, NY
Jurish, Kenneth M. ....Chicago, IL
Jurisich, Richard Blaise ....New Orleans, LA
Jurisich, Richard Blaise, Jr.
New Orleans, LA
Jurist, Bruce H. ....Baltimore, MD
Jurist, Howard C. ....Garden City, NY
Jurist, Kenneth F. ....White Plains, NY
Jurista, Alan P. ....Canton, MA
Jurista, Steven Z. ....Millburn, NJ
Jurith, Edward H.
Executive Office Of The President,
Office of National Drug Control Policy, GV
Jurjans, Peteris ....Cleveland, OH
Jurkacek, Elizabeth ....Chicago, IL
Jurkanin, Giselle A. ....Walnut Creek, CA
Jurkat, M. Alexander ....Albany, NY
Jurkevich, Jason L. ....Newark, NJ
Jurkiewicz, David J. ....Indianapolis, IN
Jurkiewicz, Thomas W. ....Bristol, CT
Jurkoic, Paul M. ....Irvine, CA
Jurkovich, Michael J. ....Fresno, CA
Jurkovich, Patti J. ....Minneapolis, MN
Jurkowicz, Jacqueline Rudman
North Woodmere, NY
Jurkowitz, Daniel S. ....Tucson, AZ
Jurkowitz, Harvey ....Tucson, AZ
Jurkowitz, Jed W. ....Phoenix, AZ
Jurkowski, Joseph T., Jr. ....Washington, DC
Jurman, Rory Eric ....New York, NY
Jurman, Stephen J. ....Moon Township, PA
Jurmu, Stephen I. ....Lansing, MI
Jurnecka, Sheri L. ....San Francisco, CA
Jurney, Kathryn V. ....West Palm Beach, FL
Jurney, Thomas F. ....Portland, OR
Jurnovoy, Holly V. ....Pensacola, FL
Juro, Richard ....Omaha, NE
Juroe, Susan E. ....Washington, DC
Juroe, Theodore C. ....Rochester, NY
Juron, Marc B. ....New York, NY
Juron-Schiffman, Reena ....Buffalo Grove, IL
Juroszek, John O. ....Lansing, MI
Jurovich, Ronald P. ....Thermopolis, WY
Juroviesky, Henry ....Treasury Department,
Internal Revenue Service, GV
Jurow, Bill Ian ....Huntington Station, NY
Jurow, George L. ....New York, NY
Jurow, Irving H. ....Chevy Chase, MD
Jurow, Martin A. ....Dallas, TX
Jurrens, M. Randall ....Saginaw, MI
Jurrius, Cynthia M. ....Greenbelt, MD
Jurs, Peter B. ....Cincinnati, OH
Jurs, Stephen Andrew ....Gastonia, NC
Jursich, John T. ....North Chicago, IL
Jursik & Jursik ....Cudahy, WI
Jursik, Patricia D. ....Cudahy, WI
Jursik, Robert J. ....Cudahy, WI
Jursinski, Kevin F. ....Fort Myers, FL
Jursinski, Kevin J., P.A., Law Office of
Fort Myers, FL
Jurus, John A. ....Oak Forest, IL
Jurus, John A., Ltd. ....Oak Forest, IL
Jurus, Stanley R. ....Columbus, OH
Jurusik, Tracy K. ....Chicago, IL
Jurva, Mark A. ....Portland, OR
Jury & Ahrens ....Appleton, WI
Jury, Clifford S. ....Minneapolis, MN
Jury, David R. ....Pittsburgh, PA
Jury, Don L. ....Appleton, WI
Jury, Jeffrey R. ....Austin, TX
Jury, Meredith A., (P.C.) ....Riverside, CA
Jury, William H. ....Phoenix, AZ
Jusek, Frank R. ....Strongsville, OH
Jusino, Phillip J. ....Coram, NY
Jusis, Helen ....Kenosha, WI
Jusk, Jerry A. ....New York, NY
Juska, William L., Jr. ....New York, NY
Juskewitch, Steven A. ....Portland, ME
Juskie, JoAnn ....Palo Alto, CA
Fort Collins, CO
Juskie, Robert M. ....San Diego, CA
Jusko, James A. ....Santa Monica, CA
Juson, Justine S. ....San Francisco, CA
Jussel, Philip W. ....Casper, WY
Jussim, Jared ....Burbank, CA
Jussim, Noah E. ....Los Angeles, CA
Just, Charles C. ....Idaho Falls, ID
Just, Chas. P. ....Sacramento, CA
Just, Chester A. ....Edison, NJ
Just, David L. ....New York, NY
Just, Joseph A. ....Tacoma, WA
Just, Joshua J. ....New York, NY
Just Law Office ....Idaho Falls, ID
Just, Lawrence E. ....Des Plaines, IL
Just, Marjorie ....Washington, DC
Just, Nicholas J. ....Ballwin, MO
Just, Raymond A. ....San Francisco, CA
Just, Vernon D. ....Wichita, KS
Just/Pratt, LLP ....San Francisco, CA
Justak, Martine H., (Mrs.) ....Indianapolis, IN
Justak, Raymond J. ....Indianapolis, IN
Juste, Jerry A. ....New York, NY
Justen, Frank A. ....Sylvania, OH
Juster, Charles P. ....New York, NY
Juster, David A. ....Treasury Department,
Internal Revenue Service, GV
Juster, Joseph K. ....Cleveland, OH
Juster, Kenneth I. ....Washington, DC
Juster, Leonard T. ....Minneapolis, MN
Juster, Mark L. ....Chicago, IL
Juster, Michael ....Newton, MA
Juster, Sara A. ....Omaha, NE
Juster, Sherman ....Philo, CA
Justesen, Kristina J. ....Northbrook, IL
Justesen, Wayne Q., Jr. ....Greenwood, SC
Justh, Bruce ....Department of Labor,
Office of the Solicitor, GV
Justh, Carolyn ....Coeur d'Alene, ID
Justham, Larry D. ....Fort Myers, FL
Justian, Charles F. ....Grand Rapids, MI
Justice, A. Doyle ....Lubbock, TX
Justice, Arthur E., Jr. ....Florence, SC
Justice & Brown ....Delphi, IN
Logansport, IN
Justice, Cheryl D. ....Los Angeles, CA
Justice, Courtney B. ....Delphi, IN
Logansport, IN
Justice, David ....Ashland, KY
Justice, Deets D. ....Austin, TX
Justice, Della M. ....Lexington, KY
Justice, Elizabeth A. ....Crawfordsville, IN
Justice, Eve & Edwards, P.A. ....Charlotte, NC
Justice For All Law Center, The, L.L.C.
Gretna, LA
New Orleans, LA
Justice, Gary L. ....Los Angeles, CA
Justice, J. Steven ....Cincinnati, OH
Justice, Jack B. ....Philadelphia, PA
Justice, James F. ....Charlotte, NC
Justice, James T. ....Manchester, MA
Justice, James W. ....Knoxville, TN
Justice, Jeff ....Decatur, IL
Justice, Jennifer L. ....New York, NY
Justice, Jessica ....Morgantown, WV
Justice, John B. ....Albany, NY
Justice, John E. ....Olympia, WA
Justice, John R. ....Chester, SC
Justice, Joseph W. ....Pikeville, KY
Justice, Judy Turner ....Knoxville, TN
Justice, Kathleen E. ....Larkspur, CA
Justice, Lawrence P. ....Albany, NY
Justice, M. Flynn, III ....Costa Mesa, CA
Justice, Malcolm F., Jr. ....Salt Lake City, UT
Justice, Marina C. ....Oak Park, IL
Justice, Max Edward ....Charlotte, NC
Justice, Michael L. ....Woodland Hills, CA
Justice, Noel & Burks ....Knoxville, TN
Justice, Patricia ....Las Vegas, NV
Justice, Paul G. ....Savannah, GA
Justice, Rebecca L. ....Richmond, IN
Justice, Robert L. ....Logansport, IN
Justice, Rodney S. ....Ashland, KY
Justice, Roy C. ....New York, NY
Justice, Samuel C. ....Portland, OR
Justice, Samuel H., Jr. ....Atlanta, GA
Justice, Samuel R. ....McMinnville, OR
Justice, Scott A. ....Orlando, FL
Justice, Scott T. ....Columbia, SC
Justice, Shirley Mahan ....Mobile, AL
Justice, Tanya Y. ....Atlantic City, NJ
Justice, Thomas H., III ....Winter Park, FL
Justice, William R. ....Columbiana, AL
Justice, William Wayne ....Tyler, TX
Justicia-Soto, Jessica Esther ....Vega Baja, PR
Justin, Beatriz E. ....Tampa, FL
Justin, Dan ....Tustin, CA
Justin, Edward L. ....Stamford, CT
Justin, James M. ....Jackson, MI
Justin, Jeffrey T. ....Vancouver, WA
Justin, Meryl S. ....Newark, NJ
Justin, Robert M. ....Rochester, MI
Justin, Roger C. ....St. Cloud, MN
Justin, W. Dyke ....Sault Ste. Marie, MI
Justinich-Cushing, Linda ....Mount Holly, NJ
Justino, Stephen A. ....Englewood, CO
Justin-Reed, Denise L. ....Alamo, CA
Justis, E. Bernard ....Columbia, MD
Justis, Gary D. ....Kansas City, MO
Justis, L. Ellis, Jr. ....Baltimore, MD
Justiss & Hornsey, P.L.C. ....Fayetteville, AR
Justiss, William B. ....Fayetteville, AR
Justl, David G. ....Oxnard, CA
Justman, Anthony J. ....San Francisco, CA
Justman, Harold A. ....San Mateo, CA
Justman, Jennifer ....Los Angeles, CA
Justman, Jonathan S. ....Los Angeles, CA
Justrabo, Alwyn J. ....New Orleans, LA
Justus, Craig D. ....Asheville, NC
Justus, James K. ....Forsyth, MO
Justus, Jo Lynne ....Topeka, KS
Justus, Jolie L. ....Kansas City, MO
Justus, Leslie-Ann M.
New Brunswick, NJ
Justus & McCullah ....Forsyth, MO
Justus, Michael K. ....Dallas, TX
Justus, Stacy M. ....Little Rock, AR
Justvig, Howard ....New York, NY
Juten, J. Russell ....West Orange, NJ
Jutila, Edwin J. ....East Hartford, CT
Jutila, Sharon M. ....Eugene, OR
Jutkowitz, J. David ....White Plains, NY
Jutkowitz, J. David ....Yonkers, NY
Jutkowitz, Stanley S. ....Washington, DC
Jutras, Allise K. ....Alexandria, VA
Jutras, Elizabeth E. ....Providence, RI
Jutras, Robert A. ....Haverhill, MA
Jutry, James A. ....Tucson, AZ
Jutze, Robert G. ....Cincinnati, OH
Juvan, Catherine M. ....Doylestown, PA
Juvan, Frank T. ....Ottumwa, IA
Juvelier, Martin D. ....New York, NY
Juvelis, Antigone E. ....Washington, DC
Juvier, Christin Jarvis ....Charlotte, NC
Juvier, Cristina ....Houston, TX
Juviler, Amy ....New York, NY
Juviler, Michael R. ....Brooklyn, NY
Juvkam-Wold, Per E. ....Washington, DC
Juvrud, Duane O. ....El Paso, TX
Juvrud, William Owen ....Plainview, TX
Juza, Wm. J. ....Salem, OR
Juzumas, Richard E. ....New York, NY
Juzwiak, Jeffrey M. ....Sayville, NY

Ka, Mimi Mei-Shen ....New York, NY
Kaake, Richard H. ....Colorado Springs, CO
Kaanehe, Blue H. ....Kailua, HI
Kaap, Keith J. ....Madison, WI
Kaapcke, Wallace L. ....San Francisco, CA
Kaapu, David B. ....Kailua-Kona, HI
Kaapuni, Gregory J. ....Westlake Village, CA
Kaar, Jason F. ....Bethesda, MD
Kaar, R. Michael ....Milton, PA
Kaardal, Erick G. ....Minnetonka, MN
Kaare, Linda Sue ....Muskegon, MI
Kaarsberg-Handrus, Marianne
Chula Vista, CA
Kaas, Brian S. ....Milwaukee, WI
Kaas, Carolyn Wilkes ....Hamden, CT
Kaas, Donald G. ....Blue Bell, PA
Kaas, Glenn ....Hartford, CT
Kaase, Robert P. ....Wytheville, VA
Kaasik, Raimo H. ....Los Angeles, CA
Kaatz, Leon M. ....Hartford, CT
Kaatz, Margo J. ....Whittier, CA
Kaatz & Peikes ....Hartford, CT
Kaatz, Sarah L. ....Monterey, CA
Kaba, Moises, III ....Miami, FL
Kaba, Richard A. ....Chicago, IL
Kaba and Shade, P.A. ....Miami, FL
Kaback, Alan W. ....Fort Lauderdale, FL
Kaback, Gilbert P. ....Colchester, CT
Kaback, Gilbert P., P.C., Law Offices of
Colchester, CT
Kaback, Hoffer ....New York, NY
Kaback, Hoffer, P.C. ....New York, NY
Kaback, Michelle A. ....Modesto, CA
Kabacoff, Lester E. ....New Orleans, LA
Kabacoff, Pres ....New Orleans, LA
Kabacy, Robert E. ....Portland, OR
Kabahar, Bryan A. ....Los Angeles, CA
Kabak, Bernard ....New York, NY
Kabak, Edward M. ....Danbury, CT
Kabak, Wayne S. ....New York, NY
Kabaker, Richard A. ....Chicago, IL
Kabaker, Richard Z. ....Madison, WI
Kabaker, William L. ....Chicago, IL
Kabakoff, Ronald M. ....Middletown, OH
Kabala, Edward J. ....Pittsburgh, PA
Kabala & Geeseman, A Professional
Corporation ....Pittsburgh, PA
Kabalka, Stephen G. ....Chattanooga, TN
Kabalkin, Barry E. ....Washington, DC
Kabanek, Susan E. ....San Jose, CA
Kabanuck, Glenn D. ....San Rafael, CA
Kabanuck, Terry C. ....Seattle, WA
Kabara, Christina J. ....Green Bay, WI
Kabat, Alan R. ....Washington, DC
Kabat, Andrew A. ....Cleveland, OH
Kabat, David L. ....Chicago, IL
Kabat, Gary B. ....Beachwood, OH
Kabat, Heidi A. ....Minneapolis, MN
Kabat, Jules L. ....Los Angeles, CA
Kabat, Michael D. ....Atlanta, GA
Kabat, Mielziner, Sobel and Janice
Beachwood, OH
Kabatchnick, Craig M. ....Durham, NC
Kabatchnick, Neil B. ....Washington, DC
Kabateck, Brian S. ....Los Angeles, CA
San Diego, CA
Kabb, Kenneth S. ....Cleveland, OH
Kabb, Kenneth S., Co., L.P.A.
Cleveland, OH
Kabbes, David G. ....Wichita, KS
Kabbes, John T. ....Jackson, MS
Kabboord, John J., Jr. ....Cocoa Beach, FL
Kabboord, John J., Jr., A Professional
Association ....Cocoa Beach, FL
Kabcenell, Martin J. ....Sarasota, FL
Kabeiseman, John R. ....Yankton, SD
Kabeiseman & Pollard ....Yankton, SD
Kabeiseman, William Karl ....Salem, OR
Kabel, Gregory W. ....Chicago, IL
Kabel, Janice ....New York, NY
Kabel, Robert J. ....Washington, DC
Kabel-Barmat, Lisa E. ....Cherry Hill, NJ
Kabele, Stacy L. ....Minneapolis, MN
Kabella, Chris R. ....Inver Grove Heights, MN
Kaber, Steven C. ....Chagrin Falls, OH
Kaberon, Seth N. ....Chicago, IL
Kabert-Gerson, Marlene ....Los Angeles, CA
Kabili, Janet Feldman ....Boulder, CO
Kabisch, Robert E. ....Fort Wayne, IN
Kablack, Mark A. ....Wellesley, MA
Kablack, Wayne A. ....Indiana, PA
Kable, Edward E. ....New York, NY
Kable, Kenneth W. ....Saginaw, MI
Kable, William H. ....Baltimore, MD
Kabler, Philip N. ....Gainesville, FL
Kabler, Stephen L. ....Denver, CO
Kabler, Steven Robert ....Englewood, CO
Kabler, Wm. M. ....Alexandria, VA
Kablik, Richard A., (P.C.) ....Newington, CT
Kablik, Thomas M. ....Wethersfield, CT
Kabnick, Lisa D. ....Philadelphia, PA
Kabodian, Janice Anne ....Pontiac, MI
Kaboolian, Nancy ....New York, NY
Kabot, Alvin A. ....New York, NY
Kabot, Byron E. ....New Canaan, CT
Kabot, Steven L. ....Visalia, CA
Kaboth, Kurt R. ....New York, NY
Kabrick, Larry E. ....Quincy, IL
Kabrick, Renee J. ....Jasper, IN
Kabrins, Ronald M. ....Beverly Hills, CA
Kabumoto, Cary K., (Mr.) ....Chicago, IL
Kacal, Jerry ....Houston, TX
Kacavas, John P. ....Concord, NH
Kacena, James L. ....Atlanta, GA
Kacer, Denise D. ....Santa Ana, CA
Kacer, Jayne Taylor ....Costa Mesa, CA
Kacer, Peter ....Atlanta, GA
Kacerovskis, William T. ....St. Louis, MO
Kachadoorian, James W. ....New York, NY
Kachadourian, Corinne V. ....Binghamton, NY
Kachadourian & Kachadourian
Binghamton, NY
Kachadourian, Mark H. ....Binghamton, NY
Kachagian, Gregory C. ....Northbridge, MA
Kachalsky, Alan ....Rye, NY
Kachel, Linda L. ....Los Angeles, CA
Kachel, Lynn Morris ....Richmond, VA
Kachelhoffer, Scott S. ....Aurora, IL
Chicago, IL
Kachigian, Amerik A. ....Granite City, IL
Kachigian, Mark G. ....Oklahoma City, OK
Tulsa, OK
Kachinsky, Joel ....Summertown, TN
Kachline, James E. ....Chattanooga, TN
Kachmar, George M., III ....Hackensack, NJ
Kachmar, James ....Reno, NV
Kachmar, Lillian S. ....Villanova, PA
Kachmar, Lori A. ....Allentown, PA
Kachmar, Shawn A. ....Atlanta, GA
Kachmar, Steven ....Pottsville, PA
Kachmarik, Ronald M. ....Cleveland, OH
Kachmarsky, John ....Charleston, SC
Kachmarsky, John, P.C. ....Charleston, SC
Kachnykewych, Vera O. ....New York, NY
Kachor, Mark A.
National Labor Relations Board,
Office of Board Members, GV
Kachulis, George P. ....Pittsburgh, PA
Kachulis, Paul G. ....Pittsburgh, PA
Kachur, John R. ....Harrisburg, PA
Kachur, Stephen B. ....Tucson, AZ
Kachuriak, Kristie M. ....Pittsburgh, PA
Kacic, Glenn D. ....Columbus, OH
Kacin, Alvin Richard ....Elko, NV
Kacin, Joanne V. ....Fort Lauderdale, FL

Kacir, Barbara B. ... Providence, RI
Kacir, George Sidney ... Temple, TX
Kacir, Sidney ... Temple, TX
Kack, Thomas P. ... Prescott, AZ
Kackley, Debra L. ... Mayfield Heights, OH
Kackley, Steve D. ... Sebring, FL
Kacmar, Donald E. ... Cleveland, OH
Kacmarcik, Sharon K. ... Atlanta, GA
Kacoyanis, Dennis C.
Consumer Product Safety Commission, Office of Compliance, GV
Kacoyannakis, John C. ... Boston, MA
Kacvinsky, John F. ... Washington, DC
Kacy & Associates ... Clarkston, MI
Kacy, Dennis M. ... Clarkston, MI
Kaczala, Larry A. ... Toledo, OH
Kaczanowska, Laurie Smith ... Denver, CO
Kaczanowski, Christine ... Cleveland, OH
Kaczensky, Tobey W.
Commodity Futures Trading Commission, Division of Trading and Markets, GV
Kaczka, Thomas C. ... Cherry Hill, NJ
Kaczka, Thomas M. ... Elmwood Park, NJ
Kaczmar, Michael J. ... Syracuse, NY
Kaczmarek, Carla ... Hamtramck, MI
Kaczmarek, Chester J. ... Hamtramck, MI
Kaczmarek, Christopher E.
Washington, DC
Kaczmarek, Jan M. Z. ... Princeton, NJ
Kaczmarek, John C., (P.A.) ... Boca Raton, FL
Kaczmarek, Kaczmarek & Kaczmarek
Hamtramck, MI
Kaczmarek, Lili C. ... Columbus, OH
Kaczmarek, Matthew R. ... South Bend, IN
Kaczmarek, Nancy J. ... Madison, WI
Kaczmarek, Robert L. ... Saginaw, MI
Kaczmarek, Robert Z. ... Hamtramck, MI
Kaczmarek, Thomas L. ... Saginaw, MI
Kaczmarek-Corrigan, Teresa ... Brooklyn, NY
Kaczmarski, Jeffrey A. ... Watertown, WI
Kaczmarski, Karen R. ... Buffalo, NY
Kaczor, David L. ... Grand Rapids, MI
Kaczor, Kathleen M. ... Buffalo, NY
Kaczor, Maria S. ... San Francisco, CA
Kaczorowski, Robert John ... New York, NY
Kaczorowski, Stanley J. ... Elizabeth, NJ
Kaczynski, Mark H. ... New York, NY
Kaczynski, Michelle A. ... Boston, MA
Kaczynski, Paola Tripodi ... Media, PA
Kaczynski, Ronald C. ... Andover, MA
Kaczynski, Stephen J. ... Cleveland, OH
Kaczynski, William C. ... Pittsburgh, PA
Kadaba, Vaibhav P. ... Atlanta, GA
Kadala, Ana E. ... Houston, TX
Kadan, O. Danl. ... Timonium, MD
Kadanoff, Jacqueline Felice ... Brooklyn, NY
Kadanoff, Peri ... Kew Gardens, NY
Kadanoff, Philip G. ... Brooklyn, NY
Kadar, Geza, Jr. ... Santa Rosa, CA
Kadas, Madeleine Boyer ... Washington, DC
Kaddaras, James C., Jr. ... Boston, MA
Kadden, Ronald S. ... New York, NY
Kadden, Steven L. ... Aurora, IL
Kaddo, James A. ... Los Angeles, CA
Kaddoura, Marwan S. ... Norton, MA
Kade, Barry ... Montgomery, VT
Kade, Paul M. ... Miami, FL
Kadel, Edward E., Jr. ... Concord, CA
Kadel, Susan M. ... Lancaster, PA
Kadela, David A. ... Columbus, OH
Kadell, Samuel L. ... Chicago, IL
Kademenos, Victor P. ... Mansfield, OH
Sandusky, OH
Kaden, Alan S. ... Washington, DC
Kaden, Ellen Oran ... Camden, NJ
Kaden, Gerald ... Freehold, NJ
Kaden, Hayden J. ... Gustavus, AK
Kaden, Jeffrey M. ... New York, NY
Kaden, Lawrence A. ... Pensacola, FL
Kaden, Lewis B. ... New York, NY
Kader, David ... Tempe, AZ
Kaderabek, Lisa M. ... Chicago, IL
Kaderly, Edison ... Lamar, MO
Kaderly & Kaderly ... Lamar, MO
Kaderly, Steven H. ... Lamar, MO
Kades, Matthew D. ... Akron, OH
Kades, Michael B.
Federal Trade Commission, Bureau of Competition, GV
Kadet, Samuel ... New York, NY
Kadets, Andrew J. ... Cambridge, MA
Kadi, William J. ... San Francisco, CA
Kadian, Mark A. ... Southfield, MI
Kadick, Scott T. ... Syracuse, NY
Kadievitch, Natalie D. ... Minneapolis, MN
Kadilak, Susan Elaine ... Beaver, PA
Kadin, David C. ... Redondo Beach, CA
Kadin, Howard G. ... New York, NY
Kadin, Jacqueline L. ... New York, NY
Kadin, Lisa E. ... New York, NY
Kadin, Ronald ... Woodbury, NY
Kading, George P. ... Sun City, AZ
Kading, Linda King ... West Des Moines, IA
Kading, Mary L. ... Brooksville, FL
Kading, Matthew J. ... Milwaukee, WI
Kading, R.B., Jr. ... Boise, ID
Kading, Scott D. ... Sioux Falls, SD
Kadinger, Richard A. ... Denver, CO
Kadir, Safia S. ... Gaithersburg, MD
Kadis, Gary M. ... Chesterland, OH
Kadis, Jeffrey A. ... Charlotte, NC
Kadis, Suellen S. ... Chagrin Falls, OH
Kadish, Aaron ... Baltimore, MD
Kadish, Abbe L. ... New York, NY
Kadish, Allen G. ... Waldwick, NJ
New York, NY
White Plains, NY
Kadish, Bethany T. ... Rockville, MD
Kadish, Craig M. ... Baltimore, MD
Kadish, Craig M., Chartered ... Baltimore, MD
Kadish, Darren L. ... Baltimore, MD
Kadish, David A. ... San Francisco, CA
Kadish, Eric J. ... Philadelphia, PA
Kadish, Eugene M. ... Tempe, AZ
Kadish, Eugene M., Ltd. ... Tempe, AZ
Kadish & Fiordaliso ... Buffalo, NY
Kadish, Gerald ... New York, NY
Kadish, Glenn W. ... Everett, WA
Kadish, Hinkel & Weibel, A Legal Professional Association ... Cleveland, OH
Kadish, Jed S. ... Princeton, NJ
Kadish, Jeffrey M. ... Livingston, NJ
Kadish, Joanne ... Lakewood, CO
Kadish, Joshua ... Portland, OR
Kadish & Kadish, P.C. ... Baltimore, MD
Kadish, Keith I. ... Buffalo, NY
Kadish, Kenneth F. ... Syracuse, NY
Kadish, Marc R. ... Chicago, IL
Kadish, Matthew F. ... Washington, DC
Kadish, Michael B. ... Lawrenceville, GA
Kadish, Michael L. ... Los Angeles, CA
Kadish, Richard L. ... Rockville, MD
Kadish, Sanford H. ... Berkeley, CA
Kadish, Scott P. ... Cincinnati, OH
Kadish, Stephen L. ... Cleveland, OH
Kadish, William L. ... New York, NY
Kadison, Charles G., Jr. ... Acton, MA
Kadison, Joseph L. ... Chicago, IL
Kadison, Steven J. ... Chicago, IL
Kadison, Stuart L. ... Los Angeles, CA
Kadjan, Daniel N. ... Chicago, IL
Kadle, Ranjana ... Buffalo, NY
Kadlec, Cindy S. ... Columbia, MO
Kadlec, Daniel T. ... Minneapolis, MN
Kadlec, Keith Daniel ... Winston-Salem, NC
Kadlec, Kevin O. ... Cleveland, OH
Kadlec, Randall J. ... Chicago, IL
Kadlec, Robert W. ... Los Angeles, CA
Kadlec, Shane R. ... Houston, TX
Kadletz, Diane Stavenhagen ... Santa Ana, CA
Kadletz, Kim F. ... Santa Ana, CA
Kadlic, Carl E. ... San Francisco, CA
Kadlic, John J. ... Reno, NV
Kadlick, Richard F. ... New York, NY
Kadlubek, Brian ... Pittsburgh, PA
Kadlubowski, Marian F. ... Iselin, NJ
Kadoch, Laurie C. ... Portland, ME
Kadon, Karl P. ... Cincinnati, OH
Kadosh, Orit ... New York, NY
Kadotani, Cheri A. ... Fullerton, CA
Kadow, Joseph J. ... Tampa, FL
Kadre, Manuel ... Miami, FL
Kaduboski, Mark S. ... New York, NY
Kadue, David D. ... Los Angeles, CA
Kadunce, Darrell L. ... Butler, PA
Kadushin, A. Donald ... Pontiac, MI
Kadushin, Jeffrey D.
Rockville Centre, NY
Kadushin, Karen D. ... Monterey, CA
Kadwell, Laura D. ... St. Paul, MN
Kady, Louis J.R., P.A. ... Carteret, NJ
Kady, Louis J.R. ... Carteret, NJ
Kadyk, D. James ... Tampa, FL
Kadyk, David J. ... Tampa, FL
Kadzielski, Mark A. ... Los Angeles, CA
Kadzik, Peter J. ... Washington, DC
Kaechele, Lawrence D. ... Lansing, MI
Kaeder, Kennan Edward ... San Diego, CA
Kaeding, Michael A. ... Chicago, IL
Kaeding, Patricia J. ... Rockville, MD
Kaeding, Robert H. ... Lake Forest, IL
Kaehler, James A. ... Hopkins, MN
Kaehler, William J. ... Schenectady, NY
Kaeiser, Clayton R. ... Miami, FL
Kaelber, Donald D. ... St. Petersburg, FL
Kaelin, Debra A. ... Clifton Park, NY
Kaelin, Doris A. ... Palo Alto, CA
Kaelin, George H., III ... San Diego, CA
Kaelin, Gerard J. ... Danvers, MA
Kaelin, Henry M. ... Louisville, KY
Kaelin, John Norman, III ... Glenolden, PA
Kaelin, Lynne D. ... San Diego, CA
Kaelin, Michael P. ... Stamford, CT
Kaelin, Robert E. ... Hartford, CT
Kaelin, Thomas A. ... Bethel, CT
Waterbury, CT
Kaelin, William G. ... Fairfield, CT
Kaem, Lewis Y. ... Brentwood, NY
Kaemmerer, Michael E. ... St. Louis, MO
Kaemper, Michael ... Albuquerque, NM
Kaempf, John T. ... Portland, OR
Kaempf, Victoria N. ... Palo Alto, CA
Kaempfer, Christopher L. ... Las Vegas, NV
Kaeo, George K. K., Jr. ... Honolulu, HI
Kaer, Diane ... Red Bluff, CA
Kaercher, Kathleen A. ... Washington, DC
Kaercher, Robert M. ... Fairdale, KY
Kaergard, Kenneth L. ... St. Charles, IL
Kaesebier, Carol C. ... Notre Dame, IN
Kaeser, Carin C. ... Sacramento, CA
Kaeser, Clifford R. ... Buffalo, NY
Kaeser, Hans F. ... New York, NY
Kaeser, Richard R. ... Cherry Hill, NJ
Kaeser, Steven D. ... Glastonbury, CT
Kaesgen, Derek ... Cleveland, OH
Kaeske, Caroline E. Kirksey ... Dallas, TX
Kaeske, Michael Louis ... Dallas, TX
Kaess, Charles J. ... Old Bridge, NJ
Kaess, Warren V. ... Cuyahoga Falls, OH
Kaestner, James A.
South San Francisco, CA
Kaestner, Joseph W. ... Richmond, VA
Kaestner, Matthew G. ... Long Beach, CA
Kaestner, Richard D. ... Elm Grove, WI
Kaestner, Richard D., Law Offices of, S.C.
Elm Grove, WI
Kaestner, Steven D. ... Oklahoma City, OK
Kafader, Edward F. ... Wilmington, DE
Kafader, Edward F., P.A. ... Wilmington, DE
Kafafian, Martin W. ... Montvale, NJ
Kafalenos, Vivian P. ... Washington, DC
Kafantaris, George Nicholas ... Warren, OH
Kafarski, Erik M. ... Madison Heights, MI
Kafer, Charles William ... New Bern, NC
Kafer, Michael S. ... New York, NY
Kafer, Susan M. ... Brooklyn, NY
Kaffee, Stephen ... Washington, DC
Kaffee, Stephen, P.C., Law Offices of
Washington, DC
Kaffen, Ronald O. ... Akron, OH
Kaffenbarger, James A., Jr. ... Bethesda, MD
Kaffenberger, Howard W. ... Houston, TX
Kaffer & Hannan ... Mobile, AL
Kaffun, Howard ... Keizer, OR
Kafin, Robert J. ... New York, NY
Kafka, Alfred H. ... Sharon, MA
Kafka, Benjamin S. ... Dedham, MA
Kafka, Bernard R. ... Sharon, MA
Kafka, Bradley G. ... St. Louis, MO
Kafka & Budman ... Garden City, NY
Kafka, Gerald A. ... Washington, DC
Kafka, Joseph R. ... San Jose, CA
Kafka, Julie L. ... Irvine, CA
Kafka & Kaufman, P.C. ... Sharon, MA
Kafka, Lindsay Smith ... Boston, MA
Kafka, M. Milton ... Sharon, MA
Kafka, Steven M. ... Garden City, NY
Kafkas, Demetrios ... Lowell, MA
Kafkas, T. ... Brookfield, WI
Kafker, Arlene ... Washington, DC
Kafker, Serena L. ... Cincinnati, OH
Kaforey, Melville ... Akron, OH
Kafoury, Gregory ... Portland, OR
Kafoury, John P. ... St. Louis, MO
Kafoury, Michael A. ... St. Louis, MO
Kafrissen, Arthur S. ... Philadelphia, PA
Kafrissen, Carole F. ... Philadelphia, PA
Kafrissen, Terri J. ... Boulder, CO
Kaftan, Andrew C. ... Cashton, WI
Sparta, WI
Kaftan, Frederick B. ... West Bend, WI
Kaftan, G. Jane ... Appleton, WI
Kaftan, Van Egeren & Gilson, S.C.
Green Bay, WI
Kaftarian, Melissa A. ... New York, NY
Kaften, Timothy W. ... Los Angeles, CA
Kagan, Amber L. ... New York, NY
Kagan, Andrew B. ... Lincolnwood, IL
Kagan, Arthur L. ... Bronx, NY
Kagan, Barbara K. ... Washington, DC
Kagan, Barton D. ... Randolph, MA
Kagan, Benjamin ... North Hollywood, CA
Kagan, Carole F.
Department Of Health And Human Services, Office of the General Counsel, GV
Kagan, Charles G. ... Revere, MA
Kagan, Daniel ... Rockville, MD
Kagan, Daniel G. ... Lewiston, ME
Kagan, David B. ... Minneapolis, MN
Kagan, David H. ... New York, NY
Kagan, Debra M. ... Worcester, MA
Kagan, Edwin B. ... Tampa, FL
Tampa, FL
Kagan, Edwin B., P.A. ... Tampa, FL
Kagan, Elena
Executive Office Of The President, GV
Kagan, Eugene M. ... Farmington, CT
Kagan, Faye ... Rockville, MD
Kagan, Gerald B., (P.C.) ... Santa Monica, CA
Kagan, H. George ... West Palm Beach, FL
Kagan, Harvey M. ... Carmel, IN
Kagan, Howard ... Brooklyn, NY
Kagan, J. Harlan ... Edwardsburg, MI
Kagan, Jeffrey F. ... Tarzana, CA
Kagan, Jonathan P. ... Annapolis, MD
Kagan, Jonathan S. ... Los Angeles, CA
Kagan & Kagan ... Rockville, MD
Revere, MA
Kagan, Kenneth S. ... Seattle, WA
Kagan, Linda S. ... Chicago, IL
Kagan, Linda S. ... New York, NY
Kagan & Lubic ... New York, NY
Kagan, Martin L. ... New York, NY
Kagan, Matthew H. ... Woodland Hills, CA
Kagan, Nancy A. ... New York, NY
Kagan, Rachelle A. ... Washington, DC
Kagan, Rebecca Appenzeller ... Dayton, OH
Kagan, Richard E. ... Baltimore, MD
Kagan, Richard G. ... Randolph, MA
Kagan, Robert ... New York, NY
Kagan, Robert A. ... Berkeley, CA
Kagan, Robert A., The Law Offices of
Plattsburgh, NY
Kagan, Rory L. ... Washington, DC
Kagan, Rosalyn H. ... Chicago, IL
Kagan, Sarah A. ... Washington, DC
Kagan, Seymour ... Los Angeles, CA
Kagan, Seymour J. ... Toms River, NJ
Kagan, Spencer M. ... Revere, MA
Kagan, Stewart A. ... New York, NY
Kagan, Stuart A. ... Los Angeles, CA
Kagarise, Wade Alan ... Hollidaysburg, PA
Kagawa, Carlton M. ... Danville, IL
Kagay, Albert & Diehl ... Columbus, OH
Kagay, Charles M. ... San Francisco, CA
Kagay, Jerry A. ... McKinney, TX
Kagay, Joji ... Torrance, CA
Kagei & Matsunaga LLP
Los Angeles, CA
Torrance, CA
Kagel, Ina P. ... Los Angeles, CA
Kagel, John ... Redwood City, CA
Kagel, Joseph H. ... Huntington Beach, CA
Kagel, Peggy M. ... San Rafael, CA
Kagel, Sam ... San Francisco, CA
Kagele, Jerry L. ... Spokane, WA
Kagels, Edward G. ... Cleveland, OH
Kagen, Alan M. ... Arlington, VA
Kagen, Andrew F. ... York, PA
Kagen, J. Stuart ... New York, NY
Kagen, MacDonald & France, P.C.
York, PA
Kages, C. Gus ... Chicago, IL
Kagesa, Elisse H. ... Honolulu, HI
Kagesa, Elisse H., A Law Corporation
Honolulu, HI
Kagey, Lyn ... San Diego, CA
Kagey, Lynda L. ... Alexandria, VA
Kagi-Larrivee, Thomasina J ... Missoula, MT
Kagimoto, Elton S. ... Honolulu, HI
Kagiwada, Cynthia A. ... San Francisco, CA
Kagler, Robert W. ... Moundsville, WV
Kagnoff, Michael S. ... San Diego, CA
Kagon, A. David ... Los Angeles, CA
Kagon, Robert L. ... Malibu, CA
Kah, Helmut ... Woodinville, WA
Kah, Jong-Hyun ... New York, NY
Kahalas, David A., (P.C.) ... Needham, MA
Kahalas, Howard M., (P.C.) ... Boston, MA
Kahalas, Jason ... Needham, MA
Kahalas, Warshaw & Friend, P.C.
Needham, MA
Kahale, George, III ... New York, NY
Kahalley, Karol L.
Greenwood Village, CO
Kahan, Allan R. ... Silver Spring, MD
Kahan, Ari ... Cupertino, CA
Kahan, Barry H. ... Chicago, IL
Kahan, Dan M. ... Chicago, IL
Kahan, David ... Fort Lauderdale, FL
Kahan, David A. ... Reno, NV
Kahan, David D. ... Cleveland, OH
Kahan, Douglas E. ... New York, NY
Kahan, Eric Howard ... New York, NY
Kahan, James ... Santa Barbara, CA
Kahan, James L. ... Seattle, WA
Kahan, Jeffrey J. ... Troy, MI
Kahan, Jeffrey M. ... Glen Rock, NJ
Kahan, Joel ... Half Moon Bay, CA
Kahan, Jonathan S. ... Washington, DC
Kahan, Julian ... Cleveland, OH
Kahan, Kerensky & Capossela, L.L.P.
Hartford, CT
Vernon, CT
Kahan, Lawrence ... San Diego, CA
Kahan, Linda S. ... Rockville, MD
Kahan, Marc A. ... Chicago, IL
Kahan, Marcel ... New York, NY
Kahan, Mark L. ... Pico-Rivera, CA
Kahan, Mark S. ... Silver Spring, MD
Kahan, Martin J. ... New York, NY
Kahan, Penny Nathan ... Chicago, IL
Kahan, Penny Nathan, & Associates, Ltd.
Chicago, IL
Kahan, Robert ... Westbury, NY
Kahan, Robert L. ... Los Angeles, CA
Kahan, Rochelle L. ... Houston, TX
Kahan, Sanford M. ... Morris Plains, NJ
Kahan, Sheldon ... Poughkeepsie, NY
Kahan, Shimon B. ... Chicago, IL
Kahan, Steven E. ... Cleveland, OH
Kahan, Stuart E. ... Irving, TX
Kahan, Tehilah Berman ... New York, NY
Kahan, Theodore F. ... Santa Monica, CA
Kahana, Peter R. ... Philadelphia, PA
Kahana, Shraga F. ... Spring Valley, NY
Kahane, Deborah ... Piedmont, CA
Kahane, Dennis Spencer ... San Ramon, CA
Kahane, Karen M. ... Fort Lauderdale, FL
Kahane, Lynda ... Santa Rosa, CA
Kahane, Robert S. ... Miami, FL
Kahane, Tammy L. ... Woodland Hills, CA
Kahanek, Daniel L. ... Austin, TX
Kahanek, John, III ... Bellaire, TX
Kahaner, Eileen L. ... Washington, DC
Kahaner, Nancy Sue ... Westminster, CO
Kahaner, Paula Sue ... Fairfax, VA
Kahaner, Paula Sue, P.C. ... Fairfax, VA
Kahaner, Steven M. ... New York, NY
Kahaner, Vicki R. ... New Haven, CT
Kahanowicz, Alex ... Los Angeles, CA
Kahanowitch, Richard ... Woodland Hills, CA
Kaharick, Jerome J. ... Johnstown, PA
Kaharick, Jerome J., and Associates
Johnstown, PA
Kahdeman, Richard J. ... Glendale, CA
Kahelin, William J. ... Westfield Center, OH
Kahen, Behnam ... Floral Park, NY
Kahen, David E. ... New York, NY
Kahen, Harold I. ... New York, NY
Kaheny, John M. ... Chula Vista, CA
Kahill, Charles J. ... South Portland, ME
Kahl, Andrew H. ... Des Moines, IA
Kahl, Barbara E. ... Department of Labor, Office of the Solicitor, GV
Kahl, Christian M. ... Towson, MD
Kahl, David B. ... Corning, NY
Kahl, Dick L. ... Powell, WY
Kahl, Donald L. ... Tulsa, OK
Kahl, James A. ... Washington, DC
Kahl, Kevin C. ... Palmdale, CA
Kahl, Kevin H. ... Springfield, IL
Kahl, Leah A. ... Charlotte, NC
Kahl, Malcolm H. ... Fort Lauderdale, FL
Kahl, Mary K. ... South Portland, ME
Kahl, Michelle L. ... Minneapolis, MN
Kahl, Richard C. ... Lewiston, NY
Kahl, Robb Bradford ... Appleton, WI
Kah-Lai Ip, Joanna ... Burlingame, CA
Kahlbaugh, Richard S. ... York, PA
Kahle, A. Dana ... Wheeling, WV
Kahle, Bridget Hayward ... Columbus, OH

Kahle, Douglas Aaron .... Chicago, IL
Kahle, Douglas E. .... Virginia Beach, VA
Kahle, Gail W., Law Office of
Wheeling, WV
Kahle, Gary A. .... Port Charlotte, FL
Kahle & Hartle .... Bradford, PA
Kahle, Jay Paul .... Bradford, PA
Kahle, John H. .... Jasper, IN
Kahle, Kara M. .... West Palm Beach, FL
Kahle, Karen E. .... Wheeling, WV
Kahle Law Offices .... Wheeling, WV
Kahle, Melvin W., Jr. .... Wheeling, WV
Kahle, Neill R., Jr. .... Tampa, FL
Kahle, Richard F., Jr. .... Honolulu, HI
Kahle, Thomas W. .... Cincinnati, OH
Kahlenbeck, Howard, Jr. .... Indianapolis, IN
Kahlenberg, Steven Jay .... Atlanta, GA
Kahler, Camille Tauroney .... Rome, NY
Utica, NY
Kahler, Frederick W. .... East Norwich, NY
Kahler, H. Richard .... Peoria, IL
Kahler, James G. .... Lyons, KS
Kahler, John M., II .... Tiffin, OH
Kahler, Judith Fine .... Larchmont, NY
Kahler and Kahler .... Tiffin, OH
Kahler, L. William, Jr. .... Reedsburg, WI
Kahler Law Offices .... Reedsburg, WI
Kahler, Mark P. .... Round Rock, TX
Kahler, Ray W. .... Hoquiam, WA
Kahler, Richard A. .... Tiffin, OH
Kahler, Steven J. .... Maquoketa, IA
Kahler, Timothy I. .... New York, NY
Kahlert, George D. .... Sarasota, FL
Kahlert, Vera I. .... Toms River, NJ
Kahley, Stephen W. .... Rushford, MN
Kahlmus, Maurice F. .... Meridian, MS
Kahlon, Tejindar Singh .... North Merrick, NY
Kahme, Michael .... Princeton, NJ
Kahn, A. David .... Atlanta, GA
Kahn, A. Michael, Jr. .... Humble, TX
Kahn, Aaron B. .... Treasury Department,
Office of Thrift Supervision, GV
Kahn, Adam P. .... Boston, MA
Kahn, Alan .... Philadelphia, PA
Kahn, Alan E. .... New York, NY
Kahn, Alan M. .... Chicago, IL
Kahn, Andrea L. .... Newark, NJ
Kahn, Andrew H. .... Baltimore, MD
Kahn, Ann R. .... Reisterstown, MD
Kahn, Anthony C. .... New York, NY
Kahn, Anthony F. .... New York, NY
Kahn, Arnold D. .... Los Angeles, CA
Kahn, Arnold E. .... Palm Beach, FL
Kahn, Arthur H. .... Philadelphia, PA
Kahn, Arthur M. .... Kingston, NY
Kahn, Arthur S. .... Memphis, TN
Kahn, Barbara E. .... Springfield, MA
Kahn, Benita A. .... Columbus, OH
Kahn, Benjamin A. .... Greensboro, NC
Kahn, Benjamin Alexander .... Denver, CO
Kahn, Bernard L. .... Canton, OH
Kahn, Bernard S. .... Rancho Viejo, TX
Kahn, Bert L. .... Skokie, IL
Kahn, Bert L., Ltd. .... Skokie, IL
Kahn, Bertrand J. .... New York, NY
Kahn, Beth A. .... Los Angeles, CA
Kahn, Beth E. .... Mount Holly, NJ
Kahn and Block, LLP .... New York, NY
Kahn, Brian J. .... Helena, MT
Kahn, Brian J. .... New York, NY
Kahn, Bruce M. .... Memphis, TN
Kahn, Bruce S. .... Southfield, MI
Kahn, Bruce W. .... New York, NY
Kahn, Burt M. .... Greenbelt, MD
Kahn, Carole S. .... Los Angeles, CA
Kahn, Charles F., Jr. .... Milwaukee, WI
Kahn, Charles H. .... Los Angeles, CA
Kahn, Charles J., Jr. .... Tallahassee, FL
Kahn, Cheryl .... North Chicago, IL
Kahn, Claude B. .... Chicago, IL
New Lenox, IL
Kahn, Corinne B., P.A. .... Boca Raton, FL
Plantation, FL
Kahn, Cynthia C. .... Denver, CO
Kahn, Cynthia L. .... New York, NY
Kahn, D. Barry .... Santa Monica, CA
Kahn, Dana Selig .... Stony Point, NY
Kahn, David B. .... Northfield, IL
Kahn, David B., & Associates, Ltd.
Northfield, IL
Kahn, David E. .... Mercer Island, WA
Kahn, David L. .... Los Angeles, CA
Kahn, David M. .... Collinsville, IL
Kahn, David Miller .... New York, NY
White Plains, NY
Kahn, David O. .... Los Angeles, CA
Kahn, David S. .... San Francisco, CA
Kahn, David S. .... Washington, DC
Kahn, David V. .... Chicago, IL
Kahn, Deborah Ann .... Cohoes, NY
Kahn, Deborah Beth .... New York, NY
Kahn, Dees, Donovan & Kahn
Boonville, IN
Evansville, IN
Jasper, IN
Mt. Vernon, IN
Princeton, IN
Henderson, KY
Owensboro, KY
Kahn, Dennis Alan .... Buffalo, NY
Kahn, Dennis I. .... New Brunswick, NJ
Kahn, Dona Seeman .... New York, NY
Kahn, Donald J. .... Miami Beach, FL
Kahn, Donald W. .... Libertyville, IL
Kahn, Douglas A. .... San Francisco, CA
Kahn, Douglas A. .... Ann Arbor, MI
Kahn, Edmund D. .... Tucson, AZ
Kahn, Edward J. .... Chicago, IL

Kahn, Edward S. .... Lawrenceville, NJ
Kahn, Edwin L. .... Washington, DC
Kahn, Edwin S. .... Denver, CO
Kahn, Elaine S. .... Chevy Chase, MD
Kahn, Ellen I. .... San Francisco, CA
Kahn, Ellis I. .... Charleston, SC
Kahn, Eric G. .... Springfield, NJ
Kahn, Erik W. .... New York, NY
Kahn, Evan L. .... New York, NY
Kahn, Evans .... Stamford, CT
Kahn, F. Warren .... Lewiston, NY
Kahn, Faith Stevelman .... New York, NY
Kahn, Freeman & LaForge, P.A.
Phoenix, AZ
Kahn, Fritz R. .... Washington, DC
Kahn, Fritz R., P.C. .... Washington, DC
Kahn, Gail Mason .... Rancho Viejo, TX
Kahn, Garry L. .... Portland, OR
Kahn, Gary I. .... Mahwah, NJ
Kahn, Gary K. .... Portland, OR
Kahn, Geoffrey A. .... Philadelphia, PA
Kahn, Gerald .... New York, NY
Kahn, Gerald H. .... New Haven, CT
Kahn, Gerald J. .... Milwaukee, WI
Kahn, Geri Nadine .... San Francisco, CA
Kahn, Glen I. .... Denver, CO
Kahn, Glenn .... New Lenox, IL
Kahn, Gordon B. .... Mobile, AL
Kahn, Gregg S. .... Newark, NJ
Kahn, Gregory H. .... Houston, TX
Kahn & Gutter .... Plantation, FL
Kahn, Harlan D. .... Chicago, IL
Kahn, Harold E. .... San Francisco, CA
Kahn, Harold E., Law Offices of
San Francisco, CA
Kahn, Harry H. .... San Francisco, CA
Kahn, Heidi M. .... New York, NY
Kahn, Henry D. .... Baltimore, MD
Kahn, Herbert L. .... Floral Park, NY
Kahn, Hilde Elisabeth .... Washington, DC
Kahn & Horwitz, P.C. .... New York, NY
Kahn, Howard M. .... Houston, TX
Kahn, Howard M., P.C. .... Houston, TX
Kahn, Howard N. .... Hollywood, FL
Kahn, Ilene A. .... Baltimore, MD
Kahn, Ira M. .... Huntington, NY
Kahn, Irving B. .... Milwaukee, WI
Kahn, Irwin .... New York, NY
Kahn, James C. .... White Plains, NY
Kahn, James F. .... Phoenix, AZ
Kahn, James R. .... Philadelphia, PA
Kahn, James T. .... New York, NY
Kahn, Jan L. .... Hanford, CA
Kahn, Jane E. .... San Rafael, CA
Kahn, Jaymee .... New York, NY
Kahn, Jeffrey B. .... Fort Lauderdale, FL
Kahn, Jeffrey D. .... Philadelphia, PA
Kahn, Jeffrey H. .... Department of Agriculture,
Office of the General Counsel, GV
Kahn, Jeffrey H. .... Chicago, IL
Kahn, Jeffrey J. .... Longmont, CO
Kahn, Jeffrey S. .... Boca Raton, FL
New York, NY
Kahn, Jeffrey S. .... Plymouth Meeting, PA
Kahn, Jeremy .... Washington, DC
Kahn, Joann .... Houston, TX
Kahn, Joel H. .... Midland, MI
Kahn, John M. .... Boston, MA
Kahn, John R. .... San Jose, CA
Kahn, Jolie G. .... Mineola, NY
Kahn, Jonathan E. .... New York, NY
Kahn, Jonathan S. .... Kansas City, KS
Kahn, Jordan C. .... San Francisco, CA
Kahn, Joshua N. .... El Paso, TX
Kahn, Joyce Adler .... Glen Rock, NJ
Kahn, Judith Gaies .... New York, NY
Kahn, Judith S. .... St. Petersburg Beach, FL
Kahn, Julius, III .... San Ramon, CA
Kahn, Justin S. .... Charleston, SC
Kahn and Kahn .... Washington, DC
Kahn, Kahn, Gibson & Roosen, P.C.
Detroit, MI
Troy, MI
Kahn & Kahn, P.C. .... Hillsboro, OR
Portland, OR
Kahn, Kahn & Scutieri .... White Plains, NY
Kahn, Kalvin .... Philadelphia, PA
Kahn, Kandis M. .... New York, NY
Kahn, Karen H. .... Oakland, CA
Kahn, Kenneth F. .... Troy, MI
Kahn, Kenneth F. .... Horsham, PA
Kahn, Kenneth P. .... Sunderland, MA
Kahn, Kleinman, Yanowitz & Arnson Co., L.P.A. .... Cleveland, OH
Kahn, Larry .... Atlanta, GA
Kahn, Laurence H. .... Cedar Grove, NJ
Kahn, Laurence M. .... La Jolla, CA
Kahn, Laurence S. .... Chicago, IL
Kahn Law Firm .... Charleston, SC
Kahn, Lawrence B. .... Great Neck, NY
Kahn, Lawrence E. .... Albany, NY
Kahn, Lawrence J. .... New York, NY
Kahn, Lawrence M. .... Shaker Heights, OH
Kahn, Lawrence P. .... Milwaukee, WI
Kahn, Lawrence P., Ltd., Law Offices of
Milwaukee, WI
Kahn, Lawrence S. .... New York, NY
Kahn, Leigh Baseheart .... New York, NY
Kahn, Leo .... Linden, NJ
Kahn, Leon E. .... Department of State,
Foreign Service Officers (Overseas), GV
Kahn, Leonard M. .... Boca Raton, FL
Kahn, Lessing A. .... Cambridge, MA
Kahn & Licker .... New City, NY
Kahn, Linda G. .... Washington, DC
Kahn, Lis L. Cohen .... New Orleans, LA
Kahn, Lisa .... Los Angeles, CA

Kahn, Lisa Ann .... Department of Justice,
Criminal Division, GV
Kahn, Lisa H. .... Los Angeles, CA
Kahn, Lisa H. .... Pittsburgh, PA
Kahn, Lisa J. .... New City, NY
Kahn, Lori S. .... New York, NY
Kahn, Louis .... New York, NY
Kahn, Louis E. .... San Francisco, CA
Kahn, Marc A. .... Miami, FL
Kahn, Marcy L. .... New York, NY
Kahn, Marguerite R. .... New York, NY
Kahn, Maria Araujo .... Hartford, CT
Kahn, Martin D. .... Miami, FL
Kahn, Martin K. .... Brooklyn, NY
Kahn, Martin L. .... Irving, TX
Kahn, Melissa J. .... Secaucus, NJ
Kahn, Michael A. .... Los Angeles, CA
San Francisco, CA
Kahn, Michael A. .... St. Louis, MO
Kahn, Michael H. .... Melbourne, FL
Kahn, Michael H., P.A. .... Melbourne, FL
Kahn, Michael I. .... Addison, TX
Kahn, Michael L. .... Leawood, KS
Kahn, Michael S. .... Palm Springs, CA
Kahn, Michele .... New York, NY
Kahn, Michele, P.C. .... New York, NY
Kahn, Michelle D. .... San Francisco, CA
Kahn, Mitchel B. .... Oxnard, CA
Kahn, Mitchell .... New York, NY
Kahn, Murray Z. .... Atlanta, GA
Kahn, Myles H. .... New York, NY
Kahn, Myron .... New York, NY
Kahn, Nancy L. .... Farmington Hills, MI
Kahn, Neil C. .... Baltimore, MD
Kahn, Orlee E. .... Minneapolis, MN
Kahn, Orville S. .... Decatur, IL
Kahn, Owen Ellison .... Coral Gables, FL
Kahn, Paul .... Suffern, NY
Kahn, Paul H. .... Philadelphia, PA
Kahn, Penny .... Rockville, MD
Kahn, Peter J. .... Washington, DC
Kahn, Philip A. .... Parsippany, NJ
Kahn, Philip J. .... Paramus, NJ
Kahn, Philip J. .... New York, NY
Kahn, Randall B. .... St. Louis, MO
Kahn, Raymond Lee .... Camarillo, CA
Kahn, Reiter & Matlin .... New Brunswick, NJ
Kahn, Rene M., III .... Riverside, CA
Kahn, Richard .... Morristown, NJ
Kahn, Richard Alan .... Dallas, TX
Kahn, Richard D. .... Boston, MA
Kahn, Richard D. .... New York, NY
Kahn, Richard G. .... San Francisco, CA
Kahn, Richard M. .... Spartanburg, SC
Kahn, Richard R. .... Hackensack, NJ
Kahn, Richard S. .... Minneapolis, MN
Kahn, Richard S. .... Princeton, NJ
Kahn and Richardson .... Albany, NY
Saratoga Springs, NY
Kahn, Robert .... San Francisco, CA
Kahn, Robert A. .... Calabasas, CA
Kahn, Robert A. .... Bronx, NY
Kahn, Robert L. .... Knoxville, TN
Kahn, Robert M. .... Plantation, FL
Kahn, Robert N. .... St. Louis, MO
Kahn, Robert P., A Prof. Corp., Law Offices of .... Menlo Park, CA
Kahn, Robert P., (P.C.) .... Menlo Park, CA
Kahn, Robert S. .... Los Gatos, CA
Kahn, Robert S. .... Atlanta, GA
Kahn, Robert W. .... Albany, NY
Kahn, Roberta .... Brooklyn, NY
Kahn, Roberta, The Law Firm of
Brooklyn, NY
Kahn, Robin A. .... Danbury, CT
Kahn, Roger M. .... Newark, NJ
Kahn, Ronald H. .... San Francisco, CA
Kahn, Ronald H., The Law Offices of
San Francisco, CA
Kahn, Ronald L. .... Rancho Santa Fe, CA
Kahn, Ronald L. .... Cleveland, OH
Kahn, Ronald M. .... New City, NY
Kahn, Ronald S. .... New York, NY
Kahn, Ronald S. .... Cleveland, OH
Kahn, Roy J. .... Miami, FL
Kahn, Roy J., P.A. .... Miami, FL
Kahn, Russell B. .... Lafayette, LA
Kahn, Ruth D. .... Los Angeles, CA
Kahn, Ruth E. .... Southfield, MI
Kahn, Ruth E., P.C. .... Southfield, MI
Kahn, S. Reid .... Hackensack, NJ
New York, NY
Kahn, Samuel D. .... Riverside, CA
Kahn, Sandra E. .... Boston, MA
Kahn, Sanford .... Chicago, IL
Kahn, Sanford A. .... Denver, CO
Kahn, Sanford B. .... Houston, TX
Kahn, Sanford C. .... Chicago, IL
Kahn, Sanford, Ltd. .... Chicago, IL
Kahn, Sarah Elizabeth .... Washington, DC
Kahn, Scott H. .... Cleveland, OH
Kahn, Sharon Nelson .... Northfield, IL
Kahn, Shepard L. .... Cleveland, OH
Kahn, Sidney J. .... Rancho Mirage, CA
Kahn, Smith & Collins, P.A.
Baltimore, MD
Kahn, Soares & Conway, LLP
Fresno, CA
Hanford, CA
Sacramento, CA
Kahn and Stark, LLC .... New Haven, CT
Kahn, Stephen B. .... Carmel, CA
Kahn, Stephen B. .... New York, NY
Kahn, Stephen D. .... Washington, DC
Kahn, Stephen D. .... New York, NY
Kahn, Stephen H. .... Fort Lee, NJ
Kahn, Stephen R. .... Beverly Hills, CA
Kahn, Stern & Blaney .... Los Angeles, CA

Kahn, Steven A. .... Portland, OR
Kahn, Steven C. .... Washington, DC
Kahn, Steven J. .... Santa Ana, CA
Kahn, Steven L. .... Stony Point, NY
Kahn, Stewart M. .... Virginia Beach, VA
Kahn, Stuart L. .... Kansas City, MO
Kahn, Susan R. .... Concord, MA
Kahn, Tina J. .... Beverly Hills, CA
Kahn, Todd .... New York, NY
Kahn, W. Barry .... Houston, TX
Kahn, Warren B. .... Montville, NJ
Kahn & Waxman, P.A. .... Boca Raton, FL
New York, NY
Kahn, Wendy Berliant .... Chicago, IL
Kahn, Wendy Beth .... Boston, MA
Kahn, Wendy L. .... Washington, DC
Kahn, William A. .... Baltimore, MD
Kahn, William D. .... Troy, MI
Kahn, William J. .... Encino, CA
Kahn, William M. .... New York, NY
Kahn, William M. .... New York, NY
Kahne, David A. .... Houston, TX
Kahne, Howard H. .... St. Joseph, MI
Kahng, Anthony H. .... Washington, DC
Kahng, Arlene C. .... Long Beach, CA
Kahng, David B. .... Atlanta, GA
Kahng, Jeeun P. .... Los Angeles, CA
Kahng, Leemie Jeung Lim .... New York, NY
Kahng, Lily .... New York, NY
Kahnke, Jabe .... Torrance, CA
Kahnke, Randall E. .... Minneapolis, MN
Kahn-Kothmann, Andrea M.
Philadelphia, PA
Kahoe, Frank C., Jr. .... Harrisburg, PA
Kahoe, Robert F., Jr. .... Bel Air, MD
Kahoe, Robert F., Jr., P.A. .... Bel Air, MD
Kahr, Helga .... Seattle, WA
Kahr, Stephen C. .... New York, NY
Kahre, Gregory A. .... Evansville, IN
Kahrl, Benjamin M. .... Washington, DC
Kahrl, Clyde C. .... Mt. Vernon, OH
Kahrl, Robert Conley .... Cleveland, OH
Kahrl, Thomas A. .... Falmouth, MA
Kahrs, Laurie K. .... Topeka, KS
Kahrs, Mark A. .... Wichita, KS
Kahrs, Michael .... Seattle, WA
Kahrs, Nelson, Fanning, Hite & Kellogg L.L.P. .... Wichita, KS
Kahwaty, Charles J. X. .... Hackensack, NJ
Kahwaty, Charles J. X. .... Ridgewood, NJ
Kaia, Michael A. .... Bakersfield, CA
Kaichen, John A. .... Southfield, MI
Kaicher, Francis A. .... Highland Lakes, NJ
Kaichi, Myra M. .... Honolulu, HI
Kaid, Terry C. .... Mount Carmel, IL
Kaiden, Mindy A.
Department of Justice, GV
Kaiden, Robert Allen .... Valdosta, GA
Kaido, Mark E. .... Zanesville, OH
Kaier, Edward J. .... Philadelphia, PA
Kaigh, David L. .... Detroit, MI
Kaigh, David L., P.C. .... Detroit, MI
Kaighen, Sondra .... Houston, TX
Kaighen, Sondra & Associates, P.C.
Houston, TX
Kaighn, Gregory R. .... Sacramento, CA
Kaigler, Joseph M. .... Boston, MA
Kaigler, Shirley A. Powers .... Detroit, MI
Kaihoi, Gregory P. .... Minneapolis, MN
Kaikis, Darla E. .... Columbus, OH
Kail, Elizabeth O. .... Lander, WY
Kail, F. Michael .... Washington, DC
Kail, Jack .... Glenview, IL
Kail, John .... Kansas City, MO
Kail, Joyce G. .... Philadelphia, PA
Kail & Kail, P.C. .... Grand Rapids, MI
Kail, Kenneth S. .... New York, NY
Kail, Laura Kristine .... San Diego, CA
Kail, Raymond R. .... Grand Rapids, MI
Kail, Stephen C. .... Grand Rapids, MI
Kaila, John A. .... Stafford, VA
Kailas, Christopher C. .... Milwaukee, WI
Kailas, Leo G. .... New York, NY
Kailas, Steve .... Milwaukee, WI
Kaile, Davina K. .... Palo Alto, CA
Kailer, David .... Albuquerque, NM
Kailer, W. Alan .... Dallas, TX
Kailes, Howard .... Saddle Brook, NJ
New York, NY
Kailus, Michael P. .... Chicago, IL
Kaim, Henry J. .... Houston, TX
Kaiman, Barry G., (P.C.)
Los Angeles, CA
Kaiman, Beth R. .... Bloomington, IN
Kaiman, Franklin R. .... New York, NY
Kaiman, Kenneth Z. .... Milwaukee, WI
Kaiman, Mark S. .... New York, NY
Kaiman, Stan C. .... Findlay, OH
Kaimowitz, Beth Alona .... Albuquerque, NM
Kaimowitz, Gabe .... Gainesville, FL
Kain, Christopher C. .... Harrisburg, PA
Kain, Cole S. .... Chicago, IL
Kain, David J. .... New Orleans, LA
Kain, Edward M. .... Naples, FL
Kain, George A. .... Spokane, WA
Kain, George Hay, III .... York, PA
Kain, John O. .... Houston, TX
Kain, Kevin M .... Southfield, MI
Kain, Michael R., (P.C.) .... Washington, DC
Kain, Michelle Kramish
Fort Lauderdale, FL
Kain, Michelle Kramish, P.A.
Fort Lauderdale, FL
Kain, Milton J. .... New York, NY
Kain & Reedy, P.C. .... Houston, TX
Kain, Robert C., Jr. .... Fort Lauderdale, FL

Kaleniecki, Kristin A. ......Dearborn Heights, MI
Kalenka, Phyllisan Polizzi ......Garden City, NY
Kalenscher, Evelyn ....Old Brookville, NY
Kaler, Beth M. ....Fort Myers, FL
Kaler, J. Michael ....Ontario, CA
Kaler, James L. ....Baltimore, MD
Kaler, Randall W. ....San Diego, CA
Kaler, Robert J. ....Boston, MA
Kaler, Stuart P. ....San Francisco, CA
Kaler, William T. ....Jacksonville, FL
Kalergis, David G. ....Charlottesville, VA
Kales, Ronald I. ....Las Vegas, NV
Kales, Ronald S. ....Chicago, IL
Kalesnik, Laura M. ....Dallas, TX
Kalet, Joseph E. ....Washington, DC
Kalet, Linda Barbara
Department Of Health And Human Services, Social Security Administration, GV
Kaleta, Judith S.
Department of Transportation, Research and Special Programs Administration, GV
Kaleta, Paul J. ....Wichita, KS
Kaleta, Victor J. ....Pasadena, CA
Kalett, Carolyn G. ....New York, NY
Kalette, Stephen R. ....Cleveland, OH
Kaleugher, Michael B. ....Carnegie, PA
Kaleva, Joel L. ....Helena, MT
Kalevitch, Lawrence ....Fort Lauderdale, FL
Kaley, John F. ....Garden City, NY
Kaley, Max D. ....Marietta, GA
Kaley, Rebecca A. A. ....St. Louis, MO
Kaley, Rhonda E. ....Whittier, CA
Kaley-Isley, Jonathan ....Denver, CO
Kalfa, Leda L. ....Irvine, CA
Kalfa, Nicholas ....New York, NY
Kalfaian, Isabel M ....Brooklyn, NY
Kalfas, Nahale Freeland ....Durham, NC
Kalfas, Plato John ....Lafayette, CO
New York, NY
Kalfayan, Garo ....Fresno, CA
Kalfayan, Lawrence J. ....Los Angeles, CA
Kalfayan, Ralph B. ....San Diego, CA
Kalfin, Kenneth W. ....Gold River, CA
Kalfus, A. J. ....Norfolk, VA
Kalfus and Nachman, P.C. ....Norfolk, VA
Kalfus, Suzanne L. ....Herndon, VA
Kalfuss, Ronald B. ....Palm Springs, CA
Kalgreen, Andrew J. ....Columbus, OH
Kalhammer, Barbara J.S. ....Menlo Park, CA
Kalhorn, Joan Lynn ....Independence, MO
Kalhorn, Stephen M. ....Omaha, NE
Kaliardos, Christine ....Ann Arbor, MI
Kalib, David L. ....Pittsfield, MA
Kalib, Susan B. ....New York, NY
Kaliban, Kal ....Santa Ana, CA
Kalich, John W. ....Chicago, IL
Kalichman, Lisa Joy ....New York, NY
Kalichman, Mayer C. ....Baltimore, MD
Kalick, Theodore K.
Department of Transportation, Surface Transportation Board, GV
Kalicki, James A. ....Carson City, NV
Kalicki, Jean E. ....Washington, DC
Kalidindi, Krishna ....Alexandria, VA
Kalifa, Mark ....Chicago, IL
Kaliff, Matthew A. ....Washington, DC
Kaliff, William W. ....Hartford, CT
Kalifon, David R. ....Los Angeles, CA
Kalijarvi, Chuzi & Newman, P.C.
Washington, DC
Bethesda, MD
Silver Spring, MD
Alexandria, VA
Arlington, VA
Fairfax, VA
Kalijarvi, June D. W. ....Washington, DC
Kalik, Lawrence ....New York, NY
Kalik, Mark J. ....New York, NY
Kalik, Mildred ....New York, NY
Kalik, Murry ....New York, NY
Kalik, Shari J. ....Chicago, IL
Kalik, Tracy Reichman ....Washington, DC
Kalika, Michael ....Chicago, IL
Kalikhman, David ....New York, NY
Kalikman, George H. ....San Francisco, CA
Kalikman & Masnik ....Haddonfield, NJ
Kalikman, Samuel ....Haddonfield, NJ
Kaliko, Joseph J. ....Stamford, CT
Kalikow, Alan M. ....Salem, MA
Kalikow, Edward M. ....Westbury, NY
Kalikow, Irving ....Potomac, MD
Kalikow, Joseph ....Salem, MA
Kalikow, Kalikow & Truax ....Salem, MA
Kalikow, Lawrence A. ....North Wales, PA
Kalikow, Lawrence A. ....Philadelphia, PA
Kalikow, Martin ....New York, NY
Kalikow, Richard R. ....New York, NY
Kalil, Charles James ....Midland, MI
Kalil, Craig Peter ....Miami, FL
Kalil, David T. ....Pittsburgh, PA
Kalil, Edmund H. ....Eaton, OH
Kalil, Eugene J. ....New York, NY
Kalil, John N. ....Utica, NY
Kalil, John S. ....Jacksonville, FL
Kalil & Kalil, P.C. ....Utica, NY
Kalil, Michael N. ....Utica, NY
Kalil, Susan M. ....Rockville, MD
Kalil, Thomas F. ....Department of Agriculture, Farm Service Agency, GV
Kalil, Waddie N. ....Utica, NY
Kalill & Glasser ....Springfield, MA
Kalill, Paul M. ....Springfield, MA
Kalin, Alan B. ....Palo Alto, CA
Kalin & Banner ....New York, NY
Kalin, Beatrice C. ....Monsey, NY
Kalin, Diane R. ....Cambridge, MA
Kalin, Eleanor K. ....Greenville, SC
Kalin, John E. ....San Francisco, CA
Kalin, John E., A Prof. Corp., Law Offices
San Francisco, CA
Kalin, Joseph R. ....Glendale, CA
Kalin, Laura Share ....Boston, MA
Kalin, Mary Ann Kanis ....Baltimore, MD
Kalin, Mitchell B. ....Wilmette, IL
Kalin, Neil D. ....Los Angeles, CA
Kalin, Richard S. ....New York, NY
Kalin, Stanley R. ....Silver Spring, MD
Kalina, Barbara ....Mendocino, CA
Kalina, Brett J. ....Tempe, AZ
Kalina, Gerald W. ....Hastings, MN
Kalina, Harold ....Minneapolis, MN
Kalina, Ira M. ....Chicago, IL
Kalina, Lawrence A. ....Merrillville, IN
Kalina, Mark F. ....Wheaton, IL
Kalina, Norman G. ....Randolph, NJ
Kalina, Paul J. ....Kew Gardens, NY
Kalina, R. Terence ....Wheaton, IL
Kalina, Robert I. ....New York, NY
New York, NY
Kalina, Stefan B. ....Lake Success, NY
Kalina, Wills, Gisvold & Clark
Brainerd, MN
Minneapolis, MN
Kalina, Woods & Thompson, P.A.
Minneapolis, MN
Kalinchak, Stephen G. ....Summit, NJ
Kalinec, Lawrence ....Dallas, TX
Kaliner, Bruce R. ....New York, NY
Kaliner, Daniel J. ....Philadelphia, PA
Kaliner, Michael H. ....Fairless Hills, PA
Kaliner-Garcia, Wendy ....Norristown, PA
Kalinich, Gail Chaney ....Chicago, IL
Kalinich, Kevin P. ....Chicago, IL
Kalinich, Paul T. ....Downers Grove, IL
Kalinka, Edward M. ....Birmingham, MI
Kalinkos, John B. ....Perkasie, PA
Kalinofsky, Ann K. ....San Francisco, CA
Kalinoski, Alan D. ....Orlando, FL
Kalinoski, Carol A.
Department of Commerce, GV
Kalinoski & Chaplinsky ....Des Moines, IA
Kalinoski, Charles J. ....Des Moines, IA
Kalinoski, Eileen R. ....Baltimore, MD
Kalinoski, Robert D., The Law Offices of
Baltimore, MD
Kalinoski, Robert D., The Law Offices of
Towson, MD
Kalinowski, Barbara A. ....Clawson, MI
Kalinowski, Henry J. ....Glen Cove, NY
Kalinowski, Jeffrey J. ....St. Louis, MO
Kalinowski, Katherine H. ....Fairfax, VA
Kalinowski, Neal ....Rosenberg, TX
Kalinowski, Richard M. .....West Boylston, MA
Kalinowski, Timothy Wayne ......Rosenberg, TX
Kalinski, Alexander J. ....Manchester, NH
Kalinski, Daniel J. ....Manchester, NH
Kalinski, David E. ....Washington, DC
Kalinski, George ....Los Angeles, CA
Kalinski, Jane A. ....Washington, DC
Kalinski II, Francis T. ....San Diego, CA
Kalinsky, A. Stephen ....Chevy Chase, MD
Kalinsky, Ira W. ....San Francisco, CA
Kalinsky, Robert H. ....Chicago, IL
Kalinsky, Stephen D. ....New York, NY
Kalinyak & Kuzmiak ....Johnstown, PA
Kalionzes, Peter N. ....Newport Beach, CA
Kalis, Christopher A. ....Dallas, TX
Kalis, Howard E., III ....Pottstown, PA
Kalis, Janal M. ....Minneapolis, MN
Kalis & Kleiman, P.A. ....Davie, FL
Kalis, Lucas, Gelineau & Kline ....Salem, MA
Kalis, Michael L. ....Dearborn, MI
Kalis, Neal R. ....Davie, FL
Kalis, Nicholas ....McLean, VA
Kalis, Peter J. ....Pittsburgh, PA
Kalis, Robert I. ....Salem, MA
Kalis, Stephen H. ....Pottstown, PA
Kalis, William S. ....Frederick, MD
Kalisch, Cotugno & Rust, LLP
Beverly Hills, CA
Los Angeles, CA
Kalisch, Eleni Pryles ......Department of Justice, Federal Bureau of Investigation, GV
Kalisch, Mark ....Beverly Hills, CA
Kalisch, Robert M. ....Hackensack, NJ
Kalisek, Lauren J. ....Austin, TX
Kaliser, Laura B. ....Los Angeles, CA
Kalish, Ann S. ....New York, NY
Kalish, Arthur ....New York, NY
Kalish, Barbara Barbash ....New York, NY
Kalish, Carol Ann ....Sarasota, FL
Kalish, Daniel A. ....White Plains, NY
Kalish, David D. ....Cary, NC
Kalish, David T. ....Pasadena, CA
Kalish, Deborah L. ....Newnan, GA
Kalish, Debra Stinogel ....Boulder, CO
Kalish, Edward A. ....Coral Gables, FL
Kalish, Harry A. ....Philadelphia, PA
Kalish, Herbert Warren ....Phoenix, AZ
Kalish, James R. ....Belleville, IL
Kalish, Jay S., Law Offices Of
Farmington Hills, MI
Kalish, Jay S., P.C., Law Offices of
Detroit, MI
Farmington Hills, MI
Kalish, John D. ....Newton, MA
Kalish, Joseph R. ....Tampa, FL
Kalish, Katherine McAulay ....Macon, GA
Kalish, Lawrence H. ....Lake Hiawatha, NJ
Kalish & Leavy ....San Francisco, CA
San Rafael, CA
Kalish, Leonard J. ....Miami, FL
Kalish, Loren E. ....Atlanta, GA
Kalish, Marc ....Phoenix, AZ
Kalish, Mark C. ....New York, NY
Kalish, Mark L. ....New York, NY
Kalish, Martin I. ....Tampa, FL
Kalish, Max ....Brooklyn, NY
Kalish, Melvin J. ....Mineola, NY
Kalish, Michael A. ....New York, NY
Kalish, Michael G. ....New York, NY
Kalish, Myron ....New York, NY
Kalish, Paul William ....Washington, DC
Kalish, Ralph W., Jr. ....St. Louis, MO
Kalish, Richard J. ....San Rafael, CA
Kalish, Robert B. ....The Woodlands, TX
Kalish, Robert D. ....Brooklyn, NY
Kalish, Robert P. ....
Department of Housing and Urban Development, GV
Kalish, Ronald ....Chicago, IL
Kalish, Sheila Beth ....Chicago, IL
Kalish, Stephen E. ....Lincoln, NE
Kalish, Steven J. ....Washington, DC
Kalish, Thomas J. ....Lindenhurst, NY
Kalish & Ward, Professional Association
Tampa, FL
Kalish, William ....Tampa, FL
Kalish, William K. ....Alexandria, VA
Kalishman, Amy S. ....Chicago, IL
Kalishman, Neal ....St. Louis, MO
Kalishman, Steven J. ....Gainesville, FL
Kalison, McBride & Jackson, P.A.
Liberty Corner, NJ
Kalison, Michael J. ....Liberty Corner, NJ
Kalista, Stephen J. ....Big Stone Gap, VA
Kalisz, Lucy Wanda ....Sunnyside, NY
Kalisz, Walter P., Jr. ....North Dartmouth, MA
Kalita, Arthur J. ....New York, NY
Kalita, John T., Jr. ....Holland, PA
Philadelphia, PA
Kalitowski, Thomas J. ....St. Paul, MN
Kalivas, Angela M. ....Boston, MA
Kalivoda, Fredrick F. ....Rockford, IL
Kalivoda, Kenneth ....Athens, GA
Kalivoda, Mary K. D. ....Erie, PA
Kalivoda & Shelton ....Rockford, IL
Kalk, Daniel L. ....Cleveland, OH
Kalk, Jacqueline E. ....Atlanta, GA
Kalka, Daniel S. ....Barberton, OH
Kalka, Howard A., (P.C.) ....New York, NY
Kalkanian, Gerald S., Jr. ....Villa Park, IL
Kalkas, George N. ....Cleveland, OH
Kalkbrenner, Joseph J., Jr. ....Norristown, PA
Kalkbrenner, Richard C. ....Little Rock, AR
Kalke, Rahul A. ....Boston, MA
Kalker, Lisa ....Covington, KY
Kalker, Paul ....Melville, NY
Kalker, Paul ....New York, NY
Kalker, Terri Beth ....Flushing, NY
Kalkhoff, James F. ....Waterloo, IA
Kalkhoff, Richard G. ....Milwaukee, WI
Kalkin, Alan S. ....Burbank, CA
Kalkines, Arky, Zall & Bernstein LLP
Albany, NY
New York, NY
Kalkines, George A. ....New York, NY
Kalkowski, DaNay A. ....Lincoln, NE
Kalkowski, Michael J. ....Hoffman Estates, IL
Kalkstein, Allan ....Rockville, MD
Kalkstein, Benjamin ....Philadelphia, PA
Kalkstein, Gary ....Missoula, MT
Kalkstein, Joshua A. ....Groton, CT
Kalkstein Law Firm, PLLC ....Butte, MT
Missoula, MT
Kalkstein, Michael H. ....Palo Alto, CA
Kalkunte, Sheila J. ....Naples, FL
Kalkus, Mark P. ....Littleton, CO
Kalkut, Stefanie ....New York, NY
Kall, Charles J. ....Denver, CO
Kall, Christopher A. ....Torrance, CA
Kall, David M. ....Cleveland, OH
Kall, Matthew B. ....Cleveland, OH
Kall, Patricia A. ....Holtsville, NY
Kall & Reilly ....Syracuse, NY
Kall, Sheldon G. ....Red Creek, NY
Syracuse, NY
Kalla, Mark J. ....Minneapolis, MN
Kallabat, Danny A., Law Offices of
Detroit, MI
Kallabat, Danny A., Law Offices of
Southfield, MI
Kallabat, John Z. ....Bingham Farms, MI
Kallaher, Christopher H. ....Boston, MA
Kallaher, Kathleen A. ....Shepherdsville, KY
Kallal, Amy Justine ....Brooklyn, NY
Kallal, Edward W., Jr. ....Atlanta, GA
Kallam, Michelle Rome ....Lafayette, LA
Kallam, Robert M. ....Lafayette, LA
Kallan, Gerald S., Law Offices of
El Dorado Hills, CA
Kallan, Jeffrey J. ....St. Petersburg, FL
Kallan, Kathleen Glenney ....Joliet, IL
Kallan, Lisa J. ....New York, NY
Kalland, Michael E. ....Elgin, IL
Kallander, Scott A. ....Bellevue, WA
Kallas, Christina ....New York, NY
Kallas, Colleen L. ....Kansas City, MO
Kallas, Constantine N.
Bloomfield Hills, MI
Kallas, Edith M. ....New York, NY
Kallas, Edward N., Jr. ....Chicago, IL
Kallas, Hani R. ....Cincinnati, OH
Kallas & Henk, P.C. ....Bloomfield Hills, MI
Kallas, Janice L. ....Bloomfield Hills, MI
Kallas & MacDonald, Ltd. ....Edina, MN
Kallas, Michael A. ....Milwaukee, WI
Kallas, Michael T. ....Edina, MN
Kallas, Nicholas N. ....New York, NY
Kallas, Rick D. ....Boise, ID
Kallas, Sarah E. ....Wheaton, IL
Kallas, Stephan J. ....New York, NY
Kallas, Stephan J. ....Peekskill, NY
Kallay, Thomas, Law Office of
Los Angeles, CA
Kallberg, Candace E. Ahrens
Los Angeles, CA
Kallberg, Delmer C. ....Los Angeles, CA
Kallberg, Kevin M. ....Pacific Palisades, CA
Kallbreier, Kenneth A. ....Louisville, KY
Kalle, Robert P. ....St. Petersburg, FL
Kalled, James John ....Ossipee, NH
Kalled, John Pierce ....Ossipee, NH
Kalled Law Offices ....Ossipee, NH
Kallem, Howard I.
Department of Education, GV
Kallemeyn, Hogen J. ....Blue Jay, CA
Kallemeyn, Ronald P. ....Savanna, IL
Kallen, Craig G. ....St. Louis, MO
Kallen, Daniel ....Sherman Oaks, CA
Kallen, Douglas G. ....Burlington, VT
Kallen, Edward P. ....New York, NY
Kallen, Edward P., P.C. ....New York, NY
Kallen, John D. ....North Miami Beach, FL
Kallen, Nina E. ....Cambridge, MA
Kallen, Nora L. ....Jersey City, NJ
Kallen, Norman D. ....Roseland, NJ
Kallen, Norman H. ....Los Angeles, CA
Kallenbach, Jennifer B. ....Greenwich, CT
Kallenbach, John William ....Bolivar, MO
Kallenbach, Kevin M. ....Erie, PA
Kallenbach, Terrance L. ....Racine, WI
Kallenberger, Donald W. ....Eureka, SD
Kallenberger, Paul E. ....Tulsa, OK
Kallenekos, Constantine ....New York, NY
Kaller, Adam David ....Los Angeles, CA
Kaller, Emily A. ....Woodbridge, NJ
Kaller, James L., Law Offices of
San Francisco, CA
Kaller, Paul J.
Federal Maritime Commission, Bureau of Enforcement, GV
Kalleres, Arthur P. ....Indianapolis, IN
Kallestad, John L. ....Willmar, MN
Kallet, Beth R. ....Washington, DC
Kallet, Mitchel E. ....Vernon, CT
Kallett, Calvin ....Williamsville, NY
Kallgren, Charles E. ....Oakland, CA
Kallgren, Edward E. ....San Francisco, CA
Kallheim, Cory A. ....Minneapolis, MN
Kalliagas, Maria ....Forest Hills, NY
Kallianis, James H., Jr. ....Chicago, IL
Kallianos, Chris M. ....Charlotte, NC
Kallich, Paul E. ....Princeton, NJ
Kalliche, Anthony A. ....Miami, FL
Kalliche, Carol Capri ....Fort Lauderdale, FL
Kallick, David A. ....Chicago, IL
Kallick, Ivan L. ....Los Angeles, CA
Kalliel, A. Ray ....Grand Rapids, MI
Kallina & Ackerman, L.L.P.
Baltimore, MD
Kallina, Emanuel J., II ....Baltimore, MD
Kallina, Roy Stephen ....Department of Labor, Office of Secretary, GV
Kallins, Irving ....New York, NY
Kallins, Lauren B. ....Baltimore, MD
Kallins, Maureen R. ....Brooklyn, NY
Kallins, Nicholas J. ....Bellflower, CA
Kallins, Scott B. ....Bradenton, FL
Kallins, Sigmund R. ....Baltimore, MD
Kalliomaa, Jill F. ....San Diego, CA
Kallis, James N. ....Southfield, MI
Kallis, Jeffery ....San Jose, CA
Kallis, Michael J. ....Boston, MA
Kallish, Marc Howard ....Chicago, IL
Kallison, Jo Lyn ....Austin, TX
Kallman & Cropsey ....Lansing, MI
Kallman, David A. ....Lansing, MI
Kallman, Donald H. ....East Hampton, NY
Kallman, H. Jay ....Los Angeles, CA
Kallman, John K. ....Chicago, IL
Kallman, Jonathan ....New York, NY
Kallman, Kristofer, Law Offices of
Santa Barbara, CA
Kallman, Kristofer, Law Offices of
Santa Maria, CA
Kallman, Marc S. ....Garden City, NY
Kallman, Nathan N. ....Saratoga, CA
Kallman, Paul ....Marina Del Rey, CA
Kallman, Richard M. ....Ipswich, MA
Salem, MA
Kallman, Robin L. ....San Francisco, CA
Kallman, Stanley W. ....New York, NY
Kallman, Stanley W., P.C. ....New York, NY
Kallmann, Stanley W. ....Parsippany, NJ
New York, NY
Kallmer, James S. ....Seattle, WA
Kallon, Abdul K. ....Birmingham, AL
Kallor, Bruce E. ....Bronx, NY
Kallos, Chris P. ....Chicago, IL
Kallos, Constandina A. ....Chicago, IL
Kallow, Arthur S. ....Chicago, IL
Kallow & Munchunas ....Chicago, IL
Kalls, Kenneth W. ....Detroit, MI
Kallsen, Richard ....Sioux City, IA
Kallsnick, Richard J. ....Tulsa, OK
Kallstrom, D. Ward ....San Francisco, CA
Kallstrom, James D. ....Oklahoma City, OK
Kallus, Harvey C. ....West Orange, NJ
Kallus, Mindy L. ....Chicago, IL
Kallusch, H. A., Jr. ....De Witt, NY
Kallusch & Kallusch ....De Witt, NY
Kallusky, Barbara L. ....Afton, MN
Kalm, David P. ....Newark, NJ
Kalm, Linda A., (P.C.) ....Beverly Hills, CA
Kalm, Thomas L. ....Albuquerque, NM
Kalma, Frederick J. ....Matawan, NJ
Kalman, Arnold I. ....Philadelphia, PA
Kalman, Brian A. ....New York, NY
Kalman, Edward D. ....Boston, MA
Kalman, Ilene ....Philadelphia, PA

Kalman, Joel G. ....Huntingdon Valley, PA
Kalman, Kaufman & Rosenblatt, P.C.
New York, NY
Kalman, Mannie ....El Paso, TX
Kalman, Martin B. ....Highland Beach, FL
Kalman, Newton ....Encino, CA
Kalman, Stephen ....Hawley, PA
Kalman, Sumner F. ....Plaistow, NH
Kalman, Sumner F., Attorney At Law, P.C.
Plaistow, NH
Kalman, Susan B. ....Beverly Hills, CA
Kalman, Victoria L. ....Grass Valley, CA
Kalmanowitz, Linda ....Toms River, NJ
Kalmans, Patricia A. ....San Antonio, TX
Kalmans, Raymond L. ....Houston, TX
Kalmansohn, Mark E. ....Los Angeles, CA
Kalmanson, Alvin G. ....Alpine, CA
Kalmanson, Barry ....Maitland, FL
Kalmanson, Barry, P.A. ....Maitland, FL
Kalmansson, Pall G. ....Fitchburg, MA
Kalmar, Jack ....Brooklyn, NY
Kalmbach, Brock R. ....Georgetown, TX
Kalmbach, Charles F., Jr. ....Malvern, PA
Kalmbach, Herbert W. ....Long Beach, CA
Kalmbach, John T. ....Shreveport, LA
Kalmbach, Leslie Idom ....Shreveport, LA
Kalmbach, Leslie K. ....Austin, TX
Kalmbach, R. Kerry ....Kennett Square, PA
Kalmbach, Randy L. ....Wyandotte, MI
Kalmbach, Thomas E. ....St. Louis, MO
Kalmbach, Tiffanie K. ....Oakland, CA
Kalmbach, William C., III
Shreveport, LA
Kalmbacher, Ellen Neil ....Boca Grande, FL
Kalmbacher, Ellen Neil, P.A.
Boca Grande, FL
Fort Myers, FL
Sarasota, FL
Kalmeyer, Bridgit ....Pittsburgh, PA
Kalmeyer, Gary ....Pittsburgh, PA
Kalmeyer & Kalmeyer ....Pittsburgh, PA
Kalmink, Jack O. ....Detroit, MI
Kalmink, Mary Keizer ....Detroit, MI
Kalminov, Sivon ....Costa Mesa, CA
Kalmorewenig, Debra Lynn ....New York, NY
Kalmowitz, Carey F. ....Detroit, MI
Kalmus, Attilia ....Brooklyn, NY
Kalmus, Hope R. ....Commerce, CA
Kalmus, Julia H. ....Albuquerque, NM
Kalmus, Michael ....New York, NY
Kalnay, J. Timothy" jt "...........Cleveland, OH
Kalnick, Klee & Green, LLP
New York, NY
Kalnick, Michael C. ....New York, NY
Kalnins, Ivars ....Lancaster, WI
Kalnitz, Arnold B. ....Chicago, IL
Kalnitz, Arnold B., P.C. ....Chicago, IL
Kalniz, Burton A. ....Toledo, OH
Kalniz, Iorio & Feldstein
Grand Rapids, MI
Toledo, OH
Kalniz, Jeffrey T. ....Toledo, OH
Kalnoki, Andrew G. ....Carmichael, CA
Kalnoki, Aniko T. ....Cleveland, OH
Kalny, James M. ....De Pere, WI
Kalo, John J. ....Burton, MI
Kalo, Joseph J. ....Chapel Hill, NC
Kalo, Joseph J., IV ....Burlington, NC
Kalo, Lisa A. ....Sarasota, FL
Kalo, Monica Kivel ....Durham, NC
Kalo, Zilinski & Swann, A Prof. Corp.
Burton, MI
Kalocay, Michael B. ....Pittsburgh, PA
Kalodner, Howard I. ....Springfield, MA
Kalogredis, Stephanie ....West Chester, PA
Kalogredis, Vasilios J. ....Wayne, PA
Kalogridis, Peter G. ....Winter Haven, FL
Kalokathis, Nicholas G. ....Cheyenne, WY
Kalo-Keistler, Zari Ann ....Mount Vernon, IL
Kalola, Bina ....New York, NY
Kalom & Borst ....Hebron, CT
Kalom, Bruce ....Hebron, CT
Kalomiris, Errika ....New York, NY
Kaloosdian, Robert A. ....Watertown, MA
Kalos, Gary ....Miami, FL
Kalosh, Peter ....Milwaukee, WI
Kalosieh, George A. ....Wayne, NJ
Kalousdian, Raffi ....Chicago, IL
Kaloustian, Linda T. ....Andover, MA
Kaloustian, Vatche ....Philadelphia, PA
Kalow, David A. ....New York, NY
Kalow, Henry Norr ....New York, NY
Kalow, Springut & Bressler LLP
New York, NY
Kaloyanides, David J. P.
Newport Beach, CA
Kaloyanides, Sonya M. ....New York, NY
Kalpakian, Stephen M. ....Los Angeles, CA
Kalpakis, James G. ....Mineola, NY
Kalpakis, Mark G. ....Arlington, TX
Kalperis, Thomas G.J. ....Boston, MA
Kalpin, Mark C. ....Boston, MA
Kalpitcke, Scott E. ....Powell, WY
Kalra, Amit ....Chicago, IL
Kalra, Gita ....New York, NY
Kalra, Madhu ....Los Angeles, CA
Kals, Stephen A. ....New York, NY
Kalsched, Phillip H. ....Santa Rosa, CA
Kalscheur, Bradley J. ....Milwaukee, WI
Kalscheur, Gregory A. ....Syracuse, NY
Kalshan, Vernon A. ....Cambria, CA
Kalsi, Swadesh S. ....Indianapolis, IN
Kalson, Carolyne S. ....Toms River, NJ
Kalson, David J. ....Pittsburgh, PA
Kalson, Harry S. ....Pittsburgh, PA
Kalson, Howard J. ....Greenville, SC
Kalson, Janet Ray ....New York, NY
Kalson, Lisa S. ....Dublin, OH
Kalson, Richard D. ....Pittsburgh, PA
Kalstein, Allan ....
Department of the Navy, GV
Kalstein, Michele H. ....New York, NY
Kalsu, J. Robert ....Oklahoma City, OK
Kalsy, Kavita ....Treasury Department,
Bureau of the Public Debt, GV
Parkersburg, WV
Kalt, Allan S. ....Warren, MI
Kalt, Brian C. ....Washington, DC
Kalt, Melvyn B. ....Oak Park, MI
Kalt, Michael S. ....San Diego, CA
Kalt, Owen D. ....Chicago, IL
Kalt, Scott M. ....Los Angeles, CA
Kaltenbach, C. Patrick ....Saginaw, MI
Kaltenbach, Christopher E.
Cherry Hill, NJ
Kaltenbach, Donald F. ......New Port Richey, FL
Kaltenbach, Richard T. ....Warren, NJ
Kaltenbach, Timothy J. ....Paducah, KY
Kaltenbacher, Philip D. ....Newark, NJ
Kaltenbaugh, David J. ....Ebensburg, PA
Johnstown, PA
Kaltenborn, H. Stanley, Jr. ....Albany, NY
Kaltenborn, Marilyn M. ....Albany, NY
Kaltenbronn, Jon A. ....Lake Ozark, MO
Kaltenmark, Randal J. ....Indianapolis, IN
Kaltenrieder, Mark L. ....St. Louis, MO
Kalter, Albert ....New York, NY
Kalter, Brad Stewart ....Atlanta, GA
Kalter, Ivan ....Woodbourne, NY
Kalter, John J. ....Milwaukee, WI
Kalter & Kalter ....Rutland, VT
Kalter, Kaplan and Zeiger ......Woodbourne, NY
Kalter, Karen Abatiell ....Rutland, VT
Kalter, M. Richard ....Philadelphia, PA
Kalter, Sandra Cohen ....Washington, DC
Kalter, Todd ....Rutland, VT
Kalteux, James L. ....Albany, NY
Kalteux, Sheila M. ....Seminole, FL
Kalteyer, C. Ronald ....Dallas, TX
Kaltman, Ira J. ....Montvale, NJ
Kaltman, Lillian ....New York, NY
Kaltsas & Associates ....Worcester, MA
Kaltsas, Christopher G. ....Boston, MA
Kaltsas, Nicholas G. ....Worcester, MA
Kalu, Emelike I. ....Los Angeles, CA
Kaludis, Karen M. ....Easton, MD
Kaludis, Kirk J. ....New York, NY
Kaludis, Stephen G. ....St. Louis, MO
Kaludis, William M. ....Nashville, TN
Kaluger, Michael M., Jr. ....Santa Ana, CA
Kaluk, Nick S., Jr. ....Denver, CO
Kalunian, Robert E. ....Los Angeles, CA
Kalupa, Robert J. ....Milwaukee, WI
Kalus, Susan ....Atlanta, GA
Kalustian, Richard P. ....Los Angeles, CA
Kaluszkiewicz, Suzanne R. ....Denver, CO
Kaluza, Michael E. ....Akron, OH
Kaluzniacki, Carolyn M. ....Phoenix, AZ
Kaluzny, Eugene L. ....Milwaukee, WI
Kaluzny, Gerald G. ....St. Paul, MN
Kaluzny, Judith A. ....Fullerton, CA
Kaluzny, Lawrence G. ....Bingham Farms, MI
Kaluzny, Todd Alan ....Pontiac, MI
Kalver, Brian ....Roseland, NJ
Kalvert, Seth J. ....New York, NY
Kalvig, Kenneth A ....Kalispell, MT
Kalvin, Harold R. ....White Plains, NY
Kalwa, Kathleen D. ....Ballston Spa, NY
Kalyan, Ronald P., Jr. ....Reading, PA
Kalyanaraman, Palaiyur S.
Kenilworth, NJ
Kalyna, Adrianne ....Chicago, IL
Kalytiak, Roman J ....Palmer, AK
Kalyuzhny, Maxim G. ....New York, NY
Kalyvas, James R. ....Los Angeles, CA
Kalyvas, John G. ....New York, NY
Kalzer, Karen A. ....Seattle, WA
Kam, Allan J. ......Department of Transportation,
National Highway Traffic Safety
Administration, GV
Kam, Christina L. ....Voorhees, NJ
Philadelphia, PA
Kam & Ebersbach, P.C. ....Newnan, GA
Kam, Janice D. ....New York, NY
Kam, Louanne K. L. ....Honolulu, HI
Kam, Michael G. ....Newnan, GA
Kam, Michael K. ....New York, NY
Kam, Michael S. ....Rexburg, ID
Kam, Mitchell M.T. ....Austin, TX
Kamage, R. James ....Wilkes-Barre, PA
Kamahele, Dean Bradford
San Francisco, CA
Kamai, Gordon M. ....San Francisco, CA
Kamaiko, Laurie A. ....Lake Success, NY
Kamaka, Hiram K. ....Honolulu, HI
Kamakawiwoole, Lawrence Kaaloehukai
Honolulu, HI
Kamal-Griffin, Dalila ....Santa Monica, CA
Kamali, Kris M. ....Palo Alto, CA
Kamalii, Na'unanikina'u A. ....Honolulu, HI
Kaman, Berlove, Marafioti, Jacobstein & Goldman ....Rochester, NY
Kaman, Bridget K. ....San Francisco, CA
Kaman, David W. ....Cleveland, OH
Kaman, Jack A. ....Rochester, NY
Kaman, John B. ....Rochester, NY
Kaman, Robert L. ....Fort Worth, TX
Kamangar, Robert B. ....Menlo Park, CA
Kamanski, Charles W. Paul ....San Diego, CA
Kamanski, David D. ....Orange, CA
Kamanski, James B. ....Los Angeles, CA
Kamansky, Craig S. ....San Bernardino, CA
Kamantauskas-Holder, Katrina C.
Baltimore, MD
Kamarados, John S. ....Pittsburgh, PA
Kamaras, Gail ....Albany, NY
Kamarck, Jonathan D. ....United States Senate,
Committee Legal Personnel, GV
Kamarck, Lynn G. ....Washington, DC
Kamarck, Mitchell D. ....Beverly Hills, CA
Kamarei, Ali ....Palo Alto, CA
Kamas, Albert L. ....Wichita, KS
Kamas, Frank J. ....Wichita, KS
Kamath, Patricia C. ....Iowa City, IA
Kamb, Barclay J. ....Palo Alto, CA
Kamb, John G. ....Mount Vernon, WA
Kamb, John G., Jr. ....Mount Vernon, WA
Kamb & Kamb ....Mount Vernon, WA
Kamb, Rosemary ....Mount Vernon, WA
Kamb, Thomas R. ....Mount Vernon, WA
Kambas, James W. ....Stamford, CT
Kambe, Lynn L. ....Irvine, CA
Kambe, Lynn L., Inc. ....Irvine, CA
Kamber, Cathy L. ....Lake Worth, FL
Kamber, Frayda ....Harrisburg, PA
Kamber, Paul J. ....Columbia, SC
Kamber, Scott A. ....New York, NY
Kamberg, Berman, P.C. ....Springfield, MA
Worcester, MA
Kamberian, Van ....Canoga Park, CA
Kamberos & Pappas, Ltd. ....Chicago, IL
Kamberos, Peter G. ....Chicago, IL
Kamberos, Peter N. ....Chicago, IL
Kambeseles, Peter ....New York, NY
Kambesis, Cynthia Hope ....Gary, IN
Kambic, Joseph John ....Lancaster, PA
Kambic, Karla ....Chicago, IL
Kambic, Robert B. ....New York, NY
Kambic, William J. ....Kingston, TN
Kambich, Kenneth L. ....Seattle, WA
Kambies, Kathleen A. ....Walnut Creek, CA
Kamborian, Lisbeth N. ....Arlington, MA
Kambour, Annaliese S. ....New York, NY
Kambour, Sarah L. ....Morristown, NJ
Kame, Margaret M. ....Los Angeles, CA
Kamecki, Jerzy S. ....Oakland, CA
Kameen, Elizabeth M. ....Baltimore, MD
Kameen, Joseph F. ....Milford, PA
Kamel, Alan M. ....Elizabeth, NJ
Kamel, Brian P. ....Santa Monica, CA
Kamel, Kathryn ....Everett, WA
Kamel, Steve A. ....Houston, TX
Kamelamela, Joseph K. ....Hilo, HI
Kamelhair, Bruce I. ....Coconut Creek, FL
Kamelhar, Leslie C. ....New York, NY
Kameli, Taher M. ....Chicago, IL
Kamell, Rafik Y. ....La Habra, CA
Kamen & Associates, Law Offices of
Miami, FL
Kamen, Cindi ....Miami, FL
Kamen, Harry P. ....New York, NY
Kamen, Katherine S. ....Washington, DC
Kamen, Michael A. ....West Palm Beach, FL
Kamen, Michael Robert ....Pepper Pike, OH
Kamen & Orlovsky, Professional Association
West Palm Beach, FL
Kamen, Randy J. ....Woodcliff Lake, NJ
Kamen, Steven R. ....Newark, NJ
New York, NY
Kamen, William M. ....New York, NY
Kamenar, Paul D. ....Washington, DC
Kamenear, Elliot B. ....Oak Brook, IL
Kamenear, Kadison & Anderson
Chicago, IL
Kamenec, Robert G. ....Detroit, MI
Kamenetsky, Chanie ....Brooklyn, NY
Kamenetsky, Jeffrey H.
Fort Lauderdale, FL
Miami, FL
West Palm Beach, FL
Kamenetsky, Rona ....Aventura, FL
Kamenetz, Kevin B. ....Towson, MD
Kamenir, Edward ....Los Angeles, CA
Kamenir, Sandra ....Los Angeles, CA
Kamenir-Reznik, Janice M.
Los Angeles, CA
Kamenjarin, William C. ....Carlsbad, CA
Kamens, Geremy C. ....Rome, GA
Kamens, Joel ....Beverly, MA
Kamens, Marc ....Woodland Hills, CA
Kamens, Martin ....Wayne, NJ
Kamens, Matthew H. ....Philadelphia, PA
Kamens, Theo. ....New York, NY
Kamenshine, Robert D.
Department of Justice, Civil Division, GV
Kamensky, Allan E. ....Columbus, GA
Kamensky, Andrew ....Miami, FL
Kamensky, Jerrold ....Trenton, NJ
Newtown, PA
Kamensky, Mark J. ....Port Chester, NY
Kamensky, Marvin, (Ltd.) ....Chicago, IL
Lincolnwood, IL
Kamensky, Robert N. ....Chicago, IL
Kamensky & Rubinstein ....Chicago, IL
Lincolnwood, IL
Kameoka, Mizuho ....New York, NY
Kamer, Gregory J. ....Las Vegas, NV
Kamer, Marc T. ....Toledo, OH
Kamer, Mauritia G. ....Louisville, KY
Kamer, William ....Los Angeles, CA
Kamer & Zucker ....Las Vegas, NV
Kamerer, Bruce E. ....Boston, MA
Kamerer, James P. ....Canton, OH
Kamerian, Van ....Canoga Park, CA
Kamerick, Eileen A. ....Chicago, IL
Kamerling, Joanne M. ....East Haven, CT
Kamerling, Manya L. ....Haddonfield, NJ
Kamerlink, Lydia Gross ....Chicago, IL
Kamerman, Jerome ....New York, NY
Kamerman, Jon ....Chicago, IL
Kamerman, Joshua ....New York, NY
Kamerman, Lawrence S. ....New York, NY
Kamerman, Morton ....New York, NY
Kamerman, Richard A. ....Naperville, IL
Kamerman & Soniker P.C.
New York, NY
Kamerman, Steven ....New York, NY
Kamerman, Steven, P.C. ....New York, NY
Kameron, Matthew A. ....Boston, MA
Kameros, Andrew J. ....Department of Justice,
Tax Division, GV
Kamerow, Allan L. ....Washington, DC
Alexandria, VA
Kamerow, Jacob A. ....Washington, DC
Alexandria, VA
Kamerow & Kamerow, P.C.
Washington, DC
Alexandria, VA
Kamerow, Stanley H. ....Washington, DC
Kamerow, Stephanie J. ....New York, NY
Kamerrer, W. Dale ....Olympia, WA
Kamerschen, Robert W. ....Atlanta, GA
Kameya, Darren C. ....Los Angeles, CA
Kamhi, Julius B. ....Carle Place, NY
Kamholtz, Matthew A. ....Boston, MA
Kamholz, Robert L., Jr. ....Milwaukee, WI
Kamian, Alicia E. ....Redwood City, CA
Kamiat, Walter A. ....Washington, DC
Kamida, Clayton A. ....Honolulu, HI
Kamida, Nobuki ....Honolulu, HI
Kamide, James A. ....River Grove, IL
Kamien, Kalvin ....New York, NY
Kamikawa, Janice A. ....Grass Valley, CA
Kamil, Catherine A. ....Milford, MI
Kamilar, Mark A. ....Miami, FL
Kamillatos, Nicholas ....New York, NY
Kamin, Alan S. ....Phoenix, AZ
Kamin, Chester T. ....Chicago, IL
Kamin, Elizabeth Bonvillain ....Houston, TX
Kamin, James A. ....Minneapolis, MN
Kamin, John F. ....Peoria, IL
Kamin, Jonathan M. ....Pittsburgh, PA
Kamin, Jonathan T. ....Chicago, IL
Kamin, Joshua M. ....Atlanta, GA
Kamin, Kay H. ....Chicago, IL
Kamin, Kim A. ....Chicago, IL
Kamin, Lawrence O. ....New York, NY
Kamin, Lewis P. ....Bayside, NY
Kamin, Lynn ....Houston, TX
Kamin, Malcolm S. ....Chicago, IL
Kamin, Marc ....Phoenix, AZ
Kamin, Margery G. ....Chicago, IL
Kamin, Mitchell A. ....Los Angeles, CA
Kamin, Neal M. ....Atlanta, GA
Kamin, Samuel P. ....Pittsburgh, PA
Kamin, Scott A. ....Portland, OR
Kamin, Scott A., P.C. ....Portland, OR
Kamin, Scott T. ....Chicago, IL
Kamin, Sherwin ....New York, NY
Kamin, Tiffany C. ....Phoenix, AZ
Kaminash, Benjamin H. ....Portland, OR
Kamine, Arthur ....Wayne, NJ
Kamine, Bernard S. ....Los Angeles, CA
Kamine, Charles S. ....Cincinnati, OH
Kamine, Jorge H. ....Houston, TX
Kamine, Marcia Haber ....Los Angeles, CA
Kamine, Steiner & Ungerer, LLP
Los Angeles, CA
Kaminer, Debbie ....Mineola, NY
Kaminer, Frances S. ....Berkeley, CA
Kaminer, James H., Jr. ....Atlanta, GA
Kaminer, Lillian E. ....Boca Raton, FL
Kaminer, Michael D.
Fort Lauderdale, FL
Kaminer, Sarena ....Great Neck, NY
Kaminer, Stevenson S. ....McLean, VA
Kaminetz, Lee S. ....Towson, MD
Kaminetzky, Benjamin S. ....New York, NY
Kaminetzky, Eric C. ....Durham, NC
Kaminin, Tracie H. ....Princeton, NJ
Kaminkow, Michael E. ....Baltimore, MD
Kaminky, Mark D. ....Lombard, IL
Kaminoff, Eric S. ....Bronx, NY
Kaminow, David J. ....Rockville, MD
Kamins, Aaron M. ....San Rafael, CA
Kamins, Barry ....Brooklyn, NY
Kamins, Bernard J. ....Santa Monica, CA
Kamins, Clive D. ....Chicago, IL
Kamins, David E. ....Avon, CT
Kamins, Duane H. ....Colorado Springs, CO
Kamins, Howard P. ....King Of Prussia, PA
Kamins, John M. ....Detroit, MI
Kamins, Mary Lisa ....Chicago, IL
Kamins, Morton L. ....Beverly Hills, CA
Kamins, Robert M. ....Honolulu, HI
Kamins, Scott V. ....Washington, DC
Kaminska, Glenn A. ....Albertson, NY
Kaminski, Bertram G. ....New York, NY
Kaminski, Beth A. ....Oak Brook, IL
Kaminski, Bruce D. ....West Sacramento, CA
Kaminski, Cassandra Faline
Wilmington, DE
Kaminski, David J. ....Los Angeles, CA
Kaminski, David P. ....Chicago, IL
Kaminski, Edward C. ....Akron, OH
Kaminski, Edward G. ....Utica, NY
Kaminski, Gerald F. ....Cincinnati, OH
Kaminski, Gil ....Detroit, MI
Kaminski, Harvey L. ....Fort Lee, NJ
Kaminski & Hawbaker ....Chambersburg, PA
Kaminski, Helen N. ....Chicago, IL
Kaminski, James A.
Federal Trade Commission,
Bureau of Consumer Protection, GV
Kaminski, James W. ....La Porte, IN
Kaminski, Jeffri A. ....Washington, DC
Kaminski, John S. ....Portland, ME
Kaminski, Julie Ann ....Washington, DC
Kaminski, Julie Lynn ....Chicago, IL
Kaminski, Katherine Andritsakis
Elk Grove, CA
Kaminski, Kathleen ....Lakewood, OH

Kaminski, Kathryn A. ..... Jaffrey, NH
Kaminski, Kenneth Marcel ..... San Diego, CA
Kaminski, Kerin Lyn ..... Cleveland, OH
Kaminski, Kimberly A. ..... Portland, OR
Kaminski, Lawr. V. ..... Princeton, WI
Kaminski, Leon R. ..... La Porte, IN
Kaminski, Martin A. ..... Austin, MN
Kaminski, Michael ..... Pittsburgh, PA
Kaminski, Michael D. ..... Washington, DC
Kaminski, Nathan, Jr. ..... Columbia, SC
Kaminski, Paul E. ..... Minneapolis, MN
Kaminski & Pozorski ..... Manitowoc, WI
Kaminski, Robert A. ..... New York, NY
Kaminski, Robert L. ..... Austin, TX
Kaminski, Ron A. ..... Manitowoc, WI
Kaminski, Scott H. ..... Charleston, WV
Kaminski, Stanley R., Jr. ..... Chicago, IL
Kaminski, Stephen J. ..... Minneapolis, MN
Kaminski, William F. ..... Chambersburg, PA
Kaminski, William S. ..... La Porte, IN
Kaminski, Yvonne M. ..... Chicago, IL
Kaminsky, Alan ..... New York, NY
Kaminsky, Allan H. ..... Buffalo, NY
Kaminsky, Arthur C. ..... New York, NY
Kaminsky, Borner & Smith ..... Moosup, CT
Putnam, CT
Kaminsky, Carl I. ..... New York, NY
Kaminsky, David A. ..... New York, NY
Kaminsky, David R. .....
Department of Housing and Urban Development, GV
Kaminsky, Don M. ..... Milwaukee, WI
Kaminsky, Eddie ..... Singer Island, FL
Kaminsky, Edward A. ..... New York, NY
Kaminsky, Eric B. ..... Tustin, CA
Kaminsky, Faith A. ..... New York, NY
Kaminsky, Gerald S. ..... Hamtramck, MI
Kaminsky, I. Samuel ..... Johnstown, PA
Kaminsky, Jerrold N. ..... Kendall Park, NJ
Kaminsky, John R. ..... Minneapolis, MN
Kaminsky, Joseph ..... Brooklyn Center, MN
Kaminsky, Lawrence J ..... East Rockaway, NY
Kaminsky, Martin I. ..... New York, NY
Kaminsky, Martin L. ..... Lido Beach, NY
Kaminsky, Michael J. ..... Los Angeles, CA
Kaminsky, Michael P. ..... Brunswick, OH
Kaminsky, Neal M. ..... Houston, TX
Kaminsky, Peter ..... Tampa, FL
Kaminsky, Philip G. ..... Memphis, TN
Kaminsky, Richard A. ..... Chicago, IL
Kaminsky, Robert L. ..... Treasury Department, Internal Revenue Service, GV
Kaminsky, Seth F. ..... Garden City, NY
Kaminsky, Stephanie E. ..... Washington, DC
Kaminsky, Walter M. ..... Elk River, MN
Kaminsky, Wharton, Silverman and Thomas
Johnstown, PA
Kaminsky-Meyers, Judith A. ..... New York, NY
Kaminsky-Meyers, Judith A. ..... New York, NY
Kamis, Ronald J. ..... Washington, DC
Kamisar, Gordon A. ..... Issaquah, WA
Kamisar, Jonathan R. ..... Stamford, CT
Kamisar, Yale ..... Ann Arbor, MI
Kamisher, Eric S. ..... New York, NY
Kamisher, Lawrence ..... Bellmore, NY
Kamita, Kery K. ..... Honolulu, HI
Kamitomo, Mark D. ..... Spokane, WA
Kamitsuka, P. Rebecca ..... Eugene, OR
Kamizolas, William T. ..... Los Angeles, CA
Kamlani, Sanjay S. ..... New York, NY
Kamleiter, Mark S. ..... New Port Richey, FL
Kamlet, Jay F. ..... Denver, CO
Kamlet, Leonard G. ..... New York, NY
Kamlet, Susan L. ..... San Francisco, CA
Kamlowsky, John H. ..... Weirton, WV
Wheeling, WV
Kamm, Babette Dominique ..... San Diego, CA
Kamm, Carol E. ..... Boston, MA
Kamm, David B. ..... Los Angeles, CA
Kamm, David G. ..... Grand Rapids, MI
Kamm, Gerald A. ..... South Bend, IN
Kamm, Linda Heller ..... New York, NY
Kamm, Marilyn J. ..... Juneau, AK
Kamm & McConnell, L.L.C. ..... Raton, NM
Kamm, Melvin J. ..... Bridgeview, IL
Kamm, Melvin J., Ltd. ..... Bridgeview, IL
Kamm, Paul P. ..... Los Angeles, CA
Kamm, Robert M. ..... Chicago, IL
Kamm & Shapiro, Ltd. ..... Chicago, IL
Kamm, Solomon M. ..... Los Angeles, CA
Kamm, Terrence R. ..... Raton, NM
Kamm, Thomas A. ..... Healdsburg, CA
Kamm, Warren ..... Long Beach, CA
Kamm, William E.
Department of Commerce, Patent and Trademark Office, GV
Kamman, James M. ..... Santa Ana, CA
Kamman, Robert E. ..... Phoenix, AZ
Kammann, Philip H. ..... Fairview Heights, IL
Kammann, Ronald L. ..... San Francisco, CA
Kammel, Carole R.
Department Of Veterans Affairs, Board of Veterans Appeals, GV
Kammen, Julie I. ..... Columbia, SC
Kammen, Richard ..... Indianapolis, IN
Kammer, A. Thomas ..... Syosset, NY
Kammer, Alexander S. ..... Madison, WI
Kammer, Alfred C., II ..... Alexandria, VA
Kammer, Bonita S. ..... Madison, WI
Kammer, Charles H., III ..... Shreveport, LA
Kammer, David D. ..... Cincinnati, OH
Kammer, Douglas W. ..... Portage, WI
Kammer & Huff ..... San Antonio, TX
Kammer, Joseph C. ..... Cincinnati, OH
Kammer, Karen Williams ..... Miami, FL
Kammer, Karl D. ..... Cleveland, OH
Kammer, Kevin David ..... Encino, CA
Kammer, Mark A. ..... San Antonio, TX
Kammer, Nolan ..... New Orleans, LA
Kammer, Richard E. ..... Cincinnati, OH
Kammer, Robert A., Jr. ..... Wausau, WI
Kammer, Robert J. ..... Rochester, NY
Kammer, Ronald L. ..... Miami, FL
Kammer, Stanley L. ..... Cleveland, OH
Kammer, William N. ..... San Diego, CA
Kammerait, Thomas J. ..... Milwaukee, WI
Kammerer, Clinton H. ..... Missoula, MT
Kammerer, Donald B. ..... Jefferson City, MO
Kammerer, Edward H. ..... Providence, RI
Kammerer, George T., III
Sacramento, CA
Kammerer, Keith E. ..... Hauppauge, NY
Kammerer, Kelly C.
Agency for International Development, Other Offices of A.I.D., GV
Kammerer, Matthew P. ..... Cincinnati, OH
Kammerer, Patricia A. ..... Houston, TX
Kammerer, Rudolph M. ..... Washington, DC
Kammerer, Tracey C. ..... Southport, CT
Kammerer, William ..... Dublin, OH
Kammerlander, Perri A. ..... Hopkins, MN
Kammerman, Alan L. ..... New York, NY
Kammerman, Barbara ..... Department of Justice, Civil Rights Division, GV
Kammerman, Jane A. ..... Minneapolis, MN
Kammerman, Marcy H. ..... Boca Raton, FL
Kammerman, Richard E. ..... Austin, TX
Kammeyer, Daniel M. ..... Anoka, MN
Kammeyer, Ema M. G. ..... Tucson, AZ
Kammeyer, W. Randall ..... Fort Wayne, IN
Kammholz, Bradley P. ..... Rochester, NY
Kammire, Harry M. ..... Salamanca, NY
Kamnitz, Allan H. ..... New York, NY
Kamnitz, Gail ..... New York, NY
Kamo, James H. ..... Honolulu, HI
Kamo, Kathleen N. ..... Honolulu, HI
Kamoie, Brian E. ..... Washington, DC
Kamolnick, Steven ..... La Mesa, CA
Kamon, Ellen B. ..... Los Angeles, CA
Kamon, Ralph ..... Los Angeles, CA
Kamornick, Phillip S. ..... Los Angeles, CA
Kamowitz, Sharon S. ..... Boston, MA
Kamowski, Norbert R. ..... Park Ridge, IL
Kamowski, Richard M. ..... Chicago, IL
Kamp, Allen R. ..... Chicago, IL
Kamp, Arthur J. ..... Newport News, VA
Kamp, Barbara Hays ..... Newport News, VA
Kamp, David P. ..... Cincinnati, OH
Kamp, Gary A. ..... Burfordville, MO
Kamp, Henry A. ..... Miami Beach, FL
Kamp, James F. ..... Bloomfield Hills, MI
Kamp, Joel J. ..... Fort Madison, IA
Kamp, Mark M. ..... West Palm Beach, FL
Kamp, Michael P. ..... Wallingford, CT
Kamp, Nancy B. ..... St. Louis, MO
Kamp, Paul ..... Bedford, MA
Kamp, Randall W. ..... Edmond, OK
Kamp, Randall W., P.C. ..... Edmond, OK
Kamp, Rebecca J. ..... Philadelphia, PA
Kamp, Steven M. ..... Sacramento, CA
Kamp, Susan W. ..... Cincinnati, OH
Kamp, Thomas N. ..... Davenport, IA
Kampa, Mary ..... Nashville, TN
Kampani, Dharminder L. ..... Cleveland, OH
Kampas, Bradley W. ..... San Francisco, CA
Kampe, Kurt W., III ..... Sherman Oaks, CA
Kampe, Shelly ..... Sherman Oaks, CA
Kampel, Andrew D. ..... Bronx, NY
Kampelman, Max M. ..... Washington, DC
Kampen, Cheryl A. ..... Littleton, CO
Kamper, Christopher ..... Denver, CO
Kamper, Christopher E. ..... Phoenix, AZ
Kamper, Timothy J. ..... Phoenix, AZ
Kamperschroer, George R. ..... Stoughton, WI
Kampf & Associates, P.A. ..... Minneapolis, MN
Kampf, David B. ..... Tampa, FL
Kampf, Gregg K. ..... Grand Junction, CO
Kampf, Jeffrey T. ..... West Orange, NJ
Kampf, Judith R. ..... Spokane, WA
Kampf, Schiavone & Associates
San Bernardino, CA
Kampf, W. Roger ..... San Bernardino, CA
Kampf, Warren E. ..... Philadelphia, PA
Kampf, William I. ..... Minneapolis, MN
Kampfe, John S. ..... Omaha, NE
Kampfer, Robert M. ..... Great Falls, MT
Kampfner, Roberto J. ..... San Francisco, CA
New York, NY
Kamph, Thomas F. ..... Newport Beach, CA
Kamph, Thomas F. & Associates
Newport Beach, CA
Kamphuis, Wanda G. ..... Chicago, IL
Kampinen, Leland W. ..... Minneapolis, MN
Kampinski, Charles ..... Cleveland, OH
Kampinski & Mellino Co., L.P.A.
Cleveland, OH
Kampitsis, Stamatia ..... Pearl River, NY
Kamplain, Bruce L. ..... Indianapolis, IN
Kampler, Nina L. ..... Lyndhurst, NJ
Kampler, Sherry B. ..... Universal City, CA
Kampman, John W. ..... Washington, DC
Kampman, Joseph W. ..... Cleveland, OH
Kampmann, Abigail G. ..... San Antonio, TX
Kampmann, Ike S., Jr. ..... San Antonio, TX
Kampmann, Maryanne E. ..... Burlington, VT
Kampmeyer, Michael A. ..... St. Paul, MN
Kampner-Rudin, Alissa ..... New York, NY
Kamprath, Martin J. ..... Monroe, MI
Kamps, Charles Q. ..... Milwaukee, WI
Kamps, Eugene A. ..... Parma Heights, OH
Kamps, Richard ..... Phoenix, AZ
Kamps, William J. ..... Port Orchard, WA
Kampschmidt, Kerry ..... Houston, TX
Kampschroeder, Halley E. ..... Lawrence, KS
Kampsen, Patricia J. ..... Chicago, IL
Kampton, Harvey D. ..... New York, NY
Kamraczewski, Kevin P. ..... Los Angeles, CA
Kamradt, Russell T.
West Palm Beach, FL
Kamran, Kia ..... Hollywood, CA
Kamran, Mir-Houtan Tony ..... Los Angeles, CA
Kamrany, Nake M. ..... Pacific Palisades, CA
Kamrar, John J. ..... Bellingham, WA
Kamrass, Herbert ..... New York, NY
Kamrath, Alan D. ..... Minneapolis, MN
Kamrath, Lisa R. ..... Los Angeles, CA
Kamrowski, Herman V., Jr.
Los Angeles, CA
Kams, William L. ..... Needham, MA
Kamstra, John P. ..... Philadelphia, PA
Kamstra, William H. ..... Wheaton, IL
Kamuchey, Cassandra T. ..... San Jose, CA
Kamuf, Charles J. ..... Owensboro, KY
Kamuf, Charles J., II ..... Owensboro, KY
Kamuf, Yewell & Pace ..... Henderson, KY
Owensboro, KY
Kamula, Matthew Roman ..... Miami, FL
Kamysek, Phyllis Marie ..... New York, NY
Kamysz, Edward J. ..... Buffalo, NY
Kan, Blossom ..... New York, NY
Kan, Grace S. ..... Dallas, TX
Kan, Liang Leon ..... Seattle, WA
Kan, Susan J. ..... Palo Alto, CA
Kan, W. Tetsuji ..... Honolulu, HI
Kanaan, David A. ..... Southfield, MI
Kanaan, Mitchell J. ..... Chicago, IL
Kanabis, C. George ..... New London, CT
Kanabis & Houle, P.C. ..... Colchester, CT
New London, CT
Kanaday, Thomas P., Jr. ..... Nashville, TN
Kanady, Johnson, III ..... Richmond, VA
Kanady, Mary Jo ..... Chicago, IL
Kanaga, Christopher W. ..... Orleans, MA
Kanaga, Lawrence W. ..... Orange, CT
Westport, CT
Kanaga, Lynn Thomas ..... Wilmington, DE
Kanagawa, Christopher N. ..... St. Louis, MO
Kanai, Chester M. ..... Honolulu, HI
Kanai, Mark A. ..... Modesto, CA
Kanai, Mark A., A Professional Corporation
Modesto, CA
Kanak, April H. ..... Houston, TX
Kanak, Joseph R. ..... Dayton, OH
Kanak, Thomas D. ..... Houston, TX
Kanak, Wayne I. ..... Houston, TX
Kanakaredes, Aretta H. ..... Canton, OH
Kanakis, Mark D. ..... Nashua, NH
Kanalei, B.J. ..... San Diego, CA
Kanaley, Gary M. ..... Buffalo, NY
Kanaley, Michael J., Jr. ..... Albany, NY
Buffalo, NY
Kanaley, Sean Christopher ..... Los Angeles, CA
Kanaly, Mark C. ..... Atlanta, GA
Kanamine, Ann M. ..... Department of Defense, Office of the General Counsel, GV
Kanan, Gregory B. ..... Denver, CO
Kanan, John P. ..... Detroit, MI
Kanan, Thomas L. ..... Denver, CO
Kananack, William J. ..... Melbourne, FL
Kananen, Eric J. ..... Oxnard, CA
Kananen, Kurt Edward ..... Oxnard, CA
Kananen, Ronald P. ..... Washington, DC
Kanar, Stephen P. ..... Orlando, FL
Kanar, Stephen P., Professional Association
Orlando, FL
Kanar, Wendy Davis ..... Midland, MI
Kanaras, John L. ..... Southfield, MI
Kanareff, Alexander ..... Cleveland, OH
Kanarek, Adam ..... Lawrence, NY
Kanarek, Carol M. ..... New York, NY
Kanarek, Deborah J. ..... Palo Alto, CA
Kanarek, Herbert K. ..... White Plains, NY
Kanarek, Paul B. ..... Vero Beach, FL
Kanarek, Stanley ..... North Bellmore, NY
Kanaris, Peter E. ..... Chicago, IL
Kanarish, Shelby ..... Chicago, IL
Kanarish, Shelby H., P.C. ..... Chicago, IL
Kanasky, Thomas L., Jr. ..... Bridgeport, CT
Kanassatega, Joshua J. ..... Minneapolis, MN
Kanatz, Viola M. ..... Minneapolis, MN
Kanazawa, Sidney K. ..... Los Angeles, CA
Kanbar, Edward S. ..... New York, NY
Kanberg, John H. ..... San Francisco, CA
Kanc, Maureen Urban ..... Philadelphia, PA
Kanca, Diane K. ..... New York, NY
Kancel, Felix G. ..... Kansas City, KS
Kancelbaum, Joshua J. ..... Chesterland, OH
Kancewick, Mary A. ..... Anchorage, AK
Kancher, Mark S. ..... Pleasantville, NJ
Kancilia, John R. ..... Melbourne, FL
Kancler, Edward ..... Cleveland, OH
Kandah, Sabri ..... New York, NY
Kandaras, Homer M. ..... Rapid City, SD
Kandaras, Kenneth ..... Chicago, IL
Kandaras, Mary Margaret ..... Reno, NV
Kandarian, Keith A. ..... San Francisco, CA
Kandawalla, Darius N. ..... Columbus, OH
Kandel, Alan H. ..... St. Louis, MO
Kandel, Andrew ..... New York, NY
Kandel, Ann K. ..... Nesconset, NY
Kandel, Ann K., Law Offices of , P.C.
Nesconset, NY
Kandel, Brian M. ..... San Jose, CA
Kandel, Carl S. ..... Pomona, CA
Kandel, Harry N. ..... North Canton, OH
Kandel, James R. ..... Canton, OH
Kandel, James R., Co., L.P.A. ..... Canton, OH
Kandel, Jamie ..... San Francisco, CA
Kandel, Klitenic & Chernow, LLP
Baltimore, MD
Kandel, Laurie Greenstein ..... Miami, FL
Kandel, Michael J. ..... Baltimore, MD
Kandel, Nelson R. ..... Baltimore, MD
Kandel, Randy Frances ..... Bronx, NY
Kandel, Robert A. ..... New York, NY
Kandel, Robin Frazier ..... Baltimore, MD
Kandel, Solon L. ..... Roseland, NJ
Kandel, Stanley T. ..... Los Angeles, CA
Kandel, Sydney J. ..... Brooklyn, NY
Kandel, Tyler J. ..... Morristown, NJ
New York, NY
Kandel, William L. ..... New York, NY
Kandell, Beatrice E. ..... Livingston, NJ
Kandell, Brian J. ..... Philadelphia, PA
Kandell, Ellen F.
Environmental Protection Agency, Office of Enforcement and Compliance Assurance, GV
Kandell, Michael D. ..... Manhattan Beach, CA
Kandell, Richard L. ..... Louisville, KY
Kandell, Risa L. ..... Tucson, AZ
Kandell, Robin Pilar ..... Santa Clara, CA
Kandell, Scott Evan ..... Miami, FL
Kandell, Stephen A. ..... Miami, FL
Kandelman, Steven ..... Chicago, IL
Kander, Gregg M. ..... Pittsburgh, PA
Kander, Roger A. ..... Long Beach, CA
Kandler, Edward R. ..... Fresno, CA
Kandler, Michael P. ..... New York, NY
Kando, Kenneth ..... Pawtucket, RI
Kandoian, Ellen A. ..... Portland, ME
Kando-Pineda, Carol Ann
Federal Trade Commission, Office of Congressional Relations, GV
Kandravy, Elizabeth A. ..... Washington, DC
Kandravy, John ..... Florham Park, NJ
Kandt, Anthony J. ..... Brighton, MI
Kandt, Charles A. ..... Mobile, AL
Kandt, Wm. Brett ..... Reno, NV
Kandt, Wm. C. ..... Wichita, KS
Kandutsch, Carl E.
Federal Communications Commission, Cable Services Bureau, GV
Portland, ME
Kandyba, Mary L. ..... Chicago, IL
Kandzari, Pamela Lynn ..... Charleston, WV
Kane, Alan B. ..... Norristown, PA
Kane, Alan H. ..... Seattle, WA
Kane, Alan J. ..... Floral Park, NY
Kane, Alice T. ..... New York, NY
Kane, Allan D. ..... Cedar Rapids, IA
Kane, Andrew B. ..... Denver, CO
Kane, Angelique P. ..... Lebanon, TN
Kane, Anne E. ..... Philadelphia, PA
Kane, Anthony ..... Minneapolis, MN
Kane, Anthony J. ..... Minneapolis, MN
Kane, Anthony T. ..... Monticello, NY
Kane, Arlene Diane ..... Great Neck, NY
Kane, Arthur O. ..... Chicago, IL
Kane, Ballmer & Berkman, A Law Corporation ..... Los Angeles, CA
Kane, Barbara Stewart ..... Pittsburgh, PA
Kane, Barry C. ..... Grand Rapids, MI
Kane, Berry ..... San Jose, CA
Kane, Bonnie E. ..... San Diego, CA
Kane, Brad S. ..... Los Angeles, CA
Kane, Bradley H. ..... Philadelphia, PA
Kane, Brian ..... Rochester, NY
Kane, Brian F. ..... Lewiston, NY
Kane, Brian J. ..... Dubuque, IA
Kane, Brian S. ..... Pittsburgh, PA
Kane, Carol B. ..... New York, NY
Kane, Carolyn Mitchell ..... New York, NY
Kane, Charles J., P.A. ..... Boca Raton, FL
Kane, Cheryl J. ..... Los Angeles, CA
Kane, Christina M. ..... Newtown Square, PA
Kane, Christine G. ..... Sacramento, CA
Kane, Christopher ..... Seattle, WA
Kane, Christopher A. ..... Des Plaines, IL
Kane, Christopher E. ..... Bloomfield Hills, MI
Kane, Christopher J. ..... Portland, OR
Kane, Christopher M. ..... New York, NY
Kane, Christopher J., P.C. ..... Portland, OR
Kane, Christy F. ..... New Orleans, LA
Kane, Connie R. ..... Indianapolis, IN
Kane, Cornelius H., Jr. ..... Boston, MA
Kane, Dalsimer, Sullivan & Levy, LLP
New York, NY
Kane, Daniel, and Associates, P.C.
Atlanta, GA
Kane, Daniel B. ..... Buffalo, NY
Kane, Daniel E. ..... Atlanta, GA
Kane, Daniel H. ..... New York, NY
Kane, Dara M. ..... Bronx, NY
Kane, David C. ..... Treasury Department, Office of the Comptroller of the Currency, GV
Kane, David H. T. ..... New York, NY
Kane, David L. ..... Mobile, AL
Kane, David N. ..... San Rafael, CA
Kane, David W. ..... Chicago, IL
Kane, Deborah B. ..... Walterboro, SC
Kane, Deborah Elizabeth Sanders
Lanham, MD
Kane, Donald H. ..... Stuart, FL
Kane, Donald V. ..... Hempstead, NY
Kane, Donley & Johnson, P.C.
Colorado Springs, CO
Kane, Douglas C. ..... Santa Cruz, CA
Kane, Doy & Harrington, Ltd.
Chicago, IL
Kane, E. Peter ..... McLean, VA
Kane, Edmund J. ..... Farmington, CT
Kane, Edward F. ..... Norristown, PA
Philadelphia, PA
Kane, Edward J. ..... Portland, ME
Kane, Edward L. ..... San Diego, CA
Kane, Edward M. ..... Greenwich, CT
Kane, Edward M. ..... Wampsville, NY
Kane, Edward R. J., Chtd. ..... Las Vegas, NV
Kane, Edward R. J. ..... Las Vegas, NV
Kane, Elizabeth ..... New York, NY

Kane, Elizabeth A. .... Honolulu, HI
Kane, Eneas A. .... Phoenix, AZ
Kane, Eric .... Manchester, NH
Kane, Eric Alexander .... Atlanta, GA
Kane, Frances F. .... Washington, DC
Kane, Francis E. .... Shaker Heights, OH
Kane, Frank E. .... Toledo, OH
Kane, G. Donohue .... Denver, CO
Kane, G. Kevin .... Sioux Falls, SD
Kane, G. Robert .... Burlingame, CA
Kane, Gail M. .... San Francisco, CA
Kane, Gail Rose .... Cleveland, OH
Kane, Gary P. .... Raleigh, NC
Kane, George W., III .... Raleigh, NC
Kane, Gerald H. B. .... Hermosa Beach, CA
Kane, Gerald R. .... Nyack, NY
Kane, Gregory C. .... San Diego, CA
Kane, Gregory M. .... Spokane, WA
Kane, Harley N. .... Boca Raton, FL
Kane, Harold M. .... Lake Ariel, PA
Kane, Harris J. .... Beverly Hills, CA
Kane, Harry C. .... New York, NY
Kane, Harry J., Jr. .... Philadelphia, PA
Kane, Harry N. .... Los Angeles, CA
Kane, Hartley & Katz, P.C. .... Glastonbury, CT
Kane, Hayden W. .... Colorado Springs, CO
Kane, Hayden W., II
Colorado Springs, CO
Kane, Howard E. .... Chicago, IL
Kane, H. W. .... Ravenna, OH
Kane, Ingrid L. .... Duluth, MN
Kane, Ira O. .... Hebron, OH
Kane, Irvin H. .... Milwaukee, WI
Kane, Irving E. .... Lynn, MA
Kane, Ivan P. .... Chicago, IL
Kane, J. Christopher .... Chicago, IL
Kane, J. Jerry .... Mount Carroll, IL
Kane, James B., Jr. .... Buffalo, NY
Kane, James E. .... Richmond, VA
Kane, James F. .... New Britain, CT
Kane, James F. .... Peoria, IL
Kane, James J. .... Des Moines, IA
Kane, James J. .... Pottsville, PA
Kane, James L., Jr. .... McLean, VA
Kane, James M. .... Atlanta, GA
Kane, James M. .... Chicago, IL
Kane, James M. .... Chicago, IL
Kane, James P. .... New York, NY
Kane, James P., Jr .... Chicago, IL
Kane, James R., (P.C.) .... Boston, MA
Kane, James S. .... Rockville, MD
Kane, James T. .... Tempe, AZ
Kane, Jane Ennis .... Philadelphia, PA
Kane, Jane M. .... Winston-Salem, NC
Kane, Jas. L. .... Buffalo, NY
Kane, Jeffrey A. .... Fremont, OH
Kane, Jeffrey J. .... Katonah, NY
Kane, Jeffrey P. .... Fresno, CA
Kane, Jeffrey W. .... Winnetka, IL
Kane, Jeffries, Gayle, McGrath & Cooper
Richmond, VA
Kane, Jennifer .... Washington, DC
Kane, Jeremiah F., III .... West Chester, PA
Kane, Jill C.
Securities and Exchange Commission, Office of Compliance Inspections and Examinations, GV
Kane, Jim .... Spokane, WA
Kane, Jo Ellen .... Fort Myers, FL
Kane, Jo Ellen, P.A., The Law Office of
Fort Myers, FL
Kane, Joelle Segawa .... Honolulu, HI
Kane, John A. .... Brea, CA
Kane, John A., Jr. .... Detroit, MI
Kane, John B. .... Bel Air, MD
Kane, John B., Jr. .... Red Hook, NY
Kane, John C. .... Algonac, MI
Kane, John C., Jr. .... Boston, MA
Kane, John Clarke .... Boston, MA
Kane, John F. .... Wilmington, DE
Kane, John F. .... Dayton, OH
Kane, John H. .... Hartford, CT
Kane, John J. .... Wilbraham, MA
Kane, John J. .... North Brunswick, NJ
Kane, John J. .... Trenton, NJ
Kane, John K. .... New York, NY
Kane, John L., Jr. .... Denver, CO
Kane, John N., Jr. .... Washington, DC
Kane, John P. .... Huntington Station, NY
Kane, John Paul .... Hartford, CT
Kane, John S. .... Lansing, MI
Kane, John W., Jr. .... Thornton, PA
Kane, Jon E. .... Orlando, FL
Kane, Jonathan .... Berwyn, PA
Kane, Jonathan J. .... Hartford, CT
Kane, Jonna M. .... Franklin, IN
Kane, Joseph E. .... Cincinnati, OH
Kane, Joseph E., II .... Cincinnati, OH
Kane, Joseph P. .... Scranton, PA
Kane, Joseph P. .... Williamsport, PA
Kane, Joseph R. .... Mountainside, NJ
Kane, Joseph T. .... Northbrook, IL
Kane, Julia K. .... Denver, CO
Kane, Julie Braman .... Miami, FL
Kane, Julie M. .... Summit, NJ
Kane, Kane & Kane, LLP .... Pawhuska, OK
Skiatook, OK
Kane, Kane, Kane & Roark .... Bartlesville, OK
Kane, Karen A. .... Wilmington, DE
Kane, Karen J. .... Pomona, CA
Kane, Karen R. .... St. Paul, MN
Kane, Kathleen .... Philadelphia, PA
Scranton, PA
Kane, Kathleen A. .... Paoli, PA
Kane, Kathleen E. .... Lansing, MI
Kane, Kathleen L. .... San Francisco, CA
Kane, Kathleen W. .... Williamsburg, VA
Kane, Kenneth P. .... New York, NY
Kane Kessler, P.C. .... Hackensack, NJ
New York, NY
Kane, Kevin I. .... Bethesda, MD
Kane, Kevin J. .... Chicago, IL
Kane, Kevin M. .... Phoenix, AZ
Kane, Kevin M. .... Waukegan, IL
Kane, Kevin P. .... Beverly Hills, CA
Kane, Kevin T. .... New London, CT
Kane and Koltun .... Maitland, FL
Kane and Koons .... Bethesda, MD
Kane, Larry J. .... Indianapolis, IN
Kane, Larry R., (P.C.) .... Chicago, IL
Kane, Larry S. .... Keene, NH
Kane, Laura .... Rockville, MD
Kane, Laura A. .... Chicago, IL
Kane, Laura, P.A. .... Rockville, MD
Kane Law Office .... St. Paul, MN
Kane, Lawrence J. .... Lynbrook, NY
Kane, Lawrence T. .... San Francisco, CA
Kane, Leah A. .... Las Vegas, NV
Kane Legal Group, LLC .... Stamford, CT
Kane, Leo J. .... Washington, DC
Kane, Leonard P., Jr. .... Pittsburgh, PA
Kane, Leslie .... San Francisco, CA
Kane, Leslie J. .... New York, NY
Kane, Linda Connor .... Jacksonville, FL
Kane, Lisa F. .... Madison, WI
Kane, M. John, IV .... Pawhuska, OK
Skiatook, OK
Kane, M. Lynne .... Bethesda, MD
Kane, Madeleine B. .... Bayside, NY
Kane, Malcolm B. .... Ellicott City, MD
Kane, Mara Leiding .... Hampton, VA
Kane, Marc Morley .... Pittsburgh, PA
Kane, Marc Morley, A Professional Corporation .... Pittsburgh, PA
Kane, Margaret McDonald
Los Angeles, CA
Kane, Margaret O'Sullivan .... St. Paul, MN
Kane, Marianne F. K. .... Boston, MA
Kane, Maritoni D. .... Chicago, IL
Kane, Mark .... Los Angeles, CA
Kane, Mark .... Bartlesville, OK
Kane, Mark H. .... Colorado Springs, CO
Kane, Mark M. .... North Woodmere, NY
Kane, Martin D. .... Kew Gardens, NY
Kane, Martin J. .... Binghamton, NY
Kane, Mary .... Portland, OR
Kane, Mary A. .... Tallahassee, FL
Kane, Mary Clare .... Bronx, NY
Kane, Mary Kathleen .... Hauppauge, NY
Kane, Mary Kay .... San Francisco, CA
Kane, Maryanne S.
Federal Trade Commission, Office of the General Counsel, GV
Kane, Matthew A. .... Bethesda, MD
Kane, Matthew A., Jr. .... Bradenton, FL
Kane, Matthew C. .... Beverly Hills, CA
Kane, Matthew I. .... Parsippany, NJ
Kane, Matthew N. .... Boston, MA
Kane, Maureen P. .... Mesa, AZ
Kane, Maurice S., Jr. .... Los Angeles, CA
Kane, Max L.
Federal Energy Regulatory Commission, Office of the General Counsel, GV
Kane, McClean & Mengshol .... Fresno, CA
Kane, Melissa E. .... Roanoke, VA
Kane, Meredith J. .... New York, NY
Kane, Michael .... Boise, ID
Kane, Michael .... Maquoketa, IA
Kane, Michael .... Arlington, VA
Kane, Michael C. .... Philadelphia, PA
Kane, Michael G. .... Washington, DC
Kane, Michael J. .... Chicago, IL
Kane, Michael J. .... St. Paul, MN
Kane, Michael J. .... Doylestown, PA
Kane, Michael J. .... Jenkintown, PA
Kane, Michael P. .... Lancaster, PA
Kane, Michael S.
Department of Justice, GV
Kane, Michele C. .... Burbank, CA
Kane, Michele B. .... Winter Park, FL
Kane, Michelle D. .... Chicago, IL
Kane, Michelle L.
Department Of Veterans Affairs, Board of Veterans Appeals, GV
Kane, Milton B. .... Sacramento, CA
Kane, M'Liss Jones .... Irvine, CA
Kane, Murray O. .... Los Angeles, CA
Kane, Nancy A. .... Philadelphia, PA
Kane, Nancy Warren .... Newport News, VA
Kane, Nora M. .... Omaha, NE
Kane, Norby & Reddick, P.C.
Dubuque, IA
Kane, Owen P. .... Boston, MA
Kane, Pamela M. .... Fort Lauderdale, FL
Kane, Pamela S. .... Washington, DC
Kane, Patricia .... Stamford, CT
Kane, Patricia A. .... Chicago, IL
Kane, Patricia Lisehora .... Rockville, MD
Kane, Patricia Quain .... Scottsdale, AZ
Kane, Patrick J. .... New York, NY
Kane, Patrick J. .... Williamsville, NY
Kane, Patrick J. .... Sioux Falls, SD
Kane, Paul A. .... Tulsa, OK
Kane, Paul M. .... Boston, MA
Kane, Paula .... Los Angeles, CA
Kane, Peggy M. .... Chicago, IL
Kane, Peter E. .... Richmond, VA
Kane, Philip M. .... San Francisco, CA
Kane, Pugh, Knoell & Driscoll, LLP
Norristown, PA
Philadelphia, PA
Kane, Raymond J. .... Dallas, TX
Kane, Raymond J., Jr. .... Ellicott City, MD
Kane, Regina N. .... Atlanta, GA
Kane, Regina Yvonne .... Norfolk, VA
Kane, Richard .... Rochester, NY
Kane, Richard .... Bartlesville, OK
Kane, Richard F. .... Hallandale Beach, FL
Kane, Richard F. .... Charlotte, NC
Kane, Richard F. .... Columbus, OH
Kane, Richard J. .... New York, NY
Kane, Robert .... Dansville, NY
Kane, Robert B. .... Alpena, MI
Kane, Robert E., Jr. (Kane & Jeffries, P.C.)
Richmond, VA
Kane, Robert F. .... San Francisco, CA
Kane, Robert F. .... San Mateo, CA
Kane, Robert F.
National Labor Relations Board, Office of Board Members, GV
Kane, Robert H. .... Brooklyn, NY
Kane, Robert J. .... Newport Beach, CA
Kane, Robert K. .... New York, NY
Kane, Robert M. .... San Francisco, CA
Kane, Robert M. .... Bronx, NY
Kane, Robert M. .... Bartlesville, OK
Kane, Robert M. .... Tacoma, WA
Kane, Robert M., Jr. .... Seattle, WA
Kane, Robert R., III .... Pearisburg, VA
Kane, Robert T. .... Munhall, PA
Kane, Roger C. .... Denver, CO
Kane, Ronald G. .... Bethesda, MD
Kane, Ronald J. .... Ravenna, OH
Kane, Ronald P. .... Chicago, IL
Kane, Russell, Coleman & Logan, A Professional Corporation .... Dallas, TX
Kane, Russell L. .... Boston, MA
Kane, Sandra R. .... Phoenix, AZ
Kane, Scott A. .... Cincinnati, OH
Kane, Scott M. .... East Wenatchee, WA
Kane, Sean F. .... New York, NY
Kane, Shannan M. .... Washington, DC
Kane, Sicuro & Simon .... Ravenna, OH
Kane, Siegrun D. .... New York, NY
Kane & Silverman, Professional Corporation
Philadelphia, PA
Kane, Singer, Planck, Donoghue, Clark & Mixson, P.A. .... Melbourne, FL
Orlando, FL
Kane, Stephen J. .... Fresno, CA
Kane, Stephen J. .... Irvine, CA
Kane, Stephen M. .... Irvine, CA
Kane, Stephen M. .... Boston, MA
Kane, Stephen R. .... Atlanta, GA
Kane, Steven H. .... Maitland, FL
Kane, Steven H. .... Orlando, FL
Kane, T. Paul .... Cobleskill, NY
Kane, Terence M. .... San Jose, CA
Kane, Terrence D. .... Arlington Heights, IL
Kane, Terry G. P. .... Ravenna, OH
Kane, Terry Richard .... Charlotte, NC
Kane, Thomas .... Philadelphia, PA
Kane, Thomas E. .... Federal Trade Commission, Bureau of Consumer Protection, GV
Kane, Thomas G. .... Melbourne, FL
Orlando, FL
Kane, Thomas J. .... Washington, DC
Kane, Thomas J. .... Boston, MA
Kane, Thomas Kelly .... Colorado Springs, CO
Kane, Thomas P. .... Glastonbury, CT
Kane, Thomas P. .... St. Paul, MN
Kane, Timothy E. .... York, PA
Kane, Timothy J. .... Buffalo, NY
Kane, Timothy L. .... Buffalo, NY
Kane, Timothy R.
Securities and Exchange Commission, Division of Investment Management, GV
Kane, Tracy Anne .... Boston, MA
Kane, Walter M. .... New York, NY
Kane, Walter S. .... Morristown, NJ
Kane, Wilbur P. .... Silver Spring, MD
Kane, William B. .... Glenwood, IL
Kane, William D. .... Fort Worth, TX
Kane, William M. .... Grand Junction, CO
Kane, William R. .... Philadelphia, PA
Kane, William T. .... Silver Spring, MD
Kane, William Vail .... San Francisco, CA
Kane, Willner & Holman .... Philadelphia, PA
Kane, Yvette .... Harrisburg, PA
Kane Curreri, Nancy .... Birmingham, AL
Kaneda, Joseph .... Newport Beach, CA
Kaneen, Christina
Environmental Protection Agency, Office of the General Counsel, GV
Kanef, Gail Oxfeld .... Newark, NJ
Kanefield, Howard L. .... St. Louis, MO
Kanefield, Joseph .... Phoenix, AZ
Kanefsky, David H. .... New York, NY
Kanefsky, E. Paul .... New York, NY
Kanehl, Beth .... Deerfield, IL
Kaneko, Chiori .... New York, NY
Kaneko, Lani Anne I. .... Los Angeles, CA
Kaneko, Miyuki .... Princeton, NJ
Kaneko, Stuart A. .... Honolulu, HI
Kanel, David L. .... San Francisco, CA
Kanelidis, Nick B. .... Fort Lauderdale, FL
Kanell, Leo G. .... Beaver, UT
Kanell, Theodore E. .... Salt Lake City, UT
Kanellis, Dean W. .... Cleveland, OH
Kanellis, William G. .... Richmond, VA
Kanelos, Frank S. .... Brookfield, IL
Kanemaru, Donna Y. .... Honolulu, HI
Kanemitsu, Cyril S. .... Hilo, HI
Kanemitsu, Frank T. .... Honolulu, HI
Kanengiser, Amy D. .... New York, NY
Kanengiser, Gerold .... Millburn, NJ
Kanengiser, Irwin .... Lake Hiawatha, NJ
Kanengiser & Kalish .... Lake Hiawatha, NJ
Kanengiser, Sandra Gerson
Los Angeles, CA
Kanengiser, William A. .... Cape May, NJ
Kaner, Cem .... Santa Clara, CA
Kaner, Debra M. .... Jamaica, NY
Kaner, Harvey S. .... St. Paul, MN
Kaner, Jon C. .... Warren, MI
Kaner, Lisa A. .... Portland, OR
Kaner, Morton E. .... New Rochelle, NY
Kaner, Robert M. .... Duluth, MN
Kaner, Robert M. .... New York, NY
Kane-Ritsch, Julie .... Burbank, CA
Kanerviko, Arthur W., Jr. .... Syracuse, NY
Kanes, John P. .... Atlanta, GA
Kanes, Panos J. .... Atlanta, GA
Kanes, Steven R. .... Boston, MA
Kanes, Yolanda .... New York, NY
Kaneshige, Everett S. .... Honolulu, HI
Kaneshige, Melvin Y. .... Honolulu, HI
Kaneshige, Velma S. .... Honolulu, HI
Kaneshiro, Gale Eiko, (Ms.) .... San Diego, CA
Kaneshiro, Jacqueline L. Z. .... Honolulu, HI
Kaneshiro, Kelvin H. .... Honolulu, HI
Kaneshiro, Wynn Cross .... Los Angeles, CA
Kanetake, Stanley T. .... Kailua, HI
Kanetsky, Moore & DeBoer, P.A.
Venice, FL
Kanetsky, Murray .... Venice, FL
Kanev, Carl P. .... New York, NY
Kane-Vanni, Patricia R. .... Philadelphia, PA
Kaney, Frank N. .... Kissimmee, FL
Kaney, J. Lester .... Daytona Beach, FL
Kaney, Jonathan D., III
Daytona Beach, FL
Kaney, Jonathan D., Jr.
Daytona Beach, FL
Kanfer & Gritz, L.L.C. .... Rockville, MD
Kanfer, Ilene G. .... Rockville, MD
Kanfer, Kenneth A. .... New York, NY
Kanfer, Martin .... New York, NY
Kanfer, Susan .... San Diego, CA
Kang, Andrew D. .... Boston, MA
Kang, Angela K. .... San Francisco, CA
Kang, Anna Park .... Los Angeles, CA
Kang, Anthony Donghun .... Boston, MA
Kang, Brian A. .... Honolulu, HI
Kang, Chung Eok .... Los Angeles, CA
Kang, Cindy .... Dallas, TX
Kang, Edward C. .... New York, NY
Kang, Franklin D. .... Los Angeles, CA
Kang, Gail M. .... Honolulu, HI
Kang, Grant D. .... St. Louis, MO
Kang, Gregory B. .... Washington, DC
Kang, Helen H. .... San Francisco, CA
Kang, Jeannie S. .... New York, NY
Kang, Jian-Xiao .... San Diego, CA
Kang, John C. .... Newport Beach, CA
Kang, John J. .... St. Louis, MO
Kang, John M. .... Port Washington, NY
Kang, Jonathan Y. .... Los Angeles, CA
Kang, Joo R. .... Irvine, CA
Kang, Joo-Yung .... Englewood, CO
Kang, Melvin R. .... Seattle, WA
Kang, Peter H. .... San Jose, CA
Kang, Rana .... Madison, WI
Kang, Randhir S. .... Fremont, CA
Kang, Reesha May .... Kansas City, MO
Kang, Sungjin .... New York, NY
Kang, Susan S. .... New York, NY
Kang, Wan-Mo .... Trenton, NJ
Kangas, Dianne E. .... Sheridan, OR
Kangas, Jeanne S. .... Concord, MA
Kangas, Nicole P. .... Philadelphia, PA
Kangas, Roger W. .... Marquette, MI
Kangerga, Spikes .... Austin, TX
Kangesser, Hedy .... Cleveland, OH
Kang-Huneke, Myung .... New York, NY
Kangles, Constantine N., Ltd. .... Chicago, IL
Kangles, Constantine N. .... Chicago, IL
Kangun, Robert I. .... Houston, TX
Kangur, Tonu T., Jr. .... Winston-Salem, NC
Kania, Arthur J. .... Bala Cynwyd, PA
Kania, Edward David .... Washington, DC
Kania, Jay A. .... Skyland, NC
Kania, John F. .... Southington, CT
Kania, John T. .... Uniondale, NY
Kania, Karen Ann .... Newtown Square, PA
Kania, Lindner, Lasak and Feeney
Bala Cynwyd, PA
Media, PA
Norristown, PA
Philadelphia, PA
Kania, Nancy L. .... Buffalo, NY
Kania, Paul J. .... Wilmington, DE
Kania, Robert M. .... Jacksonville, FL
Kanian, Mark A. .... New York, NY
Kanichy, Ioanes .... Kolonia, TT
Kaniewski, John A. .... Newport Beach, CA
Kanige, Jeffrey C. .... Newark, NJ
Kanin, Dennis R. .... Boston, MA
Kanin, Donna L.
Federal Communications Commission, GV
Kanin, Paul R. .... Los Angeles, CA
Kanios, Chris G. .... San Francisco, CA
Kanis, Bret M. .... St. Louis, MO
Kaniuga-Golad, Ludmila .... New York, NY
Kaniuk, David J. .... Ames, IA
Kaniuk, Ronald J. .... New York, NY
Kanji, Ilyse Levine .... Boston, MA
Kanji, Riyaz A. .... Washington, DC
Kanji, Shari .... New York, NY
Kanjian, Robert J. .... West Palm Beach, FL
Kanjo, Christopher A. .... Los Angeles, CA
Kanjorski, Russell P. .... Washington, DC
Kanjuparamban, Maria .... Plymouth, MI
Kann, Aaron Kenan .... Department of Justice, Civil Division, GV
Kann, James M. .... Garnavillo, IA
Kann, Kenneth L. .... San Francisco, CA
Kann, Lewis A. .... Baltimore, MD
Kann, Robert L. .... Boston, MA
Kann, Simon .... Washington, DC
Kann, Terence J. .... Gainesville, FL
Kann, Terence J., P.A. .... Gainesville, FL

Kannaday, Walter Carlisle, III ... Columbia, SC
Kannan, Robert H. ... Rochester, NY
Kannarr, Tina L. ... Cerritos, CA
Kannas, Donald A. ... St. Paul, MN
Kannatt, Nina A. ... Salinas, CA
Kanne, Francine Marie ... Fresno, CA
Kanne, Frank J., Jr. ... Los Angeles, CA
Kanne, Jeffrey J. ... Washington, DC
Kanne, Michael F. ... Santa Ana, CA
Kanne, Michael S. ... Lafayette, IN
Kanne, Roger K. ... Indianapolis, IN
Kannebecker, Charles ... Port Jervis, NY
Kannee, Bruce N.
Department Of Veterans Affairs, Board of Veterans Appeals, GV
Kannel, William W. ... Boston, MA
Kannen, Bernard A. ... Brick, NJ
Kannen, Karen A. ... Costa Mesa, CA
Kannensohn, Fredric A. ... Canfield, OH
Youngstown, OH
Kannensohn, Jeffrey S. ... Naples, FL
Kannensohn, Kimberly J. ... Chicago, IL
Kannensohn, Margaret H. ... Lexington, KY
Kanner, Allan ... New Orleans, LA
Kanner, Allan, & Associates, P.C.
New Orleans, LA
Kanner, Bernard ... St. Petersburg, FL
Kanner, Brian G. ... Portland, ME
Kanner, Daniel J. ... Fort Lauderdale, FL
Kanner, Edward ... Atlanta, GA
Kanner, Edward, P.C., Law Offices of
Atlanta, GA
Kanner, Frederick W. ... New York, NY
Kanner, Gideon ... Santa Monica, CA
Kanner, Harry ... East Rutherford, NJ
Kanner, Jacob ... New York, NY
Kanner, James R. ... Atlanta, GA
Kanner, Jason ... New York, NY
Kanner, John M., Sr. ... Imperial Beach, CA
Kanner, Lewis M. ... Miami, FL
Kanner, Meni ... Pinellas Park, FL
Kanner, Michael A. ... Alhambra, CA
Kanner, Richard A. ... Miami, FL
Kanner, Richard L. ... Longboat Key, FL
Bloomfield Hills, MI
Kanner, Ronald H. ... Running Springs, CA
Kanner, Sheree R.
Department Of Health And Human Services, Office of the General Counsel, GV
Kanner, Sheri ... Fairfield, CT
Kanner, Steven A. ... Chicago, IL
Kanner, Ted, Law Office, The
Charleston, WV
Kanner, Ted M. ... Charleston, WV
Kanner, Terri Hinsley ... Woodland Hills, CA
Kannett, Mark S. ... Emeryville, CA
Kanniainen, J. ... St. Paul, MN
Kanninen, Michael L. ... Fremont, CA
Kanning, Philip T. ... Chaska, MN
Kannow, William Paul ... Los Angeles, CA
Kannry, Jack S. ... New York, NY
Kanny, Matthew P. ... Los Angeles, CA
Kano, Kazumune V. ... Chicago, IL
Kanode, Delno G. ... Culver City, CA
Kanoff, Debra S. ... Santa Monica, CA
Kanoff, Mary Ellen ... Los Angeles, CA
Kanoff, Richard A. ... Boston, MA
Kanofsky, Alan L. ... Freehold, NJ
Kanofsky, Martin A. ... Chicago, IL
Kanoski & Associates ... Bloomington, IL
Macomb, IL
Peoria, IL
Quincy, IL
Rushville, IL
Springfield, IL
Kanoski, Ronald J. ... Bloomington, IL
Macomb, IL
Peoria, IL
Quincy, IL
Rushville, IL
Springfield, IL
Kanoskie, Judith A. ... Cypress, CA
Kanouff, John P. ... Denver, CO
Kanouff, Kevin J. ... Denver, CO
Kanouff, Patrick John ... Denver, CO
Kanouse, Keith J. ... Boca Raton, FL
Kanouse, Keith J., P.A. ... Boca Raton, FL
Kanouse, Valerie G. ... Boca Raton, FL
Kanouse, Valerie G., P.A. ... Boca Raton, FL
Kanov, Jonathan E. ... Miami, FL
Kanovitz, Jacqueline R., (Mrs.)
Louisville, KY
Kanovitz, Michael I. ... Washington, DC
Kanovsky, Helen R. ... Alexandria, VA
Kanovsky, Lisa J. ... Los Angeles, CA
Kanovsky, Stephen M. ... Collegeville, PA
Kanovsky, Yaakov ... Brooklyn, NY
Kanowitz, Edward ... Greenwich, CT
Kanowitz, Howard Z. ... Marlton, NJ
Kanowitz, Leo ... San Francisco, CA
Kanowitz, Richard S. ... New York, NY
Kanowsky, Carl J. ... Valencia, CA
Kanrek, Victoria Jane ... New York, NY
Kansas, Alan F. ... Houston, TX
Kansas, George P. ... Delmar, NY
Kansas, Jacob ... New Orleans, LA
Kanski, Andrea M. ... Detroit, MI
Kansky, Bernard A. ... Boston, MA
Kansler, Adam J. ... New York, NY
Kansteiner, Gary W. ... Austin, TX
Kansteiner, Linda L., Law Office of
Pleasant Hill, CA
Kanstoroom, Bernard H., Jr. ... Bethesda, MD
Kant, Dean A. ... Chicago, IL
Kant, Deborah Ruth ... Department of Justice, Civil Division, GV
Kant, Douglas O. ... Boston, MA
Kant, Harlan R. ... Occidental, CA

Kant, Harold S. ... Reno, NV
Kant, Robert S. ... Phoenix, AZ
Kantack, Keith Curtis ... Montgomery, AL
Kantack, Ramona K. ... McAllen, TX
Kantack, Robert B. ... Bronxville, NY
Kantany-Casartello, Carol J. ... Westfield, MA
Kantargis, Sia Marie ... Birmingham, AL
Kantarian, Harry K. ... Washington, DC
Kantarjian, Karl G. ... Santa Monica, CA
Kantaros, David ... Boston, MA
Kantas, Robert A. ... Charlottesville, VA
Kanter, Aaron ... Washington, DC
Kanter, Alan M. ... Bloomfield Hills, MI
Kanter, Alan N. ... Baltimore, MD
Kanter, Alex ... St. Louis, MO
Kanter, Allen ... Chicago, IL
Kanter, Andrew ... New York, NY
Kanter, Ann L. ... Sacramento, CA
Kanter, Arlene S. ... Syracuse, NY
Kanter, Arnold B. ... Chicago, IL
Kanter, Arthur ... Maplewood, NJ
Kanter, Bernard E. ... Columbus, OH
Kanter, Bernstein & Kardon ... Cherry Hill, NJ
Philadelphia, PA
Kanter, Burton W. ... Chicago, IL
Kanter, Carl I. ... Montvale, NJ
Kanter, Catherine McNichols ... Chicago, IL
Kanter, Charles H., (A Professional Corporation) ... Irvine, CA
Kanter, Craig A. ... Chicago, IL
Kanter, Dale E. ... Sunland, CA
Kanter, David A. ... Chicago, IL
Kanter, David M. ... Washington, DC
Kanter, Edward J. ... Chicago, IL
Kanter, Elliott N. ... San Diego, CA
Kanter, Elvin ... Albuquerque, NM
Kanter, Ethan Baruch
Department of Justice, Civil Division, GV
Kanter & Everage, P.A. ... Albuquerque, NM
Kanter, Gary A. ... Los Angeles, CA
Kanter, Gregg H. ... New York, NY
Kanter, H. Lee ... Virginia Beach, VA
Kanter, Herbert ... Chicago, IL
Kanter, Jane A. ... Washington, DC
Kanter, Jill Ann ... New York, NY
Kanter, Joel E. ... Southport, CT
Santa Fe, NM
Kanter, Jonathan S.
Federal Trade Commission, Bureau of Competition, GV
Kanter, Jordan Elliott ... Melville, NY
Kanter, Joshua S. ... Chicago, IL
Kanter, Leslie G. ... New York, NY
Kanter, Lois H. ... Brookline, MA
Kanter, Marc Jeffrey ... Melville, NY
Kanter, Mark S. ... Cincinnati, OH
Kanter & Mattenson, Ltd. ... Chicago, IL
Kanter, Mayer ... Sioux City, IA
Kanter, Myron A. ... Melville, NY
Kanter, Paul A. ... Walnut Creek, CA
Kanter, Peter B. ... San Francisco, CA
Kanter, Richard M. ... Woodlawn, MD
Kanter, Richard S. ... Washington, DC
Kanter, Richard V. ... Melville, NY
Kanter, Ricki P. Slacter ... Vienna, VA
Kanter, Robert J. ... Detroit, MI
Kanter, Samuel I. ... Columbus, OH
Kanter, Sandra M. ... Los Angeles, CA
Kanter, Scott R. ... Sacramento, CA
Kanter, Seymour ... Philadelphia, PA
Kanter, Stacy J. ... New York, NY
Kanter, Stanley J. ... Providence, RI
Kanter, Stephanie Gale ... Philadelphia, PA
Kanter, Stephen ... Portland, OR
Kanter, Suzanne Rubens ... Chicago, IL
Kanter, William ... Department of Justice, Civil Division, GV
Kanter, William ... Skokie, IL
Kanter & Wishnow, Chartered
Washington, DC
Kanter-Forrest, June ... Trenton, NJ
Kanterman, Lawrence R. ... New York, NY
Kanterman, Paul Philip ... New York, NY
Kanterman & Taub, P.C.
Lake Hiawatha, NJ
New York, NY
Kanthak, Christopher W. ... Galesburg, IL
Kanthatham, Rujiporn Tita
Palo Alto, CA
Kantianis, Jeanne C. ... Newton, MA
Kantner & Associates ... Ann Arbor, MI
Kantner, John M. ... Columbus, OH
Kantner, John R. ... Harrisburg, PA
Kantner, Karen ... Fort Lauderdale, FL
Kantner, Perry M. ... Ann Arbor, MI
Kantner, Richard I., Jr. ... Largo, FL
Kantner, Robert W. ... Dallas, TX
Kantoff, Sheldon L. ... Highland Park, IL
Kantor, Adam L. ... Boston, MA
Kantor, Alesia J. ... New York, NY
Kantor, Allyn D. ... Ann Arbor, MI
Kantor, Andrea D. ... New York, NY
Kantor & Apter, Ltd. ... Northbrook, IL
Kantor, Barry ... Virginia Beach, VA
Kantor, Bertram M. ... New York, NY
Kantor, Charles ... Aventura, FL
Kantor, David ... Minneapolis, MN
Kantor, Davidoff, Kass & Glick, P.A.
North Miami, FL
Kantor, Davidoff, Kass, P.A.
Boca Raton, FL
Kantor, Davidoff, Wolfe, Mandelker & Kass, P.C. ... New York, NY
Kantor, DeMarco & Korobkin
New York, NY
Kantor, Dennis N. ... Avon, CT
East Hartford, CT
Kantor, Dowd ... Bridgeport, CT

Kantor, Eli M. ... Beverly Hills, CA
Kantor, Eric B. ... Cincinnati, OH
Kantor, Errol K. ... Minneapolis, MN
Kantor, Glenn R. ... Encino, CA
Kantor, Hal H. ... Orlando, FL
Kantor, Harris D. ... Lake Success, NY
Kantor, Henry ... Portland, OR
Kantor, Herbert C. ... New York, NY
Kantor, Isa Doppelt ... Hicksville, NY
Kantor, J. Jerry ... Norfolk, VA
Kantor, Joel M. ... Los Angeles, CA
Kantor, John A. ... Arlington Heights, IL
Kantor, Jonathan D. ... Chicago, IL
Kantor & Kopman ... Hicksville, NY
Kantor, Lawrence D. ... Keyport, NJ
Kantor, Lawrence, Jr. ... Newark, NJ
Kantor & Linderoth ... Keyport, NJ
Kantor, Lisa S. ... Los Angeles, CA
Kantor, Lynn ... Indianapolis, IN
Kantor, Marianne ... Fort Myers, FL
Kantor, Mark A. ... Washington, DC
Kantor, Mark B. ... Seattle, WA
Kantor, Marvin ... Phoenix, AZ
Kantor, Michael ... Washington, DC
Kantor, Michael A. ... Scarsdale, NY
Kantor, Michelle F., Law Offices of
Chicago, IL
Kantor, Mickelson and Meyers, P.C.
Avon, CT
East Hartford, CT
Kantor, Myron ... Northbrook, IL
Kantor, Norris ... Bluefield, WV
Kantor, Patricia L. ... New York, NY
Kantor, Philip A. ... Las Vegas, NV
Kantor, Philip A., Prof. Corp., Law Offices of
Las Vegas, NV
Kantor, Philip J. ... Miami, FL
Kantor, Philip L. ... Trenton, NJ
Kantor, Robert A. ... Ketchum, ID
Kantor, Robert A. ... New York, NY
Kantor, Robin J. ... Spring Valley, NY
Kantor, Sandra F. ... Ketchum, ID
Kantor, Sanford S. ... New York, NY
Kantor, Stanley W. ... Owings Mills, MD
Kantor, Stephen E., (P.C.) ... Portland, OR
Kantor, Steven J. ... Burlington, VT
Kantor, Steven L. ... Buffalo, NY
Kantor, Sudha Tiwari ... Princeton, NJ
Kantor, Susan ... New York, NY
Kantor, Susanne ... White Plains, NY
Kantor Taylor McCarthy & Britzmann, P.C.
Seattle, WA
Kantor, Theodore S. ... Rochester, NY
Kantor & Winegrad ... Owings Mills, MD
Kantor Conway, Patricia Anna
San Francisco, CA
Kantorczyk, Todd D. ... Washington, DC
Kantorowitz, Steven R. ... New York, NY
Kantosky, William H. ... Dayton, OH
Kantowitz, Jeffrey L. ... West Orange, NJ
Kantowitz, Robert I. ... New York, NY
Kantra, Andrew E. ... Philadelphia, PA
Kantra, Emil W., II ... Allentown, PA
Kantro, Mark M. ... Norfolk, VA
Kantrovitz & Brownstein, P.C.
New Haven, CT
Kantrovitz, Howard E. ... New Haven, CT
Kantrovitz, Martin, Law Offices of
Boston, MA
Hudson, MA
New Bedford, MA
Kantrovitz, Steven H. ... Boston, MA
Kantrow, Byron R., Jr. ... Baton Rouge, LA
Kantrow, David R. ... San Diego, CA
Kantrow, Josh M. ... Chicago, IL
Kantrow, Lee C. ... Baton Rouge, LA
Kantrow, Spaht, Weaver & Blitzer, A Professional Law Corporation
Baton Rouge, LA
Kantrowitz, Allan S. ... Englewood, CO
Kantrowitz, Barry S. ... Montvale, NJ
Spring Valley, NY
Kantrowitz, Goldhamer & Graifman, P.C.
Montvale, NJ
Kantrowitz, Goldhamer, Graifman, P.C.
Spring Valley, NY
Kantrowitz, Howard A. ... Secaucus, NJ
Kantrowitz, Jack I. ... New York, NY
Kantrowitz, Jonathan D. ... Fairfield, CT
Kantrowitz, R. Marc ... Boston, MA
Kantrowitz, Sharon ... New York, NY
Kantrowitz, Stan ... Pasadena, CA
Kantrowitz, Steven B. ... Philadelphia, PA
Kantrowitz, Walter L. ... Montvale, NJ
Spring Valley, NY
Kantrud, Hugh Alan ... St. Paul, MN
Kantruss, Mackenzie A. ... Mount Airy, MD
Kantz, Mary Kay ... Cleveland, OH
Kantz, S. Sanford ... New Castle, PA
Kantz, Stephen M. ... Otsego, MI
Kanu, Anita C. ... Los Angeles, CA
Kanu, Isatu ... New York, NY
Kanuch, Bruce M. ... Midland, MI
Kanuck, Sean P. ... New York, NY
Kanuit, Robert R. ... Superior, WI
Kanuk, Donald W. ... Treasury Department, Internal Revenue Service, GV
Kanuru, Raj. K. ... Atlanta, GA
Kanusher, Lawrence A. ... New York, NY
Kanusky, Rosemarie ... San Antonio, TX
Kanute, Michael J. ... Chicago, IL
Kanvik, Joel W. ... Reedsburg, WI
Kanwal, Ravi ... Denver, CO
Kanwischer, Gary D. ... Minneapolis, MN
Kanwisher, William ... Baltimore, MD
Kanwit, Glen H. ... Chicago, IL
Kanwit, Marianna ... Portland, OR
Kanwit, Stephanie W. ... Washington, DC

Kany, Lori Feinberg ... New York, NY
Kany, Steven C. ... New York, NY
Kany, William S. ... Saco, ME
Kanyock, Thomas J. ... Chicago, IL
Kanyuck, Scott ... Los Angeles, CA
Kanyuk, Amy K. ... Concord, NH
Kanz, Jack A. ... Dallas, TX
Richardson, TX
Kanzaki, Brian Akira ... Bronx, NY
Kanzaki, Kim ... Palo Alto, CA
Kanzer, Alan ... New York, NY
Kanzer, Lawrence ... Miami, FL
Kanzer, Neil L. ... Garden City, NY
Kanzer, Stephen R. ... Tampa, FL
Kanziger, Robert A. ... Miami, FL
Kanzler, Catherine Healy ... Melville, NY
Kanzler, Christopher L. ... St. Louis, MO
Kanzler, Jay Lee, Jr. ... St. Louis, MO
Kanzler, John S. ... Mineola, NY
New York, NY
White Plains, NY
Kao, Annie ... New York, NY
Kao, Carol K. ... San Diego, CA
Kao, Charles J. ... San Francisco, CA
Kao, Florence ... Washington, DC
Kao, Hilary R. ... Washington, DC
Kao, John K. ... San Francisco, CA
Kao, John, Law Corporation
San Francisco, CA
Kao, Kenneth J. ... Los Angeles, CA
Kao, Loan Anh Tran ... Houston, TX
Kao, Nancy S. ... Department of Agriculture, Office of the General Counsel, GV
Kao, Stephen ... Charlottesville, VA
Kaolulo, Archibald C. K. ... Honolulu, HI
Kaolulo & Shinmura ... Honolulu, HI
Kaough, Mimi Ginott ... New York, NY
Kaoui, Michael R. ... Mobile, AL
Kaouris, Christina ... New York, NY
Kaouris, Demetrios G. ... Easton, MD
Kapacinskas, Heidi E. ... Minneapolis, MN
Kapacinskas, John F. ... St. Paul, MN
Kapadia, Heena ... New Haven, CT
Kapadia, Neil B. ... Charlotte, NC
Kapai, Meenu ... San Francisco, CA
Kapala, Frederick J. ... Rockford, IL
Kapalka, Robert J. ... Wilmington, DE
Kapalko, Paul A. ... Trenton, NJ
Kapaloski, Lee ... Salt Lake City, UT
Kapanjie, Kelly A. ... Chicago, IL
Kapanka, Richard A. ... Greensboro, NC
Kapantais, Thomas P. ... Huntington, WV
Kapas, Eleni H. ... Yorkville, IL
Kapastin, Marc ... Hyattsville, MD
Kapatkin, Fred ... Westbury, NY
Kapel, James R. ... Los Angeles, CA
Kapelke, Robert J. ... Denver, CO
Kapell, Bernard L. ... Wayne, NJ
Kapell, Jennifer L. ... Newark, NJ
Kapell, William A. ... New York, NY
Kapella, Arthur J. ... Danville, IL
Kapelman, David A. ... New York, NY
Kapelman, David A., P.C. ... New York, NY
Kapelman, Gilbert M. ... Lincoln, RI
Kapelner, David I. ... Northborough, MA
Kapelsohn, Emanuel ... Allentown, PA
Kapen, Alon Y. ... New York, NY
Kapenstein, James M. ... Burbank, CA
Kaper, Michael J. ... New York, NY
Kaper, Terry J. ... Delta, OH
Kapetan, Alex N. ... Pittsburgh, PA
Kapetan, Alex N., Jr. ... Miami, FL
Kapetan, Eugene V. ... Los Angeles, CA
Kapetan, Jon Nick ... Fresno, CA
Kapetan, Kristi R. Culver ... Fresno, CA
Kapetan Meyers Rosen & Louik, P.C.
Greensburg, PA
Hollidaysburg, PA
Johnstown, PA
Pittsburgh, PA
Kapetan, Peter N. ... Fresno, CA
Kapetanakos, Anna ... San Francisco, CA
Kapetanovic, Vera Kaye ... Chicago, IL
Kapfer, Sergio ... Department of Education, Office of the General Counsel, GV
Kapikian, Garo G. ... Yorktown Heights, NY
Kapilian, Scott H. ... Boston, MA
Kapiloff, Arnold Y. ... Stamford, CT
Boca Raton, FL
New York, NY
Kapiloff, Lawrence ... San Diego, CA
Kapiloff, Paula E. ... Macon, GA
Kapiloff, Steven ... Hartford, CT
Kapin, Laureen ... Department of Justice, Civil Division, GV
Kapinos, Ellen Joy ... Cambridge, MA
Kapitz, Paul A. ... Reno, NV
Kapke, George A. ... Milwaukee, WI
Kapke, George E. ... Independence, MO
Kapke & Kapke ... Milwaukee, WI
Kapke, Thomas O. ... Milwaukee, WI
Kapke, Willerth & Wood, LLC
Independence, MO
Kaplain, Leonard R. ... Forest Hills, NY
Kaplan, Abbey L. ... Miami, FL
Kaplan, Abraham ... Santa Rosa, CA
Kaplan, Adam Devlin ... Aventura, FL
Kaplan, Adam M. ... West Orange, NJ
Kaplan, Adria G. ... New York, NY
Kaplan, Alan B. ... New York, NY
Kaplan, Alan D. ... Garden City, NY
Kaplan, Alan H. ... Washington, DC
Kaplan, Alan I. ... Boston, MA
Kaplan, Alan J.
Federal Deposit Insurance Corporation, Regulation and Legislation Section, GV
Kaplan, Alan M. ... Chicago, IL
Cincinnati, OH

Kaplan, Alan M. ....Matthews, NC
Kaplan, Alan M. ....Philadelphia, PA
Kaplan, Alan N. ....Chicago, IL
Kaplan, Alan R. ....Englewood, NJ
Kaplan, Alan S. ....Brockton, MA
Kaplan, Alexander M. ....Garden City, NY
Kaplan, Alisa Alpert ....Scarsdale, NY
Kaplan, Allan ....San Francisco, CA
Kaplan, Allen C. ....Monterey, CA
Kaplan, Allen L. ....Chicago, IL
Kaplan, Allen S. ....Howell, NJ
Kaplan, Alvin ....New City, NY
Kaplan, Alvin ....New York, NY
Kaplan, Alvin I. ....San Francisco, CA
Kaplan, Alvin L. ....Chicago, IL
Kaplan, Alvin, P.C. ....New York, NY
Kaplan, Alyne Wrubel
North Miami Beach, FL
Kaplan, Amy R. ....Chicago, IL
Kaplan, Andrew D. ....Miami, FL
Kaplan, Andrew F. ....Salem, VA
Kaplan, Andrew I. ....New York, NY
Kaplan, Andrew M. ....San Diego, CA
Kaplan, Andrew M. ....Cincinnati, OH
Kaplan, Ann Leopold ....Washington, DC
Kaplan, Ann S. ....Berkeley, CA
Kaplan, Annie Pennock ....Pittsburgh, PA
Kaplan, Anthony E. ....New Haven, CT
Kaplan, Ari L. ....New York, NY
Kaplan, Arnold J. ....New York, NY
Kaplan, Arnold R. ....Denver, CO
Kaplan, Arthur ....New York, NY
Kaplan, Arthur G. ....Baltimore, MD
Kaplan, Arthur H. ....Bala Cynwyd, PA
Philadelphia, PA
Kaplan, Arthur M. ....Atlanta, GA
Kaplan, Arthur M. ....Philadelphia, PA
Kaplan, Ashley Howell
Fort Lauderdale, FL
Kaplan, Aubrey F. ....Chicago, IL
Kaplan, B. Allan ....Santa Barbara, CA
Kaplan, B. Paul ....Plainfield, CT
Kaplan, Barbara J. ....Greensboro, NC
Kaplan, Barbara T. ....New York, NY
Kaplan, Barry M. ....New York, NY
Kaplan, Barry M. ....Seattle, WA
Kaplan, Barry S. ....Marshalltown, IA
Kaplan, Begy & von Ohlen ....Chicago, IL
Kaplan, Benj. ....Boston, MA
Kaplan, Benj. R. ....New York, NY
Kaplan, Benjamin A. ....Boston, MA
Kaplan, Benjamin E. ....San Francisco, CA
Kaplan, Benjamin L. ....Los Angeles, CA
Kaplan, Bernard E. ....Newton, MA
Kaplan, Bernard F. ....Wayne, NJ
Kaplan, Bernard M. ....Skokie, IL
Kaplan, Bernard S. ....Chicago, IL
Kaplan, Bernard S. ....Boston, MA
Kaplan & Bookbinder ....Howell, NJ
Kaplan, Brad M. ....Florham Park, NJ
Kaplan, Bradley D. ....Chicago, IL
Cincinnati, OH
Kaplan, Bradley P. ....San Francisco, CA
Kaplan and Brennan ....Plainfield, CT
Kaplan, Brent J. ....Atlanta, GA
Kaplan, Brewer & Maxey, P.A.
Little Rock, AR
Kaplan, Brian ....Taos, NM
Kaplan, Brian ....Bronx, NY
Kaplan, Brian J. ....Chicago, IL
Waukegan, IL
Kaplan, Brian S. ....Boston, MA
Kaplan, Brian S. ....New York, NY
Kaplan, Bruce H. ....Melville, NY
Kaplan, Bruce J. ....New Brunswick, NJ
Kaplan, Bruce M. ....New York, NY
Kaplan, Bruce S. ....New York, NY
Kaplan, Bruce S., (P.A.)
St. Petersburg, FL
Kaplan, Bryan R. ....New York, NY
Kaplan, Burton A. ....New Haven, CT
Kaplan, Carl E. ....New York, NY
Kaplan, Carol G. ....Department of Justice, Office of Justice Programs, GV
Kaplan, Caroline C. ....Mamaroneck, NY
Kaplan, Carolyn S. ....Boston, MA
Kaplan, Cathy M. ....New York, NY
Kaplan, Charles D. ....Louisville, KY
Kaplan, Charles H. ....New York, NY
Kaplan, Charles I. ....Fort Lauderdale, FL
Kaplan, Charles I. ....Dallas, TX
Kaplan, Cheryl A. ....Miami, FL
Kaplan, Chester B. ....Kansas City, MO
Kaplan, Constance J. ....Fort Lauderdale, FL
Kaplan, D. Kenneth ....Westlake Village, CA
Kaplan, Dana Renee ....New York, NY
Kaplan, Daniel ....Miami, FL
Kaplan, Daniel A. ....San Diego, CA
Kaplan, Daniel A. ....Minneapolis, MN
Kaplan, Daniel A. ....Madison, WI
Kaplan, Daniel D. ....Germantown, MD
Kaplan, Daniel F. ....Sioux City, IA
Kaplan, Daniel F. ....Lincoln, NE
Kaplan, Daniel G. ....Bethesda, MD
Kaplan, Daniel Lee ....Department of Justice, Civil Division, GV
Kaplan, Daniel, P.A. ....Miami, FL
Kaplan, Daniel R. ....New York, NY
Kaplan, Daniel S. ....Chicago, IL
Kaplan, Daniel S. ....Providence, RI
Kaplan, Darren T. ....New York, NY
Kaplan, David ....Los Angeles, CA
Kaplan, David ....Louisville, KY
Kaplan, David ....Louisville, KY
Kaplan, David A. ....New York, NY
Kaplan, David Allan, (P.C.)
Farmington Hills, MI
Kaplan, David B. ....Boston, MA
Kaplan, David E. ....Washington, DC
Kaplan, David G. ....Calabasas, CA
Kaplan, David H. ....Rahway, NJ
Kaplan, David H. ....Garden City, NY
Kaplan, David J. ....Santa Clara, CA
Kaplan, David J. ....Department of Justice, Environment and Natural Resources Division, GV
Kaplan, David J. ....New York, NY
Kaplan, David J. ....New York, NY
Kaplan, David J. ....Syosset, NY
Kaplan, David J. ....Dallas, TX
Kaplan, David L. ....Santa Monica, CA
Kaplan, David M. ....Lexington, KY
Kaplan, David M. ....Philadelphia, PA
Kaplan, David N. ....Pittsburgh, PA
Kaplan, David P. ....Burbank, CA
Kaplan, David R. ....Amherst, MA
Kaplan, David S. ....Sacramento, CA
Kaplan, David S. ....Denver, CO
Kaplan, David S. ....Manalapan, NJ
Kaplan, David S. ....Pottstown, PA
Kaplan, Deborah A. ....New York, NY
Kaplan, Deen ....Washington, DC
Kaplan, Diane S. ....Chicago, IL
Kaplan, Dina S. ....Peekskill, NY
Kaplan, Dona Lineberry ....Raleigh, NC
Kaplan, Donald A. ....Washington, DC
Kaplan, Donald L. ....New York, NY
Kaplan, Donald R. ....New York, NY
Kaplan, Douglas ....Merrick, NY
Kaplan, Douglas A. ....New York, NY
Kaplan, Douglas C. ....Hollywood, FL
Kaplan, Douglas S. ....Portland, ME
Kaplan, Drew P. ....Providence, RI
Kaplan, Edward A. ....Alexandria, LA
Kaplan, Edward D., (P.C.) ....Newburgh, NY
Kaplan, Edward I. ....San Francisco, CA
Kaplan, Edward M. ....Concord, NH
Kaplan, Edward M. ....Memphis, TN
Kaplan, Edward S. ....Hialeah, FL
Kaplan, Edwin ....Brooklyn, NY
Kaplan, Elaine D.
Office Of Special Counsel, GV
Kaplan, Elena ....Atlanta, GA
Kaplan, Eli ....Miami, FL
Kaplan, Eliezer C. ....Southfield, MI
Kaplan, Eliot L. ....Kansas City, MO
Kaplan, Eliot L. ....White Plains, NY
Kaplan, Elizabeth ....Louisville, KY
Kaplan, Elizabeth A. ....West Des Moines, IA
Kaplan, Elizabeth N. ....Washington, DC
Kaplan, Ellen B. ....Edgartown, MA
Kaplan, Ellen W. ....New York, NY
Kaplan, Elliot M. ....Kansas City, MO
Kaplan, Elliot S. ....Minneapolis, MN
Kaplan, Ellyn B. ....New York, NY
Kaplan, Emily ....Santa Cruz, CA
Kaplan, Eric D. ....Chicago, IL
Kaplan, Eric F. ....Columbia Falls, MT
Kaplan, Eric J. ....Miami, FL
Kaplan, Eric T. ....Greenwich, CT
Kaplan, Erica Minkoff ....Phoenix, AZ
Kaplan, Eugene Neal ....New York, NY
Kaplan, Evan K. ....Chestnut Hill, MA
Kaplan, Feingold & Kaplan ....Carteret, NJ
Kaplan, Fern B. ....San Francisco, CA
Kaplan, Francine W. ....Trenton, NJ
Kaplan, Frank, (P.C.) ....Los Angeles, CA
Kaplan & Franzman, P.C. ....Kingston, NY
Kaplan, Frederick M. ....Chicago, IL
Kaplan, Fredric M. ....Merrick, NY
Kaplan, Fredy Harrison ....New York, NY
Kaplan and Freedman, P.A. ....Miami, FL
Kaplan, Gail C. ....Santa Monica, CA
Kaplan, Garry R. ....Lexington, KY
Kaplan, Gary ....Dover, NJ
New York, NY
Kaplan, Gary H. ....Wilmington, DE
Kaplan, Gary L. ....Los Angeles, CA
Kaplan, Gary L. ....San Anselmo, CA
Kaplan, Gary L. ....New York, NY
Kaplan, Gary L. ....Pittsburgh, PA
Kaplan, Gary M. ....San Francisco, CA
Kaplan, Gary P. ....San Francisco, CA
Kaplan, Gary R. ....Los Angeles, CA
Kaplan, Gary S. ....Chicago, IL
Kaplan, Geo. J. ....North Bergen, NJ
Kaplan, George I. ....Cranbury, NJ
Kaplan, George M. ....Fort Lauderdale, FL
Kaplan, George M. ....Uniondale, NY
Kaplan, Gerald ....Morristown, NJ
Neptune, NJ
Kaplan, Gerald W. ....Mineola, NY
Kaplan, Gilbert B. ....Washington, DC
Kaplan & Gilman, L.L.P.
Woodbridge, NJ
Ossining, NY
Kaplan, Glenn ....Livingston, NJ
Kaplan, Glenn S.
Department of Justice, GV
Kaplan, Gordon G. ....La Jolla, CA
Kaplan Gottbetter & Levenson, LLP
New York, NY
Kaplan & Grant ....Portland, ME
Kaplan, Greta L. ....Oakland, CA
Kaplan, Harold E. ....Coral Springs, FL
Kaplan, Harold I. ....New York, NY
Kaplan, Harold L. ....Chicago, IL
Kaplan, Harold L. ....Bloomfield, NJ
Kaplan, Harold N. ....Westmont, NJ
Kaplan, Harold Z. ....Chicago, IL
Kaplan, Harrison J. ....Raleigh, NC
Kaplan, Harry ....Highland Park, IL
Kaplan, Harry Irvin ....Baltimore, MD
Kaplan, Harry J. ....San Jose, CA
Kaplan, Harry J., (A Professional Corporation)
San Jose, CA
Kaplan, Harvey ....Boston, MA
Kaplan, Harvey F. ....Minneapolis, MN
Kaplan, Harvey L. ....Kansas City, MO
Kaplan, Helene L. ....New York, NY
Kaplan, Henry A. ....Asbury Park, NJ
Kaplan, Henry J. ....Portland, OR
Kaplan, Henry P. ....Saratoga, CA
Kaplan, Herbert C. ....Sayreville, NJ
Kaplan, Hermia T. ....Santa Cruz, CA
Kaplan, Heyman, Greenberg, Engelman & Belgrad, P.A. ....Baltimore, MD
Kaplan, Hillary G. ....Bellevue, WA
Kaplan, Honora A. ....Boston, MA
Kaplan, Howard A. ....Beverly Hills, CA
Kaplan, Howard B. ....El Cajon, CA
Kaplan, Howard B. ....Metairie, LA
Kaplan, Howard C. ....Stamford, CT
Kaplan, Howard Gordon ....Chicago, IL
Kaplan, Howard Gordon, Ltd.
Chicago, IL
Kaplan, Howard H. ....St. Louis, MO
Kaplan, Howard J. ....New York, NY
Kaplan, Howard J. ....White Plains, NY
Kaplan, Howard L. ....St. Louis Park, MN
Kaplan, Howard M. ....Teaneck, NJ
Kaplan, Howard N. ....Omaha, NE
Kaplan, Howard S. ....Philadelphia, PA
Kaplan, Hugh B. ....Washington, DC
Kaplan, Hymen R. ....Bethesda, MD
Kaplan, Ira C. ....Hackensack, NJ
Kaplan, Ira C. ....Cleveland, OH
Kaplan, Irwin R. ....Brooklyn, NY
Kaplan, Ivan J. ....Newark, NJ
Kaplan, J. Jason ....San Diego, CA
Kaplan, J. Jason, A Professional Corporation
San Diego, CA
Kaplan, J. Michael ....Columbus, GA
Kaplan, Jack ....New York, NY
Kaplan, Jack H. ....Shreveport, LA
Kaplan & Jacobson Inc. ....Providence, RI
Kaplan, Jaffe and Gates, P.A.
Hollywood, FL
Kaplan, James A. ....Denver, CO
Kaplan, James A. ....Chicago, IL
Kaplan, James E. ....Portland, ME
Kaplan, James I. ....Chicago, IL
Kaplan, James M. ....Miami, FL
Kaplan, James Martin ....New York, NY
Kaplan, James S. ....New York, NY
Kaplan, Jamey Sutton ....Memphis, TN
Kaplan, Jane D. ....Edgartown, MA
Kaplan, Jane Gruber ....New York, NY
Kaplan, Jane R. ....Berkeley, CA
Kaplan, Janet ....Los Angeles, CA
Kaplan, Janet S. ....Albany, NY
Kaplan, Jared ....Chicago, IL
Kaplan, Jason N. ....Chicago, IL
Kaplan, Jason W. ....New York, NY
Kaplan, Jay A. ....Los Angeles, CA
Kaplan, Jay A. ....Kingston, NY
Kaplan, Jeff ....Dallas, TX
Kaplan, Jeffrey ....Federal Trade Commission, Bureau of Competition, GV
Kaplan, Jeffrey ....Woodbourne, NY
Kaplan, Jeffrey A. ....Los Angeles, CA
Kaplan, Jeffrey A. ....Wappingers Falls, NY
Kaplan, Jeffrey A. ....Houston, TX
Kaplan, Jeffrey B. ....Miami, FL
Kaplan, Jeffrey H. ....Washington, DC
Kaplan, Jeffrey H. ....New York, NY
Kaplan, Jeffrey H. ....Houston, TX
Kaplan, Jeffrey I. ....Woodbridge, NJ
Kaplan, Jeffrey L. ....Winter Park, FL
Kaplan, Jeffrey M. ....New York, NY
Kaplan, Jeffrey S. ....Los Angeles, CA
Kaplan, Jeremiah J. ....Plymouth Meeting, PA
Kaplan, Jerold, Law Office, P.C.
Phoenix, AZ
Kaplan, Jerome ....Philadelphia, PA
Kaplan, Jerome L., (P.C.) ....Atlanta, GA
Macon, GA
Kaplan, Jerome Michael ....Lenexa, KS
Kaplan, Jerrold L. ....Santa Fe Springs, CA
Kaplan, Jesse S. ....Sacramento, CA
Kaplan, Jessica S. ....Portland, ME
Kaplan, Jill Hyman ....Bala Cynwyd, PA
Kaplan, Jill T. ....Vienna, VA
Kaplan, Jo Frances ....Boston, MA
Kaplan, Joel ....Brooklyn, NY
Kaplan, Joel Alan ....Miami, FL
Kaplan, Joel H. ....Chicago, IL
Kaplan, Joel M. ....Chicago, IL
Kaplan, Joel S. ....Garden City, NY
Kaplan, Joel S. ....Portland, OR
Kaplan, John Stuart ....Seattle, WA
Kaplan, Jolie Kahn ....Buffalo Grove, IL
Kaplan, Jonathan ....Philadelphia, PA
Kaplan, Jonathan A.
Executive Office Of The President, GV
Kaplan, Jonathan D. ....Tampa, FL
Kaplan, Jonathan E. ....Memphis, TN
Kaplan, Jonathan J. ....Rockville, CT
Kaplan, Jonathan L.
Department of Transportation, Federal Railroad Administration, GV
Kaplan, Jonathan M. ....New York, NY
Kaplan, Jonathan T. ....New York, NY
Kaplan, Jonathon ....Los Angeles, CA
Kaplan, Joseph C. ....New York, NY
Kaplan, Joseph D., & Son, A Professional Corporation ....Trenton, NJ
Kaplan, Joseph H. ....Coral Gables, FL
Kaplan, Joseph H. H. ....Baltimore, MD
Kaplan, Joseph P. ....Braintree, MA
Kaplan, Joseph S. ....New York, NY
Kaplan, Joseph V. ....Washington, DC
Kaplan, Joshua ....Beverly Hills, CA
Kaplan, Julian ....Mineola, NY
Kaplan, Julie B. ....Department of Justice, Environment and Natural Resources Division, GV
Kaplan, Julie L. ....Washington, DC
Kaplan, Julie L. ....Cleveland, OH
Kaplan, Julius ....Washington, DC
Kaplan and Kaplan ....Saratoga, CA
Kaplan & Kaplan ....Vienna, VA
Kaplan & Kaplan, P.A. ....Baltimore, MD
Kaplan, Karen Stone ....Lake Forest, IL
Kaplan & Katzberg ....New York, NY
Kaplan, Keith E. ....New York, NY
Kaplan, Keith L. ....New York, NY
Kaplan, Keith W. ....Philadelphia, PA
Kaplan, Kenneth B. ....Seattle, WA
Kaplan, Kenneth J. ....New York, NY
Kaplan, Kenneth Joseph ....Glendale, CA
Kaplan, Kenneth M. ....Irvine, CA
Kaplan, Kenneth Marc ....Somerville, NJ
Kaplan, Kenneth Mitchell ....Miami, FL
Kaplan, Kenneth P. ....Washington, DC
Kaplan, Kenneth S. ....Atlanta, GA
Kaplan, Kevin C. ....Miami, FL
Kaplan, Kilsheimer & Fox, LLP
New York, NY
Kaplan, Kimberly M. ....Philadelphia, PA
Kaplan & Kingsley ....St. Louis Park, MN
Kaplan, Kirk David ....Las Vegas, NV
Kaplan, Klein & Rogen ....Los Angeles, CA
Kaplan, Krista Schoenheider ....Oak Park, IL
Kaplan, Lance ....Newport Beach, CA
Kaplan, Lane A. ....Chicago, IL
Kaplan, Larry S. ....Tustin, CA
Kaplan, Larry S. ....Chicago, IL
Kaplan, Laura J. ....Newark, NJ
Kaplan Law Corporation ....Los Angeles, CA
Kaplan Law Offices ....Columbia Falls, MT
Kaplan, Lawrence ....New York, NY
Kaplan, Lawrence D. ....Washington, DC
Kaplan, Lawrence E., (P.C.) ....Boston, MA
Kaplan, Lawrence I. ....Great Neck, NY
Kaplan, Lawrence J. ....Burbank, CA
Kaplan, Lawrence J., (P.C.)
San Diego, CA
Kaplan, Lawrence M. ....Rosemont, IL
Kaplan, Lawrence P. ....St. Louis, MO
Kaplan, Lawrence W. ....Pittsburgh, PA
Kaplan, Lee Landa ....Houston, TX
Kaplan, Lee M. ....Philadelphia, PA
Kaplan, Lee Samuel ....Boston, MA
Kaplan, Leith W. ....Pennsauken, NJ
Kaplan, Lenore Mintz ....Chicago, IL
Kaplan, Leon, (A Professional Corporation)
Los Angeles, CA
Kaplan, Leonard ....Boston, MA
Kaplan, Leonard S. ....Toledo, OH
Kaplan, Leonard V. ....Madison, WI
Kaplan, Leopold ....New York, NY
Kaplan, Leslie A. ....Washington, DC
Kaplan, Lewis A. ....New York, NY
Kaplan, Lewis B. ....Rockford, IL
Kaplan & Lieblich ....Brooklyn, NY
Kaplan, Linda M. ....Miami, FL
Kaplan, Lionel A. ....Trenton, NJ
Kaplan, Lisa ....Livingston, NJ
Kaplan, Lisa A. ....Philadelphia, PA
Kaplan, Lisa Moloff ....Phoenix, AZ
Kaplan, Lise S. ....Macon, GA
Kaplan, Lori B. ....Cos Cob, CT
Kaplan, Lori F. ....Indianapolis, IN
Kaplan, Louis I. ....Baltimore, MD
Bethesda, MD
Kaplan, Louis I. ....New York, NY
Kaplan, Louis M. ....Los Angeles, CA
Kaplan, Louis M. ....Alexandria, VA
Kaplan, Lucille R. ....Rockville, MD
Kaplan, Lynn Stofan ....New York, NY
Kaplan, Madeleine L. W. ....San Jose, CA
Kaplan, Marc Howard
Branchburg Township, NJ
Kaplan, Marc J. ....Lone Tree, CO
Kaplan, Marc Peter ....San Diego, CA
Kaplan, Marcia ....Washington, DC
Kaplan, Marcia E. ....New York, NY
Kaplan, Marcia O. ....Saratoga, CA
Kaplan, Marcia Press ....Washington, DC
Kaplan, Marcy ....New York, NY
Kaplan, Marilyn ....Berkeley, CA
Kaplan Marino, Attorneys at Law, A Prof. Corp. ....Beverly Hills, CA
Los Angeles, CA
Kaplan, Marjory A. ....Oakland, CA
Kaplan, Mark A. ....Burlington, VT
Kaplan, Mark D. ....Boston, MA
Kaplan, Mark E. ....Tallahassee, FL
Kaplan, Mark E. ....New York, NY
Kaplan, Mark G. ....Wellesley, MA
Kaplan, Mark L. ....Atlanta, GA
Kaplan, Mark N. ....New York, NY
Kaplan, Mark Vincent ....Los Angeles, CA
Kaplan, Mark Vincent, A P.C., Law Offices of ....Los Angeles, CA
Kaplan, Marla J. ....Northridge, CA
Kaplan, Marlyne (Marzi) ....Hollywood, FL
Kaplan, Marshall ....Chicago, IL
Kaplan, Marshall G. ....Brooklyn, NY
Kaplan, Marshall M.
Department of the Army, U.S. Army Court of Criminal Appeals, GV
Kaplan, Martin ....Brooklyn, NY
Kaplan, Martin D. ....Los Angeles, CA
Kaplan, Martin H. ....New York, NY
Kaplan, Martin J. ....Los Angeles, CA
Kaplan, Martin L. ....Raleigh, NC
Kaplan, Martin S., (P.C.) ....Boston, MA
Kaplan, Matthew ....Libertyville, IL
Kaplan, Matthew A. ....Newark, NJ
Kaplan, Matthew I. ....Los Angeles, CA

Kaplan, Matthew T. ....Englewood, NJ
Kaplan, McMillan & Harris ....Wichita, KS
Kaplan, Melissa D. ....Orlando, FL
Kaplan, Melvin J., & Associates
Chicago, IL
Kaplan, Meredith ....Mercer Island, WA
Kaplan, Michael ....Washington, DC
Kaplan, Michael ....Portland, ME
Kaplan, Michael A. ....San Diego, CA
Kaplan, Michael A. ....St. Louis, MO
Kaplan, Michael Alan ....Atlantic City, NJ
Cherry Hill, NJ
Northfield, NJ
Kaplan, Michael B. ....New York, NY
Kaplan, Michael C. ....Atlanta, GA
Kaplan, Michael D. ....Hollywood, FL
Kaplan, Michael D. ....Memphis, TN
Kaplan, Michael G. ....Fort Lauderdale, FL
Kaplan, Michael J. ....Buffalo, NY
Kaplan, Michael J. ....Akron, OH
Kaplan, Michael L. ....Scottsdale, AZ
Kaplan, Michael L. ....Brooklyn, NY
Kaplan, Michael L. ....Houston, TX
Kaplan, Michael L. B. ....Newark, NJ
Kaplan, Michael M. ....Chicago, IL
Kaplan, Michael M. ....Framingham, MA
Kaplan, Michael P. ....New York, NY
Kaplan, Michel G. ....Nashville, TN
Kaplan, Milton ....Baltimore, MD
Kaplan, Milton ....Buffalo, NY
Kaplan, Mitchell A. ....Chadds Ford, PA
Kaplan, Mitchell D. ....New York, NY
Kaplan, Mitchell H., (P.C.) ....Boston, MA
Kaplan, Mitchell L. ....New York, NY
Kaplan, Mitchell S. ....New York, NY
Kaplan, Mitchell S. ....Philadelphia, PA
Kaplan, Morris A. ....Phoenix, AZ
Kaplan, Morris A. ....Huntington, NY
Kaplan, Morton C. ....Chicago, IL
Kaplan, Morton L. ....Cleveland, OH
Kaplan, Muriel B. ....San Francisco, CA
Kaplan, Myriam Benhamou ....Chicago, IL
Kaplan, Myron ....New York, NY
Kaplan, Myron J. ....Omaha, NE
Kaplan, N. Dennis ....New City, NY
Kaplan, N. Dennis, & Associates, Law Offices of ....New City, NY
Kaplan, Nancy ....Boston, MA
Kaplan, Nancy Federman
West Bloomfield, MI
Kaplan, Nancy G. ....Rolling Meadows, IL
Kaplan, Natalie J. ....New York, NY
Kaplan, Nathan J. ....Longboat Key, FL
Kaplan, Neal H. ....Los Angeles, CA
Kaplan, Neil A. ....Salt Lake City, UT
Kaplan, Neil J. ....New York, NY
Kaplan & Nichols, P.C. ....Edgartown, MA
Kaplan, Niki A. ....New York, NY
Kaplan, Noel H. ....New York, NY
Kaplan, Norman A. ....Great Neck, NY
Kaplan, Norman D. ....Sunrise, FL
Kaplan, Norman J. ....Woodland Hills, CA
Kaplan, Norman J. ....Needham Heights, MA
Kaplan, O'Sullivan & Friedman
Boston, MA
Kaplan, Paige K. ....San Francisco, CA
Kaplan, Pamela D. ....New York, NY
Kaplan, Pamela R. ....Syracuse, NY
Kaplan Papadakis & Gournis, P.C.
Chicago, IL
Kaplan, Patricia Dolins ....Chicago, IL
Kaplan, Paul A. ....Washington, DC
Kaplan, Paul B. ....Miami, FL
Kaplan, Paul H. ....Charlotte, NC
Kaplan, Paul I. ....Baltimore, MD
Kaplan, Paul J. ....Atlanta, GA
Kaplan, Paul M. ....New Haven, CT
Orange, CT
Kaplan, Paul M. ....New York, NY
Kaplan, Paula G. ....Springfield, NJ
Kaplan, Peggy Crespi ....Gaithersburg, MD
Kaplan, Peter
Department of Housing and Urban Development, GV
Kaplan, Peter J. ....New York, NY
Kaplan, Peter M. ....Rochester, NY
Kaplan, Peter R. ....Los Angeles, CA
Kaplan, Peter R. ....Salem, MA
Kaplan, Peter R., P.C., Law Office of
Salem, MA
Kaplan, Philip ....New York, NY
Kaplan, Philip C. ....Boston, MA
Kaplan, Philip E. ....Little Rock, AR
Kaplan, Philip G. ....St. Louis, MO
Kaplan, Philip J. ....Los Angeles, CA
Kaplan, Philip J. ....Staten Island, NY
Kaplan, Philip S. ....Washington, DC
Kaplan, Philip T. ....New York, NY
Kaplan, Phillip R. ....Newport Beach, CA
Kaplan, Rachel D. ....Teaneck, NJ
Kaplan, Radol, Shapiro & Kaplan, L.L.P.
Hackensack, NJ
Teaneck, NJ
Kaplan, Randall ....Los Angeles, CA
Kaplan, Randall J. ....House of Representatives, Committee Legal Personnel, GV
Kaplan, Randy H. ....Jenkintown, PA
Kaplan, Randy J. ....Boston, MA
Kaplan, Raymond S. ....Los Angeles, CA
Kaplan, Regina S. ....Baldwin, NY
Kaplan, Richard A. ....Chicago, IL
Kaplan, Richard A. ....Minneapolis, MN
Kaplan, Richard D. ....Beverly Hills, CA
Kaplan, Richard E. ....Boston, MA
Kaplan, Richard E. ....Utica, NY
Kaplan, Richard H. ....Piscataway, NJ
Kaplan, Richard J. ....Los Angeles, CA

Kaplan, Richard J. ....Coral Springs, FL
Delray Beach, FL
Hollywood, FL
Kaplan, Richard J. ....New York, NY
Kaplan, Richard J. ....White Plains, NY
Kaplan, Richard J., P.A., Law Offices of
Coral Springs, FL
Delray Beach, FL
Hollywood, FL
Kaplan, Richard L. ....Champaign, IL
Kaplan, Richard L. ....Great Neck, NY
Kaplan, Richard M. ....San Francisco, CA
Kaplan, Richard M. ....Hartford, CT
Kaplan, Richard M. ....Chicago, IL
Kaplan, Richard M. ....Houston, TX
Kaplan, Richard M., Professional Corporation ....San Francisco, CA
Kaplan, Richard Michael ....Houston, TX
Kaplan, Richard N. ....Chicago, IL
Kaplan, Richard S. ....Miami Beach, FL
Kaplan, Richard S. ....New York, NY
Kaplan, Rina Francis ....Fort Lauderdale, FL
Kaplan, Risa ....New York, NY
Kaplan, Robert A. ....Washington, DC
Kaplan, Robert A. ....Department of Justice, Environment and Natural Resources Division, GV
Kaplan, Robert A. ....Miami, FL
Kaplan, Robert A. ....Forest Hills, NY
Kaplan, Robert B. ....San Francisco, CA
Kaplan, Robert B.
Securities and Exchange Commission, Division of Enforcement, GV
Kaplan, Robert B. ....Philadelphia, PA
Kaplan, Robert D. ....Boston, MA
Kaplan, Robert D. ....New York, NY
Kaplan, Robert D. ....Seattle, WA
Kaplan, Robert D. ....Seattle, WA
Kaplan, Robert E. ....Williamsburg, VA
Kaplan, Robert J. ....New York, NY
Kaplan, Robert Jacob ....Vienna, VA
Kaplan, Robert L. ....Milwaukee, WI
Kaplan, Robert M. ....Palatine, IL
Kaplan, Robert M. ....Westmont, NJ
Kaplan, Robert M. ....New York, NY
Kaplan, Robert N. ....New York, NY
Kaplan, Robert O. ....Los Angeles, CA
Kaplan, Robert Richard, Jr.
Washington, DC
Kaplan, Robert W. ....Wichita, KS
Kaplan, Roberta A. ....New York, NY
Kaplan, Robin L. ....New York, NY
Kaplan, Robt. ....Pompano Beach, FL
Kaplan, Robt. Z. ....Toledo, OH
Kaplan, Rochelle ....Southfield, MI
Kaplan, Rochelle K. ....Bethlehem, PA
Kaplan, Roger B. ....Woodbridge, NJ
Kaplan, Roger J. ....Santa Monica, CA
Kaplan, Roger S. ....Woodbury, NY
Kaplan, Rona L. ....Oceanside, NY
Kaplan, Rona Zucker ....Atlantic City, NJ
Kaplan, Ronald ....Chicago, IL
Kaplan, Ronald B., Ltd. ....Chicago, IL
Kaplan, Ronald I. ....Philadelphia, PA
Kaplan, Ronald M. ....Pompano Beach, FL
Kaplan, Ronald M. ....McMinnville, OR
Kaplan, Ronald P. ....Los Angeles, CA
Kaplan, Ronald S. ....West Orange, NJ
Kaplan, Rosalind T. ....Philadelphia, PA
Kaplan, Rosalyn B. ....Chicago, IL
Kaplan, Ross A. ....New York, NY
Kaplan, Russell D. ....Fort Lauderdale, FL
Kaplan, Russell D., P.A.
Fort Lauderdale, FL
Kaplan, S. Richard ....Hallandale Beach, FL
Kaplan, Samuel ....Carteret, NJ
Kaplan, Samuel C. ....Washington, DC
Kaplan, Samuel L. ....Minneapolis, MN
Kaplan, Sandy Mitchell
San Francisco, CA
Kaplan, Sanford David ....Fort Lee, NJ
Kaplan, Scott H. ....Atlanta, GA
Kaplan, Scott J. ....Portland, OR
Kaplan, Seth A. ....New York, NY
Kaplan, Seth L. ....Stamford, CT
Kaplan, Seth M. ....Roseland, NJ
New York, NY
Kaplan, Seth R. ....Miami, FL
Kaplan, Seymour ....Miami, FL
Kaplan, Seymour D. ....Trenton, NJ
Kaplan & Shanberg ....Kansas City, MO
Kaplan, Sheldon ....Minneapolis, MN
Kaplan, Sheldon Z. ....Bethesda, MD
Kaplan, Sherman Ian ....Los Angeles, CA
Kaplan, Sherman M. ....Dallas, TX
Kaplan, Sherwin S. ....Department of Labor, Office of the Solicitor, GV
Kaplan, Shimon ....Beaumont, TX
Kaplan, Shira B. ....New York, NY
Kaplan, Shirley ....New York, NY
Kaplan, Sidney ....Minneapolis, MN
Kaplan, Sidney M. ....Chicago, IL
Kaplan, Simon S. ....Farmington, MI
Kaplan & Singhal, P.A.
Fort Lauderdale, FL
Miami, FL
Palm Beach, FL
Kaplan, Solomon ....Bronx, NY
Kaplan, Stanley F. ....Chicago, IL
Kaplan, Stanley F., P.C. ....Chicago, IL
Kaplan, Stanley P. ....Miami, FL
Kaplan, Stanley R. ....New York, NY
Kaplan, Stanton S. ....Fort Lauderdale, FL
Kaplan & Steinberg ....Asbury Park, NJ
Kaplan, Stephanie J. ....Plainfield, VT
Kaplan, Stephanie Kalfon ....Cincinnati, OH
Kaplan, Stephen E. ....Dallas, TX

Kaplan, Stephen H. ....Denver, CO
Washington, DC
Kaplan, Stephen J. ....Albany, GA
Kaplan, Stephen L. ....Los Angeles, CA
Kaplan, Stephen M. ....Needham, MA
Kaplan, Stephen, P.C. ....Burleson, TX
Dallas, TX
Kaufman, TX
Plano, TX
Waxahachie, TX
Kaplan, Stephen R. ....Northampton, MA
Kaplan, Steve I. ....Encino, CA
Kaplan, Steven ....Washington, DC
Kaplan, Steven ....New York, NY
Kaplan, Steven ....Philadelphia, PA
Kaplan, Steven A. ....Paterson, NJ
Kaplan, Steven B. ....San Bruno, CA
Kaplan, Steven B. ....Hartford, CT
Kaplan, Steven F. ....Millburn, NJ
Kaplan, Steven G. ....Encino, CA
Kaplan, Steven H. ....Newark, NJ
New York, NY
Kaplan, Steven J. ....Los Angeles, CA
Kaplan, Steven J. ....Freehold, NJ
Kaplan, Steven J. ....Shrewsbury, NJ
Kaplan, Steven L. ....Hicksville, NY
Kaplan, Steven M. ....Washington, DC
Kaplan, Steven M. ....New York, NY
Kaplan, Steven M. ....New York, NY
Kaplan, Steven Marc ....Mount Clemens, MI
Kaplan, Steven S. ....Wayne, NJ
Kaplan, Steven S. ....Philadelphia, PA
Kaplan, Steven Z. ....Minneapolis, MN
Kaplan, Strangis and Kaplan, P.A.
Minneapolis, MN
Kaplan, Stuart D. ....New York, NY
Kaplan, Stuart M. ....San Francisco, CA
Kaplan, Stuart R. ....Pittsburgh, PA
Kaplan, Stuart R. ....Richmond, VA
Kaplan, Sue M. ....San Francisco, CA
Kaplan, Sumner Z. ....Boston, MA
Kaplan, Susan ....New York, NY
Kaplan, Susan B. ....Washington, DC
Kaplan, Susan B. ....Department of Labor, Office of the Solicitor, GV
Kaplan, Susan R. ....Charlestown, MA
Kaplan, Susan R. ....Woodbridge, NJ
Kaplan, Susan R. ....New York, NY
Kaplan, Sylvia ....Brooklyn, NY
Kaplan, Tami ....Belmont, MA
Kaplan, Tamsin R. ....Belmont, MA
Kaplan, Terry S., (A Professional Corporation) ....Los Angeles, CA
Kaplan, Theodore ....West Hempstead, NY
Kaplan, Theodore N. ....New York, NY
Kaplan, Thomas R. T. ....Pittsburgh, PA
Kaplan, Thomashower & Landau, LLP
New York, NY
Kaplan, Todd A. ....Memphis, TN
Kaplan, Todd S. ....Cambridge, MA
Kaplan, Tracey N. ....Boston, MA
Kaplan, Victor E. ....Los Angeles, CA
Kaplan, Victoria S. ....Chicago, IL
Kaplan, Warren A. ....Cambridge, MA
Kaplan, Warren K. ....Washington, DC
Kaplan, Wayne ....Boca Raton, FL
Kaplan, Wayne L. ....Dix Hills, NY
Kaplan, Wayne S. ....Chicago, IL
Kaplan, Wendy J. ....Boston, MA
Kaplan, William L. ....Rockville, MD
Kaplan, William L., P.C. ....Rockville, MD
Kaplan, William M. ....New York, NY
Kaplan, William M., (A Professional Corporation) ....Los Angeles, CA
Kaplan, William P.W. ....San Jose, CA
Kaplan, William T. ....Joliet, IL
Kaplan, Wm. ....Los Angeles, CA
Kaplan, Yale J. ....Omaha, NE
Kaplan, Zev E. ....Las Vegas, NV
Kaplan, Zev E., Ltd. ....Las Vegas, NV
Kaplan/Bond Group, The ....Boston, MA
Kaplan-Gross, Kimberley J. ....Boston, MA
Kaplanis, Anthony T. ....Canton, OH
Kaplanis & Grimm ....Los Angeles, CA
Kaplanis, Peter J. ....Los Angeles, CA
Kaplan-Katz, Rhonda D. ....Chicago, IL
Kaplansky, David ....Chicago, IL
Kaplansky, J. Ronald ....Lansing, MI
Kaplansky, John C. ....Bingham Farms, MI
Kaplansky, John C., P.C.
Bingham Farms, MI
Kaple, J. Kurt ....Tampa, FL
Kaplen, Michael V. ....New York, NY
Kaplen, Nancy ....Trenton, NJ
Kapler, Janis ....Boston, MA
Kaplin, Julian M., Jr. ....New York, NY
Kaplin, Marc B. ....Blue Bell, PA
Kaplin, Richard A. ....Brooklyn, NY
Kaplin Stewart Meloff Reiter & Stein, Professional Corporation
Cherry Hill, NJ
Blue Bell, PA
Philadelphia, PA
Kaplin, Thomas L., Jr. ....Columbus, OH
Kaplin, William A. ....Washington, DC
Kaplinsky, Alan S. ....Philadelphia, PA
Kaplinsky, Daniel ....Whitehouse, NJ
Kaplinsky, Mark H. ....New Orleans, LA
Kaplit, Michael ....Wilmington, DE
Kaplitt, Stephen B. ....New York, NY
Kaplon, Jon D. ....New York, NY
Kaplon, Joseph J. ....Encino, CA
Kaplove, Jay L. ....Tenafly, NJ
Kaplovitz and Associates, P.C.
Pontiac, MI
Kaplovitz, Ronald E. ....Pontiac, MI
Kaplow, Ann E. ....Rochester, NY

Kaplow, Charlotte M.
Federal Deposit Insurance Corporation, Liquidation Branch, GV
Kaplow, Herbert J. ....St. James, NY
Kaplow, Louis ....Cambridge, MA
Kaplow, Mark D. ....Stamford, CT
Kaplow, Richard J. ....Cleveland, OH
Kaplow, Robert D. ....Southfield, MI
Kaplowitz, Allan J. ....Hackensack, NJ
Kaplowitz, Bernard ....Delmar, NY
Kaplowitz, Brian M. ....New York, NY
Kaplowitz, Isaac ....Garden City, NY
Kaplowitz, Jack A. ....Hauppauge, NY
Kaplowitz, Jay M. ....New York, NY
Kaplowitz, Michael B. ....Katonah, NY
Kaplowitz, Richard H. ....Stamford, CT
Kaplowitz (P.C.), Karen ....Los Angeles, CA
Princeton, NJ
Kaplun, Oleg F. ....New York, NY
Kaplun, Paul T. ....Washington, DC
Kaplus, Howard L. ....South Orange, NJ
Kaplysh, Theodore P. ....Denver, CO
Kaplysh, Theodore P., (P.C.) ....Denver, CO
Kapner, Erik ....New York, NY
Kapner, Jeffrey H. ....New York, NY
Kapner, Lewis ....Boca Raton, FL
West Palm Beach, FL
Kapner, Lewis, P.A. ....Boca Raton, FL
West Palm Beach, FL
Kapner, Richard J. ....Hackensack, NJ
Kapner, Virginia Kingsley ....Boston, MA
Kapnick, Barbara R. ....New York, NY
Kapnick, Eric S. ....Livingston, NJ
Kapnick, Richard B. ....Chicago, IL
Kapnik, Stephen E. ....Denver, CO
Kapolchok, George M. ....Anchorage, AK
Kapoor, Rahul ....Palo Alto, CA
Kapor, David W. ....Cincinnati, OH
Kapor, Jeffrey H. ....Los Angeles, CA
Kapouytian, Ararat ....San Francisco, CA
Kapp, C. Terrence ....Cleveland, OH
Kapp, David S. ....Islandia, NY
Kapp, Howard A. ....Beverly Hills, CA
Kapp, J. Michael ....East Liverpool, OH
Kapp, James W., III ....Chicago, IL
Kapp, James W., Jr. ....Kansas City, MO
Kapp, Jeffrey L. ....Columbus, OH
Kapp, John P ....Galax, VA
Kapp, Jonathan E. ....Portland, ME
Kapp Law Office ....East Liverpool, OH
Kapp Law Offices ....Cleveland, OH
Kapp, M. Keith ....Raleigh, NC
Kapp, Marshall B. ....Dayton, OH
Kapp, Norman ....New York, NY
Kapp, Paul ....Cheyenne, WY
Kapp, Richard H. ....New York, NY
Kapp, Robert H. ....Washington, DC
Kapp, Sara A. ....Los Angeles, CA
Kapp, Scott H. ....Chicago, IL
Kapp, Stuart T. ....Boca Raton, FL
Kapp, Thomas D. ....Bronx, NY
Kappa, John R. ....Montrose, CO
Kappas, J. Scott ....Covington, KY
Kappel, Brett G. ....Washington, DC
Kappel, Cary S. ....New York, NY
Kappel, David A. ....Ebensburg, PA
Kappel, Henry Wilde ....Norman, OK
Kappel, James L. ....Springfield, IL
Kappel, Karl G. ....Los Angeles, CA
Kappel, Matthew J. ....Greenville, SC
Kappel, Neill & Wolff, L.L.C.
St. Louis, MO
Kappel, Robert ....Milford, CT
Kappel, Stephen B. ....Atlanta, GA
Kappelhoff, Mark J. ....Department of Justice, Civil Rights Division, GV
Kappelman, Lynn A. ....Boston, MA
Kappelman, Ronald R. ....Rapid City, SD
Kappers, Alan M. ....Troy, OH
Kappers, Stephen A. ....Cincinnati, OH
Kappes, Anne W. ....Phoenix, AZ
Kappes, Kelly A. ....Indianapolis, IN
Kappes, Kurt A. ....Sacramento, CA
Kappes, Kyle K. ....Los Gatos, CA
Kappes, Philip S. ....Indianapolis, IN
Kappes, R. Scott ....Wilmington, DE
Kappes, Robert F. ....Hartford, CT
Kappes, Timothy W. ....Bloomington, IN
Kappler, Ann M. ....Washington, DC
Kappler, Charles F.
United States Postal Service, Office of the Deputy General Counsel, GV
Kappler, Douglas D. ....Los Angeles, CA
Kappler, Elsie Bennett ....Boston, MA
Kappler, Richard N. ....Pittsburgh, PA
Kapples, John W. ....Lexington, MA
Kappock, Brian Hannon ....Hoboken, NJ
Kappock, Kevin P. ....Chicago, IL
Kappos, David J. ....San Jose, CA
Kappos, John ....Merrillville, IN
Kappos, John C. ....Irvine, CA
Kappos, John M. ....Stockton, CA
Kappos, Stephen M. ....San Diego, CA
Kappos, Stephen N. ....Mammoth Lakes, CA
Kappstatter, Jeffry A. ....Washington, DC
Kappus, David N. ....Fallston, MD
Kappus, George D. ....Uniondale, NY
Kapral & D'Amico, P.C. ....Westminster, MA
Kapral, John M. ....Boston, MA
Kapral, Stephen M., Jr. ....Boca Raton, FL
Kapralos, James G. ....East Meadow, NY
Kapranos, Richard W. ....Portland, OR
Kaprelian, Mark A. ....Milwaukee, WI
Kaprelian, Michael V. ....New York, NY
Kaprelian, Stephen H. ....White Plains, NY
Yorktown Heights, NY
Kaprielian, James M. ....Reedley, CA
Kaprielian, Lisa V. ....Boston, MA

Kariss, Lori Adamcik ... Camp Hill, PA
Kariss, Richard C. ... Harrisburg, PA
Kariv, Tomer ... Washington, DC
Kariya, Jean M. ... Chicago, IL
Kariya, Robert ... Ogden, UT
Karjala, Dennis S. ... Tempe, AZ
Karjala, John G. ... Federal Deposit Insurance Corporation, GV
Karjala, Les R. ... Bloomington, MN
Karjane, Damian ... Boston, MA
Karjeker, Christy Arden ... Seattle, WA
Karjeker, Shamema B. ... Houston, TX
Karjeker, Shaukat A. ... Phoenix, AZ
Karjola, Leon A. ... Eureka, CA
Karkanen, Alexander Michael ... Los Angeles, CA
Karkanen, Janet L. ... Los Angeles, CA
Karkela, Terry A. ... Perham, MN
Karkoska, Kim M. ... St. Paul, MN
Karkowsky, Jay J. ... Houston, TX
Karkowsky, Nancy Faye ... Silver Spring, MD
Karkula, Elizabeth A. ... Chicago, IL
Karkula, Paul A. ... Chicago, IL
Karkut, James E. ... Salt Lake City, UT
Karl, Carolyn Ann ... Oklahoma City, OK
Karl, Darrel C. ... Washington, DC
Karl, Donald E. ... Santa Monica, CA
Karl, Frank J. ... Pasadena, CA
Karl, Frederick B. ... Tampa, FL
Karl, Frederick B., Jr. ... Alachua, FL
Karl, Gary L. ... Rochester, NY
Karl, James, & Associates ... Marco Island, FL
Dennis Port, MA
Karl, James F. ... Kansas City, MO
Karl, James J. ... Lancaster, PA
Karl, James L., II ... Marco Island, FL
Dennis Port, MA
Karl, Jeffrey S. ... Cherry Hill, NJ
Karl, Jeffrey S., A Professional Corporation ... Cherry Hill, NJ
Karl, John F., Jr. ... Washington, DC
Karl, John F., Jr. ... Covington, KY
Karl, Karen E. ... Tucson, AZ
Karl, Katherine Howk ... Rochester, NY
Karl, Lucy J. ... Concord, NH
Karl, Mark A. ... Moundsville, WV
Karl, Max H. ... Milwaukee, WI
Karl, Nelson G. ... Cleveland, OH
Karl, Robert E. ... Columbus, OH
Karl, Roxanne R. ... Burnsville, MN
Karl, Russell R. ... North Andover, MA
Karl, Steven R. ... St. Louis, MO
Karl, Terry J., (Mr.) ... Hauppauge, NY
Karl, William B. ... Key Largo, FL
Karlak, Laura C. ... Bartlesville, OK
Karlan, Charlotte E. ... Miami, FL
Karlan, Charlotte E., P.A. ... Miami, FL
Karlan, Diane V. ... Bronx, NY
Karlan, Mark S. ... Santa Monica, CA
Karlan, Michael J. ... Treasury Department, Internal Revenue Service, GV
Karlan, Milan D. ... Department of Justice, Tax Division, GV
Karlan, Mitchell A. ... New York, NY
Karlan, Sandy ... Miami, FL
Karlan, Sandy, P.A. ... Miami, FL
Karlberg, Kenneth L. ... Seattle, WA
Karlberg, Richard V., Jr. ... Atlanta, GA
Karle & Green, L.L.C. ... Alabaster, AL
Karle, Gregory A. ... Erie, PA
Karle, Jill T. ... Alabaster, AL
Karle, Patricia A. ... Painesville, OH
Karle, Stuart D. ... New York, NY
Karle, Theresa Walker ... New York, NY
Karle, Thomas J. ... New York, NY
Karlebach, Roger J. ... Morristown, NJ
Karlen, Christopher ... St. Louis, MO
Karlen, Peter H. ... La Jolla, CA
Karlen, Peter H., A Professional Law Corporation ... La Jolla, CA
San Diego, CA
Karlick, Gregory J. ... Johnstown, PA
Karlik, Diane L. ... Palm Beach Gardens, FL
Karlin, Alan J. ... Baltimore, MD
Karlin, Alex S. ... Fairfax, VA
Karlin, Allan N., & Associates ... Morgantown, WV
Karlin, Amy M. ... Los Angeles, CA
Karlin, Andrew T. ... Santa Monica, CA
Karlin, Calvin J. ... Lawrence, KS
Karlin, Charles I. ... Redondo Beach, CA
Karlin, Clarita ... Laguna Hills, CA
Karlin, Dan, Ltd. ... Chicago, IL
Karlin, Daniel ... Chicago, IL
Karlin, David A. ... New York, NY
Karlin, David S. ... Albany, NY
Karlin, Denise J. ... Boston, MA
Karlin, Edward J. ... Chicago, IL
Karlin and Fleisher ... Chicago, IL
Karlin, Harvey ... Portland, OR
Karlin, Janice Miller ... Kansas City, KS
Karlin, Jeffrey H. ... Manchester, NH
Karlin, Jeffrey H., (P.C.) ... Austin, TX
Karlin, Jeremy S. ... Galesburg, IL
Karlin, Karen S. ... Chevy Chase, MD
Karlin, Kristine A. ... Park Ridge, IL
Karlin, L. Scott ... Tustin, CA
Karlin, Laurence M. ... Los Angeles, CA
Karlin, Lawrence M. ... Chicago, IL
Karlin, Leonard ... Forest Park, IL
Karlin, Louis W. ... Los Angeles, CA
Karlin, Marc A. ... Los Angeles, CA
Karlin, Michael J. A. ... Los Angeles, CA
Karlin, Nathan ... Boston, MA
Karlin, Norman ... Los Angeles, CA
Karlin, Peter A. ... Pasadena, CA
Karlin, Rhonda Michelle ... Bloomfield, CT
Karlin, Roy J. ... New York, NY
Karlin, Samuel A. ... Los Angeles, CA
Karlin, Steven D. ... New York, NY
Karliner, Samuel J. ... Brooklyn, NY
Karlins, Sheldon D., (P.A.) ... Minneapolis, MN
Karlinski, James W. ... Brick, NJ
Karlinsky, Cynthia G. ... Newton, MA
Karlinsky, Fred E. ... Fort Lauderdale, FL
Karlinsky, Martin E. ... New York, NY
Karlis, Michael G. ... Warren, NJ
Karlitz, Herbert S. ... New York, NY
Karlock, Kendra ... Dallas, TX
Karlos, Dean P. ... Chicago, IL
Karlov, Jason ... Los Angeles, CA
Karlovec, John D. ... Cleveland, OH
Karlovec, Lucien B., Jr. ... Cleveland, OH
Karlovich, Jay P. ... South St. Paul, MN
Karlovitz, Kathleen ... Syracuse, NY
Karlowicz, Peter M. ... Cassopolis, MI
Karlowitz, Bela A. ... Pittsburgh, PA
Karlowitz & Cromer, P.C. ... Pittsburgh, PA
Karls, Nanette L. ... Madison, WI
Karlsen, M. Alfred ... Encino, CA
Karlsen, Steven R. ... Dover, DE
Karlsgodt, Paul ... Kansas City, MO
Karlson, Cindy L. ... Phoenix, AZ
Karlson, Gaye J. ... Nashville, TN
Karlson, Henry C. ... Indianapolis, IN
Karlson, Karleen I. ... Hannacroix, NY
Karlson & Karlson ... East Hartford, CT
Karlson, Michael J. ... Phoenix, AZ
Karlson, Michael K. ... New York, NY
Karlson, Peter L. ... East Providence, RI
Karlson, Roy V. ... East Hartford, CT
Karlson, Steven M. ... East Hartford, CT
Karlson, Victoria A. ... Woodbridge, NJ
Karlson, Victoria L. ... Berwyn, PA
Karlsons, Justs N. ... San Francisco, CA
Karlsson, Gail V. ... New York, NY
Karlsson, Kent ... New York, NY
Karlsson & Ng, P.C. ... New York, NY
Karlsson, Peter Eric ... Moorhead, MN
Karlsson, Richard R. ... Oakland, CA
Karlstein, Debra A. ... New York, NY
Karlstein, Ira S. ... Matawan, NJ
Karlstrom, Carl G. ... Clarkston, MI
Karlstrom, Paul E. ... Champaign, IL
Karlstrom, S. Olof ... Flint, MI
Karlton, Lawrence K. ... Sacramento, CA
Karlyn, Matthew A. ... Boston, MA
Karlzen, Peter J. ... Encino, CA
Karm, Guy M. ... Arlington Heights, IL
Karm, Howard N. ... Glenview, IL
Karmali, Rashida A. ... New York, NY
Karman, Alexander F. ... Fairfax, VA
Karman, Howard H. ... Casa Grande, AZ
Karman, Kirk von ... Casa Grande, AZ
Karman Law Offices, P.C. ... Casa Grande, AZ
Karman, Mitchell A. ... Boston, MA
Karmarkar, Radhika ... Federal Communications Commission, Common Carrier Bureau, GV
Karmarkar, Radhika V. ... Federal Communications Commission, GV
Karmazin, Michael L. ... New Orleans, LA
Karmeier, Lloyd A. ... Nashville, IL
Karmel & Gilden ... Chicago, IL
Karmel, Ivan M. ... Portland, OR
Karmel, Ivan M., P.C., Law Offices of ... Portland, OR
Karmel, Jonathan Ball ... Schenectady, NY
Karmel, Jonathan D. ... Chicago, IL
Karmel, Joshua N. ... Chicago, IL
Karmel, Marianne M. ... Newton, MA
Karmel, Philip E. ... New York, NY
Karmel, Roberta S. ... New York, NY
Karmelin, Ira D. ... West Palm Beach, FL
Karmen, Robert ... New York, NY
Karmen, Zachary L. ... Syracuse, NY
Karmgard, Robert T. ... Chicago, IL
Karmilovich, Jeffrey M. ... Greenville, SC
Karmin & Adler ... Fort Lauderdale, FL
Karmin, Carl S. ... Fort Lauderdale, FL
Karmin, Elizabeth A. ... Washington, DC
Karmiol, Grace C. ... Equal Employment Opportunity Commission, Office of Legal Counsel, GV
Karmiol, Harold ... Garden City, NY
Karmiol, Ira M. ... Rio Rancho, NM
Karmol, David L. ... Alexandria, VA
Karmol, Erikson C. N. ... Westland, MI
Karmy & Associates ... Anaheim, CA
Karmy, Jamal Peter ... Anaheim, CA
Karn, David B. ... Clanton, AL
Karn, Joann ... Spring, TX
Karn, Leo H. ... West Des Moines, IA
Karn, M. Kathryn ... Erie, PA
Karn, Stephanie P. ... Richmond, VA
Karn, Stewart A. ... Pittsburgh, PA
Karn, William F. ... Richmond, VA
Karn, William S. ... Pittsburgh, PA
Karna, Angie ... New York, NY
Karna, James T. ... Houston, TX
Karnacewicz, Micheleen C. ... New York, NY
Karnakis, Andrew T. ... Bedford, MA
Karnakis, Christina Victoria ... Washington, DC
Karnas, Matthew David ... Tucson, AZ
Karnash, John S. M. ... Morristown, NJ
Karnath, Stephen B. ... Buffalo, NY
Karnatz, William E., Jr. ... Cleveland, OH
Karnatz, William E., Sr. ... Cleveland, OH
Karnavas, Constantine A. ... Philadelphia, PA
Karnavas, Sophia Madaline ... Brooklyn, NY
Karnaze, Terry ... Kansas City, MO
Karnedy, Gary F. ... Montpelier, VT
St. Johnsbury, VT
Karnegis, Theodora P. ... Chicago, IL
Karner, Cheryl S. ... Cleveland, OH
Karner, Jessica M. ... Los Angeles, CA
San Francisco, CA
Karnes, C. Daniel ... Chicago, IL
Karnes, Christina Edmondson ... Waco, TX
Karnes, David A. ... Beverly Hills, CA
Karnes, David K. ... Omaha, NE
Karnes, Elizabeth E. ... Los Angeles, CA
Karnes, Evan B., II ... Chicago, IL
Karnes, John H. ... Fort Worth, TX
Karnes, Joseph M. ... Salinas, CA
Karnes, Lanis Loretha ... Jackson, TN
Virginia Beach, VA
Karnes, Michael D. ... Bronx, NY
Karnes, Penelope S. ... Anna, IL
Karnes, R. Mark ... Dallas, TX
Karnes, Rebecca R. ... Washington, DC
Karnes, Sam B. ... Fort Worth, TX
Karnes, Vadd A. ... Winter Park, FL
Karnes, William M. ... Cleveland, OH
Karnes, William M., Co., L.P.A. ... Cleveland, OH
Karney and Karney ... Charlotte, NC
Karney, Mark A. ... Minneapolis, MN
Karney, Mark H. ... Los Angeles, CA
Karney, Michael E. ... Little Rock, AR
Miami, FL
Karney, Robert A. ... Charlotte, NC
Karney, Shari ... Sherman Oaks, CA
Karney, William M. ... Charlotte, NC
Karnezis, Louis N. ... Waukegan, IL
Karnezis, Themis N. ... Chicago, IL
Karnick, Jerome A. ... Hoffman Estates, IL
Karno, Earle S. ... Oak Lawn, IL
Karno, Jacob L. ... Metairie, LA
Karno, Mark L. ... Chicago, IL
Karno, Michael D. ... Coral Gables, FL
Karno, Norton S., (A Professional Corporation) ... Encino, CA
Karno, Schwartz & Friedman ... Encino, CA
Los Angeles, CA
Karnofsky, Jon D. ... Farmingdale, NY
Karnopp, Dennis C. ... Bend, OR
Karnopp, Martha J. ... Aurora, CO
Karnopp, Petersen, Noteboom, Hansen, Arnett & Sayeg, LLP ... Bend, OR
Karnopp Grimsley, LeAnna L. ... Peoria, IL
Karnow, Curtis E. A. ... San Francisco, CA
Karnowski, Jeanne ... Bloomington, MN
Karnowsky, Daniel ... West Bloomfield, MI
Karns, Barry W. ... Baton Rouge, LA
Karns, Christopher A. ... Washington, DC
Karns, Gregory J. ... Los Angeles, CA
Karns, John ... Los Angeles, CA
Karns, John F. ... Pittsburgh, PA
Karns, John O. ... Allentown, PA
Karns & Karabian ... Los Angeles, CA
Karns, Larry A. ... Plantation, FL
Karns, Larry G. ... Topeka, KS
Karns, Laura C. ... Tuscaloosa, AL
Karns, Mary Ann ... Stillwater, OK
Karns, Paul A. ... Tulsa, OK
Karns, Robert T. ... Middletown, RI
Karns, Robert T., Law Offices ... Middletown, RI
Karns, Ronald C. ... San Jose, CA
Karnstein, Walter W. ... Portland, OR
Karnuth, Michael R. ... Chicago, IL
Karo, Martin H. ... Philadelphia, PA
Karo, Wm. H. ... Miami, FL
Karoblis, Peter P. ... Wausau, WI
Karoblis & Petersen ... Wausau, WI
Karod, Stanley W. ... Camden, ME
Karod, Thomas S. ... Camden, ME
Karofsky, Jill J. ... Madison, WI
Karohl, Kent E. ... Clayton, MO
Karol, Bernard J. ... New York, NY
Karol, Brian Keith ... Chagrin Falls, OH
Karol, Catherine M. ... Detroit, MI
Karol, Dawn I ... Milton, MA
Karol, E. Michael ... New York, NY
Karol Hausman & Sosnik, P.C. ... Clearwater, FL
Fort Lee, NJ
Garden City, NY
New York, NY
Karol, Louis P. ... Garden City, NY
Karol, Marshall A. ... Boston, MA
Karol & Riley, P.A. ... Boston, MA
Karol, Scott J. ... Los Angeles, CA
Karol, Sheon ... Norwalk, CT
Karol, Thomas A. ... Toledo, OH
Karolczyk & Brown, P.L.C. ... Phoenix, AZ
Karolczyk, Mark E. ... Phoenix, AZ
Karolewski, Arnold E. ... Chicago, IL
Karolewski, Edmund T. ... Deerfield, IL
Karoll, Paul, (Prof. Corp.) ... Chicago, IL
Karoly, John P., Jr. ... Allentown, PA
Karoly, Richard Alan ... San Francisco, CA
Karolyi, Ronald W. ... Charlotte, NC
Karon & Dalimonte ... Boston, MA
Karon, Daniel R. ... Cleveland, OH
Karon, Jonathan A. ... Boston, MA
Karon, Mark J. ... Minneapolis, MN
Karon, Robert I. ... Plymouth, MN
Karon, Robert J. ... Duluth, MN
Karon, Sheldon ... Chicago, IL
Karon, Stanley E. ... St. Paul, MN
Karonis, Andrew ... New York, NY
Karonis, Geraldine Brotherton ... Manchester, NH
Karonis, Mario T. ... Kew Gardens, NY
Karopkin, Martin G. ... Brooklyn, NY
Karos, Constantine P. ... Beverly Hills, CA
Karos, Demetrius J. ... University Park, IL
Karos, John P. ... Wayzata, MN
Karos, Maria Katina ... Dallas, TX
Karosen, Laurence E. ... Bloomfield, NJ
Karosen, Lee Graham ... Roseland, NJ
Karosen, Lee Graham, P.C. ... Roseland, NJ
Karotkin, Don ... Houston, TX
Karotkin & Engvall, L.L.P. ... Houston, TX
Karotkin, Stephen ... New York, NY
Karoub, Richard M. ... Detroit, MI
Karoum, Hashem ... San Diego, CA
Karousatos, George ... Tinton Falls, NJ
Karow, John E. ... Scottsdale, AZ
Karow, Joseph ... New York, NY
Karowe, Marjorie E. ... Schenectady, NY
Karowsky, Charles A. ... Greeley, CO
Karowsky, Jan David ... Sacramento, CA
Karowsky, Lynn J. ... Greeley, CO
Karp, Aaron ... New York, NY
Karp, Adam Phillip ... Seattle, WA
Karp, Adrian I. ... Morris Plains, NJ
Karp, Adrian I., A Professional Corporation ... Morris Plains, NJ
Karp, Amy C. ... New York, NY
Karp, Andrew T. ... Chicago, IL
Karp, Arthur L. ... Arlington, VA
Karp, Bernhardt ... Hudson, NY
Karp, Brad S. ... New York, NY
Karp, Bruce A. ... Glenview, IL
Karp, Chad ... New York, NY
Karp & Co., Ltd. ... Reno, NV
Karp, Daniel ... Baltimore, MD
Karp, Daniel E. ... New York, NY
Karp, David ... Department of Justice, Office of Policy Development, GV
Karp, David A. ... Rockville Centre, NY
Karp, David B. ... Milwaukee, WI
Karp, David C. ... Los Angeles, CA
Karp, David C. ... New York, NY
Karp, David I. ... Encino, CA
Van Nuys, CA
Karp, David J. ... Richmond, VA
Karp, David W. ... Bethesda, MD
Karp, Donald M. ... Newark, NJ
Karp, Douglas M. ... Stamford, CT
Karp, Edward R. ... Oakland, CA
Karp, Eric H. ... Boston, MA
Karp, Eugene M. ... Albany, NY
Karp, Frosh, Lapidus, Wigodsky & Norwind, P.A. ... Washington, DC
Bethesda, MD
Rockville, MD
Alexandria, VA
Karp, Gabriel H. ... Dearborn Heights, MI
Karp, Gary J. ... Detroit, MI
Karp & Genauer, P.A. ... Coral Gables, FL
Miami, FL
Karp, George ... New York, NY
Karp, Harold ... Atlanta, GA
Karp, Harold E. ... Chicago, IL
Karp & Hart, P.C. ... West Chester, PA
Karp, Harvey L. ... East Hampton, NY
Karp, Herbert L. ... Alexandria, VA
Karp, Heurlin & Weiss, P.C. ... Tucson, AZ
Karp, Ira M. ... San Antonio, TX
Karp, Irwin ... Port Chester, NY
Karp, Irwin D. ... Sacramento, CA
Karp, Ivan M. ... Los Angeles, CA
Karp, James H. ... Santa Fe, NM
Karp, Jason ... Rochester, NY
Karp, Jay S. ... Morristown, NJ
New York, NY
Karp, Jeffrey A. ... Milwaukee, WI
Karp, Jeffrey M. ... Washington, DC
Karp, Jeffrey Randall ... New York, NY
Karp, Jeffrey S. ... New York, NY
Karp, Jeffrey S., P.C. ... New York, NY
Karp, Jeffrey T. ... Boston, MA
Karp, Jerome ... Brooklyn, NY
Karp, Jerome, P.C. ... Brooklyn, NY
Karp, Joel C. ... Milford, CT
Karp, Joel J. ... Miami, FL
Karp, Jonathan A. ... Los Angeles, CA
Karp, Jordan P. ... Baltimore, MD
Karp, Joseph M. ... San Francisco, CA
Karp, Joseph S. ... Delray Beach, FL
Palm Beach Gardens, FL
Port St. Lucie, FL
Karp, Judith ... Boston, MA
Karp, Judith R. ... West Palm Beach, FL
Karp, Judith Sturtz ... Washington, DC
Karp, Judith Subjack ... Rochester, NY
Karp, Kevin R. ... Reno, NV
Karp & Langerman, P.C. ... Milford, CT
Karp Law Firm, The, P.A.
Boynton Beach, FL
Delray Beach, FL
Palm Beach Gardens, FL
Port St. Lucie, FL
West Palm Beach, FL
Karp Law Offices, S.C. ... Milwaukee, WI
Karp, Leonard ... Tucson, AZ
Karp, Leslie R. ... Chicago, IL
Karp, Lois ... Ellicott City, MD
Karp, Louis I. ... Parsippany, NJ
Karp, Lucille Jane ... Secaucus, NJ
Karp, Marvin D. ... Tucson, AZ
Karp, Marvin L. ... Cleveland, OH
Karp, Marylou ... San Francisco, CA
Karp, Michael C. ... Mankato, MN
Karp, Michael N. ... Livingston, NJ
Karp, Michael R. ... Sarasota, FL
Karp, Miriam ... New York, NY
Karp, Mitchel ... Beverly Hills, CA
Karp, Morris M. ... New York, NY
Karp, Norris R. ... Newton, MA
Karp, Paul J. ... Newburgh, NY

Karp, Randall H. ... Burlingame, CA
Karp, Roberta J. ... West Palm Beach, FL
Karp, Roberta Schuhalter ... North Bergen, NJ
Karp, Ronald ... Dearborn Heights, MI
Karp, Ronald A. ... Washington, DC
Bethesda, MD
Alexandria, VA
Karp, Ronald I. ... Chandler, AZ
Karp, Sander N. ... Denver, CO
Karp, Scott B. ... Ellicott City, MD
Karp, Selwyn ... Far Rockaway, NY
Karp, Sheldon ... Cleveland, OH
Karp, Sheldon Co., L.P.A. ... Cleveland, OH
Karp and Sommers ... New York, NY
Karp, Stanley R. ... New York, NY
Karp, Stephen M. ... West Chester, PA
Karp, Stephen S. ... North Syracuse, NY
Karp, Steven C. ... Oak Brook, IL
Karp, Steven D. ... Beverly Hills, CA
Karp, Steven M. ... Los Angeles, CA
Karp, Susan A. ... New York, NY
Karp, Susan C. ... Westfield, NJ
Karp, Thomas B. ... San Diego, CA
Karp, Thomas B., P.C. ... San Diego, CA
Karp & Turkington, LLC ... Ellicott City, MD
Karp, Warren J. ... New York, NY
Karp, William H. ... Los Angeles, CA
Karpa, Jill L.
Department Of Health And Human Services, GV
Karpan, Frank J. ... Albia, IA
Karpan, Kathy ... Cheyenne, WY
Karpas, Bruce T. ... Englewood, CO
Karpas, Seymour ... New York, NY
Karpati, Elizabeth F. ... Houston, TX
Karpati, Suzan V. ... Atlantic City, NJ
Karpatkin, Rhoda H. ... Yonkers, NY
Karpay, Benj. F. ... Miami, FL
Karpay, Jeannette M. ... Baltimore, MD
Karpay, Kenneth D. ... Baltimore, MD
Karpe, Brian S. ... Hartford, CT
Karpe, David R. ... Madison, WI
Karpe, Karel S. ... New York, NY
Karpe, Mark A. ... Arlington, VA
Karpe, Richard ... Jericho, NY
Karpeh, Enid J. H. ... New York, NY
Karpel, Alan P. ... Chicago, IL
Karpel, Curtis J. ... Silver Spring, MD
Karpel, David N. ... Denver, CO
Karpel, Donald E. ... Beverly Hills, CA
Karpel, Ian S. ... Denver, CO
Karpel, Jeffrey E. ... Sherman Oaks, CA
Karpel, Jerome J. ... Carson, CA
Karpel, Jodi L. ... Beverly Hills, CA
Karpel, Kenneth N. ... Pawling, NY
Karpel, Linda J. ... Philadelphia, PA
Karpel, Philip ... Los Angeles, CA
Karpel, Philip F. ... Middletown, CT
Karpeles, Eli J. ... Beverly Hills, CA
Karpeles, Jack Howard ... Torrance, CA
Karpeles, Michael D. ... Chicago, IL
Karpen, Harry S. ... Clifton, NJ
Karpen, James L. ... Lansing, MI
Karpen, Judith S. ... Albany, NY
Karpen, Karen E. ... San Francisco, CA
Karpen, Michael A. ... Hackensack, NJ
New York, NY
Karpenko, Evans J. ... Euless, TX
Karpenko, Evans J., Inc. ... Euless, TX
Karpenski, Martin J. ... Clinton, NJ
Karpf, Andrew C. ... Central Islip, NY
Karpf, Beth L. ... Pleasanton, CA
Karpf, Dennis D. ... Medford, NJ
Karpf, Fredric S. ... Feasterville, PA
Karpf, Ilene P. ... Parsippany, NJ
Karpf, Jack F. ... Cherry Hill, NJ
Karpf, Jeffrey D. ... New York, NY
Karpf, Michael L. ... Savannah, GA
Karpf, Mitchell K.
North Miami Beach, FL
Karpf, Norman S. ... Kearny, NJ
Karpf, Spencer L. ... Glendale, CA
Karpiak, Jim R. ... San Francisco, CA
Karpie, Karen L. ... Bridgeport, CT
Karpin, Kevin J. ... Overland Park, KS
Karpink, Thomas A. ... Philadelphia, PA
Karpinos, Ralph D. ... Chapel Hill, NC
Karpinski, Alan W. ... Portland, OR
Karpinski, Bertin J. ... Tampa, FL
Karpinski, Charles Elwyn ... Portland, OR
Karpinski, Christopher John
Kansas City, MO
Karpinski, Gina K. ... Charleston, WV
Karpinski, Irena I. ... Washington, DC
Karpinski, Jayna P. ... Citrus Heights, CA
Karpinski, John A. ... Auburn, NY
Karpinski, John S. ... Vancouver, WA
Karpinski, Kevin Bock ... Baltimore, MD
Karpinski, Richard ... Washington, DC
Karpinski, Seth T. ... San Francisco, CA
Karpinski, Stacey Herman
Overland Park, KS
Karpinski, Stapleton & Fandrich, P.C.
Auburn, NY
Karpinsky, Jaroslaw P. ... Clawson, MI
Karplus, Curtis M. ... Berkeley, CA
Karplus, Wayne ... Urbana, IL
Karpman & Associates ... Los Angeles, CA
Karpman, Daniel ... Springfield, MA
Karpman, Diane L. ... Los Angeles, CA
Karpman, Randy ... New York, NY
Karpman, Valerie Ansel ... San Francisco, CA
Karpoff, Julian ... Arlington, VA
Karpoff, Michael S. ... Princeton, NJ
Karpoff & Title ... Arlington, VA
Karpook, Russell D. ... Baltimore, MD
Karpousis, John F ... New York, NY
Karpousis, Karen R. ... Cherry Hill, NJ
Karpousis, Karen Rose ... Cherry Hill, NJ
Karpousis, Thomas F. ... Cherry Hill, NJ
Karpouzian, Gilda O. ... Annapolis, MD
Karpowich, Leonard H. ... Chicago, IL
Karpowich, Sonya L. ... Irvine, CA
Karpowicz, Joseph R. ... Dublin, OH
Karppi, Patricia C. ... Fairfax, VA
Karpstein, Gregory A. ... Hillsboro, OR
Karpstein & Verhulst, P.C. ... Hillsboro, OR
Karpuk, Robert A. ... Malibu, CA
Karpuk, Theodore E. ... Sioux City, IA
Karpus, Mark R. ... Charleston, IL
Karr, Bernard L. ... Cleveland, OH
Karr, Carol J. ... Grand Rapids, MI
Karr, Carolyn
Agency for International Development, Other Offices of A.I.D., GV
Karr, Charles ... Fort Smith, AR
Karr, Charles, P.A., Law Offices of
Fort Smith, AR
Karr, David D. ... Denver, CO
Karr, David M. ... Columbus, OH
Karr, David R. ... Ravenswood, WV
Karr, Denise M. ... Novato, CA
Karr, Donald Lee ... Westlake Village, CA
Karr, Douglas B. ... Columbus, OH
Karr, Emily V. ... Portland, OR
Karr, F. John ... Fresno, CA
Karr, George ... Valley Stream, NY
Karr, Glennon J. ... Columbus, OH
Karr, Gwenn S. ... Columbus, OH
Karr, Harrison L. ... San Francisco, CA
Karr, Heath A. ... Butler, MO
Karr, J. David ... Davison, MI
Karr, Jeffrey S. ... Los Angeles, CA
Karr, Jennifer K. ... Chicago, IL
Karr, John W. ... Washington, DC
Karr, Judith A. ... Pennsville, NJ
Karr, Karen L. ... Phoenix, AZ
Karr, Karr & Karr, P.C. ... Webster City, IA
Karr, Keith M. ... Columbus, OH
Karr, Lawrence R. ... Dobbs Ferry, NY
Karr, Margaret P. ... Webster City, IA
Karr, Mary H. ... St. Louis, MO
Karr, Payne ... Seattle, WA
Karr, Philip R. ... Oceanside, CA
Karr, Randall A. ... Dallas, TX
Karr, Richard L. ... Webster City, IA
Karr, Richard M. ... Chicago, IL
Karr, Robert L. ... Passaic, NJ
Karr, Robert P. ... Seattle, WA
Karr, Robert W. ... Chicago, IL
Karr, Robert W. & Associates, Ltd.
Chicago, IL
Karr, Russell B. ... Hollywood, FL
Karr & Salber ... Pennsville, NJ
Karr, Samuel Scott ... Texarkana, AR
Amarillo, TX
Karr & Sherman Co., L.P.A.
Columbus, OH
Karr, Stephan David ... Nashville, TN
Karr, Stephen P. ... Winston-Salem, NC
Karr, Stephen W. ... Grand Rapids, MI
Karr, Thomas M., (P.A.) ... Miami, FL
Karr Tuttle Campbell, A Professional Service Corporation ... Portland, OR
Seattle, WA
Karr, William G. ... Ventura, CA
Karraker, Donald E. ... Altamonte Springs, FL
Karraker, Kevan L. ... Farmington, MO
Karras, Angelo W. ... Mount Prospect, IL
Karras, Christopher G. ... Philadelphia, PA
Karras, Donald G. ... Denver, CO
Karras, Frank N. ... Salt Lake City, UT
Karras, Patricia McCorvey ... Valdosta, GA
Karras, William Alexander ... Bethlehem, PA
Karré, Kathleen M. ... Lafayette, LA
Karre, Kay Marie ... Lafayette, LA
Karre, Nelson T. ... Battle Creek, MI
Karre, Richard A. ... Englewood, CO
Karren, Beth D. ... Piedmont, CA
Karren, Brad L. ... Bentonville, AR
Karren, Brent M. ... Dallas, TX
Karren, Herbert E. ... San Antonio, TX
Karren, Richard K. ... San Jose, CA
Karrenberg, Thomas ... Salt Lake City, UT
Karrenstein, Chris ... Matthews, NC
Karres, Matthew S. ... Charlotte, NC
Karrh, Heather Kendall ... Bremen, GA
Karrh, John M. ... Tuscaloosa, AL
Karrh, Randolph C. ... Swainsboro, GA
Karriem, Sandra S. ... New York, NY
Karriker, Robert G. ... Asheville, NC
Karris, Assunta A. ... Park Ridge, IL
Karris and Fio Rito, Law Firm of
Park Ridge, IL
Karris, Nicholas A., (Ltd.) ... Chicago, IL
Karrmann, Buggs & Baxter ... Cuba City, WI
Platteville, WI
Karrmann, Kristin L. ... Platteville, WI
Karrmann, W. Phil ... Cuba City, WI
Platteville, WI
Karro, David G.
United States Postal Service, Law Department, GV
Karro, Marshall H. ... Charlotte, NC
Karro Sellers & Langson ... Charlotte, NC
Karro, Terry ... Twisp, WA
Karron, Andrew T. ... Washington, DC
Karron, Elaine Tanner ... Rochester, NY
Kars, Larry ... New York, NY
Kars, Larry, P.C. ... New York, NY
Karsai, Liza Ilona ... New York, NY
Karsaz, Christopher A. ... Los Angeles, CA
Karsch, Dennis M. ... New York, NY
Karsch, Jay H. ... Doylestown, PA
Karsch, Michael D. ... Boca Raton, FL
Karsch, Mitchell W. ... New York, NY
Karsevar, Leonard J. ... Upland, CA
Karsh, Aaron
National Labor Relations Board, Office of the General Counsel, GV
Karsh, Alan E. ... Denver, CO
Karsh, Eli ... St. Louis, MO
Karsh, Fulton, Gabler & Joseph, P.C.
Denver, CO
Karsh, Joshua ... Chicago, IL
Karsh, Martha L. ... Los Angeles, CA
Karsh, Ralph D. ... Pittsburgh, PA
Karsh, Randolph M.
Colorado Springs, CO
Karshbaum, Bonnie L. ... Woburn, MA
Karshmer, Barbara E. ... Berkeley, CA
Karsky, Gloria J. ... Minneapolis, MN
Karsman, Brooks & Callaway, P.C.
Brunswick, GA
Hinesville, GA
Pembroke, GA
Savannah, GA
Springfield, GA
Statesboro, GA
Waycross, GA
Karsman, Stanley M. ... Savannah, GA
Karsner, Mark R. ... Taunton, MA
Karsner and Meehen, PC ... Taunton, MA
Karsner, Philip A. ... Herndon, VA
Karsnitz, Craig A. ... Georgetown, DE
Karsnitz, Kathi Ann ... Milton, DE
Karson, Barry M. ... New York, NY
Karson, Bonnie J. ... Minneapolis, MN
Karson, Daniel E. ... New York, NY
Karson, Emile ... Los Angeles, CA
Karson, Gil A. ... New York, NY
Karson, Jamieson A. ... New York, NY
Karson, Jeffrey A. ... Cleveland, OH
Youngstown, OH
Karson, Keir Thomas ... Lake Oswego, OR
Karson, Lisa A. ... New York, NY
Karson, Michael J. ... Chicago, IL
Karson, Miles K., Jr. ... Greenville, PA
Karson, Scott M. ... Melville, NY
Karst, Alexander ... San Francisco, CA
Karst, Kenneth L. ... Los Angeles, CA
Karst, Leslie J. ... Monterey, CA
Watsonville, CA
Karst, Mary Ellen ... Madison, WI
Karstaedt, Arthur R., III ... Englewood, CO
Karstaedt, Cheryl M. ... Boulder, CO
Karsten, Christopher R. ... Chicago, IL
Karsten, Kurt D. ... Annapolis, MD
Easton, MD
Karsten, Scott M. ... West Hartford, CT
Karsten, Theresa Salem ... Cincinnati, OH
Karstetter, Allan B. ... Franklin, MA
Karstetter, Timothy R. ... McPherson, KS
Kart, Eugene ... Chicago, IL
Kart, Gilbert ... Chicago, IL
Kart, Leslie N. ... Philadelphia, PA
Karta, Glenn E. ... Washington, DC
Kartagener, Carol A. ... Boca Raton, FL
Kartagener, Steven R. ... New York, NY
Kartalia, David E. ... Westminster, MD
Kartalopoulos, Anita Brass
New York, NY
Kartchner, Gene B. ... Carthage, MO
Kartchner, Jared A. ... Sierra Vista, AZ
Kartchner, Stanley J. ... Tucson, AZ
Karten, Alan I. ... Miami, FL
Karten, Joseph ... New York, NY
Karten, Susan M. ... New York, NY
Karter, Philip ... Bala Cynwyd, PA
Karter, Simon M. ... Madison, WI
Karter, Thomas G. ... Portland, OR
Kartheiser, Robert D., Jr. ... New York, NY
Kartholl, Robert J., Jr. ... Chicago, IL
Kartiganer, Craig I. ... Miami, FL
Kartiganer, Deborah L.
San Francisco, CA
Kartiganer, Joseph ... New York, NY
Kartiganer, Lawrence S.
Beverly Hills, CA
Kartman, Marc G. ... Seal Beach, CA
Kartman, Sande ... Philadelphia, PA
Karto, Steve ... Cadiz, OH
Karton, David S. ... Beverly Hills, CA
Karton, David S., A Law Corporation
Beverly Hills, CA
Karton, Robert M. ... Chicago, IL
Karton, Robert M., Ltd. ... Chicago, IL
Kartozian, William F. ... Danville, CA
Kartzinel, Jacob M. ... Palm Springs, CA
Kartzman, Abraham R. ... Scottsdale, AZ
Kartzman, Steven P. ... Morris Plains, NJ
Karu, Anita Elaine
Securities and Exchange Commission, Division of Corporation Finance, GV
Karutz, William Charles ... Lexington, KY
Karvay, Rudolf J. ... Brooklyn, NY
Karver, Jeffrey C. ... Boyertown, PA
Karvonen, John E. ... St. Petersburg, FL
Karvonides, Mia ... Burlington, VT
Karwacki, Robert L. ... Annapolis, MD
Karwal, Meera Dodeja ... New York, NY
Karwath, Bart A. ... Indianapolis, IN
Karweick, Betty ... St. Paul, MN
Karwin, Robert P. ... Glendale, CA
Karwoski, Gerald S. ... Homewood, IL
Karwoski, Gerald S., Ltd. ... Homewood, IL
Karwoski, Michael J. ... Lansing, MI
Karwowski, Henry M. ... West Orange, NJ
Karwowski, Roman S. ... Detroit, MI
Karydes, Argirios A. ... Montclair, NJ
Karz, Cheryl H. ... Los Angeles, CA
Karz, Laurence M. ... Canandaigua, NY
Karzag, Anna S. ... Santa Barbara, CA
Karzen, Herbert A. ... Scottsdale, AZ
Karzen, Matthew J.
Hot Sulphur Springs, CO
Karzmer, Erin E. ... Boston, MA
Karzmer, Steven C. ... Boston, MA
Karzon, Allaire Urban, (Mrs.) ... Nashville, TN
Karzon, David T., Jr. ... St. Louis, MO
Karzon, Elizabeth U. ... Treasury Department, Internal Revenue Service, GV
Karzov, Arnold J. ... Chicago, IL
Karz-Wagman, Harley I. ... New Orleans, LA
Kasab, Ann M. ... Birmingham, MI
Kasaba, Richard G. ... Dearborn, MI
Kasaback, John M. ... Pittsburgh, PA
Kasacavage, Kenneth S. ... Henderson, KY
Kasai, Jerry K. ... Columbus, OH
Kasai, Wayne T. ... Los Angeles, CA
Kasak, Cynthia J. ... Billings, MT
Kasakoff, Darragh K. ... Worcester, MA
Kasakove, David P. ... New York, NY
Kasal, Peter ... Hutchinson, MN
Kasameyer, James W. ... Portland, OR
Kasanin, Mark O. ... San Francisco, CA
Kasanov, Joel S. ... Chicago, IL
Kasanow, David ... Washington, DC
Kasapis, Theodore ... Kew Gardens, NY
Kasarjian, Levon, Jr. ... Paradise Valley, AZ
Kasarjian, Levon, Jr. ... Phoenix, AZ
Kasbee, Scott E. ... Pittsburgh, PA
Kasbeer, Terry G. ... Vista, CA
Kasbohm, Francis P. ... Chicago, IL
Kascak, Richard G., Jr. ... Trumbull, CT
Kascavage, Martin A. ... Philadelphia, PA
Kaschak, Lawrence M. ... La Salle, IL
Kaschak, Robert J. ... Mineola, NY
Kaschak, Wayne R. ... Canton, OH
Kaschak, Wayne R., Co., L.P.A. ... Canton, OH
Kaschke, Kevin D. ... Libertyville, IL
Kascht, John E. ... Milwaukee, WI
Kascle, Esther ... Los Angeles, CA
Kasdan, Abraham ... New York, NY
Kasdan, Alan R. ... General Accounting Office, Office of the General Counsel, GV
Kasdan, Alexander B. ... New York, NY
Kasdan, Howard P. ... Cleveland, OH
Kasdan, Ira T. ... Washington, DC
Kasdan, Kenneth S. ... Irvine, CA
San Jose, CA
Kasdan, Martin Z., Jr. ... Louisville, KY
Kasdan, Sheldon David ... Encino, CA
Kasdan, Simonds, McIntyre, Epstein & Martin ... Irvine, CA
San Jose, CA
Kasdan, Warren B. ... Montclair, NJ
Trenton, NJ
Kasdin, Neisen O. ... Miami, FL
Kasdin, Peter D. ... Chicago, IL
Kasdin, Peter D., Ltd. ... Chicago, IL
Kasdin, Tovah M. ... Rockville, MD
Kasdon, James E. ... Brooklyn, NY
Kasdorf, Clifford C. ... Milwaukee, WI
Kasdorf, Lewis & Swietlik, S.C.
Green Bay, WI
Milwaukee, WI
Wausau, WI
Kasdorf, Robert T. ... Madison, WI
Kase, Aaron S. ... Chicago, IL
Kase, Arthur J. ... Kansas City, MO
Kase & Assocs., P.C. ... Fairfax, VA
Kase, Beth A. ... Los Angeles, CA
Kase, C. Robert ... Savannah, GA
Kase, David A. ... New York, NY
Kase, Delia M. ... Fairfax, VA
Kase & Druker ... Garden City, NY
Mamaroneck, NY
Mineola, NY
New York, NY
Kase, Edmund H., III ... Socorro, NM
Kase, Jamieson Lee ... Dulles, VA
Kase, John L. ... Garden City, NY
Kase, Joseph, Jr. ... San Diego, CA
Kase, Kathryn M. ... Albany, NY
Kase, Kenneth ... New York, NY
Kase, Nathan E. ... Philadelphia, PA
Kase, Stephen A. ... Sturgeon Bay, WI
Kase, Susan Beth ... Trenton, NJ
Kaseberg, William G. ... Edwardsville, IL
Kaseburg, Frederick A. ... Seattle, WA
Kaseff, David M. ... Kansas City, MO
Kaseff, Fred E. ... Deerfield, IL
Kaseguma, Rod P. ... Bellevue, WA
Kaselak, Dennis J. ... Cleveland, OH
Kasell, Brian W. ... Los Angeles, CA
Kasem, George A. ... West Covina, CA
Kaseman, A. Carl, III ... Washington, DC
Kasemeyer, Pamela Metz ... Baltimore, MD
Kasen, Allan J. ... Phoenix, AZ
Kasen, David A. ... Cherry Hill, NJ
Kasen, Francine Stein ... Cherry Hill, NJ
Kasen, Kasen & Braverman, A Professional Corporation ... Cherry Hill, NJ
Kasen and Patterson, S.C. ... Wauwatosa, WI
Kasen, Thomas J. ... Wauwatosa, WI
Kasenter, Kenneth A. ... New Castle, PA
Kaser, Brian A. ... Lansing, MI
Kaser, Bruce A., P.C. ... Seattle, WA
Kaser, David L. ... Detroit, MI
Kaser, Jeffrey L. ... Chicago, IL
Kaser, Leonard H. ... Williamstown, NJ
Kaser, Martha J. ... Albuquerque, NM
Kaser, Richard S. ... Williamstown, NJ
Kaser, Stephen W. ... Roseburg, OR
Kaser, Sylvia T. ... Department of Justice, Civil Division, GV
Kaserman, David A. ... Oklahoma City, OK
Kaserman, Kay H. ... Knoxville, TN
Kaserman, Wm. Barton ... Knoxville, TN
Kaset, Simon ... Cottontown, TN
Kasey, Cornelius D. ... Dallas, TX

Kasfir, Nelson M. ....Hanover, NH
Kash, Bernard B. ....Chicago, IL
Kash, Catherine Seigneuray
Great River, NY
Kash, David L. ....Hamilton, OH
Kash, David W. ....Phoenix, AZ
Kash, Gregory M. ....Raleigh, NC
Kash, Ira H. ....Bay Shore, NY
Kash, James J. ....Chicago, IL
Kash, Jeffrey J. ....Stroudsburg, PA
Kash, Kevin ....Middletown, OH
Kash, Louis N. ....Rochester, NY
Kash, Richard M., Jr. ....Paris, IL
Kasha, Rebecca T. ....Evansville, IN
Kashani, Hamid R. ....Indianapolis, IN
Kashani, Mir Saied ....Los Angeles, CA
Kashani, Raana H. ....San Jose, CA
Kashanian, Shahriar ....Manhasset, NY
Kashar, Alexis ....Sherman Oaks, CA
Kashar, Gary A. ....Los Angeles, CA
Kashdan, Alan G. ....Washington, DC
Kashdan, Richard L. ....San Francisco, CA
Kashef, Cyrus Raamin
Farmington Hills, MI
Kasher, James F. ....Omaha, NE
Kasher, John M. ....Chicago, IL
Kasheta, Kelly Anne ....Rocky Hill, CT
Kashfian, Maurice ....Los Angeles, CA
Kashi, Joseph L. ....Soldotna, AK
Kashi, Joseph S. ....Fort Lauderdale, FL
Kashian, James ....Los Angeles, CA
Kashian, Jeremy S. ....Sacramento, CA
Kashiba, Yukio (IBA) ....New York, NY
Kashimba, Paul T. ....Boca Raton, FL
Kashin, Aura T. ....Sacramento, CA
Kashinski, Jerome J. ....Denver, CO
Kashishian, Tina L. ....Cinnaminson, NJ
Kashiwa, Genro ....Honolulu, HI
Kashiwa, Peter T. ....Honolulu, HI
Kashiwada, Lois M. ....Honolulu, HI
Kashiwahara, Royanne T. ....Santa Monica, CA
Kashkin, Mindy Weiss ....Tallman, NY
Kashman, David S. ....New York, NY
Kashman, Howard A. ....Durango, CO
Kashner, Howard J. ....New York, NY
Kashou, Mario M. ....San Francisco, CA
Kashouty, Henry David ....Hampton, VA
Kashtan, Michael F. ....Fort Lauderdale, FL
Miami, FL
Kashtan, Paula L.
Securities and Exchange Commission,
Division of Enforcement, GV
Kashtan, Robert J. ....Basking Ridge, NJ
Kashyap, Sajan ....Pasadena, CA
Kasi, Srinandan R. ....New York, NY
Kasian, Dean ....Baltimore, MD
Kasiborski, Chester ....Detroit, MI
Kasiborski, Chester E., Jr. ....Detroit, MI
Kasiborski, Ronayne & Flaska, A Professional Corporation ....Detroit, MI
Kasich, Gojko ....Crown Point, IN
Kasick & Madey ....Allentown, PA
Kasick, Samuel R. ....Allentown, PA
Kasicky, Paul A. ....Pittsburgh, PA
Kasierski, Scott P. ....Hopkinsville, KY
Kasieta Legal Group, LLC ....Madison, WI
Kasieta, Robert J. ....Madison, WI
Kasik, George B. ....Cleveland, OH
Kasilowski & Kasilowski
Tyngsborough, MA
Kasilowski, Mark W. ....Tyngsborough, MA
Kasilowski, William A. ....Tyngsborough, MA
Kasimatis, John ....Madison, WI
Kasimer & Annino, P.C.
Falls Church, VA
Leesburg, VA
Kasimer & Ittig, P.C. ....Burtonsville, MD
Kasimer, Joseph H. ....Falls Church, VA
Leesburg, VA
Kasimov, Jon M. ....Santa Monica, CA
Kasindorf, Matthew E. ....New York, NY
Kasinger, James R. ....Boston, MA
Kasirer, Robert A. ....Beverly Hills, CA
Kasischke, Louis W. ....Bloomfield Hills, MI
Kasischke, Marc E. ....Department of Energy,
Office of the General Counsel, GV
Kaska, Edward ....Austin, TX
Kaska, Ellen J. ....Bala Cynwyd, PA
Kaske, William E. ....Addison, IL
Kaskel, Daniel A. ....Morristown, NJ
Kaskel, Helaine R. ....Los Angeles, CA
Kaskell, Peter H. ....New York, NY
Kaskell, Ralph L., Jr. ....New Orleans, LA
Kaskey, John E. ....Cherry Hill, NJ
Philadelphia, PA
Kaskey, Karen ....Gladwyne, PA
Kaskie, Jay C. ....Addison, TX
Kaskie, Jay C. ....Dallas, TX
Kaskie, Sharon A. ....Arcadia, FL
Kaskinen, Kurt J. ....Kealakekua, HI
Kasko, Nancy L. ....Chicago, IL
Kaskowitz, Jerome I. ....St. Louis, MO
Kaskowitz, Rochelle ....St. Louis, MO
Kasle, Andrew R. ....Cleveland, OH
Kasle, Franklin H. ....Flint, MI
Kasle, Jill F. ....Washington, DC
Kasler, Carolyn ....North Olmsted, OH
Kasler, Kelion N. ....Washington, DC
Kasler, Paula S. ....Mountain View, CA
Kasler, Phyllis D. ....Redwood Valley, CA
Kasler, Theodore S. ....Buffalo, NY
Kasley, Helen Mary ....Half Moon Bay, CA
Kasley, William L. ....Washington, DC
Kaslick, Mary Elizabeth ....Frederick, MD
Kasling, R. Kemp ....Austin, TX
Kasloff, Stephen I. ....Memphis, TN
Kaslow, Aaron M. ....Washington, DC
Kaslow, Chernikoff & Garber
Washington, DC
Bethesda, MD
Rockville, MD
Kaslow, Clifford C. ....Bethesda, MD
Kaslow, D. Carlos ....Berkeley, CA
Kaslow, Harmon M. ....Los Angeles, CA
Kaslow, Howard J. ....Omaha, NE
Kaslow, Kenneth M. ....San Jose, CA
Kasmar, Charles D. ....Anchorage, AK
Kasmar and Slone, P.C. ....Anchorage, AK
Kasmar, Stephen R. ....Cherry Hill, NJ
Kasmarik, John, Jr. ....Elizabeth, PA
Kasmen, Andrew S. ....Jenkintown, PA
Kasmen, Lawrence C. ....Atlanta, GA
Kasmin, Jennifer A. ....New York, NY
Kasminoff, David H.
Department of Transportation,
Federal Railroad Administration, GV
Kasmire, Robert D. ....New York, NY
Kasner, Jay B. ....New York, NY
Kasner, Jerry A. ....Santa Clara, CA
Kasner, Karen Spar ....Scarsdale, NY
Kasner, Marc A. ....Houston, TX
Kasner, Stewart L. ....Miami, FL
Kasnetz, Andrew R. ....Belleville, IL
St. Louis, MO
Kasnetz, Deborah Altemore ....Irving, TX
Kasny, Roger R. ....McHenry, IL
Kasody-Coyle, Patricia A.
Birmingham, MI
Kasoff, Jerome ....Great Neck, NY
Kasofsky, Dale S. ....McAllen, TX
Kasok, Sharon Frances ....New York, NY
Kasok, Stephanie S. ....Wellesley Hills, MA
Kasolas, George C. ....Campbell, CA
Kasowitz, Benson, Torres & Friedman LLP
Newark, NJ
New York, NY
Houston, TX
Kasowitz, Jesse Erwin ....New York, NY
Kasowitz, Marc E. ....New York, NY
Kaspar, Eileen ....New York, NY
Kaspar, John A. ....Vineland, NJ
Kaspar, Karim G. ....Roseland, NJ
Kaspar, Patricia ....San Francisco, CA
Kaspar, Roland R., (Professional Corporation) ....Los Angeles, CA
Kasparek, Timothy G. ....Phoenix, AZ
Kaspari, John T. ....Clackamas, OR
Kaspari, Richard L. ....Minneapolis, MN
Kasparian, Ani H. ....New York, NY
Kasparian, Faith D. ....Washington, DC
Kasparson, Norman L. ....Holden, MA
Kasper, Alan J. ....Washington, DC
Kasper, Brenda S. ....Milwaukee, WI
Kasper, Caroline E. ....Jacksonville, FL
Kasper & Carpenter, P.L.L.C.
Walpole, NH
Kasper, Daniel M. ....Boston, MA
Kasper, David L. ....Troy, MI
Kasper, David T. ....Indianapolis, IN
Kasper, Debra L. ....San Francisco, CA
Kasper, Dennis R. ....Los Angeles, CA
Kasper, Edward ....Southfield, MI
Kasper, George J. ....Bridgeport, CT
Kasper, Gregory A. ....New York, NY
Kasper, Horst M. ....Warren, NJ
Kasper, Ian S. ....Woodstock, IL
Kasper, Jerome ....West Orange, NJ
Kasper, John ....Ellsworth, KS
Kasper, John, Jr. ....Watertown, MA
Kasper, Joseph V. ....Wilkes-Barre, PA
Kasper, Judith M. ....Norwich, VT
Kasper, Keith J. ....Burlington, VT
Kasper, Kenneth R. ....Baltimore, MD
Kasper, Kenneth S. ....Madison, NJ
Kasper, Kris D. ....Oklahoma City, OK
Kasper, Kristofer ....Austin, TX
Kasper, Mary M. ....Los Angeles, CA
Kasper, Michael J. ....Chicago, IL
Kasper, Paul E. ....Sacramento, CA
Kasper, Richard A. ....Phoenix, AZ
Kasper, Richard P. ....Mesa, AZ
Kasper, Robert J., Jr. ....Walpole, NH
Kasper, Robert L. ....Perry, OK
Kasper, Russell H. ....Atlanta, GA
Kasper, Soraya Hevia
Fort Lauderdale, FL
Kasper, Stephen M. ....New York, NY
Kasper, Thomas J. ....Schaumburg, IL
Kasper, Thomas R. ....Hartford, CT
Kasper, Warren E. ....Clemmons, NC
Kasper, Warren E., P.A. ....Clemmons, NC
Kasperek, Colleen ....Philadelphia, PA
Kasperek, Robert W. ....Detroit, MI
Kasperitis, Patrick R. ....Corpus Christi, TX
Kasperovich, Mark F. ....Fort Lauderdale, FL
Kaspers, John N. ....Farmington Hills, MI
Kaspers, William F., (P.C.) ....Atlanta, GA
Kasperski, Julia V. ....Houston, TX
Kasperson & Bittner, P.S. ....Seattle, WA
Kasperson, Richard W. ....Northbrook, IL
Kasperson, Stanley N. ....Seattle, WA
Kasperzak, R. Michael, Jr.
Mountain View, CA
Kasprenski, Michael D. ....Allentown, PA
Kasprzak, Daniel J. ....Houston, TX
Kasprzyk, Brian E. ....Fairless Hills, PA
Kasputis, Edward F. ....Cleveland, OH
Kasputys, Patricia Jeanne ....Baltimore, MD
Towson, MD
Kasraie, Bijan ....Atlanta, GA
Kass, Alan P. ....Wayne, NJ
Kass, Amram ....New York, NY
Kass, Andrew ....Chicago, IL
Kass, Anne ....Albuquerque, NM
Kass, Arthur ....Somers, NY
Kass, Benny L. ....Washington, DC
Kass, Bernard C. ....East Meadow, NY
Kass, Brian L. ....Washington, DC
Kass, Christina M. ....Los Angeles, CA
Kass, Colin R. ....Washington, DC
Kass, David A. ....House of Representatives,
Committee Legal Personnel, GV
Kass, David N. ....Roslyn Estates, NY
Kass, Deborah ....Los Angeles, CA
Kass, Dennis B. ....Los Angeles, CA
Kass, Donald J. ....Los Angeles, CA
Kass, Edna M. ....Ravenna, MI
Kass, Frederic C. ....Branford, CT
Kass, Frederic R. ....Columbus, OH
Kass, Gail D. ....Beverly Hills, CA
Kass, Gail D. ....Los Angeles, CA
Kass, Geoffrey R. ....Chicago, IL
Kass, Howard E. ....Washington, DC
Kass, Howard S. ....Carle Place, NY
Kass, Howard S., P.C. ....Carle Place, NY
Kass, Ian A. ....San Jose, CA
Kass, Ilene ....New York, NY
Kass, Ira ....North Bellmore, NY
Kass, Irwin L. ....Madison, WI
Kass, Jeanne E. ....St. Paul, MN
Kass, Jeffrey H. ....St. Louis, MO
Kass, Kathy M. ....New York, NY
Kass, Laura J. ....Chicago, IL
Kass Law Firm ....Norfolk, VA
Portsmouth, VA
Virginia Beach, VA
Kass, Lisa S. ....Chicago, IL
Kass, Lowell D. ....New York, NY
Kass, Madeline J. ....Seattle, WA
Kass, Mark A. ....Washington, DC
Kass, Mark E. ....Miami, FL
Kass, Michael ....Tampa, FL
Kass, Michael J. ....San Francisco, CA
Kass, Miriam ....Houston, TX
Kass, Mortimer H. ....Miami, FL
Kass & Moses ....Chicago, IL
Kass, Nicholas L. ....Forest Hills, NY
Kass, Philip G. ....Tarrytown, NY
Kass, Richard G. ....Mineola, NY
New York, NY
Kass, Robert E. ....Detroit, MI
Kass, Roberta E. ....Los Angeles, CA
Kass, Roger E. ....New York, NY
Kass, Rudolph ....Boston, MA
Kass, Sandra S. ....Culver City, CA
Kass, Shuler, Solomon, Spector, Foyle & Singer, P.A. ....Tampa, FL
Kass & Skalet, PLLC ....Washington, DC
Kass, Stephan ....Brooklyn, NY
Kass, Stephen B. ....Westbury, NY
Kass, Stephen L. ....New York, NY
Kass, Stephen M. ....Oakland, CA
Kass, Stephen M., P.C. ....Oakland, CA
Kass, Steven ....Miami, FL
Kass, Steven A. ....Westbury, NY
Kass, Terry Horwitz ....Chicago, IL
Kass, Thomas E. ....New York, NY
Kass, William A. ....Boca Raton, FL
Kass, William E. ....Portsmouth, VA
Kass, Zachary B. ....New York, NY
Kassa, Jote ....New York, NY
Kassab Archbold & O'Brien, L.L.P.
Wilmington, DE
Wildwood, NJ
Media, PA
Kassab, Burt S. ....Birmingham, MI
Kassab, Edward ....Media, PA
Kassab, Lance Christopher ....Houston, TX
Kassabian, Albert I. ....Annandale, VA
Kassabian, Brett Armen ....Annandale, VA
Kassabian, David ....Arlington, TX
Kassabian & Kassabian, P.L.C.
Annandale, VA
Fairfax, VA
Kassabian, Mark M. ....Los Angeles, CA
Kassabian, Tamara Hardney
Washington, DC
Kassak, Christine M. ....Chicago, IL
Kassak, Michael O. ....Westmont, NJ
Kassal, Bentley ....New York, NY
Kassamali, Reyaz A. ....New York, NY
Kassan, Alan E. ....Encino, CA
Kassan & Kassan ....Encino, CA
Kassan, Melvin E. ....Encino, CA
Kassapian, Susan M. ....New York, NY
Kassaw, Todd L. ....Lufkin, TX
Kasschau, Patricia L. ....Torrance, CA
Kassebaum, Jeanette C. ....Fishers, IN
Kassebaum, John P., II ....Charleston, SC
Kassebaum, Sonja L. ....Chicago, IL
Kassel, Alvin L. ....New York, NY
Kassel, Gregory H. ....San Bernardino, CA
Kassel, Jeffrey J. ....Madison, WI
Kassel, John B. ....Waterbury, VT
Kassel, John D. ....Columbia, SC
Kassel, Jonathan D. ....Woodland Hills, CA
Kassel, Judith ....New York, NY
Kassel, Judith B. ....Chantilly, VA
Kassel & Kassel ....San Bernardino, CA
Kassel, Mark A. ....Madison, WI
Kassel, Michael Jon ....Haddon Heights, NJ
Kassel, Penny B. ....Mineola, NY
Kassel, Philip ....San Bernardino, CA
Kassel, Philip J. ....New York, NY
Kassel, Richard A. ....New York, NY
Kassel, Richard A. ....New York, NY
Kassel, Robert P. ....Nyack, NY
Kassel, Ruth B. ....Middletown, NY
Kassel, Sanford A. ....San Bernardino, CA
Kassel, Sanford A., A Professional Law Corporation ....San Bernardino, CA
Kassel, Susan A. ....New City, NY
Kassel, Terry ....New York, NY
Kasselberg, Alfred Guy ....Nashville, TN
Kasselik, Lisa Erickson
San Francisco, CA
Kassell, Susan J. ....Treasury Department,
Internal Revenue Service, GV
Kasselman, Conrad ....Dallas, TX
Kasselman, Diane J. ....New York, NY
Kasselman, Edward B. ....Lakewood, NJ
Kasselman & McCorkindale, A Professional Corporation ....Dallas, TX
Kasselman, Stevens J. ....Sands Point, NY
Kassem, Nabil N. ....Roseland, NJ
Kassem, R. Robert ....Knoxville, TN
Kassen, Elizabeth A. Kruse ....Chesterland, OH
Kassen, Melinda ....Boulder, CO
Kassen, William J. ....Chesterland, OH
Kassenbrock, Mark R. ....Sacramento, CA
Kassenoff, Allan A. ....New York, NY
Kassenoff, David S. ....Jacksonville, FL
Kassenoff, Jarred I. ....New York, NY
Kassenoff, Melvyn M. ....Summit, NJ
Kasserman, Geo. W., Jr. ....Newton, IL
Kasserman, Ronald W. ....Wheeling, WV
Kasserman, Ronald William
Wheeling, WV
Kasserman, Shawn S. ....Chicago, IL
Kassian, Natasha ....New York, NY
Kassimir, Maurice R. ....New York, NY
Kassin, Alan R. ....Edwardsville, IL
Kassin, Harold H. ....North Miami Beach, FL
Kassin, Morris J. ....New York, NY
Kassin, Thomas J. ....Atlanta, GA
Kassing, Robert P. ....Indianapolis, IN
Kassinger, Theodore W. ....Washington, DC
Kassirer, Earle L. ....Buffalo, NY
Kassirer, Paul L. ....New York, NY
Kassirer, Steven J. ....San Francisco, CA
Kassis, James E. ....Sacramento, CA
Kassis, Kelly Ann ....North Charleston, SC
Kassis, Richard L. ....Oakland, CA
Kassler, Haskell A. ....Boston, MA
Kassly, Bone, English & Weilmuenster, P.C.
Belleville, IL
Kassman, Bruce G. ....Surfside, FL
Kassman, Bruce G., P.A. ....Surfside, FL
Kassman, Donna J. ....New York, NY
Kassman, Edward O., Jr. ....Conifer, CO
Kassman, Martin ....San Francisco, CA
Kassmeier, Randolf F. ....New Orleans, LA
Kassner, Andrew C. ....Philadelphia, PA
Kassner, Eileen B. ....Niskayuna, NY
Kassner, John A. ....Madison, WI
Kassner, Joshua J. ....Baltimore, MD
Kassner, Mark A. ....Niskayuna, NY
Kassner, Maureen Cummins
Mount Laurel, NJ
Kassner, Russell R. ....Uniondale, NY
Kassof, Andrew A. ....Chicago, IL
Kassof, Jacqueline R. ....Eatontown, NJ
Kassof, Sherman, Law Offices of
San Francisco, CA
Kassoff, Edwin ....Jamaica, NY
Kassoff, Eric S. ....Bethesda, MD
Kassoff, Mitchell J. ....South Orange, NJ
Kasson, Bruce M.
Department of Housing and Urban Development,
Office of General Counsel, GV
Kasson, Constantine D. ....Chicago, IL
Kasson, D. Patrick ....Dayton, OH
Kasson, Henry C. ....Fort Mitchell, KY
Cincinnati, OH
Kasson, Richard J. ....San Antonio, TX
Kasson, Tracy D. ....Wheaton, IL
Kassor, Eric H. ....Raleigh, NC
Kassos, John E., (P.A.) ....St. Petersburg, FL
Kassouf, Karen M. ....Houston, TX
Kassouf, LaVonne R. ....Cleveland, OH
Kassouf Prem, Jean E. ....Baltimore, MD
Kassouni, Timothy V. ....Laguna Niguel, CA
Kassover, Jeffrey M. ....Wayne, NJ
Kassover, Michael A. ....New City, NY
Kassover, Randi F. ....New York, NY
Kassow, Saul D. ....Fishkill, NY
Kassoy, Arnold D. ....Los Angeles, CA
Kassoy, David P. ....Beverly Hills, CA
Kass-Viola, Bonnie ....Toms River, NJ
Kass-Viola, Bonnie, P.C., Law Office of
Toms River, NJ
Kast, Andrea B. ....Jacksonville, FL
Kast, Daniel K. ....Hillsdale, NY
Kast, Ellen ....Clearwater, FL
Kast, Leslie A. ....Claremont, CA
Kast, Michael H. ....Fort Wayne, IN
Kast, Michael S. ....Orlando, FL
Kast, Paul E. ....Massapequa, NY
Kast, Peter A. ....White Plains, NY
Kast, Richard C. ....Charlottesville, VA
Kastama, Marlin L. ....Oakland, CA
Kastanakis, J. Reneé ....Atlanta, GA
Kastanek, Eugene E. ....Dallas, TX
Kastanes, George A. ....Gilbert, SC
Kast-Davids, Jana L. ....Santa Cruz, CA
Kastel, Howard L. ....Chicago, IL
Kastelic, David A.
Inver Grove Heights, MN
Kastelic, John A. ....Cleveland, OH
Kastelic, John W. ....Palo Alto, CA
Kastelic, Joseph M. ....Minneapolis, MN
Kastelic, Tara A. ....Cleveland, OH
Kastell, Paul Howard ....Brooklyn, NY
Kastellec, Philip ....New York, NY
Kastely, Amy H. ....Honolulu, HI
Kasten, A. Christopher, II ....Tampa, FL
Kasten, Bruce J. ....Philadelphia, PA
Kasten, Carl E. ....Carlinville, IL
Kasten, Catherine Lynn
West Palm Beach, FL

Kasten, Daniel D. ... Chicago, IL
Kasten, Elihu ... Oceanside, NY
Kasten, Herbert A., Jr. ... Columbia, MO
Kasten, Jack ... Newton, MA
Kasten, Jack ... Brooklyn, NY
Kasten, Jeffrey C. ... Chicago, IL
Kasten, Jody ... New York, NY
Kasten, John J. ... Cherry Hill, NJ
Kasten, Leslie L., Jr. ... Philadelphia, PA
Kasten, Michael Jay ... Manchester, NH
Kasten, Robert I. ... St. Petersburg, FL
Kasten, Sandra J. ... Albany, CA
Kasten, Sheila J. ... Brooklyn, NY
Kasten, Stanley H. ... Atlanta, GA
Kasten, Steven W. ... Boston, MA
Kasten, Walter H. ... Springfield, IL
Kastenbaum, Ely ... Tacoma, WA
Kastenbaum, Robert G. ... Richmond, VA
Kastenberg, Stephen J. ... Philadelphia, PA
Kastenholz, Peter A. ... Wisconsin Rapids, WI
Kastenson, Daryl A. ... Milwaukee, WI
Kaster, Bruce R. ... Ocala, FL
Kaster, Craig L. ... Baton Rouge, LA
Kaster, Daniel Ray ... Springfield, MN
Kaster, Eugene W. ... San Francisco, CA
Kaster, James H. ... Minneapolis, MN
Kaster, Kevin R. ... Palo Alto, CA
Kaster, Laura A. ... Liberty Corner, NJ
Kaster, Lewis R. ... New York, NY
Kaster, Mark R. ... Minneapolis, MN
Kaster, Paul A. ... Richfield, MN
Kaster, Robert F. ... Yreka, CA
Kaster, Suzy C. ... San Francisco, CA
Kaster, Thomas J. ... San Francisco, CA
Kastetter, Laura G. ... Littleton, CO
Kastetter, Todd E. ... Denver, CO
Kastigar, Elizabeth Ann ... Atlanta, GA
Kastin, David M. ... New York, NY
Kastin, Robert ... Mineola, NY
Kasting, Combs & Kauffman, P.C.
Bozeman, MT
Helena, MT
Kasting, Kent M. ... Bozeman, MT
Kasting, Margaret L. ... St. Paul, MN
Kasting, Peter Alan ... Portland, OR
Kastl, Robert J. ... Treasury Department, Internal Revenue Service, GV
Kastle, David A. ... Lynnwood, WA
Kastle, Michael J. ... Delray Beach, FL
Kastler, B. Z., Jr. ... Salt Lake City, UT
Kastler, Paul A. ... Raton, NM
Kastler, William V. ... Albuquerque, NM
Kastner, Adam B. ... Los Angeles, CA
Kastner, Cynthia A. ... Morristown, NJ
Kastner, Elizabeth Gelfand ... Mineola, NY
Kastner, Eric C. ... Mountain View, CA
Kastner, Harley M. ... Cleveland, OH
North Canton, OH
Kastner, Henry E. ... Seattle, WA
Kastner, Jeffrey L. ... Blue Jay, CA
Kastner, John H. ... Menomonee Falls, WI
Kastner, Joseph C. ... Norco, CA
Kastner, Kenneth M. ... Washington, DC
Kastner, Menachem J. ... New York, NY
Kastner, Mitchell ... Red Bank, NJ
Kastner, Robert B. ... New York, NY
Kastner, Samuel P. ... Washington, DC
Kastner, Steven I. ... San Diego, CA
Kastner, Stuart P. ... Seattle, WA
Kastner, Tal ... New York, NY
Kastner, Timothy E. ... St. Louis, MO
Kaston & Aberle ... Brooklyn, NY
Kaston, David E. ... Brooklyn, NY
Kaston, David M. ... New York, NY
Kaston, Rhea ... Staten Island, NY
Kastor, Bruce B. ... Albany, NY
Kastran, Stephen A. ... Allegan, MI
Kastrenakes, John S. ... West Palm Beach, FL
Kastriner, Lawrence G. ... Danbury, CT
Kastrinsky, Howard M. ... Nashville, TN
Kastrup, Amy Evans ... Dayton, OH
Kasubick, Girard ... Philipsburg, PA
Kasulis, Jeanine M. ... Philadelphia, PA
Kasunic, Carl P. ... Willoughby, OH
Kasunic, Carl P., Co., L.P.A.
Willoughby, OH
Kasunic, David E. ... Detroit, MI
Kasunic, Robert J. ... Darnestown, MD
Kasuri, Kuldip S. ... Jackson Heights, NY
Kaswan, Beth ... New York, NY
Kaswell, Joel R. ... Washington, DC
Kaswell, Sherry Kinland
Department Of The Interior, Office of the Solicitor, GV
Kaswell, Stuart J. ... Washington, DC
Kaszak, Nancy L. ... Chicago, IL
Kaszczuk, Robert E. ... San Antonio, TX
Kaszovitz, Gabriel ... New York, NY
Kaszovitz, Naomi Lynn Skolnick
Jamaica, NY
Kaszovitz, Saul M. ... New York, NY
Kasztelewicz, Jolanta A. ... Encino, CA
Kaszuba, Kim Lora ... Dunedin, FL
Kaszuba, Valentin K. ... Chicago, IL
Kaszubowski, Loren J. ... Prospect Heights, IL
Kaszynski, William P. ... St. Paul, MN
Kaszynski, William P., P.A. ... St. Paul, MN
Katague, Diosdado D. ... Martinez, CA
Katahara, Nils P. S. ... Honolulu, HI
Katahira, Wesley
Equal Employment Opportunity Commission, Office of the General Counsel, GV
Katakis, Karla W. ... Louisville, KY
Katalbas, Eduardo B. ... Encino, CA
Katalinic, Marc F. ... Chicago, IL
Katano, Wade J. ... Honolulu, HI
Kataoka, Mark M.
Environmental Protection Agency, Office of the General Counsel, GV
Katarikawe, Andrew Mutabaazi ... Denver, CO
Katarincic, Amy D. ... Milwaukee, WI
Katarincic, Joseph A. ... Pittsburgh, PA
Wheeling, WV
Katarincic Law Office ... Milwaukee, WI
Katarincic, Michael J. ... Milwaukee, WI
Katarincic & Salmon ... Pittsburgh, PA
Wheeling, WV
Katarzis, Frank L. ... Dearborn, MI
Katauskas, Anthony P. ... Chicago, IL
Katauskas, Philip J. ... Philadelphia, PA
Katayama, Alyce C. ... Milwaukee, WI
Katayama, Arthur S. ... Los Angeles, CA
Katayama, Imogene M. N. ... Los Angeles, CA
Katayama, Robert N. ... Honolulu, HI
Katayama, Yoshio ... San Jose, CA
Katcef, Neal B. ... Annapolis, MD
Katch, Michael E. ... Denver, CO
Katch, Michael E., P.C. ... Denver, CO
Katchem, Robyn I. ... Riverside, CA
Katchen, Robert C. ... Torrance, CA
Katchen, William S. ... Roseland, NJ
Katcher, Bruce S. ... Cherry Hill, NJ
Bala Cynwyd, PA
Katcher, Daryl B. ... Sacramento, CA
Katcher, Gerald ... Miami, FL
Katcher, James J. ... Sioux City, IA
Katcher, Jonathon A. ... Anchorage, AK
Katcher, Paul ... New York, NY
Katcher, Richard ... Cleveland, OH
Katcher, Richard D. ... New York, NY
Katcher, Robert A. ... Washington, DC
Katcher, Robert J. ... Port Washington, NY
Katcher, Ronald Aaron ... Cherry Hill, NJ
Media, PA
Katchka, Elizabeth H.
Federal Emergency Management Agency, Office of the General Counsel, GV
Katchke, Robert D. ... Southfield, MI
Katchmark, Michael R. ... Norfolk, VA
Katchmer, Paula B. ... Lancaster, PA
Katchur, Jeanne Boyer ... Wernersville, PA
Katcoff, Fredda ... Montclair, NJ
Katcoff, Joel ... New York, NY
Kate, Patricia Ann ... Fairfax, VA
Katel, Kenneth G. ... Los Angeles, CA
Katelman, John S. ... Omaha, NE
Kateman, Jeffrey L. ... Los Angeles, CA
Katen, Gilbert ... Los Angeles, CA
Katen, Harlan L. ... Philadelphia, PA
Katen, Michael W. ... Falls Church, VA
Kater, H. Janet ... East Liverpool, OH
Kater, Karmen M. ... Baltimore, MD
Kater, Susie J. ... San Diego, CA
Katerndahl, John P. ... San Francisco, CA
Katerndahl, Richard G. ... San Rafael, CA
Katers, Daniel J. ... Green Bay, WI
Kates, Adam C. ... Palo Alto, CA
Kates, Darryl M. ... Cincinnati, OH
Kates, David ... Philadelphia, PA
Kates, David J. ... Chicago, IL
Kates & Davis ... Bakersfield, CA
Kates, Don B., Jr. ... San Francisco, CA
Kates, Donald S. ... Rutherford, NJ
Kates, E. Laurence ... Philadelphia, PA
Kates, George W. ... Bakersfield, CA
Kates, Henry R. ... Providence, RI
Kates, Katharine A. ... Santa Monica, CA
Kates, Kenneth H. ... Houston, TX
Kates, Lawrence ... Los Angeles, CA
Kates, Lester G. ... Coral Gables, FL
Kates, Mary C. ... Yonkers, NY
Kates, Michael B. ... Hackensack, NJ
Kates, Nathan ... Encino, CA
Kates, Raymond C. ... Bradenton, FL
Kates, Richard M. ... Chicago, IL
Kates, Rick D. ... Cincinnati, OH
Kates, Robert J. ... Boston, MA
Kates, Roy A. ... Calabasas, CA
Kates, Thomas C. ... Ludington, MI
Kates, Wrenn Terrill ... St. Louis, MO
Katevatis, Peter ... Cherry Hill, NJ
Kath, R. Scott ... Powell, WY
Kath, Susan M. ... New York, NY
Kathan, Ann Nicole ... Alexandria, VA
Kathawala, Rene ... New York, NY
Kathe, Steven R. ... Palatine, IL
Kathe, Thomas ... Costa Mesa, CA
Katheder, Thomas ... Lake Buena Vista, FL
Katherman, Briggs & Greenberg
York, PA
Katherman & Heim, P.C. ... York, PA
Katherman, J. Robert ... York, PA
Katherman, R. Elliot ... York, PA
Katherman, Ralph D. ... Norfolk, VA
Katherman, Ralph D., P.C. ... Norfolk, VA
Kathiwala, Penelope A. ... Worcester, MA
Kathka, Alvin R. ... Merced, CA
Kathman, Debra G. ... Bethesda, MD
Kathman, William J., Jr. ... Florence, KY
Kathrein, Reed R. ... San Francisco, CA
Kathren, Daniel F. ... Richland, WA
Katibah, John Tyler ... Medford, OR
Katic, Peter ... Hammond, IN
Katica, Lorna Sills ... Atlanta, GA
Katich, Douglas J. ... Fair Haven, NJ
Katich, Nick ... Merrillville, IN
Katich, Werse and Petillo ... Fair Haven, NJ
Katich, William M. ... Staunton, IL
Katila, Ronald H. ... Pittsburgh, PA
Katims, Joel D. ... South Setauket, NY
Katims, Joel D., P.C. ... South Setauket, NY
Katims, Neil A. ... Miami, FL
Katims, Robert W. ... Burlington, VT
Katina, Michele Russell
Department Of Veterans Affairs, Office of the General Counsel, GV
Katinas, Anastasia ... Chicago, IL
Katine, Mitchell ... Houston, TX
Katine, Sanford D. ... Knoxville, TN
Katinsky, David M. ... Department of Justice, Tax Division, GV
Katirai, Mahmoud ... Washington, DC
Katkin, Alan S. ... Staten Island, NY
Katkin, Burton K. ... New York, NY
Katkin, Elizabeth L. ... Washington, DC
Katkin, Faith Sharon ... Bothell, WA
Katkin, Kenneth D. ... Washington, DC
Katkish, Cynthia ... Washington, DC
Katkowsky, Lawrence S.
Bingham Farms, MI
Katkowsky, Lawrence S., P.C.
Bingham Farms, MI
Katlein, Daniel M. ... Detroit, MI
Katleman, Steven, (P.C.)
Beverly Hills, CA
Katler, Deborah M. ... Camarillo, CA
Katlic, Diane Kopcha ... Dallas, PA
Katlin, Andrew J. ... Wilmette, IL
Katlowitz, Moshe Y. ... New York, NY
Katner, Kevin J. ... New Orleans, LA
Katnik, Andrew P. ... Santa Ana, CA
Katnik, Eugene F. ... Santa Ana, CA
Katnik & Katnik ... Santa Ana, CA
Katnik, Norman Paul ... Santa Ana, CA
Kato, Allen M. ... San Francisco, CA
Kato, Ayano ... New York, NY
Kato, Berton T. ... Honolulu, HI
Kato, Christopher M. ... Nashville, TN
Kato, Dean M. ... Los Angeles, CA
Kato, Hiroshi ... Honolulu, HI
Kato, James T. ... Rancho Palos Verdes, CA
Kato, Joan S. ... Palo Alto, CA
Kato, Keith K. ... Honolulu, HI
Kato, Kenly K. ... Los Angeles, CA
Kato, Kenneth H. ... Spokane, WA
Kato, Maurice S. ... Honolulu, HI
Kato, Pamela K. ... Santa Cruz, CA
Kato, Russell S. ... Honolulu, HI
Kato, Sheila S. ... Beverly Hills, CA
Kato, Yoshihiro ... Washington, DC
Katofsky, Jeff ... Los Angeles, CA
Katon, Glenn M. ... Department of Justice, Tax Division, GV
Katon, Thomas E. ... New Haven, CT
Katona, Gabriel P. ... New York, NY
Katona, Les, Jr. ... San Antonio, TX
Katona, Raymond M. ... Herndon, VA
Katona, Scot A. ... Tappahannock, VA
Kator, Irving ... Washington, DC
Kator, Michael J. ... Washington, DC
Kator, Scott & Parks P.L.L.C.
Washington, DC
Austin, TX
Katos, Donna J. ... Houston, TX
Katovich, Kathleen D. ... Los Angeles, CA
Katowitz, Sarah P. ... Philadelphia, PA
Katrick, Joseph P. ... White Marsh, MD
Katriel, Roy A. ... Washington, DC
Katrinak, R. Paul ... Los Angeles, CA
Katris, Basileios ... Chicago, IL
Katris, Darcy M. ... New York, NY
Katron, Barbara A.
Federal Deposit Insurance Corporation, Criminal Restitution, GV
Katrosh, K. Scott ... Lexington, SC
Kats, James S. ... West Islip, NY
Kats, Jamison, Van Der Veen, & Associates
Cherry Hill, NJ
New York, NY
Feasterville, PA
Kats, Marina ... New York, NY
Feasterville, PA
Katsafanas, Vasilis C. ... Orlando, FL
Katsampes, Theodore P. ... Rochester, NY
Katsanis, James A. ... Cincinnati, OH
Katsantonis, Joanne ... Chicago, IL
Richmond, VA
Katsantonis, Vivian ... McLean, VA
Katsaounis, Christos A. ... Harrisburg, PA
Katsarakes, George P. ... Woburn, MA
Katsaros, Peter M. ... Chicago, IL
Katsas, Gregory G. ... Washington, DC
Katsell, Jerome H. ... Irvine, CA
Katsenes, Andrea ... Boston, MA
Katsenes, Chris W. ... Orland Park, IL
Katsenes, Sylvia ... Newton, MA
Katsenes, Wm. A. ... Newton, MA
Katsh, M. Ethan ... Amherst, MA
Katsh, Salem M. ... New York, NY
Katsiaficas, Donna M. ... Portland, ME
Katsiavelos, Linda ... Chicago, IL
Katsidhe, Katherine L. ... New York, NY
Katsiff, Timothy D. ... Philadelphia, PA
Katsinas, Scott A. ... Tucson, AZ
Katsis, Kevin G. ... Forest Park, IL
Katske, Kevin T. ... Stamford, CT
Katskee, Henatsch & Suing ... Omaha, NE
Katskee, Jerry W. ... Omaha, NE
Katskee, Melvin R. ... Omaha, NE
Katskee, Milton A. ... Omaha, NE
Katsky, David L. ... New York, NY
Katsky & Lyon, L.L.P. ... Los Angeles, CA
Katsky, Ronald L. ... Los Angeles, CA
Katsman, Aaron I. ... Far Rockaway, NY
Katsman, Abraham I. ... New York, NY
Katsman, Mark ... Miami, FL
Katsock, Andrew J., III ... Scranton, PA
Katsonis, Nicholas ... Worcester, MA
Katsorhis, Kerry J. ... Flushing, NY
Katsoris, Constantine M. ... Wellesley, MA
Katsoris, Constantine N. ... New York, NY
Katsoris, Louis C. ... New York, NY
Katsoris, Nicholas C. ... New York, NY
Katsos, Barbara H. ... New York, NY
Katsoudas, George K. ... Chicago, IL
Katsoulos, John ... Sterling Heights, MI
Katsufrakis, M. Peter ... Tarzana, CA
Katsumes, T. David ... Elgin, IA
Katsurinis, Stephen A. ... Washington, DC
Katsuyama, Michael ... Chicago, IL
Katt, Faye L. ... Deerfield, IL
Katt, Peter A. ... Roanoke, VA
Katt, Peter W. ... Lincoln, NE
Katt, William J. ... Milwaukee, WI
Kattan, Joseph ... Washington, DC
Kattan, Susan J. ...
Administrative Office Of The United States Courts, GV
Kattar, Candace A. ... Washington, DC
Kattas, Paul L. ... Newark, NJ
Kattelman, Louis ... Philadelphia, PA
Kattelman, Michael V. ... Reno, NV
Kattelman, Stephanie ... Philadelphia, PA
Kattelmann, James G. ... Orlando, FL
Katten, Betsy L. ... Chicago, IL
Katten, Judith ... New York, NY
Katten, Melvin L., (P.C.) ... Chicago, IL
Katten, Mitchell B. ... Chicago, IL
Katten Muchin & Zavis ... Los Angeles, CA
Washington, DC
Chicago, IL
New York, NY
Katten, Pamela B. ... Trenton, NJ
Katten, Steven E. ... Fort Worth, TX
Kattenburg, P. Clark ... Fairfax, VA
Kattenburg, P. Clark, P.C. ... Fairfax, VA
Katter, Ronald J. ... New York, NY
Katterheinrich, Ted R. ... Seattle, WA
Katterle, Paul R. ... Cleveland, OH
Katterman, Lisa C. ... Harrisburg, PA
Kattman, John F. ... Jacksonville, FL
Kattman, John F., P.A. ... Jacksonville, FL
Kattner, Conrad O. ... Philadelphia, PA
Kattner, Kenric D. ... Houston, TX
Kattner, Steve ... Longview, TX
Kattwinkel, Linda Joy ... San Francisco, CA
Katubig, Belle L. ... Chicago, IL
Katula, Sharon E. ... Washington, DC
Katulak, Francis J. ... Mattituck, NY
Katyal, Neal ... Department of Justice, Office of the Deputy Attorney General, GV
Katz, A. Alexander ... Phoenix, AZ
Katz, A. Larry ... Minneapolis, MN
Katz, A. Sidney ... Chicago, IL
Arlington, VA
Katz, Aaron H. ... San Diego, CA
Katz, Aaron I. ... Houston, TX
Katz, Aaron L. ... Saratoga, CA
Katz, Adam ... Great Neck, NY
Katz, Adam J. ... New York, NY
Katz, Adam Louis ... Philadelphia, PA
Katz, Adam M. ... New York, NY
Katz, Alan ... Boston, MA
Katz, Alan ... New York, NY
Katz, Alan ... Richmond, VA
Katz, Alan A. ... Encino, CA
Katz, Alan A., A Professional Law Corporation
Encino, CA
Katz, Alan B. ... Farmingdale, NY
Katz, Alan B. ... New York, NY
Katz, Alan Charles ... Westminster, CO
Katz, Alan D. ... Chicago, IL
Katz, Alan E. ... New York, NY
Katz, Alan F. ... Garden City, NY
Katz, Alan G. ... New York, NY
Katz, Alan H. ... New Orleans, LA
Katz, Alan H. ... Boston, MA
Katz, Alan M. ... Springfield, MA
Katz, Alan R. ... Islandia, NY
Katz, Alayne ... Irvington, NY
Katz, Alfred B. ... Cincinnati, OH
Katz, Aliza F.
Federal Communications Commission, Office of the General Counsel, GV
Katz, Allan ... Philadelphia, PA
Katz, Allan J. ... Tallahassee, FL
Katz, Allan S. ... Indianapolis, IN
Katz, Allen J. ... Gaithersburg, MD
Katz, Alvin Charles ... Chicago, IL
Katz, Amy B. ... New York, NY
Katz, Amy Lynn ... New York, NY
Katz, Amy Lynn ... New York, NY
Katz, Andrew ... Westwood, NJ
Katz, Andrew B. ... Washington, DC
Katz, Andrew E., (A Professional Corporation) ... Los Angeles, CA
Katz, Andrew S. ... Washington, DC
Katz, Anne ... New York, NY
Katz, April L. ... West Orange, NJ
Katz, Argenio & Powers ... Springfield, MA
Katz, Arie P. ... Newport Beach, CA
Katz, Arlene E. ... Bronx, NY
Katz, Arnold I. ... New York, NY
Katz, Aron B. ... Boulder, CO
Katz, Arthur ... New York, NY
Katz, Arthur A. ... New York, NY
Katz, Arthur H. ... Toledo, OH
Katz, Arthur J. ... Los Angeles, CA
Katz, Arthur M. ... Los Angeles, CA
Katz, Arthur P. ... San Bernardino, CA
Katz, Arthur S. ... Brooklyn, NY
Katz, Arthur S. ... New York, NY
Katz, Arthur Stanley ... Paso Robles, CA
Katz, Ascher ... White Plains, NY
Katz & Associates ... Los Angeles, CA
Katz & Associates ... Englewood, CO
Katz & Associates ... Rockville, MD
Katz & Associates ... Boston, MA
Katz, Audrey S. ... New York, NY

Katz, Avery ... Ann Arbor, MI
Katz, Avi ... New York, NY
Katz, B. Kaye ... Brunswick, GA
Katz, B. Paul ... Palm Coast, FL
Katz, B. Paul, P.A. ... Palm Coast, FL
Katz & Baehre ... Buffalo, NY
Katz, Balch, Lefstein, Fieweger & Edwards, P.C. ... Rock Island, IL
Davenport, IA
Katz, Barbara A. ... Sacramento, CA
Katz, Barbara E. ... Decatur, GA
Katz, Barbara F. ... Boston, MA
Katz, Barbara Hadley ... New Haven, CT
Katz, Barbara J.
Securities and Exchange Commission, Division of Enforcement, GV
Katz, Barbara Silber ... San Diego, CA
Katz, Barron, Squitero, Faust & Berman, P.A. ... Fort Lauderdale, FL
Miami, FL
Katz, Barry L. ... Atlanta, GA
Katz, Barry M. ... Kansas City, MO
Katz, Barry M. ... New York, NY
Katz, Barry R. ... Chicago, IL
Katz, Belinda I. ... Mineola, NY
New York, NY
White Plains, NY
Katz, Benjamin Robert ... White Plains, NY
Katz, Bennett ... West Paterson, NJ
Katz, Bennett L. ... Los Angeles, CA
Katz, Bennett R. ... San Francisco, CA
Katz, Bennett R. ... New York, NY
Katz, Bernard ... Chicago, IL
Katz, Bernard ... Elkhart, IN
Katz, Bernard ... Mohegan Lake, NY
Katz, Bernard N. ... Philadelphia, PA
Katz, Bertram ... Bronx, NY
Katz, Beth E. ... Dunedin, FL
Katz, Beverly I. ... New York, NY
Katz, Beverly J.Brimmer ... Huron, SD
Katz, Beverly Moses ... Treasury Department, Internal Revenue Service, GV
Katz & Brenman ... Merrillville, IN
Katz, Brian D. ... New Orleans, LA
Katz, Brian L. ... Cherry Hill, NJ
Katz, Brian M. ... Philadelphia, PA
Katz, Brian R. ... Sacramento, CA
Katz, Bruce D. ... Westport, CT
Katz, Bruce D., P.C. ... Westport, CT
Katz, Bruce David ... Great Neck, NY
New York, NY
Katz, Bruce J. ... Pawtucket, RI
Katz, Bruce Jonathan ... United States Senate, Committee Legal Personnel, GV
Katz, Bruce M. ... Chicago, IL
Katz, Bruno W. ... San Diego, CA
Katz, Burton ... Hauppauge, NY
Katz, Burton A. ... Cleveland, OH
Katz, Carl R. ... Washington, DC
Katz, Carol Hecht ... San Francisco, CA
Katz, Carol Smith ... Memphis, TN
Katz, Carole S. ... Pittsburgh, PA
Katz, Caroline S. ... Atlanta, GA
Katz, Charles B. ... Palo Alto, CA
Katz, Charles J., Jr. ... Seattle, WA
Katz, Charles L. ... Houston, TX
Katz, Charles R., (P.C.) ... Tamarac, FL
Katz, Charles S., Jr. ... Philadelphia, PA
Katz, Charles W. ... McLean, VA
Katz, Cherol B. ... Cypress, CA
Katz, Chester N. ... Silver Spring, MD
Katz, Clifford A. ... Gibbsboro, NJ
New York, NY
Katz, Clifford E. ... New York, NY
Katz, Craig Dean ... Washington, DC
Katz, Curtis ... Great Neck, NY
Katz, Cynthia Lynn ... Allentown, PA
Katz, Daniel E. ... Riverside, CA
Katz, Daniel E. ... Washington, DC
Katz, Daniel E. ... New York, NY
Katz, Daniel Franklin ... Washington, DC
Katz, Daniel J. ... Rockville, MD
Katz, Daniel J. ... Milwaukee, WI
Katz, Daniel M. ... Washington, DC
Katz, Daniel M. ... Cleveland, OH
Katz, Daniel R. ... Cambridge, MA
Katz, Daniel S. ... Baltimore, MD
Katz, Daniel S. ... New York, NY
Katz, Darren J. ... Atlanta, GA
Katz, David ... Northbrook, IL
Katz, David ... New York, NY
Katz, David A. ... Los Angeles, CA
Katz, David A. ... New York, NY
Katz, David A. ... Cleveland, OH
Katz, David A. ... Toledo, OH
Katz, David C. ... New York, NY
Katz, David H. ... San Francisco, CA
Katz, David H. ... Brooklyn, NY
Katz, David J., (A Professional Corporation)
Los Angeles, CA
Katz, David L. ... San Diego, CA
Katz, David L. ... Washington, DC
Katz, David, Ltd. ... Northbrook, IL
Katz, David M. ... New York, NY
Katz, David M. ... Bluefield, WV
Katz, David S. ... Washington, DC
Katz, David S. ... Newton, MA
Katz, David S. ... Norristown, PA
Katz, Dawn Ross ... Louisville, KY
Katz, Deborah ... Treasury Department, Office of the Comptroller of the Currency, GV
Katz, Deborah A. ... Burlington, MA
Katz, Deborah Ann ... Columbus, OH
Katz, Deborah J. ... Washington, DC
Katz, Debra Susan ... Washington, DC
Katz, Dennis R. ... New York, NY
Katz, Diane ... Chicago, IL
Katz, Diane S. ... Rochester, NY
Katz, Donald ... Cranbury, NJ
Katz, Donald H. ... Boston, MA
Katz, Donald L. ... Turnersville, NJ
Katz, Donald L., A Professional Corporation
Turnersville, NJ
Katz, Douglas J. ... Mineola, NY
Katz, Duane M. ... Omaha, NE
Katz, Edward C. ... Valley Stream, NY
Katz, Edward Michael ... San Francisco, CA
New York, NY
Katz, Eileen ... Buffalo, NY
Katz, Eileen Giordano ... Philadelphia, PA
Katz, Elai E. ... New York, NY
Katz, Eli ... Roslyn Heights, NY
Katz, Eli M. ... Moreno Valley, CA
Katz, Elin Swanson ... Hartford, CT
Katz, Eliot J. ... Rochester, NY
Katz, Elissa B. ... Philadelphia, PA
Katz, Elkan M. ... Philadelphia, PA
Katz, Ellen C. ... Brooklyn, NY
Katz, Ellen D. ... Department of Justice, Environment and Natural Resources Division, GV
Katz, Elliott A. ... Wilmington, DE
Katz, Elliott L. ... Bernardsville, NJ
New York, NY
Katz, Ellis H. ... Doylestown, PA
Katz, Eric D. ... Livingston, NJ
Katz, Eric M. ... Baltimore, MD
Katz, Eric R. ... Marietta, GA
Katz, Erica S. ... New York, NY
Katz, Erwin I. ... Chicago, IL
Katz, Ettin, Levine, Kurzweil & Weber, P.A. ... Cherry Hill, NJ
Katz, Eugene J. ... Wellington, OH
Katz, Eugene M. ... Charlotte, NC
Katz, Evan H. ... New York, NY
Katz, Farley P. ... San Antonio, TX
Katz, Flatau, Popson & Boyer, L.L.P.
Macon, GA
Katz, Francine Halushka ... Morristown, NJ
Katz, Francine I. ... St. Louis, MO
Katz, Frank D. ... Santa Fe, NM
Katz, Friedman, Schur & Eagle, Chartered ... Chicago, IL
Katz, Gail ... Chicago, IL
Katz, Gary J. ... New York, NY
Katz, Gary M. ... New York, NY
Katz, George Ira ... Greenwood Village, CO
Katz, George L. ... Los Angeles, CA
Katz, Gerald I. ... Washington, DC
Rockville, MD
Vienna, VA
Katz, Gerald J. ... New York, NY
Katz, Gerald M. ... Towson, MD
Katz, Geraldine Foucault
Treasury Department, Internal Revenue Service, GV
Katz, Gilbert ... New York, NY
Katz, Glenn L. ... Jacksonville, FL
Katz, Gloria J. ... Los Angeles, CA
Katz, Golden & Sullivan, LLP
Los Angeles, CA
Katz, Gordon P. ... Boston, MA
Katz, Greenberger & Norton
Covington, KY
Cincinnati, OH
Katz, Gregory ... New York, NY
Katz, Gregory S. ... New York, NY
Katz, Greta ... Jamaica Plain, MA
Katz & Griffin, LLP, The Law Offices of
Sacramento, CA
Katz, H. Alan ... Indio, CA
Katz, Hadrian R. ... Washington, DC
Katz, Hal S. ... Austin, TX
Katz, Harold A. ... Chicago, IL
Katz, Harriet ... Albany, NY
Katz, Harriet N. ... Camden, NJ
Katz, Harry I. ... Fresh Meadows, NY
Katz, Harry, Jr. ... Jacksonville, FL
Katz, Harvey A. ... Glastonbury, CT
Katz, Harvey M. ... New York, NY
Katz, Henry ... Hartford, CT
Katz, Henry D. ... Sharon, MA
Katz, Henry H. ... Pawtucket, RI
Katz, Henry J. ... Suffern, NY
Katz, Herbert ... Los Angeles, CA
Katz, Herbert ... Fort Lee, NJ
Katz, Herbert ... Pawtucket, RI
Katz, Herbert D. ... Hollywood, FL
Katz, Herbert W. ... New York, NY
Katz, Howard E. ... Arlington, VA
Katz, Howard F. ... Northridge, CA
Katz, Howard G. ... Warren, NJ
Katz, Howard J. ... Los Angeles, CA
Katz, Howard J. ... West Long Branch, NJ
Katz, Howard L. ... Houston, TX
Katz, Howard M. ... Farmingdale, NY
Katz, I. Jay ... Wilmington, DE
Katz, Ira Benjamin ... Los Angeles, CA
Katz, Ira Benjamin, A Prof. Corp., Law Offices of ... Los Angeles, CA
Katz, Ira Jay ... New York, NY
Katz, Isadore B. ... Washington, DC
Katz, Israel C. ... Memphis, TN
Katz, Ivan M. ... New Haven, CT
Katz, J. Michael ... Merrillville, IN
Katz, Jack ... Los Angeles, CA
Katz, Jack ... San Diego, CA
Katz, Jack ... Canton, MA
Katz, Jack ... Seattle, WA
Katz, James ... Cherry Hill, NJ
Northfield, NJ
Katz, James L. ... Rockville, CT
Katz, James L. ... Chicago, IL
Katz, James Lee ... Owings Mills, MD
Katz, James M. ... Secaucus, NJ
Katz, James V. ... Department of Justice, Criminal Division, GV
Katz, Jamie W. ... Boston, MA
Katz, Janet F. ... Department of Justice, Civil Division, GV
Katz, Janyce ... Columbus, OH
Katz, Jared M. ... Los Angeles, CA
Katz, Jason H. ... Chicago, IL
Katz, Jason L. ... Los Angeles, CA
Katz, Jason M. ... Milwaukee, WI
Katz, Jay A. ... New York, NY
Katz, Jeffrey A. ... Phoenix, AZ
Katz, Jeffrey A. ... Los Angeles, CA
Katz, Jeffrey A. ... Miami, FL
Katz, Jeffrey A. ... New York, NY
Katz, Jeffrey A. ... New York, NY
Katz, Jeffrey B. ... Michigan City, IN
Katz, Jeffrey C. ... New York, NY
Katz, Jeffrey D. ... Rockville, MD
Katz, Jeffrey H. ... Englewood, CO
Katz, Jeffrey H. ... Springfield, NJ
Katz, Jeffrey H. ... Buffalo, NY
Katz, Jeffrey H., P.C. ... Englewood, CO
Katz, Jeffrey L. ... Dresher, PA
Katz, Jeffrey M. ... New York, NY
Katz, Jeffrey Mark ... Clearwater, FL
Katz, Jeffrey S. ... Tucson, AZ
Katz, Jeffrey S. ... Arlington Heights, IL
Katz, Jennifer L. ... Albany, NY
Katz, Jeremy W. ... Burlingame, CA
San Francisco, CA
Katz, Jerome C. ... New York, NY
Katz, Jerome I. ... New York, NY
Katz, Jerome M. ... Chicago, IL
Katz, Jerome M. ... Baltimore, MD
Katz, Jerome M. ... Lawrenceville, NJ
Katz, Jerrold C. ... Englewood, CO
Boston, MA
Katz, Jerry A. ... Manhattan Beach, CA
Katz, Jerry P. ... Springfield, MA
Katz, Jesse L. ... Pittsburgh, PA
Katz, Jessica L. ... Washington, DC
Katz, Jill M. ... Kansas City, MO
Katz, Joan K. ... Greenfield, MA
Katz, Joel A. ... Atlanta, GA
Katz, Joel H. ... Raleigh, NC
Katz, Joel L. ... Annapolis, MD
Katz, Joel L., P.A. ... Annapolis, MD
Baltimore, MD
Katz, John ... New York, NY
Katz, John S. L.
Federal Energy Regulatory Commission, Office of the General Counsel, GV
Katz, John W. ... Washington, DC
Katz, Jonas B. ... Cincinnati, OH
Katz, Jonas B., Co., L.P.A. ... Cincinnati, OH
Katz, Jonathan ... New Haven, CT
Katz, Jonathan D. ... Poughkeepsie, NY
Katz, Jonathan E. ... New York, NY
Katz, Jonathan G.
Securities and Exchange Commission, Executive Staff, GV
Katz, Jonathan L. ... Silver Spring, MD
Katz, Jonathan S. ... New York, NY
Katz, Joseph ... Mineola, NY
Katz, Joshua ... Santa Rosa, CA
Katz, Joshua R. ... Coral Springs, FL
Katz, Joy A. ... Stamford, CT
Katz, Judith I.
National Labor Relations Board, Office of the General Counsel, GV
Katz, Judith T. ... Indianapolis, IN
Katz, Julie A. ... Chicago, IL
Katz, Julie Frances ... Birmingham, AL
Katz, Julie Kechner ... Belleville, IL
Katz, K. Dianne ... Albuquerque, NM
Katz, Kantor & Perkins ... Bluefield, WV
Princeton, WV
Katz, Kara S. ... New City, NY
Katz, Karen ... Miami, FL
Katz, Karen ... Boston, MA
Katz, Karen E. ... Oakland, CA
Katz, Katheryn D. ... Albany, NY
Katz & Katz ... Hartford, CT
Jacksonville, FL
New York, NY
Toledo, OH
Katz, Kenneth B. ... Hartford, CT
Katz, Kenneth B. ... West Hartford, CT
Katz, Kenneth M. ... Bayside, NY
Katz, Keri G. ... San Diego, CA
Katz, Kerry-Lynn ... Melville, NY
Katz & Klein ... Croton-On-Hudson, NY
White Plains, NY
Katz & Korin, Professional Corporation
Indianapolis, IN
Katz, Kutter, Haigler, Alderman, Bryant & Yon ... Orlando, FL
Tallahassee, FL
Katz & Lapides, A Prof. Corp. ... Capitola, CA
Katz, Larry ... Baltimore, MD
Katz, Larry A. ... San Jose, CA
Katz, Laura L. ... Baltimore, MD
Katz, Laurence M. ... Baltimore, MD
Katz Law Offices ... San Francisco, CA
Katz, Lawrence ... Denver, CO
Katz, Lawrence ... New York, NY
Katz, Lawrence A. ... Phoenix, AZ
Katz, Lawrence A. ... Washington, DC
Katz, Lawrence A. ... Bala Cynwyd, PA
Katz, Lawrence D. ... Wayne, NJ
Katz, Lawrence E. ... Newton, MA
Katz, Lawrence G. ... Martinez, CA
Katz, Lawrence H. ... New York, NY
Katz, Lawrence H., (P.A.) ... Maitland, FL
Katz, Lawrence K. ... Garden City, NY
Katz, Lawrence M. ... Washington, DC
Baltimore, MD
Katz, Lawrence, P.C. ... Denver, CO
Katz, Lawrence R. ... Boston, MA
Katz, Lawrence S. ... Miami, FL
Katz, Lawrence S. ... Sterling Heights, MI
Katz, Lawrence S. ... Milwaukee, WI
Katz, Lawrence S., P.A. ... Miami, FL
Katz, Lawrence W. ... Arlington, VA
Katz, Lawrence William ... Prescott, AZ
Katz, Lawrence William, Lawyer, Ltd.
Prescott, AZ
Katz, Leigh Julia ... Kew Gardens, NY
Katz, Leo ... Ann Arbor, MI
Katz, Leon ... Los Angeles, CA
Philadelphia, PA
Katz, Leon W. ... White Plains, NY
Katz, Leonard S. ... Santa Fe, NM
Katz, Leslie Panzer ... Livingston, NJ
Katz, Leslie R. ... San Francisco, CA
Katz, Lester ... Hartford, CT
Katz, Lester A. ... Washington, DC
Katz, Lester A., Chartered
Washington, DC
Katz, Lewis ... Cherry Hill, NJ
Katz, Lewis R. ... Cleveland, OH
Katz, Linda Badash ... Newark, NJ
New York, NY
Katz, Linda F. ... Forest Hills, NY
Katz, Linda G. ... Boston, MA
Katz, Linda S. ... Miami, FL
Katz, Lisa B. ... New York, NY
Katz, Look & Moison, Professional Corporation ... Denver, CO
Katz, Lori B. ... New York, NY
Katz, Lori E. ... Hackensack, NJ
New York, NY
Katz, Louis ... San Francisco, CA
Katz, Louis C. ... Boston, MA
Katz, Louis E. ... Poland, OH
Katz, Louis H. ... Cincinnati, OH
Katz, Louis Meyer ... Hollywood, FL
Katz, Lucy V. ... Fairfield, CT
Katz, Lynn D. P. ... Hartford, CT
Katz, M. Marvin ... Houston, TX
Katz, M. Taylor ... Santa Ana, CA
Katz & Manka, Ltd. ... Minneapolis, MN
Katz, Marc D. ... San Francisco, CA
Katz, Marc D. ... Dallas, TX
Katz, Marc P. ... King Of Prussia, PA
Katz, Marc S. ... Los Angeles, CA
Katz, Marcel ... Lafayette, IN
Katz, Marjorie A. ... Westborough, MA
Katz, Mark D. ... Leawood, KS
Kansas City, MO
Katz, Mark D. ... Cleveland, OH
Katz, Mark F. ... Stamford, CT
Katz, Mark L. ... Kew Gardens, NY
Katz, Mark M. ... Washington, DC
Katz, Mark S. ... Los Angeles, CA
Katz, Mark S. ... Las Vegas, NV
Katz, Mark S. ... New York, NY
Katz, Martha Lessman ... Baltimore, MD
Columbia, MD
Katz, Martin B. ... Glenside, PA
Katz, Martin D. ... Los Angeles, CA
Katz, Martin D. ... Wayne, NJ
Katz, Martin H. ... Phoenix, AZ
Katz, Martin H. ... Rock Island, IL
Katz, Martin J. ... Denver, CO
Katz, Martin L. ... Chicago, IL
Arlington, VA
Katz, Martin L. ... Bloomfield Hills, MI
Katz, Martin S. ... Chicago, IL
Katz, Martin V. ... West Palm Beach, FL
Katz, Martin Z. N., A Professional Corporation ... Santa Monica, CA
Katz, Martin Z. N. ... Santa Monica, CA
Katz, Marvin ... New York, NY
Katz, Marvin ... Philadelphia, PA
Katz, Marvin E. ... Miami, FL
Katz, Marvin S., (A Professional Law Corporation) ... Los Angeles, CA
Katz, Mary Lou ... Los Angeles, CA
Katz, Mary Mendel ... Macon, GA
Katz, Matthew D. ... Fort Lauderdale, FL
Katz, Maureen M. ... Department of Justice, Environment and Natural Resources Division, GV
Katz, Maurice H. ... Los Angeles, CA
Katz, Maurice H., A Professional Law Corporation ... Los Angeles, CA
Katz, Melinda M. ... Thomasville, GA
Katz, Melinda McKeon ... Thomasville, GA
Katz, Melvin ... New York, NY
Katz, Melvin ... New York, NY
Katz, Melvin ... New York, NY
Katz, Melvin J. ... New York, NY
Katz, Melvin S. ... Hartford, CT
Katz, Meredith S. ... New York, NY
Katz, Michael ... Los Angeles, CA
Katz, Michael ... Cherry Hill, NJ
Katz, Michael A. ... Collinsville, IL
Katz, Michael A. ... Summit, NJ
Katz, Michael A. ... New York, NY
Katz, Michael A. ... New York, NY
Katz, Michael A. ... Murray, UT
Katz, Michael B. ... Springfield, MA
Katz, Michael B. ... St. Louis, MO
Katz, Michael D. ... Fort Lauderdale, FL
Miami, FL
Katz, Michael E. ... New Orleans, LA
Katz, Michael G. ... Denver, CO
Katz, Michael I. ... Oxnard, CA
Katz, Michael I. ... New York, NY
Katz, Michael J. ... Denver, CO
Katz, Michael L. ... Miami, FL
Katz, Michael L. ... White Plains, NY
Katz, Michael M. ... Denver, CO
Katz, Michael N. ... Philadelphia, PA

Katz, Michael P. .... **Minneapolis, MN**
Katz, Michael S. .... Avondale Estates, GA
Katz, Michele A. .... **New York, NY**
Katz, Michelle .... **Los Angeles, CA**
Katz, Michelle M. .... Universal City, CA
Katz, Michelle R. .... Jackson, NJ
Katz, Michelle S. .... **State College, PA**
Katz, Milton .... San Francisco, CA
Katz, Minna K. .... West Bloomfield, MI
Katz, Mitchell A. .... **Atlanta, GA**
Katz, Mitchell J. .... **Syracuse, NY**
Katz, Mitchell L. .... **New York, NY**
Katz, Mitchell R. .... **Miami, FL**
Katz, Mitchell W. .... **New York, NY**
Katz, Mordecai D. .... Englewood, NJ
Katz, Mortimer .... Maplewood, NJ
Katz, Mortimer .... New York, NY
Katz, Morton A. .... Flushing, NY
Katz, Morton H., (A Professional Law Corporation) .... **New Orleans, LA**
Katz, Morton N. .... Avon, CT
Katz, Murphy & Greenwald, A Professional Corporation .... **Pittsfield, MA**
Katz, Murray .... Glendale, NY
Katz, Myron B. .... Milwaukee, WI
Katz, Nancy J. .... Chicago, IL
Katz, Nancy S. .... **Detroit, MI**
Katz, Naomi .... Mahopac, NY
Katz, Naomi F. .... **Chicago, IL**
Lincolnwood, IL
Katz, Natalie L. .... Philadelphia, PA
Katz, Nathaniel .... New York, NY
Katz, Neal B. .... New York, NY
Katz, Neil B. .... **Torrance, CA**
Katz, Neil B. .... **Washington, DC**
Bethesda, MD
Katz, Neil B. .... **Rockville, MD**
Katz, Neil D. .... Westbury, NY
Katz, Norman .... **New York, NY**
Katz, Norman D. .... Birmingham, MI
Katz, Norman H. .... Baltimore, MD
Katz, Owen W. .... **Pittsburgh, PA**
Katz, P. André .... **Chicago, IL**
Katz, Pamela S. .... Albany, NY
Katz & Pantirer, A Professional Corporation
Deal, NJ
Union, NJ
Katz, Patrina .... Van Nuys, CA
Katz, Paul A. .... Phoenix, AZ
Katz, Paul D. .... Chicago, IL
Katz, Paul E. .... Santa Monica, CA
Katz, Paul N. .... **Houston, TX**
Katz, Paul R. .... **Santa Monica, CA**
Omaha, NE
Katz, Paul R. .... Kansas City, MO
Katz, Paula .... **New York, NY**
Katz, Peter .... **Boston, MA**
Katz, Peter A. .... St. Joseph, MI
Katz, Peter L. .... Tuckahoe, NY
Katz, Philip .... **Washington, DC**
Katz, Philip .... New York, NY
Katz, Philippe D. .... New York, NY
Katz, Phyllis C. .... **Richmond, VA**
Katz, Phyllis S. .... Chappaqua, NY
Katz, Ralph .... Oak Park, MI
Katz, Ralph P. .... Ardsley, NY
Katz Randall Weinberg & Richmond
Chicago, IL
Lombard, IL
Katz, Randolf W. .... **Irvine, CA**
Katz, Randolph S. .... Toledo, OH
Katz & Ranzman, P.C. .... **Washington, DC**
Katz, Rebecca M. .... **New York, NY**
Katz, Reuven J. .... **Cincinnati, OH**
Katz, Rhonda D. Kaplan .... Chicago, IL
Katz, Richard A.
Farm Credit Administration, Regulatory Enforcement Division, GV
Katz, Richard A. .... Atlanta, GA
Katz, Richard A. .... **Mamaroneck, NY**
Katz, Richard A. .... **New York, NY**
Katz, Richard A. .... Lancaster, PA
Katz, Richard A., P.C. .... Atlanta, GA
Katz, Richard Alan .... Leawood, KS
Katz, Richard B. .... **Kansas City, MO**
Katz, Richard B. .... Cleveland, OH
Katz, Richard C. .... **Tucson, AZ**
New York, NY
Katz, Richard C. .... Malvern, PA
Katz, Richard L. .... **Larkspur, CA**
Katz, Richard L. .... Coral Gables, FL
Katz, Richard L. .... New Orleans, LA
Katz, Richard L. .... **Cincinnati, OH**
Katz, Richard L., Co., L.P.A.
Cincinnati, OH
Katz, Richard L., Inc., Law Offices of
Larkspur, CA
Katz, Richard M. .... Pasadena, CA
Katz, Richard M. .... **Macon, GA**
Katz, Richard S. .... New York, NY
Katz, Richard W. .... **New York, NY**
Katz, Risa B. .... **Winter Park, FL**
Katz, Robert .... San Francisco, CA
Katz, Robert .... Westbury, NY
Katz, Robert A. .... Van Nuys, CA
Katz, Robert A. .... New Orleans, LA
Katz, Robert A. .... Bayside, NY
Katz, Robert B. .... **Hartford, CT**
Katz, Robert B. .... Chicago, IL
Katz, Robert D. .... Oxnard, CA
Katz, Robert D. .... **New York, NY**
Katz, Robert F. .... Los Angeles, CA
Katz, Robert H. .... **Columbus, OH**
Katz, Robert J. .... Washington, DC
Katz, Robert J. .... **New York, NY**
New York, NY
Katz, Robert J., P.C. .... Washington, DC
Katz, Robert Jay .... Capitola, CA
Katz, Robert M. .... New York, NY
Katz, Robert Neal .... **Atlanta, GA**
Katz, Robert S. .... Trumbull, CT
Katz, Robert S. .... **Washington, DC**
Katz, Robert S. .... **Honolulu, HI**
Katz, Robert S. .... New York, NY
Katz, Robert W. .... **Baltimore, MD**
Katz, Roberta Miller .... Suffern, NY
Katz, Roberta R. .... Palo Alto, CA
Katz Roberts & Baudier .... New Orleans, LA
Katz, Robin C. .... Newark, NJ
Katz, Robin J. .... **New York, NY**
Katz, Rochelle .... New York, NY
Katz, Roger J. .... **Augusta, ME**
Katz, Roger N. .... New York, NY
Katz, Ronald B. .... Owings Mills, MD
Katz, Ronald M. .... **Indianapolis, IN**
Katz, Ronald S. .... Beverly Hills, CA
Katz, Ronald S. .... **Palo Alto, CA**
San Francisco, CA
Katz, Ronald S. .... **New York, NY**
Katz & Ross .... **New York, NY**
Katz, Ross .... **New York, NY**
Katz & Rudnick, P.C. .... **Boston, MA**
Katz, Russell S. .... New York, NY
Katz, S. David .... Newton, MA
Katz, Samuel .... New York, NY
Katz, Sandra B. .... Tucson, AZ
Katz, Sandra C. .... **New York, NY**
Katz, Sanford M. .... New York, NY
Katz, Sanford N. .... Boston, MA
Katz, Sasson, Hoose & Turnbull
Springfield, MA
Katz, Saul S. .... Great Neck, NY
Katz, Scott S. .... **Tampa, FL**
Katz and Seligman .... **Hartford, CT**
Katz, Seth A. .... **New York, NY**
Katz, Seth H. .... Inglewood, CA
Katz, Seth M. .... **New York, NY**
Katz, Seth S. .... **Atlanta, GA**
Katz, Seymour .... Omaha, NE
Katz, Shalom Zev .... Los Angeles, CA
Katz, Sharon .... **New York, NY**
Katz, Shelby L. .... **Washington, DC**
Katz, Sheldon D. .... Riverhead, NY
Katz, Sherman A. .... **Fort Lauderdale, FL**
Katz, Sherman E. .... **Washington, DC**
Katz, Sherri L. .... **Flint, MI**
Katz, Sherri L., P.C. .... **Flint, MI**
Katz, Sheryl E. .... New York, NY
Katz, Sheryl L. .... Chatsworth, CA
Katz, Shlomo D. .... **Washington, DC**
Katz, Shoshana .... Baltimore, MD
Katz, Sidney Jack .... Minneapolis, MN
Katz, Sidney L. .... New York, NY
Katz, Sidney M. .... Memphis, TN
Katz, Solomon .... University Heights, OH
Katz, Stacey L. .... **Fort Wayne, IN**
Katz, Staci Flaxman .... **Raleigh, NC**
Katz, Stacy M. .... Monroe, NY
Katz, Stanley .... New York, NY
Katz, Stanley B. .... New York, NY
Katz, Stanley D. .... Houston, TX
Katz, Stanley H. .... Baltimore, MD
Katz, Stanley I. .... **New York, NY**
Katz, Stanley M. .... White Plains, NY
Katz, Stanley R. .... Deal, NJ
Katz, Stephanie A. .... Trenton, NJ
Katz, Stephen A. .... Lowell, MA
Katz, Stephen A. .... **San Antonio, TX**
Katz, Stephen F. .... **Fort Lauderdale, FL**
Katz, Stephen G. .... Chicago, IL
Katz, Stephen J. .... **Bastrop, LA**
Katz, Stephen K. .... Miami, FL
Katz, Stephen L. .... San Francisco, CA
Katz, Stephen M. .... **Atlanta, GA**
Katz, Stephen P. .... **New York, NY**
Katz, Stephen R. .... New York, NY
Katz, Steven .... **Los Angeles, CA**
Katz, Steven .... **Boston, MA**
Katz, Steven A. .... **East St. Louis, IL**
Katz, Steven B. .... **Los Angeles, CA**
Katz, Steven B. .... New York, NY
Katz, Steven D. .... Celebration, FL
Houston, TX
Katz, Steven D., A Prof. Corp., Law Offices of .... Celebration, FL
Houston, TX
Katz, Steven F. .... **Chicago, IL**
Katz, Steven H. .... **Sonoma, CA**
Katz, Steven Ian .... Los Angeles, CA
Katz, Steven J. .... **Springfield, MA**
Katz, Steven Jay .... **Chicago, IL**
Katz, Steven L. .... Hartford, CT
Katz, Steven L. .... **Chicago, IL**
Katz, Steven M. .... Bakersfield, CA
Katz, Steven M. .... **San Francisco, CA**
Katz, Steven M. .... **Rockville, MD**
Katz, Steven M. .... New York, NY
Katz, Steven M., P.A. .... **Bethesda, MD**
Chevy Chase, MD
Rockville, MD
Katz, Steven R. .... **Minneapolis, MN**
Katz, Steven R. .... New York, NY
Katz, Steven S. .... **Newark, NJ**
New York, NY
Katz, Steven W. .... Deal, NJ
Union, NJ
Katz, Stewart .... **Sacramento, CA**
Katz, Stewart J. .... **Bingham Farms, MI**
Detroit, MI
Katz & Stone, L.L.P. .... **Washington, DC**
Rockville, MD
Vienna, VA
Katz & Strausbaugh L.C.
Kansas City, MO
Katz, Stuart A. .... **Newport Beach, CA**
Katz, Stuart B. .... New York, NY
Katz, Stuart B. .... New York, NY
Katz, Stuart C. .... Chicago, IL
Katz, Stuart E. .... Newport News, VA
Katz, Stuart M. .... **Bridgeport, CT**
Katz, Stuart Z. .... **New York, NY**
Katz, Sumner J. .... Washington, DC
Katz, Susan J. .... **New York, NY**
Katz, Susan L. .... New Haven, CT
Katz, Susan S. .... Stoughton, MA
Katz, Susan Stanton .... Youngstown, OH
Katz, Teller, Brant & Hild .... **Covington, KY**
Cincinnati, OH
Katz, Terry I. .... Lake Success, NY
Katz, Thomas O. .... **Fort Lauderdale, FL**
Katz, Tilden .... **Chicago, IL**
Katz, Todd H. .... Naples, FL
Katz, Todd J. .... Braintree, MA
Katz, Tracy F. .... Los Angeles, CA
Katz, Victor & Yolles, P.C. .... Birmingham, MI
Katz, Victoria Layne .... **San Diego, CA**
Katz, Walter .... Westfield, NJ
Katz, Wayne D. .... **New York, NY**
Katz, William .... Los Angeles, CA
Katz, William B. .... River Edge, NJ
Katz, William M., Jr. .... **Dallas, TX**
Katz, Wittenberg, Levine & Silverman
New York, NY
Katzakis, Joan Glenn .... Cleveland, OH
Katzan, Stephan Z. .... Los Angeles, CA
Katzav, Barbara .... Bethpage, NY
Katzban, Jo Ann .... **Montclair, NJ**
Katzberg, Robert F. .... **New York, NY**
Katz-Crank, Sherry .... **Lansing, MI**
Katze, Edward .... **Atlanta, GA**
Katze, Margaret .... Brooklyn, NY
Katzel, Aaron J. .... **New York, NY**
Katzell, Bruce R. .... **West Palm Beach, FL**
Katzelnick, Jeffrey I. .... Whippany, NJ
Katzen, Alan .... Baltimore, MD
Katzen, Amelia Welt .... Boston, MA
Katzen, Bruce A. .... **Miami, FL**
Katzen, Carl I. .... St. Louis, MO
Katzen, David I. .... Walnut Creek, CA
Katzen, Diane Wagner .... **Miami, FL**
Katzen, Hirsh .... New Orleans, LA
Katzen, Jerry B. .... Miami, FL
Katzen, Joshua W. .... Newton, MA
Katzen, Leon .... **Rochester, NY**
Katzen, Linda R. .... **Walnut Creek, CA**
Katzen, Michael A. .... Richmond, VA
Katzen, Simon J. .... San Jose, CA
Katzen, Susan A. .... Huntington Beach, CA
Katzenbach, Christopher W.
San Francisco, CA
Katzenbach, Daniel G. .... **Raleigh, NC**
Katzenbach, G., Jr. .... Pasadena, CA
Katzenbach and Khtikian
San Francisco, CA
Katzenbach, Nicholas deB. .... Princeton, NJ
Katzenberg, Alex S. .... Baltimore, MD
Katzenberg, Barbara J. .... Worcester, MA
Katzenberg, Carla Goldman .... Baltimore, MD
Katzenberg, Pamela M. .... Tucson, AZ
Katzenberger, George L. .... Troy, OH
Katzenelson, Judith D. .... Buffalo, NY
Katzenmeyer, Dale L. .... Akron, OH
Katzenmoyer, Robert D. .... **Reading, PA**
Katzenstein, Andrew M. .... **Los Angeles, CA**
Katzenstein, Charles B. .... New York, NY
Katzenstein, Charles J., Jr. .... **Gastonia, NC**
Katzenstein, Courtney Slatten .... **Dallas, TX**
Katzenstein, David M. .... **Princeton, NJ**
Katzenstein, Lawrence P. .... **St. Louis, MO**
Katzenstein & Lorance .... **Gastonia, NC**
Katzenstein, Michael E. .... Dallas, TX
Katzenstein, Robert J. .... **Wilmington, DE**
Katzenstein, Robert L. .... Holland, PA
Katzenstein, William C. .... Riverside, CA
Katzin, Lawrence R. .... **San Francisco, CA**
Katzin, Michael F. .... Indianapolis, IN
Katzinski, William .... Louisville, KY
Katzive, Marion C. .... **New York, NY**
Katzive, Richard A. .... White Plains, NY
Katzke, Michael S. .... **New York, NY**
Katz-Mallory, P.C. .... Memphis, TN
Katzman, Abby A. .... Northport, NY
Katzman, Abby A., P.C. .... Northport, NY
Katzman, Alan .... Old Tappan, NJ
Katzman, Alex L. .... San Antonio, TX
Katzman, Alfred H. .... Atlantic City, NJ
Katzman, Alvin J. .... **Indianapolis, IN**
Katzman, Amy .... Cincinnati, OH
Katzman & Associates .... Belleville, IL
Katzman, Barry Lee .... **San Francisco, CA**
San Jose, CA
Katzman, Bernard, (Inc.)
Long Beach, CA
Katzman, Brooks H. .... Brentwood, TN
Katzman, David I. .... **Broomfield, CO**
Troy, MI
Katzman, Deborah Naomi Kahn
New York, NY
Katzman, Gerald H. .... **Troy, NY**
Katzman, Harlene G. .... New York, NY
Katzman, Harvey L. .... Pasadena, CA
Katzman, Irwin .... San Jose, CA
Katzman, Irwin .... Cincinnati, OH
Katzman, Jamie .... **Fresno, CA**
Katzman, Jerome F. .... Beverly Hills, CA
Katzman, Julie E. .... United States Senate, Committee Legal Personnel, GV
Katzman, Karen E. .... **New York, NY**
Katzman & Katzman .... San Antonio, TX
Katzman Katzman & Pylitt, A Professional Corporation .... **Indianapolis, IN**
Katzman, Kelly Allbritton .... **Dallas, TX**
Katzman, Larry .... Seattle, WA
Katzman, Lawrence .... Carthage, NY
Watertown, NY
Katzman, Leigh C. .... Margate, FL
Katzman, Logan, Halper & Bennett
Cincinnati, OH
Katzman, Marc J. .... **Los Angeles, CA**
Katzman, Mariellen .... **Indianapolis, IN**
Katzman, Mark L. .... Espanola, NM
Katzman, Martin .... Mineola, NY
Katzman, Melvin S. .... New York, NY
Katzman, Monica .... Washington, DC
Katzman, Paul D. .... Milwaukee, WI
Katzman, Richard L. .... San Diego, CA
Katzman, Robert L. .... Saratoga Springs, NY
Katzman, Ronald M. .... Sherman Oaks, CA
Katzman, Ronald M. .... **Harrisburg, PA**
Katzman, Ronald M., P.C.
Sherman Oaks, CA
Katzman, Sarah Harris .... San Diego, CA
Katzman, Scott H. .... **Washington, DC**
Katzman, Sheri B. .... Oak Park, MI
Katzman, Shirley A. .... San Antonio, TX
Katzman, Stanley .... **New York, NY**
Katzman, Stephen D. .... East Hanover, NJ
Katzman, Stephen R. .... **Parsippany, NJ**
Katzman, Steven .... Littleton, CO
Katzman, Steven E. .... Belleville, IL
Katzman, Steven J. .... **Costa Mesa, CA**
Katzman, Steven M.
West Palm Beach, FL
Katzmann, Gary Stephen .... Boston, MA
Katzmann, Robert A. .... Washington, DC
Katznelson, Cary L. .... Chicago, IL
Katznelson, Deborah Hager .... San Diego, CA
Katznelson, Leslie J. .... **San Francisco, CA**
Katznelson, Steven N. .... Tarzana, CA
Katzoff, Howard S. .... Huntingdon Valley, PA
Katzoff, Jeffrey N. .... Santa Ana, CA
Katzoff, Kenneth S. .... **Berkeley, CA**
Katzoff & Riggs .... **Berkeley, CA**
Cobb, CA
Katzoff, Susan R. .... Albany, NY
Katzovitz, Paul Michael .... Scottsdale, AZ
Katz-Pearlman, Sharon .... New York, NY
Katz Yehia, Laurie R. .... Austin, TX
Kau, Lorrin A. .... Honolulu, HI
Kau, Randall K.C. .... **New York, NY**
Kaucher, James W. .... **Tucson, AZ**
Kauder, Lois N. .... Maplewood, NJ
Kauder, Louis M. .... Washington, DC
Kauder, Saul C. .... Flushing, NY
Kauderer, Beth Susan .... New York, NY
Kauderer, Bruce M. .... Croton-On-Hudson, NY
Kauderer, Ira A. .... **Philadelphia, PA**
Kauderer & Pack, P.C.
Croton-On-Hudson, NY
Kauders, A. Eric, Jr. .... **Richmond, VA**
Kauders, Christopher P. .... Boston, MA
Kaudy, Richard M. .... **Denver, CO**
Kauer, Franc J. .... Centreville, VA
Kauer, John A. .... Estherville, IA
Kauerauf, John A. .... **Springfield, IL**
Kaufelt, Jonathan D. .... **Los Angeles, CA**
Kaufer, Alvin H. .... New York, NY
Kaufer, Alvin S. .... **Los Angeles, CA**
Kaufer, Howard M.
Department of Defense, GV
Kaufer, Jason M. .... **New York, NY**
Kaufer, Julie M. .... **Los Angeles, CA**
Kaufer, Laurel G. .... Calabasas, CA
Kaufer, Stephen G. .... West Palm Beach, FL
Kauff, Jerome B. .... **New York, NY**
Kauff, McClain & McGuire
San Francisco, CA
New York, NY
Kauff, Norman B. .... Red Bank, NJ
Kauff, Russell G. .... **Stamford, CT**
Kauff, Scott E. .... **Washington, DC**
Kauffelt, James D. .... **Charleston, WV**
Kauffelt & Kauffelt .... **Charleston, WV**
Huntington, WV
Kauffelt, Mark E. .... **Charleston, WV**
Kauffelt, T. D. .... **Charleston, WV**
Kauffman, A. James .... **Richmond, VA**
Kauffman, Alan C. .... **Boca Raton, FL**
Kauffman, Alan C., & Associates, P.A.
Boca Raton, FL
Fort Lauderdale, FL
Kauffman, Albert C. .... Pennsauken, NJ
Kauffman, Allan R. .... Reading, PA
Kauffman, Andrew C. .... Los Angeles, CA
Kauffman, Andrew M. .... Columbus, OH
Kauffman, Bishop N. .... York, PA
Kauffman, Bradley L. .... Freeport, ME
Kauffman, Bruce E. .... **Towson, MD**
Kauffman, Bruce W. .... Philadelphia, PA
Kauffman, Caryn A. .... **Minneapolis, MN**
Kauffman, Charles .... New York, NY
Kauffman, D. Stephen .... Los Angeles, CA
Kauffman, Danna Lubrani .... Baltimore, MD
Kauffman, David B. .... **Washington, DC**
Kauffman, David Brad .... Bethesda, MD
Kauffman, David S. .... **Irving, TX**
Kauffman, Douglas B. .... **Birmingham, AL**
Kauffman, Earl G. .... **Philadelphia, PA**
Kauffman, Eric A. .... **Pittsburgh, PA**
Kauffman, Fredric H. .... **Lincoln, NE**
Kauffman, Gary .... New York, NY
Kauffman, Gregory R. .... Albuquerque, NM
Kauffman, Howard D. .... Harrisburg, PA
Kauffman, Howard J. .... **Minneapolis, MN**
Kauffman, James Ray .... Foster City, CA
Kauffman, Jane L. .... **Warsaw, IN**
Kauffman, Jay C. .... York, PA
Kauffman, Jay E. .... Seminole, FL
Kauffman, Jay L. .... **Jacksonville, FL**
Kauffman, Jeffrey C. .... **Chicago, IL**
Kauffman, John F. .... Springfield, IL

Kauffman, John M. ....Bozeman, MT
Kauffman, John W. ....Pontiac, IL
Kauffman, John W. ....Philadelphia, PA
Kauffman, Joseph W. ....Media, PA
Kauffman, Kathleen D. ....Birmingham, AL
Kauffman, Keith Alan ....Baltimore, MD
Kauffman, Kenneth D. ....Marion, IN
Kauffman, Kreg A. ....Rochester, MN
Kauffman Law Firm ....Rochester, MN
Kauffman, Lisa B. ....Missoula, MT
Kauffman, Louise Ann ....Johnstown, NY
Kauffman, Madeline H. Kibrick
Albany, NY
Kauffman, Michael W. ....Rockville, MD
Kauffman, Mindy ....Sarasota, FL
Kauffman, Naomi A. ....Overland Park, KS
Kauffman, Peter H. ....Chicago, IL
Kauffman, Philip S.
Department Of Veterans Affairs, Office of the General Counsel, GV
Kauffman & Polashuk, L.L.P.
Baltimore, MD
Kauffman, R. Craig ....Buffalo, NY
Kauffman, R. Scott
Whitehouse Station, NJ
Kauffman, Ralph M. ....Des Moines, IA
Kauffman, Randal A. ....Houston, TX
Kauffman, Robert A. ....Philadelphia, PA
Kauffman, Robert H. ....Reading, PA
Kauffman, Robert J. ....Douglasville, GA
Kauffman, Robert J. ....Peoria, IL
Kauffman, Robert K. ....Libertyville, IA
Kauffman, Roland B. ....Dalton, OH
Kauffman, Ronald H. ....Miami, FL
Kauffman, Ronald P. ....Columbus, OH
Kauffman, Rosadele ....State College, PA
Kauffman, S. Blair ....De Kalb, IL
Kauffman, Samuel C. ....Portland, OR
Kauffman, Scott F. ....San Francisco, CA
Kauffman, Stephen P. ....Baltimore, MD
Kauffman, Stephen R. ....Sacramento, CA
Kauffman, Susan G. ....Vallejo, CA
Kauffman, Thomas A. ....Indiana, PA
Kauffman, Victoria H.
Department of Transportation, Federal Aviation Administration, GV
Kauffman, Warren J. ....Philadelphia, PA
Kauffman, William R. ....St. Louis, MO
Kauffmann, Ellen O. ....Denver, CO
Kauffmann, Galen K. ....Chalfont, PA
Kauffmann, Henry M. ....Louisville, KY
Kauffmann, Kristine ....Atlanta, GA
Kauffroath, Kathleen A. ....Sacramento, CA
Kaufhold, John R. ....New Brighton, MN
Kaufhold, Kevin C. ....Belleville, IL
Kaufhold, Steven S. ....San Francisco, CA
Kaufler, Philip ....Beverly Hills, CA
Kauflin, Robert J. ....Clinton Township, MI
Kaufman, Aaron S. ....Dallas, TX
Kaufman, Adam B. ....New York, NY
Kaufman, Adam D. ....Buffalo, NY
Kaufman, Alan B. ....Scottsdale, AZ
Kaufman, Alan H. ....New York, NY
Kaufman, Alan Jay ......Farmington Hills, MI
Grand Rapids, MI
Kaufman, Alan L. ....Rego Park, NY
Kaufman, Alan M. ....San Francisco, CA
Kaufman, Alan S. ....Albany, NY
Kaufman, Albert I. ....Encino, CA
Kaufman, Albert M. ....Jamaica, NY
Kaufman, Allen S. ....Oakland Park, FL
Kaufman, Allen S., P.A., Law Offices Of
Oakland Park, FL
Kaufman, Amy R. ....Highland Park, IL
Kaufman, Andrea J. ....Minneapolis, MN
Kaufman, Andrea S. ....Washington, DC
Kaufman, Andrew B. ....New York, NY
Kaufman, Andrew H. ....Kew Gardens, NY
Kaufman, Andrew Jay ....Beverly Hills, CA
Kaufman, Andrew L. ....Cambridge, MA
Kaufman, Andrew M. ....Chicago, IL
Kaufman, Andrew R. ....Philadelphia, PA
Kaufman, Andrew S. ....New York, NY
Kaufman, Ann P. ....Colorado Springs, CO
Kaufman, Ann P., P.C.
Colorado Springs, CO
Kaufman, Anne S. J. ....Boston, MA
Kaufman, Anthony H. ....Los Angeles, CA
Kaufman, Arthur M. ....Cleveland, OH
Kaufman, Arthur R. ....Jericho, NY
Kaufman, Arthur S. ....New York, NY
Kaufman, Arthur S. ....New York, NY
Kaufman & Associates ....Atlanta, GA
Kaufman & Associates, Inc.
San Antonio, TX
Kaufman, Barbara ....Sacramento, CA
Kaufman, Barbara ....Mount Vernon, NY
Kaufman, Barry B., Law Offices of
Encino, CA
Kaufman, Barry L. ....Hackensack, NJ
Kaufman, Barry M. ....Deerfield Beach, FL
Kaufman, Barry M. ....Springfield, MA
Kaufman, Barry M., P.A.
Deerfield Beach, FL
Kaufman, Bart D. ....Van Nuys, CA
Kaufman, Barton L. ....Indianapolis, IN
Kaufman, Benjamin ....Santa Ana, CA
Kaufman, Benjamin Y. ....New York, NY
Kaufman, Bennet Z. ....Frederick, MD
Kaufman, Bernard M. ....New York, NY
Kaufman, Bernard R. ....Hidden Hills, CA
Kaufman, Beth F. ....Athens, OH
Kaufman, Beth L. ....New York, NY
Kaufman, Beth S. ....Treasury Department, Departmental Offices, GV
Kaufman, Bonni Fine ....Washington, DC
Kaufman, Borgeest & Ryan
New York, NY
Kaufman, Bradford D., (P.A.)
West Palm Beach, FL
Kaufman, Bradley A. ....New York, NY
Kaufman, Brent J. ....Garden City, NY
Kaufman, Brian ....Beverly Hills, CA
Kaufman, Brian N. ....Kansas City, MO
Kaufman, Brian P. ....Department of Justice, Tax Division, GV
Kaufman, Bruce E. ....Santa Fe, NM
Kaufman, Bruce M. ....Sherman Oaks, CA
Kaufman, Bruce S. ....Washington, DC
Kaufman, Bruce S. ....Daytona Beach, FL
Kaufman, Bruce S. ....Ormond Beach, FL
Kaufman, C. Bernard ....San Marino, CA
Kaufman, C. Jeffrey ....Atlanta, GA
Kaufman & Canoles, A Professional Corporation ....Chesapeake, VA
Newport News, VA
Norfolk, VA
Virginia Beach, VA
Williamsburg, VA
Kaufman, Catherine P. ....Mechanicsville, VA
Kaufman, Celeste P. ....Hicksville, NY
Kaufman, Chaiken, Miller & Klorfein, A Professional Corporation ....Atlanta, GA
Kaufman, Charles ....Plymouth, MI
Kaufman, Charles L., Jr. ....Chesapeake, VA
Kaufman, Charles S. ....Los Angeles, CA
Kaufman, Cheryl Julien, (P.A.)
Miami, FL
Kaufman, Chet ....Tallahassee, FL
Kaufman, Christopher L.
Menlo Park, CA
Kaufman, Clarice D. ....Los Angeles, CA
Kaufman, Colin E. ....New York, NY
Kaufman, Colin K. ....Corpus Christi, TX
Kaufman, Coren, Ress & Weidman, P.C.
Haddonfield, NJ
Philadelphia, PA
Kaufman & Coxon ....Conneaut, OH
Kaufman, Craig H. ....Tucson, AZ
Kaufman, Craig I. ....Cuyahoga Falls, OH
Kaufman, Craig R. ....Menlo Park, CA
Kaufman & Cumberland Co., L.P.A.
Cleveland, OH
Kaufman, Cynthia A. ....Chicago, IL
Kaufman, D. William ....Minneapolis, MN
Kaufman, Dana M. ....Hollywood, FL
Kaufman, Daniel .....Federal Trade Commission, Bureau of Consumer Protection, GV
Kaufman, Daniel A. ....Chicago, IL
Kaufman, Daniel I. ....Deerfield Beach, FL
Kaufman, Daniel J. ....Bryn Mawr, PA
Kaufman, Daniel J. ....King Of Prussia, PA
Kaufman, Daniel L. ....Miami Lakes, FL
Kaufman, David A. ....Northbrook, IL
Kaufman, David A. ....Cleveland, OH
Kaufman, David B. ....Little Rock, AR
Kaufman, David H. ....New York, NY
Kaufman, David I., P.C. ....Royal Oak, MI
Kaufman, David J. ....Washington, DC
Kaufman, David J. ....Fort Lauderdale, FL
Kaufman, David J. ....Chicago, IL
Kaufman, David J. ....Philadelphia, PA
Kaufman, David M. ....Santa Fe, NM
Kaufman, David M. ....Brooklyn, NY
Kaufman, David M. ....New York, NY
Kaufman, David S. ....South Miami, FL
Kaufman, David S. ....Verona, NJ
Kaufman, David S., P.A. ....South Miami, FL
Kaufman, Dean Stewart ....Drain, OR
Eugene, OR
Kaufman, Deborah Ann ....Berkeley, CA
Kaufman, Debra G. ....San Diego, CA
Kaufman, Dennis A. ....Syracuse, NY
Kaufman, Denver ....Minneapolis, MN
Kaufman, Donald B. ....East Brunswick, NJ
Kaufman, Donald B. ....Harrisburg, PA
Kaufman, Donald James
Glenwood Springs, CO
Kaufman, Donald L. ....Cuyahoga Falls, OH
Kaufman, Dora F. ....Fort Lauderdale, FL
Kaufman, Douglas E. ....Tillamook, OR
Kaufman, Edmund M., (P.C.)
Los Angeles, CA
Kaufman, Edward A. ....Miami, FL
Kaufman, Edward L. ....Stamford, CT
Kaufman, Edwin ....New York, NY
Kaufman, Eileen R. ....Huntington, NY
Kaufman, Elizabeth ....Los Angeles, CA
Kaufman, Elizabeth ....Northridge, CA
Kaufman, Elizabeth A. ....Philadelphia, PA
Kaufman, Elliot M. ....Cleveland, OH
Kaufman, Englett and Lynd
Altamonte Springs, FL
Orlando, FL
Kaufman, Eric J. ....San Francisco, CA
Kaufman, Esther M. ....New York, NY
Kaufman, Ethan E. ....Dallas, TX
Kaufman, Eugene M. ....New Rochelle, NY
Kaufman, Felicia B. ....Miami, FL
Kaufman, Fern Jill Feil
Federal Labor Relations Authority, Office of Collaboration and Alternative Dispute Resolution, GV
Kaufman & Florence ....Lebanon, OH
Kaufman, Francine R. ....Teaneck, NJ
Kaufman, Frank J. ....New York, NY
Kaufman, Fred ....Boston, MA
Kaufman, Fred J. ....Seattle, WA
Kaufman, Frederic D. ....Coral Springs, FL
Kaufman, Fredrick S. ....Richmond, VA
Kaufman, Fremont M. ....La Salle, IL
Kaufman Friedman Plotnicki & Grun, LLP
New York, NY
Kaufman, Gaileen A. ....Bridgeport, CT
Kaufman, Gal N. ....Washington, DC
Kaufman, Garrison W. ....Denver, CO
Kaufman & Garshall ....Verona, NJ
Kaufman, Gary D. ....Santa Monica, CA
Kaufman, Gary, Law Offices of
New York, NY
Kaufman, Gary Lee ....Great Bend, KS
Kaufman, Gelbert & Bern ....Fort Lee, NJ
Hackensack, NJ
New York, NY
Kaufman, George A. ....Manhattan Beach, CA
Kaufman, George B. ....Somerset, PA
Kaufman, George W. ....Washington, DC
Kaufman, Gerald A. ....Huntington Station, NY
Kaufman, Gerald S. ....New York, NY
Kaufman, Gideon ....Aspen, CO
Kaufman, Glen ....Chicago, IL
Kaufman Goldstein & Gartner, P.C.
New York, NY
Kaufman & Green, L.L.P.
Wilmington, NC
Kaufman, Gregory S. ....Washington, DC
Kaufman, Harley D. ....New York, NY
Kaufman, Harold F. ....Philadelphia, PA
Kaufman, Harry L. ....Philadelphia, PA
Kaufman, Harvey ....Palm Beach Gardens, FL
Kaufman, Hattie E. ....Tuscaloosa, AL
Kaufman, Henry R. ....New York, NY
Kaufman, Herman ....Old Greenwich, CT
Kaufman, Herman ....Scranton, PA
Kaufman & Horner, Chtd. ....Great Bend, KS
Kaufman, Howard ....New York, NY
Kaufman, Howard J.
United States Postal Service, Law Department, GV
Kaufman, Howard J. ....Philadelphia, PA
Kaufman, Howard R. ....Naples, FL
Kaufman, Ian Jay ....New York, NY
Kaufman, Ira Robert ....Quincy, CA
Kaufman, Irving ....Bronx, NY
Kaufman, Irwin ....Miami Beach, FL
Kaufman, Jack ....Department of Justice, Civil Division, GV
Kaufman, Jack ....Cleveland, OH
Kaufman, Jack E. ....Sherman Oaks, CA
Kaufman, Jacob J. ....Chicago, IL
Kaufman, James ....New York, NY
Kaufman, James B. ....Arlington, VA
Kaufman, James H. ....Scarsdale, NY
Kaufman, James H. ....Colfax, WA
Kaufman, James J. ....Sacramento, CA
Kaufman, James J. ....Wilmington, NC
Kaufman, James M. ....Oklahoma City, OK
Kaufman, James P. ....Boise, ID
Kaufman, James S. ....Boston, MA
Kaufman, Janet Robertson
Solana Beach, CA
Kaufman, Janice B. ....Highland Park, IL
Kaufman, Jay C., (Ltd.) ....Buffalo Grove, IL
Kaufman, Jay C., P.C. ....Buffalo Grove, IL
Kaufman, Jeffrey ....San Francisco, CA
Kaufman, Jeffrey A. ....Palo Alto, CA
Kaufman, Jeffrey H. ....New York, NY
Kaufman, Jeffrey H. ....Arlington, VA
Kaufman, Jeffrey S. ....Scottsdale, AZ
Kaufman, Jeffrey S. ....Merced, CA
Kaufman, Jeffrey S., Jr.
Altamonte Springs, FL
Kaufman, Jennifer Brodkey .....Sacramento, CA
Kaufman, Jerry ....Los Angeles, CA
Kaufman, Jerry J. ....Las Vegas, NV
Kaufman, Jerry R. ....Miami, FL
Kaufman, Jessica Berman ....Baltimore, MD
Kaufman, Jill E. ....Palm Beach, FL
Kaufman, Joel
Federal Communications Commission, Office of the General Counsel, GV
Kaufman, Joel A. ....Santa Barbara, CA
Kaufman, Joel D. ....Washington, DC
Kaufman, Joel H. ....Farmington Hills, MI
Kaufman, John F. ....Baltimore, MD
Kaufman, John G. ....Norristown, PA
Kaufman, John M. ....Pittsfield, MA
Kaufman, John M. ....West Orange, NJ
Kaufman, Jon M. ....New York, NY
Kaufman, Jonathan Herman .....Huntington, NY
Kaufman, Jonathan Myles
San Francisco, CA
Kaufman, Joseph ....Rochester, NY
Kaufman, Joseph D. ....Neenah, WI
Kaufman, Joseph H. ....New York, NY
Kaufman, Joseph L. ....Babylon, NY
Kaufman, Joseph Q. ....Fremont, CA
Kaufman, Joseph S. ....Baltimore, MD
Kaufman, Joshua ....New York, NY
Kaufman, Joshua J. ....Washington, DC
Kaufman, Joshua P. ....New York, NY
Kaufman, Jules L. ....Cleveland, OH
Kaufman, Jules P. ....New York, NY
Kaufman, Julie Fink ....Orlando, FL
Kaufman, Karen R. ....Clear Lake, IA
Kaufman, Katheryn K. ....Oklahoma City, OK
Kaufman, Kathleen ....Grayling, MI
Kaufman, Kathleen Cobb ....Mobile, AL
Kaufman & Kaufman
Glenwood Springs, CO
Kaufman and Kaufman, A Professional Law Corporation ....Sherman Oaks, CA
Kaufman, Kaufman & Associates
Sandusky, OH
Kaufman & Kaufman, P.C. ....Babylon, NY
Kaufman, Kenneth B. ....Hartford, CT
Kaufman, Kenneth M. ....Washington, DC
Kaufman, Kenneth S. ....Washington, DC
Kaufman & Kerker ....Bronx, NY
Kaufman, Kevin Edward ....Burlington, IA
Kaufman, Kim E. ....Albuquerque, NM
Kaufman, Kim I. ....Cleveland, OH
Kaufman, Kurt A. ....Lima, OH
Kaufman, Laura E. ....Bluffton, IN
Kaufman, Lauren D. ....Boston, MA
Kaufman Law Firm, P.C.
Colorado Springs, CO
Kaufman, Lawrence A. ....Baltimore, MD
Kaufman, Leonard A. ....Los Angeles, CA
Kaufman, Leonard L. ....Kalispell, MT
Kaufman, Leslie K. ....Santa Ana, CA
Kaufman, Lewis ....Westbury, NY
Kaufman, Linda S. ....West Hartford, CT
Kaufman, Lisa J. ....Houston, TX
Kaufman, Lisa N. ....Washington, DC
Kaufman, Lissa K. ....Woodburn, OR
Kaufman, Lita C. ....Bohemia, NY
Kaufman, Lloyd G. ....Lexington, NE
Kaufman & Logan LLP
San Francisco, CA
Kaufman, Louis P. ....Newark, NJ
Kaufman, Lynn J. ....Los Angeles, CA
Kaufman, Lynne Drohlich
Los Angeles, CA
Kaufman, Lynne Levin ....Atlantic City, NJ
Kaufman, Madeleine R. ....Bensalem, PA
Kaufman, Marc A. ....Boca Raton, FL
Fort Lauderdale, FL
Miami, FL
Kaufman, Marc S. ....McLean, VA
Kaufman, Marc S. ....Bellevue, WA
Kaufman, Marchman, Kirby & Squire
New York, NY
Kaufman, Marcus M. ....Costa Mesa, CA
Los Angeles, CA
Kaufman, Marjorie Hope ....Los Angeles, CA
Kaufman, Mark A. ....Houston, TX
Kaufman, Mark D. ....Glendale, CA
Kaufman, Mark D. ....Atlanta, GA
Kaufman, Mark E. ....New York, NY
Kaufman, Mark H. ....Washington, DC
Kaufman, Mark S. ....Stamford, CT
Kaufman, Mark S. ....Atlanta, GA
Kaufman, Mark S. ....New York, NY
Kaufman, Marshall F., III ....Louisville, KY
Kaufman, Marti L. ....Memphis, TN
Kaufman, Martin ....Forest Hills, NY
Kaufman, Martin S. ....Scarsdale, NY
Kaufman, Marvin A. ....New York, NY
Kaufman, Mathew ....Glenwood Springs, CO
Kaufman, Matthew A. ....New York, NY
Kaufman, Max ....Philadelphia, PA
Kaufman and McMinimee ....Tillamook, OR
Kaufman, Michael ....St. James, NY
Kaufman, Michael A. ....San Francisco, CA
Kaufman, Michael A. ....New Brunswick, NJ
Kaufman, Michael A. ....Jericho, NY
Kaufman, Michael A. C. ....Beverly Hills, CA
Kaufman, Michael B. ....Washington, DC
Kaufman, Michael B. ....New York, NY
Kaufman, Michael D. ....Atlanta, GA
Kaufman, Michael D. ....Sandusky, OH
Kaufman, Michael L. ....Dallas, TX
Kaufman, Michael R. ....Danbury, CT
Kaufman, Michael S. ....Miami, FL
Kaufman, Michael S. ....New York, NY
Kaufman, Michelle Stark
Kansas City, MO
Kaufman Miller Dickstein & Grunspan, P.A.
Miami, FL
Kaufman, Mitchell ....Brooklyn, NY
Kaufman, Mitchell F. ....Sherman Oaks, CA
Kaufman, Monty D. ....Stamford, CT
Kaufman & Moomjian, LLC
Uniondale, NY
Kaufman, Nancy B. ....Santa Ana, CA
Kaufman, Nancy E. ....Boston, MA
Kaufman, Nancy H. ....St. Louis, MO
Kaufman, Nathan B. ....University City, MO
Kaufman, Nathan L. ....Cameron Park, CA
Kaufman, Neal S. ....New York, NY
Kaufman, Neil M. ....Uniondale, NY
Kaufman, Neil R. ....Sunrise, FL
Kaufman, Nellie C. ....Denver, CO
Kaufman, Norman L. ....Boynton Beach, FL
Kaufman, Oran ....Amherst, MA
Kaufman, Orval J. ....Wichita, KS
Kaufman, Page M. ....Atlanta, GA
Kaufman, Patricia Ann ....Tantallon, MD
Kaufman, Patrick C. ....Brunswick, GA
Kaufman, Paul ....Knoxville, TN
Kaufman, Paul C. ....Fort Lee, NJ
New York, NY
Kaufman, Paul J. ....Dubuque, IA
Kaufman, Paul M. ....Cleveland, OH
Kaufman, Paul S. ....Somerville, MA
Kaufman, Paul S., P.C. ....Somerville, MA
Kaufman, Paul W. ....Los Angeles, CA
Kaufman and Payton ....Detroit, MI
Farmington Hills, MI
Grand Rapids, MI
Kaufman, Peter S. ....New York, NY
Kaufman & Peterson, P.C. ....Aspen, CO
Kaufman, Philip B. ....Columbus, OH
Kaufman, Philip R. ....Edison, NJ
Kaufman, Philip S. ....Los Angeles, CA
Kaufman, Philip S. ....New York, NY
Kaufman, Phyllis C. ....Atlantic City, NJ
Kaufman, R. David ....Jackson, MS
Kaufman, Rachelle C. ....New City, NY
Kaufman, Randy A. ....New York, NY
Kaufman, Raymond ....Fort Myers, FL
Kaufman, Rebecca Nell ....Los Angeles, CA
Kaufman, Richard A. ....Purchase, NY
Kaufman, Richard A. ....Wheeling, WV
Kaufman, Richard B. ....Indianapolis, IN
Kaufman, Richard B. ....Blacksburg, VA
Kaufman, Richard C.
Farmington Hills, MI
Kaufman, Richard D. ....Buffalo, NY
Kaufman, Richard N. ....Trumbull, CT
Kaufman, Richard P. ....Englewood, CO

Kawala, Susan J. ....Los Angeles, CA
Kawalec, Thomas P. ....Buffalo, NY
Kawalec, Walter F., III ....Philadelphia, PA
Kawalsky, Michele B. ....Dallas, TX
Kawamoto, Craig A. ....McLean, VA
Kawamoto, Edwin H. ....San Francisco, CA
Kawamoto, Lynne ....Chicago, IL
Kawamoto, Roy Y. ....Honolulu, HI
Kawamura, Akiko ....Salt Lake City, UT
Kawamura, Eric K. ....San Francisco, CA
Kawamura, Jennifer M. ....San Francisco, CA
Kawamura, Kerry F. ....San Diego, CA
Kawamura, Koji ....Golden, CO
Kawamura Lobdell & Moniz ....Honolulu, HI
Kawamura, Robert D. ....Honolulu, HI
Kawamura, Scott K. ....Los Angeles, CA
Kawamura, Taro J. ....New York, NY
Kawana, Richard S. ....Honolulu, HI
Kawana, Teiji R. ....Los Angeles, CA
Kawanabe, Kenzo ....Denver, CO
Kawananakoa, Quentin K. ....Honolulu, HI
Kawano, Arnold H. ....New York, NY
Kawano, Carmel K. ....San Jose, CA
Kawano, Nancy ....San Diego, CA
Kawano, Roy K. ....Honolulu, HI
Kawar, Dorian C. ....Houston, TX
Kawas, Paul T. ....Rye, NY
Kawasaki, Lawrence I. ....Honolulu, HI
Kawash, Janet N. ....Charleston, WV
Kawash, Michael A. ....Charleston, WV
Kawashima, James, (Atty. At Law, A Law Corp.) ....Honolulu, HI
Kawashima, James S. ....Honolulu, HI
Kawashima, Jared N. ....Honolulu, HI
Kawashima, Neil T. ....Chicago, IL
Kawashiri, Roy N. ....South Pasadena, CA
Kawata, Mark S. ....Honolulu, HI
Kawata, Yukako ....New York, NY
Kawatani, Eric T. ....Honolulu, HI
Kawauchi, Diane T. ....Honolulu, HI
Kawczynski, John E. ....Philadelphia, PA
Kawecki, Lynn E.
Treasury Department, GV
Kawesch, Lance A. ....Boston, MA
Kawin, Warren H. ....St. Louis, MO
Kawinski, Mark ....Wheaton, IL
Kawior & Feldman, P.C. ......Silver Spring, MD
Kawior, Shraga ....Silver Spring, MD
Kawitt, Alan ....Chicago, IL
Kawles, Terrance L. ....New York, NY
Kawula, Walter J., Jr. ....Chicago, IL
Kay, Abraham ....Cleveland, OH
Kay, Alan
United States District Court For The District Of Columbia, GV
Kay, Alan C. ....Honolulu, HI
Kay, Alan S. ....Seminole, FL
Kay, Alfred N., Jr. ....Dallas, TX
Kay, Allan, P.A. ....Seminole, FL
Kay, Allison L. ....Boca Raton, FL
Kay & Andersen, S.C. ....Madison, WI
Kay, Andrew B. ....Washington, DC
Kay, Barbara Metzger
Rancho Cucamonga, CA
Kay, Bart ....Beverly Hills, CA
Kay, Brian P. ....Plantation, FL
Kay, Brian T. ....Worcester, MA
Kay Casto & Chaney PLLC
Charleston, WV
Morgantown, WV
Kay, Catherine A. ....Los Angeles, CA
Kay, Catherine M. ....Northampton, MA
Kay, Christopher K. ....Orlando, FL
Kay Collyer & Boose LLP ......New York, NY
Kay, Craig M. ....Charleston, WV
Kay, Cynthia C. Antwine ....Wichita, KS
Kay, Daniel G. ....Colorado Springs, CO
Kay, David A. ....San Diego, CA
Kay, David G. ....Irvine, CA
Kay, David N. ....Chicago, IL
Kay, David R. ....New York, NY
Kay, Deborah S. ....Boston, MA
Kay, Debra J. ....Simi Valley, CA
Kay, Dennis F. ....University City, MO
Kay, Donald L. ....San Jose, CA
Kay, Douglas R. ....McLean, VA
Kay, Edward M. ....Fort Lauderdale, FL
Kay, Edward M. ....Chicago, IL
Kay, Edward M., P.A. ....Fort Lauderdale, FL
Kay, Emanuel M. ....Uniondale, NY
Kay, Eric M. ....New York, NY
Kay, Fredie D. ....Boston, MA
Kay, Fredric F. ....Tucson, AZ
Kay, Gerald A. ....Denver, CO
Kay, Gregg E. ....Englewood, CO
Kay, Gronek & Latham, LLP
Orlando, FL
Kay, Harold W. ....North Platte, NE
Kay, Harris L. ....Richmond, VA
Kay, Herma H. ....Berkeley, CA
Kay, Howard I. ....Lakeland, FL
Lake Wales, FL
Kay, J. Benjamin, III ....Augusta, GA
Kay, James D., Jr. ....Nashville, TN
Kay, James G. ....Foothill Ranch, CA
Kay, James P. ....Far Rockaway, NY
Kay, James R. ....West Palm Beach, FL
Kay, Jeffrey H. ....Fort Lauderdale, FL
Kay, Jeffrey T. ....Cleveland, OH
Kay, Jerome M. ....Brooklyn, NY
Kay, Jerry L., (A Professional Corporation)
Santa Monica, CA
Kay, Joanne D. ....Wildwood, NJ
Kay, Joel P. ....Houston, TX
Kay, John ....Buffalo Grove, IL
Kay, John C. ....Sacramento, CA
Kay, John F., Jr. ....Richmond, VA
Kay, John Ross, Inc. ....Lufkin, TX

Kay, John S. ....Columbia, SC
Kay, John T. ....California, MO
Kay, John T., Jr. ....Charleston, WV
Kay, Joseph J., Jr. ....Reno, NV
Kay, Joseph L. ....East Greenbush, NY
Kay, Karen R. ....Boston, MA
Kay, Kathleen ....Lake Charles, LA
Kay, Kathleen, A Professional Law Corporation ....Lake Charles, LA
Kay & Kay ....North Platte, NE
Kay & Kay ....Wildwood, NJ
Kay, Kenneth Dean ....Fresno, CA
Kay, Kevin M. ....Monrovia, CA
Kay, Lane S. ....Las Vegas, NV
Kay, Larry ....Albuquerque, NM
Kay, Larry Alan ....Glendale, CA
Kay, Laurence D. ....San Francisco, CA
Kay, Lawrence H. ....Sacramento, CA
San Francisco, CA
Kay, Lawrence W., P.A. ....Albuquerque, NM
Kay, Leslie N. ....Portland, OR
Kay, Lynne M. ....Raleigh, NC
Kay, Mark W. ....Miami, FL
Kay, Marvin ....Los Angeles, CA
Kay, Mary E. ....Cranston, RI
Kay & Merkle ....Oakland, CA
San Francisco, CA
Kay, Michael B. ....Memphis, TN
Kay, Michael T. ....Midland, MI
Kay, Minta E., (P.C.) ....Boston, MA
Kay, Mitchell N. ....Garden City, NY
Kay, Neil A. ....Southfield, MI
Kay, Pamela Kristen
West Palm Beach, FL
Kay, Paul Edward ....Washington, DC
Kay, Paul G. ....Pittsburgh, PA
Kay, Paula Elaine ....New York, NY
Kay, Ped C., III ....Lafayette, LA
Kay & Povinelli, P.C. ....Washington, DC
Kay, Randall E. ....San Francisco, CA
Kay, Randall Evan ....San Diego, CA
Kay, Raymond ....Great Neck, NY
Kay, Rebecca L. ....Fort Lauderdale, FL
Kay, Rhonda E. ....New York, NY
Kay, Richard A. ....Grand Rapids, MI
Kay, Richard B. ....Tequesta, FL
Kay, Richard B., P.A. ....Tequesta, FL
Kay, Richard C. ....Baltimore, MD
Kay, Richard L. ....New York, NY
Kay, Robert A. ....Madison, WI
Kay, Robert B. ....Clarion, IA
Kay, Robert B. ....New York, NY
Kay, Robert B. ....Columbia, SC
Kay, Robert J. ....Ketchikan, AK
Kay, Robert J. ....Madison, WI
Kay, Robert M. ....Woodland Hills, CA
Kay, Robert T.C. ....Wheaton, IL
Kay, Ross A. ....Palo Alto, CA
Kay, Sara C. ....Brooklyn, NY
Kay, Saul ....Memphis, TN
Kay, Sheldon L. ....Farmington Hills, MI
Kay, Shirley K. ....Elmont, NY
Kay, Stanley B. ....Boston, MA
Kay, Stanley B. ....Newton, MA
Kay, Stanley L. ....New York, NY
Kay, Stephen H. ....New York, NY
Kay, Stephen W. ....North Platte, NE
Kay, Steven ....San Francisco, CA
Kay & Stevens ....Palo Alto, CA
Kay, Stewart F. ....Wildwood, NJ
Kay, Stuart S., Jr. ....De Ridder, LA
Kay, Susan L. ....Nashville, TN
Kay & Tawasha LLP ....San Francisco, CA
Kay, Terrence A. ....Salem, OR
Kay, Thomas J. ....Brookfield, WI
Kay, Thomas L. ....Layton, UT
Kay, Timothy J. ....Irvine, CA
Kay, W. Richard, Jr. ....Richmond, VA
Kay, Wendell R. ....Honesdale, PA
Kay, William F. ....Palo Alto, CA
Kay, William T., Jr. ....Arcata, CA
Kay, William V. ....Cedarhurst, NY
Kaya, Randall Y. ....Honolulu, HI
Kayagil, Joan Lewis
Department of Housing and Urban Development, Office of General Counsel, GV
Kayaian, Richard T. ....Los Angeles, CA
Kayaian, Richard T., A Professional Corporation ....Los Angeles, CA
Kayajanian, Jack J. ....Costa Mesa, CA
Kayajanian Law Firm ....Costa Mesa, CA
Kayajanian, Linda S. ....Los Angeles, CA
Kayajanian, Patricia A. ....Los Angeles, CA
Kayal, Dev A. ....Washington, DC
Kayan, S. Michael ....Richmond, VA
Kayar-MacGregor, Eishe ....Yakima, WA
Kayashima, Ben T. ....Rancho Cucamonga, CA
Kayatta, William J., Jr. ....Portland, ME
Kay-Decker, Courtney M.
Rock Island, IL
Kayden, Bernard H. ....Harrison, NY
Kayden, James W. ....Atlanta, GA
Kaydouh, Michael D. ....McLean, VA
Kaye, A. Paul ....Towson, MD
Kaye, Alan F. ....Springfield, MA
Kaye, Alan R. ....Lansdale, PA
Kaye, Alexander ....New York, NY
Kaye, Alfred H. ....Newton, NJ
Kaye, Allan H. ....Gainesville, FL
Kaye, Allen E. ....New York, NY
Kaye, Allen E., P.C. ....New York, NY
Kaye, Amy L. ....Atlanta, GA
Kaye, Andrew J. ....New York, NY
Kaye, Anthony C. ....Salt Lake City, UT
Kaye, Barbara A. ....Los Angeles, CA
Kaye, Barbara A. ....Detroit, MI
Kaye, Barry D. ....Beverly Hills, CA

Kaye, Barry P. ....Los Angeles, CA
Kaye, Bethany M. ....San Francisco, CA
Kaye, Brenda Maya ....Malden, MA
Kaye, Bruce J. ....Denver, CO
Kaye, Carole Penny ....Washington, DC
Kaye, Carolyn A. ....Bloomington, IN
Kaye, Carolyn J. ....San Diego, CA
Kaye, Claudia ....Los Angeles, CA
Kaye, Corey B. ....Mineola, NY
Kaye, Daniel ....New York, NY
Kaye, Daniel Evan ....Reading, PA
Kaye, Daniel L. ....Grand Island, NY
Kaye, David A. ....Department of State, Office of the Legal Adviser, GV
Kaye, David L. ....Washington, DC
Kaye, David M. ....Denver, CO
Kaye, David N. ....New York, NY
Kaye, Debbie ....Los Angeles, CA
Kaye, Deborah H. ....New York, NY
Kaye, Donald Michael ....Washington, DC
Kaye, Douglas M. ....Los Angeles, CA
Kaye, E. Donald ....Santa Fe, NM
Kaye, Elissa M. ....Boston, MA
Kaye, Fialkow, Richmond & Rothstein
Boston, MA
Kaye, Franklin M. ....Santa Monica, CA
Kaye, George ....Paxton, IL
Kaye, George S. ....San Antonio, TX
Kaye, Geri M. ....San Ramon, CA
Kaye, Gordon D. ....New York, NY
Kaye, Harvey ....Washington, DC
Kaye, Helaine M. ....New York, NY
Kaye and Hennessey, LLC
Greenwich, CT
Kaye, Henry L. ....West Palm Beach, FL
Kaye, Henry M. ....Lacey, WA
Kaye, Ira S. ....Federal Trade Commission, Office of the General Counsel, GV
Kaye, James E. ....New York, NY
Kaye, Janice A.
Federal Housing Finance Board, Office of General Counsel, GV
Kaye, Jeffrey A. ....Los Angeles, CA
Kaye, Jeffrey M. ....Lawrence, MA
Kaye, Jeremy E. ....Greenwich, CT
Kaye, Joel M. ....Greenwich, CT
Greenwich, CT
Kaye, Johanna L. ....Hartford, CT
Kaye, John ....Freehold, NJ
Kaye, John R. ....Columbia, MD
Kaye, Jonathan ....Kew Gardens, NY
Kaye, Jonathan M. ....Washington, DC
Kaye, Joseph Mitchell ....Greenwich, CT
Kaye, Judith Mani ....Worcester, MA
Kaye, Judith S. ....New York, NY
Kaye, June H. ....Baltimore, MD
Kaye, Kenneth C. ....League City, TX
Kaye, Kenneth R. ....Los Altos, CA
Kaye, Laura K. ....Madison, WI
Kaye, Laurie Kammler ....New York, NY
Kaye, Lawrence A. ....St. Louis, MO
Kaye, Lawrence M. ....New York, NY
Kaye, Lawrence W. ....Los Angeles, CA
San Diego, CA
Kaye & Lenchner ....Mineola, NY
Kaye, Leonard M. ....Los Angeles, CA
Kaye, Leslie Block ....Denver, CO
Kaye, Lori-Nan ....Boynton Beach, FL
Kaye, Louis D. ....Orlando, FL
Kaye, Marc M. ....Short Hills, NJ
Kaye, Marcy E. ....San Diego, CA
Kaye, Marjorie N., Jr ....Bronx, NY
Kaye, Martin B. ....Denver, CO
Kaye, Marvyn E. ....Los Angeles, CA
Kaye, Michael ....Topeka, KS
Kaye, Michael A. ....Brooklyn, NY
Kaye, Michael Bruce ....San Diego, CA
Kaye, Michael J. ....Indianapolis, IN
Kaye, Mitchell A. ....Bala Cynwyd, PA
Kaye • Moser ....San Francisco, CA
Kaye, Rebecca K. ....Cincinnati, OH
Kaye, Rhonda S. ....Dallas, TX
Kaye, Richard Allan ....Atlanta, GA
Kaye, Richard P. ....New York, NY
Kaye, Richard S. ....New York, NY
Kaye, Robert A. ....Secaucus, NJ
Kaye, Robert L. ....Fort Lauderdale, FL
Kaye, Robert N. ....Brooklyn, NY
Kaye, Robert P. ....Miami, FL
Kaye, Ronald O. ....Los Angeles, CA
Kaye, Rose & Partners, LLP
Los Angeles, CA
San Diego, CA
San Francisco, CA
Miami, FL
Kaye, Sally Katherine ....Pittsburgh, PA
Kaye, Sandra ....Atlanta, GA
Kaye, Scholer, Fierman, Hays & Handler, LLP ....Los Angeles, CA
Washington, DC
West Palm Beach, FL
New York, NY
Kaye, Seymour P. ....New York, NY
Kaye, Sheldon A. ....South Euclid, OH
Kaye, Stephen R. ....New York, NY
Kaye, Stephen S. ....Washington, DC
Kaye, Steven A. ....Philadelphia, PA
Kaye, Steven E. ....Santa Monica, CA
Kaye, Steven M. ....Boston, MA
Kaye, Stuart M. ....La Mesa, CA
Kaye, Susan ....Stuart, FL
Kaye, Susan E. ....San Francisco, CA
Kaye, Tonya J. ....Golden, CO
Kaye, Vera ....Chicago, IL
Kaye, Walter M. ....Pasadena, CA
Kaye, William H. ....Chambersburg, PA
Kayes, Dennis S. ....Detroit, MI
Kayes, Henry M. ....Huntington, WV

Kayes, Karen L. ....Muskegon, MI
Kayes, Robert B. ....Bloomfield Hills, MI
Kayfetz, Lael ....Napa, CA
Kayfetz, Paul D. ....Bolinas, CA
Kayhan, Nicholas D. ....Oakland, CA
Kayle, Bruce E. ....New York, NY
Kayle, Milton P. ....New York, NY
Kayler, Stephanie Corin ....Roswell, GA
Kaylian, Mark G. ....Southfield, MI
Kaylie, Rachel L., Law Office of
New York, NY
Kaylor, Anne H. ....Bartow, FL
Kaylor, Courtney A. ....Seattle, WA
Kaylor, Daniel ....San Jose, CA
Kaylor, Jamie Z. Scott ....Columbus, OH
Kaylor, John D. ....Sebring, FL
Winter Haven, FL
Kaylor & Kaylor, P.A. ....Sebring, FL
Winter Haven, FL
Kaylor, L. Mark ....Sebring, FL
Winter Haven, FL
Kaylor, L. Quinn ....Harrisonburg, VA
Kaylor, Leigh A. ....Birmingham, AL
Kaylor, Mitchell D. ....Orange, CA
Kaylor, Omer T., Jr. ....Hagerstown, MD
Kaylor, Robert W. ....Raleigh, NC
Kaylor, Robert W., P.A. ....Raleigh, NC
Kaylor, Stephen D. ....Shelby, NC
Kaylor, Teresa Dorow ....Kettering, OH
Kayman, Emanuel L. ....West Hempstead, NY
Kayman, Michael L. ....Chicago, IL
Kayman, Paul S. ....Chicago, IL
Kayman, Philip M. ....Chicago, IL
Kayman, Steven M. ....New York, NY
Kaynard, Gerald A. ....Charleston, SC
Kaynard, Meryl R. ....New York, NY
Kaynard, Samuel M. ....Hempstead, NY
Kayne, Bernard J. ....Chicago, IL
Kayne, Daniel J. ....Columbus, OH
Kayne, Joseph S. ....Chicago, IL
Kayne, Martin R. ....Paterson, NJ
Kayne, Marvin S. ....Berkeley, CA
Kayne, Michele S. ....Roseland, NJ
Kayne, Robert R. ....Longmont, CO
Kayner, David J. ....Chicago, IL
Kaynor, Peter J. ....Mexico, ME
Kaynor, Sanford B. ....Darien, CT
Kaynor, Sanford B., Jr. ....New York, NY
Kaynor, William A. ....New York, NY
Kays, Catherine C. ....Dallas, TX
Kays, David A. ....Palo Alto, CA
Kays, David Gregory ....Lebanon, MO
Kays, Douglas B. ....Los Angeles, CA
Kays, Douglas B. ....Springfield, MO
Kays, Gregg L. ....San Jose, CA
Kays, John H. ....Newport Beach, CA
Kays, Scott L. ....Fairfield, CA
Kays, Shelley A. ....Phoenix, AZ
Kays, Shepard ....Sparta, NJ
Kayser, Bruce D. ....Portland, OR
Kayser, C. Dallas ....Point Pleasant, WV
Kayser, C. Dallas, L.C. ....Point Pleasant, WV
Kayser, Christopher J. ....Washington, DC
Kayser, Joan Bradbury ....Sarasota, FL
Kayser, Kenneth W. ....East Hanover, NJ
Kayser Law Office ....Webster City, IA
Kayser, Lawrence R., Jr. ....Webster City, IA
Kayser, Leo, III ....New York, NY
Kayser, Maria ....Denver, CO
Kayser & Redfern ....New York, NY
Kayser, Robert S. ....Colorado Springs, CO
Kayser, Ronald M. ....Des Moines, IA
Kayser, Susan M. ....Chicago, IL
Kayser, Susan V. ....New York, NY
Kayser, Thomas C. ....Minneapolis, MN
Kayser, Victor P. ....Burr Ridge, IL
Kayser, William A. ....San Jose, CA
Kayton, Alan B. ....Dix Hills, NY
Kayton, David ....Houston, TX
Kayton & Kayton ....Houston, TX
Kayton, Mark ....Houston, TX
Kayuha, Bruce A. ....Charleston, WV
Kayuha, Thomas A. ....Akron, OH
Kayukov, Edward V. ....Los Angeles, CA
Kayusa, Michael F. ....Fort Myers, FL
Kaywell, James W. ....Port Charlotte, FL
Kaywell, James W. ....Punta Gorda, FL
Tallahassee, FL
Kaywood, Sam K., Jr. ....Atlanta, GA
Kayyem, Juliette N. ....Department of Justice, Civil Rights Division, GV
Kazaglis, Ted N. ....San Leandro, CA
Kazak, Kerri Ann ....New York, NY
Kazakevitch, Olga L. ....Miami, FL
Kazakis, Georgia ....Washington, DC
Kazaks, Julia M. ....Washington, DC
Kazamias, Michael A. ....Atlanta, GA
Kazan, Alan J., (P.A.) ....Miami, FL
Kazan, Barry M. ....New York, NY
Kazan, James B. ....Manchester, NH
Kazan, Kenneth ....Encino, CA
Kazan, Lawrence Ian ....Phoenix, AZ
Kazan, McClain, Edises, Simon & Abrams, A Professional Law Corporation
Oakland, CA
Kazan, Philip Y. ....San Francisco, CA
Kazan, Steven ....Oakland, CA
Kazan, Wayne ....Beverly Hills, CA
Kazanas, Christine M. ....Phoenix, AZ
Kazanas, Dan J. ....St. Louis, MO
Kazanas, Klar, Izsak & Stenger, L.L.C.
St. Louis, MO
Kazanas, Steve ....West, TX
Kazanchy, Joseph J. ....Union City, NJ
Kazanchy, Ronald R. ....Union City, NJ
Kazandjian, Yeznik O. ....Glendale, CA
Kazandjieff, Nick ....Pasadena, CA
Kazanis, Maria-Daphne ....Parsippany, NJ

Kazanjian, Debra J. .... Fresno, CA
Kazanjian, John H. .... New York, NY
Kazanjian, Larry M. .... Sacramento, CA
Kazanjian & Martinetti .... Glendale, CA
Kazanjian, Phillip .... Glendale, CA
Kazanjian, Victor M. .... Silver Spring, MD
Kazanoff, Paul E. .... New York, NY
Kazanoff, Peter E. .... New York, NY
Kazanowski, Joseph C. .... Braintree, MA
Kazanski, Claude J. .... Madison, WI
Kazansky, Evy L. .... White Plains, NY
Kazantzis, Kyra A. .... San Jose, CA
Kazanzas, Leon G., III .... Orlando, FL
Kazaras, Paul J. .... Philadelphia, PA
Kazaras, Peter D. .... New York, NY
Kazares, Jill M. .... Los Angeles, CA
Kazarian, Charles P. .... Boston, MA
Kazarian, Charles P., P.C. .... Boston, MA
Kazarian, David J. .... West Hartford, CT
Kazarian, Gregory N. .... Chicago, IL
Kazarian, Michele (Halberian
East Providence, RI
Kazarian, Thomas E. .... San Francisco, CA
Kazarosian, Marsha V. .... Haverhill, MA
Kazarosian, Paul .... Haverhill, MA
Kazary, John C. .... Revere, PA
Kazary, Robert Owen .... Cumberland, MD
Kazazian, Nina H. .... New York, NY
Kazazis & Alimaras .... Long Island City, NY
Kazazis, George .... Long Island City, NY
Kazdin, Gary A. .... Cleveland, OH
Kazdin, Gary A., Co., L.P.A. .... Cleveland, OH
Kazdoy, Alan C. .... Dallas, TX
Kaze, James M. .... Havre, MT
Kazee, D. B. .... Prestonsburg, KY
Kazee, Kinner & Chafin .... Paintsville, KY
Prestonsburg, KY
Kazee, N. Bruce .... Irving, TX
Kazemba, Mark E. .... Dallas, TX
Kazemzadeh, Farhad .... Los Angeles, CA
Kazen, Barbara Anne .... El Paso, TX
Kazen, David A. .... Austin, TX
Kazen, E. Jas. .... Austin, TX
Kazen, George P. .... Laredo, TX
Kazen, Gregory S. .... McAllen, TX
Kazen, John A. .... Laredo, TX
Kazen, Meurer & Pérez .... Laredo, TX
Kazenoff, Laurie B. .... Huntington, NY
Kazenoff, Suzanne R. .... New York, NY
Kazense, Jonathan L. .... Morton, IL
Kazepis, Christina J. .... Lake Success, NY
Kazer, Michael C. .... Jersey City, NJ
Kazer, Robert Craig .... Santa Ana, CA
Kazer, William G., Jr. .... Chicago, IL
Kazielski, Joseph P. .... Pittsburgh, PA
Kazik, Danielle .... Milwaukee, WI
Kazimer, Mary Ellen .... San Francisco, CA
Kazimiroff, Emelia .... Bronx, NY
Kazimirsky, Irina M. .... Menlo Park, CA
Kazin, Gary M. .... Decatur, GA
Kazin, Philip M. .... Hauppauge, NY
Kazlauskas, Charles F. .... New York, NY
Kazlauski, Daniel A. .... Chicago, IL
Kazlouskas, Anthony .... Akron, OH
Kazlow, Alan L. .... New York, NY
Kazlow, Gene R. .... New York, NY
Kazlow, Glenn R. .... Hackensack, NJ
Kazlow, Ira .... Forest Hills, NY
Kazlow, Todd Charles .... Baltimore, MD
Kazmann, Hollis Beem .... Houston, TX
Kazmarek, Edward A. .... Atlanta, GA
Kazmer, Carol E. .... Newton, MA
Kazmer, Janice Pastryk .... Chicago, IL
Kazmerski, Nicholas Stephan .... Southfield, MI
Kazmierczak, Lawrence E. .... Oakland, NJ
Kazmierski, Stefan .... Denver, CO
Kazon, Leslie .... New York, NY
Kazon, Peter M. .... Washington, DC
Kazragis, Gary W. .... Sedona, AZ
Kazubowski, Dennis James .... San Jose, CA
Kazul & Associates, P.C. .... Southfield, MI
Kazul, Stan C., P.C. .... Southfield, MI
Kea, Arleas Upton
Federal Deposit Insurance Corporation, Corporate Affairs Section, GV
Kea, John L., II .... Murfreesboro, TN
Keable, Edward T.
Department Of The Interior, Office of the Solicitor, GV
Keable, James E. .... Plattsburgh, NY
Keable, Steven J. .... Exeter, NH
Keable, Thomas J. .... Buffalo, NY
Keach and Buckley .... Easton, MA
Keach, Eckley M. .... Las Vegas, NV
Keach, Elmer R., III .... Albany, NY
Keach, John A., Jr. .... Easton, MA
Keach, Robert J. .... Portland, ME
Keadle, Jennifer A. .... Wheeling, WV
Keadle, Thomas H. .... Buckhannon, WV
Keady, Deirdre .... Newton, MA
Keady, George C., Jr. .... Longmeadow, MA
Keady, J. Vincent, Jr. .... St. Louis, MO
Keady, William C., Jr. .... Oxford, MS
Keagy, Bonnie-Ann Brill .... Ambler, PA
Keagy, Bonnie-Ann Brill
Fort Washington, PA
Keagy, Pilar G. .... Atlanta, GA
Keagy, Roscoe D. .... San Diego, CA
Keagy, Rose A. .... Dallas, TX
Keahey, G. Patterson, Jr.
Birmingham, AL
Keahey, Hazel C.
United States Tax Court, GV
Keahey, James H. .... Austin, TX
Keahey, Michael J. .... Las Vegas, NV
Keahey, Michael J. .... Las Vegas, NV
Keahey, Ronnie E. .... Grove Hill, AL
Keahon, Douglas P. .... Phoenix, AZ
Keal, Jeffrey C. .... Independence, MO
Keal, Robert Thaddeus (Thad)
Louisville, KY
Keal, Timothy J. .... Sun Prairie, WI
Keale, Christopher J. .... Trenton, NJ
Keale, James H. .... Newark, NJ
Keale, John E. .... Newark, NJ
Kealey, James A. .... Sacramento, CA
Kealey, Warren D. .... Norwalk, CT
Kealey, William P. .... Lafayette, IN
Kealhofer, G. Michael .... Des Moines, IA
Perry, IA
Kealing, James L. .... Kansas City, MO
Kealy, John C. .... Cleveland, OH
Kealy, Joseph V., Jr. .... Jersey City, NJ
Kealy, Luke J. .... Woodbridge, NJ
Kealy, Michael R. .... Reno, NV
Kealy, Robert L. .... Milwaukee, WI
Kealy, Robert M. .... East Orange, NJ
Kealy, Susan M. .... Boston, MA
Keamy, Leilah Anne .... Boston, MA
Kean, Barret E.
Department of the Air Force, Office of the General Counsel, GV
Kean, Cynthia A. .... Brooklyn, NY
Kean, David W. .... El Segundo, CA
Kean, Frank H., III .... Baton Rouge, LA
Kean, Gene Paul .... Sioux Falls, SD
Kean, Hamilton F. .... New York, NY
Kean, James C. .... Houston, TX
Kean, Jeffrey P .... Department of Agriculture, Farm Service Agency, GV
Kean, John V. .... Sylvania, OH
Kean, John V. .... Providence, RI
Kean, Joseph A. .... Los Angeles, CA
Kean, Lewis B. .... Long Beach, CA
Kean, Margaret Anne .... Mahwah, NJ
Kean, Michael I. .... Miami, FL
Kean, Michael R. .... Fort Washington, PA
Kean, Miller, Hawthorne, D'Armond, McCowan & Jarman, L.L.P.
Baton Rouge, LA
Covington, LA
Lake Charles, LA
New Orleans, LA
Plaquemine, LA
Kean, Milton .... New York, NY
Kean, Nicola J. .... Atlanta, GA
Kean, Paul H. .... Larchmont, NY
Kean, Robert J. .... Pierre, SD
Kean, Sharon B. .... Chatham, NJ
Kean, Suzanne B. .... Houston, TX
Kean, Warren P. .... Charlotte, NC
Keane, Alice D. .... New York, NY
Keane, Alison Ann .... Annapolis, MD
Keane, Amy Hertzberg .... Albany, NY
Keane, Anne T. .... Seattle, WA
Keane, Austin W. .... Worcester, MA
Keane & Beane, P.C. .... New York, NY
Rye, NY
White Plains, NY
Keane, Brady & Burns .... Jersey City, NJ
Keane, Brendan J. .... New York, NY
Keane, Brian P. .... Boston, MA
Keane, Brian T. .... Hackensack, NJ
Keane, Charles D. .... Vestal, NY
Keane, Christopher G. .... New York, NY
Keane, Christopher P., Jr.
East Brunswick, NJ
New York, NY
Keane, Christopher S.
Department of Transportation, U. S. Coast Guard, GV
Keane, Cornelius W. .... White Plains, NY
Keane, Cynthia .... New York, NY
Keane, Denise F. .... New York, NY
Keane, Edward A. .... Red Bank, NJ
New York, NY
Keane, Edward J. .... Sioux City, IA
Keane, Edward W. .... New York, NY
Keane, Frank W. .... Scarsdale, NY
Keane, George Michael, Jr. .... Chicago, IL
Keane, Gerald B. .... Sarasota, FL
Keane, Gregory G., (P.A.) .... Stuart, FL
Keane, Honora M. .... New York, NY
Keane, J. Timothy .... St. Louis, MO
Keane, James G. .... Hoffman Estates, IL
Keane, James J. .... Boulder, CO
Keane, James L. .... Los Angeles, CA
Keane, James M. .... Washington, DC
Keane, James P. .... Charlestown, MA
Keane, Jeffrey G. .... Palm Springs, CA
Keane, Jennifer .... Austin, TX
Keane, John B. .... Hartford, CT
Keane, John J. .... Johnstown, NY
Keane, John K., Jr. .... Washington, DC
Keane, John P. .... Lewiston, MN
Keane, Josh I. .... Los Angeles, CA
Keane, Kathleen M. .... Syosset, NY
Keane, Kevin G. .... Brookfield, WI
Keane, Lawrence G. .... White Plains, NY
Keane, Marc J. .... Jersey City, NJ
Keane, Margaret A. .... Pittsburgh, PA
Keane, Margaret E. .... Louisville, KY
Keane, Maria H. .... New York, NY
Keane & Marlowe .... East Brunswick, NJ
New York, NY
Keane, Martin E. .... Washington, DC
Keane, Martin F. .... Rego Park, NY
Keane, Mary C. .... Philadelphia, PA
Keane, Michael J. .... St. Petersburg, FL
Keane, Michael J. .... Great Neck, NY
Keane, Michael J. .... New York, NY
Keane, Michael J. .... Cleveland, OH
Keane & Murphy .... Naples, FL
Stuart, FL
Keane, Nancy A. E. .... San Mateo, CA
Keane, Nancyellen .... Richmond, VA
Keane, Patricia DeJonge .... Dallas, TX
Keane, Patricia M. .... Thousand Oaks, CA
Keane, Patrick C. .... Alexandria, VA
Keane, Paul M. .... New York, NY
Keane, Paul R. .... Boston, MA
Keane, Peter G. .... San Francisco, CA
Keane, Peter L. .... New York, NY
Keane, Peter R. .... Albany, NY
Keane, Raymond T. .... Plainsboro, NJ
Keane, Reese & Vesely, P.A.
Palm Harbor, FL
St. Petersburg, FL
Keane, Robert J. .... New York, NY
Keane, Robert M., Jr. .... Los Angeles, CA
Keane, Sally A. .... Oakland, CA
Keane, Steven E. .... Milwaukee, WI
Keane, Steven W. .... Milwaukee, WI
Keane, T. Jeffrey .... Seattle, WA
Keane, Thomas F. .... New York, NY
Keane, Thomas J. .... White Plains, NY
Keane, Thomas M. .... Portsmouth, NH
Keane, Thomas M. .... New York, NY
Keane, Timothy J. .... Minneapolis, MN
Keane, Timothy J. .... New York, NY
Keane, Vincent .... East Williston, NY
Keane, William K. .... Washington, DC
Keane, William P. .... San Francisco, CA
Keane, William T. .... Phoenix, AZ
Keane, William T., P.C. .... Phoenix, AZ
Keaney, J. David .... Springfield, MA
Keaney, James B. .... New York, NY
Keaney, Kevin J. .... Alexandria, VA
Keaney, Mark T. .... St. Louis, MO
Keaney, Patrick M. .... Muskogee, OK
Keaney, Robert E. .... St. Louis, MO
Keany, Sutton .... New York, NY
Kear, Fergus M. .... Indianapolis, IN
Kear, Frank E. .... San Diego, CA
Kear, J. G. .... Chillicothe, OH
Kear Law Firm, The .... Fairfax, VA
Kear, Maria M. .... Fairfax, VA
Kear, Russell H., Jr. .... Indianapolis, IN
Kearby, Jennings H. .... Scottsburg, IN
Keare, Stacey K. .... San Francisco, CA
Kearfott, Clarence P. .... Martinsville, VA
Kearfott, Joseph C. .... Richmond, VA
Kearin, Kathy H. .... Lebanon, OH
Kearing, Samuel J., Jr .... Centerport, NY
Kearl, Jane Grilliot .... Irvine, CA
Kearl, Kurtis J. .... Petaluma, CA
Kearl, Matthew E. .... Pasadena, CA
Kearl, Russell C. .... Salt Lake City, UT
Kearn, James J. .... Daytona Beach, FL
Kearney Alvarez, LLP .... Los Angeles, CA
Kearney, Anne Berleman .... Milwaukee, WI
Kearney, Arthur P. .... Bellevue, WA
Kearney, Barry J.
National Labor Relations Board, Office of the General Counsel, GV
Kearney, Bernadette A. .... Lansdale, PA
Kearney & Brady, P.C. .... Haddon Heights, NJ
Kearney, Brian J. .... New York, NY
Kearney, Brian J. .... Lexington, VA
Kearney, Caroline .... Brooklyn, NY
Kearney, Cauleen Ross .... Springfield, MA
Kearney, Charles E., Jr. .... Aberdeen, MD
Bel Air, MD
Kearney, Christina E. .... Richmond, VA
Kearney, Christopher C.
San Francisco, CA
Kearney, Christopher J., III
Muskegon, MI
Kearney, David B. .... Richmond, VA
Kearney, David L. .... Oklahoma City, OK
Kearney, Deborah Kaveney .... Tallahassee, FL
Kearney, Dennis J., (P.C.) .... Boston, MA
Kearney, Dennis T. .... Morristown, NJ
Kearney, Donna White .... Norfolk, VA
Kearney, Edward F. .... Washington, DC
Kearney, Elizabeth Lamb .... Denver, CO
Kearney, Eric H. .... Cincinnati, OH
Kearney, Frances .... Auburn, CA
Kearney, Francis X., Jr. .... Baltimore, MD
Kearney, Frank J. .... Baltimore, MD
Kearney, Frank R. .... Washington, DC
Kearney, Franklin R. .... New York, NY
Kearney, Frederick T. .... Oakland, CA
Kearney, Frederick T., P.C. .... Oakland, CA
Kearney, Gary W. .... Los Angeles, CA
Kearney, Gary W. .... Pasadena, CA
Kearney & Gleason, Professional Corporation
Boston, MA
Kearney, Henry F. .... West Roxbury, MA
Kearney, J. Mitchell .... Towson, MD
Kearney, James A. .... Neenah, WI
Kearney, James F. .... Jacksonville, FL
Kearney, James K. .... Washington, DC
Kearney, James M. .... Portland, OR
Kearney, James R. .... Fairfax, VA
Kearney, James V. .... New York, NY
Kearney, Jan E. .... Tucson, AZ
Kearney, Jeffrey A. .... Fort Worth, TX
Kearney, Jennifer L. .... Media, PA
Kearney, Jeremiah J. .... Minneapolis, MN
Kearney, John B. .... Cherry Hill, NJ
Kearney, John B. .... Haddon Heights, NJ
Kearney, John D. .... Atlanta, GA
Kearney, John D. .... Philadelphia, PA
Kearney, John F. .... Washington, DC
Kearney, John F. .... Lexington, MA
Kearney, John F., III .... Moorestown, NJ
Kearney, John J., Jr. .... Garden City, NY
Kearney, John L. .... Pine Bluff, AR
Kearney, John L., Jr. .... Solana Beach, CA
Kearney, John M. .... Roseland, NJ
Kearney, John P. .... Chicago, IL
Kearney, Jon .... Kearny, NJ
Kearney, Joseph J. .... Garden City, NY
Kearney, Joseph J. .... New Castle, PA
Kearney, Jude .... Washington, DC
Kearney, Julie M. .... Arlington, VA
Kearney, Kathleen A. .... Tallahassee, FL
Kearney & Kearney, LLP .... New York, NY
Kearney, Keith R. .... Dayton, OH
Kearney, Kerry A. .... Pittsburgh, PA
Kearney, Kevin M. .... Newark, NJ
New York, NY
Kearney, Kevin M. .... Brooklyn, NY
Melville, NY
Kearney, Kevin W. .... South Bend, IN
Kearney, Kimbley A. .... Chicago, IL
Kearney, Linda Marie
Corpus Christi, TX
Kearney, Marci .... Denver, CO
Kearney, Mark A. .... Blue Bell, PA
Kearney & Marshall .... York, PA
Kearney, Mary M. .... Washington, DC
Kearney, Melissa E. .... McLean, VA
Kearney, Michael E. .... Las Vegas, NV
Kearney, Michael J. .... Pittsburgh, PA
Kearney, Michael J., Jr. .... Stamford, CT
Kearney, Michael K. .... Virginia, MN
Kearney, Michael P. .... Eugene, OR
Kearney, Michael P., P.C. .... Eugene, OR
Kearney, Patrick J. .... Washington, DC
Kearney, Philip .... San Francisco, CA
Kearney, Philip F., Jr. .... Dayton, OH
Kearney, Rex T., Jr. .... Sacramento, CA
Kearney, Richard V. .... New York, NY
Kearney, Sean P. .... Minneapolis, MN
Kearney, Smith, Chustz & Minogue
New Roads, LA
Kearney, Stephanie K. .... Chicago, IL
Kearney, Stephen W. .... Charlotte, NC
Kearney, Terrence J. P. .... Palo Alto, CA
Kearney, Thomas A. .... Los Angeles, CA
Kearney, Thomas J. .... Los Angeles, CA
Kearney, Thomas L., III .... York, PA
Kearney, W. Daniel .... Palmetto, FL
Kearney, Wendy S. .... Frederick, MD
Kearney & Westfall .... Fort Worth, TX
Kearney, William J., Jr. .... Louisville, KY
Kearney, Wm. G. .... Baltimore, MD
Kearney-Wood, Annmarie .... New York, NY
Kearns, B. Thomas .... St. Louis, MO
Kearns, Benedict, Harp & Brumby
Atlanta, GA
Kearns, Burtsell J. .... Trumbull, CT
Kearns, C. Dant .... Louisville, KY
Kearns, Christine Nicolaides
Washington, DC
Kearns, Christopher J. .... San Diego, CA
Kearns & Coyle .... Liberty Corner, NJ
Kearns, Daniel H. .... Portland, OR
Kearns, Darren K. .... Overland Park, KS
Kearns, David E. .... New York, NY
Kearns, Deborah R. .... Westport, CT
Kearns, Dennis A. .... Austin, TX
Kearns, Dennis E., (P.C.) .... St. Louis, MO
Kearns, Donald N. .... Covington, LA
Kearns & Duffy, P.C. .... Liberty Corner, NJ
Kearns, Edwin N. .... Raleigh, NC
Kearns, Ellen B. .... Willingboro, NJ
Kearns, Ellen C. .... Boston, MA
Kearns, Frederick E. .... Bullhead City, AZ
Kearns, George H. .... Cincinnati, OH
Kearns, Greta M. .... Columbus, OH
Kearns, J. Bradley .... Pittsburgh, PA
Kearns, James A., III .... St. Louis, MO
Kearns, James C. .... Urbana, IL
Kearns, James Patrick .... Brooklyn, NY
Kearns, Jennifer A. .... San Diego, CA
Kearns, Jerome H. .... Cincinnati, OH
Kearns, John F., III .... West Hartford, CT
Kearns, John J. .... Gainesville, FL
Kearns, John J., III .... Pittsburgh, PA
Kearns, John S. .... Washington, DC
Kearns, John T. .... Englewood, CO
Kearns, Joseph P. .... Millington, NJ
Kearns, Joseph P., Jr. .... Ashland, OH
Kearns & Kearns, P.C.
West Hartford, CT
Kearns, Kevin L. .... Department of State, Foreign Service Officers (Overseas), GV
Kearns, Marion M. .... Boston, MA
Kearns, Mark A. .... Wells, ME
Kearns, Michael Allen .... Cincinnati, OH
Kearns, Michael B. .... Manhattan, KS
Kearns, Michael J. .... Department of Justice, Tax Division, GV
Kearns, Michael P. .... Libertyville, IL
Kearns, Michael Scott .... Cincinnati, OH
Kearns, Michael T. .... New Brunswick, NJ
Kearns, Peter D. .... Point Pleasant Beach, NJ
Kearns, Peter F. .... Manchester, NH
Kearns, Phil H. .... Winston-Salem, NC
Kearns, Raymond J. .... Atlanta, GA
Kearns, Richard L. .... Harrisburg, PA
Kearns, Ronald R. .... Braintree, MA
Kearns & Ryan, P.C. .... Englewood, CO
Kearns, Scott A. .... Bannockburn, IL
Kearns, Scott G. .... New York, NY
Kearns, Steven T. .... Hackensack, NJ
Kearns, Thomas C., Jr. .... Denver, CO
Kearns, Thomas Daniel .... New York, NY
Kearns, Thomas P. .... Denver, CO
Kearns, Thomas W. .... Houston, TX
Kearns, Thomas William .... Hampstead, MD
Kearns, Vassallo, Guest & Kearns
Mount Holly, NJ
Willingboro, NJ
Kearns, Virginia L. .... Lake Forest, IL
Kearns, William G. .... Chester, VT
Kearns, William J. .... Liberty Corner, NJ
Kearns, William John, Jr.
Willingboro, NJ

Kearny, Adelia W. .... Albuquerque, NM
Kearon, Kevin T. .... Westbury, NY
Kearon, Pamela .... New York, NY
Kearon, Robert V. .... Ronkonkoma, NY
Kearse, Amalya Lyle .... New York, NY
Kearse, Anne McGinness .... Charleston, SC
Kearse, Bernard V., III .... Atlanta, GA
Kearse, Brendan P. .... New York, NY
Kearse, Edward P. .... Albany, NY
Kearse, George H. .... Allendale, SC
Kearse, Kelvin R. .... Easley, SC
Kearse, Lamond W. .... New York, NY
Kearse, Michael J. .... New York, NY
Kearsey, Mary Sorrell .... Neptune Beach, FL
Kearsley, David A. .... Worcester, MA
Kearsley, Richard B. .... Kennebunk, ME
Keary, Ann O'Regan .... Washington, DC
Keary, Grant C. .... Irvine, CA
Keary, John E. .... Fairhaven, MA
Keary, Merle .... Reseda, CA
Keary, Thomas J. .... Department of Justice, Civil Rights Division, GV
Keas, William W., Jr. .... Corpus Christi, TX
Keasler, Frank R., Jr. .... Jacksonville, FL
Keasler, Michael E. .... Dallas, TX
Keast, Anthony F. .... Missoula, MT
Keast, David S. .... Novi, MI
Keast, Douglas A. .... Troy, MI
Keaster, Robert W. .... Los Angeles, CA
Keate, Kenneth E. .... St. Paul, MN
Keate Law Office, P.A. .... St. Paul, MN
Keaten, James H. .... Atlanta, GA
Keathley, C. Kevin .... Waco, TX
Keathley, David W. .... Van Buren, MO
Keathley, H. James .... Newport Beach, CA
Keathley, Katherine D. Newport Beach, CA
Keathley, Roy .... Memphis, TN
Keathley, Stephen A. .... Corsicana, TX
Keating, Alexander F., Jr. .... Flemington, NJ
Keating, Alysia M. .... Fort Lauderdale, FL
Keating, Amanda L. .... Boise, ID
Keating, Anne E. .... Clive, IA
Keating, Anne E. .... Frankfort, KY
Keating, Anthony E. .... Olympia, WA
Keating, Anton J. S. .... Baltimore, MD
Keating, Brendan .... Warren, OH
Keating, Brian .... New York, NY
Keating, Bucklin & McCormack, Inc., P.S. Seattle, WA
Keating, Bumb, Vowels, LaPlante & Kent, P.C. .... Evansville, IN
Keating, Catherine M. .... Philadelphia, PA
Keating, Cathleen M. .... Oak Brook, IL
Keating, Charles J. .... Springfield, IL
Keating, Christopher .... Keene, NH
Keating, Con M. .... Lincoln, NE
Keating & Conklin, P.A. .... Woodstock, NH
Keating, Cornelius F. .... New York, NY
Keating, D. Patrick .... Opelousas, LA
Keating, Daniel G. .... Warren, OH
Keating, Daniel J. .... Melrose, MA
Keating, Daniel L. .... St. Louis, MO
Keating, David C. .... Atlanta, GA
Keating, David C. .... Milwaukee, WI
Keating, Deirdre A. .... Albany, NY
Keating, Diana Marie .... Hudson, OH
Keating, Dominic J. Department of Commerce, Patent and Trademark Office, GV
Keating, Dominic J. .... Scranton, PA
Keating, Duane F. .... Albuquerque, NM
Keating, Duane F., P.A. .... Albuquerque, NM
Keating, E. Lyle .... Palo Alto, CA
Keating, E. Michael, III .... Philadelphia, PA
Keating, Edward M. .... Chicago, IL
Keating, Elizabeth Ann .... New City, NY
Keating, Elizabeth Davis .... Chicago, IL
Keating, Elizabeth J. .... Island Heights, NJ
Keating, Eugene .... Minneapolis, MN
Keating, Francis A., II .... Oklahoma City, OK
Keating, Francis J. .... Wilmette, IL
Keating, Francis J. .... Saginaw, MI
Keating, Geoffrey T. .... Washington, DC
Keating, Gerald R. .... Minneapolis, MN
Keating, Gerard F. .... Daytona Beach, FL
Keating, Gregory C. .... Boston, MA
Keating, Hugh D. .... Gulfport, MS
Keating, J. Michael, Jr. .... Cambridge, MA Providence, RI
Keating, Jaime M. .... Carlisle, PA
Keating, James A. .... Hartford, CT
Keating, James M., Jr. .... Trenton, NJ
Keating, James M., Jr. .... Philadelphia, PA
Keating, James R. .... Faribault, MN
Keating, James T. J. .... Chicago, IL
Keating, Jennifer A. .... Atlantic City, NJ
Keating, Joanne P. .... Boston, MA
Keating, John .... Las Vegas, NV
Keating, John C. .... Rockville, MD
Keating, John F. .... Lake Arrowhead, CA
Keating, John F., Jr.(A Professional Corporation) .... New Fairfield, CT **New York, NY**
Keating, John Kingman .... Orlando, FL
Keating, John R. .... Pittsburgh, PA
Keating, John S. .... Boston, MA
Keating, John Thomas .... Wooster, OH
Keating Jones Bildstein & Hughes, P.C. Portland, OR
Keating, Joseph A. .... Pompano Beach, FL
Keating, Joseph R. .... Los Angeles, CA
Keating, Karen M. .... Philadelphia, PA
Keating, Karen Maloy Department Of The Interior, Office of the Solicitor, GV
Keating, Kathleen A. .... Kingston, NY
Keating, Kathleen D. .... Harrisburg, PA
Keating, Kathleen O'Connell .... Newark, NJ
Keating, Keating & Kuzman .... Warren, OH
Keating, Keating & Pipal, P.C. Chicago, IL
Keating, Kenneth D. .... Springvale, ME
Keating, Kent Wilcox .... Woodland Hills, CA
Keating, Kevin J. .... Garden City, NY
Keating, Kevin M. .... Omaha, NE
Keating, Kevin R. .... Phoenix, AZ
Keating, Kevin S. .... New York, NY
Keating, Kevin T. .... Chicago, IL
Keating, Kirsten E. .... Washington, DC
Keating Law Offices .... Wooster, OH
Keating, Lawrence J. .... Lancaster, PA
Keating, Lisa J. .... Newport Beach, CA
Keating, Loren J. .... Kenosha, WI
Keating, Louise Walsh .... Wooster, OH
Keating, M. Hope .... Tallahassee, FL
Keating, Margaret F. .... Kansas City, MO
Keating, Marshall P. .... New York, NY
Keating, Martin J. W. .... Palatine, IL
Keating, Mary P. .... Darien, CT
Keating, Mary T. .... Baltimore, MD
Keating, Marylin A. .... Raleigh, NC
Keating, Matthew J. .... Yonkers, NY
Keating, Michael .... White Plains, NY
Keating, Michael B. .... Boston, MA
Keating, Michael C. .... Evansville, IN
Keating, Michael G. .... Hackensack, NJ New York, NY
Keating, Michael J. .... St. Louis, MO
Keating, Michael J. .... Cranford, NJ
Keating, Michele R. .... Houston, TX
Keating, Muething & Klekamp Covington, KY Florence, KY Cincinnati, OH
Keating, Nancy L. .... Boston, MA
Keating, Neil M. .... Knoxville, TN
Keating, O'Gara, Davis & Nedved, P.C. Lincoln, NE
Keating, P. Blake .... Kansas City, MO
Keating, Pamela M. .... Plymouth Meeting, PA
Keating, Patrick D. .... Dallas, TX
Keating, Patrick J. .... Chicago, IL
Keating, Patrick J. .... Detroit, MI
Keating, Patrick J. .... Akron, OH
Keating, Paul Raynor .... San Francisco, CA
Keating, Peter .... Daytona Beach, FL
Keating, Philip M. .... Alexandria, VA
Keating, R. Daniel .... Washington, DC
Keating, Ray M., Jr. .... Falls Church, VA
Keating, Richard M. .... Wooster, OH
Keating, Richard P. .... Willingboro, NJ
Keating, Robert A. .... Newton, MA
Keating, Robert C. .... Seattle, WA
Keating, Robert E. .... Pueblo, CO
Keating, Robert G. M. .... New York, NY
Keating, Robert M. .... Woodstock, NH
Keating, Robert M. .... Portland, OR
Keating, Ruth Anne .... Buffalo, NY
Keating, Sarah Peachey .... Philadelphia, PA
Keating, Scott R. .... Valencia, CA
Keating, Shana .... San Francisco, CA
Keating & Shure, Ltd. .... Chicago, IL
Keating, Sonja S. .... Lexington, KY
Keating, Stephen J. .... Miami, FL
Keating, Stephen J. .... New York, NY
Keating, Susan M. .... Chicago, IL
Keating, Suzanne Elizabeth .... Naperville, IL
Keating, Terrence E. .... Detroit, MI
Keating, Thomas A., Jr. .... Norwalk, CT
Keating, Thomas F., Jr. .... San Rafael, CA
Keating, Thomas H. Grosse Pointe Farms, MI
Keating, Thomas J. .... Marina Del Rey, CA
Keating, Thomas J., IV .... Centreville, MD
Keating, Thomas M. .... Chicago, IL
Keating, Thomas T. .... Sedalia, MO
Keating, Thomas T. .... New Rochelle, NY
Keating, Thomas T. .... Cincinnati, OH
Keating, Van D. .... Columbus, OH
Keating, Victoria A. .... Detroit, MI
Keating, W. Leo .... Warren, OH
Keating, William F. .... Haddonfield, NJ
Keating, William H. .... Dublin, OH
Keating, William J. .... Cincinnati, OH
Keating, William J. .... Carlisle, PA
Keating, William J., Jr. .... Cincinnati, OH
Keating, William L. .... Denver, CO
Keatinge, Robert R. .... Denver, CO
Keating-McKeon, Joan B. West Hartford, CT
Keatley, Robert E. .... Boulder, CO
Keaton, Edwin A. .... Camden, AR
Keaton, Forrest G. .... Jacksonville, IL
Keaton, Jo .... Plano, TX
Keaton, Karen S., (P.A.) St. Petersburg, FL
Keaton and Keaton, P.C. .... Rushville, IN
Keaton, Patrick J .... Lansing, MI
Keaton, R. Mark .... Fort Wayne, IN
Keaton, Reggie E. .... Knoxville, TN
Keaton, Stacy .... Corpus Christi, TX
Keaton, Tammy B. .... Bogalusa, LA Mandeville, LA
Keaton, Turner & Spitzer Hohenwald, TN
Keaton, Wayne Darrin .... Marietta, GA
Keaton, William B. .... Rushville, IN
Keaton, William C. .... Romney, WV
Keaton, Wm. C. .... Hohenwald, TN
Keats, Anthony M. .... Beverly Hills, CA
Keats, Craig M. Department of Transportation, Surface Transportation Board, GV
Keats, Ellen .... Greenwich, CT
Keats, H. James, Jr. Federal Communications Commission, Cable Services Bureau, GV
Keats, Joelle R. .... Pittsburgh, PA
Keats, John A. .... Fairfax, VA
Keats, McFarland & Wilson Beverly Hills, CA Los Angeles, CA
Keats, Michael C. .... New York, NY
Keats, Robert W. .... Louisville, KY
Keats, Schwietz & O'Donnell Louisville, KY
Keats & Shapiro .... Mineola, NY
Keats, Steven L. .... Mineola, NY
Keats, Wendy M. .... Department of Justice, Civil Division, GV
Keats, William Perry .... East Hampton, NY
Keatts, John C., Jr. .... Seattle, WA
Keaty & Keaty .... Lafayette, LA New Orleans, LA Beaumont, TX
Keaty, Robert Burke, Sr., (A Professional L.L.C.) .... Lafayette, LA New Orleans, LA Beaumont, TX
Keaty, Thomas St. Paul, II, (A Professional Corporation) .... Lafayette, LA New Orleans, LA Beaumont, TX
Keavany, Donald C., Jr. .... Worcester, MA
Keaveney, Eileen M. .... Newton, MA
Keaveney, James P. .... Cherry Hill, NJ
Keaveney, Kathleen A. .... Braintree, MA
Keaveny, Amanda Bethea .... Charleston, SC
Keaveny, Joseph P. .... St. Louis, MO
Keaveny, Kevin Patrick .... West New York, NJ
Keaveny, Thomas J., II .... Charleston, SC
Keavney, Richard P. .... Torrance, CA
Keay, Christopher W. .... Tacoma, WA
Keay, David H. .... Wheaton, IL
Keay, John C. .... San Jose, CA
Keays, Anne C. .... Chicago, IL
Kebbe, Timothy P. .... Uniondale, NY
Kebe, William M., Jr. .... Butte, MT
Keber, Anthony J. .... Boston, MA
Keber, Kathleen A. .... Sacramento, CA
Keberle, Ronald D. .... Wausau, WI
Kebler, Richard W. .... Tucson, AZ
Kebler, William A. .... St. Petersburg, FL
Kebodeaux, Charles K. .... Beaumont, TX
Kebrdle, Jerry F., II .... White Plains, NY
Kechejian, Haig .... Sherman Oaks, CA
Keck, Allan L. .... Maquoketa, IA
Keck, Ann I. .... St. Davids, PA
Keck, Anne L. .... Santa Rosa, CA
Keck, Anthony G. .... Boston, MA
Keck, C. L. .... San Francisco, CA
Keck, Darla J. .... Missoula, MT
Keck, David M. .... Evansville, IN
Keck, Donald W. .... Richardson, TX
Keck, Emerson R. .... Dayton, OH
Keck & Folz .... Evansville, IN
Keck, Harry B. .... Pittsburgh, PA
Keck, J. Bradley .... Chicago, IL
Keck, Jeffrey J. .... Harvard, IL
Keck, John A. .... Milwaukee, WI
Keck, John S. .... Louisville, KY
Keck, Karen R. .... Glendale, CA
Keck, Kathy J. .... Fairbanks, AK
Keck, Kenneth .... House of Representatives, Congressional Assistants, GV
Keck, Ladye H. .... Mount Pleasant, TX
Keck, Linda M. .... Cincinnati, OH
Keck, Mahin & Cate .... Chicago, IL
Keck, Marcella L. .... Salt Lake City, UT
Keck, Margaret D. .... Denver, CO
Keck, Michael Scott .... San Francisco, CA
Keck, Patricia A. .... Springfield, MO
Keck, Richard .... Atlanta, GA
Keck, Richard C. .... Fairbanks, AK
Keck, Robert C., Jr. .... Chicago, IL
Keck, Thomas C. .... Brick, NJ
Keck, Timothy E. .... Hiawatha, KS
Keck, Warren R., III .... Greenville, PA
Keck, Warren R., Jr. .... Greenville, PA
Keck, William C. .... Hamilton, OH
Keckeissen, F. Gordon .... Dresher, PA
Keckemet, John .... Seattle, WA
Keckhaver, Karla Zahorik .... Madison, WI
Keckler, Charles R., III .... Memphis, TN
Keckley, J. David .... South Bend, IN
Keckonen, Jon C. .... Sheboygan, WI
Keco, Laurie A. .... Cleveland, OH
Kecskemethy, Joseph M. .... Butler, PA
Kecskes, Kenneth A. .... San Diego, CA
Kecskes, Stephen J. .... Virginia Beach, VA
Keddie, Caeli A. .... Fairfax, VA
Keddie, Robert B. .... Pittsburgh, PA
Keddie, Robert W., III .... Princeton, NJ
Keddy, Michael F. .... Sacramento, CA
Kedeshian, Claire Siran .... Brooklyn, NY
Kedia, Sarita .... New York, NY
Kedron-Lyn, Lucea Suzan .... Dallas, TX
Kedrowski, John R. .... Minneapolis, MN
Kedson, David .... Philadelphia, PA
Kedzie, Glen Paul Environmental Protection Agency, Office of Enforcement and Compliance Assurance, GV
Kedzielawa, Frank S. .... Buffalo, NY
Kedzierski, Thaddeus J. .... Detroit, MI
Kedzior, John D. .... Cleveland, OH
Kee & Archer .... Duncan, OK
Kee, Burnice C. .... Denton, TX
Kee, Conrad Shawn .... Stamford, CT
Kee, David W. .... Bucksport, ME
Kee, Deborah L. .... Boston, MA
Kee, Diane K. .... Boynton Beach, FL
Kee, Donald E. .... Searcy, AR
Kee, James A., Jr. .... Birmingham, AL
Kee, James E. .... Rock Island, IL
Kee, James E. .... Salt Lake City, UT
Kee, James H. .... Memphis, TN
Kee, James L. .... Duncan, OK
Kee, John L., III .... Dallas, TX
Kee, Leland B. .... Angleton, TX
Kee & Neal .... Angleton, TX
Kee, R. Tyrone .... Norfolk, VA
Kee, Robert J. .... Beaver, OK Hooker, OK
Kee, Susan A. .... Waltham, MA
Kee, Terry M. .... San Francisco, CA
Kee, Tom H. .... Waco, TX
Kee, V. Patton .... Auburndale, FL
Keebaugh, Todd M. .... Garland, TX
Keeble, Allen B. .... La Grange, GA
Keeble, Charles C., Jr. .... Dallas, TX
Keeble, Floyd W., Jr. .... Lavonia, GA
Keeble, Sydney F., Jr. .... Nashville, TN
Keebler, Joseph H., Jr. .... Oil City, PA
Keebler, Michael J. .... Alameda, CA
Keech, Barry A. .... Kirkland, WA
Keech, Edward M. .... San Francisco, CA
Keech, Kevin .... Little Rock, AR
Keech, Sarah K. .... Atlanta, GA
Keech, Thomas W. .... Baltimore, MD
Keechl, Kenneth E. .... Fort Lauderdale, FL
Keedy, Brian D. .... Camdenton, MO
Keedy, Christian D. .... Miami, FL
Keedy, James A. .... Traverse City, MI
Keedy, James F. .... Leesburg, FL
Keedy, James F., P.A. .... Leesburg, FL
Keedy, John R. .... San Antonio, TX
Keedy, Michael H. .... Kalispell, MT
Keedy, Thomas J. .... Unionville, MO
Keef, Larry A. .... Milford, MI
Keefauver, William L. .... New Vernon, NJ
Keefe & Associates .... Wellesley, MA
Keefe and Associates .... Eastpointe, MI
Keefe & Brodie .... St. Louis, MO
Keefe, Carol A. .... Narragansett, RI
Keefe, Catherine W. .... St. Louis, MO
Keefe, Christopher H. .... St. Louis, MO
Keefe, Christopher Patrick .... Boston, MA
Keefe, Claudia J. .... Philadelphia, PA
Keefe, Colin .... Springfield, MA
Keefe, Dan J. .... Seattle, WA
Keefe, Dan W. .... Spokane, WA
Keefe, David F. .... Northampton, MA
Keefe, David G. .... Marshfield, WI
Keefe, David J. .... Waukegan, IL
Keefe, Deborah .... Auburn, ME
Keefe, Deirdre A. .... Braintree, MA
Keefe, Dennis R. .... Lincoln, NE
Keefe & DePauli, P.C. .... Fairview Heights, IL
Keefe, Donald J. .... Denver, CO
Keefe, Edgar S. .... Midland, TX
Keefe, Edward .... Rock Island, IL
Keefe, Ellen F. .... Boston, MA
Keefe, Eugene F. .... Chicago, IL
Keefe, F. Barry .... Cleveland, OH
Keefe, F. Michael .... Manchester, NH
Keefe, Frank D. .... Ellisville, MO
Keefe, Gregory .... Mount Kisco, NY
Keefe, Heidi .... San Francisco, CA
Keefe, Hope F. .... Blue Island, IL
Keefe, Hugh F. .... New Haven, CT
Keefe, James F., Jr. .... Cairo, NY
Keefe, James J., Jr. .... Garden City, NY
Keefe, James K. .... Fairview Heights, IL
Keefe, James N. .... Quincy, IL
Keefe, Jennifer Leigh .... Dallas, TX
Keefe, Jo-Anwyl F. .... Manchester, NH
Keefe, John E. .... Hutchinson, MN
Keefe, John E. .... Rochester, NY
Keefe, John E., Jr. .... North Brunswick, NJ
Keefe, John E., Sr. .... New Brunswick, NJ
Keefe, John F. .... Chicago, IL
Keefe, John F. .... Boston, MA
Keefe, John J. .... Lincoln, NE
Keefe, John J., Jr. .... New Haven, CT
Keefe, John L. .... Wellesley, MA
Keefe, John Miles .... Wilton, NH
Keefe, John T. .... Blue Island, IL
Keefe, John W. .... Dayton, KY
Keefe, Joseph C. .... Decorah, IA
Keefe, Joseph F. .... Torrington, CT
Keefe, Joseph F. .... Portsmouth, NH
Keefe, Joseph W. .... Buffalo, NY
Keefe, Kasal & Newman .... Hutchinson, MN
Keefe, Katherine M. .... Philadelphia, PA
Keefe, Kathleen M. .... San Bernardino, CA
Keefe & Keefe, P.A. .... Wilton, NH
Keefe, Kenneth M., Jr. .... Jacksonville, FL
Keefe, Kevin .... Seattle, WA
Keefe, King & Bowman, P.S. Coeur d'Alene, ID Spokane, WA
Keefe, Kirsten .... Philadelphia, PA
Keefe, Lawrence .... Fort Walton Beach, FL
Keefe, Liza .... Brick, NJ
Keefe, Marcia K. .... Rodeo, CA
Keefe, Margaret W., Law Offices of San Francisco, CA
Keefe, Maureen T. .... Indianapolis, IN
Keefe, Michael C. .... Murray Hill, NJ
Keefe, Michael J. .... Wellesley, MA
Keefe, M.J. .... Albuquerque, NM
Keefe, Patrick M. .... Fairview Heights, IL
Keefe, Patrick M. .... Caledonia, NY
Keefe, Paula M. .... Manchester, NH
Keefe, Peter D. .... Eastpointe, MI
Keefe, R. Michael .... New Brunswick, NJ
Keefe, Richard E., (P.S.) .... Seattle, WA
Keefe, Richard H. .... Dover, NH
Keefe, Richard L. .... Tucson, AZ

Keefe, Richard W. ... Fallbrook, CA
Keefe, Robert D. ... Boston, MA
Keefe, Robert H. ... Fullerton, CA
Keefe, Robert M. ... Seattle, WA
Keefe, Ronald D. ... Marquette, MI
Keefe, Ronald W. ... Boston, MA
Keefe, Stephen T., Jr. ... Weymouth, MA
Keefe, Thomas E. ... Lincoln, NE
Keefe, Thomas F. ... East Amherst, NY
Keefe, Thomas K. ... Albany, NY
Keefe, Thomas P., Jr. ... United States Senate, Committee Legal Personnel, GV
Keefe, Thomas Q. ... Fairview Heights, IL
Keefe, Thomas Q., Jr. ... Belleville, IL
Keefe, Thomas Q., Jr., P.C. ... Belleville, IL
Keefe, William A. ... Denver, CO
Keefe, William J. ... Wilton, NH
Keefe, William P. ... Boston, MA
Keefe-Garner, Ellen M. ... Ann Arbor, MI
Keefer, Barbara J. ... South Charleston, WV
Keefer, Christopher L. ... McLean, VA
Keefer, Elizabeth J. ... New York, NY
Keefer, J. Michael ... Fort Wayne, IN
Keefer, James O. ... Grass Valley, CA
Keefer, Jan Kepley ... Indianapolis, IN
Keefer, John M. ... Bartlesville, OK
Keefer, Mary M. ... St. Paul, MN
Keefer, Neil S. ... Billings, MT
Keefer, O'Reilly & Ferrario
Las Vegas, NV
Keefer, Patricia L. ... Norco, CA
Keefer, Robert F. ... Harrisonburg, VA
Keefer, Roy A. ... Gettysburg, PA
Keefer, Scott K. ... Woonsocket, RI
Keefer, Sean F. ... Mount Pleasant, SC
Keefer, Sophie J. ... Washington, DC
Keefer, Timothy J. ... Chicago, IL
Keefer, Timothy J. ... Bluefield, WV
Keefer, Wendy Johnson ... Charleston, SC
Keefer, William J. ... St. Paul, MN
Keefer, William P. ... Buffalo, NY
Keefer Wood Allen & Rahal, LLP
Camp Hill, PA
Carlisle, PA
Harrisburg, PA
Hershey, PA
York, PA
Keeffe, Alan M. ... Denver, CO
Keeffe, David B. ... Sayre, PA
Keeffe, J.A., P.C. ... Scarsdale, NY
Keeffe, John A. ... Scarsdale, NY
Keeffe, Stephen Daniel ... Washington, DC
Keegan, Anita DeLuca ... New Orleans, LA
Keegan, Anne E. ... Marietta, OH
Keegan & Brown ... Helena, MT
Keegan, Carla B. ... Seattle, WA
Keegan, Charles J. ... New Haven, CT
Keegan, Christopher C. ... Smithtown, NY
Keegan, Christopher J. ... New York, NY
Keegan, Colleen M. ... New York, NY
Keegan, D. Douglas ... Salinas, CA
Keegan, David C. ... Duluth, MN
Keegan, David V. ... Garden City, NY
Port Washington, NY
Keegan, Despina ... New York, NY
Keegan, Druanne ... Oakland, CA
Keegan, F. Patrick ... Sacramento, CA
Keegan & Fábregas ... Silver Spring, MD
Keegan, Francis A. ... Washington, DC
Keegan, Frank Joseph ... Shelton, CT
Keegan, Gary Sean ... Albany, NY
Keegan, Gerald S. ... West Paterson, NJ
Keegan, Gerard C., Jr. ... New York, NY
Keegan, Glenn F. ... Yonkers, NY
Keegan, Henry T. ... Atlanta, GA
Silver Spring, MD
Silver Spring, MD
Keegan & Horowitz ... Garden City, NY
Port Washington, NY
Keegan, James F. ... West Orange, NJ
Keegan, James F. ... Houston, TX
Keegan, James Michael ... Baltimore, MD
Keegan, James R.
Federal Energy Regulatory Commission, Office of the General Counsel, GV
Keegan, Jeffrey J. ... White Plains, NY
Keegan, Jennifer L. ... Chicago, IL
Keegan, John E. ... Seattle, WA
Keegan, John K. ... Flemington, NJ
Keegan, John M. ... Garden City, NY
Keegan, John M. ... Toledo, OH
Keegan, John P. ... Shrewsbury, NJ
New York, NY
Keegan, John R. ... Boston, MA
Keegan, John W. ... White Plains, NY
Keegan, John W., Jr. ... White Plains, NY
Keegan, Joseph M. ... Passaic, NJ
Keegan, Karen A. ... Dallas, TX
Keegan, Karen K.
General Accounting Office, Office of the General Counsel, GV
Keegan & Keegan ... Patchogue, NY
Keegan, Keegan & Strutt, LLP
New York, NY
White Plains, NY
Keegan, Kevin E. ... Chelmsford, MA
Keegan, Kevin M. ... Deerfield, IL
Keegan, Kyle M. ... Baton Rouge, LA
Keegan, Marcia Kenny ... Hartford, CT
Keegan, Mark S. ... Stamford, CT
Keegan, Mary Ann ... Rochester, NY
Keegan, Mary Ellen ... Cincinnati, OH
Keegan, Mary Sorensen ... San Francisco, CA
Keegan, Maureen A. ... Kingston, NY
Keegan & Myers, Law Office of, P.C.
Sacramento, CA
Keegan, Owen D. ... Arlington, VA
Keegan, Patricia M. ... Sacramento, CA
Keegan, Patrick N. ... San Diego, CA
Keegan, Raymond H. ... Elk Grove Village, IL
Keegan, Raymond J. ... White Plains, NY
Keegan, Raymond J., & Assoc., LLP
New York, NY
White Plains, NY
Keegan, Robert E. ... New York, NY
Keegan, Robert J. ... Boston, MA
Keegan, Robert L. ... Richland Center, WI
Keegan, Robert R. ... Fayetteville, AR
Keegan, Susan M. ... Chicago, IL
Keegan, Thomas B. ... Chicago, IL
Keegan, Thomas J. ... Patchogue, NY
Keegan, Thomas J., Jr. ... Patchogue, NY
Keegan, Thomas M. ... Helena, MT
Keegan, Thomas P. ... San Jose, CA
Keegan, Thomas W. ... Albany, NY
Keegan, Timothy L. ... Washington, DC
Keegan, Vincent J. ... Fairfax, VA
Keegan, Wendy A. ... Staten Island, NY
Keegan, Werlin & Pabian, LLP
Boston, MA
Keegan, William J. ... San Jose, CA
Keegan, William M. ... Fort Lee, NJ
Keegan, William P. ... Clifton Park, NY
Keegan, Wm. ... Flushing, NY
Keegin, Stafford W. ... San Rafael, CA
Keehan, Francis J. ... Albany, NY
Keehan, Michael B. ... Wilmington, DE
Keehan, Timothy E. ... Washington, DC
Keehley, Jay T. ... Starkville, MS
Keehn, Arnold H. ... King Of Prussia, PA
Keehn, Benjamin H. ... Boston, MA
Keehn, David C. ... Allentown, PA
Keehn, David H. ... Schenectady, NY
Keehn, Gary ... Seattle, WA
Keehn, Holly Coates ... San Diego, CA
Keehn, L. Scott ... San Diego, CA
Keehn, Lisa L. ... San Diego, CA
Keehn, Robert F. ... Los Angeles, CA
Keehnel, Stellman ... Seattle, WA
Keehner, Cannady & Katz ... Belleville, IL
Keehner, Jim D., Ltd. ... Belleville, IL
Keehr, Tara E. ... Olivia, MN
Keel, A. B. ... Hawthorne, CA
Keel, Alice R. ... Culver City, CA
Keel, Alison D. ... Gladwyne, PA
Keel, C. J., P.A., Jr. ... Tampa, FL
Keel, C. J., Jr. ... Tampa, FL
Keel, J. Michael ... Birmingham, AL
Keel, James W., Jr. ... Rocky Mount, NC
Keel, Jeffrey Scott ... Tampa, FL
Keel, Jimmie R. ... Tarboro, NC
Keel, Katherine Axson ... Chase City, VA
Keel, Lassiter & Duffy ... Rocky Mount, NC
Keel, Mark A. ... Columbia, SC
Keel, Patrick O. ... Austin, TX
Keel, R. Colin ... Dallas, TX
Keel, Robert T. ... Oklahoma City, OK
Keel, Rudy O. ... Paducah, KY
Keel, Susan I. ... Mill Valley, CA
Keelan, Kevin J. ... Larchmont, NY
Keelan, Terrence P. ... Culver City, CA
Keeland, Robert L. ... Atlanta, GA
Keele, Anna Maria Sparke
Shreveport, LA
Keele & Associates ... Salem, IL
Keele, Christopher A. ... San Francisco, CA
Keele, Daniel R. ... Salem, IL
Keele, David A. ... Chelmsford, MA
Keele, Garry Lynn, II ... Tulsa, OK
Keele, George M. ... Carson City, NV
Minden, NV
Keele, James R. ... West Liberty, IA
Keele Law Offices, P.C. ... West Liberty, IA
Keele, Leah P. ... Tulsa, OK
Keele, Michael D. ... Indianapolis, IN
Keelean, Edward V. ... Detroit, MI
Keelen, Jerome P. ... Trenton, NJ
Keeler, Brian ... Boston, MA
Keeler, C. Addison, Jr. ... Binghamton, NY
Keeler, Charles C. ... Media, PA
Keeler, Charles L. ... Torrance, CA
Keeler, Christopher D. ... Escondido, CA
Keeler, David J. ... Newton, MA
Keeler, Davis E. ... Menlo Park, CA
Keeler, Dennis C. ... Portland, ME
Keeler, Dianne L. ... Toledo, OH
Keeler, Eugene ... Hudson, NY
Keeler, Frederic S., Jr. ... Long Beach, CA
Keeler, James W., Jr. ... Chaska, MN
Keeler, Jean Marie ... Doylestown, PA
Keeler, John K. ... Buffalo, NY
Keeler, John M. ... Binghamton, NY
Keeler, John S. ... Indianapolis, IN
Keeler, Judith A.
Department of Housing and Urban Development, GV
Keeler, Karen E. ... Hagåtña, GU
Keeler & Keeler
Rancho Santa Margarita, CA
Keeler, Kelly Anne ... Chicago, IL
Keeler, Kevin L. ... Milwaukee, WI
Keeler, Kevin P. ... Louisville, KY
Keeler, Marie B.
Rancho Santa Margarita, CA
Keeler, Paul B. ... Houston, TX
Keeler, R. Hayes ... San Francisco, CA
Keeler, Robert B. ... Rosemead, CA
Keeler, Robert T. ... Cincinnati, OH
Keeler, Ronald ... Everett, PA
Keeler, Ronald F. ... Burbank, CA
Keeler, Shirley Ward ... Kansas City, MO
Keeler, Steven J. ... Richmond, VA
Keeler, Thomas P. ... Greenville, SC
Keeler, William J., Jr. ... Fresno, CA
Keeley, Anne Fohne ... Belleville, IL
Keeley, Carolyn I. ... Monterey, CA
Keeley, Charles F. ... Lansing, MI
Keeley, Charlotte L. ... Sacramento, CA
Keeley, Dennis ... San Francisco, CA
Keeley, Doris B. ... New York, NY
Keeley, Edward L. ... Wichita, KS
Keeley, Elizabeth ... New York, NY
Keeley, Elizabeth A. ... Cambridge, MA
Keeley, George W. ... Chicago, IL
Keeley, Hayes, Dudley & Garrett
Boca Raton, FL
Keeley, Irene M. ... Clarksburg, WV
Keeley, Irene P. ... Charleston, WV
Keeley, James E. ... Providence, RI
Keeley, James W. ... Tulsa, OK
Keeley, Joseph F., (P.A.) ... Boca Raton, FL
Keeley, Kuenn & Reid ... Chicago, IL
Keeley, Margaret A. ... Washington, DC
Keeley, Marie ... Philadelphia, PA
Keeley, Michael ... Dallas, TX
Keeley, Michael F. ... Los Angeles, CA
Keeley, Michael G. ... Dallas, TX
Keeley, Michael L. ... New York, NY
Keeley, Mike ... Great Bend, KS
Keeley, Patrick C. ... Wheaton, IL
Keeley, Patrick J. ... Washington, DC
Keeley, Robert Paul ... Hollywood, FL
Keeley, Terence J. ... Yuba City, CA
Keeley, Terri J. ... Minneapolis, MN
Keeley, Theresa Budenholzer
Scottsdale, AZ
Keeley, Therese M. ... Cherry Hill, NJ
Philadelphia, PA
Keeley, Wayne J. ... Yonkers, NY
Keeley-Cain, Thomas M. ... Cherry Hill, NJ
Keeling, Byron C. ... Houston, TX
Keeling, Daniel L. ... Fresno, CA
Keeling, Daryl B. ... Richmond, VA
Keeling, Douglas J. ... Wichita, KS
Keeling, Edward J. ... San Francisco, CA
Keeling, Gailen L. ... Salem, OR
Keeling, Ingelisa Haskins ... Houston, TX
Keeling, J. Michael ... Washington, DC
Keeling, James W. ... Rockford, IL
Keeling, John W. ... Columbus, OH
Keeling, Joyce Walker ... Prairie Village, KS
Keeling, Kenneth A. ... Houston, TX
Houston, TX
San Antonio, TX
Keeling, Kermit O. ... Baltimore, MD
Keeling Law Firm ... Houston, TX
Keeling, Lynn ... Phoenix, AZ
Keeling, Mary Ann ... Baltimore, MD
Keeling, Richard D.
Christiansted, St. Croix, VI
Keeling, Robert R. ... Sacramento, CA
Keeling, Roy D. ... Fresno, CA
Keeling, Sheri L. ... Buffalo, NY
Keeling, Thomas H. ... Stockton, CA
Keeling, W. Lee ... Victoria, TX
Keeling, Warren F. ... Newport News, VA
Keeling, William F., Jr. ... San Angelo, TX
Keeling, William Kent ... Gainesville, FL
Keelor, Robert K. ... Dayton, OH
Keels, William C. ... Chester, SC
Keelty, Lana M. ... Arlington, VA
Keely, Allen R. ... Norristown, PA
Keely, James Leo ... Ottawa, IL
Keely, Sean Thomas ... New York, NY
Keely, Shari A. ... Dallas, TX
Keely, T. Loren ... Tacoma, WA
Keen, Andrew N. ... New York, NY
Keen, C. Matthew ... Raleigh, NC
Keen, Charles H. ... Department of Justice, Tax Division, GV
Keen, D. Michael ... Atlanta, GA
Keen, Darla Lynn ... West Palm Beach, FL
Keen, Dwight D. ... Winfield, KS
Keen, Gordon L., Jr. ... Radnor, PA
Keen, Joette Stambaugh ... Tampa, FL
Keen, Joseph W. ... Peoria, IL
Keen, Keen & Good ... Downingtown, PA
Keen, Laureen J. ... Stockton, CA
Keen, Linda Ann ... Sarasota, FL
Keen, Lori J. ... Memphis, TN
Keen, Malcolm D. ... Fairfax, VA
Keen, Patrick A. ... New Orleans, LA
Keen, Paul R. ... Cleveland, OH
Keen, Philip T. ... McDonough, GA
Keen, Ralph A. ... Houston, TX
Keen, Ralph F. ... Muskogee, OK
Keen, Ralph S., III ... Farmington, CT
Keen, Randall L. ... Jonesboro, GA
Keen, Randall W. ... Los Angeles, CA
Keen, Richard ... Odessa, TX
Keen, Richard A. ... West Chester, PA
Keen, Robert T., Jr. ... Fort Wayne, IN
Keen, Roger A. ... West Hills, CA
Keen, Ronni G. ... Orange, CA
Keen, Ruth M. ... Raleigh, NC
Keen, Stephen A. ... Pittsburgh, PA
Keen, Thomas H. ... Dallas, TX
Keen, Thomas W. ... Cleveland, OH
Keen, Victor F. ... Philadelphia, PA
Keen, W. Hampton ... West Palm Beach, FL
Keen, W. H. Clay ... Harrisburg, PA
Keen, William J. ... Mason City, IA
Keen, William R., Jr. ... Downingtown, PA
Keen, William T. ... Downingtown, PA
Keena, Christian W. ... Mission Viejo, CA
Keena, Claire E. ... Woodbridge, VA
Keena, J. Robert ... Minneapolis, MN
Keena, Kathryn M. ... Bellingham, WA
Keena, Kevin T. ... Los Angeles, CA
Keenaghan, Daniel J. ... New York, NY
Keenan, Alexander S. ... San Francisco, CA
Keenan, Andrew J. ... Philadelphia, PA
West Chester, PA
Keenan, Arthur J. ... Newport, ME
Keenan & Austin, P.C. ... Novi, MI
Pontiac, MI
Redford, MI
Keenan, Bernard V., Jr. ... Boston, MA
Keenan & Boeckman Law Firm, P.A.
Great Bend, KS
La Crosse, KS
Keenan, Brian David ... Hillsdale, NJ
Keenan, Bryan E. ... Wilmington, DE
Keenan, C. Robert, III ... Pittsburgh, PA
Keenan, Carol S. ... Yonkers, NY
Keenan, Catherine L. ... Gresham, OR
Keenan, Charles B., Jr. ... Bel Air, MD
Havre de Grace, MD
Keenan, Charles E. ... St. Paul, MN
Keenan, Cheryl ... Sanatoga, PA
Keenan, Christopher P. ... Mount Kisco, NY
Keenan, Christopher W. ... Portsmouth, NH
Keenan, Ciccitto & Brant ... Collegeville, PA
Keenan, Clifford T. ... Washington, DC
Keenan & Dabbous ... Memphis, TN
Keenan, Daniel T. ... Fullerton, CA
Keenan, David C. ... Columbus, OH
Keenan, David L. ... Warren, NJ
Keenan, David Michael ... Des Moines, IA
Keenan, David T. ... Norwood, MA
Keenan, Dennis J. ... Great Bend, KS
Keenan, Don C. ... Atlanta, GA
Keenan, Elizabeth C. ... Baltimore, MD
Keenan, Francis A. ... Cincinnati, OH
Keenan, Frank J. ... New York, NY
Keenan, G. Michael ... West Palm Beach, FL
Keenan, Gary M. ... Albuquerque, NM
Keenan, George A. ... Roslyn Heights, NY
Keenan, George K. ... Bethlehem, PA
Keenan, Gloria ... Garden City, NY
Keenan, Gregory A. ... Meadville, PA
Keenan, J. Sean ... Canton, OH
Keenan, James B. ... Newark, NJ
Keenan, James F. ... Portland, ME
Keenan, James F. ... Niles, MI
Keenan, James F., Jr. ... Portland, ME
Keenan, James G. ... York, PA
Keenan, James I., Jr. ... Baltimore, MD
Keenan, James J., Jr. ... Orange, CA
Walnut Creek, CA
Keenan, James L. ... Sacramento, CA
Keenan, James P. ... Houston, TX
Keenan, James W. ... Fayetteville, WV
Keenan, Jan Austin ... Redford, MI
Keenan, Jefferson ... Tucson, AZ
Keenan, Jeffrey A. ... Myrtle Beach, SC
Keenan, Jeffrey J. ... New York, NY
Keenan, Joan W. ... New York, NY
Keenan, John A. ... Houston, TX
Keenan, John C. ... Nampa, ID
Keenan, John E., Jr. ... Worcester, MA
Keenan, John E., Jr., P.C. ... Worcester, MA
Keenan, John F. ... Quincy, MA
Keenan, John F. ... Worcester, MA
Keenan, John F. ... New York, NY
Keenan, John J. ... Redford, MI
Keenan, John J. ... Gouverneur, NY
Keenan, John L. ... Rochester, NY
Keenan, John R. ... Nashville, TN
Keenan, John Thomas, III ... Albany, NY
Keenan, Joseph D., III ... Chicago, IL
Keenan, Joseph F. ... Garden City, NY
Keenan, Judy ... New York, NY
Keenan, Juliann L. ... Baton Rouge, LA
Keenan, Kathleen M. ... Seattle, WA
Keenan, Kelly P. ... Riverside, CA
Keenan, Kevin D. ... Houston, TX
Keenan, Kevin J. ... Los Angeles, CA
Keenan, Kevin P. ... Minneapolis, MN
Keenan, Kevin W. ... Phoenix, AZ
Keenan, Larry E. ... Great Bend, KS
Keenan, Laura Marie ... Stamford, CT
Keenan, Laura N. ... Hackensack, NJ
Keenan, Laurie E. ... Washington, DC
Keenan, Leo J. ... Laurel, MD
Keenan, Linda R. ... New York, NY
Keenan, Lisa A. ... Washington, DC
Keenan, Lora E. ... Salem, OR
Keenan, Loren G. ... Farmington Hills, MI
Keenan, Marcie A. ... San Francisco, CA
Keenan, Margaret Ann ... Boston, MA
Keenan, Mark A. ... Madison, NE
Norfolk, NE
Keenan, Mark L. ... Atlanta, GA
Keenan, Martin J. ... Great Bend, KS
Keenan, Martin James ... Cleveland, OH
Keenan, Mary J. ... Southwick, MA
Keenan, Mary W. ... Boulder, CO
Keenan, Matthew D. ... Kansas City, MO
Keenan, Matthew David ... Chicago, IL
Keenan, Maureen O'Mara ... Boston, MA
Keenan, Michael ... San Francisco, CA
Keenan, Michael G. ... Boston, MA
Keenan, Michael J. ... Anchorage, AK
Naknek, AK
Keenan, Michael J. ... Phoenix, AZ
Keenan, Michael J. ... Albany, NY
Keenan, Michael J. ... Arlington, VA
Keenan, Neese & Porter, P.C.
Phoenix, AZ
Keenan and O'Connell ... Millbury, MA
Keenan, P. Dennis ... Glendale, CA
Keenan, Pamela P. ... Raleigh, NC
Keenan, Patrick A. ... Detroit, MI
Keenan, Patrick J. ... Philadelphia, PA
Keenan, Paul ... Roosevelt, NY
Keenan, Paul A. ... Albany, GA
Keenan, Paul A. ... New York, NY
Keenan, Paul David ... Philadelphia, PA
Keenan, Peter C. ... New Orleans, LA
Keenan, Peter F., Jr. ... Millbury, MA
Keenan, Peter J. ... New York, NY

Keenan, Peter M. .... Clarkston, MI
Keenan, Philip V. .... Denver, CO
Keenan, Powers & Andrews, P.C.
New York, NY
Keenan, R. Mark .... New York, NY
Keenan, Richard .... Los Angeles, CA
San Francisco, CA
Keenan, Richard A. .... Rochester, NY
Keenan, Richard B. .... Denver, CO
Keenan, Richard J. .... Minneapolis, MN
Keenan, Richard S. .... New York, NY
Keenan, Robert J. .... Irvine, CA
Keenan, Robert M., III .... Atlanta, GA
Keenan, Robert M., Jr. .... Mount Carmel, IL
Keenan, Robert P. .... Great Bend, KS
Keenan, Robert W. .... Oakland, CA
Keenan, Rosemary G. .... Atlanta, GA
Keenan, Sarah M. .... Garden City, NY
Keenan, Shawn C. .... Augusta, ME
Keenan, Thomas A. .... Hackensack, NJ
Keenan, Thomas E. .... Farmington Hills, MI
Traverse City, MI
Keenan, Thomas J. .... Neponsit, NY
Keenan, Thomas J. .... Cleveland, OH
Keenan, Thomas M. .... Westport, CT
Keenan, Thomas M. .... Collegeville, PA
Keenan, Timothy J. .... Wayzata, MN
Keenan, Timothy R. .... Great Bend, KS
Keenan, William F. .... Buffalo, NY
Keenan, William J., Jr. .... Hartford, CT
Keenan, William P. .... Atlanta, GA
Asheville, NC
Keenan, William P., A Professional Corporation
Atlanta, GA
Keenan III, John E. .... Boston, MA
Keene, Betty Josephson .... Waverly, NY
Keene, C. Alexis .... Houston, TX
Keene, Christopher J. .... Los Angeles, CA
Keene & Currall, A Professional Corporation
Ketchikan, AK
Keene, D. Brennen .... Richmond, VA
Keene, Daniel W. .... Dallas, TX
Keene, Danny C. .... Flint, MI
Keene, David A. .... Alexandria, VA
Keene, David Robert, II
Federal Labor Relations Authority,
Authority Member Staff, GV
Keene, Deborah S. .... Lansing, MI
Keene, Dennis B. .... Savannah, GA
Keene, Elizabeth Ann .... Frankfort, KY
Keene, Galvin R. .... Costa Mesa, CA
Keene, Gareth D. .... Oradell, NJ
Keene, Gerald A. .... Waverly, NY
Keene, Glen E. .... Great Neck, NY
Keene, H. Clay .... Ketchikan, AK
Keene, Henry C., Jr. .... Ketchikan, AK
Keene, Herbert G., Jr. .... Philadelphia, PA
Keene, Irving F. .... Franklin, MI
Keene, J. Ransdell .... Shreveport, LA
Keene, James W. .... San Antonio, TX
Keene, Jerald P. .... Portland, OR
Keene, John C. .... Philadelphia, PA
Keene, John J., Jr. .... Concord, MA
Keene, John M. .... New York, NY
Keene, K. Grant .... Cleveland, GA
Keene & Keene .... Waverly, NY
Keene, Kenneth C. .... Indianapolis, IN
Keene, Kenneth L., Jr. .... Denver, CO
Keene, Kenneth P. .... Colorado Springs, CO
Keene, K. Grant .... Cleveland, GA
Keene, Kirk W. .... Atlanta, GA
Keene, Laura E. .... Pensacola, FL
Keene, Mark Alan .... Austin, TX
Keene, Mark L. .... Boston, MA
Keene, Richard C. .... Neptune Beach, FL
Keene, Richard Edward .... Novato, CA
Keene, Richard J. .... Chico, CA
Keene, Robert B. .... Indianapolis, IN
Keene, Robert W., Jr. .... Rockville, MD
Keene, Ross A. .... Pensacola, FL
Keene, Ruth Ann .... San Francisco, CA
Keene, Sandra F. .... Louisville, KY
Keene, Scott R. .... San Francisco, CA
Keene, Sherri Lee .... New York, NY
Keene, Stephen W. .... Boston, MA
Keene, Susan .... Fort Lee, NJ
Keene, Thomas H. .... Montgomery, AL
Keene, Thomas J. .... Dos Palos, CA
Keene, Tom J. .... Dallas, TX
Keene, William K. .... Ottawa, IL
Keener, Allan W. .... Washington, DC
Keener, Amy Bisese .... Pittsburgh, PA
Keener & Associates .... Houston, TX
Keener, B. Nowlin .... Pensacola, FL
Keener, Carmella Piscopo
Wilmington, DE
Keener, Craig R. .... Houston, TX
Keener, Cynthia L. .... Los Angeles, CA
Keener, Dana Marks .... San Francisco, CA
Keener, Donald E. .... Department of Justice,
Civil Division, GV
Keener Doucher Curley & Patterson, A Legal Professional Association
Columbus, OH
Keener, Douglas N. .... Fairfield, CA
Keener, E. Barlow .... Boston, MA
Keener, Edison W. .... Pittsburgh, PA
Keener, Gaither M., Jr.
North Wilkesboro, NC
Keener, Hurshell H. .... Hickory, NC
Keener, Irby A., Jr. .... Centre, AL
Keener, Karl A. .... Santa Monica, CA
Keener & Keener .... Centre, AL
Keener, Larry A. .... Mansfield, PA
Keener, Larry H. .... Gadsden, AL
Keener, Mark P. .... Baltimore, MD
Keener, Rex C. .... Toledo, OH
Keener, Robert M. .... Waynesburg, PA

Keener, Ronald D. .... New Lebanon, OH
Keener, Russell G. .... Atlanta, GA
Keener, Susan Wilson .... Grand Rapids, MI
Keener, Tab H. .... Dallas, TX
Keener, Thomas J. .... Columbus, OH
Keener, U. Grant, Jr. .... Houston, TX
Keener, William H. .... Mill Valley, CA
Keener, William L. .... Bethel, OH
Cincinnati, OH
Keener-Farley, Lawrence E. .... Camp Hill, PA
Keeney, Brian J. .... New York, NY
Keeney, E. Andrew .... Kitty Hawk, NC
Keeney, E. Ludlow, Jr. .... San Diego, CA
Keeney, Frank J. .... Los Angeles, CA
Keeney, Gregory D. .... Narberth, PA
Keeney, Huey C., Jr. .... Tyler, TX
Keeney, James D. .... Sarasota, FL
Keeney, Jeffrey H. .... Portland, OR
Keeney, John C. .... Department of Justice,
Criminal Division, GV
Keeney, John C., Jr. .... Washington, DC
Keeney, Karen L. .... Portland, OR
Keeney, Kathleen Barlage .... Cincinnati, OH
Keeney, Kris R. .... Norfolk, VA
Keeney, Melanie Gurley .... St. Louis, MO
Keeney, Michael E. .... Memphis, TN
Keeney, Randolph V. .... Houston, TX
Keeney, Regina Markey .... Round Rock, TX
Keeney, Robert C. .... San Francisco, CA
Keeney, Robert L., Jr. .... Vallejo, CA
Keeney, Steven H. .... Louisville, KY
Keeney, Stewart E. .... Birmingham, MI
Keeney, Susan Carbone
San Francisco, CA
Keeney, Waite & Stevens, A Professional Corporation .... San Diego, CA
Keenheel, Mark S. .... Philadelphia, PA
Keeno, Francis Paul K. A. .... Honolulu, HI
Keeno, Laurie E. .... Honolulu, HI
Keenom, Jill F. .... Dallas, TX
Keenon, Una H. R. .... Brooklyn Heights, OH
Keenon, Wade R. .... Portland, OR
Keens, James A. .... Glendale, CA
Keens, James A. .... Santa Ana, CA
Keens, William C. .... Arlington, VA
Keenum, Gregory D. .... Booneville, MS
Keenum, Gregory D., P.A. .... Booneville, MS
Keenum, Thomas D., Jr. .... Booneville, MS
Keenum and Tutor, P.A. .... Booneville, MS
Keep, Alfred R. .... Simi Valley, CA
Keep, C. Russell, III
Hilton Head Island, SC
Keep, Judith N. .... San Diego, CA
Keep, Oscar J. .... Miami Beach, FL
Keep, Scott .... Department Of The Interior,
Office of the Solicitor, GV
Keep, William A. .... Oakland, CA
Keepers, Eric L. .... Lancaster, PA
Keephart, Lydia Fabbro .... Princeton, NJ
Keepnews, Robert L. .... Hartford, CT
Southport, CT
Keer, Gregory A. .... Cincinnati, OH
Kees, Ian .... Milwaukee, WI
Kees, Lester P. .... Leesville, LA
Kees, Nicholas A. .... Milwaukee, WI
Keesal, Samuel A., Jr. .... Long Beach, CA
San Francisco, CA
Keesal, Young & Logan, A Professional Corporation .... Anchorage, AK
Long Beach, CA
San Francisco, CA
Seattle, WA
Keese, Robert M. .... Los Angeles, CA
San Bernardino, CA
Keese, Thomas J. .... Ada, MI
Keese, W. David .... Denison, TX
Frisco, TX
Sherman, TX
Keese, William J. .... Sacramento, CA
Keesee, Herbert L. .... Louisville, KY
Keesee, Michael F. .... Port Chester, NY
Keesee, R. Neal, Jr. .... Roanoke, VA
Keesee, Sheila R. .... Harrisonburg, VA
Keesee, Yvette G. .... Denver, CO
Keesen, Susan .... Englewood, CO
Keesey, C. Laurence .... Naples, FL
Keeshan, James H., Jr. .... Conroe, TX
Keeshan, John J. .... Encino, CA
Keeshan, Lawrence W. .... New York, NY
Keeshan, Robert E. .... Topeka, KS
Keeshen, Kathleen M. .... Fairfield, CA
Keeshin, Scott A. .... Edina, MN
Keesing, Ralph K. .... Manhasset, NY
Keesing, Wouter .... Cherry Hill, NJ
Keesler, David C. .... Charlotte, NC
Keesler, Patricia K. .... Atlanta, GA
Keesley, William P. .... Edgefield, SC
Keesling, Karen R. .... Peoria, AZ
Keester, Michael T. .... Tulsa, OK
Keet, James H., Jr. .... Springfield, MO
Keet, Margaret O. .... Little Rock, AR
Keetch, Andrew D. .... Fort Worth, TX
Keetch, Von G. .... Salt Lake City, UT
Keeter, Aden .... Gainesville, FL
Keeter, Bob .... Mena, AR
Keeter, Bob J. .... Springfield, MO
Keeter, Bob, P.A. .... Mena, AR
Keeter, James W. .... Orlando, FL
Keeter, Jeffrey P. .... Wilmington, NC
Keeter, Melvin R. .... Sacramento, CA
Keeter, Morris W. .... Gastonia, NC
Keeter, Robert A. .... Gainesville, FL
Keeter, Shanley .... Annandale, VA
Keethe, Lawrence K. .... Sacramento, CA
Keetle, Roger S. .... Lincoln, NE
Keeton, Carter D. .... McLean, VA
Keeton, Charles H. .... Jackson, MS
Keeton, Charles R. .... Louisville, KY

Keeton, Edward C., Jr. .... West Liberty, KY
Keeton & Embry .... Grenada, MS
Keeton, John D., Jr. .... Westborough, MA
Keeton, John H. .... Winchester, KY
Keeton, John T. .... Grenada, MS
Keeton, Laura A. .... Huntingdon, TN
Keeton, Lori R. .... Charlotte, NC
Keeton, Paul C. .... Lewiston, ID
Keeton, Richard P. .... Houston, TX
Keeton, Robert T., III .... Huntingdon, TN
Keeton, Robert T., Jr., Law Offices of
Huntingdon, TN
Keeton, Robt. E. .... Boston, MA
Keeton, Stanley E. .... San Antonio, TX
Keeton & Tait .... Lewiston, ID
Keettel, William D. .... Scottsdale, AZ
Keeve, Vernon, Jr. .... Fredericksburg, VA
Keeven, Paul F. .... St. Louis, MO
Keeven, Richard D. .... Indianapolis, IN
Keever, A. Elizabeth .... Fayetteville, NC
Keever, Charles J. .... Honolulu, HI
Keever, David C. .... Cartersville, GA
Keever, Dina A. .... Miami, FL
Keever, Gregory .... Los Angeles, CA
Keever, J. Thomas, Jr. .... Greensboro, NC
Keever, Nathan A. .... Grand Junction, CO
Keever, Thomas F. .... Dallas, TX
Keever, William M. .... Birmingham, AL
Keevers, Suzanne P. .... Metairie, LA
Keevers, Thomas J. .... Park Ridge, IL
Keevican, Leo A., Jr. .... Washington, DC
Bloomfield Hills, MI
Harrisburg, PA
Pittsburgh, PA
Keevil, Jeffrey A. .... Columbia, MO
Keezel, Edward F., II .... Winter Park, FL
Keezel, Robert E. .... Cape Coral, FL
Keezel, Roy .... Houston, TX
Keezel, Roy, P.C. .... Houston, TX
Keezer, Ellen R. .... New York, NY
Kefalos, George J. .... Charleston, SC
Kefalos, George J., P.A. .... Charleston, SC
Kefauver, James M. .... Rockville, MD
Kefer, Deborah L. .... New York, NY
Keffer, E. Brooks, Jr. .... Philadelphia, PA
Keffer, Hugh A. .... Cranford, NJ
Keffer, James D. .... Ashland, KY
Keffer, Jeffery L. .... Boston, MA
Keffer, John L. .... Houston, TX
Keffer, Richard A. .... St. Louis, MO
Keffer, William R. .... Dallas, TX
Keffer, William W. .... Kennett Square, PA
Malvern, PA
Keffler, James P. .... Boca Raton, FL
Keffler, Richard A., Jr. .... Amarillo, TX
Keffler, Robert J. .... Fort Worth, TX
Kefgen, Robert W. .... Dearborn, MI
Kegan, Bernard M. S.
Mendota Heights, MN
Kegan, Daniel L. .... Chicago, IL
Kegan, Esther O. .... Chicago, IL
Kegan & Kegan, Ltd. .... Chicago, IL
Kegans, Nettie Joe .... Houston, TX
Kegel, Clarence C., Jr. .... Lancaster, PA
Kegel, Craig .... Irvine, CA
Kegel, Debra L. .... Irvine, CA
Kegel, Jacob David .... Plymouth, MN
Kegel, Kathleen .... New York, NY
Kegel Kelin Almy & Grimm LLP
Lancaster, PA
Kegel, Kurt A. .... Atlanta, GA
Kegel, Kurt A. .... Dalton, GA
Kegel, Margaret .... Santa Fe, NM
Kegel, Robert A. .... Long Beach, CA
Los Angeles, CA
San Diego, CA
Kegel, Tobin & Truce .... Van Nuys, CA
Long Beach, CA
Los Angeles, CA
Rancho Cucamonga, CA
San Diego, CA
Ventura, CA
Kegelman, Joan B. .... Jersey City, NJ
Kegelman, Lynn B. .... Trenton, NJ
Kegerreis, Melissa A. .... Dayton, OH
Kegerreis, Nancy R.
Department Of Veterans Affairs,
Board of Veterans Appeals, GV
Kegerreis, Sharon L. .... Miami, FL
Kegler, Brown, Hill & Ritter
Columbus, OH
Delaware, OH
Dublin, OH
Marion, OH
Kegler, Charles J. .... Columbus, OH
Kegler, Kimberly N. .... Raleigh, NC
Kegler, Todd M. .... Columbus, OH
Keglewitsch, Josef .... Columbus, OH
Kegley, Clinton Sherwood .... Wytheville, VA
Kegley, Delwyn H. .... Philadelphia, PA
Kegley, Jack N. .... Charlottesville, VA
Kegley, James A. .... Lexington, KY
Kegley, Robin J. .... Blacksburg, VA
Pulaski, VA
Kegley, Russell D. .... Portsmouth, OH
Keglovits, David Edward .... Tulsa, OK
Keglovits, Jennifer J. .... Tulsa, OK
Kegowicz, Kimberly
Department of Defense, GV
Kehagiaras, Andrew D. .... Detroit, MI
Kehart, Michael J. .... Decatur, IL
Kehart, Shafter & Webber, P.C.
Decatur, IL
Kehayas, George J. .... New York, NY
Kehe, David O. .... New York, NY
Kehew, Roger N., Jr. .... San Bernardino, CA
Kehiayan, Haig .... Canyon Country, CA
Kehinde, Ann Celeste .... Lutherville, MD

Kehir, Paul H. .... Atlanta, GA
Kehl, D. Goelet .... Albuquerque, NM
Kehl, Diane M. .... Chicago, IL
Kehl, Jeffrey A. .... New York, NY
Kehl, Jeffrey Edward .... Chicago, IL
Kehl, Larry B. .... Cheyenne, WY
Kehl, Shelley Sanders .... New York, NY
Kehl, Stanley E. .... Seattle, WA
Kehl, William W. .... Greenville, SC
Kehlenbeck, Vickery Hall .... Boston, MA
Kehler, Christopher D. .... Warsaw, IN
Kehler, Daniel R. .... West Berlin, NJ
Kehler, Laura Katherine .... Little Rock, AR
Kehlhof, Joan, (P.C.) .... Houston, TX
Kehm, Dennis J. .... Hillsboro, MO
Kehn, James M. .... Cleveland, OH
Kehn, Robert M. .... Cazadero, CA
Kehne and Adams Law Office .... Boise, ID
Kehne, Jeffrey P. .... Department of Justice,
Office of Legal Counsel, GV
Kehne, Melanie McNeill .... Montpelier, VT
St. Johnsbury, VT
Kehne, Rolf M. .... Boise, ID
Kehner, John T. .... West Chester, PA
Kehoe, Bridget C. .... Grand Rapids, MI
Kehoe, Brien E. .... Washington, DC
Kehoe, Christopher B. .... Easton, MD
Kehoe, Christopher G. .... Wakefield, RI
Kehoe, D. Bruce .... Connersville, IN
Indianapolis, IN
Richmond, IN
Kehoe, Danea M. .... Washington, DC
Kehoe, David J. .... Warwick, RI
Kehoe, Deborah H. .... Mobile, AL
Kehoe, Dennis J. .... Aptos, CA
Kehoe, Dennis J., A Law Corporation
Aptos, CA
Santa Cruz, CA
Kehoe, Dennis M. .... Lyons, NY
Kehoe & DeRose .... Olean, NY
Kehoe, E. Christopher .... Boston, MA
Kehoe, Edw. T. .... Washington, DC
Kehoe, Edward G. .... New York, NY
Kehoe, Edward J., Jr. .... Belmont, MI
Kehoe, G. Roth, II .... Atlanta, GA
Kehoe, George E., Jr. .... Hendersonville, NC
Kehoe, Gerald J. (IBA) **....... Boston, MA**
Kehoe, Gregory W. .... Tampa, FL
Kehoe, J. Michael .... Lyons, NY
Kehoe, James E. .... Olean, NY
Kehoe, James F. .... Utica, NY
Kehoe, James P., Jr. .... Rome, NY
Kehoe, Jennifer J. .... Minneapolis, MN
Kehoe, Joan A. .... Albany, NY
Kehoe, John A. .... New York, NY
Kehoe, John D. .... Naples, FL
Kehoe, John E. .... Atlanta, GA
Kehoe, John E. .... Ironton, OH
Kehoe, John F. .... Boston, MA
Kehoe, Joseph F. .... Oneonta, NY
Kehoe, Kerry S. .... Boston, MA
Kehoe, Kevin L. .... Decatur, IL
Kehoe, L. Paul .... Rochester, NY
Kehoe, Larissa A.J. .... Palo Alto, CA
Kehoe, Leslie S. .... Atlanta, GA
Kehoe, Loryn Joan .... Redwood City, CA
Kehoe, Mark A. .... Grand Rapids, MI
Kehoe, Mark R. .... Evesham, NJ
Philadelphia, PA
Kehoe, Mary P. .... Burlington, VT
Kehoe, Matthew H. .... Hillsboro, OR
Kehoe & Merzig .... Oneonta, NY
Kehoe, Michael A. .... New Bedford, MA
Kehoe, Michael E. .... Kenosha, WI
Kehoe, Michael J. .... Howell, MI
Kehoe, Michael W. .... Pensacola, FL
Kehoe, Patrick .... Albany, NY
Kehoe, Patrick E. .... Washington, DC
Kehoe, Patrick G., Jr. .... New Orleans, LA
Kehoe, Peter R. .... Troy, NY
Kehoe, Randall E. .... Albany, NY
Kehoe, Rebecca L. .... Washington, DC
Kehoe, Richard O'C. .... Utica, NY
Kehoe, Robert E., Jr. .... Chicago, IL
Kehoe, Robert F. .... Seattle, WA
Kehoe, Ronald F. .... Boston, MA
Kehoe, Sean P. .... Washington, DC
Kehoe, Sharon M. .... Brockport, NY
Kehoe, Stephen G. .... Chicago, IL
Kehoe, Stephen H. .... Easton, MD
Kehoe, Stephen J. .... Lynn, MA
Kehoe, Susan E.
National Labor Relations Board,
Office of Board Members, GV
Kehoe, Terrence E. .... Orlando, FL
Kehoe, Thomas J. .... Groton, CT
Kehoe, Ty E. .... Las Vegas, NV
Kehoe, William A., III
Federal Communications Commission,
Common Carrier Bureau, GV
Kehoe, William F. .... Boston, MA
Kehoe, William F. .... Sussex, NJ
Kehoe, William K. .... Utica, NY
Kehr, Edward C. .... Solon, OH
Kehr, Ellen Birnbaum .... Los Angeles, CA
Kehr, Janie W. .... New Orleans, LA
Kehr, Jeffrey A. .... Bloomington, IN
Kehr, Joanne Betlem .... York, PA
Kehr, Kent D. .... St. Louis, MO
Kehr, Linda Moorey .... Beulah, MI
Kehr, Robert L. .... Los Angeles, CA
Kehr, Schiff & Crane, LLP
Los Angeles, CA
Kehr, Thomas F. .... Concord, NH
Kehr, Thomas W. .... Chillicothe, IL
Kehr, William M. .... Derby, KS
Kehrer, Andrew D. .... Buffalo, NY

Kehrer, Bettye Hynson ... Austell, GA
Lago Vista, TX
Kehres, Grant W. ... Boca Raton, FL
Kehres, Grant W., P.A. ... Boca Raton, FL
Kehres, Julie Schimpf ... Cincinnati, OH
Kehres, Robert A. ... Cleveland, OH
Kehres, Robert W. ... Lansing, MI
Kehrig, Katie E. ... New York, NY
Kehrli, David ... Cypress, CA
Kehrli, Todd M. ... Concord, CA
Kehrwald, Frank J. ... Overland Park, KS
Keib, John W. ... De Witt, NY
Keidaish, Philip Frederic, Jr. ... Orlando, FL
Keidan, Dara J. ... Chicago, IL
Keidan, Edward B. ... Chicago, IL
Keidan, Harry W. ... Phoenix, AZ
Keidan, Harry W., P.C. ... Phoenix, AZ
Keidan, Herbert S. ... Bloomfield Hills, MI
Keidan, Jacob L. ... Farmington Hills, MI
Keidan, Milford ... Farmington Hills, MI
Keidatz, Thomas L. ... De Pere, WI
Keidel, James C. ... Stamford, CT
Keidel, Leslie Ann ... Glendale, CA
Keidel, Richard J. ... Garden City, NY
Keiderling, Thomas G. ... Des Moines, IA
Keidser, Kari A. ... Los Angeles, CA
Keif, Brian S. ... Miami, FL
Keif, Brian S., P.A. ... Miami, FL
Keifer, Brian P. ... Los Angeles, CA
Keifer, Eugene V. ... Iowa City, IA
Keifer, Teri L. ... Columbia, MO
Keiffer, E. Paul ... Dallas, TX
Keiffer, Johnston & Reinstein
Camp Springs, MD
Keiffer, Sebert H. ... Camp Springs, MD
Keiffer, Thomas Michael, Sr. (P.C.)
New Orleans, LA
Keiffner, John D., III. ... Indianapolis, IN
Keig, Elizabeth Johnson ... San Antonio, TX
Keig, Joseph, Jr. ... Chicago, IL
Keig, Lowell A. ... San Antonio, TX
Keig, Patrick G. ... Flagstaff, AZ
Keiger, John A. ... Winston-Salem, NC
Keiger, R. Kason ... Winston-Salem, NC
Keigher, John J. ... Rochester, NY
Keigher, Raymond ... Potomac, MD
Keighron, Brian P. ... Oxnard, CA
Keightley, James J.
Pension Benefit Guaranty Corporation, Office of the General Counsel, GV
Keightley, Ralph D., Jr. ... Lewisburg, WV
Keightly, David A. ... Lansdale, PA
Keihner, Bruce W., P.A. ... Palm Beach, FL
Keijonen, Robert D. ... Glendora, CA
Keil, A. Bartlett ... Chesapeake, VA
Keil, Bradley S. ... Minneapolis, MN
Keil, Charles K. ... Wilmington, DE
Keil and Connolly ... San Francisco, CA
Keil, Dale L. ... Conrad, MT
Keil, Daniel M. ... Hialeah, FL
Keil, Dennis M. ... Toledo, OH
Keil, Gerald W. ... West Orange, NJ
Keil & Goodson ... Texarkana, AR
Keil, Herbert B. ... Washington, DC
Keil, James J., Jr. ... Denver, CO
Keil, John S. ... Tulsa, OK
Keil, Julie A. ... Midland, MI
Keil & Keil ... Glendale, AZ
Keil, Lisa A. ... Greenville, DE
Keil, Martin F. ... Glendale, AZ
Keil, Martin F., Jr. ... Glendale, AZ
Keil, Matt ... Texarkana, AR
Keil, Monica L. ... Cleveland, OH
Keil, Ralph F. ... Wilmington, DE
Keil, Richard M. ... Oakhurst, NJ
Keil, Robert P. ... Flint, MI
Keil, Timothy P. ... Little Rock, AR
Keil, Vincent M. ... St. Louis, MO
Keil & Weinkauf ... Washington, DC
Keilbach, John J. ... Pueblo, CO
Keiler, Alan D. ... Washington, DC
Keiler, Joel I. ... Reston, VA
Keiler, Jonathan F. ... Bethesda, MD
Keiler, Leroy H. ... Williamsport, PA
Keiler, Louis C. ... Chicago, IL
Keiler, William G. ... San Antonio, TX
Keiley, Anthony J., III ... Monterey, CA
San Jose, CA
Keiley, Anthony J. III, A Professional Law Corporation ... Monterey, CA
San Jose, CA
Keiley, Elizabeth ... Chicago, IL
Keilin, Nina ... New York, NY
Keiling, Richard ... Blairstown, NJ
Keilitz, Kirsten L. ... Traverse City, MI
Keillor, Jamie P. ... Brighton, MI
Keillor, Kevin J. ... Bend, OR
Keilly, Michael S. ... Lafayette, CO
Keilman, Gerard T. ... Roseland, NJ
Keilp, Joe ... Phoenix, AZ
Keilp, Joe, P.C. ... Phoenix, AZ
Keils and Fulcher ... Teague, TX
Keils, Lucinda ... Taylor, MI
Keils, W. A., Jr. ... Teague, TX
Keilson, Joseph ... Valley Stream, NY
Keilson & Keilson ... Valley Stream, NY
Keilson, Robert C. ... Garden City, NY
Keilty, Bryan P. ... Hartford, CT
Keilty, John R. ... Peabody, MA
Keilty, Michael ... Torrington, CT
Keily, David L. ... Boston, MA
Keily, Paul A. ... West Hartford, CT
Keily, Robert A. ... New Orleans, LA
Keim, David Brent ... Cary, NC
Keim, Donald W. ... Detroit, MI
Keim, Donna ... Gainesville, FL
Keim, Elaine Velisaris ... Warrendale, PA
Keim, Judy G. ... Escondido, CA
Keim, Krista K. ... Cleveland, OH
Keim, R. Kenneth, (P.C.) ... Houston, TX
Keim, Robert B. ... Kansas City, MO
Keim, S. Clay ... Spartanburg, SC
Keim, Thomas E., Jr. ... Chicago, IL
Keim, Thomas H., Jr. ... Spartanburg, SC
Keimig, Emily F. ... Denver, CO
Kein, Donald G. ... Union, NJ
Kein, Pollatschek & Greenstein ... Union, NJ
Keinarth, Art ... Smithville, TX
Keiner, Charles H. ... New York, NY
Keiner, Christian M., PC
Sacramento, CA
Keiner & Dumont, P.C. ... Middlebury, VT
Keiner, Jeffrey D. (IBA) ... Orlando, FL
Keiner, Marilyn Malerba ... Pleasantville, NJ
Keiner, R. Bruce, Jr. ... Washington, DC
Keiner, Robert P. ... Middlebury, VT
Keiner, Suellen Terrill ... Washington, DC
Keinz, Donald E. ... Utica, NY
Keiper, Jeffrey B. ... Cleveland, OH
Keipert, Gerald F. ... Annapolis, MD
Fort Washington, MD
Waldorf, MD
Keir, David S. ... Washington, DC
Keir, Diana J. ... Bloomfield, CT
Keir, Duncan W. ... Greenbelt, MD
Keir, James M. ... Los Angeles, CA
Keir, John C. ... Oreland, PA
Keir, Loyal E. ... Riverside, CA
Keire, Fred A. ... New York, NY
Keirn, Edward A. ... Indianapolis, IN
Keirnan, John P. ... Houston, TX
Keirs, Christopher D. ... Houston, TX
Keis, R. Brent ... Fort Worth, TX
Keis, William H., Jr. ... Cleveland, OH
Keisch, Lillian ... Bronx, NY
Keiser, Alan D. ... Philadelphia, PA
Keiser, Clarence C., Jr. ... Bozman, MD
Keiser, George A. ... Harrisburg, PA
Keiser, Howard T. ... Cincinnati, OH
Keiser, Ingrid J. ... Keystone, CO
Keiser, J. Alan ... Swanton, OH
Keiser, Janet L. ... Lincoln, NE
Keiser, Jeffrey D. ... St. Louis, MO
Keiser, Jeffrey M. ... Haddonfield, NJ
Keiser, Judith Lavori
Fort Lauderdale, FL
Keiser & Keiser ... Livingston Manor, NY
Keiser, Larry S. ... Wilkes-Barre, PA
Keiser, Laurence ... White Plains, NY
Keiser, Matthew D. ... Washington, DC
Keiser, Matthew R. ... Department of the Army, Office, Chief of Engineers/Headquarters, U.S. Army Corps of Engineers, GV
Keiser, Michael S. ... Livingston Manor, NY
Keiser, Ray E. ... Fort Lauderdale, FL
Keiser, Richard M. ... Houston, TX
Keiser, Susan ... Livingston Manor, NY
Keiser, Thomas ... Arcadia, CA
Keiser, Vernon R. ... Brandon, FL
Keiser, W. Jack ... Kalamazoo, MI
Keiser, William B., Jr. ... Ridgely, TN
Keiser, William H. ... Long Beach, CA
Keish, Rodney D. ... Dayton, OH
Keisler, Peter D. ... Washington, DC
Keisler, Robert L., Jr. ... Louisville, KY
Keisler, Shirley F. ... Fairfax, VA
Keisler, Susan Gomory ... Bethesda, MD
Keisler, William B. ... Little Rock, AR
Keisling, Erica Heide ... Doylestown, PA
Keisling, Raymond F. ... Carnegie, PA
Keisling Schmitt Coletta & Deitrick, P.C.
Carnegie, PA
Keisling, Trent ... Fayetteville, AR
Keisling-Duca, Megan R. ... Carnegie, PA
Keisman, Howard I. ... New York, NY
Keisner, David A. ... Los Angeles, CA
Keist, Michelle L. ... Denver, CO
Keist, Steven D. ... Glendale, AZ
Keister, David L. ... Columbus, OH
Keister, David W. ... Baltimore, MD
Keister, Garry N. ... Tempe, AZ
Keister & McPherson ... Freeport, IL
Keister, Paul H. ... Pasco, WA
Keister, Ralph F. ... Sidney, OH
Keister, Stephen E. ... Van Wert, OH
Keita, Sylvia ... Oakland, CA
Keitel, David ... Los Angeles, CA
Keitel, Karin A. ... Minneapolis, MN
Keitel, William E. ... Los Angeles, CA
Keitelman, Charis R. ... Washington, DC
Keitelman, Jeffrey R. ... Washington, DC
Keiter, Aaron ... Houston, TX
Keiter, David C. ... York, PA
Keiter, Jeffrey A. ... Hershey, PA
Keiter, John W. ... Wilmington, DE
Keiter, Leon G. ... Wichita, KS
Keiter, Mitchell ... Los Angeles, CA
Keiter, Sheila A. T. ... Los Angeles, CA
Keiter, Timothy S., Law Office of
Portland, ME
Keitges & Bangle, A Professional Law Corporation ... Fairfield, CA
Sacramento, CA
Keitges, Cyril A., Jr. ... Fairfield, CA
Sacramento, CA
Keith, Alan C. ... Birmingham, AL
Keith, Alan G. ... Kansas City, MO
Keith, Alexander M. (Sandy)
Rochester, MN
Keith, Alexandra B.
National Credit Union Administration, Office of Inspector General, GV
Keith, Alston, Jr. ... Selma, AL
Keith, A. M. ... St. Paul, MN
Keith, Amy ... Johnson City, TX
Keith, Arnold Pennington, Jr.
New York, NY
Keith, Barrymore O. ... Lubbock, TX
Keith, Bonnie L. ... Atlanta, GA
Keith, Brenda E. ... Derry, NH
Keith, Bruce ... Albuquerque, NM
Keith, Bruce, P.C. ... Albuquerque, NM
Keith, C. David ... Bath, ME
Keith, Calvin L. ... Portland, OR
Keith, Carol M. ... St. Louis, MO
Keith, Charles L. ... Hilliard, OH
Keith, Cheryl A. ... Salt Lake City, UT
Keith, Christine M. ... Kalamazoo, MI
Keith, Christopher J. ... Fort Lauderdale, FL
Keith, Christopher J.
Fort Lauderdale, FL
Keith, Clegg & Epley ... Magnolia, AR
Keith, Courtney S. ... Fort Worth, TX
Keith, Craig B. ... Oklahoma City, OK
Keith, D. Judith ... Department of Justice, Civil Rights Division, GV
Keith, Dale W. ... Cherry Hill, NJ
Philadelphia, PA
Keith, Damon J. ... Detroit, MI
Keith, Danielle M. ... Midland, MI
Keith, Darrell L. ... Fort Worth, TX
Keith, Darrell, P.C., Law Firm of
Fort Worth, TX
Keith, Debra L. ... Omaha, NE
Keith, Edward Ray, Jr. ... Texarkana, TX
Keith, F. Wayne ... Birmingham, AL
Keith, George G. ... Cuyahoga Falls, OH
Keith, Gerald P. ... El Paso, TX
Keith, Gregory Daulton ... Charleston, SC
Keith, Gregory Dean ... Wichita, KS
Keith & Hall ... Richmond, VA
Keith & Hamm, A Professional Corporation
Montgomery, AL
Keith, Harold F. ... Hartford, CT
Keith, Heather C. ... Fort Lauderdale, FL
Keith, Helyn L. ... Memphis, TN
Keith, India Early ... Charlotte, NC
Keith, J. Parke ... Selma, AL
Keith, J. Patrick ... Richmond, VA
Keith, J. Paul, III ... Louisville, KY
Keith, J. Russell ... Columbus, OH
Keith, James A. ... Jackson, MS
Keith, James A. ... Long Beach, MS
Keith, James S. ... Virginia Beach, VA
Keith, Jamie Lewis ... Boston, MA
Keith, Jennifer M. ... Rancho Cucamonga, CA
Keith, Jerry E. ... Washington, DC
Keith, John A. C. ... Fairfax, VA
Keith, John H. ... Olympia, WA
Keith, John, III ... Great Falls, MT
Keith, John M., Jr. ... Cynthiana, KY
Keith, John T. ... Bloomington, IN
Keith, Joni ... Ottumwa, IA
Keith, June M. ... Hayward, CA
Keith, Karen L. ... Louisville, KY
Keith and Keith ... Selma, AL
Keith, Kelvin H. ... Miami Springs, FL
Keith, Kenneth L. ... Ottumwa, IA
Keith, Kenneth M. ... Garden City, NY
Keith, Kent M. ... Honolulu, HI
Keith, Kevin J. ... Dallas, TX
Keith, Kimberly S. ... Baltimore, MD
Keith, L. Rondie ... Englewood, CO
Corpus Christi, TX
Keith, Langford, Jr. ... Silver City, NM
Keith, Laura M. ... Dallas, TX
Keith Law Firm, A Professional Corporation
Ottumwa, IA
Keith, Lloyd E. ... Ottumwa, IA
Keith, M. Langhorne ... Fairfax, VA
Keith Mack LLP ... Miami, FL
Keith Mack, LLP ... West Palm Beach, FL
Keith, Maxwell ... San Francisco, CA
Keith, Michael A. ... Miami, FL
Keith and Miller, P.A. ... Rogers, AR
Keith, Patricia E. ... Department of Labor, Office of Secretary, GV
Keith, Paul ... Monticello, AR
Keith, Penrod W. ... Salt Lake City, UT
Keith, Peter E. ... Baltimore, MD
Keith, Philip ... San Francisco, CA
Keith, Phillip E. ... Christiansburg, VA
Keith, R. Fred ... Fairfax, OH
Keith, Ralph E., Jr. ... Needham, MA
Keith, Rebekah ... Huntsville, AL
Keith, Richard K. ... Montgomery, AL
Keith, Robert E.
Department Of Health And Human Services, Office of the General Counsel, GV
Keith, Robert Gary ... Charlotte, NC
Keith, Robert P. ... Chicago, IL
Keith, Robert Q. ... Johnson City, TN
Keith, Robert S., II ... Omaha, NE
Keith, Roy W. ... Pound, WI
Keith, Russell T. ... Peru, IN
Keith, Sally ... Raleigh, NC
Keith, Sean T. ... Rogers, AR
Keith, Seymour D. ... Miami, FL
Keith, Shannon R. ... Encino, CA
Keith, Sidney R. ... San Francisco, CA
Keith, Stephen Donald ... Birmingham, AL
Keith, Susan Roux ... Ocala, FL
Keith, Susan S. ... Dallas, TX
Keith, Terrance A. ... Troy, MI
Keith, Thomas A. ... Peru, IN
Keith, Thomas J. ... Winston-Salem, NC
Keith, Tom J. ... Bentonville, AR
Keith, Vanessa Kay Robinson
St. Louis, MO
Keith, W. David ... Manchester, CT
Keith & Weber, P.C. ... Johnson City, TX
Keith, William D. ... Naples, FL
Keith, William W., III ... Chatsworth, GA
Keith, William W., III, P.C.
Chatsworth, GA
Dalton, GA
Keith, Winters & Wenning
Bradley Beach, NJ
Keithley, Bradford G. ... Dallas, TX
Keithley, Jay C. ... Washington, DC
Keithley, Roger L. ... Denver, CO
Keithley, Roger L., P.C. ... Denver, CO
Keithline, Jeffrey A. ... Washington, DC
Keithline, W. Wilson ... Hartford, CT
Keithly, Bruce A. ... Snohomish, WA
Keithly & English ... Anthony, NM
Keithly, John E. ... Anthony, NM
Keithly & Keithly ... San Diego, CA
Keithly, Lisa M. ... St. Louis, MO
Keithly, Roger M., Jr. ... San Diego, CA
Keithly, Sandra L. ... San Diego, CA
Keith-Miller, Verlaine ... Seattle, WA
Keitt, John K., Jr. (IBA) ... New York, NY
Keitt, Lawrence ... Orangeburg, SC
Keizer, Bruce A. ... Juneau, AK
Keizer, Kathleen A. ... Seattle, WA
Keizer, M. John ... Arlington, TX
Keizer, M. John, P.C. ... Arlington, TX
Fort Worth, TX
Kekac, Nancy A. ... Stamford, CT
Kekel, David A. ... Portland, OR
Kekel, Eric A. ... Portland, OR
Keker, John W. ... San Francisco, CA
Keker & Van Nest, L.L.P.
San Francisco, CA
Kekich, Barbara ... Los Angeles, CA
Kekich, John ... Kalamazoo, MI
Kekina, Clarence S.K. ... Honolulu, HI
Kekina, Wayne K. ... Honolulu, HI
Kekoa, Curtis ... Kailua, HI
Kekow, Franklin A. ... Milwaukee, WI
Kekow-Keaton, Carola ... Danville, CA
Kekst, David J. ... Beverly Hills, CA
Kelaghan, Richard P. ... Cranston, RI
Kelaher, Connell & Connor, P.C.
Conway, SC
Georgetown, SC
Myrtle Beach, SC
Surfside Beach, SC
Kelaher, Edward T. ... Surfside Beach, SC
Kelaher, Garvey, Ballou & Van Dyke, A Professional Corporation
Toms River, NJ
Kelaher, James P. ... Orlando, FL
Kelaher Law Offices, P.A. ... Orlando, FL
Kelaher, Neva M. ... Winter Park, FL
Kelaher, Thomas F. ... Toms River, NJ
Kelakos, George M. ... Boston, MA
Kelash, Mary F. ... Benson, MN
Kelber, Bruce C. ... Crystal Lake, IL
Kelber, Michael G. ... Chicago, IL
Kelber, Philip H. ... Upland, CA
Kelber, Richard J. ... Minneapolis, MN
Kelber, Robt. ... Minneapolis, MN
Kelber, Steven B. ... Washington, DC
Kelber, Tamar B. ... Chicago, IL
Kelberg, Brian R. ... Los Angeles, CA
Kelberg, Childress and Flax
Virginia Beach, VA
Kelberg, Howard S. ... New York, NY
Kelberg, Lee ... Virginia Beach, VA
Kelberg, Paul R. ... White Plains, NY
Kelberman, Dale P. ... Severna Park, MD
Kelble, David L., Jr. ... Lakewood, CO
Kelble, Glenn C. ... Los Angeles, CA
Kelbley, Jeffrey P. ... Columbus, OH
Kelbley, Michael P. ... Tiffin, OH
Kelbon, Edward J., Jr. ... Philadelphia, PA
Kelbon, Marcia S. ... Seattle, WA
Kelbon, Regina Stango ... Philadelphia, PA
Kelby, David E. ... Minneapolis, MN
Kelch, Donald F., Jr. ... Columbus, OH
Kelch, Max J. ... Nebraska City, NE
Kelch, Thomas G. ... Costa Mesa, CA
Kelchner, Hannelore V.M. Hasl
Durham, NC
Kelchner, John B. ... Columbia, SC
Kelchner, Kristina S. ... Palo Alto, CA
Kelcourse, Kevin M. ... Department of Justice, Tax Division, GV
Kelcy, Michael C. ... Los Angeles, CA
Kelder, Rebecca ... New York, NY
Keldermans, Francis L. ... Chicago, IL
Keldsen, Kenneth W., (P.C.) ... Rawlins, WY
Kelecius, Linas J. ... Chicago, IL
Kelecius, Ramune Rita ... Chicago, IL
Kelegian & Associates ... Beverly Hills, CA
Newport Beach, CA
Kelegian, Mark A. ... Beverly Hills, CA
Newport Beach, CA
Kelehan, Kevin J. ... Columbia, MD
Kelehear, L. Stephen ... Dalton, GA
Keleher & Brunner ... Manistee, MI
Keleher, Dennis L. ... Manistee, MI
Keleher & Eastman ... Gladstone, MO
Keleher, James F. ... Manhattan Beach, CA
Keleher & McLeod, P.A.
Albuquerque, NM
Keleher, Michael J. ... Rock Island, IL
Keleher, Michael L. ... Albuquerque, NM
Keleher, Michael P. ... Gladstone, MO
Keleher, Thomas D. ... Syracuse, NY
Keleher, Thomas F. ... Albuquerque, NM
Keleher, William B. ... Albuquerque, NM
Keleher, William R. ... Albuquerque, NM
Kelemen, Andrea L. ... Rockledge, FL
Kelemen, Gabor J. ... Washington, DC
Kelemen, George S., Jr ... Phoenix, AZ
Kelemen, Joseph A. ... Buffalo, NY
Kelepecz, Betty P. ... Long Beach, CA
Keler, Marianne M. ... Reston, VA

Keles, Elif ... Los Angeles, CA
Kelesis, George P. ... Las Vegas, NV
Keleske, Joshua T. ... Milwaukee, WI
Keleti, S. Martin ... Los Angeles, CA
Kelety, Julia Craig ... San Diego, CA
Kelety, Theresa K. ... Washington, DC
Kelhart, Joanne ... Bethlehem, PA
Kelhoffer, Alan C. ... New York, NY
Kelhoffer, Charles I. ... Phoenix, AZ
Keligian, David L. ... Irvine, CA
Keliher, Cynthia B. ... Boston, MA
Keliher, Michael J. ... Dallas, TX
Kelin, Howard L. ... Lancaster, PA
Kelin, Richard S. ... West Orange, NJ
Kelinske, Darryl L. ... Austin, TX
Kelinsky, Allen Edward ... Rosemead, CA
Kelinson, Craig A. ... Des Moines, IA
Kelinson, Joseph H., (P.A.) ... Key West, FL
Kelk, William A. ... Stowe, VT
Kelker & Andrascik ... Rochester, PA
Kelker, Frank S. ... Rochester, PA
Kell, Alterman & Runstein, LLP
Portland, OR
Kell, Barry J. ... Anchorage, AK
Kell, C. LaTain ... Atlanta, GA
Kell, C. Lina ... Miami, FL
Kell, C. D. ... Murdo, SD
Kell, Christopher J. ... New York, NY
Kell, E. Dennis ... Atlantic City, NJ
Kell & Flach ... St. Charles, MO
Kell, George W. ... Modesto, CA
Kell, Gerald C. ... Department of Justice, Civil Division, GV
Kell, Herbert W., Jr. ... Rogers, AR
Kell, Janice K. ... Knoxville, TN
Kell, John Mark ... St. Charles, MO
Kell, John R. ... Media, PA
Kell, Kenneth H. ... Haddon Heights, NJ
Philadelphia, PA
Kell, Lee Davis ... Portland, OR
Kell & Lynch, P.C. ... Birmingham, MI
Detroit, MI
Kell, Mark Edward ... Baltimore, MD
Kell, Mary Kate ... Houston, TX
Kell, Michael V. ... Birmingham, MI
Kell, Philip W. ... Sacramento, CA
Kell, Randal B. ... Alexandria, VA
Kell, Robert A. ... Knoxville, TN
Kell, Scott, Jr., (P.C.) ... Hermann, MO
Kell, Vette E. ... Woodstock, IL
Kellahan, Jennifer Rose ... Kingstree, SC
Kellahin and Kellahin ... Santa Fe, NM
Kellahin, W. Thomas ... Santa Fe, NM
Kellam, Deborah G. M. ... Cheyenne, WY
Kellam, Floyd E., Jr. ... Virginia Beach, VA
Kellam, James L. ... Riverside, CA
Kellam, James R. ... Sandusky, OH
Kellam, John L. ... New Castle, IN
Kellam, Leroy B. ... Kew Gardens, NY
Kellam, Mary M. ... Virginia Beach, VA
Kellam, Newton W. ... Aliso Viejo, CA
Kellam, Pickrell, Cox & Tayloe, A Professional Corporation ... Norfolk, VA
Virginia Beach, VA
Kellam, Richd. B. ... Norfolk, VA
Kellam, W. J., Jr. ... Cornelius, NC
Kellam, W. J., Jr. ... Charlotte, NC
Kellams, Barbara DiFiglio ... Burbank, CA
Kellams, Marc R. ... Bloomington, IN
Kellan, Ronald L. ... Portland, ME
Kellar, Christopher J. ... Newark, NJ
Kellar, Curtis B. ... New York, NY
Kellar, James G. ... Allentown, PA
Kellar, Karl L. ... Washington, DC
Kellar & Kellar ... Kingston, NY
Kellar, Larry David ... Pensacola, FL
Kellar, Michael C. ... Los Angeles, CA
Kellar, Norman ... Kingston, NY
Kellar, Paul T. ... Kingston, NY
Kellas, Elizabeth ... Winchester, VA
Kellas, Ross J. ... Fairfax, VA
Kelleghan, Thomas C. ... Wheaton, IL
Kellegrew, Kent M. ... Ventura, CA
Kellegrew, Wallace R., Jr. ... Andover, MA
Kelleher, Arlynn K. ... Pittsburgh, PA
Kelleher, Brian E. ... Farmington, CT
Kelleher, Brian M. ... Basking Ridge, NJ
Kelleher, Christopher G.
Chesterfield, MO
St. Louis, MO
Kelleher, Cyril A. ... New York, NY
Kelleher, D. Ring ... Arlington, MA
Kelleher, Daniel F. ... Wilmington, DE
Kelleher, Daniel H. ... Boston, MA
Kelleher, Daniel J. ... Scranton, PA
Kelleher, David L. ... Washington, DC
Kelleher, David R. ... Dearborn, MI
Kelleher, Deirdre K. ... Springfield, MA
Kelleher, Denis P. ... Brooklyn, NY
Kelleher, Dennis M. ... Boston, MA
Kelleher, Diane ... New York, NY
Kelleher, Duane J. ... Columbus, OH
Kelleher, Edward J. ... Portland, ME
Kelleher, Edward J. ... Haddonfield, NJ
Kelleher, Elizabeth A. ... Providence, RI
Kelleher, Ellen ... Chicago, IL
Kelleher, Frank G. ... Boston, MA
Kelleher, Glenn W. ... New City, NY
Stony Point, NY
Kelleher, Grant W. ... Goshen, NY
Kelleher, Herbert D. ... San Antonio, TX
Kelleher, J. Michael, Jr. ... Buffalo, NY
Kelleher, Jacqueline M. ... Pittsburgh, PA
Kelleher, James E. ... Warwick, RI
Kelleher, James F. ... Wilmington, DE
Kelleher, James F. ... Boston, MA
Kelleher, James J. ... Orlando, FL
Kelleher, James J., V ... New Orleans, LA
Kelleher, James P. ... New York, NY
Kelleher, James P. ... Koror, TT
Kelleher, James W. ... Dayton, OH
Kelleher, J.D. ... Los Angeles, CA
Kelleher, Jeffry F. ... Cleveland, OH
Kelleher, Jeffry F., & Associates Co.
Cleveland, OH
Kelleher, Jennifer A. L. ... Washington, DC
Kelleher, Joellen M. ... Washington, DC
Kelleher, John A. ... Somerville, NJ
Kelleher, John C., Jr. ... Beverly, MA
Kelleher, John F. ... Providence, RI
Kelleher, John H. ... Boston, MA
Kelleher, John J. ... Treasury Department, United States Secret Service, GV
Kelleher, John J. ... Albany, NY
Kelleher, John M. ... Bryn Mawr, PA
Kelleher, John P. ... Boston, MA
Kelleher, John P. ... Las Vegas, NV
Kelleher, John T. ... Las Vegas, NV
Kelleher, Joseph J. ... New York, NY
Kelleher, Joseph T., Jr. ... Edwardsville, IL
Kelleher, Karen E. ... Boston, MA
Kelleher, Karen Kathleen
San Francisco, CA
Kelleher, Kathleen Megan ... Boston, MA
Kelleher, Kevin Barry ... Fort Lauderdale, FL
Kelleher, Kevin J. ... Bethlehem, PA
Kelleher, Kevin M. ... Catskill, NY
Kelleher, Leslie M. ... Richmond, VA
Kelleher, Louise A. ... New York, NY
Kelleher, Mark ... Montgomery, AL
Kelleher, Mary Beth ... West Liberty, OH
Kelleher, Mary E. ... New Bedford, MA
Kelleher, Maureen T. ... Immokalee, FL
Kelleher, Michael F. ... Los Angeles, CA
San Francisco, CA
Kelleher, Michael F. ... Washington, DC
Kelleher & Moore ... Somerville, NJ
Kelleher, Nancy ... Denver, CO
Kelleher, Nannette R. ... Albany, NY
Kelleher & Olivera ... Chico, CA
Kelleher, Patricia A. ... Darien, CT
Kelleher, Patrick J. ... Chicago, IL
Kelleher, Richard J. ... Newburyport, MA
Kelleher, Richard P. ... East Dennis, MA
Kelleher, Robert J. ... Los Angeles, CA
Kelleher, Robert J. ... Chicago, IL
Kelleher, Robin N. ... Minneapolis, MN
Kelleher, Rory ... New York, NY
Kelleher, Shannon Elizabeth ... New York, NY
Kelleher, Terence L. ... Brooklyn, NY
Kelleher, Thomas J., Jr. ... Atlanta, GA
Kelleher, Thomas M. ... Milford, CT
Kelleher, Thomas More ... Spokane, WA
Kelleher, Thomas R. ... San Diego, CA
Kelleher, Timothy C., III ... Boston, MA
Kelleher, Timothy M. ... Chico, CA
Kelleher, Timothy P. ... Latham, NY
Kelleher, Vincent F. ... Middlefield, OH
Kelleher, W. Sean ... Worthington, OH
Kelleher, William A. ... Bronxville, NY
Kelleher, William E., Jr. ... Pittsburgh, PA
Kelleher, William J. ... Augusta, ME
Kelleher, William J., Jr.
Rockville Centre, NY
Kelleher, William J., P.A., Law Offices of
Augusta, ME
Kelleher, William M.
Department of Transportation, U. S. Coast Guard, GV
Kelleher, William T. ... Somerville, NJ
Kelleher, William T., Jr. ... Somerville, NJ
Kellem, Steven J. ... Hull, MA
Kellems, W. Brady ... Brookhaven, MS
Kellen, Karen S. ... Philadelphia, PA
Kellen, William G. ... Cora, WY
Kellenberg, Conrad L. ... Notre Dame, IN
Kellenberger, Edward R. ... Boulder, CO
Kellenberger, Gene V. ... Ames, IA
Kellenberger, Gordon E. ... Severna Park, MD
Kellenberger, Jack C. ... Chillicothe, OH
Keller, Aimee L. ... Cincinnati, OH
Keller, Allison M. ... Los Angeles, CA
Keller, Allison Warren ... Jacksonville, FL
Keller, Andrew R. ... New York, NY
Keller, Anne Derbes ... New Orleans, LA
Keller, Anson M. ... Washington, DC
Keller, Arthur ... New York, NY
Keller, Barbara L. ... Los Angeles, CA
Keller, Bennett S. ... St. Louis, MO
Keller, Bernie W. ... Indianapolis, IN
Keller, Brad P. ... Atlanta, GA
Keller, Bradley A. ... Baytown, TX
Keller, Bradley S. ... Seattle, WA
Keller, Brenda A. Schrader ... Houston, TX
Keller, Brian M. ... Houston, TX
Keller, Bruce E. ... Dixon, IL
Keller, Bruce P. ... New York, NY
Keller, Bryan J. ... Buffalo, NY
Keller, Charlene M.
Department of Transportation, Office of the Secretary, GV
Keller, Charles C. ... Washington, PA
Keller, Charles E. ... Bloomfield Hills, MI
Keller, Charles H. ... Jacksonville, FL
Keller, Charles P. ... Phoenix, AZ
Keller, Charles R. ... Monterey, CA
Keller, Charles R. ... Church Point, LA
Keller, Charles W. ... Orlando, FL
Keller, Chester M. ... Newark, NJ
Keller, Chester R. ... Villa Grove, IL
Keller, Christine ... Galveston, TX
Keller, Christine E. ... Hartford, CT
Keller, Christine L. ... Treasury Department, Internal Revenue Service, GV
Keller, Christopher C. ... Phoenix, AZ
Keller, Christopher J. ... Oakland, CA
Keller, Christopher J. ... New York, NY
Keller, Christopher W.
Federal Trade Commission, Bureau of Consumer Protection, GV
Keller, Clifford B. ... Woodbury, NY
Keller, Coby N. ... Irvine, CA
Keller, Craig C. ... West Palm Beach, FL
Keller, Craig L. ... Tempe, AZ
Keller and Curtin Co., L.P.A. ... Akron, OH
Cleveland, OH
Elyria, OH
Keller, D. David ... Fort Lauderdale, FL
Keller & Dangerfield ... Lafayette, LA
Keller, Daniel C. ... Price, UT
Keller, Daniel L. ... Stockton, CA
Keller, David G. ... Eagan, MN
Keller, David Hill ... Greenville, SC
Keller, David M. ... Chicago, IL
Keller, David R. ... Chambersburg, PA
Hanover, PA
Harrisburg, PA
Lancaster, PA
Reading, PA
York, PA
Keller, David S. ... Waynesboro, PA
Keller, David W., Jr. ... Florence, SC
Keller, David Wm. ... Galion, OH
Keller, Deborah A. ... New York, NY
Keller, Debra E. ... Walnut Creek, CA
Keller, Dee Ann ... Golden, CO
Keller, Dennis F. ... Holland, OH
Keller, Dennis H. ... Auburn, CA
Keller, Dewey L. ... Lenoir, NC
Keller, Diane E. ... Baltimore, MD
Keller, Donald A. ... Mount Clemens, MI
Keller, Donald M., Jr. ... Menlo Park, CA
Keller, Donald R. ... Columbus, OH
Keller, Donald T., Jr. ... Houston, TX
Keller, Dorothy M. ... New York, NY
Keller, Dwight K. ... Burnt Hills, NY
Keller, Eddie T. ... Sacramento, CA
Keller, Edgar C. ... San Bernardino, CA
Keller, Edward L. ... Mount Clemens, MI
Keller, Edward M. ... East Tawas, MI
Keller, Edward O. ... Cincinnati, OH
Keller, Edwin A., Jr. ... Las Vegas, NV
Keller, Edwin L. ... Stephenville, TX
Keller, Elizabeth A. ... Moberly, MO
Keller, Ellen Holland ... Cleveland, OH
Keller, Eric L. ... Vienna, VA
Keller, Eric R. ... Washington, DC
Keller, Eugene E. ... Phoenix, AZ
Keller, Eugene Edward, II ... Phoenix, AZ
Keller, Evelyn ... Santa Monica, CA
Keller, E. W. ... Oklahoma City, OK
Keller, Fernald & Keller
Oklahoma City, OK
Keller, Gailey C. ... Bloomsburg, PA
Keller, Gary H. ... Irving, TX
Keller, Geoffrey R. ... Billings, MT
Keller, George A. C., Jr. ... Wayland, MA
Keller, George H. ... San Francisco, CA
Keller, George J. ... Santa Rosa, CA
Keller, George R. ... Bellwood, IL
Keller, George S. ... St. Joseph, MI
Keller, Gerald D. ... Southfield, MI
Keller, Glen E., Jr. ... Denver, CO
Keller, Grant W. ... Turnersville, NJ
Keller, Gregory E. ... Navarre, MN
Keller, Gregory E. ... New York, NY
Keller, Gregory T. ... Livingston, NJ
Keller, H. Michael ... Salt Lake City, UT
Keller, Harold S. ... Brooklyn, NY
Keller, Harvey W. ... Portland, OR
Keller and Heckman LLP
Washington, DC
Keller, Henry R. ... Monticello, IL
Keller, Homer W. ... Peoria, IL
Keller & Houck, A Professional Association
Fort Lauderdale, FL
Key West, FL
Miami, FL
Port Canaveral, FL
Keller, Howland G. ... New York, NY
Keller, Irwin E. ... San Francisco, CA
Keller, J. Clarke ... Lexington, KY
Keller, J Phillip ... Silver Spring, MD
Keller, J. Richard ... Ashton, IL
Dixon, IL
Keller, J. Warren ... London, KY
Keller, Jack T. ... Orlando, FL
Keller, Jacqueline ... New York, NY
Keller, James ... Chicago, IL
Keller, James A. ... Philadelphia, PA
Keller, James E. ... Oakland, CA
San Francisco, CA
Keller, James E. ... Lexington, KY
Keller, James Eugene ... Houston, TX
Keller, James F. ... Cincinnati, OH
Keller, James G. ... Topeka, KS
Keller, James H. ... Southfield, MI
Keller, James K. ... Cincinnati, OH
Keller, James L. ... Baltimore, MD
Keller, James M. ... Grand Rapids, MI
Keller, James R. ... Marathon, FL
Keller, James R. ... Bloomfield Hills, MI
Keller, James R. ... St. Louis, MO
Keller, James R., P.C.
Bloomfield Hills, MI
Keller, Jana Kim ... Little Rock, AR
Keller, Jane E. ... New York, NY
Keller, Janice N. ... Santa Maria, CA
Keller, Jay ... New York, NY
Keller, Jeffrey F. ... San Francisco, CA
Keller, Jennifer Ann ... Chicago, IL
Keller, Jennifer L., Law Offices of
Newport Beach, CA
Keller, Jennifer P. ... Johnson City, TN
Keller, Jeralyn B. ... Pasadena, CA
Keller, Jesse A. ... Florence, AL
Keller, Jill B. ... Billings, MT
Keller, Jo Anne Wells ... Berkeley, CA
Keller, Joell M. ... New Orleans, LA
Keller, John D. ... Bloomingdale, IL
Keller, John D., & Associates, Ltd.
Bloomingdale, IL
Keller, John E. ... Terre Haute, IN
Keller, John G. ... Bethesda, MD
Keller, John J. ... Allentown, PA
Keller, John K. ... Columbus, OH
Keller, John M. ... Brooksville, FL
Keller, John M. ... Kansas City, MO
Keller, John M. ... Portland, OR
Keller, John N. ... Waynesboro, PA
Keller, John P. ... Miami, FL
Keller, John R. ... Fort Lauderdale, FL
Keller, John S. ... New Orleans, LA
Keller, John T. ... Cincinnati, OH
Keller, John W. ... Huron, SD
Keller, John W., III ... Miami, FL
Port Canaveral, FL
Keller, Jordan S. ... Nashville, TN
Keller, Joyce Ann ... Goldsboro, NC
Keller, Juan D. ... St. Louis, MO
Keller, Julie C. ... Decatur, IL
Keller, K. Rick ... Effingham, IL
Keller, Katherine A. ... Cincinnati, OH
Keller, Kathleen R. ... Waukegan, IL
Keller, Keenan R. ... Washington, DC
Keller and Keller ... San Bernardino, CA
Keller & Keller ... St. Joseph, MI
Keller & Keller ... Huron, SD
Keller, Keller & Frey ... Waynesboro, PA
Keller & Keller, P.C. ... Portland, OR
Keller & Keller, P.L.L.C. ... Phoenix, AZ
Keller, Kelley M. ... Houston, TX
Keller, Kelli R. ... Indianapolis, IN
Keller, Kenneth C. ... Rochester, NY
Keller, Kenneth E. ... San Francisco, CA
Keller, Kenneth J., Sr. ... Milwaukie, OR
Keller, Kenneth R. ... Greensboro, NC
Keller, Kent ... Los Angeles, CA
Keller & Keroff, P.A. ... West Palm Beach, FL
Keller, Kevin E. ... Palo Alto, CA
Keller, Kevin L. ... Norfolk, VA
Keller, Kristen Judith ... Purchase, NY
Keller, Kristen Leigh ... Beckley, WV
Keller, Kristina S. ... Santa Monica, CA
Keller, Kurt J. ... Joliet, IL
Keller, Kym Krystyna ... New Orleans, LA
Keller, L. Charles
Federal Communications Commission, Common Carrier Bureau, GV
Keller, Larry ... Cincinnati, OH
Keller, Larry M. ... Philadelphia, PA
Keller, Larry R. ... Salt Lake City, UT
Keller & Lathe ... Ashton, IL
Dixon, IL
Keller, Laura D. ... Lexington, KY
Keller Law Firm, The ... Woodland, CA
Keller Law Offices, P.C. ... Allentown, PA
Keller, Lawrence P. ... Rochester, NY
Keller, Lawrence R. ... La Jolla, CA
Keller, Lee J. ... Minneapolis, MN
Keller, Lee J. ... Houston, TX
Keller, Lewis J. ... Sacramento, CA
Keller, Linda Marie ... New York, NY
Keller & Lokken, P.A. ... St. Paul, MN
Keller, Loretta A. ... Plano, TX
Keller & Lundgren, L.C. ... Salt Lake City, UT
Keller, Marc D. ... Springfield, NJ
Keller, Margo T. ... Seattle, WA
Keller, Maria M. ... Santa Monica, CA
Keller, Marilyn B. ... Kansas City, MO
Keller, Mark A. ... Albuquerque, NM
Keller, Mark D. ... Columbus, OH
Keller, Martha J. ... Grand Haven, MI
Keller, Martin E. ... San Bernardino, CA
Keller, Marvin E. ... Toledo, OH
Keller, Mary Beth ... Department of Justice, Executive Office for Immigration Review, GV
Keller, Mary F. ... Austin, TX
Keller, Mary G. ... Huron, SD
Keller, Matthew J., Jr. ... Chicago, IL
Keller, Max A. ... St. Paul, MN
Keller, Max A., (A P.C.) ... Sherman Oaks, CA
Keller, Michael B. ... Martinsburg, WV
Keller, Michael C. ... New Orleans, LA
Keller, Michael E. ... Larimore, ND
Keller, Michael E. ... Houston, TX
Keller, Michael E. ... Lynnwood, WA
Keller, Michael J. ... Des Moines, IA
Keller, Michael L. ... Los Angeles, CA
Keller, Michael Lee ... Charleston, WV
Keller, Michael R. ... Seattle, WA
Keller, Michelle M. ... Newport, KY
Keller, Nalda L. ... Sacramento, CA
Keller, Natalie Hoyer ... Chicago, IL
Keller, Neil R. ... Seattle, WA
Keller, O'Reilly & Watson ... Woodbury, NY
Keller, P. Keith ... Helena, MT
Keller, Pamela C. ... Fort Lauderdale, FL
Keller, Pamela D. ... Port Charlotte, FL
Keller, Pamela V. ... Indianapolis, IN
Keller, Patrick L. ... Baton Rouge, LA
Keller, Paul A. ... Troy, MI
Keller, Paul B. ... New York, NY
Keller, Paul B. ... San Antonio, TX
Keller, Paul C. ... Price, UT
Keller, Paul D. ... Wilmette, IL
Keller, Paul J., Jr. ... Birmingham, MI
Keller, Paul N. ... Park Ridge, IL
Keller, Paul T. ... Helena, MT
Keller, Paul V. ... Cleveland, OH
Keller, Paula L. ... Summit, NJ

Kelley, Kevin J. ....Three Lakes, WI
Kelley, Kevin L. ....Dallas, TX
Kelley, Kevin R. ....Tulsa, OK
Kelley, Kimberly H. ....Boston, MA
Kelley, Kirkland M. ....Norfolk, VA
Kelley, Kristin J. ....Austin, TX
Kelley, Kronenberg, Kelley, Gilmartin, Fichtel & Wander, P.A.
Fort Lauderdale, FL
Miami Lakes, FL
Orlando, FL
West Palm Beach, FL
Kelley, Kyle P. ....Beverly Hills, CA
Kelley, L. Patrick ....Lake Milton, OH
Kelley, Lara Chapman ....Washington, DC
Kelley, Laraine ....Buffalo, NY
Kelley, Laura W. ....North Reading, MA
Kelley Law Associates ....Boston, MA
Kelley Law Firm ....Rogers, AR
Kelley, Lawrence Patrick ....Cleveland, OH
Kelley, Lehan & Hall, P.C. ....Omaha, NE
Kelley, Leigh B. ....Eureka, MT
Kelley, Leonard A. ....Hingham, MA
Kelley, Leonard T. ....Anchorage, AK
Kelley, Leslie A. ....Kingshill, St. Thomas, VI
Kelley, Linda Damico ....Pittsburgh, PA
Kelley, Lisa Ann ....Malden, MA
Kelley & Lovett, P.C. ....Albany, GA
Kelley, Luann M. ....San Diego, CA
Kelley, Lydia R. B. ....Chicago, IL
Kelley, Lynn Arko ....Cleveland, OH
Kelley, Lynn M. ....Germantown, OH
Kelley, Manda McMichael
San Antonio, TX
Kelley, Margaret B. ....New York, NY
Kelley, Margaret M. ....Boston, MA
Kelley, Marianne E. ....San Diego, CA
Kelley, Mark A. ....Atlanta, GA
Kelley, Mark W. ....San Francisco, CA
Kelley, Mark W. ....Charleston, WV
Kelley, Marla Lamedman
Costa Mesa, CA
Kelley, Martha D. ....Portland, ME
Kelley, Martin C. ....Schaumburg, IL
Kelley, Mary C. ....Dubuque, IA
Kelley, Mary Katherine L. ....Los Altos, CA
Kelley, Mary Kathryn ....San Diego, CA
Kelley, Mary Page ....Cambridge, MA
Kelley, Matthew X. ....Schaumburg, IL
Kelley, Maureen S. ....Boston, MA
Kelley, McCann & Livingstone, LLP
Cleveland, OH
Kelley, Melissa A. ....Pittsburgh, PA
Kelley, Mercedes K.
Federal Trade Commission, Bureau of Consumer Protection, GV
Kelley, Michael A. ....Omaha, NE
Kelley, Michael C. ....Los Angeles, CA
Kelley, Michael E. ....Kearney, NE
Kelley, Michael E. ....New York, NY
Kelley, Michael J. ....Columbus, OH
Kelley, Michael J. ....Youngstown, OH
Kelley, Michael J. ....Salt Lake City, UT
Kelley, Michael K. ....Portland, OR
Kelley, Michael O. ....Fort Morgan, CO
Kelley, Michael R. ....Harrisburg, PA
Kelley, Michael S. ....Berkeley, CA
Kelley, Michael S. ....Knoxville, TN
Kelley, Michael S. ....Dallas, TX
Kelley, Michael V. ....Cleveland, OH
Kelley, Michaela ....Anchorage, AK
Kelley, Michelle Hawk ....Union City, PA
Kelley, Misty Smith ....Chattanooga, TN
Kelley, Monica Z. ....Salt Lake City, UT
Kelley & Murphy ....Blue Bell, PA
Norristown, PA
Philadelphia, PA
Kelley, Nancy A. ....Williams, AZ
Kelley, Nancy J. ....Waltham, MA
Kelley, Nancy L. ....Cleveland, OH
Kelley, N. F. ....Walla Walla, WA
Kelley, Nicholas, Jr. ....Little Compton, RI
Kelley, Nicholas M. ....Boston, MA
Kelley, Nora K. ....Rapid City, SD
Kelley, Norman F. ....Salem, OR
Kelley, O'Brien ....Washington, DC
Kelley, Oliver ....Belton, TX
Kelley & Osetek, P.C. ....Ann Arbor, MI
Kelley, Page ....Cambridge, MA
Kelley, Palisa R. ....New York, NY
Kelley, Pamela F. ....Newport, RI
Kelley, Patricia Hill ....Denver, CO
Kelley, Patrick ....Tyler, TX
Kelley, Patrick C. ....Metairie, LA
Kelley, Patrick G. ....Fort Lauderdale, FL
Kelley, Patrick J. ....Carbondale, IL
Kelley, Patrick M. ....Eden Prairie, MN
Kelley, Patrick W. ....Department of Justice, Federal Bureau of Investigation, GV
Kelley, Patrick W. ....Springfield, IL
Kelley, Paul ....Austin, TX
Kelley, Paul A. ....Orlando, FL
Kelley, Paul E. ....Providence, RI
Kelley, Paul E., Jr. ....Austin, TX
Kelley, Paul L. ....Chicago, IL
Kelley, Paul M. ....Los Angeles, CA
Kelley, Paul R. ....Cambridge, MA
Kelley, Paula F. ....Fort Myers, FL
Kelley, Peter C. ....Los Angeles, CA
Kelley, Peter J. ....Ann Arbor, MI
Kelley, Peter J. ....New York, NY
Kelley, Peter M. ....Boston, MA
Kelley, Peter S. ....Caribou, ME
Kelley, Phillip G. ....Arden, NC
Kelley, R. Pierce, Jr. ....Clearwater, FL
North Miami, FL
Kelley, Ralph B. ....Greenwich, CT
New York, NY

Kelley, Ralph H. ....Chattanooga, TN
Kelley, Ralph J. ....Dearborn Heights, MI
Kelley, Randall J. ....Encino, CA
Kelley, Randall W. ....Belleville, IL
Kelley & Rich, P.C. ....Englewood, CO
Kelley, Richard ....Austin, TX
Kelley, Richard A. ....Willimantic, CT
Kelley, Richard B. ....Garrett Park, MD
Kelley, Richard C., (P.C.) ....Oakland, CA
Kelley, Richard J. ....Olympia, WA
Kelley, Richard" Nick " ....Kissimmee, FL
Kelley, Richard S. ....Everson, WA
Kelley, Robert A. ....Las Vegas, NV
Kelley, Robert B. ....Las Cruces, NM
Kelley, Robert C. ....Bellevue, WA
Kelley, Robert E. V., Jr. ....Tampa, FL
Kelley, Robert F. ....Littleton, CO
Kelley, Robert F. ....Lawrence, MA
Kelley, Robert H. ....Randolph, MA
Kelley, Robert H. ....St. Louis, MO
Kelley, Robert J. ....Farmington, CT
Kelley, Robert J. ....Northborough, MA
Kelley, Robert J., Jr.
Merit Systems Protection Board, Office of Appeals Counsel, GV
Kelley, Robert Lane ....Camarillo, CA
Kelley, Robert O. ....Manchester, NH
Kelley, Robert P. ....Rapid City, SD
Kelley, Robert V., Jr. ....Charlottesville, VA
Kelley, Robert W. ....Fort Lauderdale, FL
Kelley, Robert W. ....Braintree, MA
Kelley, Rohan ....Fort Lauderdale, FL
Kelley, Rosemarie A.
Environmental Protection Agency, Office of Enforcement and Compliance Assurance, GV
Kelley, Rosemary F. ....Sacramento, CA
Kelley, Roy Elizabeth ....Russellville, AR
Kelley & Ryan, A Professional Corporation
Houston, TX
Kelley, Sam L. ....Austin, TX
Kelley, Scott L. ....Hanover, PA
Kelley, Scott M. ....Portland, OR
Kelley, Scott V. ....Vienna, VA
Kelley, Scott W. ....Woodland Hills, CA
Kelley, Scritsmier & Byrne, P.C.
North Platte, NE
Kelley, Sean P. ....New York, NY
Kelley, Sean W. ....Fort Lauderdale, FL
Kelley, Shane J. ....Fort Lauderdale, FL
Kelley, Shane R. ....Minneapolis, MN
Kelley, Shannon Ann ....Los Angeles, CA
Kelley, Sharon B.
Federal Communications Commission, Office of the General Counsel, GV
Kelley, Sharon D. Elvidge ....Indianapolis, IN
Kelley, Sheila Ann ....Colonial Heights, VA
Kelley, Sheila Doyle ....San Francisco, CA
Kelley, Sheila K. ....Norwood, MA
Kelley, Sheila Stuart ....Platteville, WI
Kelley, Stephen J. ....Manhattan Beach, CA
Kelley, Stephen M.
Grosse Pointe Woods, MI
Kelley, Stephen P. ....Minneapolis, MN
Kelley, Stephen W. ....Chicago, IL
Kelley, Steven B. ....Thomasville, GA
Kelley, Steven D. ....Minneapolis, MN
Kelley, Steven K. ....Cleveland, OH
Kelley, Stuart J. ....Cincinnati, OH
Kelley, Susan M. ....Austin, TX
Kelley, Susan R. ....San Francisco, CA
Kelley, Susan V. ....Madison, WI
Kelley, Suzanne Woods ....Monson, MA
Kelley, Teke ....San Francisco, CA
Kelley, Terence J. ....Cincinnati, OH
Kelley, Theresa ....Dallas, TX
Kelley, Thomas ....Akron, OH
Kelley, Thomas A. ....Department of Justice, Federal Bureau of Investigation, GV
Kelley, Thomas B. ....Denver, CO
Kelley, Thomas E. ....Denver, CO
Kelley, Thomas G. ....Cleveland, OH
Kelley, Thomas H. ....York, PA
Kelley, Thomas J. ....Pasadena, CA
Kelley, Thomas J. ....Schaumburg, IL
Kelley, Thomas J. ....Detroit, MI
Kelley, Thomas J. ....Omaha, NE
Kelley, Thomas J. ....Toledo, OH
Kelley, Thomas J., Jr. ....Wellesley Hills, MA
Kelley, Thomas J., Jr. ....Arlington, VA
Kelley, Thomas M. ....Glendale, CA
Kelley, Thomas P.
Department Of Veterans Affairs, Veterans Health Administration, GV
Kelley, Thomas R. ....Minneapolis, MN
Kelley, Thos. X. ....Fort Dodge, IA
Kelley, Timothy D. ....San Diego, CA
Salt Lake City, UT
Kelley, Timothy E. ....Baton Rouge, LA
Kelley, Timothy E. ....Dallas, TX
Kelley, Timothy E., P.C. ....Dallas, TX
Kelley, Timothy J. ....Washington, DC
Kelley, Timothy J. ....Reading, MA
Kelley, Timothy J. ....Green Bay, WI
Kelley, Timothy M. ....Columbus, OH
Kelley, Timothy M. ....Milwaukee, WI
Kelley, Tom ....Topeka, KS
Kelley, Troy X. ....Glendale, CA
Kelley, Vicky J. ....Anchorage, AK
Kelley, Victor ....Birmingham, AL
Kelley, Vincent F. ....Anderson, IN
Kelley, W. Michael ....Phoenix, AZ
Kelley, W. Patrick ....Palo Alto, CA
Kelley, Walter A. ....Huntsville, AL
Kelley, Walter C. ....Cleveland, OH
Kelley, Walter D., Jr. ....Norfolk, VA
Kelley, Walter W. ....Albany, GA
Kelley, Wardell & Craig ....Haddonfield, NJ

Kelley & Warren, P.A.
West Palm Beach, FL
Kelley, Weber, Pietz & Slater, S.C.
Wausau, WI
Kelley, Wendy A. ....Boston, MA
Kelley, William A., Jr. ....Philadelphia, PA
Kelley, William B. ....Chicago, IL
Kelley, William B. ....Oklahoma City, OK
Kelley, William F. ....Chicago, IL
Schaumburg, IL
Kelley, William F., Jr. ....Montgomery, AL
Kelley, William G. ....Santa Ana, CA
Kelley, William H. ....Bloomington, IN
Kelley, William H. ....Manchester, NH
Kelley, William H., P.A. ....Manchester, NH
Kelley, William J. ....Houston, TX
Kelley, William J., II ....Batesville, IN
Versailles, IN
Kelley, William J., III ....Los Angeles, CA
Kelley, William K. ....Washington, DC
Kelley, William L. ....Austin, TX
Kelley, William M. ....Chicago, IL
Kelley, William R. ....Ann Arbor, MI
Kelley, William V. ....Spokane, WA
Kelley-Bergerson, Suellen
Evergreen Park, IL
Kelley Bronner, Tae ....Sun City Center, FL
Tampa, FL
Kelley-Claybrook, Susan ....Waco, TX
Kellick, Donna M. ....Chicago, IL
Kelligher, W. Chad ....Warren, OH
Kelligrew, John R. ....White Plains, NY
Kelliher, Brendan Joseph ....Norwood, MA
Kelliher, Brian D.
United States Court Of Appeals District Of Columbia Circuit, GV
Kelliher, Carolyn A. ....Quincy, MA
Kelliher, Daniel P. ....Annapolis, MD
Kelliher, Diane M. ....Norwood, MA
Kelliher, Ellen R. ....Boston, MA
Kelliher, John ....House of Representatives, Committee on House Administration, GV
Kelliher, John F., Jr. ....Sierra Vista, AZ
Kelliher, John J. ....Albany, NY
Kelliher, Miriam J. ....Boston, MA
Kelliher, Patricia J. ....Placerville, CA
Kelliher, Richard J. ....Newton, MA
Kelliher, Thomas W. ....Manchester, NH
Kelliher, Timothy J. ....Manomet, MA
Kelliher, Walter J. ....Malden, MA
Kelling, Erin E. ....Winter Park, FL
Kelling, Gilbert V., Jr. ....Akron, OH
Kelling, Gregory A. ....Independence, MO
Kelling, Kathryn Mitchell ....Charlotte, NC
Kelling, Robert S., Jr. ....Danville, CA
Kellington, Bruce ....Medford, OR
Kellington, Daniel F. ....Medford, OR
Kellington, Jeannette C.
Point Pleasant Beach, NJ
Kellington, Krack, Richmond, Blackhurst & Sutton, LLP ....Medford, OR
Kellington, Wendie L. ....Portland, OR
Kellis, Basil L. ....Sanford, ME
Kellis, Eugene E. ....Bensalem, PA
Kellis, Steven E. ....Atlanta, GA
Kellis, Totaro & Soffer ....Bensalem, PA
Kellish, Thomas J. ....Tully, NY
Kellison, Craig M. ....Susanville, CA
Kellison, J. Bruce ....Washington, DC
Kellison, Lee G. ....Jacksonville, FL
Kellison, N. Keith, Ltd. ....Reno, NV
Kellison, Sylvia E. ....Los Angeles, CA
Kellman, Alan ....Detroit, MI
Kellman, Alise M. ....San Diego, CA
Kellman, Arthur ....Margate, FL
Kellman, Barbara S. ....Boston, MA
Kellman, Barry D. ....Los Angeles, CA
Kellman, Carolyn ....Miami, FL
Kellman, Colleen Lundwall
White Plains, NY
Kellman, David A. ....New York, NY
Kellman, Donald A. ....Spokane, WA
Kellman, Harvey ....Washington, DC
Kellman, Hope B. ....Evanston, IL
Kellman, Ira S. ....New York, NY
Kellman, Joel D. ....Palo Alto, CA
Kellman, Joel D. ....Detroit, MI
Kellman, Mark A. ....Irvine, CA
Kellman, Nancy D. ....New York, NY
White Plains, NY
Kellman, Robert C. ....Hayward, CA
Kellman, Sandra Y. ....Chicago, IL
Kellman, Steven R. ....San Diego, CA
Kellman, Susan G. ....New York, NY
Kellmeyer, Joseph M. ....St. Louis, MO
Kellndorfer, Emily M. ....Ann Arbor, MI
Kellner, Andrew J. ....New York, NY
Kellner, Chehebar & Deveney
New York, NY
Kellner, Christopher J. ....Atlanta, GA
Kellner, Cynthia MacBride ....Rochester, NY
Kellner, Douglas A. ....New York, NY
Kellner, Elizabeth Krob ....New York, NY
Kellner, Frances L. ....New York, NY
Kellner, Gayle Thomasson
Baton Rouge, LA
Kellner, George K., Jr. ....Lancaster, OH
Kellner, Gretchen Lea ....New York, NY
Kellner, Herbert Steven ....Smithtown, NY
Kellner, James L. ....Torrance, CA
Kellner, John L. ....Middlebury, VT
Kellner, Katherine C. ....Portland, OR
Kellner, Kenneth E. ....Department of Justice, Environment and Natural Resources Division, GV
Kellner, Lauren Sara Fisher
Valley Forge, PA

Kellner, Leland I. ....Mount Laurel, NJ
Philadelphia, PA
Kellner, Leon B. ....Washington, DC
Kellner, Nancy J. ....Washington, DC
Kellner, Paul ....Boynton Beach, FL
Kellner, Reed W. ....West Palm Beach, FL
Kellner, Richard L. ....Pasadena, CA
Kellner, Robert C. ....Baltimore, MD
Kellner, Stuart A. ....Warren, NJ
Kellner, Stuart L. ....Helena, MT
Kellner, Susan J. ....West Palm Beach, FL
Kellner, Victor E. ....Lafayette, LA
Kellner, William E. ....Lafayette, LA
Kellogg, Alfred C. ....Stamford, CT
Kellogg, Amy Elizabeth ....Cleveland, OH
Kellogg, Arthur E. ....St. Paul, MN
Kellogg, Barbara E. ....Great Barrington, MA
Kellogg, Carol D. ....Burbank, CA
Kellogg, Carol D. ....Los Angeles, CA
Kellogg, Clarence A., Jr. ....San Jose, CA
Kellogg, Clifton G. ....Chicago, IL
Kellogg, Cynthia Anne ....Summit, NJ
Kellogg, Daniel F. ....St. Joseph, MO
Kellogg, Daniel O. ....Renton, WA
Kellogg, David S. ....Albany, NY
Kellogg, Dennis J. ....Chicago, IL
Kellogg, Desiree Icaza ....San Diego, CA
Kellogg, Edmund H. ....South Royalton, VT
Kellogg, Edward H., Jr., (P.C.)
Atlanta, GA
Kellogg and Evans ....Kill Devil Hills, NC
Manteo, NC
Nags Head, NC
Kellogg & George, A Professional Corporation ....Boston, MA
Wellesley, MA
Kellogg, Huber, Hansen, Todd & Evans, P.L.L.C. ....Washington, DC
Philadelphia, PA
Kellogg, James C. ....Chicago, IL
Kellogg, Jarvis P. ....Boston, MA
Kellogg, John C. ....Westminster, CA
Kellogg, John H. ....Wellesley, MA
Kellogg, John H., Jr. ....Omaha, NE
Kellogg, John L. ....Kansas City, MO
Kellogg, John S. ....Denver, CO
Kellogg, John W. ....Denver, CO
Kellogg, John W. ....Missouri Valley, IA
Kellogg, Kenyon P. ....Seattle, WA
Kellogg, L. Edmund ....Burbank, CA
San Clemente, CA
Kellogg Law Firm, P.C. ....Missouri Valley, IA
Kellogg, Lawrence A. ....Miami, FL
West Palm Beach, FL
Kellogg, L. Edmund, A Professional Corporation ....San Clemente, CA
Kellogg, Leigh R. ....Durham, NC
Kellogg, LeRoy L. ....Anaheim, CA
Kellogg, Leslie R. ....Buffalo, NY
Kellogg, Lisa B. Cella ....San Diego, CA
Kellogg, Luke C. ....San Antonio, TX
Kellogg, Margaret L. ....Parsippany, NJ
Kellogg, Mark E. ....Lansing, MI
Kellogg, Mark E., P.C. ....Springfield, VA
Kellogg, Martin, Jr. ....Manteo, NC
Kellogg, Martin N. ....Stillwater, MN
Kellogg, Michael K. ....Washington, DC
Kellogg, Michael T. ....New York, NY
Kellogg, Nancy A. ....Olympia, WA
Kellogg & Palzer, P.C. ....Omaha, NE
Kellogg, Peter ....Jacksonville, FL
Kellogg, Philip L. ....Washington, DC
Kellogg, R. James ....New York, NY
Kellogg, Robert D. ....Oklahoma City, OK
Kellogg, Robert L. ....Austin, TX
Kellogg, Rosemary P. ....Englewood, CO
Kellogg, Saccoccia & Sigelman
Atlanta, GA
Decatur, GA
Kellogg, Sarah C. ....Boston, MA
Kellogg, Scott E. ....Chicago, IL
Kellogg, Stephen ....Buffalo, NY
Kellogg, Steven E. ....St. Louis, MO
Kellogg, Thomas O. ....Berlin, CT
Kellogg, Thomas R.
Plymouth Meeting, PA
Kellogg, Virginia Elaine ....Denver, CO
Kellogg, Wendell W. ....Salina, KS
Kellogg, Williams & Lyons
Washington, DC
Vienna, VA
Kellogg, Wm. Bradley ....Westport, CT
Kellogg-Martin, Kimberly
Bellefontaine, OH
Kellon, Anthony J. ....Cleveland, OH
Kellough, Berner ....Darien, IL
Kellough, Rex W. ....Newport Beach, CA
Kellough, Steven ....Miami, FL
Kellough, Steven, P.A. ....Miami, FL
Kellough, William C. ....Tulsa, OK
Kellow, Kevin C. ....Santa Monica, CA
Kellow, Linda R. ....West Bend, WI
Kellow, V. Elizabeth ....Dallas, TX
Kelloway-Martin, Sheri Jean ....Concord, NH
Kells, Richard B., Jr. ....Oklahoma City, OK
Kellstrom, Sharon Wright ....Manhattan, KS
Kellum, Arthur C. ....St. Louis, MO
Kellum, David C. ....San Antonio, TX
Kellum, David C., P.C. ....San Antonio, TX
Kellum, Henry M. ....Atlanta, GA
Kellum, Jerry L. ....Winona, MN
Kellum & Jones, P.A. ....Jacksonville, NC
New Bern, NC
Kellum, J. W. ....Sumner, MS
Kellum Law Office ....Winona, MN
Kellum, Nathan W. ....Memphis, TN
Kellum, Norman B., Jr. ....Jacksonville, NC
New Bern, NC

Kellum, Richard J. ... **Los Angeles, CA**
Kellum, Stephanie R. ... **Dallas, TX**
Kelly, A. David ... **Minneapolis, MN**
Kelly, A.J. ... **Little Rock, AR**
Kelly and Albers ... Louisville, KY
Kelly, Alice Ann ... **St. Louis, MO**
Kelly, Alicia Brokars ... Philadelphia, PA
Kelly, Alicia Colarte ... Boston, MA
Kelly, Alicia M. Colarte, (P.C.)
Boston, MA
Kelly, Alison R. ... **New York, NY**
Kelly, Amber Lee ... **San Francisco, CA**
Kelly, Amelia J. ... **Garden City, NY**
Kelly, Amy Campbell ... **Charleston, SC**
Kelly, Amy Kelly ... Sparta, NJ
Kelly, Anastasia D. ... **Hoffman Estates, IL**
Kelly, Andrea F. ... Baltimore, MD
Kelly, Andrea I. ... Department of Justice, Civil Division, GV
Kelly, Andrew C. ... **Albany, NY**
Kelly, Andrew J. ... Manasquan, NJ
Kelly, Andrew P. ... **Phoenix, AZ**
Kelly, Andria Simone ... **Albertson, NY**
Kelly, Ann E. ... **Santa Monica, CA**
Kelly, Ann H. ... **Jackson, MS**
Kelly, Anna M. ... Chicago, IL
Kelly, Anne M. ... Morris Plains, NJ
Kelly, Anne Team ... Charlotte, NC
Kelly, Annice M. ... Chicago, IL
Kelly, Arthur Daniel ... Springfield, KY
Kelly, Arthur L. ... Newton, MA
Kelly & Associates, P.S. ... Seattle, WA
Kelly, Augustine J., Jr. ... Toms River, NJ
Kelly, Aurel M. ... Arvada, CO
Kelly, Barbara A. Hopkinson ... **Newark, NJ**
Kelly, Barbara J. ... **New York, NY**
Kelly, Barbara Jane ... Port Jefferson, NY
Kelly, Barbara Krasa ... **New York, NY**
Kelly, Barry L. ... Zachary, LA
Kelly, Bauersfeld, Lowry & Kelley, LLP
Los Angeles, CA
Woodland Hills, CA
Kelly, Benjamin H. ... Baltimore, MD
Kelly & Berens, P.A. ... **Minneapolis, MN**
Kelly, Bernard J. ... Oak Forest, IL
Kelly, Bernard M. ... Keyser, WV
Kelly, Bernard P. ... Anchorage, AK
Kelly, Bernard P., & Associates, A Prof. Corp.
Anchorage, AK
Kelly, Bernard V. ... Manahawkin, NJ
Kelly, Beth Ann ... Department of Energy, Office of the General Counsel, GV
Kelly, Biruta P. ... **Washington, DC**
Kelly, Bradley L. ... **Washington, DC**
Kelly and Brady ... Metamora, IL
Peoria, IL
Kelly, Brendan A. ... Jamaica, NY
Kelly, Brendan J. ... **Chicago, IL**
Kelly, Brendan M. ... Greeley, CO
Kelly, Brian A. ... **San Francisco, CA**
Kelly, Brian C. ... **Chicago, IL**
Kelly, Brian C. ... **Reno, NV**
Kelly, Brian C. ... New York, NY
Kelly, Brian E. ... Staten Island, NY
Kelly, Brian J. ... El Segundo, CA
Kelly, Brian J. ... Sharon, MA
Kelly, Brian J. ... **Cleveland, OH**
Kelly, Brian J. ... **Chehalis, WA**
Kelly, Brian S. ... **Palo Alto, CA**
San Francisco, CA
Kelly, Brian S. ... **Santa Monica, CA**
Kelly, Brian T. ... **Jacksonville, FL**
Kelly, Brian T. ... Chicago, IL
Kelly, Brian T. ... Boston, MA
Kelly, Bridget A. ... Chicago, IL
Kelly, Bruce A. ... Taos, NM
Kelly, Bruce M. ... Rochester, MN
Kelly, Bruce R. ... **New York, NY**
Kelly, Bruce R. ... **Pawtucket, RI**
Kelly, Bryan A.C. ... New York, NY
Kelly, Burnett S. ... Midland, MI
Kelly, C. Mark ... **Charlotte, NC**
Kelly & Callahan ... Tenafly, NJ
Kelly, Candace ... Department of Justice, Office of the Attorney General, GV
Kelly, Carl N. ... Wichita, KS
Kelly, Carlos A. ... **Fort Myers, FL**
Kelly, Carol A. ... Department of Labor, Pension and Welfare Benefits, GV
Kelly, Carol A. ... **Boston, MA**
Kelly, Carol A. ... Maplewood, NJ
Kelly, Caroline M. ... Decatur, GA
Kelly, Carolyn J. ... **Cherry Hill, NJ**
Kelly, Carolyn P. ... **Groton, CT**
Kelly, Carolyn V. ... **Dallas, TX**
Kelly, Carroll J. ... Miami, FL
Kelly, Chantel L. ... **Springfield, MO**
Kelly & Chapman ... **Portland, ME**
Kelly, Charles ... Postville, IA
Kelly, Charles ... **Pittsburgh, PA**
Kelly, Charles A. ... **Chicago, IL**
Kelly, Charles E. ... Buffalo, NY
Kelly, Charles F., III ... Edina, MN
Kelly, Charles G. ... **Port Huron, MI**
Kelly, Charles J. ... **Cincinnati, OH**
Kelly, Charles, Law Office, P.C.
Postville, IA
Kelly, Charles M. ... Palmetto, FL
Kelly, Charles M., Jr. ... **Naples, FL**
Kelly, Charles P. ... Farmington Hills, MI
Kelly, Charles P. ... Garden City, NY
Kelly, Charles P., P.C. ... Farmington Hills, MI
Kelly, Charles S. ... Dyersburg, TN
Kelly, Charles T. ... Houston, TX
Kelly, Charles W. ... **Houston, TX**
Kelly, Cheryl A. ... **St. Louis, MO**
Kelly, Christina W. ... **Phoenix, AZ**
Kelly, Christine A. ... **Boston, MA**
Kelly, Christopher ... **Washington, DC**
Kelly, Christopher ... Memphis, TN
Kelly, Christopher E. ... **Omaha, NE**
Kelly, Christopher G. ... **New York, NY**
Kelly, Christopher J. ... Department of Justice, Antitrust Division, GV
Kelly, Christopher L. ... **Muskegon, MI**
Kelly, Christopher M. ... **Elkhart, IN**
Kelly, Christopher M. ... **Cleveland, OH**
Kelly, Christopher M. ... **Scranton, PA**
Kelly, Christopher M. ... **Greenville, SC**
Kelly, Christopher P. ... Westfield, NJ
Kelly, Christopher P. ... **Philadelphia, PA**
Kelly, Christopher P. ... Dallas, TX
Kelly, Christopher R. ... New York, NY
Kelly, Christopher R. ... **Nashville, TN**
Kelly, Christopher R., (P.C.)
Washington, DC
Kelly, Christopher S. ... Enid, OK
Kelly, Christopher W. ... **Los Angeles, CA**
Kelly, Christpher J. ... Naugatuck, CT
Kelly, Cindy Caranella ... **New York, NY**
Kelly, Clifford P. ... **Hartford, CT**
Kelly, Clifton M. ... Lakeland, FL
Kelly, Clinton L. ... **Hendersonville, TN**
Kelly, Colleen P. ... Florham Park, NJ
Kelly, Constance R. ... Cleveland, OH
Kelly, Copely T. ... **New York, NY**
Kelly, Cornelius Joseph ... Cincinnati, OH
Kelly, Cornelius P. ... Bridgeport, CT
Kelly, Craig E. ... **Santa Clara, CA**
Kelly, Craig F. ... New York, NY
Kelly, Craig S. ... Columbia, SC
Kelly, Cynthia A. ... Chicago, IL
Kelly, D. Alton ... **Los Angeles, CA**
Kelly, D. Cortland ... **Orlando, FL**
Kelly, D. Mathias ... Pasadena, CA
Kelly, D. Michael ... **Columbia, SC**
Myrtle Beach, SC
Kelly, D. Tyler ... Jackson, TN
Kelly, Dana E. ... **Jackson, MS**
Kelly, Daniel ... **Milwaukee, WI**
Kelly, Daniel C., III ... Springfield, KY
Kelly, Daniel E. ... Des Moines, IA
Kelly, Daniel G., Jr. ... **New York, NY**
Kelly, Daniel J. ... **San Francisco, CA**
Kelly, Daniel J. ... **San Francisco, CA**
Kelly, Daniel J. ... **Boston, MA**
Kelly, Daniel J. ... **Detroit, MI**
Kelly, Daniel J. ... Port Huron, MI
Kelly, Daniel M. ... **Nantucket, MA**
Kelly, Daniel M. ... **Springfield, MA**
Kelly, Daniel M. ... Alexandria, VA
Kelly, Daniel R. ... **Minneapolis, MN**
Kelly, Daniel S. ... **Upper Saddle River, NJ**
Kelly, Daniel W. ... **Terre Haute, IN**
Kelly, Danny C. ... **Salt Lake City, UT**
Kelly, Danny P. ... Minneapolis, MN
Kelly & Davenport ... New Orleans, LA
Kelly, David ... Colorado Springs, CO
Kelly, David A. ... **Phoenix, AZ**
Kelly, David A. ... **Glastonbury, CT**
Kelly, David A. ... **Boston, MA**
Kelly, David Andrew ... **Kansas City, MO**
Kelly, David B. ... **Aspen, CO**
Kelly, David B. ... **Bluefield, WV**
Kelly, David C. ... **Seattle, WA**
Kelly, David J. ... **Bridgeport, CT**
Kelly, David J. ... Minnetonka, MN
Kelly, David J., P.A., Attorney at Law
Minnetonka, MN
Kelly, David L. ... **Roseville, CA**
Kelly, David L. ... **Sacramento, CA**
Kelly, David L. ... **Paducah, KY**
Kelly, David L. ... Kenner, LA
Kelly, David M. ... **Washington, DC**
Kelly, David P. ... **Chicago, IL**
Kelly, David R. ... **Baton Rouge, LA**
Kelly, David R. ... **Minneapolis, MN**
Kelly, David S. ... **New Orleans, LA**
Kelly, David S. ... **Buffalo, NY**
Kelly, David W. ... **Durant, OK**
Kelly, Dawn A'Cay ... Fayetteville, NC
Kelly, Dawn K. ... New York, NY
Kelly, Deanna H. ... Wilmington, DE
Kelly, Deborah A. ... **Greenwich, CT**
Kelly, Deborah L. ... **Albany, NY**
Kelly, Deborah Mattson ... **Boulder, CO**
Kelly, Deborah P. ... **Washington, DC**
Kelly, Debra ... New York, NY
Kelly, Debra L. ... Pagosa Springs, CO
Kelly, Debra S. ... **Stamford, CT**
Kelly, Dee J. ... **Fort Worth, TX**
Kelly, Dee J., Jr. ... **Fort Worth, TX**
Kelly, Deirdre M. ... **Costa Mesa, CA**
Kelly, Denise T. ... Rochester, MN
Kelly, Dennis B. ... Houston, TX
Kelly, Dennis E. ... New Orleans, LA
Kelly, Dennis E., P.L.C. ... New Orleans, LA
Kelly, Dennis J. ... San Francisco, CA
Kelly, Dennis J. ... **San Francisco, CA**
Kelly, Dennis J. ... **Denver, CO**
Kelly, Dennis J. ... **Chicago, IL**
Kelly, Dennis J. ... Rockville, MD
Kelly, Dennis J. ... **Boston, MA**
Kelly, Dennis J. ... Mineola, NY
Woodhaven, NY
Kelly, Dennis M. ... **Cleveland, OH**
Kelly, Dennis P. ... San Marcos, CA
Kelly, Diana H. ... New York, NY
Kelly, Don V. ... **St. Louis, MO**
Kelly, Donald G. ... **Natchitoches, LA**
Kelly, Donald J. ... **Louisville, KY**
Kelly, Donald N. ... Manhattan Beach, CA
Kelly, Donald R. ... North Dartmouth, MA
Kelly, Donna ... Trenton, NJ
Kelly, Donna Colberg ... **Charleston, WV**
Kelly, Donna L. ... Great Barrington, MA
Kelly, Donna M. ... **Mount Kisco, NY**
Kelly, Dori P. ... **Boston, MA**
Kelly, Dorothy Powers ... Omaha, NE
Kelly, Douglas L. ... St. Louis, MO
Kelly, Douglas A. ... **Orlando, FL**
Kelly, Douglas R. ... **Bloomfield Hills, MI**
Kelly, E. Glenn ... **Asheville, NC**
Kelly, E. Michael ... **Chicago, IL**
Kelly, E. Paul ... Manchester, NH
Kelly, Edmund J. ... Purchase, NY
Kelly, Edward E. ... **Boston, MA**
Kelly, Edward F. ... Department of Justice, Executive Office for Immigration Review, GV
Kelly, Edward F. ... Indianapolis, IN
Kelly, Edward J. ... Park Ridge, IL
Kelly, Edward J. ... **Boston, MA**
Kelly, Edward J. ... Quincy, MA
Kelly, Edward J. ... Johnson City, TN
Kelly, Edward J. ... Falls Church, VA
Kelly, Edward J., III ... New York, NY
Kelly, Edward J., IV ... Mineola, NY
Kelly, Edward J., P.C. ... Quincy, MA
Kelly, Edward L. ... **Jacksonville, FL**
Kelly, Edward L., Jr. ... Sarasota, FL
Kelly, Edward M.
Securities and Exchange Commission, Division of Corporation Finance, GV
Kelly, Edward Matthew ... Massapequa, NY
Kelly, Edward P. ... **Spring Lake, NJ**
New York, NY
Kelly, Edward P. ... **New York, NY**
Kelly, Edward S. ... Miami, FL
Kelly, Edward S., Jr. ... **Nashville, TN**
Kelly, Edward W. ... Cranston, RI
Kelly, Edwin W. ... Concord, NH
Kelly, Edwin Z. (Zack), Jr. ... **Jasper, TN**
Kelly, Edythe H. ... Tempe, AZ
Kelly, Eileen Ann ... Boston, MA
Kelly, Eileen M. ... Albany, NY
Kelly, Eileen McChesney ... **Chicago, IL**
Kelly, E. J. ... **Des Moines, IA**
Kelly, Elizabeth K. ... **Erie, PA**
Kelly, Elizabeth M. ... New York, NY
Kelly, Elizabeth M. ... Columbus, OH
Kelly, Elizabeth M. ... **Harrisburg, PA**
Kelly, Ellen ... Lake Bluff, IL
Kelly, Ellen L. ... Brookhaven, MS
Kelly, Ellen M. ... Seattle, WA
Kelly, Emily J. ... Wheaton, IL
Kelly, Eric Damian ... Pueblo, CO
Kelly, Erin ... **Wilmington, DE**
Kelly, Erin E. ... **Chicago, IL**
Kelly, Erin E. ... Edina, MN
Kelly, Erinn C. ... **Kansas City, MO**
Kelly, Ernest G., Jr. ... **Memphis, TN**
Kelly, Eugene J. ... Bronx, NY
Kelly, F. Dulin ... **Hendersonville, TN**
Kelly, F. Patrick ... **Cumberland, MD**
Kelly, F. Patrick ... **Rockville, MD**
Kelly, Faith A. ... Los Angeles, CA
Kelly, Francine B. ... **Los Angeles, CA**
Kelly, Francis D. ... Milwaukee, WI
Kelly, Francis J. ... San Francisco, CA
Kelly, Francis T. ... Fort Worth, TX
Kelly, Francis X. ... San Francisco, CA
Kelly, Francis X. ... Westmont, NJ
Philadelphia, PA
Kelly, Frank A., Jr. ... Newington, CT
Kelly, Frank P., III ... **San Francisco, CA**
Kelly, Frank V. ... South Salem, NY
Kelly, Frank X. ... **Washington, DC**
Kelly, Fred A., III ... Gallatin, TN
Kelly, Fred A., Jr. ... **Boston, MA**
Kelly, Frederick D." Rick " ... **Roanoke, VA**
Kelly, Frederick L. ... Annapolis, MD
Kelly, Frederick P. ... Memphis, TN
Kelly, G. Frederick, III ... New Orleans, LA
Kelly, Gail ... Westport, CT
Kelly, Gail M. ... **New York, NY**
Kelly, Gary R. ... Pittsburgh, PA
Kelly & Gault, LLP ... **Jackson, MS**
Kelly, Gaus & Holub ... Newton, NJ
Kelly, Genevieve M. ... Boston, MA
Kelly, Geoffrey P. ... Pittsburgh, PA
Kelly, George D. ... Braintree, MA
Kelly, George E., III ... Raleigh, NC
Kelly, George F. ... Springfield, MA
Kelly, George G. ... Chicago, IL
Kelly, George J., Jr. ... **Hartford, CT**
Kelly, George L. ... Department of State, Foreign Service Officers (Overseas), GV
Kelly, George T. ... Long Beach, CA
Kelly, George T., Jr. ... Greenville, MS
Kelly, George W. ... **Baltimore, MD**
Eugene, OR
Kelly, Gerald D. ... Olympia, WA
Kelly, Gerald J. ... Denville, NJ
Kelly, Gerald J., P.C. ... Denville, NJ
Kelly, Gerald W., Jr. ... Bethesda, MD
Kelly, Gerard D. ... **Chicago, IL**
Kelly, Gill, Sherburne & Herrera
San Francisco, CA
Kelly, Ginaia D.B. ... Santa Cruz, CA
Kelly, Grace Park ... **Cleveland, OH**
Kelly, Graham M., Jr. ... San Diego, CA
Kelly, Gregory ... Phenix City, AL
Kelly, Gregory Francis ... Chicago, IL
Kelly, Gregory J. ... **Orlando, FL**
Kelly, Gregory L. ... Smyrna, TN
Kelly, Gregory W. ... **Abingdon, VA**
Kelly, Gretchen Gates ... Plymouth, MN
Kelly, Gretchen L. ... Pittsburgh, PA
Kelly, Grimes, Pietrangelo and Vakil, P.C.
Media, PA
Kelly, H. Dennis ... **Dallas, TX**
Kelly, H. Wise, III ... Fairfax, VA
Kelly, H. Wise, Jr. ... Fairfax, VA
Kelly & Hammers, A Professional Corporation ... **Los Angeles, CA**
Santa Monica, CA
Kelly, Hannaford & Battles, P.A.
Minneapolis, MN
Kelly, Harold T., Jr. ... **Chicago, IL**
Kelly, Harold V. ... Massillon, OH
Kelly, Harry G. ... Houston, TX
Kelly, Harry J. ... **Washington, DC**
Kelly, Hart & Hallman, A Professional Corporation ... **Austin, TX**
Fort Worth, TX
Kelly, Heather Jean ... Washington, DC
Kelly, Helen ... Brooklyn, NY
Kelly, Helen A. ... San Francisco, CA
Kelly, Helen B. ... Batesville, MS
Kelly, Helen Zoellner ... La Crosse, WI
Kelly, Henkel & David, P.C.
Grand Rapids, MI
Kelly, Henry A. ... **Albuquerque, NM**
Kelly, Henry T. ... **Chicago, IL**
Kelly, Herbert V. ... **Newport News, VA**
Kelly, Herbert V., Jr. ... **Newport News, VA**
Kelly, Herlihy, Advani & Klein
San Diego, CA
San Francisco, CA
West Los Angeles, CA
Kelly, Hilary L. ... **Bridgewater, NJ**
Kelly, Hilliard F., III ... Covington, LA
Kelly, Howard H., Jr. ... Frederick, MD
Kelly, Hubert E. ... Phoenix, AZ
Kelly, Hubert E., Law Offices of, Ltd.
Phoenix, AZ
Kelly, Hugh J. ... United States Senate, Senatorial Assistants, GV
Kelly, Hugh J. ... Ardsley, NY
Kelly, Hugh Rice ... **Houston, TX**
Kelly & Hulme, P.C.
Westhampton Beach, NY
Kelly, Ilyse Marks ... South Miami, FL
Kelly, J. Bart, III ... New Orleans, LA
Kelly, J. Claibourne ... **Detroit, MI**
Kelly, J. Clinton ... **Baltimore, MD**
Kelly, J. Crilley ... Pittsburgh, PA
Kelly, J. Don, Jr. ... **New Orleans, LA**
Kelly, J. Lawrence ... Quincy, MA
Kelly, J. Michael ... **San Francisco, CA**
Kelly, J. Michael ... **Santa Monica, CA**
Kelly, J. O'Neil ... **Suffern, NY**
Kelly, J. Richard ... **Greenville, SC**
Kelly, J. Stephen ... San Antonio, TX
Kelly, J. Trent ... Tupelo, MS
Kelly, Jacob H., III ... St. Petersburg, FL
Kelly & Jacobson ... Minneapolis, MN
Kelly, Jacqueline ... Austin, TX
Kelly, Jacqueline Asher ... **Southfield, MI**
Kelly, James A. ... Scranton, PA
Kelly, James A. ... Upper Darby, PA
Kelly, James A., Jr. ... **New York, NY**
Kelly, James A. C. ... Highland Park, IL
Kelly, James Anthony ... Fullerton, CA
Kelly, James B. ... Stamford, CT
Kelly, James B. ... North Las Vegas, NV
Kelly, James D. ... **Washington, DC**
Kelly, James D. ... Chatham, IL
Springfield, IL
Kelly, James D. ... South Hackensack, NJ
Kelly, James E. ... Dade City, FL
Kelly, James E. ... Buffalo, NY
Kelly, James E. ... **Buffalo, NY**
Eden, NY
Kelly, James E. ... New York, NY
Kelly, James F. ... **New York, NY**
Kelly, James F. ... Tulsa, OK
Kelly, James G. ... **Washington Depot, CT**
Kelly, James G. ... New York, NY
Kelly, James H. ... Farmington, MO
Kelly, James H., Jr. ... **Winston-Salem, NC**
Kelly, James J. ... Fountain Valley, CA
Kelly, James J. ... Iselin, NJ
Kelly, James J. ... Brooklyn, NY
Kelly, James J. ... Deer Park, NY
Kelly, James Joseph, Jr. ... New York, NY
Kelly, James L. ... **Brandon, MS**
Kelly, James L. ... **Reno, NV**
Kelly, James L., A Professional Corporation
Brandon, MS
Kelly, James Leverty, Jr. ... **Baltimore, MD**
Kelly, James M. ... Department of Agriculture, Office of the General Counsel, GV
Kelly, James M. ... Port Huron, MI
Kelly, James M. ... Republic, MO
Kelly, James M. ... **Cincinnati, OH**
Kelly, James M. ... Philadelphia, PA
Kelly, James Michael ... Peoria, IL
Kelly, James O., III ... Houston, TX
Kelly, James P. ... Boynton Beach, FL
Kelly, James P. ... **Atlanta, GA**
Kelly, James P. ... Providence, RI
Kelly, James R. ... Tallahassee, FL
Kelly, James R. ... Mansfield, MA
Kelly, James R. ... New York, NY
Kelly, James S. ... Houston, TX
Kelly, James T., Jr. ... Sunnyvale, CA
Kelly, James Tynan ... Houston, TX
Kelly, James V. ... **Providence, RI**
Kelly, James W. ... **Geneva, AL**
Kelly, James W. ... Avon Park, FL
Kelly, James W. ... Coral Gables, FL
Kelly, Jane F. ... Trenton, NJ
Kelly, Jane E. ... Melville, NY
Kelly, Janet L. ... **Madison, WI**
Kelly, Janet Langford ... **Chicago, IL**
Kelly, Janice Averill ... **Orlando, FL**
Kelly, Janice M. ... Pensacola, FL
Kelly, Janine M. ... **Stamford, CT**
Kelly, Jas. F. ... Kings Park, NY
Kelly, Jason S. ... **Seattle, WA**

Kelly, Jay B. ... St. Paul, MN
Kelly, Jean M. ... Washington, DC
Kelly, Jean Masten ... Bowling Green, VA
Kelly, Jeanne Doyle ... Chicago, IL
Kelly, Jeffrey B. ... Cincinnati, OH
Kelly, Jeffrey G. ... Lake Grove, NY
Kelly, Jeffrey P. ... Stamford, CT
Kelly, Jeffrey T. ... Huntsville, AL
Kelly, Jennifer M. ... Jackson, MI
Kelly, Jennifer McCombs ... San Diego, CA
Kelly, Jennifer Sevier ... Nashville, TN
Kelly, Jerome F. ... Milwaukee, WI
Kelly, Jerome P. ... Indianapolis, IN
Kelly, Jerry D. ... Dallas, TX
Kelly, Jerry L. ... Lexington, KY
Kelly, Jill Bridgett ... Toledo, OH
Kelly, Joanne ... Monterey, CA
Kelly, Joanne ... Philadelphia, PA
Kelly, Joanne M. ... Washington, DC
Kelly, Jo-Anne M. ... Long Island City, NY
Kelly, Joe E. ... Victoria, TX
Kelly, Joel P. ... Los Angeles, CA
Kelly, John A., Jr. ... Chicago, IL
Kelly, John B. ... Bellefontaine, OH
Kelly, John Barry, II ... Pensacola, FL
Kelly, John Brooke ... Annapolis, MD
Kelly, John C. ... Phoenix, AZ
Kelly, John C. ... Long Beach, CA
Kelly, John C. ... West Palm Beach, FL
Kelly, John C. ... Portland, OR
Kelly, John D. ... Duluth, MN
Kelly, John D. ... Mineola, NY
Riverhead, NY
Kelly, John D. ... New York, NY
Kelly, John D. ... Harrisburg, PA
Kelly, John E. ... Woodland Hills, CA
Kelly, John E. ... Northfield, IL
Kelly, John E. ... Bel Air, MD
Kelly, John E. ... Rockville, MD
Kelly, John E. ... Springfield, MO
Kelly, John E. ... Las Vegas, NV
Kelly, John E. ... Rochester, NY
Kelly, John E., & Associates, A Professional Corporation ... Las Vegas, NV
Kelly, John E., P.A. ... Baltimore, MD
Bel Air, MD
Elkton, MD
Kelly, John F. ... Tucson, AZ
Kelly, John F. ... Fullerton, CA
Kelly, John F. ... Upper Marlboro, MD
Kelly, John F. ... Worcester, MA
Kelly, John F. ... Grosse Pointe Park, MI
Kelly, John F. ... Eagan, MN
Kelly, John F. ... Fonda, NY
Kelly, John F. ... Mineola, NY
Kelly, John F. ... New York, NY
Kelly, John F. ... Richmond, VA
Kelly, John Fleming ... Denver, CO
Kelly, John G. ... Washington, DC
Kelly, John G. ... New York, NY
Kelly, John G., Law Offices of ... Chicago, IL
Kelly, John H. ... Department Of The Interior, Office of Hearings & Appeals, GV
Kelly, John H. ... Wheaton, IL
Kelly, John H. ... New York, NY
Kelly, John I. ... Bakersfield, CA
Kelly, John J. ... Orange, CT
Kelly, John J. ... Boston, MA
Kelly, John J. ... Albuquerque, NM
Kelly, John J. ... Arlington, VA
Kelly, John J., Jr. ... Denver, CO
Kelly, John J., Jr. ... New York, NY
Kelly, John K. ... Toms River, NJ
Kelly, John L. ... New York, NY
Kelly, John M. ... Menlo Park, CA
Kelly, John M. ... Bloomfield, CT
Kelly, John M. ... Dumont, NJ
Kelly, John M. ... Oshkosh, WI
Kelly, John Michael ... Chicago, IL
Kelly, John N. ... Portland, ME
Kelly, John P. ... Palo Alto, CA
Kelly, John P. ... San Diego, CA
Kelly, John P. ... Fort Lauderdale, FL
Kelly, John P. ... Atlanta, GA
Kelly, John P. ... Chicago, IL
Wheaton, IL
Kelly, John P. ... Northville, MI
Kelly, John Pearson ... New York, NY
Kelly, John Quinlan ... New York, NY
Kelly, John R. ... Tenafly, NJ
Kelly, John T. ... Joliet, IL
Kelly, John T. ... Wilmette, IL
Kelly, John T. ... St. Paul, MN
Kelly, John T. ... Woodbridge, NJ
Kelly, John T. ... Columbus, OH
Kelly, John T., III ... Cincinnati, OH
Kelly, John Thomas ... Aspen, CO
Kelly, John V. ... The Dalles, OR
Kelly, John W. ... Stratford, CT
Kelly, John W. ... Springfield, KY
Kelly, John W., III ... Selma, AL
Kelly, John W., Jr. ... Metairie, LA
Kelly, John W., Jr. ... Bellaire, TX
Kelly, Jon F. ... Columbus, OH
Kelly, Jon L. ... Cortez, CO
Kelly, Jon M. ... Fort Worth, TX
Kelly, Jonathan J. ... New York, NY
Kelly, Jon-Peter F. ... New York, NY
Kelly, Joseph ... Bay St. Louis, MS
Kelly, Joseph A. ... Providence, RI
Kelly, Joseph Allen ... Nashville, TN
Kelly, Joseph B. ... Carlisle, PA
Kelly, Joseph C. T. ... Treasury Department, Bureau of the Public Debt, GV
Kelly, Joseph E., Jr. ... New York, NY
Kelly, Joseph F. ... Washington, DC
Kelly, Joseph J. ... Denver, CO
Kelly, Joseph J. ... Tarrytown, NY
Kelly, Joseph L. ... Burnsville, MN
Kelly, Joseph L. ... Knoxville, TN
Kelly, Joseph L. ... Norfolk, VA
Kelly, Joseph M. ... Liverpool, NY
Kelly, Joseph P. ... Essex Fells, NJ
Kelly, Joseph P. ... Kearny, NJ
Kelly, Joseph P. ... Victoria, TX
Kelly, Joseph R. ... Minneapolis, MN
Kelly, Joseph S., Jr. ... Tempe, AZ
Kelly, Joseph T., Jr. ... Pleasantville, NJ
Kelly, Joshua Oscar, III ... Huntsville, AL
Kelly, Joy M. ... New York, NY
Kelly, Judith Z. ... Ottawa, IL
Kelly, Karen M. ... St. Petersburg, FL
Kelly, Karen Vanessa ... Boston, MA
Kelly, Karla R. ... San Diego, CA
Kelly, Kate M. ... Ocean City, NJ
Norristown, PA
Kelly, Katherine M. ... Department of Justice, Civil Division, GV
Kelly, Kathleen A. ... La Jolla, CA
Kelly, Kathleen A. ... Honolulu, HI
Kelly, Kathleen M. ... Denver, CO
Kelly, Kathleen M. ... Providence, RI
Kelly, Kathleen Marie ... Sacramento, CA
Kelly, Kathleen P. ... Washington, DC
Kelly, Kathleen R. ... Naples, FL
Kelly, Kathryn ... Washington, DC
Kelly, Kathryn A. ... Wilmington, DE
Kelly, Kathryn L. ... Naperville, IL
Kelly, Katie ... Department of Transportation, Research and Special Programs Administration, GV
Kelly, Katrina M. ... Wheaton, IL
Kelly, Katrina Robertson ... Seattle, WA
Kelly, Keenan K. ... Natchitoches, LA
Kelly, Keith A. ... Salt Lake City, UT
Kelly, Kelleher, Reilly & Simpson
Narragansett, RI
Providence, RI
Kelly and Kelly ... Hebron, IL
Kelly & Kelly ... Montrose, PA
Kelly & Kelly ... Hendersonville, TN
Nashville, TN
Kelly & Kelly ... Fairfax, VA
Kelly, Kelly & Kelly ... Jackson, MI
Kelly and Kelly, P.C. ... Northville, MI
Kelly & Kelly, P.C. ... Jasper, TN
Kelly, Kendall L. ... Atlanta, GA
Kelly, Kenneth J. ... West Simsbury, CT
Kelly, Kenneth J. ... Newark, NJ
New York, NY
Kelly, Kerin E. ... Elgin, IL
Kelly, Kerriann ... Riverhead, NY
Kelly, Kerry A. ... Palo Alto, CA
Kelly, Kevin ... Cumberland, MD
Kelly, Kevin ... Kansas City, MO
Kelly, Kevin C. ... Bridgeport, CT
Kelly, Kevin D. ... La Salle, IL
Kelly, Kevin D. ... Newton, NJ
Kelly, Kevin F. ... United States Senate, Committee Legal Personnel, GV
Kelly, Kevin F. ... Media, PA
Kelly, Kevin F. ... Seattle, WA
Kelly, Kevin G. ... Redwood City, CA
Kelly, Kevin J. ... San Jose, CA
Kelly, Kevin J. ... New York, NY
Kelly, Kevin L. ... Chicago, IL
Kelly, Kevin L. ... New York, NY
Kelly, Kevin M. ... Denver, CO
Kelly, Kevin M. ... La Salle, IL
Kelly, Kevin M. ... Dearborn, MI
Kelly, Kevin M. ... Las Vegas, NV
Kelly, Kevin M. ... Glen Mills, PA
Kelly, Kevin P. ... Orlando, FL
Kelly, Kevin P. ... Hackensack, NJ
Kelly, Kevin P. ... Philadelphia, PA
Kelly, Kevin P. ... Port Orchard, WA
Kelly, Kevin Paul ... Traverse City, MI
Kelly, Kevin, P.C. ... Kansas City, MO
Kelly, Kevin R. ... Hazelwood, MO
Kelly, Kevin Wm. ... Brick, NJ
Kelly, Keyta ... Leavenworth, KS
Kelly, Kimberly A. ... Washington, DC
Kelly & Krupp ... Bartlett, IL
Kelly, Krysten ... Chicago, IL
Waukegan, IL
Kelly, Kurt ... Rawlins, WY
Kelly, L. Todd ... Newport News, VA
Richmond, VA
Kelly, Larry E. ... Austin, TX
Kelly, Laura Ann ... Morristown, NJ
Kelly, Laura Anne ... Boston, MA
Kelly, Lauren D. ... New York, NY
Kelly, Lawrence E. ... Manchester, NH
Kelly, Laurence M. ... Montrose, PA
Kelly, Laurie ... East Haven, CT
Kelly, Laurie J. ... Bethesda, MD
Kelly Law Firm ... Miles City, MT
Kelly Law Firm, A Professional Corporation
Atlanta, GA
Kelly Law Firm, L.L.C., The
Pagosa Springs, CO
Kelly Law Firm, PLC ... Little Rock, AR
Kelly Law Office ... Excelsior, MN
Kelly, Lawrence ... Sayville, NY
Kelly, Lawrence A. ... Hanover, NH
Kelly, Lawrence E. ... Christiansburg, VA
Kelly, Lawrence J. ... Denver, CO
Kelly, Lawrence M. ... Sunnyvale, CA
Kelly, Lawrence M.
Grosse Pointe Farms, MI
Kelly, Lawrence M. ... Ellwood City, PA
New Castle, PA
Kelly, Lawrence M. ... Philadelphia, PA
Kelly, Lawrence V. ... Cumberland, MD
Kelly, Lawrence W. ... Chattanooga, TN
Kelly, Leal & Kelly, A Professional Corporation
Sunnyvale, CA
Kelly, Leo John ... Pittsburgh, PA
Kelly, Leon F., Jr. ... Birmingham, AL
Kelly, Leslie M. ... Denver, CO
Kelly, Lillian Garcia ... Bartow, FL
Kelly, Lin A. ... Hollywood, FL
Kelly, Linda Ann ... Miami, FL
Kelly, Linda J. ... Hartford, CT
Kelly, Linda L. ... Houston, TX
Kelly, Lisa Ann ... Pine Bluff, AR
Kelly, Lisa T. ... Charlotte, NC
Kelly, Loretta M. ... Philadelphia, PA
Kelly, Lorry Kohrs ... Kansas City, MO
Kelly, Louis H. ... Dallas, TX
Kelly, Lowell M. ... Union City, MI
Kelly, Lucas & Pacifico, LLP
Locust Valley, NY
Kelly, Luglio & Arcuri ... Deer Park, NY
Kelly, Lynette C. ... New York, NY
Kelly, Lynn M. ... New York, NY
Kelly Lytton Mintz & Vann LLP
Los Angeles, CA
Kelly, M. Douglas ... Clinton, WA
Kelly, M. Eileen ... New York, NY
Kelly, Mairen C. ... Atlanta, GA
Kelly, Marci ... San Francisco, CA
Kelly, Marcus M. ... Spokane, WA
Kelly, Margaret Flanagan ... New York, NY
Kelly, Margaret J. ... St. Louis, MO
Kelly, Marian I. ... Woodbury, NJ
Kelly, Marielise ... Boston, MA
Kelly, Marilyn Jean ... Southfield, MI
Kelly, Marion C. ... Anchorage, AK
Kelly, Marita A. ... New Rochelle, NY
Kelly, Mark C. ... New York, NY
Kelly, Mark D. ... Adelphi, MD
Kelly, Mark D. ... Milaca, MN
Kelly, Mark E. ... Liberty, MO
Kelly, Mark F. ... Tampa, FL
Kelly, Mark H. ... Montvale, NJ
Kelly, Mark Lawrence ... San Francisco, CA
Kelly, Mark P. ... Tampa, FL
Kelly, Mark P. ... Atlanta, GA
Kelly, Mark R. ... Port Lavaca, TX
Kelly, Mark W. ... Excelsior, MN
Kelly, Mary A.
Federal Energy Regulatory Commission, Office of the Commissioners, GV
Kelly, Mary A. ... Oklahoma City, OK
Kelly, Mary C. ... Fargo, ND
Kelly, Mary Elizabeth ... Detroit, MI
Kelly, Mary Ellen ... Dedham, MA
Kelly, Mary F. ... Livingston, NJ
Kelly, Mary J. ... Denver, CO
Kelly, Mary J., P.C. ... Denver, CO
Kelly, Mary Jo ... Wheaton, IL
Kelly, Mary Katherine Line Thompson
Charlotte, NC
Kelly, Mary Kathryn ... Chicago, IL
Kelly, Mary Quella ... San Antonio, TX
Kelly, Mary Roy ... Port Huron, MI
Kelly, Mary-Michael ... Prairie Village, KS
Kelly, Matthew ... New York, NY
Kelly, Matthew A, III ... Philadelphia, PA
Kelly, Matthew J. ... Boston, MA
Kelly, Matthew J. ... Albany, NY
Kelly, Matthew Joseph ... Chicago, IL
Kelly, Matthew W. ... Alton, IL
Kelly, Maura E. ... Yonkers, NY
Kelly, Maura O'Donnell ... Pittsburgh, PA
Kelly, Maura Patrice ... St. Louis, MO
Kelly, Maureen A. ... Oakland, CA
Kelly, Maureen E. ... Scranton, PA
Kelly, Maureen P. ... Chicago, IL
Kelly, Maureen P. ... Pittsburgh, PA
Kelly, Maureen T. ... Dayton, OH
Kelly & McClure ... Muskogee, OK
Kelly & McKee, P.A. ... Tampa, FL
Kelly, McLaughlin & Foster
Collingswood, NJ
Philadelphia, PA
Plymouth Meeting, PA
Kelly and Meenagh ... Poughkeepsie, NY
Kelly, Megan A. ... Atlanta, GA
Kelly, Megyn M. ... New York, NY
Kelly, Melissa A. ... Overland Park, KS
Kansas City, MO
Kelly, Michael A. ... San Francisco, CA
Kelly, Michael A. ... Canton, MA
Kelly, Michael B. ... San Diego, CA
Kelly, Michael B. ... Spring Lake, NJ
New York, NY
Kelly, Michael C. ... Philadelphia, PA
Kelly, Michael D. ... Waltham, MA
Kelly, Michael E. ... Phoenix, AZ
Kelly, Michael E. ... Yellville, AR
Kelly, Michael E. ... Boise, ID
Kelly, Michael E. ... Bartlett, IL
Kelly, Michael E. ... Leavenworth, KS
Kelly, Michael E. ... Greensboro, NC
Kelly, Michael E. ... Muskogee, OK
Kelly, Michael E. ... Wheeling, WV
Kelly, Michael E., P.A.
Mountain Home, AR
Yellville, AR
Kelly, Michael F. ... San Anselmo, CA
Kelly, Michael F. ... Marksville, LA
Kelly, Michael F. ... Grand Rapids, MI
Kelly, Michael F. ... Grand Rapids, MI
Kelly, Michael F. ... Brooklyn, NY
Kelly, Michael F., Jr. ... Minneapolis, MN
Kelly, Michael G. ... Whitesboro, NY
Kelly, Michael G. ... Odessa, TX
Kelly, Michael H. ... Everett, MA
Kelly, Michael J. ... Oxnard, CA
Kelly, Michael J. ... Denver, CO
Kelly, Michael J. ... Stamford, CT
Kelly, Michael J. ... Chicago, IL
Kelly, Michael J. ... Boston, MA
Providence, RI
Kelly, Michael J. ... Boston, MA
Kelly, Michael J. ... Flint, MI
Kelly, Michael J. ... Jackson, MI
Kelly, Michael J. ... Southfield, MI
Kelly, Michael J. ... New York, NY
Kelly, Michael J. ... Perry, NY
Kelly, Michael J. ... Riverhead, NY
Kelly, Michael J. ... Rochester, NY
Kelly, Michael J. ... Williston Park, NY
Kelly, Michael J. ... Philadelphia, PA
Kelly, Michael J. ... Richmond, VA
Kelly, Michael J. ... Burlington, WI
Salem, WI
Kelly, Michael J. ... Milwaukee, WI
Kelly, Michael J., A Professional Corporation
Oxnard, CA
Kelly, Michael J., P.C. ... Richmond, VA
Kelly, Michael James ... Timonium, MD
Kelly, Michael John ... Washington, DC
Kelly, Michael K. ... Phoenix, AZ
Kelly, Michael K. ... Hauppauge, NY
Uniondale, NY
Kelly, Michael K. ... Laramie, WY
Kelly, Michael L. ... Los Angeles, CA
Kelly, Michael M. ... Victoria, TX
Kelly, Michael P. ... Wilmington, DE
Kelly, Michael P. ... Mt. Orab, OH
Kelly, Michael P. ... Langhorne, PA
Kelly, Michael R. ... Sacramento, CA
Kelly, Michael R. ... Sacramento, CA
Kelly, Michael S. ... Claremont, CA
Kelly, Michael S. ... Washington, DC
Kelly, Michael S. ... Houston, TX
Kelly, Michael T. ... New York, NY
Kelly, Michael T. ... Arlington, TX
Kelly, Michael T. ... Fort Worth, TX
Kelly, Michael T. ... Houston, TX
Kelly, Michael W.
Department of Agriculture, Office of the General Counsel, GV
Kelly, Michael W. ... Lake Providence, LA
Kelly, Michael W. ... Cleveland, OH
Kelly, Michele ... Doylestown, PA
Kelly, Michele D. ... Northville, MI
Kelly, Mike ... Louisville, KY
Kelly, Mike ... Charleston, WV
Kelly, Millar and Strawn ... Dyersburg, TN
Kelly & Monighan ... Salamanca, NY
Kelly, Monroe, III ... Virginia Beach, VA
Kelly, Morgan F. ... Glens Falls, NY
Kelly, Morgan P. ... Omaha, NE
Kelly, Nancy ... Boston, MA
Kelly, Nancy ... Peabody, MA
Kelly, Neil D. ... Houston, TX
Kelly, Nevin J. ... Washington, DC
Kelly, Nicholas J., III ... Media, PA
Kelly, Nima Jacobs ... Clark, NJ
Kelly, Nora C. ... Albuquerque, NM
Kelly, Nora V. ... Denver, CO
Kelly, Norman R. ... Salina, KS
Kelly, Olson, Michod & Siepker
Chicago, IL
Kelly, Owen B. ... Glendale, MO
Kelly, P. Timothy ... Scranton, PA
Kelly, Palmer
Environmental Protection Agency, Office of Enforcement and Compliance Assurance, GV
Kelly, Pamala Sue ... Jackson, MI
Kelly, Pamela Bannon ... Wantagh, NY
Kelly, Pamela Brown ... Los Angeles, CA
Kelly, Parker S. ... Redwood City, CA
Redwood City, CA
Kelly & Passidomo, LLP ... Naples, FL
Kelly, Patric J. ... Campbell, CA
Kelly, Patrice M.
Department of Transportation, Federal Aviation Administration, GV
Kelly, Patrice P. ... San Bernardino, CA
Kelly, Patricia ... Palatine, IL
Kelly, Patricia ... Harlingen, TX
Kelly, Patricia J. ... St. Petersburg, FL
Kelly, Patricia L. ... Wilmington, DE
Kelly, Patricia L. ... Boston, MA
Kelly, Patricia M. ... Oakland, CA
Kelly, Patricia M. ... Chicago, IL
Kelly, Patricia M. ... New York, NY
Kelly, Patricia Stewart ... Austin, TX
Kelly, Patrick ... Beverly Hills, CA
Kelly, Patrick B. ... Norfolk, VA
Kelly, Patrick D. ... Kansas City, MO
Kelly, Patrick D. ... St. Louis, MO
Kelly, Patrick D. ... Charleston, WV
Kelly, Patrick E. ... Tucson, AZ
Kelly, Patrick E. ... Charlotte, NC
Kelly, Patrick F. ... Wichita, KS
Kelly, Patrick Hill ... San Jose, CA
Kelly, Patrick J. ... San Francisco, CA
Kelly, Patrick J. ... Minneapolis, MN
Kelly, Patrick J. ... St. Paul, MN
Kelly, Patrick J. ... Miles City, MT
Kelly, Patrick J. ... Hackensack, NJ
Kelly, Patrick J. ... Syracuse, NY
Kelly, Patrick J. ... Eugene, OR
Kelly, Patrick Jeremiah ... Hopkins, MN
Kelly, Patrick John ... Philadelphia, PA
Kelly, Patrick M. ... Los Angeles, CA
Kelly, Patrick M. ... Buffalo, NY
Kelly, Patrick Michael ... Austin, TX
Kelly, Patrick W. ... Woodbury, MN
Kelly, Patrick W. ... New York, NY
Kelly, Paul ... New York, NY
Kelly, Paul A. ... Montrose, PA
Kelly, Paul B. ... Olean, NY
Kelly, Paul C. ... Boston, MA

Kelly, Paul D. ...Anchorage, AK
Kelly, Paul D. ...Woodbury, NJ
Kelly, Paul D. ...New York, NY
Kelly, Paul D. ...Rochester, NY
Kelly, Paul D., Jr. ...Jasper, TN
Kelly, Paul F. ...Santa Barbara, CA
Kelly, Paul F. ...Boston, MA
Kelly, Paul G. ...New York, NY
Kelly, Paul J. ...Milwaukee, WI
Kelly, Paul J., Jr. ...Baltimore, MD
Kelly, Paul J., Jr. ...Santa Fe, NM
Kelly, Paul Scott, Jr. ...Kansas City, MO
Kelly, Paul V. ...Boston, MA
Kelly, Paula A. ...Providence, RI
Kelly, Paula Campbell ...Dearborn, MI
Kelly, Paula J. ...Chicago, IL
Kelly, Peter A. ...New Haven, CT
Kelly, Peter B. ...Monroe, WI
Kelly, Peter C. ...Los Angeles, CA
Kelly, Peter C., II ...Phoenix, AZ
Kelly, Peter D. ...Los Angeles, CA
Kelly, Peter E. ...Fort Myers, FL
Kelly, Peter E. ...Sanibel, FL
Kelly, Peter G. ...Hartford, CT
Alexandria, VA
Kelly, Peter J. ...Stockton, CA
Kelly, Peter J. ...Tampa, FL
Kelly, Peter J. ...Chicago, IL
Kelly, Peter J. ...Trenton, NJ
Kelly, Peter J. ...Jamaica, NY
Kelly, Peter K. ...Mineola, NY
Kelly, Peter M., II ...Chicago, IL
Kelly, Peter O'Connell ...Winnetka, IL
Kelly, Philip C. ...Gallatin, TN
Kelly, Philip H. ...Santa Rosa, CA
Kelly, Philip J. ...Glen Burnie, MD
Towson, MD
Kelly, Philip M. ...Scottsbluff, NE
Kelly, Phillip ...Torrance, CA
Kelly, Quentin P. ...New Orleans, LA
Kelly, R. Brett ...New York, NY
Kelly, R. Donald ...Sarasota, FL
Kelly, R. Keith ...Spartanburg, SC
Kelly, R. Michael ...Louisville, KY
Kelly, R. Patrick (Pat) ...Cleveland, OH
Kelly, Ralph ...Venice, FL
Kelly, Ralph C. ...Oakland, CA
Kelly, Ralph J. ...Philadelphia, PA
Kelly, Ralph L. ...Bennettsville, SC
Kelly, Rammelkamp & Muehlenweg, A Professional Association
Albuquerque, NM
Kelly, Randall ...Washington, DC
St. Louis, MO
Kelly, Randall M. ...New York, NY
Kelly, Raymond A., Jr. ...Albany, NY
Kelly, Raymond B. ...Tulsa, OK
Kelly, Raymond B., III ...Fort Worth, TX
Kelly, Raymond J., Jr. ...Chicago, IL
Kelly, Raymond J., Law Office of
Fairfield, CT
Kelly, Regan E. ...Foothill Ranch, CA
Kelly, Regina ...Roslindale, MA
Kelly, Regina F. ...White Plains, NY
Kelly, Regina V. ...Brooklyn, NY
Kelly, Reginald B. ...Lillington, NC
Kelly, Reid ...Pagosa Springs, CO
Kelly, Remmel & Zimmerman
Portland, ME
Kelly, Rex L. ...Seattle, WA
Kelly, Richard ...New York, NY
Kelly, Richard A. ...Marietta, GA
Kelly, Richard B. ...Phoenix, AZ
Kelly, Richard B. ...Locust Valley, NY
Kelly, Richard C. ...Hebron, IL
Kelly, Richard C. ...Whitewater, WI
Kelly, Richard D. ...Dumont, NJ
Kelly, Richard D. ...Arlington, VA
Kelly, Richard E.
Federal Energy Regulatory Commission, Office of the General Counsel, GV
Kelly, Richard F. ...Redwood City, CA
Kelly, Richard F. ...Federal Trade Commission, Bureau of Consumer Protection, GV
Kelly, Richard J. ...Portland, ME
Kelly, Richard J. ...Eau Claire, WI
Kelly, Richard L. ...Mankato, MN
Kelly, Richard L. ...Pittsburgh, PA
Kelly, Richard M. ...San Mateo, CA
Kelly, Richard R. ...Boston, MA
Kelly, Richard R. ...Portsmouth, VA
Kelly, Richard S. ...Chicago, IL
Kelly, Richard W., Jr. ...Pittsburgh, PA
Kelly, Richard W., Sr. ...Pittsburgh, PA
Kelly, Rita ...Pittsburgh, PA
Kelly, Robert ...Amsterdam, NY
Kelly, Robert A. ...Thousand Oaks, CA
Kelly, Robert A. ...Columbia, MO
Kelly, Robert A. ...Westhampton Beach, NY
Kelly, Robert A. ...Pittsburgh, PA
Kelly, Robert A., Jr.
Westhampton Beach, NY
Kelly, Robert B. ...Monterey, CA
Kelly, Robert B. ...Washington, DC
Kelly, Robert C. ...Denver, CO
Kelly, Robert C. ...Columbia, SC
Kelly, Robert C. ...Madison, WI
Kelly, Robert D. ...Naperville, IL
Kelly, Robert D., (P.C.) ...Lakewood, CO
Kelly, Robert Dale, Sr. ...Oklahoma City, OK
Kelly, Robert E. ...Bloomfield Hills, MI
Kelly, Robert E. ...Philadelphia, PA
Kelly, Robert E. ...Burke, VA
Kelly, Robert E., Jr. ...Los Angeles, CA
Kelly, Robert E., Jr. ...Harrisburg, PA
Kelly, Robert E., Jr. ...Houston, TX
Kelly, Robert F. ...Philadelphia, PA
Kelly, Robert F. ...Philadelphia, PA
Kelly, Robert G. ...Cincinnati, OH
Kelly, Robert G., Jr. ...Collingswood, NJ
Philadelphia, PA
Plymouth Meeting, PA
Kelly, Robert H. ...Windsor Locks, CT
Kelly, Robert Hamilton
Colorado Springs, CO
Kelly, Robert J. ...Clearwater, FL
Kelly, Robert J. ...Lake Forest, IL
Kelly, Robert J. ...Boston, MA
Kelly, Robert J. ...Hernando, MS
Kelly, Robert J. ...Morristown, NJ
Kelly, Robert J. ...Newark, NJ
Kelly, Robert J. ...Greenville, SC
Kelly, Robert K. ...Quincy, MA
Kelly, Robert L. ...Bloomfield Hills, MI
Kelly, Robert L. ...Kerrville, TX
Kelly, Robert M. ...Denver, CO
Kelly, Robert M. ...New York, NY
Kelly, Robert M. ...Saratoga Springs, NY
Kelly, Robert M. ...Syosset, NY
Kelly, Robert N. ...Washington, DC
Baltimore, MD
Rockville, MD
Kelly, Robert P. ...Fort Lauderdale, FL
Kelly, Robert P. ...Hallandale Beach, FL
Kelly, Robert P. ...Braintree, MA
Kelly, Robert P. ...Harrison, NY
Kelly, Robert P. ...New York, NY
Kelly, Robert P. ...Pawhuska, OK
Kelly, Robert T. ...Springfield, VA
Kelly, Robert T., Jr. ...Scranton, PA
Kelly, Robert V. ...Cleveland, OH
Kelly, Robert W.
Department of Defense, GV
Kelly, Robert W., II ...Edmond, OK
Kelly, Robin Cass ...New York, NY
Kelly, Robt. F. ...New York, NY
Kelly, Robt., P.C. ...Kerrville, TX
Kelly, Rode & Kelly, LLP ...Mineola, NY
Riverhead, NY
Westbury, NY
Kelly, Roger A. ...Winter Park, FL
Kelly, Roger E. ...Los Angeles, CA
Kelly, Roger J. ...Chicago, IL
Kelly, Roger W. ...Morristown, NJ
Kelly, Roland T. ...Los Angeles, CA
Kelly, Ronald F. ...Bronx, NY
Kelly & Roth ...New York, NY
Kelly & Rowe, P.A. ...Asheville, NC
Kelly, Roy A. ...Carrollton, AL
Kelly, Roy R., III ...Monticello, GA
Kelly & Rubin, LLP ...New York, NY
Kelly, Ruth M. ...Albany, NY
Kelly, Ryan E. ...Phoenix, AZ
Kelly & Ryberg, S.C. ...Eau Claire, WI
Kelly, Samuel C. ...Jackson, MS
Kelly, Sandra K. ...Plainsboro, NJ
Kelly, Sandra Maurer ...Cleveland, OH
Kelly, Sarah A. ...Philadelphia, PA
Kelly, Scott A. ...College Station, TX
Kelly, Scott D. ...Lincoln, NE
Omaha, NE
Kelly, Scott J. ...Cleveland, OH
Kelly, Scott M. ...Long Branch, NJ
Kelly, Scott M., P.C. ...Long Branch, NJ
Kelly, Scott V. ...Mankato, MN
Kelly, Scott W., (P.C.) ...Augusta, GA
Kelly, Sean D. ...Minneapolis, MN
Kelly, Sean F. ...Lansing, MI
Kelly, Sean P. ...Department of Agriculture, Office of the General Counsel, GV
Kelly, Sean P. ...Tampa, FL
Kelly, Sean P. ...Vienna, VA
Kelly, Sean R. ...Newark, NJ
Kelly, Sean Xavier ...Westmont, NJ
Philadelphia, PA
Kelly, Shannon A. ...Wichita, KS
Kelly, Sharon ...Portland, OR
Kelly, Sharon M. ...Ann Arbor, MI
Kelly, Sharon M. ...Buffalo, NY
Kelly, Sharon P. ...Denver, CO
Kelly, Shawn F. ...San Diego, CA
Kelly, Shawn L. ...Morristown, NJ
Kelly, Shawn P. ...Mineola, NY
Riverhead, NY
Kelly, Sheryl K. ...Cleveland, OH
Kelly, Sidney ...Bloomfield Hills, MI
Kelly, Sienie ...Buffalo, NY
Kelly & Smith ...Gallatin, TN
Kelly, Spencer H. ...Charlotte, NC
Kelly, Spicer & Sidle, P.A. ...Baltimore, MD
Timonium, MD
Kelly, Stacey A. ...Phoenix, AZ
Kelly, Stacy L. ...Pittsburgh, PA
Kelly, Stacy L. ...Houston, TX
Kelly, Steffan H. ...Clemson, SC
Kelly, Stephen ...St. Paul, MN
Kelly, Stephen ...West Chester, PA
Kelly, Stephen C. ...Seattle, WA
Kelly, Stephen D. ...Brooklyn, NY
Kelly, Stephen F., Jr. ...Avon, MA
Kelly, Stephen P. ...Springfield, IL
Kelly, Stephen Robert ...Oregon City, OR
Kelly, Steven A. ...Waxahachie, TX
Kelly, Steven W. ...Denver, CO
Kelly, Sue Ann ...New Orleans, LA
Kelly, Suedeen Gibbons ...Albuquerque, NM
Kelly, Susan M. ...St. Louis, MO
Kelly, Susan N. ...Washington, DC
Kelly, Susan N. ...Waco, TX
Kelly, Sutter, Mount & Kendrick, P.C.
Houston, TX
Kelly, Suzanne M. ...San Francisco, CA
Kelly, T. Christopher ...Madison, WI
Kelly, T. Mark ...Houston, TX
Kelly, T. Paine, Jr. ...Tampa, FL
Kelly, Tara K. ...Los Angeles, CA
Kelly, Terence M. ...Los Angeles, CA
Kelly, Terence M. ...Palo Alto, CA
Kelly, Teresa M. ...Baltimore, MD
Kelly, Terrance R. ...Denver, CO
Kelly, Terry M. ...Spokane, WA
Kelly, Theresa A. ...Morristown, NJ
Kelly, Therese A. ...Clarendon Hills, IL
Kelly, Thomas A., III
Middleburg Heights, OH
Kelly, Thomas B. ...Chesapeake, VA
Kelly, Thomas C. ...West Caldwell, NJ
Kelly, Thomas D. ...Hopkinsville, KY
Kelly, Thomas E. ...Santa Cruz, CA
Kelly, Thomas E. ...Topeka, KS
Kelly, Thomas E. ...Spring Lake, NJ
Kelly, Thomas E. ...Amsterdam, NY
Kelly, Thomas E. ...Salt Lake City, UT
Kelly, Thomas E. ...Everett, WA
Kelly, Thomas E., Jr. ...Seattle, WA
Kelly, Thomas F. ...Arvada, CO
Kelly, Thomas F. ...Holmdel, NJ
Kelly, Thomas Francis, III
Poughkeepsie, NY
Kelly, Thomas G. ...Cheyenne, WY
Kelly, Thomas G., III ...Yuma, AZ
Kelly, Thomas J.
Commodity Futures Trading Commission, Division of Enforcement, GV
Kelly, Thomas J. ...Chicago, IL
Kelly, Thomas J. ...Boston, MA
Kelly, Thomas J. ...Brewster, NY
Kelly, Thomas J. ...Brooklyn, NY
Kelly, Thomas J. ...Buffalo, NY
Kelly, Thomas J. ...Spring Green, WI
Kelly, Thomas J., Jr. ...Washington, DC
Kelly, Thomas J., Jr. ...Short Hills, NJ
Kelly, Thomas K. ...Prescott, AZ
Kelly, Thomas L. ...Media, PA
Kelly, Thomas L., Jr. ...Dallas, TX
Kelly, Thomas Lauren ...Bessemer, AL
Kelly, Thomas M. ...Minneapolis, MN
Kelly, Thomas M. ...Woodbridge, NJ
Staten Island, NY
Kelly, Thomas M. ...New York, NY
Kelly, Thomas M. ...Barre, VT
Kelly, Thomas N. ...Buffalo, MN
Kelly, Thomas O., III ...Minneapolis, MN
Kelly, Thomas P. ...Baltimore, MD
Kelly, Thomas P. ...Rochester, MN
Kelly, Thomas P. ...Trenton, NJ
Kelly, Thomas P., Jr. ...Santa Rosa, CA
Kelly, Thomas P., Jr., Inc.
Santa Rosa, CA
Kelly, Thomas Patrick ...Marlton, NJ
Philadelphia, PA
Kelly, Thomas R. ...Portland, ME
Kelly, Thomas R. ...Akron, OH
Kelly, Thomas S.
Department Of Veterans Affairs, Board of Veterans Appeals, GV
Kelly, Thomas T.
Government Printing Office, Office of General Counsel, GV
Kelly, Thomas W. ...Newport, RI
Kelly, Thos. J. ...Springfield, MA
Kelly, Timothy C. ...Helena, MT
Kelly, Timothy D. ...Minneapolis, MN
Kelly, Timothy F. ...St. Petersburg, FL
Kelly, Timothy F. ...Munster, IN
Kelly, Timothy F., Law Offices of
Chicago, IL
Crown Point, IN
Hammond, IN
Munster, IN
Valparaiso, IN
Kelly, Timothy G. ...Northbrook, IL
Kelly, Timothy J. ...Washington, DC
Kelly, Timothy J. ...New York, NY
Kelly, Timothy J. ...Mt. Orab, OH
Kelly, Timothy M. ...Chicago, IL
Kelly, Timothy P. ...Jacksonville, FL
Kelly, Timothy P. ...Salem, OR
Kelly, Timothy P. ...Port Orchard, WA
Kelly, Timothy P., P.A. ...Jacksonville, FL
Kelly, Timothy W. ...Chicago, IL
Kelly, Timothy W. ...St. Louis, MO
Kelly, Timothy W., & Associates
Bloomington, IL
Kelly, Todd P. ...Dallas, TX
Kelly, Townsend & Thomas
Natchitoches, LA
Kelly, Tracy L ...Springfield, VT
Kelly & Traul ...Bellefontaine, OH
Kelly, Valerie Lynn ...Little Rock, AR
Kelly, Vanessa M. ...Morristown, NJ
Kelly, Veronica M. ...Pittsburgh, PA
Kelly, Vic ...Dallas, TX
Kelly, W. Davis ...Anderson, SC
Kelly, W. Donald ...Columbus, GA
Kelly, W. James, P.A. ...Lakeland, FL
Kelly, W. Michael ...New York, NY
Kelly, W. Richard, Jr. ...Charlotte, NC
Kelly, Wade N. ...Lake Charles, LA
Kelly, Walter ...Tallahassee, FL
Kelly, Walter F. ...Milwaukee, WI
Kelly, Walter M. ...Chicago, IL
Kelly, Walter M., II ...Littleton, CO
Kelly, Walter M., Jr. ...Chicago, IL
Kelly & Walthall, P.C. ...Utica, NY
Kelly, Warren ...Middletown, NY
Kelly, Warren D. ...Los Angeles, CA
Kelly, Warren, P.C. ...Middletown, NY
Kelly & Weaver, A Professional Corporation
Washington, DC
Kelly, Wendy A. ...Greenwich, CT
Kelly & West ...Lillington, NC
Sanford, NC
Kelly, William A. ...Chicago, IL
Kelly, William A. ...Galena, IL
Kelly, William A. ...Lawrence, KS
Kelly, William A. ...New City, NY
Kelly, William Booker ...Santa Fe, NM
Kelly, William Bradley ...Cleveland, OH
Kelly, William C. ...New York, NY
Kelly, William C. ...Rochester, NY
Kelly, William C., Jr. ...Washington, DC
Kelly, William David, III ...Camden, SC
Kelly, William E. ...Hartford, CT
Kelly, William E. ...Boston, MA
Kelly, William E. ...New York, NY
Kelly, William E., III ...Canyon, TX
Kelly, William G., Jr. ...Washington, DC
Kelly, William H., Jr. ...Chicago, IL
Kelly, William J. ...Independence, KS
Kelly, William J. ...Jackson, MI
Kelly, William J. ...Bay Shore, NY
Kelly, William J. ...Philadelphia, PA
Kelly, William J. ...Corpus Christi, TX
Kelly, William J., III ...New Orleans, LA
Kelly, William J., Jr. ...Columbus, OH
Kelly, William J., Jr. ...Erie, PA
Kelly, William J., Sr. ...Erie, PA
Kelly, William M. ...Mountain View, CA
Kelly, William O. ...Arlington, TX
Kelly, William O., Jr. ...Flint, MI
Kelly, William P. ...Madison, NJ
Kelly, William P. ...West End, NC
Kelly, William Paul ...Philadelphia, PA
Kelly, William R. ...Metamora, IL
Peoria, IL
Kelly, William R. ...Greenlawn, NY
Kelly, William S. ...Unity, ME
Kelly, William V. ...Toms River, NJ
Kelly, William W. ...Utica, NY
Kelly, Wm. D. ...Chicago, IL
Kelly, Wm. Franklin, Jr. ...Houston, TX
Kelly, Wm. G., Jr. ...Monroe, LA
Kelly, W. T. ...Little Rock, AR
Kelly/Haglund/Garnsey & Kahn LLC
Denver, CO
Kelly-Bundle, Thea E. ...Indianapolis, IN
Kelly-Hollister, Lorene ...Pleasanton, CA
Kelly-Ivory, Moraima A. ...Sacramento, CA
Kelly-Judd, Leeann K. ...Baltimore, MD
Kelly-Kobayashi, Eleanore
Washington, DC
New York, NY
Kelly-Schilling, Sandra D. ...Cincinnati, OH
Kelly-Smethurst, Andrea
San Francisco, CA
Kelm, George ...Chicago, IL
Kelm, Jeffrey N. ...Houston, TX
Kelm, Marilynn B. ...Atlanta, GA
Kelm, Mary Kay B. ...Norristown, PA
Kelm, Robt. B. ...Baltimore, MD
Kelm, Russell A. ...Columbus, OH
Kelmachter, Barry L. ...New Haven, CT
Kelmachter, Leslie Debra ...New York, NY
Kelman, Abigail J. ...Baltimore, MD
Kelman, Abigail T. ...St. Louis, MO
Kelman, Alyssa ...New York, NY
Kelman, Barry M. ...Southfield, MI
Kelman, Bruce H. ...Three Rivers, CA
Kelman, Edward M. ...New York, NY
Kelman, Ellen M. ...Denver, CO
Kelman, George A. ...Morristown, NJ
Kelman, Howard ...Plymouth, MA
Kelman, Lane Foster ...Doylestown, PA
Kelman, Loria, Will, Harvey & Thompson
Detroit, MI
Kelman, Mark G. ...Palo Alto, CA
Kelman, Matthew S. ...New York, NY
Kelman, Maurice ...Troy, MI
Kelman, Paul ...Farmington Hills, MI
Kelman, Peter B. ...Boston, MA
Kelman, Robert A. ...Chicago, IL
Kelmans, Richard N. ...New York, NY
Kelmen, Ronel Quinn ...Los Angeles, CA
Kelner, Howard M. ...Los Angeles, CA
Kelner, John D. ...Hollywood, FL
Kelner, Joseph ...New York, NY
Kelner & Kelner ...New York, NY
Kelner, Marvin I. ...Cleveland, OH
Kelner, Milton ...Miami, FL
Kelner, Richard W. ...Long Beach, CA
Kelner, Robert K. ...Washington, DC
Kelner, Robert S. ...New York, NY
Kelner, Samuel H ...New York, NY
Kelnhofer, Joseph ...Bedford, MA
Kelroy, Jason J. ...Columbus, OH
Kelsall, Samuel, IV ...Phoenix, AZ
Sun City, AZ
Kelsall, Samuel, V ...Carlsbad, CA
Kelsay, Kenneth E. ...Oklahoma City, OK
Kelsay, Morris A. ...Marion, IN
Kelsay, Ron
Hot Springs National Park, AR
Kelsay, William M. ...Santa Cruz, CA
Kelsberg, Daniel W. ...San Diego, CA
Kelsberg, William G. ...Los Angeles, CA
Kelsch Kelsch Ruff & Kranda
Bismarck, ND
Mandan, ND
Kelsch, Kristan ...Jackson, CA
Kelsch, Mary Kae ...Mandan, ND
Kelsch, Thomas D. ...Mandan, ND
Kelsch, Thomas F. ...Mandan, ND
Kelsch, William C. ...Mandan, ND
Kelsen, David S. ...Waterloo, IA
Kelsen, Michael R. ...Philadelphia, PA
Kelsen, Peter Foster ...Philadelphia, PA
Kelsey, Alan R. ...Montvale, NJ
Kelsey, Andrea Lee ...Guilderland, NY
Kelsey, Angela M.
Department Of The Interior, Office of the Solicitor, GV

Kelsey, Arthur S. ... Petersburg, VA
Kelsey, Bitterman & Apicelli ... Trenton, NJ
Kelsey, Bruce R. ... West Chicago, IL
Kelsey, Carmen Y. ... San Antonio, TX
Kelsey, Charles E., Jr. ... Columbus, OH
Kelsey, D. Arthur ... Norfolk, VA
Kelsey, Darrel A. ... Tulsa, OK
Kelsey, David B. ... Los Angeles, CA
Kelsey, David H. ... Albuquerque, NM
Kelsey, David John, Sr. ... Palm Coast, FL
Kelsey, Dawn P. ... Salem, NH
Kelsey, Dawn S. ... Henderson, KY
Kelsey, George W. ... Ann Arbor, MI
Kelsey, George W., P.C. ... Ann Arbor, MI
Kelsey, H. Burr ... Montclair, NJ
Kelsey, Ingrid N. ... Malibu, CA
Kelsey, Jane S. ... Parsippany, NJ
Kelsey, Joan S. ... Wilsonville, OR
Kelsey, John E. ... Louisville, KY
Kelsey, John E. ... Denton, TX
Kelsey, John N. ... Saginaw, MI
Kelsey, John R., III ... Lebanon, PA
Kelsey, John W. ... Greenville, IL
Kelsey & Kelsey, P.C. ... Denton, TX
Kelsey, Kimberly Phelan ... Rochester, NY
Kelsey, Lamar H., III ... Chester, SC
Kelsey, Lloyd M. ... Willits, CA
Kelsey, Margaret C. ... Milwaukee, WI
Kelsey, Mark G. ... Columbus, OH
Kelsey, Michael A. ... Hayward, WI
Kelsey, Michael D. ... Wilmington, DE
Kelsey, Richard H. ... Denton, TX
Kelsey, Robert Jeffery ... Memphis, TN
Kelsey, Robert T. ... Sandusky, OH
Kelsey, Roger D. ... Dover, DE
Kelsey, Sally G. ... Lawrence, KS
Kelsey, Sidney H., Jr. ... Virginia Beach, VA
Kelsey, Susan E. ... Calabasas, CA
Kelsey, Thomas F. ... Glastonbury, CT
Kelsey, Thomas R. ... Houston, TX
Kelsey, Ward T. ... Pittsburgh, PA
Kelsh, James V. ... Charleston, WV
Kelsh, John C. ... New York, NY
Kelsh, John P. ... Chicago, IL
Kelsky, Brad E. ... West Palm Beach, FL
Kelso, Amy S. ... Asheville, NC
Kelso, C. Douglas, III ... Memphis, TN
Kelso, C. Kevin ... Palo Alto, CA
Kelso, Charles ... Atlanta, GA
Kelso, Christine W. ... El Paso, TX
Kelso, Daniel J. ... Columbus, OH
Kelso, David Mark ... Charlotte, NC
Kelso, Dennis D. ... Juneau, AK
Kelso, Donald I. J. ... Denver, CO
Kelso, Douglas J. ... Portland, OR
Kelso, John G. ... Asheville, NC
Kelso, Kristin L. ... San Bernardino, CA
Kelso, Linda Yayoi ... Jacksonville, FL
Kelso, Lloyd Thomas ... Charlotte, NC
Gastonia, NC
Nashville, TN
Kelso, M. Jane ... Indianapolis, IN
Kelso, Nancy L. ... Acton, CA
Kelso, Robert A. ... New Albany, IN
Kelso, Robert B. ...
Department of Labor, GV
Kelso, Robert C. ... Carlsbad, CA
Kelso, Robert M. ... Indianapolis, IN
Kelso, Starr ... Coeur d'Alene, ID
Kelso, Steven Matthew
Colorado Springs, CO
Kelso, Thomas R. ... Champaign, IL
Chicago, IL
Kelso, Wesley R. ... Lancaster, PA
Kelso, William R. ... Denver, CO
Kelso, Winchester, Jr. ... San Antonio, TX
Kelso & Young ... Acton, CA
Kelsoe, Anderson, Khoury & Clark, P.C.
Dallas, TX
Kelsoe, G. H., Jr. ... Dallas, TX
Kelsoe, Robert L. ... Dallas, TX
Kelson, Anne Therese ... Golden, CO
Kelson, Bruce B. ... San Francisco, CA
Kelson, John M. ... San Francisco, CA
Kelson, John W. ... Tulsa, OK
Kelson, Mark J. ... Los Angeles, CA
Kelson, Richard B. ... Pittsburgh, PA
Kelson, Sanford ... Pittsburgh, PA
Kelson & Slomski ... Pittsburgh, PA
Kelson, Todd A. ... Newburgh, NY
Kelson, Zachary D. ... Monticello, NY
Kelston, David L. ... Boston, MA
Kelston, Henry J. ... Valley Cottage, NY
Kelsven, Frederick D. ... Worthington, OH
Keltch, Peter M. ... Oklahoma City, OK
Kelter, Gerhard E. W., Jr., A Prof. Corp., Law Offices ... Chicago, IL
Kelter, Gerhard, Jr. ... Chicago, IL
Keltner, Alan L. ... Milwaukee, WI
Keltner, Cecil G. ... Memphis, TN
Keltner, D. Thomas ... Dallas, TX
Keltner, David E. ... Fort Worth, TX
Keltner, Donald H. ... Aspen, CO
Keltner, Donald H., A Professional Corporation ... Aspen, CO
Keltner, Edgar H., Jr. ... Fort Worth, TX
Keltner, Gary G. ... Phoenix, AZ
Keltner, Gregory S. ... Fairview Heights, IL
Keltner, Kristin B. ... Indianapolis, IN
Keltner, Thomas N. ... Oklahoma City, OK
Keltner, Thomas N., Jr. ... New York, NY
Kelton, Clyde B., Jr. ... Boston, MA
Kelton, David A. S. ... Santa Monica, CA
Kelton, David D. ... Dallas, TX
Kelton, David G. ... Mineola, NY
New York, NY
White Plains, NY
Kelton, Erika Armitage ... Washington, DC

Kelton, George M. ... Odessa, TX
Kelton & Kelton ... Santa Monica, CA
Kelton, Lisa ... Los Angeles, CA
Kelton, Margaret M. ... Austin, TX
Kelton, Michael S. ... New York, NY
Kelton, Richard I. M. ... Santa Monica, CA
Kelton, Stanley M. ... Huntington Beach, CA
Kelton, Stanton C., III ... Bensalem, PA
Langhorne, PA
Kelty, Jessica M. ... Alexandria, VA
Kelty, John C. ... New York, NY
Kelty, Stephen G. ... Jackson, MS
Kelty, Thomas W. ... Springfield, IL
Kelty, Timothy J., Jr. ... Hightstown, NJ
Kelty, William J., III ... Chicago, IL
Keltz, Karen ... Dallas, TX
Keltz, Steven ... New York, NY
Kelvasa, Anthony ... Middletown, NY
Kelvie, Patrick J. ... Los Altos, CA
Kelvin, David ... Oakland, CA
Kelvin, Jeffrey B. ... Philadelphia, PA
Kemalyan, Richard S. ... Los Angeles, CA
Kemalyan & Richland ... Los Angeles, CA
Kembel, David A. ... Lexington, MA
Kembel, Kleath A. ... San Bruno, CA
Farmington Hills, MI
Kembel, Kleath A., P.C.
Farmington Hills, MI
Kemble, Donn ... Irvine, CA
Kemble, Edward L. ... Fort Worth, TX
Kemble, Heather A. ... Dallas, TX
Kemble, Karen D. ... Bangor, ME
Kemble, Sarah Boucher ... Charlotte, NC
Kemby, Donald C. ... Twentynine Palms, CA
Kemenczy, John L. ... Bloomfield, NJ
Kemeness, Lon. P. ... Tifton, GA
Kemer, Frank C. ... Hillsdale, NY
Kemerer, David C. ... Chicago, IL
Kemery, Barbara ... St. Louis, MO
Kemether, Redmond P. ... Oklahoma City, OK
Kemether, Sean V. ... Media, PA
Kemezys, K. Peter ... Gaithersburg, MD
Kemins, Robert A. ... Department of Justice, Tax Division, GV
Kemler, Lisa Bondareff ... Alexandria, VA
Kemler, Michele Kilar ... Royal Oak, MI
Kemler, R. W. ... Marshalltown, IA
Kemm, Karl P. ... North Brunswick, NJ
Kemm, Larry R. ... Dallas, TX
Kemme, David A. ... Cleveland, OH
Kemmel, William A., Jr.
Woodland Hills, CA
Kemmer, Dennis J. ... Indianapolis, IN
Kemmer, Kyle ... Wilmington, DE
Kemmer, Mel ... Troy, OH
West Milton, OH
Kemmer, Melissa M. ... Charlotte, NC
Kemmer, Randolph T. ... Chicago, IL
Kemmer, Richard M." Mitch ", Jr.
Centreville, AL
Kemmer, Sherman J. ... Strongsville, OH
Kemmer, Stephanie Woodham
Centreville, AL
Kemmerle, Toni L. ... Brunswick, ME
Kemmerley, Erica R. ... Denver, CO
Kemmerlin, Thomas, Jr. ... Beaufort, SC
Kemmerly, McNeil J. ... Metairie, LA
Kemmerly, Peter A. ... Anaheim, CA
Kemmerly-Weber, Nanette L. ... Humboldt, KS
Kemmeter, James A. ... Madison, WI
Kemming, Richard L. ... Des Moines, IA
Kemmins, Jeanne ... Missoula, MT
Kemmis, Daniel ... Missoula, MT
Kemmler, Carolyn L. ... Sacramento, CA
Kemmler, Eric L. ... Bristol, CT
Kemmy, Michael J. ... Charlotte, NC
Kemna, Donald J. ... Kansas City, MO
Kemner, John E. ... Jacksonville, FL
Kemner, Matthew J. ... San Francisco, CA
Kemner, Nancy E. ... Jacksonville, FL
Kemnitz, Christian T. ... Chicago, IL
Kemnitz, D'Arcy ... Washington, DC
Kemnitz, Jerami D. ... Kansas City, MO
Kemnitz, Ralph A., Law Offices of
Kadoka, SD
Philip, SD
Wall, SD
Kemnitz, Walter Robert, Jr. ... Toledo, OH
Kemnitzer, Anderson, Barron & Ogilvie
Sacramento, CA
San Francisco, CA
Kemnitzer, Bryan ... San Francisco, CA
Kemon, Solon B. ... Arlington, VA
Kemp, A. Jeff ... Houston, TX
Kemp, A. Jeff, P.C. ... Houston, TX
Kemp, Aaron J. ... Troy, MI
Kemp, Albert L., Jr. ... Atlanta, GA
Kemp, Alson R., Jr. ... San Francisco, CA
Kemp, Ann C. ... Honolulu, HI
Kemp, Austin J., II ... Warner Robins, GA
Kemp, Barrett G. ... St. Marys, OH
Kemp, Bernard W. ... Washington, DC
Kemp, Bruce B. ... Houston, TX
Kemp, Carla R. ... Springfield, MO
Kemp, Carroll A. ... Destin, FL
Hazlehurst, MS
Kemp, Christopher L. ... Minneapolis, MN
Kemp, Clinton W. ... Lancaster, PA
Kemp, Clive J. ... Riverside, CA
Santa Ana, CA
Kemp, Crawley M., II ... Warner Robins, GA
Kemp, Daniel W. ... Columbus, OH
Kemp, David O. ... Dallas, TX
Kemp, Deborah A. ... Berkeley, CA
Kemp, Deborah J. ... Fresno, CA
Kemp, Dennis W. ... Palatine, IL
Kemp, Donna M. ... Philadelphia, PA
Kemp, Donna N. ... Norcross, GA

Kemp, Dorothy Lendaris ... Portland, OR
Kemp, Duckett, Spradley, Curry & Arnold
Little Rock, AR
Kemp, Duncan S., III ... Hammond, LA
Kemp, E. David ... Orlando, FL
Kemp, E. Thomas ... Richmond, IN
Kemp, Edward G. ... Akron, OH
Kemp, Ellen H. ... Albany, NY
Kemp, Gail M. ... Wilton, CT
Kemp, Gary L. ... Boston, MA
Kemp, Gaylen D. ... Atlanta, GA
Kemp, George W., Jr. ... Mill Valley, CA
Kemp, Grzelakowski & Lorenzini, Ltd.
Oak Brook, IL
Kemp, Hal Joseph, (P.A.) ... Little Rock, AR
Kemp, Harold R. ... Columbus, OH
Kemp, Harton & Tilley ... Hopkinsville, KY
Kemp, Helen Lewis ... Richmond, VA
Kemp, Helen M. ... Hartford, CT
Kemp, J. Daniel ... Hopkinsville, KY
Kemp, J. Hovey ... Washington, DC
Kemp, J. Michael ... Kalamazoo, MI
Kemp, Jacqueline L. ... Columbus, OH
Kemp, James Bradley, Jr.
New Orleans, LA
Kemp, James F. ... Sonoma, CA
Kemp, James J., Jr. ... Oak Brook, IL
Kemp, James M. ... Louisville, KY
Kemp, James S. ... Seattle, WA
Kemp, Janice Tomie Ueoka ... Honolulu, HI
Kemp, Janice Werner ... Tampa, FL
Kemp, Jeffrey W. ... Dallas, TX
Kemp, Jerylle ... New York, NY
Kemp, Jim ... Ada, OK
Kemp, John B. ... Troy, MI
Kemp, John D., Jr. ... Mountain View, AR
Kemp, John L. ... Glenwood Springs, CO
Kemp, John M. ... Marina Del Rey, CA
Kemp, John M. ... Oakland, CA
Kemp, John Paul ... Atlanta, GA
Kemp, Joseph R. ... Pell City, AL
Kemp, Julian Tyrone ... Miami, FL
Kemp, K. Lawrence ... New Kensington, PA
Kemp, Karlton H., Jr. ... Texarkana, AR
Kemp, Karol J. ... Bay Minette, AL
Kemp, Kathleen Nagy ... Murrysville, PA
Kemp, Kathryn M. ... Chicago, IL
Kemp, Klein, Umphrey & Endelman, Professional Corporation ... Detroit, MI
Troy, MI
Kemp, Kristopher W. ... Nashville, TN
Kemp, L. Hugh, (P.C.) ... Dalton, GA
Kemp, Larry A. ... St. Paul, MN
Kemp, Laurie Goetz ... Louisville, KY
Kemp Law Firm ... Dallas, TX
Kemp, Lori D. ... Miami, FL
Kemp, Marc David ... Lawrence, NY
Kemp, Margaret J. ... Redwood City, CA
Kemp, Mark A. ... Las Vegas, NV
Kemp, Mark A., Professional Corporation
Las Vegas, NV
Kemp, Maurice ... Middletown, CA
Palo Alto, CA
Kemp, Michael F. ... Savannah, GA
Kemp, Michael L. ... Holly Springs, MS
Kemp, Michael M. ... Hines, OR
Kemp, Nicholas ... Denver, CO
Kemp, Pamela ... Santa Ana, CA
Kemp, Paul B. ... San Jose, CA
Kemp, Paul F. ... Rockville, MD
Kemp, Paul J. ... Arlington, VA
Kemp, Peggy Sloan ... Cambridge, MA
Kemp, Raymond W. ... Phoenix, AZ
Kemp, René D. ... Hinesville, GA
Kemp, René D., P.C. ... Hinesville, GA
Kemp, Robert F. ... Chicago, IL
Kemp, Robert M. ... Wellsboro, PA
Kemp, Robert P. ... Metairie, LA
Kemp, Roger L. ... Chicago, IL
Kemp, Roland C. ... Houston, TX
Kemp, Roland L. ... Irvine, CA
Kemp, Russell W. ... Denver, CO
Kemp, Schaeffer, Rowe & Lardiere Co., L.P.A.
Columbus, OH
Kemp, Smith, Duncan & Hammond, A Professional Corporation ... Austin, TX
El Paso, TX
Kemp, Stephen M. ... Peoria, AZ
Kemp, Stewart W. ... Boston, MA
Kemp, Susan Michelle ... Hempstead, NY
Kemp, T. Aubrey ... Hagerstown, MD
Kemp, Terence P. ... Columbus, OH
Kemp, Thomas H. ... Department of Energy, Office of the General Counsel, GV
Kemp, Thomas P. ... Findlay, OH
Kemp, Thomas W. ... Ross, CA
San Francisco, CA
Kemp, Thos. M. ... Kansas City, MO
Kemp, Timothy V. ... Santa Ana, CA
Kemp, Traci D. ... Warner Robins, GA
Kemp, W. Robert ... Providence, RI
Kemp, Wallace B. ... Riverside, IL
Kemp, Wendi J. ... Hartford, CT
Kemp, Will ... Las Vegas, NV
Kemp, William F. ... Austin, TX
Kemp, William G. ... Denver, CO
Kemp, William G. ... Holly Springs, MS
Kemp, William J., Jr. ... Detroit, MI
Kemp, William S. ... Bamberg, SC
Kempainen, James M. ... Bloomington, MN
Kempainen, Paul R. ... St. Paul, MN
Kempaner, Richard A. ... Huntsville, AL
Kempe, Enid L. ... Berwyn, IL
Kempe, John R. ... St. Paul, MN
Kempe, Joseph C. ... Jupiter, FL
Stuart, FL
Vero Beach, FL

Kempe, Joseph C., Professional Association
Jupiter, FL
Stuart, FL
Vero Beach, FL
Kempel, Peter M. ... Lansing, MI
Kempenich, William James
San Francisco, CA
Kempe-Olinger, Elisabeth ... Colton, CA
Kemper, Ann-Kelley ... Washington, DC
Kemper & Barlow ... Madison, IN
Vevay, IN
Kemper, Bernard F. ... Los Angeles, CA
Kemper, Brian William ... New York, NY
Kemper, Carolyn V. ... Monterey Park, CA
Kemper, Edward A. ... Toledo, OH
Kemper, Edward C. ... Honolulu, HI
Kemper, Ellen Rhona ... Santa Fe, NM
Kemper, G. Kenneth ... Coral Gables, FL
Kemper, G. Whitney ... Nashville, TN
Kemper, Gary K. ... Madison, IN
Kemper, Gerald T. ... Frankfort, KY
Kemper, James D. ... Indianapolis, IN
Kemper, James H. ... Phoenix, AZ
Kemper, James S., Jr. ... Long Grove, IL
Kemper, James W. ... Eugene, OR
Kemper, John-Garrett ... Norfolk, VA
Kemper, J. R. ... Fort Myers, FL
Kemper, K. Timothy ... Miami, FL
Kemper, Keith A. ... Seattle, WA
Kemper, Kevin M. ... Los Angeles, CA
Kemper, Kim Ray ... Richmond, IN
Kemper, Kimberley S. ... Seattle, WA
Kemper, Kurt C. ... Los Angeles, CA
Kemper, Margaret-Ray ... Naples, FL
Tallahassee, FL
Kemper & McLemore ... Nashville, TN
Kemper, Richard F. ... Littlestown, PA
Kemper, Richard J. ... Wilmette, IL
Kemper, Richd. J. ... Dayton, OH
Kemper, Talfourd H. ... Roanoke, VA
Kemper, Talfourd H. (Fourd), Jr.
Roanoke, VA
Kemper, T. M. ... Houston, TX
Kemper & Watts ... Honolulu, HI
Kemper, William C. ... Lansing, MI
Kemper, William D. ... Butler, PA
Kemper, W. L., Jr. ... Magnolia, TX
Kempers, David S. ... Grand Rapids, MI
Kempes, Richard S., Law Offices of
Doylestown, PA
Kempf, Cheryl A. ... Juno Beach, FL
Kempf, Christopher J. ... Columbus, OH
Kempf, Debra Mangus ... Philadelphia, PA
Kempf, Donald G., Jr., (P.C.) ... Chicago, IL
New York, NY
Kempf, Douglas P. ... Minneapolis, MN
Kempf, James D. ... Bloomington, MN
Kempf, John Frederick, Jr.
Oklahoma City, OK
Kempf, Joseph J., Jr. ... Shelton, CT
Kempf & McKinley ... Indianapolis, IN
Kempf, Paul P. ... Minneapolis, MN
Kempf, Richard A. ... Indianapolis, IN
Kempf, Richard A. ... Minneapolis, MN
Kempf, Robert J. ... Lansing, MI
Kempf, Robin J. ... Topeka, KS
Kempf, Steven J. ... Washington, DC
Kempfert, Amy E. ... Tulsa, OK
Kemph, Carleton Richard
West Orange, NJ
Kemph, Stephen A. ... Chicago, IL
Kempic, Annamarie ... Rockville, MD
Kempin, Pamela J. ... Wilmette, IL
Kempinen, B.K. ... Madison, WI
Kempinen, LaVerne M. ... Tempe, AZ
Kempinsky, Louis E. ... Los Angeles, CA
Kempisty, Raymond P. ... Baltimore, MD
Kempke, Robert E. ... Cleveland, OH
Kempker-Cloyd, Agnes ... Grand Rapids, MI
Kempkes, Bruce L. ... Des Moines, IA
Kempkes, Jas. D. ... Des Moines, IA
Kemple, Mark D. ... Irvine, CA
Kempler, Cecelia ... Washington, DC
New York, NY
Kempler, David I. ... Washington, DC
Kempler, Gail M. ... Tarrytown, NY
Kempler, Harry D.
Small Business Administration, Office of the General Counsel, GV
Kempler, Joseph P. ... Columbia, MD
Kempler, Roger ... Costa Mesa, CA
Kempler, William B. ... Dallas, TX
Kempley, Christopher C. ... Phoenix, AZ
Kemplin, D. Randall ... Bradenton, FL
Kempner, Brian G. ... New York, NY
Kempner, David E. ... Ann Arbor, MI
Kempner, Jonathan L. ... Washington, DC
Kempner, Juli ... New York, NY
Kempner, Lawrence P. ... Bensalem, PA
Kempner, Maria ... Brooklyn, NY
Kempner, Michael F. ... Phoenix, AZ
Kempner, Stanley A., Jr. ... Spokane, WA
Kempner, Susan ... Houston, TX
Kemppainen, John P., Jr. ... St. Louis, MO
Kemppel, Huffman and Ellis, P.C.
Anchorage, AK
Kemppel, Roger R. ... Anchorage, AK
Kemprowski, Chris William
Florham Park, NJ
Kemprowski, Noel A. ... Newark, NJ
Kemps, Loreen M. ... Duncansville, PA
Kemps, Robert T. ... Appleton, WI
Kemps, Steven J. ... Dallas, TX
Kempske, Alan W. ... Baltimore, MD
Kempski, John B. ... Grand Rapids, MI
Kempsky, Nelson P. ... Sacramento, CA
Kempson, Barry B. ... Asheville, NC
Kempson, Kenneth E. ... Stamford, CT

Kempson, Marsha L. .... Santa Monica, CA
Kempster, Donald B., (P.C.) .... Chicago, IL
Kempston, David Brian .... Anoka, MN
Kempter, Joseph M. .... Haddonfield, NJ
Kempton, Bruce C. .... Southfield, MI
Kempton, J. Wayne .... Oklahoma City, OK
Kempton, James S. .... Seattle, WA
Kempton, Lawrence R. .... San Diego, CA
Kempton, Mark T. .... Sedalia, MO
Kempton, Robert G. .... Mesa, AZ
Kempton and Rosenberger, P.S.
Seattle, WA
Kempton, Timothy R. .... Beaverton, OR
Kemp-Williams, Margaret E. .... Whittier, CA
Kemsley, F. Jared .... Springville, NY
Kemsley, George G. .... Detroit, MI
Ken, Catherine, Law Offices of
Arcadia, CA
Kenady, Charles W. .... San Francisco, CA
Kenady, Christine Ratliff .... Eastsound, WA
Kenady, D. Brent .... Spokane, WA
Kenady, Patrick M. .... Martinez, CA
Kenaga, Michael L. .... Chicago, IL
Kenagy, David R. .... Salem, OR
Kenagy, R. Brooks .... Steelville, MO
Kenagy, Reed B., Jr. .... Liberty, MO
Kenagy, Robert T. .... Benton Harbor, MI
Kenan, James G. .... Atlanta, GA
Kenan, Richard M. .... Newberry, SC
Kenan, Robert C., Jr. .... Burgaw, NC
Kenan, S. Reginald .... Warsaw, NC
Kenan, Thomas J. .... Oklahoma City, OK
Kenary, Joseph .... Bethesda, MD
Kenaston, James M., Jr. .... Silver Spring, MD
Kenawell, J. William A. .... Pittsburgh, PA
Kencel, Kenneth J. .... New York, NY
Kenchelian, Mark L. .... Burbank, CA
Kenda, Maureen C. .... Manchester, NH
Kendall, Adrian P. .... Portland, ME
Kendall, Ann Hall B. .... Richmond, VA
Kendall, Anne M. .... Pittsfield, MA
Kendall, Aubrey V., (P.A.) .... Miami, FL
Kendall, Blair M. .... Randolph, WI
Kendall, Bradford C. .... Kansas City, MO
Kendall, Cheryl Ann .... Palo Alto, CA
Kendall, Christopher C. .... Chicago, IL
Kendall, Christopher Jay .... Morrisville, NY
Kendall, Clarence E., Jr. .... Houston, TX
Kendall, Clarence F., II .... Houston, TX
Kendall, Clarence F., II & Associates, P.C.
Houston, TX
Kendall, Craig S. .... Topeka, KS
Kendall, Dara M. .... Cincinnati, OH
Kendall, Darin G. .... Columbus, OH
Kendall, David Benjamin
Charlottesville, VA
Fredericksburg, VA
Harrisonburg, VA
Kendall, David E. .... Washington, DC
Kendall, David J. .... New York, NY
Kendall, David L. .... Chicago, IL
Kendall, David M. .... Austin, TX
Kendall, David P. .... Ramsey, NJ
Kendall, Deborah .... Berkeley, CA
Kendall, Donald B. .... Rogers, AR
Kendall, Donald G. .... Bakersfield, CA
Kendall, Douglas T. .... Washington, DC
Kendall, Earl D., Sr. .... Lincoln, CA
Kendall, Edward Perry .... Montgomery, AL
Kendall, Elson P. .... Union, NJ
Kendall, Everett A., II .... Columbia, SC
Kendall, F. Russell .... Houston, TX
Kendall, Frederic S. .... Watertown, NY
Kendall, Gail .... New York, NY
Kendall, Gary W. .... Charlottesville, VA
Richmond, VA
Kendall, Gaynor .... Austin, TX
Kendall, George H. .... Newark, NJ
Kendall, Glenn W. .... Baltimore, MD
Kendall, Hatten & Glasser, P.L.C.
Richmond, VA
Kendall, Heather .... Anchorage, AK
Kendall, Henry M. .... Jackson, MS
Kendall, Hugh F. .... Chattanooga, TN
Kendall, Hugh F., Attorney, P.C.
Chattanooga, TN
Kendall, J. Clarke, II .... Tulsa, OK
Kendall, Jack L. .... Sylmar, CA
Kendall, Jack O.
Federal Energy Regulatory Commission,
Office of the General Counsel, GV
Kendall, James A. .... Midland, MI
Kendall, James H. .... Linwood, NJ
Kendall, Janelle P. .... St. Cloud, MN
Kendall, Jeffrey D. .... Pittsburgh, PA
Kendall, Joe .... Dallas, TX
Kendall, John A. .... Marshall, MI
Kendall, John A. .... Houston, TX
Kendall, John D. .... Tucson, AZ
Kendall, John R. .... Culver City, CA
Kendall, John S. .... Chicago, IL
Kendall, John W. .... Green Valley, AZ
Kendall, John W., Jr. .... Atlanta, GA
Kendall, Joseph E. .... Washington, DC
Kendall, Juliana T. .... Tacoma, WA
Kendall, Karen L. .... Peoria, IL
Kendall, Karl K. .... Houston, TX
Kendall, Katherine K. .... Greenup, KY
Kendall, Keith A. .... San Antonio, TX
Kendall, Keith Edward .... Harrisburg, PA
Kendall, Kevin S. .... Carlsbad, CA
Kendall, Leon
Department Of Health And Human Services,
Office of Community Services, GV
Kendall, Lloyd W., Jr. .... Oakland, CA
Kendall, Mark Alan .... Phoenix, AZ
Kendall, Mary-Ellen Alexander
Richmond, VA
Kendall, Michael C. .... Atlanta, GA
Kendall, Michael C. .... Indianapolis, IN
Kendall, Michael D. .... Boston, MA
Kendall, Michael J. .... Boston, MA
Kendall, Nancy G. .... San Diego, CA
Kendall & Osborn .... Austin, TX
Kendall, Paul F. .... Department of Justice,
Office of Justice Programs, GV
Kendall, Paul S. .... Arlington, TX
Kendall, Paul W. .... Springfield, VA
Kendall, Peter W. .... Philadelphia, PA
Kendall, Phillip A. .... Colorado Springs, CO
Kendall, Prescott J., III .... Monterey, CA
Kendall, Richard B. .... Los Angeles, CA
Kendall, Richard J. .... Washington, DC
Kendall, Robert A. .... Costa Mesa, CA
Kendall, Robert C. .... Bristol, WI
Kendall, Robert G., III .... Mobile, AL
Kendall, Robert, Jr. .... District Heights, MD
Kendall, Robert L., Jr. .... Atlanta, GA
Philadelphia, PA
Kendall, Robert T., III .... Jackson, MI
Kendall, Robert T., Jr. .... Jackson, MI
Kendall, Robert W., Jr. .... Rosemead, CA
Kendall, Rock Olney .... Laguna Beach, CA
Kendall, Ross P. .... Duluth, GA
Kendall, S. Riley .... Valdosta, GA
Kendall, Sara Schreiner .... Tacoma, WA
Kendall, Scott M., Law Offices of
Elk Grove, CA
Kendall, Scott M., Law Offices of
Sacramento, CA
Kendall, Sherry L. .... Baltimore, MD
Kendall, Steven Carroll .... Pauls Valley, OK
Kendall, Stuart O. .... Lake Oswego, OR
Kendall, Stuart W. .... Westerville, OH
Kendall, Susan Fay .... Boston, MA
Kendall, Terrence .... Austin, TX
Kendall, Thomas E. .... Claremont, CA
Kendall, Thomas W. .... Dallas, TX
Kendall, Travis L. .... Mc Connellsburg, PA
Kendall, W. Alexander, Jr .... Charlotte, NC
Kendall, Walter J., III .... Chicago, IL
Kendall, William E. .... Brenham, TX
Kendall, William F., III .... Jackson, TN
Kendall, William G. .... Columbus Grove, OH
Lima, OH
Kendall, William K. .... Salt Lake City, UT
Kendall, William R., Jr. .... Reno, NV
Kendall, Winston D. .... Boston, MA
Kendall, Wood, Lowry & Kessinger
Danville, IN
Indianapolis, IN
Kendall-Sage, Heidi .... Madison, IN
Kende, Christopher B. .... New York, NY
Kende, Lauren .... Newark, NJ
Kende, Mark .... Lansing, MI
Kendel, Walter A., Jr. .... Little Rock, AR
Kendell, Ann Holden .... Des Moines, IA
Kendell, Gary W. .... Indianola, IA
Kendell, Kenneth E.
General Services Administration,
Office of Regional Counsel, GV
Kendellen, Lindsey E. .... Hartford, CT
Kendellen, Rosalind .... Mountainside, NJ
Kender, Frank A. .... Cleveland, OH
Kender, Randall F. .... Beverly Hills, CA
Kenderdine, Henry S., Jr. .... Lancaster, PA
Kenderdine, Nancy I. .... Oklahoma City, OK
Kendermore, Drake R. .... Seattle, WA
Kendhammer & Holden LLC
Phoenix, AZ
Kendhammer, Joseph A. .... Phoenix, AZ
Kendig, A. Edw. .... Wheatland, WY
Kendig, David E. .... Costa Mesa, CA
Kendig, Dennis A. .... Los Angeles, CA
Kendig, Ellsworth H., Jr. .... Los Angeles, CA
Kendig, Holly E. .... Los Angeles, CA
Kendig, James J. .... Nashville, TN
Kendig, Julie Pauline .... Orlando, FL
Kendig, Robert E. .... Aspen, CO
Kendig & Ross .... Los Angeles, CA
Kendig, Russ .... Canton, OH
Kendig, William F., Jr. .... Shreveport, LA
Kendinger, Jackie M. .... Augusta, GA
Kendis, Allyn D. .... Cleveland, OH
Kendis, Alvin M. .... Cleveland, OH
Kendis, Harold J. .... Los Angeles, CA
Kendis, James D. .... Cleveland, OH
Kendis, L. S. .... Cleveland, OH
Kendis, Robert D. .... Cleveland, OH
Kendle, David J. .... Chicago, IL
Kendle, Louise R. .... Long Beach, CA
Kendler, Paulette .... New York, NY
Kendo, Thomas W., Jr. .... Springfield, OH
Kendra, Gary A. .... Detroit, MI
Kendree, Michael K. .... Georgetown, SC
Kendric, Christopher .... Albertson, NY
Kendrick, Alan .... Moss Beach, CA
Kendrick, Allison Roseman .... Seattle, WA
Kendrick, Anthony W. .... Ann Arbor, MI
Kendrick, Benjamin N. A. .... Arlington, VA
Kendrick, Bert M. .... Tulsa, OK
Kendrick, Carolyn .... Fallon, NV
Kendrick, Cheri A. .... Albany, OR
Kendrick, Christine .... Palo Alto, CA
Kendrick, Christopher V.
Santa Monica, CA
Kendrick, Claborn L. .... Cincinnati, OH
Kendrick, Cynthia .... Washington, DC
Kendrick, David A. .... Bainbridge, GA
Kendrick, E. Craig .... Abingdon, VA
Kendrick, Edmund H. .... Boston, MA
Kendrick, Edmund H. .... Santa Fe, NM
Kendrick, Elizabeth A. .... Long Beach, CA
Kendrick, Elwood S. .... Los Angeles, CA
Kendrick, Elwood S., Inc.
Los Angeles, CA
Kendrick, Francis W. .... Portland, OR
Kendrick, Gardner S. .... San Antonio, TX
Kendrick, Gary L. .... Minden, NV
Kendrick, Helen M. .... Hamilton, OH
Kendrick, J. Richard .... Saginaw, MI
Kendrick, J. Vincent .... Houston, TX
Kendrick & Jackson .... Irvine, CA
Kendrick, James M. .... Birmingham, AL
Kendrick, James M. .... New York, NY
Kendrick, James M. .... Conroe, TX
Kendrick, John A. .... Grinnell, IA
Kendrick, John J., Jr. .... Irvine, CA
Kendrick, John J., Jr. .... Dallas, TX
Kendrick, Joy A. .... Buffalo, NY
Kendrick, Karen L. .... Seattle, WA
Kendrick, Katherine S. .... Universal City, CA
Kendrick, Kathryn B. .... Lexington, KY
Kendrick, Ken E. .... Houston, TX
Kendrick, Kim .... Washington, DC
Kendrick, Kip B. .... Yakima, WA
Kendrick, Kristine Bradt
New Orleans, LA
Kendrick, L. Craig .... Covington, KY
Kendrick, Leslie E. .... Omaha, NE
Kendrick, Martha M. .... Washington, DC
Kendrick, Matthew J. .... Hamilton, OH
Kendrick, Michael G. .... Birmingham, AL
Kendrick, Nisbet S., III .... Atlanta, GA
Kendrick, R. Mark .... Colby, KS
Kendrick, R. Troy, Jr. .... St. Louis, MO
Kendrick, Robert A. .... Saginaw, MI
Kendrick, Robert M. .... Greenville, SC
Kendrick, Suzanne .... Brunswick, ME
Kendrick, Thomas A. .... Birmingham, AL
Kendrick, Vaiden P. .... Wilmington, NC
Kendrick, Victoria R. .... Whittier, CA
Kendrick & Wheeler, L.L.P.
New Orleans, LA
Kendrick, William J. .... Tallahassee, FL
Kendrick, William S. .... Prestonsburg, KY
Kendrick-Gaffney, Mary .... Syracuse, NY
Kendrick-Hands, Karen D. .... Detroit, MI
Kendrick-Holmes, Thomas C. .... Macon, GA
Kendricks Bordeau, P.C. .... Marquette, MI
Kendris, Thomas N. .... East Hanover, NJ
Kendt, Amy N. .... Munster, IN
Kenduck, Melvin I. .... Morganville, NJ
Kenduck, Neil G. .... Santa Ana, CA
Kendzior, Lawrence J. .... Meriden, CT
Kendziorra, Heidi C .... Cape Coral, FL
Kendziorski, Thomas F. .... Troy, MI
Kenealey, Andrea C. .... Chicago, IL
Kenealey, George M. .... Minneapolis, MN
Kenealey, George M., Ltd.
Minneapolis, MN
Kenealey, Kevin P. .... Chicago, IL
Kenealey, Robert A. .... San Francisco, CA
Keneally, Catherine P. .... Houston, TX
Keneally, James M. .... New York, NY
Keneally, Joseph Patrick .... Smithtown, NY
Keneally, Kathryn .... New York, NY
Keneally, Paul F. .... Rochester, NY
Keneally, Walter S. .... Houston, TX
Kenealy, Barry H. .... North Hollywood, CA
Kenealy, David J. .... Washington, DC
Kenealy, Deborah Bowers .... Boston, MA
Kenealy, Edmund C. .... Waltham, MA
Kenealy, Jack .... Redding, CA
Kenealy, James N., Jr.
North Hollywood, CA
Kenealy, Kathleen A. .... Washington, DC
Kenealy, William R. .... Louisville, KY
Kenedy, Jennifer A. .... Chicago, IL
Kenefick, Andrew M. .... Seattle, WA
Kenefick, Annette Sepulveda .... Houston, TX
Kenefick, Christine L. .... Troy, NY
Kenefick, James G., Jr. .... Guilford, CT
Kenefick, James L. .... Needham, MA
Kenefick, John R. .... St. Paul, MN
Kenefick, John S. .... Dallas, TX
Kenefick, Lisabritt L. .... Lowell, MA
Kenefick, Mary H. .... St. Louis, MO
Kenefick, Paul William .... Vienna, VA
Kenefick, Thomas A., III .... Springfield, MA
Kenefick, Thomas A., III, P.C., Law Offices of .... Springfield, MA
Kenefick, William F. .... Sacramento, CA
Kenegos, Joan E. .... Beverly Hills, CA
Kenehan, Edward F., Jr. .... Washington, DC
Kenehan, Grace .... Denver, CO
Kenehan & Huckaby .... Milwaukee, WI
Kenehan, J. Kenneth .... Milwaukee, WI
Kenehan, John W. .... Las Vegas, NV
Keneipp, David M. .... Los Angeles, CA
Kenelly, Orville A. .... Colorado Springs, CO
Kenemore, Max J. .... Indianapolis, IN
Kenen, Reynold L. .... Solon, OH
Kenen & Snider Co., L.P.A .... Solon, OH
Kenepaske, Linda Marie .... New York, NY
Kenerly, William D. .... Salisbury, NC
Kenerson, David R., Jr. .... New York, NY
Kenerson, Marcy L. .... Beverly Hills, CA
Kenerson, Martha Lynne .... New York, NY
Kenesey, John W. .... Deerfield, IL
Kenety, William H., V
Department of Justice,
Criminal Division, GV
Kenevan, Brooke M. .... Chicago, IL
Kenfield, Ann .... Oakland, CA
Keng, Pearl P. .... Waldorf, MD
Keng, Steven W. .... Giddings, TX
Kengla, Richard V. .... Grants Pass, OR
Kengle, Robert A. .... Department of Justice,
Civil Rights Division, GV
Kenig, Scott H. .... Chicago, IL
Kenigsberg, Jay D. .... Uniondale, NY
Kenik, Caryn M. .... Chicago, IL
Kenin, David S. .... Miami, FL
Kenin, Melissa M. .... Los Angeles, CA
Kenion, Edmund O. .... Candor, NC
Keniry, David I. .... Framingham, MA
Keniry, Shannon P. .... Washington, DC
Keniry, William H. .... Ballston Spa, NY
Keniry, William J. .... Albany, NY
Kenis, Stephen M. .... Beverly Hills, CA
Kenison, Frank E. .... Concord, NH
Kenison, Howard .... Denver, CO
Kenison, John B., Jr. .... Manchester, NH
Kenison, Katherine L. .... Ephrata, WA
Kenison, Keven K. .... Atlanta, GA
Greenville, SC
Kenison, Keven K., P.C. .... Atlanta, GA
Greenville, SC
Kenison, Ralph B., II .... Moses Lake, WA
Kenison, Rebecca Gatchet .... Seattle, WA
Kenison, Robert S.
Department of Housing and Urban
Development,
Office of General Counsel, GV
Kenison, Shane L. .... Moses Lake, WA
Kenison, William D. .... Riverside, CA
Keniston, Patrick J. .... Washington, DC
Kenkel and Associates .... Washington, DC
Kenkel, Elizabeth Anne .... Palo Alto, CA
Kenkel, James E. .... Davidsonville, MD
Kenkel, Jerry J. .... Chico, CA
Kenkel, John B. .... Washington, DC
Kenkel, John J. .... Washington, DC
Kenkel, Kenneth R. .... Lexington, KY
Kenkel, Paul J. .... Chicago, IL
Kenkel, Stephen A. .... Toledo, IA
Kenkelen, Rosemarie T. .... Philadelphia, PA
Kenlan, A. Jay .... Rutland, VT
Kenlan, Edward O., Jr. .... Millburn, NJ
Kenley, John .... Portland, OR
Kenley, John R. .... Rockville, IN
Kenley & Kenley .... Rockville, IN
Kenley, Nancy K. .... Memphis, TN
Kenley, Stephen P. .... Olathe, KS
Kenmore, Christine F. .... Los Angeles, CA
Kenn, Edward J. .... Winnetka, IL
Kenn, Stefan A. .... Vance, AL
Kenna, Bruce E. .... Manchester, NH
Kenna, David B. .... Arlington, MA
Kenna, David W. .... New York, NY
Kenna, Francis K. .... Sunnyside, NY
Kenna & Hickcox, P.C. .... Durango, CO
Kenna, Joanne .... Tampa, FL
Kenna, Johnston and Sharkey
Manchester, NH
Kenna, Joseph E. .... Atlanta, GA
Kenna, Joseph J. .... Exton, PA
Kenna, Larry C., (P.C.) .... Boston, MA
Kenna, Loretta A. .... West Palm Beach, FL
Kenna, Matthew G. .... Durango, CO
Kenna, Thomas D., Jr. .... Arlington, MA
Kenna, Timothy W., (Professional Corporation) .... Los Angeles, CA
Kennaday, Courtney McKenzie
Columbia, SC
Kennaday, Kelli M. .... Sacramento, CA
Kennady, Emmett Hubbard, III
College Station, TX
Kennalley, J. Michael .... Wichita, KS
Kennamer, Alison D. .... Brownsville, TX
Kennamer, Crystal .... Charlottesville, VA
Kennamer, Frank B. .... San Francisco, CA
Kennamer, James Rayburn
Huntsville, AL
Kennamer, John H. .... Winnie, TX
Kennamer, Stephen M. .... Scottsboro, AL
Kennan, Brian Mathieson .... Seattle, WA
Kennan, Gregory M. .... Boston, MA
Kennan, W. Gary .... Bentonville, AR
Kennar, Elizabeth Butler .... Seattle, WA
Kennard, Alan L. .... Chicago, IL
Kennard, Carlton W. .... Pittsburg, KS
Kennard, J. Todd .... Columbus, OH
Kennard, Jeffrey A. .... Overland Park, KS
Kennard, Karen L. .... San Francisco, CA
Kennard, Mary E. .... Washington, DC
Kennard, Norman James .... Harrisburg, PA
Kennard, Raeburn G. .... Salt Lake City, UT
Kennard, Robert Scott .... Sacramento, CA
Kennard, Wayne M. .... Boston, MA
Kennard, William E.
Federal Communications Commission,
Office of the Commissioners, GV
Kenneally, Colin John .... Albany, NY
Kenneally, Dori D. .... Beverly Hills, CA
Kenneally, Francis V. .... Boston, MA
Kenneally, James X. .... Medford, MA
Kenneally, Kevin G. .... Boston, MA
Kenneally, Lynn Anne .... Manasquan, NJ
Kenneally, Patrick J., Ltd. .... Chicago, IL
Kenneally, Scott W. .... Brick, NJ
Toms River, NJ
Kenneally, Susan A. .... Randolph, MA
Kenneally & Tarantino .... Glens Falls, NY
Kenneally, Terrence J. .... Cleveland, OH
Kenneally, Timothy G. .... Wellesley Hills, MA
Kenneally, William J. .... Schenectady, NY
Kennebeck, Paul F. .... Denver, CO
Kennedy, Alan J.
National Aeronautics And Space
Administration,
Office of the General Counsel, GV
Kennedy, Albert N. .... Portland, OR
Kennedy, Alexis R. .... Chicago, IL
Kennedy, Alison D. .... Jacksonville, FL
Kennedy, Alois D., Jr. .... St. Paul, MN
Kennedy, Altomease Rucker
Washington, DC
Kennedy, Alyssa T. .... Los Angeles, CA
Kennedy, Amber D. .... Indianapolis, IN
Kennedy, Andrew .... New York, NY

Kennedy, Andrew J. ....**Altoona, PA**
Kennedy, Angela Sadie-Edith
Washington, DC
Kennedy, Ann ....Gainesville, FL
Kennedy, Ann E. ....**Minneapolis, MN**
Kennedy, Ann I. ....Royal Oak, MI
Kennedy, Ann Munro ....**Newark, OH**
Kennedy, Annie Brown ....Winston-Salem, NC
Kennedy, Anthony M. ....
Supreme Court Of The United States, GV
Kennedy & Archer, LLP ....**Monterey, CA**
Kennedy, Arlene E. ....Milwaukee, WI
Kennedy, Arthur L. ....Newton, MA
Kennedy & Associates ....Uniondale, NY
Kennedy, Barbara A. ....**Dallas, TX**
Kennedy, Barbara J. ....San Francisco, CA
Kennedy, Barbara J. ....Grosse Pointe Park, MI
Kennedy, Baris & Lundy, L.L.P.
Washington, DC
Bethesda, MD
San Antonio, TX
Kennedy, Barnes ....Dallas, TX
Kennedy, Beatrice D. ....Buffalo, NY
Kennedy Berkley Yarnevich & Williamson, Chartered ....**Salina, KS**
Kennedy, Bernard J. ....**Buffalo, NY**
Kennedy, Bernard P. ....Uniondale, NY
Kennedy, Bernard T. ....Branford, CT
Kennedy, Beth B. ....Los Angeles, CA
Kennedy, Beverly K. ....Woodland Hills, CA
Kennedy, Bill ....Palo Alto, CA
Kennedy & Black, P.A. ....Denver, NC
Kennedy Bowles, P.C. ....**Portland, OR**
Kennedy, Boyd ....Austin, TX
Kennedy, Bradley ....Schofield, WI
Kennedy, Brenda P. ....Austin, TX
Kennedy, Brendan J. ....Beverly, MA
Mount Vernon, NY
Kennedy, Brian G. ....Department of Justice, Civil Division, GV
Kennedy, Brian J. ....Los Angeles, CA
Kennedy, Brian J. ....Putnam, CT
Kennedy, Brian M., (P.C.) ....Bay City, MI
Kennedy, Brian R. ....**Washington, DC**
Kennedy, Brian Richard ....Atlanta, GA
Kennedy, Brian T. ....Sea Girt, NJ
Kennedy, Brian V. ....Alexandria, VA
Kennedy, Brigid E. ....**Chicago, IL**
Kennedy, Brigid F. ....**Oklahoma City, OK**
Kennedy, Bruce ....**Amityville, NY**
Kennedy, Bruce A. ....**Clarksville, TN**
Kennedy, Bruce D. ....St. Paul, MN
Kennedy, Bruce M. ....Ithaca, NY
Kennedy, Bruce, P.C. ....**Amityville, NY**
Massapequa, NY
Kennedy, Bryce S., Jr. ....Enid, OK
Kennedy, Bryce S., P.C. ....Enid, OK
Kennedy, Byry Daniel ....Concord, NH
Kennedy, C.F., III, Co., L.P.A.
Van Wert, OH
Kennedy, Cannon & Devinney, L.L.P.
Pittsburgh, PA
Kennedy, Carolyn ....Department of Justice, Office of Justice Programs, GV
Kennedy, Carrie ....Rochester Hills, MI
Kennedy, Carrie A.S. ....West Chester, PA
Kennedy, Catherine ....Sacramento, CA
Kennedy, Catherine Chambers
Indianapolis, IN
Kennedy, C. F., III ....Van Wert, OH
Kennedy, Charles ....**Arlington, TX**
Fort Worth, TX
Kennedy, Charles A. ....**Wooster, OH**
Kennedy, Charles D. ....Houston, TX
Kennedy, Charles E. ....**Memphis, TN**
Kennedy, Charles H. ....**Washington, DC**
Kennedy, Charles J. ....Wilmington, DE
Kennedy, Charles M. ....**Cleveland, OH**
Kennedy, Charles P. ....**Westfield, NJ**
Kennedy, Charles R. ....**Wadena, MN**
Kennedy, Charles W. ....**Wadena, MN**
Kennedy, Charles W., Jr. ....Houston, TX
Kennedy, Chas. H. ....Sun Prairie, WI
Kennedy, Christian Michael ....**Raleigh, NC**
Kennedy, Christina ....**Orlando, FL**
Kennedy, Christopher L. ....Marion, IN
Kennedy, Christopher M. ....Anchorage, AK
Kennedy, Christopher M. ....**Chicago, IL**
Kennedy, Christopher N. ....Houston, TX
Kennedy, Christopher P. ....**Baltimore, MD**
Kennedy & Christopher, P.C. ....**Denver, CO**
Kennedy, Cicconetti & Knowlton, L.P.A.
Millersburg, OH
Wooster, OH
Kennedy, Coleen H. ....Wausau, WI
Kennedy, Colleen Mary ....Washington, DC
Kennedy, Collon C. ....Golden, CO
Kennedy, Cornelia G. ....Detroit, MI
Kennedy, Cornelius B. ....McLean, VA
Kennedy Covington Lobdell & Hickman, L.L.P. ....**Charlotte, NC**
Raleigh, NC
Rock Hill, SC
Kennedy, Craig A. ....**Yankton, SD**
Kennedy, Craig P. ....Costa Mesa, CA
Kennedy, Cruise, Anderson & Frey, L.L.P.
Iowa City, IA
Kennedy, Crystal M. ....**St. Louis, MO**
Kennedy, Curtis L. ....Paris, TX
Kennedy, Cynthia D. ....**Atlanta, GA**
Kennedy, Cynthia T. ....Lafayette, CO
Kennedy, Danette L. ....**Des Moines, IA**
Kennedy, Daniel H., Jr. ....Rocky Hill, CT
Kennedy, Daniel L. ....Joliet, IL
Kennedy, Daniel Lennon ....Joliet, IL
Kennedy, Daniel L. M. ....St. Paul, MN
Kennedy, Daniel M., III ....**Rockville, MD**
Kennedy, Daniel O. ....**Atlanta, GA**

Kennedy, Daryl E. ....**Redding, CA**
Kennedy, David Allen ....Dunwoody, GA
Kennedy, David C. ....Phoenix, AZ
Kennedy, David C. ....**Overland Park, KS**
Kansas City, MO
Kennedy, David C. ....Harrisburg, PA
Kennedy, David D. ....Somers, NY
Kennedy, David D. ....**Oklahoma City, OK**
Kennedy, David H. ....**Palo Alto, CA**
Kennedy, David J. ....**Minneapolis, MN**
Kennedy, David L. ....Melbourne, FL
Kennedy, David L. ....**Troy, MI**
Kennedy, David M. ....Sherman, TX
Kennedy, David R. ....Norton, OH
Kennedy, David R. ....Hermitage, TN
Kennedy, David S. ....Memphis, TN
Kennedy, David W. ....Chico, CA
Kennedy, David W. ....Wichita, KS
Kennedy, Davis & Hodge, P.C.
Atlanta, GA
Kennedy, Dawn M. ....Phoenix, AZ
Kennedy, Deborah D. ....**Fairfax, VA**
Kennedy, Deborah McKay ....Chicago, IL
Kennedy, Denise H. ....North Miami, FL
Kennedy, Denise W. ....**Denver, CO**
Kennedy, Dennis J. ....Hauppauge, NY
Kennedy, Dennis L. ....**Las Vegas, NV**
Kennedy, Dennis M. ....St. Louis, MO
Kennedy, Dennis M. ....Alexandria, VA
Kennedy, Dermot F. ....Quakertown, PA
Kennedy, Deseriee A. ....Philadelphia, PA
Kennedy, Diane Hubbard ....Indianapolis, IN
Kennedy & Dolan ....Silver Spring, MD
Kennedy, Don M., (P.C.) ....**Boston, MA**
Kennedy, Don W. ....Kansas City, MO
Kennedy, Donald A., Jr. ....Estill, SC
Kennedy, Donald C. ....Los Angeles, CA
Kennedy, Donald D., Jr. ....Valley Forge, PA
Kennedy, Donald G. ....**St. Louis, MO**
Kennedy, Donald J. ....Palo Alto, CA
Kennedy, Donald J. ....Lansing, MI
Kennedy, Donald J. ....**New York, NY**
Kennedy, Donald M. ....**New York, NY**
Kennedy, Donald P. ....Santa Ana, CA
Kennedy, Donald R. ....Redding, CA
Kennedy, Donald R. ....Westfield, NJ
Kennedy, Dorian B. ....**Atlanta, GA**
Kennedy, Douglas M. ....**Columbus, OH**
Kennedy, Douglas M. ....**Corpus Christi, TX**
Kennedy, Douglas R. ....Poplar Bluff, MO
Kennedy, Douglas S. ....Minneapolis, MN
Kennedy, E. Craig ....**Wichita, KS**
Kennedy, E. Richard ....Montville, NJ
Kennedy, E. Stanton ....Bridgeport, CT
Kennedy, Edward G. ....Fairmont, WV
Kennedy, Edward I. ....Tucson, AZ
Kennedy, Edward J. ....Lafayette, CO
Kennedy, Edward J. ....Melbourne, FL
Kennedy, Edward J. ....Albany, NY
Kennedy, Edward J., III ....**Birmingham, AL**
Kennedy, Edward L. ....Lafayette, IN
Kennedy, Edward M. ....Boston, MA
Kennedy, Edward M., Jr. ....**New Haven, CT**
Kennedy, Edwin A. ....**Cleveland, OH**
Kennedy, Eileen ....**Philadelphia, PA**
Kennedy, Eileen P. ....**San Jose, CA**
Kennedy, Elena F. ....Treasury Department, Office of Regulations and Rulings, GV
Kennedy, Elizabeth Gregg
Des Moines, IA
Kennedy, Elizabeth Page ....Anchorage, AK
Kennedy, Ellen R. ....**Washington, DC**
Kennedy, Erika L. ....**Portland, ME**
Kennedy, Erin J. ....**Rochelle Park, NJ**
Kennedy, Eugene M. ....Fort Lauderdale, FL
Kennedy & Evans, L.L.C.
Colorado Springs, CO
Kennedy, Faye Collier ....Seattle, WA
Kennedy, Florynce R. ....New York, NY
Kennedy, Francis H., Jr. ....St. Louis, MO
Kennedy, Francis X. ....Rochester, NY
Kennedy, Frank E. ....Sibley, IA
Kennedy, Frank R. ....**Denver, CO**
Kennedy, Frank S. ....**Shreveport, LA**
Kennedy, Franklin M. ....**Dallas, TX**
Kennedy, Fred ....Boise, ID
Kennedy, Fred M., (P.C.) ....Augusta, GA
Kennedy, Frederick, III ....West Point, NY
Kennedy, Fuller & Goodson
South Daytona, FL
Kennedy, Fulton, Koontz & Farinash
Chattanooga, TN
Kennedy, Galvin B. ....**Houston, TX**
Kennedy, Gene D. ....**Portland, OR**
Kennedy, Geoffrey W. ....Cuyahoga Falls, OH
Kennedy, George C., Jr. ....Greenville, GA
Kennedy, George L., Jr. ....Jewett City, CT
Kennedy, George W. ....San Jose, CA
Kennedy, Gerald A. ....**Chicago, IL**
Kennedy, Gerald A. ....Minneapolis, MN
Kennedy, Gerald M., (P.C.) ....Stockton, CA
Kennedy, Gerald P. ....**San Diego, CA**
Kennedy, Gina B. ....**Chicago, IL**
Kennedy, Glen P. ....**New York, NY**
Kennedy, Grace C. ....Norristown, PA
Kennedy, Grafton S. ....Dover, NH
Kennedy & Graven, Chartered
Minneapolis, MN
Kennedy, Gregory D. ....New York, NY
Kennedy, Gregory G. ....**Los Angeles, CA**
Kennedy, Gregory L. ....**Jackson, MS**
Kennedy, Guy L., Jr. ....Clearwater, FL
Kennedy, Gwendolyn Thomas
Montgomery, AL
Kennedy, H. Mark ....Montgomery, AL
Kennedy, Harold L., III ....Winston-Salem, NC
Kennedy, Harold L., Jr. ....Winston-Salem, NC

Kennedy, Harris, Miller, Ferguson & Jones
Seattle, WA
Kennedy, Harry ....**Minneapolis, MN**
Kennedy, Harvey J., Jr. ....Barnesville, GA
Kennedy, Harvey L. ....Winston-Salem, NC
Kennedy, Heather L. ....St. Louis, MO
Kennedy, Helen M. ....Seattle, WA
Kennedy, Henry H., Jr. ....
United States District Court For The District Of Columbia, GV
Kennedy, Henry J. ....**New York, NY**
Kennedy, Herbert J. ....Garden City, NY
Kennedy, Hunter L. ....Honolulu, HI
Kennedy, J. Christopher ....**Los Angeles, CA**
Kennedy, J. Donald ....Rockville Centre, NY
Kennedy, J. Joseph ....Norcross, GA
Kennedy, J. Kelly ....Winter Haven, FL
Kennedy, J. Steven ....Pasadena, CA
Kennedy, J. Terry ....Cincinnati, OH
Kennedy, J. Todd ....Rockford, IL
Kennedy, Jack E. ....Denver, CO
Kennedy, Jack E. ....Reno, NV
Kennedy, Jack G. ....Sherman, TX
Kennedy, Jack L. ....**Portland, OR**
Kennedy, Jack S. ....**Hartford, CT**
Kennedy, James A. ....Freehold, NJ
Kennedy, James B. ....**St. Louis, MO**
Kennedy, James B. ....El Paso, TX
Kennedy, James C. ....**New York, NY**
Kennedy, James C. ....**Cincinnati, OH**
Kennedy, James C., III ....Los Alamos, NM
Kennedy, James D. ....**Russellville, AR**
Kennedy, James E. ....Pittsburgh, PA
Kennedy, James E. ....Seattle, WA
Kennedy, James E., Jr. ....St. Petersburg, FL
Kennedy, James G. ....**Charleston, SC**
Kennedy, James G. ....Laurens, SC
Kennedy, James H. ....San Diego, CA
Kennedy, James J. ....New Holland, PA
Kennedy, James J., III ....**Tampa, FL**
Kennedy, James L. ....Bloomington, IN
Kennedy, James L., Jr. ....**Ketchum, ID**
Kennedy, James L., Jr. ....**Dallas, TX**
Kennedy, James M. ....San Rafael, CA
Kennedy, James M. ....**Lexington, KY**
Kennedy, James M. ....Albuquerque, NM
Kennedy, James M. ....**Portland, OR**
Kennedy, James M., II
Westlake Village, CA
Kennedy, James M., III ....San Francisco, CA
Kennedy, James P. ....Buffalo, NY
Kennedy, James P. ....**Columbus, OH**
Kennedy, James R., Jr. ....St. Petersburg, FL
Kennedy, James S. ....Arlington, TX
Kennedy, James T. ....Alameda, CA
Kennedy, James W. ....Chicago, IL
Kennedy, James W. ....Toms River, NJ
Kennedy, James W. ....**New York, NY**
Kennedy, Jane M. ....**Tampa, FL**
Kennedy, Janice ....Columbus, OH
Kennedy, Janice M., Co., L.P.A.
Columbus, OH
Kennedy, Jason L. ....**Chicago, IL**
Kennedy, Jay A. ....**Detroit, MI**
Kennedy, Jay P. ....**Indianapolis, IN**
Kennedy, Jeanne E. ....**Victorville, CA**
Kennedy, Jeff ....**Wichita, KS**
Kennedy, Jeffrey G. ....Latham, NY
Kennedy, Jeffrey W. ....**New Haven, CT**
Kennedy, Jeffrey W. ....Eagan, MN
Kennedy, Jennifer L. ....Sacramento, CA
Kennedy, Jerry R. ....Salt Lake City, UT
Kennedy, Jessica W. ....St. Charles, MO
Kennedy, Jill M. ....Oklahoma City, OK
Kennedy, Joan Theresa ....Boston, MA
Kennedy, Joe R. ....Muskogee, OK
Kennedy, John ....Wheaton, IL
Kennedy, John B. ....**Washington, DC**
Kennedy, John B. ....**New York, NY**
Kennedy, John C. ....West Orange, NJ
Kennedy, John C. ....**New York, NY**
Kennedy, John E. ....Peekskill, NY
Kennedy, John E. ....**Houston, TX**
Kennedy, John F. ....**Chicago, IL**
Kennedy, John F. ....Trenton, NJ
Kennedy, John F. ....**Santa Fe, NM**
Kennedy, John F. ....**Wilkes-Barre, PA**
Kennedy, John F., Jr. ....Baltimore, MD
Kennedy, John Fitzgerald ....**Miami, FL**
Kennedy, John Fitzgerald ....Silver Spring, MD
Kennedy, John Flanders ....**Macon, GA**
Kennedy, John Francis, Law Offices of
Gig Harbor, WA
Kennedy, John H. ....Forty Fort, PA
Kennedy, John I. ....Monsey, NY
Kennedy, John J. ....New Canaan, CT
Ridgefield, CT
Kennedy, John J. ....Bloomfield, NJ
Kennedy, John J. ....New York, NY
Kennedy, John J., Jr. ....**New Haven, CT**
Kennedy, John M. ....Venice, CA
Kennedy, John M. ....New Paltz, NY
Kennedy, John M., Jr. ....**St. Paul, MN**
Kennedy, John N. ....Kennett Square, PA
Kennedy, John Neely ....Baton Rouge, LA
Kennedy, John P.
Department of Housing and Urban Development, Office of General Counsel, GV
Kennedy, John P. ....Garden City, NY
Kennedy, John P. ....Columbus, OH
Kennedy, John P. ....Glendale, WI
Kennedy, John Paul ....**Salt Lake City, UT**
Kennedy, John R. ....San Jose, CA
Kennedy, John R. ....Denver, CO
Kennedy, John R. ....Canandaigua, NY
Kennedy, John S. ....**Cherry Hill, NJ**
Kennedy, John S. ....York, PA

Kennedy, John T. ....**Denver, CO**
Kennedy, John T. ....Chicago, IL
Kennedy, John T. ....Chicago, IL
Kennedy, John T., III ....**Sacramento, CA**
Kennedy, John T., The Injury Law Offices of
Stuart, FL
Kennedy, John W. ....Oakland, CA
Kennedy, John W. ....**Columbus, OH**
Kennedy, John W. ....Austin, TX
Kennedy, John W., Jr. ....San Bernardino, CA
Kennedy, Johnson, D'Elia & Gillooly
New Haven, CT
Kennedy, Jon L. ....Wakefield, MA
Kennedy, Jonathan M. ....**San Francisco, CA**
Kennedy, Jos. W. ....Schenectady, NY
Kennedy, Joseph B. ....Washington, DC
Kennedy, Joseph C., Jr., (P.C.)
Boston, MA
Kennedy, Joseph J., IV ....Pittsburgh, PA
Kennedy, Joseph M. ....Hartford, CT
Kennedy, Joseph M. ....**Hackensack, NJ**
Kennedy, Joseph M., P.C., The Law Offices
Hartford, CT
Kennedy, Joseph P. ....**Albuquerque, NM**
Kennedy, Joseph Patrick ....Laurel, MD
Kennedy, Joseph T. ....**New York, NY**
Kennedy, Joseph T. ....The Woodlands, TX
Kennedy, Joseph W. ....**Wichita, KS**
Kennedy, Judith R. ....**Lafayette, LA**
Kennedy, Julia S. ....Fort Wayne, IN
Kennedy, Julie M. ....**Los Angeles, CA**
San Francisco, CA
Kennedy, Karen ....Corpus Christi, TX
Kennedy, Karen C. ....**Albuquerque, NM**
Kennedy, Karen J. ....Valrico, FL
Kennedy, Karen S. ....**New York, NY**
Kennedy, Katharine B. ....Los Angeles, CA
Kennedy, Katherine E. ....**St. Paul, MN**
Kennedy, Katherine See ....**Seattle, WA**
Kennedy, Kathlin Persinger ....Seattle, WA
Kennedy, Kathy ....Philadelphia, PA
Kennedy, Kay Karen ....Wynnewood, OK
Kennedy, Keith S. ....Cleveland, OH
Kennedy, Keith W. ....Dallas, TX
Kennedy, Kendra M. ....**Plano, TX**
Kennedy & Kennedy ....Marietta, GA
Kennedy and Kennedy ....Lawler, IA
New Hampton, IA
Kennedy & Kennedy ....Poplar Bluff, MO
Kennedy & Kennedy ....Bloomfield, NJ
Kennedy & Kennedy Co., A Legal Professional Association ....Cincinnati, OH
Kennedy, Kennedy, Kennedy and Kennedy
Winston-Salem, NC
Kennedy & Kennedy LLP ....**Portland, OR**
Kennedy & Kennedy, P.C. ....Lafayette, CO
Kennedy, Kenneth H., Jr ....Hartford, CT
Kennedy, Kenneth K., Jr. ....San Jose, CA
Kennedy, Kermit B.
Securities and Exchange Commission, Office of the General Counsel, GV
Kennedy, Kerry A. ....New York, NY
Kennedy, Kerry E. ....Redwood City, CA
Kennedy, Kevin ....Colchester, CT
Kennedy, Kevin ....Buffalo, NY
Kennedy, Kevin C. ....East Lansing, MI
Kennedy, Kevin C. ....**Clarksville, TN**
Kennedy, Kevin E. ....Neptune, NJ
Kennedy, Kevin G. ....San Diego, CA
Kennedy, Kevin J. ....**New Hampton, IA**
Kennedy, Kevin J. ....Mason, MI
Kennedy, Kevin J. ....**Minneapolis, MN**
Kennedy, Kevin M. ....**New Haven, CT**
Kennedy, Kevin O. ....Rye, NY
Kennedy, Kevin P. ....**Menlo Park, CA**
San Francisco, CA
Kennedy, Kevin P. ....**San Diego, CA**
Kennedy, Kevin P. ....Topeka, KS
Kennedy, Kevin P. ....**Rockville, MD**
Kennedy, Kevin P. ....**San Antonio, TX**
Kennedy, Kevin T. ....**Detroit, MI**
Kennedy, Kevin W. ....**Little Rock, AR**
Kennedy, Kim A. ....Jackson, MI
Kennedy, Kirk A. ....**Dallas, TX**
Kennedy, Kobi J. ....Charlotte, NC
Kennedy, Kurt M. ....Tulsa, OK
Kennedy, L. Neal ....**Detroit, MI**
Kennedy, Laura H. ....**Phoenix, AZ**
Kennedy, Laura K. ....**Washington, DC**
Kennedy, Laurie Schnarrs ....Harrisburg, PA
Kennedy Law Firm, The ....**Clarksville, TN**
Nashville, TN
Kennedy, Lawrence J. ....**New York, NY**
Kennedy, Lawrence X. ....Goshen, NY
Kennedy, Leonard Jervey
Washington, DC
Kennedy, LeRoy E. ....Shorewood, WI
Kennedy, Lillian B. ....Auburn, ME
Kennedy Lillis Schmidt & English
Newark, NJ
New York, NY
Kennedy, Linda D. ....**Chicago, IL**
Kennedy, Lionel ....Department of Justice, Office of Intelligence Policy and Review, GV
Kennedy, Lisa S. ....**Dallas, TX**
Kennedy, Loan B. ....**West Palm Beach, FL**
Kennedy, Loretto M. ....**Chicago, IL**
Kennedy, Louis L. ....Elmont, NY
Kennedy and Lucadamo, P.C. ....Hazleton, PA
Kennedy, Lyndal R. ....Vidalia, GA
Kennedy, Madeleine Maney ....**Albany, NY**
Kennedy, Marc C. ....San Juan Capistrano, CA
Kennedy, Marc J. ....**Dallas, TX**
Kennedy, Margaret A. ....**Cleveland, OH**
Kennedy, Maria I. ....**Nutley, NJ**
Kennedy, Maria Savasta ....Carrboro, NC
Kennedy, Marianna R. ....**Newburgh, NY**

Kennedy, Marianne E. ... Arlington, VT
Kennedy, Marie C. ... Detroit, MI
Kennedy, Mark A. ... Poplar Bluff, MO
Kennedy, Mark F. ... Denver, CO
Kennedy, Mark P. ... Weymouth, MA
Kennedy, Mark S. ... Dallas, TX
Kennedy, Mark W. ... Phoenix, AZ
Kennedy, Marsha C. ... Charlotte, NC
Kennedy, Martin J. ... Chicago, IL
Kennedy, Mary C. ... Washington, DC
Kennedy, Mary J. ... Springfield, MA
Kennedy, Mary Jane ... Weston, MA
Kennedy, Mary Katherine ... Houston, TX
Kennedy, Mary Kay ... San Francisco, CA
Kennedy, Mary L. ... Sacramento, CA
Kennedy, Mary Louise ... Providence, RI
Kennedy, Mary-Ellen ... Boston, MA
Kennedy, MaryGay ... Topsham, ME
Kennedy, Matthew ... Boca Raton, FL
Kennedy, Matthew J. ... Houston, TX
Kennedy, Matthew S.
San Luis Obispo, CA
Santa Maria, CA
Kennedy, Mavis W. ... St. Louis, MO
Kennedy, Max C. ... Charlottesville, VA
Kennedy, Maxine D. ... High Point, NC
Kennedy, Melanie Ann ... Owensboro, KY
Kennedy, Melina Maniatis
Indianapolis, IN
Kennedy, Melvin D. ... St. Louis, MO
Kennedy, Melvin L. ... Oakland, CA
Kennedy, Michael ... New York, NY
Kennedy, Michael A. ... Bucyrus, OH
Kennedy, Michael A. ... Austin, TX
Kennedy, Michael B. ... Rigby, ID
Kennedy, Michael D. ... Troy, MI
Kennedy, Michael D. ... Portland, OR
Kennedy, Michael E. ... Norwich, CT
Kennedy, Michael E. ... Washington, DC
Kennedy, Michael Edwin ... Pittsburgh, PA
Kennedy, Michael F. ... Hempstead, NY
Kennedy, Michael H. ... Mankato, MN
Kennedy, Michael J. ... Palo Alto, CA
Kennedy, Michael J.
West Palm Beach, FL
Kennedy, Michael J. ... Chicago, IL
Kennedy, Michael J. ... St. Francisville, LA
Kennedy, Michael J. ... Cherry Hill, NJ
Kennedy, Michael K. ... Phoenix, AZ
Kennedy, Michael K. ... Lawler, IA
New Hampton, IA
Kennedy, Michael P. ... Columbus, OH
Kennedy, Michael Patrick ... Menlo Park, CA
Kennedy, Michael S. ... Shelby, NC
Kennedy, Michael W. ... Iowa City, IA
Kennedy, Michael William ... Omaha, NE
Kennedy, Michele C. ... Monterey, CA
Kennedy, Michelle M. ... Greenfield, IN
Kennedy, Minshew, Campbell and Morris, P.C.
Sherman, TX
Kennedy, Moira White ... Santa Barbara, CA
Kennedy, Morgan ... New York, NY
Kennedy, Moulton & Wells, P.C.
Albuquerque, NM
Kennedy, Murry D. ... Houston, TX
Kennedy, Nancy E. ... Seattle, WA
Kennedy, Nancy Meissner ... Milwaukee, WI
Kennedy, Neal A. ... Marble Falls, TX
Kennedy, Neal R. ... Oklahoma City, OK
Kennedy, Nervig & Carlisle, LLP
Wadena, MN
Kennedy, Nicholas L., III ... Clovis, NM
Kennedy, Nicole Brown ... Dallas, TX
Kennedy, Noah ... Corpus Christi, TX
Kennedy, Nolan M. ... Monterey, CA
Kennedy, O'Brien, McCormack & Mulcahey
Scranton, PA
Kennedy, Olywn E. ... Portland, OR
Kennedy, P. Todd ... West Palm Beach, FL
Kennedy, Pamela D. ... Albuquerque, NM
Kennedy, Pat Winston
Winston-Salem, NC
Kennedy, Patricia A. ... Reseda, CA
Kennedy, Patricia A. ... Charleston, SC
Kennedy, Patricia J. ... Philadelphia, PA
Kennedy, Patricia M. ... Ithaca, NY
Kennedy, Patricia M., (P.A.) ... Miami, FL
Kennedy, Patrick ... McLean, VA
Kennedy, Patrick C. ... Berkeley, CA
Kennedy, Patrick D. ... Trenton, NJ
Kennedy, Patrick F. ... Seattle, WA
Kennedy, Patrick G. ... Daytona Beach, FL
Kennedy, Patrick H. ... Silver City, NM
Kennedy, Patrick J. ... Orlando, FL
Kennedy, Patrick J. ... Boston, MA
Kennedy, Patrick J. ... San Antonio, TX
Kennedy, Patrick J., Jr. ... San Antonio, TX
Kennedy, Patrick L. ... East Hartford, CT
Kennedy, Paul E. ... Sharon, MA
Kennedy, Paul E. ... Dallas, TX
Kennedy, Paul H. ... Yorktown Heights, NY
Kennedy, Paul J. ... Phoenix, AZ
Kennedy, Paul J. ... Washington, DC
Kennedy, Paul J. ... Albuquerque, NM
Kennedy, Paul J. ... Philadelphia, PA
Kennedy, Paula E. ... Bethpage, NY
Kennedy, Peter C. ... Philadelphia, PA
Kennedy, Peter D. ... Austin, TX
Kennedy, Peter J. ... Los Angeles, CA
Kennedy, Peter Lawson ... Boston, MA
Providence, RI
Kennedy, Philip H. ... Baton Rouge, LA
Kennedy & Price, Attorneys ... Columbia, SC
Kennedy, Purdy, Hoeffel & Gernert
Bucyrus, OH
Kennedy, Quentin J. ... Montvale, NJ
Kennedy, R. Eric ... Cleveland, OH
Kennedy, R. Michael ... South Daytona, FL

Kennedy, R. Michael ... Cherry Hill, NJ
Kennedy, Ralph E. ... St. Louis, MO
Kennedy, Ralph W., Jr. ... Alexandria, LA
Kennedy, Randy M. ... Bristol, TN
Kennedy, Raoul D. ... San Francisco, CA
Kennedy, Reba Bennett ... San Antonio, TX
Kennedy, Reid G. ... Marietta, GA
Kennedy, Reid W. ... Marietta, GA
Kennedy, Rhonda W. ... Portland, OR
Kennedy, Richard C. ... Chattanooga, TN
Kennedy, Richard D. ... Ironton, OH
Kennedy, Richard D. ... Lisbon, OH
Kennedy, Richard Dudley ... Wise, VA
Kennedy, Richard J. ... Colorado Springs, CO
Kennedy, Richard J. ... Sterling, VA
Kennedy, Richard L. ... Denver, NC
Kennedy, Richard M., III ... Columbia, SC
Kennedy, Richard M., Jr. ... Columbia, SC
Kennedy, Richard R. ... Lafayette, LA
Kennedy, Richard R., A Professional Law Corporation ... Lafayette, LA
Kennedy, Richard T. ... Pittsburgh, PA
Kennedy, Richelle S. ... Boston, MA
Kennedy, Rick W. ... Buffalo, NY
Kennedy, Robert A. ... Westlake Village, CA
Kennedy, Robert A. ... Crandon, WI
Kennedy, Robert A. P., Jr. ... Crandon, WI
Kennedy, Robert B. ... Atlanta, GA
Kennedy, Robert Dunn ... Houston, TX
Kennedy, Robert E. ... Woodbury, NJ
Kennedy, Robert E. ... El Paso, TX
Kennedy, Robert F. ... New York, NY
Kennedy, Robert G. ... Columbus, OH
Kennedy, Robert G., Co., L.P.A.
Columbus, OH
Kennedy, Robert H. ... Tallahassee, FL
Kennedy, Robert J. ... Chicago, IL
Kennedy, Robert J. ... Oak Lawn, IL
Kennedy, Robert, Jr ... Shreveport, LA
Kennedy, Robert L. ... Kansas City, KS
Kennedy, Robert L. ... Colfax, LA
Kennedy, Robert L., III ... Tallahassee, FL
Kennedy, Robert M. ... St. Louis, MO
Kennedy, Robert M. ... Dallas, TX
Kennedy, Robert M., Jr. ... Washington, DC
Kennedy, Robert P. ... Merrillville, IN
Kennedy, Robert S. ... San Diego, CA
Kennedy, Robert S., Jr. ... Monroe, LA
Kennedy, Robert T. ... Scottsdale, AZ
Kennedy, Robert T. ... Tampa, FL
Kennedy, Robert T. ... Seattle, WA
Kennedy, Robert V. ... Okeechobee, FL
Kennedy, Robert W., Jr. ... Pittsburgh, PA
Kennedy, Robin B. ... Menlo Park, CA
Kennedy, Robin M. ... Cleveland, OH
Kennedy, Robin S. ... Dallas, TX
Kennedy, Roderick T. ... Albuquerque, NM
Kennedy, Roger ... Sunnyvale, CA
Kennedy, Roger C. ... New York, NY
Kennedy, Roger P. ... Sunnyvale, CA
Kennedy, Ronald Dane ... Amarillo, TX
Kennedy, Ronald F. ... Buffalo, NY
Kennedy, Rosalie O. ... Moraga, CA
Kennedy, Ross D. ... Dallas, TX
Kennedy, Ruth A. ... Seattle, WA
Kennedy, S. Craig ... Selmer, TN
Kennedy, Sam D. ... Columbia, TN
Kennedy, Sandra Denise
Fort Lauderdale, FL
Kennedy, Sandra G. ... Orange, CA
Kennedy, Sara L. ... Brooklyn, NY
Kennedy, Sarah A. ... Chicago, IL
Kennedy and Schum ... Spencerport, NY
Kennedy Schwartz & Cure ... New York, NY
Kennedy, Scott A. ... San Diego, CA
Kennedy, Scott F. ... Pittsburgh, PA
Kennedy, Sean A. ... Buffalo, NY
Kennedy, Sean F. ... Philadelphia, PA
Kennedy, Sean P. ... Jackson, MI
Kennedy, Sharon ... Kansas City, MO
Kennedy, Sharon A. ... Jacksonville, FL
Kennedy, Sharon C. ... Santa Barbara, CA
Kennedy, Sharon C. ... New York, NY
Kennedy, Shayne ... Costa Mesa, CA
Kennedy, Sheila Berner ... Kenilworth, IL
Kennedy, Stanley W. ... Olyphant, PA
Kennedy, Stefan P. ... San Jose, CA
Kennedy, Stephen A. ... Dallas, TX
Kennedy, Stephen C. ... Lockport, NY
Kennedy, Stephen J. ... Oakland, CA
Kennedy, Stephen J. ... Seattle, WA
Kennedy, Stephen M. ... New York, NY
Kennedy, Steven C. ... Minneapolis, MN
Kennedy, Steven E. ... Dallas, TX
Kennedy, Steven L. ... Greenwood, IN
Kennedy, Steven Marshall
San Bernardino, CA
Kennedy, Steven P. ... Munster, IN
Kennedy Stoeckl & Martin, P.C.
Buffalo, NY
Kennedy, Susan D. ... Orlando, FL
Kennedy, Susan D. ... New York, NY
Kennedy, Susan Lorraine ... Chicago, IL
Kennedy, Susan Lynn
Department Of Veterans Affairs, Board of Veterans Appeals, GV
Kennedy, Susan Marie ... Philadelphia, PA
Kennedy, Susan S. ... Lexington, KY
Kennedy, Suzanne E. ... Minneapolis, MN
Kennedy, T. Michael ... Boulder, CO
Kennedy, T. Richard ... New York, NY
Kennedy, Terance P. ... Philadelphia, PA
Kennedy, Terence M. ... Cleveland, OH
Kennedy, Terence P. ... Schaumburg, IL
Kennedy, Teresa T. ... Atlanta, GA
Kennedy, Terrence, Jr. ... Chicago, IL
Kennedy, Terri Jo ... Tallahassee, FL
Kennedy, Theresa M. ... Houston, TX

Kennedy, Thomas A. ... Bolingbrook, IL
Kennedy, Thomas A. ... Baltimore, MD
Kennedy, Thomas D. ... Houston, TX
Kennedy, Thomas E., III ... East St. Louis, IL
Kennedy, Thomas F. ... San Francisco, CA
Kennedy, Thomas G. ... Telluride, CO
Kennedy, Thomas H. ... Palo Alto, CA
New York, NY
Kennedy, Thomas H. ... Annandale, VA
Kennedy, Thomas J. ... Phoenix, AZ
Kennedy, Thomas J. ... Salina, KS
Kennedy, Thomas J., (A P.L.C.)
Glendale, CA
Kennedy, Thomas L. ... Colorado Springs, CO
Kennedy, Thomas L. ... Hazleton, PA
Kennedy, Thomas M. ... Chicago, IL
Kennedy, Thomas M. ... New York, NY
Kennedy, Thomas P. ... Providence, RI
Kennedy, Thomas Ray ... Denver, CO
Kennedy, Thomas V. ... Louisville, KY
Kennedy, Thomas W. ... Montclair, NJ
Kennedy, Thos. A. ... Portland, OR
Kennedy, Thos. M. ... Cleveland, OH
Kennedy, Tia M. ... Birmingham, AL
Kennedy, Timothy F. ... Philadelphia, PA
Kennedy, Timothy J. ... Indianapolis, IN
Kennedy, Timothy J. ... Cedar Rapids, IA
Kennedy, Timothy J. ... Mission Woods, KS
Kennedy, Timothy M. ... Cleveland, OH
Kennedy, Timothy P. ... Bethel, CT
Trumbull, CT
Kennedy, Timothy W. ... Indianapolis, IN
Kennedy, Todd E. ... Las Vegas, NV
Kennedy, Tracey A. ... Los Angeles, CA
Kennedy, Tricia E. ... Dallas, TX
Kennedy, Trlica Lanette Cosby
Houston, TX
Kennedy, Vekeno ... San Diego, CA
Kennedy, Victor N. ... Des Moines, IA
Kennedy, W. James ... Yakima, WA
Kennedy, Wade M. ... Charlotte, NC
Kennedy, Walbert H. ... Parsons, TN
Kennedy, Walker, III ... Salt Lake City, UT
Kennedy, Wallace W. ... West Palm Beach, FL
Kennedy, Walter J. ... Boulder, CO
Kennedy, Walter J., Jr. ... Lenexa, KS
Kennedy, Walter R. ... Harrison, NJ
Kennedy, Walter W., III ... Pell City, AL
Kennedy, Watts, Arellano & Ricks LLP
Portland, OR
Kennedy, Wendy S. ... Hartford, CT
Kennedy, Wesley G.S. ... Chicago, IL
Kennedy, William ... McLean, VA
Kennedy, William C. ... Riverside, CA
Kennedy, William C. ... Pittsburgh, PA
Kennedy, William D. ... Ironton, OH
Kennedy, William D. ... Paoli, PA
Kennedy, William E. ... Grosse Pointe, MI
Kennedy, William E., III ... Manhattan, KS
Kennedy, William F. ... Washington, DC
Kennedy, William F., Jr. ... Lafayette, IN
Kennedy, William F., Jr. ... Boston, MA
Kennedy, William H. ... Tuscaloosa, AL
Kennedy, William H., III ... Little Rock, AR
Kennedy, William H., Jr. ... Roanoke, VA
Kennedy, William J. ... Anaheim, CA
Kennedy, William J. ... Philadelphia, PA
Kennedy, William J., Jr. ... North Haven, CT
Kennedy, William K. ... Buffalo, NY
Kennedy, William M. ... Lexington, KY
Kennedy, William P. ... New York, NY
Kennedy, William R. ... Minneapolis, MN
Kennedy, William Thomas ... Quincy, MA
Kennedy, William V. ... Bloomfield, NJ
Kennedy, Willie May Alexander
Winston-Salem, NC
Kennedy, Wm. John ... New York, NY
Kennedy, Wm. R. ... Toledo, OH
Kennedy-Bowden, Ansley
West Palm Beach, FL
Kennedy-Calo, Sally Marie ... Boston, MA
Kennedy-Gurnee, Elizabeth ... Fayetteville, NC
Kennedy III, Charles S. ... Detroit, MI
Kennedy-Luczsak, Kathleen ... Riverwoods, IL
Kennedy-Rogoza, Deborah
Grand Island, NY
Kennedy-Voise, Sarah J. ... Perry, OK
Kenneff, John A. ... Millersville, PA
Kennel, Peter M. ... Houston, TX
Kennell, James S. ... Washington, DC
Kennelly, Amy Rankin ... Indianapolis, IN
Kennelly, Anne Marie ... Palo Alto, CA
Kennelly, Beth A. ... New York, NY
Kennelly, Cheryl C. ... Atlanta, GA
Kennelly, Clyde B. ... Richmond, TX
Kennelly, Cornelius R. ... Anchorage, AK
Kennelly, David L., Law Offices of
Laguna Beach, CA
Kennelly, Dennis Lawrence, Law Office of
Menlo Park, CA
Kennelly, Donald P. ... New York, NY
Kennelly, Edward James ... New York, NY
Kennelly, Ellen M. ... New York, NY
Kennelly, Eugene J. ... Wheaton, IL
Kennelly, John B. ... Hartford, CT
Kennelly, John G. ... Detroit, MI
Kennelly, John J. ... Chicago, IL
Kennelly, John J. ... Mattituck, NY
Kennelly, John J. ... Rutland, VT
Kennelly, John M. ... Oak Park, IL
Kennelly, John P. ... Truckee, CA
Kennelly, John R. ... Fargo, ND
Kennelly, John Sherman
Fort Lauderdale, FL
Kennelly, Joseph P., Sr. ... Chicago, IL
Kennelly, Katherine T. ... San Francisco, CA
Kennelly, Lawrence W. ... Newton, NJ
Kennelly, Martin J., Sr. ... Chicago, IL

Kennelly, Mary E. ... Madison, WI
Kennelly, Matthew F. ... Chicago, IL
Kennelly, Nancy M. ... Chicago, IL
Kennelly, Sandy Sargent ... Madison, WI
Kennelly, Thomas A. ... Washington, DC
Kennemer, John Maclin ... Tuscumbia, AL
Kennemer, R. Victor, III ... Wewoka, OK
Kennemore, Jas. E. ... Memphis, TN
Kennemuth, Jerald ... Cleveland, OH
Kenner, Brian T. ... Boston, MA
Kenner, Carol J. ... Boston, MA
Kenner, David E. ... Encino, CA
Kenner, David V. ... Kansas City, MO
Kenner, Frank J. ... New Orleans, LA
Kenner, Harris P. ... Minot, ND
Kenner, James & Kavanaugh, P.C.
Kansas City, MO
Kenner, Julia Beck ... Austin, TX
Kenner, Lynn E. ... New York, NY
Kenner, Maurice ... Decatur, GA
Kenner, Nancy E. ... Kansas City, MO
Kenner, Phillip L. ... Akron, OH
Kenner & Speck, LC ... Kansas City, MO
Kenner, Spencer L. ... Woodland, CA
Kenner Sturdevant Peterson & Cresap, P.C.
Minot, ND
Kennerly, Angela Agee ... Dallas, TX
Kennerly, B. Franklin, IV ... Del Mar, CA
Kennerly, Christopher W. ... Dallas, TX
Kennerly, Clifford W. ... Roseburg, OR
Kennerly, Dan ... Houston, TX
Kennerly, James B. ... Houston, TX
Kennerly, Joan ... Irving, TX
Kennerly & Kennerly, P.C. ... Houston, TX
Kennerly, Montgomery & Finley, P.C.
Knoxville, TN
Kennerly, Paul S. ... San Diego, CA
Kennerly, Rebecca J. ... Dallas, TX
Kennerly, T. Everton ... Houston, TX
Kennerly, Thomas H. ... Houston, TX
Kennerly-Miller, Nancy N.
Los Angeles, CA
Kennerson, Paul R. ... San Diego, CA
Kennerson Schwartz Semerdjian & Haile LLP ... San Diego, CA
Kennett, Christie Shih ... Peoria, IL
Kennett, Dan P. ... Little Rock, AR
Kennett, Dan P., P.A. ... Little Rock, AR
Kennett, David H. ... Dayton, OH
Kennett, David S. ... Durham, NC
Kennett, Edward R. ... Lancaster, PA
Kennett, John H., Jr. ... Roanoke, VA
Kennett, Jon B. ... Chicago, IL
Kennett, Robert K. ... Englewood, FL
Kenney, Alan A. ... Louisville, CO
Kenney, Alton D. ... Freehold, NJ
Kenney, Andi S. ... Chicago, IL
Kenney, Becker, Solicitors LLP
New York, NY
Kenney, Brian F. ... McLean, VA
Kenney, Brian P. ... Philadelphia, PA
Kenney, Brigid E. ... Baltimore, MD
Kenney, Bruce A. ... Tulsa, OK
Kenney, Carol A. ... Falmouth, MA
Kenney, Chad F. ... Media, PA
Kenney, Charles S. ... Woodland, MI
Kenney, Christopher ... Oklahoma City, OK
Kenney, Christopher A. ... Boston, MA
Kenney, Christopher P. ... Denver, CO
Kenney, Colleen M. ... Chicago, IL
Kenney, Crane H. ... Chicago, IL
Kenney, Daniel E. ... Los Angeles, CA
Kenney, Danl. J. ... South Dennis, MA
Kenney, David E. ... Los Angeles, CA
Kenney, Deborah L. ... Newark, OH
Kenney, Dolores T. ... Chicago, IL
Kenney, Donald H. ... Dexter, MI
Kenney, Edward A. ... Phoenix, AZ
Kenney, Edward P. ... Chicago, IL
Kenney, Eileen ... Philadelphia, PA
Kenney, Francis B. ... Norwell, MA
Kenney, Francis L., III ... St. Louis, MO
Kenney, Frank D. ... Chicago, IL
Kenney, Frederic H. ... Wilmington, DE
Kenney, Frederic Lee ... Decatur, IL
Kenney, Frederick J. ... Boston, MA
Kenney, George W. ... Springfield, IL
Kenney, Gerald P. ... Chicago, IL
Kenney, Gerald T. ... Philadelphia, PA
Kenney, Glenn F. ... Helena, MT
Kenney, Gregory T. ... Houston, TX
Kenney, Gross & McDonough
Red Bank, NJ
Kenney, Herbert ... Oklahoma City, OK
Kenney, J. Ernest ... Alexandria, VA
Kenney, J. Timothy ... Atlanta, GA
Kenney, James A. ... Brooklyn, NY
Kenney, James A., III ... Leonardtown, MD
Kenney, James D., III ... Louisville, KY
Kenney, James J. ... Pflugerville, TX
Kenney, James W. ... St. Paul, MN
Kenney, Jane A. ... Cherry Hill, NJ
Kenney, Jay P. K. ... Denver, CO
Kenney, Jeffrey T. ... Cincinnati, OH
Kenney, John A. ... Oklahoma City, OK
Kenney, John A., Jr. ... Narberth, PA
Kenney, John F. ... Media, PA
Kenney, John H. ... San Francisco, CA
Kenney, John J. ... New York, NY
Kenney, John J., Jr. ... Philadelphia, PA
Kenney, John Joseph, Jr. ... Boston, MA
Kenney, John M. ... Kentfield, CA
Kenney, John M. ... Fairless Hills, PA
Kenney, John M., P.C. ... Fairless Hills, PA
Kenney, John R. ... Hartford, CT
Kenney, John T. ... Northville, MI
Kenney, Joseph A., Jr. ... Philadelphia, PA
Kenney, Joseph F. ... Omaha, NE

Kenney, Joseph H. ... Cherry Hill, NJ
Kenney, Joseph T. ... Haddonfield, NJ
Kenney, Judith ... Miami, FL
Kenney, Judith P. ... Addison, TX
Kenney, Judith P., & Associates, P.C.
Addison, TX
Dallas, TX
Kenney, Kanaley, Shelton & Liptak, L.L.P.
Albany, NY
Buffalo, NY
Syracuse, NY
Kenney, Kathleen M. ... Denver, CO
Kenney, Kathleen M. ... Department of Justice, Bureau of Prisons, GV
Kenney & Kearney LLP ... Cherry Hill, NJ
Kenney, Kelly C. ... Chicago, IL
Kenney, Kevin J. ... Sylvania, OH
Kenney, Kevin Wayne ... Kansas City, MO
Kenney, Kirby K. ... Hardin, MT
Kenney, Kristi L. ... Clinton, MO
Kenney, Laura F. ... Cleveland, OH
Kenney, Laura R. ... Martinez, CA
Kenney Law Offices ... Triadelphia, WV
Kenney, Lawrence J., Jr. ... Boston, MA
Kenney, Lawrence M. ... Smithtown, NY
Kenney, Linda B. ... Red Bank, NJ
Kenney, Lynne J. ... Lanham, MD
Kenney & Maciolek ... Medway, MA
Kenney, Malachi J. ... Red Bank, NJ
Kenney, Margaret C. ... Winthrop, ME
Kenney, Mark Joseph ... San Francisco, CA
Kenney, Mark S. ... Elkins Park, PA
Kenney, Mark S. ... Philadelphia, PA
Kenney & Markowitz L.L.P.
San Francisco, CA
Kenney, Martin J., Jr. ... Hampstead, NH
Kenney, Mary ... Chicago, IL
Kenney, Mary Anne ... Cleveland, OH
Kenney, Mary Whitney ... Los Angeles, CA
Kenney, Matthew R. ... Seattle, WA
Kenney, Maureen B. ... Malvern, PA
Kenney, Maureen G. ... Cedar Rapids, IA
Kenney, Michael J., III ... Los Angeles, CA
Kenney, Michael P. ... Baltimore, MD
Kenney, Michael P. ... New York, NY
Kenney, Michelle D.
Mendota Heights, MN
Kenney, Nat M., III ... Addison, TX
Kenney, Nicholas J. ... Chicago, IL
Kenney, P. Joseph ... Medway, MA
Kenney, Patricia A. ... Chicago, IL
Kenney, Patricia J. ... San Francisco, CA
Kenney, Patrick B. ... Detroit Lakes, MN
Kenney, Patrick E. ... Billings, MT
Kenney, Patrick F. ... Denver, CO
Kenney, Patrick L. ... Kansas City, MO
Kenney, Patrick S. ... Albany, NY
Buffalo, NY
Kenney, Paul R. ... San Francisco, CA
Kenney, Paul V. ... Medway, MA
Kenney & Pearson ... Springfield, IL
Kenney, Peter B., Jr. ... Eagan, MN
Kenney, Peter C. ... Dearborn, MI
Kenney, Raymond J., Jr. ... Boston, MA
Kenney, Robert E.
Environmental Protection Agency, Office of Enforcement and Compliance Assurance, GV
Kenney, Robert J. ... Falls Church, VA
Kenney, Robert J., Jr. ... Washington, DC
Kenney, Robert J., Jr. ... New York, NY
Kenney, Robert S. ... St. Louis, MO
Kenney, Scott M. ... Fort Pierce, FL
Kenney, Shaun P. ... Leawood, KS
Kansas City, MO
Kenney, Shawn F. ... Columbus, OH
Kenney & Solomon, P.C. ... Atlanta, GA
Duluth, GA
Kenney, Stephen C. ... San Francisco, CA
Kenney, Stephen J. ... Medway, MA
Kenney, Stephen M. ... Triadelphia, WV
Kenney, Stuart D. ... Bloomington, IL
Kenney, Terence H. ... San Francisco, CA
Kenney, Teresa ... Rockville, MD
Kenney, Theresa L. ... Kirksville, MO
Kenney, Theresa M. ... Jacksonville, FL
Kenney, Thomas E. ... Boston, MA
Kenney, Thomas E. ... Reston, VA
Kenney, Thomas H. ... Marina Del Rey, CA
Kenney, Thomas J., III ... Cherry Hill, NJ
Kenney, Thomas J., Jr., (P.C.)
Baltimore, MD
Kenney, Thomas Joseph
Environmental Protection Agency, Office of Enforcement and Compliance Assurance, GV
Kenney, Thomas M. ... Omaha, NE
Kenney, Thomas R. ... Santa Rosa, CA
Kenney, Thomas R., A Prof. Corp., Law Offices of ... Santa Rosa, CA
Kenney, Thomas S. ... Duluth, GA
Kenney, Thomas V., Jr. ... Troy, NY
Kenney, Timothy H.
West Palm Beach, FL
Kenney, Timothy H., P.A.
West Palm Beach, FL
Kenney, Valerie W. ... Denver, CO
Kenney, Warren A. ... Madison, WI
Kenney, William F. ... Naples, FL
Kenney, William F., Inc. ... San Mateo, CA
Kenney, William H. ... Haddonfield, NJ
Kenney-Smith, Melissa A. ... Boulder, CO
Kenngott, Glenn S. ... Fort Lauderdale, FL
Kenniasty, Frank W.
Indian Harbour Beach, FL
Kennick, David Michael ... Edgewood, MD
Kennick, Michael Todd ... Long Beach, CA
Kennicott, Donald ... Atlanta, GA

Kennifer, Frederick L. ... Monterey, CA
Kenniff, T. Charles ... Naperville, IL
Kenning, Charles B. ... Pittsford, NY
Kenning, Kevin K. ... Chicago, IL
Kenninger, David E. ... Danville, IN
Kennington, C. Alan ... Charleston, SC
Kennington, L. Michael ... Houston, TX
Kennington, Ray T. ... Ozark, AL
Kennis, Robert H. ... San Francisco, CA
Kennison, Judith L. ... Houston, TX
Kennison, Patrick W., Jr. ... Omaha, NE
Kenniston, Kristi A. ... Washington, DC
Kenno, Mary Ann B. ... Gaithersburg, MD
Kennon, A. William ... Durham, NC
Kennon, Amy R. ... Oakland, CA
Kennon, C. Read ... San Antonio, TX
Kennon, Hans ... Orlando, FL
Kennon, James C. ... Memphis, TN
Kennon, Jerry A. ... Nashville, TN
Kennon, Kenneth W. ... St. Francisville, LA
Kennon, Lawrence E. ... Chicago, IL
Kennon, Linda Sue ... Dallas, TX
Kennon, Maureen Healey ... Boca Raton, FL
Kennon, Maureen Healey, P.A.
Boca Raton, FL
Kennon, Randall H. ... Los Angeles, CA
Kennon, Rick J. ... Austin, TX
Kennon, Robert F., Jr. ... Baton Rouge, LA
Kennon, Thomas J., III ... Lake City, FL
Kennon, Thomas J., Jr. ... Live Oak, FL
Kennon, Warner L. ... Columbus, GA
Kennon, Warner L., P.C. ... Columbus, GA
Kennon, William R. ... Tustin, CA
Kenny, Adam ... Parsippany, NJ
Kenny, Alfreida B. ... New York, NY
Kenny, Ann T. ... New York, NY
Kenny, Anthony E.
Grosse Pointe Woods, MI
Kenny, Anthony E., P.C.
Grosse Pointe Woods, MI
Kenny, Arthur ... Palo Alto, CA
Kenny, Austin M. ... Asbury Park, NJ
Kenny, Barbara J. ... Riverhead, NY
Kenny, Bernard F., Jr. ... Hoboken, NJ
Kenny, Brimmer, Melley & Mahoney
Hartford, CT
Kenny, Camille M. ... Newark, NJ
Kenny, Charles D. ... Beverly Hills, CA
Kenny, Charles F. ... River Edge, NJ
New York, NY
Kenny, Charles F. ... Port Jefferson, NY
Kenny, Charles J., Jr. ... Hyattsville, MD
Kenny, Cheryl A. ... Washington, DC
Kenny, Christina M. ... Newark, NJ
New York, NY
Kenny, Christopher G. ... Albuquerque, NM
Kenny, Colm William ... Pittsburgh, PA
Kenny, Craig P. ... Las Vegas, NV
Kenny, Dana Livingstone ... Seattle, WA
Kenny, Daniel E. ... Old Lyme, CT
Kenny, David C. ... San Francisco, CA
Kenny, David J. ... Hamilton, NJ
Kenny, Denis S. ... Oakland, CA
Kenny, Dennis E. ... Seattle, WA
Kenny, Dennis J. ... Purchase, NY
Kenny, Diane Dray ... Seattle, WA
Kenny, Douglas Grant ... Indianapolis, IN
Kenny, Edward F., III ... New York, NY
Kenny, Edward T. ... New Smyrna Beach, FL
Kenny, Elissa B. ... Armonk, NY
Kenny, Elizabeth A. ... Newark, NJ
Kenny, Eugene P. ... San Diego, CA
Kenny, Eugene P. ... Jersey City, NJ
Kenny, Francis E. ... Rochester, NY
Kenny, George J. ... Roseland, NJ
Kenny, Gerard J. ... Irvine, CA
Kenny, Howard A. ... New York, NY
Kenny, Hugh L. ... Cheyenne, WY
Kenny, James E. ... Milwaukee, WI
Kenny, James J. ... Miami, FL
Kenny, James J., Jr. ... Claremont, CA
Kenny, James M. ... Newark, NJ
New York, NY
Kenny, James P. ... Chicago, IL
Kenny, Jas. P. ... Chicago, IL
Kenny, John C. ... New York, NY
Kenny, John C. ... Richmond, VA
Kenny, John C., Law Offices of
Tallahassee, FL
Kenny, John J. ... Baltimore, MD
Kenny, John J. ... New York, NY
Kenny, John L. ... Narberth, PA
Kenny, John R. ... San Jose, CA
Kenny, John S. ... Redding, CA
Kenny, John S. ... Syracuse, NY
Kenny, John W. ... Staten Island, NY
Kenny, Jos. T. ... San Antonio, TX
Kenny, Joseph G. ... Brooklyn, NY
Kenny, Joseph W. ... Nashua, NH
Kenny, Kathleen M. ... Wheaton, IL
Kenny, Kelly S. ... Fremont, CA
Kenny, Kendra M. ... New York, NY
Kenny & Kenny ... Wheaton, IL
Kenny, Kevin B. ... Hartford, CT
Kenny, Kevin M. ... Tampa, FL
Kenny, Leigh A. ... Tijeras, NM
Kenny, Linda Nichols ... Indianapolis, IN
Kenny & Lupia ... Syracuse, NY
Kenny, M. Bernadette ... Tarrytown, NY
Kenny, Mary A. ... Staten Island, NY
Kenny, Mary Alice ... Bridgeview, IL
Oak Lawn, IL
Kenny, Maureen Sheridan ... Cleveland, OH
Kenny, Michael A. ... Iron Mountain, MI
Kenny, Michael A., Jr. ... Cleveland, OH
Kenny, Michael H. ... Wheaton, IL
Kenny, Michael J. ... Huntington Station, NY
Kenny, Michael J. ... New Rochelle, NY

Kenny, Michael J. ... Scranton, PA
Kenny, Michael P. ... Stockton, CA
Kenny, Michael P. ... Atlanta, GA
Kenny, Michael P. ... Syracuse, NY
Kenny, Molly B. ... Seattle, WA
Kenny Nachwalter Seymour Arnold Critchlow & Spector, Professional Association ... Miami, FL
Rogersville, TN
Kenny, Pamela M. ... New York, NY
Kenny, Patrick J. ... St. Louis, MO
Kenny, Patrick J. ... New York, NY
Kenny, Paul J. ... Ridgewood, NY
Kenny, Paul L. ... Medford, MA
Kenny, Paul R. ... Newark, NJ
Kenny, Peter J. ... New York, NY
Kenny, Peter J. ... New York, NY
Kenny, Peter J. ... Charlottesville, VA
Kenny, Peter W. ... Red Bank, NJ
Whiting, NJ
Kenny, Peter Warren ... Fort Pierce, FL
Kenny, Philip S. ... Ogden, UT
Kenny, Philip W. ... Poughkeepsie, NY
Kenny, Raymond J. ... Chappaqua, NY
Kenny, Richard J. ... Hartford, CT
Kenny, Richard J., Jr. ... Philadelphia, PA
Kenny, Robert ... Basking Ridge, NJ
Kenny, Robert C. ... Chicago, IL
Kenny, Robert E., III ... Cleveland, OH
Kenny, Robert E., Jr. ... Oak Lawn, IL
Kenny, Robert G. ... New Brunswick, NJ
Kenny, Robert I. ... Charlotte, NC
Kenny, Robert L. ... San Diego, CA
Kenny, Robert M. ... Belmont, MA
Kenny, Sandra A. ... Orlando, FL
Kenny, Sheila B. ... Newark, NJ
Kenny, Stacey L. ... Tallahassee, FL
Kenny, Stanley M. ... Dodge City, KS
Kenny & Stearns ... Newark, NJ
New York, NY
Kenny, Sue-Ellen ... West Palm Beach, FL
Kenny, Susan J. ... Boston, MA
Kenny, Tamara A. ... St. Louis, MO
Kenny, Terence J ... Red Bank, NJ
Kenny, Teresa M. ... Nanuet, NY
Kenny, Terry Albright ... Gastonia, NC
Kenny, Thomas C. ... Falmouth, MA
Kenny, Thomas G. ... Wheaton, IL
Kenny, Thomas J. ... Southfield, MI
Kenny, Thomas J. ... Omaha, NE
Kenny, Thomas P. ... Omaha, NE
Kenny, Timothy M. ... Detroit, MI
Kenny, Timothy M. ... Minneapolis, MN
Kenny, Timothy M. ... Omaha, NE
Kenny, William J. ... Portland, OR
Kenny, William W. ... Oak Lawn, IL
Kenoe, Andrew S. ... Chicago, IL
Kenoff, Jay S. ... Los Angeles, CA
Kenoff & Machtinger ... Los Angeles, CA
Kenowski & Kenowski ... Scranton, PA
Kenowski, Romwald ... Scranton, PA
Kenrich, John L. ... Savannah, GA
Kenrick, John R. ... Pittsburgh, PA
Kensel, N. Michael ... Fort Worth, TX
Kensinger, George L. ... Altoona, PA
Kensinger, Karl A.
Federal Communications Commission, International Bureau, GV
Kensinger, Loren L. ... Fremont, CA
Kensington, Costa N. ... New York, NY
Kensington, Nicolas A. ... Boston, MA
Kensington & Ressler LLC
New York, NY
Kenski, Robert Richard ... Algonquin, IL
Kensler, Mindy J. ... Downey, CA
Kensok, Thomas J ... Martinez, CA
Kenswil, Lawrence ... Universal City, CA
Kent, Adam C. ... Redwood City, CA
Kent, Alan H. ... Washington, DC
Kent, Allen J. ... San Francisco, CA
Kent, Amy R. ... Portland, OR
Kent, Andrew G. ... Scottsdale, AZ
Kent, Andrew S. ... Roseland, NJ
Kent, Arnold R. ... Florham Park, NJ
Kent, Arnold R., A Professional Corporation
Florham Park, NJ
Kent, Arthur G. ... Atlanta, GA
Kent & Associates, P.C. ... Portland, OR
Kent, Barbara ... New York, NY
Kent, Beatty & Gordon, LLP
New York, NY
Kent, Bernard S. ... Detroit, MI
Kent, Bettina J. ... New York, NY
Kent, Brian C. ... Baltimore, MD
Kent, Bruce A. ... Baltimore, MD
Kent, Bruce W. ... Salina, KS
Kent, Burgin H. ... Birmingham, AL
Kent, Candace Hewitt ... Phoenix, AZ
Kent, Caroline J. ... New York, NY
Kent, Carolyn V. ... Albany, NY
Kent, Charlene Elizabeth ... Peabody, MA
Kent, Charles A. ... Santa Barbara, CA
Kent, Charles E. ... Burbank, CA
Kent, Christopher E. ... Riverhead, NY
Kent, Christopher H. ... Portland, OR
Kent, Christopher R. ... Los Angeles, CA
Kent, Clayton W. ... Novato, CA
Kent, Crawford & Gooding, P.A.
Jacksonville, FL
Kent, Cynthia D. ... Sacramento, CA
Kent, Cynthia J. ... Bloomfield, CT
Kent, Cynthia Stevens ... Tyler, TX
Kent, Daniel A. ... Atlanta, GA
Kent, Daniel H. ... Hollywood, FL
Kent, Daniel H., P.A. ... Hollywood, FL
Kent, David C. ... Dallas, TX
Kent, David L. ... Plymouth, NH
Kent, David W. ... Evansville, IN

Kent, Diane Nowak ... Boca Raton, FL
Kent, Don W. ... Tyler, TX
Kent, Donald ... Lafayette, LA
Kent, Donald H. ... Des Moines, IA
Kent, Doris Cirignano ... New York, NY
Kent, Douglas A. ... Newark, NJ
Kent, Douglas J. ... Philadelphia, PA
Kent, Edw. R. ... Chicago, IL
Kent, Edward ... Willingboro, NJ
Kent, Edward A., Jr. ... Oakland, CA
Kent, Edward A., Jr. ... Palo Alto, CA
Kent, Edward A., Jr. ... San Francisco, CA
San Jose, CA
Kent, Elizabeth ... Honolulu, HI
Kent, Elizabeth B. ... Dallas, TX
Kent, Evan M. ... Los Angeles, CA
Kent, Felix H. ... New York, NY
Kent, Fred H., Jr., P.A. ... Jacksonville, FL
Kent, Frederic D. ... San Diego, CA
Kent, Frederick H., III ... Jacksonville, FL
Kent, Frederick H., Jr. ... Jacksonville, FL
Kent, G. Marshall, Jr. ... Atlanta, GA
Kent, Gene ... Orange, CA
Kent, Geoffrey ... Tarrytown, NY
Kent, George A. ... Montgomery, AL
Kent, Gordon L. ... Little Falls, NJ
Kent, Gordon M. ... Altavista, VA
Kent, Grayer & Rosenberg, P.C.
Willingboro, NJ
Kent, Hazzard, Jaeger, Greer, Wilson & Fay
New York, NY
Scarsdale, NY
White Plains, NY
Kent, Howard J. ... Atlanta, GA
Kent, Hugh C. ... Ithaca, NY
Kent, Irvin M. ... Aurora, CO
Kent, J. Laurence ... Rockville, MD
Kent, James A. ... San Diego, CA
Kent, James L. ... Fort Worth, TX
Kent, James P., Jr. ... Altavista, VA
Kent, Jason L. ... San Diego, CA
Kent, Jason W. ... Albuquerque, NM
Kent, Jeffrey A. ... Los Angeles, CA
Kent, Jeffrey B. ... Atlanta, GA
Kent, Jeffrey D. ... La Habra, CA
Kent, Jeffrey P. ... Dallas, TX
Kent, Jennifer J. ... Milwaukee, WI
Kent, Jerri Ryan ... San Diego, CA
Kent, Joel J. ... Bend, OR
Kent, Joel Scott ... Columbus, OH
Kent, John ... Seattle, WA
Kent, John B. ... Jacksonville, FL
Kent, John F. ... Philadelphia, PA
Kent, John F., Jr. ... Old Greenwich, CT
Kent, John J. ... Baltimore, MD
Kent, John J., Jr. ... Baltimore, MD
Kent, John M. ... Anaheim, CA
Kent, John P. (Pat) ... Frederick, OK
Kent, John S. ... Los Gatos, CA
Kent, Jonathan F. ... Chattanooga, TN
Kent, Joseph F. ... Mount Pleasant, SC
Kent, Judith K. ... Sacramento, CA
Kent, K. Andrew ... Santa Barbara, CA
Kent, K. Wayne ... Evansville, IN
Kent, Karlyn R. ... La Jolla, CA
Kent, Kathleen M. ... Wichita, KS
Kent and Kent ... Altavista, VA
Kent, Kevin K. ... Virginia Beach, VA
Kent, Kimberly A. ... Phoenix, AZ
Kent, Kristin H. ... Arlington, VA
Kent, Larry J. ... Long Beach, CA
Kent, Leon E. ... Beverly Hills, CA
Kent, Lewis ... Palm Desert, CA
Kent, Lisa Kasden ... Bridgeport, CT
Kent, Lorraine R. ... Houston, TX
Kent, Love B. ... Columbus, GA
Kent, M. Elizabeth ... Washington, DC
Kent, Mark A. ... Milwaukee, WI
Kent, Martha Lucille ... Grand Junction, CO
Kent, Martin ... Savannah, GA
Kent & Martin, P.C. ... Albuquerque, NM
Kent, Mary M. ... Ocean City, MD
Kent, Marylou Lowder ... Springfield, IL
Kent & McBride, P.C. ... Wilmington, DE
Cherry Hill, NJ
Philadelphia, PA
Kent, Megan V. ... Columbus, OH
Kent, Melissa E. ... Encino, CA
Kent, Melissa P.
Department of Commerce, GV
Kent, Michael Alan ... Chattanooga, TN
Kent, Michael B. ... New York, NY
Kent, Michael M. ... Alpharetta, GA
Kent, Monett B. ... Jacksonville, FL
Kent, Morris R. ... Flint, MI
Kent, Norman Elliott ... Fort Lauderdale, FL
Kent, Patricia ... Missoula, MT
Kent, Paul David ... Easley, SC
Kent, Paul G. ... Madison, WI
Kent, Paula Susie ... Dallas, TX
Kent, Perrin A. ... Rockville, MD
Kent, Peter M. ... Stamford, CT
Kent, Peter V. ... Peabody, MA
Kent, Rachael D. ... Washington, DC
Kent, Rahel Eden ... Los Angeles, CA
Kent, Rebecca L. ... Oshkosh, WI
Kent, Richard A. ... Phoenix, AZ
Kent, Richard G. ... Bridgeport, CT
Stamford, CT
Westport, CT
Kent, Richard J. ... Doylestown, PA
Kent, Richard M. ... Encino, CA
Kent, Richard T. ... Moultrie, GA
Kent, Richard V. ... Detroit, MI
Kent, Robert A. ... Albany, NY
Kent, Robert B. ... Ithaca, NY
Kent, Robert E. ... Los Angeles, CA
Kent, Robert J. ... Fort Lee, NJ

Kent, Robert J. ... Parkersburg, WV
Kent, Robert S. ... Pecos, TX
Kent, Robert W. ... Chester, NJ
Kent, Robert W., Jr. ... Chicago, IL
Kent, Robin M. ... Jamaica, NY
Kent, Robt. L. ... Ravenna, OH
Kent, Roland C. ... Denton, MD
Kent, Roma A. ... New Orleans, LA
Kent, Ronald D. ... Los Angeles, CA
Kent, Ronald H., Jr. ... Birmingham, AL
Kent, Ronda K., (A Law Corporation)
Honolulu, HI
Kent, Ronda L. ... Treasury Department, Financial Management Service, GV
Kent, Roy W. ... Tacoma, WA
Kent, Russell S. ... Atlanta, GA
Kent, Ruth E. ... Washington, DC
Kent, Ryan A. ... San Francisco, CA
Kent, Samuel B. ... Galveston, TX
Kent & Scheufele ... Baltimore, MD
Kent, Stanley B. ... Cleveland, OH
Kent, Stanley C. ... Colorado Springs, CO
Kent, Stephen S. ... Reno, NV
Kent, Steven ... New York, NY
Kent, Susan J.W. ... New York, NY
Kent, Thomas C. ... New York, NY
Kent, Thomas D. ... Morristown, NJ
Kent, Thomas E. ... Grand Rapids, MI
Kent, Thomas I ... Atlanta, GA
Kent, Thomas L. ... New York, NY
Kent, W. Wallace, Jr. ... Caro, MI
Kent, William A. ... Irvine, CA
Kent, William J., III ... Central Islip, NY
Kent, William M. ... Jacksonville, FL
Kent, William N. ... Eugene, OR
Kent & Wittekind, P.C. ... Phoenix, AZ
Kent, Worsham & Smart ... Hinesville, GA
Savannah, GA
Kentch, James B. ... Anchorage, AK
Kentch, Jim ... Anchorage, AK
Kenter, Jerrold ... Independence, MO
Kenter, Jonathan A. ... New York, NY
Kenter, Michael L. ... Dallas, TX
Kent-Friedman, Alison Lindsay
New York, NY
Kent-Marshall, Piper ... Alameda, CA
Kentner, Jace ... Kansas City, MO
Kentoff, David R. ... Washington, DC
Kentoff, Michael C. ... Washington, DC
Kentoffio, Joseph S. ... Hartford, CT
Kenton, Carolyn L. ... Lexington, KY
Kenton, Glenn C. ... Wilmington, DE
Kenton, Jas. K. ... Waukegan, IL
Kenton, Melanie ... Santa Fe, NM
Kenton, Victor B. ... Los Angeles, CA
Kenton-Walker, Janet ... Boston, MA
Kentor, Eric S. ... Sylmar, CA
Kentos, Mark D. ... Ocean Township, NJ
Kentov, Rochelle, (Ms.) ... New York, NY
Kentra, Christopher E. ... Chicago, IL
Kentris, Brown & Powell ... Findlay, OH
Kentris, George L. ... Findlay, OH
Kentros, Arthur G. ... Somers, NY
Kent-Smith, Henry L. ... Princeton, NJ
Kenty, David E. ... Philadelphia, PA
Kentz, Andrew W. ... Washington, DC
Kentz, Frederick C., III ... Nutley, NJ
Kentz, Frederick C., Jr. ... Elizabeth, NJ
Kentz, Gilson & O'Hara ... Summit, NJ
Kentzel, William T., III ... Covington, LA
Kenvin, Helene Schwartz ... Esopus, NY
Kenward, Christopher F. ... Redwood City, CA
Kenway & Crowley ... Marblehead, MA
Kenway, Kimball L. ... Portland, ME
Kenwood, Joel D. ... Boca Raton, FL
Kenworthy, Charles N. ... Los Angeles, CA
Kenworthy, Craig T. ... Overland Park, KS
Kansas City, MO
Kenworthy, David M. ... Olympia, WA
Kenworthy, Diana L. ... Chicago, IL
Kenworthy, Gary D. ... Circleville, OH
Kenworthy, James H. ... New York, NY
Kenworthy, James L. ... Arlington, VA
Kenworthy, K. Randall ... Santa Rosa, CA
Kenworthy, Kevin L. ... Washington, DC
Kenworthy, Kraig A. ... Indianapolis, IN
Kenworthy, Lawrence C. ... Yuma, AZ
Kenworthy, Lise ... Seattle, WA
Kenworthy, Martin J. ... Des Moines, IA
Kenworthy, Patricia G. ... Washington, DC
Kenworthy, Thomas B. ... Philadelphia, PA
Kenworthy, William E. ... Washington, DC
Kenworthy, William P. ... Memphis, TN
Kenwright, M. Helen H. ... Roswell, GA
Keny, Linda B. ... San Diego, CA
Kenyon, A. Richard ... Gainesville, GA
Kenyon, Allen F. ... Ladysmith, WI
Kenyon, Allen S. ... Belen, NM
Kenyon, Andrea M. ... New York, NY
Kenyon, Archibald B., Jr. ... Wakefield, RI
Kenyon, Arnold O., II ... Creston, IA
Kenyon, Arnold O., II, A Prof. Corp.
Creston, IA
Kenyon, Arnold O., III ... Creston, IA
Kenyon and Aukerman ... Wakefield, RI
Kenyon, Cameron M. ... Arvada, CO
Kenyon, Carole ... Scotch Plains, NJ
Kenyon, Charity ... Sacramento, CA
Kenyon, David G. ... Novato, CA
Kenyon, Douglas Wayne ... Raleigh, NC
Kenyon, Edward C. Russ
Canandaigua, NY
Kenyon, Edward T. ... Summit, NJ
Kenyon, Geoffrey R. T. ... Boston, MA
Kenyon, Gregory L. ... West Des Moines, IA
Kenyon, Jay A. ... San Diego, CA
Las Vegas, NV
Kenyon, John F. ... Wakefield, RI
Kenyon, Jonathan Mark ... Florence, KY
Kenyon, Joseph K, Jr ... Boston, MA
Kenyon, Karl L. ... Anderson, SC
Kenyon, Kathryn M. ... Pittsburgh, PA
Kenyon & Kenyon ... San Jose, CA
Washington, DC
Kenyon & Kenyon ... Canandaigua, NY
Kenyon & Kenyon ... New York, NY
Kenyon, Kyle, Law Office ... Irvine, CA
Kenyon, Lisa M. ... Marion, IA
Kenyon & Lusk ... Anderson, SC
Kenyon, Mark A. ... Binghamton, NY
Kenyon, Michael P. ... Boston, MA
Kenyon, Michelle ... Atlanta, GA
Kenyon, Michelle Marchetta
Oakland, CA
Kenyon, Rosemary Gill ... Raleigh, NC
Kenyon, Sean E. ... South Bend, IN
Kenyon & Sproull, P.C. ... Austin, TX
Kenyon, Stephen B. ... Wakefield, RI
Kenyon, Stephen O. ... Seattle, WA
Kenyon, Terry F. ... Austin, TX
Kenyon, Timothy R. ... Creston, IA
Kenyon, Todd P. ... Brooklyn, NY
Kenyon, William R. ... Canandaigua, NY
Kenyon, William S., III ... Adrian, MI
Keogh, Anthony J. ... White Plains, NY
Keogh, Brad K. ... Phoenix, AZ
Keogh, Burkhart & Vetter ... Norwalk, CT
Keogh, Cox & Wilson, Ltd.
Baton Rouge, LA
Keogh, D. Webster ... Philadelphia, PA
Keogh, D. Webster, Associates, P.C.
Philadelphia, PA
Keogh, Elizabeth M. ... New York, NY
Keogh, Eugene L. ... Secaucus, NJ
Keogh and Forman ... Hagåtña, GU
Keogh, John R. (Reggie)
Baton Rouge, LA
Keogh, Kathleen ... Cleveland, OH
Keogh, Keith J. ... Chicago, IL
Keogh, Kevin ... New York, NY
Keogh, Kevin R. ... Cleveland, OH
Keogh, Linda J. ... Boston, MA
Keogh, Michael T. ... Le Center, MN
Keogh, Robert A. ... Dickinson, ND
Keogh, Robert L. ... Hagåtña, GU
Keogh & Santangelo ... White Plains, NY
Keogh, Stephen B. ... Norwalk, CT
Keogh, William J., III ... Augusta, GA
Aiken, SC
Keogh, William T. ... Palo Alto, CA
Keohane, Arthur Christopher, Jr.
Somerville, MA
Keohane, Brian W. ... Beach, ND
Keohane, David P. ... North Quincy, MA
Keohane, Harold J. ... Boston, MA
Keohane, Jeffrey R.
Environmental Protection Agency, Office of the General Counsel, GV
Keohane, John J. ... New York, NY
Keohane, Laura ... Durham, NC
Keohane, Paul J. ... Placitas, NM
Keohane, Stephen ... Cambridge, MA
Keolker, Robert A. ... Seattle, WA
Keolker & Swerk ... Seattle, WA
Keon, Barbara D. ... Danvers, MA
Keon, Barbara E. ... Atlanta, GA
Keon, Martha J. ... Minneapolis, MN
Keon, Peter Andrew ... Philadelphia, PA
Keong, Gail M.
National Labor Relations Board, Office of the General Counsel, GV
Keosaian, Dickran ... Belmont, MA
Keosian, Armand ... Encino, CA
Keosian, Christopher ... Encino, CA
Keosian, Gregory ... Encino, CA
Keosian & Keosian ... Encino, CA
Keough, Barbara A. ... San Bernardino, CA
Keough, Carol P. ... Houston, TX
Keough, Christopher L. ... Washington, DC
Keough, Daniel G. ... Summit, NJ
Keough, Dennis J. ... Orange, CA
Keough, Hugh J., Jr. ... Fort Lauderdale, FL
Keough, James E. ... Pacific Grove, CA
Keough, James E., Prof. Corp.
Pacific Grove, CA
Keough, James J. ... Fort Lauderdale, FL
Keough, Jane Boland ... Washington, DC
Keough, John J. ... Seattle, WA
Keough, John M. ... Boston, MA
Keough, John R., III ... New York, NY
Keough, Joseph A., Jr. ... Boston, MA
Pawtucket, RI
Keough, Kathleen B. ... Hummelstown, PA
Keough, Lawrence E. ... Land O'Lakes, FL
Keough, Mary Ann ... Moline, IL
Keough, Michael T. ... New Port Richey, FL
Keough, Paul G. ... Boston, MA
Keough, Paul J. ... Natick, MA
Keough, Richard D. ... Hartford, CT
Keough, Richard J. ... West Palm Beach, FL
Keough, Robert D. ... Frostproof, FL
Orlando, FL
Keough, Robert D. ... Boston, MA
Keough, Robert J., Jr. ... Tupelo, MS
Keough, Sara B. ... St. Clair Shores, MI
Keough, Sean Z. ... Waltham, MA
Keough, Steven J. ... Minneapolis, MN
Keough & Sweeney ... Boston, MA
Dedham, MA
Pawtucket, RI
Keough, Teresa Ann ... Rockville, MD
Keough, Thomas G. ... San Diego, CA
Keough, Timothy S. ... Tavares, FL
Keowen, James C. ... Sacramento, CA
Keown, Allan H. ... Sacramento, CA
Keown, Jennifer R. ... Memphis, TN
Keown, Linda H. ... Montgomery, AL
Keown, Wayne A. ... Boston, MA
Keown, William R. ... Chesterfield, VA
Keown, William S. ... Haddonfield, NJ
Kepchar, Karol A. ... Philadelphia, PA
Kepecs, Milton ... Aberdeen, WA
Kepes, Arthur J. ... Aiken, SC
Kepesky, Michael E. ... Little Rock, AR
Kepfield, Sam S. ... Hutchinson, KS
Kepford, Kirby ... Hickory, NC
Kephart, A. Evans ... Philadelphia, PA
Kephart & Fisher ... Columbus, OH
Kephart, James W. ... Philadelphia, PA
Kephart, Roger E. ... Columbus, OH
Kepics-Ulizio, Karel L. ... Zelienople, PA
Kepke, Allen N. ... Bowling Green, OH
Kepke, Carlos E., Law Office of
Houston, TX
Kepke, John R. ... Reseda, CA
Keplar, J. Andrew ... Cincinnati, OH
Kepler, Asenath Main ... Santa Fe, NM
Kepler, Charles G. ... Cody, WY
Kepler, Courtney Robert ... Casper, WY
Kepler, Craig A. ... San Francisco, CA
Kepler, John W. ... St. Louis, MO
Kepler, Karen Brown ... Oakland, CA
Kepler, Karen J. ... Boston, MA
Kepler, Loretta B. ... Seattle, WA
Kepler, Michael ... Madison, WI
Kepler, Patricia E. ... Grass Valley, CA
Kepler, Stephen J. ... Irvine, CA
Kepler, Thomas E. ... Lincoln, NE
Kepler, Turrey A. ... Norristown, PA
Kepley, Brett A. ... Champaign, IL
Kepley, Gilligan & Eyrich, A Legal Professional Association ... Cincinnati, OH
Kepley, James D., Jr. ... Richmond, VA
Kepley, Vance I. ... Champaign, IL
Keplinger, Bruce ... Overland Park, KS
Kansas City, MO
Keplinger, Helen B.
Environmental Protection Agency, Program Office Attorneys, GV
Keplinger, Michael S.
Department of Commerce, Patent and Trademark Office, GV
Kepner, Anne Jones ... San Jose, CA
Kepner, Craig R. ... Phoenix, AZ
Kepner, Daniel E. ... Springfield, IL
Kepner, Danny L. ... Pensacola, FL
Kepner, Donald ... Camden, NJ
Kepner, Franklin E. ... Berwick, PA
Kepner, Franklin E., Jr. ... Berwick, PA
Kepner, J. Hayden, Jr. ... Houston, TX
Kepner, Jas. H. ... Houston, TX
Kepner, John C. S. ... Philadelphia, PA
Kepner & Kepner ... Springfield, IL
Kepner, Kepner & Corba, P.C. ... Berwick, PA
Kepner, Kevin R. ... Rochester, NY
Kepner, Maurice W. ... Springfield, IL
Kepner, Raymond R. ... Los Angeles, CA
Kepner, Stephen A., Jr.
Oklahoma City, OK
Kepniss, Stephen A. ... Short Hills, NJ
Keppel, Arthur B. ... Philadelphia, PA
Keppel, Kathryn A. ... Milwaukee, WI
Keppel, William J. ... Minneapolis, MN
Keppeler, H. K. Bruss ... Honolulu, HI
Keppelman, Judith M. ... Hartford, CT
Keppelman, Nancy ... Ann Arbor, MI
Keppelman, Richard T. ... Farmington, CT
Keppen, Arthur A. ... Michigan City, IN
Kepper, James H., Jr. ... New Orleans, LA
Kepper, Karl W. ... Hattiesburg, MS
Kepper, Kimberlee R. ... Wilmette, IL
Kepper, Marie A. ... Hattiesburg, MS
Kepper, Stewart J., Jr. ... New Orleans, LA
Kepple, Eugene C. ... Pekin, IL
Kepple, George R. ... Kittanning, PA
Kepple, James Ray ... Ness City, KS
Kepple, Karen P. ... Mahtomedi, MN
Kepple, Lloyd G., II ... Minneapolis, MN
Kepple, Mark A. ... Wheeling, WV
Kepple, Nicholas F. ... Pawcatuck, CT
Keppleman, Richard D.
San Luis Obispo, CA
Keppler, Abbey L. ... New York, NY
Keppler, Caryn B. ... New York, NY
Keppler, Daniel L. ... Portland, OR
Keppler, Ernest C. ... Sheboygan, WI
Keppler, Joan E. ... Great Neck, NY
Keppler, Mark J. ... Fresno, CA
Keppler, Rosalind Denise ... St. Paul, MN
Kepplinger, Gary L.
General Accounting Office, Office of the General Counsel, GV
Kepros, Chad A. ... Iowa City, IA
Kera, David J. ... Arlington, VA
Kera & Graubard ... New York, NY
Kera, Martin S. ... New York, NY
Keramidas, Thomas J. ... New London, CT
Keranen, Thomas M.
Bloomfield Hills, MI
Marquette, MI
Sault Ste. Marie, MI
Kerans, Susan A. ... Los Angeles, CA
Keravuori, Jennifer ... Boston, MA
Kerbawy, Richard A. ... Lansing, MI
Kerbel, Dennis A. ... New York, NY
Kerbel, Susan Getz ... Columbia, MD
Kerben, Alan J. ... Tampa, FL
Kerben, David ... Orlando, FL
Kerben, Jason ... McLean, VA
Kerben, Jason Marc ... McLean, VA
Kerben, Lawrence S. ... Kew Gardens, NY
Kerber, Andrew G. ... Wilmington, DE
Kerber, Anthony W. ... Lakewood, OH
Kerber, Anthony W., Co., L.P.A.
Lakewood, OH
Kerber, David W. ... Denver, CO
Kerber Firm, The ... Denver, CO
Kerber, Grant D. ... Troy, OH
Kerber, Jack C. ... Columbus, OH
Kerber, Joyce B. ... Independence, MO
Kerber, Joyce B., P.C. ... Independence, MO
Kerber, Justin S. ... Boston, MA
Kerber, Lori Lynn ... Kalamazoo, MI
Kerber, Mark A. ... Chicago, IL
Kerber, Steven R. ... Columbus, OH
Kerbeshian, Lynn A. ... Grand Forks, ND
Kerbey, McFall, III ... Arlington, MA
Kerbin, Wm. G., Jr. ... Snow Hill, MD
Kerbleski, John F. ... San Francisco, CA
Kerbow, Alison R. ... Sugar Land, TX
Kerbs, Glenn I. ... Dodge City, KS
Kerbs, Michael G. ... Riverside, CA
Kerby, Brad L. ... Phoenix, AZ
Kerby, Charles K., III ... Washington, DC
Kerby, D. Christopher ... San Francisco, CA
Kerby, John H. ... Arlington, VA
Kerby, Katherine S. ... Columbus, MS
Kerby, Kathryn E. ... Pleasanton, CA
Kerby, Russell T., Jr. ... Summit, NJ
Kerby, Yale L. ... Uvalde, TX
Kerchansky, Kathleen Carr ... Springfield, OH
Kercher, Kevin K. ... Allentown, PA
Kercher, Kevin M. ... Peoria, IL
Kercher, Kristen D. ... Menlo Park, CA
Kercheville, Marlise Aimone
San Antonio, TX
Kerchman, Marc C. ... Newburgh, NY
Kerchner, Barry W. ... Pottstown, PA
Kerchner, Wayne C. ... Boston, MA
Kerckhoff, A. Jason ... Carlsbad, CA
Kerckhoff, Anton W. ... Covina, CA
Kerckhoff & Cleavinger ... Carlsbad, CA
Kerckhoff, Laurence H. ... Covina, CA
Kerckhoff, Martin D. ... San Antonio, TX
Kercsmar, Geoffrey S. ... Wilmington, DE
Kerdock, John S. ... Quakertown, PA
Kerdus, Richard H. ... Vinton, IA
Kereiakes, Ann Toni ... Louisville, KY
Kereiakes, Annette ... Cincinnati, OH
Kerek, Wayne Lewis ... Cleveland, OH
Kerekes, Diana Wechsler ... Wayne, PA
Kerekes, Robert J. ... Clark, NJ
Kerekes, Steven W. ... Beverly Hills, CA
Kerekes, William J. ... Yuma, AZ
Kerekes, Zoltan ... King Of Prussia, PA
Kerelo, Patricia Farrell ... Philadelphia, PA
Kerendian, R. Joseph ... Los Angeles, CA
Kerendian, Shahbod ... Los Angeles, CA
Kerensky Law Firm, The ... Houston, TX
Kerensky, Michael W. ... Houston, TX
Kerensky, Solomon ... Vernon, CT
Kerenyi, Mark ... Marietta, OH
Keresey, Richard E. ... Montclair, NJ
Keressi, John S., Jr. ... Amherst, OH
Kerestenzis, Constantinos
Sacramento, CA
Kerester, Charles J. ... Cleveland, OH
Kerester, Dale C. ... Boston, MA
Kerestes, Michal Jean, (Ms.)
Los Angeles, CA
Kerestine, Julia A. ... Fort Worth, TX
Kerfeld, Keith J. ... Minneapolis, MN
Kerfoot, Donna L. ... Clearwater, FL
Kerford, Leo L. ... Orangeburg, SC
Kerger, Cary J. ... Oakbrook Terrace, IL
Kerger, Jessica C. ... Toledo, OH
Kerger & Kerger ... Toledo, OH
Kerger, Richard M. ... Toledo, OH
Keri, Brian C. ... Tallahassee, FL
Keri, Julianne M. ... Somerset, PA
Keriakedes, John H. ... Omaha, NE
Keriakos, Mary Jane ... Annapolis, MD
Kerian, Jon R. ... Minot, ND
Kerin, Anthony J., III ... Palo Alto, CA
Kerin & Canty, P.C. ... Milford, CT
Kerin, James J. ... New York, NY
Kerin, Michael R. ... Milford, CT
Kerin, Theodore F. ... Hackensack, NJ
Mineola, NY
New York, NY
Kerins, David P. ... Newport, RI
Kerins, John C. ... Falls Church, VA
Kerins, John E. ... Brooklyn, NY
Kerins, Martin J. ... Patchogue, NY
Kerins, Michael J. ... San Francisco, CA
Kerins, Patricia M. ... Newark, NJ
Kerins, Richard T. ... Mineola, NY
Keris, Matthew P. ... Doylestown, PA
Philadelphia, PA
Kerivan, William R. ... Fairfax, VA
Kerka, Kathryn A. ... Detroit, MI
Kerkam, Stowell, Kondracki & Clarke, P.C.
Arlington, VA
Fairfax, VA
Falls Church, VA
Kerkam, William B., III ... Richmond, VA
Kerkam, William B., Jr. ... Lewes, DE
Kerker, Howard J. ... New York, NY
Kerker, Howard J., P.C. ... New York, NY
Kerker, Lawr. L. ... Bronx, NY
Kerker, Susan J. ... New York, NY
Kerker, Susan Wynne ... New York, NY
Kerker, Valerie ... Albany, NY
Kerkhof, Jerry L. ... Indianapolis, IN
Kerkhove, Albert B. ... Omaha, NE
Kerkhove, James Anthony ... Orlando, FL
Kerkhover, R. Jeffrey ... Chester, IL
Kerkman, Jerome R. ... Milwaukee, WI
Kerkonian, Saro K. ... Pasadena, CA
Kerkorian, Gary ... Fresno, CA
Kerkorian, John G. ... Fresno, CA

Kerl, Jerald W. ... Lecanto, FL
Kerl, Ron ... Pocatello, ID
Kerlan, Milton, Jr. ... Thousand Oaks, CA
Kerle, Kirk B. ... Prairie Village, KS
Kerley, Brian P. ... Mineola, NY
Kerley, Christopher J. ... Coeur d'Alene, ID
Spokane, WA
Kerley, J. Edward ... San Francisco, CA
Kerley, James K. ... Sierra Vista, AZ
Kerley, John E. ... Springfield, IL
Kerley, J. V. ... Paducah, KY
Kerley, Michael L. ... Washington, DC
Kerley, Michael L. ... Springfield, MA
Kerley, Sierra & Broom ... Sierra Vista, AZ
Tucson, AZ
Kerley-Schwartz, Karen ... Washington, DC
Kerlick, I. Ray ... Houston, TX
Kerlin, Gilbert ... New York, NY
Kerlin and Harvey ... Mc Connellsburg, PA
Kerlin, Karla D. ... Los Angeles, CA
Kerlin, Mahlon ... Delphi, IN
Kerlin, Merrill W. ... Mc Connellsburg, PA
Kerlin, Stanley J. ... Mc Connellsburg, PA
Kerlinsky, Jo Saxe ... Oakland, CA
Kerlinsky, Norma Saxe ... Longmeadow, MA
Kerlogue, Paul C. ... New York, NY
Kerman, Arline S., (Mrs.) ... La Jolla, CA
Kerman, Bryan Jacob ... Methuen, MA
Kerman, David D. ... Lawrence, MA
Kerman, David J. ... Boston, MA
Kerman, Edward H. ... Rockville, MD
Kerman, Kerman & Kerman ... Methuen, MA
Kerman, Larry ... Buffalo, NY
Kerman, Leslie J. ... Washington, DC
Kerman, Michael G. ... Atlanta, GA
Kerman, Norman ... Methuen, MA
Kerman, Peter F. ... Menlo Park, CA
Kerman, Peter W. ... Berkeley, CA
Kerman, Sean D. ... Detroit, MI
Kerman, Shirley B. ... Methuen, MA
Kerman, Thea J. ... Los Angeles, CA
Kermisch, Nira T. ... Rochester, NY
Kermish, Nicole C. ... Wrentham, MA
Kermode, Jeffery John ... Irvine, CA
Kermode, John D. ... Lexington, KY
Kermott, Gary L. ... Santa Ana, CA
Kermott, Lois T. ... Phoenix, AZ
Kern, Albert ... Aspen, CO
Kern, Anna M. ... Cleveland, OH
Kern Augustine Conroy & Schoppmann, A Professional Corporation ... Bridgewater, NJ
Kern, B. Scott ... Erie, PA
Kern, Barbara Jean ... Allentown, PA
Kern, Candace ... Santa Fe, NM
Kern, Carol J. ... Walnut Creek, CA
Kern, Charles E., II ... United States Senate, Committee Legal Personnel, GV
Kern, Chet W. ... New York, NY
Kern, Christina L. Benson ... Indianapolis, IN
Kern, Christopher ... Mobile, AL
Kern, Christopher O. ... Washington, DC
Kern, Clifford H., Jr. ... New Orleans, LA
Kern, Cynthia S. ... New York, NY
Kern, Daniel H. ... Pleasanton, CA
Kern, David ... Akron, OH
Kern, David A. ... Tucson, AZ
Kern, David B. ... Milwaukee, WI
Kern, David F. ... Clearwater, FL
Kern, David L. ... El Paso, TX
Kern, David M. ... Charlotte, NC
Kern, Debra Csik ... Haddonfield, NJ
Philadelphia, PA
Kern, Dennis L. ... New Britain, CT
Kern, Dwight A. ... New York, NY
Kern, Ellen S. ... Denver, CO
Kern, Frank Norton ... Santa Fe, NM
Kern, Frank W., III ... Tucson, AZ
Kern, Gayle A. ... Reno, NV
Kern, George C., Jr. ... New York, NY
Kern, George W., V ... Wilmington, DE
Mount Laurel, NJ
Philadelphia, PA
West Chester, PA
Kern & Gonzalez, A Professional Corporation ... Los Angeles, CA
Kern, Hana A. ... Seattle, WA
Kern, Howard E. ... Lahaina, HI
Kern, Howard J. ... Los Angeles, CA
Kern, Irving J. ... Bridgeport, CT
Stamford, CT
Kern, Iver J. ... San Francisco, CA
Kern, James A. ... Scottsdale, AZ
Kern, Janine M. ... Pierre, SD
Kern, Jay H. ... New Orleans, LA
Kern, Jeffrey A. ... Miami, FL
Kern, Jeffrey T. ... Brooklyn, NY
Kern, Jerome H. ... New York, NY
Kern, Jerry K. ... Delray Beach, FL
Kern, John A. ... Department of Transportation, Federal Railroad Administration, GV
Kern, John B. ... Charleston, SC
Kern, John F. ... Chicago, IL
Kern, John McD. ... Oakland, CA
Kern, John S. ... Alexandria, VA
Kern, John W. ... Washington, DC
Kern, John W., III ... Washington, DC
Kern, Joseph G. ... Orlando, FL
Kern, Joseph P. D. ... Fillmore, CA
Kern, Jurgen ... Boston, MA
Kern, Karen L. ... Clovis, CA
Kern, Keith W. ... Cleveland, OH
Kern, Kevin W. ... Beverly Hills, CA
Memphis, TN
Kern, Kristina ... Indianapolis, IN
Kern, Kurt C. ... Dallas, TX
Kern, Laura M. Urbik ... Hinsdale, IL
Kern, Lawrence E. ... San Francisco, CA
Kern, Lawrence M. ... Chicago, IL
Kern, Lawrence W. ... Memphis, TN
Kern, Lee Ann ... Los Angeles, CA
Kern, Leila R. ... Lexington, MA
Kern, Lillian M. ... Dayton, OH
Kern, Linda Geiger ... Brooklyn, NY
Kern, Lisa M. ... Martinsburg, WV
Kern, Lorena J. ... New York, NY
Kern, Lowell D. ... New York, NY
Kern, Margaret H. ... Covington, LA
Kern, Margaret M. ... White Plains, NY
Kern, Matthew D. ... Des Moines, IA
Kern, Michael ... Palo Alto, CA
Kern, Michael N. ... St. Louis, MO
Kern, Michael Sue ... Tucson, AZ
Kern, Michael W. ... Evanston, IL
Kern, Michelle Ann ... Deerfield, IL
Kern, Noda, Devine & Segal, A Law Corporation ... San Francisco, CA
Kern, Owen S. ... Indianapolis, IN
Kern, Paul J. ... Lake Andes, SD
Kern, Raymond ... Bedford, IN
Kern, René J., Jr. ... Los Angeles, CA
Kern, Richard F. ... Caro, MI
Kern, Richard J. ... Fresno, CA
Kern, Robert C., Jr. ... New York, NY
Kern, Robert J., Law Offices of
Houston, TX
Kern, Robert L. ... Pomona, CA
Kern, Robert M. ... Los Angeles, CA
Kern, Robert M. ... West Hills, CA
Kern, Robert R., Jr. ... Baltimore, MD
Kern, Robert W. ... Cleveland, OH
Kern, Robin K. ... Pawtucket, RI
Kern, Ronald A. ... San Antonio, TX
Kern & Rosenauer, Ltd. ... Reno, NV
Kern, Ruth Graham ... Englewood, CO
Kern, Scott C. ... Farmington, CT
Kern, Stacey T. ... Charlotte, NC
Kern, Stacey Tobin ... Chicago, IL
Kern, Stephen A. ... Greenville, SC
Kern, Stephen F. ... New York, NY
Kern, Stephen R. ... Harrisburg, PA
Kern, Stephen V. ... Atlanta, GA
Kern, Steven H. ... Bronx, NY
Kern, Steven I. ... Bridgewater, NJ
Kern, Steven Ted ... New York, NY
Kern, Stuart G. ... Washington, DC
Kern, Sue E. ... Fresno, CA
Kern, Sylvie K. ... San Francisco, CA
Kern, Terry C. ... Tulsa, OK
Kern, Thomas F., Jr. ... Fort Lauderdale, FL
Kern, Timothy J. ... Columbus, OH
Kern, Timothy L. ... Lafayette, IN
Kern, Tobin D. ... Denver, CO
Kern, Toni L. ... Los Angeles, CA
Kern, William F. ... Springfield, MA
Kern, William M. ... Clarion, PA
Kern, William R. ... West Bend, WI
Kern and Wooley LLP ... Los Angeles, CA
Kennesaw, GA
Dallas, TX
Irving, TX
Kernaghan, Brian F. ... Charleston, SC
Myrtle Beach, SC
Kernaghan, Edward O., A Professional Law Corporation ... Shreveport, LA
Kernaghan, Herbert E., Jr. ... Augusta, GA
Kernaghan, Kathleen ... Treasury Department, Internal Revenue Service, GV
Kernal, Todd E. ... Norman, OK
Kernan, Audriann ... Woodbury, NJ
Kernan, Daniel J. ... North Syracuse, NY
Kernan, David H. ... Buffalo, NY
Kernan, Frank J. ... Pittsburgh, PA
Kernan & Henry ... Southbury, CT
Waterbury, CT
Kernan, James E. ... Waterbury, CT
Kernan, James M. ... New York, NY
Oriskany, NY
Kernan, James S., Jr. ... Utica, NY
Kernan, John D. ... Hamden, CT
Kernan, Joseph R., Jr. ... Red Wing, MN
Kernan and Kernan, P.C. ... Utica, NY
Kernan, Kevin A. ... Alexandria, VA
Kernan, Kimberly J. ... San Jose, CA
Kernan, Leslie W., Jr. ... Rochester, NY
Kernan, Lisa R. ... St. Louis, MO
Kernan, Michael ... Albany, NY
Kernan, Michael E. ... Chicago, IL
Kernan, Patrick H. ... Tulsa, OK
Kernan, Patrick J. ... Pleasanton, CA
Kernan Professional Group, LLP
New York, NY
Oriskany, NY
Utica, NY
Kernan, S. Michael ... Los Angeles, CA
Kernan, Stephen M. ... Belleville, IL
Kernan, Susan Dalgleish ... Las Vegas, NV
Kernan, Thomas Spratt ... Utica, NY
Kernan, Tina L. ... Clarkston, WA
Kernan, William Kerry ... Washington, DC
Kernats, Charles M. ... Madison, WI
Kernbach, Michael A. ... Fairfax, VA
Kernell, Terry D. ... Houston, TX
Kernell, Thomas J. ... St. Louis, MO
Kernen, Joseph ... Princeton, NJ
Philadelphia, PA
Kernen, Will ... Logan, OH
Kerner, Arthur ... Somers, NY
Kerner, Bradley D. ... Armour, SD
Corsica, SD
Kerner, Debra Terry ... Secaucus, NJ
Kerner, Denise Marie ... Clovis, CA
Kerner, Dora ... Gainesville, FL
Kerner, Douglas K. ... Sacramento, CA
Kerner, Francine J. ... Treasury Department, Departmental Offices, GV
Kerner, Gerald ... New York, NY
Kerner, Glenn S. ... New York, NY
Kerner, J. Thomas ... Boston, MA
Kerner, James B. ... Avon Lake, OH
Kerner, Jordan R. ... Culver City, CA
Kerner, Karen E. ... San Francisco, CA
Kerner, Kenneth T. ... New York, NY
Kerner & Kerner ... New York, NY
Kerner, Louise G. ... Hastings-On-Hudson, NY
Kerner, Marcus M. ... Santa Ana, CA
Kerner, Marty-Ann ... Pound Ridge, NY
Kerner, Michael P. ... Benicia, CA
San Francisco, CA
Kerner, Patricia P. ... Raleigh, NC
Kerner, Richard A. ... New York, NY
Kerner, Ricki L. ... San Francisco, CA
Kerner, Robert C., Jr. ... Raleigh, NC
Kerner, Robert L., Jr. ... New York, NY
Kerner, Rochelle ... Delray Beach, FL
Kerner, S. Douglas ... San Diego, CA
Kerner, Sarah M. ... Dallas, TX
Kerner, Seymour L. ... Flushing, NY
Kerner, Shann ... Boston, MA
Kerner, Stuart M. ... Bronx, NY
Kerner, Todd M. ... Albany, NY
Kerner, William J., Sr. ... Avon Lake, OH
Kerner, William R. ... Milwaukee, WI
Kerness, Eric M. ... Albany, NY
Kerney, Carey G.B. ... Washington, DC
Kerney, James P. ... Seattle, WA
Kerney, John M. ... Towson, MD
Kerney, Sheri Lund ... Orlando, FL
Kerney, Thomas F. ... Orlando, FL
Kerney, Thomas F., P.A. ... Orlando, FL
Kernick, Brooke Malody ... Palo Alto, CA
Kernick, Cynthia E. ... Pittsburgh, PA
Kernie, Pamela W. ... Dallas, TX
Kernion, Richard J., Jr. ... New Orleans, LA
Kernis, Irving C. ... New Rochelle, NY
Kernis, Lainie L. ... New York, NY
Kerno, Ivan V. ... New York, NY
Kerno, Raymond E. ... Mineola, NY
Kernochan, Blair Glennon ... Needham, MA
Kernochan, John M. ... New York, NY
Kernodle, Kimberly P. ... Memphis, TN
Kernodle, Obra S., III ... Philadelphia, PA
Kernodle, Obra S., III, P.C., Law Office of
Philadelphia, PA
Kernodle, Trent M. ... Charleston, SC
Kern-Rappy, Michele E. ... New York, NY
Kerns, Alice Fleury ... Washington, DC
Kerns, Allan D. ... Dickson, TN
Kerns, Amy T. ... Columbus, OH
Kerns, Aronda Strutt ... Wichita, KS
Kerns, Arthur J. ... North Little Rock, AR
Kerns, Bennett ... Santa Monica, CA
Kerns, Cedric A. ... Las Vegas, NV
Kerns, Christianne F. ... Los Angeles, CA
Kerns, Christopher ... Chicago, IL
Kerns, David V. ... Tallahassee, FL
Kerns, Deborah J. ... Sacramento, CA
Kerns, Diane C. ... Portland, OR
Kerns, Dianne C. ... Tucson, AZ
Kerns, F. Gibbs ... Mayville, NY
Kerns, John Adam, Jr. ... Philadelphia, PA
Kerns, Jos. D. ... Urbana, OH
Kerns, Kathleen K. ... Philadelphia, PA
Kerns, Kenneth L. ... Great Bend, KS
Kerns & Kerns ... Columbus, OH
Kerns, Kevin T. ... Chicago, IL
Kerns, Kurt Patrick ... Wichita, KS
Kerns, Lawrence A. ... Chicago, IL
Kerns, Mark E. ... Columbus, OH
Kerns, Maureen E. ... Trenton, NJ
Kerns, Mia K.
Pension Benefit Guaranty Corporation, Office of the General Counsel, GV
Kerns, Michael Edwin ... Park Ridge, IL
Kerns, Paul J. ... Waltham, MA
Kerns, R. Kevin ... Columbus, OH
Kerns, Ralph A. ... Columbus, OH
Kerns, Rhonda L. ... Chicago, IL
Kerns, Richard C. ... Newport News, VA
Kerns, Richard P. ... Anchorage, AK
Kerns, Robert J. ... Lansdale, PA
Kerns, Robert M. ... Hartford, CT
Kerns, Shawn R. ... Lakeville, MN
Kerns, Timothy ... Philippi, WV
Kerns, Timothy G. ... Fort Morgan, CO
Kerns, Trent S. ... Mechanicsville, VA
Kerns, Trevilian A., Jr. ... Richmond, VA
Kerns, William C. ... Bellevue, WA
Kerns, William C., P.S. ... Bellevue, WA
Kerns, Young & Zanghi ... Mayville, NY
Kernutt, Kristin E. ... Eugene, OR
Kero, Diane J. ... Seattle, WA
Keroack, Henriette B. ... Lynn, MA
Keroes, Amy N. ... San Francisco, CA
Keroff, Stephen R. ... West Palm Beach, FL
Keron, Henry M. ... Seattle, WA
Kerosky & Bradley ... San Francisco, CA
Kerosky, Christopher A. ... San Francisco, CA
Kerpan, Allen M. ... Albuquerque, NM
Kerpan, Paul D. ... Chicago, IL
Kerpel, David S. ... Lake Forest, IL
Kerpel, Martin D. ... Chicago, IL
Kerpelman, Saul E. ... Baltimore, MD
Kerper, Janeen ... San Diego, CA
Kerper, Robert E., Jr. ... Akron, OH
Kerpon, Jane Scribner ... Boston, MA
Kerpsack, Robert W., Jr. ... Columbus, OH
Kerr, Alexander ... Philadelphia, PA
Kerr, Alexander D., Jr. ... Chicago, IL
Kerr, Andrew L. ... San Antonio, TX
Kerr, Andrew P. ... Portland, OR
Kerr, Ann Loughridge ... Clearwater, FL
Tampa, FL
Kerr, Anne Leigh ... Richmond, VA
Kerr, Arthur R., II ... Newton, MA
Kerr & Associates ... Las Vegas, NV
Kerr, Aubrey M., Jr. ... Oklahoma City, OK
Kerr, Baine P. ... Boulder, CO
Kerr, Baine P. ... Houston, TX
Kerr, Ben J., III ... Quitman, TX
Kerr, Brian C. ... New York, NY
Kerr, Brian D. ... Hingham, MA
Kerr, Bruce L. ... Sacramento, CA
Kerr, Carla A. ... New York, NY
Kerr, Carol Roecker ... Los Angeles, CA
Kerr, Carolyn H. ... Columbia, MO
Kerr, Catherine Lenette ... Malibu, CA
Kerr, Charles L. ... Moody, AL
Kerr, Charles L. ... New York, NY
Kerr, Charles M. ... Baltimore, MD
Kerr, Christopher C. ... Buffalo, NY
Kerr, Christopher D. ... New York, NY
Kerr, Christopher Lee ... Detroit, MI
Kerr & Conger ... Sacramento, CA
Kerr, Coretta Watkins ... Lubbock, TX
Kerr, Cori ... Salt Lake City, UT
Kerr, Crawford S., Jr. ... El Paso, TX
Kerr, David C. G. ... Tampa, FL
Kerr, David J. ... Dallas, TX
Kerr, David K. ... Denver, CO
Kerr, David L. ... Cincinnati, OH
Kerr, David Patrick ... San Francisco, CA
Kerr, Dennis C. ... San Diego, CA
Kerr, Diane G. ... New York, NY
Kerr, Don M. ... Washington, DC
Kerr, Dorothy C.
National Aeronautics And Space Administration, Goddard Space Flight Center, GV
Kerr, Douglas B. ... Irvine, CA
Kerr, Dudley Randall ... Los Angeles, CA
Kerr, E. Burton ... Haddonfield, NJ
Kerr, Edwin L. ... Hartford, CT
Kerr, Eleanor Owen ... Baton Rouge, LA
Kerr, Elizabeth H. ... Oklahoma City, OK
Kerr, Elizabeth Sturdivant
Fort Worth, TX
Kerr, Felice Glennon ... Wilmington, DE
Kerr, Frank C. ... Farmington Hills, MI
Kerr, Frank H. ... West Des Moines, IA
Kerr Friedrich Brosseau Bartlett, LLC
Denver, CO
Kerr, Gary E., Ltd. ... Springfield, IL
Kerr, George R. ... Rochester, MN
Kerr, Gerald L., III, (P.C.)
Virginia Beach, VA
Kerr, Gordon W. ... Point Pleasant, NJ
Kerr, Gregory J. ... Morristown, NJ
Kerr, Gregory M. ... Salt Lake City, UT
Kerr, Guy H. ... Dallas, TX
Kerr, H. Sinclair, Jr. ... San Francisco, CA
Kerr, Harris E. ... Midland, TX
Kerr, Henry V. ... Cleveland, OH
Kerr, Irvine, Rhodes & Ables, A Professional Corporation ... Oklahoma City, OK
Kerr, Ivin E. ... Detroit, MI
Kerr, J. Brice ... Pascagoula, MS
Kerr, J. Chester ... Kissimmee, FL
Kerr, J. Craig ... Syracuse, NY
Kerr, J. Crawford ... El Paso, TX
Kerr, J. David ... Mount Pleasant, MI
Kerr, J. Kent ... Chicago, IL
Kerr, J. Martin ... Independence, MO
Kerr, J. Martin, Prof. Corp.
Independence, MO
Kerr, J. Robinson ... Houston, TX
Kerr, Jack E. ... Saginaw, MI
Kerr, James D. ... Schenectady, NY
Kerr, James E. ... Bonita Springs, FL
Kerr, James E. ... Tracy, MN
Kerr, James H. ... New Paltz, NY
Kerr, James H., Jr. ... Houston, TX
Kerr, James Knox, Jr. ... Jacksonville, FL
Kerr, James L. ... Lexington, KY
Kerr, James L. ... New York, NY
Kerr, James P. ... Boston, MA
Kerr, James Yancey, II ... Raleigh, NC
Kerr, Jane G. ... San Francisco, CA
Kerr, Janet E. ... Malibu, CA
Kerr, Janet K. ... Topeka, KS
Kerr, Janice E. ... San Francisco, CA
Kerr, Jason Max ... Salt Lake City, UT
Kerr, Jeffrey A. ... Walpole, MA
Kerr, Jeffrey S. ... Virginia Beach, VA
Kerr, Jennifer A. ... Miami, FL
Kerr, John G. ... Encino, CA
Kerr, John H., III ... Goldsboro, NC
Kerr, John J. ... Charleston, SC
Kerr, John J., Jr. ... New York, NY
Kerr, John L. ... Cambridge, MA
Kerr, John P. ... Tulsa, OK
Kerr, John P., P.C. ... Tulsa, OK
Kerr, John S. ... Oklahoma City, OK
Kerr, John W., Jr. ... Virginia Beach, VA
Kerr, Jonathan Glen ... Fort Worth, TX
Kerr, Judith Mottl ... La Grange, IL
Kerr, Karen ... Hempstead, NY
Kerr, Karen A. ... Washington, DC
Kerr, Karen I. ... Bethesda, MD
Kerr, Kathleen A. ... Woodstock, GA
Kerr, Ken D., Jr. ... Oklahoma City, OK
Kerr, Kenneth D. ... Quincy, MA
Kerr, Kenneth P. ... Charlotte, NC
Kerr, Kevin G. ... Valparaiso, IN
Kerr, Kevin T. ... Martinez, CA
Kerr, Kristine Allen ... St. Louis, MO
Kerr, Lacy Elizabeth ... Biloxi, MS
Kerr, Lance N. ... Hollywood, CA
Kerr, Larry L. ... Medford, OR
Kerr Law Office, Chartered ... Blackfoot, ID
Kerr, Lawrence D. ... Greensburg, PA
Kerr, Lawrence J. ... Miami, FL
Kerr, Leland B. ... Kennewick, WA

Kerr, Leonard E. ...Lynnwood, WA
Kerr, Liane E. ...Albuquerque, NM
Kerr, Liane E., P.C. ...Albuquerque, NM
Kerr, Lisa M. ...Los Angeles, CA
Kerr, Margaret E. ...Las Vegas, NV
Kerr, Mark F. ...St. Paul, MN
Kerr, Marsha B. ...San Diego, CA
Kerr, Mary Brock ...Decatur, GA
Kerr McDonald, LLP ...Baltimore, MD
Kerr, Meg G. ...Miami, FL
Kerr, Michael A. ...Sacramento, CA
Kerr, Michael F. ...Los Angeles, CA
Kerr, Michael H., (P.C.) ...Chicago, IL
Kerr, Michael J. ...Fort Lauderdale, FL
Kerr, Michael R. ...Sacramento, CA
Kerr, Nancy Nowlin ...San Antonio, TX
Kerr, Nelson R., Jr. ...Williamsburg, VA
Kerr, Nicole Arfaras ...Tampa, FL
Kerr, Orin S. ...Department of Justice, Criminal Division, GV
Kerr, P. Sterling ...Las Vegas, NV
Kerr, Patricia A. ...Syracuse, NY
Kerr, Paul B., III ...Newport News, VA
Kerr, Peggy L. ...New York, NY
Kerr, Peter A. ...Jamaica Plain, MA
Kerr, Peyton A., III ...Phoenix, AZ
Kerr, Philip A. ...Sacramento, CA
Kerr, R. Bruce ...Oklahoma City, OK
Kerr, Raymond C. ...Houston, TX
Kerr, Richard F. ...Braintree, MA
Kerr, Richard L. ...San Antonio, TX
Kerr, Richard N. ...Baltimore, MD
Kerr, Robert A ...Portland, OR
Kerr, Robert A., Jr. ...Charleston, SC
Kerr, Robert Alexander
La Canada Flintridge, CA
Kerr, Robert M., Jr. ...Blackfoot, ID
Kerr, Robert S., Jr. ...Oklahoma City, OK
Kerr, Russell and Weber, PLC
Bloomfield Hills, MI
Detroit, MI
East Lansing, MI
Kerr, Samuel D. ...Rapid City, SD
Kerr, Samuel W. ...Steubenville, OH
Kerr, Sonja D. ...Inver Grove Heights, MN
Kerr, Stacy D. ...Brick, NJ
Kerr, Steven D. ...Atlanta, GA
Kerr, Steven S. ...Oklahoma City, OK
Kerr, Susan E. ...Goldsboro, NC
Kerr, Suzanne H. ...Houston, TX
Kerr, Theodore M. ...Midland, TX
Kerr, Thomas E. ...Pittsburgh, PA
Kerr, Thomas J. ...Houston, TX
Kerr, Thomas M.
Environmental Protection Agency, Program Office Attorneys, GV
Kerr, Thomas M. ...Pittsburgh, PA
Kerr, Thomas R. ...Covington, KY
Kerr, Thomas R. ...Warren, NJ
Kerr, Timothy S. ...Blue Bell, PA
Kerr, Todd R. ...Phoenix, AZ
Kerr, Tom A. ...Los Angeles, CA
Kerr, Troy ...Overland Park, KS
Kerr, Tym J. ...Kewanee, IL
Kerr, W. Bruce ...Aspen, CO
Kerr, W. Gregg ...Pittsburgh, PA
Kerr & Wagstaffe LLP, LLP
San Francisco, CA
Kerr, Walter L. ...Cleveland, OH
Kerr & Ward, L.L.P. ...Midland, TX
Kerr & Weiss ...New Paltz, NY
Kerr, Whitney E., Sr. ...Kansas City, MO
Kerr, William A. ...Malibu, CA
Kerr, William A. ...Indianapolis, IN
Kerr, William A., A Prof. Corp. ...Malibu, CA
Kerr, William B. ...New York, NY
Kerr, William D. ...Chicago, IL
Kerr, William F. ...Philadelphia, PA
Kerr, William G. ...Jackson, WY
Kerr, William K. ...New York, NY
Kerr, William M., Jr. ...Midland, TX
Kerr, William T. ...Towson, MD
Kerr & Wilson, P.C. ...San Antonio, TX
Kerr, Wm. H. ...Boston, MA
Kerr, Wm. Monroe ...Midland, TX
Kerrane, Jeffrey P. ...San Diego, CA
Kerrick, Carl B. ...Lewiston, ID
Kerrick, David E. ...Boise, ID
Kerrick, David E. ...Caldwell, ID
Kerrick, Grise & Stivers
Bowling Green, KY
Elizabethtown, KY
Kerrick, Robert V. ...Phoenix, AZ
Kerrick, Sandra S. ...Crystal Lake, IL
Kerrick, Thomas N. ...Bowling Green, KY
Elizabethtown, KY
Kerridge, Douglas C. ...Charlotte, NC
Kerridge, Kathy J. ...Martinez, CA
Kerridge, Ronald D. ...Dallas, TX
Kerrigan, Boller, Stevenson & Goettemoeller Co., L.P.A. ...Sidney, OH
Kerrigan, Cameron K. ...San Jose, CA
Kerrigan, Daniel J. ...Washington, DC
Kerrigan, David L. ...Irvine, CA
Kerrigan, David R. ...Boston, MA
Kerrigan, Dennis F., Jr. ...Hartford, CT
Kerrigan, Devin S. ...Washington, DC
Kerrigan, Elizabeth E. ...Decatur, GA
Kerrigan, Estess, Rankin & McLeod
Crestview, FL
Destin, FL
Fort Walton Beach, FL
Marianna, FL
Milton, FL
Panama City, FL
Pensacola, FL
Kerrigan, Estess, Rankin, McLeod & Hightower ...Mobile, AL
Kerrigan, George L. ...Seymour, IN
Kerrigan, James M. ...Ithaca, NY
Kerrigan, John F. ...Fremont, NE
Kerrigan, John J., Jr. ...Newtown, PA
Kerrigan, Joseph M. ...Nashua, NH
Kerrigan, Kathleen A. ...Princeton, NJ
Kerrigan, Kathy P. ...Baltimore, MD
Kerrigan, Kevin J. ...New York, NY
Kerrigan, Lori M. Allegri ...San Jose, CA
Kerrigan, Marli J.P. ...Washington, DC
Kerrigan, Mary Beth ...Waltham, MA
Kerrigan, Mary Dennard
New Orleans, LA
Kerrigan, Michael C. ...McLean, VA
Kerrigan, Nancy J. ...Santa Cruz, CA
Kerrigan, Patricia J. ...Houston, TX
Kerrigan, Paul B. ...Philadelphia, PA
Kerrigan, Robert E., Jr., (P.L.C.)
New Orleans, LA
Kerrigan, Robert G.
Fort Walton Beach, FL
Panama City, FL
Pensacola, FL
Kerrigan, Robert M. ...New York, NY
Kerrigan, Robert Wade ...Kansas City, MO
Kerrigan, Sarah V. ...Houston, TX
Kerrigan, Suzanne E. ...New York, NY
Kerrigan, Thomas P. ...New York, NY
Kerrigan, Thomas S. ...Los Angeles, CA
Kerrigan, Thomas W., II ...Sidney, OH
Kerrigan, Thomas W., Sr. ...Sidney, OH
Kerrigan, Timothy G. ...Nashua, NH
Kerrigan, Ursula M. ...New York, NY
Kerrigan, Wade ...Kansas City, MO
Kerrigan & Wallace ...Ithaca, NY
Kerrigan, Walter F. ...San Diego, CA
Kerrigan, William K. ...Nyack, NY
Kerrine, T. Michael ...Washington, DC
Kerrins, Michael P. ...Revere, MA
Kerrison, Karen W. ...Charleston, SC
Kerrison & Kerrison ...Charleston, SC
Kerrison, Lee ...Charleston, SC
Kerrissey, Paul M. ...Newton, MA
Kerruish, David S. ...Seattle, WA
Kerr-White, Kathleen L.
Half Moon Bay, CA
Kerry, Cameron F. ...Boston, MA
Kerry, Garcia & Lewis ...Long Beach, CA
Los Angeles, CA
Kerry, Henry E. ...Fort Worth, TX
Kerry, Jack T. ...Los Angeles, CA
Kerry, John F. ...Boston, MA
Kerry, Melinda E. ...Exton, PA
Kerry, Richard J. ...Manchester, MA
Kerry, Robert A. ...Tucson, AZ
Kerry, Robert A., P.C. ...Tucson, AZ
Kerry, William H. ...Long Beach, CA
Kersch, Kenneth I. ...Ithaca, NY
Kerschenbaum, Steven A. ...Gaithersburg, MD
Kerscher, John F. ...Racine, WI
Kerscher, William F. ...Simpsonville, SC
Kerschner, Barry J. ...New York, NY
Kerschner, Michael J. ...Indianapolis, IN
Kerschner, Stephen L. ...Chicago, IL
Kersenbrock, Sara A. ...Waterloo, IA
Kersey, Andrew J. ...Fairfax, VA
Kersey, B. Franklin ...Washington, DC
Kersey, David M. ...Bluefield, WV
Kersey, Gary E. ...Kerrville, TX
Kersey, Gary E., P.C. ...Kerrville, TX
Kersey, George E. ...Lynnfield, MA
Meredith, NH
Kersey, James M. ...Cleveland, OH
Kersey, Kimberly ...Haddonfield, NJ
Kersey, Laura Lynn ...Washington, DC
Kersey, Paul S. ...Southfield, MI
Kersey, Robert ...Granbury, TX
Kersey, Robert C. ...Washington, DC
Kersh, Candice Stein ...New York, NY
Kersh, Carrie W. ...Clarksville, TN
Kersh, DeWitte T., Jr. ...Providence, RI
Kersh, John D., Jr. ...Gastonia, NC
Kersh, John T. ...Laurel, MS
Kersh, Karol W., (Mr.) ...Salem, OR
Kersh, Nina Greene ...Miami, FL
Kershaw, Anne E. ...Tarrytown, NY
Kershaw, Brandon Kyle ...Baton Rouge, LA
Kershaw, Edward Lee ...Greeneville, TN
Kershaw, Jack ...Nashville, TN
Kershaw, James B. ...Bastrop, TX
Kershaw, James J., III ...Los Angeles, CA
Kershaw, James L. ...Fort Lauderdale, FL
Kershaw, Jeffery M. ...Dallas, TX
Kershaw and Jenkins ...Bastrop, TX
Kershaw, John W. ...Providence, RI
Kershaw, Leonard R. ...Albany, NY
Kershaw, Michael ...Fresno, CA
Kershaw, Michael ...Philadelphia, PA
Kershaw, Michele A.
Commodity Futures Trading Commission, Division of Enforcement, GV
Kershaw, Newton H., Jr. ...Manchester, NH
Kershaw, Robert B. ...Baltimore, MD
Kershaw, Robert D., Jr. ...Austin, TX
Kershaw, Thomas D., Jr. ...Twin Falls, ID
Kershaw, Walter Scott ...Uniondale, NY
Kershaw, William A. ...Sacramento, CA
San Francisco, CA
Kershek, Dennis J. ...San Diego, CA
Kershek, E. Joseph ...Milwaukee, WI
Kershek, Eugene A. ...Milwaukee, WI
Kershek Law Offices ...Milwaukee, WI
Kershek, Mark E. ...Milwaukee, WI
Kershen, Drew L. ...Norman, OK
Kershen, Harry ...Massapequa, NY
Kershenblatt, Eric S. ...Atlantic City, NJ
Kershnar, Harris Edwin ...Santa Ana, CA
Kershnar, Stephen P. ...Lincoln, NE
Kershner, A. Daniel ...Bel Air, MD
Kershner, Cheryl R. ...Los Altos, CA
Kershner, Craig D. ...Dighton, KS
Kershner, Edwin H. ...Reading, PA
Kershner, Gary R. ...Oakland, CA
Kershner, H. Morrison ...Fergus Falls, MN
Kershner, Hawkins & Polen, P.C.
Virginia Beach, VA
Kershner, Lisa A. ...Baltimore, MD
Kershner, Louis W. ...Virginia Beach, VA
Kershner, Marilyn K. ...Tampa, FL
Kershner, Mary Steck ...Detroit, MI
Kershner, Rodger A. ...Dearborn, MI
Kershner, William F. ...Berwyn, PA
Kershow, Michael R. ...Washington, DC
Kersker, Linda B. ...Akron, OH
Kerson, Edward W. ...New York, NY
Kerson, Paul E. ...Forest Hills, NY
Kerss, Brian E. ...Oakland, CA
Kerst, Dan ...Glenwood Springs, CO
Kerst, Marilyn E. ...Washington, DC
Kerstein & Associates, P.C. ...Quincy, MA
Kerstein, David A. ...New Orleans, LA
Kerstein, David A., A Professional Law Corporation ...New Orleans, LA
Kerstein, Joshua M. ...Denver, CO
Kerstein, Mark A. ...Houston, TX
Kerstein, Neil M. ...Quincy, MA
Kerstein, Philip M. ...New York, NY
Kersten Brownlee Hendricks, LLP
Fort Dodge, IA
Kersten, Carol J. ...Palo Alto, CA
Kersten, E. Campion ...Milwaukee, WI
Kersten, Ernest ...Fort Dodge, IA
Kersten, George P. ...Milwaukee, WI
Kersten, James K. ...Flat Rock, MI
Kersten, John C. ...Waynesville, NC
Kersten, Julius R. ...Buffalo, NY
Kersten, Katherine A. ...Minneapolis, MN
Kersten, Kenan J. ...Milwaukee, WI
Kersten, Kent L. ...Kansas City, MO
Kersten, Kurt G. ...Grosse Ile, MI
Kersten, Lee D. ...Eugene, OR
Kersten & McKinnon, S.C.
Milwaukee, WI
Kersten, Michael J. ...Sacramento, CA
Kersten, Montgomery ...Santa Clara, CA
Kersten, Richard G. ...Solvang, CA
Kersten, Stephen G. ...Fort Dodge, IA
Kersten, Steven A. ...Chicago, IL
Kersten, William C. ...Irvine, CA
Kerstetter, Ralph A. ...San Francisco, CA
Kerstetter, Todd P. ...Shamokin, PA
Kerstetter, Wayne A. ...Chicago, IL
Kerstiens, Kevin F. ...Portland, OR
Kerstine, Edwin E. ...Jackson, MS
Kersting, Andrew S. ...Washington, DC
Arlington, VA
Kersting, Christopher J. ...Washington, DC
Kersting, Joan M. ...St. Louis, MO
Kert, Arnold L. ...Garden City, NY
Kert, Caroline R. ...Boston, MA
Kertell, Charles A. ...Los Angeles, CA
Kertez, Jay M. ...Chicago, IL
Kerth, David M. ...Baton Rouge, LA
Kerth, Kristin Hennes ...University City, MO
Kerth, Leslie Shawn ...San Francisco, CA
Kerth, Norman R. ...New Orleans, LA
Kerth, Peter D. ...St. Louis, MO
Kerth, Samantha ...Belleville, IL
Kertman, Paul B. ...Phoenix, AZ
Kertscher, Douglas R. ...Atlanta, GA
Kertscher, Elizabeth Thompson
Atlanta, GA
Kertz, Consuelo L. ...Atlanta, GA
Kertz, Daniel J. ...St. Louis, MO
Kertzman, David K. ...Wellesley, MA
Kervel, Jana L. ...Miami Springs, FL
Kervick, David L. ...Westfield, NJ
Kervick, J. Christopher ...Windsor Locks, CT
Kerwick, Ann M. ...Rochester, NY
Kerwick, Constance R. ...Baldwin, NY
Kerwick, Stephen M. ...Wichita, KS
Kerwick, William G. ...Baldwin, NY
Huntington, NY
Kerwin, Ada Snyder ...Birmingham, MI
Kerwin, Adrienne ...Albany, NY
Kerwin, Brian P. ...Chicago, IL
Kerwin, Dennis C. ...San Francisco, CA
Kerwin, Frank J. ...St. Clair Shores, MI
Kerwin, Gregory J. ...Denver, CO
Kerwin, Gregory M. ...Harrisburg, PA
Kerwin, Harriet
Consumer Product Safety Commission, Office of the General Counsel, GV
Kerwin, Holly McClure ...Harrisburg, PA
Kerwin, J. Eugene ...Livonia, MI
Kerwin, James W. ...Naples, FL
Kerwin, Jane M. ...Fort Lauderdale, FL
Kerwin, Jeffrey ...Oakland, CA
Kerwin, John E. ...Olathe, KS
Kerwin, John M. ...Omaha, NE
Kerwin, Joseph D. ...Harrisburg, PA
Kerwin, Joseph E. ...Marco Island, FL
Kerwin, Keith M. ...Bingham Farms, MI
Kerwin & Kerwin ...Harrisburg, PA
Kerwin & Kerwin, L.L.P. ...Menlo Park, CA
Kerwin, Kristina M. ...Houston, TX
Kerwin, Marcia Jackson ...Liberty, MO
Kerwin, Mary Ann Collins
Cherry Hills Village, CO
Kerwin, Melvin C. ...Menlo Park, CA
Kerwin, Michael J. ...Camillus, NY
Kerwin, Patrick C. ...Menlo Park, CA
Kerwin, Richard A. ...Chicago, IL
Kerwin, Robert J. ...Boston, MA
Kerwin, Sheila T. ...Minneapolis, MN
Kerwin, Stephen M. ...Albany, NY
Kerwin, Sydney L. ...Southfield, MI
Kerwin, Terrence J. ...Harrisburg, PA
Kerwin, Thomas M. J.
Securities and Exchange Commission, Division of Investment Management, GV
Kerwin, Timothy L. ...Cleveland, OH
Kerwood, Gary S. ...Portland, OR
Kerwood, Mark W. ...Buffalo, NY
Kerxton, Alan S. ...Rockville, MD
Kerxton, Amy L. ...San Francisco, CA
Kerxton, Jill K. ...Washington, DC
Kery, Susan C. ...Albuquerque, NM
Keryczynskyj, Leo ...Chicago, IL
Kerzner, Debbie ...Boston, MA
Kerzner, Neil S. ...Philadelphia, PA
Kerzner, Paul A. ...Ridgewood, NY
Kesala, Victoria Ann ...Vancouver, WA
Kesaris, George P. ...Bar Harbor, ME
Kesaris, George P., P.A. ...Bar Harbor, ME
Kesaris, Philip A.
Department of Housing and Urban Development, Office of the Inspector General, GV
Kesatie, William J., Law Offices of
Thousand Oaks, CA
Keschner, Irving ...Torrance, CA
Kesecker, John E. ...Monterey, CA
Salinas, CA
Keselenko, Jonathan A. ...Boston, MA
Keshen, Nelson C. ...Miami, FL
Keshen, Nelson C., P.A. ...Miami, FL
Keshian, James H. ...Westborough, MA
Keshian & Reynolds, P.C. ...Arlington, MA
Keshian, Richard ...Arlington, MA
Keshian, Richard J. ...Winston-Salem, NC
Keshishian, Arousiag (Alyce)
Philadelphia, PA
Keshishian, Matthew M. ...Oradell, NJ
Keshner, J. Lawrence ...Edwardsville, IL
Kesinger, G. Ronald ...Jacksonville, IL
Kesinger, Heidi J. ...Denver, CO
Kesinger, Terry L. ...Santa Ana, CA
Keskey, Don L. ...Lansing, MI
Kesler, Christopher A. ...Houston, TX
Kesler, David B. ...Chattanooga, TN
Kesler, Debra M. ...Metairie, LA
Kesler, John A., II ...Terre Haute, IN
Kesler, John A., Sr. ...Terre Haute, IN
Kesler, John T. ...Salt Lake City, UT
Kesler, Julie A. ...Seattle, WA
Kesler and Kesler ...Terre Haute, IN
Kesler, Martin L., Jr. ...Taylorsville, NC
Kesler, Morton A. ...Jacksonville, FL
Kesler, Rex L. ...Houston, TX
Kesler, Robert E. ...Danville, IL
Kesler, Robert M., Jr. ...Norfolk, VA
Kesler, Robin R. ...Lancaster, CA
Kesler & Rust, A Professional Corporation
Orem, UT
Salt Lake City, UT
Kesler, Thomas L., P.A. ...Columbus, MS
Kesler, Tracy ...Houston, TX
Kesler, Vibert L., Jr. (IBA)
Salt Lake City, UT
Kesler, William R. ...Danville, IL
Kesluk, Brian S. ...Los Angeles, CA
Kesmodel & Mason ...Duluth, GA
Kesmodel, W. Paul, Jr. ...Duluth, GA
Kesner, Alan R. ...Madison, WI
Kesner, Brent K. ...Charleston, WV
Kesner, David W. ...New Haven, CT
Kesner, Harvey J. ...New York, NY
Kesner, Kesner & Bramble ...Charleston, WV
Kesner, Kim C. ...Clearfield, PA
Kesner, Michael A. ...Sutherlin, OR
Kesner, Royce G. ...Newport Beach, CA
Kesner, Stephen D. ...Central Islip, NY
Kesner, Tanya M. ...Charleston, WV
Kesoglou, Thomas ...New York, NY
Kess, Avrohom J. ...New York, NY
Kess, Jeffrey H. ...Atlanta, GA
Kess, Kenneth M. ...Boston, MA
Kess, Lydia E. ...New York, NY
Kess, Stephanie S. ...Cleveland, OH
Kessack, Philip D. ...Lexington, KY
Kessel, Alan Jules ...Irvine, CA
Kessel, Amy G. ...Glendora, CA
Kessel, Bart L. ...Los Angeles, CA
Kessel, Charles V., Jr. ...Cocoa Beach, FL
Kessel, Edward ...Philadelphia, PA
Kessel, Elizabeth M. ...Los Angeles, CA
Kessel, Eric David ...McLean, VA
Kessel, Glenn R. ...Minneapolis, MN
Kessel, Harry C. ...Santa Barbara, CA
Kessel, Herbert A. ...Chicago, IL
Kessel, I. Michael ...Parsippany, NJ
Kessel, J. Philip ...Bethesda, MD
Kessel, Jamie Zalkin ...New York, NY
Kessel, Jeffry M. ...Pittsburgh, PA
Kessel, Jon M. ...Mount Sinai, NY
Kessel, Linda J. ...Eugene, OR
Kessel, Mark ...New York, NY
Kessel, Michael H. ...New York, NY
Kessel, Renee F. ...Chicago, IL
Kessel, Roger H. ...Tampa, FL
Kessel, Roy D., Law Offices of
Chicago, IL
Kessel & Splitt ...La Moure, ND
Kessel, Steven L. ...Red Bank, NJ
Kessel, Theodore F. ...La Moure, ND
Kessel, Theodore, Jr. ...La Moure, ND
Kesselhaut, Glenn D. ...New York, NY
Kesselhaut, Martin ...Livingston, NJ
Kessell, Gregory R. ...Doylestown, PA
Kessell, Richard W. ...Watsonville, CA
Kessell, Steven C. ...Hagerstown, MD
Kessell, Steven C., P.C. ...Hagerstown, MD

Kesselman, Arthur ... Stoughton, MA
Kesselman, Barry J. ... Stamford, CT
Kesselman, Burton A. ... Cresskill, NJ
Kesselman, Deborah ... New York, NY
Kesselman, Dov ... New York, NY
Kesselman, Edward C. ... New York, NY
Kesselman, Elayne Beth ... New York, NY
Kesselman, H. Stephen ... Philadelphia, PA
Kesselman, Howard M. ... Phoenix, AZ
Kesselman, Irwin M. ... Glenview, IL
Kesselman, Jeffrey R. ... Denver, CO
Kesselman, Lawrence M. ... New York, NY
Kesselman, Leo ... Los Gatos, CA
Kesselman, Marc L. ... Washington, DC
Kesselman, Paul R. ... Wilmette, IL
Kesselman, Paul R., The Law Firm of
Wilmette, IL
Kesselman, Richard ... Parsippany, NJ
Kesselman, Sol L. ... Delray Beach, FL
Kesselman, Stanley ... New York, NY
Kesselman, Stanley W. W.
Sherman Oaks, CA
Kesselman, Stephen E. ... New York, NY
Kesselring, Leo J. ... Rochester, NY
Kessenich, J. Fredrick ... New Orleans, LA
Kessenick, Laurence W.
San Francisco, CA
Kessenides, Elizabeth T. ... New York, NY
Kesser, Janis Wild ... Memphis, TN
Kesser, Lewis K. ... Norfolk, VA
Kesser, Peter H. ... Memphis, TN
Kessie, Charles L. ... Canadian, TX
Kessing, Kerrie C. ... Kennesaw, GA
Kessing, Kerrie C., P.C. ... Kennesaw, GA
Kessinger, Ben L., Jr. ... Lexington, KY
Kessinger, Benjamin Lee, III
Lexington, KY
Kessinger, C. Steven ... Ada, OK
Kessinger, Carl ... St. Louis, MO
Kessinger, Carolyn C. ... Oxford, MS
Kessinger, James A. ... Kansas City, MO
Kessinger, Jennifer F. ... Chicago, IL
Kessinger, Kevin J. ... Cleveland, OH
Kessinger Law Firm ... Oxford, MS
Kessinger, Ralph F. ... Lexington, KY
Kessinger, Terry M. ... Danville, IN
Kessinger, Thomas J. ... Pittsburgh, PA
Kesslen, Mark P. ... New York, NY
Kessler, Alan ... Canton, OH
Kessler, Alan C. ... Philadelphia, PA
Kessler, Alan M. ... Hackensack, NJ
Kessler, Albert H. ... Oakland, CA
Kessler, Albert I. ... Union, NJ
Kessler, Amanda Gay ... New York, NY
Kessler, Amy Broecker ... Louisville, KY
Kessler, Andrea L. ... Fort Lauderdale, FL
Kessler, Andrew ... Philadelphia, PA
Kessler, Andrew N. ... New Brunswick, NJ
Kessler, Andrew S. ... Roseland, NJ
Kessler, Andrew S. ... New York, NY
Kessler, Andrew S. ... Philadelphia, PA
Kessler, Arnold H., (P.C.) ... Beverly Hills, CA
Kessler, Arnold L. ... Berkeley, CA
Kessler, Arnold M. ... Philadelphia, PA
Kessler, Arthur ... Granada Hills, CA
Kessler, Avery B. ... Muskego, WI
Kessler, Averyell A. ... Jackson, MS
Kessler & Ballenger Co., L.P.A.
Columbus, OH
Kessler, Barbara M. ... Bethpage, NY
Kessler, Barbara R. ... New York, NY
Kessler, Barry C. ... Chicago, IL
Kessler, Bernard ... Hyde Park, NY
Kessler, Bernard J. ... Boca Raton, FL
Kessler, Bertram E. ... New York, NY
Kessler, Betty ... Miami, FL
Kessler, Bradford ... St. Louis, MO
Kessler, Bruce S. ... Houston, TX
Kessler, Carl R.
Department Of Health And Human Services,
Office of the General Counsel, GV
Kessler, Carl T. ... Livingston, NJ
Kessler, Chanan Elliot ... Palo Alto, CA
Kessler, Cheryl A. ... Annandale, VA
Kessler, Christopher C. ... Tarboro, NC
Kessler, Claudia M. ... Garden City, NY
Kessler, Cohen & Roth, A Professional Corporation ... Philadelphia, PA
Kessler & Collins, A Professional Corporation ... Dallas, TX
Kessler, Craig L. ... St. Louis, MO
Kessler, Cynthia S. ... Johnson City, TN
Kingsport, TN
Kessler, D. Keith, Jr. ... Centralia, IL
Kessler, Daniel J. ... San Diego, CA
Kessler, Daniel J. ... New York, NY
Kessler, Daniel T. ... Madison, NJ
Kessler, Darren J. ... El Cerrito, CA
Kessler, Daryl I. ... New York, NY
Kessler, David ... New York, NY
Kessler, David ... Grand Forks, ND
Kessler, David ... McArthur, OH
Kessler, David I. ... Clifton, NJ
Kessler, David Jason ... Philadelphia, PA
Kessler, David Lewis ... Miami, FL
Kessler, David S. ... Madison, NJ
Kessler, David S. ... Dublin, OH
Kessler, Deirdre G. ... New York, NY
Kessler, DiGiovanni & Jesuele ... Westfield, NJ
Kessler, Donald A. ... Florham Park, NJ
Kessler, Donn G. ... Phoenix, AZ
Kessler, Douglas W. ... Atlanta, GA
Kessler, Douglas W., P.C. ... Atlanta, GA
Kessler & Doyle ... Mesa, AZ
Kessler, Edward J. ... Washington, DC
Kessler, Edwina V. ... Fort Lauderdale, FL
Kessler, Elise J. ... White Plains, NY

Kessler, Elizabeth A. ... Department of Justice,
Immigration and Naturalization Service, GV
Kessler, Elizabeth P. ... Columbus, OH
Kessler, Ellen F. ... Mineola, NY
Kessler, Ellen Widen ... New Orleans, LA
Kessler, Ellyn D. ... New York, NY
Kessler, Emanuel ... New York, NY
Kessler, Eric W. ... Mesa, AZ
Kessler, Ernest A. ... Laguna Hills, CA
Kessler & Ex ... Chicago, IL
Kessler, Florence Asnes ... Mobile, AL
Kessler, Frank A. ... Cookeville, TN
Kessler, Fred H. ... Hammond, IN
Kessler, Frederic S. ... Newark, NJ
Kessler, Frederick D. ... Lewisburg, PA
Kessler, Frederick P. ... Milwaukee, WI
Kessler, Frederick R. ... New York, NY
Kessler, Frederick S. ... Wilmington, DE
Kessler, Fredric W. ... Los Angeles, CA
Kessler, Gail D. ... Crownsville, MD
Kessler, Gary L. ... Richmond, VA
Kessler, Gary R. ... Atlanta, GA
Kessler, Gary S. ... Dallas, TX
Kessler, Gary S. ... Waterbury, VT
Kessler, George H. ... Brooklyn, NY
Kessler & Gindin ... Philadelphia, PA
Kessler, Gladys ...
United States District Court For The District
Of Columbia, GV
Kessler, Gordon M. ... New York, NY
Kessler, Greg S. ... St. Louis, MO
Kessler, Gregory S. ... Cincinnati, OH
Kessler, Hal Ross ... Chicago, IL
Kessler, Hal S. ... San Francisco, CA
Kessler, Harold I. ... Providence, RI
Kessler, Henry B. ... Bordentown, NJ
Kessler, Herbert J. ... Westfield, NJ
Kessler, Herbert R. ... San Francisco, CA
Kessler, Howard S. ... Ardsley, NY
Kessler, Irving L. ... Rochester, NY
Kessler, Jack J. ... Pittsburgh, PA
Kessler, James L. ... Birmingham, AL
Kessler, James M. ... Springfield, MA
Kessler, Jeffrey I. ... Department of the Army,
Army Materiel Command, GV
Kessler, Jeffrey L. ... New York, NY
Kessler, Jeffrey V. ... Moundsville, WV
Kessler, Jerald A. ... Highland Park, IL
Kessler, Jerome M. ... Rockville Centre, NY
Kessler, Jerry ... Valencia, CA
Kessler, Joan B. ... Los Angeles, CA
Kessler, Joan B. ... Hackensack, NJ
New York, NY
Kessler, Joan F. ... Milwaukee, WI
Kessler, Joel ... Chicago, IL
Kessler, Joel M. ... Waterford, CT
Kessler, John A. ... Charleston, WV
Kessler, John A., Jr. ... Boston, MA
Providence, RI
Kessler, John D. ... Oakland, CA
Kessler, John D. ... Princeton, NJ
Kessler, John E. ... Holland, MI
Kessler, John J. ... Rockville, MD
Kessler, John L. ... Malvern, PA
Kessler, John W. ... Dayton, OH
Kessler, Jonathan A. ... St. Louis, MO
Kessler, Jonathan L. ... Denver, CO
Kessler & Jones ... Charleston, WV
Kessler, Joseph F. ... Cherry Hill, NJ
Philadelphia, PA
Kessler, Judd L. ... Washington, DC
Kessler, Julie L. ... Beverly Hills, CA
Kessler, Katherine Allen ... New York, NY
Kessler, Keith L. ... Hoquiam, WA
Kessler, Kenneth L. ... Des Moines, IA
Kessler, Kenneth S. ... Tacoma, WA
Kessler & Kessler ... New York, NY
Kessler & Kessler ... Mc Keesport, PA
Kessler & Kessler ... San Antonio, TX
Uvalde, TX
Kessler & Kessler, A Law Corporation
Los Angeles, CA
Kessler, Kevin R. ... Warrenton, VA
Kessler, Kirsten L.
Department of Transportation,
Federal Highway Administration, GV
Kessler, Kristi E. ... Charlotte, NC
Kessler, Laura T. ... Baltimore, MD
Kessler, Laurence G. ... Richmond, VA
Kessler, Lawrence B. ... New York, NY
Kessler, Lawrence P. ... Rochester, NY
Kessler, Lawrence W. ... Hempstead, NY
Kessler, Leonard ... Goshen, NY
Kessler, Leslie M. ... Alameda, CA
Kessler, Lillian R. ... Morristown, NJ
Kessler & Lombardi ... Plymouth Meeting, PA
Kessler, Lorence L. ... Washington, DC
Kessler, Louis ... Passaic, NJ
Kessler, Marc J. ... Columbus, OH
Kessler, Margaret Lyons ... New York, NY
Kessler, Marie E. ... Grand Rapids, MI
Kessler, Mark K. ... Philadelphia, PA
Kessler, Mark S. ... Jacksonville, FL
Kessler, Mark S., P.A. ... Jacksonville, FL
Kessler, Mark Steven ... Rancho Bernardo, CA
Kessler, Martin ... Tampa, FL
Kessler, Martin, P.A. ... Tampa, FL
Kessler, Matthew R. ... Rosemont, PA
Kessler, Maureen C. ... New York, NY
Kessler, Melissa B. ... Philadelphia, PA
Kessler, Merle J. ... Atlanta, GA
Kessler, Meryl ... Boston, MA
Kessler, Michael A. ... Cumming, GA
Kessler, Michael J. ... Fort Pierce, FL
Kessler, Michael J., P.A. ... Fort Pierce, FL
Kessler, Michael L. ... Alexandria, VA
Kessler, Michael P. ... Houston, TX
Kessler, Michael W. ... Albany, NY

Kessler, Michele A. ... Lawrence, KS
Kessler, Mitchell D. ... New York, NY
Kessler, Mullkoff & Hooberman
Ann Arbor, MI
Kessler, Muriel S. ... New York, NY
Kessler, Murray J. ... New Milford, CT
Kessler, Nancy
Department of Transportation,
Office of the General Counsel, GV
Kessler, Nathan N. ... Arlington Heights, IL
Kessler, Neil S. ... Richmond, VA
Kessler, Nicholas A. ... Washington, DC
Kessler, Patricia A. ... Garden City, NY
Kessler, Paula C. ... Fort Lauderdale, FL
Kessler, Paulette Steinberg ... Bethesda, MD
Kessler, Philip J. ... Detroit, MI
Kessler, Phyllis J. ... Hackensack, NJ
New York, NY
Kessler, Ralph K. ... New York, NY
Kessler, Randall M. ... Atlanta, GA
Kessler, Remy ... Los Angeles, CA
Kessler, Richard A. ... Philadelphia, PA
Kessler, Richard F. ... Fairfax, VA
Kessler, Richard Hand ... New York, NY
Kessler, Richard M. ... Knoxville, TN
Kessler, Richard N. ... Chicago, IL
Waukegan, IL
Kessler, Richard P., Jr. ... Atlanta, GA
Kessler, Richard S. ... Memphis, TN
Kessler, Richard W. ... Philadelphia, PA
Kessler, Robert A. ... Brooklyn, NY
Kessler, Robert A. ... New York, NY
Kessler, Robert H. ... Boca Raton, FL
Kessler, Robert J. ... Baltimore, MD
Kessler, Robert Jay, P.C., Law Offices of
Baltimore, MD
Kessler, Robert Lee ... Denver, CO
Kessler, Robert M. ... Los Angeles, CA
Kessler, Robert M. ... New Haven, CT
Kessler, Robert M. ... New York, NY
Kessler, Robert S. ... Lorain, OH
Kessler, Robert T. ... Houston, TX
Kessler, Robert W. ... Rochester, NY
Kessler, Roger L. ... Indianapolis, IN
Kessler, Ronald W. ... Austin, TX
Kessler, Russell W. ... Columbus, OH
Kessler & Schwarz, P.C. ... Atlanta, GA
Kessler, Scott P. ... Rahway, NJ
Kessler & Seecof, LLP ... San Diego, CA
Kessler, Sheila J. ... Montello, WI
Kessler, Siegfried F. ... Niceville, FL
Kessler Smith & Powen ... Chicago, IL
Kessler, Stanton A. ... Chicago, IL
Kessler, Stephen F. ... Coral Gables, FL
Kessler, Stephen W. ... Topeka, KS
Kessler, Steven F. ... Mc Keesport, PA
Kessler, Steven H. ... Brooklyn, NY
Kessler, Steven L. ... New York, NY
Kessler, Steven L. ... New York, NY
Kessler, Steven L. ... New York, NY
Kessler, Steven M. ... New York, NY
Kessler, Steven P. ... New York, NY
Kessler, Steven R. ... New York, NY
Kessler, Stuart ... Ardsley, NY
Kessler, Stuart M. ... Arlington Heights, IL
Kessler, Stuart M., P.C.
Arlington Heights, IL
Kessler, Stuart Warren
Plymouth Meeting, PA
Kessler, Susan Ann ... Richmond, VA
Kessler, Susan D ... Indianapolis, IN
Kessler, Suzanne H. ... Universal City, CA
Kessler, Tamara J. ... Department of Justice,
Office of the Inspector General, GV
Kessler, Tedd ... New York, NY
Kessler, Terrence P. ... Canton, OH
Kessler, Terry A. ... Princeton, NJ
Kessler, Thomas G. ... Cherry Hill, NJ
Philadelphia, PA
Kessler, Tutek and Gladfelter
Bordentown, NJ
Kessler, W. Jack ... Beverly Hills, CA
Kessler, W. A. ... Uvalde, TX
Kessler, Walter F. ... Mesa, AZ
Kessler, Warren J. ... Los Angeles, CA
Kessler, Wilbur K. ... Fresno, CA
Kessler, William A., Jr. ... Uvalde, TX
Kessler, William F., Jr. ... San Antonio, TX
Kessman, Stephen T. ... Stoughton, MA
Kessmeier, Catherine Lavelle
Department of Commerce,
Office of the General Counsel, GV
Kessner, Audrey Bernstein
Department of Housing and Urban
Development,
Office of General Counsel, GV
Kessner Duca Umebayashi Bain & Matsunaga, Attorneys At Law, A Law Corporation ... Honolulu, HI
Kessner, Lawrence A. ... Bethesda, MD
Kessner, Neil H. ... New York, NY
Kessner, Robert C. ... Honolulu, HI
Kessner, Theodore L. ... Lincoln, NE
Kest, John Marshall ... Orlando, FL
Kest, Sally Dee Millward ... Orlando, FL
Kestan, Michael D. ... New York, NY
Kestel, Jean M. ... Garden City, NY
Kestelik, Robert J. ... Houston, TX
Kesteloot, Melany L. ... Deerfield, IL
Kesten, Daniel L. ... Lexington, KY
Kesten, Gerald L. ... Arlington, VA
Kesten, Leonard H. ... Boston, MA
Kesten, Linda A. ... Hartford, CT
Kesten, Marc J. ... Burbank, CA
Kesten, Matthew C. ... New York, NY
Kesten, Norton A. ... Van Nuys, CA
Kesten, Robert M. ... Chester, NY
Kesten, Steven M. ... Greenbrae, CA

Kestenband, Jeffrey C. ... Hartford, CT
Kestenbaum, Alan C. ... Bayside, NY
Kestenbaum, Alfred K. ... New York, NY
Kestenbaum, Barbara A. ... Rockville, MD
Kestenbaum, Brian S. ... Philadelphia, PA
Kestenbaum, Dannenberg & Klein, LLP
New York, NY
Kestenbaum, David S. ... Van Nuys, CA
Kestenbaum, Elise B. ... Great Neck, NY
Kestenbaum, Harold L. ... Garden City, NY
Kestenbaum, Harold L., P.C.
Garden City, NY
Kestenbaum & Hoffman LLP
Beverly Hills, CA
Kestenbaum, Jane ... Cary, NC
Kestenbaum, Janis C. ... Washington, DC
Kestenbaum, Jeffrey Kenneth ... Brooklyn, NY
Kestenbaum, Leon M. ... Washington, DC
Kestenbaum, M. Robert ... Albuquerque, NM
Kestenbaum & Mark ... Roseland, NJ
Great Neck, NY
Kestenbaum, Martin E. ... South Plainfield, NJ
Kestenbaum, Mary E. ... Tampa, FL
Kestenbaum, Michael ... White Plains, NY
Kestenbaum, Paul T. ... Beverly Hills, CA
Los Angeles, CA
Kestenbaum, Richard ... New York, NY
Kestenbaum, Richard S. ... Great Neck, NY
Kestenbaum, Susan M. ... Hackensack, NJ
Kestenblatt, Herman ... Rochester, NY
Kester, Charles F. ... Woodland Hills, CA
Kester, Charles M. ... Fayetteville, AR
Kester, Charles M., P.L.C.
Bentonville, AR
Fayetteville, AR
Kester, Dolores A. ... Madison, WI
Kester, Grier S., Jr. ... Columbia, SC
Kester, H. Paul ... Doylestown, PA
Kester, John G. ... Washington, DC
Kester, Kelly L. ... Sunrise, FL
Kester, Kerry L. ... Lincoln, NE
Kester, Krista L. ... Lincoln, NE
Kester, Mary Osgood ... Santa Cruz, CA
Kester & Quinlan LLP
Corona Del Mar, CA
Kester, Randall B. ... Portland, OR
Kester, Randy S. ... Springville, UT
Kester, Robert G. ... Boston, MA
Kester, Ronald C. ... Salisbury, NC
Kester, Ronald G. ... Sacramento, CA
Kester, Shelley A. ... Traverse City, MI
Kester, Steven L. ... Corona Del Mar, CA
Kester-Meyer, Lynne ... Boulder, CO
Kesterson, James C. ... Dallas, TX
Kesterson, James V. ... Vaughn, WA
Kesterson, Linda L. ... Anchorage, AK
Kesterson, Ronald W. ... Houston, TX
Kesterson, Tera Futrell ... Nashville, AR
Kestin, Howard H. ... Hackensack, NJ
Kestin, Patricia T. ... New York, NY
Kestler, Hal A. ... Pittsburgh, PA
Kestler, Jeffrey L. ... Berkeley Heights, NJ
Kestner, David W. ... Suitland, MD
Kestner, Mark P. ... Rockville, MD
Kestner, R. Steven ... Cleveland, OH
Kestner, Susan E. ... McLean, VA
Kestner, Tara J. ... Holland, OH
Keston, Joan A. ... Miami, FL
Keszler, Michael S. ... Wall Township, NJ
Keta, Mishel ... Chicago, IL
Ketai, Lisa A. ... Houston, TX
Ketaineck, Stephen R. ... West Haven, CT
Ketaineck, Stuart M. ... Hamden, CT
Ketay, Staci L. ... Chicago, IL
Ketch, Andrea M. ... Denver, CO
Ketcham, Bruce E. ... Troy, MI
Ketcham, Carleton P., Jr. ... Birmingham, AL
Ketcham, Chester S. ... Middlebury, VT
Ketcham, Christina D. ... Chicago, IL
Ketcham, Dan H. ... Omaha, NE
Ketcham, James R. ... Montauk, NY
Ketcham, John M. ... Fort Wayne, IN
Ketcham, John T. ... Department of Energy,
Office of the General Counsel, GV
Ketcham, Kenneth P. ... Memphis, TN
Ketcham & Ketcham ... Columbus, OH
Ketcham, Lori W.
National Labor Relations Board,
Office of the General Counsel, GV
Ketcham, Matthew J. ... Fort Smith, AR
Waldron, AR
Ketcham, Orman W. ... Williamsburg, VA
Ketcham, Paula M. ... Chicago, IL
Ketcham, Platt V. ... Charlotte, NC
Ketcham, Richard S. ... Columbus, OH
Ketcham, Robert C. ... Bethesda, MD
Ketcham, Stephen E. ... Naples, FL
Ketcham, Victor A. ... Columbus, OH
Ketcham, Walter A., Jr. ... Orlando, FL
Ketcham, William F. ... Newburgh, NY
Ketcham, William L. ... Tucson, AZ
Ketcham, William R. ... Elgin, IL
Ketcham, William T., Jr. ... Lawrence, NY
Ketcham-Colwill, Nancy A.
Environmental Protection Agency,
Office of the General Counsel, GV
Ketchand, Robert L. ... Houston, TX
Ketchel, Edwin J. ... Chagrin Falls, OH
Ketchel, Hyman ... New York, NY
Ketchel, Terrance R. ... Fort Walton Beach, FL
Ketchel, Terrance R., P.A.
Fort Walton Beach, FL
Ketchen, Edward G., Jr.
Department of the Army,
Office, Chief of Engineers/Headquarters,
U.S. Army Corps of Engineers, GV
Ketchersid, Timothy O. ... Dallas, TX

Khachigian, Elizabeth M.
San Francisco, CA
Khachigian, Kenneth L. ....**Los Angeles, CA**
San Clemente, CA
Khadavi, Steven ....New York, NY
Khadder, Nicholas ....**Palo Alto, CA**
Khadem, Ali ....Lake Ronkonkoma, NY
Khadem, Vanda Marie ....**Brookline, MA**
Khadilkar, Miloslav ....**Santa Ana, CA**
Khadiri, Gita ....**Washington, DC**
Khairi, Saba A. ....New York, NY
Khajezadeh, Dina R. ....Toms River, NJ
Khakee, Nitin ....**New York, NY**
Khalaf, Maha ....**Palo Alto, CA**
Khalaf, Samer E. ....**Hackensack, NJ**
Khaleel, Yasmeen Sabina ......**Moorestown, NJ**
Philadelphia, PA
Khalil, Carl J. ....**Virginia Beach, VA**
Khalil, Emad H. ....**New York, NY**
Khalil, Manal Zakhary
Salt Lake City, UT
Khalil, Margaret ....Scottsdale, AZ
Khalil, Mark E. ....San Jose, CA
Khalil, Mona Ali ....New York, NY
Khalili, Sandra ....**Los Angeles, CA**
Khalili-Esfahani, Houtan ....Washington, DC
Khalsa, Amrit Kaur ....Anchorage, AK
Khalsa, Hari Nam S. ....Salem, OR
Khalsa, Kartar S.
Pension Benefit Guaranty Corporation, Office of the General Counsel, GV
Khalsa, Kirtan K. ....**Albuquerque, NM**
Khalsa Law Firm, The, P.C. ....New York, NY
Khalsa, S. J. ....New York, NY
Khambati, Mohsin ....**Tucson, AZ**
Khami, James D. ....Troy, MI
Khan, Aasma A. ....New York, NY
Khan, Amiena A. ....New York, NY
Khan, Amman ....**Los Angeles, CA**
Khan, Arshad Q. (Paku) ....**Nashville, TN**
Khan, Asad U. ....**Charleston, WV**
Khan, Asman ....Campbell, CA
Khan, Asmat A. ....Department of Commerce, Patent and Trademark Office, GV
Khan, Ayesha N. ....Manassas, VA
Khan, Azra J. ....**Newburgh, NY**
Khan, D. Barry ....Santa Monica, CA
Khan, Farzana Z. ....**New York, NY**
Khan, Ismael G., Jr. ....San Francisco, CA
Khan, Kamran Q. ....**Kansas City, MO**
Khan, Karen A. ....**Washington, DC**
Khan, L. Ali ....Topeka, KS
Khan, Lailah N. ....Washington, DC
Khan, Lori J. ....**Houston, TX**
Khan, Lynda J. ....Chicago, IL
Khan, M. Major ....Weehawken, NJ
Khan, Margaret Jost ....Sacramento, CA
Khan, Masud E. ....**Milwaukee, WI**
Khan, N. Shaheen ....Fairfax, VA
Khan, Nadira ....**Totowa, NJ**
Khan, Naseem ....Treasury Department, Internal Revenue Service, GV
Khan, Nazir F. ....Sherman Oaks, CA
Khan, Ned C. ....Aurora, IL
Khan, Raazia A. ....**Atlanta, GA**
Khan, Rex D. ....**Beverly Hills, CA**
Khan, Safia ....**Chicago, IL**
Khan, Tariq A. ....**Houston, TX**
Khaneja, Anita ....Chicago, IL
Khang, Joon M. ....**Los Angeles, CA**
Khani, James J. ....New York, NY
Khanna, Dhruv ....Palo Alto, CA
Khanna, Melanie ....Department of State, Office of the Legal Adviser, GV
Khanna & Narain ....**Berkeley, CA**
Khanna, Padam Kumar ....**Berkeley, CA**
Khanna, Rajiv ....New York, NY
Khanna, Rakesh ....Chicago, IL
Khanwalkar, Arundhati ....**Allentown, PA**
Kharal, Asaf ....New York, NY
Kharasch, Ira D. ....**Los Angeles, CA**
Kharasch, Robert N. ....**Washington, DC**
Kharazmi, Massoumeh ....Orange, CA
Kharcheva, Yaekaterina ....New York, NY
Khare, Sanjay K. ....**Menlo Park, CA**
Kharouf, A. Ammar ....**Los Angeles, CA**
Khashiun, Karamah M. ....New York, NY
Khastoo, S. Shawn ....Beverly Hills, CA
Khatcherian, Sylvia (IBA) ....**New York, NY**
Khatchikian, Carin V. ....**New York, NY**
Khater, Tony S. ....Washington, DC
Khatibloo, Miriam ....**San Francisco, CA**
Khatri, Prakash Ishverlal ....Orlando, FL
Khatri, Prakash, P.A., Law Offices of
Orlando, FL
Khattab, Mohab T. ....**Washington, DC**
Khawly, Marianne H.
Securities and Exchange Commission, Division of Market Regulation, GV
Khazarian, Roxanne ....**Danbury, CT**
Kheder, May Shallal ....**Springfield, VA**
Khederian, Richard ....Bloomfield Hills, MI
Kheel, Alan J. ....Camarillo, CA
Kheel, Daniel ....**New York, NY**
Kheel, Robert J. ....**New York, NY**
Kheel, Shirley Dungan ....New York, NY
Kheel, Theodore W. ....**New York, NY**
Kheel, Thomas H. ....Ithaca, NY
Khera, Farhana Yasmin ....Washington, DC
Kherdekar, Avani ....**Boston, MA**
Kherkher, Steven J. ....**Houston, TX**
Khero, Tariq A. ....**Santa Monica, CA**
Khiel, Diane Albert ....Orono, ME
Khil, John C. ....**Honolulu, HI**
Khim, Charles K. Y. ....Honolulu, HI
Khimji, Mahmood ....Irving, TX
Khinda, Philip S. ....**Washington, DC**
Khirallah, Ray T. ....**Dallas, TX**

Khiterer, Vladimir ....Irvine, CA
Khlopin, Derek R.
Federal Communications Commission, Wireless Telecommunications Bureau, GV
Khodadad, Camille N. ....**Chicago, IL**
Khoei, Sayeh ....Sherman Oaks, CA
Khokhryakova, Anastasia G. ....**Denver, CO**
Kholos, Alan S. ....**San Diego, CA**
Khonsari, Arezou ....**Los Angeles, CA**
Khoo, Ee-Chuan ....Westlake Village, CA
Khoo, John ....Sacramento, CA
Khorana, Adit M. ....**Palo Alto, CA**
Khorey, David E. ....**Grand Rapids, MI**
Khorrami, Mina N. ....Columbus, OH
Khorrami, Shawn, Law Offices of
Los Angeles, CA
Khorsandi, Marilyn R. ....**Pasadena, CA**
Khoshbin, S. A. ....**Dallas, TX**
Khoshbin, Terrie DePratt ....**Dallas, TX**
Khoshbin, V. Allan ....Sherman Oaks, CA
Khosla, Anil ....**Boston, MA**
Khosla, Anita ....New York, NY
Khosla, Reena B. ....Chicago, IL
Khosravi, Kourosh Cyrus ....Schaumburg, IL
Khoudary, Maryann ....East Brunswick, NJ
Khoudary, Nicholas ....East Brunswick, NJ
Khougaz, Gregory J. ....**Los Angeles, CA**
Khourey, Louis H. ....Moundsville, WV
Khouri, Jack A. ....**San Jose, CA**
Khouri, John G. ....Westwood, MA
Khouri, Michael J. ....**Irvine, CA**
Khourie, Crew & Jaeger
San Francisco, CA
Khourie, James N. ....Tulsa, OK
Khourie, Michael N. ....Mill Valley, CA
Khoury, Alvin G ....Longview, TX
Khoury, Andrea Crowder ....**Columbia, IL**
Khoury, Andrea M. ....Riverdale, MD
Khoury, Andrew G., P.C. ....Longview, TX
Khoury, Andrew George ....Longview, TX
Khoury, Arthur M. ....Lawrence, MA
Khoury, Charles R., Jr. ....Wilton, NH
Khoury, Colleen A. ....Portland, ME
Khoury, Coreen B. ....**Lancaster, SC**
Khoury, Daniel D. ....Kill Devil Hills, NC
Khoury, Diana M. ....**San Diego, CA**
Khoury, Hani ....Fairview, NJ
Khoury, Isam C. ....**San Diego, CA**
Khoury, Jason P. ....Fort Washington, PA
Khoury, John A. ....**Los Angeles, CA**
Khoury, Karen E. ....Dallas, TX
Khoury, Kenneth F. ....**Atlanta, GA**
Khoury, Lisa A. ....Washington, DC
Khoury, Louis J. ....Los Angeles, CA
Khoury, Maha ....Santa Fe, NM
Khoury, Michael A. ....**Boston, MA**
Khoury, Michael K. ....Department of Justice, Civil Rights Division, GV
Khoury, Michael R. ....Waco, TX
Khoury, Michael S. ....Ann Arbor, MI
Khoury, Naif Samuel ....Fort Smith, AR
Khoury, Pamela J. ....Salem, NH
Khoury, Paul F. ....**Washington, DC**
Khoury, Robert P. ....**Los Angeles, CA**
Khoury, Rollin ....Waco, TX
Khoury, Stephen A. ....**Dallas, TX**
Khouzam, Marie-Joëlle C. ....**Columbus, OH**
Khouzam, Nelly N. ....Clearwater, FL
Khtikian, W. Kent ....**San Francisco, CA**
Khudari, Samia ....Seattle, WA
Khuong, Quyen H. ....**Santa Ana, CA**
Khurana, Anju ....Los Angeles, CA
Khuri, Walid A. ....**Washington, DC**
Khutorsky, Alexander ....New York, NY
Khutorsky, Gary ....**Miami, FL**
Khuu, Tuan Anh ....Oklahoma City, OK
Khuzami, Robert S. ....New York, NY
Khwaja, Sulaiman Yousuf ....Maitland, FL
Khyltash, Ann E. ....Torrance, CA
Kiacz, Joseph R. ....Bryan, OH
Kiaie, Bita M. ....Woodland Hills, CA
Kiamie, Robert A. ....Wayne, NJ
Kian, David L. ....Tampa, FL
Kiang, Lindsey C. Y. ....Maynard, MA
Kiang, Samuel Kuo-Liang ....Alhambra, CA
Kiang, William K. T. ....Los Angeles, CA
Kiar, Monroe D. ....**Davie, FL**
Kias, Michael J. ....Indianapolis, IN
Kiash, David D. ....Rochester, NY
Kiatta, David W. ....**Houston, TX**
Kiaunis, Gertrude A. ....**Bridgeport, CT**
Kibbe, David R. ....**South Bend, IN**
Kibbe, Giles R. ....**Beaumont, TX**
Kibbe, Guy G. ....Indianapolis, IN
Kibbe, John R. ....Yorktown Heights, NY
Kibbe, Jonathan ....**New York, NY**
Kibbe, King & Moran ....Attica, NY
Kibbe, Ronald J. ....Hutchinson, KS
Kibbey, Jeffrey William ....Louisville, KY
Kibbey, Mary Louise ....**Amarillo, TX**
Kibbey, Richard D. ....Stuart, FL
Kibbie, Kelly S. ....**New York, NY**
Kibble, James G. ....**Seattle, WA**
Kibble-Smith, Brian G. ....Chicago, IL
Kibby, Lori S. ....Englewood, OH
Kibby, Richard D., Law Offices of
Anchorage, AK
Kibby, Robert R. ....**Dallas, TX**
Kibby, Steven G. ....**Peoria, IL**
Kibe, Gerald H. ....Honolulu, HI
Kibel, Paul Stanton ....**Oakland, CA**
Kibel, Shari B. ....**New York, NY**
Kibelstis, Teresa E. ....**Philadelphia, PA**
Kiblan, Malea ....McLean, VA
Kibler, B. Chase ....**Knoxville, TN**
Kibler, Barbara Helen ....Frankfort, KY
Kibler, D. Burke, III ....**Lakeland, FL**
Tampa, FL

Kibler, James R., Jr. ....**Richmond, VA**
Kibler, John W. ....New York, NY
Kibler, Karen ....San Anselmo, CA
Kibler, Keith W. ....Marion, IL
Kibler, Rhoda Smith ....Tallahassee, FL
Kibler, William S. ....Syracuse, NY
Kiblinger, Cindy J. ....**Charleston, WV**
Kibre, Joseph ....**Los Angeles, CA**
Kiburz, Arnold J., III ....**Wausau, WI**
Kice, Warren B. ....**Dallas, TX**
Kicenuik, Maryann Dougherty
Morristown, NJ
Kichaven, Jeffrey G. ....**Los Angeles, CA**
Kichler, Benita K. ....**Atlanta, GA**
Kichline, Edwin G. ....**Washington, DC**
Kichline, John P. ....Palm Beach Gardens, FL
Kichline, Michael L. ....**Philadelphia, PA**
Kicinski, Christine J. ....Brooklyn, NY
Kicinski, John ....Detroit, MI
Kick, Michael J. ....Kankakee, IL
Kickbush, Raymond D. ....Valparaiso, IN
Kickham, Charles J., Jr. ....**Brookline, MA**
Kickham, Constance K. ....**Brookline, MA**
Kickham, Edward F. ....**Royal Oak, MI**
Kickham, Gabrielle Honore ....**Dallas, TX**
Kickham, George A. ....**Brookline, MA**
Kickham, James A. ....Jefferson City, MO
Kickham, James M. ....**Brookline, MA**
Kickham Law Offices ....**Boston, MA**
Brookline, MA
Kickham, Mary Anne ....Bloomfield Hills, MI
Kickham, Mary C. ....**St. Louis, MO**
Kickham, William D. ....**Brookline, MA**
Kickingbird, K. Kirke ....Oklahoma City, OK
Kicklighter, Claude M., Jr. ....Springfield, GA
Kicklighter, Kurt L. ....**San Diego, CA**
Kicklighter & Persse ....Springfield, GA
Kickliter, George D. ....Auburn, AL
Kickliter, George K., (P.A.)
St. Petersburg, FL
Kickliter, George P. ....Tampa, FL
Kicz, John Allen ....Youngstown, OH
Kiczek, Charles R. ....**Troy, MI**
Kiczek, Leonard P. ....Bayonne, NJ
Kida, Nancy Ann ....Beulah, MI
Kidambi, Vaman B. ....New York, NY
Kidani, Grant K. ....**Honolulu, HI**
Kidani - Marshall, A Law Corporation
Honolulu, HI
Kidd, A. Scott ....**Houston, TX**
Kidd, Anita M. ....**St. Louis, MO**
Kidd, Anthony R. ....**Dayton, OH**
Kidd, Byron L. ....Austin, TX
Kidd, Charles Martin ....Indianapolis, IN
Kidd, Craig ....Houston, TX
Kidd, Daniel E. ....Knoxville, TN
Kidd, Daryl L. ....**Marietta, GA**
Kidd, Daryl L., P.C. ....**Atlanta, GA**
Marietta, GA
Kidd, Don R. ....Lubbock, TX
Kidd, Donnie D. ....Prestonsburg, KY
Kidd, Doug ....United States Senate, Senatorial Assistants, GV
Kidd, Edward B. ....**Richmond, VA**
Kidd, Edward S., Jr. ....Roanoke, VA
Kidd, Genna Driscoll ....**Philadelphia, PA**
Kidd, Grant ....Concord, NH
Kidd, James F. ....**Orlando, FL**
Kidd, Janet Engel ....Chicago, IL
Kidd, Jas. M., Jr. ....Mountain Brook, AL
Kidd, Jas. S. ....Fayetteville, TN
Kidd, J. L., Jr. ....**Little Rock, AR**
Kidd, John B. ....Austin, TX
Kidd, John E. ....**New York, NY**
Kidd, Joseph A. ....**Toledo, OH**
Kidd, Joyce Marie ....Falls Church, VA
Kidd, Judith Lorraine ....Locust Hill, VA
Kidd, Judson C. ....**Little Rock, AR**
Kidd, Kim M. ....St. Martinville, LA
Kidd, Mack ....Austin, TX
Kidd, Marilyn K. ....Austin, TX
Kidd, Mark D. ....**Roanoke, VA**
Kidd, Mary Dolores ....Catonsville, MD
Kidd, Patricia Tierney ....Louisville, KY
Kidd, Patricia Tierney, P.S.C.
Louisville, KY
Kidd, Paul Henry ....Monroe, LA
Kidd, R. Hopkins ....Decatur, GA
Kidd, Robert C. ....Houston, TX
Kidd, Robert F. ....**Oakland, CA**
Kidd, Robert H., IV ....Houston, TX
Kidd, Robert W. ....West Springfield, MA
Kidd, Roger C., (P.A.) ....Wichita, KS
Kidd, Ronald C. ....**Springfield, MA**
Kidd, Ronald F. ....Haddon Heights, NJ
Philadelphia, PA
Kidd, Scott R. ....**Austin, TX**
Kidd, Shannon L. ....Houston, TX
Kidd, Teresa M. ....Kansas City, KS
Kidd, Timothy E. ....Beverly Hills, CA
Kidd & Vaughan ....**Atlanta, GA**
Kidd, William L. ....**Duluth, GA**
Kidd, William L., P.C. ....**Atlanta, GA**
Duluth, GA
Kidd, William W. ....**Austin, TX**
Kidd, Winston L. ....Jackson, MS
Kidd & Witcher ....Decatur, GA
Kiddé, Thomas S. ....**Los Angeles, CA**
Kidder, Bradley F. ....Laconia, NH
Kidder, Charles L. ....Columbus, OH
Kidder, Curtis S. ....Oakland, CA
Kidder, David S. ....**Dallas, TX**
Kidder, Donald L. ....San Diego, CA
Kidder, Donald L., A Professional Corporation
San Diego, CA
Kidder, Fred D. ....**Wickliffe, OH**
Kidder, George H. ....**Boston, MA**
Kidder, Hugh G. ....Missoula, MT

Kidder, Jacquelyn F. ....**Chicago, IL**
Kidder, Linda J. ....Waterford, CT
Kidder, Linda K. ....Ann Arbor, MI
Kidder, Marc A. ....Grand Rapids, MI
Kidder, Rex E. ....**Chicago, IL**
Kidder, Rolland E. ....Ashville, NY
Kidder, Stephen W. ....**Boston, MA**
Kidder, Steven S. ....Victoria, TX
Kidder, Vance W. ....Tallahassee, FL
Kiddoo, Jean L. ....**Washington, DC**
Kiddy, Kenneth L. ....Stockton, CA
Kideckel, Arnold ....**New York, NY**
Kider, Mitchel H. ....**Washington, DC**
Kidera, Geralyn A. ....Alexandria, VA
Kidman, Arthur G., (P.C.)
Costa Mesa, CA
Sacramento, CA
Kidman, Joan M. ....Portland, ME
Kidman, Kerry D. ....**Seattle, WA**
Kidman, Scott B. ....**Los Angeles, CA**
Kidman, Victoria K. ....Murray, UT
Kidnay, Brian ....**Castle Rock, CO**
Kidneigh, Jon F. ....Denver, CO
Glenwood Springs, CO
Kidneigh & Kaufman, P.C. ....Denver, CO
Glenwood Springs, CO
Kidner, Graham H. ....**McLean, VA**
Kidner, Rebecca Batson ....**Dover, DE**
Kidney, David F. ....Barre, VT
Kidney, James A., Jr. ....Newport, KY
Kidney, Michael L. ....**Washington, DC**
Kido, Alan Takashi ....**Honolulu, HI**
Kido, Grace Nihei ....**Honolulu, HI**
Kidokord, Harumi ....**New York, NY**
Kidon, Catherine E. ....Naples, FL
Kidston, Marlowe A. ....Park Ridge, IL
Kidston, Roger G. ....Kalamazoo, MI
Kidwell, Brent E. ....**Chicago, IL**
Kidwell, Brian F. ....**St. Paul, MN**
Kidwell, Carl J. ....Orange, CA
Kidwell, Charles Y., Jr. ....**Dayton, OH**
Kidwell, Dicken E. ....**Murfreesboro, TN**
Kidwell, Edward J. ....San Antonio, TX
Kidwell, Eric J. ....Wichita, KS
Kidwell, Gerald A. ....Alexandria, VA
Kidwell, H. Kent ....Fairfax, VA
Kidwell, John A. ....Madison, WI
Kidwell, Jos. D., Jr. ....Spring Branch, TX
Kidwell, Kent & Curran ....**Rockville, MD**
Fairfax, VA
Kidwell, Paul A. ....Poplar Bluff, MO
Kidwell, Richard P. ....Baltimore, MD
Kidwell, Robert D. ....**Greensboro, NC**
Kidwell, Scott M. ....**Midland, TX**
Kidwell, Sheila M. ....**Lubbock, TX**
Kidwell & South ....**Murfreesboro, TN**
Kidwell, Thomas B. ....San Jose, CA
Kidwell, Wayne L. ....Boise, ID
Kiebert, Irene V. ....San Francisco, CA
Kiechel, Doane F., III ....**Washington, DC**
Kieck, Patricia A. ....Hackensack, NJ
Kiecke, Roy E. ....**Austin, TX**
Kieckhafer, Marvin O. ....**North Platte, NE**
Kieckhefer, Frederick B., JR. ....McArthur, OH
Kieckhefer, James R. ....**Kohler, WI**
Kiecolt, Edward H. ....Norman, OK
Kiedaisch & Bernstein
Greenwood Lake, NY
Kiedaisch, Robert F. ....Greenwood Lake, NY
Kiedaisch, Ronald A. ....Lansing, IL
Kiedrowski, Michael ....Brooklyn Center, MN
Kief, Fuller, Baer & Wallner, Ltd.
Bemidji, MN
Kief, Paul A. ....Bemidji, MN
Kief, Robert S. ....Pontiac, MI
Kiefel, John Howard ....Downingtown, PA
Kiefer, Alfred G., Jr. ....**Bethpage, NY**
Kiefer, Allen, Cavanagh & Toohey
Ann Arbor, MI
Kiefer, Beverly L. ....Fairfax, VA
Kiefer, Bollermann & Kaplowitz
Hackensack, NJ
Kiefer, Bryan James ....**Destin, FL**
Kiefer, Charles F., Jr. ....**Springfield, MO**
Kiefer, Daniel ....**Torrance, CA**
Kiefer, Daniel A. ....**Marietta, GA**
Kiefer, Daran ....**Cleveland, OH**
Columbus, OH
Kiefer, David ....Norcross, GA
Kiefer, David W. ....**Washington, DC**
Charlotte, NC
Kiefer, Donald R. ....Greenwich, CT
Kiefer, Donna J. ....Boston, MA
Kiefer, Dudley ....Vacaville, CA
Kiefer, Gerald A. ....Kewaskum, WI
Kiefer, Ignatz G., Jr. ....Metairie, LA
Kiefer, J. Richard ....**Indianapolis, IN**
Kiefer, James P. ....**Lansing, MI**
Kiefer, John B. ....Ann Arbor, MI
Kiefer, Joseph S. ....Tucson, AZ
Kiefer, Joseph T. ....**Honolulu, HI**
Kiefer, Karen L. ....Scottdale, PA
Kiefer, Kathleen S. ....Carmel, IN
Kiefer and Kiefer ....Metairie, LA
Kiefer, Kimberly B. ....**Washington, DC**
Kiefer, Kris P. ....Metairie, LA
Kiefer, Louis ....Hartford, CT
Kiefer, Louis C. ....Seattle, WA
Kiefer, Louis M., Jr. ....New Orleans, LA
Kiefer, Mark Emerson ....Fort Wayne, IN
Kiefer, Mark L. ....**Los Angeles, CA**
Kiefer, Matthew J. ....**Boston, MA**
Kiefer, Maura J. ....St. Petersburg, FL
Kiefer, Maura J., P.A. ....St. Petersburg, FL
Kiefer and McGoff ....**Indianapolis, IN**
Kiefer, Michael A. ....**Indianapolis, IN**
Kiefer, Michael L. ....Minneapolis, MN
Kiefer, Neil G. ....St. Petersburg, FL

Kiefer, Peter H. ... **Washington, DC**
Kiefer, Reginald R., Jr. ... Phoenix, AZ
Kiefer, Richard ... **Honolulu, HI**
Kiefer, Sarah E. ... Culver City, CA
Kiefer, Scott B. ... **New Orleans, LA**
Kiefer, Stephanie A. ... Boston, MA
Kiefer, Timothy David ... Kewaskum, WI
Kiefer, William K. ... Minneapolis, MN
Kiefer, William R. ... Weirton, WV
Kiefer, Stephen H. ... Lanham, MD
Kieff, F. Scott ... **Chicago, IL**
Kieffer, Efraim Zvi ... Baltimore, MD
Suffern, NY
Kieffer, George David ... **Los Angeles, CA**
Kieffer, Gregory C. ... Manhattan, KS
Kieffer and Hahn LLP ... **New York, NY**
Kieffer, Howard O. ... Santa Ana, CA
Kieffer, James M. ... **Buffalo, NY**
Kieffer, James M. ... Pittsford, NY
Kieffer, James R. ... Waukesha, WI
Kieffer, John E. ... **Bristol, VA**
Kieffer, John E., P.C. ... **Bristol, VA**
Kieffer, Jon C. ... St. Petersburg, FL
Kieffer, Jonathan P. ... **Kansas City, MO**
Kieffer, Joseph D. ... Los Angeles, CA
Kieffer, Joseph S., III ... Wichita, KS
Kieffer, Kenneth G. ... **Tacoma, WA**
Kieffer, Kevin J. ... **Irvine, CA**
Kieffer, Michael J. ... Rochester, NY
Kieffer, Paul V. ... **Minnetonka, MN**
Dallas, TX
Kieffer and Rahter, P.A. ... St. Petersburg, FL
Kieffer, Robert C. ... **Minnetonka, MN**
Kieffer, Robert W. ... Orlando, FL
Kieffer, Thomas J. ... La Crosse, WI
Kiefner, John R., Jr. ... **St. Petersburg, FL**
Kiefor, Louis V. ... Calumet City, IL
Kieft, David W. ... Cincinnati, OH
Kiegel, Frederick A. ... Philadelphia, PA
Kiehl, Victoria A. ... St. Louis, MO
Kiehlmeier, John C. ... Los Alamitos, CA
Kiehn, Roland W. ... **Panama City, FL**
Kiehne, Julie M. ... Los Angeles, CA
Kiehnhoff, Thomas N. ... Beaumont, TX
Kiek, Robert Martin ... Encino, CA
Kiekhofer, William H., III
Los Angeles, CA
Kieklak, Kenneth J. ... **Fayetteville, AR**
Kiel, Bruce ... Brooklyn, NY
Kiel, Cindy M. ... Salt Lake City, UT
Kiel, David F. ... **Allegan, MI**
Kiel, Donald W. ... **Morristown, NJ**
Kiel, Douglas B. ... **San Antonio, TX**
Kiel, Duane D. ... Seattle, WA
Kiel, Edward R. ... **Springfield, VT**
Kiel, Edward S. ... **Hackensack, NJ**
Kiel & Ellis ... **Springfield, VT**
Kiel, Frederick O. ... **Cincinnati, OH**
Kiel, Gerald H. ... **New York, NY**
Kiel, Gerald S. ... Charlotte, NC
Kiel, Joseph ... Englewood, CO
Kiel, Lawrence J. ... **Farmington, CT**
Torrington, CT
Kiel, Paul E. ... **Hackensack, NJ**
Kiel, Paul N. ... McDonough, GA
Kiel, Paul P. ... Princeton, NJ
Kiel, Robert F. ... Tamarac, FL
Kiel, Sharon ... Little Rock, AR
Kiel & Trueax, P.C. ... Englewood, CO
Kiel, William ... Memphis, TN
Kielb, Janice S., P.C. ... Ann Arbor, MI
Kielb, Janice Seale ... Ann Arbor, MI
Kielbania, Kenneth F. ... Pompano Beach, FL
Kielczewski, Daniel G. ... **Detroit, MI**
Kielczewski, Joanna M. ... **Chicago, IL**
Kieler, Benjamin M. ... Overland Park, KS
Kielian, Gerald G. ... Joliet, IL
Kielian, Robert C. ... Chicago, IL
Kielian & Walther ... Chicago, IL
Kielkopf, Andrew John ... **Columbus, OH**
Kielkopf, Douglas W. ... Roanoke, VA
Kielkopf, Douglas W., A Professional Corporation ... Roanoke, VA
Kielman, George ... **McLean, VA**
Kielpinski, Jan C. ... Stevenson, WA
Kielpinski & Lourne, P.C. ... Stevenson, WA
Kielty, Arthur G. ... **Rockford, IL**
Kielty, Ellen ... Indianapolis, IN
Kielty, John J. ... Indianapolis, IN
Kielty, Michael J. ... **San Diego, CA**
Kielty, Timothy J. ... Omaha, NE
Kieltyka, Michael J. ... Troy, MI
Kiely, Bruce F. ... **Washington, DC**
Kiely, Carolyn M. ... Carlisle, MA
Kiely, Christopher M. ... Miller Place, NY
Kiely, Christopher P. ... **Redwood City, CA**
Kiely, David Dwight ... Evansville, IN
Kiely, Dennis Daniel ... **New York, NY**
Kiely, Dennis M. ... Long Beach, NY
Kiely, Elise P.W. ... **Washington, DC**
Kiely, G. Kevin ... **Portland, OR**
Kiely, James F. ... Sarasota, FL
Kiely, James L. ... Evansville, IN
Kiely, John C. ... Chicago, IL
Kiely, John J. ... Chicago, IL
Kiely, Lorena L. ... **Tampa, FL**
Kiely, Margaret M. ... Philadelphia, PA
Kiely, Matthew E. ... **Baltimore, MD**
Kiely, Michael J. ... **Los Angeles, CA**
Kiely, Michael J., Jr. ... **New York, NY**
Kiely, Peter G. ... **Teaneck, NJ**
Kiely, Philip G. ... Cambridge, MA
Kiely, Robert E. ... **Boston, MA**
Kiely, Stephen J. ... Boston, MA
Kiely, Thomas F. ... Great Falls, MT
Kiely, Thomas P.F.
Department of Transportation, Federal Aviation Administration, GV

Kiem, Barbara J. ... Menlo Park, CA
Kiemele, Linda D. ... **Milwaukee, WI**
Kien & Levay ... Chicago, IL
Kienast, Karen Brandstetter ... Dubuque, IA
Kienbaum, Karen Smith, & Associates
Detroit, MI
Kienbaum, Karen Smith, & Associates
Flint, MI
Grand Rapids, MI
Lansing, MI
Pontiac, MI
Kienbaum Opperwall Hardy & Pelton, P.L.C. ... **Birmingham, MI**
Detroit, MI
Kienbaum, Thomas G. ... **Birmingham, MI**
Detroit, MI
Kiendl, William R. ... **Seattle, WA**
Kiene, Joseph T., Jr. ... North Charleston, SC
Kiener, John L. ... Johnson City, TN
Kiener, Mary E. ... **Des Moines, IA**
Kienitz, Kathleen E. ... Lewiston, ME
Portland, ME
Kienker, Anne-Marie ... **St. Louis, MO**
Kienle, Jenifer L. ... **Costa Mesa, CA**
Kienle, Richard W. ... **Norfolk, VA**
Kienlen, J. Laurence ... **Chicago, IL**
Wheaton, IL
Kienlen, Ronald A. ... Department of Defense, Armed Services Board of Contract Appeals, GV
Kientz, Robert E. ... **Houston, TX**
Kientz, Val W. ... Houston, TX
Kientz, Val W., Law Offices Of, P.C.
Houston, TX
Kienz, Glenn C. ... Secaucus, NJ
Kienzl, William P. ... Cleveland, OH
Kienzle, A. Paul, Jr. ... Bridgeton, NJ
Kienzle, Larth ... Oklahoma City, OK
Shawnee, OK
Kienzle, Paul M., III ... **Albuquerque, NM**
Kienzle, Roger W., Jr. ... Wooster, OH
Kienzle, Susan Smart ... Toledo, OH
Kienzle, Talley & Grant, P.C.
Oklahoma City, OK
Shawnee, OK
Kiep, Sigrid Berglund ... **Haddonfield, NJ**
Kiepe, Diane ... Memphis, TN
Kiepen, Scott J. ... Pleasanton, CA
Kieper, Carl A. ... **Binghamton, NY**
Kiepura, Frank ... Albany, NY
Kiepura, Frank C., & Associates, P.C.
Albany, NY
Kiepura, Thomas A. ... **Chicago, IL**
St. Louis, MO
Kier, Charles Thomas ... **Marysville, KS**
Kier, Isaac ... New York, NY
Kier, Michael W. ... Lisle, IL
Kieran, Meg E. ... **Springfield, OR**
Kierce, James B., Jr. ... **Bessemer, AL**
Kierce, Robert F. ... Lowell, MA
Kierig, Paul N. ... **Northbrook, IL**
Kierkegaard, J. Michael ... York, PA
Kiern, Lawrence I. ... **Washington, DC**
Kiernan, Anne B. ... Rochester, NY
Kiernan, Brian ... **Morristown, NJ**
Kiernan, Brian ... Morristown, NJ
Kiernan, Catherine A. ... South Orange, NJ
Kiernan, Cathie A. ... Austin, TX
Kiernan, Christopher D. ... La Quinta, CA
Kiernan, David C. ... **Washington, DC**
Kiernan, Douglas M. ... Boston, MA
Kiernan, Edward M. ... Wareham, MA
Kiernan, Edwin A., Jr. ... Sanibel, FL
Kiernan, F. Patrick ... Boise, ID
Kiernan, Frank J. ... Alexandria, VA
Kiernan, Gladys M. ... Jericho, NY
Kiernan, James A. ... Flushing, NY
Kiernan, Jessica A. ... Boston, MA
Kiernan, John A. ... **Boston, MA**
Kiernan, John D. ... **St. Petersburg, FL**
Kiernan, John E. ... New York, NY
Kiernan, John G. ... Westbury, NY
Kiernan, John M. ... Miami, FL
Kiernan, John S. ... **New York, NY**
Kiernan, Joseph W. ... Washington, DC
Kiernan, Josephine A. ... San Diego, CA
Kiernan, Kerry ... **Albuquerque, NM**
Kiernan, Leonard A., Jr. ... **Providence, RI**
Kiernan, Leslie Berger ... **Washington, DC**
Kiernan, Mary Lee A. ... New York, NY
Kiernan, Matthew G. ... Riverhead, NY
Kiernan, Michael K. ... **St. Petersburg, FL**
Kiernan, Michael S. ... **Providence, RI**
Kiernan, Michael W. ... Albuquerque, NM
Kiernan, P. Barrett, Jr. ... **San Diego, CA**
Kiernan, Paul J. ... **Washington, DC**
Kiernan, Peter J. ... New York, NY
Kiernan, Peter S.
Securities and Exchange Commission, Executive Staff, GV
Kiernan, Plunkett & Redihan
Providence, RI
Kiernan, Sara J. ... **Washington, DC**
Kiernan, Stephen M. ... **Albany, NY**
Kiernan & Strenk ... **Morristown, NJ**
Kiernan, Theresa M. ... Topeka, KS
Kiernan, Thomas B., III ... Philadelphia, PA
Kiernan, Thomas E. ... Annandale, MN
Kiernan, Thomas J. ... Hampton Bays, NY
Kiernan, Thomas Michael ... Falls Church, VA
Kiernan, Vincent M. ... **Stamford, CT**
Kiernan, William J., Jr. ... **Tampa, FL**
Milwaukee, WI
Kiernan, Winifred ... Boston, MA
Kiernat, Bruce E. ... **Minneapolis, MN**
Kiernat, Bruce E. ... **St. Paul, MN**
Kiernat, Elizabeth H. ... **Minneapolis, MN**
Kierney, Roberta C. ... Grass Valley, CA

Kierney and Thomsen, A Ptnrshp. incl. A Prof. Corp ... Grass Valley, CA
Kierniesky, Nicholas ... **Vineland, NJ**
Kieronski, Joseph A., Jr. ... **Meridian, MS**
Kierr, Raymond H. ... **New Orleans, LA**
Kiersch, Lawrence ... Chicago, IL
Kierscht, Charles M. ... Chicago, IL
Kiersh, Steven R. ... **Washington, DC**
Kiersh, Warren R. ... Melville, NY
Kiersnowski, Cynthia ... **Santa Fe, NM**
Kierst, Peter S. ... **Albuquerque, NM**
Kierstead, Andrew ... **Los Angeles, CA**
Portland, OR
Kierstead, Nancy L. ... Milford, CT
Kiersz, Gregory L. ... **Greencastle, PA**
Waynesboro, PA
Kierszenbaum, Adriana E. ... Mamaroneck, NY
Kies, David M. ... **New York, NY**
Kies, Jean M. ... Milwaukee, WI
Kies, Kenneth J.
Joint Committees And Commissions, GV
Kieschnick, Cynthia L. ... St. Louis, MO
Kieschnick, Jonathan C. ... Houston, TX
Kieschnick, Rebecca R.
Corpus Christi, TX
Kiesel, Amy B. ... **Washington, DC**
Kiesel, Boucher & Larson, LLP
Beverly Hills, CA
Kiesel, Christine Sabino ... Rome, NY
Kiesel, Diana Lynn ... Tacoma, WA
Kiesel, Diana Lynn, Inc. P.S. ... Tacoma, WA
Kiesel, Diane ... New York, NY
Kiesel Hughes & Johnston
Fort Myers, FL
Kiesel, Michael T. ... **New York, NY**
Kiesel, Paul R. ... **Beverly Hills, CA**
Kiesel, Robert R. ... **New York, NY**
Kiesel, Thomas F. ... **Fort Myers, FL**
Kiesel, William David ... **Baton Rouge, LA**
Kieselbach, Thomas P. ... **Minneapolis, MN**
Kieselstein & Lee, L.L.P. ... **New York, NY**
White Plains, NY
Kieselstein, Marc ... **Chicago, IL**
Kieselstein, Steve ... **White Plains, NY**
Kieser, Chas. W. ... Menlo Park, CA
Kieser, Fred, Jr. ... Metuchen, NJ
Kieser, Fred, Jr., A Prof. Corp.
Metuchen, NJ
Kieser, William S. ... Williamsport, PA
Kiesewetter, Jay W. ... **Memphis, TN**
Kiesewetter, Jennifer S. ... **Memphis, TN**
Kiesewetter, Mark W. ... St. Louis, MO
Kiesewetter Wise Kaplan Schwimmer & Prather, PLC ... **Memphis, TN**
Kiesey, Cassandra E. ... Hamilton, OH
Kiesey, D. Bradley ... **Washington, IA**
Kieskowski, Peggy ... Vestavia Hills, AL
Kiesler & Berman ... **Chicago, IL**
Joliet, IL
Waukegan, IL
Wheaton, IL
Kiesler, David J. ... **Chicago, IL**
Waukegan, IL
Kiesler, Robert L. ... **Chicago, IL**
Kiesling, Bob R. ... New Braunfels, TX
Kiesling, Donald F. ... **Milwaukee, WI**
Kiesling, Donald F., Jr. ... Milwaukee, WI
Kiesling and Mathis ... New Braunfels, TX
Kiesling, William G. ... Philadelphia, PA
Kieson, Ryan Kirk ... Bemidji, MN
Kiess, Stephen D. ... Greenville, NC
Kiesselbach, Theodore S. ... **New York, NY**
Kiessling, B. Robbins ... **New York, NY**
Kiessling, Kurt M. ... **Amelia, OH**
Kiessling, Laura S. ... Annapolis, MD
Kiessling & Lesperance ... Lake Mills, WI
Kiessling, William E., Jr. ... Lake Mills, WI
Kiester, Geo. P. ... Butler, PA
Kiester, Gordon L., Jr ... Tampa, FL
Kies-Tokarz, Audrey ... Oak Brook, IL
Kiesz, ReDoy ... Lindsay, CA
Kiesz, Robert A. ... **Wenatchee, WA**
Kiesz, Todd M. ... **Wenatchee, WA**
Kietzman, Paul R. ... Albany, NY
Kieval, Eliot T. ... White Plains, NY
Kieve, Loren ... **Washington, DC**
Kiever, Paul K. ... Johnstown, PA
Kieves, Sidney J. ... Brooklyn, NY
Kieves, Tama J. ... Denver, CO
Kieviet, Thomas G. ... **Anaheim, CA**
Kievit, Kelly & Odom ... **Panama City, FL**
Pensacola, FL
Kievit, Kyle T. ... Northfield, NJ
Kievit, Robert W. ... **Pensacola, FL**
Kievits, Jules ... Santa Monica, CA
Kievlan, Patricia H. ... Belleville, IL
Kievsky, Marina ... **Miami, FL**
Kiewel & Harris, P.C. ... Brattleboro, VT
Kiewel, Jean Anne ... Brattleboro, VT
Kiewicz, Jeanne D. ... Los Angeles, CA
Kiewit, Peter, Jr. ... **Phoenix, AZ**
Kiey, Michael ... Burlington, VT
Kifer, James E. ... Oklahoma City, OK
Kifer, Larry L. ... **Clarion, PA**
Kifer, Stephen C. ... Pittsburgh, PA
Kifer, Thane H. ... Bolivar, MO
Kiff, Caroline R. ... Gretna, LA
Kiffel, Chaim T. ... **Chicago, IL**
Kifferstein, Warren M. ... Bloomfield Hills, MI
Kiffin, Charles W. ... Kansas City, MO
Kiffin, Matthew R. ... Rahway, NJ
Kiffner, Paul M. ... Bloomfield Hills, MI
Kift, Bonnie L. ... Ligonier, PA
Kift, Philip S., Jr. ... Rockwood, PA
Kifuthu, Susan M. ... Trenton, NJ
Kigawa, Susan S. ... **Redmond, WA**
Kiger & Alpern ... **Pittsburgh, PA**
Kiger, David V. ... Washington C. H., OH

Kiger, Douglas N. ... **Tacoma, WA**
Kiger, James A. ... Valdosta, GA
Kiger, James A. ... Washington C. H., OH
Kiger, James D. ... Maumee, OH
Kiger, Jerome W. ... **Pittsburgh, PA**
Kiger, Robert C. ... **Columbus, OH**
Kiger, Stephenie Pho-Poe
Albuquerque, NM
Kiger, William E. ... **Parkersburg, WV**
Kiger, William T. ... Prescott, AZ
Kigerl, Jack J. ... St. Clairsville, OH
Kiggans, Thomas H. ... **Baton Rouge, LA**
Kiggins, Constance B.
Securities and Exchange Commission, Division of Market Regulation, GV
Kiggins, David J. ... Melrose, MA
Kiggins, Robert J. ... **White Plains, NY**
Kight, Bennett L. ... **Atlanta, GA**
Kight, David M. ... Independence, MO
Kight, Douglas P. ... **Seattle, WA**
Kight, Jeffrey H. ... **Columbus, GA**
Kight, John ... Dallas, TX
Kight, John C. ... **Dallas, TX**
Kight, John, III ... Department of Commerce, Patent and Trademark Office, GV
Kight, Joshua Eric ... **Los Angeles, CA**
Kight, Katrina Y. ... Defiance, OH
Kight, Leo J., Jr. ... Forsyth, GA
Kight, Mason T. ... Long Beach, CA
Kight, Megan J. ... **Indianapolis, IN**
Kight, Milburn D. ... **Wenatchee, WA**
Kight, Paula Thrun ... Indianapolis, IN
Kight, R. Larry ... Columbia, SC
Kight, R. Michael ... **Everett, WA**
Kight, Sarah B. ... **Dallas, TX**
Kightlinger, Erle A. ... Indianapolis, IN
Kightlinger & Gray ... **Evansville, IN**
Indianapolis, IN
New Albany, IN
Kightlinger, Harry J. ... Glendale, CA
Kightlinger, Jeffrey ... Los Angeles, CA
Kightlinger, John D. ... Inverness, IL
Kightlinger, Kelly A. ... **Los Angeles, CA**
Kightlinger, Stephen ... **San Francisco, CA**
Kightlinger, Stephen M. ... Glen Ellyn, IL
Kightlinger, Wilhelmina F. ... **Tampa, FL**
Kigin, Thomas J. ... St. Paul, MN
Kiguchi, Mark ... Los Angeles, CA
Kihata, Kathy Davisson ... Bay City, MI
Kihl, Joseph G ... Buffalo, NY
Kihle, Donald A. ... **Tulsa, OK**
Kihm, Eric O. ... Kalamazoo, MI
Kihm, Nicholas C. ... Trevose, PA
Kihyet, David E. ... **Pascagoula, MS**
Kiibler, John S., Jr. ... La Porte, TX
Kiibler & Kiibler ... La Porte, TX
Kijewski, Joseph A. ... Department of Justice, Civil Division, GV
Kijewski, Kevin J. ... Louisville, KY
Kikel, Armin J. ... Ridgewood, NY
Williston Park, NY
Kikel, David A. ... **Washington, DC**
Kikel, Diana Gouveia ... Pittsburgh, PA
Kikel, Matthew John ... Pueblo, CO
Kikel, Michael J. ... Pueblo, CO
Kiken, Dale A. ... Irvine, CA
Kiker, Cadman Robb, Jr.
Clarkesville, GA
Kiker, David B. ... **Aurora, CO**
Kiker, Dennis R. ... **Richmond, VA**
Kiker, Jane Elizabeth ... **Minneapolis, MN**
Kiker, Jane S. ... **Seattle, WA**
Kiker, John E. ... Richardson, TX
Kikes, Nicholas S. ... Walnut Creek, CA
Kikkawa, Kaz Christopher ... **Atlanta, GA**
Nashville, TN
Kiklis, Michael L. ... **Washington, DC**
Kiko, Colleen Duffy ... **McLean, VA**
Kiko, Philip G. ... Arlington, VA
Kikol, John C. ... Cleveland, OH
Kikoler, Stephen P. ... **Chicago, IL**
Kikuchi, John M. ... San Francisco, CA
Kikuta, Anthony T. ... **Palo Alto, CA**
Kikuta, Peter Y. ... **Honolulu, HI**
Kil, William O. ... Los Angeles, CA
Kilander, Robert K. ... Wheaton, IL
Kilar, Kathleen A. ... **Fort Wayne, IN**
Kilarjian, George G. ... New York, NY
Kilb, Brian D. ... **Los Angeles, CA**
Kilb, Karl P. ... New York, NY
Kilb, Linda D. ... Berkeley, CA
Kilbane, Anne L. ... Cleveland, OH
Kilbane, Brian J. ... **Grand Rapids, MI**
Kilbane, Catherine M. ... **Cleveland, OH**
Kilbane, Grace A. ... Columbus, OH
Kilbane, James Patrick ... North Olmsted, OH
Kilbane, James V. ... Rocky River, OH
Kilbane, Thomas J. ... Delaware, OH
Kilbane, Thomas M., Jr. ... **Seattle, WA**
Kilbane, Thomas S. ... **Cleveland, OH**
Kilberg, Howard E. ... Chicago, IL
Kilberg, Lori E. ... **Atlanta, GA**
Kilberg, William J. ... **Washington, DC**
Kilbert, Colleen Noga ... **Pittsburgh, PA**
Kilbert, Kenneth K. ... **Pittsburgh, PA**
Kilborn, Benjamin H., Jr. ... **Mobile, AL**
Kilborn, Jason J. ... **Washington, DC**
Kilborn, Peter W. ... Boston, MA
Kilborn, Roebuck & Kilborn ... Mobile, AL
Kilborn, Vincent F., III ... Mobile, AL
Kilborn, Vincent F., IV ... Mobile, AL
Kilborne, Robert S., IV, Law Offices of
Rancho Santa Fe, CA
Kilbourn, Joseph A. ... **New York, NY**
Kilbourn, Samuel C. V. D.
South Freeport, ME
Kilbourn, William Douglas, Jr.
Minneapolis, MN

Kilbourne & Dart ....St. Francisville, LA
Kilbourne, Dean B. ....Bristol, CT
Kilbourne, Diane Rotering .....Falls Church, VA
Kilbourne, Douglas M. ....Ann Arbor, MI
Kilbourne, George W. ....Moraga, CA
Kilbourne, James C. ....Department of Justice, Environment and Natural Resources Division, GV
Kilbourne, James W., Jr. ....Raleigh, NC
Kilbourne, John H. ....New York, NY
Kilbourne, Richard ....Clinton, LA
Kilbourne, Richard, Jr. ....Clinton, LA
Kilbreath, Kenneth M. ....Kent, WA
Kilbreth, James T., III ....Portland, ME
Kilbride, Daniel M., Jr. ....Tallahassee, FL
Kilbride, Elizabeth (BJ) ....Houston, TX
Kilbride, Elizabeth H., P.C. ....Houston, TX
Kilbride, John G. ....Springfield, NJ
Kilbride, Randall J. ....Columbus, OH
Kilbride, Richard R. ....Newport, OR
Kilbride, Robert J. ....Marshalltown, IA
Kilbride, Robert L. Palm Beach Gardens, FL
Kilbride, Terence M. ....Ventura, CA
Kilbride, Terry M. ....Raleigh, NC
Kilbride, Wendy K. ....Los Angeles, CA
Kilbridge, Barbara A. ....Buffalo, NY
Kilburg, Paul J. ....Cedar Rapids, IA
Kilburg, Sally ....Oakland, CA
Kilburn, Casey Goscinak & Coombs Boston, MA
Kilburn, Edwin A. ....Washington, DC
Kilburn, Frank W. ....Boston, MA
Kilburn, James R. ....Austin, TX
Kilburn, Jones, Gill & Campbell, L.L.P. Houston, TX
Kilburn, Kerry A. ....Houston, TX
Kilburn, Mark A. ....Reno, NV
Kilburn, Ralph M. ....Canton, CT
Kilburn, Richard W., Jr. ....Rochester, NY
Kilbury, Deborah L. ....Madison, WI
Kilby, Bradford L. ....Fall River, MA
Kilby, Gerald W. ....Pound Ridge, NY
Kilby, Hodges & Hurley ....Jefferson, NC
West Jefferson, NC
Kilby, John T. ....West Jefferson, NC
Kilby, Marianne B. ....Essex, CT
Kilby, Pamela A. ....Oak Brook, IL
Kilby, Philip D. ....Bel Air, MD
Kilby, Randall J. ....Knoxville, TN
Kilcarr, Andrew J. ....Washington, DC
Kilcarr, John E. ....Arlington, VA
Kilcline, Edwin C. ....Boston, MA
Kilcline, Leigh S. ....Seattle, WA
Kilcommons, Kevin M. ....Annandale, NJ
Kilcommons, Shanahan & Martini, LLC Annandale, NJ
Kilcoyne, Dennis M. ....Washington, NC
Kilcoyne, James F. ....Cleveland, OH
Kilcoyne, John A. ....Treasury Department, Departmental Offices, GV
Kilcoyne, John J. ....Norristown, PA
Kilcoyne, John M. ....Skillman, NJ
Kilcoyne, John W. ....Cincinnati, OH
Kilcoyne, Thomas C. ....Cincinnati, OH
Kilcoyne, Thomas J. ....Jersey City, NJ
Kilcrease, Dawn B. ....Wilmington, DE
Kilcrease, Irvin H., Jr. ....Nashville, TN
Kilcullen, John F. ....Eugene, OR
Kilcullen, Katherine M. ....Orlando, FL
Kilcullen, Kathleen G. ....Moses Lake, WA
Wenatchee, WA
Kilcullen, Kevin M. ....Florham Park, NJ
Kilcullen, Nicole Perkins .....Philadelphia, PA
Kilcullen, Peter M. ....Washington, DC
Kilcullen, Richard J. ....Danbury, CT
Kilcullen, Thomas J. ....Emmitsburg, MD
Kilcullen, Wilson and Kilcullen, Chartered Washington, DC
Kilcur, James F. ....Philadelphia, PA
Kilday, Bruce A. ....Sacramento, CA
Kilday, G. Douglas ....Austin, TX
Kilday, Loretta ....Chicago, IL
Kilday, Pattee C. ....St. Paul, MN
Kilday, Thomas L. ....Greeneville, TN
Kildea, Dennis J. ....Flushing, NY
Kildea, Jennifer A. ....Lansing, MI
Kildee, Brian T. Nuclear Regulatory Commission, Office of the General Counsel, GV
Kildow, Alan L. ....Minneapolis, MN
Kildow, Jeanne Glader ....Rochester, MN
Kildow, Todd M. ....Wheeling, WV
Kilduff, Carolee ....Sacramento, CA
Kilduff, Daniel W. Department Of The Interior, Office of the Solicitor, GV
Kilduff, Douglas M. ....Sacramento, CA
Kilduff, James K. ....Chicago, IL
Kilduff, Jane ....Princeton, NJ
Kilduff, Jeffrey W. ....Washington, DC
Kilduff, John ....New York, NY
Kilduff, Kevin J. ....Boston, MA
Kilduff, Lee White ....Richmond, VA
Kilduff, Mark B. ....Norfolk, VA
Kilduff, Patrick J. ....New York, NY
Kilduff, Philip T. ....San Francisco, CA
Kilduff, Vincent J. ....San Jose, CA
Kilduff, W. Leslie, Jr. ....Kilmarnock, VA
Kilduff, William B. ....Richmond, VA
Kile, Bradford E. ....Washington, DC
Kile, Carol A. ....Elyria, OH
Kile, Daniel M. ....New Berlin, WI
Kile, Deborah Ann ....Jackson, MI
Kile, Edward B. ....Palo Alto, CA
Kile, Emily Blum ....Scottsdale, AZ
Kile, Emily Blum ....Downers Grove, IL
Kile, Janis L. ....Baton Rouge, LA
Kile, Mary Michelle ....Washington, DC
Kile McIntyre & Harbin ....Atlanta, GA
Kile McIntyre Harbin & Lee Washington, DC
New York, NY
Kile, Nicholas K. ....Indianapolis, IN
Kile, Paul Richard ....Springboro, OH
Kile, Rose Ann ....Knoxville, TN
Kilenda, Daniel L. ....Bedford, MA
Kilene, Jason S. ....Minneapolis, MN
Kilens, Kearney W. ....Chicago, IL
Kiley, Ann C. ....Denver, CO
Kiley, Anne Campbell ....Los Angeles, CA
Kiley, Daniel J. ....Phoenix, AZ
Kiley, Danl. P., Jr. ....Andover, MA
Kiley, David L., Sr. ....Marion, IN
Kiley, Donald T. ....Great Neck, NY
Kiley, Donald T., Jr. ....Great Neck, NY
Kiley, Edward ....Melville, NY
Kiley, Edward J. ....Washington, DC
Kiley, Feldmann, Whalen, Devine & Patane, P.C. ....Canastota, NY
Kiley, Francis C. Environmental Protection Agency, Program Office Attorneys, GV
Kiley, James J. ....Boston, MA
Kiley, James W. ....Rochester, NY
Kiley, John E. ....New York, NY
Kiley, Kevin ....Indianapolis, IN
Kiley, Kevin F. ....Randolph, MA
Kiley, Kevin J. ....Great Neck, NY
Kiley, Kiley, Harker, Michael & Certain Marion, IN
Kiley Kiley & Kiley ....Great Neck, NY
Kiley, Kristina ....Fremont, MI
Kiley, Lance ....Sacramento, CA
Kiley Law Firm, P.C. ....Oneida, NY
Kiley, Michael J. ....Marion, IN
Kiley, Michael J. ....East Lansing, MI
Kiley, Michael P. ....Shelbyville, IL
Kiley, Philip F. ....Peabody, MA
Kiley, Raymond J., Jr. ....Monterey, CA
Kiley, Robert E. ....Hartford, CT
Kiley, Roger A. ....Saratoga Springs, NY
Kiley, Roger J., Jr. ....Chicago, IL
Kiley, Stephen F. ....New Bedford, MA
Kiley, Thomas D. ....Hillsborough, CA
Kiley, Thomas F. ....Lynn, MA
Kiley, Thomas M. ....Andover, MA
Kiley, Thomas M., P.C. & Associates Andover, MA
Boston, MA
Kiley, Thomas R. ....Boston, MA
Kiley, Wm. A. ....Cincinnati, OH
Kilgallen, Honora O'Brien ....Hazlet, NJ
Kilgallen, Kevin G. ....Hazlet, NJ
Kilgallen, Michael A. ....Brooklyn, NY
Kilgallen, William ....New York, NY
Kilgallon & Carlson ....Chicago, IL
Wheaton, IL
Kilgallon, John M. ....Central Islip, NY
Kilgallon, Michael B. ....Chicago, IL
Wheaton, IL
Kilgannon, Frank X. ....Mineola, NY
Kilgannon, John C. ....Philadelphia, PA
Kilgannon, Mary Beth ....White Plains, NY
Kilgannon & Steidl ....Bronxville, NY
Mount Kisco, NY
New York, NY
Scarsdale, NY
White Plains, NY
Kilgannon, Thomas J., Jr. ....New City, NY
Kilgannon, William Forster Bronxville, NY
Kilgard, Peter C. ....Phoenix, AZ
Kilgard, Ron ....Phoenix, AZ
Kilgare, Danielle Suezette ....Harrisburg, PA
Kilgarif, Jos. A. ....San Diego, CA
Kilgariff, John J. ....Department of Justice, Tax Division, GV
Kilgariff, Martin J. ....San Francisco, CA
Kilgarlin, William W. ....Austin, TX
Kilgarriff, Mary E. ....Cincinnati, OH
Kilger, Kraig C. ....Costa Mesa, CA
Kilgo, David M. ....Harrison, OH
Kilgo, John W. ....Tallapoosa, GA
Kilgo Law Firm ....Darlington, SC
Kilgo, Robert L., Jr. ....Darlington, SC
Kilgore, Cada T., III ....Atlanta, GA
Kilgore, Carrol D. ....Nashville, TN
Kilgore, Charles Kelly ....Los Angeles, CA
Kilgore, Christina Diane ....Birmingham, AL
Kilgore, Christopher S. ....Dallas, TX
Kilgore, Collins, Jr. ....Little Rock, AR
Kilgore, Deborah Ann ....Houston, TX
Kilgore, Debra A. ....Princeton, WV
Kilgore, Don C. ....Tampa, FL
Kilgore, Donald C. ....Portsmouth, VA
Kilgore, Donald L. ....Philadelphia, MS
Kilgore, Frank ....St. Paul, VA
Kilgore, Gary L. ....Austin, TX
Kilgore, H. Maddox ....Marietta, GA
Kilgore, J. Daniel ....Wise, VA
Kilgore, J. Patrick ....Bowling Green, KY
Kilgore, James L. ....Denver, CO
Kilgore, James V. ....Plant City, FL
Kilgore, Jeffrey H. ....Galveston, TX
Kilgore, Jerry W. ....Richmond, VA
Kilgore, Jery Neal ....Buford, GA
Kilgore, John D. ....St. Louis, MO
Kilgore, Joseph P. ....Amherst, VA
Kilgore, Keith L. ....Lebanon, PA
Kilgore & Kilgore, A Professional Corporation ....Dallas, TX
Kilgore, Lanna Martin ....Bowling Green, KY
Kilgore, Lawrence A. ....Birmingham, MI
Kilgore, Leila H. ....Fredericksburg, VA
Kilgore, Leonard L., III ....Baton Rouge, LA
Kilgore, M. Karen ....Santa Fe, NM
Kilgore, Martha K. ....Ada, OK
Kilgore, Mary Ann ....Omaha, NE
Kilgore, Michael A. ....Atlanta, GA
Kilgore, Michael A., P.C. ....Atlanta, GA
Kilgore, Mima ....Fayetteville, AR
Kilgore, Nicole M. ....Ventura, CA
Kilgore, Paul B. ....Duluth, MN
Kilgore, Paul J. ....Ripon, WI
Kilgore, Paul W. ....Lebanon, PA
Kilgore, Peter G. ....Washington, DC
Kilgore, Phillip A. ....Greenville, SC
Kilgore, R. Lamar ....West Chester, PA
Kilgore, R. Scott ....Washington, DC
Kilgore, Richard T. ....Hollywood, FL
Kilgore, Robert D. ....San Antonio, TX
Kilgore, Robert J. ....Erie, PA
Kilgore, Ronald W. ....Charlotte, TN
Kilgore, Sarah J. ....Denver, CO
Kilgore & Scott ....West Chester, PA
Kilgore & Smith ....Fredericksburg, VA
Kilgore, Susan Cone ....Washington, DC
Kilgore, Terry Gene ....Gate City, VA
Kilgore, Terry L. ....Columbus, OH
Kilgore, Thomas C. ....Ripon, WI
Kilgore, Wentworth L. ....Sun City, AZ
Kilgore, Whayland W. ....Victoria, TX
Kilgore, William K. ....Clearwater, FL
Kilgriff, Stephen P. ....Eden Prairie, MN
Kilgus, Walter C. ....Morrison, IL
Kilguss, Frederick C., Jr. ....Warwick, RI
Kilhenny, Thomas T. ....New York, NY
Kilhenny, Valerie J. ....New York, NY
Kilian, Charles T. ....Cupertino, CA
Kilian, Frederick R. ....Rochester, NY
Kilian, J. Christopher ....San Antonio, TX
Kilian & Lentine ....Billerica, MA
Kilian, Patricia D. ....Billerica, MA
Kilian, Paul C. ....Billerica, MA
Kilian, Philip C. ....Melville, NY
Kilkeary, Martin J. ....Stamford, CT
Kilkelly, Francis J. ....Douglaston, NY
Kilkelly, Francis J. ....New York, NY
Kilkelly, H. Robert ....Madison, WI
Kilkelly, Michael F. ....Malden, MA
Kilkelly, Susan K. ....Malden, MA
Kilkenny, Daniel G. ....Delavan, WI
Kilkenny & Donelson, P.C. ....Denver, CO
Kilkenny, Gregory J. ....Denver, CO
Kilkenny, James M., Jr. ....Jersey City, NJ
Kilkenny, John J. ....New York, NY
Kilkenny Law Office ....Delavan, WI
Kilkenny, Russell R. ....Portland, OR
Kilkenny, Sara Gardiner ....Boston, MA
Kilker, James R. ....Girardville, PA
Pottsville, PA
Kilker, Mary C. ....Yonkers, NY
Kilker, Patrick F. ....Pittsburgh, PA
Kilker, Patrick M. ....Glendale, CA
Kilker, Robert S. ....St. Louis, MO
Kilkowski, James M. ....Los Angeles, CA
Kilkuskie, A. Anthony ....Ephrata, PA
Kill, Erika Leigh ....Newark, NJ
Kill, James L. ....Lima, OH
Kill, Lawrence ....New York, NY
Kill, Lisa K. ....New York, NY
Kill, Luke A. ....Atlanta, GA
Kill & Pedlow ....Lima, OH
Killalea, David B. ....Washington, DC
Killam, Adrian K. ....Laredo, TX
Killam, Catherine H. ....Toledo, OH
Killam, David A. ....Palo Alto, CA
Killam, Elton W. ....Pensacola, FL
Killam, James W., III ....Malden, MA
Killam, Radcliffe ....Laredo, TX
Killam, Thomas P. ....Toledo, OH
Killarney, John P. ....New York, NY
Killarney & Salmon ....New York, NY
Killbary, Virginia J. ....Saranac Lake, NY
Kille, Dennis G. ....Camden, NJ
Killea, John J. ....Somers, NY
Killea, John L. ....Port Chester, NY
Killea, Michael F. ....Jacksonville, FL
Killean, James J. ....Milwaukee, WI
Killeavy, Kathleen M. ....Satellite Beach, FL
Killebrew, Antonia C. ....Las Vegas, NV
Killebrew, Denise W. ....Birmingham, AL
Killebrew, Don J. ....Neosho, MO
Killebrew, Kimberly P. ....Dallas, TX
Killebrew, Kimberly P., P.C. ....Dallas, TX
Fort Worth, TX
Killebrew, Larry E. ....Memphis, TN
Killebrew, Ralph M., Jr. .....Chattanooga, TN
Killebrew, William W. ....St. Clair Shores, MI
Killeen, Allithea E. ....East Aurora, NY
Killeen and Bradt ....Schenectady, NY
Killeen, Denis ....New Haven, CT
Killeen, Elizabeth Virginia Fredericksburg, VA
Killeen, Eugene M. ....Cleveland, OH
Killeen & Fierro ....Houston, TX
Killeen, Frederick W. ....Schenectady, NY
Killeen, Gene A. ....Lake Oswego, OR
Killeen, George ....Flint, MI
Killeen, Henry W., III ....Orchard Park, NY
Killeen, James Charles ....Orange, CA
Killeen, Jeffrey B. ....Pittsburgh, PA
Killeen, Joanne F. ....St. Petersburg, FL
Killeen, John H. ....Atlanta, GA
Killeen, John P. ....Santa Rosa, CA
Killeen, Karen Gaynor ....Mount Olive, NJ
Killeen, Kevin ....Katonah, NY
Killeen, Mary Ann ....Buffalo, NY
Killeen, Michael J. ....Seattle, WA
Killeen, Nancy Finnerty ....Boston, MA
Killeen, Paul ....Boston, MA
Killeen, Robert Joseph, Jr. ....Houston, TX
Killeen, Teresa A. ....Southfield, MI
Killeen, Thomas J. ....Uniondale, NY
Killeen, Thomas J., Jr. ....Grosse Pointe, MI
Killeen, William R. ....Schenectady, NY
Killefer, Campbell ....Washington, DC
Killefer, Gail ....San Francisco, CA
Killefer, Tom ....New York, NY
Killelea, James K. ....Branford, CT
Killelea, Kent L. ....Washington, DC
Killelea, Michael C. ....San Francisco, CA
Killelea, Michael J. ....Houston, TX
Killelea, Timothy K. ....San Francisco, CA
Killen, Craig N. ....Columbia, SC
Killen, Guy W. ....Woodbury, NJ
Killen, James A. ....Wallingford, CT
Killen, Joann E. ....Portage, MI
Killen, Joann E., P.C. ....Portage, MI
Killen, John J. ....Duluth, MN
Killen, Patrick Mcfadden ....Sumter, SC
Killen, Russell B. ....Raleigh, NC
Killen, Werner M. ....Detroit, MI
Killen, William M. ....McCall, ID
Killen, William M., P.A. ....McCall, ID
Killenbeck, Ann M. ....Ann Arbor, MI
Killer, C. Christopher ....Orlando, FL
Killer, Clyde ....Fort Pierce, FL
Killerlane, James J., III ....New York, NY
Killgoar, George F., Jr. ....Boston, MA
Killgore, Frank H., Jr. ....Orlando, FL
Killgore, Jacqueline L. ....Manchester, NH
Killgore, Patricia Alexander ....Jackson, MS
Killgore, Pearlman, Stamp, Ornstein & Squires ....Orlando, FL
Killheffer, Sharon C. ....Newark, DE
Killheffer, Theodore F., Jr. Wilmington, DE
Killiam, Theodore R. ....Guilford, CT
Killian, A. Dan, Jr. ....Miami, FL
Killian and Boyd, P.C. ....Brunswick, GA
Killian, Bryan G. ....Boston, MA
Killian, Charles" Skip " ....Junction City, KS
Killian, Donald W., Jr. ....Laguna Beach, CA
Killian, Donohue & Shipman, LLC Hartford, CT
Killian Donohue & Shipman, LLC Simsbury, CT
Killian, Dorothy Jean ....Rock Hill, SC
Killian, Edna S. ....Metairie, LA
Killian, Elissa Yavne ....Liberty, NY
Killian, Eugene, Jr. ....Clark, NJ
Killian, Gene P. ....Tustin, CA
Killian & Gephart, LLP ....Harrisburg, PA
Killian, Gina M. ....Cleveland, OH
Killian, Howard L. ....Tampa, FL
Killian, J. Chad ....Indianapolis, IN
Killian, J. Keith ....Grand Junction, CO
Killian, James F. ....Minneapolis, MN
Killian, John D. ....Harrisburg, PA
Killian, John M. ....San Antonio, TX
Killian, Johnny H. ....Library of Congress, Congressional Research Service, GV
Killian, Kathleen ....Grand Junction, CO
Killian, Kathleen, P.C. ....Grand Junction, CO
Killian, Keith, & Associates, P.C. Grand Junction, CO
Killian, Kelly M. ....San Antonio, TX
Killian, Kersten and Patton, P.A. Waynesville, NC
Killian, Leon M., III ....Raleigh, NC
Waynesville, NC
Killian, Lewis M., Jr. ....Tallahassee, FL
Killian, Margaret M. ....Minneapolis, MN
Killian, Mark L. ....Newton, NC
Killian, Patricia A. ....New York, NY
Killian, Paul M. ....Port Jefferson, NY
Killian, Paul W. ....Washington, DC
Killian & Reilly ....Newton, NC
Killian, Rex P. ....Indianapolis, IN
Killian, Robert K. ....Hartford, CT
Killian, Robert K., Jr. ....Hartford, CT
Simsbury, CT
Killian, Robert P. ....Brunswick, GA
Killian, Roger ....Fort Payne, AL
Killian, Roger, P.C. ....Fort Payne, AL
Killian, Rosemary K. ....Wilmington, DE
Killian & Salisbury, P.C. ....Clark, NJ
Killian, Stephen B. ....Wilkes-Barre, PA
Killian, Suzanne S. ....Houston, TX
Killian, Teena M. ....Seattle, WA
Killian, Walter H. ....Baltimore, MD
Killian, William B. ....Miami, FL
Killian, William C. ....Jasper, TN
Killian, William R. ....Brunswick, GA
Killick, Emma ....Los Angeles, CA
Killien, Catharine E. ....Seattle, WA
Killigrew, Patricia A. ....Brattleboro, VT
Killilea, Ann I. ....Stow, MA
Killilea, Colleen Kearns ....Hampton, VA
Killilea, Geraldine M. ....Providence, RI
Killin, Charles C. ....Tulsa, OK
Killin, Charles Carr, III ....Davenport, WA
Killin, Michael D. ....Denver, CO
Killin, Richard C. ....Boston, MA
Killinger, Dana W., Jr. ....Topeka, KS
Killinger, Daria L. ....Exton, PA
Killinger, Kathryn A. ....Seattle, WA
Killinger, Lee M. ....Tallahassee, FL
Killinger, Lori Ellen Handelsman Tallahassee, FL
Killinger, Mary MacNeil ....Norristown, PA
Killinger, Russell R. ....Miami, FL
Killinger, Sam S. ....Sioux City, IA
Killingham, Martin F. ....Silver Spring, MD
Killingsworth, Cynthia S. ....Baton Rouge, LA
Killingsworth, Donald F. ....Tyler, TX
Killingsworth, Georgia A. ....Victorville, CA
Killingsworth, Patricia M. ....Atlanta, GA
Killingsworth, V. Scott ....Atlanta, GA
Killion, Bruce M. ....North Haven, CT

Kim, Kay Lee ... New York, NY
Kim, Keungsuk ... Lafayette Hill, PA
Kim, Kihyun S. ... Albany, NY
Kim, Kyung Tai ... Houston, TX
Kim, Laura Y. ... Honolulu, HI
Kim, Lauren E. ... Reston, VA
Kim, Leezie ... Phoenix, AZ
Kim, Leslie Y. ... Los Angeles, CA
Kim, Lilly ... Los Angeles, CA
Kim, Linda J. ... Los Angeles, CA
Kim, Linda M. ... Los Angeles, CA
Kim, Lisa ... Cincinnati, OH
Kim, Lisa H. ... New York, NY
Kim, Lisa L. ... Los Angeles, CA
Kim, Luenna Heawan ... Worcester, MA
Kim, Margret J. ... Compton, CA
Kim, Martha V. ... Cleveland, OH
Kim, Mary ... Los Angeles, CA
Kim, Mary H. ... Santa Ana, CA
Kim, Mi K. ... Boston, MA
Kim, Mia S. ... Washington, DC
Kim, Michael ... Hackensack, NJ
Kim, Michael ... New York, NY
Kim, Michael C. ... Chicago, IL
Kim, Michael G. ... San Diego, CA
Kim, Michael H. ... Oakland, CA
Kim, Michael T. I. ... Honolulu, HI
Kim, Michelle J. ... Chicago, IL
Kim, Michelle N. ... New York, NY
Kim, Mihea ... New York, NY
Kim, Millie ... New York, NY
Kim, Min Soo ... Washington, DC
Kim, Mindy J. ... Los Angeles, CA
Kim, Mindy J. ... Cherry Hill, NJ
Kim, Mi-Ryoung ... Chicago, IL
Kim, Monica Y. ... Los Angeles, CA
Kim, Monica Yung-Min ... Menlo Park, CA
Kim, Moon Sun ... New York, NY
Kim, Moon Yung ... New York, NY
Kim, Nam Hee ... New York, NY
Kim, Nan H. ... Palo Alto, CA
Kim, Nancy ... Treasury Department, Internal Revenue Service, GV
Kim, Nancy M. ... Chicago, IL
Kim, Nancy S. ... San Francisco, CA
Kim, Nina H. ... New York, NY
Kim, Nosuk Pak ... Newport News, VA
Kim, P. Stephen ... Buffalo, NY
Kim, Patricia H. ... Wayne, NJ
Kim, Patrick S. ... Washington, DC
Kim, Paul ... Irvine, CA
Kim, Paul Jaykun ... New York, NY
Kim, Paul T. ... New York, NY
Kim, Paul Thomas ... New York, NY
Kim, Pauline ... St. Louis, MO
Kim, Penelope R. ... Department of State, Bureau of International Organization Affairs, GV
Kim, Peter Hyun ... White Plains, NY
Kim, Pio S. ... Los Angeles, CA
Kim & Powell ... Kailua-Kona, HI
Kim, Raymond B. ... Los Angeles, CA
Kim, Rena Y.
General Services Administration, GV
Kim, Rex K.C. ... Honolulu, HI
Kim, Richard C. ... San Diego, CA
Kim, Richard D. ... Los Angeles, CA
Kim, Richard K. ... New York, NY
Kim, Richard S. ... Long Beach, CA
Kim, Richard Song-Uk ... Los Angeles, CA
Kim, Richard Y. ... Department of Commerce, Patent and Trademark Office, GV
Kim, Robert C. ... Las Vegas, NV
Kim, Robert D. S. ... Kailua-Kona, HI
Kim, Robert J. ... Greenbelt, MD
Kim, Robert Min ... Los Angeles, CA
Kim, Robert S. ... New York, NY
Kim, Rodney ... Wahiawa, HI
Kim, Ronald Joseph ... Saratoga Springs, NY
Kim, Ronald W. ... Memphis, TN
Kim, Rosa H. ... Redmond, WA
Kim, Rosa S. ... Santa Clara, CA
Kim, Roy P. ... Newark, CA
Kim, Rudy Y. ... Los Angeles, CA
Kim, Ryul ... Long Beach, CA
Kim, Ryul, & Associates ... Long Beach, CA
Kim, S. Isabella ... Bellevue, WA
Kim, S. Jean ... New York, NY
Kim, S. Kristin ... New York, NY
Kim, Sally S. ... New York, NY
Kim, Sally Y. ... Walnut Creek, CA
Kim, Sandy M. ... Boston, MA
Kim, Sang Y. ... New York, NY
Kim, Sarah S. ... San Mateo, CA
Kim, S. C. Brian ... Rockville, MD
Kim, Sean ... Honolulu, HI
Kim, Seong Hwan ... Los Angeles, CA
Kim, Seoun K. ... New York, NY
Kim, Shulammite ... New York, NY
Kim, Soloman S.M. ... Everett, WA
Kim, Song K. ... Boston, MA
Kim, Sonya W. ... New York, NY
Kim, Sonya Y. ... New York, NY
Kim, Soo J. ... Santa Monica, CA
Kim, Soo Y. ... Chicago, IL
Kim, Sophia Sujin
Department of Commerce, Patent and Trademark Office, GV
Kim, Sophie S. ... Los Angeles, CA
Kim, Stanley A. ... West Palm Beach, FL
Kim, Stella J. ... San Francisco, CA
Kim, Stephanie J. ... Washington, DC
Kim, Stephanie J. ... Chicago, IL
Kim, Stephen E. ... Palo Alto, CA
Kim, Steven J. ... Honolulu, HI
Lihue, HI
Kim, Stuart Y. ... Burbank, CA
Kim, Sue S. ... Los Angeles, CA

Kim, Sue Y. ... Denver, CO
Kim, Sujung ... San Francisco, CA
Kim, Suk Y. ... New York, NY
Kim, Sukhan ... Washington, DC
Kim, Sung-Eun Stephan ... New York, NY
Kim, Sunny C. ... Seattle, WA
Kim, Susan ... Hartford, CT
Kim, Susan C. ... Chicago, IL
Kim, Susan J. ... Anaheim, CA
Kim, Susan S. ... Washington, DC
New York, NY
Kim, Susan S. ... New York, NY
Kim, Susan S. ... New York, NY
Kim, Susan Y. ... Chicago, IL
Kim, Susie ... New York, NY
Kim, S.Y. ... Fort Lee, NJ
Kim, Taehun ... New York, NY
Kim, Ted ... Washington, DC
Kim, Teena Heejung ... New York, NY
Kim, Terri Ann ... Oakland, CA
Kim, Theodore ... Beverly Hills, CA
Kim, Theodore S. ... Los Angeles, CA
Kim, Thomas J. ... Beverly Hills, CA
Kim, Thomas M. ... Denver, CO
Kim, Thomas S. ... Palo Alto, CA
Kim, Todd S. ... Department of Justice, Environment and Natural Resources Division, GV
Kim, Tony K. ... Los Angeles, CA
Kim, Tori T. ... Los Angeles, CA
Kim, Walter Y. ... La Crescenta, CA
Kim, Wan J. ... Washington, DC
Kim, Willcox, McArthur & Taylor
Memphis, TN
Kim, William Y. ... New York, NY
Kim, Won
Federal Communications Commission, Wireless Telecommunications Bureau, GV
Kim, Y. Maggie ... Los Angeles, CA
Kim, Y. Peter ... Los Angeles, CA
Kim, Yale K. ... Los Angeles, CA
Kim, Yoora ... Washington, DC
Kim, You Min ... New York, NY
Kim, Young ... Chicago, IL
Kim, Young B. ... Chicago, IL
Kim, Young II ... New York, NY
Kim, Young Yuel ... Houston, TX
Kim & Yun, P.C. ... New York, NY
Kimack, Michael A. ... Garden City, NY
Kimball, Albert B., Jr. ... Houston, TX
Kimball, Albert F. ... Claverack, NY
Kimball, Andrew G. ... Pittsburgh, PA
Kimball, Anne Giddings ... Chicago, IL
Kimball, Betsy S. ... Sacramento, CA
Kimball, Brousseau & Michon, LLP
Boston, MA
Kimball, Carol DeWitt ... Dedham, MA
Kimball, Charles H. ... Coeur d'Alene, ID
Kimball, Charles J. ... Denver, CO
Kimball, Chase ... Salt Lake City, UT
Kimball, Cheryl M. ... Boston, MA
Kimball, Christian E. ... Chicago, IL
Kimball, Claire M. ... Atlanta, GA
Kimball, Clark D. ... Belfast, ME
Kimball, Claude P. ... Bakersfield, CA
Kimball, Curtis E. ... Bangor, ME
Kimball, Dale A. ... Salt Lake City, UT
Kimball, Dale A., Jr. ... Bowling Green, KY
Kimball, David P., III ... Phoenix, AZ
Kimball, Dennis R. ... Columbus, OH
Kimball, Donald G. ... Cameron, MO
Kansas City, MO
Kimball, Dove & Simpson, P.A.
Lancaster, SC
Rock Hill, SC
Kimball, Edward K. ... Northampton, MA
Kimball, Edward L. ... Provo, UT
Kimball, Elizabeth B. ... Boston, MA
Kimball, Erik P. ... Boston, MA
Kimball, Fielding ... El Centro, CA
Kimball, Frank C. ... Mariposa, CA
Kimball, Gearon J. ... Albany, NY
Kimball, George ... Los Angeles, CA
Kimball, Glen D. ... King Of Prussia, PA
Philadelphia, PA
Kimball, Greg ... Daytona Beach, FL
Palatka, FL
Kimball, H. L. ... Grundy Center, IA
Kimball, James P. ... Hackensack, NJ
Kimball, Jane S. ... Newark, NJ
Kimball, Janine R. ... Honolulu, HI
Kimball, Jeffrey B. ... Springfield, MA
Kimball, Jennifer L. ... Los Angeles, CA
Kimball, Jerry R. ... Seattle, WA
Kimball, Jesse Dudley B. ... New York, NY
Kimball, John D. ... New York, NY
Kimball, John F. ... Cleveland, TN
Kimball, John H. ... Lynnfield, MA
Kimball, John H., Jr. ... Lynnfield, MA
Kimball, John, Jr. ... Topsfield, MA
Kimball, John R. H. ... Boston, MA
Kimball, John W. ... Cardiff-By-The-Sea, CA
Kimball, Justin H. ... Philadelphia, PA
Kimball, K. Mike ... Tribune, KS
Ulysses, KS
Kimball, Karen ... Office of Government Ethics, Office of General Counsel and Legal Policy, GV
Kimball, Katherine ... Cambridge, MA
Kimball, Keith Loren ... Virginia Beach, VA
Kimball, Kevin L. ... Dearborn, MI
Kimball & Kimball ... Lynnfield, MA
Kimball, Leyla F. ... Hartford, CT
Kimball, Marilyn ... Lynnfield, MA
Kimball, Mark A. ... Minneapolis, MN
Kimball, Matthew L. ... Baltimore, MD
Kimball, Maura Johnson ... Secaucus, NJ
Kimball, Michelle L. ... Poughkeepsie, NY

Kimball, Monty W. ... Alpine, TX
Kimball, Neil L. ... Caledonia, MI
Grand Rapids, MI
Kimball & Nespor, P.C. ... Denver, CO
Kimball, Nina Joan ... Boston, MA
Kimball, Paul C. ... Washington, DC
Kimball, Paul, Jr. ... Austin, MN
Kimball, Paul M. ... Oklahoma City, OK
Kimball, Perla Figa ... San Diego, CA
Kimball, Peter Markham ... Waukesha, WI
Kimball, Philip C. ... Louisville, KY
Kimball, Philip K. ... Springfield, MA
Kimball, Priscilla E. ... Manchester, NH
Kimball, R. Bartus ... Los Angeles, CA
Kimball, Raymond J. ... Washington, DC
Kimball, Renée ... Houston, TX
Kimball, Richard A., Jr. ... New York, NY
Kimball, Richard C. ... Lancaster, NH
Kimball, Richard N. ... Boston, MA
Kimball, Robert ... Seattle, WA
Kimball, Robert D. ... Albuquerque, NM
Kimball, Robert E.
Federal Communications Commission, Office of Engineering & Technology, GV
Kimball, Robert G. ... Scottsdale, AZ
Kimball, Robert L. ... Fresno, CA
Kimball, Robert L. ... Harrison, ME
Kimball, Robert L. ... Dallas, TX
Kimball, Robert L., & Associates
Fresno, CA
Kimball, Robert R. ... Chicago, IL
Kimball, Robert R. ... Worcester, MA
Kimball, Robert Wayne ... Dallas, TX
Kimball, Ross A. ... Boston, MA
Kimball, Ruth Irene ... Renton, WA
Kimball, S. Jackson, III ... Rock Hill, SC
Kimball, Sharon R. ... Albuquerque, NM
Kimball, Sherman P. ... Department of Energy, Office of Hearings and Appeals, GV
Kimball, Stephen C. ... Mission Viejo, CA
Kimball, Steven C. ... Cincinnati, OH
Kimball, Steven S. ... San Francisco, CA
Kimball, Susannah W. ... New York, NY
Kimball, Ted C. ... San Diego, CA
Kimball, Thomas E. ... San Carlos, CA
Kimball, Tirey & St. John ... San Diego, CA
Kimball, Walter N. ... Palo Alto, CA
Kimball & Weiner LLP ... Los Angeles, CA
Kimball, William F. ... Harlingen, TX
Kimball, William L. ... Bradenton, FL
Kimball, William M. ... New York, NY
Kimball, William W. ... Philadelphia, PA
Kimball-Matson, Cheryl M. ... Boston, MA
Kimbarovsky, Ross E. ... Chicago, IL
Kimbel, Phil ... Bowling Green, KY
Kimbel, Virginia ... San Francisco, CA
Kimbell, Alphonso ... Compton, CA
Kimbell, Charles D. ... Santa Barbara, CA
Kimbell, Daniel R. ... Pasadena, CA
Kimbell, James M. ... Houston, TX
Kimbell, Katy W. ... New Orleans, LA
Kimbell, Lillian ... Woodland Hills, CA
Kimbell, Raymond G., III ... Galesburg, IL
Kimbell, Richard L. ... Yreka, CA
Kimbell, Stephen W. ... Montpelier, VT
Kimbell & Storrow ... Montpelier, VT
Kimber, Alan A. ... Troy, MI
Kimber, Brian L. ... West Palm Beach, FL
Kimber, C. Michael ... Detroit, MI
Kimber, Donald C. ... Montrose, CA
Kimber, Michael ... Bloomfield Hills, MI
Kimberley, David A. ... Gadsden, AL
Kimberlin, Diane L. ... Los Angeles, CA
Kimberlin, James R. ... Memphis, TN
Kimberlin, Leann Kosco
Bloomfield Hills, MI
Kimberlin, Robert T. ... Oakland, CA
Kimberlin, S. Scott ... Austin, TX
Kimberlin, Sam O., Jr. ... Austin, TX
Kimberlin, Wm. M. ... Harrisonville, MO
Kimberling, David L. ... Hunt Valley, MD
Kimberling, John Farrell ... Palm Springs, CA
Kimberling, Michael S. ... Washington, DC
Kimberly, George D., Jr. ... Greensboro, NC
Kimberly, John H. ... Tulsa, OK
Kimberly, Knox ... Phoenix, AZ
Kimberly, Michael G. ... Ithaca, NY
Kimberly, Richard C. ... Bellingham, WA
Kimberly, Richard H., Jr. ... Atlanta, GA
Kimbis, Thomas P. ... Washington, DC
Kimble, Barbara L. ... Fairfax, VA
Kimble, Casey M. ... Limon, CO
Kimble, Cavender Crosby
Birmingham, AL
Kimble, David E. ... Shaker Heights, OH
Kimble, David L. ... Seward, NE
Kimble, Gerald A., Jr.
Colorado Springs, CO
Kimble, James Lawson ... Washington, DC
Kimble, James T. ... Baltimore, MD
Kimble, Jeffrey A. ... Clarksburg, WV
Kimble, Joseph ... Lansing, MI
Kimble, Karen L. ... Midland, MI
Kimble, Kelly J. ... Charleston, WV
Morgantown, WV
Kimble, Kenneth L. ... Chevy Chase, MD
Kimble, Lesher, Corradini & Toone
Tucson, AZ
Kimble, MacMichael & Upton, A Professional Corporation
Bakersfield, CA
Fresno, CA
Hanford, CA
Madera, CA
Merced, CA
Visalia, CA
Kimble, Marsha Florence
Canyon Country, CA

Kimble, Nelson, Audilett, McDonough & Molla, P.C. ... Phoenix, AZ
Tucson, AZ
Kimble, Raymond V., Jr. ... Greenville, MS
Kimble, Rick C. ... Storm Lake, IA
Kimble, Robert Chad ... Fort Worth, TX
Kimble, Stan M. ... Limon, CO
Kimble, Stephen E. ... Tucson, AZ
Kimble, Steven J. ... Parsippany, NJ
Kimble, Stevens & Clark ... Portsmouth, OH
Kimble, Thomas G., & Associates
Salt Lake City, UT
Kimble, William ... Tucson, AZ
Kimbley, J. Michael ... Russellville, KY
Kimbol, Lois ... Philadelphia, PA
Kimbol, Paul S. ... Philadelphia, PA
Kimbrel, Ron W. ... Portage, MI
Kimbrell, Alan G. ... St. Louis, MO
Kimbrell, Charles A. ... Miami, FL
Kimbrell & Hamann, Professional Association ... Miami, FL
Kimbrell, Henry Wade ... Fairfax, VA
Kimbrell, Horace W. ... Grandview, MO
Kimbrell, P. Darrell ... Atlanta, GA
Kimbriel, Debra ... Bedford, TX
Kimbro, Bradford D. ... Tampa, FL
Kimbrough, Angela L. ... Montgomery, AL
Kimbrough, Carol A.
Department Of Health And Human Services, Food & Drug Administration, GV
Kimbrough, Charles A. ... Bellevue, WA
Kimbrough, Charles R. ... Lockhart, TX
Kimbrough, Colette D. ... New York, NY
Kimbrough, Erich T. ... Atlanta, GA
Kimbrough, Hardie B. ... Grove Hill, AL
Kimbrough, J. Frank, & Associates
Fort Wayne, IN
Kimbrough, James Edward, Jr. ... Mobile, AL
Kimbrough, James M. ... Fayetteville, GA
Kimbrough, John D. ... Orange, TX
Kimbrough, Julia C. ... Birmingham, AL
Kimbrough, Kelly R. ... Austin, TX
Kimbrough, Orman L., Jr. ... Orlando, FL
Kimbrough, Rick ... Grandview, WA
Kimbrough, Robert A. ... Sarasota, FL
Kimbrough, Robin J. ... Columbia, SC
Kimbrough, Thomas M. ... Fort Wayne, IN
Kimbrough, Warren O. ... Fort Smith, AR
Kimbrough, W. H., Jr. ... Athens, GA
Kimbrough, William A., Jr. ... Mobile, AL
Kimbrough, William D. ... Austin, TX
Kimbrough, William E. ... Thomasville, AL
Kime, Barrett L. ... Tucson, AZ
Kime, Christina L. ... Piedmont, MO
Kime, Karl W. ... Los Angeles, CA
Kime, Klifton L. ... Alexandria, VA
Kime, Mary Lynn ... Dallas, TX
Fort Worth, TX
Kime, Michael D., Jr. ... St. Louis, MO
Kime, Robert C. ... Beverly Hills, CA
Kime, Robt. C. ... Blowing Rock, NC
Kime, Roy C.
Environmental Protection Agency, Office of Enforcement and Compliance Assurance, GV
Kime, Todd G. ... Cincinnati, OH
Kime-Goodwin, Sherylynn A.
Lubbock, TX
Kimel, Horace M., Jr. ... Greensboro, NC
Kimel, Martin
Securities and Exchange Commission, Office of International Affairs, GV
Kimel, Metiner G. ... Yakima, WA
Kimelman, Martin ... New York, NY
Kimelman, Steven ... New York, NY
Kimenker, Alan C. ... Needham, MA
Kimenker, Nina ... New York, NY
Kimer, Thomas L. ... Minneapolis, MN
Kimerer & LaVelle, P.L.C. ... Phoenix, AZ
Kimerer, Michael D. ... Phoenix, AZ
Kimerline, Nelfred G. ... Bucyrus, OH
Kimerling, Joshua E. ... White Plains, NY
Kimery, Kristyn Elizabeth
Indianapolis, IN
Kimes, Gary G. ... Osceola, IA
Kimes, Larry W. ... Austin, TX
Kimes, Leslie L. ... Brooklyn Park, MN
Kimes, Martha H. ... New York, NY
Kimes, Phillip R. ... Irvine, CA
Kimes, Rodney W. ... Beloit, WI
Kimes, Russell A., Jr. ... New Canaan, CT
Kimes, Shapleigh H. ... Irvine, CA
Kimes, Stephen L. ... Mercer, PA
Kimes-Brown, Trecia M. ... McArthur, OH
Kimichik, Brigitte Gawenda ... Dallas, TX
Kimitch, Michael R. ... St. Paul, MN
Kimker, Teresa J. ... Minneapolis, MN
Kimler, Andrew A. ... New York, NY
Kimler, Lewis S. ... Fort Lauderdale, FL
Kimlin, Edward C.
Department of Commerce, Patent and Trademark Office, GV
Kimlinger, Katie T. ... Minneapolis, MN
Kimlinger, Richard W. ... Rochester, MN
Kimm, Glenn D. ... Oakland, CA
Kimm, Lori-Lou ... Columbus, OH
Kimm, Michael S. ... Hackensack, NJ
New York, NY
Kimm, Robert A. ... Cedar Rapids, IA
Kimm, Samantha J. ... New York, NY
Kimm, Sandra J. ... Phoenix, AZ
Kimme, William B. ... Chicago, IL
Kimme, William D. ... Washington, MO
Kimmel, Adele P. ... Washington, DC
Kimmel, Allyson E. ... Ventura, CA
Kimmel, Andrew M. ... Cedar Knolls, NJ
Kimmel, Angela M. ... Pembroke, NC

Kimmel & Batson, Chartered, Law Offices of ... Pensacola, FL
Kimmel & Beach ... Kennebunk, ME
Portland, ME
Kimmel, Bernard M. ... Wayne, NJ
Kimmel, Brett ... New York, NY
Kimmel, Carter, Roman & Peltz, P.A. ... Wilmington, DE
Kimmel, Charles F. ... Trenton, NJ
Kimmel, Christine S. ... Berwyn, PA
Kimmel, Craig Thor ... Ambler, PA
Kimmel, Daniel M. ... Brookline, MA
Kimmel, David C. ... Baton Rouge, LA
Kimmel, E. Dan ... Murphysboro, IL
Kimmel, Edw, R. ... Wilmington, DE
Kimmel, Edward M. ... Washington, DC
Greenbelt, MD
Kimmel, Edward M. ... Silver Spring, MD
Kimmel, Edward R. ... Cape Haze, FL
Kimmel, Elisabeth M. ... San Diego, CA
Kimmel, Eugene M. ... Norwalk, CT
Kimmel, George L. ... New York, NY
Kimmel, Gregory A. ... San Diego, CA
Kimmel, Gregory S. ... Norwalk, CT
Kimmel & Hagerty, A Professional Corporation ... Cedar Knolls, NJ
Kimmel, Harold D. ... Stillwater, MN
Kimmel, Hinda K. ... New London, CT
Kimmel, Hubert D. ... Mequon, WI
Kimmel, James B. ... Princeton, NJ
Kimmel, James P., Jr. ... State College, PA
Kimmel, James R. ... Los Angeles, CA
Kimmel, James S. ... Denver, CO
Kimmel, James S. ... Littleton, CO
Kimmel, Jay ... New York, NY
Kimmel, Jeffrey A. ... Hackensack, NJ
New York, NY
Kimmel, Jeffrey Mitchel ... Bronx, NY
Kimmel, Joe H., III ... Camilla, GA
Kimmel, Jonathan L. ... New York, NY
Kimmel, Kathy S. ... Minneapolis, MN
Kimmel, Kenneth C. ... Wichita, KS
Kimmel, Kenneth E. ... Kennebunk, ME
Kimmel & Kimmel ... New York, NY
Kimmel, Lance Jon ... Los Angeles, CA
Kimmel, Leo J. ... Brooklyn, NY
Kimmel, Lisa C. ... Cleveland, OH
Kimmel, Mara ... Anchorage, AK
Kimmel, Mark E. ... Hershey, PA
Kimmel, Mary P. ... Phoenix, AZ
Kimmel, Melissa B. ... Washington, DC
Kimmel, Melvin ... Brooklyn, NY
Kimmel, Meyer ... Monsey, NY
Kimmel, Michael ... Washington, DC
Kimmel, Morton Richard ... Wilmington, DE
Kimmel, P. Michael ... Carbondale, IL
Kimmel, Richard L. ... Greenwood, MS
Kimmel, Robert M. ... Cleveland, OH
Kimmel, Robert R. ... Pensacola, FL
Kimmel, Roger A., Jr. ... Aurora, OH
Kimmel, Roger H. ... New York, NY
Kimmel, Scott L. ... New York, NY
Kimmel, Seth ... Fort Lauderdale, FL
Kimmel and Silverman, P.C. ... Ambler, PA
Kimmel, Stanley H. ... New York, NY
Kimmel, Stanley H., Law Offices of ... Northridge, CA
Kimmel, Steven A. ... Newburgh, NY
Kimmel, Susan Landay
Federal Communications Commission, Wireless Telecommunications Bureau, GV
Kimmel, Thomas C. ... Berlin, MD
Kimmel, Thomas R. ... De Vault, PA
Kimmel, Timothy C. ... Frankfort, KY
Kimmel, Tracy ... New York, NY
Kimmel, Wayne D. ... Wilmington, DE
Kimmel, William L. ... Somerset, PA
Kimmelfield, Arthur L. ... New York, NY
Kimmelfield, Neil D. ... Portland, OR
Kimmell & Cummings ... Vincennes, IN
Kimmell, James W., Jr. ... Atlanta, GA
Kimmell, Jeff ... South Bend, IN
Kimmell, Joseph W., II ... Fort Wayne, IN
Kimmell, Kenneth L. ... Boston, MA
Kimmell, P. Adam ... Portland, OR
Kimmell, Thomas J. ... Denver, CO
Kimmelman, David ... Baltimore, MD
Kimmelman, David I. ... Philadelphia, PA
Kimmelman, David Joseph ... Southfield, MI
Kimmelman, Gary A. ... Long Island City, NY
Kimmelman, Irwin I. ... Springfield, NJ
Kimmelman, Louis B. ... New York, NY
Kimmelman, Ned ... Boca Raton, FL
Kimmelman, Ned, P.A. ... Boca Raton, FL
Kimmelman, Norman ... New York, NY
Kimmelman, Ray ... Bronx, NY
Kimmelman, Simon ... Trenton, NJ
Kimmelman, Susan ... Chicago, IL
Kimmelman, William C. ... Swanton, OH
Kimmer, Jeffrey W. ... Troy, NY
Kimmerlein, John D. ... Portland, OR
Kimmerly, Thomas W. ... Oxford, MI
Kimmerly, Thomas W., P.C. ... Oxford, MI
Kimmeth, Mary Jane ... New York, NY
Kimmeth, Robert C. ... Chicago, IL
Kimmett, Charles T., Jr. ... Washington, DC
Kimmey, J. Lansing ... Atlanta, GA
Kimmey, Karen P. ... San Francisco, CA
Kimminau, Chris J. ... Tucson, AZ
Kimminau, David P. ... Independence, MO
Kimmins, Thomas W. ... Massillon, OH
Kimmitt, Gerard J., II ... Houston, TX
Kimmitt, Melinda A. ... Towson, MD
Kimmitt, Robert M. ... Washington, DC
Kimmitt, Thomas P., Jr. ... Towson, MD
Kimmons, Heather V. ... Indianapolis, IN
Kimms, Lyle ... Washington, DC

Kimose, Randall C. ... Redondo Beach, CA
Kimpel, David S. ... Syracuse, NY
Kimpel, Fuchs & Norton, LLP ... Evansville, IN
Kimpel and Gideon, P.C. ... Syracuse, NY
Kimpel, Herman C. ... Pittsburgh, PA
Kimpel, Hyland, Weinkam & Goodson, L.P.A. ... Cincinnati, OH
Kimpel, John M. ... Boston, MA
Kimpel, Scott H. ... Dallas, TX
Kimpel, Thomas J. ... Evansville, IN
Kimple, Jonathan M. ... Dallas Center, IA
Kimport, David L. ... San Francisco, CA
Kimpton, Burke, White & Heiden, P.A. ... Clearwater, FL
Tampa, FL
Kimpton, William J. ... Clearwater, FL
Kimrey, Blaine C. ... Kansas City, MO
Kimsal, Viki A. ... Minneapolis, MN
Kimsey & Associates, P.A. ... Tampa, FL
Kimsey, Paul S. ... Tampa, FL
Kimsey, R. Dale ... Oklahoma City, OK
Kimsey, Robert A. ... Salt Lake City, UT
Kimsey, Rose L. ... Laguna Beach, CA
Kimsey, William J. ... Dalton, GA
Dalton, GA
Kimura, Alma M. ... Seattle, WA
Kimura, Faye T. ... Honolulu, HI
Kimura, George Y. ... Honolulu, HI
Kimura, Glenn I. ... Honolulu, HI
Kimura, Glenn N. ... Hilo, HI
Kimura, Harlan Y. ... Honolulu, HI
Kimura, Jay T. ... Hilo, HI
Kimura, Jodi L. ... Honolulu, HI
Kimura, Ken ... San Francisco, CA
Kimura, Lily M. ... Oakland, CA
Kimura, Lisa-Ann L. ... Honolulu, HI
Kimura, Max Jiro ... San Francisco, CA
Kimura, Rodney I. ... Honolulu, HI
Kimura, Trisha M. ... Honolulu, HI
Kimura, Wendell K. ... Honolulu, HI
Kimzey, Brian M. ... Kansas City, MO
Kimzey, Heidi L. ... Phoenix, AZ
Kimzey, Kimzey & York ... Cornelia, GA
Kimzey, M. Shane ... Houston, TX
Kimzey, Ronald R. ... Atlanta, GA
Kin, James W. ... Colorado Springs, CO
Kin, Steven M. ... Midland, MI
Kinack, James F. ... Redondo Beach, CA
Kinaga, Karl ... San Jose, CA
Kinaga, Patricia ... Los Angeles, CA
Kinaka, William T. ... Wailuku, HI
Kinal, Hilary Andrew ... Beaver, PA
Kinal Law Office ... Beaver, PA
Butler, PA
New Castle, PA
Pittsburgh, PA
Kinane, Michael J. ... Oakland, CA
Kinane, William G. ... Orlando, FL
Kinard, Agnes Dodds ... Verona, PA
Kinard, Crane & Butler, P.A. ... Magnolia, AR
Kinard, J. Ernest, Jr. ... Camden, SC
Kinard, John M. ... Pascagoula, MS
Kinard, Kathy A. ... Arlington, TX
Kinard, Keith M. ... Walterboro, SC
Kinard, M. Lewis ... Dallas, TX
Kinard, Mike ... Magnolia, AR
Kinard, Patricia B. ... Hopkins, SC
Kinard, Samuel McMurry ... Lexington, SC
Kinard, Stuart E. ... Austin, TX
Kinard, W. Robert ... Charleston, SC
Kinas, Mary Hitchcock ... Phoenix, AZ
Kinas, Robert R. ... Phoenix, AZ
Kinashi, Sadao ... Washington, DC
Kinast, Christopher G. ... Beloit, WI
Kinast, Frank X. ... Beloit, WI
Kinast Law Office ... Beloit, WI
Kinasz, Thomas J. ... Chicago, IL
Kinate, Gordon M. ... Fairbury, IL
Kinate & Morgan, Professional Corporation ... Fairbury, IL
Kinateder, J. Douglas ... Salt Lake City, UT
Kinberg, Edward J. ... Melbourne, FL
Kinberg, Edward J., P.A. ... Melbourne, FL
Kinberg, Robert ... Washington, DC
Kinberger, Teresa M. ... Louisville, KY
Kinburn, Daniel ... Totowa, NJ
Kincade, Bruce C. ... Metairie, LA
Kincade, Donald H. ... Toledo, OH
Kincade, James E. ... Stafford, TX
Kincade, John P. ... Dallas, TX
Kincade, Kathleen D. ... East Hanover, NJ
Kincade Law Office ... Mountain Home, AR
Kincade, Michael J. ... Metairie, LA
Kincade, Michael J., A Professional Law Corporation ... Metairie, LA
New Orleans, LA
Kincade, Ronald P. ... Mountain Home, AR
Kincaid, Amy H. ... Greensboro, NC
Kincaid, Ariana J. ... Charleston, WV
Kincaid, Arthur R. ... Liberty, MO
Kincaid, Barbara W. ... Dallas, TX
Kincaid, Brian W. ... Parsippany, NJ
Kincaid, Cassandra L. ... McLean, VA
Kincaid, Charles M. ... Huntington, WV
Kincaid, Cohen & Swanson, P.C. ... Washington, DC
Baltimore, MD
Kincaid, Dale B. ... Massillon, OH
Kincaid, Daniel E. ... Cincinnati, OH
Kincaid, David P. ... San Francisco, CA
Kincaid, Eugene D., III ... Uvalde, TX
Kincaid, Gregory D. ... Olathe, KS
Kincaid, Gregory D., P.A. ... Olathe, KS
Kincaid, Harry G. ... Jacksonville, FL
Kincaid, Horne & Trumbo ... Fayetteville, AR

Kincaid & Horton ... Austin, TX
Kincaid, Hugh R. ... Fayetteville, AR
Kincaid, J. Donald ... Zanesville, OH
Kincaid, James G. ... Redmond, OR
Kincaid, James L. ... Tulsa, OK
Kincaid, James M. ... Detroit, MI
Kincaid, James S. ... Portland, OR
Kincaid, Jeffrey Alan ... Lenexa, KS
Kincaid, John A., Jr. ... Washington, DC
Baltimore, MD
Pittsburgh, PA
Kincaid, John B. ... Wheaton, IL
Kincaid, John M. ... McLean, VA
Kincaid, John R. ... Durham, NC
Kincaid, Joseph P. ... Chicago, IL
Kincaid, Karen A. ... Washington, DC
Kincaid, Kasey W. ... Des Moines, IA
Kincaid, Kenneth A. ... Dallas, TX
Kincaid, Kenneth E. ... Morgantown, WV
Kincaid, Linda L. ... Vidalia, LA
Kincaid, Marilyn K. ... Radnor, PA
Kincaid, Mark L. ... Austin, TX
Kincaid, Matthew C. ... Indianapolis, IN
Kincaid, Ora A., III ... Lebanon, IN
Kincaid, Randall & Craine ... Columbus, OH
Kincaid, Robert M., Jr. ... Columbus, OH
Kincaid, Steven W. ... Kokomo, IN
Kincaid, Susan M. ... Cambridge, MA
Kincaid, Taylor & Geyer ... Cambridge, OH
Newark, OH
Thornville, OH
Zanesville, OH
Kincaid, Timothy S. ... Hickory, NC
Kincaid, Valerie E. ... Los Angeles, CA
Kincaid, William H. ... Sanger, TX
Kincaide, Johnny, Jr. ... Miami, FL
Kincaid-Smith, Janet E.
Treasury Department, Office of the Comptroller of the Currency, GV
Kincannon, Allen D. ... Metairie, LA
Kincannon, Barry D. ... Fort Smith, AR
Kincannon, Charles P. ... Smyrna, GA
Kincannon, Gary L. ... Newport Beach, CA
San Diego, CA
Kincannon, John A. ... Irvine, CA
Kincannon, Karen C. ... Atlanta, GA
Kincanon, Jas. N. ... Roanoke, VA
Kincart, Joseph P. ... New York, NY
Kincer, E. Lewis, Jr. ... Richmond, VA
Kinch, Allan B. ... Escondido, CA
Kinch, E. L. Lee ... Wichita, KS
Kinch, Julie M. ... White Plains, NY
Kincheloe, Andrew H. ... Dallas, TX
Kincheloe, Duncan E., III ... Jefferson City, MO
Kincheloe, Hatcher B. ... Charlotte, NC
Kincheloe, J. Gordon ... Fairfax, VA
Kincheloe, James G., Jr. ... Fairfax, VA
Kincheloe, John T. ... Fairfax, VA
Kincheloe, Laura ... Lexington, KY
Kincheloe, Pamela Barrow ... Rockville, MD
Kincheloe, Paul C., Jr. ... Fairfax, VA
Kincheloe & Schneiderman ... Fairfax, VA
Kinchen, Brent E. ... Baton Rouge, LA
Kinchen, Gilbert H. ... Moreland Hills, OH
Kinchen, Lance J. ... Baton Rouge, LA
Kinchen, Robert ... Chicago, IL
Kincher, Harold W., Jr. ... Houston, TX
Kinchy, Gerald A. ... Sayre, PA
Kincy, William P., III ... Walnut Creek, CA
Kinczewski, Greg A. ... Chicago, IL
Kind & Dashoff ... Baltimore, MD
Kind, Edward L. ... Boca Raton, FL
Kind, Edward L., P.A. ... Boca Raton, FL
Kind, Esther Drapacz ... Great Neck, NY
Kind, Keith ... La Jolla, CA
Kind, Kenneth W. ... Bakersfield, CA
Kind & McCartney ... Bakersfield, CA
Kind, Richard M. ... Baltimore, MD
Kind, Ronald J. ... La Crosse, WI
Kinda, Margaret L. ... Santa Cruz, CA
Kindall, Clare E. ... Hartford, CT
Kindall, Eric J. ... Sacramento, CA
Kindberg, J. Eric ... Charlotte, NC
Kindel, Frederick W. ... Cincinnati, OH
Kindel, James H., Jr. ... Los Angeles, CA
Kindel, Laurie Ann ... Minneapolis, MN
Kindelan, Brian P. ... Philadelphia, PA
Kindelan, Rosemary ... New York, NY
Kindelan, Timothy P. ... San Diego, CA
Kindelin, Mark Thomas ... Chicago, IL
Kindell, Judith E. ... Treasury Department, Internal Revenue Service, GV
Kindell, Louie R. ... Piqua, OH
Kinder, Bill R. ... Richardson, TX
Kinder, Byron L. ... Jefferson City, MO
Kinder, C. David ... San Antonio, TX
Kinder, C. Jeffrey ... Northampton, MA
Kinder, Carey Patrick ... Dallas, TX
Kinder, Carr L., III ... Richmond, VA
Kinder, Carr L., Jr. ... Roanoke, VA
Kinder, Daniel K. ... Providence, RI
Kinder, Duncan C. ... St. Clairsville, OH
Kinder, E. Tupper, Jr. ... Manchester, NH
Kinder & Fogel, P.C. ... Roanoke, VA
Kinder, Gary O., Jr. ... Charleston, WV
Kinder, Gordon D. ... Cleveland, OH
Kinder, Gordon D., III ... Seattle, WA
Kinder, Gordon T. ... St. Clairsville, OH
Kinder, Harper, Hazlett & Hinzey ... St. Clairsville, OH
Wheeling, WV
Kinder, James Thomas ... Dover, MA
Kinder, Jennifer Anne ... Dallas, TX
Kinder, John C. ... St. Clairsville, OH
Kinder, Joseph G. ... Bristol, RI
Providence, RI

Kinder, Larry E. ... Daytona Beach, FL
Kinder, Martha M. ... Fort Wayne, IN
Kinder, Peter D. ... Boston, MA
Kinder, Ralph M. ... Bristol, RI
Providence, RI
Kinder, Sally A. ... Framingham, MA
Kinder, Suzette Skolka ... San Antonio, TX
Kinderlehrer, Aaron C. ... New York, NY
Kinderman, Annette Lanning ... Birmingham, AL
Kinderman, Karla ... Chicago, IL
Kinderman, Keith J. ... Tallahassee, FL
Kinderman, R. Kenneth ... Louisville, KY
Kinderman, Robert H. ... Chicago, IL
Kinderman, Spencer A. ... Birmingham, AL
Kindermann, Anna L. ... United States Senate, Committee Legal Personnel, GV
Kindermann, David E. ... Rockville, MD
Kindermann, Diane Gayle ... Sacramento, CA
Kindig, Karl K. ... Abingdon, VA
Kindig, Karl W. ... Carmel, IN
Kindig & Sloat ... Nappanee, IN
Wakarusa, IN
Kindiger, Wayde S. ... Kansas City, MO
Kindinger, Jerry H. ... Seattle, WA
Kindl, John J. ... Hartford, CT
Kindle, Glenn W. ... Clayton, NJ
Kindle, Kurt A. ... Columbus, OH
Kindleberger, David W. ... Cincinnati, OH
Kindler, Hyman E. ... New York, NY
Kindler, James M. ... New York, NY
Kindler, Jeffrey B. ... Oak Brook, IL
Kindler, Pamela P. ... Rye, NY
Kindler, Robert A. ... New York, NY
Kindler, Roger A. ... Washington, DC
Kindley, Raymond S. ... Portland, OR
Kindley, Roger J. ... Seattle, WA
Kindling, Anne M. ... Topeka, KS
Kindlon & Shanks, P.C. ... Albany, NY
Kindlon, Terence L. ... Albany, NY
Kindman, Jerry ... New York, NY
Kindman, Jerry, P.C., Law Offices of ... New York, NY
Kindness, Gary S. ... Seattle, WA
Kindorf, William A., III ... Wheaton, IL
Kindred, Alan M. ... Los Angeles, CA
Kindred, Charles A. ... Overland Park, KS
Kindred, Jack Duane, II ... Seattle, WA
Kindred, Kermit G. ... Wapakoneta, OH
Kindred, Michael ... Columbus, OH
Kindred, Sam ... Austin, TX
Kindregan, Charles P. ... Boston, MA
Kindregan, Charles P., Jr. ... Boston, MA
Kindregan, Patricia A. ... New York, NY
Kindschi, John P. ... St. Louis, MO
Kindschuh, Mary Jean ... Englewood, CO
Kindschy, Darcy Arriola ... Ontario, OR
Kindschy, Eileen F. ... Chicago, IL
Kindseth, Rachel Snow ... Hartford, CT
Kindseth, Stephen M. ... Bridgeport, CT
Kindsvater, Brian G. ... Roseville, CA
Kindsvatter, Jack H. ... Hagerstown, MD
Kindsvatter, Leo R. ... Rittman, OH
Kindt, Christopher R. ... Oshkosh, WI
Kindwald, Donald J. ... Chicago, IL
Kine, Lucinda Merry ... Chadds Ford, PA
Kine, Sidney S. ... Philadelphia, PA
Kinealy, Paul V. ... Chicago, IL
Kineavy, Jerome P. ... Shrewsbury, NJ
Kinel, Daniel R. ... Rochester, NY
Kinel, Norman N. ... New York, NY
Kiner, Michael D. ... West Palm Beach, FL
Kiner, Patrick W. ... Mitchell, SD
Kiner, Patrick W., P.C. ... Mitchell, SD
Kiner, Richard D. ... Tustin, CA
Kinerk, Beal, Schmidt & Dyer, P.C. ... Nogales, AZ
Phoenix, AZ
Tucson, AZ
Kinerk, Burton J. ... Tucson, AZ
Kinerk, Colleen L. ... Tucson, AZ
Kinerk, Laurie A. ... Seattle, WA
Kinerk, M. Colleen ... Seattle, WA
Kinevan, Marcos E. ... Colorado Springs, CO
King, A. Brent ... Richmond, VA
King, A. Duncan ... Palo Alto, CA
King, Adam Bruno ... Hailey, ID
King, Adrian R. ... Philadelphia, PA
King, Adrian R., Jr. ... Philadelphia, PA
King, Adrienne S. ... Honolulu, HI
King, Alan H. ... Boston, MA
King, Alan L. ... Birmingham, AL
King, Alan S. ... Chicago, IL
King, Alethia N. ... Washington, DC
King, Alexa Erzsebet ... Palo Alto, CA
King, Alexander F. ... Tulsa, OK
King, Alice C., Law Offices of ... San Rafael, CA
Santa Rosa, CA
King, Alice M. ... Quincy, CA
King, Allan G. ... Dallas, TX
King, Allen H. ... Austin, TX
King, Allen R. ... Los Angeles, CA
King, Alton ... Palestine, TX
King, Alvin B. ... Lake Charles, LA
King, Amy E. ... New Haven, CT
King, Amye Tankersley ... Knoxville, TN
King, Andrea ... Liverpool, NY
King, Andrew J. ... Chilton, WI
King, Angela Baryames ... Ypsilanti, MI
King, Angela Marie ... Northbrook, IL
King, Angus S., Jr. ... Augusta, ME
King, Ann C. ... Boston, MA
King, Ann M. ... New York, NY
King, Anthony A. ... Denver, CO
King, Anthony F. ... Washington, DC
King, Ariail E. ... Columbia, SC

King, Arthur D. .... Columbus, IN
King, Arthur J. .... Collegeville, PA
Royersford, PA
King, Arthur M. .... Bridgeport, CT
King, Arthur T. .... Belmont, MA
King, Arthur V. .... Rockville, MD
King, Arthur W. .... Clay, WV
King & Associates .... Newport Beach, CA
King & Associates, P.C. .... Austin, TX
King & Attridge .... Washington, DC
Rockville, MD
King, Audrey C. .... Huntington, NY
King & Ballow .... San Diego, CA
Nashville, TN
King, Barbara A. .... Washington, DC
King, Barbara J. .... Latham, NY
King, Barbara M. .... Las Vegas, NV
King, Barry E. .... New York, NY
King, Barry L. .... Detroit, MI
King, Barry P. .... Los Angeles, CA
King, Bedford, Jr. .... San Jose, CA
King, Benjamin C. .... Shreveport, LA
King, Benjamin C., Jr.
Department of Justice, Tax Division, GV
King, Benjamin P., Jr. .... Mitchell, NE
King, Benjamin T. .... Portsmouth, NH
King, Bernard M. .... Fremont, CA
King, Bernard T. .... Syracuse, NY
King, Bettye J. .... West Palm Beach, FL
King, Bill Gene .... Woodinville, WA
King, Billie A. .... Chicago, IL
King, Blackwell & Downs, P.A.
Orlando, FL
King, Blaine J. .... Enterprise, AL
King, Bobbie L., (Mrs.) .... Jackson, MS
King, Brad A. .... Cincinnati, OH
King, Bradley D. .... Myrtle Beach, SC
King, Bradley E. .... Ocala, FL
King, Brady Dean, II .... Monroe, LA
King, Brandon R. .... Syracuse, NY
King & Brennan, Chtd. .... Wichita, KS
King, Brent .... Pocatello, ID
King, Brent A. .... Decatur, AL
King, Brent F. .... Statesville, NC
King, Bret F. .... Jackson, WY
King, Brian .... Palm Harbor, FL
King, Brian A. .... Springfield, NJ
King, Brian Austin .... Dallas, TX
King, Brian E. .... Chicago, IL
King, Brian J. .... Boston, MA
King, Brian J. .... Portland, OR
King, Brian S. .... Salt Lake City, UT
King, Briana .... New York, NY
King, Bruce A. .... Seattle, WA
King, Bruce Charles .... Miami, FL
King, Bruce S. .... Lansing, MI
King, Bruce Warren .... United States Senate,
Committee Legal Personnel, GV
King, Bryan .... Palo Alto, CA
King, Bryan N.B. .... Oklahoma City, OK
King & Bryant, P.A. .... New Bern, NC
King, Byron W. .... Pittsburgh, PA
King, C. Russell .... Santa Paula, CA
King, Cameron A. .... San Francisco, CA
King, Carl K. .... Boston, MA
King, Carlile E. .... Vero Beach, FL
King, Carlton T. .... Des Moines, IA
King, Carol .... Melville, NY
King, Carol J. .... Columbus, OH
King, Carol Weld .... Washington, DC
King, Carolyn Dineen .... Houston, TX
King, Carolyn L. .... Dallas, TX
King, Carolyn M., (Mrs.) .... Fort Gaines, GA
King & Carragher .... Atlanta, GA
King, Cary Davis .... Metairie, LA
King, Cary S. .... Atlanta, GA
King, Catherine A. .... Rochester, NY
King, Catherine Rene .... San Francisco, CA
King, Cecil B. .... Mobile, AL
King, Celeste M. .... Chicago, IL
King, Chad W. .... Dallas, TX
King, Charlene Boykin .... Wilson, NC
King, Charles Abraham .... Elmsford, NY
New York, NY
King, Charles B. .... Boston, MA
King, Charles C. .... Huntsville, AL
King, Charles C., Jr. .... Covington, GA
King, Charles E. .... Englewood, CO
King, Charles E. .... Pine Knot, KY
King, Charles E. .... Neptune, NJ
King, Charles E. .... Amarillo, TX
King, Charles E., III .... New York, NY
King, Charles E., Jr. .... Charleston, WV
King, Charles G. .... Houston, TX
King, Charles H. .... Mason City, IA
King, Charles, III .... Lincoln, MA
King, Charles J. .... Plantation, FL
King, Charles J. .... Moultrie, GA
King, Charles J., Jr. .... Norristown, PA
King, Charles M. .... Phoenix, AZ
King, Charles N., III, (P.C.) .... Cumming, GA
Roswell, GA
King, Charles W. .... Tucson, AZ
King, Charles W. .... Edwardsville, IL
King, Charles W. .... San Antonio, TX
King, Charles W., & Associates, P.C., Law
Office of .... San Antonio, TX
King, Charlie .... New York, NY
King, Cheryl J.
Federal Communications Commission,
Cable Services Bureau, GV
King, Cheryl L. .... Sacramento, CA
King, Cheryl Wade .... New York, NY
King, Chester H., Jr. .... Syracuse, NY
King, Christina A. .... Doylestown, PA
King, Christina Brightmire
Department of Commerce,
Patent and Trademark Office, GV
King, Christopher A. .... Baltimore, MD
King, Christopher E. .... Grafton, NH
King, Christopher G. .... Houston, TX
King, Christopher Gene .... New York, NY
King, Christopher K. .... Benicia, CA
King, Christopher Q. .... Chicago, IL
King, Christy O. .... Portland, OR
King, Clarence C. .... Chicago, IL
King, Clarence G., Jr. .... Jacksonville, FL
King, Clarence L., Jr. .... Salina, KS
King, Clark F. .... Damascus, MD
King, Clifford M. .... Sarasota, FL
King, Coby A. .... Los Angeles, CA
King, Colin P. .... Salt Lake City, UT
King, Connie H. .... Colorado Springs, CO
King, Corbin K. .... Kokomo, IN
King, Corey Slavens .... Tampa, FL
King, Cory J. .... San Diego, CA
King, Craig S. .... Washington, DC
King & Croft, LLP .... Atlanta, GA
King, Curtis M. .... Irvine, CA
King, Curtis Randall .... Houston, TX
King, C. W. .... Lincoln City, OR
King, Cynthia A. .... Mill Valley, CA
King, Cynthia Ann .... Franklin Lakes, NJ
King, Cynthia E. .... San Francisco, CA
King, D. Brian .... Springfield, MO
King, D. Michael .... Huntley, IL
King, D. Mitchell .... New Bern, NC
King, D. Randall .... Minneapolis, MN
King & Dade .... Springfield, MO
King, Dan C., II .... Bessemer, AL
King, Dan G. ......Department of Transportation,
Surface Transportation Board, GV
King, Daniel .... Rockford, IL
King, Daniel .... New York, NY
King, Daniel A. .... Oakland, CA
King, Daniel A. .... Houston, TX
King, Daniel B. .... Gadsden, AL
King, Daniel B. .... Denver, CO
King, Daniel D. .... Houston, TX
King, Daniel, III .... Ashland, KY
King, Daniel J. .... Atlanta, GA
King, Daniel J. .... Evansville, IN
King, Daniel L. .... Columbia, SC
King, Daniel N. .... Bloomfield Hills, MI
King, Daniel P. .... Farmington Hills, MI
Traverse City, MI
King, Daniel R. .... Atlanta, GA
King, Daniel W. .... Brandon, FL
King, Darlene K. .... Lancaster, PA
King, Darrel T. .... Miami, FL
King, Darrell D. .... Stearns, KY
King, David A. .... Orange Park, FL
King, David A. .... Wheaton, IL
King, David A. .... Bath, ME
King, David A. .... Ann Arbor, MI
King, David A. .... Nashville, TN
King, David Alan .... Palo Alto, CA
King, David B. .... Orlando, FL
King, David B. .... Bartlesville, OK
King, David C. .... Petaluma, CA
King, David C. .... Bangor, ME
King, David C. .... Rochester, NY
King, David Charles .... Atlanta, GA
King, David D. .... Colebrook, NH
King, David G. .... Atlanta, GA
King, David G. .... Seattle, WA
King, David H. .... Franklin, TN
King, David J. .... Leavenworth, KS
King, David L. .... Chicago, IL
King, David L. .... Akron, OH
King, David L. G., Jr. .... Decatur, GA
King, David M. .... Redwood City, CA
King, David M. .... St. Petersburg, FL
King, David M. .... Lawrenceburg, IN
King, David M. .... Beachwood, OH
King, David M. .... Cleveland, OH
King, David N. .... Northridge, CA
King, David P. .... Glendale, CA
King, David P. .... Baltimore, MD
King, David R. .... Palo Alto, CA
King, David R. .... Princeton, NJ
New York, NY
King, David R. .... Philadelphia, PA
King, David R. .... Salt Lake City, UT
King, David V. .... West Palm Beach, FL
King, Dayatra T. .... Raleigh, NC
King, Deanie M. .... Corpus Christi, TX
King, Deborah A. .... Santa Ynez, CA
King, Deborah Lynn .... Chicago, IL
King, Debra A. .... Tampa, FL
King, Debra D. .... Des Moines, IA
King, Debra R. .... Pine Knot, KY
King, Deep and Branaman
Henderson, KY
King, Denis M. .... Boston, MA
King, Denise J. .... Chicago, IL
King, Dennis .... Dallas, TX
King, Dennis D. .... Gordon, NE
Hay Springs, NE
Rushville, NE
King, Dennis D. .... Tulsa, OK
King, Dennis G. .... Miami, FL
King, Dennis G., P.A. .... Miami, FL
King, Dennis W. .... Aurora, CO
King, Dennis W. .... Baltimore, MD
King, Dennis W., (Atty. at Law, A Law
Corp.) .... Honolulu, HI
King, Diana P. .... Fairfax, CA
King, Dianah M. .... Dallas, TX
King, Diane A. .... Truckee, CA
Reno, NV
King, Diane S. .... Denver, CO
King, Don W. .... Biloxi, MS
King, Don W., Jr. .... San Antonio, TX
King, Dona P. .... Boise, ID
King, Donald B. .... San Francisco, CA
King, Donald B. .... St. Louis, MO
King, Donald Claude .... Eugene, OR
King, Donald E. .... Westmont, NJ
King, Donald F. .... Amherst, NH
King, Donald F. .... Fairfax, VA
King, Donald L. .... Los Angeles, CA
King, Donald L. .... New Orleans, LA
King, Donita M. .... Richmond, VA
King, Donna Burdyck .... Washington, DC
King, Donna D. .... Alexandria, VA
King, Douglas .... East Palestine, OH
King, Douglas A. .... Chagrin Falls, OH
King, Douglas A., Jr. .... Houston, TX
King, Douglas B. .... Indianapolis, IN
King, Douglas R. M. .... Washington, DC
King, Douglas W. .... St. Louis, MO
King, Douglas W. .... Toledo, OH
King, Drummond & Dabbs, P.C.
Birmingham, AL
King, Dudley W. .... Albuquerque, NM
King, Durwood W. .... Helena, AR
King, Dwight L. .... Salt Lake City, UT
King, E. Drummond .... Allentown, PA
King, E. Lawson .... Lexington, KY
King, Earl R. .... Weatherford, TX
King, Edmund T., II .... San Francisco, CA
King, Edward A. .... New York, NY
King, Edward C. .... Honolulu, HI
King, Edward G. .... Ketchikan, AK
King, Edward H. .... Deerfield, IL
King, Edward H. .... Brooklyn, NY
King, Edward J., III .... Red Bluff, CA
King, Edward M. .... Louisville, KY
King, Edward Vincent, Jr.
San Francisco, CA
King, Edward W. .... Ithaca, NY
King, Edwin V., Jr. .... Dallas, TX
King, Edwin W., Jr. .... Savannah, GA
King, Eileen M. .... Portland, ME
King, Eliot .... Amsterdam, NY
King, Elisha A. .... Baltimore, MD
King, Elizabeth A. .... Santa Monica, CA
King, Elizabeth Aldridge
United States Senate,
Office of the Legislative Counsel, GV
King, Elizabeth K.
Securities and Exchange Commission,
Division of Market Regulation, GV
King, Elizabeth W. .... Houston, TX
King, Ellen McGinty .... Palo Alto, CA
King, Eric R. .... Oklahoma City, OK
King, Eric T. .... Los Angeles, CA
King, Erika .... Washington, DC
King, Erin .... New York, NY
King, Ernest W. .... Hattiesburg, MS
King, Errol J. .... Baton Rouge, LA
King, Eugene R. .... Columbus, OH
King, Evans L., Jr. .... Clarksburg, WV
King & Everhard, P.C. .... Falls Church, VA
King, F. Carlton, Jr. .... Atlanta, GA
King, F. Craig, Jr. .... St. Louis, MO
King, F.C. .... Ann Arbor, MI
King, Felshaw .... Kaysville, UT
King & Ferlauto .... Los Angeles, CA
King, Florence R. .... St. Petersburg, FL
King, Floyd A. .... Waynesburg, PA
King, Floyd H. .... Long Beach, CA
King, Floyd R. .... Jackson, WY
King, Frances A. .... Boston, MA
King, Frances E. .... Birmingham, AL
King, Frances S. .... Ocala, FL
King, Francis A. .... Pittsburgh, PA
King, Francis P. .... Denver, CO
King, Francis X. .... Grosse Pointe Woods, MI
King, Frank A. .... Las Vegas, NV
King, Frank A. .... Austin, TX
King, Frank D., Jr. .... Santa Monica, CA
King, Frank G. .... Beverly Hills, CA
King, Frank H. .... Tallahassee, FL
King, Frank N., Jr. .... Henderson, KY
King, Frank S. .... Houston, TX
King, Frank S., Jr. .... San Diego, CA
Nashville, TN
King, Franklin A. .... Ocean City, NJ
King, Franklin W. .... Orangevale, CA
King, Frederick G. .... Cincinnati, OH
King, Frederick H. .... North Little Rock, AR
King, Frederick J., Jr. .... New Orleans, LA
King, Frederick M. .... Indianapolis, IN
King, Frederick R. .... Lincoln, NE
King, Freeman, II .... Pompano Beach, FL
King, Frisch & Allen, P.C. .... Tucson, AZ
King, G. Joseph
Department of Transportation,
Federal Railroad Administration, GV
King, G. Roger .... Columbus, OH
King, G. William .... Richmond, VA
King, Gail .... Cincinnati, OH
King, Garr M. .... Portland, OR
King, Gary K. .... Moriarty, NM
King, Gary L. .... Fort Smith, AR
King, Gary P. .... Springfield, IL
King, Gary P. .... Detroit, MI
King, Gary R. .... Santa Ana, CA
King, Gary R. .... Raleigh, MS
King, George .... Oakland, CA
King, George A. .... New York, NY
King, George C. .... St. Paul, MN
King, George H. .... Phoenix, AZ
King, George H. .... Los Angeles, CA
King, George Jack, Jr. .... Washington, DC
King, George S. .... Albany, NY
King, George S., Jr. .... Columbia, SC
King, George Sheram .... Baton Rouge, LA
King, George W. .... Lancaster, PA
King, Gerald A. .... Olathe, KS
Kansas City, MO
King, Gerald L. .... Columbus, OH
King, Gerald L. .... Spring, TX
King & Gilpatric .... Boston, MA
King & Green .... San Francisco, CA
King, Greg .... Ocala, FL
King, Greg A. .... Duluth, MN
King, Gregory C. .... San Antonio, TX
King, Gregory H. .... Irvine, CA
King, Guerra, Davis & Garcia, A
Professional Corporation .... Mission, TX
King, H. Lloyd, Jr. .... Fort Lauderdale, FL
King, H. Patrick, Jr. .... Louisville, KY
King, H. Spencer .... Spartanburg, SC
King & Hardesty .... Austin, TX
King, Hargrave, Scurti & Jack
Steubenville, OH
King, Harold Kenneth, Jr. .... New York, NY
King, Harold L. .... Little Rock, AR
King, Harold T. .... Bridgehampton, NY
King, Harriet Ann .... Waitsfield, VT
King, Harriet M. .... Atlanta, GA
King, Harrison Don .... Clayton, MO
King, Harry A., Jr. .... Denver, CO
King, Heather L. .... Fort Worth, TX
King, Helena Ann
Environmental Protection Agency,
Program Office Attorneys, GV
Gaithersburg, MD
King, Henry A. .... New Orleans, LA
King, Henry B., Law Offices of
Baton Rouge, LA
King, Henry J., Jr. .... Beverly, MA
King, Henry L. .... New York, NY
King, Henry R. .... Princeton, NJ
King, Henry T., Jr. .... Cleveland, OH
King, Herman, Freund, Swartz & Reid
Allentown, PA
King Hershey Coleman Koch & Stone, A
Professional Corporation
Independence, MO
Kansas City, MO
King, H. I. .... Aberdeen, SD
King & Higgs, P.C. .... Abingdon, VA
Big Stone Gap, VA
Charlottesville, VA
Danville, VA
Harrisonburg, VA
Lynchburg, VA
Roanoke, VA
King, Hiram I. .... Aberdeen, SD
King, Homer W. .... Pittsburgh, PA
King, Howard E. .... Los Angeles, CA
King, Howard P. .... Sumter, SC
King, Hugh F. .... Fort Worth, TX
King, Hugh M. .... East Hartford, CT
King, Ilene Stacey .... Columbia, SC
King, Imogene Anderson .... Knoxville, TN
King, Ira Thomas, The Law Office of
Dallas, TX
King, Irving M. .... Chicago, IL
King & Isaacson .... Salt Lake City, UT
King, Ivonne Mena .... Washington, DC
King, J. Anthony .... Clearwater, FL
King, J. Graham .... Laurinburg, NC
King, J. Kevin .... Columbus, IN
King, J. Kevin .... Louisville, KY
King, J. Lenora .... Lakeland, FL
King, J. Michael .... Newark, OH
King, J. Patterson .... Hilton Head Island, SC
King, J. Ralph .... Lexington, KY
King, J. Scott .... Independence, MO
King, J. Scott .... Nashville, TN
King, J. Stephen, Jr. .... New York, NY
King, J. Steven, Law Offices of
Fort Worth, TX
King, J. Thomas .... Birmingham, AL
King, J. Thomas, Jr. .... Birmingham, AL
King, Jack A. .... Scottsdale, AZ
King, Jack F. .... Buena Park, CA
King, Jack F., Jr. .... Nashville, TN
King, Jack H., Sr. .... Atlanta, GA
King, Jack M. .... Tyler, TX
King, Jack M. .... Yakima, WA
King, Jack R. .... Beaumont, TX
King, Jackson T. .... New Haven, CT
King, Jackson T., Jr. .... Norwich, CT
King, Jacqueline McMahon
Kansas City, MO
King, James A. .... Honolulu, HI
King, James A. .... Columbus, OH
King, James A., Jr. .... Columbus, OH
King, James A., Jr. .... Philadelphia, PA
King, James B. .... Anderson, SC
King, James B. .... Spokane, WA
King, James C. .... Jasper, AL
King, James C. .... Haddon Heights, NJ
Philadelphia, PA
King, James C. .... Lima, OH
King, James Coyne .... Boston, MA
King, James D. .... Denver, CO
King, James E. .... San Diego, CA
King, James Edward .... Oklahoma City, OK
King, James F. .... Ukiah, CA
King, James L. .... Stanton, KY
King, James L., Jr. .... Knoxville, TN
King, James Lawrence .... Miami, FL
King, James M. .... Santa Cruz, CA
King, James M. .... Denver, CO
King, James M. .... St. Paul, MN
King, James N. .... Albuquerque, NM
King, James P. .... Chicago, IL
King, James R. .... Carlisle, MA
King, James R. .... Akron, OH
Cleveland, OH
King, James R. .... Columbus, OH
King, James R. .... Nashville, TN
King, James S. .... Albany, NY
King, James S. .... Memphis, TN
King, James T., Jr. .... Watertown, NY

King, James W. ... Birmingham, AL
King, James W. ... Atlanta, GA
King, James W. ... Beaumont, TX
King, Jan. L., Sr. ... Lakeland, FL
King, Jan, (Mr.) ... Jefferson City, MO
King, Jane ... Minneapolis, MN
King, Jane Ellen ... St. Louis, MO
King, Janet L. ... San Antonio, TX
King, Janice Burns ... Marietta, GA
King, Janice Burns, P.C. ... Marietta, GA
King, Janice M. ... Modesto, CA
King, Janna Powers ... Fort Smith, AR
King and Jaques Legal Services, L.L.C. Kansas City, MO
King, Jarrid Y. ... New York, NY
King, Jason Noah ... Chanute, KS
King, Jason S. ... Washington, DC
King, J. B. ... Indianapolis, IN
King, Jean Campbell ... Department of Justice, Executive Office for Immigration Review, GV
King, Jean Ledwith ... Ann Arbor, MI
King, Jean M. ... Portland, OR
King, Jeffrey ... Brea, CA
King, Jeffrey A. ... Phoenix, AZ
King, Jeffrey A. ... Sarasota, FL
King, Jeffrey A. ... Tulsa, OK
King, Jeffrey A., P.A. ... Sarasota, FL
King, Jeffrey B. ... Houston, TX
King, Jeffrey B. ... Houston, TX
King, Jeffrey C. ... Treasury Department, Office of the General Counsel, GV
King, Jeffrey C. ... Dallas, TX
King, Jeffrey E. ... Salina, KS
King, Jeffrey J. ... Seattle, WA
King, Jeffrey M. ... Washington, DC
King, Jeffrey P. ... Dallas, TX
King, Jeffrey R. ... Nashville, TN
King, Jeffrey S. ... Leawood, KS
King, Jeffrey S. ... Boston, MA
King, Jeffrey W. ... Washington, DC
King, Jeffrey W. ... Myrtle Beach, SC
King, Jennifer Durham ... Chicago, IL
King, Jennifer J. ... Tustin, CA
King, Jennifer L. ... Beverly Hills, CA
King, Jennifer L. ... Seattle, WA
King, Jerome N. ... Rye Brook, NY
King, Jerry D. ... San Antonio, TX
King, Jerry F. ... Vancouver, WA
King, Jessica J. Orrick ... Columbia, SC
King, Jimmy R. ... Anderson, SC
King, Joan E. ... Woodland Hills, CA
King, Joanna M. ... Washington, DC
King, Jodie ... New York, NY
King, Jody L. ... New York, NY
King, John A. ... Rockville, MD
King, John A. ... Brockton, MA
King, John A., Jr. ... Washington, DC
King, John Andrew ... Austin, TX
King, John B. ... Baton Rouge, LA
King, John B. ... Haverford, PA
King, John C. ... Phoenix, AZ
King, John C. ... Hartford, CT
King, John C. ... Marietta, GA
King, John C. ... Wichita, KS
King, John D. ... Tubac, AZ
King, John E. ... Snow Hill, MD
King, John E. ... Minneapolis, MN
King, John E. ... Warren, OH
King, John E. ... Seattle, WA
King, John F. ... Baltimore, MD
King, John F. ... New York, NY
King, John F. ... Cleveland, OH
King, John F. ... Harrisburg, PA
King, John G. ... Salem, MA
King, John H. ... Cherry Hill, NJ
King, John H., Jr. ... Portland, ME
King, John J. ... San Francisco, CA
King, John J. ... Libertyville, IL
King, John J., Jr. ... Petaluma, CA
Santa Rosa, CA
King, John J., (P.C.) ... Houston, TX
King, John K. ... Knoxville, TN
King, John L. ... Boise, ID
King, John L. ... Detroit, MI
King, John L. ... Houston, TX
King, John M. ... New Orleans, LA
King, John P. ... West St. Paul, MN
King, John P. ... St. Louis, MO
King, John P., Jr. ... Costa Mesa, CA
King, John P., Jr. ... Philadelphia, PA
King, John R. ... Newport Beach, CA
King, John R. ... Ashland, OR
King, John Robert, Law Office of McAllen, TX
King, John S. ... Weston, CT
King, John S. ... Syracuse, NY
King, John T. ... Richmond, VA
King, John W. ... Washington, DC
King, John W. ... Adel, IA
King, John W. ... Baton Rouge, LA
King, John W. ... Goffstown, NH
King, John W., Jr. ... New Bern, NC
King, John Wells ... Arlington, VA
King, Jon E. ... Houston, TX
King, Jon M. ... Lawrence, KS
King, Jonathan G.L. ... New York, NY
King, Jonathan H. ... Chicago, IL
King, Jonathan H. ... Reno, NV
King, Jonathan R. ... Ormond Beach, FL
King, Jonathan S. ... Central City, KY
King, Jonathan Z. ... New York, NY
King, Jon-Marc ... Jackson, MS
King, Joseph ... Silver Spring, MD
King, Joseph A. ... Boston, MA
King, Joseph Donald ... Cleveland, OH
King, Joseph H., Jr. ... Atlanta, GA
King, Joseph H., Jr. ... Knoxville, TN

King, Joseph R. ... Denver, CO
King, Joseph T. ... Boston, MA
King, Joseph W., Jr. ... Austin, TX
King, Joshua ... Bellevue, WA
King, Joshua M. ... South San Francisco, CA
King, J.P. Sam ... Omaha, NE
King, J. T. ... Dexter, NY
King, Judson ... Ormond Beach, FL
King, Judy C. ... Duluth, GA
King, Julian F. ... Philadelphia, PA
King, Julian M. ... Talladega, AL
King, Julie A. ... Durham, NC
King, Julie Mitrovich ... Birmingham, AL
King, Julie V. ... Costa Mesa, CA
King, Juliet U. ... Austin, TX
King, June Nalley ... Louisville, KY
King, Justice B. ... Topeka, KS
King, K. Kidwell, Jr. ... Greeneville, TN
King, Kamau J. ... Atlanta, GA
King, Karen B. ... Madison, WI
King, Karen J. ... Lafayette, LA
King, Katherine A. ... United States Senate, Committee Legal Personnel, GV
King, Katherine W. ... Baton Rouge, LA
King, Katherine Wheeler Grosse Pointe Farms, MI
King, Kathie D. ... Philadelphia, PA
King, Kathleen A. ... Boston, MA
King, Kathleen J. Singer ... Miami, FL
King, Kathleen S. ... San Francisco, CA
King, Kathryn A. ... Florence, AL
King, Kathryn A. ... Memphis, TN
King, Kathryn S. ... New York, NY
King, Kathy ... St. Paul, MN
King, Kathy A. ... Dallas, TX
King, Kay A. ... Dallas, TX
King, Keith ... Columbus, OH
King, Keith C. ... Merced, CA
King & Kelleher, LLP ... San Francisco, CA
King, Kendrick ... Welch, WV
King, Kenneth C., Jr. ... Roanoke, VA
King, Kenneth E. ... London, KY
King, Kenneth H., Jr. ... Nashville, TN
King, Kenneth J. ... New York, NY
King, Kenneth L. ... Garden City, NY
King, Kenneth W., Jr. ... Elizabethtown, NC
Fayetteville, NC
Jacksonville, NC
New Bern, NC
Shallotte, NC
Wilmington, NC
King, Kenton J. ... Palo Alto, CA
San Francisco, CA
King, Kermit S. ... Columbia, SC
King, Kernan F. ... Boston, MA
King, Kevin D. ... Houston, TX
King, Kevin Joseph ... Albany, NY
King, Kevin L. ... St. Louis, MO
King, Kevin N. ... Hardy, AR
King, Kevin S. ... Atlanta, GA
King, Kevin W. ... Atlanta, GA
King, Kim ... Houston, TX
King, Kimberly J. ... Cincinnati, OH
King, Kimberly L., Mr. ... Tallahassee, FL
King, Kimberly Nilsen ... Los Angeles, CA
King and King ... Birmingham, AL
King & King ... Atlanta, GA
King & King ... Honolulu, HI
King & King ... Pine Knot, KY
King & King ... Pittsburgh, PA
King & King ... Greeneville, TN
King & King ... Waitsfield, VT
King & King, A Professional Corporation Kaysville, UT
King & King, Chartered ... Washington, DC
King, King & Fishleder, P.C., Law Offices of Oakland, CA
King, King and Goldsack North Plainfield, NJ
King, King and King, P.C. ... Gadsden, AL
King and King, L.L.C. ... Jackson, WY
King & King, LLP ... New York, NY
King and King, P.C. ... Silver Spring, MD
King, Kirby ... Round Rock, TX
King, Kirk A. ... Waynesburg, PA
King, Kitrick, Jackson & Troncone Brick, NJ
King, Kristen ... Albany, NY
King, Kristin G. ... Abingdon, VA
King, Kristin Marie ... Dallas, TX
King, Kurt H. ... Liberty, MO
King, Kyle K. ... Greeneville, TN
King, Kyle W. ... Houston, TX
King, L. Gordon, Jr. ... Baton Rouge, LA
King, L. Kristin ... Charlotte, NC
King, L. Lansden ... Paducah, KY
King, La Bruce W. ... Santa Rosa, CA
King & Lafontant ... Greensburg, PA
King, Lancelot A. ... Washington, DC
King, Larry D. ... Houston, TX
King, Larry, Jr., (P.C.) ... Jonesboro, GA
King, Larry K. ... Sedan, KS
King, Larry P. ... Quitman, TX
King, Larry W. ... Hanalei, HI
King, Laura Davis ... Tucker, GA
King, Laura Davis, Law Firm of Tucker, GA
King, Laurel L. ... Lewisburg, TN
King, Laurence D. ... New York, NY
King Law Firm ... Oklahoma City, OK
King Law Firm ... Pittsburgh, PA
King Law Firm, P.A. ... Little Rock, AR
King, Lawrence A., (P.C.) ... Troy, MI
King, Lawrence C. ... Palo Alto, CA
King, Lawrence D. ... Miami, FL
King, Lawrence E. ... Ann Arbor, MI
King, Lawrence E. ... Bismarck, ND
King, Lawrence F. ... Westminster, CO

King, Lawrence J. ... San Francisco, CA
King, Lawrence P. ... New York, NY
King, Lawrence R. ... St. Paul, MN
King, Lawrence T. ... Birmingham, AL
King, Leah M. ... Riverside, CA
King, Leavy, Rabin & Lancaster, Professional Association ... Miami, FL
King, LeBlanc, Bland & Dardenne, L.L.P. Baton Rouge, LA
King, LeBlanc & Bland, L.L.P. New Orleans, LA
King, Leif B. ... Washington, DC
King, Leigh Ann ... Birmingham, AL
King, Leigh Ann ... San Antonio, TX
King, Leigh Reynolds ... Charlotte, NC
King, Leon A., II ... Philadelphia, PA
King, Leonard H. ... Valley Stream, NY
King, Leslie A. ... Silver Spring, MD
King, Leslie C., III ... Santa Fe, NM
King, Leslie D. ... Jackson, MS
King, Leslie E. ... Los Angeles, CA
King, Leslie Renee' ... Independence, MO
King, Levon G. ... Allen Park, MI
King, Linda ... Wichita, KS
King, Linda A. ... San Diego, CA
King, Linda A. ... Oklahoma City, OK
King, Linda A. ... Pittsburgh, PA
King, Linda C. ... Philadelphia, PA
King, Linda D. ... Houston, TX
King, Linda G. ... San Antonio, TX
King, Linda J. ... Lee's Summit, MO
King, Lindsay Brooke ... Richmond, VA
King, Lisa M. ... Philadelphia, PA
King, Lisa R. ... Orange, CA
King, Loretta ... Department of Justice, Civil Rights Division, GV
King, Lorri B. ... Cadillac, MI
King, Lucia Ann ... Chicago, IL
King, M. Christian ... Birmingham, AL
King, M. Nan ... Atlanta, GA
King, M. Todd ... Atlanta, GA
King, Malcolm Frazier, Jr. ... Houston, TX
King, Malvern F., Jr. ... Durham, NC
King, Margaret Gram ... New York, NY
King, Margaret J. ... Sun Valley, ID
Santa Fe, NM
King, Margaret M. ... New York, NY
King, Margaret Mary ... Lower Gwynedd, PA
King, Margaret Willis ... Baltimore, MD
King, Marian A. ... Sacramento, CA
King, Marian Beechen ... Santa Monica, CA
King, Marie L. ... Sudbury, MA
King, Marilou M. ... Washington, DC
King, Mark E. ... Birmingham, AL
King, Mark E. ... Northfield, IL
King, Mark F. ... Brookfield, WI
King, Mark F., S.C. ... Brookfield, WI
King, Mark J., IV ... Las Vegas, NV
King, Mark Robert ... Miami, FL
King, Marsha ... Atlanta, GA
King, Marsha K. ... Burbank, CA
King, Marshall ... Miami, FL
King, Marshall R. ... New York, NY
King, Martha ... Anchorage, AK
King, Martin E. ... Mamaroneck, NY
King, Martin J. ... North Miami Beach, FL
King, Martin J. ... Mount Kisco, NY
King, Martin J. ... New Hope, PA
Newtown, PA
King, Martin S. ... Missoula, MT
King, Marvin N. (Buddy) ... Houston, TX
King, Mary E. ... Sarasota, FL
King, Mary I. ... Minneapolis, MN
King, Mary Letitia ... Juneau, AK
King, Maryann ... Irvington, NY
King, Matthew B. ... New York, NY
King, Matthew F. ... Boston, MA
King, Matthew J. ... Springfield, MA
King, Matthew R. ... Fayetteville, AR
King, Matthew R. ... Minneapolis, MN
King, Maurice L. ... Oak Brook, IL
King, Maurice L., Jr. ... Albany, GA
King, Melanie E. ... Riverwoods, IL
King, Melanie R. ... St. Louis, MO
King, Melbourne P. ... Winter Park, FL
King, Melbourne P., P.A. ... Winter Park, FL
King, Melissa M. ... Warren, MI
King, Melvin ... Los Angeles, CA
King, Michael ... Emlenton, PA
King, Michael ... Hampton, VA
King, Michael A. ... Jackson, MS
King, Michael A. ... New York, NY
King, Michael B. ... Palo Alto, CA
King, Michael B. ... Seattle, WA
King, Michael C. ... Washington, DC
King, Michael C. ... Rolla, MO
King, Michael F. ... Brooklyn, NY
King, Michael F. ... Raleigh, NC
King, Michael G. ... Los Angeles, CA
King, Michael H. ... Chicago, IL
King, Michael H. ... Boston, MA
King, Michael H. ... New York, NY
King, Michael J. ... Washington, DC
King, Michael J. ... Atlanta, GA
King, Michael J. ... Norcross, GA
King, Michael J. ... Omaha, NE
King, Michael J. ... Tulsa, OK
King, Michael J. ... Portland, OR
King, Michael J. ... Knoxville, TN
King, Michael L. ... Salisbury, NC
King, Michael L. ... Cleveland, OH
King, Michael M. ... Miami, FL
King, Michael P. ... Los Angeles, CA
King, Michael P. ... Westmont, NJ
King, Michael P. ... New York, NY
King, Michael R. ... Phoenix, AZ
King, Michael W. ... Atlanta, GA
King, Michael W. ... York, PA

King, Michael W., Law Offices of Long Beach, CA
King, Michele L. ... Dayton, OH
King, Milton P. ... Philadelphia, PA
King, Mitchell C., Jr. Hilton Head Island, SC
King, Mitchell, Jr. ... Greenville, SC
King, Mitchell S. ... Boston, MA
King, Monica Maby ... Houston, TX
King, Monta Michelle ... Tampa, FL
King, Morgan D. ... Dublin, CA
King & Nalitz ... Waynesburg, PA
King, Nancy Barrett ... Columbus, OH
King, Nancy J. ... San Diego, CA
King, Nancy J. ... Portland, OR
King, Nancy M. Anderson ... Santa Fe, NM
King, Nat B. ... Houston, TX
King, Natalie M. ... Verona, WI
King & Navins, P.C. ... Norfolk, MA
Wellesley, MA
King, Neal ... Mission, TX
King, Neil J. ... Washington, DC
King, Nicholas N. ... Louisville, KY
King, Nick C. ... West Mifflin, PA
King, Nolan F. ... Covina, CA
King, Nora ... Fairbanks, AK
King, Norah McCann ... Columbus, OH
King & Nordlinger, L.L.P.
Washington, DC
Gaithersburg, MD
Arlington, VA
King, Norman B. ... Silver Spring, MD
King, Norman W. ... Treasury Department, Office of Regulations and Rulings, GV
King, Nye ... Huntington, WV
King, O'Gwen L. ... Pensacola, FL
King, O'Gwen L., & Associates, P.A. Pensacola, FL
King, O'Neil S. ... Washington, DC
King, Oscar R., Jr. ... New York, NY
King, Otis H. ... Houston, TX
King, P. Terrence ... Lancaster, PA
King, Pagano & Harrison
Washington, DC
New York, NY
King, Pamela P. ... San Bernardino, CA
King, Patrice Adrea ... Roseland, NJ
King, Patricia A. ... New Haven, CT
King, Patricia A. ... Washington, DC
King, Patricia D. ... Chicago, IL
King, Patricia E. ... Charlotte, NC
King, Patricia Hicks ... Murfreesboro, TN
King, Patricia Kahian ... Seattle, WA
King, Patricia Mallick ... Glen Ellyn, IL
King, Patricia R. ... Baltimore, MD
King, Patricia Smith ... Madison, WI
King, Patricia White ... Lima, OH
King, Patrick A. ... Southfield, MI
King, Patrick E. ... New York, NY
King, Patrick G. ... Chicago, IL
King, Patrick J. ... Boston, MA
King, Patrick O. ... Carson City, NV
King, Patrick O., Ltd. ... Carson City, NV
King, Patrick T. ... Aptos, CA
King, Paul A. ... Katonah, NY
King, Paul D. ... Asheville, NC
King, Paul F. ... West Palm Beach, FL
King, Paul H. ... Seattle, WA
King, Paul M. ... Pittsburgh, PA
King, Paul M. ... Salt Lake City, UT
King, Paul N. ... Washington, DC
Atlanta, GA
King, Paul W. ... Springfield, MO
King, P. C., Jr. ... Fort Gaines, GA
King & Pennington, L.L.P. ... Houston, TX
King, Peter ... Tampa, FL
King, Peter A. ... New York, NY
King, Peter B. ... Fontana, WI
King, Peter C. ... Columbus, IN
King, Peter D. ... Bridgewater, MA
King, Peter J.
Federal Maritime Commission, Bureau of Enforcement, GV
King, Peter J. ... Pittsburgh, PA
King, Peter J., Jr. ... Colorado Springs, CO
King, Peter M. ... Chicago, IL
King, Peter N. ... Los Angeles, CA
King, Peter T. ... Massapequa Park, NY
King • Peterson • Dymond LLP
Denver, CO
Englewood, CO
King, Philip R. ... Chicago, IL
King, Philip S. ... McHenry, IL
King, Philip T., Jr. ... Orlando, FL
King, Phillip E., Jr. ... Covington, KY
King, Phillip E., Sr. ... Covington, KY
King, Phillip (Phil) S. ... Weatherford, TX
King & Ponder, A Prof. Assn., Law Offices of Hardy, AR
King, Purtich, Holmes, Paterno & Berliner, LLP ... Los Angeles, CA
King, Quinton S. ... Atlanta, GA
King, R. Reed ... Cleveland, OH
King, R. Richardson ... Metairie, LA
King, R. Scott ... Livingston, NJ
King, R. Todd ... Wichita, KS
King, Rachel C. ... Washington, DC
King, Rachel S. ... Department of State, Office of the Legal Adviser, GV
King, Ralph M., Jr. ... Lawrence, KS
King, Ralph Preston, II
Ocean Springs, MS
King, Ray J. ... Gahanna, OH
King, Ray W. ... Norfolk, VA
King, Raymond ... Newport Beach, CA
King, Raymond E. ... Boston, MA
King, Raymond L. ... West Branch, MI
King, Raymond V. ... Brick, NJ

King, Rebecca A. ... **Lawrence, KS**
King, Rebecca A. ... Columbus, OH
King, Rebecca J. ... **New Orleans, LA**
King, Rebecca S. ... Campbell, CA
King, Renita D. ... Katy, TX
King, Rhett E. ... **New Orleans, LA**
King, Rhonda C. ... Richmond, VA
King, Richard A. ... **Kansas City, MO**
King, Richard B., Jr. ... Shreveport, LA
King, Richard C. ... Oak Brook, IL
King, Richard C. ... El Dorado, KS
King, Richard C. ... **Monmouth Beach, NJ**
New York, NY
King, Richard C. ... Albany, NY
King, Richard D. ... San Leandro, CA
King, Richard E. ... **New Orleans, LA**
King, Richard E. ... **Cookeville, TN**
King, Richard E., Jr. ... Irvine, CA
King, Richard E., Jr., Inc. ... Irvine, CA
King, Richard G. ... **Washington, DC**
King, Richard G. D. ... San Leandro, CA
King, Richard J. ... **New York, NY**
King, Richard J., Jr. ... Lancaster, PA
King, Richard Johnston ... **Waitsfield, VT**
King, Richard L. ... Grand Forks, ND
King, Richard L. ... Portland, OR
King, Richard L., P.C. ... **Salt Lake City, UT**
King, Richard Lee ... Dallas, TX
King, Richard M. ... Santa Ana, CA
King, Richard M. ... Cleveland, OH
King, Richard W. ... Madison, WI
King, Ricky H. ... Oklahoma City, OK
King, Rob ... Austin, TX
King, Roberson L. ... Houston, TX
King, Robert A. ... **Washington, DC**
King, Robert A. ... **Pittsburgh, PA**
King, Robert A. ... **York, PA**
King, Robert A. ... Richmond, VA
King, Robert B. ... Charleston, WV
King, Robert B., Jr. ... Anderson, SC
King, Robert C. ... Monroeville, AL
King, Robert C. ... **San Francisco, CA**
King, Robert C. ... Columbus, OH
King, Robert D. ... Tolland, CT
King, Robert D., Jr. ... **Indianapolis, IN**
King, Robert E. ... Bakersfield, CA
King, Robert E. ... **Costa Mesa, CA**
King, Robert E., Jr. ... **New York, NY**
King, Robert G. ... Freeland, MD
King, Robert H., Jr. ... **Chicago, IL**
King, Robert J. ... **Minneapolis, MN**
King, Robert J. ... **Houston, TX**
King, Robert J., III ... **Greensboro, NC**
King, Robert J., Jr. ... Boston, MA
King, Robert J., Jr. ... **Minneapolis, MN**
King, Robert K. ... West Columbia, SC
King, Robert L. ... **Fort Lauderdale, FL**
King, Robert L. ... **East St. Louis, IL**
King, Robert L. ... **New York, NY**
King, Robert L.
Charlotte Amalie, St. Thomas, VI
King, Robert N. ... Milpitas, CA
King, Robert N. ... Milpitas, CA
King, Robert Oliver ... **Greenville, SC**
King, Robert P. ... Steubenville, OH
King, Robert P. ... **Toledo, OH**
King, Robert R., Jr. ... Red Wing, MN
King, Robert T. ... **Florence, SC**
King, Robert W. ... Greenbelt, MD
King, Robert W. ... **Jackson, MS**
King, Robert W. ... Greensburg, PA
King, Robert W., Jr. ... **Charlotte, NC**
King, Robin J. ... Fort Lauderdale, FL
King, Robin M. ... **Knoxville, TN**
King, Robin Vanessa ... Kalamazoo, MI
King, Robt. H. ... Gadsden, AL
King, Robyn E. ... **Walnut Creek, CA**
King, Rockforde D. ... **Knoxville, TN**
King, Ronald ... Stamford, CT
King, Ronald A. ... Lansing, MI
King, Ronald B. ... San Antonio, TX
King, Ronald L. ... Grundy, VA
King, Ronnie P. ... Roxboro, NC
King, Ronnie P., P.A. ... Roxboro, NC
King, Rory ... **Aberdeen, SD**
King, Roy D. ... San Leandro, CA
King, Roy F. ... **Birmingham, AL**
King, Roy W. ... Rochester, NY
King, Roy W., Esq., P.C. ... Rochester, NY
King, Royal W., Jr. ... San Antonio, TX
King, Rufus ... Washington, DC
King, Rufus C. ... **Boston, MA**
King, Rufus, III ... Washington, DC
King, Rufus M. ... Montgomery, AL
King, Russell ... Stephenville, TX
King, Russell D. ... **Marietta, GA**
King, Russell L. ... **Miami, FL**
King, Russell S. ... **Seattle, WA**
King, Russell T., Jr. ... Chattanooga, TN
King, Russell Todd ... **Wichita, KS**
King, Ryan Sally ... Van Nuys, CA
King, Sally Ackerman ... **Philadelphia, PA**
King, Sally Doubet ... **Chicago, IL**
King, Sally M. ... **Midland, MI**
King, Sally S. ... Granby, CT
King, Samuel G. ... Little Compton, RI
King, Samuel P. ... **Orlando, FL**
King, Samuel P. ... Honolulu, HI
King, Samuel P., Jr. ... Honolulu, HI
King, Sandra M. ... **Asheville, NC**
King, Sandra R. ... **Los Angeles, CA**
King, Sarah B. ... Kannapolis, NC
King, Sarah C. ... Owings Mills, MD
King and Schickli ... **Lexington, KY**
King & Schoborg ... Covington, KY
King, Scott A. ... **Dayton, OH**
King, Scott N. ... Newton, MA
King, Scott R. ... **Atlanta, GA**
King, Scott W. ... Salt Lake City, UT
King, Scottow A." Scott " ... **Los Angeles, CA**
King, Sean P. ... Miami, FL
King, Sharon Davis ... **Atlanta, GA**
King, Sharon L. ... **Chicago, IL**
King, Sheila M. ... Chicago, IL
King, Sheldon A. ... **Houston, TX**
King, Shelia High ... **Boston, MA**
Providence, RI
King, Shepard ... **Miami, FL**
King, Sheryl ... Cleveland, OH
King, Sheryl S. ... **San Diego, CA**
King, Shila A. ... Garland, TX
King, Sidney A. ... Beaumont, TX
King, Smith and Boresi ... Cedar Rapids, IA
King, Snell, Mildwurm & Fox, A Professional Corporation ... **Fremont, CA**
Kansas City, MO
King, Sol C. ... New York, NY
King, Sonya E. ... Cincinnati, OH
King & Spalding ... **Washington, DC**
Atlanta, GA
New York, NY
Houston, TX
King & Spencer ... **Jackson, MS**
King, Stacey Lynn ... **Detroit, MI**
King, Stacy E. ... **Dayton, OH**
King, Stanley R. ... Tacoma, WA
King, Stanton D. ... Troy, NY
King, Stephen C. ... Brooklyn, NY
King, Stephen H. ... Kansas City, MO
King, Stephen H. ... **McLean, VA**
King, Stephen J. ... **New York, NY**
King, Stephen Jennings ... Bel Air, MD
King, Stephen L. ... Los Angeles, CA
King, Stephen M. ... Naperville, IL
King, Stephen M. ... **Cincinnati, OH**
King, Stephen R. ... **Cadillac, MI**
King, Stephen R. ... Cincinnati, OH
King, Stephen Scott ... **Santa Monica, CA**
King, Stephen Scott, A Professional Corporation ... **Los Angeles, CA**
Santa Monica, CA
King, Stephen W. ... **Farmington Hills, MI**
King, Stephen W. ... Troy, OH
King, Steve M. ... Fort Worth, TX
King, Steven Austin ... **Nashville, TN**
King, Steven B. ... **Cherry Hill, NJ**
Philadelphia, PA
King, Steven E. ... Michigan City, IN
King, Stuart H. ... **Springfield, MO**
King, Stuart W. ... Abilene, TX
King, Susan A. ... Philadelphia, PA
King, Susan B. ... San Francisco, CA
King, Susan B. ... Madison, WI
King, Susan C. ... Kankakee, IL
King, Susan J. ... **Washington, DC**
King, Susan Miller ... **Chatham, NJ**
King, Susan M. R. ... El Paso, TX
King, Susan Primus ... La Crescent, MN
King, Suzanne L. ... **Boston, MA**
King, Suzanne W. ... Hampton, NH
King, T. Scott ... Phoenix, AZ
King, Tamela L. ... Burbank, CA
King, Tammy S. ... **St. Louis, MO**
King, Tancred I. ... Worcester, MA
King, Taylor A. ... Arkadelphia, AR
King, Taylor & Ryan, P.C. ... **Tulsa, OK**
King, Taylor & Stovall, P.C. ... Tucker, GA
King, Terence M. ... Wall Township, NJ
King, Terrence J. ... Department of Justice, Drug Enforcement Administration, GV
King, Terrence M. ... **Los Angeles, CA**
King, Terri S. ... Hamilton, OH
King, Terry J. ... Anchorage, AK
King, Terry L. ... Atlanta, GA
King, Thomas A. ... Gadsden, AL
King, Thomas B. ... Chicago, IL
King, Thomas C. ... Long Beach, CA
King, Thomas C., A Law Corp., Law Offices of ... Long Beach, CA
King, Thomas E. ... Kansas City, MO
King, Thomas G. ... Chicago, IL
King, Thomas G. ... **Kalamazoo, MI**
King, Thomas J. ... Brooklyn, NY
King, Thomas J. ... Mineola, NY
King, Thomas J. ... Oshkosh, WI
King, Thomas L. ... **Houston, TX**
King, Thomas M. ... Salisbury, NC
King, Thomas R. ... **Minneapolis, MN**
King, Thomas R. ... **Salt Lake City, UT**
King, Thomas R., Jr. ... Roanoke, VA
King, Thomas W. ... Rocky Mount, NC
King, Thomas W., III ... **Butler, PA**
Cranberry Township, PA
Saxonburg, PA
King, Thos. R. ... Toledo, OH
King, Timothy A. ... **Columbus, OH**
King, Timothy J. ... Wichita, KS
King, Timothy J. ... **Bedford, MA**
King, Timothy P. ... Chicago, IL
King, Tish G. ... Winston-Salem, NC
King, Tom A. ... **Cleveland, OH**
King, Tom L. ... **Oklahoma City, OK**
King, Tom R. ... Lubbock, TX
King, Tracey D. ... **Baltimore, MD**
King, Trent Thomas ... Denver, CO
King, Tunney Lee ... Columbus, OH
King, Turnbow & Brisby ... **Franklin, TN**
Nashville, TN
King, Tyrone A. ... Maitland, FL
King, V. James, Jr. ... Pocahontas, AR
King, Vernon J. ... Pocahontas, AR
King & Vernon, P.A. ... **Charleston, SC**
Columbia, SC
King, Victor E. D. ... North Plainfield, NJ
King, Victor I. ... Los Angeles, CA
King, Victor R. ... North Plainfield, NJ
King, Victoria N. ... Atlanta, GA
King, Vincent F. ... Southampton, NY
King, Vincent J. ... **Charleston, WV**
King, Vincent W. ... **Los Angeles, CA**
Minneapolis, MN
King, Vincent W. ... Golden, CO
King, Vincent W., P.A. ... **Minneapolis, MN**
King, Vivian Radine ... Houston, TX
King, Vivian Sanks ... Newark, NJ
King, W. Barrington, Jr. ... Marietta, GA
King, W. Clay ... Fort Lauderdale, FL
King, W. Courtney, Jr. ... Roanoke, VA
King, W. David ... Paducah, KY
King, W. Gary ... Cincinnati, OH
King, W. Gregory ... **Louisville, KY**
King, W. Lee, Jr. ... Stuart, FL
King, W. Robert ... **Overland Park, KS**
Kansas City, MO
King, W. Thomas ... **Atlanta, GA**
King, W. Wayt, Jr. ... **Atlanta, GA**
King, W. Winburne, III ... **Greensboro, NC**
King, Walker, Lambe & Powell, P.L.L.C.
Durham, NC
King, Walter E." Bert ", III ... **Macon, GA**
King, Walter E." Bert ", III ... **Gray, GA**
King, Walter H. ... Santa Monica, CA
King & Warren ... **Jasper, AL**
King, Warren G. ... Houston, TX
King, Wayne D. ... Simi Valley, CA
King, Wayne T. ... Valencia, CA
King, Wilbur Branch ... Niceville, FL
King, William A. ... Ocala, FL
King, William A. ... Cambridge, MA
King, William A., Jr. ... **Quincy, MA**
King, William B. ... Denver, CO
King, William B. ... **West Palm Beach, FL**
King, William B. ... Shreveport, LA
King, William B., (P.C.) ... **Boston, MA**
King, William Barrington, Jr. ... Atlanta, GA
King, William D. ... **Jacksonville, FL**
King, William D. ... Austin, TX
King, William E. ... Rohnert Park, CA
King, William E. ... Houston, TX
King, William E. ... Norfolk, VA
King, William H. ... **San Francisco, CA**
King, William H. ... Newport News, VA
King, William H., III ... **Birmingham, AL**
King, William H., Jr. ... **Richmond, VA**
King, William J. ... Glendale, CA
King, William J. ... **Santa Ana, CA**
King, William J., Jr. ... Dauphin, PA
King, William K. ... Washington, DC
King, William K., Jr. ... Seattle, WA
King, William M. ... Austin, TX
King, William M." Skip " ... **Austin, TX**
King, William McM. ... Covington, LA
New Orleans, LA
King, William Ng ... New York, NY
King, William O. ... **Durham, NC**
King, William R. ... Luverne, AL
King, William R. ... Sarasota, FL
King, William R. ... West Palm Beach, FL
Atlanta, GA
King, William R. ... **Des Moines, IA**
King, William R. ... **Rockville, MD**
King, William T. ... **Los Angeles, CA**
King, William T. ... King Of Prussia, PA
King, Williams & Hanagami, A Law Corporation ... **Los Angeles, CA**
King, Winston E. ... Louisville, KY
King, Wm. DeJarnette ... **Carrollton, AL**
King, Woods, III ... **Cleveland, OH**
King, Woods, Jr. ... Mentor, OH
Kingan, Albert Richard ... Springfield, MA
Kingcade & Garcia, Professional Association
Miami, FL
Kingcade, Thomas E.
West Palm Beach, FL
Kingcade, Thomas E., Professional Association ... **Palm Beach, FL**
West Palm Beach, FL
Kingcade, Timothy S. ... **Miami, FL**
Kingdon, Frederick T. ... Mullens, WV
Kingdon, Grover C., Jr. ... Laguna Hills, CA
Kingdon, Kenneth Allen ... **Long Beach, CA**
Kingdon, McKenna ... **Flemington, NJ**
South Plainfield, NJ
Kingdon, V. Scott ... **Fort Wayne, IN**
Kingen, Cheryl DeMers ... Spokane, WA
Kingen, Karen Kaye ... Window Rock, AZ
Kingen, Thomas F. ... **Spokane, WA**
Kingery, Arthur R. ... **Peoria, IL**
Kingery, Clark C. ... Wilmington, DE
Kingery, Clark C., P.A. ... Wilmington, DE
Kingery Durree Wakeman & Ryan, Assoc.
Peoria, IL
Kingery, Edward E. ... Boulder, CO
Kingery, Gell R. ... Waco, TX
Kingery, Gregory D. ... Cedar Rapids, IA
Kingery, Hugh E. ... Franktown, CO
Kingery, Nathan A. ... Canal Winchester, OH
Kingery, William D., Jr. ... **Washington, DC**
Kingett, Donald L. ... Marlton, NJ
Kingfield, John F. ... Belvidere, NJ
Kingfisher, Cheryl Rios ... Tahlequah, OK
King-Gilreath, Sally A. ... Charleston, SC
Kingham, T. Barry ... **New York, NY**
Kinghorn, Clifford R., Jr. ... Nashua, NH
Kinghorn, Curtis D. ... Minneapolis, MN
Kinghorn, Darwin ... Redding, CA
Kinghorn, Gerald H. ... **Salt Lake City, UT**
King-Lautanen, Michelle R.
Los Angeles, CA
Kingloff, Mildred L. ... Decatur, GA
Kingloff & Travis ... Decatur, GA
Kingma, Antje ... Atlanta, GA
Kingma, James D. ... **Milwaukee, WI**
Kingma, Johannes S. ... **Atlanta, GA**
Kingma, Kenneth W. ... **Troy, MI**
Kingma, Todd W. ... **Bridgewater, NJ**
Kingman, Allen G. ... Wasilla, AK
Kingman, Dale L. ... **Seattle, WA**
Kingman, David M. ... Arlington Heights, IL
Kingman, Michael L. ... Hackensack, NJ
Kingman, P. Grace ... Tacoma, WA
Kingman, Philip D. ... Smithfield, RI
Kingman, William B. ... **San Antonio, TX**
Kingman, William B., P.C., Law Offices of
San Antonio, TX
King-O'Brien, Pamela J. ... Rockford, IL
Kingoff, Stuart Neal ... Forest Hills, NY
Kingrea, Richard O. ... **Mobile, AL**
Kingree, Ben, III ... **Atlanta, GA**
Kingree, Kathryn J. ... **Morristown, NJ**
Kingren, J. Fred ... **Birmingham, AL**
Kingren, Katherine Ann ... Louisville, KY
Kingrey, John P. ... St. Paul, MN
King-Robinson, Arlene ... New York, NY
King-Robinson, Arlene ... **New York, NY**
Kingsafer, John R. ... Natchez, MS
Kingsbery, Douglas E. ... **Raleigh, NC**
Kingsbery & Kingsbery, L.L.C.
Boulder, CO
Kingsbery, Stuart P. ... Boulder, CO
Kingsbery, Walter W. ... Boulder, CO
Kingsbury, Dallas G. ... Houston, TX
Kingsbury, David Reid ... Gold River, CA
Kingsbury, Debra Lyn ... Auburn Hills, MI
Kingsbury, Dorothea J. ... Lyndhurst, OH
Kingsbury, John H. ... Greenville, SC
Kingsbury, Kathleen A. ... **Greensboro, NC**
Kingsbury, Kenneth R. ... Oakland, CA
Kingsbury, Robert E. ... Medford, NJ
Kingsbury, Suzanne Nelson
South Lake Tahoe, CA
Kingsbury, Thomas R. ... North Canton, OH
Kingsbury, William L. ... Philadelphia, PA
Kingscott, Craig A. ... Santa Maria, CA
Kingsdale, David L. ... Santa Monica, CA
Kingsdorf, Bruce S. ... **New Orleans, LA**
Kingseed, C. Mark ... **Dayton, OH**
Kingsepp, Jon H. ... **Bloomfield Hills, MI**
Kingsford, Barbara A. ... **Blue Bell, PA**
Kingsford, Edward ... Soda Springs, ID
Kingsford, Leonard O. ... Soda Springs, ID
Kingsford, Robert A. ... **Orlando, FL**
Kingsford, Ronald A. ... Greeley, CO
Kingshaven, Troy A. ... **San Diego, CA**
Kingshill, Kenneth P. ... Santa Monica, CA
Kingsland, Lya R. ... **Orange, CA**
Kingsland, Robert D., Jr. ... Kansas City, MO
Kingsley, Anna L. ... **Fort Worth, TX**
Kingsley, Charles C. ... **New Haven, CT**
Kingsley, Darius R. ... **Washington, DC**
Kingsley, David J. ... Plantation, FL
Kingsley, Elizabeth J. ... Washington, DC
Kingsley, Frank H., Jr. ... Whitehall, NY
Kingsley, Gail Peters ... **South Natick, MA**
Kingsley, Gail Peters, P.C., Law Office of
South Natick, MA
Wellesley, MA
Kingsley, George R. ... Encino, CA
Kingsley, Harold M. ... Hicksville, NY
Kingsley, Howard W. ... **New York, NY**
Kingsley, James C. ... Battle Creek, MI
Kingsley, James R. ... Circleville, OH
Kingsley, Jared P. ... **Clark, NJ**
Kingsley, Joan S. ... Hicksville, NY
Kingsley, John P. ... **Catskill, NY**
Kingsley, John P., P.C. ... **Catskill, NY**
Kingsley, Karen J. ... St. Louis Park, MN
Kingsley, Kay T. ... Salinas, CA
Kingsley & Kingsley ... Plantation, FL
Kingsley, L. Jean ... **Santa Rosa, CA**
Kingsley, Linda H. ... Lakeport, CA
Kingsley, Linda P. ... Fayetteville, NY
Kingsley, Louise R. ... Plantation, FL
Kingsley, Mark S. ... **New York, NY**
Kingsley, Mary Frances ... Paxton, MA
Kingsley, Michael J. ... Huntington Woods, MI
Kingsley, Mitchell L. ... Bluffton, OH
Kingsley, Pamela L. ... **Scottsdale, AZ**
Kingsley, Patrick R. ... **Pittsburgh, PA**
Kingsley, Paul R. ... **New York, NY**
Kingsley, Renée T. ... Irving, TX
Kingsley, Richard E. ... Lebanon, OR
Kingsley, Robert I. ... Richardson, TX
Kingsley, Ronald E. ... **Skokie, IL**
Kingsley, Sanford ... **San Francisco, CA**
Kingsley, Theodore R. ... **Atlanta, GA**
Kingsley, Thomas R. ... South Bethany, DE
Kingsley, W. Charles ... Lansing, MI
Kingsley, Warren E. ... **Atlanta, GA**
Kingsley, William S., II
Department of Defense, GV
Kingsmill, Arthur G. ... **Gretna, LA**
Kingsmill, Marguerite K.
New Orleans, LA
Houston, TX
Kingsmill, Thomas H., III
New Orleans, LA
Kingsmill, Thomas H., Jr. ... New Orleans, LA
Kingsmore, Fred L., Jr. ... **Columbia, SC**
Kingsolver, Jacqueline C. ... **Owensboro, KY**
Kingsolver, Paul D. ... **Tulsa, OK**
Kingstad, David G. ... Franklin, WI
Kingstad, Jon Eric ... Burlington, WI
Kingstad Law Offices, S.C. ... Franklin, WI
Kingstad, Timothy L. ... Bismarck, ND
Kingston, Abbe Allen, & Associates
Los Angeles, CA
Kingston, Abbe Allen, & Associates
Santa Barbara, CA
Kingston, Brian L. ... Austin, TX
Kingston, Carl E. ... Salt Lake City, UT
Kingston, Charles L. ... Salt Lake City, UT

Kingston, Hilary Christen
Los Angeles, CA
Kingston & Hodnett ..... Boston, MA
Kingston, Jeffrey S. ..... San Francisco, CA
Kingston, John B. ..... Chula Vista, CA
Kingston, John D. ..... Madison, WI
Kingston, John E. ..... Mineola, NY
Kingston, Kristi Lynn ..... Kansas City, MO
Kingston, Linda Drew ..... Mount Dora, FL
Kingston, Martinez & Hogan
Santa Barbara, CA
Kingston, Mindy G. ..... Boston, MA
Kingston, Paul J. ..... Boston, MA
Kingston, Philip T. ..... Dallas, TX
Kingston, Shirley ..... Cheyenne, WY
Kingston & Smart ..... Mukwonago, WI
Kingston, Timothy C. ..... Cheyenne, WY
Kingston, William H. ..... Mukwonago, WI
Kington, J. Anthony ..... Columbus, OH
Kingue-Bonnaig, Denise ..... New York, NY
Kinhan, J. Patrick ..... Topsfield, MA
Kini, Satish M. ..... Washington, DC
Kinigstein, Noah A. ..... New York, NY
Kinikin, Sherry A. ..... Potomac, MD
Kininmonth, Daniel M. ..... Louisville, KY
Kinion, Steve W. ..... Springfield, IL
Kinirons, John J. ..... Hicksville, NY
Kiniry, Patrick T. ..... Johnstown, PA
Kiniry, William F., Jr. ..... Philadelphia, PA
Kinkade, Brent S. ..... Bend, OR
Kinkade, Joseph C. ..... Santa Rosa, CA
Kinkade, Kerry J., (Mr.) ..... Kansas City, MO
Kinkade, Kristopher A. ..... Seattle, WA
Kinkade, Lori Kay ..... St. Louis, MO
Kinkade, Wayne A. ..... Salem, OR
Kinkaid, Amy I. ..... Cleveland, OH
Kinkaid, Philip M. ..... Houston, TX
Kinkaid, Susan E. ..... Houston, TX
Kinkead, Beverly S. ..... Vero Beach, FL
Kinkead, Billy Frank ..... Amarillo, TX
Kinkead, Cassandra Lynn ..... Seattle, WA
Kinkead, Duncan ..... Bloomington, IN
Kinkead, Robert C. ..... New York, NY
Kinkead, Shelby C., Jr. ..... Lexington, KY
Kinkead, Sidney C., Jr. ..... Lexington, KY
Kinkead & Stilz ..... Lexington, KY
Kinkead, William H., III ..... Blue Bell, PA
Kinkead, William W. ..... Tazewell, VA
Kinkeade, Ed ..... Dallas, TX
Kinkel, David A. ..... Washington, DC
Kinkel, Steven G. ..... Lexington, KY
Kinkela, John F. ..... Columbus, OH
Kinkelaar, Michael J. ..... San Diego, CA
Kinker, Robt. H. ..... Frankfort, KY
Kinkle, George P., Jr. ..... Los Angeles, CA
Kinkle, J. Robert ..... Princeton, IN
Kinkle, Robert L. ..... Long Beach, CA
Kinkle, Rodiger and Spriggs, Professional Corporation ..... Indio, CA
Los Angeles, CA
Riverside, CA
San Bernardino, CA
San Diego, CA
Santa Ana, CA
Kinkler, Fredric J., Jr. ..... Philadelphia, PA
Kinkley & Cox ..... Honolulu, HI
Kinkley, D. Michael, P.S. ..... Spokane, WA
Kinkley, Gregg J. ..... Honolulu, HI
Kinkley, Michael D. ..... Spokane, WA
Kinkopf, David W. ..... Baltimore, MD
Kinkopf, Michael P. ..... Mount Laurel, NJ
Philadelphia, PA
Kinkopf-Zajac, Ingrid A. ..... Cleveland, OH
Kinlaw, Alex, Jr. ..... Greenville, SC
Kinlaw, J. Hal, Jr. ..... Lumberton, NC
Kinlaw, Sheryl Lynn ..... Austin, TX
Kinlein, Richard J. ..... Ellicott City, MD
Kinler, Douglas Robert ..... New Orleans, LA
Kinley, David D. ..... Pleasanton, CA
Kinley, John R. ..... Rockford, IL
Kinley, Mark E. ..... Wheeling, WV
Kinley, Matthew L. ..... Downey, CA
Kinley, Raymond J. ..... Des Moines, IA
Kinley & Styskal ..... Tustin, CA
Kinlin, Donald J. ..... Dayton, OH
Kinlin, Michael J. ..... Lorain, OH
Kinloch, William R. ..... Waterbury, CT
Kinman, Barry Alan ..... Alturas, CA
Kinman & Curry ..... Alturas, CA
Kinman, Joseph F., Jr. ..... Tampa, FL
Kinn, Bruce A. ..... Boston, MA
Kinn, Frank J. ..... Fostoria, OH
Kinn, Jay T. ..... Burbank, CA
Kinn, John T. ..... Sacramento, CA
Kinn, Michael J. ..... Chicago, IL
Kinnaird, Charles R. ..... Detroit, MI
Kinnaird, Dennis E., (A Professional Corporation) ..... Los Angeles, CA
Kinnaird, Eleanor G. ..... Chapel Hill, NC
Kinnaird, Kenton D. ..... Colorado Springs, CO
Springfield, CO
Kinnaird & Nieman ..... Chapel Hill, NC
Kinnaird, Roy Stephen ..... Ventura, CA
Kinnaird, Shari E. ..... Columbus, IN
Kinnaird, Stephen B. ..... Washington, DC
Kinnaird, Virgil G. ..... Sheridan, WY
Kinnaird, Webster B. ..... San Diego, CA
Kinnally, M. Therese ..... Las Vegas, NV
Kinnally, Patrick M. ..... Aurora, IL
Kinnally, Robert G. ..... New York, NY
Kinnally, Wm. Lee, Jr. ..... New York, NY
Kinnaman, Bruce E. ..... Morehead City, NC
Kinnaman, Jacqueline A. ..... Charleston, WV
Kinnaman, William A., Jr.
Poughkeepsie, NY
Kinnamon, Daniel B. ..... Omaha, NE
Kinnamon, David L. ..... Milwaukee, WI
Kinnamon, Jerald W. ..... Cedar Rapids, IA
Iowa City, IA
Kinnamon, Jon M. ..... Cedar Rapids, IA
Iowa City, IA
Kinnamon, Laurel A. ..... Martinez, CA
Kinnamon, Stacey A. ..... New York, NY
Kinnamon, William J., Jr.
Fredericksburg, VA
Kinnan, Brent E. ..... Columbus, OH
Kinnan, Jerry W. ..... Addison, IL
Kinnan, Jimmie L. ..... Columbus, OH
Kinnan, Richard P. ..... Los Angeles, CA
Kinnane, Anne M. ..... Boston, MA
Kinnane, Janet E., (Miss) ..... Bay City, MI
Kinnane, Thomas W. ..... Annapolis, MD
Fort Washington, MD
Waldorf, MD
Alexandria, VA
Kinnard, Clayton & Beveridge
Nashville, TN
Kinnard, David B. ..... Billings, MT
Kinnard, David Wood ..... Overland Park, KS
Kinnard, J. Lewis ..... Madisonville, TN
Kinnard, James H. ..... Lebanon, TN
Kinnard, Joyce K. ..... Atlanta, GA
Kinnard, Michael B. ..... Wilmington, DE
Kinnard, Randall L. ..... Nashville, TN
Kinnard, Ruth M. ..... Nashville, TN
Kinnard, Stephen D. ..... Newark, NJ
Kinne, Cathleen Lahart ..... Manchester, NH
Kinne, Charles C. ..... Hoffman Estates, IL
Kinne, Kevin M. ..... Great Barrington, MA
Pittsfield, MA
Kinne, Morris Y., Jr. ..... Phoenix, AZ
Kinne, Norman ..... Dallas, TX
Kinne, Remsen M., III ..... New London, NH
Kinne, Remsen M., IV ..... San Francisco, CA
Kinne, Susan Greenberg ..... Burlingame, CA
Kinnealey, Thomas F. ..... Hingham, MA
Kinneally, James J., III
North Brunswick, NJ
Kinnear, Brian ..... Denver, CO
Kinnear, David J. ..... Cranford, NJ
Kinnear, George C. ..... Bellevue, WA
Kinnear, James Wesley
San Francisco, CA
Kinnear, Kevin J. ..... Boulder, CO
Kinneary, Jos. P. ..... Columbus, OH
Kinneberg, Paul W. ..... St. Paul, MN
Kinnebrew, Jack M., (P.C.) ..... Dallas, TX
Kinnel, R. Jackson ..... Park Ridge, IL
Kinnell, Latresia Lewis ..... Birmingham, AL
Kinnelly, Thomas F., III ..... Raymond, ME
Kinner, Donald E. ..... Department of Justice, Civil Division, GV
Kinner, Jeremy K. ..... Chapel Hill, NC
Kinner, Miriam L. ..... Fairfax, VA
Kinner, Mitchell D. ..... Prestonsburg, KY
Kinner, Russell B. ..... Department of Justice, Civil Division, GV
Kinnerk, Patrick J. ..... Chicago, IL
Kinnett, Rebekah J. ..... Washington, DC
Kinney, Aaron ..... Paradise Valley, AZ
Kinney, Alfred R. ..... Irvington, NJ
Kinney, Ann Jouett ..... Lexington, KY
Kinney, Anthony R. ..... St. Louis, MO
Kinney, Baird ..... Forrest City, AR
Kinney, Beth Ann Fryrear ..... Louisville, KY
Kinney, Burdick, Bowman & Engeln, P.L.C.
St. Joseph, MI
Kinney, Cassie N. ..... Des Moines, IA
Kinney, Charles G. ..... Oakland, CA
Kinney, Charles L. ..... Washington, DC
Kinney & Chaumont ..... Calabasas, CA
Kinney, Clifford F., Jr. ..... Charleston, WV
Kinney, Cynthia D. ..... Long Beach, CA
Kinney, Daniel Earl ..... Sacramento, CA
Kinney, David B. ..... Arlington, VA
Kinney, David C. ..... New Haven, CT
Kinney, David L. ..... Oklahoma City, OK
Kinney, Dennis M. ..... Bentonville, AR
Kinney, Douglas M. ..... Herndon, VA
Kinney, Edward W. ..... Buffalo, NY
Kinney, Eileen R. ..... Minneapolis, MN
Kinney, Eleanor D. ..... Indianapolis, IN
Kinney, Elizabeth ..... Chicago, IL
Kinney & Ellinghausen, A Professional Law Corporation ..... New Orleans, LA
Kinney, Ernest S. ..... Fresno, CA
Kinney, Francis L. ..... Rocky Hill, CT
Kinney, Gail E. ..... Atlanta, GA
Kinney, Gerald R. ..... Joliet, IL
Kinney, Gregg A. ..... St. Louis, MO
Kinney, H. Jerome ..... Omaha, NE
Kinney, Harry A. ..... Dallas, TX
Kinney, Helen C. ..... Wheaton, IL
Kinney, Henry W. ..... New Orleans, LA
Kinney, J. Nile ..... Bakersfield, CA
Kinney, Jack M. ..... Medina, OH
Kinney, Jack M., Co. L.P.A. ..... Medina, OH
Kinney, Jacqueline R. ..... Sacramento, CA
Kinney, James A. ..... Boston, MA
Kinney, James L. ..... Buffalo, NY
Kinney, Jay C. ..... Seattle, WA
Kinney, Jean M. ..... Cincinnati, OH
Kinney, Jeffrey R. ..... Evansville, IN
Kinney, John A. ..... Omaha, NE
Kinney, John C. ..... San Francisco, CA
Kinney, John E. ..... Austin, TX
Kinney, John F. ..... Chicago, IL
Kinney, Jonathan C. ..... Arlington, VA
Kinney, Judith L. ..... Rockledge, FL
Kinney, Judith M. ..... Wilmington, DE
Kinney, June ..... Memphis, TN
Kinney, Justin N. ..... Morristown, NJ
Kinney, Karin M. ..... Malvern, PA
Kinney, Kathleen E. ..... Malibu, CA
Kinney, Keith A. ..... Indianapolis, IN
Kinney, Kelley A. ..... Richmond, VA
Kinney, Kelly S. ..... Eden Prairie, MN
Kinney, Kemp, Sponcler, Joiner & Tharpe
Calhoun, GA
Dalton, GA
La Fayette, GA
Ringgold, GA
Rome, GA
Kinney, Kerry M. ..... Calabasas, CA
Kinney, Kevin J. ..... Milwaukee, WI
Kinney, Kevin M. ..... Buffalo, NY
Kinney, Kevin P. ..... Louisville, KY
Kinney, Knox ..... Forrest City, AR
Kinney, Kyle L. ..... Birmingham, AL
Kinney, L. Douglas ..... Sacramento, CA
Kinney & Lange, P.A. ..... Minneapolis, MN
Kinney, Laurelle H. ..... San Francisco, CA
Kinney, Linda I.
Federal Communications Commission, Office of Plans and Policy, GV
Kinney, Lisa ..... Laramie, WY
Kinney, Lisa F. ..... Ironwood, MI
Minneapolis, MN
Kinney, Mark J. ..... Minneapolis, MN
Kinney, Martin H., Jr. ..... Louisville, KY
Kinney, Matthew J. ..... Spearfish, SD
Kinney, Maureen L. ..... La Crosse, WI
Kinney, Michael Bryce ..... New York, NY
Kinney, Michael E. ..... Tallahassee, FL
Kinney, Michael E., Law Office of
Santa Rosa, CA
Kinney, Michael F. ..... Omaha, NE
Kinney, Michael K. ..... Waterbury, CT
Kinney, Michael L. ..... Tampa, FL
Kinney, Michael W., (P.C.) ..... Arlington, TX
Kinney, Nicole Fleet ..... Attleboro, MA
Kinney, Patrick ..... Lancaster, WI
Kinney, Patrick J., Jr. ..... Boston, MA
Kinney, Patrick T. ..... Las Vegas, NV
Kinney, Phillip Eugene ..... Birmingham, AL
Kinney, Rees ..... Greenville, KY
Kinney, Richard G. ..... Merrillville, IN
Kinney, Richard R., Jr. ..... La Jolla, CA
Kinney, Robert E. ..... Houston, TX
Kinney, Robert E. ..... Rhinelander, WI
Kinney, Robert E., Jr. ..... Mesilla, NM
Kinney, Robert F., III ..... Detroit, MI
Kinney, Robert W. ..... Pompano Beach, FL
Kinney, Ross R. ..... Waukesha, WI
Kinney and Schenk ..... Cincinnati, OH
Kinney, Sheila ..... Grand Rapids, MI
Kinney, Stephen H., Jr. ..... New York, NY
Kinney, Sterling E. ..... Amarillo, TX
Kinney, Suzanne B. ..... Albuquerque, NM
Kinney, Teresa L. ..... Aurora, CO
Kinney, Terry M. ..... Chicago, IL
Kinney, Thomas Edward
Glenwood Springs, CO
Kinney, Tricia Ann ..... Atlanta, GA
Kinney & Urban ..... Lancaster, WI
Kinney, Van O. ..... Redding, CA
Kinney & White ..... Arlington, TX
Kinney, William M. ..... Eatontown, NJ
Kinney, William M., P.C. ..... Eatontown, NJ
Kinney, Winfield E., III, (Co., L.P.A.)
Dayton, OH
Kinney, Zachary Z.
Department of the Air Force, Office of the Judge Advocate General, GV
Kinnibrugh, Polly A. ..... Houston, TX
Kinnick, Sarah L. ..... Denver, CO
Kinnicutt, Harry S. ..... Fairfield, CA
Kinnie, Andrew R. ..... Watertown, NY
Kinnie Law Firm ..... Watertown, NY
Kinnie, Richard T. ..... Watertown, NY
Kinnier, Norman A. ..... Lynchburg, VA
Kinnier, Russell D. ..... Los Angeles, CA
Kinning, Joseph T. ..... Minneapolis, MN
Kinning, Robin Powers ..... Wayzata, MN
Kinniry, Janet Tracy ..... Walsenburg, CO
Kinnison, Dana S. ..... San Diego, CA
Kinnison, Hallard B. ..... Santa Rosa, CA
Kinnison, Sharon Lyman ..... Sheridan, WY
Kinnon, Kelly ..... Los Angeles, CA
Kinnunen, Victor J. ..... Titusville, PA
Kinnunen, Zara Kivi ..... St. Paul, MN
Kinny, Paul R. ..... Louisville, KY
Charlotte, NC
Kino, Gregory S. ..... West Palm Beach, FL
Kinoian, Gregory S. ..... Fort Lee, NJ
Kinon, Amy ..... Farmingdale, NY
Kinon, Lisa A. ..... Conway, SC
Kinon, Marion H. ..... Dillon, SC
Kinon, Victor E. ..... Secaucus, NJ
Kinoshita, Dennis K. ..... Los Angeles, CA
Kinoshita, Joseph A. ..... Honolulu, HI
Kinoshita, Joseph A., A Law Corp.
Honolulu, HI
Kinoshita, Kenneth M. ..... San Francisco, CA
Kinoshita, Nelson H. ..... Hilo, HI
Kinoshita, Raymond ..... Denver, CO
Kinosian, Craig K. ..... New York, NY
Kinosky, Barbara S. ..... Vienna, VA
Kinosky, Phillips & Lieberman, PLC
Arlington, VA
Kinoy, Arthur ..... Bethesda, MD
Kinoy, Joanne ..... Chicago, IL
Kinoy, Taren, Geraghty & Potter
Chicago, IL
Kinports, Kit ..... Champaign, IL
Kins, Juris ..... Chicago, IL
Kins, Tonya ..... Riverside, CA
Kinsch, Noelle M. ..... Albany, NY
Kinscheck, Renate
Federal Trade Commission, Bureau of Consumer Protection, GV
Kinscherff, Robert Thomson ..... Boston, MA
Kinsel, Dawn ..... Los Angeles, CA
Kinsel, Grant E. ..... Los Angeles, CA
Kinsel, J. Frank ..... Houston, TX
Kinsel, J. Frank, Jr. ..... Fort Worth, TX
Kinsel, James B. ..... McLean, VA
Kinsel, William A. ..... Seattle, WA
Kinsella, Boesch, Fujikawa & Towle, L.L.P.
Los Angeles, CA
Kinsella, Christopher J. ..... Elizabeth, NJ
Kinsella, Dale F., (Professional Corporation)
Los Angeles, CA
Kinsella, Daniel V. ..... Chicago, IL
Kinsella, David L. ..... Lexington, KY
Kinsella, Donald T. ..... Albany, NY
Kinsella, E. Megan ..... St. Louis, MO
Kinsella, Eva De La Torre ..... Temecula, CA
Kinsella, Gregory P. ..... New Haven, CT
Kinsella, James H. ..... Hartford, CT
Kinsella, James M. ..... Department of Justice, Civil Division, GV
Kinsella, John B. ..... St. Louis, MO
Kinsella, John D. ..... North Syracuse, NY
Kinsella, John J. ..... Chicago, IL
Kinsella, John J. ..... Wheaton, IL
Kinsella, Joseph L. ..... Waterbury, CT
Kinsella, Kevin M. ..... Teaneck, NJ
Kinsella, Michael R. ..... Bay City, MI
Kinsella, N. Stephan ..... Houston, TX
Kinsella, Nancy L. Bohan
New Haven, CT
Kinsella, Paul M. ..... Boston, MA
Kinsella, Peter J. ..... Denver, CO
Kinsella, Peter W. ..... St. Louis, MO
Kinsella, T. R. ..... Venice, FL
Kinsella, Wendy A. ..... Syracuse, NY
Kinsella, William P. ..... Mineola, NY
Kinsellagh, John B. ..... Medfield, MA
Kinser, Carl V. ..... Rancho Cucamonga, CA
Kinser, Cynthia D. ..... Abingdon, VA
Kinser, Henry E. ..... Lexington, KY
Kinser, James G. ..... Houston, TX
Kinser, James G., P.C. ..... Houston, TX
Kinser, Katherine A. ..... Dallas, TX
Kinser, Kenneth ..... Decatur, IL
Kinser, Kirte M. ..... Dallas, TX
Kinser, Robert R. ..... Chesapeake, VA
Kinsey, Benjamin T., Jr. ..... Petersburg, VA
Kinsey, C. Ralph, Jr. ..... Charlotte, NC
Kinsey, Carrol H., Jr. ..... Treasury Department, Bureau of Engraving and Printing, GV
Kinsey, Chanda L. ..... Fairfax, VA
Kinsey, Charles M. ..... Pearland, TX
Kinsey, Charles R., III ..... Lexington, NC
Kinsey, D. Hugh, Jr. ..... Fort Myers, FL
Kinsey, Dwight A. ..... New York, NY
Kinsey, Edward W., Jr. ..... San Diego, CA
Kinsey, Euel W., Jr. ..... Southfield, MI
Kinsey, Eugene E. ..... Seal Beach, CA
Kinsey, George P., III
Department of Transportation, Federal Aviation Administration, GV
Kinsey, Gwynn X., Jr. ..... Baltimore, MD
Kinsey, J. Andrew ..... Liberty Corner, NJ
Kinsey, James B. ..... Gainesville, GA
Kinsey, John T. ..... Boca Raton, FL
Kinsey, Kathy M. ..... Baltimore, MD
Kinsey, Leah McCaslin ..... Tulsa, OK
Kinsey, Lynch & Filipour ..... Fairfax, VA
Kinsey, Madalyn S. ..... Indianapolis, IN
Kinsey, Norman V. ..... Shreveport, LA
Kinsey, Phillip K. ..... Fort Smith, AR
Kinsey, Rebecca B. ..... Goldsboro, NC
Kinsey Ridenour Becker & Kistler
Lincoln, NE
Kinsey, Robert D., Jr. ..... Lincoln, NE
Kinsey, Robert S., III ..... Mason City, IA
Kinsey, Roger W. ..... Buffalo, NY
Kinsey, Ronald C., Jr. ..... Seattle, WA
Kinsey, Roy M., Jr. ..... Pensacola, FL
Kinsey, Scott A. ..... Kokomo, IN
Kinsey, Shirley ..... Tucker, GA
Kinsey Vincent Pyle, P.A.
Daytona Beach, FL
DeLand, FL
Kinsey, Walton S., Jr.
Securities and Exchange Commission, Division of Enforcement, GV
Kinsey, William W. ..... Portland, OR
Kinsinger, Richard E. ..... Akron, OH
Kinskey, Greg T. ..... Pittsburgh, PA
Kinsler, David A. ..... Los Angeles, CA
Kinsler, Jack H. ..... Atlanta, GA
Kinsler, Jeffrey S. ..... Chicago, IL
Kinsler, John T. ..... Omaha, NE
Kinsler, Paul F. ..... Thousand Oaks, CA
Kinsler, Warren S. ..... Cerritos, CA
Kinsley, Brian L. ..... Boston, MA
Kinsley, Curtis D. ..... Portland, OR
Kinsley, David R. ..... Baltimore, MD
Kinsley, Donald R. ..... Dover, DE
Kinsley, Frederic W. ..... Marblehead, MA
Kinsley, George J. ..... Madison, CT
Kinsley, George J., P.C. ..... Madison, CT
Kinsley, Mary-Irene ..... Los Alamos, NM
Santa Fe, NM
Kinsley, Michael E. ..... Washington, DC
Kinsley, R. Clark ..... Lutherville, MD
Kinsley, Stephen L. ..... Southfield, MI
Kinsley-Mayer, Patricia ..... Bensalem, PA
Kinslow, Henry C. ..... El Dorado, AR
Kinslow, John ..... Lawton, OK
Kinslow, Joseph A. ..... Washington, DC
Kinslow, Samuel T. ..... Waco, TX
Kinsman, J. Christopher ..... Denver, CO
Kinsman, Katharine Harsch ..... Park City, UT
Kinsman, Keith ..... Milwaukie, OR
Kinsman, N. Mark ..... Chattanooga, TN
Kinsman, Paul S ..... Pierre, SD
Kinsman, Terence J. ..... Los Angeles, CA

Kinsock, Thomas B. ... St. Louis, MO
Kinsolving, Augustus B. ... New York, NY
Kinsolving, Eric Downs ... Old Hickory, TN
Kinsolving, Laurence E. ... Tampa, FL
Kinsolving, Neal A. ... Charleston, WV
Kinsolving, Ruth Barnes ... Tampa, FL
Kinson, Michael S. ... Chelmsford, MA
Kinstler, Andrew J. ... Seattle, WA
Kinstler, Jeffrey G. ... Baltimore, MD
Kinstlick, Riva F. ... Newark, NJ
Kinstlinger, Abraham ... Hackensack, NJ
Kinstlinger, Marvin J. ... Bedford Heights, OH
Kint, Jack M., Jr. ... New York, NY
Kinter, Lawrence L. ... Erie, PA
Kintigh, Thomas F. ... Ottumwa, IA
Kintisch, Alan M. ... Philadelphia, PA
Kintner, Gaylon K. ... Manhattan, KS
Kintner, James P. ... Bremerton, WA
Kintner, Janet I. ... San Diego, CA
Kintner, Thomas W. ... Lafayette, CA
Kinton, Christina ... Chicago, IL
Kinton, David E. ... Kansas City, MO
Kintz, James L. ... Vista, CA
Kintz, John F. ... St. Louis, MO
Kintz, Peter K., Law Offices of
Atlanta, GA
Kintz, Richard L. ... San Diego, CA
Kintz, Susanna Truax ... Lake Forest, IL
Kintz, Theresa R. ... Akron, OH
Kintzel, Lee A. ... Atlanta, GA
Kintzele, John A. ... Denver, CO
Kintzele, L. T. ... Evergreen, CO
Kintzer, David M. ... Newburgh, NY
Kintzinger, Andrew R. ... Minneapolis, MN
Kintzinger, Charles A. ... Dubuque, IA
Kintzinger, David N. ... Dubuque, IA
Kintzinger Law Firm, P.L.C. ... Dubuque, IA
Kintzinger, Warren H. ... Richardson, TX
Kinum, John B. ... Albany, NY
Kinworthy, Christine ... Columbus, OH
Kinworthy, David R. ... Lima, OH
Kinyon, Gary J. ... Keene, NH
Kinyon, James R. ... Hartford, CT
Kinyon, John Donald, Jr. ... Orlando, FL
Kinyon, Kendall E. ... Orangevale, CA
Kinyon, Richard S. ... San Francisco, CA
Kinz, Douglas J. ... West Paterson, NJ
Kinz, Robert B. ... Carthage, MO
Kinzel, Allen, Skone & Searing, Inc., P.S.
Bellevue, WA
Kinzel, C. Scott ... Houston, TX
Kinzel, Jennifer ... McPherson, KS
Kinzel, JoAnne E. ... Pittsburgh, PA
Kinzel, William L. ... Bellevue, WA
Kinzelman, Gregory L. ... Washington, DC
Kinzer, Allen S. ... Columbus, OH
Kinzer, James B. ... Chicago, IL
Kinzer, James B., III ... Piper City, IL
Watseka, IL
Kinzer, James R. ... Dallas, TX
Kinzer, Mark W. ... Atlanta, GA
Kinzer, Michael A. ... Babylon, NY
Kinzer, Michael J. ... Minneapolis, MN
Kinzer, Robert W., III ... Pittsfield, MA
Kinzer, Sanford, Law Offices of
Everett, WA
Kinzer, Wallace ... West Bloomfield, MI
Kinzer, William L. ... Atlanta, GA
Kinzer-Ellington, Kathrin M. ... Santa Fe, NM
Kinzey, John S., Jr. ... New York, NY
Kinzie, Cheree Tull ... San Antonio, TX
Kinzie, Frank J., III ... Boston, MA
Kinzie, Jack L. ... Dallas, TX
Kinzie, Jan J. ... Indianapolis, IN
Kinzie, Lauren ... Austin, TX
Kinzie, Mark A. ... St. Louis, MO
Kinzie, Raymond W. ... Chicago, IL
Kinzinger, Janet L. ... Milford, MI
Kinzler, Ben ... Great Neck, NY
Kinzler, Jeffrey L. ... East Meadow, NY
Kinzler, Jeffrey L. ... New York, NY
Kinzler, Ronald G. ... Somers Point, NJ
Philadelphia, PA
Kinzler, Thomas B. ... New York, NY
Kinzler, Thomas J. ... Chicago, IL
Kinzler, Thomas M. ... Springfield, MA
Kinzler, William C. ... San Francisco, CA
Kinzy & Associates, P.C. ... Chicago, IL
Kinzy, H. Norman ... Dallas, TX
Kinzy, Kyle M. ... Chicago, IL
Kiok, Joan Stern ... New York, NY
Kionka, Edward J. ... Carbondale, IL
Kious, David W. ... Murfreesboro, TN
Kious & Rodgers ... Murfreesboro, TN
Nashville, TN
Kiousis, Pete N. ... Southfield, MI
Kioutas, Anna Paniotte ... Wilmette, IL
Kiovsky, Elizabeth I. ... Denver, CO
Kip, Ruloff F., Jr. ... Whippany, NJ
Kipel, Alice Alexandra ... Washington, DC
Kipers, Anne S. ... Dallas, TX
Kipf, Kari Beth ... Boston, MA
Kipi, Jeffery T. ... Oviedo, FL
Kipka, Ross Albin ... Indianapolis, IN
Kiple, Charles M. ... Ottumwa, IA
Kiple, James L. ... Estes Park, CO
Kiple, Joseph M. ... Englewood, CO
Kiple, Kiple, Denefe, Beaver & Gardner, L.L.P. ... Ottumwa, IA
Kipley, David M. ... Acme, MI
Kipling, James M. ... Cincinnati, OH
Kipling, Linda B. ... Woodbury, NY
Kipling, Michael E. ... Seattle, WA
Kiplinger, Robert O. ... Sun City West, AZ
Kiplinger, Roy F. ... Fort Wayne, IN
Kiplinger, Victor A. ... Indianapolis, IN
Kipnees, Glenn E. ... Roseland, NJ
Kipnees, Helane A. ... Roseland, NJ
Kipnees, Robert J. ... Woodbridge, NJ
Kipnes, Allen R. ... Princeton Junction, NJ
Kipnes, Rachel ... Philadelphia, PA
Kipnes, Wilbur L. ... Philadelphia, PA
Kipness, Jason E. ... Austin, TX
Kipness, Robert ... New York, NY
Kipnis, Alan G. ... Fort Lauderdale, FL
Kipnis, Alisa ... Cleveland, OH
Kipnis, Barbara S. ... New York, NY
Kipnis, Bruce E. ... Treasury Department, Internal Revenue Service, GV
Kipnis, Howard A. ... San Diego, CA
Kipnis, Ira A. ... Chicago, IL
Kipnis, Irwin ... Chicago, IL
Kipnis, Jason D. ... Menlo Park, CA
Kipnis, Jonathan I. ... Greenbelt, MD
Kipnis, Kahn & Bruggeman, Ltd.
Chicago, IL
New Lenox, IL
Kipnis, Laura J. ... St. Louis, MO
Kipnis, Leslie ... Chicago, IL
New Lenox, IL
Kipnis, Mark S. ... Chicago, IL
Kipnis, Nancy Swerdlow ... Miami Beach, FL
Kipnis, Neal R. ... Riverside, CA
Kipnis, Robert S. ... Chicago, IL
Kipnis, Scott R. ... Roseland, NJ
New York, NY
Kipnis Tescher Lippman & Valinsky
Fort Lauderdale, FL
Kipp, Carman E. ... Salt Lake City, UT
Kipp and Christian, P.C.
Salt Lake City, UT
Kipp, Crane D. ... Jackson, MS
Kipp, Frank S. ... Middletown, OH
Kipp, James F. ... Wilmington, DE
Kipp, Jerald B. ... Akron, OH
Kipp, John T. ... Dallas, TX
Kipp, Matthew R. ... Chicago, IL
Kipp, Ralph E. ... Fairfax, VA
Kipp, Ruth E. ... Export, PA
Kipp, Somerville & Kipp ... Rutherford, NJ
Kipp, Walter A., III ... Rutherford, NJ
Kippen, Harold ... Encino, CA
Kippen, Richard M. ... Detroit, MI
Kippen, Terence A. ... Lakewood, CO
Kippenhan, Nancy J. ... Harrisburg, PA
Kipper, David L. ... New York, NY
Kipper, David R. ... Los Angeles, CA
San Diego, CA
Kipper, Eva A. ... Marquette, MI
Kipper, Robert ... Beverly Hills, CA
Kipper, Robert N., P.C. ... Beverly Hills, CA
Kipperman, Carol A. ... Maywood, IL
Kipperman, Edward O. ... Stamford, CT
Kipperman, Fred P. ... Tucson, AZ
Kipperman, Fred, P.C. ... Tucson, AZ
Kipperman & Johns ... San Francisco, CA
Kipperman, Lawrence I. ... Chicago, IL
Kipperman, Steven M., (Professional Corporation) ... San Francisco, CA
Kippes, A. T. ... San Francisco, CA
Kippes, Christopher S. ... New York, NY
Kipphan, Michael M. ... Huntingdon, PA
Kippins, Susan A. ... New York, NY
Kipps, Clarence T., Jr. ... Washington, DC
Kipps, Don L. ... Falls Church, VA
Kippur, Merrie Margolin ... Denver, CO
Kippur, Merrie Margolin, Associates, P.C.
Denver, CO
Kiracofe, Bruce H. ... Columbus, OH
Kiracofe, Warren C. ... Mount Crawford, VA
Kirages, Christopher, Law Office of
Indianapolis, IN
Kiraly, Aniko M. ... New Orleans, LA
Kiraly, Michele A. ... Las Vegas, NV
Kirbach, Rosemary Mahar
San Francisco, CA
Kirback, Mary E. ... Jerseyville, IL
Kirban, Elise ... Purchase, NY
Kirbens, Samuel M. ... Laguna Hills, CA
Kirberger & Associates ... New York, NY
Kirberger, Elizabeth A. ... New York, NY
Kirbo, Ben ... Bainbridge, GA
Kirbo, Bruce W. ... Bainbridge, GA
Kirbo, Bruce W., Jr. ... Bainbridge, GA
Kirbo, Charles H. ... Roswell, GA
Kirbo, Glenn A. ... Albany, GA
Kirbo, Helen V. ... Albany, GA
Kirbo & Herndon ... Moultrie, GA
Kirbo & Kendrick ... Bainbridge, GA
Kirbo & Kirbo, P.C. ... Albany, GA
Kirbo, Thomas L., III ... Moultrie, GA
Kirby, Alan D. ... Toms River, NJ
Kirby, Albert D., Jr. ... Clinton, NC
Kirby, Andrew W. ... Albany, NY
Kirby, Arthur W. ... Middletown, RI
Kirby, Barbara J. ... Davie, FL
Kirby, Bobby Lex ... Lake Butler, FL
Kirby, Brian K. ... Sioux Falls, SD
Kirby, Bruce K. ... Springfield, MO
Kirby, C. Lowell ... Copperhill, TN
Kirby, Carol Eller ... Norcross, GA
Kirby, Cary D. ... Lufkin, TX
Kirby, Charles M. ... Merrill, WI
Kirby, Christopher R. ... San Antonio, TX
Kirby, Christopher W. ... Austin, TX
Kirby, Clifford R., Jr. ... Kansas City, MO
Kirby, Craig A. ... Reston, VA
Kirby, Curtis G., Jr. ... Jackson, MS
Kirby, Dan ... Sioux Falls, SD
Kirby, Dan ... Houston, TX
Kirby, David F. ... Raleigh, NC
Kirby, David V. ... Burlington, VT
Kirby, Dean T., Jr. ... San Diego, CA
Kirby, Deborah A. ... Albany, NY
Canandaigua, NY
Kirby, Derrick Shane ... St. Louis, MO
Kirby, Donald A. ... Alameda, CA
Kirby, Donna Rogers ... Long Beach, CA
Kirby, Doris R. ... Memphis, TN
Kirby, Edmond M. ... Newark, NJ
Kirby, Edw. P. ... Boston, MA
Kirby, Edward L., & Associatess, P.C.
Arlington, MA
Kirby, Edward L., Jr. ... Arlington, MA
Kirby, Edward S. ... Normandy Beach, NJ
Kirby, Edwin L., Jr. ... Columbus, OH
Kirby, Elizabeth J. ... Treasury Department, Office of the Comptroller of the Currency, GV
Kirby, Erik W. ... Boston, MA
Kirby, Eugene W. ... Louisville, KY
Kirby, F. Edward ... Durham, NC
Kirby, F. William, Jr. ... Richmond, VA
Kirby, Gary E. ... Sylva, NC
Kirby, Gerald F. ... Westbury, NY
Kirby, Glen L. ... Kountze, TX
Kirby & Holt, L.L.P. ... Cary, NC
Raleigh, NC
Kirby, Homer H. ... Vienna, VA
Kirby, Homer J. ... Dallas, TX
Kirby, Jack ... La Grange, GA
Kirby, Jack Arthur ... Wayne, PA
Kirby, James L. ... Memphis, TN
Kirby, James R., II ... Sacramento, CA
Kirby, James Thornton ... Sumter, SC
Kirby, James W. ... Ashland City, TN
Kirby, Jefferson D., III ... Atlanta, GA
Kirby, Jeffrey C. ... Birmingham, AL
Kirby, Jeffrey D. ... West Palm Beach, FL
Kirby, Jeffrey T. ... Springboro, OH
Kirby, Jennifer Rearden ... Medford, MA
Kirby, Jerome W. ... Littlefield, TX
Kirby, J. F. ... Lexington, KY
Kirby, Joe P. ... Sioux Falls, SD
Kirby, John A. ... East Stroudsburg, PA
Kirby, John D. ... San Diego, CA
Kirby, John D. ... Minneapolis, MN
Kirby, John D., A P.C., Law Offices of
San Diego, CA
Kirby, John E. ... Dallas, TX
Kirby, John J. ... Williamsburg, VA
Kirby, John J., Jr. ... New York, NY
Kirby, John K. ... Oakland, CA
Kirby, John M. ... Raleigh, NC
Kirby, John P., Jr. ... Roswell, GA
Kirby, Joseph ... Jackson, OH
Kirby, Joseph W. ... Springboro, OH
Kirby, Joyce A. ... Worcester, MA
Kirby, Karen E. ... San Francisco, CA
Kirby, Katherine A. ... Rockland, MA
Kirby, Kathleen A. ... Washington, DC
Kirby, Kenneth R. ... Buffalo, NY
Kirby, Kevin Douglas ... Atlanta, GA
Kirby, Kevin T. ... Sioux Falls, SD
Kirby, Kim ... Arlington, TX
Kirby & Kirby ... Redondo Beach, CA
Kirby & Kirby, L.P.A. ... Springboro, OH
Kirby, Ky E. ... Washington, DC
Kirby, Lance Alan ... Weslaco, TX
Kirby, Larry W. ... Chattanooga, TN
Kirby, Laurie B. ... Newport, RI
Kirby, Lee M., Jr. ... Raleigh, NC
Kirby, LeGrand C., III ... Dallas, TX
Kirby, Linda K. ... El Paso, TX
Kirby, M. Cheryl ... San Antonio, TX
Kirby, Margaret Ann ... Stamford, CT
Kirby, Margaret L. ... Redondo Beach, CA
Kirby, Mark S. ... Fort Washington, PA
Kirby, Marti B. ... Hattiesburg, MS
Kirby, Mary Lynn ... Fayetteville, GA
Kirby, Matthew T. ... Los Angeles, CA
New York, NY
Kirby, Maureen Ward ... Chicago, IL
Kirby McInerney & Squire, L.L.P.
New York, NY
Kirby, Michael D. ... Toms River, NJ
Kirby, Michael D. ... Toledo, OH
Kirby, Michael D. ... Houston, TX
Kirby, Michael E. ... Pointe a la Hache, LA
Kirby, Michael L., (A P.C.)
San Diego, CA
Kirby, Michael R. ... Miami, FL
Kirby, Monroe, (P.C.) ... Tyler, TX
Kirby, N. Jacqueline ... Quincy, MA
Kirby, P. Elise Miller ... Alexandria, VA
Kirby, Patrick J. ... Spokane, WA
Kirby, Patrick James ... San Marino, CA
Kirby, Patrick M. ... Flint, MI
Kirby, Patrick R. ... Dallas, TX
Kirby, Paul M. ... Annapolis, MD
Kirby, Paula G. ... Paradise Valley, AZ
Kirby, Peter M. ... Washington, DC
Kirby, Phillip M. ... Mason City, IL
Kirby, R. Bentz ... Columbia, SC
Kirby, R. Gregory ... Oklahoma City, OK
Kirby, Richard A. ... Washington, DC
Kirby, Richard B. ... Quincy, MA
Kirby, Richard C. ... Champaign, IL
Kirby, Richard F. ... Woonsocket, RI
Kirby, Richard M. ... Atlanta, GA
Kirby, Richard P. ... Garden City, NY
Kirby, Richard W. ... Berkeley, CA
Kirby, Richard Wayne ... Anadarko, OK
Kirby, Robert E., Jr. ... Birmingham, AL
Kirby, Robert J. ... Omaha, NE
Kirby, Robert L. ... Denver, CO
Kirby, Robert L. ... Alpharetta, GA
Kirby, Robert L. ... Canton, GA
Roswell, GA
Kirby, Robert L., Jr. ... Boston, MA
Kirby, Robert S., Jr. ... Chicago, IL
Kirby, Robert W. ... Cherryville, NC
Kirby, Robert W., Jr. ... Berkeley, CA
Kirby & Roberts, P.C. ... La Grange, GA
Kirby, Roger W. ... Gadsden, AL
Kirby, Roger W. ... New York, NY
Kirby, Roy ... Coffeyville, KS
Kirby, Sammy R. ... Raleigh, NC
Kirby, Sarah Y. M. ... Radford, VA
Kirby, Sean Patrick ... Philadelphia, PA
Kirby, Steven C. ... Redondo Beach, CA
Kirby, Steven Evans ... Santa Barbara, CA
Kirby, Steven T. ... Sioux Falls, SD
Kirby, Susan M. ... Atlanta, GA
Kirby, T. Malcolm ... Jacksonville, FL
Kirby, Terrence P. ... Indianapolis, IN
Kirby, Thomas A. ... San Diego, CA
Kirby, Thomas B., Jr. ... Springboro, OH
Kirby, Thomas J. ... Tulsa, OK
Kirby, Thomas W. ... Washington, DC
Kirby, Tom, Jr. ... Sioux Falls, SD
Kirby, Vance N. ... North Chatham, MA
Kirby, Vincent J. ... Norfolk, NE
Kirby, Wendy T. ... Dayton, OH
Kirby, William B. ... Beaverton, OR
Kirby, William B. ... Enterprise, OR
Kirby, William J. ... New York, NY
Kirby, William J. ... Columbus, OH
Kirby, William Kay ... Olympia, WA
Kirby, William L., II ... Columbus, GA
Kirby, William L., III ... Martinsville, VA
Kirby, Wm. Roy ... Coffeyville, KS
Kirby, Y. Thomas ... Jacksonville, FL
Kirch, David W. ... Aurora, CO
Kirch, David W., P.C. ... Aurora, CO
Kirch, Jacques J. ... Escondido, CA
Kirch, Patricia A. ... Oklahoma City, OK
Kirchanski, Stefan J. ... Los Angeles, CA
Kirchberg, Charles R. ... Park Ridge, IL
Kirchen, Karen J. ... New York, NY
Kirchen, Peter T. ... Los Angeles, CA
Kircher, Allen D. ... St. Charles, MO
Kircher, Andrea M. ... St. Paul, MN
Kircher, C. William, Jr., A Prof. Corp., Law Offices of ... Irvine, CA
Los Angeles, CA
Kircher, C. William, Jr., (Professional Corporation) ... Irvine, CA
Irvine, CA
Kircher, Don G. ... Camarillo, CA
Kircher, J. Scott ... San Diego, CA
Kircher, John J. ... Milwaukee, WI
Kircher, Konrad ... Cincinnati, OH
Kircher, Lisa A. ... St. Louis, MO
Kircher, Mark A. ... Milwaukee, WI
Kircher, Martin A. ... Baltimore, MD
Kircher, Mary Anne ... La Crosse, WI
Kircher, Michael P. ... St. James, MN
Kircher, Philip G. ... Philadelphia, PA
Kircher, Robert E. ... Minneapolis, MN
Kircher, Robinson & Welch ... Cincinnati, OH
Kircher, Sally J. ... Jacksonville, FL
Kircher, Stephanie ... Iowa City, IA
Kircher, Susan M. ... Pittsburgh, PA
Kircher, Thomas C. ... Waterford, WI
Kircher, Thomas J. ... Cincinnati, OH
Kircher & Vail ... Jacksonville, FL
Kircher, William B. ... Kansas City, MO
Kircher-Arden, Jeanine M. ... Rochester, NY
Kirchert, Linda M. ... Memphis, TN
Kirchgaessner, William H. ... New York, NY
Kirchheimer, Arthur E. ... La Jolla, CA
Kirchheimer, Sheila Tow
Arlington Heights, IL
Kirchheimer, Susan ... New York, NY
Kirchhoefer, Gregg ... Chicago, IL
Kirchhof, Anton C., Jr. ... Portland, OR
Kirchhofer, William D. ... Bronx, NY
Kirchhoff, Bruce C. ... Denver, CO
Kirchhoff, Henry Criss ... Fairway, KS
Kirchhoff, Herbert H. ... Bozeman, MT
Kirchhoff, Jeffrey P. ... Grand Rapids, MI
Kirchick, Calvin B. ... Cleveland, OH
Kirchick, Carol R. ... Boston, MA
Kirchick, Stuart D., Law Offices of
San Jose, CA
Kirchick, Wendy I. ... Washington, DC
Kirchick, William D. ... Boston, MA
Kirchman, Charles V. ... Silver Spring, MD
Kirchman, Eric H. ... Silver Spring, MD
Kirchman & Kirchman
Silver Spring, MD
Kirchman, Michael ... Prairie du Chien, WI
Kirchmann, Jeffrey ... San Francisco, CA
Kirchmayr, Stephen J., Jr. ... Jackson, MS
Kirchmeier, Jeffrey L. ... Flushing, NY
Kirchmer, Christopher T. ... Beaumont, TX
Kirchmeyer, D. Odie, (Mrs.) ... St. Louis, MO
Kirchner, Arthur G. ... Detroit, MI
Kirchner, Christine ... Houston, TX
Kirchner, Domenique
Department of Justice, Civil Division, GV
Kirchner, J. Philip ... Cherry Hill, NJ
Kirchner, James J. ... Lancaster, PA
Kirchner, John E. ... Colorado Springs, CO
Kirchner, John R. ... Chicago, IL
Kirchner, Mary G. ... Newark, OH
Kirchner, Paul G. ... Washington, DC
Kirchner, Paul T. ... Dakota Dunes, SD
Kirchner, Richard G. ... Stoneham, MA
Kirchner, Robert G. ... Champaign, IL
Kirchner, Robert H. ... Syracuse, NY
Kirchner, Theodore H. ... Portland, ME
Kirchner, William J. ... Tucson, AZ
Kirchoff, Brian R. ... Irvine, CA
Kirchoff, Bruce ... Vincennes, IN
Kirchoff, Colleen A. ... New York, NY
Kirchoff, Eileen L. ... New York, NY
Kirchoff, Gary H. ... Denton, TX
Kirchoff, Kevin M.
Securities and Exchange Commission, Division of Investment Management, GV

Kirkpatrick, Kent A. ... San Antonio, TX
Kirkpatrick & Keyser ... Baton Rouge, LA
Kirkpatrick & Kirkpatrick, P.C.
Fort Plain, NY
Kirkpatrick, Laird C. ... Eugene, OR
Kirkpatrick & Lockhart LLP
Washington, DC
Miami, FL
Boston, MA
New York, NY
Harrisburg, PA
Pittsburgh, PA
Kirkpatrick, Loy W. ... Department of Energy, Office of the General Counsel, GV
Kirkpatrick, Lynn Marie ... Brownsville, TX
Kirkpatrick, Margaret D. ... Portland, OR
Kirkpatrick, Martin ... Marblehead, MA
Kirkpatrick, Mary Ann ... Meadville, PA
Kirkpatrick, Mary G. ... Burlington, VT
Kirkpatrick, Melissa Gail ... Brooklyn, NY
Kirkpatrick, Michael A.
Department of Defense, Defense Legal Services Agency, GV
Kirkpatrick, Michael T.
Department of Justice, Civil Rights Division, GV
Kirkpatrick, Montgomery, Crissman & Montgomery ... Butler, PA
Kirkpatrick, Moore & Westbrook
Memphis, TN
Kirkpatrick, M. W. (Bill), Jr. ... Fairfax, VA
Kirkpatrick, Nancy M. ... Buffalo, NY
Kirkpatrick, Nina B. ... Lafayette, IN
Kirkpatrick, P.C. ... Flagstaff, AZ
Kirkpatrick, Paul K., Jr. ... Monroe, LA
Kirkpatrick, Paul L. ... Spokane, WA
Kirkpatrick, Philip M. ... Nashville, TN
Kirkpatrick, R. Mark ... Mobile, AL
Kirkpatrick, Richard C., (A Law Corporation)
San Luis Obispo, CA
Kirkpatrick, Richard L.
San Francisco, CA
Kirkpatrick, Robert R. ... Long Beach, CA
Kirkpatrick, Roderick J. ... New York, NY
Kirkpatrick, Roger M. ... New York, NY
Kirkpatrick, Roger N. ... New York, NY
Kirkpatrick, Ronald J. ... Gaylord, MI
Kirkpatrick, Sarah A. ... Shreveport, LA
Kirkpatrick, Scott L., III ... Memphis, TN
Kirkpatrick, Sharon Roos ... Chicago, IL
Kirkpatrick & Silverberg, LLP
White Plains, NY
Kirkpatrick, Stephen M. ... Palm Springs, CA
Kirkpatrick, Stewart R. ... Billings, MT
Kirkpatrick, Terri E. ... Louisville, KY
Kirkpatrick, Terry R., (Ms.) ... Fayetteville, AR
Kirkpatrick, Thad D. ... Naples, FL
Kirkpatrick, Thomas ... Buffalo, NY
Kirkpatrick, Thomas B., Jr. ... Chicago, IL
Kirkpatrick, Thomas K. ... Baton Rouge, LA
Kirkpatrick, Walter K. ... Erlanger, KY
Kirkpatrick, William A. ... La Crosse, WI
Kirkpatrick, William E. ... Ponca City, OK
Kirkpatrick, William Huntington, II
Towson, MD
Kirkpatrick, William M. ... San Jose, CA
Kirkpatrick, William P. ... Rumson, NJ
Kirkpatrick, William R. (Randy)
Manhattan Beach, CA
New York, NY
Kirkpatrick & Zeitz ... Portland, OR
Kirkscey, David A. ... Memphis, TN
Kirksey & Associates ... Jackson, MS
Kirksey, Charles ... St. Louis, MO
Kirksey, Dwight R. ... Detroit, MI
Kirksey, Gerald B. ... Brentwood, TN
Kirksey, Jerry ... Edmond, OK
Kirksey, Jerry" Jay "M. ... Bolivar, MO
Kirksey, Larry B. ... Bristol, VA
Kirksey & McNamee PLC
Brentwood, TN
Nashville, TN
Kirksey & Paluzzi ... Carrollton, AL
Kirksey, Robert A. ... Birmingham, AL
Kirksey, Robert H. ... Carrollton, AL
Kirksey, William B. ... Jackson, MS
Kirkton, John L. ... Chicago, IL
Kirkvold, Susan J. ... Sioux Falls, SD
Kirkwood, Bruce Alan ... Cumberland, MD
Kirkwood, Carole Taylor ... Tampa, FL
Kirkwood, Carolyn ... Santa Ana, CA
Kirkwood, Charles W. ... New York, NY
Kirkwood, Cheryl L. ... Treasury Department, Bureau of Alcohol, Tobacco and Firearms, GV
Kirkwood, Craig E. ... Laramie, WY
Kirkwood, Erin D. ... Fort Pierce, FL
Kirkwood, Florence M ... Mount Kisco, NY
Kirkwood, J. Scott ... Wingate, NC
Kirkwood, Jan C. ... Seattle, WA
Kirkwood, Jessica E. ... Orlando, FL
Kirkwood, Joe M. ... Del Mar, CA
Kirkwood, John B. ... Seattle, WA
Kirkwood, John H., Jr. ... Montesano, WA
Kirkwood, John R. ... Indianapolis, IN
Kirkwood, J. R. ... Valley, NE
Kirkwood, Koleen S. ... Pittsburgh, PA
Kirkwood, Lawrence R. ... Orlando, FL
Kirkwood, Martin V. ... Washington, DC
Kirkwood, Nancy Carol ... Albuquerque, NM
Kirkwood, Natalie ... Philadelphia, PA
Kirkwood, Natalie J. ... Portland, OR
Kirkwood Nelson and Vang ... Laramie, WY
Kirkwood, Peter T. ... Tampa, FL
Kirkwood, Porter L. ... Delhi, NY
Kirkwood, R. Carter ... Los Angeles, CA
Kirkwood, Robert C. ... Palo Alto, CA
Kirkwood, Robert C. ... Pleasantville, NY
Kirkwood, Thomas J. ... Cincinnati, OH
Kirleis, Alyson J. ... Pittsburgh, PA
Kirley, Charles Christian
Kansas City, MO
Kirley, Daniel P. ... Honolulu, HI
Kirley, Joseph F. ... Merrimack, NH
Kirley, Joseph P. ... White Plains, NY
Kirley, Kenneth A. ... Minneapolis, MN
Kirlin, Anne M. ... Napa, CA
Kirlin, Campbell & Keating
Stamford, CT
Washington, DC
Hoboken, NJ
New York, NY
Kirlin, John P. ... Rockville, MD
Kirlin, Kevin M. ... Des Moines, IA
Kirman, Galina A. ... New York, NY
Kirman, Igor ... New York, NY
Kirmani, Samia M. ... Boston, MA
Kirmayer, Kathryn Dean
Washington, DC
Kirmayer, Matt A. ... San Diego, CA
Kirmer, Kristen ... Denver, CO
Kirmil, Scott A. ... Washington, DC
Kirmis, Lyle W. ... Bismarck, ND
Kirmser, Olivier J. ... Florham Park, NJ
Kirmssé, Leigh A. ... Emeryville, CA
Kirn, Edward W., III ... Medford, NJ
Kirn, GayLynn Renee ... Oakland, CA
Kirn, John J., Jr. ... Cleveland, OH
Kirn, Kim L. ... Springfield, IL
Kirn, Walter N. ... Houston, TX
Kirnan, Matthew J. ... Newark, NJ
Kirnbauer, Carl W. ... Torrance, CA
Kirner & Boldt, Co., L.P.A.
North Royalton, OH
Kirner, Lee M. ... Fort Smith, AR
Kirner, Paul T. ... North Royalton, OH
Kiroff, Carole R. ... Toledo, OH
Kirpalani, Maynard M. ... Boston, MA
Kirpalani, Rohit H. ... Washington, DC
Kirpalani, Susheel ... New York, NY
Kirrane, Kevin M. ... Mashpee, MA
Kirsanow, Peter N. ... Cleveland, OH
Kirsch, Benjamin H. ... Freehold, NJ
Kirsch, Daniel E. ... Hackensack, NJ
New York, NY
Kirsch, Daniel J. ... Washington, DC
Kirsch, David A. ... New York, NY
Kirsch, Debi D. ... Glasgow, KY
Kirsch, Edward W. ... Washington, DC
Kirsch, Elaine B. ... White Plains, NY
Kirsch, Eric D. ... New York, NY
Kirsch, Florence W. ... Marblehead, MA
Kirsch, Florence W., P.C. ... Marblehead, MA
Kirsch, Gartenberg & Howard
Hackensack, NJ
New York, NY
Kirsch, Gregory J. ... Atlanta, GA
Kirsch, Gregory R. ... Concord, NH
Kirsch, Helen G. ... Washington, DC
Kirsch, Hope N. ... Montclair, NJ
Kirsch, Howard ... Brooklyn, NY
Kirsch, James S. ... Indianapolis, IN
Kirsch, James W. ... Portsmouth, OH
Kirsch, Jed Neil Kirsch ... Garden City, NY
Kirsch, Jeffrey ... Stuart, FL
Kirsch, Jeffrey ... Liberty, NY
Kirsch, Jeffrey L. ... Gladstone, NJ
Kirsch, Joe M. ... Memphis, TN
Kirsch, Joel A. ... New York, NY
Kirsch, John F. ... Reno, NV
Kirsch, Jonathan L. ... Los Angeles, CA
Kirsch, Joshua Erik ... San Francisco, CA
Kirsch, Jules P. ... New York, NY
Kirsch, Kevin W. ... Newport Beach, CA
Kirsch, Laura S. ... River Edge, NJ
New York, NY
Kirsch, Laurence S. ... Washington, DC
Kirsch, Lawrence A. ... Albany, NY
Kirsch, Lawrence H. ... Rockville, MD
Kirsch, Leonard D. ... New York, NY
Kirsch, Linda M. ... Cedar Rapids, IA
Kirsch, Lisa B. ... Southfield, MI
Kirsch, Lynn ... Las Vegas, NV
Kirsch, Marjorie H. ... Lauderhill, FL
Kirsch, Mark A. ... Bridgeport, CT
Kirsch, Mark A. ... Washington, DC
Kirsch, Mark A. ... New York, NY
Kirsch, Martin ... East Brunswick, NJ
Kirsch, Martin J. ... Washington, DC
Kirsch, Melissa Vance ... Trenton, NJ
Kirsch, Michael M. ... New York, NY
Kirsch, Michael S. ... Treasury Department, Departmental Offices, GV
Kirsch & Mitchell ... Los Angeles, CA
Kirsch, Ned, (P.A.) ... Newark, NJ
Kirsch, Paul F. ... San Francisco, CA
Kirsch, Peter J. ... Denver, CO
Washington, DC
Kirsch, Ralph M. ... Salt Lake City, UT
Kirsch, Randy A. ... Hartford, CT
Kirsch, Robert Andrew ...
Department of Justice, GV
Kirsch, Robert C. ... Boston, MA
Kirsch, Robert E. ... Ligonier, IN
Kirsch, Sharon S. ... San Jose, CA
Kirsch, Solomon D. ... Great Neck, NY
Kirsch, Steven A. ... St. Louis, MO
Kirsch, Steven J. ... St. Paul, MN
Kirsch, Susan M. ... Pittsburgh, PA
Kirsch, Thomas L. ... Munster, IN
Kirsch, Vincent F. ... Massena, NY
Kirsch, William S. ... Chicago, IL
Kirsch, William T. ... Galena, MO
Kirschbaum, Amy R. ... Hartford, CT
Kirschbaum, Frank S. ... Raleigh, NC
Kirschbaum, Gayle Fichelson
Los Angeles, CA
Kirschbaum, Gerald A. ... Skokie, IL
Kirschbaum, Gerald S. ... Montclair, NJ
Kirschbaum, Howard J. ... Chicago, IL
Kirschbaum, Jay M. ... St. Louis, MO
Kirschbaum, Joel L. ... Fort Lauderdale, FL
Kirschbaum, Joel R. ... Phoenix, AZ
Kirschbaum, Joel R., P.L.C., Law Offices of
Phoenix, AZ
Kirschbaum, Lloyd ... Los Angeles, CA
Kirschbaum, Michael R. ... Santa Ana, CA
Kirschbaum, Myron ... New York, NY
Kirschbaum, Nanney & Brown, P.A.
Charlotte, NC
Hendersonville, NC
Raleigh, NC
Taylorsville, NC
Winston-Salem, NC
Kirschbaum, Ronald I. ... Raleigh, NC
Kirschbaum, Sara Ann ... Brookline, MA
Kirschbaum, Scott D. ... Miami, FL
Kirschbaum, Stephen M. ... Kansas City, KS
Kirschbaum, Thomas A. ... Los Angeles, CA
Kirschbaum, Thomas N. ... Madison, WI
Kirschberg, Morris J. ... San Antonio, TX
Kirschbraun, Keith D. ... Wailuku, HI
Kirschen, Leigh ... New York, NY
Kirschen, Michael B. ... Rochester, NY
Kirschenbaum, Abraham I. ... New York, NY
Kirschenbaum, Alan M. ... Washington, DC
Kirschenbaum, Barbara J. ... Honolulu, HI
Kirschenbaum, Benjamin C. ... New York, NY
Kirschenbaum, Dan G. ... Cleveland, OH
Kirschenbaum, David ... Cleveland, OH
Kirschenbaum, Ellen ... Denver, CO
Kirschenbaum, Ellis B. ... Los Angeles, CA
Kirschenbaum, George ... New York, NY
Kirschenbaum, Irving ... New York, NY
Kirschenbaum, Irwin S. ... Mineola, NY
Kirschenbaum, J. Ari ... Chicago, IL
Kirschenbaum, Jack A. ... Melbourne, FL
Kirschenbaum, Jeffrey B.
San Francisco, CA
Kirschenbaum, Judith A. ... Scarsdale, NY
Kirschenbaum, Kenneth ... Garden City, NY
Kirschenbaum & Kirschenbaum, P.C.
Garden City, NY
Kirschenbaum, Larry H. ... Santa Ana, CA
Kirschenbaum Law Offices, Co., L.P.A.
Cleveland, OH
Kirschenbaum, Liza M. ... Morristown, NJ
Kirschenbaum, Malcolm R.
Melbourne, FL
Kirschenbaum, Peter C. ... New York, NY
Kirschenbaum, Roger A. ... Boca Raton, FL
Atlanta, GA
New York, NY
Kirschenbaum, Samuel ... Garden City, NY
Kirschenbaum, Seth D. ... Atlanta, GA
Kirschenbaum, Sheila R. ... San Diego, CA
Kirschenbaum, Steven A. ... New York, NY
Kirschenbaum, Terry ... Sleepy Hollow, NY
Kirschenmann, Arthur W. ... Yakima, WA
Kirscher, Ralph B. ... Missoula, MT
Kirsch-Goodwin, Lori ... Phoenix, AZ
Kirschler, Jennifer M. ... Pittsburgh, PA
Kirschling, Michael J. ... De Pere, WI
Kirschman, Deborah R. ... Boulder, CO
Kirschman, James L. ... Sacramento, CA
Kirschman, Richard J. ... Des Moines, IA
Kirschman, Robert E., Jr.
Department of Justice, Civil Division, GV
Kirschman, Scott C. ... Cincinnati, OH
Kirschner, Adam S. ... Hillside, NJ
Kirschner, Andrew R. ... Atlanta, GA
Kirschner, Anna Waldorf ... Rhinebeck, NY
Kirschner & Associates ... Marco Island, FL
Kirschner, Barry ... Tucson, AZ
Kirschner, Charles ... New York, NY
Kirschner, Charles G. ... Morro Bay, CA
San Luis Obispo, CA
Kirschner & Cohen ... Great Neck, NY
Kirschner, Daniel S. ... Chicago, IL
Kirschner, David Charles
Federal Communications Commission, Common Carrier Bureau, GV
Kirschner, David J. ... Great Neck, NY
Kirschner, Elyse Garmise ... New York, NY
Kirschner, Eric L. ... Hammond, IN
Kirschner, Eric T. ... Philadelphia, PA
Kirschner, F. Curt, Jr. ... San Francisco, CA
Kirschner & Garland ... Fort Pierce, FL
Kirschner & Gartrell, P.C. ... Washington, DC
Kirschner, Ian M. ... Livingston, NJ
Kirschner, John L. ... Buffalo, NY
Kirschner, Jonathan J. ... Fort Pierce, FL
Kirschner, Jonna D. Kauger
Oklahoma City, OK
Kirschner, Jos. H. ... Woodbury, NY
Kirschner, Kenneth ... New York, NY
Kirschner, Kenneth M. ... Jacksonville, FL
Kirschner Law Firm, The, A Professional Corportation ... Oklahoma City, OK
Kirschner Law Office ... Fargo, ND
Kirschner, Leonard ... Cincinnati, OH
Kirschner, Lisa A. ... Salt Lake City, UT
Kirschner, Lori E. ... Smyrna, GA
Kirschner, Marc S. ... New York, NY
Kirschner, Melissa ... Rochester, MN
Kirschner, Michael B. ... Wall Township, NJ
Kirschner, Michael Paul
Oklahoma City, OK
Kirschner, Mitchell B. ... Boca Raton, FL
Kirschner, Murray ... Miami Beach, FL
Kirschner, Paul D., Inc., P.S.
Bellevue, WA
Bremerton, WA
Gig Harbor, WA
Lynnwood, WA
Seattle, WA
Tacoma, WA
Tukwila, WA
Kirschner, Paul David ... Seattle, WA
Kirschner, Philip ... Kingston, NY
Kirschner, Rhonda G. ... New York, NY
Kirschner, Richard ... Washington, DC
Kirschner, Richard D. ... Belle Mead, NJ
Kirschner, Richard H. ... Los Angeles, CA
Kirschner, S. Jeannette ... Marco Island, FL
Kirschner, Samuel ... New York, NY
Kirschner, Seymour ... Monsey, NY
Kirschner, Steven B. ... Great Neck, NY
Kirschner, Steven C. ... Farmington Hills, MI
Kirschner, Steven J. ... San Francisco, CA
Kirschner, Steven J. ... Winter Park, FL
Kirschner, Steven J. ... Madison, WI
Kirschner and Venker, P.C. ... Atlanta, GA
Kirschner, William ... Fargo, ND
Kirschnik, Daniel P. ... Milwaukee, WI
Kirschnik, James L. ... Milwaukee, WI
Kirschnik, James L., S.C. ... Milwaukee, WI
Kirschstein, David B. ... New York, NY
Kirschstein, Ottinger, Israel & Schiffmiller, P.C. ... New York, NY
Kirschten, Barbara L. ... Washington, DC
Kirschten, Thomas D. ... Carrollton, MS
Kirsh & Berman, Ltd. ... Chicago, IL
Kirsh, Calvin ... Cicero, IL
Kirsh, Ellen M. ... Falls Church, VA
Kirsh, Frank Allen ... Rockville, MD
Kirsh, Jeffrey H. ... New York, NY
Kirsh, Joel D. ... Indianapolis, IN
Kirsh & Kirsh, P.C. ... Indianapolis, IN
Kirsh, Pamela ... Burbank, CA
Kirsh, Peter S. ... Wilmington, DE
Kirsh, Rachel L. ... Parsippany, NJ
New York, NY
Kirsh, S. Martin ... Cleveland, OH
Kirsh, Sanford ... Chicago, IL
Kirsh, Steven M. ... Indianapolis, IN
Kirsh, Trevor F. ... Ocean Township, NJ
Kirshbaum, Barbara ... Minneapolis, MN
Kirshbaum, Daniel R. ... Houston, TX
Kirshbaum, Howard M. ... Denver, CO
Kirshbaum, James J. ... Maple Grove, MN
Kirshbaum, James J., & Associates, P.A.
Maple Grove, MN
Kirshbaum, Jane K. ... Eden Prairie, MN
Kirshbaum & Kirshbaum, Chartered
Minneapolis, MN
Kirshbaum, Marc D. ... Foster City, CA
Kirshbaum, Mitchel I. ... Minneapolis, MN
Kirsheman, Jeffrey W. ... Orlando, FL
Kirshenbaum, Allen M. ... Warwick, RI
Kirshenbaum, David L. ... Chicago, IL
Kirshenbaum, Elizabeth J. ... New York, NY
Kirshenbaum, Evan M. ... Warwick, RI
Kirshenbaum, Isidore ... Sarasota, FL
Kirshenbaum, Karen L. ... New York, NY
Kirshenbaum & Kirshenbaum ... Cranston, RI
Kirshenbaum & Kirshenbaum, PLLC
New York, NY
Kirshenbaum Law Associates
Warwick, RI
Kirshenbaum, Lester M. ... New York, NY
Kirshenbaum, Mark D. ... New York, NY
Kirshenbaum, Sam J. ... Chicago, IL
Kirshenbaum, Scott ... Omaha, NE
Kirshenbaum, Stanley A. ... Pittsburgh, PA
Kirshenbaum, Steven L. ... New York, NY
Kirshenbaum, Stuart M. ... Hewlett, NY
Kirshenbaum, Warren A. ... New York, NY
Kirshenbaum, William B.
North Hollywood, CA
Kirshenberg, Robert J. ... New York, NY
Kirshenberg, Seth David ... Washington, DC
Kirsher, Winston & Boston, Law Corp.
Weed, CA
Mount Shasta, CA
Kirshman, Harris & Branton, A Professional Corporation ... Beverly Hills, CA
Las Vegas, NV
Kirshman, Norman H. ... Beverly Hills, CA
Las Vegas, NV
Kirshner, Charles ... Philadelphia, PA
Pittsburgh, PA
Kirshner, Daniel S. ... East Brunswick, NJ
Kirshner, Daniel S. ... Edison, NJ
Kirshner, Deborah M. ... Cincinnati, OH
Kirshner & Groff ... South Miami, FL
Kirshner, Isabelle ... New York, NY
Kirshner, Jeff ... New York, NY
Kirshner, Jeffrey ... New York, NY
Kirshner, Martin ... Staten Island, NY
Kirshner, Marvin ... New York, NY
Kirshner, Miles A. ... Philadelphia, PA
Pittsburgh, PA
Kirshner, Richard M., (P.A.)
South Miami, FL
Kirshner, Robert A. ... Washington, DC
Kirshner, Ruth D. ... Newark, NJ
Kirshner, Samuel J. ... East Meadow, NY
Kirshner, Sheldon G. ... Chicago, IL
Kirshon, Ilona M. ... New York, NY
Kirshtein, Murray J. S. ... Utica, NY
Kirsner, Bernard M. ... Chicago, IL
Kirsner, Harry ... Miami, FL
Kirsner, John M. ... Columbus, OH
Kirsner, Kenneth M. ... Houston, TX
Kirsner, Kenneth S. ... Lincolnshire, IL
Kirsner, Marvin A. ... Boca Raton, FL
Kirsner, Matthew B. ... Richmond, VA

Kirsner, Melinda H.
Steamboat Springs, CO
Kirsner, M. F. .... Baltimore, MD
Kirsner, Morris .... Boston, MA
Kirsner, William .... Dallas, TX
Kirson, Sarah E. .... Chicago, IL
Kirsons, Mark R. .... Chicago, IL
Kirst, Helga L. .... Lincoln, NE
Kirst, J. Avery" Skip ", Jr. .... Orlando, FL
Kirst, Paul R. .... Las Vegas, NV
Kirst, Robt. F. .... Milwaukee, WI
Kirst, Roger W. .... Lincoln, NE
Kirst, Surges & Wutschel .... Milwaukee, WI
Kirst, Vincent R. .... Irving, TX
Kirste, M. Meredith .... Leesburg, FL
Kirste, Robert L. .... Los Angeles, CA
Kirstein, Allan E. .... New York, NY
Kirstein, David M. .... Washington, DC
Kirstein, Gregory W. .... Worthington, OH
Kirstein, Lillian Fouché .... Plano, TX
Kirstein, Philip L. .... Plainsboro, NJ
Kirstein, Roger D. .... San Antonio, TX
Kirstein, Sidney H. .... Lynchburg, VA
Kirstein-Ezzell, Tina M.
Bullhead City, AZ
Kirsten, Jack B. .... Newark, NJ
Kirt, Kathleen M. .... Nashville, TN
Kirtane, Ammu R. .... San Francisco, CA
Kirtland, John C. .... Washington, DC
Kirtland, Matthew H. .... Washington, DC
Kirtland, Michael A. .... Montgomery, AL
Kirtland & Packard LLP
Los Angeles, CA
Kirtland, Robert A. .... Port Washington, NY
Kirtland, Robert Edward .... Wood Dale, IL
Kirtley, Alan .... Seattle, WA
Kirtley, Clyde .... Washington, DC
Kirtley, Curt L. .... Columbia, MO
Kirtley, David E. .... Indianapolis, IN
Kirtley, Jane E. .... Arlington, VA
Kirtley, John L. .... Milwaukee, WI
Kirtley, John T., III .... Houston, TX
Kirtley, Patricia Ann .... Phoenix, AZ
Kirtley, Raymond M. .... Crawfordsville, IN
Kirtley, Robert M. .... Owensboro, KY
Kirtley, Scott P. .... Tulsa, OK
Kirtley, Susan .... Blairsville, GA
Kirtley, Tom .... Houston, TX
Kirtley, Wesley Williams (Bill)
Portland, OR
Kirtley, William T. .... Sarasota, FL
Kirtley, William T., P.A. .... Sarasota, FL
Kirtner, Jeffrey D. .... Eugene, OR
Kirtner, Rachel A. .... Eugene, OR
Kirtner, Timothy Edmond
Blacksburg, VA
Pulaski, VA
Kirton & McConkie, A Professional Corporation .... Salt Lake City, UT
Kirton, Paul G. .... Department Of The Interior, Office of the Solicitor, GV
Kirton, Wilford W., Jr.
Salt Lake City, UT
Kirts, Kyle Thomas .... Springfield, OH
Kirtz, Harold Edward .... Atlanta, GA
Kirven, Christine Y. .... Santa Cruz, CA
Kirven, Dennis M. .... Buffalo, WY
Kirven, Gerald .... Louisville, KY
Kirven & Kirven, P.C. .... Buffalo, WY
Kirven, Mary Beth .... Arvada, CO
Kirven, Rogers W. .... Florence, SC
Kirven, Steven C. .... Anderson, SC
Kirven, Timothy J. .... Buffalo, WY
Kirven, William J. .... Buffalo, WY
Kirven, William J., III .... Arvada, CO
Kirwan, Adam O. .... Winter Park, FL
Kirwan & Barrett, P.C. .... Bozeman, MT
Helena, MT
Kirwan, Betty-Jane .... Los Angeles, CA
Kirwan, Charles S. .... Providence, RI
Kirwan, Christopher .... Overland Park, KS
Kirwan, Daniel M. .... Mount Vernon, IL
Kirwan, Daniel R. .... San Jose, CA
Kirwan, David P. .... Marathon, FL
Kirwan, David P., P.A. .... Marathon, FL
Kirwan, John F. .... Sandusky, OH
Kirwan, John M. .... Glendale, CA
Kirwan, John R. .... Detroit, MI
Kirwan, John R. .... Midland, TX
Kirwan, Joseph A. .... Louisville, KY
Kirwan, Joseph R. .... Bowling Green, KY
Kirwan, Kathy L. .... Brighton, MA
Kirwan, Martin J. .... Los Angeles, CA
Kirwan, Michael B. .... Jacksonville, FL
Kirwan, P. Bruce, P.C. .... Atlanta, GA
Kirwan, Patrick S. .... Treasury Department, Internal Revenue Service, GV
Kirwan, Peter H. .... San Jose, CA
Kirwan, Peter M. .... Bozeman, MT
Kirwan, R. Dewitt .... Los Angeles, CA
Kirwan, Robert J., II .... Reading, PA
Wyomissing, PA
Kirwan, Susan .... Baltimore, MD
Kirwan, Terry J., Jr. .... Liverpool, NY
Kirwan, Timothy J. .... Oswego, NY
Kirwan, William E. .... Pottsville, PA
Kirwan, William E., P.C. .... Pottsville, PA
Kirwin, Andrew .... New York, NY
Kirwin, Ann C. .... Denver, CO
Kirwin, Brian P. .... Winter Park, FL
Kirwin, Edw. J. .... Columbus, OH
Kirwin, Frederick W. .... Troy, NY
Kirwin, Gerald E. .... North Chili, NY
Kirwin, Gilbert B. .... San Francisco, CA
Kirwin, John Paul, III .... Radnor, PA
Kirwin, Kenneth F. .... St. Paul, MN
Kirwin, Martha A. .... New York, NY
Kirwin, Melanie J. .... Baltimore, MD
Kirwin, Michael J. .... McLean, VA
Kirwin, P. Mark .... Santa Barbara, CA
Kirwin, Phyllis J. .... Fridley, MN
Kirwin, Phyllis J., P.A. .... Fridley, MN
Kirwin, Stanley I. .... Ossining, NY
Kirwin, Stanley I., P.C. .... Ossining, NY
Kirzner, Jeffrey B. .... Irvine, CA
Kirzner, Leonard .... Dallas, TX
Kisailus, Clement E. .... Wilkes-Barre, PA
Kisailus, Veronica S. .... Wilkes-Barre, PA
Kisak, Kathryn J. .... Erie, PA
Kisan, Peter J. .... North Jackson, OH
Kisatsky, Michele .... Cleveland, OH
Kisch, Lori B. .... Baltimore, MD
Kisch, Raymond R. .... Bloomington, IL
Kisch, Rhona J. .... New York, NY
Kisch, Victor J. .... Portland, OR
Kisch, Wendy J. .... Department of Labor, Office of Secretary, GV
Kiscoan, Patricia O'Leary
Minneapolis, MN
Kise, Christopher M. .... Miami, FL
Tampa, FL
Kise, Christopher M., P.A. .... Tampa, FL
Kiselik, Robert I. .... La Fayette, GA
Kiselstein, Bruce, Law Offices of
Mount Prospect, IL
Kiser, Alfred C. .... Boise, ID
Kiser, B. Kelly .... Washington, DC
Kiser, Charles A. .... Martinsburg, WV
Kiser, Cherie R. .... Washington, DC
Kiser, Coy M., Jr. .... Waynesboro, VA
Kiser, Estella Christie .... Chicago, IL
Kiser, Eugene R. .... Atlanta, GA
Kiser, Eugene R., P.C. .... Atlanta, GA
Kiser, George A. .... St. Louis, MO
Kiser, Gerald .... Liberty, MO
Kiser, J. Kevin .... Truth or Consequences, NM
Kiser, Jack D. .... Lexington, KY
Kiser, Jackson L. .... Danville, VA
Kiser, James L. .... Charlotte, NC
Kiser, Jennifer R. .... Atlanta, GA
Kiser, Jerry A. .... Boise, ID
Kiser, John Daniel .... Washington, DC
Kiser, John Lee .... Louisville, KY
Kiser, Jon A. .... Piedmont, MO
Kiser, J. W. .... Charlotte, NC
Kiser, Lawrence L. .... Los Angeles, CA
Kiser, Lisa L. .... Rapid City, SD
Kiser, Loren .... San Diego, CA
Kiser, Meryl G. .... Shepherdstown, WV
Kiser, Robert L. .... Atlanta, GA
Kiser, Robert L., P.C. .... Atlanta, GA
Kiser, S. Curtis .... St. Petersburg, FL
Tallahassee, FL
Kiser, Samuel C. .... Amarillo, TX
Kiser, Steven C. .... Newport Beach, CA
Kiser, Steven C. .... Midland, TX
Kiser, Terry B. .... Phoenix, AZ
Kiser, Thomas J. .... Chicago, IL
Kiser, Timothy Braden .... Philadelphia, PA
Kiser, W. David .... Louisville, KY
Kiser, W. John .... Lexington, KY
Kiser, Wendell J. .... Orlando, FL
Kiser, William Russell .... Wise, VA
Kiser, Wm. Don .... Oklahoma City, OK
Kish, Adam Christopher .... York, PA
Kish, Imelda A.
Small Business Administration, Office of the General Counsel, GV
Kish, John J. .... Indianapolis, IN
Kish, John M. .... Pittsburgh, PA
Kish, Joseph Louis .... San Francisco, CA
Kish, Keri A. .... Garden City, KS
Kish, Kish & Yarsky .... Pittsburgh, PA
Kish, Lawrence J. .... Lansing, MI
Kish, Lynn .... Lake City, FL
Kish, Matthew S. .... Hanford, CA
Kish, Paul S. .... Atlanta, GA
Kish, Robert L. .... Point Richmond, CA
Kish, Stephanie E. .... San Diego, CA
Kish, Timothy E. .... Miami, FL
Kish, William J. .... Canfield, OH
Kishbaugh, J. Eric .... Gibbsboro, NJ
Kishbaugh, Richard D. .... Lower Gwynedd, PA
Kishbaugh, Troy A. .... Orlando, FL
Kishel, Gregory F. .... St. Paul, MN
Kishel, Joseph F. .... New York, NY
Kishel, Lori-Ann .... Paramus, NJ
Kishel, MaryJo .... Wilkes-Barre, PA
Kishi, Arlene S. .... Honolulu, HI
Kishi, Satoko .... San Francisco, CA
Kishida, Yasuhiro .... Canton, MI
Kishimoto, Diane S., (A Law Corporation)
Honolulu, HI
Kishish, Christ J., II .... Minneapolis, MN
Kishmir, Anne Greer .... Department of Justice, Executive Office for Immigration Review, GV
Kishner, Bryan W. .... New York, NY
Kishner, Irwin .... Las Vegas, NV
Kishner, Irwin A. .... New York, NY
Kishner, Joanna S. .... Burbank, CA
Kishore, Rahul .... Rockville, MD
Kisicki, Mark G. .... Phoenix, AZ
Kisicki, Ronald J. .... Rochester, NY
Kisil, Jaroslaw B. .... Sterling Heights, MI
Kisilinsky, Maxine S. .... Pittsburgh, PA
Kisio, James D. .... Orlando, FL
Kiska, Aileen M. .... Detroit, MI
Kiskaddon, Walter .... New York, NY
Kiske, Anne V. .... Jackson, MO
Kisken, Peter B. .... La Crosse, WI
Kisken, Sybil R. .... Washington, DC
Kisker, Mark A. .... Lincoln, NE
Kiskis, Nancy M. .... Minneapolis, MN
Kiskunas, George L. .... Janesville, WI
Kisliak, John .... Bridgeport, CT
Kislik, Andrew R. .... Palo Alto, CA
Kislik, Pauline Lybeck .... Hewlett, NY
Kislin, Scott A. .... New York, NY
Kisling, Dale W. .... Pocatello, ID
Kisling, Gary W. .... Akron, OH
Kisling, Stephen C. .... Cincinnati, OH
Kislinger, Edward B. .... Santa Monica, CA
Kisloff, Michelle Anne .... New York, NY
Kisluk, Bret S. .... Houston, TX
Kisluk, Dick .... Albuquerque, NM
Kisluk, Eileen W. .... Houston, TX
Kisner, Ashley Thomas .... Dallas, TX
Kisner, Daniel R. .... Newark, CA
Kisner, David W. .... Oklahoma City, OK
Kisner, Gary P. .... New Hope, PA
Kisner, John J., Jr. .... Wichita, KS
Kisner, Keith E. .... Austin, TX
Kisner, Ronald H. .... New York, NY
Kisor, Geoffrey T. .... Columbus, OH
Kisor, Hazel Theresa Rankin .... Anniston, AL
Kisor, M. Joseph .... Lawrenceburg, IN
Kisor, Valerie T. .... Birmingham, AL
Kispert, Dennis K. .... St. Paul, MN
Kispert, Jennifer A. .... Cambridge, MA
Kisro, Philip Lee .... Spokane, WA
Kiss, A. Katharine Jacob
Treasury Department, Internal Revenue Service, GV
Kiss, Benjamin .... Los Angeles, CA
Kiss, Carl G. .... Portland, OR
Kiss & Doherty, Ltd., P.C.
Carpentersville, IL
Kiss, James M. .... Carpentersville, IL
Kiss, Richard G. .... San Francisco, CA
Kiss, Robert S. .... Beckley, WV
Kissam, Luther C., IV .... St. Louis, MO
Kissam, Philip C. .... Lawrence, KS
Kissam, Roger H. .... Stamford, CT
Kissane Associates .... St. Albans, VT
Kissane & Cook, A Professional Corporation
Del Mar, CA
Kissane, Daniel J. .... Miami, FL
Kissane, Dennis P. .... Pittsburgh, PA
Kissane, Gene P. .... Miami, FL
Kissane, H. Franklin .... Los Angeles, CA
Kissane, Jean C. .... Baltimore, MD
Kissane, John G. .... New York, NY
Kissane, John G. .... St. Albans, VT
Kissane, John J. .... Murray Hill, NJ
Kissane, Joseph T. .... Jacksonville, FL
Kissane, Mary E. .... New York, NY
Kissane, Matthew T. .... Del Mar, CA
Kissane, Thomas A. .... New York, NY
Kissee, Larry Dean .... Ash Flat, AR
Kissee-Sandoval, Catherine J.
Los Angeles, CA
Kissel, Benedetta A. .... Treasury Department, Internal Revenue Service, GV
Kissel, Elena T. .... New York, NY
Kissel, James E. .... Knoxville, TN
Kissel, James W. .... Chicago, IL
Kissel, John A. .... Enfield, CT
Kissel, Jonathan J. .... Tarzana, CA
Kissel, Larry E. .... Cincinnati, OH
Kissel, Lester .... New York, NY
Kissel, Marc I. .... Ramsey, NJ
Kissel, Neal H. .... Stamford, CT
Kissel, Pamela A. .... Huntsville, TN
Kissel, Paul .... San Diego, CA
Kissel & Pesce .... Maplewood, NJ
New York, NY
Kissel, Peter C. .... Washington, DC
Kissel, Richard A. .... New York, NY
Kissel, Richard J. .... Chicago, IL
Kissel, Richard O., II .... Indianapolis, IN
Kissel, Robert M. .... Pleasant Hill, CA
Kissel, Sarah E. .... Madison, WI
Kissel, Stephen F. .... New York, NY
Kissel, Thomas L. .... Hartford, WI
Kissell, Bernard F. .... Memphis, TN
Kissell, David C. .... Tarzana, CA
Kissell Massucco & Marchica, P.C.
Bellows Falls, VT
Kissell, Susan J. .... Woodbury, NY
Kisseloff, Alan S. .... New York, NY
Kisseloff, Andrew .... Norwood, MA
Kisseloff, Samuel J. .... New York, NY
Kissh, John A., Jr. .... Findlay, OH
Kissiah & Associates .... Atlanta, GA
Kissiah, Gary F. .... Austin, TX
Kissiah, Richard C. .... Atlanta, GA
Kissick, Ralph L. .... Washington, DC
Kissin, Barry J. C. .... Frederick, MD
Kissin, Gary .... New York, NY
Kissin, Robin L. .... Quogue, NY
Kissinger, Ashley I. .... Washington, DC
Kissinger, Clyde M.
St. Petersburg Beach, FL
Kissinger, Curtis E. .... Cincinnati, OH
Kissinger, Donald T. .... Harrisburg, PA
Kissinger & Fellman, P.C. .... Denver, CO
Kissinger, Leslie Ann Ellis .... Claremore, OK
Kissinger, Richard P. .... Denver, CO
Kissinger, Ronald E. .... Marshfield, WI
Kissinger, Scott V. .... Basking Ridge, NJ
Kissinger, Thomas F. .... Milwaukee, WI
Kissinger, Wes A. .... Greenville, SC
Kissinger, William .... Youngstown, OH
Kissinger, William A. .... Milwaukee, WI
Kissinger, William D. .... Department of State, Office of the Legal Adviser, GV
Kisslan, Donald J. .... Davie, FL
Kissler, Tracy S. .... Bethesda, MD
Kissling, Alice J. .... Madison, WI
Kisslinger, Paul W. .... Washington, DC
Philadelphia, PA
Kissner, Barbara E. .... Ketchikan, AK
Kissner, Leo A. .... Houston, TX
Kissner & Sandvig, P.C. .... Houston, TX
Kissner, Todd A. .... Houston, TX
Kissoon, Clugg, Linder & Dittberner, Ltd.
Edina, MN
Kissoon, K. Worner .... Edina, MN
Kist, Dennis A., & Associates
Las Vegas, NV
Kist, Nancy A. .... Bayonne, NJ
Kistenbroker, David H. .... Chicago, IL
Kister, Robert G. .... Festus, MO
Kister, Susan .... St. Louis, MO
Kister, Thomas H. .... Milwaukee, WI
Kistin, Babitsky, Latimer & Beitman
Falmouth, MA
Kistler, Bernard F., Jr. .... Atlanta, GA
Kistler, Bradford E. .... Lincoln, NE
Kistler, Daniel Rives .... Salem, OR
Kistler, Dennis A. .... Pittsburgh, PA
Kistler, Harlan B. .... Riverside, CA
Kistler, Helen M. .... Pittsburgh, PA
Kistler, John M. .... Anna Maria, FL
Kistler, Joseph S. .... Las Vegas, NV
Kistler, Judson C. .... Lancaster, OH
Kistler, K. Page .... Boston, MA
Kistler, Robert K. .... Bellefonte, PA
State College, PA
Kistler, Sara L. .... Tampa, FL
Kistler, Stephen R. .... Stillwater, OK
Kistler, Thomas King .... Bellefonte, PA
Kistler & Welch .... Stillwater, OK
Kistler, Wm. F. .... Encino, CA
Kistner, Denise E. .... Fort Lauderdale, FL
Kistner, Denise E., P.A.
Fort Lauderdale, FL
Kistner, Elkin L. .... St. Louis, MO
Kistner, Leo M. .... Warren, MI
Kistner, Mark S. .... Warren, MI
Kistner, Michael J. .... Poughkeepsie, NY
Kistner & Troyanovich, P.C. .... Detroit, MI
Mount Clemens, MI
Pontiac, MI
Warren, MI
Kistner, Wayne T. .... Long Beach, CA
Kiszkiel, Stanley .... Miami, FL
Kit, Gordon .... Washington, DC
Kita, Christopher W. .... Lowell, MA
Kita, George .... Chicago, IL
Kita, George I. .... Los Angeles, CA
Kita, Gerald K. .... Wilmington, DE
Kita, Stanley B. .... Spring House, PA
Kita, William J. .... Buffalo, NY
Kitabayashi, Mark K. .... Los Angeles, CA
Kitaeff, Jeffrey A. .... North Andover, MA
Kitaeff, Jeffrey A., P.C. .... North Andover, MA
Kitagawa, Audrey E. .... Honolulu, HI
Kitagawa, Dawn T. .... Pasadena, CA
Kitagawa & Ebert, P.C. .... Irvine, CA
Kitagawa, Lisa M. .... Irvine, CA
Kitain, Barry H. .... Philadelphia, PA
Kitamura, Henry N. .... Honolulu, HI
Kitano, Gerald K. .... Los Angeles, CA
Kitano, Judith T. .... Los Angeles, CA
Kitaoka, Takashi .... Honolulu, HI
Kitasaki, Christopher K. .... Oxnard, CA
Kitay, Cynthia .... New York, NY
Kitay, Deborah S. .... Atlanta, GA
Kitay, Evelyn G.
Department of Transportation, Surface Transportation Board, GV
Kitay, Harvey R. .... New York, NY
Kitay, Howard Alan .... El Cajon, CA
Kitay, Michael G.
Agency for International Development, Office of the General Counsel, GV
Kitay, Theresa L. .... Atlanta, GA
Kitay, William D. .... New York, NY
Kitch, Alison .... Lexington, VA
Kitch Drutchas Wagner DeNardis & Valitutti, A Professional Corporation
Ann Arbor, MI
Detroit, MI
Grand Rapids, MI
Lansing, MI
Marquette, MI
Mount Clemens, MI
Toledo, OH
Kitch, Edmund W. .... Charlottesville, VA
Kitch, James C. .... Palo Alto, CA
Kitch, John D. .... Nashville, TN
Kitch, Marsha A. .... Denver, CO
Kitch, Michelle F. .... Grand Rapids, MI
Kitch, Paul R. .... Chicago, IL
Kitch, Richard A. .... Detroit, MI
Lansing, MI
Kitch, Thomas D. .... Wichita, KS
Kitchak, Peter R. .... Minneapolis, MN
Kitchel, Chris .... Portland, OR
Kitchel, Jan K. .... Portland, OR
Kitchel, M. Crane .... Santa Rosa, CA
Kitchel, Woodrow W. .... Oakland, CA
Kitchell, Alexandra Barbara .... Houston, TX
Kitchell, David W. .... Seattle, WA
Kitchell, Frank R. .... Seattle, WA
Kitchell & Hively, P.L.L.C. .... Seattle, WA
Kitchell, Marjorie H. .... Cleveland, OH
Kitchen, Alison M. .... Westerville, OH
Kitchen, Anne L. .... Grand Rapids, MI
Kitchen, Charles W. .... Cleveland, OH
Kitchen, David S. .... Los Angeles, CA
Kitchen, Dean W. .... Baltimore, MD
Kitchen, Denis A. .... Williamsville, NY
Kitchen, Donald R. .... Anchorage, AK
Kitchen, E. C. Deeno .... Tallahassee, FL
Kitchen, Eric C. .... Santa Barbara, CA
Kitchen, Erik L. .... Washington, DC
Kitchen, F. Damon .... Jacksonville, FL
Tampa, FL
Kitchen, George T. T., III .... Louisville, KY

Kitchen, Gerald J. ... Monterey, CA
Kitchen, Heather L. ... Poughkeepsie, NY
Kitchen, J. Denny ... Circleville, OH
Kitchen, John D. ... New Orleans, LA
Kitchen, John M. ... Indianapolis, IN
Kitchen, John S. ... Laconia, NH
Manchester, NH
Kitchen, Jonathan S. ... San Francisco, CA
Kitchen, Judkins, Simpson & High
Tallahassee, FL
Kitchen, Katherine G. ... Louisville, KY
Kitchen, Kim Louise ... Colorado Springs, CO
Kitchen & Kitchen ... Toledo, OH
Kitchen, Leonard K. ... Dexter, MI
Kitchen, Louann ... Pasadena, CA
Kitchen, Margaret Applegate ... Toledo, OH
Kitchen, Marlo A. ... Toledo, OH
Kitchen, Michael J. ... Louisville, KY
Kitchen, R. David
Department of State, GV
Kitchen, Roslyn J. ... Milwaukee, WI
Kitchen, Sandra Siel ... Powell, WY
Kitchen, Sara ... Philadelphia, PA
Kitchen, S.C. ... Graham, NC
Kitchen, Stephen E. ... Fairfax, VA
Kitchen & Thornton-Green ... Paducah, KY
Kitchen, Tim L. ... Santa Clara, CA
Kitchen and Turpin ... Santa Barbara, CA
Kitchen, Wallace Anthony ... Columbus, GA
Kitchen, William A., Jr. ... Paducah, KY
Kitchen, William Anthony, III ... Paducah, KY
Kitchenoff, Robert S. ... Philadelphia, PA
Kitchens, Benton, Kitchens & Warren, A Professional Law Corporation
Minden, LA
Kitchens, David B. ... Atlanta, GA
Kitchens, Dean J. ... Los Angeles, CA
Kitchens, Elizabeth ... Salt Lake City, UT
Kitchens & Ellis ... Jackson, MS
Pascagoula, MS
Kitchens, Fred B., Jr. ... Atlanta, GA
Kitchens, Graydon K., III ... Minden, LA
Kitchens, Graydon K., Jr. ... Minden, LA
Kitchens, James W. ... Jackson, MS
Kitchens, Joyce E. ... Atlanta, GA
Kitchens Kelley Gaynes, P.C. ... Atlanta, GA
Kitchens, Lynne B. ... Montgomery, AL
Kitchens, Michael W. ... Atlanta, GA
Kitchens, Oliver ... Roanoke, AL
Kitchens, Oliver, P.C. ... Alexander City, AL
Ashland, AL
Lafayette, AL
Roanoke, AL
Kitchens, Paul E. ... Minden, LA
Kitchens, Richard E. ... Concord, CA
Kitchens, Thomas L. ... Ventura, CA
Kitchens, Travis E., Jr ... Groveton, TX
Kitchens, Wayne ... Houston, TX
Kitchens, William H. ... Atlanta, GA
Kitchens, William H. ... Valdosta, GA
Kitchens, William H., Jr. ... Atlanta, GA
Kitchens, Wolfson, Smith & Hannan, P.C.
Valdosta, GA
Kitchin, Charles D. ... St. Louis, MO
Kitchin, Henry L. ... Hamlet, NC
Rockingham, NC
Kitchin, Henry L., Jr. ... Greensboro, NC
Kitchin, John J. ... Overland Park, KS
Kansas City, MO
Kitchin, Lee C. ... Norfolk, VA
Kitchin, Neal, Webb, Webb & Futrell, P.A.
Hamlet, NC
Rockingham, NC
Kitchin, Patrick R. ... San Francisco, CA
Kitchin, Richard K. ... Omaha, NE
Kitchin, W. Walton, Jr. ... Greenville, NC
Kitchin, William I. ... Pylesville, MD
Kitching, Dale E. ... Salt Lake City, UT
Kitchings, A. Langley ... Atlanta, GA
Kitchings, Alton D. ... Savannah, GA
Kitchings, Atley A., Jr. ... Montgomery, AL
Kitchings & Potter, LLC ... Old Lyme, CT
Kitchings, Suzanne Donnelly
Old Lyme, CT
Kitchner, Carl L. ... Port Charlotte, FL
Kite, Aaron L. ... Wichita, KS
Kite, Christopher M. ... Roanoke, VA
Kite & Day, L.L.P. ... St. Francis, KS
Kite, Donald B., Sr. ... Indianapolis, IN
Kite, Harvey T. ... Clinton, TN
Kite, J. Greg ... Wichita, KS
Kite, Jerry D. ... Oklahoma City, OK
Kite, John C. ... Terre Haute, IN
Kite, John G. ... St. Francis, KS
Kite, Kevin L. ... Burlington, VT
Kite, M. Leslie ... Chicago, IL
Kite, Marilyn S., (P.C.) ... Jackson, WY
Kite, Matthew McD. ... Cincinnati, OH
Kite, M. Leslie, & Associates, P.C.
Chicago, IL
Kite, Richard L. ... Beverly Hills, CA
Kite, Sherwin B. ... Wilmette, IL
Kite, Steven B. ... Chicago, IL
Kite, William McD. ... Cincinnati, OH
Kitei, Sol H. ... Philadelphia, PA
Kitelinger, James C. ... Saukville, WI
Kite-Powell, Julia B. ... Tampa, FL
Kite-Powell, Stephen M. ... Memphis, TN
Kitey, Alan S. ... Washington, DC
Kithas, John A. ... San Francisco, CA
Kithcart, David E. ... Harlingen, TX
Kitlas, Ronald A. ... Pottstown, PA
Kitler, Charlotte ... Jersey City, NJ
Kitley, Gloria Jean ... Beech Grove, IN
Kitley, John A. ... Beech Grove, IN
Kitley, John A., Jr. ... Beech Grove, IN
Kitley Professional Corporation
Beech Grove, IN

Kitlowski, Aaron ... New York, NY
Kitman, Jamie L. ... Palisades, NY
Kitman, Sandra L. ... Pittsburgh, PA
Kitner, David N., (P.C.) ... Dallas, TX
Kitograd, Sheldon M. ... Hauppauge, NY
Kitowski, C. T. ... Michigan City, IN
Kitrick, Mark, Co., L.P.A.
Cincinnati, OH
Cleveland, OH
Columbus, OH
Kitrick, Mark G. ... Brick, NJ
Kitrick, Mark M. ... Cincinnati, OH
Columbus, OH
Kitsilis, Peter T. ... Quincy, MA
Kitsis, Michael D. ... New York, NY
Kitslaar, Elizabeth Clough ... Chicago, IL
Kitsmiller, Robert A. ... Denver, CO
Kitson, Donald ... Riverhead, NY
Kitsoulis, Michael T. ... Rockville, MD
Kitsuse, Mari L. ... Campbell, CA
Kitt, Cheryl Fridkin ... Columbia, MD
Kitt, Doniel ... Hartford, CT
Kitt, F. Theodore ... San Francisco, CA
Kitt, Jennifer ... San Francisco, CA
Kitt, Kyle R. ... Hammond, LA
Kitt, Stacy ... Albany, NY
Kitta, John N. ... Fremont, CA
Kittaka, Mark S. ... Fort Wayne, IN
Kittay, David R. ... New York, NY
White Plains, NY
Kittay, Gold & Gershfeld, P.C.
New York, NY
White Plains, NY
Kittel, Janet MacKenzie ... Littleton, CO
Kittel, John I. ... Detroit, MI
Kittel, Peggy C. ... Lawrence, KS
Kittel, Robert N. ... Department of the Army, U.S. Army Legal Services Agency, GV
Kittel, Robert P. ... St. Paul, MN
Kittell, Christopher ... Tillamook, OR
Kittell, William C. ... Burlington, VT
Kittelsen, Barry, Ross, Wellington and Thompson ... Albany, WI
Monroe, WI
Monticello, WI
Kittelsen, Jennifer ... Minneapolis, MN
Kittelsen, Rodney O. ... Albany, WI
Monroe, WI
Kittelson, Douglas C. ... Dallas, TX
Kitterman, Gregory S. ... Little Rock, AR
Kitterman, John S. ... Little Rock, AR
Kitterman, Karen A. ... Palo Alto, CA
Kittinger, Bonnie Campbell ... Lexington, KY
Kittle, Cary M. ... New York, NY
Kittle, Cynthia Bell ... Santa Ana, CA
Kittle, Jay S. ... Tucson, AZ
Kittle, Jim, Jr. ... Indianapolis, IN
Kittle, Joseph P. ... Phoenix, AZ
Kittle, Lois Ann Spencer ... San Jose, CA
Kittle, Ralph W. ... Washington, DC
Kittle, Rita Byrnes ... Denver, CO
Kittle-Kamp, Thomas L. ... Chicago, IL
Kittleman, C. Wesley ... McAllen, TX
Kittleman, Steven C. ... Syracuse, NY
Kittleman, Thomas, Ramirez & Gonzales, PLLC ... McAllen, TX
Kittleman, Trent M. ... Washington, DC
Kittler, J. Patrick ... Maple Plain, MN
Kittles, James R. ... Athens, TX
Kittleson, Gary A. ... Boise, ID
Kittleson, Henry M. ... Lakeland, FL
Kittleson, John W. ... Irvine, CA
Kittleson, Marilyn G. ... Sonoma, CA
Kittleson, Nicholas J. ... Anchorage, AK
Kittner, David ... Philadelphia, PA
Kittner, Jo Hambrick ... Richmond, VA
Kittner, Joseph M. ... Chevy Chase, MD
Kittner, Marc R. ... Seattle, WA
Kittner, Nathan ... Hackensack, NJ
Kitto, Joanna C. ... Chicago, IL
Kitto Law Offices, S.C. ... Beloit, WI
Kitto, Richard C. J. ... Princeton, NJ
Kitto, Suzanne E. ... Beloit, WI
Kitton, Cheryl H. ... East Meadow, NY
Kittredge, Amelia C. ... Philadelphia, PA
Kittredge, C. Mark ... Phoenix, AZ
Kittredge, Charlene ... Chicago, IL
Kittredge, David N. ... New York, NY
Kittredge, Donley, Elson, Fullem & Embick, LLP ... Philadelphia, PA
Kittredge, Francis I., Jr. ... Bangor, ME
Kittredge, Geoffrey ... New York, NY
Kittredge, John W. ... Greenville, SC
Kittredge, Joseph B., Jr. ... Boston, MA
Kittredge, Joseph P. ... Needham, MA
Kittredge, Patrick W. ... Philadelphia, PA
Kittredge, Paul E., Jr. ... Sioux City, IA
Kittredge, Rachel L. ... Avon, CT
Kittredge, Robert B.
Cumberland Foreside, ME
Kittredge, Ronald E. ... Hamden, CT
Kittredge, Thomas M. ... Philadelphia, PA
Kittredge, Wm. J. ... Hudson, MA
Kittrell, B. Bruce ... Torrance, CA
Kittrell, B. Bruce, P.C., Law Offices of
Torrance, CA
Kittrell, Braxton L., Jr. ... Mobile, AL
Kittrell, C. Jerome ... Meridian, MS
Kittrell, Charles A. ... Costa Mesa, CA
Kittrell, Gary A. ... New York, NY
Kittrell, H. Tom ... Nashville, TN
Kittrell, Haldon J. ... Columbia, MS
Kittrell, Harris Tom, Jr. ... Nashville, TN
Kittrell, Jodi F. ... New York, NY
Kittrell, Pamela R. ... Sunrise, FL
Kittrell, Richard J. ... New York, NY
Kittrell, Robert G., Jr. ... Henderson, NC
Kittrell, Rosemary ... Atlanta, GA

Kittrell, Steven D. ... Washington, DC
Kittrell, Thrower & Kittrell ... Nashville, TN
Kittrell, W. Bradford ... Birmingham, AL
Kittridge, Patrick A. ... St. Paul, MN
Kittrie, Nicholas N. ... Washington, DC
Kittrie, Orde F. ... Department of State, Office of the Legal Adviser, GV
Kitts, H. Douglas ... Knoxville, TN
Kitts, Lois A. ... Pikeville, KY
Kitts, Monica Chin ... Washington, DC
Kittsley, James F. ... New York, NY
Kitty, Raymond ... Delray Beach, FL
Kitty, Steven H. ... Doylestown, PA
Kitz, Linda F. ... Morristown, NJ
Kitzen, Charles L.B. ... Yonkers, NY
Kitzes, Orin R. ... Jamaica, NY
Kitzes, Stephanie K. ... Irvine, CA
Kitzi, Kim ... Santa Ana, CA
Kitzinger, Kirk R. ... Indianapolis, IN
Kitzinger, Stanley A. ... Chicago, IL
Kitzinger, Stephen ... New York, NY
Kitzler, David L. ... Mansfield, OH
Kitzler, Patricia O'Donnell ... Mansfield, OH
Kitzman, Eleanor L. ... Winston-Salem, NC
Kitzman, Oliver S. ... Brookshire, TX
Kitzman, Tracey L. ... New York, NY
Kitzmann, John H. ... Charlottesville, VA
Kitzmann, Stuart J. ... Detroit Lakes, MN
Kitzmiller, Ann E. ... Houston, TX
Kitzmiller, Ellen ... Salt Lake City, UT
Kitzmiller, Howard L. ... Washington, DC
Kivel, Franklin Jay ... Oklahoma City, OK
Kivel, Scott N., Law Offices of
Santa Rosa, CA
Kivela, Larry E. ... Scottville, MI
Kivela, Leo E. ... Hinsdale, IL
Kivell, Gary B. ... League City, TX
Kivell, Rayment and Francis, A Professional Corporation ... Tulsa, OK
Kivell, Sheldon ... Philadelphia, PA
Kivell, Thomas D. ... Tulsa, OK
Kivell, Thomas T. ... Grand Rapids, MI
Kivett, Charles H. ... New York, NY
Kivett, Donna S. ... Greenville, SC
Kivett, Gary B. ... Spruce Pine, NC
Kivett, Joseph L. ... Indianapolis, IN
Kivett, Knickrehm & Woolley
Omaha, NE
Kivett, Lisa Renee ... Dallas, TX
Kivett, Michael F. ... Omaha, NE
Kivi, James ... Montezuma, IA
Kiviat, Theodore B. ... Los Angeles, CA
Kivimaki, Mary Laue ... St. Paul, MN
Kivinski, Margaret A. ... Fullerton, CA
Kivisaari, Peter J. W. ... Norway, MI
Kivisaari & Slagle, P.C. ... Norway, MI
Kivisto, J.K. ... Lake Worth, FL
Kivisto Law Firm ... Lake Worth, FL
Kivitz, Bebe H. ... Philadelphia, PA
Kivitz, Jay E. ... Philadelphia, PA
Kivitz & Kivitz, P.C. ... Philadelphia, PA
Kivitz, Larry P. ... East Greenbush, NY
Kivitz, Leslie E. ... Waltham, MA
Kivitz, Linda B. ... Penn Valley, PA
Kivitz & Liptz, LLC ... Washington, DC
Chevy Chase, MD
Kivitz, Marc R. ... Baltimore, MD
Kivitz, Marc R. ... Columbia, MD
Kivitz, Murray A. ... Chevy Chase, MD
Kivitz, Seymour ... Philadelphia, PA
Kivlahan, Thomas W.
Arlington Heights, IL
Kivler, Russell T. ... Trenton, NJ
Kivlin, B. Noël ... Austin, TX
Kivlin, Joseph T., Jr. ... Washington, DC
Kivo, Robert J. ... Bellflower, CA
Kivo, Steven A. ... Woodland Hills, CA
Kiwaiko, Suzanne ... Rockford, IL
Kiwala, Mary Ann ... Louisville, KY
Kiwala, Terrence E. ... Chicago, IL
Kiwan, John G. ... San Diego, CA
Kixmiller, Robert V. ... Indianapolis, IN
Ki Ying Ng, Rita ... New York, NY
Kiyohara, Glen Toshio ... Downey, CA
Kiyonaga, David J. ... Alexandria, VA
Kiyonaga, John C. ... Alexandria, VA
Kiyonaga & Kiyonaga ... Alexandria, VA
Kiyuna, Gary K. ... Nyssa, OR
Ontario, OR
Kizel, Paul ... Roseland, NJ
Kizer and Black ... Maryville, TN
Kizer, Bonds & Hughes ... Milan, TN
Kizer, Cheryl R. ... Knoxville, TN
Kizer & Clarke ... Knoxville, TN
Kizer, David Allen
South San Francisco, CA
Kizer, Edward A. ... Memphis, TN
Kizer, Hood & Morgan, L.L.P.
Baton Rouge, LA
Kizer, Jean E. ... Anchorage, AK
Kizer, Jerry D., Jr. ... Jackson, TN
Kizer, John F., Jr. ... Birmingham, AL
Kizer, John F., Jr., L.L.C. ... Birmingham, AL
Kizer, John H. ... Kansas City, MO
Springfield, MO
Kizer, John O. ... Charleston, WV
Kizer, Keith E. ... Las Vegas, NV
Kizer, Maxie G. ... Pine Bluff, AR
Kizer, Maxie G., P.A. ... Pine Bluff, AR
Kizer & Neu ... Bremen, IN
Plymouth, IN
Kizer, Robert D. ... Austin, TX
Kizer, Robert D. ... Manor, TX
Kizer, Roland C., Jr., (Ltd., A Law Corporation) ... Baton Rouge, LA
Kizer, Scott A. ... Orlando, FL
Kizer, Thomas J., Jr. ... Howell, MI
Kizer, W. Morris ... Knoxville, TN

Kizer, Wade A. ... Richmond, VA
Kiziah, Brent D. ... Chapel Hill, NC
Kiziah, Trent S. ... West Palm Beach, FL
Kizis, Lynne M. ... Woodbridge, NJ
Kizma, Richard A. ... Westerville, OH
Kizner, Gail Ann ... New York, NY
Kizner, Mitchell H. ... Cherry Hill, NJ
Vineland, NJ
Kizzia, D. Bradley ... Dallas, TX
Kizziah, Larry David ... Birmingham, AL
Kizziar, James H., Jr. ... San Antonio, TX
Kjar, James J. ... Manhattan Beach, CA
Kjar, James O. ... Warsaw, MO
Kjar, Todd ... Salt Lake City, UT
Kjeldgaard, Richard H. ... Washington, DC
Kjeldsen, J. Rayner ... Winnemucca, NV
Kjelland, Kurt M. ... La Jolla, CA
Kjellberg, Craig Brian ... Creve Coeur, MO
Kjellberg, Thomas ... New York, NY
Kjellenberg, Evan M. ... Chicago, IL
Kjellgren, Bengt H. ... New York, NY
Kjellgren, Dana H. ... Flagstaff, AZ
Kjelmyr, John P. ... Denver, CO
Kjerulff, Holly Blair ... Seattle, WA
Kjolhede, Katherine ... Dearborn, MI
Kjorlie, Eric ... Topeka, KS
Kjorvestad, Steven R. ... San Bernardino, CA
Kjos, Andrew B. ... Palo Alto, CA
Kjos, Victoria ... Phoenix, AZ
K.K.M., P.A. ... Bethesda, MD
Klaas, B. Gregory ... Denver, CO
Klaas, Bruce G. ... Denver, CO
Klaas, Deborah Ellen ... Wheaton, IL
Klaas, Heather J. ... Minneapolis, MN
Klaas, Law, O'Meara & Malkin, P.C.
Denver, CO
Klaas, Paul B. ... Minneapolis, MN
Klaasen, Terry J. ... Jackson, MI
Klaasesz, Peter E. ... Buffalo, NY
Klaassen, David R. ... Marquette, KS
Klaassen, Leslie ... Richardson, TX
Klaassen, Mark ... Washington, DC
Klabacha, Barbara C. ... Chicago, IL
Klaben, Amy D. ... Columbus, OH
Klaben, Matthew J. ... Cleveland, OH
Klaber, Andrew B. ... Philadelphia, PA
Klaber, David G. ... Pittsburgh, PA
Klaber, R. Douglass, Jr. ... Pittsburgh, PA
Klaber, Richard D. ... Pittsburgh, PA
Wheeling, WV
Klabzuba, Keyna Lowrey
Gray Summit, MO
Klaczak, Lawrence C. ... Rockville, CT
Kladder, Peter, III ... Grand Rapids, MI
Kladder, Ronald A. ... Columbus, OH
Kladder, Stephen J. ... Ada, MI
Klaeger, Robert ... Marble Falls, TX
Klaeren, Lisa A. ... Detroit, MI
Klaeren, Michael J. ... Jackson, MI
Klaers, Michael J. ... Willmar, MN
Klaessy, Susan S. ... Marshalltown, IA
Klafehn, Heise & Riley ... Brockport, NY
Klafehn, Lynn M. ... Houston, TX
Klafehn, Mark H. ... Brockport, NY
Klafehn, Rodney L. ... Laurens, NY
Klafter, Bruce S. ... San Francisco, CA
Klafter, Cary I. ... Santa Clara, CA
Klafter, Craig L. ... Marlboro, NJ
Klafter, David B. ... New York, NY
Klafter, Jeffrey A. ... New York, NY
Klafter & Mason ... Marlboro, NJ
Klafter, Mitchell K. ... Brooklyn, NY
Klafter, Samuel ... Rochester, NY
Klag, Edwin James ... Irvine, CA
Klag, Michael F. ... New York, NY
Klager, James E. ... Corpus Christi, TX
Klages, Gary W. ... Chicago, IL
Klages, John A. ... Chicago, IL
Klages, William F. ... Ballwin, MO
Klagsbrun, Edward ... New York, NY
Klahn, Robert G. ... Pendleton, OR
Klahn, Sarah A. ... Denver, CO
Klahn-Kerns, Nancy Elizabeth
Pendleton, OR
Klahr, Gary Peter ... Phoenix, AZ
Klahr, Gary Peter, P.C. ... Phoenix, AZ
Klahr, James Herman ... Jefferson City, MO
Klahr, Julie F. ... Fort Lauderdale, FL
Klahs, Curtis L. ... La Crescenta, CA
Klahs, Donald R. ... Glendale, CA
Klahs, Richard W. ... La Crescenta, CA
Klaiber, Gregory B. ... Newport, RI
Klaiber, James R. ... New York, NY
Klaif, Leonard J. ... Ojai, CA
Klaiman, Carolyn S. ... Mendham, NJ
Klaiman, David J. ... Minneapolis, MN
Klaiman, Henry S. ... New York, NY
Klaiman, Jean M. ... Washington, DC
Klaiman, Kenneth Paul ... San Francisco, CA
Klaiman, Mark J. ... San Francisco, CA
Klain, Nancy ... Ann Arbor, MI
Klain, Ronald A.
Executive Office Of The President, Office of the Vice President, GV
Klain, William G. ... Scottsdale, AZ
Klainberg, Dennis S. ... Jamaica, NY
Klaine, Franklin A., Jr. ... Cincinnati, OH
Klaine, Wiley, Hoffmann & Minutolo, A Legal Professional Association ... Cincinnati, OH
Klair, James G. ... Towson, MD
Klaisz, R. Edward, Jr. ... Woodbury, NJ
Klaits, Joel M. ... Fort Lauderdale, FL
Klaits, Joel M., P.A. ... Fort Lauderdale, FL
Klakring, Glenn D. ... Easton, MD
Klamann & Hubbard, P.A.
Overland Park, KS
Kansas City, MO
Klamann, John M. ... Overland Park, KS

Klamen, Marvin ... St. Louis, MO
Klamer, J. Mark ... St. Louis, MO
Klamer, Jane Ferguson ... St. Louis, MO
Klamert, Abigail Connor ... Austin, TX
Klamm, Kevin R. ... Rutland, VT
Klamm, Linda E. ... San Francisco, CA
Klammer, Martin A. ... Mentor, OH
Klammer, Martin A., Co., L.P.A. Mentor, OH
Klammer, Steven R. ... Cherry Hill, NJ Philadelphia, PA
Klammer, Theodore R. ... Mentor, OH
Klamo, John A. ... Camden, NJ
Klamp, Carolyn ... Washington, DC
Klampe, Delehanty & Morris Rochester, MN
Klampe, Michael D. ... Rochester, MN
Klampert, Elizabeth Henry ... New York, NY
Klamrzynski, Gregory A. ... Chicago, IL
Klancke & Cook ... Denver, CO
Klancke, Jill ... Denver, CO
Klancnik, James M. ... Dallas, TX
Klancnik, James M., P.C. ... Dallas, TX
Klancnik, Thomas E. ... Madison, WI
Klanderman, Thomas C. ... Washington, DC
Klanderud, Helen Kalin ... Aspen, CO
Klane, Murray R. ... Minnetonka, MN
Klane, Murray R., P.A., & Associates Minnetonka, MN
Klang, Jeffrey A. Department of Transportation, Federal Aviation Administration, GV
Klang, Larry F. ... Irving, TX
Klang, Lawrence C. ... Portland, OR
Klanica, Kenneth F. ... Pittsburgh, PA
Klank, C. Edward, III ... Memphis, TN
Klann, David J. ... Leesville, LA
Klann, Frederick W. ... Denver, CO
Klann, Reigh F. ... Greenwich, CT
Klapatauskas, Todd N. ... Dubuque, IA
Klaper, Martin J. ... Indianapolis, IN
Klaperman, Joel S. ... New York, NY
Klaphake, Carol M. ... St. Cloud, MN
Klaphake, Roger M. ... St. Paul, MN
Klapheke, August A. ... Louisville, KY
Klapheke, David T. ... Louisville, KY
Klapheke Law Office ... Glasgow, KY
Klapheke, William Thomas, II Glasgow, KY
Klapholz, Joseph ... Hollywood, FL
Klapinsky, Raymond J. ... Malvern, PA
Klapisch, Jutta ... Washington, DC
Klapisch, Steven ... New York, NY
Klapman, Daniel S. ... Chicago, IL
Klapman, Sander A. ... Morton Grove, IL
Klapman, William T. ... Orangeburg, SC
Klapp, Fabian G. ... Bellerose, NY
Klapp, Kittredge R. ... Flint, MI
Klapp, Victoria Zwick ... Canton, OH
Klapp, William R., Jr. ... Atlanta, GA
Klappenbach, Norman" Mark "... Fordyce, AR
Klapper, Andrew David ... Staten Island, NY
Klapper, Antony B. ... Washington, DC
Klapper, Arthur M. ... Staten Island, NY
Klapper, Benjamin S. ... New York, NY
Klapper, Bill L. ... Kansas City, KS
Klapper & Fass ... New York, NY
Klapper Firm, The ... Denver, CO
Klapper, Floyd ... New York, NY
Klapper, Gail H. ... Denver, CO
Klapper, Harold ... Miami, FL
Klapper, Howard J. ... New York, NY
Klapper, Isaac & Parish ... Indianapolis, IN
Klapper, Israel T. ... Hazleton, PA
Klapper, Jonathan H. ... Atlanta, GA
Klapper, Joshua H. ... New York, NY
Klapper, Judith N. ... Staten Island, NY
Klapper & Klapper ... New York, NY
Klapper & Klapper, P.C. ... Staten Island, NY
Klapper, Morris L. ... Indianapolis, IN
Klapper, Paul C. ... Phoenix, AZ
Klapper, Richard H. ... New York, NY
Klapper, Robert J. ... New York, NY
Klapprodt, Kevin W. ... Rapid City, SD
Klapstein, Janet A. ... Salem, OR
Klar, Brian David ... St. Louis, MO
Klar, Deborah A. ... Los Angeles, CA
Klar, Doedy Presley ... Fort Worth, TX
Klar, Edward I. ... New York, NY
Klar, Howard P. ... New York, NY
Klar, Jeffrey N. ... St. Louis, MO
Klar, John S. ... Hartford, CT
Klar, Jonathan M. ... Pacific Palisades, CA
Klar, Marilyn F. ... Sylvania, OH
Klar, Michael N. ... Garden City, NY
Klar, Richard B. ... New York, NY
Klar, Steven A. ... East Meadow, NY
Klare, Karl E. ... Boston, MA
Klare, Kathe ... Richmond, VA
Klarenbach, Fred W., Jr. ... Shasta, CA
Klarer, Fredrick ... Northport, NY
Klarfeld, Jonathan S. ... New York, NY
Klarfeld, Peter J. ... Washington, DC
Klarfeld, S. Myron ... San Diego, CA
Klarfeld, Wendy F. ... Bedford, NY
Klaric, Betty ... Cleveland, OH
Klarich, David J. ... St. Louis, MO
Klarich, Mark ... Vershire, VT
Klarich, Stephen D. ... Tustin, CA
Klarin, Richard M. ... Pasadena, CA
Klaris, Harvey J. ... New York, NY
Klarish, Noah ... New York, NY
Klarish, Noah, & Associates, P.C. New York, NY
Klark, E. Louis ... Newark, OH
Klarl, John J. ... Buchanan, NY
Klarman, Barbara ... Southfield, MI
Klarman, Frederick A. ... McKenney, VA
Klarman, Margaret A. ... Washington, DC
Klarman, Rich ... Ann Arbor, MI
Klarman, Ruth E. ... New York, NY
Klarner, William Scott ... Baltimore, MD
Klarquist, Kenneth S. ... Portland, OR
Klarquist, Kenneth S., Jr. ... Portland, OR
Klarquist, Robert L. ... Department of Justice, Environment and Natural Resources Division, GV
Klarquist Sparkman Campbell Leigh & Whinston, LLP ... Portland, OR
Klarquist, Stephen J. ... Portland, OR
Klarr, John A. ... Farmington Hills, MI
Klarreich, Joel A. ... New York, NY
Klarsfeld, S. Herman ... New York, NY
Klas, Daniel A. ... St. Paul, MN
Klas, Mary Louise ... St. Paul, MN
Klas, Terry C. ... Minneapolis, MN
Klasco, Carolyn R. ... San Francisco, CA
Klasen, Charles W. ... Madison, WI
Klasen, Paul A., Jr. ... Ephrata, WA
Klasfeld, Norman ... New York, NY
Klashke, Timothy G. ... Pasco, WA
Klasic, Donald F. ... Reno, NV
Klasing, Daniel R. ... Birmingham, AL
Klasing, Leslie Miller ... Birmingham, AL
Klasing, Murphy S. ... Houston, TX
Klasinski, Stephen R. ... Olympia, WA
Klask, Gerald R. ... Dearborn Heights, MI
Klask, Jody D. ... Dearborn Heights, MI
Klaskin, Harold C. ... Los Angeles, CA
Klaskin, Rochelle H. ... Chicago, IL Madison, WI
Klaskin, Seth C. ... New Haven, CT
Klasko, H. Ronald ... Philadelphia, PA
Klasky, Mindy L. ... Washington, DC
Klasmeier, Coleen ... Washington, DC
Klasnick, Daniel D. ... Boston, MA
Klass, Alexandra B. ... Minneapolis, MN
Klass, Amy Smith ... Greensboro, NC
Klass, Barbara J. ... Agoura Hills, CA
Klass, Helman & Ross ... Los Angeles, CA
Klass, Jack E. ... Lexington, NC
Klass, Jennifer L. ... Washington, DC
Klass, Kenneth N. ... Philadelphia, PA
Klass, Kristen I. ... New York, NY
Klass, Mark E. ... Lexington, NC
Klass, Marvin J. ... Sioux City, IA
Klass, Mary A. ... Seymour, WI
Klass, Philip ... Denver, CO
Klass, Philip, P.C. ... Denver, CO
Klass, Renate ... Southfield, MI
Klass, Richard A. ... Brooklyn, NY
Klass, Robert A. ... Agoura Hills, CA
Klass, Stoos, Stoik, Mugan, Villone & Phillips, L.L.P. ... Sioux City, IA
Klassel, Dara ... New York, NY
Klassen, Dick N. ... Nickerson, KS
Klassen, John S. ... Houston, TX
Klassen, Kathryn H. ... Rockville, MD
Klassen, Kenton J. ... Fresno, CA
Klassen & Wesley ... Nickerson, KS
Klassman, Debra Ann ... Chicago, IL
Klasson, Walter ... New York, NY
Klatch, Louis ... South Bend, IN
Klatchko & Klatchko ... Palm Springs, CA
Klatchko, Linda Stearns ... Palm Springs, CA
Klatchko, Philip S. ... Palm Springs, CA
Klatell, Robert E. ... Melville, NY
Klatskin, Andrew S. ... Denver, CO
Klatskin, Deborah E. ... Teterboro, NJ
Klatsky, Alan M. ... Red Bank, NJ
Klatsky, David L. ... Los Angeles, CA
Klatsky, Fred M. ... Red Bank, NJ
Klatsky, Gabrielle ... Burbank, CA
Klatsky, Howard J. ... Dallas, TX
Klatsky, James ... Far Rockaway, NY
Klatsky & Klatsky ... Red Bank, NJ
Klatsky, Paul ... Spring, TX
Klatsky, Stephen A. Department of the Army, Army Materiel Command, GV
Klatsky, Steven B. ... Red Bank, NJ
Klatt & Associates, P.A. ... Inverness, FL
Klatt, August E. ... Vancouver, WA
Klatt, Bradford R. ... Livingston, NJ
Klatt, Curtis J. ... Waterloo, IA
Klatt, Gregory S.G. ... Los Angeles, CA
Klatt, Kenneth A. ... Atlanta, GA
Klatt, Leonard H. ... Inverness, FL Ocala, FL
Klatt, Michael R. ... Austin, TX
Klatt, William A. ... Columbus, OH
Klatte, Edward D. ... Frankfort, KY
Klatte, Ernest W., III ... Costa Mesa, CA
Klatte, Philip ... Portland, OR
Klatzke, A. Alan ... Phoenix, AZ
Klatzkow, Jeffrey A. ... Parsippany, NJ
Klau, Arnold H. ... Hartford, CT
Klau, Daniel J. ... Hartford, CT
Klauber, Adam ... Fort Lauderdale, FL
Klauber, Amy B. ... New York, NY
Klauber, Andrew L. ... New York, NY
Klauber, Geraldine A. ... Towson, MD
Klauber & Jackson ... Hackensack, NJ
Klauber, James S. ... Greenwood, SC
Klauber & Long ... Greenwood, SC
Klauber, Mark R. ... Sanibel, FL
Klauber, Skip M. ... Atlanta, GA
Klauber, Stefan J. ... Hackensack, NJ
Klauberg, John G. ... New York, NY
Klauberg, Melissa Townsend Greenwich, CT
Klauck, Karl D. ... Department of Justice, Washington, D.C. District Office, GV
Klauder, N. Jeffrey ... Philadelphia, PA
Klaudt, David W. ... Dallas, TX
Klaudt, Kent L. ... San Francisco, CA
Klauer, Peter D. ... Fenton, MO
Klauer, Richard L. ... Phoenix, AZ
Klauer, Robert D. ... Dubuque, IA
Klauke, George F., Jr. ... Chicago, IL
Klauke, Joseph M. ... Chicago, IL
Klaum, John J. ... Gulfport, FL
Klaum, Teresa A. ... New York, NY
Klaus, Charles ... Cleveland, OH
Klaus, Clifford R. ... Sarasota, FL
Klaus, Cynthia M. ... Minneapolis, MN
Klaus, Daniel E. ... Lincoln, NE
Klaus, David M. ... Washington, DC
Klaus, Joe ... Houston, TX
Klaus, Joe, P.C. ... Houston, TX
Klaus, John R. ... Ames, IA
Klaus, J. T. ... Wichita, KS
Klaus, Julie A. ... Fort Worth, TX
Klaus, Kathleen H. ... Chicago, IL
Klaus, Kelly M. ... San Francisco, CA
Klaus, Kenneth V. ... Lansing, MI
Klaus, Kurt R., Jr. ... Miami, FL
Klaus, Laura Metcoff ... Washington, DC
Klaus, Mortimer N. ... New York, NY
Klaus, Richard P. ... Urbana, IL
Klaus, Roger D. ... Deerfield, IL
Klaus & Telford, P.A. ... Sarasota, FL
Klaus, Warren J. ... Hales Corners, WI
Klaus, William A. ... New York, NY
Klaus, William R. ... Philadelphia, PA
Klauschie, Carol A. ... Pasadena, CA
Klauschie, Jack A., Jr. ... Rancho Cordova, CA
Klausen, Ellen Reesman ... Lafayette, IN
Klausen, Stephen C. ... Long Beach, CA Santa Monica, CA
Klauser, Arthur E. ... Washington, DC
Klauser, David J. W. ... Madison, WI
Klauser, James J. ... Seattle, WA
Klauser, James R. ... Madison, WI
Klausing, Craig D. ... St. Paul, MN
Klausing, Steven E. ... Colorado Springs, CO
Klausing, Thomas A. ... Louisville, KY
Klausman, C. William ... Columbus, OH
Klausman, C. William, III ... Dublin, OH
Klausman, David L. ... Santa Clara, CA
Klausman, Glenn M. ... Altamonte Springs, FL
Klausmeier, Howard M. ... Detroit, MI
Klausner, Adam A. ... Ithaca, NY
Klausner, Allison Potter ... New York, NY
Klausner, Alyssa B. ... Burbank, CA
Klausner, Amy H. ... Lima, NY
Klausner, Andrea S. ... Chappaqua, NY
Klausner, Andrew R. ... Tucson, AZ
Klausner & Cohen, P.A. ... Plantation, FL
Klausner, Dale A. ... Chandler, AZ
Klausner, David S. ... New York, NY
Klausner, Gary E. ... Los Angeles, CA
Klausner, Gerald H. ... Marina Del Rey, CA
Klausner, Jack D. ... Phoenix, AZ
Klausner, Jennifer Tafet ... New York, NY
Klausner, Jeremy M. ... White Plains, NY
Klausner, Kenneth M. ... Henderson, NV
Klausner, Manuel S. ... Los Angeles, CA
Klausner, Margery Siegel ... Detroit, MI
Klausner, Neal H. ... New York, NY
Klausner, Peter L. ... New York, NY
Klausner, R. Gary ... Los Angeles, CA
Klausner, Robert A. ... Florham Park, NJ
Klausner, Robert D. ... Plantation, FL
Klausner, Robert H. ... South Orange, NJ
Klausner, Ronald B. ... New York, NY
Klausner, S. Barbara ... Santa Monica, CA
Klausner, Stephen E. ... Somerville, NJ
Klausner, Stephen H. ... Jackson Heights, NY
Klausner, Tonia Ouellette ... New York, NY
Klausner, William F. ... San Bernardino, CA
Klauzer, Randall W. Steamboat Springs, CO
Klauzer & Tremaine, LLC Steamboat Springs, CO
Klavan, Ellen Ivy ... Denver, CO
Klavan, Stanley ... Rockville, MD
Klavans, Glenn L. ... Glen Burnie, MD
Klavans, Lee ... Owings Mills, MD
Klavens, Jonathan S. ... Boston, MA
Klavens, Kent J. ... Los Angeles, CA
Klaver, James C. ... Kingman, KS
Klaver, Mark J. ... Scotts Valley, CA
Klaver, Mary A. ... Milwaukee, WI
Klaver, Robert F., Jr. Menomonee Falls, WI
Klaverkamp, Paul H. ... Minneapolis, MN
Klavon, Pamela Haddock ... Memphis, TN
Klaw, Margaret ... Philadelphia, PA
Klawetter, Robert L. ... Houston, TX
Klawier, Wayne B. ... Louisville, KY
Klawikofsky, John M. ... Tampa, FL
Klawiter, Anne J. ... Walnut Creek, CA
Klawiter, Donald C. ... Washington, DC
Klawiter, Marilyn ... St. Joseph, MI
Klawiter, Richard ... Chicago, IL
Klawitter, Andrew L. ... Tarrytown, NY
Klawitter, George A. ... Seattle, WA
Klawitter, Jason W. ... San Jose, CA
Klawon, Lynette ... Los Angeles, CA
Klawuhn, Philip A. ... Kansas City, MO
Klawunder, Nina D. ... Irvine, CA
Klay, Anna N. ... San Jose, CA
Klay, Veldhuizen, Bindner, De Jong & Pals Alton, IA **Orange City, IA** Paullina, IA
Klayman & Associates, P.C. Washington, DC Miami, FL
Klayman, Barry M. ... Wilmington, DE
Klayman, Craig H. ... Woodbury, NJ
Klayman, Elliot I. ... Columbus, OH
Klayman & Fairley ... San Diego, CA
Klayman, Jeffrey T. ... Boston, MA
Klayman, Kenneth S. ... San Diego, CA
Klayman, Larry ... Washington, DC Miami, FL
Klayman, Lawrence L. ... Boca Raton, FL
Klayman, Lawrence L., P.A. Boca Raton, FL
Klayman, Michelle Helene ... Boca Raton, FL
Klayman, Murray A. ... Springfield, NJ
Klayman, Robert A. ... Washington, DC
Klazkin, Julian P. General Accounting Office, Office of the General Counsel, GV
Klazmer, Gary M. ... Rydal, PA
Klc, Thomas J. ... Salt Lake City, UT
Kle, John ... Sea Cliff, NY
Kleager, Richard S. ... Scottsbluff, NE
Klearman, Gail R. ... Dubuque, IA
Klearman, Laura E. ... St. Louis, MO
Klearman, Steven J. ... Reno, NV
Kleaveland, Michael I. ... Muskegon, MI
Kleaver, James E. ... Yreka, CA
Kleban, Albert J. ... Southport, CT
Kleban, Allan J. ... Simsbury, CT
Kleban, Barry D. ... Philadelphia, PA
Kleban, Daniel Ian ... Houston, TX
Kleban, Debra Ann ... Chicago, IL
Kleban, Donald M. ... New York, NY
Kleban, Kenneth A. ... St. Louis, MO
Kleban & Samor, P.C. ... Fairfield, CT Southport, CT
Kleban & Wieselman ... Simsbury, CT
Klebanoff, Arthur M., (P.C.) ... New York, NY
Klebanoff, David L. ... Boston, MA
Klebanoff, Howard M. ... West Hartford, CT
Klebanoff, Howard M., P.C. West Hartford, CT
Klebanoff, Stanley M. ... West Hempstead, NY
Klebanov, Marianna S. ... Martinez, CA
Klebanow, Anatole ... Los Angeles, CA
Klebasko, Gretchen L. ... Baltimore, MD
Klebaum, Noel A. ... Ventura, CA
Klebaum, Pamela Price ... Ventura, CA
Klebba, James M. ... New Orleans, LA
Klebba, John F. ... Chicago, IL
Klebe, Franziska ... New York, NY
Klebe, Howard C. ... New Castle, PA
Klebe, Kurt E. ... Portland, ME
Kleber, Dale Elliott ... Franklin Park, IL
Kleber, Kendra S. ... Livonia, MI
Kleberg Law Firm, The, A Professional Corporation ... Corpus Christi, TX Houston, TX San Antonio, TX
Klecan & Childress ... Albuquerque, NM
Klecan, John A. ... Phoenix, AZ Albuquerque, NM
Klecan, Mark J. ... Albuquerque, NM
Klecha, John E. ... Marysville, MI
Kleck, Monique M. ... Austin, TX
Klecker, Kory A. ... Phoenix, AZ
Kleckley, Albert L. ... Ridgeland, SC
Kleckner, David M. ... Tyler, TX
Kleckner, Janet L. ... Medina, OH
Kleckner, Robert G., Jr. ... New York, NY
Kleczek, Andrew J. ... Peoria, IL
Kleczka, Mark D. ... Bridgewater, NJ Northport, NY Northport, NY
Klee, Albert H. ... Chicago, IL
Klee, Barbara J. ... New York, NY
Klee, Gina L. ... Santa Maria, CA
Klee, Harvey H. ... Bluffton, TX
Klee, John P. ... Carnegie, PA
Klee, Jonathan R. ... Rockville Centre, NY
Klee, Kenneth N. ... Los Angeles, CA
Klee, Kimmerly Anne ... Fort Wayne, IN
Klee, Linda A. ... San Francisco, CA
Klee, Maurice M. ... Fairfield, CT
Klee, Peter H. ... San Diego, CA
Klee, Richard ... New York, NY
Klee, Roger Paul ... Toledo, OH
Klee, Stephen E. ... Greensboro, NC
Klee, Thomas A. ... Simsbury, CT
Klee, Tuchin & Bogdanoff, LLP Los Angeles, CA
Klee, Yael N. ... Carle Place, NY
Kleeb, Robert E. ... Howell, MI
Kleebauer, Susan K. ... San Leandro, CA
Kleeberg, Charles F. ... Seattle, WA
Kleeblatt, Galler & Abramson Hackensack, NJ New York, NY
Kleeblatt, Robert J. ... Hackensack, NJ
Kleedehn, G. Rodney ... Anchorage, AK
Kleederman, Eva Susan Federal Emergency Management Agency, Office of the General Counsel, GV
Kleefield, Claude H. ... New York, NY
Kleeger, James D. ... Anaheim, CA
Kleeger, Kenneth S. ... Los Angeles, CA
Kleeh, Thomas Shawn ... Charleston, WV
Kleehamer, Melinda M. ... Chicago, IL
Kleeman, Daniel C. ... Paterson, NJ
Kleeman, Dena A. ... Beverly Hills, CA
Kleeman, Dena A., A Professional Corporation ... Beverly Hills, CA Los Angeles, CA
Kleeman, Jan ... New York, NY
Kleeman, Jennifer R. ... Philadelphia, PA
Kleeman, Karri L. ... Cincinnati, OH
Kleeman, Larry Alan ... Topeka, KS
Kleeman, R. Henry ... Chicago, IL
Kleeman, Robert J. ... Austin, TX
Kleeman, William M. ... Oakland, CA
Kleemann, Carl Lawrence ... Portsmouth, OH
Kleemann, Judith A. ... Cincinnati, OH
Kleen, Jerry G. ... Salem, OR

Kleen, William P. ... New York, NY
Kleer, Silvia M. ... Southfield, MI
Klees, Aria A. ... Philadelphia, PA
Klees, Edward H. ... Chevy Chase, MD
Klees, Robert J. ... New Orleans, LA
Kleespies, J. Timothy ... Chicago, IL
Kleess, Trude ... Longmont, CO
Kleff, Pierre A., Jr ... Killeen, TX
Kleffman, Marsha L. ... Chicago, IL
Kleger, Brett I. ... Philadelphia, PA
Kleger, Scott M. ... Wheat Ridge, CO
Klegerman, Neal A. ... Chicago, IL
Klegman, Mary B. ... Quincy, MA
Klegon, Michelle R. ... Minneapolis, MN
Kleh, William H. ... Houston, TX
Klehm, Henry, III ... New York, NY
Klehm, Paul J. ... Andover, MA
Klehr, Harrison, Harvey, Branzburg & Ellers LLP ... Wilmington, DE
Cherry Hill, NJ
Philadelphia, PA
Klehr, Leonard M. ... Philadelphia, PA
Klei, Thomas J. ... Hauppauge, NY
Klei, Thomas J., Jr. ... Hauppauge, NY
Kleibacker, Wilson M., Jr. ... Madison, SD
Kleiber, Gregory ... Philadelphia, PA
Kleiboemer, Axel ... Washington, DC
Kleid, Richard M. ... Palm Beach, FL
Kleid, Susan M. ... Denver, CO
Kleid, Wallace ... Baltimore, MD
Kleidman, Paul S. ... Fishkill, NY
Kleidon, Kevin Roy ... Centreville, MI
Kleier, George O. ... Fort Smith, AR
Kleier, James P. ... San Francisco, CA
Kleier, Kenneth J. ... San Francisco, CA
Kleier, Timothy L. ... Bakersfield, CA
Kleifield, Matthew D. ... Phoenix, AZ
Kleifield, Steven J. ... Los Angeles, CA
Kleiger, Howard L. ... Great Neck, NY
Kleiger & Kleiger ... Great Neck, NY
Kleiler, James R.
Department Of The Interior, Office of Hearings & Appeals, GV
Kleiman, Alan S. ... New York, NY
Kleiman, Alan S. ... Memphis, TN
Kleiman, Andrew A. ... Indianapolis, IN
Kleiman, Ari R. ... Los Angeles, CA
Kleiman, Bernard ... Chicago, IL
Kleiman, Chas. ... New York, NY
Kleiman, Christopher A. ... New Hope, MN
Kleiman, David H. ... Indianapolis, IN
Kleiman, David M. ... Los Angeles, CA
Kleiman, David M., (P.C.) ... Dallas, TX
Kleiman, Gary A. ... Denver, CO
Kleiman, Howard ... Buffalo, NY
Kleiman, Ira ... New York, NY
Kleiman, Janet ... Dallas, TX
Kleiman, Jeremy P. ... Newark, NJ
Kleiman, Jesse ... New York, NY
Kleiman, Karen Baime ... Eagle, CO
Kleiman, Kathleen A. ... Cedar Rapids, IA
Kleiman, Kathryn A. ... Alexandria, VA
Kleiman & Kavrukov ... Arlington, VA
Kleiman, Kimberly A. ... Kalamazoo, MI
Kleiman, Laurin Blumenthal
New York, NY
Kleiman & Lawrence, L.L.P. ... Dallas, TX
Kleiman, Louis A. ... Arlington, VA
Kleiman, M. Scott ... Davie, FL
Kleiman, Marc A. ... New York, NY
Kleiman, Mark Allen, Law Offices of
Los Angeles, CA
Kleiman, Mark Allen, Law Offices of
Santa Monica, CA
Kleiman, Mark E. ... New York, NY
Kleiman, Mary M. ... Indianapolis, IN
Kleiman, Matthew N. ... Chicago, IL
Kleiman, Melodie McLennan ... Ventura, CA
Kleiman, Michael ... Philadelphia, PA
Kleiman, Michael M. ... Mentor, OH
Kleiman, Murray ... Brooklyn, NY
Kleiman, Rachel M. ... New York, NY
Kleiman, Randall B. ... East Lansing, MI
Kleiman, S. Leslie ... Chicago, IL
Kleiman, Steven M. ... San Mateo, CA
Kleiman, Susan Sonenshein
Washington, DC
Kleiman Whitney Wolfe and Elfenbaum, P.C.
Chicago, IL
Klein, Aaron E. ... Kingston, NY
Klein, Adam I. ... New York, NY
Klein, Adam R. ... Chicago, IL
Klein, Adam T. ... New York, NY
Klein, Adrienne R. ... New York, NY
Klein, Alan ... Grand Blanc, MI
Klein, Alan ... Philadelphia, PA
Klein, Alan C. ... Dallas, TX
Klein, Alan E. ... Bakersfield, CA
Klein, Alan H. ... Chicago, IL
Klein, Alan M. ... Los Angeles, CA
Klein, Alan M. (IBA) ... New York, NY
Klein, Alan P. ... Department of the Army, U.S. Army Legal Services Agency, GV
Klein, Alan R. ... Los Angeles, CA
Klein, Alan V. ... Philadelphia, PA
Klein, Alexander B., III ... Houston, TX
Klein, Alexander S., III ... Santa Clara, CA
Klein, Alfred ... Glendale, CA
Klein, Alfred ... Los Angeles, CA
Klein, Alice J. ... Charlestown, MA
Klein, Alisa B. ... Department of Justice, Civil Division, GV
Klein, Allen ... Tulsa, OK
Klein, Allen J. ... Washington, DC
Klein, Alvin F. ... New York, NY
Klein, Amelia M. ... Albany, NY
Klein, Amy L. A. ... Danbury, CT
Klein, Amy Loeserman ... Washington, DC
Klein, Andrea M. ... Sacramento, CA
Klein, Andrew B. ... St. Louis, MO
Klein, Andrew D. ... Philadelphia, PA
Klein, Andrew F. ... Chicago, IL
Klein, Andrew G. ... Phoenix, AZ
Klein, Andrew J. ... Springfield, IL
Klein, Andrew K. ... Brighton, MI
Klein, Andrew M. ... Washington, DC
Klein, Andrew R. ... Birmingham, AL
Klein, Andrew W. ... Albany, NY
Klein, Andrew W. ... New York, NY
Klein, Anita T.
Securities and Exchange Commission, Division of Corporation Finance, GV
Klein, Ann M. ... Toledo, OH
Klein, Anne ... La Quinta, CA
Klein, Anthony J., (Inc.) ... Bakersfield, CA
Klein, Anthony R. ... Palo Alto, CA
Klein, Arlene ... New York, NY
Klein, Arnold Lewis ... San Diego, CA
Klein, Arnold N. ... Yonkers, NY
Klein, Arnold S. ... Mineola, NY
Klein, Arthur ... Columbus, OH
Klein, Arthur L. ... Chicago, IL
Klein, Arthur O. ... Westport, CT
Klein, Arthur S. ... King Of Prussia, PA
Klein, Arthur S. ... Norristown, PA
Klein & Associates ... Kingsport, TN
Klein & Associates ... Dallas, TX
Plano, TX
Klein, August ... Detroit, MI
Klein, Barbara D. ... Chicago, IL
Klein, Barbara R. ... Bethesda, MD
Klein & Barenblat ... San Antonio, TX
Klein, Barnard F. ... Coto De Caza, CA
Klein, Barry G. ... Houston, TX
Klein, Barry L. ... Philadelphia, PA
Klein, Bart J. ... Maplewood, NJ
Klein, Benson ... Gaithersburg, MD
Klein, Bernard B. ... Uniontown, PA
Klein, Bernard P.
Pension Benefit Guaranty Corporation, Office of the General Counsel, GV
Klein, Beth ... Boulder, CO
Klein, Beth, P.C. ... Boulder, CO
Klein, Beth R. ... New York, NY
Klein, Beverley J. ... Chicago, IL
Klein, Blair ... Buffalo, WY
Klein, Bonnie G. ... Philadelphia, PA
Klein, Brenda ... South Easton, MA
Klein, Brent D. ... Miami, FL
Klein, Brett C. ... Los Angeles, CA
Klein, Brian J. ... Minneapolis, MN
Klein, Bruce F. ... Oklahoma City, OK
Klein, Burton G. ... New Orleans, LA
Klein & Butler ... Santa Rosa, CA
Klein, Carl C., II ... San Francisco, CA
Klein, Carl J. ... El Cajon, CA
Klein, Carl R. ... Chicago, IL
Klein, Carl S. ... New York, NY
Klein, Carol D. ... Washington, DC
Klein, Carol Savits ... Chester, NY
Klein, Carole R. ... Washington, DC
Klein, Carrie L. ... Kalamazoo, MI
Klein, Carter H. ... Chicago, IL
Klein, Cary E. ... West Palm Beach, FL
Klein, Cathy A. ... Denver, CO
Klein, Cathy A., P.C. ... Denver, CO
Klein, Charles A. ... Warminster, PA
Klein, Charles B. ... Washington, DC
Klein, Charles C. ... Ironton, OH
Klein, Charles D. ... New York, NY
Klein, Charles H. ... New York, NY
Klein, Christian A. ... Alexandria, VA
Klein, Christine A. ... East Lansing, MI
Klein, Christine J. ... New York, NY
Klein, Christopher ... Princeton, NJ
Klein, Christopher E. ... Savannah, GA
Klein, Christopher J. ... Miami, FL
Klein, Christopher J. ... Pittsburgh, PA
Klein, Christopher M. ... Sacramento, CA
Klein, Clifford L. ... Los Angeles, CA
Klein & Cohen ... New York, NY
Klein, Coleman E. ... Southfield, MI
Klein, Coleman E., P.C. ... Southfield, MI
Klein, Conrad Lee ... Los Angeles, CA
Klein, Constance ... San Diego, CA
Klein, Corey E. ... Los Angeles, CA
Klein, Craig A. ... San Diego, CA
Klein & Cutler ... Washington, DC
Klein, Dana W. ... Dublin, OH
Klein, Daniel B. ... Boston, MA
Klein, Daniel E., Jr. ... Baltimore, MD
Klein, Daniel L. ... Wilmington, DE
Klein, Daniel L. ... Naperville, IL
Klein, Daniel L. ... New York, NY
Klein, Daniel M. ... Atlanta, GA
Klein, Daniel M. ... Toledo, OH
Klein, Daniel P. ... New York, NY
Klein, Daniel S. ... Newport Beach, CA
Klein, Darrell D. ... Omaha, NE
Klein, Darren Robert ... Boston, MA
Klein, Daryl Endy ... Paoli, PA
Klein, David ... Denver, CO
Klein, David ... Larchmont, NY
Klein, David ... New York, NY
White Plains, NY
Klein, David ... Houston, TX
Klein, David A. ... San Francisco, CA
Klein, David Alan ... Haddonfield, NJ
Philadelphia, PA
Klein, David B. ... Detroit, MI
Klein, David C. ... Los Angeles, CA
Klein, David Charles ... New York, NY
Klein, David E. ... Louisville, KY
Klein, David F. ... Washington, DC
Klein, David H. ... Morris Plains, NJ
Klein, David H. ... Yorktown Heights, NY
Klein, David I. ... Ellicott City, MD
Klein, David J. ... Roseland, NJ
Klein, David L. ... White Plains, NY
Klein, David M. ... Phoenix, AZ
Klein, David M. ... New York, NY
Klein, David M. ... Suffern, NY
Klein, David M. ... Burlington, VT
Klein, David O. ... New York, NY
Klein, David S. ... Owings Mills, MD
Klein, David Y. ... Livonia, MI
Klein, Deborah ... St. Paul, MN
Klein, Deborah E.
Federal Communications Commission, Cable Services Bureau, GV
Klein, Deborah K. ... New York, NY
Klein, Deborah L. ... Beverly Hills, CA
Klein, Deborah L. ... San Antonio, TX
Klein, DeNatale, Goldner, Cooper, Rosenlieb & Kimball, LLP ... Bakersfield, CA
Lancaster, CA
Palmdale, CA
San Luis Obispo, CA
Santa Clarita, CA
Klein, Dennis S. ... Washington, DC
Klein, Deven J. ... Teaneck, NJ
Klein, Don S. ... Allentown, PA
Klein, Donald ... Santa Ana, CA
Klein, Donald A. ... Hackensack, NJ
Klein, Donald E. ... New York, NY
Klein, Donald F. ... Rock Valley, IA
Klein, Donald, Jr. ... Socorro, NM
Klein, Donald M. ... Miami, FL
Klein, Donald M. ... New York, NY
Klein, Donald R. ... Rock Valley, IA
Klein, Donald S. ... Tucson, AZ
Klein, Donald S. ... New Orleans, LA
Klein, Donald S. ... White Plains, NY
Klein, Donald S., P.C. ... White Plains, NY
Klein, Donna Guinn ... New Orleans, LA
Klein, Doreen ... New York, NY
Klein, Douglas A. ... Washington, DC
Klein, Douglas J. ... Grand Rapids, MI
Klein, Douglas K. ... South Bend, IN
Klein Dub & Holleb, Ltd. ... Chicago, IL
Highland Park, IL
Klein, Earl ... Los Angeles, CA
Klein, Edith Miller ... Boise, ID
Klein, Edw. S. ... Miami, FL
Klein, Edward ... Fort Lauderdale, FL
Klein, Edward A. ... Santa Monica, CA
Klein, Edward C. ... Syosset, NY
Klein, Edward E. ... New York, NY
Klein, Edward W. ... Syracuse, NY
Klein, Edward W., III ... Marietta, GA
Klein, Eleazer ... New York, NY
Klein, Elise D. ... Los Angeles, CA
Klein, Elizabeth Nelson ... Ventura, CA
Klein, Elliott ... Ridgewood, NY
Klein, Enid R. ... Valley Stream, NY
Klein, Eric A. ... Los Angeles, CA
Klein, Eric A. ... New York, NY
Klein, Eric G. ... San Diego, CA
Klein, Eric N. ... Boston, MA
Klein, Eric S. ... Tustin, CA
Klein, Eric T. ... New York, NY
Klein, Erica D. ... New York, NY
Klein, Erich F., Jr. ... Neches, TX
Klein, Erika Katherine ... Boise, ID
Klein, Ernest V. ... Boston, MA
Klein, Esther E. ... San Jose, CA
Klein, Eve I. ... New York, NY
Klein, Felicia J. ... New York, NY
Klein & Folchetti ... White Plains, NY
Klein and Fortune, P.A. ... North Miami, FL
Klein, Frances R. ... Buffalo Grove, IL
Klein, Frank ... Cobleskill, NY
Klein, Frank D. ... Palm Harbor, FL
Klein, Frank H. ... New York, NY
Klein, Franklin W. ... Chicago, IL
Klein, Fred B. ... Mineola, NY
Klein, Fred C. ... New York, NY
Klein, Fred J. ... Woodbridge, NJ
Klein, Frederic Lee ... Berlin, CT
Klein, Frederic M. ... Boca Raton, FL
Klein, Frederic M., P.A. ... Boca Raton, FL
Klein, Frederic R. ... Chicago, IL
Klein, Frederick L. ... Washington, DC
Klein, Frederick M. ... New York, NY
Klein, Frederick S. ... Tucson, AZ
Klein, Gail F. ... West Bloomfield, MI
Klein, Gary ... Boston, MA
Klein, Gary A. ... Miami, FL
Klein, Gary Ethan ... Washington, DC
Klein, Gary J. ... Washington, DC
Klein, Gary R. ... New York, NY
Klein, Gary S. ... Stamford, CT
Klein, George W. ... New York, NY
Klein, Gerald ... Santa Ana, CA
Klein, Gerald E. ... Danbury, CT
Klein, Gerald J. ... Miami, FL
Klein, Gerald M. ... Hartford, CT
Klein, Gerald M. ... Croton-On-Hudson, NY
White Plains, NY
Klein, Gerald S. ... Lutherville, MD
Klein, Gerhart L. ... Marlton, NJ
Klein, Geri R. ... Brooklyn, NY
Klein, Glenn ... Eugene, OR
Klein, Gordon L. ... Calabasas, CA
Klein, Gregory A. ... Chicago, IL
Klein, Gregory B. ... Los Angeles, CA
Klein, Gregory K. ... Lafayette, LA
Klein, Gregory P. ... Danbury, CT
Klein, Gwendolyn Payton ... Seattle, WA
Klein, H. Randolph ... Ocala, FL
Klein, Hali Jane ... Oklahoma City, OK
Klein, Hans-Peter ... Ukiah, CA
Klein, Harold ... Bronx, NY
Klein, Harold E. ... Houston, TX
Klein, Harold S. ... New York, NY
Klein, Harriet Farber ... Newark, NJ
Klein, Harry ... West Bloomfield, MI
Klein, Harry L. ... Brooklyn, NY
Klein, Harvey R. ... Ocala, FL
Klein, Harvey S. ... Houston, TX
Klein, Head & Head, L.L.P.
West Chester, PA
Klein, Heidi E. ... San Francisco, CA
Klein, Heisler & Klarreich, P.C.
New York, NY
Klein, Henry ... Los Angeles, CA
Klein, Henry L. ... Memphis, TN
Klein, Henry L., A Prof. Law Corp.
New Orleans, LA
Klein, Henry M. ... Denver, CO
Klein, Herbert C. ... Hackensack, NJ
Klein, Herbert H., III ... Hattiesburg, MS
Klein, Herbert Jay ... Los Angeles, CA
Klein, Herbert L. ... Woodcliff Lake, NJ
Klein, Herbert M. ... Los Angeles, CA
Klein, Herbert M. ... Miami, FL
Klein, Herbert S. ... Aspen, CO
Klein & Hill ... New York, NY
Klein, Hinda ... Hollywood, FL
Klein, Howard B. ... Providence, RI
Klein, Howard Bruce, Law Offices of
Philadelphia, PA
Klein, Howard J. ... Irvine, CA
Klein, Howard M. ... Philadelphia, PA
Klein, Howard S. ... Los Angeles, CA
Klein, Howard S. ... Forest Hill, MD
Klein, Howard S., Associates
Philadelphia, PA
Klein, Ira Paul ... Danbury, CT
Klein, Irving ... New York, NY
Klein, Irving J. ... Miami, FL
Klein, Irwin ... New York, NY
Klein, Irwin G. ... Cedarhurst, NY
Klein, Isaac ... Baltimore, MD
Klein, J. Douglas ... Chicago, IL
Klein, J. Nicholas, III ... Keller, VA
Klein, Jack ... New York, NY
Klein, Jacqueline Redin ... Los Angeles, CA
Klein, Jacqueline S. ... Pasadena, CA
Klein, Jamee Maurer ... Kansas City, MO
Klein, James M. ... Milwaukee, WI
Klein, James M. ... Stevens Point, WI
Klein, James R. ... Floral Park, NY
Klein, James William ... Los Angeles, CA
Klein, Jamie W. ... Raleigh, NC
Klein, Jane K. ... Lincolnwood, IL
Klein, Jason ... Miami, FL
Klein, Jason C. ... Seattle, WA
Klein, Jason S. ... Roseland, NJ
Klein, Jay W. ... New York, NY
Klein, Jeff I. ... Wantagh, NY
Klein, Jeffrey A. ... Secaucus, NJ
Klein, Jeffrey I. ... Boston, MA
Klein, Jeffrey L. ... Boca Raton, FL
Klein, Jeffrey M. ... Washington, DC
Klein, Jeffrey M. ... Charlotte, NC
Klein, Jeffrey S. ... New York, NY
Klein, Jennifer G. ... Austin, TX
Klein, Jennifer M. ... Lafayette, LA
Klein, Jerome A. ... Marco Island, FL
Klein, Jerome M. ... New York, NY
Klein, Jerry A. ... St. Louis, MO
Klein, Jerry A., P.C. ... St. Louis, MO
Klein, Jessica D. ... Chicago, IL
Klein, Jewel N. ... Chicago, IL
Klein, Jill ... Pasadena, CA
Klein, Jill Swerdloff ... Washington, DC
Klein, Jill W. ... La Salle, IL
Klein, Joan Dempsey ... Los Angeles, CA
Klein, Joel A. ... Pittsburgh, PA
Klein, Joel, & Associates ... San Antonio, TX
Klein, Joel H. ... San Antonio, TX
Klein, Joel I. ... Department of Justice, Antitrust Division, GV
Klein, Jo-Ellyn Sakowitz ... Washington, DC
Klein, John A. ... Santa Rosa, CA
Klein, John A. ... Bridgeport, CT
Klein, John C., III ... Columbus, OH
Klein, John E. ... St. Louis, MO
Klein, John F., Jr. ... Dallas, TX
Klein, John H. ... Norfolk, VA
Klein, John J. ... Chicago, IL
Klein, John J. ... Dallas, TX
Klein, John R. ... Omaha, NE
Klein, John V. N. ... Mineola, NY
Klein, John W. ... Mission Viejo, CA
Klein, John W.
Department Of Veterans Affairs, Office of the General Counsel, GV
Klein, John W.
Small Business Administration, Office of the General Counsel, GV
Klein, Jonathan ... New York, NY
Klein, Jonathan Allan ... San Francisco, CA
Klein, Jonathan F. ... Vienna, VA
Klein, Jonathan I. ... University Heights, OH
Klein, Jonathan J. ... Bridgeport, CT
Klein, Jonathan S. ... Boston, MA
Klein, Jordan A. ... Chicago, IL
Klein, Josef J. ... West Los Angeles, CA
Klein, Joseph ... Springfield, NJ
Klein, Joseph A. ... Harrisburg, PA
Klein, Joseph A., A Professional Corporation
Harrisburg, PA
Klein, Joseph C. ... Seattle, WA
Klein, Joseph F. ... Central Islip, NY
Klein, Joseph J. ... Arlington Heights, IL
Klein, Joseph P. ... Media, PA
Klein, Joseph R. ... Minneapolis, MN
Klein, Joseph W. ... Pittsburgh, PA

Klein, Josh
Securities and Exchange Commission, Division of Enforcement, GV
Klein, Joshua A. ... Chicago, IL
Klein, Joyce M. ...
National Mediation Board, GV
Klein, Judah B. ... New York, NY
Klein, Judith Eva ... West Bloomfield, MI
Klein, Justin P. ... Washington, DC
Philadelphia, PA
Klein, Karen A. ... Seattle, WA
Klein, Karen K. ... Fargo, ND
Klein, Karen M. ... New York, NY
Klein, Karl T. ... Boise, ID
Klein, Katharine ... Tustin, CA
Klein, Katharine Lord ... Keene, NH
Klein, Kathryn A. ... Edwardsville, IL
Klein, Katie Pearson, (P.C.)
Brownsville, TX
McAllen, TX
Klein, Kay Neiss ... Sarasota, FL
Tampa, FL
Klein and Keenan ... Yonkers, NY
Klein, Keith D. ... Los Angeles, CA
Klein, Keith E. ... San Antonio, TX
Klein, Keith J. ... Oklahoma City, OK
Klein, Keith L. ... Thousand Oaks, CA
Klein, Kelly G. ... Minnetonka, MN
Klein, Kenneth ... Washington, DC
Klein, Kenneth ... Washington, DC
Klein, Kenneth C. ... Jeffersonville, NY
Liberty, NY
Klein, Kenneth D. ... Los Angeles, CA
Klein, Kenneth J. ... New York, NY
Klein, Kenneth J. ... New York, NY
Klein, Kenneth K. ... Roscoe, PA
Klein, Kenneth M. ... New York, NY
Klein, Kenneth S. ... San Diego, CA
Klein, Kenneth S. ... Miami, FL
Klein, Kenneth Simon ... Boston, MA
Klein, Kereth Frankel ... Los Angeles, CA
San Francisco, CA
Klein, Kerry ... New York, NY
Klein, Kevin G. ... Phillips, WI
Klein, Kevin R. ... Alexandria, VA
Klein, Kimberly ... New York, NY
Klein & Klein ... Ocala, FL
Klein & Klein ... New Orleans, LA
Klein & Klein, P.A. ... West Palm Beach, FL
Klein & Klein, P.C. ... Suffern, NY
Klein, Kurt P. ... Geneva, IL
Klein, Lance H. ... Rye, NY
White Plains, NY
Klein, Landau & Romm ... Washington, DC
Klein, Larry A. ... West Palm Beach, FL
Klein, Larry M. ... Napa, CA
Santa Barbara, CA
Klein, Larry M., Inc. ... Napa, CA
Klein, Larry S. ... Cleveland, OH
Klein, Laura A. ... Canton, CT
Klein, Laura Friedman
Federal Election Commission, Office of the General Counsel, GV
Klein, Lauren G. ... Scarsdale, NY
Klein, Lawrence A. ... Palo Alto, CA
Klein, Lawrence M. ... Newburgh, NY
Klein, Lawrence M. ... Poughkeepsie, NY
Klein, Lawrence S. ... Omaha, NE
Klein, Lee David ... Poughkeepsie, NY
Klein, Leo N. ... Bronx, NY
Klein, Leon ... Clifton, NJ
Klein, Leonard ... Monroe, NY
Klein, Leonard ... Poughkeepsie, NY
Klein, Leonard E. ... Washington, DC
Klein, Leslee ... Cambridge, MA
Klein, Lesley B. ... McLean, VA
Klein, Leslie ... Sherman Oaks, CA
Klein, Leslie A. ... Chicago, IL
Klein, Leslie A. ... New York, NY
Klein, Leslie, & Associates, A Prof. Law Corp. ... Sherman Oaks, CA
Klein, Leslie E. ... Washington, DC
Klein, Leslie W. ... Klamath Falls, OR
Klein, Lester L. ... San Antonio, TX
Klein, L. G. ... Oxford, IA
Klein, Linda A. ... Atlanta, GA
Klein, Linda B. ... New York, NY
Klein, Linda B. ... Akron, OH
Klein, Linda Booz ... New Haven, CT
Klein, Linda S. ... Charlotte, NC
Klein, Linda Z. ... Bloomfield Hills, MI
Klein, Lisa E. ... Federal Election Commission, Office of the General Counsel, GV
Klein, Lisa Hamilton ... Los Angeles, CA
Klein, Lisa R. ... Santa Monica, CA
Klein, Lori D. ... Santa Cruz, CA
Klein, Lorri J. Kolbert ... Boca Raton, FL
Klein, Louis C. ... Los Angeles, CA
Klein, Louis M ... Kingston, NY
Klein, Louis T. ... Grand Blanc, MI
Klein, Luise M. ... Manhasset Hills, NY
Klein, M. Christine ... Richmond, VA
Klein, M. David ... Mineola, NY
Klein, M. Michael ... Washington, DC
Klein, Marc D. ... New York, NY
Klein, Marc H. ... Dallas, TX
Klein, Marc S. ... Somerville, NJ
Klein, Margaret G. ... Knoxville, TN
Klein, Margot ... Chicago, IL
Klein, Marian M.J. ... La Crescenta, CA
Klein, Marilyn Y. ... Woodcliff Lake, NJ
Klein, Marjorie E. ... Roseland, NJ
Klein, Mark Alexander ... Beverly Hills, CA
Klein, Mark B. ... Cherry Hill, NJ
Philadelphia, PA
Klein, Mark D. ... Irvine, CA
Klein, Mark E. ... New York, NY
Klein, Mark J. ... Kansas City, MO
Klein, Mark J. ... Jamison, PA
Klein, Mark J., P.C. ... Kansas City, MO
Klein, Mark N. ... New York, NY
Klein, Mark S. ... San Francisco, CA
Klein, Mark S. ... Boca Raton, FL
Buffalo, NY
New York, NY
Klein, Marlene ... Irvine, CA
Seattle, WA
Klein, Marne J. ... Denver, CO
Klein, Martha M. ... Dallas, TX
Klein & Martin ... Los Angeles, CA
Klein, Martin ... New York, NY
Klein, Martin B. ... Bronx, NY
Klein, Martin I. ... New York, NY
Klein, Martin I., P.C. ... New York, NY
Klein, Martin S. ... New York, NY
Klein, Mary Ellen ... Far Rockaway, NY
Klein, Mary Kay ... Bemidji, MN
Klein, Mathew R., Jr. ... Covington, KY
Klein, Matthew ... Stamford, CT
Klein, Matthew ... Fort Lauderdale, FL
Klein, Matthew ... Jamaica Plain, MA
Klein, Matthew ... Minneapolis, MN
Klein, Maurice E. ... Dallas, TX
Klein, Mayer S. ... St. Louis, MO
Klein, Maynard J. ... Torrance, CA
Klein, Melvin A. ... Manhattan Beach, CA
Klein, Michael ... Des Moines, IA
Klein, Michael ... Austin, TX
Klein, Michael A. ... Chicago, IL
Klein, Michael A. ... Bloomfield, IN
Klein, Michael A. ... Boston, MA
Klein, Michael A. ... Pittsburgh, PA
Klein, Michael C. ... Holdrege, NE
Klein, Michael D. ... Harrisburg, PA
Klein, Michael D. ... Pittsburgh, PA
Klein, Michael E. ... Washington, DC
Klein, Michael E. ... North Brunswick, NJ
Klein, Michael E. ... New York, NY
Klein, Michael F. ... Los Angeles, CA
Klein, Michael F. ... Memphis, TN
Klein, Michael H. ... New York, NY
Klein, Michael J. ... Washington, DC
Klein, Michael J. ... Chicago, IL
Klein, Michael John ... Westlake Village, CA
Klein, Michael L. ... Oceanside, CA
Klein, Michael L. ... Leawood, KS
Klein, Michael L. ... Suffern, NY
Klein, Michael L. ... Midland, TX
Klein, Michael R. ... Washington, DC
Klein, Michael R. ... Garden City, NY
Klein, Michael S. ... Los Angeles, CA
Klein, Michael Stephen ... El Cerrito, CA
Klein, Michele ... White Plains, NY
Klein, Michele I. ... Department of State, Office of the Legal Adviser, GV
Klein, Mignon D. ... Burlington, NJ
Klein, Milton ... Harrison, NY
Klein, Milton D. ... Chestnut Hill, MA
Klein, Mitchell ... New York, NY
Klein, Mitchell B. ... Philadelphia, PA
Klein, Mitchell D. ... Hallandale Beach, FL
Klein, Mitchell L. ... Chicago, IL
Klein, Monte A. ... Albany, NY
Klein, Monte S. ... Bridgeport, CT
Klein, Morris ... Bethesda, MD
Klein, Morris F. ... Miami, FL
Klein, Ms. Lesley B. ... McLean, VA
Klein, Murray J. ... Princeton, NJ
Klein, Murray, (P.A.) ... West Palm Beach, FL
Klein, Murray R. ... Great Neck, NY
Klein, Murray Z. ... Miami, FL
Klein, Nan H. ... New City, NY
Klein, Nanci S. ... Bloomfield Hills, MI
Klein, Nancy Lu ... Santa Rosa, CA
Klein, Nanette Lynn ... Los Angeles, CA
Klein, Neil B. ... Long Beach, CA
Klein, Nicholas F. ... Los Angeles, CA
Klein, Nicholas W. ... Wichita, KS
Klein, Norman I. ... Clifton, NJ
New York, NY
Klein, Norman S. ... Hollywood, FL
Klein & O'Brien ... New York, NY
Klein & O'Rourke, A Law Corporation
Santa Ana, CA
Klein, Otto G., III ... Seattle, WA
Klein, P. Richard ... West Chester, PA
Klein, Pace ... New York, NY
Klein, Paul ... Monterey Park, CA
Klein, Paul B. ... Washington, DC
Klein, Paul E. ... New York, NY
Klein, Paul I. ... Charlotte, NC
Klein, Paul J. ... Los Angeles, CA
Klein, Paul L. ... New York, NY
Klein, Paul M. ... Newark, NJ
Klein, Paul W. ... Allegan, MI
Klein, Peter G. ... Buffalo, NY
Klein, Peter M. ... Elizabeth, NJ
Klein, Philip A. ... Denver, CO
Klein, Philip C. ... San Francisco, CA
Klein, Philip E. ... New York, NY
Klein, Philip I. ... Owings Mills, MD
Klein, Phillip J. ... San Francisco, CA
Klein, Phyllis A. ... New York, NY
Klein, R. Kent ... Phoenix, AZ
Klein, R. Wayne ... Boise, ID
Klein, Randall L. ... Chicago, IL
Klein, Randi Susan ... Berkeley, CA
Klein, Raquel Singer ... Garden City, NY
Klein, Raymond M., (A Prof. Law Corp.)
Los Angeles, CA
Klein, Reuven ... New York, NY
Klein, Rhonda L. ... Atlanta, GA
Klein, Richard ... New York, NY
Klein, Richard ... Williston Park, NY
Klein, Richard A. ... Aptos, CA
Klein, Richard B. ... Philadelphia, PA
Klein, Richard C. ... Haddonfield, NJ
Klein, Richard C. ... Cleveland, OH
Klein, Richard D. ... Naperville, IL
Klein, Richard D. ... Eureka, MO
St. Louis, MO
Washington, MO
Klein, Richard E. ... Jacksonville, FL
Klein, Richard E. ... St. Paul, MN
Klein, Richard F. ... Chicago, IL
Klein, Richard G. ... New York, NY
Klein, Richard J. ... New Haven, CT
New York, NY
Klein, Richard J. ... Santa Fe, NM
Klein, Richard J. ... Pittsburgh, PA
Klein, Richard L. ... New York, NY
Klein, Richard M. ... Riverhead, NY
Klein, Richard M. ... Wilmington, NC
Klein, Richard M. ... Cleveland, OH
Klein, Richard P. ... Atlanta, GA
Klein, Richard R. ... Stinson Beach, CA
Klein, Richard S. ... New York, NY
Klein, Richard W., Jr. ... Washington, DC
Klein, Robert A. ... Los Angeles, CA
Klein, Robert A. ... Mount Laurel, NJ
Philadelphia, PA
Klein, Robert C. ... New York, NY
Klein, Robert D. ... Laguna Hills, CA
Klein, Robert Dale ... Annapolis, MD
Baltimore, MD
Klein, Robert G. ... Los Angeles, CA
Klein, Robert G. ... Honolulu, HI
Klein, Robert H., Jr. ... Waukesha, WI
Klein, Robert J. ... South Elgin, IL
Klein, Robert J. ... Philadelphia, PA
Klein, Robert L. ... Newington, CT
Klein, Robert L. ... New York, NY
Klein, Robert M. ... Los Angeles, CA
Klein, Robert M. ... Chicago, IL
Highland Park, IL
Northbrook, IL
Klein, Robert M. ... Louisville, KY
Klein, Robert Michael ... Miami, FL
Klein, Robert N. ... Fresno, CA
Klein, Robert N. ... Fort Pierce, FL
Klein, Robert S. ... North Miami Beach, FL
Klein, Robert S. ... Seattle, WA
Klein, Rodney A. ... Sacramento, CA
Klein, Rodney A., A Professional Corporation
Sacramento, CA
Klein, Rodney S. ... Kingsport, TN
Klein, Roger ... Chagrin Falls, OH
Klein, Roger A. ... Greeley, CO
Klein, Roger A. ... Washington, DC
Klein, Rona ... Boston, MA
Klein, Ronald B. ... Redwood City, CA
Klein, Ronald G. ... North Miami, FL
Klein, Ronald G. ... De Kalb, IL
Genoa, IL
Klein, Ronald H. ... Berkeley, CA
Klein, Ronald J. ... Boca Raton, FL
Klein, Roseanne M. ... New York, NY
Klein, Rowan K. ... Los Angeles, CA
Klein, Roy A., Law Offices ... Melville, NY
Klein, Ruben ... Yonkers, NY
Klein, S. Lynne ... Davis, CA
Klein, S. Philip ... Bridgewater, NJ
Klein, Saml. C. ... Washington, DC
Klein, Samuel E. ... Philadelphia, PA
Klein, Sandra R. ... Los Angeles, CA
Klein, Sanford A. ... Troy, MI
Klein, Sara B. ... Ironton, OH
Klein, Sara J. ... Pittsburgh, PA
Klein, Scott Harris ... Brooklyn, NY
Klein, Scott P. ... Los Angeles, CA
Klein, Sean J. ... Washington, DC
Klein, Shamira ... Miami, FL
Klein, Sharon R. ... Philadelphia, PA
Klein, Shaun M. ... Kansas City, MO
Klein, Sheldon H. ... Washington, DC
Klein, Sherry Murray ... Phoenix, AZ
Klein & Solomon, LLP ... New York, NY
Klein, Spencer D. ... New York, NY
Klein, Stanley D. ... Encino, CA
Klein, Stanley H. ... Boca Raton, FL
Klein, Stanley M. ... New York, NY
Klein, Stanley P. ... Fairfax, VA
Klein, Stefanie M. ... Arlington, TX
Klein, Stephan E. ... San Francisco, CA
Klein, Stephen A. ... Washington, DC
Klein, Stephen A. ... Rockville, MD
Klein, Stephen A. ... Montpelier, VT
Klein, Stephen C. ... Los Angeles, CA
Klein, Stephen E. ... Vandalia, OH
Klein, Stephen L. ... West New York, NJ
Klein, Stephen L. ... Rutland, VT
Klein, Stephen M. ... Washington, DC
Klein, Stephen M. ... Seattle, WA
Klein, Stephen S.
Department Of Health And Human Services, Food & Drug Administration, GV
Klein, Steven D. ... New York, NY
Klein, Steven H. ... Chicago, IL
Klein, Steven I., (P.C.) ... New Orleans, LA
Klein, Steven J. ... Newark, NJ
Klein, Steven L. ... San Diego, CA
Klein, Steven M. ... Miami, FL
Klein, Steven R. ... Hackensack, NJ
Klein, Stewart ... New York, NY
Klein, Stoddard, Buck & Waller
De Kalb, IL
Genoa, IL
Sycamore, IL
Klein, Stuart A. ... New York, NY
Klein, Stuart B. ... West Palm Beach, FL
Klein, Stuart L. ... Los Altos, CA
Klein, Susan E. ...
Department of Energy, GV
Klein, Susan F. ... New York, NY
Klein, Susan J. ... Baltimore, MD
Klein, Susan L. ... Burbank, CA
Klein, Susan Riva ... Austin, TX
Klein & Szekeres, LLP ... Irvine, CA
Klein, Tamara S. ... Chicago, IL
Klein, Tannen & Cohen, P.A.
Hollywood, FL
Klein, Theodore ... Miami, FL
Klein, Theodore J. ... North Miami Beach, FL
Klein, Thomas Christopher ... Palo Alto, CA
Klein, Thomas I. ... Bloomfield Hills, MI
Klein, Thomas J. ... Wahoo, NE
Klein, Thomas L. ... Washington, DC
Klein, Thomas L. ... Russell, KY
Ironton, OH
Klein, Thomas M. ... Phoenix, AZ
Klein, Thomas M. ... Arlington Heights, IL
Klein, Thomas P. ... San Francisco, CA
Klein, Thorpe and Jenkins, Ltd. ... Chicago, IL
Klein, Tiffany Welch ... San Francisco, CA
Klein, Timothy J. ... Bloomingdale, IL
Klein, Tracey L. ... Milwaukee, WI
Klein, Traycee E. ... New York, NY
Klein & Vibber, P.C. ... Westport, CT
Klein, Wagner & Morris ... New York, NY
Klein, Walter ... Beverly Hills, CA
Klein, Warren J. ... West Babylon, NY
Klein & Weisz ... Los Angeles, CA
Klein, Wendy F. ... Hackensack, NJ
Klein, Wendy S. ... Chicago, IL
Klein & White ... Minnetonka, MN
Klein, Whitney A. ... Newark, NJ
Klein, William A. ... Los Angeles, CA
Klein, William D. ... Minneapolis, MN
Klein, William H., P.C. ... Pottstown, PA
Klein, William, II, (P.C.) ... New York, NY
Klein, William J. ... Chicago, IL
Klein, William J., Jr. ... Denver, CO
Klein, William P. ... San Francisco, CA
Klein, William R. ... Chicago, IL
Klein, William R. ... New Orleans, LA
Klein, William R. ... St. Joseph, MI
Klein, William S. ... San Jose, CA
Klein, Zelman, Rothermel & Dichter, L.L.P.
New York, NY
Klein - Zimet, A Professional Corporation
Aspen, CO
Kleinau, Glen R., Jr. ... Chattanooga, TN
Klein-Baker, Tina ... New York, NY
Kleinbard, Bell & Brecker LLP
Montclair, NJ
Philadelphia, PA
Kleinbard, Edward D. ... New York, NY
Kleinbart, Cynthia Wynne ... Bronx, NY
Kleinbart, Morrie I. ... New York, NY
Kleinbaum, Charles ... Old Chatham, NY
Kleinbaum, Clifford G. ... White Plains, NY
Kleinbaum, E. Aaron ... Woodcliff Lake, NJ
Kleinbaum, Gerald M. ... New York, NY
Kleinbaum, Glenn A. ... New York, NY
Kleinbaum, James E., Law Offices of
Chatham, NY
Kleinbaum, Paul L. ... Newark, NJ
Kleinbaum, Wendy Slote
Long Island City, NY
Kleinberg, Bruce M. ... Tampa, FL
Kleinberg, Charles S. ... Brooklyn, NY
Kleinberg, David ... Miami, FL
Kleinberg, David K.
Department of Transportation, Office of the Secretary, GV
Kleinberg, Deborah ... Camp Springs, MD
Kleinberg, Elaine ... New York, NY
Kleinberg, Elliott ... Los Angeles, CA
Kleinberg, Fredric A. ... New York, NY
Kleinberg & Friedman ... New York, NY
Kleinberg, Howard B. ... Uniondale, NY
Kleinberg, James P. ... Palo Alto, CA
Kleinberg, Janet Rinauro ... San Jose, CA
Kleinberg, Jerry M. ... New York, NY
Kleinberg, Joel W. H., A Professional Corporation ... Los Angeles, CA
Kleinberg, Joel W. H. ... Los Angeles, CA
Kleinberg, Judith ... Columbia, MO
Kleinberg, Julie I. ... Los Angeles, CA
Kleinberg, Kaplan, Wolff & Cohen
Hackensack, NJ
New York, NY
Kleinberg, Kenneth ... Los Angeles, CA
Kleinberg & Lerner, LLP
Los Angeles, CA
Kleinberg, Lester, Jr. ... Seattle, WA
Kleinberg, Lisa J. ... Sarasota, FL
Kleinberg, Lois H. ... Englewood Cliffs, NJ
Kleinberg Lopez Lange Brisbin & Cuddy, L.L.P. ... Los Angeles, CA
Kleinberg, Marvin H. ... Los Angeles, CA
Kleinberg, Norman C. ... New York, NY
Kleinberg, Richard D. ... Natick, MA
Kleinberg, Robert I. ... New York, NY
Kleinberg, Robert S. ... Park Ridge, NJ
Kleinberg, Ronald M. ... New York, NY
Kleinberg, Seymour R. ... Hazlet, NJ
Kleinberg, Sue E. ... Keyport, NJ
Kleinberg, Sydney H. ... Lake Worth, FL
Kleinberger, Alan E. ... New York, NY
Kleinberger, Daniel S. ... Minneapolis, MN
Kleinberger, George H. ... Voorheesville, NY
Kleinbrodt, Peter A. ... San Rafael, CA
Kleinbrook, Charles ... Detroit, MI
Kleinburd, Alan E. ... Department of Justice, Civil Division, GV
Kleindienst, Anne L. ... Phoenix, AZ
Kleindienst, Richard G. ... Prescott, AZ
Kleindorfer, J. William ... Chicago, IL
Kleindorfer, Julian Thomas Herbert
Chicago, IL
Kleine, Lisa A. ... Gaithersburg, MD

Kleine, Lorri A. .... **Norfolk, VA**
Kleine, Michael P. .... Pasadena, CA
Kleine, Richard A. .... St. Louis, MO
Kleine, Thomas C. .... **Virginia Beach, VA**
Kleiner, Barry R. .... **New York, NY**
Kleiner, Daniel E. .... Philadelphia, PA
Kleiner, Darlene D. .... **New York, NY**
Kleiner, Gregg Steven .... **San Francisco, CA**
San Jose, CA
Kleiner, H. Frances .... **New York, NY**
Kleiner, Helen E. .... **Newark, NJ**
Kleiner, Jackie .... New York, NY
Kleiner, James D. .... **New York, NY**
Kleiner, Joanne E. .... Jenkintown, PA
Kleiner, Joel I. .... Flint, MI
Kleiner, Madeleine Ann .... Irwindale, CA
Kleiner, Philip J. .... **New York, NY**
Kleiner, Risa A. .... **Woodbridge, NJ**
Kleiner, Samuel K. .... New York, NY
Kleiner, Steven Z. .... Bridgeton, NJ
Kleiner, Stuart J. .... Cleveland, OH
Kleiner, Susan Schleck .... **Princeton, NJ**
Kleinerman, Michael R. .... **New York, NY**
Kleinert, Jennifer G. .... **Santa Monica, CA**
Kleinfeld, Andrew J. .... Fairbanks, AK
Kleinfeld, Burton H. .... Boston, MA
Kleinfeld, Carl .... Sun City, CA
Kleinfeld, David E. .... **La Jolla, CA**
Kleinfeld, Denis A. .... Miami, FL
Kleinfeld & DePaola .... Boston, MA
Kleinfeld, Douglas R. .... New Providence, NJ
Kleinfeld, Eric F. .... Washington, DC
Kleinfeld, George D. .... **Washington, DC**
Kleinfeld, Harold A. .... Kingston, NY
Kleinfeld & Heiser, Inc. .... Stockton, CA
Kleinfeld, Jane G. .... New Providence, NJ
Kleinfeld, Kaplan and Becker
San Francisco, CA
Washington, DC
Kleinfeld & Kleinfeld .... New Providence, NJ
Kleinfeld Law Firm, The .... Miami, FL
Kleinfeld, Mark B. .... **Palm Beach, FL**
Kleinfeld, Mark B., P.A. .... **Palm Beach, FL**
Kleinfeld, Oscar Budd .... Stockton, CA
Kleinfeld, Ruth L.
Department of Commerce, GV
Kleinfeld, Sam W. .... East Marion, NY
Kleinfeld, Victor W. .... Brooklyn, NY
Kleinfeldt, James R. .... Oshkosh, WI
Kleinfelter, David L. .... **Nashville, TN**
Kleinfelter, Stephanie .... **Harrisburg, PA**
Kleinhandler, Neil C. .... **New York, NY**
Kleinhans, Alice .... Lowell, MA
Kleinhans, Barbara A. .... Kalamazoo, MI
Kleinhans, Edward A. .... **San Francisco, CA**
Kleinhans, Elysabeth K. .... New York, NY
Kleinhans, Kacy F. .... **Minneapolis, MN**
Kleinhardt, Charles R. .... **Garden City, NY**
Kleinhardt, Mara .... **Garden City, NY**
Kleinhaus, Edward A. .... **San Francisco, CA**
Kleinhaus, Ferdinand Herman
Cincinnati, OH
Kleinheksel, John K. .... Denver, CO
Kleinhendler, Howard .... **New York, NY**
Kleinherenbrink, Reindert J. .... Hutchinson, KS
Kleinhubert, Daniel Joseph .... Waukegan, IL
Kleinhuizen, Todd M. .... **Willmar, MN**
Kleinick, Arnold L. .... **New York, NY**
Kleinick, Jodi A. .... **New York, NY**
Kleinick, Keith A. .... **New York, NY**
Kleinjan, Mary A.
Agency for International Development,
Legal Advisers-Overseas, GV
Kleinkauf, Pamela F. .... San Diego, CA
Kleinkauf, William J. .... **Dallas, TX**
Kleinke, Bernard L. .... **San Diego, CA**
Kleinknecht, Richard B. .... Richmond, IN
Kleinknecht, Robert T. .... **Naples, FL**
Kleinkopf, David D. .... **Denver, CO**
Kleinle, Reed C. .... Morristown, NJ
Kleinlein, Mark D. .... Dearborn Heights, MI
Kleinmaier, Stephen W. .... Madison, WI
Kleinman, Abraham .... Liberty, NY
Kleinman, Abraham N. .... **Bronx, NY**
New City, NY
Kleinman, Alan H. .... New York, NY
Kleinman, Allan D. .... **Cleveland, OH**
Kleinman, Anne Kenny .... Chicago, IL
Kleinman, Arthur E. .... Santa Monica, CA
Kleinman & Associates, P.C.
Hartford, CT
New London, CT
Kleinman, Ava B. .... Basking Ridge, NJ
Kleinman, Bennet .... Cleveland, OH
Kleinman, Bernard .... **Chicago, IL**
Kleinman, Bernard, Ltd. .... **Chicago, IL**
Kleinman, Bernard V. .... White Plains, NY
Kleinman, Bruce .... **Roseland, NJ**
Kleinman, Carol S. .... Jessup, MD
Kleinman, Chester J.
Equal Employment Opportunity
Commission, GV
Kleinman, Daniel E. .... **Farmington, CT**
Kleinman, Daniel Richard
Washington, DC
Kleinman, Elliot .... Garden City, NY
Kleinman, Eric S. .... **Miami, FL**
Kleinman, Gabrielle .... **New York, NY**
Kleinman, Gary S. .... **Hackensack, NJ**
New York, NY
Kleinman, Harold F. .... **Dallas, TX**
Kleinman, Howard A. .... Wellington, FL
Kleinman, Howard L. .... Baltimore, MD
Kleinman, Howard M. .... **New York, NY**
Kleinman, Jan L. .... **Phoenix, AZ**
Kleinman, Jeffrey L. .... Portland, OR
Kleinman, Joan D. .... Chevy Chase, MD
Kleinman, Joel B. .... **Washington, DC**
Kleinman, Kenneth D. .... **Wayne, PA**
Kleinman, Kenneth W. .... **Cleveland, OH**
Kleinman, Laurence D. .... **New City, NY**
Kleinman, Lenore .... Cleveland, OH
Kleinman, Leonard L. .... **Tampa, FL**
Kleinman, Lesselyong & Novak
Phoenix, AZ
Kleinman, Linda L. .... **Deerfield Beach, FL**
Kleinman, Lisa F. .... Beverly Hills, CA
Kleinman, Mark H. .... Dallas, TX
Kleinman, Martin .... Baltimore, MD
Kleinman, Martin G. .... Garden City, NY
Kleinman, Martin I. .... **Philadelphia, PA**
Kleinman, Martin I., P.C.
Philadelphia, PA
Kleinman, Marvin .... Cincinnati, OH
Kleinman, Max L. .... Merrick, NY
Kleinman, Michael J. .... Lakewood, CO
Kleinman, Milton E. .... **Muskegon, MI**
Kleinman, Neil .... Pomona, NJ
Kleinman, Paul B. .... **Manchester, NH**
Kleinman, Ralph .... New York, NY
Kleinman, Randall L. .... **New Orleans, LA**
Kleinman, Richard .... **Chicago, IL**
Kleinman, Richard E. .... Chagrin Falls, OH
Kleinman, Robert S., (P.A.)
Deerfield Beach, FL
Kleinman, Robert W. .... **Chicago, IL**
Kleinman, Roberta S. .... Chicago, IL
Kleinman, Roger L. .... **Cleveland, OH**
Kleinman, Ronald W. .... **Washington, DC**
Kleinman, Saltzman & Bolnick L.L.P.
New City, NY
Kleinman, Sidney C. .... **Chicago, IL**
Kleinman, Stephen R. .... **Columbus, OH**
Kleinman, Steven C. .... Jericho, NY
Kleinman, Stewart F. .... **Hartford, CT**
New London, CT
Kleinman, Stuart T. .... **New York, NY**
Kleinman, Todd M. .... **New York, NY**
Kleinman, William N. .... Farmington, CT
Kleinman, Wm. S. .... **Dallas, TX**
Kleinpeter, Jennifer M. .... **Lafayette, LA**
Kleinpeter & Kleinpeter
Baton Rouge, LA
Kleinpeter, Melanie .... Baton Rouge, LA
Kleinpeter, R. Loren .... **Baton Rouge, LA**
Kleinpeter, Robert E. .... **Baton Rouge, LA**
Kleinpeter, Robert L. .... **Baton Rouge, LA**
Kleinpeter, Schwartzberg & Stevens
Baton Rouge, LA
Morgan City, LA
Kleinpeter, William T. .... Baton Rouge, LA
Kleinschmidt, Bruce L. .... Indianapolis, IN
Kleinschmidt, Gerhard .... **Fort Worth, TX**
Kleinschmidt, James B. .... Clayton, MO
Kleinschmidt, Mark A. .... **Minneapolis, MN**
Kleinschmidt, Otto .... Holbrook, NY
Kleinschmidt, Przybeck & Frayne
St. Louis, MO
Kleinschmidt, Robert H. .... Scottsdale, AZ
Kleinschmidt, Robert S., Jr.
Lake Charles, LA
Kleinschmidt, Thomas C. .... Phoenix, AZ
Kleinschmidt, Timothy A. .... Giddings, TX
Kleinsmith & Associates, P.C.
Colorado Springs, CO
Kleinsmith, Kenneth L. .... Lake Oswego, OR
Kleinsmith, Philip M.
Colorado Springs, CO
Kleinstein, Bruce H. .... Philadelphia, PA
Kleinstuber, Dorian Rowe
Rehoboth Beach, DE
Kleintop, Charles T. .... **Honolulu, HI**
Klein VandeWiele, Jennifer .... **Peoria, IL**
Kleis, Eric R.
Department of the Navy, GV
Kleiser, James A., Jr. .... Memphis, TN
Kleisle, Laura .... **Seattle, WA**
Kleissler, Thomas F. .... **Cherry Hill, NJ**
Kleist, J. Murray .... **Seattle, WA**
Kleist, Mark A. .... **Grand Haven, MI**
Klejman, Nathan G. .... Bronx, NY
Klejna, Dennis A. .... New York, NY
Klejwa, Padmavati G. .... Palatine, IL
Klekamp, Donald P. .... **Cincinnati, OH**
Klekamp, Jody T. .... **Cincinnati, OH**
Klekers, Carl I. .... Omaha, NE
Klekman, Michael R. .... **New York, NY**
Klekner, Michael L. .... Los Angeles, CA
Klekner, Pamela Ann .... Belleville, IL
Klekotka, Walter J. .... **Cherry Hill, NJ**
Klele, Steffani Lynn .... **Fredericksburg, VA**
Klem, Abigail .... **Los Angeles, CA**
Klem, Christopher A. .... **Boston, MA**
Klem & Klem .... Shattuck, OK
Klem, Laura Vinci .... Red Bank, NJ
Klem, M. Cecil .... Shattuck, OK
Klem, Stanley M. .... Chicago, IL
Klem, Steven A. .... Chicago, IL
Klema, Catherine M. .... New York, NY
Klema, Connie J. .... **Newark, OH**
Kleman, Debra E. .... **Charlotte, NC**
Kleman, Richard D. .... McLean, VA
Kleman, Rodney M. .... Salinas, CA
Klemann, Gilbert L., II .... Old Greenwich, CT
Klemanowicz, Benjamin J., Jr.
Garden City, NY
Klemanski and Honeyman, P.C. .... Troy, MI
Klemanski, James C. .... Troy, MI
Klembczyk, Jeffrey R. .... **Albany, NY**
Klembus, Nancy M. .... Roswell, GA
Klemchuk, Darin M. .... **Dallas, TX**
Klemczak, Dwight F. .... Southfield, MI
Klemens, Melissa Lin .... **Gaithersburg, MD**
Klemens, Thaddeus E. .... San Rafael, CA
Klemensic, Francis J. .... **Erie, PA**
Klement, Lynn J. .... Angleton, TX
Klementik, David C. .... Windber, PA
Klementovich, Leo F. .... **Williamsport, PA**
Klements, Joseph M. .... **Boston, MA**
Klements, Newton Leigh
Department of the Army,
Office, Chief of Engineers/Headquarters,
U.S. Army Corps of Engineers, GV
Klemer, Anthony, Jr. .... Detroit, MI
Klemesrud, Normand C. .... Nashua, IA
Klemetson, Bret R. .... **Chicago, IL**
Klemeyer, John H. .... Milford, PA
Klemick, William J. .... **Pittsburgh, PA**
Klemin, Lawrence R. .... **Bismarck, ND**
Klemkowski, Henry W. .... Baltimore, MD
Klemkowski & Klemkowski, P.A.
Baltimore, MD
Klemkowski, Ronald J. .... Baltimore, MD
Klemm, Blair, Sterling & Johnson, A Professional Corporation .... **Hagåtña, GU**
Klemm, Brian W. .... Whippany, NJ
Klemm, David Michael .... Boston, MA
Klemm, H. Ralph .... Bountiful, UT
Klemm, J. Bradley .... **Hagåtña, GU**
Klemm, Joan L. .... New York, NY
Klemm, Kenneth M. .... **New Orleans, LA**
Klemm, Paul J. .... San Diego, CA
Klemm, Russell E. .... **Brandon, FL**
Klemme, A. Christian .... **Dallas, TX**
Klemme, Amelia L. .... Denver, CO
Klemme, G. Harmon .... Little Falls, MN
Klemme, Howard C. .... Boulder, CO
Klemme, Jeffrey .... Ventura, CA
Klemme, Virginia M. .... Lawrence, KS
San Angelo, TX
Klemmensen, Todd J. .... **St. Paul, MN**
Klemmer, Joyce B. .... **Atlanta, GA**
Klemmer, Susan E. .... **Phoenix, AZ**
Klemonski, Edward S. .... West Hartford, CT
Klemow, Lawrence M. .... **Hazleton, PA**
Klemp, D. Scott .... St. Paul, MN
Klemp, Jeffrey J. .... Eau Claire, WI
Klemper, Cindy .... **Santa Barbara, CA**
Klemperer, Leslie P. .... Atlanta, GA
Klemperer, Michelle H. .... Yonkers, NY
Klemperer, Sally .... **New York, NY**
Klempner, Esther .... **Tustin, CA**
Klempner, Joseph T. .... New York, NY
Klempner & Klempner .... **Tustin, CA**
Klempner, Robert S. .... Tustin, CA
Klempner, Ronald E. .... New York, NY
Klemt, Becky N. .... **Laramie, WY**
Klemt, LeRoy C. .... Chicago, IL
Klemz, Kevin M. .... **Minneapolis, MN**
Klemz, Nicole A. .... **Milwaukee, WI**
Klenck, Paul R. .... Chicago, IL
Klenda, Gordon & Getchell, P.C. .... Tulsa, OK
Klenda, Gregory B. .... **Wichita, KS**
Klenda, John B. .... McPherson, KS
Klenda, Mitchell, Austerman & Zuercher, L.L.C. .... **Wichita, KS**
Klenda, Steven A. .... **Denver, CO**
Klenda, Thomas M. .... Tulsa, OK
Klene, Donald A. .... Denver, CO
Klene, Therese McCullough
Indianapolis, IN
Klengler, Ingolf .... Burbank, CA
Klenk, Donald R. .... Potomac, MD
Klenk, James A. .... **Chicago, IL**
Klenk, Jeffrey P. .... **Simsbury, CT**
Klenk, Marcia .... **Chicago, IL**
Klenk, Paul T. .... Attleboro, MA
Klenk, Peter L. .... **Philadelphia, PA**
Klenk, Thomas E. L. .... Elkton, MD
Klenk, Timothy C. .... **Chicago, IL**
Klenk, William C. .... Medina, OH
Klenkar, James A. .... **Winchester, VA**
Klenke, Daniel F. .... **Aurora, IL**
Klenoff, Ross .... New York, NY
Kleopfer, James D., Jr. .... Scottsburg, IN
Klepac, Christopher T.
United States Postal Service,
Law Department, GV
Klepac, Glenn E. .... **Alcoa Center, PA**
Klepak, Gary I. .... Columbus, GA
Klepak, Ralla .... Chicago, IL
Klepaski, Cynthia M. .... Fairbanks, AK
Klepatsky, Arlene Dorothy
Castro Valley, CA
Klepatz, Mark A. .... Findlay, OH
Klepec, Jos. A. .... Joliet, IL
Kleper, Ann-Louise .... Chicago, IL
Kleper, Dennis M. .... Skokie, IL
Klepesch, Stuart B. .... Morristown, NJ
Klepetar, Ronald J. .... **Los Angeles, CA**
Klepetko, Lawrence .... Sarasota, FL
Klepfer, Robert O., Jr. .... **Greensboro, NC**
Klepfish, Isaac .... New York, NY
Klepinski, Robert J. .... Minneapolis, MN
Klepner, Lawrence M. .... New York, NY
Klepner, Miriam S. .... **New York, NY**
Klepner, Philip S. .... Great Neck, NY
Klepp, Frederick W. .... **Cherry Hill, NJ**
Philadelphia, PA
Klepp, Robert G.
Environmental Protection Agency,
Program Office Attorneys, GV
Kleppe, Andrew W. .... Caldwell, NJ
Kleppe, Jennifer L. .... **Philadelphia, PA**
Klepper, Arlene Fine .... **Washington, DC**
Klepper, Cheryl Ann .... Thousand Oaks, CA
Klepper, Faith C. .... Phoenix, AZ
Klepper, Irwin .... Tucson, AZ
Klepper, Jim C. .... Oklahoma City, OK
Klepper, Lester .... New York, NY
Klepper, Martin .... **Washington, DC**
Klepper, Matthew S. .... **Chicago, IL**
Klepper, Steven L. .... **Hackensack, NJ**
Klepperich, Thomas J. .... **Sheridan, WY**
Kleppin, Fred C. .... Rockford, IL
Kleppin, Glenda L. .... Sumner, WA
Kleppinger, David M. .... **Harrisburg, PA**
Kleppinger, Kenneth W. .... **Malvern, PA**
Kleppner, Ferdinand J. .... Metairie, LA
Klepser, Mary .... Portland, OR
Kleri, Jon C. .... Cleveland, OH
Kleri, Patricia S. .... Cleveland, OH
Kleronomos, Dean J. .... Yorkville, IL
Klesaris, Karine A. .... Tewksbury, MA
Klesch, John H. .... **South Burlington, VT**
Kleschen, F. Henry, III .... Chicago, IL
Klesel, Michael F. .... La Grange, TX
Klesmith, Colleen S. .... Grand Rapids, MI
Klesner, Steven G. .... **Iowa City, IA**
Klessen, Helga .... Bedford, NY
Mount Kisco, NY
Klessig, Christine L. .... Amherst, WI
Klest, Joseph G. .... Schaumburg, IL
Klestadt, Alan R. .... **New York, NY**
Klestadt, Helmut .... New York, NY
Klestadt, Peter W. .... **New York, NY**
Klestadt, Tracy L., & Associates
New York, NY
Kleszynski, Linda C. .... Lansing, IL
Kletke, James R. .... Houston, TX
Kletscher, Bradley Allen
Minneapolis, MN
Klett, David S. .... **Pittsburgh, PA**
Klett, Edwin L. .... **Philadelphia, PA**
Pittsburgh, PA
Klett, John C., Jr. .... New York, NY
Klett Lieber Rooney & Schorling, A Professional Corporation
Wilmington, DE
Cherry Hill, NJ
Harrisburg, PA
Philadelphia, PA
Pittsburgh, PA
Klett, Peter F. .... **Nashville, TN**
Klett, Stanley Dale, Jr.
Palm Beach Gardens, FL
Klett, Taylor S. .... **Houston, TX**
Klett, William Y., III .... **San Antonio, TX**
Klette, John H., Jr. .... Covington, KY
Klette and Klette .... Covington, KY
Cincinnati, OH
Klette, V. Ruth .... Covington, KY
Cincinnati, OH
Kletter, Cary Seth .... **New York, NY**
Kletter, James C. .... Pittsburgh, PA
Kletter, Lawrence A. .... **Boston, MA**
Kletter, Matthew L. .... New York, NY
Kletzkin, Marshall Jay .... Edison, NJ
Kletzkin, Morris .... **Washington, DC**
Kletzky, Daniel S. .... **Burbank, CA**
Kletzman, Julie L. .... San Diego, CA
Kleva, Barbara M. .... Trenton, NJ
Klevan, Bryna S. .... Wayland, MA
Klevan, Mitchell H. .... **Philadelphia, PA**
Klevan, Morton .... Department of Labor,
Pension and Welfare Benefits, GV
Klevansky, Lorraine S. .... **Honolulu, HI**
Klevansky, Simon .... **Honolulu, HI**
Klevatt, David S. .... **Chicago, IL**
Kleve, Robert E. .... Grand Forks, ND
Kleveland, Jeanelle .... Lincoln, NE
Kleven, Debbie G. .... Grand Forks, ND
Kleven, Paul .... Berkeley, CA
Kleven, Richard J. .... Minneapolis, MN
Kleven, Thomas .... Houston, TX
Kleven, Thomas C. .... Kent, WA
Klevenhagen, John J., III .... **Houston, TX**
Klevens, Joel N. .... **Santa Monica, CA**
Kleveter, Lesley C. .... El Segundo, CA
Klevickis, Marsha Kellman .... **Atlanta, GA**
Klevit, Jerold G. .... Philadelphia, PA
Klevorn, Andrew G. .... **Chicago, IL**
Klevorn, Kevin G. .... Boyne City, MI
Klevorn & Klevorn .... Boyne City, MI
Klevorn, Robert J., Jr. .... St. Louis, MO
Klevorn, Robert J., P.C. .... St. Louis, MO
Klewans, Samuel N. .... **Alexandria, VA**
Kleweno, Gilbert H. .... Vancouver, WA
Kleweno, Melvin L., Jr. .... **Kent, WA**
Klewin, Jane E. .... **Chicago, IL**
Klewin, William M. .... Madison, WI
Kleyman, Howard S. .... Minneapolis, MN
Kleynenberg, Jennifer J. .... **Chicago, IL**
Klezmer, Max .... Indianapolis, IN
Klezmer, Randal M. .... Indianapolis, IN
Kliavkoff, George T. .... Seattle, WA
Klibaner, Alexander .... **San Francisco, CA**
Klibaner, David A. .... **Denver, CO**
Klibaner, Richard B. .... Cambridge, MA
Klibaner & Sabino .... Cambridge, MA
Klibanoff, Elton B. .... Reading, MA
Klibanow, David .... New Rochelle, NY
Klibanow, Linda S. .... **Los Angeles, CA**
Kliber, William R. .... Grosse Ile, MI
Klich, Adriana .... Cabin John, MD
Klich, John J., Jr. .... Chicago, IL
Klick, James C. .... **New Orleans, LA**
Klick, Norman F., Jr. .... **Greensboro, NC**
Klick, Rhonda .... Long Beach, CA
Klick, Theodore W., Jr.
Port Washington, NY
Klicka, Christopher J. .... Purcellville, VA
Klicka, William J. .... Chicago, IL
Klickstein, Barry C. .... **Boston, MA**
Klida, Dawn Ann .... Bay City, MI
Klide, Harry E. .... Canton, OH
Klie, Hamilton F. .... Sanibel, FL
Kliebard, Kenneth M. .... **Chicago, IL**
Kliebenstein, Don .... **Grundy Center, IA**
Kliebenstein, Heronimus, Schmidt & Harris
Grundy Center, IA
Kliebenstein, Neil M. .... **Minneapolis, MN**

Kliebert & Heltz, A Professional Corporation .... Gramercy, LA
Kliebert, Thomas J. .... Gramercy, LA
Kliebert, Thomas J., Jr. .... Gramercy, LA
Klied, Jerome J. .... East Meadow, NY
Kliefoth, Christopher .... Washington, DC
Klieger, Bernard P. .... New York, NY
Klieger, David M. .... Philadelphia, PA
Klieger, Louis .... New York, NY
Klieger, Robert N. .... Los Angeles, CA
Kliegman, David R. .... Kew Gardens, NY
Kliegman, Joseph H. .... Garden City, NY
Kliegman, Matthew I. .... New York, NY
Kliegman, Michael J. .... New York, NY
Klieman, Lyons, Schindler & Gross .... Boston, MA
Klieman, Rikki J. .... Boston, MA
Klien, Lori E. .... Washington, DC
Klier, Daniel J. .... Sherman Oaks, CA
Kliesmet, Mary Honzik .... Kalamazoo, MI
Kliever, Douglas E. .... Washington, DC
Kliewer, Breen, Garatoni, Patterson & Malone, Incorporated .... Austin, TX
San Antonio, TX
Kliewer, Edward, III .... San Antonio, TX
Kliewer, Edward, Jr. .... San Antonio, TX
Kliewer, John B. .... New York, NY
Kliewer, Kyndal R. .... Bethany, OK
Kliewer, Lauralyn Brown .... New York, NY
Kliewer, Lori K. .... Bend, OR
Kliewer, Marc E. .... Cimarron, KS
Kliff, Michael David .... Buffalo Grove, IL
Kliger, Garth M. .... Costa Mesa, CA
Kliger, Lesley E. .... Pasadena, CA
Kliger, Mark S. .... New Haven, CT
Kligerman, Catherine Petersen .... Hartford, CT
Kligerman, Julie .... Stratford, NJ
Kligler, Catherine Whelan .... North Easton, MA
Kligman & Fleming .... Columbia, SC
Kligman, Melton .... Columbia, SC
Kligman, Robert I. .... San Francisco, CA
Kligman, Theodore .... Washington, DC
Klijian, Sosi Biricik .... San Diego, CA
Klika, Liao, Parrish & Cochran .... Pasadena, CA
Klika, Peter .... Pasadena, CA
Klikna, John J. .... Plantsville, CT
Klikoff, W. Alexander .... Incline Village, NV
Kliks, Bernard B. .... Portland, OR
Klim, David G. .... Syracuse, NY
Klima, Barbara A. .... St. Joseph, MO
Klima & Hopkins, P.C. .... Arlington, VA
Klima & Pezzlo, P.C. .... Stafford, VA
Klima, Robert H. .... Manassas, VA
Klima, Timothy J. .... Washington, DC
Klima, William L. .... Stafford, VA
Klimacek, Stephen M. .... Atlanta, GA
Klima Liner, Katherine E. .... Los Angeles, CA
Kliman, Burton S., & Associates, P.C., Law Offices of .... Boston, MA
Kliman, Burton S., & Associates, P.C., Law Offices of .... Newton, MA
Kliman, Steven E. .... Brooklyn, NY
Klimas, Audrius Tadas .... Rochester, NY
Klimas, Elizabeth J. .... Flossmoor, IL
Klimas & Klimas .... Flossmoor, IL
Klimas, Linda A. .... Cincinnati, OH
Klimas, Michael J. .... Flossmoor, IL
Klimas, Robert J. .... Chicago, IL
Klimas, Susan .... Treasury Department, Bureau of the Public Debt, GV
Klimashousky, William J. .... Harrison, NY
Klima-Silberg, Catherine I. .... Minneapolis, MN
Klimaski, James R. .... Washington, DC
Klimaski & Miller, P.C. .... Washington, DC
Klimaszewski, Annette .... West Trenton, NJ
Klimaszewski, David C. .... Boise, ID
Klimaszewski, Sandra M. .... Sacramento, CA
Klimaszewski, Theodore Steven .... Lansing, MI
Klimczak, Beth Parker .... Battle Creek, MI
Klimczak, Ken .... Chicago, IL
Klimczuk, Christine .... North Brunswick, NJ
Klimczyk, Berta S. .... Janesville, WI
Klimczyk, Waldemar .... Janesville, WI
Klimek, Amy .... Cleveland, OH
Klimek, John M. .... Chicago, IL
Chicago, IL
Klimek, Joseph A. .... Bloomington, MN
Klimek, Kolodney & Casale, P.C. .... Washington, DC
Klimek, Mark D. .... Cleveland, OH
Klimek, Robert A., Jr. .... Washington, DC
Klimek, Robert F. .... Norridge, IL
Klimenko, Andrew M. .... San Francisco, CA
Kliment, Claudia Donnelly .... St. Charles, IL
Kliment, David P. .... St. Charles, IL
Klimerman, Edward .... New York, NY
Klimesh, Mary Kay .... Chicago, IL
Klimetz, Frederick F. .... Franklin, WI
Klimis, George N. .... Tarpon Springs, FL
Klimis, George N., P.A. .... Tarpon Springs, FL
Klimisch, Robert W. .... Yankton, SD
Klimisch, William J. .... Yankton, SD
Klimist, Bernard T., Law Offices of .... Victoria, TX
Klimjack, Stephen L. .... Mobile, AL
Klimko, Christopher T. .... Dallas, TX
Klimko, Justin G. .... Detroit, MI
Klimkowski, Marguerite Simmons .... Bonita Springs, FL
Klimon, Ellen Schmeltzer .... Philadelphia, PA
Klimon, William Michael .... Washington, DC
Klimowicz, Jason .... Madison, WI
Klimpel, Joan D. .... Milwaukee, WI
Klimpl, Michael A. .... Doylestown, PA
Klimut, David A. .... Denver, CO
Klinck, Jonathan B. .... Torrance, CA
Klinck, Robert G. .... Livingston, NJ
Klinckhardt, Barry J. .... St. Louis, MO
Klindtworth, Jason .... Lake Oswego, OR
Kline, Adam .... Seattle, WA
Kline, Alan S. .... New York, NY
Kline, Allen E. .... Zephyr Cove, NV
Kline, Allen Haber, Jr. .... Houston, TX
Kline, Amy Kushner .... Baltimore, MD
Kline, Andrea Andrews .... Knoxville, TN
Kline, Andrew .... Minneapolis, MN
Kline, Andrew J., Law Offices .... Washington, DC
Kline, Andrew P. .... Richmond, VA
Kline, Angela .... Pittsburgh, PA
Kline, Angela P. .... Schaumburg, IL
Kline, Ann Henderson .... Lebanon, PA
Kline, Ann Walker .... Harrisonburg, VA
Kline, Anthony F. .... Salem, MA
Kline, Arthur J. .... Miami, FL
Kline & Associates, LLC .... Boulder, CO
Longmont, CO
Kline, Barton L. .... Boise, ID
Kline, Bruce P. .... Brighton, MA
Kline, Charles C. .... Miami, FL
Kline, Charles E. .... Boulder, CO
Longmont, CO
Kline & Corogin, Co., L.P.A. .... Port Clinton, OH
Kline, Craig G. .... Los Angeles, CA
Kline, Craig M. .... New York, NY
Kline, Dale A. .... Port Clinton, OH
Kline, David A. .... Fayetteville, NY
Kline, David A. .... Oklahoma City, OK
Kline, David B. .... Philadelphia, PA
Kline, Deborah A. .... Environmental Protection Agency, Office of Enforcement and Compliance Assurance, GV
Kline, Dee Altfater .... Atlanta, GA
Kline, Denis S. .... Louisville, KY
Kline, Douglas J. .... Boston, MA
Kline, E. Barry .... Trenton, NJ
Kline, E. Keller, III .... Allentown, PA
Kline, Elizabeth C. .... Pacific Palisades, CA
Kline, Elyse Salinger .... West Hills, CA
Kline, Eric D. .... Pittsburgh, PA
Kline, Eugene M. .... New York, NY
Kline, Evan J. .... Harrisburg, PA
Kline, F. Randall .... Pocatello, ID
Kline, F. Randall, Chtd. .... Pocatello, ID
Kline, Frederick W., Jr. .... Corona Del Mar, CA
Kline, Gardner & O'Connor, A Professional Corporation .... Gloucester, MA
Kline, Gary A. .... Fort Worth, TX
Kline, Gary B. .... Binghamton, NY
Owego, NY
Kline, Gary H. .... Chicago, IL
Kline, Gary Reed .... New York, NY
Kline & Gast .... Edison, NJ
Kline, George H. .... Lincolnwood, IL
Kline, Gerald B. .... Atlanta, GA
Kline & Gordon .... Boston, MA
Kline, Gregory A. .... Dallas, TX
Kline, Gregory M. .... Washington, DC
Bridgeport, WV
Kline & Gripp .... Houston, TX
Kline, Harry H. .... Stamford, CT
Kline, Harry O. .... San Jose, CA
Kline, Herbert A. .... Binghamton, NY
Kline, Hibberd V. B., III .... Kansas City, MO
Kline, I. Irving .... Gloucester, MA
Kline, Ira H. .... Birmingham, AL
Kline, Ivan O. .... New York, NY
Kline, Jack H. .... Orlando, FL
Kline, James A., IV .... Richmond, VA
Kline, James E. .... Maumee, OH
Kline, James N. .... Cleveland, OH
Kline, James W. .... Winter Park, FL
Kline, Jay R. .... Dallas, TX
Kline, Jay R., Jr. .... Dallas, TX
Kline & Jenkins .... Cheyenne, WY
Kline, Jennifer A. .... York, PA
Kline, Jeremy B. .... Los Angeles, CA
Kline, Jerome N. .... Philadelphia, PA
Kline, Joel S. .... Rockville, MD
Kline, John B. .... Boulder, CO
Kline, John Kenneth .... Ann Arbor, MI
Kline, John R. .... Helena, MT
Kline, John R., P.C. .... Helena, MT
Kline, John W. .... Livonia, MI
Kline, Jonathan .... New York, NY
Kline, Jonathan H. .... Pembroke Pines, FL
Kline, Jonathan, P.A. .... Pembroke Pines, FL
Kline, Joseph W. .... Lubbock, TX
Kline, Judith M. .... Los Angeles, CA
Kline, Julie J. .... California, PA
Monongahela, PA
Kline, K. Michelle .... Margate City, NJ
Philadelphia, PA
Kline, Karen D. .... Office Of Special Counsel, GV
Kline, Karen Munay .... New York, NY
Kline, Karl H. .... Easton, PA
Kline, Kevin D. .... Detroit, MI
Kline, Kevin F. .... Miami, FL
Kline & Kline .... Oklahoma City, OK
Kline and Kline .... Allentown, PA
Kline & Kline, P.C. .... Dallas, TX
Kline, Larry L. .... Taylor, MI
Kline, Laurence J., P.C. .... Chicago, IL
Kline Law Offices .... Portland, ME
Kline, Lee G. .... St. Louis, MO
Kline, Leon H. .... Philadelphia, PA
Kline, Linda J. .... Boston, MA
Kline, Lisa W. .... New Haven, CT
Kline, Lois G. .... Pago Pago, TT
Kline, Lorri .... Columbia, MO
Kline, Lowry F. .... Atlanta, GA
Chattanooga, TN
Kline, Marc Aaron .... Florence, SC
Kline, Marilyn L. .... Princeton, NJ
Kline, Marilyn L., P.A. .... Princeton, NJ
Kline, Martin D. .... Atlanta, GA
Kline, Martin E. .... Lawrenceville, NJ
Kline, Matthew .... New York, NY
Kline, Matthew C. .... Department of Commerce, Patent and Trademark Office, GV
Kline, Michael H. .... Harrisburg, PA
Kline, Michael J. .... Trenton, NJ
Kline, Michael J. .... Pittsburgh, PA
Kline, Moore & Klein .... Miami, FL
Washington, DC
Kline, Nancy E. .... Binghamton, NY
Kline, Norman D. .... Federal Maritime Commission, Office of Administrative Law Judges, GV
Kline, Norman L. .... Edison, NJ
Kline, Paul S. .... Pittsburgh, PA
Kline, Peter A. .... San Jose, CA
Kline, Peter G. .... Tempe, AZ
Kline, Peter T. .... Boston, MA
Kline, Ralph H. .... Kingston, NJ
Kline, Rebecca L. .... Washington, DC
Kline, Richard Charles, II .... Fort Worth, TX
Kline, Richard G. .... Washington, DC
Kline, Richard J. .... Davidson, NC
Kline, Richard L. .... Mount Carmel, IL
Kline, Rick .... Palo Alto, CA
Kline, Robert A. .... Beverly Hills, CA
Kline, Robert C. .... Washington, DC
Kline, Robert C, Jr. .... Portland, OR
Kline, Robert E. .... Pittsburgh, PA
Kline, Robert G. .... Boston, MA
Kline, Robert J. .... Tampa, FL
Kline, Robert J. .... Hutchinson, KS
Kline, Robert L. .... Miami, FL
Kline, Robert L. .... Boston, MA
Kline, Robert L., III .... Reisterstown, MD
Kline, Robert M. .... Philadelphia, PA
Kline, Robert P. .... New Cumberland, PA
Kline, Robert S. .... Trenton, NJ
Kline, Robert W. .... Portland, ME
Kline, Roberta Lane .... Ocala, FL
Kline, Roger C. .... New York, NY
Kline, Roger L. .... Circleville, OH
Kline, Roger R. .... Warren, MI
Kline, Ronald C. .... Santa Ana, CA
Kline, S. Howard .... Pittsburgh, PA
Kline, Samara Lackman .... Dallas, TX
Kline, Samuel A. .... Lebanon, PA
Kline, Sara Needleman .... Washington, DC
Kline, Scot L. .... Burlington, VT
Kline, Scott M. .... Dallas, TX
Kline, Sheldon M. .... Washington, DC
Kline, Sidney D., Jr. .... Reading, PA
Kline & Smith .... Pittsburgh, PA
Kline & Specter, P.C. .... Cherry Hill, NJ
Philadelphia, PA
Kline, Stanley J. .... Memphis, TN
Kline, Stanley S. .... Las Vegas, NV
Kline, Stephen H. .... Cheyenne, WY
Kline, Stephen W. .... Malvern, PA
Kline, Steven B. .... New York, NY
Kline, Steven C. .... New York, NY
Dallas, TX
Kline, Stuart F. .... Cleveland, OH
Kline, Terrance A. .... Philadelphia, PA
Kline, Tess J. .... Princeton, NJ
Kline, Thomas E. .... Healdsburg, CA
Kline, Thomas R. .... Washington, DC
Arlington, VA
Kline, Thomas R. .... Philadelphia, PA
Kline, Timothy D. .... Oklahoma City, OK
Kline, Victor S. .... Orlando, FL
Kline, Wayne A. .... Knoxville, TN
Kline, William H. J. .... Rochester, NY
Kline, William L. .... Clinton, LA
Klineberg, Geoffrey M. .... Washington, DC
Klineberg, Margaret K. .... Houston, TX
Klineburger, Richard F., III .... Woodstown, NJ
Philadelphia, PA
Klinedinst, Arlene F. .... Norfolk, VA
Klinedinst, Charles B. .... San Francisco, CA
Klinedinst, David M. .... West Bethesda, MD
Klinedinst, Duncan S. .... McLean, VA
Klinedinst, Fliehman & McKillop
Santa Ana, CA
Los Angeles, CA
San Diego, CA
Klinedinst, John D. .... Los Angeles, CA
San Diego, CA
Santa Ana, CA
Klinefelter, Gary V. .... Phoenix, AZ
Klinefelter, J. L. .... Anniston, AL
Klinefelter, Stanard T. .... Baltimore, MD
Easton, MD
Klinek, Robert .... New York, NY
Klineman, Alan I. .... Indianapolis, IN
Klineman, James M. .... Indianapolis, IN
Klineman, Kent M. .... New York, NY
Klineman, Stephen J. .... Indianapolis, IN
Kliner, Pamela J. .... Memphis, TN
Kliner-Krenzel, Lori .... Philadelphia, PA
Klinestiver, Beverly Glass .... Palo Alto, CA
Klinestiver, David S. .... Indianapolis, IN
Klinestiver, John W. .... Indianapolis, IN
Kling, Andrew A. .... Chicago, IL
Kling, Ann Mackey .... Las Vegas, NV
Kling, Anthony .... Santa Monica, CA
Kling, Antoine J., Jr. .... Gonzales, LA
Kling, Arnold P. .... White Plains, NY
Kling, Bruce Alan .... Dalton, GA
Kling, Carl C. .... Armonk, NY
Kling, Catherine A. .... Indianapolis, IN
Kling, Celeste Holder .... Fort Collins, CO
Kling, Christopher J. .... Bryan, TX
Kling, Clifton L. .... Jackson, MS
Kling, Fred .... Albany, MO
Kling, Frederick J. .... Los Angeles, CA
Kling, J. Kirk .... Altoona, PA
Kling Law Firm .... Santa Monica, CA
Kling, Linda .... New Holland, PA
Kling, Lisa M. .... Springfield, MA
Kling, Lou R. .... New York, NY
Kling, Mark A. .... Englewood, CO
Kling, Michael W. .... Cherry Hill, NJ
Harrisburg, PA
King Of Prussia, PA
Kling, Neal J. .... New Orleans, LA
Kling, Neill C. .... Philadelphia, PA
Kling, Philip H. .... Boston, MA
Kling, Rebecca A. .... St. Louis, MO
Kling, Richard S. .... Chicago, IL
Kling, Shirley D. .... Lincoln, NE
Kling, Stephen L., Jr. .... St. Louis, MO
Kling, Stephen P. .... Annapolis, MD
Kling, Virginia A. S. .... Washington, DC
Klingaman, David B. .... Albany, NY
Klingaman, Russell A. .... Milwaukee, WI
Klingbeil, Chad A. .... Minneapolis, MN
Klingbeil, Ricky D. .... Portland, OR
Klingbeil, Robert T., Jr. .... Venice, FL
Klingbeil & Roberts, P.A. .... Venice, FL
Klingberg, Brian D. .... Minneapolis, MN
Klingberg, Douglas J. .... Wausau, WI
Klinge, Jill Vincent .... Oakland, CA
Klinge, Kent G. .... Richmond, IN
Klinge, Richard M. .... Oklahoma City, OK
Klinge, Richard M., & Associates, P.C. .... Oklahoma City, OK
Klinge, Roland P. .... Wilmette, IL
Klingeberger, J. Philip .... Dyer, IN
Klingebiel, David C. .... Portsmouth, NH
Klingebiel, Robert S. .... Manchester, NH
Klingel, Arthur W., Jr. .... Massapequa, NY
Klingel, Virginia I. .... Grimstead, VA
Klingelhofer, Carroll S., III .... Towson, MD
Klingelhofer, Victor G. .... Washington, DC
Klingelsmith, Sharon L. .... Philadelphia, PA
Klingeman, Fred V. .... San Antonio, TX
Klingeman, Nancy M. .... Morristown, NJ
Klingemann, Bill J. .... Floresville, TX
Seguin, TX
Klingen, Anne M. .... Memphis, TN
Klingenberg, Donald H. .... Painesville, OH
Klingenberg, Erik D. .... New York, NY
Klingenberg, Kenneth W. .... Oklahoma City, OK
Klingenberg, Kristin .... Pittsburgh, PA
Klingenberg, Martin F. .... Washington, DC
Klingenberg, Paul J. .... Department of Labor, Office of the Solicitor, GV
Klingenberger, Daniel K. .... Fresno, CA
Klingenburg, Robert L. .... Mountain Lakes, NJ
Klingensmith, Allen .... Newport Beach, CA
Klingensmith, H. Jack .... Sarasota, FL
Klingensmith, Jason P. .... Cleveland, OH
Klingensmith, Lynn M. .... Collingdale, PA
Klingensmith, Mark Wayne .... West Palm Beach, FL
Klingensmith, Robert D. .... Barberton, OH
Klingensmith, Robert W., Jr. .... Buffalo, NY
Klingensmith, Thomas G.
Elizabethtown, PA
Lancaster, PA
Klingenstein, Andrew D. .... United States Senate, Committee Legal Personnel, GV
Klinger, Alan M. .... New York, NY
Klinger, Andrew M. .... New York, NY
Klinger, Brenda .... Stroudsburg, PA
Klinger, Carole .... New York, NY
Klinger, David J. .... Westfield, NJ
Klinger, Dustin R. .... Portland, OR
Klinger, Edith .... Newark, NJ
Klinger, Edward F. .... Moorhead, MN
Fargo, ND
Klinger, Elaine Whiteman .... Philadelphia, PA
Klinger, Jeffery L. .... St. Louis, MO
Klinger, Jeffrey A. .... Cherry Hill, NJ
Klinger, Joseph Konrad .... Rancho Cordova, CA
Klinger, Lawrence A. .... Department of Justice, Civil Division, GV
Klinger, Leslie F. .... Maitland, FL
Klinger, Leslie S. .... Los Angeles, CA
Klinger, Lisa K. .... Topanga, CA
Klinger, Marilyn .... Los Angeles, CA
Klinger, Nanci .... Portland, OR
Klinger, Norman Ashton .... Norristown, PA
Klinger, Norman Ashton, & Associates, P.C. .... Norristown, PA
Klinger, Paul Wesley, Jr. .... Baytown, TX
Klinger, Phillip D. .... Cedar Rapids, IA
Klinger, Richard William, Jr. .... Wheaton, IL
Klinger, Robert C. .... Richardson, TX
Klinger, Robinson & Ford, L.L.P. .... Cedar Rapids, IA
Klinger, Robyn B. .... Boston, MA
Klinger, Roger M. .... Milford, CT
Klinger, Shannon Thyme .... Atlanta, GA
Klinger, Stanford N., The Law Office of .... Atlanta, GA
Klinger, Steven A. .... Fort Lauderdale, FL

Klinger, Timothy C. ... Fayetteville, AR
Klinger, Tobias G. ... North Hollywood, CA
Klinger, Tracy L. ... Austin, TX
Klingerman, Cris A. ... Covina, CA
Klingerman, Linda K. ... Florissant, MO
Klinges, Dana B. ... Philadelphia, PA
Klinges, David H. ... Bethlehem, PA
Klinges, S. Richard, III ... Bristol, PA
Langhorne, PA
Klingfuss, Jeffrey A. ... Jackson, MS
Klinghammer, Andrew J. ... St. Louis, MO
Klinghammer, Suzanne C. ... Lafayette, IN
Klingher, Leon H. ... New City, NY
Klinghoffer, Abr. ... New York, NY
Klinghoffer, Jack H. ... Los Angeles, CA
Klinghoffer, Teddy D. ... Miami, FL
Klinginsmith, Ray E. ... Kirksville, MO
Klinginsmith, Thomas E. ... Carthage, MO
Klinginsmith, Tracy D. ... Holton, KS
Klingler, David A. ... Dallas, TX
Klingler, Gwenn ... Springfield, IL
Klingler, Lidia A. ... Irvine, CA
Klingler, Richard D. ... Washington, DC
Klingler, Richard T. ... Chattanooga, TN
Klingler, Robert A. ... Cincinnati, OH
Klingler, Robert A., Co., L.P.A.
Cincinnati, OH
Klingler, Robert W. ... Denver, CO
Klingler, Timothy A. ... Evansville, IN
Klingler, Tracy L. ... Austin, TX
Klingman, Barry ... New York, NY
Klingman, Patrick A. ... Hartford, CT
Klingman, Timothy R. ... Milwaukee, WI
Klingman, W. David ... Louisville, KY
Klingner, Harold W. ... Morris, IL
Wilmington, IL
Klingon, Robert M. ... New York, NY
Klingsberg, Brian D. ... Minneapolis, MN
Klingsberg, David ... New York, NY
Klingsberg, Ethan ... New York, NY
Klingsberg, Jordan Lee ... Washington, DC
Klingshirn, Nancy A. ... Hudson, OH
Klingshirn, Neil E. ... Akron, OH
Klingsmith & Associates, P.C.
Gunnison, CO
Klingsmith, P. C." Pete " ... Gunnison, CO
Klingsmith, Phil ... Gunnison, CO
Klink, Charles Gustaf ... Los Angeles, CA
Klink, Darrell E. ... Lincoln, IL
Klink, Fredric J. ... New York, NY
Klink, George F. ... Phoenix, AZ
Klink, Gregory L. ... Pittsburgh, PA
Klink, Heather Anne ... Baltimore, MD
Klink, Jeffrey H. ... Tampa, FL
Klink, Jeffrey H., P.A. ... Tampa, FL
Klink, Richard W. W. ... Long Beach, CA
Klink, Stephen C. ... Bakersfield, CA
Klink, William D. ... Chicago, IL
Klinke, B. Carl ... Dallas, TX
Klinke, Diane G. ... Washington, DC
Klinke, Katy R. ... Dallas, TX
Klinkel, Thomas ... Tucson, AZ
Klinkenborg, C. E. ... Parkersburg, IA
Klinkenborg, Hansmann & Mansheim
Parkersburg, IA
Klinker, Henry J. ... San Diego, CA
Klinker, Leslee Sue ... New York, NY
Klinker, Mark A. ... Omaha, NE
Klinker, Martha S. ... Milwaukee, WI
Klinker, Michael J. ... Milwaukee, WI
Klinker, William K. ... Primghar, IA
Sutherland, IA
Klinkert, James E. ... Ontario, CA
Klinkert, John F. ... Seattle, WA
Klinkner, James A. ... Danville, CA
Klinkner, James Hadrian ... Danville, CA
Klinkner, Thomas F. ... Anchorage, AK
Klinknett, Jack ... Lawrence, KS
Klinkosum, Maitri" Mike "
North Wilkesboro, NC
Klinkowitz, Richard P. ... Greendale, WI
Klinner, David R. ... Medford, WI
Klinner, Mark A. ... Wausau, WI
Klinner, Thomas B. ... Montgomery, AL
Klint, Gregory J. ... Minneapolis, MN
Klint, Philip J. ... Englewood, CO
Klint, Thomas A. ... Coon Rapids, MN
Klintworth, Kerry M. ... Beaumont, TX
Klintworth, Timothy Keith ... St. Louis, MO
Klinzing, Gregg S. ... Houston, TX
Klion, Catherine B.
Pension Benefit Guaranty Corporation,
Office of the General Counsel, GV
Klion, Scott A. ... Stamford, CT
Klionsky, Stephen H. ... Boston, MA
Klipfer, Kenneth R. ... Dayton, OH
Kliphouse, Everett A. ... Atlanta, GA
Klipp, Melissa L. ... Florham Park, NJ
Klipp, Todd L. C. ... Boston, MA
Klippel, Bernhardt W., III ... St. Louis, MO
Klippel, Charles H. ... Hartford, CT
Klippel, Mason W. ... St. Louis, MO
Klippel, Scott ... Austin, TX
Klippel, Terry J. ... Milwaukee, WI
Klippen, Nona Louise ... San Jose, CA
Klipper, Michael Russell ... Washington, DC
Klippert, Barbara D. ... New York, NY
Klippert, David J. ... Saginaw, MI
Klippi, Elizabeth ... Los Angeles, CA
Klippstein, Nora Burke ... Parlin, NJ
Klipsch, Michael F. ... Indianapolis, IN
Klipsch, Ronald E. ... Knoxville, TN
Klipstein, Matthew L. ... Encinitas, CA
Klipstein, Robert A. ... New York, NY
Klipstine, James W., Jr. ... Lovington, NM
Kliros, Alex C. ... Atlanta, GA
Klis, Deborrah Ann ... Washington, DC
Klise, J. Michael ... Washington, DC
Klise, John D. ... Chicago, IL
Klishevich, Dorothy B. ... Stockton, CA
Klissas, Nicholas S.
Department of Commerce,
Office of the General Counsel, GV
Klister, Paul A. ... Appleton, WI
Kliston, Todd W. ... Plantation, FL
Klisz, Timothy J. ... Livonia, MI
Kliszewski, Mark A. ... Oakland, CA
Klitch, Barbara Johanson ... Austin, TX
Klitch, Jennifer L. ... Columbus, OH
Klitch, Richard H., Jr. ... San Antonio, TX
Klitenic, Jason ... Atlanta, GA
Klitenic, Marc A. ... Baltimore, MD
Klitenick, Richard M. ... Key West, FL
Klitgaard, Mark S. ... San Jose, CA
Klitgaard, Robert J. ... San Diego, CA
Klitgaard, Thomas J. ... San Francisco, CA
Klitsas, Loren G. ... Houston, TX
Klitsch, Charles J. ... Philadelphia, PA
Klitsner, Marvin E. ... Milwaukee, WI
Klitz, Carson D. ... Rushville, IL
Klitzke, Ramon A. ... Waukesha, WI
Klitzke, Ramon A., II ... Portland, OR
Klitzkie, Robert ... Yigo, GU
Klitzman, Lawrence S. ... Asbury Park, NJ
Klitzman, Stephen
Federal Communications Commission,
Office of Legislative and Intergovernmental
Affairs, GV
Klitzner, Herbert ... Secaucus, NJ
Klitzner, Jay M. ... Fort Lauderdale, FL
Klitzner, Steven N. ... North Miami Beach, FL
Klitzner, Steven N., P.A.
North Miami Beach, FL
Klivans, Norman R., Jr. ... San Jose, CA
Klivans, Robert L. ... Boston, MA
Klixbull, Richard J. ... Coraopolis, PA
Kliza, Nancy G. ... Livonia, MI
Kloak, Richard C. ... Oak Park, IL
Klobas, Paul T. ... El Sobrante, CA
Klobas, Thomas E. ... Phoenix, AZ
Klobasa, Alan R. ... St. Louis, MO
Klobasa, John A. ... St. Louis, MO
Kloberdanz, Daniel L. ... Phoenix, AZ
Kloberdanz, Murray A. ... Osage, IA
Kloberdanz, Steven A. ... Marshalltown, IA
Klobnak, Michael W. ... Flora, IL
Klobuchar, Amy J. ... Minneapolis, MN
Klobuchar, Peter M. ... Chicago, IL
Klobucher, John M. ... Spokane, WA
Klobucher, Richard A. ... Bellevue, WA
Kloc, Floyd P. ... Saginaw, MI
Klocek, Leslie A. ... Chicago, IL
Klocek, Shirley J. ... Burke, VA
Kloch, John E. ... Alexandria, VA
Kloch, Richard C., Sr.
North Tonawanda, NY
Klocinski, Steven P. ... Washington, DC
Klock, Brian L. ... Washington, DC
Klock, Diane R. ... Peoria, IL
Klock, George E., Jr. ... Fort Smith, AR
Klock, John H. ... Newark, NJ
Klock, Joseph P., Jr. ... Key West, FL
Miami, FL
West Palm Beach, FL
Klock, Kathy M. ... Dallas, TX
Klock, Mark Steven ... Washington, DC
Klock, Peter A. ... East Glastonbury, CT
Klock, Robert D. ... Bentonville, AR
Klock, Susan Hallock ... East Hartford, CT
Klock, Susan Marie ... Miami, FL
Klock, Susan Marie, P.A. ... Miami, FL
Klockars, Karl N. ... Chicago, IL
Klockau, Christopher J. ... Rock Island, IL
Klockau, Lori L. ... Iowa City, IA
Klockau, Marquis & Skorepa, P.C.
Rock Island, IL
Klockau, Walter J., Jr. ... Tucson, AZ
Klocke, Dale W. ... Cincinnati, OH
Klocke, Julie N. ... Boise, ID
Klocke, Wayne M. ... Countryside, IL
Klockenbrink, Paul G. ... Roanoke, VA
Klockenkemper, Joseph B., II
Nashville, TN
Klockers, Darwin K. ... Minneapolis, MN
Klocko, John J., III ... Denver, CO
Klocko, John J., III ... Crofton, MD
Klodell, Alan H. ... Columbus, OH
Klodowski, Harry F., Jr. ... Pittsburgh, PA
Kloecker, John F. ... Chicago, IL
Kloecker, Joseph B., Jr. ... St. Louis, MO
Kloeckner, Elizabeth Jane
Lee's Summit, MO
Kloeckner, Vincent W. (Bill), Jr.
Lee's Summit, MO
Kloehn, Thomas O. ... Milwaukee, WI
Kloempken, John W. ... Itasca, IL
Kloempken, Mark S. ... St. Louis, MO
Kloenhamer, Janet S. ... Novato, CA
Kloenhamer, Larry N. ... San Francisco, CA
Kloepfer, Lynn W. ... Ontario, CA
Kloepfer, Mary C. ... Denver, CO
Kloepfer, Peter K. ... Denver, CO
Kloeppel, Byron P. ... Portsmouth, VA
Kloeppel, Gregory C. ... St. Louis, MO
Kloeppel, Nicholas R. ... Eureka, CA
Kloeppel, Robert T. ... San Ramon, CA
Kloes, Christina L. ... Austin, TX
Kloess & Associates ... Montgomery, AL
Kloess, Bernard J. ... Belleville, IL
Kloess, Branch Donelson ... Montgomery, AL
Kloess, Lawrence H., Jr. ... Montgomery, AL
Kloet, Alvin R. ... Oostburg, WI
Sheboygan, WI
Kloeti, Robert J. ... Richmond, VA
Klohe, Trena Lee ... Washington, DC
Klohr, Howard E. ... Lehigh Acres, FL
Kloid, George P. ... Baltimore, MD
Klok, Rhett D. ... Albuquerque, NM
Klok, Suzanne Lafleur ... Albuquerque, NM
Kloke, Daniel C. ... San Francisco, CA
Klokow, Anne E. ... Irvine, CA
Klomann, Karl ... Chicago, IL
Klomp, David F. ... Salt Lake City, UT
Klomp, Robert P. ... Chester, CT
Klomparens, A. Craig ... Petoskey, MI
Klomparens, Robin L. ... Sacramento, CA
Kloner, Cyrus ... Rochester, NY
Kloner, Dean ... New York, NY
Kloner, Wendy
Federal Deposit Insurance Corporation,
Trial Litigation Section, GV
Klonis, Thomas L. ... Reading, PA
Klonoff, Robert H. ... Washington, DC
Klonoski, John E. ... Atlanta, GA
Klonowski, Daniel J. ... Cleveland, OH
Garfield Heights, OH
Klonowski, Stephen M.
Garfield Heights, OH
Klonsky, Edward L. ... New York, NY
Klonsky, Fred H. ... Woodland Hills, CA
Klontz, David S. ... Department of Justice,
Civil Division, GV
Klontz, Marsha A. ... Reston, VA
Kloorfain, Warren J. ... New York, NY
Kloos, Bill ... Eugene, OR
Kloos, Brenda M. ... Cincinnati, OH
Klooster, John W. ... Lake Forest, IL
Kloostra, Robert L. ... Grand Rapids, MI
Kloote, Richard J. ... Grand Haven, MI
Klootwyk, Merilee Schmink ... Syracuse, NY
Klooz, Susan ... Grand Rapids, MI
Klopf, Charles H. ... Cleveland, OH
Klopf, Gary F. ... Greenbelt, MD
Klopf, Lynne B. ... Ponte Vedra Beach, FL
Klopfenstein, Brian J. ... Kearney, MO
Klopfenstein, John F. ... Woodland, CA
Klopfenstein, Keith Allen, Jr.
Franklin Park, IL
Klopfenstein, Vaughn M. ... Sioux City, IA
Klopfer, Barry B. ... Ventura, CA
Klopfer, Eric B. ... Raleigh, NC
Klopfer, Tibor D. ... Indianapolis, IN
Klopfleisch, Bruce W. ... Morris, MN
Klopman, Benjamin A. ... Rockville, MD
Klopman, David K. ... New York, NY
Klopman, Debbi L. ... Great Neck, NY
Klopp, Frank ... Bloomington, IL
Klopp, Reid W. ... Madison, WI
Klopp-Bryant, Bethanne ... Las Vegas, NV
Kloppenburg, JoAnne ... Madison, WI
Klopper, James J. ... Boston, MA
Klopsch, Diane K. ... Dayton, OH
Klor, John L. ... Portland, OR
Klores, Bruce J. ... Washington, DC
Arlington, VA
Klores, Bruce J. & Associates, P.C.
Washington, DC
Arlington, VA
Klores, Noel H. ... Washington, DC
Klorfein, Stephen R. ... Atlanta, GA
Klos, Bryant H. ... La Crosse, WI
Klos, Flynn & Papenfuss, Chartered
La Crosse, WI
West Salem, WI
Klos, Jerome ... La Crosse, WI
West Salem, WI
Klos, John F. ... Minneapolis, MN
Klos, Katharine A.
Merit Systems Protection Board,
Office of Appeals Counsel, GV
Klos, Kayla E. (Sandway) ... Buffalo, NY
Klos, Stanley J., Jr. ... Annapolis, MD
Greenbelt, MD
Klose, Bradley J. ... Pittsfield, MA
Klose, Woody N. ... Red Hook, NY
Klosener, Tiffany B. ... Des Moines, IA
Klosheim, J. Harold ... Boca Raton, FL
Klosik, Frank J., Jr. ... Atlanta, GA
Klosinski, Scott J. ... Augusta, GA
Klosinski, Scott J., P.C. ... Augusta, GA
Klosk, Craig B. ... New York, NY
Klosk, Michael J. ... Bronx, NY
Klosk, Steven M. ... East Rutherford, NJ
Klosner, Lise H. ... New York, NY
Klosowski, Bernard S., Jr. ... Columbia, MD
Klosowski, Henry E. ... Garden City, NY
Klosowski, Mary A. ... Wyandotte, MI
Klosowski, Thomas ... Minneapolis, MN
Kloss, David W. ... Buffalo, NY
Kloss, Edward J. ... Willingboro, NJ
Kloss, James K. ... Phoenix, AZ
Kloss, John J. ... Cedar Rapids, IA
Kloss, Patrice H. ... Minneapolis, MN
Kloss, Robert E. ... Charlotte, NC
Kloss, William D. ... Columbus, OH
Kloss, William D., Jr. ... Columbus, OH
Kloss Hogan, Sharon L. ... Portland, OR
Klossner, Daniel W. ... Juneau, WI
Klossner-Allen, Jayne ... New York, NY
Kloster, Burton J., Jr. ... Wilton, CT
Kloster, Jeffrey Craig ... Austin, TX
Kloster, Judith L. ... Kansas City, MO
Kloster, Laurie K. ... Department of Justice,
Tax Division, GV
Kloster, Lorette J. ... Glendora, CA
Kloster, Nancy J. ... Crookston, MN
Kloster, Paul G. ... Dickinson, ND
Kloster, Sandra B. ... San Jose, CA
Klosterboer, David C. ... Bloomington, IL
Klosterbuer, Donald R. ... Luverne, MN
Klosterman, Arthur ... Salem, OR
Klosterman, Julie A. Brenizer ... Toledo, OH
Klosterman, M. Joan ... Kansas City, MO
Klosterman, Mark V. ... Celina, OH
Klosterman, Scott P. ... Casper, WY
Klostermann, Roy J. ... St. Louis, MO
Klostermeyer, Frederick H. ... Richmond, VA
Klothe, Robert
Department of Transportation,
Office of the General Counsel, GV
Klothen, Eve Biskind ... Philadelphia, PA
Klotnia, Diane F. ... Chicago, IL
Klots, Cynthia M. ... Milwaukee, WI
Klotsche, John C. ... Palo Alto, CA
Klott, David L. ... San Francisco, CA
Klott, Richard S. ... Deerfield, IL
Klotter, John C. ... Louisville, KY
Klotz, Adam M. ... Los Angeles, CA
Klotz, Alexander B. ... New York, NY
Klotz, Carl E. ... Hawthorne, NJ
Klotz, Criston E. ... Oxford, KS
Klotz, Daniel J. ... New York, NY
Klotz, David B. ... Shreveport, LA
Klotz, David R. ... Syracuse, NY
Klotz, Donald R., Jr. ... Metairie, LA
Klotz, Gary L. ... Indianapolis, IN
Klotz, Gary W. ... Detroit, MI
Klotz and Gould, P.C. ... New York, NY
Klotz, J. Christopher ... Jackson, MS
Klotz, James Edward ... Lowell, MA
Klotz, Jean S. ... Placerville, CA
Klotz, Jessica ... Millburn, NJ
New York, NY
Klotz, Joseph ... Mount Vernon, NY
Klotz, Kristen B. ... Tucson, AZ
Klotz, Lisa-Jane ... Woodland Hills, CA
Klotz, Martin B. ... New York, NY
Klotz, Martin F. ... Treasury Department,
Internal Revenue Service, GV
Klotz & McCann ... Hackensack, NJ
Hawthorne, NJ
Paterson, NJ
Klotz, Nancy E. ... Rochester, NY
Klotz, Paul N. ... Westerly, RI
Klotz, R. Kenneth ... Santa Ana, CA
Klotz, Rafael ... Minneapolis, MN
Klotz, Randall B. ... San Diego, CA
Klotz, Robert L. ... Costa Mesa, CA
Klotz, Robert R. ... San Francisco, CA
Klotz, Ruth B. ... Des Moines, IA
Klotz, Simmons & Reeks ... Shreveport, LA
Klotz, Suzanne ... San Francisco, CA
Klotz, Thomas J. ... Washington, DC
Klotz, W. Patrick, Jr. ... New Orleans, LA
Klotzbach, William G. ... Independence, IA
Klotzberger, K. Lane ... Charlotte, NC
Klotzberger, Kathy A. ... Raleigh, NC
Klotzbier, E. Edward ... Boston, MA
Kloud, Jay L. ... Springfield, NJ
Klove, Carole A. ... Los Angeles, CA
Klover, Kerri L. ... Minneapolis, MN
Klovers, Kris M. ... Milwaukee, WI
Klovsky, Kuby and Harris ... Philadelphia, PA
Klovsky, Sidney B. ... Philadelphia, PA
Klow, Gary J. ... Highland Park, IL
Kloze, Ida I. ... Washington, DC
Klubeck, Richard A. ... Burbank, CA
Klubenspies, Julia A. ... Springfield, NJ
Kluber, Berne C. ... Houston, TX
Klubes, Benjamin B. ... Washington, DC
Klubock, Daniel ... Boston, MA
Klucas, David L. ... Toledo, OH
Kluchenek, Matthew F. ... Chicago, IL
Klucher, Gregory W. ... Painesville, OH
Klucher, Harry J. ... Pittsburgh, PA
Kluchin, John R. ... New Orleans, LA
Kluchin, Joseph Sr., Jr. ... New Orleans, LA
Kluck, Laurence Allan ... Eureka, CA
Kluck, Michael R. ... Okemos, MI
Klucsik, John F. ... Syracuse, NY
Klucznik, James D. ... Holyoke, MA
Klucznik, Jeanne M. ... Oakland, CA
Kluczynski, Girtz & Vogelzang
Grand Rapids, MI
Southfield, MI
Kluczynski, Robert A. ... Southfield, MI
Kludt, Clarence W. ... Crookston, MN
Kludt, Douglas E. ... Huron, SD
Kludze, A. Kodzo Paaku ... Camden, NJ
Klueck, Garrison ... Santee, CA
Kluegel, Arthur E. ... Rochester, NY
Kluegel, Spencer G. ... Minnetonka, MN
Klueger, Robert F. ... Los Angeles, CA
Klueh, James R. ... Vincennes, IN
Kluender, Douglas L. ... Lincoln, NE
Kluender, Steven G. ... Milwaukee, WI
Kluener, Thomas J. ... Cincinnati, OH
Klueppel, Susan Galagan ... Wayland, MA
Kluess, Tori L. ... Green Bay, WI
Klueter, H. R. ... Wausau, WI
Kluever, Brian D. ... Chicago, IL
Kluever, David C. ... Chicago, IL
Kluever, Larry Chad ... Dallas, TX
Kluewer, Susan T. ... Garden City, NY
Kluft, Jerome M. ... Boca Raton, FL
Klug, Angela S. ... Winter Haven, FL
Klug, Charles E., Jr. ... Tampa, FL
Klug, Denise D. ... Martins Ferry, OH
Wheeling, WV
Klug, John T. ... Houston, TX
Klug, Kenneth M. ... Fresno, CA
Klug, Kevin L. ... St. Louis, MO
Klug, Margaret A. ... Glendale, CA
Klug, Martin A. ... St. Louis, MO
Klug, Paul G. ... St. Louis, MO
Klug, Paul S. ... Cleveland, OH
Klug, Steven W. ... Seattle, WA
Klug, Thomas A., (P.C.) ... Lansing, MI
Klug, Thomas L. ... New York, NY
Klug, Thomas N. ... Milwaukee, WI
Klug, William F., IV ... Akron, OH
Kluge, Graig E. ... Eastlake, OH

Kneafsey, John K. ..... Chicago, IL
Kneafsey, Sean M. ..... Los Angeles, CA
Kneale, David H. ..... Orangevale, CA
Kneale, Jean ..... Miami, FL
Kneale, Malcolm L. ..... Miami, FL
Kneale, Michael P. ..... Grand Island, NE
Knearl, Homer L. ..... Denver, CO
Knearl, Julia M. ..... Louisville, CO
Kneas, John W. ..... Portage, MI
Knebel, Donald E. ..... Indianapolis, IN
Knebel, Henry A. ..... Pasadena, CA
Knebel, Jack G. ..... San Francisco, CA
Knebel, James H. ..... Fairfax, VA
Knebel, Jeffrey T. ..... Austin, TX
Knebel, Nancy G. ..... Greenville, SC
Knebel, Robert L., Jr. ..... Dallas, TX
Knebes, William G. ..... Port Angeles, WA
Knece, P. Randall ..... Circleville, OH
Knecht, Carolyn E. ..... Chicago, IL
Knecht, Edward ..... Sun City Center, FL
Knecht, Frederick J. ..... New York, NY
Knecht & Hansen ..... Newport Beach, CA
Knecht, Harold C., III ..... St. Paul, MN
Knecht, Harold C., Jr. ..... Miami, FL
Knecht, James A. ..... Bloomington, IL
Knecht, James H. ..... Paso Robles, CA
Knecht, James H., A Professional Corporation ..... Paso Robles, CA
Knecht & Knecht, P.A. ..... Miami, FL
Knecht, Lawrence A. ..... Kansas City, MO
Knecht, Martin ..... Elizabeth, NJ
Knecht, Michael C. Palm Beach Gardens, FL
Knecht, Michael C., & Associates, P.A. Palm Beach Gardens, FL
Knecht, Patrick J. ..... Sioux Falls, SD
Knecht, Peter ..... Los Angeles, CA
Knecht, Richard E., (P.C.) Newport Beach, CA
Knecht, Richard W. ..... Berwick, PA
Knecht, Sarah J. ..... Santa Barbara, CA
Knecht, Stephen M. ..... Miami, FL
Knecht, Steven ..... Lafayette, IN
Knecht, Steven ..... New York, NY
Knecht, Steven A. ..... Silver Spring, MD
Knecht, Timothy H. ..... Flint, MI
Knecht, Todd R. ..... Grand Rapids, MI
Knecht, Wendy Ellen West Palm Beach, FL
Knecht, William L. ..... Williamsport, PA
Knecht, Wm. C. ..... Evanston, IL
Knechtel, Carleton E. ..... Dallas, TX
Knechtel, Robert G. ..... Sausalito, CA
Knechtel, Robert L. ..... Miami, FL
Chicago, IL
Chicago, IL
Knedeisen, Mark G. ..... Pittsburgh, PA
Knedlik, Lana M. ..... Kansas City, MO
Knedlik, Will ..... Kirkland, WA
Knee, Daniel E. ..... Flemington, NJ
Knee, Howard M. ..... Los Angeles, CA
Knee, Jerrold ..... Hollywood, FL
Knee, Joel S. ..... Hollywood, FL
Knee, Kathryn ..... Jacksonville, FL
Knee Law Firm, The, L.L.C. Hackensack, NJ
Knee, Leonard ..... Charleston, WV
Knee, Martina W. ..... Fairfax, VA
Knee, Peggy Sheahan ..... Hackensack, NJ
Knee, Robert A. ..... Hackensack, NJ
Knee, Robert C., Jr. ..... Duluth, GA
Knee & Ross, LLP ..... Los Angeles, CA
Knee, Stephen H. ..... Newark, NJ
Kneece, Edgar S. ..... Columbia, SC
Kneece, Rexford P. ..... Columbia, SC
Kneece, Robert E. ..... Columbia, SC
Kneece, Robert E., Jr. ..... Columbia, SC
Kneece, William Otis ..... Columbia, SC
Kneedler, Edwin S. ..... Department of Justice, Office of the Solicitor General, GV
Kneedler, H. Lane ..... Richmond, VA
Kneedy, Mark J. ..... Chicago, IL
Kneeland, Anne T. ..... Orinda, CA
Kneeland, David J., Jr. ..... Worcester, MA
Kneeland, G.R. ..... Ketchum, ID
Kneeland, Janet ..... Portland, OR
Kneeland, John P. ..... Portland, OR
Kneeland, Katherine M. ..... Boston, MA
Kneeland, Korb, Collier & Legg Ketchum, ID
Kneeland, Marilyn ..... New York, NY
Kneeland, Mishell B. ..... New York, NY
Kneeland, Robert P. ..... Orange, CA
Kneeland, William J. ..... Fort Collins, CO
Kneeland, William R. ..... Buffalo, NY
Kneen, Jeffrey D. ..... West Palm Beach, FL
Kneese, Kyle Calvin ..... Dallas, TX
Kneese, V. Scott ..... Houston, TX
Kneezel, Ronald D. ..... Menasha, WI
Knefel, Deborah P. ..... Anaheim, CA
Knego, Thomas C. ..... Los Angeles, CA
Kneidel, Jacquelyn L. ..... Newnan, GA
Kneidel, Timothy W. ..... Newnan, GA
Kneifel & Behnke ..... Hobart, IN
Kneifel, Earle L. ..... Manhattan Beach, CA
Kneifel, Harry R. ..... Hobart, IN
Kneifel, Lothar A. ..... Washington, DC
Kneip, Frederick C. ..... New York, NY
Kneip, Gary S. ..... Tucson, AZ
Kneip, Shelley E. ..... Seattle, WA
Kneipp, Donald L. ..... Monroe, LA
Kneipper, Richard K. ..... Dallas, TX
Kneisel, Edmund M. ..... Atlanta, GA
Kneisel, Jan ..... Denver, CO
Kneisel, R. Craig ..... Montgomery, AL
Kneiser, Ronald V. ..... Grosse Pointe Farms, MI
Kneisler, James R., Jr. ..... Santa Rosa, CA
Kneisler Wedmore & Schondel Santa Rosa, CA
Kneisly, L. Douglas ..... Englewood, OH
Kneiss, Jean Soltis ..... Liverpool, NY
Kneley, Deborah Davis ..... Bloomington, IN
Knell, Bradley C. ..... Chicago, IL
Knell, Charles A. ..... Palo Alto, CA
Knell, Charles A., A Professional Corporation Palo Alto, CA
Knell, Charles D. ..... Peoria, IL
Knell & Dorner ..... Mansfield, OH
Knell, Gary E. ..... United States Senate, Committee Legal Personnel, GV
Knell, George H. ..... Mansfield, OH
Knell, Gregory Scott ..... Washington, DC
Knell, Herman ..... Chicago, IL
Knell, Michael E. ..... Atlanta, GA
Knell, Robert D. ..... Rancho Cucamonga, CA
Kneller, Douglas A. ..... Daytona Beach, FL
Kneller, James P. ..... Scottsdale, AZ
Kneller, Robert W. ..... Bethesda, MD
Kneller, Susan R. ..... Washington, DC
Knellinger, Richard M. ..... Gainesville, FL
Knellinger, Richard M., P.A. Gainesville, FL
Knepel, Susan M. ..... Milwaukee, WI
Knepley, Rita E. ..... Wayne, PA
Knepp, Christopher A. ..... Austin, TX
Knepp, James P. ..... South Bend, IN
Knepp, James R., II ..... Toledo, OH
Knepp, Linda M. ..... Toledo, OH
Knepp, Orris C., III ..... Lewistown, PA
Knepp, Thomas R. ..... State College, PA
Knepp, Timothy P. ..... Baltimore, MD
Knepper, Bradley M. ..... Denver, CO
Knepper, E. Martin, Jr. ..... Wilmington, DE
Knepper, G. Jeffrey ..... Washington, DC
Knepper & Gladney ..... Chicago, IL
Knepper, Michael A. ..... Kansas City, MO
Knepper, Randi F. ..... Morristown, NJ
Knepper, Randolph C. ..... Baltimore, MD
Knepper, Richard W. ..... Toledo, OH
Knepper & Stratton ..... Dover, DE
Newark, DE
Wilmington, DE
Knepper, Thomas M. ..... Chicago, IL
Knepper, William E. ..... Columbus, OH
Knepshield, Chris B. ..... Sacramento, CA
Knerly, Stephen J., Jr. ..... Cleveland, OH
Knerly, Stephen R. ..... Tampa, FL
Knerr, Edmund L. ..... Santa Monica, CA
Knese, Patricia E. ..... Blue Bell, PA
Knesek, Yvonne Renee ..... Addison, TX
Kneski & Kneski ..... Miami, FL
Kneski, Paul J. ..... Miami, FL
Kneski, Peter ..... Miami, FL
Kness, Bruce N. ..... Worthington, MN
Knestaut, August E. ..... Blackwood, NJ
Knetsch, Elliott B. ..... Eagan, MN
Knetsch, Jeffrey M. ..... Denver, CO
Knetsch, Kermit L. ..... Duluth, MN
Kneubuhler, Kenneth K. ..... Chicago, IL
Kneuer, John M. R. ..... Washington, DC
Knevel, Mark H. ..... Cleveland, OH
Kney, Kevin J. ..... Rockford, IL
Knez, Fred J. ..... Temecula, CA
Knez & Glatz, P.C. ..... Tucson, AZ
Knezevic, Samuel R. ..... Cleveland, OH
Knezevich, Mina ..... Harrisburg, PA
Knezevich, Peter S. ..... Plantation, FL
Knezevich, Richard A. ..... Aspen, CO
Knezic-Pleše, Maria ..... Los Angeles, CA
Knezo, Stephen J. ..... Atlanta, GA
Knezovich, James B. ..... Sacramento, CA
Kniaz, Laura G. ..... Hyattsville, MD
Kniaz, Lorna Jean ..... Madison, WI
Knibbs, James J. ..... Chicago, IL
Knicely & Associates, A Professional Corporation ..... Williamsburg, VA
Knicely, Clarke A. ..... Ojai, CA
Knicely, Jack R. ..... Sidney, NE
Knicely, James J. ..... Williamsburg, VA
Knick, Michael J ..... Joliet, IL
Knickerbocker, Beth A. ..... Easton, PA
Knickerbocker, Beth Diane Treasury Department, Office of the Comptroller of the Currency, GV
Knickerbocker, Bradley J. ..... Detroit, MI
Knickerbocker, Calvin A. ..... Calistoga, CA
Knickerbocker, Daniel C., Jr. ..... Brooklyn, NY
Knickerbocker, Donald C. ..... Cortland, NY
Knickerbocker, George B. ..... Des Plaines, IL
Knickerbocker, Helaine J. ..... Brooklyn, NY
Knickerbocker, Heredia, Jasso & Stewart, P.C. ..... Eagle Pass, TX
Knickerbocker, Peter ..... Kings Park, NY
Knickerbocker, Richard L. Long Beach, CA
Los Angeles, CA
Knickerbocker, Robert P., Jr. Hartford, CT
Knickerbocker, Ronald ..... Youngstown, OH
Knickerbocker, V. F. ..... Eagle Pass, TX
Knickle, H. Norman, Jr. ..... Warwick, RI
Knickmeier, Jeffrey D. ..... McFarland, WI
Knickmeyer, Karl H., Jr. ..... Los Angeles, CA
Knickmeyer, Kenton E. ..... St. Louis, MO
Knickrehm, Craig A. ..... Omaha, NE
Knickrehm, Donald E. ..... Boise, ID
Knickrehm, J. William ..... Pocatello, ID
Knickrehm, Kate ..... Denver, CO
Knickrehm, Kathy Pate ..... Lincoln, NE
Knie, Patrick E. ..... Spartanburg, SC
Knie, Patrick E., A Professional Association Spartanburg, SC
Kniep, Linda L. ..... Des Moines, IA
Kniepkamp, Linda M. ..... Belleville, IL
St. Louis, MO
Knieps, Karla J. ..... Klamath Falls, OR
Knier, Henry L., Jr. ..... Bay City, MI
Knierim, Glenn E. ..... Bloomfield, CT
Hartford, CT
Knierim, Glenn E., Jr. ..... Avon, CT
Knierim, Matthew W. ..... Glasgow, MT
Knierim, Paul J. ..... Hartford, CT
Stamford, CT
Knierim, Timothy J. ..... Parsippany, NJ
Kniery, Angela Meyers ..... Springfield, IL
Kniery, Joseph P. ..... Chicago, IL
Knies, Henry James ..... Seattle, WA
Knies, Robert M. ..... Bellingham, WA
Kniesly, Brian W. ..... Hartford, CT
Kniess, Kurt D. ..... Sun Prairie, WI
Kniess, October S. ..... Indianapolis, IN
Kniffen, Bruce J. ..... New York, NY
Kniffen, Daniel C. ..... Brunswick, GA
Kniffen, Thomas John ..... Owego, NY
Kniffin, Margaret ..... Jamaica, NY
Kniffin, Wayne D. ..... Norwich, VT
Knifsend, Donna L. ..... Anaheim, CA
Knifton, Matthew J. ..... Austin, TX
Knigge, Kurt R. ..... Seattle, WA
Knight, Adam O. ..... Nashville, TN
Knight, Albert F. ..... Warren, NJ
Knight, Alfred B. ..... Tulsa, OK
Knight, Alfred C. ..... New York, NY
Knight, Alfred H. ..... Nashville, TN
Knight, Allan R. ..... Miami, FL
Knight, Andrew J., II ..... Jacksonville, FL
Knight, Angela M. ..... Tulsa, OK
Knight, Ann E. ..... Houston, TX
Knight, Anthony ..... Department of Commerce, Patent and Trademark Office, GV
Knight, Arthur Franklin, III Knoxville, TN
Knight, Barbara M. ..... Columbus, OH
Knight, Barney L. ..... Austin, TX
Knight, Barry R. ..... Dallas, TX
Knight, Bernard J., Jr. Department of Justice, Tax Division, GV
Knight, Bernard, Jr. ..... Atlanta, GA
Knight, Boland & Riordan Marin City, CA
San Francisco, CA
San Rafael, CA
Knight, Brent D. ..... Chicago, IL
Knight, Brian Patrick ..... Hollywood, FL
Knight, Brian T. ..... Pueblo, CO
Knight, Bruce J. ..... Washington, DC
Knight, Byron D. ..... Des Plaines, IL
Knight, C. Foster ..... Maynard, MA
Knight, C. Jared ..... Amarillo, TX
Dallas, TX
Knight, C. Robert ..... Hartford, CT
Knight, C. Robert ..... Simsbury, CT
Knight, Carolynne M. ..... New York, NY
Knight, Cassandra ..... San Francisco, CA
Knight, C. E., III ..... Hampton, VA
Knight, Chad M. ..... Jackson, MS
Knight, Charles D. ..... Chicago, IL
Knight, Charles H. ..... Pomeroy, OH
Knight, Charles K. ..... Santa Barbara, CA
Knight, Charme Prater ..... Knoxville, TN
Knight, Chris L. ..... Tulsa, OK
Knight, Christopher ..... Mobile, AL
Knight, Christopher ..... Clyde, OH
Knight, Christopher E. ..... Miami, FL
Knight, Christopher J. ..... Harrisburg, PA
Knight, Christopher N. ..... Chicago, IL
Knight, Clarence B. ..... Redwood City, CA
Knight, Claude C. ..... St. Charles, MO
Knight, Clayton S. ..... Franklinton, LA
Knight, Craig F. ..... New Canaan, CT
Knight, Dahood, McLean & Everett Anaconda, MT
Knight, Daniel J. ..... Medfield, MA
Knight, Daniel S. ..... Biddeford, ME
North Yarmouth, ME
Knight, Daniel S. ..... Chester Springs, PA
Knight, David ..... West Palm Beach, FL
Knight, David A. ..... Little Rock, AR
Knight, David H. ..... Doylestown, PA
Knight, David L. ..... Columbia, MO
Knight, David T. ..... Tampa, FL
Knight, David W. ..... Fairfield, CA
Knight, David W. ..... Muncie, IN
Knight, David W. ..... Wichita Falls, TX
Knight, David W. ..... Princeton, WV
Knight, Deborah G. ..... Montgomery, AL
Knight, Deborah M. ..... Philadelphia, PA
Knight, Deborah Poore Fort Lauderdale, FL
Knight, Dennis K. ..... San Diego, CA
Knight, Dennis S. ..... Novato, CA
Knight, Derry L. ..... Sacramento, CA
Knight, Donald B. ..... Congers, NY
Knight, Donald G. ..... Camarillo, CA
Knight, Donald K. ..... Irving, TX
Knight, Donald R. ..... Littleton, CO
Knight, Douglas K. ..... Hartford, CT
Knight, Douglas W. ..... Baltimore, MD
Knight, Edward D., III ..... Lewisburg, WV
Knight, Edward R. ..... Atlantic City, NJ
Knight, Elizabeth A. ..... Des Plaines, IL
Knight, Ellen Faith ..... New York, NY
Knight, Faith T. ..... Atlanta, GA
Knight & Firth, P.C. ..... Birmingham, MI
Knight & Fisher ..... Macon, GA
Warner Robins, GA
Knight, Ford, Atwill, Parshall & Baker Columbia, MO
Knight, Frank A., III ..... Baytown, TX
Knight, Frank D. ..... Corvallis, OR
Knight, Frederick H., 3rd ..... Philadelphia, PA
Knight, G. Lloyd, Jr. ..... Washington, DC
Knight, G. Marcus ..... Columbia, SC
Knight, G. Marlin ..... San Jose, CA
Knight, Gary ..... Austin, TX
Knight, Gary E. ..... Wichita, KS
Knight, George B. ..... Milwaukee, WI
Knight, George F. ..... Washington, DC
Knight, George L. ..... Miami, FL
Knight, George S. ..... Fairfax, VA
Knight, Gerald G. ..... Oklahoma City, OK
Knight, Gerald L. ..... Fort Lauderdale, FL
Knight, Gina Denise ..... Midwest City, OK
Knight, Gina L. ..... Chicago, IL
Knight, Ginger Carol ..... Lexington, KY
Knight, Gregory H. ..... Harrisburg, PA
Knight, Gregory R. ..... Scottsdale, AZ
Knight, Gretchen S. ..... Wilmington, DE
Knight & Griffith ..... Cullman, AL
Knight, H. Elvin, Jr. ..... Kansas City, MO
Knight, H. Warren, III ..... Orange, CA
Knight, Haven A. ..... Greenwich, CT
Knight, Henry D., Jr. ..... Columbia, SC
Knight, Henry S., Jr. ..... Columbia, SC
Knight, Holly N. ..... Memphis, TN
Nashville, TN
Knight, Hoppe, Fanning & Knight, Ltd. Des Plaines, IL
Glen Ellyn, IL
Schererville, IN
Knight, J. Douglas, Jr. ..... Evansville, IN
Knight, J. Kathryn ..... Kearneysville, WV
Knight, Jack ..... Nashville, GA
Knight, Jack Morris, Jr. ..... Charlotte, NC
Knight, James A. ..... Paintsville, KY
Knight, James A. ..... New York, NY
Knight, James C. ..... Orange, CA
Knight, James C. ..... Miami Shores, FL
Knight, James E. ..... Stuart, FL
Knight, James E., Jr. ..... Columbia, SC
Knight, James K., Jr. ..... Marietta, GA
Knight, James L. ..... Bethesda, MD
Knight, James P., Jr. ..... Jackson, MS
Knight, James R. ..... Cullman, AL
Knight, James T. ..... Jackson, MS
Knight, James T. ..... New York, NY
Knight, James Theodore, III ..... Tallahassee, FL
Knight, James W., Jr. Fort Lauderdale, FL
Knight, James W., Jr., P.A. Fort Lauderdale, FL
Knight, Jane M. ..... Long Island City, NY
Knight, Jason P. ..... Cullman, AL
Knight, Jay Adams ..... Los Angeles, CA
Knight, Jeanne E. ..... Minneapolis, MN
Knight, Jefferson P. ..... Miami, FL
Knight, Jeffrey A. ..... Washington, DC
Knight, Jeffrey A. ..... Ann Arbor, MI
Knight, Jeffrey D. ..... Houston, TX
Knight, Jeffrey W. ..... Pleasanton, CA
Knight, Jenifer Cari ..... Boston, MA
Knight, Jerry R. ..... Decatur, AL
Knight, Joel F. ..... Reading, PA
Knight, John ..... Greenville, IL
Knight, John ..... Rockland, ME
Knight, John A. ..... Chicago, IL
Knight, John Barkley, Jr. ..... Winnsboro, LA
Knight, John Barkley, Jr., (A Professional Corporation) ..... Winnsboro, LA
Knight, John D. ..... Clear Lake, SD
Knight, John David ..... Cullman, AL
Knight, John E. ..... Madison, WI
Knight, John E., III ..... Gainesville, FL
Knight, John H. ..... Wilmington, DE
Knight, John K. ..... New York, NY
Knight, John K. ..... St. Helens, OR
Knight, John L. ..... Richmond, VA
Knight, John R. ..... New York, NY
Knight, John R. ..... Houston, TX
Knight, John S. ..... Fort Wayne, IN
Knight, John W. ..... Southfield, MI
Knight, Johnny W. ..... Albany, GA
Knight, Joseph R. ..... Austin, TX
Knight, Judith C. ..... North Adams, MA
Pittsfield, MA
Knight, Karen ..... Lincoln, NE
Knight, Karen L. ..... Gretna, LA
Knight, Karen N. ..... Montgomery, AL
Knight, Katharine M. ..... Annapolis, MD
Knight, Katherine Johnson ..... Dallas, TX
Knight, Katherine M. ..... Pearl River, NY
Knight, Kathleen A. ..... Fort Worth, TX
Knight, Kelly J. ..... Orange, CA
Knight, Kenneth D. ..... Madison, NC
Knight, Kenneth E. ..... Crown Point, IN
Knight, Kenneth F. ..... Chicago, IL
Knight, Kenneth M. ..... Parker, CO
Knight, Kerre L. ..... Kansas City, MO
Knight, Kevin R. ..... Indianapolis, IN
Knight, Kimberly A. ..... Atlanta, GA
Knight, Kirstin T. ..... New York, NY
Knight & Knight ..... Fairfield, CA
Knight & Knight ..... Beeville, TX
Knight, Lance ..... Fort Worth, TX
Knight, Laureine ..... New York, NY
Knight, Laurie A. ..... Santa Fe, NM
Knight Law Firm, The ..... Miami, FL
Knight, Lendall B. ..... Sanford, ME
Knight, Leonardo R. ..... Washington, DC
Knight, Leslie Annette ..... Davis, CA
Knight, Linda K. ..... Kansas City, MO
Knight, Linda M. ..... Seal Beach, CA
Knight, Linda Whitlow ..... Nashville, TN
Knight, Lisa M. ..... New York, NY
Knight, Lois H. ..... Boston, MA
Knight, Louise A. ..... Harrisburg, PA
Knight, Louise O. ..... Lewisburg, PA
Knight, Lynn ..... Irvington, NY
Knight, M. Kathryn ..... Mobile, AL

Knight, M. Lisa
Environmental Protection Agency,
Office of Administrative Law Judges, GV
Knight, Manzi, Nussbaum & LaPlaca, P.C.
Greenbelt, MD
Upper Marlboro, MD
Knight, Marianne E. ... Plantation, FL
Knight, Mark A. ... Lawrence, KS
Knight, Mark D. ... Somerset, KY
Knight, Markin R. ... Williamsport, PA
Knight, Mary Ann ... Philadelphia, PA
Knight & Masar, PLLP ... Deer Lodge, MT
Missoula, MT
Knight, Matthew A. ... Kenosha, WI
Knight, Matthew W. ... Thousand Oaks, CA
Knight, Micah Dawn ... Durant, OK
Knight, Michael D. ... Mobile, AL
Knight, Michael E. ... Albuquerque, NM
Knight, Michael H. ... Department of Justice,
Antitrust Division, GV
Knight, Michael J. ... Albany, NY
Knight, Michael J. ... Beeville, TX
Knight, Michael S. ... Needham, MA
Knight, Michael V. ... Eden Prairie, MN
Knight, Michelle M. ... Lawrenceville, GA
Knight, Milton F. ... Perrysburg, OH
Knight, Molly M. ... Cincinnati, OH
Knight, Montgomery, Jr. ... Norfolk, VA
Knight, Nancy Morse
Newport Beach, CA
Knight, Neal W., Jr. ... Palm Beach, FL
Knight, Newel B. ... Reno, NV
Knight, Nicola R. ... Oakland, CA
Knight, Patricia ... San Francisco, CA
Knight, Patrick H. ... Manassas, VA
Knight, Patrick J. ... Milwaukee, WI
Knight, Patrick L. ... Washington, DC
Knight, Patrick W. ... Miami, FL
Knight, Paul A. ... Austin, TX
Knight, Paul L. ... Washington, DC
Knight & Peddycord ... San Diego, CA
Knight, Peggy Berning ... Denver, CO
Knight, Perry Dallas ... Cullman, AL
Knight, Peter B. ... Hendersonville, NC
Knight, Peter C. ... Boston, MA
Knight, Peter L. ... Las Vegas, NV
Tonopah, NV
Knight, Peter R. ... Hartford, CT
Knight, Peter S. ... Washington, DC
Knight, Philip J. ... Blountstown, FL
Knight, Phillip W. ... Coral Gables, FL
Knight, Phyllis G. ... Denver, CO
Knight, Ralph H. ... Phoenix, AZ
Knight, Randal S. ... Dayton, OH
Knight, Reuben B. ... Wichita Falls, TX
Knight, Richard E. ... Arlington, VA
Knight, Richard Finley ... Bogalusa, LA
Mandeville, LA
Knight, Richard H., Jr. ... Nashville, TN
Knight, Richard J. ... Appleton, WI
Knight, Richard W. ... Austin, TX
Knight, Robert A. ... Metairie, LA
Knight, Robert B. ... Birmingham, MI
Knight, Robert C. ... Duluth, MN
Knight, Robert E. ... Austin, TX
Knight, Robert G. ... Florence, SC
Knight, Robert H. ... New York, NY
Knight, Robert Lionel ... Port Washington, NY
Knight, Robert M. ... Chicago, IL
Knight, Robert M. ... Missoula, MT
Knight, Robert W. ... Tampa, FL
Knight, Rodney A. ... Scottsdale, AZ
Knight, Roger, Jr. ... Madisonville, TX
Knight, Roger Weldon ... Raleigh, NC
Knight, Ronald G. ... Fort Worth, TX
Knight, Ronald T. ... Macon, GA
Knight, Ruby L. ... Atlanta, GA
Knight, Ruth P. ... Charlottesville, VA
Knight, Sam David ... Mobile, AL
Knight, Sandy Henderson
Albuquerque, NM
Knight, Sharon A. ... New York, NY
Knight, Sharon J. ... Baton Rouge, LA
Knight, Sherman L. ... Bellevue, WA
Knight, Sherrian Patricia
National Labor Relations Board,
Office of Board Members, GV
Knight, Sherry L. ... Kimberton, PA
Knight, Stacey D. McKee
Los Angeles, CA
Knight, Stacey L. ... Lafayette, LA
Knight, Stephen ... Marina Del Rey, CA
Knight, Stephen ... Tallahassee, FL
Knight, Stephen D. ... Washington, DC
Knight, Stephen E. ... San Diego, CA
Knight, Steve ... Columbus, GA
Knight, Stewart R. ... Salt Lake City, UT
Knight, Stuart W. ... Tustin, CA
Knight, Susan Ann ... Oklahoma City, OK
Knight, Susan P. ... Denver, CO
Knight, Sydney M.
Federal Trade Commission,
Bureau of Consumer Protection, GV
Knight, T. Kevin ... Orlando, FL
Knight, Tammy L. ... Fort Lauderdale, FL
Knight, Tara L. ... New Haven, CT
Knight, Ted A. ... Poteau, OK
Knight, Thelma Harris ... Los Angeles, CA
Knight, Thomas E. ... Washington, DC
Knight, Thomas J. ... Anniston, AL
Knight, Thomas J. ... Fort Wayne, IN
Knight, Thomas L. ... Wheaton, IL
Knight, Thomas L. N. ... Chattanooga, TN
Knight, Thomas R. ... Orland Park, IL
Knight, Timothy P. ... Chicago, IL
Knight, Timothy W. ... Birmingham, AL
Knight & Tomich ... St. Charles, MO
Knight, Townsend J. ... New York, NY
Knight, Tracy L. ... Baltimore, MD
Knight, Troy G. ... Orangeburg, SC
Knight, Victoria S. H. ... Edgefield, SC
Knight, Vinson J. ... New Orleans, LA
Knight, W. Bruce ... Birmingham, MI
Knight, W. Donald, Jr. ... Atlanta, GA
Knight, W. Ronald ... Charlotte, NC
Knight, W. Scott ... Tyler, TX
Knight, W. Thomas ... Providence, RI
Knight, W. Wilder, II ... New York, NY
Knight, Wayne A. ... Fairfield, CA
Knight, Wayne B. ... Tacoma, WA
Knight, Wayne D. ... Tallahassee, FL
Knight, W. D. (Jack), Sr. ... Nashville, GA
Knight, Webster T. ... Washington, DC
Knight, W. H., Jr. ... Iowa City, IA
Knight, Wilkerson, Parrish, Wassall & Warman
Tulsa, OK
Knight, William A. ... Tyler, TX
Knight, William C., Jr. ... Birmingham, AL
Knight, William D., Jr. ... Rockford, IL
Knight, William E. ... Upper Marlboro, MD
Knight, William F. ... Little Rock, AR
Knight, William F. ... Newton, MA
Knight, William G. ... Long Beach, CA
Knight, William J. ... Franklinton, LA
Knight, William N. ... Jennings, LA
Knight, William R., Jr.
Clinton Township, MI
Knight, W. J., Jr. ... Cat Spring, TX
Knight, Yvonne T. ... Boulder, CO
Knightly, J. William ... Hutchinson, KS
Knightly, Robert John ... Kew Gardens, NY
Knighton, Alton L., Jr. ... Roanoke, VA
Knighton, Christopher G. ... Atlanta, GA
Knighton, Cynthia L. ... Sacramento, CA
Knighton, Herbert V. ... Harrisburg, PA
Knighton, Judson R. ... Marietta, GA
Knighton, Petree A. ... San Francisco, CA
Knighton, Philip M. ... Wichita, KS
Knights, David M. ... Louisville, KY
Knights, Gregory P. ... Glendale, CA
Knights, Robert W. ... New Orleans, LA
Knights & Summer ... Glendale, CA
Knightstep, Kim R. ... Dallas, TX
Kniha, Randy C. ... Fairmont, WV
Knipe, Anne F. ... Minneapolis, MN
Knipe, Brian Jonathan ... Pittsburgh, PA
Knipe, Francis G. ... Torrance, CA
Knipe, Jon W. ... New York, NY
Knipe, Peter R. ... Princeton, NJ
Knipe, Quentin M. ... Boise, ID
Knipel, Lawrence Steve ... Brooklyn, NY
Knipfer, Shellie L. ... Des Moines, IA
Knipling, Richard F. ... Richmond, TX
Knipmeyer, Lowell L. ... Kansas City, MO
Knipmeyer, McCann, Smith, Manz & Gotfredson ... Kansas City, MO
Knipp, Barbara ... Houston, TX
Knippa & Kral ... Houston, TX
Knippa, Larry D. ... Houston, TX
Knippel, C. J. ... Minneapolis, MN
Knippen, Gary R. ... Oroville, CA
Knippen, James H., II ... Wheaton, IL
Knippen, Michael S. ... Chicago, IL
Knippenberg, Julian W. ... Lexington, KY
Knipprath, Joerg-Werner ... Los Angeles, CA
Knipps, Susan K. ... New York, NY
Knipstein, Julie E. ... Chicago, IL
Knisbacher, Alden Jay ... Oakland, CA
Kniseley, Lucy E. ... York, PA
Kniseley, Anne M. ... Grove City, OH
Knisely, Beth Ann ... Long Beach, CA
Knisely, David S. ... Boston, MA
Knisely, Gary T. ... Hanover, PA
Knisely, Harry L. ... San Clemente, CA
Knisely, Howard F. ... Lancaster, PA
Knisely, Kathleen L.
Securities and Exchange Commission,
Division of Investment Management, GV
Knisely, Marc O. ... Austin, TX
Knisely, Paul E. ... Austin, TX
Knisely & Prehoditch, P.C. ... Austin, TX
Knisely, Sherrice A. ... Philadelphia, PA
Knisely, Steven M. ... Marble Canyon, AZ
Knish, Andrea ... Hammond, IN
Knish, Michael A. ... San Bernardino, CA
Knishkowy, David S. ... Hartford, CT
Knishkowy, Jeffrey A.
Department of Agriculture,
Office of Civil Rights Enforcement, GV
Kniskern, C. B., Jr. ... Winter Springs, FL
Kniskern, Douglas ... Miami, FL
Kniskern, Joseph Warren ... Coral Gables, FL
Kniskern, Leigh ... Sanford, FL
Knisley, Daniel S. ... Columbus, OH
Knisley, David L. ... Columbus, OH
Knisley, Dean A. ... Columbus, OH
Lima, OH
Knisley, Douglas C. ... Columbus, OH
Knisley, James W. ... Dayton, OH
Knisley, Melinda E. ... Cincinnati, OH
Knisley, Nancy ... Towson, MD
Knisley, R. Jeffrey ... Providence, RI
Knisley, Scott M. ... Columbus, OH
Knisley, Wilhelm & Knisley
Columbus, OH
Lima, OH
Knispel, Jay S. ... Brooklyn, NY
Knispel, Lisa Anne ... San Francisco, CA
Knispel, Susan J. ... Trenton, NJ
Kniss, Jon R. ... Torrance, CA
Knister, Russell E. ... Bloomfield Hills, MI
Knister, Terrence K. ... Lake Charles, LA
New Orleans, LA
Houston, TX
Knitter, David G. ... Fairfield, CA
Napa, CA
Knittig, Joseph H. ... Kansas City, MO
Knittle, Charles H. ... Chicago, IL
Knittle, Duane R. ... Yakima, WA
Knittle, Steven D. ... Cincinnati, OH
Knivila, K. Bruce ... Salem, OR
Knivila, Kelly ... Salem, OR
Knize, Wesley G. ... Waxahachie, TX
Knizley, Dennis J. ... Mobile, AL
Knizley, Dennis J., P.C. ... Mobile, AL
Knobbe, Edw. A. ... Granite City, IL
Knobbe, Kyler G. ... Cimarron, KS
Knobbe, Louis J., (P.C.)
Newport Beach, CA
Knobbe, Martens, Olson & Bear, LLP
Los Angeles, CA
Newport Beach, CA
Riverside, CA
San Diego, CA
San Francisco, CA
Knobbe, Paul L. ... Granite City, IL
Knobel, Barry W. ... Anderson, SC
Knobel, James A. ... St. Paul, MN
Knobel, Mark W. ... Reno, NV
Knobeloch, John Fulton ... Charleston, SC
Knobelsdorf, John C., II ... Bellaire, TX
Knobil, Carole W. ... Austin, TX
Knoblauch, Byron M. ... Sierra Madre, CA
Knoblauch, Diane J. ... Toledo, OH
Knoblauch, Leo N. ... Warwick, NY
Knoblauch, Martin ... Philadelphia, PA
Knoblauch, Mary L. ... Minneapolis, MN
Knoble, John L. ... Philadelphia, PA
Knoble & Yoshida, LLC ... Philadelphia, PA
Knobler, Igal ... Orlando, FL
Knobles & Klingemann, Inc.
Floresville, TX
San Antonio, TX
Seguin, TX
Knobles, William L. ... Floresville, TX
Seguin, TX
Knoblich, Marvin M. ... Mishawaka, IN
Knobloch, Bernard L. ... Thibodaux, LA
Knobloch, Don ... Bellville, TX
Knobloch, Iris Nataly ... Burbank, CA
Knobloch, John F. ... Glen Ellyn, IL
Knobloch, Kathlyn A. ... Houston, TX
Knobloch, Lawrence Thomas
Sacramento, CA
Knoblock, Carolyn J. ... Tucson, AZ
Knoblock, Elizabeth M. ... Fort Lauderdale, FL
Knoblock, Erick P. ... Greenfield, IN
Knoblock, Henry E., III ... Belmont, MA
Knoblock, Henry M. ... Miami, FL
Knoblock, Kenneth E. ... Vista, CA
Knoblock, M. Richard ... Bad Axe, MI
Knoblock, Steven C. ... San Diego, CA
Knoblow, Carol J. ... Los Angeles, CA
Knoche, Karl I.
Department of Defense, GV
Knoche, William C. ... Phoenix, AZ
Knochel, Keith S., Law Offices of
Bullhead City, AZ
Knochel, Keith S., Law Offices of
Flagstaff, AZ
Kingman, AZ
Lake Havasu City, AZ
Parker, AZ
Prescott, AZ
Sedona, AZ
Knochel, Kristian ... Norcross, GA
Knochelmann, Carl E., Jr. ... Cincinnati, OH
Knock, Joseph R. ... Atlanta, GA
Knock, Rick H. ... San Diego, CA
Knocke, Laurie A. ... Minneapolis, MN
St. Paul, MN
Knocke, Peter A. ... Orlando, FL
Knockeart, Mary A. ... San Diego, CA
Knodel, John R. ... Rahway, NJ
Knodel, Maureen ... Clifton, NJ
Knodell, David R. ... Minneapolis, MN
Knodell, John D., III ... Ephrata, WA
Knodell, John D., Jr. ... Bellevue, WA
Knodell, Joyce E. ... Baltimore, MD
Knodell Law Office ... Minneapolis, MN
Knodle, Cheryl M. ... Lafayette, IN
Knoebel, Robert S., Jr. ... Nyack, NY
Knoebel, William G. ... Augusta, KY
Florence, KY
Maysville, KY
Knoeckel, Mary Ann ... Washington, DC
Knoell, George H., III ... Norristown, PA
Philadelphia, PA
Knoeller, Michael J. ... Milwaukee, WI
Knoeller, William A. ... Alexandria, VA
Knoepfel, Richard R.
Charlotte Amalie, St. Thomas, VI
Knoepfle Law Office ... Columbus, NE
Knoepfle, Melanie ... Columbus, NE
Knoepfler, Carol C. ... Omaha, NE
Knoepfler, Jas. C. ... Sioux City, IA
Knoepp, Terry J. ... San Diego, CA
Knoer, Dennis L. ... Kansas City, MO
Knoer, Robert E. ... Buffalo, NY
Knoernschild, Eric M. ... Muscatine, IA
Knoerr, Doretta M. ... Fort Lauderdale, FL
Knoerr, Stephen E. ... Fort Lauderdale, FL
Knoerzer, Michael A. ... New York, NY
Knoerzer, Suzanne M ... Melville, NY
Knoester, David ... Grand Rapids, MI
Knoff, David D. ... Yankton, SD
Knohl, Kevin C. ... Chicago, IL
Knoke, Gregory E. ... Monroe, WI
Knoke & Ingebritsen ... Monroe, WI
Knokey, David J. ... Los Angeles, CA
Knol, Kathleen P. ... Detroit, MI
Knoles, Christina G. ... Flagstaff, AZ
Knoles, Christina G., A Professional Corporation ... Flagstaff, AZ
Knoles, Diane P. ... San Francisco, CA
Knoles, James R. ... Newport Beach, CA
Knoles, Jere M. ... Omaha, NE
Knoll, Alan M. ... New York, NY
Knoll, Alfred P. ... Oakland, CA
Knoll, Amy ... Roseland, NJ
Knoll, Bradley S. ... Holland, MI
Knoll, Bruce Evans ... Troy, NY
Knoll, Charles A., Jr. ... Pittsburgh, PA
Knoll, David A. ... Sacramento, CA
Knoll, David B. ... Southfield, MI
Knoll, David D. ... Houston, TX
Knoll, David J. ... Holland, MI
Knoll, David M. ... Denver, CO
Knoll, Douglas S. ... Santa Monica, CA
Knoll, E. Joseph ... Washington, DC
Knoll, E. Joseph, III ... Washington, DC
Knoll, Edward P. ... Chicago, IL
Knoll, Franklin J. ... Minneapolis, MN
Knoll, Gregory E. ... San Diego, CA
Knoll, James L. ... Portland, OR
Knoll, Jay B. ... Detroit, MI
Knoll, Jeannette Theriot ... Marksville, LA
Knoll, Jeffrey ... Canoga Park, CA
Knoll, Jeffrey A. ... Denver, CO
Knoll, Jeffrey A., P.C. ... Denver, CO
Knoll, Jeffrey G. ... Naperville, IL
Knoll, Jeffrey T. ... Akron, OH
Knoll, Jerold Edward ... Marksville, LA
Knoll, Joan R. ... Topeka, KS
Knoll, Jocelyn Lorna ... Minneapolis, MN
Knoll, John J. ... Topeka, KS
Knoll, John P. ... San Diego, CA
Knoll, Kirk A. ... Indianapolis, IN
Knoll, Kolger, Sowers & Metzger
Richmond, IN
Knoll Law Firm, The ... Marksville, LA
Knoll, Lawrence I. ... New York, NY
Knoll, Mark S. ... Freedom, NH
Knoll, Mona ... Cedar Rapids, IA
Knoll, Persinger, Knoll & Bedevia, P.C.
Holland, MI
Knoll, Peter F. ... Yreka, CA
Knoll, Raymond P. ... Evansville, IN
Knoll, Richard ... Bingham Farms, MI
Knoll, Richard, P.C., Law Office of
Bingham Farms, MI
Knoll, Robert R. ... Milwaukee, WI
Knoll, Ronald J. ... Moorhead, MN
Fargo, ND
Knoll, Susan K. ... Houston, TX
Knoll, Terry F. ... Charlotte, MI
Knoll, Thomas G. ... Akron, OH
Knoll, Thomas H. ... Milwaukee, WI
Knoll, Thomas R., Sr. ... Staunton, VA
Knoll, Triston K. ... Marksville, LA
Knolla, Peter ... Omaha, NE
Knolle, Henry K. ... Houston, TX
Knolle, Livingston & Holcomb, A Professional Corporation ... Austin, TX
Knolle, William M. ... Austin, TX
Knoller, Guy David ... Phoenix, AZ
Knoller, Guy David, P.C. ... Phoenix, AZ
Knollmeyer, Michael J. ... Jacksonville, AR
Knolton, Robert W. ... Knoxville, TN
Oak Ridge, TN
Knoop, Stephen J. ... Cleveland, OH
Knop, Kelly C. ... Tucson, AZ
Knop, Kenneth H. ... Houston, TX
Knop, Kenneth H., P.C. ... Houston, TX
Knop, Peter J. ... Chantilly, VA
Knop, Todd J. ... Austin, TX
Knopes, T. Marty ... Crestview, FL
Knopf, Alvin N. ... Chicago, IL
Knopf, Amy S. ... Boston, MA
Knopf, Barry A. ... Saddle Brook, NJ
Knopf & Brown ... Washington, DC
Rockville, MD
Knopf, Carrie Suzanne
San Francisco, CA
Knopf, Christopher D.
Cleveland Heights, OH
Knopf, Evelyn J. ... Augusta, ME
Knopf, Fred ... New York, NY
Knopf, Gerald S. ... Stamford, CT
Knopf, James S. ... San Francisco, CA
Knopf, Judith Margulies ... Jersey City, NJ
Knopf, Karen L. ... St. Louis, MO
Knopf, Kenneth E. ... Charleston, WV
Knopf, Kevin Paul ... Treasury Department,
Departmental Offices, GV
Knopf, Kimberlee S. ... Blue Bell, PA
Knopf, Larry P. ... Mobile, AL
Knopf, Lawrence J. ... Natick, MA
Knopf, Matthew J. ... New York, NY
Knopf, Morris E. ... Minneapolis, MN
Knopf, Norman G. ... Washington, DC
Knopf, Paul V. ... Hartford, CT
Knopf, R. Eugene ... Baxter, IA
Newton, IA
Knopf, Robert I. ... St. Louis, MO
Knopf, Robert M. ... Closter, NJ
Knopf, Sharon L. ... San Jose, CA
Knopf, Shirley Fuld ... Los Angeles, CA
Knopf, Siegfried P. ... New York, NY
Knopf, Thomas J. ... Louisville, KY
Knopf, Travor ... Long Beach, CA
Knopf, William L. ... Louisville, KY
Knopf, William S. ... Phoenix, AZ
Knopfler, George ... Los Angeles, CA
Knopfler & Robertson, LLP
Camarillo, CA
Irvine, CA
Los Angeles, CA
Pleasanton, CA
Woodland Hills, CA
Knopik, Christopher S. ... Tampa, FL
Knopke, Carl G. ... Sacramento, CA

Knopke, William C. ... Tampa, FL
Knoploh, Greg H. ... Des Moines, IA
Knopoff, Katherine A. ... San Francisco, CA
Knopp, Alex A. ... Norwalk, CT
Knopp, Cheryl J. ... New York, NY
Knopp, Gregory W. ... New York, NY
Knopp, Joseph A. ... Manhattan, KS
Knopp, Matthew G. ... Seattle, WA
Knopp, Susan E. ... Toms River, NJ
Knopp, Ted E. ... Wichita, KS
Knopp, Ted E., Chtd. ... Wichita, KS
Knopp, Timothy J. ... Overland Park, KS
Knopp, William H. ... Chicago, IL
Knopping, Lester G. ... Lido Beach, NY
Knopping, Owen A. ... Philadelphia, PA
Knops, Barbara A. ... Kansas City, MO
Knops, Mark Crispin ... Phoenix, AZ
Knops, Peter C. ... Kansas City, MO
Knorek, John L. ... Honolulu, HI
Knorpp, John C. ... Clarendon, TX
Knorr, Annette E. ... Charlottesville, VA
Knorr, Gene A. ... Washington, DC
Knorr, Gerard K. ... Troy, MI
Knorr, John A. ... Pittsburgh, PA
Knorr, John G., III ... Harrisburg, PA
Knorr, John, Law ... Pittsburgh, PA
Knorr, Lincoln M. ... Franklin, MI
Knorr, Michele L.
Environmental Protection Agency, Office of the General Counsel, GV
Knorr, Stephen J. ... Tulsa, OK
Knorr, William J. ... Keene, NH
Knoshaug, Dale A. ... Des Moines, IA
Knoshaug, Dewayne A. ... Clarion, IA
Knoshaug, Kimberly P. ... Des Moines, IA
Knosher, Norris ... Montpelier, VT
Knospe, Elizabeth A. ... Chicago, IL
Knospe, Marvis ... Boston, MA
Knostman & Foster ... Dayton, OH
Knostman, Richard G. ... Dayton, OH
Knot, Alvan P. ... East Lansing, MI
Knot, Craig A. ... Chicago, IL
Knotek, Ann Z. ... Chicago, IL
Knoten, Thomas P. ... St. Louis, MO
Knoth, Mark C. ... Detroit, MI
Knoth, Richard M. ... Cleveland, OH
Knoth, Thomas A. ... Dayton, OH
Knothe, Barbara D. ... Great Neck, NY
Knothe, Charles S. ... Wilmington, DE
Knothe, Charles S., P.A. ... Wilmington, DE
Knothe, Thomas E. ... La Crosse, WI
Knott, Alvin D. ... New York, NY
Knott, Barry C. ... Stratford, CT
Knott, Bradley W. ... Greenwood, SC
Knott, Conley W. ... Birmingham, AL
Knott, Daniel A. ... Dallas, TX
Knott, Douglas S. ... Milwaukee, WI
Knott, Francis J., Jr. ... Baltimore, MD
Knott, George H. ... Fort Myers, FL
Knott, George L. ... San Jose, CA
Knott & Hartwig ... Macon, GA
Knott, Heather L. ... Hague, NY
Knott, Illyse Zesch ... Los Angeles, CA
Knott, James R. ... West Palm Beach, FL
Knott, Jay L.
Agency for International Development, Legal Advisers-Overseas, GV
Knott, Joe Thomas, III ... Raleigh, NC
Knott, John K., Jr. ... Bethany, CT
Knott, John K., Jr. ... Cheshire, CT
Knott & Knott ... Stratford, CT
Knott, Lee E., Jr. ... Washington, NC
Knott, Lisa A. ... Knoxville, TN
Knott, Loren R. ... Minneapolis, MN
Knott, Margaret M. ... Dallas, TX
Knott, Paul ... Willoughby, OH
Knott, Paul H. ... Palatine, IL
Knott, Paul M. ... Macon, GA
Knott, Richard ... Houston, TX
Knott, Rick ... Corrales, NM
Knott, Robert T. ... Kapaa, HI
Knott, Robert T., Jr. ... Las Vegas, NV
Knott, Roderick ... Miami, FL
Knott, Sanford ... Jackson, MS
Knott, Scott A. ... Washington, DC
Knott, Steven E. ... Los Angeles, CA
Knott, William C., Jr. ... Erin, TN
Knotter, James D. ... San Diego, CA
Knottnerus, John W. ... Portland, OR
Knottnerus, Wilfred O.
Newport Beach, CA
Knotts, David W. ... Boise, ID
Knotts, Elizabeth H. ... Indianapolis, IN
Knotts, H. Spencer ... Indianapolis, IN
Knotts, Joseph B., Jr. ... Washington, DC
Knotts, Marcus M. ... Pacific Palisades, CA
Knotts, Michael Ann ... Morristown, NJ
Knouft, Allen H. ... Lake Mary, FL
Knouse, John P. ... Dallas, TX
Knouse-Snyder, Denise H. ... Wheeling, WV
Knowdell, Christopher C.
Redwood City, CA
Knowlan, Jack H., Jr. ... Cape Girardeau, MO
Knowlden, Erik K. ... Mendham, NJ
Knowlden, Ethan K. ... Dallas, TX
Knowles, Andrew T.
Research Triangle Park, NC
Knowles, Anne R. ... San Francisco, CA
Knowles & Associates, LLC ... Carmel, IN
Indianapolis, IN
Knowles, B. B. ... Atlanta, GA
Knowles & Bissonnette ... Warwick, RI
Knowles, Brenda E. ... South Bend, IN
Knowles, Brenda Lee ... San Antonio, TX
Knowles, Charles T. ... Warwick, RI
Knowles, Christina Lee Dasinger
Gadsden, AL
Knowles, Clayton P., Jr. ... New York, NY

Knowles, Daniel E., III ... New Orleans, LA
Knowles, David E. ... Fresno, CA
Knowles, David K. ... Kansas City, MO
Knowles, David L. ... Fayetteville, NC
Knowles, David L. ... Ogden, UT
Knowles, David R. ... Cleveland, OH
Knowles, Dean ... Bowie, MD
Knowles, Don L. ... Atlanta, GA
Knowles, Donald L. ... Omaha, NE
Knowles, Douglas P. ... Baltimore, MD
Knowles, E. Clifton ... Nashville, TN
Knowles, Elizabeth A. ... Salem, MA
Knowles, Faye ... Minneapolis, MN
Knowles, Gary W. ... San Diego, CA
Knowles, Gearold L. ... Washington, DC
Knowles, Harold M. ... Tallahassee, FL
Knowles, H. L. George ... Bothell, WA
Knowles, James W. ... Bradenton, FL
Knowles, James W. ... Tyler, TX
Knowles, James W., Jr. ... Omaha, NE
Knowles, James W., Sr. ... Omaha, NE
Knowles, Jeffrey D. ... Washington, DC
Knowles, Jeffrey G. ... San Francisco, CA
Knowles, Jeremy ... Alexander City, AL
Knowles, John C. ... Sparta, TN
Knowles, John F. ... Alexandria, VA
Knowles, John H. ... Sacramento, CA
Knowles, John L. ... Geneva, AL
Knowles, John S. ... Portland, OR
Knowles, John W. ... Richmond, VA
Knowles, Kavita Srikant ... Clifton, VA
Knowles, Kay D. ... Austin, TX
Knowles, Kenneth ... Dallas, TX
Knowles Law Office ... Omaha, NE
Knowles, Leo A. ... Omaha, NE
Knowles, Lucy M. ... Aiken, SC
Knowles, Lyndon O. ... Denver, CO
Knowles, Mark B. ... Dallas, TX
Knowles, Marks & Randolph, P.A.
Tallahassee, FL
Knowles, Myles H. ... Port Huron, MI
Knowles, Patricia French ... Providence, RI
Knowles, Ralph I., Jr. ... Atlanta, GA
Knowles, Richard J. ... Albuquerque, NM
Knowles, Robert ... Los Angeles, CA
Knowles, Robert M. ... Omaha, NE
Knowles, Robert S. ... Chicago, IL
Knowles, Sherry M. ... Atlanta, GA
Knowles, Stephen L. ... Milwaukee, WI
Knowles, Steven ... Los Angeles, CA
Knowles, Stuart A. ... Diablo, CA
Knowles, Susan B. ... St. Louis, MO
Knowles, T. Cowin ... Montgomery, AL
Knowles, Tara Beth ... Lanham, MD
Knowles, Thomas C. ... Oakland, CA
Knowles, Thomas P. ... Hemet, CA
Knowles, Timothy A. ... Bradenton, FL
Knowles, Trayci D. ... The Woodlands, TX
Knowles, W. James ... Heber City, UT
Knowles, W. Thomas ... Portsmouth, VA
Knowles, William B. ... Seattle, WA
Knowles, William C. ... Portland, ME
Knowles, William F. ... Seattle, WA
Knowles, William W. ... Carmel, IN
Knowling, Stephen D. ... Millersburg, OH
Knowlson, Arthur R., Jr., (P.C.)
Los Angeles, CA
Newport Beach, CA
Knowlson, Mary M. ... Santa Ana, CA
Knowlton, Adam I. ... Los Angeles, CA
Knowlton, Anita Christine ... Orinda, CA
Knowlton, Benjamin P. ... Salt Lake City, UT
Knowlton & Bennett ... Cambridge, OH
Knowlton, Carol L. ... Trenton, NJ
Knowlton, Daniel D. ... Cambridge, OH
Knowlton, David C. ... Denver, CO
Knowlton, David C. ... Wooster, OH
Knowlton, David J. ... Ogden, UT
Knowlton, Dexter A. ... Freeport, IL
Knowlton, Donald D., II ... Birmingham, AL
Knowlton, Douglas H. ... Honolulu, HI
Knowlton, Francis B. B. ... Columbia, SC
Knowlton, Harold M. ... Crystal Lake, IL
Knowlton, Hugh E. ... Los Angeles, CA
Knowlton, James A. ... Aspen, CO
Knowlton, James A., P.C. ... Aspen, CO
Knowlton, Jeffrey D. ... Melbourne, FL
Knowlton, John M. ... Winnetka, IL
Knowlton, John O. ... Walla Walla, WA
Knowlton, John S. ... Los Angeles, CA
Knowlton, Jos. S. ... Salt Lake City, UT
Knowlton, Keith M. ... Chandler, AZ
Knowlton, Kevin C. ... Lakeland, FL
Lake Wales, FL
Winter Haven, FL
Knowlton, Kristine M. ... Salt Lake City, UT
Knowlton, Leah J. ... Atlanta, GA
Knowlton, Michael H. ... Cookeville, TN
Knowlton, Michael M. ... Muskegon, MI
Knowlton, Miles & Merica, P.A.
Lewiston, ID
Knowlton, Paul E. ... Atlanta, GA
Knowlton, Peter M. ... Springfield, OH
Knowlton, Richard K. ... Pleasanton, CA
Knowlton, Richard W. ... Santa Monica, CA
Knowlton, Robert Y. ... Columbia, SC
Knowlton, Sanderson Law Offices
Akron, OH
Knowlton, Sarah B. ... Manchester, NH
Knowlton, Scott ... Muskegon, MI
Knowlton, Steven P. ... New York, NY
Knowlton, Steven S. ... Englewood, CO
Knowlton, Suzy ... Carlsbad, CA
Knowlton, Timothy Sawyer ... Lansing, MI
Knowlton, Willard B. ... Lambertville, NJ
Knowlton, William A. ... Boston, MA
Knowlton, William D. ... Dallas, TX
Knox, Alison Douglas ... Philadelphia, PA

Knox, Allen R. ... Atlanta, GA
Knox, Anderson & Blake ... San Jose, CA
Knox, Anissa D. ... Washington, DC
Knox, Barbara G. ... Palm Springs, CA
Knox, Baxter N., Jr. ... New Albany, MS
Knox, Brace L. ... Jackson, MS
Knox, Brian K. ... Seattle, WA
Knox, Carl D. ... Bellevue, NE
Knox, Carol S. ... Albany, NY
Knox, Carolyn A. ... San Francisco, CA
Knox, Charles E. ... Charlotte, NC
Knox, Charles G. ... Pittsburgh, PA
Knox, Claudia Valdez ... Novato, CA
Knox, Cynthia B. ... Newburgh, NY
Knox, Daniel B. ... Fairfield, CA
Knox, Daniel F. ... Portland, OR
Knox, David L. ... Georgetown, KY
Knox, Diane ... New York, NY
Knox, D. J. ... Kirtland, OH
Knox, Donna D. ... Roanoke, VA
Knox, Donna M. ... White Plains, NY
Knox, E. Phillips ... Urbana, IL
Knox, Elinor Sandau, (Mrs.)
Zephyr Cove, NV
Knox, Frances S. ... Charlotte, NC
Cornelius, NC
Knox, Frank H. ... Cleveland, OH
Knox, Frank R. ... Jackson, MI
Knox, Frank T. ... Fargo, ND
Knox, Franklin L., Jr. ... Los Angeles, CA
Knox, Fumi ... San Francisco, CA
Knox, George E., Jr. ... Huntsville, AL
Knox, George R. ... Lafayette, LA
Knox, George R., Jr. ... Washington, DC
Knox & Givens ... Tampa, FL
Knox, Glen E. ... Santa Rosa, CA
Knox, Gordon, Jr. ... Hazlehurst, GA
Knox, H. Edward ... Charlotte, NC
Cornelius, NC
Knox, Hollie B. ... Philadelphia, PA
Knox, Howard A., Jr. ... Rocky Mount, NC
Knox, J. Craig ... Tallahassee, FL
Knox, Jack D. ... Dallas, TX
Knox, James A., Jr. ... Chicago, IL
Knox, James A., (P.C.) ... Dallas, TX
Knox, James E. ... Skokie, IL
Knox, James H. ... Clinton, NJ
Knox, James L. ... San Bernardino, CA
Knox, James M. ... Chicago, IL
Knox, James P. ... Tampa, FL
Knox, James R. ... Palo Alto, CA
Knox, Janis I. ... Roseville, CA
Knox, John A. ... Seattle, WA
Knox, John H. ... San Francisco, CA
Knox, John M. ... Lawrence, KS
Knox, John P. ... Fort Washington, PA
Knox, John T. ... San Francisco, CA
Knox & Jones, L.L.P. ... Concord, NC
Knox, Joyce H., The Law Offices of
Baltimore, MD
Knox, Joyce Hanks ... Baltimore, MD
Knox, Julie H. ... Murfreesboro, TN
Knox, Kenneth A., (P.A.)
Fort Lauderdale, FL
Knox, Kenneth N. ... Houston, TX
Knox, Kenneth N., P.C. ... Houston, TX
Knox, Kimberly A. ... Hartford, CT
Knox, Knox, Freeman & Brotherton
Charlotte, NC
Cornelius, NC
Knox, Kornegay & Bennett, L.L.P.
Rocky Mount, NC
Knox, Kris ... Baxley, GA
Knox, Kris, P.C. ... Baxley, GA
Knox, Larry D. ... Altoona, IA
Knox, Larry W. ... Chesterfield, SC
Knox, Laura M. ... Santa Ana, CA
Knox Lemmon & Anapolsky, LLP
Sacramento, CA
Knox, Leslie Qvale ... Lake Charles, LA
Knox McLaughlin Gornall & Sennett, P.C.
Erie, PA
Knox, Melanie N. Aska ... Milwaukee, WI
Knox, Michael G. ... Concord, NC
Knox, Michael R. ... Fort Worth, TX
Knox, Michael S. ... Northbrook, IL
Knox, N. Gordon ... Baltimore, MD
Knox, Noel Hollis ... Fort Wayne, IN
Knox, Paul A. ... Rock Hill, SC
Knox, Peter L. ... Brookline, MA
Knox, Philip M., Jr. ... Sacramento, CA
Knox, R. James ... Orlando, FL
Knox, Randall G. ... San Francisco, CA
Knox, Randall S. ... Fort Atkinson, WI
Knox, Rheba J. ... Fort Wayne, IN
Knox, Richard A. ... Ukiah, CA
Knox, Richard E. W. ... Calabasas, CA
Knox, Richard H. ... Philadelphia, PA
Knox Ricksen LLP ... Fairfield, CA
Oakland, CA
Knox, Robert A. ... Santa Ana, CA
Knox, Robert E., Jr. ... Thomson, GA
Knox, Robert G. ... San Jose, CA
Knox, Robert, Jr. ... White Plains, NY
Knox, Ronald J. ... Seattle, WA
Knox, Ruth A. ... Atlanta, GA
Knox, Sally Magnani ... Sacramento, CA
Knox, Samuel J., Jr. ... Bath, NY
Knox, Sandra L. ... Charlotte, NC
Knox, Sandra P. ... Palo Alto, CA
Knox, Scott E. ... Cincinnati, OH
Knox, Stacey N. ... Los Angeles, CA
Knox, Stephen J. ... Orlando, FL
Knox, Stephen R. ... Parsippany, NJ
Knox, Steven Larsen ... Southfield, MI
Knox, Susan R. ... New York, NY
Knox and Swan ... Thomson, GA

Knox, Terry W. ... Spring City, PA
West Chester, PA
Knox, Thomas J. ... McLean, VA
Knox, Thomas S. ... Sacramento, CA
Knox, Tracy D. ... Elkhart, IN
Knox, W. David, II ... Milwaukee, WI
Knox, W. John, III ... Erie, PA
Knox, Wallace J., II ... Erie, PA
Knox, William A. ... Jefferson City, MO
Knox, William D., III ... Cleveland, OH
Knox, William O. ... Los Angeles, CA
Knox, William P., Jr. ... West Trenton, NJ
Knox, William T. ... Dallas, TX
Knox, Wyck A., Jr. ... Augusta, GA
Knox-Chosy, Julianne J.
Minneapolis, MN
Knuchel, Karl G. ... Livingston, MT
Knuck, Francis X. ... Hialeah, FL
Knuck, Theodore ... Tucson, AZ
Knuckey, Arthur E. ... San Bernardino, CA
Knuckey, Donald D. ... Lacon, IL
Knuckey, Kenneth S. ... Baltimore, MD
Knuckles ... Pineville, KY
Knuckles, Dolores Clarizio ... Hackensack, NJ
Knuckles and Jagel ... Naperville, IL
Knuckles, Jeffry J. ... Naperville, IL
Knuckles, Mark R. ... White Plains, NY
Knuckles, R. Whitcomb ... Pineville, KY
Knuckles, Susan Forester ... Pineville, KY
Knuckles, Tracey J. ... New York, NY
Knudsen, Adrienne Hartzell ... Newton, MA
Knudsen, Arthur K., Jr. ... Fort Myers, FL
Knudsen, Barrett J. ... Oklahoma City, OK
Knudsen, Berkheimer, Richardson & Endacott ... Lincoln, NE
Knudsen, Chris A. ... San Diego, CA
Knudsen, Curtis E. ... Riverside, CA
Knudsen, Derek T. ... San Francisco, CA
Knudsen, Donald P. ... Rapid City, SD
Knudsen, Eric ... Burlington, VT
Knudsen, Geoffrey P., Law Offices of
Seattle, WA
Knudsen, Greg ... Torrington, WY
Knudsen, Harry J. ... Muskegon, MI
Knudsen, James D. ... Minneapolis, MN
Knudsen, James R. ... Lynnfield, MA
Knudsen, Jeannette L. ... Akron, OH
Knudsen, John B. ... Kansas City, KS
Knudsen, John C. ... Denver, CO
Knudsen, John E. ... Uniondale, NY
Knudsen, K. Sam ... Eugene, OR
Knudsen, Karl E. ... Raleigh, NC
Knudsen, Kit L. ... Los Angeles, CA
Knudsen, Kris D. ... Lake Oswego, OR
Knudsen, Kristin S. ... Anchorage, AK
Knudsen, Kurt D. L. ... Syracuse, NY
Knudsen, Larry J. ... Vancouver, WA
Knudsen, Marilyn B. ... St. Paul, MN
Knudsen, Michael B. ... Wilton, CA
Knudsen, Michael K.
Hilton Head Island, SC
Knudsen, Peter J. ... New York, NY
Knudsen, Philip H. ... Oakland, CA
Knudsen & Pozega ... Raleigh, NC
Knudsen, Richard A. ... Lincoln, NE
Knudsen, Robert E. ... Claremont, CA
Knudsen, Stephen Maurice ... New York, NY
Knudsen, Stephen T. ... Fresno, CA
Knudsen, Tara ... Bluffton, SC
Knudsen, Terrence K. ... Milwaukee, WI
Knudsen, Thomas H. ... Irvine, CA
Knudsen, Vicki ... Roundup, MT
Knudsen, Wasiura & Associates, P.C.
Muskegon, MI
Knudsen & Weiss ... San Francisco, CA
Knudsen, William G. ... Bellingham, WA
Knudsen, William J., Jr. ... Portland, OR
Knudsen, William K. ... Oak Brook, IL
Knudsen-Farrell, Wendy ... New York, NY
Knudson, Alvin J. ... Napa, CA
Knudson & Brady ... Marcus, IA
Remsen, IA
Knudson, Carlyn D. ... Minneapolis, MN
Knudson, Charles F. ... Marcus, IA
Remsen, IA
Knudson, David L. ... Sioux Falls, SD
Knudson, David N. ... Fresno, CA
Knudson, David N., A Professional Corporation ... Fresno, CA
Knudson, David S. ... Topeka, KS
Knudson, Deanne M. ... Bedford, TX
Knudson, Gary D. ... Rhinelander, WI
Knudson, Gerald R., Jr. ... San Marino, CA
Knudson, Harvey B., Jr. ... Alexandria, VA
Knudson, James A. ... Covina, CA
Knudson, James I. ... Rockledge, FL
Knudson, James T. ... South Beach, OR
Knudson, Jennifer L. ... Milwaukee, WI
Knudson, John F. ... Playa Del Rey, CA
Knudson, Karl G. ... Decorah, IA
Knudson, Kathryn L. ... Atlanta, GA
Knudson, Kenneth A. ... Superior, WI
Knudson, Martha ... Salt Lake City, UT
Knudson, Maureen J. ... Tulsa, OK
Knudson & McGreal, P.A. ... Rockledge, FL
Knudson, Randy ... Clovis, NM
Portales, NM
Knudson, Scott G. ... St. Paul, MN
Knudson, Steven A. ... La Crosse, WI
Knudson, Steven L. ... Burlington, VT
Knudson, Virginia J. ... Brainerd, MN
Knudson, Warren T., (P.C.) ... Petaluma, CA
Knudson, William H. ... Las Vegas, NV
Knudson, William R. ... Sacramento, CA
Knudson, Wm. ... Madison, WI
Knudten, Herbert J., Jr. ... Cedar Rapids, IA
Knudtson, Gigi M. ... Sacramento, CA
Knudtson, Timothy L. ... Rapid City, SD

Knuepfer, Robert C., Jr. ... Chicago, IL
Knueve, Mark A. ... Columbus, OH
Knuff, John W. ... Milford, CT
Knull, Charles H. ... New York, NY
Knull, Ralph E. ... Cleveland, OH
Knull, William H., III ... Houston, TX
Knull, Yolanda Chávez ... Houston, TX
Knupfer, Nancy, (A Professional Corporation) ... Los Angeles, CA
Knupp, Emily Lynn ... Hillsboro, OR
Knupp, Jacquelyn A. ... Youngwood, PA
Knupp & Kodak, P.C. ... Harrisburg, PA
Knupp, Larry S. ... Whittier, CA
Knupp, Robert L. ... Harrisburg, PA
Knuppel, Carole E. ... Chilton, WI
Knuppel, Grosboll, Becker & Tice Beardstown, IL; Havana, IL; Petersburg, IL; Virginia, IL
Knuppel, Neil W. ... Irvine, CA
Knuppel, Shelly Davis ... Springfield, IL
Knuppel, William H. ... Havana, IL
Knupp-Walker, Melinda San Francisco, CA
Knurr, Timothy S. ... Racine, WI
Knust, Chris R. ... Omaha, NE
Knust, Daniel Max ... Marshfield, MO
Knust, Fritz K. ... San Antonio, TX
Knust, Jac E. ... Columbia, MD
Knust, Jac E. ... Ellicott City, MD
Knuteson, John W. ... Racine, WI
Knuteson, Powers & Wheeler, S.C. Racine, WI
Knuth, Adrian T. ... Anamosa, IA
Knuth, Ann E. ... Cleveland, OH
Knuth, Conrad J. ... Ohio, IL
Knuth, Eric J. ... Iron Mountain, MI
Knuth, June C. ... Newport Beach, CA
Knuth, Margot O. ... Juneau, AK
Knuth, Randall J. ... Fort Wayne, IN
Knuth, Randall J., P.C. ... Fort Wayne, IN
Knuth, Richard L. ... Charlotte, NC
Knuth, Rick L. ... Salt Lake City, UT
Knuth, Sherri L. ... St. Paul, MN
Knuth, Thomas J. ... Peotone, IL
Knuthe, Maxwell J. ... Marlboro, NJ
Knuths, Michael S. ... Dallas, TX
Knuths, William R. ... Portland, OR
Knuti, Robert A. ... Chicago, IL
Knutsen, Clarence D. ... Stockton, CA
Knutsen, Dwayne N. ... Montevideo, MN
Knutsen, Karl D. ... Department of Justice, Antitrust Division, GV
Knutsen, Maria M. ... West Palm Beach, FL
Knutsen, Thomas E. ... Newark, CA
Knutson, Becky S. ... Des Moines, IA
Knutson, Carl Edward, Jr. ... Irvine, CA
Knutson, Colt ... Manhattan, KS
Knutson, Conrad T. ... Coral Gables, FL
Knutson, Craig ... Port Angeles, WA
Knutson, Dana F. ... Newport Beach, CA
Knutson, Darron C. ... Minneapolis, MN; St. Paul, MN
Knutson, David M. ... Spokane, WA
Knutson, Dawn M. ... Minneapolis, MN
Knutson, Douglas K. ... Idaho Falls, ID
Knutson, Elaine J. ... Tiffin, OH
Knutson, Flynn, Deans & Olsen, Professional Association ... Mendota Heights, MN
Knutson, Gregg A. ... Little Rock, AR
Knutson, Heidi J. ... Minneapolis, MN
Knutson & Heino, S.C. ... Brookfield, WI
Knutson, James A. ... Milwaukee, WI
Knutson, James E. ... Mendota Heights, MN
Knutson, Janell Marie ... Madison, WI
Knutson, Jeffrey E. ... Great Falls, MT
Knutson, John A. ... Santa Cruz, CA
Knutson, Julie A. ... Omaha, NE
Knutson, Karen Yetka ... United States Senate, Senatorial Assistants, GV
Knutson, Karsten Isaac ... Manhattan, KS
Knutson, Kathleen Ann ... Minnetonka, MN
Knutson, Kathleen M. ... St. Paul, MN
Knutson, Kent G. ... Moorhead, MN
Knutson, K. M. ... Minot, ND
Knutson, Kristal Wiitala ... Olympia, WA
Knutson, LeRoy W. ... La Mesa, CA
Knutson, LeRoy W., A Professional Corporation La Mesa, CA
Knutson, Loren G. ... Nez Perce, ID
Knutson, Lorne S. ... St. Paul, MN
Knutson, Mark C. ... Fridley, MN
Knutson, Mark L. ... Duluth, MN
Knutson, Mark Leland ... San Diego, CA
Knutson, Mark S. ... Brookfield, WI
Knutson, Martha Ann ... Washington, DC; Baltimore, MD
Knutson, Randall G. ... Hawley, MN
Knutson, Richard A. ... Seattle, WA
Knutson, Richard D. ... San Antonio, TX
Knutson, Rodney D. ... Denver, CO
Knutson, Roger N. ... Eagan, MN
Knutson, Sarah K. ... Department of Justice, Tax Division, GV
Knutson, Scott M. ... Irvine, CA
Knutson, Sherry A. ... Milwaukee, WI
Knutson, Stephanie H. ... Costa Mesa, CA
Knutson, Stephen M. Mendota Heights, MN
Knutson, Tracey L. ... Anchorage, AK
Knutter, Dorothy F. ... Kansas City, MO
Knutti, Randall W. ... Columbus, OH
Knutzen, Ernest W. ... Anahola, HI
Knutzen, Sarah C. Gemmill ... St. Paul, MN
Knuuttila, Kristin M. ... Boston, MA
Knych, Peter W. ... Syracuse, NY
Knyper, Melvin W. ... New York, NY
Ko, Ada ... Seattle, WA
Ko, Andrew W. ... Everett, WA
Ko, Anita H. ... Treasury Department, Bureau of Alcohol, Tobacco and Firearms, GV
Ko, Betty ... Bedminster, NJ
Ko, Chung Won ... Tenafly, NJ
Ko, Derek N. ... Seattle, WA
Ko, Esther P. ... San Jose, CA
Ko, Harry K. ... Verona, NJ
Ko, Henry Y. ... New York, NY
Ko, Jenny Ae-Ru ... Los Angeles, CA
Ko, Jenny G. ... San Francisco, CA
Ko, Kathy ... Chicago, IL
Ko, Raymond P. ... New York, NY
Ko, Selene S. ... Washington, DC
Ko, Un Suk ... Ridgefield Park, NJ
Koa, Christopher M. ... Redmond, WA
Koach, John H. ... New York, NY
Koach, Jules N. ... Cleveland, OH
Koach, Kraig H. ... Sarasota, FL
Koach, Kraig H., P.A. ... Sarasota, FL
Koatz, Fernando ... New York, NY
Koatz, Ronald A. ... Edgewater, NJ
Kob, Arline L. ... Manhasset, NY
Kob, Jeffrey S. ... San Diego, CA
Koba, Nancy Quinn ... White Plains, NY
Kobach, Kris William ... Kansas City, MO
Koback, Christopher P. ... Portland, OR
Koback, Peter G. ... Washington, DC
Koback, Robert ... Naperville, IL
Koback, Scott ... New York, NY
Kobak, James B., Jr. ... New York, NY
Kobak, Scott ... New York, NY
Kobak, Vickie Germain ... New York, NY
Kobal, Brenda M. ... Moosic, PA
Kobal, Steven G. ... St. Charles, MO
Kobalka, Walter S. ... Columbus, OH
Koban, Theodore J. ... Attleboro, MA
Kobasic, Dena M. ... Cleveland, OH
Kobasuk, Mark A. ... Cincinnati, OH
Kobata, Mark T. ... Los Angeles, CA
Kobayashi, Anne Mori ... New York, NY
Kobayashi, Bert T., Jr., (Atty. At Law, A Law Corp.) ... Honolulu, HI
Kobayashi, Bert T., Sr. ... Honolulu, HI
Kobayashi, Charles C. ... Sacramento, CA
Kobayashi, Christopher T. ... Honolulu, HI
Kobayashi, Craig T. ... Seattle, WA
Kobayashi, Derek R. ... Honolulu, HI
Kobayashi, Duane S. ... Washington, DC
Kobayashi, Eiji ... Houston, TX
Kobayashi, John M. ... Denver, CO
Kobayashi, Jonathan A. ... Honolulu, HI
Kobayashi, Joseph N. ... Kapaa, HI
Kobayashi, Karl K. ... Honolulu, HI
Kobayashi, Kenneth ... Kalamazoo, MI
Kobayashi Law Firm, The, P.C. Denver, CO
Kobayashi, Matthew H. ... Honolulu, HI
Kobayashi, Naho ... Atlanta, GA
Kobayashi, Naomi H. ... Los Angeles, CA
Kobayashi, Sugita & Goda ... Honolulu, HI
Kobayashi, Toshiko ... Glendale, CA
Kobayashi, Toshiko ... Glendale, CA
Kobb, Frank J. ... Nanuet, NY
Kobb, Frederick L. ... Baltimore, MD
Kobb, James S. ... Nanuet, NY
Kobbe, C. Kevin ... Baltimore, MD
Kobdish, G. Charles ... Dallas, TX
Kobdish, Richard M., Jr. ... Dallas, TX
Kobe, James A. ... Framingham, MA
Kobel, Harry ... Sylvan Lake, MI
Kobelak, William A. ... Ashtabula, OH
Kobelan, Thomas F. ... Austin, TX
Kobelin, Jerry F. ... Clackamas, OR
Kobelinski, Mark T. ... Miami, FL
Kobelinski, Mark T., & Associates, P.A. Miami, FL
Kobell, Gerald ... Pittsburgh, PA
Kobelt, Teresa K. ... Madison, WI
Kobelt, W. Hans ... New York, NY
Kober, Dale P. ... Waukegan, IL
Kober, David M. ... New York, NY
Kober, Jane ... New York, NY
Kober, John A. ... Dallas, TX; Fort Worth, TX
Kober, Karilyn E. ... Omaha, NE
Kober, K. L. ... Waterloo, IA
Kober, Louis J., II ... Greensburg, PA; North Huntingdon, PA
Kober, Peter C. ... Boston, MA
Kober, Sara ... New York, NY
Kober, Thomas W. ... New York, NY
Koberg, Jeffrey L. ... Cleveland, OH
Koberg, MaryEllen G. Daytona Beach, FL
Koberlein, Frederick L. ... Lake City, FL
Koberna, Mark R. ... Cleveland, OH
Kobernick, Todd E. ... San Diego, CA
Koberstein, John P. ... Madison, WI
Koberstein, Mary B. ... Chicago, IL
Koberstein, Nicholas R. Federal Trade Commission, Bureau of Competition, GV
Kobert, Joel A. ... Hackettstown, NJ; Morristown, NJ; Trenton, NJ
Kobert, Roger S. ... Miami, FL
Kobert, Roy S., (P.A.) ... Orlando, FL
Kobetitsch, John Frederick ... Coventry, CT
Kobetz, Philip C. ... Lafayette, LA
Kobetz, Seymour ... West Palm Beach, FL
Kobey, Theodore H., Jr. ... Fair Oaks, CA
Kobialka, Karen ... Chicago, IL
Kobialka, Lisa ... Palo Alto, CA
Kobiashvili, Zurab S. ... Houston, TX
Kobil, Daniel T. ... Columbus, OH
Kobil, Gerald M. ... Perrysburg, OH
Kobil, Walter ... Toledo, OH
Kobiljak, Kurt M. ... Taylor, MI
Kobin, Arthur R. ... Morristown, NJ
Kobin, Charles L. ... Portland, OR
Kobin & Kobin ... Portland, OR
Kobin, Robert Douglas ... Succasunna, NJ
Kobin, Thomas R. ... Secaucus, NJ
Kobiolka, Michael L. ... Hamburg, NY
Kobis, Ronne R. ... East Aurora, NY
Koblegard, Rupert N., III ... Fort Pierce, FL
Koblegarde, B. Rupert ... Portland, OR
Koblenc, Miriam ... Staten Island, NY
Koblentz, Gerald ... Seattle, WA
Koblentz & Koblentz ... Cleveland, OH
Koblentz, Richard S. ... Cleveland, OH
Koblentz, Robert A. ... Columbus, OH
Koblentz, Steven B. ... Cleveland, OH
Koblenz, Andrew D. ... Washington, DC
Koblenz, Mark L. ... Albany, NY; Cedarhurst, NY
Koblenz, Michael R. ... New York, NY
Koblenz, N. Herschel ... Cleveland, OH
Koblenz, Sidney L. ... Albany, NY
Kobler, George P. ... Huntsville, AL
Kobler, Scott A. ... Newark, NJ
Kobleur, James R. ... Savannah, GA
Koblick, Maury A. ... San Rafael, CA
Koblin, Jack L. ... Bloomfield Hills, MI
Koblin, James ... Jersey City, NJ
Koblinski, Ralph E. ... Clarkston, MI
Koblinski, Richard L. ... Birmingham, MI
Koblish, Vincent A. ... Meriden, CT
Kobliska, Mathew ... Farmington Hills, MI
Koblitz, Paul F. ... Newport, RI
Kobluk, Gerald ... Spokane, WA
Kobluk, Yvonne Leveque ... Spokane, WA
Kobly, Elizabeth A. ... Canfield, OH
Kobokovich, William J., Jr. Baltimore, MD
Kobos, Steven M. ... Tulsa, OK
Kobren, Martin E. ... Silver Spring, MD
Kobrick, Eric S. ... New York, NY
Kobrick, Gregory M. ... New York, NY
Kobrick, Jacob I. ... Philadelphia, PA
Kobrick, Jeffrey W. ... Oakland, CA
Kobrick, Saul ... Garden City, NY
Kobriger, Richard R. ... Waukesha, WI
Kobrin, David ... Miami, FL
Kobrin, David A., P.A. ... Miami, FL
Kobrin, Helena Kempner ... Los Angeles, CA
Kobrin, Janet A. ... Burbank, CA
Kobrin, John P., Jr. ... Jackson, MI
Kobrin, Kenneth ... Fairfield, CA
Kobrin, Lawrence A. ... New York, NY
Kobrin, Robyn R. ... Meriden, CT; Springfield, MA
Kobrin, Todd F. ... Orlando, FL
Kobrine, Nicole L. ... Washington, DC
Kobrovsky, Lawrence C. ... Charleston, SC
Kobrow, Ernst W. ... Sugar Grove, IL
Kobs, Jeffrey Huffman ... Fort Worth, TX
Kobuke, Linda Reiko ... Honolulu, HI
Kobus, John Jacob, Jr. ... Chicago, IL
Kobus, Theodore J., III ... Philadelphia, PA
Kobussen, Kip J. ... Sun Prairie, WI
Kobussen, Sheryl ... Rockford, IL
Koby & Associates ... Louisville, KY
Koby, Charles L. ... Louisville, KY
Koby, Colette Marie ... San Francisco, CA
Koby, Elizabeth Burns ... Herndon, VA
Koby, James R. ... La Crosse, WI
Koby, Ray F. ... Great Falls, MT
Koby, Richard H. ... New York, NY
Koby, Trude I. ... Miami, FL
Koby, William Anthony ... Houston, TX
Kobylak, Robert John ... Gaston, SC
Kobylak, Wesley ... Tuscarora, NY
Kobyljanec, William ... Aurora, OH
Kobylowski, Kenneth E. ... Princeton, NJ; New York, NY
Kobza, James J. ... Muskegon, MI
Kobza, Kim Patrick ... Naples, FL
Kobza, Lawrie J. ... Madison, WI
Koc, Lorraine Kiessling ... Philadelphia, PA
Kocab, Brooke F. ... Cleveland, OH
Kocab, David C. ... Detroit, MI
Kocab, Gregory J. ... Detroit, MI
Kocak, Richard A. ... Treasury Department, Internal Revenue Service, GV
Kocan, Sheila Tolgyesi ... Erie, PA
Kocel, Michael S. ... Colorado Springs, CO
Kocen, Sheri L. ... New York, NY
Kocer, Juliann ... Aberdeen, WA
Kocevar, Frank C. ... Charleroi, PA; Washington, PA
Koch, Adrienne B. ... New York, NY
Koch, Albert E. ... Lone Rock, WI
Koch, Amelia Williams ... New Orleans, LA
Koch, Amy S. ... Washington, DC
Koch, Annette R. ... Harrison, NY
Koch, Arthur D. ... Washington, DC
Koch, Arthur L., Jr. ... Costa Mesa, CA
Koch, Barry M. ... New York, NY
Koch, Barry Randolph ... Virginia Beach, VA
Koch, Beth Elaine ... Chicago, IL
Koch, Bonnie B. ... Woodstock, IL
Koch, Bradley T. ... Rockford, IL
Koch, Bruce J. ... New York, NY
Koch, C. John ... Chicago, IL
Koch, Calvin S., Jr. ... Kearny, NJ
Koch, Carl J. ... Mitchell, SD
Koch, Carl S. ... Glendale, CA
Koch, Carol B. ... New York, NY
Koch, Catherine F. ... Miami, FL
Koch, Charles F. ... Van Wert, OH
Koch, Charles F. ... Newtown, PA
Koch, Charles H., Jr. ... Williamsburg, VA
Koch, Christopher T. ... Detroit, MI
Koch, Clarence E. ... Wichita, KS
Koch, Conrad N. ... Roseland, NJ
Koch, Cora S. ... Newark, NJ; New York, NY
Koch & Corboy ... Cherry Hill, NJ; Jenkintown, PA; Philadelphia, PA
Koch, Curtis J. ... Norwalk, OH
Koch, D. Paul, Jr. ... Providence, RI
Koch, Dale Richard ... Portland, OR
Koch, Daniel L. ... Miami, FL
Koch, Daniel S. ... Bethesda, MD
Koch, David B. ... Anchorage, AK
Koch, David B. ... Dallas, TX
Koch, David G. ... Baton Rouge, LA
Koch, David G. ... Mineola, NY
Koch, David W. ... Washington, DC
Koch, Delrose Ann ... Wheaton, IL
Koch, Dennis L. ... Highland, IL
Koch, Donna Bruce ... Los Angeles, CA
Koch, Donna S. ... Tampa, FL
Koch, Edna M. ... Indianapolis, IN
Koch, Edward I. ... New York, NY
Koch, Edward M. ... Miami, FL
Koch, Edward M. ... Paoli, PA
Koch, Edward R. ... New Milford, NJ
Koch, Ehrich L. ... Minneapolis, MN
Koch, Elaine Drodge ... Kansas City, MO
Koch, Elizabeth C. ... Washington, DC
Koch, Elizabeth M. ... Cincinnati, OH
Koch, Eric Allan ... Bloomington, IN
Koch, Erna J. ... Boston, MA
Koch, Foust & Martin ... Milton, PA
Koch, Francis A. ... Franklin, NJ
Koch, Frank G. ... Hilton Head Island, SC
Koch, Frank T. ... Columbia, MO
Koch & Garvis ... Minneapolis, MN
Koch, Gary D. ... Tampa, FL
Koch, Gary W. ... New Ulm, MN
Koch, Geo. W., Jr. ... Wauwatosa, WI
Koch, Glen J. ... Brooklyn, NY
Koch, Graham R. E., (P.C.) ... Dallas, TX
Koch, Gregory M. ... Houston, TX
Koch & Harrington, P.A. ... Clearwater, FL
Koch, Harvey C. ... New Orleans, LA
Koch, Henry M., Jr. ... Reading, PA
Koch, Irene ... Brooklyn, NY
Koch, Irving H. ... New Orleans, LA
Koch, J. Michael, & Associates Silverdale, WA
Koch, Jacqueline L. ... Portland, OR
Koch, James A. ... Chicago, IL
Koch, James B. ... Chicago, IL
Koch, James P. ... Baltimore, MD
Koch, James W. ... Silver Spring, MD
Koch, Jan P. ... Las Vegas, NV
Koch, Janeen Beth ... Richmond, VA
Koch, Jeffery Robin ... Houston, TX
Koch, Jeffrey S. ... Billings, MT
Koch, John B. ... Department of Agriculture, Office of the General Counsel, GV
Koch, John C. ... Berlin, WI
Koch, John D. ... Baton Rouge, LA
Koch, John P. ... Chicago, IL
Koch, John R. ... St. Cloud, MN
Koch, Johnson, Weber & Goheen, P.L.L.P. Hamilton, MT
Koch, Jonathan C. ... Tampa, FL
Koch, Jonathan C., P.A. ... Tampa, FL
Koch, Judith Kilbane ... Cleveland, OH
Koch, Judith R. ... St. Petersburg, FL
Koch, Julie E. ... Washington, DC
Koch, Karl J. ... Baton Rouge, LA
Koch, Kathleen D. ... Department of Justice, Federal Bureau of Investigation, GV
Koch, Kathleen K. ... Tampa, FL
Koch, Kathryn M. ... St. Louis, MO
Koch, Keith D. ... Cedar Rapids, IA
Koch, Kelly L. ... Corpus Christi, TX
Koch, Kenneth ... Van Wert, OH
Koch, Kenneth A. ... New York, NY
Koch, Kenneth H. ... Dublin, OH
Koch, Kenneth R. ... New York, NY
Koch, Kevin D. ... Mantorville, MN
Koch, Kevin E. ... Kansas City, KS
Koch, Kevin W. ... Negaunee, MI
Koch, Kevin Wm., P.C. ... Negaunee, MI
Koch, Kimberly L. ... Treasury Department, Internal Revenue Service, GV
Koch & Koch ... Reading, PA
Koch, Koch and Bennett ... Kearny, NJ
Koch, Koch, Clark & Goldner Elm Grove, WI
Koch & Koch, L.L.C. ... New Orleans, LA
Koch, Kristin Ahr ... West Palm Beach, FL
Koch, Ky M. ... Clearwater, FL
Koch, L. Michael ... Indianapolis, IN
Koch, Larry A. ... Minneapolis, MN
Koch Law Offices ... Van Wert, OH
Koch, Linda B. ... Kansas City, MO
Koch, Lisa Z. ... Englewood, CO
Koch, Lori R. ... St. Louis, MO
Koch, M. Alexander ... Washington, DC
Koch, Marilyn A. ... Lake Forest, IL
Koch, Marilyn Porter ... Charlotte, NC
Koch, Martin S. ... Perth Amboy, NJ
Koch, Mary Kathleen ... Denver, CO
Koch, Matthew Allan ... Milwaukee, WI
Koch, Matthew J. ... Akron, OH
Koch, Michael R. ... Newberg, OR
Koch, Michael S. ... Alexandria, LA
Koch, Monica E. ... Westbury, NY
Koch, Nancy J. ... Emeryville, CA
Koch, Nancy L. ... Parsippany, NJ
Koch, Nathan D. ... Chicago, IL
Koch & Nelson ... Franklin, NJ
Koch, Paul A. ... St. Louis, MO

Koch, Paul F. ... **Franklin, NJ**
Koch, Paul F., II ... Morris Plains, NJ
Koch, Paul M. ... Grosse Pointe Park, MI
Koch, Peter C. ... **Chicago, IL**
Koch & Phelps ... Norristown, PA
Koch, Priscilla F. ... Hartford, CT
Koch, R. Joshua, Jr. ... **Metairie, LA**
Koch, Ray A. ... Nashville, TN
Koch & Regal ... Akron, OH
Koch, Richard A. ... **Las Vegas, NV**
Koch, Richard A., Ltd. A Professional Corporation ... **Las Vegas, NV**
Koch, Richard D. ... Sandusky, OH
Koch, Richard F. ... Minneapolis, MN
Koch, Richard P. ... Oakland, CA
Koch, Robbie N. ... Washington, DC
Koch, Robert ... Van Wert, OH
Koch, Robert A. ... Allendale, NJ
Koch, Robert C. ... **Bartlesville, OK**
Koch, Robert E. ... White Plains, NY
Koch, Robert F. ... **Port Charlotte, FL**
Koch, Robert J. ... **Washington, DC**
Koch, Robert J. ... Monroeville, PA
Koch, Robert M. ... Elm Grove, WI
Koch, Robert M., Jr. ... Concord, NH
Koch, Robert O. ... Kerrville, TX
Koch, Robert P. ... Valley Stream, NY
Koch, Robt. C. ... Elm Grove, WI
Koch, Ron ... **Albuquerque, NM**
Koch, Ron, P.A. ... **Albuquerque, NM**
Koch and Rouse, LLC ... **New Orleans, LA**
Koch, Roxsen E. ... **Kansas City, MO**
Koch, Sarah A., Law Office of ... Monrovia, CA
Koch, Stacey A. ... **Miami, FL**
Koch, Stephen A. ... **Tampa, FL**
Koch, Stephen P. ... **Houston, TX**
Koch, Steven ... **New York, NY**
Koch, Steven A. ... **Elkhorn, WI**
Koch, Sumner J. ... **Rosemead, CA**
Koch, Sumner S. ... Santa Fe, NM
Koch, Susan F. ... **Houston, TX**
Koch, Susan G. ... **New Orleans, LA**
Koch, Susan M. ... Eagan, MN
Koch, Tara B. ... **Tampa, FL**
Koch, Theodore M. ... Indianapolis, IN
Koch, Thomas F. ... Barre, VT
Koch, Thomas H. ... **Milwaukee, WI**
Koch, Thomas J. ... **Chicago, IL**
Koch, Thomas P. ... Hamilton, MT
Koch, Victor G. ... Sidney, MT
Koch, Victoria Jane ... Fairfield, CT
Koch, Walter O. ... **Troy, MI**
Koch, Wendy H. ... **Jenkintown, PA**
Koch, Wendy L. ... **Tampa, FL**
Koch, William A. ... Lancaster, CA
Koch, William B. ... Norristown, PA
Koch, William C., Jr. ... Nashville, TN
Koch, William E. ... Scottsdale, AZ
Koch, William H. ... **Sacramento, CA**
Koch, William L. ... Bellingham, WA
Koch, William Maurice ... New Brunswick, NJ
Kocha, Stuart E. ... West Palm Beach, FL
Kocha, Stuart E., P.A. ... West Palm Beach, FL
Kochajda, Paul L. ... Troy, MI
Kochalski, Edward M. ... Columbus, OH
Kochan, Andrea A. ... **Philadelphia, PA**
Kochan, Deborah ... **San Francisco, CA**
Kochan & Stephenson ... **San Francisco, CA**
Kochanek, Colleen ... Cary, NC
Kochanek, Joseph J. ... **Detroit, MI**
Kochanowski, Andrew ... **Southfield, MI**
Kochanski, David M. ... **Rockville, MD**
Kochanski, Paul H. ... **Westfield, NJ**
Koche, David Lawrence ... **Tampa, FL**
Kochel, Patricia Ross ... Ventura, CA
Kochell, Douglas J. ... Indianapolis, IN
Kochell, Howard E. ... **Indianapolis, IN**
Kochems, Georgann Ryan ... Mercer, PA
Kochen, Madeline Sara ... Mamaroneck, NY
Kochenbach, Carrie ... **Pittsburgh, PA**
Kochenburger, John E. ... Fort Collins, CO
Kochenburger, Peter Ralph ... Hartford, CT
Kochenderfer, Kay Ellen ... **Los Angeles, CA**
Kochenderfer, S. Ross, Jr. ... Auburn, CA
Kochenderfer, William H. ... **Walnut Creek, CA**
Kochendorfer, Tracy Falck ... **Minneapolis, MN**
Kochenthal, Robert J., Jr. ... **New York, NY**
Kocher, B. Keith ... Topeka, KS
Kocher, Bryan D. ... **Pittsburgh, PA**
Kocher, Charles R. ... Oregon City, OR
Kocher, Daniel J. ... Menlo Park, CA
Kocher, Eric G. ... Atlanta, GA
Kocher, Gary J. ... **Seattle, WA**
Kocher, Heidi A. ... **Amarillo, TX**
Kocher, James F. ... Marion, IN
Kocher, James K. ... Eugene, OR
Kocher, Jennifer L. ... **Washington, DC**
Kocher, John A. ... Winamac, IN
Kocher, John A. ... Port Clinton, OH
Kocher, John J. ... Enid, OK
Kocher, Kim ... **Philadelphia, PA**
Kocher, Paula L. ... Atlanta, GA
Kocher, Walter W. ... Columbus, OH
Kocher, William F. ... Palmyra, NY
Kochersberger, Donald F., III ... Albuquerque, NM
Koches, Paul A. ... **Washington, DC**
Kochheiser, Keith A. ... Marion, OH
Kochi, Dan T. ... Honolulu, HI
Kochinke, Clemens ... **Washington, DC**
Kochis, John P. ... Rancho Cucamonga, CA
Kochis, Joseph ... **Grand Blanc, MI**
Kochis, Joseph A. ... Cleveland, OH
Kochis, Stephen T. ... Chicago, IL
Kochis, William R. ... Treasury Department, GV
Kochiss, Deborah A. ... Stratford, CT
Kochlacs, Charles George ... **Ashland, OR**
Kochlacs, Charles George ... **Medford, OR**
Kochlefl, William M. ... Chicago, IL
Kochler, Keith W. ... **Atlanta, GA**
Kochler, Sylvia King ... **Atlanta, GA**
Kochman & Braun PLC ... **West Palm Beach, FL**
Kochman, David H. ... **Millburn, NJ**
New York, NY
Kochman, Howard C. ... Palm Springs, CA
Kochman, Howard C., A Law Corp. ... Palm Springs, CA
Kochman, Jane ... Washington, DC
Kochman, Neal M. ... **Washington, DC**
Kochman, Paula B. ... Houston, TX
Kochman, Philip J. ... Houston, TX
Kochman & Piper, P.C. ... Houston, TX
Kochman, Randi Weller ... **Hackensack, NJ**
Kochman, Ronald S. ... **West Palm Beach, FL**
Kochman, Rosalind A. ... Brooklyn, NY
Kochman, Tedd J. ... **Roseland, NJ**
New York, NY
Kochmann, Kenneth S. ... Sherman Oaks, CA
Kocho, Mirijana ... **New York, NY**
Kochosky, Krista M. ... **Pittsburgh, PA**
Kochsmeier, Susan E. ... Encinitas, CA
Kochuba, Edward L., Jr. ... Pittsburgh, PA
Koch-Weser, Kathleen R. ... Los Angeles, CA
Koci, Susan Kurzydlo ... **Chicago, IL**
Kocialski, Mollybeth R. ... Jamestown, NY
Williamsville, NY
Kocian, David A. ... Houston, TX
Kocian, Jeffrey ... Cleveland, OH
Kocian & Morgan ... Cleveland, OH
Kocian, Patrick W. ... **Chicago, IL**
Kocian, Timothy F. ... **Chicago, IL**
Kocienda, Jonathan ... **Hartford, CT**
Kocinski, Joseph J., Jr. ... Cleveland, OH
Kociol, Stephen M. ... **Palo Alto, CA**
Kociolek, Peter W., Jr. ... Harrisburg, PA
Kociubes, Joseph L. ... **Boston, MA**
Kociubes, S. Melvin ... Boynton Beach, FL
Kock, Arlene D. ... Hayward, CA
Kock, Arlene D., Law Offices of, A Professional Law Corporation ... Hayward, CA
Kocka, Frank P. ... Las Vegas, NV
Kockritz, Janis Helen ... Department of Justice, Criminal Division, GV
Koclanes, Peter G. ... **Denver, CO**
Kocmur, Marcus J. ... Helena, MT
Kocol, Elizabeth A. ... **Brookfield, WI**
Kocol, Mark S. ... Chicago, IL
Koconis, Deborah L. ... **Milwaukee, WI**
Koconis, James ... Milwaukee, WI
Kocontes, Lonnie L. ... **Los Angeles, CA**
Kocoras, Charles P. ... Chicago, IL
Kocoras, John C. ... **Chicago, IL**
Kocoras, Peter J. ... **Chicago, IL**
Kocot, Christine M. ... **St. Louis, MO**
Kocot, S. Lawrence ... Alexandria, VA
Kocour, Patricia S. ... **Chicago, IL**
Kocourek, John W. ... Council Bluffs, IA
Kocourek, Kenneth C. ... Corona, CA
Kocourek, Todd ... Tallahassee, FL
Kocovsky, Thomas E., Jr. ... **Cleveland, OH**
Kocs, Frank E. ... Cambria, CA
Paso Robles, CA
Kocsis, Alexander S. ... Columbus, OH
Kocsis, Brian Michael ... **Naperville, IL**
Kocsis, John, III ... Athens, PA
Kocsis, Louis P. ... **Bristol, CT**
Kocur, Ana M. ... Department of Justice, Executive Office for Immigration Review, GV
Kocur, David W. ... St. Louis Park, MN
Kocur, John A. ... Arnold, MD
Kocur, Michael ... Yonkers, NY
Kocurek & Associates, P.C. ... Houston, TX
Kocurek, Kelly C. ... **Austin, TX**
Kocurek, Randell A. ... Houston, TX
Kocurek, Richard A. ... Berwyn, IL
Kocurek, Thomas M. ... San Antonio, TX
Kocurek, Willie I. ... Austin, TX
Koczaja, Joseph S. ... Albany, NY
Koczan, Paula A. ... **Pittsburgh, PA**
Koczanowicz, Martin David ... Fresno, CA
Koczela, Mark L. ... Milwaukee, WI
Koczkur, Paul S. ... **Detroit, MI**
Koczot, Walter C. ... Louisville, KY
Koda, H. Henry ... Los Angeles, CA
Koda, John S. ... **Venice, FL**
Koda, Paul W. ... Washington, DC
Koda, Samuel M. ... **New York, NY**
Koda, Steven P. ... Bainbridge Island, WA
Kodachi, John A. ... Honolulu, HI
Kodadek, John R. ... Treasury Department, Bureau of Alcohol, Tobacco and Firearms, GV
Kodak, George ... Canton, OH
Kodak, Robert D. ... **Harrisburg, PA**
Kodama, Kahei ... Brisbane, CA
Kodani, Jon A. ... Santa Monica, CA
Kodani, Roy M. ... Honolulu, HI
Kodani, Timothy John ... San Francisco, CA
Koday, James ... **Fort Wayne, IN**
Kodeck, Ned S. ... Baltimore, MD
Koder, Stephen D. ... Toledo, OH
Kodesh-Baragaño, Rafael ... **San Juan, PR**
Kodiak, K. Thomas ... **Naperville, IL**
Kodis, Gaither M. ... Spokane, WA
Kodish, Jeffrey A. ... Athens, OH
Kodish, Joan Allyn ... Cleveland, OH
Kodish, Joan Allyn, Co., L.P.A. ... Cleveland, OH
Kodish, Joseph S. ... **Akron, OH**
Kodish, Martin H. ... Calabasas, CA
Kodish, Stuart M. ... **Honolulu, HI**
Koditek, Robert A. ... **Quincy, MA**
Kodjayan, Nicole J. ... Chicago, IL
Kodner, Mark C. ... **St. Louis, MO**
Kodner, Ross L. ... Milwaukee, WI
Kodner, Watkins, Muchnick & Dunne, L.C. ... **St. Louis, MO**
Kodosky, Keith M. ... **Charleston, WV**
Kodousek, Kim R. ... St. Francis, WI
Kodroff, Cathy Ann ... **Spring House, PA**
Kodroff, Jeffrey L. ... **Philadelphia, PA**
Kodsi, Neil D. ... **Winston-Salem, NC**
Kodzis, Richard F. ... Millersville, MD
Koe, Karen L. ... Los Angeles, CA
Koebbe, Lisa K. ... **West Conshohocken, PA**
Koebe, Bruce A. ... **Jensen Beach, FL**
Koebel, Delmar O. ... O'Fallon, IL
Koebel, Gregory J. ... **Saipan, TT**
Koebel, LaDonna Lynn ... **Lexington, KY**
Koebele, C. Todd ... **St. Paul, MN**
Koebele, Courtney M. ... **Bismarck, ND**
Koebele, Diane Schmidt ... St. Paul, MN
Koebele, Stephen Patrick ... Austin, TX
Koeberle, Brian E. ... Pittsburgh, PA
Koeblitz, Robert M. ... **Irvine, CA**
Koechel, John C. ... **Austin, TX**
Koecher, James R. ... **Houston, TX**
Koeck, George A. ... Minneapolis, MN
Koeck, Rick M. ... Prairie Du Sac, WI
Koeck de Schmidt, Adriana ... Miami, FL
Koeckeritz, Steven N. ... Red Feather Lakes, CO
Koederitz & Bohrer, A Professional Law Corporation ... **Baton Rouge, LA**
New Orleans, LA
Koederitz, Gary P. ... **Baton Rouge, LA**
New Orleans, LA
Koeffler, Deborah P., (A Professional Corporation) ... **Los Angeles, CA**
Koefod, Richard G. ... **Flint, MI**
Koegel, J. William, Jr. ... **Washington, DC**
Koegel, James J. ... Spring City, PA
Koegel, John B. ... **New York, NY**
Koegel, Robert B. ... **Rochester, NY**
Koegel & Rosenthal LLP ... **New York, NY**
Koegel, Thomas F. ... **Los Angeles, CA**
San Francisco, CA
Koegel, William H. ... **Kansas City, MO**
Koegen, Roy J. ... **Spokane, WA**
Koegler, Carolyn A. ... **Concord, NH**
Koegler, Claire Ann ... West Orange, NJ
Koegler, Gordon ... **Miami, FL**
Koegler, Keith S. ... **Palo Alto, CA**
Koegler, Steven C. ... Ponte Vedra Beach, FL
Koegler, Walter A. ... Pittsburgh, PA
Koehl, Edward J., Jr. ... **New Orleans, LA**
Koehl, Thomas J. ... Union City, NJ
Koehler, A. Jay, III ... **Chicago, IL**
Koehler, Alan W. ... Miamisburg, OH
Koehler, Allison P. ... **Palo Alto, CA**
Koehler, Anne C. ... Houston, TX
Koehler, Arnold R. ... **Rice Lake, WI**
Koehler, Barbara B. ... Wheat Ridge, CO
Koehler, Bruce A. ... **El Paso, TX**
Koehler, C. Herbert, Jr. ... Newark, OH
Koehler, Charles D. ... **Appleton, WI**
Koehler, Christine A. ... Atlanta, GA
Koehler, Christopher C. ... **Cleveland, OH**
Koehler, Clytie ... Merced, CA
Koehler, Cynthia L. ... San Francisco, CA
Koehler, Cynthia R. ... **Boston, MA**
Koehler, David K. ... **Washington, DC**
Koehler, Dennis P. ... West Palm Beach, FL
Koehler, Dennis P., P.A. ... West Palm Beach, FL
Koehler, Douglas T. ... Chicago, IL
Koehler, Ellen L. ... **Tampa, FL**
Koehler, Ernest K. ... Chicago, IL
Koehler, Fritz K. ... **Mountain View, CA**
Koehler, George A. ... Freeport, IL
Koehler, Henry James, IV ... Beverly Hills, CA
Koehler, James F. ... **Cleveland, OH**
Koehler, John H. ... Findlay, OH
Koehler, Joseph E. ... Tucson, AZ
Koehler, Julie Ann ... Chicago, IL
Koehler, Julie Ann ... Peoria, IL
Koehler, Kathleen M. ... Erie, PA
Koehler, Kathryn F. ... Brier, WA
Koehler, Kristin E. ... **Albany, NY**
Koehler, Kristin G. ... **Washington, DC**
Koehler, Kurt D. ... **New Haven, CT**
Koehler, Lee Ann Blackaby ... El Paso, TX
Koehler, Lee B. ... East Stroudsburg, PA
Koehler, Lee N. ... **Towson, MD**
Koehler, Lester W. ... Hamilton, OH
Koehler, Margaret M. ... Mineral Point, WI
Koehler, Martha K. ... Tampa, FL
Koehler, Michael J. ... Erie, PA
Koehler, Pamela K. ... **Indianapolis, IN**
Koehler, Patricia Carlson ... Pittsburgh, PA
Koehler, Paul Edward ... Denver, CO
Koehler, Paul R. ... Atlanta, GA
Koehler, Peter H., Jr. ... **Portland, OR**
Koehler, Philip J. ... **Irvine, CA**
Koehler, Reginald S., III ... **Seattle, WA**
Koehler, Richard A. ... Minneapolis, MN
Koehler, Richard A. ... Butler, MO
Koehler, Richard C. ... Mineola, NY
Koehler, Richard E. ... West Orange, NJ
Koehler, Richard J. ... New York, NY
Koehler, Richard N. ... Middletown, OH
Koehler, Richard N., II ... Hamilton, OH
Koehler, Robert A. ... Newtown, CT
Koehler, Robert F., Jr. ... Sacramento, CA
Koehler, Robert H. ... **Washington, DC**
Koehler, Robert P. ... Denver, CO
Koehler, Robert W. ... Pittsburgh, PA
Koehler, Ronald J. ... Akron, OH
Koehler, Stephen D. ... **Charlotte, NC**
Koehler, Steven J. ... **Metairie, LA**
Koehler, Steven J. ... **York, PA**
Koehler, Steven M. ... **Minneapolis, MN**
Koehler, Thomas J. ... **Kansas City, MO**
Koehler, Thomas L. ... Cedar Rapids, IA
Koehler, Walter C. ... Kerrville, TX
Koehler, Ward L. ... El Paso, TX
Koehler & West, Chartered ... **Towson, MD**
Koehler, William D. ... Studio City, CA
Koehler, William D., A P.C. ... Studio City, CA
Koehlinger, Denis L. ... Fort Wayne, IN
Koehmstedt, Karen C. ... Kennewick, WA
Koehmstedt, Rick L. ... **Casper, WY**
Koehn, Donald E. ... Sheboygan Falls, WI
Koehn, Janet M. ... Ventura, CA
Koehn, John D. ... Sturgeon Bay, WI
Koehn, Kellye R. ... **Houston, TX**
Koehn, Mark Allen ... Rapid City, SD
Koehn, Mark R. ... **Washington, DC**
Koehn, Richard W. ... Oregon, OH
Koehn, Susan B. ... Bronx, NY
Koehn, Susan R. ... Bethesda, MD
Koehn, Travis J. ... Bellville, TX
Koehn, William J. ... **Des Moines, IA**
Koehne, Julie ... Tallahassee, FL
Koehnke, Phillip E. ... San Diego, CA
Koehr, Jack L. ... St. Louis, MO
Koehr, Jeanne ... Bedford, MA
Koehser, David W. ... Minneapolis, MN
Koeijmans, Anthony F. ... Irving, TX
Koelbel, Kevin ... **Scottsdale, AZ**
Koelbl, Christian G., III ... **Buffalo, NY**
Koelbl, James A. ... **Milwaukee, WI**
Koelemay, James M., Jr. ... **Atlanta, GA**
Koelewyn, Herman L. ... Sacramento, CA
South Lake Tahoe, CA
Koelker, Kelly J. ... **Atlanta, GA**
Koella, Carl, Jr. ... Maryville, TN
Koella and Dixon ... Maryville, TN
Koelle, Arthur G. ... Santa Ana, CA
Koelle, Peter Brampton ... Bryn Mawr, PA
Koeller, Keith D. ... **Irvine, CA**
Koeller, Lynn Garver ... Dayton, OH
Koeller, Robert M. ... **Indianapolis, IN**
Koelling & Crawford, P.C. ... Kansas City, MO
Koelling, Demetra ... San Antonio, TX
Koelling, Gerald R. ... Hillsborough, NC
Koelling, Peter M. ... San Antonio, TX
Koelling, Peter M., P.C. ... San Antonio, TX
Koelling, Thomas W. ... Kansas City, MO
Koelsch, David C. ... **Detroit, MI**
Koelsch, Frederick J. ... **Mount Kisco, NY**
Koelsch, John C. ... Fort Collins, CO
Koelsch, Robert S. ... Houston, TX
Koeltl, John G. ... New York, NY
Koelz, John L. ... Memphis, TN
Koelzer, C. Michael ... Doylestown, PA
Koelzer, George J. ... **Los Angeles, CA**
Koelzer, James P. ... **San Francisco, CA**
Koemel, John E., Jr. ... **Stillwater, OK**
Koemel, Tina Mooney ... **Stillwater, OK**
Koempel, Alice T. ... West Union, IA
Koempel, Michael L. ... Washington, DC
Koen, Elizabeth A. ... Los Angeles, CA
Koen, Karl W. ... **Dallas, TX**
Koen, Kenneth F. ... New York, NY
Koen, Robert G. ... **New York, NY**
Koenck, Alan M. ... **Minneapolis, MN**
Koenderman, Elisa Spatola ... Bronx, NY
Koenecke, Brett M. ... **Pierre, SD**
Koeneke, Patrice J. ... New York, NY
Koeneke, Thomas D. ... **McAllen, TX**
Koeneman, D. Paul ... Chester, IL
Koeneman, Don P. ... Chester, IL
Koeneman & Koeneman ... Chester, IL
Koenen, Erin Kathleen ... New York, NY
Koenen, Frederick K. ... **San Francisco, CA**
Koenen, James J. ... Port Washington, WI
Koenen & Meyer ... Port Washington, WI
Koenen, Nita H. ... Grover City, CA
Koenen, Patrick F. ... **Appleton, WI**
Koenen, Rod J. ... Racine, WI
Koenenn, Alfred R. ... Gulfport, MS
Koener, Ronald S. ... Brookfield, WI
Koenes, Michele Rae ... Grand Rapids, MI
Koenick, Leonard J. ... **Chevy Chase, MD**
Koenig, Alan S. ... Berkeley, CA
Koenig, Alfred C. ... **Houston, TX**
Koenig, Allen B. ... **Boston, MA**
Koenig, Amy L. ... **Chicago, IL**
Koenig, Andrew L. ... Houston, TX
Koenig, Andrew T. ... **Ventura, CA**
Koenig, Arnold ... Rockville Centre, NY
Koenig, Barbara J. ... Albuquerque, NM
Koenig, Brian C. ... **Garden City, NY**
Koenig, C. Frederick, III ... **Philadelphia, PA**
Koenig Caprile & Berk ... Sacramento, CA
Koenig, Carl J. ... Richardson, TX
Koenig, Carol A. ... Half Moon Bay, CA
Koenig, Carol L. ... **San Jose, CA**
Koenig, Charles A. ... Columbus, OH
Koenig, Claudia Ivonne ... Laurel, MD
Koenig, Daniel H. ... Longview, WA
Koenig, Daniel W. ... **Greensboro, NC**
Koenig, Darlene M. ... Cincinnati, OH
Koenig, David A. ... Florence, KY
Koenig, David C. ... Titusville, FL
Koenig, David F. ... **Tampa, FL**
Koenig, David G. ... Washington, DC
Koenig, David S. ... Indianapolis, IN
Koenig, Deborah Bland ... Fayetteville, NC

Kohaut, Deborah Ann .... Short Hills, NJ
Kohen, Bruce M. .... Chicago, IL
Kohen, David M. .... Boston, MA
Kohen, Kathy L. .... Dallas, TX
Kohen, Lynn A. .... Baltimore, MD
Kohen, Roselea .... Southfield, MI
Kohen, Stefanie W. .... Morristown, NJ
Kohfield, David E. .... Anchorage, AK
Kohl, Adam J. .... Jacksonville, FL
Kohl, Barbara S. .... New York, NY
Kohl, Benedict M. .... Roseland, NJ
Kohl, Bruce R. .... Santa Fe, NM
Kohl, Cecile .... Southfield, MI
Kohl, Christine N. .... Department of Justice,
Civil Division, GV
Kohl, Daniel A. .... Milwaukee, WI
Kohl, David D. .... Novi, MI
Kohl, Deborah G. .... Brockton, MA
Kohl, Denis W. .... McLean, VA
Kohl, Donald L. .... St. Charles, MO
Kohl, Donald P. .... West Palm Beach, FL
Kohl, Donald P., P.A. .... West Palm Beach, FL
Kohl, Frank E. .... Leavenworth, KS
Kohl, George A., 2nd .... Newburgh, NY
Kohl, George H. .... Hammond, IN
Kohl, George J. .... Buffalo, NY
Kohl, Glen A. .... Palo Alto, CA
Kohl, Harris & Peters, P.C. .... Metamora, MI
Kohl, Jacquelyn M. .... Hammond, IN
Kohl, James A. .... Las Vegas, NV
Kohl, James K. .... St. Paul, MN
Kohl, James Louis .... Walnut Creek, CA
Kohl, James R. .... Bloomfield Hills, MI
Kohl, Jeffrey R. .... Nashville, TN
Kohl, John J. .... Omaha, NE
Kohl, John R. .... Fort Myers Beach, FL
Kohl, John W. .... Pennsauken, NJ
Kohl, Jonathan M. .... New York, NY
Kohl, Kenneth C. .... Washington, DC
Kohl, Konrad D. .... Metamora, MI
Kohl, Lawrence D. .... Farmington Hills, MI
Kohl, Leonard F. .... Chicago, IL
Kohl, Marian L. .... Nashville, TN
Kohl, Mary E. .... Minneapolis, MN
Kohl, Metzger & Spotts, P.A. .... Stuart, FL
Kohl, Michael J. .... St. Petersburg, FL
Kohl, N. Dean, Jr. .... Stuart, FL
Kohl, Phillip A. .... Albert Lea, MN
Ellendale, MN
Kohl, Richard L. .... Taylor, MI
Kohl, Robert L. .... New York, NY
Kohl, Secrest, Wardle, Lynch, Clark and Hampton .... Farmington Hills, MI
Kohl, Sidney A. .... Milwaukee, WI
Kohl, Steven C. .... Sioux City, IA
Kohl, Steven C. .... Bloomfield Hills, MI
Kohl, Thomas W. .... Hillsboro, OR
Kohla, Donald S. .... Atlanta, GA
Kohlberg, Jerome, Jr. .... Mount Kisco, NY
Kohlberg, Kenneth R. .... Boston, MA
Kohlbrand, R. John .... Westlake Village, CA
Kohlbrenner, Edwin Paul .... Port St. Lucie, FL
Kohlbusch, Jay E. .... La Follette, TN
Kohleffel, Bill .... Houston, TX
Kohlenberg, A. Max .... Providence, RI
Kohlenberg, Tracy Lee .... San Diego, CA
Kohler, A. Elizabeth .... Raleigh, NC
Kohler, Alan C. .... Harrisburg, PA
Kohler, Alison Daryl .... Baltimore, MD
Kohler, Andrea S. (Wall) .... Bakersfield, CA
Kohler, Anthony E. .... Springfield, OH
Kohler, Anthony J. .... Denver, CO
Kohler & Barnes, P.C. .... New York, NY
Kohler, Barry L. .... Brunswick, ME
Kohler, Ben, Jr. .... Atlanta, GA
Kohler & Black, PLC .... Traverse City, MI
Kohler, Charles W. .... Columbus, OH
Kohler, Christopher P.
Bloomfield Hills, MI
Kohler, David C. .... Atlanta, GA
Kohler, David R.
Small Business Administration,
Office of the General Counsel, GV
Kohler, Dion Y. .... Atlanta, GA
Kohler, Donald A. .... Rochester, NY
Kohler, Donald F., Jr. .... West Chester, PA
Kohler, Edward G. .... Chicago, IL
Kohler, Elizabeth A. .... Raleigh, NC
Kohler, Elizabeth L. .... Colchester, VT
Kohler, Ellen J. .... Traverse City, MI
Kohler, Erika K. .... Atlanta, GA
Kohler, Erin Connolly .... New York, NY
Kohler, Gregory J. .... Bakersfield, CA
Kohler, Harrison .... Tucker, GA
Kohler & Hart .... Milwaukee, WI
Kohler, James E. .... Brooklyn, NY
Kohler, Jay A. .... Idaho Falls, ID
Kohler, Jeanne M. .... New York, NY
Kohler, Jeffrey R. .... Spooner, WI
Kohler, Jessie A. .... Los Angeles, CA
Kohler, John E. .... Lakewood, OH
Kohler, John F. .... Dallas, TX
Kohler, John F., Jr. .... St. Louis, MO
Kohler, J. W. .... Golden, CO
Kohler, Kathryn D. .... Charlotte, NC
Kohler, Kenneth E. .... Los Angeles, CA
Kohler, Kenneth J. .... Worthington, MN
Kohler, Kristin .... Manchester, NH
Kohler Law Office .... Bakersfield, CA
Kohler, Mark D. .... Hunt Valley, MD
Kohler, Mark F. .... Hartford, CT
Kohler, Martin E. .... Milwaukee, WI
Kohler, Mary R. .... Philadelphia, PA
Kohler, Michael T. .... New York, NY
Kohler, Michele Lynne .... Portland, OR
Kohler, Patrick J. .... Atlanta, GA
Kohler, Pauline Felice .... Reading, PA
Kohler, Rainer M., (P.C.) .... Needham, MA
Kohler, Randall C. .... Redford, MI
Kohler, Raymond L. .... Austin, TX
Kohler, Robert R. .... Mill Valley, CA
Kohler, Roy .... San Diego, CA
Kohler, Sharon T. .... Boston, MA
Dedham, MA
Kohler, Shayne R. .... Salt Lake City, UT
Kohler, Steven A. .... West Bloomfield, MI
Kohler, Thomas C. .... Newton, MA
Kohler, Thomas D. .... Palo Alto, CA
Kohler, Thomas E. .... Farmington Hills, MI
Kohler, Thomas Wayne .... Tulsa, OK
Kohler, W. Lee .... New Orleans, LA
Kohler, William J. .... Atlantic City, NJ
Kohler, William Louis .... Greenbelt, MD
Kohler, William R. .... New York, NY
Kohler, William W. .... Charlotte, NC
Kohles, David Allan .... Seattle, WA
Kohles, Katharine H. .... Beverly Hills, CA
Kohlhaas, Ian B. .... Indianapolis, IN
Kohlhaas, Michael R. .... Bloomington, IN
Kohlhaas, Robert F. .... Falls Church, VA
Kohlhaas & Webb, P.C. .... Falls Church, VA
Kohlhas, Jeffrey M. .... Downingtown, PA
Kohlhase, William R. .... Peoria, IL
Kohlhausen, Frederick W., Jr. .... Houston, TX
Kohlhausen, F. W. .... Houston, TX
Kohlhepp, Keith D. .... Fort Worth, TX
Kohlhepp, William G. .... Cincinnati, OH
Kohlhepp, William J., Jr. .... Somerset, NJ
Kohlhoff, Elizabeth S. .... Chesterton, IN
Kohlhoff, Michael E. .... Wilsonville, OR
Kohlhoff, Theresa M. .... Wilsonville, OR
Kohlhoss, Charles E., III .... Bethesda, MD
Kohli, Gary A. .... Oak Harbor, OH
Kohli, Laurie Doran .... Seattle, WA
Kohli, Vineet .... New York, NY
Kohlligian, Ann Marie .... San Francisco, CA
Kohlman & Mack, P.A. .... Miami, FL
Kohlman, Richard J. .... San Francisco, CA
Kohlman, Robert F. .... Miami, FL
Kohlman, W. Gary .... Washington, DC
Kohlman, Walter D. .... Forest Hill, MD
Kohlmann, Henry G. .... Irvine, CA
Kohlmann, Kathryn L. .... Minneapolis, MN
Kohlmann, Susan J. .... New York, NY
Kohlmyer, Ernest H., III .... Orlando, FL
Kohls, B. E. .... Okanogan, WA
Kohls, Daniel V. .... Sacramento, CA
Kohls, Kevin .... Royal Oak, MI
Kohls, Robert A., Jr. .... Evansville, IN
Kohls, Shirley F. .... Juneau, AK
Kohls, Timothy Brandon .... Minneapolis, MN
Kohlstedt, James A.
Oakbrook Terrace, IL
Kohlstrand, Norman C. .... Allen Park, MI
Kohlus, Robert W. .... Wading River, NY
Kohlweck, Carl E. .... Los Angeles, CA
Kohlwey, Jane E. .... Portage, WI
Kohm, James A. .... Federal Trade Commission,
Bureau of Consumer Protection, GV
Kohm, Joseph A., Jr. .... Virginia Beach, VA
Kohman, Paulette Lynn .... Helena, MT
Kohn, Aaron M. .... New Orleans, LA
Kohn, Adam M. .... Washington, DC
Kohn, Alan C. .... St. Louis, MO
Kohn, Alisa Jancu .... New York, NY
Kohn, Andrea D. .... Palo Alto, CA
Kohn, Andrew J. .... Chicago, IL
Kohn, Andrew N. .... Los Angeles, CA
San Diego, CA
Kohn, Arnold J. .... North Bethesda, MD
Kohn, Arthur H. .... New York, NY
Kohn & Associates .... Farmington Hills, MI
Kohn, Audrey R. .... Atlanta, GA
Kohn, Barry D. .... Los Angeles, CA
Kohn, Barry J. .... San Diego, CA
Kohn, Bookstein & Karp, P.C. .... Albany, NY
Kohn, Bruce A. .... Minneapolis, MN
Kohn, Cari N. .... Philadelphia, PA
Kohn, Carole J. .... Chicago, IL
Kohn, Catherine Kriegshauser
St. Louis, MO
Kohn, Christopher P. .... New York, NY
Kohn, Daniel .... Chicago, IL
Kohn, Daniel R. .... Calumet City, IL
Kohn, Debra A. .... Treasury Department,
Internal Revenue Service, GV
Kohn, Dexter M. .... Washington, DC
Kohn, Dorine Ruiz .... Oakland, CA
Kohn, Douglas W. .... Chantilly, VA
Kohn, Elaine N. .... Los Angeles, CA
Kohn, Elizabeth J. .... Fort Worth, TX
Kohn, Ellen .... Washington, DC
Kohn, Evan W. .... Bronx, NY
Kohn, Frank E. .... Dallas, TX
Kohn, Gabriel S. .... Mineola, NY
Kohn, Gary P. .... Beverly Hills, CA
Beverly Hills, CA
Kohn, Gary P. .... Los Angeles, CA
Kohn, Gerald L. .... Buffalo, NY
Kohn, Hadas .... Boca Raton, FL
Kohn, Henry .... Chicago, IL
Kohn, Henry .... Brooklyn, NY
Kohn, Henry .... New York, NY
Kohn, Herbert M. .... Kansas City, MO
Kohn, Howard M. .... Cleveland, OH
Kohn, Howard S. .... Raleigh, NC
Kohn, Ilana .... San Francisco, CA
Kohn, Immanuel .... New York, NY
Kohn, Irving .... New York, NY
Kohn, J. Christopher .... Department of Justice,
Civil Division, GV
Kohn, James A., (A Professional Corporation) .... Los Angeles, CA
Kohn, Janet Goldrich .... Washington, DC
Kohn, Jeff .... Montgomery, AL
Kohn, Jeffrey A. .... Los Angeles, CA
Kohn, Jeffrey I. .... New York, NY
Kohn, Jeffrey L. .... Columbus, OH
Kohn, Jennifer B. .... Roslyn Heights, NY
Kohn, Jerome M. .... Billings, MT
Kohn, Jerrold H. .... Chicago, IL
Kohn, Jonathan .... Newark, NJ
Kohn, Joseph C. .... Philadelphia, PA
Kohn, Karen Michele .... Washington, DC
Rockville, MD
Kohn, Kenneth I. .... Farmington Hills, MI
Kohn, Kevin J. .... Bronx, NY
Kohn, Kimberley M. .... Tampa, FL
Kohn, Kohn & Colapinto, P.C.
Washington, DC
Kohn, Laurie S. .... Washington, DC
Kohn Law Firm S.C. .... Milwaukee, WI
Kohn, Lawrence Abram .... Atlanta, GA
Kohn, Leonard C. .... Beverly Hills, CA
Kohn, Leslie M. .... Southfield, MI
Kohn, Leslie S. .... New York, NY
Kohn, Lisa Palfy .... Philadelphia, PA
Kohn, Lisa Salkovitz .... Chicago, IL
Kohn, Louis M. .... Clayton, MO
Kohn, Margaret A. .... Washington, DC
Kohn, Margaret H. .... Bryan, TX
Kohn, Marilyn G. .... Miami, FL
Kohn, Martin S. .... Philadelphia, PA
Kohn, Mary L. .... South Bend, IN
Kohn, Meyer J. .... Cleveland, OH
Kohn, Michael D. .... Washington, DC
Kohn, Michael E. .... St. Louis, MO
Kohn, Michael Eliot .... Culver City, CA
Kohn, Michael G. .... Cincinnati, OH
Kohn, Michael J. .... Albany, NY
Kohn, Michael J. .... Flushing, NY
Kohn, Michelle S. .... Palm City, FL
Kohn and Moseman .... Remsen, NY
Kohn, Murray .... Brighton, MA
Kohn & Needle .... Maplewood, NJ
Kohn, Pamela L. .... Naperville, IL
Kohn Partnership, The .... Tucson, AZ
Clayton, MO
St. Louis, MO
Kohn, Peter Russell .... Philadelphia, PA
Kohn, Philip D. .... Costa Mesa, CA
Kohn, Philip J. .... Las Vegas, NV
Kohn & Rath .... Hinesburg, VT
Kohn, Richard A. .... Albany, NY
Kohn, Richard F. .... Schaumburg, IL
Kohn, Richard I. .... Bethesda, MD
Kohn, Richard L. .... Lincoln, NE
Kohn, Richard L. .... Columbus, OH
Kohn, Richard M. .... Chicago, IL
Kohn, Richard M. .... Trenton, NJ
Kohn, Richard S. .... Greenbrae, CA
Kohn, Richard S. .... Morristown, NJ
Kohn, Robert .... Honolulu, HI
Kohn, Robert A. .... Arlington Heights, IL
Kohn, Robert A. .... Louisville, KY
Kohn, Robert Alexander .... Atlanta, GA
Kohn, Robert E. .... Los Angeles, CA
Kohn, Robert H. .... Santa Clara, CA
Kohn, Robert N. .... Fort Worth, TX
Kohn, Robert W. .... Milwaukee, WI
Kohn, Roger E. .... Hinesburg, VT
Kohn, Roger L. .... Manhattan Beach, CA
Kohn, Rose Ellen .... Wellesley Hills, MA
Kohn, Roy E., III .... El Paso, TX
Kohn, Russell S. .... Oceanside, CA
Kohn, Samuel I. .... St. Louis, MO
Kohn, Sandra E. .... Los Angeles, CA
Kohn, Sandra L. .... Portland, OR
Kohn, Shalom L. .... Chicago, IL
Kohn, Shands, Elbert, Gianoulakis & Giljum, LLP .... St. Louis, MO
Kohn, Sharon E. .... Oak Brook, IL
Kohn, Sheldon B. .... Southfield, MI
Kohn, Sidney Y. .... Tucson, AZ
Kohn, Stephen M. .... Washington, DC
Kohn, Steven M. .... Oakland, CA
Kohn, Stuart J. .... Chicago, IL
Kohn, Susan B. .... New Orleans, LA
Kohn, Susan R. .... New York, NY
Kohn, Susan S. .... Los Angeles, CA
San Diego, CA
Kohn, Swift & Graf, P.C.
Philadelphia, PA
Kohn, Theodore J. .... Walled Lake, MI
Kohn, Thomas D. .... Baltimore, MD
Kohn, Valorie L. .... Milwaukee, WI
Kohn, Vilma Lavetti .... South Euclid, OH
Kohn, Walter C. .... Redwood City, CA
Kohn, Warren A. .... Columbia, SC
Kohn, Wendy L. .... Tarzana, CA
Kohn, William B. .... Chicago, IL
Kohn, William B. .... Roseland, NJ
Kohn, William I. .... Chicago, IL
Kohne, Kenyon K. .... San Bernardino, CA
Kohnen, Daniel J. .... Chicago, IL
Kohnen, Elizabeth A. .... Phoenix, AZ
Kohnen, Monica Donath .... Cincinnati, OH
Kohnen & Patton LLP .... Covington, KY
Cincinnati, OH
Kohnen, Ralph B. .... Cincinnati, OH
Kohnen, Ralph W. .... Cincinnati, OH
Kohner, David E. .... New Hope, MN
Kohner, Edwin J. .... St. Louis, MO
Kohner, Mann & Kailas, S.C.
Milwaukee, WI
Kohnke, Edward F., IV .... New Orleans, LA
Kohnke, Ernest W. .... Houston, TX
Kohnke, John J. .... Glen Ellyn, IL
Kohnstamm, P. Kenneth .... St. Paul, MN
Kohorn, Jay M. .... Los Angeles, CA
Kohorn, Larry S. .... Culver City, CA
Kohorst, Kathleen Schomer .... Harlan, IA
Missouri Valley, IA
Kohorst Law Firm .... Harlan, IA
Missouri Valley, IA
Kohorst, Robert .... Harlan, IA
Missouri Valley, IA
Kohout, Jenifer A. .... Anchorage, AK
Kohout, Jerry Michael .... Metter, GA
Kohout, Joan S. .... Rochester, NY
Kohout, Paul S. .... Boston, MA
Kohoutek, Mark D. .... Great Falls, MT
Kohr, Charles W. .... Decatur, IL
Kohr, John W. C. .... Spring Mount, PA
Kohr, William E. .... Detroit, MI
Kohring, John H. .... Minneapolis, MN
Kohring, Kraig M. .... Kansas City, MO
Kohrman, Daniel B. .... Department of Justice,
Civil Rights Division, GV
Kohrman Jackson & Krantz P.L.L.
Cleveland, OH
Kohrman, S. Lee .... Cleveland, OH
Kohrs, Conrad .... Santa Monica, CA
Kohrs, Edward J. .... Tampa, FL
Kohrs & Fiske .... Los Angeles, CA
Santa Monica, CA
Kohrt, Douglas H. .... Fairfax, VA
Kohs, David J. .... Winter Park, FL
Kohten, Leann F. .... Tacoma, WA
Kohtz, Donald A. .... Lincoln, NE
Kohut, Gene R. .... Southfield, MI
Kohut & Kohut LLP .... Irvine, CA
Santa Rosa, CA
Kohut, Laura L. .... Santa Rosa, CA
Kohut, Paul A. .... Charlotte, NC
Kohut, Ronald J. .... Santa Rosa, CA
Kohut, Sarah K. .... Irvine, CA
Kohutanycz, Margaret M. .... Washington, DC
Koide, Brian M. .... Washington, DC
Koide, George, (P.C.) .... Los Angeles, CA
Koinis, George F. .... Albuquerque, NM
Kois, George S. .... Wheaton, IL
Kois, Lisa M. .... Milwaukee, WI
Koizim, Harvey L. .... New Haven, CT
Koizim, John D. .... Westport, CT
Kojaku, Jon Shaw .... Irvine, CA
Kojancik, Mary L. .... Wibaux, MT
Kojelis, Daina E. .... Schaumburg, IL
Koji, Brian .... Tampa, FL
Koji, Sabine R. .... Casselberry, FL
Kojima, Gordon N. .... Sherman Oaks, CA
Kojima, J. Christopher A. .... New York, NY
Kojima, Robert Masao .... Los Angeles, CA
Kojima, Robin Dale .... San Francisco, CA
Kojnok, Ondrej M. .... San Jose, CA
Kojnok, Ondrej M., A Professional Corporation
San Jose, CA
Kok, Andrew J. .... Grand Rapids, MI
Kok, Cynthia R. .... Denver, CO
Kok, Edward W. .... Coeur d'Alene, ID
Kok, Peter J. .... Grand Rapids, MI
Kok, Sammye Oden .... Birmingham, AL
Kokakis, David B. .... New York, NY
Kokal, Michael T. .... Springfield, IL
Kokalis, Peter John .... Sacramento, CA
Kokas, Adam R. .... New York, NY
Koke, Robert E., III .... St. James, NY
Koke, Roland T. .... White Plains, NY
Kokel, Richard W. .... New York, NY
Koken, M. Diane .... Philadelphia, PA
Kokenakes, Frank J. .... Livonia, MI
Kokenge, Patrick A. .... Miami, FL
Kokes, A. Harold .... Ocean City, NJ
Kokesh, Michael O. .... San Mateo, CA
Kokie, Emily E. .... Richmond, VA
Kokiko, Christopher G. .... Quakertown, PA
Kokinda, Dennis A. .... Hines, IL
Kokinis, Carol G. .... Wonder Lake, IL
Kokish, John .... Castle Rock, CO
Kokish, John, P.C. .... Castle Rock, CO
Parker, CO
Kokka, Ralph T. .... San Francisco, CA
Kokkinakis, Barbara .... Torrance, CA
Kokkines, George C. .... Chicago, IL
Kokko, Kurt N. .... Sterling Heights, MI
Kokkoris, Constantine P. .... New York, NY
Kokoczka, Christopher J. .... Jackson, MI
Kokodis, Alice A. .... Boston, MA
Kokolakis, Joseph J. .... Tarpon Springs, FL
Kokolis, Aphrodite .... Chicago, IL
Kokolis, Jerry .... Chicago, IL
Kokonos, John S. .... Mount Laurel, NJ
Kokonos, John S., & Associates
Mount Laurel, NJ
Kokonos, Spieros John .... Mount Laurel, NJ
Kokontis, William .... Cedar Rapids, IA
Kokores, Roger P. .... Palo Alto, CA
Kokores, Roger P., A Professional Corporation .... Palo Alto, CA
Kokoris, Anne Brixie .... Chicago, IL
Kokoris, Nicholas P. .... Naperville, IL
Kokoruda, Thomas G. .... Kansas City, MO
Kokoszka, Frank J. .... Chicago, IL
Kokot, Arthur .... New York, NY
Kokot, Eugene V. .... New York, NY
Kokozian, Bruce Z. .... Los Angeles, CA
Kokrda, Robert F. .... Omaha, NE
Koksal, Ronald C. .... Knoxville, TN
Kokulis, Paul N. .... Washington, DC
Kokus, George A. .... Denver, CO
Kola, Arthur A. .... Cleveland, OH
Kolacke, F. Robert .... Minneapolis, MN
Kolaczek, Karen Gurley .... Birmingham, AL
Kolaga, John T. .... Buffalo, NY
Kolaitis, Laura Anastasia .... Rockland, MA
Kolaja, Darlene Kay .... Houston, TX
Kolak, Raymond P. .... Chicago, IL
Kolakosky, Mary Brann .... El Segundo, CA
Kolakowski, Pierre-Yves .... Greenwich, CT
New York, NY
Kolakowski, Victoria S. .... Oakland, CA

Kolman, Timothy M., and Associates
Langhorne, PA
Philadelphia, PA
Kolmar, Jay R. ... Parsippany, NJ
Kolmin, Kenneth G. ... Chicago, IL
Kolniak, Steven P. ... Lansing, MI
Kolnick, Alice ... Lincolnwood, IL
Kolnik, Michael John ... St. Louis, MO
Kolobaric, William Z. ... Southfield, MI
Kolod, Alan ... New York, NY
Kolod, Leonard ... Los Angeles, CA
Kolod, Scott M. ... Los Angeles, CA
San Diego, CA
Santa Ana, CA
Kolod, Wager & Gordon, LLP
Los Angeles, CA
Kolod, Wager & Gordon LLP
San Francisco, CA
Kolod, Wager & Gordon, LLP
Santa Ana, CA
Santa Barbara, CA
Kolod •Wager, LLP, Law Offices
San Diego, CA
Koloda, Richard J. ... Seven Hills, OH
Kolodey, Fred J. ... Dallas, TX
Kolodgy, Kathleen W. ... Toledo, OH
Kolodinsky, Rick ... New Smyrna Beach, FL
Kolodinsky, Seitz & Tresher
Daytona Beach, FL
New Smyrna Beach, FL
Kolodisner, Chad H. ... Phoenix, AZ
Kolodka, Joseph J. ... Princeton, NJ
Kolodkin, Herbert S. ... Atlanta, GA
Kolodkin, Susan J. ... Atlanta, GA
Kolodner, Bernard B. ... Philadelphia, PA
Kolodner, Deborah E. ... Philadelphia, PA
Kolodner, Elinore O'Neill ... Philadelphia, PA
Kolodner, F. Kirk ... Baltimore, MD
Kolodner, Michael L.
Cold Spring Harbor, NY
Kolodney, Lawrence K. ... Boston, MA
Kolodney, Robert ... Washington, DC
Kolodney, Robert ... New York, NY
Kolodny & Anteau ... Beverly Hills, CA
Kolodny, David S. ... New York, NY
Kolodny, Debra Ruth ... Washington, DC
Kolodny, Elliot Alan ... Doylestown, PA
Kolodny, Howard ... Bethesda, MD
Kolodny, Jeffrey B. ... New York, NY
Kolodny, Joel A. ... Denver, CO
Kolodny, Karen F. ... New York, NY
Kolodny, Lee ... Newport Beach, CA
Kolodny, Linda H. ... Stamford, CT
Kolodny & Pressman, A Professional Corporation ... San Diego, CA
Kolodny, Richard S. ... Bay Shore, NY
Kolodny, Robert J. ... San Diego, CA
Kolodny, Stephen A. ... Beverly Hills, CA
Kolodny, Steven ... New York, NY
Kolodny, Steven R. ... Woodland Hills, CA
Kolodny, Victor M. ... Cincinnati, OH
Kolodny, Virginia W. ... New York, NY
Kolody & Kolody, P.A. ... Fort Myers, FL
Kolody, Richard A. ... Fort Myers, FL
Kolody, Stephen G. ... Bonita Springs, FL
Fort Myers, FL
Kolodz, Thomas J. ... Palatine, IL
Kolodzie, Annette T. ... Portland, OR
Kolodziej, Edwin A. ... Parlin, NJ
Kolodziej, J. Paul ... Gloversville, NY
Kolodziej, Paul A. ... Quincy, IL
Kolodziej, Stephen A. ... Chicago, IL
Kolodziejczak, Michael
New Kensington, PA
Koloff, Kevin ... Los Angeles, CA
Kologi, Edward J. ... Linden, NJ
Kologinsky, Kevin W. ... Philadelphia, PA
Kolojeski, Gregory J. ... Winter Park, FL
Kolokotronis, Matina R. ... Sacramento, CA
Kolom, Alfred J. ... Olathe, KS
Kolomayets, Andrew G. ... Chicago, IL
Kolomejec, Richard S. ... San Francisco, CA
Kolomietz, Galina V. ... Washington, DC
Kolomitz, M. Jon ... La Junta, CO
Koloms, Harvey X. ... Arlington Heights, IL
Kolondra, Andrew G. ... Coral Springs, FL
Kolondra, Andrew G., P.A.
Coral Springs, FL
Kolos, Chris N. ... Orlando, FL
Kolosi, Mary Beth ... Boston, MA
Koloski, Raymond S. ... Charlotte, NC
Koloski, Steven M. ... Trevose, PA
Kolosky, Kevin J. ... Minneapolis, MN
Kolosky, Richard W. ... Bethlehem, PA
Kolostian, Richard G. ... Van Nuys, CA
Kolovos, Peter J. ... Boston, MA
Kolovson, Mark J. ... Windsor, CT
Kolowrat, Henry ... Philadelphia, PA
Kolozvary, Stephen P. ... Akron, OH
Kolpacoff, Thomas D.
South Lake Tahoe, CA
Kolpan, Kenneth I. ... Boston, MA
Kolpan, Kenneth I., P.C. ... Boston, MA
Kolpen, Jack L. ... Trenton, NJ
Kolpin, Lori J. ... Ida Grove, IA
Kolpitcke, Scott ... Laramie, WY
Kolsby, Gordon, Robin & Shore, A Professional Corporation
Philadelphia, PA
Kolsby, Herbert F. ... Philadelphia, PA
Kolshorn, William V., Jr. ... Freehold, NJ
Kolski, Stephen J. ... Miami, FL
Kolski, Stephen J. ... Orlando, FL
Kolsky, Jay M. ... Miami, FL
Kolsky, Leonard S. ... Washington, DC
Kolsky, Ronald S. ... New Brunswick, NJ
Kolson, Kenneth P. ... Washington, DC
Kolsrud, Russell A. ... Phoenix, AZ

Kolstad, Charles K. ... Los Angeles, CA
Kolstad, J. Christopher ... Palestine, TX
Kolstad, Richard S. ... Fullerton, CA
Kolstein, Engle & Prince ... Cincinnati, OH
Kolstein, Marvin N. ... Cincinnati, OH
Kolsun, Barbara ... New York, NY
Kolt, Jeffrey A. ... Solon, OH
Koltai, Mikael ... Calabasas, CA
Koltak, Ronald J. ... Columbus, OH
Kolter, Dana R. ... Louisville, KY
Kolter, Mark H. ... Stowe, VT
Kolter, Raymond Kirk ... Los Angeles, CA
Kolthoff, Erick E. ... San Juan, PR
Koltis, Tom J. ... New York, NY
Koltnow, Amy L. ... Fort Lauderdale, FL
Koltnow, H. Robert ... Plantation, FL
Koltnow, H. Robert, P.A. ... Plantation, FL
Kolton, Barbra Marcus ... Washington, DC
Kolton, Eleanor A. ... Washington, DC
Kolton, Gregory S. ... New York, NY
Kolton, Jeffrey E. ... Washington, DC
Kolton, Kevin L. ... Chicago, IL
Kolton, Timothy D. ... Arlington, TX
Koltonow, Leonard M. ... Southfield, MI
Koltos, E. Philip
Department Of The Interior, Office of the Solicitor, GV
Kolto-Wininger, Ed ... San Francisco, CA
Kolts, James Greely ... Altadena, CA
Kolts, Jas. G. ... Los Angeles, CA
Kolts, Kathlene Landgraf ... Glendale, CA
Kolts, Raymond G. ... Glendale, CA
Koltun, Dennis A. ... Miami, FL
Koltun, Dennis A., P.A.
Fort Lauderdale, FL
Miami, FL
Koltun, Elizabeth ... New York, NY
Koltun, Gregory B. ... Los Angeles, CA
Koltun, Jeffrey M. ... Maitland, FL
Koltun, Joseph J. ... New York, NY
Koltun, Joshua ... San Francisco, CA
Koltun & King, P.C. ... Washington, DC
Koltun, Lawrence W. ... Washington, DC
Koltun, Scott A. ... Deer Park, NY
Koltun, Timothy M. ... Detroit, MI
Koltz, Charles J, Jr ... Rocky Mount, NC
Kolvet, Brent Thomas ... Reno, NV
Kolvik, Nancy E. ... Wilkes-Barre, PA
Kolvoord, Overton and Wilson
Essex Junction, VT
Kolvoord, Philip A. ... Essex Junction, VT
Kolwe, John W. ... Lafayette, LA
Kolyer, Peter R. ... New York, NY
Kolyer, Steven T. ... New York, NY
Kolyn, Paul D. ... Santa Barbara, CA
Kolz, Tamara E. (Goulston) ... Boston, MA
Komada, Paul C. ... Charleston, IL
Koman, Christine M. ... Chicago, IL
Koman, Leigh Emerson ... Raleigh, NC
Komanduri, Janaki ... Los Angeles, CA
Komanecky, Bradley W. ... Rochester, NY
Komansky, Daniel S.
Huntington Station, NY
Komar, Candice L. ... Pittsburgh, PA
Komar, Jack ... San Jose, CA
Komar, John ... San Jose, CA
Komar, John J. ... Pearl River, NY
Komar, Michael S. ... New York, NY
Komar, William P. ... Mineola, NY
Komarek, Paul A. ... Cincinnati, OH
Komarek, Paul G. ... Panama City, FL
Komaridis, Alexis ... Auburn, NH
Komarjanski, Stephen ... Willowick, OH
Komarnicki, Victoria M. ... Philadelphia, PA
Komarnyckyj, Oksana M. ... Irvine, CA
Komaroff, Mitchell ... Manassas, VA
Springfield, VA
Komaroff, Stanley ... New York, NY
Komaroff, William C. ... New York, NY
Komaromi, Andrew D. ... Cleveland, OH
Komarow, Gary ... Washington, DC
Komarow, Jeffrey D. ... Washington, DC
Komarow, Michael S. ... Kingston, NY
Komas, Jay S. ... Palo Alto, CA
Komatsubara, Kerry M. ... Honolulu, HI
Komblevitz, Andrew ... Ypsilanti, MI
Komblevitz, Andrew, P.C. ... Ypsilanti, MI
Kombol, Barry ... Black Diamond, WA
Komeiji, John T., (Atty. At Law, A Law Corp.) ... Honolulu, HI
Komeily, Fariba N. ... Miami, FL
Komen, Berger & Cohen, L.C.
St. Louis, MO
Komen, Edwin ... Washington, DC
Komen, Leonard ... St. Louis, MO
Komensky, Alan M. ... Riverwoods, IL
Komer, Mark E. ... Santa Fe, NM
Komer, Nancy E. ... Southfield, MI
Komer, Richard L. ... Southfield, MI
Komesar, Neil K. ... Madison, WI
Komeya, Geoffrey K.S. ... Honolulu, HI
Komichak, Raymond M. ... Pittsburgh, PA
Komie and Associates, Law Offices of
Chicago, IL
Komie, James L. ... Chicago, IL
Komie & Kaplan ... Chicago, IL
Komie, Lowell B. ... Chicago, IL
Komie, Stephen M. ... Chicago, IL
Kominers, Abbot ... Chevy Chase, MD
Kominers, Jeffrey K. ... McLean, VA
Kominers, Odell ... Washington, DC
Kominers, William ... Bethesda, MD
Kominiarek, Michael C. ... Chicago, IL
Kominkiewicz, Laura J. ... Wilmington, DE
Kominos, Bill ... Ozark, AL
Kominoth, Tony P.
Federal Maritime Commission, Other Offices of the Commission, GV

Komins, Deborah J. ... Wilmington, DE
Komins, M. Richard ... Philadelphia, PA
Kominski, John ... Alexandria, VA
Kominsky, Adam G.L. ... New York, NY
Kominsky, Allen S. ... Ormond Beach, FL
Kominsky, Susan R. ... Bangor, ME
Komisar, Bruce Michael ... Birmingham, MI
Komisar, David I. ... Nashville, TN
Komisar, Howard D. ... Westport, CT
Komisar, Maureen S. ... Milwaukee, WI
Komisar, William L. ... Milwaukee, WI
Komisarek, Randall F. ... Denver, CO
Komisarow & Baach ... Fort Wayne, IN
Komisarow, Marvin L. ... Fort Wayne, IN
Komiss, David S., II ... Bellaire, TX
Komiss & Hutchison ... Bellaire, TX
Komissaroff, Carol L. ... Staten Island, NY
Komissaroff, Julius ... Wilmington, DE
Komitee, Eric R. ... New York, NY
Komitee, Ira ... Rockville Centre, NY
Komitor, Robert I. ... New York, NY
Komitzky, Seth M. ... Philadelphia, PA
Komives, Paul J. ... Detroit, MI
Komjathy, Laszlo, Jr. ... West Hills, CA
Komkov, Leon V. ... Austin, TX
Komkov, Rebecca Crosby ... Austin, TX
Komline, Judith Denton ... Gladstone, NJ
Komlossy, Emily C. ... Fort Lauderdale, FL
Kommel, Jody A. ... Clinton, MI
Kommer, John S. ... New Rochelle, NY
Kommers, James M. ... Bozeman, MT
Kommers, Richard W. ... Annapolis, MD
Kommers, Steele & Bentson, PLLP
Billings, MT
Bozeman, MT
Kommers, Theodore F. ... Chicago, IL
Kommerstad, Robert M. ... Pasadena, CA
Kommor, Maury D. ... Louisville, KY
Komo, Richard R. ... Wailuku, HI
Komoll, Michael S. ... Chicago, IL
Komori, Arthur S. ... Lihue, HI
Komoroske, Frances E.
Santa Barbara, CA
Komoroski, Kenneth S. ... Pittsburgh, PA
Komoroski, Mark J. ... Kansas City, MO
Komorowski, James J. ... Cleveland, OH
Komorowski, Michele ... Longview, TX
Komorsky, Jason B. ... Los Angeles, CA
Komosa, Edward J. ... Chicago, IL
Komotos, Morfia J ... Chicago, IL
Kompa, Mark A., Law Offices of
Newport Beach, CA
Kompare, Bernard J. ... Lemont, IL
Kompier, Nels A. ... Hammond, IN
Komray, Mark R. ... Fort Myers, FL
Komrower, Stuart ... Hackensack, NJ
Komsiski, Peter O. ... Indianapolis, IN
Komsky, Lawrence J. ... Flushing, NY
Komson, Richard C. ... New York, NY
Komuves, Flavio L. ... Woodbridge, NJ
Komyatte & Freeland, A Professional Corporation ... Highland, IN
Komyatte, Richard P. ... Highland, IN
Kon, Elissa Garber ... Washington, DC
Konami, Neal H. ... San Francisco, CA
Konapelsky, Paul M., Jr.
Newport Beach, CA
Konar, Howard E. ... Rochester, NY
Konash, Richard A. ... Carteret, NJ
Konat, Kimberly Ann (Marsh)
Seattle, WA
Koncan, Roland M. ... Santa Monica, CA
Koncelik, Amy L. ... Columbus, OH
Koncelik, Lawrence J., Jr.
East Hampton, NY
Konchan, James E. ... Cleveland, OH
Konchar, Robert E. ... Cedar Rapids, IA
Konchel, Matthew Christopher
Philadelphia, PA
Koncilja & Associates, P.C. ... Denver, CO
Koncilja, Frances A. ... Denver, CO
Koncilja, James R. ... Pueblo, CO
Koncilja, Joseph A. ... Pueblo, CO
Koncilja and Koncilja, P.C. ... Pueblo, CO
Koncius, Jeffrey A. ... Los Angeles, CA
Koncz, Lawrence J. ... San Francisco, CA
Konczal, David S. ... Washington, DC
Kondas, Brian E. ... Cleveland, OH
Kondas, Dale R. ... Painesville, OH
Kondé, Alex D. ... Washington, DC
Kondell, Karen Post ... Miami, FL
Kondo, Amy R. ... Honolulu, HI
Kondo, Leslie H. ... Honolulu, HI
Kondo, Peter H. ... Rochester, NY
Kondo, Ralph W. ... Las Vegas, NV
Kondo, Steven S. ... Vista, CA
Kondo, Teri Y. ... Honolulu, HI
Kondo, Wray H., (Atty. At Law, A Law Corp.) ... Honolulu, HI
Kondoleon, Nicholas L. ... Los Angeles, CA
Kondon, Christopher J. ... Beverly Hills, CA
Kondon, Hayley J. ... Los Angeles, CA
Kondos, Carol Chapman ... Richardson, TX
Kondos, Daniel P. ... Milwaukee, WI
Kondos, Peter J. ... Milwaukee, WI
Kondoudis, Michael E. ... Indianapolis, IN
Kondracki, Edward A. ... Cherry Hill, NJ
Kondracki, Edward J. ... Falls Church, VA
Kondrad, Karen H. ... Wilmington, DE
Kondrad, Michele Lynne ... Pittsburgh, PA
Kondrak, Thomas Edward ... Montgomery, AL
Kondras, Robert P., Jr. ... Terre Haute, IN
Kondrick, H. Paul ... San Diego, CA
Kondrick, H. Paul, A Professional Corporation ... San Diego, CA
Kondritz, Gregory Kent ... Houston, TX
Kondritzer, Kenneth D. ... Clarksville, GA
Kondrup, Teresa A. ... Freehold, NJ

Konduros, Aphrodite ... Columbia, SC
Konduros, James S. ... Columbia, SC
Kondzer, Thomas A. ... Westlake, OH
Kone, Allen J. ... New York, NY
Kone, Carolyn W. ... New Haven, CT
Kone, Helen R. ... West Hartford, CT
Kone, Helen R., P.C., Law Offices of
West Hartford, CT
Koneck, John M. ... Minneapolis, MN
Konecke, Eric J. ... Bedminster, NJ
Konecky, John P. ... Rock Island, IL
Konecky, Ronald S. ... New York, NY
Konecny, Frank A. ... San Francisco, CA
Konecny, Jerry N. ... Bryan, TX
Konefsky, Alan ... Philadelphia, PA
Konefsky, Albert ... Philadelphia, PA
Konefsky, Alfred S. ... Buffalo, NY
Konefsky, Leonard S. ... Jenkintown, PA
Konefsky, Samuel ... Elkview, WV
Konell, Cheryl R. ... Los Angeles, CA
Konell, Jerome J. ... Woodland Hills, CA
Konell, Suzan Vida ... Pasadena, CA
Konen, Betty J. ... Akron, OH
Konenkamp, John K. ... Rapid City, SD
Kones, Hyman I. ... Hollywood, FL
Koneski, Veronica L. ... San Francisco, CA
Konet, Thomas J. ... Cleveland, OH
Konetski, James J. ... Wheaton, IL
Konevich, Marian Malovos ... Los Altos, CA
Konevich, Robert W. ... Los Altos, CA
Konezny, Jeryn A. ... Minneapolis, MN
Konfala, John A. ... St. Louis, MO
Kong, Christine M. ... Philadelphia, PA
Kong, Clement J. ... Sacramento, CA
Kong, Diane P. ... San Francisco, CA
Kong, Helen H. ... San Francisco, CA
Kong, Jacqueline ... Honolulu, HI
Kong, John P. ... Washington, DC
Kong & Kong ... Oakland, CA
Kong, Myongsu ... New York, NY
Kong, Richter W. ... Oakland, CA
Kong, Sabrina ... Los Angeles, CA
Kong, Stephen D. ... New York, NY
Kong, Stephen T. ... Palo Alto, CA
Kong, Stewart J. ... New York, NY
Kong, Tonya C. ... Honolulu, HI
Kong, Tung-On ... San Francisco, CA
Kongable, Kirby D. ... Yuma, AZ
Kong-Brown, Barbara ... Oakland, CA
Kongsgaard, Thos. ... Napa, CA
Kong-Sivert, Jillian ... Baltimore, MD
Konheim, Halpern & Bleiwas
New York, NY
Konheim, Jon M. ... Los Angeles, CA
Kon-Herrera, Sheree ... Honolulu, HI
Konicek, Carolyn R. ... Dallas, TX
Konicek, Christopher J. ... Tampa, FL
Konicek, Colleen ... Chicago, IL
Konicek, Daniel F. ... Chicago, IL
Geneva, IL
Konicek, Kaiser and Scholze, S.C.
Burlington, WI
Konicek, Milton C. ... Burlington, WI
Konicek, Thomas Kevin ... Santa Rosa, CA
Konick, David L. ... Washington, DC
Konieczny, Edward C. ... Atlanta, GA
Konieczny, Joseph M. ... Valley Forge, PA
Konieczny, Timothy A. ... Adrian, MI
Toledo, OH
Konieczny, Timothy F. ... Lansing, MI
Konig, Michelle A. ... West Palm Beach, FL
Konig, Richard W. ... Stockton, CA
Konigar, Adrienne D. ... Los Angeles, CA
Konigsberg, Alan J. ... New York, NY
Konigsberg, Charles S.
Executive Office Of The President, Office of Management and Budget, GV
Konigsberg, Elisa M.
Hasbrouck Heights, NJ
Konigsberg, Fred S. ... San Francisco, CA
Konigsberg, Jay M. ... New City, NY
Konigsberg, Karen B. ... New York, NY
Konigsberg, N. Sandy ... Coral Springs, FL
Konigsberg, N. Sandy, P.A.
Coral Springs, FL
Konigsberg, Neil J. ... Tucson, AZ
Konigsberg, Paul J. ... New York, NY
Konigsberg, Steven I. ... Bronx, NY
Konigsburg, Dale A.
Palm Beach Gardens, FL
Konikow, Marlo ... Southfield, MI
Konin, Edmond M. ... Princeton, NJ
Koning, Harvey, III ... Grand Rapids, MI
Koning, James H. ... Kalamazoo, MI
Koning, Kirk E. ... Danville, CA
Koning, Michael A. ... Las Vegas, NV
Koning, Paul M. ... Dallas, TX
Konish, James J. ... Gainesville, FL
Konishenko, Angela C. ... Peoria, IL
Koniuszy, Thomas E., (P.C.) ... Mesa, AZ
Koniuta, Ronald John ... Waterbury, CT
Konjolka, Walter J. ... Wellesley, MA
Konjoyan, Kimberlee A. ... Los Angeles, CA
Konka, Veera V. ... Staten Island, NY
Konkel, Jerome A. ... Milwaukee, WI
Konkol, Chris P. ... Rochester, NY
Konkol, Daniel L. ... Milwaukee, WI
Konkol, Joliene D. ... Phoenix, AZ
Konkol, Robert F. ... Plover, WI
Konkol-Myers, Kim R. ... Cleveland, OH
Konkoly, Anthony D. ... Brecksville, OH
Konle, Donald F. ... Milwaukee, WI
Konner, Dennis A. ... New York, NY
Konner, Kenneth L. ... Butler, NJ
Konner, Scott C. ... New York, NY
Konner, Teitelbaum, LLP ... New York, NY
Konnersman, David ... Indianapolis, IN
Konney, Paul E. ... Irving, TX

Kopf, Kenneth A. .... **San Diego, CA**
Kopf, Patricia Nicely .... **Palo Alto, CA**
Kopf, Paul A. .... **Los Angeles, CA**
Kopf, Randy .... Hawthorne, NJ
Kopf, Richard G. .... Lincoln, NE
Kopf, Richard O. .... **Dallas, TX**
Kopf, Richard S. .... **San Francisco, CA**
Kopf, Robert Y., Jr. .... Pittsburgh, PA
Kopf, Rodger C. .... **Morristown, NJ**
Kopf, Rodger C., A Professional Corporation
Morristown, NJ
Kopf, Spencer W. .... Addison, TX
Kopf, Thomas W. .... Tyler, TX
Kopff, Frederick L. .... **Albany, NY**
Kopff, Nardelli & Dopf LLP .... New York, NY
Kopff, Peter C. .... New York, NY
Kopfler & Hermann .... Houma, LA
Kopfler, John D. .... Hammond, LA
Kopfler, Joseph G. .... Houma, LA
Kopfli, Christian W. .... **New York, NY**
Kopf Scott, Candace R. .... **Morristown, NJ**
Kopicki, Kenneth J. .... **Honolulu, HI**
Kopicki, Michael Jesse
Department Of Health And Human Services,
Social Security Administration, GV
Kopidlansky, Mark A. .... **Dallas, TX**
Kopidlansky, Victor R. .... Schaumburg, IL
Kopilak, David .... **Portland, OR**
Kopilow, Stanley R. .... Garden City, NY
Kopin, Jonathan A. .... **Baltimore, MD**
Kopinski, Michael D. .... Grand Rapids, MI
Kopis, William F. .... **Belleville, IL**
Kopish & Sequin Law Offices
Marinette, WI
Kopish, William P. .... Marinette, WI
Kopistansky, Patrice I. .... Washington, DC
Kopit, Alan S. .... **Cleveland, OH**
Kopit, Barry S. .... **Washington, DC**
Rockville, MD
Kopit, William G. .... **Washington, DC**
Kopito, Ira M., Law Office of
Brooklyn, NY
Kopito, Ira M., Law Office of
New York, NY
Kopitopoulos, Christina
Treasury Department,
Office of Regulations and Rulings, GV
Kopits, Laszlo I. .... **New York, NY**
Kopitsky, Harvey S. .... Wellston, MO
Kopitzke, Cheryl L. .... **Los Angeles, CA**
Kopitzke, Christine L. .... **San Francisco, CA**
Kopitzke, Henry W. .... Angwin, CA
Kopiwoda, Jeffrey E. .... **Chicago, IL**
Kopka, Christopher J. .... **Minneapolis, MN**
New York, NY
Kopka, Daniel D. .... Ann Arbor, MI
Kopka, Landau & Pinkus .... **Chicago, IL**
Vernon Hills, IL
Crown Point, IN
Indianapolis, IN
South Bend, IN
Farmington Hills, MI
Kopka, Robert J. .... **Chicago, IL**
Crown Point, IN
Kopkas, Andrew J. .... Cleveland, OH
Kopke, Alan N. .... San Francisco, CA
Kopke, Larry L. .... Great Bend, KS
Kopke, Warren H. .... Great Bend, KS
Kopkin, Andrew H. .... Los Angeles, CA
Kopko, Andrew J. .... **Merrillville, IN**
Kopko, Edward E. .... Providence, RI
Kopko, Frederick H., Jr. .... **Chicago, IL**
Kopko Genetos & Retson LLP
Merrillville, IN
Kopko, Mary Elizabeth .... **Chicago, IL**
Koplan, Andrew B. .... **Atlanta, GA**
Koplan, Michael S. .... **Washington, DC**
Koplan, Sharon W. .... **Dallas, TX**
Koplas, David W. .... Lockport, NY
Koplen, Michael A. .... New York, NY
Kopleton, Richard S. .... Paterson, NJ
Wayne, NJ
Kopley, Catherine S. .... South Plainfield, NJ
Koplien, Chad W. .... **Milwaukee, WI**
Koplik, Marc S., & Associates
Albany, NY
Koplik, Marc S., & Associates
New York, NY
Koplik, Pamela A. .... **New York, NY**
Koplin, Bernice J. .... Boca Raton, FL
Haddonfield, NJ
Philadelphia, PA
Koplin, Caroline .... Chicago, IL
Koplin, Gail M. Latt .... Philadelphia, PA
Koplin, Kevin S. .... Bronx, NY
Koplin, Ross .... Denver, CO
Koplin, Ryan R. .... Cherokee, IA
Koplof, Norman G. .... Los Angeles, CA
Koplove, Jay S. .... Beverly, MA
Koplove, Steven .... Philadelphia, PA
Koplovitz, Joshua N. .... **Kingston, NY**
Woodstock, NY
Koplovitz, Mayer .... Syracuse, NY
Koplovitz, Sholom B. .... **Albany, NY**
Koplow, David A. .... Department of Defense,
Office of the General Counsel, GV
Koplow, James B. .... Cleveland, OH
Koplow, Laurence N. .... Deerfield, IL
Koplow, Meyer G. .... **New York, NY**
Koplowitz, Edward A. .... **San Francisco, CA**
Kopman, Barbara H. .... Hicksville, NY
Kopman, Bryan .... **Joliet, IL**
Kopman, Charles E. .... **St. Louis, MO**
Kopman, Nancy J. .... Baltimore, MD
Kopman, Sharon M. .... **Los Angeles, CA**
Kopnicki, Robert A. .... Mountainside, NJ
Kopnitsky, Vic J., Jr. .... **Syracuse, NY**
Kopnski, Michelle L. .... **Pittsburgh, PA**

Kopocis, Christine M.
Department of Defense,
Defense Legal Services Agency, GV
Kopolow, John L. .... Baltimore, MD
Kopolow, Leroy .... St. Louis, MO
Kopon, Andrew, Jr. .... **Chicago, IL**
Koponen, Alex .... Fairbanks, AK
Kopowski, Leonard L. .... Newport, KY
Kopp, Angela Johnson .... Hinsdale, IL
Kopp, Arena & Bishop .... Milwaukee, WI
Kopp, Byron E. .... Allentown, PA
Kopp, Charles G. .... **Philadelphia, PA**
Kopp & Conner, P.C. .... Waycross, GA
Kopp, Daniel J. .... **Chicago, IL**
Kopp, David C. .... Hartford, CT
Kopp, David G. .... Greensboro, GA
Kopp, David G., P.C. .... Greensboro, GA
Kopp, David I. .... Rochester, NY
Kopp & Di Franco .... **San Francisco, CA**
Kopp, Donald A. .... **Portland, ME**
Kopp, Eugene P. .... **Washington, DC**
Washington, DC
Kopp, Fred R. .... Alma, GA
Kopp, Fred R., P.C. .... Alma, GA
Kopp, Frederick P. .... Rock Island, IL
Kopp, Howard R. .... Phoenix, AZ
Kopp, J. Brian .... **Rochester, NY**
Kopp, James O. .... San Antonio, TX
Kopp, Jay A. .... **Minneapolis, MN**
Kopp, Jeffrey S. .... **Detroit, MI**
Kopp, John G. .... Waycross, GA
Kopp, John H. .... Clifton, NJ
Kopp, John J., Jr. .... Windsor, MO
Kopp, John W., Jr. .... Coronado, CA
Kopp, Kathleen M. .... **Houston, TX**
Kopp, Kennard B. .... Rockford, IL
Kopp, Kevin P. .... **New York, NY**
Kopp, Leonard H. .... Bethesda, MD
Kopp, Mark D. .... **Janesville, WI**
Kopp, McKichan, Geyer & Skemp, LLP
Platteville, WI
Kopp, Melisande .... New York, NY
Kopp, Michael .... **San Francisco, CA**
Kopp, Philip David .... **Fresno, CA**
Kopp, Phyllis S. .... Del Mar, CA
Kopp, Quentin L. .... San Francisco, CA
Kopp, Robert E. .... Department of Justice,
Civil Division, GV
Kopp, Robert W. .... **Syracuse, NY**
Kopp, Ronald S. .... **Akron, OH**
Kopp, Sarah M. .... **Washington, DC**
Kopp, Shea Sperling .... Montrose, CO
Kopp, Shepard S. .... **Los Angeles, CA**
Kopp, Steven L. .... **New York, NY**
Kopp, Suzanne M. .... **Chicago, IL**
Kopp, W. Roy .... **Platteville, WI**
Kopp, William J. .... Cleveland, OH
Koppa, David M. .... **Colorado Springs, CO**
Koppa, David Michael .... Buffalo Grove, IL
Koppa, Patricia A. .... Manitowoc, WI
Koppe, Brenda M. .... Battle Creek, MI
Koppe, Bruce A. .... Seattle, WA
Koppe, Gregory A. .... Las Vegas, NV
Koppe, Gregory J. .... St. Louis, MO
Koppe & Koppe .... Las Vegas, NV
Koppe, Peter F. .... Las Vegas, NV
Koppe, Peter J. .... Platte Woods, MO
Koppe, Robyn L. .... Tacoma, WA
Koppekin, Stephen M. .... Los Angeles, CA
Koppel, Ann Redlich .... **New York, NY**
Koppel, Bruce S. .... Englewood, NJ
Koppel, Carol S. .... Greybull, WY
Koppel, Erwin .... Morristown, NJ
Koppel, Ezell, Jackson & Kimball, L.L.P.
Brownsville, TX
Harlingen, TX
Koppel, Gary .... Oakley, CA
Koppel, Glenn S. .... Fullerton, CA
Koppel, Grace A. .... Potomac, MD
Koppel, Irving .... Skokie, IL
Koppel & Jacobs .... Thousand Oaks, CA
Ventura, CA
Koppel, John S. .... Department of Justice,
Civil Division, GV
Koppel, Richard S. .... Thousand Oaks, CA
Koppel, Richard U. .... New York, NY
Koppel, Robert S. .... Rockville, MD
Koppel, Rollins M. .... **Harlingen, TX**
Koppel, Rosa M. .... Treasury Department,
Office of the Comptroller of the Currency,
GV
Koppel, Scott M. .... **Torrance, CA**
Koppel, Stanton R. .... **San Francisco, CA**
Koppel, Steven .... **New York, NY**
Koppel, Wayne S. .... **Plantation, FL**
Koppele, Jeffrey H. .... **New York, NY**
Koppell, Edward G. .... Brooklyn, NY
Koppell, G. Oliver .... **New York, NY**
Koppelmaa, Jeffrey S. .... **San Francisco, CA**
Koppelman, Andrea L. .... Arlington, VA
Koppelman, Andrew .... Princeton, NJ
Koppelman, David .... Chicago, IL
Koppelman, Jack .... Pagosa Springs, CO
Koppelman, James C. .... **Merrill, WI**
Koppelman, Jos. B. .... New York, NY
Koppelman, Mark S. .... Southfield, MI
Koppelman, Robert .... New York, NY
Koppelman, Ronald S. .... Nanuet, NY
Koppen, Margaret E. .... **Phoenix, AZ**
Koppen, R. Daniel .... Miami, FL
Koppen, Robert A. .... Miami, FL
Koppenaal, Richard D. .... Hackensack, NJ
Koppenheffer, Kent E. .... Northglenn, CO
Koppenheffer, Shiela T. .... Denver, CO
Koppenheffer, William K. .... **Lebanon, NH**
Koppenhofer, Andrea .... St. Charles, IL
Kopper, W. Bruce .... Colorado Springs, CO
Kopper, William D. .... Davis, CA

Kopperud, Eddie G. .... Grafton, ND
Kopperud, Noel H. .... Wasilla, AK
Kopperud, Ross A. .... Anchorage, AK
Koppes, Richard H. .... **Los Angeles, CA**
Koppes Conway, Rebecca A. .... **Greeley, CO**
Koppisch, Claude B. .... Ocean City, MD
Kopple & Klinger, LLP .... **Los Angeles, CA**
Kopple, Madelynn .... **Santa Monica, CA**
Kopple, Madelynn, A Law Corporation
Los Angeles, CA
Santa Monica, CA
Kopple, Robert C., (P.C.)
Los Angeles, CA
Kopplin, Carl J. .... Madison, WI
Kopplow & Flynn, P.A. .... Miami, FL
Kopplow, Ronald C. .... Miami, FL
Koppman, Edward S., (P.C.) .... **Dallas, TX**
Kopps, Tanya S. .... Chicago, IL
Koppy, Allen .... Mandan, ND
Koppy, David L. .... West Bloomfield, MI
Koppy, Jeffry A. .... **Chicago, IL**
Kopriva, James W. .... **Chicago, IL**
Kopriva, Jolene Grubb .... Hollidaysburg, PA
Kopriva Law Office, P.C. .... Lander, WY
Kopriva, Ron M. .... Lander, WY
Kopriva, Teresa C. .... **Chicago, IL**
Koprowicz, Kenneth M. .... **Denver, CO**
Koprowski, Debra T. .... Pembroke Pines, FL
Koprowski, Debra T., P.A.
Pembroke Pines, FL
Koprowski, Donald J. .... **Irvine, CA**
Koprowski, Wayne M. .... Glenview, IL
Koprucki, Jane .... Columbus, OH
Kops, Dennis H. .... East Setauket, NY
Kops, John Michael .... Manalapan, FL
Kops, Mitchell R. .... **Portland, ME**
Kops, Robert D. .... Brookville, NY
Kops, Stanley P. .... Philadelphia, PA
Kopshever, Thomas F. .... **San Francisco, CA**
Kopsick, Michael J. .... **Vernon, CT**
Kopsick, Richard S. .... Waukegan, IL
Kopsick, Steven C. .... New York, NY
Kopsky, Carolyn M. .... **St. Louis, MO**
Kopsky & Heck, P.C. .... **Chesterfield, MO**
St. Louis, MO
Kopsky, Paul W. .... **Chesterfield, MO**
Kopson, John E. .... Boca Raton, FL
Kopson, Mark S. .... **Rochester, MI**
Kopson, Mark S., PLC .... **Detroit, MI**
Rochester, MI
Kopstein, Alexander S.
Department of the Navy, GV
Kopstein, David M. .... Greenbelt, MD
Kopta, Gregory J. .... **Seattle, WA**
Kopta, Joseph R. .... Gig Harbor, WA
Kopta, William F. .... Downers Grove, IL
Kopti, Daniel R. .... **Atlanta, GA**
Kopycienski, Dawn M. .... Maple Glen, PA
Kor, Robert J. .... West Hartford, CT
Korab, Edward W. .... Saratoga, CA
Korach, Kenneth A. .... Philadelphia, PA
Korachis, John F. .... Detroit, MI
Korade, Carol A. .... Alameda, CA
Korade, Henry W. .... Middletown, NY
Koral, Alan M. .... **New York, NY**
Koral, Jason M. .... **New York, NY**
Koral, Kahn & Koral, P.C. .... Philadelphia, PA
Koral, Margaret M. .... Philadelphia, PA
Koral, Mark A. .... Philadelphia, PA
Koral, Richard I. .... Los Angeles, CA
Koral, Richard L. .... **New York, NY**
Koral, Timothy J. .... Cleveland, OH
Koralchik, Joseph .... **Kansas City, MO**
Koran, Isaac B. .... Pensacola, FL
Koran, Janet M. .... Chicago, IL
Koranda, Charlotte R. .... Lincoln, NE
Koranda, Hugo .... Hinsdale, IL
Koranda, Kenneth A. .... Chicago, IL
Koranda, Kenneth R. .... Naperville, IL
Koranda, Michael A. .... Harrisburg, PA
Korando, Kimberly J. .... **Raleigh, NC**
Koransky, Henry A. .... Los Angeles, CA
Koransky, Peter G. .... **Merrillville, IN**
Koransky Pothier, Katherine
San Diego, CA
Koratsky, Kim .... **Springfield, IL**
Korb, Daniel R., Jr. .... **Florham Park, NJ**
Korb, Donald L. .... **Cleveland, OH**
Korb, Joan M. .... Racine, WI
Korb, Jonathan L. .... Boston, MA
Korb, Kenneth A. .... **Boston, MA**
Korb, Mark L. .... **Fort Collins, CO**
Korb, Michael A., Jr. .... Newport News, VA
Korb, Orry Phillip .... Los Gatos, CA
Korb, Philip B. .... **Philadelphia, PA**
Korb, Robert, III .... **Ketchum, ID**
Korb, Sheila L. .... **Fort Worth, TX**
Korb, Timothy L.
Merit Systems Protection Board,
Office of Appeals Counsel, GV
Korb, Todd R. .... **Milwaukee, WI**
Korb, William R. (Butch), Jr.
Fort Worth, TX
Korba, Robert W. .... Dallas, TX
Korba, Rosemary .... Dallas, TX
Korba, Steven J. .... Hennepin, IL
Korbakes, Lee C. .... Wilmette, IL
Korbakis, Raina Ioanna .... Lansing, MI
Korbas, Neil H. .... Spokane, WA
Korbatov, Igor .... Los Angeles, CA
Korbee, Harold G. .... **Cincinnati, OH**
Korbee, Thomas C. .... **Cincinnati, OH**
Korbel, Diane .... **San Francisco, CA**
Korbel, George M. .... Breckenridge, MN
Korbel, Todd M. .... **New Orleans, LA**
Korber, Jeffrey W. .... Chico, CA
Korber, Mark F. .... **Hartford, CT**
Korbey, John A. .... Auburn, NH

Korbholz, Michael L. .... San Francisco, CA
Korbin, Ronee F. .... Phoenix, AZ
Korbol, John J. .... Riverside, CA
Korby, Mary R. .... **Dallas, TX**
Korchek, Jeffrey Alan .... Universal City, CA
Korchin, Judith M. .... **Miami, FL**
Korda, Johnson & Wall .... **San Jose, CA**
Korda, Lawrence L. .... Fort Lauderdale, FL
Korda, Michael J. .... **San Jose, CA**
Korda, Peter J. .... **New York, NY**
Kordas, Andrew F. .... **Norwalk, CT**
Kordas, Anne M. .... **Cleveland, OH**
Kordas, Nicholas .... Bayside, NY
Korde, Margaret G. .... Chelmsford, MA
Korde, Rukesh .... **Washington, DC**
Korde, Sanjit S. .... **Boston, MA**
Kordek, Kathleen A. .... Falls Church, VA
Kordeleski, Kathleen M. .... **Cleveland, OH**
Kordeliski, Terry Don, II
Oklahoma City, OK
Kordell, Kathryn Conway .... **Dubuque, IA**
Kordelski, Terry D., II
Oklahoma City, OK
Kordenbrock, Jean E. .... **Lansing, MI**
Kordenbrock, Richard R. .... St. Louis, MO
Korder, Mitchell L. .... Bronx, NY
Larchmont, NY
Kordes, Henry E. .... **Asbury Park, NJ**
Kordestani, Jennifer J.
San Francisco, CA
Kordestani, Said C. .... **San Francisco, CA**
Kordic, Bruce D. .... Los Angeles, CA
Kordic, Gregory L. .... Euclid, OH
Kordich, Donald C. .... **Los Angeles, CA**
Kordich, Kyle N. .... **Albany, NY**
Kordich, Roy A. .... Covina, CA
Kordick, Lloyd C. .... Colorado Springs, CO
Kordik, Daniel J. .... Elmhurst, IL
Kordik, Ellen R. .... Champaign, IL
Kordik, James G. .... **Dayton, OH**
Kordisch, Steven E. .... Ridgewood, NY
Kordish, Dennis E. .... Grand Rapids, MI
Kordof, Kathryn P. .... Denver, CO
Kordons & Co., L.P.A. .... **Cincinnati, OH**
Kordons, Uldis .... **Cincinnati, OH**
Korduba, George B. .... Montville, NJ
Kordula, Chantal E. .... **New York, NY**
Korduner, David J. .... Los Angeles, CA
Korduner, Debra L., Law Offices of
Los Angeles, CA
Kordyban, Emily E. .... **Los Angeles, CA**
Kordys, Richard A. .... Chicago, IL
Kordziel, Kevin M. .... **Washington, DC**
Kordziel, Linda Liu .... **Washington, DC**
Kordzik, Kelly K. .... **Austin, TX**
Korea, Kenneth S. .... **San Jose, CA**
Korecki, Richard J. .... Denver, CO
Korein, Michael H. .... **East St. Louis, IL**
Korein, Sandor .... **East St. Louis, IL**
St. Louis, MO
Korek, Jeff S. .... **New York, NY**
Korell, Bailey J. .... **New York, NY**
Korell, Bradley G. .... **Dallas, TX**
Koreman, Harold E. .... **Albany, NY**
Koren, Bennet Scott .... **New Orleans, LA**
Koren, Bertell & Hoey .... Buffalo, NY
Koren, Bruce Kevin .... Buffalo, NY
Koren, Edward F. .... **Lakeland, FL**
Tampa, FL
Koren, Harriet J. .... **Philadelphia, PA**
Koren, Jay A. .... Miami, FL
Koren, Joanne Harvest .... Miami, FL
Koren, Lindy Korn .... Brooklyn, NY
Koren, Neil J. .... **San Francisco, CA**
Koren, Philip F. .... Department of Defense,
Defense Commissary Agency, GV
Koren, Richard A. .... Carle Place, NY
Koren, Samuel M. .... Scarborough, ME
Koren, Shelley H. .... **St. Louis, MO**
Korenbaum, Laurie A. .... New York, NY
Korenblat, Steven D. .... **St. Louis, MO**
Korenblatt, Jeffrey S. .... **Washington, DC**
Korenchuk, Keith M. .... **Charlotte, NC**
Korengold, Howard .... Chicago, IL
Korengold, Jerry T. .... Santa Monica, CA
Korengold, Michael A.G.
New Orleans, LA
Korenkiewicz, Robert A. .... Chicago, IL
Korens, Joel A. .... Tulsa, OK
Kores, Katharine Wolf .... Memphis, TN
Koresko & Associates, A Professional Corporation .... **King Of Prussia, PA**
Koresko, John J., V .... **King Of Prussia, PA**
Koretoff, Robert J. .... Marina Del Rey, CA
Koretz, Amy S. .... **Colorado Springs, CO**
Koretz, Eileen .... Bronx, NY
Koretz, Joseph S. .... Farmington, MI
Koretz, Michael P. .... Brockton, MA
Koretz, Robert F. .... Syracuse, NY
Koretzky, David A. .... Miami, FL
Koretzky, David B. .... Humble, TX
Koretzky, I. Harold .... **New Orleans, LA**
Koretzky, Marsha E. .... Goshen, NY
Koretzky, Roselyn B., (P.C.)
New Orleans, LA
Korey, Carter Andrew .... **Chicago, IL**
Korey, Frederick A. .... Cleveland, OH
Korey, Gerald W. .... Lansing, IL
Korey, Ilene M. .... **Chicago, IL**
Korey, Martin S. .... **Chicago, IL**
Korey, Philip J. .... **Cleveland, OH**
Korey, Robert Kit .... **Ormond Beach, FL**
Korey, Sweet, McKinnon, Simpson & Vukelja .... **Ormond Beach, FL**
Korey, Vincent P. .... Columbus, OH
Korey, William R. .... Philadelphia, PA
Korf, Gene R. .... **Morristown, NJ**
Korf, John .... Freeport, IL

Korslund, Willet & Liekhus ....Beatrice, NE
Wymore, NE
Korsman, Thomas M. ....Minneapolis, MN
Korsmeyer, Julie ....San Diego, CA
Korsmeyer, Mary Drake ....Washington, PA
Korsmo, Elizabeth K ....Albuquerque, NM
Korsmo, John T. ....Fargo, ND
Korsmo, Kevin M. ....Spokane, WA
Korson, Michael S. ....New York, NY
Korsower, Rachel B. ....Baltimore, MD
Korst, Eugene J. ....Lockport, IL
Korst, Michael J. ....Lockport, IL
Korstad, Ardys ....Mankato, MN
Korstad, Dorothy C. ....Wheaton, IL
Korstad, Gregory E. ....Minneapolis, MN
Korstad, Stephen W. ....Minneapolis, MN
Korstad, William B. ....Minneapolis, MN
Korsten, Lisa M. ....New York, NY
Korsunski, Tola ....Santa Monica, CA
Korszen, Dorothy L. ....Venice, FL
Kort, Cindy D. ....Sherman Oaks, CA
Kort, Diane L. ....Palo Alto, CA
Kort, Jordan R. ....Los Angeles, CA
Kort, Kevin James ....Baldwin, MI
Kort, Richard A. ....Asheville, NC
Kort, Robert M. ....Phoenix, AZ
Kort, Stephen D. ....Kansas City, MO
Kortanek, Steven K. ....Wilmington, DE
Kortan-Sampson, Maria A.
Cleveland, OH
Korte, B. Michael ....St. Louis, MO
Korte, Chelsea C. ....Ellensburg, WA
Korte, David C. ....Dayton, OH
Korte, Edward J. ....Department of the Army, Army Materiel Command, GV
Korte, Frank L. ....Wellington, KS
Korte, George W. ....San Francisco, CA
Korte, Nancy J. ....Columbus, OH
Korte, Peter B. ....Cleveland, OH
Korte, R. Frederick ....Decatur, IL
Korte, R. Frederick, Ltd. ....Decatur, IL
Korte, Roy Robert ....Madison, WI
Korte and Smallwood ....St. Louis, MO
Korte, Terry Lee ....West Sacramento, CA
Korteling, David P. ....Bethesda, MD
Kortemier, William F., II ....Dallas, TX
Korten, Charles R. ....Rives Junction, MI
Korten, Douglas R. ....San Jose, CA
Korten, Lance E. ....El Centro, CA
Kortenhaus, Daniel J. ....St. Petersburg, FL
Kortenhof & Ely, A Professional Corporation
St. Louis, MO
Kortenhof, Joseph M. ....St. Louis, MO
Kortenhoven, Marilyn H. ....Crown Point, IN
Kortepeter McPherson Freihofer & Minton, A Legal Professional Association
Indianapolis, IN
Kortepeter, Paul F. ....Indianapolis, IN
Kortering, David B. ....Muskegon, MI
Kortering Law Firm ....Muskegon, MI
Kortering, Vernon D. ....Muskegon, MI
Korth, Arthur ....Atlantic City, NJ
Korth, Christopher S. ....Kansas City, MO
Korth, Donna-Marie ....East Meadow, NY
Korth, Fred ....Washington, DC
Korth, Fritz-Alan ....Washington, DC
Korth, James W. ....Springfield, OR
Korth, Jay F. ....Lynbrook, NY
Korth, Jay T. ....Lynbrook, NY
Korth, Kenneth A. ....Victoria, TX
Korth, Kevin W. ....St. Petersburg, FL
Korth & Korth ....Washington, DC
Korth & Korth ....Lynbrook, NY
Korth, Lorraine M. ....Lynbrook, NY
Korth, Theodore J. ....Orange, VA
Korth, Timothy W. ....New York, NY
Korth, William B. ....Madeira Beach, FL
Korth, William R. ....Alexandria, VA
Korthals, Candace D.
Fort Lauderdale, FL
Korthals, John L. ....Pompano Beach, FL
Korthamar, Aryeh ....Santa Clara, CA
Korthaus-Vos, Ellen J.
Federal Energy Regulatory Commission, Office of the General Counsel, GV
Korth Williams, Molly M. ....Kansas City, MO
Kortick, Linda R. ....Providence, RI
Kortkamp, Peter W. ....Boston, MA
Kortlandt, Catherine E. M. ....Danbury, CT
Kortlandt, Donald A. ....Pittsburgh, PA
Kortmansky, Jonathan G. ....New York, NY
Kortokrax, Susan M. ....Chicago, IL
Kortrey, Wendy ....Woodbridge, NJ
Kortright, Richard T. ....New York, NY
Korts, Janet H. ....Pittsford, NY
Kortsch, Gerald V. ....Milwaukee, WI
Kortum, Alfred J. ....Gering, NE
Kortum, Daniel J. ....Pittsburgh, PA
Kortum, Frank D. ....Los Angeles, CA
Kortum, John L. ....San Francisco, CA
Kortz, Donald L. ....Denver, CO
Kortz, Jack ....Whittier, CA
Kortz, Virginia M. ....Long Beach, CA
Kortze, Dale E., Jr. ....Harrisburg, PA
Korum, David M. ....St. Louis, MO
Korval, Neal I. ....New York, NY
Korvick, Michael ....Miami, FL
Korvick, Tony ....Miami, FL
Korwek, Edward L. ....Washington, DC
Korwek, Jane F. ....Hartford, CT
Kory, Marianne Greene ....Burlington, VT
Korycinski, Kathleen A. ....Albany, NY
Koryl, Robert T. ....Niagara Falls, NY
Korytkowski, Susan L. ....Washington, DC
Korytnyk, Peter G. ....Alexandria, VA
Koryto, John F. ....Kalamazoo, MI
Korzec, Arthur ....New York, NY
Korzec, Colin M. ....Boston, MA

Korzec, Rebecca ....Baltimore, MD
Korzen, Alan L. ....New York, NY
Korzen, John J. ....Greensboro, NC
Korzeniewicz, Cesar Alejandro
Department of Justice, Office of Justice Programs, GV
Korzeniewski, Lawrence F. ....Buffalo, NY
Korzenik, Armand A. ....Hartford, CT
Korzenik, David S. ....New York, NY
Korzenik, Deborah B. ....New York, NY
Korzenik, Jeremy F. ....Department of Justice, Environment and Natural Resources Division, GV
Korzenik, Sidney S. ....New York, NY
Korzeniowski, Walter J. ....South Easton, MA
Korzenowski, Scott E. ....Minneapolis, MN
Korzilius, Erik V. ....Venice, FL
Korzilius, Erik V., P.A. ....Venice, FL
Korzun, Timothy J. ....Pennington, NJ
Kos & Associate ....Fort Wayne, IN
Kos, Edmund P. ....Fort Wayne, IN
Kos, Leon ....Bainbridge Island, WA
Kos, Michael R. ....Chicago, IL
Kos, Richard J. ....Chicopee, MA
Kos, Shannon M. ....Southfield, MI
Kosa, Stephen A. ....Eagan, MN
Kosach, Steven R. ....Reno, NV
Kosack, Kurt Overton ....Nashville, TN
Kosack, Rexford C. ....Saipan, TT
Kosacz, Barbara A. ....Palo Alto, CA
Kosak, Mark S. ....Melville, NY
Kosaka, Glenn M. ....Wailuku, HI
Kosakoff, David B. ....Garden City, NY
Kosakoff, Debra G. ....New York, NY
Kosakow, James M. ....Westport, CT
Kosakowski, Aaron E. ....Fairfield, CT
Kosakowski, Abbey B. ....Atlanta, GA
Kosakowski, Thomas A. ....Los Angeles, CA
Kosan, Cheryl Koshetz ....White Plains, NY
Kosan, E. Michael ....White Plains, NY
Kosanda, Frank J. ....Grand Forks, ND
Kosanda, John D. ....Minneapolis, MN
Kosanke, Gregory L. ....Lynden, WA
Kosanovich, Daniel N. ....Dayton, OH
Kosanovich, Laurie G.
Mayfield Village, OH
Kosanovich, Wendy L. ....Menlo Park, CA
Kosar, Joseph J. ....Chesterland, OH
Kosar, Karen A.
Federal Communications Commission, Cable Services Bureau, GV
Kosar, Michael A. ....Philadelphia, PA
Kosarek, Chester ....Newton, NJ
Kosarek, Joseph C. ....Abbeville, LA
Kosarek, Joseph C., A Professional Law Corporation ....Abbeville, LA
Kosasky, Mel J. ....Northridge, CA
Kosberg, Alan H. ....West Hartford, CT
Kosberg, Alison ....Edison, NJ
Kosbie, Gretchen V. ....Redmond, WA
Kosc, Jeffrey ....Chicago, IL
Koscal, Gina Terrano ....Chicago, IL
Koscelansky, Aphrodite C.
Monmouth Junction, NJ
Koscelansky, Brian P. ....Scranton, PA
Wilkes-Barre, PA
Koscelnik, Jacqueline A. ....Pittsburgh, PA
Kosch, James A. ....Newark, NJ
Kosch, Lois M. ....San Diego, CA
Koschik, Alan M. ....Cleveland, OH
Koschik, David N. ....New York, NY
Koschineg, Ernest F., III ....Philadelphia, PA
Koscianski, John P. ....Parma Heights, OH
Koscinski, Joseph S. ....Pittsburgh, PA
Kosciolek, James F. ....Chicago, IL
Kosciuszko, Anthony J. ....New Castle, PA
Kosco, Keith J. ....Woodland Hills, CA
Koscs-Fleming, Mary Ellen
Whitehouse Station, NJ
Kose, William Henrik ....Findlay, OH
Kosefas, Geo. P. ....New York, NY
Kosek, Albert F. ....Minneapolis, MN
Kosek, Kurt R. ....Tustin, CA
Koseki, Lori Ann K. ....Honolulu, HI
Kosel, Janice E. ....San Francisco, CA
Kosel, Roger T. ....Yreka, CA
Koselka, Harvey A. ....Adrian, MI
Koselka, John J. ....Ann Arbor, MI
Koselka, Natalia M. ....Adrian, MI
Kosene, Milton ....Delray Beach, FL
Koser, Robin Shawn ....Binghamton, NY
Koserowski, Frank T. ....Bayonne, NJ
Kosewski, Paul R. ....Veradale, WA
Kosh, Adam S. ....Chicago, IL
Kosh, Christopher P. ....Austin, TX
Kosh, Michael ....Scranton, PA
Kosh, Richard J. ....New York, NY
Koshalek, John A. ....Madison, WI
Koshenina, Charles A. ....Eden Prairie, MN
Koshewa, Angela D. ....Louisville, KY
Koshgarian, Julie A. ....Boston, MA
Koshgarian, Lauren Z. ....Providence, RI
Koshgarian, Robert J. ....Albany, NY
Koshi, George M. ....Seattle, WA
Koshian, Jacqueline M. ....Niagara Falls, NY
Koshiba Agena & Kubota ....Honolulu, HI
Koshiba, James E. T. ....Honolulu, HI
Koshivas, Ann P. ....Salem, MA
Koshkin, Catherine M." Cat " ....Arcata, CA
Koshkin, Catherine M." Cat "
Eureka, CA
Koshland, James M. ....Palo Alto, CA
Koshliek, John M. ....Yarmouth, ME
Koshmrl, Michael J. ....St. Paul, MN
Koshner, Alan Jay ....St. Louis, MO
Koshner, Andrew J. ....Macomb, IL
Koshnick, Joseph Walter ....Baltimore, MD
Koshollek, Mary J. ....Milwaukee, WI

Koshuta, Cheryl R. ....Boise, ID
Koshy, Anil ....Washington, DC
Koshy, Suresh ....Washington, DC
Kosiak, Daryl J. ....Kansas City, KS
Kosiak, Mary Ann ....Chicago Ridge, IL
Kosiba, Louis W. ....Oak Brook, IL
Kosich, Jon A. ....Greenville, NY
Kosick, Peter H. ....St. Joseph, MI
Kosid, Janet E. ....Fairfield, CA
Kosieradzki, Arthur C. ....Lakeville, MN
Minneapolis, MN
Kosieradzki & Associates ....Minnetonka, MN
Kosieradzki, Mark R. ....Minnetonka, MN
Kosiewicz, Joy D. ....Akron, OH
Kosik, Edwin M. ....Scranton, PA
Kosik, John F. ....Akron, OH
Kosik, Michael E. ....Harrisburg, PA
Kosik, Robert A. ....Arlington, VA
Kosik, Thomas H. ....Bloomfield Hills, MI
Kosin, Donald G. ....La Grange Park, IL
Kosin, Donald G., Jr.
Department Of Health And Human Services, Office of the General Counsel, GV
Kosin, Paul C. ....Chicago, IL
Kosin, Robert S., (Ltd.) ....Chicago, IL
Kosineski, Denise L. ....Boston, MA
Kosinski, George R. ....Palos Park, IL
Kosinski, Gerard A. ....Philadelphia, PA
Kosinski, J. Gary ....Pittsburgh, PA
Kosinski, James N. ....Reno, NV
Kosinski, John A., Jr. ....Amsterdam, NY
Kosinski, Maria L. ....Chicago, IL
Kosinski, Peter S. ....Albany, NY
Kosinski, Raymond A.
Dearborn Heights, MI
Kosinski, Richard H. ....New Britain, CT
Kosinski, Robert E. ....Tucson, AZ
Kosior, Dana L. ....Hartford, CT
Koska, Rudolph A., Jr. ....Houston, TX
Koska, William K. ....San Diego, CA
Koskella, Michelle L. ....San Francisco, CA
Koski, Arthur C. ....Boca Raton, FL
Koski, Arthur C., P.A., Law Offices of
Boca Raton, FL
Koski, David D. ....Rockford, IL
Koski Firm, The ....Decatur, GA
Koski, Howard A. ....West Springfield, MA
Koski, John C. ....Chicago, IL
Koski & Kearns LLP ....Boston, MA
Koski, Michael C. ....Santa Ana, CA
Koski, Philip C. ....Boston, MA
Koski, Richard ....Secaucus, NJ
Koski, Robert C. ....Decatur, GA
Koski, William T. ....Boston, MA
Koskinas, Arthur F. ....Worcester, MA
Koskinen, David J. ....Oldsmar, FL
Kosko, George C., (P.A.)
Pawleys Island, SC
Kosko, John R. ....Cleveland, OH
Koskoff, David E. ....Plainville, CT
Koskoff, Joshua D. ....Bridgeport, CT
Koskoff, Karen E. ....Bridgeport, CT
Koskoff, Koskoff & Bieder, P.C.
Bridgeport, CT
Danbury, CT
Stamford, CT
Koskoff, Michael P. ....Bridgeport, CT
Koskoff, Milton M. ....Plainville, CT
Koskoff, Richard B. ....Torrance, CA
Koskoff, Rosalind J. ....Bridgeport, CT
Kosky, John Edward ....Chicago, IL
Kosky, Kenneth A. ....Deerfield, IL
Koslo, William N. ....Arcadia, WI
Kosloff, Alan M. ....West Hartford, CT
Kosloff, Andrew ....New York, NY
Kosloff & Harding ....Hartford, CT
West Hartford, CT
Kosloff, Laura H. ....Portland, OR
Kosloff, Michael L. ....Beverly Hills, CA
Kosloff, Michael L., P.C. ....Beverly Hills, CA
Koslofsky, Joanne ....New York, NY
Kosloske, John E. ....Department of Justice, Civil Division, GV
Kosloske, Verleah Brown, (Mrs.)
Washington, DC
Koslov, John ....Agoura Hills, CA
Koslov Law Office, The ....Agoura Hills, CA
Koslov, Tara Isa ......Federal Trade Commission, Offices of Commissioners, GV
Koslovsky, Allen J. ....Waynesburg, PA
Koslovsky, Steven W. ....St. Louis, MO
Koslow, Alan B. ....Fort Lauderdale, FL
Koslow, Alan J. ....Northbrook, IL
Koslow, Barry N. ....Danvers, MA
Koslow, Christopher G. ....Indianapolis, IN
Koslow, Jack E. ....St. Louis, MO
Koslow, Jonathan L. ....New York, NY
Koslow, Lawrence E. ....Minneapolis, MN
Koslow, Milton S. ....Charleston, WV
Koslow, Stephen W. ....Aurora, IL
Koslowe, Jamin R. ....New York, NY
Koslowe, Mark A. ....Edison, NJ
New York, NY
Koslowe, Neil H. ....Department of Justice, Civil Division, GV
Koslowski, Barbara A. ....San Jose, CA
Koslowsky, John C. ....Milton, MA
Kosluchar, Colleen A. ....Fairbanks, AK
Koslyn, Pamela ....Los Angeles, CA
Kosma, Montgomery N. ....Washington, DC
Kosmal, Edward J. ....Beverly Hills, CA
Kosmal, Rachel E. ....Palo Alto, CA
Kosmala, Joseph R. ....Mount Clemens, MI
Kosmala, Thomas J. ....Towanda, PA
Kosmala, Weneta M. A. ....Costa Mesa, CA
Kosman, Francis J. ....Staten Island, NY
Kosman, Joseph J. ....Chicago, IL
Kosman, Thomas ....Hyannis, MA

Kosmark, Mary L. ....Brooklyn, NY
Kosmas, James M. ....New Smyrna Beach, FL
Kosmas, John ....San Diego, CA
Kosmas, William P. ....New York, NY
Kosmerl, John K. ....Arcade, NY
Kosmerl, Mary T. ....Buffalo, NY
Kosmerl, Wayne T. ....Annapolis, MD
Kosmin, Jill C. ....Flossmoor, IL
Kosminskas, Mark J. ....Chicago, IL
Kosmitis, Georgia P." Gia " ....Shreveport, LA
Kosmo, Frederick W. ....Ventura, CA
Kosmo, Frederick W., Jr. ....San Diego, CA
Kosmond, James N. ....Chicago, IL
Kosmowski, Audra M. ....Sharon, PA
Kosmowski, Edward J. ....Wilmington, DE
Kosnett & Durchfort ....Beverly Hills, CA
Kosnett, James Victor ....Beverly Hills, CA
Kosnic, Kenneth J. ....Sterling Heights, MI
Kosnik, Richard M. ....New York, NY
Kosnitzky, Michael ....Miami, FL
Kosnoff, Amy E. ....Indianapolis, IN
Kosnoff, Kathy S. ....Minneapolis, MN
Kosnoff, Scott M. ....Indianapolis, IN
Kosnoff, Timothy D. ....Bellevue, WA
Kosobucki, John E. ....Milwaukee, WI
Kosoff, Clifford G. ....Northbrook, IL
Kosoff, Marvin ....Totowa, NJ
Kosoff-Roth, Karen L. ....Fairport, NY
Kosofsky, Jaime A. ....Davidson, NC
Kosofsky, Joseph ....White Plains, NY
Kosofsky, Mark ....White Plains, NY
Kosojet, Joseph L. ....Timonium, MD
Kosonen, Craig C. ....Wallace, ID
Kosove, Daniel B. ....New York, NY
Kosovec, Julie Lyons ....Birmingham, MI
Kosover, Irwin S. ....Brooklyn, NY
Kosowicz, Francis G., Jr. ....Newington, CT
Kosowsky, Bernice Reisner ....Stamford, CT
Kosowsky, Earl A. ....Shiremanstown, PA
Kosowsky, Harold B. ....Omaha, NE
Koss, Abe ....Miami, FL
Koss, Amara Leslie ....Walnut Creek, CA
Koss, Charles A. ....Danville, CA
Koss, David A. ....Wynnewood, PA
Koss, David R. ....Kelso, WA
Koss, Dominique T. ....Phoenix, AZ
Koss, Elizabeth L. ....Brookline, MA
Koss, Hugh Richard ....San Francisco, CA
Koss, Jennifer ....Los Angeles, CA
Koss, Jeremy A. ....Hollywood, FL
Koss, John T., Jr. ....San Francisco, CA
Koss, Judith C. ....Wynnewood, PA
Koss, Larry R. ....Brockport, NY
Koss, Laura Debora
Federal Trade Commission, Bureau of Consumer Protection, GV
Koss, Mark D. ....Brookfield, WI
Koss, Mark T. ....Oklahoma City, OK
Koss, Michelle D. ....Philadelphia, PA
Koss, Robert A. ....Van Nuys, CA
Koss, Roberta ....Washington, DC
Koss, Russell S. ....Sarasota, FL
Koss, Theodore, Jr. ....Oklahoma City, OK
Kossacoff, Sandra E. ....Encino, CA
Kossak, Adam ....Blythewood, SC
Kossak, Julia A. ....Phoenix, AZ
Kossally, Constance A. ....Philadelphia, PA
Kossar, Ronald S. ....Middletown, NY
Kossar, Stephen B. ....New York, NY
Kosse, Robert B. ....Vista, CA
Kosseff, Robert ....Hollidaysburg, PA
Philadelphia, PA
Kosseff, Robert A., & Associates, P.C.
Stratford, NJ
Hollidaysburg, PA
Philadelphia, PA
Kossek, Regina M. ....Chicago, IL
Kossen, Kay E. ....Battle Creek, MI
Kossen, Michael L. ....San Francisco, CA
Kossen, Michael T. ....Highlands Ranch, CO
Kossick, Robert M., Jr. ....San Antonio, TX
Kossin, Darin ....White Plains, NY
Kossin, Warren P. ....Nanuet, NY
Kossis, Jeffrey L. ....Fort Lauderdale, FL
Kossitch, Paul J. ....El Segundo, CA
Kosslak, Renee M. ....San Francisco, CA
Kossler and Associates ....Irvine, CA
Kossler, Douglas H. ....Anchorage, AK
Kossler, George F. ....Palm Springs, CA
Kossman, L. Paul ....Cleveland, MS
Kossman, Nancy Pace ....Clarksdale, MS
Kossmann, Alfred L. ....New York, NY
Kossoff, Alan R. ....Los Angeles, CA
Kossoff, Alice ....New York, NY
Kossoff, Kenneth W. ....Beverly Hills, CA
Kossoff, Kenneth W.
Westlake Village, CA
Kossoff, Sinclair ....Chicago, IL
Kosson, Leonard H. ....Cliffside Park, NJ
Kossoris, Amy V. ....Milwaukee, WI
Kossoris, Peter D. ....Ventura, CA
Kossove, Scott Evan ....Garden City, NY
Kossover, Andrew ....New Paltz, NY
Kossover, Victoria E ....New Paltz, NY
Kossow, Daniel H. ....White Plains, NY
Kossow, Debra J. ....Department of Justice, Civil Division, GV
Kossow, Gerald L. ....Sacramento, CA
Kossow, Julian R. ....St. Petersburg, FL
Kossow, Kenneth D. ....Miami, FL
Kossow, Mark R. ....Trenton, NJ
Kossow, Richard E. ....Kneeland, CA
Kossow, Todd M. ....Chicago, IL
Kossoy, Small & Conrad ....New York, NY
Kossuth, Heidi A. ....Wheeling, WV
Kossy, Phillip L. ....San Diego, CA
Kost, Bryan Louis ....San Antonio, TX
Kost, John G. ....Minneapolis, MN

Kost, Keith K. ... **Rhinelander, WI**
Kost, Keith R. ... Cleveland, OH
Kost, Kelly K. ... **Chicago, IL**
Kost, Leslie M. ... Mendota Heights, MN
Kost, Oral C. ... Canton, IL
Kost, Susan Smith ... **Cincinnati, OH**
Kosta & Associates ... St. Louis, MO
Kosta, George F. ... St. Louis, MO
Kostak, William Michael ... Treasury Department, Internal Revenue Service, GV
Kostakos, George P. ... **Boston, MA**
Kostakos, Gustav G. ... Seattle, WA
Kostant, Arlene ... **San Francisco, CA**
Kostant, Peter C. ... Kansas City, MO
Kostant, Ralph B. ... **Los Angeles, CA**
Kostantacos, Charles P. ... **Rockford, IL**
Kostantacos, Peter C. ... **Rockford, IL**
Kostantacos, Traum, Reuterfors & McWilliams, P.C. ... **Rockford, IL**
Kostas, Angelo A. ... **Indianapolis, IN**
Kostas, George J. ... New York, NY
Kostas, James S. ... Palmdale, CA
Kostas, Jude J. ... Dedham, MA
Kostas, Socrates J. ... Cleveland, OH
Kostbar, Otto James ... Jamesburg, NJ
Kostbar, Otto James, P.A. ... Jamesburg, NJ
Kosteck, Steve, Jr. ... Tucson, AZ
Kostecka, Robert C. ... **Bethesda, MD**
Kostecke, Keith W. ... **Appleton, WI**
Kostecki, Gabriel A. ... Chicago, IL
Kostecki, Mark ... Waterbury, CT
Kostel, George E. ... **Falls Church, VA**
Kostel, Harry J. ... Newport News, VA
Kostel, Mary E. ... **Washington, DC**
Kostel, W. Alan ... Irving, TX
Kostelaba, Michael C. ... Wilkes-Barre, PA
Kostelac, Joseph F., Jr. ... Kansas City, MO
Kostelac, Yvette M. ... Harrisburg, PA
Kostelanetz, Boris ... **New York, NY**
Kostelanetz & Fink, LLP ... **New York, NY**
Kostelansky, Michael R. ... Wilkes-Barre, PA
Kostelecky, Anthony ... Manassas, VA
Kostelecky, Cynthia M. ... **Chicago, IL**
Kostelka, Robert W. ... Monroe, LA
Kostello, Dyann L. ... **Milwaukee, WI**
Kostelny, Albert J., Jr. ... New York, NY
Kostelny, Marmarie J. ... Elgin, IL
Kosten, Alan L. ... **Memphis, TN**
Kostenbauder, Daniel ... **Palo Alto, CA**
Kostenboym, Ilya A. ... **Los Angeles, CA**
Koster, Arnold L. ... Rahway, NJ
Koster, Bernard J. ... **Hackensack, NJ**
Koster, Caroline Aiken ... **New York, NY**
Koster, Christian ... **Sacramento, CA**
Koster, Edward H. ... Ann Arbor, MI
Koster, Eric D. ... **White Plains, NY**
Koster, Erika S. ... **Minneapolis, MN**
Koster, Eugene S. ... Washington, DC
Koster, Evan M. ... **New York, NY**
Koster, Gregory E. ... Eastchester, NY
Koster, Henry ... Milwaukee, WI
Koster, Henry W. ... Plandome, NY
Koster, Jeannette Arlin ... New York, NY
Koster, John C. ... **New York, NY**
Koster, Judy ... Chicago, IL
Koster, Karen E. ... **West Paterson, NJ**
Koster, King, Hellmich & Hentz, L.L.C. ... St. Louis, MO
Koster, Marcel J. ... Cranbury, NJ
Koster, Martha J. ... **Boston, MA**
Koster, Paul R. ... United States Court Of Appeals District Of Columbia Circuit, GV
Koster, Robert J. ... St. Louis, MO
Koster, Ronald J. ... **Tampa, FL**
Koster, Ronald J., P.A. ... **Tampa, FL**
Koster, Stephen P. ... **Newton, MA**
Koster, Warren S. ... **Shrewsbury, NJ** / **New York, NY**
Koster, William N. ... **Minneapolis, MN**
Kosterlitz, Amy L. ... **Seattle, WA**
Kosterlitz, David S. ... Treasury Department, Internal Revenue Service, GV
Kosterlitz, Mary J. ... Dayton, OH
Kostic, Thomas F. ... **San Francisco, CA**
Kostich, Nada ... Oak Brook, IL
Kostich, Nikola P. ... Milwaukee, WI
Kostick, Renee M. ... Alexandria, VA
Kostik, Peter J. ... Arlington, VA
Kostin, Dane R. ... **Farmington, CT**
Kostin, Michele G. ... **Hartford, CT**
Kostiw, Alexandra O. ... Chicago, IL
Kostka, Fred P. ... Coloma, MI
Kostka, Gregory M. ... House of Representatives, Office of Legislative Counsel, GV
Kostka, Kent M. ... Austin, TX
Kostka, Stephen L. ... **Walnut Creek, CA**
Kostka, Timothy L. ... **Wausau, WI**
Kostman, David B. ... **New York, NY**
Kostmayer, Joseph D. ... San Jose, CA
Kostner, Bruce J. ... Arcadia, WI
Kostner, Joseph O. ... Chicago, IL
Kostner, Koslo & Brovold ... Arcadia, WI
Kostner & Kostner ... Bloomer, WI
Kostner, Richard J. ... Bloomer, WI
Kostner, Thomas N. ... Bloomer, WI
Kosto, Gale S. ... **Hartford, CT**
Kosto, Lawrence M. ... **Orlando, FL**
Kosto, Morton ... Maitland, FL
Kosto & Rotella, P.A. ... **Jacksonville, FL** / **Orlando, FL**
Kosto, Seth Barney ... **Boston, MA**
Kostoff, DeVere ... Philadelphia, PA
Kostoff, James R. ... Claremont, CA
Kostoff, Peter M. ... **Akron, OH**
Kostoff, Thomas W. ... Fairlawn, OH
Kostolansky, Kris J. ... **Denver, CO**
Kostolansky, Thomas Bernard ... Donora, PA
Kostopoulos, K. Dino ... **Birmingham, MI**
Kostopulos & Associates ... Washington, DC / Annapolis, MD / McLean, VA
Kostopulos, N. Peter ... Washington, DC / Annapolis, MD / McLean, VA
Kostorizos, Maria-Elena ... Arlington, MA
Kostos and Lamer, P.C. ... Philadelphia, PA
Kostos, Theodore M. ... Philadelphia, PA
Kostos, Thomas J. ... Glendale, CA
Kostovski, Suzanna ... **Detroit, MI**
Kostrenich, Robert S. ... Los Alamitos, CA
Kostrinsky, Albert ... Great Neck, NY
Kostrinsky, Hallie ... **New York, NY**
Kostrinsky, Michael E. ... **Las Vegas, NV**
Kostrinsky, Shelley ... Seattle, WA
Kostritsky, Juliet P. ... Cleveland, OH
Kostro, Nancy A. ... **Chicago, IL**
Kostro, Paul G. ... Westfield, NJ
Kostro, Victor S. ... Melbourne, FL
Kostrubanic, John A. ... **Boston, MA**
Kostrubanic, Linda D. ... Beverly, MA
Kostrzewa, Kate ... Mountain View, CA
Kostuch, Erna B. ... Chicago, IL
Kostura, Judy ... **Austin, TX**
Kosturakis, Irene ... **Houston, TX**
Kosturko, William T. ... Bridgeport, CT
Kostyack, John F. ... Washington, DC
Kostyla, Michael J. ... Lawrence, MA
Kostyn, Kevin F. ... **Newark, NJ**
Kostyo, John F. ... Findlay, OH
Kostyrka, Jeanette P. ... Lynbrook, NY
Kosub, Bruce E. ... **Washington, DC**
Kosub, James A. ... Eldorado, TX
Kosub, Phil Steven ... **San Antonio, TX**
Kosuri, Praveen ... Chicago, IL
Kosut, Kenneth P. (IBA) ... **Houston, TX**
Kosydar, Christine A. ... **Portland, OR**
Kosydar, Robert J. ... Columbus, OH
Kosydar, Walter J. ... Toledo, OH
Kosylo, John D. ... Turnersville, NJ
Koszdin & Fields ... Van Nuys, CA
Koszdin, Jack P. ... Van Nuys, CA
Koszdin, Kenton D. ... Van Nuys, CA
Koszewski, Andrew B. ... **Minneapolis, MN**
Koszkul, Christine L. ... Harrison, NY
Koszorus, Frank, Jr. ... **Washington, DC**
Kosztarab & Clark, P.C. ... Fairfax, VA
Kosztarab, Eva E. ... Fairfax, VA
Kot, Carla A. ... Waukesha, WI
Kot, John J. ... **Secaucus, NJ** / New York, NY
Kot, Raymond P., II ... Grand Island, NY
Kot, Veronika ... Woodland, CA
Kota, J. Michael ... **Miami, FL**
Kota, Robert C. ... St. Clairsville, OH
Kotab, Dominic M. ... **Palo Alto, CA**
Kotada, Kelly K. ... Honolulu, HI
Kotake, Donna L. ... **Palo Alto, CA**
Kotake, Mervyn M. ... Honolulu, HI
Kotal, David S. ... Jackson, MI
Kotalik, Emil J., Jr. ... **Phoenix, AZ**
Kotansky, William J. ... Baltimore, MD
Kotapish, William J. ... Washington, DC
Kotara, Gary M. ... **Washington, DC**
Kotara, Stephen W. ... Dallas, TX
Kotarba, Richard G. ... **Pittsburgh, PA**
Kotarba, Steven R. ... **Rockford, IL**
Kotarek, Douglas J. ... **Englewood, CO**
Kotarski, Joseph C. ... Ponca City, OK
Kotarski, Kenneth A. ... **Los Angeles, CA**
Kotarski, Michael J. ... Flint, MI
Kotary, Christopher J. ... Webster, NY
Kotas, Gerianne ... **Cruz Bay, St. John, VI**
Kotas & Hogroian, P.C. ... **Cruz Bay, St. John, VI** / **Charlotte Amalie, St. Thomas, VI**
Kotaska, Gary F. ... **Buffalo, NY**
Kotch, A. Branton ... **Houston, TX**
Kotch, George T. ... Mount Holly, NJ
Kotch, Kevin J. ... **Philadelphia, PA**
Kotchek, Patricia L. ... Petersburg, WV
Kotchen, Daniel ... Federal Trade Commission, Bureau of Competition, GV
Kotchen & Ripper, P.C. ... Rocky Hill, CT
Kotchen, William J. ... Rocky Hill, CT
Kotchick, J. Robert ... Arcadia, CA
Kotchick, John L., III ... Binghamton, NY
Kotchka, Malani L. ... **Las Vegas, NV**
Koteas, George R. ... Bridgeport, CT
Kotecki, Donna J. ... Glen Ellyn, IL
Kotecki & Kotecki ... Glen Ellyn, IL
Kotecki, Roger G. ... Glen Ellyn, IL
Koteen, Bernard ... **Washington, DC**
Koteen, Jos. G. ... White Plains, NY
Koteen, Mark A. ... Orlando, FL
Koteen & Naftalin, L.L.P. ... **Washington, DC**
Koteff, Mitchell ... Chula Vista, CA
Koteff, Stephen N. ... Anchorage, AK
Kotel, Ira L. ... **New York, NY**
Kotel, Kathryn M. ... **Oak Brook, IL**
Kotel, Randy D. ... Englewood, CO
Kotelanski, Jorge ... **Washington, DC**
Kotelez, Richard M. ... Yonkers, NY
Kotelly, John T. ... **Washington, DC**
Kotelman, Laura Mary ... **Des Plaines, IL**
Kotenberg, Kenneth C. ... **Cincinnati, OH**
Kotfila, Timothy M. ... Springfield, MA
Kothari, Aparna P. ... Millburn, NJ
Kothe, Charles A. ... **Tulsa, OK**
Kothe, Howard K. ... New York, NY
Kothe, Karen L. ... **Phoenix, AZ**
Kothe, Karl M. ... **Rome, GA**
Kothe, Lisa D. ... **New Orleans, LA**
Kothman, David M. ... **Cincinnati, OH**
Kothmann, Don W. ... Austin, TX
Kotich, Anthony J. ... Topeka, KS
Kotick, Charles M. ... **New York, NY**
Kotick, Joel M. ... New York, NY
Kotik, Lawrence H. ... **New York, NY**
Kotila, Mark W. ... Department of Justice, Environment and Natural Resources Division, GV
Kotila, Richard B. ... Andover, OH
Kotila, William R. ... Ann Arbor, MI
Kotin, Crabtree & Strong, LLP ... **Boston, MA**
Kotin, Daniel M. ... **Chicago, IL**
Kotin, Elaine J. ... New York, NY
Kotin, Gabriel G. ... Scottsdale, AZ
Kotin, Lawrence ... **Boston, MA**
Kotin, Merritt R. ... Lincolnwood, IL
Kotin, Michael J ... **Albany, NY**
Kotin, Sandra M. ... **Monticello, NY**
Kotis, Linda L. ... Oakland, CA
Kotiswaran, Prabha ... **New York, NY**
Kotite, Albert E. ... **New York, NY**
Kotite, Edward A. ... **New York, NY**
Kotite & Kotite, LLP ... **New York, NY**
Kotjarapoglus, George A. ... Greensburg, PA
Kotke-Partington, Karen ... Littleton, CO
Kotkin, David ... Hartford, CT
Kotkin, David J. ... **Garden City, NY**
Kotkin, Edward Z. ... Riverside, CA
Kotkin, Minna J. ... Brooklyn, NY
Kotkins, Henry L., Sr. ... Seattle, WA
Kotlar, Adam M. ... Cherry Hill, NJ
Kotlar, John J. ... Fort Myers, FL
Kotlar, John M. ... Detroit, MI
Kotlarchuk, Ihor ... Department of Justice, Criminal Division, GV
Kotlarsic, Liza A. ... Cincinnati, OH
Kotlarski, Ann ... **Los Angeles, CA**
Kotlarsky, Mark ... **Washington, DC**
Kotlarz, George J. ... Somers, NY
Kotler, A. Stephen ... **Miami, FL**
Kotler, Avery Ben-Zion ... **New York, NY**
Kotler, Barry L. ... **San Ramon, CA**
Kotler, Bradley E. ... **Chicago, IL**
Kotler, Bruce ... La Jolla, CA
Kotler, Carol Weiss ... Boston, MA
Kotler, David A. ... **Princeton, NJ**
Kotler, Gary A. ... **Chatham, NJ**
Kotler, Helen R., Law Offices of ... **Pittsburgh, PA**
Kotler, Herbert ... Melville, NY
Kotler, Jeffrey D. ... Metuchen, NJ
Kotler, Jennifer ... **Chicago, IL**
Kotler, Joel R. ... Philadelphia, PA
Kotler, Jonathan ... Calabasas, CA
Kotler, K. Kenneth ... Los Angeles, CA
Kotler, Lawrence J. ... **Philadelphia, PA**
Kotler, Lawrence Z. ... **Secaucus, NJ**
Kotler, Lynn R. ... Mineola, NY
Kotler, Michael I. ... Boca Raton, FL
Kotler, Nancy ... Glencoe, IL
Kotler, Richard L. ... Newhall, CA
Kotler, Scott F. ... Miami, FL
Kotler, Stuart B. ... New York, NY
Kotlikoff, Louis J. ... Sarasota, FL
Kotlowitz, Steven ... Sherman Oaks, CA
Kotnik, Donald Patrick ... Canton, OH
Kotnik, Ronald J. ... **Madison, WI** / Poynette, WI
Kotob, Robert I. ... Downey, CA
Kotob, Robert I., Inc. ... Downey, CA
Kotok, Jack B. ... Bridgeton, NJ
Kotok, Lester ... Fort Lauderdale, FL
Kotok & Romeo, P.C. ... Fort Lauderdale, FL
Koton, Steven Z. ... Brooklyn, NY
Kotoshirodo, Ronald K. ... Honolulu, HI
Kotouc, Otto ... Humboldt, NE
Kotouc, Thomas O. ... **Montgomery, AL**
Kotouc, Thomas O., P.C. ... **Montgomery, AL**
Kotovsky, Stanley K., Jr. ... **Albuquerque, NM**
Kotowski, Adrienne Walker ... **Worcester, MA**
Kotowski, Christina M. ... **Palo Alto, CA**
Kotowski, Gail S. ... **Guilford, CT**
Kotowski, Martin J. ... Sherman Oaks, CA
Kotran, Beth ... **New York, NY**
Kotran, Michael J. ... **Florham Park, NJ**
Kotran, Stephen M. ... **New York, NY**
Kotroco, Timothy Michael ... Baltimore, MD
Kotschenreuther, Philip J. ... Towson, MD
Kotseas, Harry P. ... Worcester, MA
Kotsis, Chrysanthe A. ... Novi, MI
Kotsonis, George N. ... Milwaukee, WI
Kotsonis, Nick G. ... **Milwaukee, WI**
Kott, A. Tyrrell, Law Offices of, P.C. ... San Antonio, TX
Kott, Alfred Tyrrell ... San Antonio, TX
Kott, Alison Mellor ... Irvine, CA
Kott, Andrea H. ... **Chicago, IL**
Kott, Brian J. ... **Detroit, MI**
Kott, David R. ... **Newark, NJ**
Kott, Douglas G. ... **Lexington, MA**
Kott, Irwin E. ... Miami, FL
Kott, Jeffrey S. ... San Francisco, CA
Kott, Joseph A. ... **New Orleans, LA**
Kott, Joseph H. ... **Parsippany, NJ**
Kott, Marcelle R. ... Chicago, IL
Kott, Reagan ... **Houston, TX**
Kott, Richard B. ... Brea, CA
Kott, Robert W. ... **McLean, VA**
Kott, Stephen J. ... **Washington, DC**
Kottaras, Demetrios G. ... Chicago, IL
Kottaras, James ... Chicago, IL
Kottaras, James, P.C., Law Office of ... Chicago, IL
Kottas, Leo J., Sr. ... Helena, MT
Kottcamp, Glenn M. ... Nevada City, CA
Kotte, Fred S., Jr. ... Columbus, OH
Kotte, John D. ... Chicago, IL
Kottemann, Stanley C., Jr. ... Metairie, LA
Kottemann, Timothy Peter ... Biloxi, MS
Kottenstette, Eileen S. ... **Denver, CO**
Kottenstette, Eugene J., Jr. ... Denver, CO
Kotthoff, Sara E. ... **St. Louis, MO**
Kottis, Nick C. ... **Hoffman Estates, IL**
Kottkamp, Andrew L. ... **Wenatchee, WA**
Kottkamp, Jeffrey D. ... **Fort Myers, FL**
Kottkamp, John H. ... Pendleton, OR
Kottkamp & O'Rourke, LLP ... **Pendleton, OR**
Kottke & Brantz ... Boulder, CO
Kottke, Jon F. ... Boulder, CO
Kottke, Jon S. ... Costa Mesa, CA
Kottle, Richard M. ... **Los Angeles, CA**
Kottler, Ethan M. ... Las Vegas, NV
Kottler, Miriam ... Los Angeles, CA
Kottler, Stephen ... Lewiston, ME
Kottman-Gregory, Janet ... Westerville, OH
Kottmeier, Stephen J. ... **San Jose, CA**
Kottmeyer, Richard ... O'Fallon, IL
Kottmyer, Alice M. ... Department of State, Office of the Legal Adviser, GV
Kottmyer, Diane M. ... Boston, MA
Kotto, Natasha A. ... Los Angeles, CA
Kotula, Diane A. ... **Phoenix, AZ**
Kotula, Michael A. ... **Uniondale, NY**
Kotula, Peter T. ... Detroit, MI
Kotulak, Bernard J., II ... Wilkes-Barre, PA
Kotulak, Richard M. ... Maynard, MA
Kotulak, Steven B. ... **Los Angeles, CA**
Kotulic, Irene M. ... Cleveland, OH
Kotur, Sandra ... **Daytona Beach, FL**
Kotwal, Sujit B. ... **Palo Alto, CA**
Kotwick, Mark D. ... **New York, NY**
Kotwicki, David A. ... Traverse City, MI
Kotyk, Frank P. ... **Boise, ID**
Kotz, Daniel J. ... Rockville, MD
Kotz, H. David ... Washington, DC
Kotz, James C. ... Burbank, IL
Kotz, Jeffrey M. ... Towson, MD
Kotz, Jeffrey M., P.A. ... Towson, MD
Kotz, Robert C. ... **Detroit, MI**
Kotz, Sangster, Wysocki and Berg, P.C. ... **Detroit, MI** / **Mount Clemens, MI** / **Pontiac, MI**
Kotz, Sidney C. ... Walnut Creek, CA
Kotz, Stephen R. ... Albuquerque, NM
Kotzamanis, Dimitri ... Bayside, NY
Kotzan, Bruce A. ... Indianapolis, IN
Kotzas, Stephen B. ... Toms River, NJ
Kotzebue, Margaret L. ... Concord, CA
Kotzen, Jay L. ... North Miami Beach, FL
Kotzen, Jennifer Wallis ... **New York, NY**
Kotzen, Stanley R. ... **Media, PA**
Kotzen, Wendi L. ... **Philadelphia, PA**
Kotzian, David A. ... **Southfield, MI**
Kotzky, Brian M. ... Bayside, NY
Kotzmann, Warren C. ... Phoenix, AZ
Kou, Julia C. ... **New York, NY**
Kouba, Jon Henry ... **San Francisco, CA**
Kouba, Patrick J. ... **Eugene, OR**
Kouba, Patrick J., A Professional Corporation ... **Eugene, OR**
Koubourlis, Koren T. D. ... **Seattle, WA**
Koubourlis, Yana ... **Seattle, WA**
Koucky, Joseph P. ... Chicago, IL
Koucky & Koucky ... Chicago, IL
Koudelka, Suzanne McMains ... Phoenix, AZ
Kouffman, Robert H. ... East Hampton, NY
Koufman, Victor ... **Salem, MA**
Koufman, Williams & DeIulis, LLP ... **Salem, MA**
Koufos, Peter N. ... **Washington, DC**
Kough, Ann ... Los Angeles, CA
Kough, Thomas J. ... Mooresville, IN
Kouimelis, Eleni Skoulikas ... **Chicago, IL**
Koujakian, Terenik ... Encino, CA
Koukios & Fortsas, Ltd. ... Palatine, IL
Koukios, Steven S. ... Palatine, IL
Kouklis, John C. ... **Tacoma, WA**
Koukol, Daniel D. ... **Omaha, NE**
Koukol, David J. ... **Omaha, NE**
Koukos, George K. ... Forked River, NJ
Koukoutchos, Brian Stuart ... Bedford, MA
Kouletsis, Nicholas M. ... **Cherry Hill, NJ**
Koulian, Vera ... Los Angeles, CA
Koulikourdis, Peter J. ... Bronx, NY
Koulouras, Dean ... Livonia, MI
Koumas, Elizabeth J. ... **San Diego, CA**
Koumourdas, Paul ... Garden City, NY
Koundakjian, Donald K. ... Lexington, MA
Koundakjian, Stephen J. ... South Pasadena, CA
Kounitz, Lisa J. ... Irvington, NY
Kounoupis, George S. ... Bethlehem, PA
Kouns, Lawrence J. ... **San Diego, CA**
Kouns, Mark E. ... Columbus, OH
Kountoupes, Cary G. ... Royal Oak, MI
Kountouris, Louis E. ... Toledo, OH
Kountz, Charles E., Jr. ... **Baltimore, MD**
Kountze, Elizabeth K. ... Omaha, NE
Kourakos, Hippocrates P. ... Eastchester, NY
Kourany, Edgar, Jr. ... Indianapolis, IN
Kourasis, Tina D. ... **Chicago, IL**
Kouray, Athena C. ... **Schenectady, NY**
Kouray, Christian X. ... **Schenectady, NY**
Kouray and Kouray ... **Albany, NY** / **Schenectady, NY**
Kouray, Steven X. ... **Schenectady, NY**
Koures, Antonio D. ... Kennewick, WA
Kouretas, James L. ... Sacramento, CA
Kouretchian, Seyamack ... New York, NY

Kouri, Dennett F. .... **Los Angeles, CA**
Kouri, Dennett F., Jr. .... **Irvine, CA**
Kouri, Douglas M. .... New Baltimore, MI
Kouri, Gerard M., Jr. .... Davie, FL
Kouri, Gerard M., Jr., P.A. .... Davie, FL
Kouri, Harry J. (Trey), III
Oklahoma City, OK
Kouri, Joseph A. .... Palo Alto, CA
Kouri, Lon J. .... **Sioux Falls, SD**
Kouri, Stephen A. .... **Peoria, IL**
Kouri, Syrus S. .... Minneapolis, MN
Kourides, Peter T. .... New York, NY
Kouril, Cindy .... Carle Place, NY
Kouris, John R. .... Chicago, IL
Kourlis, Rebecca Love .... Craig, CO
Kourofsky, Kevin P. .... Rochester, NY
Kouros, Chris P. .... Schererville, IN
Kouros, Joan .... Schererville, IN
Kouros & Kouros .... Schererville, IN
Kouroupas, Paul .... Staten Island, NY
Kourtesis, Nikolaos Panagiotis
Washington, DC
Kourtis, Nicholas F. .... **Boston, MA**
Koury & Abraham .... **Lafayette, LA**
Koury, Allison J. .... Providence, RI
Koury, David L. .... **Chicago, IL**
Koury, Donald C. .... Lebanon, NH
Koury, E. G." Leo ", (Co., L.P.A.)
Lorain, OH
Koury, Ellis Glenn .... **Dallas, TX**
Koury, George I., Jr. .... Lorain, OH
Koury, Joel C. .... Los Angeles, CA
Koury, John A., Jr. .... **Pottstown, PA**
Koury, Joseph A. .... **Lafayette, LA**
Koury, Joseph M. .... **Memphis, TN**
Koury, Joseph S. .... **Washington, DC**
Koury, Kenneth P. .... Woodland Hills, CA
Koury, Lee M. .... **Cleveland, OH**
Koury, Michael J., Jr. .... Davenport, IA
Koury, Peter L. .... Stone Harbor, NJ
Koury, Philip A. .... Kansas City, MO
Koury, Richard J., II .... Independence, MO
Koury, Robert G., II .... **Portland, OR**
Koury, Tighe, Lapres, Bisulca & Somers, P.C.
Northfield, NJ
Koury, Victoria J. .... **Denver, CO**
Kouser, David S. .... Cherry Hill, NJ
Kousi, John D. .... New York, NY
Kouskoutis, N. Michael .... Tarpon Springs, FL
Kousoubris, Evelyn D. .... Philadelphia, PA
Kousoulas, Antonia .... New York, NY
Kousoulas, James P. .... **Irvine, CA**
Koustmer, Thomas R. .... Cincinnati, OH
Koustoubardis, Chris .... Dallas, TX
Kousz, Carolyn G. .... Waco, TX
Kout, Hylan H. .... Miami Beach, FL
Kout, Norman .... Miami Beach, FL
Koutchak, Robin L. .... Anchorage, AK
Koutcher, Jonathan B. .... **Media, PA**
Koutchis, Peter M. .... Sacramento, CA
Koutoujian, Peter J. .... Newton, MA
Koutoulakos, Louis .... Arlington, VA
Koutouras, George C. .... **Chicago, IL**
Koutouzos, Georgia D. .... Riverwoods, IL
Koutrakos, Demetri K. .... **Columbia, SC**
Koutras, Charles .... Pensacola, FL
Koutras, James George .... **Baltimore, MD**
Koutsandreas, Peter D. .... Bethesda, MD
Koutsky, Kenneth F. .... Chicago, IL
Koutsogiane, Charles M. .... Smithfield, RI
Koutsogiane, Phillip C. .... Woonsocket, RI
Koutsogiane, Wallis McCann
Cumberland, RI
Koutsos, John C. .... Los Angeles, CA
Koutsouftikis, Leon .... **Washington, DC**
Koutsouvas, Thomas .... **Chicago, IL**
Koutz, Jos. G. .... Lutherville, MD
Kouvatas, Michael N. .... Haddonfield, NJ
Kouwe, Kenneth V. .... **Rochester, NY**
Kouwe, Robert E. .... **Rochester, NY**
Kouyoumdjian, Aram .... **Sacramento, CA**
Kouyoumdjian, Linda MacRae
Sacramento, CA
Kouyoumdjian, Natalie A.
Los Angeles, CA
Kouyoumdjian, Philip Y. .... **Brooklyn, NY**
Kouznetsov, Vladimir V. .... Washington, DC
Kouzouian, Susan S. .... Cambridge, MA
Kouzoujian, Lisa B. .... Stamford, CT
Kovac, Albert P. .... Kansas City, KS
Kovac, Deborah Brown .... Plano, TX
Kovac, Frederick J. .... Akron, OH
Kovac, George .... **Washington, DC**
Kovac, James E. .... Cleveland, OH
Kovac, James W. .... Seattle, WA
Kovac, John .... Winchester, VA
Kovac, John D. .... **Maplewood, NJ**
Kovac Law Offices .... Milwaukee, WI
Kovac, Leonard J., Jr. .... Milwaukie, OR
Kovac, Michael .... **St. Louis, MO**
Kovac, Peter J. .... Milwaukee, WI
Kovac & Puhl .... Plano, TX
Kovac, Stephen J. .... St. Louis, MO
Kovacev, Robert John .... **Los Angeles, CA**
Kovacevic, Biljana .... San Diego, CA
Kovacevic, Cynthia S. .... **Skokie, IL**
Kovacevich, George J. .... Santa Cruz, CA
Kovacevich, Robert E. .... Spokane, WA
Kovacevich, Robert E., P.S. .... Spokane, WA
Kovach, Albert A. .... Uniontown, PA
Kovach, Anthony J. .... Uniontown, PA
Kovach, Christopher .... **Boston, MA**
Kovach, David J. .... **Akron, OH**
Kovach, David S. .... Washington, DC
Kovach, Dennis E. .... Pleasanton, CA
Kovach, Dennis J. .... Johnstown, PA
Kovach, Donald L. .... Franklin, NJ
Kovach, Edward M. .... San Francisco, CA
Kovach, Ellen Shirer .... New Orleans, LA
Kovach, F. Michael .... **Seattle, WA**
Kovach, Fitzgibbons & Goovaerts, P.A.
Franklin, NJ
Kovach, Gerald J. .... Washington, DC
Kovach, James A. .... Woodbridge, NJ
Kovach, James F. .... Houston, TX
Kovach, Jennifer L. .... Franklin, NJ
Kovach, Karen S. .... Dayton, OH
Kovach, Karl D. .... Arlington, VA
Kovach, Kathleen A. B. .... **Wyomissing, PA**
Kovach, Kimberlee K. .... Houston, TX
Kovach, Kimberly D. .... Uniontown, PA
Kovach & Kovach .... Uniontown, PA
Kovach, Mary Ann M. .... Medina, OH
Kovach, Michael J. .... Bowie, MD
Kovach, Michael T. .... Inverness, FL
Kovach, Peter D. .... Harrisburg, PA
Kovach, Thomas G. .... **Cleveland, OH**
Kovach, Thomas H. .... **Wilmington, DE**
Kovach, William M. .... Seven Hills, OH
Kovachevich, Elizabeth A. .... Tampa, FL
Kovachich, Jennifer S.
National Labor Relations Board, Office of the General Counsel, GV
Kovacic, Gary A. .... **Los Angeles, CA**
Kovacic-Fleischer, Candace S.
Washington, DC
Kovacich, Michael J. .... Tucker, GA
Kovacich, Thomas W. .... **Cerritos, CA**
Kovacik, Nancy L. .... Merrick, NY
Kovacik, Stephen J., Jr. .... Sacramento, CA
Kovack, Mark J. .... **Greenwich, CT**
New York, NY
Kovacs, Alan L. .... **Boston, MA**
Kovacs, Alexander J. .... Rutherford, NJ
Kovacs, Carol P. .... Burlington, NJ
Kovacs, David L. .... **New York, NY**
Kovacs, Francis A., Jr. .... **Dayton, OH**
Kovacs, Gary W. .... **Boca Raton, FL**
Kovacs, George C. .... Cleveland, OH
Kovacs, James H. .... Upper Lake, CA
Kovacs, Jamie L. .... Minneapolis, MN
Kovacs, John J. .... Elyria, OH
Kovacs, Joseph .... Mentor, OH
Kovacs, Julia T. .... Ellicott City, MD
Kovacs, Julius E. .... Cleveland, OH
Kovacs, Julius E., & Associates Co., L.P.A.
Cleveland, OH
Kovacs, Karen T. .... Washington, DC
Kovacs, Kathryn E. .... Department of Justice, Environment and Natural Resources Division, GV
Baltimore, MD
Kovacs, Kevin .... **Bedminster, NJ**
Kovacs, Laverne M. .... **Altoona, PA**
Kovacs, Leanora A. .... Kingston, NY
Kovacs, Oliver, P.C. .... Perth Amboy, NJ
Kovacs, Oliver R. .... Perth Amboy, NJ
Kovacs, Paul E., (P.C.) .... **St. Louis, MO**
Kovacs, Peter S. .... **Indianapolis, IN**
Kovacs, Richard P. .... **Easton, PA**
Kovacs, Robert J. .... Livingston, NJ
Kovacs, William L. .... Washington, DC
Kovacs, William P. .... Carmel, IN
Kovak, Richard M. .... Seattle, WA
Kovaka, Michael .... **Washington, DC**
Kovakas, James M. .... Department of Justice, Civil Division, GV
Koval, Charles B. .... Boca Raton, FL
Koval, David E. .... **Phoenix, AZ**
Koval & Featherly, P.C. .... **Anchorage, AK**
Koval, Joseph P. .... Carlinville, IL
Koval, Kristin M.E. .... **New York, NY**
Koval, LouAnn .... **Milwaukee, WI**
Koval, Mark I. .... Garden City, NY
Koval, Melvin A. .... Rockville Centre, NY
Koval, Paul W. .... **Anchorage, AK**
Koval, Stephen C. .... **New York, NY**
Koval, Steven H. .... Atlanta, GA
Koval, Susan D. .... **Detroit, MI**
Koval, Thomas A. .... Sarasota, FL
Koval, Timothy J. .... **Greene, NY**
Koval, William J., Jr. .... Akron, OH
Kovalak, Drew J. .... **Clarksburg, WV**
Kovalan, Amy S. .... Chicago, IL
Kovalchik, Kevin S. .... **Atlanta, GA**
Kovalchuk and Cutshall, P.A.
Minneapolis, MN
Kovalchuk, Mark P. .... Minneapolis, MN
Kovalcik, Anthony R. .... **Orlando, FL**
Kovalcik, Kenneth A. .... Wayne, NJ
Kovalcik & Pondelick .... Wayne, NJ
Kovalcik, William A., Jr. .... **Wellsboro, PA**
Kovaleski, Charles J. .... Orlando, FL
Kovalick, Vincent P. .... **Washington, DC**
Kovalik, Daniel M. .... **Pittsburgh, PA**
Kovalik, David K. .... Tucson, AZ
Kovalik, Marcia Sullivan .... **Portsmouth, NH**
Kovalovska, Adriana .... Boca Raton, FL
Kovalsky, Karen L. .... **Indianapolis, IN**
Kovalsky, Laura Gorman
Department of Commerce, Patent and Trademark Office, GV
Kovalsky, Martin S. .... Encino, CA
Kovalsky, Mary E. .... Marietta, GA
Kovalsky, Robert M. .... Encinitas, CA
Kovaly, Cheryl L. .... Harrisburg, PA
Kovan, Christine M. .... **Philadelphia, PA**
Kovanda, Gary L. .... Rockford, IL
Kovanda, Keith J. .... Burwell, NE
Kovanda, Ralph D. .... Cleveland, OH
Kovar, Elyse Lori Dranoff .... New York, NY
Kovar, Jeffrey D. .... Department of State, Office of the Legal Adviser, GV
Kovar, Shirley L. .... **San Diego, CA**
Kovar, Stuart C. .... White Plains, NY
Kovarcik, Thomas J. .... Edgewater, NJ
Kovar-Donohue, Amelia S. .... **Kingman, KS**
Kovar-Hersh, Marlene .... Chicago, IL
Kovari, David .... **Miami, FL**
Kovarik, Andrew J. .... **Chicago, IL**
Kovarik, Craig A. .... **Kansas City, MO**
Kovarik, John A. .... West Palm Beach, FL
Kovarik, John F. .... Bellevue, WA
Kovarik, Joseph E. .... **Denver, CO**
Kovarik, Leland K. .... **Gering, NE**
Kovarik, Stephen V. .... **Los Angeles, CA**
Kovarovics, Susan M. C. .... **Washington, DC**
Kovars, Joseph C. .... **Baltimore, MD**
Kovary, Damien W. .... Huntington Station, NY
Kovas, Jeanne Marr .... Dallas, TX
Kovash, Robin R. .... **Denver, CO**
Kovata, J. Peter .... New Orleans, LA
Kovats, Douglas J. .... Red Bank, NJ
Kove, Joseph F. .... Los Angeles, CA
Kove & Kosakow, LLC .... **Westport, CT**
New York, NY
Kove, Myron .... **New York, NY**
Kovel, Alexander .... Brookline, MA
Kovel, Martha L. .... New York, NY
Kovel, Rod E. .... Woodmere, NY
Kovelant, Barbara H. .... Laurel, MD
Kovelant & Kovelant .... Laurel, MD
Kovelant, Richard I. .... **Laurel, MD**
Fairfax, VA
Kovell, Stanley P. .... Arlington, VA
Kovelman, Gilbert G. .... **Los Angeles, CA**
Kovelman, Paul H. .... Sylmar, CA
Kovelman, Robert L. .... **Los Angeles, CA**
Koven, Andrew I. .... Morris Plains, NJ
Koven, Edward L. .... Chicago, IL
Koven, Lisa M. .... **Los Angeles, CA**
Koven, Murray T. .... New York, NY
Koven, Vance R. .... **Boston, MA**
Koverman, John R., Jr. .... **Dayton, OH**
Koves, Ivan P. .... Boulder, CO
Koves, Scott E.
Federal Energy Regulatory Commission, Office of the General Counsel, GV
Kovey, Mark H. .... **Washington, DC**
Kovich, Don Edmond .... Dayton, OH
Kovilaritch, Jacqueline M.
Cincinnati, OH
Kovin, John F. .... Washington, DC
Kovinsky, Allen J. .... **Southfield, MI**
Kovinsky, Mark L. .... **Los Angeles, CA**
Kovinsky, Milton I. .... **Detroit, MI**
Kovis, Charles E. .... Lewiston, ID
Kovit, Charles Stewart .... Hewlett, NY
Kovitch, Elizabeth .... **New York, NY**
Kovitz, Alan D. .... Buffalo Grove, IL
Chicago, IL
Kovitz, Philip M. .... New York, NY
Kovitz Shifrin & Waitzman, A Professional Corporation .... Buffalo Grove, IL
Chicago, IL
Kovler, Elyse H. .... Briarcliff Manor, NY
Kovler, Mark A. .... Briarcliff Manor, NY
Kovler, Ronald A. .... Philadelphia, PA
Kovnat, Ruth L. .... Albuquerque, NM
Kovner, Jeffrey T. .... New York, NY
Kovner, Marcia Theresa .... Shirley, MA
Kovner, Mark L. .... **Washington, DC**
Kovner, Paul .... **New York, NY**
Kovner, Victor A. .... **New York, NY**
Kovnot, Ronald M. .... Miami, FL
Kovschak, Matthew J. .... Lakeland, FL
Kovschak, Matthew J., P.A. .... Lakeland, FL
Kovski, Christopher J. .... **Erie, PA**
Kovsky, Charles E. .... Livonia, MI
Kovsky, Robert .... Oakland, CA
Kow, Jane .... **San Francisco, CA**
Kowach, Kerrin McCormick
Pittsburgh, PA
Kowal, Christine A. .... Detroit, MI
Kowal, David P. .... **Los Angeles, CA**
Kowal, Dorothy A. .... **Hackensack, NJ**
Kowal, Edward M., Jr. .... **Huntington, WV**
Kowal, Harold F. .... Newton, MA
Kowal, James D. .... **Santa Fe Springs, CA**
Kowal, Jennifer M. .... **Los Angeles, CA**
Kowal, Karen J. .... **Chicago, IL**
Kowal, Karen L. .... Basking Ridge, NJ
Kowal, Lewis D. .... Phoenix, AZ
Kowal, Mark J. .... **New York, NY**
Kowal, Paul S. .... **Mount Clemens, MI**
Kowal, Paul S. .... **Sterling Heights, MI**
Kowal, Sanford A. .... Newton, MA
Kowal, Steven M. .... **Chicago, IL**
Kowal, Susan G. .... **Birmingham, MI**
Kowal, Vernon A. .... Western Springs, IL
Kowalchick, Henry .... Norfolk, VA
Virginia Beach, VA
Kowalchik, Walter .... **Englewood, CO**
Kowalchuk, Orest .... Philadelphia, PA
Kowalchyk, Alan W. .... **Minneapolis, MN**
Kowalchyk, Dean Clinton .... Tallahassee, FL
Kowalchyk, Katherine M.
Minneapolis, MN
Kowalchyn, Nichols W. .... New York, NY
Kowalchyn, Theodore Victor .... Linden, NJ
Kowalcik, Joseph A. .... West St. Paul, MN
Kowalcyk, Karla K. .... Sacramento, CA
Kowalczewski, Raymond A., Jr.
Kansas City, MO
Kowalczuk, Renata .... Buffalo, NY
Kowalczyk, Andrew S., III .... Utica, NY
Kowalczyk, Andrew S., Jr. .... Utica, NY
Kowalczyk, Bradley M. .... Utica, NY
Kowalczyk, Darlene Rohr .... San Diego, CA
Kowalczyk, George .... Fort Wayne, IN
Kowalczyk, John R. .... Fort Wayne, IN
Kowalczyk, John T. .... **Syracuse, NY**
Kowalczyk, John William .... Columbus, OH
Kowalczyk, Joseph M., Jr.
White Plains, NY
Kowalczyk, Karen E. .... Utica, NY
Kowalczyk, Larry S. .... **Chicago, IL**
Kowalczyk, Laura P. .... Orlando, FL
Kowalczyk, Mark E. .... Wheaton, IL
Kowalczyk, Mark Gerard
Mount Pleasant, MI
Kowalczyk, Noelle .... **New York, NY**
Rochester, NY
Kowalczyk, Robert P. .... New Haven, CT
Kowalczyk, Teresa .... Warsaw, NY
Kowalczyk, Thomas A. .... **Clinton, NJ**
Kowalczyk, Thomas J. .... Traverse City, MI
Kowalczyk, Tolles, Deery & Johnston
Utica, NY
Kowalczyk, Walter W. .... St. Louis, MO
Kowald, Kenneth .... Richmond Hill, NY
Kowalenko, Susan C. .... Westfield, NJ
Kowaleski, Patrick E. .... Denver, CO
Kowalewski, Amy .... **Philadelphia, PA**
Kowalewski, Edward, Jr. .... Clifton Park, NY
Kowalewski, John B. .... Philadelphia, PA
Kowalewski, John P. .... Oakdale, CT
Kowalewski, Richard Paul
Kansas City, MO
Kowalick, W. Frederick .... **Los Angeles, CA**
Kowalik, Dennis J. .... Victoria, TX
Kowalik, Francis C.M. .... **Deerfield, IL**
Kowalik, James S. .... **Indianapolis, IN**
Kowalik, John J. .... Chicago, IL
Kowalik, Lisa J. .... Warwick, RI
Kowalke, Todd W. .... **Cresco, IA**
Kowalko, Michael A. .... Flint, MI
Kowalkowski, Frank W. .... Green Bay, WI
Kowalkowski, Jeffrey N. .... Elmhurst, IL
Kowall and Associates .... **Pittsburgh, PA**
Kowall, Carol .... **Pittsburgh, PA**
Kowaloff, Dorothy R. .... New York, NY
Kowals, Anthony D. .... South Bend, IN
Kowalske, John Robert .... Amarillo, TX
Kowalski, Alexandra M. .... **Cleveland, OH**
Kowalski, Amy Miles .... **McLean, VA**
Kowalski, Barry F. .... Department of Justice, Civil Rights Division, GV
Kowalski, Bill .... **Blue Bell, PA**
Kowalski, Brian P. .... **Trenton, NJ**
Kowalski, Daniel M. .... **Seattle, WA**
Kowalski, David .... Buffalo, NY
Kowalski & Derfel, P.A.
Daytona Beach, FL
Kowalski, Edward John .... **Rockville, MD**
Kowalski, Edward Raymond .... Denver, CO
Kowalski, Frank X., Jr. .... **Naples, FL**
Kowalski, Gerald R. .... **Toledo, OH**
Kowalski, Gerard John .... New York, NY
Kowalski, Gregory P. .... Harrison, NJ
Kowalski, Henry J., III .... Vineland, NJ
Kowalski, Jack G. .... **Birmingham, AL**
Kowalski, James A., Jr. .... **Jacksonville, FL**
Kowalski, Joanne M. .... Berkeley, CA
Kowalski, John F. .... Alpena, MI
Kowalski, Juliane .... **New York, NY**
Kowalski, Kathiann M. .... Fairview Park, OH
Kowalski, Kenneth J. .... Cleveland, OH
Kowalski, Kirsten Hunt .... **Birmingham, AL**
Kowalski, Leann .... Pittsburgh, PA
Kowalski, Leonhard J. .... Lansing, MI
Kowalski, Maureen .... **Pittsburgh, PA**
Wheeling, WV
Kowalski, Michael .... **San Francisco, CA**
Kowalski, Michael J. .... **Riverside, CA**
Kowalski, Michael J. .... **Wilkes-Barre, PA**
Kowalski, Michael V. .... **Washington, DC**
Kowalski, Monica .... **Woodbridge, NJ**
Kowalski, Nathan J. .... Burbank, CA
Kowalski, Raymond A. .... **Washington, DC**
Kowalski, Robert J. .... Rolling Meadows, IL
Kowalski, Ronald E. .... Daytona Beach, FL
Kowalski, Ronald E., II .... **Stamford, CT**
Kowalski, Sarah L. .... **San Francisco, CA**
Kowalski, Scott W. .... **McLean, VA**
Kowalski, Stuart M. .... **Wichita, KS**
Kowalski, Suzanne Gross .... **Chicago, IL**
Kowalski, Theodore R. .... Fairview Park, OH
Kowalski, Theresa M. .... **Minneapolis, MN**
Kowalski, Thomas J. .... **New York, NY**
Kowalski, Thomas M. .... Mission, KS
Kowalski, Walter J. .... Chicago, IL
Kowalski, William J. .... **Boulder, CO**
Kowalski, Wm. A. .... East Chicago, IN
Kowalski-Garza, Adela .... Brownsville, TX
Kowalsky, Avrum M. .... Bel Air, MD
Kowalsky, Carlyn Harper .... **Apopka, FL**
Kowalsky, Deborah S. .... **Hollywood, FL**
Kowalsky, Deborah S., P.A., Law Offices of
Hollywood, FL
Kowalsky & Hirschhorn, P.A. .... Bel Air, MD
Kowalsky, Joseph Z. .... Lathrup Village, MI
Kowalsky, Mark L. .... **Bloomfield Hills, MI**
Kowalyshyn, Kathleen J. .... **Hartford, CT**
Kowantz, Robyn A. .... **Hackensack, NJ**
Kowar, Joseph Albert .... Aspen, CO
Koweek, Cranna, Agata & McEvoy, P.C.
Hudson, NY
Koweek, Richard M. .... **Hudson, NY**
Koweek, Toni G. .... Albany, NY
Kowen, Richard J. .... **Honolulu, HI**
Kowen & Walker .... **Honolulu, HI**
Kowert, David G. .... **St. Louis, MO**
Kowert, Robert C. .... **Austin, TX**
Kowey, Dorothy F. .... Bryn Mawr, PA
Kowieski, Jeffrey W. .... **Wausau, WI**
Kowis, Kelly M. .... **Houston, TX**
Kowis, Patrick M., Jr. .... New Orleans, LA
Kowit, Jonathan R. .... Jenkintown, PA
Kowitt, Arthur J. .... Evanston, IL
Kowitt, Stephen E. .... **New York, NY**

Kowitz, Jack ... Baltimore, MD
Kowitz, Julie F. ... New York, NY
Kown, Charles L. ... Brentwood, TN
Kownacki, David P. ... New York, NY
Kownacki, David P., P.C. ... New York, NY
Kownacki, Diane ... Seattle, WA
Kowolowski, Fred A. ... Redmond, OR
Kowsari, Michael M. ... Columbus, OH
Kowtko, Lisa M. ... Westport, CT
Kowtna, Paul E. ... Mineola, NY
Koya, Mansukhlal A., P.C. ... Forest Hills, NY
Koya, Mansukhlal A. ... Forest Hills, NY
Koyama, Julie K. ... Glendale, CA
Koyanagi, Faye M. ... Honolulu, HI
Koyanagi, Stan H. ... New York, NY
Koyanis, Melinda T. ... Cambridge, MA
Koyasako, Steven K. ... Sacramento, CA
Koyfman, Isaac ... New York, NY
Koykar, Frank J., P.C. ... Elmhurst, IL
Koykar, Frejlich & Associates ... Elmhurst, IL
Koyner, Andrea L. ... Washington, DC
Koza, Bart M. ... Honolulu, HI
Koza, Edw. M. ... Sun City, AZ
Koza, Thomas A. ... Dallas, TX
Kozac, Karen ... Larchmont, NY
Kozachek, James A. ... Florham Park, NJ
Kozachenko, Paul ... Fremont, CA
Kozachok, Stephen K. ... Minneapolis, MN
Kozacik, Susan M. ... Chicago, IL
Kozacki, Jerome S. ... Florence, SC
Kozacky, Paul J. ... Chicago, IL
Kozacky, Paul J., & Associates, P.C.
Chicago, IL
Kozak, Alexandria ... Trenton, NJ
Kozak, Charles R. ... Kaneohe, HI
Kozak, Christopher ... Newark, NJ
Kozak, Daniel J. ... Grand Rapids, MI
Kozak, David M. ... Scottsdale, AZ
Kozak, David M. ... Westport, CT
Kozak, Dennis M. ... Houston, TX
Kozak, Ellen M. ... Milwaukee, WI
Kozak, Frank J. ... Chicago, IL
Kozak, Fred R. ... Richmond, VA
Kozak, Gayer & Brodek, P.A. ... Augusta, ME
Bangor, ME
Portland, ME
Kozak, Harry T. ... Costa Mesa, CA
Kozak, Henry ... Pepper Pike, OH
Kozak, John H. ... Charleston, WV
Kozak, John J. ... Tampa, FL
Kozak, John W. ... Chicago, IL
Kozak, Jonathan M. ... White Plains, NY
Kozak, Joseph M. ... Augusta, ME
Portland, ME
Kozak, Mark A. ... Park City, UT
Kozak, Maryalice ... New York, NY
Kozak, Michael P. ... Chesterfield, VA
Kozak, Peter Joseph ... Cameron Park, CA
Kozak, Peter P. ... Green Bay, WI
Kozak, Robert C. ... Prescott, AZ
Kozak, Scott K. G. ... St. Louis, MO
Kozak, Troy Steven ... Vienna, VA
Kozak, Warren D. ... Portsmouth, VA
Kozakewich, Michael, Jr.
Clarksburg, WV
Kozakiewicz, Robert F. ... Riverhead, NY
Kozakiewicz, Vincent J. ... Dillon, MT
Kozakowski, Lisa ... Mandeville, LA
Columbus, OH
Kozak Roberts, Kathy S. ... Minnetonka, MN
Kozal, Kevin V. ... Santa Monica, CA
Kozan, Margaret" Amie " ... Orlando, FL
Kozar, Carol A. ... Raleigh, NC
Kozar, Mark E. ... Pittsburgh, PA
Kozar, Ronald J. ... Dayton, OH
Kozarek, Linda Jane ... Mercer Island, WA
Kozaruk, Lawrence G. ... Birmingham, MI
Kozay, Nicholas, Jr. ... Philadelphia, PA
Kozberg, Joel M. ... Los Angeles, CA
Kozberg, Lindsey C. ... Los Angeles, CA
Kozek, Neil E. ... New York, NY
White Plains, NY
Kozel, Alexander ... Pensacola, FL
Kozel, Edward J., Jr. ... Chicago, IL
Kozel, James R. ... Omaha, NE
Kozel & Rady ... San Diego, CA
Kozel, Richard J. ... Clifton, NJ
Kozel, Timothy J. ... San Diego, CA
Kozel-Carbone, Donna ... Baltimore, MD
Kozeliski, George W. ... Gallup, NM
Kozelka, Frank C. ... Broadview Heights, OH
Kozelka, Frank J. ... Independence, OH
Kozelka, Kay J. ... Broadview Heights, OH
Kozelka & Kozelka ... Broadview Heights, OH
Kozely, Joseph E., Jr. ... Detroit, MI
Kozeny, David J. ... St. Louis, MO
Kozeny, Evamarie ... St. Louis, MO
Kozeny & McCubbin, L.C. ... St. Louis, MO
Kozeny, Susan L. ... Seattle, WA
Kozeny, Wesley T. ... St. Louis, MO
Kozer, Stephen J. ... Bellingham, WA
Kozera, Daniel J., Jr. ... Grand Rapids, MI
Kozera, Virginia U. ... Blue Bell, PA
Kozerski, Danna M. ... San Francisco, CA
Kozerski, Theodore M.
Bloomfield Hills, MI
Kozey, Stephen G. ... Plainfield, IN
Koziacki, Mary Elizabeth ... Emporia, KS
Koziar, Stephen F., Jr. ... Dayton, OH
Koziboski, Edward J. ... Chicago, IL
Kozich, John H. ... Columbus, OH
Kozich, S. David ... Huntington Beach, CA
Kozicki, Steven A., & Associates
Arlington Heights, IL
Kozicki, Steven A., & Associates
Chicago, IL
Kozicky, Roman G. ... Yonkers, NY
Kozik, Kenneth F. ... Manchester, NH
Portsmouth, NH
Kozik, Mark ... Denver, CO
Kozik, Mary Ann J. ... Cleveland, OH
Kozik, Michael T. ... South Windsor, CT
Kozikowski, Paul M. ... Chicopee, MA
Kozimer, Kenneth G. ... Cincinnati, OH
Kozina, Vladimir F. ... Stockton, CA
Koziner, Pablo M. ... New York, NY
Kozinn, Marshall H. ... Closter, NJ
Kozinn, Paul ... New York, NY
Kozinski, Alex ... Pasadena, CA
Kozinski, Jane ... Princeton, NJ
Kozinski, Kathleen Gilmore
West Palm Beach, FL
Koziol, Christopher S. ... Chicago, IL
Koziol, Courtney E. ... Omaha, NE
Koziol, Frank S., Jr. ... Anchorage, AK
Koziol, Kristian M. ... Washington, DC
Koziol, Leon R. ... Utica, NY
Koziol, Michael G. ... Des Plaines, IL
Koziolkowsky, Peter ... New York, NY
Kozisek, Mark ... Ainsworth, NE
Kozlak, Jodeen A. ... Minneapolis, MN
Kozlakowski, Louis J. ... Baltimore, MD
Kozlik, Joseph W. ... Rutland, VT
Kozlik, Michael D. ... Omaha, NE
Kozloff, David M. ... Reading, PA
Kozloff, Diener, Payne & Fegley, Professional Corporation ... Reading, PA
Kozloff, John S. ... Parsippany, NJ
Kozloff, Louis H. ... Washington, DC
Kozloff, Theodore J. ... San Francisco, CA
New York, NY
Kozloski, Aaron J. ... Columbia, SC
Kozloski, Walter B. ... New Britain, CT
Kozlov, Herbert F. ... New York, NY
Kozlov, Hersh ... Cherry Hill, NJ
Kozlov, Scott A. ... Arlington Heights, IL
Kozlov, Seaton, Romanini, Brooks & Greenberg ... Cherry Hill, NJ
Kozlovsky, Donald Victor ... Milwaukee, WI
Kozlovsky, Janette Marie ... Alexandria, VA
Kozlow, Elisabeth D. ... Miami, FL
Kozlow, Jeffrey S. ... New York, NY
Kozlow, Warren J. ... Boca Raton, FL
Kozlow, Warren J., P.A. ... Boca Raton, FL
Kozlowski, Amy K. ... Chicago, IL
Kozlowski, Brian J. ... Chicago, IL
Kozlowski, David A. ... Columbia, TN
Kozlowski, David J. ... Napa, CA
Kozlowski, David P. ... West Des Moines, IA
Kozlowski, David R. ... Joliet, IL
Kozlowski, Hadas Z.
Federal Energy Regulatory Commission, Office of the General Counsel, GV
Kozlowski, Holly D. ... Cincinnati, OH
Kozlowski, James C. ... Fairfax Station, VA
Kozlowski, James J. ... Boulder, CO
Kozlowski, John F. ... Columbus, OH
Kozlowski, Jos. J. ... Willow Springs, IL
Kozlowski, Joseph F. ... Kansas City, MO
Kozlowski, Karen M. ... Morristown, NJ
Kozlowski, Kathe ... Coral Gables, FL
Kozlowski, Kathleen C. ... Dearborn, MI
Kozlowski, Kenneth S. ... Cleveland, OH
Kozlowski, Kimberly F. ... Chicago, IL
Kozlowski, Kristin T. ... Boulder, CO
Kozlowski, Laura Bare ... Westminster, MD
Kozlowski, Lucille ... Nashua, NH
Kozlowski, Mark Anthony ... Baltimore, MD
Kozlowski, Michael T. ... Richland, WA
Kozlowski, Nancy E. ... Arlington, VA
Kozlowski, Nanette M. ... Jersey City, NJ
Kozlowski, Peter J. ... New York, NY
Kozlowski, Phyllis A. ... Grosse Pointe, MI
Kozlowski, Raymond S. ... Prairie Village, KS
Kozlowski, Richard E. ... Columbus, OH
Kozlowski, Richard G. ... Washington, DC
Kozlowski, Richard W. ... Burlington, VT
Kozlowski, Robert ... Chicago, IL
Kozlowski & Smith ... Willow Springs, IL
Kozlowski, Steven R. ... Miami Beach, FL
Kozlowski, Susan Hayest ... Columbus, OH
Kozlowski, Susan M. ... Chicago, IL
Kozlowsky, Henry L. ... Reading, PA
Kozma, Daniel S. ... Washington, DC
Kozma, David P. ... Denver, CO
Kozma, Gary A. ... Detroit, MI
Kozma, John Powers ... Charleston, SC
Kozma, Kevin J. ... White Cloud, MI
Kozma, Larence R. ... Clarkston, MI
Kozminske, Ronald L. ... St. Louis, MO
Kozminski, Brian K. ... Chicago, IL
Kozminski, Peggy B. ... Chicago, IL
Kozminski, Penelope Ann
Grand Rapids, MI
Kozminsky, Ellen C. ... New York, NY
Kozmor, James D. ... Beverly Hills, CA
Kozodoy, David E. ... Boston, MA
Kozodoy, Fong & Ostreicher ... Boston, MA
Kozol, Catherine M. ... Fort Pierce, FL
Kozol, David M. ... Boston, MA
Kozol, Eric J. ... Andover, MA
Kozol, Joel A. ... Boston, MA
Kozol, Lee H. ... Boston, MA
Kozol, Matthew S. ... Boston, MA
Kozol, P.C. ... Andover, MA
Kozol, William V. ... Joliet, IL
Kozolchyk, Boris ... Tucson, AZ
Kozon, Joan Elizabeth ... Albuquerque, NM
Kozub, Diane M. ... Fort Worth, TX
Kozub, Katherine M. ... Boston, MA
Kozub, Timothy R. ... Pontiac, MI
Kozub, William A. ... Phoenix, AZ
Kozub, William G. ... Doylestown, PA
Kozubek, S. Michael ... Chicago, IL
Kozuch, Carolyn J. ... Los Angeles, CA
Kozuch, James J. ... Philadelphia, PA
Kozupsky, Allen J. ... New York, NY
Kozupsky, Deborah Lee ... New City, NY
Kozupsky, Harold ... New York, NY
Kozupsky & Lebowitz, LLP
New York, NY
Kozupsky, Roy P. ... New York, NY
Kozusko, Donald D. ... Washington, DC
Kozyak, John W. ... Miami, FL
Kozyak Tropin & Throckmorton, P.A.
Miami, FL
Kozyra, Barry A. ... Roseland, NJ
Kozyris, P. John ... Columbus, OH
Kra, Leo D. ... New York, NY
Kraai, Gerald M. ... Kansas City, MO
Kraatz, Julie ... Fort Worth, TX
Kraatz, Ken ... Fort Worth, TX
Kraatz, Theresa Ann ... Austin, TX
Kraayeveld, James W. ... Grand Rapids, MI
Krabacher, B. Joseph ... Aspen, CO
Krabacher Law Offices ... Aspen, CO
Krabbe, Donna M. ... Cincinnati, OH
Krabbe, JoAnne L. ... Milwaukee, WI
Krabbe, M. Kent ... Owings Mills, MD
Krabbendam, Deborah J.
Mount Laurel, NJ
Philadelphia, PA
Krabbenhoft, Douglas H. ... Boston, MA
Krabbenhoft, William A. ... Sacramento, CA
Krabbenschmidt, Henry ... Hillsborough, CA
Krabill, Laura E. ... Philadelphia, PA
Kracen, Scott A. ... Sycamore, IL
Krach, Donald A. ... Baltimore, MD
Krach, Kenneth F. ... Baltimore, MD
Krache, Martha E. ... Boston, MA
Krachman, Albert B. ... Washington, DC
Krachmer, Edward B.
Federal Communications Commission, Common Carrier Bureau, GV
Kracht, Carol L. ... Milwaukee, WI
Kracht, Danelia F. ... North Platte, NE
Kracht, Dominic ... Los Angeles, CA
Kracht, Eric A. ... Baton Rouge, LA
Kracht & Graves, L.L.P.
Baton Rouge, LA
Kracht, James K. ... Miami, FL
Kracht, Michael D. ... West Chester, PA
Kracht, Richard W. ... Iselin, NJ
Kracht, Robert L. ... San Diego, CA
Kracht, Robert R. ... Cleveland, OH
Kracht, Torsten M. ... New York, NY
Kracik, Deborah Kashul ... Chicago, IL
Krack, Carl R. ... Medford, OR
Kracke, Frederick C. ... Walnut Creek, CA
Kracke, Robert R. ... Birmingham, AL
Kracke, Thompson & Ellis, P.C.
Birmingham, AL
Krackeler, Christine Kirwin ... Albany, NY
Krackenberger, John H. ... Chicago, IL
Krackenberger, Mary P. ... Skokie, IL
Kracker, Erica Z. ... Palmer, AK
Krackov, Michael B ... Bethesda, MD
Kracoff, Cheryl ... Norristown, PA
Philadelphia, PA
Kracoff, Richard J. ... Los Angeles, CA
Kracov, Daniel A. ... Washington, DC
Kracov, Eric S. ... Washington, DC
Kracov, Gideon ... Los Angeles, CA
Kracov, Karen B. ... Department of Labor, Office of the Solicitor, GV
Kracum, David R. ... Eden Prairie, MN
Kraczkowsky, Mark P. ... Hartford, CT
Kradel, Eileen C. ... Fort Smith, AR
Kradel, John F. ... Ligonier, PA
Krader, Eugene M. ... New York, NY
Kradjel, Richard J. ... Franklin Center, PA
Kradolfer, Kimberly A. ... Helena, MT
Kraebel, Barbara ... New York, NY
Kraege, Richard C. ... Indianapolis, IN
Kraeger, Dorothea P. ... Phoenix, AZ
Kraeger, Dorothea P., P.C. ... Phoenix, AZ
Kraeger, Kristin M. ... Boston, MA
Kraeger, Susan Jill ... Lowville, NY
Kraeger, Thomas G. ... New London, NH
Kraehe, George C. ... Brownsville, TX
Kraemer, Alan G. ... College Point, NY
Kraemer, Alan J. ... College Point, NY
Kraemer, Andrew L. ... Merrillville, IN
Kraemer, Ann M. ... Minneapolis, MN
Kraemer, Barry E. ... Clawson, MI
Kraemer, Bradley M. ... Hamilton, OH
Kraemer, Brett A. ... San Antonio, TX
Kraemer, Burns, Mytelka, Lovell & Kulka, P.A. ... Elizabeth, NJ
Morristown, NJ
Newark, NJ
Paterson, NJ
Springfield, NJ
Kraemer, David A. ... Westbury, NY
Kraemer, Donald L. ... Huntsville, TX
Kraemer, Dwight D. ... Westbury, NY
Kraemer, Elizabeth Opper ... Chicago, IL
Kraemer, Gary A. ... Sparta, NJ
Kraemer, Glen E. ... Los Angeles, CA
Kraemer, J Kurt ... Lake Oswego, OR
Kraemer, James L. ... Lawrenceville, GA
Kraemer, Jay R. ... Washington, DC
Kraemer, Jenifer L. ... Madison, WI
Kraemer, Jill M. ... Lafayette, LA
Kraemer, John Richard ... San Diego, CA
Kraemer Kendall & Benson, Professional Corporation ... Colorado Springs, CO
Kraemer, Kenneth ... Portland, OR
Kraemer, Laurence A. ... Massapequa, NY
Kraemer, Lillian E. ... New York, NY
Kraemer, Lisa R. ... Beachwood, OH
Kraemer, Mary K. ... Destin, FL
Kraemer, Michael F. ... Philadelphia, PA
Kraemer & Mulligan ... Westbury, NY
Kraemer, Richard ... Fort Collins, CO
Kraemer, Richard A. ... Philadelphia, PA
Kraemer, Robert J., Jr. ... Mount Juliet, TN
Kraemer, Samuel H. ... Los Angeles, CA
Kraemer, Sandy F. ... Colorado Springs, CO
Kraemer, Steven A. ... Portland, OR
Kraemer, Steven Joseph ... Irvine, CA
Kraemer, Tammy H.
Colorado Springs, CO
Kraemer, Teresa M. ... Tigard, OR
Kraemer, Thomas R. ... Dayton, OH
Kraemer, Tyler D. ... Colorado Springs, CO
Kraemer, Waldron ... Springfield, NJ
Kraepel, Timothy E. ... Bloomfield Hills, MI
Kraeski, Sara ... Boulder, CO
Kraetz, Howard ... West Hempstead, NY
Kraetzer, John F. ... Oakland, CA
Kraetzer, Priscilla C. ... Irvine, CA
Kraeuter, R. Scot ... Savannah, GA
Kraeutler, Eric ... Philadelphia, PA
Kraeutler, Jacqueline M. ... Philadelphia, PA
Krafchak, Christopher E. ... Los Angeles, CA
Krafchak, Stephanie L. ... Los Angeles, CA
Krafchick, Celestine M. ... Philadelphia, PA
Krafchick Law Firm ... Seattle, WA
Krafchick, Steven P. ... Seattle, WA
Krafcik, Jamie R. ... Parma, OH
Krafcisin, John R. (Jack) ... Cicero, IL
Krafczek, Adam B. ... Reading, PA
Krafczek, Adam B., Jr. ... Reading, PA
Krafczek, J.D. ... Reading, PA
Krafft, Gary G. ... Ephrata, PA
Lancaster, PA
Willow Street, PA
Krafft, M. Sue, Law Offices of
Covina, CA
Krafft, M. Sue, Law Offices of
Los Angeles, CA
Pomona, CA
Krafft, Stephen P. ... Phoenix, AZ
Krafka, Mary Baird ... Ottumwa, IA
Krafka, Robert G. ... Fremont, NE
Krafsig, John J., Jr. ... Harrisburg, PA
Krafsig, John J., Jr., Inc. ... Harrisburg, PA
Krafsky, Kurt D. ... San Jose, CA
Krafsur, Andrew B. ... El Paso, TX
Krafsur, Gordon, Mott, Davis & Woody, P.C.
El Paso, TX
Krafsur, Jay V. ... Chicago, IL
Kraft, Alan J. ... New York, NY
Kraft & Associates, P.C. ... Dallas, TX
Kraft, Barbara ... Washington, DC
Kraft, Barbara Simpson ... Anchorage, AK
Kraft, Bernard ... Baltimore, MD
Kraft, Bernice ... Chelsea, MA
Kraft, Bruce A. ... Brookline, MA
Kraft, C. William, III ... Conifer, CO
Kraft, Carl D. ... St. Louis, MO
Kraft, Carl S. ... Pahrump, NV
Kraft, Carlan J. ... Rugby, ND
Kraft, Carol L. ... Milwaukee, WI
Kraft, Christine Kerper ... Newark, NJ
Kraft, Christine V. R., P.C. ... Chicago, IL
Kraft, Christine V. R. ... Chicago, IL
Kraft, Christopher R. ... Montgomery, NY
Kraft, Claire I. ... Woodridge, IL
Kraft, Daniel L. ... Lansing, MI
Kraft, Danya L. ... Wilmington, DE
Kraft, David A. ... Kansas City, MO
Kraft, David W. ... Seattle, WA
Kraft, Debra J. ... Milwaukee, WI
Kraft, Dennis O. ... Dallas, TX
Kraft, Douglas, & Associates
Sacramento, CA
Kraft, Eleanor M. ... Cutten, CA
Kraft, Ellen M. ... Bethlehem, PA
Kraft & Friedman ... St. Louis, MO
Kraft, Gary B., Jr. ... Tucson, AZ
Kraft, George W., Jr. ... El Cajon, CA
Kraft, Henry R. ... Tustin, CA
Kraft, Herbert R. ... Hermosa Beach, CA
Kraft, Howard Bradley
Haddon Township, NJ
Kraft, I. L. ... Kansas City, MO
Kraft & Jacobson, P.A. ... Baltimore, MD
Kraft, James A. ... Seattle, WA
Kraft, James B. ... Columbia, MD
Kraft, James L. ... Woodbridge, NJ
Kraft, James M. ... Department of Labor, Office of the Solicitor, GV
Kraft, Jeffrey G. ... Chicago, IL
Kraft, Jennifer L. ... Philadelphia, PA
Kraft, Joe ... Nashville, TN
Kraft, John A. ... New Albany, IN
Kraft, John H. ... Hutchinson, MN
Olivia, MN
Renville, MN
Kraft, John L. ... Roseland, NJ
Kraft, Joseph M. ... Briarcliff Manor, NY
Kraft, Julius B. ... Austin, TX
Kraft, K. Eugene ... Conroe, TX
Kraft, Kathleen McDonald
Bloomington, IL
Kraft, Kenneth A. ... Washington, DC
Kraft, Kenneth H. ... Atlanta, GA
Kraft & Kraft, P.C. ... Philadelphia, PA
Kraft, Kristine K. ... St. Louis, MO
Kraft, Larry ... Grand Forks, ND
Kraft Law Firm, A Professional Corporation
Kansas City, MO
Lake Ozark, MO
Kraft, Lee ... Bellevue, WA
Kraft, Marcia L., Law Offices of
Simi Valley, CA
Woodland Hills, CA
Kraft, Marcijane ... New York, NY
Kraft, Mark Alexander ... Houston, TX

Kraft, Martin ....East Brunswick, NJ
Kraft, Mary Therese ....Bloomington, IL
Kraft, Matthew H. ....Norfolk, VA
Kraft, Michael ....Deerfield Beach, FL
Kraft, Michael ....Chicago, IL
Kraft, Michael A. ....Peoria, IL
Kraft, Michael A. ....Tulsa, OK
Kraft, Michael D. ....Seattle, WA
Kraft, Michael S. ....New York, NY
Kraft, Mitchell S. ....Tamarac, FL
Kraft, Paul ....Chestnut Ridge, NY
Kraft, Paul ....Philadelphia, PA
Kraft, Paul A. ....Indianapolis, IN
Kraft, Peter R. ....Portland, ME
Kraft, Ralph E. ....Lafayette, LA
New Orleans, LA
Kraft, Ralph F. ....Johnstown, PA
Kraft, Raymond S. ....Loomis, CA
Kraft, Richard E. ....Los Angeles, CA
Kraft, Richard L. ....Roswell, NM
Kraft, Richard W. ....San Francisco, CA
Kraft, Robert A. ....Dallas, TX
Kraft, Robert F. ....Livonia, MI
Kraft, Robert L. ....New York, NY
Kraft, Robert M. ....Seattle, WA
Kraft, Robert S. ....San Francisco, CA
Kraft, Robt. S. ....Cincinnati, OH
Kraft, Ronald L. ....Kansas City, MO
Kraft, Rudolph G., Jr. ....Cupertino, CA
Kraft, Ruth B. ....New York, NY
Kraft, Sandra ....Arnold, CA
Kraft, Saul P. ....Chelsea, MA
Kraft, Shaughn E. ....Mill Creek, WA
Kraft, Stephen P. ....Omaha, NE
Kraft, Steven R. ....Moline, IL
Kraft & Stone, LLP ....Roswell, NM
Kraft, Sumner ....Malden, MA
Kraft, Theodore M. ....Cape Coral, FL
Kraft, Thomas J. ....Bellevue, WA
Kraft, Todd A. ....Dallas, TX
Kraft, Walser, Hettig & Honsey, PLLP
Hutchinson, MN
Olivia, MN
Renville, MN
Kraft, Warren G. ....Cold Spring Harbor, NY
Kraft, Warren P. ....Oshkosh, WI
Kraft & Winger ....Portland, ME
Kraftchick, Stacey L. ....Georgetown, SC
Krafte, Conrad W. ....Hackensack, NJ
Krafte, Jill H. ....Columbia, MD
Krafthefer, Keri-Lyn J. ....Chicago, IL
Krafts, Andrew J. ....Pittsburgh, PA
Krafts, Ivars J. ....Circle Pines, MN
Kraftson, Daniel J. ....Reston, VA
Kraftson, Raymond H. ....Villanova, PA
Krag, Donald R. ....Corvallis, OR
Krag, Thomas R. ....Los Angeles, CA
Krage, Ben L. ....Dallas, TX
Krage & Janvey, L.L.P. ....Dallas, TX
Fort Worth, TX
Plano, TX
Waxahachie, TX
Kragel, Bradley W. ....Sacramento, CA
Kragen, Adrian A. ....Berkeley, CA
Kragen, Jules M. ....Emeryville, CA
Kragen, Marshall ....Rockville, MD
Krages, Bert P., II ....Portland, OR
Kragh, Cheryl Bruce ....Tampa, FL
Kragh, Thomas A. ....Polson, MT
Kragie, Mary E. ....Austin, TX
Kragie, Scott T. ....Washington, DC
Kragnes, Christopher, Sr. ....Des Moines, IA
Kragnes, Christopher A., Sr., P.C., Law Offices of ....Des Moines, IA
Kragness, Duane Alan ....Wahpeton, ND
Kragness & Sandberg, Ltd. ....Wahpeton, ND
Kragt, Jeffrey S. ....Bloomfield Hills, MI
Kragt, Timothy Alan ....St. Joseph, MI
Kragulac, Robert Paul ....La Crescenta, CA
Kraguljac, Petar ....Cleveland, OH
Kraham, Bonnie Hosier ....Middletown, NY
Kraham, Kevin M.
Equal Employment Opportunity Commission,
Office of Federal Operations, GV
Kraham, William E. ....Brattleboro, VT
Kraham, William R. ....Ijamsville, MD
Krahe, Linda DeNero ....Pittsburgh, PA
Krahe, William T. ....Pittsburgh, PA
Krahelski, L. Thomas ....San Bernardino, CA
Krahelski, Michael A. ....Foothill Ranch, CA
Krahenbuhl, Glen A. ....Albuquerque, NM
Krahenbuhl, Kim D. ....Oregon, IL
Krahl, Kevin E. ....Oklahoma City, OK
Krahl, William F. ....Chicago, IL
Krahmer, Alyssa Y. ....Dallas, TX
Krahmer & Bishop ....Truman, MN
Fairmont, MN
Krahmer, Bruce A. ....Fairmont, MN
Krahmer, Donald L., Jr. ....Portland, OR
Krahmer, Fred C. ....Fairmont, MN
Truman, MN
Krahmer, Johannes R. ....Wilmington, DE
Krahmer, John E. ....Lubbock, TX
Krahmer & Shaffer, Ltd. ....Fairmont, MN
Krahn, Joseph ....Topeka, KS
Krahulec, James E. ....Harrisburg, PA
Krahulik, David C. ....Indianapolis, IN
Krahulik, Emil R. ....Middletown, NY
Krahulik, Jon D. ....Indianapolis, IN
Krahulik, Robert E. ....Middletown, NY
Kraich, Christopher Peter ....Garden City, NY
Kraidin, Adam E. ....New York, NY
Kraiem, Ruben ....New York, NY
Kraig, Jerry B. ....Cleveland, OH
Kraig, Thomas L. ....Darien, CT
Kraig, Thomas L., Jr. ....Barrington, RI
Kraimer, Robert H., Jr. ....New Castle, KY
Krain, Donald A. ....Philadelphia, PA
Krain, Jeffery L. ....Philadelphia, PA
Krain, John ....Sun City, AZ
Kraines, Merrill M. ....New York, NY
Krainess, Gerald S. ....Cleveland, OH
Krainess, Simon & Ehrenreich
Cleveland, OH
Krainik, Ralph B. ....Baraboo, WI
Krainin, Daniel M. ....Washington, DC
Krainin, Harold L. ....New York, NY
Krainin & McKenzie ....New York, NY
Krainin, Richard J. ....New York, NY
Krainin, Sylvia A. ....Miami, FL
Krais, William A. ....Brick, NJ
Morristown, NJ
New York, NY
Kraisinger, Jerome J. ....Bethesda, MD
Kraiterman, Roselyn S. ....Boston, MA
Kraiza, Michael A. ....New Windsor, NY
Kraizman, J. J. ....Detroit, MI
Kraizman & Kraizman ....Detroit, MI
Kraizman, Sidney ....Detroit, MI
Krajack, Dana Robert ....Columbia, SC
Krajci, Joseph R., Jr. ....New York, NY
KraJec, Phil ....Atlanta, GA
Krajec, William A. ....Springfield, IL
Krajewski, Gary J. ....Ogallala, NE
Krajewski, Henry L. ....Chicago, IL
Krajewski, J. Phillip ....Peoria, IL
Krajewski, Jeffrey Gerald ......Des Plaines, IL
Krajewski, Jeffrey S. ....Buffalo, NY
Krajewski, Joan ....Dallas, TX
Krajewski, John K. ....Akron, OH
Krajewski, Kenneth A. ....Buffalo, NY
Krajewski, Lance J. ....Modesto, CA
Krak, Kelly M. ....Garden City, NY
Krakar, Michael J. ....Orlando, FL
Krakar, Michael J., Law Office of
Orlando, FL
Krakauer, Bryan ....Chicago, IL
Krakauer, Castaldi, Bystrom & McClaugherty
Simi Valley, CA
Krakauer, Fred ....Simi Valley, CA
Krakauer, Melissa B. ....Austin, TX
Krakauer, Wendy ....Seattle, WA
Krakaur, Keith D. ....New York, NY
Krakaur, Peter R. ....San Francisco, CA
Krake, Allen A. ....Colfax, LA
Kraker, David L. ....Minneapolis, MN
Kraker, Michael D. ....Glen Ellyn, IL
Kraker, Michael J. ....Mahnomen, MN
Kraker, Randall W. ....Grand Rapids, MI
Krakman, Daniel H. ....Chicago, IL
Krako, Walter J. ....Trenton, NJ
Krakoff, David S. ....Washington, DC
Krakoff, Jere ....Pittsburgh, PA
Krakora, Joanne M. ....San Diego, CA
Krakora, Joseph E. ....Morristown, NJ
Krakow, Aaron D. ....Boston, MA
Krakow, David ....Teaneck, NJ
Krakow, Dennis W. ....Troy, MI
Krakow, Joshua ....Brooklyn, NY
Krakow & Kaplan ....Los Angeles, CA
Krakow, Lisa E. ....Los Angeles, CA
Krakow, Marvin E. ....Los Angeles, CA
Krakow, Mary M. ....Minneapolis, MN
Krakow, Robert B. ....Dallas, TX
Krakow, Robert J. ....New York, NY
Krakow, Robert M. ....Silver Spring, MD
Krakower, Bernard M. ....Miami, FL
Krakower, Daniel S. ....Rockville, MD
Krakower, Ira J. ....Stamford, CT
Krakower & Mason ....Philadelphia, PA
Krakower, Reina ....Trenton, NJ
Krakower, Robert L. ....Roseland, NJ
Krakower, Stanley R. ....Philadelphia, PA
Krakowski, M. E. ....Constableville, NY
Krakowski, Richard J. ....Chicago, IL
Krakowsky, Robert L. ....Highland Park, IL
Krakusin, Roger K. ....Jackson, MI
Kral, Clerkin, Redmond, Ryan, Perry & Girvan ....Morristown, NJ
Huntington, NY
Mineola, NY
New York, NY
Riverhead, NY
Smithtown, NY
Kral, Dennis G. ....Homewood, IL
Kral, Donald J. ....Shaker Heights, OH
Kral, Franklin I. ....Chicago, IL
Kral, Joseph A., III ....Houston, TX
Kral, Kenneth H. ....New York, NY
Kral, Marijana ....Los Angeles, CA
Kral, Timothy J. ....Irvine, CA
Kral, William G. ....Mineola, NY
New York, NY
Smithtown, NY
Kralick, Christopher P. ....Santa Ana, CA
Kralick, Richard L. ....Adrian, MI
Kralik, Gabriel P. ....Kenilworth, NJ
Kralik, John J., IV ....Los Angeles, CA
Kraljic, John P. ....Great Neck, NY
Krall, Andrew F. ....Worcester, MA
Krall, David G. ....Cincinnati, OH
Krall, Jay H. ....Augusta, ME
Krall, John B. ....Harrisonburg, VA
Staunton, VA
Winchester, VA
Krall, John T. ....Friday Harbor, WA
Krall, Mark L. ....Delray Beach, FL
Krall, Martin D. ....Washington, DC
Krall, Martin P., Jr. ....Roseville, MI
Krall, Robert J. ....Wheeling, WV
Krall, Roy A. ....Akron, OH
Krall, Shelley H. ....Encino, CA
Krall, Tony R. ....Minneapolis, MN
Kralovec, Celeste Ebers ....Chicago, IL
Kralovec, Jambois & Schwartz
Chicago, IL
Kralovec, John ....Chicago, IL
Kralovec, John B. ....Chicago, IL
Kralovec & Marquard, Chartered
Chicago, IL
Wheaton, IL
Kralovec, Michael J. ....Chicago, IL
Kralovec, William P. ....Portland, OR
Kralowec, Arthur C. ....Porterville, CA
Kralowec, Kimberly A.
San Francisco, CA
Kraly, Edward F. ....Westminster, CA
Kraly, Stacie L. ....Juneau, AK
Kram, Elbert J. ....Columbus, OH
Kram, Lorie D. ....Littleton, MA
Kram, Nancy ....Olive Branch, MS
Kram, Nancy L. ....Tavernier, FL
Kram, Paul ....Aurora, CO
Kram, Peter ....Tacoma, WA
Kram, Richard C. ....Syracuse, NY
Kram, Ronald W. ....Los Angeles, CA
Kram, Shirley W. ....New York, NY
Kram, Steven H. ....New York, NY
Kramar, Mark H. ....Leesville, LA
Kramar, Samuel J. ....Bradenton, FL
Kramar, Steven D. ....Encino, CA
Kramarsky, Stephen M. ....New York, NY
Kramarz, Kenneth Alan ....San Francisco, CA
Kramarz, Walter J. ....Detroit, MI
Krambeck, James L. ....Des Moines, IA
Krambeer, Richard J. ....Minneapolis, MN
Krambs, Robert E. ....Viroqua, WI
Krame, Evan J. ....Washington, DC
Krame, Jodi Mintzer ....Washington, DC
Kramer, Aaron J. ....Chicago, IL
Kramer, Adam Miles ....Houston, TX
Kramer, Alan H. ....Marblehead, MA
Kramer, Alan M. ....New York, NY
Kramer, Alan S. ....New York, NY
Kramer, Alan S., P.C. ....New York, NY
Kramer, Alan T. ....Fort Lauderdale, FL
Kramer, Albert D. ....Bartlesville, OK
Kramer, Albert H. ....Washington, DC
Kramer, Albert L. ....Swampscott, MA
Kramer, Alfred N. ....Aberdeen, MD
Kramer, Alfred R. ....South China, ME
Kramer, Ali, Fleck, Carothers & Hughes, P.A. ....Jupiter, FL
West Palm Beach, FL
Kramer, Alice L. C. ....Hillsboro, MO
Kramer, Allen ....New York, NY
Kramer, Amanda L. ....San Francisco, CA
Kramer, Amy M. ....Brooklyn, NY
Kramer, Amy Marie ....Overland, MO
Kramer, Amy Schimmel ....Armonk, NY
Kramer, Andrea C. ....Boston, MA
Kramer, Andrea R. ....Malvern, PA
Kramer, Andrea S. ....Chicago, IL
Kramer, Andrew B. ....Hagerstown, MD
Kramer, Andrew B. ....Camp Hill, PA
Kramer, Andrew J. ....Norristown, PA
Philadelphia, PA
Kramer, Andrew L. ....New Orleans, LA
Kramer, Andrew L. ....New York, NY
Kramer, Andrew M. ....Washington, DC
Kramer, Andrew M. ....New York, NY
Kramer, Anita S. ....Coral Springs, FL
Kramer, Anke Christina
Whitehouse Station, NJ
Kramer, Ann V. ....New York, NY
Kramer, Anne K. ....Stevenson, MD
Kramer, Arthur B. ....New York, NY
Kramer, Arthur S. ....Philadelphia, PA
Kramer & Associates ....Cleveland, OH
Kramer & Associates, P.C. ....Atlanta, GA
Kramer, Barbara H. ....Rydal, PA
Kramer, Barry ....Stamford, CT
Kramer, Barry D. ....Schenectady, NY
Kramer, Barry J. ....Palo Alto, CA
Kramer, Barry N. ....Philadelphia, PA
Kramer, Bauer E. ....Oakland, CA
Kramer, Benjamin P. ....Aurora, CO
Colorado Springs, CO
Englewood, CO
Kramer, Benjamin P., P.C. ....Aurora, CO
Colorado Springs, CO
Kramer, Bennette D. ....New York, NY
Kramer, Bernard ....Alexandria, LA
Kramer, Bernard S. ....Chicago, IL
Kramer, Beth A. ....Treasury Department,
Financial Management Service, GV
Kramer, Beth L. ....Larkspur, CA
San Francisco, CA
Kramer, Beth M. ....Washington, DC
Kramer, Beth R. ....Indianapolis, IN
Kramer, Beth R. ....New York, NY
Kramer, Betsy ....New York, NY
Kramer, Bob A. ....New York, NY
Stony Point, NY
Kramer, Boris B. ....Seattle, WA
Kramer, Brad A. ....Cambridge, MA
Kramer, Bradley A. ....Glendale, CA
Kramer, Brian J. ....Los Angeles, CA
Kramer, Brian J. ....St. Cloud, MN
Kramer, Brian S. ....Bradenton, FL
Kramer, Brownlee & Infield ....Fennimore, WI
Kramer, Bruce E. ....Washington, DC
Kramer, Bruce S. ....Memphis, TN
Kramer, C. William ....Independence, MO
Kramer, Charles B. ....New York, NY
Kramer, Charles E. ....McKinney, TX
Kramer, Charles L. ....Armonk, NY
Kramer, Charles M. ....Santa Clara, CA
Kramer, Charles R., Jr. ....Millburn, NJ
Kramer, Charles S. ....St. Louis, MO
Kramer, Charles W. ....Alexandria, VA
Kramer, Charles W. ....Waukesha, WI
Kramer, Cheryl ....Chicago, IL
Kramer, Cheryl J. ....Somerset, NJ
Kramer, Claudia D. ....Naperville, IL
Kramer, Colleen A. ....Detroit, MI
Kramer, Connie S. ....El Monte, CA
Kramer, Curt A. ....Stamford, CT
Kramer, Dan R. ....Tulsa, OK
Kramer, Daniel ....New York, NY
Kramer, Daniel J. ....Yorkville, IL
Kramer, Daniel J. ....New York, NY
Kramer, Darryl J. ....New York, NY
Kramer, David ....White Plains, NY
Kramer, David H. ....Palo Alto, CA
Kramer, David J. ....Washington, DC
Kramer, David J. ....Quincy, MA
Kramer, David J. ....Novi, MI
Kramer, David J. ....Omaha, NE
Kramer, David J., P.C. ....Novi, MI
Kramer, David M. ....Los Angeles, CA
Kramer, David V. ....Covington, KY
Kramer, Dean C. ....St. Louis, MO
Kramer, Debra ....New York, NY
Kramer & DeVries ....New York, NY
Kramer, Dillof, Tessel, Duffy & Moore
New York, NY
Kramer, Donald B. ....St. Louis, MO
Kramer, Donald W. ....Philadelphia, PA
Kramer, Donna R. ....Lake Worth, FL
Kramer, Douglas B. ....Greensboro, NC
Kramer, Douglas C. ....Milwaukee, WI
Kramer, Douglas D. ....Hailey, ID
Kramer, Douglas J. ....New York, NY
Kramer, Douglas M. ....Miami, FL
Kramer, Douglas M., P.A., Law Offices of
Miami, FL
Kramer & Durkin, P.C. ....Brattleboro, VT
Kramer, Edward B. ....Baton Rouge, LA
Kramer, Edward C. ....New York, NY
Kramer, Edward G. ....Cleveland, OH
Kramer, Edward I. ....Jericho, NY
Kramer, Edward N., III ....Petal, MS
Kramer, Eileen ....Los Angeles, CA
Kramer, Elaine F. ....Pasadena, CA
Kramer, Ellen W. ....Hackensack, NJ
Kramer, Elliot I. ....Roseland, NJ
Kramer, Elliot P. ....Southfield, MI
Kramer, Eric M. ....Uniondale, NY
Kramer, Eugene ....Los Angeles, CA
Kramer, Eugene F. ....Monona, IA
Kramer, Eugene L. ....Los Angeles, CA
Kramer, Eugene L. ....Cleveland, OH
Kramer, Evan ....Newark, NJ
Kramer, Evan N. ....Houston, TX
Kramer, Evelyn Ann ....Los Angeles, CA
Kramer, F. Richard ....Elkhart, IN
Kramer, Feingold & Castrovinci, PLLC
Commack, NY
Kramer & Figman, P.C. ....Dedham, MA
Kramer, Frank G. ....Lawrenceburg, IN
Kramer & Frank, P.C. ....Kansas City, MO
St. Charles, MO
St. Louis, MO
Kramer, Franklin D.
Department of Defense, GV
Kramer, Franklin J. ....Parsons, TN
Kramer, Fredda J. ....New York, NY
Kramer, Frederic S. ....Plandome, NY
Kramer, Frederick C. ....Marco Island, FL
Kramer, Frederick J. ....Farmingdale, NY
Kramer, Frederick W., III ....Savannah, GA
Kramer, Fredric E. ....Cleveland, OH
Kramer, G. Alan ....Houston, TX
Kramer, Gary M. ....Denver, CO
Kramer, Gary P. ....Hillsboro, MO
Kramer, George A. ....Bethesda, MD
Kramer, George P. ....New York, NY
Kramer, George R. ....Washington, DC
Kramer, Georgia D. ....White Plains, NY
Kramer, Gerald L. ....Arlington Heights, IL
Kramer, Gerard C. ....Harrisburg, PA
Kramer, Gerson B. ....Washington, DC
Kramer, Gilbert ....Pikesville, MD
Kramer, Gilbert, P.A. ....Pikesville, MD
Kramer, Gilda L. ....Philadelphia, PA
Kramer & Golden, P.A. ....North Miami, FL
Kramer & Goldwasser ....Los Angeles, CA
Kramer & Gorney, Chartered
Oxon Hill, MD
Upper Marlboro, MD
Kramer, Green, Zuckerman, Kahn & Greene, P.A. ....Hollywood, FL
Kramer, Gregory P. ....Floral Park, NY
Kramer, H. Henry ....Fort Mitchell, KY
Kramer, Henry E. ....Charleston, IL
Kramer, Herbert ....West Orange, NJ
Kramer, Herbert ....Brooklyn, NY
Kramer, Herbert ....Hauppauge, NY
Kramer, Herbert ....New York, NY
Kramer, Herbert J. ....Cleveland, OH
Kramer, Herbert L. ....Virginia Beach, VA
Kramer, Hillary ....Burlington, VT
Kramer, Howard A. ....Raleigh, NC
Kramer, Howard L. ....Washington, DC
Kramer, Ian L. ....Los Angeles, CA
Kramer, Ilene B. ....San Antonio, TX
Kramer, Irving ....Santa Rosa, CA
Kramer, Irwin R. ....Owings Mills, MD
Kramer, Ivan ....Cleveland, OH
Kramer, J. Devitt ....Cleveland, OH
Kramer, J. Scott ....Philadelphia, PA
Kramer, Jack A. ....Merrillville, IN
Kramer, Jack F., (P.C.) ....New York, NY
Kramer, Jackson G. ....Knoxville, TN
Kramer, James L. ....Fort Dodge, IA
Kramer, James M. ....Oak Brook, IL
Kramer, James N. ....San Francisco, CA
Kramer, James R. ....Alabaster, AL
Kramer, James R. ....Tampa, FL

Kramer, Jay D. ... New York, NY
Kramer, Jay S. ... Phoenix, AZ
Kramer, Jeffrey A. ... Roseland, NJ
Kramer, Jeffrey D. ... Bay Harbor Islands, FL
Kramer, Jeffrey G. ... Newark, NJ
Kramer, Jeffrey J. ... St. Louis, MO
Kramer, Jeffrey M. ... Brooklyn, NY
Kramer, Jeffrey N. ... Mansfield, OH
Kramer, Jeffrey S. ... Irvine, CA
Kramer, Jeffrey S. ... Miami, FL
Kramer, Jeffrey W. ... Los Angeles, CA
Kramer, Jennifer ... Marietta, GA
Kramer, Jennifer A. ... Seattle, WA
Kramer, Jeremy J. ... Chicago, IL
Kramer, Jeremy T. ... Hopkins, MN
Kramer, Jerome F. ... Seminole, FL
Kramer, Jill S. ... Orange, CA
Kramer, Joanne H. ... Owings Mills, MD
Kramer, Joel A. ... Laurel, MD
Kramer, John ... Sacramento, CA
Kramer, John A. ... Madison, WI
Kramer, John B. ... Belleville, IL
Kramer, John C. ... Toledo, OH
Kramer, John E. ... Treasury Department, Internal Revenue Service, GV
Kramer, John F. ... Cleveland, OH
Kramer, John M. ... Chicago, IL
Kramer, John N. ... Fennimore, WI
Kramer, John N., Jr. ... New York, NY
Kramer, John R. ... New Orleans, LA
Kramer, John R., II ... Department of Justice, Antitrust Division, GV
Kramer, John T. ... Minneapolis, MN
Kramer, Joseph R. ... Detroit, MI
Kramer, Joyce ... St. Louis, MO
Kramer, Joyce L. ... New York, NY
Kramer, Judith ... Newark, NJ
Kramer, Judith E. ... Department of Labor, Office of the Solicitor, GV
Kramer, Judith T. ... New York, NY
Kramer, Judy ... New York, NY
Kramer, Julie A. ... Oklahoma City, OK
Kramer, Karen ... Ventura, CA
Kramer, Karen ... Washington, DC
Kramer, Karen W. ... Washington, DC
Kramer, Karin ... San Francisco, CA
Kramer, Karl J. ... Palo Alto, CA
Kramer & Kaslow, P.C. ... Los Angeles, CA
Kramer, Katherine ... Los Angeles, CA
Kramer, Kathleen M. ... Philadelphia, PA
Kramer, Kelly B. ... Washington, DC
Kramer, Kenneth A. ... Hayward, CA
Kramer, Kenneth B. ... United States Court Of Veterans Appeals, GV
Kramer, Kenneth B. ... Wichita Falls, TX
Kramer, Kenneth E. ... Floral Park, NY
Kramer, Kenneth J. ... Austin, TX
Kramer, Kenneth M. ... New York, NY
Kramer, Kenneth N. ... Mount Clemens, MI
Kramer, Kenneth S. ... Irvine, CA
Kramer, Kenneth S. ... Denver, CO
Kramer, Kenneth S., (P.C.) ... Washington, DC
Kramer & Kenyon ... Binghamton, NY
Kramer, Kim Michelle ... Environmental Protection Agency, Program Office Attorneys, GV
Kramer, Kimberly A. ... Bay City, MI
Kramer & Kramer ... Los Angeles, CA
Santa Monica, CA
Kramer & Kramer ... Newark, NJ
Kramer & Kramer ... New York, NY
Kramer, Kristine L. ... Chicago, IL
Kramer, Kurt E. ... Haddonfield, NJ
Philadelphia, PA
Kramer, Lawrence J. ... Fort Washington, PA
Kramer, Lawrence M. ... Silver Spring, MD
Kramer, Lawrence M. ... New York, NY
Kramer, Lee H. ... Treasury Department, Office of Regulations and Rulings, GV
Kramer, Lee S. ... Phoenix, AZ
Kramer, Lenore ... New York, NY
Kramer, Leonard G. ... Islip, NY
Kramer, Leonard S. ... New York, NY
Kramer, Leroy ... New York, NY
Kramer, LeRoy, III ... Harbor Springs, MI
Kramer, Leslie J. ... Midland, TX
Kramer, Leslie P. ... Denver, CO
Kramer, Letha S. ... Indianapolis, IN
Kramer Levin Naftalis & Frankel LLP
New York, NY
Kramer, Linda C., Law Offices of
Los Altos, CA
Kramer, Linda Cecchin ... Chicago, IL
Kramer, Linzie E. ... Citrus Heights, CA
Kramer, Lori ... New York, NY
Kramer, Louis ... Brooklyn, NY
Kramer, Lynne Adair ... Commack, NY
Kramer, Lynne Adair, Law Offices of
Commack, NY
Kramer, Lynne P. ... Edison, NJ
Nutley, NJ
Kramer, Marc B. ... Roseland, NJ
Kramer, Marc L. ... Chicago, IL
Kramer, Marc L., Ltd. ... Chicago, IL
Kramer, Marc S. ... St. Louis, MO
Kramer, Marc Z. ... New York, NY
Kramer, Marie Handrich
Fort Washington, PA
Kramer, Mark ... Portland, OR
Kramer, Mark D. ... Santa Monica, CA
Kramer, Mark R. ... Brookfield, WI
Kramer, Martin R. ... Brooklyn, NY
Kramer, Martynetz & Verbesey
New York, NY
Kramer, Marvin E. ... Garden City, NY
Kramer, Mary Beth ... Woodbury, NJ
Kramer, Mary Louise ... Richmond, VA
Kramer, Mary Morton ... Baltimore, MD
Kramer, Matthew I. ... New York, NY
Kramer Mellen, P.C. ... Bloomfield Hills, MI
Kramer, Melody A. ... Lincoln, NE
Kramer, Merrill L., (P.C.)
Washington, DC
Kramer, Meyer ... Brooklyn, NY
Kramer, Michael A. ... Los Angeles, CA
Kramer, Michael A. ... St. Louis, MO
Kramer, Michael A. ... White Plains, NY
Kramer, Michael C. ... Fairbanks, AK
Kramer, Michael D. ... Kankakee, IL
Kramer, Michael E. ... Winnsboro, LA
Kramer, Michael J. ... Denver, CO
Kramer, Michael J. ... Marietta, GA
Kramer, Michael L. ... Portland, OR
Kramer, Michael M. ... Dedham, MA
Kramer, Michael R. ... Bloomfield Hills, MI
Kramer, Milton D. ... Flushing, NY
Kramer, Milton E. ... New York, NY
Kramer, Milton S. ... Newark, NJ
Kramer, Mitchell A., & Associates
Philadelphia, PA
Kramer, Mitchell A., & Associates
Rydal, PA
Kramer, Morris J. ... New York, NY
Kramer, Morris L. ... New York, NY
Kramer, Morton P. ... Hazlet, NJ
Kramer and Murray, P.C.
Mount Clemens, MI
Kramer, Myron N. ... Atlanta, GA
Kramer, Nancy W. ... Chagrin Falls, OH
Kramer, Nat ... San Anselmo, CA
Kramer, Nathaniel D. ... Tarrytown, NY
Kramer, Neil S. ... New York, NY
Kramer, Noel Anketell ... Washington, DC
Kramer, Nordling & Nordling, LLC
Hugoton, KS
Kramer, Oswald I. ... Burlington, VT
Kramer, Pamela O. ... Deerfield, IL
Kramer, Patricia ... Gold River, CA
Kramer, Paul ... Syosset, NY
Kramer, Paul A. ... Boston, MA
Kramer, Paul A., Jr. ... Woodland, CA
Kramer, Paul D. ... Newport Beach, CA
Kramer, Paul D. ... Bloomfield Hills, MI
Detroit, MI
Kramer, Paul R. ... Baltimore, MD
Kramer, Paul R. ... Mount Holly, NJ
Kramer, Paul R. ... Stroudsburg, PA
Kramer, Paul R., P.A. ... Baltimore, MD
Kramer, Peter L. ... Lake Success, NY
Kramer, Peter M., (P.A.) ... Miami, FL
Kramer, Philip A. ... Los Angeles, CA
Kramer, Philip J. ... Binghamton, NY
Kramer, Phillip A. ... St. Louis, MO
Kramer, Prudence Willett ... St. Louis, MO
Kramer, R. Brian ... Los Angeles, CA
Venice, CA
Kramer, Randall H. ... Seattle, WA
Kramer, Randall J. ... Des Moines, IA
Kramer, Randolph J.
Altamonte Springs, FL
Kramer, Randolph J., P.A.
Altamonte Springs, FL
Daytona Beach, FL
Orlando, FL
Kramer, Randy ... Norwalk, CA
Kramer, Randy, A Law Corporation
Norwalk, CA
Kramer and Rassner, P.A. ... Miami, FL
Kramer, Raymond E. ... New York, NY
Kramer, Raymond E., III
West Palm Beach, FL
Kramer, Rayson, Leake, Rodgers & Morgan, LLP ... Knoxville, TN
Maryville, TN
Oak Ridge, TN
Kramer, Reginald S. ... Akron, OH
Kramer, Richard A. ... San Francisco, CA
Kramer, Richard A. ... Oxon Hill, MD
Kramer, Richard B. ... Springfield, MA
Kramer, Richard P. ... Flushing, NY
Kramer, R. K. ... Lake Worth, FL
Kramer, Robert ... Palo Alto, CA
Kramer, Robert A. ... Pensacola, FL
Kramer, Robert A. ... Houston, TX
Kramer, Robert A., P.A. ... Pensacola, FL
Kramer, Robert F. ... Plainfield, IL
Kramer, Robert J. ... Phoenix, AZ
Kramer, Robert L. ... Palm Springs, CA
Kramer, Robert L. ... Naperville, IL
Kramer, Robert L. ... Trenton, NJ
Bensalem, PA
Kramer, Robert M. ... Hollywood, FL
Kramer, Robert M. ... King Of Prussia, PA
Kramer, Robert M., & Associates, P.C.
King Of Prussia, PA
Kramer, Robert S. ... Stuart, FL
Kramer, Robert S. ... Elgin, IL
Kramer, Robert S., P.C. ... Elgin, IL
Kramer, Roberta J. ... Woodland Hills, CA
Kramer, Robin A. ... Kansas City, MO
Kramer, Roger L. ... St. Paul, MN
Kramer, Roger S. ... Cleveland, OH
Kramer, Ron J. ... Salt Lake City, UT
Kramer, Rona E. ... Silver Spring, MD
Kramer, Ronald A. ... Worthington, OH
Kramer, Ronald J. ... Chicago, IL
Kramer, Ronald S. ... Los Gatos, CA
Kramer, Ross E. ... Minneapolis, MN
Kramer, S. Michele ... Shelbyville, IN
Kramer, Samuel E. ... New York, NY
Kramer, Samuel G. ... Chicago, IL
Kramer, Samuel L. ... Elma, IA
Kramer, Samuel R. ... New York, NY
Kramer, Sanford H. ... North Miami, FL
Kramer, Saul G. ... New York, NY
Kramer, Scott ... Jupiter, FL
Kramer, Scott ... Memphis, TN
Kramer, Scott A. ... Washington, DC
Kramer, Scott H. ... North Miami, FL
Kramer, Seth Daniel ... Los Angeles, CA
Kramer, Sewell, Sopko & Levenstein, P.A.
Stuart, FL
Kramer, Shane ... San Luis Obispo, CA
Kramer, Sharon G. ... Chicago, IL
Kramer, Shelley A. ... San Francisco, CA
Kramer & Shulman ... New York, NY
Kramer, Sidney ... East Greenwich, RI
Kramer, Sidney B. ... Westport, CT
Kramer, Sidney I. ... Boston, MA
Kramer & Smiles, P.C. ... Naperville, IL
Kramer, Stacey B.
Securities and Exchange Commission, Division of Corporation Finance, GV
Kramer, Stacy J. ... Irvine, CA
Kramer, Stanley R. ... New York, NY
Kramer, Stephen D. ... New York, NY
Kramer, Stephen L. ... Miami, FL
Kramer, Stephen P. ... New York, NY
Kramer, Stephen R. ... Chicago, IL
Kramer, Stephen W. ... Los Angeles, CA
Kramer, Steven ... Brooklyn, NY
Kramer, Steven B. ... Department of Justice, Antitrust Division, GV
Kramer, Steven E. ... Kingsport, TN
Kramer, Steven M. ... Washington, DC
Kramer, Steven M., & Associates
Beverly Hills, CA
Wayne, NJ
New York, NY
Kramer, Steven O. ... Costa Mesa, CA
Kramer, Steven P. ... Phoenix, AZ
Kramer, Steven R. ... White Plains, NY
Kramer, Susan D. ... Oakland, CA
Kramer, Susan W. ... Atlanta, GA
Kramer, Susan Werner ... Atlanta, GA
Kramer, Susanna M.
Fort Lauderdale, FL
Kramer, Susannah W. ... White Plains, NY
Kramer, Suzanne R. ... Whittier, CA
Kramer, Sybil B. ... Caldwell, NJ
Kramer, Talbot B., Jr. ... Cherry Hill, NJ
Kramer, Terry L. ... Chicago, IL
Kramer, Terry S. ... Albuquerque, NM
Kramer, Theodore C., Sr. ... Brattleboro, VT
Kramer, Theodore D. ... Arlington, VA
Kramer, Thomas E. ... St. Cloud, MN
Kramer, Thomas G. ... Granite Falls, MN
Kramer, Thomas G. ... Fairborn, OH
Kramer, Thomas I. ... Portland, OR
Kramer, Thomas J. ... Port Huron, MI
Kramer, Thomas P. ... Marshfield, MA
Kramer, Thomas W. ... Merrillville, IN
Kramer, Timothy C. ... Wichita Falls, TX
Kramer, Timothy E. ... Woonsocket, RI
Kramer, Timothy J. ... Rock Valley, IA
Kramer, Timothy J. ... Detroit, MI
Kramer, Tracy L. ... Miami, FL
Kramer, Trina Lynn ... Tallahassee, FL
Kramer, Valerie L. ... Tustin, CA
Kramer, Victor H. ... Washington, DC
Kramer, Vincent R., Jr. ... Livingston, NJ
Kramer, Walter J. ... St. Louis, MO
Kramer, Wayne R. ... Knoxville, TN
Kramer, Wendy E. ... New York, NY
Kramer, Wendy W. ... Morro Bay, CA
Kramer, Wendy W. ... Santa Monica, CA
Kramer, William ... Blue Bell, PA
Kramer, William A. ... Dallas, TX
Kramer, William D. ... Washington, DC
Kramer, William D., (P.A.) ... Naples, FL
Kramer, William J. ... San Francisco, CA
Kramer, William J. ... Chicago, IL
Kramer, William K. ... Los Angeles, CA
Kramer, William S. ... Boca Raton, FL
Kramer, William W. ... Alexandria, VA
Kramer, Wm. A., II ... Jupiter, FL
Kramer, Wm. J. ... Brooklyn, NY
Kramer, Yale ... Des Moines, IA
Kramerich, Leslie B. ... Washington, DC
Kramer-Wilt, James L. ... Treasury Department, Bureau of the Public Debt, GV
Kramish, Marc E. ... Miami, FL
Kramlich, Joan L. ... Kalamazoo, MI
Kramm, Deborah L. ... Chicago, IL
Kramm, John D. ... Minneapolis, MN
Krammer, Marlene G. ... New York, NY
Krammer, Reinhold F. ... Chicago, IL
Kramnick, Rebecca K. ... New York, NY
Kramoltz, N. Mark ... Scottsdale, AZ
Kramon & Graham, P.A.
Washington, DC
Baltimore, MD
Towson, MD
Kramon, James M. ... Baltimore, MD
Kramp, Mark L. ... Bloomington, IL
Krampf, John E. ... Philadelphia, PA
Krampien, Geo. V. ... Sun City, AZ
Krampitz, Thomas L. ... Austin, TX
Krampner, Fuller and Hambrick, L.L.C.
Casper, WY
Krampner, Michael J. ... Casper, WY
Krampner, Robert ... New York, NY
Krams, Alan G. ... New York, NY
Kramsky, Elliott N., Law Offices of
Los Angeles, CA
Kramsky, Elliott N., Law Offices of
Woodland Hills, CA
Kramsky, Les R. ... Staten Island, NY
Kramzyk, Henry S. ... Chicago, IL
Krancer, Michael L. ... Cherry Hill, NJ
Philadelphia, PA
Kranczer, Lori R. ... New York, NY
Kranda, Todd D. ... Mandan, ND
Krandel, Craig S. ... Woodstock, IL
Krandle & Mier, P.C. ... Livonia, MI
Krandle, Richard F. ... Livonia, MI
Krane, Daniel W. ... Philadelphia, PA
Krane, Deborah Ann ... Los Angeles, CA
Krane, Hilary K. ... San Francisco, CA
Krane, Howard G., (P.C.) ... Chicago, IL
Krane, Marie Campbell ... Chicago, IL
Krane, Melodie Elizabeth ... Austin, TX
Krane, Peter J. ... St. Louis, MO
Krane, Ralph J. ... Cleveland, OH
Krane, Samuel ... Encino, CA
Krane & Smith ... Encino, CA
Krane, Steven C. ... New York, NY
Kraner, Lisa Greenman ... St. Louis, MO
Kraner, Neil W. ... East Granby, CT
Kraner, Richard F. ... St. Louis, MO
Kraner, Richard L. ... White Plains, NY
Kranert, Lawrence F., Jr., (P.A.)
Chattahoochee, FL
Krangle, David B. ... New York, NY
Kranich, Ashley H. ... State College, PA
Kranich, Richard D. ... New York, NY
Kranidas, Thomas T. ... Littleton, CO
Kraniotis, Patricia ... Department of Commerce, National Oceanic and Atmospheric Administration, GV
Kranis, David J. ... New York, NY
Kranis, Jay A. ... New York, NY
Kranitz, Ephraim P. ... Los Angeles, CA
Kranitz, Ephraim P., P.C. ... Los Angeles, CA
Kranitz, Hugh D. ... St. Joseph, MO
Kranitz & Kranitz, P.C. ... St. Joseph, MO
Kranitz, Lisa E. ... Santa Monica, CA
Kranitz, Michael ... Columbus, OH
Kranitz, Michael E. ... Phoenix, AZ
Kranitz, Richard A. ... Grafton, WI
Kranitz, Theodore M. ... St. Joseph, MO
Kranjac, Mario M. ... New York, NY
Kranker, Gary S. ... Long Beach, CA
Kranovich, Thomas E. ... Lake Oswego, OR
Krans, Allan B. ... Dover, NH
Krans, Hamilton R., Jr. ... Dover, NH
Krans, Heather E. ... Concord, NH
Krans and Krans ... Dover, NH
Kransdorf, Andrew P. ... New York, NY
Kransdorf, Ronald J. ... Boston, MA
Kransdorf, William B., Law Offices of
Oakland, CA
Kranseler, Lawrence M. ... Pawtucket, RI
Kranseler, Robert S. ... Placentia, CA
Kransen, Harry J. ... Skokie, IL
Kranson, Gerald I. ... Roseland, NJ
Kranson, Michael ... Detroit, MI
Kranstuber, Charles W. ... Columbus, OH
Krant, Elisabeth Bloeme ... Visalia, CA
Krantz, Alvin C. ... Philadelphia, PA
Krantz & Berman LLP ... New York, NY
Krantz, Brett S. ... Cleveland, OH
Krantz, Brian D. ... Los Angeles, CA
Krantz, Bryan D. ... Kansas City, MO
Krantz, Byron S. ... Cleveland, OH
Krantz, Clarence A. ... Kansas City, MO
Krantz & Cohen, P.A. ... Somers Point, NJ
Krantz, David S. ... Los Angeles, CA
Krantz, Edw. G. ... Marion, IL
Krantz, Howard I. ... Lake George, NY
Krantz, Howard J. ... Cleveland, OH
Krantz, Jason G. ... New York, NY
Krantz, Jeremy J. ... New York, NY
Krantz, JoAnn Jacob ... Boonville, IN
Krantz, Kevin R. ... Chicago, IL
Krantz, Larry H. ... Hackensack, NJ
New York, NY
New York, NY
Krantz, Marc C. ... Cleveland, OH
Krantz, Michele L.S. ... Cleveland, OH
Krantz & Phillips, LLP ... New York, NY
Krantz, Powers & Friedman, P.L.L.
Cleveland, OH
Krantz, Randy C. ... Bedford, VA
Krantz, Richard A. ... Stamford, CT
Krantz, Samuel ... Somers Point, NJ
Krantz, Sheldon ... Washington, DC
Krantz, Stefan M. ... Washington, DC
Krantz, Steve ... Brooklyn, NY
Krantz, Steven L. ... Commack, NY
Krantz, Stuart H. ... Parkland, FL
Krantz, Timothy J. ... Brook Park, OH
Krantzow, Lee D. ... Teaneck, NJ
Kranwinkle, C. Douglas ... Los Angeles, CA
New York, NY
Kranyak, John T. ... Columbus, OH
Kranyak, Joseph J. ... Arlington, TX
Kranz, Alexander J. ... Stuart, FL
Kranz, Allen M. ... Hauppauge, NY
Kranz, Beverly Babcock ... Minneapolis, MN
Kranz, Charles ... Phoenix, AZ
Kranz, Charles A. ... Darlington, WI
Kranz, Denise Mortner ... New York, NY
Kranz, Elizabeth Schulman ... Merrick, NY
Kranz, Frederick D. ... Naples, FL
Kranz, Frederick H. ... Los Angeles, CA
Kranz, Geoffrey S. ... Knoxville, TN
Kranz, Jonathon L. ... New York, NY
Kranz, Kenneth D. ... Tallahassee, FL
Kranz, Kenneth H. ... New York, NY
Kranz, Lisa C. Barton ... Washington, DC
Kranz, Margaret D. ... New York, NY
Kranz, Michael T. ... West Palm Beach, FL
Kranz, Michelle L. ... Toledo, OH
Kranz, Paul ... Berkeley, CA
Kranz, Ronald E. ... Sterling Heights, MI
Kranz, Shelley L. ... Lansing, MI
Kranz, Stephen M. ... Westminster, MD
Kranz, Stephen P. ... Department of Justice, Tax Division, GV
Kranz, Thomas F. ... Beverly Hills, CA

Kranz, William C. ....Lakeport, CA
Kranz, William J. ....South St. Paul, MN
Kranz, Worthy B. ....Sullivan, IL
Kranzberg, Jason A. ....New York, NY
Kranzberg, Joshua A.
Department of the Army,
Army Materiel Command, GV
Kranzdorf, Jeffrey P. ....Tarzana, CA
Kranzdorf, Norman M. ....Conshohocken, PA
Kranzel, Isador ....Philadelphia, PA
Kranzlein, Harvard H., Jr. ....Dalton, GA
Kranzler, Richard M. ....Lakewood, CO
Kranzley, Evan ....Pottstown, PA
Kranzow, Ronald R. ....Plano, TX
Kranzthor, Bryce A. ....San Francisco, CA
Krapes, Morris ....Hicksville, NY
Krapf, Alan F. ....Danville, IL
Krapf, Daniel H. ....Wilmington, DE
Krapf, Robert J. ....Wilmington, DE
Krapf, Stephanie E. ....San Francisco, CA
Krapf, Wiley E., Jr. ....Chicago, IL
Krapf Greenhoe, Gerhild ....Iowa City, IA
Krapfl, Terry ....Des Moines, IA
Krapohl, Warren F. ....Levering, MI
Krappman, Andrew J., Jr. ....Pasadena, CA
Krasberg, Lisa J. ....Chicago, IL
Krase, Brian ....Philadelphia, PA
Krase, Morton ....Philadelphia, PA
Krase, Robert ....Porterville, CA
Kraselsky, Robert L. ....Albany, GA
Kraselsky, Robert L., P.C. ....Albany, GA
Krashes, Bertram P. ....Spring Valley, NY
Krashes, Ross, Gess & Brown
Spring Valley, NY
Krashin, Jeffrey B. ....Alexandria, VA
Krashna, David ....Oakland, CA
Krasicky, Eugene ....Lansing, MI
Krasik, Carl ....Pittsburgh, PA
Krasik, Curtis B. ....Pittsburgh, PA
Krasik, Elaine B. ....Pittsburgh, PA
Krasik, Margaret K. ....Pittsburgh, PA
Krasik, Rawley F. ....Pittsburgh, PA
Krasik, Steven L. ....Salem, OR
Krasilovsky, M. William ....New York, NY
Krasinski, Leon G.
Upper Saddle River, NJ
Krasinski, Monica G. ....East Hartford, CT
Krasity, Kenneth A. ....Bingham Farms, MI
Krask, Sylvia Jo ....Burbank, CA
Kraska, David T. ....San Francisco, CA
Kraska, James ....Sautee-Nacoochee, GA
Kraske, Anna N. ....New York, NY
Kraske, Paul S. ....New York, NY
Krasker, Bruce ....Boston, MA
Krasker, Gerald ....Boston, MA
Krasker, Paul Andrew
West Palm Beach, FL
Kraskin, Stephen G. ....Washington, DC
Krasle, Eric K. ....Athens, GA
Kraslow, Larry S. ....Miami, FL
Kraslow, Richard A. ....Mineola, NY
Kraslow, Richard A., P.C. ....Mineola, NY
Kraslow, Walter ....Boca Raton, FL
Krasna, Gary M. ....Boca Raton, FL
Krasna, Gary M., P.A. ....Boca Raton, FL
Krasnauskas, Lynne H. ....Plainville, MA
Krasne, Albert S. ....Richfield, OH
Krasne, Hale Ansberry ....Washington, DC
Krasne, James L. ....Beverly Hills, CA
Krasne, Robert M. ....Washington, DC
Krasnecki, Marrigan S. ....Chelmsford, MA
Krasnegor, Daniel G. ....Washington, DC
Krasner, Alissa Joy ....Brooklyn, NY
Krasner, Amy R. ....Austin, TX
Krasner, Bennett David ....Atlantic Beach, NY
Krasner, Bonnie Ellen ....Atlantic Beach, NY
Krasner, Daniel J. ....Los Angeles, CA
Krasner, Daniel W. ....New York, NY
Krasner, Dennis R. ....New York, NY
Krasner, Emmanuel P. ....Farmington, NH
Krasner, Fred ....Ashland, OR
Krasner, Harvey I. ....New York, NY
Krasner & Iaulus ....New York, NY
Krasner, Jay R. ....Newton, MA
Krasner, Jeffrey M. ....Sycamore, IL
Krasner, Jeffrey M. ....New York, NY
Krasner, Joshua M. ....Raleigh, NC
Krasner, Kenneth A. ....New York, NY
Krasner, Lawrence S. ....Philadelphia, PA
Krasner, Mark A. ....La Jolla, CA
Krasner, Mary ....Wheaton, IL
Krasner & Restrepo ....Philadelphia, PA
Krasner, Steven P. ....New York, NY
Krasner, Tina A. ....Raleigh, NC
Krasner, Wendy L. ....Washington, DC
Krasney, Keith L. ....New York, NY
Krasney, Reginald A. ....Wayne, PA
Krasney, Robert A. ....San Bernardino, CA
Krasney, Robert L. ....Los Angeles, CA
Krasniewicz, William Ike ....Boulder, CO
Krasniewski, Walter J. ....Oak Harbor, OH
Krasno, Isadore E. ....Pottsville, PA
Krasno, Krasno & Quinn ....Pottsville, PA
Krasno, Lester ....Pottsville, PA
Krasnoff, Brad ....Los Angeles, CA
Krasnoff, Helene T. ....Washington, DC
Krasnogor, Julie B. ....Stamford, CT
New York, NY
Krasnogor & Krasnogor ....New York, NY
Krasnogor, Norine F., Law Offices of
Stamford, CT
New York, NY
Krasnoo, James B., Law Offices of
Andover, MA
Krasnor, William S. ....New York, NY
Krasnove, Edward ....Torrance, CA
Krasnow, Beth Dworken ....Cleveland, OH
Krasnow, C. Harold ....Brookline, MA
Krasnow, David M. ....Raleigh, NC
Krasnow, Donald B. ....New York, NY
Krasnow, Edward ....Bridgeport, CT
Krasnow, Eileen Kramer ....Bridgeport, CT
Krasnow, Erwin G. ....Washington, DC
Krasnow, Frances H. ....Chicago, IL
Krasnow, Harriet ....New York, NY
Krasnow, Henry C. ....Chicago, IL
Krasnow, Jeffrey H. ....Roanoke, VA
Krasnow, Jeffrey H., & Associates, P.C.
Roanoke, VA
Krasnow, Jennifer S. ....Bridgeport, CT
Krasnow, Joel I. ....New York, NY
Krasnow, Jordan P. ....Boston, MA
Krasnow, Keller, Boris & Hughes, P.C.
Boston, MA
Framingham, MA
Krasnow, Lauren G. ....New York, NY
Krasnow, Lawrence L. ....Framingham, MA
Krasnow, Marc A. ....Bridgeport, CT
Krasnow, Melissa J. ....Chicago, IL
Krasnow, Michael E. ....Oklahoma City, OK
Krasnow, Michael E., A Professional
Corporation ....Oklahoma City, OK
Krasnow, Richard P. ....New York, NY
Krasnow, Robert L. ....New York, NY
Krasnow, Ronald S. ....Pittsburgh, PA
Krasnow Sanberg Cornblath & Hobbs
Chicago, IL
Krasnow, Willard ....Boston, MA
Providence, RI
Krasnowiecki, Jan Z. ....Philadelphia, PA
Krasny and Dettmer ....Melbourne, FL
Krasny, James R. ....Chicago, IL
Krasny, Kenneth M. ....Houston, TX
Krasny, Leslie T. ....San Francisco, CA
Krasny, Marvin ....Philadelphia, PA
Krasny, Myron S. (Mike), (P.A.)
Melbourne, FL
Krasny, Nicole E. ....Los Angeles, CA
Krasny, Paula J. ....Chicago, IL
Krasny, Philip ....Chicago, IL
Krasny, Scott ....Melbourne, FL
Krasny, Scott A. ....Trenton, NJ
Krason, Stephen M. ....Steubenville, OH
Krasovec, Frank C., Jr. ....Cleveland, OH
Krasovec, Jay E. ....Akron, OH
Krasovec, Joseph J., III ....Chicago, IL
Krasow, Garlick & Hadley, LLC
Hartford, CT
Krasow, Herbert A. ....Hartford, CT
Krass, Allen M. ....Ann Arbor, MI
Birmingham, MI
Krass, Barrett L. ....Avon, CT
Krass, Caroline D. ....Department of Justice,
Office of Legal Counsel, GV
Krass, Errol A. ....Department of Commerce,
Patent and Trademark Office, GV
Krass, Karl Joseph ....Philadelphia, PA
Krass & Lund, P.C. ....New York, NY
Krass, Marc S. ....Cincinnati, OH
Krass Monroe, P.A. ....Bloomington, MN
Minneapolis, MN
Shakopee, MN
Krass, Norbert C. ....Cincinnati, OH
Krass, Phillip R. ....Minneapolis, MN
Krass, Stephen J. ....New York, NY
Krassa, Gerald F. ....Boulder, CO
Krassa, Madsen & Miller, LLC ....Boulder, CO
Pueblo, CO
Krassa, Robert F. T., (P.C.) ....Boulder, CO
Pueblo, CO
Krassas, Ariadne M. ....Woodbury, NY
Krassen, Glenn S. ....Cleveland, OH
Krassenstein & Associates, P.C.
Wexford, PA
Krassenstein, Jonathan T. ....Wexford, PA
Krassenstein, Juliet Boniface ....Wexford, PA
Krassin, Don R. ....Wahpeton, ND
Krassner, Albert ....New York, NY
Krassner, Amy L. ....New York, NY
Krassner, Cherry ....White Plains, NY
Krassner, David M. ....North Haven, CT
Krassner, Mark ....New York, NY
Krassy, Joseph G. ....New York, NY
Krastin, Karl ....Boca Raton, FL
Kratch, Lee Paul ....Minneapolis, MN
Kratchman, D. Michael ....Southfield, MI
Kratchman, Paul M. ....Washington, DC
Kratchmer & Kloberdanz ....Osage, IA
Kratchmer, Vernon E. ....Osage, IA
Kratcoski, Peter C. ....Kent, OH
Kratenstein, William C. ....New York, NY
Krathen, David, A Prof. Assoc., The Law
Offices of ....Fort Lauderdale, FL
Krathen, David H. ....Fort Lauderdale, FL
Krathwohl, Eric J. ....Boston, MA
Kratina & Ellis ....Omaha, NE
Kratina, Mark D. ....Omaha, NE
Kratka, Joshua R. ....Boston, MA
Kratka, Rebecca J. ....Roxbury, MA
Kratochvil, Gerald L. ....Omaha, NE
Kratochvil, L. Glen ....Houston, TX
Kratochvil, Otto ....Kerrville, TX
Kratochvil & Powell ....Houston, TX
Kratochvil, Thomas J. ....New York, NY
Kratochvil, Wm. Mark ....Brookings, SD
Kratochwill, James P. ....Basking Ridge, NJ
Kratochwill, Lyndon L. ....Elbow Lake, MN
Kratofil, Gregory M., Jr.
Kansas City, MO
Kratofil, Gregory M., Sr. ....Kansas City, MO
Kratovil, Bonnie H. ....Charles Town, WV
Kratovil, Connie L. ....Riverdale, MD
Kratovil, Emil A., Jr. ....New York, NY
Kratovil, Frank M. ....Upper Marlboro, MD
Kratovil, James T. ....Charles Town, WV
Kratovil, Kurt L. ....Cedar Rapids, IA
Kratovil, Vicki L. ....Phoenix, AZ
Kratsa, Peter ....West Chester, PA
Kratsch, P. Steven ....Atlanta, GA
Kratt, Edward M. ....New York, NY
Kratt, Edward M., P.C. ....New York, NY
Kratt, Emil F. ....Charlotte, NC
Kratt, Emil William ....Raleigh, NC
Kratt, Jennifer I. ....Cleveland, OH
Kratt, Kimberly C. ....Madera, CA
Kratt, Peter G. ....Cleveland, OH
Krattenmaker, Charles G., Jr.
Boston, MA
Krattenmaker, Richard W. ....Marmora, NJ
Krattenmaker, Thomas G. ....Washington, DC
Kratter, David E. ....Bellevue, WA
Kratter, Leslie M. ....Hillsborough, CA
Krattli, John F. ....Los Angeles, CA
Kratus, Eugene A. ....Cleveland, OH
Kratville, Michael Burdic ....Omaha, NE
Kratz, A. Charles ....Alexandria, VA
Kratz, Barbara B. ....Omaha, NE
Kratz, Bryson M. ....Bishop, CA
Pasadena, CA
Kratz, Cynthia M. ....Rockville, MD
Kratz, D. Bruce ....New York, NY
Kratz, Dean G. ....Omaha, NE
Kratz, George F. ....Indianapolis, IN
Kratz, Jane Ann R. ....Riverhead, NY
Kratz, Janet S. ....Dallas, TX
Kratz, John E., Jr. ....Baltimore, MD
Kratz, Kathryn C. ....St. Paul, MN
Kratz, Kenneth R. ....Chilton, WI
Kratz, Kent P. ....Omaha, NE
Kratz, Millard C., Jr. ....Oklahoma City, OK
Kratz, Paul D. ....Omaha, NE
Kratz, Peter F. ....Department of Commerce,
Patent and Trademark Office, GV
Kratz, Philip L. ....Olympia, WA
Kratz, Rudy ....Chicago, IL
Kratz, Susan G. ....St. Paul, MN
Kratz, Timothy H. ....Atlanta, GA
Kratz, Timothy M. ....Denver, CO
Kratz, William G., Jr. ....Pittsburgh, PA
Kratze, David R. ....Bloomfield Hills, MI
Kratze, David R., P.C. ....Bloomfield Hills, MI
Kratzenberg, Holly Foster ....Louisville, KY
Kratzenberg & Lazzaro ....White Oak, PA
Kratzenberg, T.J. ....White Oak, PA
Kratzer, Charles S. ....Lexington, KY
Kratzer, John L., Jr. ....Wichita, KS
Kratzer, Malcolm M. ....New York, NY
Kratzer, Maria S. ....New York, NY
Kratzig, Paul G., Law Offices of
Corpus Christi, TX
Kratzke, William P. ....Memphis, TN
Kraucunas, Terry R. ....Milwaukee, WI
Krauel, Francesca Mecia ....San Diego, CA
Krauel, Roger W. ....San Diego, CA
Krauel, Thomas W. ....White Bear Lake, MN
Krauft, Conrad C. ....Fayetteville, AR
Krauja, George O. ....Tucson, AZ
Krauland, Edward J. ....Washington, DC
Krauland, Elke M. ....Washington, DC
Kraunelis, Matthew A. ....Andover, MA
Kraus, Alan E. ....Morristown, NJ
Kraus, Alan H. ....Cleveland, OH
Kraus, Amy D. ....Salt Lake City, UT
Kraus, Anna D.
Department Of Health And Human Services,
Office of the General Counsel, GV
Kraus, Anthony W. ....Baltimore, MD
Kraus, Audrey A. ....Los Angeles, CA
Kraus, Bonnie G. ....Solon, OH
Kraus, Bradley J. ....Johnsonburg, PA
Kraus, Bruce R. ....New York, NY
Kraus, Charles J. ....Charlotte, NC
Kraus, Cheryl R. ....Naples, FL
Kraus, Cheryl R., P.A. ....Naples, FL
Kraus, Christian D. ....New York, NY
Kraus, Christine M. ....Wauwatosa, WI
Kraus, Christopher E. ....Cincinnati, OH
Kraus, Colleen Young ....Chicago, IL
Kraus, Craig A. ....New York, NY
Kraus, Daniel J. ....Chicago, IL
Kraus, Daniel L. ....Chicago, IL
Kraus, David C. ....New York, NY
Kraus, David L. ....Louisville, KY
Kraus, David P. ....Los Angeles, CA
Kraus, David R. ....Harrisburg, PA
Kraus, Donna J., Law Offices of
Fairfax, VA
Kraus, Doug ....Chicago, IL
Kraus, Douglas M. ....New York, NY
Kraus, Edward ....Chicago, IL
Kraus, Edward A. ....San Jose, CA
Kraus, Edward H. ....Cleveland, OH
Kraus, Elena ....Deerfield, IL
Kraus, Eric J. ....Washington, DC
Kraus, Eric M. ....New York, NY
Kraus, Erwin H. ....Pacific Palisades, CA
Kraus, Eugene S. ....Chicago, IL
Kraus, Evan Marc ....Chicago, IL
Kraus, F. E. ....Elmont, NY
Kraus, Franklyn J. ....Glenview, IL
Kraus, Frederick H. ....Atlantic City, NJ
Kraus, F. W. Grant
National Labor Relations Board,
Office of Board Members, GV
Kraus, Gary P. ....Lafayette, LA
Kraus, Gary P. ....Jefferson City, MO
Kraus, Grace ....Elmhurst, IL
Kraus, Hans-Michael ....Atlanta, GA
Kraus, Heather Holt ....Baltimore, MD
Kraus, Heidi L. ....Washington, DC
Kraus, Helen R. ....Huntington Beach, CA
Kraus, Helen R., A Professional Law
Corporation ....Huntington Beach, CA
Kraus, Herb ....Albuquerque, NM
Kraus, Herbert ....Los Angeles, CA
Kraus, J. Mark ....Tallahassee, FL
Kraus, James A. ....Bronx, NY
Kraus, James A., Law Offices of
Temecula, CA
Kraus, James B. ....San Francisco, CA
Kraus, James D. ....Akron, OH
Kraus, James D. ....Vienna, VA
Kraus, James V. ....Morristown, NJ
Kraus, James W. ....Pittsburgh, PA
Kraus, Jason R. ....Minneapolis, MN
Kraus, Jeffrey T. ....Chicago, IL
Kraus, Jennifer Lynn ....New York, NY
Kraus, Jerome S. ....St. Louis, MO
Kraus, Jody S. ....Charlottesville, VA
Kraus, John J., Jr. ....Clinton Township, MI
Kraus, John L. ....Pittsburgh, PA
Kraus, Joseph M. ....Rutland, VT
Kraus, Joshua L. ....New York, NY
Kraus, Karen Kelly
Environmental Protection Agency,
Office of the General Counsel, GV
Kraus, Karl E. ....Bad Axe, MI
Kraus, Keith A. ....St. Louis, MO
Kraus, Keith R. ....Cleveland, OH
Kraus, Kenneth ....Washington, DC
Kraus, Kenneth A. ....Cleveland, OH
Kraus, Kenneth E. ....Chicago, IL
Kraus, Kenneth L. ....Nashville, TN
Kraus & Kraus ....Cleveland, OH
Kraus, Lawrence B. ....Washington, DC
Kraus, Lawrence E. ....Hartsdale, NY
Kraus, Lawrence M. ....Boston, MA
Kraus, Leslie J. ....Edina, MN
Kraus, Loren Homer ....Los Angeles, CA
Kraus, Marla B. ....Santa Monica, CA
Kraus, Marvin H. ....Cincinnati, OH
Kraus, Melvin ....Arlington, VA
Kraus, Michael Lewis ....Naples, FL
Kraus, Mitchell M. ....Rockville, MD
Kraus, Nanette M. ....Lawrence, KS
Kraus, Paul M. ....Toledo, OH
Kraus, Paul R. ....New Haven, CT
Kraus, Peter A. ....Dallas, TX
Kraus, Philip S. ....San Fernando, CA
Kraus, Phillip ....Palos Verdes Peninsula, CA
Kraus, Rainer K. ....Washington, DC
Kraus, Regina Duchin ....Milford, CT
Kraus, Richard C. ....East Lansing, MI
Kraus, Richard D. ....Hackensack, NJ
Kraus, Richard I. ....Pleasantville, NY
Kraus, Robert B. ....Port Chester, NY
Kraus, Robert D. ....New York, NY
New York, NY
Kraus, Robert D. ....New York, NY
Kraus, Robert G. ....Short Hills, NJ
Kraus, Robert H. ....Scotch Plains, NJ
Kraus, Robert J. ....Tarrytown, NY
Kraus, Roberta ....New York, NY
Kraus, Roberta A. ....Irvine, CA
Kraus, Roger W. ....Plano, TX
Kraus, Sallie B. ....New York, NY
Kraus, Seymour ....Southfield, MI
Kraus, Seymour, Professional Corporation
Southfield, MI
Kraus, Sherry S. ....Rochester, NY
Kraus, Stefanie S. ....New York, NY
Kraus, Stephen W. ....Washington, DC
Kraus, Steven G. ....Watchung, NJ
Kraus, Steven M. ....Los Angeles, CA
Kraus, Thomas H. ....Denver, CO
Kraus, Thomas J. ....Waseca, MN
Kraus, Thomas J. ....Cleveland, OH
Kraus, Virginia A. ....Hastings, MN
Kraus, Warren J. ....Granite City, IL
Kraus, William J. ....Cleveland, OH
Kraus, William M. ....Cleveland, OH
Kraus, William R. ....Cranford, NJ
Kraus, Allen H. ....Lebanon, PA
Krause, Amy M. ....San Francisco, CA
Krause, Andrew J. ....Naples, FL
Krause, Avrum ....Chicago, IL
Krause, Barbara ....St. Louis, MO
Krause, Barbara L. ....Ithaca, NY
Krause, Barbara L. ....Pittsburgh, PA
Krause & Baskin ....San Francisco, CA
San Rafael, CA
Krause, Bernard S. ....Oxnard, CA
Krause, Carl R. ....Rochester, NY
Krause, Carolyn H. ....Mount Prospect, IL
Krause, Charles F. ....Irvine, CA
New York, NY
Dallas, TX
Arlington, VA
Krause, Charles F., III ....Union City, NJ
Krause, Dale M. ....Iron Mountain, MI
Krause, Daniel J. ....Keshena, WI
Krause, Darcia ....Portland, OR
Krause, David E. ....Minneapolis, MN
Krause, David M. ....Miami, FL
Krause, David S. ....Mount Prospect, IL
Krause, Dawn Marie ....Cleveland, OH
Krause, Dean Luca ....San Francisco, CA
Krause, Don ....San Antonio, TX
Krause, Donald C. ....Ventura, CA
Krause, Douglas P. ....San Marino, CA
Krause, Douglas R. ....Cleveland, OH
Krause, Drew D. ....Short Hills, NJ
Krause, Dwight A., Jr. ....Fort Lauderdale, FL
Krause, Edward B. ....Asheville, NC
Mars Hill, NC
Krause, Elise M. Shebelut ....Fresno, CA
Krause, Ernest R. ....San Francisco, CA
Krause & Ferris ....Washington, DC
Annapolis, MD
Baltimore, MD
Krause, Floyd E. ....Miami, FL
Krause, Frank B. ....Ponte Vedra Beach, FL

Krebs, Robert P., Law Offices of
Bay St. Louis, MS
Biloxi, MS
Gulfport, MS
Krebs, Robert P., Law Offices of
Pascagoula, MS
Krebs, Ryan A. ....Austin, TX
Cameron, TX
Krebs, Scott T. ....Willoughby, OH
Krebs, Stephen ....Houston, TX
Krebs, Thomas G. ....Chicago, IL
Krebs, Thomas L. ....Birmingham, AL
Krebs, Thomas P. ....Chicago, IL
Krebs, Warren D. ....Indianapolis, IN
Krebs, William F. ....Washington, DC
Krebsbach, Frederich J. ....Santa Ana, CA
Krebsbach and Haik, Ltd.
Minneapolis, MN
Krebsbach, Jeffrey L. ....Alexandria, LA
Krebsbach, Theodore A. ....New York, NY
White Plains, NY
Krebsbach, Theodore A., & Associates, P.C.
New York, NY
White Plains, NY
Krebsbach, Walter T. ....Minneapolis, MN
Krebs-Markrich, Julia ....Falls Church, VA
Krech & Cole ....Oakland, CA
Krech, David H.
Federal Communications Commission,
Wireless Telecommunications Bureau, GV
Krech, David L. ....Providence, RI
Krech, Judith L. ....Bakersfield, CA
Krech, Richard Joseph ....Oakland, CA
Krechevsky, Curtis ....Stoughton, MA
Krechevsky, Robert L. ....Hartford, CT
Kreck, Kay B. ....Houston, TX
Krecke, Kathryn A. ....Tempe, AZ
Kreckel, Jennifer F. ....Rumford, ME
Kreckman, Alfred H., Jr. ....Paris, IL
Kreckman and Anderson ....Paris, IL
Kreckman, Thomas I. ....Gladwin, MI
Kreckman, Todd A. ....Birmingham, MI
Kredell, George S. ....Austin, TX
Fort Worth, TX
Houston, TX
Kredens, Kenneth A. ....Palos Heights, IL
Kreder, Brooks, Hailstone & Ludwig
Scranton, PA
Stroudsburg, PA
Wilkes-Barre, PA
Kreder, Joseph C. ....Scranton, PA
Kreditor, Eoin L. ....Los Angeles, CA
Kredo, Brian J. ....Philadelphia, PA
Kreeble, Kenneth T. ....San Bernardino, CA
Kreeck, Karen Bullock
Salt Lake City, UT
Kreegar, Richard E. ....Chesterfield, IN
Kreegar, William C. ....Anderson, IN
Kreeger, Christopher L. ....Sacramento, CA
Kreeger, David M. ....Washington, DC
Kreeger, George H. ....Marietta, GA
Kreeger, Judith L. ....Miami, FL
Kreeger, Julian H. ....Miami, FL
Kreeger, Lisa Robin ....Miami, FL
Kreeger, Margaret Ryan ....Los Angeles, CA
Kreeger, Matthew I. ....San Francisco, CA
Kreeger, Peter L. ....Potomac, MD
Kreeger, Susan L. ....New York, NY
Kreek, Louis F., Jr. ....Akron, OH
Kreel, Laura D. ....New York, NY
Kreep, Gary G. ....Escondido, CA
Krefman, Mark B. ....East Lansing, MI
Krefman, Stephen ....Benton Harbor, MI
Kregel, Ronald D. ....Mason, MI
Kreger, Brian F. ....Seattle, WA
Kreger, Brian S. ....San Francisco, CA
San Jose, CA
Kreger, Charles A. ....Conroe, TX
Kreger, Donald J. ....Chicago, IL
Kreger, Elizabeth Walsh ....Princeton, NJ
Kreger, Herbert M. ....Wayne, NJ
Kreger, Mark A. ....Chicago, IL
Kreger & McBride ....Chesapeake, VA
Kreger, Melvin J. ....North Hollywood, CA
Kreger, Melvin J., A Law Corporation
North Hollywood, CA
Kreger, Michael E. ....Anchorage, AK
Kreger, Richard L. ....Chesapeake, VA
Kreger & Stein ....Los Angeles, CA
Kreger, Stephen W. ....Greenville, SC
Kreger, Wayne S. ....Los Angeles, CA
Kreger-Grella, Cheryl L ....Garden City, NY
Kreglo, Roberta Kohn
Charlotte Amalie, St. Thomas, VI
Kreglow, Alan F., Jr. ....Fairfield, IA
Kregstein, Stephen P. ....Lakewood, CO
Krehbiel, Anne Einspanier ....Lebanon, OH
Krehbiel, Bannerman & Horn, P.A.
Albuquerque, NM
Krehbiel, Constance M. ....Stamford, CT
Krehbiel, David L. ....Westlake Village, CA
Krehbiel, Lorri ....Albuquerque, NM
Krehbiel, Phil ....Albuquerque, NM
Krehbiel, Robert J. ....St. Louis, MO
Krehbiel, Thomas R. ....San Francisco, CA
Krehbiel-Baskfield, Allison
Minneapolis, MN
Krehely, Albert T., Jr. ....Edgewood, MD
Krehely, Kimberly
Department of Commerce,
Patent and Trademark Office, GV
Kreher, Elizabeth A. ....San Francisco, CA
Kreher, Erich ....Lincroft, NJ
Kreher, Gail T., (Mr.) ....New Orleans, LA
Kreher, Julia S. ....Buffalo, NY
Krehl, Gerard S. ....Maitland, FL
Ocala, FL
Kreid, Christopher" Kit " ....Chicago, IL
Kreida, Alan N. ....Long Beach, CA
Kreider, David A. ....Lancaster, PA
Kreider, David H. ....Merrillville, IN
Kreider, David P. ....Gainesville, FL
Kreider, Gary P. ....Cincinnati, OH
Kreider, Karen E. ....Cincinnati, OH
Kreider, Kenneth P. ....Cincinnati, OH
Kreidle, Kevin Z. ....Littleton, CO
Kreidle, Renée Vigil ....Littleton, CO
Kreidler, Frank A. ....Lake Worth, FL
Kreidler, John E. ....Montrose, CO
Kreidler, Michael S. ....Minneapolis, MN
Kreidler, Robert L. ....Cincinnati, OH
Kreidman, Melvin ....New York, NY
Kreidman, Perry I. ....New York, NY
Kreidman, Ronald ....New York, NY
Kreidman & Slater ....New York, NY
Kreienberg, William L. ....Rochester, NY
Kreienkamp, Raymond S. ....St. Louis, MO
Kreifels, Frank A., & Associates
Omaha, NE
Kreig, Andrew T. ....Washington, DC
Kreig, James J. ....Princeton, NJ
Kreig, Larry W. ....Sacramento, CA
Kreiger, Amy T. ....Washington, DC
Kreiger, Arthur P. ....Cambridge, MA
Kreiger, Bruce D. ....Greenwich, CT
Kreiger, Leon E. ....Fair Lawn, NJ
Kreikemeier, Kevin D. ....St. Louis, MO
Kreikemeier Law Offices ....West Point, NE
Kreikemeier, Russell J. ....West Point, NE
Kreiker, Bernard ....Holtsville, NY
Kreiker, Nancy Diane ....Smithtown, NY
Kreil, Allan E., Jr. ....Roseland, NJ
Kreilick, Kristine R. ....New York, NY
Kreiling, Edward Paul ....Weston, FL
Kreiling, Kenneth R. ....South Royalton, VT
Kreiman, Keith A. ....Centerville, IA
Kreimeier, Paul ....Redmond, WA
Kreimendahl, Charles W. ....Dodgeville, WI
Kreimer, Seth F. ....Philadelphia, PA
Kreimer, Stan, Jr. ....Atlanta, GA
Kreimeyer, James H. ....Belton, TX
Kreimeyer, James H. ....Killeen, TX
Krein, Bari Susan ....Philadelphia, PA
Krein, James Scott ....Woodbridge, VA
Kreinberg, Joshua A. ....Los Angeles, CA
Kreinberg, Mitchell S. ....Livingston, NJ
Kreinbring, Daniel W. ....Encino, CA
Kreinces, Howard W. ....Hicksville, NY
Kreinces, Leonard ....Westbury, NY
Kreinces, Matthew R. ....Garden City, NY
Kreinces & Rosenberg, P.C.
Westbury, NY
Kreindel, Burton ....Newton, MA
Kreindler, Charles L. ....Los Angeles, CA
Kreindler, Donald L. ....New York, NY
Kreindler, James P. ....New York, NY
Kreindler & Kreindler ....New York, NY
Kreindler, Lee S. ....New York, NY
Kreindler, Marla J. ....Chicago, IL
Kreindler, Mitchell R. ....West Chester, PA
Kreindler, Peter M. ....Morristown, NJ
Kreindler, Robert S. ....Brooklyn, NY
Kreiner, Christopher A.
Winston-Salem, NC
Kreiner, Dennis W. ....Baltimore, MD
Kreiner, Fred J. ....Cleveland, OH
Columbus, OH
Kreiner, Frederick J. ....Cleveland, OH
Kreiner, Joel ....Santa Barbara, CA
Kreiner, Margaret H. ....Cuyahoga Falls, OH
Kreiner & Peters Co., L.P.A.
Cincinnati, OH
Cleveland, OH
Columbus, OH
Kreines, Charles W. ....New York, NY
Kreines & Engelberg ....Mineola, NY
Kreines, Melvyn ....Mineola, NY
Kreinheder, Ralph O. ....Buffalo, NY
Kreinik Aaron & Gersh, L.L.P.
New York, NY
Kreinik, Gary A. ....New York, NY
Kreinik, Steven M. ....New York, NY
Kreins, Claudia T. ....Los Angeles, CA
Kreipe, Laurine R. ....Topeka, KS
Georgetown, TX
Kreis, David Alan ....Huntington Woods, MI
Kreis, Elizabeth S. ....Arvada, CO
Kreis, Enderle, Callander & Hudgins, A Professional Corporation
Battle Creek, MI
Kalamazoo, MI
Kreis, John P., Law Offices of
Los Angeles, CA
Kreis, Kenneth O. ....Boise, ID
Kreis, Lawrence F., Jr. ....Bel Air, MD
Havre de Grace, MD
Kreis, Robert R. ....Jacksonville, FL
Kreis, Russell A. ....Kalamazoo, MI
Kreis, Susan L. ....Port Huron, MI
Kreisberg, Barrett G. ....White Plains, NY
Kreisberg, Beebe, Grossman, Bergins & Mancuso, LLP ....Buffalo, NY
Clifton Park, NY
Rochester, NY
White Plains, NY
Kreisberg, Edward L. ....San Leandro, CA
Kreisberg, Howard L. ....Chicago, IL
Kreisberg, Jeffrey L. ....New York, NY
Kreisberg, Jonathan B. ....Hartford, CT
Kreisberg, Julian ....Miami, FL
Kreisberg & Maitland, P.C. ....New York, NY
Kreisberg, Monroe N. ....Flushing, NY
Kreischer, Albert C., Jr. ....Tampa, FL
Kreisel, June E. ....Los Angeles, CA
Kreiser, Craig A. ....Wichita, KS
Kreiser, Donna L. ....Harrisburg, PA
Kreiser, Karl ....Columbia, PA
Kreiser, Mark L. ....Bethesda, MD
Kreiser, Mark L., P.A. ....Bethesda, MD
Kreiser, Travis L. ....Marlton, NJ
Philadelphia, PA
Plymouth Meeting, PA
Kreisheimer, John P. ....Denver, CO
Kreisher and Gregorowicz ....Bloomsburg, PA
Kreisher, William S. ....Bloomsburg, PA
Kreisinger, Paul D. ....Rutherford, NJ
Kreisler, Alfred ....Miami Beach, FL
Kreisler, Barry B. ....Chicago, IL
Kreisler, David ....Cleveland, OH
Kreisler, David P. ....Boston, MA
Kreisler, Lewis J. ....Nutley, NJ
Kreisler & Matanky ....Chicago, IL
Kreisler, Richard M. ....Los Angeles, CA
Kreisman, Barbara A.
Federal Communications Commission,
Mass Media Bureau, GV
Kreisman, Bruce S. ....Chicago, IL
Kreisman, Erika P. ....Pittsburgh, PA
Kreisman, Norman J. ....Los Angeles, CA
Kreisman, Robert D. ....Chicago, IL
Kreisman, Robert D., P.C., Law Offices of
Chicago, IL
Kreisman, Ronald A. ....Augusta, ME
Kreisman, Sarah Jill ....Jersey City, NJ
Kreismann, Ronald K. ....New York, NY
Kreisner, Peter M. ....Austin, TX
Kreiss, Robert A. ....Dayton, OH
Kreissl, J. F., Jr. ....Chicago, IL
Kreissman, James G. ....Palo Alto, CA
Kreiswirth, Barry ....Washington, DC
Kreitenberg, Ernie B. ....Los Angeles, CA
Kreitenberg, Mitchell H. ....Los Angeles, CA
Kreitenberg, Rena E. ....Beverly Hills, CA
Kreiter, Kristine L. ....Sioux Falls, SD
Kreiter, Mitchell D. ....Chicago, IL
Kreiter, Robert D. ....Columbus, OH
Kreiter, Ron L. ....Oklahoma City, OK
Kreiter, Shelley M. ....Highland Park, IL
Kreithen, Baron & Carpey, P.C.
Philadelphia, PA
Kreithen, Martin ....Philadelphia, PA
Kreitler, John E. ....Hartford, CT
Kreitlow, Margaret L. ....Rockford, IL
Kreitman, Lenore R. ....New York, NY
Kreitman, Mark
Securities and Exchange Commission,
Division of Enforcement, GV
Kreitman, Mark A. ....New York, NY
Kreitman, Michael E. ....New York, NY
Kreitman, Robert M. ....New York, NY
Kreitman, Shelley ....Potomac, MD
Kreitz, Robert R. ....Oley, PA
Reading, PA
Kreitzberg, Anthony R. ....Salem, OR
Kreitzberg, Benjamin I. ....West Orange, NJ
Kreitzberg, Donna C. ....Portland, OR
Kreitzberg, Ellen S. ....Santa Clara, CA
Kreitzberg, Leonard R.
Department of Agriculture,
Office of the General Counsel, GV
Kreitzer, Elizabeth A. ....San Diego, CA
Kreitzer, Gary Allen ....San Diego, CA
Kreitzer, Ilene S. ....Melville, NY
Kreitzer, Judith Epstein
Fort Lauderdale, FL
Kreitzer, Michael N. ....Miami, FL
Kreitzer, Steven W. ....Rossville, GA
Kreitzman, David ....New York, NY
Kreitzman, Mortensen, Simon & Irgang
New York, NY
Kreitzman, Ralph J. ....New York, NY
Kreivenas, Algirdas J. ....Durham, NC
Kreizenbeck, Randy J.
Mayfield Village, OH
Kreizinger, Loreen I. ....Fort Lauderdale, FL
Kreizinger, Loreen I., P.A.
Fort Lauderdale, FL
Kreizman, Ira E. ....Freehold, NJ
Kreizman, Joel N. ....Ocean Township, NJ
Krejci, Michael D. ....Clarendon Hills, IL
Krejci, William G. ....Brooklyn, NY
Krejs, Oliver B. ....Dallas, TX
Krek, Nenad ....Honolulu, HI
Krek, Raymond E. ....Jefferson, WI
Krekel, Gene R. ....Burlington, IA
Krekelberg, Charles A. ....Pelican Rapids, MN
Krekelberg, Skonseng & Lindberg, PLLP
Fergus Falls, MN
Pelican Rapids, MN
Krekeler, J. David ....Madison, WI
Krekeler & Scheffer, S.C. ....Madison, WI
Krekorian, Paul M. ....Los Angeles, CA
Krekstein, Gerald ....North Palm Beach, FL
Krekstein, Michael H. ....Philadelphia, PA
Krekstein, William O. ....Spring House, PA
Krell, Anne Graziano ....Woodbury, NJ
Krell, Barry ....Charleston, SC
Krell, Bruce E. ....San Francisco, CA
Krell, Bruce E., Inc., Law Offices of
San Francisco, CA
Krell, David E. ....Bridgeton, NJ
Krell & Jensen, L.C. ....Clive, IA
Krell, Jonathan M. ....Washington, DC
Krell, Joshua D. ....Boston, MA
Krell, Lawrence C. ....Omaha, NE
Krell, LeAnne ....Clive, IA
Krell, Raymond A., (P.C.) ....Houston, TX
Krell, Raymond L. ....Detroit, MI
Krell, Steven ....Los Angeles, CA
Krell, Susan K. ....Hartford, CT
Krell, Timothy Glenn ....Spokane, WA
Krell & Torigian ....Houston, TX
Austin, TX
Krelle, Ronald F. ....San Andreas, CA
Krellen, Joshua N. ....Fairfield, NJ
Carle Place, NY
Krellenstein, Jason M. ....Rye Brook, NY
Kreller, Joseph L., Jr. ....Gretna, LA
Kreller, Thomas R. ....Los Angeles, CA
Krellwitz, Michael W. ....Flint, MI
Kreloff, Michael A. ....Chicago, IL
Krelstein, Ronald D. ....Memphis, TN
Krem, Janice ....Portland, OR
Krema, C. Nicholas ....Boise, ID
Kremblas, Foster, Millard & Pollick
Reynoldsburg, OH
Kremblas, Frank T. ....Reynoldsburg, OH
Krembs & Alkire LLP ....Cleveland, OH
Krembs, Andrew P. ....Cleveland, OH
Krembs, James W. ....Savannah, GA
Krembs, Peter J. ....Cleveland, OH
Kremen, Andrea S. ....New York, NY
Kremen, Brian J. ....Seattle, WA
Kremen, David F. ....Pittsburgh, PA
Kremen, Hattie Bratzel ....Salem, OR
Kremen, Michael ....Jersey City, NJ
Kremen, Morris G. ....Redmond, WA
Kremen, Richard M. ....Baltimore, MD
Kremen, Ruth S. ....Beverly Hills, CA
Kremen, Seymour S. ....Coronado, CA
Kremenezky, Tina C. ....New York, NY
Kremens, Daniel E. ....New York, NY
Kremer, Alfred P. ....Rochester, NY
Kremer, Amy L. ....Boston, MA
Kremer, Arthur J. ....New York, NY
Uniondale, NY
Kremer, Brian S. ....Albany, NY
Kremer, Dale E. ....Seattle, WA
Kremer, Daniel J. ....San Diego, CA
Kremer, David H. ....San Francisco, CA
Kremer, Dean C. ....Greenbelt, MD
Kremer, Ellen T. ....Bellevue, WA
Kremer, Eric A. ....San Diego, CA
Kremer, Erica H. ....Bowling Green, OH
Kremer, James D. ....Minneapolis, MN
Kremer, Jim ....Eden Prairie, MN
Kremer, John M. ....Huntington Beach, CA
Kremer, Joseph T. ....Buffalo, NY
Kremer, J. W. ....Irvine, CA
Kremer, Kristin L. ....Annapolis, MD
Kremer, Linda K. ....San Rafael, CA
Kremer, Mark D. ....Santa Monica, CA
Kremer, Matthew M. ....San Diego, CA
Kremer, Paul E. ....Elkhorn, WI
Kremer, Richard H. ....Memphis, TN
Kremer, Scott H. ....Boston, MA
Kremers, Jeffrey A. ....Milwaukee, WI
Kremeyer, Frederick L., Jr. ....Baltimore, MD
Kremian, F. Terry ....Seattle, WA
Kremidas, Lori J. ....Hartford, CT
Kremin, David K. ....Chicago, IL
Kremin, David K. & Associates, P.C.
Chicago, IL
Kremin, Mark J. ....New York, NY
Kremins, Michael F. ....New York, NY
Kremkoski, Joe E. ....Racine, WI
Kreml, Melanie Ann ....Lake Forest, IL
Kremmel, Donn A. ....Troy, OH
Kremnick, Richard L. ....Philadelphia, PA
Kremnitzer, Ronald B. ....New York, NY
Kremp, Jennifer L. ....Indianapolis, IN
Krempa, Leslie J., (Mrs.) ....Daphne, AL
Krempasky, Richard W.
Department Of Veterans Affairs,
Board of Contract Appeals, GV
Krems, Kenneth A. ....Boston, MA
Krems, William N. ....Denver, CO
Kremser & Howard ....Santa Barbara, CA
Kremser, Mark E. ....Cleveland, OH
Kremser, Paul E., Jr. ....Santa Barbara, CA
Kremski, Julius J. ....New Britain, CT
Kremski, Victoria V. ....Owosso, MI
Kremzner, Mark T. ....Saco, ME
Krendel & Stone ....Lynbrook, NY
Krendel, Veronica Sympson ....Lynbrook, NY
Krendl, Cathy S. ....Denver, CO
Krendl, James R. ....Denver, CO
Krendl Krendl Sachnoff & Way, P.C.
Denver, CO
Krenek, Eddie M. ....Katy, TX
Krenek, Melvin A. ....San Antonio, TX
Krenek, Melvin A., & Associates, A Prof. Corp.
San Antonio, TX
Krenek, Sue A. ....San Francisco, CA
Krengel, Barry W. ....Philadelphia, PA
Krengel, Herbert B. ....St. Paul, MN
Krengel, Jennifer G. ....San Francisco, CA
Krening, Eric T. ....Honolulu, HI
Krenitsky, Albert G. ....Rochester, NY
Krenitsky, John C. ....Buffalo, NY
Krenitsky, Joseph G. ....Buffalo, NY
Krenkel, David A. ....Ocean City, NJ
Krenn, John L. ....Minneapolis, MN
Krenn, Thomas W. ....Minneapolis, MN
Krennerich, Erica L. ....Houston, TX
Krensky, Michael Ian ....Rockville, MD
Krent, Eugene P. ....Cleveland, OH
Krent, Harold J. ....Chicago, IL
Krent, Nancy Fredman
Arlington Heights, IL
Krentel, John B. ....Metairie, LA
Krentsa, Donald E. ....Fort Lauderdale, FL
Krentz, Daniel J. ....Forest Hills, NY
Krentz & Krentz ....Plano, IL
Krentz, Paul G. ....Aurora, IL
Krentz, Peter L. ....Plano, IL
Krentz, Richard J. ....Lakeville, MN
Krentz, Stephen L. ....Plano, IL
Krentzman, Beth J. ....Lexington, MA
Krentzman, Donald A. ....Los Angeles, CA
Krentzman, Jessica L. ....Philadelphia, PA
Krentzman, John A. ....Clearwater, FL

Krier, Stephen T. .... **Lubbock, TX**
Kries, Randall J. .... Phoenix, AZ
Kriesant, Carl W. L. .... Yorba Linda, CA
Kriesberg, Carol N. .... New York, NY
Kriesberg, Lois A. .... Syracuse, NY
Kriesberg, Simeon M. .... **Washington, DC**
Krieser & Bieniek .... Minnetonka, MN
Krieser, Jason D. .... **Dallas, TX**
Krieser, Michelle Douglas .... **Dallas, TX**
Krieser, Peter J. .... Minnetonka, MN
Kriessler, Lynn A. .... **Cleveland, OH**
Kriete, Debra M. .... **Harrisburg, PA**
Kriete, Peter F. .... **Harrisburg, PA**
Kriete, Susan E. .... New York, NY
Kriete, Vance R. .... Tulsa, OK
Kriete, Wilbur .... Cincinnati, OH
Krietz, Albin R. .... Tucson, AZ
Krietzman, Fredrick R. .... **Minneapolis, MN**
Krietzman, Mark H.
Palos Verdes Estates, CA
Kriezelman, Jeffrey .... Chicago, IL
Kriftcher, Eric L. .... **New York, NY**
Krigbaum, Mary K. .... **Chicago, IL**
Krigbaum, Matthew .... Cedar Rapids, IA
Krigbaum, Stephen J. .... **New York, NY**
Krigel, Erlene W. .... Kansas City, MO
Krigel, Jack Z. .... Kansas City, MO
Krigel & Krigel, P.C. .... Kansas City, MO
Krigel, Sanford P. .... Kansas City, MO
Kriger, Alvin H. .... Brookfield, WI
Kriger, Brian E. .... **New York, NY**
Kriger, James S. .... **Portland, ME**
Kriger, Joel M. .... La Mesa, CA
Ontario, CA
Temecula, CA
Kriger, Mark J. .... **Detroit, MI**
Southfield, MI
Kriger, Martin R. .... Memphis, TN
Kriger, Morris J. .... Memphis, TN
Kriger, Richard E. .... Post Falls, ID
Kriha, Darcy L. .... **Chicago, IL**
Krikava, Michael C. .... **Minneapolis, MN**
Krikawa, Charles, IV .... Silver Spring, MD
Krikelis, Basil S. .... Wilmington, DE
Krikelis, Costas S. .... **Wilmington, DE**
Krikis, Maria .... Brockton, MA
Krikorian, Adrienne L. .... **Calabasas, CA**
Encino, CA
Krikorian, Betty Linn .... Boston, MA
Krikorian, Brian H. .... **Seattle, WA**
Krikorian, Charles R. .... **Chicago, IL**
Krikorian, David M. .... Pasadena, CA
Krikorian, Elaine E. .... Watertown, MA
Ithaca, NY
Krikorian, Erica .... **Seattle, WA**
Krikorian, Joy L. .... Fresno, CA
Krikorian & Krikorian .... **Seattle, WA**
Krikorian, Priscilla D. .... Harrison, NY
Krikorian, Rosanne Joy .... Costa Mesa, CA
Krikorian, Tamara .... **Morristown, NJ**
Krikorian, Van Z. .... **New York, NY**
Kriksciun, Curt .... Denver, CO
Kril, Lisa A. .... Amherst, NY
Krilich, Thomas G. .... Tacoma, WA
Krill, Albert .... **Cleveland, OH**
Krill, Andrea M. .... Lafayette Hill, PA
Krill, Denis W. .... **Erie, PA**
Krill, Edward J. .... **Washington, DC**
Krill, John P., Jr. .... **Harrisburg, PA**
Krill, Karen E. .... Clarendon Hills, IL
Krill, Pamela M. .... **Milwaukee, WI**
Krill, R. Jeffrey .... **Milwaukee, WI**
Krill, Richard P. .... Renfrew, PA
Krill, Scott Douglas .... Elgin, IL
Krim, Daphna .... Department of Education,
Office of the General Counsel, GV
Krim, Frederick J. .... **Ocala, FL**
Krim, Gary M. .... New York, NY
Krim, Todd M. .... Westlake Village, CA
Krimbel, Rosemary .... Chicago, IL
Krimbill, Jack B. .... San Antonio, TX
Krimel, Stephen B. .... Santa Rosa, CA
Krimen, Marc Stryk .... Chicago, IL
Krimen, Richard A. .... San Francisco, CA
Krimm, John J., Jr. .... **Cleveland, OH**
Dublin, OH
Krimmel, Herbert T. .... Los Angeles, CA
Krimmel, John P. .... **Kansas City, MO**
Krimmer, Matthew .... **Los Angeles, CA**
Krimminger, Michael H.
Federal Deposit Insurance Corporation,
Liquidation Branch, GV
Krimshtein, Anna A. .... **Miami, FL**
Krimsky, Beth-Ann Ellenberg
Fort Lauderdale, FL
Krimsky, Martin M. .... **Philadelphia, PA**
Krimstock, Gary A. .... **Philadelphia, PA**
Kriner, Robert J., Jr. .... **Wilmington, DE**
Kriner, William C. .... Clearfield, PA
Kring & Brown .... Phoenix, AZ
Irvine, CA
Ontario, CA
San Diego, CA
Kring, Kristine .... **Bristol, VA**
Kring, Kyle D. .... **Irvine, CA**
Kring, Lucille Eileen .... Anaheim, CA
Kringel, Eric .... Washington, DC
Kringel, Jerome H. .... **Milwaukee, WI**
Kringlie, A. Roger .... Northwood, ND
Krings, Jerome D. .... **Milwaukee, WI**
Krinick, Cathy E. .... Hampton, VA
Krinick, Evan H. .... **Uniondale, NY**
Krinsk, J. Robert .... San Diego, CA
Krinsky, Adam D.
Federal Communications Commission,
International Bureau, GV
Krinsky, Andrew N. .... **New York, NY**
Krinsky, Daniel R. .... San Diego, CA
Krinsky, David A. .... **Newport Beach, CA**
Krinsky, Glenn Lorin .... Duarte, CA
Krinsky, Mark P. .... **San Francisco, CA**
Krinsky, Mary M. .... **New Haven, CT**
Krinsky, Michael .... **New York, NY**
Krinsky, Miriam A. .... Los Angeles, CA
Krinsky, Mitchell S. .... **Lexington, MA**
Krinsky, Richard M. .... Brooklyn, NY
Krinsky, Robert M. .... Tacoma, WA
Krinsky, Scott .... **New York, NY**
Krinsky, Steven P. .... Chicago, IL
Krinsly, Stuart Z. .... **New York, NY**
Krinsman, Allan Neil .... **New York, NY**
Krintzman, B. J. .... Newton, MA
Krintzman, David A. .... **Santa Monica, CA**
Krinzman, Alan E. .... **Miami, FL**
Krinzman, Richard N. .... **Miami, FL**
Kripalani, Eva M. .... Portland, OR
Kripalani, Sanjiv N. .... **Portland, OR**
Kripetz, Tanya M. .... **Rockville, MD**
Kripke, Joan Miriam .... Chicago, IL
Kripke, Kenneth N. .... San Diego, CA
Krippel, Darrolyn C. .... Gahanna, OH
Krippendorf, Evelyn K. .... Roanoke, VA
Krippendorf Firm, The .... Roanoke, VA
Krippner, George E., (P.C.) .... St. Charles, IL
Krippner, Timothy L. .... **Chicago, IL**
Krips, Cynthia R. .... **Columbia, MD**
Towson, MD
Krips, Richard .... Department of Justice,
Justice Management Division, GV
Kris, David S. .... Department of Justice,
Criminal Division, GV
Kris, Howard I. .... East Meadow, NY
Kris, Jody Manier .... **Washington, DC**
Krisa, John .... Blakely, PA
Krisa, Michael N. .... Blakely, PA
Krisan, Paul C. .... Elmwood Park, NJ
Krisberg, Brian C. .... **New York, NY**
Krisch, Stephen M. .... Trenton, NJ
Krischak, James R. .... **Zanesville, OH**
Krischer, Alan S. .... **Miami, FL**
Krischer, David E. .... Atlanta, GA
Krischer, Gordon E. .... **Los Angeles, CA**
Krischer, Jason .... **Los Angeles, CA**
Krischer, Joel E. .... **Los Angeles, CA**
Krisciunas, Richard Thomas .... Detroit, MI
Kriscunas, Robert A. .... **Dallas, TX**
Krise, Thomas H. .... Indianapolis, IN
Krisel, Andrew M. .... **Brooklyn, NY**
Kriseman, Richard D. .... St. Petersburg, FL
Krishan, Manoj .... Arcadia, CA
Krishel, Daniel L. .... Beverly Hills, CA
Krisher, Efrem R. .... Seattle, WA
Krisher, Howard Penn, II .... **Dayton, OH**
Krisher, Ralph E., III .... **Chicago, IL**
Krisher, Ralph E., Jr. .... Fort Wayne, IN
Krishna, Savita N. .... **San Francisco, CA**
Atlanta, GA
Krishnamurthy, Aneal .... **Washington, DC**
Krishnan, K. Harsha .... **Denver, CO**
Krishnan, Shuba
Department of Labor, GV
Krishok, Edward M. .... **Milwaukee, WI**
Krisik, Catherine A. .... **Minneapolis, MN**
Krisik, Dennis J. .... Chicago, IL
Krisjanis, Elisabeth E. .... Saugerties, NY
Krisjansons, Brigita S. .... **Thermopolis, WY**
Krisko, Kenneth J. .... **Washington, DC**
Krisky, Daniel B. .... **Fairfax, VA**
Herndon, VA
Krisky, Daniel B., P.C. .... **Fairfax, VA**
Herndon, VA
Krisle, Geo. M., Jr. .... Knoxville, TN
Krislov & Associates, Ltd. .... **Chicago, IL**
Krislov, Clinton A. .... **Chicago, IL**
Krislov, Maureen D. .... Los Angeles, CA
Krisnik, Anne F. .... St. Paul, MN
Krisor, Alphons S., Jr. .... Northbrook, IL
Krisor, Edward J., Jr. .... Denver, CO
Krisor, John D., Jr. .... South Bend, IN
Krisor & Nussbaum .... South Bend, IN
Krispin, Donald A. .... **Detroit, MI**
Krispin, James G. .... St. Louis, MO
Krispin, Paul T., Jr. .... St. Louis, MO
Kriss, Barbara H. .... Newton, MA
Kriss, Charles T. .... Albany, NY
Kriss, David S. .... **New York, NY**
Kriss, Debra Lynn .... New York, NY
Kriss, Edward W. .... Lenexa, KS
Kriss & Feit, P.C. .... Livingston, NJ
New York, NY
Kriss, Hillary S. .... **New York, NY**
Kriss, Jerald G. .... Littleton, CO
Kriss, Joel R. .... Colby, KS
Kriss, John P. .... Lawrence, KS
Kriss, Kriss & Brignola, LLP .... Albany, NY
Kriss, Mark C. .... Albany, NY
Kriss, Robert J. .... **Chicago, IL**
Kriss, Ronald A. .... **Miami, FL**
Krissman, Joel .... **Long Beach, CA**
Krissoff, Joel E. .... **Grand Rapids, MI**
Krissoff, Keith .... Annapolis, MD
Krissoff, Robert L. .... New York, NY
Krist, Diane Hammer .... Houston, TX
Krist, Kevin D. .... **Houston, TX**
Krist Law Firm, The, P.C. .... **Houston, TX**
Krist, Ronald D. .... **Houston, TX**
Krist, Scott C. .... **Houston, TX**
Krist, Stanley J., & Associates .... Houston, TX
Schulenburg, TX
Kristakis, Michele M. .... Pittsburgh, PA
Kristal, Alene Sue .... New York, NY
Kristal, Barbara E. .... Rancho Mirage, CA
Kristal, Barbara E., A Prof. Law Corp.
Rancho Mirage, CA
Kristal, Carolyn R., Law Office of
Fort Lee, NJ
Kristal, Deborah N. .... Boise, ID
Kristal & Feldman .... Fort Lee, NJ
Kristal, Jerry .... **Cherry Hill, NJ**
New York, NY
Kristal, Lisa J. .... New York, NY
Kristal, Martin C. .... **Los Angeles, CA**
Kristal, Peter L. .... Rochester, NY
Kristal, William L. .... Detroit, MI
Kristall, Wayne .... Cadillac, MI
Kristensen, Cummings, Phillips & Carroll, P.C. .... **Brattleboro, VT**
Kristensen, Debora K. .... **Boise, ID**
Kristensen, Douglas A. .... Minden, NE
Kristensen, John G. .... **Brattleboro, VT**
Kristensen, Michael K. .... Metairie, LA
Kristiansen, Brian .... New York, NY
Kristiansen, Janet L. .... Quincy, MA
Kristiansen, Kari .... **Anchorage, AK**
Kristiansen, Mark S. .... **Washington, DC**
Kristiansen, Sandra Skains .... Medford, OR
Kristianson, Larry M. .... Colville, WA
Kristich, Daria .... Port Jefferson, NY
Kristinik, Don Lawrence, III
Columbia, SC
Kristjan, Anna H. .... Tallahassee, FL
Kristjansdottir, Edda .... **New York, NY**
Kristjanson, Johann D. .... Dana Point, CA
Kristl, Kenneth T. .... **Chicago, IL**
Kristl, Timothy O. .... **Kansas City, MO**
Kristobak, Ronald D. .... **Uniontown, PA**
Kristofak, Stephen G., Jr. .... Wethersfield, CT
Kristofco, Michael D. .... **Blue Bell, PA**
Kristofer, John .... Apache Junction, AZ
Kristoff, Carol A. .... Scranton, PA
Kristoff, Christopher A. .... **Greenwich, CT**
Kristoff, Karl W. .... **Buffalo, NY**
Kristoff, Lawrence E., II .... Clayton, NC
Kristoff, Michael, Sr. .... Akron, OH
Kristoff, Robert P. .... **San Francisco, CA**
Kristoff, Sharon H. .... Clayton, NC
Kristofik, Joseph M. .... Tarentum, PA
Kristol, Daniel M. .... **Wilmington, DE**
Kristol, Howard G. .... **New York, NY**
Kristovich, Andrew F. .... San Francisco, CA
Kristovich, Baldo M. .... Los Angeles, CA
Kristovich, Marlene .... Los Angeles, CA
Kristovich, Stephen M. .... **Los Angeles, CA**
Kristovich, Theresa A. .... **Los Angeles, CA**
Kristovich, Thomas B. .... Los Angeles, CA
Kristufek, Lynne .... Downers Grove, IL
Kristufek, Matthew M. .... **Atlanta, GA**
Kristul, Gene .... San Francisco, CA
Kristy, Bobby L. .... Overland Park, KS
Kristy, John M. .... Department of Education,
Office of the General Counsel, GV
Kristy, Laura Stine .... Belvedere-Tiburon, CA
Krisztal, Ruben J. .... **Overland Park, KS**
Krisztal, Ruben J. .... **Kansas City, MO**
Krit, Jonathan J. .... **Chicago, IL**
Kritek, James J. .... Downers Grove, IL
Kriteman, Laura H. .... **Atlanta, GA**
Kritenbrink, Lawrence E. .... **Omaha, NE**
Krithades, Christine .... Alexandria, VA
Kritikos, Nicholas J. .... Lincolnwood, IL
Kritlow, Colleen M. .... Kalamazoo, MI
Kritscher, Alfred J. .... Santa Monica, CA
Kritselis, William N. .... Lansing, MI
Kritske, Lisa L. .... **Sheboygan, WI**
Kritt, Evi E. .... **Los Angeles, CA**
Kritt, Lisa Helene .... Chicago, IL
Krittman, Irwin M. .... Princeton, NJ
Kritz, David J. .... **Washington, DC**
Kritz, Paul .... Baldwin, NY
Kritz, Paul M. .... **Coffeyville, KS**
Kritzalis, Alexander S. .... **New York, NY**
Kritzberg, Joan H. .... San Bernardino, CA
Kritzer, Albert H. .... White Plains, NY
Kritzer, Craig H. .... **Atlanta, GA**
Kritzer, David Marc .... **Los Angeles, CA**
Kritzer, David S. .... Garden City, NY
Kritzer, Derek R. .... **Madison, WI**
Kritzer, Glenn B. .... **Miami, FL**
Kritzer, Harry A. .... Westport, CT
Kritzer, Howard S. .... New York, NY
Kritzer, Jeffrey M. .... **Austin, MN**
Kritzer, Joseph A. .... Torrance, CA
Kritzer, Paul E. .... Milwaukee, WI
Kritzer, Stuart A. .... **Denver, CO**
Kritzer, Stuart A., Law Offices of
Denver, CO
Kritzman, David R. .... **Manchester, CT**
Kritzman, Robert M. .... Miami, FL
Kriva, James J. .... **Milwaukee, WI**
Krivatsy, Elizabeth C. .... **San Francisco, CA**
Krivcher Magids PLC .... **Germantown, TN**
Memphis, TN
Krivetsky, Henry C. .... San Francisco, CA
Krivicic, Eleanor Anna .... Boston, MA
Krivicich, John A. .... **Chicago, IL**
Krivis, Jeffrey L. .... Encino, CA
Krivis, Spile & Siegal, LLP .... **Encino, CA**
Krivisky, Barry M. .... **Rye Brook, NY**
Krivit, Daniel H. .... Washington, DC
Krivit, David W. .... **Denver, CO**
Krivit & Krivit, P.C. .... Washington, DC
Krivitzky, Jerrold S. .... Newark, NJ
Krivitzky, Lawrence I. .... Jersey City, NJ
Krivitzky, Richard A. .... Glenview, IL
Krivitzky & Springer .... Jersey City, NJ
Krivok, James N. .... **West Palm Beach, FL**
Krivonos, Boris A. .... Forest Hills, NY
Krivonyak, J. Christopher .... Charleston, WV
Krivonyak, John C. .... Charleston, WV
Krivosha, Norman .... **Lincoln, NE**
Krivosha, Terri .... **Minneapolis, MN**
Krivoshekov, Igor L. .... **Chicago, IL**
Krivoshey, Robert M. .... Columbus, OH
Krivoshia, Eli, Jr. .... Pittsburgh, PA
Krivoshik, David P. .... **Newark, NJ**
Krivoy, Clara .... **New York, NY**
Kriynovich, Wayne S. .... Cleveland, OH
Kriz, Barbara A. .... **Lexington, KY**
Kriz, Jama M. .... **Eden Prairie, MN**
Kriz, John M. .... **New York, NY**
Kriz, Judith Anne .... Chagrin Falls, OH
Kriz, Karin Michelle .... Oklahoma City, OK
Kriz, Paul P. .... **Lexington, MA**
Krizack, Marc L. .... Berkeley, CA
Krizan, Gerald F. .... Department of Labor,
Office of Secretary, GV
Krizan, Lisa M. .... **Richmond, VA**
Krizek, Claudette Reid .... Wesley Chapel, FL
Krizek, Curtis A. .... Prairie Village, KS
Krizek, Paul E. .... Lorton, VA
Krizensky, F. David .... Menasha, WI
Krizman, Frederick E. .... Cleveland, OH
Krizman, Lisa Kopf .... **New York, NY**
Krizman, Tracy Hensler .... Chicago, IL
Krizner, Frank P. .... Butler, PA
Krizner, William T. .... **Fort Lauderdale, FL**
Krkljes, Stevan .... Chicago, IL
Krkuc Perkins, Jean F .... New Castle, PA
Krmpotic, J. Stephanie
San Francisco, CA
Krna, Steven P. .... Whitney Point, NY
Krncevic, Raymond .... **Cleveland, OH**
Kroack, Laurel L. .... Springfield, IL
Krob, Brian E. .... **Chicago, IL**
Kroberger, Jeffrey A. .... **Erdenheim, PA**
Krobert, Kenneth B. .... Metairie, LA
Kroboth, Jan T. .... Goldsboro, NC
Kroboth Law Office .... Charlotte, NC
Kroboth, Timothy R. .... Charlotte, NC
Krochalis, William J. .... Cranbury, NJ
Krochka, James J. .... San Francisco, CA
Krochmal, Gary A. .... Southfield, MI
Krochmal, Kenneth J. .... Dayton, OH
Krochmalny, Jane C. .... **Brattleboro, VT**
Krochmalny, Michael W. .... Wethersfield, CT
Krochta, Nicholas L. .... **Somerville, NJ**
Krochta, Thomas G. .... Boonville, IN
Krock, David C. .... **Toledo, OH**
Krock, Earl J. .... Cleveland, OH
Krock, Gregory J. .... **Pittsburgh, PA**
Krock, Kenneth M. .... Houston, TX
Krocker, Dan .... **Houston, TX**
Krockey, Robert S. .... **Joliet, IL**
Kroculick, George J. .... **Moorestown, NJ**
Philadelphia, PA
Krodel, Natalie L. .... **New York, NY**
Kroe, Amy I. .... **New York, NY**
Kroeger, Cynthia Panciera .... Sacramento, CA
Kroeger, David M. .... **Chicago, IL**
Kroeger, Derek .... **Los Angeles, CA**
Kroeger, John R.
Federal Energy Regulatory Commission,
Office of the General Counsel, GV
Kroeger, Karrieann Couture .... Chicago, IL
Kroeger, Lauren K. .... **Valparaiso, IN**
Kroeger, Linda L. .... Port Clinton, OH
Kroeger, Paul R. .... Wendell, ID
Kroeger, Tia M. .... Columbus, OH
Kroeger, W. Richard .... **Ironwood, MI**
Kroeger, Wilbur L. .... **Freeport, IL**
Kroeker, Dennis W. .... Nevada City, CA
Sacramento, CA
Kroeker, Kevin B. .... **Los Angeles, CA**
Kroeker, Robert D. .... **Kansas City, MO**
Kroemer, J. Albert .... **Dallas, TX**
Kroemer, Lisa M. .... Batavia, NY
Kroener, William F., III
Federal Deposit Insurance Corporation,
Supervision and Legislation Branch, GV
New York, NY
Kroenert, Robert M. .... **Kansas City, MO**
Kroening, Linda Marie .... Treasury Department,
Internal Revenue Service, GV
Kroening, Robert W. .... St. Louis, MO
Kroenke, Frederick, Jr. .... Baton Rouge, LA
Kroenlein, David F. .... **New York, NY**
Kroeper, Jon Eric
Securities and Exchange Commission,
Division of Market Regulation, GV
Kroes, R. Chris .... **Santa Barbara, CA**
Kroesch, Douglas A. .... **Sacramento, CA**
Kroesch, Stuart C. .... Joliet, IL
Kroesche, Guy P. .... **Salt Lake City, UT**
Kroesche, Jane B. .... **San Francisco, CA**
Kroesche, John E. .... Costa Mesa, CA
Kroesche, Thomas R. .... **Costa Mesa, CA**
Kroese, Jay A. .... Wayzata, MN
Kroese, Kurt .... **Tucson, AZ**
Kroessler, Andrew A. .... Garden City, NY
Krofcheck, Glenn P. .... Pittsburgh, PA
Kroff, Steven .... Los Altos, CA
Kroft, Stephen A. .... **Los Angeles, CA**
Krogdahl, Paula Jeanne .... Salem, OR
Kroger & Associates .... **Houston, TX**
Kroger, Christine Leigh .... **Stockton, CA**
Kroger, Christopher M. .... **Greensboro, NC**
Kroger, Donald J. .... Lincoln, NE
Kroger, Edward J. .... **Houston, TX**
Kroger, Elizabeth Mata .... **Houston, TX**
Kroger, Gardis & Regas .... **Indianapolis, IN**
Kroger, James .... **Muskegon, MI**
Kroger, Kristen L. .... **Grand Rapids, MI**
Kroger, Kurt B. .... San Francisco, CA
Kroger, R. McDonald .... **Indianapolis, IN**
Kroger, Richard C. .... **Houston, TX**
Kroger, Stephanie Anne .... **Austin, TX**
Kroger, William Karl .... **Houston, TX**
Kroger, William S., Jr. .... **Los Angeles, CA**
Kroger-Diamond, Catharine E.
San Diego, CA
Krogh, A. Lynne .... Boise, ID
Krogh, David L. .... Mission Viejo, CA

Krogh, Egil (Bud) ... Seattle, WA
Krogh, Frank W. ... Washington, DC
Krogh, Guy K. ... Ithaca, NY
Krogh, Harlan B. ... Billings, MT
Krogh & Leonard ... Seattle, WA
Krogh, Richard A. ... Lawrence, KS
Krogh, Timothy R. ... Toledo, OH
Krogmann, David B. ... Glens Falls, NY
Krogmeier, Charles J. ... Des Moines, IA
Krogmeier, Kevin G. ... Laguna Niguel, CA
Krogsrud, James ... Detroit, MI
Krogsrud, James, P.C. ... Detroit, MI
Krogstad, L. Kenneth ... Baton Rouge, LA
Krogstad, Robert K. ... Pierre, SD
Krogue, Karl K ... Spokane, WA
Kroha, Daniel J., Jr. ... Alexander, AR
Krohley, William A. ... New York, NY
Krohmer, Leigh R. ... Philadelphia, PA
Krohn, Adam J. ... Chicago, IL
Krohn, Alan I. ... Ventura, CA
Krohn, Carole A. ... Steamboat Springs, CO
Krohn, Charles H. ... Los Angeles, CA
Krohn, Clayton B. ... Greensboro, NC
Krohn and D'Amour, A Professional Corporation ... Evansville, IN
Krohn, Daniel A. ... Houston, TX
Krohn, Donald K. ... Baltimore, MD
Krohn, Douglas Keith ... Palo Alto, CA
Krohn, Gary J. ... Seattle, WA
Krohn & Jenkins ... Chicago, IL
Krohn, Karol H. ... Indianapolis, IN
Krohn, Kathy S. ... Oakland, CA
Krohn & Krissoff, P.A. ... Annapolis, MD
Krohn, Laura Marie ... Westwood, NJ
Krohn, M. David ... New York, NY
Krohn, Mark A. ... Walden, NY
Krohn, Mark E. ... Akron, OH
Krohn, Micah R. ... Chicago, IL
Krohn & Moss, Ltd. ... Chicago, IL
Krohn, R. Steven ... Evansville, IN
Krohn, Richard H. ... Grand Junction, CO
Krohn, Robert G. ... Corinth, MS
Krohn, Robert G. ... Edgerton, WI
Krohn, Rosenblum, & Hametz ... Merrick, NY
Krohn, Sally S. ... Philadelphia, PA
Krohn, Stanley W. ... Annapolis, MD
Krohn, Stephen P. ... Annapolis, MD
Krohn, Steven H. ... Council Bluffs, IA
Krohn, Theodore L. ... Kingston, PA
Krohn, Thomas C. ... Racine, WI
Krohn, William O. ... Chicago, IL
Krohne, Steven W. ... Indianapolis, IN
Krohner, Martin P. ... Farmington Hills, MI
Krohngold, Walter H. ... Cleveland, OH
Krohnke, Duane W. ... Minneapolis, MN
Kroiz, Michelle ... Boston, MA
Krokidas & Bluestein LLP ... Boston, MA
Krokidas, Maria J. ... Boston, MA
Krol, Anthony J. ... Philadelphia, PA
Krol, Casimar T. ... Crystal Lake, IL
Krol, Frederic B. ... Chicago, IL
Krol, Gina B. ... Chicago, IL
Krol, Igor ... New York, NY
Krol, John ... Rolling Meadows, IL
Krol, John J. P. ... Rockville Centre, NY
Krol, Joseph D. ... Daytona Beach, FL
Krol, Kenneth A. ... Chicago, IL
Krol, Kenneth H. ... Cleveland, OH
Krol, Margaret Irene ... Washington, DC
Krol, Steven D. ... Parsippany, NJ
Krol, Theodore J. ... Altoona, PA
Krolczyk, Dennis E. ... Manistee, MI
Kroleski, Steven L. ... Mount Vernon, NY
Krolewski, Martin A. ... New York, NY
Krolian, Dennis E. ... Elmsford, NY
Krolick, Jordan E. ... Chicago, IL
Krolick, Marshall D. ... Chicago, IL
Krolick, Ronald S. ... New York, NY
Krolik, Day, III ... New York, NY
Krolik, Maurice M. ... New York, NY
Krolikowski, Charles S. ... Irvine, CA
Krolikowski, John P. ... Pittsburgh, PA
Krolikowski, Joseph ... Philadelphia, PA
Krolikowski, Joseph C. ... Nashua, NH
Krolikowski, Suzanne B.
Environmental Protection Agency, Office of the General Counsel, GV
Kroll, Alan D. ... New York, NY
Kroll, Amy K. ... Walnut Creek, CA
Kroll, Amy N. ... Washington, DC
Kroll, Arnold H. ... New York, NY
Kroll, Barry L. ... Chicago, IL
Kroll & Blachor LLP ... Garden City, NY
Kroll, Carrie Welbaum ... Tallahassee, FL
Kroll, Catherine A. ... Wickliffe, OH
Kroll, Charles R. ... Weiser, ID
Kroll, Daniel Harris ... Houston, TX
Kroll, Daniel J. ... Emeryville, CA
Kroll, David C. ... Austin, TX
Kroll, David G. ... Topeka, KS
Kroll, David K. ... San Diego, CA
Kroll, Douglas A. ... San Rafael, CA
Kroll, Eileen E. ... Detroit, MI
Kroll, Elliott M. ... New York, NY
Kroll, Geo. L. ... Houston, TX
Kroll, Gerald L. ... Beverly Hills, CA
Kroll, Howard A. ... Los Angeles, CA
Kroll, Irving ... Southfield, MI
Kroll, James J., Jr. ... Modesto, CA
Kroll, Janice M. ... Los Angeles, CA
Kroll, Jeffrey J. ... Chicago, IL
Kroll, Joanne ... Rockland, ME
Kroll, Jonathan E. ... Garden City, NY
Kroll, Jules B. ... New York, NY
Kroll, Kathleen J. ... West Palm Beach, FL
Kroll, Loren H. ... Rochester, NY
Kroll, Martin N. ... Garden City, NY
Kroll, McNamara & Evans, LLP
Greenwich, CT
Hartford, CT
West Hartford, CT
Kroll, Merwyn M. ... Rochester, NY
Kroll, Michael I. ... Syosset, NY
Kroll, Michael R. ... Minneapolis, MN
Kroll, Milton P. ... Washington, DC
Kroll, Richard Alan ... Rochester, NY
Kroll, Robert A. ... Chicago, IL
Kroll, Robert E. ... Oakland, CA
Kroll, Rolf E. ... Harrisburg, PA
Kroll, Rubin & Fiorella LLP
Los Angeles, CA
Newark, NJ
Garden City, NY
New York, NY
White Plains, NY
Kroll & Rubin, Ltd. ... Chicago, IL
Kroll, Russell W. ... Tulsa, OK
Kroll, S. Robert ... Merrick, NY
Kroll, Samuel M. ... Richmond, VA
Virginia Beach, VA
Kroll, Shelley A. ... Greenwich, CT
West Hartford, CT
Kroll, Shelley B. ... Boston, MA
Kroll, Sol ... New York, NY
Kroll, Stephen R. ... Treasury Department, Financial Crimes Enforcement Network, GV
Kroll, Steven E. ... Crystal Bay, NV
Kroll, Steven L. ... Arlington Heights, IL
Chicago, IL
Kroll, Thomas J. ... Milwaukee, WI
Kroll, W. Rainer ... Osprey, FL
Krollman, Anne-Marie ... Smithfield, RI
Krolls, Egils H. ... Tucson, AZ
Kroloff, Belcher, Smart, Perry & Christopherson ... Stockton, CA
Kroloff, Mark W. ... Anchorage, AK
Kroloff, Micah N. ... Hackensack, NJ
Kroloff, Steven J. ... Deerfield, IL
Krom, Chester G. ... Kingston, NY
Krom, David B. ... Lincoln City, OR
Krom, Don C. ... Milwaukee, WI
Krom, Mickey L. ... Everett, WA
Kroman, Jennifer L. ... New York, NY
Kroman, Jonathan A. ... Seattle, WA
Kromash, Keith S. ... Boca Raton, FL
Kromash, Seliena ... Tampa, FL
Krombach, Charles K. ... Brookfield, WI
Krombein, Karlissa B.
Department of the Army, Office, Chief of Engineers/Headquarters, U.S. Army Corps of Engineers, GV
Kromelow, Marc R. ... Chicago, IL
Kromer, Beth Suzanne ... Grand Rapids, MI
Kromer, Bruce M. ... Phoenix, AZ
Kromer, James A. ... San Francisco, CA
Kromer, Sarah J. ... Charlotte, NC
Kromer, Sarel K. ... Chevy Chase, MD
Kromer, Thomas R. ... Columbus, OH
Kromholz, Joseph A. ... Brookfield, WI
Kromkowski, John D. ... Baltimore, MD
Kromkowski, Mark A. ... Chicago, IL
Kromm, Randall E. ... Boston, MA
Kromminga, Lynn R. ... Bowie, MD
Krompier, Jeffrey A. ... Florham Park, NJ
Kron, Barry ... Brooklyn, NY
Kron & Correale ... Succasunna, NJ
Kron, David P. ... Boca Raton, FL
Kron, Edward A. ... Philadelphia, PA
Kron, Jason A. ... Louisville, KY
Kron, JoAnne L. ... Northbrook, IL
Kron, Jonathan D. ... Milwaukee, WI
Kron, Larry I. ... Succasunna, NJ
Kron, Lawrence ... West Bloomfield, MI
Kron, Michael ... Anaheim, CA
Kron, Norman Fredrick, Jr. ... Denver, CO
Kron, Richard A. ... Miami, FL
Kron, Theodore L. ... Iowa City, IA
Kron, Walter V. ... Lansing, MI
Krona, Jack B., Jr. ... Dallas, TX
Kronau, Kathleen M. ... Roanoke, VA
Kronau, Roger W. ... Roanoke, VA
Kronberg, Brenda M. ... Boston, MA
Kronberg, Chris ... Boise, ID
Kronberg, G. Christian ... Chicago, IL
Kronberg, Lisa J. ... Boise, ID
Kronberg, Martin F. ... Millburn, NJ
Kroncke, Barbara J. ... Boston, MA
Kroncke, D'Arcangelo, Sutter & Furey
Toledo, OH
Kroncke, Heather Richmond
Wye Mills, MD
Kroncke, William G. ... Toledo, OH
Krone, Bruce A. ... Cincinnati, OH
Krone, Dean W. ... Chicago, IL
Krone, Gilbert L. ... Columbus, OH
Krone, Mark J. ... New York, NY
Krone, Michael P. ... Wellesley, MA
Krone, Norman Bernard ... Beachwood, OH
Krone, Paula Helene ... Atlanta, GA
Krone, Russell E. ... Tucson, AZ
Krone, Stacey J. ... New York, NY
Krone, Stephen R. ... Harrisburg, PA
Krone, Steven G. ... Beverly Hills, CA
Krone, Thomas R. ... Downers Grove, IL
Kronegold, Sheldon H. ... Englewood, NJ
Kronemer, Barry J. ... Hartford, CT
Kronemyer, Daniel R. ... San Diego, CA
Kronemyer, David E. ... Los Angeles, CA
Kronemyer, Robert E. ... La Jolla, CA
Kronen, Leif C. ... Lincoln, NE
Kronen, Sheldon H. ... Bronx, NY
Kronenberg, Alison B. ... New York, NY
Kronenberg, Angie W. ... Washington, DC
Kronenberg, Chet A. ... New York, NY
Kronenberg, Donald B. ... Seattle, WA
Kronenberg, Franklin W. ... Jamaica, NY
Kronenberg, George A. ... Huntsville, AL
Kronenberg, Hale ... Berkeley, CA
Kronenberg, Jacob A. H. ... Cleveland, OH
Kronenberg, James L. ... New York, NY
Kronenberg, Janet L. ... Cleveland, OH
Kronenberg, Jerry ... Memphis, TN
Kronenberg & Kronenberg ... Cleveland, OH
Kronenberg, Martin J. ... Flushing, NY
Kronenberg, Robert B. ... New York, NY
Kronenberg, Steven P. ... Miami Lakes, FL
Kronenberg, William S.
San Francisco, CA
Kronenberger, Donald R., Jr. ... Atlanta, GA
Kronenberger, Gregg R.
Baton Rouge, LA
Kronenberger, John B. ... Dallas, TX
Kronenberger, Karl S. ... Mansfield, OH
Kronenberger, M. Jane ... New York, NY
Kronengold, Amy L. ... Fort Lauderdale, FL
Kronengold, Jeffrey L.
Fort Lauderdale, FL
Kronengold, Ronald D. ... Hauppauge, NY
Kronenwetter, Patrick J. ... Chicago, IL
Kroner, Craig Arthur ... San Jose, CA
Kroner, James L., Jr. ... La Crosse, WI
Kroner, Jonathan Evan ... Miami, FL
Kroner, Mitchell E. ... Georgetown, MA
Kroner, Robert B. ... West Orange, NJ
Kroner, Robert J. ... Charlottesville, VA
Krones, Fred H. ... New York, NY
Krones, Mark P. ... San Diego, CA
Krones, Susan ... Lakeport, CA
Kroney • Mincey, Inc. ... Dallas, TX
Kroney, Robert H. ... Dallas, TX
Kronfeld, Bart P. ... Fort Bragg, CA
Kronfeld, Edwin ... Tulsa, OK
Kronfeld, Harvey S. ... Bala Cynwyd, PA
Kronfeld, Nicholas A. ... New York, NY
Kronfeld, Penny ... New York, NY
Krongard, Howard J. ... New York, NY
Krongold, Bass and Todd, P.A. ... Miami, FL
Krongold, Gerald ... Cleveland, OH
Krongold, Jeffrey B. ... New York, NY
Krongold Law Firm, The ... Costa Mesa, CA
Krongold, M. Ronald ... Miami, FL
Krongold, Randi M. ... Coral Gables, FL
Krongold, Sheryl ... Washington, DC
Krongold, Steven L. ... Costa Mesa, CA
Kronheim, Milton S., Jr. ... Washington, DC
Kronheim, Steven R. ... Morristown, NJ
Kronholm, Candace A. ... New York, NY
Kronick, Arnold S. ... White Plains, NY
Kronick, Brian W. ... East Orange, NJ
Kronick, Craig H. ... Garden Grove, CA
Kronick, Geoffrey M. ... Portland, OR
Kronick, Moskovitz, Tiedemann & Girard, A Professional Corporation
Sacramento, CA
San Francisco, CA
Kronick, Robert A., Law Offices of
Bakersfield, CA
Kronick, Stanley W. ... Sacramento, CA
Kronick, Stephen A. ... Sacramento, CA
Kroning, Linda J. ... Chicago, IL
Kroninger, Robert H. ... Inverness, CA
Kroninger, Timothy K. ... Troy, MI
Kronisch, Elizabeth ... Livingston, NJ
Kronisch, Matthew L.
Department of the Navy, Office of the Judge Advocate General, GV
Kronisch, Myron W. ... Livingston, NJ
Kronisch, Schkeeper and Lesser, A Professional Corporation ... Livingston, NJ
Kronish, Arnold ... New City, NY
Kronish, Herbert ... New York, NY
Kronish, Isidore ... New York, NY
Kronish Lieb Weiner & Hellman LLP
New York, NY
Kronk, Beuerle & Bowron
Traverse City, MI
Kronk, Catherine ... Burlington, VT
Kronk, Edward M. ... Detroit, MI
Kronk, Michael A. ... Traverse City, MI
Kronk, Richard F. ... Charlotte, NC
Kronk, Thomas A. ... Lansing, MI
Kronlage, Charles A., Jr. ... New Orleans, LA
Kronland, Scott A. ... San Francisco, CA
Kronlund, Michael C. ... Stockton, CA
Kronman, Ariel Z. ... New York, NY
Kronman, Carol J. ... New York, NY
Kronman, Craig H. ... San Francisco, CA
Kronmiller, Theodore G. ... Great Falls, VA
Kronovet, Alan B. ... Charlotte, NC
Kronovet, Steven Z. ... New York, NY
Kronowitz, Maurice H. ... Brooklyn, NY
Kronowitz, Rachel S. ... Washington, DC
Kronowitz, Ronald A. ... Savannah, GA
Kronquist, Kathryn A. ... Milwaukee, WI
Kronquist, Timothy E. ... Milwaukee, WI
Kronsberg, Abram J. ... Baltimore, MD
Kronsberg and Bluestein, LLP
Charleston, SC
Kronsberg, Edward ... Charleston, SC
Kronschnabel, William M. ... St. Paul, MN
Kronsnoble, Joseph M. ... Chicago, IL
Kronstadt, John A. ... Los Angeles, CA
Kronstein, Werner ... Washington, DC
Kronthal, Barry A. ... Harrisburg, PA
Kronthal, Richard H. ... New York, NY
Krontz, Kenneth W. ... Douglasville, GA
Krontz, Kenneth W., P.C.
Douglasville, GA
Kronz, Richard F. ... Pittsburgh, PA
Kronzek, Charles M. ... Lansing, MI
Kronzek, Charles M., P.C. ... Lansing, MI
Kronzer, Joann M. ... Tampa, FL
Kronzer, W. James ... Spring, TX
Krooks, Bernard A. ... New York, NY
White Plains, NY
Krooks, Howard S. ... New York, NY
Kroon, David C. ... Sioux Falls, SD
Kroon, H. Clifton ... Minneapolis, MN
Kroon, Herbert C. ... Mankato, MN
Kroon, Michael ... Palo Alto, CA
Kroon, Stephanie N. ... Palo Alto, CA
Kroontje, Mark K. ... Herreid, SD
Kroontje, Maury A. ... Seattle, WA
Kroop, Elizabeth F. ... Department of Justice, Civil Division, GV
Kroop, Gary A. ... Perth Amboy, NJ
Kroop, Jordan A. ... Phoenix, AZ
Kroop, Richard I. ... Miami Beach, FL
Kroopf, Kenneth J., (A P.C.) ... Monterey, CA
Kroopnick, David I. ... San Francisco, CA
Kroopnick, Meyer N. ... Garden Grove, CA
Kroopnick, Richard E.
Bloomfield Hills, MI
Kroos, Arthur G., III ... Wilsonville, OR
Kroot, Kenneth A. ... Chicago, IL
Kroot, M David ... San Francisco, CA
Krooth & Altman ... Washington, DC
Columbia, MD
Sterling, VA
Krooth, John D. ... Washington, DC
Krooth, Stephen ... New York, NY
Krop, Linda J. ... Santa Barbara, CA
Krop, Nancy G. ... San Francisco, CA
Krop, Pamela S. ... Eden Prairie, MN
Kropach, William J. ... Encino, CA
Kropelnicki, Steven, Jr. ... Asheville, NC
Kropf, John W. ... Department of State, Office of the Legal Adviser, GV
Kropf, John W. ... Orrville, OH
Kropf, Marcos A. ... Sacramento, CA
Kropf, Ramsey L. ... Aspen, CO
Kropf, Robert C. ... Kalamazoo, MI
Kropf, Rodney C. ... Livonia, MI
Kropf, Wagner & Hohenberger ... Orrville, OH
Kropff, James B. ... Los Angeles, CA
Kropid, David Allan ... Superior, WI
Kropiewnicki, Mark E.
Plymouth Meeting, PA
Kropik, Chas. T. ... Chicago, IL
Kropilak, Mark J. ... Bryn Mawr, PA
Kropitzer, Harold ... Portland, OR
Kropke, Amy ... Needham, MA
Kropkowski, Gary T. ... Poughkeepsie, NY
Kroposki, Edgar P., Jr. ... Greenville, SC
Kropoth, Madeline Schillaci ... Rahway, NJ
Kropp, Allen L. ... Department of Education, Office of the General Counsel, GV
Kropp, David H. ... Pittsburgh, PA
Kropp, Edith M. ... Rockville, MD
Kropp, Janet U. ... North Hollywood, CA
Kropp, Jeffrey M. ... Chicago, IL
Kropp, John J. ... Cincinnati, OH
Kropp, Joseph D. ... Boston, MA
Kropp, Karen Lautz ... Atlanta, GA
Kropp, Lawrence P. ... Jamestown, ND
Kropp, Norman W. ... Jamaica, NY
Kropp, Richard T. ... Albany, OR
Kropp, Richard V. ... Hendersonville, NC
Kropp, Robert J. ... New York, NY
Kropp, Robert, Jr. ... Burbank, CA
Kropp III, William J. ... Fort Smith, AR
Kros, Frank J. ... San Diego, CA
Kroschel, Kurt W. ... Billings, MT
Kroschel & Yerger ... Billings, MT
Krosin, Kenneth E. ... Washington, DC
Krosin, Stanley E. ... Baltimore, MD
Krosner, David R. ... Milwaukee, WI
Kross, Edward J. ... Clinton, IA
Kross, Jeffrey S. ... Oakland, CA
Kross, Michael ... San Francisco, CA
Krosschell, Stephen C. ... Clearwater, FL
Krostar, E. Stanley ... Reisterstown, MD
Krostue, Sigurd W. ... New London, WI
Krotec, Peter J. ... Sarasota, FL
Krotenberg, Deborah G. ... Atlanta, GA
Krotick, Glenn A. ... Philadelphia, PA
Krotick & Meyer ... Philadelphia, PA
Krotine, David L. ... Sacramento, CA
Krotinger, Andrew S. ... Wellesley, MA
Krotinger, Eve ... Sacramento, CA
Krotinger, Jonathan H.
San Francisco, CA
Krotinger, Myron N. ... Cleveland, OH
Krotki, Carl ... New York, NY
Krotman, Max T. ... Melville, NY
Krotman, Michael S. ... Gaithersburg, MD
Kroto, Frank L., Jr. ... Erie, PA
Krotoski, Mark L. ... Sacramento, CA
Krotoszynski, Ronald J., Jr. ... Indianapolis, IN
Krotseng, Richard Van M. ... Richmond, VA
Krouk, David B. ... St. Petersburg, FL
Krouk, Ivan J. ... Philadelphia, PA
Kroum, Robert J. ... Bellevue, WA
Krouner, Leonard W. (IBA) ... Albany, NY
Krouner, Shari Kahn ... New York, NY
Krouner, Todd J. ... New York, NY
Kroupa, Diane L. ... St. Paul, MN
Krouse, Allen J., III ... New Orleans, LA
Krouse, Bradley A. ... Philadelphia, PA
Krouse, Geoffrey R. ... New York, NY
Krouse, George E. ... Wheaton, MD
Krouse, George R., Jr. ... New York, NY
Krouse, Gwin M. ... Allentown, PA
Krouse, James E. ... Cincinnati, OH
Krouse, Lisa A. ... Fort Lauderdale, FL
Krouse, Lori Lynn ... Roseburg, OR
Krousel, Karl E. ... Baton Rouge, LA
Krousel, Walter R., III ... Baton Rouge, LA
Krousel, Walter R., Jr. ... Baton Rouge, LA
Krousel, Walter R., Jr., and Associates, A Prof. Law Corp. ... Baton Rouge, LA

Krouss, John R. ...Baudette, MN
Krout, Dale E., Jr. ...Naples, FL
Krout, John E. ...Radnor, PA
Krout, Michael J. ...York, PA
Krout, Michael S. ...San Luis Obispo, CA
Krout, Michael S., A Law Corp.
San Luis Obispo, CA
Krovatin & Associates, LLC ...Newark, NJ
Krovatin, Gerald ...Newark, NJ
Krovatin, William
Whitehouse Station, NJ
Krovitz Law Firm, The, P.C. ...Denver, CO
Englewood, CO
Krovitz, Rochelle G. ...Englewood, CO
Krow, Grant R. ...Philadelphia, PA
Krow, Judith E. ...Minneapolis, MN
Krowen, Edward ...West Palm Beach, FL
Krowen, Jerril J. ...Saugus, MA
Krowiak, Edward G. ...Scranton, PA
Krowicki, Ben M. ...Hartford, CT
Krown, Kenneth J. ...Los Angeles, CA
Krowski, Joseph F. ...Brockton, MA
Kroyer, Stephen T. ...Napa, CA
Krpan, Larry D. ...Des Moines, IA
Krpata, Kyle C. ...Dallas, TX
Krsul, John A., Jr. ...Bloomfield Hills, MI
Krsul, Timothy C. ...Minneapolis, MN
Krtil, Ernest James ...Sacramento, CA
Krubeck, Richard T., Law Offices of
Itasca, IL
Krubel, Frederick J. ...Riverside, IL
Krubiner, Alan M. ...Palo Alto, CA
Krubit, Martin J. ...Bethesda, MD
Kruce, Hilary A. ...New York, NY
Kruchek, Joseph Wm. ...Phoenix, AZ
Kruchko & Fries ...Washington, DC
Baltimore, MD
Towson, MD
McLean, VA
Kruchko, John G. ...Washington, DC
Baltimore, MD
McLean, VA
Kruchten, Gary J. ...Quantico, VA
Kruck, Frederick H., Jr. ...Warrenton, VA
Kruckemeyer, Robert J. ...Houston, TX
Krucks, William N. ...Chicago, IL
Skokie, IL
Krucoff, Neal E. ...Washington, DC
Kruczynski, Steven R. ...Boston, MA
Krudys, Kent M. ...Washington, DC
Krudys, Mark J. ...Richmond, VA
Krudys, Mark J., PLC ...Richmond, VA
Krudys, Suzanne
Securities and Exchange Commission,
Division of Investment Management, GV
Krueckeberg, John H. ...Naples, FL
Krueger, Allyson S. ...Portland, OR
Krueger, Andrew L. ...St. Louis, MO
Krueger & Aranda ...Cottonwood Falls, KS
Emporia, KS
Krueger, Ben J. ...San Antonio, TX
Krueger, Blake W. ...Grand Rapids, MI
Krueger, Brandon ...Madison, WI
Krueger, Bruce H. ...Muskegon, MI
Krueger, Carl ...Menomonee Falls, WI
Krueger, Carl S. ...Muskegon Heights, MI
Krueger, Charles E. ...San Francisco, CA
Krueger, Charles R. ...Lexington, NC
Krueger, Charles Z. ...Secaucus, NJ
Krueger, Christopher E. ...Sacramento, CA
Krueger, Christopher W. ...San Diego, CA
Krueger, Craig A. ...Silver Spring, MD
Krueger, David A. ...Brooklyn, NY
Krueger, David S. ...Eureka, CA
Krueger, Dennis A. ...Kailua-Kona, HI
Krueger, Dennis R. ...Waukesha, WI
Krueger, Donald C. ...Emporia, KS
Krueger, Donald F. ...Sacramento, CA
Krueger, Donald S. ...New York, NY
Krueger, Edward G. ...Madison, WI
Krueger, Elizabeth Ann ...Bloomington, MN
Krueger, Elizabeth L. ...Wheaton, IL
Krueger, Elizabeth L., P.C. ...Wheaton, IL
Krueger, Everett H. ...Delaware, OH
Krueger, Garrett R. ...Seattle, WA
Krueger, George E. ...San Francisco, CA
Krueger, George J. ...Philadelphia, PA
Krueger, Harvey M. ...New York, NY
Krueger, Herbert W. ...Chicago, IL
Krueger, James ...Wailuku, HI
Krueger, James A. ...Tacoma, WA
Krueger, James, Attorney at Law, A Law Corporation ...Honolulu, HI
Lihue, HI
Krueger, James, Attorney at Law, Attorney at Law, A Law Corporation
Wailuku, HI
Krueger, James P. ...Chicago, IL
Krueger, Jane L. ...Palo Alto, CA
Krueger, Jeffrey A. ...Brandon, FL
Krueger, Jeffrey A., P.A. ...Brandon, FL
Krueger, Jeffrey M. ...Portland, OR
Krueger, Jeffrey W. ...Cleveland, OH
Krueger, Jerome R. ...Frankfort, KY
Krueger, John ...St. Paul, MN
Krueger, John W. ...Rhinelander, WI
Krueger, Karen ...Washington, DC
Krueger, Karen G. ...New York, NY
Krueger, Katherine ...Freeport, TX
Krueger, Kathryn L. ...River Forest, IL
Krueger, Keith R. ...Jefferson City, MO
Krueger, Kevin P. ...Belleville, IL
St. Louis, MO
Krueger, Kris W. ...Detroit, MI
Krueger, Kurt ...Butte, MT
Krueger, Kurt J. ...Charlottesville, VA
Krueger, L. Brant ...Arlington, TX
Krueger, Larry E. ...Spokane, WA
Krueger & Lesica ...Muskegon Heights, MI
Krueger, Mark A. ...Richmond, VA
Krueger, Mark J. ...Westbury, NY
Krueger, Mark L. ...Baraboo, WI
Krueger, Matthew K. ...Streator, IL
Krueger, Maureen H. ...Carthage, NC
Krueger, Michael J. ...Kingsville, TX
Krueger, Michelle R. ...St. Paul, MN
Krueger, Moria ...Madison, WI
Krueger, Nancy J. ...Appleton, WI
Krueger, Nancy K. ...Delaware, OH
Krueger, Nicole V. ...Washington, DC
Krueger, Pamela Weidler ...Bellevue, WA
Krueger, Patrick M. ...Brainerd, MN
Krueger, Paul D. ...Sartell, MN
Krueger, Paul H. ...Salem, OR
Krueger, Paul M. ...Beverly Hills, CA
Krueger, Phillip G. ...Parker, AZ
Krueger, Rand ...Wausau, WI
Krueger, Raymond R. ...Milwaukee, WI
Krueger, Richard J. ...Oconto, WI
Krueger, Richard P. ...Linden, NJ
Krueger, R. J., Jr. ...Aberdeen, SD
Krueger, Robert ...Mexico, MO
Krueger, Robert B. ...Los Angeles, CA
Krueger, Robert J., Jr. ...Detroit, MI
Krueger, Robin H. ...Detroit, MI
Krueger, Scott David ...Gainesville, FL
Krueger, Steven C. ...Kansas City, MO
Krueger, Steven Philip ...Chicago, IL
Krueger, Stuart J. ...River Falls, WI
Krueger, Susan E. ...Elkhorn, WI
Krueger, Thomas A. ...Emporia, KS
Krueger, Thomas J. ...Chicago, IL
Krueger, Thomas R. ...Roselle, NJ
Krueger, Valerie G. ...Olathe, KS
Krueger, Vernon L. ...Dallas, TX
Krueger, Victoria ...Brentwood, TN
Krueger, Victoria ...Nashville, TN
Krueger, Victoria Lwin ...Brentwood, TN
Krueger, Walter R. ...Kirkland, WA
Krueger, William J. ...New Brighton, MN
Krueger, William J. ...Independence, OH
Krueger, William J., P.A.
New Brighton, MN
Krueger, William W., III ...Austin, TX
Krueger-Brophy, Carol ...Franklin, TN
Kruegler, Richard P. ...Richmond, VA
Kruelle, Henry F. ...Baltimore, MD
Kruer & Associates, P.S.C. ...Covington, KY
Kruer, David A. ...Covington, KY
Kruer, James R. ...Covington, KY
Kruer, Jay C. ...La Mesa, CA
Krufka, Marci M. ...Moorestown, NJ
Philadelphia, PA
Kruft, Corinne D. ...Lancaster, PA
Kruft, Stephen R. ...New York, NY
Krug, Andrew J. ...Baltimore, MD
Krug, Anita K. ...Boston, MA
Krug, Anthony E. ...Dallas, TX
Krug, Arthur J. ...Jamaica, NY
Krug, Barbara Jean Wilson ...Conway, SC
Krug & Beckelman ...Cedar Rapids, IA
Krug, Bob N. ...Redlands, CA
Krug, Daniel W. ...Russell, KS
Krug, E. Wayne ...Springdale, AR
Krug, Edward J. ...Cedar Rapids, IA
Krug, Frederick W. ...Waterbury, CT
Krug, Gene G. ...Medford, WI
Krug, Gregory G. ...Medford, WI
Krug, Howard B. ...Harrisburg, PA
Krug, Ivan D. ...La Crosse, KS
Krug, James B. ...Los Angeles, CA
Krug, John B. ...Cranford, NJ
Krug, John C. ...Cincinnati, OH
Krug, John L.
Securities and Exchange Commission,
Division of Corporation Finance, GV
Krug, John S. ...Burlingame, CA
Krug, Kenneth ...Santa Monica, CA
Krug, L. Wayne ...Sugar Land, TX
Krug Law Offices ...Medford, WI
Krug, Leonard A. ...Chicago, IL
Krug, Lyle A. ...Freeport, IL
Orangeville, IL
Krug, Marc S. ...Boxborough, MA
Krug, Michael P. ...Sacramento, CA
Krug, Michel S. ...St. Paul, MN
Krug, Paul J. ...San Francisco, CA
Krug, Philip T. ...New York, NY
Krug, Rachel M. ...Chicago, IL
Krug, Rob A. ...Dover, PA
Krug, Robert ...Tampa, FL
Krug, Robert D. ...Toms River, NJ
Krug, Robert F., Jr. ...Chicago, IL
Krug, Sandra Willis ...Oklahoma City, OK
Krug & Sobel, LLC ...Denver, CO
Krug, Stewart L. ...Clearwater, FL
Krug, Thomas E. ...Buffalo, NY
Krug, Warren J. ...Prince Frederick, MD
Krugel, Joel M. ...Bloomfield Hills, MI
Krugel, Robert J. ...New York, NY
Kruger, Allen J. ...Laurel, MD
Kruger, Allen J., P.A. ...Laurel, MD
Kruger, Andrew C. ...Milford, CT
Kruger & Benoit, L.L.C. ...Clayton, MO
St. Louis, MO
Kruger, Brian J. ...Gainesville, FL
Kruger, Bruce ...Minneapolis, MN
Kruger, Daniel Y. ...San Antonio, TX
Kruger, Daniel Y., P.C. ...San Antonio, TX
Kruger, David W. ...Madison, WI
Kruger, Donald G. ...Prentiss, MS
Kruger, Elizabeth J. ...Sherman Oaks, CA
Kruger, Elizabeth L.
General Services Administration,
Office of Regional Counsel, GV
Kruger, Eric W. ...Omaha, NE
Kruger, Frederick B. ...St. Louis, MO
Kruger, Gary I. ...Akron, OH
Kruger, Gilbert N. ...Costa Mesa, CA
Kruger, Henry & Hunter ...Karnak, IL
Metropolis, IL
Mound City, IL
Vienna, IL
Kruger, Howard K. ...Winona, MN
Kruger, Jodi L. ...Calabasas, CA
Kruger, Joel L. ...Tulsa, OK
Kruger, John E. ...Memphis, TN
Kruger, John F. ...Seattle, WA
Kruger, Karen J. ...Baltimore, MD
Kruger, Lewis ...New York, NY
Kruger, Louis T. ...San Francisco, CA
Kruger, Marc L. ...Minneapolis, MN
Kruger, Mark H. ...St. Louis, MO
Kruger, Mark R. ...Sacramento, CA
Kruger, Marvin J. ...Chicago, IL
Kruger, Monica Green ...Omaha, NE
Kruger, Murray C. ...Alexandria, VA
Kruger, Patricia R. ...Pitman, NJ
Kruger, Paul Arthur ...Norman, OK
Kruger, Philip M. ...Clifton, NJ
Kruger, Rand Eric ...Louisville, KY
Kruger, Richard ...Metropolis, IL
Kruger, Richard E. ...Southfield, MI
Kruger, Richard J. ...St. Paul, MN
Kruger, Robert ...New York, NY
Kruger, Robert J. ...Fultonville, NY
Kruger, Roland H. ...Sonoma, CA
Kruger, Rolf D. ...Lafayette, CA
Kruger, Schwartz & Morreau
New Albany, IN
Louisville, KY
Kruger, Sharla ...San Antonio, TX
Kruger, Stephen P. ...Jackson, MS
Kruger, Steven A. ...Sterling Heights, MI
Kruger, Steven R. ...Minneapolis, MN
Kruger, Stuart A. ...Washington, DC
Kruger, Stuart G. ...Jackson, MS
Kruger, Susan Laiken ...Washington, DC
Kruger, Thomas E. ...New York, NY
Kruger, Treva K. ...Norman, OK
Kruger, Walter J., III ...Atlanta, GA
Krugh, John R. ...Houston, TX
Krugh, Timothy D. ...Toledo, OH
Krugler, David ...Atlanta, GA
Krugler, Margaret Beth ...Fort Worth, TX
Krugler, Mark E. ...Giddings, TX
Krugliak, Samuel ...Canton, OH
Salem, OH
Krugliak, Wilkins, Griffiths & Dougherty Co., L.P.A. ...Akron, OH
Alliance, OH
Canton, OH
New Philadelphia, OH
Salem, OH
Krugly, Ruth E. ...Chicago, IL
Krugman, Edward B. ...Atlanta, GA
Krugman, Edward P. ...New York, NY
Krugman, Gary D. ...Washington, DC
Krugman, James D. ...Saddle Brook, NJ
New York, NY
Krugman & Kailes LLP
Saddle Brook, NJ
New York, NY
Krugman, Kimberly A. ...Chicago, IL
Krugman, Murray S. ...Thetford Center, VT
Krugman, Neil B. ...Nashville, TN
Krugman-Kadi, Eilon ...Gainesville, FL
Kruh, Joel R. ...Baltimore, MD
Kruh, Louis ...Hempstead, NY
Kruidenier, Elizabeth ...Des Moines, IA
Kruis, Elizabeth E. ...Santa Monica, CA
Kruis, John M. ...Grand Rapids, MI
Kruis, Katherine S. ...San Diego, CA
Kruis, Steven H. ...San Diego, CA
Kruit, Mary Ellen ...Chicago, IL
Kruizenga, Lori J. ...Sycamore, IL
Kruk & Campbell, P.C. ...Lima, NY
Kruk, Gregory M. ...Brockway, PA
Punxsutawney, PA
Kruk, Richard A. ...Mesa, AZ
Kruk, Stephen M. ...Lima, NY
Kruka, B. Scott ...Dallas, TX
Krukiel, Charles E. ...Wilmington, DE
Krukowski & Costello, S.C.
Washington, DC
Milwaukee, WI
Krukowski, Deborah A. ...Milwaukee, WI
Krukowski, Thomas P. ...Milwaukee, WI
Krul, Michael H. ...Fort Lauderdale, FL
Krula, David W. ...Naperville, IL
Krulewich, Helen D. ...Boston, MA
Krulewich, Lawrence T. ...Chicago, IL
Krulewich, Leonard M. ...Boston, MA
Krulewich, Leonard M., Law Offices of
Boston, MA
Krulewitch, Beth L. ...Denver, CO
Kruley, Harold ...Chicago, IL
Kruley, Michael F. ...Chicago, IL
Krulik, Holly Debra ...Fort Lauderdale, FL
Krulin, Stephen E., Law Offices of
North Miami, FL
Krulisky, Paul A. ...Phoenix, AZ
Kruljac, Michael V. ...Washington, DC
Krull, Charles R. ...Phoenix, AZ
Krull, Curtis J. ...Des Moines, IA
Krull, Deborah ...Media, PA
Krull, Douglas A. ...Northwood, IA
Krull, Frederick John ...Chicago, IL
Krull, Gregory P. ...Buffalo, NY
Krull, John A. ...Buffalo, NY
Krull, Kyle E. ...Overland Park, KS
Krull, Kyle E., P.A. ...Overland Park, KS
Krull, Robert J. ...Chicago, IL
Krull, Stephen K. ...Toledo, OH
Krulla, Rhett R. N.
Federal Trade Commission,
Bureau of Competition, GV
Krulwich, Andrew S. ...Washington, DC
Krulwich, David S. ...New York, NY
Krum, Eugene W. ...Fresno, CA
Krum, Jean A. ...Columbus, OH
Krum, Mark G. ...Los Angeles, CA
Krum, Mark Jay ...Boca Raton, FL
Philadelphia, PA
Krum, Melissa R. ...Oakland, CA
Krum, Neil M. ...Abington, PA
Krum, Philip J., Jr. ...El Centro, CA
Krum, Richard W. ...Fresno, CA
Krum, Sidney D. ...New York, NY
Kruman, Donna ...Pittsburgh, PA
Kruman, Eric ...Pittsburgh, PA
Kruman, Martin J. ...Malverne, NY
Krumbein, Mark S. ...Cincinnati, OH
Krumbein, Richard M. ...Denver, CO
Krumbhaar, George D.
Joint Committees And Commissions, GV
Krumbholz, Walter O., Jr. ...Portland, OR
Krumdick, Candace ...Wheaton, IL
Krumdick, Eric A. ...Chicago, IL
Krumeich, Edward T., Jr. ...Greenwich, CT
Krumeich, Elizabeth Kneisel
Middlebury, CT
Krumenacker, Kelli A. ...Martinsville, VA
Krumenacker & Krumenacker
Johnstown, PA
Krumenacker, Norman A., III
Johnstown, PA
Krumenacker, Norman A., Jr.
Johnstown, PA
Krumenauer, Harry W. ...Marietta, GA
Krumhansl, Brigitte S. ...San Juan, PR
Krumholtz, Michael W. ...Dayton, OH
Krumholz, Arnold H. ...Westfield, NJ
Krumholz, Dennis J. ...Morristown, NJ
Krumholz, Francine ...Baltimore, MD
Krumholz, George R. ...Jericho, NY
Krumholz, Joshua C. ...Boston, MA
Krumholz, Marjorie F. ...Washington, DC
Krumholz, Peter J. ...Denver, CO
Krumholz, Richard S. ...Dallas, TX
Krumins, Girts ...Montrose, CO
Kruml, Thomas S. ...Ord, NE
Krumland, Gary G. ...Lincoln, NE
Krumlauf, Martin ...Columbus, OH
Krumm, Jeffrey D. ...Nevada City, CA
Krumm, Kathleen Ellen ...Jackson, MI
Krumm, Nancy Marakas ...Columbus, OH
Krumm, Roger P. ...Fulton, MO
Krumm, Ross W. ...Harrisonburg, VA
Krumm & Shryock ...Fulton, MO
Krumm, Stephen H. ...Encino, CA
Krumm, Timothy J. ...Iowa City, IA
Krumm, Victor C. ...Sarasota, FL
Krumme, Gregg C. ...Austin, TX
Krumme, Robin I. ...Austin, TX
Krummel, Ann C. ...Lodi, WI
Krummen, Craig S. ...Minneapolis, MN
St. Paul, MN
Krump, Gary J.
Department Of Veterans Affairs,
Office of Management, GV
Krumpe, Jeffrey E. ...Peoria, IL
Krumpe, Stephen C. ...Dubuque, IA
Krumpelbeck, Gerald W. ...Cincinnati, OH
Krumpelt, Andrew ...Naperville, IL
Krumpfes, Austin ...Chicago, IL
Krumrei, Daniel D. ...Oshkosh, WI
Krumreich, Ted A. ...Denver, CO
Krumsiek, James H. ...Boston, MA
Krumstok, Deborah J. ...Chicago, IL
Krumtum, Maria Kathryn
Virginia Beach, VA
Krumtum, Matthew G. ...Williamsburg, VA
Krup, I. Steven ...Hallandale Beach, FL
Krup, Leonard G. ...Willows, CA
Krup, Oleh A. ...Stamford, CT
Krup, Robert J. ...Newport Beach, CA
Krupa, James A. ...Amery, WI
Krupa, John A. ...Flossmoor, IL
Krupa, John R. ...Flossmoor, IL
Krupa, Lori L. ...San Diego, CA
Krupa, Michael J. ...Denver, CO
Krupanski, Susan M. ...Boston, MA
Krupansky, Blanche E. ...Fairview Park, OH
Krupansky, Robt. B. ...Cleveland, OH
Krupar, William G. ...Grand Rapids, MI
Krupczak, Norberta Fuller ...Amsterdam, NY
Krupen, Karen I. ...South San Francisco, CA
Kruper, Paul D. ...Pittsburgh, PA
Krupicka, Lisa A. ...Memphis, TN
Krupin, Charles ...Melville, NY
New York, NY
Krupin Greenbaum & O'Brien, LLC
Washington, DC
Krupin, Jay P. ...Washington, DC
Krupin, John ...New York, NY
Krupin, Stewart ...Rocky Point, NY
Krupinsky, Peter J. ...Los Angeles, CA
Krupka, Catherine M. ...Washington, DC
Krupka, James D. ...Santa Rosa, CA
Krupka, Keith M. ...Woodland Hills, CA
Krupka, Kimberly Gobla ...Allentown, PA
Krupka, Robert G., (P.C.)
Los Angeles, CA
Chicago, IL
Krupka, Robert J. ...Saginaw, MI
Krupkin, Beatrice ...Syracuse, NY
Krupkin, Gary P. ...Dallas, TX
Krupkin & Wilson, L.L.C. ...Dallas, TX
Krupman, Victor S. ...Columbus, OH
Krupman, William A. ...New York, NY

Krupnick Campbell Malone Roselli Buser Slama Hancock McNelis Liberman & McKee, P.A. ... Fort Lauderdale, FL
Krupnick Campbell Malone Roselli Buser Slama & Hannock McNelis Liberman & McKee, P.A. ... Miami, FL
Krupnick Campbell Malone Roselli Buser Slama Hancock McNelis Liberman & McKee, P.A. ... Palm Beach, FL
Krupnick & Goldman ... Garden City, NY
Krupnick, Jerold B. ... Stony Brook, NY
Krupnick, Jon E. ... Fort Lauderdale, FL
Krupnick, Laurence A. Huntingdon Valley, PA
Krupnick, Marshall P. ... Hollywood, FL
Krupnick, Marshall P., P.A. ... Hollywood, FL
Krupnick, Matt J. ... Dallas, TX
Krupnick, Michael B. ... Philadelphia, PA
Krupnick, Neil & Associates, P.C. Westlake Village, CA
Krupnick, Neil Lawrence Westlake Village, CA
Krupnick, Scott ... Buffalo Grove, IL
Krupnick, Shauna B. ... Berwyn, PA
Krupnick, Sheldon M. ... Garden City, NY
Krupnikoff, Jeffrey M. ... Meriden, CT
Krupnow, Mary M. ... Raleigh, NC
Krupp, Alvin F. ... Safford, AZ
Krupp, Christian G., II ... Grand Rapids, MI
Krupp, Clarence W. ... Scottsdale, AZ
Krupp, David J. ... Chicago, IL
Krupp, Debra S. ... Boston, MA
Krupp, Elizabeth D. ... Naperville, IL
Krupp, Frederick S. ... Lake City, MI
Krupp, George T. ... Grand Rapids, MI
Krupp, Gerald ... Encino, CA
Krupp, Harvey J. ... Pompano Beach, FL
Krupp, Harvey J., P.A. ... Pompano Beach, FL
Krupp, James P. ... St. Louis, MO
Krupp & Krupp ... De Kalb, IL
Krupp & Langell ... Lake City, MI
Krupp Law Office, P.C. ... Grand Rapids, MI
Krupp, Lynda ... Highland Park, MI
Krupp, Nancy Black ... Dallas, TX
Krupp, Peter B. ... Boston, MA
Krupp, Peter C. ... Chicago, IL
Krupp, Robert J. ... Bartlett, IL
Krupp, Robert J. ... De Kalb, IL
Krupp, Spencer J. ... Atlanta, GA
Krupp, Stephen A. ... Plymouth, MN
Krupp, Stephen P. ... Freeport, TX
Krupp, Thomas J. ... De Kalb, IL
Kruppe, Michael A. ... Los Angeles, CA
Kruppenbacher, Frank ... Orlando, FL
Kruppenbacher, Frank, P.A. ... Orlando, FL
Kruppstadt, Adam L. ... Iron Mountain, MI
Krupsaw, Fulton H. ... Washington, DC
Krupsaw, Samuel M. ... Waynesboro, PA
Krupski, John S. ... Concord, NH
Krupsky, Amy Eisen National Archives And Records Administration, General Counsel Staff, GV
Krupsky, Joseph F. ... Basking Ridge, NJ
Krupsky, Kenneth J. ... Washington, DC
Krus, Cynthia M. ... Washington, DC
Krusch, Alan R. ... Charlotte, NC
Krusch, Joseph G. ... New York, NY
Kruschke, Linda L. ... Lake Oswego, OR
Kruse, Alan Garnet ... Houston, TX
Kruse, Alvin L. ... Chicago, IL
Kruse, Ann E. ... Redwood City, CA
Kruse, Bradley R. ... Chicago, IL
Kruse, C. Thomas ... Houston, TX
Kruse, Clifton B., Jr. Colorado Springs, CO
Kruse, Corinne R. ... Chicago, IL
Kruse, Daniel A. ... Cincinnati, OH
Kruse, David A. ... Auburn, IN
Kruse, Derald D. ... Auburn, IN
Kruse, Desmond H. ... Pago Pago, TT
Kruse, Douglas R. ... Valparaiso, IN
Kruse, Edward C. ... St. Louis, MO
Kruse, Edward H. ... Fort Lauderdale, FL
Kruse, Erika L. ... Chicago, IL
Kruse, Erika Leigh ... Providence, RI
Kruse, Fredrickcus M. ... Pago Pago, TT
Kruse, Gary A. ... Merrillville, IN
Kruse, Harold C. ... Fortuna, CA
Kruse, Howard L. ... Chicago, IL
Kruse, J. Henry, Jr. ... Albany, CA
Kruse, James R. ... Salt Lake City, UT
Kruse, Jane Y. ... Jefferson City, MO
Kruse, Jeffrey A. ... Kansas City, MO
Kruse, John A. ... Troy, MI
Kruse, John A. ... Marshfield, WI
Kruse, John A., Jr. ... Hamilton, OH
Kruse, John C. ... Department of Justice, Civil Division, GV
Kruse, Jordon L. ... Chicago, IL
Kruse, Joy A. ... San Francisco, CA
Kruse, Karen P. ... Seattle, WA
Kruse, Kelly A. ... Troy, MI
Kruse, Kenneth D. ... Allen Park, MI
Kruse, Kevin J. ... Des Moines, IA
Kruse, Kevin J. ... Overland Park, KS
Kruse, Landa & Maycock, L.L.C. Salt Lake City, UT
Kruse, Layne E. ... Houston, TX
Kruse, Leonard W. ... Port Orchard, WA
Kruse, Lorie A. ... Monterey, CA
Kruse & Luccia, L.L.P. ... Houston, TX
Kruse & Lynch, P.C. Colorado Springs, CO
Kruse, M. Russell, Jr. Newport Beach, CA
Kruse, Margaret A. ... Louisville, KY
Kruse, Margaret E. ... Ann Arbor, MI
Kruse, Marion Woodrow, Jr. ... Houston, TX
Kruse, Mark E. ... San Diego, CA
Kruse, Mark F. ... Cleveland, OH
Kruse, Patrick G. ... Detroit, MI
Kruse, Paul S. ... Indianapolis, IN
Kruse, Paul W. ... Washington, DC
Kruse, Paul W. ... Brenham, TX
Kruse, Reinker & Hamilton, L.L.C. St. Louis, MO
Kruse, Renae S. ... Rock Rapids, IA
Kruse, Richard A., III ... Smyrna, GA
Kruse, Richard J., Jr. ... Houston, TX
Kruse, Robert G. ... Sacramento, CA
Kruse, Robert L., Jr. ... Alamosa, CO
Kruse, Robert M. ... Grand Rapids, MI
Kruse, Roland R. ... Payson, AZ
Kruse, Russell J. ... Palmyra, MO
Kruse, Sara M. ... Detroit, MI
Kruse, Scott August ... Los Angeles, CA
Kruse, Thomas C. ... Everett, WA
Kruse, William E. ... Sacramento, CA
Kruse, William F. ... Pasadena, CA
Krusen, Robert P. ... Washington, DC
Krushenski, Kenneth R. ... La Follette, TN
Krushinski, Michael J. ... Scranton, PA
Kruska, Kristin L. ... Chicago, IL
Kruskal, Karen L. ... Cambridge, MA
Krusniak, Connie P. ... Ludington, MI
Krusor, Mark W. ... Winfield, KS
Krusos, Denis A. ... Lloyd Harbor, NY
Kruss, Richard S. ... Chicago, IL
Krustapentus, Stephanie ... Athol, MA
Krusz, Keith E. ... Hartford, CT
Kruszewski, George H. ... Detroit, MI
Kruszynski, Laura A. ... San Mateo, CA
Krut, Joshua D. ... Chicago, IL
Krut, Michael P. ... Farmington Hills, MI
Krut, Michael P., P.C. ... Farmington Hills, MI
Kruta, James M. ... Newburgh, NY
Krutch Lindell, A Professional Service Corporation ... Seattle, WA
Krutch, Richard F. ... Seattle, WA
Krutcik, James A. ... Mission Viejo, CA
Krute, Robert E. ... Montrose, CO
Kruteck, Laurence R. ... New York, NY
Kruth, Harold E. ... Menlo Park, CA
Kruthers, Mark D. ... Fresno, CA
Kruthoffer, Kurt ... Paintsville, KY
Krutman, Michael W. ... Trenton, NJ
Krutman, Robert ... Woodridge, NY
Krutoff, Glenn S. ... White Plains, NY
Krutter, Forrest N. ... Omaha, NE
Kruttschnitt, Donald B. ... De Witt, NY
Kruttschnitt, Herbert, III ... Brick, NJ
Krutz, David A. ... Milwaukee, WI
Krutz, Fred, III ... Jackson, MS
Krutzel, Martin ... New York, NY
Krutzfeldt & Jones ... Miles City, MT
Krutzfeldt, William J. ... Miles City, MT
Krutzsch, Andrew S., (P.C.) ... Brawley, CA
Krutzsch, Joseph M. ... St. Louis, MO
Krutzsch, Stephen G. ... Brea, CA
Kruvant, Beth Toni Gelber ... Montclair, NJ
Kruvant, Cathy G. ... South Orange, NJ
Kruy, Catherine A. ... Costa Mesa, CA
Kruzel, Gregory M. ... Scottsdale, AZ
Kruzhkov, Marlen ... New York, NY
Kruzynski, Michael G. ... Garden City, NY
Kruzynski, Peter G. ... New Haven, CT
Krycia, Frank ... Mount Clemens, MI
Kryda, Frank J. ... Cicero, IL
Kryder, Andrew ... Milpitas, CA
Kryder, George M., III ... Dallas, TX
Kryger, Alexander, Egan & Elmer, P.C. Albany, OR
Salem, OR
Kryger, J. David ... Albany, OR
Kryger, Ralph S. ... Lincoln, NE
Krygier, Kathleen M. ... Stratford, CT
Krygowski, Walter J. ... Dayton, OH
Kryle, Sanford I. ... New York, NY
Krylov, Nikolai ... New York, NY
Krymowski, John J. ... Cleveland, OH
Krynski, Peter ... Falls Church, VA
Krynski, William A. Department of Commerce, Patent and Trademark Office, GV
Krys Boyle Freedman & Sawyer, P.C. Denver, CO
Krys, Joseph F. ... Denver, CO
Krysa, Stanley F. ... Department of Justice, Tax Division, GV
Krysak, Robert E. ... San Diego, CA
Kryshak, Gary J. ... Wisconsin Rapids, WI
Kryshak, Robert V. Wisconsin Rapids, WI
Kryshak, Thad F. ... Milwaukee, WI
Krysiak, Charles J. ... Baltimore, MD
Krysinski, Mark P. ... Detroit, MI
Krysl & Cikanek ... Stockton, KS
Krysl, Stanley ... Stockton, KS
Krystal, Alan ... Jamaica, NY
Krystal, Donna Bleiberg ... New York, NY
Krystal, Sidney D. ... Los Angeles, CA
Krystek, Dennis J. ... Long Beach, MS
Krystowski, Dean S. ... San Francisco, CA
Krystowski-Enright, Dawn A. ... Holland, PA
Kryvoruka, Kenneth J. Equal Employment Opportunity Commission, Office of Federal Operations, GV
Krywucki, Michael A. ... Dallas, TX
Kryzan, Alice J. ... Hamburg, NY
Kryzan, Frank X. ... Youngstown, OH
Kryzanski, Daniel H. ... Stratford, CT
Kryzovic, John F. ... Everett, MA
Krzak, Michael S. ... Chicago, IL
Krzanowicz, Ella L. ... Rochester, NY
Krzanowicz, Lisa A. ... Rochester, NY
Krzanowski, Edward F. ... Hartford, CT
Krzanowski, Ralph J. ... Bridgeview, IL
Krzanowski, Ronald A. ... Easthampton, MA
Krzastek, Walter R., Jr. ... Roseland, NJ
Krzemien, Louis J., Jr. ... Pittsburgh, PA
Krzewicki and Kreswick ... Chelsea, MA
Krzewicki, Walter S. ... Chelsea, MA
Krzewinski, Aaron M. ... Appleton, WI
Krzisnik, William A. ... Allen Park, MI
Krzoska, Darla A. ... La Crosse, WI
Krzton & Krzton ... Tarentum, PA
Krzton, Nancy L. ... Tarentum, PA
Krzton, William T. ... Tarentum, PA
Krzton, Wm. J. ... Tarentum, PA
Krzykowski, Brian P. ... Clifton Park, NY
Krzyminski, Edward J. ... Oak Brook, IL
Krzyminski, James M., Law Offices of Beverly Hills, CA
Krzynowek, Kerry A. ... New York, NY
Krzys, Robert J. ... Amsterdam, NY
Krzywicki, Anthony P. ... Harrisburg, PA
Krzywicki, Clausen J. ... Falls Church, VA
Krzyzaniak, Leonard A., Jr. Dearborn, MI
Krzyzanowski, Richard L. Philadelphia, PA
Ksander, Karen Beth ... Chicago, IL
Kschinka, Chas. M. ... Laporte, PA
Ksenak, Stephen M. ... New York, NY
Ksidakis, Andreanna ... Sacramento, CA
Ksieniewicz, Charles F. ... Northampton, MA
Ktorides, Stanley ... Danbury, CT
Ktsanes, Basil D. ... Barrington Hills, IL
Ku, Edward Y. ... Los Angeles, CA
Ku, Ernest C. ... Bloomfield Hills, MI
Ku, Fong & Chen, LLP ... Los Angeles, CA
Ku, Jay ... Chattanooga, TN
Ku, Jay, (Ms.) ... Chattanooga, TN
Ku, Peter C. ... Redmond, WA
Ku, Portia ... New York, NY
Kuan, Julia P. ... New York, NY
Kuan, Shirley A. ... Boston, MA
Kuba, Dennis M. ... Santa Rosa, CA
Kuba, Donald L. ... New York, NY
Kuba, Edward M. ... Honolulu, HI
Kuba, Henry I. ... Honolulu, HI
Kuba, Jonathan S. ... Honolulu, HI
Kuba, Lisa Kahan ... New York, NY
Kubacki, Joseph, Jr. ... Pittsburgh, PA
Kubacki, Michael ... Philadelphia, PA
Kubacki, Robert W. ... Riverside, CA
Kubal, Patricia Tobin ... Redwood City, CA
Kubala, Karen M. ... San Jose, CA
Kubala, Lisa A. ... Killeen, TX
Kubalak, Marie A. ... Columbus, OH
Kubalanza, Joan M. ... Chicago, IL
Kubale, Bernard S. ... Milwaukee, WI
Kubancik, Joseph J. ... Walnut Creek, CA
Kubani, Thomas L. ... Los Angeles, CA
Kubanis, Albert J. ... Ukiah, CA
Kubar, Susan ... Naples, FL
Kubarek, Joseph P. ... Buffalo, NY
Kubasek, Nancy J. ... San Francisco, CA
Kubasek, Nancy K. ... Bowling Green, OH
Kubasiak, Cremieux, Fylstra, Reizen & Rotunno, Professional Corporation Chicago, IL
Kubasiak, Daniel J. ... Chicago, IL
Kubasiak, Gerald E. ... Chicago, IL
Kubasiewicz, Edward E. ... Washington, DC
Kubasta, Kelly J. ... Dallas, TX
Kubasta, Rathjen & Bickford ... Wautoma, WI
Kubasta, Thomas M. ... Wautoma, WI
Kubat, Cynthia M. ... Omaha, NE
Kubat, David A. ... Seattle, WA
Kubat, Denise M. ... Canton, OH
Kubat, Joseph J., Jr. ... Omaha, NE
Kubat, Joseph P. ... Arlington, VA
Kubat, Rod ... Des Moines, IA
Kubay, Jeffrey A. ... Pittsburgh, PA
Kube, Barbra A. ... Bloomington, IL
Kube, James G. ... Norfolk, NE
Kube, Michael R. ... Cleveland, OH
Kube, Paul S. ... Wenatchee, WA
Kube, Robyn W. ... Boulder, CO
Kubec, Edward M. ... Los Angeles, CA
Kubec, Edward Michael ... Los Angeles, CA
Kubec, Kristin M. ... Los Angeles, CA
Kubecka, Wanda K. Sells ... Edna, TX
Kubehl, Douglas M. ... Dallas, TX
Kubek, Gary W. ... New York, NY
Kubelun, Walter H. ... Los Angeles, CA
Kuber, Douglas A. ... New York, NY
Kubersky, Zave ... New York, NY
Kubes, Eugene L. ... St. Paul, MN
Kubes, Jeffrey T. ... Chicago, IL
Kubes, Kelly Lynn ... Atlanta, GA
Kubes, Kristine A. ... St. Paul, MN
Kubes, Troy George ... Atlanta, GA
Kubetz, Bernard J. ... Bangor, ME
Kubey, Craig H. ... Davis, CA
Kubiak, Christopher M. ... New York, NY
Kubiak, Craig A. ... Green Bay, WI
Kubiak, Daniel R. ... Grand Rapids, MI
Kubiak, Deborah P. ... New York, NY
Kubiak, Fonda Dawn ... Buffalo, NY
Kubiak, Kelly L. ... Tampa, FL
Kubiak, Michele P. ... Doylestown, PA
Kubiak, Ron M., P.A. ... Collingswood, NJ
Kubiak, Walter M. ... Narberth, PA
Kubiatowski, Lucia Anne ... Chicago, IL
Kubiatowski, Steve A. ... Chicago, IL
Kubic, Carl J. ... Flushing, NY
Kubic, Joseph A. ... Milford, CT
Kubic, Thomas A. ... Northport, NY
Kubicek, C. James ... Little Rock, AR
Kubicek, David W. ... Cedar Rapids, IA
Kubicek, Donald ... Sinton, TX
Kubicek, Robert E. ... Washington, NC
Kubicek, Terrence L. ... Lincoln, NE
Kubicek, Theodore L. ... Cedar Rapids, IA
Kubicek, Wayne J. ... Houston, TX
Kubick, Richard A. ... New York, NY
Kubicki, Charles J., Jr. ... Cincinnati, OH
Kubicki Draper ... Fort Lauderdale, FL
Miami, FL
West Palm Beach, FL
Kubicki, Gene ... Miami, FL
Kubicki, Margaret G. ... Cincinnati, OH
Kubicki, Richard R. ... Kennewick, WA
Kubicsek, Debra ... Gainesville, FL
Kubiczky, Stephen R. ... Riverside, IL
Kubida, William J. ... Colorado Springs, CO
Kubie, Kevin P. ... Pueblo, CO
Kubie, Robert H. ... St. Louis, MO
Kubier, Julius E., Jr. ... Oklahoma City, OK
Kubiesa, Kenneth T. Oakbrook Terrace, IL
Kubiesa, Spiroff, Gosselar & Pieper, P.C. Oakbrook Terrace, IL
Kubik, Bogner, Ridl & Selinger Dickinson, ND
Kubik, Brooks D. ... Louisville, KY
Kubik, Dawn R. ... Colorado Springs, CO
Kubik, Frederick J. ... Los Angeles, CA
Kubik, James J. ... Chicago, IL
Kubik, Jas. F. ... Wichita, KS
Kubik, Joseph H. ... Dickinson, ND
Kubik, Keith M. ... Seattle, WA
Kubik, Mary J. ... Minneapolis, MN
Kubilus, Ingrid V. ... Lake Orion, MI
Kubilus, Richard J. ... Canton, OH
Kubin, Karen J. ... San Francisco, CA
Kubin, Kip A. ... Overland Park, KS
Kubin, Rebecca Deloria ... Norfolk, VA
Kubin, Rudolph Michael ... Crosby, TX
Kubinec, Jeffrey S. South San Francisco, CA
Kubinec, John R. ... Rochester, NY
Kubiniec, Julian F. ... Buffalo, NY
Kubiniec, Richard J. ... Buffalo, NY
Kubinski & Associates, P.C. ... El Paso, TX
Kubinski, Mark A. ... Boise, ID
Kubinski, Paul J. ... El Paso, TX
Kubinski, Thomas S. ... Erie, PA
Kubis, Edward A. ... Silver Spring, MD
Kubis, Scott K. ... Orange, CA
Kubisiak, Amy B. ... Pittsburgh, PA
Kubista, Kimberly M. ... Clearfield, PA
Kubiszyn, John J. ... Birmingham, AL
Kubiszyn, Margaret Smith Birmingham, AL
Kubit, Donald E. ... Miami, FL
Kubit, John T. ... Vineland, NJ
Kubit, Joseph E. ... Butler, PA
Kubitschek, Carolyn A. ... New York, NY
Kubitschek, Kevin J. ... Belleville, IL
Kubitz, Kermit R. ... San Francisco, CA
Kubitz, Walter E. ... Arlington, VA
Kubler, Frank L. ... Fort Lauderdale, FL
Kubler, Rick E. ... Minneapolis, MN
Kubli, David F. ... Columbus, OH
Kublick, Jan S. ... Syracuse, NY
Kublicki, Nicolas M. ... Beverly Hills, CA
Kublin, Rhonda B. ... Manlius, NY
Kubly, Dale A. ... St. Louis, MO
Kubo, Edward H., Jr. ... Honolulu, HI
Kubo, Junichi ... New York, NY
Kubo, Larry A. ... San Jose, CA
Kuborn, Joseph D. ... Milwaukee, WI
Kuborn, Michael J. ... Sheboygan, WI
Kubosh & Associates ... Houston, TX
Kubosh, Ernest L. ... Sugar Land, TX
Kubosh, Paul ... Houston, TX
Kubota, Christine A. ... Honolulu, HI
Kubota & Constantino ... Burlingame, CA
Kubota, Ernest H. ... Hilo, HI
Kubota, Glenn M. ... Los Angeles, CA
Kubota, Howard T. ... San Bernardino, CA
Kubota, Noell K. ... Burlingame, CA
Kubota, Peter K. ... Hilo, HI
Kubota, Russell T. ... Oakland, CA
Kubota, Scott E. ... Honolulu, HI
Kubota, Yoshiaki C. ... Riverside, CA
Kubovcik & Kubovcik ... Washington, DC
Kubovcik, Ronald J. ... Washington, DC
Kuboviak, J. M. ... Bryan, TX
Kubrick, Kenneth W. ... Weirton, WV
Kubu, Teresa Lynn ... San Diego, CA
Kubulak, Karen Ann ... Perth Amboy, NJ
Kuby, Benjamin ... Philadelphia, PA
Kuby, Raymond ... Chicago, IL
Kuby, Ronald L. ... New York, NY
Kubyn, R. Russell ... Painesville, OH
Kuc, Gary W. ... Baltimore, MD
Kucera, Christine A. ... St. Paul, MN
Kucera, Clement M. ... Hallettsville, TX
Kucera, Daniel J. ... Chicago, IL
Kucera, Dennis E. ... Thousand Oaks, CA
Kucera, George R. ... Reno, NV
Kucera, Gerald J. ... Cedar Rapids, IA
Kucera, Jeffrey T. ... Miami, FL
Kucera, Jill E. ... Riverton, WY
Kucera, John M. ... Redding, CA
Kucera, Philip E. ... New York, NY
Kucera, Randall R., (P.C.) ... Dallas, TX
Kucera, Richard T. ... Cicero, IL
Kucera, Robert C. ... Minneapolis, MN
Kucera & Wilson ... Redding, CA
Kuch, Bailin L. ... Shelburne, VT
Kuch, Norman G. ... Rosemead, CA
Kuch, Stacey A. ... San Francisco, CA
Kucha, Helen Anne ... Broadview Heights, OH
Kuchan, Rudy F. ... Kansas City, MO
Kuchar, Melonie I. ... Fort Lauderdale, FL

Kucharek, Mary M. .... Bloomfield Hills, MI
Kucharski, Edward R. .... Santa Ana, CA
Kucharski, Richard L. .... Cullowhee, NC
Kucharski, Timothy J. .... Cleveland, OH
Kuchel, Jeff .... Remsen, IA
Kuchel, Terrence G. .... Tucson, AZ
Kuchenberg, Thomas C.
Department Of Health And Human Services, Food & Drug Administration, GV
Kucher, Leon .... Glendale, CA
Kuchevar, Gwen .... Prescott, WI
River Falls, WI
Kuchinos, David M. .... Philadelphia, PA
Kuchins, Harry L., Jr. .... San Mateo, CA
Kuchinski, Edward .... Tampa, FL
Kuchinski, John J. .... Woodland Hills, CA
Kuchinski, Joseph A., Jr. .... Boston, MA
Kuchinski, William A. .... Albany, NY
Troy, NY
Kuchinsky, Andrew E. .... Brooklyn, NY
Kuchinsky, Dori Anne .... Washington, DC
Kuchinsky, Gerald M. .... Pompano Beach, FL
Kuchinsky, Neil .... Colonial Heights, VA
Kuchinsky, Neil, & Associates, P.C.
Colonial Heights, VA
Kuchinsky, Robert I. .... Flemington, NJ
Kuchinsky and Rotunno, A Professional Corporation .... Flemington, NJ
Kuchka, John M. .... Berwick, PA
Kuchle, Jo A. .... Fairbanks, AK
Kuchler, Deborah D. .... Lake Charles, LA
New Orleans, LA
Kuchler, Gerard F. .... Waukesha, WI
Kuchler, Mark A. .... Chicago, IL
Kuchler, Ralph R. .... Monterey, CA
Kuchmay, Jason M. .... Fort Wayne, IN
Kuchno, John J. .... Baltimore, MD
Kuchta, Traci L. .... San Diego, CA
Kucik, Barry M. .... Cocoa Beach, FL
Kucik, George R. .... Washington, DC
Kucik, Hyacinth Grey .... McLean, VA
Kucik, Karen C. .... Department of Commerce, Office of the General Counsel, GV
Kucik, Kim M. .... Juneau, WI
Kucinic, William E. .... Joliet, IL
Kucinski, Paul W. .... Charlotte, NC
Kuck, Charles H. .... Atlanta, GA
Kuck, Ernst W. .... Southfield, MI
Kuck, Lea Haber .... New York, NY
Kuck, Richard W. .... Cincinnati, OH
Kuck, Scott Thomas .... Aberdeen, SD
Kuckelman, Dean .... Wichita, KS
Kuckelman, Gerald R. .... Atchison, KS
Kuckelman, Karl .... Overland Park, KS
Kuckelman, Kristopher C. .... Olathe, KS
Kuckelman, Michael J.
Overland Park, KS
Kucker, Alan D. .... New York, NY
Kucker, Fred R. .... Boulder, CO
Kucker Kraus & Bruh, LLP
New York, NY
Kucker-Horland, Alix Fredrika
Kew Gardens, NY
Kuckes, Niki .... Washington, DC
Kuckleburg, Martha J. .... Atlanta, GA
Kucklick, JoAnn F. .... Jacksonville, FL
Kucko, Sally J. .... Anchorage, AK
Kuckro, Lee G. .... Hartford, CT
Kucy, Lawrence J. .... Charlotte, NC
Kuczak, Konrad .... Dayton, OH
Kuczek, Theodore D. .... Deerfield, IL
Kuczma, Linda A. .... Chicago, IL
Kuczmarski, Edward J. .... Cheektowaga, NY
Kuczmarski, John P. .... West Bend, WI
Kuczwara, Thomas P. .... Chicago, IL
Kuczynski, Edward L. .... Hagerstown, MD
Kuczynski, John R. .... Rockford, IL
Kuczynski & Kuczynski, P.A.
Hagerstown, MD
Kuczynski, Robert E. .... Hagerstown, MD
Kudart, Arthur R. .... Cedar Rapids, IA
Mechanicsville, IA
Mt. Vernon, IA
Kudart-Joy Law Offices .... Cedar Rapids, IA
Mechanicsville, IA
Mt. Vernon, IA
Kudasik, James A. .... Somerset, PA
Kudatzky, Steven, Chartered .... Marlton, NJ
Kudatzky, Steven K. .... Marlton, NJ
Kudej, Lawrence D. .... Cedar Rapids, IA
Kudenholdt, Stephen S. .... New York, NY
Kuder, Armin U. .... Washington, DC
Kuder, Hugh B., Jr. .... Kansas City, MO
Kuder, John P. .... Pensacola, FL
Kuder, Keith .... Washington, DC
Kuder, Smollar & Friedman, P.C.
Washington, DC
Rockville, MD
Kuderer, Elton A. .... Fairmont, MN
Kuderer, Gregory E. .... Fairmont, MN
Kuderer, Patricia E. .... Eden Prairie, MN
Kuderer, Robert E. .... Minneapolis, MN
Kuderko, J. Ted .... Waukegan, IL
Kudia, Frank S. .... Oak Brook, IL
Kudirka & Jobse, LLP .... Boston, MA
Kudirka, Paul E. .... Boston, MA
Kudisch, Alan E. .... Kew Gardens, NY
Kudisch, Selwyn A. .... Brookline, MA
Kudla, M. Susan, P.C. .... Denver, CO
Kudla, Richard A. .... Southfield, MI
Kudla, Richard A., & Associates
Southfield, MI
Kudlac, Kevin S. .... Austin, TX
Kudlacz, Charles J. .... Omaha, NE
Kudlick, Susan Bittel .... Cambridge, MA
Kudman, Stuart R. .... Hackensack, NJ
New York, NY
Kudman, Tama Beth .... Hackensack, NJ
New York, NY
Kudman, Trachten, Kessler, Tacopina & Newman, LLP .... Hackensack, NJ
New York, NY
Kudner, Kathrin E. .... Detroit, MI
Kudo, Benjamin A. .... Honolulu, HI
Kudo & Daniels, LLP .... Los Angeles, CA
Kudo, Richard K. .... Los Angeles, CA
Kudon, H. Kenneth .... Washington, DC
Kudon Law Firm .... Washington, DC
Kudravetz, David W. .... Charlottesville, VA
Kudriavetz, Debra L. .... Morristown, NJ
Kudrle, Larry A. .... Plattsburgh, NY
Kudrna, Jonathan J. .... Great Falls, MT
Kuduk, David G. .... Grand Rapids, MN
Kudzma, Daniel E. .... Norwell, MA
Kuebel, Omer F., III .... New Orleans, LA
Kuebel, Omer F., Jr. .... New Orleans, LA
Kueber, Michael A. .... Huntsville, TX
Kuebler, Christopher D. .... Avon Lake, OH
Kuebler, Donald A. .... Flint, MI
Kuebler, Jeffrey J. .... Lexington, KY
Kuebler, John W. .... Jefferson City, MO
Kuebler, Robert W., Jr. .... Prescott, AZ
Kuebrich, Sarah A. .... St. Louis, MO
Kuech, John W. .... Oshkosh, WI
Kuechenberg, Cheryl A. .... Merrillville, IN
Kuechenberg, Cheryl A. .... Merrillville, IN
Kuechenmeister, Charles A. .... Denver, CO
Kuechle, Gerrit C. .... Cleveland, OH
Kuechle, John M., (A Professional Corporation) .... Los Angeles, CA
Kuechler, Maria M. .... Canton, MI
Kueck, Dianne M. .... Denver, CO
Kueffner, Eric A. .... Juneau, AK
Kueffner, Friedrich .... New York, NY
Kueffner, Friedrich, P.C. .... New York, NY
Kueffner, William C., Jr.
St. Louis Park, MN
Kueh, Tan-Yuan .... New York, NY
Kuehhas, Steven J. .... Southampton, NY
Kuehl, Albert R. .... Riesel, TX
Kuehl, David C. .... Milwaukee, WI
Kuehl, James R. .... South Bend, IN
Kuehl, Mary Ritter .... Philadelphia, PA
Kuehl, Robert S. .... Wilmington, DE
Kuehl, Sarah J. .... Sioux City, IA
Kuehl, Sheila James .... Sacramento, CA
Kuehl, Thomas D. .... Milwaukee, WI
Kuehl, Todd F. .... Baltimore, MD
Kuehler, Anthony M. .... Fort Worth, TX
Kuehling & Kuehling .... Madison, WI
Kuehling, Mark W. .... Oklahoma City, OK
Kuehling, Robert W. .... Madison, WI
Kuehling, William J. .... St. Louis, MO
Kuehm, Robert C. .... Houston, TX
Kuehn, Andrea R. .... Sioux Falls, SD
Kuehn, Angelika .... Oak Park, IL
Kuehn, Arnold V. .... Plymouth, MN
Kuehn, Carolie Balder .... Wausau, WI
Kuehn, Charles E. .... Green Bay, WI
Kuehn, Charlotte R. .... Green Bay, WI
Kuehn, Christopher K. .... Cutchogue, NY
Kuehn, Clyde L. .... Belleville, IL
Kuehn, Dianne L. .... Mequon, WI
Kuehn, Edward R. .... South Windsor, CT
Kuehn, George E. .... Detroit, MI
Kuehn, Gerald A. .... Des Moines, IA
Kuehn, Jayne K. .... Madison, WI
Kuehn, John C., (P.A.) .... Minneapolis, MN
Kuehn, John L. .... New York, NY
Kuehn & Keppler .... St. Paul, MN
Kuehn, Kristopher A. .... Overland Park, KS
Kuehn, Mark S. .... Morristown, NJ
Kuehn, Michael A. .... Des Moines, IA
Kuehn, Rebecca E. .... Falls Church, VA
Kuehn, Robert F. .... Wausau, WI
Kuehn, Robert H. .... Anaheim, CA
Kuehn, Robert O. .... Barrington, IL
Chicago, IL
Kuehn, Robert R. .... New Orleans, LA
Kuehn, Roger W. .... St. Paul, MN
Kuehn, Roger William, Sr. .... St. Paul, MN
Kuehn, Ronald W. .... Madison, WI
Kuehn, William C. .... Bomoseen, VT
Kuehn, William R. .... Barrington, IL
Chicago, IL
Kuehne, Benedict P. .... Fort Lauderdale, FL
Miami, FL
Kuehne, Carl W. .... Green Bay, WI
Kuehne, Ernest W., Jr. .... Dallas, TX
Kuehne & Foote, A Professional Law Corporation .... Baton Rouge, LA
Kuehne, G. Bruce .... Baton Rouge, LA
Kuehne & Moore, L.L.P. .... Dallas, TX
Kuehnel, Kathi A. .... Chicago, IL
Kuehnel, Norman E. .... Hamburg, NY
Kuehner, D. Brian .... Lakeland, FL
Kuehner, David B. .... Eau Claire, WI
Kuehner, George W. .... St. Paul, MN
Kuehner, Herman O. .... San Antonio, TX
Kuehnert, Cecil W. .... Conyers, GA
Kuehnert, Daniel A. .... Morganton, NC
Kuehnle, Bruce M., Jr. .... Natchez, MS
Kuehnle, G. Wesley, Jr. .... Ottsville, PA
Kuehnle, George, Jr.
Department of Transportation, Federal Transit Administration, GV
Kuehnle, Jeffrey T. .... Houston, TX
Kuehnle, John L. .... Mechanicsville, IA
Kuehnle, Kenton L. .... Columbus, OH
Kuehnle, R.D. .... New Orleans, LA
Kuehnle, Roger
Treasury Department, GV
Kuehnle, William H.
Securities and Exchange Commission, Division of Enforcement, GV
Kuehnlein, Christopher T. .... St. Louis, MO
Kuehr, Michael A. .... San Antonio, TX
Kuelbs, John T. .... Los Angeles, CA
Kuelker, Gates & Schaumann, A Prof. Corp.
St. Louis, MO
Kuelker, H. Carl .... St. Louis, MO
Kuelling, Christopher J. .... Englewood, CO
Kuelper, Jean Dudek .... Chicago, IL
Kuelthau, Camron R. .... Boulder, CO
Kuelthau, Paul S. .... St. Louis, MO
Kuelthau, Robert E. .... Milwaukee, WI
Kuemmel, Joseph K. .... Madison, WI
Kuemmel Law Offices, S.C. .... Madison, WI
Kuemmerlein, Marc L. .... Kansas City, MO
Kuenhold, O. John .... Alamosa, CO
Kuenn, Neil J. .... Chicago, IL
Kuenning, Brad, Law Offices of
Los Angeles, CA
Kuenning, Brad, Law Offices of
Pasadena, CA
Kuenning, Keith Urban Stack .... Bow, NH
Kuenster, Jennifer .... San Francisco, CA
Kuenstler, John F. .... Chicago, IL
Kuentz, Leonard C. .... Upper Marlboro, MD
Kueny, Barbara A. .... Omaha, NE
Kueny, Barbara Sheridan
Philadelphia, PA
Kueny, Bernard E., III .... Voorhees, NJ
Kueny, Ellen Hatch .... Mount Laurel, NJ
Philadelphia, PA
Kueny, Jay V. .... Carlsbad, CA
Kuenzel & Associates .... San Rafael, CA
Kuenzel, Byron K. .... Grand Forks, ND
Kuenzel, Calvin A. .... St. Petersburg, FL
Kuenzel, Diane V. .... Land O'Lakes, FL
Kuenzel & Ewell LLP .... Ashland, OR
Kuenzel & Lutes, P.A. .... Land O'Lakes, FL
Kuenzel, Robert V. .... San Rafael, CA
Ashland, OR
Kuenzel, Steven P. .... Washington, MO
Kuenzi, Hans C. .... Cleveland, OH
Kuenzi, Hans C., Co., L.P.A. .... Cleveland, OH
Kuenzinger, Bill J. .... Bakersfield, CA
Kuenzli, David P. .... Findlay, OH
Kuenzli, Kevin D. .... Fort Worth, TX
Kueper, Marilyn A. .... Springfield, IL
Kuepper, Emerald Erickson .... Trenton, NJ
Kuepper, Richard R. .... Cleveland, OH
Kueppers, Barbara R. .... Minneapolis, MN
Kueppers, Fred A., Jr. .... St. Paul, MN
Kueppers, Hackel & Kueppers, P.A.
St. Paul, MN
Kueppers, Joseph F. .... St. Paul, MN
Kuerbis, Erica L. .... Palo Alto, CA
Kuerbis, Lawrence, Jr. .... El Cajon, CA
Kuerbitz, Ronald J. .... Northbrook, IL
Lexington, MA
Kuergeleis, Thomas H. .... Fairview Heights, IL
Kuerner, Harry J., Jr. .... Department of Justice, Federal Bureau of Investigation, GV
Kuerschner, Caroline E. .... Portland, OR
Kuersteiner, Richard L. .... San Mateo, CA
Kuerzi, Kenneth L. .... Mullica Hill, NJ
Kuesel, Jane Lembeck .... New York, NY
Kuesel, Jeffery T. .... Madison, WI
Kuesel, Thomas S. .... Bemidji, MN
Kuesel, William B. .... New York, NY
Kuester, Allan C. .... Kankakee, IL
Kuester, Erin L. .... Red Wing, MN
Kuester, Jeffrey R. .... Atlanta, GA
Kuester, Noel J. .... Houston, TX
Kuester, Timothy J. .... Kansas City, MO
Kuester, William D. .... Lincoln, NE
Kuesters, Eckhard H. .... Arlington, VA
Kuestner, Denise A. .... Philadelphia, PA
Kueter, David J. .... Steelville, MO
Kueter, David Lawrence .... Denver, CO
Kueter, Lawrence R. .... Denver, CO
Kuether, John F. .... Topeka, KS
Kuettel, David L. .... Corte Madera, CA
Kuffel, John C. .... Baltimore, MD
Kuffel, Klashke & Shea, L.L.P. .... Pasco, WA
Kuffel, Mark P. .... Pasco, WA
Kuffel, Therese P. .... Chicago, IL
Kuffer, Dorene A. .... Wheaton, IL
Kuffler, Alfred J. .... Philadelphia, PA
Kuffler, David J. .... New York, NY
Kuffler, Joseph .... Philadelphia, PA
Kuffner, Alan C. .... Phoenix, AZ
Kuffner, Charles A., Jr. .... New York, NY
Kuffner, John F. .... St. Marys, OH
Kuffner, Kenneth E. .... Houston, TX
Kuffner, Mary L. .... Washington, DC
Kuffner and Pierce, Law Office
St. Marys, OH
Kuflik, Madeline B. .... Secaucus, NJ
Kuflik, Melina .... New York, NY
Kuflik, Sidney H. .... New York, NY
Kufta, Richard J. .... Pittsford, NY
Kufus, Steven R. .... St. Paul, MN
Kugal, Douglas A. .... Jericho, NY
Kugel, Dina G. .... Neshanic Station, NJ
Kugel, Robert W. .... Chicago, IL
Kugele, Norbert F. .... Grand Rapids, MI
Kugell, Jaclyn L. .... Boston, MA
Kugell, Karen .... Fort Lauderdale, FL
Kugelman, Harvey .... Cleveland, OH
Kugelman, Jerry E. .... Cleveland, OH
Kugelman, Paul, Jr. .... Virginia Beach, VA
Kugelman, William R. .... Fairfield, NJ
Kugelmann, Joan M. .... Red Bank, NJ
Kugelmann, Kathleen M. .... Tewksbury, MA
Kugelmas, Jerry .... New York, NY
Kugisaki, Craig T. .... Honolulu, HI
Kugisaki, Craig T., Attorney at Law, A Law Corporation .... Honolulu, HI
Kugiya, Neal J. .... Honolulu, HI
Kugle, Gregory W. .... Honolulu, HI
Kugle, J. Alan .... Honolulu, HI
Kugle, Robert A. .... Fort Worth, TX
Kugle & Skelton .... Athens, TX
Kugler, Andrew T. .... Los Angeles, CA
Kugler, Bruce A. .... Denver, CO
Kugler, C. Brenton .... Dallas, TX
Kugler, Carl R. .... Milwaukee, WI
Kugler, Charles D. .... Kansas City, KS
Kugler, Claire Swift .... Houston, TX
Kugler, Craig W. .... Woodstown, NJ
Kugler & Dickerson .... Kansas City, KS
Kugler, Ellen B. .... Copiague, NY
Kugler, Fred J. .... Silver Spring, MD
Kugler, George F., Jr. .... Haddonfield, NJ
Kugler, Heidi L. .... Tarzana, CA
Kugler, Jerry A. .... Chicago, IL
Kugler, John B. .... Pocatello, ID
Kugler, John R. .... Wells, ME
Kugler, John Thomas .... Tacoma, WA
Kugler, Karen A. .... St. Paul, MN
Kugler, Kip M., J.D. & Associates
Dallas, TX
Kugler, Laura E. .... Dallas, TX
Kugler, Manuel L. .... Chula Vista, CA
Kugler, Mark W. .... Silver Spring, MD
Kugler, Michelle Shandera .... Lincoln, NE
Kugler, Paul F. .... Treasury Department, Internal Revenue Service, GV
Kugler, Paul R., II .... Boston, MA
Kugler, Robert B. .... Camden, NJ
Kugler, Robert R. .... Haddonfield, NJ
Kugler, Robert T. .... Minneapolis, MN
Kugler, Sandra W. .... Philadelphia, PA
Kuglitsch, Jeffrey S. .... Shawano, WI
Kuh, Richard H. .... New York, NY
Kuh, Steven H. .... Chicago, IL
Kuh, Steven H., P.C. .... Chicago, IL
Kuha, Jan .... Dickson City, PA
Kuhar, Deviani M. .... Cleveland, OH
Kuhar, Fred .... Eastlake, OH
Kuhar, Gary G. .... Seattle, WA
Kuhar, Ludwig J. .... Joliet, IL
Kuhar, Mark J. .... Erie, PA
Kuharevicz, Jean .... Tacoma, WA
Kuhary, Craig M. .... Waukesha, WI
Kuhary, Sheryl L. .... West Allis, WI
Kuhbach, Robert G. .... New York, NY
Kuhens, Jacquelyn Jess .... Dayton, OH
Kuhfahl & Bailly .... White Plains, NY
Kuhfahl, Ingo .... White Plains, NY
Kuhfal, David P. .... La Mesa, CA
Kuhfeldt, Kirk A. .... Grand Rapids, MI
Kuhfuss, Kuhfuss & Kepple .... Pekin, IL
Kuhfuss, W. Thad .... Pekin, IL
Kuhl, Albert F. .... Lenexa, KS
Kuhl, Arthur D. .... Wilmington, DE
Kuhl, Carolyn B. .... Los Angeles, CA
Kuhl, Charlene M. .... East Meadow, NY
Kuhl, David L. .... Toledo, OH
Kuhl, Eric A. .... Washington, DC
Kuhl, Gareth W. .... Indianapolis, IN
Kuhl, Harold N. .... Merrick, NY
Kuhl, John A. .... Davenport, IA
Kuhl, John H. .... Los Angeles, CA
Kuhl, John R. .... Toledo, OH
Kuhl, John R., Jr. .... Bath, NY
Kuhl, Larry R. .... Grosse Pointe, MI
Kuhl, Lesley H. .... North Andover, MA
Kuhl, Lewis D. .... Louisville, KY
Kuhl, P. Beach .... San Francisco, CA
Kuhl, P. John, Jr., P.C. .... Houston, TX
Kuhl, Richard S. .... Washington, DC
Kuhl, Robert W. .... Wellsboro, PA
Kuhl, Shannon M. .... Cincinnati, OH
Kuhle, Roger J. .... West Des Moines, IA
Kuhle, Roger J., P.C., Law Office of
Des Moines, IA
West Des Moines, IA
Kuhlengel, Kimberly K. .... Nashville, IL
Kuhlik, Bruce N. .... Washington, DC
Kuhling, Richard W. .... Spokane, WA
Kuhlke, Lois A. .... Duluth, MN
Kuhlman, Bradley Dean .... Lexington, MO
Kuhlman, Calvin R. .... Bettendorf, IA
Kuhlman, Catherine Kirgis .... Austin, TX
Kuhlman, Darlene V. .... St. Louis, MO
Kuhlman, David B. .... San Diego, CA
Kuhlman, Denise S. .... Seattle, WA
Kuhlman, Frederick S. .... Los Angeles, CA
Kuhlman, George A. .... Chicago, IL
Kuhlman, Gina A. .... Cleveland, OH
Kuhlman, Jack D. .... Columbiana, OH
Kuhlman, Jack F. .... Hinsdale, IL
Kuhlman, Jonathan R. .... Morristown, NJ
New York, NY
Kuhlman, Kenton H. .... Englewood, CO
Kuhlman, Kerry J. .... Hartford, CT
Kuhlman, Lawrence J.
Rancho Cucamonga, CA
Kuhlman, Margaret N. .... St. Louis, MO
Kuhlman, Michelle M. .... Oakland, CA
Kuhlman, Michone J. .... Waukegan, IL
Kuhlman, P. Wayne .... Liberty, MO
Kuhlman, Patricia F. .... Tampa, FL
Kuhlman, Reddoch, Sullivan & Roberts, P.C.
Liberty, MO
Kuhlman, Richard H. .... St. Louis, MO
Kuhlman, Richard L. .... Fremont, NE
Kuhlman, Richard S. .... Chicago, IL
Kuhlman, Robert A. .... Pemberville, OH
Kuhlman, Theodore J. .... Englewood, CO
Kuhlman, Timothy C. .... Toledo, OH
Kuhlmann, Brian S. .... Columbia, MO
Kuhlmann, Fred L. .... St. Louis, MO
Kuhlmann, Gary G. .... St. George, UT
Kuhlmann, Katrin A. .... New York, NY
Kuhlmann, Kerri S. .... Washington, DC
Kuhlmann, Sherri Heckel .... Denver, CO

Kuhlmann, Steven K. ... **Denver, CO**
Kuhlmann, William C. ... **Minneapolis, MN**
Kuhlmann, William D., Jr. ... Fort Worth, TX
Kuhlmann, William E. ... Houston, TX
Kuhlmann-Macro, Venessa F.
Washington, DC
Kuhls, Joseph C. ... **Lansdale, PA**
Kuhlthau, John S. ... New Brunswick, NJ
Kuhlwilm, Frederick C. ... **Denver, CO**
Kuhn, Anna Conyers ... **Austin, TX**
Kuhn, Augusta" Shea "P. ... **Charleston, SC**
Kuhn, Barbara J. ... Minneapolis, MN
Kuhn, Barry W. ... Memphis, TN
Kuhn & Belz ... **Irvine, CA**
Laguna Niguel, CA
Newport Beach, CA
Kuhn, Benjamin R. ... **Raleigh, NC**
Kuhn, Bill ... Dallas, TX
Kuhn, Bowie K. ... Ponte Vedra Beach, FL
Kuhn, Brent M. ... Omaha, NE
Kuhn, Brian L. ... **Memphis, TN**
Kuhn, Carl W. ... Glen Ellyn, IL
Kuhn, Chandlee Johnson ... Wilmington, DE
Kuhn, Christopher G. ... Horsham, PA
Kuhn, Christopher L. ... Greenbelt, MD
Kuhn, Christopher S. ... Largo, FL
Kuhn, Clifford N., Jr. ... Edison, NJ
Kuhn, Clifford R. ... Longview, WA
Kuhn, Cynthia T. ... **Tucson, AZ**
Kuhn, Daniel D. ... **Staten Island, NY**
Kuhn, Daniel L. ... **Naperville, IL**
Kuhn, David A. ... Rocky River, OH
Kuhn, David L. ... Sterling Heights, MI
Kuhn, David N. ... Piedmont, CA
Kuhn, David R. ... **Orlando, FL**
Kuhn, David W. ... Portsmouth, OH
Kuhn, Deborah L. ... **Chicago, IL**
Kuhn, Denise A. ... Philadelphia, PA
Kuhn, Donald S. ... Santa Barbara, CA
Kuhn, Douglas W. ... Orchard Park, NY
Kuhn, Doyle & Kuhn, P.C. ... Austin, TX
Kuhn, Edna Berk ... Bronx, NY
Kuhn, Edward M., III
Lake Buena Vista, FL
Kuhn, Ellen L. ... Baltimore, MD
Kuhn, Engle and Stein ... Brackenridge, PA
Pittsburgh, PA
Kuhn, Eric David ... Boston, MA
New York, NY
Kuhn, Eric K. ... **Wichita, KS**
Kuhn, Ernest ... Los Angeles, CA
Oxnard, CA
Kuhn, Eugene P. ... Waterford, PA
Kuhn, Fred W. ... Department of the Air Force, Office of the General Counsel, GV
Kuhn, Frederick ... **Boston, MA**
Kuhn, G. Wayne ... Franklinton, LA
Kuhn, George M., Jr. ... Houston, TX
Kuhn, George M., Jr., A Professional Corporation ... Houston, TX
Kuhn, Gerald A. ... Napoleon, ND
Kuhn, Gregory B. ... **Overland Park, KS**
Kuhn, Gretchen ... Houston, TX
Kuhn, H. Fred, Jr. ... Beaufort, SC
Kuhn, Hartley M. ... **San Francisco, CA**
Kuhn, H. G. ... Houston, TX
Kuhn, Hubert R. ... Wichita, KS
Kuhn, Irwin J. ... **Nashville, TN**
Kuhn, James C., III ... Brackenridge, PA
Pittsburgh, PA
Kuhn, James E. ... Baton Rouge, LA
Kuhn, James F. ... Pittsburgh, PA
Kuhn, James I. ... Miami Beach, FL
Kuhn, James Michael ... Chicago, IL
Kuhn, Janet L., and Associates
McLean, VA
Kuhn, Jas. R., Jr. ... Portland, OR
Kuhn, Jeffrey A. ... Trenton, NJ
Kuhn, Jeffrey D. ... Glenwood, MN
Starbuck, MN
Kuhn, Jennifer ... Washington, DC
Kuhn, Jim L. ... Omaha, NE
Kuhn, John C. ... Austin, TX
Kuhn, John D. ... **Chicago, IL**
Kuhn, John D. ... Gettysburg, PA
Kuhn, John E., Jr. ... Louisville, KY
Kuhn, John F. ... Huntington, NY
Kuhn, John J. ... Detroit, MI
Kuhn, John M. ... **Miami, FL**
Kuhn, John R. ... Charleston, SC
Kuhn, John S. ... Canton, OH
Kuhn, Kevin J. ... **Denver, CO**
Kuhn, Kevin J. ... **Chicago, IL**
Kuhn, Kris J. ... Wichita, KS
Kuhn, Kurt H. ... Dallas, TX
Kuhn, Lawrence D. ... Shoreline, WA
Kuhn & Levy, P.C. ... **San Rafael, CA**
Kuhn, Linda S. ... Houston, TX
Kuhn, Loraine R. ... **Southfield, MI**
Kuhn, Lydia ... North Brunswick, NJ
Kuhn, Martha ... Orlando, FL
Kuhn, Martin D. ... Colorado Springs, CO
Kuhn, Mary Anne Frazier ... Lutherville, MD
Kuhn, Mary Julia ... **Louisville, KY**
Kuhn, Michael ... **Houston, TX**
Kuhn, Michael K. ... **Houston, TX**
Kuhn, Michael P. ... **Richmond, VA**
Kuhn and Muller ... New York, NY
Kuhn, Nancy Ortmeyer ...
Treasury Department, GV
Kuhn, Nancy R. ... **Washington, DC**
Kuhn and O'Toole, LLP ... **New York, NY**
Staten Island, NY
Kuhn, Patricia Anne ... **New York, NY**
Kuhn, Perla M. ... **New York, NY**
Kuhn, Peter J. ... Salt Lake City, UT
Kuhn, Phillip E. ... Lakeland, FL
Kuhn, R. Edward ... **Traverse City, MI**
Kuhn, Reginald S. ... Hickman, NE
Lincoln, NE
Kuhn, Richard D. ... Pontiac, MI
Kuhn, Richard D. ... **New York, NY**
Staten Island, NY
Kuhn, Richard D., Jr.
Bloomfield Hills, MI
Kuhn, Richard J. ... **Portland, OR**
Kuhn, Richard R. ... **San Rafael, CA**
Kuhn, Richard R. ... Canton, OH
Kuhn, Richard W. ... Naperville, IL
Kuhn, Robert E. ... Los Angeles, CA
Kuhn, Robert F. ... **Philadelphia, PA**
Kuhn, Robert J. ... Austin, TX
Kuhn, Robert W. ... New York, NY
Kuhn, Rocky L. ... United States Senate, Committee Legal Personnel, GV
Kuhn, Russell P. ... Visalia, CA
Kuhn, Sandra A. ... Manchester, NH
Kuhn, Spicer & Mills ... Heppner, OR
Kuhn, Stacia D. ... **Denver, CO**
Kuhn, Stephen B. ... **New York, NY**
Kuhn, Stephen L. ... **Springfield, MA**
Kuhn, Steven James ... **Portland, OR**
Kuhn, Steven P. ... Hauppauge, NY
Kuhn, Steven R. ... **Laguna Niguel, CA**
Kuhn, Ted B., (P.C.) ... Houston, TX
Kuhn, Terrence F. ... Huntington, NY
Kuhn, Thomas ... Utica, NY
Kuhn, Thomas E. ... Detroit, MI
Kuhn, Thomas E. ... **Erie, PA**
Kuhn, Thomas J. ... New York, NY
Kuhn, Thomas R. ... Lima, OH
Kuhn, Timothy C. ... Overland Park, KS
Kuhn, W. Jeffrey ... **San Antonio, TX**
Kuhn, William C. ... Hermitage, PA
Kuhn, William E. ... Shoreline, WA
Kuhn, William J. ... Heppner, OR
Kuhn, William O. ... **Wilson, NC**
Kuhn, Willis E. (" Bill "), II ... Dallas, TX
Kuhne, Alexander E. ... Bingham Farms, MI
Kuhne, Cecil C. ... **Lubbock, TX**
Kuhne, Cecil C., III ... **Dallas, TX**
Kuhne, William J. ... Atlanta, GA
Kuhnel, Paul C. ... **Roanoke, VA**
Kuhnell, Ludolf R., III ... Altus, OK
Kuhnen, Richard F. ... Binghamton, NY
Kuhner, Chris D. ... **Oakland, CA**
Kuhner, Harry E., II ... **New Orleans, LA**
Kuhner, Harry E., II, Ltd.
New Orleans, LA
Kuhner, John David ... Walnut Creek, CA
Kuhner, Patrick J. ... Orinda, CA
Kuhnhausen, Steven ... Salt Lake City, UT
Kuhnke, Carol Anne ... **Ann Arbor, MI**
Kuhnke, Nancy R. ... East St. Louis, IL
Kuhnle, Carl A. ... Toledo, OH
Kuhnle, Thomas Eilif ... **Palo Alto, CA**
Kuhnmuench, Helen M. ... Lansing, MI
Kuhnmuench, John R., Jr. ... Milwaukee, WI
Kuhnmuench, Mary M. ... Milwaukee, WI
Kuhns, David Brian ... Salem, OR
Kuhns, Everett G. ... Indianapolis, IN
Kuhns, Jason W. ... **San Francisco, CA**
Kuhns, Joyce A. ... **Baltimore, MD**
Kuhns, Keven J. ... Columbus, OH
Kuhns, Kirk D. ... **Raleigh, NC**
Kuhns, M. Edward ... Dayton, OH
Kuhns, Martha ... Sacramento, CA
Kuhns, Richard B. ... St. Louis, MO
Kuhns, Robert A. ... **Minneapolis, MN**
Kuhns, Thomas Otman ... **Chicago, IL**
Kuhns, William G. ... Parsippany, NJ
Kuhr, Harvey N. ... Los Altos, CA
Kuhr, John B. ... **Havre, MT**
Kuhr, Marilyn T. ... Chicago, IL
Kuhr, Robert A. ... Grosse Pointe Farms, MI
Kuhrau, Edward W., (P.C.) ... **Seattle, WA**
Kuhrt, Richard L. ... Elizabeth, NJ
Kuhs, Muriel ... **Chicago, IL**
Kuhs, Parker & Stanton ... **Bakersfield, CA**
Kuhs, Robert G. ... **Bakersfield, CA**
Kuhs, William C. ... **Bakersfield, CA**
Kuiken, Richard A. ... Carlyle, IL
Kuiken, Timothy B. ... **Fairfield, IA**
Kuiland, Walter ... Los Angeles, CA
Kuilema, Amy D. ... Sacramento, CA
Kuiper, David L. ... **Costa Mesa, CA**
Kuiper, Gary A. ...
Federal Deposit Insurance Corporation, GV
Kuiper, Joseph Andrew
Grand Rapids, MI
Kuiper, Thomas A. ... **Grand Rapids, MI**
Kuirsky, Dennis J. ... Waterford, MI
Kuis, Ronald L. ... Pittsburgh, PA
Kuist, Gary G. ... **Santa Monica, CA**
Kuitunen, Richard H. ... Honolulu, HI
Kujaca, Linda M. ... **Chicago, IL**
Kujawa, John A. ... **Oak Brook, IL**
Kujawa, Kenneth T. ... Sylvania, OH
Kujawa, Michael E. ... Park Ridge, IL
Kujawa, Patricia A. ... Milwaukee, WI
Kujawa, Philip Reed ... **Chicago, IL**
Kujawa, Thomas ... Eagle, MI
Kujawa, Warren P. ... San Francisco, CA
Kujawski, Bryan P., (P.C.) ... Deer Park, NY
Kujawski & Faerber, P.C.
North Little Rock, AR
Belleville, IL
Kujawski, John P. ... North Little Rock, AR
Belleville, IL
Kujawski, Michael R. ... Wauwatosa, WI
Kujawski, Peter T. ... New York, NY
Kujawsky, Paul ... Studio City, CA
Kukainis, Ginta D. ... **Southfield, MI**
Kukankos, John A. ... **Chicago, IL**
Kukasawa, John F., Jr. ... Mountain View, CA
Kukec, Kenneth J. ... Miami, FL
Kukec, Kenneth J., P.A. ... Miami, FL
Kuker, Alan M. ... Miami, FL
Kuker, David J. ... **Fort Wayne, IN**
Kuker, Diane K. ... Miami, FL
Kuker, Howard L. ... Miami, FL
Kuker, Robert J. ... **Chicago, IL**
Kuker, Ronald P. ... **Valparaiso, IN**
Kukey, Lawrence M.
Palm Beach Gardens, FL
Kukin & Bieg, P.C. ... Livingston, NJ
Kukin, Jonathan ... Livingston, NJ
Kukkonen, Carl A., III ... **Los Angeles, CA**
Kukkonen, Phillip L. ... Houghton, MI
Kukla, Karen K. ... Fayetteville, NY
Kukla, Robert J. ... Park Ridge, IL
Kuklin, Anthony B. ... **New York, NY**
Kuklin, Bailey H. ... Brooklyn, NY
Kuklin, Jeffrey P. ... Beverly Hills, CA
Kuklin, Susan B. ... San Jose, CA
Kuklis Smith, Eileen ... **Albany, NY**
Kuknyo, John R. ... Urbana, IL
Kukoff, Ian J. ... **Miami, FL**
Kukol, Albert B. ... **Binghamton, NY**
Kukor, Kevin J. ... Mequon, WI
Milwaukee, WI
Racine, WI
Kukovich, Allen G. ... Greensburg, PA
Kukowski, Barbara F. ... Hawthorne, NY
Kukowski, Eric G. ... **St. Louis, MO**
Kukowski, Richard D. ... West Des Moines, IA
Kukowski, Thomas H. ... **Stamford, CT**
Elmsford, NY
New York, NY
Kukreja, Rajesh K. ... **Denver, CO**
Kukta, Stephen H. ... **Kansas City, MO**
Kukuca, Kathleen Ende ... Cleveland, OH
Kukuk, Terry L. ... Bainbridge Island, WA
Kukula, Ted J. ... San Francisco, CA
Kukuljan, Robert A. ... **Minneapolis, MN**
Kukunas, Theodore J. ... Pittsburgh, PA
Kukura, Meryl A. ... South Natick, MA
Kukura, Thomas V. ...
Department of Justice, GV
Kukuvka, Cynthia M. ... Palmyra, NY
Kula, David P. ... Chicago, IL
Kula, Donald J. ... **Los Angeles, CA**
Kula, Elliot B. ... **Miami, FL**
Kula, James R. ... **Pasadena, CA**
Kula, Keith M. ... Chicago, IL
Kula, Kenneth P. ... **Dallas, TX**
Kula, Michael G ... St. Paul, MN
Kula, Richard J. ... Eureka, CA
Kula, Stacy Charlotte ... **Louisville, KY**
Kulak, Abraham W. ... Brooklyn, NY
Kulak, Andrew H. ... New York, NY
Kulak, Barnett L. ... New York, NY
Kulak, Bryan M. ... Middletown, NY
Kulak, Daniel B. ... Peabody, MA
Kulak, Gail Geisinger ... **Walden, NY**
Kulak, Gregory W. ... Hartford, CT
Kulak, Kenneth M. ... Department of Justice, Civil Division, GV
Kulak & Zaslowsky ... New York, NY
Kulakis, Christopher George ... Astoria, NY
Kulakoff, David S. ... Massapequa Park, NY
Kulakofsky, Daniel P. ... West Hartford, CT
Kulakowski, Henry J., Jr. ... Palm Harbor, FL
Kulakowski, Joseph O. ... Mobile, AL
Kulas, Andreas A. ... Merritt Island, FL
Kulas, Charles J. ... **San Francisco, CA**
Kulas, James A. ... Chicago, IL
Kulas, John Noel ... Belmont, MA
Kulas, Julian E. ... Chicago, IL
Kulas, Ludwik ... Grand Forks, ND
Kulas, Paul J. ... Chicago, IL
Kulas, Robert J. ... Port St. Lucie, FL
Kulas, Robert J., P.A. ... Port St. Lucie, FL
Kulas, Steven P. ... Seymour, CT
Kulasza, Kathleen M. ... **Denver, CO**
Kulat, Randall S. ... **Schaumburg, IL**
Kulawik, Mary Morse ... Anchorage, AK
Kulawitz, Harvey J. ... **Ridgefield, CT**
Kulawiz, JoAnne Kiely ... Hartford, CT
Kulb, Amy T. ... **Garden City, NY**
Kulbaski, James J. ... **Arlington, VA**
Kulber, Terry ... Palm Desert, CA
Kulchak, J. Michael ... **Boise, ID**
Kulchin, Sydney ... **Encino, CA**
Kulcsar, Roy R. ... New York, NY
Kulczak, Michael J. ... Washington, DC
Kulczycki, Eve M. ... Phillipsburg, NJ
Kule, Christopher A., (P.C.)
New York, NY
Kuleck, Edward J. ... Ottawa, IL
Kule-Korgood, Michele ... Forest Hills, NY
Kulerman, Michele A. ... **Washington, DC**
Kulerski, J. Richard ... **Oak Brook, IL**
Kulerski, J. Richard, P.C. ... **Chicago, IL**
Oak Brook, IL
Wheaton, IL
Kulesa, Amy H. ... Columbus, OH
Kulesh, Carrie J. ... **Sun City, AZ**
Kulesh, Carrie J., P.C. ... **Sun City, AZ**
Kulesz, David T. ... Arlington, TX
Kulesz, Elizabeth A. ... Detroit, MI
Kulesza, Joseph D., Jr. ... **Wilmington, DE**
Kulesza, Robert John ... Hackensack, NJ
Kulevich, Deidre C. ... Hingham, MA
Kulevich, Frederick J.
Hoffman Estates, IL
Kulewicz, John J. ... **Columbus, OH**
Kulhanek, Carl D., Jr. ... **Houston, TX**
Kulhanjian, Laura L. ... **San Francisco, CA**
Kulick, Andrew Jay ... Saugus, CA
Kulick, Andrew M. ... **Somerville, NJ**
Kulick & Associates ... **Biloxi, MS**
Gulfport, MS
Jackson, MS
Kulick, Brennan & Krochta, P.A.
Bridgewater, NJ
Elizabeth, NJ
Freehold, NJ
Hackensack, NJ
Jersey City, NJ
Newark, NJ
New Brunswick, NJ
Paterson, NJ
Somerville, NJ
Toms River, NJ
Kulick, Gail T. ... Milaca, MN
Kulick, Irving J. ... White Plains, NY
Kulick, Leslie Ava ... Topeka, KS
Kulick, Lizbeth B.
Department of Commerce, Patent and Trademark Office, GV
Kulick, Lora A. ... Harrisburg, PA
Kulick, Michael S. ... Avon, CT
Kulick, Neil M. ... Cambridge, MA
Kulick, Richard S. ... Williamsville, NY
Kulick, Susan Goldsmith ... Cincinnati, OH
Kulick, William M. ... **Biloxi, MS**
Kulig, Edw. J. ... Independence, WI
Kulig, Frank H. ... Omaha, NE
Kulig, Janet ... **Burlingame, CA**
Kulig, John J. ... Parma Heights, OH
Kulig, Lawrence R. ... **Boston, MA**
Kulig, Michalak & Franklin
Independence, WI
Kulig, Paul S. ... **Rutland, VT**
Kulig, Stephen T. ... Pomfret Center, CT
Kulik, Bernard
Small Business Administration, GV
Kulik, David J. ... **Washington, DC**
Kulik, Ellen Gottmann ... Syracuse, NY
Kulik, Glen L. ... **Los Angeles, CA**
Kulik, Gottesman & Mouton, LLP
Los Angeles, CA
Kulik, Joseph M. ... McKees Rocks, PA
Kulik, Joseph P. ... Greenville, TX
Kulik, Kevin J. ... Fort Lauderdale, FL
Kulik, Michael G. ... **Des Moines, IA**
Kulik, Robert F. ... Jacksonville, FL
Kulik, Teresa ... Yakima, WA
Kulik, Thomas Alexander ... **Dallas, TX**
Kulikov, Maxim S. ... **New York, NY**
Kulikowski, John F., III ... Fairfield, CT
Kulikowski, John M. ... Albuquerque, NM
Kulinski, Paul F. ... **Cherry Hill, NJ**
Kulinsky, Lois ... Wheeling, IL
Kulinsky, Lois, & Associates, Ltd.
Wheeling, IL
Kulis, Gregory E. ... Chicago, IL
Kulis, James M. ... **Chicago, IL**
Kulis, Merrillyn Erskine ... Long Beach, CA
Kulisch, David A. ... **Spokane, WA**
Kulish, Christopher J. ... **Boulder, CO**
Kulish, Dennis J. ... **Morristown, NJ**
Kulish, Jon N. ... **San Francisco, CA**
Washington, DC
Kulish, Jonathan A. ... **New York, NY**
Kulka, Ellen B. ... **Springfield, NJ**
Kulka, Sean C. ... **Atlanta, GA**
Kulkarni, Cynthia L. ... Chicago, IL
Kulkarni, Dilip ... **Indianapolis, IN**
Kulkarni, Manjusha P. ... Los Angeles, CA
Kulkarni, Sima Singadia ... **Atlanta, GA**
Kulkarni, Sunil R. ... **Palo Alto, CA**
Kulkoski, Glen B. ... New Berlin, WI
Kulkoski, Michael B. ... Green Bay, WI
Kulkoski, William B. ... Green Bay, WI
Kull, Alexander E. ... Evanston, IL
Kull, Andrew ... Atlanta, GA
Kull, Dana Smith ... **Atlanta, GA**
Kull, David L. ... **Farmington Hills, MI**
Kull, Gary S. ... **Gladstone, NJ**
Kull, Geary W. ... Chicago, IL
Kull, James Fitzmorris ... **Dallas, TX**
Kull, John E. ... Dallas, TX
Kull, L. Lee ... Maryville, TN
Kull, Robert F. ... **Los Angeles, CA**
Kull, Robert J. ... **Farmington Hills, MI**
Kull, Stanley J. ... **Philadelphia, PA**
Kulla, Mark A. ... **Las Vegas, NV**
Kulla, Michael Q. ... Atlanta, GA
Kulla, Norman S. ... Beverly Hills, CA
Kulla, Raymond J. ... Terre Haute, IN
Kulla, Stephen D. ... Waynesboro, PA
Kulla & Weisbrod, P.C. ... Waynesboro, PA
Kullas, Joel Robert ... Rockville, CT
Kullby, Laurie Z. ... Evergreen, CO
Kulle, David A. ... **Hartford, CT**
Kullen, John A. ... Birmingham, MI
Kullen, Paul H. ... Southfield, MI
Kullen, Richard C., Jr. ... **New York, NY**
Kuller, Alan S. ... Norwalk, CT
Kuller, Barbara ... Cincinnati, OH
Kuller, Hart ... **Minneapolis, MN**
St. Paul, MN
Kuller, Henry M. ... **Philadelphia, PA**
Kuller, Jonathan M. ... Livingston, NJ
Kuller, Mark A. ... **Washington, DC**
Kuller, Mark D. ... **Wilmington, DE**
Kulleseid, Lars I. ... **New York, NY**
Kullgren, Robert D. ... **Grand Rapids, MI**
Kullick, Ronald H. ... Hamilton, MT
Kullman, Aimee P. ... **New Orleans, LA**
Kullman, David G. ... Creve Coeur, MO
Kullman Firm, The, A Professional Law Corporation ... **Birmingham, AL**
New Orleans, LA
Jackson, MS
Memphis, TN
Kullman, Frederick S. ... New Orleans, LA
Kullman, Jack R., Jr. ... Columbus, OH
Kullman, Lawrence S. ... **New Orleans, LA**
Kullman, Mary C. ... **St. Louis, MO**

Kullman, Paul W. .... West Seneca, NY
Kullman, Thomas M. .... Springfield, VA
Kullman, William F. .... Treasury Department, Bureau of Alcohol, Tobacco and Firearms, GV
Kullmann, Chas. W. .... St. Louis, MO
Kullmann, Sandra C. .... Charlotte, NC
Kully, David C. .... Washington, DC
Kully, Leonard A. .... Walnut Creek, CA
Kully, Russel I. .... Los Angeles, CA
Kully & Snyder, P.C. .... Walnut Creek, CA
Kulmala, E. Pete .... Barnwell, SC
Williston, SC
Kulman, Bradley G. .... New York, NY
Kulon, Leila T. .... Chicago, IL
Kulongoski, Theodore R. .... Salem, OR
Kulowiec, David .... New York, NY
Kulp, Christopher G. .... Richmond, VA
Kulp, Dolores Rocco .... Philadelphia, PA
Kulp, F. Bruce .... Dearborn, MI
Kulp, James E. .... Richmond, VA
Kulp, James Scott .... Richmond, VA
Kulp, Linda McQuillen .... Tulsa, OK
Kulp, Robert E., Jr. .... Louisville, KY
Kulp, Stephen M. .... Dearborn, MI
Kulp, Timothy A. .... Philadelphia, PA
Kulp, Timothy Clay
North Charleston, SC
Kulp, Victor K. .... Tulsa, OK
Kulp, Willis K. .... Greeley, CO
Kulpa, Lorraine A. .... Chicago, IL
Kulpaca, Bruce C. .... Milwaukee, WI
Kulper, Douglas E. .... Ventura, CA
Kulperger, Robert J. .... Washington, DC
Kulseth, Denice Brown .... Santa Fe, NM
Kulseth, John R., Jr. .... Santa Fe, NM
Kulseth, Reagen .... Tucson, AZ
Kult, Gregory P. .... Indianapolis, IN
Kultala, John E. .... Keokuk, IA
Kultgen, David B. .... Waco, TX
Kultgen, Pamela A. ....
Department of Labor, GV
Kulunas, Joseph J. .... West Palm Beach, FL
Kuluva, Carol D. .... Los Angeles, CA
Kuluva, Randy W. .... Glendale, CA
Kulvin, Dana Robin .... San Jose, CA
Kulvinskas, Mary .... Los Angeles, CA
Kulwicki, David A. .... Cleveland, OH
Kulwicki, David A., Co., L.P.A.
Cleveland, OH
Kulwicki, Joseph F., III .... Meadville, PA
Kulwicki, Mark A. .... Silver Spring, MD
Kulwin & Associates .... Chicago, IL
Kulwin, Hollis L. .... Los Angeles, CA
Kulwin, Jeffrey R. .... Chicago, IL
Kulwin, Shelly B. .... Chicago, IL
Kulyk, Carl .... Lake Forest, CA
Kulynych, Jennifer J. .... Washington, DC
Kulys, Margarita T. .... Chicago, IL
Kulzer, Barbara A. .... Haddonfield, NJ
Kulzer & DiPadova, A Professional Corporation .... Camden, NJ
Haddonfield, NJ
Kulzer, Michael A. .... Haddonfield, NJ
Kulzick, Kenneth E. .... Los Angeles, CA
Kum, Robert .... Westlake Village, CA
Kumabe, Lawrence D. .... Honolulu, HI
Kumada-Lawrence, Naoko .... New York, NY
Kumagai, Duane .... Los Angeles, CA
Kumagai, Susan T. .... San Francisco, CA
Kumagai, Toru T. .... El Toro, CA
Kumagai, Wesley S. .... Buena Park, CA
Kumamoto, Brian A. .... Costa Mesa, CA
Kumamoto, Don F. .... Santa Clara, CA
Kumar, Aneeta .... Los Angeles, CA
Kumar, Anjali .... Rockville, MD
Kumar, Aradhana .... Washington, DC
Kumar, Becky Christina
Office of Personnel Management, Merit Systems Division, GV
Kumar, Chandran D. .... Houston, TX
Kumar, Jai-Prakash (J.P.) Philip
Houston, TX
Kumar, Jeri L. .... Asheville, NC
Kumar, Johnny A. .... Washington, DC
Kumar, Mita N.
Department Of Health And Human Services, Office of the General Counsel, GV
Kumar, Nisha R. .... Department of Energy, Office of the General Counsel, GV
Kumar, Rajat .... Washington, DC
Kumar, Sanjay T. .... Los Angeles, CA
Kumble, Jennifer Stein .... New York, NY
Kumble, Steven J., (P.C.) .... New York, NY
Kumbula-Fraser, Mandinema R.
Washington, DC
Kumer, Kathleen Patricia .... Rosemont, IL
Kumetz, Barbara A. .... Los Angeles, CA
Kumetz, Fred J. .... Los Angeles, CA
Kumiega, Bonnie Drumm .... Ellington, CT
Kumiega, Brian B. .... Buffalo, NY
Kumiega, Edward J. .... Oklahoma City, OK
Kumin, Daniel J. .... Needham, MA
Kumin, Jane S. .... Palo Alto, CA
Kumin, Laura A. .... Chevy Chase, MD
Kumin, Lisa J. .... Los Angeles, CA
Kumin, Max H. .... Boston, MA
Kumin, Robert A. .... Mission, KS
Kumin, Robert A., P.C. .... Mission, KS
Kansas City, MO
Kumin, Shari C. .... Salem, MA
Kumins, Steven M. .... Providence, RI
Kumley, Lloyd S. .... Salem, OR
Kumli, Karl F., III .... Boulder, CO
Kumli, Kurt E. .... San Jose, CA
Kumli, Susan Gillett .... San Francisco, CA
Kumlin, Richard L. .... Chicago, IL
Kumm, Kelly .... Pocatello, ID
Kummel, Patricia E. .... New York, NY
Kummer, Daniel M. .... New York, NY
Kummer, Dixon G. .... Bakersfield, CA
Kummer, Donna Endreson .... Milwaukee, WI
Kummer, Janis Gorby .... Los Angeles, CA
Kummer, John R. .... Covington, KY
Kummer Kaempfer Bonner & Renshaw
Las Vegas, NV
Kummer, Knox, Naughton & Hansbury, A Professional Corporation
Morristown, NJ
Parsippany, NJ
Kummer, Lee H. .... Manitowoc, WI
Kummer, Martin A. .... Milwaukee, WI
Kummer, Richard E. .... Parsippany, NJ
Kummer, Rita J. .... Denver, CO
Kummer, Thomas F. .... Las Vegas, NV
Kummer, Thomas L. .... Reno, NV
Kummer, Victoria A. .... New York, NY
Kummer, William A. .... Monroe, NY
Kummerer, J. Michael .... Columbus, IN
Kummerer, William A. .... Chicago, IL
Kummert, Richard O. .... Seattle, WA
Kummings, William W.
Department of Justice, Immigration and Naturalization Service, GV
Kumor, Kenneth M.
Department of Agriculture, Rural Utilities Service, GV
Kumorowski, Edward M. .... Hutchinson, KS
Kumorowski & Kumorowski
Hutchinson, KS
Kumorowski, Victoria M. .... Hutchinson, KS
Kump, Edward R. .... Washington, DC
Kump, Jeffrey J. .... Elko, NV
Kump, Kary R. .... Carpinteria, CA
Kump, Lee N. .... Richmond, VA
Kump, Lon Rodney .... Salt Lake City, UT
Kump, Michael J. .... Los Angeles, CA
Kump, William T. .... Newport News, VA
Kumpe, David E. .... San Antonio, TX
Kumpe, Peter G. .... Little Rock, AR
Kumpf, Scott D. .... Castle Rock, CO
Kumpis, Philip Bruno .... Los Angeles, CA
Kumpula, Elaine M. .... Minneapolis, MN
Kumro, Richard A. .... New York, NY
Kumta, Jyoti A. .... Baltimore, MD
Kun, Albert M. .... San Francisco, CA
Kun, Joan-Margaret .... White Plains, NY
Kun, Michael S. .... Atlanta, GA
Kun, Sigrid E. .... New Haven, CT
Kun, Steve J. .... Dallas, TX
Kuna, Edward J. .... Pittsburgh, PA
Kuna, John Richard .... Tyler, TX
Kunak, John N. .... Encino, CA
Kunard, Barnett, Kakeldey & Gates, Ltd.
Mankato, MN
Mapleton, MN
Kunard, Marlin R. .... Mankato, MN
Mapleton, MN
Kunath, Dwayne .... Eugene, OR
Kunath, George M. .... New York, NY
Kunath, John F., Jr. .... Irvine, CA
Kunath, Pamela L. .... Los Angeles, CA
Kunau, Andrew R. .... San Antonio, TX
Kunau, Richard D. .... Preston, IA
Kunberger, Katherine J. .... Los Angeles, CA
Kunberger, Paul H. .... Richmond, VA
Kunc, Clarence C. .... Wilber, NE
Kunc, Michaela C. .... Chicago, IL
Kunce, James E. .... Overland Park, KS
Kunce, Peyton H. .... Murphysboro, IL
Kuncik, William A. .... Boston, MA
Kuncz, Timothy A. .... San Diego, CA
Kunczt, Robert M. .... San Antonio, TX
Kunda, Catherine Hill .... Philadelphia, PA
Kunda, Kevin P. .... Rhinelander, WI
Kunda, Walter E. .... King Of Prussia, PA
Kundahl, Griffith A. .... Denver, CO
Kundar, Kathleen M. .... New York, NY
Kunde, Grace L. .... San Antonio, TX
Kunderer, Charles W. .... New Orleans, LA
Kundert, Lisabeth Ryan .... Boston, MA
Kundert, Thomas L. .... Dayton, OH
Kundid, Michael Anton
Daytona Beach, FL
Kundin, Joel B. .... Pittsburgh, PA
Kundin, Robert H. .... New City, NY
Kundinger, Carrie L. .... De Pere, WI
Kundinger, Mathew H. .... Los Angeles, CA
Kundinger, Ravelle Rainey .... Denver, CO
Kundinger, Vicki P. .... Traverse City, MI
Kundl, Judith .... South Deerfield, MA
Kundla, Mark S. .... Springfield, NJ
Kundra, Chaya .... Rockville, MD
Kundra, Chaya, P.C. .... Rockville, MD
Kundra, Kevin P. .... Philadelphia, PA
Kundrat & Associates .... Harrisburg, PA
Kundrat, Douglas A. .... Palo Alto, CA
Kundrat, Frank J. .... St. Cloud, MN
Kundrat, George J. .... Westfield, NJ
Kundrat, John S. .... Harrisburg, PA
Kundtz, Alan J. .... Columbus, OH
Kundtz, John Andrew .... Cleveland, OH
Kundtz, Paul J. .... Seattle, WA
Kundupoglu, Yoncha L. .... Washington, DC
Kunec, Robert J. .... Wilkes-Barre, PA
Kunego, Todd M. .... New York, NY
Kunen, Eve .... New York, NY
Kunert, Bernard I. .... Florida, NY
Kunert, Gregory M. .... Los Angeles, CA
Kunert, Paul .... Minneapolis, MN
Kunes, G. Gerald .... Tifton, GA
Kunes, G. G. Joseph, Jr. .... Tifton, GA
Kunes and Kunes .... Tifton, GA
Kunes, Robert M. .... Charleston, SC
Kunesh, Patrice .... Boulder, CO
Kunetka, Julie A. .... Chicago, IL
Kuney, David R. .... Washington, DC
Kuney, George W. .... San Diego, CA
Kuney, Kenneth A. .... Visalia, CA
Kuney, Robert M. .... Washington, DC
Kuney, Scott K. .... Bakersfield, CA
Kuney, Steven R. .... Washington, DC
Kung, Alice S. .... Reno, NV
Kung, Alice S. .... East Hanover, NJ
Kung, Catherine .... New York, NY
Kung, David C. .... Chicago, IL
Kung, Felicia H.
Securities and Exchange Commission, Division of Corporation Finance, GV
Kung, Huai Han .... New York, NY
Kunian, Alan E. .... Framingham, MA
Kunian, Stephen T. .... Boston, MA
Kuniansky, Harry S. .... Atlanta, GA
Kuniansky, Harry S., P.C. .... Atlanta, GA
Kuniansky, Richard B. .... Houston, TX
Kunick, James M. .... Chicago, IL
Kunick, Leslie Thullen .... Ketchum, ID
Kunihiro, Gary N. .... Honolulu, HI
Kuniholm, Elizabeth F. .... Raleigh, NC
Kunik, Mary Gail .... Trenton, NJ
Kunimoto, Valri Lei .... Honolulu, HI
Kunimoto, Warren Y. .... Honolulu, HI
Kunin, Brett K. .... Livingston, NJ
Kunin, Christy C. .... Washington, DC
Kunin, Douglas S. .... Minneapolis, MN
Kunin, Israel L., A Professional Corporation
Las Vegas, NV
Kunin, Israel L." Ishi " .... Las Vegas, NV
Kunin, Joel A. .... East St. Louis, IL
Kunin, Lawrence .... New York, NY
Kunin, Lawrence H. .... Miami, FL
Kunin, Louis .... New York, NY
Kunin, Mark & Associates, P.C.
Collinsville, IL
Kunin, Mark H. .... Collinsville, IL
Kunin, Max B. .... New York, NY
Kunin, Michelle A. .... East St. Louis, IL
Kunin, Peter B. .... Burlington, VT
Kunin, Stephen G.
Department of Commerce, Patent and Trademark Office, GV
Kunisaki, Eric H. .... Honolulu, HI
Kunitz, Norman N. .... Washington, DC
Kuniyuki & Chang .... Honolulu, HI
Kuniyuki, Ken T. .... Honolulu, HI
Kunkel, Andrea R. .... Tulsa, OK
Kunkel, Christopher M. .... Doraville, GA
Kunkel, Daniel H. .... Fort Myers, FL
Sarasota, FL
Tampa, FL
Kunkel, Daniel James .... Honolulu, HI
Kunkel, Edward L. .... Pasadena, CA
Kunkel, Elmer M. .... Tulsa, OK
Kunkel, Eric B. .... Santa Barbara, CA
Kunkel, Gregory T. .... Pittsburgh, PA
Uniontown, PA
Kunkel, Joe .... St. Paul, MN
Kunkel, Jonathan W. .... Camp Hill, PA
Kunkel, Kenneth E. .... Birmingham, MI
Kunkel, Leah R. .... Northampton, MA
Kunkel, Lewis S., Jr. .... Harrisburg, PA
Kunkel Miller & Hament .... Bradenton, FL
Fort Myers, FL
Naples, FL
Sarasota, FL
Tampa, FL
Kunkel, Phillip L. .... St. Cloud, MN
Kunkel, Richard G. .... St. Paul, MN
Kunkel, Scott S. .... Salt Lake City, UT
Kunkel, Shelly J. .... Harrisburg, PA
Kunkel, Stephen F. .... Fairfax, CA
Kunkel, William R. .... Chicago, IL
Kunken, Kenneth James .... Mineola, NY
Kunken, Stephen .... Commack, NY
Kunkes, Eric L. .... New York, NY
Kunkin, Marc I. .... New York, NY
Kunkis, Martha H. .... New York, NY
Kunkis, Roger M. .... New York, NY
Kunkle, Brendan M. .... San Francisco, CA
Kunkle, Gary J. .... Exton, PA
Kunkle, J. Richard .... Oklahoma City, OK
Kunkle, Jean L. .... Salem, OR
Kunkle, John H., Jr. .... Pittsburgh, PA
Kunkle, Kenneth L. .... St. Paul, MN
Kunkle, Lisa K. .... Cleveland, OH
Kunkle, Regina V. .... Santa Monica, CA
Kunkle, Stephen C. .... Paoli, PA
Kunkle, William J., Jr. .... Chicago, IL
Kunkleman, Gregory L. .... Charlotte, NC
Kunkler, Mark A. .... Sunnyside, WA
Kunmann, Edmond J. .... Boca Raton, FL
Kunmann, Herbert H. .... Boca Raton, FL
Kunmann & Kunmann, P.A.
Boca Raton, FL
Kuno, Cynthia A. .... Seattle, WA
Kunofsky, William F. .... Dallas, TX
Kunold, Robert, Jr. .... Seattle, WA
Kunowski, Herbert P. .... Los Angeles, CA
Kunreuther, Judith Berry
White Plains, NY
Kuns, Gary F. .... Maumee, OH
Kuns, Owen K. .... Sacramento, CA
Kunsberg, Sandra P. .... Los Angeles, CA
Kunsch, Harold E. .... Santa Ana, CA
Kunsch, J. Michael .... Philadelphia, PA
Kunsch, John M. .... Philadelphia, PA
Kunsch, Kelly, (Mr.) .... Seattle, WA
Kunselman, Harry F. .... Pittsburgh, PA
Kunselman, Robert E. .... Beaver, PA
Kunshek, Rudy .... Chicago, IL
Kunst, John M., Jr. .... Cincinnati, OH
Kunst, M. Andica .... New York, NY
Kunst, Mark W. .... Washington, DC
Kunstadt, R., P.C. .... New York, NY
Kunstadt, Robert M. .... New York, NY
Kunstle, Howard J., (P.C.)
Colorado Springs, CO
Kunstle, William D. .... Sioux Falls, SD
Kunstler, Marilyn C. .... New York, NY
Kunstler, Peter M. .... Los Angeles, CA
Kunstlinger, Joseph .... Monsey, NY
Kunstmanas, Raymond .... Dyer, IN
Kuntz, April .... Tampa, FL
Kuntz & Bonesio, L.L.P. .... Dallas, TX
Kuntz, C. Edward .... Atlanta, GA
Kuntz, Charles P. .... Napa, CA
Kuntz, Daniel S., P.C. .... Bismarck, ND
Kuntz, David E. .... Blaine, MN
Kuntz, Donald W. .... Mount Prospect, IL
Kuntz, Eugene .... Oklahoma City, OK
Kuntz, Glenn J. .... Alexandria, VA
Kuntz, Henry N., Jr. .... Dayton, OH
Kuntz, J. Daniel .... Alexandria, VA
Kuntz & Jambor, L.L.C. .... Blaine, MN
Kuntz, James W. .... Dallas, TX
Kuntz, Janet Rice .... San Bernardino, CA
Kuntz, Jill M. .... Philadelphia, PA
Kuntz, Joel D. .... Lebanon, OR
Kuntz, John A. .... San Bernardino, CA
Kuntz, John D. .... Houston, TX
Kuntz, John F. .... Summit, NJ
Kuntz, Keenan & Laughlin .... Des Moines, IA
Kuntz & Kuntz .... Mount Prospect, IL
Kuntz, Laura R. .... Roseland, NJ
Kuntz, Lee A. .... New York, NY
Kuntz, Leslie Iams .... Canton, OH
Salem, OH
Kuntz, Mark E. .... Kokomo, IN
Kuntz, Melanie Kay .... Salem, IN
Kuntz, Michael D. .... Seattle, WA
Kuntz, Peter F. .... Orleans, MA
Kuntz, Raymond G. .... Bedford, NY
Poughkeepsie, NY
Kuntz, Raymond G., III .... Red Lodge, MT
Kuntz, Raymond G., P.C. .... Bedford, NY
Poughkeepsie, NY
Kuntz, Richard A. .... New Orleans, LA
Kuntz, Richard M. .... Chicago, IL
Kuntz, Robert J., Jr. .... Miami, FL
Kuntz, Ronald W. .... Des Moines, IA
Kuntz, Sandra K. .... Dickinson, ND
Kuntz, Scott C. .... Mount Prospect, IL
Kuntz, Stephen A. .... Houston, TX
Kuntz, Steven M. .... Jefferson City, MO
Kuntz, Stuart M. .... Washington, DC
Kuntz, Timothy J. .... South St. Paul, MN
Kuntz, Walter N., III .... Dallas, TX
Kuntz, William E. .... Jacksonville, FL
Kuntz, William F., II .... New York, NY
Kuntz, William Henry .... Connersville, IN
Kuntz, William M. .... San Bernardino, CA
Kuntz, William R., Jr. .... San Diego, CA
Kuntze, Richard K. .... Cape Girardeau, MO
Kuny, K. Martin .... Independence, MO
Kuny, K. Martin, P.C. .... Independence, MO
Kunz, Adam Seymour .... Phoenix, AZ
Kunz, Armand D. .... Lathrup Village, MI
Kunz & Associates, P.A. .... Douglasville, GA
Kunz, Brent R. .... Cheyenne, WY
Kunz, C. Thomas .... New York, NY
Kunz, Carl N., III .... Wilmington, DE
Kunz, Carol L. .... Manchester, NH
Kunz, Carolee Burton .... Wilmington, DE
Kunz, Christina L. .... St. Paul, MN
Kunz, Daniel H. .... Indianapolis, IN
Kunz, David F. .... Albany, NY
Kunz, David R. .... Philadelphia, PA
Kunz, David Robertson, & Associates
Philadelphia, PA
Kunz, David S. .... Ogden, UT
Kunz, Donald J. .... Detroit, MI
Kunz, Donald R. .... Phoenix, AZ
Kunz, Earl G. .... Rancho Palos Verdes, CA
Kunz, Edward A. .... New Orleans, LA
Kunz, Elizabeth H. .... Mattapoisett, MA
Kunz, Germain B. .... Ortonville, MN
Kunz, Halbert W. .... Indianapolis, IN
Kunz, John E. .... Pittsburgh, PA
Kunz, John R. .... Lakewood, CO
Kunz, Kate M. .... Dallas, TX
Kunz, Kathryn .... Indianapolis, IN
Kunz, Kirsten J.
Department Of Veterans Affairs, Board of Veterans Appeals, GV
Kunz and Kunz .... Indianapolis, IN
Kunz, Marco B. .... Salt Lake City, UT
Kunz, Michael J. .... New York, NY
Kunz & Opperman .... Indianapolis, IN
Kunz, Paul T. .... Ogden, UT
Kunz, Richard F. .... Westlake Village, CA
Kunz, Richard L. .... Lexington, KY
Kunz, Robert A. .... Douglasville, GA
Kunz, Stephen M. .... Tampa, FL
Kunz, Thomas Eagan .... Toms River, NJ
Kunz, Warren .... Wilmington, MA
Kunz, Willis K. .... Indianapolis, IN
Kunza, Christina C. .... Clayton, MO
Kunze, Germain E. .... Stevens Point, WI
Kunze, Kaaren A. .... Chicago, IL
Kunze, Karl W. .... Batavia, NY
Rochester, NY
Kunze, Mary Bone .... Jackson, OH
Kunzel, Frederick K. .... San Diego, CA
Kunzelman, George J. .... Newport Beach, CA
Kunzeman, Joseph J. .... Mineola, NY
Kunzi, Brian T. .... Reno, NV
Kunzi, S. Gregg .... Washington, DC
Kunzier, Frank J. .... Parsippany, NJ
Kunzig, Anne E. .... Irvine, CA
Kunzke, Katja .... Madison, WI
Kunzler, Brian C. .... Salt Lake City, UT
Kunzler, Ron R. .... Brigham City, UT

Kurtz, Barry ....Los Angeles, CA
Kurtz, Barry, A Professional Corporation Encino, CA Los Angeles, CA
Kurtz, Becky A. ....Atlanta, GA
Kurtz, Birgit ....New York, NY
Kurtz, Brian J. ....Memphis, TN
Kurtz, Bryan D. ....Palo Alto, CA
Kurtz, Carol E. ....Malibu, CA
Kurtz, Charles J., III ....Columbus, OH
Kurtz, Charles W. ....Frankfort, KY
Kurtz, Christopher F. ....Miami, FL
Kurtz, Christopher T. ....Louisville, KY
Kurtz, D. Scott ....Brooklyn, NY
Kurtz, Daniel L. ....New York, NY
Kurtz, David A. ....Everett, WA
Kurtz, David C. ....Boston, MA
Kurtz, David L. ....Phoenix, AZ
Kurtz, David M., Jr. ....Detroit, MI
Kurtz, David R. ....Ventura, CA
Kurtz, David S. ....Chicago, IL
Kurtz, Deborah S. ....Levittown, NY
Kurtz, Dennis E. ....Louisville, KY
Kurtz, Derek A. ....Orlando, FL
Kurtz, Donald R. ....Irvine, CA
Kurtz, Eric ....New York, NY
Kurtz, Eric M. ....Kingston, NY
Kurtz, Frank L. ....Yakima, WA
Kurtz, Gary A. ....Los Angeles, CA
Kurtz, George ....Torrance, CA
Kurtz, Glenn M. ....New York, NY
Kurtz, Harvey A. ....Milwaukee, WI
Kurtz, Howard A. ....Fayetteville, NC
Kurtz, J. Jack ....Forest Hills, NY
Kurtz, Jack M. ....Charleston, SC
Kurtz, James A. ....Madison, WI
Kurtz, James L. ....Chicago, IL
Kurtz, James P. ....Detroit, MI
Kurtz, Jane E. ....Kansas City, MO
Kurtz, Janell M. ....St. Cloud, MN
Kurtz, Jeffrey M. ....Omaha, NE
Kurtz, John D. ....West Palm Beach, FL
Kurtz, John F., Jr. ....Boise, ID
Kurtz, John K. ....Cut Bank, MT
Kurtz, John W. ....Kansas City, MO
Kurtz, John W. ....Warren, OH
Kurtz, Jon Brenner ....Winston-Salem, NC
Kurtz, Joseph W. ....Traverse City, MI
Kurtz, J. S. ....Bellingham, WA
Kurtz, Judith E. ....San Francisco, CA
Kurtz, Julia L. ....Houston, TX
Kurtz, Katharine D. ....Denver, CO
Kurtz, Kevin F. ....Dallas, TX
Kurtz and Kurtz Attorneys PLLC Louisville, KY
Kurtz, Leigh ....Vienna, VA
Kurtz, Lisa ....Phoenix, AZ
Kurtz, Louis L. ....Eugene, OR
Kurtz, L. S., Jr. ....Anchorage, AK
Kurtz, Lyn Ann ....Sterling, VA
Kurtz, M. David ....New Orleans, LA
Kurtz, Marcy E. ....Houston, TX
Kurtz, Margaret U. ....Atlanta, GA
Kurtz, Maurice ....Bronx, NY
Kurtz, Maxine ....Denver, CO
Kurtz, Melissa M. ....New Bern, NC **Wilmington, NC**
Kurtz, Melissa M. ....Nashville, TN
Kurtz, Melvin H. ....Greenwich, CT
Kurtz, Michael ....Redwood City, CA
Kurtz, Michael L. ....Cincinnati, OH
Kurtz, Nat ....New York, NY
Kurtz, Norman I. ....Mount Prospect, IL
Kurtz, Normand R. ....New York, NY
Kurtz, Pamela L. ....Ann Arbor, MI
Kurtz, Patricia A. ....New York, NY
Kurtz, Paul L. ....Coral Gables, FL
Kurtz & Peckham ....Denver, CO
Kurtz, Philip M. ....Beverly Hills, CA
Kurtz, Philip M., A Law Corp. Beverly Hills, CA
Kurtz, Quentin E. ....Wichita, KS
Kurtz & Revness, P.C. ....Cherry Hill, NJ **Wayne, PA**
Kurtz, Richard E. ....Philadelphia, PA
Kurtz, Richard E., II ....Tysons Corner, VA
Kurtz, Richard J. ....New York, NY
Kurtz, Richard J. ....New York, NY
Kurtz, Robert J. ....Houston, TX
Kurtz, Robert K. ....Hayward, CA
Kurtz, Robin S. ....Beverly Hills, CA
Kurtz, Ronald D. ....Los Angeles, CA
Kurtz, Ruth G. ....New York, NY
Kurtz, Ryan A. ....Nashville, TN
Kurtz, Sanders L. ......Port Jefferson Station, NY
Kurtz, Sandra Koss ....White Plains, NY
Kurtz, Sarah Elizabeth ....Redwood City, CA
Kurtz & Schuster, P.A. ....Marietta, GA
Kurtz, Sharron M. ....Greensboro, NC
Kurtz, Sheldon F. ....Iowa City, IA
Kurtz, Spencer C. ....Durham, NC
Kurtz, Steven D. ....Los Angeles, CA
Kurtz, Steven E. ....New York, NY
Kurtz, Steven N. ....Encino, CA
Kurtz, Stewart L., II ....Huntingdon, PA
Kurtz, Stuart Alan ....Marietta, GA
Kurtz, Stuart B. ....Cherry Hill, NJ **Wayne, PA**
Kurtz, Ted ....South Paris, ME
Kurtz, Theodore J. ....Las Vegas, NV
Kurtz, Thomas G. ....Las Vegas, NV
Kurtz, Toby ....Mineola, NY
Kurtz, Walter C. ....Nashville, TN
Kurtz, William A. ....Chicago, IL
Kurtz, William A. ....Cleveland, OH
Kurtz, William D. ....Baltimore, MD
Kurtz, William J. ....Syracuse, NY
Kurtz, William L. ....Phoenix, AZ

Kurtzberg, Bradley W. ....Melville, NY
Kurtzberg, Deborah E. ....New York, NY
Kurtzberg, Howard ....Jericho, NY
Kurtzberg, Ira B. ....Melville, NY
Kurtzberg and Kurtzberg, P.C. ....Melville, NY
Kurtzberg, Linda A. ....Melville, NY
Kurtzer, Stuart M., (P.A.) ....Nutley, NJ
Kurtzhalts, Joel R. ....East Aurora, NY
Kurtzman, Alvin M. ....Los Angeles, CA
Kurtzman, Bryant S. ....Niagara Falls, NY
Kurtzman Cohen Matera & Gurock Montvale, NJ New York, NY Spring Valley, NY White Plains, NY
Kurtzman, Daniel M. ....Haddonfield, NJ
Kurtzman, Eben Lee ....San Jose, CA
Kurtzman, Eric Charles ....Montvale, NJ New York, NY Spring Valley, NY White Plains, NY
Kurtzman, Eric S. ....Los Angeles, CA
Kurtzman, Ilene Wendy ....Calabasas, CA
Kurtzman, James E. ....Aurora, CO
Kurtzman, Jeffrey ....Philadelphia, PA
Kurtzman, Jill E. ....New York, NY
Kurtzman, John L. ....Massillon, OH
Kurtzman, Melissa B. ....Ambler, PA
Kurtzman, Raymond ....Beverly Hills, CA
Kurtzman & Sarfaty, A Law Corporation Los Angeles, CA
Kurtzman, Sidney D. ....Delray Beach, FL
Kurtzon, Michael S. ....Chicago, IL
Kurtz-Phelan, James L. ....Denver, CO
Kurtzweil, Terrence J. ....Reedsburg, WI
Kuruc, Michele ....Department of Commerce, National Oceanic and Atmospheric Administration, GV
Kurucz, John ....New York, NY
Kurucza, Robert M. ....Washington, DC
Kuruk, Paul ....Birmingham, AL
Kurumada, Kevin J. ....Salt Lake City, UT
Kuruppillai, Sangeeta S. ....Dallas, TX
Kurvin, Stephen H. ....Sarasota, FL
Kury, Bernard E. ....New York, NY
Kury, Channing ....Commack, NY
Kury, Franklin L. ....Harrisburg, PA
Kuryk, David N. ....Baltimore, MD
Kuryla, Matthew L. ....Houston, TX
Kury Latorre, Marta M. ....San Juan, PR
Kurylo, Walter ....Arlington, VA
Kurys, Barbara Elaine ....Bridgewater, NJ
Kurz, Andrew A. ....Cardiff-By-The-Sea, CA
Kurz, Charles G. ....Bethesda, MD
Kurz, Daniel L. ....Monsey, NY
Kurz and Dick ....New York, NY
Kurz, Douglas L. ....Mineola, NY
Kurz, Edward Philip ....Aurora, CO
Kurz, Edward V. ....San Francisco, CA
Kurz, Eleanor H. ....Sands Point, NY
Kurz, Jacquelyn M. ....Portland, ME
Kurz, James S. ....Falls Church, VA
Kurz, Jules I. ....New York, NY
Kurz, Mark R. ....Belleville, IL **St. Louis, MO**
Kurz, Mary Elizabeth ....College Station, TX
Kurz, Michael J. ....Long Beach, CA
Kurz, Michael J., Law Office of Long Beach, CA
Kurz, Raymond A. ....Washington, DC
Kurz, Rebecca L. ....Kansas City, MO
Kurz, Stanley ....New York, NY
Kurz, Theodore A. ....New York, NY
Kurz, Thomas P. ....Houston, TX
Kurz, Warren W. ....Miami, FL
Kurz, William C. F. ....New York, NY
Kurzawa, David J. ....Hamden, CT
Kurzban, Ira J. ....Miami, FL
Kurzban Kurzban Weinger and Tetzeli, P.A. Miami, FL
Kurzban, Marvin ....Miami, FL
Kurzeja, Paul E. ....Charlotte, NC
Kurzeja, Ronald ....Saddle Brook, NJ Toms River, NJ
Kurzeka, Paul W. ....Oxnard, CA
Kurzer, Amy ....San Francisco, CA
Kurzer, Martin J. ....Miami, FL
Kurzinger, Arnold F. ....Boynton Beach, FL
Kurzman & Associates, P.C. Bloomfield Hills, MI
Kurzman & Eisenberg, LLP Brooklyn, NY New York, NY Scarsdale, NY White Plains, NY
Kurzman, Grant & Ojala Law Office,, Chtd. Minneapolis, MN
Kurzman, Jayne M. ....New York, NY
Kurzman Karelsen & Frank, LLP New York, NY
Kurzman, Marc G. ....Minneapolis, MN
Kurzman, Marc J. ....Westport, CT
Kurzman, Michael J. ....Miami, FL
Kurzman, Robert G. ....New York, NY **White Plains, NY**
Kurzman, Stephen ....Washington, DC
Kurzmann, Mark J. ....New York, NY
Kurzner, Christopher L. ....Dallas, TX
Kurzner, Wayne D. ....New York, NY
Kurzon, Jennifer L. ....Los Angeles, CA
Kurzweg, Anne Salzman ....Pittsburgh, PA
Kurzweil, David B. ....Atlanta, GA
Kurzweil, Deborah Fleischer ....Atlanta, GA
Kurzweil, Harvey ....New York, NY
Kurzweil, Howard E. ....Coral Gables, FL
Kurzweil, Howard E., P.A. Coral Gables, FL
Kurzweil, Jeffrey ....Washington, DC

Kurzweil, Judith ....Long Island City, NY
Kurzweil, Lanny S. ....Newark, NJ
Kurzweil, Robert B. ....Cherry Hill, NJ
Kurzweil, Sean Edward ....Los Angeles, CA
Kurzweil, Vivianne V. ....Miami, FL
Kurzynski, Thomas W. ....Greenfield, WI
Kus, Edward J. ....Chicago, IL
Kus, Martin W. ....La Porte, IN
Kus, Michael A. ....Troy, MI
Kusak, Albert S. ....Canandaigua, NY Rochester, NY
Kusak, Walter R. ....Wallingford, CT
Kusaka, Dan H. ....Seattle, WA
Kusakabe, Perry T. ....Kirkland, WA
Kusbach, Paul B. ....South Bend, IN
Kusch, Fred A. ....Sun City West, AZ
Kusch, Kenneth B. ....Central City, KY
Kusch, Robert E. ....Vero Beach, FL
Kuschner, Herbert ....New Rochelle, NY
Kuschner, Jeffrey R. ....Montclair, NJ
Kusek, Laurence A. ....Glenn, MI
Kusel, Elaine Simek ....New York, NY
Kuselias, Eric ....Hartford, CT
Kuselias, Jason ....Hartford, CT
Kuser, Debra Tantum ....Millburn, NJ
Kuser, J. Kerney, II ....Princeton, NJ
Kuseski, Richard B. ....Lake Forest, IL
Kush, Alice K. ....Lisle, IL
Kushan, Jeffrey P. ....Washington, DC
Kushel, Barry J. ....Riverhead, NY
Kushel, Glenn E. ....Atlanta, GA
Kushel, Stephen J. ....New York, NY
Kushen, Allan S. ....Madison, NJ
Kushen, Robert A. ....New York, NY
Kushi, Herbert I. ....Hilo, HI
Kushi, Hisao T. ....Pasadena, CA
Kushi & Kushi, Attys. at Law, A Law Corp. Hilo, HI
Kushi, Lynne K. ....Hilo, HI
Kushi, Masanori ....Hilo, HI
Kushibab, Peter D. ....Tempe, AZ
Kushida, Yayoi ....Granite Bay, CA
Kushinka, Calhoun and Godwin, LLP Warner Robins, GA
Kushinka, George ....Warner Robins, GA
Kushinsky, Gans & Chaplick Toms River, NJ
Kushinsky, R. Richard ....Toms River, NJ
Kushiyama, Dwight A. ....Honolulu, HI
Kushlefsky, Noah H. ....New York, NY
Kushman, Camille Kathleen Cincinnati, OH
Kushman, Irving A. ....Miami Beach, FL
Kushman, James A. ....Southfield, MI
Kushman, Moshe J. ....Los Angeles, CA
Kushner, Alexander ....Jersey City, NJ
Kushner, Andrew B. ....Cherry Hill, NJ
Kushner, Barry A. ....Keego Harbor, MI
Kushner, Beatrice J. ....San Francisco, CA
Kushner, Beth J. ....Milwaukee, WI
Kushner, Charles ....Florham Park, NJ
Kushner, Colleen A. ....Chicago, IL
Kushner, David ....Greensboro, NC **Raleigh, NC**
Kushner, David A. ....Estacada, OR
Kushner, Elliott ....Los Angeles, CA
Kushner, Enid L. ....Cleveland, OH
Kushner, Ervan F. ....Paterson, NJ
Kushner, Franklyn H. ....Boynton Beach, FL
Kushner, Gary Jay ....Washington, DC
Kushner, Gary M. ....Carle Place, NY
Kushner, Harold B. ....Birmingham, AL
Kushner, Howard J. ....San Diego, CA
Kushner, Howard L. ....Niagara Falls, NY
Kushner, Howard W. ....Freehold, NJ
Kushner, Ivy L. ....Scottsdale, AZ
Kushner, J. Ronald ....Oil City, PA
Kushner, James A. ....Los Angeles, CA
Kushner, Jay ....New York, NY
Kushner, Jeffrey ....Fort Myers, FL
Kushner, Jennifer L. ....Detroit, MI
Kushner, Jordan S. ....Minneapolis, MN
Kushner, Joseph M. ....Longboat Key, FL
Kushner & Kushner ....Fort Myers, FL
Kushner, Kushner & Roscetti, P.C. Niagara Falls, NY
Kushner, L. Stephen ....Charlotte, NC
Kushner, Larry ....Reseda, CA
Kushner, Les S. ....Hollywood, FL
Kushner, Lester ....New York, NY
Kushner, Louis B. ....Pittsburgh, PA
Kushner, Manuel ....Fort Lauderdale, FL
Kushner, Marc A. ....New York, NY
Kushner, Margaret Baumgardner Portland, OR
Kushner, Marvin W. ....Wellesley, MA
Kushner, Michael B. ....Irvine, CA
Kushner, Michael E. ....Albuquerque, NM
Kushner, Michael F. ....Los Angeles, CA
Kushner, Michael F., A Professional Corporation ....Los Angeles, CA
Kushner, Michael G. ....Washington, DC
Kushner, Michael S. ....New York, NY
Kushner, Morris J. ....Santa Monica, CA
Kushner, Philip S. ....Cleveland, OH
Kushner, Phillip J. ....Miami, FL
Kushner, Rachel Stephanie ....Fort Myers, FL
Kushner, Rita ....Los Angeles, CA
Kushner, Robert A. ....Pittsburgh, PA
Kushner, Robert E. ....New York, NY
Kushner, Roberta D. ....Fort Myers, FL
Kushner, Samuel A., Jr. ....Danville, VA
Kushner, Sanders & Krone, LLP Wellesley, MA
Kushner, Sandra Reiter ....Pittsburgh, PA
Kushner, Shari L. ....New York, NY
Kushner, Sherrill J. ....Santa Monica, CA
Kushner, Stefanie L. ....New York, NY

Kushner, Steven E. ....Los Angeles, CA
Kushner, Steven E. ....St. Louis, MO
Kushner, Steven M. ....Atlanta, GA
Kushner, Steven P. ....Fort Myers, FL
Kushner, Steven P., P.A. ....Fort Myers, FL
Kushner, Susan M. ....Albany, NY
Kushner, William M. ....Menlo Park, CA
Kushnick, Alan E. ....Santa Maria, CA
Kushnick & Associates ....Melville, NY
Kushnick, Lawrence A. ....Melville, NY
Kushnick, Martin J. ....Huntington, NY
Kushnick, Michael G. ....Washington, DC
Kushnick, Norman L. ....Baltimore, MD
Kushnir, David M. ....Chicago, IL
Kushnir, Kathy J. ....Providence, RI
Kushnir, Michael E. ....Andover, MA
Kushnir, Stephen J. ....Arlington, VA
Kushon, Jane Korein ....Philadelphia, PA
Kusiak, Kurt S. ....Boston, MA
Kusiak, Patrick J. ....Rancho Cordova, CA
Kusic, Arthur A. ....Harrisburg, PA
Kusic, Arthur A., P.C. ....Harrisburg, PA
Kusic, Gregory F. ....South Amboy, NJ
Kusic, John B. ....Denver, CO
Kusic, Marta ....Department of Labor, Office of the Solicitor, GV
Kusin & Hoover ....Texarkana, TX
Kusin, Michael B. ....Houston, TX
Kusin, Sherman A. ....Texarkana, TX
Kusin, Stuart V. ....Houston, TX
Kusinitz, Alan R. ....New York, NY
Kusinitz, Barry J. ....Providence, RI
Kusinski, Arthur J. .... Federal Deposit Insurance Corporation, GV
Kusion & Campana ....Lawndale, CA
Kusion, Eugene L. ....Lawndale, CA
Kusior, Robert ....Redondo Beach, CA
Kuskin, Harold A. ....Morristown, NJ
Kuskin, Judith Rutberg ....Summit, NJ
Kusko, Jonathan S. ....New York, NY
Kusko, Karen Y. ....New York, NY
Kuslansky, Allan J. ....Cornwall, NY
Kuslansky & Dorfman ....Brooklyn, NY
Kuslansky, Milton ....Brooklyn, NY
Kusman, George D. ....Chicago, IL
Kusmer, Toby H. ....Boston, MA
Kusmiss, John H. ....Pasadena, CA
Kusner, Andrew T. ....Cleveland, OH
Kusnerus, Wendell G. ....Portland, OR
Kusnetz, Dan A. ....New York, NY
Kusnetzky, Leon G., P.C. ....Kansas City, MO
Kusnetzky, Phillip A. ....Kansas City, MO
Kusnick, Howard A. ....Fort Lauderdale, FL
Kusnir, J. Michael ....San Diego, CA
Kusnirik, Andrew M., III ....Hamilton, NJ
Kusnitz, H. Norman ....Bridgeport, CT
Kusper, Joseph G. ....Rosemont, IL
Kusper & Raucci, Chartered ....Chicago, IL
Kusper, Stanley T., Jr. ....Chicago, IL
Kusper, Stewart T. ....Chicago, IL
Kuss, Christine L. ....Philadelphia, PA
Kuss, Herbert ....Fairbanks, AK
Kuss, Joseph P. ....Tampa, FL
Kuss, Mark D. ....Terrytown, LA
Kuss, Rudolf L. ....New Milford, CT
Kuss, Susan L. ....Indianapolis, IN
Kuss, William E. ....Pittsburgh, PA
Kussel, William F. ....Keshena, WI
Kusske, Kathryn A. ....Washington, DC
Kussman, Catherine E. ....San Francisco, CA
Kussman, Joshua D. ....San Francisco, CA
Kussman, Russell S., (A Professional Corporation) ....**Los Angeles, CA**
Kussman & Whitehill ....Los Angeles, CA
Kussmann, Patricia C. ....Brentwood, TN
Kussmann, Roy F. ....Tacoma, WA
Kussmaul, John A. ....Lancaster, WI
Kussner, Stephen L. ....Tampa, FL
Kussoy, Eric G. ....New York, NY
Kussoy, Marisa R. ....New Providence, NJ
Kussy, Edward V.A. Department of Transportation, Federal Highway Administration, GV
Kust, Susan G. ....Orland Park, IL
Kust, Susan G., Ltd. ....Orland Park, IL
Kusta & Boan, P.C. ....Bolingbrook, IL
Kusta, Edward D. ....Bolingbrook, IL
Kustell, Carl B. ....Buffalo, NY
Kustell, Carl Patrick ....Buffalo, NY
Kuster, Ann McLane ....Concord, NH
Kuster, Bradford W. ....Concord, NH
Kuster, Charles W., Jr. ....Cynthiana, KY
Kuster, Heidi ....Chicago, IL
Kuster, John J. ....New York, NY
Kuster, Larry D. ....Jacksonville, IL
Kuster, Michael J. ....Jefferson City, MO
Kuster, Michele P. ....Sherman Oaks, CA
Kuster, Thomas W. ....Hermitage, PA New Wilmington, PA **Sharon, PA**
Kustin, Carl, Jr. ....Los Angeles, CA
Kustoff, Daniel O. ....San Antonio, TX
Kustoff, David F. ....Memphis, TN
Kustoff & Strickland, PLLC ....Memphis, TN
Kustra, Lawrence W. ....Pittsburgh, PA
Kustron, Konnie Gerlyn ....Ypsilanti, MI
Kusturiss, Dennis J. ....Pittsburgh, PA
Kusturiss, John E., Jr. ....Philadelphia, PA
Kusturiss, Michael E. ....Canonsburg, PA
Kusuda, Hiroko ....New Orleans, LA
Kusyk, Douglas A. ....Portland, OR
Kusz, Michael J. ....Iron Mountain, MI
Kuszaj, James M. ....Raleigh, NC
Kuszewski, Alexander R. ....Milwaukee, WI
Kuta, Alexander E., Jr. ....Chicago, IL
Kuta, Ann Marie ....Chicago, IL
Kuta, Christine M. ....Boston, MA
Kuta, Jeffrey ....Chicago, IL

Kyle, Harold K., III .... Woodland Hills, CA
Kyle, Henry C. .... San Marcos, TX
Kyle, Henry C., III .... San Marcos, TX
Kyle, J. Timothy .... Decatur, AL
Kyle, James F. .... Memphis, TN
Kyle, James M., III .... Hayward, CA
Kyle, Jean Elaine .... Gainesville, FL
Hamilton, MT
Kyle, Jeffrey S. .... Austin, TX
Kyle, Jerry V., Jr. .... Austin, TX
Kyle, Jessica .... Hackensack, NJ
Kyle, Jessica L. .... Woodbridge, NJ
Kyle, John B. .... Dallas, TX
Kyle, John M. .... Noblesville, IN
Kyle, John M., III .... Indianapolis, IN
Kyle, John S. .... San Diego, CA
Kyle, Joseph F. .... Las Vegas, NV
Kyle, Judith S. .... Orlando, FL
Kyle, Karen S. .... Jetmore, KS
Kyle, Kathryn Wright .... Pittsfield, MA
Kyle, Keith B. .... Providence, RI
Kyle, Keith R. .... Fort Myers, FL
Kyle, Kevin A. .... Fort Myers, FL
Kyle, Kimme Smith .... Wylie, TX
Kyle & Kyle .... Las Vegas, NV
Kyle, Marcia A. .... Harrisburg, PA
Kyle, Mark L. .... Alameda, CA
Kyle & Martin .... Clarksburg, WV
Kyle & Mathis, L.L.P. .... Dallas, TX
Kyle, Michael E. .... Pleasanton, CA
Kyle, Paige C. .... San Antonio, TX
Kyle, Pamela Hornett .... Miami, FL
Kyle, Patricia J. .... Bozeman, MT
Kyle, Penelope Ward .... Richmond, VA
Kyle, Philip T. .... Jetmore, KS
Kyle, Philip W. .... Tulsa, OK
Kyle, Pugh E. .... Atlanta, GA
Kyle, R. Douglas .... Tacoma, WA
Kyle, R. Kelly .... Jackson, MS
Kyle, R. Matthew .... New Braunfels, TX
Kyle, Richard H. .... St. Paul, MN
Kyle, Robert D.
Executive Office Of The President, Office of Management and Budget, GV
Kyle, Robert P. .... Richmond, VA
Kyle, Robert W. .... Shreveport, LA
Kyle, Roy W. .... Tucson, AZ
Kyle, Sara .... Nashville, TN
Kyle, Shellie Deffendall .... Evansville, IN
Kyle, Stephan E. .... San Francisco, CA
Kyle, Stephen M. .... Kansas City, MO
Kyle, Steven J., (P.C.) .... Atlanta, GA
Kyle, Ted L. .... Tempe, AZ
Kyle, Terry L. .... San Antonio, TX
Kyle, Walker & Gossett .... San Marcos, TX
Kyler, Daniel R. .... Tacoma, WA
Kyler, David J. .... Tucson, AZ
Kyler, William A. .... New Philadelphia, OH
Kyle-Reno, Shelia A. .... Worthington, OH
Kyles & Associates, P.C. .... Memphis, TN
Kyles, John H. .... Houston, TX
Kyles, Keith C. .... Memphis, TN
Kyllo, Jamie Alin .... Albert Lea, MN
Kym, Jiyoung .... Los Angeles, CA
Kyman, Alan B. .... St. Louis, MO
Kyman, Alan M. .... Phoenix, AZ
Kyman, David S. .... Los Angeles, CA
Kyman, Roberta H. .... Los Angeles, CA
Kyme, Gary P. .... Larchmont, NY
Kynard, Horace W. .... Bessemer, AL
Kyndberg, Kathleen A. .... Carbondale, IL
Kyne, Heidi L. .... Monterey, CA
Kyne, James P. .... Miami, FL
Kyne, Stephen P. .... New York, NY
Kyner, Jennifer Putman .... Kansas City, MO
Kynerd, Stanley Lee .... Jackson, MS
Kynes, C. Allen, Jr. .... Clearwater, FL
Kynes, Deborah Pointer .... Clearwater, FL
Kynes, Markman & Felman, P.A.
Tampa, FL
Kynett, Kenneth D. .... Wildwood, NJ
Media, PA
Kyono, Steven J. .... Roseland, NJ
Kyper, James R. .... Pittsburgh, PA
Kypreos, Spiro T. .... Pensacola, FL
Kypta, Richard J. .... Boston, MA
Kyre, Kenneth, Jr. .... Greensboro, NC
Kyreakakis, Andrew J. .... Bloomfield, NJ
Kyreakedes, John H. .... Dobbs Ferry, NY
Kyres, Catherine A. .... St. Petersburg, FL
Kyres, Peter .... Tampa, FL
Kyriakakis, Jeffrey L. .... Charlotte, NC
Kyriakidis, Despina .... Medford, MA
Kyriakodis, Harry G. .... Philadelphia, PA
Kyriakos, Theodore C. .... Sioux Falls, SD
Kyriakou, Christos S. .... Atlanta, GA
Kyriazis, Arthur (Athanasios) John
Ocean City, NJ
Lansdowne, PA
Kyriazis and Associates .... Ocean City, NJ
Lansdowne, PA
Kyriazos, Charles S. .... Hollywood, FL
Kyrios, Helen .... Fairfield, OH
Kyröläinen, Annika .... Richmond, VA
Kyropoulos, Adriane .... New York, NY
Kyros, Dennis P. .... Chicago, IL
Kyros, Konstantine William, P.C., Law Offices of .... Boston, MA
Kyros, Konstantine William .... Boston, MA
Kyros, Thomas G. .... Grand Rapids, MI
Kyrouac, Scott M. .... Terre Haute, IN
Kyrouz, Michele F. .... San Francisco, CA
Kysela, Sussan Mahallati .... Washington, DC
Kysella, William H., Jr.
Department of Commerce, Office of the General Counsel, GV
Kyser, John M. .... Austin, TX
Kyser, Kenneth D. .... Moberly, MO
Kyser, Nickolas J. .... Detroit, MI
Kyser & Nordyke .... Butler, MO
Kansas City, MO
Kyser, Patricia Ann .... Jacksonville, FL
Kysilka, Karin J. .... Washington, DC
Kysor, Charles C. .... Gowanda, NY
Kysor & Della Posta .... Gowanda, NY
Kystad, Laura M. .... Southfield, MI
Kyte, Donald J. .... Oklahoma City, OK
Kyte, Janet M. .... Chicago, IL
Kyte, Lawrence H., Jr. .... Cincinnati, OH
Kyte, Richard E., Jr. .... Woonsocket, RI
Kyte, Richard E., Jr., P.C. .... Woonsocket, RI
Kyte, Robert E. .... Boise, ID
Kytle, James W. .... Atlanta, GA
Kytle, Kevin G. .... Kenner, LA
Kyttle, Stuart F. .... Rockville, MD
Kyyhkynen, Paul A. .... St. Paul, MN
Kyzar & Celles .... Natchitoches, LA
Kyzar, Van H. .... Natchitoches, LA
Kyzivat, Thomas A. .... Bronx, NY
Kyzmir, Anne K. .... Buffalo, NY

La, Carolyn Y. .... Los Angeles, CA
La, Esther H. .... Palo Alto, CA
La, Huy Q. .... Seattle, WA
Laabs, Gerald W. .... Black River Falls, WI
Laager, John C. .... Malvern, PA
Laak, Michael J. .... Minneapolis, MN
Laak, William G. .... Minneapolis, MN
Laake, Edward J. .... Norcross, GA
Laake, Walter E., Jr. .... Greenbelt, MD
Laaker, James A. .... St. Louis, MO
Laakso, Bonnie S. .... Elkton, MD
Laakso, Kim E. .... Denver, CO
Laakso, Raymond L. .... Hattiesburg, MS
Laaksonen, Rex W. .... Cloquet, MN
Laaksonen, II, Albert W. .... Paw Paw, MI
Laam, Barbara C. Y. .... Santa Clara, CA
Laanciloti, Daniel .... Roselle, IL
Laane, M. Sean .... Washington, DC
Laarman, Jill Clark .... Chicago, IL
Laarman, Linda M. .... Kansas City, MO
Laas, Elizabeth T. L. .... Cohasset, MA
Laas, Frederick H. .... Joplin, MO
Laas, Marek L. .... Boston, MA
Laasanen, Mary T. .... Stuart, FL
Laasch, Jon W. .... Edmond, OK
LaAsmar, Ronald G. .... Zanesville, OH
Laats, Alexander .... Cambridge, MA
Laatsch, Gary K. .... Chicago, IL
Rockford, IL
Laatsch, Morris H. .... Akron, OH
Laatsch, Susan W. .... Carbondale, CO
Lab, Charles E. .... Minooka, IL
Lab, Mark T. .... New York, NY
Laba, Jonathan T. .... Martinez, CA
Laba, Kerrie A. .... Bloomfield Hills, MI
Labach, Kenneth J. .... Washington, DC
LaBach, William A. .... Lexington, KY
Labadie, Craig .... Oakland, CA
Labadie, Dwight D. .... Detroit, MI
Labadie, Montie J. .... Trenton, MI
Labadie, Montie J., P.C. .... Trenton, MI
Labadie, Tim, Law Office of .... Austin, TX
Labadie, Timothy M. .... Detroit, MI
LaBaer, A. Jackson .... Phoenix, AZ
LaBahn, David R. .... Santa Ana, CA
La Bahn, William S. .... Anchorage, AK
Eugene, OR
Labaj, Pamela J. .... Newark, NJ
Labaj, Susan .... Oak Park, IL
Labaki, Paul F. .... Buffalo, NY
Labalme, Guy E. .... Apollo Beach, FL
Labanca, Leslie Gordon (IBA)
San Antonio, TX
Labanowski & Associates .... Houston, TX
Labanowski, Elizabeth J. .... Houston, TX
Labanowski, Ellen M. .... Deer Park, NY
Labanowski, Lawrence F. .... Houston, TX
Labanowski, Paul A. .... Houston, TX
Labanowski, Robert A. .... Rochester, NY
Labanowsky & Associates, S.C.
Kenosha, WI
Labanowsky, Charles J., III .... Kenosha, WI
LaBant, Terrence M. .... Chicago, IL
LaBar, Donald A. .... Great Falls, MT
LaBar, Robert G. .... Morrisville, PA
La Barba, Frank S., Jr. .... Dallas, TX
LaBarbera, Barry T. .... San Luis Obispo, CA
LaBarbera, Campbell and Leto
Tampa, FL
La Barbera, Deana A.
Securities and Exchange Commission, Division of Market Regulation, GV
LaBarbera, Dennis G. .... Monterey, CA
LaBarbera, Joseph J. .... New York, NY
La Barbera, Mario R. .... New Milford, NJ
LaBarbera, Michael D. .... Tampa, FL
La Barbera & Myers, A Prof. Corp.
Santa Ana, CA
LaBarbera, Salvatore J. .... Chicago, IL
La Barbera, Thomas J. .... Syosset, NY
LaBarbera, Vincent John, Jr. .... Santa Ana, CA
LaBarbiera, Ingrid R. .... New York, NY
La Barbiera, Joseph .... Cliffside Park, NJ
LaBarbiera, Leonard A.
New Brunswick, NJ
New York, NY
Labarca, Joseph Jude .... Staten Island, NY
LaBarca, Kenneth A. .... New York, NY
Labarga, Jorge .... West Palm Beach, FL
LaBarge, Campbell & Lyon, L.L.C.
Chicago, IL
La Barge, Claralou Ahlen .... Bloomington, CA
La Barge, Emery K. .... Tucson, AZ
LaBarge, Gerald L. .... Waukesha, WI
LaBarge, J. Russell, Jr.
Farmington Hills, MI
St. Clair Shores, MI
LaBarge, James A. .... Chicago, IL
LaBarge, Jeffrey .... Binghamton, NY
LaBarge, Lisa K. .... Binghamton, NY
LaBarge, Michael R. .... Chicago, IL
Labarge, Neil C. .... Phoenix, AZ
LaBarge, Richard M. .... Chicago, IL
Labarge, Sandra A. .... Seattle, WA
Labarge, Sandra A., PLLC, Law Office of
Seattle, WA
LaBarr, Karl K. .... Easton, PA
LaBarre, Alfred B." Pete " .... Springfield, IL
LaBarre, Christine Ghislaine .... Buffalo, NY
LaBarre, David Q. .... Durham, NC
LaBarre, Dennis W. .... New York, NY
Cleveland, OH
LaBarre, Donald L., Jr. .... Allentown, PA
LaBarre, Edward J. .... Colorado Springs, CO
LaBarre, Elviria A. C. .... Bangor, PA
Stroudsburg, PA
LaBarre, James A. .... Alexandria, VA
LaBarre, Jerome, A Professional Corporation .... Portland, OR
LaBarre, Jerome E. .... Portland, OR
LaBarre, Oscar P. .... Vicksburg, MS
LaBarre, Scott .... Metairie, LA
LaBarre, William R. .... Hollandale, MS
LaBarre & Young .... Springfield, IL
LaBarthe, Christopher .... Irvine, CA
Labarthe, Patricia McCarthy
Oklahoma City, OK
Labarthe, Richard C.
Oklahoma City, OK
Labasi, Philip G., (P.C.) .... Edison, NJ
Labasky, Ronald A. .... Tallahassee, FL
Labasky, Susan K. .... Miami, FL
Labat, GermainD., III .... Palo Alto, CA
LaBat, Joseph M. .... Minneapolis, MN
Labat, Keith J. .... Thibodaux, LA
Labat, Terry Smith
Department of Commerce, GV
Labate, Greg S. .... Costa Mesa, CA
LaBate, Mark J. .... Fort Lauderdale, FL
Labate, Robert J. .... Chicago, IL
Labaton, Edward .... New York, NY
Labaton, Mark .... Palo Alto, CA
Labaton, Stephen .... Washington, DC
Labatte, Leta .... Seattle, WA
LaBauda & Goulart, LLC .... Boulder, CO
LaBauve, Donald James .... Kansas City, MO
LaBauve, Melissa S. .... New Orleans, LA
LaBauve, Randall R. .... North Palm Beach, FL
LaBaw, Jeffrey S. .... Austin, TX
Labay, Eugene B. .... San Antonio, TX
Labay, Joan M. .... Carrollton, TX
Labbadia, Pat, III .... Clinton, CT
L'Abbate, Balkan, Colavita & Contini, L.L.P. .... Livingston, NJ
Garden City, NY
New York, NY
White Plains, NY
L'Abbate, Donald R. .... Garden City, NY
Labbate, Kenneth M. .... New York, NY
Labbe, Charla Bizios .... Manchester, NH
Labbe, Robert L. .... Newport Beach, CA
Labbee, Michael F. .... Venice, CA
Labbienti, Jo-Nell .... Denver, CO
Labe, L. Jay .... Denver, CO
Labe, Monica J. .... Detroit, MI
Labe, Robert B. .... Southfield, MI
Labe, Robert B., P.C. .... Southfield, MI
LaBeau, Benjamin J. .... Billings, MT
LaBeau & Dietchweiler .... Kankakee, IL
LaBeau, Michael W. .... Monroe, MI
LaBeau, Robert B. .... Kankakee, IL
Labeaune, Todd D. .... Los Angeles, CA
Labeck, Monica Irene .... Redmond, WA
Labedz, Chester S., Jr. .... Providence, RI
Labedz, Ronald F. .... Chicago, IL
Labell, Joseph S. .... New York, NY
Labell, Mark .... New York, NY
LaBell, Oldric J., Jr. .... Newport News, VA
Labella, Anthony A., Jr. .... Brooklyn, NY
LaBella, Charles G. .... San Diego, CA
LaBella, Frank .... Sacramento, CA
LaBella, Jason L. .... Chicago, IL
Lincolnwood, IL
Labella, John A. .... Brooklyn, NY
LaBella, Joseph M. .... Bloomfield Hills, MI
Labella, Rocco J. .... Hackensack, NJ
LaBella, Tara Ann .... Baldwin, NY
LaBelle, Amy L. .... Boston, MA
La Belle & Associates, P.A.
Palm Harbor, FL
LaBelle, Charles J. .... Saratoga Springs, NY
LaBelle, Clifford W. .... Zion, IL
LaBelle, Dan E. .... Westport, CT
LaBelle, Jeanne A. .... McLean, VA
LaBelle, John D. .... Manchester, CT
LaBelle, John D., Jr. .... Manchester, CT
Labelle, Krista .... Washington, DC
LaBelle & LaBelle .... Saratoga Springs, NY
LaBelle, LaBelle, Naab & Horvath, P.C.
Hartford, CT
Manchester, CT
LaBelle, Lance A. .... Irvine, CA
LaBelle, Lawrence J. .... Saratoga Springs, NY
LaBelle, Molly A. .... Seattle, WA
LaBelle, Paul J. .... Scranton, PA
LaBelle, R. Michael .... Washington, DC
La Belle, Richard D., III .... Palm Harbor, FL
LaBelle, Robert A. .... Bloomfield Hills, MI
Labelle, Robert J. .... Oconomowoc, WI
La Belle, Terrence L. .... Fort Lauderdale, FL
Labensart, Irving .... Tucson, AZ
Labensky, Steven J. .... Phoenix, AZ
Labenz, Robert C. .... Columbus, NE
Laber, Christopher T. .... Cincinnati, OH
Laber, Edward Harris .... Tucson, AZ
Laber, Edward Harris, Ltd. .... Tucson, AZ
Laber, Michael L. .... Dearborn, MI
Laber, Stephen C. .... Covington, KY
Laberee, Peter W. .... Philadelphia, PA
LaBerge, Andre S. .... Maple Grove, MN
Laberge, Cynthia L. .... San Francisco, CA
Laberge, Ellen T. .... North Syracuse, NY
LaBerge, Robert A. .... Syracuse, NY
LaBerge, Robert V. .... San Diego, CA
LaBerge, Stephen M. .... Santa Cruz, CA
LaBerge, Suzanne .... St. Petersburg, FL
Labert, Louis S. .... Palm Beach Gardens, FL
Labertew, Michael L. .... Salt Lake City, UT
Labes, Robert D. .... Cleveland, OH
Labgold, Marc R. .... Washington, DC
Labhart, Sigmund V., Jr. .... Evansville, IN
LaBianca, Michael F. .... San Francisco, CA
LaBiche, Franck F., Jr. .... Harahan, LA
Labin & Buffomante .... Williamsville, NY
Labin, Paul D. .... Encino, CA
Labin, Thomas S. .... Williamsville, NY
Labin, Tracy Anne .... Boulder, CO
Labine, Mark A. .... St. Paul, MN
Labine, Robert J., & Associates
East Grand Forks, MN
Labine, Robert J., & Associates
Grand Forks, ND
Labiner, Howard Mark .... Matthews, NC
Labiner, Paul S. .... Boca Raton, FL
Labinger, Jerome .... Brooklyn, NY
Labinger, Lynette .... Providence, RI
Labis, Keith L. .... Brewster, NY
La Bissonniere, Joel R.
Department of Commerce, National Oceanic and Atmospheric Administration, GV
Labkoff, William M. .... Philadelphia, PA
Labkon, Jordan R. .... Chicago, IL
Labmeier, John F. .... Cincinnati, OH
Laboda, Alane C. .... Fort Myers, FL
LaBoda, Barry C. .... Orlando, FL
LaBoda, Janel E. .... Minneapolis, MN
LaBoda, John J., Jr. .... Saratoga Springs, NY
Laboda, Katherine D. .... Saratoga Springs, NY
Labode, Evelyn .... Lincoln, NE
Laboe & Collins, Legal Counsel, PLLC
Concord, NH
Laboe, John E. .... Concord, NH
Laboe, Norman J. .... San Francisco, CA
Laboe, Ronald F. .... St. Louis, MO
LaBollita, Mark .... Boston, MA
Labonski, Peter M. .... New York, NY
Labonte, Andrea Q. .... Goffstown, NH
LaBonte, Clarence V., Jr. .... Lexington, MA
La Bonte, Philip E. .... Milton, MA
LaBoon, John A. .... Houston, TX
LaBoon, R. Bruce, (P.C.) .... Houston, TX
Labor, Frank A., III .... Philadelphia, PA
LaBorde, Andre T. .... San Francisco, CA
Laborde, Cliffe C., III .... Shreveport, LA
Laborde, Cliffe E., III (P.C.)
Lafayette, LA
Laborde, Cliffe F. .... New Orleans, LA
Laborde, David C. .... Lafayette, LA
LaBorde, Dennis M. .... New Orleans, LA
Laborde, Edward T., Jr. .... Houston, TX
Laborde, Elmo J., Jr. .... Lafayette, LA
Laborde, Gary L. .... Baton Rouge, LA
New Orleans, LA
Laborde, Gregory J. .... Lafayette, LA
Laborde, Jeanne Marie .... Lafayette, LA
Laborde, John P. .... New Orleans, LA
Laborde, Kenneth H. .... New Orleans, LA
Laborde & Laborde .... Lafayette, LA
Laborde, Larry .... Santa Barbara, CA
Laborde Law Firm, The, L.L.C.
Lafayette, LA
LaBorde, Margaret Ann Sicard .... Metairie, LA
Laborde & Neuner .... Lafayette, LA
Laborde and Nguyen .... Santa Barbara, CA
Laborde, Pamela Roger .... Houston, TX
LaBorde, Patricia A. .... McLean, VA
Laborde, Paulin J., Jr. .... Lafayette, LA
Laborde, Stephanie B. .... Baton Rouge, LA
Laborde, Stephen J. .... New Orleans, LA
La Borde, William P. .... Seattle, WA
Tacoma, WA
La Bore, Carla K. .... Mound, MN
LaBore, Lee L. .... Hopkins, MN
LaBosco, Teresa E. .... New York, NY
LaBoskey, Peter .... Palo Alto, CA
Labosky, Jennifer A. .... Lexington, NC
Labosky, John J. .... St. Paul, MN
La Bouff, Anthony J. .... Auburn, CA
LaBounty, Debra S. .... Eugene, OR
LaBounty, Eric B. .... Los Angeles, CA
LaBounty, Mark E. .... Los Angeles, CA
Labov, Andrea L. .... New York, NY
Labov, Daniel A. .... Ridgefield, NJ
LaBovick, Brian F. .... Jupiter, FL
LaBovick, Esther U. .... Jupiter, FL
LaBovick & LaBovick, P.A. .... Jupiter, FL
Labovitch, Gerald .... Los Angeles, CA
Labovitz, Albert L. .... Atlanta, GA
Labovitz, Daniel M. .... New York, NY
Labovitz, David J. .... Gurnee, IL
Labovitz, Harvey .... Cleveland, OH
Labovitz, Irving D. .... Springfield, MA
Labovitz, Irving D., P.C. .... Springfield, MA
Labovitz, John R. .... Washington, DC
Labovitz, Judah I. .... Philadelphia, PA
Labovitz, Laurence B. .... Los Angeles, CA
Labovitz, M. Natasha .... New York, NY
Labovitz, Neal H. .... Southaven, MS
Labovitz, Priscilla .... Washington, DC

Labovitz, Sheri S. .... Atlanta, GA
Labovitz, Steven J. .... Atlanta, GA
Labovitz, William J. .... Pittsburgh, PA
Labovitz, Zelda .... Sunflower, MS
Labovsky, Maxine S. .... Newark, DE
Labow, Joseph .... Alexandria, VA
Labow, Scott A. .... Hammond, IN
Labowe, Labowe & Hoffman
Los Angeles, CA
Labowe, Richard W. .... Los Angeles, CA
Labowe, Ronald B. .... Los Angeles, CA
Labowitz, Allan M.
Department of State, GV
Labowitz, Daniel I. .... Pittsford, NY
Labowitz, Edward S. .... Los Angeles, CA
Labowitz, Kenneth Edward
Alexandria, VA
LaBoy, Jose A. .... Vineland, NJ
Labrador, Edward George .... Tallahassee, FL
Labrador, Peter C. .... Mission Viejo, CA
San Francisco, CA
LaBran, Ronald M. .... Pasadena, CA
Labranche, Frans J., Jr. .... New Orleans, LA
LaBranche & Lejeune .... Baton Rouge, LA
LaBranche, Maxime (Max) G.
Baton Rouge, LA
LaBrant, Robert S. .... Lansing, MI
LaBre, William L. .... Edwardsburg, MI
LaBrec, David J. .... Dallas, TX
LaBreche, Stephen O. .... San Marcos, CA
LaBrecque, Alexander T. .... Elmira, NY
La Brecque, Alfred E., Jr. .... Red Bank, NJ
LaBrecque, Koreen R. .... Bridgeport, CT
Labrecque, Theodore J. .... Red Bank, NJ
Labrecque, Theodore J., Jr. .... Freehold, NJ
La Bree, Craig J. .... Hobbs, NM
La Bree, Craig J., & Associates, P.C.
Hobbs, NM
Labree, Robert W., (P.C.)
Colorado Springs, CO
LaBresh, Jason J. .... Washington, DC
La Bret, Steven M. .... Orlando, FL
La Bret, Steven Michael, P.A.
Orlando, FL
LaBrie, D. Victoria .... Santa Monica, CA
LaBrie, Michael J. .... Oklahoma City, OK
Labrie, Michael R. .... Chicopee, MA
Labrie, Paula D. .... Sacramento, CA
LaBrie, Raquiba N. .... New York, NY
Labrie, Roger E. .... Chicopee, MA
Labriola, David K. .... Naugatuck, CT
Labriola, Gerald, Jr. .... Naugatuck, CT
Labriola & Labriola, LLC .... Naugatuck, CT
Labriola, Lisa C. .... Pittsburgh, PA
Labriola, Michael A. .... Pittsburgh, PA
Labriola, Michael Joseph
Department of State,
Foreign Service Institute, GV
Labriola, Ronald T. .... Santa Monica, CA
La Briola, Stephen T. .... Atlanta, GA
Labrit, Suzanne Youmans .... Miami, FL
Labros, Arthur .... Brookfield, WI
La Brosse, Luc R. .... Central Falls, RI
Labrousse, Carl F. .... Fitchburg, MA
LaBrucherie, Roger A. .... El Centro, CA
LaBrucherie, Timothy J. .... El Centro, CA
Labrum, Mark C. .... Trevose, PA
Labrum, Michael R. .... Richfield, UT
Labrum, Michael R., P.C. .... Richfield, UT
LaBrun, Henry A. .... Charlotte, NC
Labruna, Carol Jean .... Buffalo, NY
La Bruno, David M. .... Newark, NJ
Labrusciano, Tina M. .... Bridgeton, NJ
LaBruyere, Joana Ortego .... Opelousas, LA
LaBruyere, Pamela .... San Diego, CA
Labson, Courtenay M. .... Washington, DC
Labson, Michael Scott .... Washington, DC
Labson Freeman, Beth .... Redwood City, CA
Labuda, Frank J., Jr. .... Monticello, NY
Labuda, Genevie F. .... Chicago, IL
Labuda, Jayne Marie .... St. Clair Shores, MI
LaBuda, John P. .... Rock Springs, WY
Labuda, Joseph M. .... New York, NY
LaBuda, Judy L. .... Boulder, CO
Labuda, Thomas A., Jr. .... Chicago, IL
LaBudde, Frank .... Montgomery, AL
LaBudde, Roy C. .... Milwaukee, WI
Labudde, Susan A. .... Milwaukee, WI
La Bue, Anne Marie .... Columbus, OH
LaBue, Anthony C. .... Rochester, NY
LaBue, Anthony F. .... West Orange, NJ
La Bue, Eugene P. .... Rochester, NY
La Bue, Michael J. .... Webster, NY
LaBue, Richard H. .... Webster, NY
LaBuhn, Matthew A. .... Columbus, OH
LaBunski, Julie A. .... Chicago, IL
Labush, Gerald M. .... New York, NY
Laby, Arthur B. .... Washington, DC
LaCabe, Alvin J. .... Denver, CO
LaCagnin, Stephen M. .... Clarksburg, WV
Morgantown, WV
Lacagnina, Gina L. .... San Diego, CA
Lacagnina, Michael A. .... Tucson, AZ
Lacagnina, Michael A. .... Rochester, NY
Lacaire, John A. .... Bedford, MA
Lacal, Emilio H. .... Miami, FL
Lacallade, Charles L. .... Austin, TX
Lacampagne, Suzanne .... Portland, OR
LaCapra, John R. .... Coral Gables, FL
La Caprucia, Cynthia M. .... New York, NY
Lacara & Galvez, P.C. .... West Sayville, NY
Lacara, Garrett R. .... West Sayville, NY
LaCaria, Philip A. .... Welch, WV
Lacasa, Armando .... Miami, FL
Lacasa, Eduardo R. .... Miami, FL
LaCascia, Michael J. .... Boston, MA
LaCascia, Patricia L. O'Leary
Worcester, MA

LaCasse, Barry K. .... North Attleboro, MA
Lacasse, Daniel L. .... Calais, ME
LaCasse, Leonard J. .... Ukiah, CA
LaCasse, Marc L. .... Boston, MA
LaCasse, William O. .... Portland, ME
Lacau, Adrienne H. .... San Francisco, CA
Lacau & Compton .... San Francisco, CA
LaCava, Daniel F. .... Pittsburgh, PA
LaCava, Daniel F., Law Firm, The, P.C.
Pittsburgh, PA
LaCava, Frederick William .... Indianapolis, IN
LaCava, John J. .... Stamford, CT
La Cava, John R. .... White Plains, NY
LaCava, Louis J. .... Tampa, FL
LaCava, Richard .... Syosset, NY
La Cava, Richard A. .... San Francisco, CA
LaCava, Susan .... Madison, WI
LaCava, Susan, S.C. .... Madison, WI
Lacaz Martins, Srour & Fischer LLP
New York, NY
Laccavole, Dennis M. .... Bridgeport, CT
Westport, CT
Lacchia, Thomas W. .... San Francisco, CA
Lacci, John V. .... West Lafayette, IN
Lace, Sharon McCurdy .... Verona, PA
Lacek, Michael J. .... Boston, MA
Lacelle, Erik C. .... Rochester, NY
Lacera, Francisco J. .... Union City, NJ
LaCerra, Traci Harris .... Little Rock, AR
North Little Rock, AR
Lacerte, Arthur J. G., Jr. .... Albuquerque, NM
Lacerte, Dennis A. .... Denver, CO
LaCerva, Anthony J. .... Cleveland, OH
La Cesa, Mary M. .... Santa Monica, CA
Lacewell, Linda A. .... New York, NY
Lacewell, Tonya Marie .... Murfreesboro, NC
Lacey, Alisa C. .... Phoenix, AZ
Lacey, Allen L., Jr. .... Commerce, GA
Lacey, Brian E. .... Boston, MA
Lacey, Darren L. .... Houston, TX
Lacey, David M. .... Houston, TX
Lacey, Dennis V. .... Wichita, KS
Lacey, Douglas A. .... Houston, TX
Lacey, Edward J. .... Ventura, CA
Lacey, Eleanor Baldwin .... San Rafael, CA
Lacey, Forrest W. .... Knoxville, TN
Lacey, Francis T. .... Rockville, MD
Lacey, Frank M. .... Bartlesville, OK
Lacey, Frederick B. .... Newark, NJ
Lacey, Gary E. .... Lincoln, NE
Lacey, Gregory L. .... Chicago, IL
Lacey, Heather A. .... Boston, MA
Lacey, Henry B. .... Phoenix, AZ
Portland, OR
Lacey, Hugh J., Jr. .... Nipomo, CA
Lacey, J. Ronald .... Chesterfield, MO
Lacey, James R. .... Morristown, NJ
Lacey, Jeffrey T. .... Syracuse, NY
Lacey, John F. .... Helena, MT
Lacey, John P. .... Roseland, NJ
Lacey, John R. .... Department of Justice,
Foreign Claims Settlement Commission of
the United States, GV
Lacey, Jonathon P. .... San Diego, CA
Lacey & Jones, LLP .... Ann Arbor, MI
Birmingham, MI
Detroit, MI
Grand Rapids, MI
Jackson, MI
Lacey, Kevin C. .... Los Angeles, CA
Lacey, Kevin S. .... Pasadena, CA
Lacey, Laurence A. .... Jackson, CA
Lacey, LeRoy M. .... Kokomo, IN
Lacey, Mary Kay .... San Francisco, CA
Lacey, Michael C. .... Anderson, IN
Lacey, Michael F., Jr. .... Des Moines, IA
Lacey, O'Mahoney, Mahoney, King & McCann .... Kokomo, IN
Lacey, Pamela A. .... Washington, DC
Lacey, Pamela G. .... Santa Ana, CA
Lacey, Pamela Sue .... Benton, IL
Lacey, Patricia M. .... Albany, NY
Lacey, Patrick H. .... Sioux Falls, SD
Lacey, Philip C. .... Atchison, KS
Lacey, Philip C. .... McPherson, KS
Wichita, KS
Lacey, R. Bruce .... Newland, NC
Lacey, Richard C. .... Fairhope, AL
Lacey, Richard E. .... Bristol, CT
Lacey, Robert H. .... Newland, NC
Lacey, Thomas A., A Professional Corporation
Modesto, CA
Lacey, Thomas C., Jr. .... Jackson, MS
Lacey, Thomas J. .... Collingdale, PA
Lacey, Trisha .... Glenwood Springs, CO
Lacey, Walter Alonzo .... Cherry Hill, NJ
Lacey & Ziogas .... Bristol, CT
Lach, Dana Marie .... Milwaukee, WI
Lach, David J. .... Little Rock, AR
Lach, Donna M. .... Chicago, IL
Lach, Herbert F., Jr. .... Dennis Port, MA
Lach, JoAnn .... Long Beach, CA
Lach, Joseph A. .... Wilkes-Barre, PA
Lach, Linda E. F. .... Lihue, HI
Lach, Michael J. .... Belleville, IL
Lach, Susan M. .... Minneapolis, MN
Lachall, Brion, Cohen & Lawson
West Chester, PA
Lachall, John L. .... West Chester, PA
Lachance, Andre J. .... Washington, DC
LaChance, James M. .... Atlanta, GA
La Chance, James T. .... Los Angeles, CA
LaChance, John H. .... Framingham, MA
La Chance, John P. .... Land O'Lakes, WI
LaChance, Kevin K. .... Topeka, KS
LaChapelle, Charmaine C. .... Chicago, IL
La Chapelle, Harold J.
Wisconsin Rapids, WI

La Chapelle, Hartley E. .... Milwaukee, WI
LaChapelle, Kinga M. .... Albany, NY
La Charite, George J. .... Assumption, IL
Lachat, Frederick T., Jr. .... Philadelphia, PA
La Chaussee, Charles Brian .... New York, NY
Lachcik, Terry M. .... Chicago, IL
LaCheen, Cary .... New York, NY
LaCheen, Stephen Robert, & Associates
Philadelphia, PA
Lachenauer, Robert B. .... New York, NY
Lachenauer, Stephen P. .... Howell, NJ
Lachenmaier, Courtenay A.
Las Vegas, NV
Lachenmeier, Enloe & Rall .... Portland, OR
Vancouver, WA
Lachenmeier, Rudy R. .... Portland, OR
Lacher, Alan E. .... New York, NY
Lacher, Elizabeth M. .... Millburn, NJ
Lacher, Frederick K., Co., L.P.A.
Akron, OH
Lacher, Frederick K., Co. (L.P.A.)
Akron, OH
Lacher & Lovell-Taylor, P.C.
New York, NY
Lacher, Michael A. .... New York, NY
Lacher, Richd. W. .... Jackson Springs, NC
Lacher, Stanley J. .... Huntington, NY
Lacher, Stephen J. .... Buffalo, NY
Lachey, Robert E. .... Dayton, OH
Lachiatto, Alexander M. .... Franklin, NH
Lachicotte, Althea M. .... Atlantic Beach, FL
Lachina, Andrew C. .... Los Alamitos, CA
Lachini, Jos. .... New York, NY
Lachman, Arthur J. .... Seattle, WA
Lachman, Branton G. .... Running Springs, CA
Lachman, Carol .... San Diego, CA
Lachman, Edwin .... Endicott, NY
Lachman, Gary M. .... Hackensack, NJ
Lachman, Gary S. .... Landover, MD
Lachman, Gerson H. .... Dallas, TX
Lachman & Gorton .... Endicott, NY
Lachman, Janice K. .... Sacramento, CA
Lachman, Marlene F. .... Philadelphia, PA
Lachman, Marshall G. .... Miamisburg, OH
Lachman, Moses .... New York, NY
Lachman, Ronald A. .... Santa Monica, CA
Lachman, Roy E. .... Cleveland, OH
Lachman, Theodore D. .... Lake Oswego, OR
Lachman, Theodore D., P.C.
Lake Oswego, OR
Lachmann, Richard H. .... Honolulu, HI
Lachmar, Barbara .... Logan, UT
Lachner, Geoffrey N. .... Laguna Hills, CA
Lachner, Ronald K., Law Offices of
Long Beach, CA
Lachow, Andrew B. .... New York, NY
Lachowicz, Mark T. .... Southfield, MI
Lachowicz, Mary Ellen .... New Canaan, CT
Lachs, Aileen L. .... Burlington, VT
Lachs, Samuel .... Elizabeth, NJ
Lachs, Sheila Marie .... Washington, DC
Lachs, Stephen M. .... Los Angeles, CA
Lachs, Susanna E. .... Philadelphia, PA
Lachter, Sidney N. .... Phoenix, AZ
Lachter, Sidney N. .... Scottsdale, AZ
Lachter, Stephen H., Law Offices of
Washington, DC
Lachterman, Steven J. .... Coral Gables, FL
Lachtman, David R. .... New York, NY
Lachuk, Michael B. .... San Diego, CA
Lachut, Joseph F. .... Cranston, RI
Lacich, Christopher P. .... Youngstown, OH
LaCien, Richard A. .... Flossmoor, IL
La Cilento, Michael J. .... Corona, CA
Costa Mesa, CA
Lacina, Charles F. .... New York, NY
Lacina, John W. .... Port Huron, MI
Lacina, L. J., Jr. .... Brenham, TX
Lacina, Milton E. .... New York, NY
Lacina, Thomas A. .... Grinnell, IA
LaCivita, Anthony J. .... Stamford, CT
LaCivita, David M. .... Landover, MD
LaCivita, Richard J. .... Hubbard, OH
Lack & Cogan .... Boston, MA
Lack, Edward I. .... Fort Lauderdale, FL
Lack, James H. .... Palmer, AK
Lack, James J. .... Huntington, NY
Lack, Jeremy .... Franklin Lakes, NJ
Lack, John J. .... Camden, NJ
Lack, Jonathan D. .... Fort Lauderdale, FL
Lack, Jonathan H. .... Anchorage, AK
Lack and Lack, Chartered
Fort Lauderdale, FL
Lack, Michael J. .... Boston, MA
Lack, Robert J. .... Newark, NJ
New York, NY
Lack, Walter J. .... Los Angeles, CA
Lackard, Angela L. .... Boston, MA
Lackay, William E. .... Bushnell, FL
Lackaye, Edward J., Jr. .... Poughkeepsie, NY
Lackaye, Robert J. .... Poughkeepsie, NY
Lackenbach, Carol K. .... Staten Island, NY
Lackenbach Siegel Marzullo Aronson & Greenspan, P.C. .... New York, NY
Scarsdale, NY
White Plains, NY
Lacken-Geers, Kimberly M. .... Trenton, NJ
Lackeos, Dorothy Kelley .... Mobile, AL
Lackert, Clark W. .... New York, NY
Lackey, Anne W. .... San Francisco, CA
Lackey, Cary L. .... Phoenix, AZ
Lackey, Charles Y. .... Winston-Salem, NC
Lackey, Chester T. .... Bellingham, WA
Lackey, Craig A. .... Phoenix, AZ
Lackey, David L. .... Groveport, OH
Lackey, David S. .... Lenoir, NC
Lackey, Doug .... Austin, TX
Lackey, Douglas K. .... Woodland Hills, CA

Lackey, Gary D. .... Sharon, PA
Lackey, Gary W. .... Scottsboro, AL
Lackey, George C. .... Centralia, IL
Lackey, Gerald B. .... Toledo, OH
Lackey, Henry L. .... Calhoun City, MS
Lackey, Jack N., Jr. .... Hopkinsville, KY
Lackey, James G., III .... Nashville, TN
Lackey, James H. .... Mobile, AL
Lackey, Jane L. .... Holland, OH
Lackey, John D. .... Centralia, IL
Lackey, John F. .... Richmond, KY
Lackey, Joseph H. .... Grosse Pointe Farms, MI
Lackey, Joseph L., Jr. .... Nashville, TN
Lackey, Kester D., Jr. .... Oklahoma City, OK
Lackey & Lackey .... Shelby, NC
Lackey & Lackey, P.C. .... Centralia, IL
Lackey, Lance T. .... College Station, TX
Lackey Law Office .... Richmond, KY
Lackey, L. C. .... Greensboro, NC
Lackey, Mark D. .... Shelby, NC
Lackey, Melissa Cecil .... Rockville, MD
Lackey, Meredith M. .... Washington, DC
Lackey, Michael E., Jr. .... Washington, DC
Lackey, N. Dixon, Jr. .... Shelby, NC
Lackey, Nusbaum, Harris, Reny & Torzewski, A Legal Professional Association .... Toledo, OH
Lackey, Patricia S. .... Scottsboro, AL
Lackey, Paul B. .... Dallas, TX
Lackey, R. Douglas .... Atlanta, GA
Lackey, Robert E. T. .... Chicago, IL
Lackey, Robert L. .... Sharon, PA
Lackey, Rodgers, Price and Snedeker
Nashville, TN
Lackey, Ronald L. .... Danville, VA
Lackey, Samuel Allen .... Houston, TX
Lackey, Sandra L. .... San Diego, CA
Lackey, Seth N. .... Shelby, NC
Lackey, Stacy L. .... Scottsdale, AZ
Lackey, Stacy L., P.C. .... Scottsdale, AZ
Lackey, Steve .... Chapel Hill, NC
Lackey, Thomas L. .... Bowie, MD
Lackey, Vaden M., Jr. .... Nashville, TN
Lackey, William B. .... New Orleans, LA
Lackey, Wm. Lee .... Savannah, TN
Lacki, Ralph S. .... Canton, OH
Lackie & Dammeier LLP
Rancho Cucamonga, CA
Lackie, H. Terrence .... Spokane, WA
Lackie, James R. .... Baton Rouge, LA
Lackie, Michael D. .... Rancho Cucamonga, CA
Lackier, Seymour .... Wynnewood, PA
Lackland & Heyward .... Atlanta, GA
Lackland, Theodore H. .... Atlanta, GA
Lacklen, John E. .... Oakland, CA
Lackman, Barbara A. .... Burbank, CA
Lackman, James S. .... Cambridge, MA
Lackman, Jared .... Fort Worth, TX
Lackman, Lawrence H. .... Long Beach, CA
Lackman, Lawrence H., Law Offices of
Long Beach, CA
Lackman, Melissa Morton
Granada Hills, CA
Lackmann, Chris G. .... Albuquerque, NM
Lackmeyer, Michael R. .... Killeen, TX
Lackner, James E. .... Minneapolis, MN
Lackner, Marc A. .... San Francisco, CA
Lackner, Michael .... Los Angeles, CA
Lackner, Richard J. .... Downers Grove, IL
Lackner, Robin Perlstein .... Minneapolis, MN
Lackore, Ramona C. .... Willmar, MN
Lackritz, Marc E. .... Washington, DC
Lacks, David B. .... St. Louis, MO
Lacks, Monica Levine .... New Orleans, LA
Lacks, Newman & Wynne .... St. Louis, MO
Lacks, Stanton M. .... Bensalem, PA
Lackshin, Herbert N. .... Houston, TX
Lacksonen, Todd .... Deerfield, IL
Lacktman, Eric .... Philadelphia, PA
Lacktman, Morrey .... Maple Shade, NJ
La Clair, Craig .... Boston, MA
LaClair, Paul L. .... New York, NY
Laco, John A. .... Los Angeles, CA
Lacobelle, Jerome A. .... West Haven, CT
Lacobelle, Jerome A., Jr. .... West Haven, CT
Lacobelle, Jerome A., LLC, Law Offices of
West Haven, CT
Lacobelle, Robert A. .... Fairfield, CT
La Coe, Norm .... Gainesville, FL
LaCombe, Alexandra V., P.C. .... Troy, MI
LaCombe, Alexandra Valleri .... Troy, MI
LaCombe, Daniel J. .... Detroit, MI
Lacombe, Deborah C. .... Charleston, SC
Lacomis, Bernard J. .... Cambridge, MA
Lacon, Harvey .... Mount Vernon, NY
LaCon, Walter J. .... Atlantic City, NJ
LaConte, Lisa A. .... Peoria, IL
La Conte, Mark S. .... Boston, MA
La Conte, Thomas J. .... Hackensack, NJ
LaCorte, Brian W. .... Phoenix, AZ
La Corte, Bundy & Varady .... Elizabeth, NJ
La Corte, James S. .... Elizabeth, NJ
LaCorte, Jerome James .... Berlin, MD
La Corte, Samuel M. .... Clifton, NJ
LaCost, Julie A. .... Iron Mountain, MI
Lacosta, Anthony W. .... Washington, DC
LaCosta, Joseph J. .... North Brunswick, NJ
Lacosta, Susan M. .... Whitefish, MT
LaCosta-Davino, Lucille .... Newark, NJ
La Costa Gonzalez, Carlos E. .... San Juan, PR
LaCoste, Anne Dishuck .... Tuscaloosa, AL
Lacoste, Rodney J., Jr. .... Slidell, LA
Lacoste, Steven E. .... New Orleans, LA
Lacoste, Todd L. .... Metairie, LA
LaCount, Karen Ann .... Baton Rouge, LA
LaCount, Stephen H. .... Irvine, CA
LaCour, Adrienne A. .... Metairie, LA
Lacour, Albert A., III .... Charleston, SC

LaCour, Barry L. ... Harahan, LA
LaCour, Cherie L. ... Albuquerque, NM
LaCour, Jeffrey W. ... Menlo Park, CA
LaCour, Jenny Brown ... New Orleans, LA
La Cour, Louis Bernard ... Columbus, OH
LaCour, Louis C., Jr. ... New Orleans, LA
LaCour, Marcia M. ... San Bernardino, CA
LaCour, T. Robert ... Kenner, LA
Lacour, Vanue B. ... Baton Rouge, LA
Lacourciere, Paul C. ... Los Angeles, CA
LaCourse, Joel A. ... Tulsa, OK
LaCourse, Nancy L. ... Austin, TX
La Course, Russell J. ... Duluth, MN
LaCourse, William R. ... Center Harbor, NH
LaCoursiere, Michael L.
Red Lake Falls, MN
Lacouture, Paul E. ... Dayton, OH
Lacouture, Paul M. ... Dayton, OH
Lacouture, Peter V. ... Providence, RI
Lacovara, Kirsten M. ... Boston, MA
Providence, RI
Lacovara, Michael ... New York, NY
Lacovara, Philip Allen ... Washington, DC
New York, NY
Lacroce, Eugene A., Jr. ... Boston, MA
Lacroix, Barry J. ... Chelsea, MA
LaCroix, Burke & Hand, P.C.
Grand Junction, CO
LaCroix, Charles ... Alexandria, LA
Lacroix, Charlotte A. ... Yardley, PA
LaCroix, Chris ... New York, NY
LaCroix, Christopher J. ... Basalt, CO
La Croix, David ... Punta Gorda, FL
LaCroix, Dennis J. ... Cambridge, MA
La Croix, Edward R. ... San Jose, CA
Lacroix, Ellen M. ... Northampton, MA
Lacroix & Fuller ... Springfield, MA
LaCroix, Jean R. ... Springfield, MA
LaCroix & Levy ... Alexandria, LA
LaCroix, M. Steven ... Fort Lauderdale, FL
La Croix, Strohe D. ... Los Angeles, CA
LaCroix, Thomas R. ... Grand Junction, CO
Lacroix, William J. ... Boulder, CO
LaCroix-Tighe, Corrine ... Short Hills, NJ
Lacross, David ... Jackson, MI
LaCross, Thomas J. ... Alpena, MI
La Crosse, Louis J. ... San Antonio, TX
LaCues, Jerry A. ... Chino, CA
Lacy, Alan E. ... San Francisco, CA
Lacy, Albert S. ... Chicago, IL
Lacy, Ben R., IV ... Richmond, VA
Lacy, Benjamin H. ... Boston, MA
Lacy, Campbell and Associates, P.C.
Wytheville, VA
Lacy, Cara A. ... Portland, OR
Lacy, Charles C. ... Wytheville, VA
Lacy, D. Patrick, Jr. ... Richmond, VA
Lacy, David W. ... Kailua-Kona, HI
Lacy, David W. ... Austin, TX
Lacy, Don P. ... Jackson, MS
Lacy, Edward M., Jr. ... Modesto, CA
Lacy, Elaine Marzetta
Department of Justice, Civil Division, GV
Lacy, Eldridge D. ... Orlando, FL
Lacy, Elizabeth ... Pittsburgh, PA
Lacy, Elizabeth Bermingham ... Richmond, VA
Lacy, Ford, (P.C.) ... Dallas, TX
Lacy, Gary L. ... Placerville, CA
Lacy, Glenn B. ... Aransas Pass, TX
Lacy, Graham G., Jr. ... Rocky Mount, NC
Lacy, J. Michael ... Kansas City, MO
Lacy, James V. ... Laguna Niguel, CA
Lacy, Janet Bledsoe ... Oceanside, CA
Lacy, Janice A. ... Laguna Niguel, CA
Lacy, Jeffrey A. ... Fort Worth, TX
Lacy, John C. ... Tucson, AZ
Lacy, John E. ... Springfield, MO
Lacy, John R. ... Honolulu, HI
Lacy, Julie A. Branstad ... Hingham, MA
Lacy & Kane, P.S. ... East Wenatchee, WA
Lacy, Katzen, Ryen & Mittleman, LLP
Rochester, NY
Lacy and Lacy ... Laguna Niguel, CA
Lacy, Leslie Wright ... Boulder, CO
Lacy, Lisa M. ... Savannah, GA
Lacy, Maricarol ... Chicago, IL
Lacy & Moseley, P.C. ... Farragut, TN
Knoxville, TN
Lacy, N. Duane
United States Postal Service,
Law Department, GV
Lacy, Paul Antonio ... Oklahoma City, OK
Lacy, Paul E. ... Gold River, CA
Lacy, Paul E. ... Sacramento, CA
Lacy, Paul E. ... Minneapolis, MN
Lacy, Peyton, Jr. ... Birmingham, AL
Lacy, Philip T. ... Columbia, SC
Lacy, Raymond E. ... Farragut, TN
Knoxville, TN
Lacy, Robinson B. ... New York, NY
Lacy, Rodney L. ... Minneapolis, MN
Lacy, Stanford E. ... Columbia, SC
Lacy, Steven C. ... East Wenatchee, WA
Lacy, Steven E. ... New Bern, NC
Lacy, Steven R. ... Wheeling, WV
Lacy, Terri ... Houston, TX
Lacy, Theo ... Santa Ana, CA
Lacy, Thomas C. ... Cypress, CA
Lacy, Thomas R. ... Hastings, MN
Lacy, Thomas William ... Taylorville, IL
Lacy, Virgil A., III ... Metairie, LA
New Orleans, LA
Lacy, Virginia Gordon ... Birmingham, AL
Lacy, Wayne D. ... Dallas, TX
Lacy, William Hershel ... Celina, TN
Lacy, William N. ... Yates Center, KS
Lacy, William R. ... Conway, AR
Lacy, William Thomas, Jr. ... Atlanta, GA

Laczewski, John M. ... Pompano Beach, FL
Laczko, John P. ... Youngstown, OH
Ladak, Imtiaz T. ... Washington, DC
Ladanyi, Robert A. ... Middletown, NY
Ladar, Jerrold M. ... San Francisco, CA
Ladar, Joyce B. ... San Francisco, CA
Ladar & Ladar ... San Francisco, CA
LaDart, Peter C. ... Gretna, LA
Ladas, Christos G. ... West Seneca, NY
Ladas, Hoopes, & Associates
North Muskegon, MI
Ladas, J. Stephen ... Hanover, MA
Ladas & Parry ... Los Angeles, CA
Chicago, IL
New York, NY
Ladas, Paul M. ... North Muskegon, MI
Ladd, Allen C. ... Spartanburg, SC
Ladd, Allen C., Immigration Law Office,
P.C. ... Asheville, NC
Spartanburg, SC
Ladd, Ann M. ... Minneapolis, MN
Ladd, Ann T. ... New York, NY
Ladd, B. Ernest ... Tulsa, OK
Ladd, Carolyn H. ... Seattle, WA
Ladd, Charles H., Jr. ... Oakhurst, NJ
Ladd, Charles J. ... Ann Arbor, MI
Ladd, Christine R. ... Bethesda, MD
Ladd, Cynthia J.
South San Francisco, CA
Ladd, D. Alan ... Indianapolis, IN
Ladd, Daniel W., III ... Stamford, CT
Ladd, David ... Denver, CO
Ladd, Dennis W. ... Jefferson, IA
Ladd, Donald F. ... Philadelphia, PA
Ladd, Donald M., Jr. ... Los Altos, CA
Ladd, Dorin J. ... Fresno, CA
Ladd, Edwin V., Jr. ... Avon, CT
Ladd, Elisabeth S. ... Toledo, OH
Ladd, F. Van D. ... Schenectady, NY
Ladd, Ford C. ... Department of Justice,
Civil Division, GV
Ladd, Frank A. ... Amarillo, TX
Ladd, Gretchen M. ... Portland, OR
Ladd, Heidi ... Urbana, IL
Ladd, J. Scott ... Gardiner, ME
Ladd, Jack D. ... Midland, TX
Ladd, Jeffrey R. ... Chicago, IL
Ladd, Jessica A. ... Sharon, MA
Ladd, John Curran, Law Offices of
San Francisco, CA
Ladd, Jon K. ... La Jolla, CA
Ladd, Jonathan E. ... New York, NY
Ladd, Joseph M. ... Union, MO
Ladd, Kathryn J. ... Nashville, TN
Ladd, Leah P. ... Mobile, AL
Ladd, Maribeth ... Boston, MA
Ladd, Nancy K. ... Mobile, AL
Ladd, Nancy Kirchberger
Bloomfield Hills, MI
Ladd, Patricia E. ... Los Gatos, CA
Ladd, Renee Dawn ... St. Paul, MN
Ladd, Richard D. ... Lubbock, TX
Ladd, Richard E. ... Bristol, TN
Ladd, Richard E., Jr. ... Abingdon, VA
Bristol, VA
Ladd, Robert J. ... Andover, MA
Ladd, Robert P. ... Port Huron, MI
Ladd, Robert S. ... Houston, TX
Ladd, Thomas A. ... Midland, MI
Ladd, Thomas W. ... Newark, NJ
Ladd, Vincent O. ... Warsaw, NY
Ladd, William M. ... Milford, NH
Ladd & Yackey ... Indianapolis, IN
Laddaga, Beth ... Charleston, SC
Laddaga, Drachman & Garrett, P.A.
Charleston, SC
West Columbia, SC
Laddaga, Lawrence A. ... Charleston, SC
West Columbia, SC
Ladden, Douglas S. ... Milpitas, CA
Ladden, Richard M. ... Milpitas, CA
Laddey, Brian M. ... Sparta, NJ
Laddey, Clark & Ryan ... Sparta, NJ
Laddin, Darryl S. ... Atlanta, GA
Laddish, Timothy Graves ... Oakland, CA
Laddon, Warren M. ... Merion, PA
Laddusaw, Marci L. ... Kingsley, IA
Laddusaw, Mark J. ... Algona, IA
Laddy, Donna L. ... Chicago, IL
Lade, Jeffrey R. ... Indianapolis, IN
LaDeane, E. Frederick ... Sacramento, CA
La Deau, Michael H ... Camden, NJ
Ladegaard, James C. ... Spirit Lake, IA
Ladegaard, Maahs & Owens
Spirit Lake, IA
Ladegaillerie, Denis ... New York, NY
Ladegast and Heffner ... Louisville, KY
Ladegast, Lawrence C., Jr. ... Louisville, KY
Ladeira, Ernest Martin ... Fall River, MA
Ladell, Ronald S. ... Florham Park, NJ
Lademan, Carrie E. ... Naples, FL
Laden, Adam ... New York, NY
Laden, Gilbert B. ... Mobile, AL
Laden, Gilbert B., P.C. ... Mobile, AL
Laden, John J. ... Garden City, NY
Laden, Kristan Quinn ... Chicago, IL
Laden, Larry ... Austin, TX
Laden, Michael J. ... Meriden, CT
Laden, Patrick R. ... Richmond, VA
Laden, Y. Paulette
Federal Communications Commission,
Mass Media Bureau, GV
Ladenberger, Erin Marie ... Glen Ellyn, IL
Ladenburg, Frank B., Jr. ... Tacoma, WA
Ladenburg, John W. ... Tacoma, WA
Ladenburg, John W., Jr. ... Tacoma, WA
Ladendorf, Barry D. ... San Diego, CA
Ladendorf, Daniel Allen ... Indianapolis, IN

Ladendorf, Mark C., & Associates
Indianapolis, IN
Ladendorff, G. Henry ... Scottsdale, AZ
Ladenheim, C. Jacob ... Fincastle, VA
Ladenheim, Janet ... Hackensack, NJ
Ladenheim Law Offices ... Fincastle, VA
Ladenson, Melissa A. ... San Bernardino, CA
Ladenson, Robert F. ... Chicago, IL
Lader, Irvin M. ... Fort Lauderdale, FL
Lader, Philip ... Washington, DC
Lader, Wendy S. ... Department of Commerce,
National Telecommunications & Information
Administration, GV
Laderberg, Jerry C. ... Treasury Department,
Office of Regulations and Rulings, GV
Laderer & Fischer, P.C. ... South Bend, IN
Laderer, Lewis C., Jr. ... South Bend, IN
Laderman, Gerald ... Houston, TX
Laderman, Gerald L. ... Los Angeles, CA
Laderman, Leslye G. ... St. Louis, MO
Laderman, Louis N. ... Brentwood, TN
Laderman, Samuel ... Cleveland, OH
Laderoute, Laurin L., Jr. ... Melville, NY
Ladesh, Katherine E. ... Liberty, MO
Ladestro, Gregory ... Stamford, CT
Ladewig, Brock L. ... San Diego, CA
Ladewig and Rechlicz
Menomonee Falls, WI
Ladewig, William G. ... Menomonee Falls, WI
Ladewski, Gregory B. ... Milwaukee, WI
LaDier, Tovah ... Missoula, MT
Ladieu, Kevin ... Hartford, CT
Ladig, Peter B. ... Wilmington, DE
Ladik, Steven M. ... Dallas, TX
Ladin, Timothy E. ... New York, NY
Ladine, Wray F. ... Modesto, CA
Ladinig, Benjamin T. ... Santa Ana, CA
Ladino, Michael J. ... Washington, DC
Ladinsky, Stanley ... West Islip, NY
Ladizki, David A. ... Agawam, MA
Ladizki, David A., P.C. ... Agawam, MA
Ladle, John L., Jr. ... Chicago, IL
Ladle, John L., Jr., P.C. ... Chicago, IL
Ladley, Candace K. ... Burbank, CA
Port Orchard, WA
Ladley, Edward Michael ... Phoenix, AZ
Ladley, James D. ... Vancouver, WA
Ladner, Benjamin David ... Atlanta, GA
Ladner, Carol ... Gulfport, MS
Ladner, Christine M.T. ... Wichita, KS
Ladner, Dempsey ... Jackson, MS
Ladner, Elizabeth S. ... New York, NY
Ladner, Frederick H. ... Minneapolis, MN
Ladner, Gordon L. ... Montgomery, AL
Ladner, Gregory W. ... Wilmington, DE
Ladner, James William Abbott ... St. Paul, MN
Ladner, John ... Los Angeles, CA
Ladner, John A. ... Tulsa, OK
Ladner, Karen M. ... San Diego, CA
Ladner, Kirk Gavin ... Jackson, MS
Ladner, Leslie N. ... New Orleans, LA
Ladner, Marian E. ... Fort Lauderdale, FL
Ladner, Mark P. ... New York, NY
Ladner, Stanford G. ... New York, NY
Ladner, Susan Rachel ... New York, NY
Ladner, Thomas M. ... Tulsa, OK
Ladner, Tracey R. ... Chicago, IL
Ladney, Nicholas C. ... Auburn Hills, MI
Ladnier & Elliott, P.L.C. ... Fairfax, VA
Ladnier, Patricia ... Fairfax, VA
LaDolce, Deborah L. ... Park Ridge, IL
Ladon, Richard J. ... Chicago, IL
Ladouceur and Ladouceur, L.L.C.
New Orleans, LA
Ladouceur, Lindsey M. ... New Orleans, LA
Ladouceur, Mary Ellen ... Albany, NY
Ladouceur, Raymond P. ... New Orleans, LA
LaDouceur, Todd M. ... Pensacola, FL
Ladov & Bernbaum ... Norristown, PA
Philadelphia, PA
Plymouth Meeting, PA
Ladov, David L. ... Plymouth Meeting, PA
Ladov, E. Donald ... Pittsburgh, PA
Ladov, Joshua B. ... Philadelphia, PA
Ladov, Sayde J. Markowitz ... Philadelphia, PA
Ladow, Daniel A. ... New York, NY
LaDow, David E. ... Kirkland, WA
Ladra, Michael A. ... Palo Alto, CA
LaDriere, Raymond E., II ... Dallas, TX
Ladrigan, Terrence F. ... Cincinnati, OH
Ladson, M. Brice ... Savannah, GA
Ladson & Suthers, LLP ... Savannah, GA
LaDuca, Anthony J. ... Rochester, NY
LaDuca, Heidi E. ... Rochester, NY
LaDuca, John J. ... Rochester, NY
LaDuca, McGinn & Burbank ... Rochester, NY
LaDuca, Robert F., Jr. ... Niagara Falls, NY
LaDue, Charles W. ... Coon Rapids, MN
LaDue, David N. ... Walnut Creek, CA
Ladue, Gerald H. ... Southfield, MI
LaDue & Goldston ... Walnut Creek, CA
LaDue, John D. ... South Bend, IN
LaDuke, Donald J. ... Louisville, KY
LaDuke, Nancie W. ... Troy, MI
LaDuke, Sharon J. ... Detroit, MI
LaDuke, Stanley F. ... Knoxville, TN
Ladutko, D. Link ... Oceanside, CA
Laduzinski, Nicholas H. ... New York, NY
Laduzinsky, Steven M. ... Chicago, IL
Ladwig, David S. ... Kansas City, MO
Ladwig, Glenn P. ... Gainesville, FL
Ladwig, Gordon R. ... Monroe, WI
Ladwig, Marion C.
National Labor Relations Board,
Division of Administrative Law Judges, GV
Ladwig, Patti Heidler ... Wellington, FL
Ladwig, Patti Heidler, P.A. ... W[illegible]ngton, FL
Ladwig, Theodore M. ... [illegible] CT

Lady, David R. ... Ann Arbor, MI
Lady, James E. ... Charleston, SC
Lady, Pauline Mcalister ... Charleston, SC
Lady, Shirley S. ... Indianapolis, IN
Ladyman, W. Andrew ... Abilene, TX
Ladyman, W. Tim ... Abilene, TX
Ladzinski, Peter J. ... Baltimore, MD
La Eace, Julie E. ... Chicago, IL
Laechelin, Suzanne V. ... Conroe, TX
Laedeke, Randy S. ... Billings, MT
Laedlein, Charles E., III ... Arlington, VA
Laemers, Peter J. ... Newton, NJ
Laemmle, Ann K. ... New York, NY
Laemmle, Laura Frick ... Washington, DC
Laeser, Abraham ... Miami, FL
Laeser, Joyce Hester ... Los Alamos, NM
Laessig, Walter B. ... Washington, DC
Laethem, Nancy L. ... Chicago, IL
Laface, Joseph J. ... Garden City, NY
LaFace, Ronald C. ... Tallahassee, FL
LaFace-Sapienza, Laura ... Huntington, NY
LaFache, Anthony J. ... Utica, NY
Lafair, Michael S. ... Philadelphia, PA
Lafakis, Gregory J. ... Chicago, IL
LaFalce, Frank A., Jr. ... Washington, DC
LaFalce, John A. ... Flint, MI
LaFalce, John J. ... Buffalo, NY
LaFar, W. Marshall ... Gastonia, NC
Lafarga, David ... Detroit, MI
LaFarga, Jeannene ... Claremont, CA
La Farge, Richard E. ... Bourne, MA
Lafargue, Carol M. ... Baton Rouge, LA
Lafargue, David E. ... Marksville, LA
Lafargue, Edwin L. ... Marksville, LA
Lafargue, James F. ... Newark, NJ
Lafargue, Julie Mobley ... Shreveport, LA
Lafargue & Lafargue ... Marksville, LA
Lafargue, Norman I. ... Shreveport, LA
LaFarlette, Barry J. ... Jonesboro, AR
Lafaro, Lawrence J. ... Morristown, NJ
Lafata, Joseph M. ... Troy, MI
LaFata, Richard Thomas ... Baltimore, MD
LaFauci, Thomas J. ... Syosset, NY
LaFauci, Thomas V. ... Bayside, NY
La Fauci, Willard G. ... Rockville Centre, NY
Lafave, Arthur J., III ... Washington, DC
Lafave, Arthur J., Jr. ... Cleveland, OH
LaFave, Cynthia S. ... Delmar, NY
La Fave, Daniel J. ... Milwaukee, WI
LaFave, E. Joseph ... Minneapolis, MN
LaFave & Higgins, LLP ... Delmar, NY
LaFave, James E. ... St. Paul, MN
LaFave, Jeffrey F. ... San Diego, CA
LaFave, John F. ... Rochester, NY
LaFave, Julie A. ... Washington, DC
LaFave, LeeAnn Larson ... Sioux Falls, SD
La Fave, Lloyd ... Milwaukee, WI
Lafave, Mary Ferguson ... Minneapolis, MN
LaFave, Melanie ... Detroit, MI
LaFave & Rice ... San Diego, CA
LaFave, Thomas W. ... Milwaukee, WI
LaFave, Wayne R. ... Champaign, IL
LaFaver, Jon F. ... New Cumberland, PA
La Fay, Anthony P. ... Rochester, NY
La Fay Byrne & La Fay, P.C.
Rochester, NY
La Fay, Joseph H. ... Rochester, NY
La Fay, Joseph W. ... Syracuse, NY
Lafaye, George E., III ... Columbia, SC
Lafaye, George E., IV ... Greenville, SC
West Columbia, SC
Lafayette, Elissa J. ... New Orleans, LA
Lafayette, Francis, Jr. ... Palmer, MA
Lafayette, Gary T. ... San Francisco, CA
Lafayette, Gerald W. ... Rockford, IL
LaFayette, Gregory P. ... Trenton, MI
LaFayette, John C. ... Palm Harbor, FL
Lafayette & Kumagai LLP
San Francisco, CA
Lafayette, Mark S. ... New York, NY
La Fayette, Paul-Michael ... Columbus, OH
LaFayette Professional Association
Palm Harbor, FL
La Fayette, Renee ... Prince Frederick, MD
LaFazia, Jeanne E. ... Providence, RI
LaFazia, Raymond A. ... Providence, RI
LaFazia, Raymond Alan ... Providence, RI
Lafazman, Stanley J. ... New York, NY
Lafeber, Michael M. ... Minneapolis, MN
LaFemina, Rose Marie
Fort Lauderdale, FL
Lafer, A. David ... Department of Justice,
Civil Division, GV
Lafer, Barry S. ... New York, NY
Lafer, Fred S. ... Roseland, NJ
LaFerrara, Charles A. ... Trenton, NJ
Laferrera, Joseph J. ... Boston, MA
Laferty, Samuel ... Akron, OH
La Fetra, Deborah J. ... Sacramento, CA
LaFever, M. Gary ... McLean, VA
LaFevers, J. Gregory ... Tulsa, OK
LaFevor, J. Randall ... Nashville, TN
LaFevor, James R. ... Knoxville, TN
Laff, Alan D. ... Denver, CO
Laff, Charles A. ... Chicago, IL
Laff, Joshua F. ... Moorestown, NJ
Philadelphia, PA
Laff, Kenneth M. ... Denver, CO
Laff Stein Campbell Tucker & Delaney, LLP
Denver, CO
Laff & Tuber ... Chicago, IL
Laff, Whitesel & Saret, Ltd., A Professional Corporation ... Chicago, IL
Laffan, James R. ... Lebanon, NH
Laffan, Maura V. ... New York, NY
Laffan, William F., Jr. ... New York, NY
Syosset, NY
La[illegible], Henry ... Fort Lauderdale, FL

Laffer, Henry, P.A. ....Fort Lauderdale, FL
Laffer, Phyllis ....Boston, MA
Laffer, Renee F. ....Port Washington, NY
Laffer, Susan K. ....Calabasas, CA
Lafferrandre, Robert S.
Oklahoma City, OK
Lafferre, Luke A. ....Charleston, WV
Huntington, WV
Laffert, Donald A. ....Washington, DC
Lafferty, Charles N. ....Conneaut, OH
Lafferty, Cynthia Morgan ....Kansas City, MO
Lafferty, David S. ....Fort Lee, NJ
Lafferty, Gayle P. ....Wilmington, DE
Lafferty, Helen Haney ....Philadelphia, PA
Lafferty, James M. ....Philadelphia, PA
Lafferty, Jane G. ....New Brunswick, NJ
Lafferty, John C. ....Grand Junction, CO
Lafferty, Jon A. ....Toledo, OH
Lafferty, Karen M. ....Decatur, GA
Lafferty, Lawrence E. ....Boca Raton, FL
Lafferty, Michelle A. ....Cleveland, OH
Lafferty, Randolph C. ....Atlantic City, NJ
Pleasantville, NJ
Lafferty, Richard E. ....Pittsburgh, PA
Lafferty, Richard Q. ....Charlotte, NC
Lafferty, Richard W. ....Branford, CT
Lafferty, Scott W. ....Cleveland, OH
Lafferty, Sheila Gay ....Dayton, OH
Lafferty, Stephen W. ....Baltimore, MD
Lafferty, Steven M. ....Philadelphia, PA
Lafferty, Tammy L. ....Upper Marlboro, MD
Lafferty, Todd O. ....Amarillo, TX
Lafferty, William ....Pittsburgh, PA
Lafferty, William Brook ....Atlanta, GA
Lafferty, William J. ....San Francisco, CA
Lafferty, William J. ....Burlington, MA
Lafferty, William M. ....Wilmington, DE
Laffey, James T. ....Chicago, IL
Laffey, Jane A. M. ....Boiling Springs, PA
Laffey, Jeffrey F. ....Philadelphia, PA
Laffey, John J. ....Elizabeth, NJ
Laffey, John J. ....Milwaukee, WI
Laffey, Kathryn J. ....Wilmington, DE
Laffey & Kerr, P.A. ....Dover, DE
Wilmington, DE
Laffey, Lissa D. ....Hermosa Beach, CA
Laffey, Michael J. ....Pittsburgh, PA
Laffey, Michael P. ....Holmdel, NJ
Laffey, Myles J. ....Hartford, CT
Laffey, Regina F. ....Colts Neck, NJ
Laffey, Thomas M. ....Minneapolis, MN
Laffey, Thomas P. ....Los Angeles, CA
Laffey, W. Thomas, Jr. ....Pittsburgh, PA
Laffey-Ferry, Marion ....Butler, PA
Laffin, Patricia A. ....Auburn, CA
Laffitte, Hector M. ....San Juan, PR
Laffitte, Miguel G. ....San Juan, PR
Laffitte, Rebecca ....Columbia, SC
LaFiandra, Aldo L. ....Atlanta, GA
LaFiandra, Catherine H. ....Alpharetta, GA
La Fiandra, Dino C. ....Baltimore, MD
Towson, MD
La Fiandra, Dino V. ....New York, NY
La Fiandra, Jacqueline C. ....Baltimore, MD
LaFiandra, Kenneth J. ....Moorestown, NJ
Philadelphia, PA
LaFiandra, Maria Mancini
East Brunswick, NJ
Lafield, Ray ....Baker, LA
Lafionatis, Arthur F. ....Bethesda, MD
Lafionatis, Arthur F., P.C., Law Offices of
Washington, DC
Bethesda, MD
Vienna, VA
Lafitte, David E. ....Newport Beach, CA
Lafitte, Gene W. ....New Orleans, LA
Lafitte, Gene W., Jr. ....Tucson, AZ
Lafitte, Ramon ....Shreveport, LA
LaFiura, Charles D. ....Morristown, NJ
LaFiura, Dennis R. ....Morristown, NJ
Lafko, Margaret A. ....San Diego, CA
Lafky, Elton T. ....Salem, OR
Lafky, Kevin T. ....Salem, OR
Laflamme, Brian ....Waltham, MA
Laflamme & Davis ....Manchester, NH
Laflamme, Elaine M. ....New York, NY
LaFlamme, Gerard R., Jr. ....Haverhill, MA
La Flamme, Joseph A. ....Reading, PA
LaFlamme & Mauldin, P.C. ....Jackson, MI
LaFlamme, Migliori, Barron & Chabot
Haverhill, MA
LaFlamme, Richard N. ....Jackson, MI
Laflamme, W. Jean ....Manchester, NH
La Fleur, Brian De ....Scotia, NY
La Fleur, Catherine A. ....Milwaukee, WI
La Fleur, Catherine L. ....New Orleans, LA
LaFleur, Cheryl A. ....Westborough, MA
La Fleur, Deborah Lynn ....Orlando, FL
LaFleur, Ernest G., Jr. ....Alexandria, LA
LaFleur, Frances P. ....Chicago, IL
LaFleur, Gary T. ....Anoka, MN
LaFleur, J. Ricky ....Abbeville, LA
La Fleur, Jon J. ....Rapid City, SD
LaFleur, Joseph F. ....Marysville, OH
Lafleur, Judith ....El Centro, CA
LaFleur, L. Caroline ....Atlanta, GA
La Fleur, La Fleur & La Fleur, P.C.
Rapid City, SD
La Fleur Law Office, S.C. ....Milwaukee, WI
La Fleur, Mitchell C. ....Rapid City, SD
La Fleur, Monique J. ....Washington, DC
LaFleur, Nina M. ....Jacksonville, FL
Lafleur, Paul M. ....Alexandria, LA
LaFleur, Randi W. ....Minneapolis, MN
La Fleur, Richard J. ....San Jose, CA
LaFleur, Robert A. ....Minneapolis, MN
La Fleur, Robert F. ....Rapid City, SD

Lafleur, Ward F. ....Lafayette, LA
New Orleans, LA
LaFleur-Spawn, Stacey ....New Orleans, LA
Laflin, Jane A. ....Albuquerque, NM
Laflin, John D. ....Albuquerque, NM
Laflin, Lieuwen, Tucker, Pick, Heer & Neerken, P.A. ....Albuquerque, NM
Laflin-Kyman, Katherine ....Santa Monica, CA
LaFoe, Lauri A. ....Harrisburg, PA
La Follett, Thomas L. ....Canby, OR
LaFollette, Amy Sherman ....Omaha, NE
LaFollette, Christine B. ....Houston, TX
LaFollette, Elizabeth V. ....Greensboro, NC
LaFollette, Ernest C. ....Fairfield, CT
LaFollette, Gene P. ....Oakland, CA
LaFollette, James E. ....Fresno, CA
La Follette, Johnson, De Haas, Fesler, Silberberg & Ames, A Professional Corporation ....Los Angeles, CA
Riverside, CA
San Diego, CA
San Francisco, CA
Santa Ana, CA
LaFollette, Mary F. ....Anchorage, AK
LaFollette, Robert M. ....Laingsburg, MI
LaFollette, Robin R. ....Shawnee, KS
LaFollette Sinykin, LLP ....Madison, WI
Sauk City, WI
Stoughton, WI
LaFon & Hall ....Alpharetta, GA
Cumming, GA
Roswell, GA
LaFon, Timothy J. ....Charleston, WV
LaFon, Tommy L. ....Houston, TX
LaFon, W. Courtney ....Roswell, GA
LaFon, Whit ....Jackson, TN
Lafond, Catherine Elizabeth
Johns Island, SC
Lafond, Gerard A., Jr. ....Los Angeles, CA
Lafond, John D. ....Champaign, IL
LaFond, John Q. ....Tacoma, WA
LaFond, Melanie J. ....Tampa, FL
LaFond, Michel A. ....Concord, NH
LaFond, Michelle Jodoin ....Portland, ME
LaFond, Monica P. ....Boston, MA
LaFond, Peter B. ....Portland, ME
LaFond, Richard C. ....Denver, CO
LaFond, Stephen D. ....Norfolk, VA
LaFond & Sweeney, L.L.C. ....Denver, CO
LaFond, Thomas J. ....Boston, MA
LaFond, Thomas J. ....Cleveland, OH
LaFont, Harold M. ....Plainview, TX
Lafont, Richard A. ....Morristown, NJ
LaFont, Tunnell, Formby, LaFont & Hamilton, L.L.P. ....Lubbock, TX
Plainview, TX
LaFont, William Harold ....Plainview, TX
LaFontaine, Earl J. ....Southfield, MI
La Fontaine, Frank R. ....Gilbert, AZ
La Fontaine, Mark R. ....Hartford, CT
LaFontaine, Monique M.
New Orleans, LA
LaFontaine, Richard M. ....Brooklyn, NY
Lafontant, Monique J. ....Greensburg, PA
La Fontisee, Louis L., III ....Miami, FL
La Fontisee, Louis L., Jr. ....Miami, FL
LaForce, Jeffrey R. ....San Mateo, CA
La Force, Norman C. ....El Cerrito, CA
LaForce, Pierre J. ....Washington, DC
LaForce, Ronald L. ....Modesto, CA
LaForest, Robert J. ....Benton Harbor, MI
La Forge, Amanda S. ....Annapolis, MD
La Forge, Binder & Betancourt
Hackensack, NJ
La Forge, Curtis J. ....Hackensack, NJ
LaForge, David P. ....St. Joseph, MI
LaForge, Gladys C. ....Goshen, NY
LaForge, Gregory M. ....Hollister, CA
La Forge, James C. ....New York, NY
LaForge, Julie A. ....Phoenix, AZ
LaForge, Lisa ....Boulder, CO
LaForge, Raymond A.
Federal Communications Commission,
Office of Engineering & Technology, GV
LaForge, Robert M. ....Santa Rosa, CA
LaForge, Steven G. ....Columbus, OH
La Forge, Thomas J. ....Danbury, CT
LaForge, William N. ....Washington, DC
LaForgia, A. Barry ....San Diego, CA
LaForgia, Frank S. ....Whitehouse Station, NJ
LaForgia, Michelina Darcy ....Pine Beach, NJ
LaForte, George F. ....Olympia Fields, IL
LaForte, George F., Jr.
Oakbrook Terrace, IL
LaForte, Stephen J. ....Seattle, WA
La Forte, William N. ....Rochester, NY
LaFortune, Georgiana Betses ....Andover, MA
LaFortune & LaFortune ....Andover, MA
LaFortune, Robert R. ....Winchendon, MA
LaFortune, Steven M. ....Andover, MA
LaFortune, William D. ....Tulsa, OK
Lafountain, Lloyd P. ....Biddeford, ME
Lafountain, Lloyd P, III ....Biddeford, ME
LaFountaine, Frank S. ....Sumner, WA
LaFountaine, Michael D. ....St. Cloud, MN
LaFountaine, Ralph R. ....Honolulu, HI
Lafourcade, Caroline D.
New Orleans, LA
LaFourcade, Lisa M. ....Costa Mesa, CA
LaFoy, Randall A. ....Birchwood, MN
LaFrance, Arthur B. ....Portland, OR
La France, Christopher G. ....Carmel, NY
New York, NY
LaFrance, Claudine M. ....Fort Lauderdale, FL
LaFrance & Crawford ....Durango, CO
LaFrance, James F. ....Laconia, NH
LaFrance, Marie Diane ....Syracuse, NY
LaFrance, Mary ....Tallahassee, FL

LaFrance, Michael R. ....Cedar Rapids, IA
LaFrance, Peter R. ....Freehold, NJ
LaFrance, Shannon Martin ....Hudson, NY
Poughkeepsie, NY
LaFrance, Timothy A. ....Durango, CO
Lafranchi, Arthur L. ....Santa Rosa, CA
Lafranchi, Arthur L., P.C. ....Santa Rosa, CA
Lafranchi, Robert J. ....Menlo Park, CA
La Franchi, Timothy S. ....Sacramento, CA
Lafranchise, Paul ....Bakersfield, CA
LaFrankie, Robert L. ....Washington, DC
LaFratta, John Gregory ....Richmond, VA
La Fratta, Mark J. ....Richmond, VA
LaFray, Warren T. ....Clearwater, FL
LaFray, Warren T., P.A. ....Clearwater, FL
Lafreniere, Joanne M. ....San Francisco, CA
LaFreniere, Kevin F. ....Hartford, CT
LaFreniere, Pamela F. ....New Bedford, MA
LaFreniere, Patricia E. ....New York, NY
Lafrenz, Andrew W. ....Oakland, CA
LaFrey, Timothy L. ....Austin, TX
Lafuente, Cynthia B. ....Dayton, OH
LaFuria, David A. ....Washington, DC
Lafuse, Christopher L. ....Indianapolis, IN
Lafuze, Ralph O. ....Hagerstown, IN
LaFuze, William L. ....Houston, TX
Lafving, Brian D. ....Dallas, TX
Lag, John J. ....Chicago, IL
Lagalante, Louis M. ....New York, NY
Lagaly, Thomas C. ....Duncan, SC
Lagan, John F. ....New York, NY
Lagana, Beth Broidy ....Columbus, OH
Laganaro, Samuel Thomas, Jr.
Poughkeepsie, NY
Laganelli, Ralph A. ....Somerset, MA
Lagano, Christopher ....Stamford, CT
LaGarde, Ben L., Jr. ....Glenmoore, PA
Lagarde, Charlotte A. ....New Orleans, LA
Lagarde, Chas. S., Jr. ....Luling, LA
Lagarde, Frank W., Jr. ....Metairie, LA
Lagarde, Jesse P. ....Amite, LA
Lagarde, Lawrence L., Jr. ....New Orleans, LA
Lagarde, Lynne A. ....Phoenix, AZ
Lagarde, Paul V. ....Mobile, AL
Lagarde, Richard L. ....Houston, TX
Lagarenné, Lawrence E. ....Monticello, NY
LaGarenne, Robert J. ....Woodhaven, NY
Lagarias, Peter C. ....San Rafael, CA
Lagasi, Anthony J. ....Cedar Grove, NJ
Lagasse, David R. ....New York, NY
LaGasse, Denise A. ....Kittery Point, ME
Lagassé, Jacques J. ....South Windsor, CT
Lagasse, Paul A. ....Hartford, CT
Lagasse, Traci S. ....San Francisco, CA
Lagattuta, John M. ....Schaumburg, IL
Lagattuta, Nicholas J. ....Arlington Heights, IL
Lagattuta, Paula J. ....Midland, MI
Lagay, Christopher P. ....Newtown, PA
Lage, Gonzalo R. ....Hialeah, FL
Lage, Gustavo D. ....South Miami, FL
Lage, Scott W. ....Algona, IA
Lagemann, Jonathan Kord, Law Offices of
Ghent, NY
New York, NY
Lager, Dennis P. ....Indianapolis, IN
Lager, H. Jacob ....Los Angeles, CA
Lager, J. Victor ....Virginia, MN
Lager, James M. ....General Accounting Office,
Office of the General Counsel, GV
Lager, Linda K. ....New Haven, CT
Lager, Marvin M. ....Los Angeles, CA
Lager, Thomas W. ....Tallahassee, FL
Lager, Vivian D. ....Naples, FL
Lagerberg, Jon Oscar ....Walters, OK
LaGere, Shelley ....Dallas, TX
Lagergren, Brent ....Kansas City, MO
Lagergren, Walter B. ....Pensacola, FL
Lagerlöf & Leman ....New York, NY
New York, NY
Lagerlof, Senecal, Bradley, Gosney & Kruse, LLP ....Los Angeles, CA
Pasadena, CA
Lagerman & Associates, P.C. ....Reston, VA
Lagerman, Bruce K. ....Washington, DC
New York, NY
Reston, VA
Lagerman, Lars O. ....Phoenix, AZ
Lagerman, Susan L.B. ....Phoenix, AZ
Lagerquist, Edwin C. ....Seattle, WA
Lagerquist, Jerry C. ....Chicago, IL
Lagerquist, McConnell & McDonough, Inc., P.S. ....Seattle, WA
Lagerquist, Thomas E. ....San Francisco, CA
Lagerquist, Walter G., Jr. ....San Antonio, TX
Lagerstrom, Thomas J. ....Lincoln, NE
Lageschulte, Roger E. ....Seattle, WA
Lagesen, Frank H. ....Portland, OR
Lageson, Angela D. ....Minneapolis, MN
Lageson, Ernest B. ....Walnut Creek, CA
Lageson, Richard D. ....St. Louis, MO
Lageson, Robb M. ....St. Paul, MN
Lagestee, Tad Alan ....Clarendon Hills, IL
Laggis, Paul S. ....American Falls, ID
Laggis, Stratton P. ....Ketchum, ID
Lagin, Eric L. ....Los Angeles, CA
Laginess, Thomas J. ....Livonia, MI
Lagioia, Salvatore M. ....Niles, IL
Lagios, Louis P. ....Clifton, NJ
Lagitch, Kellie E. ....Mineola, NY
Lagle, John F. ....Los Angeles, CA
Lagman, Albert ....Phoenix, AZ
Lagman, Henry E. ....Birmingham, AL
Lagnado, Michael P. ....New York, NY
Lagner, Stephen J., III ....Erie, PA
Lagnese, Joyce A. ....Hartford, CT
Lagnese, Paul A. ....Pittsburgh, PA
Lagno, Christopher J. ....New York, NY
Lago, Jose Luis ....Miami, FL

Lago, Maria Louise (Marisa)
Securities and Exchange Commission,
Office of International Affairs, GV
Lago, Peter L. ....Downey, CA
Lago, Philip V. ....Holiday, FL
Lago, Victor A. ....Washington, DC
Lagoa, Barbara ....Miami, FL
Lagod, Alan M. ....San Jose, CA
Lagod, Martin L. ....Palo Alto, CA
Lagomarcino, John P., Jr. ....Los Angeles, CA
Lagomarcino, Leslie K.
Department of Agriculture,
Office of the General Counsel, GV
Lagomarsino, Mark S. ....Newton, IA
Lagomarsino, Andre M. ....Las Vegas, NV
Lagomarsino, Anthony G. ....Fullerton, CA
Lagomarsino, George A. ....Sacramento, CA
Lagomarsino, Joanne N. ....Philadelphia, PA
Lagomarsino, Robert J. ....Ventura, CA
Lagomasino, Leonor M. ....Miami, FL
Lagona, James F. ....Buffalo, NY
Lagoni, William O. ....Bridgman, MI
Lagonia, Salvatore A.
Yorktown Heights, NY
LaGorga, Anne M. ....Saugerties, NY
Lagorio, Anthony ....Los Altos, CA
Lagorio, John D., Jr. ....Nokomis, FL
Lagorio, Peter A. ....Boston, MA
LaGory, Dennis G. ....Chicago, IL
Lagos, George P. ....Manchester, NH
Lagos, James H. ....Springfield, OH
Lagos & Lagos ....Springfield, OH
Lagos, Panos ....Oakland, CA
Lagos, Thomas H. ....Springfield, OH
Lagoski, Diane M. ....Mount Sterling, IL
Lagoulis & Clark ....Newburyport, MA
Lagoulis, James ....Newburyport, MA
Lagousakos, Athanasia ....Joliet, IL
LaGow, J. Christopher ....Richmond, VA
LaGow, Nancy Glaser ....Richmond, VA
Lagowski, John R. ....Chicago, IL
Lagoy and Lyons ....Chadds Ford, PA
Media, PA
West Chester, PA
Lagoy, Stephen P. ....Chadds Ford, PA
LaGrange, Frank C. ....Minneapolis, MN
Lagrange, Patrick C. ....Metairie, LA
La Grange, Richard L. ....Franklin, IN
LaGrave, Charles W. ....San Francisco, CA
LaGreca, Linda C. ....Kew Gardens, NY
LaGreca, Vincent J. ....New York, NY
LaGrone, Daniel E. ....New Orleans, LA
La Grone, J. Clayton ....Longview, TX
LaGrone, Mary J. Chukinas ....Nashville, TN
LaGrone, Rodney L. ....Texarkana, TX
LaGrone, T. Gaines ....Orlando, FL
Lagrone, Wade H. ....Tupelo, MS
LaGrone, W. T. ....Dallas, TX
La Grone, Yvonne Spradley ....Chicago, IL
LaGrosse, John B. ....Cape May, NJ
LaGrotta, Thomas ....Pleasantville, NY
LaGrotteria, Francisco R. ....Pittsfield, MA
Lagrotteria, Joseph F. ....Newark, NJ
Lagrou, Francis J. ....Detroit, MI
LaGrou, Stephen E. ....Rochester, NY
Laguarda, Fernando R. ....Washington, DC
Laguarda, Wendy R.
Farm Credit Administration,
Legal Counsel Division, GV
La Guardia, Maryanne ....Los Angeles, CA
Lague, Alice Graham ....Plymouth, MA
Lague, Newman & Irish, A Professional Corporation ....Grand Haven, MI
Grand Rapids, MI
Holland, MI
Ludington, MI
Muskegon, MI
Lague, Richard C. ....Muskegon, MI
LaGuerre, Danie V. ....Stuart, FL
LaGuerre, Danie V., P.A. ....Stuart, FL
LaGueux, Jeffrey E. ....New York, NY
Lagueux, Linda Twing ....Garden City, NY
Lagueux, Ronald R. ....Providence, RI
La Guire, Kris Alan ....Hilo, HI
LaGumina, John Joseph ....Purchase, NY
Laguna, Carlos ....Austin, TX
Laguna, Francisco A. ....Miami, FL
Laguzza, James R. ....Santa Ana, CA
Laguzza, Jennifer L. ....Norcross, GA
Lah, Robert D. ....New York, NY
Lahab, Ishmael ....New York, NY
Lahaderne, Paul B. ....San Francisco, CA
Lahaderne, Teresa C. ....Piedmont, CA
LaHaie, Donn P. ....Chicago, IL
LaHaie, Gerald P. ....Washington, DC
LaHaie, Henry I. ....Department of Justice,
Civil Division, GV
LaHaie, John P. ....Tarzana, CA
La Hait, Robert P. ....Boston, MA
Laham, Carol A. ....Washington, DC
Lahammer, Douglas E. ....Los Angeles, CA
Lahammer, Margaret K. ....Eagan, MN
Lahan, P. Michael ....Norwich, CT
Lahanas, Demetri D. ....San Diego, CA
Lahart, F. Vern ....Allen, TX
Lahart, John E. ....San Rafael, CA
Lahart, John E., P.C. ....San Rafael, CA
LaHart, Marcy L. ....West Palm Beach, FL
Lahat, Gal ....Dallas, TX
Houston, TX
LaHatte, Joseph F., Jr. ....New Orleans, LA
Lahav, Alexandra D. ....New York, NY
LaHaye, Daniel N. ....New Orleans, LA
La Haye, Jos. A. ....Opelousas, LA
LaHaye, Michael P. ....Rochester, NY
Lahde, Bernard P. ....San Jose, CA
Lahendro, A. Lewis ....Lomita, CA
Laher, Linda S. ....Ashland, MS

Laher, Robert Sneed ... Booneville, MS
Laherty & Associates ... Salt Lake City, UT
Laherty, John E. ... Salt Lake City, UT
Lahey, Ann ... Iowa City, IA
Lahey & Associates, P.C. ... Denver, CO
Lahey, Barbara Birch ... Denver, CO
Lahey, Edward V., Jr. ... Purchase, NY
Lahey, Frank J., Jr. ... St. Louis, MO
Lahey, James A., Jr. ... Bakersfield, CA
Lahey, John H. ... Washington, DC
Lahey, Judith A. ... Hartford, CT
Lahey, Karen E. ... Hartford, CT
Lahey, Kate ... Salt Lake City, UT
Lahey, Kerry Ann ... Birmingham, AL
Lahey, Leo Jerome ... Lafayette, LA
Lahey, Lucy J. ... St. Louis, MO
Lahey, Matthew J. ... Laconia, NH
Lahey, Paul A. ... Poughkeepsie, NY
Lahey, Ruah Donnelly ... Boston, MA
Lahey, Timothy G. ... Wichita, KS
Lahey, William E. ... St. Louis, MO
Lahey, William L. ... Boston, MA
Lahey, William R. ... Denver, CO
Lahiff, Christin ... Burlington, VT
Lahiff, Christopher M. ... Washington, DC
LaHiff, Dennis P. ... Fair Lawn, NJ
Lahiff, Lisa Kay ... Chicago, IL
Lahiff, Robert G. ... Detroit, MI
Lahiff, Sean P. ... Goshen, NY
Lahiff, Thomas M., Jr. ... Elizabeth, NJ
Lahiri, Indra ... Bakersfield, CA
Lahiri, Yasho ... New York, NY
Lahive & Cockfield, LLP ... Boston, MA
Lahive, Mark S. ... Los Angeles, CA
Lahm, Gunther K. ... Columbus, OH
Lahm, Robert E. ... Syracuse, NY
Lahman, Carol Hambrick ... Enid, OK
Lahman, Jack R. ... Lake Havasu City, AZ
Lahman, Janice A. ... Rochester, NY
Lahman, Larry D. ... Enid, OK
Lahmers, Nancy K. ... Springfield, MO
Lahmers, Nancy K., P.C. ... Springfield, MO
Lahn, Peter D. ... Grinnell, IA
Lahne, Daniel R. ... Norfolk, VA
Lahne, Philip L. ... Honolulu, HI
Lahne, Richard K. ... Department of State, Office of the Legal Adviser, GV
Lahne, Susan G. ... Silver Spring, MD
Lahner, Joanne ... West Point, PA
Lahner, Ronald B. ... Minneapolis, MN
Lahners, Ronald D. ... Omaha, NE
Lahoda, Constance Petroni
Cherry Hill, NJ
La Hood, Maria C. ... Oakland, CA
La Hood, Michael T. ... San Antonio, TX
La Hood, Michael T., P.C. ... San Antonio, TX
Lahoud, Nina J. ... New York, NY
Lahoud, Ronald J. ... Littleton, NH
Lahout, Joseph H., Jr. ... Littleton, NH
Lahr, Dillon, Manzulli, Kelley & Penett, P.C.
Staten Island, NY
Lahr, Fred C. ... Staten Island, NY
Lahr, J. Gregory ... New York, NY
Lahr, Jack L. ... Washington, DC
Lahr, Janice H. ... Tucson, AZ
Lahr, Jeffrey F. ... New Haven, CT
Lahr & Lahr ... Allentown, PA
Lahr, Leslie K. ... Indianapolis, IN
Lahr, Marilyn K. ... Dallas, TX
Lahr, Michael S. ... Helena, MT
Lahr, Rick E., Jr. ... Plano, TX
Lahr, Robin L. ... Allentown, PA
Lahr, Todd Harold ... Allentown, PA
Lahr, William V. ... St. Paul, MN
Lahring, Karl ... Department of Education, Office of the General Counsel, GV
Lahrman, Jeanne M. ... Roswell, NM
Lahrman, Lisa L. ... Department of Labor, Office of Secretary, GV
Lahti, Bette J. ... Birmingham, MI
Lahti, Bette Jean, Prof. Immig.Servs., Law Offices of ... Birmingham, MI
Lahti, Bruce M. ... St. Augustine, FL
Lahti, Lynn M. ... Menomonie, WI
Lahti, Maria H. ... Northborough, MA
Lahti, Michael Toivo ... Hyannis, MA
Lahtinen, John A. ... Plattsburgh, NY
Lahtinen, Robert W. ... Rochester, MN
LaHue, William B. ... Atlanta, GA
Lahy, Donald A. ... Richmond, VA
Lai, Christina Y. ... Menlo Park, CA
Lai, Cynthia ... New York, NY
Lai, Edward M. ... Emeryville, CA
Lai, Fernanda ... Los Angeles, CA
Lai, Harold Gun, Jr.
Rancho Cucamonga, CA
Lai, Hon ... Brooklyn, NY
Lai, Janice D. ... Hartford, CT
Lai, Jonathan W. Y. ... Honolulu, HI
Lai, Josephine H. ... Beverly Hills, CA
Lai, King-Fun Ho ... Houston, TX
Lai, Lisa B. ... San Francisco, CA
Lai, Lydia C. ... New York, NY
Lai, Rhonda Iwalani ... Wailuku, HI
Lai, Suet F. ... Burbank, CA
Lai, Suzanne E. ... New York, NY
Lai, T. Eric ... Washington, DC
Lai, Teresa L. ... San Francisco, CA
Lai, Vicki W. W. ... Seattle, WA
Laiblin, William W. ... Evanston, IL
Laibstain, Linda S. ... Norfolk, VA
Laibstain, Richard H. ... Ashland, VA
Laicato, Christine ... Santa Ana, CA
Laichas, James N. ... Glendale, CA
Laiche, Barry Ray ... Houma, LA
Laiche, Calvin J. ... Westwego, LA
Laiche, Stephen L. ... Grand Junction, CO
Laiderman, Steven M. ... St. Louis, MO
Laidhold, Stephen J. ... Pittsburgh, PA
Laidig, Craig A. ... Thousand Oaks, CA
Laidig, Samuel L. ... Pasadena, CA
Laidlaw, Andrew R. ... Chicago, IL
Laidlaw, Bruce W. ... San Francisco, CA
Laidlaw, Carleton Bruce, Jr. ... Syracuse, NY
Laidlaw, Earl S. ... Norway, ME
Laidlaw, H. David ... Adrian, MI
Laidlaw, R. Bruce ... Ann Arbor, MI
Laidlaw, Robert R. ... Pinehurst, NC
Laidlaw, Sally J. ... Oakland, CA
Laidlaw, Sharee M. ... Salt Lake City, UT
Laidlaw, Trina Eubank ... Eugene, OR
Laidley, Forrest D. ... Lincolnshire, IL
Laidley Sutter & Porter ... Lincolnshire, IL
Laidman, Daniel H. ... Los Angeles, CA
Laidman, David G. ... Seattle, WA
Laifer, Daniel M. ... New York, NY
Laifer, Mark S. ... New York, NY
Laifman, Jay S. ... Calabasas, CA
Laigaie, David M. ... Philadelphia, PA
Laikin & Laikin, S.C. ... Milwaukee, WI
Laikin, Michael B. ... Milwaukee, WI
Laiks, Richard Jon ... Passaic, NJ
Lail, Brandon W. ... Southaven, MS
Lail, Cindy Kay ... Brook, IN
Lail, Patrick L. ... Atlanta, GA
Lail, Rick D. ... Charlotte, NC
Lail, Warren K. ... Morganton, NC
Laiminger, Mark A. ... Spokane, WA
Lain, Ann M. ... Westerly, RI
Lain, Dallas ... Denver, CO
Lain, J. Michael ... Oak Ridge, TN
Lain, Jacqueline F. ... Austin, TX
Lain, John M. ... Richmond, VA
Lain, Rose Mary ... New Orleans, LA
Lain, Sir Clyde, II ... Monroe, LA
Lain, Sir Clyde, II, A Professional Law Corp., Inc. ... Monroe, LA
Lain, W. Keith ... Houston, TX
Laine, Barry ... Youngstown, OH
Laine, Edward M. ... Minneapolis, MN
Laine, Frank J. ... Mineola, NY
Laine, Harold J., Jr. ... Beaumont, TX
Laine, Kevin S. ... Beaumont, TX
Laine, Michele R. ... Miami, FL
Laine, Paige Flowers ... Atlanta, GA
Laine, Reino O. ... Roseville, MN
Laine, Susan C. ... Minneapolis, MN
Lainer, Allyson B. ... Millburn, NJ
New York, NY
Lainer, Ilene F. ... Los Angeles, CA
Roseland, NJ
New York, NY
Lainer & Lainer ... Van Nuys, CA
Lainer, Luis ... Van Nuys, CA
Lainer, Mark ... Van Nuys, CA
Lainer, Randall S. ... Somerville, NJ
Lainez, Pamela S. ... Framingham, MA
Laing, Andrew O'Reilly ... Glenview, IL
Laing, David A. ... Columbus, OH
Laing, David J. ... Washington, DC
Laing, Dean P. ... Milwaukee, WI
Laing, Dennis O. ... Richmond, VA
Laing, Edward A. ... New Rochelle, NY
Laing, Edwin L. ... Santa Barbara, CA
Laing, Harley F. ... Boston, MA
Laing, Harold ... Wilmington, NC
Laing, James S. ... St. Joseph, MI
Laing, John B. ... Mission Hills, CA
Laing, John C., Jr. ... Portland, OR
Laing, Kenneth ... East Lansing, MI
Laing Law Offices ... San Francisco, CA
San Rafael, CA
Laing, Lynda L. ... Providence, RI
Laing, Mercedes A. ... Chicago, IL
Laing, Michael A., (P.A.) ... Miami, FL
Laing, R. Bruce ... San Rafael, CA
Laing, Raymond W. ... San Geronimo, CA
Laing, Robert Bruce ... San Rafael, CA
Laing, Robert R., Jr. ... Overland Park, KS
Laing, Sheryl L. ... Alexandria, LA
Laing, Susan K. ... Chicago, IL
Laing, Verne M. ... Wichita, KS
Lainhart, Angela A. ... New York, NY
Lainhart, Betty S. ... Cincinnati, OH
Laino, Kenneth J. ... Cleveland, OH
Laino, William P. ... Garden City, NY
Lainof, Cohen & Weinstein ... Alexandria, VA
Lainoff, Michael A.
Securities and Exchange Commission, Executive Staff, GV
Lainoff, Steven R. ... Washington, DC
Lainson, Margaret T. ... Iowa City, IA
Laipson, Saml. M. ... Worcester, MA
Laipson, Samuel M. ... Worcester, MA
Lair, Anthony R. ... Dayton, OH
Lair, Craig S. ... Little Rock, AR
Lair, Eric G. ... Tulsa, OK
Lair, Gregory A. ... Moses Lake, WA
Wenatchee, WA
Lair, John ... Cynthiana, KY
Lair, John H. ... Birmingham, AL
Lair, Mark T. ... Chanute, KS
Lair, Montgomery Loyd ... Tulsa, OK
Lair, R. Matt ... San Antonio, TX
Laird, Barbara J. ... Princeton, NJ
Laird, Benjamin W. ... Green Bay, WI
Laird, Carol L. ... Visalia, CA
Laird, Chin & Schwartz, P.C.
Ann Arbor, MI
Laird, Christine J. ... Nashville, TN
Laird, Craig Stephen ... Mission, KS
Kansas City, MO
Laird, Dallas J. ... Casper, WY
Laird, David A. ... Denver, CO
Laird, Donald R. ... Eugene, OR
Roseburg, OR
Laird, Douglas S. ... Kansas City, MO
Laird, Edward C. ... Haddonfield, NJ
Laird, Edward D., Jr. ... Albany, NY
Laird, Edward L. ... Santa Ana, CA
Laird, E. E., III ... Jackson, MS
Laird, Evalyn Walsh, (Mrs.)
New Buffalo, MI
Laird, Fiona Campbell ... New York, NY
Laird, Fred G. ... Albuquerque, NM
Laird, Glendon L. ... Denver, CO
Laird, Gregory Wayne ... Tulsa, OK
Laird, H. Gray, III ... Jackson, MS
Laird & Hallberg, P.C. ... Phoenix, AZ
Laird, Heiny, McManigal, Winga, Duffy & Stambaugh, P.L.C. ... Mason City, IA
Laird, Henry F., Jr. ... Gulfport, MS
Laird, Janine A. ... Minneapolis, MN
Laird, Jeff R., Jr. ... Oklahoma City, OK
Laird, Jo Backer ... New York, NY
Laird, John C. ... Monroe, LA
Laird, John R. ... Ann Arbor, MI
Laird, Jules L., Jr. ... Houston, TX
Laird, June Baker ... Denver, CO
Laird, Katherine Kramer ... Seattle, WA
Laird & Laird ... Waverly, IA
Laird, Lisa Ayumi ... San Francisco, CA
Laird, Martin L., III ... Alexandria, LA
Laird, Michael J. ... Chicago, IL
Laird, Michael J. ... Whitewater, WI
Laird, Michael S. ... Oklahoma City, OK
Laird, Mitchell C. ... Phoenix, AZ
Laird, Morris E. ... Mason City, IA
Laird, Paul C., II ... Irving, TX
Laird, Peter F. ... Los Angeles, CA
Laird, Philip B., Jr. ... Visalia, CA
Laird, Phillip A. ... Jasper, AL
Laird, R. Joel, Jr. ... Anniston, AL
Laird, Ralph E. ... Sacramento, CA
Laird, Ralph E., III ... Waverly, IA
Laird, Rebecca H. ... Washington, DC
Laird, Richard A. ... Baldwin Park, CA
Laird, Robert D. ... Coos Bay, OR
Laird, Robert D., P.C. ... Coos Bay, OR
Laird, Robert E., Jr. ... Princess Anne, MD
Laird, Robert M. ... Somerville, MA
Laird, Russell H. ... Des Moines, IA
Laird, Scott D. ... Fresno, CA
Laird, Sherry S. ... New York, NY
Laird, Stephanie L. ... Houston, TX
Laird, Steven C. ... Fort Worth, TX
Irving, TX
Laird, Steven R. ... Gillette, WY
Laird, Vanessa A. ... Department of State, Office of the Legal Adviser, GV
Laird, Wesley L. ... Andalusia, AL
Laird & Wiley, P.C. ... Jasper, AL
Laird, William P. ... Rock Island, IL
Laird, Woodard & Baker ... Andalusia, AL
Lais, Ronald E. ... Anaheim, CA
Lais, Ronald E., Inc., Law Offices of
Anaheim, CA
Laishley, John Harold ... Huntington, WV
Laisure, Paul Skip ... New York, NY
Laisy, Albert W. ... Bel Air, MD
Lait, Hayden D. ... Memphis, TN
Laite, David A. ... Cincinnati, OH
Laite, Gilbert C., III ... Raleigh, NC
Laites, Sandra L. ... Los Angeles, CA
Laitinen, Sari K. M. ... Minneapolis, MN
Laitinen, Stephen P. ... St. Paul, MN
Laitinen, William H., Jr. ... Detroit, MI
Laitman, Daniel E. ... New York, NY
Laitman, Joel P. ... New York, NY
Laitman, Samuel H. ... New York, NY
Laitner, Morton R. ... Cooper City, FL
Laitos, Jan G. ... Denver, CO
Laitos, Mary V. ... Denver, CO
Laitsch, Lowell C. ... Alexandria, VA
Laity, Eric T. ... Oklahoma City, OK
Laizer, Edwin C. ... New Orleans, LA
Laizure, Anthony M. ... Tulsa, OK
Laizure, Kathy Laughter ... Memphis, TN
Lajara-Borelli, Luis ... San Juan, PR
Lajcik, Thomas ... Thousand Oaks, CA
LaJeunesse, Raymond J., Jr.
Springfield, VA
LaJeunesse, Richard M. ... Salt Lake City, UT
La Jeunesse, Richard T. ... Cincinnati, OH
Lajewski, Leslie Ann ... Los Angeles, CA
Roseland, NJ
New York, NY
Lajoie, Bernadette ... New York, NY
Lajoie, David E. ... Richardson, TX
Lajoie, James R. ... Marblehead, MA
Lajoie, John T. ... Tallahassee, FL
LaJoie, Roger W. ... Vero Beach, FL
Lajoie, Ronald J. ... Manchester, NH
La Jolla Law Group ... San Diego, CA
LaJone, Jay A. ... Dallas, TX
LaJone, Lynne M. ... Park Ridge, IL
Lajoy, Marcel J. ... Albany, NY
Lak, Richard S. ... Dover, NH
La Kam, Bruce H. ... Deerfield Beach, FL
Lakat, Cathy R. ... Mount Olive, NJ
Lakatos, Alex ... Washington, DC
Lakatta, Edward Alexander ... New York, NY
Lake, Adriana B. ... Springfield, VA
Lake, Ann W. ... Dedham, MA
Lake, Barry ... Lincoln, NE
Lake, Bernice Lynn ... San Francisco, CA
Lake, Brent C. ... McMinnville, OR
Lake, Brian C. ... New York, NY
Lake, Brian D. ... Raleigh, NC
Lake, Brian J. ... South Bend, IN
Lake, C. William ... La Grange, IL
Lake, Carolyn A. ... Seattle, WA
Lake, Charles ... Washington, DC
Lake, Charles E. (Ted), Jr. ... Atlanta, GA
Lake, Charles H. ... Louisville, KY
Lake, Charles W. ... New York, NY
Lake, Christian D. ... Tallahassee, FL
Lake, Christopher M. ... Plano, TX
Lake, Clifton A. ... Chicago, IL
Lake, David ... Lincoln, NE
Lake, David A. ... Tyler, TX
Lake, David G. ... Warren, OH
Lake, David N. ... Santa Monica, CA
Lake, Diane ... Franklin, MI
Lake, Don ... Tarzana, CA
Lake, Elizabeth A. ... San Francisco, CA
Lake, Ellen ... Oakland, CA
Lake, F. David, Jr. ... Washington, DC
Lake, Frederick A. ... Kalamazoo, MI
Lake, Gay M., Jr. ... Tuscaloosa, AL
Lake, Gregory E. ... Englewood, NJ
Lake, Gregory J. ... Abington, PA
Lake, Heather Dawn ... Oklahoma City, OK
Lake, Holly R. ... Los Angeles, CA
Lake, Howard O. ... Huntsville, TX
Lake, Hymen ... Orlando, FL
Lake, I. Beverly, Jr. ... Raleigh, NC
Lake, I. Beverly, Sr. ... Wake Forest, NC
Lake, J. Gregory ... Phoenix, AZ
Lake, J. Richard ... Topeka, KS
Lake, James B. ... Tampa, FL
Lake, James E. ... Mesa, AZ
Spokane, WA
Lake, Jas. A., Sr. ... Lincoln, NE
Lake, Jay B. ... Los Angeles, CA
Lake, Jay V. ... Pacific Palisades, CA
Lake, Jeffrey A. ... San Diego, CA
Lake, Jeffrey M. ... Eugene, OR
Lake, John F. ... Michigan City, IN
Lake, John F. ... Barnstead, NH
Lake, John H. ... Jefferson City, MO
Lake, John V., Jr. ... Gillette, WY
Lake, John W. ... Pittsfield, MA
Lake, Jonathan M. ... New Orleans, LA
Lake, Julia
Federal Energy Regulatory Commission, Office of the General Counsel, GV
Lake, Katherine C. ... Tampa, FL
Lake, Kathleen C. ... Houston, TX
Lake, Kenneth G. ... Los Angeles, CA
Lake, Kevin J. ... New York, NY
Lake, Kevin T. ... St. Louis, MO
Lake, Kimberley M. ... Lawrenceville, NJ
Trenton, NJ
Lake, Kimberly J. ... Westport, CT
Lake, L. Robert
Department Of Health And Human Services, Food & Drug Administration, GV
Lake & Lake ... Michigan City, IN
Lake & Lake ... Newberry, SC
Lake, Leonard M. ... New York, NY
Lake, Leslie Wolcott ... Bridgewater, MA
Lake & Levine ... Tarzana, CA
Lake, María Patricia ... San Juan, PR
Lake, Mark G. ... New York, NY
Lake Markham Pennachio ... Englewood, NJ
Lake, Marna M. ... Grand Junction, CO
Lake, Marsha S. ... Norcross, GA
Lake, Mary J. ... Hillsboro, MO
Lake, Mary J., L.C. ... Hillsboro, MO
Lake, Michael ... New Canaan, CT
Lake, Micheal D. ... Chicago, IL
Lake, Monte B. ... Washington, DC
Lake, P. Frank ... Austin, TX
Lake, Patrick W. ... Los Angeles, CA
Lake, Paul Martin ... Marion, IN
Lake, Peter S. ... Norfolk, VA
Lake, Philip G. ... Concord, NH
Lake, R. Alexander, Jr. ... New York, NY
Lake, R. Henry ... Houston, TX
Lake, R. Howard ... Winthrop, ME
Lake, Ralph B. ... Memphis, TN
Lake, Richard W. ... Round Rock, TX
Lake, Robert C., III ... Newberry, SC
Lake, Robert C., Jr. ... Newberry, SC
Lake, Robert D. ... Norcross, GA
Lake, Robert D. ... Broomall, PA
Lake, Robin F. ... San Diego, CA
Lake, Robin R. ... Chicago, IL
Lake, Ronald M. ... Rolling Meadows, IL
Lake, Rutherford C., Jr. ... Newport News, VA
Lake, Sally Lu ... Yorktown Heights, NY
Lake, Sara M. ... Lafayette, CA
Lake & Schau, P.C., Law Offices of
Kalamazoo, MI
Lake, Scott ... Prior Lake, MN
Lake, Sean B. ... Mesa, AZ
Lake, Shirlie Norris ... Baltimore, MD
Lake, Simeon T., III ... Houston, TX
Lake, Stephanie E. ... Phoenix, AZ
Lake, Stephen W. ... Tulsa, OK
Lake, Steven ... Palm Beach Gardens, FL
Lake, Steven R. ... Chicago, IL
Lake, Sue L. ... Stanwood, MI
Lake, Susan A. ... Columbia, SC
Lake, Thomas A. ... Santa Maria, CA
Lake, Thomas H. ... St. Louis, MO
Lake, Thomas M. ... Waukegan, IL
Lake, Timothy D. ... Los Angeles, CA
Lake, Timothy W. ... Dearborn, MI
Lake Tindall ... Paducah, KY
Cleveland, MS
Greenville, MS
Greenwood, MS
Grenada, MS
Indianola, MS
Jackson, MS
Oxford, MS
Lake, Toback & Yavitz ... Chicago, IL
Lake, Warren F. ... Sanbornton, NH
Lake, Wendy M. ... Omaha, NE
Lake, William M. ... Trenton, NJ

Lake, William T. ... Washington, DC
Lakel, Francis R. ... West Chester, PA
Lakeland, Albert A., Jr ... Bethesda, MD
Lakeman, Arend E. ... Mobridge, SD
LaKemper, Daniel A. ... Peoria, IL
Lake Potter, Barbara R. ... Morristown, NY
Laker, Gregory L. ... Indianapolis, IN
Lakerdas, James G. ... Chicago, IL
Lakes, Anthony O. ... Atlanta, GA
Lake-Smith, Nancy J. ... St. Paul, MN
Lakey, Carl E., Jr. ... Walnut Creek, CA
Lakey, Gayle B. ... Memphis, TN
Lakey, J. Robert W. ... Sayre, OK
Lakey, Jonathan P. ... Memphis, TN
Lakey, Patrick J. ... Bellingham, WA
Lakey, Randy A. ... Rantoul, IL
Lakey, Robert F. ... New Orleans, LA
Lakey, Theodore R. ... Oakland, CA
Lakhani, Farooq ... Corpus Christi, TX
Lakhdhir, David K. ... New York, NY
Lakhia, Patricia Ermel ... Wilkes-Barre, PA
Lakidis, Stella ... New Bedford, MA
Lakin, Andrew H. ... Savannah, GA
Lakin, Arlene Hechter ... Margate, FL
Lakin, Bradley M. ... Wood River, IL
Lakin, Cecilia J. ... Southfield, MI
Lakin, Garry ... Naples, FL
Lakin, James R. ... Rensselaer, IN
Lakin, John F. ... Andover, MA
Boston, MA
Lakin & Jones ... Jeffersontown, KY
Lakin, Kenneth A. ... Andover, MA
Boston, MA
Lakin, L. Thomas ... Wood River, IL
St. Louis, MO
Lakin, Larry L. ... Jeffersontown, KY
Lakin Law Firm, The, P.C.
Edwardsville, IL
Wood River, IL
St. Louis, MO
Lakin, Leonard ... Briarcliff Manor, NY
Lakin, Leonard S. ... Wellesley, MA
Lakin, Marc R. ... Detroit, MI
Lakin, Robert F. ... Wellesley, MA
Lakin, Sanford N. ... Southfield, MI
Lakin, Scott A. ... North Andover, MA
Lakin • Spears, LLP ... Palo Alto, CA
Lakin, Thomas J. ... Cincinnati, OH
Lakin, Worsham & Victor, P.C.
Southfield, MI
Lakind, Arnold C. ... Lawrenceville, NJ
Lakind, Howard P. ... New Brunswick, NJ
New York, NY
LaKind, Steven M. ... Evanston, IL
Lakis, Dean J. ... New York, NY
Lakis, William E. ... New York, NY
Lakner, Patricia S. ... Emeryville, CA
San Francisco, CA
Lakoff, Lincoln L. ... Nashville, TN
LaKoma, Matthew W. ... Oak Brook, IL
Lakomy, Michelle L. ... Elizabeth, NJ
Lakovitch, Joseph B. ... Dania, FL
Lakritz, Alfred J. ... Encino, CA
LaKritz, Barry F. ... Farmington Hills, MI
LaKritz, Barry F., P.C. ... Farmington Hills, MI
Lakritz, Gerald H. ... Bingham Farms, MI
Lakritz, Herman & Wissbrun, P.C.
Bingham Farms, MI
Lakritz, Ira ... Hackensack, NJ
Lakritz, Robb M. ... Washington, DC
Lakritz, Simeon ... San Diego, CA
Laks, Carl L. ... Miami, FL
Laks, Eugene M. ... Albany, NY
Laks, Jason ... New York, NY
Laks, Joseph J. ... Princeton, NJ
Laks, Perry M. ... Chicago, IL
Lakshmanan, Joseph L. ... Decatur, IL
Laky, Lisa Ott ... Austin, TX
Lal, Arvind K.
Securities and Exchange Commission, Office of the General Counsel, GV
Lal, Christopher M. ... Newport Beach, CA
Lal, Paul J. ... Las Vegas, NV
Lalafarian, Daniel ... Glendale, CA
Lalak, Lori Ann ... Cleveland, OH
Lalama, Anthony J. ... Pittsburgh, PA
Lalama, Jeffrey R. ... Pittsburgh, PA
LaLancette, Robert R. ... Fitchburg, MA
LaLanne, Thomas J. ... San Francisco, CA
Laliberte, Antonio M. ... San Jose, CA
Laliberte, Dana J. ... Portland, ME
Laliberte, Gerard R. ... Woonsocket, RI
La Liberte, John C. ... Boston, MA
Laliberte, Judith C. ... Rumford, RI
Laliberte, Kimberly J. ... Walnut, CA
Laliberte, Margaret G. ... Palo Alto, CA
Laliberte, Robert J. ... Plymouth, MA
LaLiberty, James M. ... Waterville, ME
Lalich, Gayle L. ... Boulder, CO
Lalich, George S. ... Chicago, IL
Lalik, Elizabeth A. ... McLean, VA
Lalikos, John J. ... Peabody, MA
Lalikos, Michael S. ... Danvers, MA
LaLima, David J. ... Boston, MA
Lalime, Richard A. ... Lowell, MA
Laline, Daniel G., Jr. ... Stamford, CT
Lalk, Margaret U. ... Bryan, TX
Lall, Arvind ... Jericho, NY
Lall, Indrani ... New York, NY
Lall, Parshotam S.
Department of Commerce, Patent and Trademark Office, GV
Lalla, Anthony P. ... Washington, DC
Lalla, Jeffrey G. ... St. Paul, MN
Lalla, Thomas R., Jr. ... New York, NY
Lallana, M. Isabel C. ... Woodland Hills, CA
Lallande, M. Lawrence ... Long Beach, CA
Lallas, Peter L.
Environmental Protection Agency, Office of the General Counsel, GV
Lallas, Tom, (P.C.) ... Los Angeles, CA
Lallatin, Gerald J. ... Provo, UT
Lalle, A. Wayne, Jr. ... McLean, VA
Lalle, Frank A. ... Redwood City, CA
Lalley, Edward P. ... Westport, CT
Lalley, John D. ... Scranton, PA
Lalley, Robert L., Jr. ... Grand Rapids, MI
Lalley, William D. ... Indianapolis, IN
Lalli, Daniel F. ... McAlester, OK
Lalli, Dennis A. ... New York, NY
Lalli, Matthew L. ... Salt Lake City, UT
Lalli, Michael A. ... White Plains, NY
Lalli, Paul Vincent ... Atlanta, GA
Lalli, Sharon Frances ... Brockton, MA
Lallier, Gregg J. ... Farmington, CT
Lallier, Paula M. ... Salida, CO
Lallier, Thomas J. ... Minneapolis, MN
Lallier, Thornton E. ... Amesbury, MA
Lalliss, Keith R. ... Mesa, AZ
Lallo, Christopher Joseph ... Houston, TX
Lallo, Ernest A. ... Cleveland, OH
Lallo, John F. ... Providence, RI
Lallo, Jon D. ... Westerly, RI
Lallos, Donatos E. ... Boston, MA
Lally, Carol Williams ... Washington, DC
Lally, Charles J. ... Cleveland, OH
Lally, Cynthia Davis ... Orlando, FL
Lally, Daniel W. ... Chicago, IL
New York, NY
Lally, David B. ... Newport Beach, CA
Lally, Douglas R. ... Jenkintown, PA
Lally, Elizabeth Nunziato ... Cleveland, OH
Lally, Emmett W. ... Las Vegas, NV
Lally, Gerald P. ... New York, NY
Lally, Gerald Patrick ... Middletown, NJ
Lally, Grant M. ... Mineola, NY
Lally, Holtzman, Gilligan, Duffin & Quasti, P.C. ... Philadelphia, PA
Lally, Holtzman, Gilligan & Quasti, P.C.
Cherry Hill, NJ
Linwood, NJ
Turnersville, NJ
Lally, J. Robert ... Sacramento, CA
Lally, John ... Chicago, IL
Lally, John A. ... St. Louis, MO
Lally, John K. ... Springfield, VA
Lally, John M. ... Louisville, KY
Lally, Joseph P. ... St. Paul, MN
Lally, Joseph P. ... Austin, TX
Lally, Joseph R. ... Margate City, NJ
Lally, Karen M. ... Boston, MA
Lally, Kevin D. ... San Ramon, CA
Lally, Kevin M. ... Washington, DC
Lally & Lally ... Sacramento, CA
Lally and Lally ... Mineola, NY
Lally and Lally, LLP ... Kinderhook, NY
Lally, Laura E. ... Chicago, IL
Lally, Lawrence D. ... Cherry Hill, NJ
Lally, Lawrence M. ... Mineola, NY
Lally, Maria Anne ... Kinderhook, NY
Lally, Mark S. ... Columbus, OH
Lally, Marlene N. ... Cleveland Heights, OH
Lally, Maryann D. ... Wilton, CT
Lally, Michelle H. ... Pittsburgh, PA
Lally, Patricia C. ... Seattle, WA
Lally, Paul T. ... Oakton, VA
Lally, Regan U. ... Mineola, NY
Lally, Robert C. ... Brookfield, WI
Lally, Robert J. ... Cleveland, OH
Lally, Robt. J. ... Cleveland, OH
Lally, Sean P. ... Kinderhook, NY
Lally, Thomas William ... Canton, OH
Lally, Ute Wolff ... Hempstead, NY
Lally, William F., Jr. ... Kinderhook, NY
Lally, William H. ... Sacramento, CA
Lally, William K. ... Jacksonville, FL
Lally-Green, Maureen E. ... Pittsburgh, PA
Lalo, Deborah Kartoz ... Atlanta, GA
Lalomia, Santo J. ... Pompton Plains, NJ
La-Londe, Alexa Richman
Morristown, NJ
Lalonde, Andrew Venant ... Rome, NY
Lalonde, Cheryl A. ... Lexington, KY
LaLonde, Eugene A. ... Billings, MT
LaLonde, Gregory T. ... Washington, DC
LaLonde, John L. ... Vancouver, WA
LaLonde, John P. ... Coarsegold, CA
LaLonde, Lori L. ... Costa Mesa, CA
LaLonde, Martin J. ... Department of Justice, Environment and Natural Resources Division, GV
Lalonde, Michelle T. ... Atlanta, GA
Lalonde, Paul G. ... Hadley, MA
LaLonde, Robert R. ... Ithaca, NY
LaLone, Douglas P. ... Troy, MI
Lalone, Theresa Lynn ... Spokane, WA
Lalor, Daniel K. ... Catskill, NY
Lalor, Daniela M. ... Binghamton, NY
Lalor, Edward D. D. ... St. Cloud, MN
Lalor-Lueders, Cathy ... New York, NY
Lalos & Keegan ... Washington, DC
Lalos, Peter N. ... Washington, DC
Laluk, Susan Schultz ... Rochester, NY
Lalumia, Matthew Paul ... Towson, MD
La Luzerne, Larry ... Waukegan, IL
Lal-Wadia, Zenobia ... Novato, CA
Lam, B. Lynne ... Norman, OK
Lam, Bonnie A. ... Klamath Falls, OR
Lam, Bradford J. ... Denver, CO
Lam, Brian E. J. ... Dulles, VA
Lam, Christine S. ... Palo Alto, CA
Lam, Christopher S. ... Philadelphia, PA
Lam, Cloris L. ... Arcadia, CA
Lam, Conner ... Grapevine, TX
Lam, Conner, P.C. ... Grapevine, TX
Lam, Cynthia C. ... Los Angeles, CA
Lam, David S.C. ... Houston, TX
Lam, Dennis C. ... Seattle, WA
Lam, Edward W. ... Washington, DC
Lam, Eric W. ... Cedar Rapids, IA
Lam, Fei F. ... Edison, NJ
New York, NY
Lam, Gregory B. ... Kansas City, MO
Lam, Henry L., Jr. ... Virginia Beach, VA
Lam, Howard D. ... Minneapolis, MN
Lam, J. Gerard ... Honolulu, HI
Lam, James ... Houston, TX
Lam, James F. ... Irvine, CA
Lam, James Wolcott ... Virginia Beach, VA
Lam, Judy ... Atlanta, GA
Lam, Judy Man-Ling ... Los Angeles, CA
Lam, L. Andre ... Fountain Valley, CA
Lam, Leo L. ... San Francisco, CA
Lâm, MaivânClech ... Flushing, NY
Lam, Margaret J. ... Houston, TX
Lam, Mee Lon ... Department of Justice, Civil Division, GV
Lam, Michael ... New York, NY
Lam, Michael L. ... Honolulu, HI
Lam, Nam-Yeng Mark ... Newport Beach, CA
Lam, Ngoc H. ... Washington, DC
Lam, Philip H. ... Los Angeles, CA
Lam, Phuong T. ... Chicago, IL
Lam, Q. Gwynn ... New York, NY
Lam, Shirley F. ... Novato, CA
Lam, T. Maria ... Boston, MA
Lam, Timothy L. ... Monticello, GA
Lam, Tony Y. ... Washington, DC
Lam, Tuan A. ... Fresno, CA
Lam, Valerie J. ... Honolulu, HI
Lam, Winston K.C. ... Deerfield, IL
Lama, Albert J. ... Santa Fe, NM
Lama, Alfred M. ... Riverhead, NY
Lama, Luciano L. ... Ithaca, NY
LaMacchia, Lori A. ... Paso Robles, CA
LaMacchia, Philip ... Berlin, MD
LaMacchia, Sally F. ... Oxnard, CA
LaMacchia, Thomas F. ... New York, NY
Lamade, Barbara Spencer ... Arlington, VA
Lamade, Lawrence L. ... Washington, DC
LaMadrid, Marisol ... Washington, DC
LaMagna, Donna L. ... New York, NY
Lamagna, Joseph A. ... Pawtucket, RI
Lamal, Christopher T. ... New York, NY
Laman, Charley ... Topeka, KS
Laman, Debra K. ... House of Representatives, Committee Legal Personnel, GV
Laman, Hevron & Hines ... Plano, TX
Laman, Luke, Jr. ... Plano, TX
Laman, Steven D. ... Edwardsville, IL
Laman & Swenson Law Offices
Eau Claire, WI
Laman, William F. ... Eau Claire, WI
Lamancusa, Carmen F. ... New Castle, PA
Lamancusa & Cilli, P.C. ... New Castle, PA
Lamancusa, Frank G.
Federal Communications Commission, Common Carrier Bureau, GV
LaMancuso, John L. ... Jamestown, NY
LaManna, Eugene C. ... Reading, PA
LaManna, Jeanmarie ... Jacksonville, FL
LaManna, Judith A. ... Syracuse, NY
Lamanna, Julia ... New York, NY
LaManna, Kathleen M. ... Hartford, CT
La Manna, Lynn L. ... Los Angeles, CA
Lamanna, Michael A. ... Cleveland, OH
Lamanna, Nick M. ... Priest River, ID
Sandpoint, ID
Lamanna, Paul L. ... New York, NY
LaManna & Swavely ... Reading, PA
Lamanna, Vincent L., Jr. ... Sea Isle City, NJ
Lamantia, Anthony Philip, III ... Freehold, NJ
Lamantia, Carl H. ... Indianapolis, IN
La Mantia, Joseph A. ... Salinas, CA
La Mantia, Joseph A., A Professional Corporation ... Salinas, CA
LaMantia, Louis J. ... Hamburg, NY
La Mantia, Mark A. ... Raleigh, NC
Lamantia, Stephen R. ... Buffalo, NY
LaMantia, Victor A. ... Riverwoods, IL
Lamar, Archer & Cofrin ... Atlanta, GA
La Mar, Ben F., Jr. ... Redwood City, CA
Lamar, Burgess, Hale, Miller, Norris & Feldman, P.C. ... Birmingham, AL
LaMar, Carl O. ... Duncan, OK
Lamar, Charles L. ... Owensboro, KY
Lamar, Charles W., III ... Baton Rouge, LA
Lamar, David W. ... Owensboro, KY
Lamar, Douglas George ... Concord, CA
Lamar, Edward D. ... Greenville, MS
LaMar & Grasso, P.C. ... Scottsdale, AZ
Lamar & Hannaford, P.A. ... Senatobia, MS
Lamar, Hector A. ... Coral Gables, FL
Lamar, Hilary L. ... San Francisco, CA
Lamar, Howard H., III ... Nashville, TN
Lamar, Jayna Partain ... Birmingham, AL
Lamar, Jeanne M. ... Chicago, IL
Lamar, John T., Jr. ... Senatobia, MS
Lamar, Kipler S. ... Augusta, GA
LaMar, Kristena A. ... Portland, OR
Lamar, L. Wardlaw ... Nashville, NC
Lamar, Lawson L. ... Orlando, FL
Lamar, Lewis W., Jr. ... Nashville, NC
LaMar, Margery S. ... Annapolis, MD
Lamar, Marilyn ... Chicago, IL
Lamar, Mario ... Coral Gables, FL
Lamar, Mario A. ... Miami, FL
Lamar, Mary Ellen ... Decatur, AL
La Mar, Michelle M. ... Los Angeles, CA
Lamar, P. Camille ... Birmingham, AL
Lamar, Patricia W. ... Atlanta, GA
Lamar, Patrick M. ... Huntsville, AL
Lamar, Patrick M., LLC ... Huntsville, AL
Lamar, Paul W. ... Elizabethtown, IL
LaMar, Philip S. ... Charlottesville, VA
Lamar, R. David ... Kansas City, KS
Lamar, Ralph E., IV ... Savannah, GA
Lamar, Robert C. ... Atlanta, GA
Lamar, Robert S., Jr. ... Birmingham, AL
Lamar, Sandra J. ... Chestnut Hill, MA
Lamar, Sarah H. ... Savannah, GA
LaMar, Steven A. ... Scottsdale, AZ
LaMar, Sylvia F. ... Santa Fe, NM
Lamar, Timothy J. ... Portland, ME
La Marca, Anthony J. ... Oyster Bay, NY
Lamarca, Darren J. ... Clinton, MS
LaMarca, George A. ... Islamorada, FL
Sarasota, FL
West Des Moines, IA
LaMarca & Landry, P.C. ... Islamorada, FL
Des Moines, IA
West Des Moines, IA
LaMarca, Robert M. ... Boston, MA
LaMarca, Susan F.
Commodity Futures Trading Commission, Division of Enforcement, GV
La Marca, Thos. J. ... Cleveland, OH
LaMarca, William ... Department of Commerce, Patent and Trademark Office, GV
LaMarca, William ... Springfield, IL
La Marca, William R. ... Garden City, NY
LaMarche, Margaret G. ... Des Moines, IA
Lamar-Hart, Cynthia G.
Birmingham, AL
Lamari, Joseph P. ... Rockville, MD
Lamarine, Paul A. ... Southbridge, MA
Lamarine, Peter C. ... Southbridge, MA
LaMarr, Catherine E. ... New Haven, CT
La Marr, Jack P., (P.A.) ... Fort Lauderdale, FL
Lamarre, David R. ... San Francisco, CA
Lamarre, Stephanie Simonds
San Francisco, CA
LaMartina, Timothy J. ... Tucson, AZ
Lamas, Patricia H. ... Ventura, CA
Lamas, Sergio D. ... Roslyn, NY
Lamasa, Charles ... Baltimore, MD
Lamason, Fielding E., Jr.
Environmental Protection Agency, Office of Enforcement and Compliance Assurance, GV
Lamaster, Teresa K. ... Towson, MD
LaMastra, Anne Maher ... Atlanta, GA
Lamastra, John E. ... Florham Park, NJ
Lamastra, Joseph M. ... Morristown, NJ
Lamatina, Louis J. ... Paramus, NJ
New York, NY
LaMay, Michael I. ... Danville, CA
Lamb, Adam J. ... Miami, FL
Lamb, Andrea L. ... San Diego, CA
Lamb, Anthony B. ... Burlington, VT
Lamb, Archie C., Jr. ... Birmingham, AL
Lamb, Archie C., Jr., LLC, Law Offices of
Birmingham, AL
Lamb, Arthur J., & Co. ... Amarillo, TX
Lamb, B. Michele ... Seattle, WA
Lamb & Barnosky, LLP
Central Islip, NY
Huntington, NY
Melville, NY
Lamb & Baute LLP ... Los Angeles, CA
Lamb, Bradford H. ... Portland, OR
Lamb, Bradley Robert ... Pittsboro, NC
Lamb, Brian J. ... Cleveland, OH
Lamb, Brockenbrough, Jr. ... Richmond, VA
Lamb, Bruce Douglas ... Tampa, FL
Lamb, Bruce G. ... Seattle, WA
Lamb, Bryan D. ... San Francisco, CA
Lamb, Carl Paul ... Bloomington, IN
Lamb, Celeste Y. ... Warren, NJ
Lamb, Charles D. ... Kansas City, KS
Lamb, Charles G. ... Louisville, KY
Lamb, Charles P. ... Grosse Pointe Farms, MI
Lamb, Christine Kessler ... Denver, CO
Lamb, Christopher J. ... Wilmington, DE
Lamb, Clay J. ... Louisville, KY
Lamb, Colin D. ... Portland, OR
Lamb, Crystal R. ... San Diego, CA
Lamb, Cynthia D. ... Crystal Lake, IL
Lamb, Dale A. ... Grinnell, IA
Lamb, Daniel G., Jr. ... San Diego, CA
Lamb, Daniel N. ... Saugerties, NY
Lamb, Daniel N., Jr. ... Saugerties, NY
Lamb, Davey ... Dallas, TX
Lamb, David A. ... Los Angeles, CA
Lamb, David A. ... Denver, CO
Lamb, David B. ... Washington, DC
Rockville, MD
Lamb, David C. ... Cleveland, OH
Lamb, David W. ... Los Angeles, CA
Lamb, Deanna F. ... Santa Clara, CA
Lamb, Deanna R. ... Utica, NY
Lamb, Deborah E. ... Baton Rouge, LA
Lamb, Diane M. ... Mount Laurel, NJ
Lamb, Donald E. ... Centerville, MO
Lamb, Douglas Edward ... Clarksburg, WV
Lamb, Douglas Martin ... Louisville, KY
Lamb, Edward A. ... Spartanburg, SC
Lamb, Eric M. ... Louisville, KY
Lamb, Eric N. ... Baltimore, MD
Lamb, Eugene G. ... Syosset, NY
Lamb, Eugene K. ... Brooklyn, NY
Lamb, Frederic D. ... Wilton, CT
Lamb, George C., III ... Dallas, TX
Lamb, George S. ... Decatur, GA
Lamb, George T. ... Santa Cruz, CA
Lamb, George W. ... Springfield, VT
Lamb, Gmerice H. ... Decatur, GA
Lamb, Gwenda Reneé ... Alexandria, LA
Lamb, Harold W. ... Brookline, MA
Lamb, Harry T. ... Philadelphia, PA

Lamb, Hartung, Kretzer, Reinman & De Pascale ... Elizabeth, NJ
Hackensack, NJ
Jersey City, NJ
Newark, NJ
Paterson, NJ
Lamb, Heidi J. ... Boston, MA
Lamb, Iven S., Jr. ... Jacksonville, FL
Lamb, J. Patrick ... Decatur, AL
Lamb, J. Wyman ... Tucker, GA
Lamb, James B. ... Waco, TX
Lamb, James C. ... Washington, DC
Lamb, James L. ... Grand Forks, ND
Lamb, James M. ... Tulsa, OK
Lamb, James R. ... Morristown, NJ
Lamb, James R., P.C. ... Morristown, NJ
Lamb, James T., Jr. ... Houston, TX
Lamb, Jane Deterding ... Wichita, KS
Lamb, Jerome A. ... Ypsilanti, MI
Lamb, Joan Gudesblatt ... Kingston, NY
Lamb, Joe B., Jr. ... Richmond, VA
Lamb, John A. ... Los Angeles, CA
Lamb, John D. ... New York, NY
Lamb, John F. P. ... New York, NY
Lamb, John G., Jr. ... Richardson, TX
Lamb, John J. ... Montvale, NJ
Lamb, John J. ... Philadelphia, PA
Lamb, John N. ... Holbrook, AZ
Lamb, Joseph T., III ... Kitty Hawk, NC
Norfolk, VA
Lamb, Joyce Ann ... Alliance, OH
Lamb, Joyce K. ... Paterson, NJ
Lamb, Karen K. ... Norwich, CT
Lamb, Katherine Dalman ... Kalamazoo, MI
Lamb, Kathleen E. ... Houston, TX
Lamb, Kathleen M. ... Minneapolis, MN
Lamb, Kathy R. ... Buffalo, NY
Lamb, Kenneth R. ... Anchorage, AK
Lamb, Kenneth R. ... San Francisco, CA
Lamb, Kevin J. ... Los Angeles, CA
Lamb, Kevin T. ... Boston, MA
Lamb, Kristen A. ... Menlo Park, CA
Lamb & Lamb ... Tallahassee, FL
Lamb & Lamb ... Louisville, KY
Lamb & Lamb ... Watervliet, NY
Lamb, Larry E. ... Monroe, MI
Lamb Law Offices, P.A. ... Shelby, NC
Lamb & Lerch ... New York, NY
Lamb, Lewis E., III ... Atlanta, GA
Lamb, Lewis R. ... Albany, GA
Lamb, Madeline H. ... West Chester, PA
Lamb, Madelyn J. ... Alton, IL
Lamb, Marcus N. ... New York, NY
Lamb, Margaret C. ... Johnson City, TN
Lamb, Margaret W. ... Questa, NM
Lamb, Marion D., III ... Tallahassee, FL
Lamb, Marion D., Jr. ... Tallahassee, FL
Lamb, Martin A. ... Holliston, MA
Lamb, Mary Ann ... Los Gatos, CA
Lamb, Matthew R. ... East Meadow, NY
Lamb, Maureen ... Rochester, NY
Lamb, Melissa E. ... Washington, DC
Lamb, Merrill I. ... Miami, FL
Lamb, Metzgar, Lines & Dahl, P.A.
Albuquerque, NM
Lamb & Michael, A Professional Corporation
Modesto, CA
Lamb, Michael T. ... Chicago, IL
Lamb, Michael V. ... Los Angeles, CA
Lamb, Micheal F. ... Helena, MT
Lamb, Morris & Lobello, LLP
Pomona, CA
San Dimas, CA
Lamb, Nancy B. ... Elizabeth City, NC
Lamb, Nancy R. Axelrod ... Katonah, NY
Lamb, Nicholas J. ... St. Louis, MO
Lamb, Norman A. ... Enid, OK
Lamb, Owen H. ... New York, NY
Lamb, Patricia A. ... Tulsa, OK
Lamb, Patrick C. ... Philadelphia, PA
Lamb, Patrick D. ... Chicago, IL
Lamb, Patrick J. ... Chicago, IL
Lamb, Patrick R. ... Seattle, WA
Lamb, Philip A. ... Yakima, WA
Lamb, P. L. ... Melville, NY
Lamb, R. Gregory ... Dallas, TX
Lamb, Randall ... Houston, TX
Lamb, Randy S. ... Alamo, TN
Lamb, Raymond A. ... Fargo, ND
Lamb, Raymond G. ... San Dimas, CA
Lamb, Rex M., III ... Atlanta, GA
Lamb, Richard Ryan ... Kalamazoo, MI
Lamb, Robert C. W. ... Dallas, TX
Lamb, Robert G., Jr. ... Rochester, NY
Lamb, Robert H. ... Washington, DC
Lamb, Robert H. ... Seattle, WA
Lamb, Robert J., III ... Tullahoma, TN
Lamb, Robert J., Jr. ... Charlotte, NC
Lamb, Robert M. ... Cincinnati, OH
Lamb, Robert O. ... Dallas, TX
Lamb, Robert W. ... Cartersville, GA
Lamb, Roland J. ... Tampa, FL
Lamb, Ronald D. ... Tacoma, WA
Lamb, Ronald R. ... Sacramento, CA
Lamb, Roscoe L. ... Ridgewood, NJ
Lamb, Sara Hay ... Tallahassee, FL
Lamb & Shaffer, P.C. ... Holliston, MA
Lamb, Sharon P. ... Richmond, VA
Lamb, Sherri Renee ... Chicago, IL
Lamb, Sidney ... Sacramento, CA
Lamb, Stephen A. ... Charlotte, NC
Lamb, Stephen P. ... Wilmington, DE
Lamb, Steven A. ... Irvine, CA
Lamb, Steven F. ... Fargo, ND
Lamb, Su Zann ... Department of Justice, Criminal Division, GV
Lamb, Theodore C. ... Little Rock, AR
Lamb, Thomas E. ... Watervliet, NY
Lamb, Thomas F. ... Pittsburgh, PA
Lamb, Thomas J. ... Wilmington, NC
Lamb, Thomas J., P.A., Law Offices of
Wilmington, NC
Lamb, Thomas R. ... Lincoln, NE
Lamb, Timothy J. ... Anchorage, AK
Lamb, Timothy J. ... Denver, CO
Lamb, Timothy J., P.C. ... Denver, CO
Lamb, Todd V. ... New York, NY
Lamb, Victor T. ... Sonora, CA
Lamb, Vincent A. ... Watervliet, NY
Lamb, William ... Baldwin, WI
Lamb, William E., Jr. ... Shelby, NC
Lamb, William F. ... New Brunswick, NJ
Lamb, William H. ... West Chester, PA
Lamb, William P. ... Little River, CA
Lamb, William R. ... Oxford, MS
Lamb, William S. ... New York, NY
Lamb, Windle & McErlane, P.C.
West Chester, PA
Lamb, Zee B. ... Elizabeth City, NC
Lamba, Sanjay ... Washington, DC
Lambacher, William G. ... Springfield, OH
Lambariello, Joseph A. ... Mountainside, NJ
Lambarth, Douglas D. ... Newport, WA
Lambarth & Geissler ... Newport, WA
Spokane, WA
Lambden and Gardner, P.C. ... Rye, NY
Lambden, James R. ... San Francisco, CA
Lambden, Ronald J. ... Greeley, CO
Lambdin, Candace Newell ... Austin, TX
Lambdin, Donald E. ... Wichita, KS
Lambdin, Jerome T. ... Baltimore, MD
Lambdin, John J. ... Baltimore, MD
Lambdin, Johnson, Herlocker, Soderberg & Lambdin, Chartered ... Wichita, KS
Lambdin, Keith J. ... Davie, FL
Lambdin, Lisa L. ... Wichita, KS
Lambdin, Suzanne J. ... Denver, CO
Lambe, Deborah C. ... Los Angeles, CA
Lambe, James F. ... Western Springs, IL
Lambe, James P. ... Fresno, CA
Lambe, Malcolm D. ... Chicago, IL
Lambe, Richard L. ... Seattle, WA
Lambe, William H., Jr. ... Durham, NC
Lambeck, Debra Tilson ... Los Angeles, CA
Lambek, Bernard D. ... Montpelier, VT
Lambek, Debra J. ... Albany, NY
Lambek, Jules K. ... Hewlett, NY
Lamber, Dennis M. ... Phoenix, AZ
Lamber, Julia C. ... Bloomington, IN
Lamber, Marc H. ... Phoenix, AZ
Lamberg, David H. ... Hillsborough, NJ
Lamberg, Heather P. ... Washington, DC
Lamberg, Samantha F. ... Torrance, CA
Lambergman, Barry ... Washington, DC
Lamberis, Anthony B. ... Evanston, IL
Lamberis, Anthony Byron, Ltd.
Evanston, IL
Lambers, August G. ... Dillingham, AK
Lambers, Benjamin E. ... Tampa, FL
Lamberski, John ... Atlanta, GA
Lamberson, Elise S. ... Tualatin, OR
Lamberson, Gary R. ... Charleston, SC
Lamberson, James W. ... Denver, CO
Lamberson, Kevin J. ... Glen Cove, NY
Lamberson, Phillip L. ... Dallas, TX
Lamberson & Schneider ... Charleston, SC
Lamberson, Stephen M.
Coeur d'Alene, ID
Spokane, WA
Lambert, Amy ... Baton Rouge, LA
Lambert, Amy J. ... San Jose, CA
Lambert, Andrew J. ... Anchorage, AK
Lambert, Antone L. ... Livonia, MI
Lambert, Arthur N. ... New York, NY
Lambert, Arthur V. ... Dallas, TX
Lambert and Associates ... Richmond, VA
Lambert, Barron P., III ... Brockton, MA
Lambert & Beggs ... Harrisburg, IL
Lambert, Benjamin D., Jr.
Woodbridge, NJ
Lambert, Benjamin F. ... New Brunswick, NJ
Lambert, Bettyanne" Betsy " ... New York, NY
Lambert, Bettye J. ... Houston, TX
Lambert, Bettye J., Law Offices of
Houston, TX
Lambert, Beverly A. ... Ocala, FL
Lambert & Boeder ... Minneapolis, MN
Lambert, Brett J. ... Longmont, CO
Lambert, Brian D. ... Ocala, FL
Lambert, Brian D., P.A. ... Ocala, FL
Lambert, Caralee A. ... Boise, ID
Lambert, Carl Jay ... Santa Monica, CA
Lambert, Carl L. ... Mountain View, CA
Lambert, Carl M. ... Miami, FL
Lambert, Carol McKinney ... Henderson, KY
Lambert, Charles G. ... San Francisco, CA
Lambert, Charles S., Jr.
Baton Rouge, LA
Lambert, Christine A. ... Grand Rapids, MI
Lambert, Christopher ... Providence, RI
Lambert, Coffin, Rudman & Hochman
Portland, ME
Lambert, Connie J. ... Chicago, IL
Flossmoor, IL
McHenry, IL
Lambert, Craig ... Little Rock, AR
Lambert, Craig S. ... Appleton, WI
Lambert, Cynthia Sleder ... Omaha, NE
Lambert, D. David ... Provo, UT
Lambert, Dale J. ... Salt Lake City, UT
Lambert, Daniel S. ... Chicago, IL
Lambert, David ... San Francisco, CA
Lambert, David G. ... Cleveland, OH
Lambert, David L. ... Washington, DC
Lambert, David M. F. ... Washington, DC
Lambert, David P. ... Charleston, WV
Lambert, David W. ... Alexandria, LA
Lambert, David W. ... West Point, MS
Lambert, Denise A. ... Boston, MA
Lambert, Dennis H. ... Burke, VA
Lambert, Donald B. ... Lexington, KY
Lambert, Donald R. ... Oklahoma City, OK
Lambert, Douglas P.
North Palm Beach, FL
Palm Beach, FL
Lambert, Douglas W. ... Columbus, OH
Lambert, Earle ... Encino, CA
Lambert, Edmund G. ... Evergreen, CO
Lambert, Edwin F., Jr. ... New York, NY
Lambert, Elan C. ... Walnut Creek, CA
Lambert, Elynn C. ... New York, NY
Lambert, E. R. ... Madison, GA
Lambert, Eugene I. ... Washington, DC
Lambert, Floyd & Conger
Bainbridge, GA
Lambert, Frederick W. ... San Francisco, CA
Lambert & Furlow ... Washington, DC
Chevy Chase, MD
Lambert, G. Steven ... Los Angeles, CA
Lambert, Gabriela V. ... Boston, MA
Lambert, Gail M. ... Lexington, KY
Lambert & Garrison, PLLC ... Boston, MA
Lambert, Gary E. ... Boston, MA
Lambert, George R. ... Philadelphia, PA
Lambert, Gina ... Austin, TX
Lambert, Gregory A. ... Gonzales, LA
Lambert, Harold ... Bainbridge, GA
Lambert, H. E. ... Camden, OH
Lambert, Henry M. ... New Orleans, LA
Lambert, Hugh P. ... New Orleans, LA
Lambert, J. Laird ... Rockford, IL
Lambert, Jack W., Jr. ... San Antonio, TX
Lambert, James A., II ... New York, NY
Lambert, James H. ... Mount Vernon, KY
Lambert, James M. ... Tulsa, OK
Lambert, James P. ... Lafayette, LA
Lambert, James R. ... Staten Island, NY
Lambert, James W. ... Mount Vernon, KY
Lambert, Janna L. ... Hayward, CA
Lambert, Jason P. ... Knoxville, TN
Lambert, Jay ... Louisville, KY
Lambert, Jay J. ... Philadelphia, PA
Lambert, Jayne M. ... Tampa, FL
Lambert, Jeffrey S. ... San Diego, CA
Lambert, Jeffrey S. ... Boston, MA
Lambert, Jeffrey S., P.C. ... Boston, MA
Lambert, Jeffrey W. ... Minneapolis, MN
Lambert, Jeremiah D. ... Washington, DC
Lambert, Jerry L. ... Chicago, IL
Flossmoor, IL
Lake In The Hills, IL
Lambert, Jesse D. ... Lafayette, LA
Lambert, Jo Lynn ... San Francisco, CA
Lambert, Joanne ... Raleigh, NC
Lambert, Joanne Braddock ... Orlando, FL
Lambert, Jodi E. ... San Diego, CA
Lambert, Joel C. ... Houston, TX
Lambert, John ... Kalamazoo, MI
Lambert, John C. M. ... San Francisco, CA
Lambert, John D. ... Akron, OH
Lambert, John D., Jr. ... New Orleans, LA
Lambert, John E. ... Carson City, NV
Lambert, John F. ... Greenwich, CT
Lambert, John F., Jr. ... Portland, ME
Lambert, Joseph E. ... Phoenix, AZ
Lambert, Joseph E. ... Mount Vernon, KY
Lambert, Joseph J. ... New York, NY
Lambert, Judith A. ... New York, NY
Lambert, Karl R. ... Minneapolis, MN
Lambert, Katherine J. ... Hartford, CT
Lambert, Katherine W. ... Milwaukee, WI
Lambert, Kathleen Diane ... New Orleans, LA
Lambert, Kathryn L.W. ... Bozeman, MT
Lambert, Kelly B. ... Denver, CO
Lambert, Kenneth H., Jr. ... Norfolk, VA
Lambert, Kenneth J. ... Dallas, TX
Lambert, Kent A. ... New Orleans, LA
Lambert, Kim A. ... Chicago, IL
Lambert, Kristine M. ... Memphis, TN
Lambert, L. Bruce ... Arlington, TX
Lambert & Lambert, A Law Corporation
New Orleans, LA
Lambert, Lambert & Duncan
Mount Vernon, KY
Lambert, Lanneau William, Jr.
Columbia, SC
Lambert, Larry ... Wichita Falls, TX
Lambert, Laurent P. ... Haverhill, MA
Lambert Law Corporation, PLLC
San Diego, CA
Lambert, Lawrence B. ... Miami, FL
Lambert, Lawrence B. ... New York, NY
Lambert, L. Bruce ... Fort Worth, TX
Lambert, Lenore ... Tarzana, CA
Lambert, Leonard W. ... Richmond, VA
Lambert, LeRoy ... New York, NY
Lambert, Leser, Cook, Giunta & Smith, P.C.
Bay City, MI
Lambert, Lindsay L. ... Houston, TX
Lambert, Lloyd F. ... Palm Beach Gardens, FL
Lambert, Lon Keith ... Norfolk, VA
Lambert, Loren M. ... Midvale, UT
Lambert, Loyce D. ... Memphis, TN
Lambert, Lucille B. ... Arlington, VA
Lambert, Lyndall M. ... Miami, FL
Lambert, Mark A. ... Los Angeles, CA
Lambert, Mark F. ... Menlo Park, CA
Lambert, Martin D. ... Bozeman, MT
Lambert, Mary B. ... Alameda, CA
Lambert, Mary M. ... Santa Barbara, CA
Lambert, Meghan ... New York, NY
Lambert, Melissa Lazarich ... Bel Air, MD
Lambert, Michael C. ... New York, NY
Lambert, Michael E. ... Manitowoc, WI
Lambert, Michael H. ... Daytona Beach, FL
Lambert, Michael H., P.A.
Daytona Beach, FL
Lambert, Michael J. ... Manchester, NH
Lambert, Michael J. ... Middleton, WI
Lambert, Michael K. ... White Plains, NY
Lambert, Michael P. ... Los Angeles, CA
Lambert, Michael T. ... Denver, CO
Lambert, Mikal S. ... Wichita Falls, TX
Lambert, Mollie Cohn ... Houston, TX
Lambert & Nelson, A Professional Law Corporation ... New Orleans, LA
Lambert, Nolan P. ... New Orleans, LA
Lambert, Norma J. ... San Francisco, CA
Lambert, Norman Ward ... Greenville, SC
Lambert, Pamela ... Columbia, MO
Lambert, Pamela A. ... Pineville, WV
Lambert, Patricia A. ... Cambridge, MA
Lambert, Patricia McHugh ... Towson, MD
Lambert, Patrick Henry ... Cherokee, NC
Lambert, Paul C. ... New York, NY
Lambert, Paul J. ... Washington, DC
Lambert, Paul M. ... Scottsdale, AZ
Lambert, Paul Richard ... Hattiesburg, MS
Lambert, Paul Richard ... Hattiesburg, MS
Lambert, Paul Watson ... Tallahassee, FL
Lambert, Peter C. ... San Rafael, CA
Lambert, Phelps L. ... Henderson, KY
Lambert, Phyllis ... Dallas, TX
Lambert, R. Bradley ... Birmingham, MI
Lambert, R. Bradley, P.C.
Birmingham, MI
Rochester Hills, MI
Lambert, R. Larry ... Virginia Beach, VA
Lambert, Randall L. ... Ironton, OH
Lambert, Raymond E. ... West Warwick, RI
Lambert, Richard A. ... Bethesda, MD
Lambert, Richard A. ... Dayton, OH
Lambert, Richard Alan ... New York, NY
Lambert, Richard Gordon ... Marion, IL
Lambert, Richard J. ... New York, NY
White Plains, NY
Lambert, Richard J., Jr. ... Somerville, NJ
Lambert, Rick L. ... Dallas, TX
Lambert, Robert D., (P.C.) ... Davenport, IA
Lambert, Robert J. ... Worcester, MA
Lambert, Robert J., Jr. ... Springdale, AR
Lambert, Robert L., Jr. ... Valdosta, GA
Lambert, Robert W. ... Indiana, PA
Lambert & Roffman, L.L.C.
Madison, GA
Lambert, Roger C. ... West Palm Beach, FL
Lambert, Roger T. ... Wauwatosa, WI
Lambert and Rogers ... El Cajon, CA
Lambert, Roy D. ... Portland, OR
Lambert, Sally Hardin ... Louisville, KY
Lambert, Samuel W., III ... Princeton, NJ
Lambert, Sanda K. ... Washington, DC
Lambert, Sandra A. ... San Rafael, CA
Lambert, Sandra L. ... Waltham, MA
Lambert, Scott C. ... San Francisco, CA
Lambert, Sheila M. ... Candler, NC
Lambert, Sherri Dark ... Maplewood, NJ
Lambert, Sherry J. ... Dayton, OH
Lambert, Sophie B. ... New York, NY
Lambert, Stanford L. ... Chicago, IL
Lambert, Stephen F. ... El Cajon, CA
Lambert, Steven C. ... Washington, DC
Lambert, Stewart K. ... Cherokee Village, AR
Lambert, Suellen Powers ... Montgomery, AL
Lambert, Suzanne M. ... Boston, MA
Lambert, Thomas A. ... Woodbury, NY
Lambert, Thomas C. ... New York, NY
Lambert, Thomas H. ... San Diego, CA
Lambert, Thomas P. ... Westport, CT
Lambert, Thomas P., (A Professional Corporation) ... Los Angeles, CA
Lambert, Timothy J. ... Joliet, IL
Lambert, Todd D. ... Harrisburg, IL
Lambert, W. Clair, III ... Miami, FL
Lambert, Wayne W., Jr. ... Bainbridge, GA
Lambert & Weiss ... New York, NY
Lambert, William D., III ... St. Louis, MO
Lambert, William E. ... Wilmington, DE
Lambert, William F. ... Lewiston, ID
Lambert, William H. ... Lafayette, LA
Lambert, William M. ... Marco Island, FL
Lambert, William R. ... Lakewood, CO
Lambert, William W. ... Dayton, OH
Lambert, Yolonda G. ... Wheeling, WV
Lamberta, Joseph B. ... Massapequa, NY
Lamberta and Laurencelle ... Massapequa, NY
Lambert-Dean, Deborah
Treasury Department, Internal Revenue Service, GV
Lamberth, Bonapfel, Cifelli & Stokes, P.A.
Atlanta, GA
Lamberth, J. Michael ... Atlanta, GA
Lamberth, James A. ... Atlanta, GA
Lamberth, Jeff C. ... Houston, TX
Lamberth, Kelley Pirnie ... Montgomery, AL
Lamberth, R. Edwin ... Montgomery, AL
Lamberth, Rebecca McLemore
Atlanta, GA
Lamberth, Royce C. ...
United States District Court For The District Of Columbia, GV
Lamberti, Gerald F. ... Kansas City, MO
Lamberti, John M. ... North Billerica, MA
Lamberti, Matthew A. ... Washington, DC
Lamberti, Michael ... Inverness, FL
Lamberti, Michael T. ... Hicksville, NY
Lamberti, Nicholas J. ... Harrisburg, PA
Lamberti, Thomas M. ... New York, NY
Lamberto & Kreger ... San Jose, CA
Lamberto, Peter N. ... San Francisco, CA
San Jose, CA
Lamberton, Benjamin P. ... Washington, DC

Lampe, Ronald L. ..... Oshkosh, WI
Lampe, Ross ..... Sacramento, CA
Lampe, Thomas R. ..... Walnut Creek, CA
Lampear, Bernard ..... Southfield, MI
Lampel, Arthur H. ..... San Diego, CA
Lampel, Carey ..... Schaumburg, IL
Lampen, David A. .....
United States Court of Federal Claims, GV
Lampen, Richard J. ..... Miami, FL
Lampenfeld, Gary ..... Johnstown, PA
Lamper, Mark H. ..... Laconia, NH
Lamperski, Blaine A. ..... Pittsburgh, PA
Lampert, Alan G. ..... Chelmsford, MA
Lampert, Andrea A. ..... Portland, OR
Lampert, Andrew F. ..... Chicago, IL
Lampert, Brian J. ..... Breckenridge, CO
Englewood, CO
Lampert, Bruce A. ..... Broomfield, CO
Troy, MI
Lampert, Charles E. ..... Harbor Springs, MI
Lampert, Daniel ..... Fort Lauderdale, FL
Miami, FL
Lampert, Darren ..... New York, NY
Lampert, Donald E. ..... Cleveland, OH
Lampert, Donna N., & Associates
Washington, DC
Lampert, Elise Louise ..... Sherman Oaks, CA
Lampert, Elizabeth ..... Fort Lauderdale, FL
Lampert, Gary D. ..... Woodland Hills, CA
Lampert, Gregory S. ..... Pasadena, CA
Lampert, Irwin S. ..... New York, NY
Lampert, J. Marc ..... Alexandria, LA
Lampert, James B. ..... Boston, MA
Lampert, Jeffrey B. ..... Royal Palm Beach, FL
Lampert, Jeffrey M. ..... Harwood Heights, IL
Lampert, John F. ..... Fort Atkinson, WI
Lampert & Lampert ..... New York, NY
Lampert, Lauren D. ..... Alexandria, VA
Lampert, Loren M. ..... Alexandria, LA
Lampert, Michael A.
West Palm Beach, FL
Lampert, Michael A. ..... Princeton, NJ
New York, NY
Lampert, Michael A., P.A., Law Offices of
West Palm Beach, FL
Lampert, Mitchell L. ..... New York, NY
Lampert, Patricia G ..... West Palm Beach, FL
Lampert, Scott L. ..... Deerfield Beach, FL
Lampert, Steven A. ..... Chicago, IL
Lampert, Susan M. ..... Chicago, IL
Lampert, Todd H. ..... New Canaan, CT
Lampert, Todd H. ..... Stamford, CT
Lampert, Wayne A. ..... Oakland, CA
Lampert, Wayne M. ..... Fort Lauderdale, FL
Lampertius, James P.
Farmington Hills, MI
Lampf, Lipkind, Prupis, Petigrow & LaBue, A Professional Corporation
Morristown, NJ
Newark, NJ
West Orange, NJ
Lampf, Stephen E. ..... West Orange, NJ
Lamph, Max D. ..... Ogden, UT
Lamphere, Gordon W. ..... Bloomfield Hills, MI
Lamphere, James C. ..... Lincoln, NE
Lamphere, Michael O. ..... San Francisco, CA
Lamphere, Paul O. ..... Martinez, CA
Lamphere, Richard M.
Colorado Springs, CO
Lampi, Bill H. ..... Hayward, CA
Lampi, Gephart & Silverman
Mammoth Lakes, CA
Lampi, John B. ..... Harrisburg, PA
Lampi, William R. ..... Mammoth Lakes, CA
Lampiasi, Jeffrey M. ..... New York, NY
Lampin, Charles E., Jr. ..... St. Charles, MO
Lampinen, Timothy J. ..... Chicago, IL
Lamping, Kathryn S. ..... Dearborn, MI
Lamping, Leslie D. ..... Washington, IA
Lamping, William J., Jr.
Bloomfield Hills, MI
Lampke, Haskell A. ..... Hingham, MA
Lampke, James B. ..... Hingham, MA
Lampke, Matthew J. ..... Columbus, OH
Lampkin, Ben T. ..... Oklahoma City, OK
Lampkin, Bertina E. ..... Chicago, IL
Lampkin, David P. ..... Los Angeles, CA
Lampkin, David P. ..... Studio City, CA
Lampkin, James W., II ..... Mobile, AL
Lampkin, Margy J. ..... Oregon City, OR
Lampkin, Odella ..... Columbus, OH
Lampkin-Isabel, Robin ..... Dublin, OH
Lampl, David W. ..... Pittsburgh, PA
Lampl, Sanford M. ..... Greer, SC
Lampley, C. Joy ..... Atlanta, GA
Lampley, Danny R. ..... Tupelo, MS
Lampley, Dawn M. ..... Cincinnati, OH
Lampley, G. H., Law Firm, P.C.
San Angelo, TX
Lampley, G. H. ..... San Angelo, TX
Lampley, Judith A. ..... Washington, DC
Lampley, Nathaniel, Jr. ..... Cincinnati, OH
Lampley, Paula D. ..... Mason, OH
Lampman, Kathleen Marie Killingstad
Ridgway, PA
Lampón, Santiago F., & Associates
Guaynabo, PR
Lampone, Leah M. ..... Milwaukee, WI
Lampón-González, Santiago F.
Guaynabo, PR
Lamport, Allan H. ..... Framingham, MA
Lamport, Stanley W. ..... Los Angeles, CA
Lamprecht, Lynne W. ..... Fort Myers, FL
Lamprey, Wayne T. ..... San Francisco, CA
Lamprich, Julie E. ..... Tulsa, OK
Lampron, Shawn E. ..... Menlo Park, CA
Lamproplos, George W. ..... Greensburg, PA
Lampros & Deneka, P.C. ..... Roanoke, VA

Lampros, John N. ..... Roanoke, VA
Lampros, Lisa P. ..... San Jose, CA
Lampros, Nicholas L. ..... Roanoke, VA
Lampros, R. G. Wilmot ..... Portland, OR
Lamprou, Chrisoula ..... San Diego, CA
Lampson, Elizabeth E. ..... Portland, OR
Lampson, R. Wayne ..... Kansas City, KS
Lampton, Dudley F. ..... Hazlehurst, MS
Lampton, Dunn O. ..... Magnolia, MS
Lampton, Kenneth R., Jr. ..... Conifer, CO
Lampton Law Firm, The, P.C.
Conifer, CO
Lampton, Mark I. ..... Oxford, MS
Lamrouex, Floyd L. ..... San Antonio, TX
Lamsens, Catherine E. ..... Chicago, IL
Lamski, Dale F. ..... Hastings, NE
Lamson, Carole C. ..... New York, NY
Lamson, David C. ..... Salt Lake City, UT
Lamson, David H. ..... Rockland, MA
Lamson, Donald N. ..... Treasury Department,
Office of the Comptroller of the Currency,
GV
Lamson, Donald W. ..... Encinitas, CA
Lamson, Dugan & Murray
Council Bluffs, IA
Lincoln, NE
Omaha, NE
Lamson, Jeffrey E. ..... Des Moines, IA
Lamson, Larry D. ..... Prince Frederick, MD
Lamson, Michael A. ..... Houston, TX
Lamson, Norman H. ..... Charlottesville, VA
Lamson, Robert W. ..... Lafayette, CA
Lamson, Susan E. ..... Encinitas, CA
Lamson, William M., Jr. ..... Omaha, NE
Lamstein, Matthew C. ..... Melville, NY
Lamun, Mock, Featherly, Kuehling & Cunnyngham ..... Oklahoma City, OK
Lamunyon, Justin L. ..... Enid, OK
LaMura, Robert E. ..... Morganville, NJ
LaMure, Jamie A. ..... Twin Falls, ID
Lamutis, Donald F. ..... Rochester, NY
Lamvik, Nancy M. ..... Portland, OR
Lamy, Harold J. ..... New Orleans, LA
Lamy, Timothy K. ..... New Orleans, LA
Lamz, James ..... Slidell, LA
Lan, Donald P., Jr. ..... Dallas, TX
Lan, Dong ..... New York, NY
Lana, Anthony J. ..... Buffalo, NY
Lana, Christina M. ..... Buffalo, NY
Lana, Edgar J. ..... Orinda, CA
Lana, Edgar J., A Professional Corporation
Orinda, CA
Lanahan, Barbara Pattillo ..... Jacksonville, FL
Lanahan, Daniel J. ..... Los Angeles, CA
San Francisco, CA
Santa Rosa, CA
Lanahan, Fred P. ..... Phoenix, AZ
Lanahan, John O. ..... San Diego, CA
Lanahan, Joseph A. ..... Kansas City, MO
Lanahan, Lawrence S., Jr. ..... Bel Air, MD
Lanahan, Patrick M. ..... Columbus, OH
Lanahan & Reilley LLP ..... Los Angeles, CA
Sacramento, CA
San Francisco, CA
Santa Rosa, CA
Lanak, Francis J. ..... Santa Ana, CA
Lanak, Frank M. ..... Santa Ana, CA
Lanak & Hanna, P.C. ..... Santa Ana, CA
Lanam, John D. ..... Chico, CA
Paradise, CA
Lanam, Linda L. ..... Washington, DC
Lanam, Reneé F. ..... Menlo Park, CA
Lanam, William F. ..... San Mateo, CA
Lanan, Kathryn Bradfield ..... Galveston, TX
Texas City, TX
Lanane, Timothy S. ..... Anderson, IN
Lanao, Jairo Ernesto ..... Miami, FL
LaNasa, August J. ..... New Orleans, LA
LaNasa, Philip J. ..... New Orleans, LA
Lancaster, Alan D. ..... Jackson, MS
Winona, MS
Lancaster, Alex P. ..... Sarasota, FL
Lancaster, Anne E. ..... Berkeley, CA
Lancaster, Arthalu ..... Flushing, MI
Lancaster, Baxter & Lancaster
Tallulah, LA
Lancaster, Ben ..... Centreville, AL
Lancaster, Bland, Eisele and Herring
Hyattsville, MD
Upper Marlboro, MD
Lancaster, Brad A. ..... Edmonds, WA
Lancaster, C. Alan ..... Brentwood, TN
Lancaster, C. Calvert ..... Cheverly, MD
Lancaster, Carrie C. ..... Houston, TX
Lancaster, Charles L. ..... Grapevine, TX
Lancaster, Christopher J. ..... Moorhead, MN
Lancaster, Clifford R. ..... Alameda, CA
Lancaster, Colin M. ..... Minneapolis, MN
Lancaster, Daphne M. ..... Hattiesburg, MS
Lancaster, David P. ..... Bellevue, WA
Lancaster, Deborah D. ..... New York, NY
Lancaster, Deborah M. ..... Marco Island, FL
Inverness, IL
Lancaster, Debra O. ..... Gainesville, FL
Lancaster, Dennis W. ..... Evanston, WY
Lancaster, Dianne L. ..... Salem, OR
Lancaster, Donald L. ..... Boston, MA
Lancaster, Douglas ..... Overland Park, KS
Lancaster, E. Patrick ..... Memphis, TN
Lancaster, E. Preston, Jr. ..... Farmville, VA
Lancaster, Edgar H., Jr. ..... Tallulah, LA
Lancaster, Edward K. ..... Columbia, TN
Lancaster & Eure, P.A. ..... Sarasota, FL
Lancaster, Frank H. ..... Charlotte, NC
Lancaster, Gary L. ..... Pittsburgh, PA
Lancaster, Gary L. ..... Houston, TX
Lancaster, George H., Jr. ..... Columbus, OH

Lancaster, Gregory Wayne
Lawrenceville, GA
Lancaster, H. Martin
Department of the Army,
Office of the Secretary, GV
Lancaster, J. Justin ..... Lexington, MA
Lancaster, James R. ..... Dallas, TX
Lancaster, James R., Jr. ..... Lansing, MI
Lancaster, Janette Boyd ..... Austin, TX
Lancaster, Jas. D. ..... Gadsden, AL
Lancaster, Joan Ericksen ..... St. Paul, MN
Lancaster, John Joseph ..... Lakeland, FL
Lancaster, John L., III ..... Dallas, TX
Lancaster, John M. ..... Department of Justice,
Criminal Division, GV
Lancaster, John M. ..... Oak Grove, LA
Lancaster, Judith E. ..... Canton, OH
Lancaster, Kathryn McLeod ..... Gainesville, FL
Lancaster, Kenneth G. ..... Miami, FL
Lancaster, Kevin ..... San Francisco, CA
Lancaster, Kristina Geister ..... Omaha, NE
Lancaster, Lisette Ann ..... Sacramento, CA
Lancaster, Louise Bruce ..... Wilmington, DE
Lancaster, Marika ..... Department of Justice,
Tax Division, GV
Lancaster, Marjorie Ellen Herr ..... Houston, TX
Lancaster, Mark D. ..... Pittsburgh, PA
Lancaster, Mary Dale ..... West Redding, CT
Lancaster, Michael A. ..... Sterling, IL
Lancaster, Michael E. ..... Tallulah, LA
Lancaster, Michael J. ..... Santa Ana, CA
Lancaster, Miriam D. ..... Atlanta, GA
Lancaster, N. G. ..... Arlington, VA
Lancaster, Pamela S. ..... Austin, TX
Lancaster, Patricia Corey ..... Seminole, FL
Lancaster, Patricia M. ..... Rutland, VT
Lancaster, Patrick S. ..... Detroit, MI
Lancaster, Paul K. ..... Benton, AR
Lancaster, Peter M. ..... Minneapolis, MN
Lancaster, Phyllis Smith ..... Macon, GA
Lancaster, R. Paul ..... Midland, TX
Lancaster, Ralph I., Jr. ..... Portland, ME
Lancaster, Raymond L. ..... Charlotte, NC
Lancaster, Robert G. ..... St. Louis, MO
Lancaster, Robert J. ..... St. Petersburg, FL
Lancaster, Robert L. ..... Columbus, MS
Lancaster, Robert N., Jr. ..... Springfield, OH
Lancaster, Robin P.
Environmental Protection Agency,
Office of Enforcement and Compliance
Assurance, GV
Lancaster, Robt. S. ..... Sewanee, TN
Lancaster, Ronny B. .....
Office of Personnel Management, GV
Lancaster, Scott J., (P.A.) ..... Little Rock, AR
Lancaster, Sheree H. ..... Trenton, FL
Lancaster, Sheree H., P.A. ..... Trenton, FL
Lancaster, Stephen Nicholas ..... Denver, CO
Lancaster, Stephen O. ..... Daytona Beach, FL
Lancaster, Stephen R. ..... Little Rock, AR
Lancaster, Susan M. ..... Birmingham, MI
Lancaster, Todd W. ..... Madison, NE
Lancaster & Trotter ..... Charlotte, NC
Lancaster, Walter R. ..... Chicago, IL
Lancaster, William H. ..... Los Angeles, CA
Lancaster, William J. ..... Chicago, IL
Lancaster, William R. ..... Mobile, AL
Lancaster, William W., III
Great Neck, NY
Lance, Alan G. ..... Boise, ID
Lance, Alden S. ..... Savannah, MO
Lance, Andrew A. ..... New York, NY
Lance & Associates, P.C. ..... Conyers, GA
Lance, Bradley D ..... Eden Prairie, MN
Lance, Brent A. ..... St. Charles, MO
Lance, Brent Edward ..... Palm Desert, CA
Lance, Bruce J., Jr. ..... Ontario, CA
Lance, Charles E. ..... Cameron, TX
Lance, Cynthia A. ..... Chicago, IL
Lance, Donna L. ..... Wichita, KS
Lance, Forrest Jack ..... Conyers, GA
Lance, Frederick M. ..... Johnson City, TN
Lance, Gerald P. ..... Houston, TX
Lance, H. James ..... Ukiah, CA
Lance, Harold J. ..... Dunlap, TN
Lance, I. Glenn ..... Laguna Niguel, CA
Lance, James R. ..... San Diego, CA
Lance, James W. ..... Washington, DC
Lance, James W. ..... Clinton, NJ
Lance, Jean F. ..... Maple Grove, MN
Lance, John D. ..... Jamaica, NY
Lance, Lisa D. ..... Woodland, CA
Lance, Lisa Watson ..... Oklahoma City, OK
Lance, Miles A. ..... Dunedin, FL
Lance, Nicole ..... Palo Alto, CA
Lance, Wesley L. ..... Clinton, NJ
Lance, William C., (P.C.) ..... Boston, MA
Lancefield, Robert K. ..... Palo Alto, CA
Lancella, Roxanne H. ..... Miami, FL
Lancelle, Cora J. ..... San Rafael, CA
Lancelloti, Albert ..... East Orange, NJ
Lancellotta, Amy B.R. ..... Washington, DC
Lancellotta, Steven A. ..... Washington, DC
Lancellotti, Albert ..... Ringwood, NJ
Lancelot, John E. ..... Denver, CO
Lancelotta, Dominic A. ..... Baltimore, MD
Lancer, M. Jay ..... Sarasota, FL
Lancer, Phillip C. ..... Los Angeles, CA
Lancetti, Luisa L. ..... Washington, DC
Lanchantin, Kristine Amodeo ..... Albany, NY
Lanchester, Michelle ..... Washington, DC
Lanchner, Bertrand M. ..... New York, NY
West Nyack, NY
Lanci, Karen E. ..... Armonk, NY
Lancia, Maurizio D. ..... New York, NY
Lancia, Paul A. ..... Providence, RI
Lancia, Thomas M. ..... New York, NY
Lancianese, Frank W. ..... Canton, OH

Lancianese, Richard L. ..... Huntington, WV
Lanciano, Gaetano C. ..... Princeton, NJ
Lanciault, Bertrand R., III
Washington, DC
Lanciloti, Daniel F. ..... Chicago, IL
Lanciloti, Richard F. ..... Roselle, IL
Lanciloti, Richard M. ..... Roselle, IL
Lancione, Bernard G. ..... Westerville, OH
Lancione, David ..... Columbus, OH
Lima, OH
Lancione, Davis & Lloyd, L.P.A.
Bellaire, OH
Lancione, John A. ..... Cleveland, OH
Lancione, John G. ..... Cleveland, OH
Lancione & Lancione, PLL
Cleveland, OH
Lancione Law Offices ..... Columbus, OH
Lima, OH
Lancione, Richard L. ..... Bellaire, OH
Lancione, Robert M. ..... Columbus, OH
Lanciotti, David J. ..... Wheaton, IL
Lanckton, A. Van C. ..... Boston, MA
Lancman, Rory I. ..... New York, NY
Lancome, Claude G. ..... Lynnfield, MA
Lancour, Anne Marie J. ..... Washington, DC
Lancour, Robert F. ..... Feeding Hills, MA
Lancto, Michael R. ..... Denver, CO
Lanctot, Catherine J. ..... Wilmington, DE
Lanctot, David J. ..... Detroit, MI
Lanctot, Denis W. ..... Morrisville, PA
Lanctot, Lawrence R. ..... San Francisco, CA
Lanctot, Robert E. ..... San Francisco, CA
Lanctot, Stephen T. ..... San Francisco, CA
Lanctot, Thomas E. ..... Chicago, IL
Lancy, John S. ..... Phoenix, AZ
Lancy, Oliveann ..... Stuart, FL
Lancz, David E. ..... Miami, FL
Land, Aaron J. ..... Columbus, GA
Land, Alan E. ..... Palmdale, CA
Land, Alissa ..... Alexandria, VA
Land, Arthur W. ..... Okemos, MI
Land, Benjamin A. ..... Columbus, GA
Land, Brian R. ..... Washington, DC
Land, Bryon L. ..... Eugene, OR
Land, Charles E. ..... Norfolk, VA
Land, Clark, Carroll, Mendelson & Blair, P.C. ..... Alexandria, VA
Fairfax, VA
Land, Clay D. ..... Columbus, GA
Land, Cohen & Keon, LLP ..... Atlanta, GA
Land Conservation Legal Services
Bernard, ME
Land & Cramer ..... New Haven, CT
Land, David P. ..... New York, NY
Land, Dean P. ..... Portland, OR
Land, Douglas S. ..... Secaucus, NJ
Land, Evan L. ..... San Francisco, CA
Land, Frank R. ..... Island Park, NY
Land, Gregory E. ..... Cincinnati, OH
Land, H. Carter, III ..... Alexandria, VA
Land, Hans A. ..... Washington, DC
Land, Harlow H., Jr. ..... Mayo, FL
Land, Hazel M. ..... Brooksville, FL
Land, James E. ..... Worth, IL
Land, Janet E. ..... Memphis, TN
Land, Janet L. ..... Indianapolis, IN
Land, Jeffrey A. ..... Atoka, TN
Land, John C., III ..... Manning, SC
Land, John Calhoun, IV ..... Manning, SC
Land, John F. ..... La Jolla, CA
Land, John H. ..... Columbus, GA
Land, John W. (Jack) ..... Hattiesburg, MS
Land, Jolee ..... Tampa, FL
Land, Karen M. ..... San Francisco, CA
Land, Katherine T. ..... Boston, MA
Land, Korine L. ..... South St. Paul, MN
Land, Laurence K. ..... Norfolk, VA
Land & Lemle ..... Washington, DC
Land, Lucinda M. ..... Findlay, OH
Land, Mark Allen ..... Austin, TX
Land, Michael G. ..... Modesto, CA
Land, Murphey C. ..... Vincennes, IN
Land, Neil E. ..... Kennett Square, PA
Land, Parker & Reaves, P.A.
Manning, SC
Land, Paula ..... San Francisco, CA
Land, Penny A. ..... Chicago, IL
Land, Peter G. ..... Chicago, IL
Land, Richard J. ..... Providence, RI
Land, Richard S. ..... Danbury, CT
Land, Robert ..... Tuscaloosa, AL
Land, Robert ..... Philadelphia, PA
Land, Robert, P.C. ..... Philadelphia, PA
Land, S. Marc ..... Baltimore, MD
Land, Stephen A. ..... Atlanta, GA
Land, Stephen B. ..... New York, NY
Land, Stuart J. ..... Washington, DC
Land, Susan J. ..... Lutherville, MD
Land, Suzanne Prieur ..... Cincinnati, OH
Land, Thornton R. ..... Branchville, NJ
Land, Vicki E. ..... Los Angeles, CA
Land, Wilbur J. ..... New Haven, CT
Land, William Ceth ..... Manning, SC
Landa, Adam B. ..... New York, NY
Landa, Aida Margarita ..... Miami, FL
Landa, Albert G. ..... Ann Arbor, MI
Landa, Elissa Beth ..... New York, NY
Landa, Howard M. ..... New York, NY
Landa, Howard S. ..... Salt Lake City, UT
Landa, Jay, Law Offices of ..... Garden City, NY
Landa, John C., Jr. ..... Houston, TX
Landa, Leor S. ..... New York, NY
Landa, Marjorie B. ..... New York, NY
Landa, Mark ..... Des Moines, IA
Landa, Martin L. ..... Melville, NY
Landa, Michael M. ..... Washington, DC
Landa, Norman ..... Dallas, TX
Landa, Norman, P.C. ..... Dallas, TX

Landa, Samuel ... Pittsfield, MA
Landa, Scott J. ... Grand Forks, ND
Landa, Scott R. ... Waukegan, IL
Landa, Solomon ... Brooklyn, NY
Landaal, Steven R. ... Santa Monica, CA
Landan, Barbara A. ... Ventura, CA
Landau, Allan J. ... Boston, MA
Landau, Amy ... Albuquerque, NM
Landau & Anderson ... Baldwin, NY
Landau, Arnold S. ... Crystal Bay, NV
Landau, Barry S. ... Treasury Department, Internal Revenue Service, GV
Landau, Bernard D. ... Great Neck, NY
Landau, Beth A. ... Northbrook, IL
Landau, Brenda R. Department Of The Interior, Office of the Solicitor, GV
Landau, Bruce G. ... Beverly Hills, CA
Landau, Byron L. ... Chicago, IL
Landau, Caroline H. ... New York, NY
Landau, Cecil ... Boston, MA
Landau, Charles R. ... Sacramento, CA
Landau, Christopher ... Washington, DC
Landau, David ... Springfield, NJ
Landau, David E. ... Philadelphia, PA
Landau, David H. ... New York, NY
Landau, David M. ... Seattle, WA
Landau, David P. ... Washington, DC
Landau, Dean J. ... East Brunswick, NJ
Landau, Debbi ... New York, NY
Landau, Deborah J. ... New York, NY
Landau, Douglas K. W. ... Fairfax, VA
Landau, Edmund A., III ... Albany, GA
Landau, Edward J. ... New York, NY
Landau, Eric N. ... Los Angeles, CA
Landau, Eric R. ... Baldwin, NY
Landau, Eric R. ... New York, NY
Landau, Felix ... Bellevue, WA
Landau, Gail B. ... Rockville, MD
Landau, Gail B., P.C. ... Washington, DC
Bethesda, MD
Rockville, MD
Landau, Gary M. ... Bronx, NY
Landau, Gary R. ... Indianapolis, IN
Landau, Geoffrey I. ... Scarsdale, NY
Landau, Harriet I. ... Atlanta, GA
Landau, Harvey G. ... White Plains, NY
Landau, Helene M. ... New York, NY
Landau, Herbert H. ... Dallas, TX
Landau, Hortense R ... New York, NY
Landau, Hyman ... Scarsdale, NY
Landau, James K. ... New York, NY
Landau, Jeffrey M. ... Miami, FL
Landau, Jennifer Altfeld ... Los Angeles, CA
Landau, Jerome ... Teaneck, NJ
Landau, Jerry G. ... Phoenix, AZ
Landau, Jodi M. ... Boston, MA
Landau, Joel M. ... Lakeland, FL
Landau, Jonathan S. ... Palm Desert, CA
Landau, Jonathan S., A Professional Law Corporation ... Palm Desert, CA
Landau, Julie B. ... San Francisco, CA
Landau, Julie Ellen, Law Office of
Baltimore, MD
Landau, Karen L. ... Oakland, CA
Landau, Kenneth J. ... Mineola, NY
Landau, Kevin S. ... New York, NY
Landau & Landau ... Boston, MA
Landau and Landau, P.A. ... Rockville, MD
Landau, Laura R. ... Jersey City, NJ
New York, NY
Landau, Lauren S. ... New Rochelle, NY
Landau, Lee E. ... Rockville, MD
Landau, Leslie G. ... San Francisco, CA
Landau, Lewis R. ... Los Angeles, CA
Landau, Lynn Ackerman ... Memphis, TN
Landau, Maggi ... New York, NY
Landau, Malcolm E. ... New York, NY
Landau, Marina ... San Francisco, CA
Landau, Mark ... New York, NY
Landau, Mark G. ... Farmington Hills, MI
Landau, Mark S. ... New York, NY
Landau, Melvin M. ... Chicago, IL
Landau, Norman J. ... Alexandria, VA
Landau & O'Connor ... Worcester, MA
Landau Omahana Tucker Progar & Siebenhaar, L.L.C. ... Chicago, IL
Farmington Hills, MI
Orange, CA
Landau Omahana & Tyra, P.C.
Indianapolis, IN
Landau, Paul H. ... Los Angeles, CA
Landau, Paul K. ... New York, NY
Landau, Pearl Sandra ... Irving, TX
Landau, Richard D. ... White Plains, NY
Landau, Richard J. ... Ann Arbor, MI
Landau, Robert J. ... Plymouth Meeting, PA
Landau, Robert M. ... Washington, DC
Landau, Robert P. ... Providence, RI
Landau, Robert T. ... San Francisco, CA
Landau, Robert W. ... Anchorage, AK
Landau, Rodger M. ... Los Angeles, CA
Landau, Ronald W. ... Woodbury, NY
Landau, Rue ... Philadelphia, PA
Landau, Ruth L. ... Overland Park, KS
Landau, Ruth S. ... Dallas, TX
Landau, Samuel ... Costa Mesa, CA
Landau, Samuel J. ... New York, NY
Landau, Sandra S. ... Worcester, MA
Landau, Scott ... New York, NY
Landau, Shawn P. ... New York, NY
Landau, Sherman ... Dunwoody, GA
Landau, Sidney S. ... Hartford, CT
Landau, Stephen M. ... Troy, MI
Landau, Stephen R., (A Prof. Law Corp.)
Los Angeles, CA
Landau, Steven J. ... Vernon Hills, IL
Landau, Steven M. ... Lake Success, NY
Landau, Sybil H. ... New York, NY
Landau, Todd M. ... New York, NY
Landau, Vincent R. Department of Housing and Urban Development, Office of General Counsel, GV
Landau, W. Loeber ... New York, NY
Landau, Warren S. ... Smithtown, NY
Landau, William ... Boston, MA
Landau, Yvette E. ... Las Vegas, NV
Landauer, Andrew T. ... Durham, NC
Landauer, Carl H. ... San Francisco, CA
Landauer, Craig L. ... Washington, DC
Landauer, Sally C. ... Portland, OR
Landauer, Tracy Green ... New York, NY
Landaw, Jared L. ... Wayne, NJ
Landay, Andrew ... San Diego, CA
Santa Monica, CA
Landay, Bruce M. ... Boston, MA
New York, NY
Landay, David M. ... Pittsburgh, PA
Landay, David S. ... New York, NY
Landay & Leblang ... Boston, MA
New York, NY
Landay, William S. ... Cambridge, MA
Landback, Sally E.O. ... Wichita Falls, TX
Landbeck, John S., Jr. ... Aberdeen, MD
Landberg, Kevin William ... St. Paul, MN
Lande, Arnold ... Brooklyn, NY
Lande, Charles A. ... Chicago, IL
Lande, David ... Los Angeles, CA
Lande, David H. ... Edison, NJ
Lande, David S. ... New York, NY
Lande, David S., P.C. ... New York, NY
Lande, Gary E. ... Los Angeles, CA
Lande, Jack J. ... Palm Springs, CA
Lande, James A. ... San Francisco, CA
Lande, James R. ... Minneapolis, MN
Lande, Jonathon G. ... Austin, TX
Lande, Laura J. ... Morristown, NJ
Lande, Melissa P. ... Bend, OR
Lande, Michael J. ... Seattle, WA
Lande, Philip M. ... Renton, WA
Lande, Robert L. ... Davenport, IA
Muscatine, IA
Lande, Roger L. ... Davenport, IA
Muscatine, IA
Lande, Stephen C. ... Pittsburgh, PA
Lande, Steven A. ... Los Angeles, CA
Landeck, Bruce F. ... Overland Park, KS
Landeck, Katherine A. ... Chicago, IL
Landeck, Ronald J. ... Moscow, ID
Landeck, Westberg, Judge & Graham, P.A.
Moscow, ID
Landecker, David J. ... Santa Barbara, CA
Landeen, Jerry H. ... Seattle, WA
Landefeld, Anne M. ... Shaker Heights, OH
Landefeld, Charles W. ... Cleveland, OH
Landefeld, David L. ... Lancaster, OH
Landefeld, Stewart M. ... Seattle, WA
Landegger, Alfred J. ... Sherman Oaks, CA
Landegger, Alfred J., A Professional Corporation ... Sherman Oaks, CA
Landells, Michael B. ... Newark, NJ
Landels Ripley & Diamond, LLP
San Francisco, CA
Landen, Everett E. ... Cincinnati, OH
Landen, F. Gifford ... Cleveland, OH
Landen, J. Jeffrey ... Florence, KY
Cincinnati, OH
Landen, Leslie S. ... Middletown, OH
Landen, Michael T. ... Miami, FL
Landen, Paul B. ... Houston, TX
Landen, Pennington Parker ... Edgewood, KY
Landen, Robert K. ... Fresno, CA
Landen, Walter J. ... Montoursville, PA
Landen, Walter J., Jr. ... Denver, CO
Landenberger, Eugen K. ... Palos Hills, IL
Landenberger, James T. ... Chicago, IL
Landenberger, Keith U. ... El Segundo, CA
Lander, Al ... Clarion, PA
Lander, Barbara Brown ... Melville, NY
Lander & Berkowitz, P.C. ... St. Louis, MO
Lander, Daryl A. ... Washington, DC
Lander, Daryl J. ... Cameron Park, CA
Lander, David A. ... St. Louis, MO
Lander, Edward ... St. Louis, MO
Lander, Gary D. ... Chattanooga, TN
Lander, George ... New York, NY
Lander, Gregg ... Los Angeles, CA
Lander, Guy P. ... New York, NY
Lander, Jay J. ... Framingham, MA
Lander, John E. ... Babylon, NY
Lander, John P. ... Mason City, IA
Lander, Jonathan H. ... Philadelphia, PA
Lander, Kenneth M. ... St. Louis, MO
Lander & Lander, P.C. ... Boston, MA
Framingham, MA
Lander, Larry D. ... Tulsa, OK
Lander, Marcia L. ... Albuquerque, NM
Lander, Michael J. ... Washington C. H., OH
Lander, Michael L. ... Minneapolis, MN
Lander, Michelle H. ... Framingham, MA
Lander & Paul, Law Offices of
Cameron Park, CA
Lander, Robert M., II ... Wurtsboro, NY
Lander, Stephen N. ... Framingham, MA
Lander, Steven E. ... University Heights, OH
Lander, Steven M. ... Santa Rosa, CA
Lander, Todd M. ... Los Angeles, CA
Landergan, Walter L., III ... Brookline, MA
Landergan, Walter L., Jr. ... Boston, MA
Landerholm, Arthur S. ... Washington, DC
Landerholm, Dovy C. ... Vancouver, WA
Landerholm, Irwin C. ... Vancouver, WA
Landerholm, Memovich, Lansverk & Whitesides, P.S. ... Portland, OR
Longview, WA
Stevenson, WA
Vancouver, WA
Landerman, Alan J. ... Orlando, FL
Landeros, Jose G. ... Dana Point, CA
Landeros, Roberto R. ... Oakland, CA
Landeros, Vincent P. ... Pasadena, CA
Landers, Amy ... Menlo Park, CA
Landers & Associates ... Memphis, TN
Landers & Boggs, LLP ... Waycross, GA
Landers, Colette M. ... Rego Park, NY
Landers, Daniell S. ... Waycross, GA
Landers, Daniella D. ... Detroit, MI
Houston, TX
Landers, David Michael ... Washington, DC
Landers, David S. ... Tulsa, OK
Landers, Denise ... Washington, DC
Landers, Diann J. ... Grand Rapids, MI
Landers, Edwin F., Jr. ... Boston, MA
Landers, Gary ... Tyler, TX
Landers, James E., Jr. ... Winston-Salem, NC
Landers, Jeffrey S. ... Albuquerque, NM
Landers, Jerry A., Jr. ... Marietta, GA
Landers, John B. ... Hackensack, NJ
Landers, Jonathan M. ... San Francisco, CA
Landers, Joseph W., Jr. ... Tallahassee, FL
Landers, Kelly V., P.A.
West Palm Beach, FL
Landers, Kelly Vincent
West Palm Beach, FL
Landers, Lori A. ... Springfield, MA
Landers, Margaret M. ... Indianapolis, IN
Landers, Melvin H. ... Miami, OK
Landers, Michael R. ... El Dorado, AR
Landers, Michelle C. ... Charlotte, NC
Landers, Neal H. ... Atlanta, GA
Landers & Parsons ... Tallahassee, FL
Landers, Patrick B. ... Providence, RI
Landers, Renée M. ... Boston, MA
Landers, Ronald E. ... Ventura, CA
Landers, Roy Lee ... San Diego, CA
Landers, Sharon L. ... Pearl River, NY
Landers, Suzanne ... Memphis, TN
Landers, William D. ... Rittman, OH
Landers, William F. ... Indianapolis, IN
Landers, William Joseph, II ... Memphis, TN
Landeryou, Christina A. ... Durango, CO
Landes, Angela Hochmeister
Harrisonburg, VA
Landes, Annette P. ... Nazareth, PA
Landes, Crystal L. ... Dallas, TX
Landes, Daniel A. ... White Plains, NY
Landes, David J. ... New York, NY
Landes, Donald H. ... Coos Bay, OR
Landes, Dwight R. ... Denver, CO
Landes, Irwin J. ... New York, NY
Landes, Jeffrey M. ... New York, NY
Landes, John ... Maspeth, NY
Landes, Mark ... Columbus, OH
Landes, Michael S. ... New York, NY
Landes, Rebecca ... Sacramento, CA
Landes, Rebecca M. ... Philadelphia, PA
Landes, Richard J. ... New York, NY
Landes, Richard L. ... Long Beach, CA
Landes, Robert G. ... Briarcliff Manor, NY
Landes, Roger W. ... El Dorado, AR
Landes, Scott S. ... Huntingdon Valley, PA
Landes, Stanley J. ... Los Angeles, CA
Landes, Stephen J. ... Chicago, IL
Landes, Steven R. ... Walnut Creek, CA
Landes, Wendy R. ... Pacific Palisades, CA
Landes, William L., III ... Goshen, KY
Landesberg, Janet Rubin ... Falls Church, VA
Landesberg, Lee J. ... Bethesda, MD
Landesberg, Martha K.
Federal Trade Commission, Bureau of Consumer Protection, GV
Landesman, Burton M. ... New York, NY
Landesman, Charles H. ... Kearny, NJ
Landesman, Jill A. ... New York, NY
Landesman, Jonathan ... Harrisburg, PA
Landesman, Judith L. ... Chicago, IL
Landesman, Laura ... Los Angeles, CA
Landesman, Marcia L. ... New York, NY
Landesman, Robert ... Evanston, IL
Landesman, Wayne R. ... New York, NY
Landess, Elizabeth Gong ... San Jose, CA
Landess, Fred S. ... Charlottesville, VA
Landess, Jason G., (Chartered)
Las Vegas, NV
Landess, Robert C. ... Des Moines, IA
Landever, Arthur R. ... Shaker Heights, OH
Landever, Carolyn M. ... Chapel Hill, NC
Landever, David ... Cleveland, OH
Landew, Lori T. ... New York, NY
Landey & Associates ... Atlanta, GA
Landey, Benjamin ... Atlanta, GA
Landey, Lisa Lynne ... San Rafael, CA
Landfair, Stanley W. ... San Francisco, CA
Landfield, Richard ... Washington, DC
Landfield, Stephen D. ... Morris Plains, NJ
Landgraf, Bruce J. ... Milwaukee, WI
Landgraf, Christina M. ... Chicago, IL
Landgraf, David C. ... Philadelphia, PA
Landgraf, H. F. ... San Diego, CA
Landgraf, James H. ... Mount Laurel, NJ
Landgraf, Laurie K. ... St. Louis, MO
Landgraf, Robert L., Jr. ... Niles, MI
Landgraf, William R. ... Niles, MI
Landgraff, Chris D. ... Chicago, IL
Landgraff, Donald N. ... Charlotte, NC
Landgraff, Frank A. ... Atlanta, GA
Landgraff, Lawrence F.
Pension Benefit Guaranty Corporation, Office of the General Counsel, GV
Landgrebe, Francis C. ... Woodbury, NJ
Landgren, James F. ... Arlington Heights, IL
Landgren & Sabin ... Arlington Heights, IL
Landheer, Robert F. ... Santa Barbara, CA
Landherr, Curtis C. ... Kansas City, MO
Landherr, Gretchen Elizabeth
Kansas City, MO
Landi, Albert J. ... Stow, OH
Landi, August J., Jr. ... Red Bank, NJ
Landi, Dianne S. ... New York, NY
Landi, Joseph D. ... New York, NY
Landicino, Carl J. ... Brooklyn, NY
Landin, D. Craig ... Sugar Land, TX
Landin, David Craig ... Richmond, VA
Landin, Dennis J. ... Los Angeles, CA
Landin, Thomas M. ... Valley Forge, PA
Landini, Louis F. ... San Francisco, CA
Landis, Adam G. ... Wilmington, DE
Landis, Angela H. ... Harrisonburg, VA
Landis, Anne L. ... Seattle, WA
Landis, Arnold H. ... Chicago, IL
Landis, August B. ... Des Moines, IA
Landis & Bailey ... Portland, OR
Landis, Betty E. ... Indianapolis, IN
Landis, Black & Schorpp ... Carlisle, PA
Landis, Carl David ... Jonesboro, AR
Landis, Christopher A. ... Santa Cruz, CA
Landis, Cullen H. ... Houston, TX
Landis, Daniel A. ... Marietta, GA
Landis, Daniel M. ... Boca Raton, FL
Landis, David C. ... Portland, OR
Landis, David H. ... Hamilton, OH
Landis, David M. ... Orlando, FL
Landis, Deborah E. ... New York, NY
Landis, Deborah M. Wotring
Houston, TX
Landis, Donald E., Jr. ... Santa Ana, CA
Landis, Donald M. ... New York, NY
Landis, Edwin C., Jr. ... Newark, NJ
Landis, Elizabeth H. ... Gladwyne, PA
Landis, Elizabeth S. ... New York, NY
Landis, Frank E., Jr. ... Lincoln, NE
Landis, Graham, French, Husfeld, Sherman & Ford, P.A. ... Daytona Beach, FL
DeLand, FL
Deltona, FL
Landis, Gregory P. ... Redmond, WA
Landis, Herbert J. ... Spokane, WA
Landis, J. Peter ... Reading, PA
Landis, Jack Alan ... Moncks Corner, SC
Landis, Jahn R. ... Chalfont, PA
Landis, James H. ... Prescott, AZ
Landis, James M. ... Tampa, FL
Landis, James P. ... Palo Alto, CA
Landis, Jeffrey K. ... Souderton, PA
Landis, Jeffry L. ... Southfield, MI
Landis, John C. ... Bellflower, CA
Landis, John E. ... Lansdale, PA
Landis, John M. ... New Orleans, LA
Landis, John R. ... Chicago, IL
Landis, Joseph ... Belmont, MA
Landis, Joseph ... Boston, MA
Landis, Judith ... San Francisco, CA
Landis, Kathleen M. ... Dallas, GA
Landis, Keehn ... Harbor Springs, MI
Landis, Kenneth R., Jr. ... Chicago, IL
Landis, Kenneth W. ... Haddon Township, NJ
Landis, Kerns & Associates ... Lansdale, PA
Landis, Kipp A. ... Los Angeles, CA
Landis, Laurence R. ... Braddock, PA
Landis, Linda Turner ... Manchester, NH
Landis & Louden, P.C. ... Moncks Corner, SC
Landis, Lynn I. ... Los Angeles, CA
Landis, Marc A. ... New Brunswick, NJ
New York, NY
Landis, Marc Andrew, P.L.L.C.
New Brunswick, NJ
New York, NY
Landis, Marcy H. ... Philadelphia, PA
Landis, Mark L. ... New York, NY
Landis, Martin S. ... Basking Ridge, NJ
Landis, Mary Catherine ... Wilmington, DE
Landis, Mary Jennifer ... Baltimore, MD
Landis, Michael H. ... Trevose, PA
Landis, Peter J. ... Portland, ME
Landis, Raymond L. ... Troy, OH
West Milton, OH
Landis, Richard F., II ... Kinston, NC
Landis, Richard M. ... Silver Spring, MD
Landis, Richard M. ... Cincinnati, OH
Landis, Robert K., III ... New York, NY
Landis, Robert M. ... Philadelphia, PA
Landis, Ryan S. ... Irvine, CA
Landis, Scott F. ... Lancaster, PA
Landis & Setzler, P.C. ... West Chester, PA
Landis, Steven S. ... New York, NY
Landis, Susan Sheppard ... New York, NY
Landis, Thomas A. ... Lansdale, PA
Landis, Todd E. ... Dallas, TX
Landis, Valerie Ann ... Des Moines, IA
Landis, Vern K. ... Warsaw, IN
Landis, Verna ... Carmel Valley, CA
Landis, W. Robert, II ... West Chester, PA
Landis, William ... Los Angeles, CA
Landis, William B. ... New York, NY
Landisburg, Rozalyn ... Hollywood, FL
Landisburg, Rozalyn, P.A., Law Offices of
Hollywood, FL
Landish, Joshua M. ... Las Vegas, NV
Landish, Joshua M., Ltd. ... Las Vegas, NV
Landman, Alan H. ... Melbourne, FL
Landman, Alan H., P.A. ... Melbourne, FL
Landman & Beatty ... Indianapolis, IN
Landman, Catherine R. ... Dallas, TX
Landman Corsi Ballaine & Ford
Newark, NJ
Landman Corsi Ballaine & Ford P.C.
New York, NY
Landman, Daniel S. ... Farmington Hills, MI

Landman, Edith A. ... Grand Rapids, MI
Landman, Eric C. ... New Brunswick, NJ
Landman, Georgina B. ... St. Peters, MO
Landman, Helene Glick ... Pittsburgh, PA
Landman, Jessica C. ... Washington, DC
Landman, Lynn K. ... Chicago, IL
Landman, Marcia ... New York, NY
Landman, Mark S. ... New York, NY
Landman, Pamela ... New York, NY
Landman, Richard E. Fort Lauderdale, FL
Landman, Richard M. ... New York, NY
Landman, Robert M. ... Kansas City, MO
Landman, Scott P. ... New York, NY
Landman, William A. ... Philadelphia, PA
Landmann, Walter O., Jr., (P.A.) Titusville, FL
Landmark, Nancy K. ... Paynesville, MN
Landmeier, Allen L. ... Geneva, IL
Landmeier, Lisa M. ... Washington, DC
Lando, Idelcy L. ... Bronx, NY
Lando, Maxine Cohen ... Miami, FL
Lando, Michael S. ... Pittsburgh, PA
Lando, Michelle B. ... Billerica, MA
Lando, Peter C. ... Boston, MA
Lando, Peter R. ... Dallas, TX
Lando, Rebecca Livingston Pittsburgh, PA
Lando, Robert E. ... Fairfield, CA
Lando, S. Dov ... New York, NY
Landoe, Brown, Planalp, Braaksma & Reida, P.C. ... Bozeman, MT
Landolfi, John L. ... Columbus, OH
Landolfo, Maria ... Washington, DC
Landolina, Carl ... Windsor Locks, CT
Landolina, Joseph A. ... Pittsburgh, PA
Landoll, Eric M. ... Nevada, MO
Landolt, Joseph M. ... St. Louis, MO
Landolt, Keith R. ... Albuquerque, NM
Landolt, Robert G. ... Columbia, MD
Landon, Abby Wool ... Lake Oswego, OR
Landon, Alex ... San Diego, CA
Landon, Alexander Louis ... San Diego, CA
Landon, Benjamin E. ... Williamsport, PA
Landon, Bradford E. ... Allentown, PA
Landon, Carolyn ... Birmingham, AL
Landon, Dion C. ... Wausau, WI
Landon, Doris C. ... Oxford, MS
Landon, Douglas E. ... Amsterdam, NY
Landon, Eleanor D. ... Plano, TX
Landon, Gerald James ... Austin, TX
Landon, J. Herbert ... Chicago, IL
Landon, James A. ... Tucson, AZ
Landon, James H. ... Atlanta, GA
Landon, Jas. A. ... Las Cruces, NM
Landon, John C. ... Houston, TX
Landon, Kim R. ... Houston, TX
Landon, Laurence B. ... Columbus, OH
Landon, Lilie Lundberg, (P.A.) Fort Lauderdale, FL
Miami, FL
Landon, Marilynn W. ... Dallas, TX
Landon, Raymond J. ... Lancaster, PA
Landon, Rick A. ... Indio, CA
Landon, Robert D. W., II ... Miami, FL
Naples, FL
Landon, Robert D.W., III ... Miami, FL
Landon, Robt. D. W. ... Vestal, NY
Landon, Roger D. ... Wilmington, DE
Landon, Scott ... Wagoner, OK
Landon, Stephen C. ... Sioux Falls, SD
Landon, Thomas W. ... Cincinnati, OH
Landon & Wickersty, Ltd. ... Chicago, IL
Landou, Jeffrey A. National Archives And Records Administration, General Counsel Staff, GV
Landow, Ian N. ... New York, NY
Landowe, Karen A. ... Pasadena, CA
Landow-Esser, Janine M. ... Chicago, IL
Landowne, Kate B. ... New York, NY
Landreau, Linda A. ... Los Alamitos, CA
Landreau, Sidney Gene (Buster) Phenix City, AL
Landreneau, F. Steve ... De Ridder, LA
Landreneau, Johanna R. Baton Rouge, LA
Landreneau, Kevin P. ... Baton Rouge, LA
Landres, Jeffrey T. ... Ventura, CA
Landres, Linda Grey ... Coronado, CA
Landres, Norman ... New York, NY
Landress, James V. ... Corpus Christi, TX
Landress, Sanford R. ... Portland, OR
Landress, Shlomo ... New York, NY
Landress, S. M. ... Dallas, GA
Landreth, Duane P. ... Orleans, MA
Landreth, Ivan K., Jr. ... Seattle, WA
Landreth, Joseph F. ... Salinas, CA
Landreth, Lloyd W. ... Tulsa, OK
Landreth, Michael C. ... Greensboro, NC
Landrey, David R. ... Philadelphia, PA
Landrey, Floyd A. ... Beaumont, TX
Landrey, Francis D. ... New York, NY
Landrey, Margaret M. ... Irving, TX
Landrieu, Madeleine M. New Orleans, LA
Landrieu, Martin E. ... New Orleans, LA
Landrieu, Maurice E. ... New Orleans, LA
Landrieu, Mitchell J. ... New Orleans, LA
Landrieu, Moon ... New Orleans, LA
Landrigan, Elizabeth J. ... Memphis, TN
Landrigan, Phillip C. ... White Plains, NY
Landrigan, Richard F. ... Somerville, MA
Landrith, Kevin S. ... San Diego, CA
Landrith, Kris L. ... Arlington, TX
Landrith & Kulesz, L.L.P. ... Arlington, TX
Landron, Michel J. ... New York, NY
Landrón-Guardiola, Eileen ... San Juan, PR

Landrum, Alisa Bearov ... Norfolk, VA
Landrum, Anne M. ... Atlanta, GA
Landrum, Billy Joe ... Laurel, MS
Landrum, Bruce D. ... Tallahassee, FL
Landrum, Craig N. ... Jackson, MS
Landrum, Dana Maloch ... Little Rock, AR
Landrum, David A. ... Salem, OR
Landrum, Douglas F. ... Irvine, CA
Landrum, Gayle L. ... Detroit, MI
Landrum, Hal B., Jr. ... San Antonio, TX
Landrum, Jane Ann ... Kansas City, MO
Landrum, John S. ... Houston, TX
Landrum, Julius C. ... Fort Worth, TX
Landrum, Kimbra L. ... Baton Rouge, LA
Landrum, L. Clark ... Tifton, GA
Landrum & Landrum ... Ellijay, GA
Jasper, GA
Landrum, Lee W. ... Carlsbad, CA
Landrum, Lori A. ... Cincinnati, OH
Landrum, Marquis C. ... Columbia, MO
Landrum, Michael L. ... Houston, TX
Landrum, Phil M., Jr. ... Jasper, GA
Landrum, Philip E., Jr. ... Portsmouth, VA
Landrum, Phillip M., III ... Jasper, GA
Landrum, R. Mason ... Waukesha, WI
Landrum, Rhonda Murrah ... Clarksdale, MS
Landrum, Richard C. ... Lakewood, CO
Landrum, Rick J. ... Cincinnati, OH
Landrum, Roger C. ... Jackson, MS
Landrum, Shawn E. ... Las Vegas, NV
Landrum & Shouse ... Lexington, KY
Louisville, KY
Landrum, Susan ... Jasper, GA
Landrum, Terrill V. ... Muskogee, OK
Landrum, Whitefield M. ... Evans, GA
Landrum, William W. ... Mount Pleasant, TX
Landry, Alfred Smith ... New Iberia, LA
Landry, Alfred Smith, Jr. ... Lafayette, LA
Landry, Alison Paige ... Richmond, VA
Landry, Alvin F. ... Port Allen, LA
Landry, A.M." Andy ", III ... Houston, TX
Landry, Amy L. ... New Orleans, LA
Landry, Andrew ... Bangor, ME
Landry, Andrew M. ... Brandon, MS
Landry, Arthur W. ... New Orleans, LA
Landry, Ashton J. ... Lafayette, LA
Landry, Barbara Burnes ... Amherst, NH
Landry, Barry J. ... Reserve, LA
Landry, Brenda M. ... Houston, TX
Landry, Brian D. ... Shreveport, LA
Landry, Brock R. ... Washington, DC
Landry, Carole D. ... Honolulu, HI
Landry, Catherine B. ... New Orleans, LA
Landry, Charles A. ... Baton Rouge, LA
Landry, Charles Benjamin New Iberia, LA
Landry, Charlotte Coleman New Orleans, LA
Landry, Cheryl A. ... Plano, TX
Landry, Cheryl Ann ... Foxboro, MA
Landry, Christopher M. ... Metairie, LA
New Orleans, LA
Landry, Craig J. ... Shreveport, LA
Landry, D. Scott ... Baton Rouge, LA
Landry, Dallari Lynne ... San Marcos, TX
Landry, Darrell C. ... Houston, TX
Landry, David B. ... Farmington Hills, MI
Landry, David L. ... Thibodaux, LA
Landry, David S. ... Kenai, AK
Landry, David S. ... New Orleans, LA
Landry, Diane ... Santa Cruz, CA
Landry, Diane K. ... La Grange, IL
Landry, Donald D. ... Erath, LA
Lafayette, LA
Landry, Edward A. ... Los Angeles, CA
Landry, Edward J. ... Houston, TX
Landry, Edward P. ... New Iberia, LA
Landry, Eva Marie ... Topeka, KS
Landry, Frances L., (Mrs.) Baton Rouge, LA
Landry, Francis J. ... Toledo, OH
Landry, Francis W. ... Albany, NY
Landry, Gregory W. ... West Des Moines, IA
Landry, Jacob S. ... New Iberia, LA
Landry, James D. ... Crowley, LA
Landry, James Lowell, Jr. ... Lafayette, LA
Landry, James Lowell, Jr., A Prof. Law Corp. Lafayette, LA
Landry, Jean M. ... San Bernardino, CA
Landry, Jody A. ... San Diego, CA
Landry, Joel D. ... Providence, RI
Landry, John A. ... Toledo, OH
Landry, John B., Jr. ... Monroe, LA
Landry, John M. ... Los Angeles, CA
Landry, John T., Jr. ... New York, NY
Landry, Joseph B. ... New Orleans, LA
Landry, Joseph Pierre, III ... Beaumont, TX
Landry, J. W., Jr. ... Crowley, LA
Landry, Keith G. ... Atlanta, GA
Landry, Keith M. ... New Orleans, LA
Landry, Kent J. ... Aiken, SC
Landry, Kim S. ... Baton Rouge, LA
Landry, Kirk L. ... Baton Rouge, LA
Landry and Landry ... Baton Rouge, LA
Landry & Landry ... Crowley, LA
Landry, Larry J., Jr. ... Dallas, TX
Landry, Laurel D. ... St. Augustine, FL
Landry & Lavelle, L.L.P. ... New Orleans, LA
Landry, Lawrence R. ... Atlanta, GA
Landry, Lawrence R. ... Decatur, GA
Landry & Ludewig, L.L.P. Albuquerque, NM
Landry, Marc A. ... Philadelphia, PA
Landry, Margaret M. ... New Orleans, LA
Landry, Mark C. ... Metairie, LA
Landry, Mark Cullerton ... Dallas, TX
Landry & Meilus, LLP ... Barre, MA
Landry, Michael D. ... New Orleans, LA

Landry, Michelle L. ... San Francisco, CA
Landry, Mickey P. ... Baton Rouge, LA
Landry, Myka Marie ... Kiowa, CO
Landry, Nan M. ... Lafayette, LA
Landry, Neville M. ... New Orleans, LA
Landry, Paul A. ... Lafayette, LA
Landry, Paul B., Jr. ... Port Allen, LA
Landry, Paul L. ... Minneapolis, MN
Landry, Paul T. ... Morgan City, LA
Landry, Percy J., Jr. ... Baton Rouge, LA
Landry, Peter A. ... Lafayette, LA
Landry, Philip J., III ... Troy, NY
Landry, Raymond B. ... Metairie, LA
Landry, Richard J. ... Philadelphia, PA
Landry, Robert B., III ... New Orleans, LA
Landry, Robert E. ... Lake Charles, LA
Landry, Robert J. ... Tampa, FL
Landry, Robert J., (P.C.) ... New Orleans, LA
Landry, Robt. W. ... Glendale, WI
Landry, Ronald J. ... La Place, LA
Landry, Scott D. ... Chesterfield, VA
Landry, Scott P. ... Denver, CO
Landry, Scott P., P.C., Law Office of Denver, CO
Landry & Shea ... Lafayette, LA
Landry, Sherry S. ... New Orleans, LA
Landry, Sidney P., III ... Lafayette, LA
Landry, Stephanie ... Albuquerque, NM
Landry, Steven Y. ... Baton Rouge, LA
Landry, Susan M. ... Barre, MA
Landry, Sylvia ... Metairie, LA
Landry, Terry R. ... Dallas, TX
Landry, Thomas A. ... Sudbury, MA
Landry, Thomas E. ... Worcester, MA
Landry, Thomas G. F. ... Mobile, AL
Landry, Thomas K. ... Bronxville, NY
Landry, Thomas W., Jr. ... Dallas, TX
Landry, Virginia L. ... Irvine, CA
Landry, Virginia L., Inc. ... Irvine, CA
Landry & Watkins ... Lafayette, LA
New Iberia, LA
Landry, William N., Jr. ... Gretna, LA
Landry, William R. ... Providence, RI
Lands, Alan M. ... Pleasantville, NJ
Landsbaum, Scott ... Los Angeles, CA
Landsberg, Alan L. ... Hollywood, FL
Landsberg, Barry S. ... Los Angeles, CA
Landsberg, Bill E. ... Colorado Springs, CO
Landsberg, Brian K. ... Sacramento, CA
Landsberg, Donnamarie Kansas City, MO
Landsberg, Dorothy S. ... Sacramento, CA
Landsberg, Erica M. ... Chicago, IL
Landsberg, Howard S. ... New Brunswick, NJ
Landsberg, Ian S. ... Santa Monica, CA
Landsberg, James D. ... Troy, MI
Landsberg, Jill W. ... Chicago, IL
Landsberg, Perry L. ... Los Angeles, CA
Landsberg, William ... Niceville, FL
Landsburg, Norman ... Huntingdon Valley, PA
Landsburg, William L. ... Blue Bell, PA
Landset, Ellis S. ... Amherst, MA
Greenfield, MA
Landsgaard, Olaf A. ... Rosamond, CA
Landskroener, Cristina Harding Chestertown, MD
Landskroener, Paul M. ... St. Paul, MN
Landskroner, Jack ... Cleveland, OH
Landskroner Law Firm, Ltd. The Cleveland, OH
Landskroner, Lawr. ... Cleveland, OH
Landsman, Arnold E. ... Chicago, IL
Landsman, Arnold E., Ltd. ... Chicago, IL
Landsman, David M. ... Bethesda, MD
Landsman, Gail R. ... Bethesda, MD
Landsman, J. Philip ... Hollywood, FL
Landsman, Jeffrey L. ... Madison, WI
Landsman, Jonathan M. ... New York, NY
Landsman, Kim J. ... New York, NY
Landsman, Laurence M. ... Chicago, IL
Landsman, Lisa A. ... Washington, DC
Landsman, Lisa B. ... Trenton, NJ
Landsman, Lisa Cortney ... North Miami, FL
Landsman, M. Zeb ... New York, NY
Landsman, Mark E., (A P.L.C.) San Diego, CA
Landsman, Maury S. ... Minneapolis, MN
Landsman, Paul ... New York, NY
Landsman, Paul A. ... New York, NY
Landsman, R. Broh ... Seattle, WA
Landsman, Robert S. ... Bethesda, MD
Landsman, Ron M. ... Bethesda, MD
Landsman, Ron M., P.A. ... Washington, DC
Bethesda, MD
Landsman, Ronald S. ... Baltimore, MD
Landsman, Scott B. ... Eden Prairie, MN
Landsman, Sheldon I., (P.C.) Washington, DC
Landsman, Spencer J. ... Urbana, IL
Landsman, Stephan A. ... Chicago, IL
Landsman, Stephen A. ... Chicago, IL
Landsman, Stephen N. ... Naperville, IL
Landsman, Tracy Dibble ... Mercer Island, WA
Landsman, Warren P. ... Chicago, IL
Landsmark, Theodore C. ... Boston, MA
Landsness, Roland K. ... Atlantic, IA
Griswold, IA
Landsteiner, Karl C., (P.A.) Fort Myers, FL
Landstrom, Karl S. ... Arlington, VA
Landstrom, Mark R. ... Baldwin Park, CA
Landstrom, Ruth H. ... Monroe, NY
Landsverk, Wayne D. ... Portland, OR
Landt, Frederick E., III ... Belleview, FL
Ocala, FL
Landt and Landt ... Ocala, FL
Landt, Mary Catherine ... Ocala, FL
Landt, Robert E. ... Ocala, FL

Landt, Wiechens, LaPeer & Ayres Belleview, FL
Ocala, FL
Landuyt, Stephen T. ... San Diego, CA
Landwehr, Darryl T. ... New Orleans, LA
Landwehr, Dawn L. ... Bourbonnais, IL
Landwehr & Hof ... New Orleans, LA
Landwehr, John D. ... Jefferson City, MO
Landwehr, John F. ... Perrysburg, OH
Landwehr, John T. ... Toledo, OH
Landwehr, Merrill T. ... New Orleans, LA
Landwehr, Roderick E. ... Gunnison, CO
Landwehr, Roderick E., P.C. Gunnison, CO
Landwehr, Theodore C. ... Minneapolis, MN
Landwehr, Vicki E. ... St. Cloud, MN
Landwer, Michael ... Indianapolis, IN
Landwerlen, James B. ... Shelbyville, IN
Landwerlen, Thomas L. ... Indianapolis, IN
Landy, Brian ... Englewood, CO
Landy, Brian R. ... Rye, NY
Landy, Burton A. ... Miami, FL
Landy, Charles J. ... Washington, DC
Landy, Craig A. ... New York, NY
Landy, Daryl S. ... San Francisco, CA
Landy, Douglas ... New York, NY
Landy, Eli H. Overseas Private Investment Corporation, GV
Landy, Eric W. ... Morristown, NJ
Landy, Eugene W. ... Eatontown, NJ
Landy, Gene K. ... Boston, MA
Landy, Joni L. ... Pittsburgh, PA
Landy, Joseph Brian West Palm Beach, FL
Landy & Landy ... Eatontown, NJ
Landy & Landy ... Sayre, PA
Towanda, PA
Landy, Lawrence K. ... Newton, MA
Landy, Lisa A. ... Miami, FL
Landy, Meredith Nelson ... Palo Alto, CA
Landy, Morton ... Charlestown, MA
Landy, Nanci S. ... Fort Lauderdale, FL
Miami, FL
Landy, Norman ... Arlington, VA
Landy, R. Joseph ... Sayre, PA
Landy, Ralph L. Pension Benefit Guaranty Corporation, Office of the General Counsel, GV
Landy, Robert J. ... Sayre, PA
Landy, Robin S ... Minneapolis, MN
Landy, Roy H. ... Great Neck, NY
Landy, Samuel A. ... Eatontown, NJ
Landy & Seymour ... New York, NY
Landy, Steven ... New York, NY
Landy, Steven A. ... Miami, FL
Landy, Susan L. ... Lakeland, FL
Landy, Thomas ... Mount Clemens, MI
Landye, Thomas M. ... Portland, OR
Landzberg, Alan J. ... New York, NY
Lane, A. Thomas, Jr. ... Harrisonburg, VA
Lane, A. H. ... Lakeland, FL
Lane, Aitken & McCann, L.L.P. Washington, DC
Lane, Allen T. ... Pittsburgh, PA
Lane Altman & Owens LLP ... Boston, MA
Lane, Alton & Horst ... Columbus, OH
Lane, Alvin S. ... New York, NY
Lane, Andi ... Houston, TX
Lane, Andrew B. ... West Seneca, NY
Lane, Andrew F. ... Boston, MA
Lane, Ann E. ... Denver, CO
Lane, Ann M. ... Portland, OR
Lane, Anne M. ... New York, NY
Lane, Arline ... White Plains, NY
Lane, Arnold S. ... Bridgton, ME
Lane, Arthur A. ... Melville, NY
New York, NY
Lane, Arthur L. ... Fayetteville, NC
Lane & Associates, P.A. ... Orlando, FL
Lane, B. Patrick, Inc. ... San Clemente, CA
Lane, Barbara A. ... Ventura, CA
Lane, Barret W.S. ... Minneapolis, MN
Lane, Benjamin H., III ... Kansas City, MO
Lane & Bentley ... Keene, NH
Lane, Bill ... Fort Worth, TX
Lane, Blair C., Sr. ... Cherry Hill, NJ
Lane, Bonnie ... Studio City, CA
Lane, Bradley G. ... Chicago, IL
Lane, Brian J. Securities and Exchange Commission, Division of Corporation Finance, GV
Lane, Brigid A. ... Houston, TX
Lane, Bruce S. ... Washington, DC
Lane, Bryan D. ... Bellingham, WA
Lane, Byrl R. ... Phoenix, AZ
Lane, Byron R. ... San Pedro, CA
Lane, C. Page ... Coral Gables, FL
Lane, C. Wesley, II ... Oklahoma City, OK
Lane, Carl J. ... Encino, CA
Lane, Carlisle B. ... San Francisco, CA
Lane, Carol M. ... Washington, DC
Lane, Caswell P. ... Mount Sterling, KY
Lane, Charles A. ... San Francisco, CA
Lane, Charles A. ... Portland, ME
Lane, Charles C. ... Tampa, FL
Lane, Charles H. ... Clinton Township, MI
Lane, Charles R." Chuck " New Orleans, LA
Lane, Charles T. ... Rocky Mount, NC
Lane, Charles W., III ... New Orleans, LA
Lane, Charles W., IV ... Olympia, WA
Lane, Charlotte R. ... Charleston, WV
Lane, Christopher ... Denver, CO
Lane, Christopher Decker North Wilkesboro, NC
Lane, Christopher E. ... Dallas, TX
Lane, Clair W., (Ltd.) ... Tempe, AZ

Lanford, Charles M. .... Jackson, MS
Lanford, David B. .... Fort Worth, TX
Lanford, Holly B. .... Atlanta, GA
Lanford, J. Scott .... Melbourne, FL
Lanford, J. Scott, P.A. .... Melbourne, FL
Lanford, Jarrett B. .... Anderson, SC
Lanford, Kathryn S., Law Office of
Fort Worth, TX
Lanford, Norman E. .... Wimberley, TX
Lanford, Rhonda L. .... Madison, WI
Lanford, Smith and Kapiloff .... Macon, GA
Lanfranco, Jennifer L. .... Portland, OR
Lanfredi, Muriel Ainsworth .... Tiverton, RI
Lanfrit, Liscinski & Rosenwasser, P.C.
Somerset, NJ
Lanfrit, Peter U. .... Somerset, NJ
Lang, Ainsley H. .... Little Rock, AR
Lang, Allan E. .... Dallas, TX
Lang, Amy Sargeant .... Stamford, CT
Lang, Andrea J. .... Los Angeles, CA
Lang, Andrea M. .... Fort Myers, FL
Lang, Andrew L. .... Cincinnati, OH
Lang, Angela R. .... Indianapolis, IN
Lang, Anne-Marie Raffa .... Decatur, GA
Lang, Annette M. .... Department of Justice, Environment and Natural Resources Division, GV
Lang, Anthony K. .... Department of Justice, Federal Bureau of Investigation, GV
Lang, Arthur P. .... Columbia, MO
Lang & Baker, P.L.C. .... Phoenix, AZ
Scottsdale, AZ
Lang, Barbara T. .... New Brunswick, NJ
Lang, Barry D. .... Boston, MA
Providence, RI
Lang, Broughton K. .... Miami, FL
Lang, Carl C. .... St. Louis, MO
Lang, Catherine B. .... Glendale, CA
Lang, Chad K. .... Miami, FL
Lang, Charles Victor .... Moreland Hills, OH
Lang, Christopher J. .... St. Louis, MO
Lang, Conrad H., Jr. .... Troy, NY
Lang, Cornelius J. .... Buffalo, NY
Lang, Craig N. .... Palo Alto, CA
Lang, D. Andrew .... New Orleans, LA
Lang, Dan H. .... Palo Alto, CA
Lang, Daniel Patrick .... Parma, OH
Lang, Daniel R. .... Anahuac, TX
Lang, Danny R. .... Roseburg, OR
Lang, Darin J. .... Lincoln, NE
Lang, David H. .... Media, PA
Lang, Donald W. .... Sylacauga, AL
Lang, Donna K. .... Willoughby Hills, OH
Lang, Douglas B. .... Westmont, NJ
Dallas, TX
Lang, Douglas S. .... Dallas, TX
Lang, Dudley M. .... Los Angeles, CA
Lang, E. Brian .... Pensacola, FL
Lang, E. Christopher .... Denver, CO
Lang, E. Thomas .... Waukegan, IL
Lang, Eaton A., Jr. .... Gulfport, MS
Lang, Edmund J. .... Albuquerque, NM
Lang, Edward G. .... Middlefield, CT
Lang, Ellen F. .... Winnetka, IL
Lang, Ellen M. .... Houston, TX
Lang, Eric Charles .... Atlanta, GA
Lang, Eugene A., Jr. .... Denver, CO
Lang, Frank H. .... Fresno, CA
Lang, Frank W. .... Albany, NY
Lang, Gabriella I. .... Portland, OR
Lang, Gary M. .... Pittsburgh, PA
Lang, George E. .... Munfordville, KY
Lang, Glenn F. .... Tallahassee, FL
Lang, Gordon, Jr. .... Chicago, IL
Lang, Gordon L. .... Washington, DC
Lang, Greer S. .... Lawrence, KS
Lang, Gregory F. .... Stamford, CT
Lang, Hans J. .... Tenafly, NJ
Lang, Hope Susan .... Southampton, PA
Lang, Howard A., Jr. .... Houston, TX
Lang, Howard M. .... Libertyville, IL
Lang, Huey Parker, II .... Biloxi, MS
Lang, I. Ward .... Decatur, GA
Lang, Isa, (Mrs.) .... Philadelphia, PA
Lang & Ishee, PLLC .... Pascagoula, MS
Lang, J. Elmo .... Pascagoula, MS
Lang, James A. .... Jeffersonville, IN
Lang, James C. .... Tulsa, OK
Lang, James D. .... Portland, OR
Lang, James E. .... Omaha, NE
Lang, James F. .... Gainesville, FL
Lang, James F. .... Cleveland, OH
Lang, James P. .... Fairfield, CA
Lang, James & Wheeler, Inc. A Professional Corporation .... Tulsa, OK
Lang, Jane .... Washington, DC
Lang, Jay A. .... New York, NY
Lang, Jeffrey A. .... New London, CT
Lang, Jeffrey I. .... New York, NY
Lang, Jeffrey I. .... New York, NY
Lang, Jeffrey M. .... Washington, DC
Lang, Jeffrey R. .... Kansas City, MO
St. Louis, MO
Lang, Jeffrey S. .... Cranbury, NJ
Lang, Joe Allen .... Wichita, KS
Lang, John A. .... Rice Lake, WI
Lang, John C. .... Sun City, AZ
Lang, John D. .... Woodland Hills, CA
Lang, John E. .... Wamego, KS
Lang, John F. .... Atlanta, GA
Lang, John F. .... New York, NY
Lang, John F. .... New York, NY
Lang, John J. .... Lynnfield, MA
Lang, John M. .... Atlanta, GA
Lang, John W. .... Minneapolis, MN
Lang, Jon J. .... Kansas City, MO
Lang, Jonathan .... New York, NY
Lang, Jos. A. .... Redford, MI

Lang, Joseph H. .... St. Petersburg, FL
Lang, Joseph Hagedorn, Jr
St. Petersburg, FL
Lang, Joseph R. .... Trenton, NJ
Lang, Joseph W. .... Chicago, IL
Lang, Joseph W., Jr. .... Washington, DC
Lang, Judy A. .... Bronx, NY
Lang, Jules .... Norwalk, CT
Lang, Karen S. .... Woodbridge, VA
Lang, Kathleen A. .... Detroit, MI
Lang, Kathleen R. .... Racine, WI
Lang, Kay Templeton .... Nashville, TN
Lang, Kenneth H. .... Moreland Hills, OH
Lang, Kenneth R. .... Wichita, KS
Lang, Kent A. .... Scottsdale, AZ
Lang, Kevin M. .... Albany, NY
Lang, Kimberly A. .... Millersburg, OH
Lang & Kustoff, L.L.P. .... San Antonio, TX
Lang, Laurie G. .... Dallas, TX
Lang, Leighton W. .... Atlanta, GA
Lang, Leslie Jeddis .... Woodbridge, NJ
Lang, Lila V. .... Marblehead, MA
Lang, Lindsey B. .... Washington, DC
Lang, Lisa .... Flint, MI
Lang, Lisa L. .... Philadelphia, PA
Lang, Louis H. .... Columbia, SC
Lang, Louis I. .... Chicago, IL
Lang, Marcus G. .... Seattle, WA
Lang, Marie Duesing .... Alexandria, VA
Lang, Mark .... Orlando, FL
Lang, Mark J. .... Astoria, OR
Lang, Marsha M. .... Sacramento, CA
Lang, Mary Sue .... East Liverpool, OH
Lang, Melissa .... Philadelphia, PA
Lang, Michael .... New York, NY
Lang, Michael B. .... Portland, ME
Lang, Michael D. .... Yellow Springs, OH
Lang, Michael E. .... Wexford, PA
Lang, Michael J. .... Woodland Hills, CA
Lang, Michael J. .... Seattle, WA
Lang, Michael L. .... Dayton, OH
Lang, Michael O. .... Huntington Woods, MI
Lang & Morgera, L.L.P. .... Boston, MA
Providence, RI
Lang, Neil S. .... Washington, DC
Lang, Nicholas F. .... St. Petersburg, FL
Lang, Nicholas F., P.A. .... St. Petersburg, FL
Lang, Niles .... New York, NY
Lang & O'Neal .... Dayton, OH
Lang, Pamela A. .... Seattle, WA
Lang, Paul A. .... Cleveland, OH
Lang, Paul A. .... Uniontown, OH
Lang, Paul B. .... Philadelphia, PA
Lang, Paul R. .... Washington, DC
Lang, Pauly, Gregerson & Rosow, Ltd.
Eden Prairie, MN
Minneapolis, MN
St. Paul, MN
Lang, R. Michael .... Tulsa, OK
Lang, Richard A. .... Chicago, IL
Lang, Richard A., Jr. .... Burlington, VT
Lang, Richard David .... Chattanooga, TN
Lang, Richard J. .... Chicago, IL
Lang, Richard L. .... Cadillac, MI
Lang, Richard L. .... Portland, OR
Lang, Richard V. .... Syracuse, NY
Lang, Richard W. .... Sacramento, CA
Lang, Richert & Patch, A Professional Corporation .... Fresno, CA
Madera, CA
Merced, CA
Visalia, CA
Lang, Robbie D. .... Mount Clemens, MI
Lang, Robert A. .... Winston-Salem, NC
Lang, Robert B. .... Culver City, CA
Lang, Robert D. .... New York, NY
Lang, Robert H. .... Chicago, IL
Lang, Robert I. .... Minneapolis, MN
Lang, Robert P. .... Atlantic City, NJ
Lang, Robert Todd, (P.C.) .... New York, NY
Lang, Robert W. .... Clearwater, FL
Lang, Robert W. .... New York, NY
Lang, Roberta L. .... Roselle, IL
Lang, Rodney P. .... Laramie, WY
Lang, Ronald A. .... Dearborn, MI
Lang, Scott H. .... Chicago, IL
Lang, Scott W. .... New Bedford, MA
Lang & Smith, Law Offices of
Levittown, PA
Lang, Stephen A. .... Livonia, MI
Lang, Stephen B. .... Providence, RI
Lang, Stephen, Neill Boldrick, Jr. & Benjamin F. Youngblood, III, Law Offices of .... San Antonio, TX
Lang, Stephen, P.C. .... San Antonio, TX
Lang, Stephen R. .... New York, NY
New York, NY
Lang, Steven A. .... Wayne, NJ
Lang, Steven C. .... Houston, TX
Lang, Straus, Xifaras & Bullard, P.A.
New Bedford, MA
Lang, Sue N. .... Levittown, PA
Lang, Susan Barsh .... Atlantic City, NJ
Pleasantville, NJ
Lang, Susan G. .... New Orleans, LA
Lang, Sylvan S., Jr. .... San Antonio, TX
Lang, Teal Carroll .... Dallas, TX
Lang, Terry O. .... Detroit, MI
Lang, Thomas A. .... Santa Maria, CA
Lang, Thomas A. .... Harrisburg, PA
Lang, Thomas E. .... Houston, TX
Lang, Thomas F. .... Orlando, FL
Lang, Thomas J. .... Phoenix, AZ
Lang, Thomas J. .... Washington, DC
Lang, Thomas J. .... Cleveland Heights, OH
Lang, Thomas M. .... St. Louis, MO
Lang, Thomas P. .... York, PA
Lang, Thomas P. .... Fort Worth, TX

Lang, Timothy Norman .... Seattle, WA
Lang, Vaughn D. .... Fayetteville, NY
Lang, Venita M. .... Tacoma, WA
Lang, Victoria .... San Francisco, CA
Lang, Virgil D. .... Dallas, TX
Lang, Walter F., Jr. .... Portsmouth, NH
Lang, Wesley M. .... Ogden, UT
Salt Lake City, UT
Lang, Wilbur S. .... Dayton, OH
Lang, William .... Waycross, GA
Lang, William A. .... Dallas, TX
Lang, William A. .... Olympia, WA
Lang, William E. .... Sidney, OH
Lang, William F. .... Albuquerque, NM
Lang, William F., III .... Newark, NJ
Lang, William F., IV .... Arlington, VA
Lang, William P. .... Avon Lake, OH
Lang, Yvonne E. .... Agoura Hills, CA
Langa, Brian D. .... Los Angeles, CA
Langa, Melissa .... Boston, MA
Langa, Ronald J. .... Orlando, FL
Langa, Ronald J., P.A. .... Orlando, FL
Langa, Sanford J. .... Wailuku, HI
Langabeer, Richard J. .... Bellingham, WA
Langabeer, Tull & Lee, P.S.
Bellingham, WA
Langacker, Ronald S. .... Danville, IL
Langan, Alf R.H.R. .... Green Bay, WI
Langan, Anthony J. .... De Witt, NY
Langan, Dempsey and Brodigan
Boston, MA
Langan, Elena B. .... Miami, FL
Langan, Elena B., P.A.
Fort Lauderdale, FL
Miami, FL
Langan, Eugenia .... Washington, DC
Langan, Gerard W., Jr. .... Pittston, PA
Scranton, PA
Langan, Gregory J. .... Brooklyn, NY
Langan, James Andrew .... Chicago, IL
Langan, James M., Jr. .... Boston, MA
Langan, Jane F. .... Lincoln, NE
Langan, Jeffrey .... Los Angeles, CA
Langan, John B. .... Boston, MA
Langan, John J. .... Staten Island, NY
Langan, John J., Jr. .... Teaneck, NJ
Langan, John P. .... Syracuse, NY
Langan, Joseph N. .... Mobile, AL
Langan, Kathleen H. .... Los Angeles, CA
Langan, Keith E. .... Novato, CA
Langan, Kenneth J. .... Los Angeles, CA
Langan and Langan .... De Witt, NY
Langan, Larry .... Bardstown, KY
Langan, Mark A. .... Burlington, VT
Langan, Michael D. .... Mobile, AL
Langan, Michael G. .... Washington, DC
Langan, Michael G. .... Newark, NJ
Langan, Michael J. .... Valhalla, NY
Langan, Richard F., Jr. .... New York, NY
Langan, Terence A. .... De Witt, NY
Langan, Thomas A. .... Phoenix, AZ
Langan, Thomas R. .... Peekskill, NY
Langan, Timothy J. .... Clinton, NJ
Langan, Virginia .... San Diego, CA
Langan-Feirson, Mary Kay
Department of Transportation, Office of the General Counsel, GV
Langbaum, Gerald I. .... Annapolis, MD
Langbein, Evan J. .... Miami, FL
Langbein, John H. .... New Haven, CT
Langbein & Langbein, P.A. .... Miami, FL
Langbein, Leslie W. .... Miami, FL
Langbein, Stanley I. .... Coral Gables, FL
Langbein, Stuart M. .... Washington, DC
Langberg, Barry B. .... Los Angeles, CA
Langberg, George .... New York, NY
Langberg, Harvey S., (P.A.) .... Sunrise, FL
Langberg, Henry .... Bingham Farms, MI
Langberg, Henry, P.C. .... Bingham Farms, MI
Langberg, Mitchell J. .... Los Angeles, CA
Langbord, Peter B. .... Pasadena, CA
Langbord, Roy .... New York, NY
Lang-Caditz, KiSong Kim .... Seattle, WA
Langdale, Mark .... Dallas, TX
Langdale, Vallotton, Linahan & Wetherington .... Valdosta, GA
Langdale, William P., III .... Valdosta, GA
Langdale, William P., Jr. .... Valdosta, GA
Langdon, Amy Rickner .... Charlotte, NC
Langdon, Betty J. .... Depoe Bay, OR
Langdon, Brent M. .... Texarkana, TX
Langdon, Carolyn L.G. .... Danville, PA
Langdon, Daniel J. .... Flint, MI
Langdon, Dean A. .... Lexington, KY
Langdon, Donald A. .... Council Bluffs, IA
Langdon, Douglas W. .... Louisville, KY
Langdon, Emison, Kuhlman & Evans, LLC
Lexington, MO
Langdon, Herschel G. .... Des Moines, IA
Langdon, J. Howard .... Muncy, PA
Langdon, Jack A. .... St. Augustine, FL
Langdon, Jack A., P.A. .... St. Augustine, FL
Langdon, James C., Jr. .... Washington, DC
Langdon, James K., II .... Minneapolis, MN
Langdon, James R. .... Charlotte, NC
Langdon, Jeanne L. .... Dover, DE
Langdon, John E. .... Fort Worth, TX
Langdon, John O. .... Dallas, TX
Langdon, Karen E. .... Tulsa, OK
Langdon, Kim Dorine .... Tucson, AZ
Langdon, Monroe N. .... Sutter Creek, CA
Langdon, Olive B. .... Birmingham, AL
Langdon, Peter C. .... Omaha, NE
Langdon, Richard G. .... Des Moines, IA
Langdon, Robert L. .... Lexington, MO
Langdon, Wesley M. .... St. Petersburg, FL
Lange & Anderson .... Bloomington, MN
Lange, Andrew G. .... San Francisco, CA

Lange, Anne Elouise .... Lincoln, NE
Lange, Anne M. .... Washington, DC
Lange, B. John, III .... Houston, TX
Lange, Barbara .... San Francisco, CA
Lange, Becky B. .... Santa Maria, CA
Lange & Behm .... Tiffin, OH
Lange, Bjorn R. .... Concord, NH
Lange, C. Dan .... San Francisco, CA
Lange, C. William .... Cuba, MO
Lange, Carol Z. .... Metairie, LA
Lange, Caroline Ruth .... Sacramento, CA
Lange, Catherine L. .... Cuba, MO
Lange, Charles J., Jr. .... Palisades Park, NJ
Lange & Cholack, P.C. .... Troy, MI
Lange, Christoph .... New York, NY
Lange, Christopher J. .... New York, NY
Lange, Craig W. .... Troy, MI
Lange, Cynthia Juarez .... Irvine, CA
Los Angeles, CA
Lange, D. Frank .... San Clemente, CA
Lange, David L. .... Prescott, AZ
Lange, David L. .... Raleigh, NC
Lange, David L. .... La Crosse, WI
Lange, David M. .... New York, NY
Lange, David R. .... Charlotte, NC
Lange, Denise S. .... Des Moines, IA
Lange, Desiree M. .... Baltimore, MD
Lange, Douglas A. .... Chicago, IL
Lange, Edward C. .... Fort Worth, TX
Lange, Edward N. .... Seattle, WA
Lange, Eric L. .... Perth Amboy, NJ
Lange, Francis J. .... Dubuque, IA
Lange, Fred A. .... Houston, TX
Lange, Fred M. .... Houston, TX
Lange, Gary H. .... St. Louis, MO
Lange, Gene C. .... Washington, DC
Lange, Gregory J. .... Brainerd, MN
Lange, Gregory L. .... Hazen, ND
Lange, G. W. .... Burlington, VT
Lange, Heather J. .... Philadelphia, PA
Lange, Howard W. .... Bay Shore, NY
Lange, James .... Pittsburgh, PA
Lange, James E. T. .... Silver Spring, MD
Lange, James King .... Savannah, GA
Lange, James King, P.C. .... Savannah, GA
Lange, Jennifer L. .... Salt Lake City, UT
Lange, Jill J. .... Cleveland, OH
Lange, John C. .... Southfield, MI
Lange, John D. .... Savannah, GA
Lange, John E., III .... Newport, KY
Lange, John E., IV .... Newport, KY
Lange, John P. .... Denver, CO
Lange, John R. .... Seattle, WA
Lange, Joseph J. .... Springfield, MA
Lange, Joseph J. M. .... Los Angeles, CA
Lange, Katherine Thompson
Charlotte, NC
Lange, Kathleen Hennessy .... Chicago, IL
Lange, Kathleen P. .... North Aurora, IL
Lange, Kathryn E. .... San Diego, CA
Lange, Keith A. .... Kenton, OH
Lange, Kenneth E. .... San Diego, CA
Lange, Kenneth H. .... White Plains, NY
Lange & Koncius, LLP .... Los Angeles, CA
Lange and Lange .... Cuba, MO
Lange and Lange, P.A. .... Fort Lauderdale, FL
Lange, Leif E. .... Sacramento, CA
Lange, Leonard .... Marina Del Rey, CA
Lange, Lisa K. .... Cape Girardeau, MO
Lange, Lori Ann .... Washington, DC
Lange, Maggie A. .... Boston, MA
Lange, Mark R. .... Indianapolis, IN
Lange, Mark S. .... Atlanta, GA
Lange, Marvin R. .... New York, NY
Lange, Meryl .... Harrisonville, MO
Lange, Michael B. .... Tucson, AZ
Lange, Michael B. .... Tiffin, OH
Lange, Michael G. .... Boston, MA
Lange, Miné B. .... Fort Lauderdale, FL
Lange & Minnott .... San Clemente, CA
Lange, Morton K. .... Cuba, MO
Lange, Noel C. .... Avondale, LA
Lange, Norbert H. .... Venice, FL
Lange & Park, P.A. .... Charlotte, NC
Lange, Patricia Lamkin .... Rochester, NY
Lange, Paul A., Law Offices of
Stamford, CT
Lange, Paul A., Law Offices of
Stratford, CT
New York, NY
Lange, Paul E. .... Tampa, FL
Lange, Paul K. .... Rochester, NY
Lange, Paul M. .... Fresno, CA
Lange, Quill & Powers, P.S.C.
Newport, KY
Lange, Richard M. .... Columbus, OH
Lange, Rick D. .... Lincoln, NE
Lange, Robert D. .... Indianapolis, IN
Lange, Robert E., III .... Madison, WI
Lange, Robert G. .... Lincoln, NE
Lange, Robert J. .... Walnut Creek, CA
Lange, Robert J. .... Bloomington, MN
Lange, Robert M. .... Los Angeles, CA
Lange, Roberto A. .... Sioux Falls, SD
Lange, Robt. E. .... Tucson, AZ
Lange, Roger A. .... Flint, MI
Lange, Ronald A. .... Grass Valley, CA
Lange, Russell D. .... Simi Valley, CA
Lange, Sidney T. .... Dallas, TX
Lange, Simpson, Robinson & Somerville LLP .... Anniston, AL
Birmingham, AL
Huntsville, AL
Montgomery, AL
Lange, Stephan P. .... Fort Lauderdale, FL
Lange, Steven Z. .... Minneapolis, MN
Lange, Susan Kagan .... Wellesley, MA
Lange, Tamara .... Los Angeles, CA

Langston, Lundy Ruffles
Fort Lauderdale, FL
Langston, Malinda L. ....Cincinnati, OH
Langston, Mark T. ....Boulder, CO
Langston, Mark T., P.C. ....Boulder, CO
Langston, Mary Sprague
New Orleans, LA
Langston, Michael J. ....Santa Rosa, CA
Langston, Pamela D. ....Tulsa, OK
Langston, Richard L. ....Frankfort, IN
Langston, Robert Bruce ....Houston, TX
Langston, Robert T. ....Irving, TX
Langston, Sally J. ....Houston, TX
Langston, Scott H. ....Lakeland, FL
Langston, Shane F. ....Jackson, MS
Port Gibson, MS
Langston, Thomas M. ....Lakeland, FL
Langston, W. Dortch, Jr. ....Goldsboro, NC
Langston, Walter S. ....Springfield, MO
Langston, William H., III ....New York, NY
Langston, Yancey F. ....Pensacola, FL
Langston-Ames, Susan ....Columbia, MO
Langston-Cox, Pamela D.
San Francisco, CA
Langthorn, Edward A. ....Danville, CA
Langton, Alan J., II ....Boston, MA
Langton, Charles E. ....Sterling Heights, MI
Langton, Derek ....Salt Lake City, UT
Langton, Diane ....Rochester, MN
Langton, Dorothy S. .... Marlton, NJ
Media, PA
Philadelphia, PA
Langton, Frank R. ....Sterling Heights, MI
Langton, Frank R., & Associates, P.C.
Sterling Heights, MI
Langton, Gerre S. ....St. Louis, MO
Langton, Grant T. ....Pasadena, CA
Langton, Jeffrey H. ....Hamilton, MT
Langton, Jennifer Anne .....Sterling Heights, MI
Langton, Kazer & Block ....Santa Ana, CA
Langton, Keith D., (P.C.) ....Santa Ana, CA
Langton, Michael E. ....Reno, NV
Langton, Stephen ....Lower Burrell, PA
Langtry, Virgil ....Maupin, OR
Languedoc, Ronald S. ....Brooklyn, NY
Languirand, Janie E. ....Baton Rouge, LA
Langum, David J. ....Birmingham, AL
Langus, Alan L. ....New York, NY
Langus, Sandra ....White Plains, NY
Langvardt, Arthur R. ....Hastings, NE
Langway, Robert E., Jr. ....Brockton, MA
Langweber, Denise R. ....Merrick, NY
Langweiler, Bernard ....Great Neck, NY
Langwig, J. Russell, III ....Schoharie, NY
Langwiser, Cynthia A. .....Treasury Department, Office of the Inspector General, GV
Langworthy, Elisabeth A.
Washington, DC
Langworthy, John A. ....Freeport, TX
Langworthy, Leslie M. ....Staten Island, NY
Langworthy, Lucinda Minton
Washington, DC
Langworthy, Mark A. ....Columbia, MO
Langworthy, Robert B. ....Kansas City, MO
Langworthy, Timothy H. ....Fort Collins, CO
Langworthy, William B.
The Woodlands, TX
Lanham, Chas. W., Jr. ....Daytona Beach, FL
Lanham, Donna M. ....Buffalo, NY
Lanham, Eric Thomas ....Kansas City, KS
Lanham, James J. ....Wooster, OH
Lanham, John C. ....Majuro, TT
Lanham, John F. ....Leesburg, VA
Lanham, Kara W. ....Santa Monica, CA
Lanham, Kyle E. ....Indianapolis, IN
Lanham, Michael F. ....Miami, FL
Lanham, Sally A. ....Seattle, WA
Lanham, Sam W. T., III ....Kerrville, TX
Lanham, Samuel W., Jr. ....Bangor, ME
Lanham, Thomas H. ....Melbourne, FL
Lanham, Thomas H., P.A. ....Melbourne, FL
Lanham, William C. ....Atlanta, GA
Lanham-Patrie, Elizabeth A. ......Orlando, FL
Laniado, David ....Brooklyn, NY
Laniado, Ely ....Jackson, NJ
Laniado, Sam M. ....Albany, NY
Lanich, Clarence L. ....Buffalo, NY
Lanier, A. Christian, III ....Chattanooga, TN
Lanier, Addison ....Cincinnati, OH
LaNier, Angie ....Medford, OR
Lanier, Barbara L. ....El Cerrito, CA
Lanier, Becky J. ....Houston, TX
Lanier, Beth ....Atlanta, GA
Lanier, Charles M., Jr. ....New Orleans, LA
Lanier, Charles S. ....Jacksonville, NC
Lanier, Clinton W. ....Vero Beach, FL
Lanier, Daniel R. ....Baltimore, MD
Lanier, David F. ....Avon Park, FL
Lanier, Dean A. ....Leavenworth, KS
Lanier, Elizabeth K. ....Schenectady, NY
Lanier Ford Shaver & Payne, P.C.
Huntsville, AL
Lanier, George H. ....Atlanta, GA
Lanier, Grady O., III ....Andalusia, AL
Lanier, H. Jeff ....Lilburn, GA
Lanier, J. Mitchell ....Moncks Corner, SC
Lanier, James A., II ....Miami, FL
Lanier, James C., Jr. ....Greenville, NC
Lanier, James E. ....Dyersburg, TN
Lanier, James T. ....Bakersfield, CA
Lanier, John L., Law Office of
Thibodaux, LA
Lanier, Julie Ann ....New Bern, NC
Lanier, Kenneth E. ....Houston, TX
Lanier, Lance A. ....Cleveland, OH
Lanier & Lanier ....Statesboro, GA
Lanier, Lewis C. ....Orangeburg, SC
Lanier, Lisa ....Durham, NC
Lanier, Lorelei M. ....Columbus, OH
Lanier, Marcie A. ....Birmingham, AL
Lanier, Margaret Leah ....Baltimore, MD
Lanier, Marjorie E. ....Boston, MA
Lanier, Mary Elizabeth ....Atlanta, GA
Lanier, M. H. ....Huntsville, AL
Lanier, N. Shannon Gentry ....Augusta, GA
Aiken, SC
Lanier, Nancy P. ....Indianapolis, IN
Lanier, Parker & Sullivan, P.C.
Houston, TX
Lanier, Patrick ....Austin, TX
Lanier, Philip M. ....Louisville, KY
Lanier, Randolph H. ....Birmingham, AL
Lanier, Robert A. ....Memphis, TN
Lanier, Robert C." Bob " ....Houston, TX
Lanier, Robert S. ....Statesboro, GA
Lanier, Robert W. ....Buena Vista, VA
Lanier, Ronald E. ....Beaumont, TX
Lanier, Russell J. ....Wrightsville Beach, NC
Lanier, Russell J., Jr. ....Kenansville, NC
Lanier, Samuel H. ....Jacksonville, FL
Lanier, Sidney ....Torrance, CA
Lanier, Suzanne D. ....Naples, FL
Lanier, T. Shawn ....Atlanta, GA
Lanier, Tharan Gregory ....Palo Alto, CA
Lanier, Troy A. ....Augusta, GA
Lanier, W. Mark ....Houston, TX
Lanier, Walter I., III ....Thibodaux, LA
Lanier-Jones, B. Kai, (Ms.) ....Southfield, MI
Lanigan, Christopher John ....Melville, NY
Lanigan, David C. ....Tampa, FL
Lanigan, Edward J., III ....Memphis, TN
Lanigan, Eric A. ....Orlando, FL
Lanigan, James S., Jr. ....New York, NY
Lanigan, Jeffrey M. ....Albany, NY
Lanigan, John J. ....Orland Park, IL
Lanigan, Kevin J. ....Washington, DC
Lanigan, Kevin N. ....Park Ridge, NJ
Lanigan, Michael F. ....Chicago, IL
Lanigan, Patrick ....Coram, NY
Lanigan, Susan S. ....Irving, TX
Lanigan, Thomas P. ....Miami, FL
Lanigan, William W. .... Carefree, AZ
Somerville, NJ
New York, NY
Lanigan, William W., Law Offices of
Carefree, AZ
Bridgewater, NJ
Flemington, NJ
Morristown, NJ
New York, NY
Lanigar, Edward F. ....La Mesa, CA
Lanik, James C. ....Englewood, CO
Laning, Ann Cheri ....Napa, CA
Laning, Davidson L. ....Birmingham, AL
Laning & Laning ....Birmingham, AL
Laning, Paul F. ....Birmingham, AL
Lanis, Nancy F. ....Melville, NY
Lanius, John W., Jr. ....Dallas, TX
Lanius, P. Baxter, III ....New York, NY
Lanius, Patrick A. ....Rancho Cordova, CA
Lank, Aubrey B. ....Wilmington, DE
Lank, David Allan ....Baltimore, MD
Lank, David S. ....Wilmington, DE
Lank, Dorothy E. ....Monterey, CA
Watsonville, CA
Lank, James A. ....Houston, TX
Lank, John J., Jr. ....San Francisco, CA
Lankarani, Nazanin ....New York, NY
Lankau, Charles A, III ....Ithaca, NY
Lankenau, Jeffrey R. ....Napoleon, OH
Lankenau, John C. ....New York, NY
Lankenau, Ronald P. ....Napoleon, OH
Lankenau, Susan M. ....Buffalo, NY
Lankenau, Wesche & McColley
Napoleon, OH
Lanker, Alan S. ....Salem, OR
Lanker, Gary W. ....Memphis, TN
Lanker, Lois L. ....Columbus, OH
Lanker & Samuels ....Salem, OR
Lankes & MacMillan ....Salinas, CA
Lankes, Stephen A. ....Salinas, CA
Lankfer, Marilyn A. ....Grand Rapids, MI
Lankford, Alex F., IV ....Mobile, AL
Lankford, Alexander F., III ....Mobile, AL
Lankford, Cara E. ....San Francisco, CA
Lankford & Coffield ....Alexandria, VA
Lankford, David J. ....Troy, MI
Lankford, David Wayne ....Bethesda, MD
Lankford, E. Joe ....Norman, OK
Lankford, Frank E. ....Mountain Brook, AL
Lankford, Frank E., Jr. ....Birmingham, AL
Lankford, George L. ....Dallas, TX
Lankford, Howell L. ....Milwaukie, OR
Lankford, James C. ....North Brunswick, NJ
Lankford, Jefferson L. ....Phoenix, AZ
Lankford & Klipfer ....Dayton, OH
Lankford, Patrick S. ....Houston, TX
Lankford, Paul V. ....San Francisco, CA
Lankford, R. Bruce ....Lexington, KY
Lankford, Richard B. ....Washington, DC
Lankford, Richard E. ....Annapolis, MD
Lankford, Sara E. ....Dallas, TX
Lankford, V. Thomas, Jr. ....Alexandria, VA
Lankford, Wayne H. ....Farmington, MN
Lankler, Alexander M.
Bay Harbor Islands, FL
Lankler, Beth Mennies ....Brooklyn, NY
Lankler, Douglas M. ....New York, NY
Lankler, Roderick C. ....New York, NY
Lankler Siffert & Wohl LLP
New York, NY
Lankler, Tracey Splaine
Department of Justice, Executive Office for United States Attorneys, GV
Lankowsky, Zenon Paul ....Woonsocket, RI
Lankton, Milton C. ....Portland, OR
Lanman, Charles B., Jr. ....Bethesda, MD
Lanman, Henry A. ....New York, NY
Lanman, Maurice H. ....Kensington, MD
Lann, John W. ....Wichita, KS
Lann, Lisa M. ....Des Moines, IA
Lanna & Coppola ....Yonkers, NY
Lanna, Vincent W. ....Yonkers, NY
Lannak, Andrea ....Islandia, NY
Lannan, Kathleen A. ....Washington, DC
Lannan, Robert E., II ....Charleston, WV
Lannen, Patrick J. ....Grand Rapids, MI
Lannen, Thomas J. ....Hagåtña, GU
Lanners, Alan J. ....Plymouth, MN
Lanners & Olson, P.A. ....Plymouth, MN
Lannes, Roman M. ....Coral Gables, FL
Lanney, Robert J. ....Concord, NH
Lanni, Paul A. ....Jericho, NY
Lanni, Sandra A. ....Warwick, RI
Lannie, P. Anthony ....Houston, TX
Lannie, Scott C. ....Baytown, TX
Lannin, Robert S. ....Omaha, NE
Lanning, Allen P. ....Great Falls, MT
Lanning, Chad A. ....Elkhart Lake, WI
Lanning, Christopher G. ....Richmond, VA
Lanning, Forrest H. ....Kenner, LA
Lanning, Geoffrey B. ....Washington, DC
Lanning, Geoffrey J. ....Detroit, MI
Lanning, James C., Jr. ....Chicago, IL
Lanning, James E. ....Charlotte, NC
Lanning, Jeffrey S.
Federal Communications Commission, Office of the General Counsel, GV
Lanning, Jerome K. ....Birmingham, AL
Lanning, Jessica K. ....San Francisco, CA
Lanning, Jodde Olsen .....Overland Park, KS
Lanning, John G. ....Bartlesville, OK
Lanning, John M. ....Chestnut Hill, MA
Lanning, Linda L. ....Jefferson City, MO
Lanning, Mark Edward ....Viera, FL
Lanning, Maureen C. ....Richmond, VA
Lanning, Michael K., (A Professional Law Corporation) ....Los Angeles, CA
Lanning, Oliver W. ....Fort Wayne, IN
Lanning, Ronald N., Jr. ....New York, NY
Lanning, Royston ....Round Rock, TX
Lannis, Sandra L. ....Pittsburgh, PA
Lannis, Walter E. ....Pittsburgh, PA
Lannom, Frank ....Lebanon, TN
Lannom, John Montgomery
Dyersburg, TN
Lannon, Cecilia D. ....San Rafael, CA
Lannon, Lannon & Barr, Ltd. ....Chicago, IL
Lannon, Lawrence E. ....Irvine, CA
Lannon, M. Catherine ....Tallahassee, FL
Lannon, Mark W. ....Santa Barbara, CA
Lannon, Michael E. ....Louisville, KY
Lannon, Patrick J. ....Miami, FL
Lannon, Paul G., Jr. ....Boston, MA
Lannon, Peter K., Jr. ....Costa Mesa, CA
St. Louis, MO
Lannon, R. James, Jr. ....La Salle, IL
Lannon-Kus, Patricia C. ....Chicago, IL
Lannus, Paul ....Menlo Park, CA
Lano, James D. ....Columbia, MD
Lano, Neal ....Grand Rapids, MN
Lano, Nelson, O'Toole & Bengtson, Ltd.
Grand Rapids, MN
Lanocha, N. Frank ....Baltimore, MD
Lanoff, Ian D. ....Washington, DC
Lanoff, Samuel M. ....Chicago, IL
Lanoie, David A. ....Greenfield, MA
Lanois, Jill Ramirez ....Charlotte, NC
Lanosa, Linda S. Brehmer ....Orlando, FL
Lanosa, Stephen F. ....Orlando, FL
Lanotte, Michael Anthony ....Albany, NY
Lanoue, Betty J. ....Concord, CA
Lanoue, John D. ....Adams, MA
Lanoue, Michael J. ....Hartford, CT
LaNoue, Robert E. ....Sacramento, CA
Lanouette, Kevin P. ....Boston, MA
Lanoux, Louis B. ....Jackson, MS
Lanphar, Anne Nelson ....Santa Ana, CA
Lanphear, David A. ....Bowling Green, KY
Lanphear & Dillon ....Cranston, RI
Lanphear, Jeffrey A. ....Cranston, RI
Lanphear, Lisa Hwang ....Philadelphia, PA
Lanphear, Martha J. ....Roanoke, VA
Lanphear, Thomas J. ....Atlanta, GA
Lanpher, John D. ....Rockford, IL
Lanpher, Lawrence Coe ....Washington, DC
Lanphere, Andrew ....San Francisco, CA
Lanphere & Associates
Colorado Springs, CO
Lanphere, Eric D. ....Albuquerque, NM
Lanphere, Gregory S. ....Colorado Springs, CO
Lanphere, Michael A. ....Irvine, CA
Lanphier, David J. ....Lincoln, NE
Lanphier, E. Paul ....Elmhurst, IL
Lanphier, E. Paul, Ltd. ....Elmhurst, IL
Lanphier, James R. ....Elk Grove Village, IL
Lanphier, Sean ....Milwaukee, WI
Lanquist, Edward D., Jr. ....Nashville, TN
Lanquist, Robert C., P.A. ....Jacksonville, FL
Lans, Asher B. ....New York, NY
Lans, Deborah E. ....New York, NY
Lans, Jared M. ....Hackensack, NJ
Lans, Sherman B. ....Pasadena, CA
Lans, Stephen M. ....Pasadena, CA
Lansangan, Pio C. ....Glendale, CA
Lansat, William ....Birmingham, MI
Detroit, MI
Lansberg, Justin J. ....Beverly Hills, CA
Lansberry, Debra Klinck ....Boston, MA
Lansberry, Kyle A. ....Indianapolis, IN
Lansberry & Lansberry ....Doylestown, PA
Lansberry, Lee B. ....Spartanburg, SC
Lansberry, Robert L. ....Doylestown, PA
Lansburgh, Matthew S. ....New York, NY
Lansburgh, Richard ....Woodland, CA
Lansche, John E. ....Charlotte, NC
Lansdale, Daryl Louis, Jr.
San Antonio, TX
Lansdale, John, Jr. ....Washington, DC
Lansdale, Richard B. ....Naples, FL
Lansdale, Richard Bivins, P.A. ....Naples, FL
Lansdell, Carroll deG., (Mr.) ....Newark, NJ
Lansdell, G. Alan ....Decatur, AL
Lansden, Charles D. ....Charlotte, NC
Lansden, Joe P. ....Simi Valley, CA
Lansden, John S. ....Murfreesboro, TN
Lansden, Mitchell Baylor ....Houston, TX
Lansdown, Myrna ....Bartlesville, OK
Lansdown, Scott ....Houston, TX
Lansdowne, Dennis R. ....Cleveland, OH
Lansdowne, John R. ....Albuquerque, NM
Lansdowne, Patricia Joan ....Rohnert Park, CA
Lanser, Adrian F., III ....Cartersville, GA
Lanser, Brian G. ....Milwaukee, WI
Lansford, Edwin G. ....Crossville, TN
Lansford, Jamie Kathryn
Kansas City, MO
Lansford, Steven D. ....Los Angeles, CA
Lanshe, Barbara G. ....Miami, FL
Lanshe, Frederick J. ....Allentown, PA
Lanshe, James C. ....Phoenix, AZ
Lanshe, James C., Sr. ....Allentown, PA
Lanshe, Lanshe and Collins
Allentown, PA
Lanshe, Stephen A. ....Allentown, PA
Lansing, Brian C. ....Department of the Navy, Office of the Judge Advocate General, GV
Lansing, Carl F. ....Denver, CO
Lansing, Carl F., P.C. ....Denver, CO
Lansing, David S. ....Chicago, IL
Lansing, Ellyn M. ....Chicago, IL
Lansing, Harriet ....St. Paul, MN
Lansing, Jay F. ....Billings, MT
Lansing, Joseph G. ....Chicago, IL
Lansing, Karen L. ....Boise, ID
Lansing, Lisa L. ....Florham Park, NJ
Lansing, Mark A. ....Grants Pass, OR
Lansing, Mark D. ....Albany, NY
Lansing, Mark, P.C. ....Grants Pass, OR
Lansing, Mary C. ....La Crosse, WI
Lansing, Neil D. ....Costa Mesa, CA
Lansing, Ronald B. ....Portland, OR
Lansinger, John R. ....New Castle, IN
Lansky, David L. ....Phoenix, AZ
Lansky, David L. ....Palo Alto, CA
Lansky, Donald M. ....Farmington Hills, MI
Lansky, Louise M. ....Purchase, NY
Lansky, Marc A. ....Churubusco, IN
Fort Wayne, IN
Lansky, Maryna ....New York, NY
Lansky, Mitchell I. ....Memphis, TN
Lansky, Myra Jane ....Wheat Ridge, CO
Lansky, Sidney ....New Bedford, MA
Lansner, David J. ....New York, NY
Lansner & Kubitschek ....New York, NY
Lansner, Ruth L. ....New York, NY
Lanson, Don E. ....Sherman Oaks, CA
Lanson, Stephen C. ....Lansing, MI
Lanspa, Joseph R. ....Santa Ana, CA
Lansverk, Duane ....Vancouver, WA
Lansverk, Eric D. ....Seattle, WA
Lant, Graham C. ....Bloomington, MN
Lantelme, James T.
Federal Deposit Insurance Corporation, Liquidation Branch, GV
Lanter, Brian F. ....Albuquerque, NM
Lanter, Edward Charles ....Fort Wright, KY
Lanter, Frank D. ....Houston, TX
Lanter, James ....Fort Worth, TX
Lanter, James E. ....Chicago, IL
Lanter, Marvin S. ....Los Angeles, CA
Lanter, Ottis P. ....Williamstown, KY
Lanter, Robert L. ....Cheyenne, WY
Lanterman, Daniel C. ....Springfield, IL
Lanterman, Jeffrey F. ....San Jose, CA
Lanterman, Stephen D. ....Topeka, KS
Lantermo, Deborah Ann ....Pocatello, ID
Lantero, Lisa ....Chicago, IL
Lanthier, Veronique ....Washington, DC
Lanthorn, Jeff R. ....Bellevue, WA
Lantier, Brendan J. ....New York, NY
Lantier, James D. ....Syracuse, NY
Lantieri, Paul F. ....Lancaster, PA
Philadelphia, PA
Lantinberg, Richard J. ....Jacksonville, FL
Lanting, James ....South Holland, IL
Lanting, Steven ....Adrian, MI
Lanting, Todd K. ....Holland, MI
Lantis, Edgar R., III ....Indianapolis, IN
Lantner, Andrew Mark ....Annapolis, MD
Lantner, Gary H. ....Spring, TX
Lanto, Reino C., Jr. ....Rantoul, IL
Lanton, Edward A. ....Oregon City, OR
Lantor, Todd Bradley ....Alexandria, VA
Lantos, Yvonne K. ....United States Senate, Committee Legal Personnel, GV
Lantrip, William E. ....Clinton, TN
Lantry, Daniel B. ....Los Angeles, CA
Lantry, Glenn E. ....Belleair Bluffs, FL
Lantry, Kevin T. ....Los Angeles, CA
Lantry, Kimber J. ....Hercules, CA
Lantry, Michael L. ....Cook, MN
Lantry, Terry L. ....Fort Collins, CO
Lantz, Adam L. ....Philadelphia, PA
Lantz, Andrea Sue ....Charlottesville, VA
Lantz, Arthur L., Jr. ....San Mateo, CA
Lantz, Barbara L. ....Boston, MA
Lantz, Benjamin J. ....Seattle, WA
Lantz, Chandra D. ....Richmond, VA
Lantz, Charles ....Rochester, MN
Lantz, Charles J. ....Lancaster, OH

Lantz, Clifford G. ... Institute, WV
Lantz, Constantine P. ... South Miami, FL
Lantz, Delano M. ... Harrisburg, PA
Lantz, Duane F. ... Columbus, OH
Lantz, F. Tenney ... North Dartmouth, MA
Lantz, George E. ... Parkersburg, WV
Lantz, Gregory D. ... Tucson, AZ
Lantz, Heidi ... Seattle, WA
Lantz, Herbert J., Jr. ... Belleville, IL
Lantz, James A. ... Lancaster, OH
Lantz, Jeffery L. ... Evansville, IN
Lantz, Jennifer M. ... San Jose, CA
Lantz, John H. ... Decatur, GA
Lantz, Kevin A. ... Dayton, OH
Lantz, Lantz & Lipp Co., L.P.A.
Lancaster, OH
Lantz, Leanne M. ... Crete, IL
Joliet, IL
Lantz & Luscomb ... North Dartmouth, MA
Lantz, Michael W. ... Richmond, VA
Lantz, Raymond C., Jr.
North Dartmouth, MA
Lantz, Rick P. ... Palm Springs, CA
Lantz, Robert D. ... Kansas City, MO
Lantz, Robert H. ... Washington, DC
Lantz, Ronald K. ... West Palm Beach, FL
Lantz, Stuart H. ... West Caldwell, NJ
Lantz, Susan M. ... Columbus, OH
Lantz & Tebay ... Parkersburg, WV
Lantz, Thomas J. ... Seymour, IN
Lantz, W. Charles ... Rochester, MN
Lantz, William H., Jr.
Department of Justice, Criminal Division, GV
Lantzas, George S. ... Glen Burnie, MD
Lantzy, Gary P. ... Milwaukee, WI
Lantzy, Leroy V. ... Auburn Hills, MI
Lantzy & Parsons ... Falls City, NE
Lantzy, Patricia A. ... Cleveland, OH
Lantzy, Robert J. ... Royal Oak, MI
Lanum, Robert W. ... Jeffersonville, IN
Lanum, Steven G. ... San Francisco, CA
Lanusse, Leslie A. ... New Orleans, LA
Lanuti, James A. ... Ottawa, IL
Lanuti, Joseph E. ... Ottawa, IL
Lanuto, Alfio S. ... Little Ferry, NJ
Lanway, Erin ... Grove, OK
Lany, James A. ... Edina, MN
Lany, Mary Ambler ... Eden Prairie, MN
Lanyard, Eric M. ... Los Angeles, CA
Lanyi, Rex G. ... Ypsilanti, MI
Lanyi, William D. ... Fond du Lac, WI
Lanyon, Janet E. ... Troy, MI
Lanyon, Robert E. ... Fort Valley, GA
Lanz, Brian P. ... Santa Rosa, CA
Lanz, Charles S. ... Youngstown, OH
Lanz, Jeffrey W. ... Des Moines, IA
Lanz, John E., Jr. ... Cleveland, OH
Lanz, Linda L. ... Hackensack, NJ
Lanz, Sabrina Katherine ... Boston, MA
Lanza, Andrew Joseph ... New York, NY
Lanza, Anthony L. ... Irvine, CA
Lanza, Beth A. ... Nashua, NH
Lanza, Carl F. ... Leominster, MA
Lanza, David J. ... Lemoyne, PA
Lanza, Donald C. ... White Plains, NY
Lanza, Elena R. ... Hempstead, NY
Lanza, George V. ... Miami, FL
Lanza, George V., P.A. ... Miami, FL
Lanza, Guy J. ... Palisades Park, NJ
Lanza, Guy J., Jr. ... Palisades Park, NJ
Lanza, James A. ... Bellevue, WA
Lanza, John D. ... Boston, MA
Lanza, John R. ... Flemington, NJ
Lanza, Kathy McGill ... Boston, MA
Lanza & Lanza ... Palisades Park, NJ
Lanza, Michael H. ... Hartford, CT
Lanza, Michael J. ... South Windsor, CT
Lanza, Nicholas J. ... Houston, TX
Lanza, Richard E. ... Mamaroneck, NY
Lanza, Robt. F. ... Cleveland, OH
Lanza, Salvatore F. ... Fulton, NY
Lanza, Shelley B. ... Seattle, WA
Lanza, Steven C. ... Lafayette, LA
Lanza, Steven J. ... Fort Lee, NJ
Lanza, Thomas J. ... Flemington, NJ
South Plainfield, NJ
Lanza, Timothy A. ... Lancaster, PA
Lanza, William A. ... Newington, CT
Lanzafame, Mary Jo ... San Diego, CA
Lanzafame, Philip F. ... Pasadena, CA
Lanzafame, Ross P. ... Rochester, NY
Lanza-Huber, Magda ... Daytona Beach, FL
Lanzara, Gary M. ... McLean, VA
Lanzarone, Michael R. ... New York, NY
Lanzel, Marvin G. ... La Grange, IL
Lanzer, Kenneth C. ... Escondido, CA
Lanzer & Myers, Law Offices of
Escondido, CA
Lanzetta, Donna J. ... Nyack, NY
Lanzetta, James P. ... Livonia, MI
Lanzilli, Carl A., Jr. ... Revere, MA
Lanzillo, Dana C. ... Boston, MA
Lanzillo, Richard A. ... Erie, PA
Lanzillotta, A. Paul ... Arlington, VA
Lanzillotti, Gribben & Marchuk ... Berwyn, IL
Lanzillotti, Joseph J. ... Berwyn, IL
Lanzilotta, Nicholas M. ... Salt Lake City, UT
Lanzinger, Joshua W. ... Toledo, OH
Lanzinger, Judith Ann ... Toledo, OH
Lanznar, Howard S. ... Chicago, IL
Lanzner, Craig P. ... Somerville, NJ
Lanzo, Douglas J. ... Washington, DC
Lanzo, Frank C. ... Mineola, NY
Lanzo, James R. ... Youngstown, OH
Lanzon, Christine E. ... Washington, DC
Lanzon, Paul J. ... New York, NY
Lanzone, Anthony M. ... Nyack, NY
Lanzone, Anthony M., A Professional Corporation ... Nyack, NY
Lanzone, Mary Geissler ... Fremont, CA
Lanzone, Robert J. ... San Carlos, CA
Lanzone, Shannon P. ... Decatur, GA
Lanzone, Suzanne B. ... Irvine, CA
Lanzoni, Dennis C. ... Meriden, CT
Lanzoni, Dennis C., P.C. ... Meriden, CT
Lao, Marina ... Newark, NJ
Laorr, Jill B. ... Minneapolis, MN
Lap, Benjamin P. ... Newport Beach, CA
Lapacek, James V. ... Chicago, IL
Lapadat, Stephen C. ... Minneapolis, MN
Lapadula, Elizabeth S. ... New York, NY
La Padula, Paschal R. ... Washington, DC
Bethesda, MD
La Paglia, Vincent J. ... Union City, NJ
LaPalme, Robert S. ... New York, NY
LaPan, James E. ... Saranac Lake, NY
Lapan, Joseph ... Bixby, OK
La Pan, Richard A. ... Downey, CA
Lapan, Roger D. ... Bloomington, IL
Lapan, Rosanne F. ... Tucson, AZ
LaPann, J. Robert ... Queensbury, NY
LaPann, James L. ... Glens Falls, NY
LaParl, John R., Jr. ... Kalamazoo, MI
LaParl, Roy L. ... Chicago, IL
LaParo, John B. ... Syracuse, NY
Lapas, Adrian M. ... Goldsboro, NC
Lapas, Adrian M., P.A. ... Goldsboro, NC
Lapat, Andrew ... Haverford, PA
Lapat, Michael J., Law Offices of
Coral Springs, FL
Chicago, IL
Lapatin, Joseph ... New York, NY
Lapatin Lewis & Kaplan, P.C.
New York, NY
Lapatin, Philip S. ... Boston, MA
Lapatine, Kenneth A. ... New York, NY
Lapayover, Shari P. ... New York, NY
Lapayowker, Andrew ... Baltimore, MD
Lapayowker, Stewart H.
Fort Lauderdale, FL
Lapciuc, Marcos J. ... Miami, FL
Lape, Gary M. ... Costa Mesa, CA
Lape, Kathleen S. ... Cincinnati, OH
Lape, Raymond E., Jr. ... Covington, KY
Lape, Robert W., Jr. ... Roaring Spring, PA
Lape, Rodd B. ... Columbus, OH
Lape, Timothy J. ... Missoula, MT
LaPedis, Jack M. ... Los Angeles, CA
LaPeer, Russell W. ... Belleview, FL
Ocala, FL
Lapekas, Ronald C. ... Glendale, CA
Lapelle, William J. ... Northfield, IL
Lapenn, James A. ... New York, NY
LaPenna, Alex. V. ... Poughkeepsie, NY
LaPenna & Associates, P.C. ... Clifton, NJ
LaPenna, Jerome J. ... Clifton, NJ
LaPenotiere, Angelina ... Dallas, TX
La Penta, John ... Charlotte, NC
LaPenta, Philip S. ... New York, NY
Lapenta, Susan M. ... Pittsburgh, PA
Lapera, Nancy DeFonce ... Bridgeport, CT
Lapera, Patrick J. ... Shelton, CT
La Pera, Richard A. ... Hempstead, NY
LaPerle, Thomas R. ... Palo Alto, CA
LaPerna, Anthony A. ... Cleveland, OH
Laperouse, Edward (Ted) J., II
Dallas, TX
Laperouse, Lambert M. ... New Orleans, LA
LaPetina, Gary M. ... Oak Brook, IL
Lapetina, Gerardo A. ... New York, NY
Lapeyre, Etienne C., (P.L.C.)
New Orleans, LA
Lapeyre, F. Henri, Jr. (P.L.C.)
New Orleans, LA
Lapeyre, Felix H. ... New Orleans, LA
Lapeyre, James M., Jr. ... New Orleans, LA
Lapeyre and Lapeyre, L.L.P.
New Orleans, LA
LaPeyronnie, Adrian F., III ... Gretna, LA
Lapeyrouse, Michael L. ... Mobile, AL
Lapeyrouse, Paul A. ... Chauvin, LA
Lapeza, David H. ... Gambier, OH
Lapeze, Keith W. ... Houston, TX
Lapham, Anthony A. ... Washington, DC
Lapham, Arthur L. ... Victoria, TX
Lapham, Barbara R. ... Vineland, NJ
Lapham and Doyle ... Farmington, MI
Lapham, Edwin S. ... Wading River, NY
Lapham, Elizabeth (Beth) J.
Northbrook, IL
Lapham, Harry L., Jr. ... Farmington, MI
Lapham, John J., III ... Seattle, WA
Lapham, R. Steven ... Sacramento, CA
Lapham, Rebecca Borden ... Boston, MA
Lapham, Samuel Peyre ... Houston, TX
Lapham, Stephen F. ... Charlotte, NC
Laphen, Frank M. ... Austin, TX
LaPiana, Jeanne M. ... Providence, RI
Lapiana, John K. ... Washington, DC
LaPiana, William P. ... New York, NY
Lapic, Jeffrey R. ... San Francisco, CA
Lapica, Larry S. ... Riverside, CA
Lapica, Ray ... Riverside, CA
Lapicola, Michael B. ... Minneapolis, MN
Lapid, Ronald A. ... New York, NY
Lapides, Barbara B. ... Memphis, TN
Lapides, David L. ... Tampa, FL
Lapides, Gordon D. ... Kentfield, CA
Lapides, Julian L. ... Baltimore, MD
Lapides, Leola ... Capitola, CA
Lapides, Renée ... New York, NY
Lapidos, Manny M. ... Skokie, IL
Lapidow, Seth J. ... New York, NY
Lapidus, Allan E. ... Chicago, IL
Lapidus, Anita Lynn ... New York, NY
Lapidus, Cary S. ... San Francisco, CA
Lapidus, Darryl E. ... New York, NY
Lapidus, Douglas J. ... Addison, TX
Lapidus, Elise R. ... Arlington, VA
Lapidus, Gregory Drake ... Beverly Hills, CA
Lapidus, Howard L. ... Bayside, NY
Lapidus, Jack David ... Washington, DC
Lapidus, Jeffrey H. ... Boca Raton, FL
Lapidus, Karen C. ... New York, NY
Lapidus, Kevin S. ... Washington, DC
Lapidus, Laura R. ... Melville, NY
Lapidus, Lawrence S. ... Washington, DC
Bethesda, MD
Lapidus, Mark A. ... Denver, CO
Lapidus, Mark B. ... Baltimore, MD
Lapidus, Mark R. ... Houston, TX
Lapidus, Melanie S. ... St. Louis, MO
Lapidus, Michael H. ... Los Angeles, CA
Lapidus, Michael H., Inc. ... Los Angeles, CA
Lapidus, Mitchell ... New York, NY
Lapidus, Myra P. ... Wantagh, NY
Lapidus, Nancy S. ... Washington, DC
Lapidus, Richard L. ... Miami, FL
Lapidus, Riva B. ... New York, NY
Lapidus, Robert D. ... San Diego, CA
Lapidus, Rodney S. ... Wantagh, NY
Lapidus, Rodney S., P.C. ... Wantagh, NY
Lapidus, Ryan D. ... Los Angeles, CA
Lapidus & Smith, LLP ... New York, NY
Lapidus, Steven B. ... Miami, FL
Lapidus, Steven M. ... Newark, NJ
Lapidus, Steven R. ... New York, NY
LaPierre, D. Bruce ... St. Louis, MO
LaPierre, John L. ... New York, NY
Lapierre, Leon ... East Hartford, CT
Lapierre, Nancy ... Hollywood, FL
Lapierre, Neil R. ... Woburn, MA
Lapierre, René Charles ... Sioux City, IA
LaPietra, Lauren M. ... Oakland, CA
La Pietra, Pasquale A. ... Jamaica, NY
Lapin, Andrew W. ... Chicago, IL
Lapin & Associates, P.C. ... Denver, CO
Lapin, David A. ... Los Angeles, CA
Lapin, David A., P.C. ... Los Angeles, CA
Lapin, Deborah S. ... Bronx, NY
Lapin, Harvey I. ... Northbrook, IL
Lapin, Herbert R. ... Los Angeles, CA
Lapin, Ian S. ... Los Angeles, CA
Lapin, Jack A., (P.C.) ... Houston, TX
Lapin, James B. ... Denver, CO
Lapin, Jeffrey B. ... Lincoln, NE
Lapin, Jeffrey C. ... Los Angeles, CA
Lapin, Jeffrey S. ... Miami, FL
Lapin, Jonathan B. ... New York, NY
Lapin, Juli E. ... Denver, CO
Lapin, Martaine J. L. ... Bangor, ME
Lapin, Michael E. ... Seattle, WA
Lapin, Michael L. ... Costa Mesa, CA
Lapin, Norman C. ... Tarzana, CA
Lapin, Paula A. ... Syracuse, NY
Lapin, Robert E. ... Houston, TX
Lapin, Sharon L. ... Grass Valley, CA
Lapin, Steven B. ... Stamford, CT
Lapin, Susan R. ... Sioux Falls, SD
Lapine, Felix V. ... Rochester, NY
Lapine, Jay M. ... Atlanta, GA
La Pine, John E. ... Chicago, IL
Lapine, Kenneth M. ... Cleveland, OH
Lapine, Lawrence M. ... Stamford, CT
Lapins, Aldis
Securities and Exchange Commission, Office of Investor Education and Assistance, GV
Lapins, David A. ... Chicago, IL
Lapins, Scott M. ... Chicago, IL
Lapinskas, Aras ... Boston, MA
Lapinski, Alexander J. ... Elmhurst, NY
Lapinski, Ann ... Schenectady, NY
Lapinski, John A. ... Los Angeles, CA
Lapinski, John C. ... Milwaukee, WI
Lapinski, Paul A. ... Philadelphia, PA
La Pinta, Anthony M. ... East Islip, NY
Lapis, Julia ... Los Angeles, CA
Lapkin, Tricia S. ... Oak Park, IL
Lapka, Sheryl R. ... Chicago, IL
Lapka, Theodore A. ... Chicago, IL
Lapka, Thomas L. ... Lansing, MI
Lapke, John H. ... St. Paul, MN
Lapkin, Mary Royce ... Phoenix, AZ
Lapkovitch, Larry E. ... Jasper, AL
LaPlaca, Anthony C. ... Elyria, OH
LaPlaca, Damian R. ... Boston, MA
LaPlaca, Daniel A. ... Upper Marlboro, MD
LaPlaca, M. Michael ... Washington, DC
LaPlaca, Raymond G.
Upper Marlboro, MD
La Placa, Salvatore G. ... Lombard, IL
LaPlace, Angie Rogers ... Baton Rouge, LA
LaPlace, Anne Marie ... Irvine, CA
La Place, Christine M. ... Garden City, NY
LaPlace, Jeannine ... New York, NY
La Place, Maxine L. ... Newark, DE
LaPlace, Michael T. ... Baton Rouge, LA
LaPlace, Seana F. ... New York, NY
Laplace-Smith, Lisa Jill ... New York, NY
LaPlant, Carol P. ... Carmel, CA
San Diego, CA
LaPlant, David E. ... Malone, NY
Laplante, Andrew ... Bessemer, AL
La Plante, Ann M. ... Greeley, CO
Laplante, Arthur J. ... Fort Lauderdale, FL
LaPlante, Brian ... Providence, RI
LaPlante, Edward A., III ... Holyoke, MA
LaPlante, Gary P. ... Denver, CO
LaPlante, George R. ... Arlington, VA
Laplante, John M. ... Sacramento, CA
LaPlante, Joseph A. ... West Hartford, CT
Laplante, Joseph N. ... Nashua, NH
LaPlante, Kathleen R. ... Suisun City, CA
LaPlante, R. Stephen ... Evansville, IN
Laplante, Stephen S. ... Detroit, MI
LaPlata, George H. ... Birmingham, MI
Lapoff, Lucinda Odell ... Rochester, NY
LaPointe, Brenda L. ... Nashua, NH
Lapointe, Dennis G. ... Clearwater, FL
LaPointe, Douglas J. ... Orlando, FL
LaPointe, Ellen L. ... San Francisco, CA
LaPointe, George A., Jr. ... Albany, NY
LaPointe, Gregory P. ... New Haven, CT
Lapointe, Jon-Paul ... Boston, MA
Lapointe, Joseph R. ... Mason City, IA
Lapointe & Lapointe ... Mason City, IA
LaPointe, Martin K. ... Chicago, IL
Lapointe, Mary Jane ... Indianapolis, IN
Lapointe, Matthew J. ... Manchester, NH
Lapointe, Monique ... New York, NY
LaPointe, Richard A. ... Marco Island, FL
LaPointe, Robert ... Rumford, RI
LaPointe, Robert L., Jr. ... Manchester, NH
LaPointe, Scott W. ... Exeter, NH
LaPointe, Sharon F. ... Worcester, MA
LaPointe, Sharon L. ... Okemos, MI
Lapointe, Timothy ... Mason City, IA
Lapointe, Vincent D. ... Los Angeles, CA
LaPointe, William E. ... Sharon, MA
La Poll, Francis A. ... Palo Alto, CA
La Polla, Ann E. ... Salt Lake City, UT
La Polla, Ann E., P.C. ... Salt Lake City, UT
LaPolla, Charles P. ... New York, NY
LaPolla, Regina ... New York, NY
LaPolla, Thomas A. ... Warren, OH
LaPolt, Monica ... Princeton, WV
Lapon, Albert I. ... Springfield, MA
Laponsky, Mark D. ... Washington, DC
Baltimore, MD
LaPook, Gary J. ... Westlake Village, CA
Laport, Frank L. ... Bridgeview, IL
LaPorta, Alfred ... Bronx, NY
LaPorta, Anthony J. ... Parsippany, NJ
New York, NY
LaPorta, Edward ... Bronx, NY
LaPorta, Jeanne M. ... Stamford, CT
LaPorta & LaPorta ... Bronx, NY
Laporta, Patrick J. ... Utica, NY
Laporta, Peter R. ... Henderson, NV
LaPorta, Robert A. ... San Francisco, CA
LaPorta, Robert J. ... Atlanta, GA
Laporte, Adele P. ... Ann Arbor, MI
Laporte, Anthony L. ... Houston, TX
Laporte, Claire ... Boston, MA
Laporte, Cloyd, Jr. ... New York, NY
Laporte, Craig A. ... Port Richey, FL
LaPorte, Dale C. ... Cleveland, OH
LaPorte, Daniel G. ... Coraopolis, PA
LaPorte, David L. ... Chicago, IL
LaPorte, Dennis J. ... Tacoma, WA
La Porte, Donna L. ... Newport Beach, CA
Laporte, Elizabeth D. ... San Francisco, CA
Laporte, Gerald J. S. ... Washington, DC
LaPorte, Katherine M. ... Baton Rouge, LA
LaPorte, Kelly G. ... Honolulu, HI
LaPorte, Lawrence R. ... Los Angeles, CA
Laporte, Michael J. ... Daytona Beach, FL
LaPorte, Michael R. ... Chicago, IL
Laporte & Norris ... Elizabethton, TN
La Porte, Peter F. ... Fort Lauderdale, FL
Laporte & Plaszner, P.C. ... Ann Arbor, MI
LaPorte, Richard G. ... Los Angeles, CA
LaPorte, Roc E. ... Philadelphia, PA
LaPorte, Sam J. ... Elizabethton, TN
Laporte, Susan R. ... New Orleans, LA
LaPorte, Wm. Howard ... Crestview, FL
Lapota, Jeffrey ... Los Angeles, CA
Lapowsky, Robert ... Philadelphia, PA
Wayne, PA
Lapp, Charles E., III ... Cedarhurst, NY
Lapp, Charles E., Jr. ... Cedarhurst, NY
Lapp, Dale E. ... Lancaster, PA
Lapp, Daryl J. ... Boston, MA
Lapp, Deborah A. ... Medina, OH
Lapp, Dennis R. ... Cincinnati, OH
Lapp, Ira H. ... White Plains, NY
Lapp, Joseph L. ... Harrisonburg, VA
Lapp, Katherine N. ... Brooklyn, NY
Lapp & Lapp ... Cedarhurst, NY
Lapp, Laurie, Libra, Abramson & Thomson, Chartered ... Minneapolis, MN
Lapp, Marc A. ... St. Louis, MO
Lapp, Mark F. ... Brooksville, FL
Lapp & Pontz, LLP ... Lancaster, PA
Lapp, Richard B. ... Chicago, IL
Lapp, Richard N. ... Dallas, TX
Lapp, Stuart W. ... Los Angeles, CA
Lapp, Stuart W. ... The Woodlands, TX
Lapp, Stuart W., P.C. ... The Woodlands, TX
Lapp, Timothy C. ... South Holland, IL
Lapp, William S. ... Minneapolis, MN
Lappan, James Edward ... Penfield, NY
Lappano, Frank C. ... Glen Cove, NY
Lappas, Frank P. ... Fort Lauderdale, FL
Lappas, Marcia I. ... Herndon, VA
Lappas, Spero T., The Law Offices of
Harrisburg, PA
Lappas, Theodore, Jr. ... Fort Lee, NJ
Lappe, Donnie ... Brownwood, TX
Lappe, Ronnie ... Brownwood, TX
Lappegaard, Jennifer L. ... Red Wing, MN
Lappen, Arthur L. ... Bethesda, MD
Lappen, Cheryl ... New York, NY
Lappen, Chester I., (A Professional Corporation) ... Los Angeles, CA
Lappen, Jeremy A. ... Los Angeles, CA
Lappen, Jonathan Bailey ... Los Angeles, CA
Lappen, Louis D. ... Philadelphia, PA
Lappen, Myron G. ... Allentown, PA
Lappen, Robin D. ... Encino, CA

Lappen, Susan E. ..... Milwaukee, WI
Lappen, Timothy ..... Los Angeles, CA
Lappen, William A. ..... Encino, CA
Lappenga, Wendy K. ..... New Orleans, LA
Lapperre, Ruth M. ..... Evanston, IL
Lappert, Stephen F. ..... New York, NY
Lappin, Claudia Carroll ..... Bloomington, IN
Lappin, Debra R. ..... Englewood, CO
Lappin, Frederick M. ..... Livingston, NJ
Lappin, Greg I. ..... Houston, TX
Lappin, James Brian ..... Parsippany, NJ
Lappin, John Christopher ..... Armonk, NY
Lappin & Kusmer LLP ..... Boston, MA
Lappin, Lawrence B. ..... New York, NY
Lappin, Mark G. ..... Boston, MA
Lappin, Michael ..... Milwaukee, WI
Lappin, Michael A. ..... Dracut, MA
Lappin, Wendy Edwards
Plymouth Meeting, PA
Lapping & Bukuras, P.A. ..... Boston, MA
Lapping, Hans ..... San Francisco, CA
Lapping & Lapping ..... Carthage, NC
Lapping, Norman E. ..... Chicago, IL
Lapping, Richard A. ..... San Francisco, CA
Lapping, Robert A. ..... Boston, MA
Lapping, Robert K. ..... Syosset, NY
Lapping, Shale P. ..... Chicago, IL
Lapping, Sherwood Foster ..... Carthage, NC
Lapping, Stephan F. ..... Carthage, NC
Lapple, Kirk F. ..... Los Alamitos, CA
Lapple, Matthew C. ..... Los Angeles, CA
Lapps, Brian A., Jr. ..... Nashville, TN
LaPrade, F. Grey, Jr. ..... Mount Airy, NC
La Prade, Frank G. ..... Glen Allen, VA
La Prade, Jennie L. ..... Los Angeles, CA
Laprade, Kenneth I. ..... Easthampton, MA
Laprade, Steven E. ..... Rochester, NY
Laprade, Thomas V. ..... Portland, ME
La Pratt, Roger D. ..... Lansing, MI
La Pré, John-Paul ..... Marlborough, MA
Lapres, Marie T. ..... Chicago, IL
Lapresi, Dominic M. ..... Rochester, NY
Lapsley and DePoy ..... Harrisonburg, VA
Lapsley, Norvell A. ..... Harrisonburg, VA
Laptook, Eric J. ..... New York, NY
Laptook, Kenneth N. ..... Roseland, NJ
Lapuk, Marvin H. ..... Farmington, CT
La Puma, Christopher P. ..... Washington, DC
LaPunzina, Carol J. ..... Secaucus, NJ
Laputka, Bayless, Ecker & Cohn, P.C.
Hazleton, PA
Laputka, Dolores A. ..... Allentown, PA
Laputka and Pedri ..... Hazleton, PA
Laputka, Theodore R. ..... Hazleton, PA
Laputka, Theodore R., Jr. ..... Hazleton, PA
Lapuyade, Keith Dale ..... Denver, CO
Lapuyade, Washington & Molk, LLC
Denver, CO
LaPuzza, Paul J. ..... Omaha, NE
Lapworth, Kimberly A. ..... Philadelphia, PA
La Qua, John F. ..... Langdon, ND
Laqua, Lisa Marie ..... San Diego, CA
Laqua, Scott J. ..... San Diego, CA
La Qua, Vincent A. ..... Hankinson, ND
LaQuay, Christopher R. ..... Los Angeles, CA
LaQuay, Kathryn E. ..... Los Angeles, CA
Laquer, Christopher M. ..... Pasadena, CA
Laquer, Urban, Clifford & Hodge LLP
Pasadena, CA
Bellevue, WA
Laquercia, Thomas Michael
New York, NY
Laquerre, Ann M. ..... Boston, MA
Laquey, Diana ..... Dallas, TX
Laquidara, Pamela F. ..... Framingham, MA
Lara, Art B., Jr. ..... Amarillo, TX
Lara, Aurelio Leo ..... McAllen, TX
Lara, Constance H. ..... Chicago, IL
Lara, Constance H., P.C. ..... Chicago, IL
Lara, Elizabeth Yelland
San Francisco, CA
Lara, Germán M. ..... Houston, TX
Lara, J. Adin ..... Nashville, TN
Lara, Julianne K. ..... Davie, FL
Lara, Julianne K., P.A. ..... Davie, FL
Lara, Maria E. ..... Sacramento, CA
Lara, Michelle A. ..... San Diego, CA
Lara, Pam ..... Milwaukee, WI
Lara, Patricia ..... Austin, TX
Lara, Richard David ..... Miami, FL
Lara, Roberto ..... Irvine, CA
Lara, Shapiro & Vitek, S.C.
Milwaukee, WI
Lara, Stacey A. ..... New York, NY
Lara, Yamil ..... New Haven, CT
Larabee, Dale R. ..... San Diego, CA
Larabee, Erin H. ..... Key West, FL
Larabee, Jennifer
Commodity Futures Trading Commission,
Division of Enforcement, GV
Larabee and Loadman ..... San Diego, CA
Laracey, Melvin C. ..... Ann Arbor, MI
Larach, Richard L. ..... Washington, DC
Laracuente, Lenore Boyarin ..... Edison, NJ
Laracy, Ward C. ..... Saddle Brook, NJ
New York, NY
Laragy, Christopher J. ..... Rochester, NY
Laragy, William S. ..... New Orleans, LA
LaRaia, Henry A. ..... Herkimer, NY
Laraia & Hubbard, P.C. ..... Wheaton, IL
Laraia, Joseph M. ..... Wheaton, IL
LaRaia, Laura C. ..... Dallas, TX
LaRaia, Robert F. ..... Houston, TX
Laraja and Kanaga, P.C. ..... Orleans, MA
Laraja, Richard A. ..... Orleans, MA
Laramee, Robert P. ..... Gloucester, MA
Laramey, Thomas A., Jr. ..... Austin, TX
Laramie, James R. ..... Washington, DC

Laramie, Michael J. ..... Troy, MI
Laramie, Robert E. ..... Southfield, MI
Laramore, Herman D. ..... Marianna, FL
Laramore, James E.
Cape Girardeau, MO
Laramore, James R. ..... Bowling Green, KY
Laramore, Jon ..... Indianapolis, IN
Laramore, Sandra Jean ..... Tallahassee, FL
Lara-Moscardini, Nancy Ann ..... Millbrae, CA
Laramy, James E. ..... Rancho Cordova, CA
Larance, Gregory M. ..... Savannah, GA
LaRance, Jill Deann ..... Billings, MT
LaRance Law Firm, Inc. ..... Billings, MT
Larason, Timothy M.
Oklahoma City, OK
LaRatta, Anthony R. ..... Haddonfield, NJ
La Raus, David William ..... Chicago, IL
LaRaus, Lawrence B. ..... White Plains, NY
Laravuso, John J. ..... Minneapolis, MN
Larcade, Jodee Sparkman ..... Raleigh, NC
Larche, James G., Jr. ..... Gainesville, FL
Larche, W. Lawrence ..... Boca Raton, FL
Larcher, Carol ..... Chicago, IL
Larchez, Lawrence F. ..... Quincy, MA
Larchuk, Kathleen B. ..... Pittsburgh, PA
Larchuk, Steven B. ..... Wexford, PA
Larcombe, Valerie Goodwin
West Palm Beach, FL
Lard, Bradley W. ..... Nashville, TN
Lard, Todd A. ..... Oklahoma City, OK
Lardakis, Moira Gambrill
Mayfield Village, OH
Lardakis, Terry E. ..... Akron, OH
Lardent, Esther F. ..... Washington, DC
Larder, Robert H. ..... Woonsocket, RI
Lardi, Paul F. ..... Great Neck, NY
Lardiere, Christopher L. ..... Columbus, OH
Lardiere, Eric G. ..... Beverly Hills, CA
Lardiere, Garrett A. ..... Point Pleasant, NJ
Lardiere, Sylvia P. ..... Beverly Hills, CA
Lardieri, Anthony G. ..... Baltimore, MD
Lardieri, Cheryl ..... Baltimore, MD
Lardin, Joan C. ..... Decatur, GA
Lardin, Thomas D. ..... Fort Lauderdale, FL
Lardin, Thomas D., P.A.
Fort Lauderdale, FL
Lardizabal, Carlos A. ..... Los Angeles, CA
Lardner, John G. ..... Little Rock, AR
Lardner, Kathy G. Merveldt ..... Houston, TX
Lare, Gregory B. ..... New York, NY
Lareau, Douglas J. ..... Minneapolis, MN
Lareau, Gail M. ..... Lynn, MA
Lareau, Hector L. ..... Rock Island, IL
Lareau, Margaret A. ..... Granby, CT
Lareau, Richard G. ..... Minneapolis, MN
Laredo, Carolyn ..... Pomona, NY
Laredo, David C. ..... Pacific Grove, CA
Laredo, Marc C. ..... Boston, MA
Laremont, Anita W. ..... New York, NY
Laren, Anders F. ..... Philadelphia, PA
Laren, Cara A. ..... New York, NY
Laren, Guy ..... Philadelphia, PA
Laret, Joffre Scott ..... Columbus, OH
Larew, James C. ..... Iowa City, IA
Larew Law Office ..... Iowa City, IA
Larew, Melvin G. ..... Draper, UT
Larey, Lance L. ..... Tulsa, OK
Largay, Christopher R. ..... Bass Harbor, ME
Largay Law Offices, P.A. ..... Bass Harbor, ME
Largay, Richard P. ..... Hyannis, MA
Largay, Timothy L. ..... Hartford, CT
Large, Allen W. ..... Lawrenceville, IL
Large, Donald W. ..... Portland, OR
Large, Douglas B. ..... Santa Barbara, CA
Large, E. Ray ..... Birmingham, AL
Large, Elizabeth Morley ..... Portland, OR
Large, Gary F. ..... Titusville, FL
Large, Howard G. ..... Wichita Falls, TX
Large, Jack M. ..... Fort Lauderdale, FL
Large, John H. ..... Niles, OH
Large, Mary Jane ..... Sacramento, CA
Large, Michael E. ..... Bristol, TN
Large, Michael S. ..... Philadelphia, PA
Large, Raymond D. ..... Sylva, NC
Large, Ronald E. ..... Holmdel, NJ
Large, Russell M. ..... Coeburn, VA
Large, Scammell & Danziger, A Professional Corporation ..... Flemington, NJ
Somerville, NJ
Large, Wendell G. ..... Portland, ME
Large, William F. ..... Anchorage, AK
Large, William W. ..... Orlando, FL
Largen, Ginger J. ..... Abingdon, VA
Largen, Karen Lynn ..... St. Louis, MO
Largent, George W. ..... Miami, OK
Largent, H. William ..... Charleston, WV
Largent, Jeffrey W. ..... Cleveland, OH
Largent, Pinkney C., Jr. ..... Waurika, OK
Largess, Stephen Luke ..... Charlotte, NC
Largesse, Claire M. ..... Boulder, CO
Largey, James P. ..... New York, NY
Largey, Thomas L. ..... Quincy, MA
Lari, Ayla A. ..... Pittsburgh, PA
Lari, David P. ..... Los Angeles, CA
Laria, Jon M. ..... Baltimore, MD
Laribee, Hertrick & Kray ..... Brunswick, OH
Lodi, OH
Medina, OH
Laribee, Michael Lee ..... Medina, OH
Laribee, Ray E. ..... Medina, OH
Laribee, Richard L. ..... Medina, OH
Lariccia, John E.
Department of the Air Force,
Office of the General Counsel, GV
LaRiche, Anthony A., Jr.
Willoughby Hills, OH
Larick, Barbara Doane ..... Findlay, OH
Larick, Jo E. ..... San Bernardino, CA

Larigan, John S. ..... Wichita, KS
Larimer, Ann ..... Phoenix, AZ
Larimer, David G. ..... Rochester, NY
Larimer, Jake A. ..... Chesterfield, MO
Larimer, John T. ..... Yuba City, CA
Larimer, John T. ..... Cincinnati, OH
Larimer, Linda A. ..... Boise, ID
Larimer, Louie V. ..... Colorado Springs, CO
Larimer, Louie V., P.C.
Colorado Springs, CO
Larimer, Rae Skirvin ..... Cincinnati, OH
Larimer, Tracy J. ..... West Palm Beach, FL
Larimer, William F. ..... Chapel Hill, NC
Larimore, James K. ..... Oklahoma City, OK
Larimore, Jolene ..... Carpinteria, CA
Larimore, Mary Nold ..... Indianapolis, IN
Larimore, Paul D. ..... St. Louis, MO
Larimore, Steven M. ..... Martinez, CA
Larimore, Tim A. ..... Higginsville, MO
Larimore, Tom L. ..... Fort Worth, TX
Larin, Anne T. ..... Detroit, MI
Larin, Daniel Joseph ..... Bloomfield Hills, MI
Larin, Deanne B. ..... St. Paul, MN
Larin & Leonard ..... Bloomfield Hills, MI
Larin, Michael J. ..... Los Angeles, CA
Larin, Robert W. ..... Bloomfield Hills, MI
Lario, Anthony M. ..... Camden, NJ
Lario, Frank M., Jr. ..... Camden, NJ
Lario, Marc A. ..... Haddonfield, NJ
Lario, Michael J. ..... Haddonfield, NJ
Lario, Wendy Johnson ..... Morristown, NJ
Larios, Brian D. ..... Kansas City, MO
Larios, Deborah W. ..... Nashville, TN
Larisa, Joseph S., Jr. ..... Providence, RI
Lariscy, Earl Allan ..... Washington, DC
Lari" 2 h, Inge A. ..... Dallas, TX
Larish, James P. ..... New York, NY
Larish, Kenneth M. ..... Dallas, TX
Larison, Dorraine A. ..... St. Cloud, MN
Larison, Dwight L. ..... Kansas City, MO
Larison, Scott T. ..... St. Cloud, MN
Laritz, Kenneth F. ..... Clinton Township, MI
Larivee, Alan J. ..... Grand Forks, ND
Larivee, John J ..... Andover, MA
Lariviere, Denise L. ..... Pasadena, CA
Lariviere & Dickerson ..... San Jose, CA
LaRiviere, F. David ..... Monterey, CA
San Jose, CA
LaRiviere, Grubman & Payne, LLP
Monterey, CA
San Jose, CA
Lariviere, Leah ..... Miami, FL
Lariviere, Margie R. ..... San Francisco, CA
Lariviere, Maurice J., Jr. ..... Methuen, MA
Lariviere, Norman ..... San Jose, CA
LaRiviere, Wendy ..... San Francisco, CA
Larizza, Raymond M.
Department of Justice, Civil Division, GV
Larizza, Silvia Simpson ..... New York, NY
Lark, Eric I. ..... Detroit, MI
Lark & Folts ..... Cutchogue, NY
Lark, Frederick J. ..... New York, NY
Lark, J. Andrew ..... Summit, NJ
New York, NY
Lark, J. Peter ..... Lansing, MI
Lark, James D. ..... West Bloomfield, MI
Lark, Raymon E., Jr. ..... Columbia, SC
Lark, Richard F. ..... Cutchogue, NY
Lark, Stuart J. ..... Colorado Springs, CO
Lark, Tonya Feit ..... Colorado Springs, CO
Larke, George J., Jr. ..... Houma, LA
Larken, Joan K. ..... Tucson, AZ
Larkin, Adrienne ..... Larkspur, CA
Larkin, Amy W. ..... San Clemente, CA
Larkin, Arthur G. ..... White Plains, NY
Larkin, Axelrod, Trachte & Tetenbaum, L.L.P. ..... Newburgh, NY
Larkin, Barbara Ann ..... Alpharetta, GA
Larkin, Barbara Mills ..... United States Senate,
Senatorial Assistants, GV
Larkin, Benjamin C. ..... Hillsborough, NH
Larkin, Benjamin T. ..... Birmingham, AL
Larkin, Brent W. ..... Sagamore Hills, OH
Larkin, Brian K. ..... Rockford, IL
Larkin, Brian O. ..... New York, NY
Larkin, Charles J. ..... San Bernardino, CA
Larkin, Christine E. ..... Dallas, TX
Larkin, Christopher C. ..... Los Angeles, CA
Larkin, Daniel E. ..... Chicago, IL
Larkin, Daniel P. ..... El Cajon, CA
Larkin, David ..... Walnut Creek, CA
Larkin, David C. ..... Tempe, AZ
Larkin, David C., P.C. ..... Tempe, AZ
Larkin, David G. ..... Melbourne, FL
Larkin, David M. ..... Vista, CA
Larkin, Donald A. ..... Palo Alto, CA
Larkin, Donna M. ..... Baltimore, MD
Larkin, E. Daniel, III ..... Merion Station, PA
Larkin, Edward T. ..... Boston, MA
Larkin, Edward W. ..... New York, NY
Larkin, Edwin M. ..... New York, NY
Larkin, Edwin M. ..... Rochester, NY
Larkin, Ellen M. ..... New York, NY
Larkin, Frances J. ..... Memphis, TN
Larkin, Francis J. ..... Boston, MA
Larkin, Francis J. ..... North Dartmouth, MA
Larkin, Gayle Blaine ..... Lawrence, KS
Larkin, Girard C., Jr. ..... Virginia Beach, VA
Larkin, Hoffman, Daly & Lindgren, Ltd.
Bloomington, MN
Minneapolis, MN
Larkin, Holly L. ..... Memphis, TN
Larkin, Jack M. ..... Tampa, FL
Larkin, James C., Jr. ..... Houston, TX
Larkin, James J. ..... Boston, MA
Larkin, James M. ..... Chicago, IL
Larkin, James P. ..... Minneapolis, MN
Larkin, James P. ..... Purchase, NY

Larkin, Jane S. ..... New York, NY
Larkin, Jerome P. ..... Salem, OR
Larkin, Joan Kupersmith
Los Angeles, CA
Larkin, Jocelyn D. ..... Oakland, CA
Larkin, Joel L. ..... Marietta, GA
Larkin, John E. ..... Stuart, FL
Larkin, John F., III ..... New York, NY
Larkin, John J. ..... Washington, DC
Larkin, John R. ..... Media, PA
Larkin, Jon A. ..... Chadds Ford, PA
Larkin, Jon S. ..... Dade City, FL
Larkin, Joseph P. ..... Rahway, NJ
Larkin, Joseph P., III ..... Tavares, FL
Larkin, Katherine Shand ..... Denver, CO
Larkin, Kathleen Herzog ..... Paoli, PA
Larkin, Laura A. ..... Louisville, KY
Larkin, Lee Marshall, (P.C.) ..... Houston, TX
Larkin, Lee R. ..... Houston, TX
Larkin, Leo P., Jr. ..... New York, NY
Larkin, Linda J. ..... Portland, OR
Larkin, Lisa A. ..... St. Louis, MO
Larkin, Lisa W. ..... Tucson, AZ
Larkin, Lloyd G. ..... Tulsa, OK
Larkin, Lynne A. ..... Vero Beach, FL
Larkin, Mary E.
Department Of Veterans Affairs,
Board of Veterans Appeals, GV
Larkin, Michael E. ..... Tucson, AZ
Larkin, Michael E. ..... Lansing, MI
Larkin, Michael E. ..... Reese, MI
Larkin, Michael F. ..... New York, NY
Larkin, Michael T. ..... Houston, TX
Larkin, Michael W. ..... Miami, FL
Larkin, Murl A. ..... Lubbock, TX
Larkin, Patricia A. ..... Boston, MA
Larkin, Patrick B. ..... Houston, TX
Larkin, Patrick J. ..... St. Cloud, MN
Larkin, Patrick J. ..... Dallas, TX
Larkin, Patrick V. ..... Media, PA
Larkin, Paul M. ..... Myrtle Beach, SC
Larkin, Paul R., Jr. ..... Fort Lauderdale, FL
Larkin, Peter ..... San Pedro, CA
Larkin, Peter J. ..... New York, NY
Larkin, Randall F. ..... Lawrence, KS
Larkin, Richard W. ..... Chicago, IL
Larkin, Richard W. ..... Ayer, MA
Larkin, Robert E. ..... Tallahassee, FL
Larkin, Robert F., Jr. ..... Boston, MA
Larkin, Robert G., Jr. ..... Boston, MA
Larkin, Robert M. ..... Greene, NY
Larkin, Robert X. ..... Huntington, NY
Larkin, Rosemary Filter ..... Chicago, IL
Larkin, Sharon L. ..... McLean, VA
Larkin, Shaye ..... San Francisco, CA
Larkin, Stephen W. ..... Media, PA
Larkin, Terrence B. ..... Troy, MI
Larkin, Thomas A. ..... Tampa, FL
Larkin, Thomas A. ..... Portland, OR
Larkin, Thomas B., Jr. ..... Newport Beach, CA
Larkin, Thomas P. ..... Tacoma, WA
Larkin, Tom L. ..... Birmingham, AL
Larkin, Twila B. ..... Albuquerque, NM
Santa Fe, NM
Larkin, W. Kevin ..... Cambridge, MA
Larkin, Walter N. ..... Skokie, IL
Larkin, William A. ..... Los Angeles, CA
Larkin, William A. ..... Chicago, IL
Larkin, William J., III ..... Newburgh, NY
Larkins, James M., III ..... Washington, DC
Larkins, John K., Jr. ..... Atlanta, GA
Larkins, Kathryn A. ..... Kansas City, MO
Larkins, Nelson J ..... Portland, ME
Larkins, Richard G. ..... Washington, DC
Larkins, Thomas F. ..... Torrance, CA
Larkins Vacura, LLP ..... Portland, OR
Larkins, W. Haywood ..... West Palm Beach, FL
Larkins, William L., Jr. ..... Portland, OR
Larko, Arlene Gahagan ..... Atwater, OH
Larko, John ..... Cuyahoga Falls, OH
Larkosh, Daniel J. ..... Edgartown, MA
Larkowich, Peter, Law Offices of
Wellesley, MA
Larks, Laura A. ..... Rosemead, CA
Larky, Sheldon G. ..... Bingham Farms, MI
Larm, Richard P. ..... Department of Justice,
Antitrust Division, GV
Larman, Barry W. ..... Portland, ME
Larmann, Kevin O. ..... Metairie, LA
Larmann, Laurence E., (P.L.C.)
Metairie, LA
Larmee, Donald H. ..... Arlington Heights, IL
Larmer, Robert C. ..... Escondido, CA
Larmer, Robin L. ..... New York, NY
Larmi, Allan R. ..... Warren, OH
Larmore, David G. ..... Chicago, IL
Larmore, Philip H. ..... Fort Wayne, IN
Larmore, Scarlett, Myers & Temple
Kennett Square, PA
Larmore, Scott D. ..... Phoenix, AZ
Larmore, Thomas R. ..... Santa Monica, CA
Larmoyeux, Christopher M.
West Palm Beach, FL
Larned, Nancy C. ..... Denver, CO
Larner, H. LeRoy ..... Philadelphia, PA
Larner, Henry A. ..... Short Hills, NJ
Larner, Keith S. ..... Clayton, MO
Larner, Mark D. ..... Short Hills, NJ
Larner, Robin C. ..... Rochester, NY
Larner, Samuel A. ..... Short Hills, NJ
Larney, Ann Fitzpatrick ..... Concord, NH
Larney, Keith L. ..... Dallas, TX
Laro, David .....
United States Tax Court, GV
Laro, Marlene Ellen ..... Washington, DC
LaRobardier, Genevieve K.
Florham Park, NJ
New York, NY

Larobina, Michael D. ... Stamford, CT
La Rocca, Angel F. ... Elizabeth, NJ
LaRocca, Anthony J. ... Washington, DC
Larocca, Dominick X. ... Atlanta, GA
La Rocca, F. Craig ... Lansdale, PA
LaRocca, Francis P., Jr. ...
National Aeronautics And Space Administration, GV
LaRocca, Frank J. ... Birmingham, MI
LaRocca, Frank J. ... Paramus, NJ
Larocca, James L. ... Brooklyn, NY
LaRocca, John D. ... Philadelphia, PA
LaRocca, John William ... New York, NY
LaRocca, Leo M. ... San Francisco, CA
LaRocca, Michele ... Riverdale, MD
LaRocca, N. Dante ... New York, NY
LaRocca, Nicholas F., Jr.
Morgan City, LA
LaRocca, Nicholas F., Jr., Ltd., A Prof. Law Corp. ... Morgan City, LA
LaRocca, Nicholas J. ... Union City, NJ
LaRocca, Paul J. ... East Hartford, CT
La Rocca, Phillip ... Indio, CA
LaRocca, Robert J. ... Philadelphia, PA
LaRocca, Robert R. ... Irvington, NY
Larocca, Ronald M. ... Brooklyn, NY
La Rocca, Stephen S. ... New York, NY
La Rocca, Tony F. ... East Orange, NJ
Linden, NJ
La Rocca, Tony F., & Associates, P.C.
East Orange, NJ
Linden, NJ
Newark, NJ
La Rocco, Anthony P. ... Newark, NJ
La Rocco, August F., Jr. ... Hollywood, FL
LaRocco, John B. ... Sacramento, CA
LaRocco, Joseph B. ... New Canaan, CT
LaRocco, Joseph J. ... Chicago, IL
La Roche, Bruce E. ... Philadelphia, PA
LaRoche, David G.
Securities and Exchange Commission, Division of Investment Management, GV
LaRoche, George Simons ... Takoma Park, MD
Laroche, Mark B. ... Providence, RI
LaRoche, Richard F., Jr. ... Murfreesboro, TN
LaRoche, Richard F., Sr.
Murfreesboro, TN
LaRoche, W. Michael ... Sacramento, CA
LaRochelle, Dawn R. ... New York, NY
LaRochelle, Dennis ... New York, NY
LaRochelle, Dennis, The Law Offices of
Ventura, CA
LaRochelle, Fernand ... Augusta, ME
Larochelle, John P. ... Providence, RI
LaRock, Jacqueline Trojnar
Simsbury, CT
La Rock, Jane G. ... Canton, NY
LaRocque, Daniel J. ... Madison, WI
La Rocque, Donald P., The Law Offices of
San Diego, CA
LaRocque, James E. ... Chicago, IL
Larocque, Jeremy P. ... Monroe, NC
LaRocque, Kathleen A. ... Santa Rosa, CA
LaRocque, Ronald R. ... Chicopee, MA
LaRocque, Thomas C. ... Malone, NY
Larocque, Tracy M. ... Clifton Park, NY
Laroe, James K. ... Dallas, TX
Laroe, James K., P.C. ... Dallas, TX
Laroe, Kenneth E. ... Leesburg, FL
Laroe, Nicolette M. ... Dallas, TX
LaRoe, Winn, Moerman & Donovan
Washington, DC
LaRoque, Elizabeth L. ... Rochester, MN
La Rosa, Anthony C. ... Indianapolis, IN
LaRosa, Carla M. ... Denver, CO
LaRosa, Cynthia Kassab ... Media, PA
La Rosa, Gregory C.
National Aeronautics And Space Administration, Goddard Space Flight Center, GV
LaRosa, Jeffrey T. ... Morristown, NJ
LaRosa, Joseph J. ... Kenilworth, NJ
LaRosa, Katherine Hairston ... Tallahassee, FL
LaRosa, Lillian J. ... Winchester, MA
La Rosa, Maria F. ... Union, NJ
LaRosa, Mariella ... Waterbury, CT
LaRosa, Richard A. ... Staten Island, NY
LaRosa, Robert S. ... Mount Laurel, NJ
LaRosa, Roseann J. ... New York, NY
La Rosa, Shara L. ... New York, NY
Larose, Andree ... Helena, MT
Larose, Cynthia J. ... Boston, MA
LaRose, David E. ... Knoxville, TN
LaRose, David R. ... Olympia, WA
LaRose, Edward C. ... Tampa, FL
La Rose, Elizabeth A. ... Chicago, IL
La Rose, Erwin A. ... Baton Rouge, LA
Larose, F. Hugh ... Thibodaux, LA
Larose, J. Browne, III ... New Orleans, LA
LaRose, Judith C. ... Jefferson City, MO
LaRose, Keith V. ... Poughkeepsie, NY
LaRose & LaRose ... Poughkeepsie, NY
Larose, Lawrence A. ... New York, NY
LaRose, Mark A. ... Chicago, IL
LaRose, Paul J. ... Columbia, MO
LaRose, Robert M. ... St. Louis, MO
LaRose, Roger J. ... Harper Woods, MI
LaRose, Shelley Ann ... Poughkeepsie, NY
Larose, Stuart J. ... Syracuse, NY
Larosiliere, Jean D. ... Washington, DC
LaRosiliere, Marthe ... Arlington, VA
Laroski, Joseph A., Jr ... Washington, DC
La Rossa, James M. ... New York, NY
La Rossa & Ross ... New York, NY
LaRossa, Susan G. ... New York, NY
LaRotonda, James J., Jr.
Stone Mountain, GA
Larotonda, Jerry ... Miami, FL
La Roue, Larry A. ... Minneapolis, MN
Larounis, Thomas ... Melville, NY
LaRovere, Francis J., III ... Everett, MA
LaRowe, Gerlach & Roy, S.C.
Madison, WI
Reedsburg, WI
Sauk City, WI
Wonewoc, WI
LaRowe, Myron E. ... Reedsburg, WI
LaRowe, William Clair ... Toledo, OH
Larpenteur, Dana K. ... Plaquemine, LA
Larpenteur, James A., Jr. ... Portland, OR
Larr, Robert Scott ... Orlando, FL
Larr, William Ray, (P.C.) ... Pasadena, CA
Larrabee, Arthur M. ... Philadelphia, PA
Larrabee & Associates ... San Diego, CA
Larrabee, Bryce A. ... New York, NY
Larrabee & Burchanowski ... Williamsport, PA
Larrabee, Charles B. ... Albuquerque, NM
Larrabee, Christine J.C. ... Lynn, MA
Larrabee & Cunningham ... Philadelphia, PA
Larrabee, Diane Wear ... San Francisco, CA
Larrabee, Don M., II ... Williamsport, PA
Larrabee, J. Whitfield ... Brookline, MA
Larrabee, Jennifer A. ... New York, NY
Larrabee, Jon ... Houston, TX
Larrabee, Leonard P., III ... New York, NY
Larrabee, Matthew L. ... San Francisco, CA
Larrabee, Paige Black ... Houston, TX
Larrabee, Peter N. ... San Diego, CA
Larrabee, Philip A. ... Berkeley, CA
Larrabee, Steven H. ... Walnut Creek, CA
Larrabee, Susan B. ... Ardsley, NY
Larrabee, Susan Nobes ... Brooklyn, NY
Larrabee, Sylvia V. ... Washington, DC
Larracuente, Jerome J. ... Bridgeport, CT
Larraga, Angelo D. ... Dedham, MA
Larragoite, Philip P. ... Albuquerque, NM
Larralde, Diana ... Rowland Heights, CA
Larramore, Randall D. ... Chattanooga, TN
Larrauri, Elizabeth M. ... New York, NY
Larraz, Jose J., Jr. ... Miami, FL
Larré, Eric C. ... San Francisco, CA
Larre, James G. ... New Orleans, LA
Larrea, Jeanine Marie ... San Francisco, CA
Larrea, John G. ... Sacramento, CA
Larrew, Joseph W. ... St. Louis, MO
Larrick, J. Randolph ... Winchester, VA
Larrick, James K. ... Wilmington, NC
Larrick, James R., Jr. ... Winchester, VA
Larrick, Larrick & Drown, P.C.
Winchester, VA
Larrick, Scott A. ... Chesterland, OH
Larrick, S. Y. ... Kalispell, MT
Larrimer, Courtney Ann ... Columbus, OH
Larrimer, Gavin R. ... Columbus, OH
Larrimer, James S. ... Pittsburgh, PA
Larrimer, John B. ... Dallas, TX
Larrimer, John H. ... Columbus, OH
Larrimer, Kevin J. ... Columbus, OH
Larrimer and Larrimer ... Columbus, OH
Larrimer, Marilyn J. ... Pittsburgh, PA
Larrimer, Terrence W. ... Columbus, OH
Larrimer, Thomas G. ... Columbus, OH
Larrimore, Dale G. ... Philadelphia, PA
Larrimore, James B. ... Lutherville, MD
Larrimore, Jeffery J. ... San Diego, CA
Larrinaga, Erin M. ... Tampa, FL
Larrinaga, Joseph L. ... Tampa, FL
Larrinaga, Robert M. ... Tampa, FL
Larrison, David W. ... Syracuse, NY
Larrison, Kathleen A. ... St. Petersburg, FL
Larriva, G. A. ... Tucson, AZ
Larriva, Phillip H. ... Tucson, AZ
Larriva, Richard P. ... Tustin, CA
Larrivee, Tina J. ... Missoula, MT
Larroca, Jeffrey W. ... Washington, DC
Larroca, Ray ... San Francisco, CA
Larroca, Raymond G. ... Washington, DC
Larrouy, David R. ... Ann Arbor, MI
Larry, David ... Milwaukee, WI
Larry, David H. ... Boone, NC
Larry, Dennis K. ... Pensacola, FL
Larry, Jeffery ... Chicago, IL
Larscheid, Buchanan & Zeff
Sacramento, CA
Larscheid, Kristine A. ... Topeka, KS
Larsen, Alan S. ... Portland, OR
Arlington, VA
Larsen, Anne Edelman ... Chicago, IL
Larsen, Anne F. ... Minneapolis, MN
Larsen & Associates ... Costa Mesa, CA
Larsen, Barbara A. ... Chicago, IL
Larsen, Bea V. ... Cincinnati, OH
Larsen, Bradley James ... Minneapolis, MN
Larsen, Brent A. ... Las Vegas, NV
Larsen, Brooks M. ... Seattle, WA
Larsen, Bruce A. ... Hobbs, NM
Larsen, Caitlin M. ... Santa Barbara, CA
Larsen, Carl R. ... Punta Gorda, FL
Larsen, Celia ... Dublin, GA
Larsen, Charles R. ... McFarland, WI
Larsen, Chris R. ... Milwaukee, WI
Larsen, Christopher ... Encinitas, CA
Larsen, Christopher A. ... Portland, OR
Larsen, Constance, Law Offices of
Escondido, CA
Larsen, Craig A. ... Annandale, MN
Larsen, Craig N. ... Wenatchee, WA
Larsen, Craig S. ... Berlin, NJ
Larsen & Crickmore, A Professional Association ... Encinitas, CA
Larsen, Curtis E. ... Helena, MT
Larsen, Cynthia J. ... Sacramento, CA
Larsen, Daniel P. ... Portland, OR
Larsen, Darrell R., Jr. ... Chicago, IL
Larsen, Darrell W. ... Yuba City, CA
Larsen, Darren M. ... Camarillo, CA
Larsen, David A. ... Birmingham, AL
Larsen, David C. ... Honolulu, HI
Larsen, David C., (P.C.) ... Costa Mesa, CA
Larsen, David J. ... Alamo, CA
Larsen, David M. ... Minneapolis, MN
Larsen, David P. ... Detroit, MI
Larsen, David W. ... Boise, ID
Larsen, Dexter A. ... Duluth, MN
Larsen, Diane R. ... Avon, CO
Larsen, Diane R., P.C. ... Avon, CO
Vail, CO
Larsen, Diane Ruisch ... Waterloo, IA
Larsen, Dirk ... Great Falls, MT
Larsen, Donald H. ... Roseland, NJ
Larsen, Douglas M. ... Fresno, CA
Larsen, Douglas P. ... Madison, WI
Larsen, Douglas P., Jr. ... Arlington, VA
Larsen & Edlund ... Park Ridge, IL
Larsen, Edward L. ... Neptune, NJ
Staten Island, NY
Larsen, Edward V. ... Ronkonkoma, NY
Larsen, Elaine D. ... Salt Lake City, UT
Larsen, Elaine Murphree
Oklahoma City, OK
Larsen, Eric A. ... Tucson, AZ
Larsen, Eric O. ... Sacramento, CA
Larsen, Erick S. ... Baltimore, MD
Larsen, Erik C. ... Winter Park, FL
Larsen, Erik C., P.A. ... Winter Park, FL
Larsen, Esther ... Spokane, WA
Larsen, Feist, Hess & May, P.C.
St. Louis, MO
Larsen, Gary H. ... Sarasota, FL
Larsen, George N. ... Salt Lake City, UT
Larsen, Gerald L. ... Costa Mesa, CA
Larsen, Gregory S. ... Chesapeake, VA
Larsen, Hans L. ... Cleveland, OH
Larsen, Harold S. ... Beaufort, SC
Larsen, Howard M. ... Newport Beach, CA
Larsen, Howard M., Incorporated
Newport Beach, CA
Larsen, J. Allen ... New York, NY
Larsen, J. David ... San Francisco, CA
Larsen, Jack ... Park Ridge, IL
Larsen, James C. ... Port Isabel, TX
Larsen, James Paul ... Orinda, CA
Larsen, Jan A. ... Fort Collins, CO
Larsen, Jay L. ... Kansas City, MO
Larsen, Jeffrey R. ... Boston, MA
Larsen, Joan L. ... Washington, DC
Larsen, John C. ... Cedar Falls, IA
Larsen, John J., Jr. ... St. Louis, MO
Larsen, Jonathan S. ... San Francisco, CA
Larsen, Joseph R. ... Houston, TX
Larsen, Joseph Y., Jr. ... Irvine, CA
Larsen, Julie Dean ... Los Angeles, CA
Larsen, Karen L. ... Washington, DC
Larsen, Karen M. ... St. Paul, MN
Larsen, Kari S.
Commodity Futures Trading Commission, Division of Enforcement, GV
Larsen, Keith G. ... Salt Lake City, UT
Larsen, Keith P. ... Omaha, NE
Larsen, Kenneth R. ... Ridge Manor, FL
Larsen, Kent F. ... Las Vegas, NV
Larsen, Kent W. ... Salt Lake City, UT
Larsen, Kerry Elizabeth ... Washington, DC
Larsen, Kirsten S. ... Kansas City, MO
Larsen, Kory ... Great Falls, MT
Larsen, Kyle ... Great Falls, MT
Larsen, Lance D. ... Greenwich, CT
Larsen, Larry C. ... Sacramento, CA
Larsen Law Firm, The, PLLC
Great Falls, MT
Larsen, Lee A. ... Papillion, NE
Larsen, Linda L. ... Flagstaff, AZ
Larsen, Lloyd M. ... Fountain Valley, CA
Larsen, Louis N. ... Stuart, FL
Larsen, Lyman L. ... Omaha, NE
Larsen, Lynda ... Pasadena, CA
Larsen, Lyndon F. ... International Falls, MN
Larsen, Lynn B., (Mr.)
Salt Lake City, UT
Larsen, Lynn Rowe ... Cleveland, OH
Larsen, Marcella ... Aspen, CO
Larsen, Mark A. ... Chicago, IL
Larsen, Mark A. ... Salt Lake City, UT
Larsen, Mary Johnson ... Columbia, SC
Larsen, Matthew L. ... Dallas, TX
Larsen, Melissa W. ... Huntsville, AL
Larsen, Melodie K. ... Los Angeles, CA
Larsen, Michael D. ... Santa Rosa, CA
Larsen, Michael L. ... Salt Lake City, UT
Larsen, Michael L. ... Kennewick, WA
Larsen & Mooney Law ... Hollywood, CA
Salt Lake City, UT
Larsen, Norman W. ... Minneapolis, MN
Larsen, Olaf ... Westfield, MA
Larsen, Patrick H. ... Coudersport, PA
Larsen, Paul A. ... Pasadena, CA
Larsen, Paul A. ... Elk River, MN
Larsen, Paul D. ... Fargo, ND
Larsen, Paul E. ... Las Vegas, NV
Larsen, Paul J. ... Washington, DC
Larsen, Paula Kurko ... Dallas, TX
Larsen, Peter O. ... Jacksonville, FL
Larsen, R. Chip ... Phoenix, AZ
Larsen, R. Paul ... Saginaw, MI
Larsen, Ralph C. ... Huntington Park, CA
Larsen, Reed W. ... Pocatello, ID
Larsen, Reid K. ... Blackfoot, ID
Larsen, Richard A. ... Davenport, IA
Larsen, Richard A. ... Dallas, TX
Larsen, Richard E., P.A. ... Orlando, FL
Larsen, Richard Erik ... Orlando, FL
Larsen, Richard G. ... Aurora, IL
Larsen, Richard G. ... Park Ridge, IL
Larsen, Robert A. ... Elburn, IL
Larsen, Robert D. ... Las Vegas, NV
Larsen, Robert E. ... Kansas City, MO
Larsen, Robert L. ... Wheaton, IL
Larsen, Robert M. ... Concord, NH
Larsen, Roger B. ... Colorado Springs, CO
Larsen, St. John & Johnson, P.C.
Meriden, CT
Larsen, Scott ... Chicago, IL
Larsen, Scott C. ... Dallas, TX
Larsen, Shelby S., (Mrs.)
Pacific Palisades, CA
Larsen, Stanley L. ... Salt Lake City, UT
Larsen, Stephenie L. ... New York, NY
Larsen, Steven J. ... Spokane, WA
Larsen, Steven P. ... Des Moines, IA
Larsen, Stuart L. ... Cleveland, OH
Larsen, Susan ... San Diego, CA
Larsen, Susan ... El Paso, TX
Larsen, Suzanne L. ... Salt Lake City, UT
Larsen, Suzanne M. ... Seattle, WA
Larsen, Thomas A. ... San Francisco, CA
Larsen, Timothy A. ... Novato, CA
Larsen, Tracy T. ... Grand Rapids, MI
Larsen, Walter R. ... Santa Barbara, CA
Larsen, Wayne E. ... Cudahy, WI
Larsen, Wendy U. ... Boca Raton, FL
Chicago, IL
Larsen, William H. ... Macon, GA
Larsen, William L. ... Washington, DC
Larsen, William P., III ... New York, NY
Larsen, William W. ... San Jose, CA
Larsen, Wm. Washington, Jr. ... Dublin, GA
Larsen, Wm. Washington, Jr., P.C.
Dublin, GA
Larsen-Harper, Carole A. ... Mesa, AZ
Larson, A. Bruce ... Soda Springs, ID
Larson, A. Russell ... Jackson, TN
Larson, Aaron R. ... Ann Arbor, MI
Larson, Adam A. ... Boston, MA
Larson, Adrienne L. ... Tampa, FL
Larson, Alan J. ... Seattle, WA
Larson, Albert H., III ... San Francisco, CA
Larson, Aleron H., Jr. ... Denver, CO
Larson, Aleron H., Sr. ... Highlands Ranch, CO
Larson, Allan G. ... Staten Island, NY
Larson, Allan L. ... Salt Lake City, UT
Larson, Allen R. ... Yarmouth Port, MA
Larson, Alvin E. ... Phoenix, AZ
Larson, Amy M. ... Monterey, CA
Larson, Amy Wright
Federal Maritime Commission, Office of the General Counsel, GV
Larson, Anita F. ... New York, NY
Larson, Ann A. ... Fort Dodge, IA
Larson, Ann H. ... Walnut Creek, CA
Larson, Anne E. ... Chicago, IL
Larson, Arlen R. ... Bagley, MN
Larson, Arnold D. ... Los Angeles, CA
Larson, Arnold W. ... Duluth, MN
Larson, Arthur B. ... Manassas, VA
Larson, B. A. ... Edmond, OK
Larson, Baxter ... Billings, MT
Larson, Bernadette T. ... Ashtabula, OH
Larson, B. G. (Skip) ... Dodge City, KS
Larson, Bianca G. ... Hillsborough, CA
Larson, Brad ... Portland, OR
Larson, Bradford Ulrich ... St. Petersburg, FL
Larson, Bradley R. ... Sacramento, CA
Larson, Bradley V. ... Monticello, MN
Larson, Brian A. ... Las Vegas, NV
Larson, Brian G. ... Nogales, AZ
Larson, Bruce A. ... Hilo, HI
Honolulu, HI
Kailua-Kona, HI
Larson, Bruce E. ... Seattle, WA
Larson, Bruce R. ... Atlanta, GA
Roanoke, VA
Larson, Bruce W. ... Minneapolis, MN
Larson, Bryan A. ... Salt Lake City, UT
Larson, Bryan E. ... Nashville, TN
Larson & Burnham, A Professional Corporation ... Oakland, CA
Larson, C. Gregg ... St. Joseph, MO
Larson, C. Gregg, P.C. ... St. Joseph, MO
Larson, C. Ingrid ... Santa Rosa, CA
Larson, Calvin F. ... Reston, VA
Larson, Carl A. ... Rancho Santa Fe, CA
Larson, Carl A. ... Spring Valley, CA
Larson, Carl J. ... Mayville, ND
Larson, Carl R. ... Minneapolis, MN
Larson, Carla J. ... Miami, FL
Larson, Carol K. ... Minot, ND
Larson, Carolyn L. ... Portland, OR
Larson, Catherine M. ... Salt Lake City, UT
Larson, Charles A. ... Los Angeles, CA
Larson, Charles, Jr. ... Anamosa, IA
Larson, Charles W. ... Des Moines, IA
Larson, Cheston J. ... San Diego, CA
Larson, Childs, Hall & Christensen, P.C.
Elk Horn, IA
Harlan, IA
Larson, Chris ... Irvine, CA
Larson, Christine E. ... Fort Myers, FL
Larson, Christopher P. ... Peoria, IL
Larson, Craig D. ... Champlin, MN
Larson, Craig E. ... Rochester, NY
Larson, Craig S. ... Salt Lake City, UT
Larson, Cullen C. ... Dahlonega, GA
Larson, D. Erik ... Salem, OR
Larson, Dale I. ... St. Paul, MN
Larson, Daniel A. ... Phoenix, AZ
Larson, Daniel A. ... Tampa, FL
Larson, Daniel N. ... Ontario, CA
Larson, Darin W. ... Rapid City, SD
Larson, Darrell E. ... Grand Forks, ND
Larson, Darryl L. ... Eugene, OR
Larson, David A. ... Tillamook, OR
Larson, David A. ... Federal Way, WA

Larson, David A., P.S. ....Federal Way, WA
Larson, David Allen ....Omaha, NE
Larson, David C. ....Department of Justice,
Federal Bureau of Investigation, GV
Larson, David C. ....Spirit Lake, IA
Larson, David D., Jr. ....Raleigh, NC
Larson, David E. ....Kansas City, MO
Larson, David E. ....Dayton, OH
Larson, David J. ....Marietta, GA
Larson, David J. ....Avoca, IA
Larson, David J. ....Minneapolis, MN
Larson, David J. ....Chamberlain, SD
Larson, David K. ....Jackson, WY
Larson, David L. ....Palo Alto, CA
Larson, David L. ....El Paso, TX
Larson, David N. ....Minneapolis, MN
Larson, David O. ....San Francisco, CA
Larson, David P. ....Port Angeles, WA
Larson, David W. ....Minneapolis, MN
Larson, David W. ....St. Paul, MN
Larson, Dennis G. ....Decorah, IA
Larson, Dennis R. B. ....Playa Del Rey, CA
Larson, Derek V. ....Albuquerque, NM
Larson, Diana S. ....Elgin, IL
Larson, Dohn S. ....Austin, TX
Larson, Donald B ....Belvidere, IL
Larson, Donald L. ....Fridley, MN
Larson, Donald R. ....Riverdale, IL
Larson, Douglas E. ....Grand Junction, CO
Larson, Douglas N. ....Los Angeles, CA
Larson, Douglas R. ....Mesquite, TX
Larson, Dwane A. ....Brainerd, MN
Larson, E. Richard ....Los Angeles, CA
Larson, Earl R. ....Minneapolis, MN
Larson, Edward ....Topeka, KS
Larson, Elisa M. ....Portland, OR
Larson, Ellen Roucek ....Naperville, IL
Larson, Eric C. ....Portland, OR
Larson, Eric D. ....Rochester, MN
Larson, Eric J. ....San Diego, CA
Larson, Eric J. ....Wichita, KS
Larson, Eric J. ....Waukesha, WI
Larson, Eric K. ....San Francisco, CA
Larson, Erik N. ....San Francisco, CA
Larson, Erik V. ....San Antonio, TX
Larson, Evan H. ....Austin, MN
Larson, Evangeline J. ....San Diego, CA
Larson & Fischer ....Astoria, OR
Larson, Fred A. ....Hartford, CT
Larson, Fred A. ....Story City, IA
Larson, Frederick A. ....Jamestown, NY
Larson, Frederick A. ....College Station, TX
Larson, G. Chris ....Auburn, CA
Larson, Gary B. ....Mesa, AZ
Larson, Gary R. ....Minneapolis, MN
Larson, Gary W. ....Santa Fe, NM
Larson, George R. ....Evansville, MN
Larson, Gerald Keith ....Akron, OH
Larson, Glenn E. ....Dallas, TX
Larson, Gloria Cordes ....Boston, MA
Larson, Gregg M. ....St. Paul, MN
Larson, Gregory A. ....Mesa, AZ
Larson, Gregory C. ....Bismarck, ND
Larson, Gregory D. ....San Diego, CA
Larson, Gregory D. ....Park Rapids, MN
Larson, Gregory K. ....Little Falls, MN
Larson, Gregory L. ....Calabasas, CA
Larson, Gregory S. ....San Diego, CA
Larson, Grethe Ann ....Vancouver, WA
Larson, Gustave W. ....Miami Shores, FL
Larson, H. William ....Largo, FL
Larson, Harms, Bibeau & Reynolds, P.C.
Farmington Hills, MI
Larson, Harold A. ....Farmington Hills, MI
Larson Hart & Shepherd, P.L.L.C.
Seattle, WA
Larson, Helen B. ....San Francisco, CA
Larson, Herbert V., Jr. ....New Orleans, LA
Larson, Herbert W. ....Largo, FL
St. Petersburg, FL
Larson, J. Herbert ....Pontiac, MI
Larson, Jack E. ....Fort Worth, TX
Larson - Jackson, P.C., Law Firm of
Washington, DC
Larson, Jacqueline S. ....Santa Clara, CA
Larson, James ....San Francisco, CA
Larson, James A. ....Denver, CO
Larson, James A. ....Chicago, IL
Larson, James D., (P.A.) ....Minneapolis, MN
Larson, James E. ....Littleton, CO
Larson, James Edward ....Largo, FL
Larson, James F. ....Prineville, OR
Larson, James L. ....Fort Bragg, CA
Larson, James M. ....Helena, MT
Larson, James M., Esq.
Glenwood Springs, CO
Larson, James R. ....Wakefield, MN
Larson, Jan C. ....Buffalo, MN
Larson, Jane J. ....St. Paul, MN
Larson, Jeanenne B. ....Salt Lake City, UT
Larson, Jeff A. ....Sioux Falls, SD
Larson, Jeff L. ....Galveston, TX
Larson, Jeffrey D. ....Longmont, CO
Larson, Jeffrey D. ....Woonsocket, SD
Larson, Jeffrey E. ....Cambridge, MN
Larson, Jeffrey L. ....Harlan, IA
Larson, Jeffrey S. ....Greenbelt, MD
Larson, Jeffrey S. ....Boston, MA
Larson, Jeffrey V. ....Tacoma, WA
Larson, Jeffry J. ....Emporia, KS
Larson, Jeremy R. ....Seattle, WA
Larson, Jerry D. ....Fargo, ND
Larson, Jerry G. ....Larned, KS
Larson, J. L. ....Des Moines, IA
Larson, Joanne E. K. ....Novato, CA
Larson, John A. ....Williamsport, IN
Larson, John A. ....Lincoln, NE
Larson, John B. ....Los Angeles, CA

Larson, John B. ....Severna Park, MD
Larson, John C. ....San Francisco, CA
Larson, John D. ....Madison, WI
Larson, John E. ....Essex, CT
Larson, John E. ....Lenexa, KS
Larson, John F. ....Portland, OR
Larson, John Farr ....Salt Lake City, UT
Larson, John H. ....Sacramento, CA
Larson, John K. ....Portland, OR
Larson, John R. ....Minneapolis, MN
Larson, John S. ....Cleveland, OH
Larson, John W. ....San Francisco, CA
Larson, John W. ....Walnut Creek, CA
Larson, John W. ....Tallahassee, FL
Larson, John W. ....Missoula, MT
Larson, John W. ....Chamberlain, SD
Larson, Jon C. ....Portland, OR
Larson, Jon H. ....Inver Grove Heights, MN
Larson, Jon R. ....Nome, AK
Larson, Jon S. ....Lexington, KY
Larson and Jones ....Miami Shores, FL
Larson, Joni ....Treasury Department,
Internal Revenue Service, GV
Larson, Joseph D. ....New York, NY
Larson, Joseph F., II ....Jamestown, ND
Larson, Joseph H. ....Livonia, MI
Larson, J. R. ....Atlantic, IA
Larson, Julie A. ....Chicago, IL
Larson, Julie M. ....Cleveland, OH
Larson, K. Ruth ....New Brunswick, NJ
Larson, Karen A. ....Marco Island, FL
Larson, Karen A., P.A. ....Marco Island, FL
Larson, Karin L. ....Portland, ME
Larson, Karin L. ....Kent, WA
Larson, Katherine B. ....Darien, CT
Larson, Kathleen H. ....Morrisville, PA
Larson, Keil M. ....Chicago, IL
Larson, Kelly ....Chicago, IL
Larson, Kenneth A. ....Minneapolis, MN
Larson, Kenneth W. ....San Francisco, CA
Larson, Kenneth W., (A Professional
Corporation) ....San Pablo, CA
Larson, Kent W. ....Burnsville, MN
Larson • King, LLP ....San Francisco, CA
Miami, FL
Boston, MA
Minneapolis, MN
St. Paul, MN
Larson, Kirkham & Turner
Salt Lake City, UT
Larson, Konrad K. ....Anaheim, CA
Larson, Kristin J. ....Port Orchard, WA
Larson, K. Ruth, A Professional Corporation
New Brunswick, NJ
Larson, Kurt D. ....Duluth, MN
Larson, Kurt J. ....Springfield, MO
Larson, Kyle I. E. ....Belvidere, IL
Larson, Larry C. ....Kansas City, MO
Larson, Larry W. ....Moses Lake, WA
Larson & Larson, P.A. ....Largo, FL
Larson & Larson, P.C. ....Kansas City, MO
Larson, Lary C. ....Department of Justice,
Environment and Natural Resources
Division, GV
Larson, Lary S. ....Idaho Falls, ID
Larson, Lauren A. ....Alexandria, VA
Larson, Laurie W., Jr. ....Belvidere, IL
Larson Law Firm, P.C. ....Minot, ND
Larson Law Office ....Decorah, IA
Larson Law Office ....Watertown, SD
Larson, Lawrence E. ....Greenwich, CT
Larson, Lee A. ....Spokane, WA
Larson, Lee E. ....Avon Lake, OH
Larson, Lennart V. ....Dallas, TX
Larson, Leslie L. ....Cleveland, OH
Larson, Lex K. ....Durham, NC
Larson, Lilienthal & Morris ....Reston, VA
Larson, Linda R. ....Seattle, WA
Larson, Lindsay A., III ....New Orleans, LA
Larson, Lisa F. ....St. Paul, MN
Larson, Lori R. ....Treasury Department,
Internal Revenue Service, GV
Larson, Lyle David ....Birmingham, AL
Larson, Marc W. ....Decatur, IL
Larson, Marcia A. ....Escondido, CA
Larson, Marina T. ....Frisco, CO
Larson, Marion V. "Mick" ....Seattle, WA
Larson, Mark A. ....Pittsburgh, PA
Larson, Mark C. ....Detroit, MI
Larson, Mark E. ....Milwaukee, WI
Larson, Mark E., Jr. ....Naperville, IL
Larson, Mark J. ....Washington, DC
Larson, Mark R. ....Seattle, WA
Larson, Mark S. ....Minneapolis, MN
Larson, Mark S. ....Gulfport, MS
Larson, Mark V. ....Minot, ND
Larson, Mary Jo ....Detroit, MI
Larson, Mary Vandelicht ....Kansas City, MO
Larson, Max W. ....Lancaster, CA
Larson & Melcher ....Fridley, MN
Larson, Meria E. ....Detroit, MI
Larson, Michael ....Watertown, SD
Larson, Michael A. ....Seattle, WA
Larson, Michele M. ....Stockton, CA
Larson, Michelle M. ....Milwaukee, WI
Larson, Michelle, P.C. ....Laurel, MD
Larson, Michelle VonSenden ....Dallas, TX
Larson, Mundy & Evenson ....Iowa City, IA
Larson, Nancy J. ....Syracuse, NY
Larson, Nancy R. ....Belleville, IL
Larson & Nipe ....Mitchell, SD
Woonsocket, SD
Larson, Norman T. ....San Francisco, CA
Larson, O. Bruce ....Conroe, TX
Larson, Olive E. ....Boston, MA
Larson, Orval A., (Ltd.) ....Orland Park, IL
Larson & Owen, P.C. ....Portland, OR

Larson, Pamela J., (Atty. At Law, A Law Corp.) ....Honolulu, HI
Larson, Patricia A. ....Palm Desert, CA
Larson, Patricia J. ....Philadelphia, PA
Larson, Patricia Shea ....Pacific, MO
Larson, Patrick C. ....Ellsworth, ME
Larson, Paul E. ....Des Moines, IA
Larson, Paul M. ....Yakima, WA
Larson, Paul T. ....New Milford, CT
Larson, Peder A. ....St. Paul, MN
Larson & Perkins, P.L.L.C. ....Yakima, WA
Larson, Perry & Ward ....Naperville, IL
Larson, Peter N. ....San Francisco, CA
Larson, Philip B. ....Minneapolis, MN
Larson, Philip C. ....Washington, DC
Larson, Phillip K. ....Denver, CO
Larson, R. William ....Buffalo, NY
Larson, Rachel A. ....Seattle, WA
Larson, Raeder ....Minneapolis, MN
Larson, Ralph E. ....Long Beach, CA
Larson, Randy ....Iowa City, IA
Larson, Ray ....Lexington, KY
Larson, Rebecca L. ....West Palm Beach, FL
Larson, Rebecca M. ....Tacoma, WA
Larson, Regina A. ....Ada, MN
Larson, Reneé Michelle ....Laurel, MD
Larson, Richard A. ....St. Paul, MN
Larson, Richard A. ....Helena, MT
Larson, Richard D. ....De Kalb, IL
Larson, Richard J. ....St. Charles, IL
Larson, Richard L. ....Eugene, OR
Larson, Richard M. ....Covington, LA
Larson, Robert D. ....Alton, IL
Larson, Robert G. ....Bountiful, UT
Larson, Robert H. ....Seattle, WA
Larson, Robert J. ....Essex, CT
Larson, Robert J. ....Eugene, OR
Larson, Robert L. ....Cleveland, OH
Larson, Robert P. ....Minneapolis, MN
Larson, Roberta L. ....Sacramento, CA
Larson, Roger A. ....Clearwater, FL
Larson, Roma Barksdale ....Springfield, IL
Larson, Ronald ....St. Helena, CA
Larson, Ronald D. ....Washington, DC
Larson, Ronald E. ....Chicago, IL
Larson, Ronald F. ....Sun City, AZ
Larson, Ronald F., P.C. ....Peoria, AZ
Phoenix, AZ
Sun City, AZ
Larson, Ronald V. ....Riverside, CA
Larson, Rosemary A. ....Bellevue, WA
Larson, Roy B. ....Stamford, CT
Larson, Roy J. ....Miami, FL
Larson, Rozanna C. ....Minot, ND
Larson, Sandra Twiss ....Encino, CA
Larson, Sarah Richardson
Sioux Falls, SD
Larson, Sarah Yates ....Birmingham, AL
Larson & Schainost, LLC ....Wichita, KS
Larson, Scott A. ....Dallas, TX
Larson, Scott P. ....Geneva, IL
Larson, Scott R. ....Denver, CO
Green Lake, WI
Larson, Scott R., P.C. ....Denver, CO
Green Lake, WI
Larson, Scott T. ....Denver, CO
Larson, Sharon D. ....Fort Pierce, FL
Larson, Sheldon S. ....Winthrop, MN
Larson & Simpson, P.C. ....Batavia, IL
Larson, Sonja A. ....Minneapolis, MN
Larson, Stephen C. ....Denver, CO
Larson, Stephen G. ....Los Angeles, CA
Larson, Stephen H. ....St. Louis, MO
Larson, Stephen P. ....Seattle, WA
Larson, Stephen R. ....Portland, OR
Larson, Stephen R. ....Richmond, VA
Larson, Steve D. ....Portland, OR
Larson, Steven K. ....Chandler, AZ
Larson, Steven L. ....Waukegan, IL
Larson, Steven L. ....Tacoma, WA
Larson, Stuart A. ....Hillsboro, ND
Larson, Stuart A., P.C. ....Hillsboro, ND
Larson, Sundall, Larson, Schaub & Fox, P.C.
Chamberlain, SD
Kennebec, SD
Larson & Taylor ....Washington, DC
Alexandria, VA
Arlington, VA
Larson, Theadore A. ....Lyons, OR
Larson, Thomas A. ....Minneapolis, MN
Larson, Thomas Dean ....St. Louis, MO
Larson, Thomas E. ....Erie, PA
Larson, Thomas M. ....Casa Grande, AZ
Larson, Thomas R. ....Kansas City, MO
Larson, Tim J. ....Wichita, KS
Larson, Timbers & Van Winkle, Inc.
Nome, AK
Larson, Timothy A. ....Mission Hills, CA
Larson, Timothy D. ....Austin, TX
Larson, Todd S. ....Louisville, CO
Larson, Valerie N. ....San Diego, CA
Larson, Van A. ....Batavia, IL
Larson, Vandersloot & Rivers
San Pablo, CA
Larson, Vicki J. ....Washington, DC
Larson, Vincent R. ....Seattle, WA
Larson, W. Louis ....Astoria, OR
Larson, Wallace L. ....Phoenix, AZ
Larson, Wallace L. ....New York, NY
Larson, Ward J. ....Glen Ellyn, IL
Larson, Warren H. ....Rockford, IL
Larson, Warren H., P.C. ....Rockford, IL
Larson, Wayne ....Willmar, MN
Larson & Weisinger ....Conroe, TX
Larson, Wendy Lisa Coretz ....Rockford, IL
Larson, William A. ....Topeka, KS
Larson, William G. ....Laguna Niguel, CA
Larson, William L. ....Beverly Hills, CA

Larson, William P. ....Azusa, CA
Larson-Jackson, Laurie
Federal Deposit Insurance Corporation,
Liquidation Branch, GV
Larson-Jackson, Steve ....Washington, DC
Larsson, David J. ....Philadelphia, PA
Larsson, Gustav J. ....Phoenix, AZ
Larsson, John A. ....Eugene, OR
Lartigue, C.W., IV ....Metairie, LA
Lartz, John A. ....Chicago, IL
LaRue, Adrian J. ....Harrisburg, PA
La Rue, Ann E. ....New York, NY
La Rue, Annette ....Fresno, CA
La Rue, Beth Z. ....Cleveland, OH
LaRue, Carl F. ....Toledo, OH
LaRue, Dan F. ....Portland, OR
LaRue, Dan F., P.C. ....Portland, OR
LaRue, David A. ....Steubenville, OH
LaRue, Denise K. ....Indianapolis, IN
La Rue, Edward R. ....Cleveland, OH
Larue, Homer C. ....Washington, DC
LaRue, Hugh F., III ....Greeneville, TN
LaRue, James D. ....Boise, ID
LaRue, Janis M. ....Maynard, MA
LaRue, John B. ....Muncie, IN
La Rue, Joseph E. ....Phoenix, AZ
LaRue Law Firm ....Daytona Beach, FL
LaRue, Lawrence B. ....Toledo, OH
LaRue, Lewis H. ....Lexington, VA
LaRue, Mary Kay ....Colorado Springs, CO
LaRue, Michelle L. ....Fort Lauderdale, FL
LaRue, Patricia ....Arlington, TX
LaRue, Paul H. ....Chicago, IL
LaRue, Paul H., Jr. ....Chicago, IL
Larue, Roger J., Jr. ....Metairie, LA
LaRue, Sharon Elaine ....Memphis, TN
LaRue, Terrill J. ....Daytona Beach, FL
LaRue, William W. ....Kansas City, MO
La Ruffa, Francis V. ....Highland Beach, FL
LaRuffa, Mary Elizabeth ....New York, NY
Larus, Christopher K. ....Minneapolis, MN
LaRusch, James P. ....West Seneca, NY
LaRussa, Dennis A., (P.A.)
Key Biscayne, FL
LaRussa, James P. ....Tampa, FL
LaRussa, Ronald ....Boston, MA
LaRussa, Rudy G. ....Tampa, FL
Larussa, Salvatore S. ....Philadelphia, PA
LaRussa, Stephen M. ....Houma, LA
La Russo, Anthony J. ....Westfield, NJ
La Russo, Gerard M. ....Rochester, NY
Larvadain, Edward, Jr. ....Alexandria, LA
Larvick, Matthew P. ....Chicago, IL
Larvie, Veronica I.
Department Of The Interior,
Office of the Solicitor, GV
Larvik, Cory ....Portland, OR
Larwill & Wolfe ....Los Angeles, CA
Larwood, David J. ....Livermore, CA
Lary, Camm C., Jr. ....Burnet, TX
Lary, Camm C. "Trey", III ....Houston, TX
Lary, Michael R. ....Cedar Park, TX
Lary, Mike R., P.C. ....Cedar Park, TX
Larywon, Kenneth R. ....New York, NY
Larzelere, H. T., Jr. (P.A.)
Little Rock, AR
Larzelere & Picou, L.L.P. ....Metairie, LA
New Orleans, LA
Larzelere, Stephen M. ....Metairie, LA
Larzelere, William J., III ....New Orleans, LA
Larzelere, William J., Jr. ....Metairie, LA
Lasa, Monroig & Veve ....Washington, DC
Lasa, Monroig & Veve ....Guaynabo, PR
Lasa Ferrer, Armando ....Guaynabo, PR
Lasagna, Mary Angela ....Overland Park, KS
LaSaine, Dorian B. ....Peoria, IL
Lasak, John ....Bala Cynwyd, PA
Lasala, Anthony J. ....New Haven, CT
La Sala, Bruce ....Englewood, NJ
LaSala, Jake ....Kew Gardens, NY
LaSala, James E. ....Riverdale, NJ
Lasala, John P. ....New York, NY
LaSala, Joseph A., Jr. ....Fort Worth, TX
LaSala, Joseph F. ....Newark, NJ
La Sala, Joseph P. ....Morristown, NJ
La Sala, Lawrence J. ....New York, NY
LaSala, Marie A. ....San Diego, CA
LaSala, Stephen R. ....Fairfax, VA
LaSala, Todd A. ....Kansas City, MO
Lasala, Walsh & Wicklow ....New Haven, CT
La Salle, Brandon E. ....Englewood, CO
LaSalle, Faith A. ....Wellesley, MA
Providence, RI
LaSalle, Frank J. ....New York, NY
Lasalle, Hector Daniel ....Mineola, NY
LaSalle, James ....Kansas City, MO
LaSalle, John D. ....Aspen, CO
La Salle, Lawrence ....Columbus, OH
La Salle, LeRoy ....Carthage, TX
LaSalle, Michael E. ....Hanford, CA
LaSalle, Nina S. White ....Fall River, MA
LaSalle, Raymond M. ....Marlton, NJ
La Salle, Richard ....Jackson Heights, NY
LaSalle, Richard C. ....Sacramento, CA
LaSalle, Richard N. ....Fall River, MA
LaSalle, Robert C. ....West Paterson, NJ
LaSalle, Susan Laurea ....Dallas, TX
LaSalle, Thomas L. ....Fort Lauderdale, FL
LaSalle & White ....Fall River, MA
LaSalle, William J. ....Richardson, TX
LaSalvia, Anthony J. ....Akron, OH
Lasar, Daniel ....Washington, DC
Lasarow, Jerald M. ....South Lake Tahoe, CA
Lasarow, William J. ....Los Angeles, CA
Lasarte, Felix M. ....Miami, FL
LaSasso, James F. ....Portland, OR
La Sata, Charles J. ....Niles, MI
LaSata, Charles T. ....St. Joseph, MI

Lasater & Associates, P.C. ... Denver, CO
Lasater, F. Wilbert ... Tyler, TX
Lasater, Ike K. ... San Francisco, CA
Lasater, J. Scott ... Denver, CO
Lasater, John R. ... St. Louis, MO
Lasater, Marceline L. ... Austin, TX
Lasater, Mary Meghan ... Kansas City, MO
Lasater, Melinda J. ... San Diego, CA
Lasater, Nancy E., The Law Office of ... Washington, DC
Lasater, Richard W., II ... Los Angeles, CA
Lasater, Thomas J. ... Wichita, KS
Lasater, W. Robert, Jr. ... Albuquerque, NM
La Scala, Paul B. ... Irvine, CA
La Scala, Robert F. ... San Diego, CA
La Scala, Stacy L. ... San Diego, CA
Lascara, Dominic P. ... Chesapeake, VA
Lascara, William A. ... Norfolk, VA
Virginia Beach, VA
Lascari, Scott C. ... Chicago, IL
Lascell, Daniel M. ... McLean, VA
Lascell, David M. ... Rochester, NY
Lasch, Debora S. ... Cleveland, OH
Lasch, Doreen E. ... Miami, FL
Lasch, Frank J. ... Albany, NY
Lasch, Moira Kehoe ... West Palm Beach, FL
Lascheid, Elizabeth M. ... Los Angeles, CA
Lascher, Alan A. ... New York, NY
Lascher & Lascher, A Professional Corporation ... Los Angeles, CA
Santa Barbara, CA
Ventura, CA
Lascher, Lascher & Kintzer ... Newburgh, NY
Lascher, Susan B. ... Ventura, CA
Lascher, Wendy Cole ... Ventura, CA
Laschet, Jana W. ... Atlanta, GA
Laschever, Eric S. ... Seattle, WA
Laschever, Richard B. ... East Hartford, CT
Laschewer, Heather Leigh ... New York, NY
Lasco, Laura L. ... East Rutherford, NJ
Lasco, Robt J. ... Lorain, OH
Lascoe, Jerry ... Birmingham, MI
Columbus, OH
Lascoe, John S. ... Sterling Heights, MI
Lascoe, John S., P.C. ... Sterling Heights, MI
lascone, Peter M. ... Newport, RI
Lascurettes, Tod M. ... Utica, NY
Lasday, H. Robert ... Harrisburg, PA
Lasdon, Douglas H. ... New York, NY
Lasee, Lawrence J. ... Green Bay, WI
Lasee, Mark E. ... Phoenix, AZ
Laser, Adam M. ... Chicago, IL
Laser, Alvin ... Houston, TX
Laser, David M. ... San Francisco, CA
Laser, David N. ... Jonesboro, AR
Laser, Gail E., Law Offices of ... New York, NY
Laser, Gary S. ... Chicago, IL
Laser, Jennifer E. ... Los Angeles, CA
Laser, Jules M. ... Chicago, IL
Laser, Pokorny, Schwartz, Friedman & Economos, P.C. ... Chicago, IL
Laser, Proctor & Cole, P.C. ... Houston, TX
Laser, Rachel K. ... Boston, MA
Laser, Sam ... Little Rock, AR
Laser, Wilson, Bufford & Watts, P.A. ... Little Rock, AR
Laser-Bair, Susan E. ... Cheyenne, WY
Lasersohn, Helen H. ... New York, NY
Lasersohn, Thomas D. ... New York, NY
Laserson, Lillian J. ... New York, NY
La Serte & Associates, LLC ... Fairfax, VA
Falls Church, VA
Herndon, VA
La Serte, Robert Edmund ... Fairfax, VA
Laseter, James W. ... Honolulu, HI
Laseter, John R. ... Monroe, GA
Laseter, W. Scott ... Atlanta, GA
Lasezkay, George M. ... Irvine, CA
Lash, Alan D. ... Miami, FL
Lash, Alice Jacobson ... Miami, FL
Lash, Arthur G. ... Princeton, NJ
Lash, David A. ... Los Angeles, CA
Lash, David L. ... Beachwood, OH
Lash, Donald A. ... New York, NY
Lash, Douglas S. ... Omaha, NE
Lash & Goldberg LLP ... Miami, FL
Lash, Jonathon O. ... Chicago, IL
Lash, Joseph W. ... Southfield, MI
Lash, Karen A. ... Los Angeles, CA
Lash, Kathleen Davis ... Arlington, VA
Lash, Kelli Lester ... Charlotte, NC
Lash, Lawrence G. ... Olney, MD
Lash, Lester S. ... Columbus, OH
Lash, Michael E. ... Fresno, CA
Lash, Nancy B. ... Fairfax, VA
Lash, Peter Ross ... Miami, FL
Lash, Richard A. ... Fairfax, VA
Lash, Robert L. ... San Francisco, CA
Lash, Scott E. ... Reading, PA
Lash, Stephen H. ... Boston, MA
Lash, William H., III ... Arlington, VA
Lashaw, Robert J. ... New York, NY
Lashaway, Jeff R. ... Lubbock, TX
Lashay, Jill M. ... Pittsburgh, PA
Lashbrook, John B. ... Indianapolis, IN
Lashbrook, Linda ... Woodbridge, NJ
Lashbrook, Paul N. ... Fort Lauderdale, FL
Lashbrooke, Elvin C., Jr. ... East Lansing, MI
Lashenske, Andrew J. ... Cambridge, MA
Lasher, Alan D. ... Staten Island, NY
Lasher, Allan ... Los Angeles, CA
Lasher, Alvin W. ... Akron, OH
Lasher, Cheryl D. ... Oklahoma City, OK
Lasher, Earl P., III ... Seattle, WA
Lasher, Harold P. ... San Diego, CA
Lasher Holzapfel Sperry & Ebberson, PLLC ... Seattle, WA
Lasher, Howard L. ... New York, NY
Lasher, Humes T. ... Fort Lauderdale, FL
Lasher, Lisa S. ... New York, NY
Lasher, Lori Leigh ... Philadelphia, PA
Lasher, Michael David ... Oakland, CA
Lasher, Nancy I. ... Highland Park, NJ
Lasher, S. Scott ... Denver, CO
Lasher, Steven H. ... Lansing, MI
Lasher, William W., III ... New York, NY
Lashford, David ... Texarkana, TX
Lashgari, David T. ... Atlanta, GA
LaShier, Richard D. ... Environmental Protection Agency, Program Office Attorneys, GV
Lashin, Arthur ... Philadelphia, PA
Lashinger, Joseph A., Jr. ... Wyomissing, PA
Lashinsky, Ilene J. ... Phoenix, AZ
Lashinsky, Larry D. ... Hollidaysburg, PA
Lashinsky, Samuel J. ... Bayonne, NJ
Lashkari, Leily ... New York, NY
Lashlee, Butler & Darling, P.A. ... Rogers, AR
Lashlee, C. Timothy ... Long Beach, CA
Lashlee, K. R. ... Rogers, AR
Lashley, Allen ... Brooklyn, NY
Lashley, Curtis D. ... Independence, MO
Lashley, Douglas L. ... San Antonio, TX
Lashley, Gary J. ... Edmond, OK
Lashley, K. Michele ... Durham, NC
Lashley, Lenore ... Los Angeles, CA
Lashley, Lisa G. ... Brooklyn, NY
Lashley-Greenbaum, Jill ... New York, NY
Lashly & Baer, P.C. ... St. Louis, MO
Lashman, Deborah ... St. Albans, VT
Lashman, Shelley B. ... Camden, NJ
Lashmit, Dianne E. ... Knoxville, TN
Lashner, Gary A. ... Philadelphia, PA
Lashner, Michael A. ... Newtown, PA
Lashner, Parker & Giannone ... Philadelphia, PA
Lashner, William ... Wynnewood, PA
Lashnits, George R. ... Stuart, FL
Lashnits, Nancy M. ... Portland, OR
Lashomb, Laurie A. ... Cocoa, FL
Lashuk, Beth Anne S. ... Columbus, OH
Lashus, Kevin Robert ... Austin, TX
Lashutka, Gregory S. ... Columbus, OH
Lashway, David ... Washington, DC
Lashway, J. Lee ... Eugene, OR
Lashway, Patricia K. ... Olympia, WA
Lasica, Donald P. ... Hinsdale, IL
Lasich, A. Robert, Jr. ... Des Moines, IA
Lasich, Michael F. ... Sacramento, CA
Lasics, Jean M. ... Oak Brook, IL
Wheaton, IL
Lasics-Parker, Julie ... Warrenville, IL
Lasine, Andrew S. ... High Point, NC
Lasitter, Moses Dow ... New Bern, NC
Lask, Andrew ... Brooklyn, NY
Lask, Kathryn Ulrich ... Kansas City, KS
Lask, Michael D. ... Southfield, MI
Lask, Susan Chana ... New York, NY
Laska, Alan J. ... New York, NY
Laska, Casimir F. ... Milwaukee, WI
Laska, George ... Warren, MI
Laska, George, P.C. ... Warren, MI
Laska, Gerald W. ... Cheyenne, WY
Laska, Jeffery H. ... New York, NY
Laska, Kenneth John ... Plainville, CT
Laska, Lewis L. ... Nashville, TN
Laska, Meghan Seale ... Boston, MA
Laska, Walter J. ... Lakewood, OH
Laskaris, Nancy Yost ... Minneapolis, MN
Laskay, C. Mark ... New York, NY
Laske, Arthur C., III ... Bridgeport, CT
Laske, Arthur C., III ... Trumbull, CT
Laske, Dawn K. ... Mineola, NY
Lasken, Glen J. ... Portland, OR
Lasken, Jesse E. ... National Science Foundation, Office of the General Counsel, GV
Lasker, Arthur E. ... New York, NY
Lasker, David E. ... Madison, WI
Lasker, Eric G. ... Washington, DC
Lasker, Helene C. ... Washington, DC
Lasker, Joel M. ... Princeton, NJ
New York, NY
Lasker, Judith Olson ... Brea, CA
Lasker, Kenneth M. ... Jamestown, NY
Lasker, Kristen ... Cambridge, MA
Lasker, Morris E. ... Boston, MA
Lasker, Richard S. ... New York, NY
Lasker, Robert J. ... Arlington, VA
Laskey, Dona Scott ... Southfield, MI
Traverse City, MI
Laskey, Henry Brook ... Albuquerque, NM
Laskey, James H. ... Somerville, NJ
Laskey, John L. ... Cherry Hill, NJ
Laskey, Kimberly B. ... Cherry Hill, NJ
Laskey, Lawrence A. ... Schaumburg, IL
Laskey, Norman P. ... Mystic, CT
Laskey, Richard C. ... White Plains, NY
Laskey, Robert M. ... Portland, ME
Laski, Cornell ... San Diego, CA
Laski, Frank J. ... Salem, MA
Laski, Frank J. ... Kenmore, NY
Laski & Gordon ... Los Angeles, CA
Laski, James E. ... Chicago, IL
Laski, James R. ... Ketchum, ID
Laski, Mortimer L. ... Los Angeles, CA
Laski, Warren C. ... Chicago, IL
Laskin, Alan M. ... Sacramento, CA
Laskin, Andrew M. ... New York, NY
Laskin, Edward S. ... New York, NY
Laskin, Franklin Theo. ... Angels Camp, CA
Laskin & Graham ... Glendale, CA
Los Angeles, CA
Santa Ana, CA
Laskin & Guenard ... Sacramento, CA
Laskin, Herbert ... Los Angeles, CA
Laskin, Herbert, A Law Corporation ... Los Angeles, CA
Laskin, Jared ... Los Angeles, CA
Laskin, Jeffrey L. ... Phoenix, AZ
Laskin, Jeffrey L., P.C. ... Phoenix, AZ
Laskin, Jonathan B. ... Brooklyn, NY
Laskin, Lee B. ... Camden, NJ
Laskin, Michelle F. ... Mineola, NY
Laskin, Nicole A. ... New York, NY
Laskin, Richard ... Glendale, CA
Laskin, Sheldon H. ... Washington, DC
Laskin, Stephen E. ... Wellesley, MA
Laskin, Wendy S. ... Phoenix, AZ
Laskis, Michael G. ... Madison, WI
Lasko, Bennett W. ... Chicago, IL
Lasko, John J., Jr. ... Cleveland, OH
Lasko, Norman ... Chicago, IL
Lasko, Richard P. ... New York, NY
Lasko, Ronald H. ... Cleveland, OH
Lasko, William E., II, P.C. ... Chicago, IL
Lasko, William E., II (P.C.) ... Chicago, IL
Lasko, William E., Sr. ... Chicago, IL
Laskody, Lee ... Graham, NC
Laskoff & Associates ... Lewiston, ME
Laskoff, Leo L. ... New York, NY
Laskoff, Robert A. ... Lewiston, ME
Laskoff, Susan I. ... New York, NY
Laskow, Mark J. ... Pittsburgh, PA
Laskow, Paul J. ... Philadelphia, PA
Laskowska, Malgorzata ... San Jose, CA
Laskowski, Edward J. ... Littleton, CO
Laskowski, John J. ... Milwaukee, WI
Laskowski, Joseph M. ... Kansas City, KS
Laskowski, Joseph M., P.A. ... Kansas City, KS
Laskowski, Robert C. ... Portland, OR
Laskowski, Ronald J. ... Topeka, KS
Laskowski, Stanley J. A. ... Harrisburg, PA
Lasky, Allan N. ... Chicago, IL
Lasky, Arnold ... New York, NY
Lasky, Barry M. ... Garden City, NY
Lasky, Beth S. ... New York, NY
Lasky, Bigge & Rodriguez, P.A. ... Fort Lauderdale, FL
Miami, FL
Lasky, Carolyn S. ... York, PA
Lasky, Charles L. ... Lansing, MI
Lasky and Cohen ... Newark, NJ
Lasky, David C. ... Columbus, OH
Lasky, Edward ... St. Louis, MO
Lasky, Eleanor A. ... Roanoke, VA
Lasky Fifarek & Hogan, P.C. ... Lansing, MI
Lasky, Floria V. ... New York, NY
Lasky, George J. ... Newark, NJ
Lasky, Gilbert P. ... Newport Beach, CA
Lasky, Haas & Cohler, Professional Corporation ... San Francisco, CA
Lasky, Harvey L. ... Miami, FL
Lasky, Helaine B. ... Oakland, CA
Lasky, Henry B. ... San Francisco, CA
Lasky, Herbert ... Fairfield, CA
Lasky, Howard ... San Francisco, CA
Lasky, Jeffrey W. ... Savannah, GA
Lasky, Jerome M. ... New York, NY
Lasky, Joseph A. ... San Francisco, CA
Lasky, Kenneth J. ... Roanoke, VA
Lasky, Laurence Alan ... Dayton, OH
Lasky, Laurence D. ... Chicago, IL
Lasky, Leigh R. ... New York, NY
Lasky, Lewis A. ... Worcester, MA
Lasky, Lynn M. ... Miamisburg, OH
Lasky, Manuel ... St. Louis, MO
Lasky, Marc B. ... Morristown, NJ
Lasky, Matthew J. ... New York, NY
Lasky, Michael B. ... Minneapolis, MN
Lasky, Michael C. ... New York, NY
Lasky, Monica B. ... Chicago, IL
Lasky, Moses ... San Francisco, CA
Lasky, Paul H. ... Fawnskin, CA
Lasky & Rifkind, Ltd. ... Chicago, IL
New York, NY
Lasky, Robert F. ... Miami, FL
Lasky, Robert J. ... Chicago, IL
Lasky, Robert L. ... New York, NY
Lasky, Robert S. ... New York, NY
Lasky, Robert T. ... Washington, DC
Lasky, Ronald E. ... New London, CT
Lasky & Scharrer ... Dayton, OH
Lasky, Sean R. ... New York, NY
Lasky & Semons ... Columbus, OH
Lasky, Sondra V. ... Newark, NJ
Lasky, Steve M. ... Denver, CO
Lasky, Susan D. ... Fort Lauderdale, FL
Lasky, Thomas D. ... Bingham Farms, MI
Lasky-Levine, Terry Ann ... Sherman Oaks, CA
Lasley, Candis D. ... Knoxville, TN
Lasley, Dana A. ... St. Louis, MO
Lasley, Donald M. ... Soddy-Daisy, TN
Lasley, Edward Lee ... Louisville, KY
Lasley, Francine Kay ... Cleveland, OH
Lasley, John W. ... Cocoa, FL
Lasley, Jonathan G. ... Baltimore, MD
Lasley, Lee Ann ... Topeka, KS
Lasley, Linda M. ... Pasadena, CA
Lasley, Peter J. ... Carthage, MO
Lasley, T. Terrell ... Houston, TX
Lasley, Thomas L. ... Kansas City, MO
Lasley, Wilbur M. ... Minneapolis, MN
Lasley, William Joseph ... Carthage, MO
Laslie, Melinda Milby ... Campbellsville, KY
Laslo, Ruth G. ... Stamford, CT
Lasman, Edwin I., (P.C.) ... Los Angeles, CA
Newport Beach, CA
Lasner, Harvey R. ... East Syracuse, NY
Lasner, Richard F. ... Department of Housing and Urban Development, Office of General Counsel, GV
Lasnick, David P. ... Stamford, CT
Lasnik, Robert S. ... Seattle, WA
Lasof, Edward L., (P.C.) ... Houston, TX
Lasoff, Laurence J. ... Washington, DC
Lasorella, William T. ... Peru, IL
La Sorsa & Beneventano ... New York, NY
La Sorsa, Gregory M. ... New York, NY
Lasorsa, Joseph F. ... Milford, MA
LaSorsa, William G. ... Tulsa, OK
LaSorte, Alfred A., Jr. ... West Palm Beach, FL
LaSota, A. Douglas ... Phoenix, AZ
LaSota, A. Douglas, & Associates, A Prof. Corp. ... Phoenix, AZ
LaSota, David J. ... Chicago, IL
LaSota, Douglas C. ... Pittsburgh, PA
LaSota, John A., Jr. ... Phoenix, AZ
Lasota, Marie C. ... Philadelphia, PA
La Sota, Melanie M. ... Pittsburgh, PA
LaSovage, Michael E. ... Lima, OH
Lasover, Morris ... Baltimore, MD
La Soya, Ray ... Los Angeles, CA
LaSpada, Anthony J. ... Tampa, FL
LaSpada, Anthony J., P.A. ... Tampa, FL
LaSpada, Anthony P. ... Montvale, NJ
Laspia, Tessa M. ... Baltimore, MD
LaSpina, Gregory M. ... Whitestone, NY
La Spina, Mark S. ... Austin, TX
Laspisa, Vincent, III ... New York, NY
Lasris, Lee F. ... Miami, FL
Lasris, Roy H. ... Yorktown, VA
Lasris & Vannan, P.C. ... Yorktown, VA
Lasry, Lynne R. ... San Diego, CA
Lass, Adam Bennett ... New York, NY
Lass, Christina M. L. ... Wheaton, IL
Lass, David R. ... Breckenridge, CO
Lass, Robert A. ... Hackensack, NJ
Lass, Steven C. ... Denver, CO
Lassa, Dennis R. ... St. Louis, MO
Lassagne, Theodore H. ... Walnut Creek, CA
Lassalette, John M. ... Aspen, CO
Lassalle, Annette M. ... Baton Rouge, LA
Lassalle, Jane Marie ... Northborough, MA
Lassar, Scott R. ... Chicago, IL
Lassar, Stephen D. ... New York, NY
Lassart, James A. ... San Francisco, CA
Lassaw, Donald A. ... Boise, ID
Lasseigne, Janis M. ... Thibodaux, LA
Lasseigne, Ted A. ... Haines City, FL
Lasseigne, Ted A., P.A. ... Haines City, FL
Lassen, Abby H. ... San Francisco, CA
Lassen, Albert B. ... Albuquerque, NM
Lassen, Barbara J. ... Sterling Heights, MI
Lassen, Elizabeth ... Davis, CA
Lassen, Gary L. ... Phoenix, AZ
Lassen, J. Kai ... Wilmington, DE
Lassen & Jaffe ... Albuquerque, NM
Lassen, Nancy B. G. ... Harrisburg, PA
Philadelphia, PA
Lassen, Richard L. ... Phoenix, AZ
Lassen, Svein J. ... Newport News, VA
Lassen, Wendy A. ... Washington, DC
Lasser, Alyse I. ... Chicago, IL
Lasser, Donald M. ... Del Mar, CA
Lasser, Herbert S. ... Merrillville, IN
Lasser Hochman, L.L.C. ... Hackensack, NJ
Newark, NJ
Roseland, NJ
Lasser, Lawrence L. ... Pottersville, NJ
Lasser, Mark L. ... San Francisco, CA
Lasser, Miles L. ... Jamestown, NY
Lasser, Mitchel D. ... New Haven, CT
Lasser, Myron G. ... Staten Island, NY
Lasser, Myron G., P.C. ... Staten Island, NY
Lassers, Willard J. ... Chicago, IL
Lasseter, Alan B. ... Pell City, AL
Lasseter, Earle F. ... Atlanta, GA
Columbus, GA
Lasseter, Edward L., Jr. ... Tuscaloosa, AL
Lasseter, Jack H. ... Tucson, AZ
Lasseter, R. Jeff ... Macon, GA
Lassetter, Scott D. ... Houston, TX
Lassey, John A. ... Manchester, NH
Lassi, Peter ... Harrisburg, PA
Lassig, Paulette-Gail ... St. Paul, MN
Lassila, Carol J. ... Helena, MT
Lassinger, Dora M. ... Cedarhurst, NY
Lassise, Robin K. ... Winona, MN
Lassiter, A. Lee, Jr. ... Treasury Department, Office of Thrift Supervision, GV
Lassiter, Andrew A. ... Morehead City, NC
Lassiter, Barbara M. ... Atlanta, GA
Lassiter, Duane L. ... Philadelphia, PA
Lassiter, Herbert C. ... Chicago, IL
Lassiter, Horace A., Jr. ... Greenbelt, MD
Lassiter, J. Donnell ... Charlotte, NC
Lassiter, Jack T. ... Little Rock, AR
Lassiter, James M. ... Murray, KY
Lassiter, Joe F., Jr. ... Duncan, SC
Lassiter, John M., Jr. ... Mobile, AL
Lassiter, John Wells ... Charlotte, NC
Lassiter, Joseph R., Jr. ... Norfolk, VA
Lassiter, Lawrence R. ... Dallas, TX
Lassiter, Leah D. ... Elizabethtown, NC
Fayetteville, NC
Jacksonville, NC
New Bern, NC
Shallotte, NC
Wilmington, NC
Lassiter, Mark E. ... Mesa, AZ
Lassiter, Nicole ... New York, NY
Lassiter, Richard W. ... Orlando, FL
Lassiter, Robert, Jr. ... Charlotte, NC
Lassiter, Samuel D. ... Valdosta, GA

Lassiter & Sessions ... Jacksonville, FL
Lassiter, T. Michael ... Statesville, NC
Lassiter, T Michael, Jr. ... Statesville, NC
Lassiter, Tidwell & Hildebrand
Brentwood, TN
Nashville, TN
Lassiter, Will H., III ... Rocky Mount, NC
Lassiter, William H., Jr. ... Nashville, TN
Lassiter, William T., Jr. ... Jacksonville, FL
Lassleben, William M., Jr. ... Whittier, CA
Lassman, Donald R. ... Boston, MA
Lassman, Edwin A. ... Hartford, CT
Lassman, Garry W. ... Pittsburg, KS
Lassman, Malcolm, (P.C.)
Washington, DC
Lassman, Mark J. ... Hartford, CT
Lassman, Prescott M. ... Washington, DC
Lassman, Richard ... Seattle, WA
Lassmann, Robert Charles ... Cuero, TX
Lassner, John C. ... Sacramento, CA
Lassner, Kip O. ... Fort Lauderdale, FL
Naples, FL
Lasso, David R. ... McLean, VA
Lasso, Jilma M. ... Miami, FL
Lasso, Ricardo A. ... Washington, DC
Lasso, Rogelio A. ... Topeka, KS
Lasso, Scott J. ... Raleigh, NC
Lasson, Kenneth L. ... Baltimore, MD
Lasson, Lori B. ... New York, NY
Lassota, Michael A. ... Craig, CO
Lassow, Dina R. ... Washington, DC
Lassus, Edward J., Jr. ... New Orleans, LA
Lassus, Kenneth J. ... Department of the Army, Office of the Judge Advocate General, GV
Lasswell, Bryan R. ... Galveston, TX
Lasswell, Gerald D. ... Wichita, KS
Lasswell, Michelle Marie ... Olivia, MN
Lasswell, Roberta Lee ... Roseburg, OR
Lasswell, Roy S. ... Hinckley, IL
Lasswell, William L. ... Roseburg, OR
Last, Andrew, The Law Offices of
Sacramento, CA
Last, Bennett H. ... Greenwich, CT
New York, NY
Last, Fred B. ... Woodbury, NJ
Last, Harrelson & Faoro
San Francisco, CA
San Mateo, CA
Last, Meyer ... New York, NY
Last, Michael P. ... Boston, MA
Last, Richard S. ... New York, NY
Last, Walter J. ... Newport Beach, CA
Last, William C., Jr. ... San Mateo, CA
LaStaiti, Elizabeth O'Neill
New Bedford, MA
Lastelic, Robert E. ... Overland Park, KS
Lastelick, Jerry ... Dallas, TX
Lastella, Vito M. ... Jamaica, NY
Laster, Alan M. ... Portland, OR
Laster, Anita ... Cleveland, OH
Laster, Charles M. ... Shawnee, OK
Laster, Daniel ... Redmond, WA
Laster, Dorothea E. ... Denton, TX
Laster, Earlean A. ... Milwaukee, WI
Laster, G. A. ... San Mateo, CA
Laster, Gerald A. ... San Mateo, CA
Laster, Hubert D. ... Houston, TX
Laster, J. Travis ... Wilmington, DE
Laster, John L. ... Washington, DC
Falls Church, VA
Laster, John W. ... Panorama City, CA
Laster, Jonathan E. ... Suwanee, GA
Laster, Judith Eve ... Boston, MA
Laster, Marvin J. ... Plainview, NY
Laster & McKenzie ... Houston, TX
Laster, Michael W. ... Overland Park, KS
Laster, Robert T., Jr. ... Grenada, MS
Lasting, Richard Paul ... Santa Monica, CA
Lastomirsky, Steven R. ... Portland, OR
Lastorino, Carol ... Uniondale, NY
Lastorino, Kevin M. ... New York, NY
Lastova, John R. ... Arlington, VA
Lastovich, Lee A. ... Minneapolis, MN
Lastovich, Steven D. ... St. Cloud, MN
Lastovka, Terri A. ... Olmsted Falls, OH
Lastowka, James A. ... Washington, DC
Lastowka, Joseph E., Jr. ... Media, PA
Lastowka Messick & Malady P.C.
Media, PA
Lastowski, Julian T., Jr. ... San Francisco, CA
Lastowski, Michael R. ... Philadelphia, PA
Lastra, Amir ... Bayamon, PR
Lastra, Carlos M. ... Miami, FL
Lastra, Carlos M., P.A. ... Miami, FL
Lastra, Carmen C. ... Huntington Beach, CA
Lastra, David ... Department of Justice, Environment and Natural Resources Division, GV
Lastrapes, J. Stephen ... Houston, TX
Lastrapes, Paula Caruso ... Kittanning, PA
Lastrapes, Richard L., Jr.
Rio Rancho, NM
Lastrapes & Spangler, P.A.
Albuquerque, NM
Rio Rancho, NM
Lastrapes & Weiss ... New Orleans, LA
Lastrapes, Wiley G. ... New Orleans, LA
Lastrapes, Wiley G., Jr. ... New Orleans, LA
Lastreto, Rene, II ... Fresno, CA
La Suer, Gene R. ... Des Moines, IA
LaSusa, Barbara E. ... Chicago, IL
LaSusa, Deanna M. ... Chicago, IL
LaSusa & LaSusa, P.C. ... Des Plaines, IL
LaSusa, Lawrence R. ... Milwaukee, WI
LaSusa, Matthew A. ... Des Plaines, IL
Lasusa, Peter R., Jr. ... New York, NY
LaSusa, Samuel A. ... Des Plaines, IL
Laswell, Claudia A. Nelson ... Houston, TX
Laswell, Dixie L. ... Chicago, IL
Laswell, Gregg C. ... Houston, TX
Laswell, William T. ... Fort Lauderdale, FL
Laszcz, Joseph S. ... Cleveland, OH
Laszlo, John B. ... Merrillville, IN
Laszlo, Sandra S. ... Norcross, GA
Laszlo, Theodore E., Jr. ... Richfield, OH
Laszynski & Moore ... Lafayette, IN
Laszynski, Robert S. ... Lafayette, IN
Lata, Celia G. ... Raleigh, NC
Lataille, Michele M. ... Providence, RI
Smithfield, RI
Latane, Lawr. W., Jr.
Washington's Birthplace, VA
Latanick, David G. ... Columbus, OH
La Tanzi, Spaulding & Landreth, P.C.
Hyannis, MA
Orleans, MA
La Tanzi, Thomas A. ... Orleans, MA
Latas, Mark ... Youngstown, OH
Latas, Milan ... Youngstown, OH
Latasso, Joseph A. ... Garden City, NY
Latcham, Franklin C. ... San Francisco, CA
Latchaw, Jill H. ... Fairfield, CA
Sacramento, CA
Latchem, Edna Ayliffe ... Baton Rouge, LA
Latchford, George P. ... River Forest, IL
Latchford, Paul C. ... Baltimore, MD
Latchney, John D. ... Cleveland, OH
Latchum, James L. ... Wilmington, DE
Latchum, Joseph H., Jr.
Newport News, VA
Lateef, Michael Y. ... San Francisco, CA
Lateer, James W. ... Belvidere, IL
Lateer, Jane R. ... Richmond, VA
Lateiner, Emanuel ... Livermore, CA
Latek, Kevin P. ... Washington, DC
Latella, John W. ... Pittsburgh, PA
Latella, Leo A. ... Hazleton, PA
Latella & Nerone ... Pittsburgh, PA
Latella, Robert N. ... Rochester, NY
La Tempa, Catherine K. ... Irvine, CA
Latenser, David B. ... Omaha, NE
Latenser & Johnson, P.C. ... Omaha, NE
Later, Chester J. ... Wethersfield, CT
Later, Michael M. ... Salt Lake City, UT
Later, Stephen F. ... Pinehurst, NC
Laterman, Barry ... Boston, MA
Laterman, Joshua Paul ... New York, NY
Laterza, B. Franco ... Chicago, IL
Laterza, B. Franco, Law Offices of, P.C.
Chicago, IL
Laterza, Nancy Rae ... Schaumburg, IL
Laterza, Peter ... Glen Allen, VA
Latez, Glenn A. ... Toledo, OH
Latham, B. Mills ... San Antonio, TX
Latham, Bert E. ... Centre, AL
Latham, Bobby L., Jr. ... Tulsa, OK
Latham, Britt K. ... Dallas, TX
Latham, Byrd R. ... Athens, AL
Latham, Cherly A. ... Albuquerque, NM
Latham, Chilton B. ... Albany, NY
Latham, Christopher B. ... San Diego, CA
Latham, Daniel W. ... Minneapolis, MN
Latham, Darrell E. ... Altus, OK
Latham, Darren R. ... St. Petersburg, FL
Latham, David C. ... Orlando, FL
Latham, David H. ... Chicago, IL
Latham, David J. ... Reading, MA
Latham, David M. ... New Orleans, LA
Latham, Debbie Fair ... Santa Rosa, CA
Latham, Felicia ... Seattle, WA
Latham, Gregory D. ... New Orleans, LA
Latham, J. Al, Jr. ... Los Angeles, CA
Latham, James D. ... Boston, MA
Latham, James F. ... Burlington, NC
Graham, NC
Latham, John L. ... Atlanta, GA
Latham, Joseph W. ... Bath, NY
Latham, Kenneth C. ... Reading, MA
Latham, L. Paul ... Midland, TX
Latham & Latham ... Washington, DC
Latham, Latham & Lamond, P.C.
Reading, MA
Latham Law Firm ... Jackson, MS
Latham, Mark A. ... Chicago, IL
Latham, Mark D. ... New Orleans, LA
Latham, Marsha Henley ... Huntsville, AL
Titusville, FL
Latham, Mary ... Dallas, TX
Latham, Myrna Schack
Oklahoma City, OK
Latham, Nelson & Thomas ... Altus, OK
Latham, O. Bradley ... Reading, MA
Latham, Patricia Horan, (Mrs.)
Washington, DC
Latham, Paul L. ... Conway, AR
Latham, Peter G. ... Orlando, FL
Latham, Peter S. ... Washington, DC
Latham, Richard B. ... Rockville, MD
Latham, Robert A., III ... Los Angeles, CA
Latham, Robert C. ... Natchez, MS
Latham, Robert P. ... Dallas, TX
Latham, Sheryl Brantley ... Dallas, TX
Latham, Stephen B. ... East Hampton, NY
Riverhead, NY
Latham, Steve ... Whitney, TX
Latham, Steven L. ... Bismarck, ND
Latham, Thomas W. ... San Francisco, CA
Latham, Walter T. ... Santa Fe, NM
Latham & Watkins ... Costa Mesa, CA
Los Angeles, CA
Menlo Park, CA
Newport Beach, CA
San Diego, CA
San Francisco, CA
Washington, DC
Chicago, IL
Newark, NJ
New York, NY
Latham, W. D. Shane ... Springfield, OH
Latham, Weldon H. ... Washington, DC
Latham, William C. ... Naperville, IL
Latham, William D. ... Clanton, AL
Latham, William Ellis, II
Winston-Salem, NC
Latham, William H. ... Columbia, SC
Latham, William L. ... Fort Worth, TX
Latham, William Larry ... Jackson, MS
Latham, W. J., Jr. ... Marshalltown, IA
Latham, Wood & Dorrestein, L.L.P.
Burlington, NC
Graham, NC
Lathan & Barbare, Professional Association
Greenville, SC
Lathan, Milton ... Oakland, CA
Lathan, Ray D. ... Greenville, SC
Lathan, Terri L. ... Dallas, TX
Lathan, William R., Jr. ... New Bern, NC
Raleigh, NC
Lathe, Douglas E. ... Dixon, IL
Lathem, Donald N. ... Alabaster, AL
Lathem, Jeffery J. ... Daytona Beach, FL
Lathen, Deborah A.
Federal Communications Commission, Cable Services Bureau, GV
Lathen, Neil F. ... Salem, OR
Lather, Kenneth L. ... Findlay, OH
Lather & Koehler ... Findlay, OH
Latherow, David F. ... Ashland, KY
Latherow, Jerry A. ... Chicago, IL
Latherow, Jerry A., Ltd. ... Chicago, IL
Lathi, Anjali B. ... San Mateo, CA
Lathouris, Peter V. ... Stamford, CT
Lathram, J. Brook ... Memphis, TN
Lathram, Robert Gregory ... London, KY
Lathram, Steven M. ... San Francisco, CA
Lathram, Thomas W. ... San Francisco, CA
Lathrom, Alan Dean ... Fort Worth, TX
Lathrop, Alexander J. ... Washington, DC
Lathrop, Anthony T. ... Charlotte, NC
Lathrop, Bruce ... Redlands, CA
Lathrop, Carl L. ... Cheyenne, WY
Lathrop, Carolyn D. ... Cumberland, MD
Lathrop & Clark, LLP ... Belleville, WI
Lodi, WI
Madison, WI
Poynette, WI
Lathrop, David N. ... San Francisco, CA
Lathrop, David S., Jr. ... Omaha, NE
Lathrop, Diane M. ... Cheyenne, WY
Lathrop, F. Steven, (P.S.) ... Ellensburg, WA
Lathrop & Gage ... St. Louis, MO
Lathrop & Gage L.C. ... Overland Park, KS
Jefferson City, MO
Kansas City, MO
Springfield, MO
Lathrop & Gage PLLC ... Washington, DC
Lathrop, Gary T. ... Bethlehem, PA
Harrisburg, PA
Lathrop, Jerry ... Boise City, OK
Lathrop, Kyle W. ... Athens, GA
Lathrop, Mary B. ... Houston, TX
Lathrop, Matthew A. ... Omaha, NE
Lathrop, Mitchell L. ... New York, NY
Lathrop, Peter K. ... New York, NY
Lathrop, Richard J. ... Cupertino, CA
Lathrop, Robert G. ... Morgantown, WV
Lathrop, Roger A. ... Davenport, IA
Lathrop & Rutledge, A Professional Corporation ... Cheyenne, WY
Lathrop, Scott A. ... Boston, MA
Lathrop, Scott A., P.C. ... Boston, MA
Lathrop, Stephen M. ... Redondo Beach, CA
Lathrop, Steven M. ... Omaha, NE
Lathrop, Stirling ... Wallingford, PA
Lathrop, Victor G. ... Ames, IA
Lathrop & Villa ... Redondo Beach, CA
Lathrop, Winbauer, Harrel & Slothower L.L.P. ... Cle Elum, WA
Ellensburg, WA
Lathrope, Daniel J. ... Gainesville, FL
Lathrop-Roberts, Carol ... Howell, MI
Lathum, Margaret L. ... Birmingham, AL
Latici, Steven M. ... Gilford, NH
Latiff, Michael G. ... Detroit, MI
Latimer, Aimee D. ... Richmond, VA
Latimer, Arthur H. ... Bethany, CT
Látimer, Biaggi, Rachid & Godreau
San Juan, PR
Latimer, Brian P. ... Oakhurst, NJ
Latimer, Caesar C. ... Tulsa, OK
Látimer, Carlos G. ... San Juan, PR
Latimer, Cary R. ... Chicago, IL
Latimer, Clay L. ... Houston, TX
Latimer, Dennis M. ... Chico, CA
Latimer, E. Douglas ... Albuquerque, NM
Latimer, Earl O., II ... Dallas, TX
Latimer, Edward B. ... Columbia, SC
Latimer, Edwin P. ... Manassas, VA
Latimer, Erik M. ... New Orleans, LA
Latimer, F. Clayton ... New Orleans, LA
Latimer, George A.
Department of Housing and Urban Development, GV
Latimer, Gretchen W. ... San Francisco, CA
Latimer, Henry ... Fort Lauderdale, FL
Latimer, Hugh ... Washington, DC
Latimer, James E. ... Walnut Creek, CA
Latimer, Jerome C. ... Seminole, FL
Latimer, John A., Jr. ... Williamsport, MD
Latimer, Kate ... St. Paul, MN
Latimer, Katharine R. ... Washington, DC
Latimer & Kenkel, A Professional Corporation
Chico, CA
Latimer, Kenneth A. ... Chicago, IL
Latimer, L. Patrice ... Washington, DC
Latimer, Marzella B. ... Chicago, IL
Latimer, Matthew D. ... Seattle, WA
Latimer, Michael ... San Antonio, TX
Latimer, R. Michael ... Overland Park, KS
Latimer, Randolph E., Jr.
Charlotte Amalie, St. Thomas, VI
Latimer, Richard K. ... Falmouth, MA
Latimer, Stephen M. ... Hackensack, NJ
Latimer, Suzanne L. ... Latham, NY
Latimer, Timothy B. ... Jackson, TN
Latimer, Walter G. ... Miami, FL
Latimer, William H., Jr. ... Delray Beach, FL
Latimer, William P. ... Carmel, IN
Latimore, Alicia L. ... Orlando, FL
Latimore, D. W., Jr. ... Atlanta, GA
Latimore, D. W., Jr., P.C. ... Atlanta, GA
Latin, Michael A. ... Los Angeles, CA
Latin, Monica Wiseman ... Dallas, TX
Latin, Oscar B. ... Columbus, OH
Latin, Richard G. ... Jamaica, NY
Latin, Shelley ... Melfa, VA
Latin, Thomas D. ... Albany, NY
Latin, Vito J. ... Rochester, NY
Latiner, Forrest ... Los Angeles, CA
Latini, John M. ... Sacramento, CA
Latini, Sandra Marie Gleixner
Pittsburgh, PA
Latino, Heather M. ... Missoula, MT
Latino, Joseph P. ... East Hartford, CT
Latinsky, Martin C. ... Haworth, NJ
Latiolais, Clifton J., Jr. ... Denver, CO
Latiolait, Anthony F. ... Los Angeles, CA
Latker, Norman J. ... Washington, DC
Latman, Abraham ... Borger, TX
Latman, Marc D. ... Washington, DC
Latman, Stanley E. ... Dallas, TX
Latner, Irwin M. ... New York, NY
Latney, Harvey, Jr. ... Bowling Green, VA
Latoff, Clinton Geesaman ... Coatesville, PA
Latoff, Marie A. ... Valley Forge, PA
Latoff, Thomas J., II ... Rosemont, PA
Laton, Donald W. ... Raleigh, NC
Latona, Anthony J. ... Buffalo, NY
Latona, Carmen ... Inkerman, PA
Latona, Joseph ... Islandia, NY
LaTona, Joseph M. ... Buffalo, NY
Latona, Kay ... Fort Lauderdale, FL
Latona, Lydia S. ... Millburn, NJ
Latona, Salvatore M. ... Amherst, NY
Latoni, Demetrio Luis ... Bayamon, PR
Latoof, Joseph ... Trenton, NJ
Latore, Lawrence ... Parsippany, NJ
LaTorella, Charles A., Jr. ... Little Neck, NY
La Torraca and Goettsch
Long Beach, CA
La Torraca, Henry B. ... Long Beach, CA
LaTorraca, Kimberly Gail ... Cohasset, MA
Latorre, Lisa I. ... Washington, DC
Latorre, M. Catherine ... New York, NY
LaTorre, Michael J. ... Lewiston, ME
La Torre, Pamela A., R.N. ... Media, PA
Latorre, Stefan R. ... Charlotte, NC
LaTorre, Yvonne ... Albany, NY
Latos, Andrew ... Bayside, NY
Latou, Bernice Lynne ... Baltimore, MD
Latouf, Charbel G. ... Erie, PA
Latouf, Gail M. ... Westbrook, ME
Latour, Ann D. ... Lafayette, LA
Latour, Edmund S. ... Metairie, LA
Latour, Eduardo R. ... Tarpon Springs, FL
Latour, José E. ... Gainesville, FL
Latour, José E., & Associates, P.A.
Gainesville, FL
Latour, Oliver J., Jr. ... Foley, AL
LaTour, Randall D. ... Columbus, OH
Latour & Sidlosca, P.A. ... Miami, FL
La Tour, Stephanie ... Boston, MA
Latourette, Audrey Wolfson ... Woodbury, NJ
LaTourette, Brainerd W., III
St. Louis, MO
LaTourette, Brainerd W., Jr.
St. Louis, MO
Latourette, Edward D. ... Oregon City, OR
LaTourette, Harry B., Jr. ... Tyler, TX
Latourette, John R., Jr. ... Cherry Hill, NJ
Philadelphia, PA
Latourette, Laurence R. ... Washington, DC
LaTourette, Steven C. ... Painesville, OH
Latovick, Paula R. ... Lansing, MI
Latray, Michelle ... Charleston, SC
Latreille, Stanley J. ... Howell, MI
LaTremouille, Robert J. ... Cambridge, MA
Latrenta, Nicholas D. ... New York, NY
Latrobe, Osmun R. ... Oklahoma City, OK
Latrone, Robt. A. ... Philadelphia, PA
Latronica, Robert R., Jr. ... Jamaica, NY
Latronico, Kenneth A. ... Boston, MA
Latsch, Patricia Burnett ... Olympia, WA
Latsey, Christine J. ... Washington, DC
Latsha Davis & Yohe, P.C.
Mount Laurel, NJ
Harrisburg, PA
Malvern, PA
Latsha, Kimber L. ... Harrisburg, PA
Latshaw, James W. ... Wilmington, NC
Latshaw, John H., Jr.
Jacksonville Beach, FL
Latshaw, K. Michael ... Decatur, IL
Latshaw, Krista ... Richmond, VA
Latshaw, Paula A. ... Dallas, TX
Latshaw, Ralph S., Jr. ... Leawood, KS
Latsinova, Margarita V. ... Seattle, WA
Latsios, C. Dean ... Fairfax, VA
Latsko, John M. ... Columbus, OH
Latsko, Michael G. ... Charlottesville, VA
Latson, Jack W. ... Austin, TX
Latson, Marya R. ... Ocala, FL

Latt, Paul G. ... Chesterfield, MO
Latta & Brown ... Prestonsburg, KY
Latta, Clifford B. ... Prestonsburg, KY
Latta, Donna Hughes ... Norfolk, VA
Latta, Forrest S. ... Mobile, AL
Latta, Gil H. ... Fresno, CA
Latta, James R. ... Chicago, IL
Latta, Jennie D. ... Memphis, TN
Latta, John L., (P.C.) ... Denver, CO
Latta, Kurt A. ... Menlo Park, CA
Latta, Leroy K., Jr. ... Anchorage, AK
Latta, Lucille T. ... Vicksburg, MS
Latta, Lynda ... Albuquerque, NM
Latta, Meena Kang ... Seattle, WA
Latta, Peter A. ... West Chester, PA
Latta, Richard A. ... Madison, WI
Latta, Robert E. ... Bowling Green, OH
Latta, Robert P. ... Palo Alto, CA
Latta, Thomas A. ... San Francisco, CA
Latta, W. B., Jr. ... Boise, ID
Latta, William A. ... Monroe, OR
Lattaker, Pearl ... Los Angeles, CA
Lattal, Frank A. ... Roseland, NJ
Lattan, Lisa Hund ... Kansas City, MO
Lattanza, John C. ... Charlotte, NC
Lattanzi, Gregory T. ... New Haven, CT
Lattanzi, Richard E. ... Baltimore, MD
Lattanzio, Douglas E. ... Dallas, TX
Lattanzio, Frank ... Franklin Square, NY
Lattarulo, Donna M. ... Norwalk, CT
New York, NY
Lattavo, Philip E. ... Canton, OH
Latter, Bruce E. ... Cincinnati, OH
Latter, Byron F. ... Flint, MI
Latter, Daniel S. ... Encino, CA
Latter, Thomas C. ... Houston, TX
Latterman and Associates, P.C. ... Lansing, MI
Latterman, Carol Ann
General Services Administration,
Office of Regional Counsel, GV
Latterman, Mark A. ... Lansing, MI
Latterman, Paul E. ... Mount Holly, NJ
Lattes, Conrad R. ... Boulder, CO
Lattes, Lisa Jane ... Beckley, WV
Latti Associates ... Boston, MA
Gloucester, MA
New Bedford, MA
Latti, Carolyn M. ... Boston, MA
Latti, Michael B. ... Boston, MA
Gloucester, MA
New Bedford, MA
Lattiboudere, Perry L. ... Park Ridge, NJ
Lattie, David L. ... Grand Blanc, MI
Lattie, Jonathan G. ... Las Vegas, NV
Lattie, Lyndon J. ... Grand Blanc, MI
Lattie, Lyndon J., P.C. ... Grand Blanc, MI
Lattier, Joseph Martin ... Shreveport, LA
Lattier, Michael S. ... Key West, FL
Greeneville, TN
Kingsport, TN
Lattier, Ronald F. ... Shreveport, LA
Lattime, Suzanne ... Lake Success, NY
Lattimer, Gregory M., (P.C.) ... Golden, CO
Lattimer, John Mangan
Environmental Protection Agency,
Office of Enforcement and Compliance
Assurance, GV
Lattimer, Richard M., Jr
Pension Benefit Guaranty Corporation,
Office of the General Counsel, GV
Lattimore, Don M. ... St. Paul, MN
Lattimore, Hal M. ... Fort Worth, TX
Lattimore, Mark D. ... Charlotte, NC
Lattimore & Mooney,, P.A. ... St. Paul, MN
Lattimore, Phillip A., III ... Williamsburg, VA
Lattimore, Rachel G. ... Washington, DC
Lattin, Alexander P. ... Cincinnati, OH
Lattin, Donald A. ... Reno, NV
Lattin, John E., IV ... Newport Beach, CA
Lattin, Robert W. ... Independence, KS
Lattin, Stephanie T. ... Washington, DC
Latting, James T. ... Mercer Island, WA
Latting, Joseph ... Austin, TX
Latting, Trimble B. ... Oklahoma City, OK
Lattinville, Robert H. ... St. Louis, MO
Lattis, Jennifer S. ... Madison, WI
Lattner, Edward B. ... Rockville, MD
Latto, Aaron B. ... Minneapolis, MN
Latto, Douglas A. ... Morristown, NJ
New York, NY
Latto, Harrison ... Portland, OR
Latto, Lawrence J. ... Washington, DC
Lattof & Lattof, P.C. ... Mobile, AL
Lattof, Mitchell G., Jr. ... Mobile, AL
Lattof, Mitchell G., Sr. ... Mobile, AL
Lattomus, Tara L. ... Wilmington, DE
Latton, Howard W. ... Portage, WI
Latts, Leatrice Lynne ... Pasadena, CA
Latts, Leatrice Lynne, A P.C.
Pasadena, CA
Lattuga, Robert L. ... Menlo Park, CA
Latturner, James O. ... Chicago, IL
Latty, Theodore H. ... Los Angeles, CA
Latuga, Diane M. ... East Williston, NY
Laturno, Gary M. ... San Diego, CA
Laturno & Graves ... San Diego, CA
Latus, Gerard M. ... Chicago, IL
Latus, Lisa L. ... Joliet, IL
Latwesen, David G. ... Spokane, WA
Latwin, Joseph L. ... White Plains, NY
Latz, Holly ... San Francisco, CA
Latz, J. Kelly ... Austin, TX
Latz, Martin E. ... Phoenix, AZ
Latz, Peter J. ... Oak Park, IL
Latz, Robert ... Minneapolis, MN
Latz, Robert C. ... Kansas City, MO
Latz, Robert, P.A. ... Minneapolis, MN
Latz, Ronald S. ... St. Paul, MN

Latza, William D. ... New York, NY
Latzanich, John J., II.
Sherman Oaks, CA
Latzer, Bertram J. ... Morristown, NJ
Latzer, Donald H. ... Fair Oaks, CA
Latzer, Thos. F. ... St. Louis, MO
Latzes, Michael Alan ... Lauderhill, FL
Latzko, David M. ... Newark, DE
Latzman, Patricia Miller
Port Washington, NY
Latzman, Stephen I. ... New York, NY
Lau, Alan K. ... Honolulu, HI
Lau, Alana W. ... Honolulu, HI
Lau, Ben ... Honolulu, HI
Lau, Bernard ... Danbury, CT
Lau, Burt T. ... Honolulu, HI
Lau, Calvin ... Carlsbad, CA
Lau, Catherine L. ... San Jose, CA
Lau, Cheryl A. ... Carson City, NV
Lau & Choi, P.C. ... Denver, CO
Lau, Christopher L. ... Honolulu, HI
Lau, Collin ... Livermore, CA
Lau, Collin K. C. ... Honolulu, HI
Lau, Corianne W. ... Honolulu, HI
Lau, David L. ... San Francisco, CA
Lau, Edward C.Y. ... San Francisco, CA
Lau, Edward H. ... Columbus, OH
Lau, Edward Y. ... Chicago, IL
Lau, Elaine Y. ... San Francisco, CA
Lau, Elise K.Y. ... Los Angeles, CA
Lau, Emily S. ... Palo Alto, CA
Lau, Estella M. ... New York, NY
Lau, Eugene W. I. ... Honolulu, HI
Lau, Gayle John ... Honolulu, HI
Lau, Gene K. ... Honolulu, HI
Lau, Girard D. ... Honolulu, HI
Lau, Herbert B. K. ... Honolulu, HI
Lau, James V. ... Tampa, FL
Lau, Jeffrey D. ... Honolulu, HI
Lau, Jennie ... San Francisco, CA
Lau, Karen ... Washington, DC
Lau, Kenneth G. ... Encino, CA
Lau, Kenneth K. ... Honolulu, HI
Lau, Kenneth K. S. ... Honolulu, HI
Lau, Kevin J. ... Haddonfield, NJ
Lau, Kimberly A. ... Baltimore, MD
Lau, Lane, Pieper, Conley & McCreadie,
P.A. ... Cape Canaveral, FL
Tampa, FL
Lau, Laura Schmidt ... Waukesha, WI
Lau, Laurence K. ... Honolulu, HI
Lau, Laurie L. ... Brooklyn, NY
Lau, Lawrence B. L. ... San Mateo, CA
Lau, L.C. ... San Mateo, CA
Lau, Lucius Bernard ... Department of Justice,
Civil Division, GV
Lau, Marco A. ... New York, NY
Lau, Marjorie A. ... Honolulu, HI
Lau, Mark W. ... Los Angeles, CA
Lau, Mary A. ... Tampa, FL
Lau, Michael H. Q. L. ... Honolulu, HI
Lau, Michael N. ... Washington, DC
Lau, Norman K. K. ... Honolulu, HI
Lau, Norman K.K., A Law Corp.
Honolulu, HI
Lau, Patrick K. ... Honolulu, HI
Lau, Peter W. ... Los Angeles, CA
Lau, Philip K. ... Washington, DC
Lau, Richard ... Brewster, NY
Lau, Robert K. ... Portland, OR
Lau, Ronald Duk-Sing ... Honolulu, HI
Lau, Ronald Hing ... Atlanta, GA
Lau, Sandra K. ... Los Angeles, CA
Lau, Serena ... Bridgeport, CT
Lau, Shannon M.I. ... Honolulu, HI
Lau, Shawn J. ... Cherry Hill, NJ
Reading, PA
Lau, Shawn J., P.C. ... Cherry Hill, NJ
Lau, Sheila Yee ... Honolulu, HI
Lau, Sherman ... New York, NY
Lau, Stanford Y. K. ... Redondo Beach, CA
Lau, Stephen Y. ... Honolulu, HI
Lau, Steve ... San Francisco, CA
Lau, Steven L. ... San Francisco, CA
Lau, Steven R. ... Stamford, CT
Lau, Susan ... San Francisco, CA
Lau, Terence Joseph ... Dearborn, MI
Lau, Una ... Houston, TX
Lau, Vincent W. ... Worcester, MA
Lau, Wai Kit ... New York, NY
Lau, Wesley K. C. ... Kaneohe, HI
Lau, Woon Ki ... Denver, CO
Lau, Ying-Kit ... Los Angeles, CA
Laub, Alfred C. ... White Plains, NY
Laub, Arnold ... San Francisco, CA
Laub, Arnold, A Prof. Corp., Law Offices of
Oakland, CA
San Francisco, CA
San Jose, CA
Laub, David C. ... Buffalo, NY
Buffalo, NY
Laub, David W. ... Philadelphia, PA
Laub & Franchino, L.L.C., Law Offices of
Raritan, NJ
Somerville, NJ
Laub, Graham R. ... Philadelphia, PA
Laub, Hyman S. ... Baldwin, NY
Laub, Jeffrey M. ... Rockville, MD
Laub, Joe M. ... South Lake Tahoe, CA
Truckee, CA
Carson City, NV
Reno, NV
Laub, Joseph M. ... Chicago, IL
Laub, Kenneth A. ... Lake Hiawatha, NJ
New York, NY
Laub & Laub ... South Lake Tahoe, CA
Truckee, CA
Carson City, NV

Reno, NV
Laub, Linda J. ... Harrisburg, PA
Laub, M. Joel ... New York, NY
Laub, Melvin ... South Lake Tahoe, CA
Truckee, CA
Carson City, NV
Reno, NV
Laub, Michael J. ... New York, NY
Laub, Patricia D. ... Cincinnati, OH
Laub, Peter N. ... Raritan, NJ
Laub, Sam ... Mountain View, CA
Laub, Seidel, Cohen and Hof, L.L.C.
Allentown, PA
Bethlehem, PA
Easton, PA
Laub, Soyeon (Karen) Pak
Newport Beach, CA
Laub, Thomas J. ... Okmulgee, OK
Laub, Tom J. ... Okmulgee, OK
Laubach, Andrew C. ... Encinitas, CA
Laubach, Dawn M. ... Friendswood, TX
Laubach, Edward J. ... St. Cloud, MN
Laubach, Edward J., Jr. ... Pittsburgh, PA
Laubach & Fulton, LLC ... Carnegie, PA
Laubach, Gregory L. ... Washington, DC
Rockville, MD
Laubach, John A. ... Phoenix, AZ
Laubach, Larry P. ... Cherry Hill, NJ
Philadelphia, PA
Laubach, Timothy C. ... Orlando, FL
Laubach, Timothy C., P.A. ... Orlando, FL
Laubach, Vincent A. ... Las Vegas, NV
Laubach, Wendy K. ... Houston, TX
LauBach, William M. ... St. Petersburg, FL
Laube, Bonnie L. ... Vineland, NJ
Laube, Thomas R. ... San Diego, CA
Laube, William T. ... Laguna Hills, CA
Laubengayer, Robert E. ... Stockton, CA
Laubenstein, Kathleen M.
Washington, DC
Philadelphia, PA
Laubenstein, Richard W. ... Park Ridge, IL
Laubenstein, William H., III ... Augusta, ME
Laubenthal, Robert J. ... Council Bluffs, IA
Laubenthal, Thomas J. ... Cleveland, OH
Lauber, Albert G., Jr. ... Washington, DC
Lauber, Daniel M. ... River Forest, IL
Lauber, Douglas R. ... Sanford, FL
Lauber, Paul H. ... Edwardsville, IL
Lauber, Robert C. ... Wauseon, OH
Lauber, William G. ... Lima, OH
Laubhan, Alan J. ... Woodward, OK
Laubhan, Daniel B. ... Chicago, IL
Laubich, Lori M. ... New York, NY
Laubin, Michelle C. ... Milford, CT
Laubner, F. Paul, Law Offices of
Allentown, PA
Laubner, Philip E. ... Peabody, MA
Laubscher, Barry R. ... Irvine, CA
Laubscher & Laubscher ... Arlington, VA
Laubscher, Lawrence E., Jr.
Arlington, VA
Laubscher, Lawrence E., Sr.
Arlington, VA
Laucella, Patricia L. ... Burbank, CA
Laucello, Michael J. ... Utica, NY
Lauchengco, José Y., Jr. ... Los Angeles, CA
Lauchlan, Robert J., Jr. ... San Diego, CA
Lauchli, Linda Diane ... Loveland, CO
Lauchli, Mary Szto ... Malibu, CA
Lauchmen, Carol M. ... Harleysville, PA
Harleysville, PA
Lauchmen, Carol M., Associates
Lansdale, PA
Lauck, Claude M. ... Roanoke, VA
Lauck, Frederick W. ... Farmington Hills, MI
Lauck, Frederick W., Professional Corporation
Farmington Hills, MI
Lauck, James G. ... Indianapolis, IN
Lauck, Robert G. ... Reston, VA
Lauck, Scott G. ... Little Rock, AR
Laucks, David M. ... Red Lion, PA
York, PA
Laucks & Laucks, LLP ... Red Lion, PA
York, PA
Laucks, Samuel S., Jr. ... Red Lion, PA
York, PA
Laudadio, Brian ... Rochester, NY
Lau Dan, Jose A. ... New York, NY
Laudani, Anthony ... Beachwood, OH
Laudano, Paul C. ... Boston, MA
Laudati, Hector D. ... Providence, RI
Laudati, John L. ... Farmington, CT
Torrington, CT
Laudato, Paul J. ... Albany, NY
Laudeman, Arthur N. ... Bloomington, IL
Laudeman, Arthur N., Ltd. ... Bloomington, IL
Laudeman, Kirk W. ... Springfield, IL
Laudeman, Robert A. ... Treasury Department,
Internal Revenue Service, GV
Laudeman, William D. ... Evansville, IN
Laudenbach, Jeffrey D. ... Moorestown, NJ
Philadelphia, PA
Laudenslager, Kenneth H. ... Kalamazoo, MI
Lauder, Leona L. ... San Francisco, CA
Lauder, William T. ... Amityville, NY
Lauderbach, Jonathan E. ... Midland, MI
Lauderback, Greg L. ... Kingsport, TN
Lauderback, J. Eddie ... Johnson City, TN
Lauderback, J. Klyne ... Bristol, TN
Lauderback & Lauderback ... Kingsport, TN
Lauderback, Lynn ... Kingsport, TN
Lauderdale, D. Christopher
Greenville, SC
Lauderdale, Helen J. ... Los Angeles, CA
Lauderdale, James H. ... Weslaco, TX
Lauderdale, James M., Jr. ... Monterey, CA
Lauderdale, J. G. ... Lexington, MO

Lauderdale, Katherine S. ... Chicago, IL
Lauderdale Law Offices ... Monterey, CA
Lauderdale, Mary Jane ... Oklahoma City, OK
Lauderdale, Melissa L. ... Washington, DC
Lauderdale, Michael F.
Oklahoma City, OK
Lauderdale, Robert V. ... Pasadena, CA
Lauderdale, Ronald A. ... Somers, NY
Lauderdale, Virginia H. ... Monterey, CA
Laudermilk, Jack ... Randolph, MA
Laudig George Rutherford & Sipes
Indianapolis, IN
Laudig, Stephen ... Indianapolis, IN
Laudise, Thomas M. ... Short Hills, NJ
Laudo, Philip L. ... Garden City, NY
Laudon, Jack W. ... Brooklyn, NY
Laudone, Vincent A. ... Norwich, CT
Laudor, Richard S. ... Hackensack, NJ
Laudumiey, Fernand L., III
New Orleans, LA
Laudumiey, Fernand L., IV
New Orleans, LA
Laue, Bradley D. ... Greeley, CO
Laue, Brant M. ... Kansas City, MO
Laue, Robert P. ... Minneapolis, MN
Laue, Thomas D. ... Chicago, IL
Lauenstein, Douglas C. ... Perry Hall, MD
Lauenstein, Douglas C., P.A.
Perry Hall, MD
Lauenstein, Norman W. ... Essex, MD
Lauer, Andrew J. ... New York, NY
Lauer, Ari J. ... Los Angeles, CA
Lauer, Barbara L. ... Laramie, WY
Lauer, Bernard ... Los Angeles, CA
Lauer, Carla J. ... Dayton, OH
Lauer, Daniel L. ... Fort Wayne, IN
Lauer, David W. ... San Francisco, CA
Lauer, Debra ... Encino, CA
Lauer, E. Steven ... Vero Beach, FL
Lauer, Elias ... New York, NY
Lauer, Eliot ... New York, NY
Lauer, Ethan Breneman
House of Representatives,
Office of Parliamentarian, GV
Lauer, Gregory Scott ... Bloomington, IN
Lauer, Gregory T. ... Martinsville, IN
Lauer, Harrison S. ... Pittsburgh, PA
Lauer, Herbert ... New York, NY
Lauer, Jay ... South Bend, IN
Lauer, John A. ... Erie, PA
Lauer, Joletta C. ... Fort Wayne, IN
Lauer, Joseph I. ... New York, NY
Lauer, Katherine A. ... San Diego, CA
Lauer, Kurt A. ... Department of Agriculture,
Farm Service Agency, GV
Lauer, Laura Ann Lauritzen ... McLean, VA
Lauer, Lawrence ... New York, NY
Lauer, Louis ... New York, NY
Lauer, Mark M. ... Tulsa, OK
Lauer, Michael J. ... Menomonee Falls, WI
Lauer, Perkins & Pagliari, P.C.
Sewickley, PA
Lauer, Philip D. ... Easton, PA
Lauer, Philip D., P.C. ... Allentown, PA
Bethlehem, PA
Easton, PA
Lauer, Rebecca J. ... Chicago, IL
Lauer, Richard T. ... Cincinnati, OH
Lauer, Robert A. ... Dallas, TX
Lauer, Robert J. ... Milwaukee, WI
Lauer, Stephen J. ... Santa Fe, NM
Lauer, Steven A. ... Maplewood, NJ
Lauer, Steven Lee ... Norfolk, VA
Richmond, VA
Lauer, Theodore E. ... Laramie, WY
Lauer, Thomas G. ... Apple Valley, MN
Lauer, Warren A. ... Laramie, WY
Lauer, Wayne F. ... Englewood, CO
Lauer, Wesley A. ... West Palm Beach, FL
Lauer, William R. ... Sewickley, PA
Lauerhass, Theresa ... Bethesda, MD
Lauerman, Colleen M. ... Washington, DC
Lauerman, David L. ... Salinas, CA
Lauerman, E. Anthony, III ... Chicago, IL
Lauerman, Marc S. ... Chicago, IL
Lauerman, Thomas C. ... Washington, DC
Lauersdorf, Andrew C. ... Portland, OR
Lauersdorf, Jeffrey L. ... Overland Park, KS
Laufenberg, Dennis L. ... Arena, WI
Laufenberg, Jeffrey J. ... Gardena, CA
Laufenberg, Lynn R. ... Brookfield, WI
Laufenberg, Peter ... Oakland, CA
Laufenberg, Walter P. ... Morristown, NJ
Laufer, Alan S. ... Little Neck, NY
Laufer, Albert L. ... Philadelphia, PA
Laufer, Alexander ... Fairfax, VA
Laufer, Barry ... New York, NY
Laufer, Cory S. ... Miami, FL
Laufer, Daniel A. ... Manchester, NH
Laufer, David ... Woodland Hills, CA
Laufer, David D. ... Torrance, CA
Laufer, Deborah Schick
Federal Mediation and Conciliation Service,
GV
Laufer, Donald L. ... New York, NY
Laufer & Halberstam, LLP
New York, NY
Laufer, Harold A. ... Milwaukee, WI
Laufer, Jacob ... Brooklyn, NY
Laufer, Jacob ... New York, NY
Laufer, Janet A. ... Treasury Department,
Internal Revenue Service, GV
Laufer, Joel ... Denver, CO
Laufer, Joseph ... Sarasota, FL
Laufer & Katcher ... Port Washington, NY
Laufer, Keith A. ... Anchorage, AK
Laufer, Laurence D. ... New York, NY
Laufer, Leslie Ann ... Raleigh, NC

Laufer, Linda E. ....New York, NY
Laufer, Michael M. ....Port Washington, NY
Laufer, Robert L. ....New York, NY
Laufer, Rochelle ....Mineola, NY
Laufer, Samuel P. ....New York, NY
Laufer, Sidney ....Liberty, NY
Laufer, William M. ....Hackettstown, NJ
Morristown, NJ
Trenton, NJ
Lauffer, Andre M. ....Brooklyn, NY
Lauffer, Charles E., Jr. ....Tyler, TX
Lauffer, Daniel R. ....Durham, NC
Lauffer, John W. ....Jenkintown, PA
Lauffer, Michael A. M. ....Sacramento, CA
Laufman, Alan K. ....Dallas, TX
Laufman, Alan K., J.D., M.D., A Prof. Corp., Law Offices of ....Dallas, TX
Laufman, Mark S. ....Washington, DC
Laufman, Paul M. ....Cincinnati, OH
Laufman, Rauh & Gerhardstein
Cincinnati, OH
Laufman, Robert F. ....Cincinnati, OH
Laugen, Kent D. ....Red Wing, MN
Laugesen, Richard W. ....Denver, CO
Laugges, Linda L. ....Champaign, IL
Laughbaum, Carol A. ....Royal Oak, MI
Laughbaum, Rolland E. ....Galion, OH
Laughead, G. Ross ....San Antonio, TX
Laughead, James M. ....Austin, TX
Laughery, Bridget J. ....Pittsburgh, PA
Laughinghouse, Durwood S. ....Raleigh, NC
Laughland, David A. ....Lebanon, NJ
Laughland, Lauri J. ....Kansas City, MO
Laughlin, Alexander M. ....Alexandria, VA
Laughlin and Bowen ....Beaufort, SC
Hilton Head Island, SC
Laughlin, Bradford ....St. Joseph, MI
Laughlin, Brian L. ....Omaha, NE
Laughlin, Brian M. ....Chicago, IL
Laughlin, Charles Timothy ....Clinton, OK
Laughlin, Charles W. ....Richmond, VA
Laughlin, Craig S. ....Hazlet, NJ
Laughlin, David J. ....Painesville, OH
Laughlin, Dillard C. ....Kinsale, VA
Laughlin, Drew A.
Hilton Head Island, SC
Laughlin, Eddie L. ....Temple, TX
Laughlin, Evan Rorke ....Phoenix, AZ
Laughlin, Everett E. ....Green Valley, AZ
Laughlin, Falbo, Levy & Moresi LLP
Fresno, CA
Irvine, CA
Pasadena, CA
Redding, CA
Sacramento, CA
San Bernardino, CA
San Diego, CA
San Francisco, CA
San Jose, CA
Walnut Creek, CA
Laughlin, Felix B. ....Washington, DC
Laughlin, Fontaine D. ....Dallas, TX
Laughlin, Gary E. ....Topeka, KS
Laughlin, Gary M. ....Los Angeles, CA
Laughlin, Gerald P. ....Omaha, NE
Laughlin, Glenn E. ....Stillwater, OK
Laughlin, Gregory H. ....Washington, DC
Laughlin, Gregory K. ....Lima, OH
Laughlin, Harry W., III ....Memphis, TN
Laughlin, J. Bruce ....Manhattan, KS
Laughlin, Jack M. ....Sacramento, CA
Laughlin, James H. ....Bartlesville, OK
Laughlin, James H., Jr. ....Arlington, VA
Laughlin, James, III ....Chester, NJ
Laughlin, James P. ....New York, NY
Laughlin, James R. ....Morristown, NJ
Laughlin, James W. ....Fairfield, CA
Laughlin, Jerry W. ....Greeneville, TN
Laughlin, Jo Ann A. ....Swedesboro, NJ
Laughlin, John F. ....Chicago, IL
Laughlin, John G., Jr. ....Fairfax, VA
Laughlin, John R. ....Frederick, MD
Laughlin, Kathleen A. ....Omaha, NE
Laughlin, Kevin B. ....Midland, TX
Laughlin & Laughlin ....Freeport, IL
Laughlin, Lois S. ....Tustin, CA
Laughlin, LouCinda ....Los Angeles, CA
Laughlin, Mark C. ....Omaha, NE
Laughlin, Mark L. ....Omaha, NE
Laughlin, Matthew E. ....Des Moines, IA
Laughlin, Merida A. ....Houston, TX
Laughlin, Michael J. ....San Diego, CA
Laughlin, Michael J. ....Des Moines, IA
Laughlin, Michael J. ....New Orleans, LA
Laughlin, Michael W., (A Professional Corporation) ....San Francisco, CA
Laughlin, Neil M. ....Newark, OH
Laughlin, Owen W. ....Woodward, OK
Higgins, TX
Laughlin, Paul F. ....Allentown, PA
Laughlin, Paul F. ....Pittsburgh, PA
Laughlin, Paul J. ....Chicago, IL
Laughlin & Peabody ....San Diego, CA
Laughlin, Peter M. ....Morristown, NJ
Laughlin, Peterson & Lang ....Omaha, NE
Laughlin, R. Gordon ....Brentwood, CA
Laughlin, Richard T. ....Morristown, NJ
Laughlin, Robert A. ....Omaha, NE
Laughlin, Robert J. ....Hobbs, NM
Laughlin, Robert J. ....New York, NY
Laughlin, Ronald L., Jr. ....Clackamas, OR
Laughlin, Sheri G. ....Laguna Beach, CA
Laughlin, Shirl B. ....Freeport, IL
Laughlin, Stanley Ira ....North Babylon, NY
Laughlin, Stanley K., Jr. ....Columbus, OH
Laughlin, Theresa B. ....Wausau, WI
Laughlin, Thomas ....St. Paul, MN
Laughlin, Thomas E. ....Rockford, IL
Laughlin, Thomas G. ....Oklahoma City, OK
Laughlin, Vonda M. ....Knoxville, TN
Laughlin, Whitney M. ....San Diego, CA
Laughlin, William G. ....Houston, TX
Laughlin, William J. ....Great Bend, KS
Laughlin-Schopis, Susan K. ....Columbus, OH
Laughman, Mark E. ....Chicago, IL
Laughnan, Monti S. ....
Office of Personnel Management, GV
Laughner, Catherine A. ....Helena, MT
Laughon, C. Joseph, II ....New York, NY
Laughren, Sheryl A. ....Detroit, MI
Laughrey, Nanette K. ....Kansas City, MO
Laughridge, Don E. ....Napa, CA
Laughrun, George V., II ....Charlotte, NC
Laughter, Bennie M. ....Dalton, GA
Laughter, Britton P., Jr. ....Kemah, TX
Laughton, John D. ....Monterey, CA
Laughton, Steven D. ....Treasury Department, Community Development Financial Institutions, GV
Laugier, Francois G. ....Redwood City, CA
Lauhead, Mary Catherine ....St. Paul, MN
Lauher, Paul K. ....Palo Alto, CA
Lauhon, Gregory T. ....Redwood City, CA
Lauinger, Lisa Dawn ....Fargo, ND
Lauinger, Marita Murphy ....San Diego, CA
Lau-Kee, Glenn ....Ardsley, NY
Lau-Kee, Norman ....Ardsley, NY
Laukenmann, Chris B. ....Los Angeles, CA
Laukhuf, Stanley D. ....Dallas, TX
Laukien, Robyn L. ....Billerica, MA
Laukitis, Richard V. ....Chillicothe, IL
Laula, Otto W. ....Santa Barbara, CA
Lauletta, Frank A., III ....Cherry Hill, NJ
Philadelphia, PA
Lauletta, Thomas K. ....Riverwoods, IL
Laulicht, Murray J. ....Morristown, NJ
New York, NY
Laumann, Eric K. ....Chicago, IL
Laumann, J. Michael ....Cincinnati, OH
Laumann, Joseph ....Annapolis, MD
Laumann, Richard D. ....Liberty Corner, NJ
Laumas, Kevin ....Owensboro, KY
Laumbach, Ronald L. ....Minneapolis, MN
Laumer, J. Kevin ....Fredonia, NY
Jamestown, NY
Laumer, Mary Kay ....Columbiana, AL
Laun, Arthur H., Jr. ....Milwaukee, WI
Laun, Ernest A. ....Dallas, TX
Laun, John I. ....Kiel, WI
Madison, WI
Laun Law Offices ....Kiel, WI
Madison, WI
Laun, Max W. ....Pittsburgh, PA
Laun, Peter D. ....Pittsburgh, PA
Launay, Gerard D. ....Berkeley, CA
Launay, Jeanine M. ....New York, NY
Launder, Pamela D. ....Los Angeles, CA
Laundon, Averill ....Waterbury, VT
Laundry, Melburn E. ....Lake Forest, IL
Laundy, Henry H. ....Cleveland, OH
Launer, Chaffee & Schulman ....Fullerton, CA
Launer, Charlene A. ....Emeryville, CA
Launer, Elizabeth E. ....San Francisco, CA
Launer, Jeannette M. ....Vancouver, WA
Launer, Lawrence B. ....Los Angeles, CA
Launer, Leland C. ....Newport Beach, CA
Launer, Susan L.
Federal Communications Commission, Office of the General Counsel, GV
Launey, Donald J., Jr. ....Ville Platte, LA
Launhardt, Greg A. ....St. Louis, MO
Lauper, Edward C. ....Boston, MA
Lauper, John B. ....Stockton, CA
Lauper, Marc D. ....Pomona, CA
Laupheimer, Ann Blair ....Philadelphia, PA
Laupheimer, F. Ronald ....Oakland, CA
Laur, G. David ....Albion, IN
Kendallville, IN
Laur, James D. ....Los Angeles, CA
Laur, Morgan J. ....Merritt Island, FL
Laur, Morgan J., P.A. ....Merritt Island, FL
Laura, Anthony J. ....Newark, NJ
Laura, Joni A. ....Carlsbad, CA
Laura, Joseph M. ....Staten Island, NY
Laura, Lisa M. ....Philadelphia, PA
Laura, Peter F. ....Los Angeles, CA
Laura, Rosemary M. ....Newark, NJ
Laura, Wesley J. ....Houston, TX
Laurance, Leo M. ....Suffern, NY
Laurano, Joseph A. ....Boston, MA
Laurano, Michael A. ....Boston, MA
Laurans, Jonathan L. ....Kansas City, MO
Lauranzano, Michael C. ....Beverly, MA
Laureano, Robert A. ....Bronx, NY
Laureano, Robert A. ....Bronx, NY
Laureda and Associates ....Philadelphia, PA
Laureda, Juan J. ....Philadelphia, PA
Laurel, Oscar M. ....Laredo, TX
Laurel, Oscar M., Jr. ....Laredo, TX
Laurel, Ricardo ....Corpus Christi, TX
Laurel, Sandra D. ....San Antonio, TX
Laurel, Wendy S. ....Lahaina, HI
Laureles, Saul R. ....San Antonio, TX
Lauren, Barbara
Merit Systems Protection Board, Office of Appeals Counsel, GV
Lauren, Charles B. ....New York, NY
Lauren, Jason F. ....Oakland, CA
Lauren, Nadine Permutt ....Pleasanton, CA
Laurence, Daniel R. ....Seattle, WA
Laurence, David L. ....Dania, FL
Laurence, Elaine S. ....New York, NY
Laurence, Gerard R. ....Worcester, MA
Laurence, James P. ....Dallas, TX
Laurence, Jodi B., (P.A.) ....Boca Raton, FL
Laurence, Kenneth ....Boston, MA
Laurence, Kevin B. ....Salt Lake City, UT
Laurence, L. E. ....Houston, TX
Laurence, Margaret A. ....Wakefield, RI
Laurence, Margaret M. ....Richland, MI
Laurence, Michael ....San Francisco, CA
Laurence, Steven L.
Altamonte Springs, FL
Laurence, Stuart G. ....New York, NY
Laurence, Suzanne M. ....Walnut Creek, CA
Laurencelle, Adrien E., Jr. ....Massapequa, NY
Laurendeau, Amy J. ....Newport Beach, CA
Laurendine, Chase R. ....Mobile, AL
Laurenson, Edwin C. ....New York, NY
Laurenson, James A. ....Cleveland, OH
Laurenson, Michael A. ....San Francisco, CA
Laurenson, Robert C. ....La Jolla, CA
Laurent, Bernard ....Chicago, IL
Laurent, Carl E. ....Independence, MO
Laurent, David ....Edwardsville, IL
Laurent, David J. ....Pittsburgh, PA
Laurent, Donna A. ....Encino, CA
Laurent, Holly C. ....Boston, MA
Laurent, James J. ....Minneapolis, MN
Laurent, John F. ....Bartow, FL
Laurent, Kathleen Simmons ....Park Ridge, NJ
Laurent, Larry J. ....Austin, TX
Laurent, Larry J., P.C. ....Austin, TX
Laurent, Linda L. ....Houston, TX
Laurent, Reginald J. ....Slidell, LA
Laurent, Stephen J. ....Laconia, NH
Laurentano, Anthony A. ....Boston, MA
Laurentino, JoAnn L. ....New York, NY
Laurento, Wendy S. ....Blue Bell, PA
Laurents, Renee ....Los Angeles, CA
Laurenza, Paul M. ....Washington, DC
Laurenzano, Elizabeth L. ....Newark, NJ
Laurenz-Bogue, Cheryl ....Dupree, SD
Laurenzi, Eugene A. ....Memphis, TN
Laurenzi, Mark V. ....New York, NY
Laurenzo, Brian J. ....Des Moines, IA
Laures, Ann ....Kansas City, MO
Lauret, Douglas J. ....Chicago, IL
Laureta, Alfred ....Saipan, TT
Lauretano, Daniel A. ....El Paso, TX
Laureti, Anthony R. ....San Diego, CA
Lauretti, David G. ....Hartford, CT
Lauri, Andrew M. ....East Meadow, NY
Lauri, Kenneth J. ....Melville, NY
Lauri, Kevin G. ....New York, NY
Lauria, Anthony D. ....Sacramento, CA
Lauria, Christopher J. ....Canoga Park, CA
Lauria, Joseph M. ....Jamaica, NY
Lauria, Thomas E ....Miami, FL
Laurian, Anthony E. ....Stateline, NV
Lauriat, Peter M. ....Boston, MA
Laurice, Douglas M. ....Palo Alto, CA
Lauricella, Anthony G. ....Greenwich, CT
Lauricella, J. Travis ....Lakewood, WA
Lauricella, John E. ....Woodland, CA
Lauricella, John R. ....San Francisco, CA
Lauricella, Leonard J. ....Jersey City, NJ
Lauricella, Paul A. ....Philadelphia, PA
Lauricella, Peter A. ....Albany, NY
Lauricella, Richard W. ....Hagerstown, MD
Lauricella, Richard W., P.A.
Hagerstown, MD
Lauricella, Thomas J. ....Greenwich, CT
Laurich, Eugene J. ....Hilton Head Island, SC
Laurich, Eugene J., P.A.
Hilton Head Island, SC
Laurich, Linda L. ....Schaumburg, IL
Laurick, James P. ....Portland, OR
Lauridsen, David W. ....Columbia Falls, MT
Lauridsen, Jeffrey T. ....Tustin, CA
Lauridsen, Lee T. ....Kansas City, MO
Lauridsen, Vernon C. ....Monterey, CA
Laurie, Anna M. ....Bremerton, WA
Laurie, Charles R., Jr. ....Brecksville, OH
Laurie, Gerald T. ....Minneapolis, MN
Laurie, Ian S. ....Minneapolis, MN
Laurie, James P., III, Law Office of ....Raleigh, NC
Laurie, John David ....Los Angeles, CA
Laurie, John G. ....Chicago, IL
Laurie, Maloney & Wheatley
Cameron Park, CA
Folsom, CA
Placerville, CA
Sacramento, CA
Laurie, Oscar F. ....Red Bank, NJ
Laurie, Robert A. ....Cameron Park, CA
Laurie, Robin G. ....Montgomery, AL
Laurie, Ronald S. ....Palo Alto, CA
Laurie, S. J. ....Chatom, AL
Laurie, Ty D. ....Chicago, IL
Lauriello, Anthony ....New York, NY
Lauriello, Josephine ....New York, NY
Laurilliard, Kevin ....Albany, NY
Laurin, Christa States ....Canton, MI
Laurin, Keith U. ....Louisville, KY
Laurin, Kristin K. ....New York, NY
Laurin, Paul J. ....Encino, CA
Laurin, Richard K., Jr. ....Dallas, TX
Laurin, V. Samuel, III ....Indianapolis, IN
Lauring, John P. ....Worcester, MA
Laurino, Carl J., Jr. ....Brooklyn, NY
Laurino, Clare ....New York, NY
Laurino & Laurino ....Garden City, NY
Laurino, Louis D. ....Garden City, NY
Laurino, Louis M. ....Garden City, NY
Laurino, Maria D. ....Harrington Park, NJ
Laurino, Onofrio F. ....Harrington Park, NJ
Laurino, Paul ....Boston, MA
Laurino, Robert D. ....Newark, NJ
Laurion, Joseph A. ....Lynn, MA
Laurita, Alan J. ....Hamburg, NY
Laurita, Nee Marie ....Morgantown, WV
Lauritano, Armando T. ....Clearwater, FL
North Palm Beach, FL
Orlando, FL
Lauritano, Catherine T. O'Toole
New City, NY
Laurito, Jeffrey V. ....Dayton, OH
Laurito, Kerry Riordan ....Hackensack, NJ
Lauritsen, Brownell, Brostrom, Stehlik & Thayer ....Grand Island, NE
Lauritsen, John C., and Associates
Santa Barbara, CA
Lauritsen, Marc R. ....Cambridge, MA
Lauritsen, Thomas C. ....Omaha, NE
Lauritzen, Andrew R. ....Milwaukee, WI
Lauritzen, Arden W. ....Logan, UT
Lauritzen, David K. ....Salt Lake City, UT
Lauritzen, David W. ....Midland, TX
Lauritzen, Paul G. ....Tucson, AZ
Lauritzen, Peter B. ....Menlo Park, CA
Lauro, Clara A. ....Great Neck, NY
Lauro, Jennifer L. ....Boston, MA
Lauro, John F. ....Tampa, FL
Lauro, John F., P.A. ....Tampa, FL
Lauro, Linda M. Boswell ....Greenwood, IN
Lauro, Lino J. ....Los Angeles, CA
Lauro, Philip H. ....Springfield, MA
Lauro, Sandra K. ....Dallas, TX
Lauro, Thomas S. ....Brooklyn, NY
Lauroesch, Janice Mulligan ....Washington, DC
Lauroesch, Mark W. ....Washington, DC
Lauron, Michelle A. ....Victorville, CA
Laursen, Gary A. H. ....Dunedin, FL
Laursen, Lisa K. ....Los Angeles, CA
Laursen, Thomas E. ....Tucson, AZ
Laury, Everett L. ....Danville, IL
Lausa, Paula A. ....Houston, TX
Lausch, Connie Cline ....Cincinnati, OH
Lausch, Eugene W. ....Indianapolis, IN
Lausch, John R., Jr. ....Chicago, IL
Lausche, Louis F. ....Cincinnati, OH
Lause, Christopher A. ....Chicago, IL
Lause, Michael F. ....St. Louis, MO
Lausell, Carlo, Gaztambide & Plaza
San Juan, PR
Lausell, Michael L. ....Geneva, NY
Lausell, Miguel D. ....San Juan, PR
Lausell, Steven C. ....San Juan, PR
Lausen, Carrie J. ....Chicago, IL
Lausier, Paul L. ....Marblehead, MA
Lausman, Carri Ann ....Chicago, IL
Lauson, Robert J. ....Santa Monica, CA
Laussel, Joseph C. ....Miami, FL
Lausterer, Wayne R. ....Omaha, NE
Laustsen, David ....Doylestown, PA
Trevose, PA
Laut, Steven ....Los Angeles, CA
Lautanen & Stanley, A Professional Law Corporation ....La Jolla, CA
San Diego, CA
Lautanen, W. Alan ....La Jolla, CA
Lautemann, John E. ....Los Angeles, CA
Lauten, David M. ....Medfield, MA
Lauten, Frederick J., Jr. ....Orlando, FL
Lauten, Heather Liddell ....Baltimore, MD
Lauten, John H. ....Camarillo, CA
Lauten, Max H. ....Baltimore, MD
Lauten, Nancy A. ....Tampa, FL
Lauten, William R. ....Mobile, AL
Lautenbaugh, Scott A. ....Omaha, NE
Lautenberg, Melissa B. ....New York, NY
Lautenschlaeger, Lester J., Jr.
New Orleans, LA
Lautenschlager, Edward W. ....Salem, VA
Lautenschlager, Kenneth T.
Charlotte, NC
Lautenschlager, Lea L. ....Roanoke, VA
Lautenschlager, Peggy A. ....Madison, WI
Lautenschlager, Tracy H.
Fort Lauderdale, FL
Lauter, John J. ....New York, NY
Lauter, Kenneth E. ....Indianapolis, IN
Lauter, Leonard H. ....Skokie, IL
Lauter, Richard S. ....Chicago, IL
Lauter, Robert S. ....Ross, CA
Lauter, Ronald J. ....San Diego, CA
Lauterbach, Barbara A. ....Houston, TX
Lauterbach and Garfinkel, LLP ....Yonkers, NY
Lauterbach, Hans D. ....Irvine, CA
Lauterbach, John C., Jr. ....Suffolk, VA
Lauterbach, Joseph C. ....Harlan, IA
Woodbine, IA
Lauterbach, Leon A. ....Yonkers, NY
Lauterbach, Richard Spencer ....New City, NY
Lauterbach, Theresa M. ....Juneau, AK
Lauterer, Eric ....Garden Grove, CA
Lauterjung, Larry Edward ....Marion, IL
Lautermilch, John D. ....Plano, TX
Lauterstein, Henry W. ....New York, NY
Lauterstein, Lincoln W. ....Rockport, MA
Lauth, David J. ....Minneapolis, MN
Lauth, James E. ....San Diego, CA
Lauth, M. Katherine ....San Francisco, CA
Lauth, Thomas P., III ....Atlanta, GA
Lautin, Stuart A. ....Dallas, TX
Lautman, Kenneth Z. ....Los Angeles, CA
Lauto and Garabedian ....Commack, NY
Lauto, Paul A. ....Commack, NY
Lauto, Robert D. ....Commack, NY
Lautrup, Crystal D. ....Los Angeles, CA
Lautrup, Greer O. ....Washington, DC
Lautsch, John C. ....Newport Beach, CA
Lautsch Law Corporation
Newport Beach, CA
Lautsch, Sylvia D. ....Beverly Hills, CA
Lautt, Jonathan J. ....Kansas City, MO
Lautz, Donald G. ....Racine, WI
Lautz, Fredrick G. ....Milwaukee, WI
Lautz, Karl R. ....Tucson, AZ

Lautz, Thad E. ....Bel Air, MD
Lautzenheiser, Michael W. ....Bluffton, IN
Markle, IN
Lautzenheiser, Myers & Holdman
Bluffton, IN
Markle, IN
Lautzenhiser, John G. ....Whittier, CA
Lautzenhiser, Roger E. ....Columbus, OH
Lauve, Lewis O. ....Alexandria, LA
Lauve, Lewis O., Jr. ....Alexandria, LA
Lauver, E. Eugene ....Houston, TX
Lauver, J. Richard ....Pittsburgh, PA
Lauver, Linda B. ....Greensboro, NC
Lauver, Lynn D. ....Topeka, KS
Lauver, Robert A. ....Kernersville, NC
Lauver, Robert A., P.A. ....Kernersville, NC
Lauwers, Steven J. ....Concord, NH
Laux, Bonnie V. ....Salem, OR
Laux, Colleen B. ....Cincinnati, OH
Laux, Jill J. ....St. Louis, MO
Laux, Joanmarie ....Norristown, PA
Laux, Michael A. ....Westport, CT
Laux, Richard T. ....Elyria, OH
Laux, Robert B. ....Marietta, GA
Laux, Timothy J. ....Osceola, WI
Lauzon, Debra A. ....Manhattan Beach, CA
Lauzon, Michael L. ....Chicago, IL
Lauzon, Peter A. ....Los Angeles, CA
Lava, Brian R. ....Hauppauge, NY
Lava, Leslie M. ....San Francisco, CA
Lava, Levine & Lava ....Hauppauge, NY
Lava, Marvin S. ....Hauppauge, NY
Lavacot, Carol E. ....Santa Ana, CA
Lavaglia, Frank A. ....New York, NY
Lavake, Stephanie Michelle ....Fort Worth, TX
Lavalette, Peter N. ....Toledo, OH
Lavalle, Anthony C. ....Syracuse, NY
Lavalle, Brown & Ronan, P.A.
Boca Raton, FL
LaValle, David C. ....Boston, MA
Lavalle, Dennis P. ....Mineola, NY
Lavalle, John Jay ....Centereach, NY
LaValle, Kathleen M. ....Dallas, TX
La Valle, Kenneth ....New York, NY
Lavalle, Kevin A. ....Flint, MI
Lavalle, Lawrence L. ....Boca Raton, FL
Lavalle, Paul Houston ....Texas City, TX
La Valle, Peter J. ....Texas City, TX
Lavalle, Ralph E. D. ....Ormond Beach, FL
La Valle, William J. ....Jamaica, NY
Lavallee, Adrienne C.
Executive Office Of The President, GV
Lavallee, Claude Bernard ....Lexington, MA
LaVallee, Courtland R. ....Buffalo, NY
LaVallee, Diane M. ....Buffalo, NY
Lavallee, Fernand A. ....Washington, DC
Lavallee, Keith ....Farmingdale, NY
Lavallee, Nicole ....San Francisco, CA
Lavallee, Norman G.
Huntington Station, NY
Lavallée, Peter J. ....Washington, DC
Lavallee, Raymond G. ....Freeport, NY
LaVallee, Roland J. ....Tempe, AZ
LaVallee, Therese M. ....Portland, OR
Lavallee, Thomas J. ....Bay Shore, NY
LaValley, Daniel J. ....Toledo, OH
LaValley, Frederick J. M.
Philadelphia, PA
LaValley, LaValley, Todak & Schaefer Co., L.P.A. ....Toledo, OH
LaValley, Melvin ....Los Angeles, CA
LaValley, Richard G. ....Toledo, OH
LaValley, Richard G., Jr. ....Toledo, OH
Lavalleye, Jean-Paul P.M. ....Arlington, VA
Lavalleye, Marie A. ....Washington, DC
LaVallo, Richard ....Austin, TX
Lavan, Brian ....Brighton, MI
Lavan, Brian, & Associates, P.C.
Brighton, MI
LaVan, Byron R. ....Lafayette Hill, PA
LaVan, Justin E. ....West Des Moines, IA
Lavan, Maryanne R. ....Bethesda, MD
Lavan, Noreen M. ....New York, NY
Lavan, Robert E. ....Cleveland, OH
Lavandeira, Barbara Antonia
Hicksville, NY
Lavandera, Henry W. ....Tampa, FL
Lavandero Latimer, Fernando J.
San Juan, PR
LaVanier, William R. ....New Albany, OH
LaVardera, Lisa Marie ....Hempstead, NY
Lavargna, Carrie S. ....Miami, FL
LaVarnway, Richard L. ....Auburn, NY
LaVarre, Donald J. ....Northbrook, IL
LaVaute, James R. ....Syracuse, NY
Lavayen, Gustavo E. ....Santa Barbara, CA
Lavdas, George
Securities and Exchange Commission,
Office of International Affairs, GV
Lavdiotis, Chris P. ....Oakland, CA
Lave, Steven H. ....Fremont, CA
Lave, Tamara R. ....Vista, CA
Lavecchia, Carolyn C. ....Richmond, VA
La Vecchia, John B. ....Roseland, NJ
LaVecchio, Lawrence D. ....Miami, FL
LaVeck, Arthur Lee ....Syracuse, NY
LaVela, Joseph A. ....Basking Ridge, NJ
Lavelle, Anne M. ....Pittsburgh, PA
Lavelle, Brian F. D. ....Asheville, NC
Lavelle, Charles J. ....Louisville, KY
Lavelle, Charles P. ....Holyoke, MA
Lavelle, Dominick W. ....Mineola, NY
La Velle, Edward H., III ....Lakeport, CA
Lavelle, Edward L. ....Warren, OH
Lavelle, Eleissa C. ....Las Vegas, NV
Lavelle, Felicity T. ....Philadelphia, PA
Lavelle, Francis A. ....Chevy Chase, MD
Lavelle, Francis (Frank) A. ....Athens, OH
Lavelle, Gregory J. ....Macedonia, OH
Lavelle, James V., III ....Las Vegas, NV
Lavelle, Jas R. ....Louisville, KY
LaVelle, John C. ....Covington, KY
Lavelle, John H. ....Albany, NY
Lavelle, John J. ....New York, NY
Lavelle, John P. ....Athens, OH
Lavelle, John P. ....Jim Thorpe, PA
Lavelle, John P., Jr. ....Cherry Hill, NJ
Philadelphia, PA
Lavelle, Joseph P. ....Washington, DC
Lavelle, Kerry M. ....Chicago, IL
Lavelle & Lavelle Co., L.P.A.
Cleveland, OH
Lavelle Law Offices, L.P.A. ....Athens, OH
Lavelle Legal Services, Ltd. ....Chicago, IL
Lavelle, Linda ....Orlando, FL
Lavelle, Lisa A. ....Washington, DC
Lavelle, Lisa M. ....Pittsburgh, PA
Lavelle, Lydia E. ....Durham, NC
Lavelle, Marceline A. ....Pittsburgh, PA
Lavelle, Marianne S. ....Lehighton, PA
Lavelle, Martin P. ....New York, NY
LaVelle, Matthew K. ....Phoenix, AZ
Lavelle, Michael E. ....Franklin Park, IL
LaVelle, Michael J. ....Phoenix, AZ
LaVelle, Michael N. ....Bridgeport, CT
Lavelle, Motta, Klopfenstein and Saletta, Ltd.
Franklin Park, IL
Lavelle, Neal P. ....Cleveland, OH
Lavelle, Patrick J. ....Clarks Summit, PA
Lavelle, Patrick S. ....Cleveland, OH
Lavelle, Paul K. ....Birmingham, AL
Lavelle, Paul M. ....New Orleans, LA
Lavelle, Richard J. ....Sacramento, CA
Lavelle, Robert P. ....San Luis Obispo, CA
Lavelle, Sheilah Anne ....Phoenix, AZ
Lavelle, Thomas ....Timonium, MD
Lavelle, Thomas G. J. ....Minneapolis, MN
LaVelle, Thomas J. ....Worthington, MN
Lavelle, Thomas R. ....Santa Clara, CA
Lavelle, William A. ....Athens, OH
Lavelle, William J. ....Chicago, IL
Lavelle, William Scott ....Columbus, OH
LaVelle, William Troy ....Holtsville, NY
Lavelle-Stubberud & Associates, A Professional Corporation ....Las Vegas, NV
Reno, NV
Lavely, John H., Jr. ....Los Angeles, CA
Lavely & Singer, Professional Corporation
Los Angeles, CA
Lavely, Steven G. ....Bradenton, FL
Laveman, Marlene G. ....Florham Park, NJ
Laveman, Robin S. ....Westbury, NY
Laven, Bernard B. ....Los Angeles, CA
Laven & Laven ....Los Angeles, CA
Laven, Peter J. ....Los Angeles, CA
Laven, Stuart A. ....Cleveland, OH
Lavenant, Michael S. ....Camarillo, CA
Lavenant, Rene P., Jr. ....Houston, TX
Lavenberg, Robert A. ....Fort Washington, PA
Lavenburg, David A. ....Springfield, MA
Lavenda, Diane M. ....Newark, NJ
Lavender, Barbara A. ....Oberlin, OH
Lavender, Bradford B. ....New York, NY
Lavender, Carmen H. ....Albuquerque, NM
Lavender, Carol K.
La Canada Flintridge, CA
Lavender, Deborah E. ....New Orleans, LA
Lavender, Dennis ....Neptune, NJ
Lavender, G. William ....Texarkana, AR
Lavender, George William, III
Charleston, WV
Lavender, Jason E. ....San Francisco, CA
Lavender, Jay L. ....Warsaw, IN
Lavender, Joel R. ....Fort Lauderdale, FL
Lavender & Kehler ....Warsaw, IN
Lavender & Lavender ....Elberton, GA
Lavender, Phillip N. ....Norcross, GA
Lavender, Robert E. ....Oklahoma City, OK
Lavender, Robert W. ....Elberton, GA
Lavender, Rochelle & Barnette, PLC
Texarkana, AR
Lavender, Rosanne ....Santa Ana, CA
Lavender, Thomas E., III ....Atlanta, GA
Lavender, Thomas Wade, II ....Ashland, KY
Lavender, Timothy R. ....Chicago, IL
Lavender, W. Thomas, Jr. ....Columbia, SC
Lavender, Wesley M. ....Decatur, AL
Lavender-Che, Joyce C. ....Cincinnati, OH
Lavengood, Kirk L. ....Detroit, MI
Lavenstein, Terry S. ....Baltimore, MD
Laventhal, Nahum D. ....Metairie, LA
Laventhall, Donald I. ....New York, NY
Laventhall & Zicklin ....New York, NY
Laventis, George P. ....Gloucester, MA
Laventis, Geri ....Holyoke, MA
Laventure, Michelle M. ....Columbia, SC
Lavenue, Lionel M. ....Washington, DC
Lavenue, Roxanne W. ....Mobile, AL
Lavenue, Teresa A. ....Washington, DC
Lavenue, Teresa Ann Floyd
United States Court Of Appeals For The
Federal Circuit, GV
Laver, Edith G. ....Bethlehem, PA
Laver, Gerald D. ....Napoleon, OH
Laver, Miriam ....Philadelphia, PA
Laver, Roberto ....Boston, MA
Laver, Steven G. ....Philadelphia, PA
Lavera, Michael S. ....Louisville, KY
Laveran-Stiebar, Peter A. ....New York, NY
Laverde, Maria M. ....Las Cruces, NM
LaVerdi, Barbara J. ....Rochester, NY
LaVerdiere, Charles C., Jr. ....Wilton, ME
LaVerdiere, Charles C., P.A. ....Wilton, ME
LaVerdiere, Donald A. ....Amherst, MA
Laverdiere, Marc Gaston ....Arlington, VA
LaVerdiere, Richard A. ....Hastings, MN
Laverdure, Donald E. ....Milwaukee, WI
Laverdure, Mary Frances ....Minneapolis, MN
LaVere, Raymond L. ....Glen Ellyn, IL
La Verghetta, Joseph C. ....Lutherville, MD
Lavergne, Edwin N. ....Washington, DC
LaVergne, Eugene M. ....Asbury Park, NJ
LaVergne, Luke A. ....Baton Rouge, LA
Lavergne-Ramirez, Alicia I. ....San Juan, PR
Lavering, Daniel C. ....Charlottesville, VA
Laveris, Nicholas A. ....New York, NY
Laverly, Bruce ....West Chester, PA
LaVerne, Carol L. ....Colfax, WA
Lavernoich, Valerian J. ....Berlin, NH
Laveroni, Paul J. ....San Francisco, CA
Laverriere, Kenneth J. ....New York, NY
Lavers, Richard M. ....Elkhart, IN
Lavertu, L. James ....Madawaska, ME
Laverty, Anne M. ....Cedar Rapids, IA
Laverty, Dana C. ....Seattle, WA
Laverty, David A. ....Chicago, IL
Laverty, David V. ....West Palm Beach, FL
Laverty, Joanne Heslin ....Hartford, CT
Laverty, Joseph H. ....Davenport, IA
Laverty, Lisa Glenn ....Boston, MA
Laverty, Roger M., III ....Los Angeles, CA
Laverty, Sarah G. ....Ann Arbor, MI
Lavery, Daniel C. ....Encino, CA
Lavery, Edward G. ....Dallas, TX
Lavery, Edward W. ....Skaneateles, NY
Lavery, Frank J., Jr. ....Harrisburg, PA
Lavery, Harry D. ....Sarasota, FL
Lavery, Hugh A., Jr. ....Ossining, NY
Lavery, Hugh J. ....Bridgeport, CT
Lavery, James G. ....Brockton, MA
Lavery, Joan S. ....Hackettstown, NJ
Lavery, John C. ....St. Petersburg, FL
Lavery, John Patrick ....Las Vegas, NV
Lavery, John R. ....Clearwater, FL
Lavery, Joseph ....Trenton, NJ
Lavery & Kain, P.C. ....Harrisburg, PA
Lavery & Lavery ....Skaneateles, NY
Lavery, Liam Burgess ....Seattle, WA
Lavery, Linda C. ....Skaneateles, NY
Lavery, Michael B. ....Hackettstown, NJ
Lavery, Michael J. ....Boynton Beach, FL
Lavery, Michael J. ....New York, NY
Lavery, Michael J., P.A. ....Boynton Beach, FL
Lavery, Richard L. ....Evanston, WY
Lavery, Robert G. ....Alliance, OH
Lavery, William D., Jr. ....Cherry Hill, NJ
Lavery, William G. ....Elkhart, IN
Laves, Alan L., (P.C.) ....Dallas, TX
Laves, Benjamin S. ....Maplewood, NJ
Laveson, Jeffrey D. ....Seattle, WA
Lavespere, Jerry L., Jr. ....Alexandria, LA
Lavespere, Jerry L., Law Corporation
Alexandria, LA
Lavet, Robert S. ....Reston, VA
Lavette, Dennis R. ....Hartford, CT
Lavette, John H. ....Birmingham, AL
Lavette, John R. ....Birmingham, AL
Lavette, Patrick M. ....Birmingham, AL
La Vetter, Toby ....Tucson, AZ
Lavey & Burnett ....Little Rock, AR
Lavey, David ....Cleveland, OH
Lavey, Jeffrey C. ....Braintree, MA
Lavey, John P. ....St. Louis, MO
Lavey, John T. ....Little Rock, AR
Lavey, Stewart E. ....Florham Park, NJ
Lavey, Warren G. ....Chicago, IL
Lavey, Wendlene M. ....Cleveland, OH
Lavezzo, Albert M. ....Vallejo, CA
Lavi, Donald L. ....Los Angeles, CA
Lavi, Laura Ann ....Auburn, WA
LaVia, Jennifer P. ....Tallahassee, FL
LaVia, John T., III ....Tallahassee, FL
Lavian, Susan ....Los Angeles, CA
Laviana, Robert ....Hartford, CT
Laviano, Andrew C. ....Charlestown, RI
Laviano, William M. ....Ridgefield, CT
Lavick, Neil A. ....Beverly Hills, CA
LaVie, Kevin J. ....New Orleans, LA
Lavien, David ....Boston, MA
Lavien & Tveekrem ....Boston, MA
Lavieri & Dougherty, LLC ....Winsted, CT
Lavieri, João Vicente ....Plano, TX
Lavieri, Richard R. ....Winsted, CT
Lavieri, Vincent A. ....Chicago, IL
Lavietes, Steven A. ....New York, NY
Lavigna, Lisa ....Atlantic City, NJ
Lavigna, Michael P. ....Euclid, OH
LaVigne, A. W. David ....Eastham, MA
Lavigne, Eileen M. ....New York, NY
Lavigne, Evariste G. ....Albany, NY
Lavigne, Francis C. ....Massena, NY
Lavigne, Gary D. ....Willimantic, CT
Lavigne, James R. ....Orlando, FL
Lavigne, James W. ....Clinton, MI
LaVigne, Jay ....Greenwood Village, CO
Lavigne, John J. ....Greensboro, NC
Lavigne, Lawrence N. ....Edison, NJ
New York, NY
LaVigne, Mark Stephen ....St. Louis, MO
Lavigne, Michael T. ....Morristown, NJ
Lavigne, Peter M. ....Gladstone, OR
LaVigne, Peter W. ....New York, NY
Lavigne, Ronald L. ....Olympia, WA
Lavigne, Thomas ....Midland, MI
LaVignera, Guy G. ....Newark, NJ
Lavik, A. Roy
Commodity Futures Trading Commission,
GV
Lavik, Bricker L. ....Minneapolis, MN
LaVille, Daniel M. ....Grand Rapids, MI
LaVille, Jeanine Nemesi ....Grand Rapids, MI
Lavin, Allen S. ....Chicago, IL
Lavin, Andrew T. ....Fort Lauderdale, FL
Lavin, Barbara ....Portsmouth, VA
Lavin, Coleman, O'Neil, Ricci, Finarelli & Gray ....Mount Laurel, NJ
New York, NY
Philadelphia, PA
Lavin, Daniel ....New York, NY
Lavin, David M. ....Chicago, IL
Lavin, Donald S. ....Northbrook, IL
Lavin, Edward M. ....San Antonio, TX
Lavin, Ellen ....Hopkins, MN
Lavin, Francesca ....New York, NY
Lavin, Frederick M. ....Orchard Park, NY
Lavin, George J., III ....Mount Laurel, NJ
Philadelphia, PA
Lavin, George J., Jr. ....Philadelphia, PA
Lavin & Hansen, LLP ....Silverado, CA
Lavin, Howard S. ....New York, NY
Lavin, James R. ....Silverado, CA
Lavin, Jerald A. ....Elgin, IL
Lavin, Jerold R. ....Chicago, IL
Lavin, John J. ....Buffalo, NY
Lavin, Joseph B. ....Port Angeles, WA
Lavin, Joseph F. ....Baltimore, MD
Lavin, Karen M. ....McHenry, IL
Lavin, Kevin J. ....Washington, DC
Lavin & Kleiman, P.C. ....Buffalo, NY
Lavin, Laurence M. ....Los Angeles, CA
Lavin, Lawrence M., Jr. ....St. Louis, MO
Lavin, Luis A. ....Los Angeles, CA
Lavin, Marvin M. ....Calabasas, CA
Lavin, Maureen C. ....Mineola, NY
New York, NY
White Plains, NY
Lavin, Michael H. ....Chicago, IL
Lavin, Michelle C. ....Encino, CA
Lavin, Patrick D. ....Anchorage, AK
Lavin, Richard R. ....Boston, MA
Lavin, Richard W. ....Dayton, OH
Lavin, Ross G. ....St. Louis, MO
Lavin, Scott A. ....New York, NY
Lavin, Stacy D. ....Moses Lake, WA
Lavin, Stanley ....New York, NY
Lavin, Steven H. ....Chicago, IL
Lavin, Terrence J. ....Chicago, IL
Lavin, Thomas J. ....Bronx, NY
Lavin, Timothy J. ....Kansas City, MO
Lavin, Todd Elliot ....Encino, CA
Lavin, Todd Elliot, A Prof. Corp.
Encino, CA
Lavin & Waldon, P.C. ....Chicago, IL
Lavinder, David L. ....Franktown, CO
Lavine, Alan S. ....Trenton, NJ
Lavine, Bryan B. ....Atlanta, GA
Lavine, Carol Vogt ....Portland, OR
Lavine, Charles D. ....Forest Hills, NY
Lavine, Henry W. ....Washington, DC
Lavine, Howard D. ....Baltimore, MD
Lavine, Irvin A. ....Washington, DC
Lavine, Jim E. ....Houston, TX
Lavine, J. M. ....Brooklyn, NY
Lavine, Joan C. ....Los Angeles, CA
LaVine, Jordan ....Philadelphia, PA
Lavine, Karen S. ....New York, NY
LaVine, Kenneth N. ....New York, NY
Lavine, Mark A. ....Miami, FL
Lavine, Matt P. ....Silver Spring, MD
Lavine, Michael E. ....Washington, DC
Lavine, Nancy B. ....Windsor, CT
Lavine, Rachel ....New York, NY
Lavine, Robert J. ....Rockville, MD
La Vine, Robert L. ....San Francisco, CA
Lavine, Ruth J. ....Beverly Hills, CA
Lavine, Stuart A. ....Coventry, CT
Lavinger, Michael B. ....New York, NY
Lavinski, Joseph M. ....Springfield, MA
Lavinsky, Corey Myles ....St. Louis, MO
Lavinsky, Jordan ....San Francisco, CA
Lavinsky, Larry M. ....New York, NY
Lavinsky, Michael B. ....Denver, CO
Lavinsky, Rick A. ....Columbus, OH
Lavinsky, Roger N. ....New York, NY
Lavinthal, Edwin M. ....Livingston, NJ
Lavinthal, Fredric P. ....Livingston, NJ
Lavintman, Joel W. ....St. Paul, MN
LaViolette, Diana Jane ....Greencastle, IN
LaViolette, John S. ....Beverly Hills, CA
Lavis, Charles E., Jr. ....New Orleans, LA
Lavis, Charles E., Jr., Professional Law Corporation ....New Orleans, LA
LaVista, Anthony F. ....Belleville, NJ
La Vista, Nancy L. ....West Palm Beach, FL
Lavit, Theodore H. ....Lebanon, KY
Lavit, Theodore H., & Associates, P.S.C.
Lebanon, KY
LaVita, Ronald J. ....East Setauket, NY
Lavitt, Joseph ....Los Angeles, CA
Lavitt, Kathy A. ....Salt Lake City, UT
Lavitt, Robert M. ....Seattle, WA
Lavllo, Frank Joseph ....Cleveland, OH
Lavner, Stephen B. ....Philadelphia, PA
LaVoie, Anne E. ....Chicago, IL
Lavoie, Christopher R. ....Boston, MA
Lavoie, Estelle A. ....Portland, ME
Lavoie, James A. ....Minneapolis, MN
Lavoie, John G. ....McLean, VA
Lavoie, John T. ....Bennington, VT
Lavoie, Larry R. ....New York, NY
Lavoie, Margaret C. ....Portland, ME
Lavoie, Mariam Alexanian ....Providence, RI
Lavoie, Mark B. ....Boston, MA
Lavoie, Mark G. ....Portland, ME
Lavoié, Marylou J. ....Springfield, MA
Lavoie, Michael J. ....Detroit, MI
Lavoie, Richard L. ....New York, NY
Lavoie, Robert L. ....Anaheim, CA
Lavoie, Robert W. ....Andover, MA
La Voie, Theresa M. ....Sacramento, CA
Lavoipierre, Xavier A.M. ....Sonoma, CA
Lavolette, Richard D. ....Lansing, MI

Lavorata, Richard, Jr. ....Brentwood, NY
Lavorato, Charles S. ....Des Moines, IA
Lavorato, House, Chilton & Lavorato, A Professional Corporation ....Salinas, CA
Lavorato, John C. ....Washington, DC
Lavorato, Sam A., Sr. ....Salinas, CA
Lavorato, Sam, III ....Salinas, CA
Lavorgna, Gregory J. ....Philadelphia, PA
Lavori, Nora ....New York, NY
LaVoy, Ann E. ....San Diego, CA
LaVoy, Christopher A. ....Phoenix, AZ
LaVoy, Jill M. ....Monroe, MI
LaVoy, Jonathan A. ....Milwaukee, WI
La Voy, Kenneth R., Jr. ....New York, NY
LaVoy, Thomas O. ....San Diego, CA
LaVoy, William F. ....Monroe, MI
Lavra, John A. ....Sacramento, CA
LaVrar, Franklyn C., Jr. .....Fort Lauderdale, FL
Lavrenchik, Peter G. ....Riverhead, NY
Lavrich, Frank G. ....Chardon, OH
Lavrin, Cecilia I. ....Stevensville, MD
Lavrisha, Anton M. ....Cleveland, OH
Lavroff, Jay ....Westfield, NJ
Lavy, Glen E. ....Dallas, TX
Law, Alfred J. ....Owings, MD
Law & Arthur ....San Francisco, CA
Law, Benjamin B. ....Menlo Park, CA
Law, Beth L. ....Deerfield, IL
Law, Carole A. ....Danville, CA
Law, Carter C. ....St. Louis, MO
Law, Casey R. ....McPherson, KS
Law, Charles B., Jr. ....New York, NY
Law, Charles M. ....Montgomery, AL
Law, Christine J. ....Aurora, CO
Law, Cynthia L. ....Fredericksburg, VA
Law, Dare ....Los Angeles, CA
Law, David B. ....Denver, CO
Law, David Bradford ....Washington, DC
Law, David M. ....Concord, NH
Law, Dennis D. ....San Luis Obispo, CA
Law, Dennis M. ....Monterey, CA
Law, Donald L. ....Olympia, WA
Law, Donna J. ....Niskayuna, NY
Law, Douglas D. ....San Diego, CA
Law, Douglas J. ....Omaha, NE
Law, E. Janice ....Houston, TX
Law, Edmund W. ....Frederick, MD
Law, Ellen M. Tepedino ....Boca Raton, FL
Law, Erving G. ....Yorba Linda, CA
Law Firm For Businesses, The, A Professional Corporation
Chesterfield, MO
St. Louis, MO
Law, Franklin N. ....San Antonio, TX
Law, Fred H., Jr. ....Elmhurst, IL
Law, Froelich & Landesman ....Kearny, NJ
Law, G. Hammond, III ....Gainesville, GA
Law, George A. ....Portland, CT
Law, George T. ....New Bedford, MA
Law, Glenn ....Washington, DC
Law, H. Grant ....San Francisco, CA
Law, Howard B. ....Dallas, TX
Law, Hugh R. ....St. Louis, MO
Law, Janet ....Cherry Hill, NJ
Law, John F. ....Panama City, FL
Law, John F., P.A., Law Office of
Panama City, FL
Law, John M. ....Denver, CO
Law, John P. ....Monterey Park, CA
Law, Judy ....Oakland, CA
Law, Julia R. ....Groveland, FL
Law, Katharine S. J. ....New York, NY
Law, Kenneth T. ....Palo Alto, CA
Law, Kerri Ann ....New York, NY
Law, Kevin S. ....Garden City, NY
Law, L. William, Jr. ....Weston, MA
Law, Lester B. ....Naples, FL
Law, Lillard Eugene ....Atlantic City, NJ
Law, Linda S. ....Portland, OR
Law, Lyman, Daniel, Kamerrer & Bogdanovich, P.S. ....Olympia, WA
Law, Madelyn C. ....Parsippany, NJ
Law, Marcia T. ....Rosemead, CA
Law, Maria Holland ....Manchester, NH
Law and Mediation Office of Kate Warner
San Rafael, CA
Law, Michael R. ....Rochester, NY
Law, Moni T. ....Yakima, WA
Law, Nancy W. ....Wilmington, DE
Law, Nicholas B. ....Indianapolis, IN
Law Office of Barbara Suskind, The
Walnut Creek, CA
Law Office, The, Ltd. ....Grafton, ND
Law, P. Cole ....Cartersville, GA
Law Partners, L.L.C. ....Birmingham, AL
Law, Patricia A. ....Riverside, CA
Law, Patrick B. ....Washington, DC
Law, Peter A. ....Atlanta, GA
Law, Philip S. ....Sugar Land, TX
Law, R. Zebulon ....Newport Beach, CA
Law & Resource Planning Associates, P.C.
Albuquerque, NM
Torreon, NM
Law, Rhea F. ....Tampa, FL
Law, Richard M. ....Houston, TX
Law, Richard S. ....Canoga Park, CA
Law, Robert C. ....Bloomfield Hills, MI
Lansing, MI
Law, Robert E. ....Martinez, CA
Law, Robert H. ....Bowie, MD
Law, Robert H., III ....Armonk, NY
Law, Robert J. ....Liberty Lake, WA
Law, Robert O., III ....Fernandina Beach, FL
Law, Robert S. ....Sioux Falls, SD
Law, Robert T., III ....Cohoes, NY
Law, Robt. D. ....Cedarville, IL
Law, Roger ....Shelby, MI
Law, Roger P. ....Treasury Department,
Internal Revenue Service, GV
Law, Ronald D. ....Dallas, TX
Law, Samuel C. ....San Diego, CA
Law, Sandra K. ....Weirton, WV
Wheeling, WV
Law, Sarah Frances ....Durango, CO
Law, Scott A. ....Oklahoma City, OK
Tulsa, OK
Law, Sharon J. ....Fayetteville, GA
Law, Snakard & Gambill ....Arlington, TX
Dallas, TX
Fort Worth, TX
Abilene, TX
Law, Stuart A., Jr. ....Princeton, NJ
Law, Susan Kelty ....New York, NY
Law, Sylvia A. ....New York, NY
Law, Teresa Gillis ....Lansing, MI
Law, Theodore W., III ....Columbia, SC
Law, Thomas A. ....Farmington Hills, MI
Law, Thos. H. ....Fort Worth, TX
Law, Timothy A. ....Seattle, WA
Law, Timothy E. ....Hartford, CT
Law, Timothy P. ....Philadelphia, PA
Law, Tsiwen M. ....Philadelphia, PA
Law, Walter J. ....Warrensburg, NY
Law, Weathers & Richardson, P.C.
Grand Rapids, MI
Law, William A. (Andy) ....Kingsport, TN
Law, William G., Jr. ....Brooksville, FL
Law, Yuk Kwong ....Los Angeles, CA
LaWall, Barbara ....Tucson, AZ
Lawall, Francis J. ....Philadelphia, PA
Lawall, Patrice ....Madison, NJ
Lawatsch, Frank E., Jr. ....Newark, NJ
Lawbaugh, Emanuel S., Jr. ....Fayetteville, AR
Law-Bennett, L. Kimberly ....Allentown, PA
Bethlehem, PA
Jim Thorpe, PA
Lawcewicz, Maria H. ....Arlington, MA
Lawch, Richard S. ....Washington, DC
Lawder, Fortis M. ....St. Louis, MO
Lawder, Joseph S. ....Minneapolis, MN
Lawder, Michael A. ....Belleville, IL
Lawder, Shawn Elizabeth ....St. Louis, MO
Lawdermilk, Rocky ....Beaumont, TX
Lawent, Paul D. ....Madison, WI
LaWer, Thomas G. ....Palo Alto, CA
Lawes, Charles O., III ....Hartford, CT
Lawfer, Martha A. ....Louisville, KY
Lawhead, Alan ....Washington, DC
Lawhead, Brandon V. ....Austin, MN
Lawhead, Janice M. ....Mandan, ND
Lawhead, Joshua B. ....Memphis, TN
Lawhead, Lawrence E. ....Indianapolis, IN
Lawhn, James H. ....Honolulu, HI
Lawhon, James B. ....Sacramento, CA
Lawhon, John E. ....Shreveport, LA
Lawhon, John E. ....Denton, TX
Lawhon, Joseph R. ....Albuquerque, NM
Lawhon, M. Jane ....Oakland, CA
Lawhon, Susan H. ....Houston, TX
Lawhorn, Charles A. ....Washington, DC
Lawhorn, Christopher J. ....Chicago, IL
Lawhorn, John M. ....Knoxville, TN
Lawhorn, Louis P. ....Loganville, GA
Lawhorn, M. Shawn ....Tulsa, OK
Lawhorn, Victor R. ....Oakland, CA
Lawhorne, Edward S. ....Media, PA
Lawhorne, Ernest G. ....Columbia, SC
Lawhun, Linda L. ....Bridgeton, NJ
Lawing, Douglas L. ....Houston, TX
Lawing, Jack L. ....Atlanta, GA
Lawing, Jim ....Wichita, KS
Lawing, Linda E. ....Charlotte, NC
Lawing, Robert J. ....Winston-Salem, NC
Lawing, Sally A. ....Greensboro, NC
Lawing Sharpless & Stavola, P.A.
Greensboro, NC
Lawing, Stephen E. ....High Point, NC
Lawing & Yu, P.L.L.C. ....High Point, NC
Lawinger, Jane M. ....Vandalia, IL
Lawit, Jason A. ....New York, NY
Lawit, John W. ....Albuquerque, NM
Lawit, John W., P.C. ....Albuquerque, NM
Lawitz, Alan J. ....Albany, NY
Lawko, Wm. A. ....Cleveland, OH
Lawlace, J. Randolph ....Philadelphia, PA
Lawler, Andrew M. ....New York, NY
Lawler, Andrew M., P.C. ....New York, NY
Lawler, Ann ....Arlington, TX
Lawler, Anne DeVoe ....Seattle, WA
Lawler, Anne Kathryn ....Deephaven, MN
Lawler, Betty A. ....Bala Cynwyd, PA
Lawler, Betty L. ....Oklahoma City, OK
Lawler, Brian E. ....Seattle, WA
Lawler & Burroughs, P.C. ....Seattle, WA
Lawler, Byron J. ....Ventura, CA
Lawler, Christopher E. ....Chicago, IL
Lawler, Christopher E. ....Metairie, LA
Lawler, Colin G. ....Chicago, IL
Lawler, Colleen Ann ....Irvine, CA
Lawler, Daniel ....Chicago, IL
Lawler, Daniel J. ....Doylestown, PA
Lawler, David A. ....Houston, TX
Lawler, David V. ....Hyannis, MA
Lawler, Denis James ....Philadelphia, PA
Lawler, Dennis M. ....Clearwater, FL
Lawler, Donald K. ....Omaha, NE
Lawler, Edward E., Jr. ....Jackson, MS
Lawler, Francis J., (P.C.) ....Boston, MA
Lawler, George Joseph, Law Offices of
Trumbull, CT
Lawler, George S. ....Towson, MD
Lawler, George V. ....Cromwell, CT
Lawler, James F. ....Salem, OR
Lawler, James F., Jr. ....Fort Worth, TX
Lawler, James W. ....Centralia, WA
Lawler, Jean M. ....Los Angeles, CA
Lawler, John E. ....Yonkers, NY
Lawler, John F.X. ....Boston, MA
Lawler, John H. ....West Union, OH
Lawler, John L. ....Mobile, AL
Lawler, John P. ....Stroudsburg, PA
Lawler, Judd ....Washington, DC
Lawler, Julie Kerwin ....Palos Heights, IL
Lawler, Kathy A. ....Morristown, NJ
Lawler, Larry E. ....Lakewood, CO
Lawler & Lawler ....San Francisco, CA
Lawler, Lilia E. ....Philadelphia, PA
Lawler, Marion R., III ....Brownsville, TX
Lawler, Martin J. ....San Francisco, CA
Lawler, Mary ....Burbank, CA
Lawler, Mary G. ....Philadelphia, PA
Lawler, Megan J. ....New York, NY
Lawler, Michael B. ....Los Angeles, CA
Lawler, Michael R., Jr. ....Newport Beach, CA
Lawler, Nancy F. ....Atlanta, GA
Lawler, Patrick W. ....San Francisco, CA
Lawler, Paul R. ....Memphis, TN
Lawler, Peter C. ....McLean, VA
Lawler, Raymond ....Marion, IL
Lawler, Richard A. ....Lakewood, CO
Lawler, Richard F. ....Greenwich, CT
New York, NY
Lawler, Robert B. ....Philadelphia, PA
Lawler, Robert H. ....De Witt, NY
Lawler, Robert H., P.C. ....De Witt, NY
Lawler, Stewart C., II
Federal Trade Commission,
Bureau of Competition, GV
Lawler & Swanson, PLC .....Parkersburg, IA
Lawler & Tanner, P.C. ....Atlanta, GA
Lawler, Theresa A. ....Towson, MD
Lawler, Thomas A. ....Parkersburg, IA
Lawler, Thomas C. ....San Diego, CA
Lawler, Thomas C., III ....Lawrenceville, GA
Lawler, Thomas J. ....Saginaw, MI
Lawler, Thomas James ....Chicago, IL
Lawler, Thomas M., Jr. ....Washington, DC
Lawler, Timothy G. ....Palos Heights, IL
Lawler, W. Gale ....Chicago, IL
Lawler, William E., III ....Washington, DC
Lawler, William F., Jr. ....Anderson, IN
Lawler, William H. ....Brookfield, WI
Lawless, Barbara A. ....San Francisco, CA
Lawless, Bleu Kuwanyantiwa
Washington, DC
Lawless, Bonnie J. ....Bethesda, MD
Lawless, Donald P. ....Grand Rapids, MI
Lawless, Douglas P. ....Sarasota, FL
Lawless, Fran I. Lepper ....New York, NY
Lawless, Horowitz & Lawless
San Francisco, CA
Lawless, J. Mark ....Austin, TX
Houston, TX
Lawless, J. Martin ....Peoria, IL
Lawless, James J., Jr. ....Philadelphia, PA
Lawless, Jeffrey Scott ....Somerset, KY
Lawless, Jo Ellen ....Louisville, KY
Lawless, John H., Jr. ....Petaluma, CA
Lawless, John J. ....Springfield, IL
Lawless, John J. ....Richmond Hill, NY
Lawless, Kevin W. ....Newburyport, MA
Lawless & Lawless, P.C. ....Barnstable, MA
Orleans, MA
Lawless, Lawrence C. ....Norfolk, VA
Lawless, Lee T. ....St. Louis, MO
Lawless, Maria I. ....San Francisco, CA
Lawless, Mark J. ....New York, NY
Lawless, Matthew E. ....Hempstead, NY
Lawless, Megan A. ....New York, NY
Lawless, Michael R. ....Overland Park, KS
Lawless, Monica Rose ....New York, NY
Lawless, Patrict T. ....Albany, NY
Lawless, Paul A., Jr. ....East Brunswick, NJ
Westmont, NJ
Philadelphia, PA
Lawless, Paul R. ....Cedar Grove, NJ
Lawless, Paul Thomas
Bowling Green, KY
Lawless, Richard G. ....Mineola, NY
Lawless, Robert C. ....Barnstable, MA
Orleans, MA
Lawless, Robert T. ....Florham Park, NJ
New York, NY
Lawless, Stephen F. ....Albuquerque, NM
Lawless, Sue ....Baltimore, MD
Lawless, Susan ....Bedminster, NJ
Lawless, Therese M. ....San Francisco, CA
Lawless, Thomas D. ....Phoenix, AZ
Lawless, Thomas W., Jr. ....Westwood, MA
Lawless, William B. ....Barnstable, MA
Orleans, MA
Lawless, William F. ....Altamonte Springs, FL
Lawless, William F., P.A.
Altamonte Springs, FL
Lawley, Don E. ....Montgomery, AL
Lawley, H. Cannon ....Birmingham, AL
Lawley, Leslie Joan ....Kensington, MD
Lawley, M. Bridgit ....Oakland, CA
Lawley, Patricia M. ....Gates Mills, OH
Lawley, Robert T. ....Springfield, IL
Lawlis, Gerald L. ....Indianapolis, IN
Lawlis, J. Hunter ....New York, NY
Lawlis, Monte D. ....Jasper, TX
Lawliss & Cantwell ....Plattsburgh, NY
Lawliss, Kathleen Weaver ....Plattsburgh, NY
Lawliss, Timothy J. ....Plattsburgh, NY
Lawlor, Andrew ....Dedham, MA
Lawlor, Brian E. ....Albany, NY
Lawlor, Brian P. ....San Francisco, CA
Lawlor, Brian Patrick ....Sacramento, CA
Lawlor, Bruce M. ....Arlington, VA
Lawlor, Christopher L. ....Mequon, WI
Lawlor, David F. ....Rochester, NY
Lawlor, Dianne R. ....Hanover, MA
Lawlor, E. Scott ....Eugene, OR
Lawlor, E. Scott, P.C. ....Eugene, OR
Lawlor, Eugene K. ....El Cerrito, CA
Lawlor & Fortin, LLP ....Chelmsford, MA
Lawlor, H. Seward ....Norfolk, VA
Richmond, VA
Lawlor, J. Michael ....Towson, MD
Lawlor, James D. ....Silver Spring, MD
Lawlor, James H., III ....Chicago, IL
Lawlor, James J. ....Waterbury, CT
Lawlor, James N. ....Newark, NJ
Lawlor, James S. ....Philadelphia, PA
Lawlor, John B., Jr. ....East Providence, RI
Lawlor, John E., III ....Jacksonville, FL
Ponte Vedra Beach, FL
Lawlor, John F. ....Chicago, IL
Lawlor, John J. ....Chicago, IL
Lawlor, John K. ....Miami, FL
Lawlor, Jonathan S. ....Department of Justice,
Civil Division, GV
Lawlor, Karen L. ....Los Angeles, CA
Lawlor, Kerri E. ....New York, NY
Lawlor, Leila Ann Greiff ....Atlanta, GA
Lawlor, Marie M. ....Brighton, MA
Lawlor, Mariellyn ....Palo Alto, CA
Lawlor, Martin J., Jr. ....Bethel, CT
Lawlor, Mary Ann V. ....Crozet, VA
Lawlor, Michael E. ....Baltimore, MD
Lawlor, Miles G. ....Syracuse, NY
Lawlor, Patrick M. ....Massapequa, NY
Lawlor, Paul A. ....Hagåtña, GU
Lawlor, Peter V. ....Chelmsford, MA
Lawlor & Polidor ....Springfield, VT
Lawlor, Rebecca Yuan ....Los Angeles, CA
Lawlor, Richard D. ....Baltimore, MD
Lawlor, Richard J. ....Indianapolis, IN
Lawlor, Richard P. ....Hartford, CT
Lawlor, Richard P. ....Crozet, VA
Lawlor, Richard W. ....Rockville, MD
Lawlor, Richard W., P.A. ....Rockville, MD
Lawlor, Roberta S. ....Natick, MA
Lawlor, Rosalie ....Swarthmore, PA
Lawlor, Rosemary ....Atlanta, GA
Lawlor, Timothy M. ....Spokane, WA
Lawlor, William F., III ....Dana Point, CA
Lawlor, William G. ....Philadelphia, PA
Lawlor, William J., III ....New York, NY
Lawlyes, Brian C. ....Champaign, IL
Lawn, Lawrence E. ....Haworth, NJ
Lawn, Ronald K. ....Bangor, ME
Lawn, Timothy R. ....Philadelphia, PA
Lawner, Ivan ....White Plains, NY
Lawner, Leslie J. ....Houston, TX
Lawniczak, Brandon D. ....Chicago, IL
Lawniczak, James M. ....Cleveland, OH
Lawniczak, Jon J. ....Grand Blanc, MI
Lawonn, Michele M. ....Denver, CO
Lawrance, H. Irvin ....Pasadena, CA
Lawrason, Pamela Knowles
Cumberland Center, ME
Lawrence, Adam H. ....Miami, FL
Lawrence, Albert ....Brooklyn, NY
Lawrence, Albert B. ....Albany, NY
Lawrence, Albert F. ....Utica, NY
Lawrence, Alexander L. ....San Francisco, CA
Lawrence, Allegra ....Atlanta, GA
Lawrence, Allen S., Jr. ....Aransas Pass, TX
Lawrence, Allen S., Jr., P.C., A Professional Corporation ....Aransas Pass, TX
Lawrence, Allison K.
National Aeronautics And Space Administration,
Goddard Space Flight Center, GV
Lawrence, Amy B. ....Los Angeles, CA
Lawrence, Andrea J. ....New York, NY
Lawrence, Andrea S. ....Philadelphia, PA
Lawrence, Andrew D.
Department of Commerce,
Patent and Trademark Office, GV
Lawrence, Andrew G. ....Fairfax, VA
Lawrence, Andrew W. ....Dallas, TX
Lawrence, Andrew W., Jr. ....Huntington, NY
Lawrence, Anne R. ....Cold Spring, NY
Lawrence, Antonia, (Mr.) ....Rocky Mount, NC
Lawrence, Arthur G. ....Los Angeles, CA
Lawrence & Associates ....Los Angeles, CA
Lawrence, Baca & Donohue PLLC
Houston, TX
Lawrence, Barbara ....Morristown, NJ
Lawrence, Barry G. ....Salt Lake City, UT
Lawrence, Barry H. ....Los Angeles, CA
Lawrence, Betty Tenn ....Asheville, NC
Lawrence, Brent A. ....Sacramento, CA
Lawrence, Bruce A. ....Sikeston, MO
Lawrence, C. Bruce ....Lapeer, MI
Lawrence, C. Bruce ....Rochester, NY
Lawrence, C. Stephen
Newport Beach, CA
Lawrence, Carl M. ....Huntington, NY
Lawrence, Carol Joy ....Brooklyn, NY
Lawrence, Charles A., Jr. ....St. Louis, MO
Lawrence, Charles David ....Irvine, CA
Lawrence, Charles F. ....Berkeley, CA
Lawrence, Charles P. ....Frankfort, KY
Lawrence, Chester C. ....Dearborn, MI
Lawrence, Clarence B.
Farmington Hills, MI
Lawrence, Clifford A., Jr. ....Dallas, TX
Lawrence, Clifford L., Jr. ....Monroe, LA
Lawrence, Cynthia G. ....Redwood City, CA
Lawrence, Cyril L. ....Merced, CA
Lawrence, D. Michael ....Salinas, CA
Lawrence, Damon ....Encino, CA
Lawrence, Daniel W. S. ....Los Angeles, CA
Lawrence & Daniels ....Miami, FL
Lawrence, Darryl Kim ....Southfield, MI
Lawrence, David A. ....Detroit, MI

Lawson, Catherine A. ... Cameron Park, CA
Lawson, Catherine D. ... Portland, OR
Lawson, Charles D. ... Chattanooga, TN
Lawson, Cheri A. ... Brooklyn, NY
Lawson, Christopher L. Department Of Veterans Affairs, Board of Veterans Appeals, GV
Lawson, Chrysa Ann ... Woodbridge, NJ
Lawson, Clark T. ... Marshfield, MO
Lawson, Craig M. ... Lincoln, NE
Lawson, Craig M. ... Kirkland, WA
Lawson, Craig S. ... Greenwood, IN
Lawson, Dana Marie ... Los Angeles, CA
Lawson, Daniel C. ... Pittsburgh, PA
Lawson, David ... Dallas, TX
Lawson, David E. ... Danville, IN
Lawson, David J. ... Palo Alto, CA
Lawson, David L. ... Washington, DC
Lawson, David M. ... Birmingham, AL
Lawson, David M. ... Birmingham, MI
Lawson, David M. ... Minneapolis, MN
Lawson, David N. ... Palo Alto, CA
Lawson, David N. ... Marshfield, MO
Lawson, David R. ... San Diego, CA
Lawson, Davis, Pickren & Seydel, L.L.P. Atlanta, GA
Lawson, Debra Murphy ... Oakland, CA
Lawson, Dennis J. ... Washington, DC
Lawson, Dirk P.C. ... Washington, DC
Lawson, Donald A. ... Phoenix, AZ
Lawson, Douglas A. ... Simsbury, CT
Lawson, Douglas E. ... Cleveland, OH
Lawson, Durenda Lundy ... Barbourville, KY
Lawson, Earl H., Jr. ... Birmingham, AL
Lawson, Edward ... Springboro, OH
Lawson, Edward A. ... Ketchum, ID
Lawson, Edward E. ... Laconia, NH
Lawson, Edward G., Jr. ... Pawtucket, RI
Lawson, Edward, Jr. ... New York, NY
Lawson, Edward R., Jr. ... Milwaukee, WI
Lawson, Elaine L. ... Houston, TX
Lawson, Ellen M. ... Buffalo, NY
Lawson, Erik F., Jr. ... Delmont, PA
Lawson, Eugene E. ... Jonesboro, GA
Lawson, Eugene M., Jr. ... Washington, DC
Arlington, VA
Lawson, Evan T. ... Boston, MA
Brewster, MA
Providence, RI
Lawson, F. Dean ... Minneapolis, MN
Lawson, F. Dean, P.A. ... Minneapolis, MN
Lawson & Fields, P.C. ... Dallas, TX
Lawson, Floyd E. ... Paris, MO
Lawson & Frank, A Professional Corporation ... Arlington, VA
Fairfax, VA
Lawson, Fred ... Chicago, IL
Lawson, Gary B. ... Dallas, TX
Lawson, Gary D. ... Houston, TX
Lawson, Gary S. ... Chicago, IL
Lawson, George M. ... Atlanta, GA
Lawson, Gerald J. ... Ticonderoga, NY
Lawson, Glenn V. ... Sacramento, CA
Lawson, Grace A. ... Davis, CA
Lawson, Grace W. ... Washington, DC
Lawson, Guy ... Omaha, NE
Lawson & Gwin ... Conway, SC
Myrtle Beach, SC
Lawson, Harold Lewis ... Pittsburg, KS
Lawson, Harry G. ... Appomattox, VA
Lawson, Heidi A. ... New York, NY
Lawson, Herman L. ... Mansfield, LA
Lawson, Hugh ... Macon, GA
Lawson, J. Allen ... Macon, GA
Lawson, J. Allen, P.C. ... Macon, GA
Lawson, J. Paul ... Atlanta, GA
Lawson, Jack W. ... Fort Wayne, IN
Lawson, Jack W., Jr. ... Florence, SC
Lawson, Jack W., Jr., P.A. ... Florence, SC
Lawson, James A. ... Chicago, IL
Lawson, James D. ... Little Rock, AR
North Little Rock, AR
Lawson, James D. ... Los Angeles, CA
Lawson, James D. ... Lexington, KY
Lawson, James Eric ... Indianapolis, IN
Lawson, James M. ... Albany, KY
Lawson, James P. ... Peoria, IL
Lawson, James P. ... Southfield, MI
Lawson, James W. ... Boston, MA
Lawson, Janice E. ... Boise, ID
Lawson, Jean B. ... Charlotte, NC
Lawson, Jeanne M. ... Los Angeles, CA
Lawson, Jeffrey B. ... Grand Rapids, MI
Lawson, Jeffrey S. ... San Jose, CA
Lawson, Jennifer K. ... Hartford, CT
Lawson, Jerry A. National Archives And Records Administration, Office of the Inspector General, GV
Lawson, Jerry H. ... Cincinnati, OH
Lawson, Jerry L., Jr. ... Portland, OR
Lawson, Jerry W. ... Phoenix, AZ
Lawson, John F. ... El Monte, CA
Lawson, John F. ... Sarasota, FL
Lawson, John James ... Philadelphia, PA
Lawson, John R. ... Dallas, TX
Lawson, John R., Jr. ... Clearwater, FL
Tampa, FL
Lawson, John T. ... Coalgate, OK
Lawson, John W. ... Indianapolis, IN
Lawson, Joseph H. ... New Orleans, LA
Lawson, Joseph L. ... Naples, FL
Akron, OH
Lawson, Julie A. ... Detroit, MI
Lawson, Karen D. ... Painesville, OH
Lawson, Karyl McCurdy ... Houston, TX
Lawson, Keith D. ... Washington, DC
Lawson, Kenneth L. ... Cincinnati, OH
Lawson, Kent R. ... Madison, WI
Lawson, Kindall T. ... Rogersville, TN
Lawson, Kipp, Forbes & Ayres Fairfax, VA
Lawson, Kurt L.P. ... Washington, DC
Lawson, L. David ... Flint, MI
Lawson, Lance A. ... Charlotte, NC
Lawson, Laura B. ... Topeka, KS
Lawson, Laura E. ... New Port Richey, FL
Lawson, Lawrence M. ... Freehold, NJ
Lawson and Lawson ... Marshfield, MO
Lawson & Lawson ... Ticonderoga, NY
Lawson & Lawson ... Chattanooga, TN
Lawson & Lawson ... Dyersburg, TN
Lawson, Leonard J. ... Trenton, NJ
Lawson, Linda A. ... Naples, FL
Lawson, Linda M. ... Los Angeles, CA
Lawson, Lisa G. ... San Francisco, CA
Lawson, Louis W. ... Santa Monica, CA
Lawson, Louis W., Inc. ... Santa Monica, CA
Lawson, M. Juliet ... Pascagoula, MS
Lawson & Macrae ... Santa Ana, CA
Lawson & Marcus ... Grand Rapids, MI
Lawson, Margaret Avril ... Cincinnati, OH
Lawson, Marjorie M. ... Washington, DC
Lawson, Mark Gates ... Tallahassee, FL
Lawson, Mark M. ... Bristol, VA
Lawson, Mark McCarroll Birmingham, AL
Lawson, Mark R. ... Maquoketa, IA
Lawson, Mark R., P.C. ... Maquoketa, IA
Lawson, Marshall, McDonald & Galowitz, P.A. ... Lake Elmo, MN
Stillwater, MN
Lawson, Mary K. ... Beckley, WV
Lawson, Matthew J. ... St. Louis, MO
Lawson & McLean ... Cincinnati, OH
Lawson, Michael A. ... Los Angeles, CA
Lawson, Michael J. ... San Francisco, CA
Lawson, Michael J. ... Sandusky, OH
Lawson, Michael Scott ... Springfield, MO
Lawson, Michele ... Phoenix, AZ
Lawson, Miriam E. ... Department of Justice, Immigration and Naturalization Service, GV
Lawson, Nancy A. ... Cincinnati, OH
Lawson, Pamela R. ... Las Vegas, NV
Lawson, Patricia J. ... Charleston, WV
Lawson, Paul D. ... Columbus, IN
Lawson, Philip J. ... Cookeville, TN
Knoxville, TN
Morristown, TN
Lawson & Philpot, P.C. ... Laconia, NH
Lawson, Pushor, Mote, Coriden & Gamso Columbus, IN
Lawson, Quentin A. Federal Energy Regulatory Commission, Office of the General Counsel, GV
Lawson, R. Christopher, (P.A.) Little Rock, AR
Lawson, Ralph I. ... Dyersburg, TN
Lawson, Rebecca G. ... Front Royal, VA
Winchester, VA
Lawson, Richard A. ... Atlanta, GA
Lawson, Richard Brooke, III Montgomery, AL
Lawson, Richard C. ... United States Senate, Senatorial Assistants, GV
Lawson, Richard H. ... West Chester, PA
Lawson, Richard M. ... Wausau, WI
Lawson, Richard Polk ... Tampa, FL
Lawson, Robert D. ... Chattanooga, TN
Lawson, Robert D., Jr. ... Chattanooga, TN
Lawson, Robert E. ... Cupertino, CA
Lawson, Robert W., III ... Charleston, WV
Lawson, Roderick A. ... Lake Elmo, MN
Lawson, Rodney H. ... Dallas, TX
Lawson, Ronald H. ... Spiro, OK
Lawson, Rush D. ... Dyersburg, TN
Lawson, Scott E. ... Mayfield Village, OH
Lawson, Scott G. ... Palo Alto, CA
Lawson, Scott R. ... Department of Justice, Tax Division, GV
Lawson, Sharon Dubin Securities and Exchange Commission, Division of Market Regulation, GV
Lawson and Silek, P.L.C. Front Royal, VA
Winchester, VA
Lawson, Slade A. ... Mesa, AZ
Lawson, Stanley R. ... Cleveland, GA
Lawson, Stanley R., P.C. ... Cleveland, GA
Lawson, Stephen C. ... Ravenna, OH
Lawson, Steve L. ... Oklahoma City, OK
Lawson, Steven ... Chicago, IL
Lawson, Susan C. ... Harlan, KY
Lawson, Susan L. ... Tampa, FL
Lawson, Tanya M. ... Atlanta, GA
Lawson, Thomas A. ... Grand Rapids, MI
Lawson, Thomas B. ... Washington, DC
Lawson, Thomas M. ... Glens Falls, NY
Lawson, Thomas Moore ... Front Royal, VA
Winchester, VA
Lawson, Thomas O. ... Fairfax, VA
Lawson, Thomas S. ... West Palm Beach, FL
Lawson, Thomas S., Jr. ... Montgomery, AL
Lawson, Thomas T. ... Roanoke, VA
Lawson, Thomas W. ... Appomattox, VA
Lawson, Timothy C. ... Indianapolis, IN
Lawson, Virginia L. ... Lexington, KY
Lawson, W. Henry ... Pineville, KY
Lawson, Wade C. ... Lexington, KY
Lawson, Walter M., III ... Lima, OH
Lawson, Walter M., Jr., Law Office of Lima, OH
Lawson, Warner, Jr. ... Washington, DC
Lawson, Weitzen & Bankert, LLP Brewster, MA
Lawson & Weitzen, LLP ... Boston, MA
Lawson, Weitzen, Pfarr & Bridges, LLP Providence, RI
Lawson, William B. ... Erwin, TN
Lawson, William B. ... Arlington, VA
Lawson, William B., Jr. ... Arlington, VA
Lawson, William E. ... Buffalo, NY
Lawson, William E. ... Conway, SC
Myrtle Beach, SC
Lawson, William H. ... Atlanta, GA
Lawson, William H. ... Aiea, HI
Lawson, William H. ... Honolulu, HI
Lawson, William H., III ... Santa Ana, CA
Lawson, William J., Jr. ... Plymouth, MI
Lawson, William M. ... St. Louis, MO
Lawson, William M., Jr. ... Phoenix, AZ
Lawson, William M., Jr., P.A. Phoenix, AZ
Lawson, William S. ... Tupelo, MS
Lawson, William T., III ... Norristown, PA
Lawson, William T., III ... Philadelphia, PA
Lawson, Willie ... Fort Lauderdale, FL
Lawson, Wm Bret ... Coffeyville, KS
LawTech, P.A. ... Jacksonville, FL
Lawter, Anne E. ... Detroit, MI
Lawter, Dianne Whitehorn ... Houston, TX
Lawter, J. Mike ... Tulsa, OK
Lawter, Jack W. ... Piedmont, OK
Lawter, Jack W., Jr. ... Houston, TX
Lawter, Joe B. ... Norman, OK
Lawter & Lawter ... Houston, TX
Lawter & Pitts ... Tulsa, OK
Lawther, Brian N. ... San Jose, CA
Lawther, Francis Rivers, Jr. Salisbury, NC
Lawther, Jennifer L. ... Cleveland, OH
Lawther, Robert M. ... Cleveland, OH
Lawton, Andrew S. ... Spooner, WI
Lawton, Angus M. ... Mount Pleasant, SC
Lawton, Anne ... Oxford, OH
Lawton, Barbara G. ... St. Paul, MN
Lawton, Bettina M. ... Washington, DC
Lawton & Cates, S.C. ... Madison, WI
Lawton, Christine E. ... Universal City, CA
Lawton, Dan ... San Diego, CA
Lawton, Daniel G. ... North Chicago, IL
Lawton, David B. ... New Orleans, LA
Lawton, Donald P. ... Portland, OR
Lawton, Eric ... Los Angeles, CA
Lawton, Eric, A Professional Corporation Los Angeles, CA
Lawton, Fred, III ... Anniston, AL
Lawton, Gregory G. ... Philadelphia, PA
Lawton, James A. ... Atlanta, GA
Lawton, James F., Jr. ... Woburn, MA
Lawton, James J., III ... St. Paul, MN
Lawton, James P. ... New York, NY
Lawton, James R. ... Brockton, MA
Lawton, Jeff ... New York, NY
Lawton, Jerome J. ... New York, NY
Lawton, John C. Commodity Futures Trading Commission, Division of Trading and Markets, GV
Lawton, John F. ... Syracuse, NY
Lawton, Joseph J., Jr. ... Syracuse, NY
Lawton, Julie D. ... Washington, DC
Lawton, Kathleen M. ... Kalamazoo, MI
Lawton, Kenneth R. ... Los Angeles, CA
Lawton, Larry ... San Francisco, CA
Lawton Law Firm ... San Diego, CA
Lawton & Lawton ... St. Paul, MN
Lawton, L. B. ... Henderson, KY
Lawton, Louie J., (Miss) ... Orchard Lake, MI
Lawton, Mark D. ... Winchester, MA
Lawton, Mark E. ... Boston, MA
Lawton, Mary R. ... Chicago, IL
Lawton, Michael J. ... Madison, WI
Lawton, Paul Mathew ... Brockton, MA
Lawton, R. Hanson ... Friendswood, TX
Lawton, Richard L. ... St. Louis, MO
Lawton, Rick, Law Office of ... Fallon, NV
Lawton, Robert J. ... St. Paul, MN
Lawton and Rodgers, L.L.C. Mount Pleasant, SC
Lawton, Samuel T., Jr. ... Chicago, IL
Lawton, Shan A. ... Danvers, MA
Lawton, Spencer, Jr. ... Savannah, GA
Lawton, Stephan E. ... Washington, DC
Lawton, Stephen E. ... Palmdale, CA
Lawton, Thomas D. ... Bridgewater, MA
Lawton, Thomas E., Jr. ... Boston, MA
Lawton, Thomas Oregon, III ... Raleigh, NC
Lawton, Thomas P., III ... Pittsburgh, PA
Lawton, William C. ... Raleigh, NC
Lawton, William E. ... Orlando, FL
Lawton, Winston A., Jr. ... Estill, SC
Lawty, Thomas Miller ... Dallas, TX
Lawver, Joseph W. ... Minneapolis, MN
Lawwell, Dale & Graham ... Columbia, TN
Lawwell, T. Edward ... Columbia, TN
Lawyer, Bobby C. ... San Francisco, CA
Lawyer, C. Martin, III ... Tampa, FL
Lawyer, Catherine A. ... Chicago, IL
Lawyer, David J. ... Bellevue, WA
Lawyer, David Mark ... West Des Moines, IA
Lawyer, Dennis M. ... Des Moines, IA
Lawyer, Dougherty & Palmer, P.L.C. West Des Moines, IA
Lawyer, Emily W. ... Tampa, FL
Lawyer, Gary E. ... Colorado Springs, CO
Lawyer, James ... West Des Moines, IA
Lawyer, James R. (Jim) West Des Moines, IA
Lawyer, Jeffrey T. ... Winston-Salem, NC
Lawyer, John D. ... Carbondale, CO
Lawyer, Lawyer, Dutton & Drake Des Moines, IA
West Des Moines, IA
Lawyer, Lynne H. ... Anderson, IN
Lawyer, Steven Verne, Law Offices of Des Moines, IA
Lawyer, Vivian Jury ... Des Moines, IA
Lawyer, Vivian Moore ... Rockville, MD
Lawyer-Smith, Majorie ... Indianapolis, IN
Lax, Andrew W. ... Charlotte, NC
Lax, Barry R. ... New York, NY
Lax, Charles M. ... Southfield, MI
Lax, Emil ... New York, NY
Lax, Fred M. ... New York, NY
Lax, Gary A., (P.C.) ... Washington, DC
Lax, Gary M. Hot Springs National Park, AR
Lax, George ... New York, NY
Lax, Howard A. ... Southfield, MI
Lax, Jerold ... Ann Arbor, MI
Lax, Joanne R. ... Detroit, MI
Lax, Jonathan A. ... Manchester, NH
Lax, Kathleen T. ... Woodland Hills, CA
Lax, Martin ... Palm Desert, CA
Lax, Michael F. ... Little Rock, AR
Lax, Michael H. ... Miami, FL
Lax, Michael H., P.A. ... Miami, FL
Lax & Noll ... New York, NY
Lax, Paul A. ... Los Angeles, CA
Lax, Robert I. ... New York, NY
Lax, Sandra P. ... Bridgeport, CT
Lax, Stephen ... Media, PA
Lax, Stephen A. ... Los Angeles, CA
Lax, Thelma M. ... Santa Cruz, CA
Lax, Vaughan, Evans & Fortson, P.A. Little Rock, AR
Laxa, Rowena E. ... Washington, DC
Laxalt, Bruce R. ... Reno, NV
Laxalt, Monique ... Reno, NV
Laxalt & Nomura, Ltd. South Lake Tahoe, CA
Carson City, NV
Las Vegas, NV
Reno, NV
Laxalt, Peter D. ... Reno, NV
Laxer, Nancy E. ... Brooklyn, NY
Laxson, Bradley E. Department of Housing and Urban Development, Office of General Counsel, GV
Laxson, David C. ... Honolulu, HI
Lay, Andrew J. ... St. Louis, MO
Lay and Bjornstad, LLP ... Knoxville, TN
Lay, Carol Buchanan ... Denver, CO
Lay, Carroll T. ... Summersville, WV
Lay, Charles F. ... Gardner, KS
Lay, Cheryl S. ... El Paso, TX
Lay, Christine A. ... Detroit, MI
Lay, David M. ... Richmond, VA
Lay, Donald P. ... St. Paul, MN
Lay, Dorothea B. ... Department of Justice, Immigration and Naturalization Service, GV
Lay, Douglas T. ... Atlanta, GA
Lay, Elizabeth A. ... Washington, DC
Lay, Frank ... Borger, TX
Lay, Gregory A. ... London, KY
Lay, Howard D. ... Kansas City, MO
Lay, James P., III ... Erie, PA
Lay, Jeffrey L. ... Dyersburg, TN
Lay, John B. ... Austin, TX
Lay, John Thomas, Jr. ... Columbia, SC
Lay, Kenneth F. ... Secaucus, NJ
Lay, Kenneth J. ... Birmingham, AL
Lay, Kenneth S. ... Clayton, MO
Lay, Kimberly Carpenter ... Sylva, NC
Lay, Kristine Rasmussen ... Denver, CO
Lay, Lisa A. ... Toledo, OH
Lay, Norvie L. ... Louisville, KY
Lay, Patti Jane ... Knoxville, TN
Lay, Paul J. ... Farmington Hills, MI
Lay, R. Thomas ... Oklahoma City, OK
Lay, Skipper ... Austin, TX
Lay, Thomas F. ... Houston, TX
Lay, Tillman L. ... Washington, DC
Lay, Wood W. ... Charlotte, NC
Layber, Lynne A. ... Milwaukee, WI
Laybourne, Robert B. ... Akron, OH
Laycock, Charles M. ... Chicago, IL
Laycock, Claudia ... Provo, UT
Laycock, Colette M. ... Dallas, TX
Laycock, H. Douglas ... Austin, TX
Laycock, Larry R. ... Salt Lake City, UT
Laycoe, Juliet C. ... Vancouver, WA
Layde, Joseph B. ... Milwaukee, WI
Layden, Amanda S. ... Milwaukee, WI
Layden, Bill ... McAlester, OK
Layden, Charles Max ... Lafayette, IN
Layden, Daniel J. ... Philadelphia, PA
Layden, David C. ... Chicago, IL
Layden, David J. ... Worcester, MA
Layden, Donald W., Jr. ... Milwaukee, WI
Layden, Edward F. ... Hudson Falls, NY
Layden, Inc. ... McAlester, OK
Layden, James D. ... Los Angeles, CA
Layden, John J. ... Hudson Falls, NY
Layden, Joseph L. ... McAlester, OK
Layden & Layden ... Lafayette, IN
Layden & Layden ... Hudson Falls, NY
Layden, Leon M. ... Denver, CO
Layden, Leon M., Jr. ... Hudson Falls, NY
Layden, Lionel L. ... Mobile, AL
Layden, Lynn M. ... Lafayette, IN
Layden, Michael T. ... Chicago, IL
Layden, Robert A. ... McAlester, OK
Layden, Stephen M. ... Hudson Falls, NY
Layden, Thomas J. ... Rutland, VT
Layden, William H. ... McAlester, OK
Laye, Dennis J. ... Riderwood, MD
Layer, George L. ... Schaumburg, IL
Layer, Jayne K. ... Beaumont, TX

Layer, Rodriguez & Associates
McAllen, TX
San Antonio, TX
Layer, Ronald B. ..... McAllen, TX
Layer, Ronald F. ..... Hammond, IN
Layfer, Seymour J. ..... Chicago, IL
Layfield, L. DeWayne ..... Akron, OH
Layfield, L. M., III ..... Columbus, GA
Layher, Barbara J. ..... Mountain Home, ID
Laykind, Marc Bennett ..... Franklin Square, NY
Laylin, Peter R. ..... Renton, WA
Layman, Christopher A. ..... Melbourne, FL
Layman, Daniel F., Jr. ..... Roanoke, VA
Layman, David M. ..... West Palm Beach, FL
Layman, Elizabeth Waterhouse
Houston, TX
Layman, Jenifer Amy ..... Baltimore, MD
Layman, John G. ..... Spokane, WA
Layman, John R. ..... Seattle, WA
Spokane, WA
Layman, Joseph A., Jr. ..... Harrisburg, PA
Layman, Joseph M. ..... Waco, TX
Layman, Katherine M. ..... Philadelphia, PA
Layman, Layman & Fennessy
Seattle, WA
Spokane, WA
Layman, Lempert & Winslow
San Francisco, CA
Layman, Lois C. ..... Yakima, WA
Layman, M. Carol ..... Spring, TX
Layman, Michael D. ..... Greenville, SC
Layman, Michael Lee ..... Harrisonburg, VA
Layman, Nancy Staats ..... Columbia, SC
Layman, Neil F. ..... Tulsa, OK
Layman & Nichols, A Professional Corporation
Harrisonburg, VA
Layman, Patrick J. ..... Redmond, WA
Layman, Peter C. ..... Bangor, PA
Layman, Ralph E., III ..... Denver, CO
Layman, Randall J. ..... Farmington Hills, MI
Layman, Richard P. ..... Cleveland, OH
Layman, Roy F. ..... Huntington, WV
Layman, Sabrina A. ..... Everett, WA
Layman, T. Rodman ..... Pulaski, VA
Layman, Vicki L. ..... Fairfax, VA
Layman, Wilbur D. ..... Irvine, CA
Layman, William K. ..... Washington, DC
Laymon, John W. ..... Boston, MA
Laymon, Ronald E. ..... Columbus, OH
Laynas, Steven ..... Philadelphia, PA
Layne, Alan N. ..... Brooklyn, NY
Layne, Alan P. ..... Lyons, GA
Layne, Bradley H. ..... Point Pleasant, WV
Layne, Charles Michael ..... Manchester, TN
Layne, Ford Nelson ..... Tracy City, TN
Layne, Jonathan K. ..... Los Angeles, CA
Layne, Judith Fertel ..... Bloomfield Hills, MI
Layne, Judith L. ..... Cleveland, OH
Layne, Kenda
Environmental Protection Agency,
Office of Enforcement and Compliance
Assurance, GV
Layne and Layne, P.C. ..... Lyons, GA
Layne, Michele ..... Los Angeles, CA
Layne, Paul J. ..... Miami, FL
Layne, Richard M. ..... Portland, OR
Layne, Robert C. ..... Nashville, TN
Layne, Robert Jeffrey ..... Washington, DC
Layng, Edwin T., III ..... New York, NY
Layng, Karen P. ..... Chicago, IL
Layng, Mark E. ..... Lilburn, GA
Layng, Mark E., Esq., P.C. ..... Lilburn, GA
Layng, William J., Jr. ..... Atlanta, GA
Laynor, Anne Kelly ..... Baltimore, MD
Laynor, Jeffrey Y. ..... Baltimore, MD
Layon, Cronin, Clark & Kaiser, A Professional
Association ..... Tulsa, OK
Layon & Holck, A Prof. Law Corp., Law
Offices of ..... Vista, CA
Layon, Richard H. ..... Vista, CA
Layon, Thomas A., Jr. ..... Tulsa, OK
Layrisson, Jean-Paul ..... New Orleans, LA
Ponchatoula, LA
Layser, Derek R. ..... Philadelphia, PA
Layson, David A. ..... Corydon, IN
Layson, H. Franklin ..... Atlanta, GA
Layson, Jeff V., Jr. ..... Paris, KY
Layson, Jefferson V., III
Bowling Green, KY
Laystrom, C. William, Jr. (P.C.)
Fort Lauderdale, FL
Laystrom, C. William, Sr.
Fort Lauderdale, FL
Laytham, Raymond A. ..... Keyport, NJ
Laytin, Jeffrey L. ..... New York, NY
Laytin, William M. ..... Chicago, IL
Layton, Alfred H. ..... Orinda, CA
Layton, Amy L. ..... Raleigh, NC
Layton Brooks & Hecht LLP
Lakeville, CT
New York, NY
White Plains, NY
Layton, Chad J. ..... Chicago, IL
Layton, Charles M. ..... Cincinnati, OH
Layton, Christiane E. ..... Sacramento, CA
Layton, David A. ..... Gastonia, NC
Layton, David A. ..... Medina, OH
Layton, David K. ..... Lancaster, KY
Layton, David M. ..... Baltimore, MD
Layton, Deborah Sutton ..... Philadelphia, PA
Layton, Duane W. ..... Washington, DC
Layton, E. Grant ..... Maywood, NJ
Layton, Elaine L. ..... Coraopolis, PA
Layton, Elisabeth ..... Washington, DC
Layton, Fran M. ..... San Francisco, CA
Layton, H. F. ..... Orinda, CA
Layton, Jennifer Adina ..... Pawhuska, OK
Layton, John A. ..... Cape Girardeau, MO
Layton, Jonathan ..... Wilmington, DE
Layton, Kenneth A. ..... Seymour, IN
Layton, Kenneth C. ..... Maywood, NJ
Layton, Kipling F. ..... Corpus Christi, TX
Layton, Lana L. ..... Duluth, GA
Layton, Larry H. ..... Acton, CA
Layton & Layton, P.A. ..... Maywood, NJ
Layton, Linda Thater ..... Baltimore, MD
Layton, Mariko T., P.C. ..... Pagosa Springs, CO
Layton, Mariko Tatsumoto
Pagosa Springs, CO
Layton, Michael J. ..... Seattle, WA
Layton, Paul Thomas ..... New York, NY
Layton, Phillip James ..... San Diego, CA
Layton, Powell A., Jr. ..... Shreveport, LA
Layton, R. Kevin ..... Tulsa, OK
Layton, Robert ..... Washington, DC
New York, NY
Layton, Robert H. ..... Goodyear, AZ
Layton, Robert L. ..... Los Angeles, CA
Layton, Robert P. ..... New Canaan, CT
Layton, Rona P. ..... San Jose, CA
Layton, Samuel G., Jr. ..... Charlotte, NC
Layton, Stanley R. ..... Somerville, NJ
Layton, Thomas E. ..... Raleigh, NC
Layton, Timothy C. ..... Washington, DC
Layton, William M. ..... Lake Worth, FL
Layton, William R. ..... Washington, DC
Layva, Bittorf & Santa Barbara, P.L.L.C.
Charles Town, WV
Martinsburg, WV
Layva, David ..... Charles Town, WV
Martinsburg, WV
Lay Watson, Rayni ..... San Antonio, TX
Layzell, Thomas D. ..... Springfield, IL
Laz, Anita ..... Houston, TX
Laz, Creighton B. ..... Costa Mesa, CA
Laz, David M. ..... Westmont, IL
Lazaar, Allison ..... Elizabeth, NJ
Lazala, Virginia A. ..... Roseland, NJ
Lazan, David M. ..... Bay Harbor Islands, FL
Lazan, Lisa E. ..... Vero Beach, FL
Lazan, Trute & Robbins
Bay Harbor Islands, FL
Lazansky, Elyse ..... Philadelphia, PA
Lazar, Alan H. ..... Los Angeles, CA
Lazar, Alan S. ..... Santa Ana, CA
Woodland Hills, CA
Lazar, Alyse M. ..... Westlake Village, CA
Lazar, Bart A. ..... Chicago, IL
Lazar, Bruce D. ..... Sylvania, OH
Lazar, Bruce E. ..... Miami Beach, FL
Lazar, Bruce J. ..... Farmington Hills, MI
Lazar, Charles S. ..... Rockville, MD
Lazar, Cheri R. ..... Miami, FL
Lazar, Dale S. ..... Washington, DC
Lazar, Daniel Bennett ..... Miami, FL
Lazar, Dennis R. ..... Flint, MI
Lazar, Eileen Moran ..... San Diego, CA
Lazar, Ellen W. ..... Columbia, MD
Lazar, Ellyn H. ..... Worcester, MA
Lazar, Gary R. ..... Warren, MI
Lazar, George C. ..... San Diego, CA
Lazar, Herbert L. ..... New York, NY
Lazar, Howard A. ..... Anchorage, AK
Lazar, James P. ..... Dallas, TX
Lazar, James S. ..... Auburn, CA
Lazar, Janet G. ..... New York, NY
Lazar, Jason A. ..... River Edge, NJ
Lazar, Jay L. ..... Bethlehem, PA
Lazar, Jodi R. ..... Portland, OR
Lazar, Joey B. ..... Department of Justice,
United States Marshals Service, GV
Lazar, John D. ..... Royal Oak, MI
Lazar, John I. ..... Los Angeles, CA
Lazar, John P. ..... Akron, OH
Lazar, Joseph ..... Boulder, CO
Lazar, Joseph D. ..... New York, NY
Lazar, Kara G. ..... New York, NY
Lazar, Kathryn S. ..... Hopewell Junction, NY
Lazar, Kathy P. ..... Cleveland, OH
Lazar, Larry ..... New York, NY
Lazar, Marc D. ..... Boston, MA
Lazar, Maria S. ..... Milwaukee, WI
Lazar, Mary Tamara ..... Flint, MI
Lazar, Michael A. ..... Greeley, CO
Lazar, Nancy L. ..... New York, NY
Lazar, Paul ..... Flint, MI
Lazar, Raymond M. ..... Minneapolis, MN
Lazar, Richard A. ..... Portland, OR
Lazar, Robert J. ..... Chicago, IL
Lazar, Ruth E. ..... New York, NY
Lazar, S. Alan ..... Phoenix, AZ
Lazar & Schwartz ..... Hopewell Junction, NY
Lazar, Scott ..... Miami, FL
Lazar, Seymour M. ..... Palm Springs, CA
Lazar, Stephanie D. ..... New York, NY
Lazar, Steven R. ..... Cambridge, MA
Lazar, Stuart ..... Providence, RI
Lazar, Theodore A. ..... Worthington, OH
Lazar, Thomas, (P.C.) ..... Farmington Hills, MI
Lazar, Thomas Samuel ..... San Diego, CA
Lazar, Victoria V. ..... Plano, TX
Lazar, Vincent E. ..... Chicago, IL
Lazar, Wendi ..... New York, NY
Lazar, William H. ..... Santa Fe, NM
La Zara, Joseph A. ..... Chicago, IL
Lazaran, Mary A. ..... Encino, CA
Lazarczyk, Laura J. ..... Chicago, IL
Lazard, Barbara M. ..... Austin, TX
Lazard, Kathleen R. ..... Susanville, CA
Lazard & Lazard ..... Susanville, CA
Lazard, Ridgely L. ..... Susanville, CA
Lazare, Bennett S. ..... Wood Ridge, NJ
Lazare, Melinda Tell
Pension Benefit Guaranty Corporation,
Office of the General Counsel, GV
Lazare Potter Giacovas & Kranjac LLP
New York, NY
Lazare, Stephen M. ..... New York, NY
Lazares, Danny E. ..... Tacoma, WA
Lazares, Nicholas W., (P.C.) ..... Boston, MA
Lazares, Pamela J. ..... Boston, MA
Lazarescu, Alan E. ..... New York, NY
Lazarini, Andrea M. ..... Memphis, TN
Lazarini, Christopher G. ..... Memphis, TN
Lazar-Meyn, Heidi Ann .....
Department of Labor, GV
Lazaro, Avelino Bill ..... Los Angeles, CA
Lazaro, Charles L. ..... Visalia, CA
Lazaro, Joaquina ..... New York, NY
Lazaro, Louis Daniel ..... St. Petersburg, FL
Lazaroff, Cathy A. Glaser ..... Northbrook, IL
Lazaroff, Daniel E. ..... Los Angeles, CA
Lazaroff, Joseph L. ..... Rowayton, CT
Lazaroff, Michael ..... St. Louis, MO
Lazaroff, Michael S. ..... New York, NY
Lazaroff, Thomas A. ..... Pittsburgh, PA
Lazaroff, Vern S. ..... Port Jervis, NY
Lazaroff, Walter ..... Philadelphia, PA
Lazaron, Terry L. ..... Washington, DC
Fairfax, VA
Lazaron, Thos. F. ..... Cincinnati, OH
Lázaro-San Miguel, Rosa M.
San Juan, PR
Lazarov, Craig J. ..... Memphis, TN
Lazarov, Sidney ..... Memphis, TN
Lazarow, Benjamin W. ..... Tucson, AZ
Lazarow, Edythe ..... Hackensack, NJ
Lazarow, Jeffrey W. ..... Middletown, OH
Lazarow, Joseph ..... Atlantic City, NJ
Lazarow & Lazarow ..... Tucson, AZ
Lazarow, Martin S. ..... Clifton Park, NY
Lazarow, Robin S. ..... Florham Park, NJ
Lazarow, Sheldon ..... Tucson, AZ
Lazarow, Warren T. ..... Palo Alto, CA
Lazarow, William S. ..... Columbus, OH
Lazarow, Wm. W. ..... New York, NY
Lazarowitz, Harvey O. ..... Brooklyn, NY
Lazarowitz & Manganillo ..... Brooklyn, NY
Lazarowitz, Michael S. ..... Brooklyn, NY
Lazarre, Mark M. ..... Baton Rouge, LA
Lazarte, Frank A. ..... Corpus Christi, TX
Lazaruk, Kenneth H. ..... New York, NY
Lazarus, Alan J. ..... San Francisco, CA
Lazarus, Albert S. ..... Irvine, CA
Lazarus, Arleen ..... Pembroke Pines, FL
Lazarus, Arthur, Jr. (P.C.)
Washington, DC
Lazarus & Associates ..... Washington, DC
Lazarus & Associates, A Professional
Corporation ..... Phoenix, AZ
Lazarus, Barrett S. ..... Tamarac, FL
Lazarus, Barrett S., P.A. ..... Tamarac, FL
Lazarus, Barry ..... Minneapolis, MN
Lazarus & Billek, A Professional Association
Edison, NJ
Lazarus, Bruce I. ..... West Lafayette, IN
Lazarus, Burton A. ..... New York, NY
Lazarus, Carol ..... Boston, MA
Lazarus, Charles S. ..... Bronx, NY
Lazarus, Daniel F. ..... Chicago, IL
Lazarus, David ..... Cincinnati, OH
Lazarus, David M. ..... Boca Raton, FL
Hollywood, FL
Lazarus, Donald ..... Brooklyn, NY
Lazarus, Doris E. ..... Mason, OH
Lazarus, Edmond P. ..... Baltimore, MD
Lazarus, Edward M. ..... Los Angeles, CA
Lazarus, Elise N. ..... Cherry Hill, NJ
Lazarus, Ellen M. ..... Library of Congress,
Congressional Research Service, GV
Lazarus, Ellyn K. ..... San Francisco, CA
Lazarus & Fogelsong ..... Tucson, AZ
Lazarus, Gary ..... New York, NY
Lazarus, Gustav ..... White Plains, NY
Lazarus, H. Michael ..... Miami, FL
Lazarus, Howard J. ..... New York, NY
Lazarus, Ira S. ..... Department of Commerce,
Patent and Trademark Office, GV
Lazarus, James A. ..... Buffalo, NY
Lazarus, Jason D. ..... Jacksonville, FL
Lazarus, Jennifer Hughes ..... Ann Arbor, MI
Lazarus, Jerome K. ..... Fremont, CA
Lazarus, Jessica D. ..... Los Angeles, CA
Lazarus, Joel D. ..... Newport Beach, CA
Lazarus, John Kiva ..... Tucson, AZ
Lazarus, Kenneth A. ..... Washington, DC
Lazarus, L. Jackson ..... Natchez, MS
Lazarus, Larry S. ..... Phoenix, AZ
Lazarus, Laura A. ..... Minneapolis, MN
Lazarus, Laura O. ..... New York, NY
Lazarus, Leland J. ..... San Francisco, CA
Lazarus, Leonard ..... Uniondale, NY
Lazarus, Leonard Harvey
Woodland Hills, CA
Lazarus, Lester A. ..... New York, NY
Lazarus, Lewis H. ..... Wilmington, DE
Lazarus, Linda .....
Department of Energy, GV
Lazarus, Lisa F. ..... Washington, DC
Lazarus, Maggi A. ..... Washington, DC
Lazarus, Mark D. ..... Bronx, NY
Lazarus, Maurice U. ..... Minneapolis, MN
Lazarus, Michael H. ..... Miami, FL
Lazarus, Michael L. ..... Edison, NJ
Lazarus, Michael R. ..... New York, NY
Lazarus, Mitchell ..... Washington, DC
Lazarus, Monte ..... Marco Island, FL
Lazarus, Norman F. ..... Newton, MA
Lazarus, Paul D. ..... Miami, FL
Lazarus, Paul F. ..... Phoenix, AZ
Lazarus, Paul F., P.C. ..... Phoenix, AZ
Lazarus, Peter M. ..... Los Angeles, CA
Lazarus, Ralph E. ..... Los Angeles, CA
Lazarus, Randi Klayman ..... Miami, FL
Lazarus, Richard B.
Department of Commerce,
Patent and Trademark Office, GV
Lazarus, Richard H. ..... Rockville Centre, NY
Lazarus, Robert S. ..... Jackson, MS
Lazarus, Robyn Berg ..... Lancaster, PA
Lazarus, Ronald H. ..... Annandale, VA
Lazarus, Ronna ..... Baltimore, MD
Lazarus, Rosalind Avnet
Department of Transportation,
Office of the General Counsel, GV
Lazarus, Samuel ..... Plymouth, MA
Lazarus, Sarah R. ..... Towson, MD
Lazarus, Scott R. ..... New York, NY
White Plains, NY
Lazarus, Shelley N. ..... Gurnee, IL
Lazarus, Simon, III ..... Washington, DC
Lazarus, Stephen R. ..... Cleveland, OH
Lazarus, Stephen S. ..... West Palm Beach, FL
Lazarus, Stephen S. ..... Cincinnati, OH
Lazarus, Steven Wayne ..... Los Angeles, CA
Lazarus, Wayne H. ..... Atlanta, GA
Lazarus, Wendy J. ..... Newark, NJ
Lazarus, William B. ..... Department of Justice,
Environment and Natural Resources
Division, GV
Lazarz, Mark G. ..... Houston, TX
Lazas, Ronald C., Jr. ..... Louisville, KY
Lazear, Arthur William ..... Oakland, CA
Lazear, Bruce C. ..... Columbus, OH
Lazear, Robert L. ..... Minneapolis, MN
Lazear, Sherri Blank ..... Columbus, OH
Lazega, Jay S. ..... Atlanta, GA
Lazenby, D. Alan ..... Spartanburg, SC
Lazenby, George William ..... Tampa, FL
Lazenby, Henry H., Jr. ..... Salem, OR
Lazenby, K. Bruce ..... Beckley, WV
Lazenby, Marc B. ..... Princeton, WV
Lazenby, R. Blake ..... Talladega, AL
Lazenby, Richard A. ..... Los Angeles, CA
Lazenby, Robert A., (P.A.) ..... Melbourne, FL
Lazenski, David P. ..... New York, NY
Lazer, Aptheker, Feldman, Rosella & Yedid,
P.C. ..... Melville, NY
Lazer, David ..... Melville, NY
Lazer, Leon D. ..... Melville, NY
Lazer, Michael L. ..... Omaha, NE
Lazerov, Manuel H. ..... Highland, MD
Lazerow, Andrew ..... Washington, DC
Lazerow, Herbert I. ..... San Diego, CA
Lazerson, Wendy M. ..... San Francisco, CA
Lazerus, Bruce ..... San Diego, CA
Lazerus, Gilbert ..... New York, NY
Lazerwith, Mark A. ..... Glenview, IL
Lazerwitz, Alison R. ..... Allentown, PA
Lazerwitz, David J. ..... Boulder, CO
Department of Justice, GV
Lazerwitz, Michael R. ..... Washington, DC
Lazetera, Lianne ..... New York, NY
Lazewski, Jennifer A. ..... Milwaukee, WI
Lazich, Patricia D. ..... Columbus, OH
Lazin, Malcolm L. ..... Philadelphia, PA
Lazin, Terry W. ..... Chicago, IL
Lazinger, Samuel J. ..... Bridgeport, CT
Lazinsky, Steven ..... Indianapolis, IN
Lazio, Rick A. ..... Babylon, NY
Laznovsky, Frank T. ..... Washington, DC
Annapolis, MD
Owings Mills, MD
Lazo, Avida R. ..... Nashville, TN
Lazo, Conrad J. ..... Palm Harbor, FL
Lazo, Ignacio J. ..... Irvine, CA
Lazo, Jacqui Fiske ..... Pittsburgh, PA
Lazo, Kristin A. ..... Memphis, TN
Lazo, Robert E. ..... San Francisco, CA
Lazo, Theodore R. ..... Washington, DC
Lazof & Coss ..... Newport Beach, CA
Lazof, Ronald C. ..... Newport Beach, CA
Lazoff, Joyce ..... New York, NY
Lazofsky, Miriam ..... Brooklyn, NY
Lazo-Miller, Teresa ..... Harrisburg, PA
Lazonby, J. Lance, Jr. ..... Hawthorne, FL
Lazor, Allan R. ..... Houston, TX
Lazor, John ..... Culver City, CA
Lazor, Stephen F. ..... San Antonio, TX
Lazorcheck, Sandra M. ..... Charlotte, NC
Lazorisak, Alex ..... Succasunna, NJ
Lazorisak, Theresa H. ..... Costa Mesa, CA
Lazorishak, Karen L. ..... Columbus, OH
Lazos, Nicholas J. ..... Manchester, NH
Lazos, Pamela J. ..... Philadelphia, PA
Lazos, Sylvia R. ..... Tallahassee, FL
Lazour, Paul A. ..... Worcester, MA
Lazovich, Jennifer ..... Las Vegas, NV
Lazris, Mitchell J. ..... Washington, DC
Lazris, Yale I. ..... West Orange, NJ
Lazroe, Jeffrey A. ..... Buffalo, NY
Corfu, NY
Lazrus, Jay N. ..... Washington, DC
Lazuk, Robert H. ..... Springfield, MA
Lazun, Stephen R. ..... Lancaster, PA
Lazuran, Catherine R. ..... San Rafael, CA
Lazzara, Bennie, Jr. ..... Tampa, FL
Lazzara, Beth A. ..... Pittsburgh, PA
Lazzara, Daniel E. ..... Monroeville, PA
Lazzara, Elizabeth Olen ..... Chicago, IL
Lazzara, John J. ..... Tallahassee, FL
Lazzara, Joseph Anthony ..... Westminster, CO
Lazzara, Lisa Boutelle
San Luis Obispo, CA
Lazzara, Michael D. ..... Pittsburgh, PA
Lazzara, Philip R., P.A. ..... Tampa, FL
Lazzara, Richard A. ..... Tampa, FL
Lazzareschi, Craig A. ..... Walnut Creek, CA
Lazzari, Cindi C. ..... Austin, TX
Lazzari, Lisa ..... Johnstown, PA
Lazzari, Sean M. ..... La Grange, IL

Lazzari, Stephen .... **West Trenton, NJ**
Lazzarini, Lorne .... San Diego, CA
Lazzarini, Robert T. .... **San Francisco, CA**
Lazzarini, Robert W. .... Walnut Creek, CA
Lazzaris, Diane E. .... Pittsburgh, PA
Lazzaro, Carol J. .... Waukegan, IL
Lazzaro, Charles B. .... Cleveland, OH
Lazzaro, Clifford E. .... Newark, NJ
Lazzaro, D. Vincent .... Blackwood, NJ
Lazzaro, Glen Duncan .... **Baltimore, MD**
Towson, MD
Lazzaro, Henry .... Waukegan, IL
Lazzaro, James .... Princeton, NJ
Lazzaro, Joseph W. .... White Oak, PA
Lazzaro and Kraus .... **Cleveland, OH**
Lazzaro & Lazzaro, P.C. .... Waukegan, IL
Lazzaro, Lynn A. .... **Cleveland, OH**
Lazzaro, Martin E. .... **Pittsburgh, PA**
Lazzaro, Michele M. .... **Cleveland, OH**
Lazzaro, Patrick G. .... Cleveland, OH
Lazzaro, Randall C. .... New York, NY
Lazzaro, Robert W. .... Towson, MD
Lazzaro, S. Robert E. .... Lakewood, OH
Lazzaro, Stephen J. .... Central Islip, NY
Lazzeri, James J. .... **Dover, DE**
Lazzeroni, Stephanie W. .... Racine, WI
Lazzio, Stephen M. .... Flint, MI
Lazzo, Mark J. .... **Wichita, KS**
Lazzo, Susan J. .... Boston, MA
Le, An T. .... Los Angeles, CA
Le, Angie D. H. .... **New York, NY**
Le, Bich-Vi Thi .... Oklahoma City, OK
Le, Christine P. .... **Irvine, CA**
Le, Dien .... **Oxnard, CA**
Le, Duc Tri .... **Los Angeles, CA**
Le, Edward K. .... Seattle, WA
Le, Hao P. .... San Antonio, TX
Le, Hientrinh M. .... **Boston, MA**
Le, K. Margaret .... Department of Commerce, Patent and Trademark Office, GV
Le, Khanh .... Department of Commerce, Patent and Trademark Office, GV
Le, Lisa N. .... **Ontario, CA**
Le, Patty H. .... **Irvine, CA**
Le, Quan .... Boston, MA
Le, Quan S. .... **Wheeling, WV**
Le, Son K. .... **New York, NY**
Le, Tan H. .... **Chicago, IL**
Le, Thong (Tom) D. .... **Newport Beach, CA**
Le, Tuyen Dinh .... Seattle, WA
Le, Van P.T. .... **Boston, MA**
Le, Viet V. .... **Phoenix, AZ**
Lea, Arden J., Law Offices of
Fort Walton Beach, FL
New Orleans, LA
Lea, Arlene C. .... **Culver City, CA**
Rancho Cucamonga, CA
Lea & Arruti .... Sacramento, CA
Lea & Chamberlain .... **Austin, TX**
San Antonio, TX
Lea, Christopher G. .... Chicago, IL
Lea, Clyburn & Rhine .... **Wilmington, NC**
Lea, Clyde W. .... **Bartlesville, OK**
Lea, E. Garland .... **Cartersville, GA**
Lea, Edwin P. .... Houston, TX
Lea, Ellen Bradford .... Nashville, TN
Lea, Gale Reddie .... **Charleston, WV**
Lea, Glen Andrew .... **Richmond, VA**
Lea, Gordon .... **Fort Lauderdale, FL**
Lea, Haynes P. .... **Charlotte, NC**
Lea, J. Peyton, III .... Orlando, FL
Lea, James F. .... **Houston, TX**
Lea, James G. .... Sunnyvale, CA
Lea, James W., III .... **Wilmington, NC**
Lea, Joe Edward, Jr. .... **Austin, TX**
San Antonio, TX
Lea, John C. .... Seattle, WA
Lea, Kelly B. .... Tyler, TX
Lea and Lea .... **Allentown, PA**
Lea, Lola S. .... Freeport, ME
Lea, Lyman G. .... **San Francisco, CA**
Lea, Melissa E. .... **Philadelphia, PA**
Lea, Michael R. .... Anaheim, CA
Lea, Paul A., Jr. .... Covington, LA
Lea, Paul A., Jr., A Prof. Corp.
Covington, LA
Lea, Richard C. .... Montgomery, MN
Lea, Richard N. .... Atlanta, GA
Lea, Robert .... Sacramento, CA
Lea, Robert C. .... Dallas, TX
Lea, Robert C., Jr. .... Queen Anne, MD
Lea, Robin .... **Miami, FL**
Lea, Royal B., III .... **San Antonio, TX**
Lea, Stephen R. .... Phoenix, AZ
Lea, Susan J. .... Berkeley, CA
Lea, Susan M. .... **Allentown, PA**
Lea, Victor N. .... **Allentown, PA**
Lea, W. Clark .... **Midland, TX**
Lea, W. E. .... Crystal Beach, TX
Leaberry, John F. .... Fort Lauderdale, FL
Leabman, Scott H. .... Somerville, MA
Leabres, Rosalie .... Hermosa Beach, CA
Lea-Brown, Bonnie H. .... Department of State, Foreign Service Officers (Overseas), GV
Leace, Benjamin E. .... **Valley Forge, PA**
Leace, Elyse .... Philadelphia, PA
Leach, Alicemary O.
House of Representatives, Committee on Veterans Affairs, GV
Leach & Ames, P.C. .... **Hurst, TX**
Southlake, TX
Leach, Anne C. .... **Salinas, CA**
Leach, Anthony C., Jr. .... Leesville, LA
Leach, Arthur W. .... Atlanta, GA
Leach, Betty .... Washington, DC
Leach, Brenda Lee .... New York, NY
Leach, Brian E. .... **Geneva, IL**
Leach, Bruce A. .... **Providence, RI**

Leach, Buddy H. .... Guymon, OK
Leach, Chris A. .... **Chicago, IL**
Leach, Christopher H. .... **Kansas City, MO**
Leach, Courtnay Stallings .... **Memphis, TN**
Leach & Cummins .... Franklin, KY
Leach, Danforth H. .... Naples, FL
Leach, Daniel E. .... San Francisco, CA
Washington, DC
Las Vegas, NV
Reno, NV
Leach, David E. .... **Syracuse, NY**
Leach, David E., III .... New York, NY
Leach, David G. .... **Mission Viejo, CA**
San Francisco, CA
Leach, David H. .... New Bedford, MA
Leach, Daylin B. .... Allentown, PA
Leach, Deborah L. .... **San Antonio, TX**
Leach, Donald B. .... Columbus, OH
Leach, Donald B., Jr. .... **Columbus, OH**
Leach, Donald F. .... **Monterey, CA**
Leach, Donald L. .... Ventura, CA
Leach, Edmond K. .... Bloomfield Hills, MI
Leach, Edmund J., Jr. .... Bend, OR
Leach, Edward J. .... Revere, MA
Leach, Ellen C. .... Columbus, OH
Leach & English .... San Francisco, CA
Washington, DC
Las Vegas, NV
Reno, NV
Leach, Eric L. .... **Jacksonville, FL**
Leach, F. Keith .... Noblesville, IN
Leach, F. Richard .... Houston, TX
Leach, Frank C., Jr. .... Lexington, KY
Leach, G. William, Jr. .... Franklin, KY
Leach, Garret .... **Chicago, IL**
Leach, George .... Guymon, OK
Leach, George R. .... Williamsburg, VA
Leach, Harold H., Jr. .... **Boston, MA**
Leach, Howard O. .... **Hazlehurst, MS**
Leach, J. Robert .... **Everett, WA**
Leach, James D. .... Rapid City, SD
Leach, James H. .... Denver, CO
Leach, James R. .... Vienna, WV
Leach, Jami E. .... **Detroit, MI**
Leach, Jeanne .... Austin, TX
Leach, Jeryl F. .... **Morocco, IN**
Leach, John E. .... **Las Vegas, NV**
Leach, John K. .... **New Orleans, LA**
Houston, TX
Leach, John N., Jr. .... **Mobile, AL**
Leach, John R., III .... **Houston, TX**
Leach, John W. .... **Memphis, TN**
Leach, Karen K. .... **Atlanta, GA**
Leach, Kathryn L. .... Cambridge, MA
Leach, Kenneth C. .... **Albuquerque, NM**
Leach, Kenneth C., P.C.
Albuquerque, NM
Santa Fe, NM
Leach, Kenneth H. .... Penn Valley, CA
Leach, Kevin M. .... **Manchester, NH**
Leach, Larry M. .... Denver, CO
Leach, Leslie G. .... Lafayette, LA
Leach, Lisa Lichterman .... **Memphis, TN**
Leach, Marie F. .... **Wheaton, IL**
Leach, Marion D. .... Houston, TX
Leach, Mark A. .... Winston-Salem, NC
Leach, Marlo Orlin .... **Atlanta, GA**
Leach, Martin E. .... **Miami, FL**
Leach, Mary McElroy
Department of Justice, Civil Division, GV
Leach, McGreevy & Bautista, LLP
Chino, CA
Mission Viejo, CA
San Francisco, CA
Leach, Michael .... **Allentown, PA**
Leach, Michael E., (P.A.)
Fort Lauderdale, FL
Leach, Nicholas N. .... Roswell, GA
Leach, Nikki G. .... Perry, OK
Leach, Parker O. .... Bozeman, MT
Leach, Patrick .... St. Louis Park, MN
Leach, Patrick J. .... Brooklyn, NY
Leach, Phillip M. .... Lufkin, TX
Leach, Phyllis G. .... **Kansas City, MO**
Leach, Ray .... **San Antonio, TX**
Leach, Rex N. .... **McAllen, TX**
Leach, Richard A.
Department Of Health And Human Services, GV
Leach, Rob G. .... San Diego, CA
Leach, Robert S. .... **Los Angeles, CA**
Leach, Robert S. .... Wickliffe, OH
Leach, Ronald L.
Research Triangle Park, NC
Leach, Russell .... Columbus, OH
Leach, Sally A. .... **Columbus, OH**
Leach, Sarah .... San Rafael, CA
Leach, Shelton B. .... Bloomington, IL
Leach, Sid .... **Phoenix, AZ**
Leach, Stephen E. .... **Washington, DC**
Leach, Steven C. .... **Drexel Hill, PA**
Leach, Steven D. .... **Phoenix, AZ**
Leach, Stuart .... **Birmingham, AL**
Leach, Sullivan, Sullivan & Watkins
Duncan, OK
Leach, Susan K. .... **New York, NY**
Leach, Terry J. .... Lake Oswego, OR
Leach, Terry R. .... **Hurst, TX**
Leach, Thad N. .... **St. Louis, MO**
Leach, Thomas J. .... Philadelphia, PA
Leach, Timothy G. .... Huntington, WV
Leach, Timothy P. .... **Los Angeles, CA**
Leach, Timothy T. .... **Charlotte, NC**
Leach, Warren B., Jr. .... Houston, TX
Leach, William S. .... **Tulsa, OK**
Leachman, Bernard D., Jr. .... Louisville, KY
Leachman, Charles D. .... Fort Lauderdale, FL
Leachman, Marcy Kelley .... Houston, TX

Leachman, Margaret F. .... El Paso, TX
Leachman, Mark Alan .... Boulder, CO
Leachman, Pennie Cannon .... Sequim, WA
Leachman, Ronald Van .... Tracy, CA
Leachman, Russell D. .... **El Paso, TX**
Leachman, Tamsen L. .... **Boise, ID**
Leacock, David .... **West Palm Beach, FL**
Leacock, Stephen J. .... Chicago, IL
Leacox, Jeffrey .... **Sacramento, CA**
Leacy, Laura A. .... **Newark, NJ**
Leacy, Rosanne .... **New York, NY**
Leadabrand, Thomas D. .... Golden, CO
Leadbeater, Lea .... **Chicago, IL**
Philadelphia, PA
Leadbetter, Bonnie Brigance .... Blue Bell, PA
Leadbetter, Charles K. .... Augusta, ME
Leadbetter, Denise Ann
San Francisco, CA
Leadbetter, Gary R. .... Norristown, PA
Leadbetter, Jeffrey K. .... Lisbon, ND
Leadbetter, Paris I. .... Hopewell, VA
Leadbetter, Philip P. .... Woodside, CA
Leadbetter, Ronald C. .... Knoxville, TN
Leadem, Bonita C. .... Eatontown, NJ
Leaden, Christopher S. .... **Falls Church, VA**
Leader, Allison B. .... **Washington, DC**
Leader, Arnold L. .... Beverly Hills, CA
Leader & Associates, Ltd. .... Northbrook, IL
Leader, Bennett .... Williamsville, NY
Leader & Berkon LLP .... **New York, NY**
Leader, Cornelius .... Oklahoma City, OK
Leader, Dennis J. .... San Francisco, CA
Leader, Edward J. .... **Cleveland, OH**
Leader, Emily J. .... Harrisburg, PA
Leader, G. Michael, 3rd .... Hershey, PA
Leader, George N. .... North Miami Beach, FL
Leader, Henry B. .... **York, PA**
Leader, Henry J. .... **Gouverneur, NY**
Leader, Howard .... New York, NY
Leader, Jack G. .... **Rock Hill, SC**
Leader, James K. .... **New York, NY**
Leader, James L. .... **Houston, TX**
Leader, Janet H. .... **San Francisco, CA**
Leader, Jeffrey N. .... **Ventura, CA**
Leader, John P. .... Tucson, AZ
Leader, Jon M. .... **Beverly Hills, CA**
Leader, Joshua K. .... **New York, NY**
Leader, Joshua M. .... Miami, FL
Leader, Judith K.
Department of State, GV
Leader, Laurie E. .... Northbrook, IL
Leader & Leader, A Professional Corp.
Beverly Hills, CA
Leader, Leonard .... **Stamford, CT**
Leader, Martin R. .... **Washington, DC**
Leader, Mary J. .... Phoenix, AZ
Leader, Rhonda .... New York, NY
Leader, Rita J. .... **Houston, TX**
Leader, Robert B. .... Carmel, NY
Leader, Robert J. .... **Gouverneur, NY**
Leader, Robin B. .... Burlington, MA
Leader, Sylvia M. .... Beverly Hills, CA
Leader, T. Philip .... **Worcester, MA**
Leader, William D., Jr. .... **Nashville, TN**
Leaderman, Arthur I. .... **Vienna, VA**
Leaderman, Maurice .... Baltimore, MD
Leader-Picone, Malcolm .... **Oakland, CA**
San Francisco, CA
Leaders, Ronald R. .... **Seattle, WA**
Leadingham, Charles C. .... Flatwoods, KY
Leadlove, Mark B. .... **St. Louis, MO**
Leadlove-Plant, Elaine F.B. .... Alameda, CA
Leadon, Marilynne P. .... San Diego, CA
Leadroot, Don .... Portland, OR
Leaf, Frederick P. .... **New Haven, CT**
Leaf, Jonathan W. .... Minneapolis, MN
Leaf, Jonathan W., P.A. .... Minneapolis, MN
Leaf, Karen .... Sacramento, CA
Leaf & Mahoney, P.A. .... **Bel Air, MD**
Leaf, Maralyn D. .... **Miami, FL**
Leaf, Marc A. .... **New York, NY**
Leaf, Marc J. .... Chicago, IL
Leaf, Marc J., P.C. .... Chicago, IL
Leaf, Martin N. .... **New York, NY**
Leaf, Matthew A. .... Beverly Hills, CA
Leaf, Michael E. .... **Bel Air, MD**
Leaf, Ron .... San Mateo, CA
Leaf, Samuel M. .... **New York, NY**
Leaf, Shalom .... **New York, NY**
Leaf, Sharon A. .... Libertyville, IL
Leaf, Wallace A. .... Lopez, WA
Leafe, Joseph A. .... Norfolk, VA
Leaffer, Karen Schauble .... **Denver, CO**
Leafstedt, Ann M. .... **San Antonio, TX**
Leager, Samuel R. .... Raleigh, NC
Leago, Regina A. .... Los Angeles, CA
Leagre Chandler & Millard LLP
Indianapolis, IN
Leagre, Richard M. .... **Indianapolis, IN**
League, Alice P. .... **Minneapolis, MN**
League, Barbara Jane .... Treasury Department, Internal Revenue Service, GV
League, David W. .... Oak Brook, IL
League, James William .... **Huntsville, AL**
League, Jason G. .... Towson, MD
League, Mary Sowell .... **Columbia, SC**
League, Richard N. .... Raleigh, NC
Leah, Scott R. .... **Pittsburgh, PA**
Leaheey, J. Bradford .... Westlake, OH
Leahey, Anne C. .... Shoreham, NY
Leahey, Eva-Marie .... Odessa, TX
Leahey, Francis J., Jr. .... Ebensburg, PA
Leahey, George B. .... Lowell, MA
Leahey, John M., Jr. .... Hopkins, MN
Leahey & Johnson, P.C. .... **Bronx, NY**
Brooklyn, NY
New York, NY
White Plains, NY

Leahey, Jonathan D. .... Kansas City, MO
Leahey, Mary Ellen .... Red Bank, NJ
Leahey, Matthew A. .... Toms River, NJ
Leahey, Richard C. .... Shrewsbury, NJ
Leahey, Richard C., Jr. .... **Red Bank, NJ**
Leahey, Thomas M. .... **Washington, DC**
Leahy, Alan J. .... **Riverside, CA**
Leahy, Albert D., Jr. .... **Claremont, NH**
Leahy, Anne .... **Bellevue, WA**
Leahy, Arthur C. .... **San Diego, CA**
Leahy & Associates, P.C. .... Dallas, TX
Leahy, B. Thomas .... Newark, NJ
Leahy, Beth J. .... **Fort Lauderdale, FL**
Leahy, Brian D. .... Vancouver, WA
Leahy, Carrie .... **Chicago, IL**
Leahy, Catherine Elizabeth .... Hudson, NY
Leahy, Charles E. .... **Detroit, MI**
Leahy, Charles F. .... **Concord, NH**
Leahy, Christine A. .... **Chicago, IL**
Leahy, Christopher B. .... Louisville, CO
Leahy, Constance A. .... **San Francisco, CA**
Leahy, Cynthia L. .... San Francisco, CA
Leahy, Daniel J. .... Chicago, IL
Leahy, Daniel P. .... Lowell, MA
Leahy, Daniel P., P.C. .... Lowell, MA
Leahy, David M. .... **Washington, DC**
Leahy, David W. .... San Jose, CA
Leahy, Deborah B.
Federal Energy Regulatory Commission, Office of the General Counsel, GV
Leahy, Debra L. .... Bethel, VT
Leahy & Denault, LLP .... **Claremont, NH**
Concord, NH
Leahy, Dennis L. .... Rockford, IL
Leahy, Edward H. .... Arlington Heights, IL
Leahy, Edward J. .... San Francisco, CA
Leahy, Edward J. .... Chicago, IL
Leahy, Edward R. .... **Washington, DC**
Leahy, Eileen T.
Department of Transportation, National Highway Traffic Safety Administration, GV
Leahy, Eisenberg & Fraenkel, Ltd.
Chicago, IL
Leahy, Eugene A. .... Omaha, NE
Leahy, George F. .... **Boston, MA**
Leahy, Gina A. .... **Boston, MA**
Leahy, Gregory P. .... **New York, NY**
Leahy, Harriet Friday .... New York, NY
Leahy, J. Brooks .... **Westminster, MD**
Leahy, James E. .... Fargo, ND
Leahy, James F. .... Chicago, IL
Leahy, James P. .... Elgin, IL
Leahy, James R. .... **Houston, TX**
Leahy, Jeannie A. .... **Seattle, WA**
Leahy, Jerry M. .... San Diego, CA
Leahy, John E. .... **Indianapolis, IN**
Leahy, John F., Jr. .... Braintree, MA
Leahy, John H. .... Los Angeles, CA
Leahy, John J. .... Newton, MA
Leahy, John J., Jr. .... Springfield, MA
Leahy, John M. .... Louisville, KY
Leahy, John M. .... **Lima, OH**
Leahy, John Michael .... **Lima, OH**
Leahy, John P. .... **Springfield, IL**
Leahy, John T. .... Worthington, MA
Leahy, John W. .... Franklin, MA
Leahy, Joseph J. .... **Springfield, OR**
Leahy, Joseph K. .... Washington, DC
Leahy, Joseph L. .... Omaha, NE
Leahy, Joseph L., Jr. .... **Omaha, NE**
Leahy, Joseph M. .... South Weymouth, MA
Leahy, Joyce A. .... Brooklyn, NY
Leahy, Kevin F. .... Burlington, VT
Leahy, Kevin L. .... **Roseland, NJ**
Leahy, Kevin M. .... **St. Louis, MO**
Leahy, Mark A. .... **Palo Alto, CA**
Leahy, Mark A. .... Quincy, MA
Leahy, Mary C. .... New York, NY
Leahy, Mary Hill .... **Waukesha, WI**
Leahy, Mary L. C. .... Springfield, IL
Leahy, Mary Susan .... **Concord, NH**
Leahy, Michael H. .... **Washington, DC**
Leahy, Michael J. .... **Santa Monica, CA**
Leahy, Michael J. .... **Omaha, NE**
Leahy, Michael V. .... **Los Angeles, CA**
Leahy, Michael W. .... **New York, NY**
Leahy, Monique C.M. .... Kansas City, MO
Leahy, Nyberg, Curto & D'Apice
Yonkers, NY
Leahy, Patrick J. .... Burlington, VT
Leahy, Patrick J. .... Tacoma, WA
Leahy, Patrick T. .... New York, NY
Leahy, Paul J. .... Tempe, AZ
Leahy, Paul J. .... Sudbury, MA
Leahy, Peter J. .... Concord, NH
Leahy, Phillip .... Elizabeth, NJ
Leahy, Richard J. .... **Yonkers, NY**
Leahy, Robert F. .... Stoneham, MA
Leahy, Robert J. .... Santa Rosa, CA
Leahy, Stephen G. .... Yonkers, NY
Leahy, Stephen J. .... Boston, MA
Leahy, Susan .... **Bethesda, MD**
Leahy, Terrence A. .... Bellevue, WA
Leahy, Terrence J. .... Milwaukee, WI
Leahy, Thomas G. .... **Portland, ME**
Leahy, Thomas J. .... Woodstock, IL
Leahy, Thomas M. .... Stoneham, MA
Leahy, Timothy Bruce .... St. Petersburg, FL
Leahy, Timothy J. .... Dallas, TX
Leahy, Timothy P. .... San Antonio, TX
Leahy, Tom .... Chicago, IL
Leahy, Tracy A. .... **Detroit, MI**
Leahy, W. Daniel .... Chicago, IL
Leahy, Walter R. .... Columbus, OH
Leahy & Ward .... Boston, MA
Leahy, William B. .... **Cleveland, OH**
Leahy, William Christopher .... Washington, DC

Leahy, William F. ... **Washington, DC**
Leahy, William J. ... **Philadelphia, PA**
Leahy-Fucheck, Andrea ... Annapolis, MD
Leair, Rebecca ... **Milwaukee, WI**
Leak, Douglas G. ... **Cleveland, OH**
Leak, G. Wade ... New York, NY
Leak, J. Elwyn ... Ocala, FL
Leak, Joe L. ... **Birmingham, AL**
Leak, Kathleen A. ... **San Francisco, CA**
Leak, Keith L. ... Saginaw, MI
Leakakos, Renie M. ... Los Angeles, CA
Leake, Alexandra ... Boston, MA
Leake, Andersson & Mann, L.L.P.
New Orleans, LA
Leake, David F. ... Memphis, TN
Leake, Donelson M. ... **Knoxville, TN**
Leake, James C., Jr. ... Tulsa, OK
Leake, Larry B. ... **Asheville, NC**
Marshall, NC
Leake Law Firm, The ... Memphis, TN
Leake, Loncy L. ... Mesquite, TX
Leake, Nolan C. ... **Atlanta, GA**
Leake, Paul D. ... **New York, NY**
Leake, Paul R. ... Mesquite, TX
Leake, Raymond C. ... **Durango, CO**
Leake, Robert E., Jr. ... **New Orleans, LA**
Leake, Robert S. ... Baton Rouge, LA
Leake, Thomas J. ... **Austin, MN**
Leake, W.T. Skip ... **Arlington, TX**
Dallas, TX
Fort Worth, TX
Leake, Warren Thomas (Skip), Jr.
Arlington, TX
Leal, Aaron ... **Holland, MI**
Leal, Alan G. ... Houston, TX
Leal, Alfred G. ... Houston, TX
Leal & Bratt, P.C. ... Redmond, WA
Leal, Carlos, III ... **Denver, CO**
Leal, Charles E. ... West Palm Beach, FL
Leal, Chrisann ... **Boston, MA**
Leal, Dolores Y. ... Los Angeles, CA
Leal, George C. ... **San Francisco, CA**
Leal, H. Francisco ... **Los Angeles, CA**
Leal, Heather N. ... **San Francisco, CA**
Leal, Hector J., Jr. ... Redmond, WA
Leal, Jas. D. ... River Ridge, LA
Leal, Jennifer D. ... Jacksonville, FL
Leal, John R ... **Fort Wayne, IN**
Leal, Joseph M., III ... Mesa, AZ
Leal, Leandro O. ... Miami, FL
Leal, Manuel D. ... Houston, TX
Leal, Mercedes ... Houston, TX
Leal, Olivas & Jauregui, LLP
Los Angeles, CA
Leal, Omar J. ... **Corpus Christi, TX**
Leal, Peter R. ... **Palo Alto, CA**
Leal, Stanley F. ... Sunnyvale, CA
Leal, Stephen A. ... **Tampa, FL**
Leal & Vela ... Laredo, TX
Leal, Victor L. ... Griffith, IN
Leal-Gamba, Ana M. ... **San Juan, PR**
Leaman, Donna L. ... San Francisco, CA
Leaman, John G. ... Hudson, NY
Leamer, Norris G. ... Norfolk, NE
Leamer, Robert E. ... Brooklyn, NY
Leaming, BethAnn Wiley
Philadelphia, PA
Leaming, Brian P. ... **Hartford, CT**
Leaming, John C. ... Bay City, MI
Leaming, Judith A. ... Window Rock, AZ
Leaming, Judy ... Towaoc, CO
Leaming, Margaret A. ... Big Rapids, MI
LeaMond, Deborah Kelly ... Goose Creek, SC
Leamons, Spence A. ... Fort Smith, AR
Leamy, Charles J. ... **New York, NY**
Leamy, Jane M. ... **Philadelphia, PA**
Leamy, Richard J., Jr. ... **Chicago, IL**
Lean, Charles W. ... **Olympia, WA**
Leander, Joel M. ... **Winston-Salem, NC**
Leanders, Christopher J. ... **Irvine, CA**
Leanders, Heidi Knapp ... **Irvine, CA**
Leanderson, Gretchen M. ... Olympia, WA
Leaness, Charles ... New York, NY
Leano, James E. ... Jacksonville, FL
Leanos, James A. ... San Jose, CA
Leanos, Stephen D. ... **San Francisco, CA**
Leanse, David V. ... Malibu, CA
Leanse, Thomas J. ... **Los Angeles, CA**
Leanza & Agrapidis ... Hackensack, NJ
New York, NY
Leanza, Anthony J. ... Riverhead, NY
Leanza, Anthony V. ... Lyndhurst, OH
Leanza, Cheryl A. ... Washington, DC
Leanza, Frank M., (P.C.) ... Hackensack, NJ
New York, NY
Leanza, Frank P. ... **Millburn, NJ**
Leape, James P. ... Washington, DC
Leaphart, Ben G., P.A. ... **Greenville, SC**
Pickens, SC
Leaphart, Ben Gibbs ... **Greenville, SC**
Leaphart, C. W., Jr. ... **Helena, MT**
Leaphart, J. Alvin, Jr. ... Jesup, GA
Leaphart, Jerry V. ... **Danbury, CT**
Red Bank, NJ
Leaphart, Jerry V., & Associates, P.C.
Danbury, CT
Red Bank, NJ
Leaphart & Johnson, P.C. ... Jesup, GA
Leaphart Law Firm ... **Helena, MT**
Leaphart, W. William ... Helena, MT
Leapheart, DeLois T. ... Midland, MI
Leapheart, DeLois T., P.C. ... Midland, MI
Leapley, Robert A., Jr. ... **Jacksonville, FL**
Lear, Adele ... Modesto, CA
Lear, Allen L. ... Washington, DC
Lear, Carol L. ... **Hartford, CT**
Lear, Christopher ... Fountain Valley, CA
Lear, Coates ... **Washington, DC**
Lear, Dwight O. ... Salem, OR
Lear, Edward O. ... Beverly Hills, CA
Lear, Elizabeth D. ... **Palo Alto, CA**
Lear, Elizabeth T. ... Gainesville, FL
Lear, Gerard R. ... **Arlington, VA**
Lear, Holly Parkhurst ... **Reston, VA**
Lear, Jennifer M. ... Falls Church, VA
Lear, Lewis R. ... **Boston, MA**
Lear, Lisa Elayne ... **Portland, OR**
Lear, Mark C. ... Houston, TX
Lear, Nancy N.C. ... **Kansas City, MO**
Lear, Phillip Wm. ... **Salt Lake City, UT**
Lear, Rhonda K. ... Madison, MS
Lear, Richard E. ... **Washington, DC**
Lear, Robert C. ... **Stroudsburg, PA**
Lear, S. Michael ... **Cleveland, OH**
Lear, Sherry Anne ... Torrance, CA
Lear, Steven D., (P.A.) ... **Miami, FL**
Lear, Tom ... San Angelo, TX
Lear, William H. ... **Riverside, CA**
Lear, William M., Jr. ... **Lexington, KY**
Leara, Stephen P. ... **Birmingham, AL**
Learch, Sharon Strayer ... **Jacksonville, FL**
Leard, David C. ... Torrington, CT
Lear-Johnson, Patricia L. ... Kansas City, MO
Learman, John F. ... **Saginaw, MI**
Learman, Patricia L. ... Saginaw, MI
Learman, Peters, Sarow and McQuillan, PLC ... **Bay City, MI**
Learman, Richard B. ... **Bay City, MI**
Learman, Richard C. ... **Bay City, MI**
Learman, Susan ... Birmingham, MI
Learmonth, Doloris F. ... **Cincinnati, OH**
Learmonth, Laurel E. ... **Minneapolis, MN**
Learn, Gerald M. ... Oakland, CA
Learn, Gordon W. ... Elmhurst, IL
Learn, June M. ... **San Diego, CA**
Learn, Mark D. ... **Washington, DC**
Learn, Michael C. ... Margate City, NJ
Learned, Daniel C. ... East Lansing, MI
Learned, Jeffrey R. ... **Bingham Farms, MI**
Learned, Kevin R. ... **New York, NY**
Learned, Philip C. ... **Elmira, NY**
Learned, Reilly & Learned ... **Elmira, NY**
Learned, Samuel M., Jr. ... York, PA
Learned, Scott J. ... **Elmira, NY**
Learner, David ... Morganton, NC
Learner, Howard A. ... Chicago, IL
Learner, James L. ... **Chicago, IL**
Learner, Nathan ... Boca Raton, FL
Learsy, Serge A. ... **New York, NY**
Leary, A. Pearson ... Chagrin Falls, OH
Chardon, OH
Leary, A. Peter ... **Boston, MA**
Leary, Anne L. ... **Phoenix, AZ**
Leary, Brian F. ... Fort Lauderdale, FL
Leary, Brian G. ... Needham, MA
Leary, Brian O. ... Oakland, CA
Leary, Bride, Tinker & Moran
Newark, NJ
Cedar Knolls, NJ
Morristown, NJ
Leary, Bryan J. ... **Minneapolis, MN**
Leary, Daniel F. ... **White Plains, NY**
Leary, Daniel P. ... **Atlanta, GA**
Leary, Denise B. ... Washington, DC
Leary, Douglas J. ... **Washington, DC**
Leary, Edward J. ... Dunwoody, GA
Leary, Erin ... Omaha, NE
Leary, Francis D. ... Newburyport, MA
Leary, Francis X. ... **Baltimore, MD**
Leary, Frank M. ... Auburn, NY
Leary, Gary L. ... Burbank, CA
Leary, George F. ... Worcester, MA
Leary, George J., Jr. ... **Boston, MA**
Leary, George W. ... Springfield, MA
Leary, Gerald P. ... **Albany, NY**
Leary and Holland ... **Little Compton, RI**
Tiverton, RI
Leary, J. Kevin ... Boston, MA
Leary, Jack C. ... Baton Rouge, LA
Leary, James C. ... **Rutland, VT**
Leary, James D., Jr. ... Cocoa Beach, FL
Leary, James Dennis ... Salem, MA
Leary, James E. ... Memphis, TN
Leary, James H. ... **Nashua, NH**
Leary, Jane S. ... **Glenview, IL**
Leary, Jeremiah R. ... **Tiverton, RI**
Leary, J. J., Jr. ... **Seattle, WA**
Leary, John ... **Washington, DC**
Leary, John A. ... Hudson Falls, NY
Leary, John D. ... **Eau Claire, WI**
Leary, John J., Jr. ... Herndon, VA
Leary, Joseph A. ... Glendale, NY
Leary, Joseph P. ... Bethesda, MD
Leary, Justin W. ... Auburn, ME
Leary, Kenneth A. ... New London, CT
Leary and Leary ... Newburyport, MA
Leary, Linda S. ... Albany, NY
Leary, Lisa Schmandt ... **St. Louis, MO**
Leary, Lynn Walter ... Parma, OH
Leary, Margaret A. ... Ann Arbor, MI
Leary, Marguerite Anne
Cedar Knolls, NJ
Leary, Marie
Federal Judicial Center, GV
Leary, Mary Lou ... Department of Justice, Office of the Associate Attorney General, GV
Leary, Mary W. ... Jackson, MS
Leary, Maureen F. ... Albany, NY
Leary, Michael J. ... Marshall, MN
Leary, Michael P. ... **Washington, DC**
Leary & Miller ... Oakland, CA
Leary, Oyer G. ... Thornton, CO
Leary, Patricia ... Costa Mesa, CA
Leary, Patricia M. ... **Los Altos, CA**
Leary, Patricia S. ... **Troy, MI**
Leary, Patrick J. ... Marshall, MN
Leary, Regina D. ... Fresno, CA
Leary, Richard T. ... Midlothian, VA
Leary, Robert D. ... **Buffalo, NY**
Leary, Robert G. ... New York, NY
Leary, Roxanne C. ... Cambridge, MA
Leary, Scott F. ... Jackson, MS
Leary, Shawn Pennell, (Ms.) ... **Lee, MA**
Leary, Steven W. ... Springfield, MA
Leary, Thomas A. ... San Diego, CA
Leary, Thomas B. ... **Washington, DC**
Leary, Thomas J. ... **Newport Beach, CA**
Leary, Thomas P. ... Omaha, NE
Leary, Timothy D. ... Treasury Department, Office of Thrift Supervision, GV
Leary, Virginia A. ... Buffalo, NY
Leary, W. Stephen ... **Cedar Knolls, NJ**
Leary, William C. ... Windsor, CT
Windsor Locks, CT
Leary, William H., III ... **St. Paul, MN**
Leary, William R. ... Houma, LA
Leas, Catherine, Law Office of
Sun City, AZ
Leas, Harry E. ... **Pittsburgh, PA**
Leas, James Marc ... Essex Junction, VT
Leas, Mark Charles ... Carmichael, CA
Leas, Michael R. ... **Jacksonville, FL**
Ponte Vedra Beach, FL
Leas, Philip J. ... **Honolulu, HI**
Leas, R. W. ... Jacksonville, NC
Leas, Stephen T. ... McAllen, TX
Lease, Andrew Charles ... Miami, FL
Lease, Charles H. ... Columbus, OH
Lease, Daniel H. ... Fremont, OH
Lease, David W. ... **Rockville, MD**
Lease, Lawrence M. ... Benicia, CA
Lease, Michael M. ... Scarsdale, NY
Lease, Robert K. ... **Cleveland, OH**
Leasendale, Jeffrey F. ... **Atlanta, GA**
Leasia, Nancy A. ... Saratoga, CA
Leasia, Richard A. ... **San Jose, CA**
Leason, Chris S. ... **Washington, DC**
Leason, David ... **New York, NY**
Leason, Wendy Z. ... **New York, NY**
Leasum, H. Jay ... Sturgeon Bay, WI
Leasure, Charles E., III ... **Philadelphia, PA**
Leasure, Diane O. ... Ellicott City, MD
Leasure, Gary G. ... Cumberland, MD
Leasure, Gow, Munk & Rizzuto
Endicott, NY
Leasure, Jeffrey W. ... Fort Myers, FL
Leasure, Joanne L. ... Washington, DC
Leasure, Kenneth S. ... Johnson City, NY
Leasure, Kevin P. ... **Jacksonville, FL**
Leasure, Linda L. ... Department of Labor, Office of Secretary, GV
Leasure, Russell ... **Cleveland, OH**
Leasure, Stanley A. ... **Fort Smith, AR**
Leasure, Virginia A. ... Syracuse, NY
Leasure, W. Bruce ... **Little Rock, AR**
Leate-Varney, Shannon Lisa ... Lowell, MA
Leath, Alex B., III ... **Birmingham, AL**
Leath, Bouch & Crawford, L.L.P.
Charleston, SC
Columbia, SC
Leath, Thomas E. ... Myrtle Beach, SC
Leath, Tom J. ... Fresno, CA
Leath, W. Jefferson, Jr. ... **Charleston, SC**
Leath, William B. ... Panama City, FL
Leatham, Nancy Lee ... San Francisco, CA
Leatham, Nile ... **Las Vegas, NV**
Leatham, Stephen G. ... Vancouver, WA
Leathe, Jeremy P. ... **Miami, FL**
Leathem, William W. ... Rosemont, IL
Leather, James L. ... **Phoenix, AZ**
Leather, Karen E. ... **Denver, CO**
Leatherbarrow, Elizabeth J. ... Washington, DC
Leatherberry, Jon C. ... **Dallas, TX**
Leatherberry, Roy J., IV ... **Austin, TX**
Leatherberry, Wilbur C. ... Cleveland, OH
Leatherberry, William J. ... **Dallas, TX**
Leatherbury, Douglas C. ... Indianapolis, IN
Salem, IN
Leatherbury, Gregory L., Jr. ... **Foley, AL**
Mobile, AL
Leatherbury, Thomas S. ... **Dallas, TX**
Leatherby, Joann ... Newport Beach, CA
Leatherman, C. E. ... Lincolnton, NC
Leatherman, Dania Long ... Knoxville, TN
Leatherman, Frederick D., Jr.
Seattle, WA
Leatherman, John B., Jr. ... Anderson, IN
Leatherman, Leland F. ... **Little Rock, AR**
Leatherman, L.J. ... **Topeka, KS**
Leatherman, Robertson M., Jr.
Jackson, MS
Memphis, TN
Leatherman, Todd Evan ... Versailles, KY
Leatherman, Wayne M. ... **Perrysburg, OH**
Leatherman, Witzler, Dombey & Hart
Bowling Green, OH
Perrysburg, OH
Leathers, A. Wade ... Fayette, AL
Winfield, AL
Leathers, Bill F. ... Lake Jackson, TX
Leathers, Clarence L., Jr. ... College Park, GA
Leathers, H. Rowan, III ... **Nashville, TN**
Leathers, James G., Jr. ... Walnut Creek, CA
Leathers, John R. ... **Lexington, KY**
Leathers, Kevin P. ... New York, NY
Leathers, LeeAnne ... **Livingston, NJ**
Leathers, M. Lionel ... Winfield, AL
Leathers, Patrick D. ... Sacramento, CA
Leathers, Ramsey B. ... Nashville, TN
Leathers, Raymond S. ... **Nashville, TN**
Leathers, Timothy J. ... Little Rock, AR
Leathers, Wade S. ... **Seattle, WA**
Leatherwood, Felix E. ... Los Angeles, CA
Leatherwood, Harris Lee ... Oakdale, LA
Leatherwood, Judith A. ... **Greenville, SC**
Leatherwood, Valerie L. ... **Dallas, TX**
Leatherwood Walker Todd & Mann, P.C.
Greenville, SC
Spartanburg, SC
Leaton, Barry R. ... Houston, TX
Leaton, Thomas U., II ... Glendale Heights, IL
Leatzow, M. Penny ... Kalispell, MT
Leavell and Associates ... Albuquerque, NM
Leavell, Barry C. ... **Montgomery, AL**
Leavell, Carroll B. ... Washington, GA
Leavell, Craig D. ... **Chicago, IL**
Leavell, George B. ... **Palo Alto, CA**
Leavell, George G. ... **Memphis, TN**
Leavell, Hugh M. ... **Charlottesville, VA**
Leavell, Jeffrey L. ... **Racine, WI**
Leavell, Jeffrey, S.C. ... **Racine, WI**
Leavell, Julita Ann ... Albuquerque, NM
Leavell, Robert F. ... Bellflower, CA
Leavell, Robert N. ... New Orleans, LA
Leavell, Stephen K. ... Nampa, ID
Leavengood, Joseph A.
Greenwood Village, CO
Leavens, Amy Susan ... **Washington, DC**
Leavens, Andrew A. ... **Shamokin, PA**
Leavens, Arthur B. ... Springfield, MA
Leavens, Ladd B. ... **Seattle, WA**
Leavens & Roberts ... **Shamokin, PA**
Leaventon, Adam ... **New York, NY**
Leavenworth, David, Jr. ... Boulder, CO
Leavenworth, Loyal E.
Glenwood Springs, CO
Leavenworth, Melody Ruth
Grand Rapids, MI
Leavenworth, Philip G. ... St. Paul, MN
Leavenworth, Simone S. ... Austin, TX
Leavenworth & Tester, P.C. ... **Aspen, CO**
Glenwood Springs, CO
Leaver, James R. ... Medina, OH
Leaver, Robert J. ... Santa Barbara, CA
Leaver, Walter C., Jr. ... Nashville, TN
Leaverton, Bruce W. ... **Seattle, WA**
Leaverton, David G. ... La Jolla, CA
Leaverton, Jack D. ... Boise, ID
Leaverton, Mark K. ... **Austin, TX**
Leaverton, Susan H. ... Seattle, WA
Leavey, Christopher L. ... Trenton, NJ
Leavey, James H. ... Providence, RI
Leavey, Joseph J. ... Walnut Creek, CA
Leavey, Kathleen ... Detroit, MI
Leavine, Barbara A. ... **Miami, FL**
Leavis, Paul F. ... **Boston, MA**
Leavis and Rest, P.C. ... **Boston, MA**
Leavitt, Andrea R. ... San Diego, CA
Leavitt, Brent E. ... Las Vegas, NV
Leavitt, Bruce ... Santa Rosa, CA
Leavitt, Cori L. ... **New York, NY**
Leavitt, Curtis ... Sacramento, CA
Leavitt, Dane O. ... Cedar City, UT
Leavitt, David ... Brockton, MA
Leavitt, David Keene ... Beverly Hills, CA
Leavitt, David O. ... **Provo, UT**
Leavitt, Donald G. ... **St. Louis, MO**
Leavitt, Douglas M. ... **Philadelphia, PA**
Leavitt, Elwin C. ... Las Vegas, NV
Leavitt, I. Martin ... Roanoke, VA
Leavitt, Ilona S. ... Chesterfield, MO
Leavitt, Ira D. ... Palatine, IL
Leavitt, Ira D., Ltd. ... Palatine, IL
Leavitt, J. Patrick, Jr. ... Shakopee, MN
Leavitt, J. Patrick, Jr., Professional Association
Shakopee, MN
Leavitt, Jack ... Berkeley, CA
Leavitt, James Patrick, II ... Shakopee, MN
Leavitt, James T., Jr. ... **Honolulu, HI**
Leavitt, Jeffrey H. ... New York, NY
Leavitt, Jeffrey M. ... **New York, NY**
Leavitt, Jeffrey S. ... **Cleveland, OH**
Leavitt, John H. ... Forest Grove, OR
Leavitt, John N. ... Bellevue, WA
Leavitt, Josh M. ... **Chicago, IL**
Leavitt, K. Michael, (Chartered)
Las Vegas, NV
Leavitt, Laura Ann ... Los Angeles, CA
Leavitt, Laurence H. ... **Portland, ME**
Leavitt, Lawrence R. ... Las Vegas, NV
Leavitt, Linda M. ... San Francisco, CA
Leavitt, Marc Crawford ... Woodside, NY
Leavitt, Margaret Gibson ... Sacramento, CA
Leavitt, Mark R. ... **Orlando, FL**
Leavitt, Martin J. ... **Novi, MI**
Leavitt, Marvin ... Chicago, IL
Leavitt, Mary Hannah ... **Harrisburg, PA**
Leavitt, MaryAnn ... Grand Forks, ND
Leavitt, Maurice J. ... Somerville, MA
Leavitt, Melanie A. ... Metairie, LA
Leavitt, Michael J. ... **Novi, MI**
Leavitt, Michael L. ... New York, NY
Leavitt, Michael W. ... Yakima, WA
Leavitt, Myron E. ... Las Vegas, NV
Leavitt, Neil ... Bellevue, WA
Leavitt, Neil, P.S. ... Bellevue, WA
Leavitt, Nelson S. ... Lansing, MI
Leavitt, Paul D. ... Atlanta, GA
Leavitt, Peter M. ... White Plains, NY
Leavitt, Randal C. ... El Cajon, CA
Leavitt, Randy T. ... **Austin, TX**
Leavitt, Richard A. ... Las Vegas, NV
Leavitt, Richard B. ... Los Angeles, CA
Leavitt, Robert D. ... Chicago, IL
Leavitt, Samson B. ... Great Neck, NY
Leavitt, Scott M. ... **Los Angeles, CA**
Leavitt, Sully & Rivers ... **Las Vegas, NV**
Leavitt, Terry V. ... Las Vegas, NV
Leavitt, Thomas E. ... Bellevue, WA
Leavitt, Wendy S. ... **Miami, FL**
Leavitt, William S. ... Northbrook, IL

Leavitt, Yamane & Soldner, Attorneys at Law, A Law Corporation ... Honolulu, HI
Leavitt-Gruberger, Edwin S. Princeton, NJ
Leavoy, Leslie R., Jr. ... De Ridder, LA
Leavoy, Lindsey J. ... Baton Rouge, LA
Leavy, Adrienne T. ... Phoenix, AZ
Leavy, Charles W. ... Virginia Beach, VA
Leavy, Edward ... Portland, OR
Leavy, Elizabeth G. ... Greenbrae, CA; San Rafael, CA
Leavy, Jane R. ... Miami, FL
Leavy, Laurence F., (P.A.) ... Miami, FL
Leavy, Michael G. ... Rockville Centre, NY
Leavy, Michael S. ... New York, NY
Leavy, Morton L. ... New York, NY; White Plains, NY
Leavy, Peter H. ... Miami, FL
Leavy, Richard A. ... New York, NY
Leavy Rosensweig & Hyman New York, NY
Leavy, Schultz, Davis & Fearing, P.S. Kennewick, WA; Pasco, WA; Richland, WA
Leavy, Zad ... Carmel, CA
Leazenby, Dean E. ... Elkhart, IN
Leb, Arthur S. ... Canton, OH
Leb, Cheryl Poulin ... Fort Worth, TX
Leb, Michael H. ... Pleasanton, CA
Leb, Silvia ... Worcester, MA
Leban, Abbott A. ... Wilmington, DE
Leban, Mark King ... Miami, FL
Leban, Michael F. ... Norfolk, VA
Lebar, Daniel A. ... Metuchen, NJ
Le Bar, David W. ... Southgate, MI
LeBar, Loretta G. ... Crestwood, KY
LeBar, Paul W. ... St. Louis, MO
Lebar, Robert N. ... Richmond, VA
LeBari, D. Sean ... Houston, TX
Lebario, Norma ... Florence, AZ
LeBaron, C. Frederick, Jr. ... Chicago, IL
LeBaron, C. Steven ... Philadelphia, PA
LeBaron, Edward W., Jr. ... Sacramento, CA
LeBaron, Elizabeth Z. ... Chicago, IL
LeBaron, Michael B. ... Minneapolis, MN
LeBaron, Shirl Don ... Moab, UT
LeBaron, Shirl Don, & Associates, Law Offices of ... Moab, UT
LeBarron, Barbara J. ... Houston, TX
LeBarron, Graham W. ... Eau Claire, WI
Le Barron, Lisa J. ... Eau Claire, WI
LeBarron, Poquette & Lokken Eau Claire, WI
LeBas, David L. ... Amarillo, TX
LeBas, Henry H. ... Lafayette, LA
LeBas, Sean O. ... Ansonia, CT
Lebau & Neuworth ... Baltimore, MD
Lebau, Stephen B. ... Baltimore, MD
Lebb, Edward R. ... Honolulu, HI
Lebbin, Deborah H. ... Rockville, MD
Lebe & Finer ... Los Angeles, CA
Lebe, Melvin S. ... Los Angeles, CA
LeBeau, Bernard G., Jr. ... Bakersfield, CA
Le Beau, Charles J. ... Solvang, CA
LeBeau, Charles P., Law Offices of San Diego, CA
LeBeau, F. William ... Washington, DC
LeBeau, James V. ... Passaic, NJ
LeBeau, Jeffrey O. ... Long Beach, CA
LeBeau, Joseph H., III ... Monroe, LA
Lebeau, Michelle J. ... Bloomfield Hills, MI
LeBeau, Morgan M. ... San Diego, CA
LeBeau, Thelen, Lampe, McIntosh & Crear, LLP ... Bakersfield, CA
Lebeaux, Susan L. Securities and Exchange Commission, Division of Enforcement, GV
Lebeck, Albert O., Jr. ... Gallup, NM
Lebeck, Kathleen Davison Albuquerque, NM
Lebeda, John W. ... Caldwell, NJ
Lebedeker, Michael D. West Palm Beach, FL
Lebedev, Gennady L. ... Los Angeles, CA
Lebedev, Marsha ... New York, NY
Lebedoff, David M. ... Minneapolis, MN
Lebedoff, Jonathan ... Minneapolis, MN
Lebedoff, Randy Miller ... Minneapolis, MN
Lebed-Rofes, Ruth J. ... Racine, WI
LeBel, Antoinette Patterson ... Bethesda, MD
LeBel, Carolyn S. ... Brooklyn, NY
Le Bel, Christine Y. ... Los Angeles, CA
LeBel & Gaulke ... Los Angeles, CA
LeBel, Lionel B., Jr. ... Los Angeles, CA
LeBel, Paul A. ... Williamsburg, VA
Lebel, Richard A. ... Denver, CO
Lebel, Ronald A. ... Portsmouth, RI
Lebel, Ronald P. ... Auburn, ME
Lebel, Stephen J. ... Colorado Springs, CO
Lebell, Jeanette L. ... Novato, CA
Le Bell, Robert G. ... Milwaukee, WI
Leben, Richard ... Tamarac, FL
Leben, Steve A. ... Olathe, KS
Lebenbaum, Alan G. ... Far Rockaway, NY
Lebenberg, Margot T. ... Dallas, TX
Lebenbom, David ... Troy, MI
Lebenbom, David, P.C. ... Troy, MI
Lebenbom, Michael J. ... Troy, MI
Lebenger, Aaron Louis ... New York, NY
Lebenkoff, Abraham ... New York, NY
Lebenkoff & Coven ... New York, NY
Lebens, Susan ... Omaha, NE
Lebens, Thomas F. ... San Diego, CA
Lebensbaum, Louis "Leon" ... Levittown, NY
Lebensburger, Scott E. ... Hendersonville, NC
Lebensfeld, Alan M. ... Red Bank, NJ; New York, NY
Lebensfeld Borker & Sussman LLP Red Bank, NJ; New York, NY
Lebensohn, Alisa R. ... New York, NY
Lebensold, Kenneth ... New York, NY
Lebensold, Linda R. ... New York, NY
Lebenstein, David N. ... New York, NY
Lebental, Miriam J. ... San Pedro, CA
Lebenzon, Farrel F. ... Los Angeles, CA
LeBeouf, David R. ... Stockton, CA
Leber, Alan D. ... New York, NY
Leber, Bartlett F. ... Andover, MA
Leber, Bernice K. ... New York, NY
Leber, Bradley J. ... York, PA
Leber, Celia H. ... Boston, MA
Leber, Frank J. ... Harrisburg, PA
Leber, Jeff ... Coudersport, PA
Leber, Jill E. ... Covington, LA
Leber, Michael A. ... Baltimore, MD
Leber, Richard B. ... New York, NY
Leber, William E. ... Cape Haze, FL
Leberman, Peter W. ... Concord, NH; Manchester, NH
Leberman, Robert L. ... San Francisco, CA
Leberman, Susan M. ... San Francisco, CA
Leberman, William J. ... Syracuse, NY
Le Berthon, Adam ... Los Angeles, CA
Le Berthon, Edward L. ... Chatsworth, CA
Le Berthon, James L. ... Glendale, CA
Lebetkin, Corynne A. ... New York, NY
Lebetsamer, Ronald A. ... Torrance, CA
Lebeuf, Ronald A. ... Battle Creek, MI
Lebewitz, Joel A. ... Minneapolis, MN
Lebewohl, Jacob J. ... New York, NY
LeBey, Barbara S. ... Atlanta, GA
LeBey, Daniel M. ... Richmond, VA
Lebherz, Christopher G. ... Falmouth, MA
Lebherz, George H., Jr. ... Falmouth, MA
Lebit, Michael A. ... Hauppauge, NY
LeBlanc, A. Paul, Jr. ... Houston, TX
LeBlanc, Alfred P., Jr. ... Houston, TX
LeBlanc, Alvin A., Jr.(Professional Law Corporation) ... Metairie, LA
LeBlanc, Ann Marie ... New Orleans, LA
LeBlanc, Belinda B. ... Baton Rouge, LA
LeBlanc, Bertrand, II ... San Francisco, CA
LeBlanc, Charles J. ... Thibodaux, LA
LeBlanc, Chris J. ... Baton Rouge, LA
Leblanc, Collin J. ... Baton Rouge, LA
LeBlanc, Danl. W. ... Baton Rouge, LA
Le Blanc, David ... Galveston, TX
LeBlanc, Frank V., III ... Metairie, LA
LeBlanc & Iennaco ... Orlando, FL
LeBlanc, J. Burton, IV ... Baton Rouge, LA
LeBlanc, J. Burton, Jr. ... Baton Rouge, LA
LeBlanc, J. Dwight, III ... New Orleans, LA
LeBlanc, J. Dwight, Jr. ... New Orleans, LA
Le Blanc, J. Louis ... New Bedford, MA
LeBlanc, James G. ... Boston, MA
LeBlanc, James L. ... Columbia, SC
LeBlanc, Jean B., II ... Los Angeles, CA
Le Blanc, Jeffrey L. ... Lockport, LA
Le Blanc, Jesse E., II ... New Orleans, LA
LeBlanc, Jill E. ... Baton Rouge, LA
LeBlanc, Joan A. ... Palo Alto, CA
LeBlanc, John E. ... Thibodaux, LA
Le Blanc, John M. ... Los Angeles, CA
LeBlanc, Jonathan M. ... Dallas, TX
LeBlanc, Joseph E., Jr. ... New Orleans, LA
Leblanc, Jude Normand ... Denver, CO
LeBlanc, Jules B., III ... Baton Rouge, LA; Monroe, LA; New Orleans, LA; Shreveport, LA
LeBlanc, Jules B., IV ... Baton Rouge, LA
LeBlanc, K. Bradleigh ... Plano, TX
LeBlanc, Lee Anne ... Hallandale Beach, FL
LeBlanc, Lee Anne, P.A., Law Office of Hallandale Beach, FL
LeBlanc, Maples & Waddell, L.L.C. Baton Rouge, LA; Monroe, LA; New Orleans, LA; Shreveport, LA
LeBlanc, Marc Alan ... Pulaski, VA
LeBlanc, Margaret A. "Peggy" New Orleans, LA
LeBlanc, Marianne Camille ... Boston, MA
Le Blanc, Matthew J. ... Santa Rosa, CA
LeBlanc, Michelle Gaudet ... Houston, TX
LeBlanc, Miranda & deLaup, A Professional Law Corporation ... Metairie, LA; New Orleans, LA
Le Blanc, Nancy E. ... Wilmington, NY
LeBlanc, Patricia Schuster ... Metairie, LA; New Orleans, LA
LeBlanc, Richard B. ... Philadelphia, PA
LeBlanc, Richard D. ... Pittsfield, MA
LeBlanc, Richard P. ... Portland, ME
Leblanc, Ricky A. ... Malden, MA
Leblanc, Robert E. ... Washington, DC
LeBlanc, Robert F. ... Tulsa, OK
Leblanc, Robert Joseph Crowley Methuen, MA
LeBlanc, Robert Paul ... Orlando, FL
LeBlanc, Robert R. ... Boston, MA
Le Blanc, Roger J. ... St. Gabriel, LA
LeBlanc, Sam A., III ... New Orleans, LA
LeBlanc & Sans ... Gardner, MA
Le Blanc, Stacia Davis Department of Commerce, Office of the General Counsel, GV
Le Blanc, Stephen J. ... San Francisco, CA
Le Blanc, Steve ... Baton Rouge, LA
LeBlanc, Steven R. ... Columbia, SC
LeBlanc, Ted P. ... Prince Frederick, MD
Le Blanc, Thomas A. ... Tulsa, OK
LeBlanc, Thomas P. ... Lake Charles, LA
LeBlanc, Vicki Ann ... Pewaukee, WI
LeBlanc, Wayne M. ... Worcester, MA
LeBlanc, Wilfrid, Jr. ... Springfield, NJ
LeBlanc, William E. ... Donaldsonville, LA
LeBlanc & Young ... Portland, ME
LeBlanc, Yvon J.R.J. ... Los Angeles, CA
LeBlancq, Richard W. ... Hackensack, NJ
Leblang, Clay, Sobel & Ashbaugh Tulsa, OK
Leblang, Kevin B. ... New York, NY
Leblang, Mark J. ... Tulsa, OK
Leblang, Russell D. ... Boston, MA; New York, NY
Leblang, S. Alan ... New York, NY
Leblang, Stuart E. ... New York, NY
Leblang, Theodore R. ... Springfield, IL
Lebleu, Alison Zollo ... Franklin, MA
LeBleu, Floyd ... Lafayette, LA
LeBleu, John H., Sr. ... Lake Charles, LA
LeBleu, Nick Clarence E. ... Orange, TX
LeBlon, Vincent ... Florham Park, NJ
LeBlond, John F. ... Pittsburgh, PA
Lebman, Marvin ... San Antonio, TX
Lebo, Andrew M. ... Anchorage, AK
Lebo, Diane ... Washington, DC
Lebo, Karen L. ... Richmond, VA
Lebo, Louis S. ... Toledo, OH
Lebo, Todd ... New York, NY
LeBoeuf, Bradley S. ... Washington, DC
LeBoeuf, Dean R. ... Tallahassee, FL
LeBoeuf, Denise ... New Orleans, LA
LeBoeuf, Jacques B. ... Oakland, CA
LeBoeuf, Lamb, Greene & MacRae, L.L.P. Los Angeles, CA; San Francisco, CA; Denver, CO; Hartford, CT; Washington, DC; Jacksonville, FL; Boston, MA; Newark, NJ; Albany, NY; New York, NY; Portland, OR; **Harrisburg, PA; Pittsburgh, PA; Houston, TX; Salt Lake City, UT**
Leboeuf, Loree Peacock ... New Orleans, LA
LeBoeuf, MaryGaye ... Oklahoma City, OK
Leboeuf, Michael A. ... Little Rock, AR
LeBoeuf, Nicole T. ... Dallas, TX
LeBoeuf, Robert J. ... Brockton, MA
LeBoeuf, Robert L. ... Angleton, TX; Houston, TX
Leboeuf, Roger N. ... Providence, RI
LeBoeuf, Wittenmyer & Underwood, P.C. Angleton, TX; Houston, TX
Leboff, Beth R. ... Fort Lauderdale, FL
Leboff, Eric S. ... Waltham, MA
Leboff, Susan ... New York, NY
Leboffe, Paul A. ... Menlo Park, CA
Lebofsky, Howard ... Fort Washington, PA
Lebofsky, Stanley ... Philadelphia, PA
Lebold, Deborah E. ... Chicago, IL
Lebold, John W. ... Cleveland, OH
LeBold, Sandra J. ... Flossmoor, IL
Lebold, Sheldon L., & Associates Orland Hills, IL
Lebold, Susan M. ... Framingham, MA
Lebon, Alan E. ... St. Louis, MO
Lebon, Kenneth M. ... St. Paul, MN
Le Bon, Patricia Richmond Mount Holly, NJ
LeBon, Raymond T. ... Philadelphia, PA
Lebor, David ... Philadelphia, PA
Lebos, Richard J., Jr. ... Dallas, TX
LeBost, Paulette M. ... Detroit, MI
LeBouef, John F. ... Los Angeles, CA
LeBourgeois, Cynthia C. ... Lafayette, LA
Lebovic, Ira D. ... Newport Beach, CA
LeBovici, Jacqueline R. ... Kew Gardens, NY
LeBovici & LeBovici ... Kew Gardens, NY
LeBovici, Ronald S., (P.C.) Kew Gardens, NY
Lebovici, Victor B. ... Boston, MA
LeBovit, Lisa A. ... Yorktown Heights, NY
Lebovits & David, A Professional Corporation ... Los Angeles, CA
Lebovits, Dianne Caplan ... Santa Monica, CA
Lebovits, Gerald ... New York, NY
Lebovits, Moses ... Los Angeles, CA
Lebovits, Ronald N. ... Sacramento, CA
Lebovitz, Amy S. ... Hackensack, NJ
Lebovitz, Arthur E. ... Maplewood, NJ
Lebovitz, Emily J. ... Hartford, CT
Lebovitz, Gilbert ... Hartford, CT
Lebovitz, James A. ... Philadelphia, PA
Lebovitz, Jamie R. ... Cleveland, OH
Lebovitz & Lebovitz, P.A. ... Pittsburgh, PA
Lebovitz, Margot S. ... Rancho Santa Fe, CA
Lebovitz, Michael ... Arlington Heights, IL
Lebovitz, Richard D. ... Pittsburgh, PA
Lebovitz, Richard M. ... Arlington, VA
Lebovitz, Robert A. ... Pittsburgh, PA
Lebovitz, Stephen H. ... Pittsburgh, PA
Lebow, Carol A. ... Los Angeles, CA
Lebow, Cynthia C. Department of Justice, GV
Lebow, Edward M. ... Washington, DC
Lebow, Joan Moeckel ... Chicago, IL
Lebow, Larry J. ... Pittsburgh, PA
Lebow, Lawrence N. ... Fairfax, VA
Lebow, Mark ... Jacksonville, FL
Lebow, Mark D. ... New York, NY; New York, NY
Lebow, Melvin L. ... Bellerose, NY
Lebow, Michael J. ... West Bloomfield, MI
Lebow, Patricia, (P.A.) West Palm Beach, FL
Lebow, Ronald M. ... Marina Del Rey, CA
Lebow, Susan ... Fort Lauderdale, FL
Le Bow, Susan M. ... Commack, NY
Lebow and Tobin, PLLC Farmington Hills, MI
Lebowich, Michael J. ... New York, NY
Lebowitz, Alan D. ... Department of Labor, Pension and Welfare Benefits, GV
Lebowitz, Alan G. ... New York, NY
Lebowitz, Alan P. ... New York, NY
Lebowitz, Albert ... St. Louis, MO
Lebowitz, Ann C. ... Philadelphia, PA
Lebowitz, Brian E. ... Washington, DC
Lebowitz, David A. ... New York, NY
Lebowitz, Don ... New York, NY
Lebowitz, Donna S. ... Los Angeles, CA
Lebowitz, Henry C. ... New York, NY
Lebowitz, J. Leon ... Austin, TX
Lebowitz, Jack D. ... Owings Mills, MD
Lebowitz, Jack R. ... Saratoga Springs, NY
LeBowitz, Jerome D. ... New York, NY
Lebowitz, Karen M. ... Austin, TX
Lebowitz, Laurence J. ... New York, NY
Lebowitz, Lawrence M. ... Pittsburgh, PA
Lebowitz, Linda S. General Accounting Office, Office of the General Counsel, GV
Lebowitz, Lisa ... New York, NY
Lebowitz, Louis ... Palm Beach Gardens, FL
Lebowitz, Louis H. ... Dallas, TX
Lebowitz, Marc A. ... New York, NY
Lebowitz, Mark A. ... Glens Falls, NY
Lebowitz, Maxine J. ... Long Beach, CA
Lebowitz, Molly K. ... Burlington, VT
Lebowitz & Mzhen, LLC ... Baltimore, MD; Owings Mills, MD
Lebowitz, Neil H. ... Glens Falls, NY
Lebowitz, Neil R. ... Baltimore, MD
Lebowitz, Philip H. ... Philadelphia, PA
Lebowitz, Ronald A., (P.C.) ... Phoenix, AZ
Lebowitz, Samuel ... Rockville, MD
Lebowitz, Sidney E. ... Washington, DC
Lebowitz, Stephen E. ... Pittsburgh, PA
Lebowitz, Stephen Mark ... New York, NY
Lebowitz, Todd H. ... Cleveland, OH
Lebowitz, Walter B. ... Lawrence, MA
Lebowitz-Prager, Wendy ... New York, NY
Lebowski, Steven J. ... Milford, MI
Lebowsky, Lawrence M. ... Los Angeles, CA
LeBoyer, Donald A. ... Chicago, IL
Lebrato, Gary D. ... Fort Wayne, IN
Lebrato, Kenneth J. ... New Brunswick, NJ
LeBre, Kristin Peterson ... Minnetonka, MN
Lebrecht, Brian A. ... Newport Beach, CA
LeBreton, Edward F., III New Orleans, LA
Le Breton, Rose McCabe New Orleans, LA
LeBrocq, Lawrence A. ... Edison, NJ
LeBrocq, Lawrence A., Law Offices of Edison, NJ; New Brunswick, NJ
Lebron, Marion T. Department Of Health And Human Services, GV
Lebron, Roberto ... Bronx, NY
LeBrón-González, Ernesto ... San Juan, PR
Lebrón-Nieves, Gloria L. ... San Juan, PR
Lebron-Velazquez, J. R. ... San Juan, PR
Le Brun, Christian G. ... New York, NY
Le Brun, Douglas D. ... Burlington, VT
Lebrun, Gene N. ... Rapid City, SD
LeBrun, John P. ... Concord, NH
LeBrun, M. David ... Baltimore, MD
LeBrun, Michael A. ... Florence, AL
LeBrun, William K. ... Torrance, CA
LeBrun Mackles, Judy ... Metairie, LA
Lebsack, Chester W., (A Professional Corporation) ... Redwood City, CA
Lebsack, John ... Denver, CO
Lebsack, Raymond L. ... Greenacres, WA
Lebsack, Ronald A. ... Fort Morgan, CO
Lebsack, Todd D. ... St. Louis, MO
Lebsock, Christopher L. San Francisco, CA
Lebson, Daniel Peter ... New York, NY
Lebson, James D. ... Tenafly, NJ
Lebson, Judith F. ... Englewood, NJ
Lebson, Prigoff & Baker ... Englewood, NJ
Lebson, Sean E. ... New York, NY
Lebster, Allyn R. ... Grand Rapids, MI
LeBurkien, Michael P. ... Houston, TX
LeBus, Betty V. ... Bloomington, IN
Lebwith, David Laurence ... Boston, MA
Lebwohl, Linda S. ... Kew Gardens, NY
LeCarner, Thomas M. ... Los Angeles, CA
Lecaroz, Suzanne ... Boston, MA
LeCarpentier III, Edward C. ... Raleigh, NC
LeCates, Byron H. ... York, PA
LeCates, William B. ... Plantation, FL
LeCates, William B., P.A. ... Plantation, FL
Lecce, Gail M. Agency for International Development, Other Offices of A.I.D., GV
Lecce, Luigi ... Latham, NY
Leccese, Anthony L. ... Boston, MA
Leccese, Joseph J. ... Garden City, NY
Leccese, Joseph M. ... New York, NY
Lecci, John C. ... Hartford, CT
Lecci, Salvatore A. ... Bay Shore, NY
LeCesne, Alvarez L., Jr. ... Reston, VA
Le Cesne, Blaine ... New Orleans, LA
Lech, Robert J. ... Grosse Pointe Woods, MI
Lech, Robert R. ... Columbus, OH
Leche, Charles E. ... New Orleans, LA

Leche, Paul A. ....Austin, TX
Lecher, Donald J. .....Department of Commerce, Patent and Trademark Office, GV
Lecher, Steven M. ....New York, NY
Le Chevallier, Robert T. ....Lake Oswego, OR
LeChien, Brenda S. ....Belleville, IL
LeChien, Elaine Louise ....Belleville, IL
LeChien & LeChien, Ltd. ....Belleville, IL
LeChien, Robert P. ....Belleville, IL
LeChien, Thomas A. ....Belleville, IL
Lechleiter, Gerard ....Mamaroneck, NY
Lechleitner, Thomas M. ....Deer Park, NY
Lechman, Bradley C. ....Portland, OR
Lechman, Joseph ....Camarillo, CA
Lechner, Albert H. ....Columbia, MD
Lechner, Alfred J., Jr. ....Newark, NJ
Lechner, Bernard J. ....Clearwater, FL
Lechner, David C. ....Chicago, IL
Lechner, Edward J. ....Edina, MN
Lechner, Ira M. ....Washington, DC
Lechner, Jennifer M. ....Augusta, ME
Lechner, Joyce P. ....Wheeling, WV
Lechner, Paul A. ....Tinley Park, IL
Lechner, Robert L. ....Seattle, WA
Lechner, Scott W. ....Richmond, VA
Lechner, Stanley F. ....Washington, DC
Lechnowsky, Orest J. ....Cleveland, OH
Lechowicz, Alan E. ....Naperville, IL
Lechowicz & Davis ....Annapolis, MD
Glen Burnie, MD
Lechowicz, Edwin A. ....Glen Burnie, MD
Lechowicz, Mark A. ....Glen Burnie, MD
Lechowicz, Robert A. ....Telford, PA
Lechowicz, Robert A., Law Offices
Sellersville, PA
Lechtenberg, Penelope M. ....Rockford, IL
Lechtenberger, Joseph D. ....Houston, TX
Lechtenberger, Kirk F. ....Dallas, TX
Lechter & Lechter, P.C. ....Norristown, PA
Philadelphia, PA
Lechter, Lynne Kessler ....Norristown, PA
Lechter, Mark E. S. ....New York, NY
Lechter, Michael A. ....Phoenix, AZ
Lechter, Stephen A. ....Attleboro, MA
Lechter, Stephen A. ....Taunton, MA
Lechtman, Arthur Thomas
Federal Communications Commission, Wireless Telecommunications Bureau, GV
Lechtman, Michael L. ....Miami, FL
Lechtman, Michael L.
North Miami Beach, FL
Lechtman, Vladimir ....Washington, DC
Lechtner, Neal Brian ....Hollywood, FL
Lechtrecker, George E. ....Patchogue, NY
Lechtrecker, Norman F.
Center Moriches, NY
Patchogue, NY
Lechtzin, Eric ....Cherry Hill, NJ
Philadelphia, PA
Leck, Brian C. ....Los Angeles, CA
Leck, Robert B., III ....Santa Monica, CA
Leckar, Bonnie Erbe ....Arlington, VA
Leckar, Stephen C. ....Washington, DC
Washington, DC
Leckart, Julie D. ....Key West, FL
Leckband, Carl A. ....Lake Charles, LA
Leckemby, William R., Jr. ....Frederick, MD
Lecker, Wendy Carolyn ....Stamford, CT
Leckerling, E. William, III
Burlington, VT
Leckerling, Richard E. ....Albany, NY
Leckey, Kathryn D. ....McLean, VA
Leckey, Lenk & Luketina, L.L.C.
Fairfax, VA
McLean, VA
Leckie, Bernard A. ....Irvine, CA
Leckie, Bruce C. ....Charleston, WV
Leckie, Cabell T. ....Salem, VA
Leckie, David A. ....Lovettsville, VA
Leckie, David John ....Chicago, IL
Leckie, E. Loyd ....Fairmont, WV
Leckie, Elizabeth A. ....New York, NY
Leckie, J. Scott ....Washington, PA
Leckie, Lisa ....Helena, MT
Leckie, V. Joe ....Billings, MT
Lecklider, Timothy A. ....Columbus, OH
Lecklikner, Jan M. ....San Francisco, CA
Leckman, Henry T. ....Coalinga, CA
Leckman, Terry K. ....Mc Keesport, PA
Pittsburgh, PA
Leckow, Derek W. ....Chicago, IL
Leckrone, Daniel E. (IBA) ....San Jose, CA
Leckrone, James David ....Nashville, TN
Leckrone Law Corporation ....San Jose, CA
Leckstein, Michael R. ....Little Silver, NJ
Leckszas, Manfred W. ....Baltimore, MD
Lecky, Paul S. ....Oakland, CA
Lecky, Robert J. ....New Brunswick, NJ
Le Clainche, Janice ....West Palm Beach, FL
LeClainche, Stephan A.
North Palm Beach, FL
LeClair, Brian A. ....New London, CT
Le Clair, Brian J. ....St. Paul, MN
LeClair, Brian W. ....Boston, MA
LeClair, Gary D. ....Richmond, VA
LeClair, L. Richard ....Waltham, MA
LeClair, Lawrence ....Elmira, NY
LeClair, Leon R., Jr. ....Waltham, MA
LeClair, Lewis Titus ....Dallas, TX
LeClair, Malena R. ....Santa Ana, CA
Leclair, Mark F. ....Springfield, MA
Leclair, Paul L. ....Rochester, NY
LeClair, Quinn Scimone, Noonan & Connors
Waltham, MA
LeClair, Rachael A. ....Lenoir, NC
Le Clair, Robert J. ....Honolulu, HI

LeClair Ryan, A Professional Corporation
Alexandria, VA
Blacksburg, VA
Charlottesville, VA
Glen Allen, VA
Norfolk, VA
Richmond, VA
LeClair, Stephen A. ....Hollywood, FL
Leclair, Thomas J. ....Columbia, SC
LeClaire, Charles J. ....Pittsburgh, PA
LeClaire & Griewahn, L.L.C. ....Pittsburgh, PA
LeClaire, John R., (P.C.) ....Boston, MA
LeClaire, Sarah E. ....Presque Isle, ME
Leclaire, Stephanie ....New York, NY
LeClaire, Thomas L. ....Washington, DC
LeClair-Sommer, Cheryl ....Minneapolis, MN
LeClerc, Bryan L. ....Bridgeport, CT
Le Clerc, Desiree ....Redwood City, CA
Leclerc, Jeffrey L. ....Minneapolis, MN
St. Paul, MN
Leclerc, Lawrence A. ....Fargo, ND
LeClerc & LeClerc ....Oroville, CA
Le Clerc, Mark C. ....Walnut Creek, CA
LeClerc, Michel C. ....Redding, CA
LeClerc, Raoul J. ....Oroville, CA
Le Clercq, Ben Whaley ....Charleston, SC
LeClercq, Frederic S. ....Knoxville, TN
Le Clercq, Frederic Theodore
Metairie, LA
LeClere, David A. ....Baton Rouge, LA
LeClere Law Firm ....Baton Rouge, LA
Leclere, Roger F. H. ....Esmont, VA
Lecocke, Suzanne E. ....Houston, TX
LeColst-Johnston, Michelle
Los Angeles, CA
LeCompte, Charles M. ....Rogersville, MO
Le Compte, James W., II ....Cassville, MO
Le Compte, James W., II, P.C.
Cassville, MO
LeCompte, Morris A. ....St. Petersburg, FL
LeCompte, Morris A., P.A.
St. Petersburg, FL
LeCompte, Norman J., Jr. ....Eugene, OR
Lecomte, Emanuelson, Motejunas & Doyle
Boston, MA
Quincy, MA
Providence, RI
Lecomte, John E. ....Quincy, MA
LeComte, John R. ....Savanna, IL
LeComte, Samantha R. ....Pittsburgh, PA
LeCoq, Mark M. ....Portland, OR
LeCoque, Alain G. ....Chicago, IL
LeCorgne, Livaudais & Baus, A Professional Corporation ....New Orleans, LA
LeCorgne, R. Parker ....New Orleans, LA
LeCount, Lori ....St. Paul, MN
Lecount-McClanahan, Sonya A.
Morristown, NJ
LeCouris, Leah C. ....St. Petersburg, FL
LeCours, Alan R. ....Saratoga Springs, NY
LeCours, Brian R. ....Albany, NY
LeCover, Michael ....Grover City, CA
LeCraw, Linda L. ....Washington, DC
LeCren, Pamela E.F.
Federal Deposit Insurance Corporation, Regulation and Legislation Section, GV
LeCrone, Adam B. ....Sherman, TX
LeCrone, Douglas C. ....Covina, CA
Le Crone, Hayward P. ....Santa Ana, CA
LeCrone, John P. ....Los Angeles, CA
LeCrone, Laura D. ....Sherman, TX
LeCrone, Noel B. ....Waco, TX
LeCrone, William M. ....Chicago, IL
LeCroy, Charles L., III ....Glendale, CA
LeCroy, Daryl G. ....Atlanta, GA
Le Croy, David P. ....San Antonio, TX
Lecroy, Mark A. ....Morganton, NC
LeCroy-Schemel, Cynthia A.
Chattanooga, TN
Lecso, Madeleine L. ....Bedford, OH
L'Ecuyer, Eleanor C. ....Ruskin, FL
L'Ecuyer, Paul A. ....Honolulu, HI
LeCuyer, Stephen T. ....Shiprock, NM
Lecznar, Robert H. ....New Port Richey, FL
Ledahl, Brian D. ....Los Angeles, CA
Ledakis, James M. ....Los Angeles, CA
San Diego, CA
Ledakis, Sherry L. ....San Diego, CA
Ledbetter & Associates ....Englewood, CO
Ledbetter & Associates, Ltd. ....Harrison, AR
Ledbetter, Beverly E. ....Providence, RI
Ledbetter, Bill ....Gainesville, TX
Ledbetter & Buck ....Cookeville, TN
Ledbetter, Bureon E., Jr. ....Atlanta, GA
Ledbetter, Calvin R., Jr. ....Little Rock, AR
Ledbetter, Charles C. ....Denver, CO
Ledbetter, Charles R. ....Fort Smith, AR
Ledbetter, Charles R. ....Denver, CO
Ledbetter, Cogbill, Arnold & Harrison, LLP
Bentonville, AR
Fayetteville, AR
Fort Smith, AR
Harrison, AR
Mena, AR
Russellville, AR
Texarkana, AR
Ledbetter, David G. ....Caledonia, MI
Ledbetter, David Lee ....Waynesboro, VA
Ledbetter, David O. ....Richmond, VA
Ledbetter, David W. ....Cookeville, TN
Ledbetter, Don W. ....Dallas, TX
Ledbetter, Don W., PLLC ....Dallas, TX
Ledbetter, Edwin ....Savannah, TN
Ledbetter, Fred F., Jr. ....Birmingham, AL
Ledbetter, Garry D., Jr. ....Los Angeles, CA
Ledbetter, George H. ....Danielsville, GA
Ledbetter, H. J. "Jay", Jr. ....Englewood, CO
Ledbetter, Jack W. ....Austin, TX

Ledbetter, Jack W. & Associates, P.C.
Austin, TX
Ledbetter, James D. ....Southfield, MI
Ledbetter, James E. ....Cottonwood, AZ
Flagstaff, AZ
Sedona, AZ
Ledbetter, James E. ....Washington, DC
Ledbetter, James F. ....Calhoun, GA
Ledbetter, Janet L. ....Troy, MI
Ledbetter, Jeffrey L. ....Evansville, IN
Ledbetter, Jeffrey Taylor ....Asheville, NC
Ledbetter, John N. ....Boynton Beach, FL
Ledbetter, John N.C. ....Destin, FL
Ledbetter, Judith F. ....Williamsburg, VA
Ledbetter, Judy M. ....St. Louis, MO
Ledbetter, Larry D. ....Atlanta, GA
Ledbetter, Little & Smith ....Calhoun, GA
Ledbetter, Lloyd S. ....Chattanooga, TN
Ledbetter, Melisa G. ....Harrisonburg, VA
Ledbetter, Michael R. ....Santa Barbara, CA
Ledbetter, P. Mark, (P.A.) ....Memphis, TN
Ledbetter, Richard J. ....San Diego, CA
Ledbetter, Samuel E. ....Little Rock, AR
Ledbetter, Steven K. ....Los Angeles, CA
Ledbetter, Thomas D. ....Harrison, AR
Ledbetter, Thomas Larry ....Memphis, TN
Ledbetter, V. Elizabeth
Corpus Christi, TX
Ledbetter, W. Dale ....Houston, TX
Ledbetter, William H., Jr.
Bossier City, LA
Ledbetter, William H., Jr. ....Spotsylvania, VA
Ledden, C. Earl ....Pulaski, NY
Ledden, Collette A. ....Costa Mesa, CA
Ledden, Jay H. ....Baldwinsville, NY
Ledden Law Offices ....Baldwinsville, NY
Leddin, Brian J. ....Newark, NJ
Ledding, Mary S. ....Universal City, CA
Leddy, Albert M. ....Los Osos, CA
Leddy, Alexander ....Portland, ME
Leddy, Bruce E. ....Portland, ME
Leddy, Daniel D., Jr. ....Staten Island, NY
Leddy, Edward F. ....Wesley Chapel, FL
Leddy, Francis J., Jr. ....Wayne, NJ
Leddy, James F. ....Los Osos, CA
Leddy, John F. ....Minneapolis, MN
Leddy, John H. ....Philadelphia, PA
Leddy, John T. ....Burlington, VT
Leddy, Lorey Rives ....Stamford, CT
Leddy, Mark ....Washington, DC
Leddy, Patrick J. ....New York, NY
Leddy, Patrick J. ....Cleveland, OH
Leddy, Robert Carten ....Saginaw, MI
Ledebur, Joan B. ....Alexandria, VA
Ledebur, Lawrence F. ....Alexandria, VA
Ledecky, David ....Washington, DC
Leder, Amy Serper ....New York, NY
Leder, Andrew R. ....New York, NY
Leder, Bruce D. ....Kenilworth, NJ
Leder, Charles P. ....Denver, CO
Leder, Deborah ....Miami, FL
Leder, Debra M. ....Miami, FL
Leder, Howard ....New York, NY
Leder, Karen R. ....Sacramento, CA
Leder, Mark R. ....Waterbury, CT
Leder, Nathan I. ....Miami, FL
Leder, Paul A. ....Washington, DC
New York, NY
Leder, Richard M. ....New York, NY
Leder, Steven E. ....Baltimore, MD
Leder, William T. ....Floral Park, NY
Lederach, James S. ....Scottdale, PA
Lederberg, Michael S. ....Miami, FL
Lederberg, Tobias M. ....Providence, RI
Lederberg, Victoria ....Providence, RI
Lederer, Amy B. ....Hartford, CT
Lederer, Ann E. ....Santa Monica, CA
Lederer, Brian J. H. ....Washington, DC
Lederer, Bruce C. ....Brooklyn, NY
Lederer, Calvin M. .....Department of the Army, Office of the Judge Advocate General, GV
Lederer, Caren A. ....Chicago, IL
Lederer, Courtney A. ....New York, NY
Lederer, David J. ....Los Angeles, CA
Lederer, Elizabeth J. ....New York, NY
Lederer, Eugene G. ....Beverly Hills, CA
Lederer, Eugene W. ....State College, PA
Lederer, Fredric I. ....Williamsburg, VA
Lederer, George W. ....Houston, TX
Lederer, George W., Jr. ....Houston, TX
Lederer, Gregory M. ....Cedar Rapids, IA
Lederer, Howard Michael
Huntingdon Valley, PA
Lederer, Irvin ....New York, NY
Lederer, Jan Perry ....San Antonio, TX
Lederer, Joel O. ....Port Charlotte, FL
Lederer, John B. ....Dallas, TX
Lederer, John H. ....Madison, WI
Lederer, Karen F. ....New York, NY
Lederer, Karen S. ....Bronx, NY
Lederer, Lawrence J. ....Philadelphia, PA
Lederer, Les E. ....Los Angeles, CA
Lederer, Les E, A Professional Law Corporation ....Los Angeles, CA
Lederer, Leslie T. ....Chicago, IL
Lederer, Margaret E. ....Orlando, FL
Lederer, Margaret E., P.A. ....Orlando, FL
Lederer, Michael L. ....New York, NY
Lederer, Paul R. ....Glencoe, IL
Lederer, Peter D. ....New York, NY
Lederer, Philip C. ....Chicago, IL
Lederer, Robert A. ....Downers Grove, IL
Lederer, Robert D. ....Altus, OK
Lederer, Steven L. J.
North Miami Beach, FL
Lederer, Stuart R. ....Mahwah, NJ
Lederer, Susan E. ....Hershey, PA
Lederer, William J. ....Wheeling, IL

Lederer, William M. ....Greenville, NC
Lederer, Wm. J. ....Philadelphia, PA
Lederhouse, Rebecca B. ....Chicago, IL
Lederkramer, David M. ....New York, NY
Lederle, Neal P. ....New York, NY
Lederleitner, Joseph B. ....Chicago, IL
Lederman, Alan S., (P.A.) ....Miami, FL
Lederman, Andrew P. ....New York, NY
Lederman, Andrew P., P.C. ....New York, NY
Lederman, Barbara W. ....Shaker Heights, OH
Lederman, Bonnie G. ....Chicago, IL
Lederman, Bruce H. ....New York, NY
Lederman, Bruce N. ....New York, NY
Lederman, Bruce R. ....Los Angeles, CA
Lederman, Charles O. ....White Plains, NY
Lederman, David E. ....Los Angeles, CA
Lederman, David M. ....Walnut Creek, CA
Lederman, David P. ....Miami, FL
Lederman, Diane E. ....New York, NY
Lederman, Georges G. ....New York, NY
Lederman, Gordon ....Washington, DC
Lederman & Graves, LLP ....New York, NY
Lederman, Harold N. ....Massapequa, NY
Lederman, Henry D. ....Walnut Creek, CA
Lederman, Herman ....New York, NY
Lederman, Ira S. ....Greenwich, CT
Lederman, Irving I. ....Brooklyn, NY
Lederman, Jeanine Emily
West Palm Beach, FL
Lederman, Jeffrey J. ....Palo Alto, CA
Lederman, Jonathan L. ....New York, NY
Lederman, Kevin ....Seattle, WA
Lederman, Lawrence ....New York, NY
Lederman, Leslie Anne ....Sacramento, CA
Lederman, Linda ....Bridgeport, CT
Lederman, Martin S. ....Department of Justice, Office of Legal Counsel, GV
Lederman, Maury E. ....Boston, MA
Lederman, Michael J. ....Mission Viejo, CA
Lederman, Peter H. ....Piscataway, NJ
Lederman, Peter H., P.A. ....Piscataway, NJ
Lederman, Phyllis R. ....Staten Island, NY
Lederman, Pia Rebecca Desiree
Department of Education, Office of the General Counsel, GV
Lederman, Rachel ....San Francisco, CA
Lederman, Robert Elliot ....Coral Gables, FL
Lederman, Robert J. ....Tucson, AZ
Lederman, Ronald S. ....Southfield, MI
Lederman, Russell F. ....Minneapolis, MN
Lederman, Sander S. ....Brockton, MA
Lederman, Scott J. ....Chicago, IL
Lederman, Sema E. ....Chapel Hill, NC
Lederman, Sheryl R. ....West Bloomfield, MI
Lederman, Steven F. ....Virginia Beach, VA
Lederman, Stuart M. ....Morristown, NJ
Lederman, Thomas C.
Department of Justice, Civil Division, GV
Ledermann, David J. ....Tampa, FL
Ledesma, Bruce R. ....Berkeley, CA
Ledesma & Diaz ....Union City, NJ
Ledesma, Hector ....Chicago, IL
Ledesma, Jose Joaquin ....Washington, DC
Ledesma, Luis, Jr. ....Angleton, TX
Le Desma, Michael G.
Environmental Protection Agency, Office of the General Counsel, GV
Ledesma, Oscar U. ....Union City, NJ
Ledesma, Randel L. ....Beverly Hills, CA
Ledesma-Gonzalez, Rosa Lilia ....McAllen, TX
Ledesma-Mouzon, Linda
Woodland Hills, CA
Ledet, Craig J. ....Houston, TX
Ledet, Edei Pippin ....Atlanta, GA
Ledet, Eugene A., Jr. ....Alexandria, LA
Ledet, Marc ....Houston, TX
Ledet, Rosemary ....New Orleans, LA
Ledet, Zacharias ....San Jose, CA
LeDew, Andrea Wiegel ....Jacksonville, FL
Ledewitz, Bruce S. ....Pittsburgh, PA
Ledford, Bob A. ....Morganton, NC
Ledford, Brent R. ....Redding, CA
Ledford, Clara J. ....Ontario, CA
Ledford, Connie ....Greenville, SC
Ledford & Edwards ....Morganton, NC
Ledford, Edwin D. ....Cumming, GA
Ledford, George W. ....Englewood, OH
Ledford, J. Patrick ....Kingsport, TN
Ledford, James F. ....Baton Rouge, LA
Ledford, James W. ....Ormond Beach, FL
Ledford, John W. ....Charleston, SC
Ledford, Joseph L. ....Charlotte, NC
Ledford, Julie Ann ....London, KY
Ledford, Kenneth F. ....Cleveland, OH
Ledford, Kris T. ....Tulsa, OK
Ledford Law Corporation ....Visalia, CA
Ledford, Lee B. ....Putnam Valley, NY
Ledford, Lynn M. ....Brea, CA
Ledford, M. Leonard ....Greenville, SC
Ledford, Mayfield and Ogle
Ormond Beach, FL
Ledford, Merl, III ....Visalia, CA
Ledford & Murray, P.C. ....Charlotte, NC
Ledford, Pamela J. ....Louisville, KY
Ledford, Paul A. ....Minneapolis, MN
Ledford, Paul B. ....Vincennes, IN
Ledford, Paul B., Professional Corporation
Vincennes, IN
Ledford, Thomas G. ....Albany, GA
Ledford, Todd Brown ....Greenville, SC
Ledgard, John F. ....San Rafael, CA
Ledger & Associates ....Carlsbad, CA
Los Angeles, CA
Newport Beach, CA
San Diego, CA
Ledger, Brett Emery ....Carlsbad, CA
Los Angeles, CA
Newport Beach, CA

Ledger, Brett Emery—Continued
San Diego, CA
Ledger, Brian M. ....San Diego, CA
Ledger, Darrell J. ....St. Paul, MN
Ledger, David Patrick ....Hagåtña, GU
Ledger, William D. ....Newport Beach, CA
Ledger, William Steele ....Palm Springs, CA
Ledgerwood, Deborah A. ....Belleville, IL
St. Louis, MO
Ledgerwood, Ronald K. ....Denver, CO
Ledgerwood, Steven T.
Oklahoma City, OK
Ledgerwood, Thomas D. ....Norman, OK
Ledgerwood, Thomas L. ....Clarkston, WA
Ledgerwood, Thomas P. ....Bloomington, IL
Ledgewood Law Firm, A Professional Corporation ....Philadelphia, PA
Ledgin, David H. ....Mineola, NY
Ledgin, Elana Gol ....Mineola, NY
Ledic, Helena M. ....St. Paul, MN
Ledig, Kathryn A. ....Washington, DC
Fairfax, VA
Ledig, Robert H. ....Washington, DC
Ledin & Hofstad ....Hinckley, MN
Pine City, MN
Ledin, Howard N. ....Hinckley, MN
Pine City, MN
Ledin, Robert N. ....Iron River, WI
Ledin, Steven J. ....St. Paul, MN
Ledin, Steven J. ....Superior, WI
Ledina, Burton ....Monticello, NY
Ledingham, T.M. ....Las Vegas, NV
Le, Dirksen, Flipse & Doran ....Seattle, WA
Ledley, James R. ....New York, NY
Ledlin, Ian ....Spokane, WA
Ledman, David E. ....Willoughby Hills, OH
Ledman & Hamm, P.A. ....Panama City, FL
Ledman, James H. ....Columbus, OH
Ledman, Thomas W. ....Panama City, FL
Ledner, Sherri L. ....Washington, DC
Lednicer, Oliver ....New York, NY
Lednick, Joseph E., Jr. ....Dallas, TX
Ledo, Michele A. ....Philadelphia, PA
Ledogar, Edward J. ....West Islip, NY
Ledogar, Frederick G. ....Rocky Point, NY
Ledogar, Leslie W. ....Camden, NJ
Philadelphia, PA
Ledogar, Stephen J. ....Department of State, Foreign Service Officers (Overseas), GV
LeDonne, Eugene ....New York, NY
LeDonne, James J. ....New Haven, CT
Le Donne, Nancy White ....New York, NY
Ledoux, Amy E. ....Washington, DC
Ledoux, Bruce G. ....Marlborough, MA
Ledoux, Conrad C. ....Washington, DC
LeDoux, Dean A. ....Minneapolis, MN
LeDoux, Gabrielle R. ....Kodiak, AK
Ledoux, Josette Marie ....Houston, TX
LeDoux & LeDoux ....Kodiak, AK
Ledoux, Robert A. ....Salem, MA
Ledoux, Stephen R. ....San Francisco, CA
LeDoux, William J. ....Worcester, MA
Le Doux, William M. ....Boston, MA
Ledray, Patrick W. ....Fridley, MN
Ledridge, Sam H. ....La Grande, OR
Ledsinger, Jere ....Manchester, TN
Ledsky, Jonathan N. ....Chicago, IL
LeDu, Bradley J. ....San Ramon, CA
LeDuc, Charles H. ....International Falls, MN
LeDuc, Denis R. ....Mount Clemens, MI
LeDuc, Don ....Lansing, MI
LeDuc, Edward J. ....Department of Energy, Office of the General Counsel, GV
LeDuc, John André.........................Chicago, IL
LeDuc, Laura ....Norcross, GA
Leduc, Louise A. ....Boston, MA
LeDuc, Mark B. ....Augusta, ME
LeDuc, Robert J. ....Boston, MA
LeDuc, Susan L. ....Lansing, MI
Leduc, Thomas Charles ....Dearborn, MI
Leduc, Tracy E. ....St. Petersburg, FL
LeDuc, Vickie E. ....Annapolis, MD
Le Duy, Sharon A. ....San Francisco, CA
Ledva, Stephen, Jr. ....Philadelphia, PA
Ledward, Gail M. ....Mesa, AZ
Ledwidge, Chris P. ....Portland, OR
Ledwidge & Ledwidge ....Portland, OR
Ledwidge, Patrick J. ....Detroit, MI
Ledwidge, Patrick J. ....Portland, OR
Ledwidge, Paul M. ....Bloomfield Hills, MI
Ledwin, Mark G. ....White Plains, NY
Ledwith, James R. ....Berwyn, PA
Ledwith, John F. ....Philadelphia, PA
Ledwith, Peter K. ....Garden City, NY
Ledwitz, Wendi S. ....Springfield, NJ
Ledwon, Clarence H. ....Southfield, MI
Ledwon & Gardner ....Southfield, MI
Ledwon, Lenora P. ....Miami, FL
Ledy, Clayton Barry ....Wyoming, MI
Ledyard, David E. ....Avondale, AZ
Ledyard, David W. ....Beaumont, TX
Ledyard, Goodman G. ....Mobile, AL
Ledyard, Lewis C., III ....Wilmington, DE
Ledyard, Michael M. ....Wilmington, DE
Ledyard, Quitman R. ....Memphis, TN
Ledyard, Robert E., III ....Huntsville, AL
Ledyard, Robins H. ....Nashville, TN
Ledy-Gurren & Blumenstock, L.L.P.
New York, NY
Ledy-Gurren, Nancy ....New York, NY
Ledynh, Bot ....Department of Commerce, Patent and Trademark Office, GV
Lee, A. Mark ....Savannah, GA
Lee, A. Michael ....Atlanta, GA
Lee, A. Scott ....Wheaton, IL
Lee, Aaron A. ....Aiea, HI
Lee, Adam ....Honolulu, HI
Lee, Adams C. ....Washington, DC
Lee, Adele G. ....New York, NY
Lee, Adrian J. ....Salt Lake City, UT
Lee, Aileen A. ....Phoenix, AZ
Lee, Alan ....New York, NY
Lee, Alan ....Madison, WI
Lee, Alan C. ....Morristown, TN
Lee, Alan J. ....Newport News, VA
Lee, Alan M. ....Portland, OR
Lee, Albert, Law Offices of ....Pasadena, CA
Lee, Albert S. ....Philadelphia, PA
Lee, Albert S. ....Pittsburgh, PA
Lee, Alexander M. ....Palo Alto, CA
Lee, Alexandra H. ....White Plains, NY
Lee, Alexandra J. ....Chantilly, VA
Lee, Alexandria J. ....New York, NY
Lee, Alfred S. ....Carol Stream, IL
Lee, Alice F. ....Monroeville, AL
Lee, Alison Renee ....Columbia, SC
Lee, Alissa ....Menlo Park, CA
Lee, Allen ....San Francisco, CA
Lee, Allen ....Helena, MT
Lee, Allen C. ....Ingleside, TX
Lee, Allison B. ....Long Beach, CA
Lee, Allison H. ....Denver, CO
Lee, Amanda E. ....Seattle, WA
Lee & Amtzis, LLP ....Staten Island, NY
Lee, Amy E. ....Austin, TX
Lee, Amy J. ....Topeka, KS
Lee, Amy Toy ....San Francisco, CA
Lee, Amy Y. ....Washington, DC
Lee, Andrea White ....Richmond, VA
Lee, Andrew B. ....Los Angeles, CA
Lee, Andrew B. ....Washington, DC
Lee, Andrew H. ....Boston, MA
Lee, Andrew L. ....New York, NY
Lee, Andrew P. ....Minneapolis, MN
Lee, Andrew R. ....New Orleans, LA
Lee, Andrew R. ....Birmingham, MI
Lee, Angela ....New York, NY
Lee, Angela T. ....Bend, OR
Lee, Anita D. ....Los Angeles, CA
Lee, Ann On-Yee ....Dearborn, MI
Lee, Ann S. ....Los Angeles, CA
Lee, Anna ....Silver Spring, MD
Lee, Anna ....New York, NY
Lee, Anna Blackmon ....Bluefield, WV
Lee, Anna Chou ....New City, NY
Lee, Anson K. ....Hilo, HI
Lee, Anthony A. ....Paxton, IL
Lee, Anthony B. ....Johnson City, TN
Lee, Anthony K. ....San Francisco, CA
Lee, Anthony T. ....Rochester, NY
Lee, Antony H. ....New York, NY
Lee, Arlene F. ....Centreville, MD
Lee, Arlene V.H. ....Oakland, CA
Lee, Armon D., Jr. ....Aberdeen, MS
Lee, Art M. ....Denver, CO
Lee, Arthur I. ....Yorktown Heights, NY
Lee and Associates, P.C. ....Denver, CO
Lee, Audrey ....Los Angeles, CA
Lee, Austin M. ....Jenkintown, PA
Lee, Ayleen Ito ....Palo Alto, CA
Lee, B. Christopher ....Philadelphia, PA
Lee, Baldwin J. ....San Francisco, CA
Lee, Barbara A. ....New Brunswick, NJ
Lee, Barbara A. ....New York, NY
Lee, Barbara S. ....Johnstown, NY
Lee, Barry W. ....San Francisco, CA
Lee, Bartholomew ....San Francisco, CA
Lee, Belinda S. ....Los Angeles, CA
Lee, Benita ....Houston, TX
Lee, Benjamin ....Seattle, WA
Lee, Benjamin S. ....New York, NY
Lee, Benjamin T. ....Los Angeles, CA
Lee, Bennett J. ....McLean, VA
Lee, Benson ....Las Vegas, NV
Lee, Benson, and Associates, Ltd.
Las Vegas, NV
Lee, Bernadette Rocco ....New Orleans, LA
Lee, Bernard ....Philadelphia, PA
Lee, Bertha Claire ....Miami, FL
Lee, Betsy P. ....Department of Commerce, Patent and Trademark Office, GV
Lee, Betty L. ....Weirsdale, FL
Lee, Beverly H. ....Atlanta, GA
Lee, Bill Lann ....Department of Justice, Civil Rights Division, GV
Lee, Black, Scheer & Hart, P.C.
Savannah, GA
Lee, Bob H. ....San Jose, CA
Lee, Bobby Y. ....Rockville, MD
Lee, Bonda E. ....New York, NY
Lee, Bradford H. ....Oakland, CA
Lee, Brandy Murphy ....Birmingham, AL
Lee, Brendan M. ....Tampa, FL
Lee, Brian C. ....Washington, DC
Lee, Brian D. ....Fresno, CA
Lee, Brian D. ....Newark, NJ
Lee, Brian Donald ....Saratoga Springs, NY
Lee, Brian E. ....Lake Success, NY
Lee, Brian F. ....Owings Mills, MD
Lee, Brian J. ....Ocala, FL
Lee, Brian Kenneth ....Washington, DC
Lee, Brian P. ....Owings Mills, MD
Lee, Brian S. ....Los Angeles, CA
Lee, Brian Y. ....San Francisco, CA
Lee & Broussard ....Monroe, LA
Lee, Bruce A. ....Greensboro, NC
Lee, Bruce E. ....Billings, MT
Lee, Bryan E. ....Issaquah, WA
Lee, Bryan W. ....Austin, TX
Lee, Bucchino & Lee ....Omaha, NE
Lee & Burchett, P.A. ....Nokomis, FL
Sarasota, FL
Venice, FL
Lee, Burns & Cossell, LLP ......Indianapolis, IN
Lee, Burton ....Macon, GA
Lee, Byron G. ....Houston, TX
Lee, Byrum C., Jr. ....Denver, CO
Lee, Byung Min ....Portland, OR
Lee, Byung-Il ....New York, NY
Lee, C. Dixon, III ....Columbia, SC
Lee, C. Theodore ....Tucker, GA
Lee, Calvin ....Glenwood Springs, CO
Lee, Calvin A. ....New York, NY
Lee, Calvin B. T. ....Newark, NJ
Lee, Carl B., (P.C.) ....Dallas, TX
Lee, Carl D. ....Phoenix, AZ
Lee, Carl W. ....Belleville, IL
Lee, Carley D.
Equal Employment Opportunity Commission, Office of Federal Operations, GV
Lee, Carmen ....San Francisco, CA
Lee, Carol F. ....Washington, DC
Lee, Carol K. ....Red Wing, MN
Lee, Carol M. ....Honolulu, HI
Lee, Caroline S. ....Sherman Oaks, CA
Lee, Carolyn Joy ....New York, NY
Lee, Carolyn S. ....New York, NY
Lee, Cary L. ....Washington, DC
Lee, Caryl A. ....Santa Ana, CA
Lee, Catherine A. ....Portland, ME
Lee, Catherine A. ....Richmond, VA
Lee, Catherine L. ....Palo Alto, CA
Lee, Catherine M. ....Oakland, CA
Lee, Catherine W. ....Jackson, MS
Magee, MS
Lee, Celia Anne ....San Marcos, TX
Lee, Celia W. ....San Francisco, CA
Lee, Chaemin Michael ....Melville, NY
Lee, Cha-Hee Nagashima
Los Angeles, CA
Lee, Chak Yin ....New York, NY
Lee, Chan H. ....Whitehouse Station, NJ
Lee, Chandra T. ....Jackson, MS
Lee, Chanwoo ....Kew Gardens, NY
Lee, Charles A. ....Orinda, CA
Lee, Charles A., Jr. ....Clayton, MO
Lee, Charles B. ....Chattanooga, TN
Lee, Charles B., Jr. ....Charlotte, NC
Lee, Charles C. ....Los Angeles, CA
Lee, Charles D. ....Hutchinson, KS
Lee, Charles Dudley, Jr. ....San Diego, CA
Lee, Charles (Ed) ....Springfield, MO
Lee, Charles F. ....Novato, CA
Lee, Charles F. ....House of Representatives, Committee Legal Personnel, GV
Lee, Charles F. ....Roseburg, OR
Lee, Charles G., III ....Asheville, NC
Lee, Charles H. ....Willows, CA
Lee, Charles Hoon ....Chicago, IL
Lee, Charles J. ....Red Wing, MN
Lee, Charles M. ....Hackettstown, NJ
Lee, Charles M ....Bronx, NY
Lee, Charles S. ....New York, NY
Lee, Charles T. ....Stamford, CT
Lee, Charlie ....Vienna, VA
Lee, Charlotte C. ....New York, NY
Lee & Cheng ....New York, NY
Lee, Cherng-Tsong Mark ....New York, NY
Lee, Chester P. ....New York, NY
Lee, Chiao ....Chicago, IL
Lee, Chilton H. ....Palo Alto, CA
Lee, Chisoon ....Menlo Park, CA
Lee, Chou-Il ....Terre Haute, IN
Lee, Christina Burks, Law Offices
New York, NY
Lee, Christina Silva ....Roseland, NJ
Lee, Christine C. ....Fort Lauderdale, FL
Lee, Christine M. ....Washington, DC
Lee, Christopher A. ....Walnut Grove, CA
Lee, Christopher B. ....New York, NY
Lee, Christopher C. ....Beverly Hills, CA
Lee, Christopher D. ....Evansville, IN
Lee, Christopher J. ....Chicago, IL
Lee, Christopher Martin ....Baltimore, MD
Lee, Christopher N. ....Tarzana, CA
Lee, Christopher P. ....New York, NY
Lee, Christopher T. ....Lafayette, LA
Lee, Christopher T. ....Pittsburgh, PA
Lee, Chung H., Law Offices of ....Boston, MA
Lee, Cindy ....San Francisco, CA
Lee, Cindy S. ....Pasadena, CA
Lee, Claire Ervin ....San Francisco, CA
Lee, Clarice Parrish ....Los Angeles, CA
Lee, Claude L. ....Topeka, KS
Lee, Clendon H., Jr. ....United States Senate, Committee Legal Personnel, GV
Lee, Clinton W. ....Topeka, KS
Lee, Connie ....Boston, MA
Lee, Corinne ....Los Angeles, CA
Lee, Corrine H. ....San Francisco, CA
Lee, Craig M. ....Los Angeles, CA
Lee, Craig M. ....Pittsburgh, PA
Lee, Cristine ....Santa Ana, CA
Lee, Cyrus F. ....Wilson, NC
Lee, Dale W. ....Diboll, TX
Lee, Dale W., (Atty. At Law, A Law Corp.)
Honolulu, HI
Lee, Dan C. ....Pulaski, TN
Lee, Dan E. ....Minneapolis, MN
Lee, Dan M. ....Jackson, MS
Lee, Daniel F. S. ....Honolulu, HI
Lee, Daniel W. ....Greenville, GA
La Grange, GA
Lee, Daniel W., P.C. ....Greenville, GA
La Grange, GA
Lee, Dara A. ....Alexandria, MN
Lee, Darrell E. ....Vancouver, WA
Lee, Darren W. ....Eugene, OR
Lee, Darryl J. ....Salt Lake City, UT
Lee, Darryl J. ....Waukesha, WI
Lee, David A. ....Birmingham, AL
Lee, David A. ....Hanford, CA
Lee, David A. ....Department of Defense, Defense Legal Services Agency, GV
Lee, David A. ....Syracuse, NY
Lee, David A. ....Arlington, TX
Lee, David B. ....Washington, DC
Lee, David B. ....Plano, TX
Lee, David B., Jr. ....Orange Park, FL
Lee, David C. ....Menlo Park, CA
Lee, David C. ....Oakland, CA
Lee, David C. ....San Francisco, CA
Lee, David C. ....Naples, FL
Lee, David C. ....Knoxville, TN
Lee, David G. ....Sacramento, CA
Lee, David H. ....Boston, MA
Lee, David H. C. ....Honolulu, HI
Lee, David H. C. ....Chicago, IL
Lee, David J. ....Inglewood, CA
Lee, David J. ....Lake Forest, CA
Lee, David J. ....Boulder, CO
Lee, David J. ....Boise, ID
Lee, David J. ....Pontiac, MI
Lee, David K. ....Indianapolis, IN
Lee, David L., Law Offices of ......Chicago, IL
Leawood, KS
Lee, David M. ....New York, NY
Lee, David O. ....Bismarck, ND
Lee, David P. ....Irvine, CA
Lee, David P. ....Washington, DC
Lee, David R. ....Menlo Park, CA
Lee, David R. ....Albuquerque, NM
Lee, David S. ....Orange, CA
Lee, David S. ....New York, NY
Lee, David S. ....Arlington, VA
Lee, David V. ....Los Angeles, CA
Lee, David W. ....Monterey Park, CA
Lee, David W. ....St. Petersburg, FL
Lee, David W. ....Richfield, MN
Lee, David W. ....Oklahoma City, OK
Lee, David W., P.A. ....St. Petersburg, FL
Lee, Deanna ....Los Angeles, CA
Lee, Debbie Ling ....Los Angeles, CA
Lee, Deborah ....Atlanta, GA
Lee, Deborah A. ....San Francisco, CA
Lee, Deborah T. ....Los Angeles, CA
Lee, Debra L. ....Washington, DC
Lee, Deidre W. ....Fairhope, AL
Lee, Denis ....Honolulu, HI
Lee, Denise A. ....Cupertino, CA
Lee, Dennis A. ....San Francisco, CA
Lee, Dennis E. ....Kansas City, MO
Lee, Dennis K. ....Chicago, IL
Lee, Dennis P. ....Omaha, NE
Lee, Dennis Y. ....Portola Valley, CA
Lee, Desmond C. ....Los Angeles, CA
Lee, Dewey ....Poughkeepsie, NY
Lee, Diana C. ....Framingham, MA
Lee, Diana J. ....New York, NY
Lee, Diana Jessup ....Santa Barbara, CA
Lee, Diana L. ....San Francisco, CA
Lee, Diane M. L. ....San Francisco, CA
Lee, Dick ....Sarasota, FL
Lee, Dick R. ....Miami, FL
Lee, Dickson C. H. ....Honolulu, HI
Lee, Dina C. ....New York, NY
Lee, Dolly M. ....Mountain View, CA
Lee, Don R. ....Shelby, MT
Lee, Donald ....Los Angeles, CA
Lee, Donald B. ....Scarsdale, NY
Lee, Donald D. ....Arlington, TX
Lee, Donald E. ....Bellefonte, PA
State College, PA
Lee, Donald E., Jr. ....Virginia Beach, VA
Lee, Donald H. ....Bogalusa, LA
Lee, Donald J. ....Pittsburgh, PA
Lee, Donald R., Jr. ....Richmond, VA
Lee, Donald S. ....Washington, DC
Lee, Donald W. (Fred) ....Albany, GA
Lee, Donna ....New York, NY
Lee, Donna A. ....Los Angeles, CA
Lee, Donna David ....Long Beach, CA
Lee, Donna H. ....Denver, CO
Lee, Donna H. ....New York, NY
Lee, Donna M. ....Raleigh, NC
Lee, Donna Wright ....Baton Rouge, LA
Lee, Doreen ....Boston, MA
New York, NY
Lee, Dorothy L. ....Coronado, CA
Lee, Douglas A.
Administrative Office Of The United States Courts, GV
Lee, Douglas D. ....Springfield, MO
Lee, Douglas E. ....Dixon, IL
Lee, Douglas E., Law Offices of ......Decatur, IL
Lee, Douglas G. ....Charleston, WV
Lee, Douglas J. ....Placentia, CA
Lee, Douglas M. ......Department of Commerce, Office of the General Counsel, GV
Lee, Douglas T. Y. ....Honolulu, HI
Lee, Duane R.
Administrative Office Of The United States Courts, GV
Lee, Duncan Rogers, II ....Upper Nyack, NY
Lee, Durocher, Kisner, Walker & Reid
Oklahoma City, OK
Lee, Dyana ....New York, NY
Lee, Eadon, Isgett and Powell, P.A.
Columbia, SC
Lee, Edmund S. ....Cincinnati, OH
Lee, Edquon ....Honolulu, HI
Lee, Edw. A. ....Attleboro, MA
Lee, Edward B. ....Englewood, CO
Lee, Edward B., III ....Pitcairn, PA
Lee, Edward F. ....San Jose, CA
Lee, Edward H. ....Savannah, GA
Lee, Edward H. ....Springfield, NJ
Lee, Edward J. ....Boston, MA
Lee, Edward J. ....Bloomfield Hills, MI
Lee, Edward J. ....Norwich, NY

Lee, Edward M. ....Westfield, MA
Lee, Edward M., Jr. ....Los Angeles, CA
Lee, Edward O. ....San Jose, CA
Lee, Edward O. ....Edmond, OK
Lee, Edward S. ....Washington, DC
Lee, Edward T. ....Palo Alto, CA
Lee, Edward U., III ....Towson, MD
Lee, Edward W. ....Los Angeles, CA
Lee, Edward Y. ....New Bern, NC
Lee, Edwin A. ....Paola, KS
Lee, Edwin P. ....Phoenix, AZ
Lee, Eileen C. ....Washington, DC
Silver Spring, MD
Lee, Elaine K. ....Chicago, IL
Lee, Elisa S. ....San Francisco, CA
Lee, Elizabeth C. ....Washington, DC
Lee, Elizabeth Haemi ....Honolulu, HI
Lee, Elizabeth Kwei-Lan ....San Francisco, CA
Lee, Elizabeth R. ....Jackson, MS
Lee, Ellen L. ....Gaithersburg, MD
Lee, Ellen Ma ....Los Angeles, CA
Lee, Ellen Moore ....Gibson City, IL
Lee, Ellin Jiyoung ....Oakland, CA
Lee, Elwyn C. ....Houston, TX
Lee & Emerson, LLP ....Norwich, NY
Lee, Emma H.C. ....New York, NY
Lee, Engel E. ....Seattle, WA
Lee, Eric ....Fort Lauderdale, FL
Lee, Eric G. ....San Francisco, CA
Lee, Eric H. M. ....United States Senate, Committee Legal Personnel, GV
Lee, Eric M. ....Franklin Lakes, NJ
Lee, Eric P., (P.C.) ....Salt Lake City, UT
Lee, Eric R. ....Minneapolis, MN
Lee, Ernest R. ....Jacksonville, NC
Lee, Erter, Wilson, Holler & Smith, L.L.C.
Bishopville, SC
Camden, SC
Kingstree, SC
Manning, SC
Sumter, SC
Lee, Esther Cohen ....Utica, NY
Lee, Euffi D. ....Los Angeles, CA
Lee, Eugene D. ....New York, NY
Lee, Eugene M. ....Washington, DC
Lee, Eugene T. ....New York, NY
Lee, Eugene Y. ....New York, NY
Lee, Eun Young (amy) ....San Francisco, CA
Lee, Eunice E. ....Boston, MA
Lee, Eva J. ....New York, NY
Lee, Evan T. ....San Francisco, CA
Lee, Evelyn C. ....San Francisco, CA
Lee, F. Drake, Jr. ....Shreveport, LA
Lee, F. Gordon ....Washington, DC
Lee & Fishman, LLP ....Boulder, CO
Denver, CO
Lee, Florence E. ....Bronx, NY
Lee, Francis X. ....Cincinnati, OH
Lee, Frank ....Beverly Hills, CA
Lee, Frank ....Sacramento, CA
Lee, Frank ....New York, NY
Lee, Frank E. ....Nashville, TN
Lee, Frank-Roy ....New York, NY
Lee, Freddie F. ....Bridgton, ME
Lee, Frederick D., (Mrs.) ....Ellabell, GA
Lee, Frederick H ....Minneapolis, MN
Lee, Futrell & Perles, L.L.P.
New Orleans, LA
Lee, G. Michael ....Challis, ID
Lee, G. Roger ....Boston, MA
Lee, G. Thomas ....Raleigh, NC
Lee, Garrett Jorgen ....Boston, MA
Lee, Garrett L. ....Washington, DC
Lee, Gary ....Philadelphia, PA
Lee, Gary A. ....New Orleans, LA
Lee, Gary B. K. T. ....Honolulu, HI
Lee, Gary E. ....Houston, TX
Lee, Gary H. ....Minot, ND
Lee, Gary J. ....Oakland, CA
Lee, Gary M. ....Norwood, MA
Lee, Gary S. ....New York, NY
Lee, Geena ....Sacramento, CA
Lee, Gene Ming ....New York, NY
Lee, Gene W. ....New York, NY
Lee, George D. ....Los Angeles, CA
Lee, George Evander ....Atlanta, GA
Lee, George I. ....Martinez, CA
Lee, George I. ....Chicago, IL
Lee, George K. C. ....New York, NY
Lee, George M. ....Stamford, CT
Lee, George T., III ....Houston, TX
Lee, George T., Jr., (P.C.) ....Dallas, TX
Lee, Georgette B. ....Naples, FL
Lee, Gerald A. ....White Plains, NY
Lee, Gerald Bruce ....Alexandria, VA
Lee, Gerald D. ....Springdale, AR
Lee, Gerald R. ....Pryor, OK
Lee, Gilbert W. ....Los Angeles, CA
Lee, Glenn M. ....Fruitland, ID
Lee, Goddard & Duffy LLP ....Irvine, CA
Lee & Gooch, P.C. ....Oklahoma City, OK
Lee, Gordon H. ....Jacksonville, FL
Lee, Grace H. ....Dedham, MA
Lee, Grace Kim ....San Diego, CA
Lee, Graham J. ....East Moline, IL
Lee, Gregory ....Washington, DC
Lee, Gregory A. ....Orange, CA
Lee, Gregory A. ....Topeka, KS
Lee, Gregory A. ....New York, NY
Lee, Gregory D. ....Orlando, FL
Lee, Gregory P. ....North Attleboro, MA
Lee, Gregory P. ....Houston, TX
Lee, Gregory & Sternberg, P.C.
Birmingham, MI
Lee, Gregory T. H. ....San Francisco, CA
Lee, Gwenn B. ....Albany, NY
Lee, H. Clifford ....Winter Park, FL

Lee, H. Greg ....Nokomis, FL
Sarasota, FL
Lee, H. Owen ....Columbus, GA
Lee, Hae-Joon Joseph ....New York, NY
Lee, Hancock & Lasitter, P.A.
New Bern, NC
Lee, Harold B. ....Van Nuys, CA
Lee, Harold Eugene ....Canoga Park, CA
Lee, Harold S. ....Chicago, IL
Lee, Harriet Whitman ....Berkeley, CA
Lee, Harry ....Washington, DC
Lee, Harry ....Metairie, LA
Lee, Harry F. ....Boston, MA
Lee, Harry M. ....Clinton, NC
Lee, Harry O. ....Troy, NY
Lee & Hayes, P.L.L.C. ....Spokane, WA
Lee, Hazel I. ....Denver, CO
Lee & Healy, L.L.P. ....El Paso, TX
Lee, Heather B. ....Sacramento, CA
Lee, Helen ....Lexington, MA
Lee, Helen C. ....Woodbridge, NJ
Lee, Helen C. ....Langhorne, PA
Lee, Helen Shores ....Birmingham, AL
Lee, Helena ....Brooklyn, NY
Lee, Helge K. ....Overland Park, KS
Lee, Henry ....Los Angeles, CA
Lee, Henry E. ....Sarasota, FL
Lee, Henry F. (Buddy), III ....Geneva, AL
Lee, Henry M. ....Los Angeles, CA
Lee, Henry P. ....Birmingham, MI
Lee, Herbert, Jr. ....Jackson, MS
Lee, Herman W.H. ....Honolulu, HI
Lee & Hollander ....Boston, MA
Lee, Hoon-Suk ....San Jose, CA
Lee, Hosoon ....Portland, OR
Lee, Howard C. ....Houston, TX
Lee, Howard C., Jr. ....Houston, TX
Lee, Howard E. ....West Orange, NJ
Lee, Hsiang-Lin Henry ....Gladstone, MO
Lee, Huey-Fun ....New York, NY
Lee, Hugh A. ....Rockingham, NC
Lee, Hugh H. ....Bushnell, FL
Lee, Hugh T. ....Dover, NH
Lee, Hugh W. ....Cerritos, CA
Lee, Hyang-Sook ....New York, NY
Lee, Hyeon ....New York, NY
Lee, In ....Palo Alto, CA
Lee, Ingram, III ....Houston, TX
Lee, In-Young ....New York, NY
Lee, Irwin ....San Diego, CA
Lee, J. Arthur, Jr. ....Atlanta, GA
Lee, J. Bachman ....Monroe, LA
Lee, J. Bachman, P.C. ....Monroe, LA
Lee, J. Gary ....Lexington, KY
Lee, J. Mark ....Lebanon, TN
Lee, J. Oliver, Jr. ....Dallas, TX
Lee, J. Rodney ....Waco, TX
Lee, J. Stan ....Lexington, KY
Lee, Jack B. ....San Antonio, TX
Lee, Jack H. ....Reno, NV
Lee, Jack P. ....Houston, TX
Lee, Jack W. ....San Francisco, CA
Lee, Jack W. ....Mason, TX
Lee, Jacob D. ....Beverly Hills, CA
Lee, Jacqueline C. ....Washington, DC
Lee, Jacquelyn I. ....Smithfield, NC
Lee, Jae ....Fort Lee, NJ
Lee, Jae K. ....New York, NY
Lee, Jae M. ....Honolulu, HI
Lee, Jae W. ....New York, NY
Lee, Jae Y. ....Los Angeles, CA
Lee, Jaeho ....New York, NY
Lee, James A. ....Port Washington, NY
Lee, James B. ....Salt Lake City, UT
Lee, James C. ....Los Angeles, CA
Lee, James C. ....Columbus, OH
Lee, James C. ....Chattanooga, TN
Lee, James C., P.C. ....Chattanooga, TN
Lee, James D. ....San Francisco, CA
Lee, James D. ....Tuscola, IL
Lee, James F. ....Binghamton, NY
Lee, James F., Jr. ....Washington, DC
Lee, James H. ....Fairfield, CT
Lee, James Henry ....Eagan, MN
Lee, James H. Q. ....Honolulu, HI
Lee, James J. ....Las Vegas, NV
Lee, James J. ....Kingsport, TN
Lee, James J. ....Dallas, TX
Lee, James J., P.C., Law Offices of
Las Vegas, NV
Lee, James K. ....Los Angeles, CA
Lee, James L ....Jackson, MS
Lee, James L. ....New York, NY
Lee, James M. ....Oakland, CA
Lee, James M. ....Newark, NJ
Lee, James Mitchell ....Los Angeles, CA
Lee, James N. ....Bunkie, LA
Lee, James P. ....Oakland, CA
Lee, James P. ....Houston, TX
Lee, James T. ....Covina, CA
Lee, James T. ....Bunkie, LA
Lee, James V. ....Redwood City, CA
Lee, James W. ....Oakhurst, CA
Lee, James W. ....Louisville, KY
Lee, James W., III ....Dallas, TX
Lee, James Y. ....New York, NY
Lee, Jameson ....Department of Commerce, Patent and Trademark Office, GV
Lee, Jamie F. ....Bennettsville, SC
Lee, Jane ....Valhalla, NY
Lee, Jane E. ....New York, NY
Lee, Jane M. ....Richmond, CA
Lee, Jane M. ....San Francisco, CA
Lee, Jane Y. ....Seattle, WA
Lee, Janet ....Palo Alto, CA
Lee, Jang W. ....Los Angeles, CA
Lee, Janice B. ....Los Angeles, CA
Lee, Janice M. ....New York, NY

Lee, Jas. W. ....Forest, MS
Lee, Jason E. ....Oakland, CA
Lee, Jason W. ....Kansas City, MO
Lee, Jay J. ....Riverside, CA
Lee, Jay Sung ....Hackensack, NJ
New York, NY
Lee, J. D. ....Biloxi, MS
Lee, J. D. ....Knoxville, TN
Lee, Jeannine L. ....Minneapolis, MN
Lee, Jeanny K. ....Washington, DC
Lee, Jeff M. ....Manhattan Beach, CA
Lee, Jeffrey A. ....Birmingham, AL
Lee, Jeffrey C. ....Pasadena, CA
Lee, Jeffrey F. ....San Francisco, CA
Lee, Jeffrey J. ....Charlotte, NC
Lee, Jeffrey K. ....Washington, DC
Lee, Jeffrey M. ....Los Angeles, CA
Lee, Jeffrica Jenkins ....Department of Justice, Civil Division, GV
Lee, Jennifer Davis ....Tulsa, OK
Lee, Jennifer H. ....Wheaton, IL
Lee, Jennifer M. ....Washington, DC
Lee, Jennifer S. ....Phoenix, AZ
Lee, Jenny ....Costa Mesa, CA
Lee, Jere R. ....Nashville, TN
Lee, Jerold W. ....Twin Falls, ID
Lee, Jerome E. ....Waukegan, IL
Lee, Jerome G. ....New York, NY
Lee, Jerry F. ....Union City, GA
Lee, Jessica ....Denver, CO
Lee, Jessica B. ....Pittsburgh, PA
Lee, Jim ....Ennis, TX
Lee, Jim D. ....Hanford, CA
Lee, Jim W. ....Oklahoma City, OK
Lee, Jimmie F. Y. ....Houston, TX
Lee, Jiyun Cameron ....Los Angeles, CA
San Francisco, CA
Lee, Jo Ann ....Houston, TX
Lee, Joan Sarles ....Portland, ME
Lee, Jocelyn ....Boston, MA
Lee, Joe ....Lexington, KY
Lee, Joe E. ....Emporia, KS
Lee, Joel S. ....Milwaukee, WI
Lee, Johann ....Detroit, MI
Lee, John ....Houston, TX
Lee, John A. ....Palm Springs, CA
Lee, John A. ....Pittsburgh, PA
Lee, John C. ....Los Angeles, CA
Lee, John D. ....Lisle, IL
Lee, John Doechung ....Las Vegas, NV
Lee, John Doechung, Chtd. ....Las Vegas, NV
Lee, John E. ....New Haven, CT
Lee, John E. ....Boonton, NJ
Lee, John E. ....Fayetteville, WV
Lee, John E., III ....Edmond, OK
Lee, John G. ....Coffeeville, MS
Lee, John H. ....Livermore, CA
Lee, John J. ....Asbury Park, NJ
Lee, John J. ....New York, NY
Lee, John J., Jr. ....New Orleans, LA
Lee, John J., Jr. ....Bronxville, NY
Lee, John J., Jr. ....Warwick, NY
Lee, John Jin ....San Francisco, CA
Lee, John Jody ....New York, NY
Lee, John Joseph ....St. Louis, MO
Lee, John K. ....Los Angeles, CA
Lee, John K. ....Greensboro, NC
Lee, John M. ....Atlanta, GA
Lee, John M. ....Minneapolis, MN
Lee, John M., Jr. ....Cleveland Heights, OH
Lee, John Michael ....San Fernando, CA
Lee, John Michael ....Fort Worth, TX
Lee, John N. ....Irvine, CA
Los Angeles, CA
Lee, John P. ....Attleboro, MA
Lee, John Penn ....Fresno, CA
Lee, John Peter ....Las Vegas, NV
Lee, John Peter, Ltd. ....Las Vegas, NV
Lee, John R. ....Williston, ND
Lee, John R. ....Lubbock, TX
Lee, John T. ....Fayetteville, AR
Siloam Springs, AR
Lee, John T. ....Fort Worth, TX
Lee, John V. ....Mobile, AL
Lee, John W., III ....Williamsburg, VA
Lee, John Y. ....Washington, DC
Lee, John Y. E. ....Chicago, IL
Lee, John Z. ....Chicago, IL
Lee, Johnny E. ....Morristown, NJ
Lee, Jo-Lynne Q. ....Oakland, CA
Lee, Jonathan D. ....Department of Justice, Antitrust Division, GV
Lee, Jonathan L. ....San Jose, CA
Lee, Jonathan U. ....San Francisco, CA
Lee, Jong ....New York, NY
Lee, Jong H. ....New York, NY
Lee, Joni A. ....Los Angeles, CA
Lee, Joseph ....Los Angeles, CA
Lee, Joseph ....Tampa, FL
Lee, Joseph A. ....Scottsboro, AL
Lee, Joseph C. ....New Haven, CT
Lee, Joseph C. ....Tulsa, OK
Lee, Joseph D. ....Los Angeles, CA
Lee, Joseph D. ....West Palm Beach, FL
Lee, Joseph D. ....Seattle, WA
Lee, Joseph Gerard ....Newark, NJ
Lee, Joseph H. ....Irvine, CA
Lee, Joseph, IV ....New York, NY
Lee, Joseph K., Jr. ....Aiea, HI
Lee, Joseph M. ....Lake Worth, FL
Lee, Joseph T. ....Long Beach, NY
Lee, Joseph W. ....Wittmann, AZ
Lee, Joy Namsil ....Newton, MA
Lee, Judith A. ....Washington, DC
Lee, Judith A. ....Albany, NY
Lee, Judy ....Los Angeles, CA
Lee, Judy Jade ....Houston, TX
Lee, Judy L. ....Los Angeles, CA

Lee, Judy Y. ....Honolulu, HI
Lee, Julia Eng ....Victoria, TX
Lee, Julia H. ....New York, NY
Lee, Jun Young ....Ellicott City, MD
Lee, Junell Y. K. ....Honolulu, HI
Lee, Junius B., III ....Whiteville, NC
Lee, K. Wayne ....Oklahoma City, OK
Lee, Kahala ....San Francisco, CA
Lee, Karen D. ....Flourtown, PA
Lee, Karen E. ....Cleveland, OH
Lee, Karen J. ....Irvine, CA
Lee, Karen K. ....San Francisco, CA
Lee, Karen M. ....Chicago, IL
Lee, Karen S. ....Bethesda, MD
Lee, Karen-Denise ....Los Angeles, CA
Lee, Karyn M. ....Washington, DC
Lee and Kaser, P.C. ....Roseburg, OR
Lee, Katherine C. ....Edison, NJ
New York, NY
Lee, Katherine D. ....Milwaukee, WI
Lee, Katherine J. ....Berkeley, CA
Lee, Katherine K. ....New York, NY
Lee, Katherine Markheim ....Denver, CO
Lee, Kathie S. ....Parsippany, NJ
Lee, Kathleen E. ....Berwyn, PA
Lee, Kathleen I. ....Indianapolis, IN
Lee, Kathleen K. ....Cincinnati, OH
Lee, Kathleen M. ....Roseland, NJ
Lee, Kathryn E. ....Washington, DC
Lee, Kathryn E. ....Atlanta, GA
Lee, Kathryn K. ....Rochester, NY
Lee, Kathy Ann ....Indianapolis, IN
Lee, Kay Lynn ....Encino, CA
Lee, Keith A. ....Oakland, CA
Lee, Keith L. ....Reno, NV
Lee, Keith L., A Prof. Corp., Law Offices of
Reno, NV
Lee, Kelly L. ....Parkersburg, WV
Lee, Kelly Tipton ....Prattville, AL
Lee, Kelvin K. ....Sacramento, CA
Lee, Ken K. ....Santa Clara, CA
Lee, Kenneth ....Tucson, AZ
Lee, Kenneth D. ....San Jose, CA
Lee, Kenneth E. ....Carbondale, PA
Lee, Kenneth G. ....Washington, DC
Lee, Kenneth H. ....San Francisco, CA
Lee, Kenneth J. ....Phoenix, AZ
Lee, Kenneth James ....Washington, DC
Lee, Kenneth W. ....Pittsburgh, PA
Lee, Kent D. ....Phoenix, AZ
Lee, Kevin F. ....Austin, TX
Lee, Kevin L. ....Treasury Department, Office of the Comptroller of the Currency, GV
Lee, Kevin M.
Environmental Protection Agency, Office of the General Counsel, GV
Lee, Kevin T. ....Chicago, IL
Lee, Kevin W. ....Pittsburgh, PA
Lee, Kilkelly, Paulson & Younger, S.C.
Madison, WI
Lee, Kim Walters ....Colorado Springs, CO
Lee, Kim, Wong, Yee & Lau, Attorneys at Law, A Law Corporation ....Honolulu, HI
Lee, Kimberly J. ....Tampa, FL
Lee, Kimberly Yvonne ....Los Angeles, CA
Lee, Kimuel W. ....Baton Rouge, LA
Lee, Konrad S. ....Crescent City, CA
Lee, Kristen Elizabeth ....Bingham Farms, MI
Lee, Kurt E. ....Sarasota, FL
Lee, Kyung S. ....Houston, TX
Lee, Kyungwon ....New York, NY
Lee, L. Joe ....Jackson, MS
Lee, L. Tennent, III ....Huntsville, AL
Lee, Lance ....Texarkana, TX
Lee, Lani M.
Securities and Exchange Commission, Division of Enforcement, GV
Lee, Lansing B., III ....Washington, DC
Lee, Lansing B., Jr. ....Augusta, GA
Lee, Larry C. Y. ....Honolulu, HI
Lee, Larry D. ....Boulder, CO
Lee, Larry M. ....Visalia, CA
Lee, Larry Mason, & Associates
Houston, TX
Lee, Larry S. ....San Francisco, CA
Lee, Laura Dickinson ....Schaumburg, IL
Lee, Laura K. ....Los Angeles, CA
Lee, Laura K. ....Los Angeles, CA
Lee, Laurens C. ....Fort Valley, GA
Lee, Laurie J.
Commodity Futures Trading Commission, Division of Enforcement, GV
Lee, Laurie Neilson ....Portland, OR
Lee, Lawrence B. ....Savannah, GA
Lee, Lawrence H. ....Fort Wayne, IN
Lee and Lee ....East Moline, IL
Lee & Lee ....New York, NY
Lee and Lee, Attorneys at Law, P.C.
Lebanon, TN
Lee, Lee & Garner ....Whiteville, NC
Lee, Lee & Lee ....Knoxville, TN
Lee and Lee Ltd. ....Tuscola, IL
Lee & Lee, P.A. ....Forest, MS
Lee & Lee, P.C. ....New York, NY
Lee, Lee & Young ....Mason, TX
Lee, Leeton H. ....Burbank, CA
Lee, Leighton, III ....Westbrook, CT
Lee, Leighton K. ....Honolulu, HI
Lee, Lena S. K. ....Baltimore, MD
Lee, Lenore H. ....Honolulu, HI
Lee, Leon H., Jr. ....Atlanta, GA
Lee, Leroy G. ....Miami, FL
Lee, Leslie Lien ....Lexington, MA
Lee, Leslie Staehle ....Jackson, MS
Lee, Levine & Bowser ....Boston, MA
Lee, Lewey K. ....Wise, VA
Lee, Lewis C. ....Spokane, WA

Lee, Linda L.
Federal Energy Regulatory Commission, Office of the General Counsel, GV
Lee, Linda Sue .... Los Angeles, CA
Lee, Lindsey .... Houston, TX
Lee, Lisa A. .... Indianapolis, IN
Lee, Lisa Ann .... Denver, CO
Lee, Lisa Ann .... Richmond, TX
Lee, Lisa S. .... Los Angeles, CA
Lee, Lisa W. .... Ventura, CA
Lee, Lloyd C. .... Oakland, CA
Lee, Lori Ann .... San Francisco, CA
Lee, Lori M. .... Department of Justice, Executive Office for Immigration Review, GV
Lee, Lorin, (Mr.) .... Tallahassee, FL
Lee, Lorraine .... New York, NY
Lee, Louis N. (Buddy), III .... Dallas, TX
Lee, Lucinda, Law Office of
San Francisco, CA
Lee, Lucy Fong .... San Francisco, CA
Lee, Lydia W. .... Los Angeles, CA
Lee, Lynch & Ford, P.C. .... Atlanta, GA
Lee, M. Carlson .... Fresno, CA
Lee, M. David .... Columbus, OH
Lee, M. Jean .... Charleston, SC
Lee, M. Patrice .... Knoxville, TN
Lee, M. Rhea .... Philadelphia, PA
Lee & MacMillan, P.A.
Saint Simons Island, GA
Lee, Madeleine T. .... Greenwood Village, CO
Lee, Madeline J. .... Alexandria, LA
Lee, Malcolm R.
Executive Office Of The President, Office of Policy Development, GV
Lee, Man .... New York, NY
Lee, Mandy J. .... San Francisco, CA
Lee, Mann, Smith, McWilliams, Sweeney & Ohlson .... Chicago, IL
Lee, Marcia .... Louisville, KY
Lee, Marcus S. .... Charlotte, NC
Lee, Marcus W. .... Birmingham, AL
Lee, Maren D. .... Washington, DC
Lee, Margaret Mikyung .... Library of Congress, Congressional Research Service, GV
Lee, Margaret S. .... New York, NY
Lee, Margery Q. .... Walnut Creek, CA
Lee, Marguerite .... Woodland Hills, CA
Lee, Marianne J. .... Chicago, IL
Lee, Maribod L. .... Oklahoma City, OK
Lee, Marie T. .... Boston, MA
Lee, Marietta S. .... Washington, DC
Lee, Marilyn K. .... Homer, IL
Lee, Marilyn Modarelli .... Greenfield, MA
Lee, Marina .... Old Saybrook, CT
Lee, Mark D. .... Paducah, KY
Lee, Mark J. .... Bellingham, WA
Lee, Mark R. .... Carbondale, IL
Lee, Mark Randolph .... Austin, TX
Lee, Mark S. .... Los Altos, CA
Lee, Mark S. .... Los Angeles, CA
Lee, Mark T. .... San Diego, CA
Lee, Mark T. .... Brooklyn, NY
Lee, Mark Tae .... Los Angeles, CA
Lee, Mark W. .... Minneapolis, MN
Lee, Marla Dena .... Fort Worth, TX
Lee, Marlene W. .... New Canaan, CT
Lee, Marron .... Las Cruces, NM
Lee, Martin, Green & Reiter, Inc.
Bellefonte, PA
State College, PA
Lee, Martin L. .... Newport Beach, CA
Lee, Martin R. .... New York, NY
Lee, Martin T. .... Los Angeles, CA
Lee, Martin V. .... Los Angeles, CA
Lee, Martiny & Caracci, A Professional Law Corporation .... Metairie, LA
Lee, Mary E. .... Burgaw, NC
Lee, Mary Ellen .... Oklahoma City, OK
Lee, Mary Jane .... New York, NY
Lee, Mary Latta .... Manchester, KY
Lee, Mary M. .... Los Angeles, CA
Lee, Mary M. .... Oklahoma City, OK
Lee, Mary S. .... Houston, TX
Lee, Matthew .... Bronx, NY
Lee, Matthew D. .... Department of Justice, Civil Division, GV
Lee, Matthew William .... Washington, DC
Fairfax, VA
Lee, Maureen A. .... Attleboro, MA
Lee, Maurice D., III .... New York, NY
Philadelphia, PA
Lee, Mavis K. .... Los Angeles, CA
Lee, Maxine Yi Hwa .... New York, NY
Lee, Maya S. .... Bakersfield, CA
Lee & McFarland .... Camden, NJ
Lee & McInish .... Dothan, AL
Lee & McShane, PC .... Washington, DC
Lee, Melinda L. .... Saddle River, NJ
Lee, Melissa J. .... Evanston, IL
Lee, Mervyn W. .... Honolulu, HI
Lee, Mervyn W., A Law Corporation
Honolulu, HI
Lee, Mi Young .... Detroit, MI
Lee, Michael .... Mission Hills, KS
Lee, Michael A. .... Washington, DC
Lee, Michael A. .... Houston, TX
Lee, Michael B. .... Monterey, CA
Mountain View, CA
Lee, Michael B. .... Houston, TX
Lee, Michael C. .... Chicago, IL
Lee, Michael D. .... Chicago, IL
Lee, Michael D. .... Poteau, OK
Lee, Michael E. .... Huntsville, AL
Lee, Michael E. .... Mountain View, CA
Lee, Michael E. .... Raleigh, NC
Lee, Michael E. .... Houston, TX
Lee, Michael G. .... Sacramento, CA
Lee, Michael G.
Environmental Protection Agency, Office of the General Counsel, GV
Lee, Michael G. W. .... San Francisco, CA
Lee, Michael H. .... Los Angeles, CA
Lee, Michael H. .... Concord, NH
Lee, Michael K. .... Southfield, MI
Lee, Michael Kuman .... Los Angeles, CA
Lee, Michael L. .... Detroit, MI
Lee, Michael P. .... Chicago, IL
Lee, Michael Quentin .... Washington, DC
Lee, Michael R., P.A. .... Hendersonville, NC
Lee, Michael S. .... Washington, DC
Lee, Michael S. .... Chicago, IL
Lee, Michael Stuart .... Corpus Christi, TX
Lee, Michael Stuart, A Professional Corporation
Corpus Christi, TX
Lee, Michael T. .... Owensboro, KY
Lee, Michael U. .... Duluth, GA
Lee, Michael V. .... Raleigh, NC
Lee, Michael W. .... Houston, TX
Lee, Michael W. .... Colonial Heights, VA
Lee, Michael W., Law Office of
Livingston, LA
Lee, Michel .... New York, NY
Lee, Michele .... Washington, DC
Lee, Michelle A. .... Greenville, MS
Lee, Michelle B. .... New York, NY
Lee, Michelle Hopkins .... Beverly Hills, CA
Lee, Michelle K. .... Palo Alto, CA
Lee, Mimi .... New York, NY
Lee, Mimi M. .... Los Angeles, CA
Lee, Minjoo .... New York, NY
Lee, Miriam A. .... Tampa, FL
Lee, Mitchell D. .... Washington, DC
Lee, Mitzi A. .... Honolulu, HI
Lee, Molly Prichitt .... Atlanta, GA
Lee, Mona A. .... Wilmington, DE
Lee, Monica D. .... Sunnyvale, CA
Lee, Monica R. .... Fremont, CA
Lee, Monika Pleyer .... San Francisco, CA
Lee, Montgomery .... Phoenix, AZ
Lee, Moon Soo .... Washington, DC
Lee, Myung J. .... Washington, DC
Lee, N. Genell .... Birmingham, AL
Lee, N. Joseph, III .... Bel Air, MD
Lee, N. Warner .... Phoenix, AZ
Lee, Namee .... Los Angeles, CA
Lee, Nancy A. .... Los Angeles, CA
Lee, Nancy C. .... Washington, DC
Lee, Nancy M. .... San Francisco, CA
Lee, Nancy P. .... Sacramento, CA
Lee, Nathaniel .... Indianapolis, IN
Lee, Neilda C. .... Department of Labor, Office of the Solicitor, GV
Lee, Nelson J. .... San Francisco, CA
Lee, Nelson M. .... Bunkie, LA
Lee, Nelson N. .... Los Angeles, CA
Lee, Nilane A., (A Professional Corporation)
Fullerton, CA
Lee, Nona M. .... Phoenix, AZ
Lee, Oliver .... Atlanta, GA
Lee, Otis L. .... Charlottesville, VA
Lee, Otto O. .... San Jose, CA
San Marino, CA
Lee, Pa Lai .... Fresno, CA
Lee, Padraic D. .... White Plains, NY
Lee, Parvin C., Jr. .... Pontiac, MI
Lee, Patrice .... Knoxville, TN
Lee, Patricia A. .... Chatham, NJ
Lee, Patricia Chung-Yen .... New York, NY
Lee, Patricia D. .... San Jose, CA
Lee, Patricia F. .... Palo Alto, CA
Lee, Patricia M. .... St. Petersburg, FL
Lee, Patricia M. .... New York, NY
Lee, Patricia Y. .... Washington, DC
Lee, Patricia Y. .... Honolulu, HI
Lee, Patrick A. .... New York, NY
Lee, Patrick W. .... Washington, DC
Lee, Paul .... Leesburg, FL
Lee, Paul A. .... Salem, OR
Lee, Paul B. .... St. Louis, MO
Lee, Paul E. .... Pasadena, CA
Lee, Paul L. .... New York, NY
Lee, Paul S. .... Atlanta, GA
Lee, Paul W. .... Columbus, OH
Lee, Paul W., (P.C.) .... Boston, MA
Lee, Paul Y. .... Los Angeles, CA
Lee, Paula H. .... New Orleans, LA
Lee, Paula R. .... San Francisco, CA
Lee, Paulette W. .... Burbank, CA
Lee, Pauline Ng .... Las Vegas, NV
Lee, Peter A., Law Offices of
Honolulu, HI
Lee, Peter D. .... Boston, MA
Lee, Peter K. .... Chicago, IL
Lee, Peter M. .... Fort Worth, TX
Lee, Peter S. .... Yarmouth, ME
Lee, Peter W. .... Trenton, NJ
Lee, Peter Y. .... Los Angeles, CA
Lee, Philip F., II .... Bronx, NY
Lee, Philip H. .... Palo Alto, CA
Lee, Philip J. .... Omaha, NE
Lee, Philip Nelson .... Los Angeles, CA
Lee, Philip W. .... Columbus, OH
Lee, Phillip P. .... Mountain View, CA
Lee and Phipps, P.C. .... Wise, VA
Lee, Phyllis M. .... Wilmington, NC
Lee, R. Hart .... Richmond, VA
Lee, R. John .... St. Johns, AZ
Lee, R. Joneal .... Warner Robins, GA
Lee, R. Kimbark .... Orlando, FL
Lee, R. Marilyn .... Los Angeles, CA
Lee, R. May .... New York, NY
Lee, R. Randy .... Staten Island, NY
Lee, R. Stephen .... Washington, DC
Lee, R. Winston .... Montgomery, AL
Lee, Raine .... Chapel Hill, NC
Lee, Ralph B. .... Sugar Land, TX
Lee, Ralph K., Jr. .... New Iberia, LA
Lee, Ralph S. .... Palo Alto, CA
Lee, Ralph V. .... Basking Ridge, NJ
Lee, Ralph W. .... West Babylon, NY
Lee, Randal J. .... Linden, TX
Lee, Randal Kwai On .... Honolulu, HI
Lee, Randall J. .... San Francisco, CA
Lee, Randall R. .... Los Angeles, CA
Lee, Randall W. .... Charlotte, NC
Lee, Randolph Marshall .... Charlotte, NC
Lee, Randy .... El Paso, TX
Lee, Randy H. .... Grand Forks, ND
Lee, Raymond .... Honolulu, HI
Lee, Raymond A. .... Irvine, CA
Lee, Raymond J. .... Seattle, WA
Lee, Raymond R. .... San Diego, CA
Lee, Raymond Victor .... Washington, DC
Lee, Rebecca A. .... Boston, MA
Lee, Reed .... Chicago, IL
Lee, Regina S. .... New York, NY
Lee, Renee M. .... Los Angeles, CA
Lee, Rhonda P. .... Philadelphia, PA
Lee, Richard A. .... Lake George, NY
Lee, Richard A. .... Portland, OR
Lee, Richard A. .... San Juan, PR
Lee, Richard D. .... Berkeley, CA
Lee, Richard D. .... Salem, OR
Lee, Richard E. .... Pineville, LA
Lee, Richard E. .... Baltimore, MD
Lee, Richard E. .... Darlington, MO
Lee, Richard F. .... Santa Barbara, CA
Lee, Richard H. .... Phoenix, AZ
Lee, Richard H. .... Phoenix, AZ
Lee, Richard H. .... Atlanta, GA
Lee, Richard H. .... Bethesda, MD
Lee, Richard J. .... Los Angeles, CA
Lee, Richard J. .... Oakland, CA
Lee, Richard J. .... Coral Gables, FL
Lee, Richard Jarratt .... Richmond, VA
Lee, Richard K. .... Oakland, CA
Lee, Richard L., Jr. .... Midland, MI
Lee, Richard, Law Offices of
Honolulu, HI
Lee, Richard P. .... Tallahassee, FL
Lee, Richard S. .... Bronx, NY
Lee, Richard Tracy .... Sarasota, FL
Lee, Richard Ung-Jin .... Los Angeles, CA
Lee, Richard V. .... Bradenton, FL
Lee, Richard Y. .... Los Angeles, CA
Lee, Richd. J. .... Oklahoma City, OK
Lee, Robert
Federal Deposit Insurance Corporation, GV
Lee, Robert A. .... Sarasota, FL
Lee, Robert A. .... Monroe, LA
Lee, Robert B. .... Joplin, MO
Lee, Robert C. .... Chicago, IL
Lee, Robert D. .... South Bend, IN
Lee, Robert D. .... Natchez, MS
Lee, Robert D. .... Mt. Vernon, OH
Lee, Robert E. .... Montgomery, AL
Lee, Robert E. .... Palo Alto, CA
Lee, Robert E. .... Bode, IA
Humboldt, IA
Lee, Robert E. .... Lafitte, LA
Lee, Robert E. .... Caledonia, MN
Lee, Robert E. .... Akron, OH
Lee, Robert E. .... Cleveland, OH
Lee, Robert E. .... Florence, SC
Lee, Robert E. .... Lebanon, TN
Lee, Robert E. .... Richmond, VA
Lee, Robert E. .... Richmond, VA
Lee, Robert E., Jr. .... DeLand, FL
Lee, Robert E., Jr. .... Libertyville, IL
Lee, Robert E., Jr. .... Indianapolis, IN
Lee, Robert E., Jr. .... Westfield, NJ
New York, NY
Lee, Robert E., Jr. .... Buffalo, NY
Lee, Robert E., Jr. .... Winston-Salem, NC
Lee, Robert E., Jr. .... Plano, TX
Lee, Robert Edd .... Billings, MT
Lee, Robert Edward, Jr.
Murfreesboro, NC
Lee, Robert Emmett .... River Forest, IL
Lee, Robert Evans .... Lebanon, TN
Lee, Robert F. .... San Mateo, CA
Lee, Robert G. .... Dallas, TX
Lee, Robert G. .... San Antonio, TX
Lee, Robert G. .... Madison, WI
Lee, Robert J. .... Portland, OR
Lee, Robert John .... Buffalo, NY
Lee, Robert L. .... Atlanta, GA
Lee, Robert L. .... Minneapolis, MN
Lee, Robert M. .... St. Louis, MO
Lee, Robert N. .... Cavalier, ND
Lee, Robert Quan .... Miami, FL
Lee, Robert R. .... Wichita, KS
Lee, Robert S. .... Minneapolis, MN
Lee, Robert S. .... Freer, TX
Lee, Robert T. .... Riverhead, NY
Lee, Robert T. .... Nashville, TN
Lee, Robert W. .... Fort Lauderdale, FL
Lee, Robert W. .... Tyler, TX
Lee, Robert W., & Associates, P.C.
Birmingham, AL
Lee, Robert Wayne
Environmental Protection Agency, Program Office Attorneys, GV
Lee, Robert Wyeth, Jr. .... Birmingham, AL
Lee, Roger A. .... Dayton, OH
Lee, Roger A., Law Office of
Wichita Falls, TX
Lee, Roland V., Jr. .... Mobile, AL
Lee, Ron L. .... Cottonwood, AZ
Lee, Ronald B. .... Easton, MD
Lee, Ronald B. .... Akron, OH
Lee, Ronald D. .... Department of Justice, Office of the Deputy Attorney General, GV
Lee, Ronald D. .... Kansas City, MO
Lee, Ronald E. .... Sacramento, CA
Lee, Ronald E. .... Florham Park, NJ
Lee, Ronald J. .... Minneapolis, MN
Lee, Ronald Y. C. .... Honolulu, HI
Lee, Rosa H. .... New York, NY
Lee, Rosemarie Bucchino .... Omaha, NE
Lee, Rosemary .... San Rafael, CA
Lee, Ross P. .... Mesa, AZ
Lee, Ross W. .... Modesto, CA
Lee, Rotan E. .... Philadelphia, PA
Lee & Rousseau, P.C., Law Office of
Geneva, AL
Lee, Roy, III .... Seattle, WA
Lee, Roy M. .... Baton Rouge, LA
Lee, Roy Noble .... Forest, MS
Lee, Roy Noble, Jr. .... Forest, MS
Lee, Royce B. .... Idaho Falls, ID
Lee, Ryan C. .... Los Angeles, CA
Lee, Ryan J. J. .... Chicago, IL
Lee, Ryan M. .... Redding, CA
Lee, S. James .... San Francisco, CA
Lee's Law Offices .... Yankton, SD
Lee, S. Peter .... Morristown, NJ
Lee, S. Ramsdell .... Newton, MA
Lee, S. Robert .... New York, NY
Lee, Sabing H. .... Newport Beach, CA
Lee, Sabrina L. H. .... New York, NY
Lee, Sam L. .... Maitland, FL
Lee, Saml. E., Jr. .... Winnsboro, LA
Lee, Samuel J., II .... Angleton, TX
Lee, Samuel K. .... Stamford, CT
Lee, Samuel King .... Oak Ridge, TN
Lee, Samuel S. .... La Jolla, CA
Lee, Samuel S. .... Memphis, TN
Lee, Samuel SungMok .... New York, NY
Lee, San San .... Dallas, TX
Lee, Sandra D. .... New York, NY
Lee, Sandra M. .... Palo Alto, CA
Lee, Sandy V. .... Washington, DC
Lee, Sanford E. (Pete)
Colorado Springs, CO
Lee, Sangyeup .... New York, NY
Lee, Sang-yul .... Chicago, IL
Lee, Sarah .... Department of Commerce, Patent and Trademark Office, GV
Lee, Sarah Hooke .... Andover, MA
Lee, Sarah J. .... Honolulu, HI
Lee, Sarah L. .... Tacoma, WA
Lee, Scott W. .... Salt Lake City, UT
Lee, Seung Jai .... Harrisburg, PA
Lee, Sey-Hyo .... New York, NY
Lee, Sharon G. .... Madisonville, TN
Lee, Sheila Jackson .... Houston, TX
Lee, Shelly M. .... Southfield, MI
Lee, Sherman C. .... San Francisco, CA
Lee, Sheryl A. .... Buffalo, NY
Lee, Simon .... New York, NY
Lee, Smart, Cook, Martin & Patterson, P.S., Inc. .... Seattle, WA
Lee & Smith, P.C. .... Washington, DC
Lee, So Young Sarah .... New York, NY
Lee, Sondra Warner .... Arlington, TX
Lee, Sonia .... New York, NY
Lee, Sonia M. .... San Diego, CA
Lee, Sonia Y. .... Los Angeles, CA
Lee, Sonia Y. .... Los Angeles, CA
Lee, Sonja A. .... Madison, WI
Lee, Soo Jee .... New York, NY
Lee, Sook H. .... Long Beach, CA
Lee, Soo-Mi .... New York, NY
Lee, Sophia .... New York, NY
Lee, Spence Chadwick .... Roanoke, AL
Lee, Stegall & Katz, P.C. .... Phoenix, AZ
Lee, Stephanie Dea .... Boston, MA
Lee, Stephen .... Honolulu, HI
Lee, Stephen .... New York, NY
Lee, Stephen A. .... Houston, TX
Lee, Stephen B. .... Owensboro, KY
Lee, Stephen C. .... Minneapolis, MN
Lee, Stephen C. .... Cleveland, OH
Lee, Stephen E. .... Phoenix, AZ
Lee, Stephen H. .... Dallas, TX
Lee, Stephen H. .... Houston, TX
Lee, Stephen M. .... Kingman, AZ
Lee, Stephen M. .... Denver, CO
Lee, Stephen N. .... Belton, TX
Lee, Stephen W. .... Indianapolis, IN
Lee, Steven A. .... New York, NY
Lee, Steven B. .... Minneapolis, KS
Lee, Steven C. .... Orlando, FL
Lee, Steven C. .... Westlake, OH
Lee, Steven E. .... Phoenix, AZ
Lee, Steven G. .... Riverside, CA
Lee, Steven H. .... Honolulu, HI
Lee, Steven J. .... New York, NY
Lee, Steven James .... Sherborn, MA
Lee, Steven K. .... Mill Valley, CA
Oakland, CA
Lee, Steven L. .... Austin, TX
Lee, Steven M. .... Scottsdale, AZ
Lee, Steven M. .... Sacramento, CA
Lee, Steven M. .... Rockford, IL
Lee, Steven M. .... Houston, TX
Lee, Steven P. .... Miami, FL
Lee, Steven Patrick .... Santa Barbara, CA
Lee, Steven R. .... Lihue, HI
Lee, Sue M. .... Austin, TX
Lee, Sung H. .... Irvine, CA
Lee, SunMee .... Philadelphia, PA
Lee, Susan .... Kenilworth, NJ
Lee, Susan .... New York, NY
Lee, Susan .... New York, NY
Lee, Susan .... New York, NY
Lee, Susan C. .... Washington, DC
Silver Spring, MD

Lee, Susan G.
Commodity Futures Trading Commission, Executive Staff, GV
Lee, Susan J. ....Anchorage, AK
Lee, Susan Kerr ....Chattanooga, TN
Lee, Susan L.
Securities and Exchange Commission, Office of Compliance Inspections and Examinations, GV
Lee, Susan M. ....New York, NY
Lee, Susan S. ....New York, NY
Lee, Susanne M.
Environmental Protection Agency, Office of the General Counsel, GV
Lee, Suzanne ....Chicago, IL
Lee, Suzanne S. ....New York, NY
Lee, Sylvia E. ....New York, NY
Lee, T. Caice ....Jeffersonville, IN
Lee, Tahirih V. ....Minneapolis, MN
Lee, Tamara D. ....Yankton, SD
Lee, Tammy M. ....New York, NY
Lee, Tashir J. ....Washington, DC
Lee, Ted D. ....Houston, TX
Houston, TX
San Antonio, TX
Lee, Ted M. ....Newport Beach, CA
Lee, Teresa Coin ......Department of Commerce, Patent and Trademark Office, GV
Lee, Teresa L.
Department Of Health And Human Services, GV
Lee, Terrence M. ....Honolulu, HI
Lee, Terry ....Vancouver, WA
Lee, Terry H. ....Department of Commerce, Office of the General Counsel, GV
Lee, Thelma ....New York, NY
Lee, Theodora R. ....Oakland, CA
Lee, Theodore B. ....San Francisco, CA
Lee, Theodore J. ....Houston, TX
Lee, Theodore S. ....Monterey, CA
Lee, Theresa Barrett ....New York, NY
Lee, Theresa Kroll ....Kingsport, TN
Lee, Thomas ....Harahan, LA
Lee, Thomas ....New Orleans, LA
Lee, Thomas A., III ....Malvern, PA
Lee, Thomas A., Jr. ....San Francisco, CA
Lee, Thomas C. ....San Francisco, CA
Lee, Thomas C. ....Portland, OR
Lee, Thomas D. ....Forest, MS
Lee, Thomas D. ....New York, NY
Lee, Thomas E. ....Fairfield, CT
Lee, Thomas E. ....St. Paul, MN
Lee, Thomas E. ....New York, NY
Lee, Thomas E. ....Fort Pierre, SD
Lee, Thomas E., Jr. ....Jupiter, FL
Lee, Thomas F. ....Del Rio, TX
Lee, Thomas G. ....Miami, FL
Lee, Thomas H. ....Houston, TX
Lee, Thomas H., II ....Philadelphia, PA
Lee, Thomas H., Jr. ....Durham, NC
Lee, Thomas Hayden ....Nashville, TN
Lee, Thomas J. ....Saint Simons Island, GA
Lee, Thomas J. ....Chicago, IL
Lee, Thomas J. ....Cleveland, OH
Lee, Thomas J. ....San Antonio, TX
Lee, Thomas J., Ltd. ....Chicago, IL
Lee, Thomas R. ....Salt Lake City, UT
Lee, Thomas W. ....New York, NY
Lee, Tienne Elissa ....San Francisco, CA
Lee, Tiffani G. ....Miami, FL
Lee, Timothy F. ....Alhambra, CA
Lee, Timothy F. ....Houston, TX
Lee, Timothy G. ....St. Charles, MO
Lee, Timothy H. ....Phoenix, AZ
Lee, Timothy J. ....Berkeley, CA
Lee, Timothy Orin ....Cambridge, NY
Lee, Timothy R. ....Santa Monica, CA
Lee, Tin Kin ....Los Angeles, CA
Lee, Todd R. ....New York, NY
Lee, Tom ....Yale, OK
Lee, Tom S. ....Jackson, MS
Lee, Tommy R. ....Novato, CA
Lee, Tony S. ....Washington, DC
Lee, Tony S. ....Seattle, WA
Lee, Traci Fraser ....Sacramento, CA
Lee, Tracia Y. ....Austin, TX
Lee, Tracie B. ....Huntsville, AL
Lee, Troy C., Jr. ....Woodland Hills, CA
Lee, V. Vincent ....Chicopee, MA
Lee, Vanessa ....Seattle, WA
Lee, Victor A. ....Santa Ana, CA
Lee, Victor H. ....McLean, VA
Lee, Victor K. ....Palo Alto, CA
Lee, Victoria ....Pittsburgh, PA
Lee, Victoria S. ....Lancaster, PA
Lee, Victoria W-Y ....Palo Alto, CA
Lee, Violet M. ....San Francisco, CA
Lee, Virginia ....Boston, MA
Lee, Virginia Curtis ....Salt Lake City, UT
Lee, Vivian E. ....Boston, MA
Lee, Vivian Lee Foster ....Birmingham, AL
Lee, W. Brewster, (P.C.) ....Boston, MA
Lee, W. David ....Monroe, NC
Lee, W. David ....Fort Worth, TX
Lee, W. Richard ....Fresno, CA
Lee, W. Spencer, IV ....Albany, GA
Lee, W. Sperry ....Jacksonville, FL
Lee, Wallace A. ....Panguitch, UT
Lee & Walsh ....Baton Rouge, LA
Lee, Walter ....Bethesda, MD
Lee, Warren R. ....Sacramento, CA
Lee, Warrick E., Jr. ....Kenilworth, NJ
Lee, Wayman ....Springfield, MA
Lee, Wayne C. ....Colfax, CA
Lee, Wayne E. ....Dallas, TX
Lee, Wayne J., (P.C.) ....New Orleans, LA
Lee, Wayne O. ....Greenville, MS

Lee, Wendy H. ....Stamford, CT
New York, NY
Lee, Wendy L. ....Palo Alto, CA
Lee, Wenglin W. ....San Jose, CA
Lee, Wesley W. ....San Diego, CA
Lee, Whitney E. ....Murrieta, CA
Lee, William ....San Francisco, CA
Lee, William A., III ....Waterville, ME
Lee, William B. ....Rochester, NY
Lee, William B. ....Tulsa, OK
Lee, William B., Inc. ....Tulsa, OK
Lee, William C. ....Marietta, GA
Lee, William C. ....Fort Wayne, IN
Lee, William C., III ....Atlanta, GA
Lee, William D., Jr. ....Greenville, SC
Lee, William F. ....Washington, DC
Lee, William F. ....Boston, MA
Lee, William F., Jr. ....Newnan, GA
Lee, William G. ....Woodland Hills, CA
Lee, William Gentry ....Houston, TX
Lee, William H. ....Boston, MA
Lee, William J. ....New York, NY
Lee, William J. ....Howard, OH
Lee, William L., III ....Dothan, AL
Lee, William L., IV ....Dothan, AL
Lee, William M., Jr. ....Chicago, IL
Lee, William P. ....San Francisco, CA
Lee, William P. ....Boston, MA
Lee, William S. ....Santa Ana, CA
Lee, William S. ....Pittsburgh, PA
Lee, William S. ....Houston, TX
Lee, William Swain ....Georgetown, DE
Lee, William Y. ....New York, NY
Lee, Wing K. ....San Francisco, CA
Lee, Wm. Marshall ....Chicago, IL
Lee, Won K. ....Gainesville, FL
Lee, Won S. ....Las Vegas, NV
Lee & Yeh ....New York, NY
Lee, Yong ....Washington, DC
Lee, Yong G. ....New York, NY
Lee, Yong On ....Palisades Park, NJ
Lee, Yoon-Young ....Washington, DC
Lee, Yoo-Rah ....San Jose, CA
Lee, Young ....New York, NY
Lee, Young ....New York, NY
Lee, Young S. ....Fairfield, CA
Napa, CA
Lee, Younghea ....Farmington Hills, MI
Lee, Yun Gyong ....New York, NY
Lee, Yung W. ....Philadelphia, PA
Lee, Yungman F. ....New York, NY
Lee, Yun-Kyung ....White Plains, NY
Lee, Zhu ....Milwaukee, WI
Lee & Zohar LLP ....Los Angeles, CA
Leeb, Andrea Lisa ....Los Angeles, CA
Leeb, David
Securities and Exchange Commission, Division of Corporation Finance, GV
Leeb, Larry J. ....Los Angeles, CA
Leeb, Richard A. ....Portland, OR
Leeb, Steven M. ....Glendale, CA
Leebove, Lisa J. ....San Francisco, CA
Leebrick, Thomas S., P.C. ....Lynchburg, VA
Leebron, David W. ....New York, NY
Leebron, Jack ....Oklahoma City, OK
Leebron & Robinson ....Houston, TX
Leebron, W. Michael, II ....Houston, TX
Lee-Bryant, Danita C. ....Takoma Park, MD
Leece, Blithe Cravens ....Overland Park, KS
Leece, Jenifer K. ....Walnut Creek, CA
Leece & Phillips Law Offices, S.C.
Elkhorn, WI
Leece, Randall G. ....Elkhorn, WI
Leece, Robert L. ....Cleveland, OH
Leece, Wilson A., II ....Cleveland, OH
Leech, Anthony P. ....Pittsburgh, PA
Leech, Charles R., Jr. ....Toledo, OH
Leech, Colleen A. ....Los Angeles, CA
Leech, D. Wayne ....El Monte, CA
Leech, David A. ....Greenville, NC
Leech, Dean J. ....Marion, IL
Leech, Frederick C. ....Pittsburgh, PA
Leech, Gary L. ....Winchester, TN
Leech, Gordon R. ....West Palm Beach, FL
Leech, James G. ....Fort Lauderdale, FL
Leech, Jeffrey J. ....Pittsburgh, PA
Leech, John D. ....Cleveland, OH
Leech, Michael J. ....Chicago, IL
Leech, Nancy E. ....Columbus, OH
Leech, Noyes E. ....Philadelphia, PA
Leech, Paul W. ....Grand Prairie, TX
Leech, Ralph J. ....El Monte, CA
Leech, Richard E. ....Grand Junction, CO
Leech, Richard E., P.C. ....Grand Junction, CO
Leech, Scherbel & Peddicord
Coshocton, OH
Leech, Seth R. ....Albany, NY
Leech, Sidney G. ....Baltimore, MD
Leech, Stephen H., Jr. ....Jackson, MS
Leech, Thomas B. ....Coshocton, OH
Leech Tishman & Fuscaldo ....Pittsburgh, PA
Sewickley, PA
Leech, Wesla S. ....Mendenhall, MS
Leech, William H., Sr. ....Jackson, MS
Leech, William W. ....Nashville, TN
Leecock, Stephen M. ....Springfield, MA
Leecraft, Judy ....Austin, TX
Lee-Crist, Jennifer C. ....Indianapolis, IN
Leed, Arthur H. ....Athens, GA
Leed, Claudia ....Oakland, CA
Leed, Roger M., P.S. ....Seattle, WA
Leeder, Louis I. ....New York, NY
Leeder, Nancyann Pacheo, (P.C.) ....Reno, NV
Leeders, Lawrence D. ....Cleveland, OH
Leedes, Gary C. ....Richmond, VA
Leedham, Sophie van Til ....Simsbury, CT
Leedom, Charles M., Jr. ....Arlington, VA
McLean, VA

Leedom, Chester B. ....Sioux Falls, SD
Leedom, Elizabeth A. ....Seattle, WA
Leedom, Gerald B. ....Department of Justice, Tax Division, GV
Leedom, Harvey S. ....New Cumberland, PA
Leedom, John B. ....Churchville, PA
Leedom, Walter Scott ....Milwaukee, WI
Leedom, William J. ....Seattle, WA
Leeds, A. James ....Marina Del Rey, CA
Leeds, Andrea S. ....New York, NY
Leeds & Colby ....Orlando, FL
Miami, FL
Leeds, Craig B. ....Beverly Hills, CA
Leeds, Dani. ....New York, NY
Leeds, Dennis I. ....Garland, TX
Leeds, Edward Ira ....Philadelphia, PA
Leeds, Eileen M. ....Brownsville, TX
Leeds, Frederic G. ....Edison, NJ
Leeds, Gilbert S. ....Morristown, NJ
Leeds, J. Venn, Jr. ....Houston, TX
Leeds, Jacques E. ....Baltimore, MD
Leeds, James P. ....Indianapolis, IN
Leeds, Julie Ann ....Los Angeles, CA
Leeds, Karen B. ....Buffalo, NY
Leeds, Kenneth A. ....St. Louis, MO
Leeds, Kenneth B. ....San Antonio, TX
Leeds, Kenneth E. ....Sunnyvale, CA
Leeds, Kenneth W. ....Setauket, NY
Leeds, Laurence G. ....Sunrise, FL
Leeds & Leeds ....Marina Del Rey, CA
Leeds, Lenard ....Carle Place, NY
Leeds, Lizabeth A. ....Tallahassee, FL
Leeds, Mark H. ....Chicago, IL
Leeds, Martin N. ....Santa Monica, CA
Leeds, Matthew J. ....New York, NY
Leeds, Maura B. ....New York, NY
Leeds, Michael H. ....Boca Raton, FL
Leeds, Mindy R. ....Newark, NJ
Leeds & Morelli ....Carle Place, NY
Leeds, Nancy B. ....Philadelphia, PA
Leeds, Paul ....New York, NY
Leeds, Paul L. ....Chicago, IL
Leeds, Richard F. ....Newport Beach, CA
Leeds, Richard L. ....Woodland Hills, CA
Leeds, Richard W. ....Tarpon Springs, FL
Leeds, Robert H., Jr. ....Spokane, WA
Leeds, Sanford ....Washington, DC
Leeds, Sanford J. ....Yonkers, NY
Leeds, Scott W. ....Miami, FL
Orlando, FL
Leeds, Spencer A. ....Waldwick, NJ
Leeds, Stacy L. ....Skiatook, OK
Leeds, Stephen R. ....Atlanta, GA
Leeds, Stuart L. ....El Paso, TX
Leeds, Terence C. ....Portland, OR
Leeds, Thomas L. ....Las Vegas, NV
Leeds, Wm. A. ....Marina Del Rey, CA
Leedy, Christopher D. ....Canton, OH
Leedy, Daniel C. ....San Diego, CA
Leedy, Daniel W. ....Bellville, TX
Leedy, J. Stratton ....Atlanta, GA
Leedy, R. Allan, Jr. ....Portland, OR
Leedy, Richard I. ....Riverton, WY
Leedy, Richard J. ....Salt Lake City, UT
Leedy, Robert A. ....Portland, OR
Leedy & Stagg ....Terre Haute, IN
Leedy, Stephen R. ....Terre Haute, IN
Leedy, Susan S. ....Sun Lakes, AZ
Leedy, Terry L. ....Arlington, TX
Leedy, William H. ....Falls Church, VA
Leef, Jaquelin Gay "J" ....Chappell, NE
Leef, Joel L. ....Valley Stream, NY
Leefe, David W. ....New Orleans, LA
Leefe, Gibbs & Koehler ....Metairie, LA
New Orleans, LA
Leefe, Richard K. ....Metairie, LA
Leefer, Ilene Cohen ....Pittsburgh, PA
Leefer, Matthew C. ....Boonsboro, MD
Leegan, Kimberly A. ....Newark, NJ
Leegan, Michael J. ....Florham Park, NJ
Leegant, Joan ....Middleton, MA
Leegant, JoAnne ....Rochester, NY
Leegard, Lynn M. ....Bloomington, MN
Leege, William N. ....Oconto, WI
Leege, William N., S.C. ....Oconto, WI
Leeger, Luther L. ....Rancho Santa Fe, CA
Lee-Gulley, Patricia ....Los Angeles, CA
Leehey, Paul W. ....Fallbrook, CA
Leehey, Peter J. ....Cedar Rapids, IA
Leehy, Peter E. ....New York, NY
Leek, Everett P. ....Saginaw, MI
Leek, Jerry C. ....Potsdam, NY
Leek, Kevin S. ....Kansas City, MO
Leek, Shoko I. ....Seattle, WA
Leek, Thomas J. ....Daytona Beach, FL
Leeka, Jack K. ....Houston, TX
Leeka & Rice ....Houston, TX
Lee-Kaniowski, Deanna ....Southfield, MI
Leekley, John D., Jr. ....Milwaukee, WI
Leekley, John R. ....Taylor, MI
Leeland, James H. ....Houston, TX
Leeland, Randall D. ....Yakima, WA
Leeling, Gerald J. ....Lead, SD
Leeman, David M. ....Department of Education, Office for Civil Rights, GV
Leeman, Don J. ....Oklahoma City, OK
Leeman, Joel M. ....Nashville, TN
Leeman, Joel R. ....Boston, MA
Leeman, Wm. Kelly ....Logansport, IN
Lee-Martinez, Marikay ....Phoenix, AZ
Leemhuis, John P., Jr ....Erie, PA
Leemhuis, John P., Sr. ....Erie, PA
Leeming Law ....Boston, MA
Concord, NH
Manchester, NH
Leeming, Peter A. ....Santa Cruz, CA
Leeming, Rupert P. ....Hopkinton, NH

Leeming, Simon C. ....Boston, MA
Concord, NH
Manchester, NH
Leemis, Lloyd C. ....Jacksonville, FL
Leemis, Ralph B. ....Orlando, FL
Leemon, Darryl M. ....Malibu, CA
Leemon, Gary R. ....Los Angeles, CA
Leemon, John A. ....Morrison, IL
Mount Carroll, IL
Leemon, Mark ....Seattle, WA
Leemon, Norman I. ....Southfield, MI
Leemon, Philmore A. ....Las Vegas, NV
Leemon, Scott ....New York, NY
Leemon, Vicki Sherman
Department of Transportation, Federal Aviation Administration, GV
Lee-Muschong, Kimberly K. ....Southfield, MI
Leen, Carolyn B. ....Virginia Beach, VA
Leen, David A. ....La Conner, WA
Seattle, WA
Leen, David J. ....Bangor, ME
Leen, Edward J. ....New York, NY
Leen & Emery, P.A. ....Bangor, ME
Leen, Keri ....Naperville, IL
Leen, Marc H. ....Short Hills, NJ
Leen, Mark ....Glendale, CA
Leen & Moore ....La Conner, WA
Seattle, WA
Leen, Robert M. ....Seattle, WA
Leen, Thomas L. ....Las Vegas, NV
Leen, Virginia A. ....Los Angeles, CA
Lee-Navas, Edgar A. ....San Juan, PR
Leenhouts, Keith J. ....Detroit, MI
Lee-O'Halloran, Patrick
Minneapolis, MN
Leep, Ben ....Redding, CA
Leep, Daniel M. ....Milwaukee, WI
Leep & Tescher ....Redding, CA
Leeper, Andrew J. ....Orlando, FL
Leeper, Andrew R. ....Cincinnati, OH
Leeper, Bob J. ....Norman, OK
Leeper, Charles S. ....Washington, DC
Leeper, Charles S., Law Offices of
Fort Worth, TX
Leeper, David P. ....El Paso, TX
Leeper, E. Matthew, Jr. ....Houston, TX
Leeper & Farha, P.C. ....Quincy, IL
Leeper, Harold H. ....Dallas, TX
Leeper, James K. M. ....Brooklyn, NY
Leeper, John E. ....El Paso, TX
Leeper, Kevin R. ....Framingham, MA
Leeper, M. Dale ....Marietta, OH
Leeper, Norman B. ....Fullerton, CA
Leeper, Rick ....Austin, TX
Leeper, Roshell ....Columbus, OH
Leeper, Silvia Jimenez ....St. Petersburg, FL
Leeper, Thomas A. ....Huntsville, TX
Leeper, Thomas K. ....Quincy, IL
Leeper, Towner ....El Paso, TX
Leeper, Virginia ....Seattle, WA
Leepson, Brian M. ....Atlanta, GA
Leepson, Peter L. ....Westport, CT
Leepson, Peter L., P.C. ....Westport, CT
Leer, Daniel J. ....Oakland, CA
Leer, David K. O. ....Bismarck, ND
Leer, Mary Anne ....Chicago, IL
Leer, Sandra G. ....Riverside, CA
Leer, Timothy J. ....Minneapolis, MN
Leerink, Amy R. ....Wellesley Hills, MA
Leerkamp, Randolph A. ....Indianapolis, IN
Leerkamp, Sonia J. ....Noblesville, IN
Leermakers, Stephen W. ....Dublin, OH
Lees, A. Edward ....Lakewood, CO
Lees, Alan B. ....Los Angeles, CA
Lees, Aubrey ....New York, NY
Lees, C. Ray ....Oklahoma City, OK
Lees, Carlton A. ....Westport, MA
Lees, Donald H. ....Oklahoma City, OK
Lees, Earle D., Jr. ....Du Bois, PA
Lees, Frederick J. ....Washington, DC
Lees, Gail Ellen ....Los Angeles, CA
Lees, George T., III ....Wilmington, DE
Philadelphia, PA
Lees, James B., Jr. ....Charleston, WV
Lees, John ....Walnut Creek, CA
Lees, Joseph E. ....Rockville, MD
Lees, Judd H. ....Seattle, WA
Lees, Kenneth J. ....Philadelphia, PA
Lees, Martha A. ....Camden, NJ
Lees, Matthew N. ....San Diego, CA
Lees, Mindy J. ....Burbank, CA
Lees, Paul G. ....Bethlehem, PA
Lees, Paul L. ....Gloucester, MA
Lees, Rhonda ....Alexandria, VA
Lees, Richard, & Associates, P.A.
Santa Fe, NM
Lees, Richard S. ....Santa Fe, NM
Lees, Robert A., & Associates ....Denver, CO
Lees, Robert W. ....Philadelphia, PA
Lees, Susan LeSueur ....Northbrook, IL
Lees, Timothy D. ....St. Paul, MN
Leese, Holly E. ....Highland Park, MI
Leese, James K., (A Professional Corporation) ....Santa Ana, CA
Leese, William F. ....Cincinnati, OH
Leeseberg, Gerald S. ....Columbus, OH
Leeseberg Schulman & Valentine
Columbus, OH
Leeser, Ralph M. ....Closter, NJ
Leesfield & Burke, P.A. ....Miami, FL
Leesfield, Ellen L. ....Miami, FL
Leesfield, Ira H. ....Key West, FL
Miami, FL
Leesfield, Leighton, Rubio & Mahfood, P.A.
Key West, FL
Miami, FL
Leeson, Joseph F., Jr. ....Bethlehem, PA
Leeson, Leeson & Leeson ....Bethlehem, PA

Leeson, Margaret H. ... Boston, MA
Leeson, Susan Margaret ... Salem, OR
Leeson, Todd A. ... Roanoke, VA
Leeson, William P. ... Bethlehem, PA
Lee-Stevens, Kathleen Gay ... Charlotte, NC
Leet, Alan C. ... Atlanta, GA
Leet, Byron E. ... Louisville, KY
Leet, James L. ... Sacramento, CA
Leet, Lisa Patrick ... Louisville, KY
Leet, W. Carlos ... San Jose, CA
Leet, William A. ... New York, NY
Leete, Burt A. ... College Park, MD
Leete, Elizabeth B. ... Hartford, CT
Leete, John B. ... Coudersport, PA
Leete & Kosto, LLP ... Hartford, CT
Leete & Lemieux, P.A. ... Portland, ME
Leete, Virginia C. ... Chicago, IL
Leete, William H., Jr. ... Portland, ME
Leeth, Alan D. ... San Diego, CA
Leeth, Stewart T. ... Arlington, VA
Leeth, Todd A. ... Valparaiso, IN
Leetma, Ivar E. ... La Jolla, CA
Leeton, James R. ... Midland, TX
Leeton, James R., Jr. ... Midland, TX
Leetz, Paul A. ... Wheaton, IL
Leetzow, Karen B. ... Charlotte, NC
Leeuw & Doyle, Professional Corporation
Fort Wayne, IN
Indianapolis, IN
Leeuw, Gene R. ... Fort Wayne, IN
Indianapolis, IN
Leeviraphan, Americ ... Oklahoma City, OK
Leeviraphan, Eric ... Oklahoma City, OK
Leewong, James D. ... Los Angeles, CA
Lee-Wong, Wendy ... Alhambra, CA
Leezer, Patsy ... Macomb, IL
LeFaiver, William A., (Co. L.P.A.)
Hudson, OH
Lefante-Persich, Giustina ... New Orleans, LA
Lefari, Cindi A. ... New York, NY
Lefari, Donald M. ... New York, NY
LeFave, Ricki C. ... Gainesville, FL
Lefchak, Richard A. ... Philadelphia, PA
Lefco, Arthur W. ... Philadelphia, PA
Lefco & Blumenthal ... Atlanta, GA
Lefco, Stanley M. ... Atlanta, GA
Lefcoe, George ... Los Angeles, CA
Lefcourt, Gerald B. ... New York, NY
Lefcowitz, Martin ... Arlington, VA
LeFeber, Alfred C. ... Geneva, IL
Lefeber, Hope C. ... Philadelphia, PA
Lefeber, John C. ... Baytown, TX
Lefeber, Peter J. ... Hartford, CT
New Haven, CT
LeFeber, Sally ... Lake Oswego, OR
Lefebre, James B. ... Torrington, CT
Lefebvre, Alan J. ... Las Vegas, NV
LeFebvre, Andrea Orr ... Boston, MA
Lefebvre, Barron & Vivone, Chtd.
Carson City, NV
Las Vegas, NV
Reno, NV
Lefebvre, Christopher M. ... Pawtucket, RI
Lefebvre, Claude, Christopher Lefebvre, P.C.
Pawtucket, RI
Lefebvre, Claude F. ... Pawtucket, RI
Lefebvre, David M. ... Overland Park, KS
Lefebvre, Elizabeth H. ... Southfield, MI
Lefebvre, Francis, Bureau ... New York, NY
New York, NY
Lefebvre, George A. ... El Cajon, CA
Lefebvre, Gerald ... Okeechobee, FL
Lefebvre, Glenn R. ... Albany, NY
Lefebvre, Kim F., (Mr.) ... Albany, NY
Lefebvre, Maureen E. ... Miami, FL
Lefebvre, Paul E. ... Oklahoma City, OK
Lefebvre, Robert J. ... Chicopee, MA
Lefebvre, Stephen L. ... Damascus, MD
Lefebvre, Stephen L., P.C. ... Damascus, MD
Gaithersburg, MD
Germantown, MD
Lefelar, Donald E. ... Chagrin Falls, OH
Lefelar, Scott A. ... Cleveland, OH
Lefelt, Steven L. ... New Brunswick, NJ
Lefere, Alidor P., III ... Sterling Heights, MI
Lefere, Marie ... Fort Lauderdale, FL
Lefeve, David M. ... Baton Rouge, LA
Lefeve, Douglas H. ... Austin, TX
Lefever, D. Michael ... Washington, DC
LeFever, Donald E. ... Lancaster, PA
LeFever, Edward T. ... Ocala, FL
LeFever, John C. ... Chicago, IL
Lefever, Richard R. ... Harrisburg, PA
LeFever, Ronald P. ... Milwaukee, WI
Lefever, Timothy John ... Vacaville, CA
LeFever, William F.
Department Of Health And Human Services, Social Security Administration, GV
LeFevere, Charles L. ... Minneapolis, MN
Lefevere, John F. ... Chantilly, VA
LeFevour, Mark L. ... Schaumburg, IL
LeFevour, Martin T. ... Chicago, IL
LeFevour, Michael J. ... Chicago, IL
LeFevour, Terrence P. ... Chicago, IL
LeFevre, Charles A. ... Bloomfield Hills, MI
LeFevre, Christie M. ... St. Louis, MO
LeFevre, D. Thomas ... Gainesville, GA
LeFevre, Daniel J. ... Winter Park, FL
LeFevre, David E. ... Manchester, NH
LeFevre, Edouard Charles ... Boston, MA
Le Fevre, Eugene de D. ... Los Altos, CA
LeFevre, George E. ... Smithville, TN
LeFevre, Jackie ... Palatine, IL
LeFevre, John H. ... St. Paul, MN
LeFevre, John M., Jr. ... Minneapolis, MN
Lefevre, Keith H. ... Orlando, FL
LeFevre, Lance W. ... Kansas City, MO
LeFevre, Larry L. ... Vandalia, IL
Lefevre, Matthew J. ... Hartford, CT
Torrington, CT
Lefevre, Matthew J., Esq., P.C., The Law Offices of ... Hartford, CT
Torrington, CT
LeFevre, Peter G. ... House of Representatives, Office of Law Revision Counsel, GV
Lefevre, Regina ... Hartford, CT
Lefevre, Robert ... Department of Justice, Environment and Natural Resources Division, GV
LeFevre, Robert ... Okemos, MI
LeFevre, Ronald E. ... San Francisco, CA
LeFevre, Sandra J. ... Auburn Hills, MI
Lefevre, Susan M. ... Austin, TX
Lefevre, Suzanne M. ... Los Angeles, CA
LeFevre, Tamara L. ... Houston, TX
LeFevre, Zeman, Oldfield and Lawinger, Law Group, Ltd. ... Vandalia, IL
Leff, Alan R. ... Iowa City, IA
Leff, Alexander ... New York, NY
Leff, Andrew L. ... Encino, CA
Leff, Barbara J. ... Deerfield, IL
Leff, Clyde M. ... Granville, OH
Leff, Cohen & Winkler, Ltd. ... Chicago, IL
Leff, Craig M. ... Kansas City, MO
Leff, Daniel ... South Orange, NJ
Leff, David ... Englewood Cliffs, NJ
Leff, David A. ... New Haven, CT
Leff, David K. ... Hartford, CT
Leff, Edward J. ... Solon, IA
Leff, Elizabeth A. ... Washington, DC
Leff, Erin Hillary ... Philadelphia, PA
Leff, Ernest ... Beverly Hills, CA
Leff, Ernest, A Professional Corporation
Beverly Hills, CA
Leff, Haupert, Traw & Willman
Iowa City, IA
Leff, Howard B. ... Hempstead, NY
Leff, Ira Mark ... Atlanta, GA
Leff, Irwin ... San Francisco, CA
Leff, James J. ... New York, NY
Leff, Jody ... Jersey City, NJ
Leff, Karin S.
Environmental Protection Agency, Program Office Attorneys, GV
Leff, Kathryn Thickstun ... San Diego, CA
Leff, Kenneth M. ... Woodbridge, NJ
Pearl River, NY
Leff, Laurence R. ... Livingston, NJ
Leff, Lawrence B. ... Denver, CO
Leff, Marc Jay ... Brooklyn, NY
Leff, Meredith Ann ... Stamford, CT
Leff, Michael ... San Francisco, CA
Leff, Miriam W. ... New York, NY
Leff, Neil M. ... New York, NY
Leff, Peter J. ... Washington, DC
Leff, Philip ... Massapequa, NY
Leff, Philip A. ... Iowa City, IA
Leff, Randall S. ... Los Angeles, CA
Leff, Richard E. ... New York, NY
Leff, Richard I. ... Buffalo, NY
Leff, Robert A. ... Bronx, NY
Leff, Robert M. ... Hawthorne, NY
Leff, Robert M. ... Massapequa Park, NY
Leff, Samuel I. ... North Miami Beach, FL
Leff, Scott Darren ... Freehold, NJ
Leff, Sherwin H. ... Chicago, IL
Leff, Stephen M. ... Chicago, IL
Leff, Steven A. ... San Mateo, CA
Leff, Steven M. ... New York, NY
Leff, Steven M. Law Offices, P.C.
New York, NY
Leff, Thomas P. ... Wilmington, DE
Leff, Todd P. ... Fort Washington, PA
Leffak, Ellen S. ... Dayton, OH
Leffall, LaSalle D., III ... New York, NY
Leffard, Gregory W. ... Mobile, AL
Leffel, Kevin L. ... Chicago, IL
Leffel, Michael ... Washington, DC
Leffel, Russell C. ... Merriam, KS
Leffell, Daniel J. ... New York, NY
Leffell, Michael J. ... New York, NY
Leffelman, Dean J. ... Lisle, IL
Leffer, Richard S. ... Mineola, NY
Lefferdink, John J. ... Lamar, CO
Lefferdink, John S. ... Lamar, CO
Lefferdink Law Office, LLC ... Lamar, CO
Leffers, Beverly ... New York, NY
Leffert, Anthony L. ... Denver, CO
Leffert, Dennis J. ... San Diego, CA
Leffert, Kim A. ... Chicago, IL
Leffert, Linda Garelik ... Boston, MA
Leffert, Thomas W. ... Minneapolis, MN
Leffert-Heise, Elizabeth A. ... Miami, FL
Lefferts, Christopher B. ... San Jose, CA
Lefferts, Jacqueline Moore ... Houston, TX
Lefferts, Matthew C. ... New York, NY
Leffew, Billy H. ... Rockwood, TN
Leffingwell, John V. ... Guilford, CT
Leffingwell, Lisa ... Dallas, TX
Leffler, April Christine ... Miami, FL
Leffler, B. Bert ... Benkelman, NE
Leffler, Barbara E. ... Lincoln, NE
Leffler, Bruce S. ... New York, NY
Leffler, Carroll G. ... Warrensburg, MO
Leffler, David J. ... New York, NY
Leffler, Ella M. ... White Plains, NY
Leffler, Frederick W. ... Akron, OH
Leffler, Fredric C. ... New York, NY
Leffler, Fredric D. ... Columbia, MD
Leffler and Hartigan ... Newton, IL
Leffler, Hyland & Thompson, A Professional Corporation ... Fairfax, VA
Leffler, James R. ... Sugar Land, TX
Leffler, Jay H. ... Philadelphia, PA
Leffler, Karla A. ... Ottumwa, IA
Leffler, Kenneth B. ... Alexandria, VA
Leffler, Kenneth M. ... Winter Springs, FL
Leffler, Mark C. ... Richmond, VA
Leffler, Melvyn J. ... Middletown, NY
Leffler, Michael ... Milwaukee, WI
Leffler, Ray ... Memphis, TN
Leffler, Raymond G. ... New York, NY
Leffler, Rodney G. ... Fairfax, VA
Leffler, Ruth L. ... Mount Prospect, IL
Leffler, Sheldon S. ... Woodside, NY
Leffler, Stanley S. ... New York, NY
Leffler, Stephen R. ... Memphis, TN
Leffler, Stephen R., P.C., Law Office of
Memphis, TN
Leffler, Susan I. ... Lansing, MI
Leffler, Theodore F. ... Davison, MI
Leffler, William A., III ... Tallahassee, FL
Leffler, William G. ... Massillon, OH
Leffler-Wachtel, Marjorie B. ... Westfield, NJ
Leffman, David L. ... El Paso, TX
Leffmann, Ann M. ... Alexandria, VA
Lefholz, Rodney C. ... Rapid City, SD
Lefkarites, Christopher ... Kew Gardens, NY
Lefko, Lewis A. ... Dallas, TX
Lefko, Tami K. ... Los Angeles, CA
Lefkoe, Arthur ... Avalon, NJ
Lefkof, Amy ... Little Rock, AR
Lefkoff, Craig B. ... Atlanta, GA
Lefkoff, Craig B., P.C. ... Atlanta, GA
Lefkoff, Duncan, Grimes & Miller, P.C.
Atlanta, GA
Lefkoff, Joseph ... Atlanta, GA
Lefkoff, Milt ... Tallahassee, FL
Lefkofsky, Steven R. ... Bloomfield Hills, MI
Lefkofsky, William ... Farmington Hills, MI
Lefkort, Leonard J. ... New York, NY
Lefkort, Maurice M. ... New York, NY
Lefkovits, Arnold K. ... Birmingham, AL
Lefkovitz, Allen A ... Chicago, IL
Lefkovitz, Allen A, & Associates, P.C.
Chicago, IL
Lefkovitz, Arnold E. ... Cookeville, TN
Nashville, TN
Lefkovitz, Barbara J. ... Boston, MA
Lefkovitz & Lefkovitz ... Cookeville, TN
Nashville, TN
Lefkovitz, Steven L. ... Cookeville, TN
Nashville, TN
Lefkow, David M. ... Chicago, IL
Lefkow, Joan H. ... Chicago, IL
Lefkow, Michael F. ... Chicago, IL
Lefkow, Michael R. ... Chicago, IL
Lefkowitz, Alan L. ... Boston, MA
Lefkowitz, Alan Z. ... Pittsburgh, PA
Lefkowitz, Albert S. ... New York, NY
Lefkowitz, Alisa F. ... New York, NY
Lefkowitz, Barbara J. ... Hopkinton, MA
Lefkowitz, Bloom & Van Leuven, P.A.
Orlando, FL
Lefkowitz, Claire Kiehl ... Tucson, AZ
Lefkowitz, Daniel J. ... Jericho, NY
Lefkowitz, David ... Los Angeles, CA
Lefkowitz, David N. ... Atlanta, GA
Lefkowitz, David S. ... New York, NY
Lefkowitz, Dena ... Media, PA
Lefkowitz, Dennis Samuel ... Boca Raton, FL
Lefkowitz & Edelstein ... New York, NY
Lefkowitz, Elisa J. ... White Plains, NY
Lefkowitz, Ellen ... New York, NY
Lefkowitz, Eric S. ... New York, NY
Lefkowitz, Eugene E. ... Flushing, NY
Lefkowitz Firm, The, LLC ... Atlanta, GA
Decatur, GA
Lefkowitz, Gary A. ... Albany, NY
Lefkowitz, Gary H. ... Department of Labor, Pension and Welfare Benefits, GV
Lefkowitz, Helen ... Hauppauge, NY
Lefkowitz, Holloway B. ... Rockville, MD
Lefkowitz, Howard ... East Hanover, NJ
Lefkowitz, Howard M. ... New York, NY
Lefkowitz, Howard N. ... New York, NY
Lefkowitz, Ivan M. ... Orlando, FL
Lefkowitz, James E. ... Cleveland, OH
Lefkowitz, Jared M. ... New York, NY
Lefkowitz, Jay P. ... Washington, DC
Lefkowitz, Jeff D. ... Houston, TX
Lefkowitz, Jerry ... New City, NY
Lefkowitz, Joan B. ... White Plains, NY
Lefkowitz, Jon A. ... New York, NY
Lefkowitz, Julie ... New York, NY
Lefkowitz, Kathleen Kelly
South Euclid, OH
Lefkowitz & Keefe, P.C. ... Albany, NY
Lefkowitz, Kenneth A. ... New York, NY
Lefkowitz, Kim E. ... New York, NY
Lefkowitz, Lawrence ... New York, NY
Lefkowitz, Lawrence S. ... Garden City, NY
Lefkowitz, Leslie S. ... North Brunswick, NJ
Lefkowitz, Lewis M. ... New York, NY
Lefkowitz, Mark D. ... Montvale, NJ
New York, NY
Lefkowitz, Melvin E. ... Washington, DC
Lefkowitz, Michael A. ... Miami Beach, FL
Lefkowitz, Michael E. ... New York, NY
Lefkowitz, Michael G. ... Newark, NJ
Lefkowitz, Michael L. ... McLean, VA
Lefkowitz, Morris B. ... Southfield, MI
Lefkowitz, Neil ... Washington, DC
Lefkowitz, Paul S. ... Washington, DC
Cleveland, OH
Lefkowitz, Peter Franklin
Pompton Lakes, NJ
Lefkowitz, Peter M. ... Waltham, MA
Lefkowitz, Richard A. ... New City, NY
Lefkowitz, Richard I. ... Boston, MA
Lefkowitz, Richard S. ... New York, NY
Lefkowitz, Robert A. ... Winston-Salem, NC
Lefkowitz, Ronald W. ... Larkspur, CA
Lefkowitz, Sol ... Glen Cove, NY
Lefkowitz, Stephen ... New York, NY
Lefkowitz, Todd ... Washington, DC
Lefkowitz, Victor M. ... Winston-Salem, NC
Lefkowitz, William H., (P.A.)
Fort Lauderdale, FL
Lefland, Robert M. ... White Plains, NY
Leflar, John R. ... Sunnyvale, CA
Leflar, Robert B ... Fayetteville, AR
Lefler, Charles B., Jr. ... Albemarle, NC
Lefler, Daniel P. ... Los Angeles, CA
Lefler, Dean H. ... Houston, TX
Lefler, Derrick W. ... Princeton, WV
Lefler, E. Elizabeth ... Franklin, NC
Lefler, Elizabeth P. ... Washington, DC
Lefler, Eugene L. ... Beaumont, TX
Lefler & Franklin ... Omaha, NE
Lefler, Helen C. ... Mears, MI
Lefler, Herbert P., III ... Minneapolis, MN
Lefler, John M. ... Lincoln, NE
Lefler, John N. ... Fort Collins, CO
Lefler, M. L., Jr. (P.C.) ... Beaumont, TX
Lefler, Rochelle L. ... Tampa, FL
Lefler, Steven ... Omaha, NE
Lefler, Susan K. ... Austin, TX
Lefler, Thomas C., Jr. ... Lansing, MI
Lefler & Walker ... Beaumont, TX
Lefler, Wendy Roy ... Monterey, CA
Lefleur, Michael S. ... Miami, FL
LeFloch, Eugene M. ... Tampa, FL
LeFlore, Byron L., Jr. ... San Antonio, TX
LeFlore, Claire Priestley ... Sacramento, CA
LeFlore, Ray L. ... New York, NY
Lefoer, Dominic S. ... Austintown, OH
LeFoll & LeFoll ... Rocky Hill, CT
LeFoll, Raymond G. ... Rocky Hill, CT
LeFoll, Tammy ... Rocky Hill, CT
Lefont, Stacey N. ... New York, NY
LeForce, Carl E. ... Idabel, OK
LeForce, Clark H. ... Hugo, OK
LeForce, H. Jefferson ... Fort Worth, TX
LeForce & McCombs, P.C. ... Idabel, OK
LeFort, Daniel P. ... Houston, TX
Lefort, Mary Ann ... New York, NY
Lefrak, Joseph S. ... New York, NY
LeFrak, Richard S. ... Rego Park, NY
Lefranc-Morales, Roberto E. ... San Juan, PR
LeFrancois, Arthur G. ... Oklahoma City, OK
LeFrancois, David G. ... Derry, NH
Lefranc Romero, Roberto ... San Juan, PR
Lefsetz, Robert S. ... Santa Monica, CA
Lefstein, Lori R. ... Rock Island, IL
Lefstein, Norman ... Indianapolis, IN
Lefstein, Stuart R. ... Rock Island, IL
Lefter, Cushman, & Wilkinson, P.A.
St. Petersburg, FL
Lefter, J. Baird ... St. Petersburg, FL
Leftin, Solomon Louis ... Denver, CO
Leftoff, George ... Franklin Square, NY
Lefton, David E. ... Cincinnati, OH
Lefton, David H. ... Cincinnati, OH
Lefton, David S. ... Fort Lauderdale, FL
Lefton, David S., P.A. ... Fort Lauderdale, FL
Lefton, Ira J. ... Hempstead, NY
Lefton, Ira S. ... Philadelphia, PA
Lefton, Jerome L. T. ... St. Louis, MO
Lefton, Jimmy J. ... Cincinnati, OH
Lefton, Marie ... Boston, MA
Lefton, Nicole R. ... New York, NY
Lefton, Robert C. ... Wilmington, DE
Lefton, Ronald D. ... New York, NY
Leftridge, Gary L. ... Kansas City, MO
Leftridge, Janis M. ... Harrisburg, PA
Leftridge, Lenzie L., Jr. ... Park Hills, MO
Leftwich, Brian T. ... New Orleans, LA
Leftwich & Douglas, P.L.L.C.
Washington, DC
Leftwich, Gail M. ... Arlington, VA
Leftwich, Harold A. ... Chicago, IL
Leftwich, Helga Lura ... Raleigh, NC
Leftwich, J. Daniel ... Washington, DC
Leftwich, James A. ... Chesapeake, VA
Leftwich, James A., Jr. ... Chesapeake, VA
Leftwich, James W. ... Irving, TX
Leftwich, John T., II ... Shawnee, KS
Leftwich, Juliet A. ... San Francisco, CA
Leftwich, Kyle C. ... Richmond, VA
Leftwich, Michael B. ... Nashville, TN
Leftwich, Michelle A. ... New York, NY
Leftwich, Norma B. ... Washington, DC
Leftwich, Willie L. ... Washington, DC
Lega, Mark J. ... Jeffersontown, KY
Legaard, Paul K. ... Philadelphia, PA
Legacki, Kenneth W. ... Anchorage, AK
Legakis, Peter P. ... Stony Brook, NY
Legal Advantage, The ... Santa Ana, CA
Longwood, FL
Legal Aid of Western Missouri
Kansas City, MO
Legal Solution, The, P.C. ... Scottsdale, AZ
Farmington Hills, MI
Legal Solutions Group, The, L.L.P.
San Rafael, CA
Legal Strategies Group ... Emeryville, CA
San Francisco, CA
Legamaro, Michael J. ... Chicago, IL
Legan, Pat ... San Antonio, TX
Legare, David P. ... Billings, MT
Legaré, Hare & Smith ... Charleston, SC
Legaré, T. Allen, Jr. ... Charleston, SC
Legaré, Thomas C. R., Jr. ... Columbia, SC
Legare, Timothy Asher ... San Ramon, CA
Legarza, Richard J. ... Reno, NV
Legasey, John S. ... Salem, MA
Legaspi, Cristina G. ... Monterey Park, CA
Legaspi, Leonard S. ... Los Angeles, CA
Legat, Joseph M. ... Las Vegas, NV
Legate, Clark H. ... Presidio, TX
Legate, Claude E. ... Jackson, MS

Legate, Clifford W. ... Oklahoma City, OK
Legate, Sam J. ... El Paso, TX
Legath, R. Jeffrey ... Philadelphia, PA
Legato, Carmen D. ... Washington, DC
Legato, Gerard J. ... Somerville, NJ
Legato, Marianne ... Morristown, NJ
Legator, Sheldon P. ... Chicago, IL
Legatos, Despina M. ... Garden City, NY
Legatos, Nick S. ... Chicago, IL
Legatt, Jerome ... Great Neck, NY
Legatz, Joseph C. ... Grand Haven, MI
Legatz and Ten Cate ... Grand Haven, MI
Legault, Danielle A. ... Fort Worth, TX
Legault, Theresa S. ... Hollywood, FL
LeGaye, Daniel E. ... The Woodlands, TX
LeGaye, Marjorie Mize ... Santa Ana, CA
Legband, Donna P. ... Skillman, NJ
LeGear, Daniel H., Jr. ... St. Louis, MO
Legelis, Alfred ... Dover, MA
Le Gendre, Bertrand C. ... Lawrence, MA
LeGendre, Edward M. ... Newark, OH
Legendre, Pamela Jean ... Slidell, LA
Legendre, Ronald A. ... Kissimmee, FL
Le Gendre, Simeon E., Jr. ... Andover, MA
LeGendre, Stephen M. ... Annapolis, MD
Legenhausen, Thomas R. ... Hartford, CT
Legenza, Lawrence J. ... Kensington, CT
Legenza, Richard A. ... Cleveland, OH
Leger, Albert J. ... Lafayette, LA
Leger, Andrew J., Jr. ... Greensburg, PA
Pittsburgh, PA
Leger & Babineaux ... Lafayette, LA
Leger, Charles P. ... Meridian, MS
Leger, Christopher M. ... Caribou, ME
Leger & Coplen ... Houston, TX
Leger, D. John ... Houston, TX
Leger, Ernest H., Jr. ... Albuquerque, NM
Leger, Lindy Thomas ... Matthews, NC
Leger & Mestayer ... New Iberia, LA
New Orleans, LA
Leger, Nicolas T. ... Las Vegas, NM
Leger, Walter J., Jr., (P.C.)
New Iberia, LA
New Orleans, LA
Legere, Henry Joseph, Jr. ... East Lansing, MI
Leger-Kelley, Lesley E. ... Dallas, TX
Legernes, Bruce ... San Francisco, CA
Legernes, Norman W. ... Portland, OR
Legerski, Donald L. ... Lander, WY
Legerski, Mary L. ... Cleveland, OH
Legerton, Coleman M. ... Charleston, SC
LeGette, A. LaFon, Jr. ... Latta, SC
LeGette, Charles E., Jr. ... Washington, GA
LeGette, Charles E., Jr., P.C.
Washington, GA
Legg, Ann ... Ketchum, ID
Legg, Basil R., Jr. ... Clarksburg, WV
Legg, Benson Everett ... Baltimore, MD
Legg, Courtney B. ... Austin, TX
Legg, Erik W. ... Huntington, WV
Legg, George F. ... Knoxville, TN
Legg, J. Stephen ... Mobile, AL
Legg, James S. ... Alsip, IL
Legg, Janet S. ... Frederick, MD
Legg, Jason E. ... Clinton, TN
Legg, JoEllen Lotvedt ... Washington, DC
Legg, L. George ... Ithaca, NY
Legg, Lawrence George ... Duncan, SC
Legg, Linda S. ... San Francisco, CA
St. Louis, MO
Legg, Martin L. ... Boston, MA
Legg, Michael W. ... Farmington Hills, MI
Legg, Michele Denise ... Blue Springs, MO
Legg, Myrl E. ... Harlingen, TX
Legg, Patricia S. ... Sarasota, FL
Legg, Randy G. ... Washington, DC
Legg, Ray M. ... Torrance, CA
Legg, Reagan H. ... Kaufman, TX
Legg, Robert P. ... Baltimore, MD
Legg, Roger E. ... Parkesburg, PA
West Chester, PA
Legg, Sonya Kay ... Tulsa, OK
Legg, Thomas C. ... Coldwater, MI
Legg, William J. ... Oklahoma City, OK
Legg & Wilson ... Parkesburg, PA
West Chester, PA
Leggans, David R. ... Mount Vernon, IL
Leggat, Bonnie Jean ... Marshall, TX
Leggat, John E. ... Lowell, MA
Leggat, Richard D. ... Boston, MA
Leggat, Robert B., Jr. ... St. Louis, MO
Leggat, Thomas E. ... Boston, MA
Legge, Charles A. ... San Francisco, CA
Legge, David Frederick
Department of Justice, Civil Division, GV
Legge, Farrow, Kimmitt & McGrath, L.L.P.
Houston, TX
Legge, Glenn R. ... Houston, TX
Legge, Laura K. ... Los Angeles, CA
Legge, Myriam K. ... Houston, TX
Legge, Stephen R. ... Waterford, MI
Legge, Wendy Willson ... St. Paul, MN
Legge, Winston V., Jr. ... Athens, AL
Leggett, Carroll H. ... United States Senate,
Senatorial Assistants, GV
Leggett, Charles M. ... Waynesboro, MS
Leggett, David John ... Nantucket, MA
Leggett, Dewey B. ... Dallas, TX
Leggett, E. Sheldon ... Alexandria, VA
McLean, VA
Leggett, Ida ... Lewiston, ID
Leggett, Isiah ... Washington, DC
Leggett, James F. ... Seattle, WA
Tacoma, WA
Leggett, Jeffrey M. ... Mequon, WI
Leggett, John C. ... Conyers, GA
Leggett, John W. ... Houston, TX
Leggett, Kenneth G. ... Abilene, TX
Leggett & Kram ... Seattle, WA
Tacoma, WA
Leggett, Larry E. ... Seattle, WA
Leggett, Leslie A. ... Reno, NV
Leggett, Linda M. ... Cambridge, MA
Leggett, Paul C. ... Houston, TX
Leggett, R. Bradford ... Winston-Salem, NC
Leggett, Robert A., III ... Danville, VA
Leggett, Russell R. ... White Plains, NY
Leggett, Thad, III ... Magnolia, MS
Leggett, Thomas P., (P.A.)
Little Rock, AR
Leggett, Vicki R. ... Hattiesburg, MS
Leggett, Walter E., Jr. ... Macon, GA
Leggette, L. Poe ... Washington, DC
Leggette, Lemire ... Prospect Heights, IL
Leggette, Thomas A. ... Roanoke, VA
Leggett-Murphy, Melissa Joy ... Tampa, FL
Legghio, Brian M. ... Mount Clemens, MI
Legghio, Brian M., P.C. ... Detroit, MI
Mount Clemens, MI
Legghio, Christopher P. ... Southfield, MI
Leggio, Anthony J.
Amelia Island Plantation, FL
Leggio, Anthony L. ... Bakersfield, CA
Leggio, Suzie ... Houston, TX
Leggott, L. Kirk ... North Liberty, IA
Leghorn, Joseph J. ... Boston, MA
Leghorn, Thomas A. ... New York, NY
Legier, Ernest Philip, Jr.
New Orleans, LA
Legier, John R. ... New Orleans, LA
Legier, Kelly McNeil ... New Orleans, LA
Legin, Joel L. ... Cleveland, OH
Leginsky, Ned M. ... Hamden, CT
Legister, Nadine A. ... Kew Gardens, NY
Legler and Flynn ... Bradenton, FL
Legler, Joel Ivan ... Prescott Valley, AZ
Legler, Kennedy, III ... Bradenton, FL
Legler, Kennedy, Jr. ... Bradenton, FL
Legler, Mitchell W. ... Jacksonville, FL
Legler, Mitchell W., P.A. ... Jacksonville, FL
Legler, Paul K.
Department Of Health And Human Services, GV
Legler, Paul W. ... Chula Vista, CA
Legler & Tomlinson ... Chula Vista, CA
Legmann, Rona L. ... Culver City, CA
Legnard, Joseph F. ... Albany, NY
Legner, Edward J. ... Pontiac, IL
Legner, Gary E. ... Charlottesville, VA
Legner, James J. ... Chicago, IL
Legnon, Edwin K. ... New Orleans, LA
Lego, Raymond J. ... Denver, CO
Lego, Robbin A. ... Littleton, CO
Lego, Robert T. ... Englewood, CO
LeGoff, Patricia A. ... Parsippany, NJ
New York, NY
Legomsky, Stephen H. ... St. Louis, MO
Legon, Suzanne M. ... Coral Gables, FL
Legon, Todd R. ... Miami, FL
LeGore, Robert O. ... Linwood, NJ
Legore, Stan ... Eugene, OR
Legorius, Christine Marie ... Albany, NY
Legow, Christine Blair ... Warren, OH
Legow, Donald M. ... Livingston, NJ
Legow, Elliot P. ... Youngstown, OH
LeGoy, L. Robert, Jr. ... Reno, NV
LeGrand, Bornstein & Naylor, LLP
Columbus, OH
LeGrand, Camille E. ... Guerneville, CA
Legrand, Charles ... New York, NY
LeGrand, Charles D. ... Greenville, SC
LeGrand, Clay ... Davenport, IA
LeGrand, David G. ... Columbus, OH
LeGrand, Donald G., Jr. ... Pasadena, TX
LeGrand, George, (P.C.) ... San Antonio, TX
Legrand, Georges M. ... New Orleans, LA
LeGrand, Jean A. ... Boerne, TX
LeGrand, Leslie P., Jr. ... Humble, TX
LeGrand, Nicholas W. ... Davenport, IA
Legrand, Pierre M. ... Metairie, LA
LeGrand, Roger W. ... La Crosse, WI
Legrand, Terri E. ... Wilmington, NC
Legrand, William Gregory
New Orleans, LA
LeGrande, Barbara ... Fort Myers, FL
LeGrande, James Leray ... Fort Myers, FL
LeGrande & LeGrande, P.A. ... Fort Myers, FL
Le Grand Koehler, Renée ... Chicago, IL
Legree, Ernest W. ... Highland Heights, OH
Legreid, Donald W. ... Fargo, ND
Legris, John F. ... San Antonio, TX
Legro, Monta K., (Mr.) ... Houston, TX
Legro, Stanley W. ... Washington, DC
Le Gro, Thomas R. ... Riverside, CA
Le Gros, Buchanan & Paul, P.S.
Anchorage, AK
Seattle, WA
LeGros, Clay J. ... Metairie, LA
Le Gros, Gary F., Jr. ... Jeanerette, LA
LeGros Law Partners, P.C. ... Princeton, NJ
Berwyn, PA
LeGros, Nancy C. ... Houston, TX
LeGros, Robert R. ... Philadelphia, PA
LeGros, Susan P. ... Princeton, NJ
Berwyn, PA
Leguay, Allan P. ... Irvine, CA
Legum, Alan Hilliard ... Annapolis, MD
Legum, Barton ... New York, NY
Legum, Howard E. ... Mineola, NY
Legum, Jonas D. ... Annapolis, MD
Legum, Radine
National Labor Relations Board,
Office of Board Members, GV
Legum, Steven G. ... Mineola, NY
Legum, Steven M. ... Norfolk, VA
Legum, Terry C. ... Fairfax, VA
Legum, Terry, P.L.C., Law Offices of
Fairfax, VA
Legus, Carrie J. ... South Burlington, VT
Leh, Christopher M. ... Boulder, CO
Leh, James R. ... Sterling, CO
Leh, John M. ... Southfield, MI
Leh, Marc B. ... Los Angeles, CA
Leh, Michael B. ... Philadelphia, PA
Lehan, Jonathan M. ... Fort Bragg, CA
Lehan, Michael J. ... Omaha, NE
Lehan, Samantha J. ... Seal Beach, CA
Lehan, Thomas P. ... Omaha, NE
Lehan, Timothy P. ... Raleigh, NC
Lehane, Christopher S.
Executive Office Of The President,
Office of the Vice President, GV
Lehane, Erin M. ... South Portland, ME
Lehane, Michael C. ... Quincy, MA
Lehane, William J. ... Philadelphia, PA
Lehat, Steven B. ... Irvine, CA
Lehavi, Florence Cavanna ... New York, NY
Lehavi, Limor ... Orange, CA
Lehberg, Mark C. ... San Diego, CA
Lehberger-Richard, Ingrid E.
Springfield, MA
Lehder, Todd E. ... Towson, MD
Lehe, Linda S. ... Birmingham, AL
Lehecka, John W. ... Wichita, KS
Lehecka, William B. ... Cleveland, OH
Lehenbauer, Alan J. ... Swanton, OH
Whitehouse, OH
Leheny, Mary F. ... New York, NY
Leheny, Sandra Vilardi ... Danbury, CT
Leher, Robert C. ... Denver, CO
Lehere, Allyson L. ... Youngstown, OH
Lehfeldt, Richard ... Fairfax, VA
Lehfellner, Werner R. ... New York, NY
Lehigh, Daniel T. ... New Philadelphia, OH
Lehigh, Elizabeth ... New Philadelphia, OH
Lehigh, L. Edwin ... Springfield, PA
Lehigh & Lehigh ... New Philadelphia, OH
Lehinger, Mark E. ... Spokane, WA
Lehl, Donna J. ... Tawas City, MI
Lehlbach, Frederick B. ... Newark, NJ
Lehleitner, George H., Jr. ... Portland, OR
Lehman, Adam H. ... Dulles, VA
Lehman, Anne L. ... Harrisburg, PA
Lehman, Anthony D. ... Atlanta, GA
Lehman, Antonette Miller ... Stillwater, MN
Lehman, Arnold S. ... New York, NY
Lehman, Arthur R. ... New York, NY
Lehman, Beth A. ... Chicago, IL
Lehman, Betsy G. ... Chicago, IL
Lehman, Bob E. ... Uniondale, NY
Lehman, Burton ... New York, NY
Lehman, Carol Bellinghausen
Lakewood, CO
Lehman, Carol Bellinghausen, L.L.C.
Lakewood, CO
Lehman & Cauley LLP ... Cairo, GA
Lehman, Charles C. ... Naples, FL
Lehman, Charles H. ... Pittsburgh, PA
Lehman, Christine E. ... Washington, DC
Lehman, Craig S. ... Rainsville, AL
Lehman, David B. ... Worthington, OH
Lehman, David E. ... Harrisburg, PA
Lehman, David J. ... Pittsburgh, PA
Lehman, David O. ... Chicago, IL
Lehman, David W. ... Hudson, OH
Lehman, Dayton, Jr.
Department of Transportation,
Office of the General Counsel, GV
Lehman, Diane C. ... Ann Arbor, MI
Lehman, Donna Peurifoy ... Miami, FL
Lehman, Douglas C. ... Wabash, IN
Lehman, Douglas M. ... New York, NY
Lehman, Douglas P. ... Lancaster, PA
Lehman, Duberman & Harris
New York, NY
Lehman, Edward ... Longmont, CO
Lehman, Edward A. ... Chicago, IL
Lehman, Edward C. ... Garwood, NJ
Lehman, Edward G. ... San Diego, CA
Lehman & Eilen LLP ... New York, NY
Lehman & Eilen, LLP ... Uniondale, NY
Lehman, Emmett R., III ... Lancaster, PA
Lehman, Evelyn J. ... New York, NY
Lehman & Fox ... Chicago, IL
Lehman, Gail E. ... Morristown, NJ
Lehman, Gary Edward, (P.A.) ... Miami, FL
Lehman & Gikow, P.C. ... New York, NY
Lehman, Gregg H. ... Boulder, CO
Lehman, Heidi Bierman ... Livingston, NJ
New York, NY
Lehman, Henry H. ... Memphis, TN
Lehman, Howard N. ... Los Angeles, CA
Lehman, Imogene ... Gaithersburg, MD
Lehman, J. Michael ... Wichita, KS
Lehman, Jack ... Las Vegas, NV
Lehman, James K. ... Columbia, SC
Lehman, James M. ... Minneapolis, MN
Lehman, Jane E. ... Charlottesville, VA
Lehman, Jeanine M. ... Austin, TX
Lehman, Jeanine, P.C., Law Offices of
Austin, TX
Lehman, Jeffrey M. ... New York, NY
Lehman, Jennifer A.D. ... San Rafael, CA
Lehman, Jennifer L. ... Harrisburg, PA
Lehman, Jennifer L. ... Fort Worth, TX
Lehman, Jennifer N. ... San Diego, CA
Lehman, Jensen & Donahue, L.C.
Salt Lake City, UT
Lehman, Jody ... Coral Gables, FL
Lehman, John E. ... Treasury Department,
U.S. Customs Service, GV
Lehman, Jonathan E. ... New York, NY
Lehman, Joseph A. ... Miamisburg, OH
Lehman, Julie S. ... Chicago, IL
Lehman, Kenneth A. ... Fresno, CA
Lehman, Kenneth M. ... Boston, MA
Lehman, Kenneth R. ... Washington, DC
Lehman, Kenneth W. ... Portland, ME
Lehman, Larry L. ... Cheyenne, WY
Lehman, Laura B. ... New York, NY
Lehman, Laurie Anderson ... Dallas, TX
Lehman, Lawrence J. ... Chicago, IL
Lehman & Lehman ... Lancaster, PA
Lehman, Lehman & Gruber
Livingston, NJ
Newark, NJ
New York, NY
Lehman, Margaret Elias ... New York, NY
Lehman, Mark A. ... Danville, IL
Lehman, Mark E. ... New York, NY
Lehman, Mark E. ... Salt Lake City, UT
Lehman, Martha Reddy ... Indianapolis, IN
Lehman, Martin J. ... Dallas, TX
Palmer, TX
Lehman, Marvin ... Elizabeth, NJ
Lehman, Mary A. ... San Diego, CA
Lehman, Mary B. ... New York, NY
Lehman, Mary Kate ... Seattle, WA
Lehman, Michael E. ... Fresno, CA
Lehman, Michael E. ... Livingston, NJ
New York, NY
Lehman, Michael F. ... Fort Wayne, IN
Lehman, Michael P. ... Concord, NH
Lehman, Michael R. ... Coos Bay, OR
Lehman, Myron S. ... Livingston, NJ
New York, NY
Lehman, Nancy ... Palm Beach Gardens, FL
Lehman, Neal F. ... Bartlesville, OK
Lehman, Palmer Smith ... Montgomery, AL
Lehman, Paul H., III ... San Francisco, CA
Lehman, Peter O. ... Charleston, SC
Lehman, Philip A. ... Raleigh, NC
Lehman, Ralph E. ... Wooster, OH
Lehman, Ralph F., Jr. ... Scottsdale, AZ
Lehman, Richard H. ... Chicago, IL
Lehman, Richard L. ... Bloomfield Hills, MI
Lehman, Richard S. ... Boca Raton, FL
Lehman, Richard S., P.A. ... Boca Raton, FL
Lehman, Robert A. ... Denver, CO
Lehman, Robert C. ... Mandeville, LA
Lehman, Robert C., P.L.C. ... Mandeville, LA
Lehman, Robert E. ... Indianapolis, IN
Lehman, Robert F. ... Dayton, OH
Lehman, Robert R. ... Jupiter, FL
Lehman, Robert T. ... Haddonfield, NJ
Lehman, Roberta L. ... Redondo Beach, CA
Lehman, Ronald M. ... Tucson, AZ
Lehman, Russell M. ... Olympia, WA
Lehman, Ruth G. ... Longmont, CO
Lehman, Scott B. ... Westminster, CO
Lehman, Scott Cristopher ... Columbus, OH
Lehman, Scott F. ... Tulsa, OK
Lehman, Sharon F. ... Pittsburgh, PA
Lehman, Stan A. ... Bisbee, AZ
Lehman, Stanley J. ... Pittsburgh, PA
Lehman, Stanley P. ... New York, NY
Lehman, Stephanie F. ... New York, NY
Lehman, Stephen P. ... New York, NY
Lehman, Steven J. ... Billings, MT
Lehman, T. Jeffery ... Atlanta, GA
Lehman, Thomas L. ... Cairo, GA
Lehman, Thomas R., (P.A.) ... Miami, FL
West Palm Beach, FL
Lehman, Tracy ... New York, NY
Philadelphia, PA
Lehman & Valentino, P.C.
Bloomfield Hills, MI
Lehman, Walter M. ... Toledo, OH
Lehman, William J. ... Hartford, CT
Lehman, William J.
Administrative Office Of The United States
Courts, GV
Lehman, Zachary Gimbel ... Charlestown, MA
Lehmann, Anja ... Washington, DC
Lehmann, Carl Crosby ... Minneapolis, MN
Lehmann, Carl Harrison
Upper Marlboro, MD
Lehmann, Catherine Buchanan
Houston, TX
Lehmann, Christopher G. ... Brooklyn, NY
Lehmann, Christopher J.
South St. Paul, MN
Lehmann, Eileen Anne
National Aeronautics And Space
Administration,
Goddard Space Flight Center, GV
Lehmann, Ernest L., Jr. ... Houston, TX
Lehmann, Harry V. ... Novato, CA
Lehmann, J. Michael
Federal Election Commission,
Office of the General Counsel, GV
Lehmann, James H. ... Houston, TX
Lehmann, Jeffrey A. ... Houston, TX
Lehmann, Katie Crosby ... Minneapolis, MN
Lehmann, Kenneth H. ... Los Angeles, CA
Lehmann, Lawrence M. ... New Orleans, LA
Lehmann, Linda Carole ... Manchester, CT
Lehmann, Lynn W. ... Denver, CO
Lehmann, Mark ... San Francisco, CA
Lehmann, Mary Anne ... Binghamton, NY
Lehmann, Michael A. ... New York, NY
Lehmann, Michael P. ... San Francisco, CA
Lehmann, Norman & Marcus, L.L.P.
New Orleans, LA
Lehmann, René ... New Orleans, LA
Lehmann, Richard ... Old Tappan, NJ
Lehmann, Richard A. ... Madison, WI
Lehmann, Richard S. ... Baltimore, MD
Lehmann, Ronald A.
Colorado Springs, CO
Denver, CO
Lehmann, Ronald A. ... New York, NY

Lehmann, S. Jerry ... Pensacola, FL
Lehmann, Sidney H. ... Lawrenceville, NJ
Lehmann, Stockton ... Fairfield, OH
Lehmann, Suzan Min ... Concord, NH
Lehmann, Terry W. ... Cincinnati, OH
Lehmann, Thomas G. ... Vernon Hills, IL
Lehmann, Thomas R. ... St. Paul, MN
Lehmann, Wendy E ... Rochester, NY
Lehmbecker, Larry Alan ... Bellevue, WA
Lehmberg, Bette Branch ... Midland, TX
Lehmberg, Philip R. ... Houston, TX
Lehmberg, Rosemary ... Austin, TX
Lehmer, Francie ... San Francisco, CA
Lehmkuhl, Allen M., (Co., L.P.A.)
Springfield, OH
Lehmkuhl, Phillip D. ... Columbus, OH
Lehn, David M. ... Southport, CT
Lehn, Kenneth K. ... Hackensack, NJ
Lehn, Richard L. ... Tekoa, WA
Lehn, Richard M. ... Downey, CA
Lehnardt, Detlef G. ... Kansas City, MO
New York, NY
Lehnardt & Lehnardt, LLC
Kansas City, MO
New York, NY
Lehnardt, Stephen K. ... Kansas City, MO
New York, NY
Lehnen, George, III ... Richmond, MO
Lehner, Charles W. ... Lawrenceburg, IN
Lehner, Craig P. ... New York, NY
Lehner, Daniel P. ... San Diego, CA
Lehner, Edward H. ... New York, NY
Lehner, Emma ... Phoenix, AZ
Lehner, George A. ... Washington, DC
Lehner, Jonathan ... Washington, DC
Lehner, Mary N. ... Richmond, VA
Lehner, Michael A. ... Portland, OR
Lehner, Michael P. ... Princeton, WI
Lehner, Mitchell, Rodrigues and Sears
Portland, OR
Lehner, Paul E. ... Chicago, IL
Lehner, Peter H. ... New York, NY
Lehner, Philip ... Brookfield, WI
Racine, WI
Lehner, Randall D. ... Chicago, IL
Lehner, Richard J. ... Buffalo, NY
Lehner, Robert J. ... Miami, FL
Lehner, Steven D. ... Tampa, FL
Lehner, Tara K. ... Silver Spring, MD
Lehner, Thomas J. ... Montpelier, VT
Lehner, William T. ... Richmond, VA
Lehner, Yolanda I. ... Milwaukee, WI
Lehnert, Edgar F. ... Grand Rapids, MI
Lehnert, Ingrid ... Streamwood, IL
Lehnert, Jack Scheringson ... Bronx, NY
Lehnert, Leslie E. ... Department of Justice, Environment and Natural Resources Division, GV
Lehnert, Robert C. ... Littleton, CO
Lehnhardt, Dana Belk ... Monroe, NC
Lehnhardt, Susan K. ... New York, NY
Lehnhardt, William E. ... El Centro, CA
Lehnigk, George F. ... Washington, DC
Lehnowsky, Judith A. ... Pittsburgh, PA
Lehocky, Jerry M. ... Philadelphia, PA
LeHocky, Mark ... San Francisco, CA
Lehotsky, Marc A. ... Mansfield, OH
LeHouillier, Patric J. ... Colorado Springs, CO
Lehr, Alison M. ... New York, NY
Lehr, Alison W. ... Sunrise, FL
Lehr, Bruce H. ... Miami, FL
Lehr, Christine C. ... Atlanta, GA
Lehr, Dennis J. ... Washington, DC
Lehr, Frederick Peter ... Bethlehem, PA
Lehr, Gary M. ... Livingston, NJ
Lehr & Gasalla, P.A. ... Miami, FL
Lehr, John F., Jr. ... Irvine, CA
Lehr, Jonathan M. ... New York, NY
Lehr, Kent E. ... Menno, SD
Lehr, L. Anthony ... Chicago, IL
Lehr, Louis A., Jr. ... Chicago, IL
Lehr, Matthew B. ... Wilmington, DE
Lehr, Meredith L. ... Bellevue, WA
Lehr, Michael A. ... Kansas City, MO
Lehr, Michael K. ... Wichita, KS
Lehr, Michael L. ... Philadelphia, PA
Lehr Middlebrooks Price & Proctor, P.C.
Birmingham, AL
Decatur, AL
Lehr, Myriam ... Miami, FL
Lehr, Rachel ... Trenton, NJ
Lehr, Richard D. ... Boston, MA
Lehr, Richard G. ... Warren, MI
Lehr, Richard I. ... Birmingham, AL
Lehr, Rodger W., Jr. ... Groton, CT
Lehr, Ronald L. ... Denver, CO
Lehr, S. Ruth, Law Offices of
Kansas City, MO
Lehr, Sheila ... Oak Brook, IL
Lehr, Stephen Michael ... Gainesville, FL
Lehr, Steven R. ... Fairfield, NJ
Lehr, Steven Robert, P.C. ... Fairfield, NJ
Lehr, Susan E. ... Seattle, WA
Lehr, Terri L. ... Superior, WI
Lehr, Terry V. ... San Diego, CA
Lehrberg, Roger J. F. ... Newton, MA
Lehrburger, James F. ... St. Petersburg, FL
Lehrburger, Robert W. ... New York, NY
Lehrenbaum, Warren U. ... Washington, DC
Lehrer, Alexander D. ... Freehold, NJ
Lehrer, Andrew ... New York, NY
Lehrer, Benjamin ... Los Angeles, CA
Lehrer, Bernard ... Los Angeles, CA
Lehrer, Brian R. ... Millburn, NJ
Lehrer, David A. ... Los Angeles, CA
Lehrer, Douglas W. ... Hartford, WI
Lehrer, Flaherty & Canavan ... Wheaton, IL
Lehrer, Gaby Ferman ... New York, NY
Lehrer, Gregg R. ... Orlando, FL
Lehrer, James M. ... Rosemead, CA
Lehrer, Jeffrey B. ... Warren, NJ
Lehrer, Jeffrey K. ... Reston, VA
Lehrer, Joel ... New York, NY
Lehrer, John W. ... Sandusky, OH
Lehrer, Joseph D. ... St. Louis, MO
Lehrer, Julius M. ... Chicago, IL
Lehrer, Mark R. ... New York, NY
Lehrer, Matthew D. ... Tucson, AZ
Lehrer, Michael W. ... Tampa, FL
Lehrer, Norman E. ... Cherry Hill, NJ
Philadelphia, PA
Lehrer, Norman E., P.C. ... Cherry Hill, NJ
Philadelphia, PA
Lehrer, Norman H. ... Wheaton, IL
Lehrer, Pamela I. ... Philadelphia, PA
Lehrer & Redleaf ... Chicago, IL
Lehrer, Richard ... Morganville, NJ
Lehrer, Richard M. ... New York, NY
Lehrer, Robert E. ... Chicago, IL
Lehrer, Robert W. ... Clemmons, NC
Lehrer, Samuel M. ... Philadelphia, PA
Lehrer, Sander ... New York, NY
Lehrer, Scott E. ... New York, NY
Lehrer, Stanley I. ... New York, NY
Lehrer, William R., III ... Folsom, CA
Lehrer-Graiwer, Jonathan ... Beverly Hills, CA
Lehrer-Stein, Janice ... San Francisco, CA
Lehrfeld, Betsy Eileen ... Maitland, FL
Lehrfeld, William J. ... Bethesda, MD
Lehrfeld, William J., P.C.
Washington, DC
Bethesda, MD
Lehrfield, Aaron Y. ... New York, NY
Lehrfield, Moshe M. ... Miami, FL
Lehrhaupt, Charles M.
Gaithersburg, MD
Lehrhaupt, Liesel E. T. ... Spokane, WA
Lehrhaupt, Wayne R. ... New York, NY
Lehrhoff, Michael B. ... Washington, DC
Lehrhoff, Steven J. ... Los Angeles, CA
Lehrich, Hyman D. ... New York, NY
Lehrich & Lehrich ... New York, NY
Lehrich, Richard S. ... Cranford, NJ
Lehrkind, H. Thompson
San Francisco, CA
Lehrkinder, Donald W. ... Media, PA
Lehrkinder and Gillingham ... Media, PA
Lehrman, Andrew J. ... Austin, TX
Corpus Christi, TX
Lehrman, Douglas M. ... Sacramento, CA
Lehrman, Fredric M. ... White Plains, NY
Lehrman, Jeffrey B. ... Irvine, CA
Lehrman, Jeffrey E. ... Coral Gables, FL
Lehrman, Jerome M. ... Dearborn, MI
Lehrman, June R. ... Culver City, CA
Lehrman, Kate S., (A Professional Corporation) ... Santa Monica, CA
Lehrman, Kim J. ... Plantation, FL
Lehrman & Kronick ... White Plains, NY
Lehrman, Lewis ... Mineola, NY
Lehrman, Margie A.S. ... Washington, DC
Lehrman, Mark D. ... New York, NY
Lehrman, Michael B. ... New York, NY
Lehrman, Richard Alan
Miami Beach, FL
Lehrman, Robert A. ... New York, NY
Lehrman, Robert C. ... Washington, DC
Lehrman, Ronald J. ... New York, NY
Lehrman, Steven M. ... New York, NY
Lehrmann, Debra H. ... Fort Worth, TX
Lehrmann, Gregory A. ... Hurst, TX
Lehrmann, Kathleen F. ... Fort Worth, TX
Lehrter, Erin K. ... San Diego, CA
Lehrter, Richard John ... Oklahoma City, OK
Lehsten, Barry Jay ... Farmington Hills, MI
Lehtinen, Dexter W. ... Miami, FL
Lehtinen, O'Donnell, Vargas & Reiner, Professional Association ... Miami, FL
Lehtman, Myron S. ... Department of Justice, Civil Rights Division, GV
Lehto, Duke J. ... Wauwatosa, WI
Lehto, Michael D. ... Detroit, MI
Lehto, Neil J. ... Sterling Heights, MI
Lehto, Sheila G. ... Worcester, MA
Lehto, Steve, Law Offices of
Farmington Hills, MI
Lehtola, Patricia B. ... Dallas, TX
Lehtonen, Alfred J. ... College Station, TX
Lehtonen, Andrea J. ... Fitchburg, MA
Lehtonen, Lesla ... San Mateo, CA
Lehtonen, Todd A. ... McLean, VA
Lehtonen, Tony ... Sacramento, CA
Lehu, Joanne Seminara ... New York, NY
Lehutsky, Michael P. ... Honesdale, PA
Lehv, David G. ... New York, NY
Lehv, H. Anthony ... Washington, DC
Lehv, Hilary Z. ... Ardsley, NY
Lehv, Michael S. ... Columbus, OH
Lehv, Michael S., Co., L.P.A.
Columbus, OH
Lehv, Richard Z. ... New York, NY
Lei, Leslie A. ... Boulder, CO
Lei, Wendy H. ... New York, NY
Leib, Alton ... Los Angeles, CA
Leib, Alton ... Los Angeles, CA
Leib, Charles B. ... Palo Alto, CA
Leib, Charles R. ... Marina Del Rey, CA
Leib, Daniel C. ... Beverly Hills, CA
Leib, David ... Kensington, CT
Leib, David A. ... McLean, VA
Leib, Elisa ... Clifton, NJ
Leib, Gerald B. ... Mountain View, CA
Leib, Harold ... Clifton, NJ
Leib, Harold, P.A. ... Clifton, NJ
Leib, Howard D. ... New York, NY
Leib, Jeffrey M. ... Southfield, MI
Leib & Katt, S.C. ... Milwaukee, WI
Leib, Kraus, Grispin & Roth, A Professional Corporation ... Scotch Plains, NJ
Leib, Leib & Kramer, P.C. ... Southfield, MI
Leib, Michael S. ... Chicago, IL
Leib, Michael S. ... Southfield, MI
Leib, Rosalie ... Milwaukee, WI
Leib, Samuel J. ... Milwaukee, WI
Leib, Susan J. ... Indianapolis, IN
Leib, Walter L. ... Scotch Plains, NJ
Leiba, Arthur ... Stockton, CA
Leibel, Alan S. ... Dallas, TX
Fort Worth, TX
Leibel, Jay M. ... Madison, SD
Leibel, John M. ... St. Paul, MN
Leibel, Shelley ... Philadelphia, PA
Leibel, Steven K. ... Atlanta, GA
Leibell, David T. ... Stamford, CT
Leibell, Jeffrey N. ... New York, NY
Leibell, John J. ... Stamford, CT
Leibell, Vincent L., III ... Carmel, NY
Leibenguth, Boos & Neilsen, P.C.
Traverse City, MI
Leibenguth, James M. ... Traverse City, MI
Leibenguth, M Scott ... Portland, OR
Leibenluft, Robert F. ... Washington, DC
Leibensperger, Edward P. ... Boston, MA
Leibensperger, Patricia K. ... Newton, MA
Leibenstein, Elli ... Chicago, IL
Leibenstern, Maurice ... Islandia, NY
Leiber, Deborah Weiss
The Woodlands, TX
Leiber, Dennis B. ... Grand Rapids, MI
Leiber, James R. ... Oklahoma City, OK
Leiber, John Lee ... Tucson, AZ
Leiberan & Gazeley ... Portland, OR
Leiberan, Margaret H. Leek ... Portland, OR
Leibert, Burton M. ... New York, NY
Leibert, Matthew A. ... Ocala, FL
Leibert, Richard M. ... Hartford, CT
Leibert-Hall, Linda A. ... Fargo, ND
Leibham, Shelly A. ... Austin, TX
Leibholtz, Maria E. ... New York, NY
Leibig, Michael T. ... Washington, DC
Leibinger, Diana P. ... Missoula, MT
Leibl, Daniel ... Pasadena, CA
Leibl, Geoffrey ... Del Mar, CA
Leibl & Kirkwood ... Del Mar, CA
Leible, Charles, Jr. ... Sikeston, MO
Leible, W. Robert ... St. Louis, MO
Leibler, Elisheva S. ... New York, NY
Leibman, Alain ... Newark, NJ
Leibman, David J. ... New York, NY
Leibman, Deborah H. ... San Mateo, CA
Leibman, Jordan H. ... Indianapolis, IN
Leibman, Leonard S. ... New York, NY
Leibman, Mark ... Potomac, MD
Leibman, Neil ... Bala Cynwyd, PA
Leibman, Neil M. ... Houston, TX
Leibman & Oesch, L.L.P. ... Houston, TX
Leibman, Ronald ... Newark, NJ
Leibner, Carl A. ... Clayton, MO
Leibner & Potkin, P.C. ... Washington, DC
Leibner, Robert F. ... Washington, DC
Leibnitz, Andrew ... Palo Alto, CA
Leibold, Arthur W., Jr. ... Washington, DC
Leibold, Barbara Zeid ... Orange, CA
Leibold, Charles H. ... Des Moines, IA
Leibold, Gregory D. ... Denver, CO
Leibold, John W. ... Columbus, OH
Leibold, Peter M. ... Washington, DC
Leibold, Terence E. ... Lawrence, KS
Leibold, William J. ... Dayton, OH
Leibovic, Aaron J. ... Sherman Oaks, CA
Leibovic & Tysch ... Sherman Oaks, CA
Leibovich, Robert Joseph ... Memphis, TN
Leibovit, Louis ... Palm Beach, FL
Leibovitch, Ellen M. ... Miami, FL
Leibovitch, Jack I. ... Towson, MD
Leibovitch, Jay Byron ... Chicago, IL
Leibovitz, Norman ... Philadelphia, PA
Leibovitz, Paula ... Orinda, CA
Leibovitz, Stefanie Chirlin ... Cherry Hill, NJ
Leibovitz, William ... New York, NY
Leibow, Howard P. ... Phoenix, AZ
Leibow, Ronald L. ... Los Angeles, CA
Leibow, Sandra ... New York, NY
Leibow, Whitney H. ... Seattle, WA
Leibowicz, Barry ... Great Neck, NY
Leibowicz, Joseph ... Pittsburgh, PA
Leibowitt, S. David ... Palm Beach, FL
Leibowitz, Alan B. ... New York, NY
Leibowitz, Alan I. ... Hartford, CT
Leibowitz, Andrew S. ... Melville, NY
Leibowitz, Ann G. ... Weston, MA
Leibowitz & Associates, P.A. ... Miami, FL
Leibowitz & Band ... Wheaton, MD
Falls Church, VA
Leibowitz, Barry L. ... Wheaton, MD
Falls Church, VA
Leibowitz, Benjamin D. ... Edison, NJ
Leibowitz & Bock ... New York, NY
Leibowitz & Chehanske ... Howell, NJ
Leibowitz & Cohen ... Knoxville, TN
Leibowitz, David McQuade
San Antonio, TX
Leibowitz, David McQuade, P.C., Law Offices of ... San Antonio, TX
Leibowitz, David P., Law Offices of
Waukegan, IL
Leibowitz, Donald S. ... Newark, NJ
Leibowitz, Ellen R. ... Garden City, NY
Leibowitz, Ephraim K. ... New York, NY
Leibowitz, Gary ... Santa Ana, CA
Leibowitz, Gary H. ... Baltimore, MD
Leibowitz, George J. ... Rockville, MD
Leibowitz, Hal J. ... Boston, MA
Leibowitz, Harold L. ... New York, NY
Leibowitz, Henry J. ... New York, NY
Leibowitz, Herman M. ... New York, NY
Leibowitz, Hilary K. ... Plantation, FL
Leibowitz, Ira H. ... Port Jefferson, NY
Leibowitz, Ivy ... Hempstead, NY
Leibowitz, Joel L. ... Parsippany, NJ
Leibowitz, Jonathan D. ... United States Senate, Committee Legal Personnel, GV
Leibowitz, Kenneth M. ... New York, NY
Leibowitz, Lawrence P. ... Knoxville, TN
Leibowitz, Lawrence S. ... Uniondale, NY
Leibowitz, Lewis E. ... Washington, DC
Leibowitz, Marc ... San Diego, CA
Leibowitz, Mark A. ... Miami, FL
Leibowitz, Martin L. ... Jacksonville, FL
Leibowitz, Martin L., P.A.
Jacksonville, FL
Leibowitz, Marvin ... Pittsburgh, PA
Leibowitz, Mary Beth ... Knoxville, TN
Leibowitz, Matthew L. ... Miami, FL
Leibowitz, Melvin ... New York, NY
Leibowitz, Paul ... Denver, CO
Leibowitz, Reuben S. ... New York, NY
Leibowitz, Richard D. ... Baton Rouge, LA
Leibowitz, Robin Lynn ... Baltimore, MD
Leibowitz, Samuel ... New York, NY
Leibowitz, Saul A. ... Livingston, NJ
Leibowitz, Sheldon B. ... Howell, NJ
Leibowitz, Sherry S. ... Boston, MA
Leibowitz, Sonya ... Battle Creek, MI
Leibowitz, Stanley H. ... Boston, MA
Leibowitz, Stephen R. ... Pennsauken, NJ
Leibowitz, Stuart A. ... Norristown, PA
Leibowitz, Thomas J. ... Stafford, TX
Leibowitz, Wendy R. ... New York, NY
Leibrock, Fred A. ... Oklahoma City, OK
Leibrock, William M. ... Newport, TN
Leibsker, Donald M. ... Chicago, IL
Leibsker, Ira F. ... Chicago, IL
Leibsle, Robert C. ... Elkhorn, WI
Leibsohn, Hope ... Phoenix, AZ
Leibsohn, Mark ... Phoenix, AZ
Leibsohn, Seth ... Washington, DC
Leibson, David J. ... Louisville, KY
Leibson, James D. ... San Francisco, CA
Leibson, Michael C. ... Oak Park, MI
Leibson, Michael J. ... Louisville, KY
Leibson, Michele K. ... New York, NY
Leibson, Russell, Law Offices of
San Francisco, CA
Leibst, Mitzi D. ... Seattle, WA
Leibundgut, Peter W. ... Cherry Hill, NJ
Leiby Construction Law Firm, Professional Association ... Fort Lauderdale, FL
Miami, FL
West Palm Beach, FL
Leiby, Jack L. ... Moline, IL
Leiby, Kenneth L., Jr. ... Fairfield, NJ
Leiby, Lana L. ... Washington, DC
Leiby, Larry R. ... Fort Lauderdale, FL
Leiby, Stephen P. ... Akron, OH
Leich, Christopher M. ... Boston, MA
Leichenger, David B. ... Beverly Hills, CA
Leichenger, David B. ... Los Angeles, CA
Leichenger, Sheryl W. ... Los Angeles, CA
Leicher, Bruce A. ... Cambridge, MA
Leicher, Lewis H. ... New York, NY
Leicher, Marvin H. ... New York, NY
Leichliter, Van H., Jr. ... Wilmington, DE
Leichman, Sherry L. ... Rockville, MD
Leichner, Curtis W. ... Portland, OR
Leichner, Curtis W., P.C. ... Portland, OR
Leichnitz, Leonard P. ... Los Angeles, CA
Leicht, Donald E. C. ... Kokomo, IN
Leicht, Eric F. ... New York, NY
Leicht, F. Josiah ... White Plains, NY
Leicht, Fred, Jr., (P.C.) ... St. Louis, MO
Leicht, Gene T. ... Asheville, NC
Leicht, George P. ... Bethel, OH
Leicht, Holly Marie ... New York, NY
Leicht, Leonard C. ... Livingston, NJ
Leicht, M. Joshua ... Little Rock, AR
Leicht, Paula J. ... Harrisburg, PA
Leichter, Alexandra ... Beverly Hills, CA
Leichter, Franz S. ... New York, NY
Leichter, Helene L. ... Menlo Park, CA
Leichter, Henry O. ... New York, NY
Leichter, Joshua W. ... Boston, MA
Leichter, Kevin J. ... Los Angeles, CA
Leichter, Louis D. ... Austin, TX
Leichtfuss, David E. ... Milwaukee, WI
Leichtfuss, Peter S. ... Portland, OR
Leichtling, Adam B. ... Miami, FL
Leichtling, Ely A. ... Milwaukee, WI
Leichtling, Michael A. ... New York, NY
Leichtling, Pamela J. ... Chicago, IL
Leichtman, David ... New York, NY
Leichtman, Ira Alan ... Houston, TX
Leichtman, Lauren ... Beverly Hills, CA
Leichtman, Judith A. ... San Francisco, CA
Leichtner, Edward J. ... Rochester, NY
Leichtner, Robert S. ... Pleasant Hill, CA
Leichtner, Scott ... Palo Alto, CA
Leichty, Bruce ... Clovis, CA
Leick, Charles R. ... Steelville, MO
Leick, Christine M. ... Edina, MN
Leick, Hammons and Brittain
Barbourville, KY
Corbin, KY
Leick, Herman E. ... Corbin, KY
Leick, Robert K. ... Stevenson, WA
Leickly, James R. ... Columbus, OH
Leid, Patricia A. ... Miami, FL
Leid, Rory W., III ... Seattle, WA
Leiden & Leiden, A Professional Corporation ... Augusta, GA
Waynesboro, GA
Aiken, SC

Leiden, Terrance Patrick ... Augusta, GA
Leiden, Warren R. ... San Francisco, CA
Leiden, Zane P. ... Augusta, GA
Leidenheimer, Robert E., Jr.
Department of Justice, Civil Division, GV
Leider, Andrew B. ... Brooklyn, NY
Leider, Heidi A. ... Santa Monica, CA
Leider, Herbert J. ... Honolulu, HI
Leider, Stephanie ... Oakland, CA
Leider, Suzanne M. ... Boca Raton, FL
Leiderman, Harvey L. ... San Francisco, CA
Leiderman, Joel D. ... Great Neck, NY
Leiderman, Jonathan S. ... Miami, FL
Leiderman, Kathryn R. ... Jasper, TN
Leiderman, Mitchell R. ... Media, PA
Leiderman, Robert J. ... Jasper, TN
Leidich, Robert J. ... Houston, TX
Leidig, John J. ... Baltimore, MD
Leidigh, Barbara J. ... Sacramento, CA
Leidigh, Robert Dale ... Pittsburgh, PA
Leidigh, Robert E. ... Sacramento, CA
Leiding, Melvin D. ... Anaheim, CA
Leidl, Richard J. ... Washington, DC
Leidler, Margaret ... Boston, MA
Leidman, Frank Z. ... San Francisco, CA
Leidner, Anthony S. ... New York, NY
Leidner, Charles G. ... Denver, CO
Leidner, Ellen Beth ... Columbus, OH
Leidner, Harold E. ... Cleveland, OH
Leidner, Joel D. ... Los Angeles, CA
Leidner & Leidner, A Professional Corporation
Los Angeles, CA
Leidner, Nelson J. ... Philadelphia, PA
Leidner, Susan Whittington
New Orleans, LA
Leidner, Suzanne C. ... Los Angeles, CA
Leids, Asher M. ... Los Angeles, CA
Leidy, Antonette M. ... West Palm Beach, FL
Leidy, John D. ... Elizabeth City, NC
Leidy, Lee L. ... Elizabeth City, NC
Leidy, Thomas D. ... Boyertown, PA
Leiendecker, Mark A. ... Summerville, SC
Leiendecker, Mark A., L.L.C.
Summerville, SC
Leier, Glenn A. ... Portland, OR
Leier, Ranelle A. ... Minneapolis, MN
Leier, Robert A. ... Herndon, VA
Leif, Jason F. ... Washington, DC
Leifel, Danny J. ... Bloomington, IL
Leifer, Alan J. ... Tampa, FL
Leifer, David C. ... Santa Monica, CA
Leifer, David M. ... Washington, DC
Leifer, Deborah L. ... Laguna Niguel, CA
Leifer, Elihu I. ... Washington, DC
Leifer, Jacqueline C. ... Washington, DC
Leifer, Jane A. ... Newton, MA
New York, NY
Leifer, Joel M., & Associates
New York, NY
Leifer, Kevin ... New York, NY
Leifer, Larry L., P.C. ... Maplewood, NJ
Leifer, Max D ... New York, NY
Leifer, Max D., P.C. ... New York, NY
Leifer, Michael H. ... Irvine, CA
Leifer, Neil T. ... Boston, MA
Leifer, Roger J., Law Offices of
Westport, CT
Leifer, Sharan ... Washington, DC
Leifer, Sharan ... Gaithersburg, MD
Leifer & Sheptock ... Maplewood, NJ
Leifer, Steven L. ... Washington, DC
Leifer, Wendy ... New York, NY
Leifer, William H. ... Fresno, CA
Leiferman, Cynthia A. ... Austin, TX
Leiferman, Cynthia A., P.C. ... Austin, TX
Leifert, John L. ... New York, NY
Leifeste, Michelle T. ... Boulder, CO
Leifeste, Roger Rae ... San Angelo, TX
Leifeste, William H. ... Midland, TX
Leifheit, John A. ... De Kalb, IL
Leifker, David W. ... Dubuque, IA
Leifman, Steven ... Miami, FL
Leifman, Vera Hallemann ... Brooklyn, NY
Leifur, Katherine F. ... Minneapolis, MN
Leifz, Christopher J. ... New York, NY
Leigh, Alison ... Bronx, NY
Leigh, Benjamin D. ... Fairfax, VA
Leigh, Bruce K. ... San Francisco, CA
Leigh, Christopher K.
Fort Lauderdale, FL
Leigh, Cindie S. ... Great Neck, NY
Leigh, Cynthia Fuller ... Austin, TX
Leigh, D. Kenneth, Jr. ... Jacksonville, FL
Leigh, David E. ... Naples, FL
Leigh, Douglas M. ... San Diego, CA
Leigh, Ellen M. ... New York, NY
Leigh, G. Whitney ... San Francisco, CA
Leigh, Gary D. ... Chicago, IL
Leigh, James S. ... San Francisco, CA
Leigh, James S. ... Portland, OR
Leigh, John R. ... Dallas, TX
Leigh, John R. ... Duncanville, TX
Leigh, Keith R. ... Ottawa, IL
Leigh, Laura H. ... Leesburg, VA
Leigh, Lawrence S. ... La Jolla, CA
Leigh, Lewis, Jr. ... Fairfax, VA
Leigh, Lewis R. ... Omaha, NE
Leigh, Mari Henry ... Chicago, IL
Leigh, Monroe ... Washington, DC
Leigh, Rebecca A. ... Houston, TX
Leigh, Rebecca Kapell ... Washington, DC
Leigh, Richard A. ... Winter Park, FL
Leigh, Stephanie ... Clark, NJ
Leigh, Steven M. ... Kansas City, MO
Leigh, Todd E. ... San Diego, CA
Leigh, William C. ... Houston, TX
Leigh, William H. ... Cedar City, UT

Leighner, William ... Alexandria, VA
Leighner, William H. ... Columbus, OH
Leighninger, Sally Heinz ... Minneapolis, MN
Leigh-Suelflow, Phoebe M.
Los Angeles, CA
Leight, Arnold W. ... New York, NY
Leight, Leonard ... Palm Beach Gardens, FL
Leight, Michael E. ... Long Beach, CA
Leight, Michelle S. ... Torrance, CA
Leight, Peter ... Cheshire, CT
Leight, Robert R. ... Pittsburgh, PA
Leightman, Caryl W. ... Millburn, NJ
Leighton, A. Patrick ... St. Paul, MN
Leighton, Barry B. ... New York, NY
Leighton, C. Thomas ... Columbus, OH
Leighton, Charles J., Jr. ... Berkeley, CA
Leighton, Daniel F. ... Minneapolis, MN
Leighton, Everett W. ... Riverside, CA
Leighton, George N. ... Chicago, IL
Leighton, James Paul ... Monterey Park, CA
Leighton, Jamie L. ... Brockton, MA
Leighton, Jeanette C. ... Pensacola, FL
Leighton, Jeffrey A. ... East Hanover, NJ
Leighton, John Elliott ... Miami, FL
Leighton, John J. ... New York, NY
Leighton, John M. ... Minneapolis, MN
Leighton, Joseph F., Jr. ... Boston, MA
Leighton, Judd ... South Bend, IN
Leighton, Kathryn E. ... Brooklyn, NY
Leighton & Katz ... Rockville, CT
Leighton, Kaye L. ... Mount Sterling, KY
Leighton, Kelly A. ... Lowell, MA
Leighton, Leighton & Leighton
New York, NY
Leighton, Leonard ... San Antonio, TX
Leighton, Leonard, A Professional Corporation
San Antonio, TX
Leighton, Lewis C. ... New York, NY
Leighton, Mark D. ... Rockville, CT
Leighton, Meany, Cotter & Enger, Ltd.
Austin, MN
Leighton, Michael R. ... Hackensack, NJ
Leighton, Noble I. ... Mountain Grove, MO
Leighton, Patricia A. ... College Station, TX
Leighton, Paul A. ... Tampa, FL
Leighton, Paul J. ... Des Moines, IA
Leighton, Philip Z. ... Orlando, FL
Leighton, Richard J. ... Washington, DC
Leighton, Richard J. ... Duluth, MN
Leighton, Richard L. ... Minneapolis, MN
Leighton, Richard L., P.A.
Minneapolis, MN
Leighton, Robert ... Pasadena, CA
Leighton, Robert J., Jr. ... Austin, MN
Leighton, Robert P. ... New York, NY
Leighton, Ronald B. ... Seattle, WA
Tacoma, WA
Leighton, Sally Briggs ... Tacoma, WA
Leighton, Samuel ... New York, NY
Leighton, Scott M. ... Austin, MN
Leighton, Theodore R. ... Westbury, NY
Leighton, Walter M. ... Los Angeles, CA
Leighton-Beasley, Marcheta ... Houston, TX
Leightty, David ... Louisville, KY
Leighty, Ellis E. ... Macomb, IL
Leighty, John W. ... Olathe, KS
Leighty, Leighton L. ... East Lansing, MI
Leik, James N. ... Anchorage, AK
Leik, Kevin C. ... Eau Claire, WI
Leik, Michael G. ... Cincinnati, OH
Leiken, Ben C. ... Eureka, IL
Leiken, Earl M. ... Cleveland, OH
Leiken, Jerome ... Belhaven, NC
Leiken, Judith ... Richmond, CA
Leiken, Larry M. ... El Paso, IL
Eureka, IL
Metamora, IL
Leiken & Leiken ... Minonk, IL
Leiken, Leiken & Leiken ... Eureka, IL
Metamora, IL
Leiken, N. Ned ... El Paso, IL
Minonk, IL
Leiken, Richard W. ... El Paso, IL
Eureka, IL
Metamora, IL
Leiker, Joseph ... Topeka, KS
Leiker, Kaylene M. ... Topeka, KS
Leiker, Patricia L. ... Milwaukee, WI
Leikhim, Paul J. ... Boston, MA
Leikin, George A. ... Southfield, MI
Leikin & Ingber, P.C. ... Southfield, MI
Leikin, Jeffrey A. ... Cleveland, OH
Leikin, Jeffrey M. ... Ellicott City, MD
Leikin, Mitchell ... Chicago, IL
Leikin, William F. ... Hartford, CT
Leiman, Alan J. ... Eugene, OR
Leiman, Eugene A. ... New York, NY
Leiman, Joe ... Washington, DC
Leiman, Jose ... Washington, DC
Leiman, Leonard M. ... New York, NY
Leiman, Paul G. ... Treasury Department, Office of Thrift Supervision, GV
Leimas, Irwin ... New York, NY
Leimas, Roth & Schein ... New York, NY
Leimbach, Carol C. ... San Diego, CA
Leimbach, James D. ... Rochester, NY
Leimberg, Stephan R. ... Bryn Mawr, PA
Leimer, Gerald W. ... Eagan, MN
Leimer, Jacqueline A. ... Northfield, IL
Leimer, Randal J. ... Kansas City, MO
Leimkuhler, Mark J. ... Washington, DC
Lein, Diane Smits ... Wilmington, DE
Lein, Kristin D. ... Janesville, WI
Lein, Lorelei A. ... Montgomery, AL
Lein, Marlene A. ... Manchester, NH
Lein, Russell M. ... Milwaukee, WI
Lein, Susan C. ... Hayward, WI
Leinauer, Craig M. ... St. Louis, MO

Leinbach, Brian J. ... Los Angeles, CA
Leinbach, Eric Lester ... Washington, NJ
Easton, PA
Leinbach, Kenneth A. ... Boston, MA
Leinbach, Margaret R. K. ... Charlotte, NC
Leinbach, Michelle E. ... Boston, MA
Leinbach, O. Charles, Jr. ... Columbus, OH
Leinbach, Robert D. ... Seattle, WA
Leinback, Bruce A. ... Tallahassee, FL
Leinback, Bruce A., P.A. ... Tallahassee, FL
Leinberg, Gunnar G. ... Rochester, NY
Leinberger, Clifford A. ... New York, NY
Leinberger, Karl G. ... Chicago, IL
Leinen, Amy L. ... Phoenix, AZ
Leinen, Robert J. ... Marengo, IA
North English, IA
Leinenweber, Harry D. ... Chicago, IL
Leinenweber, Thomas M. ... Chicago, IL
Leiner, Alice D. ... Seattle, WA
Leiner, Frederick C. ... Baltimore, MD
Leiner, Helen ... Fairfax, VA
Leiner, Helen, P.C. ... Fairfax, VA
Leiner, Jonathan H. ... New York, NY
Leineweber, Edward E. ... Richland Center, WI
Leineweber, Gregory J. ... Portland, OR
Leineweber, Robert J. ... Portland, OR
Leinhardt, Jeanne E. ... New York, NY
Leinhardt, Jonathan ... Bay Shore, NY
Leinhardt, Walter F. ... New York, NY
Leinheardt, Wallace L. ... Garden City, NY
Leinicke, Shelley H. ... Fort Lauderdale, FL
Leinicke, Steven Y. ... Fort Lauderdale, FL
Leininger, Barbara A. ... Bloomington, MN
Leininger, Brian L. ... Topeka, KS
Leininger, Carri S. ... West Palm Beach, FL
Leininger, Cheryl L. ... Santa Ana, CA
Leininger, D. Steven ... Grand Island, NE
Leininger, Daniel K. ... Warsaw, IN
Leininger, George A., Jr.
Lawrenceburg, IN
Leininger, Jack H. ... Kent, WA
Leininger, Mark E. ... Millersburg, OH
Leininger, Robert C. ... Metairie, LA
Leininger, Robert E. ... Columbus, OH
Leininger, Roland Lee ... Department of Justice, Environment and Natural Resources Division, GV
Leininger, Vance E. ... Columbus, NE
Leininger, William J. ... Staten Island, NY
Leininger, William J., P.C.
Staten Island, NY
Leino, John Frank ... Alexandria, VA
Leinoff, Andrew M. ... Miami, FL
Leinoff, Andrew M., & Associates, P.A.
Coral Gables, FL
Fort Lauderdale, FL
Miami, FL
West Palm Beach, FL
Leins, Richard A. ... Ossining, NY
Leinsdorf, David I. ... Crested Butte, CO
Leinster, Ed ... Jacksonville, FL
Leinster, Ed, P.A. ... Jacksonville, FL
Leinwand, David ... New York, NY
Leinwand, Harris D. ... New York, NY
Leinwand, Jonathan D. ... Fort Lauderdale, FL
Leinwand, Martin R. ... Boston, MA
Leinwand, Robert ... San Francisco, CA
Leinwand, Robert R. ... New York, NY
Leinwand, Shari ... Los Angeles, CA
Leinweber, Katie Avery ... Scottsdale, AZ
Leinweber, Kurt A. ... Joliet, IL
Leinwohl, Arthur ... Kings Beach, CA
Leip, Lawrence D. ... Jefferson City, MO
Leiper, William C. ... Monroeville, PA
Leipham, Jay E. ... Spokane, WA
Leipheimer, Linda S. ... Oakland, CA
Leipold, Andrew D. ... Philadelphia, PA
Leipold, Calvin A. ... Decatur, GA
Leipold, Daniel A. ... Orange, CA
Leipold, Mark E. ... Chicago, IL
Leipold, Michele M. ... Rapid City, SD
Leipold, Paul A. ... Rochester, NY
Leipold, Thomas E. ... Bloomsburg, PA
Leippe, Richard A. ... Greensboro, NC
Leipply, Gerald R. ... Cuyahoga Falls, OH
Leipply & Kreiner ... Cuyahoga Falls, OH
Leipprandt, Aileen M. ... Grand Rapids, MI
Leipzig, Scott J. ... Los Angeles, CA
Leipzig, Steven D. ... Hackensack, NJ
Leipziger, David A. ... Los Angeles, CA
Leipziger, Dorrith ... Plantation, FL
Leis, Carole Sherman ... Narberth, PA
Leis, Donald G., Jr. ... Windsor Locks, CT
Leis, Simon L., Jr. ... Cincinnati, OH
Leisawitz, Alan G. ... Wyomissing, PA
Leisawitz Heller Abramowitch Phillips, P.C.
Hamburg, PA
Reading, PA
Wyomissing, PA
Leise, Christopher P. ... Westmont, NJ
Leiseca, Sergio A., Jr. ... Dallas, TX
Leisenring, Erica Bissell ... St. Louis, MO
Leiser, Allan W. ... Milwaukee, WI
Leiser, Burton M. ... Briarcliff Manor, NY
Leiser, Christie Day ... Wilmington, DE
Leiser, Erica J. ... Melbourne, FL
Leiser, G. Malcolm ... Woodland, CA
Leiser, H. Wayne ... Commerce City, CO
Leiser, Lawrence J. ... Alexandria, VA
Leiser, Phillip B. ... Washington, DC
Leiserowitz, Bruce H. ... Los Angeles, CA
Leish, Matthew A. ... New York, NY
Leishman, David M. ... Pasadena, CA
Leishman, N. Todd ... Salt Lake City, UT
Leishman, Scott A. ... New York, NY
Leising, Thomas J. ... Topeka, KS
Leisman, Ross A. ... Grand Rapids, MI

Leisner, Richard M. ... St. Petersburg, FL
Tampa, FL
Leissner-Rupp, Tracy L. ... Houston, TX
Leissing, William ... Santa Rosa, CA
Leist, Henry N. ... New Albany, IN
Leist, Jeffrey J. ... Los Angeles, CA
Leist, Nelson R. ... Cincinnati, OH
Leist, Robert C. ... Steubenville, OH
Leisten, Arthur G. ... Chicago, IL
Leisten, Karen F. ... Princeton, NJ
New York, NY
Leisten, Laurence M. ... Los Angeles, CA
Leistensnider, Ruth E. ... Albany, NY
Leister, Craig D. ... Columbus, OH
Leister, Curtis W. ... Beaumont, TX
Leister, Curtis W. ... Beaumont, TX
Jasper, TX
Leister, Leslie R. ... Napa, CA
Leistico, Gary R. ... St. Cloud, MN
Leistico, Kent R. ... Austin, TX
Leistico, Nathan H. ... Austin, TX
Leistikow, Kurt R. ... Reinbeck, IA
Leistman, Donald F. ... Mineola, NY
Leistman, Nancy J. ... Coram, NY
Leistner, Mary Porter ... Eugene, OR
Leisure, Craig M. ... Fincastle, VA
Leisure, George S., Jr. ... New York, NY
Leisure, Jodi ... Clearwater, FL
Leisure, Peter K. ... New York, NY
Leisure, Sally R. ... Portland, OR
Leisz, Lauren E. ... Redding, CA
Leisz, Scott R. ... Indianapolis, IN
Leit, David Edward ... New York, NY
Leitão, Kevin D. ... New York, NY
Leitao, Pamela Jean
Rancho Cucamonga, CA
Leitch, Andrew V. ... Irvine, CA
Leitch, Arthur E., Jr. ... College Park, MD
Leitch, B. Bryan, III ... Dallas, TX
Leitch, Brian P. ... Denver, CO
Leitch, Catherine Stronach ... Covington, VA
Leitch, Chad C. ... Dubuque, IA
Leitch, David B. ... Elyria, OH
Leitch, David D. ... New York, NY
Leitch, David G. ... Washington, DC
Leitch, Dougald B. ... Orlando, FL
Leitch, Hugh J. ... Babylon, NY
Leitch, J. Bradley ... Kansas City, MO
Leitch, John D., Jr. ... Virginia Beach, VA
Leitch, Kevin C. ... Tulsa, OK
Leitch, Laura J. ... Madison, WI
Leitch, Neil M. ... Missoula, MT
Leitch, Noel E ... Brooklyn, NY
Leitch, Pamela J. ... Portland, OR
Leitch, Powell M., III ... Roanoke, VA
Leitch, Robert N. ... Atlanta, GA
Leitch, Ryan L. ... Indianapolis, IN
Leite, Roy J., Jr. ... Atlanta, GA
Leitel, Ira ... Kamuela, HI
Leiter, Brian Russell ... Austin, TX
Leiter, Bruce L. ... Springfield, MA
Leiter, Carl H. ... Irvine, CA
Leiter Group, The, Attorneys and Counselors, P.C. ... Peoria, IL
Leiter, Irwin E. ... Oak Brook, IL
Leiter, James A. ... Syracuse, NY
Leiter, Jeffrey L. ... Washington, DC
Leiter, John M. ... Myrtle Beach, SC
Leiter, Manning K. ... Chicago, IL
Leiter, Mark A. ... Buffalo, NY
Leiter, Marvin W. ... Western Springs, IL
Leiter, Maurice A. ... Los Angeles, CA
Leiter, Peter G. ... San Francisco, CA
Leiter & Snook, P.A. ... Myrtle Beach, SC
Leiter, Stephanie K. ... New York, NY
Leiter, Steven J. ... Fort Lauderdale, FL
Leiter, Thomas E. ... Peoria, IL
Leiter, William ... Bartlesville, OK
Leiter, William ... Tulsa, OK
Leiterman, Rachel V. ... San Jose, CA
Leiterman, Sheldon B. ... Wynnewood, PA
Leitess, Earl F. ... Baltimore, MD
Alexandria, VA
Leitess Leitess & Friedberg, P.C.
Baltimore, MD
Alexandria, VA
Leitess, Steven N. ... Baltimore, MD
Alexandria, VA
Leith, Arthur H. ... New Orleans, LA
Leith, Deborah K. Smith ... Mandeville, LA
Leith, Debra K. ... Seattle, WA
Leith, Elizabeth Demberg ... Denver, CO
Leith, Heather A. ... Kansas City, MO
Leith, John A. ... Boston, MA
Leith, John R. ... Newark, NJ
Leith, Patricia M. ... Salt Lake City, UT
Leithart, Paul W., II ... Columbus, OH
Leithauser and Leithauser, P.C.
Eastpointe, MI
Leithauser, Robert C., Jr. ... Eastpointe, MI
Leithead, A. Scott ... Hilo, HI
Leithead, Heidi E. C. ... Salt Lake City, UT
Leithead, James A. ... Lake Charles, LA
Leithiser, Robert S. ... Dallas, TX
Leithner, George E. ... Deerfield, IL
Leitich, Greg H. ... Chicago, IL
Leitman, Alvin A. ... Jacksonville, FL
Leitman, Bruce T. ... Bloomfield Hills, MI
Leitman, Eddie ... Birmingham, AL
Leitman, Genay Ann ... New York, NY
Leitman, Matthew F. ... Bloomfield Hills, MI
Leitman, Siegal & Payne, P.C.
Birmingham, AL
Leitman, Tracey A. ... New York, NY
Leitman, Wendy ... Burbank, CA
Leitner, Abraham ... New York, NY
Leitner, Anthony J. ... New York, NY
Leitner, Cathy Jackson ... Harrisonburg, VA

Leitner, Christopher Brian
Ocean Township, NJ
Leitner, David K. ... New York, NY
Leitner, David L. ... Des Moines, IA
Leitner, Eric D. ... San Francisco, CA
Leitner & Getz LLP ... New York, NY
Leitner, Gregory M. ... Chattanooga, TN
Leitner, Howard ... White Plains, NY
Leitner, Jerome M. ... Brooklyn, NY
Leitner, Jerome M. ... New York, NY
Leitner, John R. ... Brainerd, MN
Leitner, Kara B. ... Washington, DC
Leitner, Mark M. ... Milwaukee, WI
Leitner, Martin L., (P.C.)
Kansas City, MO
Leitner, Patricia ... Department of Justice,
Civil Division, GV
Leitner, Paul R. ... Chattanooga, TN
Knoxville, TN
Memphis, TN
Nashville, TN
Leitner, R. Elaine ... San Francisco, CA
Leitner, Reid D. ... Nashville, TN
Leitner, Rick L. ... Seattle, WA
Leitner, Rudolph V. ... Friendswood, TX
Leitner, Stephen M. ... Woodbridge, NJ
Leitner, Williams, Dooley & Napolitan,
PLLC ... Chattanooga, TN
Knoxville, TN
Memphis, TN
Nashville, TN
Leitsch, Anne M. ... Louisville, KY
Leitson, Mark ... Chicago, IL
Leittem, Thomas J. ... Kansas City, MO
Leitten, Brian Joseph ... Batesville, IN
Leitten, Scott J. ... Jupiter, FL
Buffalo, NY
Leitz, Jane Ross ... Atlanta, GA
Leitz, M. Barry ... Atlanta, GA
Leitz, M. Richd. ... Dearborn, MI
Leitz, Rosemary Keating ... Shelton, CT
Leitze, Robert C. ... New Haven, CT
Leitzelar, Luis A. ... Baton Rouge, LA
Leitzell, Robert J. ... Media, PA
Leiva, Aldo M. ... Miami, FL
Leiva, Marlene ... Canoga Park, CA
Leive, David M. ... Washington, DC
Leiwant, David O. ... Brooklyn, NY
Leixner, Timothy C. ... Fort Lauderdale, FL
Leizerman, E.J., & Associates, LLC
Southfield, MI
Toledo, OH
Leizerman, E. J. ... Toledo, OH
Leizerman, Joseph-Jacques Sylvain
Holland, OH
Leizerman, Michael Jay ... Southfield, MI
Toledo, OH
Leizman, Amy B. ... Cleveland, OH
Leizman, Murray D. ... Atlanta, GA
Leizman, William S. ... Cleveland, OH
Leizman-Moses, Karen ... Columbus, OH
Leja, Andrew J. ... Syracuse, NY
Leja, Carolyn H. ... Springfield, IL
Leja, Edward V. ... Springfield, MA
Leja, John A. ... Chicago, IL
LeJeune, Anne D. ... Baton Rouge, LA
Lejeune, J. Michael ... Baton Rouge, LA
LeJeune, Peter Dietrich ... Birmingham, AL
Lejeune, Peter Lawrence ... St. Louis, MO
LeJeune, Raymond J. ... Mamou, LA
Lejnieks, John H. ... Huntington Beach, CA
LeJuerrne, Richard J., Jr. ... Wellington, KS
Lejuwaan, Randal J. ... San Diego, CA
Leka, Donald G. ... Boston, MA
Leka, Jill ... Chicago, IL
Leka, Tessica ... Castle Rock, CO
Lekach, Craig W. ... Fort Lauderdale, FL
Lekach & Klitzner ... Fort Lauderdale, FL
LeKachman, Richd. L. ... New York, NY
Lekarew, Leonard ... Kew Gardens, NY
Lekarew & Nimetz ... Kew Gardens, NY
Lekas, Gary J. ... Portland, OR
Lekas, John J. ... Grand Rapids, MI
Lekas, Melissa ... Brick, NJ
Lekas, Stephen ... Houston, TX
Lekas, Thomas J. ... Portland, OR
LeKashman, John Q. ... San Jose, CA
Lekhe, Arina ... Dallas, TX
Lekisch, Peter A. ... Anchorage, AK
Lekki & Crowe, P.C. ... Canton, NY
Massena, NY
Lekki, Peter B. ... Canton, NY
Leklem, John A. ... Orlando, FL
Leklem, John A., P.A. ... Orlando, FL
Lekos, Konstantine ... Treasury Department,
Internal Revenue Service, GV
Leksan, Thomas J. ... Cincinnati, OH
Leland, Arlean
Department of Agriculture, GV
Leland, Bonita Marie ... Northridge, CA
Leland, Caryn R. ... New York, NY
Leland, Clarence McDonald ... Jackson, MS
Leland, Daniel L. ... Department of Labor,
Office of Secretary, GV
Leland, David J. ... Columbus, OH
Leland, Elizabeth A. ... Seattle, WA
Leland, Gerald W. ... St. Paul, MN
Leland, Jeffrey B. ... Northborough, MA
Leland, John S. ... Buena Park, CA
Leland, Judith S. ... Downey, CA
Leland, Margaret Allen ... Charleston, SC
Leland, N. Stanley ... Los Angeles, CA
Leland, Parachini, Steinberg, Matzger &
Melnick, L.L.P. ... Los Angeles, CA
San Francisco, CA
Leland, Richard A., Jr. ... Chico, CA
Leland, Richard G. ... New York, NY
Leland, Richard M. ... Spokane, WA

Leland, Robert G. ... Dayton, OH
Leland, Robert H. ... New York, NY
Leland, Roger B. ... Northborough, MA
Leland, Schultz & Morrissey, LLP
Chico, CA
Oroville, CA
Leland, Thomas D. ... Washington, DC
LeLaurin & Adams, P.C.
Corpus Christi, TX
San Antonio, TX
LeLaurin & Kessler, L.L.P.
San Antonio, TX
LeLaurin, Louis A., III (P.C.)
San Antonio, TX
Lelchuk, Deborah E. ... Seal Beach, CA
Lelchuk, Sheldon N. ... Miami, FL
Lele, Avinash S. ... New York, NY
Lele, Sal ... Chicago, IL
LeLeiko, Marilyn Bush ... Larchmont, NY
Leleiko, Steven H. ... New York, NY
Lelen, Ronald T. ... New York, NY
LeLievre, Andre J. ... Sacramento, CA
Lelko, Andrew ... Cleveland, OH
Lelli, Craig T. ... Columbus, OH
Lelli, Ramon S. ... Redwood City, CA
Lelling, Andrew E. ... Boston, MA
Lello, Victor W. ... Chicago, IL
Lellouche, Michele D. ... Jacksonville, FL
Lelonek, Richard L. ... Baltimore, MD
Lelong, F. Rivers, Jr. ... New Orleans, LA
Lelong, Marion P. ... Falls Church, VA
LeLouis, Constance L. ... Sacramento, CA
LeLouis, Michael P. ... Sacramento, CA
Lem, Darryl R. ... Calumet City, IL
Lem, Frank ... Sacramento, CA
Lem, Howard C.
Department Of Veterans Affairs,
Office of the General Counsel, GV
Lem, Nancy ... Newark, NJ
Lem, Robert K. ... New York, NY
Lem, Theresa M. ... Thousand Oaks, CA
Lem, Victor M. ... New York, NY
Lema, Brian A. ... Milford, CT
Lema, Marlynn B. ... St. George, UT
Lemaek, Danielle B. ... Chicago, IL
Lemack, Kevin S. ... Concord, MA
Westborough, MA
Lemaire, Charles A. ... Minneapolis, MN
Lemaire, E. Lynette ... Woodland Hills, CA
Lemaire, Faunce, Pingel & Singer
Seal Beach, CA
Lemaire, Janet M. ... Brooklyn, NY
Lemaire, Leon L. ... Farmington, CT
Lemaire, Marcellus D. ... Taunton, MA
LeMaire, Michael R. ... Fort Lauderdale, FL
LeMaire, Phyllis B. ... East Hampton, CT
Lemaire, Thomas E. ... Arlington, MA
LeMaistre, George A., Jr. ... Mobile, AL
LeMaistre, Samuel A. ... Eufaula, AL
Leman, John A. ... Anchorage, AK
Leman, Joseph T. ... Dalton, GA
Leman, Kenneth W. ... New York, NY
Leman, Kenneth W. ... Roslyn Heights, NY
Lemanczyk, Lisa M. ... Austin, TX
Lemanek, Diane P. ... Detroit, MI
Lemann, Arthur A., III ... New Orleans, LA
Lemann, Catherine ... New Orleans, LA
Lemann, Monte M., II ... Los Angeles, CA
Lemann, Thomas B. ... New Orleans, LA
Lemann, Wilfrid C. ... Rancho Mirage, CA
San Bernardino, CA
Lemanowicz, Edward ... Philadelphia, PA
Lemanowicz, John L. ... Philadelphia, PA
Lemanski, David A. ... Dubuque, IA
Lemanski, Susan M. ... Washington, DC
Lemanski, Walter J. ... Milwaukee, WI
LeMar, Bruce R. ... Chicago, IL
LeMar, Harold W. ... New York, NY
Lemargie, Richard A., (P.S.) ... Ephrata, WA
Lemargie & Whitaker ... Ephrata, WA
LeMaster, Alison ... Fairfax, VA
Le Master, David A. ... Seattle, WA
LeMaster, Gary D. ... Ocala, FL
LeMaster, James G. ... Lexington, KY
LeMaster, James H. ... Florence, AL
Lemaster, John C. ... Phoenix, AZ
LeMaster, Kenneth L. ... Seattle, WA
Lemaster, L. Guy, Jr. ... Pomona, CA
Le Master, Matthew D. ... Seattle, WA
LeMaster, Ray W., Jr. ... Louisville, KY
LeMaster, Richard Y. ... Bellevue, WA
LeMaster, Roger Joe ... Washington, DC
Lemaster, Shannon Denise
Owensboro, KY
LeMaster, Smith & Malone ... Florence, AL
LeMasters, Claude Richard
Beaumont, TX
LeMasters, Joseph M., Jr. ... Checotah, OK
Lemasters, P. Reid ... Cincinnati, OH
LeMastus, Robin J. ... Louisville, KY
Le Matty, Mary P. ... Summerville, SC
LeMay, David M. ... New York, NY
LeMay, Glenn R. ... Houston, TX
LeMay, James C. ... Fairlawn, OH
LeMay, Joe D. ... Coleman, TX
LeMay, John H. ... Eagan, MN
Lemay, Marcia Lee ... Canton, NY
LeMay, Robert N. ... Dallas, TX
LeMay, Susan K. ... Fort Myers, FL
New Albany, IN
LeMay, Tandra ... New Orleans, LA
Lembach, Robert G. ... Baltimore, MD
Lembcke, Charles B. ... Jacksonville, FL
Lembeck, Anthony Jon ... Lawrence, NY
Lember, Steven C. ... Flemington, NJ
Lemberg, D. Stephen
Consumer Product Safety Commission,
Office of the General Counsel, GV

Lemberg, Frederic G. ... Battle Creek, MI
Lemberg, Howard ... Santa Ana, CA
Lemberg, Marc J. ... Warren, NJ
Lemberg, Thomas M. ... Cambridge, MA
Lemberg, William ... Manchester, MA
Lemberger, Dale ... Harrisburg, PA
Lemberger, Kenneth ... Burbank, CA
Lemberger, Ronald I. ... Hempstead, NY
Lemberger, Victoria M. ... St. Paul, MN
Lemberis, Theodore T. ... Chicago, IL
Lembesis, Paul C. ... Washington, DC
Lembitz, Edward L., Jr. ... Chicago, IL
Lembke, Kent ... Boulder, CO
Lembke, Matthew H. ... Birmingham, AL
Lembke, Matthew Robert ... Rochester, NY
Lembke, Michael J. ... Los Angeles, CA
Lembke, Raymond W. ... Cincinnati, OH
Lembke, Robert A. ... Denver, CO
Lembke, Robert G. ... Parker, CO
Lembo, Anna ... Boston, MA
Lembo, August T. ... Plainsboro, NJ
Lembo, Barbara Howie ... Charlotte, NC
Lembo, Donald R. ... North Providence, RI
Lembo, Francine E. ... Paterson, NJ
Lembo, Joseph A. ... Hartford, CT
Lembo, Karen Kleppe ... Newark, NJ
Lembo, Keith D. ... Charlotte, NC
Lembo, Loren R. ... New York, NY
Lembo, Nicholas B ... Atlantic City, NJ
Lembo, Vincent J. ... Boston, MA
Lembree, Ashlyn J. ... Concord, NH
Lembright, Mark Ryan ... Cleveland, OH
Lembright, Ronald K. ... Cleveland, OH
Lemcke, Howard R., Jr. ... Salt Lake City, UT
Lemcke, Nancy L. ... Las Vegas, NV
Lemcke, Paul A. ... Las Vegas, NV
Lemcool, Michael J. ... Las Vegas, NV
Lemcovitz, Zoe A. ... St. Louis, MO
Lemega, John W. ... Hartford, CT
LeMeilleur, Lynn B. ... Kerrville, TX
Lemein, Gregg D. ... Chicago, IL
Lemel, Gary C. ... Charlotte, NC
Lemelin, Whitney Scott ... Okemos, MI
Lemell, Phyllis E. ... Berlin, CT
LeMelle, Gerald A. ... New York, NY
LeMelle, Gertrude M. ... Wyckoff, NJ
Lemelle, Ivan L. R. ... New Orleans, LA
Lemelle, James Stanley ... Baton Rouge, LA
Le Melle, Patrice M. ... New York, NY
Lemelman, Andrew ... Boston, MA
Lemelman, Bernard ... New York, NY
Lemelman, George ... Boston, MA
Lemelman, Herbert ... Boston, MA
Lemelman & Lemelman ... Boston, MA
Lemen, G. Dale ... Baltimore, MD
Lemen, Robert T. ... Irvine, CA
Lemen, William L. ... San Juan, TX
Lemens, Christopher L. ... Austin, TX
Lemens, Robert L. ... Austin, TX
Lemens, W. Vernon, Jr. ... Austin, TX
LeMense, Robert D. ... Milwaukee, WI
Lemer, Randall S. ... Houston, TX
Lemere, Mary Ann G. ... Morristown, NJ
Lemerman, Barbara S. ... Beverly Hills, CA
Lemerman, Paula J. ... Clayton, MO
Lemert, James E. ... Washington, DC
Lemert, Robert C., Jr. ... Atlanta, GA
Lemery, John C. ... Glens Falls, NY
Saratoga Springs, NY
Lemery MacKrell LLC ... Albany, NY
Glens Falls, NY
Saratoga Springs, NY
Lemery, Neal C. ... Rockaway, OR
Lemesany, Wm. L. ... Lawrence, KS
Lemeshewsky, Andrew A., Jr.
New Orleans, LA
Lemhouse, Jad B. ... Brownsville, OR
Lemich, George E. ... Rock Springs, WY
LeMieux, Allen ... Boulder, MT
LeMieux, Dianna ... Mineola, NY
Lemieux, Donald G. ... Falls Church, VA
Le Mieux, Dotty E. ... Mill Valley, CA
LeMieux, George S. ... Fort Lauderdale, FL
Lemieux, Holly Krapf ... Easton, MA
Lemieux, James Philip ... Long Beach, CA
Lemieux, James R. ... Portland, ME
Lemieux, John N. ... Johnston, RI
Lemieux, John R. ... Augusta, ME
LeMieux, Louis H. ... La Grange, IL
LeMieux, Matthew B.
Clinton Township, MI
Lemieux & O'Neill ... Westlake Village, CA
Lemieux & Osborn ... Falls Church, VA
Lemieux, Ronald J. ... Malibu, CA
Lemieux, Ronald S. ... Palo Alto, CA
Lemieux, Wayne K. ... Westlake Village, CA
Leming, H. Clark ... Stafford, VA
Leming, Healy, Levy and Saller
Stafford, VA
Leming, Robert O. ... Cincinnati, OH
Leming, Susan M. ... Camden, NJ
Westmont, NJ
Leming, Theresa L. ... Denver, CO
Leminger, Tricia A. ... Indianapolis, IN
Lemire, Christopher R. ... Albany, NY
Lemire, Daniel J. ... Farmington, CT
LeMire, Donald F. ... Escanaba, MI
LeMire, Gerald A. ... Uxbridge, MA
Lemire, James R. ... Holden, MA
Lemire, Jennifer A. ... Portsmouth, NH
Lemire, Jerome A. ... Jefferson, OH
Lemire, John J. ... Detroit, MI
Lemire, Joseph C. ... Metairie, LA
LeMire Law Office ... Escanaba, MI
LeMire, Robert E., Jr. ... Escanaba, MI
LeMire, William A. ... Minneapolis, MN
Lemisch, Raymond H. ... Philadelphia, PA
Lemkau, Gary R. ... Wheaton, IL

Lemkau, Robert J. ... Rancho Cucamonga, CA
Lemke, Alois Ernst ... San Jose, CA
Lemke, David E. ... Nashville, TN
Lemke, Dawn R. ... Merrill, WI
Lemke, Dennis M. ... Mineola, NY
Lemke, Douglas G. ... Tucson, AZ
Lemke, Elaine M. ... Los Angeles, CA
Lemke, Jack W. ... Appleton, WI
Lemke, John R. ... Ogden, UT
Lemke, Kathy J. ... Phoenix, AZ
Lemke, Kristin Lee ... Austin, TX
Lemke, Michael C. ... Louisville, KY
Lemke & Pederson ... McKinney, TX
Lemke, Richard O. ... Troy, MI
Lemke, Scott ... McKinney, TX
Lemke, Thomas P. ... Washington, DC
Lemke, Timothy C. ... Atlanta, GA
Lemke, Todd C. ... Fond du Lac, WI
Lemke, William A. ... Hendersonville, NC
Lemke, William F. ... Seattle, WA
Lemkemeier, David B. ... St. Louis, MO
Lemkemeier, John W. ... St. Louis, MO
Lemkemeier, Ned O. ... St. Louis, MO
Lemken, Deborah L. ... Cumming, GA
Lemker, John F., Jr. ... Chicago, IL
Lemke-von Ammon, Derek
San Francisco, CA
Lemke-von Ammon, Sara
San Francisco, CA
Lemkin & Barnes Inc. ... Santa Ana, CA
Lemkin, E. Robert ... Santa Ana, CA
Lemkin, E. Robert, Inc., Law Offices
Santa Ana, CA
Lemkin, Jason M. ... San Francisco, CA
Lemkin, Jeffrey W. ... Los Angeles, CA
Lemkin, Samuel ... Westbury, NY
Lemkuil, Daniel J. ... Houston, TX
Lemkuil, Daniel J., P.C. ... Houston, TX
Lemkul, William A. ... Las Vegas, NV
Lemle, J. Stuart ... Washington, DC
Lemle, Janis W. ... New Orleans, LA
Lemle & Kelleher, L.L.P.
Baton Rouge, LA
New Orleans, LA
Lemle, Robert L. ... Reseda, CA
Lemle, Robert S. ... Bethpage, NY
Lemlech, Bernard ... Los Angeles, CA
Lemley, Alfred J. ... Fairmont, WV
Lemley, Amy S. ... Wichita, KS
Lemley, Charles C. ... Washington, DC
Lemley, Daniel C. ... Tuscaloosa, AL
Lemley, Gregg M. ... St. Louis, MO
Lemley, L. Terrell ... Mobile, AL
Lemley, Mark A. ... Menlo Park, CA
Lemley, Michael S. ... New York, NY
Lemley, Michelle M. ... San Francisco, CA
Lemley, Norma M. ... Tuscaloosa, AL
Lemley, Raymond J. ... New Haven, CT
Lemly, Thomas A. ... Seattle, WA
Lemm, Brian A. ... Washington, DC
Lemm, Robert J. ... St. Paul, MN
Lemme & Conway ... Shepherdsville, KY
Lemme, Norman R. ... Shepherdsville, KY
Lemme, Theresa ... West Palm Beach, FL
Lemmen, Larry A. ... Coopersville, MI
Lemmenes, Michael L. ... Naperville, IL
Lemmer, Catherine A. ... Chicago, IL
Lemmer, Don S. ... Los Angeles, CA
Lemmer, Gregory S. ... Menlo Park, CA
Lemmer, Thomas A. ... Denver, CO
Lemmer, William C. ... Dallas, TX
Lemmer, William P. ... Ann Arbor, MI
Lemmerman, R. Douglas
Winston-Salem, NC
Lemmer-Martens, Sonja G.
Minneapolis, MN
Lemmie, Vanessa Hall
Federal Communications Commission,
Mass Media Bureau, GV
Lemming, Raymond M. ... Chicago, IL
Lemming, Stacey M. ... Circleville, OH
Lemmink, Robert D. ... Cincinnati, OH
Lemmis, Rosemary ... Los Angeles, CA
Lemmler, Richard P., Jr. ... New Orleans, LA
Lemmo, Edward A. ... New York, NY
Lemmo, Sabine M. B. ... Santa Clara, CA
Lemmon, Andrew A. ... New Orleans, LA
Lemmon, Angela M. ... Woodbridge, VA
Lemmon, Cyrus J. ... Riverside, CA
Lemmon, Denise D. ... St. Paul, MN
Lemmon, Duncan S. ... San Francisco, CA
Lemmon, Eileen S. ... Riverside, CA
Lemmon, Harry T. ... New Orleans, LA
Lemmon, J. Roslyn ... New Orleans, LA
Houston, TX
Lemmon, Jenifer Livaccari
New Orleans, LA
LemMon, John F. ... Sonoma, CA
Lemmon, John M. ... Sacramento, CA
Lemmon, John Vincent ... Sacramento, CA
Lemmon, Julie M. ... Tempe, AZ
Lemmon, M. Gale ... Salt Lake City, UT
Lemmon, M. Lauren ... Mobile, AL
Lemmon, Mary Ann Vial ... New Orleans, LA
Lemmon, Mary K. ... Blue Bell, PA
Lemmon, Peter D. ... Ventura, CA
LemMon, Richard T. ... Redwood City, CA
Lemmon, Stella K. ... New York, NY
Lemmon, Stephen ... Sacramento, CA
Lemmon, Stephen W. ... Austin, TX
LemMon, Thomas H. ... El Sobrante, CA
Lemmon, Tracy C. ... Los Angeles, CA
Lemmon, William J. ... Haworth, NJ
Lemmond, Charles D., Jr. ... Dallas, PA
Lemmond, James W. ... Sacramento, CA
Lemmond, Martha Lorraine ... New York, NY
Lemmons, Howard M. ... Austin, TX
Lemmons, Mark ... Las Vegas, NV

Lemmons, Perry O. .... Atlanta, GA
Lemmons, Phillip C. .... Fountain Valley, CA
Lemmons, Raymond L. .... St. Paul, MN
Lemmons, Robert W. .... Dallas, TX
Lemn, Haunani S. Y. .... Wailuku, HI
Lemna, Moore & Carroll .... Tuscola, IL
Lemna, Thomas E. .... Kankakee, IL
LeMoine, Anna-Marie .... Atlanta, GA
Lemoine, Brian W.
Department Of Veterans Affairs, Board of Veterans Appeals, GV
Le Moine, Charles A. .... Chicago, IL
Lemoine, David George
Old Orchard Beach, ME
Lemoine, Dominique M. H. .... Atlanta, GA
Lemoine, France D. .... Los Angeles, CA
LeMoine, Frank E. .... Abbeville, LA
Lemoine, Gano D., III .... New Orleans, LA
Lemoine, Gano D., Jr. .... Lafayette, LA
Lemoine, Henry H., Jr. .... Pineville, LA
Lemoine, James P. .... Colfax, LA
Lemoine, Jean-Louis .... Lafayette, LA
Lemoine, John G. .... Old Orchard Beach, ME
Lemoine, Joseph L., Jr. .... Lafayette, LA
Lemoine, Michael G. .... Lafayette, LA
Lemoine, Peter J. .... Alexandria, LA
Lemoine, Rebekah B. .... Baton Rouge, LA
Lemoine, Richard G. .... Glastonbury, CT
LeMoine, Rosemarie Warren .... Bellevue, WA
Lemoine, Steven .... New Orleans, LA
Lemoine, Steven P. .... Baton Rouge, LA
Lemoine-Bui, Allison .... Costa Mesa, CA
Lemole, Paul A. .... Staten Island, NY
Le Mon, Antonio .... Metairie, LA
Lemon, Armey, Hearn & Leininger
Warsaw, IN
Lemon, Boyd S. .... Los Angeles, CA
Lemon, Bruce L. .... Olympia, WA
Lemon, C. Neel, III .... Dallas, TX
Lemon, C. Richard .... Napa, CA
Lemon, Catherine A. .... Denver, CO
Lemon, Chrys D. .... Washington, DC
Lemon, D. Brent .... Dallas, TX
Lemon, Donald J. .... Chicago, IL
Lemon, Eric V. .... St. Louis, MO
Lemon, George L. .... Lewisburg, WV
Lemon, George S., Jr. .... Winnsboro, TX
Lemon, Heather C. .... Chicago, IL
Lemon, James L. .... New London, MO
Lemon, John C. .... Alice, TX
Lemon, John F. .... New York, NY
Lemon, Joseph L. .... Sausalito, CA
Lemon, L. Gene .... Phoenix, AZ
Lemon Law, Inc. .... Bingham Farms, MI
Lemon, Loren J. .... Lexington, MA
Lemon, Marcus J. .... Harrisburg, PA
Lemon, Maureen Anichini .... Wheaton, IL
Lemon, Michael E. .... Yankton, SD
Lemon, Nancy K.D. .... Berkeley, CA
Lemon, Patrick A. .... Jackson, MS
Lemon, Philip H. .... Roanoke, VA
Lemon, Robert D. .... Perryton, TX
Lemon, Robert T., II .... New Orleans, LA
Lemon, S. Timothy .... San Francisco, CA
Lemon, Shearer, Ehrlich, Phillips & Good, A Professional Corporation .... Booker, TX
Perryton, TX
Lemon, Stephen W. .... Roanoke, VA
Lemon, Steven J. .... Geneva, IL
Lemon, Thomas G. .... Topeka, KS
Lemon, Thomas R. .... Warsaw, IN
Lemon, W. Clyde, & Associates
Houston, TX
Lemon, W. Douglas .... Warsaw, IN
Lemon, W. Tucker .... Roanoke, VA
Lemon, William De Witt
New Martinsville, WV
Lemon, William J. .... Roanoke, VA
Lemon, Willis B. .... Syracuse, NY
LeMond, Carson and Yockey Associates
Indianapolis, IN
Lemond, James M. .... Houston, TX
Lemond, Joseph M. .... Warren, NJ
LeMond, Kevin T. .... San Francisco, CA
Lemond, Scott A. .... Houston, TX
LeMond, William F. .... Indianapolis, IN
Lemond, Xavier C. .... Houston, TX
Lemonds, James P. .... St. Louis, MO
Lemongello, Daniel .... Fort Lauderdale, FL
Lemonick, John D. .... Philadelphia, PA
Lemonidis, Robin C. .... Melbourne, FL
Lemonik, Murray .... Valley Stream, NY
Lemonik, Norman .... Oklahoma City, OK
Lemons, Bruce N. .... Salt Lake City, UT
Lemons, Cheri B. .... Los Angeles, CA
Lemons, Clyde, Jr. .... Chicago, IL
Lemons, Donald W. .... Richmond, VA
Lemons, Edward J. .... Reno, NV
Lemons, Eric A. .... McMurray, PA
Lemons, Grundy & Eisenberg
Carson City, NV
Elko, NV
Reno, NV
Lemons, J. Andrew .... Atlanta, GA
Lemons, John H., Jr. .... Houston, TX
Lemons, Keith D. .... Fort Worth, TX
Lemons, Norman R. .... Canon City, CO
Lemons, R. Alan .... Portsmouth, OH
Lemons, Thomas F., Jr. .... Irving, TX
Lemons, Thomas G. .... McMurray, PA
Lemons, William H., III .... San Antonio, TX
Lemont, Eric D. .... Philadelphia, PA
Lemos, Bernard J. .... Providence, RI
Lemos, Christopher T. .... Miami, FL
Lemos, Natalie Scharf .... Miami, FL
Lemos, Robert A. .... Palo Alto, CA
Lemos, William R. .... Miami, FL
Lemoult, Brendan J. .... New York, NY
LeMoult, John E. .... Darien, CT
Lemov, Michael R. .... Washington, DC
Lemp & Anthony, P.C. .... St. Louis, MO
Lemp, William .... Fairview Heights, IL
St. Louis, MO
Lempel, J. Steven .... Fresno, CA
Lempel, J. Steven, Professional Law Corporation .... Fresno, CA
Lempel, Steven .... Scarsdale, NY
Lempel-Sander, Lisa .... New York, NY
Lempenski, Robert J. .... Carle Place, NY
Lempert, Arthur J. .... San Mateo, CA
Lempert, David Howard .... Berkeley, CA
Lempert, Dennis Alan, Law Offices of
San Jose, CA
Lempert, Dennis Alan, Law Offices of
Santa Clara, CA
Lempert, Harvey .... Baltimore, MD
Lempert, James G. .... Houston, TX
Lempert, Jeanne M. .... San Francisco, CA
Lempert, Lawrence A. .... Tampa, FL
Lempert, Lawrence S. .... Washington, DC
Lempert, Nina F. .... Boston, MA
Lempert, Richard A. .... Dallas, TX
Lempert, Richard O. .... Ann Arbor, MI
Lempert, Scott M. .... Philadelphia, PA
Lempert, Spencer N. .... Mount Laurel, NJ
Lempesis, Charles B. .... Post Falls, ID
Lempesis, J. Louis .... Charleston, SC
Lempia, Bryan J. .... Milwaukee, WI
Lempiner, Alex G. .... New York, NY
Lempke, George J. .... Chicago, IL
Lempp, Stefanie .... Boston, MA
Lempres, Matthew D. .... Oakland, CA
Lempres, Michael T. .... Washington, DC
Lempriere, Philip R. .... Seattle, WA
Lems, Wendy J. .... Salt Lake City, UT
Lemucchi, Timothy J., Law Offices of
Bakersfield, CA
Lemuth, Mary B. .... Houston, TX
Lemuth, Richard F. .... Houston, TX
Lena, Catherine M. .... Santa Monica, CA
Lena, Glory Martyn .... Hartford, CT
Lena, Jeffrey S. .... Berkeley, CA
Lena, Joseph A. .... Boston, MA
Lena, Manuel P., Jr. .... Department of Justice, Tax Division, GV
Lenaburg, Dean E. .... Valley City, ND
Lenaburg, Fitzner, Nelson, Hooper & Cruff, PLLP .... Valley City, ND
Lenack, Jack R. .... Los Angeles, CA
Lenaghan, James M. .... New York, NY
Lenagman, Robert A. .... New York, NY
Lenahan, Brian J. .... Scranton, PA
Lenahan & Dempsey, A Professional Corporation .... Scranton, PA
Lenahan, Dennis J. .... Los Angeles, CA
Lenahan, Diane Hepford .... Scranton, PA
Lenahan, George T., Jr. .... San Francisco, CA
Lenahan, Gerald M. .... Sacramento, CA
Lenahan, Gregg T. .... Glendale, CA
Lenahan, James J. .... Chicago, IL
Lenahan, John C. .... Washington, DC
Lenahan, John R., Jr. .... Scranton, PA
Lenahan, John T. .... Chicago, IL
Lenahan, John T. .... Woodstown, NJ
Lenahan, Joseph P. .... Scranton, PA
Lenahan, Kathleen A. .... Scranton, PA
Lenahan, Mary K. .... Pasadena, CA
Lenahan, Maureen Kay .... Oakland, CA
Lenahan, Michael G. .... Park Ridge, NJ
Lenahan, Robert J. .... Philadelphia, PA
Lenahan, Robert J., Jr. .... Cranford, NJ
Lenahan & Rockwell, P.A. .... Bridgewater, NJ
Freehold, NJ
Lenahan, Thomas E., Jr. .... Bridgewater, NJ
Freehold, NJ
Lenahan, Timothy G. .... Scranton, PA
Lenahan, William D. .... Harrisburg, PA
Lenain, Adam .... San Diego, CA
Lenane, Pamela A. .... Chicago, IL
Lenane, Timothy J. .... New York, NY
LeNaour, Frank L. .... New York, NY
Lenar, Jeffrey J. .... Nashville, TN
Lenard, Allen D. .... Los Angeles, CA
Lenard, Brian D. .... Hammond, LA
Lenard, Dennis J. .... Stanhope, NJ
Lenard, Edward M. .... Larchmont, NY
Lenard, George D. .... Joliet, IL
Lenard, George L. .... St. Louis, MO
Lenard & Gonzalez .... Los Angeles, CA
Lenard, Joan A. .... Miami, FL
Lenard, Lori A. .... Chicago, IL
Lenard, Louis G. .... Joliet, IL
Lenard, Mary S. .... Mamaroneck, NY
Lenard, Rhonda L. .... Fort Worth, TX
Lenard, Roland Robert .... Clarksville, TN
Lenart, Krista L. .... Ann Arbor, MI
Lenart, Robert P. .... Pittsburgh, PA
Lenarz, Robin J. .... Eagan, MN
Lenas, Peter T. .... St. Petersburg, FL
Lenavitt, Jack M. .... Toledo, OH
Lence, George E. .... New York, NY
Lence, John A. .... Kalispell, MT
Lence Law Firm, A Professional Corporation
Kalispell, MT
Lence, Robert B. .... Salt Lake City, UT
Lench & Crisci, P.C. .... Harrisburg, PA
Lench, Kenneth R.
Securities and Exchange Commission, Division of Enforcement, GV
Lench, Mary Ellen D. .... Washington, DC
Lench, Ronald G. .... Harrisburg, PA
Lenchek, Allen M. .... Rockville, MD
Lenchek, Stanley L. .... Milwaukee, WI
Lenchner, Mitchell Jay .... Mineola, NY
Lenci, David J. .... Everett, WA
Lenci, Edward K. .... New York, NY
Lencioni, Allen S. .... Evanston, IL
Lenck, Eric E. .... New York, NY
Lencki, Kevin G. .... Mineola, NY
Riverhead, NY
Lenckos, Daniel J. .... Hinsdale, IL
Lencyk, Andrew E. .... New York, NY
Lencz, Norman .... Baltimore, MD
Lenczewski, Mitchell P. .... New York, NY
Lenczewski, Susan D. .... Duluth, MN
Lenczowski, Hubert .... Oakland, CA
Lenczowski, Mark .... Chicago, IL
Lenczycka, Leona E. .... Scranton, PA
Lenczycki, Joseph A., Jr. .... New York, NY
Lenczycki, Wayne A. .... Homewood, IL
Houston, TX
Lendais, Jean-Pierre .... Houston, TX
Lender, David .... New York, NY
Lenderman, Donald B. .... Detroit, MI
Lenderman, John C. .... St. Petersburg, FL
Lenderman, John F., Jr. .... El Centro, CA
Lenderman, Lisa J. .... Baltimore, MD
Lenderman, William Rex .... Baltimore, MD
Lending, Randall Marc .... Chicago, IL
Lending, Ronald M., (P.C.) .... St. Louis, MO
Lending, Stephen A. .... Torrance, CA
Lendino, Michael J. .... New York, NY
Lendino, Robert G. .... Charlotte, NC
Lendio, Darolyn Hatsuko .... Honolulu, HI
Lendormy, Jean-Yves P. .... San Francisco, CA
Lendrum, Jeffrey P. .... San Diego, CA
LeNeave, Cortney S. .... Minneapolis, MN
LeNeave, Randal W. .... Minneapolis, MN
Lenefsky, David .... New York, NY
Lenefsky & Lenefsky .... New York, NY
Lenefsky, Selig .... New York, NY
Leneghan, Christine .... Cleveland, OH
Leneghan, David M. .... Cleveland, OH
Leneghan & Leneghan .... Cleveland, OH
Leneghan, Patrick P., JR .... Cleveland, OH
Lenehan, Daniel W., III .... Washington, DC
Lenehan, Gary S. .... Manchester, NH
Lenehan, John F. .... Dayton, OH
Lenehan, Michael .... Concord, NH
Lenehan, William J. .... Los Angeles, CA
Lenell, Jack Anderson .... Fort Collins, CO
Lenell, Meredith .... Kailua-Kona, HI
Lenenberg, Mark D. .... Chatsworth, CA
Lener, Jenifer M. .... Philadelphia, PA
Lenert, Michael Edward .... Sacramento, CA
Lenes, James A. .... New Haven, CT
Lenes, Timothy P. .... Norwich, CT
Leness, George C. .... New York, NY
Leness, John S. .... Kent, WA
Lenett, Michael G. .... Washington, DC
L'Enfant, Howard W., Jr. .... Baton Rouge, LA
Lenfestey, James A. .... Tampa, FL
Lenga, Charles F. .... Toledo, OH
Lenga, J. Thomas .... Detroit, MI
Lenga, Robert A. .... Youngstown, OH
Lengauer, Steven F. .... Orlando, FL
Lengauer, Thomas E. .... Flint, MI
Lengemann, John L. .... Imlay City, MI
Lengler, Richard C. .... Harrisburg, PA
Lengnick, Sonja L. .... Seattle, WA
Lengyel, Linda B. .... Trenton, NJ
Lengyel, Melissa A. .... Baltimore, MD
Lengyel-Leahu, Pal A. .... Newport Beach, CA
Lenhard, John E. .... Cleveland, OH
Lenhard, Joseph A. .... Department of Energy, Office of the General Counsel, GV
Lenhard, Kirk B. .... Las Vegas, NV
Lenhard, Matthew A. .... Buffalo, NY
Lenhard, William R. .... Timonium, MD
Lenhardt, David J. .... St. Michael, MN
Lenhardt, David P. .... Santa Ana, CA
Lenhardt, Eileen R. .... Vernon Hills, IL
Lenhardt, Ingrid L. .... Chicago, IL
Lenhardt, Robert J. .... Charleston, SC
Lenhardt, Robin A. .... Department of Justice, Office of Legal Counsel, GV
Lenhart, Benedict M. .... Washington, DC
Lenhart, Benjamin G. .... Portland, OR
Lenhart, Carol P. .... Alexandria, VA
Lenhart, Christy L. .... Lancaster, OH
Lenhart, Daniel A. B. .... Los Angeles, CA
Lenhart, Douglas W. .... Chicago, IL
Lenhart, Edward R. .... Atlanta, GA
Lenhart, J. Thomas, (P.C.)
Washington, DC
Lenhart, Jeffrey G. .... Harrisonburg, VA
Lenhart, Leroy M. .... Freeland, PA
Lenhart, Peter J. .... Honolulu, HI
Lenhart, Peter J. .... New York, NY
Lenhart, Sarah J. .... Fremont, CA
Lenhart, Thomas E. .... Cleveland, OH
Lenhoff, Bernard .... North Adams, MA
Lenhoff, Glen N. .... Flint, MI
Lenhoff, John .... North Adams, MA
Leni, Robert Serafino .... Rochester, NY
Lenich, John P. .... Lincoln, NE
Lenicheck, Douglas H. .... Wauwatosa, WI
Lenick, Terrence F. .... Bonita Springs, FL
Lenick, Terrence F., P.A. .... Bonita Springs, FL
Lenihan, Brian P. .... Boston, MA
Lenihan, Daniel R. .... New York, NY
Houston, TX
Lenihan, David A. .... Delmar, NY
Lenihan, F. Thomas .... Westerly, RI
Lenihan Grady & Steele .... Westerly, RI
Lenihan, Jacob P. .... Minneapolis, MN
Lenihan, James B. .... Louisville, KY
Lenihan, Joleen C. .... San Francisco, CA
Lenihan, Joseph J. .... Pueblo, CO
Lenihan, Lawrence D. .... Chappaqua, NY
Lenihan, Lisa Pupo .... Pittsburgh, PA
Lenihan, Mary Anne .... Washington, DC
Lenihan, Robert J., II .... Troy, MI
Lenihan, Stephen J. .... Tucson, AZ
Lenihan, Thomas F. .... Wilsonville, OR
Lenihan, William F. .... Seattle, WA
Lenihan, William O. .... New York, NY
Lenik, Diana S. .... Urbana, IL
Lenington, William W. .... Minneapolis, MN
Lenk, Barbara A. .... Boston, MA
Lenk, Barry R. .... McLean, VA
Lenk, Christa C. .... San Antonio, TX
Lenke, Sharon L. .... Los Angeles, CA
Lenker, Brian R. .... Roseland, NJ
Lenker, John E. .... Seattle, WA
Lenker, Stephen C., Jr. .... Columbia, SC
Lenkiewicz, Cynthia J. .... New York, NY
Lenkin, Alan M. .... Reston, VA
Lenkin, Ronald L. .... Rockville, MD
Lenkov, Jeffrey M. .... Los Angeles, CA
Lenkov, Richard W. .... Oakbrook Terrace, IL
Lenkowicz, Stanley M. .... New York, NY
Lenkowski, Joseph V., Jr. .... Sanford, ME
Lenkowsky & Ezzell .... Bullhead City, AZ
Kingman, AZ
Lake Havasu City, AZ
Needles, CA
Las Vegas, NV
Laughlin, NV
Lenkowsky, Paul .... Bullhead City, AZ
Lenkowsky, Steven .... New York, NY
Lenkszus, Donald J. .... Phoenix, AZ
Lenmark, Jacqueline T. .... Helena, MT
Lenn, Christian M. .... Evansville, IN
Lenna, Leo G. .... New York, NY
Lennahan, Charles B. .... Denver, CO
Lennahan, Rebecca C. .... Denver, CO
Lennard, Colin .... Los Angeles, CA
Lennard, Gary L. .... Monroe, MI
Lennard, Graham & Goldsmith .... Monroe, MI
Lennard, Jeffrey .... Chicago, IL
Lennard, Melvin .... Pacific Palisades, CA
Lennard, Michael J. .... Lake Forest, IL
Lennarson, Marvin R. .... Hoffman Estates, IL
Lennart, Joseph P. .... Tulsa, OK
Lennarz, Alison V. .... Richmond, VA
Lenneberg, Roger A. .... Portland, OR
Lenneman, Annette J. .... Los Angeles, CA
Lennemann, K. Erin .... Los Angeles, CA
Lennemann, Lawrence J. .... Cerritos, CA
Lennen, Joel L. .... Pittsburgh, PA
Lennen, Kevin L. .... Dayton, OH
Lennen, Michael .... Wichita, KS
Lenner, Donald J. .... Hackensack, NJ
Lenner, Richard N. .... Atlanta, GA
Lenner, Robert Scott .... Boca Raton, FL
Lennertz, C. Robert .... Cincinnati, OH
Lennes, John Burr, Jr.
Marine On St. Croix, MN
Lenney, David M. .... Albany, NY
Lenney, James R. .... Herkimer, NY
Lenney, Ronald J. .... Pelham, NY
Lenney, Thomas E. .... Verona, NJ
Lenney, Thomas M. .... Detroit, MI
Lennie, Bradley T. .... Washington, DC
Lennie, Michael R., Law Offices of
Valley Center, CA
Lennig, Edward N., III .... Stratford, CT
Lennihan, C. Joseph .... Albuquerque, NM
Santa Fe, NM
Lennihan Law Offices .... Sacramento, CA
Lennihan, Martha H. .... Sacramento, CA
Lenninger, John J. .... Winter Haven, FL
Lennington, Lana Lenore .... Nashville, TN
Lennington & Lennington .... Muncie, IN
Lennington, Peter G. .... Roseville, MI
Lennington, Wayne J. .... Muncie, IN
Lennon, Alton Y. .... Wilmington, NC
Lennon, Brian Patrick
Department of Justice, Civil Division, GV
Lennon, Cynthia .... Xenia, OH
Lennon, Daniel T. .... Washington, DC
Lennon, David P. .... New York, NY
Lennon, Duncan .... Washington, DC
Lennon, Edward G. .... Detroit, MI
Lennon, George H., III .... Kalamazoo, MI
Lennon, George W. .... Raleigh, NC
Lennon, Gerald A. .... Walden, NY
Lennon, Gerald E. .... Los Angeles, CA
Lennon, Hugh F. .... San Jose, CA
Lennon, J. Howard .... Dallas, TX
Lennon, J. Michael .... Buffalo, NY
Lennon, James K. .... Palatine, IL
Lennon, Jane E. .... Oakland, CA
Lennon, Janet J. .... Brooklyn, NY
Lennon, Jennifer Anne .... Worcester, MA
Lennon, John F. .... Brooklyn, NY
Lennon, John M. .... Simsbury, CT
Lennon, Joseph P. .... Stockton, CA
Lennon, Julie E. .... Dallas, TX
Lennon, Kathleen .... New York, NY
Lennon, Kathleen A. .... Hartford, CT
Lennon, Kenneth J. .... Treasury Department, Office of the Comptroller of the Currency, GV
Lennon, Kevin J. .... Southport, CT
Lennon & Klein, P.C. .... New York, NY
Lennon, LaRue G. .... Westminster, MD
Lennon, Laura .... New York, NY
Lennon, Margaret E. .... Los Angeles, CA
Lennon, Mary H. .... Woodstock, IL
Lennon, Michael J. .... New York, NY
Lennon, Michael P., Jr. .... Houston, TX
Lennon & Miller .... Westminster, MD
Lennon, Patricia A. .... Brockton, MA
Lennon, Patrick F. .... Southport, CT
New York, NY
Lennon, Patrick T. .... Tampa, FL
Lennon, Peter A. .... New York, NY
Lennon, Rebecca Rose .... Littleton, CO
Lennon, Robert F. .... Chicago, IL
Lennon, Robert G .... Kalamazoo, MI

Lennon, Robert H. .... Westminster, MD
Lennon, Robert J., Jr. .... Towson, MD
Lennon, Robert R. .... Kalamazoo, MI
Lennon, Roger J. .... Briarcliff Manor, NY
Lennon, Rose T. .... Washington, DC
Lennon, Susan H. .... Department of Justice, Civil Division, GV
Lennon, Susan M. .... Washington, DC
Lennon, Theresa L. .... San Jose, CA
Lennon, Thomas A. .... Edina, MN
Lennon, Thomas J. .... Hackensack, NJ
Lennon, Timothy B. .... Albany, NY
Lennon, Timothy P. .... Philadelphia, PA
Lennox, Edwin Cornell .... Deerfield, IL
Lennox, Heather .... Cleveland, OH
Lennox, Malissia R. .... Redondo Beach, CA
Lennox & Murtha, P.A. .... Berlin, NJ
Lennox, Susan L., (P.C.) .... Boston, MA
Lennox, Thomas A. .... Berlin, NJ
Lenns, Margaret Duffy .... Butler, PA
Lenny, Dave .... Los Angeles, CA
Lenny, Patricia M. .... Cherry Hill, NJ
Leno, David P. .... Valley Stream, NY
Leno, Matthew E. .... Chicago, IL
Lenobel, Jeffrey A. .... New York, NY
Le Noble, Gerald J. .... Little Chute, WI
Lenoff and Lenoff, P.A. .... Deerfield Beach, FL
Lenoff, Lester .... Bronx, NY
Lenoff, Michele M. .... Deerfield Beach, FL
Lenoff, Steven .... Deerfield Beach, FL
Lenoir, Kenneth .... Abilene, TX
Lenoir, Rachael Hetherington Jackson, MS
LeNoir, S. John .... New York, NY
Lenoir-Peek, Annick I. .... Beaufort, SC
Lenon, Lisa Stanton .... Marshfield, MA
Lenora, Larry K. .... Chandler, OK
Lenore, Charles H. .... Hartford, CT
Lenow, Edwin C. .... Memphis, TN
Lenow, Howard B. .... Boston, MA
Lenowitz, Ronald A. .... New York, NY
Lenox, Bradford R. .... Raleigh, NC
Lenox, Bryce A. .... Dayton, OH
Lenox, Calvin, III .... Winter Park, FL
Lenox, Catherine A. .... Austin, TX
Lenox, David J. .... Dillsburg, PA
Lenox, David R. .... Orlando, FL
Lenox, Edward F., Jr. .... Quincy, MA
Lenox, Jayson B. .... St. Charles, MO
Lenox, Judith W. .... Houston, TX
Lenox, Samuel D., Jr. .... Trenton, NJ
Lenox, Socey, Wilgus, Formidoni & Casey Flemington, NJ
Freehold, NJ
Mount Holly, NJ
New Brunswick, NJ
Princeton, NJ
Red Bank, NJ
Somerville, NJ
Trenton, NJ
Doylestown, PA
Lenox, Walter S. .... New York, NY
Lenox, William Securities and Exchange Commission, Office of the General Counsel, GV
Lenrow, Jay Laurence .... Baltimore, MD
Lenrow, Kohn, Howard & Oliver, A Professional Corporation .... Baltimore, MD
Lenrow, Mitchel H. .... New York, NY
Lenrow, Robert J. .... Paramus, NJ
Lensbower, Gregory .... Hanover, PA
Lenschau, James G M .... Memphis, TN
Lense, Alberto A. .... Miami, FL
Lense, Pablo E. .... Miami, FL
Lenser, Jeffrey M. .... Washington, DC
Lensing, Connie Lewis .... Memphis, TN
Lensing, Gregory J. .... Dallas, TX
Lensing, Robert W. .... Evansville, IN
Lensink, Andrew J. .... Denver, CO
Lenske, Lenske & Abramson, A Law Corporation .... Los Angeles, CA
Woodland Hills, CA
Lenske, Sherman D. .... Woodland Hills, CA
Lenske, Stephen A. .... Woodland Hills, CA
Lensky, Harry .... Milwaukee, WI
Lensky, Mark A. .... Houston, TX
Lensman, Todd A. .... Canton, OH
Lenson, Kevin L. .... Cleveland, OH
Lenson, Murray K. .... Cleveland, OH
Lenson, Todd E. .... New York, NY
Lenssen, John L. .... Santa Fe, NM
Lent & Abrams .... New York, NY
Lent, Berkeley .... Keizer, OR
Lent, Brian S. .... Pearl River, NY
Lent, Daniel .... Monroe, CT
Lent, Deborah Tymon .... Los Angeles, CA
Lent, Dennis M. .... Albany, NY
Lent, Gerri Sue .... Portland, OR
Lent, James W. .... Laguna Hills, CA
Lent, Krista R. .... Cincinnati, OH
Lent, Margaret H. .... Seattle, WA
Lent, Norman F. .... Washington, DC
Lent, Norman F., III .... Washington, DC
Lent, Richard W. .... New Paltz, NY
Lent, Robert J. .... Los Angeles, CA
Lent, Robert N. .... Williamsburg, VA
Lent, Susan Heck .... Washington, DC
Lent, Thomas M. .... Erie, PA
Lentchner, Cassandra F. .... Washington, DC
Lentchner, Harry L. .... Pittsburgh, PA
Lentell, John Leonard .... Independence, MO
Lentell Law Firm, A Professional Corporation .... Overland Park, KS
Independence, MO
Lenter, Richard A., (P.C.) .... Southfield, MI
Lentes, John R. .... Pomeroy, OH
Lenti, Arlindo D. .... Spring Valley, NY
Lenti, Bridget C. .... New York, NY
Lentine, Gerilyn A. .... Herndon, VA
Lentine, John A. .... Birmingham, AL
Lentine, Stephen J. .... Billerica, MA
Lentini, Arthur J. .... Metairie, LA
Lentini, David P. .... Emeryville, CA
Lentini, Elizabeth J. .... Milwaukee, WI
Lentini, Peter A. .... Marlton, NJ
Philadelphia, PA
Lentini, Richard P. .... Seattle, WA
Lentini, Teresa .... Shamong, NJ
Lentini, Tracy Wittenburg .... Syracuse, NY
Lentini, Vincent M. .... Danvers, MA
Lentner, Darin J. .... Fort Lauderdale, FL
Lento, Gary N. .... Kenosha, WI
Lento, Thomas J. .... Lisle, IL
Lentol, Joseph R. .... Brooklyn, NY
Lents, Charles E. .... Morris Plains, NJ
Lents, Don G. .... St. Louis, MO
Lents & Foley LLP .... Irvine, CA
Lents, Michelle M. .... Irvine, CA
Lentz, Allen D. .... Nashville, TN
Lentz, Barbara R. .... Winston-Salem, NC
Lentz, Benjamin D. .... New York, NY
Lentz, Bruce M. .... Grand Rapids, MI
Lentz, Bryan R. .... Philadelphia, PA
Lentz, Cantor & Massey, Ltd. Kennett Square, PA
Malvern, PA
Lentz, Charles O. .... Minneapolis, MN
Lentz & Clark, P.A. .... Overland Park, KS
Lentz, David D. .... Richmond, VA
Lentz, David W. .... West Bloomfield, MI
Lentz, David W. .... Livingston, NJ
Lentz, Deborah Harley .... Philadelphia, PA
Lentz, DeVere & Associates, P.A. Asheville, NC
Lentz, DeVere C., Jr. .... Asheville, NC
Lentz & Duval .... Santa Barbara, CA
Lentz, Edward J. .... Allentown, PA
Lentz, Edward T. .... Philadelphia, PA
Lentz, Edward W. .... Arlington, VA
Lentz, E. R. .... Lancaster, OH
Lentz, Eric S. .... Chatham, NJ
Lentz, Evans and King P.C. .... Denver, CO
Lentz, F. Stannard .... Overland Park, KS
Lentz & Fair, P.A. .... Palm Beach, FL
Lentz, Frank E. .... Lilburn, GA
Lentz, Frederick C. .... Columbus, OH
Lentz, Gary C. .... Joplin, MO
Lentz, Gavin P. .... Cherry Hill, NJ
Philadelphia, PA
Lentz, Gene H. .... Decatur, AL
Lentz, George M. .... Troy, MI
Lentz, Gilbert W. .... Santa Barbara, CA
Lentz, H. James .... Palm Beach, FL
Lentz, Harold S. .... Alamo, CA
Lentz, Harry A., Jr. .... Oklahoma City, OK
Tulsa, OK
Lentz, Hover T. .... Denver, CO
Lentz, James E. .... Chicago, IL
Lentz, Jennifer Beth .... Los Angeles, CA
Lentz, John C. .... Columbus, OH
Lentz, John D. .... Nashville, TN
Lentz, John H. .... Clarksville, TN
Lentz, Joseph William .... Emporia, KS
Lentz, Julius .... New York, NY
Lentz, Marguerite Munson .... Detroit, MI
Lentz, Martin R. .... Philadelphia, PA
Lentz, Mary A. .... Cleveland, OH
Lentz, Michael Joseph .... Baltimore, MD
Lentz, Nelsen L. .... Indianapolis, IN
Lentz, Nelson, Whitmire & House Decatur, AL
Lentz, Paula N. .... Topeka, KS
Lentz, Robert H. .... Los Angeles, CA
Lentz, Robert J. .... Bolingbrook, IL
Lentz, Robert W. .... Kennett Square, PA
Malvern, PA
Lentz, Sally A. .... Washington, DC
Lentz, Stephen D. .... Virginia Beach, VA
Lentz, Susan .... Madison, WI
Lentz, Susan L. .... Healdsburg, CA
Minneapolis, MN
Lentz, W. Parish .... Providence, RI
Lentz, Wesley G. .... Bangor, MI
Lentz, William D. .... Ravenna, OH
Lentz, William H. .... Oakland, CA
Lentz, William W. .... Independence, MO
Lentzner, Michelle E. .... Lake Oswego, OR
Lenvin, Nancy C. .... San Francisco, CA
Lenweaver, Thomas E. .... Rochester, NY
Lenyo, David L. .... Aspen, CO
Lenyo, Mark S. .... South Bend, IN
Lenz, David D. .... Richmond, VA
Lenz, Edward A. .... Alexandria, VA
Lenz, Eileen M. .... West Chester, PA
Lenz, F. Lawrence .... Oregon, IL
Lenz, Frederick S., Jr. .... Simsbury, CT
Lenz, George R. .... Huntington, NY
Lenz, Jolie S. .... Houston, TX
Lenz, Kenneth E. .... Orange, CT
Lenz, Kurt W. .... Pittsburgh, PA
Lenz, Laurence H., Jr. .... Chicago, IL
Lenz Law Firm, L.L.C. .... Orange, CT
Lenz, Leslie Edward .... Oklahoma City, OK
Lenz, Mark .... Chicago, IL
Lenz, Mark J. .... Reno, NV
Lenz, Marvin R. .... Taylor, TX
Lenz, Paul A., Inc. .... Santa Monica, CA
Lenz, Paul J. .... Eau Claire, WI
Lenz, Richard T. .... Milwaukee, WI
Lenz, Robert J. .... Bloomington, IL
Lenz, Stewart W. .... Lafayette, CA
Lenz, Theodore W. .... Nashville, TN
Lenz, Thomas A. .... Cerritos, CA
Lenz, Thomas M. .... Boston, MA
Lenz, Valerie A. .... San Francisco, CA
Lenz, William J. .... Chicago, IL
Lenza, Richard E. .... Kansas City, MO
Lenzen, Gerald P. .... Woodstock, IL
Lenzen, Glenn H., Jr. .... Lexington, MA
Lenzen, John C. .... Roseland, NJ
Lenzen, Louis C. .... Belvedere-Tiburon, CA
Lenzendorf, Leah Fillbach .... Enid, OK
Lenzer & Lenzer .... Norcross, GA
Lenzer, Robert W. .... Norcross, GA
Lenzer, Thomas P. .... Norcross, GA
Lenzi, Albert J., Jr. .... Chico, CA
Lenzi, Louis G. .... Armonk, NY
Lenzi, Stephen E. .... Los Angeles, CA
Lenzini, Paul A. .... Washington, DC
Lenzini, Phillip B. .... Peoria, IL
Lenzini, Robert T. .... Foothill Ranch, CA
Lenzmeier, Roger R. .... St. Paul, MN
Lenzner, Igor S. .... St. Cloud, MN
Lenzner, Lawrence P. .... New York, NY
Lenzner, Terry F. .... Washington, DC
Lenzner, Terry F., P.C. .... Washington, DC
Lenzo, Christopher P. .... Millburn, NJ
Lenzo, Daniel F. .... Boston, MA
Lenzotti, Dean M. .... Dublin, OH
Lenzser, Frederick .... Portland, OR
Lenzy, Tammy J. .... Oak Park, IL
Leo, Ann .... Cleveland, OH
Leo, Anthony N. .... East Berlin, PA
Leo and Associates .... Huntsville, AL
Leo, Charles H. .... Orlando, FL
Leo, David .... Pueblo, CO
Leo, Donald .... New York, NY
Leo, Donald W. .... Coram, NY
Leo, Doreen K. .... Centreville, MI
Leo, Eileen D. .... Springfield, MA
Leo, Elizabeth C. .... Wilkes-Barre, PA
Leo, Evan T. .... Washington, DC
Leo, Flory J., Jr. .... Des Moines, IA
Leo, Harold E. .... Baltimore, MD
Leo, Jeffrey H. .... Los Angeles, CA
Leo, John J. .... New York, NY
Leo & Johnson .... Bloomfield, NJ
Leo, Jonathan S. .... San Francisco, CA
Leo, Karen .... New York, NY
Leo, Karl W. .... Huntsville, AL
Leo, Leonard A. .... Washington, DC
Leo, Louis J. .... Metairie, LA
Leo, Louis Joseph, A Prof. Law Corp. Metairie, LA
Leo, Luigi .... Boston, MA
Leo, Matilde .... New York, NY
Leo, Michael S. .... New York, NY
Leo, Michele .... Clinton, MS
Leo, Nicholas, Jr. .... Yonkers, NY
Leo, Robert G., Jr. .... Houston, TX
Leo, Robert J. .... New York, NY
Leo, Rocco J. .... Birmingham, AL
Leo, Roger J. .... Portland, OR
Leo, Ronald B. .... San Francisco, CA
Leo, Scott E. .... Charlotte, NC
Leo, Simon S. .... Orange, CA
Leo, Steven J. .... Milford, CT
Leo, T. Scott .... Chicago, IL
Leo, Theodore J. .... Bloomfield, NJ
Leo, Thomas Glen .... Los Angeles, CA
Leo & Weber, P.C. .... Chicago, IL
Leoci, Deborah E., (P.A.) .... Fort Myers, FL
Leoci & Meisenberg .... Fort Myers, FL
Leodori, Paul A. .... Philadelphia, PA
Leomporra, Tullio Gene .... Lafayette Hill, PA
León, Alberto A. .... Miami, FL
Albuquerque, NM
León, Alberto A., Attorney and Counselor at Law, P.C. .... Albuquerque, NM
Leon, Amberson & Carroll, L.L.P. San Antonio, TX
Leon, Anthony Thomas New Port Richey, FL
Leon, Anthony Thomas .... Tampa, FL
Leon, Arnold H. .... Portsmouth, VA
Leon, Barbara A. Department of Housing and Urban Development, Office of General Counsel, GV
Leon, Bernard S. .... Newark, NJ
Leon, Carlos .... Miami, FL
Leon, Carlos .... Houston, TX
Leon, Carmen .... Miami, FL
Leon, Carmen L. .... Miami, FL
Leon, Catherine M. .... San Francisco, CA
Leon, Christopher E. .... Atlanta, GA
Winston-Salem, NC
Leon, Craig L. .... Cambridge, MA
Leon, Dana .... Warsaw, IN
Leon, Daniel B. .... Beverly Hills, CA
Leon, David .... Cambridge, MA
Leon, David F. .... Bakersfield, CA
Leon, David F. .... Orlando, FL
Leon, David L. .... Dallas, TX
Leon, David M. .... Encino, CA
Leon, David P. .... Wichita, KS
Leon, Deborah G. .... Mountain View, CA
Leon, Deborah L. .... Oakland, CA
Leon & Deffet .... Hauppauge, NY
Leon, Derek E. .... Houston, TX
Leon, Donald E. .... Arcadia, CA
Leon, Enrique J. .... New York, NY
Leon, Eric F. .... New York, NY
Leon, Francis E., Jr. .... Mobile, AL
León, Francisco .... Tucson, AZ
Leon, Geraldine E. .... Hauppauge, NY
Leon, Glenn S. .... New York, NY
Leon, Gracelyn A. .... Chicago, IL
Leon, Gus .... Cincinnati, OH
Leon, Harold B. .... Detroit, MI
Leon, Harvey R. .... Sacramento, CA
Leon & Hosmer, L.L.P. .... Dallas, TX
Leon, Jack J. .... Buffalo Grove, IL
Leon, Jack Paul .... San Antonio, TX
Leon, Jeffrey A. .... Oakland, CA
Leon, Jeffrey A. .... Chicago, IL
Leon, Joaquin E. .... Miami, FL
Leon, John P. .... Voorhees, NJ
Leon, Jorge M. .... Chicago, IL
Leon, Jose I. .... Miami, FL
Leon, Joseph Paul .... New York, NY
Leon, Julia L. .... Tucson, AZ
Leon & Leon .... Oakland, CA
Leon, Leonard .... Oakland, CA
Leon, Lisa Marcel .... St. Augustine, FL
Leon, Lori A. .... Chicago, IL
Leon, Marvin, (A Professional Corporation) Los Angeles, CA
Leon, Matthew Todd .... New York, NY
Leon, Michael A. .... Boston, MA
Leon, Norman M. .... Chicago, IL
Leon, Phillip .... Wichita, KS
Leon, Richard J. .... Washington, DC
Leon, Roland L. .... Corpus Christi, TX
Leon, Santiago G. .... Miami, FL
Leon, Sara Hardner .... Austin, TX
Leon, Stephen A. .... Tampa, FL
Leon, Stephen A. .... Portsmouth, VA
Leon, Stuart I. .... Philadelphia, PA
Leon, Tania L., (P.A.) .... Charlotte, NC
Leon, Theodore D. .... St. Paul, MN
Leon, Trino J. .... Davenport, IA
Leon, William J., Jr. .... Morgantown, WV
Leonard, A. G. .... Steubenville, OH
Leonard, Alan C. .... Rutherfordton, NC
Leonard, Alexander C. .... Plymouth, MA
Leonard, Allen J. .... Naperville, IL
Leonard, Alvin R. .... Springfield, NJ
Leonard, Alvin R. .... Oklahoma City, OK
Leonard, Amy J. .... Cincinnati, OH
Leonard, Amy Marie .... San Francisco, CA
Leonard, Andrew B. .... St. Louis, MO
Leonard, Anita Perkins .... Jonesboro, AR
Leonard, Arthur A. .... Los Angeles, CA
Leonard, Arthur D. .... Farmington, MI
Leonard, Arthur F. .... Beverly Hills, CA
Leonard, Arthur J. .... Pittsburgh, PA
Leonard, Arthur J. .... Providence, RI
Leonard, Arthur S. .... New York, NY
Leonard, Barbara M. .... San Jose, CA
Leonard, Beverly Saxon .... Napa, CA
Leonard & Biggers, P.A. .... Asheville, NC
Leonard, Billy G., Jr. .... Dallas, TX
Leonard, Bob, Jr. .... Austin, TX
Leonard, Bresci R. P. .... Pittsburgh, PA
Leonard, Brian F. .... Minneapolis, MN
Leonard, Bruce E. .... Sacramento, CA
Leonard & Butler, A Professional Corporation Morristown, NJ
Phillipsburg, NJ
Leonard, C. Glenn .... Fort Lauderdale, FL
Leonard, C. Jerome, Jr. .... Charlotte, NC
Leonard, C. Kevin .... Concord, NH
Leonard, Cameron M. .... Fairbanks, AK
Leonard, Carl A. .... Somerset, NJ
Leonard, Caroline A. .... Washington, DC
Leonard, Carolyn Jo .... Slidell, LA
Leonard, Carson M. .... New York, NY
Leonard, Cathye E. .... Oakland, CA
Leonard, Charles D. .... Albuquerque, NM
Leonard, Charles E. .... Atlanta, GA
Leonard, Charles F. .... Fort Wayne, IN
Leonard, Charles V. .... Myrtle Beach, SC
Surfside Beach, SC
Leonard, Christopher B., (A Professional Corporation) .... Los Angeles, CA
Leonard, Christopher J. .... Atlanta, GA
Leonard, Christopher K. .... Danbury, CT
Ridgefield, CT
Leonard & Clancy, P.C. .... Phoenix, AZ
Leonard Collins & Kelly, P.C. Phoenix, AZ
Leonard, Colvin T., III .... Atlanta, GA
Leonard, Craigh .... New York, NY
Leonard, Curtis N. .... Midland, TX
Leonard, D. Hywel .... Tampa, FL
Leonard, D. Mark .... Secaucus, NJ
Leonard, Daniel J. .... Andover, MA
Leonard, Daniel P. .... Santa Monica, CA
Leonard, David A. .... Dallas, TX
Leonard, David F. .... Fairbanks, AK
Leonard, David H. .... Salem, OR
Leonard, David Heerwald .... Honolulu, HI
Leonard, David J. .... Tucson, AZ
Leonard, David M. .... Atlanta, GA
Leonard, David M. .... Indianapolis, IN
Leonard, David Neal .... Dallas, TX
Leonard, David R. .... Northbrook, IL
Leonard, Dawn A. .... Newburyport, MA
Leonard, Dawson B. .... Orinda, CA
Leonard, Deborah Lynne .... Cedar Rapids, IA
Leonard, Declan C. .... Springfield, VA
Leonard, Dicker & Schreiber, Limited Liability Partnership .... Beverly Hills, CA
Los Angeles, CA
Leonard & Dively .... Pittsburgh, PA
Leonard, Don .... Fort Worth, TX
Leonard, Don J. .... Farmington, UT
Leonard, Donald H. .... East Grand Forks, MN
Leonard, Donna K. .... Cincinnati, OH
Leonard, Donna Mullen .... Chicago, IL
Leonard, Douglas C. .... Providence, RI
Leonard, Duane M. .... Berkeley, CA
Leonard, E. Gay .... Abingdon, VA
Leonard, Edward D., III .... Bangor, ME
Leonard, Edward J. .... Garden Homes, IL
Leonard, Edward J. .... Columbus, OH
Leonard, Edward J. .... Philadelphia, PA
Leonard, Edward L. .... Tulsa, OK
Leonard, Edward M. .... Foster City, CA
Leonard, Edward M., Jr. .... Morgan City, LA

Leonard, Edward R. ....Los Angeles, CA
Orange, CA
Leonard, Edward W., Jr. ....Astoria, OR
Leonard, Edwin Deane ....New York, NY
Leonard, Edwin R. ....Bloomfield Hills, MI
Leonard, Eleanor H. ....Lexington, KY
Leonard, Elizabeth M. ....Boston, MA
Leonard, Elizabeth M. "Betty"
Marietta, GA
Leonard, Elizabeth M., P.C. .....Marietta, GA
Leonard, Elizabeth Maher
Manchester, NH
Leonard, Ellen J. ....Oakland, CA
Leonard, Ellen R. ....Montgomery, AL
Leonard, Emily ....Washington, DC
Leonard, Eric W. ....Washington, DC
Leonard, Ernest W. ....Dallas, TX
Leonard, Ethan Y. ....New York, NY
Leonard, Evita A. ....Washington, DC
Leonard, F. Elliot ....New Milford, CT
Leonard Felker Altfeld Greenberg & Battaile, P.C. ....Tucson, AZ
Leonard, Francis M., Jr. ....New York, NY
Leonard, Frank M. ....Hudson, WI
Leonard, Frank P. ....Boston, MA
Leonard, Fred M. ....Bristol, TN
Leonard, G. Thomas ....Fullerton, CA
Leonard, Gary E. ....Austin, MN
Leonard, Gary H. ....Rochester, NY
Leonard, Gary L. ....Houston, TX
Leonard, Gaylord ....Springfield, VA
Leonard, Geo. A. ....Cincinnati, OH
Leonard, Geo. Stephen ....Alexandria, VA
Leonard, Geoffery W. ....Salt Lake City, UT
Leonard, Geoffrey P. ....Menlo Park, CA
Leonard, Georganne G. ....Austin, TX
San Antonio, TX
Leonard, George E. ....Kansas City, MO
Leonard, George E., III ....Hinsdale, IL
Leonard, Glenford S. ....Oak Park, MI
Leonard, Glenn T. ....North Arlington, NJ
Leonard, Gregory J. ....Macon, GA
Leonard, H. Lee ....Lafayette, LA
Leonard and Hayes ....Morgan City, LA
Leonard, Heidi W. ....New York, NY
Leonard, Holly ....Santa Ana, CA
Leonard, Hugh B. ....Binghamton, NY
Leonard, Hugh M. ....Hackensack, NJ
Leonard Hurt Frost & Lilly, A Professional Corporation ....Washington, DC
Austin, TX
Dallas, TX
Houston, TX
Leonard, Ina B. ....Birmingham, AL
Leonard, Irvin A. ....Cleveland, OH
Leonard, J. Rich ....Wilson, NC
Leonard, Jack ....Melrose, MA
Leonard, Jack D., II ....Hampstead, MD
Leonard, Jack R. ....Tallahassee, FL
Leonard, James ....Clinton, NJ
Leonard, James ....Ada, OH
Leonard, James A. ....Kansas City, MO
Leonard, James Burgess ....Ada, OH
Leonard, James D. ....Denver, CO
Leonard, James G. ....Dallas, TX
Waxahachie, TX
Leonard, James G., & Associates, P.C.
Dallas, TX
Waxahachie, TX
Leonard, James J., Jr. ....Phoenix, AZ
Leonard, James K. ....Lima, OH
Leonard, James M. ....Los Angeles, CA
Leonard, James M. ....Huntington, NY
Leonard, James P. ....St. Louis, MO
Leonard, James R. ....Newark, DE
Wilmington, DE
Leonard, James R. ....Lafayette, LA
Leonard, James R., Jr. ....Lancaster, PA
Leonard, Jane E. ....Washington, DC
Leonard, Jason D. ....Oklahoma City, OK
Leonard, Jean P. ....Riverside, CA
Leonard, Jeffrey A. ....Philadelphia, PA
Leonard, Jeffrey A. ....Dallas, TX
Leonard, Jeffrey D. ....Wichita, KS
Leonard, Jeffrey S. ....Phoenix, AZ
Leonard, Jeffrey S. ....Newark, NJ
Leonard, Jeffrey S. ....Short Hills, NJ
Leonard, Jerome M. ....Boston, MA
Leonard, Jerris ....Washington, DC
Leonard, Jerry L. ....San Francisco, CA
Leonard, J. K. ....San Antonio, TX
Leonard, Joan S. ....Chevy Chase, MD
Leonard, Joe H. ....Lexington, NC
Leonard, Joe M., III ....Greenville, TX
Leonard, Joel P. ....Portland, OR
Leonard, John ....Dublin, CA
Leonard, John ....Staten Island, NY
Leonard, John A. ....Fresno, CA
Leonard, John A. ....Wichita Falls, TX
Leonard, John B. ....Mount Sterling, IL
Leonard, John B. ....Ogdensburg, NY
Leonard, John C., Jr. ....Lewisburg, TN
Leonard, John H. ....Cocoa Beach, FL
Leonard, John J. ....Canton, OH
Leonard, John J. ....Philadelphia, PA
Leonard, John J., Jr. ....Chicago, IL
Leonard, John L. ....Chicago, IL
Leonard, John M. ....Latrobe, PA
Leonard, John M. ....Hudson, WI
Leonard, John M., Jr. ....Chicago, IL
Leonard, John P. ....Morristown, NJ
Leonard, John S. ....Boston, MA
Leonard, John W. .....Department of Commerce, Patent and Trademark Office, GV
Leonard, Joseph H. ....San Francisco, CA
Leonard, Judith B. ....Tucson, AZ
Leonard, Judith S. ....New York, NY
Leonard, Julian F. ....Jacksonville, FL

Leonard & Kaserman, PLLC ......Knoxville, TN
Leonard, Katherine G. ....Honolulu, HI
Leonard, Keith N. ....Moorestown, NJ
Philadelphia, PA
Leonard, Keitha A. ....Lafayette, LA
Leonard, Kevin ....New York, NY
Leonard, Kevin J. ....Towson, MD
Leonard, Kevin P. ....Latrobe, PA
Leonard, Kip W. ....Eugene, OR
Leonard, Kris C. ....Salt Lake City, UT
Leonard, Krista F.N. ....Durham, NC
Leonard, L. Charles ....Hempstead, NY
Leonard, Larry D. ....Tulsa, OK
Leonard, Larry E. ....Thomasville, NC
Leonard, Laura L. ....Chicago, IL
Leonard, Laurie S. ....New York, NY
Leonard, Lawrence ....New York, NY
Leonard, Lawrence S. ....Chicago, IL
Leonard, Lawrence Y. ....Vero Beach, FL
Leonard, Lee R. ....Metairie, LA
Leonard, Leigh M. ....Los Angeles, CA
Leonard & Leonard ....Linden, NJ
Lima, OH
Leonard & Leonard, Ltd., A Prof. Law Corp. ....Lafayette, LA
New Iberia, LA
Leonard, Li-An C. ....San Diego, CA
Leonard, Louis G., III
Department Of The Interior, Office of the Solicitor, GV
Leonard, Lucille S. ....Denver, CO
Leonard & Lyde ....Chico, CA
Oroville, CA
Leonard, Lynn M. ....Winter Haven, FL
Leonard, Margaret M. ....Baltimore, MD
Leonard, Margery C. ....Brighton, MA
Leonard, Marilyn ....Golden, CO
Leonard, Marjorie H. ....San Francisco, CA
Leonard, Mark F. ....Denver, CO
Leonard, Martha J. ....Star City, AR
Leonard, Martin ....Philadelphia, PA
Leonard, Mary E. ....Cortland, NY
Leonard, Mary E. ....South Milwaukee, WI
Leonard, Matthew G. ....New York, NY
Leonard, Melissa A. ....Cleveland, OH
Leonard, Michael ....Philadelphia, PA
Leonard, Michael A.
Department Of Veterans Affairs, Office of the General Counsel, GV
Leonard, Michael H. .....Department of Defense, Defense Legal Services Agency, GV
Leonard, Michael I. ....Chicago, IL
Leonard, Michael J. ....Manhattan Beach, CA
Leonard, Michael R. ....Machias, ME
Leonard, Michael S. ....Chicago, IL
Leonard, Michelle Nahon
Springfield, MO
Leonard & Morrison
Fort Lauderdale, FL
Leonard, Nancy M. ....Kansas City, MO
Leonard, Nathan & Zuckerman
San Francisco, CA
Leonard, Nicholas A. ....Doylestown, PA
Leonard, Norbert B. ....Troy, MI
Leonard, Norman ....San Francisco, CA
Leonard, O'Brien, Wilford, Spencer & Gale, Ltd. ....Minneapolis, MN
St. Paul, MN
Leonard, Patricia A. ....Washington, DC
Leonard, Patricia A. .....Department of the Navy, Office of the Judge Advocate General, GV
Leonard, Patricia A.
West Palm Beach, FL
Leonard, Patrick F. ....Philadelphia, PA
Leonard, Patrick J. ....Knoxville, TN
Leonard, Paul A., Jr. ....Highland, IN
Leonard, Paul F., Jr. ....Rockville, MD
Leonard, Paul H. ....Baton Rouge, LA
Leonard, Paul R. ....Lima, OH
Leonard, Paul S. ....Birmingham, AL
Leonard, Phillip H. ....Duncan, OK
Leonard, R. Gregory ....Morristown, NJ
Phillipsburg, NJ
Leonard, R. Michael ....Winston-Salem, NC
Leonard, R. Webb ....Hamburg, NJ
Leonard, Rachael L. ....Chicago, IL
Leonard, Ralston & Stanton, Chartered
Washington, DC
Fairfax, VA
Leonard, Rebecca L. ....Blue Springs, MO
Leonard, Remy S. ....Everett, WA
Leonard, Richard A. ....Downey, CA
Leonard, Richard C. ....Westport, CT
Leonard, Richard C., (A Professional Corporation) ....Beverly Hills, CA
Leonard, Richard E. ....North Oaks, MN
Leonard, Richard G. ....Grand Rapids, MI
Leonard, Richard J. ....Reading, MA
Leonard, Richard W. ....Nashua, NH
Leonard & Rineer, P.C. ....Tulsa, OK
Leonard, Robert A. ....Norcross, GA
Leonard, Robert F. ....Sidney, IA
Leonard, Robert G. ....Washington, IN
Leonard, Robert G. ....New York, NY
Leonard, Robert H. ....Knoxville, TN
Leonard, Robert H. ....Laramie, WY
Leonard, Robert J. ....Denver, CO
Leonard, Robert J. ....Washington, DC
Leonard, Robert K. ....Winston-Salem, NC
Leonard, Robert K. ....Lima, OH
Leonard, Robert L. ....Springfield, MA
Leonard, Robert M. ....Florham Park, NJ
Leonard, Robert S. ....Staten Island, NY
Leonard, Robert T. ....Los Angeles, CA
Leonard, Robin D. ....Berkeley, CA
Leonard, Roderick W. ....Los Angeles, CA
Leonard, Roy E. ....Pittsburgh, PA
Leonard, Russell V. ....Seattle, WA

Leonard, Sharyn M. ....El Cajon, CA
Leonard, Sheri Hecht ....West Orange, NJ
Leonard, Sheri L. ....Sacramento, CA
Leonard, Stephen C. ....Linden, NJ
Leonard, Stephen M. ....Boston, MA
Leonard, Stephen P. ....Hingham, MA
Leonard, Steven C. ....Newport Beach, CA
Leonard, Steven L. ....St. Louis, MO
Leonard, Steven L., P.C. ....St. Louis, MO
Leonard, Street and Deinard, Professional Association ....Mankato, MN
Minneapolis, MN
St. Paul, MN
Leonard, Susan Burden ....Wausau, WI
Leonard, Susan E. ....San Diego, CA
Leonard, Susan Leigh ....Landover, MD
Leonard, Susan Y. ....Roseland, NJ
Leonard, T. Bentley ....Asheville, NC
Leonard, T. A. ....Milton, FL
Leonard, Tennie C., (Mrs.) ....Memphis, TN
Leonard, Terrence E. ....Chicago, IL
Leonard, Terrence E., Chartered .....Chicago, IL
Leonard, Terrence J., Jr. ....Houston, TX
Leonard, Terry J. ....Camden, TN
Leonard, Terry L. ....McAllen, TX
Leonard, Thomas A. ....Philadelphia, PA
Leonard, Thomas B., III ....Birmingham, AL
Leonard, Thomas J. ....White Plains, NY
Leonard, Thomas J., III ....Nashua, NH
Leonard, Tillery & Sciolla, LLP
Moorestown, NJ
Philadelphia, PA
Leonard, Tim S. ....Houston, TX
Leonard, Timothy D. ....Oklahoma City, OK
Leonard, Tom ....Ponca City, OK
Leonard, Tom ....Austin, TX
Dallas, TX
Houston, TX
Leonard, Vann F. ....Jackson, MS
Leonard, Veronica C. G. ....Linden, NJ
Leonard, W. Dudley ....Independence, MO
Leonard, Wade H., Jr. ....Mocksville, NC
Leonard, Walter W. ....Fort Worth, TX
Leonard, Warren A. ....San Francisco, CA
Leonard, Wesley T. ....La Grange, GA
Leonard, Wilbur G. ....Topeka, KS
Leonard, Will E. ....Washington, DC
Leonard, William F. ....Denver, CO
Leonard, William F. ......Fort Lauderdale, FL
Leonard, William G. ....Atlanta, GA
Leonard, William J. ....Philadelphia, PA
Leonard, William L. ....Cincinnati, OH
Leonard, William L. ....Philadelphia, PA
Leonard, William M. ....North Scituate, MA
Leonard, William Robert
Fort Lauderdale, FL
Leonard-Dent, Marva J. ....South Bend, IN
Leonardi, Barbara Glynn ....Boston, MA
Leonardi, Glenn D. ....Buffalo, NY
Leonardi, John F., Jr. ....Waukegan, IL
Leonardi, Kenneth J. ....Golden, CO
Leonardi, Maria Ann ....Brooklyn, NY
Leonardi, Robert M. ....Toledo, OH
Leonardi, Stephen A. ....Plymouth, MA
Leonardi, Thomas B. ....Hillsdale, NJ
Leonardini, Ernest John ....New York, NY
Leonardini, Raymond J. ....Sacramento, CA
Leonardini, Saroya J. ....Stockton, CA
Leonard-Mayer, Patricia J. ....Minneapolis, MN
Leonardo, Anthony F., Jr. ....Rochester, NY
Leonardo, Giselle ....Dearborn, MI
Leonardo, John S. ....Tucson, AZ
Leonardo, Mark J. ....Malibu, CA
Leonardo, Mark S. ....Boston, MA
Leonardo, Robert ....Newark, NJ
Leonardo, Stephen M. ....Rochester, NY
Leonardson, John M. ....Valatie, NY
Leonart, Ralph A. ....Newark, NJ
Leonatti & Baker, P.C. ....Mexico, MO
Leonatti, Louis J. ....Mexico, MO
Leon-Benner, Terri ....Tallahassee, FL
Leone, Albert ....Uniondale, NY
Leone, Amy L. ....Rockville, MD
Leone, Anthony G. ....Andover, MA
Leone, Anthony Robert, II ....Providence, RI
Leone, Armand, Jr. ....Glen Rock, NJ
Leone, Augustine, Jr. ....New Castle, PA
Leone, Carla C. ....Arlington, MA
Leone, Carmen S. ....Rochester, NY
Leone, Catherine M. ....Tacoma, WA
Leone, Charles S. ....South Bend, IN
Leone, Claudine M. ....Princeton, NJ
Leone, Cynthia Pauley ....Charlotte, NC
Leone, David A. ....Arlington, MA
Leone, David S. ....Drexel Hill, PA
Leone, Denio Angelo ....Lakewood, OH
Leone, Dennis ....Miami, FL
Leone, Donald E., Jr. ....Norwich, CT
Leone, Donald P. ....Youngstown, OH
Leone, Edmond A. ....Orchard Park, NY
Leone, Edward S. ....Syracuse, NY
Leone, Elizabeth A. ....Dunn, NC
Leone, Eugene J. M. ....Chicago, IL
Leone, Francis ....Boston, MA
Leone, Frank A. ....East Hartford, CT
Leone, Frank, Jr. ....Washington, DC
Leone, Fred D. ....Melbourne, FL
Leone, Frederick A. ....New York, NY
Leone, Frederick, Jr., (P.A.)
Hollywood, FL
Leone, George A., Sr. ....Minneapolis, MN
Leone, George S. ....Philadelphia, PA
Leone, Gerard T., Jr. ....Boston, MA
Leone, Helene R. ....Haddonfield, NJ
Leone, James A. ....Auburn, NY
Leone, James J., Jr. ....Bay Head, NJ
Leone, James R. ....Heathrow, FL
Leone, James R. ....Orlando, FL

Leone, Joe L. ....Bethesda, MD
Leone, John ....New York, NY
Leone, John A. ....Boston, MA
Leone, John D. ....Arlington, MA
Leone, John F. ....Buffalo, NY
Leone, Joseph A. ....Indianapolis, IN
Leone, Joseph L., Jr. ....Niagara Falls, NY
Leone, Joseph M. ....Indianapolis, IN
Leone, Joseph Robert ....Framingham, MA
Leone, Joseph T. ....Madison, WI
Leone, Judy L. ....Philadelphia, PA
Leone, Kimberly A. ....Los Angeles, CA
Leone, Lawrence E. ....Los Angeles, CA
Leone & Leone ....Arlington, MA
Leone, Louis A. ....Walnut Creek, CA
Leone, Marny G. ....Pittsburgh, PA
Leone, Michael A. ....San Diego, CA
Leone, Michael A. ....Kingston, MA
Leone, Michael S. ....West Palm Beach, FL
Leone, Pasquale ....Irvine, CA
Leone, Paul F. ....Denver, CO
Leone, Paul Michael ....Garden City, NY
Leone, Peter R. ....Boston, MA
Leone, Phil H. ....Red Bank, NJ
Leone, Philip D. ....Buffalo, NY
Leone, Renay W. ....New Brighton, MN
Leone, Richard J. ....Elmsford, NY
Leone, Robert E. ....Houston, TX
Leone, Robert F. ....Rochester, NY
Leone, Robert M. ....Chicago, IL
Leone, Robert Pompei ....Waltham, MA
Leone & Rossi ....Auburn, NY
Leone, Samuel J. ....Woodbury, NJ
Leone, Sheila Marie ....San Diego, CA
Leone, Silvina ....New York, NY
Leone, Stephan R. ....Lakewood, NJ
Leone, Therese M. ....San Francisco, CA
Leone, Thomas ....Auburn, NY
Leone, Thomas G., Jr. ....Syracuse, NY
Leone, Throwe, Teller & Nagle
East Hartford, CT
Hartford, CT
Leone, Tiffany Romney
Salt Lake City, UT
Leone, Trina L. ....Charleston, WV
Leone, William A. ....East Hartford, CT
Leone, William J. ....Boulder, CO
Denver, CO
Leone-Lindner, Suzanne M. .....Cambridge, MA
Leonelli, Esther D. ....Boston, MA
Leones, Anthony M. ....Walnut Creek, CA
Leonetti, Albert F. ....Cleveland, OH
Leonetti, Douglas ....Beaverton, OR
Leonetti, Ellen M. ....Cleveland, OH
Leonetti, Frank, III ....Cleveland, OH
Leonetti, Karen M. ....Southfield, MI
Leonetti, Kenneth S. ....Boston, MA
Leonetti, Linda A. ....Chicago, IL
Leonetti, Mark A. ....Cherry Hill, NJ
León-Freire, Luis ....San Juan, PR
Leong, Allen H.Y. ....Honolulu, HI
Leong, Alvin K. ....New York, NY
Leong, Andrew M. ....New York, NY
Leong, Anna A. ....San Francisco, CA
Leong, Arnold T. ....San Mateo, CA
Leong, Christopher K.D. ....Los Angeles, CA
Leong, Denis C. H. ....Honolulu, HI
Leong, Donna Y. L. ....Honolulu, HI
Leong, Edward ....House of Representatives, Office of Legislative Counsel, GV
Leong, Elizabeth R. ....Philadelphia, PA
Leong, Emily W. S. ....New York, NY
Leong, Galen C. K., (A Law Corporation)
Honolulu, HI
Leong, Glenn R. ....Orlando, FL
Leong, James Y. ....San Francisco, CA
Leong, Jeffrey T. ....San Leandro, CA
Leong, Jonathan ....Honolulu, HI
Leong, Kimberly J. ....Mission Viejo, CA
Leong, Kimo C. ....Honolulu, HI
Leong Kunihiro & Leong, Attys At Law., A Law Corp. ....Honolulu, HI
Leong, Kurt K. ....Honolulu, HI
Leong, Lilian ....East Hanover, NJ
Leong, Linda S. ....Modesto, CA
Leong, Linda Zichittella ....Honolulu, HI
Leong, Linda-Mei Y.K. ....Honolulu, HI
Leong, Margaret Jenkins ....Honolulu, HI
Leong, Patricia A. ....Walnut Creek, CA
Leong, Randolph F. ....Honolulu, HI
Leong & Rayfield ....New York, NY
Leong, Ronald Y. K., (Atty. At Law, A Law Corp.) ....Honolulu, HI
Leong, Scott G. ....Honolulu, HI
Leong, Stacey H. ....Sacramento, CA
Leong, Susan J. ....New York, NY
Leong, T. Stephen ....Honolulu, HI
Leon-Guerrero, C. Vincent ....McLean, VA
Leon Guerrero, Jose I., P.C. ....Hagåtña, GU
Leonhaeuser, Janet C. ....Healdsburg, CA
Leonhaeuser, Raymond C.
San Francisco, CA
Leonhard, Alicia Marie ....Honolulu, HI
Leonhard, Chunlin ....Chicago, IL
Leonhardt, Arthur G., Jr. ....Orlando, FL
Leonhardt, Arthur G., Jr., P.A. ....Orlando, FL
Leonhardt, D. Leon ....Fort Lauderdale, FL
Leonhardt, Donald E. ....Los Angeles, CA
Leonhardt, Edgar C. ....Fultonville, NY
Leonhardt, Frederick W. ....Orlando, FL
Leonhardt, Harry J. ....San Diego, CA
Leonhardt & Kruger, P.C. ....Fultonville, NY
Leonhardt, Mary Alice ....Hartford, CT
Leonhardt, Ronald D. ....Milwaukee, WI
Leonhardt, Stephen H. ....Denver, CO
Leonhart, Victoria A. ....New Holland, PA

Leoni, Andrew F. ... Long Beach, CA
Los Angeles, CA
Van Nuys, CA
Leoni, Marguerite Mary ... **Mill Valley, CA**
Sacramento, CA
San Francisco, CA
Leoni, Robert J. ... **Newark, DE**
Baltimore, MD
Leonian, Leon ... Los Angeles, CA
Leonick, James F. ... Woodbury, NY
Leonick, Leslie ... **Albertson, NY**
Leonidou, Janette G. ... San Mateo, CA
Leonidov, Sergey ... Boston, MA
Leonie, Andrew D. ... Rockwall, TX
Leonnig, Henry F. ... Upper Marlboro, MD
Leonoudakis, Stephan C. ... San Francisco, CA
Leonovich, Teri Kaufman ... **Baltimore, MD**
Leons, Natalia R. ... Department of Justice, Federal Bureau of Investigation, GV
Leontakianakos, Mary ... Tallahassee, FL
Leonti, Geraldine Careccia ... Glendale, NY
Leontsinis, George J. ... **St. Louis, MO**
Leopard, G. Bailey, Jr. ... **Memphis, TN**
Leopard, John A. ... Atlanta, GA
Leopard, John K. ... Gallatin, MO
Leopard & Leopard ... Gallatin, MO
Leopardi, John A. ... Warren, OH
Leopardi, John A., Co., L.P.A. ... Warren, OH
Leopold, A. Fredric ... **Los Angeles, CA**
Leopold, Aloysius A. ... San Antonio, TX
Leopold, Brett D. ... **Kansas City, MO**
Leopold, Christopher B. ... **Burlington, VT**
Leopold, David W. ... Cleveland, OH
Leopold, David W., L.P.A. ... Cleveland, OH
Leopold, Donald G. ... New York, NY
Leopold, Elise Michelle Udolf
New York, NY
Leopold, Elizabeth A. ... Waterbury, VT
Leopold, Evelyn R. ... **Fort Worth, TX**
Leopold, G. Vernon ... Birmingham, MI
Leopold, George W., Jr. ... **New York, NY**
Leopold, Georges ... **New York, NY**
Leopold, Gregory A. ... Des Moines, IA
Leopold, Gross & Sommers, P.C.
Brooklyn, NY
Leopold, Heidi L. ... St. Louis, MO
Leopold, Howard ... Staten Island, NY
Leopold, Howard B. ... **Paramus, NJ**
Leopold, J. Harry ... Ottawa, OH
Leopold, James F. ... New City, NY
Leopold, John P. ... Englewood, CO
Leopold, Joshua W. ... Burbank, CA
Leopold, Karen S. ... **Aventura, FL**
Leopold, Kenneth E. ... New York, NY
Leopold, Larry E. ... Ottawa, OH
Leopold, Laurence Scott
Small Business Administration, GV
Leopold, Leonard ... North Miami, FL
Leopold & Leopold, P.A. ... **Aventura, FL**
Leopold, Lynn M. ... **New York, NY**
Leopold, Madelyn D. ... **Madison, WI**
Leopold, Mark F. ... **Prospect Heights, IL**
Leopold, Norman ... **Aventura, FL**
Leopold, Norman R. ... Bellevue, WA
Leopold, Petrich & Smith, A Professional Corporation ... **Los Angeles, CA**
Leopold, Robin D. ... Kew Gardens, NY
Leopold & Sipper ... New City, NY
Leopold, Stephen R. ... San Francisco, CA
Leopold, Theodore J.
West Palm Beach, FL
Leopold, Theresa S. ... Brooklyn, NY
Leopold, Valerie A. ... **Chicago, IL**
Leopold-Leventhal, Jane E.
Doylestown, PA
Leoris and Cohen ... Highland Park, IL
Leoris, Drake ... Highland Park, IL
Leoris, Drake J., Jr. ... Highland Park, IL
Leos, Lynette M. ... Salem, MA
Leotsakos, Anastasios M. ... Danielson, CT
Leotta, Michael J. ... **Washington, DC**
Leotta, Patricia A. ... Newtown Square, PA
Leotta, Richard A. ... Brooklyn, NY
Leotti, Darren J. ... **Somerville, NJ**
Leoussis, Fay ... New York, NY
Le Pack, Keith ... New York, NY
Le Page, Clifford B., Jr. ... Reading, PA
LePage, Gregory W. ... **Denver, CO**
LePage, Herbert J. ... **Rochester, NY**
LePage, John R. ... Pineville, MO
Lepage, Kenneth R. ... **Boston, MA**
LePage, Margaret Coughlin
Portland, ME
Lepage, Stephen D. ... Grand Blanc, MI
LePage, Todd E. ... Richmond, VA
LePage, William F. ... **Dallas, TX**
Lepage, Yves E. ... **New York, NY**
Lepak, Linda Stoia ... Claremore, OK
LePak, Paul L. ... Belton, TX
Lepak, Scott M. ... **Minneapolis, MN**
Lepant, David P. ... Beatrice, NE
Lepanto, Joseph C. ... **Philadelphia, PA**
Lepape, Harry L. ... Los Angeles, CA
LePar, Lori J. ... **Chicago, IL**
Lepard, Amy S. ... Seattle, WA
Lepard, John S. ... **Grand Haven, MI**
Lepardo, Rachel G. ... Boston, MA
Leparulo, Linda S. ... **West Orange, NJ**
Leparulo, Peter V. ... **Los Angeles, CA**
LePatner, Barry B. ... **New York, NY**
LePatner, Barry B., & Associates, LLP
New York, NY
Lepchitz, W. Michael ... Charlottesville, VA
Le Pelletier, Jerome A.
Old Orchard Beach, ME
Lepelstat, Joseph J. ... Brooklyn, NY
Lepelstat, Marc R. ... **New York, NY**
Lepelstat, Martin L. ... **Woodbridge, NJ**

Lependorf, Barbara R. ... Trenton, NJ
Lepene, Alan R. ... **Cleveland, OH**
Lepentis, Jennifer Gottschalk
Kansas City, MO
Lepera, Christine ... **New York, NY**
LePera, Marianne H. ... Fort Myers, FL
LePera, Ralph R. ... Bishop, CA
Lepert, Debra S. ... **Minneapolis, MN**
Lepeska, Allyn ... Madison, WI
Le Phong, John P. ... Westminster, CA
Lepiane, Donald C. ... Pittsburgh, PA
Lepidi, Lawrence J. ... Warrendale, PA
Lepie, Luba Young ... Brookline, MA
LePiere, Lawrence R. ... San Diego, CA
LePine, Patrick G. ... **Detroit, MI**
Lepinskas, Ronald M. ... **Chicago, IL**
Lepis, Anne F. ... Jersey City, NJ
Lepis, Gerald J. ... Jersey City, NJ
Lepis, James G. ... Jersey City, NJ
Lepis, Joseph M. ... Jersey City, NJ
Lepiscopo, Peter Dominick ... San Diego, CA
Lepkowski, Cynthia A. ... Greendale, WI
LePla, Charles A. ... Escondido, CA
Lepler, Gerald H. ... Boston, MA
Lepler, Shirley M. ... Detroit, MI
Lepley, Donald E., Jr. ... Albuquerque, NM
Lepley, Engelman and Yaw
Williamsport, PA
Lepley, George E., Jr. ... **Williamsport, PA**
Lepley & McDonald, P.C.
Albuquerque, NM
LePley, Patrick H. ... **Bellevue, WA**
Lepley, Richard G. ... Department of Justice, Civil Division, GV
Lepley, Stephen C. ... Scottsdale, AZ
Lepman, Carol S. ... **Chicago, IL**
Le Pochat, Maureen ... West Orange, NJ
Lepofsky, Lepofsky and Lang ... Norwalk, CT
LePome, Robert C. ... **Las Vegas, NV**
Lepon, Jeffrey M. ... Washington, DC
Lepon McCarthy White & Holzworth
Washington, DC
Leporati, Christopher J. ... Pennsauken, NJ
Leporati, Dawn A. ... **Denver, CO**
Lepore, Albert J. ... Providence, RI
Lepore, Albert J., Jr. ... Providence, RI
Lepore, Alphonse P., Jr. ... Harrisburg, PA
Lepore, Amato V. ... Medford, MA
Lepore, Anthony J. ... Evergreen Park, IL
Lepore, Anthony T. ... Coral Gables, FL
LePore & Argento ... Rochester, NY
Lepore, Bruce A., Law Office of
Oakland, CA
Lepore, Christopher ... Pittsburgh, PA
Lepore, David M. ... Arlington, MA
Lepore, Gregory F. ... Lansdale, PA
Lepore, J. Robin ... Newton, MA
LePore, James ... Brick, NJ
Lepore, James Joseph ... Providence, RI
Le Pore, John ... Juneau, AK
Le Pore, John C. ... Washington, DC
Lepore, Joseph G. ... Brick, NJ
Lepore Luizzi Lepore & Blunda ... Brick, NJ
Lepore, Maria M. ... Trenton, NJ
Lepore, Matt ... Atlanta, GA
Lepore, Matthew ... **San Francisco, CA**
Lepore, Matthew J. ... **Denver, CO**
LePore, Nicholas J., III ... **Philadelphia, PA**
Lepore, Patrick A. ... Melbourne, FL
Lepore, Ralph T., III ... **Boston, MA**
LePore, Robert M. ... Brick, NJ
Lepore, Robert T. ... Lancaster, CA
LePore, Rudolph J. ... Rochester, NY
LePore, Vincent J., III ... Long Beach, CA
Lepore, William A. ... Hammond, LA
Leporiere, David A. ... **Sacramento, CA**
Leposki, Gene A. ... **San Diego, CA**
Lepow, Cynthia Ann ... New Orleans, LA
Lepow, Donald A. ... East Longmeadow, MA
Lepow, Leslie H. ... **Washington, DC**
Lepow, Susan G.
Environmental Protection Agency, Office of the General Counsel, GV
Lepp, Aaron G. ... **Akron, OH**
Lepp, Alan W. ... Chicago, IL
Lepp, Donald A. ... **Tulsa, OK**
Lepp, Gerald P. ... Brooklyn, NY
Lepp, Heidi Ann ... **Metuchen, NJ**
Lepp, Lingle & Zapf, S.C. ... Kenosha, WI
Lepp, Lois B. ... Pensacola, FL
Lepp, Melanie ... Brentwood, TN
Lepp, Nathaniel S. ... Kenosha, WI
Lepp, Robert L. ... **Omaha, NE**
Leppanen, Ann K. ... Minneapolis, MN
Leppanen, Douglas L. ... Sheboygan, WI
Leppanen, JoAnne ... Waltham, MA
Leppek, Harry V. ... Los Angeles, CA
Lepper, Gary M. ... Walnut Creek, CA
Lepper, Gregg J. ... **St. Louis, MO**
Lepper, Jack E. ... New York, NY
Lepper, Kathryn A. ... Birmingham, AL
Lepper, Schaefer & Harrington
Walnut Creek, CA
Lepper, Steven J.
Department of the Air Force, Office of the Judge Advocate General, GV
Leppert, Charles A. ... **Milwaukee, WI**
Leppert, Cynthia L. ... **Baltimore, MD**
Leppert, Elaine M. ... **Scotia, NY**
Leppert, Kenneth D., Jr. ... **Portland, OR**
Leppert, Michael, (P.C.) ... Houston, TX
Leppert, Timothy J. ... **Albany, NY**
Lepping-Pool, Sharon ... **Oak Brook, IL**
Leppke, Wendell E. ... Sacramento, CA
Leppla Associates ... **Dayton, OH**
Germantown, OH
Leppla, Bruce W. ... San Francisco, CA

Leppla, Gary J. ... **Dayton, OH**
Germantown, OH
Leppmann, Karl F. ... **Denver, CO**
Leppo, Jeffrey W. ... **Seattle, WA**
Lepre, Michael G. ... **Washington, DC**
LePrell, Samuel L. ... **Jacksonville, FL**
Lepri, A. J. ... Northfield, OH
Lepri, Julia A. ... Chicago, IL
Lepri, Robert J. ... Chicago, IL
Leprino, Nancy ... Denver, CO
Le Prohn, Robert ... San Francisco, CA
LeProwse, Jack ... Westminster, CO
Lepson, Sandra L. ... **Santa Monica, CA**
Leque, John A. ... Juneau, AK
LeQuire, Thomas E. ... **Chattanooga, TN**
Lera, Gina Louise ... **Sacramento, CA**
Lerach, Richard F. ... Pittsburgh, PA
Lerach, William S. ... **San Diego, CA**
Lerandeau, Paul E. ... **Fresno, CA**
Leras, Todd D. ... Sacramento, CA
LeRay, Charles N. ... **Boston, MA**
Lerberg, Gary L. ... Parshall, ND
Lerblance, Richard C. ... Hartshorne, OK
Lerch, Allan ... **San Francisco, CA**
Lerch, Allan, A Prof. Corp. & Associates
San Francisco, CA
Lerch, Early & Brewer, Chartered
Washington, DC
Bethesda, MD
Frederick, MD
Fairfax, VA
Lerch, Gregory D. ... Silver Spring, MD
Lerch, Harry W. ... **Bethesda, MD**
Lerch, Jerome N. ... **San Francisco, CA**
Lerch, Joseph B. ... **New York, NY**
Lerch, Keith W. ... Indianapolis, IN
Lerch, McDaniel & DePrima, P.L.C.
Phoenix, AZ
Lerch, Richard H. ... Towson, MD
Lerch, Spencer E. ... Niagara Falls, NY
Lerch, Stanford E. ... **Phoenix, AZ**
Lerch, Stephen J. ... Fort Wayne, IN
Lerche, Robert C. ... Golden, CO
Lerche, Vivian Leung ... **San Francisco, CA**
Lerchen, Edward H., Jr. ... Birmingham, MI
Lercher, Max ... San Diego, CA
Lerda, Patti Collins ... Pittsburgh, PA
Lerdal, Mark D. ... San Francisco, CA
Lerdal, Paul M. ... St. Cloud, MN
Lerer, Bruno Dov ... **New York, NY**
Lerer, Harvey L. ... Los Angeles, CA
Lerer, Jeffrey H. ... **Atlanta, GA**
Lerer, Neal M. ... **Chelmsford, MA**
Lerer, R. O. ... Atlanta, GA
Lerer, Stephen Alan ... Dallas, TX
Lerer, Tracey L. ... Columbia, MD
Lerew, Harold ... Wichita Falls, TX
Lerg, George H. ... **San Diego, CA**
Leri, Craig A. ... Marysville, CA
Le Riche, Jeff ... **Kansas City, MO**
LeRiche, Trina Ricketts ... **Kansas City, MO**
Lericos, Perry W. ... Baltimore, MD
Lerini, Alfredo J. ... Dearborn, MI
Leritz, Christopher P. ... **St. Louis, MO**
Leritz, James C. ... **St. Louis, MO**
Leritz, Joseph L. ... **St. Louis, MO**
Leritz, Peter N. ... **St. Louis, MO**
Leritz, Plunkert & Bruning, P.C.
St. Louis, MO
Lerma, Dwayne Stephen ... Hilo, HI
Lerma & Goya ... Hilo, HI
Lerma, John J. ... Boise, ID
Lerma, José M. ... Nogales, AZ
Lerma, Robert ... Brownsville, TX
Lerma, Ruben Romeo, Jr.
Corpus Christi, TX
Lerman, Alice C. ... Chicago, IL
Lerman, Averil ... Anchorage, AK
Lerman, Barbara ... White Plains, NY
Lerman, Bart E. ... Stamford, CT
Lerman, Bradley E. ... **Chicago, IL**
Lerman, Carlos D. ... Miami, FL
Lerman, Cary B. ... **Los Angeles, CA**
Lerman, Cathy Jackson, (P.A.)
Coral Springs, FL
Lerman, David ... Vineland, NJ
Lerman, David A. ... **Berkeley, CA**
Lerman, Esther M. ... Mendota Heights, MN
Lerman, Eve C. ... West Bloomfield, MI
Lerman, Gerald F. ... South Bend, IN
Lerman, Herbert S. ... Brookline, MA
Lerman, Herschel M. ... Biddeford, ME
Lerman, Howard D. ... **Chicago, IL**
Lerman, Ilan A. ... **New York, NY**
Lerman, James ... Beverly Hills, CA
Lerman, Janet L. ... Glencoe, IL
Lerman, Jeffrey E. ... **Los Angeles, CA**
Lerman, Jeffrey G. ... **Mineola, NY**
Lerman, Jeffrey G., P.C. ... **Mineola, NY**
New York, NY
Lerman, Jeffrey H. ... Los Angeles, CA
Lerman, Jeffrey R. ... **Philadelphia, PA**
Lerman, Julie Chatz ... Chicago, IL
Lerman & Katz, P.C. ... **New York, NY**
Lerman, Kenneth B. ... **Windsor, CT**
Lerman, Kenneth B., P.C. ... **Windsor, CT**
Lerman, Lance J. ... Department of Justice, Civil Division, GV
Lerman, Lawrence G. ... **Bethesda, MD**
Lerman & Lerman ... Los Angeles, CA
Lerman, Lindsey M. ... Omaha, NE
Lerman, Lisa G. ... Washington, DC
Lerman & Mann ... Brookline, MA
Lerman, Marvin S. ... **New York, NY**
Lerman & McCarthy ... Melrose, MA
Lerman, Michelle ... Los Angeles, CA
Lerman, Moses A. ... Brooklyn, NY
Lerman, Murray ... Cincinnati, OH

Lerman, Nancy ... Chicago, IL
Lerman, Robert A. ... **York, PA**
Lerman, Roy S. ... Washington, DC
Lerman, Sally A. ... Melrose, MA
Lerman, Scott ... **New York, NY**
Lerman, Steven A. ... Beverly Hills, CA
Lerman, Steven Alman ... **Washington, DC**
Lerman, Terry ... Pittsburgh, PA
Lerminiaux, Keith J. ... **Detroit, MI**
Lermond, Jessica M. ... **New York, NY**
Lerner, Alan B. ... Dallas, TX
Lerner, Albert J., (Co., L.P.A.)
Cincinnati, OH
Lerner, Allan M. ... Fort Lauderdale, FL
Lerner, Allison C. ... Department of Commerce, Office of the Inspector General, GV
Lerner, Andrew R. ... **New York, NY**
Lerner, Andrew S. ... **New York, NY**
Lerner, Andrew Scott ... Chevy Chase, MD
Lerner, Arthur J.
Corporation for National and Community Service, Office of Human Resources, GV
Lerner, Arthur M. ... **Champaign, IL**
Lerner, Arthur N. ... **Washington, DC**
Lerner, Barbara A. ... Chicago, IL
Lerner, Barry E. ... Rye, NY
Lerner, Barry R. ... Fort Lauderdale, FL
Lerner, Belinda A. ... New York, NY
Lerner, Bennett H. ... Cambridge, MA
Lerner, Brad S. ... Treasury Department, Office of the General Counsel, GV
Lerner, Brian L. ... **Miami, FL**
Lerner, Bruce R. ... **Washington, DC**
Lerner, Bruce W. ... Jersey City, NJ
Lerner, Carl Michael ... New York, NY
Lerner, Carol L. ... Walnut Creek, CA
Lerner, Carolyn N. ... **Washington, DC**
Lerner, Chris A. ... Orlando, FL
Lerner, Christopher ... Washington, DC
Lerner & Cianfrone ... Dunedin, FL
Lerner, Cindy L. ... Miami, FL
Lerner, Craig S. ... **Washington, DC**
Lerner, David ... **New York, NY**
Lerner, David A. ... Bloomfield Hills, MI
Lerner, David G. ... **Orlando, FL**
Lerner, David, Littenberg, Krumholz & Mentlik ... **Newark, NJ**
Westfield, NJ
Lerner, David S. ... Miami, FL
Lerner, Dean A. ... Des Moines, IA
Lerner, Debbie K. ... **Chicago, IL**
Lerner, Deborah M. ... Washington, DC
Lerner, Deborah M. ... Harrisburg, PA
Philadelphia, PA
Lerner, Debra Ilene ... Boston, MA
Lerner, Donald M. ... **Cincinnati, OH**
Lerner, Edward N. ... Stamford, CT
Lerner, Eric I. ... Philadelphia, PA
Lerner, Eric M. ... **New York, NY**
Lerner, Esther R. ... Belvedere-Tiburon, CA
San Francisco, CA
Lerner, Eugene M. ... Grass Valley, CA
Lerner, Eugene M. ... Annapolis, MD
Lerner, Frank ... Jersey City, NJ
Lerner, Fred S. ... **Park Ridge, NJ**
Lerner, Frederick M. ... Chicago, IL
Lerner, Gary ... **Middle Village, NY**
Lerner, Gary I. ... **New York, NY**
Lerner, Glenn A. ... San Francisco, CA
Santa Rosa, CA
Lerner and Greenberg, P.A.
Hollywood, FL
Lerner, Gregg S. ... **New York, NY**
Lerner, Gwen M. ... Burnsville, MN
Lerner, Harold B. ... San Francisco, CA
Lerner, Helene D.
National Labor Relations Board, Office of the General Counsel, GV
Lerner, Henry ... **San Francisco, CA**
Lerner, Henry R. ... New York, NY
Lerner, Herbert J. ... Washington, DC
Lerner, Herbert Joshua ... Miami Beach, FL
Lerner, Herbert L. ... **Hollywood, FL**
Lerner & Holmes, LLP ... Boston, MA
Lerner, Howard ... Annapolis, MD
Lerner, I. Allan ... Lamarque, TX
Lerner, I. Jack ... **St. Louis, MO**
Lerner, Irving ... Jericho, NY
Lerner, Irwin H. ... Bethesda, MD
Lerner, Jack Newton ... **New York, NY**
Lerner, James F. ... **New York, NY**
Lerner, James H. ... **Boston, MA**
Lerner, Jane H. ... **Houston, TX**
Lerner, Jay N. ... Department of Justice, Criminal Division, GV
Lerner, Jeffrey D. ... Fort Worth, TX
Lerner, Jeffrey M. ... Niles, IL
Lerner, Jerome ... Northbrook, IL
Lerner, Jessica A. ... Department of Justice, Civil Division, GV
Lerner, Jill R. ... **Santa Monica, CA**
Lerner, Jody ... San Francisco, CA
Lerner, Joel D. ... Boston, MA
Lerner, Joel J. ... Dallas, TX
Lerner, Johnathan C. ... **New York, NY**
Lerner, Jonathan E. ... Skokie, IL
Lerner, Jonathan J. ... **Roseland, NJ**
New York, NY
Lerner, Jonathan J. ... **New York, NY**
Lerner, Joshua A. ... Bloomfield Hills, MI
Lerner, Joshua D. ... **Miami, FL**
Lerner, Judith ... Eugene, OR
Lerner, Karen ... Bellingham, WA
Lerner, Karen A. ... Houston, TX
Lerner, Ken ... Argonne, IL
Lerner, Kenneth ... Portland, OR
Lerner, Kenneth D. ... **Austin, TX**

Lerner & Kirchner ... Champaign, IL
Lerner, Laura B. ... Boston, MA
Lerner, Laurence R. ... San Bernardino, CA
Lerner Law Offices ... Belvedere-Tiburon, CA
San Francisco, CA
San Jose, CA
San Mateo, CA
San Rafael, CA
Lerner, Lawrence ... Kansas City, MO
Lerner, Lawrence ... New Brunswick, NJ
Lerner, Lawrence I. ... Westfield, NJ
Lerner, Leonard D. ... Encino, CA
Lerner, Leonard D., A P.C. ... Encino, CA
Lerner, Linda ... New York, NY
Lerner, Lisa A. ... Miami, FL
Lerner, Lisa B. ... New York, NY
Lerner, Lois G.
Federal Election Commission, Office of the General Counsel, GV
Lerner, Louis Robert ... Hampton, VA
Lerner, Louise A. ... Department of Justice, Civil Rights Division, GV
Lerner, Maida Oringher ... Washington, DC
Lerner, Marc ... Los Angeles, CA
Lerner, Marc A.
Department of Transportation, Surface Transportation Board, GV
Lerner, Marily P. ... San Jose, CA
Lerner, Mark ... New York, NY
Lerner, Mark D. ... Las Vegas, NV
Lerner, Mark G. ... Santa Ana, CA
Lerner, Mark J. ... Department of Labor, Office of the Solicitor, GV
Lerner, Mark S. ... Charlotte, NC
Lerner, Mark W. ... New York, NY
Lerner, Marla ... New York, NY
Lerner, Marni J. ... New York, NY
Lerner, Marshall A. ... Los Angeles, CA
Lerner, Marshall L. ... Columbus, OH
Lerner, Martin ... Mineola, NY
Lerner, Martin L. ... Garden City, NY
Lerner, Matthew D. ... Washington, DC
Lerner, Max K. ... New York, NY
Lerner & McDonald ... Santa Ana, CA
Lerner, Michael A., (Ltd.) ... Wheeling, IL
Lerner, Michael B. ... Philadelphia, PA
Lerner, Michael J. ... Newark, NJ
Lerner, Michael J. ... Mentor, OH
Lerner, Michele A. ... New York, NY
Lerner, Mick ... Overland Park, KS
Lerner, Mick, P.A. ... Overland Park, KS
Lerner, Moore, Mammano, Strasser & Silva
San Bernardino, CA
Lerner, Nancy F. ... Orange Village, OH
Lerner, Nancy Miller ... New York, NY
Lerner, Neil S. ... Los Angeles, CA
Lerner, Patricia Leib ... Dunedin, FL
Lerner, Paul A. ... Phoenix, AZ
Lerner & Pearce, P.A. ... Fort Lauderdale, FL
Lerner, Perry A. ... Beverly Hills, CA
Lerner, Peter ... New York, NY
Lerner, Peter M. ... Woodbridge, CT
Lerner, Peter S. ... New York, NY
Lerner, Philip ... Manhasset, NY
Lerner, Philip ... New York, NY
Lerner, Philip D. ... New York, NY
Lerner & Piermont, P.A. ... Jersey City, NJ
Lerner, Rachel S. ... New York, NY
Lerner, Raissa S. ... Oakland, CA
Lerner, Ralph E. ... New York, NY
Lerner, Randal J. ... Houston, TX
Lerner, Reed, Bolton & McManus, LLP
Washington, DC
Alexandria, VA
Lerner, Richard D.
Federal Communications Commission, Common Carrier Bureau, GV
Lerner, Richard E. ... New York, NY
Lerner, Richard P. ... New York, NY
Lerner, Richard S. ... Los Angeles, CA
Lerner, Richard W. ... Carle Place, NY
Lerner, Robert J. ... Milwaukee, WI
Lerner, Robert N. ... Altamonte Springs, FL
Lerner, Robert N. ... Brooklyn, NY
Lerner, Roger J. ... Washington, DC
Lerner, Sam ... Port Chester, NY
Lerner, Sampson & Rothfuss, A Legal Professional Association ... Cincinnati, OH
Lerner, Shirley ... Minneapolis, MN
Lerner, Stanley G. ... Carmichael, CA
Lerner, Stanley R., (P.C.) ... Phoenix, AZ
Lerner, Stephen D. ... Cincinnati, OH
Lerner, Stephen M. ... San Diego, CA
Lerner, Stephen M. ... Atlanta, GA
Lerner, Steven D., (P.C.) ... Houston, TX
Lerner, Steven Paul ... Rockville Centre, NY
Lerner, Susan ... Santa Monica, CA
Lerner, Susan Scrivani ... Miami, FL
Lerner, Theodore N. ... North Bethesda, MD
Lerner, Thomas A. ... Seattle, WA
Lerner & Veit, Professional Corporation
San Francisco, CA
Santa Rosa, CA
Lerner, Veronique M. ... Ann Arbor, MI
Lerner, Vicki J. ... Kula, HI
Lerner & Wilhoite ... Chicago, IL
Lerner-Wren, Ginger I. ... Fort Lauderdale, FL
Leroe, Bernard A. ... Livingston, NJ
Leroi, Christopher ... Cortez, CO
Leroux, Clayton G., Jr. ... Cleveland, OH
Leroux, James D. ... Boston, MA
LeRoux, Jan E. ... Florham Park, NJ
LeRoux, John M. ... Clearwater, FL
LeRoux, Mark F. ... Portland, OR
Le Roux, Peter W. ... Falls Church, VA
LeRoux, Thomas R. ... San Francisco, CA
LeRoy, Bryan Cameron ... Irvine, CA
Leroy, Dan G. ... Midland, TX
Leroy, David H. ... Boise, ID
LeRoy, David R. ... Ventura, CA
LeRoy, Donald C. ... Hamilton, OH
LeRoy, Erik J. ... Anchorage, AK
LeRoy, F. Scott ... Chattanooga, TN
Leroy, Gary E. ... Boston, MA
Leroy, Kenneth J. ... Omaha, NE
LeRoy, L. Neil ... Providence, RI
Le Roy, Lawrence E. ... Mission, KS
LeRoy, Lawrence K. ... Newark, NJ
LeRoy, Lloyd F. ... Novato, CA
Leroy, Martin A. ... New York, NY
Leroy, Michael D. ... Chicago, IL
LeRoy, Michael W. ... Orlando, FL
LeRoy, Spencer, III ... Chicago, IL
LeRoy, W. Wayne ... Nashville, TN
Lers, David W. ... West Allis, WI
Lert, Erika Nagy ... Boston, MA
Lert, Richard F. ... Woodbridge, NJ
Lerten, Erwin ... Beverly Hills, CA
Lertzman, Eric J. ... Los Angeles, CA
Lerud, Roger C. ... Honolulu, HI
Lerude, Eric W. ... Las Vegas, NV
Reno, NV
Lerum, Eileen Burns ... Chicago, IL
Lerum, Norman J. ... Chicago, IL
Lervick, Craig J. ... Minneapolis, MN
Lervick, John C. ... Alexandria, MN
Lervick, Timothy D. ... Bismarck, ND
Lerway, Philip R. ... Austin, TX
Les, Gary R. ... Hales Corners, WI
Lesaca, Christine R. ... New York, NY
Lesaganich, John ... Peoria, IL
Le Sage, Bernard E. ... Los Angeles, CA
Le Sage, Jeffrey A. ... Los Angeles, CA
LeSage, Joan M. ... San Diego, CA
LeSage, Joseph C., Jr. ... Shreveport, LA
Lesage, Lisa M. ... Hillsboro, OR
LeSage, Michael T., A Professional Corporation
Paso Robles, CA
LeSage, Robert T., III ... Sterling, IL
Le Sage, Tracy R. ... Santa Ana, CA
Lesak, Robert L. ... Park Ridge, IL
Lesan & Finneran ... Coos Bay, OR
Lesan, Jerry O. ... Coos Bay, OR
Lesansky & Associates ... Pasadena, CA
Lesar, A. Keith ... Aptos, CA
Lesar, James H. ... Washington, DC
LeSatz, Stephen, Jr. ... Houston, TX
Lesavich, Stephen ... Chicago, IL
Lesavoy, Bernard M. ... Allentown, PA
Lescano, Marcelo L. ... Miami, FL
Lescault, Maurice A., Jr. ... Chepachet, RI
Lesch, Barry M. ... Sacramento, CA
Lesch, David P. ... Bronx, NY
Lesch, John Foster ... Chicago, IL
Lesch, Kenneth M. ... Washington, DC
Lesch, Marjorie A. ... Bronx, NY
Lesch, Michael ... New York, NY
Lesch, Millard D. ... Seattle, WA
Lesch, Peter C. ... Washington, DC
Lesch, Richard J. ... Denver, CO
Lesch, Sara ... New York, NY
Lesch, Solomon I. ... Bronx, NY
LeSchack & Grodensky, P.C.
New York, NY
Leschensky, William L. ... Palo Alto, CA
Lescher, H. W. ... Chicago, IL
Leschins, Preston A. ... New York, NY
Leschner, Peter M. ... New York, NY
Lescht, Alan ... Washington, DC
Lescht, Alan, & Associates, P.C.
Washington, DC
Leschuck, Lisa E. ... Cheyenne, WY
Lesco, Richard A. ... Cleveland, OH
Lescoe, Richard J. ... Pasadena, CA
Lescohier, Philip R. ... Sturgeon Bay, WI
Lescoulie, Donald P. ... Fresno, CA
Lescure, Paige ... Towson, MD
Lese, Laurence S. ... Washington, DC
Lese, Peter L. ... New York, NY
Lesel, Dov S. ... Los Angeles, CA
Lesem, Judith Ann ... Portland, OR
Lesemann, Arthur J. ... Hackensack, NJ
Lesemann, Arvid R., Jr. ... Charleston, SC
Lesemann, Arvid R., Jr. ... Greenville, SC
Lesemann, Dana J.
Federal Trade Commission, Bureau of Consumer Protection, GV
Lesemann, Ellis Reed-Hill ... Greenville, SC
Lesemann, James A. ... White House, TN
Leser, William R. ... Bay City, MI
Leserman, Paul ... Los Angeles, CA
Lesrowitz, Nathaniel E. ... Brooklyn, NY
Lesesne & Connette ... Charlotte, NC
Lesesne, Louis L., Jr. ... Charlotte, NC
Lesesne, Margaret Wueste ... Dallas, TX
Lesesne, Robert H. ... Dallas, TX
LeSeur, John H. ... Washington, DC
Lesh, Casner & Miller, A Legal Professional Association ... Canton, OH
Lesh, Larry M. ... Dallas, TX
Lesh and Lesh ... San Diego, CA
Lesh, Michael D. ... New York, NY
Lesh, Newton D., II ... Woodland Hills, CA
Lesh, Peter J. ... Doylestown, PA
Lesh, Robert L. ... San Diego, CA
Lesh, W. Robert ... San Diego, CA
Lesh, William W. ... Glen Burnie, MD
Lesha, Michael A. ... Detroit, MI
Leshanski, George P. ... New York, NY
Leshanski O'Sullivan & Maybaum, LLP
Carlstadt, NJ
New York, NY
Leshaw, Gary, and Associates
Decatur, GA
Leshaw, James P. S. ... Miami, FL
Leshe, Susan L. ... New York, NY
Leshen, Joseph C. ... West Islip, NY
Leshen, Kenneth A. ... Kankakee, IL
Lesher, Arthur C., Jr. ... Houston, TX
Lesher, David William ... Norristown, PA
Lesher, Donald M. ... Denver, CO
Lesher, Frank M. ... Park Ridge, NJ
Lesher, Gerald S. ... West Palm Beach, FL
Lesher, Greta ... Cleveland, OH
Lesher, Julie L. ... Laconia, NH
Lesher, M. Mark ... Texarkana, TX
Lesher, Michael L. ... Monsey, NY
Lesher, Raymond A., II ... Honolulu, HI
Lesher, Robert O. ... Tucson, AZ
Lesher, Robert S. ... East Aurora, NY
Lesher, Stephen H. ... Tucson, AZ
Leshikar, Nancy ... Austin, TX
Leshin & Dincel, LLP ... San Francisco, CA
Leshin, Ira ... San Francisco, CA
Leshin, L. Steven ... Dallas, TX
Leshin, Michael L. ... Wellesley, MA
Leshin, Randall L. ... Pompano Beach, FL
Leshin, Richard L. ... Corpus Christi, TX
Leshinski, John J. ... Phoenix, AZ
Leshko, Gary L. ... New York, NY
Leshko, Tanya C. ... Harrisburg, PA
Leshkowitz, Chaim Herbert ... New York, NY
Leshkowitz, Naftali T. ... New York, NY
Leshman, Martin D., (P.C.) ... Southfield, MI
Leshner, David E. ... Seattle, WA
Leshner, Stephen I. ... Phoenix, AZ
Leshner, Zane ... Corona Del Mar, CA
Leshnower, Richard ... Woodmere, NY
Leshnower, Ronald M. ... New York, NY
Lesho, James T. ... Pittston, PA
Lesho, James T. ... Pittston, PA
Wilkes-Barre, PA
Lesho, Karlene M. ... Treasury Department, Internal Revenue Service, GV
Lesht, David ... Chicago, IL
Leshy, Albert ... Columbus, OH
Leshy, George V. ... Columbus, OH
Leshy, John D. ... Department Of The Interior, Office of the Solicitor, GV
Lesiak, Theodore J. ... Medina, OH
Lesica, Catherine H. ... Fayetteville, NC
Lesica, Fred J. ... Muskegon Heights, MI
Lesicko, Dan M. ... St. Louis, MO
LeSieur, Bryan ... Brownsville, KY
Lesinski, John M. ... West Palm Beach, FL
Lesinski, Kevin J., (P.C.) ... Boston, MA
Lesinski, Leon C. ... Walpole, MA
Lesinski, Roger John ... Troy, MI
Lesinski, Steven M. ... St. Clair Shores, MI
Lesk, Ann Berger ... New York, NY
Lesk, Jeffrey S. ... Washington, DC
Lesk, Sherwin M. ... Chicago, IL
Leska, Richard C. ... Palo Alto, CA
Leske, Brian J. ... Washington, DC
Leske, Corina L. ... Minneapolis, MN
Leskera, John W. ... Belleville, IL
Collinsville, IL
Leski, Dennis W. ... San Francisco, CA
Leskin, Lori B. ... New York, NY
Leskinen & Cook ... Uniontown, PA
Leskinen, Julie K. ... Chicago, IL
Leskinen, Steve P. ... Uniontown, PA
Lesko, Deborah L. ... West Mifflin, PA
Lesko, Gregory S. ... Albany, NY
Lesko, Jason M. ... New York, NY
Lesko, Joseph M. ... San Diego, CA
Lesko, Richard G. ... Golden, CO
Lesko, Robert P. ... Morristown, NJ
Lesko, Theodore D. ... Rochelle Park, NJ
Leskovec, Mark ... Cleveland, OH
Leskovsek, Andreas H. ... Washington, DC
Leskovsek, Natasha ... Washington, DC
Leskovyansky, John J. ... Youngstown, OH
Leslein, Betty Swayne ... Big Canoe, GA
Lesley, Douglas M. ... Gillette, WY
Lesley, Robert O. ... Kansas City, MO
Leslie, Ann Farrell ... Wallingford, CT
Leslie, Betsy B. ... Tampa, FL
Leslie, Bob, Law Firm, P.A.
Little Rock, AR
Leslie, Brian H. ... Miami, FL
Leslie, Brian J. ... Wallingford, CT
Leslie, Bruce A. ... Las Vegas, NV
Leslie, Carol R. ... New York, NY
Leslie, Collins & Foy ... Waverly, IA
Leslie, Craig L. ... Kerrville, TX
Leslie, David R. ... St. Paul, MN
Leslie, Donald H. ... Marion, IN
Leslie, Donald S. ... El Paso, TX
Leslie, Dwayne O. ... Washington, DC
Leslie, Fredric A. ... Jersey City, NJ
Leslie, Gregory S. ... Minneapolis, MN
Leslie, Helen W. ... St. Paul, MN
Leslie, Henry A. ... Montgomery, AL
Leslie, J. David ... Boston, MA
Leslie, J. Douglass
Commodity Futures Trading Commission, Executive Staff, GV
Leslie, J. Robert ... Charleston, WV
Leslie, J. Timothy ... Hoffman Estates, IL
Leslie, James W. ... Seattle, WA
Leslie, Jennifer Wascak ... Brighton, CO
Leslie, Jody ... Fort Lauderdale, FL
Leslie, Jody, P.A., Law Offices of
Fort Lauderdale, FL
Leslie, John A ... Gretna, LA
Leslie, John Arthur ... Quincy, MA
Leslie, John E. ... Dallas, TX
Leslie, John K. ... Chelmsford, MA
Leslie, John W. ... San Diego, CA
Leslie, Karen G. ... Syosset, NY
Leslie, Karl E. ... St. Cloud, MN
Leslie, Kathleen D. ... Towson, MD
Leslie, Lann D. ... Eugene, OR
Leslie, Lee J. ... Huntington Beach, CA
Leslie, Linda M. ... Greenville, SC
Leslie, Louise W. ... Port Isabel, TX
Leslie, Marc C. ... Boston, MA
Leslie, Mark A. ... Hilliard, OH
Leslie, Mark R. ... Pittsburgh, PA
Leslie, Melanie B. ... New York, NY
Leslie, Michael R. ... Los Angeles, CA
Leslie, Michael W. ... Boston, MA
Leslie, Mickey K. ... Tulsa, OK
Leslie, Neville Malcolm
Fort Lauderdale, FL
Leslie, O'Sullivan, McCarville & Brown
Hutchinson, KS
Leslie, Pamela S. ... Tallahassee, FL
Leslie, Pamela S. ... Fayetteville, NC
Leslie, Paul S. ... Dallas, TX
Leslie, Philip M. ... Mobile, AL
Leslie, Philip W. ... Alexandria, VA
Leslie, Phillip Bruce ... Greenup, KY
Lexington, KY
Leslie, Phillip M., P.C. ... Mobile, AL
Leslie, Powell and Hannemann
San Francisco, CA
Leslie, R. Ted ... Oklahoma City, OK
Leslie, Richard M., (P.A.) ... Miami, FL
Leslie, Richard V. ... Waverly, IA
Leslie, Robert B. ... Little Rock, AR
Leslie, Robert B. ... Seattle, WA
Leslie, Robert E. ... San Francisco, CA
Leslie, Robert L. ... Oakland, CA
Leslie, Robert P. ... Salem, NH
Leslie, Robert P. ... Glenmont, NY
Leslie, Ronald L. ... Hutchinson, KS
Leslie, Rosalie C. ... Yonkers, NY
Leslie & Rubin ... Beverly Hills, CA
Leslie, Sean F. ... Carlsbad, CA
Palm Desert, CA
Leslie & Smith, P.C. ... Las Cruces, NM
El Paso, TX
Leslie, Stephen R. ... Tampa, FL
Leslie, Susan K. ... Department of Commerce, Patent and Trademark Office, GV
Leslie, Suzanne Boyer
Newport Beach, CA
Leslie, Suzanne C. ... Dallas, TX
Leslie, Tamara M. ... Newport Beach, CA
Leslie, Thomas M. ... White Plains, NY
Leslie, Thomas N. ... Indianapolis, IN
Leslie, Thomas W. ... New Castle, PA
Leslie, Timothy C. ... Cleveland, OH
Leslie, William H. ... Weaverville, NC
Leslie-Soley, Judith ... Fresno, CA
Leslie-Soley & Nystrom-Geist, A Professional Corporation ... Fresno, CA
Lesly, John L. ... Amarillo, TX
Lesly & Russ, P.L.L.C. ... Amarillo, TX
Lesman, Michael S. ... New York, NY
Lesmes, George Scott ... Washington, DC
Lesmes, Melissa Callahan
Washington, DC
Lesmez, Arthur G. ... Los Angeles, CA
Lesnak, Teresa Mahan ... Kingsport, TN
Lesnek-Cooper, Carol H. ... Detroit, MI
Lesneski, Gary J. ... Haddonfield, NJ
Lesnett, George M. ... White Plains, NY
Lesnevich & Marzano-Lesnevich
Tenafly, NJ
New York, NY
Lesnevich, Walter A. ... Tenafly, NJ
New York, NY
Lesnewich, Alan G. ... Somerset, NJ
Lesniak, Edward J. ... Chicago, IL
Lesniak, James A. ... Springfield, IL
Lesniak, James F. ... Newport Beach, CA
Lesniak, John W. ... Albany, NY
Lesniak, Kimberly Z. ... Houston, TX
Lesniak, Raymond J. ... Parsippany, NJ
Lesniak, Robert Walter ... Petersburg, VA
Lesnick, Adam D. ... New York, NY
Lesnick, Irving I. ... Boca Raton, FL
Lesnick, Matthew A. ... Los Angeles, CA
San Francisco, CA
Lesnik, Bonita G. ... Evanston, IL
Lesnik, Larry ... Roseland, NJ
Lesnik, Leon ... Springfield, NJ
Lesnock, Joan E. ... Washington, PA
Lesoon, Stephne J. ... Pittsburgh, PA
LeSourd, Francis A. ... Seattle, WA
Le Sourd, Nancy Oliver ... McLean, VA
LeSourd & Patten, P.S. ... Seattle, WA
LeSourd, Peter ... Mission Viejo, CA
Lesousky, James R., Jr. ... Louisville, KY
Lespasio, Michelle J. ... Stoneham, MA
Lesperance, Jeannine R.
Department of Justice, Civil Division, GV
L'Esperance, John F. ... Washington, DC
Lesperance, Kevin M. ... Chicago, IL
Lesperance, Lesperance & Lesperance
Miami, FL
Lesperance, Lisa ... Miami, FL
Lesperance, Louis K. ... Miami, FL
L'Esperance, Oneida ... Las Vegas, NM
Lesperance, Robert ... Miami, FL
Lesperance, T. J. ... Lake Mills, WI
L'Esperance, William A. ... Albuquerque, NM
Lespier, Manfredo E. ... Irvine, CA
Lespier & Muñoz-Noya ... San Juan, PR
Less, Daniel A. ... Cambridge, MA
Less, Dara B. ... Cherry Hill, NJ
Philadelphia, PA
Less, Getz & Lipman ... Memphis, TN
Less, Jeffrey A. ... Philadelphia, PA
Less, Lawrence J. ... San Francisco, CA
Less, Michael I. ... Memphis, TN
Less, Peter ... Chicago, IL
Less, Phillip A. ... Arvada, CO
Less & Weaver ... San Francisco, CA

Lessa, Charles R. .... Ayer, MA
Lessa, Michael C. .... Wakefield, MA
Lessack, Michael J. .... Fort Lee, NJ
Lessack, Ross T. .... Cheshire, CT
Lessack, Susan K. .... Berwyn, PA
Lessani, Andrea M. .... Palo Alto, CA
Lessani, Tina M. .... Palo Alto, CA
Lessans, Martin B. .... Glen Burnie, MD
Lessans, Praley & McCormick
Glen Burnie, MD
Lessard, Daphne .... Concord, NH
Lessard, Gabrielle .... Boise, ID
Lessard, Karen .... Pensacola, FL
Lessard, Lori L. .... Phoenix, AZ
Plano, TX
Lessard, Richard O. .... Providence, RI
Lesse, Sylvia .... Washington, DC
Lesseg, Daniel C. .... St. Louis, MO
Lessel, John C. .... Little Rock, AR
Lesselyong, Frank .... Phoenix, AZ
Lessem, Joseph H. .... New York, NY
Lessen, Larry L. .... Springfield, IL
Lessenberry, Jack L. .... Little Rock, AR
Lessenco, Gilbert B. .... Washington, DC
Lesser & Associates .... Redondo Beach, CA
Boca Raton, FL
Honolulu, HI
Lesser, Barbara A. .... Chicago, IL
Lesser, Beatrice .... New York, NY
Lesser, Bruce R. .... Philadelphia, PA
Lesser, Craig P. .... Brenham, TX
Lesser, Daniel J. .... Chicago, IL
Lesser, Danielle C. .... New York, NY
Lesser, David I. .... Costa Mesa, CA
Lesser, David M. .... Woodbridge, CT
Lesser, David M. .... Chicago, IL
Lesser, Don A. .... San Francisco, CA
Lesser, Eric B. .... New York, NY
Lesser, Frances Shaiman .... Columbus, OH
Lesser, Fredric Bryan .... Lake Forest, IL
Lesser, Gary S. .... West Palm Beach, FL
Lesser, Gary S. .... Indianapolis, IN
Lesser, Gary T. .... West Orange, NJ
Lesser, Gregory A. .... Redondo Beach, CA
Lesser & Harrison .... New York, NY
Lesser, Henry (IBA) **.... Los Angeles, CA**
Palo Alto, CA
San Francisco, CA
Lesser, Herbert .... Evanston, IL
Lesser, Jack I. .... Baltimore, MD
Lesser, Jacqueline M. .... New York, NY
Lesser, Jeffrey A. .... New York, NY
Lesser, Jeffrey M. .... Livonia, MI
Lesser, Jeffrey M., P.C. .... Livonia, MI
Lesser, Jill A. .... Washington, DC
Lesser, Jill C. .... New York, NY
Lesser, Joan L., (P.C.) .... Los Angeles, CA
Lesser, Jonathan .... New York, NY
Lesser, Joseph .... Secaucus, NJ
New York, NY
Lesser, Katherine M. .... Brooklyn, NY
Lesser, Laurence M. .... Norwalk, CT
Lesser & Lawrence .... Cincinnati, OH
Lesser, Lawrence R. .... Philadelphia, PA
Lesser, Leonard F. .... New York, NY
Lesser & Lesser, P.A. .... West Palm Beach, FL
Lesser, Lisa Fenakel .... Albany, NY
Lesser, Lisa H. .... River Edge, NJ
Lesser, Lori E. .... New York, NY
Lesser, Marc E. .... Livingston, NJ
Lesser, Margo Rogers .... Birmingham, MI
Lesser, Maria Y. .... Boston, MA
Lesser, Michael A. .... Boston, MA
Lesser, Monroe L. .... Department of the Army, Office, Chief of Engineers/Headquarters, U.S. Army Corps of Engineers, GV
Lesser, Nancy F. .... Washington, DC
Lesser, Newman, Souweine & Nasser
Northampton, MA
Lesser, Norman H. .... Chicago, IL
Lesser, Patricia R. .... Washington, DC
Lesser, Peter A. .... Philadelphia, PA
Lesser, Peter A. .... Dallas, TX
Lesser, Peter J. .... Los Angeles, CA
Lesser, Philip J. .... Arlington, VA
Lesser & Rich, LLP .... Los Angeles, CA
Lesser, Richard A. .... Redondo Beach, CA
Honolulu, HI
Lesser, Richard F. .... Cincinnati, OH
Lesser, Robert D. .... Trumbull, CT
Lesser, Robert E. .... New York, NY
Lesser, Robert I. .... Hackensack, NJ
New York, NY
Lesser, Robert K. .... Bridgeport, CT
Lesser, Saul .... Fort Lauderdale, FL
Lesser, Scott J. .... New York, NY
Lesser, Seth R. .... New York, NY
Lesser, Seymour S. .... Valley Stream, NY
Lesser, Shepard P. .... West Palm Beach, FL
Lesser & Sobel, P.C. .... Bridgeport, CT
Lesser, Stanley C. .... New York, NY
Lesser, Stanton H. .... Bridgeport, CT
Lesser, Stephen M. .... Yuba City, CA
Lesser, Steven B. .... Fort Lauderdale, FL
West Palm Beach, FL
Lesser, Steven D. .... Columbus, OH
Lesser, Stuart M. .... Baltimore, MD
Lesser, Susan Fortin .... Syracuse, NY
Lesser, Thomas .... Northampton, MA
Lesser, Thomas M. .... Chatsworth, CA
Lesser, Trudi J. .... Los Angeles, CA
Lesser, Wayne Lewis .... San Francisco, CA
Lesser, William .... Department of Labor, Office of the Solicitor, GV
Lesser, William M. .... New York, NY
Lessick, Steven E. .... Mountain Lakes, NJ
Lessie, Jennifer Thompson
Salt Lake City, UT
Lessig, Louis R. .... Camden, NJ
Westmont, NJ
Lessig, William R., Jr. .... Reading, PA
Lessin, Jeffrey R. .... Philadelphia, PA
Lessing, David L. .... New York, NY
Lessing, Robert E., Jr. .... Elyria, OH
Lessing, White & Roig, Ltd., Attorneys at Law
Elyria, OH
Lessinger, Howard M. .... Atlanta, GA
Lessinger, Jason A. .... Sarasota, FL
Lessis, James W. .... Dallas, TX
Lessler, Arthur L. .... New York, NY
Lessler, Chester A. .... St. Louis, MO
Lessler, Jay P. .... New York, NY
Lessler, Lauren B. .... Los Angeles, CA
Lessler, Robert H. .... Norwalk, CT
Lessler, Stanley M. .... Bridgeport, CT
Lessley, Rebecca Hairston
Los Angeles, CA
Mountain View, CA
Lesslie, Gary A. .... Yardley, PA
Lessly, Larry D. .... Reno, NV
Lessman, Robert E. .... Barrington, IL
Lessman, Sarah P. .... Waukegan, IL
Lessmann, Marlin M. .... Sioux City, IA
Lessmann, Michael G. .... Omaha, NE
Lessmeier, Gregory W. .... Juneau, AK
Lessmeier, Michael L. .... Juneau, AK
Lessmeier & Winters .... Juneau, AK
Lessne, Dale Laster .... Trenton, NJ
Lessne, Scott A. .... Hartford, CT
Lessne, Steven A. .... Boca Raton, FL
Lessner, Craig M. .... Summit, NJ
Lessner, Jane E. .... Philadelphia, PA
Lessner, John Francis .... Baltimore, MD
Lessner, Jonathan I. .... Wilmington, DE
Lessner, Martin S. .... Wilmington, DE
Lessner, Ronald D. .... Los Angeles, CA
Lessow, Marc A. .... Phoenix, AZ
Lessuk, Gerald H. .... Glen Ellyn, IL
Lessy, Roy P., Jr. .... Washington, DC
Lestage, Brian S. .... De Ridder, LA
Lestage, David R. .... De Ridder, LA
Lestage, H. O., III .... De Ridder, LA
Lestch, David A. .... New York, NY
Lestelle, Andrea S. .... Metairie, LA
Lestelle & Lestelle, A Professional Law Corporation .... Metairie, LA
Lestelle, Terrence J. .... Metairie, LA
Lester, A. Willard .... Wytheville, VA
Lester, Alison A. .... Chicago, IL
Lester, Alyse R. .... New York, NY
Lester, Andrew W. .... Edmond, OK
Lester, Arnold T. .... Torrance, CA
Lester, Arthur H. .... Fort Walton Beach, FL
Lester, Belford S., III .... Orlando, FL
Lester, Betty J. .... Newark, NJ
Lester, Billy Carl .... Purcell, OK
Lester, Bruce W. .... Chicago, IL
Lester, Catherine A. .... Newton, MA
Lester, Charles G. .... Covina, CA
Lester, Charles P. .... Pasadena, CA
Lester, Charles T., Jr. .... Atlanta, GA
Lester, Dana A. .... Brownsville, TX
Lester, Danny B. .... El Cajon, CA
Lester, David A. .... Estherville, IA
Lester, David J. .... Chicago, IL
Lester, David L. .... Cleveland, OH
Lester, David Lee .... Jackson, MS
Lester, David M. .... Los Angeles, CA
Lester, David S. .... Manhasset, NY
New York, NY
Lester, Debra Ritt .... Des Plaines, IL
Lester, Don H. .... Jacksonville, FL
Lester, Edgel C., Jr. .... Tampa, FL
Lester, Edwin .... Poughkeepsie, NY
Lester, Ellen C. .... Penn Valley, CA
Lester, Elton J.
Department of Housing and Urban Development, Office of General Counsel, GV
Lester, Esther C. .... Cleveland, OH
Lester, Eugene E., III .... Greensboro, NC
Lester & Fontanetta .... Garden City, NY
Lester, Frederick .... Pittsford, NY
Lester, Frederick L., Jr. .... Cleveland, TN
Lester, G. Holland, Jr. .... Marble Falls, TX
Lester, Gary E. .... Chattanooga, TN
Lester, George N., IV .... Boston, MA
Lester, Harold D., Jr. .... Department of Justice, Civil Division, GV
Lester, Harry S. .... Nashville, TN
Lester, Helen M. .... Lafayette, CA
Lester, Helene C. .... Las Vegas, NV
Lester, Herman W. .... Pikeville, KY
Lester, Herman W., P.S.C. .... Pikeville, KY
Lester, Howard .... New York, NY
Lester, J. Morgan .... Vista, CA
Lester, Jack L. .... New York, NY
Lester, James .... Coldwater, MI
Lester, James D. .... Phoenix, AZ
Lester, James K. .... Alamosa, CO
Lester, James L. .... Augusta, GA
Lester, James L. .... Greensboro, NC
Lester, Jane A. .... Jacksonville, FL
Lester, Jeffrey A. .... Hackensack, NJ
Lester, Jeffrey D. .... Moline, IL
Lester, Jennifer C. .... Gainesville, FL
Lester, John H. .... Houston, TX
Lester, John R. .... Columbia, SC
Lester, John W. .... Hamburg, NY
Lester, Joseph S., Jr. .... St. Paul, MN
Lester, Judith A., (Ms.) .... Boston, MA
Lester, Kathleen J. .... Washington, DC
Lester, Kelly Mooney .... Albany, NY
Lester, Kenneth H. .... Columbia, SC
Lester, Kenneth R. .... Atlanta, GA
Lester, Kenneth R., Jr. .... Sanford, FL
Lester, Laine R. .... Tulsa, OK
Lester, Laura S. .... Washington, DC
Lester, Leslie Ann .... Dallas, TX
Lester & Lester .... Brockport, NY
Lester, Lester & Flynt .... Augusta, GA
Lester & Lev, P.S. .... Bellingham, WA
Lester, Linda J. .... Santa Ana, CA
Lester, Loving & Davies, P.C.
Edmond, OK
Lester, M. Ignatius .... Key West, FL
Lester, Mark A. .... Alexandria, VA
Lester, Mark S. .... Riverside, CA
Lester, Marshall N. .... New York, NY
Lester, Martha L. .... Roseland, NJ
Lester, Martin W. .... Fredericksburg, VA
Lester, Matthew B. .... Orchard Lake, MI
Lester, Michael A. .... Phoenix, AZ
Lester, Michael H. .... East Meadow, NY
Lester, Michelle N. .... Arlington, VA
Lester, Minsky & Berzak, P.C.
East Meadow, NY
Lester & Mitchell, P.A. .... Jacksonville, FL
Lester, Nat O., III .... Brockport, NY
Lester, Nat O., Jr. .... Brockport, NY
Lester, Norman E., Jr. .... Dallas, TX
Lester, Paige G. .... Richmond, VA
Lester, Pamela J. .... Lexington, KY
Lester, Pamela R. .... New York, NY
Lester, Patric, & Associates
St. Louis, MO
Lester, Paul A. .... Miami, FL
Lester, Paul D. .... New York, NY
Lester, Phillip M. .... Bastrop, LA
Lester, R. David .... Lexington, KY
Lester, Ralph J. .... Phoenix, AZ
Lester, Randall C. .... Great Falls, MT
Lester, Raymond E. .... Athens, GA
Lester, Raymond J. .... Lake Forest, IL
Lester, Richard A. .... Chicago, IL
Lester, Richard D. .... Tarzana, CA
Lester, Richard E. .... Myrtle Beach, SC
Lester, Richard M. .... Encino, CA
Lester, Robert A. .... Atlanta, GA
Lester, Robert L. .... Bayside, NY
Lester, Robert M.
Agency for International Development, Office of the General Counsel, GV
Lester, Ronald L. .... Prestonsburg, KY
Lester, Roy J. .... Garden City, NY
Lester, Sam .... Tallahassee, FL
Lester, Sandra Elkin .... Irvine, CA
Lester Schwab Katz & Dwyer
Millburn, NJ
New York, NY
Lester, Sherwin D. .... Englewood Cliffs, NJ
New York, NY
Lester, Sigmond, Rooney & Schwiesow
Alamosa, CO
Lester, Stephanie M. .... Pittsburgh, PA
Lester, Stephen K. .... Wichita, KS
Lester, Steven C. .... Phoenix, AZ
Lester, Steven C., P.C. .... Phoenix, AZ
Lester, Stuart A. .... La Mesa, CA
Lester, Thomas E. .... Bellingham, WA
Lester, Thomas J. .... Rockford, IL
Lester, Troy R. .... Washington, DC
Lester, Urban A., II .... Washington, DC
Lester, Virgil T. .... Dallas, TX
Lester & Vohra, L.L.P. .... Washington, DC
Alexandria, VA
Lester & Weisinger .... Englewood Cliffs, NJ
New York, NY
Lester, Wendi R. .... Killeen, TX
Lester, Wilbur R. .... Cincinnati, OH
Lester, William A. .... Lombard, IL
Lester, William A., Ltd. .... Lombard, IL
Lester, William H., Jr. .... San Antonio, TX
Lester, William K., Jr. .... Lakewood, CO
Lester, William M. .... Charleston, WV
Lester, William R. .... Atlanta, GA
Lestikow, James M. .... Springfield, IL
Lestina, Matthew J. .... Washington, DC
Lestitian, William Edward .... Pittsburgh, PA
Lestock, John D. .... Waco, TX
Leston, Kristine E. .... Northbrook, IL
Leston, Patrick J. .... Wheaton, IL
Lestrade, Laura M. .... New York, NY
LeStrange, J. Scott .... Santa Rosa, CA
L'Estrange, John H., Jr., (P.C.)
San Diego, CA
Lestyk, Joseph A. .... San Diego, CA
Lestz, Alan M. .... Bronxville, NY
LeSuer, Robert C. .... Erie, PA
LeSueur, David C. .... McHenry, IL
LeSueur, Leon J. .... Napoleonville, LA
Le Sueur, Robt. L., Jr. .... Americus, GA
LeSueur, Stephen J. .... Champaign, IL
Leswing, Kristi E. .... Milwaukee, WI
Lesyk, Alexander .... Chateaugay, NY
Lesyk & Virkler .... Chateaugay, NY
Lesyna, James J. .... Houston, TX
Lesz, David Edward
Farmington Hills, MI
Leszcynski, Laurence T. .... Aurora, IL
Leszczynski, Joseph John .... Charleston, WV
Leszyk, Richard A. .... Ontario, NY
Leta, David E. .... Salt Lake City, UT
Leta, David M. .... Atlanta, GA
Letang, Peter N. .... Wilmington, DE
Le Tard, Philip A. .... Vidalia, LA
LeTart, Phyllis A. .... Atlantic City, NJ
Letarte, Diane T. .... Encinitas, CA
Letarte, Lisa A. .... Kalamazoo, MI
Letbetter, Tom R. .... Houston, TX
Letcher, Ann Joyce .... Wilmington, DE
Letcher, Barbara Kozar .... Columbus, OH
Letcher, C. Scott .... St. Louis, MO
Letcher, Dawn Curran .... Owingsville, KY
Letcher, Elizabeth S. .... San Francisco, CA
Letcher, J. Clifford .... Washington, DC
Letcher, Jason L. .... Des Moines, IA
Letcher, Joseph R. .... Ho-Ho-Kus, NJ
Letcher, N. Noelle .... Wayne, NJ
Letchford, James A. .... Mount Holly, NJ
Letchford, John F. .... Philadelphia, PA
Letchinger, Gary M. .... San Diego, CA
Letchinger, John S. .... Chicago, IL
Letchinger, Michael J. .... McLean, VA
Letchinger, Robert S. .... Chicago, IL
Letchinger, Sharon Zaban .... Chicago, IL
Letchworth, Frank G. .... Columbia, SC
Letelier, Patricio A. .... San Jose, CA
Letellier, Frank P., II .... Metairie, LA
Letellier, Gina-Marie .... Springfield, MA
Letendre, George A. .... St. Paul, MN
Letham, Glenn W. .... Washington, DC
Lethbridge, Kerrie A. .... Chicago, IL
Lether, Margaret .... Orange, CA
Lether, Thomas .... Seattle, WA
Letizia & Ambrose .... New Haven, CT
Letizia, Clarice Jean .... San Diego, CA
Letizia, Daniel P. .... Oakbrook Terrace, IL
Letizia, David D. .... Oakbrook Terrace, IL
Letizia, Donald L. .... Denville, NJ
Letizia, Frances R. .... Bernardsville, NJ
Letizia, John M. .... New Haven, CT
Letizia & Letizia, Ltd. .... Oakbrook Terrace, IL
Letizia, Thomas M. .... Princeton, NJ
Letkewicz, Lawrence C. .... Chicago, IL
Letnes, Daniel S. .... Grand Forks, ND
Letnes, Marshall & Swanson, Ltd.
Grand Forks, ND
Letnes, Thomas A., II .... Tucson, AZ
Letney, Susan .... Houston, TX
Letnick, Robert S. .... Fairfax, VA
Leto, Anthony L. .... Los Gatos, CA
Leto, Bruce G. .... Philadelphia, PA
Leto, Cristie Coates .... Racine, WI
Leto, Francis J. .... Rosemont, PA
Leto, Frank P. .... Tucson, AZ
Leto, Nicholas A., Jr. .... San Diego, CA
Leto, Nora .... Sebring, FL
Winter Haven, FL
Leto, Patricia L. .... Des Moines, IA
Leto, Peter, (P.C.) .... Bloomfield Hills, MI
Leto, Salvatore J. .... Mineola, NY
Leto, Vincent A. .... Tampa, FL
Letofsky, Alan R. .... Blue Bell, PA
Letofsky & Dombrowski
Breckenridge, CO
Frisco, CO
Letofsky, Larry D. .... San Diego, CA
Letofsky, Steven F. .... Frisco, CO
Letourneau, Cynthia A. .... Taunton, MA
Letourneau, Dennis R. .... Minneapolis, MN
Letourneau, Gerald J. .... Topeka, KS
Letourneau, John P. .... New Bedford, MA
Letourneau, Keith B. .... Houston, TX
Le Tourneau, Lawrence F. .... Earlham, IA
Letourneau, Raymond A. .... New Bedford, MA
Letourneau, Steven P. .... Virginia Beach, VA
Letourneau & Surprenant
New Bedford, MA
Letsch, Daniel E. .... Springfield, MO
Letsche, Keith E. .... Chicago, IL
Letscher, Thomas A. .... Minneapolis, MN
Letsen, Royden A. .... Yonkers, NY
Letsinger, James E. .... Crown Point, IN
Letson, Daniel B. .... Warren, OH
Letson, Griffith, Woodall, Lavelle & Rosenberg Co., L.P.A. .... Warren, OH
Letson, Janet Marie "Jaye" .... Washington, DC
Letson, Laurence R. .... Lexington, KY
Letson, Thomas B. J. .... Warren, OH
Letson, Thomas C. B. .... Warren, OH
Letson, William N. .... Warren, OH
Letson, William W. .... Chattanooga, TN
Letsou, Costas G. .... Lowell, MA
Letsou, Peter V. .... Arlington, VA
Letsou, Thomas C. .... New York, NY
Lett, Adam M. .... Traverse City, MI
Lett, Daniel J. .... St. Louis, MO
Lett, Gloria J. .... Washington, DC
Lett, J. David .... Loogootee, IN
Lett, J Martin .... Atlanta, GA
Lett, Jack .... Grove City, OH
Lett, Jack, Co., LPA .... Grove City, OH
Lett and Jones .... Loogootee, IN
Lett, Katherine Partain .... Dallas, TX
Lett, Marshall I. .... Southfield, MI
Lett, Michael B. .... Loogootee, IN
Lett, Michael K. .... Ashland, KY
Lett, Rita K. .... Monroeville, AL
Lett, Robt. W. .... Ashland, OH
Lett, Sam J. .... Ashland, OH
Lett, Stacie L. .... Des Moines, IA
Lett, Steven T. .... Lansing, MI
Lett, Thomas R. .... Tipton, IN
Lette, Roger A. .... Spokane, WA
Letteau, Robert M. .... Los Angeles, CA
Letteleir, Amy E. .... Tampa, FL
Lettelleir, Diane K. .... Dallas, TX
Lettenberger, Peter J. .... Milwaukee, WI
Letteney, Scott R. .... Elkhorn, WI
Lettenmaier, Arthur J. .... Los Angeles, CA
Letter, Anita A. .... Albuquerque, NM
Letter, Douglas N. .... Department of Justice, Civil Division, GV
Letter, Gordon A. .... Los Angeles, CA
Lettera, Frank L. .... Milwaukee, WI
Letteri, John C. .... Washington, DC
Letterman, Bryce L. .... Newport Beach, CA
Letterman, G. Gregory .... Kansas City, MO
Lettes, Amy Stutz .... Atlanta, GA
Lettes, Louis .... Atlanta, GA
Lettick & Lettick, P.C. .... Hamden, CT

Lettick, Loren ... Wallingford, CT
Lettick, Sharon P. ... Hamden, CT
Lettick, Steven M. ... Hamden, CT
Lettiere, Joseph R. ... Boston, MA
Lettieri, Frank A. ... Akron, OH
Lettieri, Joan T. ... Los Angeles, CA
Lettieri, Joseph A. ... Roselle Park, NJ
Lettieri, Judith A. ... Scranton, PA
Lettieri, Michael A. ... Atlantic Highlands, NJ
Lettieri, Richard J. ... Boston, MA
Lettieri, Richard N. ... Pittsburgh, PA
Lettman, Dawn S. ... Baltimore, MD
Lettman, Robert D. ... Fort Lauderdale, FL
Letton, Harry P., Jr. ... San Marino, CA
Letton, John K. ... Weaverville, CA
Lettow, Carl F. ... Washington, DC
Lettow, Charles F. ... Washington, DC
Lettow, Donald D. ... St. Cloud, FL
Lettow, Renee B. ... Washington, DC
Lettrich, Jeffrey J. ... Pittsburgh, PA
Lettrich, Michael R. ... Pittsburgh, PA
Letts, Bradley B. ... Cherokee, NC
Letts, C. Kempton ... Redding, CA
Letts, David S. ... Washington, DC
Letts, Eileen M. ... Chicago, IL
Letts, J. Spencer ... Los Angeles, CA
Letts, Jack K. ... Lakewood, CO
Letts, Nathan P. ... New York, NY
Letts, Scott A. ... Manhattan, KS
Letts, Sophia ... West Palm Beach, FL
Lettunich, Anthony B.
Steamboat Springs, CO
Lettunich, Martin N. ... Saratoga, CA
Lettunich, Paul F. ... El Paso, TX
Lettunich & Vanderbloemen, LLC
Steamboat Springs, CO
Letty, Doreen E. ... Lackawanna, NY
Letulle, Gayle P. ... New Orleans, LA
Letulle, Raymond T. ... Philadelphia, PA
Letvin, David J. ... Chicago, IL
Letvin, Marc A. ... Southfield, MI
Letvin & Stein ... Chicago, IL
Letwat, Julie K. ... Chicago, IL
Letwin, Gerald D.
Equal Employment Opportunity Commission,
Office of the General Counsel, GV
Letwin, Jeffrey W. ... Washington, DC
Pittsburgh, PA
Letwin, Leon ... Los Angeles, CA
Letwin, Michael Zurav ... New York, NY
Letz, Carl R. ... Eldora, IA
Letz Law Firm ... Eldora, IA
Letzer, Joseph W. ... Birmingham, AL
Letzer, Norman R. ... Royal Oak, MI
Letzkus, Jeffrey E. ... Columbia, MD
Letzler, Jeffrey T. ... New York, NY
Letzler, Kenneth A. ... Washington, DC
Letzmann, Peter A. ... Troy, MI
Letzring, Kurt F. ... Battle Creek, MI
Letzring, Timothy David ... University, MS
Letzsch, William C., III ... Denver, CO
Letzter, Katherine Georgette
West Palm Beach, FL
Leu, Dennis ... Council Bluffs, IA
Leu, Leslyn S. ... San Francisco, CA
Leu, Lester Koon-Ming ... Honolulu, HI
Leu, Lori A. ... Dallas, TX
Leu, Lori A., P.C. ... Dallas, TX
Leu, Michael A. ... Goleta, CA
Leu & Okuda ... Honolulu, HI
Leu, Russell ... Honolulu, HI
Leu, Tracy Gehan ... Boston, MA
Leuba, Jennifer L. ... Liberty Corner, NJ
Leuba, Robert C. ... Hartford, CT
Leuba, Sean P. ... Peoria, IL
Leuba, Thomas R. ... Washington, DC
Leubuscher, Lynn A. ... Portland, ME
Leuby, William A. ... Columbus, OH
Leuchtag, Clyde R. ... Houston, TX
Leuchtag, Emery J. ... Cleveland, OH
Leuchtenburg, Joshua A. ... New York, NY
Leuchtman, Gary B. ... Pensacola, FL
Leuchtman, Stephen N. ... Detroit, MI
Leuchtmann, Mark R. ... St. Louis, MO
Leuck, Mark J. ... Racine, WI
Leuck, Matthias J. ... Riverside, IL
Leuckel, Sarae T. ... Washington, DC
Leudesdorff, John W. ... Sault Ste. Marie, MI
Leuenberger, Fred ... San Francisco, CA
Leuenberger, James E. ... Portland, OR
Leuenberger, Jan W. ... Topeka, KS
Leuenberger, Martin J. ... Baker City, OR
Ontario, OR
Leuer, Dennis Osborn ... San Francisco, CA
Leuffen, Erika L. ... Janesville, WI
Leufven, Donald K. ... Houston, TX
Leuin, Anthony B. ... San Francisco, CA
Leuin, Charles B. ... Chicago, IL
Leuin, Terry C. ... Los Angeles, CA
Leukart, Barbara J. ... Cleveland, OH
Leukart, Richard H., II ... Cleveland, OH
LeUnes, Chay ... Galveston, TX
Leung, Anthony S. ... Oakland, CA
Leung, Anton W. ... Los Angeles, CA
Leung, Chin-Pok "Roger"
San Francisco, CA
Leung, Darien G. ... New York, NY
Leung, David W. ... New York, NY
Leung, Diane S. ... Cleveland, OH
Leung, Dickson ... San Francisco, CA
Leung, Emily ... San Francisco, CA
Leung, Francis S. ... Palo Alto, CA
Leung, Frankie Fook-Lun
Los Angeles, CA
Leung, Jacqueline Jordan ... Oakland, CA
Leung, Jeffrey S. ... Pasadena, CA
Leung, Kelvin K. ... San Francisco, CA
Leung, Kevin K. ... Los Angeles, CA
Leung, Nhadine ... New York, NY
Leung, Patrick C. ... St. Paul, MN
Leung, Richard ... Los Angeles, CA
Leung, Robert W. ... New York, NY
Leung, Sandra ... New York, NY
Leung, Simon Y. ... San Francisco, CA
Leung, Sydney Si-ning ... San Francisco, CA
Leung, Tina ... Boston, MA
Leung, Tommy ... Rancho Cordova, CA
Leung, Tony N. ... Minneapolis, MN
Leunig, Mark W. ... Rochester, NY
Leunig, Sheila M. ... San Jose, CA
Leuning, Ross L. ... Owatonna, MN
Leuning, Scott J. Hendricks
Anchorage, AK
Leupp, Thomas A. ... Auburn, CA
Leupp, Wachob & Woodall ... Auburn, CA
Nevada City, CA
Placerville, CA
Roseville, CA
Leurck, John G. ... Indianapolis, IN
Leus, Hyacinth E. ... Los Angeles, CA
Leuschel, Jeffrey A. ... Dallas, TX
Leussing, Laura M.
Department of Transportation,
U. S. Coast Guard, GV
Leuteneker, Tom C. ... Wailuku, HI
Leutgeb, Paul F. ... Minneapolis, MN
Leutgeb, Paul F., Ltd. ... Minneapolis, MN
Leuthauser, James ... Denver, CO
Leuthold, Kenneth D. ... Sequim, WA
Leuthold, Richard R. ... Encino, CA
Leuthold, Sean E. ... Bucyrus, OH
Leuthold, Shawn T. ... San Jose, CA
Leutner, LeAnn S. ... New York, NY
Leutza, John N. ... San Francisco, CA
Walnut Creek, CA
Leutza, Stephen J. ... San Francisco, CA
Leutze, Clark B. ... Philadelphia, PA
Leuzzi, Bruce J. ... New York, NY
Leuzzi, Joseph P. ... New York, NY
Leuzzi, Paul W. ... Danbury, CT
Lev, Abraham D. ... Palo Alto, CA
Lev, Alan D. ... Chicago, IL
Lev, Allen P. ... Chicago, IL
Lev, Arthur J. ... New York, NY
Lev, Avi Meir ... Boston, MA
Lev, Berlin & Dale, P.C. ... Norwalk, CT
New York, NY
Lev, Bruce L. ... Norwalk, CT
Lev, Daniel A. ... Los Angeles, CA
Lev, Debra A. ... Bellingham, WA
Lev, Elaine Rappaport ... Chicago, IL
Lev, Leonard J. ... Montclair, NJ
New York, NY
Lev, Ori ... Federal Trade Commission,
Bureau of Consumer Protection, GV
Lev, Phillip M. ... San Mateo, CA
Lev, Phillip M., Incorporated
San Mateo, CA
Lev, Richard S. ... Rockville, MD
Lev, Robert G. ... Reston, VA
Lev, Ronald A. ... Barrington, IL
Lev, Sean A. ... Washington, DC
Lev, Steven A. ... Youngstown, OH
Lev, Tobe M. ... Orlando, FL
Leva, Harriet Beegun ... Santa Monica, CA
Leva, Marx ... Washington, DC
Levaccare, Lucien D. ... Chicago, IL
Levad, Charles H. ... Mason City, IA
LeVahn, Joel T. ... Fridley, MN
Levai, Michael I. ... New York, NY
Levaillant, Audrey S. Bretillot
New York, NY
Levak, Thomas F. ... Portland, OR
Leval, Alain ... Chicago, IL
Leval, Gerard ... Washington, DC
Leval, Pierre N. ... New York, NY
LeValley, James K. ... Phoenix, AZ
LeVally, Earl E. ... Healdton, OK
LeVally & Pinkerton, P.C. ... Healdton, OK
LeVan, Christy L. ... Chicago, IL
LeVan, Daniel G. ... Birmingham, MI
Levan, Elissa D. ... Columbia, MD
Levan, Gail Cummings ... Philadelphia, PA
Le Van, Gerald ... Baton Rouge, LA
Levan, Jarett Stephen ... Fort Lauderdale, FL
Le Van, John A. ... Santa Fe, NM
Levan, Joseph B. ... Grand Rapids, MI
Levan, LeRoy G. ... Reading, PA
LeVan, Mark S. ... Nashville, TN
LeVan, Molly S. ... Bridgeport, CT
LeVan, Peter H., Jr. ... Cherry Hill, NJ
Philadelphia, PA
Levan, Richard A. ... Washington, DC
Philadelphia, PA
Levan, Robert H. ... Columbia, MD
Le Vanda, Edward ... North Babylon, NY
Levander, Andrew J. ... New York, NY
LeVander, Bernhard W. ... Minneapolis, MN
LeVander, Gillen & Miller, P.A.
Minneapolis, MN
St. Paul, MN
South St. Paul, MN
LeVander, Harold, Jr. ... Minneapolis, MN
LeVander, Zotaley, Vander Linden & Rydland, A Professional Association
Minneapolis, MN
Levandoski, Dennis ... Falmouth, ME
Levandowski, Richard L. ... Tacoma, WA
Levandowski, Tom ... Sacramento, CA
Levangie, Michael J. ... Sacramento, CA
Levant, David B. ... Seattle, WA
Levant, John M. ... Studio City, CA
Levant, Michel
Federal Energy Regulatory Commission,
Office of the Administrative Law Judges, GV
Levant, S. Robert ... Philadelphia, PA
Levant, William J. ... Cherry Hill, NJ
Blue Bell, PA
Levanti, Ellen M. ... Jamaica, NY
Levanti, John C. ... Westerly, RI
Levantin, Amy G. ... Greenwich, CT
Levantino, Barney T. ... Hauppauge, NY
Levanway, Douglas E. ... Jackson, MS
Levao, Richard A. ... Florham Park, NJ
Levar, Alan Jeddy ... Arkadelphia, AR
Levarda, Daniela ... New York, NY
Le Varge, Lincoln S. ... Tampa, FL
LeVasseur, Arthur J. ... Detroit, MI
Levasseur & Buckel ... Cumberland, MD
Levasseur, Carol Ann ... Cambridge, MA
LeVasseur, Christopher E. ... Troy, MI
LeVasseur, Cynthia ... Las Vegas, NV
LeVasseur, Denice M. ... Southfield, MI
Levasseur, Dennis J. ... Detroit, MI
Levasseur, Elise S. ... Bloomfield Hills, MI
Levasseur, George B., Jr. ... Cumberland, MD
Levasseur, Guy J. ... New York, NY
LeVasseur & LeVasseur, P.C.
Southfield, MI
Levasseur, Luke P. ... Department of Justice,
Civil Division, GV
LeVasseur, Norman J. ... Southfield, MI
LeVasseur, Randall T. ... Birmingham, MI
Levasseur, Robert Mark ... Alexandria, MN
Levasseur, Ronald J. ... Cumberland, MD
LeVasseur, W. David ... Killingworth, CT
Levasseur, William R., Jr. ... Baltimore, MD
Frederick, MD
Towson, MD
Levasseur, William R., The Law Office of
Baltimore, MD
Frederick, MD
Levatich, Emeric ... Albany, NY
Levatino, Anthony P. ... Troy, NY
Levatino, Jerome ... Chicago, IL
Levatino & Levatino ... Chicago, IL
Levatino, Phillip C. ... Chicago, IL
Levatino, Sal ... Austin, TX
Levatino, Steven C. ... Austin, TX
Levato, Michael L. ... Canton, NY
Levavy, Bardin ... Montclair, NJ
Levay, Alexander N., Jr. ... Leesburg, VA
LeVay, Brian D. ... Chicago, IL
LeVay, Helen Fanz ... Cincinnati, OH
LeVay, Stephen ... Austin, TX
Levbarg, Mark Z. ... Austin, TX
Levbarg, Mark Z., P.C. ... Austin, TX
Levchak, Deborah Fohr ... Bismarck, ND
Levchuck, Richard S. ... Hauppauge, NY
Levchuk, Alexander ... Freehold, NJ
Levchuk, Andrew ... Springfield, MA
Levchuk, Karen ... Concord, NH
Leve, David P. ... Rochester, NY
Leve, Stephen J. ... Dayton, OH
Leve, Terrence Mitchell, Sr. ... Dallas, TX
Levee, Ira M. ... Roseland, NJ
LeVee, Janet Smerling ... Chicago, IL
LeVee, Jeffrey A. ... Los Angeles, CA
Levee, Newton H. ... Boston, MA
LeVee, Richard P. ... Atlanta, GA
Leveen, Barry G. ... Hillsdale, NJ
Leveille, Michael G. ... Atlanta, GA
Leveille, Robert R. ... Boston, MA
Leveille, Thomas M. ... Knoxville, TN
Level, Edward E. ... Everett, WA
Level, Kurt A. ... Overland Park, KS
Level, Meredith E. ... Orlando, FL
Level, Randall L. ... Seattle, WA
Levell, Gary P. ... Kirkland, WA
Levelle, Michael D. ... Portland, OR
Leven, Albert E. ... Pittsburgh, PA
Leven, Andrew D. ... Brooklyn, NY
Leven, Brian H. ... Montpelier, VT
Leven, David C. ... New York, NY
Leven, Gary E. ... Los Angeles, CA
Leven, Harris S. ... Houston, TX
Leven, Myron P. ... Southfield, MI
Leven, Paul Marshall ... Calabasas, CA
Leven, Raymond F. ... Roanoke, VA
Leven Surloff Smith & Cohen
Pittsburgh, PA
Levenback, Robert ... Bronx, NY
Levenback, Virginia C. ... Houston, TX
Levenbaum & Cohen ... Phoenix, AZ
Levenbaum, Warren G. ... Phoenix, AZ
Levenberg, Bonnie S. ... Whitestone, NY
Levenberg, Charles M. ... St. Paul, MN
Levenberg, David ... Philadelphia, PA
Levenberg, Jay R. ... Jenkintown, PA
Levenberg, Jeffrey A. ... San Bruno, CA
Levenberg, Jerome J. ... Levittown, NY
Levenberg, Joshua S ... San Francisco, CA
Levenberg, Karin ... Houston, TX
Levenberg, Peter N. ... San Francisco, CA
Levenberg, Richard S. ... Chicago, IL
Levenberg, Sanford ... Culver City, CA
Levenberg, Susan G. ... San Jose, CA
Levenberg, Thomas O. ... Chicago, IL
Levenberg, Timothy S.
Securities and Exchange Commission,
Division of Corporation Finance, GV
Levenbook, Kenneth T. ... Raleigh, NC
Levenbron, Maurice ... Huntington, NY
Levenbron & Stern ... Huntington, NY
Levender, Philip J. ... Mineola, NY
Levendis, George P. ... Washington, DC
Levendos, Thomas ... Pittsburgh, PA
Levendusky, David B. ... Washington, DC
Levene, Beth A. ... Washington, DC
Levene, David W. ... Los Angeles, CA
Levene, Douglas B. ... Stamford, CT
Levene, Elyse Beidner ... New York, NY
Levene, Gouldin & Thompson, LLP
Binghamton, NY
Levene, Louis S. ... Glen Rock, NJ
Levene, Neale, Bender & Rankin L.L.P.
Los Angeles, CA
Levene, Norman A. ... Ossining, NY
Levene, Paul R., (P.A.) ... Baltimore, MD
Levene, Ralph Michael ... New York, NY
Levene, Samuel K. ... Binghamton, NY
Levene, Stuart C. ... New York, NY
Levenfeld, Andrew W. ... Chicago, IL
Levenfeld, Andrew W., & Associates, Ltd.
Chicago, IL
Levenfeld, Gold & Rosenstein, Ltd.
Wheeling, IL
Levenfeld, M. Teresa Abad
Sacramento, CA
Levenfeld, Milton A. ... Chicago, IL
Levenfeld Pearlstein Glassberg Tuchman Bright Goldstein & Schwartz, LLC
Chicago, IL
Levenfeld, Richard B. ... Northbrook, IL
Levenfeld, Scott ... Wheeling, IL
Levenglick, Martin H. ... New York, NY
Levengood, Alan L. ... Pottstown, PA
Levengood, J. Michael ... Atlanta, GA
Levengood, Lynn E. ... Fairbanks, AK
Levengood, Robin S. ... Reading, PA
Levenhagen, Donald D. ... Indianapolis, IN
Levenhagen, T. Fritz ... Belleville, IL
Levenreich, David C. ... Clearwater, FL
Levens, Corey A. ... Palo Alto, CA
Levens, Jeffrey B. ... Chicago, IL
Levens, William P. ... Brandon, FL
Levens, William P. ... Tampa, FL
Levensohn, Betsy J. ... Department of Justice,
Federal Bureau of Investigation, GV
Levenson, Alan B. ... Washington, DC
Levenson, Alan J. ... Portland, ME
Levenson, Amy B. ... Washington, DC
Levenson, Andrew M. ... Boston, MA
Levenson, Barbara S. ... Miami, FL
Levenson, Barry M. ... Madison, WI
Levenson & Bonin ... New Orleans, LA
Levenson, Carole S. ... Piedmont, CA
Levenson, Clifford I. ... Mesa, AZ
Levenson, Daniel D. ... Boston, MA
Levenson, Daniel J. ... Miami, FL
Levenson, David J. ... Washington, DC
Levenson, Donald S. ... Marlton, NJ
Levenson, Franklyn ... Miami, FL
Levenson, Frederic L. ... Fort Lauderdale, FL
Levenson, Gary D. ... Washington, DC
Levenson, Gordon M., (P.A.)
Baltimore, MD
Levenson, Herbert ... South Orange, NJ
Levenson, Howard S. ... Brookline, MA
Levenson, Irving B. ... Miami, FL
Levenson, Jay E. ... Woburn, MA
Levenson, Judy A. ... Boston, MA
Levenson, Lee E., Jr. ... Delray Beach, FL
Levenson, Leonard H. ... Pittsburgh, PA
Levenson, Leonard J. ... New York, NY
Levenson, Leonard L. ... New Orleans, LA
Levenson, Liane P. ... Atlantic City, NJ
Levenson, Lloyd D. ... Atlantic City, NJ
Levenson, Lloyd S. ... Hingham, MA
Levenson, Louis ... Atlanta, GA
Levenson, Malcolm L. ... Southfield, MI
Levenson, Marilyn Stone ... Boston, MA
Levenson, Mark L. ... New York, NY
Levenson, Mark S. ... New York, NY
Levenson, Martin ... New York, NY
Levenson, Mary B. ... Winston-Salem, NC
Levenson, Max H. ... Baltimore, MD
Levenson, Myra K. ... Mill Valley, CA
Levenson, Paul E. ... Boston, MA
Levenson, Paul Getz ... Boston, MA
Levenson, Paul J. ... Boston, MA
Levenson, Paul R. ... New York, NY
Levenson & Pressman ... New York, NY
Levenson, Rebecca J. ... Washington, DC
Levenson, Richard B. ... Tacoma, WA
Levenson, Richard H. ... New York, NY
Levenson, Richard L. ... New York, NY
Levenson, Robert K. ... Miami, FL
Levenson, Samuel William ... Flushing, NY
Levenson, Stanton D. ... Pittsburgh, PA
Levenson, Stanton D., P.A. ... Pittsburgh, PA
Levenson, Steven S. ... Chicago, IL
Levenson, Vickerson & Beneman
Portland, ME
Levenson, Wendy J. ... Washington, DC
Levenson, Yetta ... Pittsburgh, PA
Levenstam, Barry ... Chicago, IL
Levenstein, Alan D. ... New Carrollton, MD
Levenstein, Alan M. ... Santa Monica, CA
Levenstein, David H. ... Worcester, MA
Levenstein, Gary I. ... Chicago, IL
Levenstein, Herbert ... Greenbelt, MD
Levenstein, Jay S. ... Tallahassee, FL
Levenstein, Marc ... Chicago, IL
Levenstein, Myron ... East Rockaway, NY
Levenstein, Richard H. ... Stuart, FL
Levenstein, Robert A. ... Morristown, NJ
Levenstein, Robert D. ... La Place, LA
Levenstien, Robert A. ... Morristown, NJ
Leventer, Jan C. ... Franklin, MI
Leventer, Robert E. ... Monterey Park, CA
Leventhal, A. Linda ... Albany, NY
Leventhal, Barbara W. ... Carmel, IN
Leventhal, Brian H. ... Vienna, VA
Leventhal, Cari Lyn ... Harrisburg, PA
Leventhal, Charles M. ... Deerfield Beach, FL
Leventhal, Danielle M. ... New York, NY
Leventhal, David ... Santa Clarita, CA
Leventhal, David A. ... Dix Hills, NY
Leventhal, Dinah S. ... Washington, DC

Leventhal, Donald C. ....New York, NY
Leventhal, F. Daniel ....San Francisco, CA
Leventhal, H. David ....Hartford, CT
Leventhal, Howard G. ....New York, NY
Leventhal, Ira S. ....New York, NY
Leventhal, Jacob
Federal Energy Regulatory Commission,
Office of the Administrative Law Judges, GV
Leventhal, Jeffrey R. ....Englewood, CO
Leventhal, Jess ....Langhorne, PA
Leventhal, Jim ....Denver, CO
Leventhal Law Firm, The, P.C.
Denver, CO
Leventhal, Law Offices of & Associates
Santa Clarita, CA
Leventhal, Mara ....New York, NY
Leventhal, Mark R. ....Washington, DC
Leventhal, Markham R. ....Miami, FL
Leventhal, Melvyn R. ....New York, NY
Leventhal, Melvyn R., A Professional
Corporation ....New York, NY
Leventhal, Michael D. ....Los Angeles, CA
Leventhal, Michael J. ....Westport, CT
Leventhal, Michael L., Jr. ....Chicago, IL
Leventhal, Nancy ....San Francisco, CA
Leventhal, Norman P. (IBA)
Washington, DC
Leventhal, Robert ....Yonkers, NY
Leventhal, Robert A. ....Orlando, FL
Leventhal, Robert C. ....Los Angeles, CA
Leventhal, Robert Carlson ....Trenton, NJ
Leventhal, Roberta R. ....East Hills, NY
Leventhal, S. Michael ....Los Angeles, CA
Leventhal, Samantha J. ....New York, NY
Leventhal, Senter & Lerman, P.L.L.C.
Washington, DC
Leventhal, Shari D. ....New York, NY
Leventhal, Sherry Marcus
Chestnut Hill, MA
Leventhal & Slaughter, P.A. ....Orlando, FL
Leventhal, Stanley R. ....Santa Ana, CA
Leventhal, Stephen H. ....Los Angeles, CA
Leventhal, Stephen R. ....Bethesda, MD
Leventhal, Steven G. ....Philadelphia, PA
Leventhal & Sutton ....Langhorne, PA
Leventis, Dina S. ....Springfield, PA
Leventis, James C. ....Columbia, SC
Leventis, Joni ....San Mateo, CA
Leventis, Leigh J. ....Columbia, SC
Leventon, Aileen R. ....New York, NY
Leventon & Leventon ....Pittsburgh, PA
Leventon, Martin S. ....Haverford, PA
Leventon, Nathan H. ....Pittsburgh, PA
Leventon, Paul J. ....Pittsburgh, PA
Leventritt Lewittes & Bender
New York, NY
Leventry, Timothy C. ....Johnstown, PA
Leveque, Charles ....Madison, WI
LeVeque, E. Lee ....Great Falls, MT
LeVeque, Edward A., Jr. ....Torrance, CA
Leveque, Jerome J. ....Spokane, WA
Leveque & Kirkpatrick, P.S.
Spokane, WA
LeVeque, Michelle A. ....Grand Rapids, MI
Leveque, Nicole S. ....Bloomfield Hills, MI
LeVeque, Paul D. ....San Francisco, CA
LeVeque, Roland S., II
Westlake Village, CA
Lever, A. Frank, Jr. ....Lexington, SC
Lever, Alisa Morgenthaler
Los Angeles, CA
Lever, Ann B. ....St. Louis, MO
Lever, Chauncey W., Jr. ....Jacksonville, FL
Lever, Jack Q., Jr. ....Washington, DC
Lever, Joel S. ....White Plains, NY
Lever, Kristen ....
Securities and Exchange Commission, GV
Lever, Lawrence G. ....Rye Brook, NY
Lever, Sharon E. ....Tampa, FL
Lever, Steven B. ....Long Beach, CA
Lever, Suzanne S. ....Raleigh, NC
Leverage, M. Elizabeth ....Washington, DC
Leverage, Thomas G. ....Hempstead, NY
Leverant, Barry ....Phoenix, AZ
Levere, David G. ....New York, NY
Levere, Steven D. ....Palo Alto, CA
LeVere, T. Earl ....Columbus, OH
Leverenz, Carl B. ....Chico, CA
Leverenz, Carl B., A Professional Corporation
Chico, CA
Leverenz, Emily ....Sacramento, CA
Leverett, Brad D. ....Altus, OK
Leverett, Charles M. ....Macon, GA
Leverett, Gerald M. ....Bakersfield, CA
Leverett, H. W., Jr. ....Midland, TX
Leverett, John M. ....Irvine, CA
Leverett, Mitchell L. ....Beverly Hills, CA
Newport Beach, CA
Leverett, Robert F. ....Elberton, GA
Leverett, Sarah ....Oakland, CA
Leverett, Shon ....Jeffersonville, IN
Leverette, Sarah E. ....Columbia, SC
Leverich, Bingham B. ....Washington, DC
Leverich, Chris ....Aspen, CO
Leverick and Musselman, L.L.C.
Albuquerque, NM
Taos, NM
Leverick, Richard Martin ......Albuquerque, NM
Leveridge, Aubrey T., Jr. ....East Bernard, TX
Leveridge, Richard J. ....Washington, DC
Levering, Charles B. ....Cambridge, MD
Levering, Eileen B. ....Mt. Vernon, OH
Levering, Jo Ann Dougall ....Houston, TX
Levering, John P. ....Salinas, CA
Levering, Julie ....Los Angeles, CA
Levering, Kathryn H. ....Philadelphia, PA
Levering, Mary Berghaus
Library of Congress,
Copyright Office, GV
Leverone, Joseph D. ....Manchester, NH
Leverone, Susan A.
National Labor Relations Board,
Office of Board Members, GV
Leveroni, Peter J. ....Braintree, MA
Leversen, Carol J. ....Orange, CA
Leversen, Lisa C. ....Irvine, CA
Leverson, Leonard G. ....Milwaukee, WI
Le Vert, Dwight W. ....Homewood, IL
Levert, Edward L., Jr. ....New Orleans, LA
Leverton, Lee J. ....Lake Mills, WI
Leverton, Reed ....El Paso, TX
Leverton, William R. ....El Paso, TX
Leverty & Associates Law, Chartered
San Diego, CA
Carson City, NV
Las Vegas, NV
Reno, NV
Leverty, Vernon E. ....San Diego, CA
Las Vegas, NV
Reno, NV
Levesque, Alan T. ....Farmington, CT
Levesque, David R. ....Hartford, CT
Levesque, Ellen Jo ....Boston, MA
Levesque, Jane Dominica ....Danvers, MA
Levesque, Jeanne ....Boston, MA
Levesque, Joseph N. ....Barrow, AK
Levesque, Larry P. ....New Britain, CT
Levesque, Scott D. ....Providence, RI
Levesque, Stephen P. ....Providence, RI
Levesque, Thos. H. ....Middletown, RI
Leveton, David A. ....Los Angeles, CA
Leveton, Erin Leigh ....Lakeland, FL
Leveton, Morton E. ....Toledo, OH
Levetown, Andrew S. ....Falls Church, VA
Levett, David R. ....Westport, CT
Levett, Matthew D. ....San Francisco, CA
Levett Rockwood P.C. ....Westport, CT
Levey, Andrew S. ....Beverly Hills, CA
Levey & Associates, P.A. ....Coral Gables, FL
Levey, Barry J. ....Middletown, OH
Levey, Brian C. ....Framingham, MA
Levey, Brian H. ....Santa Monica, CA
Levey, Brian R. ....Arlington, VA
Levey, Burton R. ....Miami, FL
Levey, Chas. H. ....Plainview, NY
Levey, Elan S. ....Los Angeles, CA
Levey, Ernest W. ....Yonkers, NY
Levey, Gustave S. ....Houston, TX
Levey, Harold A., Jr. ....Fairbanks, AK
Levey, Harold L. ....Cleveland, OH
Levey, Helene M. ....Detroit, MI
Levey, Jack S. ....Columbus, OH
Levey, James R. ....St. Louis, MO
Levey, Jeffrey E. ....Miami, FL
Levey, Jonathan R. ....Los Angeles, CA
LeVey, Kenneth R. ....Sturgeon Bay, WI
Levey, Kevin S. ....Washington, DC
Levey, Lewis J ....Coral Gables, FL
Levey, Lila R. ....Staten Island, NY
Levey, Lisa D. ....New York, NY
Levey, Marc M. ....New York, NY
Levey, Michael A. ....Milwaukee, WI
Levey, Michael J. ....Winthrop, ME
Levey, Phillip D. ....Chicago, IL
Levey, Robert A. ....Newburgh, NY
Levey, Robert E. ....Toledo, OH
Levey, Robert F. ....Tupelo, MS
Levey, Ross S. ....Chicago, IL
Levey, S. Jerome ....Pearl River, NY
Levey, Scott I. ....Cleveland, OH
Levey, Sherman F. ....Rochester, NY
Levey, Stephen K. ....Washington, DC
Levey, Stuart A. ....Washington, DC
Levi, Andrew K. ....New York, NY
Levi, Barbara ....New York, NY
Levi, Benjamin ....New York, NY
Levi, Beth D. ....Boston, MA
Levi, Bruce T. ....Bismarck, ND
Levi, Dafna G. ....Walnut Creek, CA
Levi, Daniel H. ....New York, NY
Levi, David F. ....Sacramento, CA
Levi, Deborah L. ....Boston, MA
Levi, Dempsey M. ....Ocean Springs, MS
Levi, Donald M. ....Cincinnati, OH
Levi, Donald R. ....Wichita, KS
Levi, Donna G. ....Sarasota, FL
Levi, Edward H. ....Chicago, IL
Levi, Emma Jean Hemby ....Chapel Hill, NC
Levi, Gary W. ....Cherry Hill, NJ
Levi, Harold L. ....Washington, DC
Levi, Harry J. ....Highland, IL
Levi, Heather M. ....New York, NY
Levi, Henry B. ....Atlanta, GA
Levi, Howard B. ....New York, NY
Levi, James S. ....Arlington Heights, IL
Levi, Jill ....New York, NY
Levi, Joel Garner ....Washington, DC
Levi, John G. ....Chicago, IL
Levi, Joseph E. ....New York, NY
Levi, Julian H. ....San Francisco, CA
Levi, Kelly B. ....New York, NY
Levi, Kenneth B. ....Houston, TX
Levi, Lloyd ....New York, NY
Levi, Louise C. ....San Mateo, CA
Levi Lubarsky & Feigenbaum LLP
New York, NY
Levi, Mark D. ....New York, NY
Levi, Michael P. ....Newberg, OR
Levi & Perry, P.C. ....Washington, DC
Levi, Peter S. ....Kansas City, MO
Levi, Richard H. ....Washington, DC
Levi, Richard K. ....Rushville, IN
Levi, Richard P. ....Knoxville, TN
Levi, Robert L. ....Detroit, MI
Levi, Robert L., P.C. ....Detroit, MI
Levi, Sara C. ....Utica, NY
Levi, Stuart D. ....New York, NY
Levi, Thomas C. ....Englewood, CO
Levi, Thomas J. ....Watertown, WI
Levi, William G. ....Kansas City, MO
Levi, Wittenberg, Harritt, Hoefer & Davis, P.A.
Sumter, SC
Levi, Zion ....Washington, DC
Leviant, Shulamit ....New York, NY
Levick, Jeffrey A. ....Chicago, IL
LeVick, John P. ....Lubbock, TX
Levick, Larry A. ....Addison, TX
Levick, Mark D. ....Fort Wayne, IN
Levick, Mark J. ....Atlanta, GA
Levick, Michael J. ....Deerfield, IL
Levick, Richard A. ....Erie, PA
Levick, Sandra K. ....Washington, DC
Le Vick, Shelly Diane ....Austin, TX
Levicoff, Avrum ....Pittsburgh, PA
Levidiotis, Thomas C. ....Oxford, MS
Levidow, Beatrice ....Springfield, NJ
Levidow, David J. ....New York, NY
Levidow, Levidow and Oberman, P.C.
Bronx, NY
Brooklyn, NY
Jamaica, NY
New York, NY
Staten Island, NY
Valley Stream, NY
Levidow, Richard D. ....New York, NY
Levie, Dewey J. ....Chino Valley, AZ
Levie, Dewey J., P.C. ....Chino Valley, AZ
Levie, Howard S. ....Newport, RI
Levie, Joseph H. ....New York, NY
Levie, Mark R. ....San Francisco, CA
Levie, W. Iain E. ....Portland, OR
Levie, Warren M. ....Bronx, NY
Levien, Craig A. ....Davenport, IA
Levien, Jane S. ....New York, NY
Levien, Jason M. ....Washington, DC
Levien, Jeffrey S. ....New York, NY
Levien, Jerold K. ....New York, NY
Levien, Lawrence D., (P.C.)
Washington, DC
Levihn, Lynne A. ....Milwaukee, WI
Levin, ...Sacramento, CA
Levin, A. Leo ....Philadelphia, PA
Levin, A. Thomas ....Mineola, NY
Levin, Abraham H. ....Silver Spring, MD
Levin, Adam, (A Professional Corporation)
Los Angeles, CA
Levin, Adam K. ....Washington, DC
Levin, Adam K. ....Westfield, NJ
Levin, Adam Kenneth ....Philadelphia, PA
Levin, Alan ....Havertown, PA
Levin, Alan A. ....Indianapolis, IN
Levin, Alan F. ....Houston, TX
Levin, Alan J. ....Santa Cruz, CA
Levin, Alan J. ....Hartford, CT
Levin, Alan M. ....Chicago, IL
Levin, Alan S. ....Newport Beach, CA
San Francisco, CA
Levin, Albert D. ....Edina, MN
Levin, Albert Z. ....Miami, FL
Levin, Ali ....Boston, MA
Levin, Alisa F. ....New York, NY
Levin, Allan E. ....Quincy, MA
Levin, Allan Earl ....Chicago, IL
Levin, Allen J. ....Port Charlotte, FL
Levin, Allen Joseph ....Lewistown, PA
Levin, Allison A. ....Dallas, TX
Levin, Alvin M. ....Los Angeles, CA
Levin, Andrea ....New York, NY
Levin, Andrea D. ....Houston, TX
Levin & Andress ....Coral Gables, FL
Miami, FL
Levin, Andrew C. ....Hilo, HI
Levin, Andrew R. ....Boston, MA
Levin, Andrew S. ....Washington, DC
Levin, Anita ....Toledo, OH
Levin, Ann R. ....Shaker Heights, OH
Levin, Ann V. ....Harrisburg, PA
Levin, Anna Hayes ....New York, NY
Levin, Annette ....College Park, MD
Levin, Arnold ....Los Angeles, CA
Levin, Arnold (IBA) **.....................Philadelphia, PA**
Levin, Arnold A. ....Ardsley, NY
Levin, Arnold B. ....West Long Branch, NJ
Levin, Arnold J. ....Peabody, MA
Levin, Arnold S. ....Sheffield Lake, OH
Levin, Asher A. ....North Hollywood, CA
Levin, Barbara B. ....Sarasota, FL
Levin, Barry ....Garden City, NY
Levin, Barry ....Chadds Ford, PA
Levin, Barry F. ....Baltimore, MD
Levin, Barry J. ....Mount Laurel, NJ
Levin, Barry L. ....Los Angeles, CA
Levin, Barry M. ....Boston, MA
Levin, Barry S. ....San Francisco, CA
Levin, Batya S. ....Bronx, NY
Levin, Benjamin A. ....Voorhees, NJ
Levin, Benjamin B. ....Bala Cynwyd, PA
Levin, Benjamin B., P.C. ....Bala Cynwyd, PA
Levin, Benjamin D. ....Milwaukee, WI
Levin, Bernard N. ....Tenafly, NJ
Levin, Bernard T. ....Annapolis, MD
Levin, Betsy ....Washington, DC
Levin, Blair
Federal Communications Commission, GV
Levin, Brad A. ....Chicago, IL
Levin, Bradley A. ....Denver, CO
Levin & Brend, P.C. ....Chicago, IL
Levin, Brian ....Newport Beach, CA
Levin, Brian T. ....Chicago, IL
Levin, Bronna G. ....Elizabeth, NJ
Levin, Bruce A. ....Las Vegas, NV
Levin, Bruce D. ....Boston, MA
Levin, Bruce L. ....Bridgeport, CT
Levin, Burton H. ....Avon, CO
Baltimore, MD
Levin, C. James ....Los Angeles, CA
Levin, Calman A. ....Baltimore, MD
Levin, Carl ....Detroit, MI
Levin, Chad S. ....Cincinnati, OH
Levin, Chaim A. ....New York, NY
Levin, Charles ....Mercerville, NJ
Levin, Charles E. ....Chicago, IL
Levin, Charles G. ....Portland, OR
Levin, Charles J. ....Tampa, FL
Levin, Charles L. ....Detroit, MI
Levin, Charles R. ....Boston, MA
Levin, Charles R. ....Needham, MA
Levin, Cheri Wyron ....Baltimore, MD
Levin, Cheryl J., P.A. ....Sunrise, FL
Levin, Cheryl Joy ....Sunrise, FL
Levin, Christine C. ....Philadelphia, PA
Levin, Clancy, Foster & Arena
Livingston, NJ
Levin, Clifford ....Brooklyn, NY
Levin, Clifford A. ....Detroit, MI
Levin & Cooper ....Philadelphia, PA
Upper Darby, PA
Levin, Craig R. ....Philadelphia, PA
Levin, Craig Stuart ....Syracuse, NY
Levin, Cynthia Zevin ....Cherry Hill, NJ
Levin, Daniel ....Los Angeles, CA
Levin, Daniel ....New York, NY
Levin, Daniel C. ....Philadelphia, PA
Levin, Daniel G. ....Ossining, NY
Levin, Daniel J. ....Denver, CO
Levin, Daniel J. ....Cleveland, OH
Levin, Daniel W. ....Hartford, CT
Levin, David A. ....Annapolis, MD
Baltimore, MD
Levin, David A. ....New York, NY
Levin, David B. ....Chicago, IL
Levin, David C. ....Quincy, MA
Levin, David E. ....New York, NY
Levin, David H. ....Sacramento, CA
Levin, David H. ....Pensacola, FL
Levin, David M. ....San Francisco, CA
Levin, David M. ....Bloomfield, CT
Levin, David M. ....Sarasota, FL
Levin, David M. ....Chicago, IL
Levin, David M., Ltd. ....Chicago, IL
Levin, David P. ....Albuquerque, NM
Levin, David P. ....New York, NY
Levin, David R. ....Washington, DC
Levin, David R. ....Pittsburgh, PA
Levin, David R. ....Portsmouth, VA
Levin, David S. ....Palo Alto, CA
Levin, David S. ....Seattle, WA
Levin, Dean J. ....Woodland Hills, CA
Levin, Debbe A. ....Cincinnati, OH
Levin, Dennis P. ....Cleveland, OH
Levin, Donald ....Philadelphia, PA
Upper Darby, PA
Levin, Donald C. ....St. Paul, MN
Levin, Donald H. ....Long Beach, NY
Levin, Donald R. ....Roslyn, NY
Levin, Donna Rice ....Westlake Village, CA
Levin, Donna S. ....New York, NY
Levin, Dorothy ....Garden Grove, CA
Levin, Edith S. ....Palo Alto, CA
Levin, Edward J. ....Baltimore, MD
Levin, Edward M.
Department of Commerce,
Economic Development Administration, GV
Levin, Edward R. ....Washington, DC
Levin, Elaine R. ....Costa Mesa, CA
Levin, Elias ....Chicago, IL
Levin, Ellen B. ....New York, NY
Levin, Elliott D. ....Indianapolis, IN
Levin, Emanuel L., P.A. ....Atlantic City, NJ
Levin, Emanuel M. ....Baltimore, MD
Levin, Emanuel M., & Associates, P.A.
Baltimore, MD
Levin, Emily R. ....New Haven, CT
Levin, Eric D ....Boston, MA
Levin, Eric D. ....Butler, PA
Cranberry Township, PA
Levin, Eugene M. ....Rockford, IL
Levin, Evanne L. ....Los Angeles, CA
Levin, Ezra G. ....New York, NY
Levin, Fishbein, Sedran & Berman
Philadelphia, PA
Levin, Ford & Paulekas, LLP
Hartford, CT
Levin, Frank ....San Diego, CA
Levin, Frank K. ....Cleveland, OH
Levin, Frank W. ....Minneapolis, MN
Levin, Fred Jay ....Cherry Hill, NJ
Levin, Fredric G. ....Pensacola, FL
Levin, Fredrick S. ....Los Angeles, CA
Levin & Freedman LLP ....Los Angeles, CA
Santa Monica, CA
Levin & Funkhouser, Ltd. ....Chicago, IL
Levin & Gann, A Professional Association
Baltimore, MD
Towson, MD
Levin, Gary H. ....Philadelphia, PA
Levin, Gary M. ....Palo Alto, CA
Levin, Gary P. ....Philadelphia, PA
Levin, Geoffrey W. ....New York, NY
Levin, George ....Erie, PA
Levin, Gerald M. ....New York, NY
Levin & Gilley ....Beaufort, SC
Charleston, SC
Hilton Head Island, SC
Levin & Ginsburg, Ltd. ....Chicago, IL
Levin & Glasser, P.C. ....New York, NY
Levin, Glenn I. ....Westport, CT
Levin, H. Debra ....Chicago, IL
Levin, Hallie B. ....New York, NY
Levin, Harold F. ....New York, NY

Levine, Arthur S. ... Los Angeles, CA
Levine, Arthur S ... New York, NY
Levine, Arthur S., A Professional Corporation ... Los Angeles, CA
Levine & Associates ... Los Angeles, CA
Seattle, WA
Levine, Audrey Hope ... New York, NY
Levine, B. Scott ... Alameda, CA
Levine, Barbara Baum ... Commack, NY
Levine, Barbara Holtz ... Baltimore, MD
Levine, Barbara J. ... Cambridge, MA
Levine, Barrie N. ... Salem, MA
Levine, Barry F. ... Erie, PA
Levine, Barry J. ... Phoenix, AZ
Levine, Barry J. ... Olivette, MO
Levine, Barry J. ... Mineola, NY
Levine, Barry M. ... Ann Arbor, MI
Saginaw, MI
Levine, Barry R. ... Wakefield, MA
Levine, Barry Wm. ... Washington, DC
Levine, Barton P. ... New York, NY
Levine, Benjamin ... Newark, NJ
New York, NY
Levine, Benjamin D. ... East Syracuse, NY
Syracuse, NY
Levine, Benjamin I., Jr.
Hollidaysburg, PA
Levine, Benjamin, Tushman, Bratt, Jerris & Stein, P.C. ... Flint, MI
Southfield, MI
Levine, Bernard ... Glen Cove, NY
Levine, Bernard ... Twinsburg, OH
Levine, Bernard B. ... Kansas City, MO
Levine, Bernard B., P.C., A Professional Corporation ... Kansas City, MO
Levine, Bernard D. ... Rochester, NY
Levine, Bernard I. ... North Attleboro, MA
Levine, Bernard L. ... Monticello, NY
Levine, Bert ... Brooklyn, NY
Levine, Beth E. ... New York, NY
Levine, Beth F. ... New York, NY
Levine, Beth L. ... San Diego, CA
Levine, Beth M. ... Chicago, IL
Levine, Betsy J. ... Tampa, FL
Levine, Betty J. ... Los Angeles, CA
Levine, Blaszak, Block & Boothby, LLP
Washington, DC
Levine & Block ... Atlanta, GA
Levine, Brandon J. ... Washington, DC
Levine, Brett ... Florham Park, NJ
Levine, Brian D. ... Staten Island, NY
Levine, Brian J. ... Livingston, NJ
Levine, Bruce ... Topeka, KS
Levine, Bruce A. ... Fairfax, VA
Levine, Bruce C.
Commodity Futures Trading Commission, Office of Proceedings, GV
Levine, Bruce H. ... Los Angeles, CA
Levine, Bruce M. ... Spring Valley, NY
Levine, Bruce P. ... New York, NY
Levine, Bruce S. ... New York, NY
Levine, Burt S. ... Great Neck, NY
Levine, Burton I. ... Florham Park, NJ
Levine, Busch, Schnepper & Stein, P.A.
Miami, FL
Levine, C. Bruce ... Los Angeles, CA
Levine, Carl F. ... White Plains, NY
LeVine, Carl R. ... Silver Spring, MD
Levine, Carl S. ... Roslyn, NY
Levine, Carl S., & Associates, P.C.
Roslyn, NY
Levine, Carol ... Juno Beach, FL
Levine, Carole ... San Francisco, CA
Levine, Caroline A. ... East Brunswick, NJ
Levine, Carolyn B. ... New York, NY
Levine, Catherine Mafee ... Chicago, IL
Levine, Cathy J. ... Bexley, OH
Levine, Charles D. ... St. Paul, MN
Levine, Charles S. ... Bronx, NY
Levine, Clifford B. ... Pittsburgh, PA
LeVine, Craig A. ... Rockville, MD
Levine, Curtis G. ... Boca Raton, FL
Levine, Dana B. ... New York, NY
Levine, Daniel B. ... Great Falls, MT
Levine, Daniel B., P.C. ... Great Falls, MT
Levine, Daniel R. ... Hollywood, FL
Levine, Darin Scott ... Oxon Hill, MD
Levine, David ... Miami, FL
Levine, David ... New York, NY
Levine, David A. ... Pittsburgh, PA
Levine, David A. ... Arlington, VA
Levine, David C. ... Columbus, OH
Levine, David E. ... Brooklyn, NY
Levine, David E. ... Niagara Falls, NY
Levine, David H. ... Miami, FL
Levine, David I. ... San Francisco, CA
Levine, David I. ... Mineola, NY
Levine, David J. ... Washington, DC
Levine, David J. ... Nashville, TN
Levine, David K. ... San Francisco, CA
Levine, David L. ... Cleveland, OH
Levine, David M. ... Bridgeport, CT
Westport, CT
Levine, David M.
Securities and Exchange Commission, Office of the General Counsel, GV
Levine, David M. ... Miami, FL
Levine, David M. ... Cleveland, OH
Levine, David N. ... Washington, DC
Levine, David N. ... Briarcliff Manor, NY
Levine, David N., (P.C.) ... Atlanta, GA
Levine, David P. ... Portland, OR
Levine, David S. ... San Francisco, CA
Levine, David S. ... Lincolndale, NY
Levine, David S. ... New York, NY
Levine, David S. ... Cincinnati, OH
Levine, David Tobias ... New York, NY
Levine, Deanna S. ... Westport, CT

Levine, Deborah
Securities and Exchange Commission, Division of Enforcement, GV
Levine, Deborah A. ... Glendale, CA
Levine, Deborah S. ... Newark, NJ
New York, NY
Levine, Debra W. ... Newark, NJ
LeVine, Dennis J. ... Tampa, FL
LeVine, Dennis J., & Associates, P.A.
Tampa, FL
Levine, Dennis P., P.C. ... Phoenix, AZ
Levine, DeSantis & Associates ... Millburn, NJ
Levine, Diane ... Morristown, NJ
New York, NY
Levine, Donald B. ... Chicago, IL
Levine, Donna P. ... West Palm Beach, FL
Levine, Donna R. ... New Haven, CT
Levine, Douglas L. ... Ferguson, MO
Washington, MO
Levine, Edmund L. ... Philadelphia, PA
Le Vine, Edw. ... Chicago, IL
Levine, Edward ... Los Angeles, CA
Levine, Edward L. ... New York, NY
Levine, Edward L. ... Alcoa Center, PA
Levine, Edward S. ... Coral Gables, FL
Levine, Edward W., & Associates
Miami, FL
Levine, Elaine G. ... Atlanta, GA
Levine, Eli ... New York, NY
Levine, Eliot S. ... Hauppauge, NY
Levine, Elliot R. ... Quincy, MA
Levine, Elliott ... Salt Lake City, UT
Levine, Elliott B. ... Schaumburg, IL
Levine, Elliott M. ... La Crosse, WI
Levine, Ellis B. ... New York, NY
Levine, Eric B. ... Westfield, NJ
Levine, Eric B. ... New York, NY
Levine, Eric David ... Charlotte, NC
Levine, Eric J. ... Roseland, NJ
Levine, Eric L., & Associates ... Boston, MA
Levine, Eric M. ... New York, NY
Levine, Eric R. ... New York, NY
Levine, Eric S. ... New York, NY
Levine, Eric T. ... Stamford, CT
Levine, Estee S. ... Washington, DC
Levine, Eugene ... Boston, MA
Levine, Eva Liang ... San Jose, CA
Levine, Ezra C. ... Washington, DC
Levine & Finger ... Miami, FL
Levine, Frank & Edgar, P.A.
Palm Beach Gardens, FL
Levine, Frederick E. ... Brookline, MA
Levine, Frederick I. ... Fair Lawn, NJ
Levine & Furman ... East Brunswick, NJ
Levine, Gail F. ... Department of Justice, Civil Division, GV
Levine, Gary A. ... Baldwin, NY
Levine, Gary H. ... Cleveland, OH
Levine, Gary J. ... Providence, RI
Levine, Gary L. ... Oklahoma City, OK
Levine, Gary M. ... Kingston, NY
Levine, Gary M. ... Rochester, NY
Levine, Gary N. ... New York, NY
Levine, Gerald ... Ardsley, NY
Levine, Gerald M. ... New York, NY
Levine, Gilbert M. ... Millburn, NJ
Levine, Glass & Miller ... Jeffersonville, NY
Monticello, NY
Levine, Glenn ... Whitestone, NY
Levine, Glenn S. ... Washington, DC
Levine & Glynn, LLC ... New Haven, CT
Levine, Gregory H. ... Washington, DC
Levine, H. Ronald ... Kendall Park, NJ
Levine, Harlan Lawrence ... Carteret, NJ
Levine, Harmon B. ... Los Angeles, CA
Levine, Harold ... New York, NY
Levine, Harold ... Dallas, TX
Levine, Harold David ... Newton, MA
Levine, Harold I. ... Chicago, IL
Levine, Harvey ... East Brunswick, NJ
Levine, Harvey, A Professional Corporation
East Brunswick, NJ
Levine, Harvey E. ... Fremont, CA
Levine, Harvey L. ... New Britain, CT
Levine, Harvey L. ... New York, NY
Levine, Harvey R. ... San Diego, CA
Levine, Heather I. ... Philadelphia, PA
Levine, Heidi ... Berkeley, CA
Levine, Heidi L. ... Baltimore, MD
Levine, Heidi Shana ... New York, NY
Levine, Helaine Damask
Woodcliff Lake, NJ
Levine, Henry ... Vienna, VA
Levine, Henry D. ... Washington, DC
Levine, Herbert ... Silver Spring, MD
Levine, Herbert ... Milwaukee, WI
Levine, Herbert B. ... Cleveland, OH
Levine, Herbert D. ... Great Neck, NY
Levine, Herbert J. ... New York, NY
Levine, Herman A. ... Poughkeepsie, NY
Levine, Herzl E. ... Chicago, IL
Levine, Hirsch, Segall & Brennan, P.A.
Tampa, FL
Levine, Hofstetter & Frangk
Poughkeepsie, NY
Levine, Hollie S. ... Binghamton, NY
Levine, Howard ... Oklahoma City, OK
Levine, Howard A. ... Boston, MA
Levine, Howard A. ... Schenectady, NY
Levine, Howard B.
Department of Commerce, Patent and Trademark Office, GV
Levine, Howard I. ... West Hartford, CT
Levine, Howard I. ... Chattanooga, TN
Levine, Howard J. ... Washington, DC
Levine, Howard J. ... Chicago, IL
Levine, Howard K. ... New Haven, CT
LeVine, Howard M. ... Homewood, IL

Levine, Howard M. ... Portland, OR
Levine, Howard R. ... Los Angeles, CA
Levine, Howard R. ... New York, NY
Levine, Howard S. ... Los Angeles, CA
Levine, Howard S. ... Tarzana, CA
Levine, Howard Warren ... Washington, DC
Levine, Hugh Anthony ... San Francisco, CA
Levine, I. Oscar ... Hartford, CT
Levine, I. Stanley ... Miami, FL
Levine, Ida L. (IBA) ... New York, NY
Levine, Ileana Aguinis ... New York, NY
Levine, Ira G. ... Mamaroneck, NY
Levine, Ira J. ... Fair Lawn, NJ
Levine, Ira S. ... Las Vegas, NV
Levine, Irving ... Farmington Hills, MI
Levine, Irving ... New York, NY
Levine, Irwin M. ... Atlanta, GA
LeVine, J. Eric ... Garden Grove, CA
Levine, Jack ... Phoenix, AZ
Levine, Jack ... Santa Monica, CA
Levine, Jack ... Denver, CO
Levine, Jack ... Boca Raton, FL
Levine, Jack ... New York, NY
Levine, Jack A. ... Tampa, FL
Levine, Jack & Associates, P.C.
Denver, CO
Levine, Jack G. ... San Anselmo, CA
Levine, Jacob ... Tarrytown, NY
Levine, Jaimy M. ... Chicago, IL
Levine, James D. ... Atlanta, GA
Levine, James H. ... Chattanooga, TN
Levine, James R. ... New York, NY
Levine, Jan Greenberg ... Santa Monica, CA
Levine, Jan M. ... Philadelphia, PA
Levine, Jan P. ... Philadelphia, PA
Levine, Jane R. ... New York, NY
Levine, Janet I. ... Los Angeles, CA
Levine, Janet Lynn ... Boston, MA
Levine, Janice E. ... New York, NY
Levine, Janine S. ... San Francisco, CA
Levine, Jared Elliott ... Los Angeles, CA
Levine, Jason A. ... Washington, DC
Levine, Jason E. ... Nutley, NJ
Levine, Jay ... New York, NY
Levine, Jay D. ... Chicago, IL
Levine, Jay L. ... Washington, DC
Levine, Jay L. ... Miami, FL
Levine, Jay Milton ... Chicago, IL
Levine, Jay Steven
Palm Beach Gardens, FL
Levine, Jeffrey A. ... Boca Raton, FL
Levine, Jeffrey A. ... Sudbury, MA
Levine, Jeffrey A. ... Farmington Hills, MI
Levine, Jeffrey A. ... Scranton, PA
Levine, Jeffrey A., P.A., Law Offices of
Boca Raton, FL
Levine, Jeffrey B. ... Bloomfield Hills, MI
Levine, Jeffrey E. ... Mission Hills, CA
Levine, Jeffrey Elliott ... New York, NY
Levine, Jeffrey H. ... Garden City, NY
Levine, Jeffrey J. ... Chicago, IL
Levine, Jeffrey Kenneth ... New York, NY
Levine, Jeffrey L. ... Los Angeles, CA
Levine, Jeffrey L. ... Dayton, OH
Levine, Jeffrey M. ... New York, NY
Levine, Jennifer Dienstag
Rolling Meadows, IL
Levine, Jerald ... Jackson Heights, NY
Levine, Jeremy P. ... Austin, TX
Levine, Jerold E. ... New York, NY
Levine, Jerome D. ... Vernon, CT
Levine, Jerome L. ... Los Angeles, CA
Levine, Jerome L. ... New York, NY
Levine, Jerry ... San Diego, CA
Levine, Jerry ... Washington, DC
Levine, Jessica B. ... Los Angeles, CA
Levine, Jodi B. ... Oklahoma City, OK
Levine, Joel ... Los Angeles, CA
Levine, Joel A. ... Los Angeles, CA
Levine, Joel A. ... Toledo, OH
Levine, Joel, A Professional Corporation
Los Angeles, CA
Levine, John ... Pompano Beach, FL
Levine, John ... Pittsburgh, PA
Levine, John D. ... Minneapolis, MN
Levine, Johnna B. ... Sherman Oaks, CA
Levine, Jonathan B. ... White Plains, NY
Levine, Jonathan B. ... Milwaukee, WI
Levine, Jonathan K. ... New York, NY
Levine, Jonathan M. ... Stamford, CT
Levine, Jonathan O. ... Milwaukee, WI
Levine, Jonathan P. ... Rochester, NY
Levine, Jonathan R. ... Atlanta, GA
Levine, Jonathan R., L.L.C. ... Atlanta, GA
Levine, Jordan S. ... Denver, CO
Levine, Joseph ... Los Angeles, CA
Levine, Joseph ... New York, NY
Levine, Joseph C. ... St. Louis, MO
Levine, Joseph C. ... Brooklyn, NY
Levine, Joseph M.
Department of Commerce, Office of the General Counsel, GV
Levine, Joseph S. ... Brooklyn, NY
Levine, Joshua ... New York, NY
Levine, Joshua A. ... New York, NY
Levine, Joshua S. ... White Plains, NY
Levine, Joyce Celnik ... New York, NY
Levine, Judith D. ... Columbus, OH
Levine, Jules B. ... Mineola, NY
Levine, Jules E. ... Great Neck, NY
Levine, Jules P., (P.C.) ... Newburgh, NY
Levine, Julius B. ... Boston, MA
Levine, Karen ... Miami, FL
Levine, Karen ... Chicago, IL
Levine, Karen ... Newark, NJ
Levine, Kari Erickson ... San Francisco, CA
Levine, Kenneth A. ... Pasadena, CA
Levine, Kenneth J. ... Farmington, CT

Levine, Kenneth J. ... Normal, IL
Levine, Kenneth L. ... Hartford, CT
Levine, Kenneth L. ... Chicago, IL
Levine, Kenneth M. ... Boston, MA
Levine, Kenneth S. ... Washington, DC
Levine, Kenneth T. ... Philadelphia, PA
Levine, Kent Jay ... Englewood, CO
Levine, Kent Jay, P.C. ... Englewood, CO
Levine, Kevin ... Los Angeles, CA
Levine, Kimberly A. ... New Hyde Park, NY
Levine, Kimberly Anne ... Newport News, VA
Levine, Kyle B. ... Los Angeles, CA
Levine, L. Andrew ... Greenwich, CT
Levine, Lance I. ... New York, NY
Levine, Larry R. ... Hartford, CT
Levine, Laura J. ... New York, NY
Levine, Laurence David
Department of Justice, Executive Office for Immigration Review, GV
Levine, Laurence H. ... Chicago, IL
Levine, Laurence J. ... Washington, DC
Levine, Laurence W. ... New York, NY
Levine Law Firm, The ... San Francisco, CA
Levine Law Office ... Erie, PA
Levine, Lawrence ... New York, NY
Levine, Lawrence A. ... Melville, NY
Levine, Lawrence D. ... Thousand Oaks, CA
Levine, Lawrence E. ... Secaucus, NJ
Levine, Lawrence E. ... Nashville, TN
Levine, Lawrence Jeffrey
East Longmeadow, MA
Le Vine, Lawrence N. ... New York, NY
Levine, Lawrence P. ... Miami, FL
Levine, Lawrence S. ... New York, NY
Levine, Lazarus I. ... Liberty, NY
Levine, Lee ... Washington, DC
Levine, Lee A. ... Atlantic City, NJ
Levine, Leigh M. ... Charlotte, NC
Levine, Leon R. ... Troy, MI
Levine, Leonard B. ... Los Angeles, CA
Levine, Leonard D. ... Virginia Beach, VA
LeVine, Leonard H., Jr. ... Lakewood, CO
Levine, Leonard J. ... Baltimore, MD
Levine, Les J. ... Newburgh, NY
Levine, Lesley F. ... Bronx, NY
Levine, Leslie J. ... Great Neck, NY
Levine, Leslie M. ... Cambridge, MA
Levine, Lester I. ... Longboat Key, FL
Levine & Levine ... Birmingham, AL
Levine & Levine ... Kalamazoo, MI
Levine & Levine ... Chatham, NJ
East Hanover, NJ
Florham Park, NJ
Livingston, NJ
Madison, NJ
Morristown, NJ
Parsippany, NJ
Levine & Levine ... Charlotte, NC
Levine & Levine ... Cleveland, OH
Levine & Levine ... New Castle, PA
Levine & Levine, P.C. ... New York, NY
Poughkeepsie, NY
Levine, Lillian C. ... Brockton, MA
Levine, Linnea J. ... Stamford, CT
Poughkeepsie, NY
Purchase, NY
Levine, Linnea J., P.C., Law Offices of
Stamford, CT
Poughkeepsie, NY
Purchase, NY
Levine, Lisa ... New York, NY
Levine, Lisa Fialkow ... Fort Lauderdale, FL
Levine, Lisa K. ... San Francisco, CA
Levine, Lisa K. ... Cleveland, OH
Levine, Lisa L. ... Washington, DC
Levine, Lisa R. ... Trenton, NJ
Levine, Lois B. ... Beverly Hills, CA
Levine, Loren F. ... New York, NY
Levine, Lori J. ... Jefferson City, MO
Levine, Lori M. ... Los Angeles, CA
Levine, Louis ... Syracuse, NY
Levine, Louis H. ... New York, NY
Levine, Lynn Iris
United States International Trade Commission, Office of Unfair Import Investigations, GV
Levine and Majorie, Ltd. ... Dallas, TX
Levine & Mandelbaum ... New York, NY
Levine, Marc B. ... San Diego, CA
Levine, Marc E. ... Los Angeles, CA
Levine, Marc S. ... Bethesda, MD
Levine, Marci R. ... Los Angeles, CA
Levine, Marci Rose ... Washington, DC
Levine, Marcia D. ... Los Altos, CA
Levine, Marcia E. ... Aventura, FL
Levine, Margo L. ... New York, NY
Levine, Marilyn Markovich
Valley Stream, NY
Levine, Marjorie ... New York, NY
Levine, Mark ... New York, NY
Levine, Mark A. ... Minneapolis, MN
Levine, Mark A. ... New York, NY
Levine, Mark E. ... Chicago, IL
Levine, Mark G. ... Highland Park, IL
Levine, Mark H. ... Los Angeles, CA
Levine, Mark J. ... Houston, TX
Levine, Mark L. ... Denver, CO
Chicago, IL
Levine, Mark L. ... New York, NY
Levine, Mark Lee ... Denver, CO
Levine, Mark M. ... Hartford, CT
Levine, Mark S. ... Los Angeles, CA
Levine, Mark S. ... Tallahassee, FL
Levine, Mark S. ... Boston, MA
Levine, Mark W. ... New York, NY
Levine, Marsha F. ... Irvine, CA
Levine, Marta S. ... Milwaukee, WI

Levine, Martin ... Los Angeles, CA
Levine, Martin ... Rockville, MD
Levine, Martin E. ... Miami, FL
Levine, Martin R. ... New York, NY
Levine, Martin R. ... New York, NY
Levine, Marva M. ... New York, NY
Levine, Marvin ... Santa Barbara, CA
Levine, Marvin ... New York, NY
Levine, Marvin J. ... New York, NY
Levine, Mary Beth ... Cleveland, OH
Levine, Mary Ellen Environmental Protection Agency, Office of the General Counsel, GV
LeVine, Mary Fabre ... Woodland Hills, CA
Levine, Mary P. ... Lansing, MI
Levine, Matthew B. ... Scottsdale, AZ
Levine, Matthew L. ... Department of Justice, Office of the Attorney General, GV
Levine, Matthew P. ... Lafayette, CA
Levine, Mattson, Orr & Geracioti Nashville, TN
Levine, Maura D. ... New York, NY
Levine, Max A. ... Pittsburgh, PA
Levine, M. Carl, Morgulas & Foreman, P.C. New York, NY
Levine, Megan Lesser ... Albany, NY
Levine, Meldon E. ... Los Angeles, CA
Washington, DC
Levine, Melissa B. ... Washington, DC
Levine, Melissa Beth ... Garden City, NY
Levine, Melissa F. ... Washington, DC
Levine, Melissa Smith ... Library of Congress, National Digital Library, GV
Levine, Melvin H. ... Florham Park, NJ
Levine, Melvin J. ... Sharon, MA
Levine, Meredith B. ... Houston, TX
Levine, Mia M. ... Department of Justice, Criminal Division, GV
Levine, Micaela H. ... Milwaukee, WI
Levine, Michael ... San Francisco, CA
Levine, Michael ... Brooklyn, NY
Levine, Michael A. ... Des Moines, IA
Levine, Michael A. ... New York, NY
Levine, Michael B. ... Los Angeles, CA
Levine, Michael C. ... Thousand Oaks, CA
Levine, Michael C. ... Lansing, MI
Levine, Michael D. ... Chapel Hill, NC
Levine, Michael Gary ... Boca Raton, FL
Levine, Michael I. ... Baltimore, MD
Levine, Michael J. ... New York, NY
Levine, Michael J. ... Houston, TX
Levine, Michael M. ... Martinez, CA
Levine, Michael Robert ... Portland, OR
Levine, Michael S. ... Washington, DC
Potomac, MD
Levine, Michael S. ... Washington, DC
Levine, Michael S. ... Melville, NY
Levine, Michael S. ... Mineola, NY
Levine, Michael S. ... New York, NY
Levine, Michele Donna ... Riverside, CA
Levine, Miles S. ... Charlotte, NC
Levine & Miller ... Beverly Hills, CA
Levine & Miller, P.A. ... Minneapolis, MN
Levine, Mindy E. ... New York, NY
Levine, Mitchell B. ... Hackensack, NJ
Levine, Mitchell J. ... Bloomfield, CT
Levine & Montana ... Peekskill, NY
Levine, Morree M. ... Niagara Falls, NY
Levine, Morrie I. ... Hollywood, FL
Levine, Morton ... Juno Beach, FL
Levine, Morton ... Larchmont, NY
Levine, Morton P. ... Atlanta, GA
Levine, Murray ... Buffalo, NY
Levine, Myron ... Jacksonville, FL
Levine, Myron ... Tenafly, NJ
Levine, Neil ... Santa Barbara, CA
Levine, Neil H. ... New York, NY
Levine, Neil J. ... Wheaton, IL
Levine, Neil L. ... Albany, NY
Levine, Nicki F. ... Charlotte, NC
Levine, Nina D. Small Business Administration, Office of the General Counsel, GV
Levine, Norman A. ... New Castle, PA
Levine, Norman E. ... Wilmington, DE
Levine, Norman H. ... Los Angeles, CA
Levine & Partners, P.A. ... Miami, FL
Levine, Paul A. ... Clearwater, FL
Levine, Paul A. ... Albany, NY
Saratoga Springs, NY
Levine, Paul Anthony ... Miami, FL
Levine, Paul H. ... Los Angeles, CA
Levine, Paul J. ... Hollywood, CA
Levine, Paul J. ... Washington, DC
Levine, Paul L. ... Lowell, MA
Levine, Paul M. ... Phoenix, AZ
Levine, Paul M., P.C. ... Phoenix, AZ
Levine, Paul Samuel ... Venice, CA
Levine, Penny ... New York, NY
Levine, Peter H. ... Hartford, CT
Levine, Peter K. ... Beverly Hills, CA
Levine, Peter K. ... United States Senate, Committee Legal Personnel, GV
Levine, Peter M. ... New York, NY
LeVine, Peter R. ... Palo Alto, CA
Levine, Peter S. ... Cleveland, OH
Levine, Philip ... Mountain Lakes, NJ
Levine, Philip ... Waynesboro, PA
Levine, Philip J. ... Palo Alto, CA
Levine, Philip J. ... Treasury Department, Internal Revenue Service, GV
Levine, Philip R. ... Los Angeles, CA
Levine, Phyllis B. ... Arlington, VA
Levine, Ralph ... New York, NY
Levine, Randall C. ... Buckhannon, WV
Levine, Randall S. ... Kalamazoo, MI
Levine, Randi ... Boston, MA
Levine, Randi ... Newton, MA
Levine, Randy L. ... New York, NY
Levine, Rebecca-Sue ... New York, NY
Levine, Rhona ... Radford, VA
Roanoke, VA
Levine, Ria A. ... New York, NY
Levine, Richard A. ... Evergreen, CO
Levine, Richard A. ... Wilmington, DE
Levine, Richard A. Securities and Exchange Commission, Office of the General Counsel, GV
Levine, Richard A. ... New York, NY
Levine, Richard C. ... Pittsburgh, PA
Levine, Richard E. ... San Francisco, CA
Levine, Richard E. ... Baltimore, MD
Levine, Richard H. ... Edina, MN
Levine, Richard I. ... North Babylon, NY
LeVine, Richard J. ... San Diego, CA
Levine, Richard L. ... Boston, MA
Levine, Richard L. ... New York, NY
Cincinnati, OH
Columbus, OH
Levine, Richard M. ... New York, NY
LeVine, Richard S. ... Chicago, IL
Levine, Robert ... Hillsdale, NJ
Levine, Robert ... Houston, TX
Levine, Robert A. ... Tampa, FL
Levine, Robert A. ... Portland, ME
Levine, Robert A. ... Milwaukee, WI
Levine, Robert B. ... Farmington, CT
Levine, Robert B. ... New York, NY
Levine, Robert B. ... New York, NY
Levine, Robert C. ... New Haven, CT
Levine, Robert C. ... Exeter, NH
Levine, Robert E. ... Woodland Hills, CA
Levine, Robert E. ... Washington, DC
Levine, Robert F. ... New York, NY
Levine, Robert J. ... Miami, FL
Levine, Robert J. ... Rockland, ME
Levine, Robert J. ... New York, NY
Levine, Robert J. ... White Plains, NY
Levine, Robert M. ... Syosset, NY
Levine, Robert M. ... Pittsburgh, PA
Levine, Robert M., P.A. ... St. Louis Park, MN
Levine, Robert P. ... New York, NY
Levine, Robert, P.C. ... Houston, TX
Levine, Robert S. ... Chicago, IL
Levine, Robert S. ... Poughkeepsie, NY
Levine, Robert Stephen ... Plantation, FL
Levine, Robin B. ... San Francisco, CA
Levine, Robin J. ... Mt. Orab, OH
Levine, Robin Paige ... Washington, DC
Levine, Robin W. ... Garden City, NY
Levine, Roger N. ... East Brunswick, NJ
New York, NY
Levine, Ronald A. ... Atlanta, GA
Levine, Ronald B. ... Westlake Village, CA
Levine, Ronald E. ... Costa Mesa, CA
Levine, Ronald H. ... Philadelphia, PA
Le Vine, Ronald I. ... Hackensack, NJ
Levine, Ronald J. ... Princeton, NJ
New York, NY
Levine, Ronald J. ... Philadelphia, PA
Levine, Ronald R. ... Poughkeepsie, NY
Levine, Ronald R., II ... Denver, CO
Levine, Rosemary T. ... New York, NY
LeVine, Roxanne H. ... New York, NY
Levine, Russell E. ... Chicago, IL
Levine, Ruth M. ... Norwalk, CT
Levine, Ruth R. ... Santa Barbara, CA
Levine, Sally Anne ... New York, NY
Levine, Sally R. ... Encino, CA
Levine, Samuel H. ... Chicago, IL
Levine, Samuel Jay ... Arlington, VA
Levine, Samuel M. ... Garden City, NY
Levine, Sandra B. ... Pittsburgh, PA
Levine, Sandra E. ... Montpelier, VT
Levine, Sanford C. ... Dobbs Ferry, NY
Levine, Sanford H. ... Albany, NY
Levine, Saul R. ... Los Angeles, CA
Le Vine, Saul S. ... Roslyn Heights, NY
Levine, Scott ... Dallas, TX
Levine, Scott A. ... Fort Lauderdale, FL
Levine, Scott D. ... San Diego, CA
Levine, Scott D. ... Fort Lauderdale, FL
Levine, Scott D. ... St. Louis, MO
Levine, Scott David ... Chicago, IL
Levine, Scott K. ... New York, NY
Levine, Seth D. ... Roseland, NJ
Levine, Seymour ... Greenwich, CT
Levine, Seymour ... New York, NY
Levine, Sharan Lee ... Kalamazoo, MI
Levine, Sharon L. ... Roseland, NJ
Levine, Sharron ... Washington, DC
Levine, Sheila J. ... New York, NY
Levine, Shelley E. ... Los Angeles, CA
Levine, Sheree F. ... New York, NY
Levine, Sherri B. ... New York, NY
Levine, Sherrie G. ... Roslyn Heights, NY
Levine, Sheryl H. ... New York, NY
Levine, Shifrin & Associates, Ltd. Schaumburg, IL
Levine, Sidney ... Sealy, TX
Levine, Sidney C. ... Des Moines, IA
Levine, Sidney M. ... Chicago, IL
Levine & Skigen ... San Francisco, CA
Levine & Slavit ... New York, NY
Levine, Sol ... Charlotte, NC
Levine, Solomon L. ... Manhasset Hills, NY
Levine & Spatz, A Professional Corporation Pittsburgh, PA
Levine, Stacey A. ... Hollis, NY
Levine, Staller, Sklar, Chan, Brodsky & Donnelly, P.A. ... Atlantic City, NJ
Levine, Stanley ... Orange, NJ
Levine, Stanley ... Hartsdale, NY
Levine, Stanley A. ... Washington, DC
Levine, Stanley A. ... Fort Wayne, IN
Levine, Stanley E. ... Pittsburgh, PA
Levine, Stanley J. ... Miami Beach, FL
Levine, Stanley L. ... San Diego, CA
Levine, Steinberg & Miller San Diego, CA
Levine, Stephen E. ... Arlington, TX
Levine, Stephen L. ... Dallas, TX
Levine, Stephen M. ... Emeryville, CA
Levine, Stephen P. ... San Bernardino, CA
Levine, Steven ... Miami, FL
Levine, Steven ... Minneapolis, MN
Levine, Steven ... New York, NY
Levine, Steven A. ... Madison, WI
Levine, Steven B. ... Boston, MA
Levine, Steven D. ... Glendale, CA
Levine, Steven D. ... Miami, FL
Levine, Steven Graff ... Torrance, CA
Levine, Steven J. ... San Diego, CA
Levine, Steven J. ... San Jose, CA
Levine, Steven J. ... Boca Raton, FL
Levine, Steven J. ... Chester, IL
Levine, Steven J. ... Baton Rouge, LA
Levine, Steven Jon ... White Plains, NY
Levine, Steven M. ... Washington, DC
Levine, Steven Marc ... Bronx, NY
Levine & Stewart ... Chapel Hill, NC
Levine, Stewart L. ... Philadelphia, PA
Levine, Stuart ... Winter Park, FL
Levine, Stuart ... Baltimore, MD
Levine, Stuart Jay ... Sarasota, FL
Levine, Stuart, L.L.C. ... Baltimore, MD
Levine, Stuart M. ... Westport, CT
Levine, Stuart M. ... Pittsburgh, PA
Levine, Stuart M., P.C. ... Pittsburgh, PA
Levine Sullivan & Koch, L.L.P. Washington, DC
Levine, Susan ... Aventura, FL
Levine, Susan Ann ... New York, NY
Levine, Susan F. ... Northfield, MA
Levine, Susan J. ... Chicago, IL
Levine, Syma Shulman ... Uniondale, NY
Levine, Tama L. ... Denver, CO
Levine, Tamara Kagan ... Farmington, CT
Levine, Tedd S. ... Bridgewater, NJ
Mineola, NY
Levine, Tema A. ... Van Nuys, CA
Levine, Teresa Z. ... Bedford, NH
Lubbock, TX
Levine Thall Plotkin & Menin, LLP New York, NY
Levine, Theodore A. ... New York, NY
Levine, Thomas ... Los Angeles, CA
Levine, Thomas M. ... Pittsburgh, PA
Levine, Thomas S. ... New York, NY
Levine & Thompson ... Wilmington, DE
Levine, Todd A. ... Fort Lauderdale, FL
Levine, Tori Smith, (P.C.) ... Dallas, TX
Levine, Tracy Ellen Federal Labor Relations Authority, Washington Regional Office, GV
Levine & Unger ... Beverly Hills, CA
Los Angeles, CA
Levine, Victoria A. Department of Agriculture, Food Safety and Inspection Service, GV
LeVine, Walter D. ... Florham Park, NJ
LeVine, Walter D., P.A. ... Florham Park, NJ
Levine, Wayne ... Lantana, FL
Levine, Wayne P. ... Miami, FL
Levine, Wayne P., P.A. ... Miami, FL
Levine, Wendy Pauling ... Columbia, SC
Levine, William A. ... Boston, MA
Levine, William A. ... Rochester, NY
Levine, William C. ... Cherry Hill, NJ
Levine, William D. ... Huntington, WV
Levine, William F., and Michael B. Grossman Mineola, NY
Levine, William G., (P.C.) Beverly Hills, CA
Levine, William M. ... Boston, MA
Levine, William M. ... New York, NY
Levine and Yates, P.C. ... Washington, DC
Arlington, VA
Levine, Zahavah ... San Francisco, CA
Levine & Zelman ... White Plains, NY
Levin-Epstein, Ethan A. ... New Haven, CT
LeViner, Bernard L. ... Ontario, NY
Levine-Rubel, Gail M. ... New York, NY
LeViness, Thomas R. ... New York, NY
Leving, Jeffery M. ... Chicago, IL
Leving, Jeffery M., Ltd., A P.C., Law Offices of Chicago, IL
Levinger, Donald A. ... Elmira, NY
Levinger, Jeffrey S. ... Dallas, TX
Levinger, Mark B. ... St. Paul, MN
Levinger, Mary Jo. ... San Jose, CA
Levings, Jacqueline K. ... Wichita, KS
Levings, Theresa L. F. ... Kansas City, MO
Levings, William F. ... Duluth, MN
Levingson, Alfred ... New York, NY
Levingston, Jeffrey A. ... Cleveland, MS
Levingston, K.D. ... Dallas, TX
Levingston, Kirsten D. ... Washington, DC
Levingston & Levingston ... Cleveland, MS
Levington, Marcy C. ... Newton, MA
Levinkind, Susan ... San Jose, CA
Levin Moulton, Cynthia R. ... Houston, TX
Levin-Muriel, Jayme ... Chicago, IL
Levin-Nussbaum, Anne ... New York, NY
Levinrad, Eric ... Los Angeles, CA
Levins, Alan S. ... San Francisco, CA
Levins, Annmarie ... Redmond, WA
Levins, Debra Homer ... Chicago, IL
Levins, James G., III ... Rutland, VT
Levins, Richard F. ... Philadelphia, PA
Levins, Stephen H. ... Honolulu, HI
Levins, Will ... Hackensack, NJ
Levinski, Albert L. ... Seattle, WA
Levinsky, Alan M. ... Phoenix, AZ
Levinsky, Barry ... Chicago, IL
Levinsky, Mitchell A. ... New York, NY
Levinsohn, Craig L. ... Hackensack, NJ
Levinsohn, Donald M. ... New York, NY
Levinsohn, Mark A. ... New York, NY
Levinsohn, Paul ... Woodbridge, NJ
Levinsohn, Robert J. ... New York, NY
Levinson, Adam P. ... Miami, FL
Levinson, Alfred A. ... Edison, NJ
Levinson, Alfred L. ... Des Plaines, IL
Levinson, Andrea S. ... Wellesley, MA
Levinson, Andrew E. ... Studio City, CA
Levinson, Andrew J. ... New York, NY
Levinson, Arlene A. ... Hudson, NY
Levinson, Arnold R. ... San Francisco, CA
Levinson, Barry P. ... New York, NY
Levinson, Brian David ... Basehor, KS
Levinson, Bryan Fielder ... Kew Gardens, NY
Levinson, Burton S. ... Beverly Hills, CA
Levinson, Cara B. ... Chicago, IL
Levinson, Cary S. ... Philadelphia, PA
Levinson, Catherine E. ... Milwaukee, WI
Levinson, David A. ... Philadelphia, PA
Levinson, David B. ... New York, NY
Levinson, David L. ... Central Valley, NY
Levinson, David S. ... San Francisco, CA
Levinson, Donald P. ... Merrillville, IN
Levinson, Doreen ... Valley Stream, NY
Levinson, Edward E. ... Miami Beach, FL
Levinson, Edward E., P.A. Miami Beach, FL
Levinson, Edward S. ... Oakland, CA
Levinson, Elinor B. ... Camarillo, CA
Levinson, Eric D. ... Oakdale, MN
Levinson, Friedman, Vhugen, Duggan & Bland, A Professional Service Corporation Seattle, WA
Levinson, Gary A. ... Miami, FL
Levinson, Gary A., P.A. ... Miami, FL
Levinson, Gary Paul ... Newport Beach, CA
Levinson, George ... Asbury Park, NJ
Levinson, Gerald M. ... Bergenfield, NJ
Levinson, Gerald S. ... Garden City, NY
Levinson, H. Brian ... Binghamton, NY
Levinson, Hal A. ... Charlotte, NC
Levinson, Harry ... New York, NY
Levinson, Harvey B. ... Mineola, NY
Levinson, Hillel S. ... Harrisburg, PA
Levinson, Holly Hickman ... Charlotte, NC
Levinson, Howard M. ... Wilkes-Barre, PA
Levinson, Irving B. ... Chicago, IL
Levinson, J. Gordon ... San Francisco, CA
Levinson, Jackie S. ... Washington, DC
Levinson, James R. ... Benson, NC
Levinson, James R. ... Dayton, OH
Levinson, Jeffrey A. ... Los Angeles, CA
Levinson, Jeffrey A. ... Boston, MA
Levinson, Jeffrey G. ... Tulsa, OK
Levinson, Jeffrey H. ... Phoenix, AZ
Levinson, Jeffrey L. ... Hanford, CA
Levinson, Jeffrey M. ... Cleveland, OH
Levinson, Jeremy P. ... Milwaukee, WI
Levinson, Jodi ... Burbank, CA
Levinson, Joel H. ... West Sacramento, CA
Levinson, Jos. H. ... Benson, NC
Levinson, Joseph ... Stamford, CT
Levinson, Judith Aronow ... Atlanta, GA
Levinson, Judith R. ... Hackensack, NJ
Levinson, Justin D. ... Palo Alto, CA
Levinson & Kaplan ... Los Angeles, CA
Encino, CA
Levinson, Karen J. ... New York, NY
Levinson, Kenneth L. ... Denver, CO
Levinson, L. David ... San Antonio, TX
Levinson, L. Harold ... Nashville, TN
Levinson, Lara ... Department of Justice, Civil Division, GV
Levinson, Laurence I. ... Wilmington, DE
Levinson, Lawrence A. ... New Haven, CT
Levinson, Lawrence E. ... Washington, DC
Levinson, Lawrence L. ... Columbus, OH
Levinson, Lawrence M. ... Boston, MA
Levinson, Lawrence M. ... New York, NY
Levinson, Lawrence R. ... Waltham, MA
Levinson, L. David, P.C. ... San Antonio, TX
Levinson, Lee I. ... Tulsa, OK
Levinson, Leslie J. ... New York, NY
Levinson & Levinson ... Benson, NC
Levinson, Lieberman & Maas, A Professional Corporation ... Beverly Hills, CA
Levinson, Lisa S. ... New York, NY
Levinson, Lizbeth R. ... Washington, DC
Levinson, Lois T. ... Denver, CO
Levinson, Lois T. ... Englewood, CO
Levinson, Lori H. ... Pittsfield, MA
Levinson, Lori R. ... New York, NY
Levinson, Louis H. ... Chicago, IL
Levinson, Marc A. ... Sacramento, CA
Levinson, Marc R. ... Miami, FL
Levinson, Marilyn W. ... Wilmington, DE
Levinson, Mark ... Plainview, NY
Levinson, Mark J. ... Boston, MA
Levinson, Mark L. ... Beverly Hills, CA
Levinson, Mark L. ... Los Angeles, CA
Levinson, Mark V. ... Tampa, FL
Levinson, Martin ... Miami, FL
Levinson, Marvin L. ... St. Louis, MO
Levinson, Michael Gregg ... Chicago, IL
Levinson, Michael H. ... Virginia Beach, VA
Levinson, Michael R. ... Chicago, IL
Levinson, Michael S. ... San Diego, CA
Levinson, Michele ... Chicago, IL
Levinson, Murray & Jensen, P.C. Chicago, IL
Levinson, Myrna A. ... New York, NY
Levinson, Myron N. ... Chicago, IL
Levinson, Neil D. ... Santa Monica, CA
Levinson, Neil H. ... Miami Beach, FL

Levinson, Patti S. ....Chicago, IL
Levinson, Paul ....Los Angeles, CA
Levinson, Paul H. ....New York, NY
Levinson, Peter J. ....
Joint Committees And Commissions, GV
Levinson, Philip Z. ....Boca Raton, FL
Levinson, Ralph W. ....Buffalo, NY
Levinson, Randi Bliss ....Fairfax, VA
Levinson, Richard J. ....Edison, NJ
Levinson, Rick B. ....Colorado Springs, CO
Levinson, Robert A. ....Encino, CA
Levinson, Robert N. ....Decatur, GA
Levinson, Robert N., P.C. ....Decatur, GA
Levinson, Robert R. ....Edison, NJ
Levinson, Roberta A. ....Chicago, IL
Levinson, Ronald E. ....Los Angeles, CA
Levinson, Ronald T. ....Albertson, NY
Levinson, Rosalie B. ....Merrillville, IN
Levinson, Scott ....New York, NY
Levinson, Scott A. ....Bronx, NY
Levinson, Scott S. ....New York, NY
Levinson, Sidney P. ....Washington, DC
Levinson & Smith ....Tulsa, OK
Levinson, Stanton J. ....Silver Spring, MD
Levinson, Stephen B. ....Anniston, AL
Levinson, Stephen M. ....Cartersville, GA
Levinson, Steven H. ....Honolulu, HI
Levinson, Tasha Dian ....Los Angeles, CA
Levinson, W. Mark ....Los Angeles, CA
Levinson, William ....Chicago, IL
Levinson, William R. ....Kent, WA
Levinson, William R., Inc., P.S. ....Kent, WA
Levinson, William S. ....Rochester, NY
Levinson, Zeccola, Reineke, Ornstein & Selinger, P.C. ....Central Valley, NY
Goshen, NY
Levinstein, Janna M. ....Norfolk, VA
Levinstein, Mark S. ....Washington, DC
Levin-Tavares, Jennifer ....New Haven, CT
Levinthal, Allen ....Harrisburg, PA
Levinthal, Angelyn E. ....Houston, TX
Levinthal, Bernard L. ....Philadelphia, PA
Levinthal, Jared I. ....Houston, TX
Levinthal, Malcolm ....Santa Barbara, CA
Levinthal, Seymour C. ....Liverpool, NY
Levinthal, William M. ......San Francisco, CA
Levintoff, Carina ....New York, NY
Levinton, Howard ....Baltimore, MD
Levintow, Nicholas J. ......Department of Labor,
Office of the Solicitor, GV
Levion, Leon L. ....Zanesville, OH
Levis & Barron ....Audubon, IA
Levis, Earl F. ....San Antonio, TX
Levis & Hull, P.A. ....Biddeford, ME
Levis, John F. ....Mount Olive, NJ
Levis, Kara M. ....Seattle, WA
Levis, Lance D. ....Audubon, IA
Levis, Marc R. ....Library of Congress,
Congressional Research Service, GV
Levis and Pinto ....Media, PA
Levis, Robert J. ....Media, PA
Levis, S. James, Jr. ....Biddeford, ME
Levis, Thomas J. ....Des Moines, IA
Levis, W. Kent ....Fresno, CA
Levis, William H. ....Denver, CO
Levis, William J. ....New York, NY
Levisohn, Lerner & Berger ....New York, NY
Levison, Andrew J. ....Brooklyn, NY
Levison, Barbara S. ....Hartford, CT
Levison, Diane L. ....San Luis Obispo, CA
Levison, Harold G. ....New York, NY
Levison, Jon B. ....New York, NY
Levison, Kathie A. ....Toledo, OH
Levison, Mark H. ....St. Louis, MO
Levison, S. Jarvin ....Atlanta, GA
Levison, Stuart L. ....Rochester, NY
Leviss, David J. ....New York, NY
Leviss, Evan S. ....Newport, RI
Leviss, Sidney ....Jamaica, NY
Leviss, Stewart M. ....Short Hills, NJ
Levister, Robert L. ....Stamford, CT
Levit, Abraham ....Bellaire, TX
Levit, Abraham ....Houston, TX
Levit, Janet K.
Export-Import Bank of The United States,
Office of the General Counsel, GV
Levit, Jay J. ....Richmond, VA
Levit, Joan M. ....Fort Lauderdale, FL
Levit, Lawrence A. ....Washington, DC
Levit, Lawrence D. ....New York, NY
Levit & Lipshutz ....Chicago, IL
Levit, Louis W. ....Chicago, IL
Levit, Mann & Halligan, P.C.
Ashland, VA
Richmond, VA
Levit, S. Daniel ....Highland Park, MI
Levit, Saul ....Norristown, PA
Philadelphia, PA
Levit, Steven B. ....Chicago, IL
Levit, Victor B. ....San Francisco, CA
Levit, William H., Jr. ....Milwaukee, WI
Levitan, A. Harry ....Philadelphia, PA
Levitan, Barbara ....New York, NY
Levitan, Daniel A.
National Labor Relations Board,
Office of the General Counsel, GV
Levitan, David M. ....Roslyn Harbor, NY
Levitan, Eve H. ....Wyncote, PA
Levitan & Frieland, P.C. ....Boca Raton, FL
Tampa, FL
Livingston, NJ
Newark, NJ
New York, NY
Levitan, Howard S. ....Prairie Village, KS
Levitan, James A. ....New York, NY
Levitan, Jeffrey ....Los Angeles, CA
Levitan, Jeffrey W. ....New York, NY
Levitan, Jonathan M. ....Los Angeles, CA
Levitan, Judith Nisenbaum ....Deerfield, IL
Levitan, Katherine ....Huntington, NY
Huntington, NY
Levitan, Kenneth B. ....Nashville, TN
Levitan, Lara M. ....Chicago, IL
Levitan, Laurence ....Annapolis, MD
Baltimore, MD
Levitan, Lynn R. ....Santa Monica, CA
Levitan, Neal P. ....Chestnut Hill, MA
Levitan & Pardes ....Huntington, NY
Levitan, Paula I. ....San Francisco, CA
Levitan, Peter A. ....Beverly Hills, CA
Levitan, Philip I. ....Livingston, NJ
New York, NY
Levitan, Rachel S. ....New York, NY
Levitan, Ralph S. ....Bensalem, PA
Philadelphia, PA
Levitan, Richard A. ....Wayne, NJ
Levitan, Roger S. ....Tucson, AZ
Levitan, Ronald M. ....Baltimore, MD
Levitan, Sandra L. ....Easton, MD
Levitan, Shari A. ....Boston, MA
Levitan, Stacy J. ....Philadelphia, PA
Levitan, Steve ....New York, NY
Levitan, Steven M. ....San Jose, CA
Levitan, Stuart D. ....Madison, WI
Levitas, Alan H. ....Department of Labor,
Pension and Welfare Benefits, GV
Levitas, Elisabeth J. ....San Jose, CA
Levitas, Elliott H. ....Washington, DC
Atlanta, GA
Levitas, Martin J. ....Camden, NJ
Levitas, Peter J. ....Department of Justice,
Antitrust Division, GV
Levitas, Phyllis B. ....New York, NY
Levitas, Steven J. ....Greensboro, NC
Raleigh, NC
Levitch, Burt ....Beverly Hills, CA
Levitch, Harry ....Spokane, WA
Levitch, Jay L. ....St. Louis, MO
Levites, Paul C. ....Boston, MA
Levites, Raymond A. ....New York, NY
Levith, Alan J. ....Hammond, LA
Levithan, Allen B. ....Roseland, NJ
Levithan, Estelle ....Flushing, NY
Levitin, Betty H. ....San Francisco, CA
Levitin, Jeffrey ....New York, NY
Levitin, Jerrold E. ....Napa, CA
Levitin, Joel H. ....New York, NY
Levitin, Martin A. ....Orangeburg, NY
Levitin, Michael J. ....Washington, DC
Levitin, Mitchell H. ....Mineola, NY
Levitin, Nancy ....Lake Success, NY
Levitine, Ilia ....Washington, DC
Leviton, Dawn ....Chappaqua, NY
Leviton, Gareth C. ....Memphis, TN
Leviton, James H. ....Minneapolis, MN
Leviton, Karen R. ....Los Angeles, CA
Leviton, Phyllis E. ....Rego Park, NY
Leviton, Rabine, Diaz & Whiting, Inc.
Santa Ana, CA
Leviton, Robin Beth ....Santa Ana, CA
Leviton, Stuart L. ....Encino, CA
Leviton, Susan P. ....Baltimore, MD
Leviton, Wendy S. ....Los Angeles, CA
Levitske, John, Jr. ....Pittsburgh, PA
Levitsky, Adam ....Detroit, MI
Levitsky, Asher S. ....New York, NY
Levitsky, Neal J. ....Wilmington, DE
Wilmington, DE
Bellmawr, NJ
Levitsky, Paul A. ....Stamford, CT
Levitsky, Ross ....Salem, NJ
Levitsky, Steven B. ....Rochester, NY
Levitsky, Steven E. ....New York, NY
Levitt, Adam J. ....Chicago, IL
Levitt, Alfred P. ....New York, NY
Levitt, Alvin T. ....San Francisco, CA
Levitt, Andrea J. ....Englewood, CO
Levitt, Andrew Jason ....Uniondale, NY
Levitt, Barry ....Santa Monica, CA
Levitt, Betsy J. ....St. Louis, MO
Levitt, Bonnie K. ....San Francisco, CA
Levitt, Bruce H. ....South Orange, NJ
Levitt, Cary A. ....Wilmington, DE
Levitt, Catherine B. ....Deerfield, IL
Levitt, Chet D. ....Washington, DC
Levitt, Cynthia Joanne ....Washington, DC
Levitt, Dana N., (P.C.) ....Los Angeles, CA
Levitt, Daniel P. ....New York, NY
Levitt, David A. ....San Francisco, CA
Levitt, David B. ....Bronx, NY
Levitt, David H. ....Chicago, IL
Levitt, Donald R. ....Fresno, CA
Levitt, Donald R., Inc. ....Fresno, CA
Levitt, Drew M. ....Deerfield Beach, FL
Levitt, Erica A. ....Sherman Oaks, CA
Levitt, Eugene J. ....Huntington, NY
Levitt, Gary E. ....Bloomfield Hills, MI
Levitt, Gary E., P.C. ....Bloomfield Hills, MI
Levitt, Gary M. ....Honolulu, HI
Levitt, Geoffrey M. ....Washington, DC
Levitt, Glenn R. ....Rochester, NY
Levitt & Gordon ....New Hartford, NY
Utica, NY
Levitt, Harriette P. ....Tucson, AZ
Levitt, Harvey J. ....Cleveland, OH
Levitt, Howard E. ....Mineola, NY
Levitt, Jack B. ....New York, NY
Levitt, Jack R. ....Bozeman, MT
Levitt, Jamie A. ....New York, NY
Levitt, Jay T. ....Beverly Hills, CA
Levitt, Jeffrey ....Amityville, NY
Levitt, Jeffrey A. ....New York, NY
Levitt, John B. ....Boca Raton, FL
Levitt, John S. ....Los Angeles, CA
Levitt, Jonathan E. ....Roseland, NJ
Levitt, Joseph A.
Department Of Health And Human Services,
Food & Drug Administration, GV
Levitt, Joseph J., Jr. ....Knoxville, TN
Levitt, Judith A. ....Los Angeles, CA
Levitt, Judith E. ....Chicago, IL
Levitt, Julian M. ....Kansas City, MO
Levitt, Julie ....Memphis, TN
Levitt, Julie M. ....Miami, FL
Levitt, Julie Melissa ....Miami, FL
Levitt, Karen J. ....Lowell, MA
Levitt, Kenneth E. ....Minneapolis, MN
Levitt, Kenneth W. ....New York, NY
Levitt, Lawrence I. ....Millburn, NJ
Levitt, Leon I. ....Commack, NY
Levitt & Levitt ....Chattanooga, TN
Levitt, Lloyd A. ....Chattanooga, TN
Levitt, Mallory D. ....New York, NY
Levitt, Marc E. ....Philadelphia, PA
Levitt, Marilyn R.
Department of Transportation,
Surface Transportation Board, GV
Levitt, Mark ....Rockville, MD
Levitt, Mark D. ....New Hartford, NY
Levitt, Mark E. ....Tampa, FL
Levitt, Mark L. ....Chicago, IL
Levitt, Mark S. ....St. Louis, MO
Levitt, Martin J. ....Chattanooga, TN
Levitt, Matthew J. ....Minneapolis, MN
Levitt, Matthew L. ....St. Paul, MN
Levitt, Melinda F. ....Washington, DC
Levitt, Meyer S. ....Los Angeles, CA
Levitt, Michael ....Chicago, IL
Levitt, Michael A.
Department of Commerce,
Office of the General Counsel, GV
Levitt, Michael A. ....New York, NY
Levitt, Michael B. ....St. Louis, MO
Levitt, Michelle A. ....New York, NY
Levitt, Neil F. ....Garland, TX
Levitt, Peter H. ....Miami, FL
Levitt, Peter K. ....Washington, DC
Levitt, Peter S. ....Department of Justice,
Civil Division, GV
Levitt, Preston C. ....Plantation, FL
Levitt, Preston C., P.A. ....Plantation, FL
Levitt, Randall J. ....Rockville, MD
Levitt, Randy M. ....West Palm Beach, FL
Levitt, Renee S. ....Chicago, IL
Levitt, Richard Alan ......Huntington Woods, MI
Levitt, Richard S. ....Rockville, MD
Levitt, Richard W. ....New York, NY
Levitt, Robert A. ....Englewood, CO
Levitt, Robert A. ....Greensboro, NC
Levitt, Ronald A. ....Birmingham, AL
Levitt, Ronald S. ....Bridgewater, NJ
New Brunswick, NJ
Levitt, Russell D. ....New York, NY
Levitt, Ruth Lerner ....Mesa, AZ
Levitt, Samuel ....New York, NY
Levitt, Sandy Alan ....Sarasota, FL
Levitt, Sandy Alan, P.A. ....Sarasota, FL
Levitt, Sarah L. ....Washington, DC
Levitt, Scott J. ....Washington, DC
Levitt, Sheldon H. ....Owings Mills, MD
Levitt, Sidney B. ....Brooklyn, NY
Levitt, Sol ....Santa Barbara, CA
Levitt, Stanley W. ....Atlanta, GA
Levitt, Steven C. ....Trenton, NJ
Levitt, Susan B. ....Scottsdale, AZ
Levitt, Thomas C. ....Davis, CA
Levitt, V. David ....Mount Vernon, NY
Levitte, Carol A. ....Plymouth, MI
Levitte, Hal K. ....Boston, MA
Levitt-Vogel, Debra M. ......North Andover, MA
LeVitus, Kurt J. ....Chicago, IL
LeVitus Law Offices ....Chicago, IL
Albuquerque, NM
Levitz, Bruce J. ....San Francisco, CA
Levitz, Dana M. ....Towson, MD
Levitz, Howard J. ....New York, NY
Levitz, Jerome M. ....Ventura, CA
Levitz, Michael S. ....Minneapolis, MN
Levitz, Michelle S. ....Denver, CO
Levitz, Robert L. ....Stoughton, MA
Levitz, Stanley A. ....San Diego, CA
Levitz & Trossman ....New York, NY
Levitzky, Kenneth R. ....Dushore, PA
Levkoff, Irving ....Charleston, SC
Levkowicz, Sam ....New Orleans, LA
Levkowitz, Elayne ....Los Angeles, CA
Levkowitz, Howard M. ....Los Angeles, CA
Levner, Lawrence H. ....New York, NY
Levner, Nathan ....North Merrick, NY
Levoff, Philip S. ....Newton, MA
Levor, L. Ruth ....Cincinnati, OH
Levorchick, Joseph D. ....Smithtown, NY
LeVorse, Alexander P. ....Atlanta, GA
LeVorse, Alexander P., P.C. ....Atlanta, GA
LeVorse, Debra E. ....Atlanta, GA
Le Vota, Michael A. ....Kansas City, MO
LeVota, Philip Andrew ....Independence, MO
Levow, Evan M. ....Cherry Hill, NJ
Levowitz, Joyce E. ....New York, NY
Levoy, George E., III ....Natick, MA
LeVoy, Katherine A. ....Englewood, CO
Levstik, Steven ....San Diego, CA
Levstik, Timothy E. ....Chicago, IL
Levun, Charles R., Ltd. ....Chicago, IL
Northbrook, IL
Levun, Goodman & Cohen ....Chicago, IL
Northbrook, IL
Levun, Loretta K. ....Simi Valley, CA
Levun, Roy A. ....Los Angeles, CA
Levush, Ruth ....Library of Congress,
Law Library, GV
Levy, Aaron ....Washington, DC
Levy, Abe F. ....Los Angeles, CA
Levy, Abigail R. ....New York, NY
Levy, Abraham M. ....Atlantic City, NJ
Levy, Adam ....Carmel, NY
Levy, Adolph J. ....New Orleans, LA
Levy, Adrian F., Jr. ....Galveston, TX
Levy, Alan ....New York, NY
Levy, Alan C. ....Mineola, NY
Levy, Alan D. ....Pittsburgh, PA
Levy, Alan L. ....New York, NY
Levy, Alan M. ....Milwaukee, WI
Levy, Albert ....Plainview, NY
Levy, Albert ....Dallas, TX
Levy, Albert E. ....Newport Beach, CA
Levy, Albert E. ....Miami Beach, FL
Levy, Albert L. ....Passaic, NJ
Levy, Albert, P.C. ....Dallas, TX
Levy & Aldrich ....Silver Spring, MD
Levy, Alene Ross ....Houston, TX
Levy, Alexander ....Glendale, CA
Levy, Allen W. ....Department of Justice,
Civil Rights Division, GV
Levy, Allonn E. ....San Jose, CA
Levy, Amos M. ....New York, NY
Levy, Amy B. ....New Haven, CT
Levy, Amy Moss ....Norfolk, VA
Levy, Anat R. ....Los Angeles, CA
Levy, Andrea F. ....Bloomfield, CT
Levy, Andrew ....Encino, CA
Levy, Andrew D. ....Washington, DC
Levy, Andrew D. ....Boca Raton, FL
Levy, Andrew D. ....Baltimore, MD
Levy, Andrew Gary ....Crofton, MD
Levy, Andrew H. ....New York, NY
Levy, Andrew L. ....White Plains, NY
Levy, Andrew L. ....Harrisburg, PA
Levy, Angstreich, Finney, Baldante, Rubenstein & Coren, P.C.
Cherry Hill, NJ
Langhorne, PA
Philadelphia, PA
Levy, Ann M. ....Houston, TX
San Antonio, TX
Levy, Annabel Shull ....Houston, TX
Levy, Anne C. ....East Lansing, MI
Levy, Arden B. ....Department of the Army,
U.S. Army Legal Services Agency, GV
Levy, Arnold ....Washington, DC
Levy, Arnold I. ....Miami, FL
Levy, Arthur ....Media, PA
Levy, Arthur A. ....San Francisco, CA
Levy, Arthur D. ....San Francisco, CA
Levy, Arthur J. ....Phoenix, AZ
Levy, Arthur J. ....Brooklyn, NY
Levy, Arthur, Jr. ....Fairfield, CT
Levy, Arthur L. ....Princeton, NJ
Langhorne, PA
Levy & Associates, P.S. ....Seattle, WA
Levy & Augustine ....Chicago, IL
Levy, Aviva L. Weinbach ......Kew Gardens, NY
Levy, B. Joseph ....Atlanta, GA
Levy, Barbara Jo ....Seattle, WA
Levy, Barbra S. ....New York, NY
Levy, Barry D. ....Cincinnati, OH
Levy, Barry I. ....New York, NY
Levy, Barry R., (A P.C.) ....Los Angeles, CA
Levy, Barton S. ....Department of Justice,
Antitrust Division, GV
Levy, Ben G. ....Houston, TX
Levy, Benjamin ....New York, NY
Levy, Benjamin D. ....Miami Lakes, FL
Levy, Benjamin F. ....Philadelphia, PA
Levy, Benjamin J. ....Chesapeake, VA
Levy, Benton J. ....New York, NY
Levy, Bernard ....Jamaica Plain, MA
Levy, Bernard F. ....Houma, LA
Levy, Bernard M. ....Portland, OR
Levy, Berthold W. ....Melrose Park, PA
Levy, Bertram L. ....Atlanta, GA
Levy, Beth Alysse ....Bronx, NY
Levy, Beth C. ....New York, NY
Levy, B. H., Jr. ....Savannah, GA
Levy, Bonnie Gail ....Syracuse, NY
Levy Boonshoft & Lichtenberg, LLP
New York, NY
Levy, Brenda G. ....Boston, MA
Levy, Brett ....Boston, MA
Levy, Brian C. ....Mandeville, LA
Levy, Brian D. ....Coconut Grove, FL
Levy, Brian M. ....New York, NY
Levy, Brian S. ....Brown Deer, WI
Levy, Bruce A. ....Pikeville, KY
Levy, Bruce A. ....Newark, NJ
Levy, Bruce A. ....New York, NY
Levy, Bruce M., (P.C.) ....Houston, TX
Levy, Bruce T. ....Bedford Park, IL
Levy, Bryan Aric ....San Francisco, CA
Levy, Bryan H. ....Southfield, MI
Levy, Buddy J. ....Tampa, FL
Levy, Burton H. ....San Francisco, CA
Levy, C. Daniel ....Los Angeles, CA
Levy, Cara L. ....Philadelphia, PA
Levy, Carl B. ....Roseland, NJ
Levy, Carol Weiner ....New York, NY
Levy, Caroline ....Northport, NY
Levy, Caroline Krass ....New York, NY
Levy, Charles ....Chicago, IL
Levy, Charles G. ....Chicago, IL
Levy, Charles L. ....Waco, TX
Levy, Charles L. & Assoc. ....Waco, TX
Levy, Charles M. ....Treasury Department,
Internal Revenue Service, GV
Levy, Charles M. ....Coral Gables, FL
Levy, Charles M., (P.C.) ....Los Angeles, CA
Levy, Charles S. ....Washington, DC
Levy, Charlotte Lois ....Frankfort, KY
Levy, Claire B. ....Golden, CO
Levy, Clifford M. ....San Diego, CA
Levy, Coleman B. ....Farmington, CT

Levy and Craig, A Professional Corporation
Overland Park, KS
Kansas City, MO
Levy, Cynthia Hogue
Federal Trade Commission, Office of the General Counsel, GV
Levy, D. Bruce ... Miami, FL
Levy, Dale Penneys ... Philadelphia, PA
Levy, Dana M. ... Phoenix, AZ
Levy, Daniel C. B. ... Chatsworth, CA
Levy, Daniel W. ... New York, NY
Levy, Danielle M. ... New York, NY
Levy, Darryl H. ... Galveston, TX
League City, TX
Levy, David ... Newport Beach, CA
Levy, David ... Boulder, CO
Levy, David ... Atlanta, GA
Levy, David ... Jamaica Plain, MA
Levy, David A. ... Burlingame, CA
Levy, David A. ... Uniondale, NY
Levy, David B. ... New York, NY
Levy, David F. ... Chicago, IL
Levy, David H., (P.C.) ... Chicago, IL
Lake Forest, IL
Levy, David J. ... Martinez, CA
Levy, David J.
Research Triangle Park, NC
Levy, David J. ... Houston, TX
Levy, David J., & Joan L. Klemm
New York, NY
Levy, David L. ... Marina Del Rey, CA
Levy, David L. ... Miami, FL
Levy, David M. ... San Luis Obispo, CA
Levy, David M. ... Walnut Creek, CA
Levy, David M. ... Washington, DC
Levy, David M. ... New York, NY
Levy, David M. ... Rochester, NY
Levy, David M. ... Fairfax, VA
Levy, David R. ... St. Louis, MO
Levy, David S. ... Los Angeles, CA
Levy, David V. ... Atlanta, GA
Levy, Davis, Maher & Klein, LLP
New York, NY
Levy, Dawn L. ... New York, NY
Levy, Deborah L. ... Oakland, CA
Levy, Deborah M. ... Washington, DC
Levy, Deena P. ... New York, NY
Levy, Donald A. ... Northbrook, IL
Levy, Donald A. ... Cedarburg, WI
Levy, Donald A., Ltd., Law Office of
Northbrook, IL
Levy, Donald M. ... Cleveland, OH
Levy, Donald M., Jr. ... Encinitas, CA
Levy, Donna L. ... West Palm Beach, FL
Levy, Donna Marie ... Baltimore, MD
Levy, Dorit ... Los Angeles, CA
Levy, Douglas B. ... Tucson, AZ
Levy & Drangel ... Great Neck, NY
Levy & Droney, P.C. ... Farmington, CT
Hartford, CT
Levy & Dubovich ... Highland, IN
Levy, E. Robert ... Trenton, NJ
Levy, Earl ... Springfield, VA
Levy, Edgar S., III ... Washington, DC
Levy, Edith Engel ... Van Nuys, CA
Levy, Edward ... Sacramento, CA
Levy, Edward P. ... Department of Energy, Office of the General Counsel, GV
Levy, Edward S. ... West Caldwell, NJ
Levy, Edwin M. ... Chestnut Ridge, NY
Levy, Edwin M. ... New York, NY
Levy, Efrat ... Los Angeles, CA
Levy, Ehrlich & Petriello, A Professional Corporation ... Newark, NJ
Levy, Eileen C. ... Hamden, CT
Levy, Elizabeth A. ... Boston, MA
Levy, Elizabeth Levine R. ... Edwardsville, IL
Levy, Elwood S. ... Sarasota, FL
Levy, Eric S. ... Dallas, TX
Levy, Eugene ... North Merrick, NY
Levy, Eugene F. ... Kew Gardens, NY
Levy, Evan R. ... New York, NY
Levy, Farrell A. ... Knoxville, TN
Levy, Francine F. ... Highland Park, IL
Levy, Franklin H. ... Boston, MA
Levy, Fred L. ... Washington, DC
Levy, Frederic J. ... West Hempstead, NY
Levy, Frederic M. ... Washington, DC
Levy, Frederick A. ... Philadelphia, PA
Levy, Frederick I. ... White Plains, NY
Levy, Fredrick J. ... New York, NY
Levy, Gail ... Seattle, WA
Levy, Gary J. ... New York, NY
Levy, Gayle P. ... New York, NY
Levy, George ... Chicago, IL
Levy, George M. ... Newburgh, NY
Levy, Gerald ... Cape Coral, FL
Levy, Gerald ... Morristown, NJ
New York, NY
Levy, Gerald J. ... Milwaukee, WI
Levy, Gilbert H. ... Seattle, WA
Levy, Ginger L. ... South San Francisco, CA
Levy, Glenn D. ... Laredo, TX
Levy & Goodwin ... Columbia, SC
Levy, Gordon H. ... Baltimore, MD
Levy & Grandinetti ... Washington, DC
Levy, Greenfield & Davidoff, LLP
San Jose, CA
Levy, Gregg H. ... Washington, DC
Levy, Gregg S. ... Cleveland, OH
Levy, Gregory T. ... Forest Hills, NY
Levy, Gutman, Goldberg & Kaplan
New York, NY
Levy, H. Ben ... Cedarburg, WI
Levy, H. Irwin ... West Palm Beach, FL
Levy, H. Mark ... Baton Rouge, LA
Levy & Hamilton ... Seattle, WA
Levy, Harlan A. ... New York, NY
Levy, Harlan E. ... Oregon City, OR
Levy, Harlee Beth ... Rockville, MD
Levy, Harold A. ... Washington, DC
Levy, Harold J. ... Los Angeles, CA
Levy, Harold J. ... New York, NY
Levy, Harold J. ... Westbury, NY
Levy, Harold L. ... San Francisco, CA
Levy, Harold L. ... Brooklyn, NY
Levy, Harold L. ... Dallas, TX
Levy, Harold M. ... Hartford, CT
Levy, Harris ... New York, NY
Levy, Harry ... Baltimore, MD
Levy, Harry ... New York, NY
Levy, Harry H. ... Skokie, IL
Levy, Harry M. ... Chicago, IL
Levy, Helen C. ... New York, NY
Levy, Herbert I. ... Fresno, CA
Levy, Herbert L. ... Brooklyn, NY
Levy, Herbert Monte ... New York, NY
Levy, Herman ... Galesville, MD
Levy, Herman D. ... Falls Church, VA
Levy, Herman M. ... Santa Clara, CA
Levy, Howard A. ... Tarzana, CA
Levy, Howard A. ... New York, NY
Levy, Howard A. ... New York, NY
Levy, Howard A. ... Cleveland, OH
Levy, Howard S. ... West Covina, CA
Levy, Howard Yale ... New York, NY
Levy, I. Harrison ... Phoenix, AZ
Levy, I. Richard ... Addison, TX
Levy, I. Steven ... Philadelphia, PA
Levy, Ira A. ... Newark, NJ
Levy, Ira F. ... Dallas, TX
Levy, Ira Jay ... New York, NY
Levy, Ira S. ... White Plains, NY
White Plains, NY
Levy, Irving H. ... Northbrook, IL
Levy, Irwin ... New York, NY
Levy, Irwin A.
Agency for International Development, Other Offices of A.I.D., GV
Levy, Isaac L. ... Jacksonville, FL
Levy, Isaac L., P.A. ... Jacksonville, FL
Levy, Israel A. ... Sepulveda, CA
Levy, Ivan M. ... St. Paul, MN
Levy, J. Bertram ... Atlanta, GA
Levy, Jack ... Beverly Hills, CA
Levy, Jack ... Bronx, NY
Levy, Jack ... New York, NY
Levy, Jack ... Portland, OR
Levy, Jack Alan ... New York, NY
Levy, Jack B. ... Birmingham, AL
Levy, Jack, Inc. ... Beverly Hills, CA
Levy, Jack S. ... New York, NY
Levy, James L. ... St. Albans, VT
Levy, James L., P.C. ... St. Albans, VT
Levy, Jane A. ... Fort Lauderdale, FL
Levy, Janet E. ... Fort Worth, TX
Levy, Jason ... Boston, MA
Levy, Jason M. ... Boston, MA
Levy, Jay E. ... Columbia, MD
Towson, MD
Levy, Jay K. ... Chicago, IL
Levy, Jay M. ... Miami, FL
Levy, Jay M., P.A. ... Miami, FL
Levy, Jay W. ... New York, NY
Levy, Jean Wm. ... Atlanta, GA
Levy, Jeffrey A. ... Minneapolis, MN
Levy, Jeffrey A. ... New York, NY
Levy, Jeffrey D. ... Toledo, OH
Levy, Jeffrey H. ... Los Angeles, CA
Levy, Jeffrey L. ... Boston, MA
Levy, Jeffrey L. ... Nashville, TN
Levy, Jeffrey N. ... Great Neck, NY
Levy, Jennifer ...
Department of Justice, GV
Levy, Jennifer E. ... Department of Justice, Criminal Division, GV
Levy, Jennifer Elizabeth ... Los Angeles, CA
Levy, Jerome ... Bayonne, NJ
Levy, Jerome S. ... Dallas, TX
Levy, Jerome T. ... New York, NY
Levy, Jerrold M. ... Boca Raton, FL
Levy, Jerry K., Law Offices of
Lawrence, KS
Levy, Jessica Stone ... Seattle, WA
Levy, Jill Brodie ... Philadelphia, PA
Levy, Jill D. ... Miami, FL
Levy, Joan Lia ... New York, NY
Levy, JoAnne ... Chesterfield, MO
Levy, Joanne D. ... Wellesley, MA
Levy, Joe L. ... Coffeyville, KS
Levy, Joel A. ... Marrero, LA
Levy, Joel F. ... New York, NY
Levy, Joel G. ... Hartford, CT
Levy, Joel H. ... Washington, DC
Levy, Joel S. ... Sacramento, CA
Levy, Joelyn Knopf ... St. Louis, MO
Levy, John C. ... Minneapolis, MN
Levy, John C. ... New York, NY
Levy, John D. ... Tucson, AZ
Levy, John J. ... Cherry Hill, NJ
Philadelphia, PA
Levy, John M. ... Williamsburg, VA
Levy, John S. ... Lighthouse Point, FL
Levy, John S., P.A. ... Lighthouse Point, FL
Levy, Jon D. ... York, ME
Levy, Jonathan ... Palo Alto, CA
Levy, Jonathan A. ... Portland, OR
Levy, Jonathan B. ... Minneapolis, MN
Levy, Jonathan D. ... Chicago, IL
Levy, Jonathan H. ... Cincinnati, OH
Levy, Jonathan T. ... West Palm Beach, FL
Levy, Jonathan W. ... Chicago, IL
Levy, Joseph ... New York, NY
Levy, Joshua B. ... Milwaukee, WI
Levy, Joshua M. ... Miami, FL
West Palm Beach, FL
Levy, Joshua S. ... Boston, MA
Levy, Joyce A. ... Deerfield, IL
Levy, Joyce W. ... San Jose, CA
Levy, Judith ... New York, NY
Levy, Judith ... New York, NY
Levy, Judith A. ... Highland, IN
Levy, Judith M. ... Atlanta, GA
Levy, Jules E. ... New York, NY
Levy, Julie A. ... New York, NY
Levy, Julius ... New York, NY
Levy, Karen B. ... Lafayette, LA
Levy, Karen M. ... Scarsdale, NY
Levy, Karen Shaffer ... Boston, MA
Levy, Karen W. ... Bethesda, MD
Levy, Karen Weinhaus ... St. Louis, MO
Levy, Katherine J. ... Lake Forest, IL
Levy, Kathryn ... Albuquerque, NM
Levy, Keith B., Law Offices of
Juneau, AK
Levy, Kelly Catherine ... Oakland, CA
Levy, Kelly Klegar
Department of Commerce, National Telecommunications & Information Administration, GV
Levy, Kenneth L. ... Decatur, GA
Levy, Kenneth S. ... Cerritos, CA
Levy, Kenneth W. ... Elmwood Park, NJ
Levy, Kerri E. ... New York, NY
Levy, Kevin M. ... Miami, FL
Levy, Kim ... Palo Alto, CA
Levy, Kim ... Fort Myers, FL
Levy, Kirk B. ... Virginia Beach, VA
Levy, Kneen, Mariani, Curtin, Kornfeld & del Russo, Professional Association
Palm Beach, FL
West Palm Beach, FL
Levy & Lambdin, P.C. ... Denver, CO
Levy, Lance B. ... Waltham, MA
Levy, Larni S. ... Boston, MA
Levy, Larry E. ... Tallahassee, FL
Levy, Larry E. ... Tacoma, WA
Levy, Lauren D. ... Stamford, CT
Levy, Laurence A. ... Bronx, NY
Levy, Laurence D. ... Great Falls, VA
Levy Law Firm, The ... Tallahassee, FL
Levy Law Offices ... Boise, ID
Levy, Lawrence ... Denver, CO
Levy, Lawrence ... Hollywood, FL
Levy, Lawrence A. ... Coral Gables, FL
Levy, Lawrence A. ... Uniondale, NY
Levy, Lawrence I. ... Bellaire, TX
Levy, Lawrence M. ... Boston, MA
Levy, Lawrence S. ... Larkspur, CA
Levy, Lazard ... Marrero, LA
Levy, Leonard J. ... Bethesda, MD
Levy, Leonard L. ... New Haven, CT
Levy, Leonard L., P.C. ... New Haven, CT
Levy, Leonard M. ... Carmichael, CA
Levy, Leopold & Associates, P.C.
Chicago, IL
Levy, Leroy ... North Miami Beach, FL
Levy, Leslie A. ... Richmond, CA
Levy, Leslie F. ... Oakland, CA
Levy, Lester A. ... Dallas, TX
Levy, Lester J. ... San Francisco, CA
Levy, Lester L. ... New York, NY
Levy, Lester L., III ... Palo Alto, CA
Levy & Levy ... North Miami Beach, FL
Levy & Levy ... New York, NY
Levy, Levy & Levy, A Professional Corporation ... Larkspur, CA
San Francisco, CA
Levy & Levy, P.A. ... Voorhees, NJ
Levy & Levy, S.C. ... Cedarburg, WI
Levy, Lewis M. ... Columbia, SC
Levy & Licata, P.C. ... Rochester, NY
Levy, Lila F. ... Milford, PA
Levy, Lillian L. ... Binghamton, NY
Levy, Linda B. ... Berkeley, CA
Levy, Linda J. ... Freeport, NY
Levy, Linda J. ... Long Beach, NY
Levy, Lisa A. ... New York, NY
Levy, Loren E. ... Tallahassee, FL
Levy, Lori C. ... Los Angeles, CA
Levy, Lori J. ... New York, NY
Levy, Louis ... Tulsa, OK
Levy, Louis, Inc., A Professional Corporation
Tulsa, OK
Levy, Louis J. ... Washington, DC
Levy, Louis K. ... Youngstown, OH
Levy, Lowell K. ... Cedarburg, WI
Levy, Lybeck, Bertele & Beck, P.C.
Springfield, NJ
New York, NY
Levy, Lynn G. ... Horsham, PA
Levy, M. Barry ... Washington, DC
New York, NY
Levy, M. Raphael ... Dallas, TX
Levy, Madeleine R. ... Anchorage, AK
Levy, Marc C. ... Seattle, WA
Levy, Marc H. ... Louisville, KY
Levy, Marc Paul ... Washington, DC
Levy, Marc R. ... Denver, CO
Levy, Marc W. ... New York, NY
Levy, Marci Robin ... Livingston, NJ
Levy, Marcus ... Hallandale Beach, FL
Levy, Margaret ... Los Angeles, CA
Levy, Margaret P. ... Hartford, CT
Levy, Margaret R. ... Johnston, RI
Levy, Marie Louise ... Philadelphia, PA
Levy, Marilyn W. ... New York, NY
Levy & Marino, P.A. ... Towson, MD
Levy, Marjorie A. ... Beverly Hills, CA
Levy, Mark ... Binghamton, NY
Levy, Mark A. ... Miami, FL
Levy, Mark A. ... Edwardsville, IL
Levy, Mark A. ... Peabody, KS
Levy, Mark A. ... New York, NY
Levy, Mark Carlisle ... Philadelphia, PA
Levy, Mark F. ... West Palm Beach, FL
Levy, Mark I. ... Washington, DC
Levy, Mark J. ... Bronx, NY
Levy, Mark P. ... Larkspur, CA
Levy, Mark P. ... Dayton, OH
Levy, Mark R. ... Denver, CO
Levy, Mark S. ... Cherry Hill, NJ
Langhorne, PA
Philadelphia, PA
Levy, Mark W. ... West Hartford, CT
Levy, Martin ... Silver Spring, MD
Levy, Martin L. ... Houston, TX
Levy, Marvin ... Thousand Oaks, CA
Levy, Marvin W. ... New York, NY
Levy, Matthew A. ... Los Angeles, CA
Levy, Matthew David
North Miami Beach, FL
Levy, Matthew L. ... Los Angeles, CA
Levy, Mauri L. ... Fort Washington, PA
Levy, Maurice, Jr. ... Los Angeles, CA
Levy, Melvin H. ... Pittsburgh, PA
Levy, Micah A. ... Washington, DC
Levy, Michael A. ... San Francisco, CA
Levy, Michael A. ... South Plainfield, NJ
Levy, Michael A. ... Manhasset, NY
Levy, Michael A. ... New York, NY
Levy, Michael B. ... Denver, CO
Levy, Michael B. ... New York, NY
Levy, Michael E. ... Stafford, VA
Levy, Michael J. ... San Francisco, CA
Levy, Michael J. ... San Francisco, CA
Levy, Michael J. ... Louisville, KY
Levy, Michael K. ... Las Vegas, NV
Levy, Michael K. ... Philadelphia, PA
Levy, Michael L. ... Philadelphia, PA
Levy, Michael M. ... Washington, DC
Levy, Michael N. ... Washington, DC
Levy, Michael N. ... Chicago, IL
Levy, Michael R. ... San Jose, CA
Levy, Michael R. ... Washington, DC
Levy, Michael S. ... Washington, DC
Levy, Michael T. ... Omaha, NE
Levy, Michael W. ... Hartford, CT
Levy, Michele ... New York, NY
Levy, Michelle R. ... Boston, MA
Levy, Mildred Blitt ... Chicago, IL
Levy, Mindy A. ... New York, NY
Levy, Miryam ... Albuquerque, NM
Levy, Mitchell ... Los Angeles, CA
Levy, Mont S. ... Clayton, MO
Levy, Monty S. ... Atlanta, GA
Levy, Morris A. ... Chicago, IL
Levy, Nancy Sue ... Atlanta, GA
Levy, Natalie Turner ... New York, NY
Levy, Nathan A., Jr. ... Houma, LA
Levy, Nathan Cook ... Albany, GA
Levy, Nazila Y. ... Beverly Hills, CA
Levy, Neil I. ... Washington, DC
Levy, Neil L. ... Washington, DC
Levy, Neil M. ... Owings Mills, MD
Levy, Neill A. ... Chatsworth, CA
Levy, Norma B. ... New York, NY
Levy, Norman ... New York, NY
Levy, Norman D. ... Great Neck, NY
Levy, Ornah ... Irvine, CA
Levy, Paige A. ... McLean, VA
Levy, Patrick S. ... Saginaw, MI
Kansas City, MO
Levy, Paul A. ... Chicago, IL
Levy, Paul Alan ... Washington, DC
Levy, Paul E. ... Boise, ID
Levy, Paul G. ... Trenton, NJ
Levy, Paul M. ... Chicago, IL
Levy, Paul R. ... Battle Creek, MI
Levy, Paul S. ... Hempstead, NY
Levy, Paul S. ... New York, NY
Levy, Pauline ... Oak Brook, IL
Levy, Peter ... Port Washington, NY
Levy, Peter A. ... Chicago, IL
Levy, Peter A. ... Basking Ridge, NJ
Levy, Peter D. ... Ashland, KY
Levy, Peter H. ... Lynbrook, NY
Levy, Peter L. ... San Francisco, CA
Levy, Philip ... New York, NY
Levy, Philip A. ... Ewing, NJ
Levy, Phillip G. ... Boston, MA
Levy Phillips & Konigsberg, L.L.P.
New York, NY
Levy, Phyllis ... Tulsa, OK
Levy, Pollack, Ratner & Behroozi, P.C.
New York, NY
Levy & Preate ... Scranton, PA
Levy, R. Geoffrey ... Columbia, SC
Levy, Ralph B. ... Atlanta, GA
Levy, Ralph, III ... St. Louis, MO
Levy, Ralph Z., Jr. ... Nashville, TN
Levy, Ram & Olson LLP
San Francisco, CA
Levy, Raymond H. ... San Francisco, CA
Levy, Raymond H., Inc. ... San Francisco, CA
Levy, Richard A. ... Los Angeles, CA
Levy, Richard A. ... Torrance, CA
Levy, Richard A. ... Chicago, IL
Levy, Richard A. ... New York, NY
Levy, Richard A. ... Alexandria, VA
Levy, Richard B. ... Beverly Hills, CA
Levy, Richard B. ... Chicago, IL
Levy, Richard F., (P.C.) ... Chicago, IL
Levy, Richard H. ... Chicago, IL
Levy, Richard, Jr. ... New York, NY
Levy, Richard M. ... West Hartford, CT
Levy, Richard M. ... Brooklyn, NY
Levy, Richard Paul ... Los Angeles, CA
Levy, Robbin D. ... Grand Rapids, MI
Levy, Robert ... Los Angeles, CA
Levy, Robert ... New York, NY
Levy, Robert A. ... San Diego, CA

Levy, Robert A. ....Port Charlotte, FL
Levy, Robert A. ....Garden City, KS
Levy, Robert A. ....Minneapolis, MN
Levy, Robert A. ....Hackensack, NJ
New York, NY
Levy, Robert B. ....Liberty Corner, NJ
Levy, Robert C. ....Kansas City, MO
Levy, Robert D. ....Albuquerque, NM
Levy, Robert E. ....Hollywood, FL
Levy, Robert E. ....Secaucus, NJ
Levy, Robert E. ....New York, NY
Levy, Robert G. ....San Francisco, CA
Levy, Robert G. ....Washington, DC
Levy, Robert G. ....Alexandria, LA
Levy, Robert H. ....Nashville, TN
Levy, Robert J. ....Los Angeles, CA
Levy, Robert J. ....Minneapolis, MN
Levy, Robert L. ....Burr Ridge, IL
Levy, Robert L. ....New York, NY
Levy, Robert L. ....Houston, TX
Levy, Robert M. ....San Rafael, CA
Levy, Robert M. ....Brooklyn, NY
Levy, Robert M. ....Huntington, WV
Levy, Robert S. ....Beverly Hills, CA
Levy, Robert S. ....West Palm Beach, FL
Levy, Robert S. ....Cherry Hill, NJ
Bala Cynwyd, PA
Levy, Robert S. ....Commack, NY
Levy, Robert S. ....New York, NY
Levy, Robert S., P.A.
West Palm Beach, FL
Levy, Robert W. ....Ruston, LA
Levy, Roberta K. ....Minneapolis, MN
Levy, Rochelle S. ....San Francisco, CA
Levy, Roger ....New York, NY
Levy, Roger A., (A Professional Corporation)
San Francisco, CA
Levy, Roger B. ....Taunton, MA
Levy, Roger M. ....New Castle, DE
Levy, Ron K. ....Thousand Oaks, CA
Levy, Ronald C. ....Slidell, LA
Levy, Ronald G. ....North Miami Beach, FL
Levy, Ronald I. ....New York, NY
Levy, Ronald S. ....Treasury Department, Office of the General Counsel, GV
Levy, Ronald W. ....New York, NY
Levy, Ronniel ....New York, NY
Levy, Rosemary Sgroi ....Goshen, NY
Levy, S. David ....Washington, DC
Levy, S. Jerome ....Chicago, IL
Levy, Sally Kaplan ....Boston, MA
Levy, Samrick & O'Donnell, P.C.
San Francisco, CA
Levy, Samuel D. ....New York, NY
Levy, Samuel L. ....Denver, CO
Levy, Samuel R. ....Brooklyn, NY
Levy, Sanford R. ....Seattle, WA
Levy, Sanford S. ....Great Neck, NY
Levy, Sarah Harberg ....Trenton, TN
Levy, Sarah R. ....Boston, MA
Levy, Sarah Salter ....Columbus, OH
Levy, Saul ....New York, NY
Levy & Schneps, P.C. ....Manhasset, NY
Levy, Scott ....Chicago, IL
Levy, Scott D. ....Houston, TX
Levy, Seth A. ....Jersey City, NJ
Levy, Seth A. ....Newburgh, NY
Levy, Shari Eisenberg ....San Francisco, CA
Levy, Shari J. ....Bismarck, ND
Levy, Sharon L. ....Fairfield, CT
Levy, Sharon L. Bulbin ....Bridgeport, CT
Levy, Shelby H. ....Albany, GA
Levy, Sherri A. ....Setauket, NY
Levy, Sheryl S. ....Philadelphia, PA
Levy, Shirley A. ....Denver, CO
Levy, Sloane ....Greenwich, CT
Levy, Small & Lallas ....Los Angeles, CA
Levy & Sonet ....New York, NY
Levy, Stanley H. ....New York, NY
Levy, Stanley J. ....New York, NY
Levy, Stanley M. ....Highland, MD
Levy, Stanley W. ....Los Angeles, CA
Levy, Stanton L. ....East Brunswick, NJ
Levy, Stanton M. ....Fresno, CA
Levy, Stanton M., Law Corporation
Fresno, CA
Levy, Stefan C. ....Columbus, OH
Levy, Stephanie M. ....Los Angeles, CA
Levy, Stephen ....Chicago, IL
Levy, Stephen A. ....San Jose, CA
Levy, Stephen A. ....New York, NY
Levy, Stephen G. ....Albany, NY
Fishkill, NY
New York, NY
Levy, Stephen J. ....Chicago, IL
Levy, Stephen J. ....Brooklyn, NY
Levy, Stephen R. ....White Plains, NY
Levy, Steven ....Memphis, TN
Levy, Steven A. ....Fairfield, CT
Levy, Steven A. ....Chicago, IL
Levy, Steven B. ....Naperville, IL
Levy, Steven B., Ltd. ....Naperville, IL
Wheaton, IL
Levy, Steven E. ....Encino, CA
Levy, Steven E. ....Los Angeles, CA
Levy, Steven E. ....Washington, DC
Levy, Steven H. ....Torrington, CT
Levy, Steven Louis ....Germantown, TN
Levy, Steven M. ....Chicago, IL
Levy, Steven Mark ....Los Angeles, CA
Levy, Steven R. ....Morgan Hill, CA
Levy, Steven R. ....Tacoma, WA
Levy, Stewart L. ....New York, NY
Levy, Stieh & Blumberg ....Milford, PA
Levy & Stopol, LLP ....New York, NY
Levy, Stuart ....Northridge, CA
Levy, Stuart P. ....Brooklyn, NY
Levy, Stuart S. ....Department of Commerce, Patent and Trademark Office, GV
Levy, Sue Barbara S. ....New York, NY
Levy, Susan B. ....Boulder, CO
Levy, Susan C. ....Chicago, IL
Levy, Susan J. ....New York, NY
Levy, Susan M. ....New York, NY
Levy, Susan M. ....New York, NY
Levy, Susan May ....Oakbrook Terrace, IL
Levy, Susan W. ....Great Neck, NY
Levy, Sylvia S. ....Houston, TX
Levy, Teresa L. ....Sacramento, CA
Levy, Teresa M. ....Milwaukee, WI
Levy, Terry R. ....Jackson, MS
Levy, Thellen, Law Offices of
San Francisco, CA
Levy, Theodore S. ....New York, NY
Levy, Thomas B. ....Columbia, SC
Levy, Thomas R. ....New York, NY
Levy, Thomas R. ....New York, NY
Levy, Timothy J. ....Washington, DC
Levy, Todd Michael ....Muttontown, NY
Levy & Tolman ....New York, NY
Levy, Tracey I. ....New York, NY
Levy, Trudy B.
Department of Transportation, Federal Transit Administration, GV
Levy, Victor ....Portland, OR
Levy, W. Byron ....San Mateo, CA
Levy, W. Byron, A Prof. Corp.
San Mateo, CA
Levy, Wallace H. ....Lowell, MA
Levy, Warren D. ....Philadelphia, PA
Levy, William ....Indianapolis, IN
Levy, William A. ....Chicago, IL
Levy, William Aran ....Las Vegas, NV
Levy, William C. ....Washington, DC
Levy, William D. ....Memphis, TN
Levy, William M. ....Towson, MD
Levy, William N. ....Voorhees, NJ
Levy, William R. ....Philadelphia, PA
Levy • Winer, P.C. ....Greenfield, MA
Levy, Yale R. ....Columbus, OH
Levy, Zachary ....Hicksville, NY
Levy & Zeewy, LLC ....Atlanta, GA
Levy-Dino, Lila F. ....Port Jervis, NY
Levy-McNamara, Deena Rachelle
West Palm Beach, FL
Levyn, Thomas S. ....Los Angeles, CA
Levy-Warren, Jay P. ....New York, NY
Levy-Weinstein, Dawn C. ....Brooklyn, NY
Lew, Avi ....New York, NY
Lew, Branch R. ....Fort Wayne, IN
Lew, Carol L. ....Newport Beach, CA
Lew, Daniel K. ....Duluth, MN
Lew, Darryl S. ....Richmond, VA
Lew, David ....River Edge, NJ
New York, NY
Lew, Debra D. ....San Francisco, CA
Lew, Edward W. ....Los Angeles, CA
Lew, Elana Teitelman ....New York, NY
Lew, Elizabeth G. ....Iowa City, IA
Lew, Ernest Paul ....San Francisco, CA
Lew, Garrick S. ....San Francisco, CA
Lew, Gary H. ....Nampa, ID
Lew, Henry ....Los Angeles, CA
Lew, Jacob J.
Executive Office Of The President, Office of Management and Budget, GV
Lew, Jeffrey C. ....Wilmington, DE
Lew, Jennifer B. ....Boston, MA
Lew, Jin N. ....Manhattan Beach, CA
Lew, Jocelyne J. Kim, A Prof. Law Corp., Law Offices of ....Redwood City, CA
Lew, Jocelyne J. K. ....Redwood City, CA
Lew, Jonathan ....Oakland, CA
Lew, Judy ....Monterey Park, CA
Lew, Kimberley M. ....Seattle, WA
Lew, Mabel ....West Sacramento, CA
Lew, Mae J. ....Boston, MA
Lew, Marilyn E. ....Buffalo, NY
Lew, Mark ....San Jose, CA
Lew, Mela ....Waltham, MA
Lew, Michael I. ....Chicago, IL
Lew, Michael S. ....Glendale, CA
Lew, Michele Marie ....New York, NY
Lew, Nancy ....Salt Lake City, UT
Lew, Oliverio ....New York, NY
Lew, Pamela ....Treasury Department, Internal Revenue Service, GV
Lew, Ronald S. W. ....Los Angeles, CA
Lew, Stephen ....Los Angeles, CA
Lew, Susan ....San Francisco, CA
Lew, Walter Gene ....Wausau, WI
Lew, Waymond ....Glendale, CA
Lew, Wayne W. ....San Jose, CA
Lewald, George H. ....Boston, MA
Lewald, Susanne ....San Francisco, CA
Lewallen, Cynthia T. ....Torrance, CA
Lewallen, David L. ....Fort Worth, TX
LeWallen, Dawn ....Denver, CO
Lewallen, Jo Betsy, Law Offices of
Austin, TX
Lewallen, Joe C., Jr. ....Oklahoma City, OK
Lewallen, Monica Suzanne ....Fisherville, VA
Lewallen, Robert Alvin, Jr.
Savannah, GA
Lewallen, Stephen B. ....Naples, FL
Lewallen, Stephen B., P.A. ....Naples, FL
Lewallen, W. Buford ....Knoxville, TN
Lewan, Daniel M. ....Brooksville, FL
Lewan, Matthew J. ....Vallejo, CA
Lewand, F. Thomas ....Detroit, MI
Lewand, Kevin O. ....Santa Ana, CA
Lewand, Kimberly E. ....Los Angeles, CA
Lewandos, Noel Anne ....Houston, TX
Lewandoski, Mark J. ....Wausau, WI
Lewandoski, Wanda M.
Department Of Health And Human Services, Social Security Administration, GV
Lewandowski, Alex M. ....Kansas City, MO
Lewandowski, Brian D. ....Denver, CO
Lewandowski, Brian N. ....Buffalo, NY
Lewandowski, Daniel F. ....Cheektowaga, NY
Lewandowski, David S. ....Hamburg, NY
Lewandowski, Dennis T. ....Norfolk, VA
Lewandowski, Dona ....Raleigh, NC
Lewandowski, James F. ....Plymouth, MI
Lewandowski, John A. ....Escanaba, MI
Lewandowski, Kurt S. ....Newark, NJ
Lewandowski Law Firm, The, A Professional Corporation ....Kansas City, MO
Lewandowski, Lynne ....Brattleboro, VT
Lewandowski, Mark C. ....Hackensack, NJ
Lewandowski, Mark S. ....Phoenix, AZ
Lewandowski, Michael T. ....New York, NY
Lewandowski, Richard G. ....Troy, MI
Lewandowski, Richard J. ....Madison, WI
Lewandowski, Rita L. ....Chicago, IL
Lewandowski, Robert G.
Birmingham, MI
Troy, MI
Lewandowski, Robert M.
Mount Pleasant, PA
Lewandowski, Susan Maria
Sterling Heights, MI
Lewandowski, Thomas P. ....Akron, OH
Lewandowski, William J. ....Buffalo, NY
Lewane, Michele S. ....Richmond, VA
Lewanski, David J., Jr ....Willoughby, OH
Lewarne, John R. ....Rock Island, IL
Lewbart, Daniel T. ....Philadelphia, PA
Lewbel, Steven I. ....Jersey City, NJ
New York, NY
Lewczak, Joseph J. ....New York, NY
Lewellan, Gail I. ....St. Paul, MN
Lewellen, Carolyn ....Hot Springs, NC
Lewellen & Frazier, P.L.L.C.
Little Rock, AR
Lewellen, George M. ....Redding, CA
Lewellen, JoAnne F. ....Minneapolis, MN
Lewellen, Marsha R. ....Kansas City, MO
Lewellen, Royce R. ....Santa Maria, CA
Lewellen, Todd A. ....Little Rock, AR
Lewellyan, Ronald L. ....Columbia, LA
Lewellyn, Bruce ....New Haven, CT
Lewellyn, Jeffrey A. ....Terre Haute, IN
Lewellyn, Larry D., Law Offices of
Los Angeles, CA
Lewellyn, Stephen K. ....Culpeper, VA
Lewellyn, Thomas G. ....Alameda, CA
Lewen, Bert J. ....New York, NY
Lewen, Stephen ....Palm City, FL
Lewenberg, Franklin ....Newton, MA
Lewenberg, Roger S. ....Boston, MA
Lewenberg, Sara ....Boston, MA
Lewenberg, Stephen S. ....Boston, MA
Lewendon, Whitney M. ....New Haven, CT
Lewengrub, Steven J. ....Atlanta, GA
Lewensohn, Leonard J. ....Milwaukee, WI
Lewerenz, Sarah ....Duluth, MN
Lewers, Catherine R.
Department of Commerce, National Oceanic and Atmospheric Administration, GV
Lewers, Cornett L. ....White Plains, NY
Lewers, Joanne C. ....Washington, DC
Lewers, Robert O. ....Wayne, PA
Lewert, Adam E. ....Wheeling, IL
Lewey, Margaret L. ....San Diego, CA
Lewey, Virginia S. ....Chicago, IL
Lewi, Christopher C. ....Costa Mesa, CA
Los Angeles, CA
Lewi, Peter A. ....Solana Beach, CA
Lewicki, Elizabeth Krystyna
Shingle Springs, CA
Lewicki, Leonard P. ....Seattle, WA
Lewicki, Margaret T. ....Truckee, CA
Lewicki, Peter S. ....Seattle, WA
Lewiecki, Paige Anders ....Arlington, TX
Lewiecki, Stanley F. ....Dallas, TX
Lewin, Alyza D. ....Washington, DC
Lewin, Andrea J. ....San Francisco, CA
Lewin, Andrew E. ....New York, NY
Lewin, Barry E. ....Phoenix, AZ
Lewin, Bradford A. ....Madison, NJ
Lewin, Chad M. ....Sherman Oaks, CA
Lewin, Cynthia M. ....Alexandria, VA
Lewin, David M. ....Chicago, IL
Lewin, Genia Stacy ....Bel Air, MD
Lewin, Geoffrey ....Los Angeles, CA
Lewin, Harley I. ....New York, NY
Lewin, Henry ....Los Angeles, CA
Lewin, Herbert M. ....Chicago, IL
Lewin, James F. ....El Cajon, CA
Lewin, Jay ....New York, NY
Lewin, Jeff L. ....Morgantown, WV
Lewin, Jeffrey D. ....San Diego, CA
Lewin, Joel ....Boston, MA
Providence, RI
Lewin, John ....New York, NY
Lewin, John Henry, Jr., (P.C.)
Baltimore, MD
Lewin, K. Tamar ....New York, NY
Lewin, Kurt J. ....Los Angeles, CA
Lewin, Lawrin S. ....Los Angeles, CA
Lewin, Lee J. ....Northbrook, IL
Lewin & Lewin, A Partnership of Professional Corp. ....Los Angeles, CA
Lewin & Lewin ....Malden, MA
Lewin, Lucien G. ....Martinsburg, WV
Lewin, Malcolm I. ....New York, NY
Lewin, Martin J. ....Washington, DC
Lewin, Matthew R. ....Chicago, IL
Lewin, Michael J. ....Redlands, CA
San Bernardino, CA
Lewin, Nathan ....Washington, DC
Lewin, Norman A. ....Glendale, CA
Lewin, Paul ....Miami, FL
Lewin, Richard H. ....Simsbury, CT
Lewin, Robert ....New York, NY
Lewin, Robert D. ....Malden, MA
Lewin, Robert S. ....Laguna Beach, CA
Lewin, Robert S., A Law Corporation
Laguna Beach, CA
Lewin, Rodney T. ....Beverly Hills, CA
Lewin, Ross A. ....Princeton, NJ
Lewin & Schneider, P.C. ....Phoenix, AZ
Lewin, Stuart F. ....Great Falls, MT
Lewin, Thomas G. ....St. Louis, MO
Lewin, Travis H. ....Syracuse, NY
Lewin, Werner S., Jr. ....Novato, CA
Lewine, Alan R. ....Washington, DC
LeWine, Jerome M. ....New York, NY
Lewine, Stuart Alan ....Westbury, NY
Lewinger, Esther D. (Shana)
New York, NY
Lewinger, Robert J. ....New York, NY
Lewington, Mark C. ....Tacoma, WA
LeWinn, Laura M. ....Cranford, NJ
LeWinn, Laura M.
Princeton Junction, NJ
Lewins, Richard A. ....Dallas, TX
Lewin Sacks, Carol ....Phoenix, AZ
Lewinski & Brewster, P.C. ....Marquette, MI
Sault Ste. Marie, MI
Lewinski, Guy W. ....Marquette, MI
Sault Ste. Marie, MI
Lewinski, Joseph M. ....Atlanta, GA
Lewinski, Michael J. ....Indianapolis, IN
Lewinski, Richard R. ....Troy, MI
Lewinson, Barbara Kaplan
East Brunswick, NJ
Lewinson, Robert C. ....Atlanta, GA
Lewinstein, Stephen R. ....Newport, RI
LeWinter, Anthony A. ....Encino, CA
Lewinter, David J. ....New York, NY
LeWinter, Jonathan S. ....New York, NY
LeWinter, Kevin M. ....Las Vegas, NV
Lewinter, Linda B. ....Roseland, NJ
LeWinter, Mark ....New York, NY
Lewinter, Mark J. ....Bala Cynwyd, PA
LeWinter & Rosman, A Professional Corporation ....Encino, CA
Lewis, A. Bart ....Birmingham, MI
Lewis, A. Camden ....Columbia, SC
Lewis, A. Churchill Ripley ....Baltimore, MD
Lewis, A. Eugene ....Tallahassee, FL
Lewis, A. Lisa Merklin ....Minneapolis, MN
Lewis, Adam A. ....San Francisco, CA
Lewis, Adam F. ....Chicago, IL
Lewis, Adam McLean ....New York, NY
Lewis, Adam N. ....Boston, MA
Lewis, Adam S. ....Chicago, IL
Lewis, A. J., Jr. ....San Antonio, TX
Lewis, Alan I. ....San Francisco, CA
Lewis, Alan L. ....Boston, MA
Lewis, Alan M. ....Stockton, CA
Lewis, Alan M. ....Stamford, CT
Lewis, Alan R. ....Newburgh, NY
Lewis, Alan S. ....New York, NY
Lewis, Albert B. ....St. Petersburg, FL
Lewis, Albert B. ....New York, NY
Lewis, Albert G., III ....Tuscaloosa, AL
Lewis, Albert L. ....Orlando, FL
Lewis, Albert M. ....Basking Ridge, NJ
Lewis, Albert Z., Jr. ....Arlington, VA
Lewis, Alden Travis ....Brooklyn, NY
Lewis, Alec M. ....Rockville, MD
Lewis, Alexander ....Huntington Park, CA
Lewis, Alexander ....New York, NY
Lewis, Alexander I., III (P.C.)
Baltimore, MD
Towson, MD
Lewis, Alfred B. ....Boston, MA
Lewis, Alfred J. ....Davis, CA
Lewis, Algie R. ....Washington, DC
Lewis, Alisa D. ....New York, NY
Lewis, Alison ....Phoenix, AZ
Lewis, Alison J. ....Hewlett, NY
Lewis, Allan M. ....Buffalo, NY
Niagara Falls, NY
Olean, NY
Lewis, Allen J. ....Gobles, MI
Lewis & Allen, P.C. ....Battle Creek, MI
Kalamazoo, MI
Lewis, Alphonse, Jr. ....Grand Rapids, MI
Lewis, Alton B., Jr. ....Hammond, LA
Lewis, Alvin B., Jr. ....Lancaster, PA
Lewis, Amy C. ....Tacoma, WA
Lewis, Amy L. ....Fairmont, WV
Lewis, Amy W. ....Los Angeles, CA
Lewis, Ancel W., Jr., (P.C.) ....Denver, CO
Fort Collins, CO
Lewis, Ancel W., Jr., P.C., Law Offices of
Fort Collins, CO
Lewis & Anderson, P.C. ....Chapel Hill, NC
Lewis, Andrew A. ....Marietta, GA
Lewis, Andrew D. ....New York, NY
Lewis, Andrew G. ....Eugene, OR
Lewis, Andrew I. ....Hollywood, FL
Lewis, Andrew J. ....Tampa, FL
Lewis, Andy D. ....Chattanooga, TN
Lewis, Anette Seltzer ....Wayland, MA
Lewis, Ann E. ....New York, NY
Lewis, Ann Marie ....Seattle, WA
Lewis, Anna ....New York, NY
Lewis, Anne E. ....Victorville, CA
Lewis, Anne Harrison ....Pittsburgh, PA
Lewis, Anne L. ....New Orleans, LA
Lewis, Anne M. ....Washington, DC
Lewis, Anne N. Awtrey ....Bethesda, MD

Lewis, Huppert & Slovak, P.C. ... **Great Falls, MT**
Lewis & Hutchison, P.C. ... **Fort Worth, TX**
Lewis, I. Norman ... Honolulu, HI
Lewis, Ira M. ... Plainsboro, NJ
Lewis, Irving ... Chicago, IL
Lewis, J. Allen, Jr. ... Florence, SC
Lewis, J. Brad ... **Portland, OR**
Lewis, J. Christian ... Lafayette, LA; New Orleans, LA; Beaumont, TX
Lewis, J. Craig ... **Birmingham, AL**
Lewis, J. Curtis, III ... **Savannah, GA**
Lewis, J. David ... **Lillington, NC**
Lewis, J. Dean ... Spotsylvania, VA
Lewis, J. Douglas ... Fairfax, VA
Lewis, J. Gordon ... Auburn Hills, MI
Lewis, J. Harvey ... Dallas, TX
Lewis, J. Kenny ... San Francisco, CA
Lewis, J. Mark ... Jonesboro, AR
Lewis, J. Michael ... Pine Bluff, AR
Lewis, J. Michael ... **Stamford, CT**
Lewis, J. Otis ... Alamosa, CO
Lewis, J. Scott ... **Wilmington, NC**
Lewis, J. Stephen ... Hollywood, CA
Lewis, J. Stephen ... **Savannah, GA**
Lewis, J. William ... **Birmingham, AL**
Lewis, J. Woodrow ... Darlington, SC
Lewis, Jack ... Brooklyn, NY
Lewis, Jack A. ... North Kansas City, MO
Lewis, Jack L. ... **Great Falls, MT**
Lewis, Jack L. ... **McLean, VA**
Lewis, Jack M. ... Clinton, AR
Lewis, Jack S. ... **Miami, FL**
Lewis, Jacob M. ... Department of Justice, Civil Division, GV
Lewis, Jacqueline ... Columbus, OH
Lewis, Jacqueline A. ... Philadelphia, PA
Lewis, Jacqueline Thorne ... Philadelphia, PA
Lewis, Jacques C. ... Hartford, CT
Lewis, James A. ... Springfield, IL
Lewis, James A. ... Helena, MT
Lewis, James A. ... **Pittsburgh, PA**
Lewis, James B. ... **Las Vegas, NV**
Lewis, James B. ... New York, NY
Lewis, James B. ... Nashville, TN
Lewis, James B. ... **Houston, TX**
Lewis, James Boyd ... **San Francisco, CA**
Lewis, James Bryan ... **Nashville, TN**
Lewis, James C. ... Isonville, KY
Lewis, James C. ... Lubbock, TX
Lewis, James C. ... **Salt Lake City, UT**
Lewis, James C. ... **Norfolk, VA**
Lewis, James D. ... Ann Arbor, MI
Lewis, James E., Jr. ... San Jose, CA
Lewis, James Edward ... **Waukesha, WI**
Lewis, James F. ... **Modesto, CA**
Lewis, James F. ... Warren, OH
Lewis, James G. ... Los Angeles, CA
Lewis, James H. ... Birmingham, AL
Lewis, James H. ... Douglasville, GA
Lewis, James H. ... Carolina Beach, NC
Lewis, James K. ... **Chicago, IL**
Lewis, James L. ... **Washington, DC**
Lewis, James L. ... Washington, DC
Lewis, James L. ... Schuylkill Haven, PA
Lewis, James M. ... **South Bend, IN**
Lewis, James M. ... Attleboro, MA
Lewis, James M. ... **McLean, VA**
Lewis, James M., P.C. ... Attleboro, MA
Lewis, James N., Sr. ... Conyers, GA
Lewis, James P. ... Dallas, TX
Lewis, James R. ... Tustin, CA
Lewis, James R. ... Denver, CO
Lewis, James R. ... **Baton Rouge, LA**; Lafayette, LA
Lewis, James S., Jr. ... Fort Lauderdale, FL
Lewis, James T. Blaine ... **Louisville, KY**
Lewis, James W. ... Los Angeles, CA
Lewis, James W. ... **Columbus, OH**
Lewis, James W. ... Jacksonville, OR
Lewis, Jan Alan ... **Hackensack, NJ**
Lewis, Jan Henrie ... Denton, TX
Lewis, Jane Kenworthy ... Boston, MA
Lewis, Janet ... Salt Lake City, UT
Lewis, Janet Quick ... **Atlanta, GA**; **Greenville, SC**
Lewis, Janice Ann ... **Hicksville, NY**
Lewis, Janith Alyssa ... Wichita, KS
Lewis, Jannie M. ... Lexington, MS
Lewis, Jason A. ... **New York, NY**
Lewis, Jason S. ... **Dallas, TX**
Lewis, Jay ... Montgomery, AL
Lewis, Jay W. ... Pittsburgh, PA
Lewis, J. D., III ... Stuart, FL
Lewis, J. D. Jeff ... Abilene, TX
Lewis, Jean Price ... Novato, CA
Lewis, Jefferson ... Petersburg, IL
Lewis, Jeffery C. ... **Texarkana, TX**
Lewis, Jeffrey ... **Irvine, CA**
Lewis, Jeffrey D. ... Los Angeles, CA
Lewis, Jeffrey D. ... Landover, MD
Lewis, Jeffrey E. ... Gainesville, FL
Lewis, Jeffrey E. ... Pensacola, FL
Lewis, Jeffrey E. ... **Chicago, IL**
Lewis, Jeffrey G. ... **Oakland, CA**
Lewis, Jeffrey I. D. ... **New York, NY**
Lewis, Jeffrey James ... **Los Angeles, CA**
Lewis, Jeffrey L. ... **Sycamore, IL**
Lewis, Jeffrey M. ... Washington, DC
Lewis, Jeffrey M. ... **Columbus, OH**
Lewis, Jeffrey O. ... **Indianapolis, IN**
Lewis, Jeffrey P. ... **Philadelphia, PA**
Lewis, Jeffrey R. ... Cincinnati, OH
Lewis, Jeffrey S. ... **New York, NY**
Lewis, Jeffrey S. ... Spring Valley, NY
Lewis, Jeffrey Y. ... **Atlanta, GA**
Lewis, Jennifer B. ... Raleigh, NC
Lewis, Jennifer Cook ... **Los Angeles, CA**
Lewis, Jennifer Lynne ... Merriam, KS
Lewis, Jennifer W. ... **Washington, DC**
Lewis, Jerome H. ... Minneapolis, MN
Lewis, Jerome J. ... New York, NY
Lewis, Jerome R. ... Sacramento, CA
Lewis, Jerome X. ... Maynard, MA
Lewis, Jerry C. ... McKinney, TX
Lewis, Jerry L. ... College Park, MD
Lewis, Jessica M. ... **Tampa, FL**
Lewis, Jill B. ... Chicago, IL
Lewis, J. K. ... Pittsburgh, PA
Lewis, Jo Ellen D. ... St. Louis, MO
Lewis, Joan ... Los Angeles, CA
Lewis, Joanne ... New Britain, CT
Lewis, Jodi M. ... **Los Angeles, CA**
Lewis, Joe, Attorney, P.C. ... **Colonial Heights, VA**
Lewis, Joe Henry ... Temple City, CA
Lewis, Joe K. ... Marion, IN
Lewis, Johanna ... Los Angeles, CA
Lewis, John ... San Francisco, CA
Lewis, John ... Houghton, MI
Lewis, John A. ... San Fernando, CA
Lewis, John A. ... Wallkill, NY
Lewis, John Alan ... **Fort Smith, AR**
Lewis, John B. ... **Sacramento, CA**
Lewis, John B. ... St. Louis, MO
Lewis, John B. ... **Cleveland, OH**
Lewis, John B. ... Hillsboro, OR
Lewis, John B., Jr. ... Raleigh, NC
Lewis, John C., III ... Hartford, CT
Lewis, John D. ... **Tempe, AZ**
Lewis, John D. ... Brooklyn, NY
Lewis, John D., P.C. ... **Tempe, AZ**
Lewis, John Dean ... Knoxville, PA; **Wellsboro, PA**
Lewis, John E. ... Reno, NV
Lewis, John F. ... **Cleveland, OH**
Lewis, John F. ... **Norristown, PA**; **Philadelphia, PA**
Lewis, John F., Jr. ... Wellesley, MA
Lewis, John G. ... **Denver, CO**
Lewis, John G. ... Alexandria, VA
Lewis, John G., Jr. ... Statesville, NC
Lewis, John H. ... **Atlanta, GA**
Lewis, John H. ... **Indianapolis, IN**
Lewis, John H. ... Grove City, OH; Westerville, OH
Lewis, John H., Jr. ... **Philadelphia, PA**
Lewis, John, Jr. ... **Kansas City, MO**
Lewis, John L., III ... Powhatan, VA
Lewis, John M. ... Seymour, IN
Lewis, John M. ... Manchester, NH
Lewis, John Malachi ... **Hickory, NC**
Lewis, John M. B., IV ... **Martinez, GA**
Lewis, John N. ... **Boston, MA**
Lewis, John N. ... **Grand Rapids, MI**
Lewis, John P. ... Grand Rapids, MI
Lewis, John P., Jr. ... **Dallas, TX**
Lewis, John Q. ... **Cleveland, OH**
Lewis, John R. ... Sacramento, CA
Lewis, John R. ... Carle Place, NY
Lewis, John R. ... Lynchburg, VA
Lewis, John R., (P.C.) ... Springfield, MO
Lewis, John Randall ... Palo Alto, CA
Lewis, John Robert, Jr. ... Natural Bridge, VA
Lewis, John S. ... Santa Clara, CA
Lewis, John S. ... Cartersville, GA
Lewis, John S. ... Schuylkill Haven, PA
Lewis, John T. ... **Houston, TX**
Lewis, John W. ... **Fort Myers, FL**
Lewis, John W. ... **Mount Pleasant, MI**
Lewis, John W. ... **Nashville, TN**
Lewis, John W., II ... **Pittsburgh, PA**
Lewis, Johs, Avallone, Aviles & Kaufman ... **Melville, NY**
Lewis, Jon E. ... **Birmingham, AL**
Lewis, Jon M. ... Kingston, NY
Lewis, Jon M. ... **Greensburg, PA**
Lewis, Jonathan C. ... Delaware, OH
Lewis, Jonathan F. ... **New York, NY**
Lewis, Jonathan H. ... **New York, NY**
Lewis, Jonathan M. ... **Hartford, CT**
Lewis, Joni Gaylor ... Houston, TX
Lewis, Jordan D. ... Terre Haute, IN
Lewis, Jordan M. ... **Minneapolis, MN**
Lewis, Joseph ... Los Angeles, CA
Lewis, Joseph D. ... **Washington, DC**
Lewis, Joseph E. ... **Reading, PA**
Lewis, Joseph F. ... Grass Valley, CA
Lewis, Joseph G. ... **Reading, PA**
Lewis, Joseph Gerard ... Duxbury, MA
Lewis, Joseph, Jr. ... Tallahassee, FL
Lewis, Joseph K., Jr. ... **Kansas City, MO**
Lewis, Joseph L. ... **Colonial Heights, VA**
Lewis, Joseph Leo ... Timonium, MD
Lewis, Joseph M. ... New Brighton, PA
Lewis, Joseph P. ... Lakewood, CO
Lewis, Josephine E. ... Irvine, CA
Lewis, Joyce Staat ... **Chicago, IL**
Lewis, Judith A. ... Pittsburgh, PA
Lewis, Judith Kemper ... Boulder, CO
Lewis, Julie ... **Rochester, NY**
Lewis, Julie E. ... Cleveland, OH
Lewis, Julie E. ... Alexandria, VA
Lewis, Julie R. ... **Dayton, OH**
Lewis, Julius ... **Chicago, IL**
Lewis Kaehler Bates & Angle LLP ... Schenectady, NY
Lewis & Kappes, Professional Corporation ... **Indianapolis, IN**
Lewis, Kara Kantor ... **Morristown, NJ**
Lewis, Karen A. ... **New York, NY**
Lewis, Karen B. ... Beaumont, TX
Lewis, Karen E. ... **Tampa, FL**
Lewis, Karen J. ... Library of Congress, Congressional Research Service, GV
Lewis, Karen Judd ... **Washington, DC**
Lewis, Karen Lee ... **New Orleans, LA**
Lewis, Karen M. ... **San Bernardino, CA**
Lewis, Karen R. ... Faribault, MN
Lewis, Karen Robbins ... **Olney, MD**
Lewis, Karen Robbins ... **Rockville, MD**
Lewis, Karen S. ... Haddonfield, NJ
Lewis, Karl B. ... Renton, WA
Lewis, Karl E., Jr. ... Houma, LA
Lewis, Katharine F. ... Boston, MA
Lewis, Katharine R. ... San Francisco, CA
Lewis, Katherine ... DeWitt, MI
Lewis, Katherine A. ... Baltimore, MD
Lewis, Katherine A. ... Vancouver, WA
Lewis, Katherine Dumas ... Department of Labor, Pension and Welfare Benefits, GV
Lewis, Katherine G. ... Atlanta, GA
Lewis, Katherine M. ... **Raleigh, NC**
Lewis, Kathleen Ann ... Cheyenne, WY
Lewis, Kathleen Gallagher ... Livonia, MI
Lewis, Kathleen McCree ... **Detroit, MI**
Lewis, Kathy Evans ... Memphis, TN
Lewis, Kay M. ... Salt Lake City, UT
Lewis, Keith M. ... Lakeville, MN
Lewis, Keith W. ... San Francisco, CA
Lewis, Kelly R. ... East Stroudsburg, PA
Lewis, Kelly W. ... **Phoenix, AZ**
Lewis, Kemp S. ... Farmington, NM
Lewis, Kenneth ... Federal Deposit Insurance Corporation, Professional Liability Section, GV
Lewis, Kenneth E. ... **Pittsburgh, PA**
Lewis, Kenneth H. ... Los Angeles, CA
Lewis, Kenneth L. ... **Detroit, MI**
Lewis, Kenneth M. ... **New York, NY**; **White Plains, NY**
Lewis, Kenneth R. ... Chillicothe, MO
Lewis, Kenneth S ... Chicago, IL
Lewis, Kenneth W. ... Beaumont, TX
Lewis, Kent S. ... Salt Lake City, UT
Lewis, Kent W. ... Burlington, IA
Lewis, Kermit W. ... **Middletown, NY**
Lewis, Kern A. ... **Fort Worth, TX**
Lewis, Kerry R. ... **Tulsa, OK**
Lewis, Kevin D. ... **New York, NY**
Lewis, Kevin H. ... Searcy, AR
Lewis, Kevin H. ... **San Francisco, CA**
Lewis, Kevin Neil ... **Ahoskie, NC**; **Rocky Mount, NC**
Lewis, Kevin P. ... **Houston, TX**
Lewis, Kevin R. ... **St. Paul, MN**
Lewis, Kim A. ... Hampton, VA
Lewis, Kim Andrew, (Mr.) ... Island Lake, IL
Lewis, Kim K. ... **Dallas, TX**
Lewis, Kim Martin ... **Cincinnati, OH**
Lewis, Kimberly B. ... Atlanta, GA
Lewis, Kimberly D. ... Beverly Hills, CA
Lewis, Kimberly Joy ... New Orleans, LA
Lewis, King, Krieg, Waldrop & Catron, P.C. ... **Bowling Green, KY**; **Knoxville, TN**; **Nashville, TN**; **Sevierville, TN**
Lewis, Kirk M. ... **Albany, NY**
Lewis & Kolton, PLLC ... **Washington, DC**
Lewis, Kristin E. ... Plaistow, NH
Lewis, Kullman & Sterbcow ... **New Orleans, LA**
Lewis, Kurt S. ... **Denver, CO**
Lewis, Kyle ... Coral Gables, FL
Lewis, Kyle ... **Dumas, TX**
Lewis, Lance David ... **Philadelphia, PA**
Lewis, Larry ... Wichita Falls, TX
Lewis, Larry A. ... **Tulsa, OK**
Lewis, Larry E. ... Pittsford, NY
Lewis, Larry H. ... Meriden, CT
Lewis, Larry O. ... **Marks, MS**
Lewis, Laura Jane ... New York, NY
Lewis, Laura L. ... Leoti, KS
Lewis, Laura Leigh ... Columbus, MS
Lewis, Laura V. ... Bronx, NY
Lewis, Laurence E. ... **Boston, MA**
Lewis, Laurie D. ... **Washington, DC**
Lewis Law Firm, P.A. ... Searcy, AR
Lewis Law Firm, The, A Professional Corporation ... **Washington, DC**; Rockville, MD; **Fairfax, VA**
Lewis Law Offices ... **Salt Lake City, UT**
Lewis, Lawrence D., (P.C.) ... **Irvine, CA**
Lewis, Lawrence J. ... Huntington, WV
Lewis, Lawrence L., III ... **Lafayette, LA**
Lewis, Lawrence S. ... Buffalo, NY
Lewis, Lawrence T. ... Pittsburgh, PA
Lewis, Lawrence W. ... Wilmington, DE
Lewis, Leah H. ... **Baltimore, MD**
Lewis, Lee A. ... Mitchell, SD
Lewis & Leeper ... Framingham, MA
Lewis, Leona E. ... **Minneapolis, MN**
Lewis, Leonard J. ... **Salt Lake City, UT**
Lewis, Leonard John, Jr. ... **Salt Lake City, UT**
Lewis, Leonard L. ... **Cleveland, OH**
Lewis, Leonard W. ... Hollywood, FL
Lewis, Leonard W. ... Cincinnati, OH
Lewis, Leonore C. ... **Newark, NJ**
Lewis, Leslee M. ... **Grand Rapids, MI**
Lewis, Leslie A. ... Salt Lake City, UT
Lewis, Leslie R. ... New Hartford, NY
Lewis, Lester A. ... **Daytona Beach, FL**
Lewis & Lewis ... Waynesboro, GA
Lewis and Lewis ... Boston, MA
Lewis & Lewis, A Professional Corporation ... **San Francisco, CA**
Lewis, Lewis & Ferraro, L.L.C. ... Bristol, CT; West Hartford, CT
Lewis & Lewis, P.A. ... Clarksdale, MS
Lewis & Lewis, P.C. ... Buffalo, NY; Jamestown, NY; Niagara Falls, NY; Olean, NY
Lewis, Lewis & Triggs ... Taunton, MA
Lewis, L. G. ... Houston, TX
Lewis, Lilly ... **Santa Monica, CA**
Lewis, Linda C. ... **Clearfield, PA**
Lewis, Linda L. ... St. Louis, MO
Lewis, Linton D., Jr. ... New Lexington, OH
Lewis, Lisa C. ... Omaha, NE
Lewis, Lisa Donk ... Boulder, CO
Lewis, Lois M. ... Newton, MA
Lewis, Longman & Walker, P.A. ... **Jacksonville, FL**; **Tallahassee, FL**; **West Palm Beach, FL**
Lewis, Loren P. ... Benton, IL
Lewis, Lori J. ... **Burlington, VT**
Lewis, Lorraine ... Silverton, CO
Lewis, Lorraine ... Office of Personnel Management, Office of the General Counsel, GV
Lewis, Lou ... **Poughkeepsie, NY**
Lewis, Louise A. ... Pasadena, CA
Lewis, Lowell S. ... Fort Washington, MD
Lewis, Luther R. ... Sacramento, CA
Lewis, Lynwood W., Jr. ... Accomac, VA
Lewis, M. Byron ... **Phoenix, AZ**
Lewis, M. Calien ... Lansing, MI
Lewis, M. Christian ... Kansas City, MO
Lewis, M. Melisse ... Bethesda, MD
Lewis, M. Richard, Jr. ... **Jacksonville, FL**
Lewis, M. Wayne ... Chandler, AZ
Lewis, M. A., Jr. ... Jackson, MS
Lewis, Marc C. ... **New York, NY**
Lewis, Marc Evan ... **Fort Wayne, IN**
Lewis, Marc Meyer ... **Washington, DC**
Lewis, Margaret C. ... **Richmond, VA**
Lewis, Margaret H. ... Burbank, CA
Lewis, Margaret W. ... Indianapolis, IN
Lewis, Margo L. ... **San Diego, CA**
Lewis, Marilea W. ... Dallas, TX
Lewis, Marilyn Gail ... Portland, OR
Lewis, Mario ... El Paso, TX
Lewis, Marion H. ... Louisville, KY
Lewis, Marjorie B. ... **Woonsocket, RI**
Lewis, Marjorie Ehrich ... **Los Angeles, CA**
Lewis, Marjorie M. ... **Columbia, MO**
Lewis, Mark ... **Denton, TX**
Lewis, Mark A. ... **Shallotte, NC**
Lewis, Mark C. ... **Tupelo, MS**
Lewis, Mark D. ... Southfield, MI
Lewis, Mark D. ... **Columbus, OH**
Lewis, Mark E. ... Beverly Hills, CA
Lewis, Mark E. ... **Houston, TX**
Lewis, Mark F. ... Tampa, FL
Lewis, Mark K. ... **Washington, DC**
Lewis, Mark R. ... Falls Church, VA
Lewis, Mark R., P.A. ... **St. Petersburg, FL**
Lewis, Mark R., Sr. ... **St. Petersburg, FL**
Lewis, Mark Stephen ... Washington, DC
Lewis, Mark W. ... Chicago, IL
Lewis, Marshall A. ... San Diego, CA
Lewis, Martin H. ... **Columbus, OH**
Lewis, Martin R., Jr. ... Hartford, CT
Lewis, Marvin H. ... **Beverly Hills, CA**
Lewis, Marvin K. ... **San Francisco, CA**
Lewis, Marvin W. ... Miami, FL
Lewis, Mary B. ... Tulsa, OK
Lewis, Mary Geiger ... **Columbia, SC**
Lewis, Mary Lynn ... Salem, OR
Lewis, MaryAnn A. ... Treasury Department, Internal Revenue Service, GV
Lewis, Maryanne ... Dedham, MA
Lewis, Mason C. ... Los Angeles, CA
Lewis, Matthew Allen ... **Orlando, FL**
Lewis, Matthew H. ... **Morristown, NJ**
Lewis, Matthew J. ... **San Francisco, CA**
Lewis, Matthew P. ... **Los Angeles, CA**
Lewis, Matthew R. ... **Washington, DC**
Lewis, Mattson D. ... Chattanooga, TN
Lewis, Maureen A. ... Washington, DC
Lewis, Maurice A. ... Falls Church, VA
Lewis, Maurice C. ... Hurlock, MD
Lewis, Max B. ... Salt Lake City, UT
Lewis, Maxine Kay ... Harrisburg, PA
Lewis & McKenna ... Tallahassee, FL; **Hackensack, NJ**; **Saddle River, NJ**; **New York, NY**
Lewis Meaden Iwanyshyn & Sargent LLC ... **Pittsburgh, PA**
Lewis, Melanie B. ... **Denver, CO**
Lewis, Melanie M. ... The Woodlands, TX
Lewis, Melissa A. ... **Detroit, MI**
Lewis, Melissa Moore ... Prestonsburg, KY
Lewis, Melton M. ... St. Louis, MO
Lewis, Meredith Kolsky ... **Washington, DC**
Lewis, Merle D. ... Huron, SD
Lewis, Merwin ... Garden City, NY
Lewis, Michael A. ... Stuart, FL
Lewis, Michael A. ... New York, NY
Lewis, Michael A. ... Eugene, OR
Lewis, Michael A. ... Portland, OR
Lewis, Michael B. ... Woodland Hills, CA
Lewis, Michael B. ... **Troy, MI**
Lewis, Michael B. ... Longview, TX
Lewis, Michael Bruce ... Bakersfield, CA
Lewis, Michael C. ... **Farmington Hills, MI**
Lewis, Michael D. ... Los Angeles, CA
Lewis, Michael D. ... **Traverse City, MI**
Lewis, Michael D. ... **Oklahoma City, OK**
Lewis, Michael G. ... **New York, NY**
Lewis, Michael H., Law Offices of ... **San Francisco, CA**
Lewis, Michael J. ... Terre Haute, IN
Lewis, Michael J. ... Silver City, NM

Lewis & White ... Tallahassee, FL
Lewis, White, Porter, Law Offices of
Oklahoma City, OK
Lewis, Willa I. ... New York, NY
Lewis, William ... Portland, OR
Lewis, William A. ... Panama City, FL
Lewis, William A., Jr. ... United States Senate, Committee Legal Personnel, GV
Lewis, William, & Associates, P.C.
Portland, OR
Lewis, William B. ... Riverside, CT
Lewis, William Bee Ravenel
Columbia, SC
Lewis, William C. ... Petersburg, AK
Lewis, William C., Jr. ... Miami, FL
Woodstock, VT
Lewis, William E. ... New Orleans, LA
Lewis, William E. ... Locust Valley, NY
Lewis, William G. ... San Francisco, CA
Lewis, William H. ... Washington, DC
Lewis, William H. ... Lincoln, NE
Lewis, William H. ... New York, NY
Lewis, William H., Jr. ... Farmville, NC
Lewis, William J. ... Huntington Beach, CA
Lewis, William J. ... Chicago, IL
Lewis, William J. ... Melville, NY
Lewis, William John, III ... Bryn Mawr, PA
Lewis, William, Jr. ... Oxford, MS
Lewis, William K. ... Richmond, VA
Lewis, William K., II ... Morristown, NJ
Lewis, William L. ... Tappahannock, VA
Lewis, William O. ... Harlan, IA
Lewis, William O. ... Lebanon, OR
Lewis, William P., II ... Wilmington, NC
Lewis, William R. ... Tampa, FL
Lewis, William R. ... North Tonawanda, NY
Lewis, William Richard ... Jackson, MS
Lewis, William S. ... Trenton, MO
Lewis, William S. ... Kingsport, TN
Lewis, William S. ... Seattle, WA
Lewis, William V. ... Ann Arbor, MI
Detroit, MI
Lewis, Williams & Caravan
Schuylkill Haven, PA
Lewis, Williams G. ... Purchase, NY
Lewis & Williams, LLP ... Galveston, TX
Lewis, Wilma A. ... Washington, DC
Lewis, Wilson, Lewis and Jones, Ltd.
Fairfax, VA
Lewis, W. M. ... Halifax, VA
Lewis, Wm. Lance ... Dallas, TX
Lewis, Wm. Thomas ... San Jose, CA
Lewis & Wood, P.C. ... Boca Raton, FL
Brielle, NJ
Trenton, NJ
Philadelphia, PA
Lewis, Woodward F., Jr. ... Wallingford, CT
Lewis, Yehudis S. ... New York, NY
Lewis & Zilaff ... Sacramento, CA
Lewis, Zipporah J. ... Chicago, IL
Lewis-Eng, Claudia A. ... Washington, DC
Lewis-Gellen, Karen ... Chagrin Falls, OH
Lewis-Heard, Joan E. ... Los Angeles, CA
Lewis-Johnston, Gail ... Philadelphia, PA
Lewisohn, Brandon K. ... Charlotte, NC
Lewisohn, Carol J. ... Hempstead, NY
Lewisohn, Ina B. ... Morristown, NJ
Lewison, Bret ... Minneapolis, MN
Lewison, Edward ... Chicago, IL
Lewison, Murray J. ... Hillside, IL
Lewison, Robert J. ... Miami, FL
Lewis-Osborne, Joan J. ... Minneapolis, MN
Lewiss & Bauerle ... Westerly, RI
Lewiss, Matthew L. ... Westerly, RI
Lewiss, Peter L. ... Westerly, RI
Lewis-Somers, Susan ... Salem, OR
Lewiston, David H. ... Southfield, MI
Lewiston, Jeffrey A. ... Los Angeles, CA
Lewiston, Michael B. ... Detroit, MI
Lewiston, Richard M. ... Oak Park, MI
Lewit, Peter M. ... New York, NY
Lewitan, Dinah H. ... New York, NY
Lewitas, Bruce ... Chicago, IL
Lewitas, Laurence T. ... New York, NY
Lewitas & Yohonn ... New York, NY
Lewites, Nisa ... New York, NY
Lewitt, Hackman, Hoefflin, Shapiro, Marshall & Harlan, A Law Corporation
Encino, CA
Los Angeles, CA
Van Nuys, CA
Westlake Village, CA
Lewitt, Leon ... Encino, CA
Lewitt, Maurice ... Encino, CA
Lewitt, Victor H. ... St. Louis, MO
LeWitter, Jody ... Oakland, CA
Lewittes, Aaron ... New York, NY
Lewittes, David I. ... New York, NY
Lewittes, Joel ... New York, NY
Lewittes, Paul M. ... White Plains, NY
Lewittes, Ronald J. ... Miami, FL
Lewke, Carl A. ... Columbus, WI
Lewko-Vermetten, Cynthia D.
Traverse City, MI
Lewkow, Victor I. ... New York, NY
Lewkowicz, Carol S. ... Fairfield, NJ
Lewkowicz, Paul E. ... San Jose, CA
Lewkowicz, Thaddeus J. ... Syracuse, NY
Lewkowitz, H. J. ... Phoenix, AZ
Lewkowitz, Richard B. ... Sacramento, CA
Lewkowski, Edward A. ... Denver, CO
Lewman, John F. ... Fremont, CA
Lewman, Ruth N. ... Houston, TX
Lewnard, Lawrence E. ... Cincinnati, OH
Lewonski, Sharon M. ... Atlanta, GA
Lewright, John A. ... Cassville, MO
Lewris, Basil J. ... Washington, DC
Lewry, Thomas A. ... Southfield, MI

Lewter, Judith Elizabeth ... Lexington, KY
Lewthwaite, Karen ... Jackson, MI
Lewton, Michael C. ... Portland, OR
Lewton, Robert J. ... Hartford, CT
Lewy, Amy B. ... Irving, TX
Lewy, Donald L. ... Fairfax Station, VA
Lewy, Lawrence E. ... Fairfax, VA
Lewy, Timothy J. ... Bakersfield, CA
Lewy, Timothy J., Inc. ... Bakersfield, CA
Lewyn, Alfred ... New York, NY
Lewyn, Michael E. ... Buffalo, NY
Lewyn, Thomas M., (P.C.) ... New York, NY
Lex, Joseph T. ... West Allis, WI
Lex, Michael L. ... Tucson, AZ
Lexa, Joseph J. ... Pompano Beach, FL
Lexa, Margery J. ... Miami, FL
Lexier, Kenneth A. ... Skowhegan, ME
Lexner, Eugene E. ... West Seneca, NY
Lexo, Mary Keysa ... Grand Island, NY
Lexow, Berbit & Associates, P.C.
Mahwah, NJ
New York, NY
Lexow, Berbit, & Associates, P.C.
Suffern, NY
Lexton, Jean D. S. ... Sarasota, FL
Lexvold, Timothy M. ... Rochester, NY
Ley, Andrew J. ... Boston, MA
Ley, David Cress ... Oklahoma City, OK
Ley, Douglas L. ... Boston, MA
Ley, Jane S. ... Office of Government Ethics, Office of the Director, GV
Ley, John M. ... Springfield, NJ
Ley, John P., Jr. ... Department of the Army, U.S. Army Legal Services Agency, GV
Ley, John R. ... Denver, CO
Ley, John R., LLC ... Denver, CO
Ley, Kari L. ... Clovis, CA
Ley, Kathleen M. ... Chicago, IL
Ley, Marshall F. ... Wheaton, IL
Ley, Nancy Moate ... Clearwater, FL
Ley, Patricia B. ... Winnetka, IL
Ley, Paul D. ... Tampa, FL
Ley, Paul S. ... Indianapolis, IN
Ley, Richard G. ... Austin, TX
Ley, Robert J. ... Buffalo Grove, IL
Ley, Rock B. ... Honolulu, HI
Ley, Roger B. ... Seattle, WA
Ley, William T., P.C. ... Austin, TX
Ley & Young, P.C. ... Boston, MA
Leyba, Kenneth P. ... Wichita, KS
Leyba, Linda ... Watsonville, CA
Leyba, Mike L. ... Great Bend, KS
Leyba, Yvonne ... San Francisco, CA
Leybold, Dennis ... Portland, OR
Leyden, Andrew Parker
House of Representatives, Committee Legal Personnel, GV
Leyden, Arthur F., III ... Toms River, NJ
Leyden, Christopher ... Hackensack, NJ
Leyden, Diana Lynn ... Boston, MA
Leyden, James G., Jr. ... Wilmington, DE
Leyden, James J. ... Philadelphia, PA
Leyden, James J., Jr. ... Smithtown, NY
Leyden, Jay S. ... Merrillville, IN
Leyden, John F. ... Wayland, NY
Leyden, John W., Jr. ... Hackensack, NJ
Leyden and Leyden ... Hackensack, NJ
Leyden, Michael R. ... Elk Grove Village, IL
Leyden, Pamela Lee ... Pittsburgh, PA
Leyden, Raymond William ... Stamford, CT
Leyden, Sean P. ... New York, NY
Leyden, Shawn P. ... Edison, NJ
Leyden, Stanley ... New York, NY
Leyder, Gary L. ... Harrisburg, PA
Leydig, C. Frederick ... Chicago, IL
Leydig, Gary W. ... Chicago, IL
Leydig, Jeralyn Adelman ... Plantation, FL
Leydig, Richard A., Law Office of
Fort Lauderdale, FL
Leydig, Voit & Mayer, Ltd.
Washington, DC
Chicago, IL
Rockford, IL
Leydiker, Eugene M. ... Los Angeles, CA
Leydon, Brenden P. ... Stamford, CT
Leydon, Edward R. ... Kenilworth, NJ
Leydon, John F., Jr. ... Stamford, CT
Leydorf, Donna M. ... Winchester, TN
Leydorf, Fred L. ... Rancho Mirage, CA
Leyel, Christopher P. ... Los Angeles, CA
Leyendecker, P. Kevin ... Houston, TX
Leyens, E. Adam ... Rochester, NY
Leyens, Jon F., Jr. ... New Orleans, LA
Leyerle, Albert H. ... Akron, OH
Leyh, Peter J. ... Haddonfield, NJ
Philadelphia, PA
Leyh, Steven A. ... Houston, TX
Leyh, Timothy G. ... Seattle, WA
Leyhane, Francis J. (Jack), III
Chicago, IL
Leyhane, Thomas B. ... Lawrenceville, NJ
Leyhe, Meyer, Leyhe & Lobel
St. Louis, MO
Leyhe, William H., III ... St. Louis, MO
Leyhow, Sharon A. ... Wilmington, DE
Leykam, William A. ... Brooklyn, NY
Leyland, Nora H. ... Washington, DC
Leylegian, J. Gregory ... Department of Justice, Federal Bureau of Investigation, GV
Ley-Mackey, Sheridan J.
Bainbridge Island, WA
Leynaud, George G. ... Peru, IL
Leynaud & Leynaud, Law Offices of
Peru, IL
Leyner, Joel A. ... Secaucus, NJ
Leys, Martha H. ... Petaluma, CA
Leyshock, Douglas Gerard
Jefferson City, MO

Leyshon, Robert Kelly ... Rock Island, IL
Leyton, Daniel L. ... Boca Raton, FL
Leyton, David S. ... Flint, MI
Leyton, Jeffrey A. ... Scottsdale, AZ
Leyton & Kasle, P.L.C. ... Flint, MI
Leyton, Peter S. ... Fairfax, VA
Leyton, Steven H. ... St. Louis, MO
Leyton, Vivian ... Fountain Valley, CA
Leyva, Cynthia Cochran ... Lompoc, CA
Leyva, Elsa ... Los Angeles, CA
Leyva, Jessica Lima ... Miami, FL
Leyva, Joe Alfred ... Diamond Bar, CA
Leyva, Leo V. ... Hackensack, NJ
Leyval, Eugene R. ... Palm Desert, CA
Leyva-Ligon, Terry ... El Paso, TX
Lezak, John F., (Atty. At Law, A Law Corp.)
Honolulu, HI
Lezak, Lawrence H. ... New York, NY
Lezak, Sidney I. ... Portland, OR
Lezama, M. Timothy ... Bensalem, PA
Lezama-Ramirez, Sharon V. ... Plattsburgh, NY
Lezamiz, John T. ... Twin Falls, ID
Lezamiz, Margaret M. ... Boise, ID
Lezar, Tex, (P.C.) ... Dallas, TX
Houston, TX
Lezcano, Abel M. ... Los Angeles, CA
Lezdey, John, and Associates
Collingswood, NJ
Lezell, Mark L. ... Washington, DC
Lezenby, Philip R., Jr. ... Barrington, NJ
Lezenby, Zane & Cure, P.A.
Barrington, NJ
LeZotte, Linda J. ... San Jose, CA
Lezotte, Mark R. ... Dearborn, MI
Lezovich, Christopher J. ... Detroit, MI
Lezy, Normand R. ... Honolulu, HI
Lhamon, Emily N. ... San Francisco, CA
Lhamon, George M. ... Redmond, WA
L'Hernault, Suzanne ... New York, NY
L'Heureux, Elisabeth ... New York, NY
L'Heureux, Robert D. ... Alexandria, VA
L'Heureux, Stephen M. ... Carlsbad, CA
Lhevine, Paul ... Denver, CO
L'Hommedieu, Edward C. ... Lewiston, ME
L'Hommedieu, Noelle ... Santa Fe, NM
L'Hommedieu, Samuel J., Jr.
Washington, DC
Lhost, John H. ... Milwaukee, WI
L'Hoste, David J. ... New Orleans, LA
Lhota, David P. ... Pompano Beach, FL
Lhota, Janna Peters ... Fort Lauderdale, FL
Lhota, John R. ... Clearfield, PA
L'Hote, Jeff ... Jersey City, NJ
Li, Albert J. ... Austin, TX
Li, Cang ... New York, NY
Li, Chi-Dooh ... Seattle, WA
Li, Christine F. ... Woodbridge, NJ
Li, Christine S. ... Morristown, NJ
Li, Chunhua ... Richmond, VA
Li, David Shao ... Brooklyn, NY
Li, David Y. ... Boston, MA
Li, Donna ... New York, NY
Li, Frances S. P. ... Minneapolis, MN
Li, J. Edward ... New York, NY
Li, James Yuanxin ... San Francisco, CA
Li, Jason Xinyu ... Los Angeles, CA
Li, Jeffrey K. ... San Francisco, CA
San Jose, CA
Li, Jennifer T. ... New York, NY
Li, Jerry Tian ... Detroit, MI
Li, John J. ... New York, NY
Li, Julie Y. ... Chicago, IL
Li, K. Thomas ... Washington, DC
Li, Kam W. ... San Diego, CA
Li, Katy C. ... Jersey City, NJ
Li, Ka-Yin ... New York, NY
Li, Kening ... Washington, DC
Li, Kenneth S. ... Monterey Park, CA
Li, Laurence L. ... New York, NY
Li, Leyi "Larry" ... Shelby, NC
Li, Li ... New York, NY
Li, Lindsay ... Norfolk, MA
Li, Luis ... Los Angeles, CA
Li, Mark K. ... San Dimas, CA
Li, Michael C. ... San Francisco, CA
Li, Michael C. ... Dallas, TX
Li, Paul M. ... Orinda, CA
Li, Peter B. ... Cleveland, OH
Li, Phillip A. ... Honolulu, HI
Li, Ruilin ... Minneapolis, MN
Li, Susan Arinaga ... Honolulu, HI
Li, Victor Hao ... Honolulu, HI
Li, Vivian Chun ... Kirkland, WA
Li, Winifred I. ... Boston, MA
Li, Yiqiang ... St. Louis, MO
Li, Yulan ... New York, NY
Lia, Catherine ... Los Angeles, CA
Lia, James D. ... Los Alamitos, CA
Liabo, Corenne M. ... Cedar Rapids, IA
Liabo, Mark E. ... Cedar Rapids, IA
Liacos, Paul J. ... Boston, MA
Liacouras, Ann Myers ... Philadelphia, PA
Liacouras, Gregory L. ... Philadelphia, PA
Liacouras, Peter J. ... Philadelphia, PA
Liacouras & Smith, LLP ... Philadelphia, PA
Liakas, Anastasia ... Los Angeles, CA
Liakas, Nicolas ... Agoura Hills, CA
Liakos & Associates ... Omaha, NE
Liakos, John G. ... Omaha, NE
Liamos, Paul T., Jr. ... Cheyenne, WY
Lian, Albert W. ... New York, NY
Lian, Chuncheng ... Washington, DC
Lian, Jos. G. ... Brooklyn, NY
Lian, Joseph, Jr. ... Worcester, MA
Lian, Malapero & Prisco ... New York, NY
Lian, Robert G. ... Worcester, MA
Lian, Robert G., Jr. ... Washington, DC
Lian, Steven C. ... Minot, ND

Lian, Zarrow, Eynon & Shea
Worcester, MA
Liang, Angela Y. ... San Francisco, CA
Liang, Elisa L. ... Brooklyn, NY
Liang, Felice P. ... San Francisco, CA
Liang, Grace C. ... Burbank, CA
Liang, J. May ... Dulles, VA
Liang, Jaime D. ... Tallahassee, FL
Liang, Kenneth ... Los Angeles, CA
Liang, Zhihai ... St. Louis, MO
Lianides, Peter ... Newport Beach, CA
Lianopoulos, Drew ... Salem, OR
Liantonio, Francis V., Jr.
New Orleans, LA
Houston, TX
Liantonio-McBride, Gaetana ... Uniondale, NY
Liao, Abraham C. ... Monterey Park, CA
Liao, Edward Ho Tung ... New York, NY
Liao, Fang-Lian ... Pacific Palisades, CA
Liao, Frank Y. ... Princeton, NJ
Liao, Gabriel ... Santa Monica, CA
Liao, Joannie H. ... Los Angeles, CA
Liao, Robert H. ... New York, NY
Liao, S. Alex ... San Jose, CA
Liao, Wayne M. ... San Francisco, CA
Liapakis, Pamela Anagnos ... New York, NY
Liapis, Georgia P. ... Boston, MA
Liapis, Gray & Stegall, L.C.
Salt Lake City, UT
Liapis, Mark T. ... Reno, NV
Liapis, Paul H. ... Salt Lake City, UT
Lias, Elizabeth A. ... Vandalia, OH
Lias, Renee ... San Francisco, CA
Lias-Booker, Ava ... Baltimore, MD
Liaskos, Peter S. ... New York, NY
Liaurado, Mireya A.R. ... Washington, DC
Liazos, Andrew C. ... Boston, MA
Liban, Theodore B. ... New York, NY
Libanoff, Ira ... Fort Lauderdale, FL
LiBassi, David P. ... Lowell, MA
Libassi, Frank Peter S. ... Hartford, CT
Libassi, Mary ... Secaucus, NJ
Libber, Jonathan D.
Environmental Protection Agency, Office of Enforcement and Compliance Assurance, GV
Libber, Sherie Brook ... Crownsville, MD
Libbey, James H. ... Martinez, CA
Libbey, Keith A. ... Minneapolis, MN
Libbey, Morton H., Jr. ... Bristol, CT
Hartford, CT
Libbey, Robert M. ... Anchorage, AK
Libbey & Suddock, P.C. ... Anchorage, AK
Libbin, Anne E. ... San Francisco, CA
Libbin, Martin R. ... Hartford, CT
Libbon, Vincent R., Jr. ... Phoenix, AZ
Libbos, Thomas M. ... Springfield, MA
Libbos, Thomas M., P.C., Law Offices of
Springfield, MA
Libby, Darald ... Franconia, NH
Libby, Debra J. ... Atlanta, GA
Libby, Diane Geiger ... Everett, WA
Libby, Douglas E. ... Elmont, NY
Libby, Eileen B. ... Chicago, IL
Libby, Frank A., Jr. ... Boston, MA
Libby, Gary W. ... Portland, ME
Libby, Gene R. ... Kennebunk, ME
Libby, Gerald E., II ... Boston, MA
Libby, Gerold W. ... Los Angeles, CA
Libby, Harold L. ... Youngstown, OH
Libby, Howard A. ... Bethesda, MD
Libby, I. Lewis ... Washington, DC
Libby, Jean C. ... Los Angeles, CA
Libby, Jeffrey T. ... Dallas, TX
Libby, Joan G. ... Hartford, CT
Libby, John A. ... Detroit, MI
Libby, John F. ... Los Angeles, CA
Libby, Joseph D. ... Houston, TX
Libby, Judith L. ... Springfield, IL
Libby, Kenneth A.
Federal Trade Commission, Bureau of Competition, GV
Libby, Kevin G. ... Portland, ME
Libby, Melvin E. ... Manhasset, NY
Libby, Patricia A. ... Los Angeles, CA
Libby, Patricia Jean ... North Conway, NH
Libby, Russell T. ... Norcross, GA
Libby, Thomas L. ... Oakland, CA
Libby, Valerie S. ... Portland, ME
Libby, Walt ... Winterset, IA
Libby, Wilfred Daniel ... Punta Gorda, FL
Libby, William L. ... Newport, MN
Liben, Judith ... Boston, MA
Libenson, Amy ... Pittsford, NY
Libenson, Clark H. ... San Diego, CA
Libenson, Daniel J. ... Cambridge, MA
Libenson, Jerome M. ... Coronado, CA
Liber, Adrianna K. ... Wheaton, IL
Liber, John D. ... Cleveland, OH
Liber, John R., II ... Chagrin Falls, OH
Liber, John R., II ... Cleveland, OH
Libera, Harold J. ... Winona, MN
Libera, Libera & Bernatz ... Winona, MN
Libera, Stephen A. ... Winona, MN
Libera, Thomas M. ... Minneapolis, MN
Liberace, Elisa Maria ... Boston, MA
Liberace, Gerald C. ... Broomall, PA
Liberati, David K. ... Martins Ferry, OH
St. Clairsville, OH
Liberati, Mark E. ... Providence, RI
Liberati & Peretti ... Providence, RI
Liberato, Deborah ... Fairfield, NJ
Liberato, Lynne ... Houston, TX
Liberatore, Edward Richard ... Golden, CO
Liberatore, Frank M. ... Los Angeles, CA
Liberatore, Joseph T. ... Portsmouth, VA
Liberatore, Lisa Winfield ... Burbank, CA

Liberatore, Michael Joseph
Coconut Grove, FL
Liberatore, Stephen J. ... San Francisco, CA
Liberchuk, Larry ... New York, NY
Liberi, Dominic S. ... Media, PA
Philadelphia, PA
Liberio, Rocco Joseph ... Pasadena, CA
Liberis & Associates, P.A. ... Pensacola, FL
Liberis, Charles S. ... Pensacola, FL
Liberman, Alex M. ... Mundelein, IL
Liberman, Arthur L. ... Union Beach, NJ
Liberman, David ... Los Angeles, CA
Liberman, Donald B. ... Hackensack, NJ
Liberman, Eric ... Millbrae, CA
Liberman, Gregory R. ... San Francisco, CA
Liberman, Howard M. ... Washington, DC
Liberman, James B. ... New York, NY
Liberman, Jason J. ... Los Angeles, CA
Liberman, Joshua Moses ... Boston, MA
Liberman, Keith G. ... St. Louis, MO
Liberman, Lenard David ... Santa Ana, CA
Liberman, Leonard J. ... Needham, MA
Liberman, Lois Jean ... New York, NY
Liberman, Martin ... Morristown, NJ
Liberman, Martin, A Professional Corporation ... Morristown, NJ
Liberman, Michael ... Richmond, VA
Liberman, Patti S. ... Morristown, NJ
Liberman, Phillip E. ... Houston, TX
Liberman, Scott A. ... Dayton, OH
Liberman, Scott S. ... Fort Lauderdale, FL
Liberman, Susan ... Lawrence, NY
Liberman, Susan R. ... Manhasset, NY
Liberman, Susan S. ... Washington, DC
Liberman, Terry W. ... Ballwin, MO
Liberson, Bloom, Bloom & Bock, P.C.
Farmington Hills, MI
Liberson, Howard S. ... Los Angeles, CA
Liberson, Joel K. ... Los Angeles, CA
Liberson, William I. ... Farmington Hills, MI
Liberstein, Arthur ... New York, NY
Liberstein, Kenneth F. ...
Department of Commerce, GV
Libert, Donald J. ... Lancaster, OH
Libert, Jack L., Law Offices of
Garden City, NY
Libert, Jeffrey A. ... Mullica Hill, NJ
Libert, Marshall C. ... Chicago, IL
Libert, Richard C. ... New York, NY
Libert, Victor E. ... Simsbury, CT
Libert, Victor E., Law Office of
Hartford, CT
Simsbury, CT
Libertelli, Christopher D.
Federal Communications Commission,
Common Carrier Bureau, GV
Liberth, Richard F. ... Newburgh, NY
Liberti, Ben M. ... Hackensack, NJ
Liberti, Michael ... Paramus, NJ
Liberti, Vincent A., Jr. ... West Haven, CT
Libertino, Teresa Anna ... Los Angeles, CA
Liberto, Charles J. ... Long Beach, CA
Liberto, James L. ... New Kensington, PA
Liberto, Mary B. ... Orlando, FL
Liberto, Nicole ... Louisville, KY
Liberto, Nicole T. ... Louisville, KY
Liberto, Peter Frank ... New Orleans, LA
Liberto, Shelley M. ... Santa Ana, CA
Santa Ana, CA
Libertucci, Linda M. ... Glendale, CA
Liberty, Arthur A. ... Evansville, IN
Liberty, Arthur R. ... Beverly Hills, CA
San Diego, CA
Liberty, Dale D., Sr. ... Salem, OR
Liberty, Frank J. ... New London, CT
Liberty, John P. ...
Treasury Department, GV
Liberty & Liberty ... Scotts Valley, CA
Liberty, Michael D. ... Burlingame, CA
Liberty & O'Neill ... Tucson, AZ
Liberty, Pamela A. ... Tucson, AZ
Liberty, Patricia A. ... Scotts Valley, CA
Liberty, Philip S. ... Scotts Valley, CA
Liberty, Robert L. ... Portland, OR
Libes, Deborah S. ... New York, NY
Libeson, Sandra J. ... New York, NY
Libet, Gayla B. ... Oakland, CA
Libetti, Alfeo P. ... Philadelphia, PA
Libeu, Aimee Meredith ... Santa Ana, CA
Libey, Gary J. ... Colfax, WA
Libhart, Wayne P. ... Bangor, ME
Libicki, Stuart ... Los Angeles, CA
Libien, James R. ... San Francisco, CA
Libiez, Elizabeth M. ... Gretna, LA
Libin, Jerome B. ... Washington, DC
Libin, Renee S. ... Cos Cob, CT
Libis, Paul H. ... Granada Hills, CA
Libit, William M. ... Chicago, IL
Liblang & Associates ... Birmingham, MI
Traverse City, MI
Liblang, Dani K. ... Birmingham, MI
Traverse City, MI
Libman, George H. ... Albuquerque, NM
Libman, Larry K. ... Madison, WI
Libman, Raquel Nurith ... Miami, FL
Libman, Robert H. ... Chicago, IL
Libman, Robert S. ... Department of Justice,
Civil Rights Division, GV
Libman, Stephen M. ... Chicago, IL
Libner, Maurice A. ... Brunswick, ME
Libner, Robert ... Muskegon, MI
Libner, Van Leuven, Evans, Portenga & Duffey, P.C. ... Holland, MI
Muskegon, MI
Libo, Andrew L. ... New York, NY
Libo, David J. ... Beverly Hills, CA
Libonati, Dominick Richard ... San Mateo, CA
Libonati, Michael E. ... Philadelphia, PA
Libonati-Ritz, Genene ... Hazleton, PA
Libor, Michael R. ... Philadelphia, PA
Libott, Robert Y. ... Rolling Hills, CA
Libow, Allen H. ... Boca Raton, FL
Libow, Brian M. ... San Pablo, CA
Libow, Daryl A. ... Washington, DC
New York, NY
Libowitz, Michael S. ... Baltimore, MD
Libowsky, David J. ... Florham Park, NJ
New York, NY
Libowsky, Stephen D. ... Chicago, IL
Libra, David A. ... Minneapolis, MN
Librach, Burton A. ... St. Louis, MO
Librach, Miriam C. ... Boston, MA
Librach & Rothman, P.C. ... St. Louis, MO
Librett, Friedland & Lieberman
Garden City, NY
Librett, Richard A. ... Garden City, NY
Libretta, Donald F. ... Washington, DC
Libretti, John P., III ... Secaucus, NJ
West Caldwell, NJ
Librie, Joseph M. ... Lake Success, NY
Librizzi, Joseph J. ... Villa Park, IL
Librizzi, Thomas G. ... Hartford, CT
Librizzi, Victor, Jr. ... Cedar Grove, NJ
Libsack, Laurence ... Odessa, WA
Spokane, WA
Libsohn, Ralph J. ... Providence, RI
Libson, Craig S. ... New York, NY
Libson, Jeffrey P. ... Berwyn, PA
Libson, Marilyn R. ... Hartsdale, NY
Libster, Mitchell A. ... Marion, OH
Liburd, Ann C. ... Anchorage, AK
Liburd, Marjorie Ann ... New York, NY
Liburt, Joseph C. ... Menlo Park, CA
Libutti, Eileen H. ... Melville, NY
Libutti, Michael R. ... Rancho Cucamonga, CA
Liby, Justin Troy ... Kansas City, MO
Liby & McVay, LLC ... Kansas City, MO
Liby, Richard J. ... Wichita, KS
Li Calsi, Anthony N. ... Peekskill, NY
Licalsi, Ernest J. ... Madera, CA
LiCalsi, Paul V. ... New York, NY
LiCalzi, Jacqueline O. ... New York, NY
LiCalzi, James N. ... Melville, NY
Licano, Michael A. ... Mesa, AZ
Licari, John F. ... Philadelphia, PA
Licari, Mary F. ... Chicago, IL
Licari, Thomas B. ... East Islip, NY
Licastro, Brian T. ... Pittsburgh, PA
Licastro, John T. ... McHenry, IL
Licata, Anthony R. ... Chicago, IL
Licata, Arthur F. ... Boston, MA
Licata, Arthur F., P.C. ... Boston, MA
Licata & Associates Co., L.P.A.
Cleveland, OH
Licata, Charles A. ... Trenton, NJ
Licata, Francis P. ... Los Angeles, CA
Licata, James D. ... Suffern, NY
Licata, James J. ... Chicago, IL
Licata, Jane Massey, Law Offices of
Marlton, NJ
Licata, Joseph ... Livingston, NJ
Licata, Joseph J., III ... Millburn, NJ
New York, NY
Licata, Lon A. ... Omaha, NE
Licata, Louis J. ... Cleveland, OH
Licata, Mark C. ... Houston, TX
Licata, Peter G. ... Lakewood, NJ
Licata, Richard V. ... New City, NY
Licata, Steven B. ... Columbia, SC
Licata, Steven V. ... Milwaukee, WI
Licata, Thomas M. ... New York, NY
Licata, Vicki S. ... New York, NY
Licata, Vincent Joseph ... New York, NY
Licata, Walter J. ... Rochester, NY
Licatesi, Anthony Joseph ... Garden City, NY
Licatovich, William T. ... Lady Lake, FL
LiCausi, Bruce C. ... Raritan, NJ
Liccardi, Crawford & Ogden, P.C.
Rutland, VT
Liccardi, John S. ... Rutland, VT
Liccardi, Joseph B. ... East Greenbush, NY
Liccardo, Cynthia A. ... Trenton, NJ
Liccardo, Laura ... San Jose, CA
Liccardo, Paul Salvatore ... San Jose, CA
Liccardo, Rossi, Sturges & McNeil, A Professional Law Corporation
San Jose, CA
Liccardo, Salvador A. ... San Jose, CA
Liccardo, Sam T. ... San Diego, CA
Licciardi, John L. ... Naples, FL
Licciardi, John L., P.A. ... Naples, FL
Liccione, Maureen T. ... Riverhead, NY
Liccione, Roxann Therese
Albuquerque, NM
Liccione, Stephen J. ... Milwaukee, WI
Licensing Strategies ... Menlo Park, CA
Lich, Herold & Mackiewicz ... Omaha, NE
Lich, Victor J., Jr. ... Bellevue, NE
Lichatin, Stephen, III ... Providence, RI
Lichauco, Faustino A. ... Boston, MA
Lichko, Gregory M. ... Cleveland, OH
Lichko & Schechter ... Cleveland, OH
Lichliter, Sharon Gruby ... Germantown, TN
Lichman, Barbara E., P.h.D. ... Irvine, CA
Lichman, Harry C. ... Keene, NH
Lichstein, Toni C. ... New York, NY
Licht, David A. ... Santa Monica, CA
Licht, David E. ... New York, NY
Licht, David G. ... Beverly Hills, CA
Licht, Doris Jami ... Boston, MA
Providence, RI
Licht, Frederick R. ... Los Angeles, CA
Licht, Jeffrey L. ... Los Angeles, CA
Licht, Jeri Wingate ... New York, NY
Licht, John H. ... Denver, CO
Licht, Kenneth D. ... Rochester, NY
Licht, Laura K. ... San Diego, CA
Licht, Louis ... Mill Valley, CA
Licht, Louis W. ... Forest Hills, NY
Licht, Louise ... New York, NY
Licht, Michele Habibi ... Hidden Hills, CA
Licht, Philip M. ... Mount Laurel, NJ
Jenkintown, PA
Licht, Raphael ... Philadelphia, PA
Licht, Renée
Federal Communications Commission,
Office of the Commissioners, GV
Licht, Richard A. ... Providence, RI
Licht, Robert A. ... Boston, MA
Licht, Roger H. ... Beverly Hills, CA
Licht, Stuart A. ... Department of Justice,
Civil Division, GV
Lichtash, Terry ... Brooklyn, NY
Lichtblau, Erich F. ... San Francisco, CA
Lichtblau, Fred ... New York, NY
Lichtblau, Joseph B. ... Boston, MA
Lichtblau, Leonard R. ... New York, NY
Lichtcsien, Bruce M. ... Chicago, IL
Lichte, Larry E. ... Madison, WI
Lichtefeld, H. John, III ... Pittsburgh, PA
Lichten, Earl B. ... Riverwoods, IL
Lichten, Harold L. ... Boston, MA
Lichten, Rachel Gordon ... New York, NY
Lichten, Stuart ... New York, NY
Lichten, Thomas R. ... Chicago, IL
Lichten, Thomas R., Ltd. ... Chicago, IL
Lichtenauer, Robert A. ... Indianapolis, IN
Lichtenbaum, Greta L.H.
Washington, DC
Lichtenbaum, Jill Amy ... New York, NY
Lichtenbaum, Peter ... Washington, DC
Lichtenberg, Alan H. ... New York, NY
Lichtenberg, Beth E. ... Chicago, IL
Lichtenberg, David B. ... Morristown, NJ
Lichtenberg & Ginach, P.C. ... New York, NY
Lichtenberg, John M. ... Grand Rapids, MI
Lichtenberg, Judith B. ... Indianapolis, IN
Lichtenberg, Karen A. ... Los Angeles, CA
Lichtenberg, Kathryn J. ... New Orleans, LA
Lichtenberg, Kurt ... Bellevue, WA
Lichtenberg, Kurt ... Seattle, WA
Lichtenberg, Lynn ... Everett, WA
Lichtenberg, Max ... New York, NY
Lichtenberg, Meredith Fein
New York, NY
Lichtenberg, Micheal G. ... Gaithersburg, MD
Lichtenberg, Murray ... Lake Success, NY
Lichtenberger, John ... Succasunna, NJ
Lichtenberger, Paul H. ... Bloomfield, CT
Lichtenberger, Vera B. ... Des Moines, IA
Lichtenberger, Vincent M. ... Chicago, IL
Lichtenegger, John P. ... Jackson, MO
Lichtenegger, Larry J. ... Monterey, CA
Lichtenfeld, Joseph J. ... Clark, NJ
Lichtenfeld, Steven L. ... New York, NY
Lichtenfeld, Susan Grob ... Chicago, IL
Lichtenfels, J. Reid ... Denver, CO
Lichtenfels, Pansing & Miller, P.C.
Denver, CO
Lichtenstein, Adam V. ... Washington, DC
Lichtenstein, Alan D. ... Mount Kisco, NY
Lichtenstein, Allen ... Las Vegas, NV
Lichtenstein, Aviva Z. ... Skokie, IL
Lichtenstein, Cynthia C. ... New York, NY
Lichtenstein, Daniel H. ... Chicago, IL
Lichtenstein, David ... Denver, CO
Lichtenstein, David G. ... Chicago, IL
Lichtenstein, David N. ... Birmingham, AL
Lichtenstein, David S. ... Rockville, MD
Lichtenstein, David S. ... Birmingham, MI
Lichtenstein, Edward S. ... Chicago, IL
Chicago Heights, IL
Lichtenstein, Edward Weil ... Philadelphia, PA
Lichtenstein, Elissa C. ... Washington, DC
Lichtenstein and Fishwick, P.L.C.
Roanoke, VA
Lichtenstein, Jason M. ... Pittsburgh, PA
Lichtenstein, Jason R. ... Chicago, IL
Lichtenstein, Joel H. ... Bridgeport, CT
Lichtenstein, John E. ... Roanoke, VA
Lichtenstein, Jon D. ... New York, NY
Lichtenstein, Jonathan G.
Philadelphia, PA
Lichtenstein, Joseph M. ... Bronx, NY
New York, NY
Lichtenstein, Joshua S. ... Iselin, NJ
Short Hills, NJ
Lichtenstein, Kari H. ... Chicago, IL
Lichtenstein, Larry B., & Associates
Chicago, IL
Lichtenstein, Lawrence R.
Saratoga Springs, NY
Lichtenstein, Lynn S.
Federal Energy Regulatory Commission,
Office of the General Counsel, GV
Lichtenstein, Mark ... Newton, MA
Lichtenstein, Mark S. ... Princeton, NJ
New York, NY
Lichtenstein, Michael David ... Roseland, NJ
Lichtenstein, Michael J. ... Washington, DC
Lichtenstein, Michael J. ... New York, NY
Lichtenstein, Nancy J. ... Denver, CO
Lichtenstein, Nancy Rabi ... Trenton, NJ
Lichtenstein, Natalie G. ... Washington, DC
Lichtenstein, Nathan H. ... Chicago, IL
Lichtenstein, Norman B. ... White Plains, NY
Lichtenstein, Robert B. ... San Francisco, CA
Lichtenstein, Robert J. ... Philadelphia, PA
Lichtenstein, Robert L. ... Hopewell, VA
Lichtenstein, Russell L. ... Atlantic City, NJ
Lichtenstein, Sande E., (Mr.)
Mamaroneck, NY
Lichtenstein, Sarah C. ... New York, NY
Lichtenstein & Schindel ... Mamaroneck, NY
Lichtenstein, Seth ... Beverly Hills, CA
Lichtenstein, Stephen D. ... Waltham, MA
Lichtenstein, Stephen F. ... Trenton, NJ
Lichtenstein, Susan R. ... Chicago, IL
Lichtenthal, Joseph A. ... White Plains, NY
Lichter & Associates, P.C. ... Boulder, CO
Denver, CO
Lichter, Cathy J. ... Washington, DC
Lichter, David H. ... Miami, FL
Lichter, David I. ... Clearwater, FL
Lichter, Erik J. ... Washington, DC
Baltimore, MD
Lichter, George S. ... Beverly Hills, CA
Lichter, Grossman, Nichols & Adler, Inc.
Los Angeles, CA
Lichter, Irwin G., (P.A.) ... Miami, FL
Lichter, Jonathan M. ... Hartsdale, NY
Lichter, Julius W. ... Baltimore, MD
Towson, MD
Lichter, Lance Alan ... Cedarburg, WI
Lichter, Laura L. ... Boulder, CO
Lichter, Leo R. ... Cedarburg, WI
Lichter, Leon J. ... New York, NY
Lichter, Leonard ... New York, NY
Lichter, Lester ... White Plains, NY
Lichter, Linda ... Los Angeles, CA
Lichter, Martin ... New York, NY
Lichter, Mayra R. ... North Miami, FL
Lichter, Richard R. ... Milwaukee, WI
Lichter, Rosalind ... New York, NY
Lichter, Sally A. ... Libertyville, IL
Lichterman, Harold R.
San Francisco, CA
Lichterman, Harvey S. ... Chicago, IL
Lichterman, Herbert ... Lauderhill, FL
Lichterman, Stuart F. ... Beverly Hills, CA
Lichterman, Susan S. ... Detroit, MI
Lichterman, Traister & Brussel
Beverly Hills, CA
Lichtfuss, Kurt E. ... Lakewood, CO
Lichtgarn, Eve ... Los Angeles, CA
Lichtig, Howard S. ... Castro Valley, CA
Lichtig, Scott ... Los Angeles, CA
Lichtig, Steven M. ... Hamilton, OH
Lichtig, William A. ... Sacramento, CA
Lichtinger, Michele M. ... Findlay, OH
Lichtman, Aaron Chess ... New York, NY
Lichtman, Arthur ... New York, NY
Lichtman, Bari Brown ... Chicago, IL
Lichtman, Charles H. ... Miami, FL
Lichtman, Charles S. ... Birmingham, AL
Lichtman, Elliott C. ... Washington, DC
Lichtman, James M. ... Burbank, CA
Lichtman, Jay L. ... Los Angeles, CA
Lichtman, Jeffrey ... New York, NY
Lichtman, Jeffrey A. ... New York, NY
Lichtman, Jeffrey E. ... Cleveland, OH
Lichtman, Jeffrey S. ... New York, NY
Lichtman, Jeffrey S. ... Philadelphia, PA
Lichtman, Joanne ... Los Angeles, CA
Lichtman, Jonathan J. ... Fort Lauderdale, FL
Lichtman, Joshua D. ... Los Angeles, CA
Lichtman, L. Savannah
San Francisco, CA
Lichtman, Lawrence A. ... Birmingham, MI
Lichtman, Marc S. ... Chicago, IL
Lichtman, Paul B. ... Studio City, CA
Lichtman, Robert M. ... San Francisco, CA
Lichtman, Shari H. ... New York, NY
Lichtman, Stephen L. ... Trumbull, CT
Lichtman, Steven ... New York, NY
Lichtman, Trister, Singer & Ross
Washington, DC
Lichtmann, Katherine J. ... Chevy Chase, MD
Lichtnegger, Payne, Weiss, Hahn & Fetterhoff, L.L.C. ... Jackson, MO
Lichtor, David T. ... St. Paul, MN
Lichtsinn & Haensel, S.C. ... Milwaukee, WI
Lichtstein, Stephen P. ... West Orange, NJ
Lichty, Glenna Kelly ... Kansas City, MO
Lichty, Michael J. ... St. Louis, MO
Lichty, Warren D., Jr. ... Lincoln, NE
Lichy, Andrew D. ... Merrick, NY
Licitra, Edward A. ... Miami, FL
Licitra, Lawrence J. ... Armonk, NY
Lick, David M. ... Lansing, MI
Lick, Fred, Jr. ... Strongsville, OH
Licke, James W. ... Bellevue, WA
Licke, Wallace J. ... Grand Rapids, MN
Licker, Donald J. ... Sacramento, CA
Licker, Douglas E. ... Boston, MA
Licker, Eugene R. ... New York, NY
Licker, Mark B. ... New City, NY
Licker, Marvin ... Downey, CA
Licker, Naomi R. ... Potomac, MD
Licker, Robert ... Sepulveda, CA
Licker, Stephen S. ... Los Angeles, CA
Licker, William ... Los Angeles, CA
Lickerman, Michael A. ... Los Angeles, CA
Lickey, Randolph H. ... Richmond, VA
Lickfelt, Gary A. ... Sandusky, OH
Lickiss, Stephen J. ... Decorah, IA
Lickness, Timothy R. ... San Diego, CA
Licko, Carol A. ... Tallahassee, FL
Lickstein, Fred K. ... Miami, FL
Lickstein, Leslie W. ... Fairfax, VA
Lickstein, Leslie W., P.C. ... Fairfax, VA
Lickstein, Scott A. ... Syracuse, NY
Lickteig, Stephen G. ... Minneapolis, MN
Lickteig, Theodore J. ... Overland Park, KS
Lico, James A. ... San Francisco, CA
Lico, Jennifer R. ... Garden City, NY
Licosati, Michael C. ... Chicago, IL
Licygiewicz, Arthur P. ... Cleveland, OH
Lida, Carl H. ... Plantation, FL
Lida, Carl H., P.A. ... Plantation, FL
Lidaka, Maris V. ... Oak Park, IL
Lidaka, Mary Jane ... Toms River, NJ

Lidawer, Annette R. ... New York, NY
Lidbury, James T. ... Chicago, IL
Lidbury, Thomas A. ... Chicago, IL
Lidd, Dorothea ... Chicago, IL
Liddane, Michael J. ... Detroit, MI
Liddell, Amber M. ... San Antonio, TX
Liddell, David B. ... Syracuse, NY
Liddell, Donald C. ... Los Angeles, CA
Liddell, Frank A., Jr. ... Houston, TX
Liddell, Gloria Washington ... Louisville, MS
Liddell, Jeanine Parshley ... Boston, MA
Liddell, Leon M. ... Houston, TX
Liddell & Liddell, P.A. ... Louisville, MS
Liddell, Patrick A. ... Glendale, CA
Liddell, Pearson, Jr. ... Louisville, MS
Liddell, Robert B. ... Syracuse, NY
Liddell, Roy H. ... Jackson, MS
Liddell, Sapp, Zivley, Hill & LaBoon, L.L.P. Austin, TX Dallas, TX Houston, TX
Liddell, Tomilou Gentry Oklahoma City, OK
Liddell, W. Kirk ... Lancaster, PA
Liddicoat, Brian ... Watsonville, CA
Liddicote, Harry, Jr. ... Crescent City, CA
Liddle, Bradway A., Jr. ... Madison, WI
Liddle, Donald J., Law Office of Antioch, CA
Liddle, George Lee, Jr. ... Glendora, CA
Liddle, Jeffrey L. ... New York, NY
Liddle, Karen C. ... Southfield, MI
Liddle, Layne L. ... Glendora, CA
Liddle & Liddle, A Prof. Corp. Glendora, CA
Liddle, Mary T. ... Leawood, KS
Liddle, Patrick W. ... Spring House, PA
Liddle, Rob ... Oak Brook, IL
Liddle & Robinson, L.L.P. ... New York, NY
Liddle, Thomas H., III Department of Justice, Antitrust Division, GV
Liddon, J. Flint ... Birmingham, AL
Liddon, Page Poerschke ... Birmingham, AL
Liddon, Robert C. ... Memphis, TN
Liddy, Dan P. ... Corona, CA
Liddy, Dianne L. ... Westminster, CA
Liddy, Donald G. ... Glendale, CA
Liddy, J. Patrick ... Cincinnati, OH
Liddy, Joseph P. ... Corona, CA
Liddy, Mary J. ... Detroit, MI
Liddy, Raymond J. ... Irvine, CA
Liddy, Sarah J. ... Holly Springs, MS
Liddy Sullivan Galway Begler & Cohen, P.C. New York, NY
Liddy, Thomas P. ... Phoenix, AZ
Lide, Melville D. ... Vineland, NJ
Lide, Montgomery & Potts, P.C. Columbia, SC
Lide, Vinton D. ... Columbia, SC
Liden, Barry Robert ... Dallas, TX
Liden & Dobberfuhl, S.C. ... Barron, WI
Liden, Gerald L. ... Barron, WI
Liden, Tracy B. ... Dallas, TX
Lider, Bruce W. ... New Bedford, MA
Lider, Ralph D. ... New Bedford, MA
Lider, Smola & Fogarty ... New Bedford, MA
Lidfeldt, Lawrence L. ... Maitland, FL
Lidgate, James A. ... Worcester, MA
Lidia, D. Daryl ... Oklahoma City, OK
Lidinsky, Frank G. ... Baltimore, MD
Lidji, Brian M. ... Dallas, TX
Lidji, I. Scott ... Houston, TX
Lidke, Lynne D. ... Indianapolis, IN
Lidl, Erich J., The Law Office of San Diego, CA
Lidman, Daniel H. ... Beverly Hills, CA
Lidman, Diane S. ... Chicago, IL
Lidman, Eric A. ... New York, NY
Lidman, James R. ... Wilmette, IL
Lidman, Scott M. ... Los Angeles, CA
Lidoff, Herbert J. ... Washington, DC
Lidon, James Peter ... Newark, NJ
Lidon, Jean S. ... Cranford, NJ
Lidowsky, Mitchel ... New York, NY
Lidschin & Lidschin ... Waukegan, IL
Lidschin, Mark R. ... Waukegan, IL
Lidsky, Carlos ... Hialeah, FL
Lidsky, Judith ... Boston, MA
Lidsky, Michael A. Department of Agriculture, Animal and Plant Health Inspection Service, GV
Lidstad, Christopher A. ... Minneapolis, MN
Lidston, Robert C. ... Baltimore, MD
Lidstone, David J. ... Princeton, NJ
Lidstone, Herrick K., Jr. ... Englewood, CO
Lidums, O. Robert ... Elkton, MD
Lidy, Adeline G. ... Walnut Creek, CA
Lidz, Diane L. ... Atlanta, GA
Lidz, Jerome ... Roseburg, OR
Lidz, Katharine G. ... Norristown, PA
Lidz, Theodore J. Administrative Office Of The United States Courts, GV
Lieb, Allan G. ... San Diego, CA
Lieb, Benjamin Baughman ... Denver, CO
Lieb, Bruce L. ... New York, NY
Lieb, Charles H. ... Easton, CT
Lieb, David ... Washington, DC
Lieb, David K. ... Center Moriches, NY
Lieb, David K., P.C. ... Center Moriches, NY
Lieb, Dawn B. ... Augusta, ME
Lieb, Donald M. ... Milwaukee, WI
Lieb, Dwight L. ... San Antonio, TX
Lieb, Ellen M. ... New York, NY
Lieb, Fred L. ... Buffalo Grove, IL
Lieb & Hayes ... Patchogue, NY
Lieb, James M. ... New York, NY
Lieb, James S. ... Dallas, TX
Lieb, Joseph ... Patchogue, NY
Lieb, Kenneth S. ... Department of Defense, Defense Legal Services Agency, GV
Lieb, L. Robert ... West Paterson, NJ
Lieb, Lester ... North Caldwell, NJ
Lieb, M. Joseph, Jr. ... Sarasota, FL
Lieb, Michael C. ... Los Angeles, CA
Lieb, Morton ... Orangeburg, NY
Lieb, Peggy R. ... San Diego, CA
Lieb, Peter M. ... Purchase, NY
Lieb, Philip S. ... Chicago, IL
Lieb, Richard ... New York, NY
Lieb, Robert D. ... Encino, CA
Lieb, Stephen J. ... New York, NY
Lieb, Steven E. ... Chicago, IL
Lieb, Victoria L. ... Syracuse, NY
Lieb, Wayne ... Olympia, WA
Lieb, William G. ... Los Angeles, CA
Liebaert, Timothy B. ... Bakersfield, CA
Liebau, Amy J. ... Wichita, KS
Liebau, Judd Alan ... Wichita, KS
Liebbe, Bill ... Dallas, TX Lindale, TX
Liebbe, Bill ... Tyler, TX
Liebbe, Michael W. ... Davenport, IA
Liebe, Annette I. ... Portland, OR
Liebel, Walter E. ... Seymour, TX
Liebel, William E. ... Oklahoma City, OK
Liebeler, Eric C. ... Los Angeles, CA
Liebeler, Lars H. ... Washington, DC Bethesda, MD Fairfax, VA
Liebeler, Susan Wittenberg ... Malibu, CA
Lieben, T. Geoffrey ... Omaha, NE
Lieben, Whitted, Houghton, Slowiaczek & Cavanagh, P.C. ... Omaha, NE
Liebenbaum, Lawrence F. Los Angeles, CA
Liebenberg, Roberta D. ... Jenkintown, PA
Liebenberg & White ... Jenkintown, PA Philadelphia, PA
Liebengood, Kirk M., P.C. ... Flint, MI
Liebengood, Paul O. ... Blue Springs, MO
Liebenson, Harold A. ... Highland Park, IL
Liebenson, Jeffrey M. ... New York, NY
Liebenson, Paul M. ... Schaumburg, IL
Liebenthal, Jon B. ... Toledo, OH
Liebentritt, Donald J. ... Chicago, IL
Lieber, Alan H. ... New York, NY
Lieber Associates, P.C. ... Pittsburgh, PA
Lieber, Barbie D. ... New York, NY
Lieber, Barry T. ... Miami Beach, FL
Lieber, Benjamin ... Washington, DC
Lieber, Bennett M. ... Arcadia, CA
Lieber, Bruce J. ... New York, NY
Lieber & Carisch ... Indianapolis, IN
Lieber, Carol N. ... Highland Park, MI
Lieber, Daniel M. ... Minneapolis, MN
Lieber, Deanna Lynn ... Topeka, KS
Lieber, Deborah A. ... Los Angeles, CA
Lieber, Eugene H. ... New York, NY
Lieber, Gary L. ... Washington, DC
Lieber, Howard L. ... Chicago, IL
Lieber, James C., Jr. ... Kansas City, MO
Lieber, James Richard ... Tulsa, OK
Lieber, Jeffrey E. ... Woodland Hills, CA
Lieber, Jerome B. ... Pittsburgh, PA
Lieber, John H. ... Tulsa, OK
Lieber, Joseph S. ... Boston, MA
Lieber, Karen ... Irvine, CA
Lieber, Kate ... Amherst, MA
Lieber, Katherine B. ... Portland, OR
Lieber, Kenneth W. ... Allen Park, MI
Lieber & Lieber ... New York, NY
Lieber, Lieber & Tarantine, P.C. Pittsburgh, PA
Lieber, Lynn D. ... Redwood City, CA
Lieber, Margery E. National Labor Relations Board, Office of the General Counsel, GV
Lieber, Mark C. ... Los Angeles, CA
Lieber, Marvin S. ... Pittsburgh, PA
Lieber, Michael R. ... Chicago, IL
Lieber, Paula A. ... Short Hills, NJ
Lieber, Penina Kessler ... Pittsburgh, PA
Lieber, Rachel Carlson ... Washington, DC
Lieber, Robert ... Boca Raton, FL
Lieber, Robert M. ... San Francisco, CA
Lieber, Ronald S. ... Indianapolis, IN
Lieber, Sheila ... Department of Justice, Civil Division, GV
Lieber, Stanley ... Woodland Hills, CA
Lieber-Alessie, Alex ... Houston, TX
Lieberbaum, William J. ... Atlanta, GA
Lieberfarb, Stanley J. ... Naples, FL
Lieberg, Jon H. ... Temecula, CA
Lieberman, A. Robt. ... New York, NY
Lieberman, Abraham ... Lorain, OH
Lieberman, Alan E. ... Hartford, CT
Lieberman, Alan M. ... Philadelphia, PA
Lieberman, Alan S. ... Chico, CA
Lieberman, Albert L. ... Detroit, MI
Lieberman, Allan M. Department of Commerce, Patent and Trademark Office, GV
Lieberman, Amy Bloom San Francisco, CA
Lieberman, Amy L. ... Scottsdale, AZ
Lieberman, Ann Dee ... Absecon, NJ
Lieberman, April ... New Haven, CT
Lieberman, Arnold & Associates Buffalo, NY
Lieberman, Arnold Lewis, (P.A.) ... Miami, FL
Lieberman, Arnold R. ... Philadelphia, PA
Lieberman, Arnold T. ... Buffalo, NY
Lieberman, Arthur M. ... New York, NY
Lieberman, Barry L. ... Las Vegas, NV
Lieberman, Bernard ... Piscataway, NJ
Lieberman, Bernard ... Cincinnati, OH
Lieberman, Boris R.Z. ... San Francisco, CA
Lieberman, Brian D. ... Secaucus, NJ
Lieberman, Bruce A. ... Walnut Creek, CA
Lieberman, Bruce A., A Prof. Corp., Law Offices of ... Walnut Creek, CA
Lieberman, Bruce H. ... Hopkins, MN
Lieberman, Bruce R. ... Scottsdale, AZ
Lieberman, Charles F. ... Milford, PA
Lieberman, Dale ... Philadelphia, PA
Lieberman, Daniel M. ... Lancaster, PA
Lieberman, David ... New York, NY
Lieberman, David ... New York, NY
Lieberman, David C. ... Treasury Department, Bureau of Alcohol, Tobacco and Firearms, GV
Lieberman, David E. ... Chicago, IL
Lieberman, David E. ... Nashua, NH
Lieberman, David H., P.C. ... Jericho, NY
Lieberman, David J. ... Southfield, MI
Lieberman, David S. ... Atlantic City, NJ
Lieberman, Deborah ... San Francisco, CA
Lieberman, Dennis A. ... Dayton, OH
Lieberman, Dodge, Sendrow & Gerding, Ltd. ... Phoenix, AZ
Lieberman, Donna ... New York, NY
Lieberman, Donna H. ... New York, NY
Lieberman, Douglas M. ... Hicksville, NY
Lieberman, Edward H. ... Washington, DC
Lieberman, Edward I. ... New York, NY
Lieberman, Edward J. ... St. Louis, MO
Lieberman, Edward L. ... Garden City, NY
Lieberman, Edward M. ... Elmsford, NY
Lieberman, Elizabeth Rae ... Bethesda, MD
Lieberman, Ellen ... New York, NY
Lieberman, Elliott B. ... Oakland, CA
Lieberman, Eric B. ... Freehold, NJ
Lieberman, Eric J. ... Wheaton, IL
Lieberman, Eric M. ... New York, NY
Lieberman, Eric N. ... Washington, DC
Lieberman, Erik R. ... Venice, FL
Lieberman, Eugene ... Wilmette, IL
Lieberman, Frederic L. ... New York, NY
Lieberman, Gary ... Los Angeles, CA
Lieberman, Gary A. ... New York, NY
Lieberman, Gary H. ... Las Vegas, NV
Lieberman, Gary L. ... Cleveland, OH
Lieberman, Gary R. ... Oakland, CA
Lieberman, George E. ... Providence, RI
Lieberman, Glenn B. ... Beverly Hills, CA
Lieberman, Hal R. ... New York, NY
Lieberman, Harold ... Cincinnati, OH
Lieberman, Heidi Atkins ... Jefferson City, MO
Lieberman, Herman ... Coconut Creek, FL
Lieberman, Howard Loren ... Stillwater, MN
Lieberman, Ilene ... Lauderhill, FL
Lieberman, Irena S. ... Falls Church, VA
Lieberman, James G. ... San Diego, CA
Lieberman, Jay M. ... Milwaukee, WI
Lieberman, Jeffrey A. ... New York, NY
Lieberman, Jeffrey B. ... Chicago, IL
Lieberman, Jethro K. ... New York, NY
Lieberman, Joan S. ... Department of Justice, Immigration and Naturalization Service, GV
Lieberman, Joan Wiesen ... New York, NY
Lieberman, Joel M. ... Philadelphia, PA
Lieberman, John B., III ... Pottsville, PA
Lieberman, John K. ... Philadelphia, PA
Lieberman, Jon ... New York, NY
Lieberman, Jonathan ... New York, NY
Lieberman, Jonathan A. ... Miami, FL
Lieberman, Jonathan A. ... New York, NY
Lieberman, Jules A. ... Cherry Hill, NJ
Lieberman, Kalman S. ... Glencoe, IL
Lieberman, Karen M. ... Chicago, IL
Lieberman, Kathleen H. ... Bensalem, PA
Lieberman, Kathy A. ... Washington, DC
Lieberman, Kraag C. ... Charlevoix, MI
Lieberman, Lance J. ... New York, NY
Lieberman, Larry D. ... Milwaukee, WI
Lieberman, Laurie ... Santa Monica, CA
Lieberman, Lawr. L. ... Newport News, VA
Lieberman, Lawrence ... Brooklyn, NY
Lieberman, Lawrence H. ... Phoenix, AZ
Lieberman, Lawrence M. ... Encino, CA
Lieberman, Lawrence R. ... Los Angeles, CA
Lieberman, Lewis E. ... New York, NY
Lieberman, Lewis I. ... Warminster, PA
Lieberman, Lisa R. ... Philadelphia, PA
Lieberman, Lyle ... Greenbelt, MD
Lieberman, Lyle ... Warren, MI
Lieberman, Lyle D., Law Offices of Miami, FL
Lieberman, Marc ... Danville, PA
Lieberman, Marc R. ... Phoenix, AZ
Lieberman, Mark C. ... Chicago, IL
Lieberman, Mark L. ... Westbury, NY
Lieberman, Mark S. ... Chicago, IL
Lieberman, Martin ... Phoenix, AZ
Lieberman, Martin ... Bronx, NY
Lieberman, Martin L. ... Jamaica, NY
Lieberman, Martin, P.C. ... Phoenix, AZ
Lieberman & Martin, P.C. ... Chesapeake, VA
Lieberman, Marvin ... Somerville, NJ
Lieberman, Marvin ... Brooklyn, NY
Lieberman, Max L., & Associates Fort Washington, PA
Lieberman, Mayer L. (Max) San Francisco, CA
Lieberman, Meryl R. ... Hawthorne, NY
Lieberman, Michael ... Cherry Hill, NJ Philadelphia, PA
Lieberman, Michael A. ... Silver Spring, MD
Lieberman, Michael D. ... Southfield, MI
Lieberman, Michael J. ... Boston, MA
Lieberman, Michael L. ... Washington, DC
Lieberman, Michael S. ... Alexandria, VA
Lieberman, Mitchell A. ... Chicago, IL
Lieberman, Mitchell P. Yorktown Heights, NY
Lieberman, Myron ... Chicago, IL
Lieberman, Nancy A. ... New York, NY
Lieberman, Nancy D. ... Jericho, NY
Lieberman, Norman ... Monterey Park, CA
Lieberman & Nowak, LLP ... New York, NY
Lieberman, Paul ... Washington, DC
Lieberman, Paul ... Department of Commerce, Patent and Trademark Office, GV
Lieberman, Paul ... General Accounting Office, Office of the General Counsel, GV
Lieberman, Paul ... Bloomfield Hills, MI
Lieberman, Paul ... Brooklyn, NY
Lieberman, Penny Ann ... New York, NY
Lieberman, Peter H. ... Chicago, IL
Lieberman, Philippe ... Miami, FL
Lieberman, Phillip H. ... Boston, MA
Lieberman, R. Michael ... San Francisco, CA
Lieberman, Rachel S. ... Philadelphia, PA
Lieberman, Raphael ... New York, NY
Lieberman, Richard ... Phoenix, AZ
Lieberman, Richard D. ... Washington, DC
Lieberman, Richard E. ... Chicago, IL
Lieberman, Richard L. ... Northbrook, IL
Lieberman, Robert A. ... Kansas City, MO
Lieberman, Robert B. ... Harrisburg, PA
Lieberman, Robert H. ... Los Angeles, CA
Lieberman, Robert L. ... Westmont, NJ
Lieberman, Rochelle ... Gaithersburg, MD
Lieberman, Ronald G. ... Haddonfield, NJ
Lieberman, Ronald J. ... Chicago, IL
Lieberman, Ronald M. ... Skokie, IL
Lieberman & Ryan ... Somerville, NJ
Lieberman, Scott D. ... Fort Lauderdale, FL
Lieberman, Seth M. ... Brooklyn, NY
Lieberman, Sidney C. ... Cincinnati, OH
Lieberman, Sol ... New York, NY
Lieberman, Stanley J. ... Exton, PA
Lieberman, Stephen B. ... Reading, PA
Lieberman, Stephen C. ... Truckee, CA
Lieberman, Stephen H. Department Of Health And Human Services, Food & Drug Administration, GV
Lieberman, Stevan H. ... Takoma Park, MD
Lieberman, Steven ... Washington, DC
Lieberman, Steven ... Chesapeake, VA
Lieberman, Steven B. ... Somerville, NJ
Lieberman, Steven Jeffrey ... Houston, TX
Lieberman, Steven P. ... Tarrytown, NY
Lieberman, Stuart J. ... Plainsboro, NJ
Lieberman, Sumner M. ... Boston, MA
Lieberman, Toby ... Los Angeles, CA
Lieberman, Valerie H. ... Philadelphia, PA
Liebermann, Amy C. ... Lexington, KY
Liebermann, Eric J. ... Wheaton, IL
Liebermann, Jane ... Rancho Santa Fe, CA
Liebers, Emily H. ... Chicago, IL
Liebers, Robert A. ... Jamestown, NY
Liebersbach, John W. ... Columbus, OH
Liebersbach, Mohun, Carney & Reed, A Professional Corporation Mammoth Lakes, CA
Liebersbach, Richard W. Mammoth Lakes, CA
Liebersohn, Arthur P. ... Philadelphia, PA
Lieberson, Alan D. ... Westport, CT New York, NY
Lieberson, Jay B. ... Yardley, PA
Lieberson, Miriam ... New York, NY
Lieberson, Rhona S. Derrin ... Greenwich, CT
Lieberson, Saml. ... Boston, MA
Lieberstein, Eugene ... New York, NY
Lieberstein, Gary A. ... Napa, CA
Lieberstein, Marc A. ... New York, NY
Lieberstein, Stanley H. ... New York, NY
Liebert, Allan H. ... Los Angeles, CA
Liebert, Cassidy & Frierson, A Professional Corporation ... Los Angeles, CA San Francisco, CA
Liebert, Frank W. ... Coffeyville, KS
Liebert, J. Michael ... Silverdale, WA
Liebert, John ... Los Angeles, CA
Liebert, Martin ... Loomis, CA
Liebert, Ronald ... Sacramento, CA
Liebert, T. Richard ... Coffeyville, KS
Liebert, Tabatha A. ... Tampa, FL
Lieberth, David A. ... Akron, OH
Lieberth/Anderson, A Legal Prof. Assoc. Akron, OH
Liebertal, David H. ... Tucson, AZ
Liebertal, Neil A. ... Bridgeport, CT
Liebert-Hall, Linda A., P.C. ... Fargo, ND
Lieberworth, David ... Seattle, WA
Liebes, Hal ... New York, NY
Liebeschuetz, Joe ... Palo Alto, CA
Liebeskind, John W. ... Springfield, PA
Liebeskind, Marc Emile ... Flourtown, PA
Liebeskind, Michelle L. ... New York, NY
Liebeskind, Richard, Jr. Federal Trade Commission, Bureau of Competition, GV
Liebesman, Lawrence R. Silver Spring, MD
Liebesman, Michelle Aldrich ... Paoli, PA
Liebesman, Peter C. ... Treasury Department, Office of the Comptroller of the Currency, GV
Liebesman, Sidney S. ... Cherry Hill, NJ Philadelphia, PA
Liebfeld, Daniel E. ... Baltimore, MD
Liebgold, Michael P. ... St. Petersburg, FL
Liebhaber, Jack M. ... Los Angeles, CA
Liebhaber, Sharon Fay ... Berwyn, PA
Liebhafsky, Andrew ... New York, NY
Liebhafsky, Douglas S. ... New York, NY

Liebhard, Sandy A. ... **New York, NY**
Liebhardt, Nadine S. ... **New York, NY**
Liebhauser, Jennifer Dawn ... **Dallas, TX**
Liebherr, Donald P. ... Sherman Oaks, CA
Liebig, Virginia L. ... North Oaks, MN
Liebke, Hope H. ... **New York, NY**
Liebl, Kenneth A. ... West Hempstead, NY
Lieblein, Mark S. ... **Burbank, CA**
Liebler, Craig M. ... **Kennewick, WA**
Liebler, Edward C. ... Lansing, MI
Liebler, Gonzalez & Portuondo, P.A. **Miami, FL**
Liebler, Ivey & Connor, P.S. **Pendleton, OR** **Kennewick, WA** **Pasco, WA** **Richland, WA** **Yakima, WA**
Liebler, J. Randolph ... **Miami, FL**
Liebler, James M. ... Moorestown, NJ
Liebler, Lewis ... Syracuse, NY
Lieblich, Alan H. ... **Philadelphia, PA**
Lieblich, Daniel Parke ... Deal, NJ
Lieblich, Herman ... Flushing, NY
Lieblich, Herman, P.C. ... Flushing, NY
Lieblich, Mark S. ... **Orlando, FL**
Lieblich, Ralph ... Brooklyn, NY
Lieblich, Sharon K. ... **Alexandria, VA**
Lieblich, Sharon K., P.C. ... **Alexandria, VA**
Lieblich, William C. ... **Washington, DC**
Liebling, Charles B. ... **New Brunswick, NJ**
Liebling, Cynthia P. ... **Newark, NJ**
Liebling, Edward ... Clearwater, FL
Liebling, Edward, P.A. ... Clearwater, FL
Liebling, Jeff H. ... **Chicago, IL**
Liebling, Scott D. ... Cherry Hill, NJ
Liebling, Scott D., P.C. ... Cherry Hill, NJ
Liebling, Tina ... Rochester, MN
Liebman, Alan S. ... **New York, NY**
Liebman, Allyson S. ... **New York, NY**
Liebman, Barry G. ... White Plains, NY
Liebman, Bennett M. ... Albany, NY
Liebman, Betsy G. ... **Mount Laurel, NJ**
Liebman, Bruce S. ... **Fort Lauderdale, FL**
Liebman, Burt H. ... New York, NY
Liebman, Carol B. ... New York, NY
Liebman, Carol F. ... Boston, MA
Liebman, Christopher J. ... Sublette, KS
Liebman, David E. ... Brooklyn, NY
Liebman, David L. ... Lincolnshire, IL
Liebman, Dayann M. ... Vancouver, WA
Liebman, Deborah R. ... Albany, NY
Liebman, Diane Fried ... Falls Church, VA
Liebman, Donald ... **New York, NY**
Liebman, Emmanuel ... **Cherry Hill, NJ**
Liebman, Emmanuel, Chartered, A Prof. Corp. ... **Cherry Hill, NJ**
Liebman, Eric B. ... **Denver, CO**
Liebman, Hanna ... **Houston, TX**
Liebman, Helen L. ... **Columbus, OH**
Liebman & Helwig ... Sudbury, MA
Liebman, Henry G. ... **Seattle, WA**
Liebman, Herbert D. ... **Frankfort, KY**
Liebman, J. David ... Miami, FL
Liebman, James Dean ... **Frankfort, KY**
Liebman, James S. ... New York, NY
Liebman, Jan Pittman ... Tampa, FL
Liebman, Jan Pittman, P.A. ... Tampa, FL
Liebman, Jay M. ... Jersey City, NJ
Liebman, Jeffrey R. ... Lincolnwood, IL
Liebman, Jerome J. ... Syosset, NY
Liebman, John B., (P.A.) ... **Orlando, FL**
Liebman, John R. ... **Los Angeles, CA**
Liebman, Jonathan ... Beverly Hills, CA
Liebman, Joseph I. ... Department of Justice, Civil Division, GV
Liebman, Judith G. ... Brooklyn, NY
Liebman, Kenneth A. ... **Minneapolis, MN**
Liebman, Kenneth R. ... Sudbury, MA
Liebman, Lauren Gentele West Palm Beach, FL
Liebman, Lawrence M. ... Jupiter, FL
Liebman and Liebman ... **Frankfort, KY**
Liebman, Lynn Abelson ... Mamaroneck, NY
Liebman, Maurice ... Chicago, IL
Liebman, Michael C. ... Department of Justice, Criminal Division, GV
Liebman, Paul A. ... Philadelphia, PA
Liebman, Paul F. ... Wichita, KS Houston, TX
Liebman, Philip A. ... Virginia Beach, VA
Liebman, Raymond L. ... New York, NY
Liebman & Reiner, A Professional Law Corporation ... Los Angeles, CA Roseville, CA San Diego, CA San Francisco, CA
Liebman, Richard ... **New York, NY**
Liebman, Richard D. ... Chicago, IL
Liebman, Richard F. ... **Portland, OR**
Liebman, Robert Franz ... Carmel, CA
Liebman, Robert L. ... Cincinnati, OH
Liebman, Ronald S. ... **Washington, DC**
Liebman, Samuel J. ... Mechanicsburg, PA
Liebman, Samuel M. ... Jenkintown, PA
Liebman, Seth L. ... **Newport Beach, CA**
Liebman, Seymour E. ... Lake Success, NY
Liebman, Sharon R. ... **Miami, FL**
Liebman, Stacey Spector ... Collegeville, PA
Liebman, Steven E. ... New York, NY
Liebman, Stewart B. ... Montgomeryville, PA
Liebman, Stuart D. ... **Paramus, NJ** New York, NY
Liebman, Stuart J. ... Los Angeles, CA
Liebman, Vance L. ... **Chicago, IL**
Liebman, William S. Commodity Futures Trading Commission, Office of the General Counsel, GV
Liebman-Mimbu, PLLC ... **Seattle, WA**
Liebmann, Beth S. ... Department of Justice, Executive Office for Immigration Review, GV
Liebmann, Bradley N. ... New York, NY
Liebmann, Conway, Olejniczak & Jerry, S.C. **Green Bay, WI**
Liebmann, Diana M. ... **San Antonio, TX**
Liebmann, Geoffrey E. ... **New York, NY**
Liebmann, George W. ... **Baltimore, MD**
Liebmann, Herbert C., III ... **Green Bay, WI**
Liebmann, Jeff S. ... **New York, NY**
Liebmann, Jeffrey A. ... **Holland, PA**
Liebmann & Shively, P.A. ... **Baltimore, MD**
Liebmann, Theodor S. ... New York, NY
Liebmann, Wilhelm E. ... **San Antonio, TX**
Liebmann, William Q. ... **Camarillo, CA**
Liebo, Stephen L. ... New Hope, MN
Liebolt, F. Lee, Jr. ... **New York, NY**
Liebov, David ... **New York, NY**
Liebovich, Theodore ... Rockford, IL
Liebovich & Weber, P.C. ... Rockford, IL
Liebovitz, Alfred S. ... Costa Mesa, CA
Liebow, Deborah A. ... Chicago, IL
Liebow, Peter A. ... **San Jose, CA**
Liebow, Wendy F. ... Lexington, MA
Liebowitz, Alan E. ... Newtown, PA
Liebowitz, Alan M. ... Englewood, NJ
Liebowitz, Alan R. ... Wayne, NJ
Liebowitz, Allison D. B. ... Newark, NJ
Liebowitz, Elise G. ... **New York, NY**
Liebowitz, Ellen ... Department of Justice, Executive Office for Immigration Review, GV
Liebowitz, Jeffrey B. ... **New York, NY**
Liebowitz, Jerome L. ... **Fort Lee, NJ**
Liebowitz, Jonathan S. ... White Plains, NY
Liebowitz & Jurecky, L.L.P. ... **Fort Lee, NJ**
Liebowitz & Liebowitz ... Englewood, NJ
Liebowitz, Milton D. ... Englewood, NJ
Liebowitz, Mitchell A. ... West Orange, NJ
Liebowitz, Ronnie F. ... **Newark, NJ**
Liebowitz, Sheldon M. ... Englewood, NJ
Liebowitz, Sidney I. ... **New York, NY**
Liebross, Audrey H. Small Business Administration, Office of the General Counsel, GV
Liebschner, Sherill L. ... Lisbon, OH
Liebschutz, Elizabeth H. ... Albany, NY
Liebschutz, John F. ... **Rochester, NY**
Liebschutz, Peter R. ... Rochester, NY
Liebschutz, Sanford J. ... **Rochester, NY**
Liebschutz, Scott N. ... Atlanta, GA
Liebson, Susan D. ... Long Beach, CA
Liebster, Jeffrey R. ... **Los Angeles, CA**
Liebzeit, Larry ... Appleton, WI
Liechty, Clinton L., P.C. ... Tucson, AZ
Liechty, Douglas C. ... **Newport Beach, CA**
Liechty, Jean Singleton ... Newport Beach, CA
Liechty, Linda C. ... Pittsburgh, PA
Liechty, Lorne O. ... Dallas, TX
Liechty, Robert M. ... **Denver, CO**
Liechty, V. Ann ... **Billings, MT**
Lieck, Charles J., Jr. ... San Antonio, TX
Lied, Erik R. ... **Seattle, WA**
Lied, Michael R. ... **Peoria, IL**
Liedberg, Douglas H. ... **Toledo, OH**
Liedecke, Lee M. ... **Los Angeles, CA**
Liedel, David M. ... **Detroit, MI**
Liedel, Deidre A. ... **Toledo, OH**
Liedel, Jason, Grinnan & Liedel, P.C. **Detroit, MI** Northville, MI
Liedel, Richard J. ... Gaylord, MI
Liedel, Steven C. ... **Lansing, MI**
Liedel, William J. ... **Detroit, MI** Northville, MI
Lieder, Dennis ... Webster, WI
Lieder, Kathleen A. ... **Cheboygan, MI**
Lieder, Michael D. ... **Washington, DC**
Liederbach, Hahn, Foy & Petri, P.C. Jamison, PA **Richboro, PA**
Liederman, Arthur J. ... New York, NY
Liederman, Carl L. ... **Washington, DC**
Liederman, Robt. ... Forest Hills, NY
Lieding & Anderson, P.C. ... **McLean, VA**
Liedl, Mark B. ... Madison, WI
Liedle, Matthew J. ... **San Diego, CA**
Liedlich, Nancy C. ... Southbury, CT
Liedtka, Jeanne M. ... **Washington, DC**
Liedtke, Mary M. ... Eau Claire, WI
Liedtke, William P. ... North Olmsted, OH
Liedy, Robert E. ... Staten Island, NY
Lief, Daniel S. ... New York, NY
Lief, Jason A. ... **New York, NY**
Lief, Stephen J. ... Riverdale, NY
Liefer, Gerald H. ... Grand Rapids, MI
Lieff, Cabraser, Heimann & Bernstein, LLP **San Francisco, CA** **New York, NY**
Lieff, Robert L. ... **San Francisco, CA**
Lieffers, Harry, Jr. ... St. Petersburg, FL
Lieffrig, Yvonne ... Smithtown, NY
Liefschultz Law Firm ... Minneapolis, MN
Liefschultz, Steven B. ... Minneapolis, MN
Liegel, Konrad J. ... **Seattle, WA**
Liegel, Robert G. ... Syracuse, NY
Liegeot, Lisa M. ... West Hartford, CT
Liegl, David B. ... Lincoln, NE
Liegl, Joseph L. ... Cleveland, OH
Liehe, Clifford J. ... San Francisco, CA
Liekar, James P. ... Canonsburg, PA
Liekar, John P. ... Canonsburg, PA
Liekar, John P., Jr. ... **Pittsburgh, PA**
Liekar & Liekar ... Canonsburg, PA
Liekhus, Lisa A. ... Beatrice, NE Wymore, NE
Liekweg, John A. ... Washington, DC
Liell, James T. ... **White Plains, NY**
Liell, Katharine C. ... Bloomington, IN
Liell & McNeil ... Bloomington, IN
Liem, Angelica S. ... **Roseland, NJ**
Liem, Michael A. ... **Bridgewater, NJ**
Lieman, Leonard ... Carmel, NY
Lien, Barbara E. ... St. Paul, MN
Lien, Christian Bruce ... Rapid City, SD
Lien, Gregg R. ... Tahoe City, CA
Lien, Henry ... **Los Angeles, CA**
Lien, Herb G. ... Oakland, CA
Lien, James A. ... Orlando, FL
Lien, Jason A. ... Pensacola, FL
Lien, John A. ... Keizer, OR
Lien, John D. ... **Chicago, IL**
Lien, Katherine M. ... Cheshire, CT
Lien, Michael W. ... Duluth, MN
Lien, Molly Warner ... Chicago, IL
Lien, Rhonda J. Federal Communications Commission, Common Carrier Bureau, GV
Lien, Ronald Andrew ... **Washington, DC**
Lien, Wallace W. ... Salem, OR
Lien, Wallace W., P.C. ... Salem, OR
Lienard, Kevin L. ... **Orlando, FL**
Lienemann, Leslie L. ... Bloomington, MN
Lienesch, Theodore D. ... **Dayton, OH**
Lienesch, Wendy Lux ... Olympia, WA
Lienhard, Henry O. ... Brea, CA
Lienhard, Jonathan Philip ... Arlington, VA
Lienhard, Rosanne ... **Sioux City, IA**
Lienhard, Tammie T. ... Oklahoma City, OK
Lienhard, W.F. ... San Diego, CA
Lienhart, Frank B. ... Fairfield, OH
Lienhoop, Mark A. ... **La Porte, IN**
Liening, Stacie L. ... **St. Louis, MO**
Lientz, John G. ... **Savannah, GA**
Liepe, Winfrid K. F. ... Eugene, OR
Liepins, Eric A. ... **Dallas, TX**
Liepins, Eric A., P.C., Law Offices of **Dallas, TX**
Liepmann, Karen L. ... **Phoenix, AZ**
Liepmann, W. Hugo ... **Boston, MA**
Liepold, Alfred J. ... Department of Agriculture, Food Safety and Inspection Service, GV
Liepold, Christina M. ... **Cincinnati, OH**
Lieppe, Frank B. ... Atlanta, GA
Lieppe, Frank B., P.C. ... Atlanta, GA
Lieppman, Liessa ... Oklahoma City, OK
Liepshutz, Gerald H. ... Albany, NY
Liepshutz, Greg M. ... Southfield, MI
Liepshutz, M. Paul ... Tallahassee, FL
Lier, Gregory C. ... Harvey, LA
Lier, Kathleen O. ... New Orleans, LA
Lier, M. Renee ... Longmont, CO
Lierely, Patrice ... Des Moines, IA
Lierly, Julie A. ... **Atlanta, GA**
Lierman, Dale O. ... Fairfield, OH
Lierman, Joseph H. ... Champaign, IL
Lierman, Owen Donald ... Springfield, IL
Liero, Steven M. ... Philadelphia, PA
Lierz, Richard K. ... Boise, ID
Lies & Bullis ... **Breckenridge, MN** **Wahpeton, ND**
Lies, Mark A., II ... **Chicago, IL**
Lies, Mary Beth ... La Grange, IL
Lies, Steven J. ... **Wahpeton, ND**
Lies, Thomas W. ... St. Cloud, MN
Lies, William J. ... San Francisco, CA
Liesch, Joseph R. ... Minneapolis, MN
Liesche, Ramona R. ... **Coeur d'Alene, ID**
Liese, E. Thomas ... **St. Louis, MO**
Liese, Richard A. ... New York, NY
Liese, Thomas A. ... New York, NY
Liesemer, Jeffrey A. ... **Washington, DC**
Liesenfeld, Vincent J. ... **Norman, OK**
Lieser, Charles D. ... Fort Worth, TX
Lieske & Kristensen ... Minden, NE
Lieske, Robert E. ... **Minneapolis, MN**
Lieske, Stephen P. ... **San Francisco, CA**
Lieske, Thomas G. ... Minden, NE
Liesman, Francis X., II ... Mason, MI
Liesveld, Barbara H. ... Cedar Rapids, IA
Lietar, Paul A. ... Providence, RI
Lieteau, Michelle L. ... **Los Angeles, CA**
Lieteau, Triste N. ... **Chicago, IL**
Lieth, William ... **Washington, DC**
Liethen, Michael A. ... Madison, WI
Lietz, David K. ... **Washington, DC**
Lietz, Gary R. ... **Champaign, IL**
Lietz, Gregory G. ... **Danville, IL**
Lietz, Robert D. ... Hampton, NH
Lietz, W. Carl, III ... **Atlanta, GA**
Lietzke, Jeffrey S. ... **Cleveland, OH**
Lietzke, Randolph C. ... Lombard, IL
Lietz-Ray, Lisa K. ... Madison, WI
Lieu, Marguerite T. ... **San Diego, CA**
Lieu, Susanne J. ... **Chicago, IL**
Lieuallen, Perry P. ... Port Washington, WI
Lieurance, Cherie L. ... **Los Angeles, CA**
Lieurance, Lovell B. ... Scottsdale, AZ
Lieuwen, James E. ... **Albuquerque, NM**
Lieuwen, John N. ... **Albuquerque, NM**
Lieux, John A. ... Gonzales, LA
Lieux, Kenneth M. ... Elyria, OH
Lieux, Meredith Hoag ... Baton Rouge, LA
Lievano, Fernando ... Miami, FL
Lievens, Gregory M. ... Aplington, IA
Lievens, Richard C. ... **Houston, TX**
Lievense, Mack D. ... Gig Harbor, WA
Liever, Hyman and Potter, P.C. ... Reading, PA
Liever, Michael H. ... **San Francisco, CA**
Lieverman, Theodore M. ... **Cherry Hill, NJ** **Northfield, NJ**
Lievers, Carolyn ... Denver, CO
Lievers, Gregory Y. ... **Escondido, CA**
Lievois, Christopher ... **Bingham Farms, MI**
Lievois, Elise L. ... Bloomfield Hills, MI
Lievois, Gerald T. ... **Bloomfield Hills, MI**
Lievois, Thomas P. ... Troy, MI
Lievy, Stefan C. ... Columbus, OH
Liewald, Lisa H. ... Berwyn, IL
Liewen, Antoinette C. ... Tarzana, CA
Life, Greg A. ... Oskaloosa, IA
Life, Jack T. ... Athens, TX
Life, Robert L. ... Indianapolis, IN
Life, Stark & Owen, P.C. ... Athens, TX
Lifebridge Family Mediation ... Bethesda, MD
Lifer, Martin W., III ... Cumming, GA
Liff, Diane R. ... Department of Transportation, Federal Highway Administration, GV
Liffers, Wendy A. ... Bethesda, MD
Lifflander, Matthew L. ... **New York, NY**
Liffman, Kenneth B. ... **Cleveland, OH**
Liffrig, Michael G. ... Bismarck, ND
Lifka, Daniel ... Downers Grove, IL
Lifland, Burton R. ... New York, NY
Lifland, Carol M. ... Los Angeles, CA
Lifland, Charles C. ... **Los Angeles, CA**
Lifland, Craig I. ... **Bridgeport, CT**
Lifland, John C. ... Newark, NJ
Lifland, Thomas A. ... Cedarhurst, NY
Lifland, William T. ... **New York, NY**
Lifschitz, Hyman ... New York, NY
Lifschitz, Jeanette ... Kew Gardens, NY
Lifschitz, Judah ... **Washington, DC** Greenbelt, MD
Lifschitz & Lifschitz ... New York, NY
Lifschitz, Morris ... New York, NY
Lifschultz, Lowell S. ... **New York, NY**
Lifschultz, Phillip I. ... Mount Prospect, IL
Lifset, Harvey M. ... **Albany, NY**
Lifset, Marc J. ... **Albany, NY**
Lifset, Milton D. ... Delray Beach, FL
Lifsey, J. Stanford ... Tampa, FL
Lifsey, J. Stanford, P.A. ... Tampa, FL
Lifsey, Jerry L. ... Chatsworth, GA
Lifsey, Laura J. ... **Philadelphia, PA**
Lifsey Portes, Susan A. ... New York, NY
Lifshey, Deborah ... **New York, NY**
Lifshitz, Benjamin ... **Beverly Hills, CA**
Lifshitz, Harris T. ... Hartford, CT
Lifshitz, Joshua M. ... **New York, NY**
Lifshitz, Marielle V. ... **Chicago, IL**
Lifshitz, Mel E. ... **New York, NY**
Lifshitz, Miriam L. ... Rocky Hill, CT
Lifshitz, Richard A. ... **Chicago, IL**
Lifshutz, Marvin L. ... New York, NY
Lifshutz & Polland, P.C. ... New York, NY
Lifson, Chrystal N. ... Richmond, VA
Lifson, Roman ... **Richmond, VA**
Lifson, Scott ... **Minneapolis, MN**
Lifson, Steven R. ... **Chicago, IL**
Lifter, Bennett M., (P.A.) ... Miami, FL
Lifter, Jean B. ... Cleveland, OH
Lifter, Jill J. ... **Oakland, CA**
Liftin, John M. ... **Newark, NJ**
Liftman, Barbara S. ... Worcester, MA
Liftman, Beverly E. ... North Brunswick, NJ
Liftman, Kimberly M. ... Chicago, IL Garden City, NY
Lifton, Barbara G. ... Hamden, CT
Lifton, Diane E. ... **New York, NY**
Lifton, Fred B. ... Chicago, IL
Lifton, Judie ... New York, NY
Lifton, Marcy ... **St. Louis, MO**
Lifton, Robert J. ... Wilmette, IL
Lifton, Robert K. ... New York, NY
Lifton, Rosen & Pastel ... Albany, NY
Lifton, Stacy D. ... Beverly Hills, CA
Lifton, Stanley S. ... Los Angeles, CA
Lifton, William S. ... Albany, NY
Lifur, Jeff ... **New York, NY**
Lifvendahl, Eric R. ... **Chicago, IL**
Lifvendahl, Susan F. ... **Chicago, IL**
Ligammari, Andrew A. ... Niagara Falls, NY
Ligammari and Caserta ... Niagara Falls, NY
Ligarde, Margaret ... Austin, TX
Ligas, Andrew ... Chicago, IL
Ligda, Matthew J. ... **Chicago, IL**
Ligda, Paul ... Vallejo, CA
Ligelis, Calliope K. ... New York, NY
Ligelis, Gregory J. ... **Stamford, CT**
Liggett, Barbara S. Federal Labor Relations Authority, Washington Regional Office, GV
Liggett, David K. ... **Raleigh, NC**
Liggett, Dennis A. ... Blue Ash, OH
Liggett, Frank R., III ... **Raleigh, NC**
Liggett, Helen ... Lubbock, TX
Liggett, Lucille G. ... Clayton, MO
Liggett, Luther L., Jr. ... **Columbus, OH**
Liggett, Martha L. ... Washington, DC
Liggett, Michael D. ... **Fort Collins, CO**
Liggett, Nora L. ... **Nashville, TN**
Liggett, Pamela J. ... Bloomfield Hills, MI
Liggett, Philip T. ... Boca Raton, FL
Liggett & Ripley ... Richland, MI
Liggett, Robert G., Jr. ... Williamston, MI
Liggett, Smith & Williams, P.C. **Fort Collins, CO**
Liggett, Thomas E. ... **Windsor, CT**
Liggett, Timothy C. ... Richland, MI
Liggett-Pelanda Co., L.P.A. ... Marysville, OH
Liggin, G. Leonard ... Montezuma, GA
Liggins, Keith G. A. ... Los Angeles, CA
Liggio, Ana O'keefe ... Park Ridge, NJ
Liggio, Benrubi & Williams, P.A. **West Palm Beach, FL**
Liggio, Carl D., Sr. ... Chicago, IL
Liggio, Jeffrey M. ... **West Palm Beach, FL**
Liggio, Paul A. ... **New York, NY**
Ligh, Randy B. ... Baton Rouge, LA
Light, Alan G. ... Lebanon, PA
Light, Alfred Robert ... Miami, FL

Light, Andrew K. ... Indianapolis, IN
Light, Barbara A. ... Annapolis, MD
Light, Bluford H. ... Westminster, CA
Light, C. Orville ... Eden, NC
Light, C. Randolph ... Toledo, OH
Light, Carol J. ... Department of State, Office of the Legal Adviser, GV
Light, C. E. ... Yankton, SD
Light, Cheryl E. ... Knoxville, TN
Light, Corey E. ... Chicago, IL
Light, Dorothy K. ... Newark, NJ
Light, Eber W., Jr. ... Charleston, WV
Light, Edward A. ... Rockford, IL
Light, Elliott B. ... Eau Claire, WI
Light, Gregory A. ... Southfield, MI
Light, Harold J., Law Office of
Santa Monica, CA
Light, Harry A., (P.A.) ... Little Rock, AR
Light, Henry D. ... Norfolk, VA
Light, Ivan I. ... Philadelphia, PA
Light, Jeffrey D. ... San Diego, CA
Light, Jeffrey D. ... Linwood, NJ
Light, Jeffrey H. ... Cleveland, OH
Light, Jeffrey Taylor ... Los Angeles, CA
Light, John K.
Equal Employment Opportunity Commission, Office of Legal Counsel, GV
Light, John P. ... Danville, VA
Light, John R. ... Los Angeles, CA
San Diego, CA
Light, Jonathan D. ... Boston, MA
Light, Jonathan D., P.C. ... Boston, MA
Light, Jonathan Fraser ... Oxnard, CA
Light, Kathryn J. ... Irving, TX
Light, Kenneth B. ... Highland Park, IL
Light, Kenneth H. ... Newton, MA
Light, Kevin P., (P.C.) ... Boston, MA
Light, Leslie W. ... Santa Monica, CA
Light, Louis "Whit" ... Little Rock, AR
Light, Maria Magallanes ... Little Rock, AR
Light, Mark N. ... St. Louis, MO
Light, Melody Layne ... Detroit, MI
Light, Neil H. ... Toledo, OH
Light, Paul T. ... Hollywood, FL
Light, R. Chambliss, Jr. ... Lynchburg, VA
Light, Randall C. ... Clarksburg, WV
Light, Robert E. ... Edison, NJ
Light, Robert M. ... Bemidji, MN
Light, Robt. M. ... Lima, OH
Light, Russell J. ... Fort Worth, TX
Light, Samuel J. ... Glenwood Springs, CO
Light, Sara Grundish ... Utica, OH
Light, Sheldon N. ... Detroit, MI
Light, Stanley R. ... Springfield, MA
Light, Susan A. ... Tucson, AZ
Light, Susan E. ... Bronx, NY
Light, Terry Barnum ... McLean, VA
Light, Terry Barnum, P.C. ... McLean, VA
Light, Terry W. ... Lewisburg, PA
Light, Wade B. ... Barrington, IL
Light, William J. ... Riverside, CA
Light, William R. ... Lynchburg, VA
Light, William R., P.C. ... Amherst, VA
Lynchburg, VA
Lightbody, Jennifer L. ... Cleveland, OH
Lightbody, John C. ... Portland, ME
Lightbody, William S. ... Cleveland, OH
Lightcap, Robert P. ... Greensburg, PA
Lightcap, Robert P. ... Latrobe, PA
Lightcap, Victoria Lieb ... Syracuse, NY
Lighter, Lawrence ... New York, NY
Lighter, Sally A. ... Knoxville, TN
Lightfoot, Benjamin A. ... Jetmore, KS
Lightfoot, C. Kelly ... Metairie, LA
Lightfoot, Claude C., Jr. ... Metairie, LA
Lightfoot, Claude C., Jr., P.C.
Metairie, LA
New Orleans, LA
Lightfoot, Franklin & White, L.L.C.
Birmingham, AL
Lightfoot, Jane ... Detroit, MI
Lightfoot, John D. ... El Dorado, AR
Lightfoot, John H., Jr. ... Manchester, NH
Lightfoot, Mark F. ... Memphis, TN
Lightfoot, Mark R. ... Fairfax, VA
Lightfoot, Mary P. ... Los Angeles, CA
Lightfoot, Michael J. ... Los Angeles, CA
Lightfoot, Michael J. ... Palatine, IL
Lightfoot & Nichols ... Luverne, AL
Lightfoot & Northup, A Professional Corporation ... Los Angeles, CA
Oceanside, CA
Pasadena, CA
Lightfoot, Richard ... Hadlyme, CT
Lightfoot, Robert A., Jr. ... Vernon, TX
Lightfoot, Robert J., II ... Madison, WI
Lightfoot, Stephen K. ... Oceanside, CA
Pasadena, CA
Lightfoot, Stephen K., II
San Francisco, CA
Lightfoot, Susan ... Larchmont, NY
Lightfoot, Thaddeus R. ... Minneapolis, MN
Lightfoot, Warren B. ... Birmingham, AL
Lightfoot, Warren B., Jr.
Birmingham, AL
Lightfoot, William P., Jr. ... Washington, DC
Lighthall, John A. ... Manchester, NH
Lighthall, Peter M. ... North Conway, NH
Lighthammer, Dwaine V. ... Ann Arbor, MI
Lighthizer, O. James ... Baltimore, MD
Lighthizer, Robert E. ... Washington, DC
Lightle, Beebe, Raney, Bell and Simpson
Searcy, AR
Lightle, Grant Clayton ... Dallas, TX
Lightman, Gary M. ... Harrisburg, PA
Lightman, Gary P. ... Haddonfield, NJ
Philadelphia, PA

Lightman, Howard M. ... Reading, PA
Lightman, James A. ... Waltham, MA
Lightman, Jonathan Robert ... Sacramento, CA
Lightman, Linda A. ... Maple Glen, PA
Lightman, Manochi & Kornilowicz
Haddonfield, NJ
Philadelphia, PA
Lightmas & Delk ... Atlanta, GA
Lightmas, Frank A., Jr. ... Atlanta, GA
Lightner, Claire B. ... San Diego, CA
Lightner, David M. ... Albany, CA
Lightner, Debra M. ... Newark, NJ
Lightner, J. Michael ... Newark, NJ
Lightner, John R. ... Springfield, MO
Lightner, John W. ... San Diego, CA
Lightner & Lightner, A Professional Corporation ... San Diego, CA
Lightner & Medvesky ... Allentown, PA
Easton, PA
Lehighton, PA
Reading, PA
Lightner, Merrie C. ... San Francisco, CA
Lightner, Merrie Turner ... San Francisco, CA
Lightner, Monte J. ... Fort Wayne, IN
Lightner, Star ... San Francisco, CA
Lightner, Thomas L. ... Allentown, PA
Easton, PA
Lehighton, PA
Reading, PA
Lightner, William F. ... San Diego, CA
Lightner, William, Jr. ... San Francisco, CA
Lightsey, Alton L. ... Orlando, FL
Lightsey & Associates, P.A. ... Orlando, FL
Lightsey, Harry M., III ... Atlanta, GA
Lightsey, Harry M., Jr. ... Columbia, SC
Lightsey, Mary Walpole ... Canandaigua, NY
Lightsey, Nancy D. ... Birmingham, AL
Lightsey, Rebecca S. ... Austin, TX
Lightsey, Regina A. ... Gulfport, MS
Lightsey, Roger S. ... San Antonio, TX
Lightsey, Thomas N., III ... Houston, TX
Lightsey, Thomas N., III, P.C., Law Offices of ... Houston, TX
Lightsey, Wallace K. ... Columbia, SC
Greenville, SC
Lightstone, Irwin ... Dallas, TX
Lightstone, Irwin, P.C., The Law Offices of
Dallas, TX
Lightstone, Marte D. ... Albuquerque, NM
Lightstone, Peter Bruce ... San Diego, CA
Lightvoet, Billee R. ... Chicago, IL
Lightvoet, Pamela L. ... Kalamazoo, MI
Lighty, Cynthia Mae ... Hershey, PA
Lighty, Donald Francis ... Beaumont, TX
Lighty, Frederick Williams ... Harrisburg, PA
Lighty, Gregory S. ... Yakima, WA
Lighty, Justin B. ... Santa Cruz, CA
Lighty • Kinda, An Association of Attorneys
Santa Cruz, CA
Ligi, Anthony V., Jr. ... Metairie, LA
Ligi, James J. ... Peckville, PA
Ligibel, Rebecca K. ... Toledo, OH
Ligman, Daniel V., (P.A.) ... Miami, FL
Ligman, James E. ... Columbia, IL
Ligman, Joseph W., (P.A.) ... Miami, FL
Ligman, Martin & Evans, P.L.
Coral Gables, FL
Fort Lauderdale, FL
Miami, FL
Pompano Beach, FL
West Palm Beach, FL
Lignoul, Timothy G. ... San Pedro, CA
Lignowski, Michael E. ... Philadelphia, PA
Ligo, Wendy K. ... Pittsburgh, PA
Ligocki, Raymond J. ... Des Plaines, IL
Ligon, Anne ... Fredericksburg, VA
Ligon, Curby ... Houston, TX
Ligon, Duke R. ... Oklahoma City, OK
Ligon, James Guthrie, Jr. ... Sonoma, CA
Ligon, James K. ... Sandy Spring, MD
Ligon, John A. ... Newark, NJ
Ligon, Keith A.
Federal Deposit Insurance Corporation, Liquidation Branch, GV
Ligon, L. Earl ... San Diego, CA
Ligon Law Office ... Clinton, LA
Ligon, Leslie D. ... Clinton, LA
Ligon, Robert D. ... Clinton, LA
Ligon, Roddey M., Jr.
Winston-Salem, NC
Ligon, Stark ... Little Rock, AR
Ligon, Tracey F.
Federal Election Commission, Office of the General Counsel, GV
Ligon, William O. ... Alpharetta, GA
Ligon, William T., Jr. ... Brunswick, GA
Ligon, William T., Jr., P.C.
Brunswick, GA
Ligon, William T., Jr., P.C.
Saint Simons Island, GA
Ligorano, Michael K. ... Flemington, NJ
Ligorio, Donald C. ... Wilkes-Barre, PA
Ligorsky, Brenda ... Sherman Oaks, CA
Ligorsky, Sharon A. ... Los Angeles, CA
Ligos, Gioia M. ... New York, NY
Ligos, Kurt G. ... Hackettstown, NJ
Ligos, Mark A. ... New York, NY
Ligotti, John ... Malden, MA
Ligouri, Louie M. ... Auburn, NE
Ligouri, Morris & Redding ... Dover, DE
Liguori, Christopher D. ... Chicago, IL
Liguori, James A. ... Toms River, NJ
Liguori, James E. ... Dover, DE
Liguori, John ... Bartow, FL
Liguori, John W. ... Albany, NY
Liguori, Patrick A. ... Providence, RI
Liguori, Robert ... Springfield, MA

Liguori, Robert E. ... Boston, MA
Providence, RI
Liguori, Thomas J., Jr. ... Westerly, RI
Liguoro, Joan L. ... Santa Monica, CA
Ligutis, Richard Adam ... Berkeley, CA
Lihani, David L. ... Washington, DC
Lihotz, Marie E. ... Haddonfield, NJ
Liibbe, H. Duane ... Encino, CA
Liinve, Mai Lutterus ... Watertown, NY
Liipfert, B. Bailey, III
Winston-Salem, NC
Liipfert, Charles J. ... Fort Valley, GA
Liipfert, Christian E. ... Houston, TX
Liipfert, Cowles ... Winston-Salem, NC
Liivak, Arno ... Camden, NJ
Lijoi, Costanzo Z. ... Detroit, MI
Lijoi, Peter B. ... Summit, NJ
Likavec, Michael A. ... Richmond, VA
Like, Gregory E. ... Tampa, FL
Like, Irving ... Babylon, NY
Like, Lance D. ... Bloomington, IN
Like, Sharon B.
Federal Housing Finance Board, Office of General Counsel, GV
Like, Steven K. ... Elkhart, IN
Liken, Charles E. ... Lansing, MI
Liken, Christopher J. ... Athens, GA
Liken, Joseph B. ... Dallas, TX
Liken, Robert L. ... Houston, TX
Likens, Christopher A. ... Sarasota, FL
Likens, Christopher A., P.A. ... Sarasota, FL
Likens, George B. ... Menlo Park, CA
Likens, Steven W. ... Memphis, TN
Liker, Alan D. ... Los Angeles, CA
Liker, Alan D., A Professional Corporation
Los Angeles, CA
Liker, Howard E. ... Bronx, NY
Liker, Keith A. ... San Diego, CA
Likes, Mary G. ... Omaha, NE
Likes, Steven C. ... Lincoln, NE
Omaha, NE
Likes, Terry Lambert ... Topeka, KS
Likins, Floyd L., Jr. ... Opelika, AL
Liko, Sharon D. ... Denver, CO
Liko, Sharon D., P.C. ... Denver, CO
Likoff, Bruce L. ... Denver, CO
Likoff, Mark H. ... Boston, MA
Likos, Mark S. ... Birmingham, AL
Likoudis, Michael ... Buffalo, NY
Likourezos, George ... Uniondale, NY
Liland, Jon S. ... Boston, MA
Lilburn, Verna B. ... Madison, CT
Lile, Charles A. ... Winchester, KY
Lile, John G. ... Little Rock, AR
Lile, Laird A. ... Naples, FL
Lile, Laird A., P.A. ... Bonita Springs, FL
Marco Island, FL
Naples, FL
Lile, Roger G. ... New Philadelphia, OH
Lile-King, Phyllis J. ... Greensboro, NC
Lilenfeld, David M. ... Atlanta, GA
Liles, Bernard ... Boynton Beach, FL
Liles, Curtis O., III ... Birmingham, AL
Liles, Davison, Davis, Tieman & Hendrix, A Professional Corporation
St. Joseph, MO
Savannah, MO
Liles, Detria J. ... Washington, DC
Liles, Donald R. ... Woodward, OK
Liles, Edward B. ... Brunswick, GA
Liles, G. Kemp ... Burlington, NC
Liles, Gary F. ... Little Rock, AR
Liles, Gavin & Costantino
Jacksonville, FL
Liles, Gerald L. ... St. Joseph, MO
Liles, Geryl Renae ... Norfolk, VA
Liles, Henry R. ... Lake Charles, LA
Liles, J. Michael, Law Office of
Fort Worth, TX
Liles, James D. ... Cincinnati, OH
Liles, Jeanne Overall ... Shreveport, LA
Liles, John H., Jr.
Federal Deposit Insurance Corporation, GV
Liles, John W., Jr. ... Raleigh, NC
Liles, Kenneth H. ... Bethesda, MD
Liles, Kevin W. ... Houston, TX
Liles & Laubhan ... Woodward, OK
Liles, Mike, Jr. ... Seattle, WA
Liles, Paul A. ... Birmingham, AL
Liles, Paul F. ... North Fort Myers, FL
Liles & Redd, L.C. ... Lake Charles, LA
Liles, Robert E., II ... Washington, DC
Liles, Robert, Jr. ... New Orleans, LA
Liles, Rutledge R. ... Jacksonville, FL
Liles, Teresa E. ... Pensacola, FL
Liles, Todd J. ... Dallas, TX
Liley, Lucia A. ... Fort Collins, CO
Lilian, Eric L. ... Philadelphia, PA
Lilien, Jason R. ... New York, NY
Lilien, Lindy M. ... San Francisco, CA
Lilien, Robert S. ... Charlotte, NC
Lilien, Shirley A. ... Tucson, AZ
Lilien, Thomas A. ... Elgin, IL
Lilien, Warren H. ... Sausalito, CA
Lilienfeld, Carol ... New York, NY
Lilienfeld, Doreen E. ... New York, NY
Liliensiek, William F.
Grosse Pointe Farms, MI
Lilienstern, Holman ... Texas City, TX
Lilienstern, O. Clayton ... Houston, TX
Lilienthal, Aymara Edwards ... Houston, TX
Lilienthal, Gary P. ... Boston, MA
Lilienthal, Julie A. ... Middlesboro, KY
Lilienthal, Philip H. ... Reston, VA
Lilienthal, Ryan H. ... Lawrenceville, NJ
Lilienthal, Scott R. ... Washington, DC
Lilja, Jonathan E. ... Boston, MA
Lilja, Scott M. ... Salt Lake City, UT

Liljeberg, Hans J. ... Metairie, LA
Liljedahl, Donald F. ... Los Angeles, CA
Liljedahl, Gerald V.
Department Of Health And Human Services, Social Security Administration, GV
Liljedahl, Linda A. ... Baton Rouge, LA
Liljedahl, Lori A. ... Des Moines, IA
Liljegren, John W. ... Portland, OR
Liljenquist, Michael D. ... Midvale, UT
Liljenquist, Robert C. ... Murray, UT
Liljenwall, Emily Harrison
San Antonio, TX
Liljequist, Jon L. ... Chicago, IL
Liljestrand, Cheryl A. ... Washington, DC
Liljestrand, Craig T. ... Chicago, IL
Liljestrom, Brent R. ... Costa Mesa, CA
Liljestrom, Roger ... Laguna Beach, CA
Lill, Daniel Coit ... Albuquerque, NM
Lill, Daniel Coit, P.A. ... Albuquerque, NM
Lill, David ... Austin, TX
Lill, Don W. ... Emporia, KS
Lill, Kathryn Ebenhahn ... Grand Forks, ND
Lilla, John M. ... Kansas City, MO
Lillard, David H., Jr. ... Memphis, TN
Lillard, Harry ... Oak Ridge, TN
Lillard, Holly K. ... Memphis, TN
Lillard, Jacqueline A. ... Boston, MA
Lillard, John F., III ... Annapolis, MD
Cambridge, MD
Chestertown, MD
College Park, MD
Easton, MD
Hollywood, MD
Prince Frederick, MD
Stevensville, MD
Waldorf, MD
Lillard & Lillard ... Annapolis, MD
Cambridge, MD
Chestertown, MD
College Park, MD
Easton, MD
Hollywood, MD
Prince Frederick, MD
Stevensville, MD
Waldorf, MD
Lillard, Louise D. ... Los Angeles, CA
Lillard, Monique C. ... Moscow, ID
Lillard, Ross N., III ... Oklahoma City, OK
Lillard, Ross W. ... Kansas City, MO
Lillard, Samuel N. ... Dublin, OH
Lillard, Thomas F. ... Dallas, TX
Lillard, Thomas M., Jr. ... Wilmette, IL
Lillard, Zack W. ... Houston, TX
Lilleberg, B. Jon ... Minneapolis, MN
Lilledahl, Linda L. ... Madison, WI
Lillegard, Chris L. ... Dallas, OR
Lillehaug, David L. ... Minneapolis, MN
Lillehaug, Duane A. ... Moorhead, MN
Lillehaugen, L. McRoy ... Minneapolis, MN
Lillenstein, Mark A. ... Delevan, NY
Lillesand, David J. ... Miami, FL
Lilleston, George R. ... Clinton, MO
Lilletvedt, J Brian ... Havre, MT
Lillevand, David E. ... Palo Alto, CA
Lillevand, Peter ... San Francisco, CA
Lilley, Charles, & Associates ... Denver, CO
Lilley, Charles W., (P.C.) ... Denver, CO
Lilley, Daniel G. ... Portland, ME
Lilley, Daniel G., P.A. ... Portland, ME
Lilley, Darla J ... Wichita, KS
Lilley, John W., III ... Dallas, TX
Lilley, Kirk A. ... Seattle, WA
Lilley, Leslie L. ... Virginia Beach, VA
Lilley, Max W. ... Springfield, MO
Lilley, Michael W. ... Las Cruces, NM
Lilley, Michael W., P.A. ... Las Cruces, NM
Lilley, Robert B. ... Atascadero, CA
Lilley, Robert B., A Professional Law Corporation ... Atascadero, CA
Lilley, Robert F. ... Orlando, FL
Lilley, Robert L. ... Logan, OH
Lilley, Robert L. Co., L.P.A. ... Logan, OH
Lilley, Robert O. ... Cincinnati, OH
Lilley, Stephanie Blessey ... Washington, DC
Lilley, Suzanne Russell ... Houlton, ME
Lilley, Vincent A. ... Salem, VA
Lilley, W. Alan ... Lafayette, LA
Lillian, Guy H., III ... New Orleans, LA
Lillianfeld, Mark ... Lafayette, IN
Lillich, Richard B. ... Charlottesville, VA
Lillich, Shane ... Kansas City, KS
Lillich, Victor L. ... Ann Arbor, MI
Lillick & Charles LLP ... Costa Mesa, CA
San Francisco, CA
Parsippany, NJ
Lillicrap, James ... Lancaster, CA
Lillie, Charisse R. ... Philadelphia, PA
Lillie, Charles C. ... Bloomfield Hills, MI
Lillie, James W. ... Raleigh, NC
Lillie, John C., III ... St. Paul, MN
Lillie, Margaret E. ... Bennington, VT
Lillie, Mark S. ... Chicago, IL
Lillie, Michael W. ... Englewood, CO
Lillie, Mildred L. ... Los Angeles, CA
Lillie, Raymond J. ... Roseland, NJ
Lillie, Richard G. ... Cleveland, OH
Cleveland, OH
Lillie, Robt. C. ... Grand Rapids, MI
Lillie, Shawn R. ... Memphis, TN
Lillie, Susan Jane ... Reno, NV
Lillien, Jeffrey S. ... Chicago, IL
Lilliendahl, John R., III ... Hartford, CT
Lillienstein, Robert D. ... New York, NY
Lillig, David J. ... Salem, OR
Lillig, Martin J. ... Oak Brook, IL
Lillig & Thorsness, Ltd. ... Oak Brook, IL
Lilling, Bruce E. ... New York, NY
White Plains, NY

Lilling, Caryn L. ...Great Neck, NY
Lilling & Lilling P.C. ...White Plains, NY
Lillington, Brenda M. ...San Francisco, CA
Lillios, Mary N. ...Chicago, IL
Lillis, Charles J. ...Coldwater, MI
Lillis, Damien P. ...San Francisco, CA
Lillis, Francis X. ...Vienna, VA
Lillis, James M. ...Reading, PA
Lillis, John T. ...New York, NY
Lillis, John T., Jr. ...New York, NY
Lillis, Marcella ...Palo Alto, CA
Lillis, Susan G. ...Ipswich, MA
Salem, MA
Lillis, William J. ...Des Moines, IA
Lilliston, Andrew W., Jr. ...Raleigh, NC
Lillquist, P. Christine ...San Francisco, CA
Lilly, Adrienne M. ...Minneapolis, MN
Lilly, Alan B. ...Sacramento, CA
Lilly, Albert J., Jr. ...Bloomfield Hills, MI
Lilly, Albert J., Jr. ...Bowling Green, VA
Lilly, C. Berkley ...Beckley, WV
Lilly, C. Craig ...Dallas, TX
Lilly, Christopher A. ...Los Angeles, CA
Lilly, Christopher L. ...Frankfort, KY
Lilly, Christopher T. ...Ayer, MA
Lilly, Claude B., Jr. ...Austin, TX
Lilly, Daniel J. ...La Crosse, WI
Lilly, Dennis P. ...Santa Clara, CA
Lilly, Donald S. ...Lynchburg, VA
Lilly, Douglas Gerard ...New Haven, CT
Lilly, Earle S. ...Houston, TX
Lilly, Edward J. ...New Orleans, LA
Lilly, Edward John ...Baltimore, MD
Lilly, Edward M. ...Elkhart, IN
Lilly, Elisabeth Bates ...Redondo Beach, CA
Lilly, Eugene R. ...Las Vegas, NV
Lilly, George M. ...Falls Church, VA
Lilly, George R., II ...Thomasville, GA
Lilly, George S. ...Detroit, MI
Lilly, Graham C. ...Charlottesville, VA
Lilly, Ivan M. ...Johnson City, TN
Lilly, J. Kevin ...Los Angeles, CA
Lilly, James E. ...Atlanta, GA
Lilly, James R. ...Detroit, MI
Lilly, James V. ...Oakdale, MN
Lilly, Jeffrey R. ...Austin, TX
Lilly, John C. ...Cleveland, OH
Lilly, John L., Jr. ...Alexandria, VA
Lilly, John P. ...Dallas, TX
Lilly, John R., II ...Upper Marlboro, MD
Lilly, John S. ...Houston, TX
Lilly, John T. ...Oklahoma City, OK
Lilly, Joseph H., III ...New York, NY
Lilly, Joyce Stamp ...Houston, TX
Lilly, Julia J. ...St. Louis, MO
Lilly, Kent, The Law Offices of
Avon Park, FL
Bartow, FL
Fort Meade, FL
Haines City, FL
Lilly, Kent, The Law Offices of
Lakeland, FL
Lake Wales, FL
Winter Haven, FL
Lilly, Kent, The Law Offices of
Sebring, FL
Wauchula, FL
Lilly, Kevin L. ...Princeton, NJ
Lilly, Lawrence G. ...St. Augustine, FL
Lilly & Lilly, P.C. ...Kalamazoo, MI
Lilly, Lisa L. ...Charleston, WV
Lilly, Lucinda L. ...Tulsa, OK
Lilly, Marie J. ...Portland, OR
Lilly, Merton B. ...Green Valley, AZ
Lilly, Michael A. ...Honolulu, HI
Lilly, Michael J. ...Bozeman, MT
Lilly, Michael J. ...Portland, OR
Lilly, N. Scott ...Louisville, KY
Lilly, Orley R., Jr. ...Jackson, MS
Lilly, Paulette J. ...Elyria, OH
Lilly, Phillip G. ...Columbus, OH
Lilly, R. G. (Bob) ...Fort Walton Beach, FL
Lilly, Robert G. ...Charleston, WV
Lilly, Robert Mason, Jr. ...Narrows, VA
Lilly, Robt. E. ...Mesa, AZ
Lilly, Roy M. ...Thomasville, GA
Lilly, Roy M., Jr. ...Thomasville, GA
Lilly, Roy M., Jr. ...Minden, LA
Lilly, S. Matthew, Jr. ...Washington, NC
Lilly, Scott B. ...Brooklyn, NY
Lilly, Scott R. ...Lakeland, FL
Lilly, Terrence J. ...Kalamazoo, MI
Lilly, Thomas G. ...Jackson, MS
Lilly, Thomas J. ...Garden City, NY
Lilly, Thomas J. ...Garden City, NY
Lilly, Thomas L. ...Salisbury, MD
Lilly, Thomas M. ...Pittsburgh, PA
Lilly, Thomas S. ...Princeton, WV
Lilly & Wise, PLLC ...Jackson, MS
Liloia, Dennis P. ...Springfield, NJ
Liloia, Gerald A. ...Morristown, NJ
Liloia, Peter, III ...Washington, NJ
Lilore, Ralph P. ...Hackensack, NJ
Lilore, Ralph T. ...Clifton, NJ
Lilyblade, Clara A. ...Winters, CA
Lilyestrom, John R. ...Washington, DC
Lilygren, John A. ...Los Angeles, CA
Lim, Angela G. ...Pleasanton, CA
Lim, Arlene ...Chicago, IL
Lim, Arnold ...Jamaica, NY
Lim, Bryant D. ...Philadelphia, PA
Lim, Byungkwon ...New York, NY
Lim, Daniel ...Houston, TX
Lim, Diana G. ...Sacramento, CA
Lim, Edwin Y. ...Columbus, OH
Lim, Elisa ...Flushing, NY
Lim, Elizabeth ...Miami, FL
Lim, Evelyn ...New York, NY
Lim, Fidelio L. ...New York, NY
Lim, Frederick B. ...New York, NY
Lim, Gene M. ...Twinsburg, OH
Lim, George S. ...Phoenix, AZ
Lim, H. Antony ...Baltimore, MD
Lim, Howard, Jr. ...New York, NY
Lim, James T. ...Los Angeles, CA
Lim, Janet G. ...Seattle, WA
Lim, Jeanette J. ...Department of Education, Office for Civil Rights, GV
Lim, Jeffery D. ...Santa Barbara, CA
Lim, Jiyeon Lee ...New York, NY
Lim, John S. C. ...Los Angeles, CA
Lim, Josephine Eun-Jung ...Pasadena, CA
Lim, Joy L. ...Santa Barbara, CA
Lim, Joyce Y. ...Washington, DC
Lim, Juliet A. ...Phoenix, AZ
Lim, K. Jin ...Detroit, MI
Lim, Kang S. ...Palo Alto, CA
Lim, Kwan Hi ...Honolulu, HI
Lim, Lawrence S. ...Columbus, OH
Lim, Lillian Y. ...San Diego, CA
Lim, Lily
United States Court Of Appeals For The Federal Circuit, GV
Lim, Lisa ...San Francisco, CA
Lim, Lloyd ...Honolulu, HI
Lim, Michael ...Oshkosh, WI
Lim, Patricia ...Boston, MA
Lim, Peter ...Boston, MA
Lim, Phillips, Hurley & Mahowald, L.L.C.
Phoenix, AZ
Lim, Ricarda L. ...Sacramento, CA
Lim, Richard ...San Francisco, CA
Lim, Roger ...San Rafael, CA
Lim, Ruger & Kim, LLP
Los Angeles, CA
Lim, Rustico L. ...Virginia Beach, VA
Lim, S. Deborah ...Los Angeles, CA
Lim, S. Young ...Los Angeles, CA
Lim, Serene Tan ...Redwood City, CA
Lim, Soo Jin ...Boston, MA
Lim, Steven ...Newburgh, NY
Lim, Steven S. C. ...Hilo, HI
Lim, Thomas E. ...New York, NY
Lim, Tillie ...Tarrytown, NY
Lim, Tomas Blaquera ...New York, NY
Lim, Velma K. ...Stockton, CA
Lim, Vincent A. ...Los Angeles, CA
Lim, Virginia ...Kensington, CA
Lim, Wonshick ...Flushing, NY
Lima, Albert P. ...Lutz, FL
Lima, Charles S., (P.C.) ...Honolulu, HI
Lima, David S. ...Chantilly, VA
Lima, Gilbert, Jr. ...Attleboro, MA
Lima, Paul X. ...White Plains, NY
Lima, Ricardo De F. ...New York, NY
Lima, Salvatore A. ...San Francisco, CA
Lima, Sara J. ...Turlock, CA
Lima, Sydney M. ...Providence, RI
Lima, Thomas J. ...San Francisco, CA
Limage, Bret L. ...Silver Spring, MD
Liman, Arthur L. ...New York, NY
Liman, Lewis J. ...New York, NY
LiMandri, Charles S
Rancho Santa Fe, CA
LiMandri, Charles S. ...San Diego, CA
Limanni, Mark Anthony ...Chicago, IL
Limar, Nick ...Harrison, NY
Limardo, Mark A. ...New York, NY
Limas, Vicki J. ...Tulsa, OK
Limauro, Michael A. ...Detroit, MI
Limb, John J. ...Seattle, WA
Limbach, Alan A. ...San Francisco, CA
San Jose, CA
Limbach, Douglas C. ...San Francisco, CA
San Jose, CA
Limbach, George C. ...San Francisco, CA
San Jose, CA
Limbach, John ...West Bend, WI
Limbach, Karl A. ...San Francisco, CA
Limbach & Limbach, L.L.P.
Menlo Park, CA
San Francisco, CA
San Jose, CA
Limbach, Lois R. ...Belvedere-Tiburon, CA
Limbacher, Robert A. ...Philadelphia, PA
Limbaugh, David S.
Cape Girardeau, MO
Limbaugh, James H. ...Allison Park, PA
Limbaugh, John M. ...Sikeston, MO
Limbaugh, Joseph T. ...Birmingham, AL
Limbaugh, L. Hunter ...Columbia, SC
Limbaugh, Russell, Payne & Howard, A Professional Corporation
Cape Girardeau, MO
Limbaugh, Stephen N. ...St. Louis, MO
Limbaugh, Stephen N., Jr.
Jefferson City, MO
Limbeck, George A. ...Sheboygan, WI
Limbeck, Randal M. ...Omaha, NE
Limber, Jack P. ...San Diego, CA
Limberg, Allen L. ...Washington, DC
Limberg, Madonna ...Kansas City, MO
Limberis, Christopher G. ...Bangor, ME
Limberis, George P. ...Bangor, ME
Limberis & Limberis, P.A. ...Bangor, ME
Limberis, Peter C. ...Bradenton, FL
Limberopoulos & Associates, P.A.
Tampa, FL
Limberopoulos, Chris M. ...Tampa, FL
Limbert, George James ...Youngstown, OH
Limbocker, Craig T. ...Kansas City, MO
Limbrick, Kimberly L. ...Baltimore, MD
Limburg, Richard P. ...Philadelphia, PA
Lime, Daniel A., II ...Raritan, NJ
Limeberry, William E. ...Greenwood, IN
Limehouse, C. Walker ...Orangeburg, SC
Limehouse & Walsh ...Orangeburg, SC
Limekiller, David P. ...Tulsa, OK
Limentato, Sam A. ...Champaign, IL
Lim-Epstein, Cerise H. ...Boston, MA
Limer, Donald E. ...Long Beach, CA
Limer, Jana K. ...Dallas, TX
Limeres, Amy W. ...Anchorage, AK
Limeres-Grau, Miguel ...Ponce, PR
Limes, Leonard ...Covington, LA
Limes, Leslie Ann ...Austin, TX
Liming, John M. ...Defiance, OH
Hicksville, OH
Liming, Roxi Ann ...Dublin, OH
Limitone, Anthony P., Jr. ...Morristown, NJ
Limitone & Hillenbrand ...Morristown, NJ
Limmer, Andrea ...Department of Justice, Antitrust Division, GV
Limmer, H. Robert ...New York, NY
Limmer, James H. ...Houston, TX
Limmer, Stephen G. ...Great Neck, NY
Limmiatis, Paul ...Syracuse, NY
Limon, Abelardo (Abe), Jr.
Brownsville, TX
Limon, Raymond A.
Office of Personnel Management, Merit Systems Division, GV
Limon, Stephen M. ...Boston, MA
Limoncelli, Gary L. ...Garden City, NY
Limoncelli, Gregory T. ...New York, NY
Limoncelli, Jerry J. ...Garden City, NY
Limond, Mark J. ...Aventura, FL
Limond, Michael L. ...Miami, FL
Limone, Gerald C. ...East Norwich, NY
Limone, Joseph P. ...Annapolis, MD
Limone, Stephen C. ...Melrose, MA
Limongelli, Adam M. ...Forty Fort, PA
Limongelli, John M. ...Philadelphia, PA
Limongelli & Limongelli ...Forty Fort, PA
Limongelli, Malcolm M. ...Forty Fort, PA
Limongelli, Victor T. ...Philadelphia, PA
Limón-Wynn, Monica A. ...Phoenix, AZ
Limor, Susan ...Nashville, TN
Limor, Susan R., A P.C. ...Nashville, TN
Limotte, John ...New York, NY
Limperes, Donna ...Northbrook, IL
Limperis, Connie P. ...Chicago, IL
Limperis, Peter T. ...Tucson, AZ
Limpert, Theodore H. ...Syracuse, NY
Limprecht, Jane E. ...Washington, DC
Limpus, Lawrence L. ...St. Louis, MO
Limsky, Michael Richard
Owings Mills, MD
Lin, Albert C. ...Department of Justice, Environment and Natural Resources Division, GV
Lin, Albert Y. ...Fort Worth, TX
Lin, Albert Yabo ...Kansas City, MO
Lin, Alexander T. ...New York, NY
Lin, Anne V. ...Department of Commerce, National Oceanic and Atmospheric Administration, GV
Lin, Audrey I. ...Los Angeles, CA
Lin, Carol Gilkey ...Worthington, OH
Lin, Christiana L. ...Washington, DC
Lin, Christopher ...New York, NY
Lin, Crystal T. ...Palo Alto, CA
Lin, David Swei-chuan ...Los Angeles, CA
Lin, Dorothy H. Patterson ...Washington, DC
Lin, Edward T. ...Los Angeles, CA
Lin, Eileen ...White Plains, NY
Lin, Elizabeth ...Washington, DC
Lin, Elizabeth Pei ...Los Angeles, CA
Lin, Francis F. ...Las Vegas, NV
Lin, George Chao-I ...Downey, CA
Lin, Grace L. ...Alhambra, CA
Lin, Jan-Yung ...Boston, MA
Lin, Jean ...Department of Justice, Antitrust Division, GV
Lin, Jeffrey ...Palo Alto, CA
Lin, Joanna Y. ...Tarzana, CA
Lin, John L. ...Palo Alto, CA
Lin, Joseph T. ...Palo Alto, CA
Lin, Judy M. ...Richmond, VA
Lin, Kenneth ...House of Representatives, Committee on the Budget, GV
Lin, Laura ...Chicago, IL
Lin Li & Jiang ...New York, NY
Lin, Margaret A. ...Washington, DC
Lin, Maria C. H. ...New York, NY
Lin, Maria Y. ...Garden City, NY
Lin, Michelle T. ...New York, NY
Lin, Patricia E. ...Houston, TX
Lin, Patrick ...Stockton, CA
Lin, Paul C. ...Irvine, CA
Lin, Philip Y. ...Philadelphia, PA
Lin, Raymond Yung ...New York, NY
Lin, Rosanne Y. ...Phoenix, AZ
Lin, Stanford M. ...New York, NY
Lin, Steven S. ...Austin, TX
Lin, Tana ...Department of Justice, Civil Rights Division, GV
Lin, Tricia T. ...Santa Clara, CA
Lin, Vincent W. ...Los Angeles, CA
Lin, Wallace E. ...Sunnyvale, CA
Lin, Weicheng ...New York, NY
Lin, Wei-Nuoo ...New York, NY
Lin, Wen-Ching, Law Offices of
San Jose, CA
Lin, Wendy J. ...San Diego, CA
Lin, William W. ...Seattle, WA
Linahan, Willie J. ...Valdosta, GA
Linam, E. William ...Knoxville, TN
Linardos, George S. ...Windsor Locks, CT
Linarducci, Gary C. ...New Castle, DE
Linares and Coviello ...Bloomfield, NJ
Linares, Francisco J. ...Charlotte, NC
Linares, Jose L. ...Bloomfield, NJ
Linares, Leonard L. ...Los Angeles, CA
Linares, Luis Carlos, Jr. ...Orlando, FL
Linares, Luisa Maria ...Miami, FL
Linares, Rodolfo ...Coral Gables, FL
Linares-Moreno, Ivette E.
Coral Gables, FL
Linbeck, Constance B. ...Houston, TX
Linberg, Pamela Banks ...Houston, TX
Lincenberg, Gary S. ...Los Angeles, CA
Linch, Bryan N. ...Odessa, TX
Linch, Keith E. ...Atlanta, GA
Linch, M. Jebb ...Westerville, OH
Linchenko, Andre A. ...Salt Lake City, UT
Linchey, Daniel M. ...San Francisco, CA
Linchitz, Peter J. ...New York, NY
Lincicome, Brian L. ...Philadelphia, PA
Lincicome, David V. C. ...Akron, OH
Lincicome, Francine T. ...Philadelphia, PA
Linck, Judith Ann ...Sacramento, CA
Linck, Leo L. ...Muskegon, MI
Linck, Susan K. ...Madison, WI
Linck, Thomas H. ...Muskegon, MI
Lincke, William P. ...Media, PA
Lincoln, Alexander, III ...Denver, CO
Lincoln, Anna C. ...Washington, DC
Lincoln, Arthur M. ...Houston, TX
Lincoln, B. Tyler ...Harrisburg, PA
Lincoln, Barbara A. ...Atlanta, GA
Lincoln, Bruce D. ...Fort Lauderdale, FL
Lincoln, Charles F. ...Marion, VA
Lincoln, Charles J., II ...Little Rock, AR
Lincoln, Danforth F. ...Santa Ana, CA
Lincoln, David B. ...Boise, ID
Lincoln, Donald E. ...Monterey, CA
Lincoln, Donald R. ...San Diego, CA
Lincoln, Edward W., Jr. ...Hartford, CT
Lincoln, Elizabeth S. ...Excelsior, MN
Lincoln, Emma S. ...Shaker Heights, OH
Lincoln, Erik C. ...Cleveland, OH
Lincoln, Frank W. ...Tuscola, IL
Lincoln, George L. ...Chicago, IL
Lincoln, Gustafson & Cercos
Los Angeles, CA
San Diego, CA
Temecula, CA
Las Vegas, NV
Lincoln, Harold W. ...Chevy Chase, MD
Lincoln, J. Alden ...Boston, MA
Lincoln, Jack N. ...Atlanta, GA
Lincoln, James W., III ...Nashville, TN
Lincoln, Jas. H. ...Harbor Beach, MI
Lincoln, Jerry D. ...Montrose, CO
Lincoln, John C. ...Phoenix, AZ
Lincoln, John T. ...Columbia, MD
Lincoln, John W. ...Rockland, MA
Lincoln, Jos. R. ...Parker, CO
Lincoln, Joseph L. ...Malvern, PA
Lincoln, Judith A. ...Saginaw, MI
Lincoln Law Group, The ...Wheaton, IL
Lincoln, Leonard T. ...Tampa, FL
Lincoln, Linda Kimmerling ...Golden, CO
Lincoln, Lucian A. ...Marion, IL
Lincoln, Marcia Brown
Albuquerque, NM
Lincoln and Markey ...Glen Rock, NJ
Lincoln, Martyn H. ...North Boston, MA
Lincoln, Mary S. ...Lincoln, MA
Lincoln, Michael P. ...Emerald Isle, NC
Lincoln, Michael R. ...Reston, VA
Lincoln, Ollie H., III ...Kensington, MD
Lincoln, Paula A. ...Department of Labor, Office of the Solicitor, GV
Lincoln, Robert A. ...Library of Congress, Office of the General Counsel, GV
Lincoln, Robert G. ...Johnson City, TN
Lincoln, Robert T. ...New York, NY
Lincoln, Robin P. ...Philadelphia, PA
Lincoln, Sara R. ...Charlotte, NC
Lincoln, Sean A. ...Menlo Park, CA
Lincoln, Sheryl J. ...Washington, DC
Lincoln, Simon Joel ...New York, NY
Lincoln, Steven F. ...San Jose, CA
Lincoln, Thomas A. ...Windermere, FL
Lincoln, Thomas D. ...Cohasset, MA
Lincoln, Thomas J. ...Los Angeles, CA
San Diego, CA
Temecula, CA
Las Vegas, NV
Lincoln, Thomas R. ...Sacramento, CA
Lincoln, Virginia M. ...Glen Rock, NJ
Lincoln, William T. ...Dayton, OH
Lincoln, Wm. A. ...Andover, MA
Lincolnhol, Paul E. ...Tallahassee, FL
Lincoln-Stewart, Kimberly A.
Washington, DC
Lind, Albert C. ...Falmouth, ME
Lind, Barry N. ...North Miami Beach, FL
Lind, Carol M. ...Chicago, IL
Lind, Cary A. ...Arlington Heights, IL
Lind, Cary A., P.C. ...Arlington Heights, IL
Lind, Charles R. ...Austin, TX
Lind, Charles W. ...Seattle, WA
Lind, Chris ...Denver, CO
Chicago, IL
Lind, Connie V. ...Seattle, WA
Lind, David C., II ...Indianapolis, IN
Lind, David D. ...Alexandria, LA
Lind, Debra Townsend ...Des Moines, IA
Lind, Dennis E. ...Missoula, MT
Lind, Eugene F. ...New Albany, IN
Lind, Frank O., Jr. ...Cumberland, RI
Lind, Frederick G. ...Greensboro, NC
Lind, Gary D. ...Naples, FL
Lind, George L. ...Oskaloosa, IA
Lind, Gregory B. ...Dallas, TX
Lind, H. Samuel ...Cincinnati, OH
Lind, Harry S. ...Dayton, OH
Lind, Harvey J. ...Beverly Hills, CA
Lind, Howard W. ...Oakland, CA

Lind, Jeffry A. .... **Terre Haute, IN**
Lind, Jensen & Sullivan, A Professional Association .... **Minneapolis, MN**
Lind, Jessica .... **Boston, MA**
Lind, Joel S. .... Dearborn, MI
Lind, John K. .... **Cleveland, OH**
Lind, Jon R. .... Chicago, IL
Lind, K. Michelle .... Phoenix, AZ
Lind, Karen G. .... New York, NY
Lind, Katherine A. .... Riverside, CA
Lind, Kathleen Marie .... Ionia, MI
Lind, Keith D. .... **Washington, DC**
Lind, Kenneth C. .... **New York, NY**
Lind, Kenneth F. .... Greeley, CO
Lind, Laron J. .... **Syracuse, UT**
Lind, Lawrence & Ottenhoff .... Greeley, CO
Lind, Leo B., Jr. .... Concord, NH
Lind, Martin .... Burlington, WA
Lind, Marvin G. .... Minneapolis, MN
Lind, Melvin R. .... Danville, IN
Lind, Michael D. .... **Orange, CA**
Lind, Michael S. .... Tacoma, WA
Lind, Norman P. .... Long Grove, IL
Lind, Patricia Anne .... **New York, NY**
Lind, Peter F. .... **Minneapolis, MN**
Lind, Peter E. .... New York, NY
Lind, Philip G. .... Minneapolis, MN
Lind, Richard A. .... **Minneapolis, MN**
Lind, Richard B. .... New York, NY
Lind, Richard J. .... **Washington, DC**
Lind, Richard J. .... Olathe, KS
Lind, Richard John .... Miami, FL
Lind, Robert C. .... Los Angeles, CA
Lind, Robert L. .... Corona, CA
Lind, Rosalind Cardone .... Shaker Heights, OH
Lind, Ruth P. .... Fresno, CA
Lind, Stanley L. .... Kansas City, KS
Lind, Stanley L. .... Milwaukee, WI
Lind, Stephen A. .... Gainesville, FL
Lind, Stephen Michael .... Whippany, NJ
Lind, Thomas O. .... New Orleans, LA
Linda, Martin S. .... **New York, NY**
Lindabury, McCormick & Estabrook, P.A.
Elizabeth, NJ
Westfield, NJ
New York, NY
Lindahl, Barry A. .... Dubuque, IA
Lindahl, Brent R. .... **St. Paul, MN**
Lindahl, George M. .... **Los Angeles, CA**
Lindahl, Gross & Lievois, P.C.
Bingham Farms, MI
Birmingham, MI
Detroit, MI
Lindahl, Judith L. .... **Boston, MA**
Lindahl, Kevin .... Eagle, CO
Lindahl, Loren L. .... **Wahoo, NE**
Lindahl, Martin L.
North Miami Beach, FL
New York, NY
Lindahl, Norman C. .... Springfield, IL
Lindahl, R. Daniel .... **Portland, OR**
Lindahl, Thomas K. .... **Bingham Farms, MI**
Lindahl-Garcia, Jeri .... **Chicago, IL**
Lindall, Robert J. .... **Minneapolis, MN**
Lindamood, Dale Jackins .... Springfield, OR
Lindamood, Donna C. .... Orlando, FL
Lindamood, Janie .... Johnson City, TN
Lindamood, John B. .... **Canton, OH**
Lindamood, Steven P. .... **Houston, TX**
Lindamood, Timothy M. .... **Boston, MA**
Lindamood, William S. .... **Tucson, AZ**
Lindamood, William S., P.C. .... **Tucson, AZ**
Lindanger, Susan Jiles .... Shreveport, LA
Lindars, Arthur P. .... Pomona, CA
Lindau, David S. .... Fishkill, NY
New York, NY
Lindau, Jules W. .... Wilmington, NC
Lindau, Mose S. .... Portland, OR
Lindau, Peter D. .... **Chicago, IL**
Lindauer, Brian T. .... **Pittsburgh, PA**
Lindauer, Curt C. .... Belleville, IL
Lindauer, Eric B. .... **Salem, OR**
Lindauer, Erik D. .... **New York, NY**
Lindauer, Jerry D. .... Austin, TX
Lindauer, Joan D. .... **Chicago, IL**
Lindauer, John A. .... Manlius, NY
Lindauer, Joyce W. .... **Dallas, TX**
Lindauer, Kathryn K. .... **Austin, TX**
Lindauer, Kenneth E. .... Haverhill, MA
Salem, MA
Lindauer, L. David .... Portsmouth, VA
Lindauer, Mitchell J. .... New York, NY
Lindauer, Patricia .... **Pittsburgh, PA**
Lindauer, Paul D., Jr. .... Ottawa, IL
Lindauer, Thayer C. .... Agoura Hills, CA
Lindauer, Vick & Welch .... Belleville, IL
Lindbeck, Kathryn B. .... St. Louis, MO
Lindbeck, Lilli K. .... San Francisco, CA
Lindberg, Ann M. .... Essex Junction, VT
Lindberg, Brian L. .... **Minneapolis, MN**
Lindberg, Bryan Robert .... Anoka, MN
Lindberg, C. Foster .... Brunswick, GA
Lindberg, C. Foster, P.C. .... Brunswick, GA
Lindberg, Charles D. .... **Cincinnati, OH**
Lindberg, Charles S. .... Brookfield, CT
Lindberg, Craig E. .... Irvine, CA
Lindberg, D. Dean .... **San Francisco, CA**
Lindberg, David B. .... Houston, TX
Lindberg, Denise Posse .... Salt Lake City, UT
Lindberg, Erik M. .... Eagan, MN
Lindberg, Erik P. .... **Charlotte, NC**
Lindberg, Gary W. .... Portland, OR
Lindberg, George W. .... Chicago, IL
Lindberg, J. Todd .... Minneapolis, MN
Lindberg, Jerry J. .... Sauk Rapids, MN
Lindberg, Kirstin G. .... **Denver, CO**
Lindberg, Kristen K. .... Seattle, WA
Lindberg, Lawrence V. .... **Cleveland, OH**
Lindberg, Marian E. .... **New York, NY**
Lindberg, Mark S. .... Toledo, OH
Lindberg, Matthew G. .... Framingham, MA
Lindberg, Merry Ellen .... **Delray Beach, FL**
Lindberg, Michael C. .... **Minneapolis, MN**
Lindberg, Neil A. .... Draper, UT
Lindberg, Roberta J. .... Eugene, OR
Lindberg, Steven C. .... Naperville, IL
Lindberg, Theodore L., Jr. .... Mill Valley, CA
Lindberg, Thomas B. .... Prescott, AZ
Lindberg, Thomas R. .... New Britain, CT
Lindberg, Thomas W. .... **Minneapolis, MN**
Lindberg, Tracey R. .... Fergus Falls, MN
Lindberg, Wesley E. .... **Rockford, IL**
Lindberg, William H. .... St. Paul, MN
Lindberg, William J., Jr. .... **Bellevue, WA**
Lindbergh, Doris C. .... New York, NY
Lindblad, Christine Nicole
Minneapolis, MN
Lindblad, Jim L. .... Paducah, KY
Lindblad, Lisa M.J. .... **Salt Lake City, UT**
Lindblom, Deborah, Law Offices of
San Francisco, CA
Lindblom, Lance E. .... New York, NY
Lindblom, Marjorie Press .... **New York, NY**
Lindbloom, Cynthia Ann
Fort Lauderdale, FL
Lindborg, Peter F. .... **Los Angeles, CA**
Lindburg, Fred .... Shenandoah, IA
Lindburg, Thomas O. .... **Davenport, IA**
Linde, Clyde J. .... Kansas City, MO
Linde, Eileen .... New York, NY
Linde, Florence .... Lynn, MA
Linde, Hans A. .... Salem, OR
Linde, John O. .... **Friday Harbor, WA**
Linde, Julian J. .... Glendale, CA
Linde, Llewellyn H. .... Stillwater, MN
Linde, Matthew A. .... Los Angeles, CA
Linde, Mitchell .... Washington, DC
Linde, Paul H. .... **Parker, SD**
Linde, Roger C. .... **New Orleans, LA**
Linde, Selena J. .... **Washington, DC**
Linde, Stephen A. .... **New York, NY**
Linde, Tamara L. .... Newark, NJ
Linde, Thomas S. .... Seattle, WA
Lindebak, Layne M. .... Des Moines, IA
Lindeen, Gordon R. .... Simi Valley, CA
Lindeen, Larry Wayne .... **Houston, TX**
Lindeen, Tracey Smith .... **Houston, TX**
Lindefjeld, Robert O. .... **Pittsburgh, PA**
Lindegren, Karl R. .... **Newport Beach, CA**
Lindeke, Craig E. .... St. Paul, MN
Lindeke, Jonathan M. .... **San Francisco, CA**
Lindekugel, Gina S. .... **Baltimore, MD**
Lindekugel, Howard J. .... Spokane, WA
Lindelef, Lisa Peck .... San Francisco, CA
Lindelien, Keli J. .... Bryan, TX
Lindell, Carla (Woodward) .... **Virginia, MN**
Lindell, Charlotte L. .... **San Francisco, CA**
Lindell, David A. .... **Washburn, ND**
Lindell, Elizabeth J. .... **San Antonio, TX**
Lindell, Eric W. .... Seattle, WA
Lindell, J. Michael .... **Jacksonville, FL**
Lindell, James E. .... Minneapolis, MN
Lindell, John Leslie .... St. Paul, MN
Lindell, Lavoie & Lowe, LLP
Minneapolis, MN
Lindell Law Office .... **Washburn, ND**
Lindell, Marisa V. .... **Seattle, WA**
Lindell, Michael P. .... **Las Vegas, NV**
Reno, NV
Lindell, Rocky V. .... **Seattle, WA**
Lindell, William F. .... **Washburn, ND**
Lindeman, Alfred
Department of Labor, GV
Lindeman, Devora L. .... **Newark, NJ**
Lindeman & Dillon .... **Houston, TX**
Lindeman, George .... Waterloo, IA
Lindeman, James P. .... Sherman Oaks, CA
Lindeman, Janet A. .... **Chicago, IL**
Lindeman, Jeffrey A. .... **Washington, DC**
Lindeman, Jim .... **Houston, TX**
Kingwood, TX
Lindeman, Lawrence E. .... Alexandria, VA
Lindeman, Lawrence E., P.C.
Alexandria, VA
Lindeman, Lisa L. .... Juneau, AK
Lindeman, Louis H., Jr. .... **Detroit, MI**
Lindeman, Michael J. .... Anchorage, AK
Lindeman, Philip, II .... **Newark, NJ**
Lindeman, Ralph H. .... Department of Justice, Environment and Natural Resources Division, GV
Lindeman, Robert J. .... Troy, OH
Lindeman, William M. .... Orlando, FL
Lindemann, Albert P., Jr.
Washington, DC
Lindemann, Andrew F. .... **Columbia, SC**
Lindemann, Barbara T. .... **Los Angeles, CA**
Lindemann, Cynthia Borsella
Roseland, NJ
Lindemann, Daniel R. .... **Cranford, NJ**
Lindemann, Eric Todd .... New York, NY
Lindemann, G. Gilbert .... Milwaukee, WI
Lindemann, Jeffrey N. .... **Columbus, OH**
Lindemann, John S. .... **Chicago, IL**
Lindemann & Lindemann .... New York, NY
Lindemann, Michael P.
Department of Justice, Civil Division, GV
Lindemann, Paul B. .... **Greenville, SC**
Lindemann, Paul F. .... **Indianapolis, IN**
Lindemann, Stephen W. .... New York, NY
Lindemann, Steven R. .... **Minneapolis, MN**
Lindemeier, Robert P. .... North Platte, NE
Lindemer, Lawrence B. .... **Lansing, MI**
Lindemood, David W. .... Midland, TX
Lindemood, Stephen R. .... San Antonio, TX
Lindemuth, Jahna M. .... **Anchorage, AK**
Linden, Bella L. .... New York, NY
Linden, David J. .... Chico, CA
Linden, David L. .... Pleasant Ridge, MI
Linden, David R. .... Tonka Bay, MN
Linden, Derek W. .... Rockville, MD
Linden and Deutsch .... **New York, NY**
Linden, Edward A. .... **Tucson, AZ**
Linden, Eric A. .... **Detroit, MI**
Linden & Gallagher .... New York, NY
Linden, Gary F. .... **Seattle, WA**
Linden, Gerald E. .... Orlando, FL
Linden, Gerald E., P.A. .... Orlando, FL
Linden, Howard T. .... Southfield, MI
Linden, Howard T., P.C. .... Southfield, MI
Linden, Jay Steven .... Woodland, CA
Linden, Jeffrey B. .... **Southfield, MI**
Linden, Jeffrey L. .... **Los Angeles, CA**
Linden, Jonathan Mark .... Nashua, NH
Linden, L. Thomas .... Wayland, MA
Linden, Lawrence M. .... New York, NY
Linden, Leonard J. .... New York, NY
Linden, Mary Kominek
Colorado Springs, CO
Linden, Michael J. .... **Cleveland, OH**
Linden, Neil P. .... **Coral Gables, FL**
Linden, Page McGuire .... **Edgewater, MD**
Linden, Peter J. .... **San Clemente, CA**
Linden, Peter S. .... **New York, NY**
Linden, R. William, Jr. .... Salem, OR
Linden, Ralph A. .... Department of Agriculture, Office of the General Counsel, GV
Linden, Richard F. .... **Chicago, IL**
Linden, Robert M. .... **Chicago, IL**
Linden, Roger B. .... Potsdam, NY
Linden, Russell S. .... **Detroit, MI**
Linden, S. Keith .... New York, NY
Linden, Scott C. .... **St. Louis, MO**
Linden, Stacy Renée .... **Washington, DC**
Linden, Thomas .... Carson City, NV
Linden, Thomas .... New York, NY
Linden, Vicent L., III
Colorado Springs, CO
Lindenau, Larry B. .... **Fresno, CA**
Lindenauer, Denise A. .... **New York, NY**
Lindenauer, Eric A. .... **Portland, OR**
Lindenauer, Susan B. .... New York, NY
Lindenauer, Victoria .... Santa Barbara, CA
Lindenbaum Coffman Kurlander & Brisky, Ltd. .... **Chicago, IL**
Lindenbaum, Herbert G. .... New York, NY
Lindenbaum, Jamie Elizabeth Som
Kew Gardens, NY
Lindenbaum, Keith .... **Milwaukee, WI**
Lindenbaum, Leon E. .... **Chicago, IL**
Lindenbaum, Samuel H. .... **New York, NY**
Lindenbaum, Sandford R. .... **New York, NY**
Lindenbaum & Young .... Brooklyn, NY
Lindenberg, Howard .... **McLean, VA**
Lindenberg, Lewis A. .... **New York, NY**
Lindenberger, Richard B. .... **Fenton, MO**
Lindenfeld, Daniel A. .... New York, NY
Lindenfeld, Harris .... **Cazenovia, NY**
Lindenfeld Law Firm, P.C.
Cazenovia, NY
Lindenfeld, Richard B. .... **St. Joseph, MI**
Lindenfeldar, Russell G. .... Philadelphia, PA
Lindenfelser, Cecilia M.E. .... **Roseland, NJ**
New York, NY
Lindenhayn, Rolf .... Martinez, CA
Lindenman, Eric H. .... **New York, NY**
White Plains, NY
Lindenmayer, Elaine A. .... San Francisco, CA
Lindenmeyer, Mark R. .... Batesville, IN
Lindenmuth, Noel C. .... **Chicago, IL**
Lindenmuth, Paul A. .... **Tacoma, WA**
Lindenmuth, Philip J.
Federal Deposit Insurance Corporation, GV
Lindenmuth, Thomas G. .... McAllen, TX
Lindensmith, Mark S. .... Charlottesville, VA
Linder, Alan .... Manchester, NH
Linder, Alan E. .... **New York, NY**
Linder, Andrew J. .... New York, NY
Linder, Barbara J. .... Beverly Hills, CA
Linder, Brian D. .... **New York, NY**
Linder, Charles W., Jr. .... **Indianapolis, IN**
Linder, Cheryl Bloethe .... **Kansas City, MO**
Linder, Craig D. .... **Los Angeles, CA**
Linder, David C. .... **St. Paul, MN**
Linder, David H. .... **Meridian, MS**
Linder, David K. .... **Athens, GA**
Linder, Debra J. .... **Minneapolis, MN**
Linder, Dennis G. .... Department of Justice, Civil Division, GV
Linder, Gary R. .... Los Angeles, CA
Linder, Gerald P. .... Hillsboro, OR
Linder, Harvey R. .... Atlanta, GA
Linder & Hollowell, A Professional Corporation .... **Indianapolis, IN**
Linder, Iris K. .... **Lansing, MI**
Linder, Irving J. .... Brooklyn, NY
Linder, Janet Karen .... Newton, MA
Linder, Jeffrey M. .... Shelbyville, IN
Linder, Jeffrey S. .... **Washington, DC**
Linder, Jeffrey T. .... **Raleigh, NC**
Linder, John J. .... Rushford, MN
Linder, Julianne M. .... **New York, NY**
Linder, Karen I. .... **Edina, MN**
Linder, Karen K. .... **Darien, CT**
Linder, Larry C. .... Wellsboro, PA
Linder, Leigh Otsuka .... **Irvine, CA**
Linder & Linder .... Brooklyn, NY
Linder, Mara G. .... Phoenix, AZ
Linder, Mark J. .... **Los Angeles, CA**
Linder, Milton .... Malibu, CA
Linder, Paul R. .... **Orlando, FL**
Linder, Phillip B .... **Metuchen, NJ**
Linder, Ray Dean .... Alva, OK
Linder, Rex K. .... **Peoria, IL**
Linder, Rita A. .... **Baltimore, MD**
Linder, Robert .... Plainfield, NJ
Linder, Robert B. .... **Englewood, NJ**
Linder, Robert D. .... Falls Church, VA
Linder, Robert G. .... Brooklyn, NY
Linder, Ronald J. .... San Francisco, CA
Linder, Sara Selbo .... San Jose, CA
Linder, Stephen G. .... **Providence, RI**
Linder, Steven A. .... **Minneapolis, MN**
Linder, Steven J.
Treasury Department, GV
Linder, Virginia L. .... Salem, OR
Linder, Walter C. .... **Minneapolis, MN**
Linder, Wendy L. .... South Pasadena, CA
Linderman, Abe M. .... Park Ridge, IL
Linderman, Jay S. .... San Francisco, CA
Linderman, John C. .... **Hartford, CT**
Springfield, MA
Linderman, Mark J. .... **San Francisco, CA**
Linderman, Marla A. .... Pinckney, MI
Linderman, Morris H. .... New York, NY
Linderman, Richard D. .... **Pottstown, PA**
Linderman, Robert .... San Francisco, CA
Linderman, Samuel S. .... Trinidad, CA
Linderman, Shirley M. .... Saco, ME
Linderoth, Gary E. .... Keyport, NJ
Lindevaldsen, Rena M. .... **New York, NY**
Lindey, Lori Nolan .... **Pittsburgh, PA**
Lindfors, P. J. C. .... San Francisco, CA
Lindfors, Robert P. .... **Phoenix, AZ**
Lindgard, Susan Elizabeth .... Jacksonville, FL
Lindgren, Adam U. .... **San Leandro, CA**
Lindgren, Arne S. .... Carlsbad, CA
Lindgren, Brent S. .... **Sacramento, CA**
Lindgren, Catherine N. .... **Portsmouth, NH**
Lindgren, Christian L. .... Hartford, CT
Lindgren, D. Kenneth, Jr.
Minneapolis, MN
Lindgren, David E. .... **Sacramento, CA**
Lindgren, James S. .... New London, WI
Lindgren, James T. .... Chicago, IL
Lindgren, Janet S. .... Buffalo, NY
Lindgren, Jay R. .... Minneapolis, MN
Lindgren, Jeffrey T. .... **San Francisco, CA**
Lindgren, Karin J. .... **Wheaton, IL**
Lindgren, Laura .... **Los Angeles, CA**
Lindgren, Leslie Bigler .... **Los Angeles, CA**
Lindgren, Mark A. .... **Minneapolis, MN**
Lindgren, Penny P. .... Scranton, PA
Lindgren, Robert R. .... Baltimore, MD
Lindgren, Robert S. .... Houston, TX
Lindgren, Steven C. .... **Midland, TX**
Lindgren, Thomas B. .... Peoria, IL
Lindgren, Thomas G. .... Columbus, OH
Lindgren, Thomas K. .... **White Plains, NY**
Lindgren, William D. .... Chicago, IL
Lindgren-Bron, Carol A.
Kansas City, MO
Lindh, Alfred J. .... Wilmington, DE
Lindh, Elizabeth J. .... **Long Beach, CA**
Lindh, Frank R. .... **San Francisco, CA**
Lindh, George H. .... Manchester, NH
Lindh, Lauren E. .... **Pittsburgh, PA**
Lindh, Paul A. .... Fall River, MA
Lindh, Peter A. .... **San Francisco, CA**
Lindheim, Carolyn C. .... **Cherry Hill, NJ**
Philadelphia, PA
Lindheim, Daniel N. .... Berkeley, CA
Lindheim, Jerry A. .... **Philadelphia, PA**
Lindheim, William S. .... Los Angeles, CA
Lindholm, David C. .... Boulder, CO
Lindholm, Donald W. .... **Phoenix, AZ**
Lindholm, Douglas L. .... Washington, DC
Lindholm, Dwight H. .... **Los Angeles, CA**
Lindholm, J. Andrew .... **New York, NY**
Lindholm, James B., Jr.
San Luis Obispo, CA
Lindholm, John A., Jr. .... **Poughkeepsie, NY**
Lindholm, John T. .... **Flint, MI**
Lindholm, Nancy S. .... Palo Alto, CA
Lindholm, Paul .... St. Paul, MN
Lindholm, Robert M. .... Jefferson City, MO
Lindholm, Thomas C. .... Woodland Hills, CA
Lindhorst & Dreidame Co., L.P.A.
Covington, KY
Batavia, OH
Cincinnati, OH
Hamilton, OH
Lebanon, OH
Lindhorst, Eric J. .... St. Louis, MO
Lindhout, Jane E. .... Topeka, KS
Pleasant Grove, UT
Lindie, Beth G. .... **Fort Lauderdale, FL**
Lindig, Charles N. .... Worthington, OH
Lindig, James R. .... Ottawa, IL
Lindig, Robert C. .... Mora, MN
Lindinger, Eileen .... Atlantic City, NJ
Lindkvist, Robert C. .... **San Francisco, CA**
Lindl, Bruce J. .... **Auburn Hills, MI**
Lindland, Kurt N. .... Chicago, IL
Lindlauf, Ronald Wayne, Jr. .... Hartford, CT
Lindleman, Linda .... **St. Louis, MO**
Lindler, H. Bright .... **Rockingham, NC**
Lindley, A. Kristine .... **Indianapolis, IN**
Lindley, Carla N. .... **Dallas, TX**
Lindley, Daniel F. .... **Wilmington, DE**
Lindley, David M. .... Fort Lauderdale, FL
Lindley, David M. .... **New York, NY**
Lindley, Doreen M. Hichey .... Peoria, IL
Lindley, Edgar L. .... Columbus, OH
Lindley, Edward E., Jr. .... San Diego, CA
Lindley, F. Haynes, Jr. .... Los Angeles, CA
Lindley, George W. .... Duncan, OK
Lindley, Gregory E. .... **Salt Lake City, UT**
Lindley, J. Daniel .... **Boston, MA**
Lindley, J. Robin .... **Houston, TX**
Lindley, James H. .... Fresno, CA
Lindley, Jearl R. .... Las Cruces, NM

Lindley, Kathryn S. ....Greensboro, NC
Lindley, Laura ....Denver, CO
Lindley, Lori Hildenbrand ....Monmouth, OR
Lindley, Malcolm G. ....Macon, GA
Lindley, Mark R. ....Lake Oswego, OR
Lindley, Martha Barbee ....Seattle, WA
Lindley, Meda B. ....Jackson, MS
Lindley, Meriel I. ....San Francisco, CA
Lindley, Peter P. ....Fort Lauderdale, FL
Lindley, Philip W. ....Chamberlain, SD
Lindley, Randall K. ....Dallas, TX
Lindley, Robert B. ....Oakhurst, CA
Lindley, Robert B., A Professional Law Corporation ....Oakhurst, CA
Lindley, Robin ....Seattle, WA
Lindley, Scales & Corbett, A Professional Corporation ....San Diego, CA
Lindley, Susan D. ....Boulder, CO
Lindley, Susan Shea ....Duncan, OK
Lindley, Thomas E. ....Portland, OR
Lindley, Todd P. ....Dallas, TX
Lindley, Wendy S. ....Laguna Niguel, CA
Lindley, Willard J. ....Warren, MI
Lindley & Wood ....San Francisco, CA
Lindley-Dominguez, Patricia M. ....The Woodlands, TX
Lindley-Myers, Chlora A. ....Parkville, MO
Lindlof, Stephen M. ....St. Paul, MN
Lindloff, P. Keith ....Bellaire, TX
Lindman, Dale B. ....Minneapolis, MN
Lindman, Darrell A. ....Lansing, MI
Lindman, Ruth Ann ....Mattawan, MI
Lindman, William R. ....Anoka, MN
Lindman, William R., P.A. ....Anoka, MN
Lindmark, Carl R. ....Woodland, CA
Lindmark, James A. ....Chicago, IL
Lindmark, Marvin L., III ....St. Louis, MO
Lindmeyer, Kermit J. ....Shakopee, MN
Lindner, Albert A. ....Bala Cynwyd, PA
Lindner, Anne M. ....Baltimore, MD
Lindner & Associates, P.C. ....Washington, DC
Lindner, Bernard I. ....Los Angeles, CA
Lindner, Bolt & Marquez ....Garden City, KS
Lindner, Burton R., (Ltd.) ....Chicago, IL
Lindner, Charles L. ....Santa Monica, CA
Lindner, Dennis G. ....Milwaukee, WI
Lindner, Don F. ....Glen Burnie, MD
Lindner, George P. ....Aurora, IL
Lindner, Irene M. ....Washington, DC
Lindner, Jack ....New York, NY
Lindner, Jack B. ....Lincoln, NE
Lindner, John M. ....Garden City, KS
Lindner, John W., II ....Slidell, LA
Lindner, K. David ....Phoenix, AZ
Lindner, Laura A. ....Chicago, IL
Lindner, Mark ....Needham, MA
Lindner & Marsack, S.C. ....Milwaukee, WI
Lindner, Martha F. ....Yardley, PA
Lindner, Meyer ....Staten Island, NY
Lindner, Michael David, Jr. ....Woodbury, NJ
Lindner, Patricia Reid ....Sugar Grove, IL
Lindner, Patrick W. ....San Antonio, TX
Lindner, Richard H. ....Pittsburgh, PA
Lindner, Russell C. ....Washington, DC
Lindner & Simpson ....Pittsburgh, PA
Lindner, Speers & Reuland ....Aurora, IL
Lindo, Margaret Gibbs ....Brooklyn, NY
Lindo, Stephen T. ....New York, NY
Lindon, James L. ....Sandusky, OH
Lindon Law Corporation ....Los Angeles, CA
Lindon, Mark L. ....Los Angeles, CA
Lindon, Timothy J. ....New York, NY
Lindor, Gerald J. M., P.A. ....Fort Lauderdale, FL
Miami, FL
Lindor, Gerald J. M. ....Fort Lauderdale, FL
Miami, FL
Lindover, Donald I. ....New York, NY
Lindow, John ....Reston, VA
Lindow, K. Richard, Jr. ....Fort Lauderdale, FL
Lindow, K. Richard ....San Francisco, CA
Lindow, Louisa R. ....Honolulu, HI
Lindow, Mark A. ....San Antonio, TX
Lindow & Treat, L.L.P. ....San Antonio, TX
Lindower, Kurt J. ....Cleveland, OH
Lindquist, Alan V. ....Chicago, IL
Lindquist, Benjamin L. ....Thomasville, GA
Lindquist, Deanna Ruddock ....Charlotte, NC
Lindquist, Donald A. ....New Orleans, LA
Lindquist, Dwight R. J. ....Minneapolis, MN
Lindquist, Eric ....New York, NY
Lindquist, Eric H. ....Omaha, NE
Lindquist, Eric Nelson ....Los Angeles, CA
Lindquist & Jeffrey, P.A. ....East Grand Forks, MN
Lindquist, John A., III ....Department of Justice, Tax Division, GV
Lindquist, Karen E. ....Washington, DC
Lindquist, Karl ....East Grand Forks, MN
Lindquist, Kent ....Gary, IN
Lindquist, Kim R. ....Boise, ID
Lindquist, Kurt E., II ....Charlotte, NC
Lindquist, Leigh Ann ....Washington, DC
Lindquist, Leonard E. ....Minneapolis, MN
Lindquist, Malcolm C. ....Tacoma, WA
Lindquist, Marian A. ....Fort Lauderdale, FL
Lindquist, Mary Lee ....Irvine, CA
Lindquist, Myron C. ....Kadoka, SD
Lindquist, Peter N. ....Colusa, CA
Lindquist, Philip M. ....Dallas, TX
Lindquist, Randall C. ....Columbus, OH
Lindquist, Reid R. ....Minneapolis, MN
Lindquist, Rick D. ....Kansas City, MO
Lindquist, Robert M. ....Santa Ana, CA
Lindquist, Robert W. ....Sacramento, CA
Lindquist, Rodney J., Jr. ....Lafayette, CA
Lindquist, Russell W. ....Minneapolis, MN
Lindquist, Scott A. ....Chicago, IL
Lindquist, Susan J. ....Anchorage, AK
Lindquist, Ted C., III ....San Francisco, CA
Lindquist, Timothy A. ....Minneapolis, MN
Lindquist, Vennum & Christensen P.L.L.P. ....Denver, CO
Lindquist & Vennum P.L.L.P. ....Minneapolis, MN
St. Paul, MN
Lindquist, Vicki Nugent ....San Francisco, CA
Lindquist, William A. ....Winona, MN
Lindquist-Kleissler, Arthur ....Denver, CO
Lindquist-Kleissler, Cooper & Moore, LLC ....Denver, CO
Lindrew, Gerald B. ....Department of Labor, Pension and Welfare Benefits, GV
Lindroos, Colleen Danehy ....Rocky Hill, CT
Lindroos, David W. ....Rocky Hill, CT
Lindroos, Michael E. ....North Canton, OH
Lindrooth, Charles H. ....Philadelphia, PA
Lindros, John E. ....Newtown Square, PA
Lindroth, Richard J. ....Charleston, WV
Lindsay, Alan ....Palm Beach, FL
Lindsay, Alexander H., Jr. ....Butler, PA
Lindsay, Alison K. ....Wichita, KS
Lindsay, Allen W., Jr. ....Milton, FL
Lindsay, Allen W., Sr. ....Milton, FL
Lindsay, Alvin F., III ....Miami, FL
Lindsay, Andrews, Leonard & Slingerland, A Professional Association ....Milton, FL
Pensacola, FL
Lindsay, Anne W. ....Chesterland, OH
Lindsay, Barbara B. ....Stamford, CT
Lindsay, Blair W. ....St. Louis, MO
Lindsay, Brenda Lea ....Knoxville, TN
Lindsay, Brian Joseph ....Meadville, PA
Lindsay, Brian S. ....Huntington, WV
Lindsay, Bruce A. ....Whittier, CA
Lindsay, C. Marshall ....Raleigh, NC
Lindsay, Carl L., Jr. ....New Hope, PA
Lindsay, Carol J. ....Carlisle, PA
Lindsay, Charles R. ....Shreveport, LA
Lindsay, Christina L. ....Englewood, CO
Lindsay, Christopher F. ....Cheboygan, MI
Lindsay, Clare ....Environmental Protection Agency, Program Office Attorneys, GV
Lindsay, Colin Hugh ....Louisville, KY
Lindsay, Daniel F. ....Omaha, NE
Lindsay, Daniel M. ....West Sacramento, CA
Lindsay, Daniel T. ....Minneapolis, MN
Lindsay, David C. ....Raleigh, NC
Lindsay, Dennis J. ....Portland, OR
Lindsay, Donald E. ....Austin, TX
Lindsay, Douglas A. ....Chicago, IL
Lindsay, Edward E. ....Houston, TX
Lindsay, Edward L. ....Fountain Valley, CA
Lindsay, Eileen A. ....Roseland, NJ
Lindsay, Francis E. ....Cheboygan, MI
Lindsay, G. Bruce ....Columbus, OH
Lindsay, G. Griffith ....Washington, DC
Lindsay, George P. ....New York, NY
Lindsay, Gregory Harry ....Media, PA
Lindsay, Gross C. ....Henderson, KY
Lindsay, Hart, Neil & Weigler, LLP ....Washington, DC
Portland, OR
Vancouver, WA
Lindsay, Hugh W. ....College Station, TX
Lindsay, J. Stewart ....Columbia, SC
Lindsay, J. Wade ....Washington, DC
Lindsay, Jackson & Martin, P.C. ....Butler, PA
Lindsay, Jacque Brawner ....Oklahoma City, OK
Lindsay, James C. ....Parkton, MD
Lindsay, James F. ....Altadena, CA
Lindsay, James G. ....Department of Justice, Criminal Division, GV
Lindsay, James M. ....Dublin, CA
Lindsay, James M. ....Toledo, OH
Lindsay, James P. ....Estes Park, CO
Lindsay, James R. ....Akron, OH
Lindsay, James R. ....Bennington, VT
Lindsay, Jas. H. ....Atlanta, GA
Lindsay, Jmaes M. ....Toledo, OH
Lindsay, John B. ....Salt Lake City, UT
Lindsay, John C. ....Lincoln, NE
Lindsay, John Drew, Jr. ....Department Of Veterans Affairs, Office of Employment Discrimination Complaints Adjudication, GV
Lindsay, John H. ....Branford, CT
Lindsay, John Raymond ....Turnersville, NJ
Lindsay, John V. ....New York, NY
Lindsay, Kathleen ....Mineola, NY
Lindsay, Keith L. ....Atlanta, GA
Lindsay, Kelly-Ann M. ....St. Paul, MN
Lindsay, Kent W. ....San Francisco, CA
Lindsay, Kevin W. ....Los Angeles, CA
Lindsay, Lawrence ....Niagara Falls, NY
Lindsay, Lawrence W. ....Cherry Hill, NJ
Lindsay & Lindsay ....Cheboygan, MI
Lindsay & Lindsay ....Omaha, NE
Lindsay, Lynn R. ....St. Cloud, MN
Lindsay, Marcel, Harris & Pugh, L.L.C. ....Baton Rouge, LA
Lindsay, Margaret P. ....Provo, UT
Lindsay, Mark ....Fayetteville, AR
Rogers, AR
Lindsay, Mark F. ....Executive Office Of The President, Office of Administration, GV
Lindsay, Mark, P.A. ....Fayetteville, AR
Lindsay, Michael A. ....Apple Valley, CA
Lindsay, Michael A. ....Minneapolis, MN
Lindsay, Michael E. ....Denver, CO
Lindsay, Michael R. ....Los Angeles, CA
Lindsay, Milton L. ....Milwaukee, WI
Lindsay, Nancy ....Jacksonville, IL
Lindsay, Nancy J. ....Chicago, IL
Lindsay, Pamela Tabor ....Charleston, WV
Lindsay, Patrick V. ....Provo, UT
Lindsay, Pickens M. ....Atlanta, GA
Lindsay, R. Scott ....Murphy, NC
Lindsay, Reginald C. ....Boston, MA
Lindsay, Robert Bruce ....Reno, NV
Lindsay, Robert E. ....Department of Justice, Tax Division, GV
Lindsay, Robert M. ....Louisville, KY
Lindsay, Robyn B. ....Englewood, NJ
Lindsay, Ronald A. ....Washington, DC
Lindsay, Ronald T. ....Charlotte, NC
Lindsay, Ross M., III ....Myrtle Beach, SC
Pawleys Island, SC
Lindsay, Sean C. ....Englewood, CO
Lindsay, Sharon W. ....Scarsdale, NY
Lindsay, Stephen E. ....Cheboygan, MI
Lindsay, Stephen P. ....Boston, MA
Lindsay, Stephen P. ....Asheville, NC
Lindsay, Suzanne A. ....Waukegan, IL
Lindsay, Theodore ....Library, PA
Lindsay, Theodore G. ....New York, NY
Lindsay & Tiller ....Myrtle Beach, SC
Pawleys Island, SC
Lindsay, Timothy W. ....Jackson, MS
Tupelo, MS
Lindsay, Tony ....Houston, TX
Lindsay, Tracy M. ....Mission Viejo, CA
Lindsay, W. Arthur ....Houston, TX
Lindsay, Walter H., Jr. ....Carol Stream, IL
Lindsay, Wendell G., Jr. ....Baton Rouge, LA
Lindsay, William C. ....Waukegan, IL
Lindsay, William J., Jr. ....Omaha, NE
Lindseth, Alfred A. ....Atlanta, GA
Lindseth, Arnold V., Jr. ....Memphis, TN
Lindseth, Erik A. ....Minneapolis, MN
Lindsey, Allison B. ....New York, NY
Lindsey, Andrew W. ....Dade City, FL
Lindsey, Bob ....Abilene, TX
Lindsey, Bruce ....Monterey, CA
Lindsey, Bruce ....Salinas, CA
Lindsey, Bruce R. ....Executive Office Of The President, GV
Lindsey, Camilla J. ....Tulsa, OK
Lindsey, Carrie Deem ....Fairfax, VA
Lindsey, Carson R. ....Charlotte, NC
Lindsey, Charles E., Jr. ....Bristol, CT
Lindsey, Christopher E. ....Houston, TX
Lindsey, Clayton L. ....Oregon, IL
Lindsey, Crockett ....Biloxi, MS
Lindsey, Cynthia M. ....Detroit, MI
Lindsey, Daniel L., Jr. ....Montgomery, AL
Lindsey, Daniel R. ....Clovis, NM
Lindsey, Daniel R., P.C. ....Clovis, NM
Lindsey, David ....Jasper, GA
Lindsey, David H. ....Kansas City, MO
Lindsey, David M. ....Miami, FL
Lindsey, Denise D. ....Slidell, LA
Lindsey, Duane S. ....Newport Beach, CA
Lindsey, Edward H., Jr. ....Atlanta, GA
Lindsey, F. H. ....Canyon, TX
Lindsey, Elizabeth Green ....Atlanta, GA
Lindsey, Gareth A. ....Elba, AL
Lindsey, Gregory A. ....Louisville, KY
Lindsey, H. Eugene, III ....Miami, FL
Lindsey, Heather B. ....Columbus, OH
Lindsey, Hubert R. ....West Palm Beach, FL
Lindsey, Ian Douglas ....Baton Rouge, LA
Lindsey & Jacobs ....Barnesville, GA
Lindsey, James B., Jr. ....Canton, OH
Lindsey, James G. ....Maitland, FL
Lindsey, James T. ....Santa Barbara, CA
Lindsey, Jefferson A. ....Rockport, IN
Lindsey, Jesse V. ....Midland, TX
Lindsey, Joanne M. ....Broomall, PA
Lindsey, John C. ....Research Triangle Park, NC
Lindsey, John R. ....Coral Gables, FL
Lindsey, John R. ....Jacksboro, TX
Lindsey, Jonathan A. ....New York, NY
Lindsey, Kathleen Joerger ....Rosenberg, TX
Lindsey, Katrina S. ....Orlando, FL
Lindsey, Kevin M. ....Minneapolis, MN
Lindsey, Kristin A. ....Manchester, NH
Lindsey, Laine D. ....Houston, TX
Lindsey, Lewis R. ....De Funiak Springs, FL
Lindsey & Lindsey ....Rockport, IN
Lindsey, Lisa Diana ....Detroit, MI
Lindsey, M. David ....Denver, CO
Lindsey, Marc A. ....Washington, DC
Lindsey, Marc A. ....Charlotte, NC
Lindsey, Mark A. ....Indianapolis, IN
Lindsey, Mary Anne ....St. Louis, MO
Lindsey, Michael D. ....Louisville, KY
Lindsey, Michael K. ....Los Angeles, CA
Lindsey, Natalie S. ....Sacramento, CA
Lindsey, Nicole D. ....Ocala, FL
Lindsey, Paul B. ....Oklahoma City, OK
Lindsey, Paul E. ....Camden, AR
Lindsey, R. Michael ....Wilmington, DE
Lindsey, Randall ....Phoenix, AZ
Lindsey, Richard C., Jr. ....Jackson, MI
Lindsey, Richard P. ....Atlanta, GA
Lindsey, Robert L., Jr. ....Charlotte, NC
Lindsey, Rochelle M. ....Los Angeles, CA
Lindsey, Roger L. ....Jeffersonville, IN
Lindsey, Ronald A. ....Long Beach, CA
Lindsey, Rosemary ....Fort Lauderdale, FL
Lindsey, R. W. ....Rosenberg, TX
Lindsey, Sarah C. ....Washington, DC
Lindsey and Schrimsher, P.A. ....Charlotte, NC
Lindsey, Scott T. ....Columbus, OH
Lindsey, Seth M. ....Department of Transportation, Federal Railroad Administration, GV
Lindsey, Shirley A. ....Hunt Valley, MD
Lindsey, Sidney R. ....Rockport, IN
Lindsey, Stephen L. ....West Covina, CA
Lindsey, Steven P. ....Annapolis, MD
Lindsey, Susan G. ....Nashville, TN
Lindsey, Thanayi J. ....Los Angeles, CA
Lindsey, Thomas H. ....Columbus, OH
Lindsey, Thomas K. ....Columbus, OH
Lindsey, Thomas T. ....Cable, WI
Washburn, WI
Lindsey, Tonya M ....New York, NY
Lindsey, Wallace H., III ....Butler, AL
Lindsey, Warren R. ....Manchester, NH
Lindsey, Warren W. ....Winter Park, FL
Lindsey, Wendi A. ....Melville, NY
Lindsey, William C. ....Port Arthur, TX
Lindsey, William D., (P.C.) ....Barnesville, GA
Lindsey, William H. ....Salem, VA
Lindsey, William H., P.C. ....Salem, VA
Lindsey, Wm. Scott ....Tallahassee, FL
Lindsey-Scott, Roberta ....Sacramento, CA
Lindsey-Scott, Roberta A. ....Woodbury, MN
Lindskog, David R. ....New York, NY
Lindsley, Byron F. ....San Diego, CA
Lindsley, H. Hays ....Dallas, TX
Lindsley, Jeremy D. ....Durham, NC
Lindsley, Joe ....Dallas, TX
Lindsley and Karcher Co., L.P.A. ....Toledo, OH
Lindsley, Stephen A. ....Riverside, CA
Lindsley, William H. ....Rochester, NY
Lindsley, William R. ....Toledo, OH
Lindsmith, Quintin F. ....Columbus, OH
Lind-Spahn, Jennifer ....Wichita, KS
Lindstedt, James B. ....Mariposa, CA
Lindstedt, Norman E. ....Rockford, IL
Lindstedt, Norman L. ....Portland, OR
Lindstedt-Simmons, Bethene A. ....Chatham, NY
Lindstrand, Laura Rae ....Camano, WA
Lindstrom, C. Timothy ....Charlottesville, VA
Lindstrom, Carol Perritt ....Eaton, OH
Lindstrom, Cary O. ....San Jose, CA
Lindstrom, Daniel L. ....Kearney, NE
Lindstrom, Deborah J. ....Norwalk, CT
Lindstrom, Diane S. ....Phoenix, AZ
Lindstrom, Edward R. ....Tacoma, WA
Lindstrom, Eric J., (Ltd). ....Minneapolis, MN
Lindstrom, Eric L. ....Midland, TX
Lindstrom, Eric S.C. ....San Francisco, CA
Lindstrom, Ernest A., (Ltd.) ....Minneapolis, MN
Lindstrom, Gregory P. ....San Francisco, CA
Lindstrom, John C. ....Willmar, MN
Lindstrom, John H. ....Minneapolis, MN
Lindstrom, John R. ....Suffern, NY
Lindstrom Law Offices ....Minneapolis, MN
Lindstrom, Lois A. ....Oakland, CA
Walnut Creek, CA
Lindstrom, Mark E. ....Olathe, KS
Lindstrom, Pamela A. ....Clearwater, FL
Lindstrom, Paul A., (Ltd) ....Minneapolis, MN
Lindstrom, Richard F. ....Baltimore, MD
Lindstrom, Robert ....Galesburg, IL
Lindstrom, Robert M. ....Minneapolis, MN
Lindstrom, Robert M., P.A. ....Minneapolis, MN
Lindstrom, Soren ....New York, NY
Lindstrom, Vieno R. ....Richland, WA
Lindstrom, Walter, Jr. ....San Diego, CA
Lindt, Marketa ....Chicago, IL
Lindteigen & Griffiths, Ltd. ....Mesa, AZ
Lindteigen, Susan R. ....Mesa, AZ
Lindvall, James C. ....Minneapolis, MN
Lindvall, Robert J. ....Rockford, IL
Lindvall, Scott G. ....New York, NY
Lindvig, Clifford L. ....Van Nuys, CA
Lindwall, Gregory B. ....Edina, MN
Lindwall, Robert R. ....Columbus, OH
Lindy, Jay H. ....Memphis, TN
Lindy, Jeffrey M. ....Philadelphia, PA
Lindy, Joel L. ....Albany, NY
Line, Billie B., Jr. ....Huntsville, AL
Line, Carolyn P. ....Minneapolis, MN
Line, David K. ....Dallas, TX
Line, Eric E. ....Eaton, OH
Line, Franklin K., Jr. ....Marshall, MI
Line, J. Edward ....Hereford, TX
Line, James G. ....Visalia, CA
Line, Jeffrey S. ....Indianapolis, IN
Line Law Firm, The, P.C. ....Dallas, TX
Line, Lisa M. ....Omaha, NE
Line, Michael Scott ....Ruidoso, NM
Line, Scott T. ....Orlando, FL
Line, Timothy C. ....Missoula, MT
Line, William G. ....Fremont, NE
Lineback, Jennifer ....Myrtle Beach, SC
Lineback, Judith Ward ....Greenville, SC
Lineback & Lewis, Professional Corporation ....Greenfield, IN
Linebarger, Dale ....Austin, TX
Linebarger, Douglas A. ....Dallas, TX
Linebaugh, Daniel B. ....Baytown, TX
Houston, TX
Linebaugh, Kent B. ....Salt Lake City, UT
Linebaugh, N. L., Jr. ....Dallas, TX
Linebaugh, Stephen P. ....York, PA
Lineberger, Carmen M. ....Philadelphia, PA
Lineberger, James A. ....Philadelphia, PA
Lineberger, John R. ....Fayetteville, AR
Lineberger, Martha E. ....Rocky River, OH
Lineberger, Peter S. ....Spokane, WA

Lineberger, Robert E.W. .... **Nashville, TN**
Lineberger, Samira Mery .... Houston, TX
Lineberry, Allen Scott .... Irving, TX
Lineberry, Charles M., Jr.
Wilmington, NC
Lineberry, Douglas Lee .... **Greenville, SC**
Lineberry, E. Scott .... **Austin, TX**
Lineberry, Margaret D. .... **Kansas City, MO**
Lineberry, Warren G. .... Floyd, VA
Lineberry & White, L.L.P.
Wilmington, NC
Lineberry, William D. .... **Birmingham, AL**
Lineen, Edward M. .... Armonk, NY
Linehan, Andrew F. .... Palm Desert, CA
Linehan, David A. .... **Kansas City, MO**
Linehan, David C. .... Downey, CA
Linehan, Erin K. .... **Tampa, FL**
Linehan, James R. .... **Edmond, OK**
Linehan, James R., P.C. .... **Edmond, OK**
Linehan, Joseph E. .... **Pittsburgh, PA**
Linehan, Joseph F. .... West Bridgewater, MA
Linehan, Karen M. .... **New York, NY**
Linehan, Kathleen Mary .... Washington, DC
Linehan, Paul W. .... **Cleveland, OH**
Linehan, Randolph .... Rancho Mirage, CA
Linehan, Richard F. .... Hingham, MA
Linehan, Wendy Zimmer .... **Detroit, MI**
Linek, Ernest V. .... **Boston, MA**
Linek, Francis M. .... St. Louis, MO
Linenberger, Marta Fisher .... **Topeka, KS**
Linenbroker, David A. .... **St. Louis, MO**
Liner, David B. .... Taylor, MI
Liner, David V. .... Winston-Salem, NC
Liner, Jay L. .... Baltimore, MD
Liner, Richard S. .... **Boston, MA**
Liner, Robert F. .... **New York, NY**
Liner, Scott K. .... **Los Angeles, CA**
Liner, Stuart A. .... **Santa Monica, CA**
Liner, Stuart A. .... Harrisburg, PA
Liner Yankelevitz Sunshine Weinhart & Regenstreif LLP .... **Los Angeles, CA**
Santa Monica, CA
Linero, William, Jr. .... Coral Gables, FL
Linert, Kathleen A. .... Boston, MA
Lines, Blucher B. .... **Quincy, FL**
Lines, Earl M. .... Mesa, AZ
Lines, Farrell L. .... Albuquerque, NM
Lines, Hinson and Lines .... **Quincy, FL**
Lines, John K. .... Greenville, SC
Lines, Kal W. .... Novato, CA
Lines, Karen R. .... **South San Francisco, CA**
Lines, L. Joseph, III .... **Detroit, MI**
Lines, M. Michele .... Beverly Hills, CA
Lines, Mimi M. .... **Hartford, CT**
Lines, Ruskin R. .... Safford, AZ
Lines, W. McLin .... Torrance, CA
Lines, William P. .... **Milaca, MN**
Linesch, David J. .... **Palm Harbor, FL**
Linesch Firm, The .... **Palm Harbor, FL**
Linet, Cynthia .... Hilo, HI
Linet, Jerome .... North Miami Beach, FL
Linet, Paul E. .... **Acton, MA**
Linet, Paul E., A Professional Corporation
Acton, MA
Boston, MA
Linett, David .... **Bridgewater, NJ**
Linett, Howard B. .... Herndon, VA
Linett, Janice Corwin
Environmental Protection Agency, Office of Enforcement and Compliance Assurance, GV
Linett, Jennifer H. .... **Princeton, NJ**
New York, NY
Linett, Schechter, Reicher & Ofsevit, LLP
New York, NY
Linett, Stephen D. .... Los Angeles, CA
Linfesty, R. Frederick .... **New York, NY**
Linfield, James C. T. .... **Boulder, CO**
Denver, CO
Linfield, John Charles .... Quincy, MA
Linfield, Seth D. .... **South Bend, IN**
Linford, Donley R. .... Evanston, WY
Linford, James T. .... San Francisco, CA
Linford, John B. .... Bakersfield, CA
Linford, Kirk M. .... Chicago, IL
Linford, Lorraine .... **Seattle, WA**
Linford, Richard W. .... Salt Lake City, UT
Linfors, Nils, Jr. .... **Miami, FL**
Ling, Andrew M. .... Phoenix, AZ
Ling, David T. .... New York, NY
Ling & Farran .... Greensboro, NC
Ling, Gary Alan .... **North Charleston, SC**
Ling, Heidi E. .... Chandler, AZ
Ling, Herman H. M. .... Wailuku, HI
Ling, Jenny C. Y. .... New York, NY
Ling, Joe .... Long Beach, CA
Ling, Karen L. .... St. Davids, PA
Ling, Ling .... **Washington, DC**
Ling, Lorraine B. .... New York, NY
Ling, Louis A. .... Carson City, NV
Ling, Michael C.C. .... Santa Barbara, CA
Ling, Nielsen & Robinson .... **Rupert, ID**
Ling, Robert M., Jr. .... Commerce, CA
Ling, Roger D. .... **Rupert, ID**
Ling, S. Tony .... **Chicago, IL**
Ling, Stella H. .... Los Angeles, CA
Ling, Stephen D. .... Greensboro, NC
Ling, Thomas S. .... Bedford, PA
Ling, Trent W. .... Orlando, FL
Ling, W.A., III .... **Memphis, TN**
Ling, Winston Det Min .... Honolulu, HI
Lingafelt, Phillip R. .... **Roanoke, VA**
Lingan, Thomas M. .... **Baltimore, MD**
Lingan, Victor Rirao .... Tujunga, CA
Lingard, Rebecca Niles .... Needham, MA
Linge, H. Kennedy .... **Pittsburgh, PA**
Lingel, Janet M. .... **San Diego, CA**
Lingelbach, Albert L. .... **New York, NY**
Lingelbach, Christina .... **Denver, CO**
Lingelbach, John M. .... **Omaha, NE**
Lingelser, Richard J. .... Oakland, CA
Lingeman, Larry J. .... Tucson, AZ
Lingenbrink, David A. .... **Los Angeles, CA**
Lingenbrink, Steven G. .... Bellevue, WA
Linger, Alexander .... Northridge, CA
Linger, David G. .... **Syracuse, NY**
Linger, James C. .... Tulsa, OK
Linger, Jerry Nelson, Jr. .... Chester, WV
Linger, Lori M. .... **New York, NY**
Lingerfeldt, Mary S. .... West Palm Beach, FL
Lingerfelt, David L. .... Richmond, VA
Lingg, A. Grant .... **Seattle, WA**
Lingg, Richard A. .... **New York, NY**
Linggi, Joseph A. .... Santa Maria, CA
Lingl, Herb .... San Francisco, CA
Lingl, James P. .... **Camarillo, CA**
Lingle, Barbara E. .... **Rogers, AR**
Lingle, Dena S. .... Fayetteville, NC
Lingle, Elizabeth A. .... Effingham, IL
Lingle, Frederick D. .... Lock Haven, PA
Lingle, Griffis & Southern, PLLC
Jackson, MS
Lingle, James G. .... **Rogers, AR**
Lingle, John R. .... Piggott, AR
Lingle, Katherine A. .... Kenosha, WI
Lingle, Kathryn Spruill .... **Richmond, VA**
Lingle Law Firm .... **Rogers, AR**
Lingle, Richard M. .... **Jackson, MS**
Lingle, Robert J. .... **Greensboro, NC**
Lingley, Robert Scott .... Bangor, ME
Lingner, John .... Chicago, IL
Lingnowski, Ruby Josephine .... Menasha, WI
Lingo, Anna K. .... Columbia, MO
Lingo, Bradley W. .... Houston, TX
Lingo, Jeffrey D. .... Toledo, OH
Lingo, John S. .... **Omaha, NE**
Lingo, Kim Joseph .... San Diego, CA
Lingo, Kristen Gardner .... **Raleigh, NC**
Lingo, R. Craig .... Redding, CA
Lingo, Robert S. .... Department of the Army, Army Materiel Command, GV
Lingreen, Margaret L. .... Decorah, IA
Lingren, David C. .... **Cloquet, MN**
Lingren, Kristin L. .... **Chicago, IL**
Linguanti, Thomas V. M. .... **Chicago, IL**
Linguiti, Francis M. .... **Philadelphia, PA**
Lingwall, Chris A. .... **Dallas, TX**
Lingys, Julia E. .... **San Mateo, CA**
Linh, Theme Sue .... **Beaumont, TX**
Linhardt, Daniel Sanders .... Sacramento, CA
Linhardt, Eric R. .... Williamsport, PA
Linhardt, Kathleen A. .... Buffalo, NY
Linhares, Gregory Joseph
Jefferson City, MO
Linhares, Kenneth A. .... **Palo Alto, CA**
Linhares, Robert J. .... **St. Louis, MO**
Linhart, Larry R. .... Columbus, OH
Linhart, Lisa A. .... Ontario, OR
Linhoff, Thomas R. .... Kansas City, MO
Linhoff, William P., Jr. .... **Costa Mesa, CA**
Linholm, Nick C. .... **Oklahoma City, OK**
Liniak, Berenato, Longacre & White, LLC
Washington, DC
Bethesda, MD
Arlington, VA
Leesburg, VA
Liniak, Thomas P. .... **Bethesda, MD**
Linick, Corey D. .... New Port Richey, FL
Linick, Steve A. .... Washington, DC
Linihan, D. Michael .... **St. Louis, MO**
Linihan, Martin G. .... **Buffalo, NY**
Lininger, Thomas D. .... San Francisco, CA
Linington, David George
Grosse Pointe Woods, MI
Link, Alan P., Law Offices of .... Westport, CT
Link, Amos E., Jr. .... Raleigh, NC
Link, Antony C. (Tony) .... Duncan, OK
Link, Bernard G. .... Lutherville, MD
Link, Bonnie .... East Meadow, NY
Link, Brian Fredrick .... Boston, MA
Link & Broderson .... Franklin, KY
Link, Christopher Noel .... Sunrise, FL
Link, Daniel H. .... Lake Success, NY
Link, David F. .... Sacramento, CA
Link, David J.
Securities and Exchange Commission, Division of Corporation Finance, GV
Link, David K. .... Hagåtña, GU
Link, David K., P.A., Law Offices of
Hagåtña, GU
Link, David T. .... Notre Dame, IN
Link, Diane B. .... Pomona, CA
Link, Elizabeth M. .... San Francisco, CA
Link, Eugene M. .... Minneapolis, MN
Link, Frederic L. .... San Diego, CA
Link, Frederick E. .... **Gainesville, GA**
Link, Frederick H. .... Hammond, IN
Link, Gary L. .... **Sacramento, CA**
Link, Gary S. .... Colorado Springs, CO
Link, George H. .... **Los Angeles, CA**
Link, J. Jason .... **Winston-Salem, NC**
Link, James E., II .... Ouray, CO
Link, James S. .... **Pasadena, CA**
Link, Janet Malloy .... **Chicago, IL**
Link, Jeffrey A. .... Denver, CO
Link, John A. .... **Merrillville, IN**
Link, John B., III .... Nashville, TN
Link, John D. .... **San Francisco, CA**
Link, Jonathan .... **Washington, DC**
Link, Jonathan H. .... Kenai, AK
Link, Josephine B. .... **New York, NY**
Link, Joyce B. .... **Columbus, OH**
Link, Katherine Carruth .... Columbia, SC
Link, Kathryn L. .... **Boston, MA**
Link, Ken M. .... Fort Worth, TX
Link, Ken M., P.C. .... Fort Worth, TX
Link, Lawrence R., Jr. .... Louisville, KY
Link, Mark D. .... **Atlanta, GA**
Link, Mary Ann .... Richmond, VA
Link, Mary Therese .... **Chicago, IL**
Link, May F., (Mrs.) .... Brooklyn, NY
Link, Melissa Robinson .... Newport News, VA
Link, Nora M. .... Uniondale, NY
Link, Norbert .... Ramona, CA
Link, Patrick John .... Hampton, NH
Link, Paul D. .... **Springfield, MO**
Link, Richard D. .... Doylestown, PA
Link, Richard J. .... Newburyport, MA
Link, Robert A. .... Birmingham, MI
Link, Robert J. .... **Jacksonville, FL**
Link, Robert O., Jr. .... **New York, NY**
Link, Robert Young .... Franklin, KY
Link, Ronald C. .... Chapel Hill, NC
Link, Scott J. .... **West Palm Beach, FL**
Link, Scott R. .... Houston, TX
Link, Sharon M. .... **Denver, CO**
Link, Stephen .... Concord, NH
Link, Stephen T. .... Evansville, IN
Link, Susan J. .... **Minneapolis, MN**
Link, Thomas H. .... Palatine, IL
Link, Tony .... Grand Junction, CO
Link, Troland S. .... **New York, NY**
Link & Warhurst .... San Francisco, CA
Link, Wendy Sartory
West Palm Beach, FL
Link, Wesley Paul .... **Houston, TX**
Link, William M. .... **Chicago, IL**
Linken, Dennis C. .... **Newark, NJ**
Linker, Alan N. .... **Louisville, KY**
Linker, Arthur S. .... **New York, NY**
Linker, Dana N. .... **San Francisco, CA**
Linker, David M. .... Philadelphia, PA
Linker, Diane S. .... **New York, NY**
Linker, Donald L. .... Scarsdale, NY
Linker, Donald Lee .... Dallas, TX
Linker, Helene M. .... San Francisco, CA
Linker, Ian Seth .... **New York, NY**
Linker, Joan S. .... New York, NY
Linker, John K. .... **Houston, TX**
Linker, Jonathan F. .... **New York, NY**
Linker, Linker & Northcutt .... Tulsa, OK
Linker, Paul J. .... Newark, NJ
Linker, Raymond O., Jr. .... **Charlotte, NC**
Linker, Rick Randall .... Richmond, VA
Linker, Russell R., II .... Tulsa, OK
Linker, Stan L. .... **Monterey, CA**
Linker, Stephen A. .... Louisville, KY
Linkert, Richard S. .... **Sacramento, CA**
Linkhauer, John W. .... Mc Keesport, PA
Linkhorst, Adam C. .... **Fort Lauderdale, FL**
Linkin, Robert E. .... **Houston, TX**
Linkin & Thomas, LLP .... **Houston, TX**
Linkkila, Timothy P. .... **Boston, MA**
Linklater, William Joseph .... **Chicago, IL**
Linklaters .... **Washington, DC**
New York, NY
New York, NY
Linklaters & Alliance .... **New York, NY**
Linkmeyer, Gene .... **Milwaukee, WI**
Linkner, Monica Farris .... Berkley, MI
Linkon, Steven K. .... **Newport Beach, CA**
Linkosky, John .... Wexford, PA
Linkosky, John R. .... Pittsburgh, PA
Linkous, Alan B. .... Charleston, SC
Linkous, Byron K. .... **Oklahoma City, OK**
Linkous, Gary G. .... Welches, OR
Linkous, Gerald R. .... Princeton, WV
Linkous, William J., III .... Atlanta, GA
Linkous, William Joseph, Jr. .... **Atlanta, GA**
Linkowski, Carol P. .... Dixon, IL
Links, Robert D. .... San Francisco, CA
Linkul, William F. .... Bradenton, FL
Linley, Michele A. (Del Grande)
Chula Vista, CA
Linley, Richard A. .... Jackson, MS
Linley, Rupert A. .... San Diego, CA
Linman, E. Kelly .... Cincinnati, OH
Linman, Ronald H. .... Minneapolis, MN
Linn, Adam C. .... Olney, MD
Linn, Alton A., Jr. .... **Pompano Beach, FL**
Linn, Anne Conzelman .... Lake Forest, IL
Linn & Blate, A Professional Association
Oakhurst, CA
Linn, Brett Peter .... Goshen, NY
Linn, Carl R. .... Seminole, FL
Linn, Charles A. .... Chicago, IL
Linn, Charles A. "Nick" .... **Plano, TX**
Linn, Courtney J. .... Sacramento, CA
Linn, Craig M. .... Waukegan, IL
Linn, Dave .... Berkeley, CA
Linn, David A. .... Oakhurst, CA
Linn, David R. .... San Francisco, CA
Linn, David R. .... Fort Myers, FL
Naples, FL
Port Charlotte, FL
Linn, Deborah A. .... **Washington, DC**
Silver Spring, MD
Linn, Debra J. .... Chicago, IL
Linn, Douglas G., II .... Butler, PA
Linn, Florence E. .... Burbank, CA
Linn, Herbert J. .... **Chicago, IL**
Linn, James B. .... Chicago, IL
Linn, James P. .... **Oklahoma City, OK**
Linn, James W. .... **Tallahassee, FL**
Linn, Janet B. .... **New York, NY**
Linn, Janice E. .... Chicago, IL
Linn, Jerry J. .... Columbia City, IN
Linn, Joanne S. .... Louisville, KY
Linn, John G. .... Mt. Pleasant, IA
Linn, John P. .... Littleton, CO
Linn, Joseph Ralph, III .... New Orleans, LA
Linn, Martin Paul .... Cleveland, OH
Linn, Matthew J. .... Milwaukee, WI
Linn, Michael D. .... **Cleveland, OH**
Linn, Nathan E. .... **Palo Alto, CA**
Linn & Neville, A Professional Corporation
Oklahoma City, OK
Linn, Paul F. .... **Milwaukee, WI**
Linn, Peter J. .... **San Francisco, CA**
Linn, Richard .... **Washington, DC**
Linn, Robert A. .... **San Diego, CA**
Linn, Robert A. .... Rochester, NY
Linn, Robert M. .... **Pittsburgh, PA**
Linn, Robert W. .... Brooklyn, NY
Linn, Roger D. .... **Sacramento, CA**
Linn, Sarah A. .... Charlotte, NC
Linn, Scott A. .... **Sacramento, CA**
Linn, Shirley J. .... **Charlotte, NC**
Linn, Stacy Anne .... **Montgomery, AL**
Linn, Stahle .... Salisbury, NC
Linn, Stanley .... Floral Park, NY
Linn, Steven R. .... Tempe, AZ
Linn, Terence J. .... **Grand Rapids, MI**
Linn, Thomas F. .... Denver, CO
Linn, Thomas W. .... **Detroit, MI**
Linnan, James D. .... Albany, NY
Linnan Law Firm .... Albany, NY
Linnan, Nancy G. .... **Tallahassee, FL**
Linnane, Brendan F. .... Orlando, FL
Linnartz, August, Jr. .... **Carrizo Springs, TX**
Eagle Pass, TX
Linnartz, Lawrence R., (P.C.)
San Antonio, TX
Linne, Marty Marie .... San Francisco, CA
Linne, Sheryl M. .... Cincinnati, OH
Linne, William V. .... **Pensacola, FL**
Linneball, John E. .... **San Francisco, CA**
Linneball, Laura Ann .... **Buffalo, NY**
Linnehan, Courtney C. .... Dedham, MA
Linnehan, Frank J. .... Newton, MA
Linnehan, Joseph A. .... **Fort Myers, FL**
Linnehan, Mary E. .... Woburn, MA
Linnehan, MaryEllen .... Port Chester, NY
Linnehan, MaryEllen .... **Port Chester, NY**
Rye, NY
Linnehan, Robert M., Jr.
Hampton Falls, NH
Linnehan, Timothy M. .... Lowell, MA
Linnehan, William F. .... Hingham, MA
Linnekens, Brian R. .... **Los Angeles, CA**
Linnell, Choate & Webber .... **Auburn, ME**
Linnell, John R. .... **Auburn, ME**
Linnell, Newhall, Martin & Schulke, P.C.
Great Falls, MT
Linnell, Norman C. .... Bloomington, MN
Linnell, Richard D. .... Bloomfield Hills, MI
Linnell, Robert S. .... Yakima, WA
Linnell, Wayne E. .... **Great Falls, MT**
Linneman, Burgess, Telles, Van Atta & Vierra .... **Dos Palos, CA**
Fresno, CA
Los Banos, CA
Merced, CA
Linneman, Dale L. .... Keytesville, MO
Linneman, James E. .... **Merced, CA**
Linnemann, Pamela .... Kew Gardens, NY
Linnemeier, Philip .... Indianapolis, IN
Linnen, Jerome T., Jr. .... Akron, OH
Linner, Andrea J. .... Eden Prairie, MN
Linnerooth, Richard James .... Fargo, ND
Linnert, Terrence G. .... Richfield, OH
Linnet, Martin J. .... Denver, CO
Linnetz, Jeffrey L. .... Los Angeles, CA
Linney, Barbara D. .... **Washington, DC**
Linney, John P. .... Clearwater, FL
Linngren, Thomas J. .... **Watertown, SD**
Linnihan, Gerald M. .... **St. Paul, MN**
Linnihan, Thomas J. .... **Minneapolis, MN**
Linning, W. Shannon .... Jacksonville, FL
Linnon, Craig M. .... Lima, OH
Linnstaedter, J. Susan .... **Dallas, TX**
Linnus, Francis P. .... Somerset, NJ
Lino, Jennifer Anne .... **Milwaukee, WI**
Linowes and Blocher LLP
Washington, DC
Annapolis, MD
Columbia, MD
Frederick, MD
Greenbelt, MD
Rockville, MD
Silver Spring, MD
Linowes, Michael J. .... **New York, NY**
Linowes, R. Robert .... **Washington, DC**
Silver Spring, MD
Linowitz, Marc N. .... Miami, FL
Linowitz, Sol M. .... Washington, DC
Linquanti, Richard C. .... **Denver, CO**
Linquist, Cindy R. .... Costa Mesa, CA
Linquist, Edwin R. .... Lawrence, KS
Lins, D. Michael .... **Tampa, FL**
Lins, Harold A. .... Arlington Heights, IL
Lins, Richard W., Jr. .... Bedford, PA
Linscheid, Jeremy K. .... Reedley, CA
Linscheid, Steven K.
Department Of The Interior, Office of the Solicitor, GV
Linscomb, Shiela J. .... Lafayette, LA
Linscott, Andrew R. .... Boston, MA
Linscott, J. Curtis .... Fort Worth, TX
Linscott, Jennifer Joy .... Kansas City, MO
Linscott, Jerry R. .... **Orlando, FL**
Linscott, Lynda Burris .... Vinita, OK
Linscott, Martin Virgil .... Lincoln, NE
Linscott, Michael S. .... **Grove, OK**
Vinita, OK
Linscott, Patricia .... **Ada, MI**
Linscott, Walt A. .... **Cleveland, OH**
Linscott, Wendy T.
Great Barrington, MA
Linse, Kirk R. .... Duluth, MN
Linsenbard, William E. .... Mission Viejo, CA
Linsenmann, William M. .... Hamilton, OH

Lippert, Eugene C. ....Madison, WI
Lippert, G. Mitchel ....Cincinnati, OH
Lippert & Humphreys, P.C. ....Saginaw, MI
Lippert, J. Richardson, II ....Franklinville, NY
Lippert, James B. ....Helena, MT
Lippert, James W. ....Cincinnati, OH
Lippert, Jas. G. ....Milwaukee, WI
Lippert, Keven K. ....San Diego, CA
Lippert, Michael A. ....New York, NY
Lippert, Nels T. ....New York, NY
Lippert, Richard H. ....Cincinnati, OH
Lippert, Roderick J. ....Madison, WI
Lippert, Scott R. ....Paramus, NJ
Lippert, Teressa K. ....Los Angeles, CA
San Francisco, CA
Lippert, Timothy J. ....Long Beach, CA
Lippert, Tobin D. ....Los Angeles, CA
Lippes, David S. ....Los Angeles, CA
Lippes, Gerald S. ....Buffalo, NY
Lippes, Harold S. ....Jacksonville, FL
Lippes, Karen L. ....Jacksonville, FL
Lippes, Richard J. ....Buffalo, NY
Lippes, Silverstein, Mathias & Wexler, LLP
Buffalo, NY
Lippett, Peter E. ....San Francisco, CA
Lippetz, Gregory L. ....San Francisco, CA
Lippin, Louise ....New York, NY
Lippincott, Edward N. ....Newark, NJ
Lippincott, Elizabeth Barrett ....Raleigh, NC
Lippincott, Elwood T., Jr. ....Miami, FL
Lippincott, Jeffrey J. ....Langhorne, PA
Lippincott & Kriegel ....Mount Holly, NJ
Lippincott, Laurence L. ....Houston, TX
Lippincott, Marc L. ....Houston, TX
Lippincott, Marcia K. ....Lake Mary, FL
Lippincott, Marcia K., P.A.
Lake Mary, FL
Orlando, FL
Lippincott, Nicholas S. ....Media, PA
Lippincott, Ruth Bale ....Allentown, PA
Lippincott, Victoria Lynn ....Washington, DC
Lippitt, Allen J. ....Detroit, MI
Lippitt, Barry L. ....Southfield, MI
Lippitt, C. Chandler ....Denver, CO
Lippitt, David W. ....Rochester, NY
Lippitt, Dennis Brooke ....Santa Cruz, CA
Lippitt, Frederick ....Providence, RI
Lippitt, Norman L. ....Birmingham, MI
Lippitt, Raymond F. ....Washington, DC
Lippitt, Robert A. ....Atlanta, GA
Lippitt, Robert H. ....Birmingham, MI
Lippitz, Charles A. ....Evanston, IL
Lippl, John E. ....Pittsburgh, PA
Lippman, Alan F. ....Brownsville, TX
Lippman, Alfred S. ....Morgan City, LA
Lippman, Amy F. ....White Plains, NY
Lippman, Amy J. ....New York, NY
Lippman, Arthur M. ....Needham, MA
Lippman, Barry M. ....Kingston, NY
Lippman, Barry M., P.C. ....Kingston, NY
Lippman, Daniel ....Department of Justice, Executive Office for Immigration Review, GV
Lippman, David S. ....Los Angeles, CA
Lippman, Davis Shalet ....Los Angeles, CA
Lippman, Donna M. ....New York, NY
Lippman, Gary E. ....Oakland, CA
Lippman, Gustave L. ....Larchmont, NY
Lippman, Harry S. ....Sherman Oaks, CA
Lippman, Harvey J. ....New York, NY
Lippman, Herbert K. ....New York, NY
Lippman, Ira H. ....New Haven, CT
Lippman, Jay M. ....New York, NY
Lippman, JoAnn ....Houston, TX
Lippman, Joanna R. ....Austin, TX
Lippman, Juliette E. ....Fort Lauderdale, FL
Lippman, Kevin M. ....Dallas, TX
Lippman Krasnow & Kelton LLP
New York, NY
Lippman, Kyle D. ....Houston, TX
Lippman, Lori S. ....Orange, CA
Lippman, Louis M. ....Houston, TX
Lippman, Mahfouz & Martin
Franklin, LA
Morgan City, LA
Lippman, Mark R. ....La Jolla, CA
Lippman, Matthew D. ....New York, NY
Lippman, Melvin ....White Plains, NY
Lippman, Michael R. ....New York, NY
Lippman, Neil A. ....New Haven, CT
Lippman & Ouellette, L.L.C.
New Haven, CT
Lippman, Peter I. ....Beverly Hills, CA
Montrose, CA
Lippman, Richard A. ....St. Louis, MO
Lippman, Robert A.
Saratoga Springs, NY
Lippman, Robert P. ....Flagstaff, AZ
Lippman, Roger L. ....Niles, IL
Lippman, Scott K. ....Orlando, FL
Lippman & Semsker, PLLC
Washington, DC
Lippman, Solaman G. ....Washington, DC
Lippman, Stephen S. ....River Vale, NJ
Lippman, Steven J. ....Phoenix, AZ
Lippman, Steven N. ....Fort Lauderdale, FL
Lippman, Susan G. ....Austin, TX
Lippman & Weisel, P.C. ....Sherman Oaks, CA
Lippman, William Jay ....New York, NY
Lippmann, Andrew E. ....New York, NY
Lippmann, Brigitte P. ....New York, NY
Lippmann, Robert D. ....New York, NY
Lippmen, Noel L. ....Almont, MI
Lippner, J. Jordan ....New York, NY
Lippold, Brian E. ....Costa Mesa, CA
Lippold, Deborah King ....Tacoma, WA
Lippold, Rod Earl ....Cambria, CA
Lippold, Sara S. ....St. Louis, MO
Lippold, Steven M. ....Salem, OR
Lippold, Yolanda ....Huntington Beach, CA
Lippoldt, Darin M. ....San Antonio, TX
Lippolis, Gregory Paul ....Boston, MA
Lipponen, Tarja Marketta ....Simsbury, CT
Lipps, Alexandra S. ....Indianapolis, IN
Lipps, Andrew L. ....Washington, DC
Lipps, Jeffrey A. ....Columbus, OH
Lipps, John C. ....Houston, TX
Lipps, Robert T. ....Cedar Hill, TX
Lipps, Thomas R. ....Cincinnati, OH
Lipps, Thomas W. ....Algona, IA
Lipresti, Peter ....Washington, DC
Vienna, VA
Lips, J. Alan ....Cincinnati, OH
Lips, Jonathan W. ....Minneapolis, MN
Lipsay, Alan W. ....Sarasota, FL
Lipscher, Gene D. ....Palm Beach, FL
Lipscher, Joel T. ....Los Angeles, CA
Lipscher, Robert D. ....Trenton, NJ
Lipschitz, Benjamin ....Brooklyn, NY
Lipschitz, Israel ....Rosemont, PA
Lipschitz, Lawrence B. ....White Plains, NY
Lipschitz, Randy K. ....Jensen Beach, FL
Lipschuetz, Jesse N. ....Denver, CO
Lipschuetz, Jesse N., P.C. ....Denver, CO
Lipschultz & Berg ....Auburn, CA
Lipschultz, Brent S. ....Chicago, IL
Lipschultz, Charles C. ....Glen Ellyn, IL
Lipschultz, Claire ....West Sacramento, CA
Lipschultz, James D. ....Los Angeles, CA
Lipschultz, Jerry R. ....Chicago, IL
Lipschultz, Jerry R., & Associates
Chicago, IL
Lipschultz, Robert N. ....Calumet City, IL
Lipschultz, William H. ....Auburn, CA
Lipschutz, Florence ....Monsey, NY
Lipschutz, Lester E. ....Philadelphia, PA
Lipschutz, Mark W. ....New York, NY
Lipschutz, Robert ....North Hills, NY
Lipschutz, Steven M. ....Philadelphia, PA
Lipschutz, Steven M., P.C. ....Philadelphia, PA
Lipscomb, Albert D. ....Bessemer, AL
Lipscomb, Barbara J. ....Austin, TX
Lipscomb, Bert ....Bessemer, AL
Lipscomb, Bobby F. ....Charleston, WV
Lipscomb, Cheryl Ann Capages
Springfield, MO
Lipscomb, Cue ....Fort Worth, TX
Lipscomb, David S. ....Duluth, GA
Lipscomb, Emory ....Cumming, GA
Lipscomb, Ernest B., III ....Charlotte, NC
Lipscomb, Eugene ....Kansas City, KS
Lipscomb, George H., Jr. ....Bay St. Louis, MS
Lipscomb, Gregory Owen
Federal Communications Commission, Office of Legislative and Intergovernmental Affairs, GV
Lipscomb, H. Powell, III ....Bessemer, AL
Lipscomb, Henry P., Jr. ....Jamaica, NY
Lipscomb, J. Randolph ....Columbus, MS
Lipscomb, James L. ....New York, NY
Lipscomb, Laura Lyn ....Los Angeles, CA
Lipscomb, Lee G. ....Los Angeles, CA
Lipscomb, Linda ....Camden, NJ
Lipscomb, Linda G. ....San Francisco, CA
Lipscomb and Lipscomb ....Bessemer, AL
Lipscomb, Mark G., Jr. ....Milwaukee, WI
Lipscomb, Michael ....Bessemer, AL
Lipscomb, Michael C. ....Bellingham, WA
Lipscomb, Michael R. ....Denton, TX
Lipscomb, Michael R., A Prof. Corp., Law Office of ....Denton, TX
Lipscomb, Nell I. ....Metairie, LA
Lipscomb, Owen Randolph ....Nashville, TN
Lipscomb, Paul J. ....Salem, OR
Lipscomb, Rebecca L. ....Los Angeles, CA
Lipscomb, Robert D. ....Glendale, CA
Lipscomb, Roderick C. ....Los Angeles, CA
Lipscomb, Steven J. ....Los Angeles, CA
Lipscomb, Steven Roy ....Los Angeles, CA
Lipscomb, Susan Batten ....Columbia, SC
Lipscomb, Thomas ....Chicago, IL
Lipscomb, Thomson ....Bristol, TN
Lipscomb, W. Kendall, Jr. ....West Point, VA
Lipscomb, William F. ....Wilkesboro, NC
Lipscomb, Willie G., Jr. ....Detroit, MI
Lipscomb, Woodrow P. ....Boydton, VA
Lipscomb & Yuknis ....Chicago, IL
Lipscombe, C. Douglas, Jr. ....Sumter, SC
Lipscombe, Derek B. ....Santa Barbara, CA
Lipscombe, Ken D. ....Wharton, TX
Lipsen, Charles B. ....Washington, DC
Lipsen, Zel E. ....Washington, DC
Lipset, Louis A. ....San Francisco, CA
Lipset, Ruth ....Paterson, NJ
Lipsett, Christopher R. ....Washington, DC
Lipsett, John G. ....New York, NY
Lipsett, Linda ....Washington, DC
Lipsett, Lisa Shook ....Newton, MA
Lipsetts, Eric S. ....Annapolis, MD
Lipsey, Alexander C. ....Kalamazoo, MI
Lipsey, Charles E. ....Washington, DC
Lipsey, Christine ....Baton Rouge, LA
Lipsey, Cully ....College Station, TX
Lipsey, Howard I. ....Providence, RI
Lipsey, Joseph, Jr. ....Alexandria, LA
Lipsey, Kirk D. ....New York, NY
Lipsey, Robert H. ....San Diego, CA
Lipsey, Robert S. ....Mount Laurel, NJ
Lipsey, Steven D. ....Knoxville, TN
Lipsher, Robert I. ....Washington, DC
Lipshie, Burton N. ....New York, NY
Lipshie, Jonathan W. ....Washington, DC
Lipshie, Ronald ....Garden City, NY
Lipshie, Samuel D. ....Nashville, TN
Lipshitz, Doron ....New York, NY
Lipshultz, Barbara Popper ....Houston, TX
Lipshultz, Frank L. ....Washington, DC
Silver Spring, MD
Lipshultz and Hone, Chartered
Washington, DC
Silver Spring, MD
Lipshultz, Jon M. ....Department of Justice, Environment and Natural Resources Division, GV
Lipshultz, Leonard L. ....Washington, DC
Silver Spring, MD
Lipshultz, Stanley L. ....Washington, DC
Silver Spring, MD
Lipshutz, Barbara J. ....New York, NY
Lipshutz, David M. ....Wellesley, MA
Lipshutz, David M. ....Stratford, NJ
Lipshutz, Donna R. ....Chicago, IL
Lipshutz, Gary S. ....Clark, NJ
Lipshutz, Greenblatt & King ....Atlanta, GA
Lipshutz, Hal A. ....Chicago, IL
Lipshutz, Patty ....New York, NY
Lipshutz, Randall M. ....Atlanta, GA
Lipshutz, Robert J. ....Atlanta, GA
Lipshutz, Robert M. ....Cape Coral, FL
Lipshutz, Robert M. ....Philadelphia, PA
Lipshutz, Stuart ....Bethesda, MD
Lipshy, Bruce A. ....Austin, TX
Lipshy, Esther R. ....Dallas, TX
Lipshy, Marc L. ....Dallas, TX
Lipshy, Morris ....Lincoln Park, MI
Lipsic, Martin ....Beverly Hills, CA
Lipsich, Jerome K. ....Plano, TX
Lipsig, Daniel A. ....Sherman Oaks, CA
Lipsig, Ethan ....Los Angeles, CA
Lipsig, Shapey, Manus & Moverman, P.C.
New York, NY
Lipsitt, Carol E. ....Bingham Farms, MI
Lipsitt, Eric H. ....Detroit, MI
Lipsitt, Paul D. ....Newton, MA
Lipsitt, Wm. W. ....Harrisburg, PA
Lipsitz, Alan J. ....Oakland, CA
Lipsitz, Alan M. ....Columbia, SC
Lipsitz, Barry R. ....Monroe, CT
Lipsitz, Benjamin ....Baltimore, MD
Lipsitz, Eleanor J. ....Baltimore, MD
Lipsitz, Green, Fahringer, Roll, Salisbury & Cambria LLP ....Beverly Hills, CA
Alden, NY
Buffalo, NY
East Aurora, NY
New York, NY
Lipsitz, Harold J. ....Chicago, IL
Lipsitz, Herman ....Pittsburgh, PA
Lipsitz, John N. ....Buffalo, NY
Lipsitz and Lipsitz ....Baltimore, MD
Lipsitz, Marc ....Miami, FL
Lipsitz, Martin M. ....St. Louis, MO
Lipsitz, Michael ....Chicago, IL
Lipsitz & Ponterio, LLC ....Buffalo, NY
North Tonawanda, NY
Lipsitz, Randy ....New York, NY
Lipsitz, Richard ....Buffalo, NY
Lipsitz, Susan L. ....Billerica, MA
Lipsius, Cheryl D. ....New York, NY
Lipsius, Harold B. ....Philadelphia, PA
Lipsius, Ira S. ....New York, NY
Lipsius, Mikelle V. ....New York, NY
Lipsker, Gregory B. ....Spokane, WA
Lipski, Christopher ....Cleveland, OH
Lipski, Clarence A. ....Grand Rapids, OH
Lipski, David B. ....Bloomfield Hills, MI
Lipski, Gerard F. ....Philadelphia, PA
Lipski, Nancy A. ....Lexington, SC
Lipski, P. Alex ....Auburn, NY
Lipskin, Kevin J. ....Beverly Hills, CA
Lipskin, Michael M. ....Nicasio, CA
Lipsky, Aaron A. ....Keene, NH
Lipsky, Abbott Bennett, Jr. ....Atlanta, GA
Lipsky, Burton G. ....New York, NY
Lipsky, David E. ....New York, NY
Lipsky, David I. ....Newport Beach, CA
Lipsky, Edward S. ....Buffalo Grove, IL
Lipsky, Edward S., P.C. ....Buffalo Grove, IL
Lipsky, Elias ....Franklin Square, NY
Lipsky, Henry I. ....Arlington, VA
Lipsky, Jason M. ....Cheshire, CT
Lipsky, Joan ....Cedar Rapids, IA
Lipsky, Joel B. ....New York, NY
Lipsky, Joseph I. ....Miami Lakes, FL
Lipsky, Joshua M. ....Seattle, WA
Lipsky, Lawrence J. ....Skokie, IL
Lipsky, Louis I. ....Philadelphia, PA
Lipsky, Merritt ....Boston, MA
Lipsky, Michael J. ....Princeton, NJ
Lipsky, Mortimer ....New York, NY
Lipsky, Nolan S. ....Petersburg, IL
Lipsky, Robyn M. ....San Francisco, CA
Lipsky, Rubin ....Keene, NH
Lipsky, Sumner L. ....Great Neck, NY
Lipsky, Tammi J. ....Philadelphia, PA
Lipsky, Victor ....Philadelphia, PA
Lipsky, Wendy L. ....Mineola, NY
Lipsman, Frank W. ....Kansas City, MO
Lipsman, Gary S. ....Las Vegas, NV
Lipsman, Richard M., Law Office of
New York, NY
Lipsman, Sandra M. ....New York, NY
Lipsman, Walter J. ....Los Angeles, CA
Lipsman, William S. ....Aurora, IL
Lipsmeyer, Dale ....Morrilton, AR
Lipson, Alan Gordon ....Cleveland, OH
Lipson, Alan T. ....Miami, FL
Lipson, Allan I. ....Denver, CO
Lipson, Allen S. ....Bridgeport, CT
Lipson, Ann L. ....Berkeley, CA
Lipson, Arthur H. ....North Miami, FL
Lipson, Ashley S. ....Beverly Hills, CA
Lipson, Barry J. ....Troy, MI
Lipson, Barry J. ....Pittsburgh, PA
Lipson, Constance R. ....Philadelphia, PA
Lipson, Dallas & Weiser, P.C. ....El Paso, TX
Lipson, David R. ....Oakland, CA
Lipson, David R. ....Washington, DC
Lipson, Donald H. ....Allentown, PA
Lipson, Eileen ....Santa Monica, CA
Lipson, Etta L. ....Detroit, MI
Lipson, Etta L., P.C. ....Detroit, MI
Lipson, Frank ....Federal Trade Commission, Bureau of Competition, GV
Lipson, Gary D. ....Miami, FL
Lipson, Gordon J. ....Rochester, NY
Lipson, Heather J. ....Philadelphia, PA
Lipson, Jack L. ....Washington, DC
Lipson, Jack S. ....Westport, CT
Lipson, Jacqueline ....New York, NY
Lipson, Jonathan C. ....Boston, MA
Lipson, Karen B. ....Washington, DC
Lipson, Kevin J. ....Washington, DC
Lipson, Lawrence J. ....New York, NY
Lipson, Leon ....New Haven, CT
Lipson, Leonard S. ....Philadelphia, PA
Lipson, Lisa Irene ....Phoenix, AZ
Lipson, Matthew A. ....Los Angeles, CA
Lipson, Merek E. ....San Francisco, CA
Lipson, Michael E. ....Garden City, NY
Lipson, Michael H. ....South Burlington, VT
Lipson, Milton ....Sea Cliff, NY
Lipson, Morris D. ....San Francisco, CA
Lipson, Myer J. ....El Paso, TX
Lipson, Nancy L. ....Denver, CO
Lipson, Nathan ....Ann Arbor, MI
Lipson, Nathan, P.C. ....Ann Arbor, MI
Lipson, Neilson, Jacobs & Cole, P.C.
Detroit, MI
Troy, MI
Lipson, Richard J. ....San Francisco, CA
Lipson, Roger R. ....Brookline, MA
Lipson, Ronald M. ....Cleveland, OH
Lipson, Scott R. ....Allentown, PA
Lipson, Sheldon R. ....Bethesda, MD
Lipson, Stephen B. ....Carlisle, PA
Lipson, Steve ....Long Beach, CA
Lipson, Warren M. ....Beverly Hills, CA
Lipson, Wayne David ....Chicago, IL
Lipstein, Bruce J. ....Clinton, MD
Lipstein, Evan S. ....Lakewood, CO
Lipstein, Freddi ....Department of Justice, Civil Division, GV
Lipstein, Howard D. ....Springfield, NJ
Lipstein, J. Arthur ....West Orange, NJ
Lipstein, Jaffe & Lawson, L.L.P.
Washington, DC
Lipstein, Kenneth N. ....Westfield, NJ
Lipstein & Mortimer, PC ....Lakewood, CO
Lipstein, Robert A. ....Washington, DC
Lipstein, Sidney D. ....New York, NY
Lipstein, Simon Paul ....Denver, CO
Lipstet & Hirsch, L.L.P. ....Houston, TX
Lipstet, Ira A. ....Austin, TX
Lipstet, Robert Leighton, (P.C.)
Houston, TX
Lipstone, Douglas M. ....Los Angeles, CA
Liptack, Diane L., (P.C.) ....Indianapolis, IN
Liptack, Suzanne ....New York, NY
Liptak, Adam ....New York, NY
Liptak, Edward J. ....Bloomington, IN
Liptak, Lester H., Jr. ....Cadott, WI
Liptak, Marshall W. ....Oviedo, FL
Liptak, Thomas E. ....Albany, NY
Buffalo, NY
Lipton, Adam S. ....Washington, DC
Lipton, Alan R. ....Chicago, IL
Lipton, Alfred R. ....Chicago, IL
Lipton, Amy N. ....Stamford, CT
Lipton, Andrew S. ....Cincinnati, OH
Lipton, Bella ....Perth Amboy, NJ
New York, NY
Lipton, Benjamin B. ....Coconut Creek, FL
Lipton, Carl E. ....Miami, FL
Lipton, Carol ....Brooklyn, NY
Lipton, Charles J. ....New York, NY
Lipton, Cheryl K. ....Chicago, IL
Lipton, Chet F. ....New York, NY
Lipton, David A. ....Washington, DC
Lipton, Douglas R. ....Campbell, CA
Lipton, Edward A. ....Grand Junction, CO
Lipton, Elisabeth A. ....Needham, MA
Lipton, Gail ....Media, PA
Lipton, Gary L. ....Nanuet, NY
Lipton, Harold A. ....Los Angeles, CA
Lipton, Harvey L. ....New York, NY
Lipton, Hillary D. ....Denver, CO
Lipton, Howard J. ....Boston, MA
Lipton, Hugh A. ....North Hollywood, CA
Lipton, Ira J. ....New York, NY
Lipton, Jack P. ....Camarillo, CA
Los Angeles, CA
Lipton, Jane S. ....Washington, DC
Lipton, Jeffrey H. ....New York, NY
Lipton, Joseph Robert
Department of Justice, Civil Division, GV
Lipton, Karen Shoos ....Bethesda, MD
Lipton, Katherine B. ....New York, NY
Lipton & Kearns ....Hackensack, NJ
Lipton, Kenneth M. ....Van Nuys, CA
Lipton, Lawrence B. ....Staten Island, NY
Lipton, Leslie V., (Ms.) ....Perth Amboy, NJ
New York, NY
Lipton & Lipton ....Southfield, MI
Lipton & Lipton ....Perth Amboy, NJ
New York, NY
Lipton, Lois ....Hackensack, NJ
Lipton, Lois J. ....Chicago, IL
Lipton, M. Steven ....San Francisco, CA
Lipton, Marc ....Southfield, MI
Lipton, Marc I. ....Hoffman Estates, IL
Lipton, Marilyn J. ....Milford, CT

Lipton, Mark D. ... San Francisco, CA
Lipton, Mark D. ... Champaign, IL
Lipton, Mark H. ... Walnut Creek, CA
Lipton, Mark K. ... Newark, NJ
Lipton, Marshall C. ... Kingston, NY
Lipton, Martin ... New York, NY
Lipton, Matthew C. ... Dallas, TX
Lipton, Michelle J. ... Beverly, MA
Lipton, Neil D. ... New York, NY
Lipton, Norman D. ... Garden City, NY
Lipton, Paul P. ... North Miami Beach, FL
Lipton, Paul R. ... Miami, FL
Lipton, Richard M. ... Chicago, IL
Lipton, Robert ... Denver, CO
Lipton, Robert S. ... Wilmington, DE
Media, PA
Lipton, Robert S. ... New York, NY
Lipton, Roger P. ... Northampton, MA
Lipton, Ruth ... New York, NY
Lipton, Stephanie S. ... New York, NY
Lipton, Stephen M. ... Poughkeepsie, NY
Lipton, Stephen N. ... Fort Lauderdale, FL
Lipton, Steven A. ... Newburgh, NY
Lipton, Stuart S. ... San Francisco, CA
Lipton, Virginia A. ... Department of Energy, Office of Hearings and Appeals, GV
Lipton, Warnlof & Hallbauer, A Professional Law Association ... Walnut Creek, CA
Lipton, Weinberger & Husick
Wilmington, DE
Media, PA
Philadelphia, PA
Lipton, William ... Southfield, MI
Liptrot, Jeffrey M. ... Providence, RI
Liptz, Irwin H. ... Chevy Chase, MD
Lipuma, Andrea A. ... Newark, NJ
LiPuma, Michael D. ... Philadelphia, PA
LiPuma, Richard T. ... Naperville, IL
Liput, Andrew L. ... Huntington, NY
Liput & Margolin, LLP ... Huntington, NY
Liquerman, Melissa C. ... Treasury Department, Internal Revenue Service, GV
Liquigli, Michael A ... Grand Rapids, MI
Liquori, Gary B. ... Springfield, MA
West Springfield, MA
Liquori, John J. ... Suffield, CT
Lira, David Militon ... Garden City, NY
Lira, David R. ... Los Angeles, CA
Lira, Jan Rasmussen ... Columbus, OH
Lira, Louis C. ... Tampa, FL
Lira, Sherri ... Los Angeles, CA
Lira, Tatia ... Walnut Creek, CA
Lirette, Danny J. ... Houma, LA
Lirette, Kathryn S. ... Houma, LA
Lirette & Shea, L.L.P. ... Houma, LA
Lirhus, Albert G. ... Seattle, WA
Lirhus, Clarence A. ... Seattle, WA
Liria, Peter, Jr. ... New York, NY
Lirocchi, Michael V. ... Santa Rosa, CA
Liroff, H. Ann ... Redwood City, CA
Liroff, Kenneth P. ... Fort Lauderdale, FL
Liroff, Lane Jay ... Department of Justice, Criminal Division, GV
Lirtzman, Nehls & Hepner, A Professional Corporation ... Boulder, CO
Lirtzman, Richard M. ... Boulder, CO
Lirtzman, Steven M. ... Roselle, IL
Lis, Daniel T. ... Detroit, MI
Lis, Janet M. ... Media, PA
Lis, John Michael ... Glen Burnie, MD
Lis, Lance M. ... Southfield, MI
Lis, Shabsa A. ... Chicago, IL
Lis, Shabsa A., P.C. ... Chicago, IL
Lisa, Carl B. ... Providence, RI
Lisa, Carl B., Jr. ... Providence, RI
Lisa, Donald J., Law Offices of
Scottsdale, AZ
Lisa, James P., Jr. ... Wilmington, DE
Lisa, Joseph F. ... Woodbury, NJ
Lisa, Julie Davis ... Atlantic City, NJ
Lisa & Sousa, Ltd. ... Providence, RI
Lisa, Steven G. ... Scottsdale, AZ
Lisa, Toni-Jean ... Owings Mills, MD
Lisabeth, Hayley A. ... East Meadow, NY
Lisabeth, Jeffrey S. ... East Meadow, NY
Lisak, Michael Loren ... Baltimore, MD
Lisanby, J. Gordon ... Princeton, KY
Lisankie, Paul F. ... Anchorage, AK
Lisann, Eric C. ... Department of Justice, Tax Division, GV
Lisansky, David R. ... Baltimore, MD
Lisante, Joan E. ... Oakton, VA
Lisante, Nicholas J. ... West Hempstead, NY
Lisanti, Melinda P. ... New York, NY
Lisbakken, James R. ... Seattle, WA
Lisbona, Albert C. ... Fairfield, NJ
Lisch, Ernie C. ... Bradenton, FL
Lisch, Howard ... New York, NY
Lisch, William R. ... Bradenton, FL
Lisch, William R., P.A. ... Bradenton, FL
Lischak, John M. ... Syracuse, NY
Lischer, Dale ... Atlanta, GA
Lischer, Donald H. ... Buffalo, NY
Lischer, Donald H., P.C. ... Buffalo, NY
Lischer, Henry J., Jr ... Dallas, TX
Lischer, James F., Jr. ... Treasury Department, Office of Thrift Supervision, GV
Lischer, Nancy G. ... Chicago, IL
Lischer, Tracy Kenyon ... Durham, NC
Lischer, W John ... Scottsdale, AZ
Lischin, Garry ... New York, NY
Lischin, Michael ... Midway, KY
Lischwe, Joseph Michael ... Durham, NC
Lischwe, Mark W. ... Phoenix, AZ
Liscinski, Theodore J., Jr. ... Somerset, NJ
Liscio, Elizabeth C. ... Scarsdale, NY
Liscio, Mark F. ... New York, NY

Liscio-Penny, Patricia Louise
Los Angeles, CA
Lisco, David A. ... Chicago, IL
Lisco, Robert F. ... Chicago, IL
Lisehora, James A.
Department of Commerce, Patent and Trademark Office, GV
Lisella, Thomas R. ... Tamaqua, PA
Lisenbery, John R. ... Los Angeles, CA
Lisenby, Jeffrey P. ... Birmingham, AL
Lisenby, Kent J. ... El Paso, TX
Lisenby, Michael B. ... Atlanta, GA
Liser, Grant ... Fort Worth, TX
Liser, Sandra Cockran ... Fort Worth, TX
Liset, J. Robert ... Los Angeles, CA
Lisewski, Nancy M. ... San Francisco, CA
Lish, Jacob C. ... West Bethesda, MD
Lish, James M. ... Chestnut Hill, MA
Lish, John W. ... Salt Lake City, UT
Lish, Mark E. ... Duncanville, TX
Lish, Mark E., P.C. ... Duncanville, TX
Lish, Randy M. ... Orem, UT
Lishawa, Allen C. ... Cincinnati, OH
Lisher, James R. ... Shelbyville, IN
Lisher, John L. ... Indianapolis, IN
Lisher, Mary Katherine ... Indianapolis, IN
Lishman, Joanne M.
Department of State, GV
Lishner, Elizabeth R. ... Santa Monica, CA
Lishner, Laurence H. ... Los Angeles, CA
Lisi, David ... Palo Alto, CA
Lisi, Dawn L. ... Harrisburg, PA
Lisi, Frank A. ... New York, NY
Lisi, Gregory S. ... Rockville Centre, NY
Lisi, Joseph M. ... Escondido, CA
Lisi, Lauren Barritt ... Ann Arbor, MI
Lisi, Mary M. ... Providence, RI
Lisi, Michael D. ... San Francisco, CA
Lisi, Nicholas J. ... Philadelphia, PA
Lisicky, Joseph G. ... Wilmington, DE
Lisiecki, Joseph P., III ... Oceanside, CA
San Diego, CA
Lisieski, Michael E. ... Worcester, MA
Lisiewski, David E. ... Los Angeles, CA
Lisitski, Clement F. ... Ocean City, NJ
Lisitski & Dipersio ... Ocean City, NJ
Lisk, Derek J. ... Houston, TX
Lisk, John F. ... Miami, FL
Lisk, Thomas A. ... Richmond, VA
Liska, Andrew J. ... San Diego, CA
Liska, Exnicios & Nungesser
New Orleans, LA
Liska, Frank J., Jr. ... Milwaukee, WI
Liska, Ione E. ... Hampton, NH
Liska, Michael E. ... Lexington, KY
Liska, Peter J. ... Tinton Falls, NJ
Lisk-Anani, Sandrine Marie ... Wichita, KS
Lisker, Deborah J. ... Philadelphia, PA
Lisker, Gary M. ... Atlanta, GA
Lisker, Joel S. ... United States Senate, Committee Legal Personnel, GV
Lisker, Marc R. ... Chicago, IL
Lisker, Steven L. ... Phoenix, AZ
Liskiewicz, Richard H. ... Lansing, MI
Lisko, David J. ... Waukesha, WI
Lisko, Elaine A. ... Houston, TX
Lisko, John M. ... Waynesboro, PA
Lisko, Rita C. ... Milford, CT
Lisko, Roy K. ... State College, PA
Liskov, Andrew S. ... Bridgeport, CT
Liskov, Richard G. ... New York, NY
Liskow, Kaara L. ... Biloxi, MS
Liskow & Lewis, A Professional Law Corporation ... Lafayette, LA
New Orleans, LA
Lisle, Charles J. ... Lexington, KY
Lisle, Charles L. ... McMinnville, OR
Lisle, Christopher J. ... Springdale, AR
Lisle, Donald R. ... Oklahoma City, OK
Lisle, Erin K. Fogarty ... Minneapolis, MN
Lisle, Henry L. ... Lamar, MO
Lisle, John ... Springdale, AR
Lisle, Kenneth E., Jr. ... Edmond, OK
Lisle Law Firm, P.C. ... Springdale, AR
Lisle, Matthew W.
Commodity Futures Trading Commission, Division of Trading and Markets, GV
Lisle, Randolph T. ... Boston, MA
Lisle, Raymond E. ... Brooklyn, NY
Lisle, Stephen A. ... Springdale, AR
Lisle, Thomas A. ... Oconto, WI
Lisle & Woodward ... Oklahoma City, OK
Lisman, Bernard ... Burlington, VT
Lisman, Carl H. ... Burlington, VT
Lisman, Carol K. ... Ellicott City, MD
Lisman, Eric I. ... Newton, MA
Lisman & Lisman, A Professional Corporation ... Burlington, VT
Rutland, VT
Lisman, Louis ... Burlington, VT
Lisman, Mary Beth ... Sudbury, MA
Lisman, Natasha C. ... Boston, MA
Lis-Milam, Julianne S. ... Indianapolis, IN
Lisnek, Paul M. ... Chicago, IL
Lisner, Sheal D. ... Newport News, VA
Lisnow, Jeffrey N. ... Staten Island, NY
Lisnow, Robert A., (A Professional Corporation) ... Los Angeles, CA
Lison & Griffin, P.C. ... Chicago, IL
Lison, John M. ... Chicago, IL
Lisonbee, Dan A. ... Cleveland, OH
Lisoni, Antoinette M. ... Castro Valley, CA
Lisovicz, James P. ... Morristown, NJ
Lisovicz, Paul A. ... Morristown, NJ
Lisowski, Brenna ... Beloit, WI
Lisowski, Diane L. ... Cherry Hill, NJ
Philadelphia, PA
Lisowski, Gregory F. ... New Haven, CT

Lisowski, Joanne M. ... Columbus, OH
Lisowski, John I. ... Livingston, NJ
Lisowski, John I., Jr. ... Livingston, NJ
Lisowski Law Offices ... Columbus, OH
Lisowski, Ronald J., Jr. ... Washington, DC
Lisowski, Sandra Jean ... Cleveland, OH
Lisowsky, Michael P., III ... El Paso, TX
Lispcome, Marie-Claire Brown
Washington, DC
Liss, Alan B. ... Philadelphia, PA
Liss, Arthur Y. ... Bloomfield Hills, MI
Liss and Associates, P.C.
Bloomfield Hills, MI
Detroit, MI
Liss, Barry ... Liberty Corner, NJ
Liss, Brenda C. ... Newark, NJ
Liss, Burton D ... Washington, DC
Liss, Burton D., P.C. ... Washington, DC
Liss, Christy ... Waterloo, IA
Liss, Cindy Rae ... Chicago, IL
Liss, Daniel Jeffrey ... Atlanta, GA
Liss, David G.
Equal Employment Opportunity Commission, Office of Legal Counsel, GV
Liss, Derek S. ... Philadelphia, PA
Liss, E. Herbert ... Williamsville, NY
Liss, Elliot M. ... Silver Spring, MD
Liss, Esther H. ... Boca Raton, FL
Liss, Franklin R. ... Washington, DC
Liss, Geri S. ... Fort Lauderdale, FL
Liss, Gilbert Y. ... Chicago, IL
Liss, Heidi T. ... New York, NY
Liss, Ira ... Palm Springs, CA
Liss, James D. ... New York, NY
Liss, Jeffrey F. ... Washington, DC
Liss, Jeffrey G. ... Chicago, IL
Liss, Jeffrey G., P.C. ... Chicago, IL
Liss, Jennifer M. ... Birmingham, MI
Liss, Joel I. ... Douglasville, GA
Liss, Kevin J. ... Houston, TX
Liss, Lauren A. ... Boston, MA
Liss, Lauren P. ... Gaithersburg, MD
Liss, Linda C. ... Roswell, GA
Liss, Lora ... Trenton, NJ
Liss & Marion, P.C. ... Philadelphia, PA
Liss, Mark I. ... Piedmont, CA
Liss, Mark J. ... Chicago, IL
Liss, Marsha B. ... Department of Justice, Criminal Division, GV
Liss, Marvin ... Washington, DC
Liss, Michael ... White Plains, NY
Liss, Michael R. ... Hinsdale, IL
Liss, Michael R., P.C. ... Hinsdale, IL
Liss, Morris ... Washington, DC
Liss, Norman, (P.C.) ... New York, NY
Liss, Perry P. ... Palm Springs, CA
Liss, Peter M. ... San Diego, CA
Liss, Randie M. ... New York, NY
Liss, Richard B. ... Fort Lauderdale, FL
Liss, Ricky L. ... Philadelphia, PA
Liss, Robert B. ... Columbus, OH
Liss, Robert F. ... Birmingham, MI
Liss, Robert F., P.C. ... Birmingham, MI
Liss, Sidney ... North Woodmere, NY
Liss, Solomon ... New York, NY
Liss, Stafford ... Brooklyn, NY
Liss, Steven A. ... Philadelphia, PA
Liss, Steven R. ... San Diego, CA
Liss, Steven R., a Professional Corporation
San Diego, CA
Liss, Stuart F., Law Office of
Lexington, MA
Liss, William J. ... Columbus, OH
Lissa, Anna A. ... Evanston, IL
Lissau, Michael ... Tulsa, OK
Lissauer, Charles W. ... Independence, OH
Lissebeck, Yosina M. ... San Diego, CA
Lisser, Justine S.
Equal Employment Opportunity Commission, Office of the General Counsel, GV
Lissitzyn, Christine Beck ... Weatogue, CT
Lissitzyn, Lawrence H. ... Hartford, CT
Lissitzyn, Oliver J. ... West Hartford, CT
Lissner, Jerry G. H. ... New York, NY
Lissner & Lissner ... New York, NY
Lissner, Michael D. ... New York, NY
Lisson, Jeffrey S. ... Winston-Salem, NC
Lissor, Marjorie D. ... Williston, VT
Lissuzzo, Russell C., II ... Oklahoma City, OK
Lissy, David H. ... Rocky Hill, CT
List, A. David ... Newark, OH
List, Andrew Alan ... Reno, NV
List, Anthony F. ... Media, PA
List, Charles P. ... Albuquerque, NM
List, D. Andrew ... Columbus, OH
List, David P. ... Chicago, IL
List, James A. ... Towson, MD
List, John J. ... Media, PA
List, John J. ... Herndon, VA
List, Julie Ann ... Parsippany, NJ
List, L. Stuart ... Sacramento, CA
List and List, A Professional Corporation
Media, PA
List, Martin S. ... Cleveland, OH
List, Robert E. ... Covington, KY
List, Robert F. ... Reno, NV
List, Robert S. ... New York, NY
List, Roy A. ... Hicksville, NY
List, Steven S. ... Chicago, IL
List, Susan A. ... Wilmington, DE
List, Suzanne K. ... Los Angeles, CA
List, Thomas M. ... Denver, CO
Listak, James A. ... Oak Brook, IL
Listati, Ezio A. ... Cleveland, OH
Listecki, Jerome E. ... Chicago, IL
Lister, David E. ... Glendale, CA

Lister, David P. ... Miami, FL
Lister & Hawkins ... Spartanburg, SC
Lister, James H. ... Washington, DC
Lister, John R. ... Irvine, CA
Lister, Jonathan L. ... Harrisburg, PA
Lister, Karen A. ... Houston, TX
Lister, Kevin S. ... Painesville, OH
Lister, Martin, Thompson & Secia
Glendale, CA
Lister, Penelope Margaret
Washington, DC
Lister, Phyllis ... Dallas, TX
Lister, R. Glenn, Jr. ... Mount Pleasant, SC
Lister, Richard J. ... San Diego, CA
Lister, Robert D. ... Chatham, NJ
Lister, Sara E. ... Key West, FL
Lister, Shaun B. ... Bangor, ME
Lister, Sherman L. ... Woodland Hills, CA
Lister, Sonia A. ... Irvine, CA
Lister, Stephen L. ... New York, NY
Lister, Steven E., (P.C.) ... Jonesboro, GA
Lister, Susan E. ... Detroit, MI
Lister, Terry L. ... St. Louis, MO
Lister, Thomas E. ... Black River Falls, WI
Lister, Toney J. ... Spartanburg, SC
Listgarten, Michael A. ... San Francisco, CA
Listhaus, Bruce L. ... Newark, NJ
New York, NY
Listick & Krall, P.A. ... Delray Beach, FL
Listick, Michael M. ... Delray Beach, FL
Listman, William R. ... Detroit, MI
Listokin, Nava ... New York, NY
Liston, Angela A. ... Bethel, AK
Liston, Brian P. ... Chicago, IL
Liston, David G. ... New York, NY
Liston, Dennis D. ... Columbus, OH
Liston, Edward F., Jr. ... Toms River, NJ
Liston, James M. ... Boston, MA
Liston, James T. ... Houston, TX
Liston, Jefferson E. ... Columbus, OH
Liston, John William ... Savannah, GA
Liston, Kalian D. ... Saline, MI
Liston, Katharina E. ... St. Paul, MN
Liston, Mary Ann ... Colorado Springs, CO
Liston, Michael J. ... Boston, MA
Liston, Pamela H. ... Dallas, TX
Liston, Paul Sperry ... Fayetteville, GA
Liston & Pinizzotto ... Toms River, NJ
Liston, Robert C. ... Wheaton, IL
Liston, Robert M. ... Sedalia, MO
Liston, William G. ... Miami, FL
Liston, William H. ... Jackson, MS
Winona, MS
Liston, William, III ... Jackson, MS
Winona, MS
Liston/Lancaster ... Grenada, MS
Jackson, MS
Winona, MS
Liston-Wakefield & Dwelle ... Moscow, ID
Liston-Wakefield, Robert ... Moscow, ID
Listrom, Anthony P. ... Carmel, NY
Listrom & Associates ... Carmel, NY
Listrom, Linda L. ... Chicago, IL
Listwa, Helene G. ... Woodbury, NY
Liszewski, Leonard L. ... Fort Myers, FL
Liszewski, Michael ... Buffalo, NY
Liszewski, Paul R. ... Chicago, IL
Liszka, Walter J. ... Chicago, IL
Liszt, Marvin A. ... Minneapolis, MN
Lit, Lester F. ... Memphis, TN
Litak, Michael J. ... Chicago, IL
Litaker, A. Danielle ... Little Rock, AR
Memphis, TN
Nashville, TN
Litay, Dalia ... New York, NY
Litch, Christopher Scott ... Washington, DC
Litch, Erich J. ... Portland, OR
Litch, Gordon & Associates, P.C.
Center Line, MI
Litch, John M. ... Center Line, MI
Litcher, Barbara E. ... Massapequa, NY
Litcher, Reed Leonard ... Littleton, CO
Litchfield, Allen ... Tulsa, OK
Litchfield, Anne-Marie L. ... Orleans, MA
Litchfield, C. Wayne ... Oklahoma City, OK
Litchfield, C. Wayne, Corp.
Oklahoma City, OK
Litchfield & Carstens, LLP ... Newport, OR
Litchfield Cavo ... Manchester, CT
Chicago, IL
Somerville, MA
Haddonfield, NJ
Shorewood, WI
Litchfield, Daniel G. ... Chicago, IL
Litchfield, E. Bradley ... Eugene, OR
Litchfield, E. John ... New Orleans, LA
Litchfield, E.P., Jr. ... Tulsa, OK
Litchfield, G. K. ... Newport, OR
Litchfield, Gregg E. ... Marietta, GA
Litchfield, Letty, Law Offices of
Sacramento, CA
Litchfield, Lou ... Atlanta, GA
Litchfield, N. Bradley
Federal Election Commission, Office of the General Counsel, GV
Litchfield, R. Wade ... Juno Beach, FL
Litchfield, Robert L., Jr. ... Auburn, CA
Litchfield, Stephen A. ... Palatine, IL
Litchford & Christopher, Professional Association ... Orlando, FL
Litchford, Hal K. ... Orlando, FL
Litchford, Jody Mateer ... Orlando, FL
Litchin, Kent C. ... Fort Wayne, IN
Litchman, John ... Los Angeles, CA
Litchman, Michael J. ... Boston, MA
Litchmann, Jean H. ... Los Angeles, CA
Litchmann, Marshall M. ... Los Angeles, CA
Litchtman, Joanne ... Washington, DC

Litchy, Patricia J. ....Mendota Heights, MN
Lite, Allyn Z. ....Newark, NJ
Lite, De Palma, Greenberg & Rivas, LLC
Newark, NJ
Lite, Justin N. ....West Islip, NY
Lite & Russell, P.C. ....West Islip, NY
Literski, Edwin J. ....Brighton, MI
Literski, Paul D. ....Greenfield, WI
Literski & Rogaczewski ....Greenfield, WI
Lites, James R. ....Detroit, MI
Lites, Scott K. ....Detroit, MI
Litfin, Todd O. ....Costa Mesa, CA
Lithco, George W. ....Walden, NY
Lither, Gabriel D. ....Las Vegas, NV
Litherland, Craig J. ....Austin, TX
Litherland, R.W., A Professional Corporation
San Jose, CA
Litherland, R.W. ....San Jose, CA
Lithgow, Bruce E. ....Chicago, IL
Lithgow, Timothy J. ....San Diego, CA
Lithman, Robert P. ....Miami, FL
Lithotomos, Valerie J. ......Treasury Department, Office of Thrift Supervision, GV
Litigation Advocates Group
Walnut Creek, CA
Litigation Solutions Law Group LLP
Redwood City, CA
Litke, Gary S. ....New York, NY
Litke, Jennifer Holland ....Fort Worth, TX
Litke, Larry L. ....Oakland, CA
Litke, Stephen W. ....Fort Worth, TX
Litman, Alfred I. ....New York, NY
Litman, Andra S. ....Dallas, TX
Litman, Arthur L. ....Redondo Beach, CA
Litman, Asche & Gioiella, LLP
New York, NY
Litman, Craig A. ....Mill Valley, CA
Litman, Donald S. ....Norristown, PA
Litman, Donna ....Fort Lauderdale, FL
Litman, Eugene ....New York, NY
Litman, Gary V. ....Washington, DC
Litman, Harry ....Department of Justice, Office of Policy Development, GV
Litman, Heather C. ....Los Angeles, CA
Litman, Heidi A. ....Brooklyn, NY
Litman, Helena ....New York, NY
Litman, Jack T. ....New York, NY
Litman & Jacobs ....New York, NY
Litman, Jeffrey E. ....New York, NY
Litman, Jessica D. ....Detroit, MI
Litman, Katherine J. ....New York, NY
Litman, Kraai and Brown, L.L.C.
Kansas City, MO
Litman Law Offices, Ltd.
Washington, DC
Arlington, VA
Litman Litman Harris & Brown, P.C.
Pittsburgh, PA
Litman, Malcolm A. ....Kansas City, MO
Litman, Mark A. ....Minneapolis, MN
Litman, Neal S., (P.A.) ....Coconut Grove, FL
Litman, Paul ....Bloomfield, CT
Litman, Peter E. ....Waltham, MA
Litman, Richard C. ....Arlington, VA
Litman, Roger K. ....Fresno, CA
Litman, Roslyn M. ....Pittsburgh, PA
Litman, Seth A. ....Atlanta, GA
Conyers, GA
Litman, Stephen R., (P.A.)
Minneapolis, MN
Litman, Todd M. ....Costa Mesa, CA
Litmans, Murray Ian ....Washington, DC
Litmer, Jack L. ....Cleveland, OH
Litner, Alan B. ....New York, NY
Litner, Jon D. ....New York, NY
Litner, Mark S. ....Chicago, IL
Litner, Steven M. ....Boston, MA
Litoff, Stuart M.
Merit Systems Protection Board, Office of Appeals Counsel, GV
Litovsky, Allan Z. ....Los Angeles, CA
Litow, Cutler & Zabludowski, LLC
Boca Raton, FL
Coral Gables, FL
Fort Lauderdale, FL
Miami, FL
Litow, George H. ....Paw Paw, IL
Litow, Laurence S., (P.A.)
Fort Lauderdale, FL
Litow, Mark I. ....Clayton, MO
Litowich, Leo H. ....Grand Rapids, MI
Litowitz, Mark E. ....Princeton, NJ
Litowitz, Robert D. ....Washington, DC
Litowitz, Ronald ....New York, NY
Litra, Gregory F. ....Morristown, NJ
Litrel, Christopher J. ....Hicksville, NY
Litrento, Anthony P. ....Bradenton, FL
Litroff, Herman ....Mount Vernon, NY
Litscher, Brian J. ....Pittsfield, MA
Litschewski, Jennafer M.
Department of Justice, Criminal Division, GV
Litschgi, Byrne ....Tampa, FL
Litschgi, Valerie Stoker ....Tampa, FL
Litsey, Calvin L. ....Minneapolis, MN
Litsey, Craig D. ....Minneapolis, MN
Litsey, James W. ....Providence, RI
Litsey, Jana Jones ....Providence, RI
Litsey, Richard O. ....Houston, TX
Litsinger, Karen M. ....Dulles, VA
Litsky, Darrin A. ....Treasury Department, Internal Revenue Service, GV
Litsky, Matthew L. ....Tampa, FL
Litsky, Thomas B. ....New York, NY
Litson, Lawrence H. ....Gove, KS
Litster, William J. ....Boise, ID
Litt, Arnold D. ....Hackensack, NJ
Litt, Barrett S. ....Los Angeles, CA
Litt, Bonnie S. ....New York, NY
Litt, Cheryl Kovsky ....Livonia, MI
Litt, Daniel M. ....Washington, DC
Litt, David G. ....Washington, DC
Litt, Gordon F. ....Columbus, OH
Litt, Herbert C. ....White Plains, NY
Litt, Jeremy A. ....New York, NY
Litt, Jody H. ....New York, NY
Litt, Joseph ....Philadelphia, PA
Litt, Kerry M. ....Doylestown, PA
Litt, Lynne E. ....Santa Monica, CA
Litt, Martin D. ....Denver, CO
Litt, Marvin S. ....San Francisco, CA
Litt, Michael S. ....Detroit, MI
Litt, Mitchell D. ....Sherman Oaks, CA
Litt, Paula E. ....Chicago, IL
Litt, Robert L. ....Farmington Hills, MI
Litt, Robert S. ....Washington, DC
Litt, Ronald A. ....Van Nuys, CA
Litt, Sara Moore ....New York, NY
Litt, Warren ....Baltimore, MD
Litt, William M. ....San Mateo, CA
Littau, Alan J. ....New York, NY
Littauer, Dwayne O. ....New Orleans, LA
Litteer, Harold H., Jr. ....Batavia, NY
Litteer, Philip A. ....Webster, NY
Littel, David L. ....Virginia Beach, VA
Littel, Suzanne C. ....Morgan Hill, CA
Littell, Ann R. ....Springfield, MO
Littell, Charles W. ....West Palm Beach, FL
Littell, David A. ....Philadelphia, PA
Littell, David P. ....Portland, ME
Littell, Harry B. ....Arlington, VA
Littell, Melinda Skinner
Federal Communications Commission, Wireless Telecommunications Bureau, GV
Littell, Richard ....Washington, DC
Littell, Susan A. ....New York, NY
Litten, Barbara Bolton
West Palm Beach, FL
Litten, Brian J. ....Trenton, NJ
Litten, Donald D. ....Harrisonburg, VA
Litten, Elizabeth G. ....Trenton, NJ
Litten, Jonathan J. ....Harrisonburg, VA
Litten & Sipe, L.L.P. ....Harrisonburg, VA
Littenberg, Joseph S. ....Westfield, NJ
Littenberg, Michael R. ....New York, NY
Litteneker, Edwin L. ....Lewiston, ID
Litteneker, Randall J. ....San Francisco, CA
Litteneker, Rebecca U. ....San Francisco, CA
Litter, Alice L. ....Harvard, MA
Litteral, Daniel P. ....Rockville, MD
Litteral, Daniel P., P.A. ....Rockville, MD
Litteral, L. Darlene Day ....Golden, CO
Litteral, Malesa A. ....Columbus, OH
Litterio, Christopher P. ....Boston, MA
Litterst Law Office, Ltd. ....Peoria, IL
Litterst, Roland N. ....Peoria, IL
Littky, Marvin S. ....West Palm Beach, FL
Littky-Rubin, Julie H.
West Palm Beach, FL
Little & Adams, P.C. ....Dalton, GA
Little, Alison C. ....Cleveland, OH
Little, Alison J. ....Boston, MA
Little, Amos R., III ....Helena, MT
Little, Anne Blythe ....Fort Worth, TX
Little, Anne C. ....Granville, OH
Little, Anthony F., & Associates
Albuquerque, NM
Little, Asa R., Jr. ....Frenchburg, KY
Little, Audrey B. ....Department of Labor, Office of the Solicitor, GV
Little & Baird, A Professional Corporation
Houston, TX
Little, Barbara B. ....Gardnerville, NV
Little, Barbara D. ....Charleston, WV
Little, Betty H. ....Amarillo, TX
Little, Bruce H. ....Minneapolis, MN
Little & Bryant ....San Jose, CA
Little, Bulman & Whitney, P.C.
Cambridge, MA
Providence, RI
Little, C. David ....Frankfort, IN
Little, C. Dean ....Seattle, WA
Little, C. Lawson ....Dothan, AL
Little, Carl J. ....New Orleans, LA
Little, Caroline H. ....Washington, DC
Little, Carroll D. ....Detroit, MI
Little, Catherine Derdeyn ....Atlanta, GA
Little, Cathryn M. ....Raleigh, NC
Little, Charles A. ....Camden, NJ
Little, Charles F., Jr. ....Latham, NY
Little, Charles L., III ....Oak Grove, LA
Little, Charles M. ....Fayetteville, AR
Little, Christine D. ....Tulsa, OK
Little, Christopher B. ....Denver, CO
Little, Christopher H. ....Cambridge, MA
Providence, RI
Little, Cicchetti & Conard, P.C.
Burlington, VT
Little, Craig ....Tallahassee, FL
Little, Craig J. ....Baltimore, MD
Little, Curtis W., Jr. ....Manchester, NH
Little, D. Scott ....Sandy, UT
Little, Dan ....Madill, OK
Tishomingo, OK
Little, Dana Suzanne ....Arlington, VA
Little, Daniel M. ....Bonita, CA
Little, Danielle K. ....New York, NY
Little, Darryl C. ....Cincinnati, OH
Little, David ....Oklahoma City, OK
Little, David A. ....Albany, NY
Little, David A. ....Lima, OH
Little, David C. ....Denver, CO
Little, David C. ....Quincy, IL
Little, David E. ....Austin, TX
Little, David H. ....Salt Lake City, UT
Little, David L., Jr. ....Rock Hill, SC
Little, David R. ....Denver, CO
Little, David R. ....Houston, TX
Little, David R. B. ....San Diego, CA
Little, David W. ....Bloomington, IN
Little, David Wilfrid ....Los Angeles, CA
Little, Deborah A. ....Pittsburgh, PA
Little, Don ....Dayton, OH
Little, Donald Blair ....Montgomery, AL
Little, Donald R. ....Canton, OH
Little, Donna A. ....San Francisco, CA
Little, Donna Michelle ....Louisville, KY
Little, Douglas B. ....St. Paul, MN
Little, Douglas E. ....Charlottesville, VA
Little, Douglas R. ....Houston, TX
Little, Douglas S. ....Seattle, WA
Little, Douglas W. ....Pomeroy, OH
Little, E. Neal, Jr. ....Decatur, GA
Little, Edward J. M. ....New York, NY
Little, Edward P., Jr. ....Montrose, PA
Little, Edward W., Jr. ....Boston, MA
Little, Elizabeth E. ....Oneonta, NY
Little, Eric Robert ....Irvine, CA
Little, F. Edward ....Sierra Madre, CA
Little, F. McCoy ....Colonial Heights, VA
Little, F. A., Jr. ....Alexandria, LA
Little, Fred A. ....Washington, DC
Little, Fredrika Quinn ....Providence, RI
Little, G. William, III ....Blue Ridge, GA
Little, G. William, III, P.C. ....Blue Ridge, GA
Little, Gary A. ....Albany, KY
Little, George B. ....Richmond, VA
Little, George J. ....Marianna, FL
Little, George L., Jr. ....Winston-Salem, NC
Little, Gilman & Velasquez, P.A.
Albuquerque, NM
Santa Fe, NM
Little, Gordon S. ....Albuquerque, NM
Little, Gordon S., P.A. ....Albuquerque, NM
Little, Gregory G. ....New York, NY
Little, H. Stennis ....Nashville, TN
Little, Harvey E. ....Blue Bell, PA
Little, Herman L., Jr. ....Houston, TX
Little, Horace W. ....Newport Beach, CA
Little, J. David ....Glens Falls, NY
Little, J. Ford ....Knoxville, TN
Little, J. Joseph ....Chicago, IL
Little, J. M., & Associates, P.C.
Houston, TX
Little, J. Matthew ....Raleigh, NC
Little, J. Wayne ....Houston, TX
Little, Jack Edward, Jr. ....Houston, TX
Little, Jack M. ....Dallas, TX
Little, Jack N. ....Big Spring, TX
Little, Jack R. ....Lewiston, ID
Little, James B., (A Professional Corporation)
San Jose, CA
Little, James D. ....Raleigh, NC
Little, James M. ....Oklahoma City, OK
Little, James M. ....Houston, TX
Little, James W. ....Evansville, IN
Little, James W. ....San Antonio, TX
Little, Jan Carol ....Seattle, WA
Little, Jan Nielsen ....San Francisco, CA
Little, Jane C. ....Vandiver, AL
Little, Jane W. ....Dallas, TX
Little, Jeannette L. ....La Grange, GA
Little, Jeffrey L., Law Office of
Shreveport, LA
Little, Jeffrey P. ....Frankfort, IN
Little, Joan Creigh ....San Diego, CA
Little, Joe H., Jr. ....Mobile, AL
Little, John B., IV ....San Diego, CA
Little, John Hubert ....Livingston, TN
Little, John J. ....Dallas, TX
Little, John L. ....Oklahoma City, OK
Little, John M. ....Tucson, AZ
Little, John Meighan ....United States Senate, Senatorial Assistants, GV
Little, John P. ....Roseland, NJ
Little, John R., Jr. ....Boulder, CO
Little, John S. ....Jackson, TN
Little, John V. ....Charlottesville, VA
Little, John W., III (P.A.)
West Palm Beach, FL
Little, Joseph D. ....Calhoun, GA
Little, Joseph G. ....Memphis, TN
Little, Joseph R. ....Dallas, TX
Little, Joshua E. ....San Diego, CA
Little, Joy Leslie ....Tucson, AZ
Little, Judithe Linse ....Houston, TX
Little, Karen S. ....O'Fallon, MO
Little, Kathleen C. ....Washington, DC
Little, Ken D. ....Walnut Creek, CA
Little, Kevin G. ....Fresno, CA
Little, Kevin S. ....Augusta, GA
Little, Laura Margaret ....Austin, TX
Little, Lawrence E. ....Knoxville, TN
Little, Lawrence L. ....Grenada, MS
Jackson, MS
New Albany, MS
Oxford, MS
Little, Leo A. ....Pittsburgh, PA
Little, Lesley E. ....Houston, TX
Little, Linda Marie ....Haverhill, MA
Little, Little, Little, Windel & Coppedge
Madill, OK
Tishomingo, OK
Little & Little, PLLC ....Raleigh, NC
Little, Loyd H., Jr. ....Huntsville, AL
Little, Lynn E. ....Los Angeles, CA
Little, Marcia A. ....McLean, VA
Little, Marcia A., P.C. ....McLean, VA
Little, Margaret ....Houston, TX
Little, Margaret A. ....Stratford, CT
Little, Marion H., Jr. ....Columbus, OH
Little, Mark W. ....Lewiston, ME
Little, Martha J. ....Philadelphia, PA
Little, Martin Alan ....Louisville, KY
Little, Mary Anne ....Denver, CO
Little, Mary Jean ....Tulsa, OK
Little, Mary Shannon ....New York, NY
Little, Max P. ....Towanda, PA
Little, Melton H. ....Bradenton, FL
Little, Melton H., P.A. ....Bradenton, FL
Little, Meredith ....Tucson, AZ
Little, Michael G. ....Clearwater, FL
Little, Michael J. ....Denver, CO
Little, Michael R. ....Liberty, TX
Little & Milligan, PLLC ....Knoxville, TN
Little, Miner & Petersen
Oklahoma City, OK
Little, Morris O., Jr. ....Atlanta, GA
Little, Nancy L. ....Lansing, MI
Little, Nancy R. ....Richmond, VA
Little and O'Connor ....Glens Falls, NY
Hudson Falls, NY
Little, Parsley & Cluverius, P.C.
Richmond, VA
Little, Patrick M. ....Florham Park, NJ
Little, Patrick R. ....Auburn, CA
Little, Paul D. ....Corpus Christi, TX
Little, Paul M. ....San Francisco, CA
Little, Pedersen, Fankhauser & Cox, L.L.P.
Dallas, TX
Little, Peggy S. ....Bettendorf, IA
Little, Philip W. ....North Hollywood, CA
Little, Phillip L. ....Paducah, KY
Little, Prudence Mae ....Madill, OK
Tishomingo, OK
Little, R. Jerry ....New Kensington, PA
Little, Randy D. ....Houston, TX
Little, Raquel, Mrs. ....St. Petersburg, FL
Little, Richard J. ....Cypress, CA
Little, Richard L. ....Treasury Department, Office of Thrift Supervision, GV
Little, Richard N., Jr. ....Bellingham, WA
Little, Robert ....Memphis, TN
Little, Robert B. ....Dallas, TX
Little, Robert C. ....Los Angeles, CA
Little, Robert C. ....Washington, DC
Little, Robert David ....Memphis, TN
Little, Robert E., III ....Wadesboro, NC
Little, Robert E., Jr. ....Burke, VA
Little, Robert H. ....Brookston, IN
Little, Robert Lee ....Carrizo Springs, TX
Little, Robert M. ....Englewood, CO
Little, Robert R. ....Dallas, TX
Little, Robert W. ....Longview, TX
Little, Robert W., (A Law Corp.)
Newport Beach, CA
Little, Rocky ....Richardson, TX
Little, Roger Skok ....Stratford, CT
Little, Ronald A. ....Rochester, NY
Little, Ronald L. ....Poplar Bluff, MO
Little, Ronald W. ....Tulsa, OK
Little, Rory K. ....San Francisco, CA
Little, Rose, & Associates, P.C.
Albuquerque, NM
Little, Rose M.R. ....Albuquerque, NM
Little, Russel T. ....San Diego, CA
Little, S. Fenn, Jr. ....Atlanta, GA
Little, S. Sylvan ....Boca Raton, FL
Little, Sam F. ....Dalton, GA
Little, Sandra Morgan ....Albuquerque, NM
Little & Saputo ....Walnut Creek, CA
Little & Schellhammer Law Firm
Poplar Bluff, MO
Little, Scott L. ....Largo, MD
Little, Shawn A. ....Columbus, OH
Little, Sheets & Warner ....Pomeroy, OH
Little, Silas ....Peterborough, NH
Little, Stacy L. ....Houston, TX
Little, Stefanie J. ....Dover, DE
Little, Stennis, P.C. ....Nashville, TN
Little, Stephen A., & Associates
Rockland, ME
Little, Stephen D. ....Bismarck, ND
Little, Stephen R. ....Marion, NC
Little, Stephen R., P.A. ....Marion, NC
Little, Sue Yielding ....Raleigh, NC
Little, Susan C. ....Albuquerque, NM
Little, Suzanne ....Alexandria, VA
Little, T. Vance ....Brentwood, TN
Little, Teri A. ....Palo Alto, CA
Little, Terrell David ....Auburn, AL
Little, Thomas A. ....Burlington, VT
Little, Thomas C. ....Clearwater, FL
Little, Thomas C., P.A. ....Clearwater, FL
Little, Thomas E. ....Decatur, IL
Little, Thomas M. ....Talladega, AL
Little, Thomas M. ....Tampa, FL
Little, Timothy G. ....New York, NY
Little, Timothy James ....Woodbridge, NJ
Little, T.J., Jr. ....Elizabethton, TN
Little, Traci R. ....Indianapolis, IN
Little, Tracy ....Houston, TX
Little, Vicki L. ....St. Louis, MO
Little, Victoria D., Mrs. ....Decatur, GA
Little, W. Ross, Jr. ....Franklin, LA
Little, Wallace A. ....Los Angeles, CA
Little, Walter M. ....White Plains, NY
Little, Walter R. ....Pittsburgh, PA
Little, William A. ....Myrtle Beach, SC
Little, William B. L. ....Raleigh, NC
Little, William C. ....Phoenix, AZ
Little, William C., Jr.
Department of the Navy, Office of the Judge Advocate General, GV
Little, William D., III ....Montgomery, AL
Little, William F., Jr. ....Rahway, NJ
Little, William G. ....Albany, NY
Little, William H., Jr. ....Columbus, GA
Little, William J., Jr. ....Jackson, MS
Little, William R. ....Waycross, GA
Little, William S. ....Baltimore, MD
Little, William T. ....Houston, TX

Little, Winfield E., Jr., (A Professional Corporation) ... Lake Charles, LA
Little, W. N. ... Brunswick, GA
Little, Zebulon Peyton ... Cullman, AL
Littlefield, A. Stanley ... Rockland, MA
Littlefield, Alex D., Jr. ... Gainesville, FL
Littlefield, Anne H. ... Hartford, CT
Littlefield, Charles A. ... Neenah, WI
Littlefield, Christina B. ... Hayward, CA
Littlefield, Christopher J. ... Scottsdale, AZ
Littlefield, David E. ... Salt Lake City, UT
Littlefield, David M. ... Muskogee, OK
Littlefield, Florence G. ... Lindenhurst, NY
Littlefield, J. Bradley ... Portland, OR
Littlefield, Jon R. ... Coos Bay, OR
Littlefield, K Clifford ... Corpus Christi, TX
Littlefield, Linda J. ... San Jose, CA
Littlefield, Margaret Joan ... Bolinas, CA
Littlefield, Martin J., Jr. ... Buffalo, NY
Littlefield, Mary Louise ... Pittsburgh, PA
Littlefield, Nick ... Boston, MA
Littlefield & Peterson ... Salt Lake City, UT
Littlefield, Richard C. ... Southfield, MI
Littlefield, Robert E., Jr. ... Albany, NY
Littlefield, Rodney Kelp ... Metairie, LA
Littlefield, Stephen A. ... Houston, TX
Littlefield, Sue Brooks ... Austin, TX
Littlefield, Suzanne A. ... Austell, GA
Littlefield, Wayne B. ... Los Angeles, CA
Littlefield, William C. ... Albuquerque, NM
Littlefield-Moreno, Sheri L. ... Albany, NY
Little-Fletcher, Sheryl L. ... Baltimore, MD
Littleford, Eugene R. ... Office of Personnel Management, GV
Littlehales, Charles P. ... Newport, OR
Littlehales, Lewis C. ... Salem, OR
Littlejohn & Adair, P.C. ... Stilwell, OK
Littlejohn, Andrea R. ... Bethesda, MD
Littlejohn, Bill C. ... Dayton, OH
LittleJohn, Blair R., III ... West Palm Beach, FL
Littlejohn, Bruce ... Spartanburg, SC
Littlejohn, Cameron B., Jr. ... Columbia, SC
Littlejohn, Carl W., Jr. ... Graniteville, SC
Littlejohn, Donald W. (Bill) ... Colusa, CA
Littlejohn, Edward J. ... Detroit, MI
Littlejohn, Erik P. ... Houston, TX
Littlejohn, Ernestine D. ... San Diego, CA
Littlejohn, J. Michael ... Washington, DC
Littlejohn, James M. ... Estes Park, CO
Littlejohn, James R. ... Dallas, TX
Littlejohn, Janet P. ... San Antonio, TX
Littlejohn, Jaymes D. ... Minneapolis, MN
Littlejohn, Joe O. ... San Diego, CA
Littlejohn, Junior Dewayne ... Stilwell, OK
Littlejohn, Kent O. ... Omaha, NE
Littlejohn, Lizabeth W. ... Landrum, SC
Littlejohn, Neal B. ... Columbus, GA
Littlejohn, Robert C. ... Manhattan Beach, CA
Littlejohn, Roy ... Washington, DC
Littlejohn, Talmadge D. ... New Albany, MS
Littlejohn, W. Rachel ... Beeville, TX
Littlejohn & Westfall ... Colusa, CA
Littlejohn, William L. ... Chicago, IL
Littlemore, Joseph ... Olympia, WA
Littlepage, Diane M. ... Annapolis, MD
Littlepage, James A. ... Norcross, GA
Littlepage & Littlepage ... Mart, TX
Littlepage, Paxton K. ... Mart, TX
Littlepage, Rose Ann ... Mart, TX
Littlepage, Samuel D. ... Washington, DC
Littlepage, Stephen C. ... Point Pleasant, WV
Littlepage, Zoe B. ... Houston, TX
Littler Mendelson, A Professional Corporation ... Phoenix, AZ
Fresno, CA
Los Angeles, CA
Oakland, CA
Sacramento, CA
San Diego, CA
San Francisco, CA
San Jose, CA
Santa Maria, CA
Santa Rosa, CA
Stockton, CA
Walnut Creek, CA
Denver, CO
Washington, DC
Atlanta, GA
Chicago, IL
Baltimore, MD
Minneapolis, MN
Morristown, NJ
New York, NY
Dallas, TX
Houston, TX
Seattle, WA
Littler, Renner, Howard & Schroeder ... Peoria, IL
Littler, Stacey R. ... Chicago, IL
Littler, Thomas E. ... Phoenix, AZ
Littles, Alvin ... Charlotte, NC
Littles, Lorenzo S. ... Chicago, IL
Littleton, Arthur R. ... Philadelphia, PA
Littleton, Charles D. ... Troy, OH
Littleton, Christine A. ... Los Angeles, CA
Littleton, David A. ... Little Rock, AR
Littleton, David L. ... Los Angeles, CA
Littleton, Denise I. ... Mobile, AL
Littleton, Donald C. ... St. Louis, MO
Littleton, Dorothy Wells ... Montgomery, AL
Littleton, Jack H. ... Atlanta, GA
Littleton, James K. ... Greenwood, MS
Littleton, John C. ... Chattanooga, TN
Littleton, John E. ... Philadelphia, PA
Littleton, Kathleen A. ... Frankfort, IL
Littleton, Paul E. ... St. Louis, MO
Littleton, Rebecca A. ... Atlanta, GA
Littleton, Robert B. ... Nashville, TN
Littleton, Robert L. ... Dickson, TN
Littleton, Robert W. ... New York, NY
Littleton & Smith ... Dickson, TN
Littleton, Susan R. ... Austin, TX
Littleton, Wilbur F., Jr. ... San Antonio, TX
Littleton, William C. ... Baltimore, MD
Littlewood, Bill ... Palo Alto, CA
Littlewood, Michelle ... Oakland, CA
Littlewood, Paula C. ... Seattle, WA
Littleworth, A. Todd ... La Habra, CA
Littleworth, Arthur L., (P.C.) ... Riverside, CA
Littman, Adam Ross ... Winter Park, FL
Littman, Allan N. ... San Francisco, CA
Littman, Amy Baldwin ... Chestnut Ridge, NY
Littman, Andrew C. ... Boulder, CO
Vail, CO
Littman, Bernice ... Honolulu, HI
Littman, David ... Denver, CO
Littman, David B. ... Linden, NJ
Littman, David, P.C. ... Denver, CO
Littman, Donald F. ... Williamsburg, OH
Littman, Eric P. ... Miami, FL
Littman, Eric P., P.A. ... Miami, FL
Littman, James A. ... Wilmington, DE
Littman, James F. ... Stuart, FL
Littman, Judith N. ... Melville, NY
Littman, Jules S. ... Freehold, NJ
Littman, Kenneth G. ... Fall River, MA
Littman Krooks Roth & Ball P.C. ... New York, NY
White Plains, NY
Littman, Louis H. ... Toms River, NJ
Littman, Madelyn C. ... Larchmont, NY
Littman, Marc J. ... Southfield, MI
Littman, Marion K. ... Somerville, NJ
Littman, Michael A., (P.C.) ... Wheat Ridge, CO
Littman, Michael I. ... San Diego, CA
Littman & Miller ... Chestnut Ridge, NY
Littman, Mitchell C. ... New York, NY
Littman, Owen S. ... New York, NY
Littman, Peter N. ... Ithaca, NY
Littman, Rachel J. ... New York, NY
Littman, Robert L. ... Birmingham, MI
Littman, Roger ... Chicago, IL
Littman & Sherlock, P.A. ... Stuart, FL
Littman, Sima ... New York, NY
Littman, Steven E. ... San Francisco, CA
Littman, Susan I. ... Allendale, NJ
Littman, Thomas W. ... Greenwich, CT
New York, NY
Littmann, Richard A. ... St. Louis, MO
Littner, Deschler & Littner ... Allentown, PA
Bethlehem, PA
Easton, PA
Littner, Jay G. ... Cincinnati, OH
Littner, Robert H. ... Bethlehem, PA
Littner, Robert V. ... Bethlehem, PA
Litton, Arthur C., II ... Fort Wayne, IN
Litton, Claude J. ... New York, NY
Litton, F. T. ... Charleston, WV
Litton & Geonetta, LLP ... San Francisco, CA
Litton, James D. ... New York, NY
Litton, James M. ... Boston, MA
Litton, Lisa H. ... Metamora, MI
Litton, Mark E. ... Oklahoma City, OK
Litton, Michael L. ... Oak Lawn, IL
Litton, Randall G. ... Grand Rapids, MI
Litton, Sean Byrne ... Washington, DC
Litton, T. Richard, Jr. ... Norfolk, VA
Litton, Ted C. ... Houston, TX
Litton, Thomas Marc ... San Francisco, CA
Litton, William E., II ... Atlanta, GA
Littorno, Richard A. ... Pittsburg, CA
Littrell, Amy Wright ... Tampa, FL
Littrell, Barry W. ... Columbus, OH
Littrell, Catherine M. ... Detroit, MI
Littrell, Herbert K. ... Louisville, KY
Littrell, Jeana M. ... Memphis, TN
Littrell, Kelson ... Louisville, KY
Littrell, Lawrence R. ... Fawnskin, CA
Littrell, Reginald ... Downieville, CA
Littrell, Rex A. ... Columbus, OH
Littrell, Robert C. ... Manhattan, KS
Litts, Jeffrey D. ... New Cumberland, PA
Litts, Marjorie F. ... Columbia, SC
Littwin, Barbara D. ... Oakland, CA
Litvack, Faith C. ... Port St. Lucie, FL
Litvack, Jeffrey S. ... Dix Hills, NY
Litvack, Mark D. ... Burbank, CA
Litvack, Sanford M. ... Burbank, CA
Litvak & Accardi ... Livingston, NJ
Litvak, Alexander ... Los Angeles, CA
Litvak, Andrew M. ... Miami, FL
Litvak, Eric A. ... Metuchen, NJ
Litvak, Kramer A. ... Pensacola, FL
Litvak, Lawrence ... Denver, CO
Litvak, Litvak, Mehrtens & Epstein, Professional Corporation ... Denver, CO
Litvak, Marlene S. ... Belmont, CA
Litvak, Matthew M. ... Chicago, IL
Litvak, Maxim B. ... Houston, TX
Litvak, Milton ... St. Joseph, MO
Litvak, Ronald D. ... Denver, CO
Litvak, Steven I. ... Livingston, NJ
Litvak, Uri ... New York, NY
Litvak, William ... Beverly Hills, CA
Los Angeles, CA
Litvak, William ... Denver, CO
Litvin, Blumberg, Matusow & Young, A Professional Association ... Philadelphia, PA
Litvin, Caren ... Philadelphia, PA
Litvin, David A. ... Salt Lake City, UT
Litvin, Dionna K. ... Philadelphia, PA
Litvin, Elizabeth Z. ... Philadelphia, PA
Litvin, Herbert G. ... Easton, PA
Litvin, Joel M. ... New York, NY
Litvin, Milton J. ... Los Angeles, CA
Litvin, Richard E. ... Hamden, CT
Litvin, Robert W. ... Cherry Hill, NJ
Philadelphia, PA
Litvin, Ruthie ... Norfolk, VA
Litvin, S. Gerald ... Philadelphia, PA
Litvin, William J. ... West Chester, PA
Litwa, Robin L. ... Horsham, PA
Litwack, Carol Kernan ... Bridgeton, NJ
Litwack, John ... Newton, MA
Litwack, Kenneth ... Flushing, NY
Litwack & Litwack ... Bridgeton, NJ
Litwack, Martin ... New York, NY
Litwack, Milton ... Livingston, NJ
Litwack, Robert ... Bayside, NY
Litwack, Robert C. ... Bridgeton, NJ
Litwack, Steven C. ... Rancho Mirage, CA
Litwak, Glenn T. ... Beverly Hills, CA
Litwak, Harris ... Woodmere, NY
Litwak, Jeffrey B. ... Portland, OR
Litwak, Lawrence ... Boston, MA
Litwak, Lawrence B. ... Boston, MA
Litwer, Bruce B. ... Lauderhill, FL
Litwer, Susan ... Mamaroneck, NY
New York, NY
Litwer, Susan, P.C. ... Mamaroneck, NY
Litwiler, Thomas J. ... Chicago, IL
Litwin, Avi Jacob ... Miami, FL
Litwin & Barouh ... Beverly Hills, CA
Litwin, Burton H. ... Chicago, IL
Litwin, Burton L. ... Dobbs Ferry, NY
Litwin, Daniel B. ... Newtown Square, PA
Litwin, Edward R. ... South San Francisco, CA
Litwin, Edward R., A Professional Corporation ... South San Francisco, CA
Litwin, Ethan E. ... New York, NY
Litwin, Frank E. ... Boston, MA
Litwin, Gerald H. ... Hackensack, NJ
Litwin, Gerald H., P.A. ... Hackensack, NJ
Litwin, Gordon N. ... Newark, NJ
Litwin, Harry ... New York, NY
Litwin, Hedda E. ... Washington, DC
Litwin, Jack L. ... Millbrae, CA
Litwin, Lawrence B. ... Morristown, NJ
Litwin, Leanne L. ... Philadelphia, PA
Litwin, Leonard D. ... Chicago, IL
Litwin, Louis L. ... Beverly Hills, CA
Litwin, Mark S. ... San Francisco, CA
Litwin, Michael J. ... Chicago, IL
Litwin, Paul J. ... Boston, MA
Litwin, Peter A. ... Litchfield, CT
Litwin, Peter A., P.C. ... Litchfield, CT
Litwin, Richard C. ... Atlanta, GA
Litwin & Salvaggio, P.C. ... Morristown, NJ
Litwin, Sharen ... Boston, MA
Litwin, Stuart M. ... Chicago, IL
Litwin, Stuart N. ... Chicago, IL
Litwinczak, Edward A. ... Minneapolis, MN
Litwinka, Michael ... Hartford, CT
Litynski, Warren E. ... St. Peter, MN
Litz, Arthur ... St. Louis, MO
Litz, Arthur ... Mineola, NY
Litz, Frank J. ... Schenectady, NY
Litz, Franz Thomas ... Boston, MA
Litz, Harriet R. ... Haddonfield, NJ
Narberth, PA
Litz, Jennifer A. ... Los Angeles, CA
Litz, Joseph L. ... Schenectady, NY
Litz, Kenneth P. ... Schenectady, NY
Litz, Kevin Y. ... Tulsa, OK
Litz & Litz ... Schenectady, NY
Litz, Paul J. ... Beverly Hills, CA
Litz, Robert D. ... St. Louis, MO
Litz, Ronald A., & Associates ... Los Angeles, CA
Litz, Steven A. ... Allentown, PA
Litz, Steven C. ... Monrovia, IN
Litz, Thomas A. ... St. Louis, MO
Litz, Victoria J. ... New York, NY
Litzelfelner, Donald L. ... Hamilton, OH
Litzenberger, Judith A. ... San Diego, CA
Litzenberger & Litzenberger, P.C. ... Williamsport, IN
Litzenberger, Marilyn E. ... Portland, OR
Litzenberger, Nancy J. ... Williamsport, IN
Litzenberger, Ralph W. ... Easton, PA
Litzenberger, Samuel A. ... Quakertown, PA
Litzenberger, Virginia P. ... Asheville, NC
Litzinger, Jerrold J. ... Cincinnati, OH
Litzinger, Tracy C. ... Peoria, IL
Litzky, Eric N. ... New York, NY
Litzler, James W. ... Sulphur Springs, TX
Litzman, Jay H. ... New York, NY
Litzow, Joan M. ... Cleveland, OH
Liu, Albert Yun-Quan ... Los Angeles, CA
Liu, Alvin Q. ... Auburn Hills, MI
Liu, Amy C. ... Los Angeles, CA
Liu, Andrew Ging ... Bronx, NY
Liu, Andy ... Washington, DC
Liu, Arthur J. ... San Francisco, CA
Liu, Barry R. ... Concord, CA
Liu, Ben T. ... Birmingham, MI
Liu, Brian P.Y. ... Los Angeles, CA
Liu, Catherine B. ... Livingston, NJ
Liu, Charles ... Newport Beach, CA
Liu, Chialing ... San Antonio, TX
Liu, Chiu-Ti ... New York, NY
Liu & Choy ... New York, NY
Liu, Cindy ... New York, NY
Liu, Clarice C. ... Emeryville, CA
San Francisco, CA
Liu, David C. ... Los Angeles, CA
Liu, David Michael ... Kailua, HI
Liu, David P. ... Dallas, TX
Liu, David W. ... Atlanta, GA
Liu, Dennis C. ... Boston, MA
Liu, Diana C. ... Philadelphia, PA
Liu, Don H. ... Malvern, PA
Liu, Edward ... San Francisco, CA
Liu, Eileen M. ... Chicago, IL
Liu, Erik J. ... San Francisco, CA
Liu, Florence R. ... Boston, MA
Liu, Frances ... Charlottesville, VA
Liu, Francis Yan ... Palo Alto, CA
Liu, Gilbert K. S. ... New York, NY
Liu, Henry ... Washington, DC
Liu, Irwin K. ... New York, NY
Liu, Jaclyn ... San Francisco, CA
Liu, Jean C. ... Chicago, IL
Liu, Jennifer Y. ... San Francisco, CA
Liu, Ji-Qing ... Indianapolis, IN
Liu, Joanne S. ... Boston, MA
Liu, John J. ... Clearwater, FL
Liu, John K. ... Palo Alto, CA
Liu, Judy G. Z. ... New York, NY
Liu, Judy Y. ... Houston, TX
Liu, Kenneth E. ... Washington, DC
Liu, Kenneth K. ... Las Vegas, NV
Liu, Kent C. ... Santa Monica, CA
Liu, Larry J.H. ... Newport Beach, CA
Liu, Laura C. ... Chicago, IL
Liu, Libby ... San Francisco, CA
Liu, Linfei ... Alexandria, VA
Liu, Margaret ... Cleveland, OH
Liu, Margaret K. ... New York, NY
Liu, Martin C. ... New York, NY
Liu, Mei (Michael) ... Princeton, NJ
Liu, Merlin ... Overseas Private Investment Corporation, GV
Liu, Michael E. ... Waukesha, WI
Liu, Michele ... Palo Alto, CA
Liu, Nancy M. ... Trevose, PA
Liu, Nancy N. ... Atlanta, GA
Liu, Polene ... Irvine, CA
Liu, Richard C. ... Cupertino, CA
Liu, Robert L. ... San Francisco, CA
Liu, Sally S. ... Los Angeles, CA
Liu, Shuang ... New York, NY
Liu, Stella S. ... New York, NY
Liu, Steven ... Palo Alto, CA
Liu, Sylvia F. ... Department of Justice, Environment and Natural Resources Division, GV
Liu, Therese T. ... New York, NY
Liu, Thomas T. ... Los Angeles, CA
Liu, Tina P. ... New York, NY
Liu, Vivien Yilan ... New York, NY
Liu, Wen ... Los Angeles, CA
Liu, Yvonne N. ... Monterey Park, CA
Lium, John D. ... Rye, NY
Lium, Sten ... St. Johnsbury, VT
Liuzza, Penny Dowd ... New Orleans, LA
Liuzzi, Angela M. ... New York, NY
Liuzzi, Frank C. ... San Francisco, CA
Liuzzi, Kathleen M. ... Salt Lake City, UT
Liuzzi, Michael D. ... San Diego, CA
Liuzzi, Robert C. ... Long Grove, IL
Liuzzo, Anthony L. ... New York, NY
Liuzzo, Peter J. ... New York, NY
Liva, Edward A. ... Philadelphia, PA
Liva, Janice B. ... Boston, MA
Livaccari, Anthony J., Jr. ... New Orleans, LA
Livaccari, Laura A. ... Washington, DC
Livaccari, Villarrubia & Timmons, L.L.C. ... New Orleans, LA
Livadary, Paul J. ... Los Angeles, CA
Livadopoulos, Irene ... Beverly Hills, CA
Livaich, Gary ... Sacramento, CA
Livak, Nick J. ... Santa Clara, CA
Livak, Paul V. ... Chicago, IL
Livanios, Helen ... Library of Congress, Copyright Office, GV
Livanos, Marc M. ... New York, NY
Livanos, Maria M. ... New York, NY
Livanos, Peter E., Jr. ... Castro Valley, CA
Livarchik, George R. ... Chesterton, IN
Livaudais, Alfred F., Jr. ... Daleville, AL
Livaudais, Charles H., Jr. ... Raleigh, NC
Livaudais, Julie D. ... New Orleans, LA
Livaudais, Marc M. ... New Orleans, LA
Livaudais, Marcel, Jr. ... New Orleans, LA
Livaudais, Marian M. ... Mandeville, LA
Livaudais, O. S., Jr. ... Chalmette, LA
Livedalen, Kristi J. ... Denver, CO
Livelli, John B. ... Newark, NJ
Lively, Craig R. ... Beaumont, TX
Lively, David W. ... San Jose, CA
Lively, Donald F. ... Raleigh, NC
Lively, F. Robert ... Indianapolis, IN
Lively, Frances Cox ... Denver, CO
Lively, James K. ... Plano, TX
Lively, Jeff W. ... Stowe, VT
Lively, John Edward ... Wewoka, OK
Lively, John H. ... Washington, DC
Lively, John R. ... Fort Worth, TX
Lively, Joseph M. ... Deer Park, NY
Lively, Kent ... Burlington, NC
Lively, Kent ... Greensboro, NC
Lively, Laban G. ... Tampa, FL
Lively, P. Susan ... Washington, DC
Lively & Padfield, L.L.P. ... Fort Worth, TX
Lively, Patricia D. ... Monte Sereno, CA
Lively, Paul J. ... Tucker, GA
Lively, Peter M. ... Los Angeles, CA
Lively, Pierce ... Danville, KY
Lively, Richard D. ... Montgomery, AL
Lively, Sam ... Austin, TX
Lively, Scott A. ... Boston, MA
Lively, Shaver & Troniani ... Indianapolis, IN
Lively, Thomas W. ... Dallas, TX

Lively, Truitt V. ....Houston, TX
Lively, W. Thomas ....Leitchfield, KY
Lively, William H., Jr. ....Tyler, TX
Lively, William R. ....Valencia, CA
Lively, William T., Jr. ....Charleston, WV
Livengood, Carter, Tjossem, Fitzgerald & Alskog, LLP ....Kirkland, WA
Livengood, Celeste D. ....Dallas, TX
Livengood, Gordon A. ....Kirkland, WA
Livengood, Larry L. ....Salina, KS
Livengood, William W., II ....Augusta, ME
Livens Law Firm, The ....Bedford, TX
Livens, Lois B. ....Arlington, TX
Livens, Stephen J. ....Bedford, TX
Livensparger, John C., Law Office of
Chicago, IL
Liverance, Wallace B., Jr. ....Summit, NJ
New York, NY
Livergood, Robert F. ....Clayton, MO
Liverman, Ralph L. ....Eutaw, AL
Liverman, Thierry J. ....Washington, DC
Livermon, James S., Jr. ....Enfield, NC
Livermon, Merrilyn B. ....Shawnee, OK
Livermont, Kirk K. ....Independence, CA
Livermore, Brian M. ....Chicago, IL
Livermore, Daniel U., Jr. ....Jacksonville, FL
Livermore, Freeman & McWilliams, P.A.
Jacksonville, FL
Livermore, Joseph M. ....Tucson, AZ
Livermore, Putnam ....San Francisco, CA
Livermore, Richard C. ....Redwood City, CA
Livermore, Samuel M. ....San Francisco, CA
Liversidge, Samuel G. ....Los Angeles, CA
Livesay, Deborah J. ....Atlanta, GA
Livesay, Jackie J. ....McLean, VA
Livesay, John L. ....Coldwater, MI
Livesay, Joseph A. ....Memphis, TN
Livesay, Keith C. ....Brownsville, TX
Livesay, Margo ....Arlington, VA
Livesay, Mark T. ....Hartford, CT
Livesay, Paul O. ....San Carlos, CA
Livesay, Roberta S. ....Tempe, AZ
Livesay, Viki ....Dallas, TX
Livesay, William L., Jr. ....Graham, NC
Livesey Associates ....Philadelphia, PA
Livesey, James E. ....Sacramento, CA
Livesey, Joseph R. ....Philadelphia, PA
Livesey, Kevin M. ....Philadelphia, PA
Livesley, George P. ....Eugene, OR
Liveson, Avi O. ....New York, NY
Livett, Richard K. ....La Jolla, CA
Livezey, Elnora Beth ....Redding, CA
Livezey, Jon Harlan ....Aberdeen, MD
Livezey, Tracy A. ....San Francisco, CA
Livezey, Tracy A. ....San Francisco, CA
Livgard, Paul A. ....Minneapolis, MN
Livick, Anthony ....Cleveland, OH
Livingood, John A., Jr. ....Philadelphia, PA
Livingood, John M. ....Philadelphia, PA
Livingood, Matthew G. ....Tulsa, OK
Livingstain, Harris Miller ....Asheville, NC
Livingston, A. Broaddus ....Tampa, FL
Livingston, A. Keith ....Greeneville, TN
Livingston, Adler, Pulda & Meiklejohn
Hartford, CT
Livingston, Alan C. ....Dothan, AL
Livingston, Andrew R. ....San Francisco, CA
Livingston, Ann ....Austin, TX
Livingston, Anne ....Oklahoma City, OK
Livingston, Anthony R. ....Daleville, AL
Livingston, Arthur ....Los Angeles, CA
Livingston & Associates, P.C.
Lakewood, CO
Livingston, B. Parker, Jr. ....Alexandria, VA
Livingston, Barbara C. ....Alexandria, VA
Livingston, Barger, Brandt & Schroeder
Bloomington, IL
Champaign, IL
Livingston, Becky Dasher ....Statesboro, GA
Livingston, Boynton P. ....Arlington, VA
Livingston, Bradford L. ....Chicago, IL
Livingston, Bruce D. ....St. Louis, MO
Livingston, Bruce R. ....Augusta, ME
Livingston, Calvin J. ....Oviedo, FL
Livingston, Carol ....Sacramento, CA
Livingston, Catherine A. ....Austin, TX
Livingston, Catherine E. ....Washington, DC
Livingston, Charles H. ....Sarasota, FL
Livingston, Clarence, Jr. ....Oakland, CA
Livingston, Clifton A. ....Tampa, FL
Livingston, Clifton A., P.A. ....Tampa, FL
Livingston, Clint G. ....Norman, OK
Livingston, Craig A. ....San Francisco, CA
Livingston, Craig Harnett ....Edison, NJ
Nutley, NJ
Livingston, D. Mark ....Norman, OK
Livingston, D. Matt ....Athens, TX
Livingston, Daniel E. ....Hartford, CT
Livingston, Daniel M. ....Irvine, CA
Livingston, David A. ....Houston, TX
Livingston, David C. ....Gadsden, AL
Livingston, David D. ....Houston, TX
Livingston, David W. ....Dallas, TX
Livingston, Deanna H. ....Houston, TX
Livingston, Debra Ann ....New York, NY
Livingston, Denise M. ....Olympia, WA
Livingston, Donald R. ....Washington, DC
Livingston, Douglas R. ....Bend, OR
Livingston, E. Robb ....Irvine, CA
Livingston, Edward H. ....White Plains, NY
Livingston, Edward M. ....Naples, FL
Winter Park, FL
Livingston, Edwin B. ....Sylacauga, AL
Livingston, Edwin B., Jr. ....Sylacauga, AL
Livingston, Edwin K. ....Montgomery, AL
Livingston, Elizabeth G. ....New York, NY
Livingston, Enid ....Birmingham, MI
Livingston, Farrand M. ....Portland, OR
Livingston, Fred Michael ....Fulton, NY
Livingston, Gary R. ....Los Angeles, CA
Livingston, Gene ....Sacramento, CA
Livingston, Gerald S. ....Orlando, FL
Livingston, Gerald W. ....Dallas, TX
Livingston, Gregory J. ....Reno, NV
Livingston, Gretchen M. ....Chicago, IL
Livingston and Hundley, P.C. ....Dallas, TX
Livingston, J. Cleve ....Sacramento, CA
Livingston, J. Richard
Grand Junction, CO
Livingston, Jack, (P.C.) ....Scottsboro, AL
Livingston, James D. ....Grand Island, NE
Livingston, James J., Jr. ....Medfield, MA
Livingston, James L. ....Los Angeles, CA
Livingston, James L. ....Sebring, FL
Livingston, James R. ....Troy, OH
West Milton, OH
Livingston, Jason P. ....Midlothian, VA
Livingston, Jeffrey D. ....Redwood City, CA
Livingston, Jeffrey E. ....South Beloit, IL
Livingston, Jeffrey E. ....New York, NY
Livingston, Jessica
Securities and Exchange Commission, Division of Corporation Finance, GV
Livingston, Joan M. ....Santa Barbara, CA
Livingston, John ....Chicago, IL
Livingston, John B. ....Boston, MA
Livingston, John H. ....Birmingham, AL
Livingston, John H. ....Morristown, NY
Livingston, John J. ....Utica, NY
Livingston, John J. ....Tulsa, OK
Livingston, John L. ....Lakewood, CO
Livingston, John R., Jr.
Department of Justice, Federal Bureau of Investigation, GV
Livingston, John S. ....Gladbrook, IA
Livingston, John T. ....Dallas, TX
Livingston, Judith A. ....New York, NY
Livingston, Julia C. ....Boston, MA
Livingston, Katharine ....Los Angeles, CA
San Francisco, CA
Livingston & Kroll ....Oakland, CA
Livingston, Laddie, (P.C.) ....Houston, TX
Livingston, Lawr., Jr.
Belvedere-Tiburon, CA
Livingston, Lionel J. ....Evanston, IL
Livingston, Lisa A. ....Denver, CO
Livingston & Livingston ....Sebring, FL
Livingston & Livingston, P.C.
Houston, TX
Livingston, Lora Jeanette ....Austin, TX
Livingston, Lori Winder
Newport Beach, CA
Livingston, Louis B., P.C. ....Portland, OR
Livingston, Louise S. ....San Francisco, CA
Livingston, Martin J. ....Newark, NJ
Livingston, Mary Counihan ....Boston, MA
Livingston, Mary J. ....Grand Island, NE
Livingston & Mattesich, Law Corporation
Sacramento, CA
Livingston, Michael A. ....Camden, NJ
Livingston, Michael K., (A Law Corporation)
Honolulu, HI
Livingston, Michael N. ....Syracuse, NY
Livingston & Miller ....Houston, TX
Livingston, Milton M., Jr. ....Paducah, KY
Livingston, Mitchell A. ....Trenton, NJ
Livingston, Nancy R. ....Chicago, IL
Livingston, Patrick M. ....Pittsburgh, PA
Livingston, Patterson, Strickland & Weiner, P.A. ....Sarasota, FL
Livingston, Patti W. ....Sugar Land, TX
Livingston, Paul H., Jr. ....Greensboro, NC
Livingston, Paul S. ....Albuquerque, NM
Livingston, Peter ....Portland, OR
Livingston, Peter I. ....New York, NY
Livingston, Peter J. ....Kalamazoo, MI
Livingston, Phillip R. ....Houston, TX
Livingston & Porter ....Fort Payne, AL
Scottsboro, AL
Livingston, R. Lee ....Charlottesville, VA
Livingston, Randall M. ....Denver, CO
Vail, CO
Livingston, Randell W., Jr. ....Austin, TX
Livingston & Reilly, P.A. ....Orlando, FL
Livingston, Renée Welze
San Francisco, CA
Livingston, Richard B. ....Springfield, NJ
Livingston, Richard F., Jr. ....Doraville, GA
Livingston, Richard M. ....Lynchburg, VA
Livingston, Robert, IV ....Gainesville, FL
Livingston, Robert L. ....Metairie, LA
Livingston, Roger A. ....Sandy, UT
Livingston, S. William, Jr.
Washington, DC
Livingston, Samuel G. ....Golden, CO
Livingston, Sandra L. ....Los Angeles, CA
Livingston, Scott A. ....Baltimore, MD
Livingston, Scott D. ....Pittsburgh, PA
Livingston & Smither ....Houston, TX
Livingston, Stephen P. ....New Albany, MS
Livingston, Stephen S. ....Dallas, TX
Livingston, Steven ....Roseland, NJ
Livingston, Stone & McGowan
San Francisco, CA
Livingston, Susan Bevill ....Birmingham, AL
Livingston, Susan D. ....Pittsburgh, PA
Livingston, Susan H. ....Portland, ME
Livingston, Terrance K. ....Chicago, IL
Livingston, Terrie ....Fort Worth, TX
Livingston, Theodore A., Jr. ....Chicago, IL
Livingston, Thomas A. ....Pittsburgh, PA
Livingston, Thomas P. ....Norwalk, CT
Livingston, Timothy L. ....Howell, MI
Livingston, Tina Kyle ....Houston, TX
Livingston, Wade ....Denver, CO
Livingston, William C. ....Charlotte, NC
Livingston, William G. ....Waterbury, VT
Livingston, William I. ....Palm Coast, FL
Livingston, William J., (P.C.)
Newport Beach, CA
Livingstone, Don R. ....South Miami, FL
Livingstone, Fred J. ....Cleveland, OH
Livingstone, Frederick H. ....Arlington, VA
Livingstone, Geo. D. ....Lake Forest, IL
Livingstone, Ivanna Marie ....Savannah, GA
Livingstone, James D. ....Washington, DC
Livingstone, John A. ....San Jose, CA
Livingstone, John M.
United States Tax Court, GV
Livingstone, Michael J. ....New Bedford, MA
Livingstone, Mueller, O'Brien and Davlin, P.C.
Springfield, IL
Livingstone, Philip ....Calais, ME
Livingstone, Wm. E., III ....Dallas, TX
Livingston-Wilson, Karen E. ....Jackson, MS
Livingway, Elaine L. ....Southfield, MI
Livio, James S. ....Lanham, MD
Liviola, George, Jr. ....Ashtabula, OH
Livitz, Ludmila ....Los Angeles, CA
Livnah, Gil ....Palo Alto, CA
Livnah, Margaret C. ....Palo Alto, CA
Livnat, Shmuel (Sandy) ....Washington, DC
Livo, Robert C. ....Cheboygan, MI
LiVolsi, Amy J. ....Norwalk, CT
LiVolsi, Frank W., Jr. ....Stamford, CT
Livoni, Norris C. ....Mesa, AZ
Livorine, R. Richard ....Brighton, MI
Livorine, R. Richard, P.C. ....Brighton, MI
Livornese, Deborah L. ....Oakland, CA
Livornese, Don F. ....Los Angeles, CA
Livornese, Ned W. ....Englewood, CO
Livornese, Victor W. ....New York, NY
Livorno & Arnett ....Columbus, OH
Livorno, John F. ....Columbus, OH
Livote, Leonard ....Kew Gardens, NY
Livoti, Anthony W. ....Columbia, SC
Livoti, Bernstein & Moraco, P.C.
New York, NY
Livoti, Frank J. ....Garden City, NY
Livoti, Robert V. ....New York, NY
Livow, Michael S. ....New York, NY
Livsey, Carole C. ....Rochester, NY
Livsey, Constance E. ....Anchorage, AK
Livsey, Herbert C. ....Salt Lake City, UT
Livsey, Kristine M. ....Elk Grove, CA
Livsey, Philip C. ....Avon, CT
Livsey, Robert C. ....San Francisco, CA
Liwacz, Robert M. ....Trenton, NJ
Liwosz, John C., Jr. ....Westlake, OH
Liz, Maria E. ....New York, NY
Lizak, Chester A. ....Park Ridge, IL
Lizak, Laura Lee ....Shallotte, NC
Lizana, Bruce H. ....Metairie, LA
Lizardi, Oscar S. ....Tucson, AZ
Lizardo, Esteban ....Los Angeles, CA
Lizarraga, Frank J., Jr., Law Offices of
Rancho Cucamonga, CA
Lizarraga, Juan J. ....New Orleans, LA
Lizee, Maurice C. ....Minneapolis, MN
Lizotte, Andrew G. ....Boston, MA
Lizotte, J. Colin ....Milford, NH
Lizza, Charles M. ....Newark, NJ
Lizza, Chris I ....Mammoth Lakes, CA
Lizza, John August ....Denver, CO
Lizza, John B. ....Detroit, MI
Lizza, Marianne K. ....Denver, CO
Lizza, Robert V. ....Boston, MA
Lizza, Thomas M. ....Grosse Pointe, MI
Lizza, Tiberio P. ....Belvedere-Tiburon, CA
Lizzi, Christopher D. ....Moncks Corner, SC
Lizzi, Thomas ....Pittsburgh, PA
Lizzul, Daniel M. ....Department of the Navy, Office of the Judge Advocate General, GV
Ljungman, Nils H., Jr. ....Greensburg, PA
Ljungquist, Carol S. ....Norwalk, CT
Ljutich, George P. ....Trenton, NJ
Llaca, Francisco G., Jr. ....Miami, FL
Llacar, Perfecto C., Jr. ....Los Angeles, CA
Llach, Salvador M. ....Chicago, IL
Llaguno, Ferman H. ....Los Angeles, CA
Llaguno, Pedro P. ....Miami, FL
Llamas, Cynthia C. ....El Paso, TX
Llamzon, Georgia Cullen ....Evanston, IL
Llanas, Maureen ....San Antonio, TX
Llanes, Andres M. ....Highland Park, IL
Llaneta, Ben M. ....San Diego, CA
Llantin, Betty A. ....Bronx, NY
Llaurado, Thadd J. ....Mequon, WI
Milwaukee, WI
Racine, WI
Llaurado, Wilfred A. ....Orange, CA
Lleras, Lorenzo M. ....Woodbridge, VA
Llerena, Ada G. ....Miami, FL
Llerena, Gustavo D. ....Miami, FL
Llerena, Jose Antonio ....Miami, FL
Llerena, Kristina M. ....Coral Gables, FL
Llewellyn, Adam K.
Department Of Veterans Affairs, Office of the General Counsel, GV
Llewellyn, Barbara A. ....Ocala, FL
Llewellyn, Charles W. ....New York, NY
Llewellyn, David J., Law Office of
Atlanta, GA
Conyers, GA
Llewellyn, David L., Jr. ....Fair Oaks, CA
Llewellyn, Don W. ....Villanova, PA
Llewellyn, James D. (Lew) ....Kinston, NC
Llewellyn, James M., Jr. ....Fort Smith, AR
Llewellyn, Jim O. ....Atlanta, GA
Llewellyn, John Carter ....Fort Worth, TX
Llewellyn, John Crawford ....Fort Worth, TX
Llewellyn, John J. ....Louisville, KY
Llewellyn, John R. ....Rockland, MA
Llewellyn, John R., Law Offices of
Olney, MD
Llewellyn, John R., Law Offices of
Rockville, MD
Llewellyn, Kathleen ....Monterey, CA
Santa Cruz, CA
Llewellyn, Leroy D. B. ....Golden, CO
Llewellyn & Llewellyn ....Fort Worth, TX
Llewellyn, Paul C. ....New York, NY
Llewellyn, Richard E., II
South Pasadena, CA
Llewellyn, Richard H., Jr. ....Los Angeles, CA
Llewellyn & Schaefer ....Rockland, MA
Llewellyn, Stephen
Equal Employment Opportunity Commission, GV
Llewellyn, Stephen E. ....Spokane, WA
Llewellyn, Susan J. ....Clarksburg, WV
Llewellyn, Thomas Sayre
Washington, DC
Llewellyn, Virginia R. ....Seattle, WA
Llewellyn, Warren H. ....New York, NY
Llewelyn, Elaine S. ....Kirkland, WA
Llop, Cristina ....San Francisco, CA
Llop, Rita J. ....Eastman, GA
Llorca, Manuel R. ....Stamford, CT
New York, NY
Lloreda, Carlos A., Jr., Law Offices of
Fillmore, CA
Lloreda, Carlos A., Jr., Law Office of
Los Angeles, CA
Lloreda, Carlos A., Jr., Law Offices of
Santa Paula, CA
Ventura, CA
Llorens, Armando ....San Juan, PR
Llorens, Hector E., Jr. ....Atlanta, GA
Llorens, Ramon L. ....San Juan, PR
Llorente, Alex J. ....Aliso Viejo, CA
Lloret, Richard A. ....Abingdon, VA
Llorian, Sergio ....New York, NY
Llorian, Sergio A. ....New York, NY
Lloveras-Otero, Ramon ....San Juan, PR
Llovet, Madeleine ....San Juan, PR
Lloyd, Alex ....Hartford, CT
Lloyd, Althea ....Brattleboro, VT
Lloyd, Andrew ....San Francisco, CA
Lloyd, Andrew F., (A Professional Corporation) ....San Diego, CA
Lloyd, Angela Marie ....New York, NY
Lloyd, Angelica D. ....Norfolk, VA
Lloyd, Ann Burke ....Baltimore, MD
Lloyd, Anna R. ....Washington, DC
Lloyd, Arthur E. ....Payson, AZ
Lloyd, Benita A. ....Kill Devil Hills, NC
Lloyd, Brent F. ....Boise, ID
Lloyd, Brian G. ....Salt Lake City, UT
Lloyd, C. Jerre ....Lake Charles, LA
Lloyd, C. Parkinson ....Salt Lake City, UT
Lloyd, Carol Hansberger ....Boise, ID
Lloyd, Charles A. ....Greensboro, NC
Lloyd, Charles Earl ....Los Angeles, CA
Lloyd, Charles Earl, A Law Corporation
Los Angeles, CA
Lloyd, Charles J. ....Minneapolis, MN
Lloyd, Charles R. ....Minneapolis, MN
Lloyd, David ....Portland, OR
Lloyd, David A. ....Charlotte, NC
LLoyd, David B. ....Menlo Park, CA
Lloyd, David J. ....Chicago, IL
Lloyd, David J. ....Chatham, NJ
Lloyd, David L., Jr. ....Cincinnati, OH
Lloyd, David O. ....New York, NY
Lloyd, David R.
Environmental Protection Agency, Office of the General Counsel, GV
Lloyd, Dean ....Menlo Park, CA
Lloyd, Debora ....Santa Ana, CA
Lloyd, Dennis Weston ....Kansas City, MO
Lloyd, Dinning, Boggs & Dinning
Demopolis, AL
Eutaw, AL
Linden, AL
Livingston, AL
Lloyd, Dominic A. ....Denver, CO
Lloyd, Don K. ....Portland, OR
Lloyd, Edward L. ....Newark, NJ
Lloyd, Edward W. ....Orange, CA
Lloyd, Francis L., Jr. ....Knoxville, TN
Lloyd, Francis P. ....Monterey, CA
Lloyd, Frank ....Hackensack, NJ
Lloyd, Frank H., Jr. ....Pittsford, NY
Lloyd, Frank V. D. ....Hackensack, NJ
New York, NY
Lloyd, Frank W. ....Washington, DC
Lloyd, Franklin T. ....San Diego, CA
Lloyd, Gary ....San Francisco, CA
Lloyd, George W. ....Boston, MA
Lloyd, Glynis
General Services Administration, Office of the General Counsel, GV
Lloyd, Gosselink, Blevins, Rochelle, Baldwin & Townsend, P.C. ....Austin, TX
Georgetown, TX
San Antonio, TX
Lloyd, Gregory M. ....Costa Mesa, CA
Lloyd, Harold ....Houston, TX
Lloyd, Harold A. ....Greensboro, NC
Lloyd, Harold, Inc., Law Offices of
Houston, TX
Lloyd, Henry M., (P.C.) ....Washington, DC
Lloyd, Hoskins & Pierce ....Fort Pierce, FL
Lloyd, Howard R., Jr. ....San Jose, CA
Lloyd, Hugh A. ....Demopolis, AL
Lloyd, J. Russell ....Louisville, KY
Lloyd, J. Vernon ....Evanston, IL
Lloyd, James D. ....Philadelphia, PA
Lloyd, James E. ....Canton, IL
Lloyd, James E., (P.C.) ....Washington, IA

Lloyd, James H., III ... Hartford, CT
Stamford, CT
Lloyd, James M. ... Jeffersonville, IN
Louisville, KY
Lloyd, James M. ... New York, NY
Lloyd, James Michael ... Asheville, NC
Lloyd, James S. ... Birmingham, AL
Lloyd, James T. ... Washington, DC
Lloyd, James T., Jr. ... Norfolk, VA
Lloyd, James T., Jr., P.C. ... Norfolk, VA
Lloyd, James Woodman ... New York, NY
Lloyd, Jaqluin M. Bickmore ... Dallas, TX
Lloyd, Jeff ... Gainesville, FL
Orlando, FL
Lloyd, Jennifer M. ... Los Angeles, CA
Lloyd, Jeremiah A. ... Louisville, KY
Lloyd, Jim ... Sand Springs, OK
Lloyd, John C. ... Raleigh, NC
Lloyd, John D. ... Osceola, IA
Lloyd, John H., IV ... Mishawaka, IN
Lloyd, John J. ... Tuscaloosa, AL
Lloyd, John, Jr. ... St. Petersburg, FL
Lloyd, John, Jr., P.A. ... St. Petersburg, FL
Lloyd, John P. ... Philadelphia, PA
Lloyd, John R. ... Teaneck, NJ
Lloyd, John S. ... Miami, FL
Lloyd, John Van ... Savannah, GA
Lloyd, Joseph A. ... Ann Arbor, MI
Lloyd, K. Anne ... Bedford, NH
Lloyd, Kane, Wieder & Willis, P.A.
Ellicott City, MD
Lloyd, Karen ... Washington, DC
Lloyd, Karen A. ... Brooksville, FL
Lloyd, Karen Ann P. ... Indianapolis, IN
Lloyd, Kurt D. ... Chicago, IL
Lloyd, L. Judson ... Deerfield Beach, FL
Lloyd, Laura Towe ... Gadsden, AL
Lloyd, Lee B. ... Birmingham, AL
Lloyd, Leona L. ... Detroit, MI
Lloyd, Leonard W. ... Robbinsville, NC
Lloyd, Linda ... Sautee-Nacoochee, GA
Lloyd, Lisa A. ... Winamac, IN
Lloyd & Lloyd ... Sand Springs, OK
Lloyd, Marcea Bland ... Irving, TX
Lloyd, Margaret M. ... Hammond, IN
Lloyd, Mark I. ... Washington, DC
Lloyd, Marshall O. ... Boca Raton, FL
Lloyd, Mary English ... Palm Desert, CA
Lloyd, Mary Kazaleh ... Houston, TX
Lloyd, Mary Margaret ... Evansville, IN
Lloyd & McDaniel ... Jeffersonville, IN
Lexington, KY
Louisville, KY
Lloyd, Michael A. ... Los Angeles, CA
Lloyd, Michael D. ... Encinitas, CA
Lloyd, Michael E. ... Pittsburgh, PA
Lloyd, Michelle Andreshak
Milwaukee, WI
Lloyd, Nancy ... Sand Springs, OK
Lloyd, Neil ... Chicago, IL
Lloyd, O. M. ... Santa Barbara, CA
Lloyd, Patricia ... Boston, MA
Lloyd, Patrick M. ... Burlington, WI
Salem, WI
Lloyd, Patrick R. ... Dallas, TX
Lloyd, Paula J. ... Columbus, OH
Lloyd, Peter A. ... Barnstable, MA
LLoyd, Peter M. ... Plano, TX
Lloyd, Phenicie, Lynch & Kelly, S.C.
Burlington, WI
Salem, WI
Lloyd, Philip A., II ... Akron, OH
Lloyd, Priscilla W. ... Irvine, CA
Lloyd, R. Douglas ... Decatur, GA
Lloyd, Raymond J. ... Treasure Island, FL
Lloyd, Richard D. ... Prince Frederick, MD
Lloyd, Rjay ... Phoenix, AZ
Lloyd, Robert A. ... Chicago, IL
Lloyd, Robert B., Jr. ... Greensboro, NC
Lloyd, Robert H. ... Austin, TX
San Antonio, TX
Lloyd, Robert J. ... Concord, NH
Lloyd, Robert James, III ... McLean, VA
Lloyd, Robert M. ... Fort Pierce, FL
Lloyd, Robert M. ... Knoxville, TN
Lloyd, Robert R., Jr. ... Glen Rock, PA
Shrewsbury, PA
York, PA
Lloyd, Robert W. ... Daytona Beach, FL
Lloyd, Robin A., Sr. ... Vero Beach, FL
Lloyd, Robin A., Sr. & Associates, P.A.
Vero Beach, FL
Lloyd, Roger F. ... Somerset, NJ
Lloyd, Ross J. ... North Andover, MA
Lloyd, Russell T. ... Houston, TX
Lloyd, Samuel T., Jr. ... Madison, MS
Lloyd, Schreiber & Gray, P.C.
Birmingham, AL
Lloyd, Scott Alan ... Bellaire, OH
Lloyd, Scott Andrew ... Chardon, OH
Lloyd, Seth M. ... Detroit, MI
Lloyd, Steven R. ... Westfield, IN
Lloyd, Terry L. ... Atlanta, GA
Lloyd, Theresa Smith ... Bloomfield Hills, MI
Lloyd, Thomas A. ... Pierre, SD
Lloyd, Thomas E. ... Ellicott City, MD
Lloyd, Thomas J. ... Akron, OH
Lloyd, Thomas P. ... Washington, DC
Lloyd, Thomas P. ... Roanoke, VA
Lloyd, Thomas R. ... The Woodlands, TX
Lloyd, Thomas W. ... Ashland, OR
Lloyd, Thos. R. ... Cambridge, OH
Lloyd, Timothy A. ... Washington, DC
Lloyd, Tracey J. ... Bellaire, OH
Lloyd, Trebor ... New York, NY
Lloyd, Vincent A. ... Fort Pierce, FL
Lloyd, W. Baldwin ... Jackson, MS
Lloyd, W. David ... Greensboro, NC
Lloyd, W. Waldan ... Salt Lake City, UT
Lloyd, Walter Daniel ... Houston, TX
Lloyd, Wendy S. ... Fresno, CA
Lloyd, William B., Jr. ... Birmingham, AL
Lloyd, William Bart ... Boston, MA
Lloyd, William E., Jr. ... Beverly Hills, CA
Lloyd, William F. ... Chicago, IL
Lloyd, William M. ... Chicago, IL
Lloyd, William P. ... Oak Brook, IL
Lloyd, William R., Jr. ... Somerset, PA
Lloyd, Winston P. ... Raleigh, NC
Lloyd Aho, Marianne ... Jacksonville, FL
Lloyd-Pittler, Bethann R. ... Pittsburgh, PA
Llusa, Pilar ... Houston, TX
Lo, Albert ... Washington, DC
Lo, Allen M. ... Palo Alto, CA
Lo, Benjamin T. ... Chicago, IL
Lo, Clifford ... Burbank, CA
Lo, David W. ... Honolulu, HI
Lo, Dobbin P. ... Rancho Cucamonga, CA
Lo, Eva ... New York, NY
Lo, Hung Kay ... Albany, NY
Lo, Josephine S. ... Washington, DC
Lo, Karl C. ... Palo Alto, CA
Lo, Lawrence ... Flushing, NY
Lo, Margaret ... East Brunswick, NJ
Lo, Paul C. ... Merced, CA
Lo, Sia ... St. Paul, MN
Lo, Siu K. ... New York, NY
Lo, Thierry K. ... Long Beach, CA
Lo, Thomas J. ... Costa Mesa, CA
Lo, Vincent ... Houston, TX
Loach, Jennifer C. ... New York, NY
Loach, Judith J. ... Oakland, CA
Loacker, John R. ... Gresham, OR
Loacker, Lynn J. ... Seattle, WA
Loadholt, Miles ... Barnwell, SC
Loadman, David J. ... San Diego, CA
Loafman, William M. ... New York, NY
Loaiza, Jacqueline (Jackie)
San Diego, CA
Loalbo & Bassetti, LLC
Florham Park, NJ
Morristown, NJ
Newark, NJ
New York, NY
Loalbo, John M. ... Florham Park, NJ
Loanzon, Tristan ... Washington, DC
Loar, Jeanne E. ... Austin, TX
Loar, Warren N., IV ... Mount Vernon, IL
Loats, Frederick G. ... Coeur d'Alene, ID
Loats, J. Timothy, Law Offices of
Aurora, IL
Lob, Ferdinand M. ... New Orleans, LA
Lobach, Jeffrey D. ... Hanover, PA
York, PA
Lobaco, Francisco ... Sacramento, CA
Lobasz, M. Thomas ... Tampa, FL
West Palm Beach, FL
Lobato, David L. ... Pueblo, CO
Lobato, Edwin J. ... Alamosa, CO
Lobato, Emmanuel J. ... Scarsdale, NY
Lobato, Emmanuel Joseph
Sleepy Hollow, NY
Lobato, Francesca ... Santa Fe, NM
Lobato Law Offices ... Sleepy Hollow, NY
Lobato, LeAnn M. ... Tulsa, OK
LoBaugh, Leslie E., Jr. ... Syracuse, NY
Lobaugh, Stacey ... Ponca City, OK
Lobb, Brandon S. ... Houston, TX
Lobb, Charles E., Jr. ... Houston, TX
Lobb, Christopher Montez ... Cincinnati, OH
Lobb Cliff & Roth, LLP ... Riverside, CA
Lobb, J. Mark ... Riverside, CA
Lobb, James T. ... Louisville, KY
Lobb, Joseph R. ... Southfield, MI
Lobb, Lawrence W. ... Monroe, MI
Lobb, William J. ... Bartow, FL
Lobban, Charles M. ... Alderson, WV
Lobben, Kathleen F. ... Riverhead, NY
Lobbin, Stephen M. ... Newport Beach, CA
Lobdell, Charles A., III ... Fort Pierce, FL
Lobdell, David W. ... Northbrook, IL
Lobdell, Emily F. ... Canandaigua, NY
Lobdell, H. Lewis, Jr. ... Pittsburgh, PA
Lobdell, Henry R. ... Honolulu, HI
Lobdell, Kara A. ... New York, NY
Lobdell, Katherine Laffey ... Pittsburgh, PA
Lobdell, Martin J. ... San Francisco, CA
Lobdell, Robert C. ... Long Beach, CA
Lobdell, Teresa M. ... Palo Alto, CA
Lobe, Joshua B. ... Burlington, VT
Lobe, Shari L. ... Hyannis, MA
Lobeck, Daniel J. ... Sarasota, FL
Lobeck & Hanson, P.A. ... Sarasota, FL
Lobel, Alan D. ... St. Louis, MO
Lobel, Arthur M. ... Philadelphia, PA
Lobel, Beth R. ... New York, NY
Lobel, Debra ... East Hampton, NY
Lobel, Douglas A. ... New York, NY
Lobel, Douglas P. ... Washington, DC
Lobel, Elliot D., P.C. ... Boston, MA
Lobel, Gary D. ... Anaheim, CA
Lobel, Ira B. ... Albany, NY
Lobel, Jodi Lynn ... Philadelphia, PA
Lobel, Jos. M. ... New York, NY
Lobel, Jules ... Pittsburgh, PA
Lobel, Lenore Zug ... Boston, MA
Lobel, Martin ... Washington, DC
Lobel, Meredith Anne ... Chatsworth, CA
Lobel, Myra E. ... New York, NY
Lobel, Novins & Lamont ... Washington, DC
Lobel & Opera LLP ... Irvine, CA
Lobel, Peter David ... New York, NY
Lobel, Rhona J. ... New York, NY
Lobel, Richard S. ... New York, NY
Lobel, Sheldon ... New York, NY
Lobel, Sheldon, P.C. ... New York, NY
Lobel, Shirley ... Dallas, TX
Lobel, Susan Jacobs ... New York, NY
Lobel, William N. ... Irvine, CA
Lobel-Angel, Meredith A. ... Los Angeles, CA
Lobell, Anne M. ... Department of Justice,
Civil Division, GV
Lobell, Beverly O. ... New York, NY
Lobell, Carl D., (P.C.) ... New York, NY
Lobell, J. Jay ... New York, NY
Lobell, Steven S. ... Topeka, KS
LoBello, Charles C. ... Las Vegas, NV
LoBello, Edward J. ... New York, NY
Lo Bello & Lo Bello ... Las Vegas, NV
LoBello, Mark A. ... Las Vegas, NV
LoBello, Michele Touby ... Las Vegas, NV
Lobello, Patricia A. ... San Dimas, CA
Lobel-Schneider, Jennifer S. ... Boston, MA
Lobenfeld, Eric J. ... New York, NY
Lobenherz, William E. ... Lansing, MI
Lobenhofer, Louis F. ... Ada, OH
Lobenthal, Joseph S., Jr. ... New York, NY
Lobenthal, Nicholas W. ... New York, NY
Lober, Anne ... Soquel, CA
Lober, Charles E. ... Greenwood, SC
Lober, James M. ... Houston, TX
Lober, Jere E. ... Viera, FL
Lober, Maureen Macy ... Litchfield, IL
Springfield, IL
Lober, Michael J. ... Macon, GA
Lober, Richard E. ... Tallahassee, FL
Lober, Terence A. ... Leavenworth, KS
Loberg, Harry J. ... Santa Barbara, CA
Loberg, Robert L. ... Ellsworth, WI
Loberman, Harry ... Claremont, CA
Lobert & Downey ... Big Rapids, MI
Lobert, James E. ... Arlington, TX
Lobert, John C. ... McLean, VA
Lobert, Keith F. ... Big Rapids, MI
Lobertini, Robert S. ... Knoxville, TN
Lobes, Loretta E. ... Pittsburgh, PA
Lobet, Ernest S. ... Glen Cove, NY
LoBianco, Joseph ... Providence, RI
Lo Bianco, Laura A. ... Tempe, AZ
LoBianco, Laura A. ... New York, NY
Lobin, Marshall E. ... Chicago, IL
Lobin & Soren, Ltd. ... Chicago, IL
Lobingier, David B., A Prof. Corp., Law
Offices of ... Fort Worth, TX
Lobingier, David Brooks ... Fort Worth, TX
LoBiondo, Anthony R. ... Middletown, NY
LoBiondo, George R. ... Rosenhayn, NJ
Lobiondo, Juliana Muyot
Poughkeepsie, NY
Lobis, Jessica R. ... San Diego, CA
Lobl, David ... New York, NY
Lobl, Herbert M. ... New York, NY
Lobl, Peter W. ... Washington, DC
Lobl, Richard T. ... Encino, CA
Loblack, Peter G. ... Fort Lauderdale, FL
Loble, C. Bruce ... Bozeman, MT
Loble, Jason P. ... Bellevue, WA
Loble, Lester H., II ... Bismarck, ND
Loble, Sarah A. ... Bellevue, WA
Lobley, Alan H. ... Indianapolis, IN
Lobley, Joseph H. ... Austin, TX
Fort Worth, TX
Houston, TX
Lobman, Carnahan, Batt, Angelle & Nader, A Professional Corporation
New Orleans, LA
Lobman, Dorian L. ... New Orleans, LA
Lobman, Edward P. ... New Orleans, LA
Lobman, Helaine F. ... Somerset, NJ
Lobner, Breton K. ... Los Angeles, CA
Lobner, Kneeland H. ... Sacramento, CA
Lobo, Alfred D. ... Cleveland, OH
Lobo, Anita C. ... Portland, OR
Lobo, Deborah E. ... Department of Commerce,
Patent and Trademark Office, GV
Lobo, Derek J. ... San Diego, CA
Lobo, Fatima T. ... Manchester, CT
Lobo, Glyndwr P. ... New York, NY
Lobo, Jason M. ... Hartford, CT
Lobo, Katherine Kendall ... Chicago, IL
Lobo, Toinette Carmen ... Winchester, VA
Loboda, Patricia ... Midland, MI
Lobodiak, Nestor ... Cedar Rapids, IA
Iowa City, IA
Lobos, Melissa S. ... Pittsburgh, PA
Lobos, Raymond J. ... Mifflinburg, PA
LoBosco, Carmine D. ... Chappaqua, NY
New York, NY
Lo Bosco, Francis ... Princeton, NJ
Lo Bosco, Francis M. ... Princeton, NJ
LoBosco, John ... New York, NY
Lobozzo, James V., Jr., (P.A.) ... Sebring, FL
Lobrano, E. P., Jr. ... Ridgeland, MS
Lobrano, Francis J. ... Belle Chasse, LA
Lobrano, John D. (IBA) ... New York, NY
Lobrano, Joyce Cossich ... Belle Chasse, LA
Lobrano & Kincaid, P.L. ... Jacksonville, FL
Lobrano & Lobrano, L.L.C.
Belle Chasse, LA
New Orleans, LA
Lobrano, Robert L. ... Belle Chasse, LA
Lobrano, Stephen D. ... Jacksonville, FL
Lobre, Mark T. ... San Francisco, CA
Lobred, Thomas L. ... Treasury Department,
Office of Regulations and Rulings, GV
Lobree, Fleur J. ... Miami, FL
Lobsenz, Charles B. ... Washington, DC
Lobsenz, James E. ... Seattle, WA
Lobsenz, James K. ... Washington, DC
Lobsenz, Theodore A. ... Haledon, NJ
Lobstein, Tim ... Fort Worth, TX
LoBue, Alan E. ... Phoenix, AZ
LoBue, Donald A. ... Springfield, IL
LoBue, Joseph W. ... Department of Justice,
Civil Division, GV
LoBue, Nancy D.
Department of Transportation,
Federal Aviation Administration, GV
LoBue, Robert P. ... Wilmington, DE
LoBue, Robert P. ... New York, NY
Lobue, Sandi Aucoin ... Lake Charles, LA
LoBue, Thomas S. ... Bremerton, WA
Lobur, John S. ... Howell, MI
Lobur, John S., P.C. ... Howell, MI
LoBurgio, Nicholas J. ... Denver, CO
Lobus, John A. ... Lakewood, CO
Localio, A. Russell ... Deerfield, MA
Locallo, Daniel M. ... Chicago, IL
Locallo, John G. ... Chicago, IL
Locallo, Joseph F., Jr. ... Chicago, IL
Locante, Frank G. ... Milwaukee, WI
Locante, Shari LePage ... Cashton, WI
Sparta, WI
Locario, Elizabeth J. ... Enfield, CT
LoCasale, Gregory T. ... Philadelphia, PA
Locascio, Anthony V. ... Red Bank, NJ
Locascio, David W. ... Houston, TX
Locascio, Dorothy Rose ... New York, NY
LoCascio, Gregg F. ... Washington, DC
LoCascio, Jeanne Allyson ... Cumming, GA
LoCascio, Joseph C. ... White Plains, NY
Locascio, Joseph H. ... Kansas City, MO
LoCascio, Joseph R., Jr.
Hastings-On-Hudson, NY
Locascio, Kristina Rak ... Roseland, NJ
Locascio, Lawrence J., Jr. ... Lockport, IL
Locascio, Lori ... Boston, MA
Locascio, Mark A. ... Northbrook, IL
LoCascio, P. Renee ... Los Angeles, CA
Locascio, Peter A. ... Red Bank, NJ
LoCascio, Thomas J. ... Akron, OH
LoCascio, Thomas Joseph, Co., L.P.A.
Akron, OH
LoCastro, Jean D. ... Wilmington, DE
Locatelli, Alexander L. ... Union City, NJ
Locatelli, Tina ... New York, NY
Richmond, VA
Loccke & Correia ... Hackensack, NJ
Loccke, Richard D. ... Hackensack, NJ
Loch, Robert A. ... Pittsburgh, PA
Lochabay, David ... Madison, TN
Lochbichler, Jennifer Lynn ... Houston, TX
Lochbihler, Frederick V. ... Chicago, IL
Lochead, James S. ... Valencia, CA
Locher, Albert C. ... Sacramento, CA
Locher, Bruce D. ... Springfield, IL
Locher, Ellis ... Houston, TX
Locher, Gabriel B. ... Bingham Farms, MI
Locher, James J. ... Mason City, IA
Locher, John F. ... Marion, IA
Locher, John M. ... Farley, IA
Locher, Landol J. ... Coon Rapids, MN
Locher, Locher & Strittmatter
Monticello, IA
Locher, Ralph E. ... Hollywood, FL
Locher, Thomas M. ... Omaha, NE
Locher, W. Scott ... Houston, TX
Locher, William D. ... Los Angeles, CA
Lochetta, Nicholas J., II ... Flemington, NJ
Lochhead, George S. ... St. Louis, MO
Lochhead, Guy R. ... Claremont, CA
Lochhead, James S.
Glenwood Springs, CO
Lochhead, Robert B. ... Salt Lake City, UT
Lochiatto, Albert A. ... Mystic, CT
Lochiatto, Anthony J. ... Boston, MA
Lochiatto & Lawrence ... Mystic, CT
Lochinger, Shawn D. ... Harrisburg, PA
Lochmann, Michael W. ... Kansas City, MO
Lochmiller, Beth Ann ... Elizabethtown, KY
Lochner, Glenn R. ... Louisville, KY
Lochner, James P. ... Pittsburgh, PA
Lochner, Jeffry W. ... San Jose, CA
Lochner, Nancy L. ... Minneapolis, MN
Lochner, Ray N. ... Pittsburgh, PA
Lochner, Scott J. ... Los Angeles, CA
Lochner, Stephen ... Mount Kisco, NY
Lochner, Thomas R. ... Buffalo, NY
Lochnicht, John G. ... Clearwater, FL
Lochray, Paul J. ... Storm Lake, IA
Lochridge, James Allen, Jr. ... Lafayette, LA
Lochridge, Lisa Curtis ... Dallas, TX
Lochridge, Lloyd ... Austin, TX
Lochridge, Patton G. ... Austin, TX
Lochridge, Robert D. ... Dallas, TX
Lochrie, Robert B., III
Fort Lauderdale, FL
Lochry, Thomas J. ... Dallas, TX
Lochry, Thomas J., P.C. ... Dallas, TX
Fort Worth, TX
Lochtan, Brian Michael ... Santa Rosa, CA
Lochte, Albert J. ... Bowie, MD
Lochte, Darrell G. ... Kerrville, TX
Lochte Law Office ... Kerrville, TX
Lo Cicero, Anthony F. ... New York, NY
LoCicero, Carol J. ... Tampa, FL
LoCicero, Joseph A. ... New York, NY
Lo Cicero, Michael Vincent ... Oak Brook, IL
Lo Cicero, Thos. V. ... St. Clair Shores, MI
Lociciro, Patricia S. ... New York, NY
Lock, Caroline Hudson ... Greensboro, NC
Lock, Charles M. ... St. Louis, MO
Lock, Connie C. ... San Antonio, TX
Lock, Cynthia A. ... Los Angeles, CA
Lock, David L. ... New York, NY
Lock, Donald W. ... Melbourne, FL
Lock, George C. ... New York, NY
Lock, Herbert F. ... Rockville, MD
Lock, Herschel ... Harrisburg, PA
Lock, James W. ... San Diego, CA
Lock, John ... Austin, TX

Lock, John P. .... Philadelphia, PA
Lock, Joshua D. .... Harrisburg, PA
Lock, Louise A. .... Baltimore, MD
Towson, MD
Lock, Reinier H. J. H. (IBA)
Washington, DC
Lock, Robert E. .... Jacksonville, NC
Lock, Robert K., Jr. .... Chicago, IL
Lock, Shmuel T. .... New York, NY
Lock, Thomas H. .... Smithfield, NC
Lock & Virr, P.C. .... Austin, TX
Lock, William J. .... Albuquerque, NM
Lockaby, Robert L., Jr. .... Chattanooga, TN
Lockard, Betty Pine .... Warrensburg, MO
Lockard & Bingham .... Memphis, TN
Lockard, Clinton E. .... Fairhope, AL
Lockard, David L. .... Philadelphia, PA
Lockard, David W. .... Las Vegas, NV
Lockard, Dennis R.
Department of the Air Force, Office of the Judge Advocate General, GV
Lockard, Frank P. .... East Hartford, CT
Lockard, H. T. .... Memphis, TN
Lockard, James Harry .... Norman, OK
Lockard, James R. .... Biloxi, MS
Lockard, John R. .... Norfolk, VA
Lockard, Leslie .... Boston, MA
Lockard, Mary E. .... Metairie, LA
Lockard, Sam P. .... Bristol, WV
Lockard, Theresa .... Chicago, IL
Lockard, William H., IV .... Los Angeles, CA
Lockard, William Stanley .... Shreveport, LA
Lockary, Lillian Harris .... Macon, GA
Locke, Andrew C. .... Oakland, CA
Locke, Arthur B. .... West Granby, CT
Locke, Aurelle S. .... West Hartford, CT
Locke, Barbara Ehrich .... Miami, FL
Locke, Berry D. .... Beverly Hills, CA
Locke, Beth Ann .... Springfield, MA
Locke, Bruce .... Sacramento, CA
Locke, Carey P. .... Corpus Christi, TX
Locke, Cathy .... College Station, TX
Locke, Charles F.A. .... Newport, NH
Locke, Charles T., (P.C.) .... Stamford, CT
New York, NY
Locke, Christopher M. .... New York, NY
Locke, Christopher Ronald .... Hockessin, DE
Locke, Colleen J. .... Jefferson, WI
Locke, Cynthia M. .... Indianapolis, IN
Locke, David A. .... Lafayette, IN
Locke, David B. .... Worcester, MA
Locke, David H. .... Wellesley, MA
Locke, Donald E. .... Milwaukee, WI
Locke, Donald T. .... Birmingham, AL
Locke, Douglas L. .... Portland, OR
Locke, Edgar R. .... Anchorage, AK
Locke, Edward B. .... New York, NY
Locke, Fullerton & Lundwall
Wellesley, MA
Locke, Gary F. .... Olympia, WA
Locke, Gene L. .... Houston, TX
Locke, George A. .... San Francisco, CA
Locke, Gordon .... New Rochelle, NY
Locke, Gregory F. .... Ashland, OH
Locke, Henry .... Ridgewood, NY
Locke & Herbert .... Stamford, CT
New York, NY
Locke, James A. .... Buffalo, NY
Locke, James A., III .... Rochester, NY
Locke, James T. .... Milwaukee, WI
Locke, James W. .... Bryan, TX
Locke, Jane Hoffman .... Chicago, IL
Locke, Jeffrey A. .... Boston, MA
Locke, Jeffrey A. .... St. Paul, MN
Locke, Jeffrey C. .... Atascadero, CA
Locke, Jennifer .... Boston, MA
Locke, Jennifer B. .... Hauppauge, NY
Locke, JoAnn R. .... Seattle, WA
Locke, Joanne Callahan .... Wellesley, MA
Locke, Joanne Maas .... Natick, MA
Locke, Joel B. .... Odessa, TX
Locke, John A. .... Wellesley, MA
Locke, John C. .... Clearwater, FL
Locke, John H. .... Roanoke, VA
Locke, John R., Jr. .... San Antonio, TX
Locke, Keltner W. .... Nashville, TN
Locke, Kevin .... Oklahoma City, OK
Locke, Kevin J. .... Cleveland, OH
Locke, Kevin R. .... Kansas City, MO
Locke, Kristin N. .... Los Angeles, CA
Locke, Larry G. .... Irving, TX
Locke, Laurence S. .... Boston, MA
Locke, Lawrence Alan .... Los Angeles, CA
Locke, Leslie D. .... Chicago, IL
Locke Liddell & Sapp LLP
New Orleans, LA
Austin, TX
Dallas, TX
Houston, TX
Locke, Marcia C. .... Tampa, FL
Locke, Mary E. .... Philadelphia, PA
Locke, Mary Gaines .... Hodgenville, KY
Locke, Maury D. .... Pittsburgh, PA
Locke, Merritt S. .... Rome, NY
Utica, NY
Locke, Nancy June .... Houston, TX
Locke, Nancy Nordstrom .... Ashland, OH
Locke, Patricia R. .... Lincoln, ME
Locke, Paul A. .... Washington, DC
Locke, Paul E. .... San Francisco, CA
Locke, Paul T. .... Woodland Hills, CA
Locke, Paulette M. .... Fayetteville, AR
Locke, Philip .... Glastonbury, CT
Locke Purnell Rain Harrell, A Professional Corporation .... New Orleans, LA
Austin, TX
Dallas, TX
Locke, R. Christopher .... San Francisco, CA

Locke Reynolds LLP .... Indianapolis, IN
Locke, Richard .... Richmond, VA
Locke, Richard F. .... San Francisco, CA
Locke, Robert .... Muskogee, OK
Locke, Robert B. .... Goleta, CA
Locke, Robert L. .... San Diego, CA
Locke, Ronald J. .... Huntingdon, PA
Locke, Ronald P. .... Bridgeview, IL
Locke, Rudman & Aberle
Beverly Hills, CA
Locke, Scott D. .... New York, NY
Locke, Shelley K. .... San Francisco, CA
Locke, Susan S. .... Cleveland, OH
Locke, Teresa D. .... Denver, CO
Locke, Thomas C. .... Independence, MO
Locke, Thomas S. .... Fort Wayne, IN
Locke, Thomas S. .... Agawam, MA
Locke, Thomas T. .... Washington, DC
Locke, Wendell T. .... Miami, FL
Locke, William Darin .... Superior, CO
Locke, William H., Jr. .... Austin, TX
Locke, William M. .... McMinnville, TN
Locke, W. O. .... Emeryville, CA
Lockeby, W. Gregory .... Orlando, FL
Lockemy, James E. .... Dillon, SC
Locken, Idean M. .... Lakota, ND
Lockenvitz, Bradley H. .... Linn, MO
Locke-Paddon, William F. .... Watsonville, CA
Locker, Aaron .... New York, NY
Locker, Alan N. .... New York, NY
Locker, Andrew S. .... Atlanta, GA
Locker, Brett .... Santa Barbara, CA
Locker, Bryan L. .... West Linn, OR
Locker, Charles .... Lincolnwood, IL
Locker, Elizabeth A. .... Summit, NJ
Locker, Greenberg & Brainin
New York, NY
Locker, Hal A. .... Midland, MI
Locker, Kingdon P. .... White Plains, NY
Locker, Laurence D .... Pompano Beach, FL
Locker, Lawrence C. .... Seattle, WA
Locker, Miles .... San Francisco, CA
Locker, Nina .... Palo Alto, CA
Locker, Paul E. .... Los Angeles, CA
Locker, Robert J. .... Fort Myers, FL
Locker, Walter A., III .... Irving, TX
Lockerbie, Brian D. .... La Grange, GA
Lockerbie, Brian D., P.C. .... La Grange, GA
Lockerby, Caroline Lowdon .... Richmond, VA
Lockerby, James R. .... San Mateo, CA
Lockerby, Michael J. .... Richmond, VA
Lockerman, Allen E., IV .... Atlanta, GA
Lockerman, Ted B. .... Clinton, NC
Lockert, Jimmy P. .... Ashland City, TN
Lockert & Lockert .... Ashland City, TN
Lockert, W. B., Jr. .... Ashland City, TN
Lockett, Cedric L. .... Overland Park, KS
Lockett, Charles D. .... Knoxville, TN
Lockett, George H. .... Harriman, TN
Lockett, Hal H. .... Wichita, KS
Lockett, James K. .... McLean, VA
Lockett, Jerry T. .... Tavares, FL
Lockett, John A., Jr. .... Selma, AL
Lockett, John R. .... Dothan, AL
Mobile, AL
Lockett, Landon J., III .... Austin, TX
Lockett, Laurel E. .... Tampa, FL
Lockett, Mark A. .... Cherry Hill, NJ
Philadelphia, PA
Lockett, Slovis, Rutherford & Weinstein
Knoxville, TN
Lockett, Tyler C. .... Topeka, KS
Lockett, William A. .... Chattanooga, TN
Lockett, William D. .... Sacramento, CA
Lockett, William S., Jr. .... Knoxville, TN
Locketti, Kathleen Ann .... New York, NY
Lockey, Donald V. .... Crofton, MD
Lockhart, Annabelle T.
Department of Labor, GV
Lockhart, Bonnie C. .... Austin, TX
Lockhart, Danny C. .... Birmingham, AL
Lockhart, David L. .... Phoenix, AZ
Lockhart, Dorothea .... New York, NY
Lockhart, Feleica Ann .... Greenville, MS
Lockhart, Frank .... Tulsa, OK
Lockhart, Frederick J., Jr. .... Denver, CO
Lockhart, Gary C. .... Bay Pines, FL
Lockhart, George G. .... Greensboro, NC
Lockhart, Greer E. .... Minneapolis, MN
Lockhart, Gregory Gordon .... Dayton, OH
Lockhart, Harvey G. .... Mineola, NY
New York, NY
Lockhart, Helen C. .... Boston, MA
Lockhart, James B. .... San Francisco, CA
Lockhart, James B. .... Minneapolis, MN
Lockhart, James D. .... Minneapolis, MN
Lockhart, James H. .... Norman, OK
Lockhart, James M. .... Minneapolis, MN
Lockhart, Joe C. .... Arlington, TX
Lockhart, John M. .... Cincinnati, OH
Lockhart, John M., III .... Geneseo, NY
Lockhart, Judith A. .... New York, NY
Lockhart, Kenneth C. .... San Francisco, CA
Lockhart, Kerry L. .... Bakersfield, CA
Lockhart, Kristin Nering .... Minneapolis, MN
Lockhart, Larry L. .... Baltimore, MD
Lockhart, Lionell M. .... Belleview, FL
Lockhart, Lisa C. .... Houston, TX
Lockhart, Margaret J. .... Ann Arbor, MI
Findlay, OH
Toledo, OH
Lockhart, Michael W. .... Beaumont, TX
Lockhart, Nathan A. .... Oklahoma City, OK
Lockhart, Page .... Poughkeepsie, NY
Lockhart, Robert A. .... Charleston, WV
Lockhart, Robert D. .... San Jose, CA
Lockhart, Ronald S. .... New York, NY
Lockhart, Steven B. .... Detroit, MI

Lockhart, Thomas Ashe .... Charlotte, NC
Lockhart, Thomas Ashe, Jr. .... Raleigh, NC
Lockhart, Thomas G. .... Minneapolis, MN
Lockhart, Thomas L. .... Grand Rapids, MI
Lockhart, Timothy J. .... McLean, VA
Lockhart, Tom A. .... Harlingen, TX
Lockhart, W. Kirby .... Little Rock, AR
Lockhart, William J. .... Salt Lake City, UT
Lockhart, William M. .... El Paso, TX
Lockhoof, W. Reed .... Austin, TX
Lockie, David B. .... Elko, NV
Lockie & MacFarlan .... Elko, NV
Lockie, R. Thomas .... Los Angeles, CA
Lockie, Thomas F. .... Orland Park, IL
Lockings, Elton R. .... Houston, TX
Lockings, Elton R., P.C. .... Houston, TX
Lockitski, Stanley A. .... Avon, OH
Locklair, John Wesley, III .... Columbia, SC
Locklair, Tanya D. .... Durham, NC
Locklar, Benjamin L. .... Montgomery, AL
Locklar, Michael G. .... Houston, TX
Locklear, Amy L. .... Washington, DC
Locklear, Arlinda F. .... Jefferson, MD
Locklear, Arnold .... Pembroke, NC
Locklear, Cynthia E. .... Buffalo, NY
Locklear, Jacobs, Sutton & Hunt
Pembroke, NC
Locklear, L. Hampton .... Phoenix, AZ
Locklear, Melanie N. .... Tampa, FL
Locklear, Richard D. .... Salisbury, NC
Locklear, W. Ross .... Stafford, VA
Lockley, John .... San Francisco, CA
Locklin, Jack, Jr. .... Milton, FL
Locklin, James H. .... Los Angeles, CA
Locklin & Jones, P.A. .... Milton, FL
Locklin, Kevin L. .... Manassas, VA
Locklin, Oscar Jackson, Jr. .... Milton, FL
Locklin, Tracy Anderson .... Washington, DC
Locklin-George, Barbara E. .... Washington, DC
Lockman, David M. .... Atlanta, GA
Lockman, John S. .... Mineola, NY
Lockman, Paul A., (Professional Corporation)
Dallas, TX
Lockman, Steven P. .... Washington, DC
Lockman, Stuart M. .... Detroit, MI
Lockner, Diane E. .... Owego, NY
Lockner, Richard W. .... Tacoma, WA
Lockner, Robert E. .... Chicago, IL
Lockney, Thomas M. .... Grand Forks, ND
Locko, Charles .... Los Angeles, CA
Lockridge, Ellen V. .... San Francisco, CA
Lockridge, Gloria M. .... Orlando, FL
Lockridge Grindal Nauen P.L.L.P.
Washington, DC
Minneapolis, MN
Lockridge, J. Eric .... Dallas, TX
Lockridge, John D. .... Knoxville, TN
Lockridge, Richard A. .... Minneapolis, MN
Lockridge, Thomas L. .... Nicholasville, KY
Lockridge, Valone & Beaty, P.L.L.C.
Knoxville, TN
Locks, Amy B. .... Santa Cruz, CA
Locks, Charles S. .... Rockville Centre, NY
Locks, Clifford D. .... Santa Ana, CA
Locks, David H. .... Chicago, IL
Locks, Gene .... Cherry Hill, NJ
Philadelphia, PA
Locks, Michael R. .... Burlingame, CA
Lockshin, Larry .... Sacramento, CA
Lockshin, Lori Caryn .... Ocala, FL
Lockshin, Mary Jo .... Akron, OH
Lockspeiser, Allan L. .... New Brunswick, NJ
Lockton, Andrew W., III
Marina Del Rey, CA
Lockwood, Alan S. .... Rochester, NY
Lockwood, Alejandro A. .... Milwaukee, WI
Lockwood, Andrew W.
Fort Lauderdale, FL
Lockwood, Bert B., Jr. .... Cincinnati, OH
Lockwood, Blair L. .... Denver, CO
Lockwood, Bradley M. .... Williamston, MI
Lockwood, Brian J. .... Riverside, CA
Lockwood, Brian R. .... Gainesville, FL
Lockwood, Brian R., P.A. .... Gainesville, FL
Lockwood, Brocton D. .... Marion, IL
Lockwood, Brocton, P.C. .... Marion, IL
Lockwood, C. Russell .... Arlington Heights, IL
Lockwood, Carol E. .... Washington, DC
Lockwood, Carolyn J. .... Macon, GA
Lockwood, Charles D. .... Treasury Department, Internal Revenue Service, GV
Lockwood, Charles H., II .... Arlington, VA
Lockwood, Chas. P. .... Tampa, FL
Lockwood, Chester R., Jr. .... Prescott, AZ
Lockwood, Christopher D.
San Bernardino, CA
Lockwood, Clyde E., (A Professional Corporation) .... Los Angeles, CA
Lockwood, Dale M. .... Monroe, MI
Lockwood, David C. .... Tampa, FL
Lockwood, David J. .... Huntington, WV
Lockwood, David L. .... Denver, CO
Lockwood, David M. .... Philadelphia, PA
Lockwood, Dominick A. .... Easton, PA
Stroudsburg, PA
Lockwood, Douglas A., III .... Lakeland, FL
Lake Wales, FL
Winter Haven, FL
Lockwood, Egnor & Vital .... Huntington, WV
Lockwood, Ellen A. .... San Antonio, TX
Lockwood, Frank T. .... Kailua, HI
Lockwood, Fred S., (P.C.) .... Chicago, IL
Lockwood, Gary E. .... Salem, OR
Lockwood, Gary E., P.C. .... Salem, OR
Lockwood, Gary L. .... Chicago, IL
Lockwood, George W. .... Fort Worth, TX
Lockwood & Golden .... Utica, NY
Lockwood, Gregory L. .... Baltimore, MD

Lockwood, Harold A., Jr. .... Philadelphia, PA
Lockwood & Harper, P.C. .... Williamston, MI
Lockwood, Harry A. .... Monroe, MI
Lockwood, J. Gregory .... Spokane, WA
Lockwood, James C. .... Los Angeles, CA
Lockwood, James E. .... Kansas City, MO
Lockwood, James H. .... East Rutherford, NJ
Lockwood, James M. .... Park Ridge, IL
Lockwood, Jeffrey A. .... Anderson, IN
Lockwood, Joan Galli
North Little Rock, AR
St. Louis, MO
Lockwood, Jodi Ellen .... Boston, MA
Lockwood, John A., (A Law Corporation)
Honolulu, HI
Lockwood, Julian .... Austin, TX
Lockwood, Karen M. .... Washington, DC
Lockwood, Kathleen M. .... Philadelphia, PA
Lockwood, Kristina S. .... Los Angeles, CA
Lockwood, Kurt W. .... Boston, MA
Lockwood, L. Brett .... Atlanta, GA
Lockwood, L. Scott .... Olympia, WA
Lockwood, Lucia A. .... Tulsa, OK
Lockwood, M. June .... Baldwinsville, NY
Lockwood, M. Laurene .... Albany, NY
Lockwood, Michael G. .... Austin, TX
Lockwood, Michael P. .... Woodland Hills, CA
Lockwood, Nona Hastie .... Charleston, SC
Lockwood, Paul J. .... Wilmington, DE
Lockwood, Pearl Chizner .... Boca Raton, FL
Lockwood, Peter Van N. .... Washington, DC
Lockwood, Randy G. .... Sacramento, CA
Lockwood, Robert H.G. .... Atlanta, GA
Lockwood, Robert K. .... Farmington Hills, MI
Lockwood, Robert K., II .... Northville, MI
Lockwood, Robert W. .... Portland, OR
Lockwood, Roy H. .... Rochester, NY
Lockwood, Russell D. .... El Cajon, CA
Lockwood, Sarah Evans .... Atlanta, GA
Lockwood, Stephen L. .... Utica, NY
Lockwood, Steven G. .... Albertson, NY
Lockwood, Suzanne .... Kalamazoo, MI
Lockwood, Thomas M., III
Baton Rouge, LA
Lockwood, Todd Cannon .... Phoenix, AZ
Lockwood, William O. .... Greenbelt, MD
Lockyear & Kornblum .... Evansville, IN
Lockyear, Krista B. .... Evansville, IN
Lockyear, Theodore .... Evansville, IN
Lockyear, Thomas .... Evansville, IN
Lockyear, Thomas A. .... Madison, WI
Lockyer, Charles W., Jr. .... Washington, DC
Lockyer, William S. .... Waltham, MA
Lococo, Alecia .... Hazard, KY
Lococo, David V., (P.A.) .... North Miami, FL
LoCoco, Francis H. .... Milwaukee, WI
LoCoco, Vincent B. .... New Orleans, LA
LoCoco, Vincent T. .... New Orleans, LA
Loconsolo, John M., Jr. .... Enfield, CT
LoConte, Carole A. .... Boston, MA
LoConti, Dennis N. .... Cleveland, OH
Loconto, Christopher Paul .... Worcester, MA
LoConto, Paul F. .... East Brookfield, MA
Locorotondo, Fausta Rose .... Bronx, NY
Locorotondo, Lucianna .... Bronx, NY
Locricchio, Michael A. .... Clinton, MI
Lo Cualio, Betty .... Boston, MA
LoCurto, C. Vincent .... Fort Lauderdale, FL
Locurto, Laura T. .... New York, NY
Lodato, Dominic J. .... Brooklyn, NY
Lodato, Gesuele J. .... Clark, NJ
Lodato, James J. .... Mineola, NY
Lodato, Joseph M. .... Stamford, CT
Lodato, Thomas A. .... Bergenfield, NJ
Lodato, Vincent James .... East Meadow, NY
Lodato, Vincent R. .... Newark, NJ
Lodde, Nicole E. .... San Antonio, TX
Lodders, Ronald R. .... Billings, MT
Lodemore, David C. .... Boston, MA
Loden, Elliot H., Law Offices of
Honolulu, HI
Wailuku, HI
Loden, Marcus S. .... Madison, WI
Loden, Stephen T. .... Houston, TX
Lodenkamper, Linda S. .... Golden, CO
Loder, David E. .... Philadelphia, PA
Loder, Janiffer E. .... Ocean City, NJ
Loder, John M. .... Boston, MA
Loder, LeRoy A. .... Tucson, AZ
Loder, Lorraine L. .... Los Angeles, CA
Loder, Reed E. .... Hanover, NH
Loder, Theresa M. .... Allentown, PA
Loder, Thomas T. .... Paoli, PA
Lodes, Carl F. .... Carmel, NY
Lodestro, Cass, Vanstrom & Edwards
Jamestown, NY
Lodestro, Lucian L. .... Jamestown, NY
Lodewick, John W. .... Dallas, TX
Lodewick, Robert J., Jr. .... White Plains, NY
Lodge, Barbara Straus .... Santa Monica, CA
Lodge, Connie M. .... Columbus, OH
Lodge, Deborah M. .... Washington, DC
Lodge, Dorothy T. .... Carlsbad, CA
Lodge, Edward J. .... Boise, ID
Lodge, Eric T., (P.C.) .... Carlsbad, CA
Pauma Valley, CA
Lodge, Frederick Z. .... New York, NY
Lodge, Gregory T. .... Toledo, OH
Lodge, Harry L. .... Cincinnati, OH
Lodge & Heller .... Carlsbad, CA
Pauma Valley, CA
Lodge, James M. .... Cleveland, OH
Lodge, Jeffrey James .... Fresno, CA
Lodge, John S. .... Gainesville, FL
Lodge, Joseph .... Santa Barbara, CA
Lodge, Kenneth M. .... Chicago, IL
Lodge, Laura Power .... Bethesda, MD
Lodge, Matthew J. .... Gladstone, NJ

Lodge, Richard ... **Nashville, TN**
Lodge, Steven G. ... Santa Monica, CA
Lodge, Steven J. ... **Anoka, MN**
Lodge, Terry Jonathan ... Toledo, OH
Lodge, Thomas E. ... **Columbus, OH**
Lodge, Thomas J. ... **Youngstown, OH**
Lodge, Thomas L. ... Vancouver, WA
Lodge, Thomas S. ... Wilmington, DE
Lodge, Timothy M. ... Bristol, CT
Lodge-Lane, Lori A. ... **Radcliff, KY**
Lodgen, Edward D. ... **Los Angeles, CA**
Lodico, Vincent J. ... **Columbus, OH**
Lodico, William J. ... Elmira, NY
Lodigiani, Karen M. ... **Philadelphia, PA**
Lodin, Lisa Diane ... St. Paul, MN
Lodine, Paul C. ... **Salem, OR**
Lodise, John P. ... **Los Angeles, CA**
Lodise, Margaret G. ... **Los Angeles, CA**
Lodish, Alvin D., (P.A.) ... **Miami, FL**
Lodmell, Douglass S. ... **Phoenix, AZ**
Lodmell, Gary L. ... **Phoenix, AZ**
Lodmell & Lodmell, P.C. ... **Phoenix, AZ**
Lodmer, Sheldon I. ... Beverly Hills, CA
Lodmer, Sheldon I., A Professional Corporation
Beverly Hills, CA
Lodoen, James A. ... **Minneapolis, MN**
LoDolce, Ann C. ... Brockton, MA
Lo Dolce, Nancy J. ... Santa Rosa, CA
Lodowski, Christian A. ... **Annapolis, MD**
Baltimore, MD
Lods, Dennis R. ... **San Francisco, CA**
San Jose, CA
Loduca, Janet C. ... **San Francisco, CA**
Lo Duca, Marcus J. ... Roseville, CA
LoDuca, Peter ... **New York, NY**
Lo Duca, Vincent J. ... Milwaukee, WI
Loduha, Michael A. ... Manitowoc, WI
Lodwick, David D. ... Excelsior Springs, MO
Lodwick, Michael W. ... **Long Beach, CA**
Lodwick, Peter A. ... **Dallas, TX**
Lodwick, Richard J. ... Amarillo, TX
Lodwick, Sheila R. ... **Cleveland, OH**
Lody & Arnold, P.A. ... Beebe, AR
Lody, Wesley G. ... Beebe, AR
Lodyga, Michelle R. ... **Minneapolis, MN**
Loe, Brian R. ... Lake Mary, FL
Loe, Cynthia M. ... **Palo Alto, CA**
Loe, David C. ... **Long Beach, CA**
Loe, James E. ... Cokato, MN
Loe, Shari ... Basking Ridge, NJ
Loe, Stephen R. ... **Dallas, TX**
Loe, W. Anthony ... Fort Lauderdale, FL
Loe, Warren, Rosenfield, Kaitcer & Hibbs, A Professional Corporation
Fort Worth, TX
Loeb, Alan M. ... **Denver, CO**
Loeb, Allan H. ... Ann Arbor, MI
Loeb, Alvin M. ... Cincinnati, OH
Loeb, Andrew G. ... **San Diego, CA**
Loeb, Andrew I. ... New York, NY
Loeb, Ann ... **Los Angeles, CA**
Loeb, B. Frank ... Montgomery, AL
Loeb, Ben F., Jr. ... Chapel Hill, NC
Loeb, Block & Partners LLP
New York, NY
Loeb, Cedric K. ... Houston, TX
Loeb, Charles W. ... **Charleston, WV**
Loeb, Charles W., Jr. ... **Charleston, WV**
Loeb & Ching, S.C. ... Madison, WI
Loeb, Christopher W. ... **Charlotte, NC**
Loeb, Claire ... New Orleans, LA
Loeb, Daniel E. ... **Washington, DC**
Loeb, Daniel N. ... Berkeley, CA
Loeb, Daniel N., Professional Corporation
Berkeley, CA
Loeb, David C. ... **Gretna, LA**
Loeb, Donald O. ... **Scottsdale, AZ**
Loeb, Dorothy P.
Department of the Air Force, Office of the General Counsel, GV
Loeb, Edward R. ... Miami, FL
Loeb, Elizabeth L. ... Department of Justice, Environment and Natural Resources Division, GV
Loeb, Ellen A. ... Boston, MA
Loeb, Eric H. ... Washington, DC
Loeb, Evelyn M.
United States Postal Service, Mid-Atlantic Office, GV
Loeb, Fred ... Mequon, WI
Loeb, G. Hamilton ... **Washington, DC**
Loeb, Hadassah S. ... New York, NY
Loeb, Harlan A. ... Milwaukee, WI
Loeb, Harry N. ... Madison, WI
Loeb, Harvey ... White Plains, NY
Loeb, Henry ... Somerville, NJ
Loeb & Herman, S.C. ... Milwaukee, WI
Loeb, Howard M. ... Calabasas, CA
Loeb, J. Scott ... **New Orleans, LA**
Loeb, James A. ... **Cleveland, OH**
Loeb, James R. ... **Newburgh, NY**
Loeb, James W.
Department Of Veterans Affairs, Board of Veterans Appeals, GV
Loeb, Jay E. ... Atlanta, GA
Loeb, Jeffrey B. ... **Danvers, MA**
Loeb, Jeffrey M. ... **Los Angeles, CA**
Loeb, Jonathan A. ... **Los Angeles, CA**
Loeb, Jordan ... Madison, WI
Loeb, Judith Holender ... Pittsford, NY
Loeb, Larry M. ... **New York, NY**
Loeb, Larry M. ... **New York, NY**
Loeb, Laura E. ... **Washington, DC**
Loeb, Lawrence R. ... Cleveland, OH
Loeb, Leonard L. ... Milwaukee, WI
Loeb & Loeb LLP ... **Los Angeles, CA**
Washington, DC
New York, NY
Nashville, TN
Loeb, Lori S. ... **Chicago, IL**
Loeb, Lynn ... **Burbank, CA**
Loeb, Malcolm ... **Phoenix, AZ**
Loeb, Marjorie Harris
Bloomfield Hills, MI
Loeb, Maurice ... Almonesson, NJ
Loeb, Michael J. ... **Palo Alto, CA**
San Francisco, CA
Loeb, Nancy C. ... **Morristown, NJ**
Loeb, Nancy H. ... Boston, MA
Loeb, Nicole Songy ... **New Orleans, LA**
Loeb, Ralph ... Denver, CO
Loeb, Ralph C. ... Los Angeles, CA
Loeb, Rhoda Leshine ... Branford, CT
Loeb, Richard Charles
Executive Office Of The President, Office of Management and Budget, GV
Loeb, Robert A. ... Chicago, IL
Loeb, Robert H. ... **Birmingham, AL**
Loeb, Robert L., Jr. ... **Denver, CO**
Loeb, Robin N. ... **Atlanta, GA**
Loeb, Rodney W. ... **Los Angeles, CA**
Loeb, Ronald I. ... **Jackson, MS**
Loeb, Ronald M., (P.C.) ... Los Angeles, CA
San Francisco, CA
Loeb, Sam F. ... Shreveport, LA
Loeb, Stanley R. ... **Portland, OR**
Loeb, Stephen A. ... New York, NY
Loeb, Stephen H. ... Flossmoor, IL
Loeb, Steven B. ... **Baton Rouge, LA**
Loeb, Steven M. ... **New York, NY**
Loeb, Steven S. ... Sherman Oaks, CA
Loeb, Susan H. ... Chicago, IL
Loeb, Teri Anne ... New York, NY
Loeb, Vollman, Harper & Friedmann
Cincinnati, OH
Loeb, Werner L. ... New York, NY
Loeb, William A. ... New York, NY
Loebe, Albert C. ... **Atlanta, GA**
Loebel, Kenneth R. ... Pewaukee, WI
Loebell, Diane A. ... **Blue Bell, PA**
Loeben, Arthur F., Jr. ... **Pottstown, PA**
Loeber, Christopher C. ... **Florham Park, NJ**
Loeber, Martin E. ... **San Antonio, TX**
Loebig, Patrick A. ... Tallahassee, FL
Loebl, James D. ... **Ventura, CA**
Loebl, James F. ... Green Bay, WI
Loebl, Jeffrey W. ... Charleston, SC
Loebl, Leah ... Department of Justice, Immigration and Naturalization Service, GV
Loebl, Richard I. ... **Detroit, MI**
Loeblein, Walter G. ... Jennings, MO
Loebner, Barbara M. ... Los Altos, CA
Loebs, Blake P. ... San Francisco, CA
Loebs, Kathryn Elizabeth ... Boston, MA
Loebsack, Christopher J. ... **Charlotte, NC**
Loechel, Angela G. ... Harrison, OH
Loecher, Murray M. ... New York, NY
Loechl, Kevin J. ... **Atlanta, GA**
Loedel, Bonnie L. ... West Harwich, MA
Loeding, Scott J. ... **Chula Vista, CA**
Loeff Claeys Verbeke ... **New York, NY**
New York, NY
New York, NY
New York, NY
Loeffelholz, Debra D. ... Norman, OK
Loeffelholz, Joel P. ... New Orleans, LA
Loeffler, A. William ... **Atlanta, GA**
Loeffler Allen & Ham ... Bristow, OK
Sapulpa, OK
Loeffler, Carl ... **Palo Alto, CA**
Loeffler, Catherine M. ... Riverhead, NY
Loeffler, Cheryl A. ... Saginaw, MI
Loeffler, D. Bowen ... Port Clinton, OH
Loeffler, David ... **Farmington Hills, MI**
Novi, MI
Milwaukee, WI
Loeffler, David H., Jr. ... Tulsa, OK
Loeffler, Douglas J. ... Clearwater, FL
Loeffler, Evan L. ... **Seattle, WA**
Loeffler, James J. ... Houston, TX
Loeffler, James M. ... **Uniondale, NY**
Loeffler, John H. ... Spokane, WA
Loeffler, Karen L. ... Anchorage, AK
Loeffler, Kevin W. ... Wichita, KS
Loeffler, Lynne ... Blanco, TX
Loeffler, Mark A. ... **Atlanta, GA**
Loeffler, Michael G. ... Modesto, CA
Loeffler, Michael S. ... **Chicago, IL**
Loeffler, Michael S. ... Bristow, OK
Sapulpa, OK
Loeffler, Paul H. ... Basking Ridge, NJ
Loeffler, Richard J. ... Chicago, IL
Loeffler, Robert H. ... **Washington, DC**
Loeffler, Robert M. ... Los Angeles, CA
Loeffler, Samuel H. ... El Reno, OK
Loeffler, Terri ... Austin, TX
Loeffler, Thomas G. ... **Washington, DC**
San Antonio, TX
Loeffler, Walter B., Jr. ... **Houston, TX**
Loegering, Janis H. ... **Dallas, TX**
Loegering, Weston C. ... **Dallas, TX**
Loegler, R. Link ... **Birmingham, AL**
Loehn, Susan Johnson ... Northampton, MA
Loehn, Thomas E., (A Law Corporation)
New Orleans, LA
Loehne, Richard A. ... Centreville, VA
Loehr, Angela N. ... **St. Louis, MO**
Loehr, Donald V. ... Kenner, LA
Loehr, Frederick K. ... San Mateo, CA
Loehr, Gerald E. ... **Yonkers, NY**
Loehr, John F. ... **Charleston, WV**
Loehr, John L. ... New York, NY
Loehr, Nicholas R. ... Sacramento, CA
Loehr, Robert A., II ... San Jose, CA
Loehr, Robert M. ... **Pensacola, FL**
Loehr, Thomas E. ... Sistersville, WV
Loehrer, Sally L. ... Las Vegas, NV
Loeks, Barrie Lawson, Ms.
Grand Rapids, MI
Loeks, John D., Jr. ... Grand Rapids, MI
Loeliger, Dawn Phillips ... Irving, TX
Loendorf, Jerome T. ... **Helena, MT**
Loengard, Janet S. ... Bethlehem, PA
Loengard, Richard O., Jr. (P.C.)
New York, NY
Loening, Albert P., Jr. ... Peterborough, NH
Loening, Michael ... **New York, NY**
Loennig, Carlton P. ... Portland, OR
Loennig, Doris ... Fairbanks, AK
Loeper, Jessica ... Powell, WY
Loepere, Carol Colborn ... **Washington, DC**
Loepker, Linda L. ... Indianapolis, IN
Loepp, Herman A. ... Overland Park, KS
Loepp, Jim, Law Office, P.C. ... Beaver, OK
Loeppke, Rhonda S. ... Independence, MO
Loerch, Kristen J. ... **West Palm Beach, FL**
Loertscher, Kenneth L. ... Indianapolis, IN
Loerzel, Lorenz F. ... Delmar, NY
Loesberg, Alan S. ... **New York, NY**
Loesberg, Matthew T. ... **New York, NY**
Loesberg, Michael J. ... **Morristown, NJ**
Loesch, Harrison ... United States Senate, Committee Legal Personnel, GV
Loesch, J. M. ... Buffalo, NY
Loesch, Kristen L. ... **Alexandria, VA**
Arlington, VA
Loesch, Lawrence F. ... Howard Beach, NY
Loesch, Martin C. ... Everett, WA
Loesch, Michelle K. ... San Jose, CA
Loesch, Robert L. ... Birmingham, MI
Loesch, Robert M. ... **Cleveland, OH**
Loesch, Steve ... East Sandwich, MA
Loesch, William R. ... **Chicago, IL**
Loesche, Marc C. ... Valparaiso, IN
Loesche, Robert K.
Administrative Office Of The United States Courts, GV
Loesche, William P. ... Philadelphia, PA
Loesche, Wm. H., Jr. ... Gladwyne, PA
Loeschen, John M. ... **Burlington, IA**
Loeschen & Loeschen Law Offices
Burlington, IA
Loeschen, Terry D. ... **Burlington, IA**
Loescher, Christina ... **Houston, TX**
Loescher, Craig S. ... Fort Myers, FL
Loescher, Joseph R. D. ... **Anchorage, AK**
Loescher, William H., Jr. ... Jenkintown, PA
Loeschorn, Carol A. ... Summit, NJ
Loesel, Pamela ... **Canton, OH**
Loeser, Bruce ... Houston, TX
Loeser, Charles M. ... South Bend, IN
Loeser, Constance Tilden ... **Greenwich, CT**
Loeser, Derek W. ... **Seattle, WA**
Loeser, Doron I. ... New York, NY
Loeser, Elaine Munson ... Pasadena, CA
Loeser, Hans F. ... Boston, MA
Loeser, Margie Lynn ... **Louisville, KY**
Loeshelle, Steven R. ... **New York, NY**
Loessberg, Shari ... Washington, DC
Loeterman, Mark ... Los Angeles, CA
Loeterman, Nancy Cole ... Los Angeles, CA
Loeterman, Shulkin & Kraemer
Los Angeles, CA
Loethen, Bartly J. ... **Chicago, IL**
Loev, Norman M. ... **Blue Bell, PA**
Loev, Robert M. ... Metairie, LA
Loevin, Robert H. ... Miami, FL
Loevinger, Lee ... **Washington, DC**
Loevy, Arthur R. ... Chicago, IL
Loew, Albert ... New York, NY
Loew, Doris ... **Chicago, IL**
Loew, Elliot M., P.C., Law Offices of
Newton, MA
Loew, Elliott M. ... Newton, MA
Loew, Jeffrey A. ... **Binghamton, NY**
Loew, John R. ... **Milwaukee, WI**
Loew, Jonathan L. ... **Chicago, IL**
Loew, Michael H. ... New York, NY
Loew, Ralph S. ... Stratford, CT
Loew, Raymond M. ... East Islip, NY
Loew, Robert B. ... Melville, NY
Loew, Steven I. ... Charleston, WV
Loew, William R. ... Willingboro, NJ
Loewald, Francis A. ... New York, NY
Loewe, Drew M. ... **Ventura, CA**
Loewen, C. Randall, (L.L.C.)
Lafayette, LA
Loewen, James V. ... **Somerville, NJ**
Loewen, Leonard A. ... Hayward, CA
Loewen, Michael R. ... Sacramento, CA
Loewen, Robert W. ... **Irvine, CA**
Loewen, Ronald F. ... Columbia, SC
Loewen, Theodore A. ... Los Angeles, CA
Loewen, Theodore W. ... Parlier, CA
Loewenberg, Deborah Wolikow
New City, NY
Loewenberg, Jean S. ... Boston, MA
Loewenberg, Jerome L. ... San Antonio, TX
Loewenberg, Peter B.
Department of Justice, Criminal Division, GV
Loewengart, Steven M. ... **Columbus, OH**
Loewenson, Carl H., Jr. ... **New York, NY**
Loewenstein, Benjamin S.
Philadelphia, PA
Loewenstein, Carol R. ... Irvine, CA
Loewenstein, Dana ... **Farmington Hills, MI**
Loewenstein, Daniel M. ... **Chicago, IL**
Loewenstein, David A. ... **New York, NY**
Loewenstein, Hagen, Oehlert and Smith, P.C.
Springfield, IL
Loewenstein, K. Karen ... **Washington, DC**
Loewenstein, Mark J. ... Boulder, CO
Loewenstein, Pamela B. ... Lincolnshire, IL
Loewenstein, Peter G. ... **Walnut Creek, CA**
Loewenstein, Ralph H. ... **Springfield, IL**
Loewenstein, Robert A. ... **Short Hills, NJ**
Loewenstein, Rudolph E. ... **Tustin, CA**
Loewenstein, Samuel ... Fair Lawn, NJ
Loewenstern, Daniel A. ... Philadelphia, PA
Loewenthal, Ann ... Atlanta, GA
Loewenthal, Barbara H. ... **New York, NY**
Loewenthal, David A. ... **Santa Barbara, CA**
Sherman Oaks, CA
Ventura, CA
Loewenthal, Glenn A. ... Atlanta, GA
Loewenthal & Jackson, LLP ... Atlanta, GA
Loewenthal, Nancy Sokol ... Moraga, CA
Loewenthal, Olive E. ... Fort Lauderdale, FL
Loewenthal, Robert J. ... Atlanta, GA
Loewenthal, Steven J. ... New City, NY
Loewentritt, Lennard S.
General Services Administration, Office of the General Counsel, GV
Loewer, Robert E. ... Chicago, IL
Loewi, Andrew W. ... **Denver, CO**
Loewinger, Andrew P. ... **Washington, DC**
Loewinger & Brand, PLLC
Washington, DC
Loewinger, Kenneth J. ... **Washington, DC**
Loewinsohn, Alan S. ... **Dallas, TX**
Loewy, Arnold H. ... Chapel Hill, NC
Loewy, Dina R. ... Baltimore, MD
Loewy, Douglas J. ... **Los Angeles, CA**
Loewy, E. Elizabeth ... New York, NY
Loewy, Edwin J. ... Hempstead, NY
Loewy, Ira N. ... **Miami, FL**
Loewy, John H. ... Lake Oswego, OR
Loewy, Peter H. ... **Irvine, CA**
Los Angeles, CA
Sacramento, CA
San Francisco, CA
Santa Clara, CA
Loewy, Richard R. ... **Providence, RI**
Loewy, Robert G. ... **Newport Beach, CA**
Loewy, Steven A. ... **Bethesda, MD**
Loewy, Steven A., P.A. ... **Washington, DC**
Bethesda, MD
Lof, Larry O. D. ... Denver, CO
Lofaro, Bennett C. ... **Mineola, NY**
New York, NY
Smithtown, NY
LoFaro, Carmine ... Hackensack, NJ
Lofaro, Dianne L. ... **Long Beach, CA**
LoFaro & Reiser, L.L.P. ... Hackensack, NJ
LoFaso, Charles A. ... Rochester, NY
Lofaso, Gerald F. ... Houma, LA
Lofchie, Steven David ... **New York, NY**
Lofdahl, Nancy E. ... San Francisco, CA
Loff, Alexander I. ... Bloomfield Hills, MI
Loff, Timothy R. ... **Boston, MA**
Loff, Timothy R. ... **Newton, MA**
Loffarelli, Clarence P. ... Sherman Oaks, CA
Loffel, Cynthia Leslie ... Philadelphia, PA
Loffel, Leo H. ... Merion, PA
Loffler, Peter ... Tallahassee, FL
Loffman, Leslie H. ... **New York, NY**
Loffredo, John L. ... Highland Park, MI
Loffredo, Pasco F. ... Cranston, RI
Loffredo, Peter A. ... **Toms River, NJ**
Loffredo & Sciotti ... Cranston, RI
Loffredo, Stephen K. ... Miami Shores, FL
Loffredo, Thomas Holland
Fort Lauderdale, FL
Loffswold, Richard D. ... Girard, KS
Loffswold, Richard D., Jr. ... Girard, KS
Lofftus & Dawdy ... Fenton, MO
Lofftus, Ervin D. ... Fenton, MO
Lofgren, Christine L. ... **Los Angeles, CA**
Lofgren, David E., Jr. ... Portland, OR
Lofgren, Douglas W. ... **Los Angeles, CA**
Lofgren, Karen R. ... Chicago, IL
Lofgren, Karl ... New York, NY
Lofgren, Kurt W. ... **Detroit, MI**
Lofgren, Mark L. ... **Washington, DC**
Lofgren, Marlon M. ... **Sioux Falls, SD**
Lofgren, Martha Clark ... Folsom, CA
Lofgren, Michael G. ... East Lansing, MI
Lofgren, Norman A. ... **Dallas, TX**
Lofgren, Richard J. ... **Chicago, IL**
Lofgren, Robert J. ... Del Mar, CA
Lofgren, Robert M. ... **San Jose, CA**
Lofgren, Zoe ... San Jose, CA
Lofholm, David M. ... **San Francisco, CA**
Lofino, Michael D. ... **New York, NY**
Lofland & Associates ... Yakima, WA
Lofland, Gary ... Yakima, WA
Lofland, William B. ... **Dallas, TX**
Lofland, Wm. I. ... Rockwall, TX
Loflin, Ann F. ... Durham, NC
Loflin, Gary L. ... Charlotte, NC
Loflin & Loflin ... Durham, NC
Loflin, Thomas F., III ... Durham, NC
Lofness-Baab, Carole ... Minneapolis, MN
Loforese, John T. ... **Greenwich, CT**
White Plains, NY
Lofrese, James J. ... **White Plains, NY**
LoFrisco, Anthony F. ... **New York, NY**
Lofrumento, Lucy A. ... **San Francisco, CA**
San Jose, CA
Lofrumento, Susan J. ... **New York, NY**
Lofstead, Gerald E., III ... **Clarksburg, WV**
Lofstead, Gregory A. ... **Charleston, SC**
Lofstedt, Ben E. ... Fullerton, CA
Lofstedt, Sally R. ... Fullerton, CA
Lofstrom, Mark D. ... Honolulu, HI
Lofstrom, Mark V. ... Minneapolis, MN
Loft, Donald A. ... **Atlanta, GA**
Loft, Kathryn K. ... **Chicago, IL**
Loft, Michael L. ... **Spokane, WA**
Loft, White & Mount ... **Spokane, WA**
Lofters, Cecilia O'Brien ... **New York, NY**

Loftesness, Tracy E. .... Walnut Creek, CA
Lofthouse, Wayne T. .... Park Ridge, IL
Lofthus, Scott W. .... Wayzata, MN
Loftin, Audrey Stephanie
Long Beach, CA
Loftin, Audrey Stephanie
Los Angeles, CA
Loftin, Billy E., Jr. .... Lake Charles, LA
Loftin, Brenda Stith .... St. Louis, MO
Loftin, C. Eugene .... Jacksonville, FL
Loftin, C. Richard .... Nantucket, MA
Loftin, Carl W. .... Asheville, NC
Loftin, Carole A. .... Austin, TX
Loftin, Dalton Hartwell .... Hillsborough, NC
Loftin, Davis H. .... West Memphis, AR
Loftin, Davis K. .... Atlanta, GA
Loftin, F. Patrick .... Phenix City, AL
Loftin, G. Bartley, III .... Huntsville, AL
Loftin, Harold R., Jr. .... Austin, TX
Loftin, Herndon & Loftin .... Phenix City, AL
Loftin, Jerry J. .... Fort Worth, TX
Loftin, Jerry J., A Professional Corporation
Fort Worth, TX
Loftin, Jerry W. .... Manchester, GA
Loftin, John D. .... Hillsborough, NC
Loftin, John G. .... Monroe, LA
Loftin, Karen L. .... Galax, VA
Loftin, L. Sue .... San Diego, CA
Loftin, Laura A. .... Los Angeles, CA
Loftin and Loftin, P.A. .... Hillsborough, NC
Loftin, Melinda J.
Department of the Air Force, Office of the General Counsel, GV
Loftin, Michael H. .... Amarillo, TX
Loftin, Monica Leigh .... Wilmington, DE
Loftin, Nancy C. .... Phoenix, AZ
Loftin, Richard A. .... Chelsea, AL
Loftin, Robert L., III .... Birmingham, AL
Loftin, Robert M. .... Greensboro, NC
Loftin, R. V., Jr. .... Houston, TX
Loftin, Sam E. .... Phenix City, AL
Loftin, Stacy B. .... Bedford, TX
Loftin, Stephen M. .... Houston, TX
Loftin, Valerie W. .... Greensboro, NC
Loftis, David E. .... New York, NY
Loftis, Harry .... Tyler, TX
Loftis, James R., III .... Washington, DC
Loftis, Jeanne F. .... Portland, OR
Loftis, Jim D. .... Norman, OK
Loftis, John Lindsey .... Tuscaloosa, AL
Loftis, Kristen Miller .... Tuscaloosa, AL
Loftis, Larry B. .... Orlando, FL
Loftis, Lori D. .... Asheville, NC
Loftis, Mark D. .... Roanoke, VA
Loftis, Maureen H. .... Orinda, CA
Loftis, Michael A. .... Chicago, IL
Loftis, Nancy L. .... Lincoln, NE
Loftis, Richard M. .... Atlanta, GA
Loftis, Robert O., Jr. .... Buies Creek, NC
Loftis, Tim C. .... Buffalo, NY
Loftis, W. O'Neil .... Midland, TX
Loftis, W. Randolph, Jr.
Winston-Salem, NC
Loftman, Guy R. .... Bloomington, IN
Loftman, Kelli .... Washington, DC
Lofton, Deborah Cleary .... Wayne, PA
Lofton De Lancie .... San Francisco, CA
Lofton, J. David .... Lafayette, LA
Lofton, James A. .... Department of Justice, Environment and Natural Resources Division, GV
Lofton, Jonathan Heath .... Muskogee, OK
Lofton, Lionel S. .... Charleston, SC
Lofton, Mellanese S. .... Benicia, CA
Lofton, Ned C. .... Wakefield, MA
Lofton, Oliver .... Newark, NJ
Lofton, Patricia .... Los Angeles, CA
Lofton, Robert W. .... Los Angeles, CA
Lofton, Rodger W. .... Paducah, KY
Lofton, Thomas D. .... Portland, OR
Kirkland, WA
Lofton, Thomas M. .... Indianapolis, IN
Lofton, William M. .... San Francisco, CA
Loftsgaarden, B. Jerome .... St. Paul, MN
Loftsgard, Lori Elizabeth .... Des Moines, IA
Loftsgard, Rick .... Clive, IA
Loftspring, Peter D. .... Houston, TX
Loftus, Ann T. .... Philadelphia, PA
Loftus, Barry L. .... Lafayette, IN
Loftus, Bianca M. .... Chicago, IL
Loftus, Brian A. .... Des Plaines, IL
Loftus, C. Michael .... Washington, DC
Loftus, Carolyn A. .... White Plains, NY
Loftus, Cole .... Libertyville, IL
Loftus, Connell A. .... Leesburg, VA
Loftus, Daniel B. .... Frederick, MD
Loftus, Daniel R. .... Nashville, TN
Loftus, David A., Jr. .... Skaneateles, NY
Loftus, Diane J. .... Milwaukee, WI
Loftus, Donald J. .... Pebble Beach, CA
Loftus, James T. .... Detroit, MI
Loftus, Jerome C. .... Warrenton, VA
Loftus, Jerome C., P.C. .... Warrenton, VA
Loftus, John A. .... Kingston, PA
Loftus, John B., III .... Keene, NH
Loftus, John M. .... Scottsville, NY
Loftus, John R. .... Long Beach, CA
Loftus, John T. .... Des Plaines, IL
Loftus, Joseph E. .... Indianapolis, IN
Loftus, Kevin .... Boston, MA
Loftus, Kevin M. .... Washington, DC
Loftus, Kevin M. .... White Plains, NY
Loftus, Leslie Wulfsohn .... Tampa, FL
Loftus, Linda A. .... Long Beach, CA
Loftus, Marilyn .... Newark, NJ
Loftus, Marleen J. .... Sioux City, IA
Loftus, Martin J. .... Spring Lake, NJ
Loftus, Martin R. .... Fairfax, VA
Loftus, Mary Eileen .... Pittsburgh, PA
Loftus, Mary Ellen .... Kansas City, MO
Loftus, Nancy Fry .... Fairfax, VA
Loftus, P. Michael .... Chicago, IL
Loftus, Patrick B. .... Chicago, IL
Loftus, Patrick J. .... New City, NY
Loftus, Patrick J. .... Philadelphia, PA
Loftus, Paul J. .... Huntington, WV
Loftus, Richard A. .... Westlake Village, CA
Loftus, Richard J., Jr. .... San Jose, CA
Loftus, Robert H. J. .... Fairfax, VA
Loftus, Terry .... San Diego, CA
Loftus, Thomas A.
Occupational Safety and Health Review Commission, Office of the General Counsel, GV
Loftus, Thomas A., III .... Wichita, KS
Houston, TX
Loftus, Thomas D. .... Seattle, WA
Loftus, Thomas J. .... Los Angeles, CA
Loftus, Thomas J. .... Springfield, MA
Loftus, Thomas M. .... Burnsville, MN
Loftus, Thomas P. .... Amherst, VA
Loftus, Thos. R. .... Philadelphia, PA
Loftus, William C. .... Phoenix, AZ
Loftus, William P., III .... Millbury, MA
Loftus, William R. .... Lebanon, NH
Loftus, William R., P.C. .... Lebanon, NH
Lofwall, Ian C. .... Washington, DC
Chicago, IL
Lofy, Thomas R. .... Scottsdale, AZ
Loga, Karen J. .... New York, NY
LoGalbo, John R. .... Herndon, VA
Logalbo, Mary Middaugh .... Boston, MA
Logan, Adrienne I. .... New York, NY
Logan, Alex G., III .... Fullerton, CA
Logan, Alexis R. .... Ann Arbor, MI
Logan, Alison Jean .... Corpus Christi, TX
Logan, Allison Freeman .... Dallas, TX
Logan, Andrew D. .... Warren, OH
Logan, Andrew J. .... Winston-Salem, NC
Logan, Ann H. .... Treasury Department, Internal Revenue Service, GV
Logan, Anthony David .... Phoenix, AZ
Logan, April C. .... Carlsbad, CA
Logan, Aubrey D. .... Houston, TX
Logan, Beatrice B. .... Detroit, MI
Logan, Ben H., III .... Los Angeles, CA
Logan, Ben H., Jr. .... Sun City West, AZ
Logan, Benjamin H., II .... Grand Rapids, MI
Logan, Benjamin M. .... Tupelo, MS
Logan and Bise .... Gulfport, MS
Logan, Brenda J. .... Calabasas, CA
Logan, Brian E. .... Albany, NY
Logan, Bruce A. .... Denver, CO
Logan, Bruce T. .... Chicago, IL
Logan, C. Maxwell .... Olathe, KS
Logan, C. Scott .... Atlanta, GA
Logan, Catherine P. .... Overland Park, KS
Logan, Charles C., II .... La Mesa, CA
Logan, Charles E. .... San Jose, CA
Logan, Charles E.
Treasury Department, GV
Logan, Charles P. .... Wheaton, IL
Logan, Charles W., Jr.
Federal Communications Commission, Mass Media Bureau, GV
Logan, D. Cal .... San Diego, CA
Logan, David G. .... Dallas, TX
Logan, David M. .... San Diego, CA
Logan, David M. .... Springfield, OR
Logan, David S. .... Chicago, IL
Logan, Deane Calhoun .... San Diego, CA
Logan, Deborah A. .... Los Altos, CA
Logan, Dennis V. .... Kansas City, MO
Logan, Donald J. .... Napa, CA
Logan, Donald L. .... Wilmington, DE
Towson, MD
Logan, Donald M. .... Carmel Highlands, CA
Logan, Douglas L. .... Houston, TX
Logan, Duncan J. .... New York, NY
Logan, Edward Anderson
Oklahoma City, OK
Logan, Edwin A. .... Frankfort, KY
Logan, Elizabeth .... Northfield, NJ
Logan, Elizabeth A. .... Bloomfield Hills, MI
Logan, F. Eugene .... Tustin, CA
Logan, F. L. Dennis .... Fort Wayne, IN
Logan, Floyd J. .... Gulfport, MS
Logan, Francine B. .... Los Angeles, CA
Logan, Francis D. .... New York, NY
Logan, Francis D., Jr. .... Irvine, CA
Logan, Fred J., Jr. .... Prairie Village, KS
Logan, G. Hunter, Jr.
Christiansted, St. Croix, VI
Logan, Gail K. .... New York, NY
Logan and Gaines .... Frankfort, KY
Logan, Gary .... Las Vegas, NV
Logan, Gary L. .... Bakersfield, CA
Logan, George G. .... Atwater, CA
Logan, George H.
Christiansted, St. Croix, VI
Logan, George, III .... Phoenix, AZ
Logan & Geotas, P.L.C. .... Phoenix, AZ
Logan, Gregory J. .... Lafayette, LA
Logan, Henri Ann .... Beaufort, SC
Logan, Henry J. .... White Plains, NY
Logan, Henry W. .... Santa Barbara, CA
Logan & Hibnick, P.A. .... Miami, FL
Logan, Huchla & Wycoff, P.C.
Riverview, MI
Logan, J. .... San Jose, CA
Logan, J. Anthony .... Dublin, OH
Logan, J. Duke .... Grove, OK
Vinita, OK
Logan, J. Emmett .... Kansas City, MO
Logan, J. Patrick .... Birmingham, AL
Logan, J. Thomas .... Pasadena, CA
Logan, James C. .... Kansas City, MO
Logan, James F., Jr. .... Cleveland, TN
Logan, James H. .... Pittsburgh, PA
Logan, James, III .... Mount Holly, NJ
Logan, James, Jr. .... Mount Holly, NJ
Logan, James K. .... Olathe, KS
Logan, James L. P., Jr. .... Phoenix, AZ
Logan, James P. .... Englewood, NJ
Logan, James P., Jr. .... Carson City, NV
Logan, James R., IV .... New Orleans, LA
Logan, James W., Jr. .... Anderson, SC
Logan, Jana .... San Diego, CA
Logan, Jean Elizabeth
Department of Commerce, Patent and Trademark Office, GV
Logan, Jeffrey R. .... Ottumwa, IA
Logan, John A. .... Denver, CO
Logan, John A., Jr. .... Houston, TX
Logan, John D. .... Flint, MI
Logan, John D. .... Warren, MI
Logan, John F. .... New York, NY
Logan, John F., II .... Bangor, ME
Logan, John Reid .... Torrington, CT
Logan, John S. .... Washington, DC
Logan, John W., Jr. .... Horsham, PA
Logan, Jolly & Smith, L.L.P. .... Anderson, SC
Logan, Jonathon E. .... Cerritos, CA
Logan, Joseph D., III .... Roanoke, VA
Logan, Joseph P. .... St. Louis, MO
Logan, Katherine J. .... Crookston, MN
Logan, Kathleen M. .... Pittsburgh, PA
Logan, Kathryn A. .... Salem, OR
Logan, Kempton P. .... Fort Myers, FL
Logan, Kenneth J. .... Riverview, MI
Logan, Kenneth R. .... New York, NY
Logan, Kevin V. .... Midlothian, VA
Logan, Kurr & Hamilton .... Bangor, ME
Logan, Laurie A. .... New York, NY
Logan Law Firm LLC .... Olathe, KS
Kansas City, MO
Logan, Leigh Taylor .... Dallas, TX
Logan, Leo L. .... Kansas City, KS
Logan, Leonard G., Jr. .... Kitty Hawk, NC
Logan, Leonard M., IV .... Grove, OK
Vinita, OK
Logan, Linda Land .... Columbus, GA
Logan, Lindsey, III, P.S.C. .... Shelbyville, KY
Logan, Lisa M. .... Durham, NC
Logan and Logan .... Englewood, NJ
Logan & Logan .... Pittsburgh, PA
Woodstock, VA
Logan and Logan, L.L.C. .... Kansas City, KS
Olathe, KS
Overland Park, KS
Prairie Village, KS
Kansas City, MO
Logan, Lorryn Daena M. .... Chevy Chase, MD
Logan, Louise A. .... Houston, TX
Logan & Lowry, LLP .... Claremore, OK
Grove, OK
Jay, OK
Miami, OK
Nowata, OK
Pryor, OK
Vinita, OK
Logan, Lyndol M. .... Pasadena, CA
Logan, Marcy R. .... Norman, OK
Logan, Margaret A. .... Silver Creek, NY
Logan, Mark A. .... Anaheim, CA
Logan, Mark Knowles .... Tallahassee, FL
Logan, Mary Frances .... Portsmouth, RI
Logan, Mary K. .... Evanston, IL
Logan & May .... Newton, MS
Logan, Merwin C. .... Springfield, OR
Logan, Michael A. .... Dallas, TX
Logan, Michael G. .... Park Ridge, IL
Logan, Michael J. .... Irvine, CA
Logan, Michael P. .... Alexandria, VA
Logan, Morgan N. .... Palmer Springs, VA
Logan, Morton & Ratliff .... Madisonville, KY
Logan, Nancy A. .... Indianapolis, IN
Logan, Nancy Opre .... Chandler, AZ
Logan, Nancy Opre, P.C. .... Chandler, AZ
Logan, Pamela Finn .... Roanoke, VA
Logan, Patricia A. .... Annapolis, MD
Logan, Patricia M. .... Quincy, MA
Logan, Paul A. .... Cherry Hill, NJ
Harrisburg, PA
King Of Prussia, PA
Logan, Paul E. .... Bradenton, FL
Logan, Peter B. .... San Francisco, CA
Logan, Peter J. .... San Francisco, CA
Logan, Peter S., Jr. .... Detroit, MI
Logan, Philip A. .... Cincinnati, OH
Logan, Phillip H. .... Sanford, FL
Logan, Ralph H. .... Louisville, KY
Logan, Richard D. .... Fort Wayne, IN
Logan, Richard G. .... Walnut Creek, CA
Logan, Richard G., Jr. .... Oakland, CA
Logan, Riley, Carson & Kaup, L.C.
Overland Park, KS
Topeka, KS
Logan, Rita H. .... Portland, ME
Logan, Robert E. .... Norman, OK
Logan, Robert H. .... Long Beach, CA
Logan, Robert I. .... Highland Park, IL
Logan, Robert J. .... Hackensack, NJ
Logan, Robert L. .... Pittsburgh, PA
Logan, Robert M., Jr. .... Newton, MS
Logan, Rodney D. .... Miami, FL
Logan, Rodney D., P.A. .... Miami, FL
Logan, Roger V., Jr. .... Harrison, AR
Logan, Ronald G. .... Dayton, OH
Logan, Ronald J. .... Phoenix, AZ
Logan, Ruth C. .... Dallas, TX
Logan, Sally B. .... Buffalo, NY
Logan, Samuel P. .... Olathe, KS
Logan, Sarah E. Tillman .... Chapel Hill, NC
Logan, Scott K. .... Prairie Village, KS
Logan, Sean C. .... Baltimore, MD
Logan, Sharon B. .... Ormond Beach, FL
Logan, Sharon B., P.A.
Daytona Beach, FL
Ormond Beach, FL
Logan & Soileau, LLC .... New Orleans, LA
Logan & Sparks .... Dallas, TX
Logan, Stanley W. .... Birmingham, AL
Logan, Stefanie C. .... West Palm Beach, FL
Logan, Stephen D. .... Birmingham, AL
Logan, Steven Mark
West Palm Beach, FL
Logan, Stewart W. .... Miami, FL
Logan & Stier .... Fort Wayne, IN
Logan, Stuart D. .... Bloomfield Hills, MI
Logan, Stuart J. .... Washington, DC
Logan, Symes & Keeling, L.L.P.
San Angelo, TX
Logan, Thomas C. .... Birmingham, AL
Logan, Thomas D. .... Fort Wayne, IN
Logan, Thomas G. .... North Tonawanda, NY
Logan, Thomas J. .... Des Moines, IA
Logan, Thompson, Miller, Bilbo, Thompson & Fisher, P.C. .... Cleveland, TN
Logan, Timothy .... Fort Wayne, IN
Logan, Timothy N. .... Waynesburg, PA
Logan, Valentine W. .... Denver, CO
Logan, W. Andrew P., III .... New York, NY
Logan, Wade H., III .... Charleston, SC
Logan, Walt .... Clearwater, FL
Logan, Wendell M. .... Philadelphia, PA
Logan, William A. .... Madisonville, KY
Logan, William A., Jr. .... San Francisco, CA
Logan, William B., Jr. .... Columbus, OH
Logan, William C. .... Bronx, NY
Logan, William E., Jr. .... Lafayette, LA
Logan, William E., Jr. & Assoc., A Prof. Law Corp. .... Lafayette, LA
Logan, William F. .... Alpine, CA
Logan, William F. .... San Diego, CA
Logan, William F. .... Topeka, KS
Logan, William H., Jr. .... Woodstock, VA
Logan, William L. .... Three Rivers, CA
Logan, William Lee, III .... Lansing, MI
Logan, William Lindsey, III .... Shelbyville, KY
Logan, William Tyler .... Keokuk, IA
Logan, William W. .... Wiscasset, ME
Logan, Willis .... Lake Dallas, TX
Logan, Wm. Malcom .... Washington, DC
Logan, W. R. .... Albuquerque, NM
Logan-Baldwin, Emmelyn S. .... Rochester, NY
Loganzo, Rondi Kline .... Hawthorne, NY
Logar, Ronald J. .... Reno, NV
Logar, Ronald J., A Prof. Corp., The Law Office of .... Reno, NV
Logas, Philip L. .... Miami, FL
LoGatto, Anthony F. .... San Diego, CA
Logback, Lawrence J. .... Wichita, KS
Loge, Orvil Lee, Jr. .... Muskogee, OK
Logee, F. Emerson .... Wooster, OH
Logee, Hostetler, Stutzman & Lehman
Millersburg, OH
Wooster, OH
Logee, Karen A. .... Brockton, MA
Logeman, Robert E. .... Ypsilanti, MI
Logerfo, Ann M. .... Seattle, WA
Logerfo, Michael F. .... Hackensack, NJ
Logering, Nancy J. .... Elk River, MN
Logerwell, Donald L. .... Seattle, WA
Loggans, Susan E. .... Chicago, IL
Loggans, Susan E., & Associates, P.C.
Chicago, IL
Loggi, Michele M. .... Northfield, NJ
Loggia, Elizabeth G. .... Rockville, MD
Loggie, Kathryn A. .... Mineola, NY
Loggins, Eugenia L. .... Andalusia, AL
Loggins, Fay R. .... Gainesville, GA
Loggins, John F. .... Long Beach, CA
Loggins, Joseph E. .... Summerville, GA
Loggins, Kathleen J.
West Palm Beach, FL
Loggins, Katie E. .... Birmingham, AL
Loggins, Sewell K. .... Atlanta, GA
Loggins, Timothy B. .... Opp, AL
Logie, Donald J., Jr. .... Hartford, CT
Logie, Flavia Elisa
Christiansted, St. Croix, VI
Logie, John H. .... Grand Rapids, MI
Logie, Thomas D. .... Front Royal, VA
Loginov, William A. .... Boston, MA
Loginsky, Marian E. .... Birmingham, MI
LoGiudice, Susan E. .... Portland, ME
Logli, Paul A. .... Rockford, IL
Loglisci, David A. .... Garden City, NY
Loglisci, Gail Beichman .... Mineola, NY
Logoluso, Timothy V. .... Fresno, CA
Kerman, CA
Logomasini, James C. .... Ballwin, MO
Logothetis, Pence & Doll .... Dayton, OH
Logothetis, Sorrell .... Dayton, OH
Logothetis, Steven .... Orange, NJ
Lograsso, Donald L. .... Blue Springs, MO
Logren, Arlen R. .... Minneapolis, MN
Logsdon, Barry G. .... Newport News, VA
Logsdon, Dawn S. .... Lexington, KY
Logsdon, Donald G. .... St. Albans, WV
Logsdon, Eve L. .... Portland, OR
Logsdon, Gary S. .... Brownsville, KY
Logsdon, Gary S., and Associates
Brownsville, KY
Logsdon, Harold L. .... Kingfisher, OK
Logsdon, James C. .... San Francisco, CA
Logsdon, Jann B. .... Louisville, KY
Logsdon, Jeffrey L. .... Frankfort, KY
Logsdon, John Michael
North Wilkesboro, NC

Logsdon, Larry Stephen ....Birmingham, AL
Logsdon, Patricia A. ....Dallas, TX
Logsdon, Richard R. ....Clearwater, FL
Logsdon, Richard R., P.A. ....Clearwater, FL
Logsdon, Robert G. ....Miamisburg, OH
Logsdon, Susan A. ....Houston, TX
Logsdon, Susan S. ....Winchester, MA
Logsdon, Tara ....Palmer, AK
Logsdon, William H. ....Pittsburgh, PA
Logstrom, Bridget A. ....Minneapolis, MN
Logue, A. Keith ....Marietta, GA
Logue, Abbi Silver ....Las Vegas, NV
Logue, Anthony A. ....Erie, PA
Logue, Bill ....Waco, TX
Logue, Daniel V ....Philadelphia, PA
Logue, Dayton ....Panama City, FL
Panama City Beach, FL
Logue, Donley C., Jr. ....Bedford, PA
Logue, Frank ....New Haven, CT
Logue, Gregory C. ....Knoxville, TN
Logue, Gregory F. ....Tacoma, WA
Logue, Holly Rolfes ....Monroe, LA
Logue, Irving A. ....Long Beach, NY
Logue, James G. ....Radnor, PA
Logue, John M. ....Philadelphia, PA
Logue, Katherine A. ....Waco, TX
Logue, Kevin C. ....New York, NY
Logue, Lawrence E., Jr. ....Santa Ana, CA
Logue, Michael B. ....Anchorage, AK
Logue, Michael R. ....Philadelphia, PA
Logue, Patricia M. ....Chicago, IL
Logue, Thomas J. ....Mattoon, IL
Logue, Thomas W. ....Miami, FL
Loguercio, Caren Lynn ....Medford, NY
Loguidice, Peter D. ....Vero Beach, FL
Logwood, Kenneth W. ....Washington, DC
Loh, Alice K. ....San Francisco, CA
Loh, Christopher E. ....New York, NY
Loh, David ....Boston, MA
Loh, David Y. ....New York, NY
Loh, Paul A. ....Philadelphia, PA
Loh, Paul J. ....Los Angeles, CA
Loh, Susan R. ....Long Beach, CA
Loh, Trudi K. Foutts ....Westlake Village, CA
Loha, Joseph ....Jefferson, OH
Lohan, Kevin P. ....Boston, MA
Lohaus, Judith D. ....St. Louis, MO
Lohe, Werner ....Boston, MA
Lohf, Ernest W. ....Denver, CO
Lohf, Shaiman & Jacobs, P.C.
Denver, CO
Lohff, John R. ....Anchorage, AK
Lohff, William ....Naperville, IL
Lohier, Raymond J. ....Department of Justice,
Civil Rights Division, GV
Lohin, Joseph R. ....Kingston, PA
Lohinski, Paul Bernard ....Baltimore, MD
Lohiser, Kenneth L. ....Cleveland, OH
Lohm, Thomas A. ....Rockville, MD
Lohman, Catherine L.
Colorado Springs, CO
Lohman, David H. ....Portland, OR
Lohman, David W. ....Coeur d'Alene, ID
Lohman, David W., P.A. ....Coeur d'Alene, ID
Lohman, Donald A. ....St. Louis, MO
Lohman, Edward F. ....West Linn, OR
Lohman, Eugene E. ....Abingdon, VA
Lohman, Geoffrey S. ....Indianapolis, IN
Lohman, James C. ....Tallahassee, FL
Lohman, James D. ....Denison, IA
Lohman, Janette M. ....St. Louis, MO
Lohman, Jennifer Slavik ....St. Louis, MO
Lohman Law Offices, The, P.S.C.
Louisville, KY
Lohman & Lohman, L.L.C.
Colorado Springs, CO
Lohman, Richard V.
Colorado Springs, CO
Lohman, Robert G., Jr. ....Louisville, KY
Lohman, Sabrina Wells ....Louisville, KY
Lohman, Thomas L. ....Anchorage, AK
Lohmann, Andrew M. ....Richmond, VA
Lohmann, Carl ....Summit, NJ
Lohmann, Danny G. ....Norman, OK
Lohmann, Glazer & Irwin ....Houston, TX
Lohmann, Janet Kay ....Rosemead, CA
Lohmann, John A.W. ....Charleston, WV
Lohmann, John, III ....Houston, TX
Lohmann, Victor F., III ....Fort Wayne, IN
Lohmann, Virginia E. ....Columbus, OH
Lohmann, Walter H., Jr. ....Washington, DC
Lohman-Oota, Lucinda K. ....Boston, MA
Lohmar, Douglas W., Jr. ....Chicago, IL
Lohmar, William T., Jr. ....St. Charles, MO
Lohmeier, George A. ....Greenfield, IN
Lohmeyer, C. William ....New Albany, IN
Lohmeyer, Charles Edward
Department of the Army,
Office of the Judge Advocate General, GV
Lohmeyer, Fred ....Dallas, TX
Lohmeyer Law Offices, The
New Albany, IN
Lohmeyer, Rhonda B. ....Gretna, LA
Lohmeyer, Steven S. ....New Albany, IN
Lohn, Andrew William ....Atlanta, GA
Lohn, D. Robert ....Portland, OR
Lohn, John J. ....Medina, OH
Lohn, Sherman V. ....Missoula, MT
Lohner, Linda T. C. ....Rochester, NY
Lohnes, Scott M. ....Fort Wayne, IN
Lohoff, Randy K. ....Russell, KY
Lohonen, Dylan ....Chicago, IL
Lohorn, James M. ....Lafayette, IN
Lohorn, Peggy ....Crawfordsville, IN
Lohr, Daniel E. ....Moorestown, NJ
Philadelphia, PA
Lohr, George E. ....Denver, CO
Lohr, Gregory N. ....Sioux City, IA

Lohr, Janet L. ....Lexington, KY
Lohr, John M. ....Monterey, VA
Lohr, John R. ....Malvern, PA
Lohr, Layne C. ....Dover, NH
Lohr, Lori E. ....Richmond, VA
Lohr, Noël C. ....Los Angeles, CA
Lohr, Philip B. ....Lexington, NC
Lohr, Richard A. ....Akron, OH
Lohr, Robert J. ....St. Louis, MO
Lohr, Terrance G.
Cape May Court House, NJ
Norristown, PA
Lohr, Walter G., Jr. ....Baltimore, MD
Lohr, William J. ....Columbus, OH
Lohre, John W. ....Brookfield, WI
Lohrentz, Carlton W. ....Arlington Heights, IL
Lohrentz, Carlton W., & Associates
Arlington Heights, IL
Lohrenz, Eric L. ....Chicago, IL
Lohrer, John P. ....Washington, DC
Lohrey, Christopher Thomas ....Bend, OR
Lohrey, Philip H., Jr. ....Towson, MD
Lohrfink, Charles D., Jr.
White Plains, NY
Lohrke, Mary ....Tulsa, OK
Lohrman, C. Richard ....Amherst, NY
Lohrmann, Henry T. ....Stephenville, TX
Lohrmann, John W. ....Walla Walla, WA
Lohrmann Law Offices ....Walla Walla, WA
Lohrmann, Rolf-Dieter Johannes
Gaithersburg, MD
Lohr-Schmidt, Berndt ....Los Angeles, CA
Lohrstorfer, John K. ....Kalamazoo, MI
Lohrstorfer, Timothy A. ....Indianapolis, IN
Lohse, Albert R. ....Houston, TX
Lohse, Ashby I. ....Tucson, AZ
Lohse, Constance B. ....Bethesda, MD
Lohse, Herman A., III
Colorado Springs, CO
Lohse, Timothy W. ....Palo Alto, CA
Lohwater, Karl W. ....Secaucus, NJ
Loiacono, James V. ....Painesville, OH
Loiacono, Joseph, II ....Austin, TX
Loiben, Alan A. ....Chicago, IL
Loidolt, Cecilie Morris ....Minneapolis, MN
Loigman, Larry S. ....Middletown, NJ
Loigman, Lynda C. ....New York, NY
Loigman, Robert S. ....New York, NY
Loignon, Michael R. ....Hardwick, VT
Loikith, D'Alessio & Kugelman, A Professional
Corporation ....Fairfield, NJ
Loikith, Thomas ....Fairfield, NJ
Loikow, Ann Hume
Federal Deposit Insurance Corporation,
Regulation and Legislation Section, GV
Lois, Dale J. ....Stamford, CT
Loiseau, Holly E. Washington
Washington, DC
Loiseaux, Pierre R. ....Davis, CA
Loisel, Michael J. ....Toledo, OH
Loiselle, Alva P. ....Hartford, CT
Loiselle, Arthur A., Jr. ....Worcester, MA
Loiselle, Darien S. ....Portland, OR
Loiselle, Sabrina P. ....Portland, OR
Loitherstein, Judy S. ....Boston, MA
Loitz, LaDonna M. ....Chicago, IL
Loitz, Steven R. ....Seattle, WA
Loizeaux, Christopher ....Chico, CA
Loizeaux, Paul C.
Department of Agriculture,
Office of the General Counsel, GV
Loizides, Christopher D. ....Philadelphia, PA
Loizzi, Michael A., Jr. ....Arlington Heights, IL
Loizzi, Nicholas V. ....Chicago, IL
Loizzo, Josephine A. ....Huntington, NY
Loizzo, Thomas F. ....Woodstock, IL
Lojek, Donald W. ....Boise, ID
Lojek Law Offices ....Boise, ID
Lojek, Michael ....Fairfax, VA
Lojewski, Cathy M. ....Erie, PA
Lojewski, Eugene A. ....Naples, FL
Lojewski, Eugene A., P.A. ....Naples, FL
Lojewski, Jeffrey D. ....Cleveland, OH
Lojo, Manuel A. ....Casper, WY
Lokant, Fred W. ....Oceana, WV
Loke, Dawn S. ....Hartland, WI
Loke, Kit Choy ....San Francisco, CA
Loke, Tien-Li ....Pacific Palisades, CA
Loken, Gregory A. ....New York, NY
Loken, James B. ....St. Paul, MN
Loken, Keith ....Department of State,
Office of the Legal Adviser, GV
Lokensgard, Mary Taylor ....Appleton, WI
Lokensgard, Michael J. ....Appleton, WI
Lokensgard, Steven Jon ....St. Paul, MN
Loker, F. Ford, Jr. ....Baltimore, MD
Loker, Joseph Q. ....Chicago, IL
Loker, Mary G. ....Timonium, MD
Loker, Michael W. ....San Diego, CA
Loke Walsh, Tien-Li ....Los Angeles, CA
Lokey, Charles M. ....Atlanta, GA
Lokey, Darlene D. ....Department of Defense,
Defense Legal Services Agency, GV
Lokey, Hamilton ....Atlanta, GA
Lokey, Helen M. ....Fort Worth, TX
Lokey, James H., Jr. ....Atlanta, GA
Lokey, Jeffrey J. ....Palo Alto, CA
Lokey, Marguerite ....Dallas, TX
Lokey, Paul E. ....Dallas, TX
Lokey and Smith ....Atlanta, GA
Lokis, Elena ....Uniondale, NY
Lokken, Jane E. ....Eau Claire, WI
Lokken, Lawrence ....Gainesville, FL
Lokken, Owen G. ....Rowlett, TX
Lokken, Paul J. ....St. Paul, MN
Lokken, Paul R. ....Eau Claire, WI
Lokken, Rachel N. ....Chicago, IL

Lokker, Brian N., Law Offices of
Clifton, NJ
Lokker, Brian N., Law Offices of
Montclair, NJ
Lokker, Ellen R. ....Washington, DC
Lokker, Laura J. ....Clifton, NJ
Lokting, David A. ....Portland, OR
Lokuta, Jan Joseph Stephen ....Port Jervis, NY
Lolan, Pamela B. ....New Orleans, LA
Loland, Lane T. ....Bothell, WA
Lolcama, Joan T. ....Washington, DC
Lolie, Allan F., Jr. ....Paris, IL
Lolio, John R., Jr. ....Pennsauken, NJ
Lolis, Gail M. ....Smithtown, NY
Loll, Robert A. ....Irvine, CA
Lollar, Bradley K. ....Dallas, TX
Lollar, Cecil E. ....Rangely, CO
Lollar, Charles M. ....Norfolk, VA
Lollar, James L. ....Fort Worth, TX
Lolley, Anne E. ....Topeka, KS
Lolley, E. Randall ....Osprey, FL
Lolley, John L. ....Monroe, LA
Lolli, Don R. ....Overland Park, KS
Kansas City, MO
Lolli, Richard J. ....Canton, OH
Lollie, Debbie A. ....Pasadena, CA
Lollin, Gene ....Somerset, NJ
Lollino, Laurie A. ....Chicago, IL
Lollis, Jane D. ....Louisville, KY
Lollis, Paula R. ....Greenville, SC
Lollman, Joseph F. ....Tulsa, OK
Lolly, Allan Scott ....San Diego, CA
Lolus, Bradley E. ....Fort Lauderdale, FL
Lom, John R. ....Department of Agriculture,
Office of the General Counsel, GV
Loman, Lori Lynn ....Ada, OK
Loman, Marianne Renjilian
Chevy Chase, MD
Loman, Mark S. ....Middletown, CT
Loman, Melissa J. ....Denver, CO
Loman, Paul ....Houston, TX
Loman, Robert B. ....Bethany, MO
Loman, Thomas G. ....Cresskill, NJ
Lomangino, Lori ....Dunlap, TN
Lomans, Patricia A. ....Boston, MA
Lomanto, Angelo D. ....Johnstown, NY
Lomanto, Concetta R. ....Albany, NY
Lomanto, Edward S. ....Gloversville, NY
Lomasney, Mary T. ....Boston, MA
Lomason, Philip E. ....Croswell, MI
Lomax, Carol P. ....San Antonio, TX
Lomax, Charles E. ....Deerfield Beach, FL
Chicago, IL
Lomax, Dionne C. ....Department of Justice,
Antitrust Division, GV
Lomax, Donald R. ....New York, NY
Lomax, Donald R., P.C. ....New York, NY
Lomax, Gregory A. ....Cherry Hill, NJ
Lomax, Henry C. ....Charlotte, NC
Lomax, Jason A. ....Washington, DC
Lomax, John D. ....Torrance, CA
Lomax, John F., Jr. ....Greenville, SC
Lomax, John R. ....Virginia Beach, VA
Lomax, Lisa A. ....Columbus, OH
Lomax, Lowry ....Pascagoula, MS
Lomax, Robert R. ....Columbus, GA
Lomax, Tarrant H. ....Washington, DC
Annapolis, MD
Lomax, Tarrant H., Esq., P.C.
Washington, DC
Lomax, Thomas P. ....Media, PA
Lomayesva, Frederick K. ....Sells, AZ
Lomazow, Michael J. ....Riverside, CA
Lomazzo, Nancy L. ....Stamford, CT
Lomb, Gregory P. ....Rochester, NY
Lombaer, Forest R., Jr. ....Chicago, IL
Lombana, Hector J. ....Miami, FL
Sarasota, FL
Lombard, Ben "Kip", Jr. ....Ashland, OR
Lombard, Benjamin G. ....Milwaukee, WI
Lombard, David N. ....Seattle, WA
Lombard, Eduardo S. ....Orlando, FL
Lombard, Frank P. ....Waterbury, CT
Lombard, Frederica B. ....Detroit, MI
Lombard, Frederick E. ....Shrewsbury, NJ
Lombard, Gardner, Honsowetz, Potter & Budge
Eugene, OR
Lombard, Herbert, P.C. ....Cottage Grove, OR
Lombard, Herbert W., Jr. (P.C.)
Cottage Grove, OR
Eugene, OR
Lombard, Jane Ann ....Philadelphia, PA
Lombard, John C. ....Dayton, OH
Lombard, John C. ....Seattle, WA
Lombard, John C., Law Firm of
Seattle, WA
Lombard, John J., Jr. ....Philadelphia, PA
Lombard, Joseph C. ....Washington, DC
Lombard, Kathleen M. ....Torrance, CA
Lombard, Leonard ....New York, NY
Lombard, Linda S. ....North Charleston, SC
Lombard, Michael A. ....Mandeville, LA
Lombard, Richard S. ....Dallas, TX
Lombard, Richard T. ....Flushing, NY
Lombard, Richard T., Jr. ....Flushing, NY
Lombard, Willard C. ....Everett, MA
Lombard-Clarke, Lisa ....Augusta, GA
Lombardero, David A. ....Los Angeles, CA
Lombardi, Albertina D. ....Allentown, PA
Lombardi, Alfred S. ....Providence, RI
Lombardi, Bonnell M. ....Danbury, CT
Lombardi, Cara H. ....Springfield, MA
Lombardi, Carlo A. ....Rosemont, PA
Lombardi, Carolina Ann ....Miami, FL
Lombardi, Christopher ....Long Beach, CA
Lombardi, Cornelius E., Jr.
Kansas City, MO
Lombardi, David E., Jr. ....San Francisco, CA

Lombardi, David G. ....Akron, OH
Lombardi, David R. ....Boise, ID
Lombardi, Dennis M. ....Honolulu, HI
Lombardi, Dino J. ....Kew Gardens, NY
Lombardi, Donald E. ....Akron, OH
Lombardi, Donna M. ....Edison, NJ
Lombardi, Floyd F. ....Jersey City, NJ
Lombardi, Francis T. ....Syracuse, NY
Lombardi, Frank D. ....Bronx, NY
Lombardi, Frederick M. ....Akron, OH
Lombardi, Gabriella A. ....Palo Alto, CA
Lombardi, Gary L. ....Albany, NY
Lombardi, George C. ....Chicago, IL
Lombardi, George L. ....Union, NJ
Lombardi, Gregg F. ....Kansas City, MO
Lombardi, James A. ....Rye, NY
Lombardi, James J. ....Upper Marlboro, MD
Lombardi, James T. ....Manchester, NH
Lombardi, James V., III ....Houston, TX
Lombardi, Janet L. ....Worcester, MA
Lombardi, Jeanette Martinez ....Naples, FL
Lombardi, Jennifer A. ....Brick, NJ
Lombardi, Jerome D. ....Wexford, PA
Lombardi, John A. ....Jersey City, NJ
Lombardi, John Anthony ....Summit, NJ
Lombardi, John R. ....Rolling Meadows, IL
Lombardi, Joseph E. ....New York, NY
Lombardi, Kevin C.
Commodity Futures Trading Commission,
Division of Enforcement, GV
Lombardi, Leonard E. ....Pleasantville, NY
Lombardi & Lombardi ....Edison, NJ
Lombardi, Loper & Conant, LLP
Oakland, CA
San Francisco, CA
Lombardi, Louis P., II
Plymouth Meeting, PA
Lombardi, M. Susan ....Westminster, CO
Lombardi, Marcie N. (IBA) ....Seattle, WA
Lombardi, Maria T. ....Cleveland, OH
Lombardi, Marianne Elizabeth
Washington, DC
Lombardi, Marilou ....Audubon, NJ
Lombardi, Mark A. ....East Quogue, NY
Lombardi, Michael F. ....Edison, NJ
Lombardi, Michael J. ....White Plains, NY
Lombardi, Michael P. ....Brooklyn, NY
Lombardi & Perry, LLP ....Long Beach, CA
Lombardi, Powers & Amster
Upper Marlboro, MD
Lombardi, Ralph A. ....Oakland, CA
Lombardi, Reinhard, Walsh & Harrison,
P.C. ....Albany, NY
Lombardi, Richard C. ....Ravenna, OH
Lombardi, Richard Edward
West Chester, PA
Lombardi, Robert ....Newark, NJ
Lombardi, Robert J. ....Ashland, OR
Lombardi, Robert P. ....Worcester, MA
Lombardi, Ronald V. ....Paramus, NJ
Lombardi, Sebastian P. ....West Orange, NJ
Lombardi, Stephen D. ....Des Moines, IA
Lombardi, Stephen F. ....Edison, NJ
Lombardi, Tarky, Jr. ....Albany, NY
Syracuse, NY
Lombardi, Thomas J. ....Canton, OH
Lombardi, Valentino D. ....Providence, RI
Lombardi, Vincent J. ....South Easton, MA
Lombardi, Vincent T. ....Seattle, WA
Lombardini, Carol A. ....Encino, CA
Lombardino, James, & Associates, A
Professional Corporation ....Houston, TX
Lombardino, James T. ....Houston, TX
Lombardo, Alfred ....Salinas, CA
Lombardo, Angelo ....Los Angeles, CA
Lombardo, Anthony ....Salinas, CA
Lombardo, Anthony M. ....Mount Prospect, IL
Lombardo, Anthony M., Ltd.
Mount Prospect, IL
Lombardo, Anthony P. ....Long Beach, CA
Lombardo, Bruce D. ....Harrisburg, PA
King Of Prussia, PA
Lombardo, Catherine M. ....Mentor, OH
Lombardo, Edw. T. ....Columbus, OH
Lombardo, Frank J. ....Seaford, NY
Lombardo, Geraldine ....Hingham, MA
Lombardo, Gerard R. ....Buffalo, NY
Lombardo & Gilles ....Hollister, CA
Monterey, CA
Salinas, CA
Santa Cruz, CA
Lombardo, J. Christopher ....Naples, FL
Lombardo, James A. ....Amsterdam, NY
Saratoga Springs, NY
Lombardo, James G. ....Closter, NJ
Lombardo, John D. ....Los Angeles, CA
Lombardo, John J. ....Shaker Heights, OH
Lombardo, Joseph F. ....Cleveland, OH
Lombardo, Joseph F. ....Philadelphia, PA
Lombardo, Joseph J. ....Lancaster, PA
Lombardo, Julie Culver ....Salinas, CA
Lombardo, Kenneth R. ....Detroit, MI
Lombardo, Louis ....New York, NY
Lombardo, Louis J. ....Annandale, VA
Lombardo, Louis K. ....Phoenix, AZ
Lombardo, Margaret C. ....Houston, TX
Lombardo, Maureen Ann ....Winchester, MA
Lombardo, Michael J. ....Willimantic, CT
Lombardo, Michael J. ....Buffalo, NY
Lombardo, Michelle M. ....Philadelphia, PA
Lombardo, Pasquale G. ....Chicago, IL
Lombardo, Paul A. ....Charlottesville, VA
Lombardo, Peter A. ....Lombard, IL
Lombardo, Peter J. ....Bradenton, FL
Lombardo, Philip C., Jr. ....Worcester, MA
Lombardo, Raymond A. ....Philadelphia, PA
Lombardo, Richard ....Hempstead, NY
Lombardo, Richard F. ....Kansas City, MO

Lombardo, Robert L.
Upper Marlboro, MD
Lombardo, Salvatore V. ... Lafayette, CA
Lombardo, Thomas E. ... Hartford, CT
Lombardo, Vincent J. ... Los Angeles, CA
Lombardo, Vincent J. ... Cleveland, OH
Lombardo, Vincent T. ... Cleveland, OH
Lombardy, Martha Lee ... Orlando, FL
Lombardy, Russell A., II ... New York, NY
Lombart, D. Reed ... Roanoke, VA
Lomberg, Paul ... Hackensack, NJ
White Plains, NY
Lomberg, Paul, P.C. ... Hackensack, NJ
Lombillo, Erik ... Clearwater, FL
Lombillo, Sybil A. ... New York, NY
Lombino, Annamaria A. ... New York, NY
Lombino, Annamaria A., P.C.
New York, NY
Lombino, Charles D. ... Studio City, CA
Lombino, Joseph J. M. ... Tacoma, WA
Lombino, Joseph K. ... Atlanta, GA
Lombino, Michelle C. ... Phoenix, AZ
Lombino, Richard M. ... New York, NY
Lombraña, David ... Houston, TX
Lombrano-Williamson & Associates
Irving, TX
Lombrano-Williamson, Barbara ... Irving, TX
Lomeli, Ann F. ... Springfield, MA
Lomeli, Patricia Ann Futter ... Hartford, CT
Lomell, Leonard G. ... Toms River, NJ
Lomell, Muccifori, Adler, Ravaschiere, Amabile & Pehlivanian, A Professional Corporation ... Toms River, NJ
Lomenick, James Robert ... Atlanta, GA
Lomenick, Otis E., Jr. ... Opelousas, LA
Lomenzo, John P. ... New York, NY
Lomenzo, Margaret E. ... Chicago, IL
Lomenzo, Philip N. ... Wood Ridge, NJ
Lomeo, James E. ... Mc Keesport, PA
Lometti, Christopher ... New York, NY
Lomhoff, Peter G. ... Oakland, CA
Lominac, Bruce Wayne ... London, KY
Lominac, Karen T. ... Ocean Isle Beach, NC
Lominick, Wesley R., Jr. ... Vicksburg, MS
Lomio, J. Paul ... Palo Alto, CA
Lomma, Anthony C. ... Scranton, PA
Lommen, A. Paul ... Minneapolis, MN
Lommen, Nelson, Cole & Stageberg, P.A.
Minneapolis, MN
Hudson, WI
Lommen, Stephanie M. ... Forest Grove, OR
Lomonaco, A. Philip ... Knoxville, TN
Lo Monaco & Lo Monaco ... Rochester, NY
LoMonaco, Paula ... Chicago, IL
LoMonaco, Peter F. ... Libertyville, IL
LoMonaco, Peter F., P.C. ... Libertyville, IL
Lo Monaco, Richard S. ... Rochester, NY
Lomonaco, Ross J. ... Marrero, LA
Lomond, Kristin M. ... Louisville, KY
LoMonte, Douglas E. ... Westport, CT
Lo Monte, Michelle ... Parsippany, NJ
Lomp, Peter Vincent ... Kew Gardens, NY
Lomupo, Kevin R. ... Pittsburgh, PA
Lomurro, Davison, Eastman & Munoz, P.A.
Freehold, NJ
Lomurro, Donald M. ... Freehold, NJ
Lomuscio, Catherine ... Douglaston, NY
Lomuscio, Frank A., Jr. ... Bronx, NY
Lona, Marie A. ... Chicago, IL
Lonabaugh, Ellsworth E. ... Sheridan, WY
Lonabaugh, Jerry M. ... Runnemede, NJ
Lonabaugh and Riggs ... Sheridan, WY
Lonardo, Angelo F. ... Cleveland, OH
Lonardo, Charles H. ... Joplin, MO
Lonardo, Joseph D. ... Washington, DC
Lonardo, Thomas T. ... Meriden, CT
Lonardo, Thomas T., P.C. ... Meriden, CT
Lonas, Leonard L., Jr. ... Manassas, VA
Lonas, Linda J. ... Manassas, VA
Lonas and Lonas ... Manassas, VA
Lonas, Webster M., Jr. ... Canton, OH
Lona-Wiant, Magdalena ... Orange, CA
Lonberger, James E. ... Indianapolis, IN
Loncar & Associates ... Dallas, TX
El Paso, TX
Tyler, TX
Wichita Falls, TX
Loncar, Brian ... Dallas, TX
El Paso, TX
Tyler, TX
Wichita Falls, TX
Loncar, George M. ... Buffalo, NY
Loncar, Ivan ... New York, NY
Loncon, Charles V. ... Savannah, GA
Loncto, Deborah A. ... Albany, NY
Lonczak, Don J. ... New York, NY
Londa, Abram D. ... Elizabeth, NJ
Londa, Bruce S. ... New York, NY
Londa, Ernest I. ... New York, NY
Londa, Felice T. ... Elizabeth, NJ
Londa, Jeffrey C. ... Houston, TX
Londa & Londa ... Elizabeth, NJ
Londa, Raymond S. ... Elizabeth, NJ
Londa and Traub LLP ... New York, NY
Londahl, Jan P. ... Salem, OR
Londe, Carl L. ... Chicago, IL
Londen, Jack W. ... San Francisco, CA
Londer, Donald H. ... Portland, OR
Londergan, Gary W. ... London, OH
Londerholm, Robert C., Sr. ... Olathe, KS
Londin, Jessica ... Long Beach, NY
Londin, Robert ... New York, NY
Londo, Darold J. ... Madison, WI
Londoff Law Firm, The, L.L.C.
St. Charles, MO
Londoff, Michael T. ... St. Charles, MO
London, Alan E. ... Pittsburgh, PA
London, Alfred L. ... Chicago, IL
London, Alice ... Austin, TX
London, Allen F. ... New York, NY
London, Alvin B. ... Baltimore, MD
London & Amburn, P.C. ... Knoxville, TN
London, Amy Goldman ... New York, NY
London, Anderson, Antolak & Hoeft, Ltd.
Minneapolis, MN
London, Arthur ... Malibu, CA
London & Associates, A Prof. Corp., Law Offices of ... Houston, TX
London, Bernard ... New York, NY
London, Betty R. ... Golden, CO
London, Brenda Lee ... Winter Park, FL
London, Brett G. ... Westminster, CA
London, Christopher Dwight Mejia
Boston, MA
London, David G. ... Bloomfield Hills, MI
London, David H. ... Boston, MA
London, David L. ... Denver, CO
London, David L. ... Washington, DC
London & Doherty LLP ... New York, NY
London, Donald H. ... Millwood, NY
London, Edwin L. ... Philadelphia, PA
London, Ephraim ... New York, NY
London, Eric D. ... Washington, DC
London, Eric H. ... Morgantown, WV
London, Eric N. ... Latham, NY
London Fischer LLP ... New York, NY
London, Fred S. ... Baltimore, MD
London, Frederick W.
Westlake Village, CA
London, Fredric S. ... New York, NY
London, Gary M. ... Birmingham, AL
London, Harriet J. ... Newark, NJ
London, Howard A. ... Chicago, IL
London, Howard M. ... Niles, IL
London, Ira D. ... New York, NY
London, J. A.(Jack) ... Mountain View, CA
London, J. Phillip, Jr. ... Falls Church, VA
London, J. Tate ... Seattle, WA
London, Jack ... New Bedford, MA
London, Jack E., (P.A.) ... Hollywood, FL
London, Jack W. ... Austin, TX
London, James D. ... Cleveland, OH
London, James H. ... Knoxville, TN
London, Jay M. ... Ambler, PA
London, Jeffrey H. ... Baltimore, MD
London, Jeffrey L. ... Chicago, IL
London, Jennifer ... White Plains, NY
London, Jeremy D. ... Washington, DC
London, Joan E. ... Reading, PA
London, Joanna ... Department of Justice, Immigration and Naturalization Service, GV
London, Joel L. ... New York, NY
London, John A., III ... Baton Rouge, LA
London, Joseph J. ... Woodland Hills, CA
London, Joyce C. ... New York, NY
London, Judith M. ... Los Angeles, CA
London, Julie Taub ... Armonk, NY
London, Kathleen B. ... Hanover, NH
London, Kevin ... Phillipsburg, NJ
London & Kisner ... Austin, TX
London, Lauri B. ... New York, NY
London, Leonard G. ... Williamsville, NY
London, Leslie Ann ... Detroit, MI
London, Leslie G. ... Newark, NJ
London, Lisa Peller ... Washington, DC
London & London ... Kensington, CT
London, Marjorie A. ... Hartford, CT
London, Mark ... Washington, DC
London, Mark J. ... Chicago, IL
London, Mark S. ... Hollywood, FL
London, Mark S., P.A. ... Hollywood, FL
London, Martin ... New York, NY
London, Maylon K. ... Cleveland, GA
London & Mead ... Washington, DC
London, Michael ... Austin, TX
London, Michael B. ... Los Angeles, CA
London, Michael D. ... San Diego, CA
London, Michael E. ... Oakland, CA
London, Michael J. ... Golden Valley, MN
London, Norman S. ... St. Louis, MO
London, Oscar S. ... New York, NY
London, Paul S. ... Bronx, NY
London, Rhoda A. ... New York, NY
London, Richard Chapman ... Birmingham, AL
London, Richard D. ... Silver Spring, MD
London, Richard S., (A Professional Corporation) ... Houston, TX
London, Robert H. ... Santa Monica, CA
London, Robert P. ... Phillipsburg, NJ
London, Ronald G. ... Washington, DC
London, Ronald S. ... Minneapolis, MN
London, Russell ... Kensington, CT
London, Sheldon I. ... Washington, DC
London, Sheldon M. ... Miami, FL
London, Sheri Faith ... Stamford, CT
London, Stefanie L. ... St. Louis, MO
London, Stephen D. ... New Orleans, LA
London, Steven J. ... New York, NY
London, Steven R. ... Boston, MA
London, Stuart ... New York, NY
London, Susan J. ... New York, NY
London, Toni B. ... Eagle River, AK
London, William A. ... Chicago, IL
London, William D. ... New York, NY
London, William D. ... White Plains, NY
London, William H. ... Chicago, IL
London, William L., III ... Durham, NC
London & Yancey, LLC ... Birmingham, AL
Montgomery, AL
Tuscaloosa, AL
London-Zeitz, Robin I. ... Cherry Hill, NJ
Londos, Katherine C. ... Roanoke, VA
Londregan, Francis T. ... New London, CT
Londregan, Jeffrey T. ... New London, CT
Londregan, Thomas J. ... New London, CT
Londrigan, James T. ... Springfield, IL
Londrigan & Londrigan ... Springfield, IL
Londrigan, Patrick J. ... Springfield, IL
Londrigan, Potter & Randle, P.C.
Springfield, IL
Londrigan, Thomas F. ... Springfield, IL
Londrigan, Thomas F., Jr. ... Springfield, IL
Londrigan, Timothy J. ... Springfield, IL
Londynsky, Paul A. ... Alamo, CA
Lone, Ronald J. ... Seattle, WA
Lonegan, Bryan ... New York, NY
Lonegro, Frank A. ... Jacksonville, FL
Lonen, Martin K. ... Washington, DC
Lonergan, Aimee ... New Orleans, LA
Lonergan, Charles R., Jr. ... Seattle, WA
Lonergan, Clint A. ... Portland, OR
Lonergan, Dana P. ... Bridgeport, CT
Lonergan, Dana P., P.C. ... Bridgeport, CT
Lonergan, Daniel G.
Federal Deposit Insurance Corporation, Appellate Litigation Section, GV
Lonergan, David C. ... Dallas, TX
Lonergan, Donna-Maria ... Hartford, CT
Lonergan, Edward J. ... Boston, MA
Lonergan, Edward J. ... Bronxville, NY
Lonergan, Gary W. ... Alexandria, VA
Lonergan, Gary W., Ltd. ... Alexandria, VA
Lonergan, James A. ... Los Angeles, CA
Lonergan, James B. ... Virginia Beach, VA
Lonergan, James F. ... Portland, OR
Lonergan, James S. ... Kingston, NY
Lonergan, John R. ... Fort Lauderdale, FL
Lonergan, Joseph W. ... Norristown, PA
Lonergan, Kelly James ... Urbana, IL
Lonergan, Kevin ... Appleton, WI
Lonergan, Lauren E. ... Minneapolis, MN
Lonergan, Lawrence R. ... New York, NY
Lonergan & Lonergan ... Portland, OR
Lonergan, M. A., Jr. ... New Orleans, LA
Lonergan, Mark D. ... San Francisco, CA
Lonergan, Mary Dick ... Portland, OR
Lonergan, Matthew C. ... Nashville, TN
Lonergan, Michael J. ... Albany, NY
Lonergan, Michael M. ... Concord, NH
Lonergan, Rebecca S. ... Los Angeles, CA
Lonergan, Richard L. ... Portland, OR
Lonergan, Robert A. ... Spokane, WA
Lonergan, Ronald C. ... Tuscaloosa, AL
Lonergan, Susan E. Schneider ... Rye, NY
Lonergan, Thomas C. ... Fort Bragg, CA
Lonergan, Thomas D. ... Clinton, IA
Lonergan, Todd M. ... Houston, TX
Lonergan, William R., Jr.
South Salem, NY
Lonero, Jay M. ... Metairie, LA
Lones, Laura L. ... Decatur, GA
Lonetz, Ronald G. ... Eastpointe, MI
Loney, Andrea E. ... Greenwood, SC
Loney, Glenn E.
Board of Governors Of The Federal Reserve System, Division of Consumer and Community Affairs, GV
Loney, Michael E. ... Annapolis, MD
Long, A. Donald ... Lancaster, CA
Long, A. Kel, III ... Atlanta, GA
Long, A. Kel, III, P.C. ... Atlanta, GA
Long, Aimee D. ... San Francisco, CA
Long, Alan J. ... Detroit, MI
Long Aldridge & Norman LLP
Washington, DC
Atlanta, GA
Long, Allison ... Philadelphia, PA
Long, Alonzo H. ... Roanoke, VA
Long, Alvin W. ... Boynton Beach, FL
Long, Alysia M. ... Atlanta, GA
Long, Amy Thoreson ... St. Paul, MN
Long, Andrea C. ... Richmond, VA
Long, Andrew J. ... University Park, IL
Long, Andrew K. ... Washington, DC
Long, Andy ... Knoxville, TN
Long, Anna M. ... Vista, CA
Long, Anne Osborne ... Sullivan's Island, SC
Long, Anthony J. ... Detroit, MI
Long, Arthur S. ... New York, NY
Long, Arthur S., III ... Charlotte, NC
Long & Associates, P.C. ... Washington, DC
Long, B. Earnest ... Greensburg, PA
Long, Badger, Sullivan & Robertson, P.A.
Salisbury, MD
Long, Baker & Tishkoff, LLP
Ann Arbor, MI
Long, Barney R. ... Sallisaw, OK
Long, Barney R., P.C., The Law Office
Sallisaw, OK
Long, Barry E. ... White Plains, NY
Long, Bernard J., Jr. ... Washington, DC
Long, Bertram M. ... Greenbrae, CA
Long, Beverly Glenn ... Providence, RI
Long, Bill I., Jr. ... Winston-Salem, NC
Long, Bobby R. ... Jackson, MS
Long, Boyd J. ... Kennebunkport, ME
Long, Brian D. ... Coeur d'Alene, ID
Long, Brian D. ... Lancaster, PA
Long, Bruce R. ... Youngstown, OH
Long, Bruce W. ... Dallas, TX
Long, Burner, Parks & Sealy, A Professional Corporation ... Austin, TX
Long, C. Thomas ... Washington, DC
Long, Calhoun A. ... Fayetteville, GA
Long, Carl Lawrence ... Colorado Springs, CO
Long, Carol Grant ... San Francisco, CA
Long, Carol Joy ... Tampa, FL
Long, Catherine E. ... Washington, DC
Long, Catherine E. ... Chicago, IL
Long, Catherine Newell ... Denver, CO
Long, Chanda L. ... Florence, AL
Long, Charla J. ... Austin, TX
Long, Charlene M. ... Denver, CO
Long, Charlene M. ... Englewood, CO
Long, Charles B. ... Washington, DC
Long, Charles E. ... Mendota Heights, MN
Long, Charles J. ... York, PA
Long, Charles S. ... Donaldsonville, LA
Long, Charles W. ... Needham, MA
Long, Cheryl Marie ... Washington, DC
Long, Christine A. ... Owatonna, MN
Long, Christine B. ... Des Moines, IA
Long, Christine E. ... Atlanta, GA
Long, Christine E. ... Albuquerque, NM
Long, Christine Graffis ... Indianapolis, IN
Long, Christine H. ... Stockton, CA
Long, Christine Mathews ... Pittsburgh, PA
Long, Christopher D. ... Indianapolis, IN
Long, Christopher F. ... Fall River, MA
Long, Clare Smith ... Cleveland, OH
Long, Clarence D., III
Department of the Air Force, Office of the General Counsel, GV
Long & Clark ... San Diego, CA
Long, Claudia Hagadus ... Walnut Creek, CA
Long, Clay C. ... Atlanta, GA
Long, Clayton A. ... Sayner, WI
Long, Clifford J. ... Independence, MO
Long, Clothilde C.J.
Administrative Office Of The United States Courts, GV
Long & Collins, P.A. ... Minneapolis, MN
Long, Connie K. ... Dallas, TX
Long, Constance M. ... Kansas City, MO
Long, C. R. "Skip", Jr.
Winston-Salem, NC
Long, Curtis M. ... Tulsa, OK
Long, Cynthia (Cindy) Jean ... Topeka, KS
Long, Cynthia K. ... San Francisco, CA
Long, Cynthia M. ... Philadelphia, PA
Long, D. Jamieson, Jr. ... Moline, IL
Long, Dale ... Tyler, TX
Long, Daniel E., Jr. ... West Alexander, PA
Long, Daniel J., Law Offices ... Etters, PA
Long, Daniel M. ... Indianapolis, IN
Long, Daniel M. ... Princess Anne, MD
Long, Daniel R ... Vacaville, CA
Long, Daniel R., Jr. ... Roxboro, NC
Long, Daniel W. ... Albuquerque, NM
Long, Daniel W. ... Chambersburg, PA
Long, David A. ... Orinda, CA
Long, David C. ... San Francisco, CA
Long, David C. ... Elyria, OH
Long, David E. ... Los Angeles, CA
Long, David H. ... Scottsdale, AZ
Long, David J. ... Morris Plains, NJ
Long, David Joseph ... Winston-Salem, NC
Long, David K. ... Northfield, NJ
Long, David M. ... Newport Beach, CA
Tustin, CA
Long, David M. ... Morrow, GA
Long, David Patrick ... Dallas, TX
Long, David R. ... Richland, WA
Long, David S. ... New York, NY
Long, David W. ... Birmingham, AL
Long, David W. ... Lafayette, CA
Long, David W. ... Ventura, CA
Long, David W. ... Washington, DC
Long, David W. ... Department of Justice, Civil Division, GV
Long, David W. ... Raleigh, NC
Long, David Wilson ... Knoxville, TN
Long, Deborah J. ... Birmingham, AL
Long, Deborah K. ... Pomona, CA
Long, Deirdre A. ... New York, NY
Long, Delapoer, Healy, McCann & Noonan, P.C. ... Albany, OR
Long, Denis ... San Diego, CA
Long, Dennis H. ... Indianapolis, IN
Long, Dennis R. ... Palm Harbor, FL
Long & Denton ... Quitman, GA
Long, Don B., Jr. ... Birmingham, AL
Long, Donald A. ... Greenwood, SC
Long, Donald C. ... Hopkins, MN
Long, Donald D. ... Charlottesville, VA
Long, Donald Garland ... Pittsburgh, PA
Long, Donna J. ... Concordia, KS
Long, Doris J. ... North Hollywood, CA
Long, Douglas E., Jr. ... Waynesville, MO
Long, Douglas P. ... Indianapolis, IN
Long, Douglas P. ... Minneapolis, MN
Long, Douglas R. ... Anderson, IN
Long, Durward J., Sr. ... Moline, IL
Long, Dwight E. ... Carson City, NV
Long, E. André ... Westlake Village, CA
Long, E. Burke ... Aptos, CA
Long, E. Crawford ... Waco, TX
Long, Earl W. ... Joplin, MO
Long, Earle W., IV ... Mobile, AL
Long, Earle W., IV, P.C. ... Mobile, AL
Long, Edgar H. ... Anderson, SC
Long, Edward, Jr. ... Killeen, TX
Long, Edward L., Jr. ... La Grange, GA
Long, Edward W. ... Torrance, CA
Long, Elisa Ann ... Pittsburgh, PA
Long, Elizabeth A. ... Boston, MA
Long, Elizabeth Anne ... Lafayette, LA
Long, Elizabeth Dale ... Coral Gables, FL
Long, Elizabeth E. ... Atlanta, GA
Long, Ella Maxwell ... Rogers, AR
Long, Eric ... Chicago, IL
Long, Ernest A. ... Sacramento, CA
Long, Ernest A., III ... Los Angeles, CA
Long, Eugene J. ... Palm Desert, CA
Long, Fletcher, Jr. (P.A.) ... Forrest City, AR
Long, Fletcher W. ... Nashville, TN
Long, Florence J. ... Chapel Hill, NC
Long, Frances L. ... Minneapolis, MN
Long, Francis A., Sr. ... Montgomery, AL
Long, Frank ... Sulphur Springs, TX
Long, Frank E. ... Cincinnati, OH

Long, Frank G. ..... Phoenix, AZ
Long, Frederick V. ..... Orleans, MA
Long, Frederick W. ..... Denver, CO
Long, G. Stephen ..... Denver, CO
Kansas City, MO
Long, G. William, III ..... Atlanta, GA
Long, Gary D. ..... Oklahoma City, OK
Long, Gary P. ..... Irvine, CA
Long, Gary R. ..... Kansas City, MO
Long, Geo. J. ..... Louisville, KY
Long, Geoffrey ..... Staten Island, NY
Long, Geoffrey A. ..... Houston, TX
Long, Geoffrey S. ..... San Francisco, CA
Long, George ..... Oakland, CA
Long, George A., Jr. ..... Killeen, TX
Long, George E. ..... Lincolnshire, IL
Long, George E., II ..... Benton, KY
Long, George Edwin ..... La Verne, CA
Long, George F., III ..... Virginia Beach, VA
Long, George G. ..... Olathe, KS
Long, George P., III ..... Pittsburgh, PA
Long, George S. ..... St. Louis, MO
Long, Gerard ..... Ebensburg, PA
Long & Giffen ..... Mission, KS
Long, Glenna Hayes ..... Albuquerque, NM
Long, Glynn A. ..... Donaldsonville, LA
Long, Gordon B. ..... Salyersville, KY
Long, Gregory A. ..... Los Angeles, CA
Long, Gregory E. ..... Columbus, IN
Long, Gregory F. ..... Denver, CO
Long, Gregory S. ..... Dallas, TX
Long, H. Quincy ..... Katy, TX
Long, Hal D. ..... Encino, CA
Long, Harlan L. ..... Mission, KS
Long, Harold, Jr. ..... Miami, FL
Long, Harris E. ..... Clearwater, FL
Long, Harrison "Gavin" ..... Los Angeles, CA
Long, Harrison K. ..... Costa Mesa, CA
Long, Harry P. ..... Anniston, AL
Long, Harry S. ..... Beaumont, TX
Long, Harry W., Jr. ..... Tampa, FL
Long, Heath M. ..... Ebensburg, PA
Long, Heidi J. ..... Oklahoma City, OK
Long, Helen Grayce ..... Los Angeles, CA
Long, Herbert W. ..... Louisville, KY
Long & Holder ..... Atlanta, GA
College Park, GA
Long & Houlden ..... Boston, MA
Long, Howard D. ..... Tupelo, MS
Long, Hubert E. ..... Lexington, SC
Long, Ira M., Jr. ..... Denver, CO
Long, J. Barrett ..... Chicago, IL
Long, J. Craig ..... Chicago, IL
Long, J. Jeffrey ..... Los Angeles, CA
Long, J. Jeffrey, A Professional Corporation
Los Angeles, CA
Long, J. Michael ..... Milwaukee, WI
Long, J. Paul, Jr. ..... Stanford, KY
Long, J. Richard ..... Beloit, WI
Long, J. Scott ..... Myrtle Beach, SC
Long, J. Scott, P.A. ..... Myrtle Beach, SC
Long, J. Steven ..... Staten Island, NY
Long, J. Thomas ..... Alton, IL
Long, James A. ..... Roxboro, NC
Long, James B. ..... Phoenix, AZ
Long, James C., Jr. ..... Philadelphia, PA
Long, James D. ..... Birmingham, AL
Long, James E. ..... Atlanta, GA
Long, James E. ..... Albany, NY
Long, James E. ..... Raleigh, NC
Long, James F. ..... Enid, OK
Okeene, OK
Seiling, OK
Long, James Francis ..... Middletown, OH
Long, James G., III ..... Columbia, SC
Long, James J. ..... Atlanta, GA
College Park, GA
Long, James J. ..... Des Moines, IA
Long, James J. ..... Wichita, KS
Long, James J. ..... Minneapolis, MN
Long, James J., Jr. ..... Woburn, MA
Long, James L. ..... Sacramento, CA
Long, James M. ..... Pilot Mountain, NC
Long, James M. ..... Columbus, OH
Long, James P. ..... Boston, MA
Long, James R. ..... Fort Myers, FL
Long, James R. ..... Appleton, WI
Long, James R., P.A. ..... Fort Myers, FL
Long, James W. ..... Columbus, IN
Long, Jan Michael ..... Circleville, OH
Long, Jane Broadwater ..... Atlanta, GA
Long, Jane M. ..... Reno, NV
Long, Jane P. ..... Memphis, TN
Long, Janie L. ..... Southern Pines, NC
Long, Janis C. ..... Department of Commerce, Patent and Trademark Office, GV
Long, Jason H. ..... Knoxville, TN
Long & Jaudon, P.C. ..... Denver, CO
Long, Jay B., Law Offices of
Long Beach, CA
Monterey, CA
Long, Jean M. ..... Manchester, NH
Long, Jeffery H. ..... Montgomery, AL
Long, Jeffrey A. ..... Portland, OR
Long, Jeffrey D. ..... Atlanta, GA
Long, Jeffrey L. ..... Nashville, TN
Long, Jeffrey P. ..... Chevy Chase, MD
Long, Jennifer L. ..... Chicago, IL
Long, Jennifer N. ..... San Diego, CA
Long, Jerald R. ..... Mission, KS
Long, Jeremiah M. ..... Bellevue, WA
Long, Jerome A. ..... Milwaukee, WI
Wausau, WI
Long, Jerry E. ..... Rowayton, CT
Long, Jesse P. ..... Punxsutawney, PA
Long, Jim R. ..... Indianapolis, IN
Long, Jimmy D., Jr. ..... Natchitoches, LA
Long, Jimmy D., Jr., L.L.C.
Natchitoches, LA
Shreveport, LA
Long, J. M., Jr. ..... Conway, SC
Long, Jo Anne C. ..... Portland, OR
Long, Joan C. ..... Binghamton, NY
Long, Joan L. ..... Chicago, IL
Long, Joann R. ..... Denver, CO
Long, Joanne L. ..... Longmont, CO
Long, Jodi Palmer ..... Seattle, WA
Long, Joe R. ..... Austin, TX
Long, Joel M. ..... Washington, DC
Long, John B. ..... Augusta, GA
Long, John B., II ..... Salisbury, MD
Long, John C. ..... Glendora, CA
Long, John D. ..... Evanston, IL
Long, John E., Jr. ..... Naples, FL
Naples, FL
Long, John E., Jr., P.A. ..... Naples, FL
Long, John J. ..... Newport Beach, CA
Long, John J., Jr. ..... Burlington, VT
Long, John O., III ..... Alexandria, VA
Long, John P. ..... Fall River, MA
Long, John P. ..... Albany, NY
Long, John R. ..... Durham, NC
Long, John R. ..... Oklahoma City, OK
Long, John T. ..... Birmingham, AL
Long, John V. ..... Alexandria, VA
Long, John W. ..... St. Louis, MO
Long, Joseph A. ..... Walnut Creek, CA
Long, Joseph C. ..... Norman, OK
Long, Joseph F. ..... Austin, TX
Long, Joseph F. ..... Bluefield, WV
Long, Joseph F., III ..... East Hartford, CT
Long, Joseph H.
Federal Energy Regulatory Commission, Office of the General Counsel, GV
Long, Joseph L. ..... Rockford, IL
Long, Joseph P. ..... Quincy, MA
Long, Joseph R., II ..... Madison, WI
Long, Joseph W. ..... Las Vegas, NV
Long, Joy S. ..... Hayes, VA
Long, Joyce D. ..... Hauppauge, NY
Long, Judith A. ..... Whittier, CA
Long, Julia B. ..... St. Louis, MO
Long, K. Garl ..... Mount Vernon, WA
Long, Karen E. ..... Raleigh, NC
Long, Karen L. ..... Tulsa, OK
Long, Karen Marple ..... Lexington, KY
Long, Kathleen D. ..... Pittsburgh, PA
Long, Kathy E. ..... Houston, TX
Long, Keith C. ..... Boston, MA
Long, Keith H. ..... Indian Wells, CA
Long, Kelly D. ..... Hillsboro, IL
Long, Kenneth E. ..... Kalamazoo, MI
Long, Kenneth G. ..... Department of Justice, Environment and Natural Resources Division, GV
Long, Kenneth O., Jr. ..... Abilene, TX
Long, Kenneth R. ..... Cleveland, OH
Long, Kenneth W., Jr. ..... Baltimore, MD
Long, Kent P. ..... Northglenn, CO
Long, Kerry B. ..... Washington, DC
Long, Kevin F. ..... Boston, MA
Long, Kevin G. ..... Gold River, CA
Long, Kevin M. ..... Milwaukee, WI
Long, L. Charles, Jr. ..... Richmond, VA
Long, L. Donald, Jr. ..... Winston-Salem, NC
Long, Lance N. ..... Provo, UT
Long, Langdon D. ..... Columbia, SC
Long, Larry ..... Odessa, TX
Long, Laura Lynne ..... Los Angeles, CA
Long, Lauriston H. ..... Department of Labor, Office of the Solicitor, GV
Long Law Firm ..... Washington, DC
Baton Rouge, LA
Long, Lawrence ..... Pierre, SD
Long, Lawrence C. ..... Holly Ridge, MS
Long, Lawrence H. ..... Albany, NY
Long, Lawrence L., Jr. ..... Kansas City, KS
Long, Lawrence S. ..... Silver Spring, MD
Long, Leonard J. ..... Hamden, CT
Long, Leonard L., Jr. ..... Washington, DC
Long, Leonard L., Jr. ..... Charleston, SC
Long, Leonora S. ..... St. Louis, MO
Long, Leslie J. ..... Arlington, VA
Long, Leslie Rankin ..... Cos Cob, CT
Long & Levit LLP ..... Los Angeles, CA
San Francisco, CA
Long, Linda L. ..... Valparaiso, IN
Long, Linnea ..... Seattle, WA
Long, Lisa J. ..... Winter Park, FL
Long, Lisa J., and Richard G. Wack
Winter Park, FL
Long, Lisa Lamoore ..... North Charleston, SC
Long, Lisa T.
Federal Energy Regulatory Commission, Office of the General Counsel, GV
Long & Long ..... Moline, IL
Long & Long ..... Donaldsonville, LA
Long & Long ..... Chapel Hill, NC
Long, Long & Kellerman, P.C.
Blacksburg, VA
Long & Long, P.C. ..... Denver, CO
Long, Louis C. ..... Pittsburgh, PA
Long, LuAn Marshall ..... Montgomery, AL
Long, Lucinda P. ..... Wayne, NJ
Long, Lundmark & Poppe, P.A.
Phoenix, AZ
Tucson, AZ
Long, Lunsford ..... Chapel Hill, NC
Long, Luther M. ..... Columbus, OH
Long, Lyn Taylor ..... Elizabethtown, KY
Long, M. Anthony ..... Columbus, OH
Long, M. Chrysa ..... Boston, MA
Long, M. Kenneth, Jr. ..... Hagerstown, MD
Long, Marcus H., Jr. ..... Blacksburg, VA
Long, Marden ..... Columbus, OH
Long, Maria G.B. ..... Charlotte, NC
Long, Maria Wood ..... Charlotte, NC
Long, Marikaye ..... St. Joseph, MI
Long, Marilyn H. ..... Johns Island, SC
Long, Marjorie J. ..... Lakewood, CO
Long, Mark A. ..... Portland, OR
Long, Mark E. ..... Pine Bluff, AR
Long, Mark J. ..... Atlanta, GA
Long, Mark W. ..... Houston, TX
Long & Marquis, LLP
Newport Beach, CA
Tustin, CA
Long, Marsha Papanek ..... Short Hills, NJ
Long, Martin E. ..... Denver, CO
Long, Martin J. ..... Natick, MA
Long, Martin P. ..... Chicago, IL
Long, Marvin M. ..... Falls Church, VA
Long, Mary A. ..... Northbrook, IL
Long, Mary Balent ..... Atlanta, GA
Long, Mary Beth ..... Santa Clara, CA
Long, Mary Beth ..... Washington, DC
Long, Mary Jo ..... Afton, NY
Long, Matthew J. ..... Santa Barbara, CA
Long, Mauri ..... Anchorage, AK
Long, Maxine Master ..... Miami, FL
Long, Melanie D. ..... Los Angeles, CA
Long, Merle A. ..... Albany, OR
Long, Michael Dell ..... Portland, OR
Long, Michael E. ..... St. Louis, MO
Long, Michael F. ..... Santa Ana, CA
Long, Michael G. ..... Irvine, CA
Long, Michael G. ..... Millville, NJ
Long, Michael G. ..... Columbus, OH
Long, Michael H. ..... Eugene, OR
Long, Michael H. ..... Fairfax, VA
Long, Michael J. ..... Orange, CA
Long, Michael J. ..... Warner Robins, GA
Long, Michael J. ..... Traverse City, MI
Long, Michael J. ..... Glencoe, MN
Long, Michael J. ..... Dayton, OH
Long, Michael Robert ..... Grand Rapids, MI
Long, Michael S. ..... Memphis, TN
Long, Michael S. ..... McLean, VA
Long, Michael T. ..... Simsbury, CT
Long, Michael W. ..... Charlotte, NC
Long, Michael W. ..... Providence, RI
Long, Michelle J. ..... Nashville, TN
Long, Misty T. ..... Mobile, AL
Long, Nancy Aliquo ..... Silver Spring, MD
Long, Nancy Hankins ..... Evansville, IN
Long, Nancy Jane ..... Sacramento, CA
Long, Nancy L. ..... White Plains, NY
Long, Nancy R. ..... Santa Fe, NM
Long, Nash E., III ..... Charlotte, NC
Long, Nathan R. ..... Boise, ID
Long, Nicholas ..... Roanoke Rapids, NC
Long, Nicholas, Jr. ..... Henderson, NC
Long, Nicholas Trott ..... Providence, RI
Long, Nick, Jr. ..... Atlanta, GA
Long, Noelle M. ..... Binghamton, NY
Long, O. Ross ..... Delaware, OH
Long, Olivier Denier ..... Fairfax, VA
Long, Ometrias Deon ..... Orlando, FL
Long, P. Eugene, II ..... Circleville, OH
Long, P. Marshall, Jr., P.A.
Stevensville, MD
Long, P. Marshall, Jr., P.A.
Stevensville, MD
Long, Pamela A. ..... Baltimore, MD
Long, Pamela M.
Merit Systems Protection Board, Office of Appeals Counsel, GV
Long, Parker, Warren & Jones, P.A.
Asheville, NC
Long, Patricia Hall ..... Knoxville, TN
Long, Patricia L. ..... Santa Rosa, CA
Long, Patrick A. ..... San Diego, CA
Santa Ana, CA
Long, Patrick D. ..... Franklin, OH
Long, Paul H. ..... Houston, TX
Long & Perkins, P.A. ..... Orlando, FL
Long, Peter A. ..... Ann Arbor, MI
Long, Quentin V. ..... Hollywood, FL
Long, R. Bruce ..... Gloucester, VA
Long, R. Bruce, P.C. ..... Hayes, VA
Long, R. Edgar ..... Evansville, IN
Long, R. Scott ..... Charleston, WV
Long, Rachell F. ..... Los Angeles, CA
Long, Ragsdale & Waters, P.C.
Knoxville, TN
Sevierville, TN
Long, Ralph B. ..... Medfield, MA
Long, Randall G. ..... Corinth, MS
Long, Randy J. ..... Enid, OK
Long, Randy M. ..... Reedley, CA
Long, Raymond J. ..... McLean, VA
Long, Regina R. ..... Seattle, WA
Long, Richard ..... Bakersfield, CA
Long, Richard A. ..... White Plains, NY
Long, Richard B. ..... Binghamton, NY
Long, Richard G., Jr. ..... Monroe, NC
Long, Richard M. ..... Bakersfield, CA
Long, Richard P. ..... Chicago, IL
Highland, IN
Long, Richard P. ..... Jamaica, NY
Long, Richard R. ..... Durant, OK
Long, Richard S. ..... Dearborn, MI
Long, Richard S. ..... Columbus, OH
Long, Rick ..... Reading, PA
Long, Robert ..... Polson, MT
Long, Robert ..... Whitehall, PA
Long, Robert A. ..... Los Angeles, CA
Long, Robert A. ..... Houston, TX
Long, Robert A., Jr. ..... Washington, DC
Long, Robert A., Jr. ..... Chicago, IL
Long, Robert A., Jr. ..... Boston, MA
Long, Robert B.
Securities and Exchange Commission, Division of Market Regulation, GV
Long, Robert B., Jr. ..... Asheville, NC
Long, Robert C. ..... Chicago, IL
Long, Robert C. ..... Minneapolis, MN
Long, Robert D. ..... Ardmore, OK
Long, Robert E. ..... La Canada Flintridge, CA
Long, Robert E. ..... Littleton, CO
Long, Robert E. ..... Burlington, NC
Long, Robert E., Jr. ..... Decatur, AL
Long, Robert E., (Ltd.) ..... Hampton, VA
Long, Robert F. ..... New York, NY
Long, Robert F., Jr. ..... Denville, NJ
Long, Robert H., Jr. ..... Harrisburg, PA
Long, Robert I. ..... Ventura, CA
Long, Robert J. ..... Antioch, IL
Long, Robert L. ..... Fresno, CA
Long, Robert M. ..... Austin, TX
Long, Robert P. ..... Pasadena, CA
Long, Robert P. ..... Visalia, CA
Long, Robert R., Jr. ..... Mechanicsburg, PA
Long, Robert W. ..... Lombard, IL
Long, Robert W. ..... Canton, MS
Long, Robert W. ..... Arlington, VA
Long, Robert W., Jr. ..... Charlotte, NC
Long, Rodney C. ..... Columbus, OH
Long, Roger A. ..... Tulsa, OK
Long, Roland E., Jr. ..... Arlington, VA
Long, Ronald A. ..... Doylestown, PA
Long, Ronald C. ..... Philadelphia, PA
Long, Ronald J. ..... Cleveland, OH
Long, Roscoe E. ..... Clearwater, FL
Long, Roy Edgar ..... Florence, AL
Long, Russell B. ..... Baton Rouge, LA
Long, Russell B. ..... Myrtle Beach, SC
Long, Russell S. ..... Milwaukee, WI
Long, S. Anthony ..... Boonville, IN
Long, Samuel C. ..... West Liberty, KY
Long, Samuel E., III ..... Meridian, MS
Long, Samuel E., Jr. ..... Dallas, TX
Long, Samuel J. ..... Riverside, CA
Long, Sandra Dionis ..... Boston, MA
Long, Sarah A. ..... Orlando, FL
Long, Scott A. ..... Kansas City, MO
Long, Scott C. ..... Overland Park, KS
Long, Scott David ..... San Francisco, CA
Long, Scott L. ..... Des Moines, IA
Long, Scott M., Jr. ..... Morristown, NJ
Long, Sean T. ..... Houston, TX
Long, Shana J. ..... Kansas City, MO
Long, Sharon R. ..... Milwaukee, WI
Long, Sheryle L. ..... Renfrew, PA
Long & Silvia ..... Fall River, MA
Long & Smith ..... Anderson, SC
Long, Speedy O. ..... Jena, LA
Long, Stanton F. ..... Eugene, OR
Long, Stefan C. ..... Alexandria, VA
Long, Stefan C., P.C. ..... Alexandria, VA
Long, Stefanie ..... Brookside, NJ
Long, Stephen C.M. ..... Albuquerque, NM
Long, Stephen D. ..... Houston, TX
Long, Stephen J. ..... New York, NY
Long, Stephen P. ..... New York, NY
Long, Stephen R. ..... Florham Park, NJ
Long, Stephen Tracy ..... Boca Raton, FL
Long, Steven A. ..... Sebastian, FL
Long, Steven B. ..... Raleigh, NC
Long, Steven F. ..... Birmingham, AL
Long, Steven K. ..... Buffalo, NY
Long, Stuart J. ..... Washington, DC
Long, Susan Alden ..... Tacoma, WA
Long, Susan E. ..... Madison, CT
Long, Susan E. ..... Liberty, MO
Long, Susan J. ..... Indianapolis, IN
Long, Suzette ..... Phoenix, AZ
Long, Sylvia V. ..... Rockville, MD
Long, Tammi S. ..... Atlanta, GA
Long, Terrance A. ..... Hagåtña, GU
Long, Terri M. ..... Homewood, IL
Long, Terry L. ..... Atlanta, GA
Long, Thad Gladden ..... Birmingham, AL
Long, Theodore J. ..... Madison, WI
Long, Thomas D. ..... Los Angeles, CA
Long, Thomas G. ..... Tampa, FL
Long, Thomas J. ..... Chicago, IL
Wheaton, IL
Long, Thomas L. ..... Columbus, OH
Long, Thomas M. ..... New Orleans, LA
Long, Thomas N. ..... Cheyenne, WY
Long, Thomas N., P.C. ..... Cheyenne, WY
Long, Thomas Patrick ..... Santa Ana, CA
Long, Thomas R. ..... Westport, CT
Long, Thomas S. ..... Lebanon, PA
Long, Thomas W. ..... Bakersfield, CA
Long, Thomas W. ..... Houston, TX
Long, Tim A. ..... Portland, OR
Long, Timothy C. ..... Columbus, OH
Long, Timothy J. ..... Sacramento, CA
Long, Timothy V. ..... McLean, VA
Long, Todd ..... Orlando, FL
Long, Tricia J. ..... Treasury Department, Financial Management Service, GV
Long, Tuminello, Besso, Seligman, Quinlan & Werner ..... Naples, FL
Bay Shore, NY
Long, Umsted & Jones ..... Memphis, TN
Long, Ursula P. ..... Roxboro, NC
Long, V. Eileen ..... Richmond, VA
Long, Valerie G. ..... Columbus, GA
Long, Valerie Wagner ..... Charlottesville, VA
Long, Vance Bradford ..... Asheboro, NC
Long, Vicki ..... Atlanta, GA
Long, Victor E. ..... Washington, DC
Upper Marlboro, MD
Fairfax, VA
Long, Virginia A. ..... Trenton, NJ
Long, W. Audie ..... San Antonio, TX

Long, W. Todd ... Orlando, FL
Long, Wallace G. ... Detroit, MI
Long, Walter C. ... Austin, TX
Long, Walter R., Jr. ... Karnes City, TX
Long, Wesley T. ... Greensburg, PA
Long & Whitehead ... Karnes City, TX
Long, William A. ... Eagle Grove, IA
Long, William A., Jr. ... Buffalo, NY
Long, William B. ... Jasper, AL
Long, William B., Jr. ... Greenville, SC
Long, William C. ... Morristown, NJ
Long, William C. ... Houston, TX
Long, William C., P.A. ... Morristown, NJ
Long, William Ellison ... Anderson, SC
Long, William F. ... Atlanta, GA
Long, William F., Jr. ... Brentwood, TN
Long, William H. ... Quitman, GA
Long, William Michael ... Chicago, IL
Long, William Randall ... Shreveport, LA
Long & Williamson, A Professional Corporation ... San Diego, CA
Santa Ana, CA
Longa & Aceto, LLC ... New Haven, CT
Woodbridge, CT
Longa, William C. ... Woodbridge, CT
Longacher, Karen M. ... Camden, NJ
Longacre & Associates ... Washington, DC
Arlington, VA
Longacre, James B. ... Washington, DC
Longacre, James R. ... Bethesda, MD
Arlington, VA
Arlington, VA
Leesburg, VA
Longacre, Joseph R., Jr. ... Walnut Creek, CA
Longacre, Kenneth ... Houston, TX
Longacre, Merrily T. ... Melbourne, FL
Longacre, Roy B. ... Abilene, TX
Longacre, Roy L. ... Anchorage, AK
Longaker, Christopher ... Sacramento, CA
Longaker, Richard P. ... Los Angeles, CA
Longaker, Richard P., Law Offices of
Los Angeles, CA
Longaker, Robert G., II ... Warren, NJ
Longaker, Shelly ... Sacramento, CA
Longan & Associates ... Kansas City, MO
Longan, S. W. "Woody", III ... Leawood, KS
Kansas City, MO
Longanecker, Stacey J. ... Washington, DC
Longano, Robert F. ... Cleveland, OH
Longano, Thomas P. ... Terrace Park, OH
Longarzo, Jerry A., Jr. ... Burbank, CA
Longaway, Russell B. ... San Francisco, CA
Longbottom, Bruce W. ... Indianapolis, IN
Longbottom, Harry W. ... Yuma, AZ
Longbrake, Suzanne T. ... Canton, OH
Longbrake, W. Bradford ... Canton, OH
Longchamp, Miriam P. ... New York, NY
Longden, R. Elliott, II ... New York, NY
Longden, Robert E., Jr. ... Worcester, MA
Longe, Francis T. ... Herkimer, NY
Longe, Janice C.
Department Of Health And Human Services,
Office of the General Counsel, GV
Longenbach, Karl F. ... Bethlehem, PA
Longenbach, Kevin F. ... Harrisburg, PA
Longenbach, Nancy A. ... Allentown, PA
Longenbaugh, Brian S. ... Sierra Vista, AZ
Longenbaugh, Leslie ... Juneau, AK
Longenberger, Stephanie ... Lancaster, PA
Longenecker & Associates, Ltd.
Covington, LA
Madisonville, LA
New Orleans, LA
Longenecker, Bruce E. ... Dallas, TX
Longenecker, Chester D. ... Dallas, TX
Longenecker, Geoffrey H.
Madisonville, LA
Longenecker, Joel V. ... Buena Park, CA
Longenecker, Karen Feryo ... Reading, PA
Longenecker, Mark H., Jr.
Cincinnati, OH
Longenecker, Nathan M. ... Denver, CO
Longenecker, Peter Chambers
Seattle, WA
Longenecker, Rachel A. ... Charlotte, NC
Longenecker, Ruth R. ... Cincinnati, OH
Longenhagen, Brian R. ... Allentown, PA
Longenhagen, Je Anne D. ... Canfield, OH
Longenhagen, Susanne L. ... Philadelphia, PA
Longer, Frederick S. ... Philadelphia, PA
Longer, Larry G., P.C. ... Houston, TX
Longer, Larry Glyn ... Houston, TX
Longer, William J. ... Hobart, IN
Longerbone, Jon A. ... Newport Beach, CA
Longeretta, A. Thomas ... Burbank, CA
Longeretta, David A. ... Utica, NY
Longeretta, John A. ... Utica, NY
Longeretta Law Firm ... Utica, NY
Longeretta, Paul M. ... Utica, NY
Longest, Brian L. ... Washington, DC
Longest, Dennis B. ... Evansville, IN
Longest, Frank A., Jr. ... Burlington, NC
Longest, Gloria M. ... Coal City, IL
Longeteig, Iver J. ... Boise, ID
Longeteig, Wilfrid W. ... Craigmont, ID
Longeway, Christopher T. ... Northbrook, IL
Longfelder, Lawrence L. ... Seattle, WA
Longfelder Tinker Kidman, Inc., P.S.
Seattle, WA
Longfellow, Ellen A. ... St. Paul, MN
Longfellow, Thomas A. ... Phoenix, AZ
Longfellow, Thomas R. ... St. Paul, MN
Longfellow, Victoria F. ... Scottsdale, AZ
Longhetto, Loretto M. ... Los Angeles, CA
Longhi, Patrick G. ... Atlanta, GA
Longhi, Robert A. ... New Brunswick, NJ
Longhi, Vincent J. ... New York, NY
Longhitano, Louis Christopher
New York, NY
Longhofer, Kyle ... Houston, TX
Longhofer, Ronald S. ... Detroit, MI
Longhofer, Stefanie K. ... Detroit, MI
Longhouse, Donna L. ... Tampa, FL
Longi, Maria A. ... Cincinnati, OH
Longietti, Mark A. ... Sharon, PA
Longin, Melissa ... Houston, TX
Longinaker, Jay W. ... Randolph, IA
Longino, Gregory L. ... Lufkin, TX
Longino, Hugh E., Jr. ... Texarkana, AR
Longino, J. Thomas, IV ... Birmingham, AL
Longino, John T. ... Ellijay, GA
Longino, Preston H. ... Raytown, MO
Longino, Preston H., Jr. ... Phoenix, AZ
Longino, Susan I. ... Phoenix, AZ
Longinotti, David C. ... San Francisco, CA
Longinotti, John E. ... Cupertino, CA
Longjohn, Julia ... Los Angeles, CA
Longjohn, Julia A. ... Los Angeles, CA
Longlett, John R. ... Quincy, IL
Longley, Carl M., Jr. ... La Jolla, CA
Longley, Christopher F. ... Wallingford, CT
Longley, Clarence M. ... Santa Ana, CA
Longley, Donald M. ... Hartford, CT
Longley, Earl T. ... Cleveland, OH
Longley, James B., Jr. ... Lewiston, ME
Longley, Joe K. ... Austin, TX
Longley, Kathryn T. ... Austin, TX
Longley, Kenton L. ... Seattle, WA
Longley, Louise ... Jackson, CA
Longley & Maxwell, L.L.P. ... Austin, TX
Longley, S. Catherine ... Portland, ME
Longley-Cook, Barbara A. ... Coronado, CA
Longley-Leahy, Kathryn M. ... Yarmouth, ME
Longman, Anne ... Tallahassee, FL
Longman, Catharine J. ... St. Louis, MO
Longman, Christopher Jon
New York, NY
Longman, Douglas C., Jr. ... Lafayette, LA
Longman, Linda A. ... San Francisco, CA
Longman, Robert A. ... New York, NY
Longman, Scott T. ... Chicago, IL
Longman, Tracie L. ... Boston, MA
Long-Martin, Kay M. ... Oakland, CA
Longmead, Doris J. ... Orange, CA
Longmeyer, John M. ... Louisville, KY
Longmeyer, John M., P.S.C. ... Louisville, KY
Longmeyer, Philip M. ... Louisville, KY
Longmire, Carl W. ... Pryor, OK
Longmire, George ... Grand Forks, ND
Longmire, George, Law Firm
Grand Forks, ND
Longmire, Joseph Y., Jr. ... Hendersonville, TN
Longmire, Robin K. ... Knoxville, TN
Longmire, Valerie A. ... Salt Lake City, UT
Longmire, Wendy Lynne ... Nashville, TN
Longmore, Christopher T.
Los Angeles, CA
Longmore, Gary L. ... Pocatello, ID
Longmuir, Jeanne E. ... Cleveland, OH
Longmuir, Shelley A. ... Washington, DC
Longmuir, Virginia ... Los Angeles, CA
Longnaker, John L. ... Hershey, PA
Longnecker, Anthony A. ... Des Moines, IA
Longo, Amy J. ... Newport Beach, CA
Longo, Amy L. ... Omaha, NE
Longo, Andrew ... White Plains, NY
Longo, Anne C. ... Phoenix, AZ
Longo, Bartholomew A.
New Brunswick, NJ
Longo, Beatrice C. ... Pittsburgh, PA
Longo & Bell ... New York, NY
Longo, Bernard E. ... Billings, MT
Longo, Biagio L. ... West Warwick, RI
Longo, Charles A. ... San Diego, CA
Longo, Charles V. ... Cleveland, OH
Longo, Charles V., Co., L.P.A.
Cleveland, OH
Longo, Christopher M.
New Brunswick, NJ
Longo, Dan L. ... Santa Ana, CA
Longo, Dana F. ... Santa Barbara, CA
Longo, David J. ... Norwalk, OH
Longo, Deanna L. ... Houston, TX
Longo, Dominic T. ... San Juan, PR
Longo, Edward R. ... Woodbridge, NJ
Longo, Elizabeth A. ... Chicago, IL
Longo, Frank A. ... New York, NY
Longo, Frank C. ... Scranton, PA
Longo, Frank J. ... Schenectady, NY
Longo, Giovanna M.
Nuclear Regulatory Commission,
Office of the General Counsel, GV
Longo, Hilary E. ... Des Moines, IA
Longo, Ivor J. ... Stone Mountain, GA
Longo, J. Michael ... Dayton, OH
Longo, John R. ... Leominster, MA
Longo, John T. ... Providence, RI
Longo, Joseph A. ... Mount Prospect, IL
Longo, Joseph C. ... Santa Monica, CA
Longo, Joseph F. ... White Plains, NY
Longo, Joseph J. ... New York, NY
Longo, Joseph J., P.C. ... New York, NY
Longo, Joseph Salvatore, Jr. ... Baltimore, MD
Longo, Joseph T. ... Grosse Pointe, MI
Longo, Joy E. ... Cleveland, OH
Longo, Julianne J. ... Jersey City, NJ
Longo, Laurel ... Yonkers, NY
Longo, Laurie S. ... Ann Arbor, MI
Longo, Marco A., Jr. ... Freeport, NY
Longo, Marisa ... Bronx, NY
Longo, Mark A. ... Brooklyn, NY
Longo, Mark J. ... Buffalo, NY
Longo, Marti E. ... Santa Monica, CA
Longo, Michael A. ... Phoenix, AZ
Longo, Nicholas A. ... Putnam, CT
Longo, Nicholas J. ... Buffalo, NY
Longo, Peter A. ... New York, NY
Longo, Philip J. ... Santa Barbara, CA
Longo, Philip J., Prof. Corp.
Santa Barbara, CA
Longo, Ronald A. ... Rye, NY
White Plains, NY
Longo, Samuel C.
La Canada Flintridge, CA
Longo, Santo ... Hartford, CT
Longo, Scott A. ... Columbus, OH
Longo, Stephen A. ... Clermont, FL
Longo, Thomas G. ... Cleveland, OH
Longo, Thomas G., Co., L.P.A.
Cleveland, OH
Longo, Vincent C. ... Pittsburgh, PA
Longo, Vivian Medinilla ... Georgetown, DE
Longo, William D. ... Philadelphia, PA
Longobardi, Cynthia J. ... Wilmington, DE
Longobardi, JoAnn M. ... New York, NY
Longobardi, Joseph F. ... Maspeth, NY
Longobardi, Joseph J. ... Wilmington, DE
Longobardi, Joseph J., III, Law Office of
Wilmington, DE
Longobardi, Laura E. ... New York, NY
Longobardo, Guy A. ... New York, NY
Longobucco, Anne Marie
Washington, DC
Longood, Ross E. ... Atlanta, GA
Longo Quiñones, Fernando E. ... San Juan, PR
Longoria, A. Federico, III ... Laredo, TX
Longoria, Alice C. ... Los Angeles, CA
Longoria, Arthur G. ... West Covina, CA
Longoria, Carlos J. ... The Woodlands, TX
Longoria, David N. ... Houston, TX
Longoria, Dennis A., Jr. ... McAllen, TX
Longoria, Diane M. ... Pensacola, FL
Longoria, Hector G. ... Houston, TX
Longoria, Janiece M. ... Houston, TX
Longoria, John A. ... San Antonio, TX
Longoria, John M. ... Houston, TX
Longoria, Malvina C. ... Miami, FL
Longoria, Michael J. ... Houston, TX
Longoria, Nora L. ... McAllen, TX
Longoria, Reneau Jean ... Salem, MA
Longoria, Roberto ... Santa Ana, CA
Longoria, S. Martina B. ... Beaumont, TX
Longoria, Salvador G. ... New Orleans, LA
Longosz, Edward J., II ... Washington, DC
McLean, VA
Longosz, Vickie Smith
Department of Housing and Urban
Development,
Office of General Counsel, GV
Longpré, Richard J. ... Santa Barbara, CA
Longroy, Sally A. ... Dallas, TX
Long-Sharp, Rhonda ... Indianapolis, IN
Longshore, Buck & Longshore, P.C.
Birmingham, AL
Longshore, Carol L. ... Florence, AL
Longshore, Ellen M. ... Alexandria, KY
Longshore, Frank S. ... Atlanta, GA
Longshore, George C. ... Birmingham, AL
Longshore, Leslie ... Tampa, FL
Longshore, William L., III
Birmingham, AL
Longshore, W. L., Jr. ... Birmingham, AL
Longson, Conway ... Lansing, MI
Longson, Sarah E. ... Baltimore, MD
Longstaff, Derek R. ... San Francisco, CA
Longstaff, Ronald E. ... Des Moines, IA
Longstaff/Mejia, LLP ... San Francisco, CA
Longstreet, Ami S. ... Syracuse, NY
Longstreet, Michael J. ... Syracuse, NY
Longstreet, Robert J. ... Hastings, MI
Longstreet, Scott P. ... Old Chatham, NY
Longstreet, Susan C. ... Washington, DC
Longstreth, Bevis ... New York, NY
Longstreth, Carolyn K. ... Southbury, CT
Longstreth, John L. ... Washington, DC
Longstreth, Robert C. ... San Diego, CA
Longstreth, Robert M. ... Honolulu, HI
Longstreth, Sarah A. ... San Francisco, CA
Longsworth, Jeanne E. ... Fort Wayne, IN
Longsworth, Jeffrey S. ... Washington, DC
Longthorne, William E. ... Toledo, OH
Longtin, Cheryl J. ... Auburn Hills, MI
Longtin, James ... Berkeley, CA
Longtin, James G. ... Walterboro, SC
Longtin, Matthew D. ... Eugene, OR
Longtin, Roger L., (P.C.) ... Chicago, IL
Longton, Paul A. ... Wyandotte, MI
Longua, Mark K. ... Milwaukee, WI
Longua, Paul J. ... Berwyn, PA
Longuet, Pascale ... New York, NY
Longville-Urquhart, Elisa A. ... Akron, OH
Longway, John M. ... Denver, CO
Longwell, A. Kelton ... New Orleans, LA
Longwell Associates, Chartered ... Chicago, IL
Longwell, Carol Brayshaw
Harrisburg, PA
Longwell, Donald E., Jr. ... Cleveland, OH
Longwell, Frances R. ... Upper Marlboro, MD
Longwell, John E. ... Effingham, IL
Longwell, Marilyn F. ... Chicago, IL
Longwell, Mark N. ... Orlando, FL
Longwell, Mark N., P.A. ... Orlando, FL
Longwell, Robert C., Jr. ... Galesville, WI
Longwill, Ben A. ... Las Cruces, NM
Longworth, Gregory Michael
New York, NY
Longworth, Gregory N.
Grand Rapids, MI
Longworth, Nancy Covault ... Indianapolis, IN
Longworth, Richard D. ... Oyster Bay, NY
Longyear, Craig A. ... Harrisburg, PA
Longyear, Dayton "Van" Vranken
Sacramento, CA
Longyear, Michael J. ... Seattle, WA
Longyear, O'Dea & Lavra, LLP
Sacramento, CA
Lonian, Andrea ... Washington, DC
Lonich, Michael E. ... San Jose, CA
Lonich & Patton ... San Jose, CA
Lonich, Thomas Alec ... Washington, PA
Loniello, Johnson & Simonini ... Madison, WI
Loniello, Nicholas J. ... Madison, WI
Lonjak, George F. ... Cleveland, OH
Lonker, Deborah Ellsworth
New Orleans, LA
Lonker, Elliot M. ... Metairie, LA
Lonn, Christopher D. ... Scottsdale, AZ
Lonnberg, Kelly Anne ... Oakland City, IN
Lonneman & Copley, PLLC
Bardstown, KY
Elizabethtown, KY
Leitchfield, KY
Lonneman, Phyllis K. ... Elizabethtown, KY
Lonner, Jonathan A. ... New York, NY
Lonnerstater, Brian H. ... Livonia, MI
Lonnes, Jerome L. ... Richmond, VA
Lonnevik, Tiffany B. ... Great Falls, MT
Lonnie, Dommond E. ... Los Angeles, CA
Lonnquist, John H. ... Denver, CO
Lonnquist, John H., P.C. ... Denver, CO
Lonnquist, Judith A. ... Seattle, WA
Lonnquist, Judith A., Law Offices of
Seattle, WA
Lonnquist, R. Ladd ... Eldersburg, MD
Lonnquist, Richard C. ... Denver, CO
Lonoff, Alice S. ... Chicago, IL
Lonon, Grady ... Jefferson, NC
Lonon, James John ... Kingsport, TN
Lonowski, Joel G. ... Lincoln, NE
Lonowski, Kathryn Sjulin
Fort Collins, CO
Lonowski, Susan C. ... Louisville, KY
Lonsberg, John V. ... St. Louis, MO
Lonschein, Arthur W. ... Jamaica, NY
Lonsdale, Fred D. ... Oakland, CA
Lonsdale, Judith A. ... New York, NY
Lonsdale, Linda ... Santa Fe, NM
Lonsdorf & Andraski ... Merrill, WI
Wausau, WI
Lonsdorf, James P. ... Wausau, WI
Lonsinger, Linda L. ... Columbus, OH
Lonski, David P. ... New Brunswick, NJ
Lonski, Michael J. ... Wauwatosa, WI
Lonski, Miriam S. ... Milwaukee, WI
Lonski, Robert D. ... Buffalo, NY
Lonson, Gunnar A., Law Offices of
Santa Barbara, CA
Lonstein, Benjamin ... Ellenville, NY
Lonstein, Julie Cohen ... Ellenville, NY
Lonstein Law Office, P.C. ... Ellenville, NY
New York, NY
Lonstein, Wayne D. ... Ellenville, NY
Lontchar, Mark N., Jr ... Tampa, FL
Lontz, Thomas J. ... Milwaukee, WI
Loo, Annie O. ... Palo Alto, CA
Loo, Blossom E. ... Baytown, TX
Loo, Christine K. ... New York, NY
Loo, Ernest J. T. ... Honolulu, HI
Loo, Eugene D. ... Manchester, NH
Loo, Frank M. ... San Bernardino, CA
Loo, George W. T. ... Honolulu, HI
Loo, Janice Szeto ... Old Bridge, NJ
Loo, John ... Los Angeles, CA
Loo, Jonathan Mun Fai ... Philadelphia, PA
Loo, Lamont C. ... Tacoma, WA
Loo, Leonardo ... Phoenix, AZ
Loo, Lisa S. K. ... Phoenix, AZ
Loo, Lori A. ... Los Angeles, CA
Loo, Lorna J. ... Honolulu, HI
Loo, Minnie ... Oakland, CA
Loo, Patricia A. ... Honolulu, HI
Loo, Thomas S. ... Santa Monica, CA
Loo, Wilson M. N. ... Honolulu, HI
Loob & Glover ... El Segundo, CA
Loob, Joan J. ... San Diego, CA
Loob, Susan B. ... El Segundo, CA
Looby, James V. ... Beverly Hills, CA
Looby, Joseph H. ... Albany, NY
Looby, Lynn S. ... Midland, MI
Looby, Mary Margaret ... Brooklyn, NY
Looby, Timothy J. ... Waconia, MN
Loochkartt, June Elizabeth ... Lauderhill, FL
Loock, Kathryn M. ... San Diego, CA
Loock, Paul W. ... Troy, MI
Loofboro, Gary L. ... Footville, WI
Loofbourrow, David T., Jr.
San Francisco, CA
Looft, Ann M. ... Minneapolis, MN
Look, Debra J. ... Warrenville, IL
Look, Harley K., Jr. ... Denver, CO
Look, Jeffrey J. ... Little Rock, AR
Nashville, TN
Look, John B. ... Dallas, TX
Look, Joseph F. ... Santa Barbara, CA
Look, Kalmbach & Look, P.C.
Wyandotte, MI
Look, Karin L. ... Department of State,
Office of the Secretary, GV
Look, Kurt K. ... Lawrence, KS
Look, Laurie-Ann Mei Inn ... Palo Alto, CA
Look, Marianne Theresa ... Oak Park, MI
Look, Morton B. ... Houston, TX
Look, William R. ... Wyandotte, MI
Lookadoo, Fred. W., Jr. ... Bentonville, AR
Lookadoo, J. Hugh, Jr. ... Arkadelphia, AR
Lookadoo, Lizabeth ... Little Rock, AR
Lookadoo, Phillip G. ... Washington, DC
Looker, Charles ... New York, NY
Looker, Ivan ... Watseka, IL
Looker, James M. ... Cincinnati, OH
Looker and Looker ... Watseka, IL

Lopez, Richard J. ... **San Francisco, CA**
Lopez, Richard P. ... Long Beach, CA
Lopez, Richard Valentine ... Boulder, CO
Lopez, Rick P ... Colorado Springs, CO
Lopez, Robert B. ... Los Angeles, CA
Lopez, Robert C. ... **Philadelphia, PA**
Lopez, Robert F. ... **Seattle, WA**
Lopez, Robert J. ... Asheville, NC
Lopez, Roger William ... Pasadena, CA
Lopez, Romulo I. ... Sacramento, CA
Lopez, Ronald ... **New York, NY**
Lopez, Ronald A. ... Medford, MA
Lopez, Ronald F. ... **San Francisco, CA**
Lopez, Rosa M. ... Hollywood, FL
Lopez, Rosemary ... **Miami, FL**
Orlando, FL
Lopez, Ruben M. ... Los Angeles, CA
Lopez, Sandra C. ... Ypsilanti, MI
Lopez, Scott P., Law Office of
Boston, MA
Lopez, Sergio M. ... Coral Gables, FL
Lopez, Simone Marie ... Miami, FL
Lopez & Smith ... San Antonio, TX
Lopez, Sonia I. ... **Edinburg, TX**
Lopez, Stephen B. ... Lafayette, CA
Lopez, Stephen E. ... **Washington, DC**
Lopez, Stephen F. ... **San Diego, CA**
Lopez, Susan A. ... Boca Raton, FL
Lopez, Susana ... San Antonio, TX
Lopez, Sylvia ... Bakersfield, CA
Lopez, Tamara K. ... San Jose, CA
Lopez, Tami L. ... Dearborn, MI
Lopez, Terry J. ... Caldwell, ID
Lopez, Theodore P. ... **Newport Beach, CA**
Lopez, Thomas H. ... **Boise, ID**
Lopez, Thomas M. ... **New York, NY**
Lopez, Tiany M.
Panama Canal Commission,
Office of the General Counsel, GV
Lopez, Tomás R. ... **Los Angeles, CA**
Lopez, Tony S. ... Laramie, WY
Lopez, Vicki A. Riccardo ... Phoenix, AZ
Lopez, Vincent, Jr. ... Sterling, IL
Lopez, Vivian Gallucci ... Trenton, NJ
Lopez, Walter M., Jr. ... Tampa, FL
Lopez, William D. ... Pittsburgh, PA
Lopez, William J. ... Metairie, LA
López-Adames, Marie Elsie ... **San Juan, PR**
Lopez-Aguiar, Henry A. ... Miami, FL
Lopez-Baralt, Clara E. ... San Juan, PR
Lopez-Campillo, Juan C. ... **Orlando, FL**
Lopez-Castro, Amadeo, III
Coral Gables, FL
Lopez-Castro, Corali ... **Miami, FL**
Lopez-Cepero, Alexis G. ... San Juan, PR
Lopez-Colon, Nelsa ... Aibonito, PR
López-Conway, Juan A. ... **San Juan, PR**
Lopez Correa, Luis E. ... **San Juan, PR**
López de Alós, Rica ... **San Juan, PR**
Lopez de Victoria, Jeannette M.
San Juan, PR
Lopez Diaz, Nellymarie ... **San Juan, PR**
Lopez-Fernandez, Manuel E.
San Juan, PR
Lopez-Garcia, Jorge L. ... Miami, FL
López García, Roberto A. ... **San Juan, PR**
Lopez-Goldberg, Astrid E.
Department of Transportation,
Research and Special Programs
Administration, GV
Lopez-Gonzalez, Sigrid ... San Juan, PR
Lopez-Guzman, Terry ... Denver, CO
Lopez-Henriquez, Gail K. ... Philadelphia, PA
Lopez-Hicks, Gloria Y.
Hacienda Heights, CA
Lopez Irizarry, Wilfredo ... San Juan, PR
Lopez-Isa, Lourdes M. ... Washington, DC
Lopez-Lay & Vizcarra ... San Juan, PR
Lopez-Martinez, Alicia ... **San Juan, PR**
López-Morales, Yldefonso ... **San Juan, PR**
Lopez-Ortiz, Bamily ... San Juan, PR
Lopez-Pritchard, Daniel E. ... San Juan, PR
Lopez-Romo, Daniel F. ... San Juan, PR
Lopez-Soto, Edwin J. ... Rochester, NY
López-Zambrana, Manuel ... **San Juan, PR**
Lo Piano, Christian C. ... Hoboken, NJ
Lopiano, George M. ... West Hartford, CT
Lo Piano, Stephen F., Jr. ... Lawrence, MA
LoPiccolo, Sal P., P.C., Law Office of
Houston, TX
LoPiccolo, Salvatore P., II ... Houston, TX
LoPilato, Joseph ... Townsend Center, MA
Lopilato, Kathleen A. ... **Lansing, MI**
Lopina, Brian C. ... **Washington, DC**
Lopinot, Vincent J. ... Belleville, IL
Lo Pinto, Schlather, Solomon & Salk
Ithaca, NY
Lopis, John E. ... **Hackensack, NJ**
Lopisi, Joseph A. ... Brockton, MA
Lopker, John K. ... Beverly Hills, CA
Lopkin, Wayne M. ... Croton-On-Hudson, NY
New York, NY
Lopo, Diana M. ... **New York, NY**
LoPorto, William J. ... Heathsville, VA
Lopossa, Paula E. ... Indianapolis, IN
Lopp, Harriette H. ... **Washington, DC**
Lopp, James D. ... Evansville, IN
Lopp, James D., Jr. ... Evansville, IN
Lopp, Jason Andrew ... Carmel, IN
Lopp, Kenneth Lynn ... English, IN
Lopp, William F. ... Raleigh, NC
Loprest, F. James, Jr. ... New York, NY
LoPresti, Alfred E. ... Boston, MA
Lopresti, Angelo P. ... **New York, NY**
Lopresti, Anthony J. ... Mineola, NY
Lo Presti & Birzon ... Mineola, NY
LoPresti, Charles A. ... **Cleveland, OH**
LoPresti, Daniel S. ... New York, NY
LoPresti, Eric R. ... **McLean, VA**
Lo Presti, John P., Jr. ... Mineola, NY
Lopresti, Joseph ... **San Juan, PR**
LoPresti, Joseph J., Jr. ... **Cleveland, OH**
LoPresti, Michael, Jr. ... Newton, MA
LoPresti, Robert W. ... **Los Angeles, CA**
Sacramento, CA
LoPresti, Salvatore J. ... Cleveland, OH
Lo Presti, Stephen J. ... Bronx, NY
LoPresti, Stephen Philip ... Carmichael, CA
LoPresti, Thomas A. ... Westbury, NY
Lo Presti, Vincent F. ... Yonkers, NY
Lopresto, Alex A., III ... **Lafayette, LA**
New Iberia, LA
Lopresto, Charles S, Jr ... Kew Gardens, NY
Lopresto, Michael D. ... New Iberia, LA
Lopresto, Thomas J. ... Astoria, NY
LoPrete, James H. ... **Bloomfield Hills, MI**
Loprete, Michael D. ... **Newark, NJ**
LoPrete, Robert D. ... **Chicago, IL**
LoPreto, Virginia A. ... New York, NY
Lopriore, William P., Jr. ... **Boston, MA**
Lopshire & Barkan ... Woodland Hills, CA
Lopshire, William J. ... Woodland Hills, CA
LoPucki, Anthony T. ... Gainesville, FL
LoPucki, Lynn M. ... Ithaca, NY
Lopus, Allen M. ... **Pittsburgh, PA**
Lopus, Lyle L. ... Fremont, CA
Lopuszynski, George ... Fort Wayne, IN
Loquaci, Stephen E. ... **San Jose, CA**
Loquet, Patricia ... New York, NY
Loquist, Sarah J. ... Topeka, KS
Loquvam, Joel J. ... Los Angeles, CA
Lora, Eugene L. ... Tenafly, NJ
Lora, Hector E. ... Coral Gables, FL
Loraas, Paul A. ... **Duluth, MN**
Loraditch, Gary C. ... Perry Hall, MD
Lorah, Tim O'Neal ... **New York, NY**
Loraine, Thomas E. ... Osage Beach, MO
Loraine, Thomas E., P.C. ... Osage Beach, MO
Lora Longoria, Jorge ... **San Juan, PR**
Loran, Joseph C. ... **Aurora, IL**
Loran, Joseph J. ... Tacoma, WA
Loran, Thomas V., III ... **San Francisco, CA**
Lorance, Joy ... **Tulsa, OK**
Lorance, Lonnie L. ... Columbus, OH
Lorance, R. Dennis ... **Gastonia, NC**
Lorance, Steven R. ... Crescent, OK
Lorance & Thompson, A Professional Corporation ... **Houston, TX**
Lorance, Tom ... Houston, TX
Lorand, John C. ... Anaheim, CA
Lorandos, Demosthene ... Ann Arbor, MI
LoRang, Gerald A. ... Nevada, IA
Lorang, Rodney F. ... San Diego, CA
Lorang, Sally M. ... San Diego, CA
L'Orange, H. Christian
San Francisco, CA
Loranger, Catherine S. ... East Freetown, MA
Loranger, Guy D. ... South Lake Tahoe, CA
Loranger, James R. ... **St. Louis, MO**
Lorans, Isabelle J. ... **New York, NY**
Lorant & Associates ... Birmingham, AL
Lorant, Charles J. ... Birmingham, AL
Lorant, Debra B. ... Chapel Hill, NC
Lorant, Etan Z. ... Encino, CA
Lorant, Jerry O. ... Birmingham, AL
Lorant, Paula K. ... Milwaukee, WI
Loranz, Kimberly A ... Yakima, WA
Lorber, Alan R. ... Bay Harbor Islands, FL
Lorber, Amy Ellen ... Los Angeles, CA
Lorber, Beddoe & Pengilly ... Las Vegas, NV
Lorber, Bruce W. ... Las Vegas, NV
Lorber, Charles S. ... Fairfield, NJ
Lorber, Greenfield, Blick & Beddoe
San Diego, CA
Lorber, Harry ... West Hempstead, NY
Lorber, Jerome Z. ... Woodside, NY
Lorber, John J. ... **South Bend, IN**
Lorber, Joseph ... **Suffern, NY**
Lorber, Lawrence Z. ... **Washington, DC**
Lorber, Leah ... **Washington, DC**
Lorber, Michael F. ... Twinsburg, OH
Lorber, Schneider, Nuzzi, Bilinkas & Mason
Fairfield, NJ
Randolph, NJ
Lorber, Sidney ... **Minneapolis, MN**
Lorber, Steve H., Law Offices of
Solana Beach, CA
Lorber, Tamara Elvove ... Buffalo Grove, IL
Lorberbaum, Ralph R. ... **Savannah, GA**
Lorberbaum, Stephen H. ... Columbia, MD
Lorbetske, Adrian J. ... Rhinelander, WI
Lorbiecki, Stefanie ... Sapulpa, OK
Lorch, Basil H., III ... New Albany, IN
Lorch, Basil H., Jr. ... New Albany, IN
Lorch, Ernest H. ... **New York, NY**
Lorch, Gary J. ... **Los Angeles, CA**
Lorch, Kenneth F. ... **Chicago, IL**
Lorch, Linda B. ... New Albany, IN
Lorch & Naville ... New Albany, IN
Lorch, Pamela S. ... Brentwood, TN
Lord, Albert J. ... Zachary, LA
Lord, Alfred ... San Diego, CA
Lord, Amy L. ... West Chester, PA
Lord, Andrew W. ... **Hartford, CT**
Lord, Angela Elsperger ... **Fargo, ND**
Lord, Barbara J. ... New York, NY
Lord, Bernard F. ... Evergreen Park, IL
Lord, Beverly B. ... Houston, TX
Lord, Bissell & Brook ... **Los Angeles, CA**
Atlanta, GA
Chicago, IL
Rockford, IL
New York, NY
Lord, Bryan P. ... **Boston, MA**
Lord, C. Jan ... **Boulder, CO**
Lord, Charles A. ... Philadelphia, PA
Lord, Cheryl B. ... Bloomfield Hills, MI
Lord, Christopher J. ... Herndon, VA
Lord, Clarence I. ... Trenton, NJ
Lord, Clark Stockton ... Houston, TX
Lord, Cristofer E. ... Chicago, IL
Lord, Daniel B. ... **Anchorage, AK**
Lord, Darrin ... Northfield, NJ
Lord, David C. ... Seattle, WA
Lord, David L. ... Hattiesburg, MS
Lord, David R. ... Seattle, WA
Lord, David S. ... Topeka, KS
Lord Day & Lord, Barrett Smith
New York, NY
Lord, Diane M. ... Wallingford, CT
Lord, Douglas E. ... **Oakland, CA**
Lord, E. June ... Great Falls, MT
Lord, Elizabeth Osenton ... **Charleston, WV**
Lord, Everett ... Beaumont, TX
Lord, Everett, Inc. ... Beaumont, TX
Lord Firm, The ... St. Louis, MO
Lord, Francis R. ... Media, PA
Lord, Frank H. ... Cleveland, OH
Lord, Frederick W. ... Housatonic, MA
Lord, G. Craig ... **Philadelphia, PA**
Lord, George E. ... Delaware, OH
Lord, Georgia Kay ... Athens, GA
Decatur, GA
Lord, Gerald A. ... York, PA
Lord, Greg R. ... Charleston, WV
Lord, Gregory Fisher ... Sterling Heights, MI
Lord, Gregory Fisher, P.C.
Sterling Heights, MI
Lord, Henry Robbins ... **Baltimore, MD**
Lord, Herbert M. ... **New York, NY**
Lord, Hilary G.D. ... Los Angeles, CA
Lord, J. Couper ... Southampton, NY
Lord, Jackson Vincent ... Beverly Hills, CA
Lord, James F. ... Chanhassen, MN
Lord, Janet W. ... **Phoenix, AZ**
Lord, John A. ... Wayne, PA
Lord, John F. ... **Seattle, WA**
Lord, John J., Jr. ... Old Saybrook, CT
Lord, John P. ... St. Louis, MO
Lord, John S., Jr. ... **Orlando, FL**
Lord, K. Lorraine ... **Richmond, VA**
Lord, Kathleen A. ... Denver, CO
Lord, Kenneth M. ... **Anchorage, AK**
Lord, Kenneth W. ... **Stamford, CT**
Lord, Kimberly M. ... Cleveland, OH
Lord, Kurt D. ... Belleville, IL
Lake Ozark, MO
St. Louis, MO
Lord, Linda L. ... Washington, DC
Lord & Lord ... Cleveland, OH
Lord, Mark W. ... **Sarasota, FL**
Lord, Mary C. ... Middletown, OH
Lord, Mary Jane ... Tallahassee, FL
Lord, Michael C. ... **Raleigh, NC**
Research Triangle Park, NC
Lord, Michael H. ... Stamford, CT
Lord, Michael W. ... **Atlanta, GA**
Lord, Miles W., & Associates Law Office
Chanhassen, MN
Lord, Monica C. ... **New York, NY**
Lord & Mulligan ... Media, PA
Lord, Nancy Hershey ... New York, NY
Lord, Nancy M. ... Lyons, NY
Lord, Nathan McAdams ... **Richmond, VA**
Lord, Nathan S. ... Louisville, KY
Lord, Patrick C. ... **Philadelphia, PA**
Lord, Philip M. ... Philadelphia, PA
Lord, Philip M., P.C. ... Philadelphia, PA
Lord, R. Earl ... Hemphill, TX
Lord, R. Gordon ... **Goshen, IN**
Lord, Randall W. ... Tampa, FL
Lord, Rebecca ... **Rockville, MD**
Lord, Rhonda E. ... **Lancaster, PA**
Lord, Richard A. ... Brunswick, ME
Lord, Richard A. ... Buies Creek, NC
Lord, Richard B. ... **Daytona Beach, FL**
Maitland, FL
Lord, Richard E., Jr. ... Braintree, MA
Lord, Richard M. ... Newport, RI
Lord, Robert A. ... Mountainside, NJ
Lord, Robert H. ... Houston, TX
Lord, Robert J. ... **Scottsdale, AZ**
Lord, Robert L. ... Salt Lake City, UT
Lord, Robert L., Jr. ... Stuart, FL
Lord, Rosa Beatty ... Atlanta, GA
Lord, Samuel Darrow ... **Roseland, NJ**
Lord, Sandra Dee ... Department of Justice,
Civil Division, GV
Lord, Scott R. ... **Los Angeles, CA**
Lord, Stephen J. ... Boise, ID
Lord, Susan M. ... Washington, DC
Lord, Terence G. ... Kansas City, MO
Lord, Terry R. ... Department of Justice,
Criminal Division, GV
Lord, Theresa Marie ... Quincy, MA
Lord, Thomas T. ... **San Diego, CA**
Lord, Timothy R. ... Department of Justice,
Civil Division, GV
Lord, W. Leighton, III ... **Columbia, SC**
Lord & Whip, A Professional Association
Baltimore, MD
Towson, MD
Lord, William D. ... Franklin, TN
Lordan, George P., Jr. ... Salem, MA
Lorden, Jessica E. ... White Plains, NY
Lorden, John J. ... Harvard, MA
Lorden & Pastor, P.C. ... Harvard, MA
Lordi, George D. ... West Caldwell, NJ
Lordi, Katherine M. ... Bloomfield, NJ
Lordi, Linda F. ... Newark, NJ
Lordi & Tafro, P.C. ... West Caldwell, NJ
Lordi, Viola S. ... **Woodbridge, NJ**
Lords, Ronald D., Jr. ... Stevensville, MT
Lo Re, Alan J. ... Department of Justice,
Civil Division, GV
Lore, Andrea Press ... Houston, TX
Lore, Irving A. ... **Milwaukee, WI**
Lore, John M. ... Dunellen, NJ
Lore, Kenneth G. ... **Washington, DC**
Lore & Levy ... **New York, NY**
Lore, Martin M. ... **New York, NY**
Lore & McClearen ... Raleigh, NC
Lore, Michael D. ... Houston, TX
Lore, Michelle Mary ... St. Paul, MN
Lore, R. James ... Raleigh, NC
Lore, Stephen M. ... **Atlanta, GA**
Lore, William H. ... Winter Park, FL
Lore, William H., P.A. ... Winter Park, FL
Lorea, Lisa D. ... San Francisco, CA
Lorea, Robert P. ... **Charleston, WV**
Loredo, Jose A. ... **Miami, FL**
Loree, James H. ... Ypsilanti, MI
Loree, Philip J., Jr. ... **New York, NY**
Loree, Robert W., Law Office of
San Antonio, TX
Lorell, Elizabeth F. ... **Hackensack, NJ**
Lorell, Jeffrey W. ... **Newark, NJ**
Lorell, Robin P. ... **New York, NY**
Lorelli, Paul J. ... Garden Grove, CA
Lorello, Salvatore F. ... Richmond, VA
Loreman, David D., Law Office of
Elko, NV
Loren, Bruce E. ... West Palm Beach, FL
Loren, Bruce M. ... Seaford, NY
Loren, Frances ... **New Brunswick, NJ**
Loren, Lewis I. ... **Hillsdale, MI**
Loren, Lydia Pallas ... Portland, OR
Loren, Norman J. ... Mora, MN
Loren, Ralph A. ... **Boston, MA**
Loren, Renee B. ... **Silver Spring, MD**
Loren, Shirk & Snell ... **Coldwater, MI**
Hillsdale, MI
Loren, Steven L. ... **Chicago, IL**
Loren, Steven M. ... New York, NY
Lorenc, Diane C. ... **New York, NY**
Lorenc, Robert W. ... Spring Valley, NY
Lorence, Barbara J. ... Orlando, FL
Lorence, David R. ... Corvallis, OR
Lorence & Dickman, P.C. ... Corvallis, OR
Lorence, Gerald M. ... Detroit, MI
Lorence, Joanne C. ... Atlantic, IA
Lorence, John J. ... Madison, WI
Lorence, Jordan W. ... Fairfax, VA
Lorence, Michael J. ... Pittsburgh, PA
Lorence, Robert W., Jr. ... Treasury Department,
Internal Revenue Service, GV
Lorenger, Jeffrey D. ... Minneapolis, MN
Lorenger, Michael J. ... **McLean, VA**
Lorens, L. Tracee ... San Diego, CA
Lorensen, Charles O. ... Charleston, WV
Lorensen, Michael D. ... Martinsburg, WV
Lorensen, Michael D. ... **Martinsburg, WV**
Lorensen, Richard H. ... Lewisburg, WV
Lorensen, Ronald W. ... **Juneau, AK**
Lorensen, Willard D. ... Morgantown, WV
Lorenson, David A. ... Glastonbury, CT
Lorenson, Lynn Annette ... Ripon, WI
Lorenson, Thomas ... Wautoma, WI
Lorente, Robert G. ... Detroit, MI
Lorenti, Pedro Miguel ... **New York, NY**
Lorentson, Gerald M. ... Seattle, WA
Lorentson, Leonard E. ... Kokomo, IN
Lorentz, Andrew J. ... **Washington, DC**
Baltimore, MD
Lorentz, Gerald P. ... San Jose, CA
Lorentz, John A. ... Phoenix, AZ
Lorentz, John M. ... Killington, VT
Lorentz, John M., P.C. ... Killington, VT
Lorentz, Karen ... New York, NY
Lorentz, Lorentz & Harnett
Killington, VT
Rutland, VT
Lorentz, Stephanie A. ... **Rutland, VT**
Lorentz, Thaddeus R. ... **Rutland, VT**
Lorentzen, James A. ... **Des Moines, IA**
Lorentzen, Jane V. ... **Des Moines, IA**
Lorentzen, John C. ... **Chicago, IL**
Lorentzen, John F. ... **Des Moines, IA**
Lorentzen, Lance P. ... Decorah, IA
Lorentzen, Lee A. ... Cleveland, OH
Lorentzen, Paula A., Law Offices of
Walnut Creek, CA
Lorentzen, Robert H. ... **Seattle, WA**
Lorenz, Brian E. ... **White Plains, NY**
Lorenz, Carl Jeffrey ... Ellicott City, MD
Lorenz, Carol M. ... Watertown, WI
Lorenz & Carter ... Houston, TX
Lorenz, Charles E., II
New Philadelphia, OH
Lorenz and Cutter ... Sacramento, CA
Lorenz, Daniel Buckley ... Sacramento, CA
Lorenz, Daniel C. ... Portland, OR
Lorenz, Dorothy W. ... **Bethesda, MD**
Lorenz, Edward J. ... Williamstown, KY
Lorenz, Eugene R. ... Bakersfield, CA
Lorenz, Francis S. ... **Crystal Lake, IL**
Lorenz, Gary ... Paducah, KY
Lorenz, Hermann E., Jr., ... Sacramento, CA
Lorenz, Hugo A. ... Chicago, IL
Lorenz, Jack C. ... Chesterfield, MO
Lorenz, James ... Berkeley, CA
Lorenz, Jill Tracie ... Walnut Creek, CA
Lorenz, Joseph D. ... Fort Walton Beach, FL
Lorenz, Joseph F. ... Bloomfield Hills, MI
Lorenz, Kevin J. ... **St. Louis, MO**
Lorenz, Lewis C. ... Tulsa, OK
Lorenz, Lewis G. ... Garden City, NY
Lorenz, M. James ... San Diego, CA
Lorenz, Margaret A. ... **Marion, NC**
Lorenz, Mark J. ... Spokane, WA
Lorenz, Milton E., Jr. ... **Corpus Christi, TX**

Lott, John J. ... Milwaukee, WI
Lott, Joseph A. ... Clayton, MO
Lott, Karl J. ... Los Angeles, CA
Lott, Lance Chad ... Baton Rouge, LA
Lott, Leslie J. ... Miami, FL
Lott & Levine ... Miami, FL
Lott, Lisa B. ... Lakeland, FL
Lott, Marley ... Houston, TX
Lott, Patricia D. ... Pensacola, FL
Lott, Philip S. ... Salt Lake City, UT
Lott, Richard I. ... Pensacola, FL
Lott, Richard L. ... Springfield, IL
Lott, Robert D. ... Dallas, TX
Lott, Roger C. ... Lincoln, NE
Lott, Roy Edgar, III ... New York, NY
Lott & Schaeffer ... Clayton, MO
Lott, Spencer L., II
Department Of Health And Human Services, Office of Community Services, GV
Lott and Surman, P.C. ... Springfield, IL
Lott, Thomas L. ... Detroit, MI
Lott, Victor H., Jr. ... Mobile, AL
Lott, W. Crews ... Dallas, TX
Lott, Warren G. ... Metairie, LA
Lott, William S. ... Georgetown, TX
Lott, Willie, Jr. ... Oakland, CA
Lott, Y. D., Jr. ... Mobile, AL
Lotter, Aline H. ... Manchester, NH
Lotter & Bailin, P.C. ... Manchester, NH
Lotter, Charles R. ... Plano, TX
Lotterhos, Fred J., Jr. ... Jackson, MS
Lotterhos, Frederick J., III
Jacksonville, FL
Lotterhos, Joseph E. ... Jackson, MS
Lotterman, Thomas R. ... Washington, DC
Lotters, Arlene June ... Albany, NY
Lottes, Kevin R. ... Naples, FL
Lottes, Lisa Carozza ... Naples, FL
Lottes, Paul F. ... Indianapolis, IN
Lotti, Diane L. ... Secaucus, NJ
Lottick, Karen A. ... Hartford, CT
Lottier, John S. ... San Francisco, CA
Lottinger, Lee P., Jr. ... Houma, LA
Lottinger, Morris A., Jr. ... Houma, LA
Lottinville, Nancy A. ... Newark, NJ
Lott-Knipe, Michael J. ... Biloxi, MS
Lottmann, Richard H. ... Tyler, TX
Lottner, Alan B. ... Denver, CO
Lotto, Henry J. ... Philadelphia, PA
Lottridge, Douglas D. ... Anchorage, AK
Lottridge, Richard Glen ... Sierra Madre, CA
Lotts, Kerry C. ... San Francisco, CA
Lotts, Richard L. ... Los Angeles, CA
Lotty, Robert W. ... Fairfield, CT
Lotuff, Shirley A. ... Orleans, MA
Loturco, John H. ... Central Islip, NY
Lotus, Michael J. ... Chicago, IL
Lotven, Howard L. ... Kansas City, MO
Lotven, Howard L., P.C.
Kansas City, MO
Lotvin, Mikhail ... New York, NY
Lotwick, Joseph N. ... Baton Rouge, LA
Lotwin, Stanford G. ... New York, NY
Lotysz, Joseph ... Libertyville, IL
Lotz, Allen ... Virginia Beach, VA
Lotz, Anita I. ... Memphis, TN
Lotz, Arthur M. ... Bloomington, IN
Lotz & Associates, A Professional Corporation
San Antonio, TX
Lotz, Ferdinand J., III ... Louisville, KY
Lotz, Gregory G. ... Montclair, NJ
Lotz, Harold J., Jr. ... San Antonio, TX
Lotz, John M. ... Costa Mesa, CA
Lotz, Julie Elizabeth ... Woodland Hills, CA
Lotz, Thomas E. ... San Diego, CA
Lotz, W. Robert ... Covington, KY
Lotz, Warren J. ... McArthur, OH
Lotzar, Charles W. ... Phoenix, AZ
Lotze, Brigitte ... Taos, NM
Lotzer, Gerald B. ... Dallas, TX
Lotzia, Emerson M. ... Jacksonville, FL
Lou, Elizabeth ... Monterey Park, CA
Lou, Raymond ... White Plains, NY
Louard, Janette McCarthy
Cleveland, OH
Louard, Kenneth A. ... New York, NY
Loub, Curtis A. ... Wichita, KS
Loube, Irving ... Oakland, CA
Loubet, Jeffrey W. ... Albuquerque, NM
Loubier, Gabriel ... New York, NY
Loubier, Gregg J. ... Los Angeles, CA
Loubriel-Murdock, Valerie Ann
New York, NY
Loucas, Penny E. ... Weirton, WV
Louchery, Daniel L. ... Clarksburg, WV
Louck, Lisa A. ... Houston, TX
Loucks, Allan D. ... Seattle, WA
Loucks & Brockbank ... Schenectady, NY
Loucks, Karlyn Anne ... Tampa, FL
Loucks & Lamb ... Seattle, WA
Loucks, Michael K. ... Boston, MA
Loucks, Nancy Barrett ... Louisville, KY
Loucks, Richard R. ... Pullman, WA
Loucks, Robert L. ... Saginaw, MI
Loucks, Thomas J. ... Chicago, IL
Loucks, Wendy R. ... Minneapolis, MN
Loucks, William E. ... Daytona Beach, FL
Loud, George A. ... Alexandria, VA
Loud, Jennifer ... Denver, CO
Loud, Kelley G. ... Houston, TX
Louden, Chris J. ... Moncks Corner, SC
Louden, Donald J. ... Missoula, MT
Louden, Forzani & Katz ... Torrington, CT
Hartford, CT
Louden, Janice H. ... Westminster, CO
Louden, Jeffrey Hadley ... Oakland, CA
Louden, John A.
Treasury Department, GV
Louden, Karen Jacobs ... Wilmington, DE
Louden, Nancy M. ... New York, NY
Louden, Shannon O. ... Hartford, CT
Louden, Thomas A. ... Fairfield, IA
Louden, Thomas E. ... Delaware, OH
Louden, Wm. Bruce ... Hartford, CT
Loudenback, Douglas ... Oklahoma City, OK
Louderback, Charles M.
San Francisco, CA
Louderback, Franklyn ... St. Petersburg, FL
Louderback, Richard J. ... San Rafael, CA
Louderman, Hayes, Van Camp, Priester, Strother & Schwartz, S.C. ... Madison, WI
Louderman, John P., III ... Madison, WI
Loudermilk, Alan R. ... Chicago, IL
Loudermilk, Brenda K. ... Fort Worth, TX
Loudermilk, Joey M. ... Columbus, GA
Loudermilk, Michele S. ... Honolulu, HI
Loud-Hayward, Elizabeth ... Red Bank, NJ
Loudon, Clayton B. ... St. Charles, IL
Loudon, Donald H., Jr.
Independence, MO
Loudon, Donald H., Sr. (Of Counsel)
Prairie Village, KS
Kansas City, MO
Loudon, Lee S. ... Lincoln, NE
Loudon, Timothy D. ... Omaha, NE
Loudon, Zethina L. ... Anchorage, AK
Phoenix, AZ
Loue, Sana ... San Diego, CA
Louey, Kristina ... New York, NY
Lougee, David L. ... Worcester, MA
Lougee, Laurence H. ... Worcester, MA
Lougee, Richard L. ... Tucson, AZ
Lough, Dean Kim ... Phoenix, AZ
Lough, Donald J. ... Dearborn, MI
Lough, Gregory W. ... Houston, TX
Lough, James P. ... Fresno, CA
Lough, Lyman W. ... Long Beach, CA
Lough, Mark H. ... Seattle, WA
Lough, Patricia ... Vinton, IA
Lough, Ray ... Vinton, IA
Lough, Rebecca Mullin ... Atlanta, GA
Lough, Sunita B. ... Washington, DC
Lough, Tracy Sue ... Wichita, KS
Loughbom, Robert D. ... Kansas City, KS
Lenexa, KS
Loughery, Don ... Burbank, CA
Loughhead, D. Jackson ... Exton, PA
Loughhead, Kathleen Parks
Philadelphia, PA
Loughlin, Charles A. ... Washington, DC
Loughlin, Daniel J. ... Central Islip, NY
Loughlin, Dennis W. ... Sterling Heights, MI
Loughlin, Edward P. ... Wallingford, CT
Loughlin, James M. ... Austin, TX
Loughlin, John D. ... Cherokee, IA
Loughlin, John P. ... Cherokee, IA
Loughlin, Johnson & Campbell
Kansas City, MO
Loughlin, Karen A. ... Worcester, MA
Loughlin, Kevin J. ... Chicago, IL
Loughlin Law Firm ... Cherokee, IA
Loughlin, Leo M. ... Albany, NY
Loughlin, Marie Walch, (Mrs.)
Andover, MA
Loughlin, Martin F. ... Manchester, NH
Loughlin, Nancy ... Norwalk, CT
Loughlin, Noonan & Henrici, P.C.
Wallingford, CT
Loughlin, P. Thomas ... Kansas City, MO
Loughlin, Peter J. ... Portsmouth, NH
Loughlin, Peter J. ... Norfolk, VA
Loughlin, Samuel D. ... Austin, TX
Loughlin, Stephanie M. ... Washington, DC
Loughlin, Stephen V. ... Cambridge, MA
Loughlin, Suzanne Rhulen ... Rock Hill, NY
Loughlin, Thomas P. ... Mishawaka, IN
Loughlin, Thos. K. ... Denver, CO
Loughlin, Vincent K. ... Westfield, NJ
New York, NY
Loughlin, Walter P. ... New York, NY
Loughlin, William E. ... Worcester, MA
Loughman, Barbara Fulton ... Salem, NH
Loughman, Cary F. ... Houston, TX
Loughman, Edward D., III
New Rochelle, NY
Loughman, Edward D., Jr.
New Rochelle, NY
Loughman & Fay ... Ventura, CA
Loughman, James R. ... Adams, MA
Loughman, John P. ... Chula Vista, CA
Loughman, Mark K. ... Boston, MA
Loughman, Michael J. ... Lorain, OH
Loughman, Patrick T. ... Oxnard, CA
Loughman, Peter B. ... Chicago, IL
Loughman, Thomas F. ... Morristown, NJ
Loughmiller, Brian S. ... Dallas, TX
Loughmiller, Deane A. ... Paris, TX
Loughmiller & DePlaza, A Professional Corporation ... Dallas, TX
Loughnan, Alan B. ... New York, NY
Loughnane, David J. ... Chicago, IL
Loughnane, John G. ... Boston, MA
Loughnane, John P. ... Rolling Prairie, IN
Loughnane, Michael D. ... New York, NY
Loughnane, William J. ... Titusville, NJ
Loughney, Mayrá Holl ... Brooklyn, NY
Loughney, Michael C.
Commodity Futures Trading Commission, Division of Enforcement, GV
Loughney, Patrick J. ... Pittsburgh, PA
Loughney, Robert M. ... Washington, DC
Albany, NY
Loughran, Alison L. ... Baltimore, MD
Loughran, Bernard T. ... Watertown, MA
Loughran, Bernard T., Jr. ... Watertown, MA
Loughran, Charles H. ... Greensburg, PA
Loughran, Charles S. ... Seattle, WA
Loughran & Corbett, Inc. ... Watertown, MA
Loughran, Dana ... New York, NY
Loughran, David P. ... Lakehurst, NJ
Loughran, Edward M. ... Joliet, IL
Loughran, F. Kevin ... Carlsbad, CA
Loughran, Gerard V. ... New York, NY
Loughran, Jas. P. ... Santa Ana, CA
Loughran, John B. ... New York, NY
Loughran, Joseph L.
West Conshohocken, PA
Loughran, Kenneth E. ... Los Angeles, CA
Loughran & Loughran ... Joliet, IL
Loughran, Mlakar & Bilik ... Greensburg, PA
Loughran, Peter J. ... New York, NY
Loughran, Regina ... New York, NY
Loughran, Robert F. ... Houston, TX
Loughran, Robert T. ... Pittsburgh, PA
Loughran, Thomas M. ... San Francisco, CA
Loughran, Virginia ... Burlington, VT
Loughren and Doyle, P.A.
Fort Lauderdale, FL
Loughren, James J. ... Albuquerque, NM
Loughren, Joseph M.
Fort Lauderdale, FL
Loughren, Louis B. ... Pittsburgh, PA
Loughrey, John F. ... Staten Island, NY
Loughrey, John G. ... San Francisco, CA
Loughrey, Kevin ... Englewood, CO
Loughrey, Raymond E.
San Francisco, CA
Loughridge, Gregory D. ... South Bend, IN
Loughridge, Gregory D., P.C.
South Bend, IN
Loughridge, John H., Jr. ... Columbia, SC
Loughrin, Brian T. ... Alpine, CA
Oklahoma City, OK
Loughry, Allen H., II ... Charleston, WV
Loughry, Daniel F. ... Los Angeles, CA
Loughry, J David ... Murfreesboro, TN
Loughry, Jayne ... San Francisco, CA
Loughry, Justin T. ... Cherry Hill, NJ
Loughry, Lois M. ... Tucson, AZ
Loui, Martin S. C. ... Palo Alto, CA
Loui, Warren R. ... Los Angeles, CA
Louie, Benjamin ... Glendale, CA
Louie, Betasha Wai Ying ... San Francisco, CA
Louie, Calvin S. ... Campbell, CA
Louie, David M. ... Honolulu, HI
Louie, Denise ... Los Angeles, CA
Louie, Dexter B. ... San Francisco, CA
Louie, Foone ... Sacramento, CA
Louie, Gary ... San Francisco, CA
Louie, George H. ... San Francisco, CA
Louie, Jamie Ann ... San Francisco, CA
Louie, Jason ... San Francisco, CA
Louie, Jay R. ... Fresno, CA
Louie, Joanne V. ... Wailuku, HI
Louie, Judy ... Los Angeles, CA
Louie, Kam C. ... Los Angeles, CA
Pasadena, CA
Louie, Kirk S. ... Sacramento, CA
Louie & Kitsuse ... Campbell, CA
Louie, Lawrence P. ... San Francisco, CA
Louie, Lily Leong ... Rockville, MD
Louie, Linda G. ... Philadelphia, PA
Louie, Michael L. ... Berkeley, CA
Mountain View, CA
Louie, Michael Y. ... San Jose, CA
Louie, Ming A. ... Northville, MI
Louie, Patricia ... New York, NY
Louie, Peter E. ... Sherman Oaks, CA
Louie, Stewart ... New York, NY
Louie, Winnie C. ... Los Angeles, CA
Louie-Pleschner, Clarissa A.
Sacramento, CA
Louik, Howard M. ... Pittsburgh, PA
Louik, Michael ... Pittsburgh, PA
Louis, Alexander ... Sugar Land, TX
Louis, Antony Andrew R. ... Dallas, TX
Louis, Bonnie R. ... Glendale, CA
Louis, Charlene A. ... Riverside, CA
Louis, Dianna Marie ... Washington, DC
Louis, Frank A. ... Toms River, NJ
Louis, Frank W. ... Hartford, CT
Louis, Fred, III ... Chicago, IL
Northbrook, IL
Louis, Fred, Jr. ... Harlan, IA
Louis, Harlan S. ... Columbus, OH
Louis, Henry I. ... Baltimore, MD
Louis, James A. ... Trenton, NJ
Louis, Joe ... Austin, TX
Louis, John C. ... Harlan, IA
Louis Law Firm, P.C. ... Harlan, IA
Louis, Leighton S. C. ... Honolulu, HI
Louis, Mario J. ... Miami, FL
Louis, Martin B. ... Chapel Hill, NC
Louis, Maureen M. ... Fabius, NY
Louis M. Druxman & Associates
Albuquerque, NM
Louis, Michael G. ... West Chester, PA
Louis, Paul A. ... Miami, FL
Louis, Philip G., Jr. ... St. Louis, MO
Louis, Robert H. ... Philadelphia, PA
Louis, Robert S. ... Modesto, CA
Louis, Roe & Wolf ... Toms River, NJ
Louis, Sandra F. ... St. Louis, MO
Louis, Stephen E. ... New York, NY
Louis, Thomas M. ... Jackson, MS
Louis-Dreyfus, William G. ... New York, NY
Louisell, John C. ... Washington, DC
Detroit, MI
Harbor Springs, MI
Louisell, Paul C. ... Royal Oak, MI
Louiselle, Bruce M. ... McLean, VA
Louis-Jacques, Lyonette ... Minneapolis, MN
Louison, Audrey C. ... Washington, DC
Richmond, VA
Louison, Bradford ... Boston, MA
Louison, Douglas I. ... Boston, MA
Louizos, John J. ... Stamford, CT
Louk, K. Dwayne ... Virginia Beach, VA
Louk, Ralph G. ... Fairfax, VA
Loukas, Elisabeth H. ... Miami, FL
Loukas, Eric P. ... St. Paul, MN
Loukas, Georgia ... Chicago, IL
Loukedis, Constantine S. ... Paterson, NJ
Loukides, Daphne ... Flushing, NY
Loukides, Mark ... Garden Grove, CA
Loula, Stanley D. ... Cicero, IL
Loulakis, Karen G. ... Great Falls, VA
Loulakis, Michael C. ... Washington, DC
Vienna, VA
Loumbas, Angelo J. ... Chicago, IL
Loumeau, Eric J. ... San Diego, CA
Loumiet, Carlos E. ... Miami, FL
Loumiet, Juan P. ... Miami, FL
Loumos, James G. ... Troy, MI
Loumos & Megel ... Troy, MI
Loun, Randy W. ... Bremerton, WA
Loundy, Christina King ... Chicago, IL
Loundy, Richard A. ... Chicago, IL
Lounibos, John B. ... Petaluma, CA
Lounibos, Leroy J., Jr. ... Petaluma, CA
Lounibos, Lounibos & Tinney
Petaluma, CA
Lounibos, Robert G. ... Petaluma, CA
Lounsberry, Elizabeth Leyttze ... Waterloo, IA
Lounsbery Ferguson Altona & Peak, LLP
Escondido, CA
San Diego, CA
Lounsbery, J. Daniel ... Escondido, CA
Lounsbery, Kenneth H. ... Escondido, CA
Lounsbery, Virgil E. ... Lake Elsinore, CA
Lounsbury, Donald A. ... Orange, CA
Lounsbury, Richard E. ... New York, NY
Lounsbury, Steven R. ... Woodland Hills, CA
Loup, Terry B. ... New Orleans, LA
Loupassi, G. Manoli ... Richmond, VA
Loupe, J. Chandler ... Baton Rouge, LA
New Orleans, LA
Loureiro, Karl R. ... Los Angeles, CA
Loureiro, Thomas A. ... Portland, ME
Lourenco, Catherine ... Philadelphia, PA
Lourenco, Jonathan C.
Independence, MO
Lourenso, Frank J. ... Brooklyn, NY
Lourie, Alan D.
United States Court Of Appeals For The Federal Circuit, GV
Lourie, Alan I. ... Philadelphia, PA
Lourie, Alexander ... Chicago, IL
Lourie & Cutler, P.C. ... Boston, MA
Lourie, David A. ... Cape Elizabeth, ME
Lourie, Donald K. ... Siasconset, MA
Lourie, Gwen J. ... New York, NY
Lourie, Isadore E. ... Columbia, SC
Lourie, Jonathan M. ... Boston, MA
Lourie, Lance D. ... Atlanta, GA
Lourie, Linda S. ... Department of Commerce, Patent and Trademark Office, GV
Lourie, Marvin H. ... Chicago, IL
Lourie, Miles J. ... Miami, FL
Lourie, Robert D. ... Greenbelt, MD
Waldorf, MD
Lourie, Robin Peek ... Atlanta, GA
Lourie & Safran ... Columbia, SC
Lourie, Vanessa Carpenter
Washington, DC
Lourim, Bernard T. ... Detroit, MI
Lourim, Lynne Olman ... Detroit, MI
Lourimore, Linda A. ... San Francisco, CA
Lourimore, Stanley M. ... Sacramento, CA
Lourmais, Patricia J. ... Lake Worth, FL
Lourmais, Patricia, P.A. ... Lake Worth, FL
Lourne, Susan K. ... Stevenson, WA
Louros, Steven ... New York, NY
Lousararian, James ... Stoughton, MA
Lousararian, Lori J. ... Boston, MA
Lousberg, Peter H. ... Rock Island, IL
Lousin, Ann M. ... Chicago, IL
Louskos, Theani Christine
San Francisco, CA
Lousteau, Kristi ... Altadena, CA
Lout, Frances A. ... Austin, TX
Loutfi, Tarick ... Chicago, IL
Louth, Kevin H. ... Fillmore, CA
Louth, Richard P. ... Fort Myers Beach, FL
Rocky River, OH
Louthan, Beverly Bogle ... Holdrege, NE
Louthan, Thomas A. ... Winchester, VA
Louthan, Thomas A., P.C. ... Winchester, VA
Louthian, Amy A. ... Columbia, SC
Louthian, Carolyn Gale ... Spokane, WA
Louthian, Herbert W. ... Columbia, SC
Louthian, Herbert W., Jr. ... Columbia, SC
Louthian and Louthian ... Columbia, SC
Louthian, Robert C., III ... Washington, DC
Louthian, Robert C., Jr. ... Fairfax Station, VA
Loutos, Peter A., (Ltd.) ... Park Ridge, IL
Loutos, William A. ... Phoenix, AZ
Louttit, Dana M. ... Buffalo, NY
Louttit, Eric J. ... Pittsburgh, PA
Louttit, Gordon J. ... El Segundo, CA
Louttit, Kathryn Hale ... Cleveland, OH
Loutzenhiser, Janice ... San Bernardino, CA
Louv, Arthur R. ... Orlando, FL
Louvier, Wayne D. ... Long Beach, CA
Louviere, Daniel J. ... Orange Park, FL
Louviere, Drew M. ... Baton Rouge, LA
Louviere, Drew M., A Professional Law Corporation ... Baton Rouge, LA
Louviere, E. J. ... Shreveport, LA
Louw, Joan E., A Professional Law Corporation
Temecula, CA
Louwagie, Joseph H. ... Marshall, MN

Louwagie, Vincent D. ... Minneapolis, MN
Louw-DeFazio, Joan ... Temecula, CA
Loux, George Ridgley ... Oakton, VA
Loux, Gordon B. ... Cleveland, OH
Loux, Helene E. ... Harrisburg, PA
Loux, Lloyd F., Jr. ... Cleveland, OH
Louzoun, Henriette Jeanne ... New York, NY
Louzoun, Malka ... New York, NY
Lovaas, Aaron D. ... Las Vegas, NV
Lovaas, Ivan ... Sterling, IL
Lovald, John S. ... Pierre, SD
Lovallo, Anthony F. ... Atlanta, GA
Lovallo, Joseph A., Ltd. ... Tucson, AZ
Lovallo, Leonard C. ... Buffalo, NY
LoVallo, Michael A. ... Chicago, IL
Lovallo, Randolph T. ... Stamford, CT
Lovallo, Timothy R. ... Buffalo, NY
Lovallo, Williams Law Firm ... Buffalo, NY
Lovan, Gregg E. ... Caldwell, ID
Lovas, Akselrad & Joseph ... Succasunna, NJ
Lovas, C. Natasha ... San Francisco, CA
Lovas, Sol ... Billings, MT
Lovas, William J. ... Succasunna, NJ
LoVasco, Eugene F. ... Warren, MI
Lovasz, Christopher M. ... Garden City, MI
Lovat, Lynn E. ... Houston, TX
Lovato, Peter F., III ... Chicago, IL
Lovato, Victoria ... Phoenix, AZ
Lovato-Farmer, Cindy J.
Albuquerque, NM
Love, Alice Spelas ... Manchester, NH
Love, Andrew ... Austin, TX
Love, Andrew J. ... Silver Spring, MD
Love, Andrew S. ... San Francisco, CA
Love, Angela M. Corbisiero
Haddonfield, NJ
Love, Anna M. ... Dallas, TX
Love & Associates, P.C. ... Fairfax, VA
Love, Barbara D. ... Norristown, PA
Love, Beal & Nixon, P.C.
Oklahoma City, OK
Love, Benjamin ... Corinth, TX
Love, Benjamin ... Dallas, TX
Love, Betty C. ... Talladega, AL
Love, Bonnie R. ... Cherry Hill, NJ
Love, Brian J. ... Minneapolis, MN
Love, Bruce W. ... Chula Vista, CA
Love, Bruce W., A P.C. ... Chula Vista, CA
Love, C. Stephen ... Pacific Palisades, CA
Love, Carl G. ... Washington, DC
Love, Carl Neprud ... Albuquerque, NM
Love, Carolyn Suzanne ... Westwood, KS
Love, Chad P. ... Honolulu, HI
Love, Charles F. ... Philadelphia, PA
Love, Charles M., III ... Charleston, WV
Love, Charles M., IV ... Charleston, WV
Love, Cheri D. ... Monterey, CA
Love, Chester A. ... St. Louis, MO
Love, Christopher C. ... Los Angeles, CA
Love, Christopher E. ... Los Angeles, CA
Love, Clifford, III ... Virginia Beach, VA
Love, Clifford, III, P.C. ... Virginia Beach, VA
Love, Colin L. ... Kailua-Kona, HI
Love, Cynthia M. ... Hubbard, OH
Love, D. Leigh ... Helena, AL
Love, Dana D. ... Coraopolis, PA
Love, Daniel J. ... Dodge City, KS
Love, Daryll ... Atlanta, GA
Love, Davia M. ... San Francisco, CA
Love, David ... Boston, MA
Love, David B. ... Chicago, IL
Love, David B. ... Baltimore, MD
Love, David B., P.A. ... Baltimore, MD
Love, David Lee ... Philadelphia, MS
Love, David M.
Hot Springs National Park, AR
Love, David M. ... Dallas, TX
Love, Dennis A. ... Idaho Falls, ID
Love, Diane ... Rochester, NY
Love, Donald P. ... Columbus, OH
Love, Douglas M. ... Seattle, WA
Love, Edgar, III ... Charlotte, NC
Love, Edward A. ... Chattanooga, TN
Love, Edward T. ... Bethesda, MD
Love, Eileen M. ... St. Louis, MO
Love, Elizabeth B. ... Boston, MA
Love, Ellsworth ... Cincinnati, OH
Love, Eric A. ... Brookfield, WI
Love, Eric V. ... Boulder, CO
Love, Fount L., Jr. ... Chattanooga, TN
Love, Francine E. ... New York, NY
Love, Frank, Jr. ... Atlanta, GA
Love, Fred W. ... Clarksville, TN
Love, G. Roland ... Dallas, TX
Love, Gary A. ... Ozark, MO
Love, Gary A., P.C. ... Ozark, MO
Love, Gary G. ... Grand Rapids, MI
Love, Gary H. ... Shreveport, LA
Love, George F.C. ... St. Louis, MO
Love, George G., II ... Boston, MA
Love, George H., Jr. ... Pittsburgh, PA
Love, George W. ... Waukesha, WI
Love, Gerald D. ... Towson, MD
Love, Gina S. ... Washington, DC
Love, Glen Scott ... Baton Rouge, LA
Love, Gregory S. ... Fort Worth, TX
Love, H. Wayne ... Anniston, AL
Love, Huel M., Jr. ... Talladega, AL
Love, Huel M., Sr. ... Talladega, AL
Love, Hugh Marshall, Jr. ... Yazoo City, MS
Love, J. Anthony ... Atlanta, GA
Love, J. David ... Forest Hills, NY
Love, J. Kenneth ... Washington, OK
Love, J. Michael ... Stamford, CT
Love, Jack L. ... Albuquerque, NM
Love, Jackson B., Jr. ... Marathon, TX
Love, James ... Birmingham, AL
Love, James C., IV ... Fairfax, VA
Love, James H. ... Pittsburgh, PA
Love, James Hogan ... Darien, CT
Love, James L. ... Wilmington, DE
Philadelphia, PA
Love, Jane E. ... Mayville, NY
Love, Jane S. ... Department of the Air Force, Office of the Judge Advocate General, GV
Love, Janet Otsuka ... Chicago, IL
Love, Jeff B., (P.C.) ... Houston, TX
Love, Jeffery J. ... Springfield, MO
Love, Jeffrey B.
Rancho Santa Margarita, CA
Love, Jeffrey M. ... Oklahoma City, OK
Love, Jeffrey S. ... Portland, OR
Love, Jennifer Stephens ... Indianapolis, IN
Love, Jimmy L. ... Sanford, NC
Love, Jimmy L., Jr. ... Sanford, NC
Love, John C. ... Bel Air, MD
Love, John C., Jr. ... Kosciusko, MS
Love, John E. ... Spokane, WA
Love, John H. ... Grosse Pointe, MI
Love, John J. ... Department of Commerce, Patent and Trademark Office, GV
Love, John J. ... Oklahoma City, OK
Love, John N. ... Boston, MA
Love, John P. ... New Canaan, CT
Love, Jon B. ... United States Senate, Senatorial Assistants, GV
Love, Jon F. ... Oklahoma City, OK
Love, Joseph D. ... Windsor Locks, CT
Love, Judith A. ... Philadelphia, PA
Love, Judy Cornels ... Walnut Creek, CA
Love, Kara Conway ... Albany, NY
Love, Kathryn Elliott ... St. Louis, MO
Love, Kenneth Alan ... Sugar Land, TX
Love, Kenneth J. ... Phoenix, AZ
Love, Kenyon D. ... Canton, OH
Love, Kevin ... Hampton, VA
Love, Kevin Bruce ... Miami, FL
Love, Kevin J. ... Clarence, NY
Love, Kimberly Lambert ... Tulsa, OK
Love, Kirsten C. ... Los Angeles, CA
Love, Larry S. ... Reisterstown, MD
Love, LaWonda ... Houston, TX
Love, Lawrence D. ... Independence, MO
Love, Leigh ... Pelham, AL
Love, Lela P. ... New York, NY
Love, LeRoy ... Key West, FL
Love, Leslie G. ... Indianapolis, IN
Love, Linda C. ... Lake Oswego, OR
Love, Lisa A. ... Fairfield, OH
Love, Lisa D. ... Newark, NJ
Love, Lisa D., P.C. ... Newark, NJ
Love, Lloyd F. ... Ferriday, LA
Love, Love & Love ... Talladega, AL
Love & Love, P.A. ... Sanford, NC
Love, Lucinda Anne ... Department of Justice, Civil Division, GV
Love, Mark A. ... San Francisco, CA
Love, Mark S. ... Tannersville, PA
Love, Martha G. ... Waynesboro, MS
Love, Martin T. ... San Rafael, CA
Love, Mary Alice ... Houston, TX
Love, Mary Bland ... Jacksonville, FL
Love, Mary F. ... Arlington, VA
Love, Matthew S. ... Indianapolis, IN
Love and McClelland ... Albuquerque, NM
Love, Michael B. ... Spokane, WA
Love, Michael H. ... San Francisco, CA
Love, Michael J. ... Clarksville, TN
Love, Michael S. ... Dallas, TX
Houston, TX
Love, Miron A. ... Houston, TX
Love, Nader & Cordill ... Shreveport, LA
Love, Nicole Denise ... Baltimore, MD
Love, Noreen V. ... Maywood, IL
Love, Patricia M. ... New Brunswick, NJ
Love, Patricia Stanford ... Hillsborough, NC
Love, Perrin R. ... Salt Lake City, UT
Love, Peter H. ... St. Louis, MO
Love, Peter J. ... Washington, DC
Love, R. Richard, III ... Tulsa, OK
Love, Randall J. ... New Port Richey, FL
Love, Randall J., P.A.
New Port Richey, FL
Love, Regina L. ... Jacksonville, FL
Love, Richard A. ... Los Angeles, CA
Love, Richard B.
South San Francisco, CA
Love, Richard H. ... Riverdale, MD
Love, Rigby, Dehan & McDaniel
Shreveport, LA
Love, Robert ... Berkeley, CA
Love, Robert A.
Securities and Exchange Commission, Division of Market Regulation, GV
Love, Robert H. ... Memphis, TN
Love, Robert L. ... Hobbs, NM
Love, Robert M. ... Cary, NC
Love, Robert P. ... Grapeview, WA
Love, Robert W. ... Wichita, KS
Love, Ronald C. ... Grand Rapids, MI
Love, Russell C. ... Seattle, WA
Love, Russell P. ... Atlanta, GA
Love, S. Michael ... El Cajon, CA
Love, Samuel P., Jr. ... Shreveport, LA
Love, Sara N. ... Arlington, VA
Love, Sarah Ellen McIntire ... Atlanta, GA
Love & Shenfeld, LLP ... Los Angeles, CA
Love, Sheryl H. ... Cleveland, OH
Love, Simon L. ... Chicago, IL
Love, Sue Ann ... Great Falls, MT
Love, Susan M. ... Milwaukee, WI
Love, Teresa Ann ... Dearborn, MI
Love, Thomas J. ... College Park, MD
Love, Thomas J., Jr. ... Hartford, CT
Love, Thornton, Arnold & Thomason, P.A.
Greenville, SC
Greer, SC
Love, Verner R. ... Syracuse, NY
Love, Virginia C. ... Chattanooga, TN
Love, Virginia Torgerson ... Winona, MN
Love, Voss, Murray & Goeschko
Waukesha, WI
Love, Walter B., Jr. ... Monroe, NC
Love, William A. ... Boulder, CO
Love, William C. ... Springfield, MO
Love, William C. ... Odessa, TX
Love, William C., Jr. ... New York, NY
Love, William E. ... Portland, OR
Love, William E., II ... Akron, OH
Love, William J., Jr. ... Buffalo, NY
Love and Willingham, LLP ... Atlanta, GA
Love, Wm. S. ... Louisville, KY
Love, Yamamoto & Motooka, A Law Corporation ... Honolulu, HI
Loveall, G. Michael ... Franklin, IN
Loveall, Jean Brown ... Amarillo, TX
Loveall and Woods ... Franklin, IN
Love-Baker, Jacqueline ... San Diego, CA
Lovecchio, Angela C. ... Williamsport, PA
Lovecchio, Marc F. ... Williamsport, PA
Loveder, James E. ... Santa Ana, CA
Lovegreen, Robert W. ... Providence, RI
Lovegren, James A. ... Fort Lauderdale, FL
Lovein, Hubert C., Jr. ... Macon, GA
Lovein, N. Daniel ... Valdosta, GA
Lovein, Robert Matthew ... Sacramento, CA
Lovejoy & Associates ... Southport, CT
Lovejoy, Chad S. ... Huntington, WV
Lovejoy, David A. ... Pittsburgh, PA
Lovejoy, David E. ... San Francisco, CA
Lovejoy, Elizabeth L. ... Northfield, MA
Lovejoy, Fred C. ... Lansing, MI
Lovejoy, Frederick A. ... Southport, CT
Lovejoy, Henry Stow ... New York, NY
Lovejoy, J. Michael ... Seattle, WA
Lovejoy, Jerry L. ... Glendale, CA
Lovejoy, Jesse Robert ... New York, NY
Lovejoy, John E. ... Manhattan Beach, CA
Lovejoy, John Steven ... Towson, MD
Harrisburg, PA
Lovejoy, Jonathan ... Norwalk, CT
Lovejoy, Lindsay A., Jr. ... Santa Fe, NM
Lovejoy, Paul R. ... New York, NY
Lovejoy, Rachel S. ... Palo Alto, CA
Lovejoy and Rimer, P.C. ... Norwalk, CT
Wilton, CT
Lovejoy, Scott C. ... Charlotte, NC
Lovejoy, Sharon Valentine ... Honolulu, HI
Lovejoy, Stephen A. ... Lincoln City, OR
Lovejoy, W. Scott, III
La Canada Flintridge, CA
Lovejoy, Wallace W. ... Cincinnati, OH
Lovekamp, Kelly ... Mexico, MO
Lovekin, Osgood S., Jr. ... Seattle, WA
Lovekin, Stephen L., & Associates
Hickory, NC
Lovelace, Barnes F., Jr. ... Decatur, AL
Lovelace, Brad ... San Diego, CA
Lovelace, Byron Keith ... Houston, TX
Lovelace, Caroline S. ... New York, NY
Lovelace, Dale E. ... Kansas City, MO
Lovelace, D. M. ... Oxford, MS
Lovelace & Dowd ... Linden, TX
Lovelace, Eddie C. ... Albany, KY
Lovelace, J. Mark ... Oklahoma City, OK
Lovelace, James G. ... Department of Justice, Federal Bureau of Investigation, GV
Omaha, NE
Lovelace, James R. ... Washington, DC
Lovelace, Jerry L. ... Springdale, AR
Lovelace, Jerry L. ... Cape Coral, FL
Lovelace, Joe D. ... Clearwater, FL
Lovelace, Joe W. ... Linden, TX
Lovelace, Julie E. ... Tallahassee, FL
Lovelace, Lisa C. ... Danville, IL
Lovelace, Mark L. ... Addison, IL
Lovelace, Rene D. ... New Orleans, LA
Lovelace, Reneé C., P.C. ... Dallas, TX
Lovelace, Reneé C., P.C. ... Dallas, TX
Lovelace, Richard M., Jr. ... Conway, SC
Lovelace & Rogers, P.A. ... Conway, SC
Georgetown, SC
Myrtle Beach, SC
Lovelace, Teri Scott ... Richmond, VA
Lovelace, Terry J. ... Lansing, MI
Lovelady, Joe R., Sr. ... Oxford, MS
Lovelady, Stephen T. ... Washington, DC
Lovelady, William N., Jr. ... Clinton, MS
Loveland & Brosius ... Columbus, OH
Loveland, Charles R. ... Brocton, NY
Loveland, Curtis A. ... Columbus, OH
Loveland, Darrcy ... Oakland, CA
Loveland, Gail M. ... Carmel, IN
Loveland & Garrett, A Professional Association ... Ocean City, NJ
Loveland, Genevra Kay
Federal Judicial Center, GV
Loveland, George W., II ... Las Vegas, NV
Loveland, Joseph A., Jr.
West Palm Beach, FL
Loveland, Keith A. ... Edina, MN
Loveland, Kim B. ... Pocatello, ID
Loveland, Kristin A. ... Dallas, TX
Loveland, L. Joseph, Jr. ... Atlanta, GA
Loveland, Lance Ardel ... Burley, ID
Loveland, Laurie J. ... Providence, RI
Loveland, Patricia A. Brock ... Neosho, MO
Loveland, R. Wardell ... Redwood City, CA
Loveland, Richard L. ... Columbus, OH
Loveland, Robyn Ruth ... Omaha, NE
Loveland, Sherri E. ... Lawrence, KS
Loveland, William L. ... Columbus, OH
Loveless, A. Scott ... Salt Lake City, UT
Loveless & Associates ... Fort Worth, TX
Loveless, Brett R. ... Albuquerque, NM
Loveless, Craig R. ... Garden City, KS
Loveless, Curtis M. ... Denton, TX
Loveless, Curtis M. ... Gainesville, TX
McKinney, TX
Loveless, Donald E. ... Atlanta, GA
Loveless, Earl D. ... Pensacola, FL
Loveless, Earle H., Jr. ... Wichita, KS
Loveless, Ernest A., Jr. ... Clinton, MD
Loveless, George G. ... Philadelphia, PA
Loveless, Jacqueline K. ... San Francisco, CA
Loveless, Jeb ... Dallas, TX
Loveless, Jim ... Fort Worth, TX
Loveless, John B. ... St. Clair, MO
Loveless, John J. A. M. ... Mineola, NY
New York, NY
Loveless & Lyons ... Mobile, AL
Montgomery, AL
Loveless, Norman W. ... La Quinta, CA
Loveless, R. Craig ... Oakbrook Terrace, IL
Loveless, Ralph P. ... Mobile, AL
Loveless, Scott A. ... Mill Valley, CA
Loveless, Scott W. ... Salt Lake City, UT
Lovelette, Claudia J. ... Chicago, IL
Loveley, A. Peter ... Providence, RI
Lovell, Arnold Buffum ... New York, NY
Lovell, Arthur F., Jr. ... Birmingham, AL
Lovell, Brian N. ... Enid, OK
Lovell, Carl E., Jr. ... Las Vegas, NV
Lovell, Carla L. ... Nashville, TN
Lovell, Celia C. ... Norfolk, VA
Lovell, Charles A. ... Providence, RI
Lovell, Charles C. ... Helena, MT
Lovell, Christopher, P.C. ... New York, NY
Lovell, Clayton E. ... Houma, LA
Lovell, Dennis G., Jr. ... Atlanta, GA
Lovell, E. Keith ... Cartersville, GA
Lovell, Gary B. ... Newport Beach, CA
Lovell, George L. ... Columbia, TN
Lovell, Glenda ... Kennebunkport, ME
Lovell, Jack V. ... Sacramento, CA
Lovell, James M. ... Paris, KY
Lovell, James R. ... Dumas, TX
Lovell, Jane Elizabeth ... San Francisco, CA
Lovell, Jean A. ... Lincoln, NE
Lovell, Jerald R. ... Mount Clemens, MI
Lovell, Joan ... Detroit, MI
Lovell, Joan A. ... Springfield, NJ
Lovell, Joe L. ... Amarillo, TX
Lovell, John F., Jr. ... Benton, AR
Lovell, John H. ... Amarillo, TX
Lovell, John Robert ... Troy, NY
Lovell, John W. ... Hilton Head Island, SC
Lovell, Joseph M. ... Honolulu, HI
Lovell, Karen B. ... Portland, ME
Lovell, Kelly D. ... Cincinnati, OH
Lovell, Kenneth D. ... Tulsa, OK
Lovell, Lance ... Big Timber, MT
Lovell, Lovell & Newsom, L.L.P.
Amarillo, TX
Lovell & Lyle, P.C. ... Dumas, TX
Lovell, Marc Allen ... Bowling Green, KY
Lovell, Maron E. "Ron"
St. Petersburg, FL
Lovell, Matthew C. ... San Francisco, CA
Lovell, Michael A. ... Danvers, MA
Lovell & Nalley ... Benton, AR
Lovell, Orlando Carlos ... Corpus Christi, TX
Lovell, Peter H. ... Farmington, CT
Lovell, Rebecca C. ... Denver, CO
Lovell, Richard A. "Drew"
West Palm Beach, FL
Lovell, Richard D. ... Chicago, IL
Lovell, Richard E. ... Preston, MD
Lovell, Richard H. ... Boston, MA
Lovell, Richard H. ... Ozone Park, NY
Lovell, Robert H. ... Salt Lake City, UT
Lovell, Russell E., II ... Des Moines, IA
Lovell, S. Mark ... Dallas, TX
Lovell & Stewart, LLP ... New York, NY
Lovell, Susan L.
Office Of Special Counsel, GV
Lovell, Tamara G. ... Dallas, TX
Lovell, Terry M. ... Miami, FL
Lovell, Thomas A. ... Clear Lake, IA
Lovell, Troy M. ... Tampa, FL
Lovell, Virginia F. ... New Orleans, LA
Lovell, Warner E., Jr.
Oklahoma City, OK
Lovell White Durrant ... Washington, DC
Chicago, IL
Chicago, IL
New York, NY
New York, NY
Lovell, William S. ... Aloha, OR
Lovellette, Anson L. ... St. Joseph, MI
Lovellette, Gary N. ... Cookeville, TN
Lovellette, Kevin R. ... Chicago, IL
Lovely, Bernard F., Jr. ... Lexington, KY
Lovely, Christine D. ... Pleasanton, CA
Lovely, F. Beirne, Jr., (P.C.) ... Boston, MA
Lovely, James W. ... Kensington, CA
Lovely, Jeffery N. ... Vanceburg, KY
Lovely, Jeffrey M. ... Foxboro, MA
Lovely, John M. ... Dedham, MA
Lovely, Stephen P. ... Salem, MA
Lovely, Victoria B. ... Chicago, IL
Loveman, Peggy J. ... Los Angeles, CA
Loven, Dean P. ... Charlotte, NC
Lovenberg, Douglas Richard ... Boston, MA
Lovendosky, Keith A. ... Santa Monica, CA
Lovendusky, Michael ... Washington, DC
Lovenheim, David A. ... Washington, DC
Rochester, NY
Lovenheim, Peter C. ... Rochester, NY
Lovensheimer, J. Anthony ... Florence, KY

Loventhal, Daniel J. ....New York, NY
Loventhal, Robert D. ....Sharon, MA
Loventhal, Scott Todd ....Short Hills, NJ
Lovenworth, Stanton J. ....New York, NY
Lovenworth, Susan H. ....Escondido, CA
Lover, Cynthia M. ....Myrtle Beach, SC
Lovercheck, Charles L. ....Erie, PA
Lovercheck, Dale R. ....York, PA
Lovercheck and Lovercheck ....Erie, PA
Lovercheck, Wayne L. ....Erie, PA
Loverde, Jos. J. ....Tempe, AZ
Loverde, Martha L. ....Brooklyn, NY
LoVerde, Vito P. ....Chicago, IL
Loverdi, Joseph R. ....Philadelphia, PA
Loverdi, Rosemary J. ....Cherry Hill, NJ
Philadelphia, PA
Loverich, Shannon Vizard ....Dearborn, MI
Loveridge, Gary F. ....Sacramento, CA
Lovering, Bruce J. T. ....Ann Arbor, MI
Lovering, Charles B. ....Summerland Key, FL
Lovering, Lealand L. ....Cocoa, FL
Lovering, Richard S. ....Columbus, OH
Lovern, Kenneth D. ....Roeland Park, KS
Lovern, Kent L. ....Milwaukee, WI
Lovern, Steven S. ....Indianapolis, IN
Lovern, Susan E. ....Milwaukee, WI
Lovernick, Richard N. ....Ann Arbor, MI
Lovero, Robert J. ....Berwyn, IL
Loverro, John F. ....East Hampton, NY
Loversky, Thomas R. ....Hermosa Beach, CA
Loverude, Russell H. ....Joliet, IL
Loverude, Russell H. ....New Lenox, IL
Loveseth, Ian G. ....San Francisco, CA
Lovesky, Jerome ....Newington, CT
Lovesky, Richard A. ....Sarasota, FL
Lovestrand, Sandra P. ....Chicago, IL
Lovett, Anthony ....San Diego, CA
Lovett, C. Douglas ....Cleveland, OH
Lovett, Carl J.S. ....Providence, RI
Lovett, Chester ....Charleston, WV
Lovett, Cowart & Ayerbe ....Macon, GA
Lovett, Daniel S. ....Memphis, TN
Lovett, Dorr F. ....Detroit, MI
Lovett, Gail E. ....Columbia, SC
Lovett, George S. ....DeLand, FL
Lovett, Glenn, Jr. ....Jonesboro, AR
Lovett & Gould ....White Plains, NY
Lovett, H. Malcolm ....Houston, TX
Lovett, J. Timothy ....Madison, WI
Lovett, James W. ....Quitman, GA
Lovett, James W. ....Chicago, IL
Lovett, Jim D. ....Clarksville, TX
Lovett, John A. ....New Orleans, LA
Lovett, John C. ....Tallahassee, FL
Lovett, John C. ....Benton, KY
Lovett, John C. ....Tulsa, OK
Lovett, John T. ....Louisville, KY
Lovett & Johnson ....Benton, KY
Lovett, Jonathan ....White Plains, NY
Lovett, Judy A. ....Stockton, CA
Lovett, L. Alexander ....Houston, TX
Lovett, L. Robert ....Macon, GA
Lovett, Laurence D. ....Jacksonville, FL
Lovett, Linda Marie ....New York, NY
Lovett, Linton R. ....Miami, FL
Lovett, Mack P. ....San Diego, CA
Lovett, Mark E. ....Lancaster, PA
Lovett, Mary Forbes ....Cleveland, OH
Lovett, Michael A. ....Los Angeles, CA
Lovett, Pamela House ....Houston, TX
Lovett, Robert B. ....Boston, MA
Lovett, Robert G. ....Pittsburgh, PA
Lovett, Roselyn G. ....Dayton, OH
Lovett, Ruth L. ....Cleveland, OH
Lovett, Sarah L. ....Forestville, CA
Lovett Schefrin Harnett ....Providence, RI
Lovett, Steven R. ....Woodland Hills, CA
Lovett, Steven T. ....Portland, OR
Lovett, Susan Carter ....Augusta, GA
Lovett, Suzanne D. T. ....New York, NY
Lovett, Thomas D. ....Albany, GA
Lovett, Thomas G., IV ....Minneapolis, MN
Lovett, Thomas G., Jr. ....Minneapolis, MN
Lovett, Thomas M. ....Florence, AL
Lovett, W. Thomas ....Orlando, FL
Lovett, Wells T. ....Owensboro, KY
Lovett, Willie J., Jr. ....Atlanta, GA
Lovette, Daniel R. ....Johnstown, PA
Lovette, Eugene S. ....Westbury, NY
Lovette, Kenneth F. ....San Francisco, CA
Lovewell, James D. ....Lansing, MI
Lovfald, Michael W. ....Houston, TX
Lovgren, Lori A. ....Boca Raton, FL
Lovgren, Richard Hannibal ....Sunnyvale, CA
Lovi, John D. ....New York, NY
Lovich & Penn ....Los Angeles, CA
Lovich, Richard A. ....Los Angeles, CA
Lovick, Sara ....Piscataway, NJ
Lovig, Paul ....Marshalltown, IA
Lovig, Richard G. ....Davenport, IA
Lovik, Mary M. ....Mason, MI
Loving, Cecilia ....New York, NY
Loving, Deborah Grey ....Medina, OH
Loving, Deborah June Pierre ....Oakland, CA
Loving, Jack R. ....Fort Lauderdale, FL
Loving, Jack R., P.A.
Fort Lauderdale, FL
Loving, Katherine G. ....New York, NY
Loving, Kimberly D. ....Dallas, TX
Loving, Kimberly L. ....St. Joseph, MO
Loving, Paul E. ....Beaverton, OR
Loving, Richard C. ....Warrenton, VA
Loving, Susan Brimer ....Edmond, OK
Loving, Walter H., III ....Sacramento, CA
Lovinger, Blythe E. ....New York, NY
Lovinger, Daniel L. ....Cleveland, OH
Lovinger, Jeffrey Scott ....Portland, OR
Lovinger, John P. ....Hillsdale, MI

Lovinger, Joseph S. ....White Plains, NY
Lovinger, Joseph S., P.C. ....White Plains, NY
Lovinger, Richard R. ....San Diego, CA
Lovinger, Todd D. ....Washington, DC
Lovingood, Katherine ....Oak Ridge, TN
Lovingood, Lisa A. ....Jacksonville, FL
Lovingood, M. Shane ....Dalton, GA
Lovington, Mark Ross ....Sacramento, CA
Lovins, Nelson P. ....Woburn, MA
Lovinsky, Ilan ....Palo Alto, CA
Loviscky, Douglas C. ....Pittsburgh, PA
Lovison, John K. ....Racine, WI
Lovit, Jeffrey ....Milbridge, ME
Lovit, Neil S. ....New York, NY
Lovitch, Fred B. ....Lawrence, KS
Lovitch, Karen S. ....Washington, DC
Lovitky, Jeffrey A. ....Washington, DC
Lovitt, Claudine M. ....Cleveland, OH
Lovitt & Hannan, Inc. ....San Francisco, CA
Lovitt, Kelly N. ....Dallas, TX
Lovitt, Ronald ....San Francisco, CA
Lovitz, Arnold ....Philadelphia, PA
Lovitz and Gold, P.C. ....Philadelphia, PA
Lovitz, Hyman ....Morristown, NJ
Philadelphia, PA
Lovitz, Kevin I. ....Philadelphia, PA
Lovitz, Michael L. ....Philadelphia, PA
Lovlace, Neal ....Centerville, TN
Lovlien, Robert S. ....Bend, OR
Lovo, Mario M. ....Miami, FL
Lovo, Mario M., Law Offices of, P.A.
Miami, FL
Lovoi, Gerald J. ....Tulsa, OK
LoVoi, Paul Vincent ....Washington, DC
Lovorn, Julia R. ....Houston, TX
Lovoy, Elena A. ....Hoffman Estates, IL
Lovoy, John E. ....Providence, RI
Lovre, Monica M. ....Wexford, PA
Lovretovich, Joseph M. ....Los Angeles, CA
Lovretovich, Joseph M.
Woodland Hills, CA
Lovrien, Christopher J. ....Washington, DC
Lovrien, Julie T. ....Aberdeen, SD
Lovrien, Lucy D. ....Boston, MA
Lovschal, Charlotte ....Chappaqua, NY
Low, Allan E. ....San Francisco, CA
Low, Andrew M. ....Denver, CO
Low, Ball & Lynch, A Professional Corporation ....Burlingame, CA
Monterey, CA
San Francisco, CA
Low & Childers, P.C. ....Phoenix, AZ
Low, Colbert K. H. ....Aiea, HI
Low, Cynthia P. ....Hackensack, NJ
Low, David G. ....Portland, OR
Low, Donald ....Woodland Hills, CA
Low, Donald A. ....Kansas City, MO
Low, Donald H. C. ....Honolulu, HI
Low, Donna W. ....Sacramento, CA
Low, Doris F. ....Baltimore, MD
Low, Esther ....Oakland, CA
Low, Evelyn A. ....San Francisco, CA
Low, Frederick Charles ....Tulsa, OK
Low, Gilbert I. ....Beaumont, TX
Low, Gordon J. ....Logan, UT
Low, Harold W. ....Port Washington, NY
Low, Harry W. ....San Francisco, CA
Low, J. Michael ....Phoenix, AZ
Low, James E., Jr. ....Marathon, WI
Wausau, WI
Low, James R., Jr. ....King George, VA
Low, Jeffrey N. ....Norwich, CT
Low, Jennifer Goldberg
Maryland Heights, MO
Low, Joan E. ....San Francisco, CA
Low, John B. ....Oxon Hill, MD
Low, John B. ....San Antonio, TX
Low, John B., & Associates, P.A.
Oxon Hill, MD
Low, John L., IV ....Jackson, MS
Low, John M. ....El Cerrito, CA
Low, John T. C. ....Jackson, MS
Low, John W. ....Denver, CO
Low, Joseph N. ....Niles, MI
Low, Keegan Graham ....Reno, NV
Low, Lawrence B. ....San Francisco, CA
Low & Low ....Hackensack, NJ
Jersey City, NJ
West New York, NJ
Low & Low ....Arlington, VA
Low, Lucinda A. ....Washington, DC
Low, Mary Alice Herman ....Oxon Hill, MD
Low, Mary E. ....East Lansing, MI
Low, Matthew A. ....Chantilly, VA
Low, Michael J. ....Walnut Creek, CA
Low, Nathan L. ....Escondido, CA
Low, Peter W. ....Charlottesville, VA
Low, Remington ....San Francisco, CA
Low, Rhonda B. ....San Antonio, TX
Low, Richard C. ....Lancaster, PA
Strasburg, PA
Low, Robert A. ....New York, NY
Low, Ronald ....Los Angeles, CA
Low, Rudolph E. ....St. Paul, MN
Low, Russell L. ....Hackensack, NJ
Jersey City, NJ
West New York, NJ
Low, Sonia ....New York, NY
Low, Stanley F. ....Houston, TX
Low, Stanley H. ....Monterey, CA
Low, Stanley W. ....Hackensack, NJ
Low, Susan A. ....Des Moines, IA
Low, Suzanne C. ....Bonita Springs, FL
Low, Terrence A. ....Springfield, MA
Low, Theodore J. ....Chicago, IL
Low, Warren N. ....Arlington, VA
Low, William H. ....Rochester, NY
Low, William M. ....San Diego, CA

Lowance, David C., Jr. ....Atlanta, GA
Lowans, Thurman W. ....Bremerton, WA
Lowary, Fred M. ....Anaheim, CA
Lowary, Mark ....Los Angeles, CA
Low-Beer, John R. ....New York, NY
Lowber Hendricks, Law Firm, P.A., The
Little Rock, AR
Lowcher, Alan Y. ....Washington, NJ
Lowden, David ....Wichita, KS
Lowden, David W. ....New York, NY
Lowden, Francis V., III ....Richmond, VA
Lowden, Kathleen L. ....New York, NY
Lowden, L. Merrill ....Juneau, AK
Lowden, Scott R. ....Plano, TX
Lowder, Carroll R. ....Monroe, NC
Lowder, Charles Lynn ....San Diego, CA
Lowder, Claudia J. ....San Francisco, CA
Lowder, Diane M. ....Richmond, VA
Lowder, Janet L. ....Cleveland, OH
Lowder, Juanda K. ....Riverside, CA
Lowder, Mark T. ....Albemarle, NC
Lowder, Michael C. ....Fort Worth, TX
Lowder, Vincent D. ....Irvine, CA
Lowdon, Jane E. ....Chicago, IL
Lowe, A. Burgess ....North Canton, OH
Lowe, A. James ....Columbus, OH
Lowe, Alan S. ....Savannah, GA
Lowe, Alicia L. ....Vancouver, WA
Lowe, Allan M. ....Alexandria, VA
Lowe, Allen J. ....Washington, DC
Lowe, Amanda R. ....Sacramento, CA
Lowe, Amy Groves ....Baton Rouge, LA
Lowe, Ashley Byrd ....Baton Rouge, LA
Lowe, Ashley E. ....Bloomfield Hills, MI
Lowe & Associates, P.C. ....Alexandria, VA
Lowe, Barbara ....Brooklyn, NY
Lowe, Barbara K. ....Missouri City, TX
Lowe, Barry Neil ....Chicago, IL
Lowe, Benny J. ....Odessa, TX
Lowe, Bethany C. ....Springfield, MA
Lowe, Bill G. ....Oklahoma City, OK
Lowe, Bruce J. L. ....Cleveland, OH
Lowe, Bryan A. ....Boulder City, NV
Las Vegas, NV
Lowe, Bryan A, & Associates, A Prof. Law Corp. ....Las Vegas, NV
Lowe, Bryan A., Professional Law Corporation
Boulder City, NV
Lowe, Cara K. ....San Francisco, CA
Lowe, Carlton ....Chicago, IL
Lowe, Cary D. ....Los Angeles, CA
Lowe, Catherine A. ....Richmond, VA
Lowe, Cathy C. ....Lexington, KY
Lowe, Cathy C., P.S.C. ....Lexington, KY
Lowe, Charles D. ....Dayton, OH
Lowe, Charles E. ....Lincoln, NE
Lowe, Charles E., Jr. ....Pikeville, KY
Lowe, Charles E., Jr. ....Plymouth, MI
Lowe, Charles E., Sr. ....Boca Raton, FL
Lowe, Charles W. ....Phoenix, AZ
Lowe, Charmaine M. ....Chicago, IL
Lowe, Chas. E. ....Pikeville, KY
Lowe, Chester C., Jr. ....Little Rock, AR
Lowe, Chip ....Des Moines, IA
Lowe, Christopher J. ....Kansas City, MO
Lowe, Coleen H. ....San Diego, CA
Lowe, Craig W. ....Shelton, WA
Lowe, Cynthia K. ....Cincinnati, OH
Lowe, Cyril G., Jr. ....New Orleans, LA
Lowe, Daniel W. ....Oklahoma City, OK
Lowe, Danny R. ....Marion, VA
Lowe, Darryl G. ....Knoxville, TN
Lowe, Darryl R. ....Omaha, NE
Lowe, David A. ....San Francisco, CA
Lowe, David A. ....Seattle, WA
Lowe, David C. ....Columbus, OH
Lowe, David E. ....Chardon, OH
Lowe, David E. ....Milwaukee, WI
Lowe, David H., IV ....Port Salerno, FL
Lowe, David J. ....Pittsburgh, PA
Lowe, David K. ....Columbus, OH
Lowe, David L. ....San Jose, CA
Lowe, David P. ....Milwaukee, WI
Lowe, David R. ....San Mateo, CA
Lowe, David William ....Fairfield, CA
Lowe, Deborah J. ....Miami, FL
Lowe, Debra A.
Federal Energy Regulatory Commission, Office of the General Counsel, GV
Lowe, Donald B., III ....Savannah, GA
Lowe, Donald V. ....North Platte, NE
Lowe, Douglas ....New York, NY
Lowe, Douglas E. ....Palestine, TX
Lowe, Douglas R. ....Woodbury, MN
Lowe, E. Clayton, Jr. ....Birmingham, AL
Lowe, E. Nobles ....Carmel, NY
Lowe, Edwin N. ....Palo Alto, CA
Lowe • Eklund • Wakefield Co., L.P.A.
Cleveland, OH
Lowe, Ellen M., (A P.C.) ....Seal Beach, CA
Lowe, Elmer, III ....Jamaica, NY
Lowe, Everett A., Jr. ....Houston, TX
Lowe, Farmer, Bacon & Roe ....Olathe, KS
Lowe, Frank A. ....Berkeley, CA
Lowe, Frank C. ....Denver, CO
Lowe, Frederick B. ....Virginia Beach, VA
Lowe, Frederick V. ....Stockton, NJ
Lowe, Garland E. ....Olney, MD
Silver Spring, MD
Lowe, Garland E., P.A. ....Washington, DC
Silver Spring, MD
Lowe, George A. ....Olathe, KS
Lowe, George H. ....Syracuse, NY
Lowe Gray Steele & Darko ....Indianapolis, IN
Lowe, Gregg A. ....Portland, OR
Lowe, Gretchen L.
Commodity Futures Trading Commission, Division of Enforcement, GV

Lowe, Harold C. ....Buffalo, NY
Lowe, Harry N., III ....Fairfax, VA
Lowe Hauptman Gopstein Gilman & Berner, L.L.P. ....Alexandria, VA
Lowe, Henry I. ....Denver, CO
Lowe, Henry T. ....Columbia, MO
Lowe, Herbert F. ....St. Petersburg Beach, FL
Lowe, Holly W. ....Overland Park, KS
Lowe, Horace Anthony ....Denver, CO
Lowe, Howard E. ....Los Angeles, CA
Lowe, Hugh S. ....Austin, TX
Lowe, Ira M. ....Washington, DC
Lowe, Irving ....Paradise Valley, AZ
Lowe, James A. ....Irvine, CA
Lowe, James A. ....Orlando, FL
Lowe, James A. ....Cleveland, OH
Lowe, James Earl, Jr. ....St. Francis, WI
Lowe, James H. ....Mercer Island, WA
Lowe, James M. ....Alexandria, VA
Lowe, James R. ....Tallahassee, FL
Lowe, James R. ....Houston, TX
Lowe, James R. ....Milwaukee, WI
Lowe, James W. ....Washington, DC
Lowe, James W. ....Silver Spring, MD
Lowe, Jeffery C. ....Washington, DC
Lowe, Jeffre T. ....Los Angeles, CA
Lowe, Jeffrey A. ....Beverly Hills, CA
Lowe, Jeffrey Alan ....Washington, DC
Lowe, Jeffrey Eugene ....Santa Ana, CA
Lowe, Jeffrey J. ....North Little Rock, AR
St. Louis, MO
Lowe, Jennifer M. ....Elkhorn, WI
Lowe, Joan M. ....Daytona Beach, FL
Lowe, John C. ....Washington, DC
Lowe, John E. ....Chicago, IL
Lowe, John H., Jr. ....Goodlettsville, TN
Lowe, John, IV ....Columbus, OH
Lowe, John K. ....Oregon City, OR
Lowe, John P., Jr. ....New York, NY
Rochester, NY
Lowe, John Patrick ....Uvalde, TX
Lowe, John Phillip ....Birmingham, MI
Lowe, John S. ....Dallas, TX
Lowe, John W. ....Haleyville, AL
Lowe, John W. ....Salt Lake City, UT
Lowe, Jon D. ....San Antonio, TX
Lowe, Jonathan B. ....Haleyville, AL
Lowe, Jonathan D. ....West Bloomfield, MI
Lowe, Jonathan W. ....Atlanta, GA
Lowe, Joseph H. ....Miami, FL
Lowe, Jung Y. ....Chicago, IL
Lowe, K. Arlette ....Hammonton, NJ
Lowe, Kathleen Dugi ....Oregon City, OR
Lowe, Kathlene W. ....Irvine, CA
Lowe, Keith A. ....Stuart, FL
Lowe, Keith A., P.A. ....Stuart, FL
Lowe, Kimberly A. ....Minneapolis, MN
Lowe, Kimberly D. ....Columbus, OH
Lowe, Kimberly Faith ....Waynesville, MO
Lowe, L. Robert, Jr. ....Indianapolis, IN
Lowe, Larry C. ....Cupertino, CA
Lowe, Laura A. ....Lincoln, NE
Lowe, Laura S. ....San Francisco, CA
Lowe, Laurence L. ....Kansas City, MO
Lowe, Lesley J. ....Albuquerque, NM
Lowe, Leslie H. ....New York, NY
Lowe & Lewandowski ....Plymouth, MI
Lowe, Lisa Arlyn ....Chicago, IL
Lowe, M. Leonard ....Rutherfordton, NC
Lowe, Marie H. ....Denver, CO
Lowe, Mark A. ....Lafayette, LA
Lowe, Mark A. ....New York, NY
Lowe, Mark David ....Des Moines, IA
Lowe, Mark T. ....Wadesboro, NC
Lowe, Marta T. ....Washington, DC
Lowe, Martha W. ....Metairie, LA
Lowe, Mary Baroody ....Washington, DC
Lowe, Mary Hatfield ....Fort Smith, AR
Lowe, Mary Lloyd ....Springfield, IL
Lowe, Michael ....Mineola, NY
Lowe, Michael B. ....Overland Park, KS
Lowe, Michael C. ....Dallas, TX
Lowe, Michael D. ....Arlington, VA
Lowe, Michael G., (P.C.) ....San Francisco, CA
Lowe, Michael M. ....Los Angeles, CA
Lowe, Michael R. ....Orlando, FL
Lowe, Michael S. ....Los Angeles, CA
Lowe, Michael T. ....Costa Mesa, CA
Lowe, Michael W. ....Louisville, KY
Lowe, Michele Marie ....St. Louis, MO
Lowe, Mobley & Lowe
Double Springs, AL
Haleyville, AL
Hamilton, AL
Lowe, Moira C. ....Hartford, CT
Lowe & Money, P.C. ....Marion, VA
Lowe, Morris ....Bowling Green, KY
Lowe, Noel Joy ....Absecon, NJ
Lowe, Norton T. ....Buffalo, NY
Lowe, Patricia A. ....Philadelphia, PA
Lowe, Peter D. ....Lewiston, ME
Lowe, Peter E. ....Los Angeles, CA
Lowe, Peter L., Jr. ....Huntsville, AL
Lowe, Philip G. ....San Luis Obispo, CA
Lowe, R. Christopher ....Nashville, TN
Lowe, R. Jeffrey ....New Albany, IN
Lowe, R. Stanley ....Casper, WY
Lowe, Ralph E. ....Aurora, IL
Lowe, Randall B. ....Washington, DC
Lowe, Randall L. ....Homewood, IL
Lowe, Rex A. ....San Clemente, CA
Lowe, Richard A. ....Fort Worth, TX
Lowe, Richard C. ....San Diego, CA
Nashville, TN
Lowe, Richard C. ....Lansing, MI
Lowe, Richard H. ....Philadelphia, PA
Lowe, Richard S. ....Norristown, PA
Lowe, Robert C. ....Anchorage, AK

Lowry, Houston Putnam ....Meriden, CT
Lowry, J. Kent ....Jefferson City, MO
Lowry, J. Kris ....Birmingham, AL
Lowry, James D. ....Conshohocken, PA
Lowry, James I., IV ....Lexington, KY
Lowry, James K., Jr. ....San Antonio, TX
Lowry, James L. ....Danville, IN
Lowry, James M. ....La Porte, TX
Lowry, James R. ....Tacoma, WA
Lowry, James Thomas ....Memphis, TN
Lowry, Jamie F. ....Hermosa Beach, CA
Lowry, Janet C. ....Texarkana, TX
Lowry, Jeffrey A. ....Santa Ana, CA
Lowry, Jeffrey A. ....Kokomo, IN
Lowry, Jeffrey L. ....Albuquerque, NM
Lowry, Joanna S.
Federal Communications Commission, GV
Lowry, John B. ....San Francisco, CA
Lowry, John P. ....Cincinnati, OH
Lowry, John S. ....Rockford, IL
Lowry, John T. ....Huntington, NY
Lowry & Johnson ....Valley Falls, KS
Lowry, Jolene Marie ....Jackson, MS
Lowry, Joseph R. ....Fairfax Station, VA
Lowry, Kelly Davis Heniford ....Columbia, SC
Lowry, Kevin ....Rockville Centre, NY
Lowry, Kirk W. ....Topeka, KS
Lowry, L. Randolph ....Malibu, CA
Lowry, L. Stanton ....Irving, TX
Lowry, Lauren M. ....Valley Falls, KS
Lowry Law Firm, The ....Little Rock, AR
Lowry, Lawrence B. ....Huntington, WV
Lowry, Leonard D. ....Rockwall, TX
Lowry, Leslie E., III ....Portland, ME
Lowry, Lynda L. ....Marcellus, MI
Lowry, Lynda L., P.C. ....Marcellus, MI
Lowry, Marcia Robinson ....New York, NY
Lowry, Mary M. ....Wheaton, IL
Lowry, Marylee A. ....Portland, OR
Lowry, Maureen E. ....Philadelphia, PA
Lowry, Meri Miller ....Portland, ME
Lowry, Michael L. ....Los Angeles, CA
Atlanta, GA
Lowry, Nicholas
Department of Transportation, Office of the General Counsel, GV
Lowry, Patricia Elaine
West Palm Beach, FL
Lowry, Patricia O. ....Cincinnati, OH
Lowry, Peter M. ....Austin, TX
Lowry, Phillip E. ....Provo, UT
Lowry, Randal A. ....Cuyahoga Falls, OH
Lowry & Reed ....Sullivan, IN
Lowry, Richard W. ....Grove, OK
Vinita, OK
Lowry, Robert B. ....Portland, OR
Lowry, Robert C. ....Little Rock, AR
Lowry, Robert D. ....Eugene, OR
Lowry, Robert G. ....Sullivan, IN
Lowry, Robert L. ....Houston, TX
Lowry, Robert N. ....San Francisco, CA
Lowry, Ronald Arthur ....Marietta, GA
Lowry, S. Lynn ....Atlanta, GA
Lowry, Scott David ....Topeka, KS
Lowry, Scott V. ....Waukesha, WI
Lowry, Shannon Kenney
New Orleans, LA
Lowry, Stephen D. ....Raleigh, NC
Lowry, Stephen G. ....Savannah, GA
Savannah, GA
Lowry, Stephen M. ....Los Angeles, CA
Lowry, Stuart O. ....Woodland Hills, CA
Lowry, Stuart S. ....Valley Falls, KS
Lowry, Susan Steinhorn ....Burbank, CA
Lowry, Ted ....Yakima, WA
Lowry, Thomas C. ....Blue Bell, PA
Lowry, Thomas C. ....Midland, TX
Lowry, Thomas C. ....Tacoma, WA
Lowry, Thomas F., III ....Northbrook, IL
Lowry, Thos. L. ....Tyler, TX
Lowry, Tracey L. ....Irvine, CA
Lowry, Van M. ....Cleveland, OH
Lowry, Vanessa Albert ....Philadelphia, PA
Lowry, W. Scott ....Walla Walla, WA
Lowry, Walter D. ....Denver, CO
Lowry, Walter S. ....Los Angeles, CA
Lowry, Wilburn G. ....Indianapolis, IN
Lowry, William E. ....Pittsfield, IL
Lowry, Wm. J. ....Hendersonville, NC
Lowry, Wm. M. ....Olympia, WA
Lowsen, Sharon ....Anaheim, CA
Lowson, Linda M. ....New York, NY
Lowson, Steven Robert ....New York, NY
Lowther, Charles M. ....Southfield, MI
Lowther, Craig F. ....Springfield, MO
Lowther, D. Keith ....Santa Clarita, CA
Lowther, Daniel J. ....San Diego, CA
Lowther, David H. ....Marion, OH
Lowther, Edwin L., Jr. ....Little Rock, AR
Lowther, Frederick M. ....Washington, DC
Hicksville, NY
Lowther, Gerald H. ....Springfield, MO
Lowther, Jocelyn E. ....Rockledge, FL
Lowther, John George ....Birmingham, AL
Lowther, John R. ....Columbus, OH
Lowther, Johnson, Joyner, Lowther, Cully & Housley, L.L.C. ....Springfield, MO
Lowther, Joseph H. ....Los Angeles, CA
Lowther, Patrick A. ....Sleepy Eye, MN
Lowther, Robert C., Jr. ....Covington, LA
Lowther & Schneider ....Southfield, MI
Lowther, Sheila C. ....Madisonville, KY
Lowther, Susan R. S. ....Glendale, AZ
Lowther, Thomas E. ....St. Louis, MO
Lowthian, Philip H. ....Portland, OR
Lowthian, Thomas C. ....Denver, CO

Lowthorp, Richards, McMillan, Miller, Conway & Templeman, A Professional Corporation ....Oxnard, CA
Lowy, Allison K. ....Brooklyn, NY
Lowy, Arthur ....Arlington, VA
Lowy, Barry G. ....Waukegan, IL
Lowy, Brett M. ....Secaucus, NJ
Lowy, Dana ....Los Angeles, CA
Lowy, Elisa ....San Francisco, CA
San Jose, CA
Lowy, Geo. ....Cleveland, OH
Lowy, George T. ....New York, NY
Lowy, James M. ....San Francisco, CA
Lowy, Jeffrey M. ....Encino, CA
Lowy, John B. ....East Brunswick, NJ
New York, NY
Water Mill, NY
Lowy, John B., P.C. ....East Brunswick, NJ
New York, NY
Water Mill, NY
Lowy, Lloyd S. ....New York, NY
Lowy, Marina O. ....New York, NY
Lowy, Martin E. ....New York, NY
Lowy, Martin L. ....Dallas, TX
Lowy, Michael J. ....Palo Alto, CA
Lowy, Milton ....Allentown, PA
Lowy, Nomi Irene ....Secaucus, NJ
Lowy, Peter A. ....Houston, TX
Lowy, Rachel Sarah ....Philadelphia, PA
Lowy, Ronald S., The Law Offices of
Miami, FL
Lowy, Ronald S., The Law Offices of
Miami Beach, FL
Lowy, Steven R. ....Beverly Hills, CA
Lowy, Susanna M. ....New York, NY
Lowy, Thomas ....New York, NY
Lowy Tinsky, Karen ....Washington, DC
Loxley, Gary A. ....Dayton, OH
Loxterman, Ann E. Langdon ....Richmond, VA
Loxterman, Kirk F. ....Mentor, OH
Loxton, George R. ....Milwaukee, WI
Loy, Carl L. ....Yakima, WA
Loy, Dennis K. ....Eastpointe, MI
Loy, Dennis K., P.C. ....Eastpointe, MI
Loy, Erik R. ....Manitowoc, WI
Loy, Frank E. ....Washington, DC
Loy, George W. ....Monticello, IN
Loy, Gerald A. ....Binghamton, NY
Loy, Holly M. ....Knoxville, TN
Loy, James C. ....Portland, OR
Loy, Jeffrey Todd ....Nashville, TN
Loy, Julia D. ....Selma, NC
Loy, Katherine Taylor
Oklahoma City, OK
Loy, K.I. ....Pittsburg, KS
Loy, Kurtis I. ....Pittsburg, KS
Loy, Marshall ....Columbia, KY
Loy, Michael A. ....Bowling Green, KY
Loy, Michael S. ....Portland, OR
Loy, Michelle Maria ....Denver, CO
Loy, Olga A. ....Chicago, IL
Loy, Rodney H. ....Pontiac, IL
Loy, Steven B. ....Lexington, KY
Loy & Tomassi, P.A. ....Pittsburg, KS
Loy, Wesley S. ....Phoenix, AZ
Loy, William A. ....Peru, IN
Loya, Anamaria C. ....San Francisco, CA
Loya, Felix W. ....Los Angeles, CA
Loya, Mervyn H. ....Eugene, OR
Loya, Pamela K. ....Monkton, MD
Loya, Paul M. ....Pleasanton, CA
Loya, Roy R. ....Monkton, MD
Loya, Thomas A. ....Covina, CA
Loyacono, Paul Kelly ....Vicksburg, MS
Loy-Bond, Patricia L. ....Orlando, FL
Loyd, Charles F. ....Salt Lake City, UT
Loyd, Christopher ....New Buffalo, MI
Loyd, Christopher C. ....Toledo, OH
Loyd, Donald P. ....Englewood, CO
Loyd, Janice D. ....Oklahoma City, OK
Loyd, Jennifer S. ....Nashville, TN
Loyd, Jere L. ....St. Joseph, MO
Loyd, Jere L., P.C. ....St. Joseph, MO
Loyd, John Bruster ....Houston, TX
Loyd, John F., Jr. ....Brunswick, ME
Loyd, K. Mark ....Franklin, IN
Loyd, Louis L. ....Malvern, AR
Loyd, Melissa E. ....Houston, TX
Loyd, Michael L. ....Bethany, OK
Loyd, Ralph R. ....Irvine, CA
Loyd, Robert W. ....Kansas City, MO
Loyd, Susan D. ....Washington, DC
Loyd, W. Paul ....Houston, TX
Loyd, Ward E. ....Garden City, KS
Loye, Benjamin R.
Occupational Safety and Health Review Commission, Administrative Law Judges, GV
Loye, Linda ....Chicago, IL
Loyens & Volkmaars ....New York, NY
New York, NY
Loyer, Kathleen M. ....San Clemente, CA
Loyer, Raymond C. ....St. Louis, MO
Loyer, Richard A. ....Medina, OH
Loynd, Thomas ....San Francisco, CA
Loyola, Guido A. ....Schenectady, NY
Loyola, Lisa ....Santa Ana, CA
Loyola, Mario ....San Juan, PR
Loy-Perez, Rosie M. ....Miami, FL
Lozada, John ....Boston, MA
Lozano, Anita G. ....Weslaco, TX
Lozano, Antonio C. ....San Antonio, TX
Lozano, C. John, Jr. ....Harrisonville, MO
Lozano, Christopher ....Fresno, CA
Lozano, Claudia ....Redwood City, CA
Lozano, Dawn M. ....Las Vegas, NV
Lozano, Deborah C. ....Houston, TX
Lozano, Diane M. ....Cheyenne, WY

Lozano, George D. ....Los Angeles, CA
Lozano, Gerry D. Abel ....San Antonio, TX
Lozano, John P. ....Saginaw, MI
Lozano, Lisa Ferguson ....Lincoln, NE
Lozano, Louis T. ....Monterey, CA
Lozano, Madelyn Simon ....Miami, FL
Lozano, Priscilla A. ....Austin, TX
Lozano, R. Norris ....Portland, OR
Lozano, Rudy ....Hammond, IN
Lozano Smith, A Professional Corporation
Escondido, CA
Fresno, CA
Monterey, CA
San Rafael, CA
Santa Monica, CA
Lozano, Wm. R. ....San Antonio, TX
Lozano-Netzel, Aleida F. ....Orland Park, IL
Lozar, Troy ....Yuma, AZ
Loze, Donald ....Pasadena, CA
Lozeau, Louis E., Jr. ....Stuart, FL
Lozenski, James L. ....Berkeley, CA
Lozes & Cambre ....New Orleans, LA
Lozes, Charles F. ....New Orleans, LA
Lozes, Christine O'Brien ....Covington, LA
Lozes, Christopher ....New Orleans, LA
Lozes, Felicien P. ....New Orleans, LA
Lozes, Jeffery P. ....New Orleans, LA
Lozes, Steven M. ....New Orleans, LA
Lozes, William C. ....Covington, LA
Lozich, Michael S.J. ....Dallas, TX
Lozicki, Peter J. ....Grand Rapids, MI
Lozier, Daniel R. ....Pensacola, FL
Lozier, David J. ....Pittsburgh, PA
Lozier, Edmund E. ....Tacoma, WA
Lozier, James E. ....Lansing, MI
Lozier, John T. ....Greenville, MS
Lozier, Kenneth W. ....Princeton, NJ
Lozier, Martin G. ....Jackson, MI
Lozier, Richard W., Jr. ....Des Moines, IA
Lozier, Tipton, Thames & Frazier, P.A.
Pensacola, FL
Lozier, William F. ....Atlanta, GA
Loznak, Daniel ....Cheboygan, MI
Loznak, Daniel J., P.C. ....Cheboygan, MI
Lozner, Reuben ....Silver Spring, MD
Lozo, Joseph J. ....Ellenton, FL
Lozoff, Gary L. ....Philadelphia, PA
Lozoff, Michael D. ....Miami, FL
Lozow, Bradley A. ....Denver, CO
Lozow, Charles ....New York, NY
Lozow, Donald L. ....Denver, CO
Lozow, Gary ....Denver, CO
Lozow, Jon P. ....Denver, CO
Lozow & Lozow, P.C. ....Denver, CO
Lozow, Susan K. ....Denver, CO
Lozowicki, Edward B. ....San Jose, CA
Lozuke, Barry N. ....Woodbury, NJ
Lozynskyj, Askold S. ....New York, NY
Lozynskyj, Askold S., P.C. ....New York, NY
Lu, Charlene ....San Francisco, CA
Lu, Chih-Pin ....Miami, FL
Lu, Curtis P. ....Washington, DC
Lu, David S. ....Cleveland, OH
Lu, David W. C. ....Buena Park, CA
Lu, Elaine ....Pasadena, CA
Lu, Fen ....New York, NY
Lu, James C. ....San Jose, CA
Lu, Ji ....New York, NY
Lu, John T. ....Lowell, MA
Lu, Karen C. ....New York, NY
Lu, Kathryn Anne ....New York, NY
Lu, Lily J. ....New York, NY
Lu, Linda Enn ....Chicago, IL
Lu, Rita D. ....Boston, MA
Lu, R.Z. Margaret ....Seattle, WA
Lu, Samuel Kai ....Los Angeles, CA
Lu, Shen-Shin, Law Offices of
Boston, MA
Lu, Shirley Sheau-Lih ....Los Angeles, CA
Lu, Wenyue ....Rockville, MD
Lua, Andrea Leigh ....Los Angeles, CA
Lua, Elvira S. ....Stockton, CA
Luaces, Angela Maria ....Miami, FL
Luaders, Earl J., III ....New London, WI
Luang, Hsin-Wei ....Houston, TX
Houston, TX
San Antonio, TX
Luarde, Frank T. ....Fort Wayne, IN
Luarde, Sharon A. ....Cleveland, OH
Luban, Edward G. ....Syracuse, NY
Luban, Kenneth A. ....Miami, FL
Luban, Nina B. ....New York, NY
Luban, Suzanne A. ....Berkeley, CA
Luband, Charles A. ....Washington, DC
Lubanski, Paul E. ....Chicago, IL
Lubar, Jessica Rutberg ....Baltimore, MD
Lubar, Marcia E., & Associates
Albuquerque, NM
Lubar, Sheldon B. ....Milwaukee, WI
Lubaroff, Martin I. ....Wilmington, DE
Lubarsky, Alexander ....San Mateo, CA
Lubarsky, Bruce M. ....San Mateo, CA
Lubarsky, Neil R. ....White Plains, NY
Lubarsky, Richard F. ....New York, NY
Lubart, David ....New York, NY
Lubart, Leonard ....Fort Lauderdale, FL
Lubart, Matthew H. ....Trenton, NJ
Lubart, Mitchell R. ....New York, NY
Lubart, Philip P. ....Brooklyn, NY
Lubas, Chad D. ....Reading, PA
Lubasch, Richard J. ....New York, NY
Lubash, Sharon June ....Stamford, CT
Lubatkin, Marc Paul ....Atlanta, GA
Lubbe, E. Johan ....White Plains, NY
Lubben, Craig H. ....Kalamazoo, MI
Lubben, David G. ....Peoria, IL
Lubben, George ....Argonne, IL
Lubben, Krissa P. ....St. Louis, MO

Lubben, Michael J. ....Newark, NJ
Lubben, Rick R. ....La Porte City, IA
Lubben, Stephen J. ....New York, NY
Lubben, Thomas C. ....Schaumburg, IL
Lubben, Vicki M. ....Minneapolis, MN
Lubber, Mindy S. ....Boston, MA
Lubbers, Edward C. ....Las Vegas, NV
Lubbers Law Group, The ....Las Vegas, NV
Lubberstedt, W. Wesley ....Lexington, NE
Lubberstedt, W. Wesley, P.C. ....Lexington, NE
Lubchenco, Carolyn ....Denver, CO
Lubcher, Frederick, (P.C.) ....New York, NY
Lubcke, Chas. C. ....Middleton, WI
Lubcke, Gilbert C. ....Madison, WI
Lubeck, Daniel J. ....Newport Beach, CA
Lubeck, Norman C., Jr. ....Boston, MA
Lubeck, P. Terry ....Department of Justice, Antitrust Division, GV
Lubecky, David ....Chardon, OH
Lubega, Stephen K. ....Beverly Hills, CA
Lubel, Alan E. ....Atlanta, GA
Lubel, Glenn H. ....Boulder, CO
Lubel, Howard J. ....Miami, FL
Lubel, Lance H. ....Houston, TX
Lubel, Manuel ....Miami, FL
Lubelchek, Douglas J. ....Chicago, IL
Lubeley, Aaron R. ....Los Angeles, CA
Lubeley, Michael D. ....Woodbridge, VA
Lubeley, Richard A. ....Reston, VA
Lubell, Allyson P. ....Jericho, NY
Lubell, Arthur ....New York, NY
Lubell, Daniel S. ....New York, NY
Lubell, David G. ....New York, NY
Lubell, Donald P. ....Thousand Oaks, CA
Lubell, Ellen B. ....Westport, CT
Lubell, Ellen C. ....Newton, MA
Lubell, Harold A. ....New York, NY
Lubell, Joel R. ....Chicago, IL
Lubell, Jonathan W. ....New York, NY
Lubell & Koven ....New York, NY
Lubell, Lewis Jay ....New York, NY
Lubell, Peter ....Yonkers, NY
Lubell, Rena Jaclyn ....Department of Justice, Office of Attorney Personnel Management, GV
Lubell, Steven K. ....Glendale, CA
Lubell, Steven L. ....Miami, FL
Lubell, Steven L., P.A. ....Miami, FL
Lubelle, Levin and Krenitsky ....Rochester, NY
Lubenow, Patrick Jon ....Milwaukee, WI
Luber, Anthony V. ....South Bend, IN
Luber, Byron D. ....Caruthersville, MO
Luber, David M. ....Los Angeles, CA
Luber, Elana A. ....Los Angeles, CA
Luber, I. Michael ....Philadelphia, PA
Luber, Joel S. ....Paoli, PA
Luber, Jordan B. ....Philadelphia, PA
Luber, Larry B. ....St. Louis, MO
Luber, Moshe ....Denver, CO
Luber, Richard A. ....Rochester, NY
Luber, Thomas J. ....Lexington, KY
Louisville, KY
Luberda & Carp ....St. Louis, MO
Luberda, George J. ....St. Louis, MO
Luberda, R. Alan ....Washington, DC
Luberecki, Leopold J., Jr. ....Bethesda, MD
Lubern, Harry ....Carteret, NJ
Luberoff, Robin Freedman ....Amherst, MA
Lubersky, William F. ....Portland, OR
Lubert, Jana I. ....Los Angeles, CA
Lubertazzi, Joseph, Jr. ....Newark, NJ
Luberto, Marcia L. ....Ann Arbor, MI
Luberto, Michael A., Jr. ....Troy, MI
Lubet, Marc L. ....Orlando, FL
Lubet, Marc L., P.A. ....Kissimmee, FL
Orlando, FL
Sanford, FL
Lubet, Steven ....Chicago, IL
Lubetkin, Beth Andrea ....Bethesda, MD
Lubetkin, Daniel I. ....Roseland, NJ
Lubetkin, Jay L. ....West Orange, NJ
Lubetkin, Paul ....Tarrytown, NY
Lubetkin, Shirley Zeitlin ....Nashville, TN
Lubetsky, Anita ....New York, NY
Lubetsky, Cary A. ....Miami, FL
Lubetsky, Steven ....Boca Raton, FL
Lubetzky, Darren H. ....Chicago, IL
Lubey, Patricia J. ....New York, NY
Lubey, Ronald P. ....San Bernardino, CA
Lubic, Bret ....Saipan, TT
Lubic, Douglas Watson ....Woodbridge, NJ
Lubic, Michael B. ....Los Angeles, CA
Lubic, Robert Bennett ....Bethesda, MD
Lubic, William James ....New York, NY
Lubich, William A. ....Quakertown, PA
Lubick, Donald C. ....Treasury Department, Departmental Offices, GV
Lubiejewski, Alois ....Erie, PA
Lubienski, Casimir A. ....Southfield, MI
Lubienski, George R. ....Dearborn, MI
Lubienski, Lubienski & Lubienski
Dearborn, MI
Lubienski, Maria L. ....Woodinville, WA
Lubienski, Paul ....Dearborn, MI
Lubienski, Walter H. ....Dearborn, MI
Lubin, Andrew R. ....New Haven, CT
Lubin, Carol J. ....San Diego, CA
Lubin, David ....New York, NY
Lubin, David A. ....Dallas, TX
Lubin, Deborah M. ....Atlanta, GA
Lubin, Donald G. ....Chicago, IL
Lubin, Edwin J. ....New York, NY
Lubin, Elaine R.
Department Of Health And Human Services, Office of the General Counsel, GV
Lubin, Emanuel ....New York, NY
Lubin & Enoch, P.C. ....Phoenix, AZ
Lubin & Glazer, P.A. ....Miami Beach, FL

Lucas, William B. ... Richmond, VA
Lucas, William J. ... Cleveland, OH
Lucas, William M., Jr. ... New Orleans, LA
Lucas & Worker, P.C. ... Onsted, MI
Lucas, Zane L., Jr. ... Peoria, IL
Lucas-Durham, Jayne Ann ... Mattoon, IL
Lucas-Fehm, Lynn M. ... Philadelphia, PA
Lucash, Gesmer & Updegrove, LLP
Boston, MA
Lucash, Richard M. ... Boston, MA
Lucashu, Pamela M. ... Durham, CT
Lucasse, Mary L. ... Honolulu, HI
Lucca, Marie J. ... Stamford, CT
Lucca, P. J. ... Haddonfield, NJ
Luccarelli, Peter A., Jr. ... Iselin, NJ
Lucchese, Angela D. ... Louisville, KY
Lucchese, David R. ... Walnut Creek, CA
Lucchese, John A. ... Lauderdale Lakes, FL
Lucchese, Robert J. ... White Plains, NY
Lucchese-Soto, Lynn ... Chicago, IL
Lucchesi, David P. ... Vallejo, CA
Lucchesi, Frank T. ... Hartford, CT
Lucchesi, Joseph L. ... Seneca Falls, NY
Syracuse, NY
Lucchesi, Kathleen K. ... Charlotte, NC
Lucchesi, Lionel L. ... St. Louis, MO
Lucchesi, Peter R. ... Norfolk, VA
Lucchesi, S. Ronald ... Memphis, TN
Lucchesi, Thomas R. ... Cleveland, OH
Lucchesi, William A. ... Memphis, TN
Lucchi, Benedict E. ... Hackensack, NJ
Lucchi & Jenifer ... Annapolis, MD
Lucchi, Leonard L. ... Annapolis, MD
Lucchini, Allan ... Pittsburgh, PA
Lucchino, Frank J. ... Pittsburgh, PA
Lucchino, Frank J., Jr. ... Pittsburgh, PA
Lucchino, Lawrence ... Washington, DC
Lucci, Eugene A. ... Mentor, OH
Lucci & Graves ... Houston, TX
Lucci, Jacqueline ... Houston, TX
Lucci, Joseph ... Philadelphia, PA
Lucci, Joseph C. ... Youngstown, OH
Lucci, Marie Mc Carthy ... San Antonio, TX
Lucci, Michael T. ... Superior, WI
Lucci, Susan Mechley ... Chicago, IL
Luccia, Frank N. ... Houston, TX
Luccio, Richard A. ... Boston, MA
Lucciola, Gerard Anthony ... New York, NY
Luccitti, Warren ... West Hempstead, NY
Lucco Brown & Mudge ... East St. Louis, IL
Edwardsville, IL
Lucco, J. William ... Edwardsville, IL
Luce, Beth Smolens ... Doylestown, PA
Luce, Bryan W. ... Chicago, IL
Luce, Charles F. ... New York, NY
Luce, Charles F., Jr., (P.C.) ... Denver, CO
Luce, David H. ... Wichita, KS
Luce, Derrel ... Waco, TX
Luce, Derrel, P.C., Law Offices of
Waco, TX
Luce, Dianna L. ... Hobbs, NM
Luce, Donald G. ... Sidney, OH
Luce, Edgar A., Jr. ... San Diego, CA
Luce, Forward, Hamilton & Scripps LLP
La Jolla, CA
Los Angeles, CA
San Diego, CA
San Francisco, CA
Chicago, IL
New York, NY
Luce, Graham N. ... Boston, MA
Luce, Gregory M. ... Washington, DC
Luce, Henderson & Lane ... Capac, MI
Port Huron, MI
Luce, James G. ... Mountain View, CA
Luce, James O., III ... Portland, OR
Luce, Joe A. ... McKinney, TX
Luce, Joe E. ... Houston, TX
Luce, John C. ... Washington, DC
Luce, Jonathan R. ... Farmington, ME
Luce, Kenyon E. ... Tacoma, WA
Luce, L. Ames ... Anchorage, AK
Luce, L. Ames, A Prof. Corp., Law Offices of
Anchorage, AK
Luce, Lombino & Riggio, P.S.
Tacoma, WA
Luce, M. Celeste ... Las Vegas, NV
Luce, Mairi V. ... Philadelphia, PA
Luce, Melissa H. ... Morristown, NJ
Luce, Michael L. ... Sioux Falls, SD
Luce, Ray W. ... Missouri City, TX
Luce, Richard A. ... Clearwater, FL
Luce, Rita E. ... Chicago, IL
Luce, Robert B. ... Burlington, VT
Luce, Robert L. ... Columbia, SC
Luce, Robin K. ... Detroit, MI
Luce, Stephen F.(Buddy) ... Grapevine, TX
Luce, Susan B. ... San Jose, CA
Luce, Susan D. ... Grand Blanc, MI
Luce, Thomas F. ... Wilmington, DE
Luce, Thomas W., III ... Dallas, TX
Luce, Timothy J. ... Waterloo, IA
Luce, W. Alan ... Kissimmee, FL
Luce, Wayne S. ... Beaver, PA
Luceno, Charles E. ... White Plains, NY
Lucente, Debra Jean ... Hickory Hills, IL
Lucente, Diane C. ... Philadelphia, PA
Lucente, Frank S. ... Meyersdale, PA
Lucente, James M. ... Gahanna, OH
Lucente, Martin M. ... New York, NY
Lucente, Rocco, II ... Buffalo, NY
Lucenti, Robert C. ... Chicago, IL
Lucere, Mary T. ... Massapequa, NY
Lucero, Arthur S. ... Denver, CO
Lucero, Carlos F. ... Denver, CO
Lucero, Charles S. ... Great Falls, MT
Lucero, Chris, Jr. ... Albuquerque, NM
Lucero, Chris, Jr., & Associates, P.A.
Albuquerque, NM
Lucero, David J. ... Cheyenne, WY
Lucero, Fred S. ... San Jose, CA
Lucero, Gene A. ... Los Angeles, CA
Lucero & George, L.L.P. ... Great Falls, MT
Lucero, Jacqueline Music ... Hayward, CA
Lucero, James Daniel ... Columbia, SC
Lucero, Katherine ... San Jose, CA
Lucero, Kathleen Kentish ... Espanola, NM
Lucero, Kathryn D. ... Albuquerque, NM
Lucero, L. E., & Associates, P.C.
Aurora, CO
Lucero, Lee E. ... Aurora, CO
Lucero, Luis A. ... Los Osos, CA
Lucero, Manuel ... Albuquerque, NM
Lucero, Matthew J. ... San Jose, CA
Lucero, Michelle M. ... Denver, CO
Lucero, Orlando ... Albuquerque, NM
Lucero, R. Antonio ... Denver, CO
Lucero, Rudolph A. ... Albuquerque, NM
Lucey, Anne C. ... New York, NY
Lucey, Brian J. ... Albany, NY
Lucey, Charles Emmet ... Murrells Inlet, SC
Lucey, David ... Milwaukee, WI
Lucey, David C. ... Burnsville, MN
Lucey, David P. ... Boston, MA
Lucey, E. Patricia ... San Francisco, CA
Lucey, Gerald F. ... Boston, MA
Lucey, Gerald P. ... Barrington, IL
Lucey, Gordon M. ... Stamford, CT
New York, NY
Lucey, James J. O. ... Washington, DC
Lucey, James W. ... Palo Alto, CA
Lucey, John D., Jr. ... Philadelphia, PA
Lucey, John F. ... Fall River, MA
Lucey, John K. ... Honolulu, HI
Lucey, Kristin ... Orinda, CA
Lucey, Laurel J. ... Atlanta, GA
Lucey, Lawrence H. ... Chicago, IL
Lucey, Margaret B. ... San Francisco, CA
Lucey, Michael T. ... San Francisco, CA
Lucey, Paul A. ... Milwaukee, WI
Lucey, Paul R. ... Washington, DC
Lucey, Peter J. ... Pleasanton, CA
Lucey, Richard A. ... Charlotte, NC
Lucey, Richard G. ... South Euclid, OH
Lucey, Stephen F. ... Lafayette, CA
Lucey, Timothy J. ... San Francisco, CA
Lucey, Watkins & Lamson, A Professional Corporation ... Lafayette, CA
Luchak, Frank A. ... Cherry Hill, NJ
Luchansky, Bruce M. ... Baltimore, MD
Luchansky, John E., Jr. ... Lambertville, MI
Lucheme, Roberto Tschudin
Glastonbury, CT
Luchenitser, Alexander J. ... Greenbrae, CA
Luchetta, Michael L.
Colorado Springs, CO
Luchetti, Lisa ... Boston, MA
Luchetti, Thomas D., (P.C.) ... Rockford, IL
Luchini, Eva M. ... Los Angeles, CA
Luchini, Joseph S. ... Falls Church, VA
Luchins, Moshe A. ... New York, NY
Luchkiw, Michael G. ... Teaneck, NJ
Luchs, Elliott, Attorney at Law
Riverside, CA
Luchs, Elliott S. ... Riverside, CA
Luchs, Erik C. ... Washington, DC
Luchs, Gregg ... Kew Gardens, NY
Luchs, Morton A. ... New York, NY
Luchs, Richard W. ... Washington, DC
Luchs, Robyn Amy ... New York, NY
Luchs, Roger D. ... Washington, DC
Gaithersburg, MD
Arlington, VA
Luchsinger, Ann L. ... Columbus, OH
Luchsinger, Daniel W. ... Washington, DC
Luchsinger, John A. ... Media, PA
Luchsinger, John F., Jr. ... Syracuse, NY
Luchsinger & O'Malley, P.C. ... Media, PA
Luchsinger, Steven J. ... Watertown, WI
Lucht, Carroll L. ... New Haven, CT
Lucht, E. James ... Erie, PA
Lucht, John C. ... New York, NY
Lucht, Julie Sherman ... Chicago, IL
Lucht, Larry C. ... Worthington, MN
Lucht, Philip H. ... Cedarburg, WI
Lucht, Robt. E. ... Harrington, WA
Lucht, Wiltrout & Ahlquist
Worthington, MN
Luchtel, Keith E. ... Des Moines, IA
Luchtenburg, Russell J. ... Park Ridge, IL
Luci, David P. ... New York, NY
Lucia, Anthony R. ... Phoenix, AZ
Lucia, Antonia T. ... Poughkeepsie, NY
Wappingers Falls, NY
Lucia, Daniel S. ... Newburgh, NY
Lucia, Daniel S. ... New Windsor, NY
Lucia, Eugene P. ... Washingtonville, NY
Lucia, Gregory E. ... Houston, TX
Lucia, Mark D. ... San Francisco, CA
Lucia, Steven A. ... New York, NY
Lucian, Dawn L. ... Santa Barbara, CA
Lucian, John Edward ... Silver Spring, MD
Luciana, Jeffrey J. ... Pittsburgh, PA
Luciana, Joseph L., III ... Pittsburgh, PA
Luciana, Joseph L., Jr. ... Oakmont, PA
Luciani, Amy Lynn ... Daytona Beach, FL
Luciani, Thomas R. ... Spokane, WA
Lucianna, Brian V. ... Haddon Heights, NJ
Lucianna, Brian V., P.C.
Haddon Heights, NJ
Lucianna, Diane M. ... Hackensack, NJ
Lucianna, Frank P. ... Hackensack, NJ
Lucianna & Lucianna, P.A. ... Hackensack, NJ
Lucianna, Nancy E. ... Hackensack, NJ
Luciano, Arnulfo U. ... Cleveland, MS
Luciano, Beth E. ... Jacksonville, FL
Luciano, Carmen A. ... Pompano Beach, FL
Luciano, Daniel F. ... Central Islip, NY
Luciano, Elizabeth ... New York, NY
Luciano, Jane ... Walnut Creek, CA
Luciano, Kenneth John ... New York, NY
Luciano, Lori E. ... Lawrence, MA
Luciano, Robert P. ... Madison, NJ
Luciano, Susan Marie ... New York, NY
Luciano, Thomas Daniel ... Hauppauge, NY
Luciano-Velez, Jose H. ... Arecibo, PR
Lucic, Robert R. ... Manchester, NH
Lucich, Nicholas Louis, Jr. ... Fresno, CA
Lucid, Albert R. ... Hanover, MA
Lucid, Philip J. ... Seattle, WA
Lucid, Rowland V., Jr. ... Morristown, NJ
Lucido, Anthony T. ... Harrisburg, PA
Lucido, Fortunato L. ... Kansas City, MO
Lucido, Lawrence J. ... De Kalb, IL
Lucido, Paul A. ... New York, NY
Lucido, Peter D. ... Oceanside, NY
Lucido, Peter J. ... Mount Clemens, MI
Lucido, Peter J., P.C. ... Mount Clemens, MI
Lucido, Rita ... Houston, TX
Lucido, Robert O., II ... Pittsfield, MA
Lucido, Sebastian ... Clinton, MI
Lucie, Jim D. ... Macomb, IL
Lucie, Mitchell K. ... Bloomington, IL
Lucie, Stephanie A. ... Palo Alto, CA
Lucien, Donald S. ... Encino, CA
Lucier, Anna M. ... Torrance, CA
Lucier, Helen ... Louisville, KY
Lucier, James G. ... Laguna Hills, CA
Lucier, Lynn Marie ... Dallas, TX
Lucier, Timothy P. ... Chicago, IL
Lucin, Laura J. ... Clearwater, FL
Lucio, Bronstein, Garbett, Stiphany & Martinez, Professional Association
Miami, FL
Lucio, Lydia Ann ... Murphysboro, IL
Lucio, Saturnino E., II ... Miami, FL
Lucio, Tonia L. ... Austin, TX
Lucious, Felicia E. ... Baton Rouge, LA
Lucius, James R. ... Milwaukee, WI
Lucius, William C. ... Greenville, SC
Lucivero, Lucretia M.
Port Jefferson Station, NY
Luciw, Eugene A. ... Bethlehem, PA
Philadelphia, PA
Luck, Aaron John ... Montgomery, AL
Luck, Anita ... Pasadena, CA
Denver, CO
Luck, Bradley J. ... Missoula, MT
Luck, Dorin E. ... Henderson, KY
Luck, Elaine ... Akron, OH
Luck, Gary M. ... Brookfield, WI
Luck, Gregory ... Wilkesboro, NC
Luck, Gregory M. ... Dallas, TX
Houston, TX
Luck, Karyl S. ... Charlottesville, VA
Luck, Kelli K. ... Los Angeles, CA
Luck, Lawrence E. ... Richmond, VA
Luck, Max M. ... Chicago, IL
Luck, Rebecca Rofsky ... Columbus, OH
Luck & Rosenthal, S.C. ... Brookfield, WI
Luck, Sarah ... Portland, ME
Luck, Sarah, P.A. ... Portland, ME
Luck, Sheila M. ... Appleton, WI
Luck, Thomas R., Jr. ... Atlanta, GA
Luck, Tiernan W., III ... Montgomery, AL
Luck, William D. ... Argonne, IL
Luck, William H. ... Memphis, TN
Luckanick, Alexander W. ... Binghamton, NY
Luckart, Bernard J. ... Bridgeport, CT
Luckasson, Ruth A. ... Albuquerque, NM
Luckau, Erik W. ... Washington, DC
Lucke, James T. ... Milwaukee, WI
Lucke, Paul V. ... Milwaukee, WI
Lucke, Robert N., Sr. ... Glen Burnie, MD
Lucke, Stephen P. ... Minneapolis, MN
Lucke, William P., Law Offices of
Oakland, CA
Piedmont, CA
Lucke, William P., Law Offices of
San Francisco, CA
Walnut Creek, CA
Luckel, Eb F., Jr. ... San Francisco, CA
Lucken, Pamela S. ... Kansas City, MO
Luckenbach, Denise M. ... Roseland, NJ
Luckenbach, Elizabeth L. ... Northbrook, IL
Luckenbacher, Frank C. ... Los Angeles, CA
Luckenbill, Paul T., Jr. ... Plattsburg, MO
Luckenbill, Susan L. ... Scranton, PA
Lucker, Howard P. ... Franklin Center, PA
Lucker, Stephanie J. ... Media, PA
Luckerath, Carl B. ... Seattle, WA
Luckerman, Ronald Paul ... Anaheim, CA
Luckern, Paul J.
United States International Trade Commission,
Office of Administrative Law Judges, GV
Luckeroth, William J. ... San Juan, PR
Luckert, Marla J. ... Topeka, KS
Luckett, Carole R. ... Vancouver, WA
Luckett, Carole R., P.S., Law Offices Of
Vancouver, WA
Luckett, John M. ... Jackson, MS
Luckett Law Firm, A Professional Association ... Clarksdale, MS
Tunica, MS
Luckett, Leonard S. ... Alpharetta, GA
Luckett, Lori Ann ... Grand Blanc, MI
Luckett, William O., Jr. ... Clarksdale, MS
Memphis, TN
Luckey, Alwyn H. ... Biloxi, MS
Gulfport, MS
Luckey, Alwyn H. ... Ocean Springs, MS
Luckey, Carabeth Stringer ... Houston, TX
Luckey, Charles D. ... Winston-Salem, NC
Luckey, Clarence E. ... Grants Pass, OR
Luckey, John R. ... Library of Congress,
Congressional Research Service, GV
Luckey, Judge C., Jr. ... Tampa, FL
Luckey, Kent M. ... Sacramento, CA
Luckey, Lori J. ... Cambridge, WI
Luckey, Owen L., Jr. ... LaBelle, FL
Luckey, Randall D. ... Houston, TX
Luckham, Richard C. ... Kailua-Kona, HI
Luckhardt, Charles E. ... San Jose, CA
Luckhardt, Jane E. ... Sacramento, CA
Luckhardt, Philip G. ... Easton, CT
Luckhardt, William G., (A Professional Corporation) ... Santa Rosa, CA
Luckhart, Elton W. ... Youngstown, OH
Luckhart, Mumaw, Zellers & Robinson
Youngstown, OH
Luckhaupt, Gerald P. ... Juneau, AK
Luckie, Charlie, & Associates, P.A.
Brooksville, FL
Dade City, FL
Luckie, Charlie, Jr. ... Brooksville, FL
Dade City, FL
Luckie, Stuart Y. ... Mobile, AL
Luckie-Anderson Law Firm, The
Austin, TX
Luckie-Anderson, Linda ... Austin, TX
Luckiesh, Robert E. ... San Francisco, CA
Luckinbill, Robert W.
Mountain View, CA
Lucking, John T. ... Danbury, CT
Lucking, William A., Jr. ... Ojai, CA
Luckman, Bruce S. ... Philadelphia, PA
Luckman, Dennis B. ... Orange, CA
Luckman, Eric H. ... West Palm Beach, FL
Luckman, Eric H., P.A.
West Palm Beach, FL
Luckman, Gerard R. ... Jericho, NY
Luckman, Gregg A. ... Great Neck, NY
Luckman, Marvin P. ... Chicago, IL
Luckman, Todd A. ... Topeka, KS
Luckner, Steven J. ... New York, NY
Luckoff, Howard N. ... Bloomfield Hills, MI
Lucks, Barbara J. ... Circleville, OH
Lucks, Edwin J. ... Thousand Oaks, CA
Lucks, Gary A. ... Walnut Creek, CA
Lucks, Irvin L. ... Thousand Oaks, CA
Lucksinger, Michael J. ... Burnet, TX
Lucksinger, Thomas S. ... Houston, TX
Luckstone, John S. ... Murray Hill, NJ
Lucky, Christian M. ... New York, NY
Lucky, Jeffrey T. ... El Paso, TX
Lucoff, Aaron Nicholas ... Caldwell, ID
Lucow, Milton ... Detroit, MI
Lucrezi, Cathy L. ... Fort Myers, FL
Lucurell, Drew D. ... Seattle, WA
Lucus, Charles R. ... Oklahoma City, OK
Lucy, Cecil B. ... Chicago, IL
Lucy, Charles R. ... Baldwinsville, NY
Lucy, Jennifer N. ... Fort Lauderdale, FL
Lucy, John B. ... Bangor, ME
Lucy, Patricia Alden ... Tulsa, OK
Lucy, Richard H. ... Chicago, IL
Lucy & Suhar ... Chicago, IL
Lucy, Terry D. ... Little Rock, AR
Lucyk, Brian M. ... Elmsford, NY
Lucyk, Gregory E. ... Richmond, VA
Lucyshyn, Peter S. ... Wood Dale, IL
Luczak, David A. ... Largo, FL
Luczak, David A., P.A. ... Largo, FL
Luczak, Gregory S. ... Chicago, IL
Luczak, M. Bradley ... Orlando, FL
Luczak, Ronald L. ... Evanston, IL
Luczak, Thomas D. ... Ann Arbor, MI
Luczkowski, Jean M. ... Columbus, OH
Ludacer, Randy ... Key West, FL
Ludaway, Natalie O. ... Washington, DC
Ludcke, George O. ... Minneapolis, MN
Ludd, Oksana M. ... Toledo, OH
Luddecke, Hugh F., Jr. ... Shelter Island, NY
Ludden, C. Thomas ... Troy, MI
Ludden, Catherine A. ... New York, NY
Ludden, Karen Libertiny
Farmington Hills, MI
Ludden, Nancy J. ... Lincoln, NE
Ludder, David A. ... Tallahassee, FL
Luddy, John Paul ... La Jolla, CA
Luddy, Marc J. ... Livonia, MI
Luddy, Robert J. ... New York, NY
Ludecke, Alan J. ... San Diego, CA
Ludecke, Denton & Bunn ... San Diego, CA
Ludeke, Todd A. ... Houston, TX
Ludeman, L. Ruth ... McLean, VA
Ludemann, Cathie Jane ... Pequannock, NJ
Ludemann, Doreen A. ... San Francisco, CA
Ludemann, Lorraine E. ... New York, NY
Ludemann, Matthew R. ... Glens Falls, NY
Ludens, Potter & Burch ... Morrison, IL
Mount Carroll, IL
Luder, Robert J. ... Overland Park, KS
Luderer, R. Dennis ... Los Angeles, CA
Ludescher, David L. ... Northfield, MN
Ludewig, Deborah J. ... Palo Alto, CA
Ludewig, Margaret Carter
Albuquerque, NM
Ludewig, Walter A. ... Albany, NY
Ludgate, Kristen M. ... Minneapolis, MN
Ludgin, David A. ... Newark, NJ
Ludgin, John Richard ... Columbus, OH
Ludgin, Robert F. ... Hartford, CT
Ludgood, Merceria ... Mobile, AL
Ludgus, Nancy Lucke ... Santa Clara, CA
Ludi, Susan L. ... Atlanta, GA
Ludick, Joseph E. ... North Miami, FL
Ludin, Eric E. ... St. Petersburg, FL
Ludin, Gary D. ... Pittsburgh, PA
Ludington, David T. ... Walnut Creek, CA

Ludington, Karen E. ....Worcester, MA
Ludington, Margaret Daley
Westlake Village, CA
Ludington, Ramsey G. ....Fulton, NY
Ludington, Richard P. ....Chapel Hill, NC
Ludington, Spencer J. ....Fulton, NY
Ludington, Thomas L. ....Midland, MI
Ludka, Lawrence M. ....Corpus Christi, TX
Ludke Cook, Sara ....Colorado Springs, CO
Ludlam, Charles E. ....United States Senate, Senatorial Assistants, GV
Ludlam, James E. ....Los Angeles, CA
Ludlam, John L. ....Cape May, NJ
Ludlam & LaGrosse ....Cape May, NJ
Ludlam, Margot L. ....New York, NY
Ludlam, Warren V., Jr. ....Jackson, MS
Ludlow, Dione J. ....Chehalis, WA
Ludlow, G. Kevin ....Sauquoit, NY
Ludlow, James F. ....Indianapolis, IN
Ludlow, John Thomas ....Bellevue, WA
Ludlow, Lisa G. ....Fresno, CA
Ludlow & Price ....Corona, CA
Ludlow, Randy S. ....Salt Lake City, UT
Ludlow, Richard T. ....Salt Lake City, UT
Ludlow, Robert H. ....Santa Cruz, CA
Ludlow, Robert H., Jr., A Prof. Corp., Law Offices of ....Santa Cruz, CA
Ludlow, Thos. H., Jr. ....Corona, CA
Ludlow, Vicki L. ....Miamisburg, OH
Ludlow, Warren J. ....Dallas, TX
Ludlum & Casteen, Professional Association
Clinton, NC
Kenansville, NC
Warsaw, NC
Ludlum, Georgia H. ....Panama City, FL
Ludlum, J. Garrett ....Warsaw, NC
Ludlum, James, Jr. ....Austin, TX
Ludlum, James N. ....Austin, TX
Ludlum, John E. ....Richmond, VA
Ludlum, Julie L. ....St. Louis, MO
Ludlum, M. P. ....Norman, OK
Ludman, Kathleen W. ....Princeton, NJ
Ludman, Kenneth ....New York, NY
Ludmerer, Nancy B. ....New York, NY
Ludmerer, Richard C. ....Long Beach, CA
Ludmerer, Victor J. ....Goshen, NY
Ludolph, Mark A. ....Peoria, IL
Ludolph, Robert C. ....Detroit, MI
Ludolph-Heikkala, Marla R. ....Vancouver, WA
Ludorf, Edward S. ....Hartford, CT
Ludovici, Clyde A. ....McKees Rocks, PA
Ludovici, Edward P. ....Miami, FL
Ludovici, Joseph L. ....East Liverpool, OH
Ludovici, Joseph P. ....St. Petersburg, FL
Ludovici, Lorena Hart, (P.A.) ....Tampa, FL
Ludovici & Ludovici ....Miami, FL
Ludovici, Philip F. ....Miami, FL
Ludovici, Susan M. ....Miami, FL
Ludovici-Lint, Joanne ....Washington, DC
Ludovico, Anthony B. ....Hartford, CT
Ludsin, Hallie G. ....New York, NY
Ludt, Veronica ....Philadelphia, PA
Ludtke, David A. ....Lincoln, NE
Ludtke, Leslie J. ....Concord, NH
Ludtke, Meghan G.
Department of Transportation, Federal Transit Administration, GV
Ludvigsen, Carl W., Jr. ....Lenexa, KS
Ludvigsen, Gregory A. ....Denver, CO
Ludvigson & Galewyrick, S.C. ....Osceola, WI
Ludvigson, Guy T. ....Osceola, WI
Ludwick, Alan L. ....Salem, OR
Ludwick, John H. ....Seattle, WA
Ludwick, Kelly D. ....Atlanta, GA
Ludwick, Kurt Stephen ....Kansas City, MO
Ludwick, Lindalea P. ....New Haven, CT
New York, NY
Ludwick, M. Kirk ....Denver, CO
Ludwick, Mary K. ....Dallas, TX
Ludwick & Poletto, L.L.C. ....Denver, CO
Ludwick, Sarah Burlison ....Milwaukee, WI
Ludwick, Steven W. ....Atlanta, GA
Ludwick, Steven W., P.C. ....Atlanta, GA
Ludwig, Alvin J. ....Pittsburgh, PA
Ludwig, Annette Scordino
New Windsor, NY
Ludwig, Arnold J. ....Brooklyn, NY
Ludwig, Brett H. ....Milwaukee, WI
Ludwig, Britt B. ....Chapel Hill, NC
Ludwig, Bruce I. ....Juneau, AK
Ludwig, Bruce M. ....Philadelphia, PA
Ludwig, Burton D. ....Columbia, MO
Ludwig, Charles F. ....Philadelphia, PA
Ludwig, Curran & Patberg, P.C.
Pittsburgh, PA
Ludwig, David A. ....Madison, WI
Ludwig, David G. ....Staunton, VA
Ludwig, David R. ....Portland, OR
Ludwig, Edmund V. ....Philadelphia, PA
Ludwig, Eric J. ....Princeton, NJ
Ludwig, Eric W., (P.A.)
Altamonte Springs, FL
Ludwig, Eugene A. ....Treasury Department, Departmental Offices, GV
Ludwig, F. Michael ....Denver, CO
Ludwig, Gene A. ....Little Rock, AR
Ludwig, Glenn A. ....Worcester, MA
Ludwig Goldberg & Krenzel, A Professional Corporation ....San Francisco, CA
Ludwig, Gordon M. ....New York, NY
Ludwig, Graham G., Jr. ....Richmond, VA
Ludwig, Herbert J., P.A.
South Portland, ME
Ludwig, James C. ....Louisville, KY
Ludwig, James M., III ....Washington, DC
Ludwig, Jeffrey R. ....Jacksonville, FL
Ludwig, Jeffrey R., P.A. ....Jacksonville, FL
Ludwig, Jeffrey W. ....Highlands Ranch, CO
Ludwig, Jon M. ....Reno, NV
Ludwig, Joseph M. ....Pittsburgh, PA
Ludwig, Kenneth D. ....Washington, DC
Ludwig, Kirk A. ....Roanoke, VA
Ludwig, Kirt J. E. ....Burlington, WI
Ludwig, Lawrence M. ....Scranton, PA
Ludwig, Lisa J. ....Portland, OR
Ludwig, Lloyd ....Ho-Ho-Kus, NJ
Ludwig, Marek W. ....Chicago, IL
Ludwig, Marilyn D. ....Wayne, NJ
Ludwig, Mark A. ....Jefferson City, MO
Ludwig, Mark H. ....Akron, OH
Ludwig, Michael ....New York, NY
Ludwig, Michael A. ....Phoenix, AZ
Ludwig, Michael L. ....Los Angeles, CA
Ludwig, Mitchell B. ....Glendale, CA
Ludwig, Monika D. ....Naples, FL
Ludwig, Paul D. ....Indianapolis, IN
Ludwig, Penelope S. ....Washington, DC
Ludwig, R. Arthur ....Milwaukee, WI
Ludwig, Robert S. ....Baker, WV
Ludwig, Robert W., Jr. ....Washington, DC
Ludwig & Robinson, P.L.L.C.
Washington, DC
Ludwig, Robt. J. ....Silver Spring, MD
Ludwig, Ronald L. ....San Francisco, CA
Ludwig, S. Peter ....New York, NY
Ludwig, Sarah H. ....Staunton, VA
Ludwig, Scot M. ....Boise, ID
Ludwig, Scott E. ....Huntsville, AL
Ludwig & Shlimovitz, S.C. ....Milwaukee, WI
Ludwig, Stacy M. ....Washington, DC
Ludwig, Stanley W. ....Springdale, AR
Ludwig, Steven K. ....Philadelphia, PA
Ludwig, Steven R. ....Washington, DC
Ludwig, Thomas ....Ridgewood, NJ
Ludwig, Thomas A. ....Jackson, MO
Ludwig, Victor V. ....Staunton, VA
Ludwig, Vincent E. ....Livingston, NJ
Ludwig, W. Rod ....Beloit, KS
Ludwigson, David R. ....St. Paul, MN
Ludwigson, John S. ....Bellingham, WA
Ludwigson, Sandra B. ....Boise, ID
Ludwigson, Susan L. ....New York, NY
Ludwigson, Thompson, Hayes & Bell
Bellingham, WA
Ludwikow, Steven J. ....New Britain, CT
Ludwikowski, Jeffrey J. ....Pittsburgh, PA
Ludwikowski, Joanne C.
Williamsport, PA
Ludwikowski, Lucy L. ....Pittsburgh, PA
Ludwin, Mitchell F. ....Milwaukee, WI
Ludwinski, Kristine B. ....Hawthorne, CA
Ludwinski, Stephen C. ....St. Louis, MO
Ludwiszewski, Christine B.
Oak Brook, IL
Ludwiszewski, Raymond B.
Washington, DC
Ludy & Bright ....Portland, IN
Ludy, Kelly D. ....Waco, TX
Ludy, Max C., Jr. ....Portland, IN
Luebbe, Lorna ....Seattle, WA
Luebbe, Verlyn ....Pierce, NE
Luebben, Philip William ....Rosemead, CA
Luebben, Thomas E. ....Albuquerque, NM
Luebben, Thomas E., Law Offices of
Albuquerque, NM
Luebbering, Thomas Blaine
Kansas City, MO
Luebberke, John M. ....Los Angeles, CA
Luebbers, Thomas A. ....Cincinnati, OH
Luebbert, Robert J. ....Omaha, NE
Luebchow, James E. ....Chicago, IL
Luebchow, Kevin H. ....Watseka, IL
Luebe, Doug Law Office, P.C.
South Sioux City, NE
Luebe, Douglas L. ....South Sioux City, NE
Luebehusen, Susan D. ....Winchester, VA
Luebehusen, Susan Luby ....Winchester, VA
Luebke, Dennis C. ....Appleton, WI
Luebke, Douglas J. ....Corsica, SD
Luebke and Kerner ....Armour, SD
Corsica, SD
Luebke, Michael J. ....Madison, WI
Luebke, Richard J. ....Columbia, MD
Columbia, MD
Luebke, Thomas N. ....Orange, CA
Luebkeman, Theodore C. ....Campbell, CA
Luebker, Monica L. ....Dallas, TX
Luebs, Jon F. ....Grand Island, NE
Luebs, Leininger, Smith, Busick, Johnson, Baack, Placzek & Steele
Grand Island, NE
Hastings, NE
Kearney, NE
Superior, NE
Luebs, Roger A. ....Riverside, CA
Lueck, Charles S. ....Madison, WI
Lueck, Christy G. ....Minneapolis, MN
Lueck, Debra A. ....Melbourne, FL
Lueck, Dwight D. ....Indianapolis, IN
Lueck, John D., Law Offices of
Rancho Cucamonga, CA
Lueck, Martin R. ....Minneapolis, MN
Lueck, Robert B. ....Oakland, CA
Lueck, Robert W. ....Las Vegas, NV
Luecke, Jerome E. ....Florham Park, NJ
Luecke, Marcia ....Akron, OH
Luecke, Mary R. ....Evanston, IL
Luecke, Tiffany M.
Plymouth Meeting, PA
Luecken, John J., Jr. ....Akron, OH
Lueckenbach, Edward A. ....Greenville, MS
Lueckenhoff, Edward H. ....Indianapolis, IN
Lueckenhoff, Terry ....St. Louis, MO
Luedde, Charles E. H. ....St. Louis, MO
Lueddeke, Ronald L. ....Spring Lake, NJ
Luedecker, Warren A. ....Trumbull, CT
Luedecker, Warren A., Jr. ....New York, NY
Luedecking, Trudy Y. ....Kalamazoo, MI
Luedeka, Neely & Graham, P.C.
Knoxville, TN
Luedeke, Harry J. ....Newport, KY
Luedeke, Jeffrey R. ....Fayetteville, NC
Luedemann, Ronald S. ....Denver, CO
Lueder, John ....Atlanta, GA
Lueder, Michael A. ....Atlanta, GA
Lueders, April F. ....Department of Commerce, Patent and Trademark Office, GV
Lueders & Boanerges, P.C. ....Houston, TX
Lueders, Daniel J. ....Indianapolis, IN
Lueders, David E. ....Houston, TX
Lueders, Dean R. ....Sacramento, CA
Lueders, Fredric J. ....Columbus, WI
Lueders, Linda M. ....Houston, TX
Lueders, Mary McArdle ....Zionsville, IN
Lueders, Matthew D. ....Los Angeles, CA
Lueders, Randall ....Columbus, WI
Lueders, Robertson & Konzen
Danville, IL
Granite City, IL
Lueders, Scott W. ....Novato, CA
Lueders, Wayne R. ....Milwaukee, WI
Luedke, Adriana S. ....Washington, DC
Luedke, Carolyn Barefield ....Houston, TX
Luedke, Charles ....Billings, MT
Luedke, John F. C. ....Washington, DC
Luedke, Scott J. ....Dallas, TX
Luedke, William H. ....Auburn, WA
Luedke, William T., IV ....Houston, TX
Luedtke, Charles G. ....Sachse, TX
Luedtke, Charles W. ....Sachse, TX
Luedtke, Eric V. ....Brea, CA
Luedtke, J. Peter ....Arlington, VA
Luedtke, Jill W. ....San Diego, CA
Luedtke, Joelle C. ....Chicago, IL
Luedtke, John R. ....Bloomington, IL
Luedtke, Katia Ann ....McLean, VA
Luedtke, Roger A. ....Portland, OR
Luedtke, Roland A. ....Lincoln, NE
Luedtke, Sherilee M. ....Tacoma, WA
Luefschuetz, Gary Steven ....Bethesda, MD
Luege, Carmen R. ....Santa Ana, CA
Lueger, Eugene ....Topeka, KS
Luehr, Paul H. ....Federal Trade Commission, Bureau of Consumer Protection, GV
Luehring, Heidi ....Madison, WI
Luehring, JoAnn ....New York, NY
Luehrman, Frances M. ....Kansas City, MO
Luehrsmann, Ronald L. ....Cedar Rapids, IA
Lueke, H Mark ....Louisville, KY
Lueke, Stephen R. ....Universal City, CA
Lueken, Francis H., Jr. ....Ferdinand, IN
Lueken, Harold W. ....New York, NY
Lueken, John S. ....Louisville, KY
Lueken Law Firm, P.A. ....Little Rock, AR
Lueken, Patty W. ....Little Rock, AR
Luekens, Jeffrey W. ....Midland, MI
Luekens, Wendell H. ....Arlington, VA
Lueking, Christopher D. ....Chicago, IL
Lueking, Jason P. ....Evansville, IN
Lueking, Paige A. ....Dallas, TX
Luelf, Stephen W. ....Mountain Home, AR
Luellen, Jack K. ....Denver, CO
Luellig, Lorrie L. ....Phoenix, AZ
Luemers, Martha C. ....Palo Alto, CA
Luenenborg, Michael ....Littleton, CO
Luengas, Judith A. ....Orlando, FL
Luepke, Ellen L. ....Chicago, IL
Luepke, Henry F., III ....Belleville, IL
St. Louis, MO
Luepke, Henry F., Jr. ....St. Louis, MO
Luepke, Paula Finlay ....St. Louis, MO
Luepker, Wayne R. ....Chicago, IL
Luer, Carl ....Seattle, WA
Luer, Kenneth A. ....Beverly Hills, CA
Lueras, Sharon A. ....Sacramento, CA
Luers, James B. ....Lincoln, NE
Luers, Margaret F., (Miss) ....Washington, DC
Luersen, Harold A. ....Fort Thomas, KY
Luersman, Paul D. ....Greenville, OH
Luerssen, Richard W. ....Plano, TX
Luesebrink, Richard W. ....Santa Ana, CA
Luessenhop, Valerie J. ....Austin, TX
Luethi, Robert M. ....Independence, WI
Luethke, K. Jeff ....Johnson City, TN
Kingsport, TN
Luetjen, Calvin H. ....Portland, OR
Luetjen, Douglas A. ....Seattle, WA
Luetke, Charles C. ....Peekskill, NY
Luetkehans, Melody ....Reno, NV
Luetkemeyer, Tom H. ....Chicago, IL
Luettgen, David G. ....Milwaukee, WI
Luettgen, Robert A. ....Dallas, TX
Luettgen, Wanda A. ....Boston, MA
Luetto, Helen M. ....Orange, CA
Luetto, John A. ....Fullerton, CA
Luevano, Daniel M. ....Los Angeles, CA
Luevano, Emma ....Los Angeles, CA
Luevano, Mark ....Los Angeles, CA
Luey, Michael L. ....Phoenix, AZ
Luff, Edw. T. ....Sarasota, FL
Luff, H. David ....Orlando, FL
Luff, Lynette M. ....New York, NY
Luff, Mark R. ....Grand Junction, CO
Luffey, John L., Jr. ....Monroe, LA
Luffman & Bledsoe, Ltd. ....Fayetteville, AR
Rogers, AR
Luffman, James M. ....Rogers, AR
Luffman, Karen E. ....Dalton, GA
Luffy, Craig J. ....Dallas, TX
Lufkin, David A. ....Knoxville, TN
Lufkin, Henley & Conner, PLLC
Knoxville, TN
Lufkin, Martha B. G. ....Lincoln, MA
Lufkin, Michael G. ....Olympia, WA
Lufkin, Paul T. ....San Francisco, CA
Lufman, Jennifer L. ....Denver, CO
Lufman, Tyrone L. ....Denver, CO
Lufrano, Michael R. ....Chicago, IL
Luft, Edward David ....
Treasury Department, GV
Luft, Jill K. ....St. Louis, MO
Luft, Julie R. ....Cleveland, OH
Luft, Martha L. ....Riverhead, NY
Luft, Robert S. ....San Jose, CA
Luftig, Murry ....San Diego, CA
Luftman, Albert J. ....Brookline, MA
Luftman, Amanda N. ....Los Angeles, CA
Luftman, Douglas B. ....Palo Alto, CA
Luftman, Michael B. ....Los Angeles, CA
Luftman, Walter ....North Palm Beach, FL
Lugar, James P. ....Kansas City, KS
Lugar, Karen S. ....San Antonio, TX
Lugar, Lynette Weiss ....San Diego, CA
Lugar and Pohl ....San Diego, CA
Lugara, Anthony J. ....Milford, NJ
Lugash, Jeffrey B. ....Encino, CA
Lugauskas, Lisa Jean ....Waterbury, CT
Lugbill, Ann ....Cincinnati, OH
Lugenbuhl, Burke, Wheaton, Peck, Rankin & Hubbard, A Law Corporation
Metairie, LA
New Orleans, LA
Gulfport, MS
Lugenbuhl, Charles E. ....New Orleans, LA
Luger, Allen Max ....Sacramento, CA
Luger, Andrew M. ....Minneapolis, MN
Luger, Helen N. ....Athens, TX
Luger, Jayne B. ....Atlantic Beach, NY
Luger, Laura Bernstein ....Durham, NC
Luger, Paul L. ....Orlando, FL
Luger, Stephen ....New York, NY
Luger, Walter G. ....Roseland, NJ
Lugert, David C. ....Denver, CO
Lugg, Allan W. ....Lock Haven, PA
Lugg and Lugg ....Lock Haven, PA
Lugg, Robert H. ....Lock Haven, PA
Lugg, Sean P. ....Wilmington, DE
Lugge, Richard Lee ....Palm Springs, CA
Lughes, Joseph A. ....Raleigh, NC
Lughezzani, Theodore A.
Birmingham, MI
Lugibihl, Lynn Summers ....Tulsa, OK
Luginbill, David H. ....Des Moines, IA
Lugli, Richard H. ....New Haven, CT
Luglio, Albert J. ....Deer Park, NY
Lugo, Adelfa A. ....New York, NY
Lugo, Angelina ....El Paso, TX
Lugo, Betty ....New York, NY
Lugo, Diana E. ....Minneapolis, MN
Lugo, Ivonne T. ....New York, NY
Lugo, Jose A. ....Brooklyn, NY
Lugo, Leslie A. ....Dallas, TX
Lugo, Ricardo ....Racine, WI
Lugo-Cox, Christina A. ....Washington, DC
Lugo-Janer, Alberto E. ....Orlando, FL
Lugo Miranda, Anibal ....San Juan, PR
Lugo-Muñoz, Julio I. ....San Juan, PR
Lugo-Rigau, Heber E. ....San Juan, PR
Lugo-Rigau, Ruben ....Houston, TX
Lugosi, Karen L. ....Phoenix, AZ
Lugo-Vilanova, Rafael ....Ponce, PR
Lugrin, George H., IV ....Houston, TX
Lugten, Paul J. ....Boston, MA
Luh, Andrew ....Palo Alto, CA
Luhe, Kathryn ....San Francisco, CA
Luhe, Thos. F. ....Denver, CO
Luhm, Edward G. ....Worland, WY
Luhman, David W. ....Lafayette, IN
Luhman, Fred W. ....San Francisco, CA
Luhman, Gary L. ....Monroe, WI
Luhman, Richard S. ....Cortez, CO
Luhman, Richard S., P.C. ....Cortez, CO
Luhmann, James D. ....Walnut Creek, CA
Luhn, Christopher N. ....Clifton Park, NY
Luhn, Christopher N., P.C., The Law Office of ....Clifton Park, NY
Luhn, Donna Pereksta ....Mahwah, NJ
Luhn, Kim M. ....Salt Lake City, UT
Luhn, V. Jerome ....Albany, NY
Luhn, Warren P. ....Knoxville, TN
Luhowiak, G. Michael ....Chattanooga, TN
Luhr, John P. ....Buffalo, NY
Luhring, John W. ....Palm Desert, CA
Luhring, Lana Lee ....Waverly, IA
Luhring, Susan E. ....Pasadena, CA
Luhrsen, Jeffrey Andrew ....Bradenton, FL
Luhrsen, Julie S. ....Bradenton, FL
Lui, Bradley S. ....Washington, DC
Lui, Christopher ....Los Angeles, CA
Lui, Courtney S. ....San Francisco, CA
Lui, David H. ....San Francisco, CA
Lui, Earl ....San Francisco, CA
Lui, Earl W. ....San Francisco, CA
Lui, Elwood ....Los Angeles, CA
Lui, Lisa ....Washington, DC
Lui, Richard ....Boston, MA
Lui, Richard, P.C., Law Offices of
Boston, MA
Lui, Tom ....New York, NY
Lui, Violet A. Pohakukuiai ....Tucson, AZ
Luibrand, Kevin A. ....Albany, NY
Luick, Robert B. ....Boston, MA
Luick, Sarah Hall ....Boston, MA
Luigs, David A. ....Washington, DC
Luikart, Loyal E., Jr. ....Cleveland, OH
Luikens, Thomas G. ....Phoenix, AZ
Lui-Kwan, Gregory L. ....Honolulu, HI
Lui-Kwan, Ivan M. ....Honolulu, HI
Lui-Kwan, Tim ....Honolulu, HI
Luing, Randy B. ....Waldwick, NJ
Luinstra, Gregory A. ....Great Falls, MT
Luinstra & Semansky, P.C. ....Great Falls, MT

Luis, Christopher .... Arlington, VA
Luis, Michael R. .... Columbus, OH
Luise, Salvatore .... Woods Cross, UT
Luise, Vincent R. .... Lynn, MA
Luisi, John V. .... New York, NY
Luisi, Rocco .... Roseland, NJ
Luizzi, Peter J. .... Brick, NJ
Lujan, Brenda L. .... Denver, CO
Lujan, David J. .... Hagåtña, GU
Lujan, David M. .... Phoenix, AZ
Lujan, Deborah A. .... Southfield, MI
Luján, Ida M. .... Santa Fe, NM
Lujan, Jennifer .... Southfield, MI
Lujan, John-Paul .... Chicago, IL
Lujan, Joseph G. .... Bloomfield Hills, MI
Lujin, Patrick A. .... Kansas City, MO
Luk, Charles K. .... New York, NY
Luk, Leon K. .... New York, NY
Luk & Luk, P.C. .... New York, NY
Luk, Mimi Chan .... Phoenix, AZ
Lukac, Diane S. .... Portland, ME
Lukacevich, Wm. J. .... Milwaukee, WI
LuKacher, Kenneth J. .... Rochester, NY
LuKacher, Martin .... Rochester, NY
Lukacovic, Perry .... Hawthorne, CA
Lukacs, Andrew Z. .... Hartford, CT
Lukacs, Cheryl .... Cleveland, OH
Lukacs, John .... Miami, FL
Lukacs, John C. .... Miami, FL
Lukacs & Lukacs .... Miami, FL
Lukacs, Norma J. .... Chambersburg, PA
Lukacs, Paul Karl .... Los Angeles, CA
Lukacs, Robin A., (Mr.) .... Miami, FL
Lukacsko, Shea H. .... Los Angeles, CA
Roseland, NJ
Lukakis, Michael J. .... Holyoke, MA
Lukakis, Nikki A. .... West Springfield, MA
Lukanich, J. Mark .... Chicago, IL
Lukanski, John O. .... Roseland, NJ
Lukas, Anne L. .... Beachwood, OH
Lukas, Bruce S. W. .... Norristown, PA
Lukas, Daniel A. .... Chicago, IL
Lukas, David J. .... Wisconsin Rapids, WI
Lukas, DeAnn M. .... St. Clair Shores, MI
Lukas, Edward W., Jr. .... Los Angeles, CA
Lukas, Edwin J. .... Detroit, MI
Lukas, Henry .... New York, NY
Lukas, Henry F., Jr. .... Cleveland, OH
Lukas, James C. .... Chicago, IL
Lukas, Joseph B. .... New Haven, CT
Lukas, Karen B. .... New York, NY
Lukas, Nace, Gutierrez & Sachs, Chartered
Washington, DC
Lukas, Paul J. .... Minneapolis, MN
Lukas, Rimas (Ray) T. .... Chicago, IL
Lukas, Robert A. .... Phoenix, AZ
Lukas, Russell D. .... Washington, DC
Lukas, Susana R. .... Chicago, IL
Lukas, Teresa N. .... Denver, CO
Lukas, Thomas William .... Phoenix, AZ
Lukas, Timothy A. .... Reno, NV
Lukas, Vitas J. .... St. Petersburg, FL
Lukashok, Edward .... New York, NY
Lukashow, Thomas .... Palatka, FL
Lukasievich, Michael .... Fort Lauderdale, FL
Lukasievich, Michael, P.A.
Fort Lauderdale, FL
Lukasiewicz, Marie L. .... Buffalo, NY
Lukasik, Daniel T. .... Buffalo, NY
Lukasik, Frank A. .... Punta Gorda, FL
Lukasik, Joan Helen .... Bainbridge Island, WA
Lukasik, Kristine .... Miami, FL
Lukasik, Lisa .... Raleigh, NC
Lukaszewski, Anthony S. .... New York, NY
Lukaszewski, Lisa A. .... Kansas City, MO
Lukats, Alexander R. .... Safford, AZ
Lukcso, Andrew J. .... Middleburg Heights, OH
Luke, Allison Keitt .... Marietta, GA
Luke, Barbara C. .... Dallas, TX
Luke & Barron .... Visalia, CA
Luke, Benjamin A. .... Marksville, LA
Luke & Casteel, P.S.C. .... Lynnwood, WA
Luke, Cheryl Denise .... Salt Lake City, UT
Luke, Colin H. .... Birmingham, AL
Luke, Colin W. .... Idaho Falls, ID
Luke & Cunliff, P.C. .... St. Louis, MO
Luke, Debra K. .... Hammond, IN
Luke, Denise J. .... Minneapolis, MN
Luke, Donald F. .... New York, NY
Luke, F. Dennis .... Allen Park, MI
Luke, Fiona G. .... Riverside, CA
Luke, Fred J. .... Pekin, IL
Luke, Gary C. .... Orange Park, FL
Luke & Genebach .... Washington, VA
Luke, George W. .... Santa Rosa, CA
Luke, Gregory C. .... Cincinnati, OH
Luke, Gregory G. .... Boston, MA
Luke, Howard K. K. .... Honolulu, HI
Luke, Jacquelyn R. .... Anchorage, AK
Luke, James A. .... Prince George, VA
Luke, Jenni M. .... Frisco, CO
Luke, John J. .... Pittsburgh, PA
Luke, John R. .... Pittsburgh, PA
Luke, Jordan .... Washington, DC
Luke, Kathleen Allen .... Purchase, NY
Luke, Kendal A. .... Honolulu, HI
Luke, Kenneth W. .... Boston, MA
Luke, Kerry Phillip .... Birmingham, AL
Luke, Laurence M. .... Troy, MI
Luke, Linda A. .... Visalia, CA
Luke, Linda K. C. .... Honolulu, HI
Luke, Lucinda J. .... Richland, WA
Luke, Maureen D. .... Wilmington, DE
Luke, Michael J. .... Springfield, IL
Luke, Michele-Lynn E. .... Honolulu, HI
Luke & Miyatake .... Honolulu, HI
Luke, Nancy A. .... Cypress, CA
Luke, Peter H. .... Washington, VA

Luke, Randall D. .... Cleveland, OH
Luke, Ricky G. .... Jackson, MS
Luke, Ringgold Hynson .... Bunkie, LA
Luke, Robert N. .... Lynnwood, WA
Luke, Robert R. .... Houston, TX
Luke, Saralee K. .... Cleveland, OH
Luke, Sharon Genebach .... Washington, VA
Luke, Sherrill D. .... Los Angeles, CA
Luke, Stanley K. .... Crestview, FL
Luke, Sylvia J. .... Honolulu, HI
Luke, Thaddeus J. .... Ilion, NY
Luke, Wayne W. S. .... Honolulu, HI
Lukehart, Catherine .... Los Angeles, CA
Lukehart, J. Kipp .... Punxsutawney, PA
Lukehart, Jack .... Brunswick, MO
Lukehart & Lundy .... Punxsutawney, PA
Lukehart, Michael C. .... Bakersfield, CA
Lukeman, Paul G. .... Columbus, OH
Luken, Clement H., Jr. .... Cincinnati, OH
Luken, John D. .... Cincinnati, OH
Luken, Joseph M. .... Cincinnati, OH
Luken, Susan J. .... Washington, DC
Luken, Thomas A. .... Cincinnati, OH
Luken, Thomas F. .... Fort Lauderdale, FL
Lukenbill, Kenneth H. .... Plymouth, IN
Lukens and Drummond
San Francisco, CA
Lukens, Elizabeth B. .... Philadelphia, PA
Lukens, Ira B. .... Plymouth, MA
Lukens, John P. .... Las Vegas, NV
Lukens, John R. .... Charleston, WV
Lukens, Joseph T. .... Philadelphia, PA
Lukens, Karl R. .... Dearborn, MI
Lukens, Ralph D. .... West Hartford, CT
Lukens, Robert .... Philadelphia, PA
Lukens, Robert A. .... Philadelphia, PA
Lukens, William E. .... Indianapolis, IN
Lukens, William H. .... Rocky River, OH
Lukens, William M. .... San Francisco, CA
Luker, Charles R., Jr. .... London, KY
Luker, Daniel P. .... Concord, NH
Luker, David S. .... Birmingham, AL
Luker, David S., & Associates, P.C.
Birmingham, AL
Luker, George P. .... Maynard, MA
Luker, J. Milton .... London, KY
Luker, James C. .... Wynne, AR
Luker, Joe C. .... Santa Barbara, CA
Luker, Lynn M. .... Boise, ID
Luker, Lynn M. .... New Orleans, LA
Luker, William H. .... Oklahoma City, OK
Lukes & Bassoni .... San Francisco, CA
Lukes, Donald J. .... Spokane, WA
Lukes, John C. .... Flint, MI
Lukes, Jos. A. .... San Francisco, CA
Lukes, Konstantina B. .... Worcester, MA
Lukes, Paul M. .... Chicago, IL
Lukes, Rita E. .... Minneapolis, MN
Lukes, Robert C. .... Missoula, MT
Lukes, Robert J. .... Minneapolis, MN
Lukesh, Linell M. .... Philadelphia, PA
Luketina, Robin M. .... McLean, VA
Lukey, Edward J. .... Boston, MA
Lukey, Joan A. .... Boston, MA
Lukey, Nancy L. .... Bloomfield Hills, MI
Lukey, Paul E. .... Cincinnati, OH
Lukhard, Ralph C. .... Richmond, VA
Lukich, Richard A. .... Cleveland, OH
Lukievics, Helen J. .... New York, NY
Lukin & Hedges .... Houston, TX
Lukin, Karen Beasley .... Houston, TX
Lukin, Lee G. .... New York, NY
Lukin, Mitchell D. .... Houston, TX
Lukingbeal, Anne .... Ithaca, NY
Lukingbeal, Eric .... Hartford, CT
Lukinovich, David J. .... Metairie, LA
Lukins & Annis, P.S. .... Coeur d'Alene, ID
Moses Lake, WA
Spokane, WA
Lukins, Denise J. .... Vancouver, WA
Lukins, Kyle B. .... Seattle, WA
Lukins, Scott B. .... Spokane, WA
Lukitsch, Paul J. .... Chicago, IL
Lukitsch, Shirley M. .... Chicago, IL
Lukjanowicz, John .... Anchorage, AK
Seattle, WA
Lukmann, L. Charles, III .... Chesterton, IN
Lukoff, David M. .... Wilmington, DE
Lukoff, Murray J. .... New Bedford, MA
Lukoff, Paul M. .... Wilmington, DE
Lukoschek, Monica E. .... Irvine, CA
Lukoski, Edward G. .... Riverhead, NY
Lukoskie, Jerry .... Shoreview, MN
Lukovic, M. Mira .... Hoboken, NJ
Lukowiak, Henry .... St. Clair Shores, MI
Lukowicz, Michelle L. .... Denver, CO
Lukowski, Jay D. .... New York, NY
Luks, Allan B. .... Long Beach, NY
Luks, Georgia C. .... South Bend, IN
Luks, Jack D. .... Fort Lauderdale, FL
Luks, Jerome M. .... Bronx, NY
Luks, Koleos & Santaniello P.A.
Fort Lauderdale, FL
Tampa, FL
Luks, Ronald P. .... Syosset, NY
Luksa, Steven M. .... Allentown, PA
Luksch, Joseph D. .... New York, NY
Luksetich, Thomas A. .... Houston, TX
Lukus, Frank W. .... Los Angeles, CA
Lulay, Patricia C. .... Lyons, OR
Lulejian, John J. .... Los Angeles, CA
Luley, John E. .... Washington, DC
Lulf, Debra Y. .... Sioux City, IA
Lulic, Joseph F. .... Minneapolis, MN
Lulich, Lawrence M. .... Chicago, IL
Lulich, Michael K. .... Indianapolis, IN
Lulich, Murphy, Dowling, & Associates, P.C.
Indianapolis, IN

Lulich, Steven .... Sebastian, FL
Lulie, Harriet E. .... Frederick, MD
Lull, David S. .... San Jose, CA
Lull, Margaret Ione .... Georgetown, DE
Lull, Robert E. .... Corning, NY
Lullo, David A. .... Chicago, IL
Lullo, Margaret J. .... Jacksonville, FL
Luloff, Gary R. .... Yakima, WA
Lulofs, Larry E. .... Oakland, CA
Lulow, Rebecca .... South Pasadena, CA
Lulucki, Mary A. .... Los Angeles, CA
Luludis, Frederick B. .... Holmdel, NJ
Lum, Albert C. .... Los Angeles, CA
Lum, Albert C. .... South Pasadena, CA
Las Vegas, NV
Lum, Albert Justin .... South Pasadena, CA
Lum, Arnold Leighton .... Honolulu, HI
Lum, Bettina W. J. .... Honolulu, HI
Lum, Dale W. .... San Francisco, CA
Lum, Danzis, Drasco, Positan & Kleinberg, LLC .... Newark, NJ
Roseland, NJ
Lum, David A. .... Cleveland, OH
Lum, David M. K. .... Honolulu, HI
Lum, Dean S. .... Seattle, WA
Lum, Dwight .... Honolulu, HI
Lum, Herman T. F. .... Honolulu, HI
Lum, Jennifer T. .... Los Angeles, CA
Lum, Lawrence H. .... New York, NY
Lum, Leslie W. S. .... Honolulu, HI
Lum, Margaret Chan .... Dixon, CA
Lum, Michael J. .... Honolulu, HI
Lum, Michael Y. W. .... Honolulu, HI
Lum, Nathaniel Y. T. .... Honolulu, HI
Lum, Raymond J. .... Rochester, NY
Lum, Richard M. C. .... Honolulu, HI
Lum, Robert K. .... Houston, TX
Lum, Rona .... Troy, MI
Lum, Ronald H. W. .... Honolulu, HI
Lum, Russell W. O. .... Honolulu, HI
Lum, Steven K. K. .... Las Vegas, NV
Lum, Virginia M. .... Department of Justice, Civil Division, GV
Lum, William Boyce .... Roseland, NJ
Luma, Daren A. .... White Plains, NY
Lumaghi, Peter .... St. Louis, MO
Luman, Arthur E. .... White Plains, NY
Luman, John F., III .... Houston, TX
Luman, Joseph C. .... Washington, DC
Luman, Joseph M. .... St. Louis, MO
Luman, Lange & Wheeler
Washington, DC
Lumannick, Gary B. .... Miami, FL
Lumb, David A.E. .... Memphis, TN
Lumb, David M. .... Los Angeles, CA
Lumb, J. Trevor .... Groton, CT
Lumb, Kathryn M. .... Chicago, IL
Lumb, Kenneth T. .... Chicago, IL
Lumb, Sharon M. W. .... Canton, NY
Lumbard, Carolyn T. .... Las Cruces, NM
Lumbard, Eliot H. .... Hollis, NH
Lumbard, Michael B. .... Penn Valley, CA
Lumbard, Thomas .... Washington, DC
Lumber, F. James .... Antioch, IL
Lumberg, Eric S. .... Birmingham, MI
Lumberg, Eugene .... Birmingham, MI
Lumbye, Paul F., III .... Denver, CO
Lumer, Joel V. .... Miami, FL
Lumer, Michael B. .... New York, NY
Lumerman, David T. .... St. Louis, MO
Lumia, Peter J. .... Jamesburg, NJ
Lumicao, Benjamin E. .... Northbrook, IL
Luminello, Stephen .... Secaucus, NJ
Lumish, B. Steven .... Miami, FL
Lumish, Douglas E. .... Menlo Park, CA
Lumish, Wendy Frank .... Miami, FL
Lumkes, Debby .... Reno, NV
Lumley, Carl J. .... St. Louis, MO
Lumley, Jacqueline N. .... Lyndhurst, NJ
Lumley, Jerry A. .... Macon, GA
Lummanick, James F. .... Cincinnati, OH
Lummis, Christopher M. .... Stevens Point, WI
Lummis, Cynthia M. .... Cheyenne, WY
Lummis, John M. .... Baltimore, MD
Lummis, Krell & Baker .... Bridgeton, NJ
Woodbury, NJ
Lummis, William R. .... Houston, TX
Lummus, Carlos M. .... Philadelphia, PA
Lummus, Charles D. .... Cleburne, TX
Lummus, Hallman, Pritchard & Baker, P.C.
Cleburne, TX
Lummus, William F., Jr. .... Atlanta, GA
Lumpe, J. Richard .... Columbus, OH
Lumpkin, Alva M. .... Columbia, SC
Lumpkin, Carol Celeiro .... Miami, FL
Lumpkin, Charles H., Jr. .... Carrollton, GA
Lumpkin, Douglas B. .... Sarasota, FL
Lumpkin, Edward B. .... Richmond, VA
Lumpkin, Gary L. .... Oklahoma City, OK
Lumpkin, Jas M. .... Richmond, VA
Lumpkin, John C. .... Norfolk, VA
Lumpkin, John C., P.C. .... Norfolk, VA
Lumpkin, John H., Jr. .... Columbia, SC
Lumpkin, John H., Sr. .... Columbia, SC
Lumpkin, Joseph H., Jr. .... Columbia, SC
Lumpkin, Julia Willcox .... Columbus, GA
Lumpkin, Kathryn A. .... Dallas, TX
Lumpkin, Mark D. .... Biloxi, MS
Lumpkin, Michael M. .... Columbia, SC
Lumpkin, Peyton White .... Miami, FL
Lumpkin, R. Hugh .... Miami, FL
Lumpkin, Robert L., Jr. .... Georgetown, SC
Lumpkin, T. Bryan .... Hinesville, GA
Lumpkin, Thomas D., II .... Coral Gables, FL
Lumpkin, William H. .... Centre, AL
Lumpkins, Debra K. .... Hugo, OK
Lumpkins, John L., Jr. .... Richmond, VA
Lumpkins, Rosemary C. .... Atlanta, GA

Lumpkins, Stuart B., Jr. .... Fort Worth, TX
Lumpp, Sarah M. .... LaBelle, FL
Hannibal, MO
Lumsdaine, Dianne N. .... Anaheim, CA
Lumsdaine, Joseph A. .... Downey, CA
Lumsden, C. David .... Atlanta, GA
Lumsden, Dana C. .... New York, NY
Lumsden, Dennis J. .... Fort Myers, FL
Naples, FL
Lumsden, Diana J. .... Boston, MA
Lumsden, Faith L. .... Seattle, WA
Lumsden, Gary L. .... Roanoke, VA
Lumsden, Margaret C. .... Raleigh, NC
Lumsden, Overstreet & Hansen
Roanoke, VA
Lumsden, Terry E. .... Tacoma, WA
Lumsden, Treve B. .... Beaufort, NC
Lumsdon, Thomas G. .... Corona Del Mar, CA
Lumumsa, Chokwe .... Jackson, MS
Lun, Ku Faye Fei .... New York, NY
Lun, Wendy .... Palo Alto, CA
Luna, Ana Maria .... Huntington Park, CA
Luna, Anthony J. .... Los Angeles, CA
Luna, B. Martin .... Wailuku, HI
Luna, Carl .... Garland, TX
Luna, César .... San Diego, CA
Luna, Charles Stephen .... Houston, TX
Luna, David A. .... Los Angeles, CA
Luna, Dennis R. .... Los Angeles, CA
Luna, Earl .... Dallas, TX
Luna, Felix G. .... Seattle, WA
Luna, Grant B. .... San Diego, CA
Luna, Gregory .... San Antonio, TX
Luna, Gregory V. .... McAllen, TX
Luna, Joe Luis .... Crystal City, TX
Luna, Jones W. .... Nashville, TN
Luna, Jorge J. .... Los Angeles, CA
Luna, Joseph Richard "Dick" .... Houston, TX
Luna, Laura J. .... Philadelphia, PA
Luna, Maria Pilar .... Laguna Niguel, CA
Luna, Michael J. .... St. Louis, MO
Luna, Rene .... Corpus Christi, TX
Luna, Robert E. .... Dallas, TX
Luna, Scott L. .... Garland, TX
Luna, Sharon Thompson .... Pleasanton, CA
Luna, Vilma .... Corpus Christi, TX
Luna-Martinez, Wanda I. .... San Juan, PR
Lunardi, Henry J. .... Media, PA
Lunardini, Lawrence M. .... Bakersfield, CA
Lunas, Michael S. .... Lakeport, CA
Lunceford, David A. .... Leoti, KS
Lunceford, Lloyd J. .... Baton Rouge, LA
Lunceford, Rhett .... Bountiful, UT
Lunceford-Hedtke, Connie A.
Minneapolis, MN
Lunch, Milton F. .... Chevy Chase, MD
Lunche, Richard J. .... Encino, CA
Lund, Allan I. .... Treasury Department, Department Offices, GV
Lund, Allan R. .... Minneapolis, MN
Lund, Amy Poskin .... Cambridge, MD
Lund, Andrew E. .... New York, NY
Lund, Arlan O. .... Richland, WA
Lund, Arthur K. .... San Francisco, CA
San Jose, CA
Lund, Benjamin W. .... Lewiston, ME
Lund, Carl A. .... Paris, IL
Lund, Charles .... Milwaukee, WI
Lund, Christian W. .... Fitchburg, MA
Lund, Clifford E. .... Elgin, IL
Lund, Cody Dale .... Newport Beach, CA
Lund, Colby B. .... Minneapolis, MN
Lund, Cory D. .... Joliet, IL
Lund, Daniel .... Culver City, CA
Lund, Daniel, (A Professional Law Corporation) .... New Orleans, LA
Lund, Daniel, III .... New Orleans, LA
Lund, Daniel P. .... New York, NY
Lund, David .... Wichita, KS
Lund, David B. .... De Forest, WI
Lund, David H. .... Los Angeles, CA
Lund, David H. .... Erie, PA
Lund, David H., Jr. .... Redmond, WA
Lund, David R. .... Boston, MA
Lund, David R., & Associates, P.C.
Boston, MA
Lund, Donald M. .... Pittsburgh, PA
Lund, Douglas R. .... Ojai, CA
Lund, Elmo .... Oberlin, KS
Lund, Eric C. .... Grand Rapids, MI
Lund, Eric James .... Los Angeles, CA
Lund, Erik K.E. .... Rancho Santa Fe, CA
Lund, Erik, P.C. .... Boston, MA
Lund, F. Jules, Jr. .... Grand Canyon, AZ
Lund, Gordon L. .... Salt Lake City, UT
Lund, Herbert A. .... Albert Lea, MN
Lund, Ilene A. .... Edmonds, WA
Lund, Jack E. .... Bakersfield, CA
Lund, Jack W. .... Gary, IN
Lund, James A. .... Minneapolis, MN
Lund, James B. .... Minneapolis, MN
Lund, James E. .... Escondido, CA
Lund, James E. .... San Diego, CA
Lund, James L. .... Los Angeles, CA
Lund, Jeffrey .... Long Beach, CA
Lund, Joan E. .... Gulfport, MS
Lund, John C. .... Fall River, MA
Lund, John E. .... Tampa, FL
Lund, John Myron .... Minneapolis, MN
Lund, John R. .... Salt Lake City, UT
Lund, John R. .... Woodruff, WI
Lund, John T. .... St. Cloud, MN
Lund, Jon A. .... Hallowell, ME
Lund, Jon B. .... Hillsboro, OR
Lund, Juli A. .... Minneapolis, MN
Lund, Julie V. .... Salt Lake City, UT
Lund, Kenneth J. .... Pittsburgh, PA
Lund, Kenneth L. .... Madison, WI

Lupas, Anthony J., Jr. .... Wilkes-Barre, PA
Lupas, David W. .... West Pittston, PA
Lupel, Warren .... Chicago, IL
Luper, Frederick M. .... Columbus, OH
Luper, Sheriff & Neidenthal, A Legal Professional Association .... Columbus, OH
Luperini, Joseph A.
Treasury Department, GV
Lupert, Leslie A. .... New York, NY
Lupescu, Sallie Moutvic .... Oak Brook, IL
Lupi, Dawn Catera .... Utica, NY
Lupia, Charles E. .... Syracuse, NY
Lupia, Joseph A. .... East Syracuse, NY
Lupia, Joseph A., Jr. .... Syracuse, NY
Lupia, Lynnette L. .... Chicago, IL
Lupia, Paul J. .... Utica, NY
Lupia, Terry A. .... Harrisburg, PA
Lupica, Cynthia A. .... Glendale, CA
Lupica, Jay A. .... Wellesley, MA
Lupica, Salvatore .... Richmond, VA
Lupica, Thomas A. .... Toledo, OH
Lupin, E. Ralph .... New Orleans, LA
Lupin, Louis J. .... New Orleans, LA
Lupin, Louis M. .... San Diego, CA
Lupin, Steven H. .... Lansdale, PA
Lupinacci, Timothy M. .... Birmingham, AL
Lupinek, Joseph J. .... Baltimore, MD
Lupinetti, Bernadette E. .... Goshen, NY
Lupino, James S. .... Key Largo, FL
Tavernier, FL
Lupkes, Margaret D. .... Minneapolis, MN
Lupkin, Jonathan D. .... New York, NY
Lupkin, Stanley N. .... New York, NY
Luplow, Dale L. .... Grangeville, ID
Luplow, Russell N. .... Birmingham, MI
Luplow, Thomas R. .... Saginaw, MI
Lupnacca, Janet S. .... Moorestown, NJ
Lupo, Anthony V. .... Washington, DC
Lupo, Ashley D. .... Marco Island, FL
Lupo, Betty .... Norristown, PA
Lupo, Cynthia B. .... Nutley, NJ
Lupo, Dane A. .... Detroit, MI
Lupo, Dane A., Jr. .... Detroit, MI
Lupo, David G. .... St. Louis, MO
Lupo, David G., P.C. .... St. Louis, MO
Lupo, Dickson M. .... Charlotte, NC
Lupo, Frank .... Pasadena, CA
Lupo, Glenn T. .... Fort Worth, TX
Lupo, Kenneth G. .... Houston, TX
Lupo & Koczkur, P.C. .... Detroit, MI
Lupo & Lupo .... Waltham, MA
Lupo, M. Adeline .... Boston, MA
Lupo, Mary E. .... West Palm Beach, FL
Lupo, Nicholas A. .... Waltham, MA
Lupo, Philip F. .... Rockledge, FL
Lupo, Philip F., P.A. .... Rockledge, FL
Lupo, Raphael V. .... Washington, DC
Lupo, Richard .... North Brunswick, NJ
Lupo, Robert N. .... Waltham, MA
Lupo, Thomas D. .... Chicago, IL
Lupoff, Jerrold I. .... Sarasota, FL
Lupold, Ray P., III .... Richmond, VA
Lupoli, Geraldine A. .... Orange, CT
Lupoli, Geraldine A., P.C. .... Orange, CT
Lupoli, Matthew M. .... Flushing, NY
Lupoli, Virginia E. M.
Cold Spring Harbor, NY
Lupone, E. Robert .... New York, NY
Lupori, James A. .... Stow, OH
Lupovitz, Joni .... Federal Trade Commission, Bureau of Consumer Protection, GV
Luppert, Sylvia .... Seattle, WA
Luppi, Henry M. .... Los Angeles, CA
Luppi, Michael D. .... Glendale, CA
Luppi, Robert W. .... Foothill Ranch, CA
Luppino, Anthony J. .... Leawood, KS
Kansas City, MO
Luppino, James R. .... Fresno, CA
Luptak, David A. .... Pittsburgh, PA
Luptak, Jerry D. .... Detroit, MI
Luptak, Richard J. .... Kings Mountain, NC
Lupton, Anne B. .... Greensboro, NC
Lupton, Harvey A. .... Winston-Salem, NC
Lupton, James M. .... Beaufort, NC
Lupton, Ralph L. .... Los Angeles, CA
Lupton, Ronald W. .... Bath, ME
Lupton, Stephen R. .... San Angelo, TX
Lupton, Stevenson, Jr. .... Greensboro, NC
Lupton, Suzann Weber .... Indianapolis, IN
Lupton, Theodore Nichols .... Spartanburg, SC
Lupton, William E. .... Overland Park, KS
Lupu, Andrew H. .... Islandia, NY
Lupul, Donald K. .... Manteca, CA
Lupuloff, Harry
National Aeronautics And Space Administration, Office of the General Counsel, GV
Luque, Nancy A. .... Washington, DC
Luque-Rosales, Mercedes .... Chicago, IL
Luquet, Michael C. .... New Orleans, LA
Luquette, Ted L. .... Lake Charles, LA
Luquire, Brace W. .... Columbus, GA
Luquis, Glenda K. .... Miami, FL
Lura, Mark J. .... Chicago, IL
Lurensky, Marcia A.
Federal Energy Regulatory Commission, Office of the General Counsel, GV
Lurey, Alfred S. .... Atlanta, GA
Lurey, Michael S. .... Los Angeles, CA
Luria, April .... Honolulu, HI
Luria, Edward M. .... Wilmington, DE
Washington, DC
Luria, Joan M. .... Washington, DC
Luria Law Firm, The .... Honolulu, HI
Luria, Mary M. .... New York, NY
Luria, Neil F. .... Cleveland, OH
Luria, Nelson J. .... New York, NY
Luria, Peter D. .... Avon, CT
Luria, Remy .... Honolulu, HI
Luria, Sydney A. .... New York, NY
Luria, Timothy .... Honolulu, HI
Luria-Cohen, Nancy .... Fort Lauderdale, FL
Lurie, Abraham M. .... Los Angeles, CA
Lurie, Alvin D. .... Larchmont, NY
Lurie, Alvin D., P.C. .... Larchmont, NY
Lurie, Andrew .... Los Angeles, CA
Lurie, Barak .... Los Angeles, CA
Lurie, Bernard J. .... Los Angeles, CA
Lurie, Bertrand F. .... San Francisco, CA
Lurie, Bruce J. .... Beverly Hills, CA
Lurie, David E. .... Boston, MA
Lurie, David J. .... Aspen Hill, MD
Lurie, David M. .... Kansas City, MO
Lurie, David R. .... New York, NY
Lurie, Donna E. .... Bothell, WA
Lurie, Elana Turoff .... Shaker Heights, OH
Lurie, Frederick A. .... Chicago, IL
Lurie, Frederick J. .... Sherman Oaks, CA
Lurie, Gerald B. .... Chicago, IL
Lurie, Herbert A. .... New York, NY
Lurie, Herbert M. .... Pittsburgh, PA
Lurie, Howard R. .... Villanova, PA
Lurie, James M. .... New York, NY
Lurie, Janet B. .... Hackensack, NJ
Lurie, Jeanne F. .... Jacksonville, FL
Lurie, Jeffrey K. .... Cincinnati, OH
Lurie, Jennifer .... Los Angeles, CA
San Francisco, CA
Lurie, Jerald B. .... Baltimore, MD
Lurie, Jonathan C. .... Los Angeles, CA
Lurie, Jordan L. .... Los Angeles, CA
Lurie, Joseph .... Philadelphia, PA
Lurie, Keith E. .... New York, NY
Lurie, Kimberly Wittenberg .... Canton, MA
Lurie & Krupp, LLP .... Boston, MA
Lurie, Leonard N. .... Cleveland, OH
Lurie, Lesley I. .... Dallas, TX
Lurie, Lloyd D. .... Baltimore, MD
Lurie, Lynn A. .... Morristown, NJ
Lurie, Maria Elena
Department Of The Interior, GV
Lurie, Mark David .... Newark, NJ
Lurie, Mark I. .... West Palm Beach, FL
Lurie, Martin D. .... San Francisco, CA
Lurie, Michael D. .... Chicago, IL
Lurie, Michael D. .... Boston, MA
Lurie, Michael H. .... Chicago, IL
Lurie, Michael I. .... Jamaica, NY
Lurie, Paul M. .... Chicago, IL
Lurie, Peter .... New York, NY
Lurie, R. Thornton .... New York, NY
Lurie, Randolph G. .... Montgomery, AL
Lurie, Robert A. .... Los Angeles, CA
Lurie, Robert N. .... Cleveland, OH
Lurie, Ruth B. .... Englewood, CO
Lurie, Samuel J. .... New York, NY
Lurie, Sanford S. .... New York, NY
Lurie, Steven J. .... Los Angeles, CA
Lurie, Stuart D. .... Philadelphia, PA
Lurie, Wendy Anne .... New York, NY
Lurie & Zepeda, A Professional Corporation
Beverly Hills, CA
Luring, Roger E. .... Troy, OH
Lurio & Associates, P.C. .... Haddonfield, NJ
Philadelphia, PA
Lurio, Douglas M. .... Philadelphia, PA
Lurio, Margaret Sherry .... Haddonfield, NJ
Philadelphia, PA
Lurker, David A. .... Newport Beach, CA
Lurker, James J. .... Malvern, PA
Lurner, Jefferey B. .... Irvine, CA
Luros, Hilary .... Palo Alto, CA
Luros, Michael S. .... Los Angeles, CA
Lurtz, Timothy E. .... Oklahoma City, OK
Lurvey, Daniel A. .... Miami, FL
Lurvey, Ira H. .... Los Angeles, CA
Lurvey, John A. .... Hollywood, FL
West Palm Beach, FL
Lurvey, John W. .... Bennington, VT
Lurvey, Jonathan B. .... New York, NY
Lurvey, Lawrence C. .... Los Angeles, CA
Lurvey & Shapiro .... Los Angeles, CA
Lury, Gemma M. .... Newark, NJ
Lury, Richard R. .... New York, NY
Lurya, Alan M. .... Washington, DC
Lurye, Richard S. .... Rockville, MD
Lurye, William .... Metairie, LA
Lurz, Beth Heier .... Wheeling, WV
Lusak, John E. .... Chicago, IL
Lusardi, Robert A. .... Springfield, MA
Lusardi, Robert C. .... Carmel, NY
Cold Spring, NY
Lusby, Gregory Thomas .... Salem, OR
Lusby, Paul H. .... Pasadena, CA
Lusby, Richard A. .... Jonesboro, AR
Lusby, Ruth A. .... Phoenix, AZ
Luschas, Alvin J. .... Bloomsburg, PA
Luschei, Erich R. .... Los Angeles, CA
Luscher, Brian A. .... Phoenix, AZ
Lusco, Louis L., II .... Jefferson, LA
Luscomb & English .... Wayland, MA
Luscomb, Harris T., III
North Dartmouth, MA
Luscombe, George A., II .... Chicago, IL
Luscombe, John B., Jr. .... Peru, NY
Luscutoff, Lendormy & Associates
San Francisco, CA
Luscutoff, Sidney A. .... San Francisco, CA
Luscy, William J., III .... Metairie, LA
Luse, Barry F. .... Marion, OH
Luse, Eric .... Washington, DC
Luse, James W. .... Lancaster, OH
Luse, Jennifer .... Baton Rouge, LA
Luse Lehman Gorman Pomerenk & Schick, A Professional Corporation
Washington, DC
Baltimore, MD
Luse, Miriam G. .... Marysville, MT
Luse, Steven M., (A Professional Corporation)
Modesto, CA
Luse, Susan S. .... Bethesda, MD
Lusero, James F. .... Longmont, CO
Lusetti, David M. .... Denver, CO
Lush, Gale E. .... Wilcox, NE
Lush, L. Anthony .... Dayton, OH
Lushanko, Larry G. .... Bonsall, CA
Lushbaugh, Bradley H. .... Fayetteville, AR
Lushbough, K. Diane .... Clovis, CA
Lushenko, E. Al .... Eugene, OR
Lusher, Bradley A. .... Pleasanton, CA
Lusher, Jill E. .... Carson City, NV
Lusher, Robert W. .... Nashville, IN
Lushin, Laddie .... Randolph, VT
Lushing, Peter .... New York, NY
Lushing, Susan C. .... Jamaica, NY
Lushis, John F., Jr. .... Bethlehem, PA
Lusiani, R. Craig .... Sacramento, CA
Lusich, Jeffrey V. .... Stockton, CA
Lusignan, Michael R.
Department of Commerce, Patent and Trademark Office, GV
Lusins, Gillian M. .... New York, NY
Lusitana, Gregory L. .... San Diego, CA
Lusk, Andrew J. .... Bloomfield Hills, MI
Lusk, Dennis L. .... Clifton, AZ
Lusk, Donald D. .... Birmingham, AL
Lusk, Drasites & Tolisano, P.A.
Cape Coral, FL
Lusk, E. Craig .... Austin, TX
Lusk, Fraley, McAlister & Simms, P.C.
Birmingham, AL
Lusk, J. Marshall, Jr. .... Jackson, MS
Arlington, VA
Lusk, Jack S. .... New York, NY
Lusk, James W. .... Lenexa, KS
Lusk, Lisa M. .... Cape Coral, FL
Lusk, Liska F. .... College Station, TX
Lusk, Louis B. .... Guntersville, AL
Lusk, Louis B., Jr. .... Atlanta, GA
Lusk & Lusk .... Guntersville, AL
Lusk, Martha Uber .... Fresno, CA
Lusk & McGhehey .... Chattanooga, TN
Lusk, Michael P. .... Chicago, IL
Lusk, Michael S. .... Anniston, AL
Lusk, Nancy E. .... Sugar Land, TX
Lusk, Neva G. .... Charleston, WV
Lusk, Payton Caldwell .... Birmingham, AL
Lusk, Robert A. .... Detroit, MI
Lusk, Robert E. .... Kansas City, MO
Lusk, Robert M. .... Portland, OR
Lusk, Robert P. .... Anderson, SC
Lusk, Stephanie E. .... Austin, TX
Lusk, Tracy Blaine .... Welch, WV
Lusk, William E., Jr. .... Wichita, KS
Luskey, Lane M. .... Washington, DC
Luski, Moses .... Charlotte, NC
Luskin, Andrew J. .... Great Neck, NY
Luskin, Bert L. .... Highland Park, IL
Luskin, John P. .... Cleveland, OH
Luskin, Joshua Dante .... Urbana, IL
Luskin, Martin .... Hackensack, NJ
New York, NY
Luskin, Michael .... New York, NY
Luskin, Richard S. .... Malibu, CA
Luskin, Robert D. .... Washington, DC
Luskin, Stern & Eisler LLP
New York, NY
Luskin, Sue K. .... Great Neck, NY
Luskin, Vladislav V. .... San Francisco, CA
Luskus, George .... Jenkintown, PA
Luskus, Lynnae L. .... Dallas, TX
Luskus and Tinucci .... Media, PA
Luskus, William T. .... Media, PA
Lusky & Associates, P.C. .... Dallas, TX
Lusky, Barbara E. .... Skokie, IL
Lusky, Herman A. .... Dallas, TX
Lusky, John A., P.C. .... Portland, OR
Lusky, Louis .... Ridgewood, NJ
Lusky, Paul M. .... Baltimore, MD
Lusnia, Kenneth J. .... Cleveland, OH
Luss, Robert D. .... Dallas, TX
Lussen, Thomas A., Jr. .... Slidell, LA
Lusser, Amber L. .... Southfield, MI
Lusser, Hughes and Lusser .... St. Louis, MO
Lusser, Rene E. .... St. Louis, MO
Lussi, Arthur S. .... Lake Placid, NY
Lussier, David G. .... West Warwick, RI
Lussier, Donald G. .... Boston, MA
Lussier, Edward F. .... Department of Defense, Armed Services Board of Contract Appeals, GV
Lussier, Ellen Staley .... Portola Valley, CA
Lussier, James R. .... Orlando, FL
Lussier, Jolynn M. .... Boston, MA
Lussier, Nella M. .... South Easton, MA
Lussier, Normand V. .... Department of Defense, Defense Legal Services Agency, GV
Lussier, Richard J.
National Labor Relations Board, Office of the General Counsel, GV
Lussier, Robert G. .... Somers, CT
Lussier, Sherin B. .... Pawtucket, RI
Lussier, Steven C. .... Davenport, IA
Lusskin, Andrew M. .... Livingston, NJ
Lusskin, Benjamin J. .... Hollywood, FL
Lussler, Kevin B. .... Los Angeles, CA
Lussnig, Monika .... Des Plaines, IL
Lusson, Douglas A. .... Los Angeles, CA
Lusson, Karen L. .... Chicago, IL
Lussow, John H. .... Janesville, WI
Lust, Connie P. .... Dallas, TX
Lust, Jeffrey M. .... Dallas, TX
Lust, Marc J. .... New York, NY
Lust, Steven E. .... Tacoma, WA
Lustbader, Brian G. .... New York, NY
Lustbader, David .... Livingston, NJ
Lustbader, Mark Adam .... Parsippany, NJ
Lustbader, Paula .... Tacoma, WA
Lustbader, Philip L. .... Norwood, MA
Lustbader, Philip M. .... Livingston, NJ
Lustbader, Philip M., & David Lustbader, A Professional Corporation
East Orange, NJ
Livingston, NJ
Morristown, NJ
Newark, NJ
Lustbader, Susan E. .... New York, NY
Lustberg, Lawrence S. .... Newark, NJ
Lustberg, Roger H. .... Los Angeles, CA
Lustenberger, Louis C., Jr. .... New York, NY
Luster & Cônine, L.L.P. .... Natchitoches, LA
Shreveport, LA
Luster, Eleanor .... Agoura Hills, CA
Luster, Gregory S. .... Oklahoma City, OK
Luster, John Patrick .... Coeur d'Alene, ID
Luster, John William .... Natchitoches, LA
Luster, Martin A. .... Ithaca, NY
Luster, Reginald .... Jacksonville, FL
Lustfeldt, Gordon L. .... Watseka, IL
Lustgarten, Annette Star .... Flagstaff, AZ
Lustgarten, Chester P. .... Brooklyn, NY
Lustgarten, Harry, Jr. .... Omaha, NE
Lustgarten, Ira H. .... New York, NY
Lustgarten, Isaac B. .... New York, NY
Lustgarten, Jodi R. .... West Palm Beach, FL
Lustgarten, Marvin .... Chicago, IL
Lustgarten, Michael B. .... Omaha, NE
Lustgarten, Ralph W. F. .... Chicago, IL
Lustgarten, Richard A. .... West Orange, NJ
Lustgarten and Roberts, P.C. .... Omaha, NE
Lustgarten, Sondra S. .... Bellevue, WA
Lustgarten, Steven J. .... Omaha, NE
Lusthaus, Meredith A. .... Brooklyn, NY
Lusthaus, Stephen J. .... New York, NY
Lusthaus, Stephen J., P.C. .... New York, NY
Lusthoff, Craig W. .... Riverside, IL
Lustick, Marc W. .... Albany, NY
Lustig, Adam D. .... Miami, FL
Lustig, Amy W. .... Department of Education, Office of the General Counsel, GV
Lustig, Andrew P. .... Dallas, TX
Lustig, Arthur F. .... Cleveland, OH
Lustig & Brown, LLP .... Stamford, CT
Buffalo, NY
New York, NY
Lustig, D. Carl, III .... New York, NY
Lustig, Douglas J. .... Rochester, NY
Lustig, Dov William .... Birmingham, MI
Lustig, Elaine Marie .... San Francisco, CA
Lustig, Eric A. .... Boston, MA
Lustig, Gerald I. .... Mineola, NY
Lustig, Glaser & Wilson, P.C. .... Newton, MA
Lustig, Harvey .... Brooklyn, NY
Lustig, Herbert J. .... Buffalo, NY
Lustig and Hermer .... Deer Park, NY
Lustig, Howard S. .... Milwaukee, WI
Lustig, Icove & Lustig Co., L.P.A.
Cleveland, OH
Lustig, Jacqueline Stanley .... Chicago, IL
Lustig, Jason P. .... Los Angeles, CA
Lustig, Jordan R. .... Bridgeport, CT
Lustig, Kevin B. .... Boston, MA
Lustig, Leonard .... Deer Park, NY
Lustig, Lyn M. .... Boston, MA
Lustig, Mary Nell .... Pittsburgh, PA
Lustig, Michelle D. .... Irvine, CA
Lustig, Mitchell S. .... New York, NY
Lustig, Norman I. .... Walnut Creek, CA
Lustig, Patrick Foran .... Chicago, IL
Lustig, Raymond J., Jr. .... New York, NY
Lustig, Richard M., P.C. .... Birmingham, MI
Lustig, Robert M. .... Cleveland, OH
Lustig, Ronald A. .... Birmingham, MI
Lustig, Ronald E. .... Newton, MA
Lustig, Roy R. .... Miami, FL
Lustig, Roy R., P.A. .... Miami, FL
Lustig, SharynL. .... New York, NY
Lustig, Sheldon H. .... Utica, NY
Lustig, Sheldon M. .... Skokie, IL
Lustig, Stanley H. .... North Palm Beach, FL
Lustig, Steven D. .... Washington, DC
Lustig, Steven D. .... Northbrook, IL
Lustig, Steven G. .... Phoenix, AZ
Lustig, Theodore D. .... Boston, MA
Lustig, Theodore S. .... Dallas, TX
Lustig, Thomas D. .... Boulder, CO
Lustiger, Richard .... Phoenix, AZ
Lustigman, Andrew B. .... New York, NY
Lustigman Firm, The, P.C. .... New York, NY
Lustigman, Sheldon S. .... New York, NY
Lustman, Jeffrey P. .... Los Angeles, CA
Lustman, Ronda C. .... New York, NY
Lustri, Philip R. .... Modesto, CA
Lustrin, Deborah Lynn .... Mineola, NY
Lustrin, Robert E. .... New York, NY
Lusty, Kirk C. .... Department of Justice, Tax Division, GV
Luszcz, Chester A. .... Deptford, NJ
Lutch, Brian P. .... Newton, MA
Lutche, Stephen W. .... Bel Air, MD
Lutche, Wayne L. .... Towson, MD
Lutcher, Gregory L. .... Walla Walla, WA
Lutcher & Phillips .... Walla Walla, WA
Lute, Mel L., Jr. .... Canton, OH
Luten, Claire K. .... Clearwater, FL
Luten, Drew W., III
Agency for International Development, Office of the General Counsel, GV
Luten, Melanie .... Atlanta, GA

Luten, Susan Burnett, Law Offices of Berkeley, CA
Luter, Edward R. ....Dallas, TX
Luter, George S. ....Jackson, MS
Luterman, Harvey S. ....Philadelphia, PA
Lutes, Barbara H. ....Denver, CO
Lutes, Billy G. ....Colfax, LA
Lutes, Brian A. ....Plymouth, MN
Lutes, Dennis L. ....Dallas, TX
Lutes, Edmund M., Jr. ....Tujunga, CA
Lutes, Mark E. ....Washington, DC
Lutes, Pamela D. ....Land O'Lakes, FL
Lutes, Scott A. ....Providence, RI
Lutey, Selmer D. ....Prescott, AZ
Lutfy, James L. ....Staten Island, NY
Lutfy, Leland E. ....Las Vegas, NV
Lutgen, Douglas A. ....San Francisco, CA
Lutgens, Christine ....Chicago, IL
Lutgring, Judy Ann ....Tucson, AZ
Luth, Nancy J. ....Great Falls, MT
Luth, Thomas E. ....Celina, OH
Luthens, August H. ....Colfax, IA
West Des Moines, IA
Luthens, Erik A. ....Colfax, IA
West Des Moines, IA
Luthens Law Offices, P.C. ....Colfax, IA
West Des Moines, IA
Luther, Albert F. ....Utica, MI
Luther, Anderson, PLLP
Chattanooga, TN
Luther & Associates, A Professional Corporation ....St. Louis, MO
Luther, Cara J. ....Washington, DC
Luther, Charles M., Jr. ....Florence, SC
Luther, Daniel W. ....Chicago, IL
Luther, David G., Jr. ....Dallas, TX
Luther, Debora G. ....Sacramento, CA
Luther, Debra K. ....St. Paul, MN
Luther, E. Eugene ....Annandale, VA
Luther, Florence J. ....Fair Oaks, CA
Luther, Frederick C. ....Waverly, NY
Luther, Gregg W. ....Edmond, OK
Luther, Heckt & Cameron ....Minnetonka, MN
Luther, Henry N., III ....Morristown, NJ
Luther, James ....Menlo Park, CA
Luther, James D. ....Nashville, TN
Luther, Jay W. ....San Anselmo, CA
Luther, Jeffrey L. ....Mobile, AL
Luther, John E., II ....Memphis, MO
Luther, John Kelly ....Pontotoc, MS
Luther, Kelly Anne ....Miami, FL
Luther, Kevin J. ....Rockford, IL
Luther, Kim Roger ....St. Louis, MO
Luther, Kurt Albert ....Washington, DC
Luther, Lance S. ....Albany, NY
Luther & Luther, A Professional Corporation
Fair Oaks, CA
Luther, Mark D., P.A. ....Minneapolis, MN
Luther, Max J., III ....Corpus Christi, TX
Luther, Max J., III & Associates, P.C.
Corpus Christi, TX
Luther, Michael M. ....Parsippany, NJ
Luther, Oldenburg & Rainey, P.C.
Mobile, AL
Luther, Paul T. ....Washington, DC
Luther, Raymond P. ....Newark, OH
Luther, Richard A. ....Columbus, OH
Luther, Richard F. ....San Diego, CA
Luther, Richard K. ....Minneapolis, MN
Luther, Richard L. ....Minnetonka, MN
Luther, Robert S. ....San Jose, CA
Luther, Shawn ....New York, NY
Luther, Susan M. ....Chicago, IL
Luther, Teresa K. ....Grand Island, NE
Luther, Wade Paul ....Fairfax, VA
Luther, William B. ....Chattanooga, TN
Luther, William D. ....Austin, TX
Luther, William P. ....Stillwater, MN
Luther-Veno, Linda S. ....Allentown, PA
Luthey, Graydon D. ....Tulsa, OK
Luthey, Graydon D., Jr. ....Tulsa, OK
Luthey, Lynn A. ....Department of Commerce, Patent and Trademark Office, GV
Luthi, Eric ....Los Angeles, CA
Monrovia, CA
Orange, CA
Luthi, Gary & Appel, A Professional Corporation ....Los Angeles, CA
Monrovia, CA
Orange, CA
Luthi, Jeffery N. ....
United States Court Of Veterans Appeals, GV
Luthin, Bonnie Claire ....Jacksonville, FL
Luthin, Henry C. ....Boston, MA
Luthin, Ruthann ....Phoenix, AZ
Luthman, David A. ....Cherry Hill, NJ
Luthra, Susan W. ....Greenwood, IN
Luthringshausen, Jacqueline R. ....Chicago, IL
Lutich, Lanette L. ....Dallas, TX
Lutin, Lewis G. ....Burlington, MA
Lutins, Harvey S., & Associates
Roanoke, VA
Lutje, Gregory G. ....Portland, OR
Lutjen, George W. ....Cleveland, OH
Lutjen, Laura J. ....Stamford, CT
Lutkenhaus, Gerald G. ....Petersburg, VA
Lutkenhaus, Gerald G. ....Richmond, VA
Lutkewitte, Thomas J. ....New Orleans, LA
Lutkus, Gerald F. ....South Bend, IN
Lutkus, Theodore A. ....Towson, MD
Lutner, Rachel E. ....Chicago, IL
Lutnick, Edith ....New York, NY
Lutnick, Jerome I. ....New York, NY
Lutnick & Swomley ....New York, NY
Lutnicki, V. A. ....Lincoln, MA
Luton, Evelyn Pollard ....Milledgeville, GA
Luton, James P. ....Marion, OH
Luton, Jesse P., Jr. ....Houston, TX
Luton, John D. ....Muskogee, OK
Luton, Richd. R. ....Houston, TX
Luton, S. Scott ....Carthage, MO
Lutrey, David M. ....Lake Forest, IL
Lutringer, Richard E. ....New York, NY
Lutsch, Keith ....Houston, TX
Lutseck, John P. ....Vienna, OH
Lutsep, Marja I. ....New York, NY
Lutsk, Bruce M. ....Hartford, CT
Lutsky, Jeffrey A. ....Philadelphia, PA
Lutt, Karen Kaplen ....New York, NY
Lutt, Steven M. ....New York, NY
Luttati, Carol M. ....New York, NY
Luttenauer, Dennis ....Kane, PA
Luttenegger, Jerry F. ....Cincinnati, OH
Lutter, Barbara Saunders ....St. Paul, MN
Lutter, Charles W., Jr. ....San Antonio, TX
Lutter, Paul A. ....Chicago, IL
Lutter, Rudolph V., Jr. ....Washington, DC
Lutteral, Margarita N. ....New York, NY
Lutterbeck, Ann G. ....Chicago, IL
Lutterbie, Lucy C. ....Fredericksburg, VA
Lutterman, Brian P. ....Minneapolis, MN
Lutterman, M. Alison ....Circle Pines, MN
Lutterman, Neal C. ....Stockton, CA
Luttier, Mark T. ....North Palm Beach, FL
Luttig, J. Michael ....Alexandria, VA
Luttinger, David A. ....White Plains, NY
Luttinger, David A., Jr. ....New York, NY
Luttinger, Kenneth R. ....Pittsburgh, PA
Luttjohann, John R. ....Topeka, KS
Luttjohann, Larry L. ....Topeka, KS
Luttmann, Roy A. ....Detroit, MI
Lutton, Claude D., Jr. ....Ashland, NE
Lutton, David N. ....Ashland, NE
Lutton, Delos N. ....Milwaukee, WI
Lutton, Elizabeth L. ....Ann Arbor, MI
Lutton, Katherine Kelly ....Menlo Park, CA
Lutton Law Office ....Ashland, NE
Lutton, Richard J., Jr. ....Menlo Park, CA
Lutton-Shields, Pamela ....Tallahassee, FL
Luttrell, Jerry A. ....East Hanover, NJ
Luttrell, Jordan D. ....San Francisco, CA
Luttrell, Leslie M. ....San Antonio, TX
Luttrell, Robert T., III
Oklahoma City, OK
Luttrell, Robert T., III P.C.
Oklahoma City, OK
Luttrell, William H. ....Monarch Beach, CA
Luttrell, William J., III ....Media, PA
Luttrell, Willis W. ....Oklahoma City, OK
San Antonio, TX
Luttringer, Wayne ....San Francisco, CA
Luttrull, James D., Jr. ....Marion, IN
Luttrull, R. Scott ....Dallas, TX
Lutts, Terry L. ....Denver, CO
Lutty, Paul F., Jr. ....Pittsburgh, PA
Lutu, L. Suesue ....Pago Pago, TT
Lutwak, Elizabeth Ann ....Beverly, MA
Lutwin, Joel M. ....New York, NY
Luty, Robert L. ....Los Angeles, CA
Luty, Robert L., A Professional Corporation
Los Angeles, CA
Lutynski, Adam M. ....Dayton, OH
Lutz, Albert S., Jr. ....Greenwood, LA
Lutz, Alfred C. ....Macdoel, CA
Lutz, Amy S. ....Atlanta, GA
Lutz, Arlene Goldfus ....Trenton, NJ
Lutz and Berkowitz, P.C. ....Denver, CO
Lutz, Boster & Cornetet ....Cincinnati, OH
Lutz, Burnett, McDermott, Jahn & King, LLP
Chilton, WI
New Holstein, WI
Lutz, Carol Lombard ....Greenwich, CT
Lutz, Charles A. ....Cherry Hill, NJ
Lutz, Charles B., Jr. ....Oklahoma City, OK
Lutz, Cheryl R. ....Madison, WI
Lutz, Christopher J. ....Boston, MA
Lutz, Christopher T. ....Washington, DC
Lutz, Daniel R. ....Orrville, OH
Lutz, Dara A. ....Washington, DC
Lutz, David ....Federal Way, WA
Tacoma, WA
Lutz, David A. ....Minneapolis, MN
Lutz, David L. ....Harrisburg, PA
Lutz, David M. ....Fort Wayne, IN
Lutz, David N. ....Minneapolis, MN
Lutz; Dawn M. ....Denver, CO
Lutz, Dawn M., P.C. ....Denver, CO
Lutz, Dora L. ....Salem, OR
Lutz, Douglas J. ....New York, NY
Lutz, Douglas L. ....Cincinnati, OH
Lutz, E. Clark ....Kerrville, TX
Lutz, Edward C. ....Morristown, NJ
Lutz, Edward J. ....Tulsa, OK
Lutz, Elizabeth M. ....Baltimore, MD
Lutz, Francis J. ....New Brunswick, NJ
Lutz, Frederick B. ....Dayton, OH
Lutz, Frederick S. ....High Point, NC
Kernersville, NC
Lutz, G. Scott ....San Diego, CA
Lutz, George D. ....Lapeer, MI
Lutz, George M. ....Reading, PA
Lutz, Gregory ....Del Mar, CA
Lutz, H. Roger ....Sarasota, FL
Lutz, Hartwell B. ....Brownsboro, AL
Lutz, Henry Jay ....Pompano Beach, FL
Lutz, Herman W. ....Alexandria, VA
Lutz, Holley Thames ....Washington, DC
Lutz, Holly ....Wausau, WI
Lutz, Holly Nelson ....Glenmont, NY
Lutz, Hugh P., Jr. ....
Department of Housing and Urban Development, GV
Lutz, Jacob Andrew, III ....Richmond, VA
Lutz, James G. ....Cincinnati, OH
Lutz, James H. ....Newtown Square, PA
Lutz, James J. ....Kansas City, MO
Lutz, James N. ....Syracuse, NY
Lutz, Jay E. ....Denver, CO
Lutz, Jeffrey W. ....East Orange, NJ
Lutz, Jerome J. ....Roscoe, IL
Lutz, Joel A. ....Detroit, MI
Lutz, John E., Jr. ....Charleston, WV
Lutz, John F., II ....Wyomissing, PA
Lutz, John R. ....Goshen, IN
Lutz, John Shafroth ....Denver, CO
Lutz, John T. ....New York, NY
Lutz, Joseph ....Palo Alto, CA
Lutz, Julie K. ....Denver, CO
Lutz, Karl E., (P.C.) ....Chicago, IL
New York, NY
Lutz, Kerry H. ....Elmsford, NY
Lutz Law Offices, P.S. ....Federal Way, WA
Tacoma, WA
Lutz, Lawrence P. ....Butler, PA
Pittsburgh, PA
Lutz & Levow, A Professional Corporation
Cherry Hill, NJ
Lutz, Lonnie R. ....Greensboro, NC
Lutz, Lori Ann ....Detroit, MI
Lutz, Marguerite Cusack ....Morristown, NJ
Lutz, Mark E. ....Cincinnati, OH
Lutz, Martin T. ....Washington, DC
Lutz, Michael A. ....Madison, WI
Lutz, Michael F. ....Chicago, IL
Lutz, Milton F., II ....Jackson, MI
Lutz, Nancy H. ....Washington, DC
Lutz and Oxley ....Ashland, OH
Lutz, Paul G. ....Shrewsbury, PA
York, PA
Lutz, Paul V. ....Houston, TX
Lutz, Paulette B. Garcia ....Fremont, CA
Lutz, Pawk & McKay ....Butler, PA
Pittsburgh, PA
Lutz, Peter C., Jr. ....Rochester, NY
Lutz, R. Gerard ....Bellevue, WA
Lutz, Randall M. ....Towson, MD
Lutz, Richard B., Jr. ....Romeo, MI
Lutz, Richard J., Jr. ....East Hanover, NJ
Lutz, Richard M. ....Newtown Square, PA
Lutz, Richard R. ....New York, NY
Lutz, Robert B. ....St. Joseph, MI
Lutz, Robert Charles ....Glendale, CA
Lutz, Robert E., II ....Los Angeles, CA
Lutz, Robert Howard ....Shelby, NC
Lutz, Robert J. ....Rome, NY
Lutz, Robert W. ....Mount Olive, NJ
Lutz, Robert W. ....Chilton, WI
Lutz, Shafranski, Gorman and Mahoney, P.A. ....New Brunswick, NJ
Somerville, NJ
Lutz, Sharon Spencer ....Detroit, MI
Lutz, Sheldon M. ....Farmington Hills, MI
Lutz, Stanley B. ....New York, NY
Lutz, Thomas P. ....Pittsburgh, PA
Lutz, Timothy G. ....Overland Park, KS
Lutz, Timothy R. ....Hinckley, OH
Lutz, Victoria L. ....White Plains, NY
Lutz, Warren C. ....Washington, DC
Baltimore, MD
Rockville, MD
Lutz, Webb & Bobo, P.A. ....Sarasota, FL
Lutz, Webb, Bobo, Telfair, Lumpkin & Haskins, P.A. ....Tallahassee, FL
Lutz, William D. ....Philadelphia, PA
Lutz, William H. ....Muncie, IN
Lutz, William H., Jr. ....Palm City, FL
Lutz, William J. ....San Francisco, CA
Lutz, William L. ....Las Cruces, NM
Lutz, William M. ....Minneapolis, MN
Lutz, William R. ....Claremont, CA
Lutze, Peter C. ....Boise, ID
Lutzel, Richard J. ....Salisbury, NC
Lutzen, Helen E. ....Washington, DC
Lutzer, A. Scott ....Stony Brook, NY
Lutzke, Bernard J. ....Milwaukee, WI
Lutzker, Dov ....Los Angeles, CA
Lutzker, Elliot H. ....New York, NY
Lutzker, Gary S. ....Washington, DC
Lutzker, Joel E. ....New York, NY
Lutzker, Lori A. ....Burlingame, CA
Lutzker, Wendy A. ....Los Angeles, CA
Lutzky, Barry I. ....New York, NY
Lutzky, Jayson ....Bronx, NY
Lutzo, Christopher J. ....New York, NY
Luu, Thai ....San Jose, CA
Luukinen, Charles E., (P.C.) ....Salem, OR
Luu-Sanders, Nhi T. ....Portland, OR
Luvaas, Cobb, Richards & Fraser, P.C.
Eugene, OR
Luvaas, John L. ....Eugene, OR
Luvaas, John L., Jr. ....Chico, CA
Luvara, David F. ....Philadelphia, PA
Luvara, Joseph L. ....Pittsburgh, PA
Wheeling, WV
Luvera, Barnett, Brindley, Beninger & Cunningham, A Professional Service Corporation ....Mount Vernon, WA
Seattle, WA
Luvera, Paul N. ....Mount Vernon, WA
Seattle, WA
Luvisi, Michael A. ....Louisville, KY
Lux, Arthur E. ....Wilmington, NC
Lux, Brenda Joyce ....Hollywood, FL
Lux, Carl A. ....Los Angeles, CA
Lux & De Croce, P.C. ....Syracuse, NY
Lux, Donald A. ....Syracuse, NY
Lux, Donna Beck ....Wilmington, NC
Lux, Douglas Steven ....Miami, FL
Lux, Douglas Steven, P.A. ....Miami, FL
Lux, Frank J. ....Belmar, NJ
Lux, Frank J., PC ....Belmar, NJ
Lux, Jerry J. ....Shelbyville, IN
Lux, John D. ....Shelbyville, IN
Lux, Joseph R. ....Rapid City, SD
Lux & Lux ....Wilmington, NC
Lux & Lux, P.A. ....Shelbyville, IN
Lux, Marshall E., Jr. ....Lincoln, NE
Lux, Paul G. ....Norwalk, OH
Lux, Paul S. ....Newtown, CT
Lux, Robert R ....San Jose, CA
Lux, Sallie Conley ....Akron, OH
Lux, Stephen Stavrum ....San Diego, CA
Lux & Timmel ....Newtown, CT
Luxa, Mary Clare ....Des Moines, IA
Luxan & Murfitt ....Helena, MT
Luxemburg, Marc J. ....New York, NY
Luxemburger, Jeremiah ....Atlanta, GA
Luxen, Robert E. ....Dallas, TX
Luxenberg, Arthur ....New York, NY
Luxenberg, Darcy B. ....Tacoma, WA
Luxenberg, Dave J. ....Tacoma, WA
Luxenberg, Deborah ....Washington, DC
Luxenberg, Garbett, Kelly & Sapienza, P.C.
Ellwood City, PA
New Castle, PA
Luxenberg, Jerry S. ....Orlando, FL
Luxenberg, Johnson & Dickens, P.C.
Washington, DC
Luxenberg, Marvin A. ....Ellwood City, PA
New Castle, PA
Luxenberg, Scott J. ....Kendall Park, NJ
Luxenberg, Steven B. ....Deerfield, IL
Luxford, Steve N., The Law Office of, P.C.
Vienna, VA
Luxon, Ross R. ....Flint, MI
Luxon, Susan Dabney ....Richmond, KY
Luxon, Susan L. ....Toledo, OH
Luxon, Timothy P. ....Southfield, MI
Luxton, Jane C. ....Washington, DC
Luxton, John W. ....Richmond, VA
Luxton, Matthew S. ....Minneapolis, MN
Luyendyk, Charles W. ....Muskegon, MI
Luyendyk, Laura J. ....Grand Rapids, MI
Luymes, Jan L. ....New York, NY
Luymes, Keith A. ....Galva, IL
Luymes, Ted H. ....Pasadena, CA
Luyombya, Juni Mirembe ....Seattle, WA
Luyster, Julia ....West Palm Beach, FL
Luysterborghs, Robert E. ....Milford, CT
Luyt, Gregory M. ....Pittsburgh, PA
Luyties, William K. ....Houston, TX
Luz, Lydia J. ....Waltham, MA
Luz, Matthew A. ....Natick, MA
Luz, Thomas J. ....New York, NY
Luzader, B. Gilbert ....Okanogan, WA
Luzaich, Stevan N. ....Millbrae, CA
Luzarraga, Alberto, Jr. ....New York, NY
Luzarraga, Jose M. ....Dallas, TX
Luzarraga, Maria Teresa ....New York, NY
Luzbetak & Caneva ....Lockport, IL
Luzbetak, Stephen B. ....Lockport, IL
Luzecky, Gregory ....St. Louis, MO
Luzecky, Harriet L. ....Springfield, MO
Luzecky, James A. ....St. Louis, MO
Luzier, William D., Jr. ....Boston, MA
Luzietti, Maria Luisa ....Miami, FL
Luzietti-Myers, Debra L. ....Washington, DC
Luzim, Ronald A. ....Coral Springs, FL
Luzim, Ronald A., P.A. ....Coral Springs, FL
Luzio, Leon R. ....Loudon, TN
Luzio, Thomas G. ....Kew Gardens, NY
Luzmore, Loren Agert Krause
New York, NY
Luzon, David J. ....Buffalo, NY
Luzuriaga, Elizabeth B. ....Charleston, SC
Luzynski, Terri Welch ....Charlottesville, VA
Luzzatto, Ernesto V. ....New York, NY
Luzzi, Gayle M. ....Bradford, PA
Luzzi, Margherita A. ....Litchfield, CT
Luzzi, Michael J. ....New Haven, CT
Luzzi, Richard T. ....Rockaway, NJ
Luzzie, Christine M. ....Iowa City, IA
Luzzie, Edward L. ....Chicago, IL
Luzzo, John T. ....Fort Lauderdale, FL
Lybarger, Barbara E. ....Lowell, MA
Lybarger, Bunin & Bunin ....Las Vegas, NV
Lybarger, Charles J. ....Las Vegas, NV
Lybarger, Jerry ....St. Louis, MO
Lybarger, Leonard F. ....Cleveland, OH
Lybbert, David L. ....Kennewick, WA
Moses Lake, WA
Lybbert, David M. ....Riverside, CA
Lybbert, L. D. ....Waterloo, IA
Lybbert, Merlin R. ....Salt Lake City, UT
Lybbert, Ruth ....Salt Lake City, UT
Lybbert, Steven H. ....Salt Lake City, UT
Lybeck, Kevin L. ....Seattle, WA
Lybeck, Lory R., P.S. ....Portland, OR
Kirkland, WA
Lybeck, Mark R. ....Springfield, NJ
Lybeck, Susan C. ....Seattle, WA
Lybecker, Martin E. ....Washington, DC
Lybrand, A. Martin ....Los Angeles, CA
Lybrand, Anna R. ....Mill Valley, CA
Lybrand, Fred Ray ....Anniston, AL
Lybrand, J. Austin, IV ....Chapel Hill, NC
Lybrand, James B., Jr. ....Columbia, SC
Lybrand, Robert D. ....Dallas, TX
Lybrand & Schutza, P.C. ....Dallas, TX
Lybrook, Michael J. ....Chicago, IL
Lybrook, Robert E. ....Martinsville, IN
Lycan, D. Eric ....Lexington, KY
Lycan, David A. ....Wayne, WV
Lycette, John P., Jr. ....Seattle, WA
Lychak, John D. ....Macungie, PA
Lychuk, Paul S. ....Las Vegas, NV
Lycke, Lawrence E. ....Seattle, WA
Lyckman, John A. ....Carthage, MO
Lyczko, Catherine M. ....Chicago, IL
Lyda, Clark E. ....Austin, TX
Lyda, Kimberly A. ....Asheville, NC

Lyda, Kirk R. .... Austin, TX
Lyda, Madelaine P. .... Farmington Hills, MI
Lyda, T. H. .... Pittsburgh, PA
Lyddan, Jeffrey D. .... Torrance, CA
Lyddane, John L. A. .... New York, NY
Lyddane, William E. .... Reston, VA
Lyddon, Phillip S. .... Agoura Hills, CA
Lyddy, Raymond C. .... Bridgeport, CT
Lyddy, Zelotus .... Kendall, WI
Lyde, Dorsett Marc .... Chico, CA
Lyde, John R. .... Edinburg, TX
Lydecker, Judith Morgan .... Pacific Grove, CA
Lydell, Jon D. .... Fair Oaks, CA
Lydell, Mark J. .... Yuba City, CA
Lydell, Sherri D. .... New York, NY
Lyden, C. Norman .... Pittsburg, KS
Lyden, Christine C. .... Calabasas, CA
Lyden, Cyndi L. .... Denver, CO
Lyden, D. Michael .... Agoura Hills, CA
Lyden, Kevin T. .... Akron, OH
Lyden & Liebenthal, Ltd. .... Toledo, OH
Lyden, Patricia G. .... Toledo, OH
Lyden, Shawn M. .... Akron, OH
Lyden, Thomas J. .... Washington, DC
Lyden, Timothy J. .... McLean, VA
Lyden, William J. .... Fairfax, VA
Lyder, Jane M. .... Department Of The Interior, Office of Legislation, GV
Lyderson, Donald J. .... Everett, WA
Lydick, Andy W. .... Dallas, TX
Lydick & Associates, P.C. .... Dallas, TX
Lydick, Howard L. .... Richardson, TX
Lydick, John A. .... Detroit, MI
Lydick, Richard K. .... Omaha, NE
Lydick, Robert W. .... Fort Worth, TX
Lydie, Pierre-Louis .... New York, NY
Lydiksen, Mary Jo Montgomery
Chicago, IL
Lyding, Christopher S. .... Philadelphia, PA
Lyding, Michael J. .... Phoenix, AZ
Lyding, Michael J., P.C. .... Phoenix, AZ
Lyding, Richard J. .... Walnut Creek, CA
Lydon & Brown, LLP .... Alexandria, VA
Lydon, Colin Kelly .... Harrisburg, PA
Lydon, Deborah R. .... Cincinnati, OH
Lydon, Gregory D. .... McLean, VA
Lydon, J. Joseph .... West Barnstable, MA
Lydon, James C. .... Alexandria, VA
Lydon, Janet M. .... Milton, MA
Lydon, John F. .... Norwood, MA
Lydon, John J. .... Chicago, IL
Lydon, John Patrick .... Pittsburgh, PA
Lydon, Leann M. .... Ramsey, NJ
Lydon, Maria-Liisa .... New York, NY
Lydon, Matthias A. .... Chicago, IL
Lydon, Maureen H. .... Chicago, IL
Lydon, Patricia .... Greenwich, CT
Lydon, Patrick D. .... Webster, NY
Lydon, Patrick J. .... Boston, MA
Lydon, Patrick M. .... Allentown, PA
Lydon, Robert F. .... St. Paul, MN
Lydon & Schubert, PC .... Pittsburgh, PA
Lydon, Thomas E. .... Columbia, SC
Lydon, Thomas J. .... United States Court of Federal Claims, GV
Lydon, Thomas P. .... Towson, MD
Lydy, R. Jeffrey .... Sylvania, OH
Lydy, R. Jeffrey .... Toledo, OH
Lyell, G. Garland, III .... Jackson, MS
Lyell, Jerry C. .... Arlington, VA
Lyell, John C., II .... Nashville, TN
Lyell, Louis J. .... Jackson, MS
Lyell, Seaman & Shelton .... Nashville, TN
Lyell, Sean A. .... Portland, OR
Lyerla, Bradford P. .... Chicago, IL
Lyerla, Ronald O. .... Redding, CA
Lyerly, Jonathan E. .... Birmingham, AL
Lyerly, Michele Fuller .... Greenville, SC
Lyerly, R. Alexander, II .... Newland, NC
Lyerly, Robert .... Melbourne, FL
Lyford, Brian R. .... Northfield, VT
Lyford, Daniel E. .... Concord, NH
Lyford, Debra K. .... Lincoln, NE
Lyford, F. Richard .... Des Moines, IA
Lyford, Gwendolyn H. .... Anchorage, AK
Lyford, Robert M. .... Little Rock, AR
Lyford, Scott .... Galveston, TX
Lyford, Stephanie Kristen .... Raleigh, NC
Lyga, Peter H. .... Thomaston, CT
Lygizos, John A. .... Detroit, MI
Lygizos, John A., P.C. .... Detroit, MI
Lygnos, Michael N. .... Mineola, NY
Lygo, James C. .... Portland, OR
Lygo & Peterson, LLP .... Portland, OR
Lyions, Michael L. .... Modesto, CA
Lyke, Jerome P. .... Champaign, IL
Lyke, Sarah R. .... Chicago, IL
Lyken, Leslie C. .... New York, NY
Lykes, Charles E., Jr. .... Clearwater, FL
Lykins, Charles W. .... Columbus, GA
Lykins, Clayton G., Jr. .... Vanceburg, KY
Lykins, Deana .... New York, NY
Lykins, Elizabeth Welch
Grand Rapids, MI
Lykins, Gary D. .... Dallas, TX
Lykins, Gerald R. .... Grand Rapids, MI
Lykins, Herbert C. .... Cincinnati, OH
Lykins, R. Daniel .... Topeka, KS
Lykins, Tally D. .... Columbus, IN
Lykkebak, Donald A. .... Orlando, FL
Lykken, Matthew A. .... Chicago, IL
Lykos, Angela .... Department of Commerce, Patent and Trademark Office, GV
Lykos, Cosmas N. .... Aliso Viejo, CA
Lykos, George J. .... West Haven, CT
Lykos, Nicholas J. .... Dallas, TX
Lykos, Patricia R. .... Houston, TX
Lykoudis, Anna Savvas .... Tampa, FL

Lykoudis & Associates .... Tampa, FL
Lykowski, Timothy S. .... Los Angeles, CA
Lyle, Carl B., II .... St. Petersburg, FL
Lyle, Charles A. .... St. Petersburg, FL
Lyle, Charles C., Jr. .... East Windsor, NJ
Lyle, David L., Jr. .... Charleston, SC
Lyle, Delbert S. .... Glen Ellyn, IL
Lyle, Dennis A. .... Toledo, OH
Lyle, E. Peck, Jr. .... Winter Park, FL
Lyle, Edward W. .... Washington, DC
Lyle, Elizabeth Evans
Federal Communications Commission, Wireless Telecommunications Bureau, GV
Lyle, Ellen Hobbs .... Nashville, TN
Lyle, Frank G. .... Denton, TX
Lyle, George .... Martinsville, VA
Lyle, George R. .... Anchorage, AK
Lyle, Hugh N. .... Lubbock, TX
Lyle, James M. .... Boston, MA
Lyle, James P. .... Albuquerque, NM
Lyle, James R. .... St. Petersburg, FL
Lyle, James R., Jr. .... St. Petersburg, FL
Lyle, Jeffrey Jon .... Hillsboro, OH
Lyle, John E. .... Houston, TX
Lyle, John F., III .... Birmingham, AL
Lyle, John Paul .... Colorado Springs, CO
Lyle, John W., Jr .... Cranston, RI
Lyle, Joseph B. .... Bristol, TN
Lyle, Joseph L., Jr. .... Virginia Beach, VA
Lyle, Margaret I. .... Dallas, TX
Lyle, Mary Frances .... Nashville, TN
Lyle, Michael J.
Executive Office Of The President, Office of Administration, GV
Chicago, IL
Lyle, Murphy, LLP .... Reno, NV
Lyle, Paul .... Plainview, TX
Lyle, Paul R. .... Fairbanks, AK
Lyle, Phillip E. .... Littleton, CO
Lyle, Richard R. .... High Point, NC
Lyle, Robert Edward .... Reno, NV
Lyle, Robert F. .... Naples, FL
Lyle, Robert F. .... Camden, NJ
Lyle, Robert L. .... Jackson, MS
Lyle, Roxana .... Ravenna, OH
Lyle, Sidney A. .... Odessa, TX
Lyle, Vernon J. .... Amissville, VA
Lyle, William F., Jr. .... Hutchinson, KS
Lyles & Associates .... Las Vegas, NV
Lyles, Darnail .... Gary, IN
Lyles, Darr & Clark .... Spartanburg, SC
Lyles, David L. .... Washington, DC
Lyles, Dennis E. .... Fort Lauderdale, FL
Tampa, FL
West Palm Beach, FL
Lyles, Don T. .... Thomasville, GA
Lyles, Donna Hayden .... Fayetteville, AR
Lyles, Eugene D. (Sonny), Jr.
College Station, TX
Lyles, Frank A. .... Spartanburg, SC
Lyles, G. Robert, III .... Gaithersburg, MD
Lyles, George R. .... Las Vegas, NV
Lyles, Harry A. .... Montgomery, AL
Lyles, Janet M. .... Beaufort, NC
Lyles, Jeanne M. .... Charleston, SC
Lyles, Joseph S. .... Greenville, SC
Lyles, Kevin D. .... Columbus, OH
Lyles, Lawrence F. .... Richardson, TX
Lyles, Marcy M. .... Houston, TX
Lyles, Robert T., Jr. .... Charleston, SC
Lyles, Ronald E. .... Hartford, CT
Lyles, Sharon F. .... Baton Rouge, LA
Lyles, Vincent P. .... Milwaukee, WI
Lyles, William C. .... Spartanburg, SC
Lyles, William G., III .... Charleston, SC
Lym, Gi Yoon .... Franklin Lakes, NJ
Lyman, Andrea Lee .... Atlanta, GA
Lyman & Ash .... Camden, NJ
Philadelphia, PA
Lyman, Beverly A. .... Cincinnati, OH
Lyman, Charles S. .... Manhattan, KS
Lyman, Charles W. .... Houston, TX
Lyman, Chester J. .... Des Moines, IA
Lyman, Chester T., Jr. .... Columbus, OH
Lyman, Christopher B. .... Atlanta, GA
Lyman, Christopher S. .... Wellesley Hills, MA
Lyman, Chuck S. .... Manhattan, KS
Lyman, Cletus P. .... Philadelphia, PA
Lyman, Cynthia Robison .... Chicago, IL
Lyman, Daniel F. .... Nashua, NH
Lyman, Daryl W. .... Salt Lake City, UT
Lyman, David K. .... Los Angeles, CA
Lyman, Edward H. .... Berkeley, CA
Lyman, Edwin F. .... Springfield, MA
Lyman, F. Frank .... Castleton-on-Hudson, NY
Lyman, Gary M. .... New York, NY
Lyman, Gregory G. .... Durango, CO
Lyman, Gregory R. .... Merrillville, IN
Lyman, Guy C., Jr., (P.C.)
New Orleans, LA
Lyman, Helen T. .... Portland, OR
Lyman, Herbert A. .... Beverly Hills, CA
Lyman, Jocelyn J. .... Olympia, WA
Lyman, John C. .... Redding, CA
Lyman, John V. .... Olympia, WA
Lyman, Jon J. .... New York, NY
Lyman, Joseph J. .... Washington, DC
Lyman, Kai W. .... Boston, MA
Lyman, Kenneth H. .... Denver, CO
Lyman, Kevin M. .... New York, NY
Lyman & Landy .... New York, NY
Lyman, Linda B. .... Boca Raton, FL
Lyman & Lyman .... Albion, NY
Columbus, OH
Lyman, Lynden .... Sudbury, MA
Lyman, Mark M. .... Chicago, IL
Lyman, Mary Ann .... Los Angeles, CA
Lyman, Mary S. .... Andover, MA

Lyman, Nathan M. .... Albion, NY
Lyman, Patricia Bast .... Virginia Beach, VA
Lyman, Paul D. .... Richfield, UT
Lyman, R. Jeffrey .... Boston, MA
Lyman, Richard W., Jr. .... Long Beach, CA
Lyman, Robert C. .... St. Paul, MN
Lyman, Robert G. .... Albany, NY
Lyman, Robert J. .... Oakland, CA
Lyman, Ronald E. .... Los Angeles, CA
Lyman, Stephen S. .... Exeter, RI
Lyman, Stephen W. .... Indianapolis, IN
Lyman, Susan J. .... Houston, TX
Lyman, Thomas J., III .... Chicago, IL
Lyman, Timothy R. .... Hartford, CT
Lyman, Walter J. .... Dallas, TX
Lyman, Webster S. .... Columbus, OH
Lyman, William D. .... Oak Brook, IL
Lyman-Askew, Brian .... Bridgeport, CT
Lymas-Johnson, Larry E.
Fort Lauderdale, FL
Lymberis, Nick S. .... San Jose, CA
Lymberis, Robin S. .... Charlotte, NC
Lymburn, Bruce .... Oakland, CA
Lymburner, John F. .... Redmond, WA
Lymn, Merry
Commodity Futures Trading Commission, Office of the General Counsel, GV
Lympus, Ted O. .... Kalispell, MT
Lyn, Denise A. .... Inverness, FL
Lyn, Kevin R. .... Raleigh, NC
Lyn, Kurt L. .... Houston, TX
Lynagh, John J. .... New York, NY
Lynam, James P. .... Shawnee, OK
Lynam, Joseph E. .... Seattle, WA
Lynam, Terence J. .... Washington, DC
Lynam, Terence V. .... Lansing, MI
Lynam, Terrance J. .... Princeton, NJ
Lynam, Thomas M. .... Arroyo Grande, CA
Lynam, William E. .... Roeland Park, KS
Lynam, William T. .... Stamford, CT
Lynas, Richard V. .... Dundalk, MD
Towson, MD
Lynaugh, Barbara .... Central Islip, NY
Lynaugh, Fitzgerald, Eiselein & Grubbs
Billings, MT
Lynaugh, John P. .... Springfield, IL
Lynaugh, Thomas J. .... Billings, MT
Lynaugh, Thomas P. .... Tenafly, NJ
Long Island City, NY
Lynberg, Charles A. .... Los Angeles, CA
Lynberg & Watkins, A Professional Corporation .... Los Angeles, CA
Santa Ana, CA
Lynch, Adrienne C. .... Massapequa Park, NY
Lynch, Alexander D. .... New York, NY
Lynch, Alice Vinson .... Treasury Department, GV
Lynch, Allen A., II .... Boston, MA
Lynch, Allison Ulin .... Chattanooga, TN
Lynch, Aloysius J. .... Lansing, MI
Lynch, Amy J. .... Paris, IL
Lynch, Andrea .... Syracuse, NY
Lynch, Andrew C. .... Washington, DC
Lynch, Andrew C. .... Antioch, IL
Lynch, Angenette M. .... Palo Alto, CA
Lynch, Anna E. .... Rochester, NY
Lynch, Anne Kennedy .... Cleveland, OH
Lynch, Anne Marie .... West Palm Beach, FL
Lynch, Anthony .... Marion, NC
Lynch, Arch E., Jr. .... Raleigh, NC
Lynch, Arnold B. .... Hopkinsville, KY
Lynch, Arthur J. .... New York, NY
Lynch & Associates, P.L.L.C. .... Boise, ID
Lynch, Barbara J. .... Chicago, IL
Lynch, Ben P. .... Winchester, TN
Lynch, Benjamin P., Jr. .... Norfolk, VA
Lynch, Blake, Law Offices of
Edwards, CO
Vail, CO
Lynch, Blake T. .... Chicago, IL
Lynch and Bloom, P.C. .... Eureka, IL
Pekin, IL
Peoria, IL
Lynch & Blum, P.C. .... Anchorage, AK
Lynch, Bob, Jr. .... Nashville, TN
Lynch, Brenda Clark .... Chagrin Falls, OH
Lynch, Brenda M. .... New York, NY
Lynch, Brendan .... Philadelphia, PA
Lynch, Brewer, Hoffman & Sands, LLP
Boston, MA
Lynch, Brian A. .... Great Neck, NY
Lynch, Brian D. .... Seattle, WA
Lynch, Brian J. .... Philadelphia, PA
Lynch, Brian P. .... Berwyn, PA
Lynch, Bryann .... Littleton, CO
Lynch & Buttery, P.C. .... Fairfax, VA
Lynch, Byron Lee .... Redding, CA
Lynch, Byron Lee, A Professional Law Corporation .... Redding, CA
Lynch, Carol M. .... Pensacola, FL
Lynch, Carol W. .... Los Angeles, CA
Lynch, Carole Sakowski .... Springfield, MA
Lynch, Carolyn J. .... Department of the Army, Office, Chief of Engineers/Headquarters, U.S. Army Corps of Engineers, GV
Lynch, Carter J., III .... Chattanooga, TN
Lynch, Carter J., Jr. .... Chattanooga, TN
Lynch, Catherine G. .... Atlanta, GA
Lynch, Chappell & Alsup, A Professional Corporation .... Midland, TX
Odessa, TX
Lynch, Charles A., III .... Springfield, MA
Lynch, Charles B. .... Trenton, NJ
Lynch, Charles D. .... Mansfield, OH
Lynch, Charles E. .... Nyack, NY
Lynch, Charles E., Jr. .... High Point, NC
Lynch, Charles H., Jr. .... Auburn, NY
Lynch, Charles S. .... Cleveland, OH

Lynch & Chisholm .... Great Falls, MT
Lynch, Christine D. .... Boston, MA
Lynch, Christopher J. .... Hartford, CT
Lynch, Christopher J. .... Miami, FL
Lynch, Christopher J. .... Niles, MI
Lynch, Christopher K. .... San Francisco, CA
Lynch, Christopher P. .... Ballston Spa, NY
Lynch, Cindy A. .... Redwood City, CA
Lynch, Colleen K. .... Pittsburgh, PA
Lynch, Con P. .... Salem, OR
Lynch, Constance L. .... Santa Barbara, CA
Lynch, Corrine D. .... Edina, MN
Lynch, Courtney M. .... San Francisco, CA
Lynch, Cox, Gilman & Mahan, P.S.C.
Jeffersonville, IN
Louisville, KY
Lynch, Craig M. .... Bakersfield, CA
San Fernando, CA
Lynch, Craig T. .... Charlotte, NC
Lynch, Dallas, Smith & Harman, P.C.
Cedar Rapids, IA
Lynch, Dana O. .... Baltimore, MD
Lynch, Daniel .... Chicago, IL
Lynch, Daniel C. .... Denver, CO
Lynch, Daniel E. .... West Hartford, CT
Lynch, Daniel E. .... Richmond, VA
Lynch, Daniel F. .... Denver, CO
Lynch, Daniel F. .... New York, NY
Lynch, Daniel F., III
Upper Marlboro, MD
Lynch, Daniel J. .... Dover, NH
Lynch, Daniel P. .... Philadelphia, PA
Lynch, Daniel P. .... Pittsburgh, PA
Lynch, Darlene C. .... Chestnut Hill, MA
Lynch, David B. .... San Francisco, CA
Lynch, David G. .... Chicago, IL
Lynch, David J. .... Des Moines, IA
Lynch, David Justin .... Santa Ana, CA
Lynch, David M. .... Peoria, IL
Lynch, David Marlborough .... Euclid, OH
Lynch, David O. .... Washington, CT
Lynch, David R. .... Glastonbury, CT
Lynch, David R., & Associates, LLC, Law Offices .... Glastonbury, CT
Lynch, David S. .... Houston, TX
Lynch, David W. .... Minneapolis, MN
Lynch, David W. .... Burlington, VT
Lynch, Dean .... Paramus, NJ
Lynch, Deborah Graham Longstaff
Seattle, WA
Lynch, Debra McVicker .... Indianapolis, IN
Lynch, Denise .... San Francisco, CA
Lynch, Dennis E. A. .... Nyack, NY
Lynch, Dennis M. .... Dallas, TX
Lynch, Dennis M., Law Offices of
Visalia, CA
Lynch, Dennis P. .... Blue Bell, PA
Lynch, Dennis R. .... Burlington, WI
Salem, WI
Lynch, DeSimone & Nylen, LLP
Boston, MA
Lynch, Diana .... Atlanta, GA
Lynch, Donald F., III .... Richmond, VA
Lynch, Donald J. .... Marlborough, MA
Lynch, Donald L. .... Albany, NY
Lynch, Donald W. .... Carlsbad, CA
Lynch, Donna J. .... Rancho Santa Fe, CA
Lynch, Donna S. McLamb .... Raleigh, NC
Lynch, Eatman & Twiddy, L.L.P.
Raleigh, NC
Lynch, Edward .... Hastings, MN
Lynch, Edward J. .... Palo Alto, CA
Lynch, Edward J. .... Union City, NJ
Lynch, Edward J. .... Cincinnati, OH
Lynch, Edward J. .... Dallas, TX
Lynch, Edward N. .... Traverse City, MI
Lynch, Edward P. .... Morristown, NJ
Lynch, Edward T., Jr. .... New Britain, CT
Lynch & Edwards, P.C. .... Burlington, VT
Lynch, Eleanor M. .... Maynard, MA
Lynch, Elizabeth B. .... New York, NY
Lynch, Elizabeth L. .... Pittsburgh, PA
Lynch, Ellen B. .... Rockford, IL
Lynch, Eric E. .... Chicago, IL
Lynch, Eugene C. .... Randolph, NY
Lynch, Eugene F. .... Ross, CA
Lynch, Eve F. .... San Francisco, CA
Lynch, F. Blake .... Edwards, CO
Lynch, F. Edmund .... Wilmington, DE
Lynch, F. Kevin .... East Brunswick, NJ
Lynch, F. H., Jr. .... Kansas City, MO
Lynch & Fierro LLP .... Boston, MA
Lynch Firm, The .... Dallas, TX
Lynch, Frances M. .... New York, NY
Lynch, Francine D. .... Chicago, IL
Lynch, Francis C. .... Boston, MA
Lynch, Francis I. .... Las Vegas, NV
Lynch, Francis J. .... Chicago, IL
Lynch, Francis J. .... Springfield, IL
Lynch, Francis J., II .... Easton, MA
Lynch, Francis J., III, (P.C.) .... Easton, MA
Lynch, Francis M. .... Evergreen Park, IL
Lynch, Francis M. .... Boston, MA
Quincy, MA
Providence, RI
Lynch, Francis X. J. .... Palm Beach, FL
Lynch, Frank C. .... Winchester, TN
Lynch, Frank J., Jr. .... Fort Pierce, FL
Lynch, Franklin E. .... Colorado Springs, CO
Lynch, Fred P. .... Santa Barbara, CA
Lynch, Fredye Long .... Texarkana, TX
Lynch & Friel .... Warwick, RI
Lynch, G. Berk .... Cool Ridge, WV
Lynch, Gail M. .... Hampton, NH
Lynch, Gallagher, Lynch & Martineau, P.L.L.C. .... Cheboygan, MI
Lansing, MI
Mount Pleasant, MI

Lynch, Gary F. ... New Castle, PA
Lynch, Gary F., P.C. ... New Castle, PA
Lynch, Gary G. ... New York, NY
Lynch, Gary W. ... Bolivar, MO
Lynch, Geoffrey P. ... Milford, NH
Lynch, George F. ... Washington, DC
Lynch, George F. ... Cleveland, OH
Lynch, George J. ... Chicago, IL
Lynch, George M. ... Latrobe, PA
Lynch, George P. ... Lisle, IL
Lynch, Gerald Lawrence ... Albany, NY
Lynch, Gerald M., Jr. ... New York, NY
Lynch, Gerard E. ... New York, NY
Lynch, Gilardi & Grummer, A Professional Corporation ... San Francisco, CA
Lynch & Greenfield ... Narragansett, RI
Providence, RI
Lynch, Greenleaf and Michael, L.L.P.
Iowa City, IA
Lynch, Gregory G. ... Los Angeles, CA
Lynch, Gregory J. ... Madison, WI
Lynch, Gregory P. ... Fairfield, CT
Lynch, Gregory P. ... Bend, OR
Lynch, H. Keith ... Houston, TX
Lynch, H. Michael ... New York, NY
Lynch, H. Robertson ... Louisville, KY
Lynch, Hanna & Boyd, PLLC
Amarillo, TX
Lynch, Harold J. ... Bronx, NY
Lynch, Helen M. ... Pittsburgh, PA
Lynch & Hensley ... Wenatchee, WA
Lynch, Herbert J. ... Boston, MA
Lynch, Humphrey J. ... Darlington, WI
Lynch Ichida Thompson & Kim, A Law Corporation ... Honolulu, HI
Lynch, J. Albert ... Pelham, NH
Lynch, J. Christopher ... Coeur d'Alene, ID
Spokane, WA
Lynch, J. Christopher ... Raleigh, NC
Lynch, J. David ... Fort Lauderdale, FL
Lynch, J. Gregory ... New York, NY
Lynch, J. Kenneth ... San Francisco, CA
Lynch, J. Richard ... Skaneateles, NY
Lynch, J. Robert ... Lowville, NY
Lynch, J. Ronald ... Fairfax, VA
Lynch, J. Shannon ... Hartford, CT
Lynch, J. Timothy ... Greer, SC
Lynch, Jacob R. ... Greenwich, CT
Lynch, James A., Jr. ... New York, NY
Lynch, James Asher ... Havertown, PA
Lynch, James Asher, III ... Havertown, PA
Lynch, James B. ... Boise, ID
Lynch, James B. ... Minneapolis, MN
Lynch, James B. ... Tacoma, WA
Lynch, James B., Jr. ... Cambridge, MA
Lynch, James C. ... Lakeview, OR
Lynch, James C. ... Wenatchee, WA
Lynch, James D. ... Mineola, NY
Lynch, James D., Jr. ... Sacramento, CA
Lynch, James F., Jr. ... Bronx, NY
Lynch, James G. ... Bangor, ME
Lynch, James J. ... Tampa, FL
Lynch, James J. ... Williston Park, NY
Lynch, James J. D., Jr. ... Philadelphia, PA
Lynch, James K. ... San Francisco, CA
Lynch, James M. ... Washington, DC
Lynch, James M ... Chicago, IL
Lynch, James M. ... Hingham, MA
Lynch, James M. ... St. Paul, MN
Lynch, James P., Jr. ... Boston, MA
Lynch, James R. ... Long Beach, CA
Lynch, James R. ... Jersey City, NJ
New York, NY
Lynch, James R., Jr. ... Norristown, PA
Lynch, James S. ... Ridgewood, NJ
Greenwood Lake, NY
Lynch, James W. ... Mineola, NY
Lynch, Jamison E. ... Chicago, IL
Lynch, Jason Craig ... Amarillo, TX
Lynch, Jeanine Maietta ... Trumbull, CT
Lynch, Jeanne B. ... Fairfax, VA
Lynch, Jeff E. ... Oklahoma City, OK
Lynch, Jeff R. ... Great Falls, MT
Lynch, Jeffery M. ... New Orleans, LA
Lynch, Jeffrey D. ... Bridgeport, CT
Lynch, Jeffrey D. ... Mount Pleasant, MI
Lynch, Jeffrey R. ... Pittsfield, MA
Lynch, Jeffrey S., P.C. ... Dallas, TX
Lynch, Jennifer L. ... San Diego, CA
Lynch, Jennifer M. ... Washington, DC
Lynch, Jennifer R. ... High Point, NC
Lynch, Jeremiah ... Boston, MA
Lynch, Jeremiah C., III ... Newport, RI
Lynch, Jeremiah J. ... Foster City, CA
Lynch, Jeri Dye ... Los Angeles, CA
Lynch, Jerome B. ... Media, PA
Lynch, Jerome E. ... La Crosse, WI
Lynch, Jerrold T. ... Grand Junction, CO
Lynch, Jessica L. ... Pittsburgh, PA
Lynch, Joann L. ... Florham Park, NJ
Lynch, Joanne ... Louisville, KY
Lynch, John A. ... North Brunswick, NJ
Lynch, John B. ... Media, PA
Lynch, John B., Jr. ... Hartford, CT
Lynch, John C. ... Washington, DC
Lynch, John C. ... Arlington, VA
Lynch, John C. ... Virginia Beach, VA
Lynch, John D. ... Union City, NJ
Lynch, John D. ... Warwick, RI
Lynch, John D., Jr. ... Warwick, RI
Lynch, John David ... Cincinnati, OH
Lynch, John E. ... New York, NY
Lynch, John E. ... Houston, TX
Lynch, John E., Jr. ... Omaha, NE
Lynch, John E., Jr. ... Houston, TX
Lynch, John F. ... Menlo Park, CA
Lynch, John F. ... Great Falls, MT
Lynch, John F. ... New York, NY
Lynch, John F., Jr. ... Newark, NJ
Lynch, John H. ... Brooklyn, NY
Lynch, John H. ... Durham, NC
Lynch, John J. ... Los Angeles, CA
Lynch, John J. ... Chicago, IL
Lynch, John J. ... Chicago, IL
Lynch, John J. ... Damariscotta, ME
Lynch, John J. ... Dennis Port, MA
Lynch, John J. ... Mount Pleasant, MI
Lynch, John J. ... Albany, NY
Lynch, John J. ... Kingston, NY
Lynch, John J. ... New York, NY
Lynch, John J. ... New York, NY
Lynch, John J., III ... Birmingham, MI
Lynch, John J., Jr. ... Kirkwood, MO
Lynch, John J., Jr. ... Youngstown, OH
Lynch, John Kennedy ... Cleveland, OH
Lynch, John Larkin ... Macon, GA
Lynch, John M. ... Department of Justice, Antitrust Division, GV
Lynch, John M. ... Boston, MA
Lynch, John P. ... San Francisco, CA
Lynch, John P. ... Chicago, IL
Lynch, John P. ... Greenbelt, MD
Lynch, John P. ... Binghamton, NY
Lynch, John P., Jr. ... Chicago, IL
Lynch, John R. ... Mineola, NY
Lynch, John R. ... Alexandria, VA
Lynch, John S. ... Bartow, FL
Lynch, John T. ... Riverdale, IL
Lynch, John T. ... Boston, MA
Lynch, John T. ... Martinsville, NJ
Lynch, John T. ... Greenfield, WI
Lynch, John T., IV ... Bedford, TX
Lynch, John T., Jr. ... Department of Justice, Criminal Division, GV
Lynch, Joseph B. ... Northfield, IL
Lynch, Joseph C.
Federal Energy Regulatory Commission, Office of the General Counsel, GV
Lynch, Joseph E. ... Washington, DC
Lynch, Joseph E. ... Auburn, NY
Lynch, Joseph E., Jr. ... Algona, IA
Lynch, Joseph G. ... Hartford, CT
Lynch, Joseph M. ... Princeton, NJ
Lynch, Joseph M., Jr. ... Canal Fulton, OH
Lynch, Joseph P. ... Norristown, PA
Lynch, Julia Kelleher ... Chicago, IL
Lynch, Karen E. ... Dallas, TX
Lynch, Karen L. ... Fresno, CA
Lynch, Karen L. ... New York, NY
Lynch, Karen M. ... Springfield, IL
Lynch, Karen M. ... Warwick, RI
Lynch, Karen Renzulli ... West Hartford, CT
Lynch, Katherine M. ... Boise, ID
Lynch, Kathleen ... Maple Shade, NJ
Lynch, Kathleen A. ... Bronx, NY
Lynch, Kathleen Ann ... Sacramento, CA
Lynch, Kathleen J. ... Boston, MA
Lynch, Kathleen M. ... Kansas City, KS
Lynch, Kathleen Mary ... McLean, VA
Lynch, Kelly Ann ... Newark, NJ
Lynch, Kelly M. ... Los Angeles, CA
Lynch, Kenneth J. ... Bethesda, MD
Lynch, Kenneth P. ... Syracuse, NY
Lynch, Kevin ... Mansfield, MA
Lynch, Kevin Brian ... New York, NY
Lynch, Kevin G. ... San Fernando, CA
Lynch, Kevin J. ... Glenview, IL
Lynch, Kevin J. ... Westwood, NJ
Lynch, Kevin W. ... Westmont, NJ
Lynch, Kim R. ... Rochelle Park, NJ
Lynch, Kimberle A. ... Los Angeles, CA
Lynch, Kimberley A. Martin ... Telluride, CO
Lynch, Kula Hoty ... Cleveland, OH
Lynch, Larry Persons ... Forsyth, GA
Monticello, GA
Lynch Law Firm, P.C. ... Atlanta, GA
Lynch Law Office ... Decorah, IA
Lynch Law Offices ... West Hartford, CT
Lynch Law Offices ... Olympia, WA
Lynch, Lawrence L. ... Iowa City, IA
Lynch, Lawrence T. ... Milwaukee, WI
Lynch, Leslie ... Oklahoma City, OK
Lynch, Leslie A. Evans ... Remsenburg, NY
Lynch, Leslie K. ... Tucson, AZ
Lynch, Leslie O. ... Corpus Christi, TX
Lynch, Linda J. ... San Francisco, CA
Lynch, Linda L. ... Knoxville, TN
Lynch, Loretta E. ... Garden City, NY
Lynch, Lucile Hooton ... Philadelphia, PA
Lynch, Luke ... New Brunswick, NJ
Lynch, Luke D., Jr. ... New York, NY
Lynch and Lynch ... Bakersfield, CA
San Fernando, CA
Lynch & Lynch ... Algona, IA
Lynch and Lynch ... Ridgewood, NJ
Greenwood Lake, NY
Lynch & Lynch ... Mineola, NY
Lynch and Lynch ... Pittsburgh, PA
Lynch & Lynch, A Professional Corporation
Easton, MA
Lynch & Lynch, Co., L.P.A. ... Auburn, OH
Bainbridge, OH
Cleveland, OH
Solon, OH
Lynch & Lynch, L.L.C. ... Telluride, CO
Lynch, Lynch & Lynch ... Winchester, TN
Lynch, Lynch, Martelon, Trembicki and Boynton ... Milford, CT
Westport, CT
Lynch, M. Joey ... Los Angeles, CA
Lynch, M. Kristine ... Newark, NJ
Lynch, M. Teri ... Akron, OH
Lynch, Maliza J.A. ... Newark, NJ
Lynch, Mann, Smith & Bibb
Beckley, WV
Lynch, Marcia Ann ... Wichita, KS
Lynch, Margaret A. ... Birmingham, MI
Lynch, Margaret Comard ... Albany, NY
Lynch, Margaret M. ... Providence, RI
Lynch, Maria M. ... Raleigh, NC
Lynch, Marianne P. ... Abington, PA
Lynch, Marilyn T. ... Washington, DC
Lynch, Marjorie K. ... Wilson, NC
Lynch, Mark ... Philadelphia, PA
Lynch, Mark A. ... Kansas City, MO
Lynch, Mark H. ... Washington, DC
Lynch, Mark P. ... Los Angeles, CA
Lynch, Mark S. ... Greenbelt, MD
Waldorf, MD
Lynch, Mark W. ... Madison, NJ
Lynch, Mark X. ... Massapequa Park, NY
Lynch, Martin Jeremy ... Albany, GA
Lynch, Martin, Kane, Kuper, Keefe & Bartels, LLC ... East Brunswick, NJ
New Brunswick, NJ
North Brunswick, NJ
South Brunswick, NJ
Trenton, NJ
Lynch, Mary A. ... Albany, NY
Lynch, Mary Ann ... Brunswick, ME
Wiscasset, ME
Lynch, Mary E. ... Costa Mesa, CA
Lynch, Matthew B. ... Pratt, KS
Lynch, Matthew H. ... Hartford, CT
Lynch, Matthew J. ... Upper Marlboro, MD
Lynch, Matthew J., Jr. ... Wilmington, DE
Lynch, Matthew Joseph DuMont
Cleveland, OH
Lynch, Matthew R. ... Boston, MA
Lynch, McKay, Moreland & Webber, P.C.
Ottumwa, IA
Lynch, Meek & Battitori
Baxter Springs, KS
Lynch, Meredith L. ... New York, NY
Lynch, Michael A. ... Davenport, IA
Lynch, Michael Brady
North Brunswick, NJ
Lynch, Michael C. ... Washington, DC
Lynch, Michael C. ... Amarillo, TX
Lynch, Michael D. ... Providence, RI
Lynch, Michael E. ... House of Representatives, Congressional Assistants, GV
Lynch, Michael F. ... New York, NY
Lynch, Michael F. ... Austin, TX
Lynch, Michael F. ... Dallas, TX
Lynch, Michael G. ... Boston, MA
Lynch, Michael J. ... Menlo Park, CA
Lynch, Michael J. ... Telluride, CO
Lynch, Michael J. ... Chicago, IL
Lynch, Michael J. ... Pittsburgh, PA
Lynch, Michael L. ... Boise, ID
Lynch, Michael P. ... Princeton, NJ
Lynch, Michael P. ... Cranston, RI
Westerly, RI
Lynch, Michael P. ... Olympia, WA
Lynch, Michael S. ... Bridgeport, CT
Lynch, Michael T. ... Detroit, MI
Lynch, Michael W. ... Yakima, WA
Lynch, Michele D. ... Department of Justice, Civil Division, GV
Lynch, Michele L. ... Irvine, CA
Lynch, Mike P. ... Winchester, TN
Lynch, Monica ... Sacramento, CA
Lynch, Myra Clark ... Albuquerque, NM
Lynch, N. Joseph, II ... Olympia, WA
Lynch, Nancy A. ... Austin, TX
Lynch, Nancy E.
Farm Credit Administration, GV
Lynch, Nancy E. ... New York, NY
Lynch, Nancy Kay ... Madison, WI
Lynch, Ned ... San Diego, CA
Lynch, Neil J. ... Butte, MT
Lynch, Niall E. ... San Francisco, CA
Lynch, Noreen A. ... Annapolis, MD
Lynch, Norman B. ... Jenkintown, PA
Lynch, Oliver Kent ... Baxter Springs, KS
Lynch, Owen B. ... Boston, MA
Lynch, P. Michael, III ... Atlanta, GA
Lynch, Pamela E. ... Boston, MA
Lynch, Patricia A. ... Boston, MA
Lynch, Patricia A. ... Reno, NV
Lynch, Patricia A. ... Toledo, OH
Lynch, Patricia Ann ... New Orleans, LA
Lynch, Patricia M. ... Oakland, CA
Lynch, Patrick ... Los Angeles, CA
Lynch, Patrick M. ... Omaha, NE
Lynch, Patrick W. ... Omaha, NE
Lynch, Patrick Winston ... Washington, DC
Lynch, Paul A. ... Honolulu, HI
Lihue, HI
Lynch, Paul A. ... Overland Park, KS
Lynch, Paul Dunn ... Evergreen Park, IL
Lynch, Paul F. ... Boston, MA
Wakefield, RI
Lynch, Paul F. ... Boston, MA
Lynch, Paul M. ... Marblehead, MA
Lynch, Paul M. ... Charleston, SC
Lynch, Paul R. ... Tampa, FL
Lynch, Paul R. ... Mount Vernon, IL
Lynch, Paul W. ... East Norwich, NY
Lynch, Peter A. ... San Diego, CA
Lynch, Peter A. ... Albany, NY
Lynch, Peter J.
Department of Transportation, Federal Aviation Administration, GV
Lynch, Peter J. ... Waldoboro, ME
Lynch, Peter M. ... Dahlonega, GA
Lynch, Peter O ... Redwood City, CA
Lynch, Peter T. ... Treasury Department, Office of Regulations and Rulings, GV
Lynch, Phillip M., Jr. ... Mandeville, LA
Lynch, Printz, Aldridge & Grammer, P.A.
Albuquerque, NM
Lynch, R. Jane ... Los Angeles, CA
Lynch, Ralph, Jr. ... Pittsburgh, PA
Lynch, Raymond F. ... San Francisco, CA
Lynch, Raymond J., Jr. ... Staten Island, NY
Lynch, Raymond M. ... Walnut Creek, CA
Lynch, Richard B. ... Des Moines, IA
Lynch, Richard C. ... Orinda, CA
Lynch, Richard J. ... Hartford, CT
Lynch, Richard P. ... Washington, DC
Lynch, Richard Standish ... Norwalk, OH
Lynch, Richard W. ... New Haven, CT
Lynch, Rick L. ... Bloomfield, IA
Lynch, Robert B. ... New York, NY
Lynch, Robert Berger ... Rancho Cordova, CA
Lynch, Robert E. ... Schenectady, NY
Lynch, Robert E., Jr. ... Washington, DC
Lynch, Robert E., Jr. ... Bethesda, MD
Lynch, Robert J. ... Irvine, CA
Lynch, Robert M. ... San Antonio, TX
Lynch, Robert P. ... Washington, DC
Lynch, Robert S. ... Phoenix, AZ
Lynch, Robert S. ... Bel Air, MD
Havre de Grace, MD
Lynch, Robert T. ... San Francisco, CA
Lynch, Robert T. ... Philadelphia, PA
Lynch, Robert Troll ... Cleveland, OH
Lynch, Robert W. ... New Haven, CT
Lynch, Robert W. ... Pennsauken, NJ
Lynch, Robin M. ... Boston, MA
Lynch, Robt. C. ... Studio City, CA
Lynch, Robt. J. ... Merrimack, NH
Lynch, Roger A. ... Shelburne Falls, MA
Lynch, Rona C. ... Waterbury, CT
Lynch Rowin, LLP ... Los Angeles, CA
Lynch Rowin LLP ... New York, NY
Lynch, Russell C. ... McLean, VA
Lynch, Ryan J. ... Algona, IA
Lynch, Sandra D. ... Hagåtña, GU
Lynch, Sandra L. ... Boston, MA
Lynch, Sarah F. ... Boston, MA
Lynch, Shawn R. ... Exton, PA
Quakertown, PA
Lynch, Sherian S. ... San Bernardino, CA
Lynch, Skip Edward ... Pascagoula, MS
Lynch, Spears & Shuman, LLC
Atlanta, GA
Decatur, GA
Lynch, Stephen A., III ... Miami, FL
Lynch, Stephen F. ... Colorado Springs, CO
Lynch, Stephen F. ... Boston, MA
Lynch, Stephen J. ... Huntington, NY
Lynch, Stephen M. ... Charlotte, NC
Lynch, Stephen Thomas
Department of Defense, GV
Lynch, Steven J. ... Pittsburgh, PA
Lynch, Steven R. ... Austin, TX
Lynch, Susan E. ... Ottumwa, IA
Lynch, Susan J. ... Chicago, IL
Lynch, Suzanne Harvey ... Denver, CO
Lynch, T. Stephen ... Columbia, SC
Lynch, Tamika D. ... Dallas, TX
Lynch, Tara E. ... Sacramento, CA
Lynch, Terence J. ... New York, NY
Lynch, Terence V. ... Seattle, WA
Lynch, Teresa Perkins ... Cincinnati, OH
Lynch, Terrance M. ... Farmington Hills, MI
Lynch, Terrance P. ... Detroit, MI
Lynch, Terri G. ... Simi Valley, CA
Lynch, Terri Morrill ... Charleston, SC
Lynch, Thomas A. ... Narragansett, RI
Providence, RI
Lynch, Thomas B. ... Milford, CT
Lynch, Thomas E. ... New York, NY
Lynch, Thomas E., III ... Frederick, MD
Lynch, Thomas G. ... Bloomfield, NJ
Lynch, Thomas H. ... Albany, NY
Lynch, Thomas J. ... Quincy, MA
Lynch, Thomas J. ... Southfield, MI
Lynch, Thomas J. ... New York, NY
Lynch, Thomas J. ... Syracuse, NY
Lynch, Thomas J., Jr. ... Uxbridge, MA
Lynch, Thomas J., P.C. ... Quincy, MA
Lynch, Thomas Lee ... Fort Collins, CO
Lynch, Thomas M. ... Chicago, IL
Lynch, Thomas M. ... Alexandria, VA
Lynch, Thomas M., IV ... Fort Lauderdale, FL
Lynch, Thomas P. ... Keene, CA
Lynch, Thomas P. ... Minneapolis, MN
Lynch, Thomas P. ... New York, NY
Lynch, Thomas S. ... Pittsburgh, PA
Lynch, Thomas W. ... Washington, DC
Lynch, Timothy C. ... Decorah, IA
Lynch, Timothy Cronin ... Baltimore, MD
Lynch, Timothy G. ... Washington, DC
Lynch, Timothy G. ... Boston, MA
Lynch, Timothy J. ... Washington, DC
Lynch, Timothy Jeremiah-Mahoney
San Francisco, CA
Lynch, Timothy M. ... Anchorage, AK
Lynch, Timothy M. ... Rochester, NY
Lynch, Timothy P. ... Hartford, CT
Lynch Tornetta & Mirabile ... Norristown, PA
Lynch & Toscano ... Mineola, NY
Lynch, Traub, Keefe and Errante
Hartford, CT
New Haven, CT
Lynch, Travis T. ... Memphis, TN
Lynch & Vandenberg ... Lakeview, OR
Lynch, Vernon S., III ... Baltimore, MD
Lynch, Victor K. ... Pittsburgh, PA
Lynch, Vincent B. ... Atlanta, GA
Lynch, Vincent J. ... New York, NY
Lynch, Vincent J. ... New York, NY
Lynch, W. Gerald ... Tacoma, WA
Lynch & Weigand ... Olympia, WA
Lynch & Wenzel, A Law Corporation
Santa Ana, CA
Lynch & White ... Norwalk, OH
Lynch, William A. ... Kansas City, MO

Lynch, William A. ... Omaha, NE
Lynch, William B. ... Jennings, LA
Lynch, William B., P.L.C. ... Jennings, LA
Lynch, William C. ... San Diego, CA
Lynch, William C. ... New Haven, CT
Lynch, William D. ... Austin, TX
Lynch, William F. ... Youngstown, NY
Lynch, William H. ... Olympia, WA
Lynch, William Isaac ... Indianapolis, IN
Lynch, William J. ... West Hartford, CT
Lynch, William J. ... Detroit, MI
Lynch, William J. ... Providence, RI
Lynch, William L. ... Seattle, WA
Lynch, William O. ... Bloomfield Hills, MI
Lynch, William O. J. ... Wilmington, NC
Lynch, William P., Jr. ... San Rafael, CA
Lynch, William R. ... Greenwich, CT
Lynch, Wm. Brennan ... Santa Barbara, CA
Lynchard, Percy L., Jr. ... Hernando, MS
Lynchard, R. Lane ... Destin, FL
Lyncheski, John E. ... Pittsburgh, PA
Lynchey, Kendall B. ... Chicago, IL
Lynch Jarrell, Mary B. ... Charlotte, NC
Lynd, Alice ... Youngstown, OH
Lynd, Craig R. ... Altamonte Springs, FL
Lynd, Deborah Titus ... Rochester, NY
Lynd, Edward J., III ... Rochester, NY
Lynd, Grant A. ... Westminster, CA
Lynd, Robert D. ... Baltimore, MD
Lynd, Staughton ... Youngstown, OH
Lyndaker, Keith A. ... Lowville, NY
Lyndall, Terri Mick ... Atlanta, GA
Lynde, Allen H. ... Honolulu, HI
Lynde, Lawrence K. ... Phoenix, AZ
Lynde, Pamela S. ... Thomasville, GA
Lyndon, John F. ... Athens, GA
Lyndon, T. Edward ... Chicago, IL
Lyndrup, Peggy B. ... Louisville, KY
Lyne, Daniel J. ... Boston, MA
Lyne, Emmett E. ... Boston, MA
Lyne, Eugene D. ... Memphis, TN
Lyne, James D. ... Vista, CA
Lyne, Robert C., Jr. ... Richmond, VA
Lyne & Van Dyke, LLP ... Vista, CA
Lyne, Woodworth & Evarts LLP
Boston, MA
Lynem, Catherine C. ... Ada, MI
Lynes, Jerome M. ... Roseland, NJ
Lynes, Steven C. ... San Jose, CA
Lynes, Timothy J. ... Washington, DC
Lynes, Wesley J. ... Birmingham, AL
Lynes, William H. ... Los Angeles, CA
Lyness, Janet M. ... Davenport, IA
Lyness, John Michael ... Salt Lake City, UT
Lyness, Nancy D. ... Red Bank, NJ
New York, NY
Lynett, Deborah D. ... Bloomfield Hills, MI
Lynett, George V. ... Scranton, PA
Lynett, John J. ... Akron, OH
Lynett, John J., Jr. ... Akron, OH
Lynett, Leo M., Jr. ... Buffalo, NY
Lynett, Michael J., (P.C.) ... Detroit, MI
Lynett, Thomas F. ... Akron, OH
Lynfield, H. Geoffrey ... Boca Raton, FL
Lynfield, Peter J. ... New York, NY
Lynford, Jeffrey H. ... New York, NY
Lyng, Catherine M. ... New York, NY
Lyng, R. Wm., III ... Kissimmee, FL
Lyng, Robert L. ... Hannibal, MO
Lyngklip, Ian B. ... Southfield, MI
Lyngklip, Ole W., III ... New York, NY
Lyngklip & Taub Consumer Law Group PLC
Southfield, MI
Lynham, John M., Jr. ... Washington, DC
Lynk, M. Jane ... Skokie, IL
Lynk, Myles V. ... Washington, DC
Lynn, Alan Hugh ... Markham, IL
Lynn, Andrew S. ... Los Angeles, CA
Lynn, Andrew S. ... New York, NY
Lynn, Andrew S. ... Memphis, TN
Lynn, Andrew W. ... Eden Prairie, MN
Lynn, Anita H. ... Atlanta, GA
Lynn, Anita H., P.C. ... Atlanta, GA
Lynn, Arthur D., Jr. ... Columbus, OH
Lynn, Barbara M. G. ... Dallas, TX
Lynn, Brian F. ... Providence, RI
Lynn, Bruce G. ... Columbus, OH
Lynn, Candice M. ... Seattle, WA
Lynn, Cecil A., III ... Los Angeles, CA
Lynn, Claude B. ... Evansville, IN
Lynn, Daniel A. ... Livingston, NJ
Lynn, Daniel E. ... Jackson, MS
Lynn, Darrell L. ... Eagan, MN
Lynn, David ... Los Angeles, CA
Lynn, David E. ... Washington, DC
Lynn, Deddo G. ... Lexington, KY
Lynn, Dick ... Oklahoma City, OK
Lynn, D. M. ... Dallas, TX
Lynn, Don A., (P.A.) ... Miami, FL
Lynn, Donald B. ... Oklahoma City, OK
Lynn, Donald B. ... Waco, TX
Lynn, Donald B., P.C. ... Waco, TX
Lynn, Donald E. ... Jamestown, NY
Lynn, Eleanor E. ... East Lansing, MI
Lynn, Eleanor M. ... Salem, MA
Lynn, Eleanor R. ... Santa Barbara, CA
Lynn, Elise Batsel ... Tampa, FL
Lynn, Elizabeth A. ... Long Beach, CA
Lynn, F. Randolph ... Tulsa, OK
Lynn, Fulkerson, Nichols and Kinkel, PLLC
Lexington, KY
Lynn, G. Dennis, Jr. ... St. Petersburg, FL
Lynn, Gary A. ... Park Ridge, IL
Lynn, George G. ... Birmingham, AL
Lynn, Giannina ... Washington, DC
Lynn, Gordon A. ... Hagerstown, MD
Lynn, H. Bailey, II
Occupational Safety and Health Review
Commission,
Office of the General Counsel, GV
Lynn, Harold S. ... Sherman Oaks, CA
Lynn, Horace N. ... Montgomery, AL
Lynn, Jack H., Law Office of ... Greenville, SC
Lynn, Jackson, Shultz & Lebrun, P.C.
Rapid City, SD
Sioux Falls, SD
Lynn, James A. ... Pittsburgh, PA
Lynn, James F. ... Philadelphia, PA
Lynn, James M. ... Columbus, OH
Lynn, James Murray ... Philadelphia, PA
Lynn, James P. ... New York, NY
Lynn, James T. ... Washington, DC
Lynn, James T., III ... Wilmington, DE
Lynn, James T., Jr. ... Dayton, OH
Lynn, Jann M. ... Costa Mesa, CA
Lynn, Jeffrey C. ... Los Angeles, CA
Lynn, Jeffrey Scott ... Irving, TX
Lynn, Jennifer R. ... St. Louis, MO
Lynn, Jennifer S. R. ... Burlington, MA
Lynn, Jesse A. ... New York, NY
Lynn, Jessica R. ... New York, NY
Lynn, John ... New York, NY
Lynn, John C. ... Boise, ID
Lynn, John D. ... St. Louis, MO
Lynn, John D. ... Palmyra, NY
Lynn, John H. ... Costa Mesa, CA
Lynn, John M. ... Homestead, FL
Lynn, John M. ... Round Rock, TX
Lynn, Jonathan S. ... Warrenton, VA
Lynn, Jonathon P. ... Fort Lauderdale, FL
Lynn, Julie G. ... Los Angeles, CA
Lynn, Karen A. ... Arlington, TX
Lynn, Katherine Lerner ... Los Angeles, CA
Lynn, Kathy A. ... Seattle, WA
Lynn, Kenneth H. ... Sylvan Lake, MI
Lynn, Kristina L. ... Wabash, IN
Lynn, Laura M. ... Howell, MI
Lynn Law Firm, PLC ... Heber Springs, AR
Lynn Law Office ... Skaneateles, NY
Syracuse, NY
Lynn, Lawrence A. ... Houston, TX
Lynn, Leslie A. ... New York, NY
Lynn, Lois A. ... Wichita, KS
Lynn, Lori J. ... Billerica, MA
Lynn & Lynn ... Costa Mesa, CA
Lynn, M. Kathleen ... Cazenovia, NY
Lynn, M. Richardson, Jr. ... San Diego, CA
Lynn, Mark J. ... Miami, FL
Lynn, Melvin E., Jr. ... Park Falls, WI
Lynn, Michael ... New Bedford, MA
Lynn, Michael A. ... New York, NY
Lynn, Michael P., (P.C.) ... Dallas, TX
Lynn, Michael R. ... Bloomsburg, PA
Lynn, Michelle Marie ... Los Angeles, CA
Lynn, Miles R., Jr. ... Emlenton, PA
Lynn, Morton M. Z. ... Albany, NY
Lynn, Nicholas J. ... Chicago, IL
Lynn, Norman S. ... Bensenville, IL
Lynn, Penny ... Denver, CO
Lynn, Phyllis Savage ... Albuquerque, NM
Lynn, Pietro J. ... Burlington, VT
Lynn, Rebecca L. ... Heber Springs, AR
Lynn, Rebecca L., P.A.
Heber Springs, AR
Lynn, Richard B. ... Laguna Niguel, CA
Lynn, Richard C. ... Oklahoma City, OK
Lynn, Richard W. ... New York, NY
Lynn, Richardson R. ... Malibu, CA
Lynn, Robert C. ... San Diego, CA
Lynn, Robert H. ... San Diego, CA
Lynn, Robert H. ... Minneapolis, MN
Lynn, Robert P., Jr. ... Mineola, NY
Lynn, Robert P., Jr., LLC ... Mineola, NY
Lynn, Robt. John ... Columbus, OH
Lynn, Sandra T. ... Homestead, FL
Key Largo, FL
Lynn, Sarah E. ... Columbus, OH
Lynn, Sarah Maria Hicks ... Durham, NC
Lynn, Scott, Hackney & Sullivan ... Boise, ID
Lynn, Scott J. ... Nashville, TN
Lynn, Shelah Fidellman ... Bethesda, MD
Lynn, Shelly M. ... Washington, DC
Lynn, Stephen W. ... Kansas City, MO
Lynn Stodghill Melsheimer & Tillotson, L.L.P. ... Dallas, TX
Lynn, Suzanne M. ... New York, NY
Lynn, Terry ... Charlottesville, VA
Lynn, Terry J. ... Heber Springs, AR
Lynn, Theodore S. ... New York, NY
Lynn, Theresa A. ... Houston, TX
Lynn, Thomas D. ... New York, NY
Lynn, Thomas Neil, III ... Oklahoma City, OK
Lynn, Timothy M. ... Syracuse, NY
Lynn, Tish E. ... Geneseo, NY
Lynn, Todd Manley ... Richmond, VA
Lynn, Wendy R. ... Armonk, NY
Lynn, William F. ... Skaneateles, NY
Syracuse, NY
Lynn, William T. ... Tacoma, WA
Lynne, Diane S.
Environmental Protection Agency,
Program Office Attorneys, GV
Lynne, Jeffrey ... Miami, FL
Lynne, Michael ... New York, NY
Lynne, Seybourn H. ... Birmingham, AL
Lynner, Terry A. ... Minneapolis, MN
Lynn-Ford, Patricia A. ... Syracuse, NY
Lynott, Bradley C. ... Portland, OR
Lynott, Daniel J. ... Tampa, FL
Lynott, Joseph A., III ... Rockville, MD
Lynott, Joseph A., Jr. ... Rockville, MD
Lynott, Keith E. ... Newark, NJ
Lynott and Lynott, P.A. ... Rockville, MD
Lynott, Michael J. ... Miami, FL
Lynott, Michael T. ... Miami, FL
Lynott, Robert J. ... Baltimore, MD
Lynskey, Kathleen M. ... Miami, FL
Lynskey, Sandra L. ... Columbus, OH
Lynt, Christopher H. ... Alexandria, VA
Lynton, Harold S. ... New York, NY
Lynton, Richard D. ... Denver, CO
Lynton, Wingrove S. ... Crofton, MD
Lynyak, Joseph T., III ... Los Angeles, CA
Lyon, Alton F. ... Pembroke, MA
Lyon, Andrew L.
Federal Energy Regulatory Commission,
Office of the General Counsel, GV
Lyon, Ann D. ... Jacksonville, FL
Lyon & Artz PLLC ... Bloomfield Hills, MI
Lyon & Artz, PLC ... Detroit, MI
Lyon & Artz PLLC ... Southfield, MI
Lyon, Barbee B., (P.C.) ... Portland, OR
Lyon, Ben H. ... San Carlos, CA
Lyon, Beverly M., (Ms.) ... Kensington, CA
Lyon, Bruce A. ... Auburn, CA
Lyon, Bruce W. ... Chicago, IL
Lyon, Carl F., Jr. ... New York, NY
Lyon & Carmel ... San Luis Obispo, CA
Lyon, Carol S. ... Irving, TX
Lyon, Cathy H. ... Marietta, GA
Lyon, Cathy Hockman, P.C. ... Marietta, GA
Lyon, Chantal vanLede ... Hopkinton, MA
Lyon, Charles B. ... Cleveland, OH
Lyon, Chas. S. ... New York, NY
Lyon, Clarke S. ... Holyoke, MA
Lyon, Daniel F. S. ... Albuquerque, NM
Lyon, Daniel P. ... Fairfax, VA
Leesburg, VA
Lyon, Danny Leon ... Oklahoma City, OK
Lyon, David G. ... Morristown, NJ
Lyon, David J. ... Las Vegas, NV
Salt Lake City, UT
Lyon, David M. ... Baltimore, MD
Lyon, David N. ... Glendale, CA
Lyon, David Pierce ... Los Angeles, CA
Lyon, Deanna Down ... Oakland, CA
Lyon, Deborah E.
National Aeronautics And Space
Administration,
Office of the General Counsel, GV
Lyon, Deborah Henscheid ... Phoenix, AZ
Lyon, Dee W. ... Thousand Oaks, CA
Lyon, Donald M. ... Cleveland, OH
Lyon, Douglas ... Los Angeles, CA
Lyon, E. Barry ... Norwalk, CT
Lyon, Edwin L. ... Washington, DC
Lyon, Eileen ... Los Angeles, CA
Lyon, Eldon D. ... Bethany, OK
Lyon, Elliott M. ... Evanston, IL
Lyon, Elmer E. ... Greeneville, TN
Lyon, Eric C. ... Houston, TX
Lyon, Faye Marie ... Rockford, IL
Lyon, Ferriter & Fitzpatrick, LLP
Holyoke, MA
Springfield, MA
Lyon, Frank B. ... Austin, TX
Lyon, Frederick C. ... Boise, ID
Lyon, Gary G. ... Carrollton, TX
Lyon, Geoffrey C. ... Huntington Beach, CA
Lyon, George C.
Department Of Health And Human Services,
Office for Civil Rights, GV
Lyon, George L., Jr. ... Washington, DC
Lyon, Gladys M. ... Atlanta, GA
Lyon & Glassman, P.C. ... Florham Park, NJ
Lyon, Gregory J. ... Phoenix, AZ
Lyon, Gregory Karl ... Norwood, MA
Lyon, H. Mark ... Palo Alto, CA
Lyon, Harllee W. ... Wilson, NC
Lyon, I. Harry ... Pelham, AL
Lyon & Ingleson ... Cheboygan, MI
Lyon, J. Barton ... Fort Wayne, IN
Lyon, James B. ... Hartford, CT
Lyon, James B. ... Coral Springs, FL
Lyon, James B., P.A. ... Coral Springs, FL
Lyon, James D. ... Lexington, KY
Lyon, James M. ... Minneapolis, MN
Lyon, James T. ... Richmond, VA
Lyon, James W., Jr. ... Greenup, KY
Lyon, James W., Sr. ... Greenup, KY
Lyon, Jeffery T. ... Cheboygan, MI
Lyon, Jeffrey J. ... Long Beach, CA
Lyon, Jeffrey S. ... Deerfield, IL
Lyon, Jesse D. ... Portland, OR
Lyon, Jim A. ... Oklahoma City, OK
Lyon, John D. ... Los Angeles, CA
Lyon, John W.
Environmental Protection Agency,
Office of Enforcement and Compliance
Assurance, GV
Lyon, Jonathan E. ... McLean, VA
Reston, VA
Lyon, Karl D. ... San Francisco, CA
Lyon, Karl H. ... Stoneham, MA
Lyon, Karla A. ... San Diego, CA
Lyon, Kathryn C. ... Topsfield, MA
Lyon and Kendall ... Greenup, KY
Lyon, Kenneth E., III ... Pocatello, ID
Lyon, Kenneth E., Jr. ... Pocatello, ID
Lyon, Kerry A. ... Los Angeles, CA
Lyon, Kevin R. ... Olympia, WA
Lyon, Kevin R., P.S., The Law Office of
Olympia, WA
Lyon Kirwin, P.A. ... Washington, DC
Orlando, FL
St. Petersburg, FL
Winter Park, FL
Lyon Law ... Huntington Beach, CA
Lyon, LeRoy E., Jr. ... Loomis, CA
Lyon, Lyman R. ... Bloomfield Hills, MI
Lyon, Lynn P. ... Denver, CO
Lyon & Lyon ... Pocatello, ID
Preston, ID
Lyon & Lyon LLP ... Costa Mesa, CA
Irvine, CA
La Jolla, CA
Los Angeles, CA
San Diego, CA
San Jose, CA
Washington, DC
White Plains, NY
Lyon, Margaret Sue ... Vero Beach, FL
Lyon, Mark S. ... Olympia, WA
Lyon, Mark W. ... Rochester, MI
Lyon, Mary F. ... Rochester Hills, MI
Lyon and McManus ... San Antonio, TX
Lyon, Michael D.
Department Of Veterans Affairs,
Board of Veterans Appeals, GV
Lyon, Michael D. ... Ogden, UT
Lyon, Michael E. ... San Diego, CA
Lyon, Michael F. ... Cincinnati, OH
Lyon, Michael Randy ... Wilkesboro, NC
Lyon, Michael T. ... Skokie, IL
Lyon, Michael V. ... Laurel, DE
Lyon, Neill B ... Warwick, RI
Lyon, P. A., III ... Odessa, TX
Lyon, Patricia H. ... San Francisco, CA
Lyon, Peter B. ... Littleton, CO
Houston, TX
Lyon, Peter C. ... San Francisco, CA
Lyon, Philip K. ... Little Rock, AR
Nashville, TN
Lyon, Randall C. ... Visalia, CA
Lyon, Rexford L. ... Florham Park, NJ
Lyon, Richard E., Jr., (A Professional Corporation) ... Los Angeles, CA
Lyon, Richard F. ... San Francisco, CA
Lyon, Richard G. ... Dallas, TX
Lyon, Richard J. ... Lexington, KY
Lyon, Richard K. ... Washington, DC
Lyon, Richard L. ... Chevy Chase, MD
Lyon, Richard M. ... Chicago, IL
Lyon, Robert, & Associates ... Rowlett, TX
Lyon, Robert B., Jr. ... Department of Justice,
Office of Professional Responsibility, GV
Lyon, Robert C. ... Rowlett, TX
Lyon, Robert E., (A Professional Corporation) ... Los Angeles, CA
Lyon, Roger ... Pasadena, CA
Lyon, Roger C., Jr. ... San Luis Obispo, CA
Lyon, Ronald A. ... Wichita, KS
Lyon, Ronald W. ... Sherman, TX
Lyon, Ronald W., P.C. ... Sherman, TX
Lyon, Samuel M., Jr. ... Ridgewood, NJ
Lyon, Scott H. ... Vienna, VA
Lyon, Stan L. ... Reno, NV
Lyon, Stanley W. ... Long Beach, CA
Lyon, Susan L. ... Menlo Park, CA
Lyon, Tanisha L. ... Columbus, OH
Lyon, Ted B., & Associates, P.C.
Dallas, TX
Mesquite, TX
Lyon, Ted B., Jr. ... Mesquite, TX
Lyon, Thomas I. ... Raleigh, NC
Lyon, Tiffany ... Los Altos, CA
Lyon, Todd ... Chicago, IL
Lyon, V. Frederic ... Winter Park, FL
Lyon, Warren C. ... Dallas, TX
Lyon, Weigand & Gustafson, P.S.
Yakima, WA
Lyon, Wendell V., Jr. ... Somerset, KY
Lyon, William M., Jr. ... Mobile, AL
Lyons, Aaron P. ... Springfield, MO
Lyons, A. L. ... Boise, ID
Lyons, Alan D. ... Oakland, CA
Oak Park, IL
Lyons, Alan R. ... New York, NY
Lyons, Alexander S. ... Shreveport, LA
Lyons, Allen W. ... Lake Oswego, OR
Lyons, Alycia K. ... Boston, MA
Lyons, Amy S. ... Blair, NE
Lyons, Amy W. ... Los Angeles, CA
Lyons, Andrew D. ... Overland Park, KS
Lyons, Andrew D. ... Lewisburg, PA
Lyons, Andrew M. ... Philadelphia, PA
Lyons, Angelique Groza ... Jacksonville, FL
Tampa, FL
Lyons, Arthur J. ... Mahopac, NY
Lyons, Barbara N. ... Doylestown, PA
Lyons, Barry S. ... Philadelphia, PA
Lyons Beaudry & Harrison, P.A.
Sarasota, FL
Lyons, Bernard E. ... Thousand Oaks, CA
Lyons, Beth Schwartz ... New York, NY
Lyons, Brandt, Cook & Hiramatsu
Honolulu, HI
Lyons, Bruce M. ... Fort Lauderdale, FL
Lyons, Champ, III ... Birmingham, AL
Lyons, Champ, Jr. ... Point Clear, AL
Lyons, Charles E. (Ed), II ... Charlotte, NC
Lyons, Charles H.S., III ... Augusta, GA
Lyons, Charles J., Jr. ... Lakewood, CA
Lyons, Charles K. ... Waltham, MA
Lyons, Charles M. ... Hartford, CT
Lyons, Charles R. ... Scranton, PA
Lyons, Charles V., Sr. ... Memphis, TN
Lyons, Charles W. ... Atlanta, GA
Lyons, Christopher B. ... Pryor, OK
Lyons, Christopher G. ... Miami, FL
Lyons, Christopher P. ... Chicago, IL
Lyons, Cindy B. ... Wilmette, IL
Lyons & Clark ... Tulsa, OK
Lyons, Clem ... Brownsville, TX
San Antonio, TX
Lyons, Clinton ... Washington, DC
Lyons, Clinton C., Jr. ... Orlando, FL
Lyons, Colleen ... Manchester, NH
Lyons, Condon A. ... Albany, NY
Lyons, Cornelius J. ... Bronx, NY
Lyons, Cynthia R. ... Naperville, IL

Lyons, Cynthia S. .... Crossville, TN
Lyons, D. Edwin .... Binghamton, NY
Lyons, Daniel A., Jr. .... West Haven, CT
Lyons, Daniel G. .... Philadelphia, PA
Lyons, Daniel J. .... Houston, TX
Lyons, Daniel J., Jr. .... Hopewell, NJ
Lyons, Daniel P. .... Fresno, CA
Lyons, Daniel P. .... Stroudsburg, PA
Lyons, Daniel W. .... Boston, MA
Lyons, David A. .... Stamford, CT
Lyons, David C. .... Indianapolis, IN
Lyons, David J. .... Wilmington, DE
Lyons, David J. .... Des Moines, IA
Lyons, David P. .... Columbus, OH
Lyons, David R. .... Mount Laurel, NJ
Lyons, David T. .... Southborough, MA
Lyons, David T. .... Seattle, WA
Lyons, Deborah B. .... Chicago, IL
Lyons, Dennis G. .... Washington, DC
Lyons, Desmond Charles Barnett
New York, NY
Lyons, Dianna J. .... Oakland, CA
Lyons, Dolores R. .... San Diego, CA
Washington, DC
Lyons, Donna L.
Department Of Health And Human Services,
Social Security Administration, GV
Baltimore, MD
Lyons, Doughty & Veldhuis, P.C.
Wilmington, DE
Mount Laurel, NJ
Philadelphia, PA
Lyons, Douglas B. .... New York, NY
Lyons, Douglas B., P.C. .... New York, NY
Lyons, Douglas F. .... Annapolis, MD
Lyons, Douglas S. .... Coral Gables, FL
Tallahassee, FL
Lyons, Douglas W., Jr. .... Houston, TX
Lyons, Duane .... Los Angeles, CA
Lyons, Edmund Daniel .... Wilmington, DE
Lyons, Edward C. .... San Francisco, CA
Lyons, Edward J. .... Clearwater, FL
Lyons, Edward T., Jr. .... Denver, CO
Lyons, Elisabeth J. .... Washington, DC
Lyons, Ellen L. .... Washington, DC
Lyons, Ellen S. .... Salinas, CA
Lyons, Ellis .... Washington, DC
Lyons, Emerson & Cone, P.L.C.
Jonesboro, AR
Lyons and Farrar, P.A. .... Coral Gables, FL
Lyons & Farrar, P.A. .... Miami, FL
Lyons and Farrar, P.A. .... Tallahassee, FL
Lyons, Francis J. .... Vienna, VA
Lyons, Francis M. .... San Mateo, CA
Lyons, Francis X .... Department of Justice,
Environment and Natural Resources
Division, GV
Lyons, Frederic .... Dobbs Ferry, NY
Lyons & Fries Co., L.P.A. .... Cincinnati, OH
Lyons, G. Sage .... Mobile, AL
Lyons, Gary F. .... Bloomington, MN
Lyons, Gary G. .... White Plains, NY
Lyons, Gary G. .... Spring, TX
Lyons, Gary W. .... Clearwater, FL
Lyons, Gary W. .... Columbus, OH
Lyons, George H. .... Phoenix, AZ
Lyons, Gina M. .... New York, NY
Lyons, Gregory .... Washington, DC
Lyons, Gregory J. .... Boston, MA
Lyons, Gregory J. .... Tacoma, WA
Lyons, Gregory S. .... Oakland, CA
Lyons, Gregory W. .... Milwaukee, WI
Lyons, Hal V. .... Shreveport, LA
Lyons, Hardy C. .... Sagle, ID
Lyons, Henry, III .... Fairfield, CT
Lyons, Herbert L. .... Tucson, AZ
Lyons, Holly L. .... Indianapolis, IN
Lyons, Irwin .... Fair Oaks, CA
Lyons, J. Austin .... New York, NY
Lyons, J. Austin, Jr. .... New York, NY
Lyons, J. Matthew .... Austin, TX
Lyons, J. Robert, Jr. .... Lexington, KY
Lyons, James A. .... Albuquerque, NM
Lyons, James A., Jr. .... Washington, DC
Lyons, James C. .... Ansonia, CT
Lyons, James D. .... New York, NY
Lyons, James E. .... Palo Alto, CA
San Francisco, CA
Lyons, James F. .... Boise, ID
Lyons, James J. .... Wappingers Falls, NY
Lyons, James L. .... Washington, DC
Lyons, James L. .... Cincinnati, OH
Lyons, James M. .... Denver, CO
Lyons, James M.
Executive Office Of The President,
Office of the U.S. Trade Representative, GV
Lyons, James M. .... Dallas, TX
Lyons, James M., Jr. .... Akron, OH
Lyons, James O. .... Seattle, WA
Lyons, James P. .... Philadelphia, PA
Lyons, James R. .... Boston, MA
Lyons, James W. .... Cincinnati, OH
Lyons, Jamie Platt .... Atlanta, GA
Lyons, Jane M. .... Washington, DC
Lyons & Jarrell, L.L.P. .... Houston, TX
Lyons, Jason P. .... Houma, LA
Lyons, Jay C. .... Bridgeport, CT
Lyons, Jeffrey S. .... Denver, CO
Lyons, Jerry .... Philadelphia, PA
Lyons, Jim .... Jonesboro, AR
Lyons, JoEllen .... Pittsburgh, PA
Lyons, John A., P.C. .... Troy, MI
Lyons, John D. .... New York, NY
Lyons, John D., Jr. .... San Francisco, CA
Lyons, John E., Jr. .... Portsmouth, NH
Lyons, John F. .... Fort Wayne, IN
Lyons, John F. .... Olney, MD
Lyons, John F. .... Hackensack, NJ
Lyons, John F. .... Rhinebeck, NY
Lyons, John F. .... Harrisburg, PA
Lyons, John F., Jr. .... Washington, DC
Lyons, John G. .... San Francisco, CA
Lyons, John H. .... Mesa, AZ
Lyons, John H. .... Washington, DC
Lyons, John J. .... Los Angeles, CA
Lyons, John J. .... San Francisco, CA
Lyons, John J. .... Sarasota, FL
Lyons, John J. .... Arlington Heights, IL
Lyons, John J. .... Boston, MA
Lyons, John J. .... Shell Knob, MO
Lyons, John K. .... Chicago, IL
Lyons, John Kenneth .... Baltimore, MD
Lyons, John M. .... Valparaiso, IN
Lyons, John T. .... Wilkes-Barre, PA
Lyons, John T., Jr. .... Newark, NJ
Lyons, John W., Jr. .... Texas City, TX
Lyons, Jon C. .... Lancaster, PA
Lyons, Jon H. .... Eureka, CA
Lyons, Joseph F. .... Boston, MA
Lyons, Joseph G. .... Chicago, IL
Lyons, Joseph S. .... Towson, MD
Lyons, Joseph S., P.A. .... Towson, MD
Lyons, Kathleen A. .... Chicago, IL
Lyons, Kathleen A. .... New York, NY
Lyons, Kathleen Liu .... Chicago, IL
Lyons, Kenneth M. .... Washington, DC
Lyons, Kevin .... New York, NY
Lyons, Kevin J. .... Boston, MA
Lyons, Kevin J. .... Milwaukee, WI
Lyons, Kevin Kemp .... Chicago, IL
Lyons, Kevin M. .... Fort Lauderdale, FL
Lyons, Kevin M., P.A. .... Fort Lauderdale, FL
Lyons, Kevin W. .... Peoria, IL
Lyons, Kipp Ian .... Palm Springs, CA
Lyons, Kirk M. H. .... Stamford, CT
Boston, MA
New York, NY
Lyons, Lance D. .... Fort Lauderdale, FL
Lyons, Lane D. .... Salem, OR
Lyons, Lauragene .... New Haven, CT
Lyons, Laurie W. .... Shreveport, LA
Lyons Law Firm, The .... Wilmington, DE
Lyons Law Offices .... Seattle, WA
Lyons, Lawrence W., Jr. .... Barnstable, MA
Lyons, Lester .... New Rochelle, NY
Lyons, Lisa A. .... Milwaukee, WI
Lyons & Lyons Co., L.P.A.
West Chester, OH
Lyons & Lyons, P.C. .... Philadelphia, PA
Lyons, Malcolm L. .... Augusta, ME
Lyons, Marc A. .... Coeur d'Alene, ID
Lyons, Marjorie M. .... Binghamton, NY
Lyons, Mark A. .... Omaha, NE
Lyons, Mark B. .... Salem, MA
Lyons, Mark D. .... Tulsa, OK
Lyons, Marsha L. .... Coral Gables, FL
Lyons, Martha A. .... Binghamton, NY
Lyons, Martin C. .... West Springfield, MA
Lyons, Martin Trevor Hughes
Newark, NJ
Lyons, Mary F. .... Roswell, GA
Lyons, Mary Margaret Callahan
Norfolk, VA
Lyons, Maryanne .... Houston, TX
Lyons, Matt G. .... Biloxi, MS
Ocean Springs, MS
Lyons, Matthew .... Palo Alto, CA
Lyons, Matthew P. .... Turnersville, NJ
Lyons, Michael D. .... Miami, FL
Lyons, Michael D. .... Nashua, NH
Lyons, Michael J. .... Palo Alto, CA
Lyons, Michael J. .... Chicago, IL
Lyons, Michael J. .... Chadds Ford, PA
Lyons, Michael K. .... Medina, OH
Lyons, Michael L. .... Los Angeles, CA
Lyons, Michael L. .... St. Louis, MO
Lyons, Michael M. .... Pittsburgh, PA
Lyons, Michael N., Jr. .... West St. Paul, MN
Lyons, Michael P. .... Dallas, TX
Lyons, Michael S. .... El Segundo, CA
Lyons, Michael W. .... Norwalk, CT
Lyons, Michael W. .... Florence, KY
Lyons, Michele Olsen .... Branford, CT
Lyons, Mitchell R. .... Stoughton, MA
Lyons, Mona .... Washington, DC
Lyons, N. David .... Los Angeles, CA
Lyons, Nance .... Boston, MA
Lyons, Pamela B. .... Boston, MA
Lyons, Pamela Chiott .... Englewood, CO
Lyons, Patrice A. .... Washington, DC
Lyons, Patrice, Chartered, Law Offices of
Washington, DC
Lyons, Patricia M. .... Wilmington, DE
Lyons, Paul B. .... New York, NY
Lyons, Paul V. .... Boston, MA
Lyons, Peter D. .... New York, NY
Lyons, Peter J. .... Detroit, MI
Taylor, MI
Lyons, Philip N. .... San Leandro, CA
Lyons, Philip P. .... McCook, NE
Lyons, Pipes & Cook, P.C. .... Mobile, AL
Lyons & Plackemeier, A Partnership of Prof.
Corp. .... Texas City, TX
Lyons, R. Michael .... Baton Rouge, LA
Lyons, Ramonda C. .... Winston-Salem, NC
Lyons, Ray .... Groton, MA
Lyons, Raymond, Jr. .... Chicago, IL
Lyons, Raymond T., Jr. .... Newark, NJ
Lyons, Redmond J. .... Streamwood, IL
Lyons & Rhodes .... Brownsville, TX
San Antonio, TX
Lyons, Rhona S. .... St. Louis, MO
Lyons, Richard A. .... Oakland, CA
Lyons, Richard D. .... Naples, FL
Lyons, Richard J. .... Syracuse, NY
Lyons, Richard J. .... Warminster, PA
Lyons, Richard N., II .... Longmont, CO
Lyons, Richard W. .... Miami, FL
Lyons, Robert B. .... Arlington, VA
Lyons, Robert D. .... West Chester, OH
Lyons, Robert G. .... Sarasota, FL
Lyons, Robert H. .... West Chester, OH
Lyons, Robert P. .... Kansas City, MO
Lyons, Robert Swayne .... Santa Barbara, CA
Lyons, Robert W. .... Hayward, CA
Lyons & Rodeberg .... Roswell, GA
Lyons, Rodney K. .... St. John, KS
Lyons, Ronald E. .... Rockville, MD
Lyons, Ronald L. .... Salt Lake City, UT
Lyons, Rory D. .... Atlanta, GA
Lyons, S. Robert .... Department of Justice,
Tax Division, GV
Lyons, Samuel A. B. .... Honolulu, HI
Lyons and Sanders, Chartered
Boca Raton, FL
Fort Lauderdale, FL
Miami, FL
West Palm Beach, FL
Lyons, Sarah J. .... Beverly Hills, MI
Lyons, Scott E. .... Chicago, IL
Lyons, Sean M. .... San Antonio, TX
Lyons, Sheri M. .... Washington, DC
Lyons, Sheryl .... New Orleans, LA
Lyons, Sidney H. .... Los Angeles, CA
Lyons, Skoufalos, Proios & Flood
Stamford, CT
Boston, MA
Englewood Cliffs, NJ
New York, NY
Lyons and Smith, P.A. .... Miami, FL
Lyons, Stephanie A. .... Milwaukee, WI
Lyons, Stephanie Beth .... Hollywood, FL
Lyons, Stephen B. .... Washington, DC
Lyons, Stephen J. .... Boston, MA
Lyons, Stephen M. .... Washington, DC
Lyons, Stephen M., III .... Philadelphia, PA
Lyons, Stephen T. .... Department of Justice,
Tax Division, GV
Lyons and Sullivan, Law Offices
Valparaiso, IN
Lyons & Supple .... Beacon, NY
Wappingers Falls, NY
Lyons, Susan B. .... Baldwin, NY
Lyons, Susan M.
Department Of Health And Human Services,
Office of the General Counsel, GV
Lyons, T. Jackson .... Jackson, MS
Lyons, T. Randall .... Montgomery, AL
Lyons, Tara .... Newington, CT
Lyons, Theodore V., Jr. .... Janesville, WI
Lyons, Theresa Brewton .... Fort Worth, TX
Lyons, Therese M. .... Brookfield, WI
Lyons, Thomas C. .... Covington, KY
Lyons, Thomas G. .... Chicago, IL
Lyons, Thomas J. .... Denver, CO
Lyons, Thomas J. .... Pocatello, ID
Lyons, Thomas J. .... St. Paul, MN
Lyons, Thomas J. .... St. Paul, MN
Lyons, Thomas J., & Associates, P.A.
St. Paul, MN
Lyons, Thomas P. .... Milwaukee, WI
Lyons, Thomas W., III .... Providence, RI
Lyons, Timothy D. .... Middletown, NJ
Lyons, Timothy F. .... Hartford, CT
Lyons, Timothy K. .... Mill Valley, CA
Lyons, Timothy L. .... Milwaukee, WI
Lyons, Tony Jack .... Pryor, OK
Lyons, Tracie Tabor .... Irwindale, CA
Lyons, Tracy A. .... Waltham, MA
Lyons, Tuccio & Gallant .... Ansonia, CT
Lyons, Virginia R. .... Riverwoods, IL
Lyons, Wendy Bush .... Pleasant Valley, NY
Lyons, William A. .... Louisville, KY
Lyons, William D. .... Omaha, NE
Lyons, William H. .... Lincoln, NE
Lyons, William H. .... Concord, NH
Lyons, William J. .... New York, NY
Lyons, William J., Jr. .... West Springfield, MA
Lyons, William M. .... Sacramento, CA
Lyons, William M. .... Kansas City, MO
Lyons, William T. .... Treasury Department,
Internal Revenue Service, GV
Lyons-Gibson, Lois M. .... New York, NY
Lyons-Leoni, Joseph .... Virginia, MN
Lyp, Patrick A. .... Valparaiso, IN
Lype, Bob E. .... Chattanooga, TN
Lyras, Alexandra G. .... New York, NY
Lyren, Philip S. .... Houston, TX
Lysaght, Brian C. .... Santa Monica, CA
Lysaght, James F. .... Bronxville, NY
Lysaght, James J. .... Lake Success, NY
Lysaght, Lysaght & Kramer, P.C.
Lake Success, NY
Lysak, Assunta .... New York, NY
Lysak, Dale C. .... San Francisco, CA
Lysak, Mary Ellen .... Savannah, GA
Lysaught, Eileen A. .... Chicago, IL
Lysaught, J. Donald .... Kansas City, KS
Lysaught, J. Donald, Jr. .... Kansas City, KS
Lysaught, Patrick .... Kansas City, MO
Lysaught, Thomas F. .... Schaumburg, IL
Lyshak, Carol J. .... Southfield, MI
Lyshak, William P. .... Livonia, MI
Lysiak, Conrad C. .... Spokane, WA
Lysiak, Robert E. .... Emerson, NJ
Lysik, David A. .... Chicago, IL
Lysko, Gregg M. .... Boston, MA
Lysko, Lisa A. .... Boston, MA
Lyskowski, Kevin .... Washington, DC
Lysle, Richard S. .... Marina Del Rey, CA
Lysohir, Alexander .... South Bend, IN
Lystad, James H. .... Rockville, MD
Lystad, Robert D. .... Washington, DC
Lyster, Christopher G. .... Fort Worth, TX
Lyster, Ronald W. .... Los Angeles, CA
Lystig, Mark .... Eagan, MN
Lystra, Edward H. .... Grand Haven, MI
Lysz, John M. .... Dearborn Heights, MI
Lytal, Lake H., III .... West Palm Beach, FL
Lytal, Lake, Jr. (P.A.)
West Palm Beach, FL
Lytal, Reiter, Clark, Fountain & Williams
West Palm Beach, FL
Belle Glade, FL
Boca Raton, FL
Port St. Lucie, FL
Lytal, Scott L. .... Cookeville, TN
Lytch, R. Allen .... Dunn, NC
Lyte, Suzanne M. .... South Plainfield, NJ
Lytel, Roger B. .... Santa Barbara, CA
Lythcott, Stephen X. .... Chicago, IL
Lythgoe, W. Scott .... Ogden, UT
Lytle, Alice A. .... Sacramento, CA
Lytle, Bradley D. .... Arlington, VA
Lytle, Brett S. .... Daly City, CA
Lytle, Craig M. .... Hermosa Beach, CA
Lytle, Diane S. .... Ashland, OH
Lytle, Douglas W. .... San Diego, CA
Lytle, E. Kent .... Charlotte, NC
Lytle, Edward L. .... Westfield Center, OH
Lytle, Erika Ritt .... Cleveland, OH
Lytle, Florence J. .... Duluth, GA
Lytle, Florence J., P.C. .... Duluth, GA
Lytle, George N. .... Winter Haven, FL
Lytle, Guy T. .... Roseland, NJ
Lytle, J. Michael .... Richmond, TX
Lytle, J. Warren, Jr. .... Washington, DC
Lytle, James W. .... Albany, NY
New York, NY
Lytle, Jeanette C. .... Madison, WI
Lytle, Joann M. .... Philadelphia, PA
Lytle, John B. .... Dillon Beach, CA
Lytle, L. Ben .... Indianapolis, IN
Lytle, Margaret M. .... Brooksville, FL
Lytle, Marilyn L. .... New York, NY
Lytle, Mary E. .... Orlando, FL
Lytle, Mary E., P.A. .... Orlando, FL
Lytle & Moore, L.L.P. .... Richmond, TX
Lytle, Patricia M. .... Newport Beach, CA
Lytle, Richard F. .... Anchorage, AK
Lytle, Richard H. .... Keosauqua, IA
Lytle, Robert B. .... Houston, TX
Lytle, Robert F. .... Overland Park, KS
Lytle, Sally A. .... Philadelphia, PA
Lytle, Shirley A. .... Findlay, OH
Lytle Soulé & Curlee, P.C.
Oklahoma City, OK
Lytle, Steven H. .... Des Moines, IA
Lytle, Thomas F. .... Sacramento, CA
Lytle, Wm. David .... Pueblo, CO
Lytten, Walter C. .... Portsmouth, OH
Lyttle, Carol, Jr. .... New York, NY
Lyttle, Constance Fox .... Damascus, PA
Lyttle, David F. .... Hawthorne, NJ
Lyttle, John W., Jr. .... Iselin, NJ
New York, NY
Lytton, Howard B., Jr. .... Jasper, IN
Lytton, Julius M. .... East Moline, IL
Lytton, Lee H., III .... San Antonio, TX
Lytton, Michael .... Boston, MA
Lytton & Ripstra .... Jasper, IN
Lytton, Sheldon H. .... Los Angeles, CA
Lytton, Stuart C. .... Los Angeles, CA
Lytton, Sutton & Zimmer .... East Moline, IL
Lytton, Timothy Daniel .... New York, NY
Lytton, Tom M. .... Moline, IL
Lytton, William B. .... Purchase, NY
Lytton LLoyd, Deborah .... Los Angeles, CA
Lytz, Karl S. .... San Francisco, CA
Lyubkin, Rina .... Miami, FL
Lyubovnaya, Yuliya .... New York, NY
Lyverse, Steven H. .... Louisville, KY
Dobbs Ferry, NY

Ma, Akana K. J. .... Portland, OR
Ma, Alan J. .... Honolulu, HI
Ma, Alan W. C. .... Honolulu, HI
Ma, Amy L. .... Charlotte, NC
Ma, Beverly M. .... San Francisco, CA
Ma, Christopher Y.W. .... Washington, DC
Ma, Edward Yeh-Kuang .... New York, NY
Ma, Jacinta S. .... Boston, MA
Ma, Jingsheng .... Alhambra, CA
Ma, Judy C. .... Los Angeles, CA
Ma, Junling .... Palo Alto, CA
Ma, Kathryn E. .... San Francisco, CA
Ma, Louise E. .... Emeryville, CA
Ma, Marlene S. .... San Francisco, CA
Ma, Mike Yuh-hung .... Washington, DC
Ma, Patricia C. .... Melville, NY
Ma, Qiang .... Alhambra, CA
Ma, Richard J. .... New York, NY
Ma, Rongjie .... San Francisco, CA
Ma, Shirley S. .... New Haven, CT
Ma, Siu L. .... San Francisco, CA
Ma, Stephen Y. .... Chicago, IL
Maag, Edward G. .... Belleville, IL
Maag, Gordon E. .... Granite City, IL
Maag, Gregory L. .... Houston, TX
Maag, Marilyn J. .... Cincinnati, OH
Maag, Stephen J. .... Seattle, WA
Maahs, Earl H. .... Spirit Lake, IA
Maahs, Kurt D. .... Kansas City, MO
Maahs, Rebecca L. .... Kansas City, MO
Maaia, William C. .... East Providence, RI
Maak, Bruce A. .... Salt Lake City, UT
Maak, Charles L. .... Salt Lake City, UT
Maalouf, John J. .... New York, NY
Maalouf, Laila .... Quincy, MA
Maan de Kok, John .... Kenosha, WI

Maan De Kok, Michele Weaver
Lake Forest, IL
Ma'ani, Sovaida .... Department of State, Office of the Legal Adviser, GV
Maas, Ann Marie .... San Diego, CA
Maas & Assocs., P.S. .... Kenmore, WA
Maas, Bertram A. .... Vienna, VA
Maas, Brian E. .... New York, NY
Maas, Brian J. .... Newport Beach, CA
Maas, Brian W. .... Sacramento, CA
Maas, Bruce L. .... Rochester, NY
Maas, Charles .... Hillsboro, MO
Maas, Colleen Rutherford .... Riverside, CA
Maas, Dale M. .... Baton Rouge, LA
Maas, Dale M., A Professional Law Corporation .... Baton Rouge, LA
Maas, David E. .... High Point, NC
Maas, Donald W. .... Houston, TX
Maas, E. Jerome .... Arlington Heights, IL
Maas, Earl H., III .... San Diego, CA
Maas, Earl H., Jr. .... Del Mar, CA
Maas, Elizabeth A. .... Jacksonville, FL
Maas, Ellen L. .... Anoka, MN
Maas, Francis S. .... Beverly Hills, CA
Maas, Frank .... New York, NY
Maas, Fredric J. .... United States Senate, Committee Legal Personnel, GV
Maas, Gary R. .... Buffalo, NY
Maas, Harrison D. .... New York, NY
Maas, Hyman T. .... Fairport, NY
Maas, Jason R. .... Kenmore, WA
Maas, Jennifer L. .... Philadelphia, PA
Maas, John .... Denver, CO
Maas, John P. .... Homestead, FL
Maas, Kathryn R. .... San Diego, CA
Maas, Kenneth J., Jr. .... Stillwater, MN
Maas, Leonard E. .... Rochester, NY
Maas, Lisa M. .... Sacramento, CA
Maas, Madonna .... St. Cloud, MN
Maas, Marty J. .... Glendale, CA
Maas, Maryann .... Des Plaines, IL
Maas, Norman B. .... Kenmore, WA
Maas, Paul A. .... San Diego, CA
Maas, Rebecca J. .... Indianapolis, IN
Maas, Robert D. .... Indianapolis, IN
Maas, Ronald H. .... San Jose, CA
Maas, Ronald J. .... Lake City, SC
Surfside Beach, SC
Maas, Steven A. .... Rochester, NY
Maas, Steven D. .... Youngstown, OH
Maas, Steven L. .... Grandville, MI
Maas, Thomas C. .... Farmington, IL
Maas, Walter M., III .... Seattle, WA
Maas, Warren J. .... Minneapolis, MN
Maas, William E. .... Wausau, WI
Maas, William K., Jr. .... San Francisco, CA
Maasch, Mark A. .... San Diego, CA
Maass, Andrew H. .... Rutland, VT
Maass, Harold G. .... Palm Beach, FL
Maass, Robb R. .... Fort Lauderdale, FL
Palm Beach, FL
Maass, Robert G. .... Glen Cove, NY
Maass, Sandra L. .... Omaha, NE
Maassel, Mark Thomas .... Michigan City, IN
Maassen, Eric L. .... Milwaukee, WI
Maassen, Peter J. .... Anchorage, AK
Maassen, Stephen J. .... Alton, IL
Maastricht, Eileen A. .... Chicago, IL
Maaswinkel, Gregory C. .... Orlando, FL
Maasz, P. Steven .... Canton, OH
Maatman, Gerald L., Jr. .... Chicago, IL
Maatman, Mary Ellen .... Philadelphia, PA
Maatsch, James T. .... Lansing, MI
Maatta, John D., Jr. .... Burbank, CA
Maazel, Ilann M. .... New York, NY
Mabanta, Melodie M. .... Joppa, MD
Mabary, John R. .... Sherman, TX
Mabb, Mark R. .... Tempe, AZ
Mabbett, Deborah .... Manchester, CT
Mabbitt, R. Curtis .... Muskegon, MI
Mabbitt, Stanley D. .... Phoenix, AZ
Mabbun, Yvette Jimenez .... Dallas, TX
Mabe, Christopher L. .... Fort Worth, TX
Mabe, Hugh P., III
Charlotte Amalie, St. Thomas, VI
Mabe, Jeffrey L. .... High Point, NC
Mabe, John I., Jr. .... Raleigh, NC
Mabee, Erskine Patterson .... Chattanooga, TN
Mabee & Kyriakos .... Sioux Falls, SD
Mabee, Meyers & Mills .... Mansfield, OH
Mabee, Robert E. .... Mansfield, OH
Mabee, Robert L. .... Sioux Falls, SD
Mabel, Robert J. .... Addison, TX
Maberry, John H. .... Alexandria, VA
Maberry, Scott .... Washington, DC
Mabery, Daniel T. .... Dallas, TX
Mabery, L. Richard .... Cottonwood, AZ
Prescott, AZ
Mabery, L. Richard, P.C.
Cottonwood, AZ
Prescott, AZ
Mabey, L. Benson .... Salt Lake City, UT
Mabey, Ralph R. .... New York, NY
Salt Lake City, UT
Mabie, Dean E. .... Milwaukee, WI
Mabie, J. Ralph .... West Palm Beach, FL
Mabie, J. Ralph, Jr. .... West Palm Beach, FL
Mabie, John C. .... Brattleboro, VT
Mabie, Lefferts L., III .... Tampa, FL
Mabie, Lefferts L., III, P.A. .... Tampa, FL
Mabie & Mabie .... West Palm Beach, FL
Mabie, Thomas H. .... Los Angeles, CA
Mabile, Heidi L. .... Thibodaux, LA
Mabile, Marc D. .... San Diego, CA
Mabile, Michael P. .... Washington, DC
Mabile, William R., III .... Tallahassee, FL
Mabinton, Loretta I. .... Brea, CA
Mabius, Wilhelm H. .... Harrisburg, PA

Mable, Pamela .... Atlanta, GA
Mable, Richard W. .... Walpole, MA
Mableson, Connie J. .... Phoenix, AZ
Mableson, Connie J., P.C. .... Phoenix, AZ
Mableson, William T. .... Spokane, WA
Mabley, Daniel H. .... Minneapolis, MN
Mabley, Frank T. .... St. Paul, MN
Mabley, John D. .... Farmington Hills, MI
Mabon, James M., Jr. .... Charlotte, NC
Mabon, Monrow .... Los Angeles, CA
Mabon, William F. .... Doylestown, PA
Mabray, Cheryll Pickering, (Mrs.)
Llano, TX
Mabrey, John G. .... Atlanta, GA
Mabrey, Kevin F. .... Los Angeles, CA
Mabrey, W. Carlisle, III .... Okmulgee, OK
Mabry, Alex G. .... Houston, TX
Mabry, Benjamin M. .... Columbia, SC
Mabry, Billy J. .... Danville, KY
Mabry, Bobby S. .... Houston, TX
Mabry, Buford S., Jr. .... Columbia, SC
Mabry, Carl E., II .... Indianapolis, IN
Mabry, Clegg W., Jr. .... Albemarle, NC
Mabry, Daniel E. .... Beaumont, TX
Mabry, Donald L. .... San Francisco, CA
Mabry, E. Speer, III .... Atlanta, GA
Mabry, Edwin S. .... Texas City, TX
Mabry, Frank L. .... Las Vegas, NV
Mabry, H. Sam, III .... Greenville, SC
Mabry, Herbeck & Chilton, L.L.P.
Galveston, TX
Texas City, TX
Mabry, Jerry Larry .... Dallas, TX
Mabry, John Porter, Jr. .... Waco, TX
Mabry, Linda A. .... San Francisco, CA
Mabry, Lynda Sue .... Las Vegas, NV
Mabry, M. Linda .... Macon, GA
Mabry, Michael D. .... Philadelphia, PA
Mabry, Philip P. .... Houston, TX
Mabry, Ralph T. .... Silver Spring, MD
Mabry, Richard C. .... Abilene, TX
Mabry & Steele .... Macon, GA
Mabry, Thomas F. .... Oak Ridge, TN
Mabry, Thomas F., P.C. .... Oak Ridge, TN
Mabry, Tracy J. .... Austin, TX
Mabry, III, William .... Santa Fe, NM
Mabus, Raymond E., Jr. .... Washington, DC
Jackson, MS
Maca, France M. T.
Commodity Futures Trading Commission, Division of Trading and Markets, GV
MacAbee, James M. .... Franklin, IN
MacAdam, James J. .... Topsham, ME
MacAdam, Regina Ciccone
Washington, DC
Rochester, NY
MacAdams, Pamela J. .... Cleveland, OH
MacAdams, Richard W. .... Providence, RI
MacAdams & Wieck Incorporated
Providence, RI
Macaddino, Dawn M. .... Detroit, MI
Macaddino, Kevin S. .... Birmingham, MI
MacAfee, James J., (P.C.) .... Salem, OR
MacAffer, Duncan S. .... Menands, NY
MacAffer, Kenneth S., Jr. .... Albany, NY
Macaione, David M. .... Los Angeles, CA
Nashville, TN
Macala, Brian J. .... Salem, OH
Macala, Ronald G. .... Akron, OH
Canton, OH
Youngstown, OH
MacAlarney, John B., II .... Leola, PA
Macalester, T. Lane .... Washington, DC
Macali, William M. .... Virginia Beach, VA
Macalka, James Michael .... Crown Point, IN
MacAllister, Alice J. .... Cupertino, CA
MacAllister, Bruce J. .... Santa Fe, NM
MacAllister, Joseph W. .... Nashua, NH
MacAllister, Linda S. .... Long Beach, CA
MacAllister, Marjorie L. .... New York, NY
MacAllister, Robert M. .... New York, NY
Mac Allister, Thomas W. .... Washington, DC
MacAloon, Donald J. .... Birmingham, MI
MacAloon, Martha A. .... Chicago, IL
MacAlpine, Robert F.
Mount Clemens, MI
Macaluso, Carla D. .... Morristown, NJ
Macaluso, Carmen J. .... Watertown, NY
Macaluso, Glenn T. .... La Jolla, CA
Macaluso, John .... New York, NY
Macaluso, Joseph A. .... Chicago, IL
Macaluso, Joseph A. .... Shippensburg, PA
Macaluso, Joseph G. .... White Plains, NY
Macaluso, Joseph P. .... San Ramon, CA
Macaluso, Judith N.
Department of Justice, GV
Macaluso, Michael J. .... Minneapolis, MN
Macaluso, Peter N. .... Tampa, FL
Macaluso, Richard C.
Denham Springs, LA
Macaluso, Richard C. .... Hammond, LA
Macaluso, Richard W. .... Hackensack, NJ
Macaluso, Ron S. .... Hammond, LA
Macaluso, Ron S., A P.C. .... Hammond, LA
Macaluso, Roy R. .... Passaic, NJ
Macaluso, Stacey M. .... Glendale, CA
Macan, W. Andrew .... Philadelphia, PA
Macan, William A., IV .... New York, NY
Philadelphia, PA
MacAnally, Melinda Hoover
Indianapolis, IN
MacAnanny, Glynis Anne .... Dover, DE
MacAniff, Thomas F. J. .... Doylestown, PA
Macaninch, Michael R. .... Norristown, PA
Macarchuk, Nicole J. .... New York, NY
Mac Argel, Donald T. .... Colonia, NJ
Macari, Gina L. .... Chicago, IL
Macari, Lisa J. .... Jackson Heights, NY

Macari, Louis J. .... Elmhurst, NY
Macari, Messina & Ingber .... Elmhurst, NY
Macari, Paul M. .... Troy, NY
Macario, Matthew J. .... Seattle, WA
Macaronis Law Firm .... Lowell, MA
Macaronis, Nicholas .... Lowell, MA
MacArthur, Andrew J. .... St. Michael, MN
MacArthur, Diane .... Chicago, IL
MacArthur, Douglas H. .... Miami, FL
MacArthur, Frederick E.
Los Angeles, CA
MacArthur, Gordon T. .... Syracuse, NY
MacArthur, J. Douglas .... Fresno, CA
MacArthur, John F. .... Mount Clemens, MI
MacArthur, Kelly Jo .... Seattle, WA
MacArthur, Kenneth J. .... Los Angeles, CA
MacArthur, Malcolm D. .... Washington, DC
MacArthur, Marjorie E. .... New York, NY
MacArthur, Mary .... Bethesda, MD
MacArthur & Neilson .... Fresno, CA
Mac Arthur, Scott D. .... Klamath Falls, OR
MacArthur, Stephen M. .... Washington, DC
MacArthur, Timothy P. .... Cheboygan, MI
MacArthur, Uribe, Hicks & Mims
Los Angeles, CA
MacArthur, Wallace F. .... Lafayette, CA
MacArthur, William A. .... Los Angeles, CA
Macartney, John T. .... St. Davids, PA
Macartney, Margaret L. .... Bisbee, AZ
Macartney, Martha I. .... Malvern, PA
MacArtor, June D. .... Dover, DE
Macary, Joseph P. .... Fort Washington, PA
Macauda, Marlene E. .... Westport, CT
Macauda, Vincent .... Cleveland, OH
Macaulay, Alexander Macdonald
Richmond, VA
Macaulay, Angus H., Jr. .... Columbia, SC
Macaulay, Brendan F. .... Beverly Hills, CA
Macaulay, Christopher T. .... Denver, CO
Macaulay, Donald W. .... Mount Kisco, NY
Macaulay, Joan M. .... Washington, DC
MacAulay, John B. .... New York, NY
Macaulay, Juliet O. .... Inglewood, CA
Macaulay, Karen Anne .... Hyannis, MA
Macaulay, Laura J. .... San Francisco, CA
Macaulay Lee Powell, P.C. .... Richmond, VA
Macaulay, Noel E. .... Los Angeles, CA
Macaulay, Robert B. .... Miami, FL
Macaulay, Robert C., Jr. .... Boston, MA
Macaulay, Susan J. .... Chicago, IL
MacAulay, Thomas E. .... Beckley, WV
Macaulay, Zoe .... Katonah, NY
Macauley, Anthony J. .... San Bernardino, CA
Macauley, Cherie L. .... Washington, DC
Macauley, Craig A. .... Boston, MA
MacAuley, Dan J. .... Laguna Hills, CA
MacAuley, James D. .... Columbus, OH
Macauley, John F. .... Buffalo, NY
MacAuley, Laury .... Pleasanton, CA
Macauley, Sandra K. .... Richmond, VA
MacAuley & Smart .... Laguna Hills, CA
Macauley, Thomas G. .... Wilmington, DE
Macauley, William F. .... Boston, MA
MacAvery, J. Terence .... New York, NY
MacAvoy, Christopher J. .... Washington, DC
MacAvoy, Janice .... New York, NY
MacAyeal, James R. .... Department of Justice, Environment and Natural Resources Division, GV
MacAyeal, John O. .... Fremont, MI
MacAyeal, Linda S.
Oakbrook Terrace, IL
MacBain, Douglas S. .... Seattle, WA
MacBain, Wallace A., III .... Milwaukee, WI
MacBan, Barry A. .... Tucson, AZ
MacBan, Laura V. .... Tucson, AZ
MacBan Law Offices .... Phoenix, AZ
Tucson, AZ
MacBeth, Alice Knetsch .... Wichita, KS
Macbeth, Angus .... Washington, DC
Macbeth, Arthur E. .... Los Angeles, CA
Macbeth, D. Brian .... Houston, TX
Macbeth, Douglas B. .... West Chester, PA
Macbeth, H. Scott .... Sebring, FL
MacBeth, James Scott .... Wichita, KS
Macbeth, JoAnn E. .... Washington, DC
Macbeth, Joseph O. .... Sebring, FL
MacBeth, Lynn E. .... Pittsburgh, PA
Macbeth, Robert J., Jr. .... Norfolk, VA
Macbeth, William H. .... Dayton, OH
Macbeth, William H., III .... Dayton, OH
MacBlain, Thomas D. .... Phoenix, AZ
MacBride, Dexter D. .... Diamond Bar, CA
MacBride, Jonathan R. .... Philadelphia, PA
MacBride, Lynn Y. .... Chambersburg, PA
MacBride, Marsha J.
Federal Communications Commission, Office of the Commissioners, GV
MacBride, Owen E. .... Chicago, IL
MacBride, Richard .... San Francisco, CA
MacBride, Thomas H. .... Claremont, CA
MacBride, Thomas J. .... Sacramento, CA
MacBride, Thomas J. .... Waynesboro, PA
MacBride, Thomas J., Jr.
San Francisco, CA
MacBride, William L., Jr. .... Helena, MT
MacCabe, Edward H. .... Chicago, IL
MacCabe & McGuire .... Chicago, IL
MacCabe, Scott .... Torrance, CA
MacCabe, Wm. J. .... Torrance, CA
MacCalla, Gordon F. .... Winter Haven, FL
MacCallum, Bernard J. .... Revere, MA
MacCallum, Duncan J. .... Portsmouth, NH
Maccallum, James A. .... Perry, NY
MacCallum, James J. .... Madison, WV
MacCallum, Neil R. .... Bad Axe, MI
MacCallum, Neil W. .... Southfield, MI
MacCallum, R. Kenneth .... New York, NY

MacCalman, Malcolm .... Deer Lodge, MT
MacCardle, Kenneth L. .... New York, NY
Maccariello & Bornstein .... Southington, CT
Maccarini, Anthony G. .... Carmel, NY
MacCarley, Lisa M. .... Glendale, CA
MacCarley, Mark .... Glendale, CA
MacCarley & Rosen, PLC .... Glendale, CA
Maccaro, James A. .... Whitestone, NY
Maccarone & Farhi .... Lodi, NJ
Long Valley, NJ
Maccarone, Gaetano D. .... Cambridge, MA
Maccarone, John L. .... Glen Cove, NY
Maccarone, Joseph T. .... Lodi, NJ
Long Valley, NJ
Maccarone, Melissa M. .... Palo Alto, CA
Maccarone, Ralph L., III
St. Clair Shores, MI
Maccarone, Robert M. .... Valhalla, NY
Maccaroni, Cheryl A. .... Trenton, NJ
Maccarrone, Eugene T. .... Farmingdale, NY
MacCartee, T. Douglas .... El Centro, CA
MacCarthy, Deirdre M. .... Baltimore, MD
MacCarthy, John L. .... Chicago, IL
MacCarthy, Kevin .... New York, NY
MacCarthy, Kevin, Associates, P.C.
New York, NY
MacCarthy, Philip J. .... Worcester, MA
MacCarthy, Pojani & Hurley, LLP
Worcester, MA
MacCarthy, Sean Patrick .... Chicago, IL
MacCarthy, Terence F. .... Chicago, IL
MacCartney, Harold Y., Jr. .... Nyack, NY
MacCartney, J. David, Jr. .... Nyack, NY
MacCartney, John D. .... Nyack, NY
MacCartney, MacCartney, Kerrigan & MacCartney .... Nyack, NY
MacCary, Karla Nefkens
Los Angeles, CA
MacCary, Kevin G. .... Littleton, CO
Macce, John C. .... Parsippany, NJ
Macchi, Alfred A. .... Framingham, MA
Macchi, Lea Jane Hunsicker .... Wrentham, MA
Macchi, Philip H. .... Norwood, MA
Macchi & Zucchi .... Framingham, MA
Macchia, George M. .... Newark, NJ
Macchia, Marilyn F. .... Scarsdale, NY
Macchia, Paul B. .... North Brunswick, NJ
Macchia, Raymond D. .... Cheyenne, WY
Macchia, Robert G. .... New York, NY
Macchia, Robert P. .... Melville, NY
Macchia, Stephanie .... San Antonio, TX
Macchia, Vincent M. .... New York, NY
Macchiagodena, Marina A. .... Pasadena, CA
Macchiarola, Frank J. .... New York, NY
Macchiarola, Joseph J. .... New York, NY
Macchiarola, Michael C. .... New York, NY
Macchiaroli, Jean A. .... Wilmington, DE
Macchiaroli, Michael A.
Securities and Exchange Commission, Division of Market Regulation, GV
Macchiarulo, Louis .... Elmhurst, NY
Macchiavelli, David E. .... Sacramento, CA
Macchiaverna, Louis .... Toms River, NJ
Macchio, Nicholas R., Jr. .... Brooklyn, NY
Macchione, Joseph M. .... Philadelphia, PA
Macchione, Lisa M. .... San Diego, CA
Macchitelli, James J. .... Chicago, IL
Macci, Lisa Marie .... Boca Raton, FL
Macci, Lisa Marie, P.A. .... Boca Raton, FL
Maccini, Kristen Sloan .... Providence, RI
MacClain, George .... Williamsburg, VA
MacClary, Michael D. .... Boston, MA
MacCloskey, G. Kimball .... Rockford, IL
MacClugage, Lisa D.
Fort Lauderdale, FL
Macco Hackeling & Stern .... Huntington, NY
Macco, Michael J. .... Huntington, NY
Maccoby, Matthew F. .... Los Angeles, CA
MacColl, E. Kimbark, Jr. .... Portland, OR
MacColl, Edward S. .... Portland, ME
MacColl, John A. .... St. Paul, MN
MacCollom, Kenneth Wallace
St. Petersburg, FL
MacConaghy, John H. .... Sonoma, CA
MacConnachie, Ian M., Jr. .... Monroe, NC
MacConnell, John C., Jr. .... DeLand, FL
MacConnell, Peter W. .... Amherst, MA
MacConnell, R. Ford .... Maitland, FL
MacConnell, Stephen T. .... Cincinnati, OH
MacCoon, John Patrick .... Chattanooga, TN
Maccora, James P. .... San Jose, CA
MacCord, Howard A., Jr.
Greensboro, NC
Maccorkle, Eleanor .... Asheville, NC
MacCorkle, John L. .... Charleston, WV
MacCorkle Lavender & Casey PLLC
Charleston, WV
Morgantown, WV
MacCorkle, Sam L. .... South Charleston, WV
MacCormac, Susan H. .... San Francisco, CA
MacCormack, Robert A. .... Canton, MA
MacCormack, Scott W. .... Seattle, WA
MacCoun, James W. .... Palo Alto, CA
MacCourt, Douglas C. .... Portland, OR
MacCracken, Alan M. .... Greenwich, CT
MacCracken, Constable .... New Canaan, CT
MacCracken, Lee M. .... Shepherdsville, KY
MacCracken, Richard Hardison
Los Angeles, CA
MacCrae, Mary Jane .... Carmel, NY
MacCrate, John, III .... New York, NY
MacCrate, Robert .... New York, NY
MacCrellish, W. Bruce .... Marlborough, MA
MacCrellish, William H., Jr. .... Boston, MA
MacCuish, David S. .... Los Angeles, CA
MacCulloch, David C. .... Santa Barbara, CA
MacCullough, Kara L. .... Miami, FL
Maccurtain, Gerald T. .... Boston, MA

MacDaniel, John M. .... Miami, FL
MacDermid, Bruce G. .... Hartford, CT
MacDermid, John S. .... Trenton, NJ
MacDermid, Liebert & Morgan, P.S.
Silverdale, WA
MacDermid, Reynolds & Glissman, P.C.
Hartford, CT
MacDermid, Robert C. .... Silverdale, WA
MacDermot, Andrea M. .... Las Vegas, NV
MacDermott, John T. .... San Francisco, CA
MacDermott, Julia Sherman
New York, NY
MacDermott, Kay T. .... Jamaica, NY
MacDermott, Michael J. .... Los Angeles, CA
MacDevitt, Catherine F. .... Great Neck, NY
MacDevitt, James C. .... Great Neck, NY
MacDevitt, William G. .... Melville, NY
MacDonald, A. Blake .... Duluth, MN
MacDonald, Alan K. .... Louisville, KY
Macdonald, Alan S. .... Washington, DC
MacDonald, Alex E. .... Columbus, OH
MacDonald, Alex H. .... Boston, MA
MacDonald, Alison M.
Board of Governors Of The Federal Reserve System,
Office of the General Counsel, GV
Macdonald, Amy Hurite .... Washington, DC
Macdonald, Andrew .... New York, NY
MacDonald, Andrew F. .... Washington, DC
Macdonald, Angelo Gerard .... Bronx, NY
MacDonald, Anthony B. .... Alexandria, VA
Macdonald, Arnold C. .... Portland, ME
MacDonald, Arthur J., Jr. .... Woodbury, NJ
Macdonald & Associates
San Francisco, CA
MacDonald & Associates, Ltd.
Las Vegas, NV
Macdonald & Associates, P.C.
Washington, DC
Fairfax, VA
MacDonald, Barbara .... Wilmington, DE
MacDonald, Barclay E. .... Kula, HI
MacDonald Beckman, LLP
San Francisco, CA
MacDonald, Bradley A. .... Newton, MA
Macdonald, Bradley S. .... Atlanta, GA
MacDonald, Brett W. .... Harrisburg, PA
MacDonald, Brian .... Buffalo, NY
MacDonald, Brian J. .... Stamford, CT
MacDonald, Bruce B.
Yorktown Heights, NY
MacDonald, Bruce G. .... Tucson, AZ
Macdonald, Bruce T. .... Cambridge, MA
MacDonald, Bruce W. .... Greenup, KY
MacDonald, Bryant C. .... Redlands, CA
MacDonald, Bryce .... Schenectady, NY
Macdonald, Cameron J. .... Baltimore, MD
MacDonald, Cara Lee .... Palm Beach, FL
MacDonald, Carl J. .... Columbus, OH
MacDonald, Cathleen .... Santa Ana, CA
MacDonald, Celine M. .... Oakland, CA
Macdonald & Chase, P.A. .... Bangor, ME
MacDonald, Cherie K. .... Belleville, IL
St. Louis, MO
Macdonald, Clare H. .... Santa Barbara, CA
MacDonald, Craig R. .... Lisle, IL
MacDonald, Cynthia M. .... St. Paul, MN
Macdonald, Cynthia P. .... Hartford, CT
Macdonald, D. Charles .... Minneapolis, MN
Macdonald, D. Lloyd .... Boston, MA
MacDonald, Daniel A. .... Madison, WI
MacDonald, Daniel F. .... Norwood, MA
MacDonald, Daniel F., P.C. .... Norwood, MA
MacDonald, Daniel J. .... Myrtle Beach, SC
MacDonald, Darcy M. .... Stoughton, MA
Macdonald, David .... Rockville, MD
MacDonald, David .... New York, NY
MacDonald, David A. .... Hempstead, NY
Macdonald, David M. .... Dallas, TX
MacDonald, David R. .... Washington, DC
MacDonald, DeWitt K. .... San Rafael, CA
MacDonald, Diane Kazmierowicz
Newcastle, WA
MacDonald, Donald, IV .... Anchorage, AK
MacDonald, Donald J. .... Walpole, MA
MacDonald, Donald P. .... Denver, CO
MacDonald, Douglas A. .... Sacramento, CA
MacDonald, Douglas R. .... Holland, MI
Macdonald, Douglas W. .... Washington, DC
MacDonald, Duncan A.
Long Island City, NY
MacDonald, Duncan D. .... Baton Rouge, LA
MacDonald, Duncan S.
San Francisco, CA
Macdonald, Edward P. .... Shelton, CT
MacDonald, Elizabeth A. .... Denver, CO
MacDonald, Ellen M. .... Washington, DC
MacDonald, Ellen R. .... Bloomfield Hills, MI
Macdonald, Eric K. .... Mesa, AZ
MacDonald, FitzGerald & MacDonald, P.C.
Flint, MI
Pontiac, MI
MacDonald, Francis J. .... Winthrop, MA
MacDonald, Frederick M.
Salt Lake City, UT
MacDonald, Gary A. .... Washington, DC
MacDonald, Geoffrey .... Miami, FL
MacDonald, George C. .... Buffalo, MN
MacDonald, George E. .... York, PA
MacDonald, George M. .... New York, NY
MacDonald, George W. .... Cleveland, OH
MacDonald, Gerald G. .... Lansing, MI
MacDonald, Gina G. .... Canyon Country, CA
MacDonald, Gordon C. .... Concord, CA
MacDonald, Gordon J. .... Manchester, NH
MacDonald, Gregory A. .... Des Plaines, IL
MacDonald, Harold C. .... Birmingham, MI

MacDonald & Hicks, Law Offices of
Denver, CO
MacDonald, Hoague & Bayless, A Professional Service Corporation
Seattle, WA
Macdonald, Iain A. .... San Francisco, CA
Macdonald, Ian A. .... Honolulu, HI
MacDonald, Ian A. .... Lafayette, LA
MacDonald, Ian G. .... Poughkeepsie, NY
MacDonald, Illig, Jones & Britton LLP
Erie, PA
MacDonald, Irving C. .... Minnetonka, MN
MacDonald, J. Brian .... Flint, MI
Mac Donald, J. Bruce .... Schenectady, NY
Macdonald, J. Coury .... Washington, DC
Fairfax, VA
MacDonald, J. Scott .... Las Vegas, NV
Macdonald, J. Thomas .... Denver, CO
MacDonald, Jack R. .... Seattle, WA
MacDonald, James A. .... Wilmington, NC
MacDonald, James B. .... Costa Mesa, CA
Macdonald, James B. .... Fullerton, CA
MacDonald, James B. .... Ocean Grove, NJ
MacDonald, James B. .... Princeton, NJ
MacDonald, James B. .... Madison, WI
Macdonald, James C. .... Los Angeles, CA
Macdonald, James E. .... Ogden, UT
Macdonald, James G. .... Austin, TX
MacDonald, James H. .... Mendham, NJ
MacDonald, James Ross, IV
New York, NY
Macdonald, James S. .... Denver, CO
MacDonald, James S. .... Moscow, ID
MacDonald, James S. .... Knoxville, TN
MacDonald, Janet A. .... Baltimore, MD
Mac Donald, Janet M. .... Kenmore, NY
MacDonald, Jeffrey S. .... New York, NY
MacDonald, Jennifer G. .... Kansas City, KS
MacDonald, Jimmy A. .... Van Nuys, CA
MacDonald, Joel G. .... Gloucester, MA
MacDonald, John A. .... Philadelphia, PA
MacDonald, John A. .... Seattle, WA
MacDonald, John B. .... Jacksonville, FL
MacDonald, John E. .... Plymouth, MI
MacDonald, John E. .... Princeton, NJ
MacDonald, John H. .... Buchanan, MI
MacDonald, John K. .... Washington, DC
MacDonald, John M. .... Hillsdale, MI
Macdonald, John P. .... New York, NY
MacDonald, Jon Robert .... West Branch, MI
MacDonald, Joseph J. .... Rumson, NJ
MacDonald, Joseph W. .... Cohasset, MA
MacDonald, Joyce Yulkey .... Edwardsville, IL
MacDonald, Judith R. .... New York, NY
MacDonald, Karen M. .... West Branch, MI
Macdonald, Katherine E. .... Gainesville, FL
MacDonald, Kathryn C. .... New York, NY
MacDonald, Kenneth A. .... Seattle, WA
Macdonald, Kevin Joseph
Jamaica Plain, MA
MacDonald, Kimberly L. .... Exton, PA
MacDonald, Kirk S. .... Glendale, CA
MacDonald, L. Lloyd .... Midland, TX
MacDonald, Lani Torres .... St. Petersburg, FL
MacDonald, Larry A. .... Harper Woods, MI
MacDonald Law Offices, P.C.
Wilkes-Barre, PA
MacDonald, Lawrence B. .... Detroit, MI
MacDonald, Lawrence D.
Wilkes-Barre, PA
Macdonald, Lena Ruth .... Louisville, KY
Macdonald, Lenore L. .... Chicago, IL
Macdonald, Leo H., Jr. .... St. Louis, MO
MacDonald, Leo H., Sr. .... St. Louis, MO
Mac Donald, Linda Silling .... New York, NY
MacDonald, Lizabeth M. .... Exeter, NH
MacDonald, Lynn C. .... Chicago, IL
MacDonald, M. Melinda .... Emeryville, CA
MacDonald, Madlyne A. .... Sacramento, CA
MacDonald, Malcolm John
Washington, DC
MacDonald, Maralee .... Laramie, WY
Macdonald, Marcy F. .... Shelton, CT
Macdonald, Margaret D. .... Washington, DC
MacDonald, Marit S. .... Palo Alto, CA
MacDonald, Mark A. .... Cincinnati, OH
MacDonald, Mark E. .... Dallas, TX
MacDonald, Mark T. .... Lexington, KY
MacDonald, Mary Byrne .... St. Louis, MO
MacDonald, Mary E. .... Oakland, CA
MacDonald, Michael A. .... Fairbanks, AK
MacDonald, Michael A. .... Grand Rapids, MI
MacDonald, Michael E. .... Pittsfield, MA
MacDonald, Michael G. .... New York, NY
MacDonald, Michael W.
Sault Ste. Marie, MI
Mac Donald, Michelle A. .... Los Angeles, CA
MacDonald, Michelle L. .... Edina, MN
MacDonald, Milford W.
Hilton Head Island, SC
MacDonald, Munger, Downs & Munger
Duluth, MN
MacDonald, Neil F. .... Kingston, PA
Scranton, PA
MacDonald, Neil Joseph .... Lanham, MD
MacDonald, Norman C. .... Van Nuys, CA
Macdonald, Patrick P. .... Malden, MA
MacDonald, Paul A. .... Wiscasset, ME
MacDonald, Paul H. .... Concord, NH
Macdonald, Peter C. .... Hopkinsville, KY
MacDonald, Peter D. .... Pleasanton, CA
Macdonald, Peter F. .... Quincy, MA
MacDonald, Peter H. .... Bridgeport, CT
Macdonald, Peter J. .... Boston, MA
MacDonald, Peter S. .... San Diego, CA
MacDonald, R. Duncan .... Flint, MI
MacDonald, Ralph F., III .... Atlanta, GA
MacDonald, Rand .... Phoenix, AZ

MacDonald, Raymond A. .... Utica, MI
MacDonald, Reina M. .... Chatsworth, CA
Macdonald, Rhonda J. .... Vienna, VA
MacDonald, Rhonda J., Esq., P.C.
Vienna, VA
MacDonald, Richard B. .... Lancaster, PA
MacDonald, Richard E.
St. Petersburg, FL
MacDonald, Rob D. .... San Jose, CA
MacDonald, Robert .... Springfield, NJ
Macdonald, Robert A. .... Provo, UT
MacDonald, Robert B. .... Minneapolis, MN
MacDonald, Robert B., Jr.
Bellefontaine, OH
MacDonald, Robert C. .... Washington, DC
Macdonald, Robert F., Jr. .... Portland, ME
Macdonald, Robert F., Sr. .... Bridgton, ME
MacDonald, Robert G. .... Suffolk, VA
MacDonald, Robert J. .... San Mateo, CA
MacDonald, Robert J .... Flint, MI
MacDonald, Robert S. .... Orlando, FL
MacDonald, Robert W. .... Chicago, IL
Macdonald, Roderick L. .... Boston, MA
MacDonald, Roderick W. .... Plano, TX
MacDonald, Roland L., Jr.
Department of Commerce, GV
MacDonald, Ronald B. .... Missoula, MT
Mac Donald, Ronald P. .... Salem, OR
MacDonald Rudy & Byrns .... Honolulu, HI
MacDonald & Schuble, L.L.P. .... Dallas, TX
Macdonald, Scott D. .... Hartford, CT
MacDonald, Scott D. .... Southfield, MI
Macdonald, Scott L. .... Los Angeles, CA
MacDonald, Scott W. .... Houston, TX
MacDonald, Shari R. .... Peabody, MA
MacDonald, Shirley J. .... Santa Ana, CA
MacDonald, Stephen B. .... Honolulu, HI
MacDonald, Stephen R. .... New York, NY
MacDonald, Steven Adair
San Francisco, CA
MacDonald, Stewart D. .... Youngstown, OH
MacDonald, Susan Pardue
Myrtle Beach, SC
MacDonald, Terry J. .... Missoula, MT
MacDonald, Theodore J., Jr.
Edwardsville, IL
MacDonald, Thomas C., Jr. .... Tampa, FL
MacDonald, Thomas G. .... New York, NY
Mac Donald, Thomas J. .... Boston, MA
MacDonald, Thomas L. .... Flemingsburg, KY
MacDonald, Thomas S. .... San Jose, CA
Macdonald, Timothy .... Denver, CO
MacDonald, Timothy J. .... Flint, MI
MacDonald, Timothy P. .... Boston, MA
MacDonald, W. Barry .... Danvers, MA
MacDonald, W. Cullen .... New York, NY
MacDonald, Walter A., Jr. .... San Jose, CA
MacDonald, Walter B. .... Algona, IA
MacDonald & Walton .... Flemingsburg, KY
Macdonald, William .... Winnemucca, NV
MacDonald, William A. .... Washington, DC
Macdonald, William C. .... San Francisco, CA
Macdonald, William E. .... Bangor, ME
Macdonald, William J. .... Denver, CO
MacDonald, William P., Jr. .... Holyoke, MA
MacDonald, William R. .... Westminster, MD
MacDonald, William R. .... New York, NY
Macdonald, Winslow H. .... Wellesley, MA
Macdonald-Bousaleh, Kateri .... Quincy, MA
Macdonald-Matthes, Paige F.
Harrisburg, PA
MacDonell, Angus G. .... Sacramento, CA
MacDonell, Janet L. .... New Orleans, LA
Macdonell, Robert A. .... Farmington Hills, MI
MacDonneil, Cori L. .... San Francisco, CA
MacDonnell, Ann Marie .... New York, NY
MacDonnell, Craig A. .... Boston, MA
MacDonnell, G. J. Stillson
San Francisco, CA
MacDonnell, Lawrence J. .... Boulder, CO
MacDonnell, Margaret S. .... Boulder, CO
MacDonnell, Mark A. .... Las Animas, CO
MacDonnell, Philip J. .... Phoenix, AZ
MacDonnell, Robert A. .... Philadelphia, PA
Macdonough, Bruce E. .... Miami, FL
MacDonough, Richard .... San Diego, CA
MacDougal, Douglas W. .... Portland, OR
MacDougald, Daniel, III .... Atlanta, GA
MacDougald, Daniel, Jr. .... Baconton, GA
MacDougald, Harry W. .... Atlanta, GA
MacDougald, Kevin .... Santa Rosa, CA
MacDougall, Allan L. .... Seattle, WA
MacDougall, Ann L. .... New York, NY
MacDougall, David J. .... Janesville, WI
MacDougall, Donald B.
San Francisco, CA
MacDougall, Francis .... Towson, MD
MacDougall, Gordon P. .... Washington, DC
MacDougall, Heather L. .... Washington, DC
MacDougall, Hugh C. .... Department of State,
Foreign Service Officers (Overseas), GV
MacDougall, Irene M. .... Cleveland, OH
Macdougall, Iver C. .... Bainbridge Island, WA
Macdougall, John S., Jr. .... Haverhill, MA
Macdougall, Joseph W., Jr. .... Worcester, MA
MacDougall, Kate B. .... Lowell, MA
MacDougall, Mark A. .... Baltimore, MD
MacDougall, Mark J. .... Washington, DC
MacDougall, M. E. .... Colorado Springs, CO
MacDougall, Michael M. .... Boston, MA
MacDougall, Vicki Lawrence
Oklahoma City, OK
MacDougall, William R. .... Sacramento, CA
MacDougall, Woldridge & Worley P.C.
Colorado Springs, CO
MacDowall, Alexis .... Chicago, IL
MacDowell, C. Frederick .... Atlanta, GA
MacDowell, Elizabeth L. .... Los Angeles, CA

MacDowell, Francesca Jeanne
Albuquerque, NM
Macdowell, G. Kendrick .... Washington, DC
MacDowell, John R. .... Santa Ana, CA
MacDuff, Sara J. .... Seattle, WA
MacDuffie, E. Allen, Jr. .... Lavallette, NJ
MacDwyer, Sara .... San Francisco, CA
Mace, Amy E. .... Minneapolis, MN
Mace, C. Robert .... Houston, TX
Mace, Damond R. .... Cleveland, OH
Mace, David M. .... New York, NY
Mace, Derek L. .... Hickory, NC
Mace, Gerald F. .... Nashville, TN
Mace, Glenn L. .... Fort Worth, TX
Mace, James S. .... Las Vegas, NV
Mace, Jeffrey H. .... New York, NY
Mace, Karen Audrey .... Miami Beach, FL
Mace, Matthew A. .... Baltimore, MD
Mace, Philip J. .... Columbia, SC
Mace, Robert A. .... Cincinnati, OH
Mace, Robert F. .... New York, NY
Mace, Russell Warren, III .... Bal Harbour, FL
Mace, Stephen A. .... St. Louis, MO
Mace, Stephen G. .... Los Angeles, CA
Mace, Teri Stewart .... Dallas, TX
Mace, Theodora M. .... Lansing, MI
Mace, Thomas J. .... Baltimore, MD
Mace, Valerie .... Somers, NY
MacEachen, John D. .... Treasury Department,
Internal Revenue Service, GV
MacEachern, Katherine A. .... St. Paul, MN
MacEachern, Kelly Walls .... Santa Ana, CA
MacEachern, Kimberly W. .... Phoenix, AZ
MacEachron, Susan .... New York, NY
Maceda, Joseph L. .... Brooklyn, NY
Macedo, Augusto D.
Securities and Exchange Commission,
Office of Investor Education and Assistance, GV
Macedo, Charles R. .... New York, NY
Macedo, Ernesto .... Brooklyn, NY
Macedo, José J. .... Somerville, MA
Macedonio, Rosemary A. .... Cleveland, OH
Macedonio & Toerek, P.L.L. .... Cleveland, OH
Maceiko, Theodore S. .... Los Angeles, CA
Macejko & Macejko .... Youngstown, OH
Macejko, Theodore T. .... Youngstown, OH
Macejko, Theodore T., Jr. .... Youngstown, OH
Macek, Edward M. .... Milford, MA
Macek, Gary M. .... St. Louis, MO
Macek, Julie A. .... Great Falls, MT
Macek, Paul L. .... Davenport, IA
Macek, Robert C. .... Ann Arbor, MI
Macek, Stephen G. .... Chardon, OH
Macel, Leanne K. .... Washington, DC
Macel, Stanley C., III .... Wilmington, DE
MacElhenney, Jane B. .... Philadelphia, PA
Macellaro, Charles J. .... Yonkers, NY
Macellaro, Theresa J. .... Los Angeles, CA
MacElree, Harvey, Gallagher, Featherman & Sebastian, Ltd. .... Exton, PA
Kennett Square, PA
Philadelphia, PA
Spring City, PA
West Chester, PA
MacElree, James P., II .... West Chester, PA
MacElhenney, Laurence D. .... West Chester, PA
MacElree, Linda Labiak
West Chester, PA
Macenka, Mark J. .... Boston, MA
Macer, B. Michael .... Evansville, IN
Macerato, Frank M. .... Reading, PA
Macerelli, Joseph A. .... Pittsburgh, PA
Macero, Rosemary A. .... Boston, MA
Maceroni & Maceroni, P.C.
Sterling Heights, MI
Maceroni, Michael .... Sterling Heights, MI
Maceroni, Peter J. .... Mount Clemens, MI
Mac Eslin, Bonnie .... Dallas, TX
Macevicz, Stephen C. .... Hayward, CA
MacEwan, Alan D. .... Portland, ME
MacEwan, Dorothy D., (Mrs.) .... Berkeley, CA
MacEwan, Kevin E. .... Austin, TX
MacEwen, Elizabeth A. .... New York, NY
MacEwen, Wilson M. .... Sumter, SC
Macey, Barry A. .... Indianapolis, IN
Macey, Eric N. .... Chicago, IL
Macey, Harry J. .... Palo Alto, CA
Macey, Joe S.
Department of Transportation,
Maritime Administration, GV
Macey, Jonathan R. .... Ithaca, NY
Macey, Julie M. .... Stockton, CA
Macey, M. William, Jr. .... New York, NY
Macey, Macey & Swanson .... Indianapolis, IN
Macey, Marilyn H. .... Birmingham, AL
Macey, Marla A. .... Philadelphia, PA
Macey, Marsha C. .... San Francisco, CA
Macey, Morris W. (IBA) .... Atlanta, GA
Macey, Nora L. .... Indianapolis, IN
Macey, Scott J. .... Somerset, NJ
Macey, Wilensky, Cohen, Wittner & Kessler, LLP .... Atlanta, GA
MacFadyen, John A., III .... Providence, RI
MacFadyen, Kenneth J. .... Baltimore, MD
MacFall, Riedl & Miskowski
Ridgewood, NJ
Macfarlan, David M. .... Horsham, PA
Macfarlan, Debbie A. .... Miami, FL
Macfarlan, John H. .... Murphy, NC
MacFarlan, Sherburne M., III .... Elko, NV
MacFarland, Alfred T.
Castalian Springs, TN
MacFarland, Richard B., (P.A.)
Boca Raton, FL
MacFarland, Ronald M. .... Woodbine, NJ
MacFarland, William H. .... Scottsdale, AZ
Macfarlane, Andrew K. .... Tampa, FL

Macfarlane, Bonnie L. ....Carpentersville, IL
MacFarlane, Bruce F. ....Detroit, MI
Macfarlane, Charles N.
San Francisco, CA
Macfarlane, Christine M.
Los Angeles, CA
MacFarlane, Earl W. ....Wilmington, DE
Macfarlane, Ellen M. ....Tampa, FL
Macfarlane, Evan L. ....Grand Rapids, MI
Macfarlane Ferguson & McMullen,
Professional Association .....Clearwater, FL
Tallahassee, FL
Tampa, FL
MacFarlane, Frances
Department of Housing and Urban Development,
Office of General Counsel, GV
Macfarlane, Hugh C. ....Tampa, FL
MacFarlane, J. Thomas ....Birmingham, MI
MacFarlane, James P. ....Butler, PA
MacFarlane, James Wry
Montgomery, AL
MacFarlane, Janet G. ....Denver, CO
MacFarlane, John D. ....Denver, CO
Macfarlane, John H. ....Battle Creek, MI
Macfarlane, Kelly H. ....Salt Lake City, UT
Macfarlane, Kira E. ....Salt Lake City, UT
Macfarlane, Kirk R. ....King Of Prussia, PA
Macfarlane, Lisa Davis ....Seattle, WA
Macfarlane, Margaret A.H.
New York, NY
MacFarlane, Margaret Anne ....Tustin, CA
MacFarlane, Margaret L. ....Beaver Dam, WI
MacFarlane, Marshall G. ....Ann Arbor, MI
Troy, MI
MacFarlane, R. Bruce ....Richmond, VA
MacFarlane, R. Todd ....Cedar City, UT
MacFarlane, Richard D. ....Mass City, MI
Mac Farlane, Robert D. .....Newport Beach, CA
MacFarlane, Ron G., Jr. ....Dallas, TX
Macfarlane, Ross A. ....Seattle, WA
MacFarlane, Stephen M. ....Sacramento, CA
MacFerrin, Kurtis D. ....Palo Alto, CA
MacFie, Keith A. ....Tacoma, WA
MacGibbon, B. Douglas
West Palm Beach, FL
MacGibbon, John E. ....Monticello, MN
Macgill, Frank S. ....Savannah, GA
Macgill, James ....Towson, MD
MacGill, Robert D. ....Indianapolis, IN
MacGill, Sue Tuohy ....Indianapolis, IN
MacGillis, James C. ....Minneapolis, MN
MacGillis, Roderick T. ....Lansing, MI
MacGillivray, Corey M. ....Dearborn, MI
MacGillivray, Douglas D. .....Bellefontaine, OH
Macgillivray, Karyn A. ....Webster, MA
MacGillivray, Kevin ....Morristown, NJ
MacGillivray, Lisa ....Halifax, MA
MacGillivray, Stephen J. ....Providence, RI
MacGillivray, William D. ......Westborough, MA
MacGilvra, Glenn E. ....Seattle, WA
MacGlashan, Cate ....St. Petersburg, FL
MacGlashan, Craig S. ....Sacramento, CA
MacGowan, Clyde L. ....Oakland, CA
MacGowan, John L. ....Coopersburg, PA
MacGrady, Barbara L. ....New York, NY
MacGrady, Glenn J. ....Hartford, CT
MacGrath, Dana C. ....New York, NY
MacGray, Douglas R. ....Bear, DE
MacGreevy, William R. ....St. Louis, MO
MacGregor, A. Bruce ....Haverhill, MA
MacGregor, Alexander G. ....Orlando, FL
MacGregor & Berthel ....Los Angeles, CA
Woodland Hills, CA
MacGregor & Carroll ....Canton, MA
MacGregor, Charles E. ....New Albany, IN
MacGregor, Clark ....Washington, DC
MacGregor, D. Gregor, III ....Marquette, MI
MacGregor, David B. ....Philadelphia, PA
MacGregor, David L. ....Milwaukee, WI
MacGregor, David W. ....Newark, NJ
Macgregor, Dawn A. ....Natick, MA
MacGregor, Elizabeth H.
Securities and Exchange Commission,
Division of Market Regulation, GV
MacGregor, Gregory Michael
Woodland Hills, CA
MacGregor, Iain D. ....Dearborn, MI
MacGregor, Katrine Benedict
Boston, MA
MacGregor, Kirk Angus ....Grangeville, ID
MacGregor, MacLaren H. ....Canton, MA
MacGregor, Malcolm D.
Minneapolis, MN
MacGregor, Malcolm L. ....Scranton, PA
Macgregor, Meichelle R. ....New York, NY
MacGregor, Rob R. ....Birmingham, MI
MacGregor, Spurling, Hart & Trakimas, P.C.
Haverhill, MA
MacGregor, Susan Douglas
Marquette, MI
MacGregor, Thomas G. ....Summerville, SC
MacGregor, Wayne C., Jr.
Grangeville, ID
MacGregor, Wm. Paul ....Seattle, WA
MacGriff, Scott A. ....Detroit, MI
MacGuigan, Patricia D.
Oklahoma City, OK
MacGuineas, D. Biard ....Washington, DC
Macgurn, Richard B. ....Carlsbad, CA
Mach, Daniel ....Washington, DC
Mach, Donald J. ....San Antonio, TX
Mach, Edwin K. ....Turlock, CA
Mach, Joseph D. ....Hackensack, NJ
Mach, Lori L. ....Philadelphia, PA
Mach, Philip L. ....Fresno, CA
Mach, Scott W. ....Kansas City, MO
Macha, Barry L. ....Wichita Falls, TX
Macha, Eugene A. ....Houston, TX
Macha, Larry L. ....Bellville, TX
Macha, Stacy L. ....Southfield, MI
Machac, George W. ....Humble, TX
Machado, Arthur, & Associates .....Windsor, CT
Machado, C. Patrick ....Walnut Creek, CA
Machado, Carlos M. ....Miami, FL
Machado, Donald C. ....Honolulu, HI
Machado, Donald Carl, Jr. ....Honolulu, HI
Machado, E. L. ....Carmel Valley, CA
Machado, Emilio E. ....Chicago, IL
Machado, Isabel ....Westfield, NJ
Machado, John B. ....San Jose, CA
Machado, John J. ....Modesto, CA
Machado, John L. ....Washington, DC
Machado, Kenneth J., Jr. ....San Jose, CA
Machado, Leslie L. ....Schaumburg, IL
Machado, Leslie P. ....Washington, DC
Machado, Luis F. ....Sturtevant, WI
Machado & Machado ....San Jose, CA
Machado, Mark S. ....Easton, MA
Machado, Michelle L. ....Boston, MA
Machado, Michelle L. ....Providence, RI
Machado, Nancy E.
Department of Transportation,
Research and Special Programs
Administration, GV
Machado, Paul David ....Boston, MA
Machado, Paul J. ....Holbrook, MA
Machado, Ramon Rafael, Jr.
Los Angeles, CA
Machado, Richard T. ....San Diego, CA
Machado, Robert A. ....San Jose, CA
Mac Haffie, Dale S. ....Portland, OR
MacHale, William M. ....Wheaton, MD
MacHale, William M., P.A. ....Wheaton, MD
Machalicky, Charles G.
Rancho Palos Verdes, CA
Machalinski, Donald G. ....Chicago, IL
Machan, Michael J. ....West Allis, WI
Machan, Mitchell A. ....Canton, OH
Machan, Sandra J. ....Akron, OH
Machan & Whalen ....Akron, OH
Machanic, David ....Charlotte, VT
Machanic, Scott L. ....Natick, MA
Machann, E. Dwaine ....Kerrville, TX
MacHare, Peter ....Department of Agriculture,
Office of the General Counsel, GV
MacHarg, Donald A. ....Slingerlands, NY
MacHarg, James C. ....Toledo, OH
MacHarg, Jean Veeder ....Washington, DC
MacHarg, Marcia L. ....Washington, DC
MacHarg, Suzan A. ....Toledo, OH
Machat, Michael ....Los Angeles, CA
Machcinski, Victor Anthony, Jr.
New York, NY
Machel, Christine ....Wellsburg, WV
Macheledt, Jean M. ....Fort Collins, CO
Machen, Arthur W., Jr. (P.C.)
Baltimore, MD
Machen & Dobson ....Sylacauga, AL
Machen, Donald E. ....Pittsburgh, PA
Machen, Harold P. ....Sacramento, CA
Machen, John P. ....Baltimore, MD
Machen, Mark R. ....Fairfax, VA
Machen, Robert B. ....Fairfax, VA
Machen, Stephen Morris ....Sylacauga, AL
Machen, William F. ....Boston, MA
MacHenry, Thomas E. ....Wakefield, MA
Macher, David J. ....Riverside, CA
Machera, Joseph ....Revere, MA
Machera, Mark A. ....Methuen, MA
Macheras, Peter G. ....Baltimore, MD
Macherson, David G. ......Colorado Springs, CO
Macherzak, Michael F. ....Mount Clemens, MI
Machesney, Lisa A. ....Houston, TX
Machetanz, Traeger ....Anchorage, AK
Seattle, WA
Machi, Angela L. ....La Crescent, MN
Machi, Mark A. ....Washington, DC
Machi, Mary Anna ....Healdsburg, CA
Machi, Peter P. ....San Francisco, CA
Machi, Renée T. ....San Francisco, CA
Machi, Robert J. ....Livingston, NJ
Machicao, Dorothy L. ....Marion, IL
Machicao, Lisa C. ....Kansas City, MO
Machida, Kenji, (A Professional Corporation)
Los Angeles, CA
Machida, Marieann Z. ....Washington, DC
Machii, Lisa N. ....Los Angeles, CA
Machin, Barbara E. ....Toledo, OH
Machin, George L. ....Hialeah, FL
Machin, Manuel A. ....Tampa, FL
Machinton, Nancy W. ....Easthampton, MA
Machion, Charles B. ....Rockville, MD
Machione, Robin A. ....Mendon, MA
Machit, Monte H. ....Long Beach, CA
Machiz, Larry H. ....Ghent, NY
Machiz, Marc I. ....Department of Labor,
Office of the Solicitor, GV
Machle, Kathi J. ....Columbus, OH
Machleder, Robert A. ....New York, NY
Machler, Susan ....Seattle, WA
Machles, Arnold ....Bala Cynwyd, PA
Machles & Ring ....Bala Cynwyd, PA
Machlin, Barry N. ....Chicago, IL
Machlin, Marc D. ....Washington, DC
Machlin, Philip A. ....Woodbridge, NJ
Machlis, Roger M. ....New York, NY
Machlowitz, David S. ....New York, NY
Machmeier, Bruce A. ....Minneapolis, MN
Machmer, Gerald A. ....Phoenix, AZ
Machmer & Schlosser, Ltd. ....Phoenix, AZ
Machnacki, David ....Birmingham, MI
Machnik, Ronald E. ....Jackson, MI
Machnik, Todd M. ....Franklin, MA
Machnik, Wendelyn M. ....Coldwater, MI
Machol, Jacques A., III ....Denver, CO
Machol, Jacques A., Jr. ....Denver, CO
Machol & Johannes, P.C. ....Denver, CO
Machol, Melynda J. ....Cincinnati, OH
Macholl, James E. ....Rosemont, IL
Machonkin, Richard A. ....Chicago, IL
Machov, Steven J. ....St. Paul, MN
Machovec, Jennifer Buchanan
Research Triangle Park, NC
Machroli, Vincent C. ....Hillside, IL
Machson, Marvin S. ....Somers, NY
Machson, Robert A., & Associates
New York, NY
Macht, Brenizer & Gingold, P.C.
Syracuse, NY
Macht, Elliot G. ....Manchester, CT
Macht, Jane ....Rockville, MD
Macht, Julie K. ....Bronx, NY
Macht, Milton ....Fayetteville, NY
Macht, Valarie H. ....Los Angeles, CA
Macht, William P. ....Hood River, OR
Machtinger, John F. ....Los Angeles, CA
Machtinger, Leonard S. ....Los Angeles, CA
Machtinger, Marc D. ....Chicago, IL
Machtinger, Sidney J. ....Los Angeles, CA
Machtmes, Todd E. ....Walnut Creek, CA
Machuga, Richard William
Youngstown, OH
Machulak, Hutchinson, Robertson & O'Dess, S.C. ....Milwaukee, WI
Machulak, John E. ....Milwaukee, WI
Macia, Alberto A. ....Miami, FL
Macia, Alexander ....Charleston, WV
Macia, Lillian C. ....Miami Lakes, FL
Maciag & Associates, A Professional
Corporation ....Newark, NJ
Somerville, NJ
Maciag, Thaddeus R. ....Newark, NJ
Somerville, NJ
Maciak, Edward J. ....Flint, MI
Maciak, Ronald S. ....Indianapolis, IN
Macias, Ernest R. ....Morgan Hill, CA
Macias, Jose F. ....Palo Alto, CA
Macias, Marianne V. ....New York, NY
Macias, Mark E. ....Austin, TX
Macias, Patricia A. ....El Paso, TX
Macias, Patrick M. ....San Rafael, CA
Macias, Richard A. ....Wichita, KS
Macias, Richard C. ....Los Angeles, CA
Macias, Xavier Alfredo ....Hawthorne, NY
Maciasz, Mark ....Chicago, IL
Macie, James J. ....Jonesboro, GA
Macie, Michael J. ....Irvine, CA
Maciejczyk, John M. ....Elkhart, IN
Maciejewski, Donald M. ....Jacksonville, FL
Maciejewski, Michael A. ....Elmhurst, IL
Oak Brook, IL
Maciel, Antonio L. ....New York, NY
Macielak, Paul F. ....Mineola, NY
Macik, Luke A. ....Gallup, NM
MacIlroy, John W. ....Midlothian, TX
MacIlwaine, Wendy L. ....Chicago, IL
Macina, Robert P. ....Lancaster, PA
Macinanti, Amy G. ....Harrisburg, PA
MacInnes, Cathryn M. ....Boston, MA
MacInnes, Douglas B. ....Tallahassee, FL
MacInnes, Ian ....Bangor, ME
MacInnes, Malcolm D. ....Salem, OR
MacInnes, Robert A. ....Austin, TX
MacInnes, Whigham, Lively & Siefken
Austin, TX
MacInnis, Donner & Koplowitz
San Francisco, CA
MacInnis, Michael S. ....Jackson, MS
Macinski, Martha Keeler
Watkins Glen, NY
Macintosh, Andrea R. ....Washington, DC
MacIntosh, Barbara D. ....Memphis, TN
MacIntosh, Bruce D., Jr. ....Broomfield, CO
MacIntosh, Donald N. ....San Francisco, CA
MacIntosh, G. Thomas, II
Minneapolis, MN
Macintosh, Mary K. ....Overland Park, KS
MacIntosh, Susanne M. ....Los Angeles, CA
MacIntosh, Victoria E., (P.A.)
St. Petersburg, FL
MacIntyre, Anne E. ....Detroit, MI
MacIntyre, Anne L. ....Helena, MT
MacIntyre, Bruce G. ....Seattle, WA
MacIntyre, Daniel I. ....Atlanta, GA
MacIntyre, David S. ....Boston, MA
Macintyre, David W. G., Jr. ....Atlanta, GA
MacIntyre, Donald D. ....Helena, MT
Macintyre, Donald S. ....Westminster, CA
MacIntyre, James D. ....Dallas, TX
MacIntyre, Joy S. ....San Francisco, CA
MacIntyre & MacIntyre ....Harrisburg, PA
MacIntyre, Marion E., (Mrs.)
Harrisburg, PA
MacIntyre, Robert B. ....Harrisburg, PA
MacIntyre, Robert S., Jr. ....Houston, TX
MacIntyre, Shona M. ....Chicago, IL
MacIntyre, Susan A. ....Washington, DC
MacIntyre, Timothy D. ....Troy, MI
MacIntyre, Tuppence ....Los Angeles, CA
Macioce, Frank M., Jr. ....New York, NY
Macioci, Joseph J. ....Newport, RI
Maciolek, John R. ....Worcester, MA
Maciolek, Kenneth J. ....Milwaukee, WI
Maciolek, Richard D. ....Medway, MA
Macione, Kyle P. ....Bristol, VA
Maciorowski, Edmund ....Bloomfield Hills, MI
Maciorowski, Edmund, P.C.
Bloomfield Hills, MI
Maciorowski, John A. ....Chicago, IL
Maciorowski, Michelle M. ....Springfield, OH
Maciorowski, Robert E. ....Chicago, IL
Macirowski, Nancy ....Chatham, NJ
MacIsaac, D. J. ....Belmont, MA
MacIsaac, James W. ....Mahwah, NJ
MacIsaac, Peter C. ....Mahwah, NJ
MacIsaac, Stephen A. ....Woodbridge, VA
MacIsaac, Suann C. ....Los Angeles, CA
MacIsaac, Vincent ....Los Angeles, CA
Maciszewski, Felix A. ....Honolulu, HI
MacIver, Anne Keyes ....Chicago, IL
MacIver, Byrnn L. ....Mount Laurel, NJ
MacIver, Christine M. ....Atlanta, GA
MacIver, Clyde H., P.C. ....Seattle, WA
MacIver, Dale ....House of Representatives,
Committee on District of Columbia, GV
MacIver, Donald J., Jr. ....Annapolis, MD
Mac Iver, Elizabeth Anne .....Chagrin Falls, OH
MacIver, J. Robertson ....Millville, NJ
MacIver, John K. ....Milwaukee, WI
MacIver, Kenneth F., Jr. ....Boston, MA
Mac Iver, Stuart J. ....Fort Lauderdale, FL
Mack, Abbey A. ....Metairie, LA
Mack, Alice C. ....Norwalk, CT
Mack, Anna E. ....Sunrise, FL
Mack, B. Bayles ....Fort Mill, SC
Mack, Barron B., Jr. ....Fort Mill, SC
Mack, Barry L. ....New York, NY
Lake Ariel, PA
Mack, Bernard F. ....Charleston, SC
Mack, Beverly J. ....Michigan City, IN
Mack, Brenda S. ....Macon, GA
Mack, Brian P. ....Chicago, IL
Mack, Bruce B. ....Houston, TX
Mack, C. Edward ....Los Angeles, CA
Mack, Carolyn D. ....Wilmington, DE
Mack, Cary ....San Diego, CA
Mack, Catherine R. ....Rockville, MD
Mack, Charles J. ....Chicago, IL
Mack, Charles R. ....Woodland, CA
Mack, Chester W. ....Arlington, MA
Mack, Christina L. ....Chicago, IL
Mack, Clayton A. ....Bakersfield, CA
Mack, Curtis L. ....Boca Raton, FL
Atlanta, GA
Mack, Cuthbert E. A. ....Las Vegas, NV
Mack, Cynthia M. ....Milwaukee, WI
Mack, David A. ....Crown Point, IN
Mack, David B. ....Boston, MA
Mack, David E. ....Cleveland, OH
Mack, David Scott ....Morristown, NJ
Mack, Deborah L. ....Mansfield, OH
Mack, Debra K. ....Philadelphia, PA
Mack, Dennis W. ....New York, NY
Mack, Diane ....Hartford, CT
Mack, Diane L. ....San Diego, CA
Mack, E. Allan ....Atlantic City, NJ
Mack, Edward N. ....Adrian, MI
Mack, Edward R. ....Tampa, FL
Mack, Elizabeth E. ....Dallas, TX
Mack, Eric ....Cleveland Heights, OH
Mack, Erin E. ....Houston, TX
Mack, Eulalia M. ....New York, NY
Mack, Francis M. ....Columbia, SC
Mack, Frank G. ....Ironton, MO
Mack, Frank J. ....Library of Congress,
Office of the General Counsel, GV
Mack, Frank P. ....Sacramento, CA
Mack, Galen J. ....Rugby, ND
Mack, Gary A. ....Belleville, IL
Mack, Gary R. ....Buffalo, NY
Mack, George M. ....Seattle, WA
Mack, Grace D. ....West Orange, NJ
Mack, Gregory C. ....Dallas, TX
Mack, Gregory D. ....Department of Defense,
Defense Legal Services Agency, GV
Mack, Greta S. ....St. Paul, MN
Mack, Hal W. ....Mesa, AZ
Mack, Hal W., P.C. ....Mesa, AZ
Mack, Hansen, Gadd, Armstrong & Brown, P.C. ....Storm Lake, IA
Mack, Harold N. ....Haverhill, MA
Mack, Henry C., Jr. ....Bakersfield, CA
Mack, Herbert A. ....St. Louis, MO
Mack, Howard I. ....Scotia, NY
Mack, J. Alan ....Dallas, TX
Mack, J. & Associates ....Joliet, IL
Mack, J. Frederick ....Boise, ID
Mack, Jack S. ....Oxnard, CA
Mack, Jacquelyn ....Englewood, FL
Mack & James ....San Francisco, CA
Mack, James A. ....Hennepin, IL
Mack, James A. ....Binghamton, NY
Mack, James E. ....Potomac, MD
Mack, James L. ....Miami, FL
West Palm Beach, FL
Mack, James R. ....Cincinnati, OH
Mack, James R. ....Beaver Dam, WI
Mack, Jamie Lynn ....Gainesville, GA
Mack, Jane ....Saipan, TT
Mack, Janice N. ....Meriden, CT
Mack, Janice N., P.C. ....Meriden, CT
Mack, Jerome J. ....Grand Forks, ND
Mack, J. H. ....Butte, MT
Mack, Joan ....Los Angeles, CA
Mack, Joanne S. ....Milwaukee, WI
Mack, Joel H. ....San Diego, CA
Mack, John M. ....Chicago, IL
Mack, John P. ....Petoskey, MI
Mack, John R. ....Villa Park, IL
Mack, Jonathan D. ....Palo Alto, CA
Mack, Jonathan F. ....Minneapolis, MN
Mack, Joseph, III ....Pittsburgh, PA
Mack, Joseph N. ....Indiana, PA
Mack, Joyce B. ....Joliet, IL
Mack, Julia Cooper ....Washington, DC
Mack, Julian S. ....Miami, FL
Mack, Julian W. ....San Francisco, CA
Mack, Julie A. ....Greenbelt, MD
Mack, Julie N. ....Washington, DC
Mack, Julie R. ....San Diego, CA
Mack, Karol P. ....Fort Wayne, IN

Mack, Kathryn S. ... Guilford, CT
Mack, Kenneth E. ... Washington, DC
Mack, Kenneth H. ... Trenton, NJ
Mack, Kerry E. ... Englewood, FL
Mack, Kerry E., P.A. ... Englewood, FL
Mack, Kevin A. ... Hartford, CT
Mack, Kevin D. ... Columbus, OH
Mack, Kristina Ann ... Washington, DC
Mack, Kristine McGee ... Belleville, IL
Mack, L. Barry ... Palm Desert, CA
Mack, Laura Redmond ... Southfield, MI
Mack, Lauren E. ... Brooklyn, NY
Mack, Laurie A. ... Miami, FL
Mack Law Offices, P.C. ... Rugby, ND
Mack, Lawrence E. ... Cleveland, OH
Mack, L. Barry, A Professional Law Corporation ... Palm Desert, CA
Mack, Leo W. ... Neenah, WI
Mack, Linda ... Trenton, NJ
Mack, Linda McCauley ... Burbank, CA
Mack, Lisa ... Minneapolis, MN
Mack, Lynn Heather ... Pacific Palisades, CA
Mack & Mack ... Fort Mill, SC
Rock Hill, SC
Mack, Mark M. ... Kingston, PA
Mack, Martin J. ... Cortland, NY
Mack, Mary C. ... Department of Commerce, Patent and Trademark Office, GV
Mack & McLean, P.A. ... Boca Raton, FL
Atlanta, GA
Mack, Michael E. ... Detroit, MI
Mack, Michael G. ... Alpena, MI
Mack, Michael Jerome ... Santa Ana, CA
Mack, Michael P. ... East Taunton, MA
Mack, Michael R. ... Fairlawn, OH
Mack, Michael R., Co., L.P.A.
Fairlawn, OH
Mack, Milton L., Jr. ... Detroit, MI
Mack, Mona Dobaran ... Boise, ID
Mack, Monte E. ... Akron, OH
Mack, Nicholas R. ... Palo Alto, CA
Mack, Nina Reid ... Columbia, SC
Mack & O'Neal ... Hammond, LA
Mack, Patricia A. ... Englewood, CO
Mack, Paul B. ... Spokane, WA
Mack, Paul R. ... Richmond, VA
Mack, Peter G. ... Washington, DC
Mack, R. Gayle ... Indianapolis, IN
Mack, Randy A. ... Corpus Christi, TX
Mack, Richard F. ... Akron, OH
Mack, Richard L. ... Charlotte, NC
Mack, Richard V. ... Phoenix, AZ
Mack, Richard W. ... Cleveland, OH
Mack, Robert ... Bartow, FL
Mack, Robert E. ... Tacoma, WA
Mack, Robert J. ... Boston, MA
Mack, Robert M. ... Springfield, MA
Mack, Ronald E. ... Dearborn, MI
Mack, Ronald K. ... Evergreen, CO
Mack, Ronald M. ... Columbus, GA
Mack, Ronald W. ... Greensboro, NC
Mack, Ruben H. ... New York, NY
Mack, Sandra Matrone ... Boston, MA
Providence, RI
Mack, Sarah E. ... Seattle, WA
Mack, Stanley J. ... Louisville, KY
Mack, Steven J. ... Las Vegas, NY
Mack, Steven M. ... Glen Ellyn, IL
Mack, Stuart A. ... Staten Island, NY
Mack, Susan D. ... Anchorage, AK
Mack, Susan E. ... Charlotte, NC
Mack, Susan J. ... Washington, DC
Mack, Theodore ... Fort Worth, TX
Mack, Theodore E. ... Tallahassee, FL
Mack, Thomas C. ... Medina, NY
Mack, Thomas C., P.C. ... Medina, NY
Mack, Thomas J.
Department Of Health And Human Services, Office of Community Services, GV
Mack, Thomas R. ... Albuquerque, NM
Mack, Thomas W. ... Washington, DC
Mack, Timothy A. ... Dallas, TX
Mack, Tracy A. ... Philadelphia, PA
Mack, Walter S., Jr. ... New York, NY
Mack, Warren E. ... Minneapolis, MN
Mack, Wayne A. ... Philadelphia, PA
Mack, Wilber H. ... Detroit, MI
Mack, William C. ... Fairfield, NJ
Mack, William D. ... Scottsdale, AZ
Mack, William F. ... Evansville, IN
Mack, William M. ... Guilford, CT
Mackall, Crounse & Moore, PLC
Minneapolis, MN
St. Paul, MN
Mackall, Donald C. ... Canton, OH
Mackall, Douglass S., III ... Fairfax, VA
Mackall, Henry C. ... Fairfax, VA
Mackall, Jane Friedman
National Transportation Safety Board, Office of the General Counsel, GV
Mackall, John R. ... Santa Barbara, CA
Mackall, Laidler B. ... Washington, DC
Mackall, Louis
Department of Transportation, Surface Transportation Board, GV
Mackall, Mackall & Gibb, A Professional Corporation ... Fairfax, VA
Mackall, Theodore E., Jr. ... Greenville, NC
Mackall, Thomas M. ... Washington, DC
Mackaman, Donald H. ... Dallas, TX
Mackaman, John R. ... Des Moines, IA
Mackanos, Donald D. ... Jacksonville, FL
Mackaoui, Linden N. ... San Luis Obispo, CA
Mackarevich, Gerard M. ... Harrisburg, PA
Mackaronis, Christopher G.
Washington, DC
Mackas, Daniel G. ... Hartford, CT
Mackasek, Robert A. ... New York, NY

Mackasek, Thomas C. ... New York, NY
Mackauf, Stephen H. ... New York, NY
Mackay, Alexander Roy ... Arlington, VA
MacKay, Andrew S. ... Oakland, CA
Mackay, Bart P. ... Redmond, WA
Mackay, Bruce M. ... Redwood City, CA
Mackay, Calder M. ... Phoenix, AZ
Mackay, Caswell & Callahan, P.C.
Syracuse, NY
Mackay, Conde F. ... Anaconda, MT
Mackay, David L. ... Ocala, FL
MacKay, Deborah J. ... Minneapolis, MN
Mackay, Donald A. ... Chicago, IL
Mackay, Donald A., P.C. ... Chicago, IL
Mackay, Donald B. ... Department of Justice, Criminal Division, GV
MacKay, Douglas G. ... Los Angeles, CA
MacKay, Duncan R. ... Berlin, CT
Mackay, Elizabeth D. ... New Orleans, LA
Mackay, Elizabeth D., PLC
New Orleans, LA
MacKay, Ellen M. ... Springfield, MA
Mackay, Greg P. ... Bellevue, WA
Mackay, Hugh R. ... Tuxedo, NY
Mackay, Hyrum J. ... Columbus, OH
Mackay, J. Michael ... Raleigh, NC
Mackay, James A. ... Decatur, GA
Mackay, James L. ... Atlanta, GA
Mackay, James R.
Treasury Department, GV
MacKay, Jill Colson ... Farmington, MO
MacKay, John N. ... Toledo, OH
MacKay, John R., 2nd ... Roseland, NJ
Mackay, John W. ... Tampa, FL
Mackay, John W. ... Salt Lake City, UT
Mackay, John W., P.A. ... Tampa, FL
MacKay, Jon C. ... Northbrook, IL
MacKay, Karen K. ... Chicago, IL
Mackay, Kathleen
Charlotte Amalie, St. Thomas, VI
MacKay, Kathleen H. ... Fairfax, VA
Mackay, Keena M. ... Morristown, NJ
MacKay, Kenneth A. ... San Francisco, CA
MacKay, Kenneth H., Jr. ... Tallahassee, FL
Mackay, Kimberly Banks ... South Orange, NJ
Mackay, Kyle D. ... Batavia, NY
Mackay, Laurel ... Boston, MA
MacKay, M. Jennifer ... New York, NY
Mackay, Michael W. ... New York, NY
MacKay, Norman E. ... Los Banos, CA
Palo Alto, CA
MacKay & Ranew, P.A. ... Ocala, FL
MacKay, Raymond L. ... Walnut Creek, CA
Mackay, Richard ... Beverly Hills, CA
Mackay, Richard Lewis, Jr. ... Gatesville, TX
MacKay, Robert F. ... Novato, CA
Mackay, S. Douglas ... Wichita, KS
Mackay, Taralynn R. ... Austin, TX
MacKay, Walter S. ... Cincinnati, OH
Mackay, William J. ... Syracuse, NY
Mackay, William J. ... Grants Pass, OR
MacKay & Wrynn ... Douglaston, NY
Macke, Frank ... Columbus, OH
Macke, Jason A. ... Lima, OH
Macke, R. Christian ... Covington, KY
Macke, Thomas F. ... Valparaiso, IN
Mackechnie, John A. ... Oklahoma City, OK
MacKechnie, Russell W., Jr. ... New York, NY
Macke Dick, Patricia A. ... Hutchinson, KS
Mackedon & McCormick ... Fallon, NV
Mackedon, Michael F. ... Fallon, NV
Mackel, Daniel J., Jr. ... New Orleans, LA
Mackel, John E., III ... Los Angeles, CA
Mackel, Marilyn H. ... Fullerton, CA
Mackela, Carol J. ... Department of Justice, Civil Rights Division, GV
Mackell, Cheryl Hamer ... New York, NY
Mackell, Heather L. ... Denver, CO
MacKelvie & Associates, P.C. ... Chicago, IL
MacKelvie, Charles F. ... Chicago, IL
Macken, Daniel D. ... Santa Barbara, CA
Macken, James L. ... Gering, NE
Macken Law Firm, Ltd. ... Albuquerque, NM
Macken, Thomas P. ... Albuquerque, NM
Macken, Thomas P. ... Wausau, WI
Mackender, Darin ... Denver, CO
MacKenna, Donna Brewer ... Boston, MA
MacKennan, Robert A. ... Poughkeepsie, NY
Mackenroth, D. Irwin, Jr. ... New Orleans, LA
Mackenroth, David E. ... Sacramento, CA
Mackenroth Ryan & Fong, A Professional Corporation ... Sacramento, CA
MacKenty, John E. ... Edgartown, MA
New York, NY
MacKenzie, Albert H. ... Alhambra, CA
MacKenzie & Albritton ... San Francisco, CA
MacKenzie, Andrew ... Carson City, NV
Mackenzie, Andrew C.
Department Of Veterans Affairs, Board of Veterans Appeals, GV
Mackenzie, Andrew Ross ... Greenville, SC
MacKenzie, Barbara B. ... Petoskey, MI
MacKenzie, Brian S. ... Littleton, CO
MacKenzie, Brian W. ... Novi, MI
MacKenzie, Bruce A. ... Great Falls, MT
MacKenzie, Budd E. ... Walnut Creek, CA
MacKenzie, Carol ... Syosset, NY
MacKenzie, Carol A. ... Marshall, MI
Mackenzie, Charles Alfred ... Waco, TX
Mackenzie, Charles Rudd
Hastings-On-Hudson, NY
MacKenzie, Christopher ... Carson City, NV
MacKenzie, David J. ... Los Angeles, CA
MacKenzie, David J. ... Wayland, MA
Mackenzie, Derek G. P. ... New York, NY
MacKenzie, Dominic C. ... Jacksonville, FL
MacKenzie, Donald N. ... Mineola, NY

MacKenzie, Douglas E. ... Palo Alto, CA
Minneapolis, MN
MacKenzie, Franklin ... Southfield, MI
Mackenzie, G. Michael ... Clearwater, FL
MacKenzie, Gordon G. ... Elkhart, IN
MacKenzie, Gregory W.
Albuquerque, NM
MacKenzie & Gustafson Ltd.
St. Peter, MN
Mackenzie & Hallberg, Professional Association ... Minneapolis, MN
Mackenzie, Harold B. ... Wheaton, IL
MacKenzie, Heather A.
Winston-Salem, NC
Mackenzie, Hendry K. ... Jamestown, ND
MacKenzie, H. W., Jr. ... Portsmouth, VA
Mackenzie, James Alec, Jr. ... Frankfort, KY
MacKenzie, Joan L.
Department of Commerce, Office of the General Counsel, GV
MacKenzie, John A. ... Norfolk, VA
Mackenzie, John D. ... Saginaw, MI
MacKenzie, John N. ... Tulsa, OK
MacKenzie, John R., (P.C.)
Clifton Park, NY
MacKenzie, John W. ... Fort Smith, AR
MacKenzie, Julie M. Arvo ... Phoenix, AZ
MacKenzie, Kara A. ... New York, NY
MacKenzie, Karen ... Pittsford, NY
MacKenzie, Katherine J. ... Reno, NV
MacKenzie, Kenneth B.
Department Of Veterans Affairs, Office of the General Counsel, GV
MacKenzie, Kenneth C. ... Morristown, NJ
MacKenzie, Kenneth E. ... Boston, MA
MacKenzie, Kevin I. ... McLean, VA
Mackenzie, Leslie J. ... Portland, OR
MacKenzie, Lisa M. ... Bourne, MA
MacKenzie, Lyle M. ... Bellflower, CA
Mackenzie, Malcolm A. ... Napa, CA
MacKenzie, Malcolm, III ... Savannah, GA
MacKenzie, Malcolm K. ... St. Peter, MN
MacKenzie, Marcia ... Madison, WI
Milwaukee, WI
MacKenzie, Mary Ann ... Key Biscayne, FL
MacKenzie, Matthew ... Palo Alto, CA
Mackenzie, Melody A. ... Albany, NY
MacKenzie, M. J. ... Rochester, NY
Syracuse, NY
MacKenzie, Pamela Maloney ... Boston, MA
MacKenzie, Paul A. ... Columbus, OH
MacKenzie & Peden, P.S.C.
Louisville, KY
Mackenzie, Peter Neil ... Arcadia, CA
Sherman Oaks, CA
MacKenzie, R. Bruce ... Santa Barbara, CA
MacKenzie, Reed K. ... Minneapolis, MN
MacKenzie, Regina M. ... Media, PA
Mackenzie & Reisnour ... Jamestown, ND
MacKenzie, Richard C. ... Hartford, CT
Mackenzie, Richard S. ... Santa Fe, NM
MacKenzie, Robert A. ... Phoenix, AZ
Mackenzie, Robert H. ... Wesley Chapel, FL
Mackenzie, Robert P., III
Birmingham, AL
Mackenzie, Roderick I. ... Minneapolis, MN
Mackenzie, Roger D. ... San Francisco, CA
Mackenzie, Ronald C. ... Burlington, MA
MacKenzie, Ross I. ... Detroit, MI
MacKenzie, Sara R. ... Winter Springs, FL
Mackenzie Smith Lewis Michell & Hughes, LLP ... Syracuse, NY
MacKenzie, Stuart C. ... Chinook, MT
MacKenzie, Stuart I. ... Newark, CA
Mackenzie, Susan T. ... New York, NY
MacKenzie & Tallent ... Albany, NY
Canajoharie, NY
Mackenzie, Thomas W. ... Milwaukee, WI
MacKenzie, Timothy G. ... Hull, MA
Mackenzie, Timothy J. ... Los Angeles, CA
MacKenzie, Warren G. ... Lakeland, FL
Mackenzie, William A. ... Jamestown, ND
MacKenzie, William B. ... Canajoharie, NY
MacKenzie, William M. ... Clearwater, FL
Mackenzie, William M. ... Providence, RI
MacKenzie, William Patrick ... Papillion, NE
MacKenzie, Wm. A. ... Louisville, KY
MacKenzie Ehrens, Doris R. ... Quincy, MA
Mackerell, Avonelle R. ... Dunnellon, FL
MacKerron, John A. ... New York, NY
Mackert, Kristin S.
Securities and Exchange Commission, Office of the General Counsel, GV
Mackesey, Daniel R. ... McLean, VA
Mackeson, Wayne ... Portland, OR
MacKethan, John A. ... Raleigh, NC
Mackevich & Burke ... Clark, NJ
Mackevich, James E. ... Clark, NJ
Mackey, Alfred W. ... Ashtabula, OH
Mackey, Ann Carr ... Indianapolis, IN
Mackey, Anthony ... Phoenix, AZ
Mackey, B. Frank, Jr. ... Little Rock, AR
Mackey, Bruce C. ... Chicago, IL
Mackey, Catherine Z. ... Bradenton, FL
Mackey, Charles M. ... Sonoma, CA
Mackey, David L. ... Prescott, AZ
Mackey, Debra Lee ... Birmingham, AL
Mackey, Deepali Nadkarni
Department of Justice, Executive Office for Immigration Review, GV
Mackey, Diane S., (P.A.) ... Little Rock, AR
Mackey, Dr. William F. ... Falls Church, VA
Mackey, Edward L., (A Professional Corporation) ... Riverside, CA
Mackey, Edward S. ... Jupiter, FL
Mackey & Foster, P.A. ... Boston, MA
Osterville, MA

Mackey, Frank J., Jr. ... Chicago, IL
Mackey, Frank J., P.C. ... Chicago, IL
Mackey, G. Nelson, Jr. ... Radford, VA
Roanoke, VA
Mackey, George B. ... Fort Worth, TX
Mackey, George F. ... Saddle River, NJ
Garden City, NY
Mackey, George G. ... Rochester, NY
Mackey, I. B., Jr. ... Adkin, TX
MacKey, James F. ... Canton, OH
Mackey, James Lee ... Murray, KY
Mackey, James M. ... Cleveland, OH
Mackey, James S. ... Philadelphia, PA
Mackey, Jason T. ... Dallas, TX
Mackey, Jeffrey D. ... Westerville, OH
Mackey, Jerry D. ... Irvine, CA
Mackey, Joel T. ... Oakland, CA
Mackey, John C. ... Lawton, OK
Mackey, John M. ... Dennis, MA
Mackey, John N. ... Canton, OH
Mackey, John S. ... Mason City, IA
Mackey, John S. ... Lansing, MI
Mackey, John S. ... Pinedale, WY
Mackey, Joseph K. ... Boston, MA
Mackey, Joshua Edward ... New York, NY
Mackey, Kirk W. ... Brooklyn, NY
Mackey, L. Michael ... Albany, NY
Mackey, Larry A. ... Indianapolis, IN
Mackey, Leonard B. ... Sarasota, FL
Mackey, Leonard B., Jr. ... New York, NY
Mackey, Lesley E. ... Los Angeles, CA
Mackey, Lester Wayne ... Bay Shore, NY
Mackey, Linda C. ... La Jolla, CA
Mackey & Mackey ... Ontario, CA
Mackey & Mackey, P.A. ... Bradenton, FL
Mackey, Malcolm H. ... San Fernando, CA
Mackey, Mary Devereaux ... Ontario, CA
Mackey, Paige L. ... Denver, CO
Mackey, Pamela Robillard ... Denver, CO
Mackey, Paul G. ... New York, NY
Mackey, Peter J. ... Bradenton, FL
Mackey, Peter S. ... Mobile, AL
Mackey Price & Williams, A Professional Corporation ... Salt Lake City, UT
Mackey, Randall A. ... Salt Lake City, UT
Mackey, Rob R. ... Point Richmond, CA
Mackey, Robert A., Jr. ... Ontario, CA
Mackey, Robert D. ... Inglewood, CA
Mackey, Roger S. ... Gaithersburg, MD
Mackey, Sarah Dryden ... Washington, DC
Mackey, Sarah E. ... Eugene, OR
Mackey, Stephen C. ... Billings, MT
Mackey, Stephen J. ... Sacramento, CA
Mackey, Stephen L. ... West Palm Beach, FL
Mackey, Stephen P. ... Lansing, MI
Mackey, Stephen P., P.C. ... Lansing, MI
Mackey, Steven R. ... Tulsa, OK
Mackey, Stuart J. ... Los Angeles, CA
San Francisco, CA
Mackey, Terry W. ... Cheyenne, WY
Mackey, Thomas G. ... Los Angeles, CA
Mackey, Tracy Davis ... Kansas City, MO
Mackey, Walter J., Jr. ... Columbus, OH
Mackey, Walter L. ... Mesquite, TX
Mackey, William K. ... Boston, MA
Osterville, MA
Mackey, William R. ... San Francisco, CA
Mackey, William R. ... Cincinnati, OH
Mack-Harris, Greta D. ... Edwards, MS
MacKidd, Martie L. ... Walnut Creek, CA
Mackie, A. William ... Jacksonville, FL
Mackie, Alexander W., Jr. ... Olympia, WA
Mackie, Bette A. ... Auburn, CA
Mackie, Carter G. ... Raleigh, NC
Mackie, Charles L. ... Austin, TX
Mackie, David ... Houston, TX
MacKie, Donald L. ... Canton, CT
Mackie, Douglas B. ... Oak Brook, IL
Mackie, Edward B. ... Olympia, WA
Mackie, Edward C. ... Baltimore, MD
Mackie, James B. ... Ithaca, MI
Mackie, James K. (Jim) ... Tucson, AZ
Mackie, Jeffrey T. ... Hickory, NC
Mackie, John G. ... Santa Rosa, CA
Mac'Kie, John G. ... Naples, FL
Mackie, John P. ... New York, NY
Mackie, M. L. Harrison ... Comptche, CA
Mac'Kie, Pamela S. ... Naples, FL
Mac'Kie, Pamela S., P.A. ... Naples, FL
Mackie, Sam A. ... Orlando, FL
Mackie, Sam A., P.A. ... Orlando, FL
Mackie, Stephen C. ... Providence, RI
Mackie, Stephen F. ... Atlanta, GA
Lawrenceville, GA
Mackie, Thomas A. ... Boston, MA
Mackiewicz, Alan J. ... Omaha, NE
Mackiewicz, Edward R. ... Washington, DC
Mackiewicz, John J. ... Philadelphia, PA
Mackiewicz, Kathelynne A. ... Kenner, LA
Mackillop, Innes Alexander Henderson
Houston, TX
Mackillop, Katherine Dudas ... Houston, TX
MacKimm, Nancy ... Dallas, TX
Mackin, Bernard John ... Houston, TX
Mackin, Daniel E. J. ... Chicago, IL
Mackin, Dennis S., Sr. ... Atlanta, GA
Mackin, F. Gerald ... Hancock, NY
Mackin, Gerard F., Jr. ... Weymouth, MA
Mackin, James A. ... Cleveland, OH
Mackin, James E. ... Syracuse, NY
Mackin, James L. ... Worthington, OH
Mackin, James L., Co. L.P.A.
Cleveland, OH
Mackin, James L., Co., L.P.A.
Worthington, OH
Mackin, Jeffrey L. ... Sellersburg, IN
Mackin, John F. ... Avon Lake, OH
Mackin, John J. ... Lake Success, NY

Mackin, John J., Jr. .... Boston, MA
Mackin, Melanie R. .... Dayton, OH
Mackin, Patrick C. .... Avon Lake, OH
Mackin, Patrick K. .... Portland, OR
Mackin, Paula B. .... Newton, MA
Mackin, Ralph R. .... North Salem, NY
Mackin, Ralph R. .... White Plains, NY
Mackin, Scott G. .... Fairfield, NJ
Mackin, Thomas G. .... Toledo, OH
Mackin, Tim J. .... Spokane, WA
Mackin, William .... Mullica Hill, NJ
Mackin, William J. .... Columbus, OH
Mackinaw, Candace Jones .... Moneta, VA
Mackinder, Douglas J. .... Hartford, MI
MacKinlay, Edgar H. .... Lexington, VA
Virginia Beach, VA
MacKinlay, Edgar H., P.C., Law Offices
Lexington, VA
Virginia Beach, VA
MacKinlay, Glenn .... Boston, MA
MacKinlay, J. Kent .... Mesa, AZ
Mackinney, Thomas R. .... Sebastopol, CA
Mackinnon, Alexander C. .... Orlando, FL
MacKinnon, Alexander F.
Los Angeles, CA
Mackinnon, Allan P. .... Washington, DC
MacKinnon, Carol L. .... Tacoma, WA
MacKinnon, Charles .... Rolling Meadows, IL
Mackinnon, Cynthia Z. .... Orlando, FL
MacKinnon, D. Scott .... Honolulu, HI
MacKinnon, Dana .... Hartford, CT
Mackinnon, Daniel J. .... Scituate, MA
Mackinnon, Dawn Michelle
Springfield, MA
MacKinnon, Ian D. .... Minneapolis, MN
MacKinnon, Ian F. .... New York, NY
MacKinnon, James D. .... South Windsor, CT
MacKinnon, James D. .... Wayzata, MN
MacKinnon, Jeanne L. .... San Diego, CA
MacKinnon, John A. .... New York, NY
MacKinnon, John H., Jr. .... Boston, MA
MacKinnon, John J. .... Columbus, OH
MacKinnon, John Noel .... Southfield, MI
Mackinnon, John T. .... Fresno, CA
MacKinnon, Katherine L., Law Office of
Minneapolis, MN
MacKinnon, Kathryn D. .... Washington, DC
MacKinnon, Kevin S. .... Chicago, IL
MacKinnon, Michael .... Greenville, SC
MacKinnon, Michael Y. .... San Diego, CA
MacKinnon, Peter P. .... Locust Valley, NY
Mackinnon, R. Gavin .... Winter Park, FL
MacKinnon, Robert A. .... Kingston, NY
MacKinnon, Robert H. .... New York, NY
MacKinnon, Roderick C. .... Chicago, IL
MacKinnon, Sandra E. .... Mountain View, CA
MacKinnon, Stephen J. .... East Hartford, CT
Mackinnon, William J. .... Montpelier, VT
Mackinson, Gail A. .... Decatur, GA
Mackinson & Katz .... Decatur, GA
Mackinson, Thomas R. .... San Francisco, CA
Mackintosh, Bruce A. .... Pittsburgh, PA
Mackintosh, J. Triplett .... Denver, CO
Mackintosh, John A., Jr. .... Dallas, TX
Mackintosh, Kristen N. .... Elyria, OH
Mackintosh, Todd Estes .... Denver, CO
Mackle, James W. .... Sun City Center, FL
Mackle, Robert Joseph
Long Island City, NY
Mackler, Bruce F. .... Washington, DC
Mackler, Daniel M. .... Fort Lauderdale, FL
Mackler and Gold, P.C. .... Stamford, CT
Mackler, Harvey K. .... New Haven, CT
Mackler, Ian .... Brockport, NY
Mackler, Isadore M. .... Stamford, CT
Mackler, James E. .... Fort Collins, CO
Mackler, Jeffrey David .... Aurora, CO
Mackler, Joni Katz .... Boston, MA
Mackler, Kenneth D. .... Atlantic City, NJ
Mackler, Mitchell G. .... Princeton, NJ
Mackley, Carter R. .... Berkeley, CA
Mackley, Jennifer Turley .... Pocatello, ID
Mackley, Kenneth J. .... Hagerstown, MD
Mackley, Mark S. .... Kalkaska, MI
Macklin, Cerene .... Los Angeles, CA
Macklin, Crofford J., Jr. .... Dayton, OH
Macklin, Dale S. .... Winslow, ME
Macklin, George K. .... Columbus, OH
Macklin, James E., Jr. .... Alexandria, VA
Macklin, John C. .... New Hyde Park, NY
Macklin, John D. .... Bellevue, WA
Macklin, Karen G.Z. .... Chapel Hill, NC
Macklin, Kenneth E. .... New York, NY
White Plains, NY
Macklin, Meryl .... Los Angeles, CA
Macklin, Michael E. .... Las Vegas, NM
Macklin, Richard G. .... Denver, CO
Macklin, Ronald J. .... Hicksville, NY
Macklin, Stacey E. .... Hicksville, NY
Macklin, William E. .... Lakeville, MN
Macklin, William F. .... El Centro, CA
Macklow, Jay E. .... Worcester, MA
Macklowitz, Michael L. .... New York, NY
Mackness, Michael D. .... Rosemead, CA
Mackniak, Michael W. .... New Haven, CT
MacKnight, David D. .... Rochester, NY
MacKnight, Kamrin T. .... Redwood City, CA
San Francisco, CA
Mac Knight, William B. .... Princeton, NJ
Mac Knight, William J., Jr.
New York, NY
Macknin, Mitchell H. .... Chicago, IL
Macko, John .... Rochester, NY
Macko, Michael J. .... Modesto, CA
Macko, Michael J. .... Connellsville, PA
Mackoff, Benjamin S. .... Chicago, IL
Mackoff, Julie B. .... San Francisco, CA
Mackoff Kellogg Law Firm .... Beach, ND
Dickinson, ND
Baker, MT
Mackolin, Elizabeth L. .... Forked River, NJ
Mackolin, William D. .... Lakewood, NJ
Morrisville, PA
Mackoul, Frank G., II .... Jacksonville, FL
MacKoul, George Joseph .... Santa Monica, CA
MacKoul, Matthew M.
North Reading, MA
MacKoul, R. John, Jr. .... Reading, PA
Mackoul, Scott A.
Federal Communications Commission,
Wireless Telecommunications Bureau, GV
Mackouse, Stephen Mitchell
San Francisco, CA
Mackowiak, Jayne E. .... Escanaba, MI
Mackowsky, Richard M. .... Westmont, NJ
Philadelphia, PA
MacKoy, Debby .... Plano, TX
Mackoy, Deborah .... Plano, TX
MacKrell, Joseph F. .... Erie, PA
MacKrell, Patrick J. .... Albany, NY
Saratoga Springs, NY
Mackrides, William C. .... Media, PA
Mackritis, Rosemary D. .... Durham, NC
Mack Rosenberg, Kimberly M.
New York, NY
Macks, Jonathan L. .... Agoura Hills, CA
Macks, Jonathan P. .... Hoffman Estates, IL
Macks, Lawrence M. .... Owings Mills, MD
Macksey, Brigit McCann .... Baltimore, MD
Macksey, David M. .... Chicago, IL
Mackson, Andrea B. .... Hollywood, FL
Mackson, Lee D. .... Miami, FL
Mackson, Murray .... Lehigh Valley, PA
Macksoud, Alexander E. .... Torrance, CA
Macksoud, Kenneth J. .... Providence, RI
Macksoud, Maria T. .... Birmingham, AL
Macksoud, Richard M., Jr. .... Teaneck, NJ
Mackston, Jack .... Mineola, NY
Macktaz, Louis M. .... Woonsocket, RI
Mackus, Eloise L. .... Orrville, OH
Mackuse, Gregg W. .... Philadelphia, PA
MacLachlan, Andrew C. .... Albany, GA
Mac Lachlan, Bruce D. .... San Bernardino, CA
Maclachlan, Christopher L. .... Boston, MA
MacLachlan, Donald S. .... Roseland, NJ
MacLachlan, John A. .... Montauk, NY
MacLaren, Alexander T. .... Honolulu, HI
MacLaren, Heidi E. .... Worcester, MA
Maclaren, Jeanne E. .... Hanover, MA
Maclaren, John Roberts .... Braintree, MA
MacLaren, Linda Carl Olson
Boca Raton, FL
MacLaren, Peter A. .... San Bruno, CA
MacLaren, Robert I., II .... Boca Raton, FL
MacLaren, Ronni B. .... Los Angeles, CA
MacLaren, Scott W. .... Dallas, TX
MacLaren, W. Breck .... Santa Ana, CA
MacLatchie, Scott D. .... Pasadena, CA
MacLaughlin, Ann K. .... Colorado Springs, CO
MacLaughlin, David J. .... Minneapolis, MN
MacLaughlin, Francis J. .... New York, NY
MacLaughlin, Harry H. .... Minneapolis, MN
MacLaughlin, Jerome William
Department of Justice,
Environment and Natural Resources
Division, GV
MacLaughlin, Lewis H., III .... Columbus, OH
MacLaughlin, Marlin V., Jr. .... Jasper, AL
MacLaughlin-Barck, Megan K.
Newton, MA
MacLaury, Joyce .... Santa Rosa, CA
MacLaury, Richard J. .... San Francisco, CA
Maclay, David S. .... Southport, CT
Maclay, Donald M. .... Philadelphia, PA
Maclay, Helena S. .... Missoula, MT
Maclay, John B., III .... New York, NY
Maclay, Kevin C. .... Washington, DC
Maclay, Kristine Dubiel .... Houston, TX
Maclay Law Firm .... Missoula, MT
Maclay, Robert H. .... Bethesda, MD
MacLean, Andrew B. .... Manchester, ME
MacLean, Andrew W. .... Montpelier, VT
MacLean, Anne B. .... Pompano Beach, FL
MacLean, Babcock .... New York, NY
MacLean & Boulware .... Cleburne, TX
MacLean, Bradley A. .... Nashville, TN
MacLean, Bruce D. .... Seattle, WA
MacLean & Burbott .... Royal Oak, MI
MacLean, C. Donald, Jr. .... Jacksonville, FL
MacLean, Charles E. .... Marshall, MN
MacLean, Colleen P. .... Nashville, TN
MacLean, Cynthia Thomas .... Boston, MA
Maclean, Daniel C. .... New York, NY
MacLean, Douglas A. .... Chicago, IL
MacLean and Ema .... Pompano Beach, FL
MacLean, Frederick R., (P.A.)
Pompano Beach, FL
MacLean, Gary T. .... Farmington Hills, MI
MacLean, George H. .... Iselin, NJ
MacLean, Hector .... Lumberton, NC
MacLean, Ian W. .... New York, NY
MacLean & Jacques, Ltd. .... Phoenix, AZ
MacLean, James P., III .... Haddonfield, NJ
MacLean, Jane A. .... Seattle, WA
MacLean, John R. .... Cleburne, TX
MacLean, John T. .... Royal Oak, MI
MacLean, Kenneth H. .... Auburn Hills, MI
MacLean, Kurt A. .... Newport Beach, CA
MacLean, Laura G. .... Pompano Beach, FL
MacLean, Lester D. .... Farmington Hills, MI
MacLean, Linda R. .... Claremont, CA
MacLean & MacLean .... Seattle, WA
MacLean, Malcolm F., III .... Danvers, MA
Maclean, Malcolm R. .... Savannah, GA
MacLean, Mark B. .... Jacksonville, FL
MacLean, Matthew S. .... Milwaukee, WI
MacLean, Merrilee A. .... Seattle, WA
MacLean, Michael J. .... Indianapolis, IN
MacLean, Michael R. .... Redwood City, CA
Maclean, Norman E. .... Torrance, CA
MacLean, Proppe, MacLean & Darnell, P.C.
Farmington Hills, MI
MacLean, Rebecca G. .... Chicago, IL
MacLean, Richard J. .... Chattanooga, TN
MacLean, Robert D. .... Providence, RI
MacLean & Schloth .... Jacksonville, FL
MacLean, Scotty .... Fort Worth, TX
MacLean Seaman Laing & Guilford, P.L.C.
East Lansing, MI
Lansing, MI
MacLean, Shian .... Monterey, CA
Macleay, Kenneth G. .... Baltimore, MD
Macleay, Lynch, Gregg & Lynch, P.C.
Washington, DC
Bethesda, MD
Fairfax, VA
MacLeid, Matthew T. .... Cincinnati, OH
MacLeish, Bruce D. .... San Diego, CA
MacLeish, Roderick, Jr. .... Boston, MA
MacLeith, Douglas Ransom
Santa Fe Springs, CA
MacLellan, Donald F. .... Arlington, MA
MacLellan, Eleanor Holmes .... Concord, NH
MacLellan, Ignatius .... Concord, NH
MacLellan, John G., III .... Lowell, MA
Maclellan, Leslie Stophel .... Nashville, TN
MacLellan, Michael John .... San Jose, CA
MacLellan, Stephen J. .... Worcester, MA
MacLennan, Alexandra M.
Jacksonville, FL
MacLennan, Carol A. .... Augusta, ME
MacLennan, Christopher S. .... Edina, MN
MacLennan, Eileen M. .... Cambridge, MA
Mac Lennan, Elliott .... Los Angeles, CA
MacLennan, Jennifer N. .... Phoenix, AZ
MacLennan, John F. .... Jacksonville, FL
Mac Lennan, Krista Smith .... La Porte, IN
MacLeod, Andrew W. .... Detroit, MI
MacLeod, Angus M. .... Bakersfield, CA
MacLeod, Angus M. .... Oakland, CA
MacLeod, Angus M. .... Sacramento, CA
MacLeod, Ann T. .... Los Angeles, CA
Macleod, Anthony M. .... Greenwich, CT
MacLeod, Bonnie H. .... Cambridge, MA
MacLeod, Bruce D. .... San Jose, CA
MacLeod, Bruce R. .... Los Angeles, CA
MacLeod, Charles D. .... Chestertown, MD
MacLeod, Charles K. .... Richland, WA
MacLeod, Daniel B., & Associates
San Diego, CA
MacLeod, David S. .... Boston, MA
MacLeod, Denise Broughton .... Windsor, VT
MacLeod, Donald .... Alameda, CA
Macleod, Edward S. .... Dallas, TX
Macleod, Glenn A. .... Department of Justice,
Civil Division, GV
MacLeod, Gordon A. .... Buffalo, NY
MacLeod, Iain-Breac .... Pleasanton, CA
Mac Leod, James A. .... Londonderry, NH
MacLeod, Janet M. .... New York, NY
Macleod, John A. .... Washington, DC
MacLeod, John A. .... Grosse Pointe Farms, MI
MacLeod, John F., Jr. .... Cranford, NJ
MacLeod, Jon W. .... Seattle, WA
MacLeod, Kendall .... Kalamazoo, MI
MacLeod, Lawrence A., Jr. .... Lebanon, NH
MacLeod, Lesley Skye .... Durham, NC
MacLeod, Linda M. .... San Jose, CA
MacLeod, Marcia Mott .... Plano, TX
MacLeod, Mary E. .... Grand Rapids, MI
MacLeod & McGinness, P.A.
Sarasota, FL
MacLeod, Melissa .... Haddonfield, NJ
MacLeod, Niall A. .... Minneapolis, MN
Macleod, Norman .... San Francisco, CA
Macleod, Peter R. .... Wilmington, DE
Macleod, Phyllis K. .... Lacey, WA
MacLeod, Richard J. (Jeff) .... Rome, GA
MacLeod, Rod B. .... Sarasota, FL
MacLeod, Roderick C. .... Mountain Home, AR
Mac Leod, Roderick J. .... Poughkeepsie, NY
Macleod, Sarah H. .... Alexandria, VA
MacLeod, Scott R. .... New York, NY
Macleod, Stephen C. .... Wenham, MA
MacLeod, Tamara E. .... Bend, OR
MacLeod, Tracy S. .... San Francisco, CA
MacLeod, Tymothy Y. .... Los Angeles, CA
MacLeod, William C. .... Washington, DC
Macleod-Ball, Michael W.
Kennebunk, ME
Maclin, A. D. .... Skokie, IL
Maclin, Alan H. .... St. Paul, MN
Maclin, Bruce .... Bakersfield, CA
Maclin, J. Mark .... Du Quoin, IL
Maclin, M. Tracey, Mr. .... Boston, MA
Maclin, Robert E., III .... Lexington, KY
MacLuckie, Sally L. .... Denver, CO
MacLure, Laurens, Jr. .... Baltimore, MD
Mac Mahon, Dermot P. .... Marathon, FL
MacMahon, Edward B., Jr.
Washington, DC
Falls Church, VA
MacMahon, Hugh G. E. .... Portland, ME
MacMahon, Jay Ross
Point Reyes Station, CA
San Rafael, CA
MacMahon, Joseph V. .... Riverdale, NJ
MacMahon, Robert D. .... Philadelphia, PA
MacMain, David J. .... Philadelphia, PA
MacManus, Donald E. .... Seekonk, MA
MacManus, Frederick O. .... San Diego, CA
MacManus, Michael .... Newark, NJ
Macmanus, Sheila .... Chicago, IL
MacMartin, J. Alexander, Jr. .... Milford, NH
MacMaster, Doug .... Martinez, CA
MacMaster, James E. .... Sacramento, CA
MacMaster, John H. .... Williston, ND
MacMaster, John P. .... New York, NY
MacMaster Law Firm, Ltd. .... Williston, ND
Macmeeken, John P., (A Professional
Corporation) .... Oakland, CA
MacMeekin, Colin D. .... McHenry, IL
MacMeekin, Daniel H. .... Washington, DC
MacMeekin, Robert W. .... Baltimore, MD
MacMeekin & Woodworth .... Washington, DC
MacMichael, James .... Skowhegan, ME
MacMichael, Shannon P. .... Washington, DC
Macmillan, Alexander .... Hingham, MA
MacMillan, Bruce E. .... Menlo Park, CA
MacMillan, Catherine Cope
San Francisco, CA
MacMillan, David D. .... Salinas, CA
Mac Millan, Debora .... Kimball, NE
MacMillan, Douglas .... Washington, DC
MacMillan, Douglas A. .... Bradford, MA
MacMillan, Douglas P. .... Charlotte, NC
MacMillan, Gary A. .... Westport, CT
MacMillan, Geoffrey J.
Walnut Creek, CA
MacMillan, Gregg M. .... San Francisco, CA
MacMillan, H.M. "Hoke", II
Laramie, WY
MacMillan, Jennifer L.
Saint Simons Island, GA
MacMillan, John C. .... Rockville, MD
MacMillan, John M. .... Detroit, MI
MacMillan, John R. .... Portland, OR
MacMillan, John T. .... Walnut Creek, CA
MacMillan, Kimberly Holtz
San Francisco, CA
MacMillan Law Offices .... Jensen Beach, FL
MacMillan & Lucas .... Westport, CT
MacMillan, Malcolm S. .... Upland, CA
MacMillan, Mary K. .... United States Senate,
Office of the Legislative Counsel, GV
MacMillan, Neil E. .... Delray Beach, FL
MacMillan, Neil W. .... Jensen Beach, FL
Macmillan, Paul M., Jr. .... Johns Island, SC
MacMillan, Peter A. .... Plymouth, MN
MacMillan, Richard A. .... Lafayette, LA
MacMillan, Richard G. .... Honolulu, HI
MacMillan, Richard S. .... Toledo, OH
MacMillan, Robert W. .... Jamesburg, NJ
MacMillan, Roderic S. .... Portland, OR
MacMillan, Scholz & Marks, P.C.
Portland, OR
MacMillan, Sobanski & Todd, L.L.C.
Livonia, MI
Perrysburg, OH
Toledo, OH
MacMillan & Stanley .... Delray Beach, FL
MacMillan, Thomas K. .... Bradford, MA
MacMillan, William W., Jr. .... Dayton, OH
MacMillin, Carrie .... Newport Beach, CA
MacMinn, William T. .... Doylestown, PA
MacMitchell, Thomas L. .... Palo Alto, CA
MacMonagle, Linda Johnson .... Erie, PA
MacMorris, John .... San Francisco, CA
MacMullan & Associates, P.C.
Pittsburgh, PA
MacMullan, Thomas D. .... Pittsburgh, PA
MacMullen, Kenneth E. .... Brockton, MA
MacMullin, Megan R. .... Concord, NH
Macmurdo, R. Bruce .... Baton Rouge, LA
Macmurdo, Walker P. .... Baton Rouge, LA
MacMurray, Ann E. .... Austin, TX
MacMurray, Frank G., Jr. .... Portland, OR
MacMurray, J. Richard .... Long Beach, NY
MacMurray, John C. .... New York, NY
MacMurray, Lauren E. .... Allentown, PA
MacMurray, Patrick A. .... New York, NY
MacMurray, Worth D. .... Sterling, VA
Mac Murren, Harold H. .... Sussex, NJ
MacNab, Charles H., Jr.
San Francisco, CA
Macnab, Janet .... Boston, MA
MacNabb, Alexander S. .... Great Falls, VA
MacNabb, Gregory W. .... Phoenix, AZ
MacNabb, Joseph P. .... Newnan, GA
Macnabb, Mary L. .... Las Vegas, NV
Macnair, A. Kennedy .... Fall City, WA
Macnamara, J. Terry .... Omaha, NE
MacNamara, Monica F. .... Chicago, IL
MacNamara, Peter M. .... Miami, FL
MacNamara, Peter M., A Professioanl Association .... Miami, FL
MacNamara, Stephen R. .... Tallahassee, FL
MacNary, Shelley A. .... New Orleans, LA
MacNaughton, Barry J. .... Beverly Hills, CA
MacNaughton, Burdzinski & Company
Bellaire, TX
MacNaughton, Donald S. .... Nashville, TN
MacNaughton, Donald T. .... New York, NY
MacNaughton, J. Robert .... Houston, TX
MacNaughton, John P. .... Atlanta, GA
MacNaughton, Philip A. .... Bellaire, TX
MacNaughton, Ruth D. .... San Francisco, CA
MacNaughton, W. James .... Woodbridge, NJ
MacNaul, M. Bruce .... Haddon Heights, NJ
MacNeal, John A. .... Traverse City, MI
MacNeal, Kelly .... New York, NY
MacNeal, Roderick V. .... Detroit, MI
MacNeal, Stacey R. .... York, PA
MacNeely, Thomas J. .... Wilkes-Barre, PA
MacNeil, Allen Donald .... Brea, CA
MacNeil, Christopher E. .... Albany, OR
MacNeil, Donald J. .... San Diego, CA
MacNeil, Donald L. .... Chicago, IL
Macneil, Hugh L. .... Pasadena, CA
Macneil, Ian R. .... Chicago, IL
MacNeil, Justin W. .... San Francisco, CA

MacNeil, Raymond J., (P.C.) ....Gaylord, MI
MacNeil, Rosa M. ....Arlington Heights, IL
Macneil, Sayre ....Santa Barbara, CA
MacNeil, Sayre ....Ventura, CA
Mac Neil, Susan Jeanne ....Hingham, MA
MacNeil, Timothy K. ....San Diego, CA
MacNeill & Buffington, P.A. ....Jackson, MS
Mac Neill, Glenn ....Malone, NY
MacNeill, Jay Scott ....Roseland, NJ
MacNeill, John B. ....Jackson, MS
MacNeill, John C., Jr. ....Charlotte, NC
MacNeill, Margaret H. ......New Providence, NJ
MacNeill, Paul L. ....West Hartford, CT
Macneill, Richard K. ....San Diego, CA
MacNeille, Douglas W.
Hilton Head Island, SC
Mac Neille, Margie ....Anchorage, AK
MacNeilly, Darlene Peterson ....Dinuba, CA
Macner, Esther Alta ....New York, NY
MacNett, Kathryn Speaker
Harrisburg, PA
MacNett, Stephen C. ....Harrisburg, PA
MacNichol, Alexander A. ....Portland, ME
MacNichol, Layton F.
Agency for International Development,
Other Offices of A.I.D., GV
MacNicholas, Henry R. ....Hershey, PA
MacNicol, Donna L. ....Greenfield, MA
Macnish, James M., Jr. ....Topeka, KS
Macnoll, Stephen W. ....Dallas, TX
Macnow, Selma ....North Hills, NY
MacNulty, Richard P. ....San Diego, CA
MacNutt, Karen L. ....Boston, MA
Maco, Frank S. ....Litchfield, CT
Maco, Paul S.
Securities and Exchange Commission,
Office of Municipal Securities, GV
Macol, Katherine M. ....Fairfield, CT
Macolini, Ruthann M. ....Lincoln, NE
Macom, Arthur R. ....Stuttgart, AR
Macom, Laura F. ....San Antonio, TX
Macomber, A. Grant ....Applegate, CA
Macomber, Donald William ....Augusta, ME
Macomber, Gary R. ....St. Paul, MN
Macomber, John A. ....Stockton, CA
MacOmber, Karl E. ....Tucson, AZ
Macomber, Martha D. ....Henderson, NV
Macomber, Mary F. G. ....Coral Springs, FL
Macomber, Michael D. ....Ukiah, CA
Macomber, Robert D. ....Riverside, CA
Macomber, Robert L. ....Quincy, MA
Macomber, S. Kingsley ....Sacramento, CA
Macomber, Thomas K. ....Riverside, CA
Macon, Ava-Lisa Frances-Ann
Baltimore, MD
Macon, Barclay T., Jr. ....Atlanta, GA
Macon, Clay L. ....Chesapeake, VA
Macon, Edward Meade ....Richmond, VA
Macon, J. Madison ....Richmond, VA
Macon, Jane H. ....San Antonio, TX
Macon, Marianne Nelms ....Richmond, VA
Macon, Nathaniel, Jr. ....Knoxville, TN
Macon, Paul M. ....St. Louis, MO
Macon, R. Laurence, (P.C.)
San Antonio, TX
Macon, Valencia N. ....New York, NY
Macone, Daniel A. ....North Miami, FL
Maconga, John W. ....Newton, MA
Macoretta, Lizabeth B. ....Philadelphia, PA
Macosky, Michele M. ....San Diego, CA
Macoubrie, Dana J. ....Chillicothe, MO
Macoubrie, David P. ....Chillicothe, MO
Macoul, John A. ....Lawrence, MA
Salem, NH
Macoy, Cecil H., Jr. ....Birmingham, AL
Macoy, Mark W. ....Birmingham, AL
Macpeak, Thomas J., (P.C.)
Washington, DC
MacPete, Wsewolod S. "Sev"
San Diego, CA
MacPhail, Barbara B. ....Schenectady, NY
MacPhail, Bruce I. ....St. Davids, PA
Macphail, Donald G. ....Abilene, TX
MacPhail, Douglas F. ....Schaumburg, IL
MacPhail, John A. ....Spartanburg, SC
MacPhail, Stephen M. ....Universal City, CA
MacPhail, William S. ....Buffalo, MN
MacPhaul, Charles H. ....Atlanta, GA
MacPhee, Bruce A.
Hot Springs National Park, AR
MacPhee, Chester Riddoch, III
San Francisco, CA
MacPhee, Dawn M. ....Great Falls, VA
MacPhee, Debra A. ....Harrisburg, PA
MacPhee, John P. ....Newark, NJ
Mac Phee, Kenneth A. ....Springfield, MA
MacPhee, Lee Stephen ....Boston, MA
MacPhee, Leonard H. ....Denver, CO
Macphee, Lisa H.
Department of Transportation,
Office of the General Counsel, GV
MacPhee, Robert C. ....San Ramon, CA
Macpherson, Alan D. ....Tacoma, WA
MacPherson, Alan H. .....Newport Beach, CA
San Jose, CA
MacPherson, Ann Marie
Kansas City, MO
MacPherson, Bruce ....Montgomery, AL
MacPherson, Bryan F.
Department of Energy,
Office of Hearings and Appeals, GV
Macpherson, Carl D., III ....Tucson, AZ
MacPherson, Catherine ....Rawlins, WY
Macpherson, Catherine R. ....La Jolla, CA
MacPherson, Cynthia Ogar
Mountain Grove, MO
Macpherson, David C. ....San Francisco, CA
MacPherson, Diana ....Hartford, CT

MacPherson, Donald C., Jr. ....St. Louis, MO
MacPherson, Donald W. ....Phoenix, AZ
MacPherson, Douglas M. ....Seattle, WA
Macpherson, Gilbert P. ....Clearwater, FL
Macpherson, Gilbert P., P.A., Law Offices of
Clearwater, FL
Macpherson, Gintner, Gordon & Diaz
Newport, OR
MacPherson, Gloria A. Jory
South Pasadena, CA
Macpherson, Gordon L. ....Newport, OR
Macpherson, Gregory H. ....Portland, OR
MacPherson Group, The ....Phoenix, AZ
MacPherson, Harry L., III ....Fairfax, VA
Macpherson, Ian A. ....Phoenix, AZ
MacPherson, J. Randolph
Washington, DC
Macpherson, James E. ....Seattle, WA
Macpherson, Janice
Federal Energy Regulatory Commission,
Office of the General Counsel, GV
MacPherson, John A. ....Rawlins, WY
MacPherson, John D. ....Hicksville, NY
MacPherson, John J. ....Monterey, CA
MacPherson, Laura N. ....Jackson, WY
MacPherson Law Offices LLC
Rawlins, WY
MacPherson, Maureen A. ....Syracuse, NY
MacPherson, Rebecca
Department of Transportation,
National Highway Traffic Safety
Administration, GV
MacPherson, Robert J. ....New York, NY
Macpherson, Roderick J., III
Minneapolis, MN
Macpherson, Sandra ....Verona, PA
Macpherson, Sean S. ....New York, NY
MacPherson, Shawn R. ....Camas, WA
MacPherson, Victoria L. ....Portland, OR
MacPherson, William M. ....Rawlins, WY
MacPherson, William T. ....Albuquerque, NM
MacQuaid, Michael S. ....Fort Worth, TX
MacQuarrie, Christopher J. ....Ocala, FL
MacQueen, Cynthia B. ....Philadelphia, PA
MacQueen, Ewan C. ....Piermont, NY
MacQueen, James R. ....Niles, OH
MacQueen, Joanna ....Oakland, CA
MacQueen, Kevin F. ....Snow Hill, NC
MacQueen, William J. ....Warren, MI
MacQueeney, V. Patrick ....Cincinnati, OH
MacQuesten, Gail ....Santa Fe, NM
Macquet, Kendra Lanata ....New Orleans, LA
MacRae, Andrew F. ....Austin, TX
Macrae, Andrew W., III ....Santa Ana, CA
MacRae, Cameron F., III (P.C.)
New York, NY
MacRae, D. Roderick, II ....Austin, TX
MacRae, Denise A. ....Los Angeles, CA
MacRae, Donald J. ....Boston, MA
Macrae, Donald Scott ....San Francisco, CA
Mac Rae, Donna S. ....Lake City, FL
MacRae, Gerald C. ....Los Angeles, CA
Macrae, Howard T., Jr. ....Richmond, VA
MacRae, James C. ....Fayetteville, NC
MacRae, James C., Jr. ....Fayetteville, NC
MacRae, James R. ....Philadelphia, PA
Macrae, John H., Jr. ....Knoxville, TN
Macrae, Lorion K. ....Raleigh, NC
MacRae, Patrick F. ....Syracuse, NY
MacRae, Perry, Pechmann, Williford &
MacRae ....Fayetteville, NC
MacRae, Roderick E. ....Chicago, IL
MacRae, Samuel H. ....Wilmington, NC
MacRae, Sharon S. ....San Antonio, TX
MacRae, Warren K. ....New York, NY
Macre, Walter F. ....Rockville Centre, NY
Macreery, John B. ....Katonah, NY
Macreery, William F. ....White Plains, NY
Macres, Philip J. ....Washington, DC
Macri, Anthony ....Denville, NJ
Macri, Catherine Cress ....Princeton, NJ
Macri, Giovanna ....Buffalo, NY
Macri, Greenspan & Moramarco
Carle Place, NY
Macri, Marc (Marcantonio) D.
Fort Lee, NJ
Macri, Mia M. ....Hackensack, NJ
Macri, Nicholas A. ....Herkimer, NY
Macri, Paul F. ....Lewiston, ME
Macri, Samuel A. ....Niagara Falls, NY
Macri, Stephen J. ....New York, NY
Macri, Vincent ....East Hanover, NJ
Macrides, Zezima & Christiano
Stamford, CT
MacRill & Associates, A Professional
Corporation ....Upland, CA
MacRill, John R., III ....Upland, CA
MacRill, John R., Jr. ....Upland, CA
Macri-Ortiz, Barbara ....Keene, CA
Macris, Michael ....New York, NY
MaCris, Steven W. ....Venice, FL
MacCris, Steven W., P.A. ....Venice, FL
MacRitchie, Brian J. ....Bend, OR
MacRitchie, Kenneth L. ....Newark, NJ
MacRitchie, William ....Hillsdale, MI
Macrito, Lisa ....Chicago, IL
Macro, Venessa ....Des Moines, IA
MacRobbie, James B. ....San Diego, CA
Macrohon, M. P. ....West Hartford, CT
Macron, Elizabeth ....Eatontown, NJ
Macron, James J. ....Elmhurst, NY
Macron, John ....New York, NY
Macron & Macron ....New York, NY
Macron, Marilyn ....New York, NY
Macron, Mark ....New York, NY
Macropoulos, Angela M. ....New York, NY
Macrorie, Richard R. ....Tracy, CA
Pueblo, CO

Macrorie, Richard R., P.C. ....Pueblo, CO
Macrory, Harry B. ....Bethany, OK
Macrory, Patrick F. J. ....Washington, DC
Macrory, Robert A. ....Montgomery, AL
Macrum, James F., Jr. ....Littleton, CO
MacSheain, Phyllis P. ....Rochester, NY
MacSporran, James M. ......Newport Beach, CA
MacSteel, Genevieve ....New York, NY
MacSwain, Gregory S. ....San Jose, CA
MacTaggart, Glenn W. ....San Antonio, TX
MacTaggart, Philip A. ....Del Rio, TX
MacTaggart-Dobbs, Suzanne R.
Elk Grove, CA
MacTarnaghan, James C. ....Depew, NY
MacTavish, Bruce A. ....Indianapolis, IN
Seymour, IN
Mac Tavish, Sharon A. ....Seattle, WA
MacTiernan, William S. ....Albany, NY
Macturk, Christopher Hunt
Glen Allen, VA
Macturk, Christopher Hunt
Richmond, VA
Macurda, William B. ....Charlotte, NC
MacVeagh, Theodore E. ....Boston, MA
MacVean, Lewis, Sherwin & McDermott,
P.C. ....Goshen, NY
Middletown, NY
Mac Veety, Glynis ....Pittsfield, MA
MacVey, John H. ....Vienna, VA
MacVey, Kendall H. ....Riverside, CA
MacVicar, Neil A. ....Lansing, MI
MacVittie, Lisa A. ....Washington, DC
MacWilliam, Diego F. ....San Jose, CA
MacWilliam, Lori Kopf ....Clinton, NJ
MacWilliams, Diane ....Woodbury, NJ
MacWilliams, Michael B. ....Baltimore, MD
Macy, Barbara J. ....Boston, MA
Macy, Cary S. ....Huntington Beach, CA
Macy, Daniel P. ....Alexandria, VA
Macy, Donald ....Denver, CO
Macy, Edwin A. ....Fall River, MA
Macy, Edwin E. ....Albuquerque, NM
Macy, Gregory L. ....Brandon, FL
Macy, Harry E. ....Fresno, CA
Macy, James A. ....San Diego, CA
Macy, James R. ....Oshkosh, WI
Macy, Jed C. ....Portland, OR
Macy, Jeffrey M. ....Southfield, MI
Macy, Jennifer ....Denver, CO
Macy, John P. ....Waukesha, WI
Macy, Joseph E. ....Garden City, NY
Macy, Judith K. ....Kansas City, MO
Macy Law Office, A Professional
Corporation ....Cheyenne, WY
Macy and Lober ....Litchfield, IL
Springfield, IL
Macy, Mark E. ....Denver, CO
Macy, Mark E. ....Cheyenne, WY
Macy, Matthew D. ....Denver, CO
Macy, Peter M. ....Newton, MA
Macy, Randall L. ....Belle Fourche, SD
Macy, Richard J. ....Cheyenne, WY
Macy, Robert H. ....Oklahoma City, OK
Macy, Robert W. ....Clinton, MI
Macy, Robert W., P.C. ....Clinton, MI
Macy, Samuel ....San Francisco, CA
Macy & Turley, LLP ....Boston, MA
Macy, Wendy G. ....Irvine, CA
Madachik, Joseph M
Middleburg Heights, OH
Madaio, John F. ....Worcester, MA
Madaio, Mark D. ....Bergenfield, NJ
Madaj, Edwin J., Jr.
United States International Trade
Commission,
Office of the General Counsel, GV
Madajczyk, Jill M. ....Merrillville, IN
Madajian, Michael ....Oakland, CA
Madalena, Ralph J. ....Long Beach, NY
Madama, Havona ....Chicago, IL
Madamba, Patrick, Jr. ....Atlantic City, NJ
Madan, Allison A. ....Washington, DC
Madan, Anil ....Boston, MA
Madan and Madan, A Professional
Corporation ....Boston, MA
Madan, Marilee A. ....Houston, TX
Madan, Paul S. ....Houston, TX
Madan, Rafael A. ....Department of Justice,
Justice Management Division, GV
Madan, Rajiv ....Washington, DC
Madan, Rosann C. ....Boston, MA
Madans, Alan S. ....Chicago, IL
Madans, Lawrence B. ....Los Angeles, CA
Madar, Alexander P. ....Arlington, TX
Madar, Brian E. ....East Lansing, MI
Madar, Michael A. ....Harrisburg, PA
Madara, Eugene E. ....Norwalk, CT
Madarang, Marilyn M.
Department of Energy,
Office of the General Counsel, GV
Madarasz, Mary Beth ....Boston, MA
Madariaga, David B. ....Long Beach, CA
Madas, Pamela M. ....Newark, NJ
Madaus, Gerald F., Jr. ....Worcester, MA
Madaus, Gerald F., Sr. ....Worcester, MA
Maday, Timothy ....Mokena, IL
Madda, Michael J. ....Palo Alto, CA
Maddalena, Aimee M. ....New York, NY
Maddalena, Gracemarie ....Arlington, VA
Maddalena, John L. ....Elizabeth, NJ
Maddalone, Joseph R., Jr. ....Melville, NY
Maddaloni, Joseph, Jr. ....Newark, NJ
New York, NY
Maddatu, Nestor P. ....New York, NY
Madden, Albert M. ....Rosemont, IL
Madden, Alice D. ....Boulder, CO

Madden, Alison, Law Offices of
San Francisco, CA
San Jose, CA
Madden, Alison, Law Offices of
Woodside, CA
Madden, Allison Turley ....Hackensack, NJ
Madden, Ann M. ....Philadelphia, PA
Madden, Anne ....Morristown, NJ
Madden, Arthur J., III ....Mobile, AL
Madden Breslin, P.C. ....Chalfont, PA
Madden, Brian ....San Jose, CA
Madden, Brian J. ....Kansas City, MO
Madden, Brian M. ....Washington, DC
Madden, Brian M. ....Front Royal, VA
Madden, C. John ....Wareham, MA
Madden, Carole ....Libertyville, IL
Madden & Crockett ....Seattle, WA
Madden, Daniel J. ....Dallas, TX
Madden, Daniel J. ....Dallas, TX
Madden, Daniel L. ....Ashtabula, OH
Madden, Daniel P. ....Chicago, IL
Madden, David P. ....Overland Park, KS
Madden, Deborah Whitlock
Southbury, CT
Waterbury, CT
Madden, Dixie F. ....Wichita, KS
Madden, Donald P. ....New York, NY
Madden, Donna S. ....North Kingstown, RI
Madden, Edward B. ....Sharon, PA
Madden, Edward B., Jr.
Treasury Department,
Internal Revenue Service, GV
Madden, Edward E. ....Boston, MA
Madden, Edward G., Jr. ....Newark, NJ
Madden, Edward J. ....Watertown, NY
Madden, Elisabeth A. ....San Francisco, CA
Madden, Eric ....Dallas, TX
Madden, Erinn M. ....Treasury Department,
Internal Revenue Service, GV
Madden, Ford Victor ....Springfield, MA
Madden, Frank, & Associates
Plymouth, MN
Madden, Frank H. ....Hendersonville, NC
Madden, Frank J. ....Plymouth, MN
Madden, Ginger B. ....Shalimar, FL
Madden, Greg ....Tempe, AZ
Madden, Gregory J. ....Washington, DC
Madden, Harold W., (P.A.)
North Little Rock, AR
Madden, Holobinko & Gehlhaus
Middletown, NJ
Madden, Hugh A. ....Phoenix, AZ
Madden, J. Christopher ....Chicago, IL
Madden, J. Thomas ....Glen Dale, WV
Madden, James A., Jr. ....New York, NY
Madden, James E. ....St. Louis, MO
Madden, James F. ....Cliffside Park, NJ
Madden, James G. ....Freeport, IL
Madden, James J. ....Haddonfield, NJ
Madden, James M. ....Helena, MT
Madden, James P. ....Los Altos, CA
Madden, Jason T. ....Des Moines, IA
Madden, Jean A. ....Canton, OH
Madden, Jean M. ....Little Rock, AR
Madden, Jennifer S. ....Lexington, KY
Madden, Jerome A.
Federal Deposit Insurance Corporation,
Appellate Litigation Section, GV
Madden, Jiganti, Moore & Sinars
Chicago, IL
Madden, John B., Jr. ....New York, NY
Madden, John D. ....Raleigh, NC
Madden, John F., Jr. ....Los Angeles, CA
Madden, John H., Jr. ....Springfield, MA
Madden, John J. ....Boston, MA
Madden, John J. ....New York, NY
Madden, John J. ....Spokane, WA
Madden, John K. ....Chicago, IL
Madden, John L. ....Medford, NJ
Madden, John P. ....Gillespie, IL
Madden, John P. ....Douglaston, NY
New York, NY
Madden, John R. ....Red Bank, NJ
Madden, John T. ....Cranston, RI
Madden, John T. ....Moundsville, WV
Madden, John W. ....Stuart, FL
Madden, John W., III ....Denver, CO
Madden, John W., IV ....Denver, CO
Madden, John-Paul ....Philadelphia, PA
Madden, Jones, Cole & Johnson, A
Professional Corporation
Long Beach, CA
Madden, Joseph M., Jr. ....Fort Myers, FL
Madden, Justin F. ....Cleveland, OH
Madden, Karen S. ....Galveston, TX
Madden, Karl L., Jr. ....Moberly, MO
Madden, Kay ....Kansas City, MO
Madden, Kelly Anne ....Anoka, MN
Madden, Kenneth P. ....Providence, RI
Madden, Kenneth V. ....Manalapan, NJ
Brooklyn, NY
Madden, Kevin P.
Federal Energy Regulatory Commission,
Office of the General Counsel, GV
Madden, Lance J. ....Buffalo, NY
Madden Law Firm, The ....Little Rock, AR
Madden, Lawrence William
Longmeadow, MA
Madden, Lynne S. ....Bloomington, IL
Madden, M. Shannon ....Rockville, MD
Madden, M. Stuart ....White Plains, NY
Madden & Madden ....Denver, CO
Madden, Madden and Del Duca, P.A.
Haddonfield, NJ
Madden, Margaret M. ....Boston, MA
Madden, Margaret M. ....Newark, NJ
New York, NY
Madden, Mark D. ....St. Louis, MO

Madden, Mark M. ....Boston, MA
Madden, Martha E. ....Kansas City, MO
Madden, Mary ....Minneapolis, MN
Madden, Maureen A. ....Troy, NY
Madden, Michael ....Washington, DC
Madden, Michael ....Seattle, WA
Madden, Michael F. ....New York, NY
Madden, Michael I. ....Cleveland, OH
Madden, Michael J. ....Stamford, CT
Madden, Michael K. ....New York, NY
Madden, Michael P. ....Haddonfield, NJ
Madden, Mitchell ....Dallas, TX
Madden, Murdaugh Stuart
Washington, DC
Madden, Murdaugh Stuart and Roger A. Kindler ....Washington, DC
Madden, Neal D. ....Rochester, NY
Madden, Norine G. ....Eugene, OR
Madden, P. Michael ....New York, NY
Madden, Palmer Brown ....Alamo, CA
Madden, Patrick F. ....Dallas, TX
Madden, Patrick H. ....Mayville, WI
Madden, Patrick J. ....Hurley, WI
Madden, Patrick J. ....Hurley, WI
Madden, Patrick J., II ....Livonia, MI
Madden, Patrick Jefferson ....Muscatine, IA
Madden, Patrick Joseph ....Haddonfield, NJ
Madden, Patrick M. ....Seattle, WA
Madden & Patton, L.L.C. ....Washington, DC
Madden, Paul C. ....Philadelphia, PA
Madden, Paul L. ....Hawesville, KY
Madden, Paul R. ....Phoenix, AZ
Madden, Paul W. ....Baltimore, MD
Columbia, MD
Madden, Peter E. ....Providence, RI
Madden, Peter J. ....Mobile, AL
Madden, Philip M. ....Long Beach, CA
Madden, Poliak, MacDougall & Williamson
Seattle, WA
Madden, R. Scott ....Manchester, KY
Madden, Raymond H., III ....Ruston, LA
Madden & Redding ....San Jose, CA
Madden, Richard D. ....Pennsauken, NJ
Madden, Richard, Jr. ....Charlotte, NC
Madden, Richard L. ....Indianapolis, IN
Madden, Richd. A., L.P.A. ....Painesville, OH
Madden, Rick C. ....Los Angeles, CA
Madden, Robert E. ....Washington, DC
Vienna, VA
Madden, Robert E. ....Cherry Hill, NJ
Madden, Robert H. ....Seattle, WA
Madden, Robert J. ....Waterford, MI
Madden, Robert J. ....Houston, TX
Madden, Roger W. ....Lexington, KY
Madden, Ross M. ....San Francisco, CA
Madden, Roy R. ....Colonial Beach, VA
Madden, Sheila A. ....Phoenix, AZ
Madden, Sheila J. ....Kansas City, MO
Madden, Shelly ....St. Louis, MO
Madden and Sisler ....Freeport, IL
Madden, Sonia ....Chicago, IL
Madden & Soto ....Mobile, AL
Madden, Stanford C. ....Kansas City, MO
Madden, Stanley J. ....San Francisco, CA
Madden, Stephan D. ....Cincinnati, OH
Madden, Stephanie Anne ....Brewerton, NY
Madden, Tamara M. ....Houston, TX
Madden, Terrence J. ....Chicago, IL
Madden, Terrence J. ....Arcadia, WI
Madden, Terrence P. ....Colorado Springs, CO
Madden, Thomas J. ....Washington, DC
Madden, Thomas J., III ....Paso Robles, CA
Madden, Thomas M. ....Florham Park, NJ
Madden, Timothy ....Newark, NJ
Madden, Timothy E. ....Greenville, SC
Madden, Timothy G. ....Topeka, KS
Madden, Timothy J. ....Reisterstown, MD
Madden, Timothy K. ....Jersey City, NJ
Madden, Timothy M. ....Mayfield Village, OH
Madden, Timothy S. ....New Orleans, LA
Madden, Tricia A. ....Altamonte Springs, FL
Madden, Tricia A., P.A.
Altamonte Springs, FL
Madden, Turner D. ....Washington, DC
Madden, Veronica M. ....Boston, MA
Madden, Wales, Jr. ....Amarillo, TX
Madden, Walter H. ....Rockville, MD
Madden, Walter J., Jr. ....Port Ludlow, WA
Madden, William C., Jr. ....Vestal, NY
Madden, William H., Jr. ....Orange, CA
Madden, William J. ....Hays, KS
Madden, William J. ....Mendota Heights, MN
Madden, William J. ....Yonkers, NY
Madden, William J. ....Sharon, PA
Madden, William J., A Professional Corporation
Sharon, PA
Madden, William J., Jr. ....Washington, DC
Madden, William K. ....Middletown, NJ
Madden, William L., Jr. ....Bozeman, MT
Madden, William L., Jr., P.C.
Bozeman, MT
Madden, William M. ....Chicago, IL
Madden, Wm. C. ....Peterborough, NH
Maddex, Robert L., Jr. ....Reston, VA
Maddex, Stephen J. ....Houston, TX
Maddi, Thomas W. ....New York, NY
Maddick, Sally M. ....Milwaukee, WI
Maddigan, Michael M. ....Los Angeles, CA
Maddigan, Richard J. ....Cupertino, CA
Maddigan, Thomas A. ....Falmouth, MA
Raynham, MA
Maddin, Hauser, Wartell, Roth, Heller & Pesses, P.C. ....Detroit, MI
Mount Clemens, MI
Southfield, MI
Maddin, John K., Jr. ....Nashville, TN
Maddin, Michael W. ....Southfield, MI
Maddin, Miller & McCune ....Nashville, TN

Maddin, Richard J. ....Southfield, MI
Maddison, Laurence B., Jr. ....Raleigh, NC
Maddix, Barry Keith ....Boston, MA
Maddock, Charles E. ....Pasco, WA
Maddock, Charles S. ....Wilmington, DE
Maddock, James P. ....Free Union, VA
Maddock, John H., III ....Richmond, VA
Maddock, Laurence R. ....Florham Park, NJ
Maddock, Patrick J. ....Grand Forks, ND
Maddock, Paul A. ....St. Louis, MO
Maddock, Raymond R., Jr. ....Lincolnshire, IL
Maddock, Thomas M. ....Sacramento, CA
Maddocks, Donald B. ....Burlington, VT
Maddow, Richard M. ....Atlanta, GA
Maddow, Robert B. ....Walnut Creek, CA
Maddox, A. Hugh ....Montgomery, AL
Maddox, Austill, Parmer & Lewis, P.C.
Birmingham, AL
Maddox, Bruce ....Montgomery, AL
Maddox, Charles J., Jr. ....Missouri City, TX
Maddox, Charles R. ....Austin, TX
Maddox, Christine ....Bellevue, WA
Maddox Cummings & Kelley, LLP
Gainesville, GA
Maddox, Cynthia Buss ....Louisville, KY
Maddox, David L. ....Nashville, TN
Maddox, David L., & Associates, P.C.
Nashville, TN
Maddox, David T. ....Phoenix, AZ
Maddox, D. D. ....Huntingdon, TN
Maddox, Don ....Hobbs, NM
Maddox, Dwayne D., III ....Huntingdon, TN
Maddox, E. Thomas, Jr. ....Greensboro, NC
Maddox, Edward S. ....Harrisburg, AR
Maddox and Gorham, P.A. ....Greensboro, NC
Maddox, Gregory A. ....Tupelo, MS
Maddox, H. Edward ....Pikeville, KY
Maddox, J. Cordell, Jr. ....Anderson, SC
Maddox, J. David ....Mena, AR
Maddox, James D. ....Rome, GA
Maddox, James G. ....Jeffersonville, GA
Maddox, James M. ....Hobbs, NM
Maddox, James W., Law Offices of
Los Angeles, CA
Maddox, Jay R. ....Rockford, IL
Maddox, J. C. ....Calhoun, GA
Maddox, John ....Mena, AR
Maddox, John D. ....Washington, DC
Maddox, John G. ....Clinton, TN
Maddox, John M. ....Dothan, AL
Maddox, John R. ....Hartford City, IN
Maddox, John R., Jr. ....Hartford City, IN
Maddox, Jon R. ....Belmont, MA
Maddox, Joseph K., Jr. ....Spartanburg, SC
Maddox, Joseph W. ....Springfield, IL
Maddox, Joy E. ....New York, NY
Maddox, Kelli Gregg ....Columbia, SC
Maddox, Kendall W., Law Offices of
Birmingham, AL
Maddox Koeller Hargett & Caruso
Indianapolis, IN
New York, NY
Maddox, L. Michael ....Jacksonville, FL
Maddox Law Firm, Professional Corporation
Hobbs, NM
Maddox, Lola P. ....Edwardsville, IL
Maddox, Lynwood A. ....Atlanta, GA
Maddox, Lynwood A., Jr. ....Atlanta, GA
Maddox, Maddox and Maddox ....Atlanta, GA
Maddox, Maddox & Maddox
Huntingdon, TN
Maddox, Marcia M. ....Vienna, VA
Maddox, Mark A. ....Campton, KY
Maddox, Mark E. ....Indianapolis, IN
Maddox, Mark R. ....Midland, MI
Maddox, Mark S. ....Columbus, OH
Maddox, Mary Elizabeth ....Knoxville, TN
Maddox, Matthew J. ....Springfield, IL
Maddox, Matthew M. ....Huntington, TN
Maddox, Matthew Morgen ....Stamford, CT
Maddox, Melinda Lee ....Brewton, AL
Maddox, Michael A. ....Pittsburgh, PA
Maddox, Michael B. ....Birmingham, AL
Maddox, Michael J. ....Lawrence, KS
Maddox, Michael Paul ....Washington, DC
Maddox, Milton E. ....Richmond, VA
Maddox, Nancy M. ....Hernando, MS
Maddox, Nathan P. ....Springfield, IL
Maddox, O. Gene ....Des Moines, IA
Maddox, Paul J. ....San Francisco, CA
Maddox, Paul R. ....Jefferson, LA
Maddox, R. Anderson ....Orlando, FL
Maddox, Robert Bruni ....Austin, TX
Maddox, Robert C. ....Rockville, MD
Maddox, Robert C. ....Reno, NV
Maddox, Robert D. ....Fort Worth, TX
Maddox, Robert L. ....Louisville, KY
Maddox, Robert L. ....Houston, TX
Maddox, Robert L., III ....Louisville, KY
Maddox, Robert W. ....Conyers, GA
Maddox, Ronald P. ....Annandale, VA
Maddox, Roy C., Jr. ....Chattanooga, TN
Maddox, Scott D. ....Huntington, WV
Maddox, Selene Dunn ....Tupelo, MS
Maddox, Shane C. ....Jacksonville, FL
Maddox, Sheila Newsome ....Newark, NJ
Maddox & Shelton ....Rockville, MD
Maddox, Starnes & Nix ....Conyers, GA
Maddox & Stearns ....Brewton, AL
Maddox, Steve ....Olympia, WA
Maddox, Steven ....Menlo Park, CA
Maddox, Tamara A. ....Fairfax, VA
Maddox, Thomas E., Jr. ....Atlanta, GA
Maddox, Thomas E., Jr., P.C.
Atlanta, GA
Decatur, GA
Maddox, Todd B. ....Medford, OR
Maddox, Tommy Lee ....Calhoun, GA

Maddox, Victor B. ....Louisville, KY
Maddox, W. Andrew ....Gainesville, GA
Maddox, William E., Jr. ....Knoxville, TN
Maddox, William G. ....Department of Justice, Civil Rights Division, GV
Maddox, W. T. ....Rome, GA
Maddox-Cook, P.J. ....Blytheville, AR
Maddrell, Donald B. ....Sandusky, OH
Maddrey, Jeffrey W. ....Treasury Department, Internal Revenue Service, GV
Maddrey, John F. ....Raleigh, NC
Maddrey, Joseph G. ....Eden, NC
Maddrey, Nicole M.
Securities and Exchange Commission, Division of Corporation Finance, GV
Maddrey, Wendell C. ....New York, NY
Maddrey, Wilson & Etringer ....Eden, NC
Wentworth, NC
Maddry, Tyler ....Schenectady, NY
Maddux, Amy Douthitt ....Houston, TX
Maddux, Cortlan H. ....Houston, TX
Maddux, David A. ....Los Angeles, CA
Maddux, Deborah L. ....Sacramento, CA
Maddux, George C. ....Gate City, VA
Maddux, H. Owen ....Chattanooga, TN
Maddux, Howard A. ....Tulsa, OK
Maddux, Jere C. ....Ames, IA
Maddux, Jerry M. ....Bartlesville, OK
Maddux, John C. ....Claremont, CA
Rancho Cucamonga, CA
Maddux, John Charles
Westlake Village, CA
Maddux, John J., Jr. ....Cookeville, TN
Maddux, Lisa Ellen ....Baltimore, MD
Maddux, Mark E. ....Springfield, MO
Maddux, Markie Hart ....Fort Worth, TX
Maddux, Michael C.
Rancho Cucamonga, CA
Maddux, Michael P. ....Tampa, FL
Maddux, Parker A. ....Portola Valley, CA
Maddux, Spencer ....Atlanta, GA
Maddux, W. Lee ....Chattanooga, TN
Maddux, W. E. ....Nowata, OK
Maddux, William D. ....Chicago, IL
Maddy, Daniel D. ....Phoenix, AZ
Duluth, MN
Maddy, Elmer C. ....Greenwich, CT
Maddy, Kenneth L. ....Fresno, CA
Madea, Frank P. ....Chicago, IL
Madea, J. Dennis ....Atlanta, GA
Madeira, Edward W., Jr.
Philadelphia, PA
Madeira, Percy C. ....Bethesda, MD
Madeiros, Pamela A. ....Albany, NY
Madej, James T. ....Chicago, IL
Madek, Gerald A. ....Boston, MA
Madeksho, Lawrence ....Houston, TX
Madel, Christopher W. ....Minneapolis, MN
St. Paul, MN
Madeley, D. Foster ....Conroe, TX
Madeley, Gregory Z. ....Conroe, TX
Madenci, Diane ....Tucson, AZ
Madenlian, Tamara ....Los Angeles, CA
Madenspacher, Joseph C. ....Lancaster, PA
Madeo, Donald Francis ....Garden City, NY
Madeo, John ....New Rochelle, NY
Mader, Brenda Taylor ....Topeka, KS
Mader, Christopher P. ....Los Angeles, CA
Mader, Diane L. ....Madison, WI
Mader, Jay W. ....Knoxville, TN
Mader, Joyce A. ....Washington, DC
Mader, Lynn R. ....Wellsboro, PA
Mader, Mark G. ....Milwaukee, WI
Mader, Monica S. ....Los Angeles, CA
Madera, Cornelius J. J., Jr. ....Florida, NY
Madera, Gregory A. ....Boston, MA
Madere, Barbara Volk ....Metairie, LA
New Orleans, LA
Madere, Rodney J. ....Metairie, LA
Maderer, William F. ....Newark, NJ
Maderious, John W. ....Santa Rosa, CA
Madewell, James D. ....Cookeville, TN
Madewell, Jared & Halfacre
Cookeville, TN
Madey, Frank J. ....Allentown, PA
Madey, Joseph A. ....Little Rock, AR
Madfes, Jason L. ....New York, NY
Madge, Leslie S. ....Littleton, MA
Madge, Leslie S., P.C. ....Littleton, MA
Madgett, Michael L. ....San Diego, CA
Madgett, Paul W. ....Omaha, NE
Madia, Frank Leonard ....Utica, NY
Madia, Marc A. ....Albany, NY
Madick, Paul H. ....Torrance, CA
Madigan, Amy Lee ....Atlanta, GA
Madigan, Arnold R. ....Denver, CO
Madigan, Brian C. ....Binghamton, NY
Deposit, NY
Madigan, Carol M. ....Oak Brook, IL
Madigan, Daniel T. ....Chicago, IL
Madigan, Dominic P. ....Richmond, VA
Madigan, Edward J. ....New York, NY
Madigan, Elizabeth R. ....Treasury Department, Internal Revenue Service, GV
Madigan & Getzendanner ....Chicago, IL
Madigan, Heather M. ....Camas, WA
Madigan, John E. ....Northbrook, IL
Madigan, John L. ....Encinitas, CA
Madigan, John S. ....Irving, TX
Madigan, John T. ....Toledo, OH
Madigan, Kathryn Grant
Binghamton, NY
Madigan, Kimberly A. ....Washington, DC
Madigan, Lawrence J. ....Houston, TX
Madigan, Lisa M. ....Chicago, IL
Madigan & Madigan ....Bath, NY
Madigan & Madigan ....Binghamton, NY
Madigan, Mark J. ....Springfield, VA

Madigan, Mark Steven ....Milwaukee, WI
Madigan & McBride ....Danvers, MA
Madigan, Michael ....New York, NY
Madigan, Michael D. ....Minneapolis, MN
Madigan, Michael J. ....Chicago, IL
Madigan, Michael J. ....Chicago, IL
Madigan, Michael J., (P.C.)
Washington, DC
Madigan, Patrick T. ....Denver, CO
Madigan, Peter J., (A P.C.)
Newport Beach, CA
Madigan, Richard M. ....Mineola, NY
Madigan, Robert J. ....Binghamton, NY
Madigan, Robert J. ....Manassas, VA
Springfield, VA
Madigan, Robert J., Jr. ....Binghamton, NY
Deposit, NY
Madigan & Scott, Inc. ....Fairfax, VA
Manassas, VA
Springfield, VA
Madigan, Shelia P. ....St. Paul, MN
Madigan, Terrell C. ....Tallahassee, FL
Madigan, Thomas C. ....Belmar, NJ
Madigan, Thomas J. ....Pittsburgh, PA
Madigan, Timothy G. ....Danvers, MA
Madigan, Timothy O. ....Urbana, IL
Madigan, William G. ....Bath, NY
Madigan-Cassidy, Mary E.
Washington, DC
Madin, Everett Howard, Jr. ....Hartford, CT
Mading, Thomas B. ....Clinton, NJ
Mading, Tricia D. ....La Jolla, CA
Madinger, Hulit L. ....Dallas, TX
Madisen, Neal E. ....Milwaukee, WI
Madison, Allen D.
United States Tax Court, GV
Madison, Benjamin V., III ....Norfolk, VA
Madison, Blake A. ....Tuscaloosa, AL
Madison, Charles A. ....Raleigh, NC
Madison, David A. ....Fort Worth, TX
Madison, Dina K. ....Beaumont, TX
Madison, Donna Britt ....Anniston, AL
Madison, Douglas G. ....Cheyenne, WY
Madison, G. Gordon ....San Diego, CA
Madison, Garrett, Brandon & Tugwell
Bastrop, LA
Madison, Gary R. ....Arlington, VA
Madison, George F. ....Bastrop, LA
Madison, George W. ....Detroit, MI
Madison, Harbour, Mroz & Brennan, P.A.
Albuquerque, NM
Santa Fe, NM
Madison, James Pierce ....Bastrop, LA
Madison, James R. ....San Francisco, CA
Madison, James R. ....Shreveport, LA
Madison, Jerrie M. ....Jackson, MS
Madison, John L. ....Syracuse, NY
Madison, John L., Jr. ....Jasper, AL
Madison, John M., Jr. ....Shreveport, LA
Madison, John P., Jr. ....Newport Beach, CA
Madison, Jonathan L. ....Denver, CO
Madison, Kellis L. ....Pearl, MS
Madison, Kenneth W. ....Roseburg, OR
Madison, Kevin R. ....Austin, TX
Madison, Kevin R., A Prof. Corp., Law Offices Of ....Austin, TX
Madison, Larry W. ....Hartselle, AL
Madison, Marshall B. ....Kalamazoo, MI
Madison, Mary E. ....Havre de Grace, MD
Madison, Michael T. ....New York, NY
Madison, Norbert T., Jr. ....Detroit, MI
Madison, Patina A. ....Orange, CA
Madison, Paul E. ....Portage Des Sioux, MO
Madison, Paul G. ....Washington, DC
Madison, Peter J. ....New City, NY
Madison, Regina ....Washington, DC
Madison, Richard J. ....New York, NY
Madison, Samuel R. ....Delmar, NY
Madison, Sara E. ....San Francisco, CA
Madison, Sarah C. ....Minneapolis, MN
Madison, Steven G. ....Los Angeles, CA
Madison, Suzanne M. ....Los Angeles, CA
Madison, Tammara C. ....Washington, DC
Madison, Timothy G. ....Winder, GA
Madison, Timothy G. ....Columbus, OH
Madison, William C. ....Albuquerque, NM
Madison, William H. ....San Francisco, CA
Madison Pratt, Vivian L. ....Iselin, NJ
Madkour, Stephen Lewis ....Portland, OR
Madler, James R. ....Chicago, IL
Madler & Peldyak ....Chicago, IL
Madlock, Clim, Jr. ....Memphis, TN
Madlock, Kathryn A. ....Tustin, CA
Madlom, Bruce L. ....Fargo, ND
Madnick, Benjamin ....Neptune, NJ
Madnick, Carla H. ....Hackensack, NJ
Madnick, Milstein, Mason, Weber, Farnsworth & Collazo, P.A. ....Brick, NJ
Neptune, NJ
Madnick, Seth B. ....Napa, CA
Madock, Daniel R. ....Chicago, IL
Madoff, David B. ....Boston, MA
Madoff, Emily ....New York, NY
Madoff, Jeffrey L. ....Chicago, IL
Madoff, Linda F. ....Walden, NY
Madoff, Ray D. ....Newton, MA
Madoff, Steven ....Los Angeles, CA
Madoian, Gregory A. ....Cranston, RI
Madok, Robert L. ....Los Angeles, CA
Madokoro, Mike Hitoshi ....Torrance, CA
Madole, Bret A. ....Dallas, TX
Madole, Cynthia E. Joyce ....Dallas, TX
Madole, Donald W. ....Rosslyn, VA
Madole, Juanita M. ....Irvine, CA
Madole, Luke ....Dallas, TX
Madole, Margo M. ....Houston, TX
Madole, Mercedes ....Washington, DC
Alexandria, VA

Magee, Neal H., II .... Columbus, OH
Delaware, OH
Magee, Negele & Associates
Round Lake, IL
Magee, Noel T. .... Columbia, MO
Magee, Norman M. .... Ferriday, LA
Magee, Pamela .... Madison, WI
Magee, Peder van Wagonen
Federal Trade Commission, Offices of Commissioners, GV
Magee, Raymond W. .... Sherman Oaks, CA
Magee, Rebecca .... Tulsa, OK
Magee, Rhonda V. .... San Francisco, CA
Magee, Richard D., Jr. .... Doylestown, PA
Magee, Richard J. .... St. Louis, MO
Magee, Richard L. .... Charlotte, NC
Magee, Robert J. .... Allentown, PA
Bethlehem, PA
Jim Thorpe, PA
Magee, Robert L., Jr. .... Sacramento, CA
Magee, Scott R. .... Long Beach, CA
Magee, Shara Garwood .... Atlanta, GA
Magee, Shawn S. .... Chicago, IL
Magee, Steven H. .... Dallas, TX
Magee, Steven H., Attorney at Law, PLLC
Dallas, TX
Magee, Theodore M. .... Minneapolis, MN
Magee, Thomas B. .... Washington, DC
Magee, Thomas H. .... Wilmington, DE
Magee, Thomas J. .... St. Louis, MO
Magee, Thomas L. .... Round Lake, IL
Magee, Thomas M. .... Emmetsburg, IA
Magee, Timothy J. .... Troy, AL
Magee, William Eugene .... Jackson, MS
Magee, William F. .... Lewisville, AR
Magee, William M. .... Covington, LA
Magee, Yada T., Ms. .... New Orleans, LA
Magel, Barbara A. .... Chicago, IL
Magel, Daniel L. .... Los Angeles, CA
Magel, Daniel L. .... Manhattan Beach, CA
Magel, John .... Boise, ID
Magelaner, Thomas L. .... Columbus, OH
Magelky, Nancy K. .... Dickinson, ND
Magen, Barbara S. .... Philadelphia, PA
Magen, Burt .... San Francisco, CA
Magen, Philip A. .... San Diego, CA
Magenau, Jeff L. .... Washington, DC
Magence, Meyer .... Niles, IL
Magendantz, Kristin Bierly .... Quincy, MA
Magenheim, Alan N. .... Houston, TX
Magenheim, Alissa J. .... San Diego, CA
Magenheim, Bateman & Helfand, PLLC
Houston, TX
Magenheim, Craig J. .... Houston, TX
Magenheim, Janet H. .... Newton, MA
Magenheimer, Stanley J. .... Miami, FL
Mager, Carol A. .... Philadelphia, PA
Mager, Clara DeMatteis .... Detroit, MI
Mager, George J., Jr. .... Detroit, MI
Troy, MI
Mager, Gerald .... Fort Lauderdale, FL
Mager, Gregory S. .... Milwaukee, WI
Mager, John J. .... Milford, CT
Mager, Joseph J. .... Milford, CT
Mager, Joseph J., Jr. .... Milford, CT
Mager Law Firm, The, P.C. .... Delran, NJ
Haddonfield, NJ
Philadelphia, PA
Mager, Lee M. .... Bronx, NY
New York, NY
Mager & Mager .... Milford, CT
Mager, Mercer & Alber, P.C. .... Detroit, MI
Pontiac, MI
Troy, MI
Mager, Michael B. .... Albany, NY
Mager, Scott A. .... Fort Lauderdale, FL
Mager, Scott A. .... New York, NY
Mager, Stanley D. .... Atlanta, GA
Mager, Steven M. .... Newark, NJ
Mager, Suzanne L. .... Boston, MA
Mager, T. Richard .... Carbondale, IL
Mager, Wendy L. .... Princeton, NJ
Magera, Diana E. .... Pittsburgh, PA
Magera, George F. .... Pittsburgh, PA
Magera, Gregg C. .... Aberdeen, SD
Magera, John M. .... Charleston, SC
Magerer, Michael .... Needham, MA
Magers, Barbara Shelley .... Philadelphia, PA
Magers, Bruce .... Winston-Salem, NC
Magers, Gail .... Houston, TX
Magers, John A. .... Kansas City, MO
Magers, M. Scott .... San Antonio, TX
Magers, Patrick F. .... Perris, CA
Magers, Thomas Vandiver .... Tampa, FL
Mages-Rankin, Deborah K. .... Berkeley, CA
Mages, Lawrence M. .... Chicago, IL
Mages, Rubie A. .... New York, NY
Magett, Carol Elyse .... Hackensack, NJ
New York, NY
Magette, Kurt Robert .... Richmond, VA
Magevney, Laura Mann .... Nashville, TN
Maggard, Darquita L. .... Gulfport, MS
Maggard, James M. .... Wilmington, NC
Maggard, Sarah E. .... Whittier, CA
Maggert, James R. .... Ankeny, IA
Maggi, David A. .... Department of Commerce, Office of the General Counsel, GV
Maggi, Philip J. .... House of Representatives, Congressional Assistants, GV
Maggi, Richard J. .... Springfield, MA
Maggi, Richard P. .... Millburn, NJ
Maggiacomo, Edward L. .... Providence, RI
Maggiacomo, Humbert Vernon
Pleasant Valley, NY
Maggiacomo, Jennifer A. .... Boston, MA
Maggiacomo, Steven W. .... Braintree, MA
Maggiani, Euclid F. .... Manhasset, NY
Maggiano, Michael J. .... Fort Lee, NJ
Maggied, Pamela N. .... Columbus, OH
Maggin, Bruce .... Flushing, NY
Maggin, Bruce R. .... Brooklyn, NY
Maggin & Swan .... Forest Hills, NY
Maggin, Wayne L. .... New York, NY
Maggini, Alfred F. .... Santa Rosa, CA
Maggini, Louis E. .... Grand Rapids, MI
Maggio, Albert B., Jr. .... Boxborough, MA
Maggio, Andrew P., Jr. .... Chicago, IL
Maggio, Andrew P., Jr. and Associates
Chicago, IL
Maggio, Angelo J. .... Salemburg, NC
Maggio, Brent M. .... Lafayette, LA
Maggio, Charles F. .... Rochester, NY
Maggio, Cornelia Farrell .... Philadelphia, PA
Maggio, Daniel F., Jr. .... Utica, NY
Maggio, Evelyn .... Flemington, NJ
Maggio, F. Michael .... Houston, TX
Maggio & Fox .... Rockford, IL
Maggio, Frank G. .... Rochester, NY
Maggio, Frank P. .... Rockford, IL
Maggio, James G. .... Towson, MD
Maggio, James M., Jr .... Paramus, NJ
Maggio, John .... New York, NY
Maggio, John J. .... New York, NY
Maggio & Kattar, P.C. .... Washington, DC
Maggio, Michael .... Washington, DC
Maggio, Michael A. .... Conway, AR
Maggio, Michael A. .... Little Rock, AR
Searcy, AR
Maggio, Patricia L. .... Catonsville, MD
Maggio, Patrick J. .... Colorado Springs, CO
Maggio, Paula C. .... Chicago, IL
Maggio, Richard .... San Francisco, CA
Maggio, Robert A. .... Columbia, MD
Maggio, Stephen J. .... Gulfport, MS
Maggio, Timothy M. .... Chicago, IL
Maggio & Wyman, P.A. .... Towson, MD
Maggiola, Stephen P. .... Fairfield, CT
Maggiolo, Allison Joseph .... Louisville, KY
Maggiolo, Walter A. .... Arlington, VA
Maggioncalda, Theresa A. .... Kalamazoo, MI
Maggioni, Cara .... Washington, DC
Maggioni, Paul D., Sr. .... Dedham, MA
Maggiore, W. Ann .... Albuquerque, NM
Maggiore-Conner, Lisa A. .... Mesa, AZ
Maggiore-Tragni, Rosa P. .... Staten Island, NY
Maggiotto, Louis J., Jr. .... Secaucus, NJ
Maggiotto, Paul A., Law Office of
Concord, NH
Maggipinto, V. Anthony .... Riverhead, NY
St. James, NY
St. James, NY
Maggipinto, V. Anthony .... St. James, NY
Maggipinto, Wm. V. .... Southampton, NY
Maggs, Gregory Eaton .... Washington, DC
Maggs, James A. .... Wall Township, NJ
Maggs, Marguerite A. .... Eatontown, NJ
Maggs, Michael K. .... Schenectady, NY
Maggs, Peter B. .... Champaign, IL
Magguilli, Michael C. .... Albany, NY
Maghamé, Taraneh .... Seattle, WA
Maghiar, Livia L. .... New York, NY
Maghie, Mark A. .... Seattle, WA
Maghrak, Monica .... Pittsburgh, PA
Maghran, Irving C., Jr. .... Buffalo, NY
Maghran, McCarthy & Flynn .... Buffalo, NY
Magid, Creighton R. .... Minneapolis, MN
Magid, James M. .... Mammoth Lakes, CA
Magid, Jeffrey A. .... Detroit, MI
Magid, Julie Manning .... Indianapolis, IN
Magid, Laurie .... Wilmington, DE
Magid, Lawrence .... Woodbury, NJ
Magid, Leonard S. .... Jacksonville, FL
Magid, Martin K. .... Detroit, MI
Magid, Paul S. .... Washington, DC
Magid, Richard J. .... Baltimore, MD
Magid, Stephen H. .... Jamaica, NY
Magid, Steven E. .... New York, NY
Magid, Terren B. .... Indianapolis, IN
Magid, Wm. H. .... Cleveland, OH
Magida, Kenneth S. .... Great Neck, NY
Magida, Lenore R. .... United States Senate, Committee Legal Personnel, GV
Magida, Stephen A. .... Stamford, CT
Magidoff, Barry G. .... New York, NY
Magidova, Alona .... Skillman, NJ
Magids, Jack Steven .... Memphis, TN
Magids, Marc J. .... Houston, TX
Magids, Samuel B. .... Houston, TX
Magidsohn, Herman E. .... Encino, CA
Magidson, Adolph .... Lake Worth, FL
Magidson, David L. .... Miami, FL
Magidson, Emma Dale .... San Diego, CA
Magidson, Hinda .... Boston, MA
Magidson, Ilene C. .... New York, NY
Magidson, Isabel R. .... St. Paul, MN
Magidson, Joshua .... Clearwater, FL
Magidson, Mark H. .... Detroit, MI
Magidson, Matthew A. .... Fort Worth, TX
Magidson, Sherman C. .... Chicago, IL
Magidson & Sullivan .... Chicago, IL
Magidson, William H. .... Chicago, IL
Magie, Andresen, Haag, Paciotti, Butterworth & McCarthy, P.A.
Duluth, MN
Magie & Palmer .... Pensacola, FL
Magie, Robert H., III .... Duluth, MN
Magie, Roderic G. .... Pensacola, FL
Magielnicki, Robert L. .... Washington, DC
Magielnicki, Robert L., Jr.
Washington, DC
Magier, Eugene M. .... Needham, MA
Magier, Heather G. .... New Orleans, LA
Magier, Leora A. .... New York, NY
Magier, Seymour .... New York, NY
Magilavy, David .... Newport Beach, CA
Magill & Atkinson LLP .... Atlanta, GA
Magill, Brad R. .... Philadelphia, PA
Magill, Crye & Cizek .... Clinton, TN
Magill, Edward L. .... Miami, FL
Magill, Frank C. .... St. Louis, MO
Magill, Frank J. .... Fargo, ND
Magill, Frank J., Jr. .... Minneapolis, MN
Magill, Goldah Brenner .... Brooklyn, NY
Magill, James L. .... Peoria, IL
Magill, Joe E. .... Clinton, TN
Magill, John P. .... House of Representatives, Congressional Assistants, GV
Magill, Kent B. .... Mission Woods, KS
Magill Law Offices .... Fresno, CA
Magill, Margaret Burns .... Minneapolis, MN
Magill, Marisa B. .... Miami, FL
Magill, Mary E. .... Charlottesville, VA
Magill, Michael K. .... Chicago, IL
Magill, Patrick M. .... Orlando, FL
Magill, Patrick M., P.A. .... Orlando, FL
Magill, R. Hugh .... Chicago, IL
Magill, Richard A. .... Philadelphia, PA
Magill, Robert F. .... Birmingham, MI
Magill, Robert F., Jr. .... Ann Arbor, MI
Magill, Robert M. .... Springfield, IL
Magill, Robert T. .... New York, NY
Magill and Rumsey, P.C. .... Ann Arbor, MI
Magill, Thomas D. .... Irvine, CA
Magill, Thomas E. .... Atlanta, GA
Magill, Thomas J. .... Chicago, IL
Magill, Timothy V. .... Fresno, CA
Magilow, Mark G. .... Dallas, TX
Maginn, William F., Jr. .... Canton, NY
Maginnis, Arthur .... Miami, FL
Maginnis, Edward J. .... Largo, MD
Maginnis, Eugene J., Jr. .... Philadelphia, PA
Maginnis & Hurley, A Professional Law Corporation .... Metairie, LA
New Orleans, LA
Maginnis, J. Patrick .... Santa Monica, CA
Maginnis, James B. .... Baltimore, MD
Maginnis, Jeanette Torrel .... Santa Monica, CA
Maginnis, John C., III .... Washington, DC
Maginnis, John T. .... Houston, TX
Maginnis, Kevin J. .... Philadelphia, PA
Maginnis & Maginnis, A Professional Corporation .... Santa Monica, CA
Maginnis, Michael J. .... New Orleans, LA
Maginniss, Christopher Lyle .... Dallas, TX
Maginot Addison & Moore
Indianapolis, IN
Maginot, Paul J. .... Indianapolis, IN
Maginot, Peter M. .... St. Louis, MO
Magioncalda, Albert J. .... Woodhaven, NY
Magioncalda, Jane M. .... New York, NY
Magis, Thomas H. .... Atlanta, GA
Magiske, Kelly A. .... Pittsburgh, PA
Magistrale, Anthony N.
Research Triangle Park, NC
Magistrale, Jean .... San Anselmo, CA
Magistrale, Samuel A. .... Buffalo, NY
Magistrali, Michael F. .... Winsted, CT
Magistre, Dervis .... New York, NY
Magit, George .... Encino, CA
Magit, Mark Gilbert
Mammoth Lakes, CA
Maglaras, Chris, Jr. .... Las Vegas, NV
Maglaras, Nicholas G. .... New York, NY
Magleby, James E. .... Salt Lake City, UT
Magleby, Linda Waters .... Provo, UT
Magleby, Steven C. .... Salt Lake City, UT
Magley, David J. .... Wabash, IN
Magley, Erin Morrae .... Grand Rapids, MI
Magley, Raymond R. .... Jacksonville, FL
Magley, Robert E. .... Wabash, IN
Magley, Stephen J. .... Pittsburgh, PA
Magliarditi, Dominic J. .... Las Vegas, NV
Magliari, Michael E. .... St. Louis, MO
Magliaro, C. L. .... South Orange, NJ
Magliato, Jeanine F. .... Woodbury, NY
Maglich, David S. .... Sarasota, FL
Maglicic Kramer, Ellen .... Cleveland, OH
Maglieri, Charles A. .... Bloomfield, CT
Maglio, Altom M. .... Sarasota, FL
Maglio, Altom M., P.A. .... Sarasota, FL
Maglio, Anthony E. .... Brooklyn, NY
Maglio, David E., & Associates
Providence, RI
Maglio, Gerald J. .... Las Vegas, NV
Maglio, Jennifer G. .... Sarasota, FL
Maglio, Michael F. .... Hartford, CT
Maglio, Michael J. .... Sewickley, PA
Maglio, Nicholas J. .... Hartford, CT
Magliocca, Gerard N. .... Washington, DC
Magliocco, Anna M. .... Cambridge, MA
Magliocco, John A. .... Brooklyn, NY
Magliocco, Michael C. .... Willimantic, CT
Magliochetti, Lisa A. .... Hartford, CT
Magliochetti, Scott D. .... Princeton, NJ
Maglione, Christine A. .... Boston, MA
Maglione, Daniel F. .... Chicago, IL
Maglione, Fred J. .... Tallahassee, FL
Magliozzi, Thomas A. .... San Diego, CA
Magliulo, Angelique M.S. .... Boston, MA
Magloff, Michael B. .... Los Angeles, CA
Maglone, Lisa A. .... Edison, NJ
Magna & Hauser .... Gurnee, IL
Magna, Rudolph F. .... Gurnee, IL
Magnan, Pierre .... New York, NY
Magnan, Pierre P. .... New York, NY
Magnan, Richard M. .... Saugus, MA
Magnani & Buck Ltd. .... Chicago, IL
Magnani, Linda Ann .... Bronx, NY
Magnani, Peter J. .... Chicago, IL
Magnanimo, Frank A. .... Granada Hills, CA
Magnanini, Robert A. .... Newark, NJ
Magnano, Joseph S. .... New York, NY
Magnano, Marco J., Jr. .... Seattle, WA
Magnant, Suzanne L. .... Indianapolis, IN
Magnarella, Paul J. .... Gainesville, FL
Magnarelli, David J. .... Syracuse, NY
Magnarelli, Dominic J. .... Wakefield, MA
Magnarelli, William B. .... Syracuse, NY
Magnarini, Gary A. .... Miami, FL
Magnatta, George T. .... Philadelphia, PA
Magner, Anne Cushing
Upper Marlboro, MD
Magner, Austin P. .... Monmouth Beach, NJ
Magner, Edward J. .... Kennesaw, GA
Magner, Elizabeth Wall .... New Orleans, LA
Magner, J. C. .... Houston, TX
Magner, Michael W. .... New Orleans, LA
Magner, Michele G. .... Chicago, IL
Magner, Philip H., Jr. .... Buffalo, NY
Magner, Richard B. .... Linden, NJ
Magner, Robert J. .... Houston, TX
Magnes, Evelyn, (Mrs.) .... San Jose, CA
Magnes, Ronald E. .... Northbrook, IL
Magness, B. Percy .... Memphis, TN
Magness, J. Gregory .... Fort Smith, AR
Magness, J.T. .... Springfield, MO
Magness, Marcus Don .... Fresno, CA
Magness, W. Bruce .... Lubbock, TX
Magnetti, Ralph E. .... Tarrytown, NY
Magnetti, Suzanne S. .... Silver Spring, MD
Magnetti, Thomas O.
Department of Commerce, Office of the General Counsel, GV
Magney, John S. .... Washington, DC
Magnier, Mary Anne .... Honolulu, HI
Magnis, Richard H. .... Dallas, TX
Magno, JoAnn V. .... Riverside, CA
Magnola, Michael L. .... Tinton Falls, NJ
Magnoli, Carolan .... New York, NY
Magnone, Joseph R. .... Alexandria, VA
Magnone, Matthew .... Newark, NJ
Magnone, Richard .... Chicago, IL
Magnotta, Anthony J. .... Hawley, PA
Magnotti, Joseph E. .... Staten Island, NY
Magnotti, Susan E.
Federal Communications Commission, Common Carrier Bureau, GV
Magnotto, Mark R. .... Westlake, OH
Magnozzi, Mark F. .... New York, NY
Magnum, Castro & Associates, P.C.
San Bernardino, CA
Magnum, Chaim .... San Bernardino, CA
Magnus, Allen F. .... Brooklyn, NY
Magnus, Cynthia .... Pleasanton, CA
Magnus, Erin L. .... Minneapolis, MN
Magnus, Ilysa M. .... New York, NY
Magnus, John R. .... Washington, DC
Magnus, Karl H. .... Arlington Heights, IL
Magnus, Karl H. .... Chicago, IL
Magnus, Lee .... White Plains, NY
Magnus, Melvin Walter .... Bakersfield, CA
Magnus, Michael G. .... Beaverton, OR
Magnus, Neal M. .... Elizabeth, NJ
Magnus, Neil D. .... Trenton, NJ
Magnus, Richard A. .... Cincinnati, OH
Magnusen, Denise Pappas .... Long Valley, NJ
Magnusen, William H., Jr. .... Gulfport, MS
Magnuson, Arnold N., Jr. .... Southfield, MI
Magnuson & Barone .... Columbus, OH
Magnuson, Carolyn M. .... Worcester, MA
Magnuson, Cathy .... St. Louis Park, MN
Magnuson, Charles H. .... Los Angeles, CA
Magnuson, David T. .... Stillwater, MN
Magnuson, Dennis C. .... Omaha, NE
Magnuson & Dieperink .... Stillwater, MN
Magnuson, Eric J. .... Minneapolis, MN
Magnuson, Gerald E. .... Minneapolis, MN
Magnuson, H. James .... Coeur d'Alene, ID
Magnuson, James A. .... Columbus, OH
Magnuson, Janet A. .... South Bend, IN
Magnuson, John David .... Minneapolis, MN
Magnuson, John F. .... Coeur d'Alene, ID
Magnuson, Kevin M. .... Cleveland, OH
Magnuson, Lee A. .... Sioux Falls, SD
Magnuson Lowell, P.S. .... Redmond, WA
Magnuson, Marcus Richard
Minneapolis, MN
Magnuson, Mark G. .... Washington, DC
Magnuson, Mary B. .... Minneapolis, MN
Magnuson, Michael S. .... Whittier, CA
Magnuson, Nels G. .... Syracuse, NY
Magnuson, Paul A. .... St. Paul, MN
Magnuson, Peter B. .... Houston, TX
Magnuson, Philip E. .... Hyannis, MA
Magnuson, Randall W. .... San Diego, CA
Magnuson, Richard G. .... Wallace, ID
Magnuson, Richard H. .... St. Paul, MN
Magnuson, Richard H., Jr. .... Lakeport, CA
Magnuson, Robert L. .... Spokane, WA
Magnuson, Robert S. .... Spokane, WA
Magnuson, Roger J. .... Minneapolis, MN
Magnuson, Ruth Ann
Charlotte Amalie, St. Thomas, VI
Magnuson, S. Thomas .... Redmond, WA
Magnuson, Scott P. .... Monroeville, PA
Magnuson, Scott P. .... Pittsburgh, PA
Magnuson, Veldon G. .... Omaha, NE
Magnuson & Wright .... Southfield, MI
Magnuson-Carson, Marrianne
Burbank, CA
Magnussen, Robert D. .... Houston, TX
Magnussen, William R. .... Fort Worth, TX
Magnusson, Craig D. .... Bellevue, WA
Magnusson, David W. .... Santa Barbara, CA
Magnusson, Keith C. .... Bismarck, ND
Magnusson, Leifur .... Metuchen, NJ
Mago, Bernard A. .... Tonawanda, NY
Mago, Jane E.
Federal Communications Commission, Office of the Commissioners, GV
Mago, Louis M. .... Bensenville, IL
Mago, Vijay .... Richmond, VA

Magoffin, James S., Jr. ... Fairbanks, AK
Magolnick, Elena M. ... Miami, FL
Magolnick, Joel S. ... Miami, FL
Magolnick, Rena K. ... Homestead, FL
Magone, Frank D. ... Washington, PA
Magone, Michael A. ... Columbia Falls, MT
Magoon, Brian A. ... Denver, CO
Magoon, Eric T. ... Coral Gables, FL
Magoon, Robt. A. ... Morrisville, VT
Magoon, Sanjeev ... Washington, DC
Magoon, Sumeet ... Washington, DC
Magori, Segal N. ... New York, NY
Magory, Vallerie Volesko ... Randolph, NJ
Magouirk, Priscilla E. ... San Antonio, TX
Magovern, Elizabeth A. ... Reading, PA
Magovern, Frederick J. ... New York, NY
Magovern, John J. ... Stamford, CT
Magovern & Sclafani ... Brooklyn, NY
New York, NY
White Plains, NY
Magowan, Stephen P. ... Burlington, VT
Magowan, Terry ... Milwaukee, WI
Magram, Edward J. ... Burlington, NJ
Magram, Martin Yale ... Baltimore, MD
Magram, Richard O. ... Los Angeles, CA
Magram, Ronald L. ... Miami, FL
Magram, Saul H. ... New York, NY
Magrames, James G. ... Crown Point, IN
Magrane, Abigail E. ... Salt Lake City, UT
Magrath, Christopher ... New York, NY
Magrath, Patricia A. ... Phoenix, AZ
Magrath, William A. S., II ... Reno, NV
Magrath, William J. ... St. Louis, MO
Magratten, Brooks R. ... Providence, RI
Magraw, Charles E. ... Helena, MT
Magraw, Daniel B., Jr.
Environmental Protection Agency, Office of the General Counsel, GV
Magre, Ed. P. ... Cameron, TX
Magri, Deborah Brennan ... Columbus, OH
Magri, Joseph D. ... Tampa, FL
Magri, Joseph J. ... Eastlake, OH
Magri, Karen A. ... Raleigh, NC
Magri, Lucian C. ... Boston, MA
Magri, Philip ... New York, NY
Magri, Richard A. ... Boston, MA
Magrini, Allen J. ... Secaucus, NJ
Magrini, Ellen ... Skokie, IL
Magrini, Joyce Manning ... New York, NY
Magrini, Lorri Duncan
Oklahoma City, OK
Magrini, Robert L. ... Oklahoma City, OK
Magrino, Joseph L., Jr. ... Cutchogue, NY
Magriples, George ... Purchase, NY
Magro, Jamy ... St. Petersburg, FL
Magro, John J. ... Barrington, IL
Magro, John J., P.C. ... Barrington, IL
Magro, Linda Zappi ... Warwick, RI
Magro & Magro ... Morgantown, WV
Magro, Michael V. ... New York, NY
Magro, Phillip M. ... Morgantown, WV
Magro, Richard D. ... Yonkers, NY
Magro, Richard L. ... White Plains, NY
Magro, Stephen M. ... Tustin, CA
Magrogan, Gerard G. ... Columbia, MD
Magruder, Anna Maria ... McLean, VA
Magruder & Associates, P.C. ... McLean, VA
Magruder, B. Lloyd ... New Orleans, LA
Magruder, Guy A., Jr. ... Kansas City, MO
Magruder, Jerrie G. ... Orlando, FL
Magruder, Kathleen E. ... Houston, TX
Magruder, Lauch M., Jr. ... Jackson, MS
Magruder, Meghan Howett
Washington, DC
Magruder, Michelle R. ... Denver, CO
Magruder, Rebecca T. ... St. Charles, MO
Magruder, Richard S. ... Kansas City, MO
Magruder, Stacy L. ... Vero Beach, FL
Magruder, Stephen R. ... San Diego, CA
Magruder & Sumner ... Cartersville, GA
Rome, GA
Magryta, Leslie K. ... Colfax, WA
Richland, WA
Spokane, WA
Yakima, WA
Magsam & Harwig ... Osseo, MN
Magsam, Loren A. ... Osseo, MN
Maguffee, Paul R. ... Jefferson City, MO
Maguffee, Sarah R. ... Jefferson City, MO
Maguigan, Holly ... New York, NY
Maguire, Alan J. ... New York, NY
Maguire, Amelia Rea ... Miami, FL
Maguire, Ann Marie ... Taunton, MA
Maguire, Ann Marie, P.C., Law Offices of
Taunton, MA
Maguire, Annemarie ... Treasury Department, Office of the General Counsel, GV
Maguire, Arthur T. ... Harrison, NY
Maguire & Ashbaugh ... San Luis Obispo, CA
Maguire, B. Todd ... Forty Fort, PA
Maguire, Brian D. ... Minneapolis, MN
Maguire, Bruce J., Jr. ... East Lansing, MI
Maguire, Bryan V. ... Holmdel, NJ
Maguire, Cecily P. ... New York, NY
Maguire, Charles D., Jr. ... Dallas, TX
Maguire, Charles J., Jr. ... Oakland, CA
Maguire, Charles M. ... Northampton, MA
Maguire, C. J., Jr. ... North Attleboro, MA
Maguire, Daniel G. ... San Rafael, CA
Maguire, Daniel H. ... San Francisco, CA
Maguire, Daniel J. ... Department of Labor, Pension and Welfare Benefits, GV
Maguire, Daniel P. ... Sacramento, CA
Maguire, Daniel W. ... Palm Desert, CA
Maguire, David H. ... Pocatello, ID
Maguire, David T. ... Richmond, VA
Maguire, Denis ... Boston, MA
Maguire, Dennis F., III ... Boston, MA
Maguire, E. Jeanne ... Clearwater, FL
Maguire, E. Thomas ... Toledo, OH
Maguire, Eugene P. ... Somerville, NJ
Maguire, Everett W. ... Los Angeles, CA
Maguire, Francis J., Jr. ... Monroe, CT
Maguire, Francis V. ... New York, NY
Maguire, Frank ... General Accounting Office, Office of the General Counsel, GV
Maguire, Frederick ... San Diego, CA
Maguire, Frederick B., Jr. ... Burlingame, CA
Maguire & Friend, P.A. ... Coral Gables, FL
Maguire & Gahan ... San Rafael, CA
Maguire, Gary A. ... Portland, OR
Maguire, George E. B. ... New York, NY
Maguire, George J. ... Garden City, NY
Maguire, Gregory M. ... Montpelier, VT
Maguire, Ian Denis ... Myrtle Beach, SC
Maguire, J. Matthew, Jr. ... Atlanta, GA
Maguire, James B. ... Portland, ME
Maguire, James B., III
San Luis Obispo, CA
Maguire, James F. ... Indianapolis, IN
Maguire, James G. ... Pleasant Hill, CA
Maguire, James G. ... New Orleans, LA
Maguire, James P. ... Elm Grove, WI
Maguire, James Robert ... Shoreham, VT
Maguire, Jane M. ... Uniondale, NY
Maguire, Jean Z. ... Trumbull, CT
Maguire, Jeffrey S. ... Cape Girardeau, MO
Maguire, Joel C. ... Boulder, CO
Maguire, John J. ... Lake Success, NY
Maguire, John K. ... Findlay, OH
Maguire, John P. ... Falls Church, VA
Maguire, John T., II ... Westminster, MD
Maguire, Joseph P. ... Indianapolis, IN
Maguire, Joyce Nagata
Department of Defense, Defense Legal Services Agency, GV
Maguire, Kate E. ... White Plains, NY
Maguire, Kenneth R. ... Albertson, NY
Maguire, Kevin Gerard ... New York, NY
White Plains, NY
Maguire, Kevin J. ... Dallas, TX
Maguire, Kevin M. ... Santa Rosa, CA
Maguire & Kress, P.C. ... Pocatello, ID
Maguire, Leah H. ... Detroit, MI
Maguire, Linda L. ... Champaign, IL
Maguire, Linda S. ... Minneapolis, MN
Maguire, Mairi Patricia ... Baltimore, MD
Maguire, Margaret M. ... Portland, OR
Maguire, Marjorie Reiley ... Milwaukee, WI
Maguire, Mark W. ... Tulsa, OK
Maguire, Matthew J. ... Berwyn, PA
Maguire, Michael A. ...
National Aeronautics And Space Administration, GV
Maguire, Michael, & Associates
Costa Mesa, CA
Maguire, Michael B. ... St. Louis, MO
Maguire, Michael H. ... Cape Girardeau, MO
Maguire, Michael P. ... Costa Mesa, CA
Maguire, Michael P. ... Coral Gables, FL
Maguire, Michael R. ... Austin, TX
Maguire, Michele D. ... Ventnor City, NJ
Maguire, Patrick D. ... Columbus, OH
Maguire, Patrick T. ... Clearwater, FL
Maguire, Paula K. ... Chicago, IL
Maguire & Pearlman, Law Corporation
Los Angeles, CA
Maguire, Perry E., (A Professional Corporation) ... Los Angeles, CA
Maguire, Raymer F., III ... Orlando, FL
Tallahassee, FL
Maguire, Raymer F., Jr. ... Orlando, FL
Maguire, Raymond M. ... Patterson, NY
Maguire, Richard A. ... Spring Lake, NJ
Maguire, Richard L. ... Jacksonville, FL
Maguire, Richard R. ... Albany, NY
Maguire, Robert D. ... Tallmadge, OH
Maguire, Samuel F. ... Augusta, GA
Maguire & Schneider, L.L.P.
Cleveland, OH
Columbus, OH
Maguire, Sharon C. ... New York, NY
Maguire, Stephen A. ... Denver, CO
Maguire, Stephen P. ... Providence, RI
Maguire, Susan K. ... Dallas, TX
Maguire, Theresa N. ... White Plains, NY
Maguire, Thomas V. ... Minneapolis, MN
Maguire, Timothy C. ... Boston, MA
Maguire, Timothy Patrick ... Ventnor City, NJ
Maguire, Timothy R. ... Atlanta, GA
Maguire, W. Terry ... McLean, VA
Maguire, William E. ... Los Angeles, CA
Maguire, William R. ... New York, NY
Magulick, Michael L. ... Pittsburgh, PA
Magur, Louis ... Los Angeles, CA
Magura, Stephen J. ... Neptune, NJ
Magurno, Richard P. ... St. Louis, MO
Magurshak, Jeanine L. ... Washington, DC
Maguschak, Elizabeth A. ... Hazleton, PA
Magut, Jeffrey P. ... Trumbull, CT
Magy, Paul S. ... Southfield, MI
Magyar, Jennifer A. ... Milford, CT
Magyar, John F. ... Dowagiac, MI
Magyar, Laura ... Chicago, IL
Magyar, Mimi Leigh ... Bethesda, MD
Magyar, Patricia J. Hunsicker ... Chelsea, MI
Magyar, Robert M. ... Moscow, ID
Magyar & Swisher, P.C. ... Dowagiac, MI
Magyar-Africk, Julie A. ... Chicago, IL
Magyaros, Anne Schaefer ... Salem, OH
Magyera, Charles P. ... Milwaukee, WI
Mah, Donald ... Daly City, CA
Mah, Gayle C. Heirshberg
Los Angeles, CA
Mah, Horace H. ... New York, NY
Mah, John K. C. ... Van Nuys, CA
Mah, Raymond Y. ... Washington, DC
Mah, Richard ... Pasadena, CA
Mah, Richard, Jr. ... Bellevue, WA
Mah, Sharon F. ... San Rafael, CA
Mah, Teresa L. ... Wichita, KS
Mahacek, Jim P. ... Santa Ana, CA
Mahady, Frank Thomas ... Albany, NY
Mahady and Mahady ... Greensburg, PA
Mahady, Patrick H. ... Greensburg, PA
Mahady, Susana M. ... San Diego, CA
Mahady, Suzanne J. ... Greensburg, PA
Mahady-Smith, Catherine M. ... Harrisburg, PA
Mahady-Smith, Catherine M., P.C.
Harrisburg, PA
Mahaffa, Walt D. ... Los Angeles, CA
Santa Ana, CA
Mahaffee, Max G. ... Charleston, SC
Mahaffey, Blair D. ... Forsyth, GA
Mahaffey, Carol ... Columbus, OH
Mahaffey, David C. ... Washington, DC
Mahaffey, David S. ... New York, NY
Mahaffey, Douglas L. ... Irvine, CA
Mahaffey & Gore, A Professional Corporation ... Oklahoma City, OK
Mahaffey, Gregory L.
Oklahoma City, OK
Mahaffey, H. William
Colorado Springs, CO
Mahaffey, J. Michael ... Corpus Christi, TX
Mahaffey, James Watson, Jr. ... Sarasota, FL
Mahaffey, Jeffrey R. ... Lawrenceville, GA
Mahaffey, John P. ... Columbus, OH
Mahaffey, Kenneth A. ... Streator, IL
Mahaffey, Kenneth L. ... San Francisco, CA
Mahaffey Law Office ... Montezuma, IA
Mahaffey & Mahaffey, P.C. ... Carthage, TX
Mahaffey, Margaret Flynn
San Francisco, CA
Mahaffey, Michael L. ... Reno, NV
Mahaffey, Michael W. ... Montezuma, IA
Mahaffey, R. Peyton ... Fairfax, VA
Mahaffey, Robert G. ... Pasadena, CA
Mahaffey, Sherry L. ... Carthage, TX
Mahaffey, Stephen C. ... Carthage, TX
Mahaffey, Sue Ann ... Rockville, MD
Mahaffey, Sylvia M. ... Washington, DC
Mahaffey, Thomas J. ...
Overseas Private Investment Corporation, GV
Mahaffey, Townes ... Corpus Christi, TX
Mahaffey, William L., Jr.
Charlotte Amalie, St. Thomas, VI
Mahaffie, Charles D., Jr. ... Washington, DC
Mahajan, Neera ... Dallas, TX
Mahale, Raj R. ... Hamden, CT
Mahaley, Peri N. ... Washington, DC
Mahalic, Drew ... Portland, OR
Mahalingam, Ravi ... Los Angeles, CA
Mahamedi, Zurvan ... Palo Alto, CA
Mahan, Armer H., Jr. ... Louisville, KY
Mahan, Charles W. ... Dayton, OH
Mahan, Christopher L. ... Granada Hills, CA
Mahan, Collis P. ... Fortuna, CA
Mahan, Constance C. ... Spartanburg, SC
Mahan, Dee ... Washington, DC
Mahan, Edward J. ... Framingham, MA
Mahan, Elizabeth K.
North Wilkesboro, NC
Mahan, Ellen M. ... Department of Justice, Environment and Natural Resources Division, GV
Mahan, Francis B. ... Rochester, NY
Mahan, Frederick ... San Francisco, CA
Mahan, Hurley D. ... Clinton, MO
Mahan, Jeffrey B. ... Seattle, WA
Mahan, Kathleen O'Sullivan
Santa Barbara, CA
Mahan, Kevin M. ... Rancho Bernardo, CA
Mahan, Lloyd J. ... Parkston, SD
Mahan, Matthew J. ... Los Angeles, CA
Mahan, Michael G. ... Dallas, TX
Mahan, O. Leland ... Leesburg, VA
Mahan, Patricia M. ... San Jose, CA
Mahan, Randolph R. ... Columbia, SC
Mahan, Robert E. ... Waterloo, IA
Mahan, Stephen C. ... Virginia Beach, VA
Mahan, Susan J. ... Ashby, MA
Mahan, William D. ... Campbell, CA
Mahan, William F. ... West Roxbury, MA
Mahanay, Bradley K. ... Dallas, TX
Mahaney, Daniel J. ... Waterbury, CT
Mahaney, F.T. Alexandra ... La Jolla, CA
Mahaney & Geghan ... Waterbury, CT
Mahaney, Gerard M. ... Natick, MA
Mahaney, John A. ... Boston, MA
Mahaney, John D. ... Waterbury, CT
Mahaney, John H. ... Huntington, WV
Mahaney, Kimberly A. ... Painesville, OH
Mahaney, Patrick ... Montgomery, AL
Mahaney, Sheryl S. ... Huntington, WV
Mahaney-Turley, Nora ... Chicago, IL
Mahan-Lamb, Nancy ... Los Angeles, CA
Mahannah, William H. ... San Francisco, CA
Mahannah, William J. ... Library of Congress, Law Library, GV
Mahany, Michael D. ... Cincinnati, OH
Mahany, Michael P. ... Boston, MA
Mahar, Amy J. ... Albany, NY
Mahar, Dennis L. ... Calais, ME
Mahar, Edward J. ... Houston, TX
Mahar, Francis X. ... Sequim, WA
Mahar, James A. ... Stamford, CT
Mahar, James E., Jr. ... Gainesville, GA
Mahar, Jennifer A. ... Vienna, VA
Mahar, Lawrence J. ... Burnt Hills, NY
Mahar, Raymond J. ... Cleveland Heights, OH
Mahar, Robert L. ... New York, NY
Mahar, Thomas D., Jr. ... Poughkeepsie, NY
Mahar, Timothy J. ... Albany, NY
Maharaj, Dhana S. ... Memphis, TN
Maharaj, Leslie C. ... Honolulu, HI
Maharaj, Mahindra ... Hamburg, NY
Maharg, John D. ... La Canada Flintridge, CA
Maharry, Rodney K. ... Des Moines, IA
Mahasa, Zakia ... Baltimore, MD
Mahathey, Ryland F. ... Lexington, KY
Mahatme, Ujwala ... New York, NY
Mahavier, R. Anthony ... San Diego, CA
Mahboubi, Kambiz K. ... Los Angeles, CA
Mahdavi, David R., (P.C.) ... Washington, DC
Falls Church, VA
Mahdavi, Maryam ... Philadelphia, PA
Mahdavi, Yassaman ... Los Angeles, CA
Mahdavian, Stacey L. ... New York, NY
Mahendra, Rupali ... New York, NY
Mahendra, Sharmila ... Haverhill, MA
Mahendran, M. Sharmini ... New York, NY
Mahendran, Nishan C. ... Aventura, FL
Mahendru, Ashish ... Austin, TX
Maher, A. Melinda ... Minneapolis, MN
Maher, Ann M. ... Milwaukee, WI
Maher, Anne H. ... Briarcliff Manor, NY
Maher, Anne M. ... Washington, DC
Maher, Anne Marie ... Detroit, MI
Maher, Anne V. ... Federal Trade Commission, Bureau of Consumer Protection, GV
Maher and Arendt ... Pierre, SD
Maher & Associates, Law Offices of
Towson, MD
Maher, Avery P. ... Boston, MA
Maher, Barbara A. ... Laurel, MD
Maher, Brendan A. ... Rockford, IL
Maher and Brofman, LLP ... Carmel, NY
Maher & Brown ... New York, NY
Maher, Cathie Beatty ... Northville, MI
Maher, Charles P. ... San Francisco, CA
San Jose, CA
Maher, Christopher A. ... New York, NY
Maher, Christopher S. ... Columbus, OH
Maher, Clarence L. ... Chickasha, OK
Maher, Colleen Carney ... Philadelphia, PA
Maher, Constance M. ... Arlington, TX
Maher and Cotnoir ... Putnam, CT
Maher, Crystal S. ... Chicago, IL
Maher, Cynthia R. ... Irvine, CA
Newport Beach, CA
Maher, Damon R. ... New York, NY
Maher, Dana D. ... Scotch Plains, NJ
Maher, Daniel F., Jr. ... Long Beach, NY
Maher, Daniel M. ... Columbus, OH
Maher, Daniel R. ... Bakersfield, CA
Maher, David J. ... Miami, FL
Maher, David W. ... Chicago, IL
Maher, Deborah Arndt ... Bloomfield Hills, MI
Maher, Debra M. ... Crystal Lake, IL
Maher, Dennis E. ... Bloomington, MN
Maher, Dennis M. ... Hackensack, NJ
Maher, Donald E. ... New York, NY
Maher, Douglas B. ... Akron, OH
Maher, Edward C. ... Worcester, MA
Maher, Edward J. ... Cleveland, OH
Maher, Edward J., Co., L.P.A.
Cleveland, OH
Maher, Edward James ... Baltimore, MD
Maher, Edward M. ... Rockford, IL
Maher, Eileen M. ... Natchez, MS
Maher, Ellen S. ... Houlton, ME
Maher, Ernest A. ... Wayland, MA
Maher, Francesca Marciniak
Elk Grove Village, IL
Maher, Frank J., Jr. ... Flossmoor, IL
Maher, Gary L. ... Bernardsville, NJ
Maher, George A. ... Tinley Park, IL
Maher, Gerard A. ... Brooklyn, NY
Maher, Gibson and Guiley, A Prof. Assn. of Lawyers ... Orlando, FL
Maher, Gregory F. ... Kansas City, MO
Maher, Gregory G. ... New York, NY
Maher, Helen Finnigan ... New York, NY
Maher, Helen M. ... White Plains, NY
Maher, Henry J. ... Mount Clemens, MI
Maher, J. Michael ... Wheaton, IL
Maher, James E. ... Alexandria, VA
Maher, James F. ... Laurel, MD
Maher, James F. ... Lewisberry, PA
Maher, James, III ... New Orleans, LA
Maher, James J. ... Houston, TX
Maher, James L. ... Portland, OR
Maher, James M. ... Hagåtña, GU
Maher, James P. ... Hartford, CT
Maher, James P. ... Sterling Heights, MI
Maher, James V. ... Lyndhurst, NJ
Maher, Jerard F. ... Morristown, NJ
Maher, Jerelyn D. ... Pekin, IL
Maher, Jerome A. ... Chicago, IL
Maher, Jerome T. ... New City, NY
Maher, John A. ... Summit, NJ
New York, NY
Maher, John D. ... Tallahassee, FL
Maher, John F. ... Chicago, IL
Maher, John F. ... Arlington, MA
Maher, John G., Jr. ... Tustin, CA
Maher, John J. ... Putnam, CT
Maher, John M. ... Cedar Rapids, IA
Maher, John R. ... Bristol, NH
Maher, John T. ... Hartford, CT
Maher, Joseph C., Jr. ... Boston, MA
Maher, Joseph D., Jr. ... Lincoln Park, NJ
Maher, Joseph P. ... Hellertown, PA
Maher, Joy E. ... Chicago, IL
Maher, Judith Miller ... Pittsburgh, PA
Maher, Karen Wojtowicz ... Chicago, IL
Maher, Katheleen Bartlett ... Newton, MA
Maher, Kathleen A. ... New Haven, CT
Maher, Kathleen Crean ... Mineola, NY
Maher, Kathleen L. ... Atlanta, GA

Maher, Kenneth W. ..... Indianapolis, IN
Maher, Kevin J. ..... Fairfield, CT
Maher, Kristi A. ..... Chicago, IL
Maher Law Firm, The ..... Arlington, TX
Fort Worth, TX
Maher, Lawrence M. ..... Kansas City, MO
Maher, Lawrence P. ..... Woodbridge, NJ
Maher, Leah ..... Andover, MA
Maher, Leslie Swift ..... Bedford Hills, NY
Maher, Linda ..... New York, NY
Maher, Lisa Lemaire ..... New Orleans, LA
Maher & Maher ..... Hackensack, NJ
Maher & Maher, Chartered ..... Laurel, MD
Maher, Maher & Goodlet, An Assn. of Indep. Attys. at Law ..... Akron, OH
Maher & Maher, LLP ..... Irvine, CA
Maher, Marianne ..... San Francisco, CA
Maher, Martin T. ..... Detroit, MI
Maher, Mary Brigid ..... Deerfield, IL
Maher, Mary F. ..... Austin, TX
Maher, Maureen T.
Department of Agriculture, Office of the General Counsel, GV
Maher, Michael ..... Orlando, FL
Maher, Michael H. ..... Gladstone, MO
Maher, Michael J. ..... San Diego, CA
Maher, Michael J. ..... Chicago, IL
Maher, Michael K. ..... Irvine, CA
Newport Beach, CA
Maher, Michael P. ..... West Palm Beach, FL
Maher, Michael T. ..... Dallas, TX
Maher & Murtha ..... Bridgeport, CT
Maher & Nidey Law Firm ..... Cedar Rapids, IA
Maher, O. Kent ..... Winnemucca, NV
Maher, Owen P. ..... Boston, MA
Maher, Pamela G. ..... Los Angeles, CA
Maher, Patricia M. ..... Towson, MD
Maher, Patricia M. ..... Towson, MD
Maher, Patrick E. ..... Towson, MD
Maher, Patrick J. ..... Fort Worth, TX
Maher, Paul R ..... Mechanicville, NY
Maher & Petrilli ..... Long Beach, NY
Maher, Ralph B. ..... Akron, OH
Maher, Raymond S., Jr. ..... New Orleans, LA
Maher, Richard B. ..... Omaha, NE
Maher, Richard L. ..... Carmel, NY
Maher, Richard M. ..... Jensen Beach, FL
Maher, Robert D. ..... Minneapolis, MN
Maher, Robert E., Jr. ..... Department of Justice, Environment and Natural Resources Division, GV
Maher, Robert F., (P.C.) ..... Houston, TX
Maher, Robert T. ..... Bonita Springs, FL
Cape Coral, FL
Maher, Robert T. ..... Fort Myers, FL
Maher, Robert V. ..... Hudson, OH
Maher, Robert W. ..... Jenkintown, PA
Maher, Robin A. ..... Waltham, MA
Maher, Robin M. ..... Minneapolis, MN
Maher, Ronald L. ..... Towson, MD
Maher, Shaun A.
Federal Communications Commission, Mass Media Bureau, GV
Maher, Stephen J. ..... Albany, NY
Maher, Stephen M. ..... Fort Myers, FL
Maher, Stephen T. ..... Miami, FL
Maher, Stephen T., P.A. ..... Miami, FL
Maher, Steven R. ..... Orlando, FL
Maher, Susan S. ..... Baltimore, MD
Maher, T. Michael ..... Roanoke, VA
Maher, Tamara B. ..... Portland, OR
Maher, Teresa R. ..... Chicago, IL
Joliet, IL
Maher, Terrence P. ..... Omaha, NE
Maher, Thomas A. ..... Detroit, MI
Maher, Thomas D. ..... Irving, TX
Maher, Thomas F. ..... Avon, CT
Maher, Thomas K. ..... Chapel Hill, NC
Maher, Thomas M. ..... Pierre, SD
Maher, Thomas R. ..... Billerica, MA
Maher & Thompson, P.C. ..... Hagåtña, GU
Maher, Timothy J. ..... South Bend, IN
Maher, Vincent F. ..... New York, NY
Maher, Walter B. ..... Washington, DC
Maher, Wendy Juracka ..... Schenectady, NY
Maher, William A. ..... New York, NY
Maher, William F. ..... Alexandria, VA
Maher, William F., Jr. ..... Washington, DC
Maher, William J. ..... Terre Haute, IN
Maher, William K. ..... Tinley Park, IL
Maher, William L. ..... Boston, MA
Maher, William L. ..... Mineola, NY
Maher, William L. ..... Peekskill, NY
Maher and Williams ..... Bridgeport, CT
Fairfield, CT
Greenwich, CT
Stamford, CT
Maher, Yvonne G. ..... Atlantic City, NJ
Maheras, Theodore G. ..... Chicago, IL
Mahesh, Dave ..... New York, NY
Maheshwari, Bitthal Das ..... Corona, CA
Maheu, Karen ..... Detroit, MI
Mahevich, Richard A., II
Harrisonburg, VA
Mahfood, George G. ..... Miami, FL
Mahfood, James E. ..... Santa Ana, CA
Mahfood, Richard A. ..... Bal Harbour, FL
Mahfouz, Thomas L. ..... Morgan City, LA
Mahida, Imtiyaz A. ..... New York, NY
Mahin, Amy R. ..... Silver Spring, MD
Mahin, Betsy Cox ..... Jacksonville, FL
Mahin, Charles B. ..... Chicago, IL
Mahin, Gregory A. .....
Administrative Office Of The United States Courts, GV
Mahin, J. Michael ..... Walnut Creek, CA
Mahin, J. Michael, & Associates, A Prof. Corp.
Walnut Creek, CA
Mahin, John E. ..... Cincinnati, OH
Mahinka, Stephen Paul ..... Washington, DC
Mahl, Cort B. ..... Stockton, CA
Mahl, David A. ..... Bettendorf, IA
Mahl, Jeffrey S. ..... Del Rio, TX
Mahl Rehon Walworth & Roberts, A Professional Corporation ..... Palo Alto, CA
San Jose, CA
Mahl, Susan J. ..... San Jose, CA
Mahlab, Vivian ..... Austin, TX
Mahlan, William C., Jr. ..... Locust Valley, NY
Mahlberg, Mark T. ..... Saginaw, MI
Mahle, David M. ..... New York, NY
Mahle, Jeffrey A. ..... Pottstown, PA
Mahle, Jeffrey A., P.C. ..... Pottstown, PA
Mahle, Stephen, (P.A.) ..... Boca Raton, FL
Mahlen, Jeffrey D. ..... Anchorage, AK
Mahler, Aloysius F. ..... Pittsburgh, PA
Mahler, Barry A. ..... New York, NY
Mahler, Benjamin H. ..... New York, NY
Mahler, Christian C ..... Laurel, MD
Mahler, Edward A. ..... San Jose, CA
Mahler, Edward J. ..... Chappaqua, NY
Mahler, Elliott J. ..... Boston, MA
Mahler, Eric A. ..... Elyria, OH
Mahler, Eric N. ..... Kingston, PA
Mahler, Frederick ..... Norwich, CT
Mahler, Gary L. ..... Beverly Hills, CA
Mahler, Harold C. ..... Greensboro, NC
Mahler, Heinz J. ..... Salt Lake City, UT
Mahler, Linda L. ..... Landover, MD
Mahler, Lyle C. ..... Uniondale, NY
Mahler, Mary B. ..... St. Cloud, MN
Mahler, Melissa A. ..... Rochester, NY
Mahler, Nancy Jane ..... Texarkana, TX
Mahler, Paul F. ..... Walnut Creek, CA
Mahler, Paul R. ..... Kingston, PA
Mahler, Paul W. ..... Levittown, NY
New York, NY
Mahler, Peter A. ..... New York, NY
Mahler, Richard A. ..... Sharon, MA
Mahler, Richard C. ..... Department of Justice, Office of Intelligence Policy and Review, GV
Mahler, Robert Mark ..... Canton, GA
Mahler, Robert S. ..... Seattle, WA
Mahler, Shaffer & Pugliese ..... Kingston, PA
Wilkes-Barre, PA
Mahler, Thomas R. ..... Minneapolis, MN
Mahler, Tim ..... Belton, TX
Mahler, William D. ..... Rochester, MN
Mahley, F. William ..... Houston, TX
Mahley, Gordon H., Jr. ..... Raleigh, NC
Mahling, Wendy B. ..... Minneapolis, MN
Mahlmeister, Karen Korkuc ..... Buffalo, NY
Mahloch, Nancy J. ..... Beatrice, NE
Mahlowitz, Edward M. ..... Belmont, MA
Mahlowitz, Naaman ..... Boston, MA
Mahlowitz, Robert M. ..... Los Angeles, CA
Mahlum, Conrad E. ..... Barstow, CA
Mahlum, Jon Kristian ..... Barstow, CA
Mahlum, Thomas C. ..... Minneapolis, MN
Mahlum, William M. ..... St. Paul, MN
Mahmood, Gulam Rafiqueuddin
Birmingham, AL
Huntsville, AL
Mahmoud, Basil ..... Houston, TX
Mahmud, Diana ..... Los Angeles, CA
Mahmud, J. Omar ..... Palo Alto, CA
Mahmud, J.Omar ..... Palo Alto, CA
Mahmud, Urooj ..... Chicago, IL
Mahn, Daniel D. ..... Wilmington, NC
Mahn, Michael J. ..... Chattanooga, TN
Mahn, Sharon ..... New York, NY
Mahn, Terry G. ..... Washington, DC
Mahn, William K.
United States Postal Service, Judicial Officer, GV
Mahnesmith, Kent E. ..... Rensselaer, IN
Mahnke, Kymric Y. ..... Greenville, SC
Mahnke, Norbert C. ..... Houston, TX
Mahnke, Robert P. ..... San Francisco, CA
Mahnken, Susan S. ..... Boston, MA
Mahnke Pavlet, Jennifer ..... Monterey, CA
Maho, Tyrone J. ..... Santa Barbara, CA
Mahon, Arthur J. ..... New York, NY
Mahon & Berger ..... Garden City, NY
Mahon, Brian P. ..... Medina, OH
Mahon, Brian T. ..... Meriden, CT
Mahon, Christy Elizabeth ..... Columbia, SC
Mahon, Cindy M. ..... Phoenix, AZ
Mahon, Dale W. ..... Elk Grove, CA
Mahon, Dixon ..... Ozona, TX
Mahon, E. Brad ..... Fort Worth, TX
Mahon, Edward M. ..... Philadelphia, PA
Mahon, Edward M., Jr. ..... Dearborn, MI
Mahon, Eldon B. ..... Fort Worth, TX
Mahon & Farley, P.A.
Fernandina Beach, FL
Jacksonville, FL
Orange Park, FL
Mahon, Francis J. ..... Skokie, IL
Mahon, Francis J. ..... Trenton, NJ
Mahon, Harry B. ..... Jacksonville, FL
Mahon, James F. ..... Foster City, CA
Mahon, James F., Jr. ..... New York, NY
Mahon, James J., Jr. ..... New York, NY
Mahon, James V. ..... New York, NY
Mahon, Jeffrey P. ..... Dallas, TX
Mahon, Jody P. ..... King Of Prussia, PA
Mahon, John F. ..... Rochester, NY
Mahon, John J. ..... Stamford, CT
Mahon, John J. ..... Department of the Army, Office, Chief of Engineers/Headquarters, U.S. Army Corps of Engineers, GV
Mahon, John J. ..... Department of Justice, Civil Division, GV
Mahon, John M., Jr. ..... Columbia, SC
Mahon, John P. ..... Garden City South, NY
Mahon, Joseph C. ..... Princeton, NJ
Mahon, Kenneth P.
Garden City South, NY
Mahon, Lacy, Jr. ..... Jacksonville, FL
Mahon, Lawrence T.
Garden City South, NY
Mahon, Leroy H. ..... Little Rock, AR
Mahon, Mahon & Healey, P.A.
Jacksonville, FL
Orange Park, FL
Ponte Vedra Beach, FL
Mahon, Mahon & Mahon, P.C.
Garden City South, NY
Mahon, Malachy T., Sr. ..... Hempstead, NY
Mahon, Mark H. ..... Jacksonville, FL
Mahon, Mary E. ..... Garden City South, NY
Mahon, Mary Emilia Jensen, (P.A.)
Tampa, FL
Mahon, Mary J. ..... New York, NY
Mahon, Mary M. ..... Fairfax, VA
Mahon, Maura E. ..... New York, NY
Mahon, Meghan Mastellon ..... Philadelphia, PA
Mahon, Michael J. ..... New York, NY
Mahon, Patrick J. ..... Hopkinton, MA
Mahon Patusky Rothblatt & Fisher
Washington, DC
Mahon, Paul A. ..... Washington, DC
Mahon, Raymond T. ..... Worcester, MA
Mahon, Richard J., Jr. ..... Lorain, OH
Mahon, Richard M., II ..... Newburgh, NY
Mahon, Robert L. ..... Seattle, WA
Mahon, Roger F. ..... Flemington, NJ
Mahon, Sean Anthony ..... San Francisco, CA
Mahon, Stephanie Mary ..... Dallas, TX
Mahon, Stephen C. ..... Cincinnati, OH
Mahon, Stephen G. ..... Birmingham, AL
Mahon, Steven Gerald ..... St. Paul, MN
Mahon, Susan P. ..... Newark, NJ
Mahon, Timothy K. ..... Fort Lauderdale, FL
Mahon, Timothy K., P.A.
Fort Lauderdale, FL
Mahon, Timothy P. ..... Huntingdon Valley, PA
Mahon, Victorine Robben
Jefferson City, MO
Mahon, William P. ..... West Chester, PA
Mahone, Glenn R. ..... Pittsburgh, PA
Mahone, Susan Leigh ..... St. Louis, MO
Mahone, William L. ..... Greenwich, CT
Mahoney, A. Franklin ..... Troy, NY
Mahoney, Ann C. ..... Center, ND
Mahoney, Ann S. ..... San Francisco, CA
Mahoney, Anne B. ..... Gary, IN
Mahoney, Anne R. ..... Newark, NJ
New York, NY
Mahoney, Anthony M. ..... Westfield, NJ
Mahoney, Arthur J. ..... Stuart, FL
Mahoney & Associates ..... Houston, TX
Mahoney & Berg ..... Buffalo, NY
Mahoney, Brandon R. ..... Wichita, KS
Mahoney, Brendan N. ..... Phoenix, AZ
Mahoney, Brian F. ..... Dedham, MA
Mahoney, Brian K. ..... Petersburg, IN
Mahoney, Brian M. ..... San Diego, CA
Mahoney, Catherine ..... Boston, MA
Mahoney, Cathleen M.
Department of Justice, Civil Rights Division, GV
Mahoney, Christopher J.
Framingham, MA
Mahoney, Christopher W.
Washington, DC
Mahoney, Colleen P. ..... Washington, DC
Mahoney Coppenrath & Jaffe LLP
Los Angeles, CA
Mahoney, Cornelius A. ..... New York, NY
Mahoney, Daniel B. ..... Wilmington, DE
Mahoney, Daniel J. ..... Boston, MA
Mahoney, Daniel J. ..... Wellesley Hills, MA
Mahoney, Daniel J., Jr.
West Palm Beach, FL
Mahoney, Daniel M. ..... Seattle, WA
Mahoney, David B. ..... Rochester, NY
Mahoney, David J. ..... Buffalo, NY
Mahoney, David J., Jr. ..... Secaucus, NJ
Mahoney, Deborah L. ..... Wichita, KS
Mahoney, Deborah Louise ..... Morris, IL
Mahoney, Dennis C. ..... Dedham, MA
Mahoney, Dennis C. ..... Cincinnati, OH
Mahoney, Dennis C. ..... Racine, WI
Mahoney, Dennis J. ..... San Bernardino, CA
Mahoney, Dennis J., III ..... Goshen, NY
Mahoney, Dennis M. ..... Lakewood, CO
Mahoney, Dennis M. ..... Westfield, NJ
Mahoney, Donal M. ..... Mineola, NY
Mahoney, Donald A. ..... Rahway, NJ
Mahoney, Donald C. ..... Hartford, CT
Mahoney, Donald T. ..... Kenmore, NY
Mahoney, Dougherty and Mahoney, P.A. Professional Association
Minneapolis, MN
Mahoney, Douglas P. ..... Bridgeport, CT
Mahoney, Edward F. ..... Boston, MA
Mahoney, Edward J. ..... Akron, OH
Mahoney, Edward M. ..... Boston, MA
Mahoney, Edward S. ..... Kokomo, IN
Mahoney, Estelle E. ..... Houma, LA
Mahoney, Eugene L. ..... Chicago, IL
Mahoney, Eugene L., & Associates, P.C.
Chicago, IL
Mahoney, F. Steven ..... Anchorage, AK
Mahoney, Francis X. ..... Freeport, IL
Mahoney, Frank W. ..... San Francisco, CA
Mahoney, G. Michael ..... Leesburg, FL
Mahoney, George F. ..... Boston, MA
Mahoney, George F., III ..... Joliet, IL
Mahoney, George L. ..... New York, NY
Mahoney, George L. ..... Richmond, VA
Mahoney, George R., Jr. ..... Charlotte, NC
Mahoney, Greg ..... Denver, CO
Mahoney, Hagberg & Rice, PLLP
Minneapolis, MN
St. Paul, MN
Mahoney, Harry G. ..... Philadelphia, PA
Mahoney, Harry T. ..... Wheaton, IL
Mahoney & Hauser, Ltd. ..... Freeport, IL
Mahoney, Hawkes & Goldings, LLP
Boston, MA
Mahoney, Helen ..... Elmhurst, NY
Mahoney, Hugh J. ..... Newark, NJ
Mahoney, Hussey & McLoone
Mineola, NY
Mahoney, J. Kevin ..... Rochester, NY
Mahoney, James E. ..... Los Angeles, CA
Mahoney, James E. ..... Chicago, IL
Mahoney, James E. ..... Hammond, IN
Mahoney, James E. ..... Boston, MA
Mahoney, James F. ..... Phoenix, AZ
Mahoney, James J. ..... Denville, NJ
Mahoney, James M. ..... Minneapolis, MN
Mahoney, James P. ..... Chicago, IL
Mahoney, James P. ..... Lynn, MA
Mahoney, James W. ..... Jacksonville, FL
Mahoney, Jane ..... Philadelphia, PA
Mahoney, Jeff ..... Flemington, NJ
Mahoney, Jennifer Reid ..... Boise, ID
Mahoney, Jerry C. D., (P.A.)
Minneapolis, MN
Mahoney, Joan ..... Springfield, MA
Mahoney, Joan A. ..... Dayton, OH
Mahoney, Joan E. ..... Norfolk, VA
Mahoney, Joanne M. ..... Rochester, NY
Mahoney, John C. ..... Minneapolis, MN
Mahoney, John D. ..... Alameda, CA
Mahoney, John E. ..... San Rafael, CA
Mahoney, John F. ..... Chicago, IL
Mahoney, John H. ..... Chicago, IL
Mahoney, John J. ..... Boston, MA
Mahoney, John J. ..... Center, ND
Mahoney, John J. ..... Berwyn, PA
Mahoney, John L. ..... New Brunswick, NJ
Mahoney, John M. ..... San Francisco, CA
Mahoney, John P. ..... Ashtabula, OH
Mahoney, John Patrick ..... Washington, DC
Mahoney, John R. ..... Providence, RI
Mahoney, John S. ..... Bethlehem, PA
Mahoney, John T. ..... Fredericksburg, VA
Mahoney, John W. ..... Hartford, CT
Mahoney, John W. C. ..... Brewster, NY
Mahoney, Joseph A. ..... Chicago, IL
Mahoney, Joseph E. ..... Jefferson, OH
Mahoney, Joseph F. ..... New York, NY
Mahoney, Joseph J. ..... Elkton, MD
Mahoney, Joseph V. ..... North Andover, MA
Mahoney, Karen F. ..... Boston, MA
Mahoney, Karen Kremer ..... Chicago, IL
Mahoney, Katherine Mary
San Francisco, CA
Mahoney, Kathlea Marie ..... Sutton, MA
Mahoney, Kathleen ..... Miami, FL
Mahoney, Kathleen Anne ..... New York, NY
Mahoney, Kathleen Derks ..... Kansas City, MO
Mahoney, Kathleen Kibler ..... Rockville, MD
Mahoney, Kathleen M. ..... St. Paul, MN
Mahoney, Kathryn Long ..... Columbia, SC
Mahoney and Keane ..... Red Bank, NJ
New York, NY
Mahoney, Kevin A. ..... Waldorf, MD
Mahoney, Kevin G. ..... Boston, MA
Mahoney, Kevin J. ..... Bel Air, MD
Mahoney, Kevin Sean ..... Lakewood, CO
Mahoney, Kevin W. ..... Evesham, NJ
Mahoney Law Office ..... Petersburg, IN
Mahoney, Lawrence C. ..... St. Paul, MN
Mahoney, Lawrence J. ..... Cotuit, MA
Mahoney, Leo E. ..... Pittsfield, MA
Mahoney, Linda Leigh ..... New York, NY
Mahoney & Mahoney ..... Kansas City, KS
Mahoney & Mahoney ..... Westfield, NJ
Mahoney & Mahoney ..... Center, ND
Mahoney & Mahoney, LLC ..... Waldorf, MD
Mahoney, Marc M. ..... New York, NY
Mahoney, Marcia Andersen ..... Chicago, IL
Mahoney, Margaret A. ..... Mobile, AL
Mahoney, Margaret Jane
Department of Justice, Civil Division, GV
Mahoney, Margaret Julie ..... Worcester, MA
Mahoney, Margaret P. ..... Bethlehem, PA
Mahoney, Margaret R. ..... Phoenix, AZ
Mahoney, Marilyn T. ..... Manchester, NH
Mahoney, Mark A. ..... Phoenix, AZ
Mahoney, Mark B. ..... Des Moines, IA
Mahoney, Mark J. ..... Buffalo, NY
Mahoney, Mark J. ..... Appleton, WI
Mahoney, Mark Joseph ..... Bay Village, OH
Mahoney, Marta Rosas ..... Lubbock, TX
Mahoney, Martha B. ..... Shelburne, VT
Mahoney, Martin F., II ..... Boston, MA
Mahoney, Mary A. ..... Madison Heights, MI
Mahoney, Mary Ann ..... New York, NY
Mahoney, Mary E. ..... White Plains, NY
Mahoney, Mary O'Toole ..... Waltham, MA
Mahoney, Mary Williams ..... Wellesley, MA
Mahoney, Matthew ..... Boston, MA
Mahoney, Maureen A. ..... Galesburg, IL
Mahoney, Maureen E. ..... Washington, DC
Mahoney, Maxwell J. ..... Boston, MA
Mahoney, Maylin Wong ..... St. Louis, MO
Mahoney, Megan ..... Las Vegas, NV
Mahoney, Michael C. ..... Minneapolis, MN
Mahoney, Michael F. ..... Boone, IA
Madrid, IA
Mahoney, Michael G. ..... Chicago, IL
Mahoney, Michael G. ..... Garden City, NY
Mahoney, Michael J. ..... Cleveland, OH
Mahoney, Michael J. ..... Houston, TX

Maino, Kathi E. ... Salem, MA
Maino, Roger L. ... Campbell, CA
Maino, Runston G. ... Vista, CA
Mainor & Harris ... Las Vegas, NV
Reno, NV
Mainor, W. Randall, (A Professional Corporation) ... Las Vegas, NV
Mainous & Grant ... Lexington, KY
Mainous, Joseph E., Jr. ... Lexington, KY
Mainous, Mart V. ... Irvine, KY
Mainprize & Mainprize ... Grand Blanc, MI
Mainprize, P. Anthony ... Grand Blanc, MI
Mainprize, Robert, Jr. ... Grand Blanc, MI
Mains, Chas. H. ... Indianapolis, IN
Mains, David D. ... Long Beach, CA
Mains, David S. ... Odessa, TX
Mains, Deborah L. ... Cherry Hill, NJ
Mains, Donald L., Jr. ... Columbus, OH
Mains, Jeffrey ... Des Moines, IA
Mains, Jon F. ... McLean, VA
Mains, Julie Brooks ... Oakland, CA
Mains & Mains, L.C. ... McLean, VA
Mains, Richard H. ... Dallas, TX
Mains, Steve A. ... Denver, CO
Mains, Steven B. ... San Francisco, CA
Mains, Thomas P., Jr. ... McLean, VA
Mains, William B. ... Morehead, KY
Mains, William Michael ... Albany, NY
Mainstain, Morris ... Los Angeles, CA
Mainz, Edward C., Jr. ... San Antonio, TX
Mainzer, David Eric ... Los Angeles, CA
Mainzer, Gertrud ... New York, NY
Mainzer, James M. ... Chicago, IL
Mainzer, Susan D. ... Minneapolis, MN
Maio, Anthony M. ... Weymouth, MA
Maio, Carl Anthony ... Philadelphia, PA
Maio, Dennis Peter ... San Francisco, CA
Maio, Duncan A. ... Randolph, MA
Maio, F. Anthony ... Milwaukee, WI
Maio, Juliana ... Beverly Hills, CA
Maio, Michael L. ... Cincinnati, OH
Maio, Stephen P. ... Danvers, MA
Maio, Steven P. ... Corning, NY
Maio, Zaira M. ... Mount Clemens, MI
Maiocchi, Anthony J. ... Brooklyn, NY
Maiocco, John P., Jr. ... Bridgeport, CT
Maioli, Jay H. ... New York, NY
Maiolo, Francis M. ... Richmond Hill, NY
Maiolo, Joseph C. ... Richmond Hill, NY
Maiolo & Maiolo ... Richmond Hill, NY
Maiolo, Sally R. ... Kew Gardens, NY
Maiolo, Tina M. ... Washington, DC
Maiona, Justin G. ... Boston, MA
Maiona, Matthew Jude ... Boston, MA
Maionchi, Paula M ... Richmond, KY
Maione, Louis J. ... New York, NY
Maione, Michael R. ... Towson, MD
Maione, William J. ... Cedar Grove, NJ
Maiorana & Acosta ... Royal Oak, MI
Maiorana, Christopher P.
St. Clair Shores, MI
Maiorana, Christopher P., P.C.
St. Clair Shores, MI
Maiorana, David M. ... Cleveland, OH
Maiorana, Frank H. ... Redondo Beach, CA
Maiorana, Kristina Schwab ... Houma, LA
Maiorano, Franca D. ... Roseland, NJ
Maiorano, Joseph G. ... San Diego, CA
Maiorano, Wayne K. ... Raleigh, NC
Maiorca, Philip R. ... Fort Myers, FL
Maioriello, John J. ... Norristown, PA
Maioriello, Joseph T. ... Bowie, MD
Maioriello, Lawrence E. ... Appling, GA
Augusta, GA
Maiorino, Pasquale F. ... Auburn, ME
Maiorino, Patricia Warren ... Mt. Vernon, OH
Maiorino, Thomas J. ... Cherry Hill, NJ
Philadelphia, PA
Mair, Alex M. ... Houston, TX
Mair, Andrew B. ... Binghamton, NY
Mair, Bruce ... Grosse Pointe Farms, MI
Mair, Camiel & Kovach, P.S. ... Seattle, WA
Mair, David A. ... Hagåtña, GU
Mair, David N. ... New York, NY
Mair, George P. ... Boston, MA
Mair, Glen M. ... Worcester, MA
Mair, Gordon M. ... East Greenville, PA
Mair, Jennifer H. ... Portland, OR
Mair, June S. ... Hagåtña, GU
Mair, Mair, Spade & Thompson, A Professional Corporation ... Hagåtña, GU
Saipan, TT
Mair, Peter K. ... Seattle, WA
Mair, Steven E. ... Rancho Cordova, CA
Mair, Todd E. ... Washington, DC
Maira, Joseph B. ... Brooklyn, NY
Maira, Octavio V. ... Salinas, CA
Maira, Thomas G. ... New York, NY
Mairanz, Theodore T. ... New York, NY
Maire, David G. ... Orlando, FL
Maire, Eric R. ... Redding, CA
Maire, Jonathan E. ... Lansing, MI
Maire, Mansell & Beasley, A Law Corporation ... Redding, CA
Maire, Richard J., Jr. ... Los Angeles, CA
Maire, Susan S. ... Halifax, MA
Maire, Wayne H. ... Redding, CA
Mairella, Steven ... Tuxedo, NY
Mairo, John S. ... Morristown, NJ
Mairone, Biel, Zlotnick & Feinberg, P.A.
Atlantic City, NJ
Mairone, Gavriel ... Chicago, IL
Mairone, Louis J., Jr. ... Philadelphia, PA
Mairone, Richard S. ... Atlantic City, NJ
Maironis, Mark D. ... Belleville, MI
Mairose, John H. ... Rapid City, SD
Mairs, Donald B. ... Jacksonville, FL
Mairs, John A. ... Charleston, WV
Mairs, Patricia Ann ... Scarsdale, NY
Mairs, Robert W. ... Minneapolis, MN
Mairs, Terryl L. ... Stanton, CA
Mairzadeh, Gabriel S. ... New York, NY
Mais, Charles, Jr. ... Lubbock, TX
Mais, Joseph E. ... Phoenix, AZ
Mais, Michael J. ... Long Beach, CA
Maisa, Susan R. ... Milwaukee, WI
Maisano, Nancy ... Seattle, WA
Maisashvili, Robin Lightner ... Houston, TX
Maisch, Donald D. ... Clinton, OK
Maisch, Gwendoline A. ... Lansing, MI
Maisch, John Allen ... Oklahoma City, OK
Maisch, Victoria U. ... Lima, OH
Maise, Willie A. ... Birmingham, AL
Maisel, Allan S. ... Miami, FL
Maisel, Drew A. ... New York, NY
Maisel, Gary S. ... Fort Lauderdale, FL
Maisel, Gregg ... Washington, DC
Maisel, John S. ... Houston, TX
Maisel, Len ... Bethesda, MD
Maisel, Margaret M. ... San Antonio, TX
Maisel, Mark ... San Diego, CA
Maisel, Minda E. ... Newark, NJ
Maisel, Seymour I. ... St. Louis Park, MN
Maisel, Tami Zay ... Saginaw, MI
Maisel, Travis G. ... Chicago, IL
Maisels, Amanda Lee ... Washington, DC
Maish, Kristine ... Tucson, AZ
Maish & Mysliwy ... Hammond, IN
Maish, Stephen M. ... Hammond, IN
Maislen, Andrea H. ... Boston, MA
Maislin, Blake R. ... Cincinnati, OH
Maislin, Sam ... Amherst, NY
Maisner, Linda J. ... Monterey Park, CA
Maisnik, M. Guy ... Los Angeles, CA
Maison, Donald J., Jr. ... Dallas, TX
Maison, Donald J., Jr., P.C. ... Dallas, TX
Maison, Robert T. ... Carey, OH
Maisonneuve, Mark D. ... Los Angeles, CA
Maiss, Lance P. ... Reno, NV
Maissel, Raina E. ... Poughkeepsie, NY
Maistelman, Michael S. ... Milwaukee, WI
Maister, Caryn L. ... Fort Lauderdale, FL
Maister, Marc S. ... Newport Beach, CA
Maisto, Barbara ... Iselin, NJ
New York, NY
Maisto, Lester J., Jr. ... Trenton, NJ
Maistrellis, Judy K. ... Crownsville, MD
Maistrellis, Maria ... Tampa, FL
Maistros, David M. ... Cleveland, OH
Maistros, Jack D. ... Cleveland, OH
Maistrow, Brad S. ... New York, NY
Mait, Wang & Simmons ... Woodbridge, NJ
New York, NY
Mait, William R. ... New York, NY
Maiter, Iris M. ... Chicago, IL
Maith, Sheila F. ... Columbia, MD
Maitin, Emily A. ... Waltham, MA
Maitin, Lawrence S. ... Raleigh, NC
Maitland, Elizabeth J. ... Norfolk, MA
Maitland, Gary ... New York, NY
Maitland, Guy E. C. ... New York, NY
Reston, VA
Maitland, Johan W. E. ... Burlington, VT
Maitland, Nancy M. ... Baltimore, MD
Maitland, Robert N., II ... Stuart, FL
Maitlin, Allan ... West Orange, NJ
Maitlin, David Eric ... West Orange, NJ
Maitner, John J. ... Kenilworth, NJ
Maitra, Jai ... New York, NY
Maitra, Raoul K. ... Farmington Hills, MI
Maitre, Gary R. ... Austin, TX
Maitre, Sherry A. ... Lake Charles, LA
Maiucci, John E. ... Stuart, FL
Maiullo, Daniel A., Jr. ... Neptune, NJ
Maiullo, Joseph A. ... Grosse Pointe, MI
Maiuri, Anna M. ... Troy, MI
Maivald, David P. ... Pittsburgh, PA
Maixner, Aloyse H. ... Lincoln, NE
Maixner, George Ann Harpole
Corpus Christi, TX
Maixner, Rick ... Bismarck, ND
Maize, Robert K., Jr. ... Santa Rosa, CA
Maizel, Mark N. ... Irvine, CA
Maizel, Samuel R. ... Los Angeles, CA
Maizels, Elliott ... Library of Congress, Congressional Research Service, GV
Maizes, Howard T. ... Bronx, NY
Maizes & Maizes ... Bronx, NY
Maizes, Michael H. ... Teaneck, NJ
Bronx, NY
Maizes, Rachel L. ... Boulder, CO
Maizes, Steven R. ... Bronx, NY
Maizlish, Greg ... San Diego, CA
Maizlish, Leonard M. ... Los Angeles, CA
Maizys, Donald J. ... Fair Lawn, NJ
Maj, JoAnn M. ... Akron, OH
Majarian, William R. ... Wilmington, DE
Majcher, Dineen J. ... Austin, TX
Majcher, Thomas H. ... Los Angeles, CA
Majczan, Frank L., Jr. ... Bethlehem, PA
Majczan & Majczan ... Bethlehem, PA
Majczan, Raymond C. ... Bethlehem, PA
Majdloch, Ellen M. ... Boston, MA
Majeed, Alli B. ... Titusville, FL
Majer, Charles ... Annandale, VA
Majer, Julie Dampier ... Savannah, GA
Majerek, Jeffrey A. ... Goshen, IN
Majernik, James J. ... Bloomfield Hills, MI
Majernik, William R., Jr. ... Sacramento, CA
Majerowicz, Thomas E.
Mount Clemens, MI
Majers, Elizabeth L. ... Chicago, IL
Majerus, Laura A. ... Palo Alto, CA
Majerus, Michael G. ... Billings, MT
Majerus, Robert P. ... Seattle, WA
Majeske, Andrew J. ... Davis, CA
Majeske, Robert S. ... Chicago, IL
Majeski, Colleen A. ... Cleveland, OH
Majeski, Eugene J. ... Redwood City, CA
Majeski, John ... Atherton, CA
Majeski, Michael B. ... Independence, OH
Majeski, Michael J. ... St. Paul, MN
Majeski, Stephen L. ... Hartford, CT
Majestic, Ann L. ... Raleigh, NC
Majestic, John A. ... New Port Richey, FL
Majestic, John A., P.A.
New Port Richey, FL
Majestic, Martin F. ... San Francisco, CA
Majestic, Maryanne ... Scottsdale, AZ
Majestic, Parsons, Siebert & Hsue, A Professional Corporation
San Francisco, CA
Santa Clara, CA
Majestro, Anthony J. ... Charleston, WV
Majestro, Cynthia A. ... Charleston, WV
Majett, Nicholas A. ... Washington, DC
Majette, R. Shawn ... Richmond, VA
Majev, Howard R. ... Washington, DC
Baltimore, MD
Majewicz, Anna T. ... New York, NY
Majewski, Alexander F. ... San Diego, CA
Majewski, Arthur J.
Grosse Pointe Woods, MI
Majewski, Dennis R. ... Terre Haute, IN
Majewski, Gregory J. ... Rexford, NY
Westerly, RI
Majewski, Jan F. ... St. Petersburg, FL
Majewski, Jennifer Bullock ... Hartford, CT
Majewski, Jerome C. ... Algonquin, IL
Majewski, Jon A. ... Metairie, LA
Majewski, Kevin E. ... Hartford, CT
Majewski, Michael ... Garden City, NY
Majewski, Raymond T. ... Roseland, NJ
Majewski, Thomas M. ... New York, NY
Majhan, Thomas J. ... Port Townsend, WA
Majikas, Jeffrey C. ... Hazleton, PA
Majka, Joseph T. ... Kenilworth, NJ
Majkowski, James P. ... Mount Clemens, MI
Majkowski, Paul V. ... New York, NY
Majkut, Paul Stevenson ... Portland, OR
Majlessi, Ardeshir ... Beverly Hills, CA
Majoe, Ben ... Honolulu, HI
Major, A. Edward, Jr. ... New York, NY
Major, Alice Jean ... Denver, CO
Major, Amanda Alexander ... Hickman, KY
Major, Barbara L. ... San Diego, CA
Major, Bruce W. ... St. Louis, MO
Major, Calvin F. ... Richmond, VA
Major, Charles T., Jr. ... Syracuse, NY
Major, David R. ... Seattle, WA
Major, Don H. ... Louisville, KY
Major, F. Lee, III ... Kansas City, MO
Major, Francis J. ... Falls Church, VA
Major, Gene A. ... Atlanta, GA
Major, Hugh G. ... San Francisco, CA
Major, Jacqueline Wilson ... Little Rock, AR
Major, John F. ... Novato, CA
Major, John H. ... Van Nuys, CA
Major, John T. ... Prairie Village, KS
Kansas City, MO
Major, Joseph E. ... Greenville, SC
Major, Joseph W. ... Pottstown, PA
Major, Julianne ... Santa Rosa, CA
Major, Karrick L. ... Chicago, IL
Major, Kevin W. ... Colorado Springs, CO
Major, Kristin ... Phoenix, AZ
Major, Kristin M. ... Winston-Salem, NC
Major, Lawrence E., (P.A.) ... Miami, FL
Major, Lynn N. ... Mayfield Village, OH
Major, Malcolm M. ... Fort Lauderdale, FL
Major, Marcia J. ... Ann Arbor, MI
Major, Mark A. ... Saratoga Springs, NY
Major, Mark W. ... Denver, CO
Major, Martin S. ... New York, NY
Major, Patricia Briggs ... Riviera Beach, FL
Major, Richard L., Jr. ... Hickman, KY
Major, Robert Allen, Jr. ... San Francisco, CA
Major, Robert R. ... Orlando, FL
Major, Roberta J. ... Wickliffe, OH
Major, Ronald D. ... Cincinnati, OH
Major, Scott J. ... Washington, DC
Major, Susan E. ... Tulsa, OK
Major, Theodore
United States Postal Service, Law Department, GV
Major, Thomas, Jr. ... Indianapolis, IN
Major, Tibor E. ... Lakeport, CA
Major, W. Glenn ... Westport, CT
Major, William A., Jr. ... Birmingham, AL
Major, William H., III ... Atlanta, GA
Majoras, John M. ... Cleveland, OH
Majorie, Francis B. ... Dallas, TX
Majoros, Elias Themistocles
Southfield, MI
Majors, Amye Bensenhaver ... Louisville, KY
Majors, B. Joseph, II ... Wadena, MN
Majors, Carrie A. ... Milwaukie, OR
Majors, Carrie Ann ... San Marcos, TX
Majors, Charles H. ... Danville, VA
Majors, Edward M. ... Louisville, KY
Majors, Fletcher H. ... Selma, AL
Majors & Fox, A Law Partnership
San Diego, CA
Majors, Gary W. ... San Diego, CA
Majors, Gene ... San Marcos, TX
Majors, James E. ... Grand Junction, CO
Majors, Jay D. ... Washington, DC
Majors, John A. ... Louisville, KY
Majors, John D. ... Atlanta, GA
Majors, Kelly L. ... San Antonio, TX
Majors, M. Mark ... Montgomery, AL
Majors, Michael S. ... Everett, WA
Majors, Ned B. ... Myrtle Beach, SC
Majors, Paul John ... Laguna Hills, CA
Majors, Raymond A. ... Ludowici, GA
Majors, Scott D. ... Frankfort, KY
Majors, Shirley F. ... Canton, OH
Majors, Stanley E. ... Fairfax, VA
Majors, Warren D. ... Oklahoma City, OK
Majors, Wm. M., Jr. ... Oklahoma City, OK
Majorski, Davor N. ... Kingston, NY
Majowka, John Martin, Jr. ... Arlington, VA
Majul-Virgen, Adriana ... San Antonio, TX
Majumdar, Malini ... New York, NY
Majumder, Indrajit Bobby ... Dallas, TX
Majzoub, Jeffrey A. ... Washington, DC
Majzoub, Mona K. ... Detroit, MI
Mak, Brian T. ... St. Paul, MN
Mak, Danton K. ... Pasadena, CA
Mak, Gina ... Los Angeles, CA
Mak, Ilene ... New York, NY
Mak, Loretta ... San Francisco, CA
Mak, Pamela J. ... Washington, DC
Mak, Raymond T. ... New York, NY
Mak, Suzanna ... Stanford, CA
Mak, Yuk-Shim ... Hackensack, NJ
Makadon, Arthur ... Philadelphia, PA
Makaitis, Nijole ... Boston, MA
Makal, Judith A. ... Brookfield, WI
Makant, Barbara W. ... Tallahassee, FL
Makar, John ... Natchitoches, LA
Makar, Margaret C. ... Denver, CO
Makar, Marjorie Conner ... Jacksonville, FL
Makar, Scott D. ... Jacksonville, FL
Makara, David S. ... Hazleton, PA
Makarechian, David A. ... Palo Alto, CA
Makarechian, Jeremy W. ... Denver, CO
Makarem, Lisa A. ... Los Angeles, CA
Makarem, Ronald W. ... Los Angeles, CA
Makarenko, Nikolai, Jr. ... Atlanta, GA
Makarevic, Stanley S. ... Trenton, NJ
Makarevich, Viktoria ... New York, NY
Makarewich, John A. ... Los Angeles, CA
Makaric, Brian S. ... Saginaw, MI
Makaroff, Michael V. ... Denver, CO
Makarowitz, Jonathan M. ... New York, NY
Makarski, Daniel P. ... Mount Clemens, MI
Makarski, David S. ... Chicago, IL
Makarski, Richard A. ... Chicago, IL
Makau, Elena K. ... Brooklyn, NY
Makauskas, Andrew R. ... Chicago, IL
Makay, Albert J. ... San Antonio, TX
Makay, Christopher L. ... San Antonio, TX
Makdisi, John ... Miami, FL
New Orleans, LA
Makdisi, June Mary Z. ... New Orleans, LA
Makdissi, Nada Michel ... Houston, TX
Makechnie, Norman H.
Peterborough, NH
Makee, Dan L. ... Cleveland, OH
Makee, Joel A. ... Cleveland, OH
Makeever, Jeffery J. ... Rockford, IL
Makeig, Thomas H. ... Fairfield, IA
Makeig, Thomas H., P.C. ... Fairfield, IA
Makel, Dennis M. ... Washington, PA
Makel, Kathleen R. ... Sacramento, CA
Makel, Larry A. ... Dallas, TX
Makela, Jane ... Dallas, TX
Makela, Sheryl-Lynn C. ... Norfolk, VA
Makemson, Leland C. ... Phoenix, AZ
Makemson, Robert R. ... Stuart, FL
Makens, Hugh H. ... Grand Rapids, MI
Makepeace, Caroline Dibona
Washington, DC
Makepeace, J. Tyler ... Colorado Springs, CO
Maker, Andrea Cianchette ... Bucksport, ME
Maker, Edward H., II ... Palo Alto, CA
Maker, Joseph A. ... Stamford, CT
Maker, Joseph E. ... Lakewood, CO
Maker, Scott T. ... Portland, ME
Maker, Walter S. ... Park Forest, IL
Maker, William, Jr. ... Larchmont, NY
Makhdoom, Saima ... Washington, DC
Makhlouf, Christina M. ... Chicago, IL
Maki, Allan O. ... Brookfield, WI
Maki, Craig R. ... Los Angeles, CA
Maki, David J. ... Seattle, WA
Maki, Durst, Ledin, Bick, Lehr & Kanuit, S.C. ... Ashland, WI
Hayward, WI
Superior, WI
Maki, E. Charles ... Ventura, CA
Maki, Eloise J. ... St. Paul, MN
Maki, Forrest O. ... Superior, WI
Maki, J. Eric ... New York, NY
Maki, Jennifer K. ... Portland, OR
Maki, Jon E. ... La Jolla, CA
Maki, Leo E. ... Hancock, MI
Maki, Linda J. ... Chicago, IL
Maki, Lisa L. ... Los Angeles, CA
Maki, Mark L. ... Kalamazoo, MI
Maki & Overom ... Duluth, MN
Maki, Paul ... Honolulu, HI
Maki, Richard W. ... Anchorage, AK
Maki, Robert C. ... Duluth, MN
Maki, Susan K. ... Minneapolis, MN
Maki, Teresa A. ... Brooklyn, NY
Maki, William O. ... Glenview, IL
Makia, Abit B. ... Silver Spring, MD
Makibe, Michael J. ... Honolulu, HI
Makich, Ann ... New York, NY
Makiewicz, Mark ... San Jose, CA
Makin & Associates ... Long Beach, CA
Makin, Cynthia C. ... Long Beach, CA
Makin, Harold LeRoy ... Long Beach, CA
Makin, James R. ... Beaumont, TX
Makin, John P. ... San Francisco, CA
Makin, Phillip S. ... Chicago, IL
Makin, Roy ... Palos Verdes Estates, CA
Makin, Sarah C. ... Philadelphia, PA
Makinen, Michael E. ... Hancock, MI
Makino, Kazuharu ... Santa Ana, CA

Makkai, Alexander, Jr. ....Westminster, CO
Makkiya, Ann B. ....Springfield, MA
Makkreel, Karen Emiko
Treasury Department,
Office of the General Counsel, GV
Makl, Glenn A. ....Department of Justice,
Tax Division, GV
Makla, Robert M. ....New York, NY
Makler, Alexandre B. ....San Francisco, CA
Makler, Julianna ....San Francisco, CA
Makler, Mark J. ....Portland, OR
Makley, Andrea J. ....Beverly Hills, CA
Makley, Robert E. ....Santa Ana, CA
Makley, Roger J. ....Dayton, OH
Makman, David A. ....Palo Alto, CA
Mako, Emery R. ....Willoughby, OH
Mako, Sue Elaine ....Leland, NC
Mako, Sue Elaine ....Wilmington, NC
Makoff, Charlotte N. ....San Francisco, CA
Makoff, Jeffrey T. ....San Francisco, CA
Makoff Kinnear Counsel P.C.
Los Angeles, CA
San Francisco, CA
Makoff, Richard P. ....Salt Lake City, UT
Makofka, Lester ....Jacksonville, FL
Makofsky, Ellen G. ....Garden City, NY
Makohin, George M. ....Oklahoma City, OK
Makol, Jennifer ....Granite Bay, CA
Makoroff, Stanley G. ....Pittsburgh, PA
Makos, Susan Smith ....Cincinnati, OH
Makoski, Mark J. ....Warren, MI
Makoski, Tara Marie ....Towson, MD
Makosky, Alexandra ....Harrisburg, PA
Makoui, Ali ....Encino, CA
Makoul, Kimberly F. ....Allentown, PA
Makoul, Richard J. ....Allentown, PA
Makoulian, Tina R. ....Philadelphia, PA
Makous, David N. ....Los Angeles, CA
Makous, Jo Ann Brady ....Los Angeles, CA
Makovic, William T. ....Peoria, IL
Makow, Lawrence S. ....New York, NY
Makow, Tracy Ellen ....Roseland, NJ
New York, NY
Makower, Alissa D. ....New York, NY
Makower, Mark F. ....Farmington Hills, MI
Makower, Mark F., P.C., & Associates
Farmington Hills, MI
Makower, Sharon H. ....New York, NY
Makowicz, Mitchell J., Jr. ....Chatham, NJ
Makowitz, Mark ....Denver, CO
Makowitz, Mark, P.C. ....Denver, CO
Makowski, Alphonse R. ....Cinnaminson, NJ
Makowski, Chester J. ....Houston, TX
Makowski, Edward J., Jr. ....Baltimore, MD
Makowski, John J. ....Macon, GA
Makowski, Joseph G. ....Buffalo, NY
Makowski, Kathleen P. ....Wilmington, DE
Makowski, Kevin D. ....Milwaukee, WI
Makowski, Marateck, Konopka & Marateck
Shamokin, PA
Makowski, Raymond E.
Jacksonville Beach, FL
Makowski, Richard J. ....Cleveland, OH
Makowski, Thomas A. ....Wilkes-Barre, PA
Makowski, Vincent B. ....Shamokin, PA
Makowski, Wojciech P. ....Santa Rosa, CA
Makowski-Rivera, Donna B. ....Chicago, IL
Makowsky, Danny A. ....Waco, TX
Makowsky, Dorold A. ....Naugatuck, CT
Makowsky, Russell E. ....New York, NY
Makowsky, Sarah M. ....Los Angeles, CA
Makransky, Jane A. ....Philadelphia, PA
Makredes, Maria ....Boston, MA
Makricostas, Dean G. ....Weirton, WV
Makridis, Irene K. ....Warren, OH
Makris, Elaine ....Houston, TX
Makris, George M. ....Memphis, TN
Makris, Harry ....Garden City, NY
Makris, Helen ....Montvale, NJ
Makris, John G. ....Troy, MI
Makris, Thomas N. ....San Francisco, CA
San Jose, CA
Makris, Victor N. ....Bellaire, TX
Makris, Victor N., P.C. ....Bellaire, TX
Makris-Gouvas, Maria ....Department of Labor,
Office of the Solicitor, GV
Makrodimitris, Pinelopi ....Baltimore, MD
Makrouer, Cary M. ....Southfield, MI
Maks, Jeffrey P. ....Rapid City, SD
Maksail, George A. ....Albany, NY
Maksimov, Lorraine ....Irvine, CA
Maksimowicz, Sheila C. ....Wichita, KS
Maksym, Ronald L. ....Scottsdale, AZ
Maksym, Walter P. ....Oak Brook, IL
Maksym, Walter P., & Assoc., Ltd.
Oak Brook, IL
Makuakane, Scott A. ....Honolulu, HI
Makuch, Frances Wiet ....Chicago, IL
Makuch, Joseph S. ....Portland, OR
Makuch, Michael A. ....Washington, DC
Makujina, Shah R.
Research Triangle Park, NC
Makunga, Sonya ....Los Angeles, CA
Makupson, Carolyn A. ....Pasadena, CA
Makupson, Walter H. ....Detroit, MI
Makus, Jerry M. ....Walla Walla, WA
Makuta, Celeste S. ....Los Angeles, CA
Makuta, Ross ....Dallas, TX
Makuta, Shirley Ann ....Vandergrift, PA
Maky, Walter ....Cleveland, OH
Makynen, Michael R. ....Hopkinton, MA
Malabonga, Daniel M. ....Washington, DC
Malacarne, C. John ....Kansas City, MO
Malach, David ....New York, NY
Malach, Herbert J. ....New Rochelle, NY
Malach, Shirley ....Southfield, MI
Malach, Solomon ....New York, NY
Malach, Steven H. ....Southfield, MI
Malach, Therese R. ....White Plains, NY
Malacina, Vicki D. ....Lansing, MI
Malacko, Richard J. ....St. Paul, MN
Malaczynski, Heidi A. ....Albany, NY
Malad, Richard M. ....Indianapolis, IN
Malady, Brian C. ....Washington, DC
Malady, Eugene J. ....Media, PA
Malady, K. James, III ....Bennington, VT
Malafi, Christine ....Melville, NY
Malafronte, Janelle M. ....Braintree, MA
Malafronte, Richard W. ....New Haven, CT
Malagiere, Richard ....New York, NY
Malagon, Evohl F. ....Eugene, OR
Malagon, Moore, Johnson & Jensen
Eugene, OR
Malagreca, Joseph ....Brooklyn, NY
Malahowski, Richard A. ....Dallas, TX
Malahowski, Roy F. ....Bakersfield, CA
Malak, Jeffrey A. ....Chicago, IL
Malak, Mark P. ....Utica, NY
Malak, Michael James ....Northridge, CA
Malak, Michael P. ....Schaumburg, IL
Malak, Pamela Croft ....Northridge, CA
Malak, Paul J. ....Pittsburgh, PA
Malaker, A. Deane ....Rocky River, OH
Malakoff Doyle & Finberg, P.C.
Pittsburgh, PA
Malakoff, Drew ....Stamford, CT
New York, NY
Malakoff, Harvey T. ....Brooklyn, NY
Malakoff, Joseph F. ....Oakland, CA
Malakoff, Louise Reiber ....Pittsburgh, PA
Malakoff, Marc Terry ....Rockville, MD
Malakoff, Michael P. ....Pittsburgh, PA
Malakoff, Murray E. ....Laredo, TX
Malali, Prem N. ....Boston, MA
Malamed, Daniel S. ....Los Angeles, CA
Malamed, David ....New York, NY
Malamed, Kenneth D. ....Los Angeles, CA
Malament, Cynthia B. ....Rockville, MD
Malamphy, Richard K.
Department Of Health And Human Services,
GV
Malamud, Brad R. ....San Clemente, CA
Malamud, Deborah C. ....Washington, DC
Malamud, Leonard J.
Department Of Veterans Affairs,
Office of the General Counsel, GV
Malamud, Richard B. ....Los Angeles, CA
Malamud, Sherwood ....Madison, WI
Malamud, Sylvia Kolkin ....Brooklyn, NY
Malamut, Michael Eric ....Boston, MA
Malamuth, Steven J. ....Oakland, CA
Malamy, Kenneth W. ....New York, NY
Malan, Chris J. ....North Salt Lake, UT
Malan, Douglas R. ....Las Vegas, NV
Malana, Jerrilyn T. ....San Diego, CA
Malanaphy, Liam R. ....New York, NY
Malanca, Albert R. ....Tacoma, WA
Malanca, Frank N. ....Montebello, CA
Malanca, Glenna ....Bremerton, WA
Maland, Donald L. ....Clara City, MN
Montevideo, MN
Maland, Kristin B. ....Minneapolis, MN
Maland, Mark M. ....Elizabeth City, NC
Maland, Robert C. ....Miami, FL
Maland, Robert C., P.A. ....Miami, FL
Malandra, Charles R., Jr. ....Stamford, CT
Malandra, Joseph J., Jr. ....San Francisco, CA
Malandra, Marco J. ....Philadelphia, PA
Malaney, Kay E. ....Troy, MI
Malaney, Wayne R. ....Tallahassee, FL
Malanga, Anthony F., Jr. ....Belleville, NJ
Malanga, Christine A. ....Towson, MD
Malanga, Gerald B. ....Los Angeles, CA
Malanga, John D. ....Fort Worth, TX
Malanga, Kevin ....New York, NY
Malanga, Lauren A. ....New York, NY
Malanga, Thomas F., Jr. ....Linden, NJ
Malany, Douglas S. ....McAllen, TX
Malany, LeGrand L. ....Springfield, IL
Malanyn, Eugene ....Harrisville, MI
Malapero, Raymond J. ....New York, NY
Malapit, Eduardo E. ....Lihue, HI
Malapit, Thomas R., Jr. ....Anderson, IN
Malaquin, Didier ....New York, NY
Malara, Anthony James, III ....Washington, DC
Malara, Joseph S. ....Hartsdale, NY
Malara, Valerie J. ....Denver, CO
Malarchick, Timothy P. ....Gig Harbor, WA
Malarcik, Donald J., Jr. ....Akron, OH
Malaret, Charles J. ....Los Angeles, CA
Malarick, Michael ....Westmont, NJ
Philadelphia, PA
Malarkey, Charles J. ....San Francisco, CA
Malarkey, John D. ....Chicago, IL
Malarkey, William E. ....New York, NY
Malarney, Jeffery ....Manteo, NC
Malarney, Michael W. ....Rochester, NY
Malartsik, Jon P. ....Chicago, IL
Malas, Mary Ellen ....Cincinnati, OH
Malaska, Stephen L. ....Seattle, WA
Malasky, Alan R. ....Washington, DC
Malasky, Ellen S. ....West Palm Beach, FL
Malaspina, Ernest M. ....Mountain View, CA
Malaspina, John M. ....Florham Park, NJ
Malaspina, Mark Alexander ....New York, NY
Malaspina, Mark J. ....Waterbury, CT
Malat, Gerald A. ....Beverly Hills, CA
Malat, Malat & Getzels ....Beverly Hills, CA
Malat, Melvin H. ....Beverly Hills, CA
Malat, Samuel A. ....Haddon Heights, NJ
Malatak, Robert J. ....New York, NY
Malatesta, Carl A. ....Wilmington, DE
Malatesta, David C., Jr. ....Wilmington, DE
Malatesta Hawke & McKeon LLP
Harrisburg, PA
Malatesta, Ian C. ....Los Angeles, CA
Malatesta, Joseph J., Jr. ....Harrisburg, PA
Malatesta, Lina ....Brooklyn, NY
Malatesta, Mary A. ....Denver, CO
Malatesta, Sean M. ....New York, NY
Malatestinic, Anthony J. ....Staten Island, NY
Malato, Stephen A. ....Chicago, IL
Malato, Stephen H. ....Chicago, IL
Malato, Thomas E. ....Geneva, IL
Malatt, Raymond E. ....Palos Heights, IL
Malatt, Richard ....Los Angeles, CA
Malatz, Stephen R. ....Hanover, PA
Malatzky, Howard L ....New York, NY
Malavé, Sally ....Santa Fe, NM
Malavia, Roger A. ....Chicago, IL
Malawer, Bennett B. ....McLean, VA
Malawer, Steven J. ....Greenwich, CT
Malawer, Stuart S. ....Fairfax, VA
Malawsky, Donald N. ....New York, NY
Malay, Janet B. ....West Orange, NJ
Malay, Mariann Zampano ....Boston, MA
Malayang, Ann E. ....Detroit, MI
Malazzo, Beverly Brademan ....Houston, TX
Malban, David J. ....Duluth, MN
Malbasa, Stephanie ....Cleveland, OH
Malbin, Jerome K. ....Port Jervis, NY
Malbin, Norman D. ....Portland, OR
Malbrough, Bobby Ray T. ....Metairie, LA
Malbrough, Joan M. ....Houma, LA
Malbrough & Joffrion, L.L.C. ....Houma, LA
Malbrough, Stephanie J.
New Orleans, LA
Malc, Elizabeth A. ....Erie, PA
Malca & Jacobs, P.A.
Fort Lauderdale, FL
Miami, FL
Malca, Ramon ....Fort Lauderdale, FL
Malca, Victor ....Miami, FL
Malcarney, Ronald L. ....Medford, NJ
Malcheski, Kim ....San Francisco, CA
Malchesky, Paul R. ....Painesville, OH
Malchman, Irving ....New York, NY
Malchodi, Eric A. ....Hartford, CT
Malchon, Richard H., Jr.
St. Petersburg, FL
Tampa, FL
Malchow, E. Lynn ....Burlingame, CA
Los Angeles, CA
Malchow, Helena G. ....Orlando, FL
Malchow, Kevin G. ....Orlando, FL
Malchow, Leland M. ....Augusta, GA
Malchow, Margaret E. ....Denver, CO
Malchow, W. Timothy ....St. Paul, MN
Malciauskas, Thomas S. ....Chicago, IL
Malcolm, Allen R. ....Chestertown, MD
Malcolm, Amy E. ....Nashville, TN
Malcolm, Cheryl A. ....Denver, CO
Malcolm, Chris R. ....Eagle, NE
Malcolm, Cisneros & Houser ....Irvine, CA
Riverside, CA
Malcolm, David J. ....Portland, OR
Malcolm, John G. ....Atlanta, GA
Malcolm, John R. ....Stockton, CA
Malcolm, Joseph J. ....Los Angeles, CA
Roseland, NJ
New York, NY
Malcolm, Lawrence D. ....Bonita, CA
Malcolm, Lawrence D., Jr. ....La Jolla, CA
Malcolm & Schroeder, L.L.P.
Atlanta, GA
Malcolm, Stacey L. ....Fresno, CA
Malcolm, Thomas O. ....West Chester, PA
Malcolm, Thomas R. ....Irvine, CA
Malcolm, William G., (A Professional
Corporation) ....Irvine, CA
Malcolm, William M. ....Clay Center, KS
Malcolm-Beeker, Janice ....Miami, FL
Malcolmson, Jas. D. ....San Francisco, CA
Malcom, Christopher ....Moulton, AL
Malcom, Douglas I. ....Rockville, MD
Malcom, J. Phillip, (P.A.) ....Little Rock, AR
Malcom, Kathryn E.R. ....Birmingham, AL
Malcom, R. Michael ....Atlanta, GA
Malcom, Stauffer P., Jr. ....Valparaiso, IN
Malcoun, Steven A. ....Stockton, CA
Maldegen, Larry D. ....Santa Fe, NM
Malden, Nigel S. ....Tacoma, WA
Maldiner, Kyle ....New York, NY
Maldjian, John P. ....Westfield, NJ
Maldonado, Amy ....Chicago, IL
Maldonado, Arthur N. ....New York, NY
Maldonado, Bernabe Q. ....San Antonio, TX
Maldonado, Daniel ....Phoenix, AZ
Maldonado, Daniel ....Miami, FL
Maldonado, David ....Woodside, NY
Maldonado, David J. ....Dallas, TX
Maldonado, Diana ....Austin, TX
Maldonado, Eduardo A. ....Washington, DC
Maldonado, Elizabeth A. ....Berlin, CT
Maldonado, Ellen ....San Francisco, CA
Maldonado, Javier N. ....San Antonio, TX
Maldonado, Jeffrey A. ....Thousand Oaks, CA
Maldonado, Jennifer D. ....Raleigh, NC
Maldonado, Jesus M. ....Oakland, CA
Maldonado, Jorge A. ....Austin, TX
Maldonado, Joseph G. ....Miami, FL
Maldonado, Juan ....Department of Justice,
Civil Rights Division, GV
Maldonado, Juan D. ....San Antonio, TX
Maldonado, Kirk F. ....Costa Mesa, CA
Maldonado, Lewis C. ....San Francisco, CA
Maldonado, Lissa G. ....San Francisco, CA
Maldonado, Maria B. ....Guaynabo, PR
Maldonado, Mary K. ....Denver, CO
Maldonado, M. E. G.
Federal Labor Relations Authority,
Authority Member Staff, GV
Maldonado, Mercedes Marie ....New York, NY
Maldonado, Michael X. ....Corpus Christi, TX
Maldonado, Michelle Lopes
Falls Church, VA
Maldonado, Robert T. ....New York, NY
Maldonado, Roberto E. ....Atlanta, GA
Maldonado, Roberto O. ....San Juan, PR
Maldonado, Roger Juan ....New York, NY
Maldonado, Rosemarie ....New York, NY
Maldonado, Solangel ....Newark, NJ
Maldonado, Victor Santiago ....Belmont, MA
Maldonado, Wayne R. ....Metairie, LA
Maldonado Ayala, Alejo ....San Juan, PR
Maldonado Carrasco, Larissa
San Juan, PR
Maldonado-Casillas, Carlos M.
San Juan, PR
Maldonado Colon, Mayra ....San Juan, PR
Maldonado Figueroa, Antonio
San German, PR
Maldonado-Matías, Elaine ....San Juan, PR
Maldonado-Nieves, Roberto O.
San Juan, PR
Maldonado-Ojeda, Pedro A.
San Juan, PR
Maldonado-Rodriguez, Julio M. ....Hatillo, PR
Maldonado Vazquez, Saul ....Fajardo, PR
Maldovan, William D. ....Buffalo, NY
Male, Michael H. ....Miami, FL
Male, Michael H., Professional Association
Miami, FL
Male, Theresa Barrett ....Harrisburg, PA
Malec, John J. ....Woodland Hills, CA
Malec, Kenneth J. ....Chicago, IL
Malec, Kris M. ....El Centro, CA
Malec, Thomas O. ....West Haven, CT
Malec, Timothy A. ....Boston, MA
Malecek, Megan E. ....San Francisco, CA
Malecek, Michael J. ....Sacramento, CA
Malecek, Robert M. ....Detroit, MI
Malech, Arnold M. ....Westerville, OH
Malech, Emily A. ....Bethesda, MD
Malech, Leonard ....Tenafly, NJ
Malech, Lloyd Alan ....Washington, DC
Malech, Robert L.
Department of Housing and Urban
Development,
Office of General Counsel, GV
Malech, Rori H. ....Washington, DC
Malech, Steven B. ....Hartford, CT
Malecha, Martin P. ....Brooklyn Park, MN
Malecha, Wayne F. ....Fort Worth, TX
Malechek, Louis A. (Trey), III ....Bryan, TX
Maleck, Paul M. ....Springfield, MA
Maleckar, Rebecca J. ....Cleveland, OH
Malecki, Donald E. ....Pittsburgh, PA
Malecki, James H. ....Mankato, MN
Malecki, Jenice L. ....New York, NY
Malecki, Mark R. ....Department of Labor,
Office of the Solicitor, GV
Malecki, William E. ....San Francisco, CA
Maledon, Marilyn P. ....Pittsburgh, PA
Maledon, Michael B. ....Phoenix, AZ
Maledon, William J. ....Phoenix, AZ
Malee, Ian ....Coral Springs, FL
Malefatto, Alfred J. ....West Palm Beach, FL
Malehorn, Donald M. ....Morristown, NJ
Malejan, Todd ....Houston, TX
Malek, Andrew M. ....Columbus, OH
Malek, Bruce J. ....Mt. Vernon, OH
Malek, Francine ....Lyons, IL
Malek, Gilda ....San Francisco, CA
Malek, Joseph A. ....Chicago, IL
Malek, Lori C. ....Irving, TX
Malek & Malek ....Irvine, CA
San Francisco, CA
Torrance, CA
San Francisco, CA
Torrance, CA
Malek, Margaret Arenas ....Boston, MA
Malek, Nate N. ....Solon, OH
Malek, Paul D. ....New York, NY
Malek, Paul F. ....Birmingham, AL
Malek, Pfundstein & Dean, LLC
Solon, OH
Malek, Philip G. ....Boston, MA
Malek, Sandra L. ....San Francisco, CA
Torrance, CA
Maleki, Joseph A. ....Aliso Viejo, CA
Maleki, Paul ....Clifton Park, NY
Malek-Yonan, Monica ....Glendale, CA
Malempati, S.R. ....Pikeville, KY
Malempati, Suparna ....Atlanta, GA
Malempati, Suparna, P.C. ....Atlanta, GA
Malemud, Franklin C. ....Cleveland, OH
Malen, Dennis S. ....Westbury, NY
Malen, Peter F., Jr. ....Salt Lake City, UT
Malena, Alfred A., Jr. ....Norcross, GA
Malenda, Irene A. ....Solon, IA
Maleng, Norman K. ....Seattle, WA
Malenka, Carol A. ....San Francisco, CA
Malenski, Dennis J. ....Clinton, NJ
Maler, Nancy A. ....Fresno, CA
Maler, Sharron A. ....Houston, TX
Malerba, Marilyn ....Bryn Mawr, PA
Malerba, Robert F. ....Huntington, NY
Malerba, Steven A. ....Garden City, NY
Males, George R. ....Silver Spring, MD
Males, Julia E. ....Colchester, VT
Males, Stephen, Jr. ....Dover, NH
Malesardi, Patricia A.
Department of Commerce,
Patent and Trademark Office, GV
Malesick, Paul H. ....Cleveland, OH
North Canton, OH
Maleski, Cynthia M. ....Pittsburgh, PA
Maleski, Nadine ....Morristown, NJ
Maleson, Alfred I. ....Boston, MA
Maleson, Diane C. ....Philadelphia, PA

Maleson, Paul ... Jenkintown, PA
Philadelphia, PA
Maleson, Stephen E. ... Elkins Park, PA
Malesovas, Jerry L. ... Richardson, TX
Malesovas, John L. ... **Waco, TX**
Malesovas, Martin & Tekell, L.L.P.
Waco, TX
Malesta, Michael ... Hartford, CT
Malestein, Robert G. ... **Vineland, NJ**
Malester, Allan J. ... **Baltimore, MD**
Malester, Ann ... Federal Trade Commission, Bureau of Competition, GV
Malet, Edwin I. ... Narberth, PA
Malet, Mary E. ... New York, NY
Malet, Philip L. ... **Washington, DC**
Maletis, James C. ... Portland, OR
Maletis, James C., P.C. ... Portland, OR
Malett, Shoshanna M. ... Larchmont, NY
Maletta, Jeffrey B. ... **Washington, DC**
Maletta, Matthew J. ... **Chicago, IL**
Maletto, Angelina M. ... **Charlotte, NC**
Maletz, Esther R. ... Boston, MA
Maletz, Herbert N. ... Baltimore, MD
Malevitis, John L. ... Chicago, IL
Malewski, Alexander J., Jr. ... Brooklyn, NY
Maley, Christopher J. ... **Boston, MA**
Maley & Dougherty ... **Collingswood, NJ**
Philadelphia, PA
Maley, Edwin J., Jr. ... Hartford, CT
Maley, Eugene O. ... **Indianapolis, IN**
Maley, Heidi ... **San Diego, CA**
Maley, James E. ... Atlanta, GA
Maley, Jody K. ... **Indianapolis, IN**
Maley, John C. ... Dallas, TX
Maley, John D. ... Okmulgee, OK
Maley, John P. ... **Burlington, VT**
Maley, John R. ... **Indianapolis, IN**
Maley, John T. ... Denver, CO
Maley, Karl A. ... **Austin, TX**
Smithville, TX
Maley, Larry M. ... Reynoldsburg, OH
Maley, M. James, Jr. ... **Collingswood, NJ**
Philadelphia, PA
Maley, Martin A. ... **St. Albans, VT**
Maley, Mary Grace ... **Philadelphia, PA**
Maley, Maureen Gimpel ... Kennett Square, PA
Maley, Philip M. ... White Plains, NY
Maley, Robert C., Jr. ... **Houston, TX**
Maley, Robert J. ... **Richmond, IN**
Maley & Schiff, P.C. ... Denver, CO
Maley, Susan Chin
Merit Systems Protection Board, Office of Appeals Counsel, GV
Malfa, Katherine A. ... Rockville, MD
Malfar, David E. ... Chicago, IL
Malfeld, Diane D. ... **Minneapolis, MN**
Malfitani, Joseph C. ... Dover, NH
Malfitano Campbell & Dickinson
Jacksonville, FL
Lakeland, FL
Tampa, FL
Malfitano, Larry P. ... **Syracuse, NY**
Malfitano, Michael D. ... **Jacksonville, FL**
Tampa, FL
Malfitano, Vincent C. ... Woodbury, NJ
Malgeri, Joseph T. ... Hyde Park, VT
Malgeri, Vincent R. ... Newburyport, MA
Malgieri, Patrick M. ... **Rochester, NY**
Malgran, G. Richard ... Flemington, NJ
New York, NY
Malham, Joseph P. ... Pasadena, CA
Malheiro, Sharon K. ... **Des Moines, IA**
Malhiot, George D. ... Wood Ridge, NJ
Malhotra, Deepak ... **Spokane, WA**
Malhotra, Gary ... **New York, NY**
Malhotra, Nick ... **Boston, MA**
Malhotra, Rahul ... Odessa, TX
Malhotra, Rajshree ... Dayton, OH
Malhotra, Sanjay B. ... **New York, NY**
Malhotra, Vivek K. ... **Los Angeles, CA**
Malia, Gerald A. ... **Washington, DC**
Malia, Glen P. ... Cortlandt Manor, NY
Malia & Kressin ... Peekskill, NY
Malia, Peter J., Jr. ... Fryeburg, ME
Malia, Thomas R. ... Rochester, NY
Malian, Kenneth M. ... Glen Ridge, NJ
Malican, Denise M. ... Buffalo, NY
Malich, Alexandar D. ... Pittsburgh, PA
Malick, Clarence W. ... Hudson, WI
Malick, Gordon R.
Department Of Health And Human Services, Social Security Administration, GV
Malick, Joseph A. ... **Dallas, TX**
Malick, Lawrence C. ... Durango, CO
Malicki, Thomas J. ... **Omaha, NE**
Malickson, Bryan S. ... Chevy Chase, MD
Malickson, Jeffrey W. ... Charlotte, NC
Malicoat, Mary T. ... **Wichita, KS**
Maliga, Kristina L. ... **Tampa, FL**
Malik, Aftab Alam ... **Santa Fe Springs, CA**
Malik, Betsy R. ... **New York, NY**
Malik, Edward C. ... Saco, ME
Malik, John J., Jr. ... St. Clairsville, OH
Malik, John S. ... **Dover, DE**
Georgetown, DE
Malik, John S. ... **Wilmington, DE**
Malik, Khalid M. ... **Dallas, TX**
Malik, M. Alim ... **Irvine, CA**
Malik, Rajeev K. ... Columbus, OH
Malik, Sabiha ... **Providence, RI**
Malik, Shahzad A. ... **Los Angeles, CA**
Malik, Terry John ... **Chicago, IL**
Malik, Thomas J. ... La Place, LA
Malik, Thomas W. ... Wauconda, IL
Malikow, Louis R. ... Clifton Park, NY
Malikowski, Paul J. ... Reno, NV
Malin, Alice J. ... Brooklyn, NY
Malin, Allison L. ... **Los Angeles, CA**

Malin, Andrea B. ... **Wappingers Falls, NY**
Malin, Barbara B. ... **McKinney, TX**
Malin, Bernard E. ... Hackensack, NJ
Malin, Charles J. ... Berkeley, IL
Malin, Christopher D. ... Fort Lauderdale, FL
Malin, Donald F., Jr. ... Canaan, NY
Malin, Garry S. ... Westlake Village, CA
Malin, Gary Louis ... New York, NY
Malin, George L. ... Great Neck, NY
Malin, Haley & DiMaggio, P.A.
Fort Lauderdale, FL
Miami, FL
West Palm Beach, FL
Malin, Jeffrey D. ... **Southfield, MI**
Malin, Jennifer L. ... **New York, NY**
Malin, Lois K. ... Garden City, KS
Malin, Madonna M. ... New Brunswick, NJ
Malin & Malin, P.C. ... **McKinney, TX**
Malin, Mark ... **Menlo Park, CA**
Malin, Martin H. ... Chicago, IL
Malin, Marvin ... Woodbury, NY
Malin, Mary Catherine ... Department of State, Office of the Legal Adviser, GV
Malin, Max ... Plainville, KS
Malin, Michael H., Jr.
King Of Prussia, PA
Malin, Robert L. ... Orange, CA
Malin, Ronald H. ... **Los Angeles, CA**
Malin, Ronald W. ... Jamestown, NY
Malin, S. Hunter ... **Jacksonville, FL**
Malin, Scott H. ... **St. Louis, MO**
Malin, Serena M. ... Columbia, SC
Malin, Shelley J. ... **Walnut Creek, CA**
Malin, Steven C. ... **McKinney, TX**
Malin, Timothy J. ... **New York, NY**
Malina, Bernard ... **New York, NY**
Malina, Craig ... **Palo Alto, CA**
Malina, Hilary R. ... Detroit, MI
Malina, Mark R. ... **New York, NY**
Malina, Michael ... **New York, NY**
Malina, Paul D. ... Springfield, OH
Malina, Paul D., Co., L.P.A.
Springfield, OH
Malina, Shifra ... **New York, NY**
Malina, Steven M. ... **Chicago, IL**
Malina & Wolson ... **New York, NY**
Malinak, Robert J. ... **Houston, TX**
Malinas, Ruth Greenfield
San Antonio, TX
Malinasky, Laura A. ... **Palo Alto, CA**
Malinchak, Nicholas ... Arlington, VA
Maline, Michael D. ... **New York, NY**
Malinen, Eric
Federal Communications Commission, Office of Communications Business Opportunities, GV
Maliner, Martin M., Jr. ... Philadelphia, PA
Malingagio, Paul S. ... **Los Angeles, CA**
Malinger, David N. ... **Chicago, IL**
Malinger, Marc Eric ... Austin, TX
Maliniak, Abbie P. ... **Los Angeles, CA**
Maliniak, Donald W. ... **Memphis, TN**
Malino, Morgan E. ... **Baton Rouge, LA**
Malinofsky, Leon W., Jr. ... Northampton, MA
Malinoski, Lynn A. ... **Philadelphia, PA**
Malinou, Martin ... Providence, RI
Malinovsky, Jennifer D. ... **Atlanta, GA**
Malinowski, Adam J. ... Malden, MA
Malinowski, Andrea V. ... **Wilmington, DE**
Malinowski, Arthur A. ... Chicago, IL
Malinowski, Daniel D. ... Allison Park, PA
Malinowski, Gerald T. ... Detroit, MI
Malinowski, James F. ... Taylor, MI
Malinowski, Johanna S. ... **Trumbull, CT**
Malinowski, Joseph M. ... **Los Angeles, CA**
Malinowski, Joseph P.
Montgomery Village, MD
Malinowski, Leonard J. ... Lansing, MI
Malinowski, Michael M. ... **Wyoming, MI**
Malinowski, S. John ... West Hartford, CT
Malinowski, S. John, P.C.
West Hartford, CT
Malinowski, Shelley ... **Chicago, IL**
Malinowski, Sybil C. ... Chicago, IL
Malinowski, Thomas Edward ... Albany, NY
Malinski, Daniel R. ... **Phoenix, AZ**
Malinski, Norman ... Miami, FL
Malinski, Norman, P.A. ... Miami, FL
Malinsky, Charles W., Jr. ... Kenosha, WI
Malinzak, Edward ... Grand Rapids, MI
Malir, Nancy Jean ... Landover, MD
Malis, Daniel ... Malden, MA
Malis, George M. ... **Detroit, MI**
Malis, Henry ... Lawrence, MA
Malis, Jonathan M. ... Washington, DC
Malis, Michelle C.
Department of Labor, GV
Malis, Robert H. ... **Philadelphia, PA**
Malis, Stuart R. ... Lexington, MA
Malis, William A. ... South Pasadena, CA
Malish, Jedd S. ... **New Orleans, LA**
Maliska, Thomas P. ... Palo Alto, CA
Maliskas, Edward G. ... Homestead, FL
Maliszewski, Edward J., Jr. ... Oak Park, IL
Maliszewski, Gerald ... **San Diego, CA**
Malito, Robert J. ... **Albany, NY**
Garden City, NY
New York, NY
Malito, Vincent A. ... Central Islip, NY
Malitz, Jeanne M. ... **San Diego, CA**
Malitz, Steven H. ... **Hartford, CT**
Malitz, Steven N. ... **Chicago, IL**
Malitzis, John F. ... Washington, DC
Maliver, Deborah ... Pittsburgh, PA
Malivert, Edens ... **New York, NY**
Malizia, Anthony M. ... Farmington Hills, MI
Malizia, Deborah A. ... **Raleigh, NC**
Malizia, Paul J. ... Emporium, PA

Malizia, Samuel J. ... **Washington, DC**
State College, PA
Malizia Spidi & Fisch, PC
Washington, DC
State College, PA
Malk, Arnold B. ... **Deerfield, IL**
Malk, Charles R. ... Chicago, IL
Malk, Steven A. ... Santa Ana, CA
Malka, Edmond S. ... Old Bridge, NJ
Malka, Joseph William ... Sarasota, FL
Malkames Law Offices ... **Allentown, PA**
Malkames, Mark ... **Allentown, PA**
Malkames, William G. ... **Allentown, PA**
Malkames, William Kurt ... **Allentown, PA**
Malkan, Jeffrey D. ... Chicago, IL
Malkani, Latika ... Oakland, CA
Malkani, Robert G. ... New York, NY
Malkani, Shirin ... **New York, NY**
Malkasian, Hicinbothem, Brigham & Stein
Boston, MA
Framingham, MA
Malkemes, Janet R.
Department of State, GV
Malkemus, Charles M. ... Boston, MA
Malkerson, Bruce D. ... **Minneapolis, MN**
Malkerson Gilliland Martin, LLP
Minneapolis, MN
Malkiewich, Lorne ... Carson City, NV
Malkiewicz, Michael J. ... **Dover, DE**
Malkin, Andrea N. ... **Memphis, TN**
Malkin, Arthur D. ... Lake Hiawatha, NJ
Malkin, Arthur N. ... **Washington, DC**
Malkin, Bradley R. ... Douglasville, GA
Malkin, Brian J.
Department Of Health And Human Services, Food & Drug Administration, GV
Malkin, Brian Samuel ... Wexford, PA
Malkin, Cary J. ... **Chicago, IL**
Malkin, David ... **New York, NY**
Malkin, David, P.C., Law Offices of
New York, NY
Malkin, Deborah A. ... Santa Cruz, CA
Malkin, Earle A. ... Chicago, IL
Malkin, Eugene ... Bardonia, NY
Malkin, Gloria J.
Administrative Office Of The United States Courts, GV
Malkin, Howard I. ... Chicago, IL
Malkin, Jay K. ... **Denver, CO**
Malkin, Jennifer ... Cleveland, OH
Malkin, Jerrold A. ... Salinas, CA
Malkin, Joel D.
General Services Administration, Office of Regional Counsel, GV
Malkin, Joseph M. ... **San Francisco, CA**
Malkin, Karen Anne
Department Of The Interior, National Park Service, GV
Malkin, Kenneth M. ... Bay City, MI
Malkin, Laurie Claire ... **New York, NY**
Malkin, Leonard M. ... **Chicago, IL**
Malkin, Martin J. ... San Rafael, CA
Malkin, Melissa
Research Triangle Park, NC
Malkin, Michael L. ... **Youngstown, OH**
Malkin, Michael M. ... **New York, NY**
Malkin, Michelle L. ... **Seattle, WA**
Malkin, Peter L. ... **New York, NY**
Malkin, Rachel E. ... **Washington, DC**
Malkin, Rachel E. ... **Bethesda, MD**
Malkin, Reed L. ... Memphis, TN
Malkin, Robert G. ... **St. Louis, MO**
Malkin, Sandra L. ... **Atlanta, GA**
Malkin, Seth ... Springfield, NJ
Malkin, Seymour F. ... Nanuet, NY
Malkin, Sherwin J. ... Chicago, IL
Malkin, Sherwin J., Ltd. ... Chicago, IL
Malkin, Stacy A. ... Dallas, TX
Malkinson, Carol E. ... Minneapolis, MN
Malkmus, Brian D. ... **Kansas City, MO**
Springfield, MO
Malkmus, Deborah A. ... Springfield, MO
Malko, Simon R. ... **New York, NY**
Malkoff, Solomon ... Youngstown, OH
Malkoff, Tamara L. ... **Columbus, OH**
Malkofsky, Laura E. ... **San Francisco, CA**
Malkoon Cammarata, Maria
Fort Lauderdale, FL
Malkoski, Kathleen M ... **Holland, OH**
Malkovich, Michael ... Northampton, MA
Malkowski, John D. ... Tampa, FL
Malkowski, Lynn Morrow ... Crown Point, IN
Malks, Chaim S. ... Brooklyn, NY
Malkus, Roger L. ... Torrance, CA
Mall, Beulah P. ... Lancaster, PA
Mall, Deborah ... Monterey, CA
Mall, James R. ... **Pittsburgh, PA**
Mall, Kenneth G. ... **Jacksonville, FL**
Mall, Loren L. ... **Denver, CO**
Mall, William J., III ... **Irvine, CA**
Mallace, Anthony N. ... Audubon, NJ
Mallafre, Consuelo Maria ... New York, NY
Mallah, Evan M. ... **New York, NY**
Mallah, John D. ... **Miami Beach, FL**
Mallah, Mark Edward ... **San Francisco, CA**
Mallam, Mansour & Hager
Niagara Falls, NY
Mallam, Whitney W. ... Niagara Falls, NY
Mallamad, Jeffery M. ... **Indianapolis, IN**
Mallamo, Herbert ... Tucson, AZ
Mallams, Rodney L. ... Houston, TX
Mallamud, Jonathan ... Camden, NJ
Mallaney, Michael P. ... **Des Moines, IA**
Mallano, Robert M. ... Los Angeles, CA
Mallard, Charles A. ... **Amarillo, TX**
Mallard, Damian B. ... **Fort Lauderdale, FL**
Mallard, David S. ... Terrell, TX
Mallard, D. D. ... Boulder, CO

Mallard, E. Earl ... Monroe, GA
Mallard, E. Earl, P.C. ... Monroe, GA
Mallard, E. Lynwood ... **Charlotte, NC**
Mallard, Heather K. ... **Raleigh, NC**
Mallard, Jack E. ... Marietta, GA
Mallard, Jay A. ... Angleton, TX
Mallard, John E. ... Fairfield, IA
Mallard, John H. ... Centerville, TX
Mallard, Richard A. ... Statesboro, GA
Mallard, Robert R. ... Charleston, SC
Mallard, Sara Beth ... Miami, FL
Mallard, Vidian C. ... **Miami, FL**
Mallard, Wade V., Jr. ... **Atlanta, GA**
Mallare, Frank L. ... Jamestown, NY
Mallare, Vincent A. ... Jamestown, NY
Mallas, George W. ... Baltimore, MD
Mallatt, James C. ... **Milwaukee, WI**
Mallea, Kenneth L. ... **Boise, ID**
Mallea & Scrivner, P.L.L.C. ... **Boise, ID**
Nampa, ID
Malleck, Joseph W. ... Dearborn, MI
Mallek, Conrad F. ... Yuma, AZ
Mallek, Robert A., Jr. (Inc.) ... **Fresno, CA**
Mallen, Barry E. ... **Los Angeles, CA**
Mallen, David A. ... Los Angeles, CA
Mallen, David E. ... Orlando, FL
Mallen, John F. ... Saratoga, CA
Mallen, Michael C. ... **Chattanooga, TN**
Mallen, Patricia L. ... El Cajon, CA
Mallen, Richard F. ... Chicago, IL
Mallen, Richard F., & Associates, Ltd.
Chicago, IL
Mallen, Richard T. ... Taunton, MA
Mallen, Ronald E. ... **San Francisco, CA**
Mallen, Toby Rose ... **Los Angeles, CA**
Mallenbaum, David N. ... New York, NY
Mallenbaum, Sandra L. ... **New York, NY**
Mallenbaum, Stephan J. ... **New York, NY**
Mallender, Fred, II ... **Bloomfield Hills, MI**
Mallender, William Drew ... **McLean, VA**
Mallender, William H. ... Phoenix, AZ
Maller, Brant K. ... **New York, NY**
Maller, Daniel K. ... Falls Church, VA
Maller, Jay A. ... New York, NY
Maller, John M. ... Pebble Beach, CA
Maller, Karen E. ... **St. Petersburg, FL**
Maller, Kevin J. ... **St. Petersburg, FL**
Mallernee & Branch, L.L.P. ... **Atlanta, GA**
Mallernee, Kenneth A. ... Atlanta, GA
Mallernee, Rollin E., II ... **Atlanta, GA**
Mallers, George A., II ... Dallas, TX
Mallers, Peter G. ... **Fort Wayne, IN**
Mallers, Thomas J. ... Chicago, IL
Mallery, Daniel C. ... **Los Angeles, CA**
Mallery, Joseph A., Jr. ... Seattle, WA
Mallery, Kevin P. ... Farmington, CT
Mallery & Mallery ... Cobleskill, NY
Mallery, Mark N. ... **New Orleans, LA**
Mallery, Michael P. ... **Fresno, CA**
Mallery, Nancy A. ... New York, NY
Mallery, Nancy B. ... Hartford, CT
Mallery, Peter C. ... Albuquerque, NM
Mallery, Richard K. ... **Phoenix, AZ**
Mallery, Roger H. ... Cobleskill, NY
Mallery & Stern ... Los Angeles, CA
Mallery, Susan J. ... Cobleskill, NY
Mallery, Terry M. ... **Monterey, CA**
Mallery, Terry M., A Professional Law Corporation ... **Monterey, CA**
Mallery, Thomas F. ... **Milwaukee, WI**
Wausau, WI
Mallery, William C., Jr. ... Lindenhurst, NY
Mallery & Zimmerman, S.C. ... **Merrill, WI**
Milwaukee, WI
Mosinee, WI
Wausau, WI
Mallet, Jerry L. ... Lafayette, LA
Mallet, William M. ... McAllen, TX
Mallett, Betty A. ... **Jackson, MS**
Mallett, Bradley H. ... **Claremore, OK**
Mallett & Brown ... Seattle, WA
Mallett, Conrad L., Jr. ... Detroit, MI
Mallett, Donald A. ... Seattle, WA
Mallett, Edward A. ... Houston, TX
Mallett, G. Kevin ... San Francisco, CA
Mallett, Jacqueline S ... Columbus, OH
Mallett, Janet Brown ... Indianapolis, IN
Mallett, J. C. ... Oklahoma City, OK
Mallett, Jeanne M. ... Columbus, OH
Mallett, Kristi A. ... **Manchester, CT**
Mallett, Richard M. ... Stockton, CA
Mallett, Robert D. ... Amarillo, TX
Mallett, Robert F. ... **Orlando, FL**
Mallett, Thomas E. ... **Monterey, CA**
Mallette, James T. ... **Jackson, MS**
Mallette, John M., Jr. ... **Atlanta, GA**
Mallette & Libonati ... San Mateo, CA
Mallette, Linda L. ... San Mateo, CA
Mallette, Malcolm Carroll
Indianapolis, IN
Mallette, Pope S. ... **Oxford, MS**
Mallette, Pozzi & Cihal ... Victoria, TX
Mallette, Thomas J. ... Jackson, MS
Mallette, Weldon B. ... Victoria, TX
Malley, Andrea L. ... Phoenix, AZ
Malley, Anne M. ... **Clearwater, FL**
Malley, Brendan J. ... **New York, NY**
Malley, Colleen C. ... Pittsburgh, PA
Malley, Eileen M. ... **San Francisco, CA**
Malley, George T. ... Hampton, VA
Malley, J. Wallace, Jr. ... Montpelier, VT
Malley, James M. ... Pittsburgh, PA
Malley, John F., III ... **San Juan, PR**
Malley, John J. ... **New York, NY**
Malley, Joseph A., III ... Media, PA
Malley, Joseph A., III, P.C. ... Media, PA
Malley, Katharine C. ... Jackson, MS
Malley, Keith ... Arlington, VA

Malley, Kingston E., Jr. ....Worthington, OH
Malley, Lynn M. ....Columbia, MO
Malley, Mark D. ....Thomaston, CT
Malley, Mary Catherine ....Buffalo, NY
Malley, Michael P. ....Ann Arbor, MI
Malley, Patricia A. ....Towanda, PA
Malley, Robert J. ....Boston, MA
Malley, Stephen A., Law Offices Of
Los Angeles, CA
Malley, Thomas E. ....Camarillo, CA
Malley, William G. ....Washington, DC
Mallgrave, Deborah ....Irvine, CA
Mallgren, Anthony K. ....Denver, CO
Mallgren & Associates, P.C. ....Denver, CO
Mallia Law Firm ....Houston, TX
Mallia, Michael P. ....Houston, TX
Mallia & Moore, P.C. ....Houston, TX
Mallia, Wayne J. ....Galveston, TX
Mallia, William E. ....Houston, TX
Malliaros, George A. ....Dracut, MA
Mallick, Brenda Anne ....Clarks Summit, PA
Mallick, Craig D. ....Pittsburgh, PA
Mallick, Earl W. ....Washington, DC
Mallick, Projit ....New York, NY
Mallick, Robert Paul ....Springfield, MA
Mallicoat, Robt. R. ....Beverly Hills, CA
Mallie, Michael J. ....Sunnyvale, CA
Denver, CO
Mallien, James C. ....Milwaukee, WI
Malliet, Jerome T. ....Wethersfield, CT
Malliet, Susan E. ....Hartford, CT
Mallin, Barry, & Associates ....New York, NY
Mallin, Christopher J. ....Bedford Heights, OH
Mallin, Harry B. ....Kansas City, MO
Mallin, Joel ....New York, NY
Mallin, Joel M. ....New York, NY
Mallin, John R. ....Hartford, CT
Mallin, Joshua L. ....New York, NY
Mallin, Kenneth J. ....St. Louis, MO
Mallin, Letitia J.
Department of Justice, GV
Mallin, Michael ....Northfield, NJ
Mallin, Robert H., P.C. ....Phoenix, AZ
Mallin, Robert S. ....Chicago, IL
Mallin, Sam Z. ....Hackensack, NJ
Mallin, Thomas W. ....Schaumburg, IL
Mallin, William B. ....Pittsburgh, PA
Mallinckrodt & Mallinckrodt
Salt Lake City, UT
Mallinckrodt, Philip A. ....Kansas City, MO
Salt Lake City, UT
Mallinckrodt, Robert R. ....Kansas City, MO
Salt Lake City, UT
Malling, Gerald V. ....Greenville, MI
Mallinger, Burton J. ....Richmond, VA
Mallinger, Jeffrey D. ....Englewood, NJ
Mallinger, Larry A. ....Riverwoods, IL
Mallinger, Martin R. ....Boca Raton, FL
Mallinger, Martin R., P.A.
Boca Raton, FL
Mallini, Joseph J., Jr. ....Columbia, SC
Mallinoff, Laura Jenifer ....Newport, RI
Mallios & Associates, P.C. ....Austin, TX
Mallios, Dimitri P. ....Washington, DC
Rockville, MD
Mallios, George J. ....Austin, TX
Mallios, John C. ....Dallas, TX
Mallios, Stoddard & Weber ....Dallas, TX
Mallis, Robert P. ....Decatur, GA
Mallis, Steven ....New York, NY
Mallison, Stanley S. ....San Francisco, CA
Mallo, Gary S. ....Boulder, CO
Mallo, George D. ....Akron, OH
Mallo, Ted A. ....Akron, OH
Mallon & Associates, P.C. ....Evergreen, CO
Mallon, Barbara A. ....Chicago, IL
Mallon & Blatcher, A Professional
Corporation ....Media, PA
Philadelphia, PA
Mallon, Clifford P. ....Chicago, IL
Mallon, David J., Jr. ....Indianapolis, IN
Mallon, Deirdre ....Newton, MA
Mallon & DiCara, P.C. ....Barrington, IL
Mallon, George E. ....Kansas City, KS
Mallon, George E., P.A. ....Kansas City, KS
Mallon, Gordon ....Burns, OR
Mallon, Gregory M. ....Folsom, PA
Mallon, James C. ....Evergreen, CO
Mallon, Jeffrey M., (P.C.) ....Birmingham, MI
Mallon, John J. ....Troy, MI
Mallon, John V. ....Secaucus, NJ
Mallon & Johnson, P.C. ....Chicago, IL
Mallon, Joseph T. ....Towson, MD
Mallon, Joseph T. ....Media, PA
Philadelphia, PA
Mallon, Keri Lyn ....Colorado Springs, CO
Mallon, Kevin ....San Francisco, CA
Mallon, Lawrence G.
Huntington Beach, CA
Mallon, Linda ....Londonderry, NH
Mallon, Lisa A. ....Ballwin, MO
Mallon, Loren J. ....Chicago, IL
Mallon, Loren J., P.C. ....Chicago, IL
Mallon, Marc A. ....Atlanta, GA
Mallon, Maureen L. ....Providence, RI
Mallon, Michael T. ....Rochelle, IL
Mallon, Patricia C. ....Dearborn, MI
Mallon, Peter ....San Francisco, CA
Mallon, Thomas J. ....Freehold, NJ
Mallon, Vincent F. ....Louisville, KY
Mallon, Vincent F. ....King Of Prussia, PA
Mallon, Virginia D. ....Elmsford, NY
Mallon, W. Barry ....Buffalo, NY
Mallone, Joseph P. ....Jefferson, OH
Mallonee, Bruce C. ....Bangor, ME
Mallonee, John D. ....Bradenton, FL
Mallonee, Paul G. ....Fayetteville, NC
Mallonee, Virginia B. ....Philadelphia, PA
Mallon-Link, Constance ....Charlotte, NC
Mallor, Andrew C. ....Bloomington, IN
Mallor Clendening Grodner & Bohrer LLP
Bedford, IN
Bloomington, IN
Nashville, IN
Mallor, Jane Pratt ....Bloomington, IN
Mallory, Arthur E., III ....Reno, NV
Mallory & Associates ....Los Angeles, CA
Mallory, Bobbi Tillmon ....Los Angeles, CA
Mallory, Bradley L. ....Harrisburg, PA
Mallory, Brenda ....Washington, DC
Mallory, C. King, III ....Washington, DC
Mallory, Carol Ann ....Memphis, TN
Mallory, Diane ....Hilliard, OH
Mallory, Earl K. ....Jupiter, FL
Mallory, Frank L. ....Irvine, CA
Mallory, George L. ....Little Rock, AR
Mallory, George L., Jr. ....Los Angeles, CA
Mallory, Gregory W. ....Portland, OR
Mallory, Harold D. ....San Antonio, TX
Mallory, James B., III ....Statesville, NC
Mallory, James R. ....Arlington, TX
Mallory, James R. ....Fort Worth, TX
Mallory, James R. ....Grapevine, TX
Mallory, Janice D. ....La Grange, GA
Mallory, Jeffrey B. ....Miami, FL
Mallory, Jennifer L. ....Columbia, SC
Mallory, Karen L. ....New York, NY
Mallory, Kim F. ....San Pablo, CA
Mallory, Lark T. ....Washington, DC
Mallory, Mark L. ....Manchester, NH
Mallory, Michael D. ....Everett, WA
Mallory, Michael W. ....New Orleans, LA
Mallory, Needham C. ....La Grange, GA
Mallory, Paul W. ....Lombard, IL
Mallory, Peter A. ....Panama City, FL
Mallory, Peter A., P.A. ....Panama City, FL
Mallory, Richard C. ....San Francisco, CA
Mallory, Richard S. ....Austin, TX
Mallory, Robert P. ....Los Angeles, CA
Mallory, Robert R. ....Detroit, MI
Mallory, Roger A. ....Orlando, FL
Mallory, Sandra L. ....Los Angeles, CA
Mallory, Sherri Denton ....Panama City, FL
Mallory, Susan L. ....Lansing, MI
Mallory, Thomas H., Jr. ....Columbus, OH
Mallory & Trice ....Thomaston, GA
Mallory, Truitt A. ....Thomaston, GA
Mallory, W. Barton, III ....Memphis, TN
Mallory and White ....Reno, NV
Mallory, William A. ....Kansas City, MO
Mallory, William A., A Professional
Corporation ....Kansas City, MO
Mallos, Paul Alexander ....Baltimore, MD
Mallot, Marie ....New York, NY
Mallouk, Peter A. ....Overland Park, KS
Mallove, Daniel P. ....Seattle, WA
Mallow, Carl S., Jr. ....Mesa, AZ
Mallow, David ....New York, NY
Mallow, Edward S. ....Jacksonville, FL
Atlanta, GA
Mallow, Gary D. ....Grove, OK
Mallow, Gary D., Inc. ....Grove, OK
Mallow, Gerald M. ....New York, NY
Mallow, Janet G. ....Tulsa, OK
Mallow, Konstam & Hager ....New York, NY
Mallow, Matthew J. ....New York, NY
Mallow, Michael L. ....Beverly Hills, CA
Mallow, Robert A. ....Miami, FL
Malloy, A. Colleen ....Trenton, NJ
Malloy, Alexandria ....Livermore, CA
Malloy, Alvin ....North Little Rock, AR
Malloy, Angela M. ....Miami, FL
Malloy & Battista, LLP ....Springfield, MA
Malloy, Charles Foster ....Dallas, TX
Malloy, Charles J. ....St. Louis, MO
Malloy, Christopher P. ....New York, NY
Malloy, Cynthia M. Danielowich
Buchanan, VA
Malloy, Dorothy A. ....Villanova, PA
Malloy, Earlie L., III ....Brooklyn, NY
Malloy, Edward A., Jr. ....Cumberland, MD
Malloy, Edward C., III ....Gladwyne, PA
Malloy, Eileen ....Washington, DC
Malloy, Elizabeth A. ....Philadelphia, PA
Malloy, Frances ....Brooklyn, NY
Malloy, George A. ....Stockton, CA
Malloy, Gerald ....Florence, SC
Hartsville, SC
Malloy, Harold C. ....Georgetown, TX
Malloy, Howard P. ....Stamford, CT
Malloy, J. Michael, III ....Troy, MI
Malloy, J. Robert ....Cleveland, OH
Malloy, James B. ....Ogden, IA
Malloy, James F. ....Philadelphia, PA
Malloy, James W. ....Chicago, IL
Malloy, Jane E. ....Fort Wayne, IN
Malloy, Jennie S. ....Fort Lauderdale, FL
Miami, FL
Malloy, John A. ....Washington, DC
Malloy, John Cyril ....Miami, FL
Malloy, John Cyril, III
Fort Lauderdale, FL
Miami, FL
Malloy, John J. ....Miami, FL
Malloy, John J. ....Williamstown, MA
New York, NY
Malloy, John P. ....Washington, DC
Malloy, Joseph H. ....Canton, MA
Malloy, Kevin Martin ....Somerdale, NJ
Philadelphia, PA
Malloy, Kevin R. ....Chicago, IL
Malloy Law Firm ....Clarion, IA
Goldfield, IA
Malloy & Malloy ....Columbia, MD
Ellicott City, MD
Malloy & Malloy, Inc. ....Tulsa, OK
Malloy & Malloy, P.A.
Fort Lauderdale, FL
Miami, FL
Malloy, Marcia Harris ....Miami, FL
Malloy, Marianne Sara ....Pittsburgh, PA
Malloy, Marie A. ....Columbus, OH
Malloy, Mark D. ....St. Paul, MN
Malloy, Martin G. ....Philadelphia, PA
Malloy, Martin L. ....Vandalia, OH
Malloy, Mary A. ....Cleveland, OH
Malloy, Mary Gene ....Pittsburgh, PA
Malloy, Marybeth ....East Meadow, NY
Malloy, Matthew M. ....Cincinnati, OH
Malloy, Michael D. ....Short Hills, NJ
Malloy, Michael E. ....Reno, NV
Malloy, Michael J. ....Media, PA
Malloy, Michael P. ....New York, NY
Malloy, Michael P. ....Philadelphia, PA
Malloy, Michael S. ....Charlotte, NC
Malloy, P. Athena ....Largo, MD
Malloy, Pat, Jr. ....Tulsa, OK
Malloy, Patrice S. ....Miami, FL
Malloy, Patrick D. ....Ellicott City, MD
Malloy, Patrick J., III ....Tulsa, OK
Malloy, Paul F. ....Newton, MA
Malloy, Paul L., Jr. ....Houston, TX
Malloy, Paul V. ....Grafton, WI
Malloy, Peter ....New York, NY
Malloy, Reginald D. ....Ellicott City, MD
Malloy, Robert J. ....Marlton, NJ
Malloy, Robert P. ....Goldfield, IA
Malloy, Robert P. ....Cincinnati, OH
Malloy, Robin Paul ....New Orleans, LA
Malloy, Robin Slapin ....Park Ridge, NJ
Malloy, Samantha D. ....Fort Lauderdale, FL
Malloy, Stephan P. ....Bethesda, MD
Malloy & Sullivan, Lawyers Prof. Corp.
Manchester, NH
Hingham, MA
Malloy, Terry P., & Associates ....Tulsa, OK
Malloy, Thomas E. ....Westlake, OH
Malloy, Timothy F. ....Tampa, FL
Malloy, Timothy J. ....Chicago, IL
Malloy, Timothy O. ....Schererville, IN
Malloy, William F. ....Springfield, MA
Malloy, William H., Jr. ....Alexandria, VA
Malloy-Good Associates ....West Chester, PA
Malloy-Good, Julia ....West Chester, PA
Malloy-Pogoda, Kelly L. ....Albany, NY
Mallozzi, Linda E. ....Union, NJ
Mallozzi, Stephen A. ....Philadelphia, PA
Mallue, Henry E., Jr. ....Williamsburg, VA
Mallue, James ....St. Petersburg, FL
Mallut, Daniel ....Encino, CA
Mally, James F. ....Chicago, IL
Mallya, Lynne E. ....Los Angeles, CA
Mallyck, E. Theodore ....Washington, DC
Malm, C. Michael ....Boston, MA
Malm, Denis R. ....Lake Havasu City, AZ
Malm, Eric S. ....New York, NY
Malm, Gilbert M. ....Atlanta, GA
Malm, Jeffrey George ....Jasper, AR
Malm, John J. ....Wheaton, IL
Malm, Richard A. ....Des Moines, IA
Malm, Robert E. ....Pacific Palisades, CA
Malm, Roger C. ....Hallock, MN
Malm, Scott ....Stockton, CA
Malm, Scott A. ....Phoenix, AZ
Malm, Stephen M. ....Portland, OR
Malm, Timothy V. ....Milwaukee, WI
Malman & Associates ....Miami, FL
Malman, David A. ....West Chester, PA
Malman, Jerome S. ....Denver, CO
Malman, Jill A. ....Miami, FL
Malman, Laurie L. ....New York, NY
Malman, Lawrence M., (P.A.)
Coral Gables, FL
Malman, Myles H. ....Miami, FL
Malman, Robert L. ....Denver, CO
Malman, Ruth Cheryl ....Denver, CO
Malman, Thomas J. ....Morristown, NJ
Malman Trattler & Dehncke, P.C.
Denver, CO
Malmberg, Constantine F., III ....Dover, DE
Malmberg, Jan P. ....Logan, UT
Malmberg, John A. ....Concord, NH
Malmberg, Kristin L. ....Dallas, TX
Malmborg, Knute E., Jr.
Department of State,
Office of the Legal Adviser, GV
Malme, Jane Hamlett ....Hingham, MA
Malmgren, Lynn ....Philadelphia, PA
Malmgren, Richard E. ....Boise, ID
Malmgren, Robert T. ....Long Beach, CA
Malmgren, William H. ....Canton, IL
Malmin, Constance ....Boise, ID
Malmo, David L. ....Los Angeles, CA
Malmo, Donald A. ....Memphis, TN
Malmon, Alvin S. ....Minneapolis, MN
Malmon, Howard I. ....St. Paul, MN
Malmon, Stuart E.
Department of Housing and Urban
Development,
Office of General Counsel, GV
Malmquist & Geiger ....Morris, IL
Malmquist, Judy C. ....Battle Creek, MI
Malmquist, Kurt A. F., II ....Houston, TX
Malmquist, Michael J. ....Salt Lake City, UT
Malmquist, Nancy S. ....St. Johnsbury, VT
Malmquist, Ralph D. ....Glendale, CA
Malmquist, Robert W. ....Morris, IL
Malmquist, Timothy P. ....Morris, IL
Malmrose, Earl ....Arcadia, CA
Malmrose, John H. ....Williamsburg, VA
Malmsten, Albert C. ....Trenton, MI
Malmsten, Lisa Peskay ....Santa Ana, CA
Malmstrom, Carl E. ....Detroit Lakes, MN
Malmud, H. Gerald ....Merrick, NY
Malmud, H. Gerald, P.C. ....Merrick, NY
Malmud, Kenneth L. ....New York, NY
Malmud, Thomas J. ....New York, NY
Malnar, Patti Jo ....Cleveland, OH
Malnati, Michael C. ....Seattle, WA
Malnick, David, A Professional Corporation
San Jose, CA
Malnick, David E. ....San Jose, CA
Malnick, William A. ....Miami, FL
Malnik, Kenneth M. ....Gainesville, FL
Plantation, FL
Malnik & Salkin, P.A. ....Gainesville, FL
Plantation, FL
Malo, Aaron J. ....Costa Mesa, CA
Maloan, Michael T. ....Oklahoma City, OK
Maloan, William M. ....Dresden, TN
Maloch, Bruce D. ....Magnolia, AR
Malocu, Frank A. ....Dayton, OH
Malodonado, Roger J. ....Brooklyn, NY
Maloff, Elisa ....Dallas, TX
Maloff, Peter C. ....Bridgewater, NJ
Malofsky, Shelley F. ....Madison, WI
Maloid, William C. ....Cedar Grove, NJ
Malolepsy, Amber L. ....Santa Ana, CA
Malon, Henry C. ....New York, NY
Malon, Paul ....New York, NY
Malone, Adeline P. ....Rhinebeck, NY
Malone, Alan D. ....Nampa, ID
Malone, Albert C., Jr. ....Orange Park, FL
Malone, Albert D. ....Ridgeland, MS
Malone, Allen T. ....Memphis, TN
Malone, Andrew F. ....Blue Bell, PA
Malone, Anne V. ....New York, NY
Malone, Ault & Farell ....Toledo, OH
Malone, Bernard "Bud" ....Dallas, TX
Malone, Bernard J. ....Little Falls, NY
Malone, Bernard J., Jr. ....Albany, NY
Malone, Bernard L., Jr. ....Baton Rouge, LA
Malone, Brenda Richardson ....Detroit, MI
Malone, Brian C. ....Washington, DC
Malone, Brian F. ....Albany, NY
Malone, Brian J. ....Canton, OH
Malone, Bryan Lee ....Westlake Village, CA
Malone, C. Cyrus, III ....Atlanta, GA
Malone, C. Stephen ....Panama City Beach, FL
Malone, Catina Lynn ....Amarillo, TX
Malone, Cecil C., Jr. ....Atlanta, GA
Malone, Charles A. ....Fairfax, VA
Malone, Charles E. ....Norfolk, VA
Malone, Charles N. ....Baton Rouge, LA
Malone, Charles R. ....Tuscaloosa, AL
Malone, Christopher M. ....Richmond, VA
Malone, Clarence J. ....Topeka, KS
Malone, Clifford B., Jr., Law Offices of
Walnut Creek, CA
Malone, Clifford L. ....Wichita, KS
Malone, Clyde W., Jr. ....Torrance, CA
Malone, Cynthia ....San Antonio, TX
Malone, D. Drew ....Jackson, MS
Malone, Dale A. ....Boston, MA
Malone, Daniel ....New York, NY
Malone, Daniel B. ....Chicago, IL
Malone, Daniel L. ....New York, NY
Malone, Daniel P. ....Detroit, MI
Malone, Daniel R. ....El Paso, TX
Malone, Dannye W. ....Shreveport, LA
Malone, Darryl W. ....Houston, TX
Malone, David A. ....Bethesda, MD
Malone, David B. ....Covington, KY
Louisville, KY
Malone, David M. ....Washington, DC
Malone, David M. ....Little Falls, NY
Malone, David R. ....Fayetteville, AR
Malone, Dean G. ....Louisville, KY
Malone, Dean, Law Offices of, P.C.
Dallas, TX
Malone, Dennis Michael ....Trinidad, CO
Malone, Dennis Michael, P.C.
Trinidad, CO
Malone, Don Ross ....Vernon, TX
Malone, Douglas J. ....Denver, CO
Malone, Dwire & Jones ....Wichita, KS
Malone, E. Phillips, (P.S.C.)
Owensboro, KY
Malone, Edward F. ....Chicago, IL
Malone, Edward F. ....West Paterson, NJ
Malone, Edward J. ....Troy, NY
Malone, E. L. (Pat) ....Wichita, KS
Malone, Elizabeth M. ....Southfield, MI
Malone, Ellen J. ....Buffalo, NY
Malone, Ernest R., Jr. ....New Orleans, LA
Malone, Francis A. ....Spokane, WA
Malone, G. Michael ....Raleigh, NC
Malone, Gail Fisk ....Bangor, ME
Malone, Gary J. ....New York, NY
Malone, Gayle Ingram, Jr. ....Nashville, TN
Malone, Gerard F. ....Boston, MA
Malone, Gilbert G. ....York, PA
Malone, H. Christopher ....Rockville, MD
Malone, Harold B. (Hal) ....Wichita, KS
Malone, Harry N., III ....Washington, DC
Malone, Hugh Frank ....Columbia, SC
Malone, J. Michael ....Orlando, FL
Malone, James F. ....St. Louis, MO
Malone, James F., III ....Wexford, PA
Malone, James L. ....Cleveland, OH
Malone, James L., III ....Chicago, IL
Malone, James R., Jr. ....Haverford, PA
Malone, Jennifer ....Santa Ana, CA
Malone, John Anthony
North Hollywood, CA
Malone, John H. ....Enfield, CT
Malone, John I., Jr. ....Greensboro, NC
Malone, John James ....Feasterville, PA
Malone, John M. ....St. Paul, MN
Malone, John P., Jr. ....Cleveland, OH
Malone, John S. ....San Francisco, CA
Malone, John W. ....Lithonia, GA

Malone, Joy A. ... Little Falls, NY
Malone, Judith A. ... Boston, MA
Malone, Julianne M. ... Lilburn, GA
Malone, Kathleen Kelly ... Cincinnati, OH
Malone, Kathleen M. ... San Francisco, CA
Malone, Kenneth L. ... San Antonio, TX
Malone, Kevin A. ... Fort Lauderdale, FL
Malone, Kevin M. ... Atlanta, GA
Malone, Kimberlyn Patrice ... Huntsville, AL
Malone, Kristina Dalton ... Louisville, KY
Malone, Larchuk & Middleman ... Wexford, PA
Malone, Laura ... Seattle, WA
Malone, Laurie A. ... Cleveland, OH
Malone Law Firm, P.C. ... El Paso, TX
Malone Law Firm, P.L.L.C. ... Ridgeland, MS
Malone, Lawrence G. ... Albany, NY
Malone, Linda A. ... Williamsburg, VA
Malone, Lois L. ... Cary, NC
Malone, Louis P., III ... Washington, DC
Malone, Lucy Fay ... Florence, AL
Malone, Lynn W. ... Waco, TX
Malone, Lynne B. ... Baltimore, MD
Malone, M. Kristin ... Philadelphia, PA
Malone & Mailander ... Slayton, MN
Malone & Malone ... Cleveland, OH
Malone & Malone, LLP ... Little Falls, NY
Malone, Margaret A. ... Columbus, OH
Malone, Margaret V. ... New York, NY
Malone, Maridelle S. ... Scottsville, VA
Malone, Marion ... Los Angeles, CA
Malone, Mark J. ... Skillman, NJ
Malone, Mark K. ... White Plains, NY
Malone, Martin R. ... Visalia, CA
Malone, Mary C. ... Virginia Beach, VA
Malone, Mary Laska ... Mount Clemens, MI
Malone, Matthew E. ... Department of Defense, Defense Legal Services Agency, GV
Malone, Maureen Gail ... Atlanta, GA
Malone, Megan Miner ... Albany, NY
Malone, Melody Y. ... Charlotte, NC
Malone, Michael D. ... Columbia, SC
Malone, Michael G. ... San Francisco, CA
Malone, Michael G. ... Charlotte, NC
Malone, Michael J. ... Department of Defense, Defense Legal Services Agency, GV
Malone, Michael J. ... Lawrence, KS
Malone, Michael J. ... Findlay, OH
Malone, Michael J. P., III ... New York, NY
Malone, Michael L. ... Dallas, TX
Malone, Michael P. ... Southampton, NY
Malone, Michael P. ... Milwaukee, WI
Malone, Neal E. ... Sparks, MD
Malone & Neubaum ... York, PA
Malone, Orba Lee ... El Paso, TX
Malone, Owen J. ... Alexandria, VA
Malone, Pamela Brown ... Tulsa, OK
Malone, Patricia A. ... Towson, MD
Malone, Patrick A. ... Washington, DC
Malone, Patrick J. ... Jupiter, FL
Malone, Patrick J. ... Austin, TX
Malone, Patrick J., P.A. ... Jupiter, FL
Malone, Patrick M. ... Santa Monica, CA
Malone, Paul M. ... Slayton, MN
Malone, Paul R. ... San Francisco, CA
Malone, P.C. ... Tuscaloosa, AL
Malone, Philip P. ... Poulsbo, WA
Malone, Phillip R. ... San Francisco, CA
Malone, Randall K. ... Great Neck, NY
Malone, Raymond M. ... Cleveland, OH
Malone, Richard A. ... Swainsboro, GA
Malone, Richard M. ... Dayton, OH
Malone, Richard R. ... Toledo, OH
Malone, Richd. T. ... St. Paul, MN
Malone, Robbie ... Addison, TX
Malone, Robert B. ... Cleveland, OH
Malone, Robert G. ... St. Paul, MN
Malone, Robert H. ... Louisville, KY
Malone, Robert H., III ... Macon, GA
Malone, Robert J. ... Milford, CT
Malone, Robert J. ... St. Louis, MO
Malone, Robert J. ... Taos, NM
Malone, Robert J. ... Little Falls, NY
Malone, Robert K. ... Florham Park, NJ
Malone, Robert P. ... Boston, MA
Malone, Robert W. ... Akron, OH
Malone, Rod ... Raleigh, NC
Malone, Ronald Hayes ... San Francisco, CA
Malone, S. Caroline ... Texarkana, TX
Malone, S. Wade ... Atlanta, GA
Malone, Stephen J. ... New York, NY
Malone, Stephen K. ... Freeport, NY
Malone, Steven C. ... San Bernardino, CA
Malone, Steven C. ... Waltham, MA
Malone, Steven E. ... Victor, NY
Malone, Susan Hileman ... Pittsburgh, PA
Malone, Susan P. ... Chicago, IL
Malone, T. Dean ... Dallas, TX
Malone, T. Omar ... Miami, FL
Malone, Tauber & Sohn, P.C. ... Freeport, NY
Malone, Teresa Dillard ... Atlanta, GA
Malone, Terrance A. ... Los Angeles, CA
Malone, Terry J. ... Dodge City, KS
Malone, Terry L. ... Wichita, KS
Malone, Theresa Ann ... St. Louis, MO
Malone, Thomas E. ... Wichita, KS
Malone, Thomas M. ... Detroit, MI
Malone, Thomas P. ... Denver, CO
Malone, Thomas P. ... Minneapolis, MN
Malone, Thomas P., & Associates, P.C. ... Denver, CO
Malone, Thomas W. ... Seattle, WA
Malone, Thomas William ... Atlanta, GA
Malone & Thompson ... Columbia, SC
Malone, Timothy E. ... Fort Worth, TX
Malone, Tracey Petriskie ... Bartlett, TN
Malone, W. Bruck ... Chicago, IL
Malone, W. Davis, III ... Dothan, AL
Malone, Wallace G. ... Houston, TX
Malone, William C., IV ... Orlando, FL
Malone, William C., IV, P.A. ... Orlando, FL
Malone, William J. ... Freeport, NY
Malone, William K. ... Littleton, CO
Malone, William K., P.C. ... Littleton, CO
Malone, William R. ... Washington, DC
Malone, William R., (P.C.) ... Madisonville, TX
Malone, Wm. G. ... Arlington, VA
Malone, Wm. T. ... Moscow, PA
Malone-Munoz, Tracie L. ... Woodland, CA
Maloney, A. Richard ... Redmond, WA
Maloney, Alyce E. ... Garden City, NY
Maloney, Amelia D. ... Chelmsford, MA
Maloney, Andrew G. ... New York, NY
Maloney, Andrew J. ... New York, NY
Maloney, Andrew J., III ... New York, NY
Maloney, Andrew K. ... House of Representatives, Congressional Assistants, GV
Maloney, Arthur J. ... Buffalo, NY
Maloney & Associates, P.C. ... New York, NY
Maloney, Barry C. ... Washington, DC
Maloney, Bean & Horn, P.C. ... Irving, TX
Maloney, Beth A. ... Bedford, MA
Maloney, Beth O'Neill ... Boston, MA
Maloney, Brian C. ... Albany, NY
Maloney, Brian E. ... Cameron Park, CA
Maloney, Brian M. ... Green Bay, WI
Maloney, Brigid ... Buffalo, NY
Maloney, C. Vincent ... Chicago, IL
Maloney, Cathy Lovejoy ... Buffalo, NY
Maloney, Christopher ... Norristown, PA
Maloney, Christopher J. ... Bedford, NY
Maloney, Collin M. ... Tyler, TX
Maloney & Craven, P.C. ... Des Plaines, IL
Maloney, Daniel J. ... Toledo, OH
Maloney, Danyi and Davis ... Bethlehem, PA; Easton, PA
Maloney, Darren M. ... Hackensack, NJ
Maloney, David J. ... Birmingham, AL
Maloney, David M. ... Tallahassee, FL
Maloney, David P. ... Charlotte, NC
Maloney & Davis ... Urbana, IL
Maloney, Denis G. ... Boston, MA
Maloney, Denis J. ... Concord, NH
Maloney, Dennis ... Aberdeen, SD
Maloney, Dennis F. ... Towson, MD
Maloney, Dennis P. ... Bartow, FL
Maloney, Douglas C. ... Bristol, PA; Langhorne, PA
Maloney, Douglas J. ... San Francisco, CA
Maloney, Douglas P. ... Chicago, IL
Maloney, E. William, Jr. ... Des Plaines, IL
Maloney, Edward G., Jr. ... Sedro Woolley, WA
Maloney, Edward M. ... Chicago, IL; Skokie, IL
Maloney, Ellen H. ... Dorset, VT
Maloney, Emily ... Santa Cruz, CA
Maloney, Erin A. ... Riverside, CA
Maloney, Eugene M. ... New York, NY
Maloney, Frances J. ... Dallas, TX
Maloney, Frances Mary ... New York, NY
Maloney, Francis E., Jr. ... Syracuse, NY
Maloney, Francis J., III ... Portland, OR
Maloney, Frank ... Austin, TX
Maloney, Frank C., III ... Richmond, VA
Maloney, Frank E., Jr. ... Macclenny, FL
Maloney, Frank E., Jr., P.A. ... Macclenny, FL
Maloney, Gay Blackburn ... Decatur, AL
Maloney, George William ... Alamo, CA
Maloney, Graham ... San Francisco, CA
Maloney & Haggart ... Anchorage, AK
Maloney, Herbert F. ... Montgomery, AL
Maloney, H. T. ... Fort Lauderdale, FL
Maloney, Huennekens, Parks, Gecker & Parsons, A Professional Corporation ... Richmond, VA
Maloney, J. Michael ... Jackson, MS
Maloney, J. William ... Santa Monica, CA
Maloney, Jacqueline F. ... New Orleans, LA
Maloney, James ... North Wilkesboro, NC
Maloney, James A. ... Loves Park, IL
Maloney, James A. ... Worcester, MA
Maloney, James C. ... Coral Gables, FL
Maloney, James D., III ... Yakima, WA
Maloney, James Edward ... Houston, TX
Maloney, James H. ... Danbury, CT
Maloney, James H. ... Falls Church, VA
Maloney, James J. ... Bakersfield, CA
Maloney, James J. ... Little Silver, NJ
Maloney, James J. ... New York, NY
Maloney, James M. ... Hoboken, NJ; New York, NY
Maloney, James M. ... Williston Park, NY
Maloney, James P. ... Milwaukee, WI
Maloney, James R. ... Buffalo, NY
Maloney, James S. ... Denver, CO
Maloney, James T. ... Washington, DC
Maloney, Janice ... San Antonio, TX
Maloney, Jeanne M. ... Boston, MA
Maloney, Jennifer C. ... Washington, DC
Maloney, Jerry B. ... Grosse Ile, MI
Maloney, Joan E. ... Chicago, IL
Maloney, Joan Ellison ... Williamsville, NY
Maloney, JoAnn H. ... Minneapolis, MN
Maloney, John C. ... Wichita, KS
Maloney, John C., Jr. ... Morristown, NJ; New York, NY
Maloney, John E. ... Urbana, IL
Maloney, John F. ... Manhattan Beach, CA
Maloney, John F. ... Milwaukee, WI
Maloney, John K. ... Rochester, MI
Maloney, John L. ... St. Petersburg, FL
Maloney, John Michael ... Upper Marlboro, MD
Maloney, John P. ... Stamford, CT; New York, NY
Maloney, John P. ... New York, NY
Maloney, John T. ... Albany, NY
Maloney, John T., Jr. ... Honolulu, HI
Maloney, John T., (P.C.) ... Williamsville, NY
Maloney, John W. ... Elmira, NY
Maloney, Joseph E. ... Sacramento, CA
Maloney, Joseph E. ... New York, NY
Maloney, Joseph J. ... Bloomfield Township, MI
Maloney, Joseph M. ... Jacksonville, AL
Maloney, Judith Mathers ... Garden City, NY
Maloney, Julie A. ... Pittsburgh, PA
Maloney, Katherine L. ... Plainfield, IL
Maloney, Kathleen C. ... San Francisco, CA
Maloney, Kathleen R. ... Boston, MA
Maloney, Kathryn Ann ... Chicago, IL
Maloney and Katzman ... Morristown, NJ; Newark, NJ; Parsippany, NJ
Maloney, Kenneth T. ... Washington, DC
Maloney, Kevin M. ... Columbus, OH
Maloney, Kevin P. ... Wilmington, DE
Maloney, Kevin P. ... Buffalo, NY
Maloney, Kimberly D. ... Boise, ID
Maloney & Knox ... Washington, DC
Maloney, Kristen W. ... San Francisco, CA
Maloney, Larry ... Riverside, CA
Maloney, Larry J. ... Hartland, WI
Maloney, Liesl A. ... Detroit, MI
Maloney, Linda L. ... Fort Worth, TX
Maloney, Lindsay & McHugh ... Toledo, OH
Maloney, Lisa M. ... Philadelphia, PA
Maloney, Loran D. ... St. Louis, MO
Maloney, Lyn ... Covina, CA
Maloney, Lynn Duffy ... Washington, DC
Maloney, M. Cassin, Jr. ... New York, NY
Maloney, M. Susan ... Milwaukee, WI
Maloney & Maloney ... Aberdeen, SD; Britton, SD; Redfield, SD; Webster, SD
Maloney & Maloney, Law Offices of ... San Antonio, TX
Maloney, Margaretha ... Commerce City, CO
Maloney, Mari Brita ... New York, NY
Maloney, Maribeth ... New York, NY
Maloney, Marilyn C. ... New Orleans, LA
Maloney, Marilyn J. ... Minneapolis, MN
Maloney, Marilyn Marshall ... Aberdeen, SD
Maloney, Mark Daniel ... Decatur, AL
Maloney, Mark M. ... Atlanta, GA
Maloney, Mark R. ... Wichita, KS
Maloney, Martin & Mitchell, L.L.P. ... Houston, TX
Maloney, Mary D. ... Cleveland, OH
Maloney, Mary L. ... Mineola, NY; New York, NY; Smithtown, NY
Maloney, Marynell Baker ... San Antonio, TX
Maloney, Matthew A. ... Princeton, IL
Maloney, Matthew G. ... Washington, DC
Maloney, Matthew P. ... Washington, DC
Maloney, Maurice J. ... Red Bank, NJ
Maloney, Mehlman & Katz ... New York, NY
Maloney, Michael ... Washington, DC
Maloney, Michael B. ... Burbank, CA
Maloney, Michael D. ... Washington, DC
Maloney, Michael D. ... San Antonio, TX
Maloney, Michael F. ... Chicago, IL
Maloney, Michael F. ... Omaha, NE
Maloney, Michael G. ... Austin, TX
Maloney, Michael G. ... Fort Worth, TX
Maloney, Michael J. ... Los Angeles, CA
Maloney, Michael J. ... Orlando, FL
Maloney, Michael J. ... Liberty, MO
Maloney, Michael J. ... Oakhurst, NJ
Maloney, Michael J. ... Seattle, WA
Maloney, Michael J., P.A. ... Orlando, FL
Maloney, Michael J., P.C. ... Houston, TX
Maloney, Michael P. ... Lafayette, LA
Maloney, Michael P. ... Briarcliff Manor, NY
Maloney, Michael Patrick ... Cleveland, OH
Maloney, Michael S. ... Louisville, KY
Maloney, Michael V. ... Niagara Falls, NY
Maloney, Michelle Padden ... Austin, TX
Maloney, Millicent B. ... Denton, MD
Maloney & Mohsen ... Washington, DC
Maloney, Moira ... West Valley, NY
Maloney, Mullen & Leck, LLP ... Los Angeles, CA; Santa Monica, CA
Maloney, Murphy & McGrane ... Williston Park, NY
Maloney, Nancy ... Viera, FL
Maloney, Neil ... Lombard, IL
Maloney, Neilyn G., (Mrs.) ... Austin, TX
Maloney, P. Dennis ... Anchorage, AK
Maloney, Pamela C. ... Chicago, IL
Maloney, Pat ... San Antonio, TX
Maloney, Pat, Jr. ... San Antonio, TX
Maloney, Pat, Law Offices of, P.C. ... San Antonio, TX
Maloney, Patrice K. ... Bethlehem, PA
Maloney, Patricia ... San Antonio, TX
Maloney, Patricia A. ... Minneapolis, MN
Maloney, Patrick Brady ... New York, NY
Maloney, Patrick C. ... Greenwich, CT
Maloney, Patrick E. ... Waterbury, CT
Maloney, Patrick E. ... Chicago, IL
Maloney, Patrick J. ... Alameda, CA
Maloney, Patrick J. ... Chicago, IL
Maloney, Patrick J. ... Amherst, NY; Buffalo, NY
Maloney, Patrick J. ... New York, NY
Maloney, Patrick J., A Professional Corporation ... Alameda, CA
Maloney, Patrick M. ... San Diego, CA
Maloney, Patrick R. ... San Jose, CA
Maloney, Paul ... Bryn Mawr, PA
Maloney, Paul H. ... New York, NY
Maloney, Paul J. ... Washington, DC
Maloney, Paul M. ... St. Louis, MO
Maloney, Peter T. ... New York, NY
Maloney, Philip J. ... Washington, DC
Maloney, Philip J., Jr. ... Atlanta, GA
Maloney, Philip L. ... Los Angeles, CA
Maloney & Porcelli ... New York, NY
Maloney, Regina G. ... Washington, DC
Maloney, Rhonda Traver ... Boston, MA
Maloney, Richard J. ... Manchester, NH
Maloney, Richard Peter ... Boston, MA
Maloney, Robert B. ... Dallas, TX
Maloney, Robert E. ... Carpinteria, CA
Maloney, Robert E., Jr. ... Cheshire, CT
Maloney, Robert E., Jr. ... Portland, OR
Maloney, Robert J. ... Watertown, NY
Maloney, Robert P. ... Boston, MA
Maloney, Ruth Ann ... Cleveland, OH
Maloney, St. John & Atkins, LLC ... Waterbury, CT
Maloney, Schell & Eisenhauer, P.C. ... Watertown, NY
Maloney, Sean P. ... Executive Office Of The President, GV
Maloney, Sean T. ... Chicago, IL
Maloney, Stephen C. ... Canton, MA
Maloney, Susan E. ... New Bedford, MA
Maloney, Teresa A. ... San Francisco, CA
Maloney, Theodore R. ... Santa Barbara, CA
Maloney, Thomas B. ... St. Louis, MO
Maloney, Thomas B., (P.S.) ... Spokane, WA
Maloney, Thomas E. ... Naples, FL
Maloney, Thomas E., Jr. ... Parsippany, NJ
Maloney, Thomas H. ... Chicago, IL
Maloney, Thomas J. ... Salisbury, MD
Maloney, Thomas J. ... New York, NY
Maloney, Thomas J. ... Bethlehem, PA
Maloney, Thomas S. ... Baton Rouge, LA
Maloney, Thos. M. ... Quincy, MA
Maloney, Timothy F. ... Greenbelt, MD
Maloney, Timothy P. ... Chicago, IL
Maloney, Timothy P. ... Youngstown, OH
Maloney & Vernon, L.L.C. ... Jacksonville, AL
Maloney, Vincent J. ... Farmington Hills, MI
Maloney, W. Jeffrey ... Kansas City, MO
Maloney, Wallace E. ... Irving, TX
Maloney, William C. ... St. Augustine, FL
Maloney, William H., Jr. ... New York, NY
Maloney, William J. ... Washington, DC; New York, NY
Maloney, William Jeffrey ... Kansas City, MO
Maloney, William P. ... New York, NY
Maloney, William Power, Jr. ... Riverhead, NY
Maloney, William T. ... Toledo, OH
Maloney & Yurachek, P.C. ... Arlington, VA; Fairfax, VA; Falls Church, VA
MaloneyHuss, Mary M. ... Wilmington, DE
Maloney-Knauff, Patrice ... Northbrook, IL
Maloney-Sarle, Sharon L. ... Brick, NJ
Maloni, Jennifer ... New York, NY
Malonis, George Christo ... Dracut, MA
Malonis, Natalie B. ... Dallas, TX
Malono, Patricia Hart ... Tallahassee, FL
Malono, Steven M. ... Tallahassee, FL
Malonson, Jeffery K. ... Houston, TX
Maloof & Browne, LLP ... New York, NY
Maloof, David T. ... New York, NY
Maloof, Donna Ajlouni ... Washington, MI
Maloof, F. Paul ... Rockville, MD; McLean, VA
Maloof, George J. ... Boston, MA
Maloof, George M. ... Cleveland, OH
Maloof, Janet L. ... Boston, MA
Maloof, Mark J. ... Atlanta, GA
Maloof, Mark J., P.C. ... Atlanta, GA
Maloof, Maurice Ted ... Atlanta, GA
Maloof, Naji P. ... Prince Frederick, MD; Upper Marlboro, MD
Maloof, Nicholas G. ... Washington, MI
Maloof, Philip K. ... Worcester, MA
Maloof, Robert J. ... Hackensack, NJ
Maloof, Theodore E. ... Hackensack, NJ
Maloof, W. Michael ... Decatur, GA
Malooly, Daniel J. ... Newark, NJ
Maloon, Douglas C. T. ... Baltimore, MD
Maloon, Jeffrey L. ... Columbus, OH
Maloon, Jeffrey L., L.L.C. ... Columbus, OH; Dayton, OH
Maloon, Jerry L. ... Columbus, OH
Maloon, Jerry L., Co., L.P.A. ... Columbus, OH; Delaware, OH
Malorzo, Thomas V. ... Dallas, TX
Malos, Elwood M. ... Easton, PA
Malos, Stanley B. ... San Jose, CA
Malott, Alan M. ... Albuquerque, NM
Malott, James R., Jr. ... Globe, AZ
Malott Law Offices, A Professional Corporation ... Albuquerque, NM
Malott, Rex A. ... Stockton, CA
Malott, Richard A. ... Nevada City, CA
Malott, Russell E. ... Nevada City, CA
Malouf, C. Eric ... Jackson, MS
Malouf, Carl E. ... Logan, UT

Malouf, Donald J. ... **Dallas, TX**
Malouf, Joseph A. ... Fairfax, VA
Malouf Lynch Jackson & Swinson, A Professional Corporation ... **Dallas, TX**
Malouf, Marcellene J. ... Dallas, TX
Malouf, Marie A. ... Dallas, TX
Malouf, Melody LaVonne ... Amarillo, TX
Malouf, Michael J. ... Jackson, MS
Malouf, Michael J., Jr. ... Jackson, MI
Malouf, Philip E. ... **Los Angeles, CA**
Malouf, Raymond N. ... Logan, UT
Malouf, Rodney ... Virginia Beach, VA
Malouf, Scott L. ... **Rochester, NY**
Malouf, Stephen F. ... Dallas, TX
Malouf, Waldense D. ... Palm Harbor, FL
Malouff, Charles J., (P.C.) ... Pueblo, CO
Malouff, Phillip F., Jr. ... La Junta, CO
Rocky Ford, CO
Malouff, Theodore J. ... Pueblo, CO
Malouin, Marcia L. ... **Lansing, MI**
Malousek, Mark John ... **Omaha, NE**
Malovance, Gregory J. ... **Chicago, IL**
Malovany, Howard ... **Chicago, IL**
Malove, Robert David ... Miami, FL
Malovos, Kenneth M. ... **Sacramento, CA**
Malovos & Konevich ... **Los Altos, CA**
Malovos, Mark M. ... **Costa Mesa, CA**
Malovrh, Samuel E. ... **Wilmington, DE**
Bridgewater, NJ
Malow, Ellen B. ... **Houston, TX**
Malowitz, Wesley M. ... **Stamford, CT**
Westport, CT
Malowney, James H. ... San Diego, CA
Maloy, Bruce ... **Atlanta, GA**
Maloy, Charles T. ... Rochester, NY
Maloy, Heather C. ... Washington, DC
Maloy, James M. ... Akron, NY
Maloy & Jenkins ... **Atlanta, GA**
Maloy, John W. ... **Alexandria, LA**
Maloy, Kelly M. ... **Red Bluff, CA**
Maloy, Kevin M. ... **Wilmington, DE**
Maloy, Linda A. ... Old Orchard Beach, ME
Maloy, Lynn M. ... Elko, NV
Maloy, Mary Rich Lewis ... **Charleston, WV**
Maloy, Paul F. ... Arlington, MA
Maloy, Roberta A. ... Brooklyn, NY
Malpas, Gene Lawrence ... Middletown, MD
Malpass, Gerald D., Jr. ... **Houston, TX**
Malpass, Mary Anna ... **Myrtle Beach, SC**
Malpass, Mary T. ... **Detroit, MI**
Malpasuto, Joseph C. ... **Los Angeles, CA**
Malpede, Scott D. ... **Washington, DC**
Malpert, Rodney A. ... **Dallas, TX**
Malpezzi, Daniel J. ... **Harrisburg, PA**
Malpezzi, Donna Memmi ... Harrisburg, PA
Malphrus, Joseph N. ... Ridgeland, SC
Malphurs, Neil A. ... Alachua, FL
Malpiede, Glenn D. ... Denver, CO
Malrick, Russell A. ... Columbus, OH
Malsbury & Armenante, A Professional Corporation ... Allentown, NJ
Malsbury, Barclay P. ... Allentown, NJ
Malsbury, James W. ... Westlake Village, CA
Malsby, Felicia A. ... **Gig Harbor, WA**
Malsch, James R. ... Shreveport, LA
Malsch, Jeffrey M. ... **New York, NY**
Malsch, Martin G. ... **Washington, DC**
Malshuk, Stephen K. ... Seattle, WA
Malsin, Steven A. ... **New York, NY**
Malski, Michael, (P.C.) ... **Amory, MS**
Malsky, Herbert ... Belmont, MA
Malsman, Iris S. ... Los Angeles, CA
Malsnee, Jon S. ... Reading, PA
Malson, Chas. E. ... Bethany, OK
Malson, David A. ... Rushville, IN
Malson, David A., Jr. ... **Grand Rapids, MI**
Malson, Laurel Pyke ... **Washington, DC**
Malson Law Office, P.C. ... Rushville, IN
Malspeis, S. Philip ... Boca Raton, FL
Malstrom, Dan R. ... San Rafael, CA
Malstrom, Edward W. ... **Chicago, IL**
Malstrom, Robert A. ... **Chicago, IL**
Malt, R. Bradford ... **Boston, MA**
Malt, Valerie ... **St. Louis, MO**
Malta, Michelle V. ... Meridian, MS
Malta, Russell J. ... **Asbury Park, NJ**
Maltagliati, Janet L. ... **St. Louis, MO**
Maltbie, Theodore M. ... West Hartford, CT
Maltby, Jean M. ... Sebastopol, CA
Maltby, Jeremy ... **New York, NY**
Maltby, Richard Terry ... Marlette, MI
Maltby, Stephen J. O. ... **New York, NY**
Malter, Arnold S. ... Los Angeles, CA
Malter, Barry L. ... Washington, DC
Malter, Mark M. ... Canoga Park, CA
Malter, Melvin C. ... Oak Brook, IL
Malter, Michael W. ... **San Jose, CA**
Malter, Philip B. ... Riva, MD
Malters, James E. ... Worthington, MN
Maltese, Carl P. ... Smithtown, NY
Maltese, Joseph J. ... Staten Island, NY
Maltese, Nicholas S. ... Glendale, NY
Maltese, Peter O. ... Sidney, MT
Maltese, Serphin R. ... Glendale, NY
Maltese, Vincent P. ... **Woodbridge, NJ**
Maltezos, Jill G. ... Hinsdale, IL
Maltin, Aaron I. ... New York, NY
Maltin, Phillip R. ... **Los Angeles, CA**
Maltman, Reed, North, Ahrens & Malnati, Inc., P.S. ... **Seattle, WA**
Maltman, William L. ... **Seattle, WA**
Maltun, Dana R. ... Harbor City, CA
Maltz, Anne ... **New York, NY**
Maltz, David S. ... **Washington, DC**
Maltz, Earl Michael ... Camden, NJ
Maltz, Ellen Marsha Mandel
Los Angeles, CA
Maltz, Gerald ... **Tucson, AZ**
Maltz, Howard M. ... Jacksonville, FL
Maltz, Janis L. ... Longmeadow, MA
Maltz, Judah ... Kew Gardens, NY
Maltz, Mark E. ... **New York, NY**
Maltz, Richard M. ... New York, NY
Maltz, Robert M. ... Alameda, CA
Maltzahn, Robert C. ... Minneapolis, MN
Maltzer, Paul E. ... San Carlos, CA
Maltzman, Anamarie Marlow ... Miami, FL
Maltzman, Jeffrey B. ... **Miami, FL**
Maltzman, Marvin S. ... Los Angeles, CA
Maltzman, Richard D. ... **San Francisco, CA**
Maltzman, Seth P. ... Bala Cynwyd, PA
Malueg, Douglas J. ... Washington, DC
Maluenda, Annette V. ... **New York, NY**
Maluf, Edward F. ... **New York, NY**
Maluf, Farid R. ... **New York, NY**
Malugen, John C. ... San Diego, CA
Malugen, J. T. ... Dothan, AL
Malur, Shrinath ... Alexandria, VA
Malus, Leonce J., III ... New Orleans, LA
Malush, Gregory S. ... Minneapolis, MN
Maluski, Anthony E. ... Houston, TX
Malvar, Maximino P. ... Oceanside, NY
Malvasi, Maurus G. ... Youngstown, OH
Malveaux, Deborah F. ... **New Orleans, LA**
Malveaux, Mark A. ... **Dallas, TX**
Malveaux, Suzette M. ... **Washington, DC**
Malven, Mark G. ... **Chicago, IL**
Malvestuto, Louis A. ... Decatur, IL
Malvey, Edward M., Jr. ... Springfield, MA
Malvey, Kenneth A. ... Hastings, MN
Malvey, Steven C. ... **San Francisco, CA**
Malvey, William J. ... Neptune, NJ
Malvik, John ... **Rock Island, IL**
Malvin, Theodore J. ... New York, NY
Maly, Bonnie C. ... Berkeley, CA
Maly, George J., Jr. ... Dayton, OH
Maly, Kristen L. ... **St. Louis, MO**
Maly, Maureen M. ... **Minneapolis, MN**
Maly, Michael Kip ... **San Francisco, CA**
Maly, Michael P. ... Wickliffe, OH
Malyarov, Kira ... **New York, NY**
Malykont, Paul ... Los Osos, CA
Malyn, Harvey A. ... Houston, TX
Malynn, Brian Joseph ... Newburyport, MA
Malynn, Steven R. ... **Cleveland, OH**
Malynn, Todd M. ... **Los Angeles, CA**
Malys, James W. ... Oil City, PA
Malyshev, Peter Y. ... **San Francisco, CA**
Malysiak, James T. ... **Chicago, IL**
Malysiak, Spencer T. ... **Gold River, CA**
Malysiak, Spencer T., Law Corporation
Gold River, CA
Sacramento, CA
Malyska, John N. ... **Newark, NJ**
Malysz, Edward F. ... Mountain View, CA
Malysz, Mary Lee ... **San Jose, CA**
Malyuk, Michael A. ... Akron, OH
Malz, Leo ... New York, NY
Malz, Sanford Robert ... Brooklyn, NY
Malzahn, Angela ... **Milwaukee, WI**
Malzahn, Mark W. ... Anoka, MN
Malzberg, Norman ... Jersey City, NJ
Malzone, F. Richard ... Bowie, MD
Mamakos, James L. ... Los Angeles, CA
Mamalakis, Andreas ... Milwaukee, WI
Mamalakis, Damon P. ... **Los Angeles, CA**
Mamalian, Paul ... **Washington, DC**
Maman, Eric D. ... Los Angeles, CA
MaMana, Frank J. ... **Cleveland, OH**
Mamana, Joseph M. ... Washington, DC
Mamann, David ... Encino, CA
Mamantov, G. Mark ... **Knoxville, TN**
Mamas, Anthony N. ... Cherry Hill, NJ
Mamat, Frank T. ... **Detroit, MI**
Mamber, Milton ... North Miami Beach, FL
Mamedalin, Marie Cicconi ... Santa Ana, CA
Mamele, Richard L. ... **Sanford, FL**
Mamer, Edmond B. ... Anaheim, CA
Mamer, Stuart M. ... **Champaign, IL**
Mamet, Bernard M. ... Chicago, IL
Mamet, Mara J. ... San Francisco, CA
Mamey, Nelson G. ... Newport Beach, CA
Mamish, Julia ... Chevy Chase, MD
Mamlet, Alfred M. ... **Washington, DC**
Mammana, Salvatore J. ... New York, NY
Mammano, Philip J., Jr. ... Gibbsboro, NJ
Mammano, Robert Michael
San Bernardino, CA
Mammarella, Thomas ... **Wilmington, DE**
Mammarella, William C.
Bethany Beach, DE
Mammel, Christopher N. ... **Chicago, IL**
Mammel, Danielle N. ... **Detroit, MI**
Mammel, David B. ... Munster, IN
Mammel, Lisa A. ... **Palo Alto, CA**
Mammen, Christian E.
San Francisco, CA
Mammen, D. Dale ... La Grande, OR
Mammon, Richard R. ... **New York, NY**
Mammone, Anthony N. ... Syracuse, NY
Mammuth, Tod I. ... Bala Cynwyd, PA
Mamolen, Lon E. ... Atlantic City, NJ
Mamolito, Guy S. ... Shiremanstown, PA
Mamone, Edward J. ... Cleveland, OH
Mamone, Joseph A. ... Cleveland, OH
Mamone, Nicholas, Jr. ... Harrisburg, PA
Mamone, Russell B.
Federal Energy Regulatory Commission, Office of the General Counsel, GV
Mamorsky, Jeffrey D. ... **New York, NY**
Mamos, George E. ... Far Rockaway, NY
Mamos & Mamos ... Far Rockaway, NY
Mamos, Philip ... Far Rockaway, NY
Mamoulides, John M. ... Metairie, LA
Mamrack, E. Daniel ... **Euclid, OH**
Mamrack, Edward ... Cleveland, OH
Mamrosh, Ronald G. ... Farmington, CT
Man, Albon P., Jr. ... Palisades, NY
Man, Christopher D. ... **Washington, DC**
Man, Joseph C. ... New York, NY
Man, Kin Lum ... **New York, NY**
Man, Thomas Y. ... **Chicago, IL**
Man, Yat T. ... New York, NY
Mana & Bugatto ... San Francisco, CA
Mana, Lawr. S. ... San Francisco, CA
Mana, Stephen L. ... San Francisco, CA
Manafort, Kathleen B. ... Alexandria, VA
Managhan, Kathleen ... **Newport, RI**
Manahan & Bluth Law Office, Chartered
Mankato, MN
Manahan, David A. ... Napoleon, OH
Manahan, Elsie ... Los Angeles, CA
Manahan, James H. ... **Mankato, MN**
Manahan, James P. ... Lawrenceville, NJ
Manahan, Jonathan ... **Los Angeles, CA**
Manahan, Marsha A. ... Toledo, OH
Manahan, Matthew D. ... **Portland, ME**
Manahan, Michael C. ... Los Angeles, CA
Manahan, Michael J. ... **Toledo, OH**
Manahan, Patrick F. ... Delphi, IN
Manahan, Peter D. ... **Roseland, NJ**
Manahan, Pietrykowski, Bamman & DeLaney ... **Port Clinton, OH**
Toledo, OH
Manahan, Vincent D., III ... **Millburn, NJ**
Manak, Joseph M. ... **New York, NY**
Manaker, Alison L. ... Bryn Mawr, PA
Manalansan, Carlos G. ... **New York, NY**
Mañalich, Ramiro ... Naples, FL
Manalli, J. Christian ... Chicago, IL
Manankichian, Caroline S. ... Northridge, CA
Manansala, Antonio M. ... St. Louis, MO
Manar, Gerald T. ... Los Angeles, CA
Manara, Robert J. ... Reading, PA
Manaras, John T. ... **Billerica, MA**
Manard & Buck ... **New Orleans, LA**
Manard, John P., Jr. ... **New Orleans, LA**
Manard, Robert L. ... **New Orleans, LA**
Manardo, Susan A. ... **Cincinnati, OH**
Manarel, Michael R. ... **New York, NY**
Manary, James D. ... Salem, OR
Manas, Lillyan J. ... Baldwin, NY
Manas, Richard I. ... Miami, FL
San Antonio, TX
Manas, Richard I., P.A. ... Miami, FL
Manasco, Hobson, Jr. ... Haleyville, AL
Manasco, J. Michael ... **Montgomery, AL**
Manasco, Jason Lee ... Wetumpka, AL
Manasco, Raymond O., Jr. ... Gainesville, FL
Manasco, Ronald D. ... **Rocky Mount, NC**
Manasevit, Leigh M. ... **Washington, DC**
Manasevit, Patricia A. ... Treasury Department, Internal Revenue Service, GV
Manasian, Paul E. ... **San Francisco, CA**
Manason, Marc J. ... **Los Angeles, CA**
Manasse, Edward W. ... Torrington, CT
Manasse, Herbert ... Rancho Santa Fe, CA
Manasse, Michael G. ... **New York, NY**
Manasse, Slaiby & Leard ... Torrington, CT
Kent, CT
Manasse, William J. ... Kent, CT
Manassero, George J. ... Stockton, CA
Manaster, Ira B. ... Chicago, IL
Manaster, Joshua D. ... **Miami, FL**
Manaster, Kenneth A. ... **Palo Alto, CA**
Manasterli, Jacqueline Bennett
Arlington, VA
Manatt, Charles T., (P.C.)
Los Angeles, CA
Washington, DC
Manatt, Phelps & Phillips, LLP
Los Angeles, CA
Menlo Park, CA
Palo Alto, CA
Sacramento, CA
Washington, DC
Nashville, TN
Manatt, Scott ... Corning, AR
Manausa, Daniel E. ... **Tallahassee, FL**
Manaut, John P. ... **Honolulu, HI**
Manayan, Anna M. Przybylski ... Milpitas, CA
Manayan & Grey ... Milpitas, CA
Manayan, Henry C., Jr. ... Milpitas, CA
Manbeck, Douglas G. ... Lakota, ND
Manbeck, Harry F., Jr., Law Offices of
Washington, DC
Manbeck, John P. ... **Harrisburg, PA**
Manbeck, Peter C. ... **New York, NY**
Manbeck, Steven V. ... Mifflintown, PA
Manber, Laurence, Ph.D. ... Princeton, NJ
Manby, Amy E. ... Kansas City, MO
Manby, C. Robert, Jr. ... Burlington, VT
White River Junction, VT
Manca, Lori A. ... Washington, DC
Manca, Paul D. ... **Washington, DC**
Manca, Susan ... New York, NY
Mancabelli, Patricia A. ... **Mesa, AZ**
Mancano, Joseph D. ... **Philadelphia, PA**
Mancari, Joseph A. ... Ann Arbor, MI
Mancasola, John A. ... Redding, CA
Mance, Jack M. ... Sewickley, PA
Mance, Robert W. ... **Washington, DC**
Manch, David E. ... **Phoenix, AZ**
Manch, Joyce J. ... Buffalo, NY
Manchak, John F. ... Columbus, OH
Manchee, James J. ... **Dallas, TX**
Manchee, William L. ... **Dallas, TX**
Manchel, Donald F. ... Philadelphia, PA
Manchel, Howard J. ... Atlanta, GA
Mancher, Lauren ... **New York, NY**
Mancher, Mark S. ... **Woodbury, NY**
Mancheski, Nancy E. ... **Philadelphia, PA**
Manchester, Bennett, Powers & Ullman, A Legal Professional Association
Youngstown, OH
Manchester, Curtis Gilbert ... **Richmond, VA**
Manchester, Cynthia Ann K.
Binghamton, NY
Manchester, Dale J. ... Springville, NY
Manchester, Douglas C. ... Orleans, MA
Manchester, Edward D. ... **New York, NY**
Manchester, Gilbert M. ... **Youngstown, OH**
Manchester, Jamie E. ... Frederick, MD
Manchester, Janine C. ... **Denver, CO**
Manchester, Jeryl A. ... Calumet, MI
Houghton, MI
Manchester, Jon H. ... New York, NY
Manchester Law Offices, Professional Corporation ... **Burlington, VT**
Montpelier, VT
St. Johnsbury, VT
Manchester McNeff ... Ypsilanti, MI
Manchester & Pignato, P.C.
Oklahoma City, OK
Manchester, Robert A., III, Law Office of
Oklahoma City, OK
Manchester, Robert C. ... Paducah, KY
Manchester, Robert E. ... **Burlington, VT**
Manchester, Robert Edward
Oklahoma City, OK
Manchester, Sarah G. ... Boston, MA
Manchester, Steven R., (Inc.)
San Jose, CA
Manchester, Susan ... Oklahoma City, OK
Manchester, Susan A. ... **Manchester, NH**
Manchester, Thomas C. ... Ypsilanti, MI
Manchester & Williams ... **San Jose, CA**
Manchik, Craig ... Chicago, IL
Manchik, Merrill H. ... **Chicago, IL**
Manchin & Aloi ... **Fairmont, WV**
Manchin, Timothy J. ... **Fairmont, WV**
Manchini, Steven G. ... North Andover, MA
Manchisi, Francis P. ... **New York, NY**
Manchur, Edward L. ... **Boston, MA**
Manci, Michael L. ... New York, NY
Manciagli, Jeffrey P. ... Atlanta, GA
Mancias, Michelle D. ... **Chicago, IL**
Mancillas, Marshall A. ... Newport Beach, CA
Mancinelli, Anthony D. ... **Buffalo, NY**
Mancinelli, Diane L. ... Tustin, CA
Mancinelli, Robert J. ... Westwood, NJ
Mancinelli, Steven ... Elizabeth, NJ
New York, NY
Mancini, A. John P. ... **New York, NY**
Mancini, Andrew M. ... Philadelphia, PA
Mancini, Anthony L. ... Lexington, MA
Mancini, C. Richard ... Naples, FL
Mancini, Charles A. ... Warren, MI
Mancini, Chris ... Miami, FL
Mancini, Cynthia H.
Department of Commerce, Patent and Trademark Office, GV
Mancini, Dara L. ... **Pittsburgh, PA**
Mancini, David C. ... **McLean, VA**
Mancini, David Charles ... McLean, VA
Mancini, Dominic J. ... Hinsdale, IL
Mancini, Dominic J., Law Offices of, P.C.
Hinsdale, IL
Mancini, Donald A. ... Paoli, PA
Mancini, Elizabeth M. ... **Dunedin, FL**
Mancini & Gallagher ... **Encino, CA**
Los Angeles, CA
Mancini & Hayko ... Guilderland, NY
Mancini, Jerianne E. ... New York, NY
Mancini, John O. ... **Providence, RI**
Mancini, Joseph ... **Costa Mesa, CA**
Mancini, Joseph J. ... Port St. Lucie, FL
Mancini, Joseph M. ... Columbus, OH
Mancini, Kelly L. ... Atlanta, GA
Mancini, Leonard A. ... Albany, NY
Mancini, Linda A. ... Long Beach, CA
Mancini, Lorenzo A. ... **Chicago, IL**
Wheaton, IL
Mancini, Lorraine ... Warwick, RI
Mancini, Marcus A. ... **Encino, CA**
Mancini, Maria Anna ... Los Angeles, CA
Mancini, Marisa A. ... Chicago, IL
Mancini, Mark A. ... **Washington, DC**
Mancini, Mary Ann ... **Washington, DC**
Mancini, Nadine N.
Occupational Safety and Health Review Commission, Office of the General Counsel, GV
Mancini, Nicholas M. ... Newtown, PA
Mancini, Paul K. ... San Antonio, TX
Mancini, Paul R., (A Law Corporation)
Kahului, HI
Mancini, Paul V. ... Cranston, RI
Mancini, Peter L. ... **New York, NY**
Mancini, Philip E., Jr. ... New Haven, CT
Mancini, Philip P. ... Rockport, ME
Mancini, Ralph G. ... Guilderland, NY
Mancini, Ralph J. ... **Dobbs Ferry, NY**
Mancini, Richard ... Beaver Falls, PA
Mancini, Rose C. ... **Prospect Heights, IL**
Mancini, Rowland & Welch ... **Hilo, HI**
Kahului, HI
Lahaina, HI
Wailuku, HI
Mancini, Schreuder, Kline & Conrad, P.C.
Warren, MI
Mancini, Stephen C. ... **Los Angeles, CA**
Mancini, Stephen J. ... Poway, CA
Mancini, Vincent B. ... Media, PA
Mancino, David A. ... **Dayton, OH**
Mancino, Douglas M. ... **Los Angeles, CA**
Mancino, Frank P. ... Hamilton Square, NJ
Mancino, James P. ... Cleveland, OH
Mancino, Mancino & Mancino
Cleveland, OH

Mancino, Paul A., Jr. .... Cleveland, OH
Mancino, Peter B. .... Great Neck, NY
Mancino, Peter B. .... Nashville, TN
Mancino, Richard .... New York, NY
Mancino, Russel V. .... Princeton, NJ
Mancino, Vincent P. .... New York, NY
Mancinoni, Paul L. .... Springfield, MA
Manck, Joseph P. .... Annapolis, MD
Mancke, John B. .... Harrisburg, PA
Mancke, Wagner, Hershey and Tully
Carlisle, PA
Harrisburg, PA
Manco, Dominick M. .... Lakewood, NJ
Manco, Martin P. .... West Chester, PA
Mancoff, Neal A. .... Chicago, IL
Mancoske, Debra R. .... St. Louis, MO
Manculich, Michele A. .... Forest Hill, MD
Mancus, Peter J. .... Sebastopol, CA
Mancusi, Antoinette .... Augusta, ME
Mancusi, Leonard A. .... New York, NY
Mancusi, Michael Andrew
Treasury Department, Office of the Comptroller of the Currency, GV
Mancusi, Peter J. .... Boston, MA
Mancusi-Ungaro, Edmund .... Montclair, NJ
Mancuso, Anthony .... Toms River, NJ
Mancuso, Anthony O. .... Gahanna, OH
Mancuso, Antonia R. .... Overland Park, KS
Mancuso, Charles S. .... Walpole, MA
Mancuso, Christina Ellen .... Dallas, TX
Mancuso, Cinthia Simmons
Baton Rouge, LA
Mancuso, Colleen .... Stroudsburg, PA
Mancuso, Dominick .... Florham Park, NJ
Mancuso, Esteban A. .... New York, NY
Mancuso, Eva Marie .... New Bedford, MA
Providence, RI
Mancuso, Gilbert M. .... Reading, PA
Mancuso, Gregory J. .... Deerfield, IL
Mancuso, Jack G. .... Reading, PA
Mancuso, James N. .... Fountain Valley, CA
Mancuso, James V. .... Incline Village, NV
Mancuso, James V., Jr. .... Palm Coast, FL
Mancuso, John H. .... Cleveland, OH
Mancuso, Joseph T. .... Syracuse, NY
Mancuso, Laura L. .... Spokane, WA
Mancuso, Louis J.
Department Of Health And Human Services, Office of the General Counsel, GV
Mancuso, Maria R. .... Lawrenceville, NJ
Mancuso, Michael L. .... New Orleans, LA
Mancuso, Nathan G. .... Miami, FL
Mancuso, Paul .... Morganville, NJ
Mancuso, Phillip J. .... Roseland, NJ
Mancuso, Phyllis Ann .... Montclair, NJ
Mancuso, R. Lynette .... Sarasota, FL
Mancuso, Richard E. .... Greenwich, CT
Mancuso, Robert J. .... White Plains, NY
Mancuso, Ross .... Slidell, LA
Mancuso, Rubin & Fufidio .... Stamford, CT
New York, NY
White Plains, NY
Mancuso, Susan A. .... White Plains, NY
Mancuso, Thomas G. .... Montgomery, AL
Mancuso, Thomas J. .... Denver, CO
Mancuso, Tony .... Syracuse, NY
Mancuso, William David .... Baton Rouge, LA
Mancz, Barry W. .... Dayton, OH
Manczak, Mary Rose C. .... Chicago, IL
Manczak, Richard P. .... Detroit, MI
Mand & Marblestone Associates
Bala Cynwyd, PA
Mand, Robert .... Bala Cynwyd, PA
Manda, M. Melissa .... Jefferson City, MO
Mandabach, Carl H. .... Sacramento, CA
Mandabach, Frederick A.
Rancho Cucamonga, CA
Mandak, Nicholas G. .... Paterson, NJ
Mandala, Lawrence B. .... Dallas, TX
Mandanas, Joy .... Columbia, SC
Mandanas, Julie Montz .... Chicago, IL
Mandanici, Francis T. .... New Haven, CT
Mandanis, Marjorie G. .... Redwood City, CA
Mandarino, Joseph C. .... Atlanta, GA
Mandarino, Samuel A. .... Chicago, IL
Mandaro, Gayle A. .... New York, NY
Mandaro, Richard S. .... Garden City, NY
Mandas, Peter G. .... Huntington Woods, MI
Mandavia, Anjani, (P.C.)
Beverly Hills, CA
Mande, Deborah H. .... St. Paul, MN
Mande, Louis R. .... Minneapolis, MN
Mandel, Aaron I. .... St. Louis, MO
Mandel, Alan J. .... Chicago, IL
Mandel, Alan J., & Associates, Ltd.
Chicago, IL
Mandel, Alan S. .... St. Louis, MO
Mandel, Allan J. .... Far Rockaway, NY
Mandel, Andrew R. .... Bronx, NY
Mandel, Barbara J. .... New York, NY
Mandel, Barry H. .... New York, NY
Mandel, Barry J. .... New York, NY
Mandel, Barry R. .... Milwaukee, WI
Mandel Berezin, LLC .... Newark, NJ
Mandel, Bruce P. .... Cleveland, OH
Mandel Buder & Verges
San Francisco, CA
Mandel, Carol Ruth .... Washington, DC
Mandel, Carole Calkins .... Beverly Hills, CA
Mandel, Carrie A. .... New York, NY
Mandel, Charles L. .... Los Angeles, CA
Mandel, Chester S. .... New York, NY
Mandel Clemente, & Associates, P.C.
Albany, NY
Latham, NY
Mandel, Daniel S. .... Boca Raton, FL
Mandel, David A., (P.C.) .... New York, NY
Mandel, David L. .... Sacramento, CA
Mandel, David M. .... Boston, MA
Mandel, David S. .... Miami, FL
Mandel, David S. .... Bala Cynwyd, PA
Philadelphia, PA
Mandel, Derek L. .... Indianapolis, IN
Mandel, Eileen R. .... Santa Fe, NM
Mandel, Elaine .... Long Beach, CA
Mandel, Elizabeth W. .... San Francisco, CA
Mandel, Elliot J. .... New York, NY
Mandel, F. Howard .... Cleveland, OH
Mandel, Franklin B. .... New York, NY
Mandel, Frederick H. .... New York, NY
Mandel, Gary B. .... New York, NY
Mandel, Gary J. .... Far Rockaway, NY
Mandel, Gregory N. .... San Francisco, CA
Mandel, Hal W. .... Woodbridge, NJ
Mandel, Harry S.
Department Of Health And Human Services, Social Security Administration, GV
Mandel, Howard M. .... New York, NY
Mandel, Jack .... New York, NY
Mandel, Jack K. .... Santa Ana, CA
Mandel, Jack R. .... St. Louis, MO
Mandel, James I. .... New York, NY
Mandel, James S. .... Vail, CO
Mandel, Jane Barclay .... Mequon, WI
Mandel, Jason Adam .... Wayne, PA
Mandel, Jay Y. .... Southfield, MI
Mandel, Jed R. .... Chicago, IL
Mandel, Jeffrey Austin .... Marlborough, CT
Mandel, Jeffrey E. .... Miami, FL
Orlando, FL
Mandel, Jeffrey E. .... Newark, NJ
Mandel, Jeffrey I. .... Metairie, LA
Mandel, Jeffrey S. .... Florham Park, NJ
Mandel, Jerome H. .... White Plains, NY
Mandel, Jerome P. .... Brooklyn, NY
Mandel, Jerome P., P.C. .... Brooklyn, NY
Mandel, Jodi L. .... Brooklyn, NY
Mandel, Joel L. .... Beverly Hills, CA
Mandel, Jonathan .... Encino, CA
Mandel, Joseph D. .... Los Angeles, CA
Mandel, Joseph M. .... Bayside, NY
Mandel, Karen J. .... New York, NY
Mandel, Katz, Manna & Brosnan, LLP
New City, NY
New York, NY
Mandel, Lawrence C. ....
Department of State, GV
Mandel, Lawrence D. .... Freehold, NJ
Mandel, Lena .... New York, NY
Mandel, Lenard H. .... New York, NY
Mandel, Leon .... New York, NY
Mandel, Leonard H. .... Hemet, CA
Mandel, Leonard H. .... Long Beach, CA
Mandel, Leonard M. .... New York, NY
Mandel, Lewis R. .... Westbury, NY
Mandel, Lipton and Stevenson Limited
Chicago, IL
Mandel, Loren .... Vista, CA
Mandel, Lorraine D. .... New York, NY
Mandel, M. Milo .... Los Angeles, CA
Mandel & Mandel .... Beverly Hills, CA
Los Angeles, CA
Mandel & Mandel, LLP .... New York, NY
Mandel & Manpearl .... Los Angeles, CA
Mandel, Marc Owen .... New York, NY
Mandel, Marcy Jo .... Culver City, CA
Mandel, Mark L. .... New York, NY
Mandel, Mark S. .... New York, NY
Mandel, Mark W. .... Oakland, CA
Mandel, Martha Pink .... Chicago, IL
Mandel, Martin L. .... San Mateo, CA
Mandel, Matthew H. .... Aventura, FL
Mandel, Maurice, II .... Newport Beach, CA
Mandel, Max A. .... Laredo, TX
Mandel & McAliley, LLP .... Miami, FL
Mandel, Melissa Anne .... San Diego, CA
Mandel, Michael J. .... San Francisco, CA
Mandel, Michael J. .... New City, NY
Mandel, Michael S. .... Washington, DC
Mandel, Miranda Kiser .... Chicago, IL
Mandel, Myron I. .... New City, NY
Mandel, Nadine C. .... Seattle, WA
Mandel, Newton W. .... New York, NY
Mandel, Newton W., P.C. .... New York, NY
Mandel, Nina Stillman .... Miami, FL
Mandel, Norman A. .... Atlanta, GA
Mandel & Norwood .... Los Angeles, CA
Santa Monica, CA
Mandel, Olga Sherr .... San Jose, CA
Mandel, Pamela C. .... Millburn, NJ
Mandel, Patricia C. .... New York, NY
Mandel, Paul D. .... Coral Springs, FL
Mandel, Paul M. .... West Bloomfield, MI
Mandel & Peslak, LLC .... Freehold, NJ
Mandel, Philip .... New York, NY
Mandel, Pryce A. .... White Plains, NY
Mandel, R. Terri .... Minneapolis, MN
Mandel, Reid A. .... Chicago, IL
Mandel & Resnik P.C. .... New York, NY
Mandel, Richard A. .... Great Neck, NY
Mandel, Richard G. .... New York, NY
Mandel, Richard H. .... Boston, MA
Mandel, Richard L. .... Chicago, IL
Mandel, Richard M. .... Union, NJ
Mandel, Richard P. .... Framingham, MA
Mandel, Richard S. .... New York, NY
Mandel, Robert .... White Plains, NY
Mandel, Robert A. .... Beverly Hills, CA
Mandel, Robert A. .... New York, NY
Mandel, Robert A. .... Sioux Falls, SD
Mandel, Robert J. .... Chicago, IL
Mandel, Robert P. .... Milwaukee, WI
Mandel, Robert S. .... Miami, FL
Mandel, Robert S., P.A. .... Miami, FL
Mandel, Roger B. .... Chicago, IL
Lincolnwood, IL
Mandel, Roger L. .... Dallas, TX
Mandel, Rolland A. .... Stamford, CT
Mandel, Ronald H. .... Van Nuys, CA
Mandel, S. Jerome .... Santa Monica, CA
Mandel, S. Sidney .... New York, NY
Mandel, Samuel .... Moorestown, NJ
Mandel, Samuel .... Albuquerque, NM
Mandel, Samuel J. .... Lubbock, TX
Mandel, SaraLynn .... Palo Alto, CA
Mandel, Scott H. .... Ann Arbor, MI
Mandel, Scott H. .... New York, NY
Mandel, Scott I. .... Lansing, MI
Mandel, Seymour M. .... Buffalo, NY
Mandel, Steven J. .... Department of Labor, Office of the Solicitor, GV
Mandel, Steven J. .... New York, NY
Mandel, Stuart Jay, (P.C.)
New Haven, CT
Mandel, Stuart K. .... Universal City, CA
Mandel, Stuart R., (P.L.C.) .... Los Angeles, CA
Mandel, Susan L. .... Brooklyn, NY
Mandel, Val .... Hackensack, NJ
New York, NY
Mandel, Val, P.C. .... New York, NY
Mandel, Weisman & Kirschner, P.A.
Boca Raton, FL
Fort Lauderdale, FL
West Palm Beach, FL
Mandel, William .... San Francisco, CA
Mandel, William S. .... Springfield, MA
Mandelbaum, Allen M., Law Offices of
Norristown, PA
Mandelbaum, Arthur E. .... Fort Wayne, IN
Mandelbaum, Barry R. .... West Orange, NJ
Mandelbaum, Charles .... Brooklyn, NY
Mandelbaum, David B.
Overland Park, KS
Kansas City, MO
Mandelbaum, David G. .... Baltimore, MD
Philadelphia, PA
Mandelbaum, David L. .... New York, NY
Mandelbaum, David M. .... West Orange, NJ
Mandelbaum, Elaine H. .... New York, NY
Mandelbaum Gentile & D'Olio
Las Vegas, NV
Mandelbaum, Gerard .... New York, NY
Mandelbaum, Harold A. .... Brooklyn, NY
Mandelbaum, Howard F. .... New York, NY
Mandelbaum, James C. .... Los Angeles, CA
Mandelbaum, Joel I. .... New York, NY
Mandelbaum, John D. .... Kansas City, MO
Mandelbaum, Kathy C. .... Philadelphia, PA
Mandelbaum, Kim Irene .... Las Vegas, NV
Mandelbaum & Mandelbaum, P.A.
West Orange, NJ
Mandelbaum, Philip .... West Orange, NJ
Mandelbaum, Randi Sue .... San Francisco, CA
Mandelbaum, Robert M. .... New York, NY
Mandelbaum, Roy I. .... Mineola, NY
Mandelbaum, Salsburg, Gold, Lazris, Discenza & Steinberg, P.A.
Boca Raton, FL
Elizabeth, NJ
West Orange, NJ
Mandelbaum, Samuel R. .... Tampa, FL
Mandelbaum, Sara L. .... New York, NY
Mandelbaum & Schweiger .... New York, NY
Mandelbaum, Thomas I. .... New York, NY
Mandelblatt, Leonard S.
North Brunswick, NJ
Mandelblatt, Marc H. .... San Diego, CA
Mandelbrot, David R. .... Santa Clara, CA
Mandel-Chall, Jodi .... Minneapolis, MN
Mandel Clemente, Linda A. .... Latham, NY
Mandelcorn, Harvey Scott
Putnam Valley, NY
Mandelcorn, Howard .... Wellesley, MA
Mandelis, Marioleni .... Wellesley, MA
Mandelker, Daniel R. .... St. Louis, MO
Mandelker, Lawrence A. .... New York, NY
Mandelkern, Harvey .... Albany, NY
Mandelkern, I. Paul .... Orlando, FL
Mandelkorn, Barry A.
Fort Lauderdale, FL
Mandell, Andrea Nancy .... New York, NY
Mandell, Andrew .... New York, NY
Mandell, Andrew J. .... Westbury, NY
Mandell, Andrew L. .... Worcester, MA
Mandell, Arnold .... New York, NY
Mandell, Barbara .... Los Angeles, CA
Mandell, Barbara Goldman
Bloomfield Hills, MI
Mandell, Charles H. .... Lakewood, NJ
Mandell, Craig J. .... Fort Lauderdale, FL
Mandell, Cuthbert H. .... Alexandria, VA
Mandell, David E. .... Norwich, CT
Mandell, David L. .... Madison, WI
Mandell, David S. .... Encino, CA
Mandell, Dennis G. .... New York, NY
Mandell, Douglas D. .... San Francisco, CA
Mandell, Edward R. .... Beverly Hills, CA
New York, NY
Mandell, Ellen .... Cleveland, OH
Mandell, Erica J. .... New Brunswick, NJ
Mandell, Floyd A., (P.C.) .... Chicago, IL
Mandell & Freedman .... New York, NY
Mandell & Ginsberg .... Madison, WI
Mandell, Gregg .... Chicago, IL
Mandell, Gregg, Law Offices of .... Chicago, IL
Mandell, Harold M. .... New York, NY
Mandell, Howard A. .... Montgomery, AL
Mandell, Irving .... Floral Park, NY
Mandell, Irving .... Lynbrook, NY
Mandell, Jack .... Newark, NJ
Mandell, Jacqueline .... White Plains, NY
Mandell, Jeffery .... Boise, ID
Mandell, Jeffrey M. .... Beverly Hills, CA
Mandell, Jennifer E. .... Washington, DC
Vienna, VA
Mandell, Jill .... New York, NY
Mandell, Joel .... Farmington, CT
Mandell, Laurence H. .... Northridge, CA
Mandell Law Firm, The, A Professional Corporation .... Washington, DC
Fairfax, VA
Vienna, VA
Mandell, Lawrence H. .... Montpelier, VT
Mandell, Lee .... Philadelphia, PA
Mandell, Lee Jay .... Los Angeles, CA
Mandell, Lee, P.C. .... Philadelphia, PA
Mandell, Leonard .... De Kalb, IL
Mandell, Lewis & Goldberg, A Professional Corporation .... McLean, VA
Sterling, VA
Mandell, Mandell & Okin
Lake Success, NY
Mandell, Mara .... Bradenton, FL
Mandell, Mara, P.A. .... Bradenton, FL
Mandell, Marc S. .... Norwich, CT
Mandell, Marie .... Bayside, NY
Mandell, Mark J. .... Lake Success, NY
Mandell, Mark P. .... La Jolla, CA
Mandell, Mark S. .... Providence, RI
Mandell, Marvin .... Orlando, FL
Mandell, Melissa K. .... Memphis, TN
Mandell, Michael S. .... Phoenix, AZ
Mandell, Michael S. .... Chicago, IL
Mandell, Mitchell G. .... New York, NY
Mandell, Mordy .... Montclair, NJ
Mandell, Paul M. .... Chicago, IL
Mandell, Philip L. .... Chicago, IL
Mandell, Rachel B. .... Baltimore, MD
Mandell, Richard E. .... Aspen, CO
Mandell, Robert .... New York, NY
Mandell, Robert A. .... Altamonte Springs, FL
Mandell, Robert G. .... Glendale, CA
Mandell, Robert J. .... Northridge, CA
Mandell, Ronald J. .... Los Angeles, CA
Mandell, Samuel W. W. .... Braintree, MA
Mandell, Schwartz & Boisclair, Ltd.
Providence, RI
Mandell, Sharyn Bernstein .... Newark, NJ
Mandell, Shelly M. .... Los Angeles, CA
Mandell, Stephan A. .... Sacramento, CA
Mandell, Steve A. .... Sterling, VA
Vienna, VA
Mandell, Steven C. .... New York, NY
Mandell, Steven J. .... Washington, DC
Baltimore, MD
Mandell, Steven L. .... Toledo, OH
Mandell, Steven P. .... Chicago, IL
Mandell, Steven R. .... Santa Monica, CA
Mandell, Stewart L. .... Detroit, MI
Mandell, Victoria Ruth .... Denver, CO
Mandell, William M. .... Boston, MA
Mandell & Wright, P.C. .... Houston, TX
Mandell-Rice, Bonnie S. .... Lafayette, CO
Mandelman, Benjamin .... Milwaukee, WI
Mandelman, Joel C. .... Arlington, VA
Mandelman, Jori K. .... San Francisco, CA
Mandelman, Marc A. .... New York, NY
Mandelman, Michael D. .... Thiensville, WI
Mandelsberg, Andrea B. Green
New York, NY
Mandelsberg, Steven J. .... New York, NY
Mandelson, Richard S. .... Denver, CO
Mandelstam, Charles L. .... New York, NY
Mandelstamm, Jerome R. .... St. Louis, MO
Mandel-Trupp, Lisa .... Rockville, MD
Mandelup, A. Scott .... Westbury, NY
Mandenberg, Robert D. .... Alpena, MI
Mander, Albert R., III .... Dade City, FL
Mander, Stephen E. .... Miami, FL
Mander, William L. .... New York, NY
Manderbach, G. M. .... Temple, PA
Manderfeld, Daniel J. .... Holland, MI
Manderfeld, Margaret R. .... St. Cloud, MN
Manderfeld, Mark J. .... Minneapolis, MN
Manderfeld, Peter J. .... Minneapolis, MN
Manderfield, Paula J. .... Lansing, MI
Manderino, Alan J. .... Monessen, PA
Manderlink, Gregory J. .... Valley Forge, PA
Manders, Elise .... Sacramento, CA
Manders, John G. .... Flint, MI
Manders, John M. .... Des Moines, IA
Manders, Joseph V., Jr. .... Houston, TX
Manders, Karen K. .... St. Louis, MO
Manders, Robert P. .... Eugene, OR
Manderscheid, David J. .... Washington, DC
Manderscheid, Marc J .... St. Paul, MN
Manderson, Ernest L. .... Westbrook, ME
Manderson, Nancy .... Houston, TX
Mandery, Edward J. .... East Meadow, NY
Mandery, Evan J. .... New York, NY
Mandery, Melanie .... New York, NY
Mandeville, David C. .... Elmira, NY
Mandeville, Gerald A. .... Dallas, TX
Mandeville, Hubert T. .... New York, NY
Mandeville, Joseph S. .... Pomona, CA
Mandeville, Mary K. .... Charlotte, NC
Mandeville, Michael A. .... Orlando, FL
Mandeville, Pamela S. .... Raleigh, NC
Mandeville, Theodore S., Jr.
Bennington, VT
Mandia, Frank J., Jr. .... Neptune, NJ
Mandia, Thomas C. .... Stamford, CT
Mandiberg, Susan B.
Rockville Centre, NY
Mandich, Tara J. .... Willmar, MN
Mandig, D. Michael .... Tucson, AZ
Mandigo, Charles E. .... Seattle, WA
Mandigo, Jennifer L. .... Washington, DC
Mandil, Daniel M. .... New York, NY

Mandina & Ginsberg, P.A. ....Key West, FL
Miami, FL
Mandina, Joseph J. ....Miami, FL
Mandina, Mario ....Kansas City, MO
Mandina, Philip J. ....Key West, FL
Miami, FL
Mandinach, Barry M. ....New York, NY
Mandio, Anthony A. ....Bristol, PA
Langhorne, PA
Mandio, Mark A. ....Riverside, CA
Mandir, Frederick M.
Department of Commerce, Patent and Trademark Office, GV
Mandir, William H. ....Washington, DC
Mandis, Katherine B. ....Grand Rapids, MI
Mandl, Alan D. ....Boston, MA
Mandl, Aron M. ....North Miami, FL
Mandl, Freda L. ....Bethesda, MD
Mandl, Leonard J. ....Norfolk, VA
Mandl, Nicolette ....El Cerrito, CA
Mandl, Regina Snow ....Boston, MA
Mandla, Janice R. ....Carmel, IN
Mandle, George J., Jr. (P.C.) ....Linden, NJ
Mandle, Shaye R. ....Batavia, IL
Mandle, Susan Lynn ....Honolulu, HI
Mandlebaum, Frank K. ....Troy, MI
Mandler, Bernard S. ....Miami, FL
Mandler, James E. ....Deerfield, IL
Mandler, Jeffrey L. ....Miami, FL
Mandler, John J. ....Washington, DC
Mandler, John P. ....Minneapolis, MN
Mandler, Mitchell W. ....Miami, FL
Mandler, Peter A. ....Westbury, NY
Mandler, Robert P. ....Santa Monica, CA
Mandler, Ronald M. ....New York, NY
Mandler, Sieger and Unger ....Westbury, NY
Mandler, Thomas Y. ....Chicago, IL
Mandles, Melanie D. ....Los Angeles, CA
Mandlman, Steven C., Law Offices of
St. Louis, MO
Mandlowitz, Gerald S. ....Phoenixville, PA
Mandly, Charles R., Jr. ....Chicago, IL
Mando, Jeffrey C. ....Covington, KY
Mandola, Anthony J. ....Houston, TX
Mandolia, Charles E. ....Washington, DC
Mandosa, Rita Sabina ....Boston, MA
Mandour, Laila A. ....Willimantic, CT
Mandra, Raymond R. ....New York, NY
Mandra, Susan D. ....Marshfield, MA
Mandracchia, Charles D. ....Trooper, PA
Mandragouras, Amy B. ....Boston, MA
Mandrell, D. Matthew ....Chicago, IL
Mandrell, Martha J. ....Harrisburg, IL
Mandrgoc, David W. ....Dixon, IL
Mandriota, M. Donna ....Ipswich, MA
Salem, MA
Mandros, Platon N. ....Alexandria, VA
Mandross, Suzanne Cotner ....Toledo, OH
Mandry, Paul W. ....New York, NY
Mandsager, Dennis L. ....Newport, RI
Mandsager, Greggory Jon ....Fort Dodge, IA
Mandt, Ann K. ....Detroit, MI
Mandt, Dawn M. ....Jacksonville, FL
Mandt, Heidi L. ....Portland, OR
Mandt, John F. ....Birmingham, AL
Mandt, John T. ....Somerset, KY
Mandt, Patricia Trott ....Birmingham, AL
Mandus, Eric H. ....Atlanta, GA
Mandus, Merryl S. ....Atlanta, GA
Mandyck, Lawrence M. ....Atlanta, GA
Maneche, Mark Darius Robert
Baltimore, MD
Maneckji, Bhikhaji M. ....Providence, RI
Maneille, P. Michael ....Lake Charles, LA
Manek, Jivraj S. ....Artesia, CA
Manekas, Jason A. ....Boston, MA
Maneke, Jean A. ....Kansas City, MO
Maneker, Meryl C. ....San Diego, CA
Maneker, Morton M. ....New York, NY
Manekin, Bernard ....Baltimore, MD
Manekin, Robert A. ....Bethesda, MD
Manela, Harley D. ....Bingham Farms, MI
Manela, Mark D. ....Houston, TX
Manela, Stewart S. ....Washington, DC
Manelis, Beresen & Baron
Framingham, MA
Manelis, Richard E. ....Framingham, MA
Manella, David L. ....Los Angeles, CA
Manella & Klapholz, LLP ....Hollywood, FL
Weston, FL
Manella, Nora M. ....Los Angeles, CA
Manella, Ross H. ....Hollywood, FL
Manella, Samuel J. ....Worth, IL
Manelli, Daniel J. ....Washington, DC
Manelli, Dennis E. ....Tampa, FL
Manelli, Julian R. ....Baltimore, MD
Manello, Joseph B. ....Boston, MA
Manello, Seymour ....Rochester, NY
Manemann, Mary C. ....Washington, DC
Maner, C. Jack ....Tulsa, OK
Maner, C. Jack, P.C. ....Tulsa, OK
Maner, Charles A., Jr. ....Knoxville, TN
Maner, Doren ....Lubbock, TX
Maner, Forbes ....Washington, DC
Maner, Richard B. ....Atlanta, GA
Manera, Joseph C., Jr. ....Cranston, RI
Manerbino, George A. ....Denver, CO
Maneri, Francis P. ....Cherry Hill, NJ
Philadelphia, PA
Manero, Anne ....Philadelphia, PA
Manero, Richard P. ....Greenwich, CT
Manes, Barbara E. ....Mineola, NY
Manes, Christopher S. ....Palm Springs, CA
Manes, Dennis L. ....Cincinnati, OH
Manes, Gregg A. ....Akron, OH
Manes, Hugh R. ....Los Angeles, CA
Manes, Louis L. ....Akron, OH
Manes, Margaret (Peggy) ....Reno, NV
Manes, Marvin G. ....Akron, OH
Manes, Michael B ....Fort Lauderdale, FL
Manes, Musitano, Schrader & Assaf, (An Assn. of Ind. Attys. & a P.C.) ....Akron, OH
Manes, Sidney L. ....Syracuse, NY
Manes, Stephen ....Phoenix, AZ
Manes, Victoria E. ....Millwood, NY
Manes & Watson ....Los Angeles, CA
Manesh, Mike S. ....Los Angeles, CA
Manesis, Dennis J. ....West Orange, NJ
Manesis, Harry P. ....New York, NY
Manesis, Mary D. ....Los Angeles, CA
Maness, Alan D. ....Bloomington, IL
Maness, Charles Anthony ....Union City, TN
Maness, Jack D. ....Norfolk, VA
Maness, Jayrene R. ....Monroe, NC
Maness, Maryrose E. ....New York, NY
Maness, Mia Lauren ....Charleston, SC
Maness, Michael A. ....Houston, TX
Maness & Miller ....Doniphan, MO
Maness, Randolph ....Doniphan, MO
Maness, Richard B. ....Sacramento, CA
Maness, Roger A. ....Clarksville, TN
Maness, Siegrid Smith ....Doniphan, MO
Maness, Thomas E. ....Beaumont, TX
Maness, Wesly Carl ....Arlington, TX
Maness, William F. ....Independence, MO
Maness, William H. ....Jacksonville, FL
Manesseh, James P. ....Baton Rouge, LA
Manestar, Cynthia ....Tinley Park, IL
Manetas, Peter M. ....Daly City, CA
Manetta, J. Lucian ....Maspeth, NY
Manetta, Richard L. ....Dearborn, MI
Manetta, Robert B. ....Roanoke, VA
Manetta, Stephen J. ....New York, NY
Manetti & Griffith, Ltd. ....Oak Brook, IL
Manetti, Mark D. ....Oak Brook, IL
Manetti, Mary G. ....Danbury, CT
Manetti, Paul D. ....South Casco, ME
Manetti, Renald A. ....Sleepy Hollow, NY
Maneval, Andrew ....Boston, MA
Maneval, Kristen Orff ....Blue Bell, PA
Maneval, Wendy Cherner
Philadelphia, PA
Manewitz, Mark L. ....Newark, NJ
Maney, Anthony S. ....East Greenbush, NY
Maney, Barbara A. ....Columbus, OH
Maney, Damsker & Jones, P.A.
Tampa, FL
Maney, David A. ....Tampa, FL
Maney, Gerard E. ....Albany, NY
Maney & Gordon, P.A. ....Orlando, FL
Tampa, FL
Maney, H. Joseph ....Lynnfield, MA
Maney, John E ....Albany, NY
Maney, John R., Jr. ....Department of Justice, Tax Division, GV
Maney, Kevin P. ....Albany, NY
Maney, Mark ....Houston, TX
Maney, McConville & Liccardi, P.C.
East Greenbush, NY
Maney, Michael M. ....New York, NY
Maney, Patrick T. ....East Greenbush, NY
Maney, Richard Henry ....Orlando, FL
Tampa, FL
Maney, T. Patterson ....Shalimar, FL
Maney, Thomas M. ....Sherman Oaks, CA
Maney, Thomas P., Jr. ....Columbus, OH
Manford, Byron Craig ....Martinsburg, WV
Manford, L. Price ....Houston, TX
Manford, Morty ....New York, NY
Manford, Thomas D., III ....Houston, TX
Manfra, Jo Ann ....Worcester, MA
Manfre, Christopher M. ....Atlanta, GA
Manfre, Richard J. ....Waldwick, NJ
Manfre, Richard J., P.A. ....Waldwick, NJ
Manfre, Roger E. ....Covington, LA
Manfred, Leo F., II ....Westerly, RI
Manfred, Robert D., Jr. ....Washington, DC
Manfreda, Antonina ....Somerville, NJ
Manfreda, John G. ....Washington, DC
Ringoes, NJ
Manfreda, John J. ....Treasury Department, Bureau of Alcohol, Tobacco and Firearms, GV
Manfreda, Michael J. ....Boston, MA
Manfreda, Robert L., Jr. ....Stamford, CT
Manfredi, Christopher J.
Los Angeles, CA
Manfredi, Francis P. ....New York, NY
Manfredi, Frank A. ....Norwich, CT
Manfredi, George A. ....Los Angeles, CA
Manfredi, Joseph A. ....Bedminster, NJ
Manfredi & Levine, A P.C.
Westlake Village, CA
Manfredi, Linda P. ....East Meadow, NY
Manfredi, Sam C. ....Westlake Village, CA
Manfredonia, Albert W. ....Peekskill, NY
Manfredonia, John M. ....McLean, VA
Mang, Amy E. ....Denver, CO
Mang, Batiza, Gaudin, Godofsky & Penzaato
Metairie, LA
Mang, Batiza, Gaudin, Godofsky & Penzato
Baton Rouge, LA
Mang, Douglas A. ....Tallahassee, FL
Mang, Herbert J., Jr. ....Baton Rouge, LA
Mang Law Firm, P.A. ....Tallahassee, FL
Mang Law Firm, The, P.A. ....Weston, FL
Mangalmurti, Vikram ....Pittsburgh, PA
Mangalo, Renée L. ....New York, NY
Mangan, Barry T. ....San Jose, CA
Mangan, Brendan T. ....Seattle, WA
Mangan, Charles E. ....Philadelphia, PA
Mangan, Elmyra M. ....New York, NY
Mangan, Evelyn Gwin ....Springfield, MO
Mangan, Evelyn Gwin, P.C.
Springfield, MO
Mangan, Frank Christopher ....Sacramento, CA
Mangan, J. Matthew ....San Francisco, CA
Mangan, J. Warren ....Long Island City, NY
Mangan, James F. ....Wilkes-Barre, PA
Mangan, Jerald M. ....Chicago, IL
Wheaton, IL
Mangan, Jim ....Dodge City, KS
Mangan, John J. ....New Britain, CT
Mangan, John J. ....Washington, DC
Mangan, John J. ....Lisle, IL
Mangan, John J., Jr. ....Congers, NY
Mangan, Joseph R. (Casey), Jr.
Northbrook, IL
Mangan, Kevin J. ....Philadelphia, PA
Mangan, Laurel D. ....Vernon, CT
Mangan, Linda ....New York, NY
Mangan, Lucy Johnson ....Orlando, FL
Mangan, Lydia A. ....Denver, CO
Mangan, Margaret Ann ....Montpelier, VT
Mangan, Michael J. ....Philadelphia, PA
Mangan, Mona ....New York, NY
Mangan, Nancy Felix ....Miami, FL
Mangan, Owen F. ....Buffalo, NY
Mangan, Pamela Rae ....Indianapolis, IN
Mangan, Patrick F. ....Columbus, OH
Mangan, Patrick J. ....Rahway, NJ
Mangan, Peter J. ....York, PA
Mangan, Richard B., Jr. ....Orlando, FL
Mangan, Robert J. ....Chicago, IL
Mangan, Sheila McVey ....Philadelphia, PA
Mangan, Stephen L. ....New Britain, CT
Mangan, Thomas C. ....Erie, PA
Mangan, Thomas J., Jr. ....York, PA
Mangan, Thomas M. ....Lewiston, ME
Mangan, Thomas M. ....Elyria, OH
Mangan, Thomas P. ....Chicago, IL
Mangan, Timothy Joseph ....Columbus, OH
Mangan, Timothy S. ....Cincinnati, OH
Manganelli, Jos. T. ....Utica, NY
Manganello, Christopher M. ....Pitman, NJ
Manganello, Janice ....Newark, NJ
New York, NY
Manganello, Thomas J.
Bloomfield Hills, MI
Manganiello, Alexander ....Boston, MA
Manganiello, Dennis J. ....Atlanta, GA
Manganiello, Edward M. ....New York, NY
Manganiello, Gabrielle
Department of Justice, Civil Division, GV
Manganiello, Susan E.
Steamboat Springs, CO
Manganiello, William A. ....Taunton, MA
Manganillo, Carlo ....Brooklyn, NY
Mangano, Antonia F. ....Brooklyn, NY
Mangano, Basil W. ....Cleveland, OH
Mangano, Edward P. ....Bethpage, NY
Mangano, Frank V. ....North Babylon, NY
Mangano, Helen M. ....Bronxville, NY
Mangano, Joseph S. ....Cinnaminson, NJ
Mangano, Joy L. ....Albuquerque, NM
Mangano, Louis ....Elmwood Park, NJ
Mangano, Shawn A. ....Las Vegas, NV
Mangapora, Michael J., (P.C.) ....Flint, MI
Mangar, Jeffrey W. ....Modesto, CA
Mangarin, Daniel J. ....San Diego, CA
Mangarpan, Tina Ivankovic
Long Beach, CA
Mangas, Cloyce Leland (Lee), Jr.
Orlando, FL
Mangas, Robert ....Washington, DC
Mange, Steven A. ....Chicago, IL
Mangefrida, David J., Jr. ....Washington, DC
Mangel, Claudia Pap
Research Triangle Park, NC
Mangel, Douglas M. ....Washington, DC
Mangel, Gary ....Northfield, NJ
Mangel, Joel M. ....Rockville, MD
Mangel, Ronald ....Egg Harbor Township, NJ
Mangels, Alan A. ....Los Angeles, CA
Mangels, Alfred J. ....Cincinnati, OH
Mangels, Robert E., (P.C.)
Los Angeles, CA
Mangelsdorf, Richard C., Jr.
Nashville, TN
Mangelson, Michael E.
Salt Lake City, UT
Mangen, Christopher, Jr. ....Billings, MT
Mangeot, Henri L. ....Louisville, KY
Mangeot, Kathy Robinson ....Frankfort, KY
Manger, David J. ....Tacoma, WA
Manger, Donald E. ....Catonsville, MD
Manger, J. Anthony ....Somerville, NJ
Manger, Richard A. ....High Point, NC
Manger, Rose Marie ....Hackensack, NJ
Manger, William J. ....Oklahoma City, OK
Mangerson, Mark A. ....Rhinelander, WI
Manges, Joseph E. ....Santa Fe, NM
Manges, Richard B. ....Fort Collins, CO
Manges, Thomas A. ....Anderson, IN
Fort Wayne, IN
Marion, IN
Manges, Timothy A. ....Fort Wayne, IN
Mangham and Davis ....Lafayette, LA
Mangham, Michael R. ....Lafayette, LA
Mangham, Randal A. ....Atlanta, GA
Mangham, Randal A., P.C. ....Atlanta, GA
Mangham, W. Glen ....Shreveport, LA
Manghera, Peter J. ....Madison, WI
Manghisi, Joseph R. ....New York, NY
Mangi, Robert C. ....Mineola, NY
Mangia, Angelo J. ....Albany, NY
Mangiafico, Edgar S., Jr. ....Atlanta, GA
Mangialardi, Arlene ....Bronxville, NY
Mangialardi, John ....Hartsdale, NY
Mangiamele, Daniel D. ....Chicago, IL
Mangiamele, Suzanne C. ....McHenry, IL
Mangiantini, Paul R. ....Redwood City, CA
Mangiaracina, Anthony J. ....Islandia, NY
Mangiaracina, Joseph ....Wantagh, NY
Mangiaracina, Vicki A. ....Newark, NJ
Mangiaratti, Robert S. ....Attleboro, MA
Mangiatordi, Frank P. ....New York, NY
Mangieri, Frank J. ....New York, NY
Mangieri, Paul L. ....Galesburg, IL
Mangiero, David ....Miami, FL
Mangin, John Albert, III ....Fort Myers, FL
Mangin, Margaret E. ....San Diego, CA
Mangin, Peter G. ....Jersey City, NJ
Mangine-Gordon, Kimberly
South Plainfield, NJ
Mangines, Brian A. ....Fairfield, CT
Mangines and Mangines ....Fairfield, CT
Mangines, Thomas E. ....Fairfield, CT
Mangini, Dena C. ....Forest Hills, NY
Mangini, Janet Carol ....San Francisco, CA
Mangini, John A. ....Daly City, CA
Mangini, John Jay ....Brielle, NJ
Mangini, John Jay, P.C. ....Brielle, NJ
Mangini, Maurizio A. ....Oceanside, CA
Mangini, Vincent J. ....Hightstown, NJ
Mangino, Brian T. ....Washington, DC
Mangino, Carl R. ....Denver, CO
Mangino, Jennifer ....New York, NY
Mangino, Joni M. ....Pittsburgh, PA
Mangino, Matthew T. ....New Castle, PA
Mangino, Robert M., Jr. ....New York, NY
Mangino, Vincent M. ....Cocoa Beach, FL
Mangione, Peter T. ....Washington, DC
Mangione, Ralph P. ....Tampa, FL
Mangione & Roisman ....Rochester, NY
Mangione, Salvatore A. ....Rochester, NY
Mangione, Samuel Joseph ....Baltimore, MD
Manglardi, Michael ....Kissimmee, FL
Orlando, FL
Mangler, Robert J. ....Wilmette, IL
Manglona, John A. ....Saipan, TT
Manglona, Ramona V. ....Saipan, TT
Mango, Anthony George ....New York, NY
Mango, Charles J. ....Scotia, NY
Mango, Dana ....Charlotte, NC
Mango, Guy T. ....New Milford, NJ
Mango, Kenneth W. ....Meriden, CT
Mango, Kimberly A. ....Hartford, CT
Mango, Lisa Ann ....San Francisco, CA
Mango, Thomas J. ....Boston, MA
Mangoba, Leo Padilla ....Vallejo, CA
Mangold, Christopher L.
White Plains, NY
Mangold, Donna S. ....Washington, DC
Mangold, Harold L. ....Poughkeepsie, NY
Mangold, Mark ....New York, NY
Mangold, Martha M. ....San Francisco, CA
Mangold, Robert G. ....Philadelphia, PA
Mangold, William J., Jr. ....Phoenix, AZ
Mangolini, Solomon R. ....Los Angeles, CA
Mangone, Ann M. ....New York, NY
Mangone, Gregory ....Naples, FL
Mangone, Louis A. ....New York, NY
Mangone, Nancy A. ....Denver, CO
Mangone, Robert Courtney
New York, NY
Mangone & Schnapp ....New York, NY
Mangonon, Philip D. ....[illegible], MI
Mangoni, August M., (Ltd.) ....Chicago, IL
Mangrum, Barbara J. Ames ....Tulsa, OK
Mangrum, Boyd ....Waco, TX
Mangrum, Dennis L. ....Salt Lake City, UT
Mangrum, Gregory D. ....Memphis, TN
Mangrum, Harold D. ....Memphis, TN
Mangrum, Jason S. ....Lebanon, TN
Mangrum, Jeffrey W. ....Oxford, MS
Mangrum & Mangrum ....Memphis, TN
Mangrum, Michelle R. ....Kansas City, MO
Mangrum, Richard Collin ....Omaha, NE
Mangrum, Robert A. ....Washington, DC
Mangrum, Timothy W. ....Spokane, WA
Mangs, Gail K. ....Farmington, CT
Mangu, Jean M. ....Jacksonville, FL
Mangum & Associates, APC
San Diego, CA
Mangum, Charles D. ....Chicago, IL
Mangum, Christopher D. ....Atlanta, GA
Mangum, D. Karl ....Salt Lake City, UT
Mangum, Darin H. ....American Fork, UT
Mangum, David G. ....Nashville, TN
Mangum, David G. ....Salt Lake City, UT
Mangum, Eugene K. ....Phoenix, AZ
Mangum, Geoffrey W. ....Salt Lake City, UT
Mangum, Glen D. ....San Antonio, TX
Mangum, Henry B., Jr. ....Greensboro, NC
Mangum, Holland G. ....Seminole, FL
Mangum, J. Kenneth ....Phoenix, AZ
Mangum, Jeff L. ....San Diego, CA
Mangum, Joanna Penland Love
Atlanta, GA
Mangum, Joe O., III ....Milledgeville, GA
Mangum, John K. ....Phoenix, AZ
Mangum, John K., Jr. ....Salt Lake City, UT
Mangum, John K., P.C. ....Phoenix, AZ
Mangum, Kevin E. ....Orlando, FL
Mangum, M. Carrington ....Charlotte, NC
Mangum, Mark Christopher ....Atlanta, GA
Mangum, Merilyn M. ....Memphis, TN
Mangum, Mildred M. ....Columbus, OH
Mangum, Ned Wilson ....Raleigh, NC
Mangum, R. Worth ....Boone, NC
Mangum, Robert E., Jr. ....Dallas, TX
Mangum, Robert L. ....Decatur, MS
Mangum, Ronald Scott ....Chicago, IL
Mangum, Smietanka & Johnson, L.L.C.
Chicago, IL
Mangum, Susan D. ....Atlanta, GA
Mangum, Wall, Stoops & Warden, P.L.L.C.
Flagstaff, AZ
Holbrook, AZ
Page, AZ
Sedona, AZ

Mangum, Wall, Stoops & Warden, P.L.L.C.—Continued
Tuba City, AZ
Williams, AZ
Winslow, AZ
Mangum, Wayne B. .... Lilburn, GA
Mangus, Jon L. .... Tiburon, CA
Manha, Antone P., Jr. .... Richmond, VA
Manhard, Elgin A., Jr. .... Edina, MN
Manhard, Virginia .... Richmond, VA
Manhardt, Kirk T. .... Department of Justice, Civil Division, GV
Manhardt, Meryl R. .... Madison, WI
Manhart, Daryl .... Phoenix, AZ
Manhart, Maria T. .... Chicago, IL
Manhart, Patricia Ann .... St. Louis, MO
Manheim, Bruce S., Jr. .... Washington, DC
Manheim, Charles M. .... Syracuse, NY
Manheim, David I. .... Torrance, CA
Manheim, Gene S. .... Westport, CT
Manheim, Harold .... New York, NY
Manheim, Jennifer Susan .... Roseland, NJ
Manheim & Manheim, P.C. .... Syracuse, NY
Manheim, Michael A. .... Syracuse, NY
Manheim, William V. .... San Francisco, CA
Manheimer, Esther E. .... Raleigh, NC
Manheimer, Hollie G. .... Atlanta, GA
Manheimer, Jacob A. .... Portland, ME
Manheimer, Jeffrey A. .... New York, NY
Manheimer, William B. .... Monmouth, ME
Manhein, Jack F., Jr. .... Jackson, TN
Manhein, Jack, Sr. .... Jackson, TN
Manhire, John T., Jr. .... Windermere, FL
Manhoff, Lawrence .... Elkins Park, PA
Mani, Lalitha .... Seattle, WA
Mani, Matthew C. .... Danville, CA
Mani, Philip C. .... Fort Worth, TX
Mani, Prētha .... Los Angeles, CA
Mani, Thomas E. .... Alexandria, VA
Mania, Joseph J., III .... Flemington, NJ
Morristown, NJ
Maniace, James V. .... Columbus, OH
Maniaci, Antonio J. .... East Lansing, MI
Maniaci, Joseph G. .... Philadelphia, PA
Maniaci, Vincent M. .... Los Angeles, CA
Manian, Victor .... Milwaukee, WI
Manias, George L. .... Concord, NH
Manias, Giles P. .... Buffalo, NY
Maniatis, George L. .... New York, NY
Maniatis, James A. .... Worcester, MA
Maniatis, James P. .... Scarsdale, NY
Maniatis, John P. .... Chicago, IL
Maniatis, Marina M. .... Los Angeles, CA
Maniatis, Victoria J. .... New York, NY
Maniatty, Philip W. .... Miami, FL
Manibog, Darren A. .... Los Angeles, CA
Manibog, G. Monty .... Los Angeles, CA
Manibusan, Joaquin V. E., Jr. .... Hagåtña, GU
Maniccia, Michelle .... New York, NY
Manich, Stephen J. .... Chicago, IL
Manick, Thomas .... Miami, FL
Manickam, Sada .... Washington, DC
Manicke, Robert T. .... Portland, OR
Manico, William M. .... Upper Marlboro, MD
Manicom, A. Dale .... San Diego, CA
Manicom, John .... Houston, TX
Manicone, Nicolas M. .... Washington, DC
Manicone, Rebecca C. .... Rockville, MD
Manier & Herod .... Nashville, TN
Manier, Jody Ann .... Washington, DC
Manier, John J. .... Universal City, CA
Manieri, Anthony J. .... Boston, MA
Manierre, William T. .... San Francisco, CA
Manifesto, Jean A. .... Pittsburgh, PA
Manifesto, William F. .... Pittsburgh, PA
Manifold, Betsy C. .... San Diego, CA
New York, NY
Manifold, Hugh D. .... York, PA
Manifold, Robert F. .... Seattle, WA
Manigan, Mark E. .... Roseland, NJ
Manigault, Arthur L. .... Columbus, OH
Manigault, Dorothy A. .... Columbia, SC
Manigault, Edward M. .... Atlanta, GA
Manikas, Donald J. .... Chicago, IL
Manikas, Nicholas Edward
Birmingham, MI
Manikas, William J. .... Boynton Beach, FL
Maniker, Howard B. .... Cleveland, OH
Maniklal, Preyesh K. .... Cordele, GA
Manikoff, V. John .... Bloomfield Hills, MI
Manikowski, Jeanne M. .... Dallas, TX
Manildi, Marta A. .... Ann Arbor, MI
Maniloff, Randy J. .... Philadelphia, PA
Maniloff, Steven .... Cherry Hill, NJ
Philadelphia, PA
Manilow, Floyd B. .... Chicago, IL
Manilow, Lewis .... Chicago, IL
Manin, Mara S. .... Greenlawn, NY
Maninger, Larry G. .... Paris, TX
Maningo, Lance A. .... Las Vegas, NV
Manioci, Gerald .... Penfield, NY
Manion, Andrew J. .... Evansville, IN
Manion, Ann W. .... Utica, NY
Waterville, NY
Manion, Brian J. .... San Jose, CA
Manion, Daniel A. .... South Bend, IN
Manion, Daniel J. .... Southfield, MI
Manion, Deborah Hunicke .... Algonquin, IL
Manion, Devens & McFetridge, Ltd.
Danville, IL
Hoopeston, IL
Manion, Douglas Kevin .... Vernon, CT
Manion, Edward D., Jr. .... Jackson, WY
Manion, Francis V. .... Avon, CT
Manion, Harry L., III .... Boston, MA
Manion, James I. .... Charles Town, WV
Martinsburg, WV
Manion, James Robert, III .... Charlotte, NC
Manion, John M. .... Brookfield, WI
Manion, Lawrence E., Jr. .... St. Louis, MO
Manion, Mark S. .... Santa Barbara, CA
Manion McDonough & Lucas, A Professional Corporation .... Pittsburgh, PA
Manion, Michael P. .... Butte, MT
Manion, Paul A. .... Pittsburgh, PA
Manion, Paul J. .... Detroit, MI
Manion, Paul T. .... Hoopeston, IL
Manion, Peter W. .... Stockton, CA
Manion, Robert A. .... Lambertville, MI
Manion, Stephen B. .... Phoenix, AZ
Manion, Thomas M., Jr. .... Lanesboro, MN
Manion, William B. .... Washington, PA
Manion, William L. .... Sewell, NJ
Maniotis, Nicholas .... West Palm Beach, FL
Manipella, Samuel P. .... Tulsa, OK
Manire, James M. .... Memphis, TN
Manire, Michael Latham .... New York, NY
Manis, Calliope .... Brooklyn, NY
Melville, NY
Manis, Calvin N. .... Hazard, KY
Manis, Christos M. .... Hudson, NH
Manis, Dean E. .... Department of Commerce, Office of the Inspector General, GV
Manis, George N. .... Annapolis, MD
Manis, Kathryn Irene .... Riverside, CA
Manis, M. Kathryn .... Lexington, KY
Pikeville, KY
Manis, Nathan .... Fond du Lac, WI
Manis, Paula K. .... Lansing, MI
Mount Pleasant, MI
Manis, Stephanie B. .... Atlanta, GA
Maniscalco, Frank .... Cambridge, MA
Maniscalco, James P. .... Los Angeles, CA
Maniscalco, Joseph A., Jr. .... Atlanta, GA
Maniscalco, Joseph A., Jr., P.C. .... Atlanta, GA
Maniscalco, Joseph S. .... Wantagh, NY
Maniscalco, Karen H. .... New York, NY
Maniscalco, Lisa A. .... Memphis, TN
Maniscalco, Mark C. .... West Orange, NJ
Maniscalco, Matthew P. .... Davis, CA
Maniscalco, Michael A. .... Tampa, FL
Maniscalco, Nicholas F. .... Chicago, IL
Maniscalco, Patrick Michael .... Falmouth, KY
Mineola, TX
Maniscalco, Peter J. .... Clayton, MO
Maniscalco, Robert A. .... Fairfield, CT
Manisero, Thomas R. .... New York, NY
Manishan, Anita G. .... Portland, OR
Manishin, Glenn B. .... Washington, DC
Manison, Nicole .... Pittsburgh, PA
Manista, Raymond J. .... Milwaukee, WI
Manito, Gustavo E. .... Miami, FL
Manitsky, Andrew D. .... New York, NY
Manitta, Lana Marie .... Springfield, VA
Manitzas, Frank S. .... San Antonio, TX
Maniwa, Kaz .... San Francisco, CA
Manix, John A. .... Spokane, WA
Manjarres, David .... Chicago, IL
Manjasek and Moore .... Daytona Beach, FL
South Daytona, FL
Manjasek, Sandra, (P.A.)
Daytona Beach, FL
Mank, Dennis J. .... Milwaukee, WI
Mank, Miles B., II .... Vero Beach, FL
Mank, R. Layton .... Miami, FL
Mank, Steven D. .... Wichita, KS
Manka, Allan R. .... San Antonio, TX
Manka, Allan R., P.C. .... San Antonio, TX
Manka, Audrey Kaiser .... St. Paul, MN
Manka, Gary L. .... Minneapolis, MN
Manka, Paul J. .... Nevada City, CA
Manka, Ronald E. .... Kansas City, MO
Manka, Simon F. .... Buffalo, NY
Mankamyer, Susan .... Somerset, PA
Manke, Dana R. .... Tacoma, WA
Manke, Hugh I. .... Hartford, CT
New Haven, CT
Manke, Robert B. .... Tulsa, OK
Manker, J. Higgins .... Pasadena, CA
Manker, Meredith J. .... Los Angeles, CA
Manker, Rives A. .... Lake Worth, FL
Manker, William M. .... Miami, FL
Mankes, Barry .... North Miami Beach, FL
Mankes, Karen M. .... Albany, NY
Mankes, Michael .... San Francisco, CA
Manket, Steven M. .... New York, NY
Mankey, Caroline Hoadley
Los Angeles, CA
Mankey, Matthew J. .... Edina, MN
Mankiewicz, Frank F. .... Washington, DC
Mankin, E. Hendrie .... Oklahoma City, OK
Mankin, John M. .... Tampa, FL
Mankin, Joyce M. .... Nyack, NY
Mankin, Leonard J. .... Clearwater, FL
Mankin, Leonard J., P.A., Law Office of
Clearwater, FL
Mankin, Peter A. .... Walnut Creek, CA
Mankin, Thomas C. .... Houston, TX
Manko, David A. .... Mineola, NY
Manko, Elizabeth R. .... New York, NY
Manko, Gold & Katcher, LLP
Cherry Hill, NJ
Bala Cynwyd, PA
Harrisburg, PA
Philadelphia, PA
Manko & Hogan .... Marietta, GA
Manko, J. Stephen, P.C. .... Marietta, GA
Manko, Joseph M. .... Bala Cynwyd, PA
Manko, Peter K. .... New Haven, CT
Manko, Stephan A. .... Lapeer, MI
Manko, Teri E. .... Manhattan Beach, CA
Manko, William M. .... Reisterstown, MD
Mankoff, Geri Lynn .... New York, NY
Mankoff, Howard .... Livingston, NJ
Mankoff, Jeffrey W. .... Dallas, TX
Mankoff, Jeffrey W., P.C. .... Dallas, TX
Mankoff, Pamela .... East Amherst, NY
Mankoff, Ronald M. .... Dallas, TX
Mankofsky, Lisa S. .... Washington, DC
Mankovitz, Roy J. .... Pasadena, CA
Mankowski, Leon A. .... Philadelphia, PA
Mankus, Theodore J. .... Holbrook, MA
Mankus, Tony .... Downers Grove, IL
Mankus, Tony, Ltd. .... Downers Grove, IL
Mankuta, David B. .... Hollywood, FL
Manlapaz, Rowena R. .... San Francisco, CA
Manley, Albert L. .... Milton, MA
Manley, Anne K. .... Allentown, PA
Manley, Barclay Arendall .... Houston, TX
Manley, Bravitt C., Jr. .... Washington, DC
Manley, Burke, Lipton & Cook, A Legal Professional Association .... Cincinnati, OH
Middletown, OH
Manley, Cheryl M. .... St. Louis, MO
Manley, Colleen C. .... Phoenix, AZ
Manley, David B., III .... Atlanta, GA
Manley, David W. .... Lakeside, CA
Manley, Douglas L. .... Schenectady, NY
Manley, Douglas R. .... La Junta, CO
Manley, Duncan Y. .... Birmingham, AL
Manley, Evelyn .... Chevy Chase, MD
Manley, Frank J., IV .... Flint, MI
Manley, Fred A., Jr. .... Morristown, NJ
Manley & Goodman .... San Diego, CA
Manley, Herbert N. .... Palm Harbor, FL
Manley, Holly J. .... Vero Beach, FL
Manley, Jack .... Ilion, NY
Manley, James A. .... Polson, MT
Manley, James B. .... Pasadena, TX
Manley, James B., Jr. .... Atlanta, GA
Manley, Jeffrey A. .... Washington, DC
Manley, Jeffrey M. .... Phoenix, AZ
Manley, Joan Marie
Commodity Futures Trading Commission, Division of Enforcement, GV
Manley, John Francis .... Orange, CA
Manley, Joseph Todd .... Charleston, SC
Manley, Karraker & Reeves
Farmington, MO
Manley, Larry Paul .... Austin, TX
Manley, Larry Paul, P.C. .... Austin, TX
Manley, Lita .... San Diego, CA
Manley, Loring K. .... New City, NY
Manley, Lucile H. .... Eureka, CA
Manley, Lucinda M. .... San Jose, CA
Manley, Lyle R. .... Helena, MT
Manley, M. Kathleen .... St. Johnsbury, VT
Manley & Manley, P.C. .... Flint, MI
Manley, Marisa L. .... New York, NY
Manley, Mark E. .... Vail, CO
Manley, Mark R. .... New York, NY
Manley, Marshall, (P.C.)
Palm Beach Gardens, FL
Manley, Mary Ellen .... White Plains, NY
Manley, Mary G. .... Menlo Park, CA
Manley, May-Lis A. .... Bethesda, MD
Manley, Melinda A. .... Los Angeles, CA
Manley, Michael P. .... Flint, MI
Manley, Michael T. .... Kansas City, MO
Manley, Nena .... Washington, DC
Manley, Norman G. .... El Dorado, KS
Manley, Philip M. .... Philadelphia, PA
Manley, Reid Stephens .... Birmingham, AL
Manley, Richard A., Jr. .... Boston, MA
Manley, Richard S. .... Demopolis, AL
Manley, Robert E. .... Cincinnati, OH
Manley, Robert L. .... Anchorage, AK
Manley, Robert Lamar, III .... Douglasville, GA
Manley, Robert M. .... Dallas, TX
Manley, Robert P. .... Olympia, WA
Manley, Robt. B. .... Farmington, MO
Manley, Robt. P. .... Olympia, WA
Manley, Stephen V. .... San Jose, CA
Manley, Steve .... Newark, NJ
Manley, Tara K. .... Seattle, WA
Manley, The, P.C. .... Washington, DC
Manley, Theodore K. .... Columbus, OH
Manley, Thomas J. .... Raleigh, NC
Manley, Timothy M. .... Akron, OH
Manley, Traeger, Perry & Stapp
Demopolis, AL
Eutaw, AL
Livingston, AL
Manley, Victoria Anne .... Ada, OH
Manley, Wallace J. .... Pasadena, CA
Manley, Wendy Lou .... San Francisco, CA
Manley, Whitman F. .... Sacramento, CA
Manley, William E. .... St. Paul, MN
Manlin, Michael A. .... Pacific Grove, CA
Manlin, Roger A. S. .... Los Angeles, CA
Manlove, Mark L. .... Garrettsville, OH
Manlowe, James, Jr. .... Tuba City, AZ
Manlowe, Robert C. .... Seattle, WA
Manly, Anne E. .... Chicago, IL
Manly, Charles M., III .... Grinnell, IA
Manly, C. M. .... Grinnell, IA
Manly, Colleen P. .... Chicago, IL
Manly, Cornelius A. .... Cleveland, OH
Manly, Donald E. .... Montrose, CO
Manly, James A. .... Fargo, ND
Manly, John C., IV .... Irvine, CA
Manly Law Firm .... Grinnell, IA
Manly & Manly .... Birmingham, AL
Manly, Marc E. .... Basking Ridge, NJ
Manly, Michael P. .... Chicago, IL
Manly, Robert E. .... New Rockford, ND
Manly, Robert G. .... Carrington, ND
Manly, Roy H., Jr. .... Birmingham, AL
Manly, Samuel, Law Offices of
Louisville, KY
Manly, William F. .... Lago Vista, TX
Mann, A. Kenneth .... Pittsburgh, PA
Mann, Alice Olsen .... Boston, MA
Mann, Alice Olsen, P.C. .... Boston, MA
Mann, Allen B. .... Dallas, TX
Mann, Allison L. .... Ann Arbor, MI
Mann, Ana L. .... Department of Justice, Executive Office for Immigration Review, GV
Mann, Arline .... New York, NY
Mann, Arthur .... Kenilworth, NJ
Mann, Arthur L. .... Champaign, IL
Mann, Arthur L. .... Urbana, IL
Mann, Arthur S., III .... New Orleans, LA
Mann, Ashlee Jennifer .... Atlanta, GA
Mann, Authur H. .... Lakeport, CA
Mann, Barbara J. .... Washington, DC
Mann, Barry D. .... Raleigh, NC
Mann, Basil P. .... Chicago, IL
Mann, Benjamin F. .... Kansas City, MO
Mann & Bent, P.C. .... White Plains, NY
Mann, Bernard .... Bronx, NY
Mann, Bernard W. .... San Diego, CA
Mann, Bill .... Rosenberg, TX
Mann, Bill R. .... Hagåtña, GU
Mann, Bobby H., Jr. .... Greenville, SC
Mann, Bobby J. .... Fort Worth, TX
Mann, Bracken, Layng and Knezo, LLC
Washington, DC
Atlanta, GA
Leesburg, VA
Mann, Brian D. .... Wetumpka, AL
Mann, Bruce Alan .... San Francisco, CA
Mann, Bruce L. .... Baltimore, MD
Mann, C. Harold .... Kansas City, MO
Mann, C. Kay .... Houston, TX
Mann, C. Scott, Jr. .... Beaumont, TX
Mann, Calvin C., Jr. .... Austin, TX
Dallas, TX
Fort Worth, TX
Houston, TX
Mann, Carolyn H. .... Port Chester, NY
Mann, Carrie Bedwell
Federal Communications Commission, International Bureau, GV
Mann, Carter M. .... Portland, OR
Mann, Charles E. .... Birmingham, MI
Mann, Charles W. .... Edinburg, TX
Mann, Cheryl L. .... Dallas, TX
Mann, Cheryl L. .... Dallas, TX
Mann, Christopher L. .... New York, NY
Mann, Christopher Ludlow .... Bath, ME
Mann, Clifton A. .... Lubbock, TX
Mann, Clyde R. .... New Smyrna Beach, FL
Mann Connelly & Hastings, P.C.
Lexington, VA
Mann & Cowan, P.C. .... Birmingham, AL
Mann, Craig T. .... San Diego, CA
Mann, Curtis J. .... Bloomfield Hills, MI
Mann, Cynthia D. .... New York, NY
Mann, Daniel J. .... New York, NY
Mann, Daniel J. .... Philadelphia, PA
Mann, Dara D. .... Minneapolis, MN
Mann, Darrlyn .... Vineland, NJ
Mann, David .... Seattle, WA
Mann, David A. .... Plantation, FL
Mann, David Alan .... Huntsville, AL
Mann, David C. .... Sikeston, MO
Mann, David G. .... Los Angeles, CA
Mann, David H. .... Orange, CA
Mann, David J. .... Suisun City, CA
Mann, David M. .... San Jose, CA
Mann, David S. .... Chicago, IL
Mann, David S. .... Cincinnati, OH
Mann, Deborah A. .... Albany, NY
Mann, Deborah E. .... Albuquerque, NM
Mann, Deborah M. .... Portland, ME
Mann, Dennis S. .... New Orleans, LA
Mann, Diane McGee .... Phoenix, AZ
Mann, Donald J. .... Haddonfield, NJ
Mann, Donegan .... Rockville, MD
Mann, Douglas A. .... Dayton, OH
Mann, Douglas E. .... Corpus Christi, TX
Mann, Douglas F. .... Milwaukee, WI
Mann, Douglas K. .... Redlands, CA
Mann, Douglas L. .... Bloomfield Hills, MI
Mann, Drake .... Little Rock, AR
Mann, Dudley R. .... El Paso, TX
Mann, Edward A. .... Farmville, VA
Mann, Edward A., P.C. .... Farmville, VA
Mann, Edwin C. .... Los Angeles, CA
Mann, Eleana Kay .... Southfield, MI
Mann & Elias .... Beverly Hills, CA
Mann, Elizabeth D. .... Los Angeles, CA
Mann, Elizabeth Davis .... Woodstock, VT
Mann, Elizabeth N. .... Bloomington, IN
Mann, Elizabeth Owen .... Greenville, SC
Mann Employers Legal Group, P.A.
Sarasota, FL
Mann, Eric D. .... Atlantic City, NJ
Mann, Eric H. .... Cleveland, OH
Mann, Eric N. .... Chicago, IL
Mann, Eugene L. .... Miami, FL
Mann, Fletcher C. .... Greenville, SC
Mann, Fletcher C., Jr. .... Greenville, SC
Mann, Floyd A. .... White Plains, NY
Mann, Francis B., Jr. .... White Plains, NY
Mann, Frank P. .... Westbury, NY
Mann, Frank W. .... Baltimore, MD
Mann, Franklin B., Jr. .... Fort Myers, FL
Mann, Franklin M. .... Spartanburg, SC
Mann, Franklin Milton, Jr.
Tallahassee, FL
Mann, Fred .... Bloomfield Hills, MI
Mann, Fred R. .... Mount Vernon, IL
Mann, Frederick Martin .... Columbus, OH
Mann, Frederick R., Jr. .... Winter Park, FL
Mann, Frederick R., Jr., P.A.
Orlando, FL
Winter Park, FL
Mann, Gabrielle Marder .... Dania, FL

Mann, Gail S. ....Maynard, MA
Mann, Gary D. ....Los Angeles, CA
Mann, Gary L. ....Austin, TX
Mann, George P. ....Farmington Hills, MI
Mann, George P., & Associates, P.C. Farmington Hills, MI
Mann, George T. "Ted" Winston-Salem, NC
Mann, George W., Jr. ....Boston, MA
Mann, Gerald ....New York, NY
Mann, Gilda S. ....Baltimore, MD
Mann, Gregory B. ....Chicago, IL
Mann, Gregory J. ....Los Angeles, CA
Mann, H. Douglas ....Louisville, KY
Mann, H. George ....Chicago, IL
Mann, Hadfield & Thorne, P.C. Brigham City, UT
Mann, Henry B. ....Louisville, KY
Mann, Henry R. ....San Diego, CA
Mann, H. F. Rick ....Tallahassee, FL
Mann, Howard ....New City, NY
Mann, Howard L. ....White Plains, NY
Mann, Howard Oliver ....Corbin, KY
Mann, Ian F., P.A. ....Fort Myers, FL
Mann, Ian Ferguson ....Fort Myers, FL
Mann, J. Cameron ....Virginia Beach, VA
Mann, J. Douglas ....Tulsa, OK
Mann, J. Edward, Jr. & Associates Brownsville, TX
Edinburg, TX
Mann, J. Edward, Jr., & Associates Harlingen, TX
Mann, J. Edward, Jr. & Associates McAllen, TX
Mann, J. Keith ....Palo Alto, CA
Mann, J. Kevin ....Dallas, TX
Mann, J. Mark ....Henderson, TX
Mann, J. Terrell ....Dallas, TX
Mann, J. Thomas ....Chattanooga, TN
Mann, Jack I. ....San Diego, CA
Mann, Jacques ....Philadelphia, PA
Mann, James C. ....Oakland, CA
Mann, James E. ....Mount Kisco, NY
Mann, James E. ....Austin, TX
Mann, James G. Securities and Exchange Commission, Division of Enforcement, GV
Mann, James H. Board of Governors Of The Federal Reserve System, Division of Consumer and Community Affairs, GV
Mann, James L. ....Chillicothe, OH
Mann, James L., Jr. ....Towson, MD
Mann, James L., Jr., P.A. ....Towson, MD
Mann, James R. ....New Orleans, LA
Mann, James R. ....Greenville, SC
Mann, Jan Maselli ....New Orleans, LA
Mann, Jason ....Harlingen, TX
Mann, Jay M. ....Phoenix, AZ
Mann, Jeanne C. ....San Rafael, CA
Mann, Jeff A. ....Los Angeles, CA
Mann, Jeffrey L. ....Decatur, GA
Mann, Jeffrey R. ....New York, NY
Mann, Jeffrey S. ....New York, NY
Mann, Jeffry S. ....San Francisco, CA
Mann, Jennifer Bonanno ....Decatur, GA
Mann, Jerri Lynn ....Lompoc, CA
Mann, Jerry H. ....Fresno, CA
Mann, Jessica ....New York, NY
Mann, Jill Elmstrom ....Middleton, MA
Mann, Jim H. ....Austin, TX
Mann, Joel E. ....New York, NY
Mann, John B. ....Richmond, VA
Mann, John B., Jr. ....Auburndale, FL
Mann, John E. ....Laredo, TX
Mann, John L. ....Lakeland, FL
Mann, John M. ....Encino, CA
Mann, John M. ....Chicago, IL
Mann, John M. ....Portland, OR
Mann, John P. ....Greenville, SC
Mann, John P., Jr. ....Greenville, SC
Mann, John R. ....Denver, CO
Mann, John R. ....Royal Oak, MI
Mann, John R. ....Winston-Salem, NC
Mann, John Scott ....El Paso, TX
Mann, John W. ....Lexington, KY
Mann, John William ....Raleigh, NC
Mann Johnson Wooster & McLaughlin, P.S. Tacoma, WA
Mann, Jonathan T. ....Boston, MA
Mann, Joseph ....New York, NY
Mann, Joy R. ....Prosperity, SC
Mann, Judith M. ....New York, NY
Mann, Judy H. ....Office of Government Ethics, Office of General Counsel and Legal Policy, GV
Mann, Julia A. ....Shreveport, LA
Mann, Julia W. ....San Antonio, TX
Mann, Julian, III ....Raleigh, NC
Mann, Julie Marie ....Stratham, NH
Mann & Just, LLP ....New York, NY
Mann, Kathleen C. ....La Crosse, WI
Mann, Kay Mercein ....Lancaster, PA
Mann, Keith A. ....Sarasota, FL
Mann, Kelly M. ....Portland, OR
Mann, Kenneth C. ....Van Nuys, CA
Mann, Kenneth L. ....Orlando, FL
Mann, Kenneth L., P.A. ....Mount Dora, FL
Orlando, FL
Sanford, FL
Tavares, FL
Mann, Kent L. ....Cleveland, OH
Mann, Kevin Elliott ....Phoenix, AZ
Mann, Kim D. ....Washington, DC
Mann, Kim Kelly ....Winston-Salem, NC
Mann, Kimberly G. ....Beckley, WV
Mann, Kimberly V. ....Washington, DC
Mann, Lane W. ....Montgomery, AL
Mann, Laura Ann ....Milford, MA
Mann, Laura J. Small Business Administration, Office of the General Counsel, GV
Mann, Laurence A. ....Lexington, VA
Mann Law Associates, P.C. Cherry Hill, NJ
Langhorne, PA
Philadelphia, PA
Mann Law Firm ....Indianapolis, IN
Terre Haute, IN
Mann Law Firm ....Greenville, SC
Mann Law Firm, The ....Los Angeles, CA
Mann, Lawrence A. ....San Francisco, CA
Mann, Lawrence A. ....New Orleans, LA
Mann, Lawrence A. ....Laredo, TX
Mann, Lawrence C. ....Detroit, MI
Mann, Lawrence E. ....Portland, OR
Seattle, WA
Mann, Lawrence M. ....Washington, DC
Mann, Lawrence P. ....Bethesda, MD
Mann, Leala Salter ....Austin, TX
Mann, Lee S. ....Fairfax, VA
Mann, Leo L. ....Encino, CA
Mann, Lesli L. ....Chicago, IL
Mann, Leslie J. ....Newark, NJ
Mann, Leslie N. ....Little Rock, AR
Mann, Lewis T., III ....Los Angeles, CA
Mann, Linda ....Westhampton Beach, NY
Mann, Lisa B. ....New York, NY
Mann, Lisa E. ....Miami, FL
Mann, Lisa F. ....Albuquerque, NM
Mann, Lisa Froimson ....Cleveland, OH
Mann, Lisa Gaye ....Houston, TX
Mann, Lloyd S. ....Tarzana, CA
Mann, Lori K. ....Boise, ID
Mann, Lowell E. ....Cherry Hill, NJ
Langhorne, PA
Philadelphia, PA
Mann, Lynne Francis ....Sherman Oaks, CA
Mann, M. Douglas ....Atlanta, GA
Mann & Mairone ....Chicago, IL
Mann & Mann ....Port Chester, NY
Mann, Mann & Lewis, P.C. ....Nyack, NY
Mann, Marcus ....Salyersville, KY
Mann, Margaret M. ....San Diego, CA
Mann, Margery Moselle ....Detroit, MI
Mann, Marilyn K. Securities and Exchange Commission, Division of Investment Management, GV
Mann, Marjorie Rowe ....Asheville, NC
Mann, Mark G. ....Denton, TX
Mann, Mark L. ....San Diego, CA
Mann, Mark R. ....Evansville, IN
Mann, Mark S. ....Alexandria, VA
Mann and Marshall, LLP ....Bethesda, MD
Mann, Martin D. ....Milwaukee, WI
Mann, Martin R. ....Falls Church, VA
Mann, Mary F. ....Birmingham, MI
Mann, Mary Jo ....Knoxville, TN
Sevierville, TN
Mann, Mary Ruth ....Seattle, WA
Mann, Matthew ....Santa Barbara, CA
Mann, Maureen E. ....Victorville, CA
Mann, Michael ....New York, NY
Mann, Michael A. ....Columbia, SC
Mann, Michael B. ....Oak Brook, IL
Mann, Michael B. ....Towson, MD
Mann, Michael D. ....Washington, DC
New York, NY
Mann, Michael D. ....Atlanta, GA
Mann, Michael J. ....Princeton, NJ
Mann, Michelle ....Glendale, CA
Mann, Michelle ....New York, NY
Mann & Mitchell ....Providence, RI
Mann, Monroe Yale ....Port Chester, NY
Mann, Monte L. ....Chicago, IL
Mann & Moore, P.C. ....Vineland, NJ
Mann, Nathan H. ....Albuquerque, NM
Mann, Neal L. ....Washington, DC
Mann, Neil R. ....Chicago, IL
Mann, Nikki J. ....Albuquerque, NM
Mann, Nikolas P. ....London, OH
Mann, Norman H. ....Providence, RI
Mann, Orville H., Jr. ....Nyack, NY
Mann, Otis R., Jr. ....Charleston, WV
Mann, Pamela A. ....New York, NY
Mann, Pamuella F. ....Geneva, IL
Mann, Pat H., Jr. ....Brownsville, TN
Mann, Patricia Ivester ....Oklahoma City, OK
Mann, Paul Eugene ....Santa Ana, CA
Mann, Pearl Gondrella ....Orange, CA
Mann, Perry E., Jr. ....Hinton, WV
Mann, Peter M. ....Leland, MI
Mann, Philip Andrew ....Swampscott, MA
Mann, Philip J. ....Chicago, IL
Mann, Philip P. ....Seattle, WA
Mann, Philip R. ....New York, NY
Mann, Phillip L. ....Washington, DC
Mann, Phyllis E. ....Alexandria, LA
Mann, R. Bronson ....Houston, TX
Mann, R. Lee, III ....Atlanta, GA
Mann, R. Seth ....Dade City, FL
Mann, R. Seth, P.A. ....Dade City, FL
Mann, Rachel B. ....Philadelphia, PA
Mann, Ralph S. ....New York, NY
Mann, Ralph W. ....Roseville, CA
Mann, Rebecca N. ....Haddonfield, NJ
Mann, Richard A. ....Indianapolis, IN
Mann, Richard A. ....Chapel Hill, NC
Mann, Richard E. ....Winchester, IL
Mann, Richard E. ....Port Orchard, WA
Mann, Richard F. ....Washington, DC
Mann, Richard G., Jr. ....McLean, VA
Mann, Richard L. ....Beverly Hills, CA
Mann, Richard L. ....Los Angeles, CA
Mann, Richard L. ....Columbus, OH
Mann, Richard N. ....Oklahoma City, OK
Mann, Richard S. ....Columbus, OH
Mann, Robert ....Detroit, MI
Mann, Robert B. ....Providence, RI
Mann, Robert C. ....Waltham, MA
Mann, Robert D. ....Bloomington, IN
Mann, Robert E. ....Boca Raton, FL
Mann, Robert E. ....Chicago, IL
Mann, Robert E., (Ltd.) ....Chicago, IL
Mann, Robert J. ....Kansas City, MO
Mann, Robert J. ....Columbus, OH
Mann, Robert L. ....Milwaukee, WI
Mann, Robert M. ....Chicago, IL
Mann, Robert N. ....Phoenix, AZ
Mann, Robert Paul ....Lutherville, MD
Mann, Robert Paul, & Associates, P.A. Lutherville, MD
Mann, Robert S. ....Los Angeles, CA
Los Angeles, CA
Mann, Robert T. ....Tarpon Springs, FL
Mann, Robert W. ....Westwood, CA
Mann, Robert W. ....Martinsville, VA
Stuart, VA
Mann, Roberta F. Joint Committees And Commissions, GV
Mann, Ronald J. ....Washington, DC
Mann, Ronald J. ....Centralia, IL
Mann, Roy H. ....Corona, CA
Mann, Russell D. ....Roswell, NM
Mann, Russell H., Jr. ....Brookline, MA
Mann, Sam H., Jr. ....St. Petersburg, FL
Mann, Samuel A. ....Wilmington, NC
Mann, Sandra K. ....Washington, DC
Mann, Sandra S. ....Edinburg, TX
Mann, Scott ....Beverly Hills, CA
Mann, Scott ....Chicago, IL
Mann, Scott J. ....Hutchinson, KS
Wichita, KS
Mann, Scott M. ....Kansas City, MO
Mann, Selma J. ....Anaheim, CA
Mann, Seymour ....Houston, TX
Mann, Seymour H. ....Sebastopol, CA
Mann & Shappell ....Denver, CO
Mann, Singh Atma ....San Jose, CA
Mann, Stanley K. ....Culver City, CA
Mann, Stephen ....New York, NY
Mann, Steven F. ....Waltham, MA
Mann, Steven L. ....Colorado Springs, CO
Orlando, FL
Mann, Stuart ....Denver, CO
Mann, Stuart Jay ....Franklin Park, IL
Mann, Sue Tannehill ....Lafayette, LA
Mann, Susan ....Walnut Creek, CA
Securities and Exchange Commission, Office of the General Counsel, GV
Mann, Susan M. ....Phoenix, AZ
Mann, Susan M. ....Indianapolis, IN
Mann, Susan S. ....Toledo, OH
Mann, Suzanne ....Tallahassee, FL
Mann, T. David ....Pensacola, FL
Mann, T. David ....Macon, GA
Mann, T. Nelson ....Overland Park, KS
Kansas City, MO
Mann, Ted L. ....Birmingham, AL
Mann, Terry J. ....Wichita, KS
Mann, Theo D. ....Newnan, GA
Mann, Theodore M. ....Cleveland, OH
Mann, Theodore M., Jr. ....Cleveland, OH
Mann, Theodore M., Jr., Law Firm Cleveland, OH
Painesville, OH
Solon, OH
Mann, Theodore R. ....Philadelphia, PA
Mann, Thomas ....Austin, TX
Mann, Thomas A. ....Cleveland, OH
Mann, Thomas A. ....Tulsa, OK
Mann, Thomas A., II ....Tampa, FL
Mann, Thomas C. ....Joplin, MO
Mann, Thomas C. ....Columbia, SC
Mann, Thomas C. ....Austin, TX
Mann, Thomas D., Jr. ....Milton, MA
Mann, Thomas J. ....Arlington Heights, IL
Mann, Thomas O. ....Department of Energy, Office of Hearings and Appeals, GV
Mann, Thomas Peter ....Fairfax, VA
Mann, Tommy C. ....Macon, GA
Mann, Tommy C. ....Milledgeville, GA
Warner Robins, GA
Mann, Travis ....Beverly Hills, CA
Mann, Ungar, Spector & Labovitz, P.C. Philadelphia, PA
Mann, V. James ....New York, NY
Mann, Valerie K. ....Department of Justice, Environment and Natural Resources Division, GV
Mann, Vicki L. ....Chicago, IL
Mann, Vijai Singh ....Chicago, IL
Mann, W. Berkeley, Jr. ....Denver, CO
Mann, W. David ....Washington, DC
Mann, W. Douglas, Jr. ....Jackson, MS
Mann, Walter & Bishop, P.C. Springfield, MO
Mann, Walter H. ....Minneapolis, MN
Mann, Wilfred R. ....Saipan, TT
Mann, William ....Washington, DC
Mann, William A. ....Raleigh, NC
Mann, William A. ....Madison, WI
Mann, William A., Law Offices of Austin, TX
Gonzales, TX
Mann, William A., Law Offices of Gonzales, TX
Mann, William Ralph ....Denton, TX
Mann, William Ralph, A Professional Corporation ....Denton, TX
Mann & Wooldridge, P.C. ....Franklin, GA
Newnan, GA
Manna, Anthony S. ....Akron, OH
Manna & Bonello ....West End, NJ
Manna, Herbert T., Jr. ....Brewster, NY
Manna, John C. ....West End, NJ
Manna, John J., Jr. ....New City, NY
Manna, Joseph J. ....Buffalo, NY
Manna, Mark Andrew ....Lawrence, KS
Manna, Michael A. ....Ridgewood, NJ
Manna, Michael A., & Associates, P.C. Ridgewood, NJ
Manna, Santo ....New York, NY
Mannakee, Nate D. ....Tacoma, WA
Mannarelli, Raymond ....Providence, RI
Mannarino, Arthur A. ....New York, NY
Mannarino, Craig P. ....Chicago, IL
Mannarino, Richard O. ....New York, NY
Mannarino, Yagerman & Greenhaus, P.C. New York, NY
Mannato, John T. ....West Chester, PA
Mannausa, Gerald B. ....East Lansing, MI
Mannausa, Gerald B., P.C. ....East Lansing, MI
Mannausa, Richard R. ....Detroit, MI
Southfield, MI
Manne, Beverly Weiss ....Greensburg, PA
Pittsburgh, PA
Manne, Burton G. ....Baytown, TX
Manne, Grace Nixon Fort Lauderdale, FL
Manne, Henry G. ....Arlington, VA
Manne, Jason W. ....Pittsburgh, PA
Manne, Karl E. ....Herkimer, NY
Manne, Kathleen Neuner ....Alexandria, VA
Manne, Kenneth C. ....Phoenix, AZ
Manne, Letty Jane ....Hillsdale, NY
Manne, Neal S. ....Houston, TX
Manne, Robert J. ....Fort Lauderdale, FL
West Palm Beach, FL
Manne, William S. ....Portland, OR
Mannear, W. Steven ....Baton Rouge, LA
Manneh, Najla A. ....Hudson, OH
Mannella, F. Anthony ....Anoka, MN
Mannella, Felix A. ....Anoka, MN
Mannella, Richard S. ....Philadelphia, PA
Mannella, Robert F. ....Anoka, MN
Mannen, Ann T. ....Cleveland, OH
Mannen, Jerry A., Jr. ....Wilmington, NC
Mannen, Richard M. ....St. Petersburg, FL
Mannen, Ted R. ....United States Senate, Senatorial Assistants, GV
Mannenbach, Peter F. ....Green Bay, WI
Mannenbach, Stephen F. ....Dallas, OR
Manner, Bobby G. ....Jackson, TN
Manner, Jennifer Abbe ....Washington, DC
Manner, Mark ....Nashville, TN
Manner, Richard L. ....St. Paul, MN
Mannerino & Briguglio Rancho Cucamonga, CA
Mannerino, John D. Rancho Cucamonga, CA
Manners, Barbara R. ....Spring Valley, NY
Manners, Don ....Oklahoma City, OK
Manners, Edward F. ....Mohegan Lake, NY
Manners, Jeffrey P. ....Miami, FL
Manners, Joseph P. ....Miami, FL
Manners & Manners ....Miami, FL
Manners, Michael W. ....Independence, MO
Manners, Michelle K. ....Adams, MA
Manners, Penny Ann ....Shrewsbury, MA
Manners, Robert A. ....New Windsor, NY
Manners, Robert Neal ....Atlanta, GA
Mannes, Michael H. ....Baltimore, MD
Mannes, Michael H., P.A. ....Baltimore, MD
Mannes, Paul ....Greenbelt, MD
Mannette, Elizabeth W. ....Brooklyn, NY
Mannheim, William David ....Raleigh, NC
Mannheimer, David ....Anchorage, AK
Mannheimer, Douglas L., (P.A.) Tallahassee, FL
Mannheimer, Michael J. ....New York, NY
Mannheimer, Richard V. ....Mineola, NY
Mannheimer, Robert A. ....Seattle, WA
Mannheimer, Robert E. ....Des Moines, IA
Mannheimer Swartling ....New York, NY
New York, NY
Manni, Frank J. ....Johnston, RI
Manni, Kenneth A. ....Oak Harbor, WA
Mannicci, Lori L. ....Bethlehem, PA
Mannick, Paul D. ....Santa Fe, NM
Mannie, Cheryl A. ....San Diego, CA
Manniello, Michael C. ....Syosset, NY
Manniello, Thomas R. ....Fairbanks, AK
Mannikko & Baris ....Palm City, FL
Mannikko, Bruce K. ....Roscommon, MI
Mannikko, Joseph L. ....Palm City, FL
Mannina, Anthony ....Wheaton, IL
Mannina, George J., Jr. ....Washington, DC
Mannina, Harrett W. ....San Jose, CA
Mannina, Harrett W., Jr. ....San Jose, CA
Mannina, Paul D. ....Department of Labor, Office of the Solicitor, GV
Manning, A. Alan ....Pensacola, FL
Manning, Alan L. ....Santa Monica, CA
Manning, Albert A. ....Albany, NY
Manning, Allison ....New York, NY
Manning, Amy B. ....Chicago, IL
Manning, Andrea ....Canton, MA
Manning, Ann ....Lubbock, TX
Manning & Associates ....Norcross, GA
Manning, B. Herbert ....Fort Worth, TX
Manning, B. Barbara Brooke ....New York, NY
Manning, Barbara M. Export-Import Bank of The United States, Office of the General Counsel, GV
Manning, Bernadette M. Albuquerque, NM
Manning, Bernard A. ....Westborough, MA
Manning, Billie ....Bronx, NY
Manning, Blanche M. ....Chicago, IL
Manning, Bobby R. ....West Monroe, LA

Manning, Brent V. ....**Salt Lake City, UT**
Manning, Brian E. ....**Wilkes-Barre, PA**
Manning, Brian K. ....**Fayetteville, NC**
Manning, Brince H., III ....Decatur, GA
Manning, Bryant L. ....Houston, TX
Manning, C. Frederick W., II
Columbia, SC
Manning, C. Wendell ....**Monroe, LA**
Manning, Carl W. ....**Knoxville, TN**
Manning, Charles H. ....Solon, OH
Manning, Charles R., Jr. ....Beeville, TX
Manning, Christopher C. S.
Kansas City, MO
Manning, Christopher Nicholas
Washington, DC
Manning, Christopher P. ....**Dallas, TX**
Manning, Christopher R. ....**Chicago, IL**
Manning, Claire A. ....Springfield, IL
Manning, Claire T. ....Columbia, SC
Manning, Colleen Ann ....**Boston, MA**
Manning, Colleen Helen ....San Diego, CA
Manning, Cory E. ....**Charleston, SC**
Manning & Crouch ....**Cary, NC**
Chapel Hill, NC
Raleigh, NC
Research Triangle Park, NC
Manning Curtis Bradshaw & Bednar, LLC
Salt Lake City, UT
Manning, D. James, Jr. ....**Pocatello, ID**
Manning, Daniel A. ....Williamston, NC
Manning, Daniel F. ....Dorchester, MA
Manning, Daniel L. ....**Des Moines, IA**
Manning, Daniel T., III ......Au Sable Forks, NY
Manning, Daryl K. ....Baton Rouge, LA
Manning, David J. ....**Pittsburgh, PA**
Manning, Deborah J. ....Glendora, CA
Manning, Denise Gaynelle ....Washington, DC
Manning, Diana C. ....**Florham Park, NJ**
New York, NY
Manning, Donald E. ....Brunswick, GA
Manning, Donald J. ....Waltham, MA
Manning, Donald O. ....**Arlington, VA**
Manning, Donald Q. ....**Rockford, IL**
Manning, Donna Dillon ....New York, NY
Manning, Donna M. ....**Olathe, KS**
Manning, Duncan M. ....Freeport, NY
Manning, Ecton R. ....Washington, CT
Manning, Edward F.
Merit Systems Protection Board,
Washington, D.C. Regional Office, GV
Manning, Edward P. ....Davis, CA
Manning, Edward P. ....Providence, RI
Manning, Elizabeth ....Palo Alto, CA
Manning, Ellen Heidingsfelder
New Orleans, LA
Manning, Elliott ....Coral Gables, FL
Miami, FL
Manning, Ellis W., Jr. ....Tarrytown, NY
Manning, E. T. ....**Amarillo, TX**
Manning, Francis X. ....**Cherry Hill, NJ**
Manning, Fred J. ....San Antonio, TX
Manning, Fred W. ....Chatham, NJ
Manning, Frederick J. ....Chicago, IL
Manning, Fulton & Skinner, P.A.
Cary, NC
Raleigh, NC
Research Triangle Park, NC
Manning, G. Stephen ....**Jacksonville, FL**
Manning, G. Stephen, P.A.
Jacksonville, FL
Manning, Guy, Law Offices of
Coachella, CA
Manning, Guy V. ....**Fort Worth, TX**
Manning, Henry ....Woodland Hills, CA
Manning, Herbert C. ....Fort Worth, TX
Manning, Howard E. ....**Raleigh, NC**
Manning, Hugh A. ....Oklahoma City, OK
Manning, Inez ....Lawton, OK
Manning, J. Frank, Jr. ....West Columbia, SC
Manning, J. Lawrence, Jr.
Washington, DC
Atlanta, GA
Manning, J. Paul ....**Lubbock, TX**
Manning, J. Richard ....**Seattle, WA**
Manning, Jack B. ....Houston, TX
Manning, Jack W. ....Dallas, TX
Manning, James B. ....**Newark, NJ**
Manning, James E. ....Chicago, IL
Manning, James H., Jr. ....Philadelphia, PA
Manning, James J. ....**Peoria, IL**
Manning, James J., Jr. ....**Riverside, CA**
Manning, James L. ....Dayton, OH
Manning, James O. ....Metairie, LA
Manning, Janis M. ....Irving, TX
Manning, Jas. A. ....Manchester, NH
Manning, Jay J. ....**Olympia, WA**
Seattle, WA
Manning, Jay P. ....Department of Defense,
Defense Commissary Agency, GV
Manning, Jean M. ....United States Senate,
Office of Senate Chief Counsel for
Employment, GV
Manning, Jeffrey A. ....Pittsburgh, PA
Manning, Jeffrey F. ....Canon City, CO
Manning, Jeffrey H. ....North Ridgeville, OH
Manning, Jennifer A.C. ....**Chicago, IL**
Manning, Jennifer Ellen ....Boston, MA
Manning, Jeremiah F. ....Delmar, NY
Manning, Jerome A. ....**New York, NY**
Manning, Jerry R. ....Sacramento, CA
Manning, Jill M. ....**New York, NY**
Manning, Joe R., Jr. ....Edmond, OK
Manning, Johann Ray, Jr. ....**Huntsville, AL**
Manning, John B. ....**Boston, MA**
Manning, John B. ....Worcester, MA
Manning, John F. ....**Norcross, GA**
Manning, John F. ....New York, NY
Manning, John G. ....Waterbury, CT
Manning, John H. ....Healdsburg, CA
Manning, John J. ....**Washington, DC**
Manning, John P. ....**St. Louis, MO**
Manning, John P. ....Beaverton, OR
Manning, John R. ....Marietta, GA
Manning, John R., Sr. ....Minneapolis, MN
Manning, John T. ....Willsboro, NY
Manning, John T. ....Greensboro, NC
Manning, John T. ....Arlington, VA
Manning, John W. ....**Great Falls, MT**
Manning, John W. ....Albany, NY
Manning, John W. ....**New York, NY**
Manning, Jonathan A. ....**Dallas, TX**
Manning, Joseph A. ....**Livingston, NJ**
Manning, Joseph J., Jr. ....Mentor, OH
Manning, Joseph R. ....**Atlanta, GA**
Manning, Julie A. ....**Hartford, CT**
Manning, Julie A. ....**Chicago, IL**
Manning, Karen B. ....Pensacola, FL
Manning, Karen N. ....Oklahoma City, OK
Manning, Karen T. ....Mentor, OH
Manning, Kathleen A. ....**New Orleans, LA**
Manning, Kathy E. ....**Greensboro, NC**
Manning, Kenneth A. ....Dyer, IN
Manning, Kenneth A. ....**Buffalo, NY**
Manning, Kerry J. ....**Kansas City, MO**
Manning, Kevin W. ....East Lansing, MI
Manning, Kimberly M. ....Wilkes-Barre, PA
Manning, Kinkead, Brooks & Bradbury, A
Professional Corporation ....Norristown, PA
Manning, Kirk R. ....**Fort Worth, TX**
Manning, L. Cleaves ....Portsmouth, VA
Manning, Laura Michelle ....**Miami, FL**
Manning, Laurance Rodney ....**Sunrise, FL**
Manning, Laverne H. ....Columbia, SC
Manning, Leaver, Bruder & Berberich
Los Angeles, CA
Manning and Leipold ....Decatur, GA
Manning, Leo ....New York, NY
Manning, Lisa E. ....**Tulsa, OK**
Manning, Mack P. ....Chicago, IL
Manning & Manning ....Pensacola, FL
Manning & Manning ....Worcester, MA
Manning, Marder & Wolfe ....**Irvine, CA**
Los Angeles, CA
San Diego, CA
San Francisco, CA
Manning, Margaret M. ....Los Angeles, CA
Manning, Marjorie E. ....**Sacramento, CA**
Manning, Mark A. ....**Paw Paw, MI**
Manning, Mark A., P.C. ....**Paw Paw, MI**
Manning, Mark C. ....**Anchorage, AK**
Manning, Mark C., P.C. ....**Anchorage, AK**
Manning, Mark W. ....**Boston, MA**
Manning, Mary Jo ....**Washington, DC**
Manning, Mary K. ....Sycamore, IL
Manning, Mary VanOsdel ....**Glendale, CA**
Manning, Mary-Ellen ....Peabody, MA
Manning, Matthew D. ....**Las Vegas, NV**
Manning, Maureen P. ....**Boston, MA**
Manning, Maureen Raiche ....Manchester, NH
Manning, Melvin R. ....**Richmond, VA**
Manning, Meredith ....Rockville, MD
Manning, Michael C. ....**Phoenix, AZ**
Manning, Michael D. ....Coshocton, OH
Manning, Michael E. ....Pasadena, CA
Manning, Michael E. ....Fort Collins, CO
Manning, Michael F. X. ....Garden City, NY
Manning, Michael H. ....Encino, CA
Manning, Michael J. ....**Washington, DC**
Manning, Michael J. ....Escanaba, MI
Manning, Michael J., P.C. ....Escanaba, MI
Manning, Michael K.
Prince Frederick, MD
Manning, Michael K. ....**Springfield, MA**
Manning, Michael L. ....**Boston, MA**
Manning, Michael P. ....**New York, NY**
Manning, Michael P., P.C. ....**New York, NY**
Manning & Murray, A Professional
Corporation ....**Arlington, VA**
Manning, Nancy ....Rapid City, SD
Manning, Nancy, Law Offices of
La Jolla, CA
Manning, Nevill ....**Lubbock, TX**
Manning, Nickay B. ....**Albuquerque, NM**
Manning, Norman W. W. ....Taylor, TX
Manning, P. Bryden ....Burlington, NC
Manning, P. Michael, Jr.
Delray Beach, FL
Manning, Paige A. ....**Boston, MA**
Manning, Paul Stephen ....Washington, DC
Manning, Paul W.
United States Information Agency,
Office of the General Counsel, GV
Manning, Philip V. ....Malverne, NY
Manning, R. Kenneth, Jr. ....Birmingham, AL
Manning, Ralph F. ....**Pittsburgh, PA**
Manning, Raymond V. ....Taylor, TX
Manning, R. E. ....Holt, MI
Manning, Richard deY. ....Wilkes-Barre, PA
Manning, Richard J., Jr. ....New Bedford, MA
Manning, Richard L. ....**Chicago, IL**
Manning, Richard V. ....Canton, NY
Manning, Richard W.
Federal Mine Safety and Health Review
Commission,
Office of the Administrative Law Judges, GV
Manning, Robert A. ....Rancho Santa Fe, CA
Columbus, OH
Manning, Robert A.
Federal Deposit Insurance Corporation, GV
Manning, Robert A. ....**Tallahassee, FL**
Manning, Robert D. ....Boston, MA
Manning, Robert E., Jr. ....Peoria, IL
Manning, Robert J. ....Woodland Hills, CA
Manning, Robert P. ....Naples, FL
Manning, Robert W. ....Jericho, NY
Manning, Ronald B. ....**Houston, TX**
Manning, Russell J. ....**Corpus Christi, TX**
Manning, Sam P. ....Spartanburg, SC
Manning, Sandra L. K. ....Trenton, NJ
Manning, Sarah M. ....**Hyannis, MA**
Manning, Shannon L. ....Reston, VA
Manning, Shannon M. ....Chesapeake, VA
Manning, Sherri L. ....Kansas City, MO
Manning & Smith ....**Olathe, KS**
Manning, Stephen R.
East Longmeadow, MA
Manning, Stephen R., P.C.
East Longmeadow, MA
Manning, Steven D. ....**Los Angeles, CA**
San Diego, CA
Manning, Susan C. ....Madison, WI
Manning, Tammy C. ....**Houston, TX**
Manning, Teresa Creef ....Richmond, VA
Manning, Thomas A. ....**Worcester, MA**
Manning, Thomas C. ....**Raleigh, NC**
Manning, Thomas G. ....**Danville, CA**
Manning, Thomas H. ....**Rome, GA**
Manning, Thomas J. ....Centerville, OH
Manning, Thomas J., Co., LPA
Centerville, OH
Manning, Thomas J., Jr. ....**Baltimore, MD**
Manning, Thomas P. ....**Oklahoma City, OK**
Manning, Timothy E. ....**Cleveland, OH**
Manning, Timothy P. ....**Nashville, TN**
Manning, Tod ....**San Francisco, CA**
Manning, Victoria A. ....**Chatham, NJ**
Manning, Vincent P. ....Freehold, NJ
Manning, Walter N. ....Clearwater, FL
Manning, Wellington M., Jr.
Greenville, SC
Manning & West ....Providence, RI
Manning, William ....**Blue Bell, PA**
Manning, William E. ....**Walnut Creek, CA**
Manning, William E. ....**Dover, DE**
Wilmington, DE
Manning, William E., Jr. ....**Kinston, NC**
Manning, William H. ....**Minneapolis, MN**
Manning, William J. ....**White Plains, NY**
Manning, William J., (P.C.) ....New York, NY
Manning, Winifred E. ....San Antonio, TX
Manning-Cabrol, Denise ....**Washington, DC**
Manning-Villar, Eileen ....**San Leandro, CA**
Mannino, Anthony V., III
Philadelphia, PA
Mannino, Edward F. ....**Philadelphia, PA**
Mannino, Frederick J. ....**Biloxi, MS**
Mannino, James A., (P.C.)
Washington, DC
Mannino, Joseph, (P.A.) ....Boca Raton, FL
Mannino, Loren M. ....Warren, MI
Mannino, Robert J. ....**Philadelphia, PA**
Mannino, Rosaline A. ....Bronx, NY
Mannion & Copani ....Syracuse, NY
Mannion, Daniel J. ....St. Louis, MO
Mannion, E. Gerard ....**San Francisco, CA**
Mannion, Elizabeth R. ....**Clearwater, FL**
Mannion, J. Timothy ....Springfield, MA
Mannion, James F. ....**Norristown, PA**
Mannion, James M. ....Bethel, CT
Mannion, James P., Jr. ....**St. Louis, MO**
Mannion, Joseph A. ....Plainview, NY
Mannion, Joseph M. ....Philadelphia, PA
Mannion & Lowe, A Professional
Corporation ....**San Francisco, CA**
Mannion, M. Matthew ....**Woodbridge, NJ**
Mannion, Malachy E. ....Scranton, PA
Mannion, Maureen A. ....**Kansas City, MO**
Mannion, Michael J. ....**New Milford, CT**
Mannion, Michael Joseph ....**Springfield, IL**
Mannion, Robert E. ....**Washington, DC**
Mannion, Terence A.J. ....Syracuse, NY
Mannion, Thomas B. ....New Brunswick, NJ
Mannion, Thomas J., Jr.
Mount Laurel, NJ
Mannion, Thomas P. ....**San Francisco, CA**
Mannion, Thomas P. ....Cleveland, OH
Mannis, Bob D. ....**Stamford, CT**
Mannis, Eric I. ....Woodbridge, NJ
Mannis, Joseph ....**Los Angeles, CA**
Mannis, Kent L. ....Berkeley, CA
Mannis, Michael D. ....Chicago, IL
Mannis & Phillips, L.L.P.
Los Angeles, CA
Mannis, Valerie S. ....Madison, WI
Mannisto, Jeffrey A. ....**Los Angeles, CA**
Mannisto, Michael J. ....Houghton, MI
Mannix, Charles R., Jr.
Department of Defense,
Defense Legal Services Agency, GV
Mannix, Colleen M. ....**Mattoon, IL**
Mannix, Daniel P., V ....**West Chester, PA**
Mannix, David R. ....Grants Pass, OR
Mannix, Edward P. ....Walpole, MA
Mannix, Gerald J. ....**Park Ridge, IL**
Mannix, James M., Jr. ....Briarcliff Manor, NY
Mannix, Joan M. ....**Chicago, IL**
Mannix, John C. ....**Glens Falls, NY**
Mannix, John C., Jr. ....Saratoga Springs, NY
Mannix, John R., Jr. ....**Chicago, IL**
Mannix, Julia D. ....**Chicago, IL**
Mannix, Kevin L. ....Salem, OR
Mannix, Lawrence S. ....**New Canaan, CT**
Mannix, Maria L. ....Dover, MA
Mannix, Michael M. ....**McLean, VA**
Mannix, Michelle A. ....Boston, MA
Mannix, Patrick J. ....Glens Falls, NY
Mannix, Paul M. ....**Pittsburgh, PA**
Mannix, Phyllis M. ....Philadelphia, PA
Mannix, Richard E. ....Larchmont, NY
Mannix, Richard J. ....**Washington, DC**
Mannix, Thomas C. ....Beaver, PA
Manno, Barbara M. ....Atlanta, GA
Manno, Christine M. ....Phoenix, AZ
Manno, Christopher E. ....**New York, NY**
Manno, David B. ....**Garden City, NY**
Manno, Joseph D. ....Staten Island, NY
Manno, Michael A. ....Rochester, NY
Manno, Michael D. ....Round Rock, TX
Manno, Michael J. ....West Des Moines, IA
Manno, Richard Jay ....**Orlando, FL**
Manno, Theodore Paul ....New York, NY
Manno, Valerie R. ....Miami, FL
Manno, Vincent P. ....Chicago, IL
Mannon, Charles B. ....**Ukiah, CA**
Mannon, Cindy ....**Lansing, MI**
Mannon & King ....**Ukiah, CA**
Mannor, Robert D. ....**Saginaw, MI**
Mannos, James G. ....Akron, OH
Canton, OH
Manns, Alphonso ....Bloomington, IN
Manns, Andrew D., Jr. ....Jersey City, NJ
Manns, Dollie Stafford ....Bloomington, IN
Manns, E. Kent ....**Dallas, TX**
Manns, F. Philip, Jr. ....San Diego, CA
Manns, George ....Los Angeles, CA
Manns & Green ....Beverly Hills, CA
Manns, James H. ....Pompano Beach, FL
Manns & Manns ....Bloomington, IN
Manns, Robert S. ....Beverly Hills, CA
Manns, Thomas E. ....St. Louis, MO
Manns, Thomas E., P.C. ....St. Louis, MO
Manns, William ....Beverly Hills, CA
Mann-Stadt, Rendi L. ....**Springfield, IL**
Mannweiler, Leah S. ....**Indianapolis, IN**
Mannweiler, Paul S. ....Indianapolis, IN
Manny, Carter H., III ....Portland, ME
Manny, Gary J. ....Fort Worth, TX
Manny, Gary J., Attorney at Law, P.C.
Fort Worth, TX
Manny, Jill S. ....New York, NY
Manny, Karen D. ....Buffalo, NY
Manny, Nicole R. ....**Boston, MA**
Mano, Joseph M., Jr. ....Chehalis, WA
Mano, McKerricher, Paroutaud, Hunt &
Sprague, Inc., P.C. ....Chehalis, WA
Manocchio, Sandra A. ....**Baltimore, MD**
Manocha, Sohan L. ....Atlanta, GA
Manocha, Sohan L., P.C. ....Atlanta, GA
Manocheo, D. Nicholas ....Chicago, IL
Manochi, Glenn A. ....**Haddonfield, NJ**
Philadelphia, PA
Manock, Charles K. ....**Fresno, CA**
Manock, Kendall L. ....**Fresno, CA**
Manoff, Dawn M. ....**Chicago, IL**
Manoff, Laurie G.
Palm Beach Gardens, FL
Manoff, Lawrence M. ....Philadelphia, PA
Manoff, Marc D. ....Malvern, PA
Reading, PA
Manoff, Marcus ....Philadelphia, PA
Manoff, Paul A. ....Boston, MA
Manoff, Stuart R. ....**West Palm Beach, FL**
Manoff, Stuart R., P.A.
West Palm Beach, FL
Manogue, David J. ....**Erie, PA**
Pittsburgh, PA
Manogue, Edward S. ....Cincinnati, OH
Manogue & Manogue ....Cincinnati, OH
Manogue, Megan M. ....Baltimore, MD
Manogue, Roy, Jr. ....Cincinnati, OH
Manoil, Colette ....Boston, MA
Manoil, Colette, Law Firm of ....Boston, MA
Manoil, Mark L. ....**Phoenix, AZ**
Manolakas, Christine ....Sacramento, CA
Manolakas, Dale E. ....Beverly Hills, CA
Manolakas, George ....**Bakersfield, CA**
Manolakas, Kathleen E. ....Houston, TX
Manolakas, Stefan L. ....Folsom, CA
Manolakas, Thomas G. ....**Sacramento, CA**
Manolakis, Margaret ....**Philadelphia, PA**
Manolas, Nicholas ....New York, NY
Manolis, Christopher G. ....**Detroit, MI**
Manolis, George N. ....**Huron, SD**
Manolis, James W. ....**New Castle, PA**
Manoliu, Andrei M. ....**Palo Alto, CA**
Manolukas, Kimon ....San Francisco, CA
Manoll, Roy E., III ....**Athens, GA**
Manoloff, Richard D. ....**Cleveland, OH**
Manolopoulos, Lynn T. ....**Bellevue, WA**
Manolukas, Nicholas G. ....Corvallis, OR
Manolukas, Nicholas P. ....**Toledo, OH**
Manon, Jay P. ....Pocatello, ID
Manon, Lora L. ....Bryan, OH
Manoog, John C., III ....**Centerville, MA**
Manoog, John C., III, Law Offices of, The
Centerville, MA
Manoogian, David C. ....Attleboro, MA
Manoogian, David E. ....**Washington, DC**
Manoogian, John E., Law Offices of
Walnut Creek, CA
Manopoli, Jane E. ....Boston, MA
Manopoli, John F. ....**Cambridge, MA**
Manor, C. Robert ....**Washington, DC**
Manor, Laura L. ....Smyrna, GA
Manor, Monika L. ....**Irving, TX**
Manor, Thomas G. (IBA) ....Cedar Rapids, IA
Manor, Timothy J. ....**Orlando, FL**
Manor, Wade G. ....**Jackson, MS**
Manore, John J., III ....Toledo, OH
Manos, Bruce J. ....**Chicago, IL**
Manos, Chris G. ....Akron, OH
Manos, Christopher B., Jr. ....**Atlanta, GA**
Manos, Christopher L. ....Big Timber, MT
Manos, Christopher B., Jr., P.C.
Atlanta, GA
Manos, C. J. ....**Charleston, SC**
Manos & Curl, LLP ....Millbrae, CA
Manos, Eli ....**Cleveland, OH**
Manos, G. Basil ....**New York, NY**
Manos, Geo. T. ....Akron, OH
Manos, Jeffrey D. ....**Millbrae, CA**
Manos, Jerry R. ....Millbrae, CA

Manos, John M. ....St. Louis, MO
Manos, John M. ....Canton, OH
Cleveland, OH
Youngstown, OH
Manos, John M. ....Cleveland, OH
Manos, John S. ....Philadelphia, PA
Manos, Karen Louise ....Washington, DC
Manos, Marcus A. ....Columbia, SC
Manos, Martin, Pergram & Dietz, L.P.A.
Columbus, OH
Delaware, OH
Marion, OH
Marysville, OH
Mt. Gilead, OH
Mt. Vernon, OH
Powell, OH
Sunbury, OH
Worthington, OH
Manos, Nicholas G. ....Chicago, IL
Manos, Pappas & Stefanski Co., L.P.A.
Canton, OH
Cleveland, OH
Youngstown, OH
Manos, Peter J. ....Columbus, OH
Delaware, OH
Manos, Robyn C. ....Los Angeles, CA
Manos, Ronald N. ....Cherry Hill, NJ
Manos, Rose Duggan ....Columbia, SC
Manos, Theodore J., and Associates
Las Vegas, NV
Manos, Theodore L. ....Charleston, SC
Manougian, Nancy J. ....Columbus, OH
Manougian, Viken ....North Andover, MA
Manoukian, Marina ....Glendale, CA
Manoukian, Milton ....Reno, NV
Manoukian, Nigol ....Glendale, CA
Manoukian, Noel E. ....Gardnerville, NV
Manoukian, Noel E., Ltd., A Professional Corporation ....Gardnerville, NV
Manoukian, Socrates Peter ....San Jose, CA
Manoushagian, Dana Davis ....Bridgeport, TX
Manoussos, Michael ....Garden City, NY
Manovich, Mark E. ....Dayton, OH
Manowitz, David B. ....New York, NY
Manown, Peter S. ....Atlanta, GA
Manpearl, Gerald T. ....Los Angeles, CA
Manpel-Scianna, Dominique ....Pawling, NY
Manring, Daniel L. ....Columbus, OH
Manring, Edward M. ....Albany, MO
Manring & Farrell ....Columbus, OH
Manring, John ....St. Joseph, MO
Manring, Nicholas J. ....Laredo, TX
Manring & Parman, P.C. ....Albany, MO
Manring, Rick L. ....San Francisco, CA
Manring, Timothy A. ....Seattle, WA
Manrique, Lydia ....Miami Lakes, FL
Manriquez, Mario, Jr. ....Santa Ana, CA
Manroel, Stuart M. ....San Diego, CA
Manrow, Melissa ....Decatur, GA
Manry, Daniel S., Jr. ....Tallahassee, FL
Manry, Heather R. ....Concord, NC
Manry, Ted R., III ....Tampa, FL
Mans, Jeffrey P. ....Newtonville, NY
Mansager, Thomas M. ....Kalamazoo, MI
Mansbach, B. Thomas ....Washington, DC
Mansbach, Florence ....Boston, MA
Mansbach, Harry H. ....Norfolk, VA
Mansbach, Peter J. ....New York, NY
Mansbach, Robert A. ....Bethesda, MD
Mansbach, Robert E., Jr. ....Orlando, FL
Mansbach, S. Ross ....Atlanta, GA
Mansch, Larry D. ....Missoula, MT
Mansdorf, Paul J. ....El Sobrante, CA
Mansell & Andrews, P.C. ....New Castle, PA
Mansell, Anthony ....Little Rock, AR
Mansell, Barbara B. ....San Antonio, TX
Mansell, Calvin E. ....San Antonio, TX
Mansell, Charles Y. ....New Castle, PA
Mansell, Donald B. ....Athens, AL
Mansell & Engel ....Oklahoma City, OK
Mansell Law Office, S.C. ....Wausau, WI
Mansell, Martha A. ....Los Angeles, CA
Mansell, Melanie E. ....Salem, OR
Mansell, Patricia A. ....San Antonio, TX
Mansell, Robert W. ....Los Angeles, CA
Mansell, Steven S. ....Oklahoma City, OK
Mansell, Thomas S. ....New Castle, PA
Mansell, Thomas V. ....New Castle, PA
Mansell, William D. ....Wausau, WI
Manser, John T. ....Jackson, MI
Manser, Lyman A. ....Phoenix, AZ
Mansfield, Alan E. ....New York, NY
Mansfield, Alan M. ....San Diego, CA
Mansfield, Ali ....Sacramento, CA
Mansfield, Alice K. ....Denver, CO
Mansfield, Andrew S. ....Los Angeles, CA
Mansfield, Angela L. ....Indianapolis, IN
Mansfield, Anne M. ....Denver, CO
Mansfield & Antalis ....Fort Wayne, IN
Mansfield & Antalis ....Delphos, OH
Mansfield, Anthony M. ....Boston, MA
Mansfield, Anthony R. ....New York, NY
Mansfield, Baden ....Manhattan Beach, CA
Mansfield, Benetta M.
National Mediation Board, GV
Mansfield, Brian T. ....Gatlinburg, TN
Pigeon Forge, TN
Mansfield, Brian T. ....Sevierville, TN
Mansfield, Bruce L. ....Hurst, TX
Mansfield, Bruce R. ....Chicago, IL
Mansfield, Carolyn I. ....Boston, MA
Mansfield, Charles F. ....Seattle, WA
Mansfield, Christopher C. ....Boston, MA
Mansfield, Darryl F. ....Sacramento, CA
Mansfield, David A. ....Islandia, NY
Mansfield, Declan P. ....New Port Richey, FL
Mansfield, Donald F. ....Tacoma, WA
Mansfield, Donna J. ....Northampton, MA
Mansfield, Douglas K. ....Boston, MA
Mansfield, Douglas M. ....New York, NY
Mansfield, Douglas M. ....Cincinnati, OH
Mansfield, Douglas M. ....Columbus, OH
Mansfield, Edward M. ....Des Moines, IA
Mansfield, Elinor W., (Mrs.) ....Palo Alto, CA
Mansfield, Elizabeth G.
St. Petersburg, FL
Mansfield, Eugenie D. ....Seattle, WA
Mansfield, Frank C. ....Springfield, MO
Mansfield, Gerald N. ....Whittier, CA
Mansfield, Harry K. ....Boston, MA
Mansfield, James M. ....Fairfax, VA
Mansfield, James N., III ....Lafayette, LA
Mansfield, Jean Baker ....Louisville, KY
Mansfield, John H. ....Cambridge, MA
Mansfield, Johnathan E. ....Seattle, WA
Mansfield, Joseph C. ....Bryn Mawr, PA
Mansfield, Kenna L., Jr. ....Jackson, MS
Mansfield, Kenneth J. ....Honolulu, HI
Mansfield, Kristen M. ....New London, CT
Mansfield, Kyle B. ....Minneapolis, MN
Mansfield, Lawrence B. ....Mansfield, PA
Mansfield, Lorraine J. ....Las Vegas, NV
Mansfield, Marsha M. ....Madison, WI
Mansfield, Martin A., Jr. ....Denver, CO
Mansfield, Martin A., Jr., P.C. ....Denver, CO
Mansfield, Melainie K. ....Los Angeles, CA
Mansfield, Michael K. ....Las Vegas, NV
Mansfield, Michael L. ....Jackson, TN
Mansfield, Michael Scott ....Charlotte, NC
Mansfield & Muse ....Washington, DC
Mansfield, Nancy R. ....Atlanta, GA
Mansfield, Oliver T. ....McMinnville, OR
Mansfield, Paul ....Fort Lauderdale, FL
Mansfield, R. Clayton ....San Francisco, CA
Mansfield, R. E. ....Okanogan, WA
Mansfield, Reinbold & Gardner
Okanogan, WA
Mansfield, Richard G. ....Palo Alto, CA
Mansfield, Richard H., III ....Washington, DC
Mansfield, Robert E. ....Salt Lake City, UT
Mansfield, Seymour J. ....Minneapolis, MN
Mansfield, Shawn W. ....Springfield, MA
Mansfield, Stephen A. ....Los Angeles, CA
Mansfield, Stephen E. ....Anacortes, WA
Mansfield, Stephen J. ....Fort Wayne, IN
Delphos, OH
Mansfield, Susan L. ....Portland, ME
Mansfield Tanick & Cohen, P.A.
Minneapolis, MN
St. Paul, MN
Mansfield, Thomas C. ....Red Hook, NY
Mansfield, Thomas W. ....Murphysboro, IL
Mansfield, Thomas W. ....Raleigh, NC
Mansfield, William A. ....Medford, OR
Mansfield, William A., P.C. ....Medford, OR
Manshardt, Patrick J. ....Los Angeles, CA
Mansheim, David ....Parkersburg, IA
Manshel, Andrew M. ....New York, NY
Manshel, Lisa ....Millburn, NJ
Manshel, Max ....West Orange, NJ
Manshio, Calvin ....Chicago, IL
Manshio & Wallace ....Chicago, IL
Manship, Penny L. ....Los Angeles, CA
Mansier, Madeleine W. ....Trenton, NJ
Mansion, Jodi Lynn ....Niskayuna, NY
Mansion, Michael Philip ....Albany, NY
Manske, Catherine L. ....Sacramento, CA
Manske, James ....Oshkosh, WI
Manske, Jeffrey C. ....Austin, TX
Manske, John G. ....Kalamazoo, MI
Manske Law Office, P.C. ....Boise City, OK
Manske & Manske, A Professional Corporation
El Campo, TX
Manske, Peggy T. ....El Campo, TX
Manske, Richard L. ....El Campo, TX
Manske, Robert W. ....Olathe, KS
Manske, Robert Y. ....Rochester, NY
Manske, Stanley Ed ....Boise City, OK
Manske, William ....Oshkosh, WI
Mansker, Gregory E. ....Lancaster, PA
Mansker, William H. ....Chicago, IL
Mansky, Adam J. ....New York, NY
Mansky, Terry P. ....Oak Park, CA
Mansmann, Carol Los ....Pittsburgh, PA
Mansmann, J. Jerome ....Pittsburgh, PA
Mansmann & Moore ....Pittsburgh, PA
Mansmann, Peter J. ....Pittsburgh, PA
Manso, Gary Austin ....Melville, NY
Manso, Richard A. ....San Jose, CA
Manson, Alexander R. ....Lockport, NY
Manson, Almon A., Jr. ....Springfield, IL
Manson, Barry ....Great Neck, NY
Manson, Brian A. ....Los Angeles, CA
Manson, Daniel D. ....Butte, MT
Manson, Dean A. ....Washington, DC
Manson, Donald B. ....Boston, MA
Manson, Douglas P. ....Tampa, FL
Manson, Gary L. ....Reno, NV
Manson, George P., Jr. ....Glen Allen, VA
Manson, Harold Craig ....Sacramento, CA
Manson, John C. ....Bradenton, FL
Manson, Joseph L., III ....Washington, DC
Manson, Karen C. ....New York, NY
Manson, Keith A. ....Indianapolis, IN
Manson, Lawrence A. ....Chicago, IL
Manson, Marcie A. ....Columbus, OH
Manson, Pamela ....Springfield, MA
Manson, Patricia A. ....Chicago, IL
Manson, Patricia Louise ....New Orleans, LA
Manson, Peter C. ....Charlottesville, VA
Manson, Philip R. ....Sioux Falls, SD
Manson, R. Hunter ....Reedville, VA
Manson, Richard C., Jr. ....Richmond, VA
Manson, Richard P. ....Los Angeles, CA
Manson, Robert G. ....New York, NY
Manson, T. Bradley, P.A. ....Aspen, CO
Overland Park, KS
Kansas City, MO
Manson, Thomas P. ....Manchester, NH
Manson, W. Gilbert ....Fort Lauderdale, FL
Manson, William D. ....Wickliffe, OH
Manson, William E.
Department of the Navy, GV
Manson, William G. ....Kansas City, MO
Manson-Tompkins, Kayo ....Santa Ana, CA
Mansoor, Mark R. ....Boston, MA
Mansori, Zubair S. ....Casselberry, FL
Mansour, Alfred A. ....Alexandria, LA
Mansour, Andrew Joseph ....Wheaton, IL
Mansour, Anthony J. ....Flint, MI
Mansour, Christine Cooney ....Cleveland, OH
Madison, WI
Mansour, Constance A. ....Chicago, IL
Mansour, David J. ....Niagara Falls, NY
Mansour, Eli W. ....Hanover, MD
Mansour, Ernest P. ....Cleveland, OH
Mansour, Gavin, Gerlack & Manos Co., L.P.A. ....Cleveland, OH
Mansour, Jana ....New York, NY
Mansour, John P. ....Rochester, NY
Mansour, Joseph G. ....Los Angeles, CA
Mansour, Lauree Elisa ....Boston, MA
Mansour, Lisa Chernev ....Cleveland, OH
Mansour & Mansour ....Greenville, MS
Mansour, Mark ....Washington, DC
Mansour, Mark S. ....Greensburg, PA
Mansour, Monzer ....Fayetteville, AR
Mansour, N. Ned ....El Segundo, CA
Mansour, Philip ....Greenville, MS
Mansour, Philip, Jr. ....Greenville, MS
Mansour, Robert G. ....Cleveland, OH
Mansour, Teresa ....Fort Worth, TX
Mansouri, Haleh ....Los Angeles, CA
Mansouri, Monica ....Encino, CA
Mansouri & Sheeno ....Encino, CA
Mansourian, Raffi K. ....Los Angeles, CA
Mansourian, Vick K. ....Santa Monica, CA
Manspeizer, David Avrum
Washington, DC
Mansueto, Daniel M. ....Los Angeles, CA
Mansueto & Sakai LLP ....Los Angeles, CA
Mansukhani, Roger M. ....San Diego, CA
Mansukhani, Sunil H. ....Washington, DC
Mansulla, Wayne M. ....Washington, DC
Mansur, Carole Ann ....Londonderry, NH
Mansur, Christopher P. ....Troy, MI
Mansur, Daniel J. ....Lowell, MA
Mansur, Jean
Department Of Health And Human Services, Food & Drug Administration, GV
Mansur, Martin J. ....St. Paul, MN
Mansur, Paul E. ....Denver City, TX
Mansur-Brown, Patricia M. ....Costa Mesa, CA
Mansuy, Bucky P. ....Philadelphia, PA
Mansuy, Christopher H. ....New York, NY
Mansuy, Jeffrey P. ....San Francisco, CA
Manta, Joseph G. ....Harrisburg, PA
Philadelphia, PA
Manta, Mark J. ....West Trenton, NJ
Philadelphia, PA
Manta and Welge, A Professional Corporation ....Wilmington, DE
West Trenton, NJ
Allentown, PA
Harrisburg, PA
Philadelphia, PA
Mantak, Ruth H. ....Hartford, CT
Mantalica & Treadwell ....Los Angeles, CA
Mantas, Joleen S. ....Salt Lake City, UT
Mantas, William J. ....Park Ridge, IL
Mantegna, Michael N. ....Cumming, GA
Mantei, Richard W. ....Jacksonville, FL
Mantel, Allan D. ....New York, NY
Mantel, Arthur S. ....New York, NY
Mantel, Donna Lee ....Maplewood, NJ
Mantel, Howard N. ....New York, NY
Mantel, Joan Licht ....Stamford, CT
Mantel, Richard C. ....Dickerson, MD
Mantel & Shapiro ....New York, NY
Mantel, Thomas D. ....Indianapolis, IN
Indianapolis, IN
Mantel, Victor ....North Miami Beach, FL
Mantell, Betsy R. ....Garden City, NY
Mantell, Bruce E. ....Short Hills, NJ
Mantell, Charles A. ....New Haven, CT
Mantell, James G. ....San Jose, CA
Mantell, Laura ....New York, NY
Mantell Law Firm, The, A Professional Corporation ....Short Hills, NJ
Mantell, Lester J. ....New York, NY
Mantell, Michael ....New York, NY
Mantell, Michael A. ....Sacramento, CA
Mantell, Nanette Weitman ....Somerville, NJ
Mantell, Rodd J. ....New Britain, CT
Manter, David G. ....Golden, CO
Manterfield, Eric A. ....Indianapolis, IN
Manteria, S. William ....Washington, DC
Manternach, Bruce W. ....Hartford, CT
Mantese, Gerard ....Troy, MI
Mantese Miller and Mantese, P.L.L.C.
Troy, MI
Mantese, Theresamarie ....Troy, MI
Manteuffel, Robert L. ....Dallas, TX
Manthas, Victoria ....New York, NY
Manthe, Joanne L. ....Minneapolis, MN
Manthei, Gayl M. ....Raleigh, NC
Manthei, John R. ....Washington, DC
Manthei, Michael ....Fort Lauderdale, FL
Manthei, Rick W. ....Woodland Hills, CA
Manthey, Christopher C.
Treasury Department, Office of the Comptroller of the Currency, GV
Manthey, Ronald E. ....Dallas, TX
Manthey, Thomas R. ....Minneapolis, MN
Manthey, Tristan E. ....New Orleans, LA
Manthorpe, Spencer A. ....Harrisburg, PA
Manthripragada, Ranganath
Upper Marlboro, MD
Mantia, Bart A. ....Webster Groves, MO
Mantilla, Felix A. ....Northbrook, IL
Mantineo, Maureen B. ....Jersey City, NJ
Mantini, John C.
Federal Housing Finance Board, Office of General Counsel, GV
Dayton, OH
Mantione, Charles J., Jr. ....Buffalo, NY
Mantione, Steven K. ....Woodbury, NY
Mantiply, M. Mallory ....Mobile, AL
Mantiply, Mary Beth ....Mobile, AL
Mantiply & Partridge ....Mobile, AL
Mantis, Hillary Jayne ....New York, NY
Mantis, Joanne ....New Orleans, LA
Mantkowski, Gary T. ....Sharon Center, OH
Mantle, Raymond A. ....New York, NY
Mantle, William E. ....Seattle, WA
Mantler, M. Andrew ....Huntsville, AL
Mantlo, Bronwen L. ....Boulder, CO
Manton, Jason R. ....Atlanta, GA
Manton, John P. ....Cumming, GA
Manton, Thomas J. ....Washington, DC
Mantoni, Raeneé K. ....Washington, NJ
Mantonya, John B. ....Newark, OH
Mantonya, John B., A Legal Professional Association ....Newark, OH
Mantooth, D. Randall ....Nashville, TN
Mantooth, Geoffrey A. ....Fort Worth, TX
Mantooth, John ....Purcell, OK
Mantooth, Mark ....Washington, DC
Mantor, Allison Donnell ....Houston, TX
Mantor, David B. ....Houston, TX
Mantovani, Bonni S. ....Los Angeles, CA
Mantovani, Elinora S. ....Cupertino, CA
Mantovani, Mark P. ....St. Louis, MO
Mantovani, Yesica ....Plantation, FL
Manty, Nauni Jo ....Minneapolis, MN
Mantyh, William J. ....Mequon, WI
Mantyla, Bruce A. ....Dallas, TX
Mantyla, Edward J. ....San Diego, CA
Mantynband, Ralph A. ....Chicago, IL
Mantz, Carl W. ....Kutztown, PA
Mantz, Jo Anne T. ....Rochelle Park, NJ
Mantz, John A.
National Labor Relations Board, Office of the General Counsel, GV
Mantz, Lisa M. ....Covington, GA
Mantz, Melvyn S., & Associates, P.C.
Doylestown, PA
Mantzaris, Adam ....Wallingford, CT
Mantzaris, Daniel F. ....Orlando, FL
Mantzas, Dino S. ....Philadelphia, PA
Mantzavinos, Megan Trocki
Wilmington, DE
Mantzoros, Geo. C. ....New York, NY
Manuel, A. Michael ....Los Angeles, CA
Monterey Park, CA
Manuel, Allan Kenneth
Federal Communications Commission, Compliance and Information Bureau, GV
Manuel, Andrew W. ....St. Louis, MO
Manuel, B. J. ....Mamou, LA
Manuel, Charles B., Jr. ....New York, NY
Manuel, D. Neil ....Mount Holly, NJ
Manuel, Dallas Lee, II ....Tampa, FL
Manuel, Donna ....Chicago, IL
Manuel, Edward A. ....New York, NY
Manuel, Elaine A. ....Dallas, TX
Manuel, Franklin James, Jr. ....Orlando, FL
Manuel, G. Wesley, Jr. ....Mount Laurel, NJ
Manuel & Gibson, Law Offices of
Redding, CA
Manuel, Herman A. ....Washington, DC
Arlington, VA
Manuel, James C., Jr. ....Columbus, OH
Manuel & James, P.L.L.C.
Chattanooga, TN
Manuel, James W. ....Jackson, MS
Manuel, Joe E. ....Chattanooga, TN
Manuel, John W. (Jay) ....Panama City, FL
Manuel, Joseph Warren ....Oakland, CA
Manuel, Kenneth W. ....New Orleans, LA
Manuel, Kimberly A. ....Lafayette, LA
Manuel, Kirk M. ....Redding, CA
Manuel, Maria F. ....Lafayette, LA
Manuel, Michael B. ....Chicago, IL
Manuel, Michael Lee ....Dover, MA
Manuel, Raymond T., Jr. ....Oakland, CA
Manuel, Rebecca J. ....Dallas, TX
Manuel, Rebecca J., P.C. ....Dallas, TX
Manuel, Scott A. ....Springfield, IL
Manuel, Scott R. ....Independence, MO
Manuel, Susan Wright ....Baton Rouge, LA
Manuel, Thomas ....North Adams, MA
Manuel & Thompson, P.A.
Panama City, FL
Manuel, Todd S. ....Baton Rouge, LA
Manuel, W. Robert ....Erwin, TN
Manuel, William L. ....San Pedro, CA
Manuel-Coughlin, Jill ....Voorhees, NJ
Manuele, Anthony J. ....Springfield, IL
Manuele, Peter J. ....Springfield, IL
Manuele, Robert L. ....Irvine, CA
Manuelian, Haig Der ....Boston, MA
Manuelian, Michael Der ....New York, NY
Manuelides, Kimberly A. ....Baltimore, MD
Manuelidis, Emmanuel E. ....New Haven, CT
Manuelli, Christina M. ....Princeton, NJ
Manugian, Aleta R. ....Groton, MA
Manuia, Marjorie Higa ....Honolulu, HI
Manuia, Stanford M. J. ....Hilo, HI
Manuia, Stanford M. J. ....Honolulu, HI

Manuia, Stanford M. J. ....Lihue, HI
Wailuku, HI
Manukian, Lloyd S. ....Jacksonville, FL
Manulik, Mark A. ....Portland, OR
Manulkin, Gary H. ....Los Angeles, CA
Manulkin, Glaser & Bennett
Los Angeles, CA
Manus, Albert H., Jr. ....Freeport, IL
Manus, Barry L. ....Mineola, NY
Manus, Deborah J. ....Boston, MA
Manus, George A. ....Thousand Oaks, CA
Manus, Justin A. ....New York, NY
Manus, Mark J. ....New York, NY
Manus, Neil ....Chicago, IL
Manus, Peter J. ....Boston, MA
Manus, Peter M. ....Boston, MA
Manus, Randall J. ....Freeport, IL
Manus, Roger ....Raleigh, NC
Manuszak, Michael J. ....Cleveland, OH
Manuszak, Ronald J. ....Dayton, OH
Manuwal, Manuwal & Sinclair, LLP
Los Angeles, CA
Manuwal, Robert I. ....Los Angeles, CA
Manuwal, Sheri S. ....Los Angeles, CA
Manville, Anna W. ....Minneapolis, MN
Manville, Daniel E. ....Ann Arbor, MI
Manville, Daniel E., P.C. ....Ann Arbor, MI
Manville, Paulette M. ....Prairie Village, KS
Manvitz, Randall Lawrence
Overland Park, KS
Manvitz, Ted W. ....Kansas City, MO
Manwaring, Albert H., IV
Philadelphia, PA
Manwaring, Jas. K. ....Edgerton, WI
Manwaring, Jed W. ....Boise, ID
Manwaring, Melissa M. ....Palo Alto, CA
Manwaring, Roger T. ....Boston, MA
Manwaring, Roy A., II ....Allentown, PA
Manweiler, David D. ....Boise, ID
Manweiler, Howard I. ....Boise, ID
Manweiler, Kay C. ....Boise, ID
Manweiler, Mark H. ....Boise, ID
Manweiler, Wilcox, Trout & Manweiler, PLLC ....Boise, ID
Manwell, Edmund R. ....San Francisco, CA
Manwell, Malcolm T. ....Santa Rosa, CA
Manwell & Milton ....San Francisco, CA
Manwell, Susan J. ....Santa Rosa, CA
Manwell, Terry R. ....Saginaw, MI
Manwell, Tom ....Conway, MA
Many, Kimberly J. ....New York, NY
Many and LoCoco ....New Orleans, LA
Many, M. Hepburn ....Mandeville, LA
Manya, Douglas S. ....McLean, VA
Manydeeds, Edmund, III ....Eau Claire, WI
Manydeeds, John F. ....Eau Claire, WI
Manyin, Kenneth R. ....Philadelphia, PA
Manyon, Peter J. ....Owego, NY
Manypenny, J. Perry ....Chester, WV
Manypenny, Lawrence L.
New Cumberland, WV
Manz, Alexandre-Cyril ....New York, NY
Manz, David L. ....Marathon, FL
Manz, David M. ....Buffalo, NY
Manz, Earl M. ....Providence, RI
Manz, Jeffrey H. ....Naples, FL
Manz, Richard S. ....Kenmore, NY
Manz, Stephen D. ....Kansas City, MO
Manz, Victor E. ....Buffalo, NY
Manz, Wendy ....Lexington, MA
Manz, William H. ....Jamaica, NY
Manza, James G. ....Tacoma, WA
Manza Moceri, P.S. ....Tacoma, WA
Manza, Patrick T. ....Tacoma, WA
Manzagol, Allan James ....Sunnyvale, CA
Manzanares, Dennis ....Taos, NM
Manzanares, F. G. ....Topeka, KS
Manzanares, Jesse ....Trinidad, CO
Manzanares, Jon N. ....Los Angeles, CA
Manzanares, Lawrence A. ....Denver, CO
Manzanetti, Anthony B. ....Sacramento, CA
Manzano, Angel, Jr. ....Los Angeles, CA
Manzano, Frank R. ....Glendale, CA
Manzano, Kristin Pernoll ....Charlotte, NC
Manzano, Stephen J. ....Charlotte, NC
Manzano-Yates, Pedro J. ....San Juan, PR
Manzari, Laura ....Brookville, NY
Manzella, Anthony C. ....Los Angeles, CA
Manzella, Jeffrey F. ....New York, NY
Manzella, Joseph ....San Francisco, CA
Manzer, Nancy L. ....Washington, DC
Manzeske, Beth Marie ....Chicago, IL
Manzi, David A. ....Charlotte, NC
Manzi, James A., Jr. ....Boston, MA
Manzi, Keith ....Orlando, FL
Manzi, Lucian A. ....Worcester, MA
Manzi, Michael ....Lawrence, MA
Manzi, Michael, III ....Lawrence, MA
Manzi, Michael T. ....New York, NY
Manzi, Robert A. ....Upper Marlboro, MD
Manzi, Rosaleen ....New York, NY
Manzini & Associates, P.A. ....Miami, FL
Manzini, Constantine I. ....New York, NY
Manzini, Nicolas A. ....Miami, FL
Manzione, Claire Marie ....Mineola, NY
Manzione, Jos. A. ....Iselin, NJ
Manzione, Michelle ....Bayside, NY
Manzione, Stuart J. ....Hempstead, NY
Manzke, Edward J. ....Naperville, IL
Manzler, Michael A. ....Cincinnati, OH
Manzo, Dena Elrod ....Decatur, GA
Manzo, Edward D. ....Chicago, IL
Manzo, Elizabeth Engert ....Westfield, NJ
Manzo, Frank M. ....Santa Ana, CA
Manzo, Joan U. ....Edison, NJ
Manzo, Jon C. ....Madison, WI
Manzo, Marilyn J. ....Matawan, NJ
Manzo, Michael J. ....Pittsburgh, PA
Manzo, Michelle L. ....New York, NY
Manzo, Natalie S. ....Los Angeles, CA
Manzo, Peter B. ....Los Angeles, CA
Manzo, Peter T. ....Edison, NJ
Manzo, Valerie S. ....Smithtown, NY
Manzoni, Carol Berlin ....Chicago, IL
Manzoni, Charles R., Jr. ....Chicago, IL
Manzonie, John, Jr. ....Las Vegas, NV
Manzulli, Michael F. ....Staten Island, NY
Mao, Cecilia Meei-Wenn
San Francisco, CA
Mao, David Sidney ....Dallas, TX
Mao, Dora ....San Francisco, CA
Mao, Edward S. ....San Jose, CA
Mao, Emily W. ....Washington, DC
Mao, John ....Palo Alto, CA
Mao, Yibing ....Washington, DC
Mapel, Frank B., III ....Houston, TX
Mapel, Jameson M. ....Angleton, TX
Mapel, Ronald M. ....San Angelo, TX
Mapelli, Paul F. ....New York, NY
Mapelli, Savanna Jackson ....Plainsboro, NJ
Mapes, Charlotte J.
Department of Justice, GV
Mapes, Christopher L. ....Fort Wayne, IN
Mapes, Glenn H., Jr. ....Allenspark, CO
Mapes, Jane R. ....Bethesda, MD
Mapes, Jane R. ....Norfolk, NE
Mapes, Jeanne E. ....Springfield, MO
Mapes, Jeffrey Colin ....Portland, OR
Mapes, J. R. ....Norfolk, NE
Mapes, Kevin S. ....Gold River, CA
Mapes, Laurie B. ....Portland, OR
Mapes, Michelle S. ....Omaha, NE
Mapes, Paul A.
Department Of Health And Human Services, GV
Mapes, Regina B. ....Philadelphia, PA
Mapes, Robert Edgar ....Pickerington, OH
Mapes, Scott Michael ....Burlington, VT
Mapes, Stephanie J. ....Burlington, VT
Mapes, William R., Jr. ....Washington, DC
Mapes-Riordan, Lynne D. ....Chicago, IL
Maphet, Gloria S. ....Mansfield, MA
Maple, Chas. A. ....Altadena, CA
Maple, Marie-Claire Boisvert
Washington, DC
Maple, Mary Alice ....Louisville, KY
Maple, Michael L. ....Louisville, KY
Maple, Stephen M. ....Indianapolis, IN
Maples, A. Richard, Jr. ....Mobile, AL
Maples, Cheryl Kathleen Smith
North Little Rock, AR
Maples, Darwin M. ....Lucedale, MS
Maples, Edward S. ....Detroit, MI
Maples, F. Gerald ....New Orleans, LA
Pascagoula, MS
Maples, Kris D'Ann ....Natick, MA
Maples, Larry ....Joplin, MO
Maples & Lomax, P.A. ....Pascagoula, MS
Maples, Lorrie A. ....Birmingham, AL
Maples, Louis W. ....Newton, MA
Maples, Mark A. ....Lucedale, MS
Maples, Michelle R. ....Austin, TX
Maples, Norman ....Fort Worth, TX
Maples, Paul A. ....St. Johns, MI
Maples, Paul A., P.C. ....St. Johns, MI
Maples, Phillip R. ....Manitowoc, WI
Maples, Richard Alan ....Fort Worth, TX
Maples, Samuel ....Birmingham, AL
Maples, Scott R. ....Mountain View, CA
Maples, Stuart Michael ....Huntsville, AL
Maples, Timothy C. ....Washington, DC
Maples, Tony L. ....Nashville, TN
Maplewood Mall Law Center
Philadelphia, PA
Mapother & Mapother ....Evansville, IN
Jeffersonville, IN
New Albany, IN
Ashland, KY
Covington, KY
Lexington, KY
Louisville, KY
Pikeville, KY
Cincinnati, OH
Huntington, WV
Mapother, William R. ....Evansville, IN
Jeffersonville, IN
Lexington, KY
Louisville, KY
Cincinnati, OH
Huntington, WV
Mapp, Calvin R. ....Miami, FL
Mapp, David E. ....Camden, NJ
Mapp, Elva A. ....Richmond, VA
Mapp, G. Nicole ....Birmingham, AL
Mapp, George Walter, Jr. ....Accomac, VA
Mapp, Harry L., Jr. ....Halifax, VA
Mapp, James D. ....Orlando, FL
Mapp, Jane L. ....Jackson, MS
Mapp & Mapp ....Accomac, VA
Mapp, Mapp & Klein ....Keller, VA
Mapp, Richard C., III ....Norfolk, VA
Mapplebeck-Darrin, Leigh K.
Sturbridge, MA
Mapson, Charles E. ....Jacksonville, FL
Mapstone, Heather ....Chicago, IL
Maquire, John K. ....Columbus, OH
Mar, Eric L. ....San Francisco, CA
Mar, Eugene ....Alexandria, VA
Mar, Linda Rose ....Cupertino, CA
Mar, Patricia S. ....San Francisco, CA
Mar, Sheralyn ....New York, NY
Mar, William F., Jr. ....Madera, CA
Mara, Daniel N. ....Hartford, CT
Mara, Dorothy ....Pittsfield, MA
Mara, James P. ....Glen Burnie, MD
Mara, John David ....Brooklyn, NY
Mara, John K. ....East Rutherford, NJ
Mara, John W. ....Katy, TX
Mara, Neil F. ....Philadelphia, PA
Mara, Steven J. ....New Milford, NJ
Mara, Susan E. ....Detroit, MI
Mara, Timothy D. ....Camp Hill, PA
Mara, Timothy G. ....Cincinnati, OH
Mara, Wayne ....Peoria, IL
Marabella, Anthony J., Jr., Law Offices of
Baton Rouge, LA
Marabito, Allen J. ....Sacramento, CA
Marable, Eugene R., Jr. ....Petersburg, VA
Marable, George F., III ....Roanoke, VA
Marable, Leland K. ....Denver, CO
Marable, Paul D., III ....Waco, TX
Marable, Sidney T. ....Phoenix, AZ
Marable, Stanley E. ....Sarasota, FL
Marable, Vincent Lee, III ....Wharton, TX
Marabondo, Charles L. ....Jersey City, NJ
Marabondo, Salvatore ....Jersey City, NJ
Maracic, Marilyn ....New York, NY
Maracini, Michele A. ....Davie, FL
Maradiegue, Jorge B. ....Cerritos, CA
Marafioti, Kayalyn A. ....New York, NY
Marafioti, Leonard D. ....Rochester, NY
Marafioti, Thomas R. ....Canandaigua, NY
Maragakis, Elaina M. ....Salt Lake City, UT
Maragas, Douglas John ....Canton, OH
Maraghy, David R. ....Richmond, VA
Maragos, Angelo ....Waterbury, CT
Maragos, Diana ....Culver City, CA
Maragos, Diana, A Professional Corporation
Culver City, CA
Maragos, Samuel C. ....Chicago, IL
Maragos, Ted ....Grand Forks, ND
Maragoudakis, Cynthia Kent
Fort Worth, TX
Maraia, John A. ....New York, NY
Maraia, Mark M. ....Highlands Ranch, CO
Marain, Allan ....New Brunswick, NJ
Maraio, Armando ....Sanford, FL
Marais, André L. ....Sunnyvale, CA
Maraist, Kevin M. ....Corpus Christi, TX
Maraist, Michelle L. ....Metairie, LA
Maraist, Patrick W.
West Palm Beach, FL
Marak, Joseph P., Jr. ....Woodward, OK
Maraldo, Danté V. ....Metairie, LA
New Orleans, LA
Maraldo, David J. ....Métairie, LA
Maraldo, David J., A Prof. Law Corp.
Metairie, LA
Maraldo, John M. ....Watsonville, CA
Maralik, Dolores S. ....Seminole, FL
Marallo, Janine N. ....Uniondale, NY
Maram, Barry S. ....Chicago, IL
Maraman, Katherine Ann ....Hagåtña, GU
Maramba, Ignacio ....Chicago, IL
Maramba, Linda T. ....Arlington, VA
Marames, William E. ....Washington, DC
Maran, David ....Newark, NJ
Maran, Joe ....Newark, NJ
Maran, John B., Jr. ....Malverne, NY
Maran & Maran ....Newark, NJ
Maran, Michael J. ....Jamaica, NY
Maran, Trudy ....Newark, NJ
Maranda, Vincent Pierre ....Greenville, SC
Maranda, Walter F. ....Palos Park, IL
Marandas, John S. ....Portland, OR
Marandas, John S. J. ....Portland, OR
Marandas & Perdue ....Portland, OR
Marandett, Eric J. ....Boston, MA
Marandett, Susan Valente ....Boston, MA
Marando, Michael G. ....Warren, OH
Marando, Michael P. ....Youngstown, OH
Maranga, Kenneth A. ....Sherman Oaks, CA
Maranga, Theophilus ....New York, NY
Marangas, Theodora A., (Ms.)
Garden City, NY
Marangas, Theresa B. ....Purchase, NY
Marangell, Adam ....Costa Mesa, CA
Marangi, Karen L. ....Washington, DC
Marangi, Leonard M., (P.C.)
Pasadena, CA
Marangi, Neill M. ....San Diego, CA
Marangi, Stefanie ....Santa Ana, CA
Marangola, Charles A. ....Moravia, NY
Marangos, C. Catherine ....Fair Haven, NJ
Marangos, John Z. ....Staten Island, NY
Marani, Mark S. ....Atlanta, GA
Marani, Mary D. ....Hanover, MA
Marano, Alfonse G. ....Kew Gardens, NY
Marano, Anthony F. ....Valley Stream, NY
Marano & Diamond ....Waterbury, CT
Marano, Eugene A. ....Coeur d'Alene, ID
Marano, James V., Jr. ....Boston, MA
Marano, Joel Elizabeth ....Orlando, FL
Marano, Lori Ann ....New York, NY
Marano, Richard M. ....Waterbury, CT
Marano, Robert J. ....Trenton, NJ
Marans, J. Eugene ....Washington, DC
Marans, Michael D. ....Los Angeles, CA
Marans, Michelle C. ....Syracuse, NY
Marans, Victor ....Rockville Centre, NY
Maransky, Michael J. ....Cherry Hill, NJ
Harrisburg, PA
King Of Prussia, PA
Marantidis, Constantine ....Pasadena, CA
Marantis, Demetrios J. ....Washington, DC
Marantis, Rosenberg & Van Nes, LLP
White Plains, NY
Marantis, Zachary ....White Plains, NY
Maranto, Robert J., Jr. ....Buffalo, NY
Marantz, Anton Peter ....Encino, CA
Marantz, Neil G. ....New York, NY
Marantz, Philip F. ....Beverly Hills, CA
Marantz, Samuel J. ....Maplewood, NJ
Maranville, David E. ....Houston, TX
Maranz, Norman A. ....Whippany, NJ
Maranzini, Victoria S. ....Philadelphia, PA
Marapese, Kenneth ....Hawthorne, CA
Maras, Guy N. ....Chicago, IL
Maras, Marcia ....Chicago, IL
Maras, Tami J. ....Culver City, CA
Marasa, Francis James ....Chicago, IL
Marasciullo, Janene M.
Department of Justice, Civil Division, GV
Marasciulo, Theodore, Jr.
Philadelphia, PA
Marasco, Amy A. ....New York, NY
Marasco, Claudio M., Jr. ....Cranston, RI
Marasco, Joseph M. ....Bradford, PA
Marasco, Joseph P. ....Providence, RI
Marasco, Lynn R. ....Kansas City, MO
Marasco, Maria ....Boston, MA
Marasco, Paul A. ....Rochester, NY
Marasco, Robert M. ....Rockledge, FL
Marasco, Suzanne M. ....Princeton, NJ
Marasco & Wilkes ....Rockledge, FL
Marashian, Mardic A. ....Boston, MA
Marashlian, Jonathan S. ....McLean, VA
Marasi, Edward N. ....West Springfield, MA
Marasigan, Martin R. G. ....Houston, TX
Maras-Roberts, Paula ....Anderson, IN
Marass, Kenneth I. ....Sanford, ME
Marasse, Richard L. ....Los Angeles, CA
Maratea, Charles ....Marlton, NJ
Maratea, Michael J. ....New York, NY
Marateck, David B. ....Shamokin, PA
Marateck, Sanford S. ....Shamokin, PA
Marathas, Peter J., Jr. ....Boston, MA
Maratto, Michelle A. ....New York, NY
Maravalli, Sharon ....Los Angeles, CA
Maravel, Alexandra ....New York, NY
Maravich, M. Sean ....Philadelphia, PA
Maravich, Melissa Ann ....Memphis, TN
Maraz, Thomas A. ....Phoenix, AZ
Marazita, Paul C. ....Stamford, CT
Maraziti, Falcon & Healey, LLP
Morristown, NJ
Short Hills, NJ
Summit, NJ
Maraziti, Joseph J., Jr. ....Short Hills, NJ
Marbach, John C. ....New York, NY
White Plains, NY
Marback, William ....Chicago, IL
Marban, Mary E. ....Paterson, NJ
Marben, Kurt J. ....Thief River Falls, MN
Marben, Robert L. ....St. Paul, MN
Marber, Judith S. ....Miami, FL
Marber, Linda ....New Rochelle, NY
Marber, Paul A. ....New York, NY
Marber, Randy S. ....Merrick, NY
Marberry, Harry C. ....Oklahoma City, OK
Marbes, Melinda A. ....Atlanta, GA
Marbin, Evan R. ....North Miami Beach, FL
Marbin, Sherrie H. Cohen ....Miami, FL
Marble, Donald R. ....Chester, MT
Marble, Gina L. ....Seattle, WA
Marble, John Dexter ....Oklahoma City, OK
Marble, John Miner Carey ....Calabasas, CA
Marble, Karen E. Vaughey
Los Angeles, CA
Marble, Kenneth R. ....Yakima, WA
Marble, Roland D. ....Jackson, MS
Marble, Susan ....Glen Burnie, MD
Marble, Timothy ....Forest Grove, OR
Marblestone, Donald L. ....Sanford, FL
Marblestone, Kenneth ....Bala Cynwyd, PA
Marblestone, Richard I. ....Elgin, IL
Marblestone, Ronald W. ....Redwood City, CA
Marbley, Algenon L. ....Columbus, OH
Marbley, Janet Green ....Columbus, OH
Marbot, Karen L. ....Albany, NY
Marbrey, Janetta D. ....New Brunswick, NJ
Marburg, Sharon ....Bethesda, MD
Marburger, David L. ....Cleveland, OH
Marburger, James H. ....Phoenix, AZ
Marburger, John D. ....La Grange, TX
Marburger, Michael D. ....Savannah, GA
Marburger, Thomas E. ....San Antonio, TX
Marburg-Goodman, Jeffrey
Agency for International Development, Office of the General Counsel, GV
Marbury, Hugh J. ....Baltimore, MD
Marbut, A. Reed ....Salem, OR
Marbut, Michael P. ....San Antonio, TX
Marca, Myrna Ytis ....Lexington, KY
Marca, Richard D. ....Riverside, CA
San Bernardino, CA
Marcaccio, Edward J. ....North Providence, RI
Marcaccio & Marcaccio
North Providence, RI
Marcaccio, Mario J., Jr. ....Cambridge, MA
Marcaccio, R. Frances ....Greenville, RI
Marcaccio, Raymond A. ....Providence, RI
Marcaccio, Thos. L., Jr. ....Cranston, RI
Marcadis, Ralph S., (P.A.) ....Tampa, FL
Marcal, Joseph N., III ....New Orleans, LA
Marcalus, Jeffrey S. ....Annapolis, MD
Marcalus, Nicholas R. ....Elmwood Park, NJ
Marcano, Hipolito ....San Juan, PR
Marcano Roman, Benjamin ....San Juan, PR
Marcantano, Deborah A. ....Schenectady, NY
Marcantel, Bernard N. ....Jennings, LA
Marcantel, D. Carson ....Baton Rouge, LA
Marcantel, David E. ....Jennings, LA
Marcantel, H. Glenn, Jr. ....Mamou, LA
Marcantel, Marcantel & Wall ....Jennings, LA
Marcantonio, Aline O.
Fort Lauderdale, FL
Tampa, FL
West Palm Beach, FL
Marcantonio, Edward ....Westport, CT
Marcantonio, Edward J. ....Abington, PA
Marcantonio, Jan ....New York, NY

Marcantonio, Laura .... Savannah, GA
Marcantonio, Richard A. .... San Rafael, CA
Marcari, Donald W. .... Virginia Beach, VA
Marcari, Wendy G. .... New York, NY
Marc-Charles, Laurel W. .... Miami, FL
Marce, Roger R. .... Phoenix, AZ
Marceau, Eva Maija .... Boston, MA
Marceau, Leroy .... Ithaca, NY
Marceau, Ronald L. .... Bend, OR
Marceau, Stephen M. .... San Antonio, TX
Marceaux, Brian J. .... Houma, LA
Marceaux, Gregory P. .... Lake Charles, LA
Marceaux & Loftin, L.L.P.
Lake Charles, LA
Marcel, Glenn P. .... Baton Rouge, LA
Marcel, Henri .... Philadelphia, PA
Marcel, Stacey Williams .... New Orleans, LA
Marcela, Paul A. .... Midland, MI
Marcelain, Thomas M. .... Newark, OH
Marcelino, David A. .... Taunton, MA
Marcella, Lucille K. .... San Dimas, CA
Marcella, Susan M. .... Los Angeles, CA
Marcelle, Dawn P. .... Washington, DC
Marcelle, Reneé M. .... Sausalito, CA
Marcelle, Thomas .... Slingerlands, NY
Marcelli, Dominic E. .... Fresno, CA
Marcelli, Mark J. .... Valley Forge, PA
Marcelli, Michael A. .... Los Angeles, CA
Marcellino, Albert J. .... Philadelphia, PA
Marcellino, James J. .... Boston, MA
Marcellino, Michael J. .... New York, NY
Marcellino, Samuel E., Jr. .... Acton, MA
Marcellino, Stephen M. .... New York, NY
Marcellino Ungerman, Beth
Philadelphia, PA
Marcello, David A. .... New Orleans, LA
Marcello, Douglas B. .... Bethlehem, PA
Harrisburg, PA
Marcello, Joseph D. .... Shelton, CT
Marcello, Matthew T., III .... Boston, MA
Providence, RI
Marcello, Michael J. .... Providence, RI
Marcello, Victor L. .... Gonzales, LA
Marcellus, Jennifer L. .... St. Paul, MN
Marcero, Martha J. .... Lansing, MI
Marcey, M. Nicole .... Los Angeles, CA
March, Aaron G. .... Kansas City, MO
March, Arthur E., Jr. .... Fort Collins, CO
March, Bruce I. .... Fort Lauderdale, FL
Miami, FL
March, Donald F. .... Miami, FL
March, Douglas J. .... Macomb, IL
March, E. Russell, III .... Mobile, AL
March, George G. .... Lawrence, MA
March, Hurwitz, DeMarco & Mitchell
Cherry Hill, NJ
Media, PA
March, J. Brad .... Fort Collins, CO
March, James W. .... New York, NY
March, Jeremy G. .... Los Angeles, CA
March, John J. .... Minneapolis, MN
March, John P. .... Oklahoma City, OK
March, John P., Jr. .... Ellsworth, ME
March, John T. .... La Follette, TN
March, Jon G. .... Grand Rapids, MI
March, Jonathan S. .... Rochester, NY
March, Kathleen P. .... Los Angeles, CA
March, Laurie .... Jericho, NY
March & Liley, P.C. .... Fort Collins, CO
March, Lori W. .... Weston, FL
March, Mary G. .... Paoli, PA
March & McMillan, P.C. .... Macomb, IL
March, Nancy J. .... Tucson, AZ
March, Peter L. .... Spokane, WA
March, Richard S. .... Bala Cynwyd, PA
March, Robyn G. .... Portland, ME
March, Samuel .... Livingston, NJ
March, Scott F. .... San Jose, CA
March, Wendy A. .... Carthage, MO
March, William D. .... Media, PA
Marchak, Claudia Jackson ...... New Milford, CT
Marchal & Brown .... Greenville, OH
Marchal, Jeffrey L. .... Indianapolis, IN
Marchal, John F .... Cincinnati, OH
Marchal, John F. .... Greenville, OH
Marchan, Karene S. .... Milwaukee, WI
Marchan, Ray R. .... Brownsville, TX
Marchand, Christopher John
Baltimore, MD
Marchand, Claire M. .... Haverhill, MA
Marchand, David M. .... Boston, MA
Marchand, David V. .... Dallas, TX
Houston, TX
Marchand, Donat C. .... Greenwich, CT
Marchand, George L. .... Oakland, CA
Marchand, Gilbert Y., Jr. .... Boulder, CO
Marchand, Harold D. .... New Orleans, LA
Marchand, James E. .... Evansville, IN
Marchand, James E. .... Baton Rouge, LA
Marchand, Joseph D. .... Bridgeton, NJ
Marchand, Kimberly M. .... Manchester, NH
Marchand, Leanna .... Dallas, TX
Houston, TX
Marchand, Michael J.
Department of the Army,
Office of the Judge Advocate General, GV
Marchand, Michele C. .... Los Angeles, CA
Marchand, Paul S. .... Palm Springs, CA
Marchand, Rheo C. .... Bloomfield Hills, MI
Marchand, Robert J. .... Fall River, MA
Marchand, Sidney A., III
Donaldsonville, LA
Marchand-Quintero, Juan R. .... San Juan, PR
Marchant, Anne F. .... San Francisco, CA
Marchant, Anyda .... Washington, DC
Marchant, Bristow .... Columbia, SC
Marchant, Byron F. .... Washington, DC
Marchant, Carol A. .... Department of Defense,
Defense Legal Services Agency, GV
Marchant, Dawn Danzeisen
Washington, DC
Marchant, Jeffrey S. .... Malvern, PA
Marchant, John B. .... San Francisco, CA
Marchant, John J. .... Omaha, NE
Marchant, Michael .... New York, NY
Marchant, Michelle M. .... Bellevue, WA
Marchant, Randy R. .... Salt Lake City, UT
Marchant, Robert J. .... Watertown, WI
Marchant, Rollo M. .... Washington C. H., OH
Marchant, Scott D. .... Buffalo, NY
Marchant, T. Eston .... Columbia, SC
Marchant, Valerie L. .... San Francisco, CA
Marchant, W. Reilly .... Richmond, VA
Marchant, William L. .... San Francisco, CA
Marchbank, Ralph L., Jr. .... Sarasota, FL
Marchbanks, Brent .... Boise, ID
Marchbanks, Daiello & Leider, P.A.
Wildwood, FL
Marchbanks, Lawrence J. .... Wildwood, FL
Marchbanks, Michael L. .... Bakersfield, CA
Marchek, Carlyle S., Jr. .... Lansing, MI
Marchek, Richard J. .... Eagan, MN
Marchel, Peter M. .... Memphis, TN
Marchello, Charles J. .... New York, NY
Marchelos, Steve J. .... New York, NY
Marchena & Graham, P.A. .... Orlando, FL
Marchena, Marcos R. .... Orlando, FL
Marchesano, Michael .... Philadelphia, PA
Marcheschi, Elena .... Chicago, IL
Marchese, Andrew F. .... Troy, NY
Marchese, Andrew J. .... Miami, FL
Marchese, Anthony B. .... Tampa, FL
Marchese, Anthony P., Jr.
Bloomfield Hills, MI
Marchese, April L. .... Pittsburgh, PA
Marchese, Charles J. .... Buffalo, NY
Marchese, Christopher S. .... La Jolla, CA
Marchese, Claudia L. .... Parsippany, NJ
Marchese, David J. .... Portland, ME
Marchese, Diane Sendek .... Dearborn, MI
Marchese, Gary James .... Waltham, MA
Marchese, George J. .... New York, NY
Marchese, George W. .... Eastpointe, MI
Marchese, John C. .... Chicago, IL
Marchese, John J. .... Buffalo, NY
Marchese, Joseph A. .... Columbus, OH
Marchese, Lisa M. .... Seattle, WA
Marchese, Matthew .... Bronx, NY
Marchese, Michael, III .... Cincinnati, OH
Marchese, Michael J. .... Boston, MA
Marchese, Michael, Jr. .... Fort Wayne, IN
Marchese, Richard A. .... Rochester, NY
Marchese, Robert K. .... Brooklyn, NY
Marchese, Theresa M. .... New Orleans, LA
Marchese, Thomas J. .... Columbus, OH
Marchese, William J. .... Paterson, NJ
Marchesi, Eugene .... Baltimore, MD
Marchesi, Peter T. .... Waterville, ME
Marchesi, Silvano B. .... Martinez, CA
Marchesiello, Phillip R. .... Washington, DC
Marchesiello, Richard R. .... Laurel, MD
Marchesini, Gregory .... Philadelphia, PA
Marchesini, Michael D. .... San Diego, CA
Marcheskie, Toni A. .... Warren, OH
Marcheso, Joseph J. .... Melbourne, FL
Marchetta, Anthony J. .... Morristown, NJ
Marchetta, Joanne S. .... San Francisco, CA
Marchetti, Anthony L., Jr.
Cherry Hill, NJ
Marchetti, Christopher J. .... Pittsburgh, PA
Marchetti, Darlene Darga
Farmington Hills, MI
Marchetti, Dianna M. .... Warren, MI
Marchetti, Frances F. .... Chicago, IL
Marchetti, Frank E. .... Los Angeles, CA
Marchetti, Frank P. .... Lawrence, MA
Marchetti, George A. .... Bolingbrook, IL
Marchetti, James G. .... Boston, MA
Marchetti, Josephine .... Hartford, CT
Marchetti, Karin F. .... Bernard, ME
Marchetti, Kathleen .... Short Hills, NJ
Marchetti, L. Gino, Jr. .... Nashville, TN
Marchetti, Lynda .... Detroit, MI
Marchetti, Michael F. .... New York, NY
Marchetti, Nancy M. .... Department of Labor,
Pension and Welfare Benefits, GV
Marchetti, R. David .... Jackson, MS
Marchetti & Radzinski .... Warren, MI
Marchetti, Richard A. .... Columbus, GA
Marchetti, Vincent A. .... Tampa, FL
Marchetti-Obrien, Lisa M. .... Chicago, IL
Marchewka, James Alan .... Pittsburgh, PA
Marchewka, Richard M. .... Fort Myers, FL
Marchi, Joanne T. .... Boston, MA
Marchi, John J. .... New York, NY
Marchi, John R. .... St. Charles, IL
Marchi, Louis J. .... Staten Island, NY
Marchi, Nicholas R. .... Eureka, CA
Marchi, Nicholas W. .... Seattle, WA
Marchi, William D. .... Auburn, CA
Marchiano, James J. .... San Francisco, CA
Marchiano, John F. .... Henderson, NV
Marchiano, Maria L. .... Staten Island, NY
Marchica, John L., Jr. .... Bellows Falls, VT
Marchick, David .... Department of State,
Bureau of Economic and Business Affairs,
GV
Marchick, Robert J. .... Department of Energy,
Office of the General Counsel, GV
Marchiel, Marc S. .... Seattle, WA
Marchigiani, Albert V. .... Bedford Hills, NY
Marchigiani, Crystal Hession .... Chicago, IL
Marchik, Diane M. .... Milwaukee, WI
Marchini, Joseph M. .... Fresno, CA
Marchio, Joni-Jean Crivello
Moorestown, NJ
Marchionda, Lisa A. .... Boston, MA
Marchiondo, Philip L. .... Santa Monica, CA
Marchiondo, William C. .... Albuquerque, NM
Marchionna, Sal B. .... Park Ridge, IL
Marchioro, Joan M. .... Olympia, WA
Marchisello, Mary Jo .... New York, NY
Marchisen, Andrew .... Paterson, NJ
Marchisio, Juvenal L. .... Syosset, NY
Marchisotto, Alan L. .... Greenwich, CT
Marchisotto, Louis J. .... Brooklyn, NY
Marchisotto, Michelle .... Yorba Linda, CA
Marchitelli, David J. .... Rochester, NY
Marchlen, L. Thomas .... Pittsburgh, PA
Marchlewski, Theresa M.
Santa Monica, CA
Marchman, Kenneth R. "Kip"
Winter Park, FL
Marchman, Robert A. .... New York, NY
Marchman, Sharon Ingram .... Monroe, LA
Marchner, Kim L. .... Atlanta, GA
Marchuck, Adam T. .... Norwalk, CT
New York, NY
Marchuk, Robert C. .... Berwyn, IL
Marci, Joan-Ellen .... Treasury Department,
Departmental Offices, GV
Marci, Vincent T., Jr. .... Novato, CA
Marcial, Sharon A. .... Rockville, MD
Marciano, Anthony L. ..... Long Island City, NY
Marciano, Charles A. .... Department of Justice,
Federal Bureau of Investigation, GV
Marciano and Conn .... Hoboken, NJ
Marciano, Frank P. G. .... Hoboken, NJ
Marciano, Joseph J. .... San Diego, CA
Marciano, Kevin R. .... Media, PA
Philadelphia, PA
Marciano, Valerie L. .... Phoenix, AZ
Marciano, Yvonne E. .... Syracuse, NY
Marciari, Sandra A. .... Universal City, CA
Marciarille, Ann Marie .... San Francisco, CA
Marcickiewicz, Richard L. .... Denville, NJ
Marcie, Jay C. .... Avon Lake, OH
Marciel, Julianna R. .... Ventura, CA
Marciello, Frank A., Jr. .... Somerville, MA
Marciello, Frank A., Jr., P.C.
Somerville, MA
Marcigliano, Frank M. .... New York, NY
Marcil, Jack G. .... Fargo, ND
Marcil, John R. .... Denver, CO
Marcil, Lorrie M. .... Washington, DC
Marcil, Michael W. .... Fort Lauderdale, FL
Marcil, Roger B. .... Annapolis, MD
Marcille, Gregory A. .... Pensacola, FL
Marcille, Holly S. .... Charlotte, NC
Marcille, R. Donald .... Appleton, WI
Marcin, Beverly A. .... St. Louis, MO
Marcin, Chester H. .... Bowling Green, OH
Marcin, Donna M. .... Boston, MA
Marcin & Dunipace .... Bowling Green, OH
Marcin, Edward W. .... Milford, OH
Marcin, John B., Law Offices of
Los Angeles, CA
Marcin, John R. A. .... Hempstead, NY
Marcin & Marcin .... Milford, OH
Marcin, Marisa P. .... Philadelphia, PA
Marcin, Melissa A. .... Milford, OH
Marcin, Michael J. .... New York, NY
Marcin, Michael P. .... Austin, TX
Marcin, Patricia C. .... Uniondale, NY
Marcin, Peter R. .... Columbia, MD
Marcin, Raymond B. .... Washington, DC
Marcincuk, Robert E. .... Southampton, NY
Marciniak, Joseph A. .... Carol Stream, IL
Marciniak, Thaddeus J. .... St. Paul, MN
Marciniszyn, Jane B. .... Cleveland, OH
Marcinko, Leonard T. .... Atlanta, GA
Marcinkoski, Gerald M. .... Birmingham, MI
Marcinkowski, Robert D. .... Chadds Ford, PA
Marcinkus, James A. .... Los Angeles, CA
Marcionese, Michael A. .... Hartford, CT
Marcis, Robert A. .... Cleveland, OH
Marcis, Robert A., II .... Cleveland, OH
Marcis, Steve J. .... Schaumburg, IL
Marckese, Jeffrey N. .... Los Angeles, CA
Marcks, Celeste B. .... West Palm Beach, FL
Marcks, R. Michael .... Bakersfield, CA
Marco, Allan J. .... Downers Grove, IL
Marco, Catherine L.
Nuclear Regulatory Commission,
Office of the General Counsel, GV
Marco, Claudia R. .... Medina, OH
Marco, Corey H. .... La Mesa, CA
Marco, Daniel J. .... Medina, OH
Marco, Frank .... Glen Ellyn, IL
Marco, Frank J. .... Hartford, CT
Marco, Kenneth J. .... Medina, OH
Marco, Lori J. .... St. Paul, MN
Marco, Marco & Bailey .... Medina, OH
Marco, Paul .... Grosse Pointe, MI
Marco, Phillip .... Petoskey, MI
Marco, Richard J., Jr. .... Medina, OH
Marco, Richard J., Sr. .... Medina, OH
Marco & Stefanos .... Downers Grove, IL
Marco, Watkins and Owsiany .... Detroit, MI
Grosse Pointe, MI
Marcolin, Carla M. .... Washington, DC
Marcoline, Thomas J. .... Boston, MA
Marcolini, Toni Ann .... Woodbridge, NJ
Marcolus, Richard J. .... Edison, NJ
Marconda, Scott M. .... Hanford, CA
Marconi, Alex B. .... Phoenix, AZ
Marconi, Dennis J. .... Los Angeles, CA
Marconi, Dennis M. .... Trenton, NJ
Marconi, Eugene A. .... Torrington, CT
Marconi, Jerome F., Jr. .... Chicago, IL
Marconi, John R. .... Akron, OH
Marconi, Joseph C. .... New York, NY
Marconi, Joseph R. .... Chicago, IL
Marconi, Michael V. .... Dallas, TX
Marconi, Robert S. .... Seattle, WA
Marconi, Thomas C. .... Wilmington, DE
Marconi, William J. .... Cherry Hill, NJ
Marconis, Carolyn M. .... Pottsville, PA
Marconnay, Marianne E. .... Dearborn, MI
Marcopulos, Stathi George .... Irvine, CA
Marcordes, Charles R. .... Chicago, IL
Marcos, Ileana .... Miami, FL
Marcos-Bodker, Hortensia ...... Kansas City, MO
Marcosson, Samuel A.
Equal Employment Opportunity
Commission,
Office of the General Counsel, GV
Marcot, Carole E. .... Santa Ana, CA
Marcotrigiano, Paul .... New York, NY
Marcott, Lori M. .... Seattle, WA
Marcott, Robert S. .... Wheaton, IL
Marcott, Ruth Silseth .... St. Paul, MN
Marcotte, Albert J. .... Lowell, MA
Marcotte, Craig O. .... Shreveport, LA
Marcotte, David P. .... Washington, DC
Marcotte, Eric J. .... Washington, DC
Marcotte, Jennifer S. .... Marietta, GA
Marcotte, Jo Ellen .... Oakland, CA
Marcotte Law Firm .... Lowell, MA
Marcotte, Megan .... San Diego, CA
Marcotte, Paul A. .... Chicago, IL
Marcotte, Paul G., Jr. .... Bethesda, MD
Marcotte, Robt. D. .... Omaha, NE
Marcotty, Louise-Annette .... Ann Arbor, MI
Marcotullio, Richard J. .... Winston-Salem, NC
Marcou, Constantin .... Northridge, CA
Marcou, Dennis A. .... La Crosse, WI
Marcou, George T. .... Washington, DC
Marcou, Louis R. .... Waterville, ME
Marcouiller, Barbara A. .... Seattle, WA
Marcouiller, D. Mark .... Des Moines, IA
Marcouiller, Sheryl A. .... Northfield, IL
Marcoux, Allen, Abbott, Schomer & Bower, P.C. .... Jackson, MI
Marcoux, J. Michel .... Washington, DC
Marcoux, Jackie M. .... St. Louis, MO
Marcoux, John J. .... Dallas, TX
Marcoux, Marie C. .... New York, NY
Marcoux, Thomas A. .... Tarrytown, NY
Marcoux, William C. .... San Francisco, CA
Marcoux, William J. .... Jackson, MI
Marcovecchio, Noel D. .... San Francisco, CA
Marcovecchio, Rosalie .... Santa Rosa, CA
Marcovich, Cochrane, Milliken & Swanson, LLP .... Superior, WI
Marcovich, Stephen .... Stamford, CT
Marcovich, Toby E. .... Superior, WI
Marcovici, Janik .... Fairfield, CT
Marcovici, Robert X. ...... Department of Justice,
United States Marshals Service, GV
Marcovis, Frank J. .... Des Moines, IA
Marcovitch, Paul B. .... Chicago, IL
Marcovitch, Robert P. .... Atlanta, GA
Marcovitz, Donald L.
West Long Branch, NJ
Marcozzi, Anthony P., Jr. .... Westmont, NJ
Marcozzi, Anthony P., Jr., Law Offices of P.C.
Westmont, NJ
Marcrum, Jill Reifinger .... Evansville, IN
Marcu, Aaron R. .... New York, NY
Marcu, Hinda G. .... Broomall, PA
Marcu, Howard Saul .... Broomall, PA
Marcucci, Anna Patricia .... Atlanta, GA
Marcucci, Donald R. .... Pittsburgh, PA
Marcucci, Frank S. .... East Haven, CT
Marcucci, John M. .... Denver, CO
Marcucci, Lawrence L. .... Des Moines, IA
Marcucci, N. Joseph .... Harrisburg, PA
Marcucci, Thomas A. .... Sterling Heights, MI
Marcuccio, Elizabeth A.
Saratoga Springs, NY
Marcucco, Elizabeth A.
Saratoga Springs, NY
Marcuis, Alan J. .... Dallas, TX
Marculewicz, Anne W. .... Baltimore, MD
Marculewicz, Stefan Jan .... Baltimore, MD
Marcum, Deidre Carroll .... Berkeley, CA
Marcum, Donald C. .... Montgomery, IL
Marcum, Gordon G., II .... Midland, TX
Marcum, James V. .... Ashland, KY
Marcum, Joseph M. .... Corpus Christi, TX
Marcum, Kent Eldon .... Cincinnati, OH
Marcum, Leo A. .... Lowmansville, KY
Marcum, Molly K. .... Portland, OR
Marcum, Stephen A. .... Huntsville, TN
Marcum, Stephen S. .... Hamilton, OH
Marcum, Tanya M. .... Grand Rapids, MI
Marcum & Triplett .... Lowmansville, KY
Marcum, William J. .... Augusta, GA
Marcus, A. Richard .... Pittsburgh, PA
Marcus, Aaron F. .... New Orleans, LA
Marcus, Aaron J. .... Binghamton, NY
Marcus, Adam Gordon .... Wallingford, PA
Marcus, Adam Jonathan .... Long Beach, NY
Marcus, Alan J. .... Bronx, NY
Marcus, Alan K., (P.A.) .... Miami, FL
Marcus, Alan R. .... Chicago, IL
Marcus, Allan M. .... New York, NY
Marcus, Amy B. .... Kansas City, MO
Marcus, Andréa M. .... Santa Barbara, CA
Marcus, Andrew T. .... Orlando, FL
Marcus, Arlene B. .... Boston, MA
Marcus, Arthur S. .... New York, NY
Marcus, Averill G. .... Miami, FL
Marcus, Averill G., P.A. .... Miami, FL
Marcus, Barbara J. .... New York, NY
Marcus, Barry .... Boise, ID
Marcus, Barry D. .... New Rochelle, NY
Marcus, Barry J. .... Hallandale Beach, FL
Marcus, Benjamin E. .... Portland, ME

Marcus, Bernard ....Potomac, MD
Marcus, Bernard D. ....Pittsburgh, PA
Marcus, Bernard, (P.L.C.)
New Orleans, LA
Marcus & Bonsib ....Greenbelt, MD
Marcus, Bradley D. ....Channel Island, CA
Marcus, Bradley S. ....Tempe, AZ
Marcus, Brian I. ....San Francisco, CA
Marcus, Bruce Lawrence ....Greenbelt, MD
Marcus, Carl ....Pittsburgh, PA
Marcus, Carol E. ....Bethesda, MD
Marcus, Carol P. ....Short Hills, NJ
Marcus, Caryn L. ....New York, NY
Marcus, Charles L. ....Portsmouth, VA
Marcus, Claude V. ....Boise, ID
Marcus, Corinne I. ....New York, NY
Marcus, Craig ....Boise, ID
Marcus, Craig E. ....Boston, MA
Marcus, Craig H. ....Los Angeles, CA
Marcus, Dana E. ....Great Barrington, MA
Marcus, Daniel ....Department of Justice, Office of the Associate Attorney General, GV
Marcus, Daniel E. ....Hartford, CT
Marcus, Daniel J. ....Hartford, CT
Marcus, David ....New York, NY
Marcus, David C. ....Boston, MA
Marcus, David E. ....El Centro, CA
Marcus, David E. ....Houston, TX
Marcus, David L. ....Kansas City, MO
Marcus, David L. ....North Bergen, NJ
Marcus, David L. ....Philadelphia, PA
Marcus, David M. ....Los Angeles, CA
Marcus, David M. ....New York, NY
Marcus, David O. ....Hackensack, NJ
Marcus, David P. ....Buffalo, NY
Marcus, David R. ....New York, NY
Marcus, Deborah Lichtenstein
New York, NY
Marcus, Debra ....New York, NY
Marcus, Debra Kramer ....Chicago, IL
Marcus, Debra M. ....Millburn, NJ
Marcus, Dorene ....Chicago, IL
Marcus, Edward L. ....New Haven, CT
Marcus, Elana S. ....New York, NY
Marcus, Elizabeth S. ....Denver, CO
Marcus, Eric P. ....New York, NY
Marcus, Errico, Emmer & Brooks, P.C.
Braintree, MA
Marcus, Felicia A. ....San Francisco, CA
Marcus, Fred H. ....New York, NY
Marcus, Fred J. ....Irvine, CA
Los Angeles, CA
San Francisco, CA
Marcus, Fred O. ....Chicago, IL
Marcus, Fredric L. ....Newark, NJ
Marcus, G. Robert ....Somerville, NJ
Marcus, Gail, Law Office of
Philadelphia, PA
Marcus, Gail W. ....New York, NY
Marcus, Gary ....Melville, NY
Marcus, Gary P. ....Eugene, OR
Marcus, Geo. ....Stamford, NY
Marcus, George J. ....Portland, ME
Marcus, Gerald D. ....San Francisco, CA
Marcus, Gerald I. ....Schaumburg, IL
Marcus, Gerald I., Ltd. ....Schaumburg, IL
Marcus, Gould & Sussman, LLP
New Rochelle, NY
New York, NY
White Plains, NY
Marcus, Gregg ....Van Nuys, CA
Marcus, Grygiel & Clegg, P.A.
Portland, ME
Marcus, H. Gwen ....New York, NY
Marcus, H. Jeffrey ....Williamsville, NY
Marcus, H. Richard ....Chattanooga, TN
Marcus, Harry C. ....New York, NY
Marcus, Harvey I. ....Saddle Brook, NJ
Marcus, Harvey W. ....Kinston, NC
Marcus, Henry D. ....Hartford, CT
Marcus, Herbert J. ....Miami, FL
Marcus, Herbert K. ....Brookline, MA
Marcus, Howard S. ....Capitola, CA
Marcus, Ilana R. ....New York, NY
Marcus, Ira ....Redondo Beach, CA
Marcus, Ira ....Fort Lauderdale, FL
Marcus, Ira B ....Livingston, NJ
Marcus, Ira J. ....Chicago, IL
Marcus, Ira, P.A. ....Fort Lauderdale, FL
Marcus, Irl. E. ....Orlando, FL
Marcus, Irving C. ....Roseland, NJ
Marcus, Isaac ....White Plains, NY
Marcus, Jack L. ....Milwaukee, WI
Marcus, Jack, (P.A.) ....Fort Lauderdale, FL
Marcus, Jacqueline ....New York, NY
Marcus, James A. ....Sandusky, MI
Marcus, James B. ....Boston, MA
Marcus, James I. ....Chicago, IL
Marcus, Jan Arthur ....Bridgeport, CT
Marcus, Janet K. ....White Plains, NY
Marcus, Janna L. ....Silver Spring, MD
Marcus, Jay B. ....Fairfield, IA
Marcus, Jay E. ....Highland Park, IL
Marcus, Jeanne Disney ....Silver Spring, MD
Marcus, Jed L. ....Los Angeles, CA
Roseland, NJ
New York, NY
Marcus, Jed S. ....Brooklyn, NY
Marcus, Jeffrey ....New York, NY
Marcus, Jeffrey H. ....Philadelphia, PA
Marcus, Jeffrey L. ....Los Angeles, CA
Marcus, Jeffrey S. ....New York, NY
Marcus, Jeremy ....Norwalk, CT
Marcus, Jeremy D. ....Washington, DC
Marcus, Jerome M. ....Philadelphia, PA
Marcus, Jerry ....Palo Alto, CA

Marcus, Joel
Federal Communications Commission, Office of the General Counsel, GV
Marcus, Joel R. ....New York, NY
Marcus, Jonathan L. ....Department of Justice, Criminal Division, GV
Marcus, Jonathan N. ....Newark, NJ
Marcus, Jonathan S. ....Fort Lauderdale, FL
Marcus, Joseph R. ....Chicago, IL
Marcus, Joy S. ....New York, NY
Marcus, Julie M. ....Springfield, IL
Marcus, K. Richard ....New York, NY
Marcus, Karen D. ....Richmond, CA
Marcus, Kathleen M. ....Costa Mesa, CA
Marcus & Katz ....Garden City, NY
Mineola, NY
Marcus, Keith B. ....Richmond, VA
Marcus, Kenneth B. ....Honolulu, HI
Marcus, Kenneth E. ....Northbrook, IL
Marcus, Kenneth J. ....Los Angeles, CA
Marcus, Kenneth L. ....Washington, DC
Marcus, Kenneth R. ....West Bloomfield, MI
Marcus, Kenneth R., P.C. ....Detroit, MI
West Bloomfield, MI
Marcus Law Firm, The ....New Haven, CT
Marcus Law Offices, S.C. ....Milwaukee, WI
Marcus, Lawrence ....San Francisco, CA
Marcus, Lawrence N. ....Albany, NY
Marcus, Lee W. ....Orlando, FL
Marcus, Leon C. ....New York, NY
Marcus, Leslie ....Hanover, MA
Marcus & Levy LLP ....New York, NY
Marcus, Lillian (Polisky) ....Oak Lawn, IL
Marcus, Lori Lowenthal ....Bala Cynwyd, PA
Marcus, Lynn S. ....New York, NY
Marcus, Marc G. ....Sacramento, CA
Marcus, Marcie N. ....Denver, CO
Marcus & Marcus, P.A. ....Homestead, FL
Marcus, Maria L. ....New York, NY
Marcus, Marilyn ....Scarsdale, NY
Marcus, Marshall M. ....St. Louis, MO
Marcus, Mary Crane ....Arlington, MA
Marcus, Melvin W. ....Boston, MA
Marcus, Merrick & Montgomery ....Boise, ID
Marcus, Micah E. ....Chicago, IL
Marcus, Michael ....New York, NY
Marcus, Michael D. ....Los Angeles, CA
Marcus, Michael H. ....Portland, OR
Marcus, Michael J. ....Homestead, FL
Marcus, Michael L. ....Warren, NJ
Marcus, Michael S. ....Washington, DC
Marcus, Michael S., (P.C.)
Washington, DC
Marcus, Michael W. ....Grand Rapids, MI
Marcus, Michele Schiffman
Somerville, NJ
Marcus, Michelle S. ....Newburgh, NY
Marcus, Mitchell Lane ....Washington, DC
Marcus, Myer M. ....Portland, ME
Marcus, Myron ....White Plains, NY
Marcus, Nancy C. ....New York, NY
Marcus, Nancy E. ....Beverly Hills, CA
Marcus, Natasha Rath ....Greensboro, NC
Marcus, Neil J. ....Monongahela, PA
Marcus, Neil R. ....Danbury, CT
Marcus, Norman ....New York, NY
Marcus, Norman E. ....Plantation, FL
Marcus, Norman E., P.A. ....Plantation, FL
Marcus, Ollman & Kommer
New Rochelle, NY
Marcus, Pamela Stettin ....Miami, FL
Marcus, Patricia R. ....York, PA
Marcus, Paul ....Williamsburg, VA
Marcus, Paul R. ....Miami, FL
Marcus, Perres, Campanale & Karamanis, P.C.
Chicago, IL
Marcus, Philip L. ....Ellicott City, MD
Marcus, Phyllis E. ....Treasury Department, Internal Revenue Service, GV
Marcus, Phyllis Hurwitz
Federal Trade Commission, Bureau of Consumer Protection, GV
Marcus, Randall B. ....Ithaca, NY
Marcus, Randi D. ....Kew Gardens, NY
Marcus & Regalado ....Sacramento, CA
Marcus, Richard ....New York, NY
Marcus, Richard Adam ....North Bellmore, NY
Marcus, Richard C. ....Buffalo, NY
Marcus, Richard H. ....Wilmette, IL
Marcus, Richard I. ....Hyattsville, MD
Marcus, Richard J. ....Long Grove, IL
Marcus, Richard L. ....San Francisco, CA
Marcus, Richard L. ....Chicago, IL
Marcus, Richard M. ....Bronx, NY
Marcus, Richard S ....Bronx, NY
Marcus, Richard S. ....Milwaukee, WI
Marcus, Robb A. ....Milwaukee, WI
Marcus, Robert B. ....New City, NY
Marcus, Robert B. ....Pittsburgh, PA
Marcus, Robert B., P.C. ....New City, NY
Marcus, Robert R. ....Greensboro, NC
Marcus, Robert S. ....Maplewood, NJ
Marcus, Robert S. ....Indiana, PA
Marcus, Roselyn ....Olympia, WA
Marcus Rosenberg & Diamond LLP
New York, NY
Marcus, Rubin H. ....New York, NY
Marcus, Ruth D. ....Woodbridge, NJ
New York, NY
Marcus, Santoro, Kozak & Melvin, P.C.
Norfolk, VA
Portsmouth, VA
Marcus, Scott H., (P.C.) ....Turnersville, NJ
Marcus, Seth L. ....New York, NY
Marcus & Shapira LLP ....Pittsburgh, PA
Marcus, Shelley A. ....New Haven, CT
Marcus, Stan ....Newark, NJ
Marcus, Stanley ....Miami, FL

Marcus, Stanley A. ....Philadelphia, PA
Marcus, Stephanie R.
Department of Justice, Civil Division, GV
Marcus, Stephen ....Department of Commerce, Patent and Trademark Office, GV
Marcus, Stephen A. ....Chicago, IL
Marcus, Stephen D. ....Chicago, IL
Marcus, Stephen D. ....Dallas, TX
Marcus, Stephen H. ....Los Angeles, CA
Marcus, Stephen H. ....Washington, DC
Marcus, Stephen H. ....New York, NY
Marcus, Stephen H. ....Milwaukee, WI
Marcus, Stephen M. ....Braintree, MA
Marcus, Steven E. ....Atlanta, GA
Marcus, Steven E. ....Toledo, OH
Marcus, Steven J. ....Libertyville, IL
Marcus, Steven J. ....New York, NY
Marcus, Sumner A. ....Brookline, MA
Marcus, Susan ....San Diego, CA
Marcus, Ted ....Atlanta, GA
Marcus, Ted, P.C. ....Atlanta, GA
Marcus, Theodore C. ....Fairfax, VA
Marcus, Thomas L. ....Novato, CA
Marcus, Todd B. ....New York, NY
Marcus, Valerie ....New York, NY
Marcus, Walter ....Norwalk, CT
Marcus, Walter F., Jr. ....New Orleans, LA
Marcus, Watanabe, Snyder & Dave, LLP
Los Angeles, CA
Marcus, Wendy S ....Los Alamos, NM
Marcus, William L. ....Los Angeles, CA
Marcus, William V. ....Hollywood, FL
Marcus, Yuval H. ....Hackensack, NJ
New York, NY
Marcusa, Fred H. ....New York, NY
Marcusa, Stephen M. ....New York, NY
Marcuse, Herman ....Department of Justice, Office of Legal Counsel, GV
Marcuse, John W. ....Baltimore, MD
Marcuse, Kenneth W. ....New York, NY
Marcuse, Peter ....Waterbury, CT
Marcuse, Philip R. ....Huntington Woods, MI
Marcuse, Steven R. ....Houston, TX
Marcuse, Yvonne ....Woodbridge, NJ
Marcusen, Linda A. ....Overland Park, KS
Marcuss, Elena D. ....Baltimore, MD
Marcuss, Stanley J. ....Washington, DC
Marcuvitz, Alan ....Milwaukee, WI
Marcuzzo, Jeffrey L. ....Omaha, NE
Marcy, Donald E. ....Seattle, WA
Marcy, Eric J. ....Woodbridge, NJ
Marcy, Gary L. ....Portland, OR
Marcy, Kristine M. ....Department of Justice, Immigration and Naturalization Service, GV
Marcy, Reed W. L. ....San Francisco, CA
Marcyan, Carlton R. ....Wheaton, IL
Marczak, Susan B. ....Chicago, IL
Marczely, Bernadette A. ....Brecksville, OH
Marczely, David W. ....Akron, OH
Marczewski, William R. ....St. Paul, MN
Marczuk, Richard A. ....Rohnert Park, CA
Marczynski, Brian A. ....Dallas, TX
Marczynski, Robert ....Memphis, TN
Mardel, James L. ....Orange, CA
Mardell, Fred R. ....Chicago, IL
Mardell, Howard ....Chicago, IL
Mardell, Howard, Ltd. ....Chicago, IL
Mardell, Irwin D.
Department Of Health And Human Services, Public Health Service, GV
Mardell, Sarah C. ....Apple Valley, MN
Marden, Barbara M. ....New York, NY
Marden, Donald H. ....Augusta, ME
Marden, Dubord, Bernier & Stevens
Waterville, ME
Marden, Earle R. ....Spartanburg, SC
Marden, Frank D. ....Camden, NJ
Marden, Jack M. ....Souderton, PA
Marden, Robert A. ....Waterville, ME
Marden, Robert M. ....Waterville, ME
Marden, Steven K. ....Minneapolis, MN
Marden, Steven M. ....Oakland, CA
Marden, Victoria L. ....Annandale, VA
Mardenborough, Harold R., Jr.
Tallahassee, FL
Marder, Alan E. ....Garden City, NY
Marder, Chris ....Waukegan, IL
Marder, David ....Boston, MA
Marder, Donald P. ....Miami, FL
Marder, Donald P., P.A. ....Miami, FL
Marder, Everett Joseph ....Boston, MA
Marder, I. David ....Vernon, CT
Marder, Jeffrey ....Jersey City, NJ
Marder, John A. ....Los Angeles, CA
San Diego, CA
Marder & Kallet ....Vernon, CT
Marder, Kenneth ....New York, NY
Marder, Kenneth A. ....Tarzana, CA
Marder, Laurence A. ....Baltimore, MD
Marder, Lilli W. ....Fort Lauderdale, FL
Marder, Mark A. ....Miami, FL
Marder, Mark A., A Professional Association
Miami, FL
Marder, Marvin A. ....Highland Park, IL
Marder, Melvin ....Scarsdale, NY
Marder, Michael ....Los Angeles, CA
Marder, Michael E. ....Fort Lauderdale, FL
Orlando, FL
Marder, Mitchell S. ....Washington, DC
Marder, Muncie D. ....Tarzana, CA
Marder, Neal R. ....Los Angeles, CA
Marder, Reyna E. ....New York, NY
Marder, Robert Irving ....Upland, CA
Marder, Robert L. ....Lynn, MA
Marder, Robert M. ....Schaumburg, IL
Marder, Robert S. ....Burlingame, CA
Marder, Scott H ....Fort Lauderdale, FL
Marder, Steven E. ....Berkeley, CA

Marder, William Lucas ....Hollister, CA
Marderosian, Gregory Alan ....Providence, RI
Marderosian, Jeff C. ....Pasadena, CA
Marderosian, Mark D. ....New York, NY
Marderosian, Michael G. ....Fresno, CA
Marderosian, Oren & Paboojian
Modesto, CA
Visalia, CA
Fresno, CA
Marderosian, Steven A. ....Chicago, IL
Mardian, Cynthia M. ....Denver, CO
Mardian, Robert C. ....Phoenix, AZ
Mardikes, George M. ....Portland, OR
Mardikian, Robert Z. ....Cambria, CA
Mardiks, Lester D. ....Falls Church, VA
Mardinly, Peter A. ....Media, PA
Mardirosian, Elaine W.
Grosse Pointe Park, MI
Mardirosian, Robert M. ....Watertown, MA
Mardirossian, Garo, & Associates
Los Angeles, CA
Mardirossian, Kathy Ann Volz
Los Angeles, CA
Mardirossian, Mickey M. ....Los Angeles, CA
Mardis, James R. ....Brownsville, TX
Mardis, Terri T. ....Springdale, AR
Mardoian, Jack C. ....Lake Forest, IL
Mardon, Andre ....New York, NY
Mardon, Kent L. ....Poughkeepsie, NY
Mardon, Lisa L. ....Kailua-Kona, HI
Mardosz, Jennifer M. ....Denver, CO
Mardula, Francis
Department of Transportation, Maritime Administration, GV
Mardula, John F. ....Reston, VA
Maready, William F., The Law Offices of
Winston-Salem, NC
Maready, William Kenan, Jr.
Charlotte, NC
Marean, Browning E., III ....San Diego, CA
Marean, Michael W. ....Arlington, VA
Marecki, Michael F. ....Dearborn, MI
Maredyth, Joan M. ....Carmichael, CA
Maree, Gerald Anthony ....Walterboro, SC
Marees, John M. ....Jacksonville, FL
Marees, Michael J. ....Jacksonville, FL
Marein, Mark B. ....Cleveland, OH
Mareiniss, Martin C. ....South Orange, NJ
Marek, Angela Diane ....Indianapolis, IN
Marek, Anna D. ....Hanover Park, IL
Marek, Brian R. ....Dallas, TX
Marek, Clarence R. ....Allen Park, MI
Marek, David A. ....Paonia, CO
Marek, Doug ....West Palm Beach, FL
Marek, Douglas R. ....Des Moines, IA
Marek, Edward F. ....North Royalton, OH
Marek, Francis & Byers, P.A.
Carlsbad, NM
Marek, Frank E., Jr. ....Los Angeles, CA
Marek, Gary A. ....Chicago, IL
Marek, Gary M. ....Mount Laurel, NJ
Marek, George J. ....Milwaukee, WI
Marek, Herbert J. ....New York, NY
Marek, Howard R. ....Victoria, TX
Marek, J. Dennis ....Kankakee, IL
Marek, John J., II ....Dallas, TX
Marek, Lezlie Ott ....Minneapolis, MN
Marek, Norbert C., Jr. ....Manhattan, KS
Marek, Peter J. ....Stockton, CA
Marek, Richard J. ....Chicago, IL
Marek, Robert J. ....Cleveland, OH
Marek, Ronald L., Law Office of
Corvallis, OR
Marek, Sherman P. ....Denver, CO
Marek, Thomas L. ....Carlsbad, NM
Marek, Thomas R. ....Minneapolis, MN
Marek, Valeree D. ....Crystal Lake, IL
Marek, William ....Montgomery, MN
Marelich, Katherine M. ....Los Angeles, CA
Marelius, Suzanne ....Salt Lake City, UT
Marell, Barry ....Liberty Corner, NJ
Marell, Corey S. ....New York, NY
Marell, Jeffrey D. ....New York, NY
Marell, Jennifer D. ....New York, NY
Marell, Leslie Sharon ....Beverly Hills, CA
Marell, Phyllis S. ....Beverly Hills, CA
Marell, Raymond J. ....Richmond, TX
Marell, Sarajane Abramson
West Palm Beach, FL
Marell, William J. ....West Palm Beach, FL
Marella, Rose Mary ....Haddonfield, NJ
Marella, Vincent J. ....Los Angeles, CA
Marema, Lenore Sue ....Schaumburg, IL
Maremont, Alan S. ....San Francisco, CA
Maremont, James K. ....Chicago, IL
Marenberg, Barry J. ....Princeton, NJ
Marenberg, Steven A. ....Los Angeles, CA
Marenda, Dale E. ....Phoenix, AZ
Marengo, Christopher J. ....Bronx, NY
Marengo, Paul C. ....Chicago, IL
Marengo, Reneé M. ....Stockton, CA
Mareno, Antonio ....Yorktown Heights, NY
Marenstein, Alan B. ....Los Angeles, CA
Marenus, Harold S. ....Los Angeles, CA
Marenus, Marjorie A. ....Los Angeles, CA
Marer, Alan G. ....Palo Alto, CA
Marer, Alison Cherry ....Palo Alto, CA
Marer, Gerald Z. ....Palo Alto, CA
Mares, Brian L. ....Oshkosh, WI
Mares, Craig P. ....Pewaukee, WI
Mares, Jan W. ....Washington, DC
Mares, Lynn B. ....Oklahoma City, OK
Mares, Milton H. ....Redwood City, CA
Mares, Moses ....San Diego, CA
Mares, Ruth S. ....Denver, CO
Mares, Stephanie S. ....Milwaukee, WI
Maresca, Ann Marie ....Brooklyn, NY

Maresca, Carla P. .... Moorestown, NJ
Philadelphia, PA
Maresca, Charles A., Jr. .... Washington, DC
Maresca, Elizabeth .... New York, NY
Maresca, Laura Marie .... Denver, CO
Maresca, Orest V. .... New York, NY
Maresca, Richard A. .... Dayton, OH
Maresca, Robert A. .... Bridgeport, CT
Maresca, Salvatore A., Jr. .... Bridgeport, CT
Maresca, Steven P. .... Naples, FL
Maresch, Kim D. .... Irons, MI
Maresh, Marquette M. .... Austin, TX
Maressa, Goldstein, Birsner, Patterson, Drinkwater & Oddo, P.C. .... Berlin, NJ
Maressa, Joseph A. .... Berlin, NJ
Maressa, Vincent A. .... Lawrenceville, NJ
Marett, James J. .... Scarsdale, NY
Marett, Louis J. .... Boston, MA
Marett, Louis Q. .... Brooklyn, NY
Marett, Stephanie L. .... Des Moines, IA
Marett, Walter W., III .... Roswell, GA
Marett, William J., Jr. .... Nashville, TN
Maretz, Heidi Skuba .... San Diego, CA
Maretz, Henry B. .... Woodbridge, CT
Maretz, Peter B. .... San Diego, CA
Marfice, Douglas S. .... Coeur d'Alene, ID
Marfisi, P. Michael, (Ltd.) .... Elko, NV
Margadant, James F. .... Rapid City, SD
Margalotti, Francis A. .... Red Bank, NJ
Margand, Christopher G.
Washington, DC
Margand, John P. .... New York, NY
Margarce, Joyce B. .... Houston, TX
Margard, Werner, III .... Columbus, OH
Margareten, Lester J. .... New York, NY
Margaris, Anastasia G. .... New York, NY
Margarit, Annette Marie .... Apple Valley, MN
Margarit, Fernando .... Miami, FL
Margarita, Richard P. .... Sacramento, CA
Margaritell, Frederick W.
Lauderdale-By-The-Sea, FL
Margaritis, Nicholas J. .... Fort Lauderdale, FL
Margelefsky, Michael P. .... Toledo, OH
Margello, Michael .... Mountainside, NJ
Margello, Sharon P. .... Morristown, NJ
Margenot, Richard J. .... Greenwich, CT
Marger, Bruce .... St. Petersburg, FL
Marger, Edwin .... Jasper, GA
Marger, Jerome S. .... Portland, OR
Marger, Johnson & McCollom, P.C.
Palo Alto, CA
Bend, OR
Portland, OR
Vancouver, WA
Marger, Joseph M. .... New York, NY
Margerum, David K. .... Indianapolis, IN
Margeson, Albert R., Jr. .... Boston, MA
Margeson, Robert M., III .... Albany, GA
Marget, George W., III .... Richmond, VA
Marget, Jonathan P. .... Washington, DC
Marget, Michael R. .... Baton Rouge, LA
Marget, Patrick J. .... Milwaukee, WI
Marget, Steven G. .... Houston, TX
Margetanski, Scarlett M. .... New York, NY
Margetis, Nicholas M. .... Madison, WI
Margetson, Carole Ann .... New York, NY
Margetts, W. Thomas .... Boca Grande, FL
Margheim, Laurice M. .... Alliance, NE
Margherio, Michael C. .... St. Louis, MO
Margid, Leonard .... New York, NY
Margiloff, Susan G. .... Klamath Falls, OR
Margin, Alan W. .... Rockville, MD
Margines, Charles .... Santa Ana, CA
Marginian, Nicole M. .... Naples, FL
Margiotta, Gary S. .... Woodbridge, NJ
Margiotta, John P. .... New York, NY
Margiotta, Joseph M. .... Uniondale, NY
Margiotta & Ricigliano .... Mineola, NY
Uniondale, NY
Margiotta, William T., Jr. .... Columbus, OH
Margiotti, Samuel J. .... Pittsburgh, PA
Margiotti, Vincent D. .... Drexel Hill, PA
Margison, Susan H. .... West Nyack, NY
Margle, Stanley J., III .... Bethlehem, PA
Marglous, Linda P. .... Boston, MA
Marglous, Ray B. .... St. Louis, MO
Marglous, Sawyer .... St. Louis, MO
Marglous, Sawyer, P.C. .... St. Louis, MO
Margo, Matthew D. .... New York, NY
Margo, Mitchell A. .... St. Louis, MO
Margo, Robert C. .... Oklahoma City, OK
Margo, Roderick D. .... Los Angeles, CA
Margol & Pennington, P.A.
Jacksonville, FL
Margol, Rodney S. .... Jacksonville, FL
Margol, Scott H. .... Fort Lauderdale, FL
Margoles, Alan D. .... St. Paul, MN
Margoles, Cheryl Speeter .... Minneapolis, MN
Margoles, Lawrence A.
San Francisco, CA
Margolies, Alan I. .... Dedham, MA
Margolies, Alexander I. .... Chicago, IL
Margolies, Brian M. .... New York, NY
Margolies, Dany .... Los Angeles, CA
Margolies, George H. .... Rockville, MD
Margolies, Hubert H. .... Washington, DC
Margolies, Jacob .... New York, NY
Margolies, Jeffrey E. .... Baltimore, MD
Margolies, Jonathan A. .... Kansas City, MO
Margolies, Jonathan H. .... Milwaukee, WI
Margolies, Larry R. .... Dallas, TX
Margolies, Leslie A. .... Philadelphia, PA
Margolies & Margolies .... Dedham, MA
Margolies, Marjorie M. .... Chicago, IL
Margolies, Marjorie S. .... Boca Raton, FL
Margolies, Marvin H. .... Dedham, MA
Margolies, Melvin .... New York, NY
Margolies, Michael Z. .... Chicago, IL
Margolies, Sarah E. .... San Francisco, CA
Margolies, Stacy B. .... Palo Alto, CA
Margolies, Stanley E. .... New York, NY
Margolies, Susan Achen .... Aberdeen, SD
Margolin, Abraham E. .... Kansas City, MO
Margolin, Amy E. .... San Francisco, CA
Margolin, Andrew S. .... Washington, DC
Margolin & Biatch .... Oakland, CA
Margolin, Bruce M., (A Prof. Law Corp.)
Los Angeles, CA
Margolin, C. Lance .... Syosset, NY
Margolin, Christopher J. .... Berkeley, CA
Margolin, Christy J. .... Wilmington, DE
Margolin, Constance Berkley
New York, NY
Margolin, Diane S. .... Hackensack, NJ
Margolin, Doreen Stamm .... Portland, OR
Margolin, E Hil .... Denver, CO
Margolin, Elissa D. .... Washington, DC
Margolin, Elyse R. .... Beverly Hills, CA
Margolin, Ephraim .... San Francisco, CA
Margolin, Eric M. .... Riviera Beach, FL
Margolin, Ginger E. .... Aspen, CO
Margolin, James S. .... Boca Raton, FL
Margolin, James S. .... Kansas City, MO
Margolin, Jeff .... Des Moines, IA
Margolin, Jesse .... New York, NY
Margolin, Jocelyn D. .... Wilmington, DE
Margolin, Joseph B. .... South Orange, NJ
Margolin, Judith R. .... New York, NY
Margolin, Kenneth N. .... Boston, MA
Margolin, Laurence S. .... Huntington, NY
Margolin, Linda U. .... Islandia, NY
Margolin, Lisa Kate .... New York, NY
Margolin and Margolin .... Boca Raton, FL
Margolin and Margolin .... Portland, OR
Margolin & Margolin, LLP .... New York, NY
Margolin, Peter W. .... Boca Raton, FL
Margolin, Phillip M. .... Portland, OR
Margolin, Randi Block .... New York, NY
Margolin, Richard A. .... Los Angeles, CA
Margolin, Richard F., (P.C) .... Houston, TX
Margolin, Richard H. .... Boca Raton, FL
Margolin, Robert J. .... Kansas City, MO
Margolin, Sam S. .... Memphis, TN
Margolin, Sanford H. .... Oakland, CA
Margolin, Seymour .... New York, NY
Margolin, Stacy A. .... Boulder, CO
Margolin, Stephen J. .... Philadelphia, PA
Margolin, Stephen M. .... Chicago, IL
Margolin, Steven T. .... Wilmington, DE
Margolin, William M. .... Encino, CA
Margolin-Klein, Eileen .... Manalapan, NJ
Margolis, Aaron .... Baltimore, MD
Margolis, Abr. .... Chestnut Hill, MA
Margolis, Alan D.
Environmental Protection Agency, Office of the General Counsel, GV
Margolis, Alan Wm. .... Philadelphia, PA
Margolis, Alexandra .... New York, NY
Margolis, Alisa R. .... New York, NY
Margolis, Andrew .... Miami, FL
Margolis, Andrew S. .... Philadelphia, PA
Margolis, Anita J. .... San Diego, CA
Margolis, Arthur L. .... Los Angeles, CA
Margolis, Barry G. .... New York, NY
Margolis, Benjamin Robert
Pacific Palisades, CA
Margolis, Beth .... New York, NY
Margolis, Brad S. .... Utica, NY
Margolis, Brian B. .... New York, NY
Margolis, Carla Y. .... Los Angeles, CA
Margolis & Cassidy .... Milwaukee, WI
Margolis, Catherine E. .... Philadelphia, PA
Margolis & Cohen, LLP .... Boston, MA
Margolis & Coppersmith .... Johnstown, PA
Margolis, Craig D. .... Washington, DC
Margolis, Daniel H. .... Washington, DC
Margolis, Daniel M. .... Cleveland, OH
Margolis, Darren .... Baltimore, MD
Margolis, David .... Department of Justice, Office of the Deputy Attorney General, GV
Margolis, Debra S. .... Pleasant Hill, CA
Margolis, Donald P. .... San Francisco, CA
Margolis, Donald W. .... Boulder, CO
Margolis, Donna P. .... New York, NY
Margolis, Duckworth & Funt, P.C.
Bethlehem, PA
Margolis, E. David .... Pittsburgh, PA
Margolis Edelstein .... Westmont, NJ
Philadelphia, PA
Pittsburgh, PA
Scranton, PA
Margolis, Edward S. .... Chicago, IL
Margolis, Ellen G. .... New York, NY
Margolis, Elliot D. .... Royal Oak, MI
Margolis, Emanuel .... Stamford, CT
Margolis, Eugene .... Department of Energy, Office of the General Counsel, GV
Margolis & Flanary LLP .... Garden City, NY
Margolis, Frances S. .... Newark, NJ
Margolis, Gail L. .... Santa Monica, CA
Margolis, George & Port .... Uniontown, PA
Margolis, Gerald A. .... Beverly Hills, CA
Margolis, Gerald A. .... Los Angeles, CA
Margolis, Gerald L. .... Monroeville, PA
Margolis, Gideon .... El Cajon, CA
Margolis, Gustave S. .... Johnstown, PA
Margolis, Harry A. .... Newark, NJ
Margolis, Harry A. .... New York, NY
Margolis, Harry S. .... Boston, MA
Margolis, Harry W. .... Richardson, TX
Margolis, Harvey .... Deerfield, IL
Margolis, Herbert .... Uniontown, PA
Margolis, Ira M. .... New York, NY
Margolis, Israel .... Binghamton, NY
Margolis, James Z. .... Berkeley, CA
Margolis, Jane E. .... Rancho Palos Verdes, CA
Margolis, Jay K. .... New York, NY
Margolis, Jeffrey A. .... New York, NY
Margolis, Jeffrey R. .... Miami, FL
Margolis, Jeremy D. .... Chicago, IL
Margolis, Jesse C. .... Gold Beach, OR
Margolis, Joan Glazer .... New Haven, CT
Margolis, Joel .... Baltimore, MD
Margolis, Joel J. .... Westminster, CA
Margolis, Joel M. .... McLean, VA
Margolis, John A. .... Miami, FL
Margolis, Jonathan .... Monterey, CA
Margolis, Jonathan D. .... New York, NY
Margolis, Jonathan J. .... Wellesley, MA
Margolis, Jonathan O. .... Garden City, NY
Margolis, Jonathan S. .... New York, NY
Margolis, Jordan .... Chicago, IL
Margolis, Kenneth A. .... New York, NY
Margolis, Kenneth R. .... Cleveland, OH
Margolis, Kevin D. .... Cleveland, OH
Margolis Law Firm, The, A Professional Corporation .... Santa Monica, CA
Margolis Law Group, The, P.C. .... Verona, NJ
Margolis, Lawrence E. .... Miami, FL
Margolis, Lawrence S.
United States Court of Federal Claims, GV
Margolis, Leonard I. .... Addison, TX
Margolis, Lisa .... Burbank, CA
Margolis, Loren J. .... Cleveland, OH
Margolis & Margolis, LL.P.
Los Angeles, CA
Margolis, Martin G. .... Verona, NJ
Margolis, Marvin .... Chicago, IL
Margolis, Marvin A. .... Milwaukee, WI
Margolis, Matthew A. .... Akron, OH
Margolis, Melanie Rosenthal .... Houston, TX
Margolis, Michael B. .... Los Angeles, CA
Margolis, Michelle K. .... Ventura, CA
Margolis, Milton D. .... Pittsburgh, PA
Margolis & Morin, LLP .... Los Angeles, CA
Margolis, Naki B. .... Los Angeles, CA
Margolis, Nancy Livers .... Philadelphia, PA
Margolis, Nathaniel I. .... Boston, MA
Margolis, P. Michael .... Hartford, CT
Margolis, Pritzker & Epstein, P.A.
Baltimore, MD
Margolis, Richard A. .... Los Angeles, CA
Margolis, Richard D. .... Cleveland, OH
Margolis, Richard J. .... Philadelphia, PA
Margolis, Robert .... Bethlehem, PA
Margolis, Robert L. .... Chicago, IL
Margolis, Roger T. .... Tucson, AZ
Margolis, Ronald A. .... Cleveland, OH
Margolis, Ronald J. .... New York, NY
Margolis, Shana J. .... San Francisco, CA
Margolis, Sheldon F. .... Jersey City, NJ
Margolis, Sidney .... Chicago, IL
Margolis, Sidney B. .... Chicago, IL
Margolis, Sidney B., Ltd. .... Chicago, IL
Margolis, Sidney K. .... Bronx, NY
Margolis, Solomon L. .... Rockville, MD
Margolis, Steven J. .... Newark, NJ
Margolis, Steven M. .... New York, NY
Margolis, Stuart A. .... New Haven, CT
Margolis, Susan L. .... Los Angeles, CA
Margolis, Theodore .... Somerville, NJ
Margolis, Vicki .... Washington, DC
Baltimore, MD
Margolis, Wendy M. .... Portland, OR
Margolius, Andrew L. .... Cleveland, OH
Margolius, Bernard .... Washington, DC
Margolius, Bruce .... Park City, UT
Margolius, Bruce, P.C. .... Park City, UT
Margolius, Edwin A. .... New York, NY
Margolius, Mallios, Davis, Rider & Tomar, LLP .... Washington, DC
Rockville, MD
Fairfax, VA
Margolius, Marcia W. .... Cleveland, OH
Margolius, Peter M. .... Catskill, NY
Margolius, Philip N. .... Washington, DC
Rockville, MD
Margolius, Richard V. .... Miami, FL
Margolius, Robye Shaw .... Baltimore, MD
Margopulos, Theodore N.
Treasury Department, Internal Revenue Service, GV
Margosian, Ara H. .... Watertown, MA
Margosian, Gary M. .... Ann Arbor, MI
Margosian, Michael J. .... Fresno, CA
Margrave Celmins, P.C. .... Scottsdale, AZ
Margrave, Celmins & Verburg, P.C.
Williams, AZ
Margrave, David J. .... Colorado Springs, CO
Margrave, David J., P.C.
Colorado Springs, CO
Margrave, David R. .... Houston, TX
San Antonio, TX
Margrave, Debra .... Omaha, NE
Margrave, Michael .... Scottsdale, AZ
Williams, AZ
Margraves, Ross D., Jr. .... Houston, TX
Margre, Gregg R. .... West Palm Beach, FL
Margrey, Daniel L. .... North Miami, FL
Marguet, Susan J. .... Delafield, WI
Marguglio, Dayne .... Dallas, TX
Margules, Darin .... Los Angeles, CA
Margules, David J. .... Wilmington, DE
Margules, Ivy M. .... Miami Beach, FL
Margules, Lenamyra .... West Bloomfield, MI
Margules, Leon R. .... Fort Lauderdale, FL
Margules, Rachel M. .... Bloomfield Hills, MI
Margules, Scott .... Miami, FL
Margules, Scott, P.A. .... Miami, FL
Margules, Susan B. .... New York, NY
Margulies, Beth Z. .... Hartford, CT
Margulies, Bruce M.
North Miami Beach, FL
Margulies, Burke W. .... Virginia Beach, VA
Margulies, Craig G. .... Tarzana, CA
Margulies, David L. .... Woodland Hills, CA
Margulies, Harold P. .... Los Angeles, CA
Margulies, Irving P. .... Washington, DC
Margulies, J. Richard .... Washington, DC
Rockville, MD
Margulies, James W. .... Cleveland, OH
Margulies, Jason R. .... Miami, FL
Margulies, Jay L. .... San Jose, CA
Margulies, Jeffrey B. .... Santa Monica, CA
Margulies, Jeffrey E. .... San Francisco, CA
Margulies, Jeffrey J. .... Cleveland, OH
Margulies, Joyce E. .... Memphis, TN
Margulies, Laura J. .... Rockville, MD
Margulies, Laura J., LLC .... Frederick, MD
Greenbelt, MD
Rockville, MD
Margulies, Mara .... Los Angeles, CA
Margulies & Margulies, P.C. .... New York, NY
Margulies, Martin B. .... Hamden, CT
Margulies, Melissa R. .... Philadelphia, PA
Margulies, Michael S. .... Minneapolis, MN
Margulies, Morton B. .... Potomac, MD
Margulies, Neil A. .... Freeport, NY
Margulies, Pamela Lee .... Columbus, OH
Margulies, Peter Simon .... Miami, FL
Margulies, Philip .... Belvidere, NJ
Margulies, Rebecca L. .... New York, NY
Margulies, Richard A. .... New York, NY
Margulies, Richard N. .... Jacksonville, FL
Margulies, Richard S. .... Philadelphia, PA
Margulies, Robert E. .... Jersey City, NJ
Margulies, Robert W. .... New York, NY
Margulies, Seymour .... Jersey City, NJ
Margulies, Sidney .... Philadelphia, PA
Margulies, Stacey Z. .... Miami, FL
Margulies, Susan C. .... Cleveland, OH
Margulies & Wagner, P.C. .... Washington, DC
Margulies, Walter .... New York, NY
Margulies, Wind, Herrington & Knopf, A Professional Corporation .... Jersey City, NJ
Margulis, Andrew L. .... New York, NY
Margulis, Arthur S. .... St. Louis, MO
Margulis Grant & Margulis, P.C.
St. Louis, MO
Margulis, Gussler, Hall & Hosterman
Ashville, OH
Circleville, OH
Margulis, Howard L. .... New York, NY
Margulis, Jeffrey E. .... Chicago, IL
Margulis, Michael H. .... New York, NY
Margulis, Phyllis .... Fort Bragg, CA
Margulis, Ralph R. .... Detroit, MI
Margulis, Randy Stuart .... Buffalo, NY
Margulis, Robert A. .... St. Louis, MO
Margulis, Shari L. .... Fairfield, NJ
Margulis, Stephen A. .... Plantation, FL
Margulis, William S. .... St. Louis, MO
Margulis-Ohnuma, Mary .... New York, NY
Margullis, Norman L. .... Tacoma, WA
Marhevka, Donna M. .... Marysville, OH
Marhoefer, Gordon J. .... Newport Beach, CA
Marhoefer, Laurence J. .... Washington, DC
Marhofer, Basil C. .... Ness City, KS
Marhofer, Michael F. .... Cleveland, OH
Marhoffer, David .... Scottsdale, AZ
Marhoffer, Susan B. .... Ridgefield, CT
Marhoun, Eric L. .... Minneapolis, MN
Mari, John J. .... Baldwin Place, NY
Mari, Manuel .... Miami, FL
Mari, Manuel & Ada G. Llerena
Miami, FL
Mari, Mathew J. .... New York, NY
Mari, Theresa A. .... Mineola, NY
Maria, Joseph A. .... White Plains, NY
Maria, Joseph A., P.C. .... White Plains, NY
Maria, Susan .... Trumbull, CT
Mariajimenez, Yvonne Elizabeth
Pacoima, CA
Mariam, Alemayehu Gebre
San Bernardino, CA
Marian, Alan P. .... Philadelphia, PA
Marianes, William B. .... Atlanta, GA
Marianetti, Donna .... Rochester, NY
Mariani, Anthony M. .... Pittsburgh, PA
Mariani, Barbara E. .... Largo, FL
Mariani, Caren L. .... Pittsburgh, PA
Mariani, Erin .... Wilmington, DE
Mariani, Ernest D. .... Salt Lake City, UT
Mariani, George E. .... Highlands, NC
Mariani, Gerardo .... San Juan, PR
Mariani, Gilda I. .... New York, NY
Mariani, Henry .... San Jose, CA
Mariani, John D. .... Minneapolis, MN
Mariani, John F. .... West Palm Beach, FL
Mariani, Linda L., & Associates
New London, CT
Mariani, Michael M. .... New York, NY
Mariani, Patricia .... Washington, DC
Mariani, Ralph A. .... Philadelphia, PA
Mariani, Ramona .... Haverford, PA
Mariani, Randy R. .... St. Louis, MO
Mariani, Raymund L. .... New York, NY
Mariani, Richard C. .... Morristown, NJ
Mariani, Robert D. .... Scranton, PA
Mariani, Scott J. .... Westfield, NJ
Mariani, Terence D. .... Waterbury, CT
Mariani, Thomas A., Jr.
Department of Justice, Environment and Natural Resources Division, GV
Mariani, Thomas E. .... Indianapolis, IN
Mariani, Timothy K. .... Clearwater, FL
Mariani-Pitalo, Elizabeth E. .... Fresno, CA
Mariano, Arthur Gregory
New Hyde Park, NY
Mariano, Carl F. .... Phoenix, AZ
Mariano, Gene R. .... Marlton, NJ

Mariano, John B. ....Camden, NJ
Mariano, John B., Jr. ....Florham Park, NJ
Mariano, John E. ....Niagara Falls, NY
Mariano, Joseph N. ....Washington, DC
Mariano, Maria C. ....Columbus, OH
Mariano, Michael A. ....Lombard, IL
Mariano, Peter E. ....Naugatuck, CT
Mariano, Randy A. ....Philadelphia, PA
Mariano, William, & Associates
White Plains, NY
Marianos, M. Pete ....Oklahoma City, OK
Marianos, Ward N. ....Concord, CA
Marias, Kenneth M. ....Las Vegas, NV
Marias, Teri M. Primack ....Tarzana, CA
Maribona, Patricia M. ....New York, NY
Maric, Vlasta ....San Francisco, CA
Marich, John G. ....Downers Grove, IL
Marichal & Hernandez ....San Juan, PR
Marichal-Aponte, Antonio E.
San Juan, PR
Marichal Morales, Isamar B.
San Juan, PR
Maricic, George ....Rancho Cucamonga, CA
Maricic & Goldstein
Rancho Cucamonga, CA
Marick, Anthony M. ....Minneapolis, MN
Marick, Michael M. ....Chicago, IL
Maricle, Anne H. ....San Ramon, CA
Maricle, Gregory D. ....Metairie, LA
Maricle, Kevin H. ....Phoenix, AZ
Maricle, Paul T. ....Denver, CO
Maricle, R. Cletus ....Manchester, KY
Maricondi, Carolyn W. ....Connellsville, PA
Marie, Ann ....Denver, CO
Marie, Raymond Leon ....New Iberia, LA
Marien, Bonnie E. ....Springfield, MA
Marien, Nicholas L. ....San Diego, CA
Marien, Richard J. ....Kansas City, MO
Marienau, Kathryn E. D. ....El Cajon, CA
Marienau, William A. ....Lincoln, NE
Marienthal, Frederic H., III ....Denver, CO
Marienthal, Paul D. ....Walnut Creek, CA
Marier, Raymond C. ....Teterboro, NJ
Marietta, Elizabeth L. ....Salina, KS
Marietta, James R. ....Atlanta, GA
Charlotte, NC
Marietta, Kellogg & Price ....Salina, KS
Marietta, Robert L. ....Salina, KS
Marietta Lyons, Beth ....Mobile, AL
Marietti, William C. ....Muskegon, MI
Marie-Victoire, Jeanine ....San Francisco, CA
Marie-Victoire, Ollie ....San Francisco, CA
Marifian, George E. ....Belleville, IL
Mariger, Craig R. ....Salt Lake City, UT
Marigliano, Jonathan ....Atlanta, GA
Marigonda, Paul M. ....Santa Cruz, CA
Marik, Wayne J. ....Racine, WI
Maril, Steven A. ....Plainfield, IL
Marilley, Richard F. ....Bonita Springs, FL
Marin, Alex A. ....Denver, CO
Marin, Ana Maria ....Miami, FL
Marin, Bayard ....Wilmington, DE
Marin, Carla L. ....Carmel, NY
Marin, Edward S. ....Rockville, MD
Marin, Gilda M. ....Miami, FL
Marin, John A. ....San Diego, CA
Wilmington, CA
Marin, John A., A Professional Corporation
San Diego, CA
Wilmington, CA
Marin, John W. (Jack) ....Raleigh, NC
Research Triangle Park, NC
Marin, Kenneth P. ....New York, NY
Marin Law Center ....Novato, CA
San Rafael, CA
Marin, Louis J. ....Manassas, VA
Marin, Mariana ....Sacramento, CA
Marin, Michael Dennis ....Austin, TX
Marin, Patricia Woods
North Palm Beach, FL
Marin, Paul J. ....Long Beach, CA
Marin, Paul M. ....Marquette, MI
Marin, Richard P. ....New York, NY
Marin, Rita C. ....New York, NY
Marin, Robert M. ....Franklin, LA
Marin, Robert S. ....Secaucus, NJ
Marin, Rosemary Morales ....El Paso, TX
Marin, Sandra D. ....Sausalito, CA
Marin, Susan Erickson ....Austin, TX
Marina, James E. ....New York, NY
Marin-Abaunza, Leandro ....Miami, FL
Marinac, Paul M. ....St. Paul, MN
Marinacci, Donna D. ....Brooklyn, NY
Marinacci, Michelle Lee ....Charleston, WV
Marinaccio, Lee A. ....Oak Brook, IL
Wheaton, IL
Marinaccio, Leonard, III ....Ormond Beach, FL
Marinaccio, Michael A. ....Englewood, NJ
Bronx, NY
White Plains, NY
Marinakis, Dean C. ....Chicago, IL
Marinakis, George G. ....Chicago, IL
Marinakis, George S. ....Cincinnati, OH
Marinakis, Marina ....Cincinnati, OH
Marinakis & Marinakis ....Cincinnati, OH
Marinakis, Patty A. ....Wilmette, IL
Marinan, John P. ....Atlanta, GA
Marinari, Lawrence T. ....Trenton, NJ
Marinaro, Anthony L. ....New Orleans, LA
Marinaro, Joseph A. ....New York, NY
Marinaro, Joseph J. ....Philadelphia, PA
Marinaro, Michael V. ....Lancaster, PA
Marindin, Julie McDonald ....White Hall, MD
Marine, Andrew C. ....Aiken, SC
Marine, Christopher H. ....Vero Beach, FL
Marine, Deborah Lynn ....Buffalo, NY
Marine, Frank J. ....Department of Justice,
Criminal Division, GV

Marine, Joni Greenberg ....Woodland Hills, CA
Marine, Meredith J. ....San Jose, CA
Marine, Michael D. ....Indianapolis, IN
Marineau, Paul K. ....Ada, MI
Marinella, G. Scott ....Dayton, WA
Marinelli, Arthur J., Jr. ....Athens, OH
Marinelli, Bernard ....Okemos, MI
Marinelli, Bonnie-Jean M.
Silver Spring, MD
Marinelli, Brian R. ....Boston, MA
Marinelli, Domenic ....Wellesley Hills, MA
Marinelli, Frances Dapice ....White Plains, NY
Marinelli, Francis C. ....New York, NY
Marinelli, Frank A. ....Braintree, MA
Marinelli, George A. ....Philadelphia, PA
Marinelli, James M. ....New Britain, CT
Marinelli, John Anthony ....Downey, CA
Marinelli, John P., (P.A.)
West Palm Beach, FL
Marinelli, John V. ....Lighthouse Point, FL
Marinelli, Kathleen ....Albany, NY
Marinelli, Marisa ....New York, NY
Marinelli, Merritt McReynolds
Houston, TX
Marinelli, Michael G.
Federal Election Commission,
Office of the General Counsel, GV
Marinelli, Michael X. ....Austin, TX
Marinelli, Raymond E. ....Albany, NY
Marinelli, Robert L. ....Buffalo, NY
Marinelli, Ronald W. ....West Chester, PA
Marinelli, Sarabeth A. ....Palo Alto, CA
Marinelli & Sauer, P.C. ....New Britain, CT
Marinello, Deborah Kae ....Aloha, OR
Marinello, James N. ....New York, NY
Marinello, Joseph A. ....Miami, FL
Marinello, Leonard P. ....Garden City, NY
Marinello, Maria C. ....New York, NY
Marinello, Mitchell L. ....Chicago, IL
Marinello, Salvatore J. ....Mineola, NY
Mariner, Mildred C. ....Pembroke Pines, FL
Mariner, Rachel A. ....Washington, DC
Mariner, Wendy K. ....Boston, MA
Maring, David H. ....Georgetown, SC
Maring, David S. ....Detroit Lakes, MN
Bismarck, ND
Fargo, ND
Maring, Elizabeth Vogelzang ....Grayslake, IL
Maring, Harry B. ....San Francisco, CA
Maring, Mary Muehlen ....Bismarck, ND
Maring Williams Law Office, P.C.
Detroit Lakes, MN
Moorhead, MN
Bismarck, ND
Fargo, ND
Maringer, Elizabeth F. ....New York, NY
Marini, David J. ....Fishers, NY
Marini, Francis L. ....Hanson, MA
Marini, Nino J. ....Captiva, FL
Marini, Ronald A. ....Miami, FL
Marini & Turner ....Hanson, MA
Mariniello, Joseph R. ....Fort Lee, NJ
Mariniello, Joseph R., P.C. ....Fort Lee, NJ
Mariniello, Joseph Richard, Jr. ....Novi, MI
Marinik, Daniel F. ....Toledo, OH
Marini Roig, Luis E. ....San Juan, PR
Marinis, Thomas P., Jr. ....Houston, TX
Marinko, Christopher M. ....Sandusky, OH
Marinko, Stephen ....New York, NY
Marinkovic, Tamara ....Dallas, TX
Marinkovich, Donald P. ....Seattle, WA
Marino, A. John ....New York, NY
Marino, Andrew A. ....Belcher, LA
Marino, Angelo, Jr. ....Fort Lauderdale, FL
Marino, Anthony ....Mineola, NY
Marino, Anthony C. ....New Orleans, LA
Marino, Anthony C. ....Milwaukee, WI
Marino, Anthony J. ....Stamford, CT
Marino, Anthony J. ....Montclair, NJ
Marino, Bernstein & La Marca, P.C.
Oyster Bay, NY
Marino, Brenda A. ....New Castle, PA
Marino, Carl A. ....Syracuse, NY
Marino, Carla ....Philadelphia, PA
Marino, Carla M. ....Bronx, NY
Marino, Carmen M. ....Cleveland, OH
Marino, Cathy A. ....Winthrop, MA
Marino, Chambers & Lou, P.C.
White Plains, NY
Marino, Daniel ....Washington, DC
Marino, Donald C. ....Philadelphia, PA
Marino, Donna A. ....Bedford, NY
Marino, Edwin, Jr. ....Dallas, TX
Marino, Ellen C. ....Winsted, CT
Marino, Fabio E. ....San Jose, CA
Marino, Frank A. ....Washington, DC
Marino, Frank A. ....Chicago, IL
Marino, Frank C. ....Chicago, IL
Rockford, IL
Marino, Frank P. ....White Plains, NY
Marino, Gerard J. ....Newburgh, NY
Marino, Hope E. ....Sunnyvale, CA
Marino, Ingrid ....Memphis, TN
Marino, J. Anthony ....Encino, CA
Marino, J. Anthony, A Professional Corporation ....Encino, CA
Marino, Jack E. ....Philadelphia, PA
Marino, Jack F. ....Chicago, IL
Marino, James A. ....Chicago, IL
Marino, James E. ....Santa Barbara, CA
Marino, James G. ....Massapequa, NY
Marino, James J. ....Princeton, NJ
Marino, James M. ....White Plains, NY
Marino, James R. ....New York, NY
Marino, Jeanne O. ....Paramus, NJ
Marino, Jesse J. ....Riverside, CA
Marino, John D. ....Los Angeles, CA
Marino, John P. ....Jacksonville, FL

Marino, John W., Jr. ....East Hartford, CT
Marino, Joseph A. ....Clearwater, FL
Marino, Joseph A. ....Verona, NJ
Marino, Joseph A., III ....Gretna, LA
Marino, Joseph D. ....Portland, CT
Marino, Joseph E., Jr. ....Winchester, MA
Marino, Joseph R. ....Scranton, PA
Marino, Julie M. ....Bridgewater, NJ
Marino, Kara Read ....Lexington, KY
Marino, Kathleen Tuthill
Los Angeles, CA
Marino, Keith R. ....Washington, DC
Marino, Kenneth J. ....Wilmington, DE
Marino, Kevin H. ....Newark, NJ
New York, NY
Marino, Kevin H., P.C. ....Newark, NJ
New York, NY
Marino, Laura C. ....Bakersfield, CA
Marino, Lawrence E. ....Lafayette, LA
Marino, Linda M. ....Brooklyn, NY
Marino, Lisa J. ....Newton, MA
Marino, Lisa Wickstrom ....Denton, TX
Marino, Louis E., Jr. ....Los Angeles, CA
Marino, Lucien R. ....University Heights, OH
Marino, Marija Tenzera ....McLean, VA
Marino, Mario J. ....Brooklyn, NY
Marino, Mark A. ....Destrehan, LA
Marino, Mark D. ....New York, NY
Marino, Mary Jo ....Riverside, IL
Marino, Matthew A. ....New York, NY
Charlotte, NC
Marino & Maurice, P.C. ....Bridgewater, NJ
Marino, Michael A. ....Pasadena, CA
Marino, Michael D. ....Norristown, PA
Marino, Michael E. ....Towson, MD
Marino, Michael F. ....McLean, VA
Marino, Michael J. ....Jacksonville, FL
Marino, Michael J. ....Brooklyn, NY
Marino, Michael V. ....Concord, MA
Marino, Michael W. ....New York, NY
Marino, Nicholas A. ....Wantagh, NY
Marino, Nicholas Jack ....Akron, OH
Marino, Nina ....Beverly Hills, CA
Marino, Patricia A. ....River Forest, IL
Marino, Paul D. ....Sunrise, FL
Marino, Paul F. ....Hackensack, NJ
Marino, Paul J. ....St. Petersburg, FL
Marino, Paul V. ....Dedham, MA
Marino, Peter G. ....Boston, MA
Marino, Peter J. ....Raleigh, NC
Marino, Ralph J. ....Oyster Bay, NY
Marino, Robert B. ....New York, NY
Marino, Robert J. ....New York, NY
Marino, Robert J. ....Pittsburgh, PA
Wheeling, WV
Marino, Robert M. ....Washington, DC
Marino, Rose A. ....Lawrence, KS
Marino, Ruche J. ....Norco, LA
Marino & Sachs, P.A.
Fort Lauderdale, FL
Miami, FL
Marino, Salvatore Louis ....Hempstead, NY
Marino, Samuel A. ....Buffalo, NY
Marino, Stephen A., Jr. ....Miami, FL
Marino, Steven F. ....Philadelphia, PA
Marino, Thomas A. ....Williamsport, PA
Marino, Thomas V. ....New York, NY
Marino, Vera Gretchyn ....Bayside, NY
Marino, Vincent J. ....Winchester, MA
Marino, Vincent L. ....Houston, TX
Marino, Vincent M. ....Bridgeport, CT
Marino, Vincent M. ....Middletown, CT
Marino, Vincent N. ....Little Falls, NJ
Marino & Walsh ....St. Petersburg, FL
Marino & Weiss, P.C. ....White Plains, NY
Marino, William A. ....Boston, MA
Marino, William R. ....Milton, MA
Marinoff, Alan ....Long Island City, NY
Marino-Potter, Maria ....Charleston, WV
Marinos, Douglas M. ....Allentown, PA
Marinos, James S. ....San Diego, CA
Marinos, James S., A Professional Corporation
San Diego, CA
Marinovic, Amy Church ....Buffalo, NY
Marinovich, Michael B. ....Denver, CO
Marinovich, William F. ....Freedom, CA
Marin-Rosa, Carlos ....Orlando, FL
Marinstein, Edward R. ....Troy, NY
Marinstein, Elliott F. ....Troy, NY
Marinstein, Jay D. ....Pittsburgh, PA
Marinstein & Marinstein ....Albany, NY
Troy, NY
Marinucci, Dominick E. ....Yonkers, NY
Marinucci, Fred J. ....Department of Education,
Office of the General Counsel, GV
Marinuzzi, Lorenzo ....New York, NY
Mario, Anthony P., Jr. ....Cocoa, FL
Mario, Carter E. ....Milford, CT
Mario, David A. ....San Ramon, CA
Mario, Richard A. ....Lake Oswego, OR
Mariolis, C. Theodore ....Fitchburg, MA
Marion, Andrew ....Gulfport, MS
Marion, Arthur J. ....Philadelphia, PA
Marion, Betty D. ....Ocala, FL
Marion, Catherine ....New York, NY
Marion, Charles S. ....Philadelphia, PA
Marion, David A. ....San Jose, CA
Marion, David H. ....Philadelphia, PA
Marion, David K. ....Irvine, CA
Marion, Edward S. ....Madison, WI
Marion, Eric M. ....Washington, DC
Marion, Geoffrey E. ....New London, CT
Marion, George S. ....Philadelphia, PA
Marion, George W. ....Springfield, MA
Marion, J. Hardin ....Baltimore, MD
Marion, James P. ....Santa Ana, CA
Marion, John B., IV
West Palm Beach, FL

Marion, Joseph R., III ....Providence, RI
Marion, Joseph W. ....Durham, NC
Marion, Kimberly I. ....Pittsburgh, PA
Marion, Matthew A. ....New York, NY
Marion, Michael B. ....Denver, CO
Marion, Michael E. ....Tarrytown, NY
Marion, Michael G. ....Plymouth, MI
Marion's Inn ....Oakland, CA
Marion, S. Jill ....Atlanta, GA
Marion, Samara C. ....Santa Cruz, CA
Marion, Sandee Bryan ....San Antonio, TX
Marion, Satzberg, Trichon & Kogan, P.C.
Philadelphia, PA
Marion, Stanley W. ....South Holland, IL
Marion, Susan G. ....Flushing, NY
Marion, Thomas D. ....Keokuk, IA
Marion, Timothy F. ....Denver, CO
Marion, W. David ....Galveston, TX
Marion, W. Francis, Jr. ....Greenville, SC
Marion, Wesley S. ....Bloomington, IN
Marion, William Lee Davidson
Chester, SC
Marioni, William H. ....Santa Rosa, CA
Marionneaux, F. Barry ....Plaquemine, LA
Marionneaux, F. Charles ....Plaquemine, LA
Marionneaux, Jack T. ....Plaquemine, LA
Marionneaux, Kyle C. ....Baton Rouge, LA
Marionneaux & Marionneaux
Plaquemine, LA
Marionneaux, Mark A. ....Baton Rouge, LA
Plaquemine, LA
Marionneaux, Rhett Wade, Jr.
Atlanta, GA
Mariorenzi-Musco, Lisa ....Cranston, RI
Mariotti, Joseph E. ....Scranton, PA
Mariotti Law Offices, P.C. ....Scranton, PA
Mariotto, Donald L. ....Gold River, CA
Mari-Roca, Santiago ....Mayaguez, PR
Maris, Charles G. ....Milwaukee, WI
Maris, Charles W., Jr. ....Jackson, MS
Maris, George P. ....Chicago, IL
Maris, Karen A.
Executive Office Of The President,
Office of Management and Budget, GV
Maris, Linda Swagger ....Milwaukee, WI
Maris, Robert F. ....Dallas, TX
Maris, Stephen S. ....Dallas, TX
Mariscal, George Edward ....Tucson, AZ
Mariscal, Jorge A., Law Office of
San Antonio, TX
Mariscal, Rudolph ....Phoenix, AZ
Mariscal, Weeks, McIntyre & Friedlander, P.A. ....Phoenix, AZ
Marischen, Kenneth J., Jr. ....Anchorage, AK
Marischen, Robert G. ....Dayton, OH
Marisie, Jill Cerone ....Chicago, IL
Marisseau, Medora A. ....Seattle, WA
Maristch, Rita M.
Department of Transportation,
Office of the General Counsel, GV
Maristuen, Keith A. ....Havre, MT
Maritime Legal Resources ....Charleston, SC
Maritote, R. Mark ....Chicago, IL
Maritote, Roger F. ....Bloomingdale, IL
Marius, Frederick S. ....Boston, MA
Mariz, Darrell J. ....Beverly Hills, CA
Marjala, Donald R. ....Eau Claire, WI
Marjama, Owen D. ....Syracuse, NY
Marjerison, Thomas S. ....Portland, ME
Marjon, Louis, Law Offices of
Santa Fe, NM
Mark, Alan S. ....Bethesda, MD
Mark, Anna K. ....Rockville, MD
Mark, Bernard S. ....Roseland, NJ
Great Neck, NY
Mark, Brian A. ....Kansas City, MO
Mark, Brian M. ....Kissimmee, FL
Mark, Brian Michael, P.A.
Kissimmee, FL
Mark, Brian, Michael, P.A. ....Orlando, FL
Mark & Burkhead ....Mission, KS
Kansas City, MO
Mark, Carol ....Mount Vernon, NY
Mark, Carolyn G. ....Department of Justice,
Civil Division, GV
Mark, Catharine ....St. Paul, MN
Mark, Cynthia ....Boston, MA
Mark, Dana L. ....New York, NY
Mark, Daniel L. ....Houston, TX
Mark, Daniel S. ....Encino, CA
Mark, David B. ....Boston, MA
Mark, David J. ....New York, NY
Mark, David N. ....Seattle, WA
Mark, Debra A. ....New York, NY
Mark, Denis H. ....Denver, CO
Mark, Diane ....Denver, CO
Mark, Donald B. ....Stratford, NJ
Mark, Donald Chance, Jr. ....Minneapolis, MN
Mark, Donald J. ....Rochester, NY
Mark, Douglas Stuart ....Burbank, CA
Mark, Elliot J. ....Cambridge, MA
Mark, Eric A. ....Phoenix, AZ
Mark, Eugene J. ....Bethesda, MD
Mark, Henry Allen ....New York, NY
Mark, James R. ....Willimantic, CT
Mark, Janet L. ....Kansas City, MO
Mark, Jason ....Boston, MA
Mark, Jennifer A. ....Alexandria, VA
Mark, Joel ....Los Angeles, CA
Mark, John P. ....Saddle Brook, NJ
Mark, Jonathan ....Stroudsburg, PA
Mark, Jonathan I. ....New York, NY
Mark, Julie T. ....New York, NY
Mark, Keith L. ....Mission, KS
Mark, Lance J. ....Medina, NY
Mark, Leonard J. ....Phoenix, AZ
Mark, Liza L.S. ....Minneapolis, MN
Mark, Loren B. ....Omaha, NE

Mark, Melvyn I. ... **San Francisco, CA**
Mark, Michael A. ... Houston, TX
Mark, Michael D. ... Union, NJ
Mark, Michael E. ... Mobile, AL
Mark, Miles ... Covington, LA
Mark, Nathan ... Brooklyn, NY
Mark & Pearlstein, P.A. ... **Phoenix, AZ**
Mark, Philip A. ... San Bernardino, CA
Mark, Priscilla H. ... **Palo Alto, CA**
Mark, Richard G. ... **Minneapolis, MN**
Mark, Richard W. ... **New York, NY**
Mark, Robert A. ... Miami, FL
Mark, Robert L. ... Hannibal, MO
Mark, Robert M. ... Warren, NJ
Mark, Ronald H. ... **Newport Beach, CA**
Mark, Sharon Rivenson ... Jersey City, NJ
Mark, Sheri ... Bloomfield Hills, MI
Mark, Stacey E. ... **Portland, OR**
Mark, Stephen S. ... Dallas, TX
Mark, Steven ... Trenton, NJ
Mark, Susann G. ... Providence, RI
Mark, Thomas E. ... New York, NY
Mark, Timothy I. ... Bethlehem, PA
Harrisburg, PA
Mark, Valarie ... San Francisco, CA
Mark, Valerie A. ... Treasury Department, Internal Revenue Service, GV
Mark, Warren W., (P.C.) ... Chicago, IL
Mark, Wayne J. ... **Omaha, NE**
Mark, Weigle & Perkins ... Shippensburg, PA
Mark, William I. ... Meriden, CT
Mark, William M. ... Coronado, CA
Mark, William Martin ... Far Rockaway, NY
Markakis, Constance ... **Washington, DC**
Markakis, Nick ... Troy, MI
Markam Group, The, Inc., P.S. ... Spokane, WA
Markantonis, Frank ... Houston, TX
Markard, Marlene M. ... **New York, NY**
Markarian, David K. ... **Miami, FL**
Markarian, Edward J. ... Kenmore, NY
Markarian, James ... New York, NY
Markarian, John ... Kenmore, NY
Markarian, Kris ... Federal Judicial Center, GV
Markason, Carolyn C. ... Newark, NJ
Markason, Joseph A. ... New York Mills, NY
Markatos, David C. ... **New York, NY**
Markbreiter, Steven C. ... New York, NY
Markcity, Michael R. ... Plantation, FL
Marke, Julius J. ... Jamaica, NY
Markee, Louis J., Jr. ... Honolulu, HI
Markee, Wendy L. ... Dallas, TX
Markel, Adam David ... **New York, NY**
Markel, Bruce S., III ... Brownstown, IN
Markel, Gregory A. ... **New York, NY**
Markel, Herbert F. ... Rye Brook, NY
Markel, Howard B. ... Cumming, GA
Markel, James W. ... **Winter Park, FL**
Markel, James Wayland, P.A. ... **Winter Park, FL**
Markel, Jason E. ... **Buffalo, NY**
Markel, Jeffrey D. ... **Los Angeles, CA**
Markel, Jim ... Poplar Bluff, MO
Markel, John F. ... Columbia, PA
Lancaster, PA
Markel, Joseph K. ... Brownstown, IN
Markel, Keith A. ... **New York, NY**
Markel, Marc D. ... **Houston, TX**
Markel & Markel ... Brownstown, IN
Markel, Michael A. ... San Bernardino, CA
Markel, Robert E. ... Denver, CO
Markel, Robinson ... **New York, NY**
Markel, Schafer & Goldman, P.C. ... **Pittsburgh, PA**
Markel, Sheldon M. ... Henderson, NV
Markel, Timothy I. ... Council Bluffs, IA
Markell, Bruce A. ... **Indianapolis, IN**
Markell, David L. ... Albany, NY
Markell, George ... San Francisco, CA
Markell, Lori A. ... Cambridge, MA
Markell, Philip ... Maynard, MA
Markello, Jeffrey P. ... Elma, NY
Markels, Gail ... New York, NY
Marken, Howard A. ... **Cleveland, OH**
Marken, Kenneth R. ... Casper, WY
Marken, Michael J. ... Oakland, CA
Marken, Roger Erik ... **Los Angeles, CA**
Markenson, Michael A. ... **St. Louis, MO**
Markenson, William D. ... **Los Angeles, CA**
Marker, Charles E. ... Greensburg, PA
Marker, Clinton C. ... Wichita, KS
Marker, David A. ... Herndon, VA
Marker, Howard S. ... **Minneapolis, MN**
Marker, Joel T. ... **Salt Lake City, UT**
Marker, Jos. B. ... Bethesda, MD
Marker, Marc L. ... Corte Madera, CA
Marker, Michael B. ... **East St. Louis, IL**
Marker, Michelle Ann ... Cody, WY
Marker, Randall L. ... **Jacksonville, FL**
Marker, Richard A. ... Beverly Hills, CA
Markert, Allan R. ... St. Paul, MN
Markert, Bobbi Jo ... Durham, NC
Markert, John F. ... St. Paul, MN
Markert, Philip John, Jr. ... **Staunton, VA**
Markert, Richard F. ... **New York, NY**
Markesbery, Junel D. ... Burlington, KY
Markesbery, Glen A. ... Cincinnati, OH
Markese, Bartholomew P. ... Joliet, IL
Markese, Paul M. ... **Chicago, IL**
Markeson, Thomas A. ... Kerman, CA
Markessinis, Barbara ... Albany, NY
Market, Gary H. ... Pleasanton, CA
Marketos, Alexander K. ... **Bloomfield Hills, MI**
Marketos, James L. ... **Washington, DC**
Marketos, Peter D. ... **Dallas, TX**
Markett, Michael J. ... **Boston, MA**

Markette, David T. ... Hamilton, MT
Marketto, Anna N. ... El Paso, TX
Markewich, Daniel ... **New York, NY**
Markewich, Eve Rachel ... **New York, NY**
Markewich Friedman & Markewich, P.C. ... **New York, NY**
Markewich, Robert ... **New York, NY**
Markewitz, Elan Abraham ... Riverhead, NY
Markey, Bradley R. ... **Jacksonville, FL**
Markey, Brian M. ... Glen Rock, NJ
Markey, Charles E., Jr. ... Trenton, NJ
Markey, Charles J. ... Brooklyn, NY
Markey, Christian E., Jr. ... Los Angeles, CA
Markey, Christopher G. ... **Chicago, IL**
Markey, David J. ... Washington, DC
Markey, Edward G. ... Fort Worth, TX
Markey, Elizabeth A. ... **Irvine, CA**
Markey & Fowler, P.A. ... Merritt Island, FL
Markey, Gavin W. ... York, PA
Markey, Howard T. ... Hinsdale, IL
Markey, Hughes & Steiner ... Corpus Christi, TX
Markey, James G. ... **New York, NY**
Markey, James K. ... Chandler, AZ
Markey, Jean L. ... Princeton, NJ
Markey, Jeanne A. ... **Philadelphia, PA**
Markey, Joan M. ... **New York, NY**
Markey, John A., Jr. ... **New Bedford, MA**
Markey, John K. ... **Boston, MA**
Markey, John P. ... Hackensack, NJ
Markey, Kevin P. ... Merritt Island, FL
Markey, Kristina A. ... **Monterey, CA**
Markey, Matthew ... Media, PA
Markey, Maureen E. ... San Diego, CA
Markey, Michael D. ... **Newark, NJ**
Markey, Mike ... Wichita Falls, TX
Markey, Patrick J. ... **Springfield, MA**
Markey, Regina M. ... Washington, DC
Markey, Richard P. ... Boston, MA
Markey, Robert G. ... **Cleveland, OH**
Markey, Robert H. ... Blue Springs, MO
Markey, Stephen A. ... **Baltimore, MD**
Bel Air, MD
Markey, Stephen A., III, P.C. ... **Baltimore, MD**
Bel Air, MD
Markey, Stephen A., Jr. ... **Greenbelt, MD**
Markey, Thomas R. ... Corpus Christi, TX
Markfield, Robert S. ... **New York, NY**
Markfield & Solomon ... **New York, NY**
Markgraf, Paul R. ... Fort Mitchell, KY
Markham, Adrienne M. ... **Boston, MA**
Markham, Allan W. ... Washington, DC
Markham, Allan W., P.C. ... Washington, DC
Markham, Anne R. ... Columbia, MD
Markham, Arthur T. ... Prescott, AZ
Markham, Barbara A. ... West Palm Beach, FL
Markham, Charles B. ... Durham, NC
Markham, Charles H. ... San Diego, CA
Markham, Charles S. ... **Washington, DC**
Markham, Craig A. ... **Erie, PA**
Markham, Daniel F. ... **New York, NY**
Markham, David K. ... **Parsons, KS**
Markham, David R. ... **San Diego, CA**
Markham, Debra Jean ... Cambridge, MA
Markham, Donald W. ... Vienna, VA
Markham, Douglas E. ... **Houston, TX**
Markham, Drew G. ... **Kirkland, WA**
Markham, Edwin T. ... **New York, NY**
Markham, Gary G. ... **Charleston, WV**
Markham, Gerald W. ... Kodiak, AK
Markham, Gregory K. ... **Honolulu, HI**
Markham, Harold ... Chicago, IL
Markham, Herbert M. ... New York, NY
Markham, James ... Malvern, PA
Markham, James J., III ... Englewood, NJ
Markham, Jesse W. ... **San Francisco, CA**
Markham, John B. ... **Parsons, KS**
Markham, John E., Jr. ... **Durham, NC**
Markham, John J.E. ... San Francisco, CA
Boston, MA
Markham, Julian E., Jr. ... **Washington, DC**
Rockville, MD
Arlington, VA
Markham, Kathleen T. ... San Diego, CA
Markham, Keevil L. ... Glendale, CA
Markham, Matthew G. ... **Riverside, CA**
Markham, Melinda S. ... **St. Louis, MO**
Markham, Michael C. ... **Clearwater, FL**
Tampa, FL
Markham, Nina Lynn ... **Jersey City, NJ**
Markham, Patrick T. ... **Sacramento, CA**
Markham, Paul F. ... Melrose, MA
Markham & Read ... San Francisco, CA
Boston, MA
Markham, Redenbacher & Brown, LLP ... **San Francisco, CA**
Santa Cruz, CA
Markham, Robert C. ... Department of Justice, Tax Division, GV
Markham, Robert C. ... Chester, VA
Markham, Rosemary ... Pittsburgh, PA
Markham, Theresa A. ... Hamburg, NJ
Markham, Tracy L. ... St. Augustine, FL
Lawrenceville, NJ
Markham, Wade T., II ... **Bowling Green, KY**
Markham, Wendolyn Ward ... **Atlanta, GA**
Markham, William A. ... **San Francisco, CA**
Markham, Zachary J. ... **Flagstaff, AZ**
Markhoff, Gottlieb, Lazarus, D'Auria & Maldonado, P.C. ... New York, NY
Markhoff, Harris ... **White Plains, NY**
Markhoff, Michael ... **White Plains, NY**
Markhoff, Nancy Allen ... Bronx, NY
Markhoff, Paul M. ... New York, NY
Markhovsky, Russ ... **Chicago, IL**
Markiewicz, Stephanie J. ... Washington, DC

Markiewicz, Steven H. ... Merrimack, NH
Markiewicz, Thomas S. ... Department of the Air Force, Office of the Judge Advocate General, GV
Markijohn, Darrell N. ... **Canton, OH**
Markiles, Murray ... **Los Angeles, CA**
Markin, Robert S. ... **Chicago, IL**
Markin, Steven B. ... Armonk, NY
Markind, Daniel B. ... Gibbsboro, NJ
Philadelphia, PA
Markind, Lloyd S. ... **Cherry Hill, NJ**
Paoli, PA
Marking, John R. ... **Costa Mesa, CA**
Marking, Philip W. ... **Santa Barbara, CA**
Markir, Marsha ... Buzzards Bay, MA
Markis, Emanuel J. ... Cambridge, MA
Markison, Kenneth A. ... Department of Housing and Urban Development, Office of General Counsel, GV
Markizon, Bellanne ... Bronx, NY
Markl, Steven R. ... Winfield, IL
Markland, Dale Gene ... **Dallas, TX**
Markland, Richard H. ... University City, MO
Markle, Brinton B. ... Helena, MT
Markle, D. Todd ... **Atlanta, GA**
Markle & Daly, A Professional Law Corporation ... New Orleans, LA
Biloxi, MS
Markle, Deanna L. ... Hanford, CA
Markle, Edward D. ... New Orleans, LA
Markle, G. Donald ... **Fairfax, VA**
Markle, James T. ... Sacramento, CA
Markle, John, Jr. ... **Berwyn, PA**
Markle, John S. ... Securities and Exchange Commission, Division of Enforcement, GV
Markle, Larry ... Coffeyville, KS
Markle, Lori L. ... Doylestown, PA
Markle, Milo M., Jr. ... Clarion, PA
Markle, Peter D. ... New Haven, CT
Markle, R. Gerald ... **South Pasadena, CA**
Markle, Ramos & Zito, A Professional Corporation ... **Houston, TX**
Markle, Robert N. ... **New Orleans, LA**
Markle, Spencer G. ... **Houston, TX**
Markle, Suzanne ... Cary, NC
Markle, Thomas J. ... **Fort Wayne, IN**
Markley, Amy E. ... Indianapolis, IN
Markley, Barbara J. ... Fort Lauderdale, FL
Markley, Brian R. ... **Kansas City, MO**
Markley, Charles R. ... **Portland, OR**
Markley, Christopher P. ... Harrisburg, PA
Markley, Frederick E. ... Kenton, OH
Markley, G. Roger ... Chicago, IL
Markley, George J. ... Fairfield, CT
Markley, Hugh P. ... St. Paul, MN
Markley, Ian Carroll ... Reston, VA
Markley, Janet S. ... **Las Vegas, NV**
Markley, John K. ... Orinda, CA
Markley, Leland J. ... New York, NY
Markley, Michael E. ... Redlands, CA
Markley, Molly B. ... **Troy, MI**
Markley, Pamela A. ... **Palm Beach, FL**
Markley, Paul R. ... El Segundo, CA
Markley, Sandra K. ... **Omaha, NE**
Markley, Sheila M. ... **Canton, OH**
Markley, Steuart G., Jr. ... **Baltimore, MD**
Markley, Theresa L. ... Staunton, VA
Markley, William C., III ... **Pasadena, CA**
Markling, Matthew J. ... **Cleveland, OH**
Markman, Christine A. ... Denver, CO
Markman, David P. ... Los Angeles, CA
Markman, Howard M. ... Northfield, NJ
Markman, James L. ... **Brea, CA**
Markman, Jeremy K. ... **Orlando, FL**
Markman, Joan L. ... Philadelphia, PA
Markman, Jody E. ... New York, NY
Markman, Joy W. ... Santa Ana, CA
Markman, Linda E. ... Farmington Hills, MI
Markman, Marla Kyle ... Los Angeles, CA
Markman, Max L. ... South Euclid, OH
Markman, Michael D. ... Forest Hills, NY
Markman, Michael M. ... **Palo Alto, CA**
Markman, Natalie A. ... Commodity Futures Trading Commission, GV
Markman, Nora S. ... New York, NY
Markman, Norman L. ... Lakewood, CO
Markman, Peter E. ... **Boston, MA**
Markman, Ronald A. ... Beverly Hills, CA
Markman, Ross Garry ... New York, NY
Markman, Sherwin J. ... **Washington, DC**
Markman, Stefanie I. ... **Los Angeles, CA**
Markman, Stephen J. ... Lansing, MI
Markman, Stephen R. ... Brooklyn, NY
Markman, Stuart C. ... **Tampa, FL**
Markman, William E. ... Dallas, TX
Markmann, David ... San Rafael, CA
Marko, Allen A. ... Bristol, CT
Marko, David Everett ... **Miami, FL**
Marko, Edward J. ... Phoenix, AZ
Marko, Edward J. ... Fort Lauderdale, FL
Marko, Paul M., III ... Fort Lauderdale, FL
Marko, Shari R. ... **Newark, NJ**
Marko, Sheila Cronin ... Redwood City, CA
Marko & Stephany ... Fort Lauderdale, FL
Marko, Thomas P. ... **Kansas City, MO**
Markoff & Boyers ... Las Vegas, NV
Markoff, Brad S. ... **Raleigh, NC**
Markoff, Gary M. ... **Boston, MA**
Markoff, Jerome H. ... Annapolis, MD
Markoff, Krasny, Goldman & Grant ... Chicago, IL
Markoff, M. Daniel ... Las Vegas, NV
Markoff, Michael J. ... Falmouth, MA
Markoff, Nancy Young ... Los Angeles, CA
Markoff, Paul F., IV ... **Chicago, IL**

Markoff, Paul H. ... Department of Transportation, Surface Transportation Board, GV
Markoff, Robert G. ... Chicago, IL
Markoff, Ronald C., Law Offices of ... **Providence, RI**
Markofski, Henry C. ... Gilbertsville, PA
Markofski, Susan M. ... Norristown, PA
Markofsky, Daniel B. ... **Denver, CO**
Markopoulos, George S. ... Lynn, MA
Markos, John J. ... Lynbrook, NY
Markosky, Edward J., Jr. ... Danbury, CT
Markotsis, James Constantine ... Hicksville, NY
Markotsis and Lieberman ... Hicksville, NY
Markou, Anastase ... **Kalamazoo, MI**
Markovich, Amy B. ... Fort Myers, FL
Markovich, Bert W. ... **Seattle, WA**
Markovich, Edward P. ... Cleveland, OH
Markovich, Maria ... **Philadelphia, PA**
Markovich, Mary M. ... New Bern, NC
Markovich, Stephen E. ... Washington, DC
Markovitch, Michael D. ... **Los Angeles, CA**
Markovitch, Michael H. ... New York, NY
Markovits & Greiwe, Co., L.P.A. ... Cincinnati, OH
Markovits & Markovits ... Middletown, NY
Markovits, Richard S. ... Austin, TX
Markovits, Robert L. ... Middletown, NY
Markovits, Ronald D. ... **Chicago, IL**
Markovits, Stephen R. ... Middletown, NY
Markovits, W. B. ... Cincinnati, OH
Markovitz, Alan F. ... Bala Cynwyd, PA
Markovitz, Bernard ... Pittsburgh, PA
Markovitz, Harry ... Pittsburgh, PA
Markovitz, Lee ... Pittsburgh, PA
Markovitz, Max K. ... Pittsburgh, PA
Markovitz, Michael E. ... Camden, NJ
Philadelphia, PA
Markovitz, Michael J. ... Northbrook, IL
Markovitz, Monroe ... Union, NJ
Markovitz, Myron L. ... Johnstown, PA
Markovitz, Philip D. ... Harrisburg, PA
Markovitz, Rhoda Elvove ... Chicago, IL
Markovs, John P. ... Rockville, MD
Markow, Ari Lorin ... **Los Angeles, CA**
Markow, Gregory S. ... Chicago, IL
Markow, Herbert L. ... Coral Gables, FL
Markow, Kevin ... **Fort Lauderdale, FL**
Markow, Peter J., Jr. ... **Jackson, MS**
Markow, Richard E. ... St. Louis, MO
Markow, Theodore J. ... Richmond, VA
Markow, Walker & Reeves, P.A. ... **Jackson, MS**
Oxford, MS
Markowitz, Alon M. ... **New York, NY**
Markowitz, Amy J. ... San Francisco, CA
Markowitz, Andrew L. ... Lahaska, PA
Markowitz, Barry I. ... Chester, NJ
Markowitz, Bruce ... **Washington, DC**
Markowitz, Carl S. ... Virginia Beach, VA
Markowitz & Chorney ... Brooklyn, NY
Markowitz, Dale H. ... **Chardon, OH**
Markowitz, Daniel J. ... **Overland Park, KS**
Markowitz, Daniel J., P.A. ... **Overland Park, KS**
Markowitz, David A. ... **New York, NY**
Markowitz, David B. ... **Portland, OR**
Markowitz, David J. ... **Bloomfield, CT**
Markowitz, Davis, Ringel & Trusty, P.A. ... **Miami, FL**
Markowitz, Dawn S. ... New York, NY
Markowitz, Deborah S. ... **New York, NY**
Markowitz, Debra L. ... **Philadelphia, PA**
Markowitz, Donald ... **Bay Shore, NY**
Markowitz & Fernandez ... **Los Angeles, CA**
Markowitz, Gerald H. ... Hartsdale, NY
Markowitz, Harold E. ... Bellmore, NY
Markowitz, Harry ... New York, NY
Markowitz, Herbold, Glade & Mehlhaf, P.C. ... **Portland, OR**
Markowitz, Ira F. ... Coral Springs, FL
Markowitz, Irwin S. ... Hackensack, NJ
Markowitz, James Whitney ... La Quinta, CA
Markowitz, Jay ... Woodland Hills, CA
Markowitz, Jean E. ... **Memphis, TN**
Markowitz, Jeffrey A. ... **Baltimore, MD**
Markowitz, Jeffrey S. ... Department of Justice, Civil Division, GV
Markowitz, Jerry M. ... **Miami, FL**
Markowitz, Joel M. ... **Melville, NY**
Markowitz, Joseph ... **Lawrenceville, NJ**
Markowitz, Joseph C. ... **Los Angeles, CA**
Markowitz, Joshua ... **Lawrenceville, NJ**
Markowitz, Juliet A. ... **Los Angeles, CA**
Markowitz, Ken M. ... **San Francisco, CA**
Markowitz & Krevsky, P.C. ... Harrisburg, PA
York, PA
Markowitz, Laurence S. ... **New York, NY**
Markowitz, Lawrence A. ... Montclair, NJ
Markowitz, Lawrence S. ... York, PA
Markowitz, Lewis H. ... York, PA
Markowitz, Lewis M. ... **Chatham, NJ**
Markowitz, Linda ... **White Plains, NY**
Markowitz, Marie E. ... Pittsfield, MA
Markowitz & Markowitz ... Lahaska, PA
Markowitz & Markowitz, P.C. ... York, PA
Markowitz, Martin L. ... New York, NY
Markowitz, Matthew A. ... Glens Falls, NY
Markowitz, Michael ... Hewlett, NY
Markowitz, Michael I. ... **New York, NY**
Markowitz, Michael J. ... **Danville, CA**
Markowitz, Michele R. ... New York, NY
Markowitz, Miles L. ... Newburgh, NY
Markowitz, Morris ... Brooklyn, NY
Markowitz, Murray R. ... **New York, NY**
Markowitz, Nancy A. ... **Washington, DC**
Markowitz, Neal J. ... **Bethesda, MD**

Markowitz, Neil G. ... **Livingston, NJ**
Markowitz, Paula R. ... Philadelphia, PA
Markowitz, Petrina M. ... **Washington, DC**
Markowitz & Piro ... Hartsdale, NY
Markowitz, Richard H. ... Philadelphia, PA
Markowitz, Richard J. ... **Miami, FL**
Markowitz, Richard J., P.A. ... **Miami, FL**
Markowitz & Richman ... Allentown, PA
Harrisburg, PA
Philadelphia, PA
Markowitz, Robert ... Bloomington, IL
Markowitz, Robert A. ... **Houston, TX**
Markowitz, Roger S. ... **River Edge, NJ**
New York, NY
Markowitz, Rudolph G. ... North Bergen, NJ
Markowitz, Scott A. ... **Fort Lauderdale, FL**
Markowitz, Scott J. ... Houston, TX
Markowitz, Scott S. ... **New York, NY**
Markowitz, Shari H. ... **New York, NY**
Markowitz, Steven H. ... Wilmington, DE
Reston, VA
Markowitz, Stuart D. ... Westbury, NY
Markowitz, Susan J. ... Lahaska, PA
Markowitz and Zindler ... **Lawrenceville, NJ**
Mount Holly, NJ
Princeton, NJ
Trenton, NJ
Markowski, Elizabeth M. ... **New York, NY**
Markowski, James J. ... **New York, NY**
Markowski, Lucille ... Northfield, OH
Markowski, Robert T. ... **Chicago, IL**
Marks, Aaron H. ... **New York, NY**
Marks, Abraham ... Providence, RI
Marks & Acalin ... Los Angeles, CA
Marks, Alan H. ... Houston, TX
Marks, Alan J. ... **Pittsburgh, PA**
Marks, Alan K. ... San Bernardino, CA
Marks, Alan R. ... San Francisco, CA
Marks, Alan R. ... Fort Lauderdale, FL
Marks, Albert P. ... **Clarksville, TN**
Marks, Alfred M. ... **New York, NY**
Marks, Alfred W. J. ... **New York, NY**
Marks, Allan T. ... **Los Angeles, CA**
Marks, Alma L. ... Haddonfield, NJ
Marks, Alvin B., Jr. ... Waynesboro, VA
Marks, Amanda M. ... New York, NY
Marks, Andrew H. ... **Washington, DC**
Marks, Andrew J. ... Allegan, MI
Marks, Andrew P. ... **Morristown, NJ**
New York, NY
Marks, Andrew W. ... Chicago, IL
Marks, Anna Kristin ... **Chicago, IL**
Marks, Ansel R. ... Middletown, NY
Marks, Anthony J. ... **Los Angeles, CA**
Marks, Anthony L. ... **Phoenix, AZ**
Marks, B. Mayes, Jr. ... Hopewell, VA
Marks, B. Mayes, Jr., P.C. ... Hopewell, VA
Marks, Barbara F. ... Seattle, WA
Marks, Barry S. ... **Birmingham, AL**
Marks, Benjamin ... **New York, NY**
Marks, Benjamin Ely ... **New York, NY**
Marks, Benjamin S., Jr. ... Greensboro, NC
Marks, Bernard B. ... **Sioux City, IA**
Marks, B.G. ... Nicholasville, KY
Marks & Brooklier ... Los Angeles, CA
Marks, Bruce S. ... **Philadelphia, PA**
Marks, Bruce W. ... Lyndhurst, OH
Marks, Burton H. ... New York, NY
Marks, C. Hardaway ... Richmond, VA
Marks, Callie ... Topeka, KS
Marks, Caroline F. ... **San Diego, CA**
Marks, Charles L. ... Perry Hall, MD
Marks & Chong, P.A. ... **Orlando, FL**
Marks, Christine F. ... **Woodbridge, NJ**
Marks, Christine W. ... **Metairie, LA**
Marks, Christopher A. ... **Denver, CO**
Marks, Christophe B. ... Portland, OR
Marks, Christophe Evan ... Los Angeles, CA
Marks, Christopher M. ... **Brooklyn, NY**
Marks, Christopher M. ... Buffalo, NY
Marks, Christopher S. ... **Seattle, WA**
Marks Clare & Richards ... **Omaha, NE**
Marks, Craig A. ... **Phoenix, AZ**
Marks, Craig S. ... Stockton, CA
Marks, Craig W. ... **Lafayette, LA**
Marks, Cynthia L. ... La Jolla, CA
Marks, D. Brett ... Tampa, FL
Marks, Danelle Miller ... **Indianapolis, IN**
Marks, Daniel ... Las Vegas, NV
Marks, Daniel C. ... Charlotte, NC
Marks, David L. ... **Towson, MD**
Marks, David L. ... New York, NY
Marks, David L., Chartered
Baltimore, MD
Towson, MD
Marks, David Lyndon ... **Falls Church, VA**
Marks, David M. ... Houston, TX
Marks, David R. ... Cambridge, MA
Marks, David T. ... **Houston, TX**
Marks, David W. ... Seattle, WA
Marks, Dean S. ... **New York, NY**
Marks, Deborah ... Fort Lauderdale, FL
Miami, FL
Marks, Dennis A. ... **Chicago, IL**
Marks, Dennis Patrick ... Council Bluffs, IA
Marks, Donald B. ... Los Angeles, CA
Marks, Donald B. ... Cleveland, OH
Marks, Donald L. ... Akron, OH
Marks, Donald W. ... Alexandria, VA
Marks, Donna L. ... **Prospect Heights, IL**
Marks, Dorothy K. ... Los Angeles, CA
Marks, Doug B. ... **Sandpoint, ID**
Marks, Douglas B. ... Sandpoint, ID
Marks, Douglas D. ... **Melbourne, FL**
Marks, E. David ... **Palo Alto, CA**
Marks, E. Michael ... Jackson, MS
Marks, Edward D. ... Pittsburgh, PA
Marks, Edward G. ... **Cincinnati, OH**
Marks, Eileen M. ... **Hartford, CT**
Marks, Eileen Mulligan ... **San Diego, CA**
Las Vegas, NV
Marks, Ellen ... New York, NY
Marks, Ellen L. ... **Chicago, IL**
Marks, Elliot L. ... Seattle, WA
Marks, Emerson Robert, Jr.
Charlottesville, VA
Marks, Emily C. ... **Montgomery, AL**
Marks, Eric B. ... **Orlando, FL**
Marks, Erik G. ... **Seattle, WA**
Marks, Evan R. ... Miami, FL
Marks, F. Raymond ... El Cerrito, CA
Marks Firm, The ... **Houston, TX**
Marks, Frank M. ... Miami, FL
Marks, Gary F. ... Joseph, OR
Marks, Gary H. ... Fort Lauderdale, FL
Marks, Gary L. ... Houston, TX
Marks, Gary N. ... **Roseland, NJ**
Marks, Geoffrey B. ... **Miami, FL**
Marks, George L. ... Glen Head, NY
Marks, Gerald A. ... Red Bank, NJ
Marks, Gerard R. ... **Christiansburg, VA**
Marks & Golia, L.L.P. ... **San Diego, CA**
Marks Gray ... **Jacksonville, FL**
Marks, Greg ... **Fort Worth, TX**
Marks, Greg ... **Irving, TX**
Marks, Greg T. ... Louisville, KY
Marks, Gregory K. ... **New York, NY**
Marks, Gregory M. ... **Miami, FL**
Marks, H. Edward, Jr. ... Stone Mountain, GA
Marks & Harrison, P.C. ... Richmond, VA
Marks, Harry L. ... **Corpus Christi, TX**
Marks, Helen M. ... **Lexington, KY**
Marks, Helene E. ... Tampa, FL
Marks, Herbert E. ... **Washington, DC**
Marks, Herman H., Jr. ... Decatur, AL
Marks, Homer H. ... **Rochester, NY**
Marks and Hostetler ... Denver, CO
Marks, Howard ... **Chicago, IL**
Marks, Howard S. ... **Winter Park, FL**
Marks, Irving B. (Buddy) ... **Columbus, OH**
Marks, Isaac ... **Greenbelt, MD**
Marks, J. Alan ... El Paso, TX
Marks, J. Barrett (Barry) ... Portland, OR
Marks, J. Barrett, P.C. ... Portland, OR
Marks, Jacquelyn A ... **Canton, OH**
Marks, James ... Tuscumbia, AL
Marks, James A. ... St. Paul, MN
Marks, James D. ... New York, NY
Marks, James O. ... Jonesville, MI
Marks, James V. ... **New York, NY**
Marks, James W. ... Chicago, IL
Marks, Jan A. ... **Pittsburgh, PA**
Marks, Jane P. ... West Chester, PA
Marks, Janine M. ... Columbus, OH
Marks, Jason ... **Fort Lauderdale, FL**
Marks, Jay S. ... Silver Spring, MD
Marks, Jeanne M. Quinn ... **New York, NY**
Marks, Jeffrey ... **Cincinnati, OH**
Marks, Jeffrey A., (P.C.) ... Tucson, AZ
Marks, Jeffrey Allan ... **Washington, DC**
Marks, Jeffrey B. ... Jacksonville, FL
Marks, Jeffrey B. ... Cleveland, OH
Marks, Jeffrey D. ... Clifton, NJ
Marks, Jeffrey H. ... **Rochester, NY**
Marks, Jeffrey I. ... New York, NY
Marks, Jeffrey L.
Palm Beach Gardens, FL
Marks, Jeffrey L. ... **Norfolk, VA**
Marks, Jeffrey M. ... Chicago, IL
Marks, Jeffrey M. ... **New York, NY**
Marks, Jeffrey N. ... Miami, FL
Marks, Jeffrey P. ... Penfield, NY
Marks, Jeffrey S. ... Boca Raton, FL
Marks, Jeffrey Scott ... **Costa Mesa, CA**
Marks, Jerome ... San Francisco, CA
Marks, Jerome ... Chicago, IL
Marks, Jerome, A P.C. ... San Francisco, CA
Marks, Jerome E. ... **Philadelphia, PA**
Marks, Jerome W. ... New York, NY
Marks, Jerry L. ... **Los Angeles, CA**
Marks, Jill M. ... Geneva, NY
Marks, Jill S. ... Richmond, VA
Marks, Joey ... Oklahoma City, OK
Marks, John G. ... Hempstead, NY
Marks, John H. ... Lansing, MI
Marks, John H., Jr. ... **Dallas, TX**
Marks, John Lewis, Jr. ... Clarksburg, WV
Marks, John R. ... Franklin, VA
Marks, John R., III ... **Tallahassee, FL**
Marks, Jonathan ... Department of Justice,
Environment and Natural Resources
Division, GV
Marks, Jonathan ... New York, NY
Marks, Jonathan J. ... San Francisco, CA
Marks, Jonathan, P.C. ... New York, NY
Marks, Joseph H. ... Boca Raton, FL
Marks, Joseph L. ... Urbandale, IA
Marks, Josh A. ... **Denver, CO**
Marks, Joshua M. ... **Elyria, OH**
Marks, Julie Ann ... Birmingham, AL
Marks, Karl L. ... Oak Brook, IL
Marks, Kathy S. ... New York, NY
Marks & Katz, LLC ... Silver Spring, MD
Marks, Keith ... Irving, TX
Marks, Keith H. ... Los Angeles, CA
Marks, Keith S. ... Hartford, CT
Marks, Kenneth G., Law Offices of
Laguna Hills, CA
Marks, Kenneth H., Jr. ... Herndon, VA
Marks, Kenneth S. ... **Houston, TX**
Marks, Kevin A. ... **Oakland, CA**
Marks, Kevin Andrew ... **New Orleans, LA**
Marks, Kevin S. ... **Beverly Hills, CA**
Marks, Kristen P. ... Pensacola, FL
Marks & Lansky ... **Memphis, TN**
Marks, Laurence M. ... **Los Angeles, CA**
Marks, Lawrence D. ... **Los Angeles, CA**
Marks, Lawrence J. ... Phoenix, AZ
Marks, Lawrence J. ... **Farmington, CT**
Marks, Leah R. ... New York, NY
Marks, Leana ... South Miami, FL
Marks & Lear, A Prof. Law Corp.
Baton Rouge, LA
Marks, Lee R. ... **Tysons Corner, VA**
Marks, Leon ... **Little Rock, AR**
Marks, Leonard H. ... **Washington, DC**
Marks, Leonard H. ... Tampa, FL
Marks, Leonard M. ... **New York, NY**
Marks, Leslie Steven ... **Los Angeles, CA**
Marks, Lester A. ... Great Neck, NY
Marks, Linda I. ... Department of Justice,
Civil Division, GV
Marks, Linda S. ... Newport Beach, CA
Marks, Lionel A. ... New York, NY
Marks, Lisa E. ... **Washington, DC**
Marks, Lisa R. ... Chicago, IL
Marks, Lloyd S. ... Miami, FL
Marks, Lori ... **New York, NY**
Marks, Louis N. ... Philadelphia, PA
Wynnewood, PA
Marks, Lynn A. ... Philadelphia, PA
Marks, Madsen & Hirschbach
Sioux City, IA
South Sioux City, NE
Dakota Dunes, SD
Marks, Manuel Stanley ... New York, NY
Marks, Marc L.
Federal Mine Safety and Health Review
Commission,
Office of the Commissioners, GV
Marks, Maria G. ... **New Orleans, LA**
Marks, Marjorie A. ... Houston, TX
Marks, Mark, (P.A.) ... Miami, FL
Marks & Marks ... Glen Head, NY
Marks & Marks ... **Clarksville, TN**
Marks, Marks and Kaplan, Ltd.
Chicago, IL
Marks and Marks, L.L.C. ... New York, NY
Marks, Marks & Marks ... Urbandale, IA
Marks, Martin E. ... Great Neck, NY
Marks, Martin T. ... Louisville, KY
Marks, Marvin ... Ironwood, MI
Marks, Mary Jo B. ... Falmouth, MA
Marks, Mary K. (Mulvaney)
New York, NY
Marks, Mary Whitten ... Austin, TX
Marks, Matthew J. ... Washington, DC
Marks, McLaughlin and Dennehy
Danville, PA
Marks, Melanie L. ... **Savannah, GA**
Marks, Merton E., (P.C.) ... **Phoenix, AZ**
Marks, Michael ... **Montpelier, VT**
Marks, Michael A. ... San Francisco, CA
Marks, Michael A. ... Philadelphia, PA
Marks, Michael B. ... New York, NY
Marks, Michael E. ... Minneapolis, MN
Marks, Michael G. ... **New York, NY**
Marks, Michael H. ... Pittsburgh, PA
Marks, Michael J. ... **Honolulu, HI**
Marks, Michael V. P. ... **New York, NY**
Marks, Michelle S. ... Washington, DC
Marks, Milton ... San Francisco, CA
Marks, Morton ... White Plains, NY
Marks, Myron B. ... Houston, TX
Marks, Nancy J. ... Treasury Department,
Internal Revenue Service, GV
Marks, Nanette Halper ... New York, NY
Marks, Neison M. ... Los Angeles, CA
Marks, Norine Bobby ... Auburn, CA
Marks, O'Neill, Reilly, O'Brien & Courtney, P.C. ... **Wilmington, DE**
Westmont, NJ
Norristown, PA
Philadelphia, PA
Pittsburgh, PA
Marks, Pamela D. ... **Baltimore, MD**
Marks, Patricia A. ... **Washington, DC**
Omaha, NE
Marks, Patti Hudson ... Denver, CO
Marks, Patti J. ... **New York, NY**
Marks, Paul D. ... Escondido, CA
Marks, Paul, Jr. ... **Baton Rouge, LA**
Marks, Paul L. ... **Goshen, NY**
Marks, Paul Robert ... Towson, MD
Marks, Paul S. ... **Los Angeles, CA**
Marks, Paul T. ... Tampa, FL
Marks, Peter V., Sr. ... Northfield, NJ
Marks, R. Adrian ... Frankfort, IN
Marks, R. Edward ... Findlay, OH
Marks, Ramon P. ... **New York, NY**
Marks, Randall D.
Federal Trade Commission,
Bureau of Competition, GV
Marks, Randolph A. ... **Atlanta, GA**
Marks, Richard A. ... **Boston, MA**
Marks, Richard D. ... Calabasas, CA
Marks, Richard D. ... **Washington, DC**
Marks, Richard D. ... Garden City, NY
Marks, Richard D., Professional Corporation
Calabasas, CA
Marks, Richard G. ... Burbank, CA
Marks, Richard H. ... **Montgomery, AL**
Marks, Richard J. ... **Baltimore, MD**
Marks, Richard S. ... Chicago, IL
Marks, Richard W. ... Clarksville, GA
Marks, Robert ... **Chicago, IL**
Marks, Robert A. ... **Honolulu, HI**
Marks, Robert A. ... Newark, NJ
Marks, Robert C. ... **Clarksville, TN**
Marks, Robert G. ... **Washington, DC**
Marks, Robert J. ... **San Diego, CA**
Marks, Robert L. ... Danville, PA
Marks, Robert L., Jr. ... Danville, PA
Marks, Robert O. ... **Orlando, FL**
Marks, Robert S. ... Coopers Mills, ME
Marks, Robert W., II ... Tukwila, WA
Marks, Roger ... New York, NY
Marks, Roger H. ... Chicago, IL
Marks, Roger M., Jr. ... New York, NY
Marks, Roger N. ... Uniondale, NY
Marks, Ronald A. ... Los Angeles, CA
Marks, Ronald A. ... Warren, OH
Marks, Ronald G. ... Minneapolis, MN
Marks, Ronald H. ... Merced, CA
Marks, Ronald H. ... Virginia Beach, VA
Marks, Ronald S. ... Woodland Hills, CA
Marks, Royal D. ... Phoenix, AZ
Marks, Russell Roberts ... **Hagerstown, MD**
Marks, S. Fredric ... Arlington Heights, IL
Marks, Samuel M., III ... **Memphis, TN**
Marks, Scott A. ... **Los Angeles, CA**
Marks, Scott C. ... **Salem, MA**
Marks, Scott Charles ... **Bowling Green, KY**
Marks, Sean A. ... **Los Angeles, CA**
Marks, Seth B. ... Cleveland, OH
Marks, Seymour ... New York, NY
Marks, Shari D. ... **Los Angeles, CA**
San Francisco, CA
Marks, Shaun Richard ... Flint, MI
Marks, Shell and Maness
Hopkinsville, KY
Clarksville, TN
Marks, Sherilynne ... Boynton Beach, FL
Marks, Spencer J. ... **Chicago, IL**
Marks, Standish B. ... San Francisco, CA
Marks, Stanley H. ... Denver, CO
Marks, Stanley J. ... **Phoenix, AZ**
Marks & Steele ... Clarksburg, WV
Marks, Stephanie D. ... **Baltimore, MD**
Marks, Stephen D., (A Professional Corporation) ... **Los Angeles, CA**
Marks, Steve K. ... Pompano Beach, FL
Marks, Steve M. ... Baton Rouge, LA
Marks, Steven C. ... **Miami, FL**
Marks, Steven G. ... Portland, OR
Marks, Steven G., P.C. ... Portland, OR
Marks, Steven H. ... Clark, NJ
Marks, Steven M. ... **Washington, DC**
Marks, Steven M. ... Miami, FL
Marks, Steven R. ... Koror, TT
Marks, Steven W. ... Woodland Hills, CA
Marks, Stuart ... **New York, NY**
Marks, Susan Landon ... Mill Valley, CA
Marks, Susan N. ... **Pensacola, FL**
Marks, Sydney A. ... **Miami, FL**
Marks, Ted E. ... Urbandale, IA
Marks, Theodore L. ... **New York, NY**
Marks, Thomas C. ... **Lexington, KY**
Marks, Thomas C., Jr. ... St. Petersburg, FL
Marks, Thomas D. ... **Orlando, FL**
Marks, Timothy F. ... **Kansas City, MO**
Marks, Valerie E. ... Los Angeles, CA
Marks, Victoria Scurlock ... Honolulu, HI
Marks, Walter N. ... Los Angeles, CA
Marks, Wayne T. ... Glen Head, NY
Marks, William H., III ... **Suwanee, GA**
Marks, William P. ... Sturgis, MI
Marks, William R. ... Washington, DC
Marks & Williams, LLC ... **Atlanta, GA**
Suwanee, GA
Marks, Wirt P., IV ... **Richmond, VA**
Marks, Wirt Peebles, III ... Stamford, CT
Marks-Barnett, Sylvia ... Oklahoma City, OK
Marksbury, Kathleen C. ... **Metairie, LA**
Markson, Aldan O. ... **Union, NJ**
Markson, Barry M. ... **Phoenix, AZ**
Markson, Brett S. ... **Los Angeles, CA**
Markson, Edouard S. ... **New York, NY**
Markson, Jane S. ... **Allentown, PA**
Philadelphia, PA
Markson, John W. ... **Madison, WI**
Markson, Kenneth S. ... Beverly Hills, CA
Markson, Michael ... **New York, NY**
Markson, Neil R. ... **Boston, MA**
Markson, Paul A., Jr. ... Denver, CO
Markson, Peggy E. ... Santa Ana, CA
Markson, William H. ... New Bedford, MA
Markson, William H., P.C.
New Bedford, MA
Markstein, D. Harry ... Birmingham, AL
Markstein, Daniel H., III
Birmingham, AL
Markstein, Paul L. ... Hackensack, NJ
Blauvelt, NY
Markstein, William E. ... **New York, NY**
Markstrom, Paul F. ... Rocky River, OH
Marksz, John A. ... Cleveland, OH
Marku, Jay Michael ... Elkins Park, PA
Markum, Alan D. ... Weatherford, OK
Markum, James B., Law Office of
Victorville, CA
Markum, Todd ... **Oklahoma City, OK**
Markun, David J. ... Washington, DC
Markun, David S. ... **Los Angeles, CA**
Markun, Rachel ... Mill Valley, CA
Markunas, John Joseph, Jr. ... Burlington, MA
Markuns, John F. ... Boston, MA
Markus, Allan L. ... Parsippany, NJ
Markus, Andrew Arthur ... Aurora, CO
Markus, Andrew J. ... **Miami, FL**
Markus, Anthony C.
Yorktown Heights, NY
Markus, Carl M. ... **Belleville, IL**
Markus, Charles A. ... Philadelphia, PA
Markus, Christina M. ... **Washington, DC**
Markus & Cohen ... Parsippany, NJ
Markus, Cynthia Ann ... Seattle, WA
Markus, David ... Atlanta, GA
Markus, David O. ... Miami, FL
Markus, Egidijus ... Cleveland, OH
Markus, Eric R. ... **Washington, DC**
Markus, Gloria E. ... Washington, DC

Markus, Ilan ... Miami, FL
Markus, Ira ... Northbrook, IL
Markus, James A. ... Dallas, TX
Markus, James T. ... Denver, CO
Markus, John F. ... Washington, DC
Markus, Joseph A. ... Yorba Linda, CA
Markus, Joshua R. ... Chicago, IL
Markus, Marilyn R. ... Miami, FL
Markus, Mark J., Law Office of
Studio City, CA
Markus, Mona E. ... Miami, FL
Markus, Richard M. ... Fairview Park, OH
Markus, Richard W. ... San Juan, PR
Markus, Robert D. ... Cleveland, OH
Markus, Scott Slater ... San Diego, CA
Markus & Smith ... Pittsburgh, PA
Markus, Stephen A. ... Cleveland, OH
Markus, Stephen P. ... Garden City, NY
Markus, Stuart A. ... Miami, FL
Markus, Taisa ... New York, NY
Markus, Terry A. ... Chicago, IL
Markus & Winter, P.A. ... Miami, FL
Markusen, Martha M. ... Duluth, MN
Markusic, Ann T. ... Fairmont, WV
Markusic, George A. ... Morgantown, WV
Markuski, V. Peter, Jr. ... Laurel, MD
Markuson, Gloria Crowley
New Rochelle, NY
Markuson, Gloria Crowley ... Scarsdale, NY
Markuson, Gloria Crowley
White Plains, NY
Markuson, Grant R. ... Oakbrook Terrace, IL
Dallas, TX
Markuson & Kalb, Chartered
Oakbrook Terrace, IL
Dallas, TX
Markussen, Christine N. ... New York, NY
Markusson, Dennis H. ... Denver, CO
Markusson, Green & Jarvis, P.C.
Denver, CO
Markva, Neil F. ... Springfield, VA
Markve, John A. ... Eden Prairie, MN
Markwalder, Dale W. ... Watseka, IL
Markwalter, R. Robider ... Macon, GA
Markwardt, John J. ... Voorhees, NJ
Markwardt, Paul W. ... Minneapolis, MN
St. Paul, MN
Markwardt & Sander, P.A. ... Voorhees, NJ
Markwardt, William J. ... Atlantic City, NJ
Markwell, James F. ... Houston, TX
Markwell, William I. ... Henderson, KY
Markwell, William I., P.S.C. ... Henderson, KY
Markwith, James W. ... Irvine, CA
San Jose, CA
Markwith, Maureen G. ... Miami, FL
Markwood, James M. ... Toledo, OH
Markwood and Markwood, Co. L.P.A.
Toledo, OH
Markwood, Theodore ... Toledo, OH
Markworth, Dale E. ... Cleveland, OH
Markworth, Lawrence ... Dover, OH
Markworth, Thomas ... Columbus, OH
Marky, Douglas W. ... East Aurora, NY
Marky, Raymond L. ... Tallahassee, FL
Marlaine, Erica ... Los Angeles, CA
Marlaire, Michael L. ...
National Aeronautics And Space
Administration, GV
Marlais, John P. ... Phoenix, AZ
Marland, Melissa Kaye ... Charleston, WV
Marlar, Dale R. ... Claremore, OK
Marlar, Donald F. ... Tulsa, OK
Marlar, James M. ... Tucson, AZ
Marlar, Kimberly ... New York, NY
Marlar, Melinda S. ... Tucson, AZ
Marlatt, Jerry R. ... New York, NY
Marlatt, Michael J. ... Riverside, CA
Marlatt, William C., Jr. ... Lake Forest, IL
Marlatt, William I. ... Gary, IN
Marlborough, Jennifer L. ... New York, NY
Marlen, Matthew J. ... Belleville, IL
Marlenga, Edward M. ... Arlington, MA
Marlenga, Susan D. G. ... Arlington, MA
Marler, Dirk A. ... Yakima, WA
Marler, Fred W., Jr. ... Sacramento, CA
Marler, Jennifer A. ... St. Louis, MO
Marler, K. A. ... Milford, OH
Marler, Laura T. ... Opelousas, LA
Marler, Renee M. ... San Francisco, CA
Marles, Blake C. ... Lehigh Valley, PA
Marlett, Charles D. ... Dallas, TX
Marlett, David R. ... Rockwall, TX
Marlett, Mary ... Fishkill, NY
Marlett, Orville L. ... Irvine, CA
Marlette, Cynthia A.
Federal Energy Regulatory Commission,
Office of the General Counsel, GV
Marlette, Edward N., Jr. ... Buffalo, NY
Marlette, Gary L. ... Baker City, OR
Marlette, George L. ... Brockton, MA
Marlette, George Lane, Law Offices of
Brockton, MA
Marlette, John G. ... Valencia, CA
Marlette, Patrick ... Sacramento, CA
Marlette, Peter S. ... Buffalo, NY
Marlette, Todd E. ... Washington, DC
Marley, A. Ray, Jr. ... Greensboro, NC
Marley, Barbara L. ... Fostoria, OH
Marley, Brett D. ... Fort Lauderdale, FL
Marley, Christopher ... Northport, NY
Marley, Clifton F. ... Robbins, NC
Marley, Francis M., Jr. ... Fostoria, OH
Marley, Howard S. ... Chesterfield, VA
Marley, John A. ... Middletown, NJ
Marley, Margaret M. ... Jersey City, NJ
Marley & Marley ... Fostoria, OH
Marley, Patricia J. ... Pittsburgh, PA
Marley, Patrick J. ... Los Angeles, CA
Marley, Robert P. ... Liberty Corner, NJ
Marley, Susan O'Hagan ... Colts Neck, NJ
Marlia, Kim B. ... San Francisco, CA
Marlin, Beth L. ... Camden, NJ
Westmont, NJ
Marlin, Gary R. ... Miami, FL
Marlin, James J., Jr. ... Columbus, OH
Marlin, James M. ... Milwaukee, WI
Marlin, James P. ... New York, NY
Marlin, Jeffrey S. ... Boston, MA
Marlin, L. Christian ... Orlando, FL
Marlin, Leslie ... Louisville, KY
Marlin, Louis M. ... Santa Ana, CA
Woodland Hills, CA
Marlin, Michael C. ... New York, NY
Marlin, Michael S. ... Columbus, OH
Marlin, Michelle ... Doylestown, PA
Marlin, Morris S. ... Miami, FL
Marlin, Richard ... New York, NY
Marlin & Saltzman, A Professional Law Corporation ... Santa Ana, CA
Woodland Hills, CA
Marlin, Scott W. ... Park City, UT
Marlin, William C. ... Denver, CO
Marling, L. Bradley ... Hurst, TX
Marling, Marc G. ... Savannah, GA
Marlinga, Carl J. ... Mount Clemens, MI
Marlis, Rand A. ... Los Angeles, CA
Marlo, John A., III ... Costa Mesa, CA
Marlor, Henry S., Jr. ... Naugatuck, CT
Marlott, John A. ... Chicago, IL
Marlow & Alrutz, P.L.L.C. ... Memphis, TN
Marlow, Connell, Valerius, Abrams, Adler & Newman ... Miami, FL
Marlow, Dan ... Lexington, SC
Marlow, David A. ... South St. Paul, MN
Marlow, David Z. ... New York, NY
Marlow, George D. ... Poughkeepsie, NY
Marlow, George H. ... Manchester, CT
Marlow, Homer L. ... Miami, FL
Marlow, Hubert A. ... Tulsa, OK
Marlow, Hubert H., Jr. ... Front Royal, VA
Marlow, Jack F. ... Memphis, TN
Marlow, James H. ... Denver, CO
Marlow, John H. ... Oakland, CA
Marlow, Kimberly A. ... San Jose, CA
Marlow, Kristal A. ... Department of Justice,
Civil Division, GV
Marlow, Lee ... New Haven, CT
Marlow, Lenard ... Garden City, NY
Marlow, Michael F. ... Yankton, SD
Marlow, Orval Lee, II (IBA) ... Houston, TX
Marlow, Roger D. ... Covington, LA
New Orleans, LA
Marlow, S. Christopher ... Washington, DC
Marlow, Sidney G., Jr. ... Independence, MO
Marlow, Susan J. ... Los Angeles, CA
Marlow, Tony ... Paso Robles, CA
Marlow, Tracy A. ... Darien, CT
Marlow, William F. C., Jr.
Washington, DC
Towson, MD
Marlow, William J. ... New York, NY
Marlow, William Kenneth ... Nashville, TN
Marlow, William R. ... Houston, TX
Marlow & Wyatt ... Washington, DC
Towson, MD
Marlowe, Appleton & Weatherford, P.A.
Orlando, FL
Winter Park, FL
Marlowe, Cecil ... Cleveland, OH
Marlowe, Charles F. ... Hammond, IN
Marlowe, Charmaine ... New York, NY
Marlowe, Daniel R. ... Santa Fe, NM
Marlowe, Darren ... Santa Monica, CA
Marlowe, David F. ... Encino, CA
Marlowe, Deborah A. ... Atlanta, GA
Marlowe, Dennis H. ... Madison, CT
Marlowe, Diane Joan ... Santa Ana, CA
Marlowe & Dickson, L.L.C. ... Athens, GA
Marlowe, Elizabeth G. ... Athens, GA
Marlowe, G. Carlton ... Boca Raton, FL
Fort Lauderdale, FL
Marlowe, G. Carlton, P.A.
Boca Raton, FL
Fort Lauderdale, FL
Marlowe, James J., II ... Downingtown, PA
Marlowe, Keith S. ... Philadelphia, PA
Marlowe, L. Dennis ... Cottonwood, AZ
Marlowe Law Firm, The, A Professional Corporation ... Santa Fe, NM
Marlowe, Leslie Carson
Fort Lauderdale, FL
Marlowe, Mary Ann C.
East Brunswick, NJ
New York, NY
Marlowe, Mary L. ... Santa Fe, NM
Marlowe & McNabb, P.A. ... Tampa, FL
Marlowe, Michael L. ... Winter Park, FL
Marlowe, Patricia J. ... Salt Lake City, UT
Marlowe, Ronald J. ... Miami, FL
Marlowe, Russell G. ... Miami, FL
New Port Richey, FL
Marlowe, Stephen D. ... Tampa, FL
Marlowe, Stephen M. ... Redding, CA
Marlowe, Steven W. ... Vancouver, WA
Marlowe, Terry J. ... Albany, GA
Marlowe, Wallace T. ... Roanoke, VA
Marmaduke, Anita Seipp
Sacramento, CA
Marmaduke, Don H., (P.C.) ... Portland, OR
Marmaduke, Stephen K. ... Sacramento, CA
Marmaduke, Susan D. ... Portland, OR
Marmalefsky, Dan ... Los Angeles, CA
Marman, Joseph H. ... Citrus Heights, CA
Marmann, Diane Pacifico ... Mineola, NY
Marmaras, Vivian ... Elmwood Park, NJ
Marmarellis, John ... Kew Gardens, NY
Marmaro, Marc, (P.C.) ... Los Angeles, CA
Marmaro, Richard ... Los Angeles, CA
Marmaros, Peter W. ... Cleveland, OH
Marmarou, Steven J. ... Somerdale, NJ
Marmelstein, Charles M. ... Washington, DC
Marmelstein, David D. ... West Suffield, CT
Marmelstein, Joel L. ... Utica, NY
Marmer, Irving ... Boston, MA
Marmer, Mark ... New York, NY
Marmer, Melvin E. ... Cincinnati, OH
Marmer, Michael K. ... Wilmington, CA
Marmer, Ronald L. ... Chicago, IL
Marmer, Sandra S. ... Oak Park, IL
Marmero, Franc J. H., P.C. ... Berlin, NJ
Marmero, Franc J. H. ... Berlin, NJ
Marmet & Armstrong ... Centerville, SD
Marmet, G. John ... Glenview, IL
Marmet, Robert A. ... Frederick, MD
Marmet, Robert Glen ... Centerville, SD
Marmins, David J. ... Atlanta, GA
Marmion, Angela S. ... Tuscumbia, MO
Marmish, Paul M. ... Miami, FL
Marmish, Paul M., P.A. ... Miami, FL
Marmo, Carol A. ... Pittsburgh, PA
Marmo, Dawn ... Newark, NJ
Marmo, Frederick J. ... Fitchburg, MA
Marmo, Jason P. ... Totowa, NJ
Marmo, Michael F. ... Pittsburgh, PA
Marmo, Ronald G. ... Paterson, NJ
Marmo, Ronald P. ... Minneapolis, MN
Marmo, Theresa A. ... New York, NY
Marmol, Nancy Behr ... San Francisco, CA
Marmolejos, Policarpio
Department of Justice,
Civil Rights Division, GV
Marmoll, Helen E. ... Haymarket, VA
Marmon, David B. ... Warren, MI
Marmon, David G. ... San Diego, CA
Marmon, James L. ... Elmsford, NY
Marmon, Victor I. ... Los Angeles, CA
Marmon, William F., Jr. ... Washington, DC
Marmor, Barbara E. ... Riverside, CA
Marmor, Colleen ... Woodland Hills, CA
Marmor, Michael P. ... Fayetteville, NY
Marmor, Randall I. ... Chicago, IL
Marmor, Richard D. ... Phoenix, AZ
Marmor, Robert E. ... Healdsburg, CA
Marmor, Sarah R. ... Chicago, IL
Marmor, Seth A. ... Fort Lauderdale, FL
Marmora, John M. ... Newark, NJ
Marmorstein, David M. ... Sherman Oaks, CA
Marmorstein, Gerald ... Philadelphia, PA
Marmorstein, Robert Joel
Hackensack, NJ
Marmorstein, Victoria E.
Los Angeles, CA
Marmorstone, Edwin ... Washington, DC
Marmur, Nathaniel Z. ... New York, NY
Marmur, Sari B. ... Atlanta, GA
Marn & Associates ... Brick, NJ
Marn, Eric Y. ... Honolulu, HI
Marn, Louis E. ... Brick, NJ
Marn, Sally A. ... Gary, IN
Marn, Stephanie L. ... Washington, DC
Honolulu, HI
Marnecheck, Phillip A. ... Cleveland, OH
Marnell, Francis X. ... Los Angeles, CA
Marnell, Francis X. ... Cincinnati, OH
Marnell, Helene Miller ... Claremont, CA
Marnell, Mark F. ... Irvine, CA
Marnell, Mary A. ... Naples, FL
Marnell, Matthew J. ... Riverside, CA
Marnell, Russell I. ... East Meadow, NY
Hauppauge, NY
Marnell, Russell I., P.C., Law Offices of
East Meadow, NY
Hauppauge, NY
Marnell, Susan P. ... East Meadow, NY
Marnen, James T. ... Erie, PA
Marner, David L., Jr. ... Cedar Rapids, IA
Marner, David L., Sr. ... Cedar Rapids, IA
Marner, James E. ... Tucson, AZ
Marnett, Marilen ... Miami, FL
Marney, Elizabeth B. ... Nashville, TN
Marney, Ronald D., II ... Kansas City, MO
Marney, Sam R., III ... Memphis, TN
Marnik, Michael P. ... Peabody, MA
Marnik & Sullivan ... Peabody, MA
Marnin, Gil ... New York, NY
Marnin, Tal B. ... New York, NY
Marnocha & Associates ... Mishawaka, IN
Marnocha, Benedict (Ben) F.
Mishawaka, IN
Marnocha, John M. ... South Bend, IN
Marnock, Marvin J. ... Houston, TX
Maro, Jack R., (P.A.) ... Coral Gables, FL
Maro, Joseph R. ... Central Islip, NY
Maroc, Phillip E. ... San Jose, CA
Maroc, Richard W. ... Crown Point, IN
Maroccia, John Phillip ... Cherry Hill, NJ
Maroccia, John Philip, A Professional Corporation ... Cherry Hill, NJ
Marocco, William ... Columbus, OH
Marod, Edward A. ... West Palm Beach, FL
Marod, Edward A., P.A.
West Palm Beach, FL
Marofsky, Lawrence P. ... Minneapolis, MN
Marohnic, Louis Z. ... Pittsburgh, PA
Marois, Kim ... San Francisco, CA
Santa Rosa, CA
Marois, Kim, A Prof. Corp., Law Offices of
San Francisco, CA
Santa Rosa, CA
Marois, Theodore M., Jr.
Sacramento, CA
Maroko, Eli ... Farmington Hills, MI
Maroko and Landau, P.C.
Farmington Hills, MI
Maroko, Michael ... Los Angeles, CA
Marola, Lydia Rocissano ... Albany, NY
Marola, Thomas J. ... Milwaukee, WI
Maroldy, Donald J. ... New York, NY
Maroldy, Margaret Millus
New Rochelle, NY
Marolf, Douglas W. ... Lincoln, NE
Marolf & Pearson ... Lincoln, NE
Marolf, Robert J. ... Manly, IA
Marolt, Judy M. ... El Cajon, CA
Marom, Steven T. ... New York, NY
Maron, Andrew W. ... Seattle, WA
Maron, August G., Jr. ... New York, NY
Maron, David F. ... Jackson, MS
Maron, Edward A. ... Hewlett, NY
Maron, Elizabeth Daniello ... Wilmington, DE
Maron, Hyman ... Pembroke Pines, FL
Maron, James J. ... Wilmington, DE
Maron, Lawrence M. ... New Brunswick, NJ
Maron, Leslie B. ... Scarsdale, NY
Maron, Marvel & Wilks, P.A.
Wilmington, DE
Maron, Milford A. ... Los Angeles, CA
Maron, Sheila K. ... Brooklyn, NY
Marone, Christopher D.
St. Petersburg, FL
Marone, Denise ... Glassboro, NJ
Marone, Douglas K. ... Oshkosh, WI
Marone, Joseph J. ... Teaneck, NJ
Marone, Karen L. ... Elroy, WI
Marone & Messina, P.C. ... Farmington, CT
Hartford, CT
Marone, Michael J. ... Morristown, NJ
Marone, Paul A. ... Towson, MD
Marone, Richard A. ... Farmington, CT
Maroney, Arthur E., III
Port St. Lucie, FL
Maroney, Barbara B. ... Sun City, AZ
Maroney, Donald J. ... Providence, RI
Maroney, H. Wallace, Jr. ... Memphis, TN
Maroney, Harry B., II ... Madison, WI
Maroney, Jack D. ... Austin, TX
Maroney, James F., III ... Houston, TX
Maroney, Michael Jeffrey ... Topanga, CA
Maroney, Patrick F. ... Tallahassee, FL
Maroney, Steven W. ... Jackson, TN
Maroney, Thomas A. ... Waupaca, WI
Maroney, Thomas J. ... Syracuse, NY
Maroney, Thomas P. ... Charleston, WV
Maroney, Thomas P. ... Wauwatosa, WI
Maroney, Thomas P., L.C. ... Charleston, WV
Maroney, Vincent J. ... New York, NY
Maroney, William D. ... Detroit, MI
Maroney-Donovan, Helen M.
Alexandria, VA
Maronich, Michael G. ... Bridgeport, CT
Maronski, William E., Jr.
Philadelphia, PA
Maroon, Samuel Allen ... Jacksonville, FL
Maroon, Sarah G. ... Jacksonville, FL
Marooney, Richard T., Jr. ... New York, NY
Maroot, Hardcastle & Hatherley
Hanford, CA
Visalia, CA
Maroot, K. Phillip ... Hanford, CA
Visalia, CA
Marootian, George A. ... Kenilworth, NJ
Marootian, Greggory M. ... Livingston, NJ
Marosan, Joseph E. ... Cleveland, OH
Marose, Evelyn J. ... West Orange, NJ
Marose, Paul J. ... Juneau, WI
Marosz, Jeffrey M. ... Dallas, TX
Marothy, Christopher A. ... New York, NY
Marotta, Alfred E. ... Norwalk, CA
Marotta, Anthony J. ... Fitchburg, MA
Marotta, Daniel C. ... New York, NY
Marotta, James S. ... Totowa, NJ
Marotta, Joseph N., Jr. ... Fort Lee, NJ
Marotta, Kimberly J. ... Revere, MA
Marotta, Lisa J. ... Waterbury, CT
Marotta, Marc J. ... Milwaukee, WI
Marotta, Mark D. ... Norristown, PA
Marotta, Mark P. ... Hackensack, NJ
Marotta, Nicholas A. ... Kew Gardens, NY
Marotta, Nicholas J. ... New York, NY
Marotta, Paul David ... Burlingame, CA
Marotta & Ramos ... Norwalk, CA
Marotta, Robert ... Detroit, MI
Marotta, Robert D. ... Columbus, OH
Marotta, Robert D. ... Virginia Beach, VA
Marotta, Susan M. ... New York, NY
Marotta, Thomas P. ... Cleveland, OH
Marotta, William A. ... Rockport, MA
Marotte, David S. ... Marietta, GA
Marotte, Michael ... West Orange, NJ
Marotti, Kris R. Macaruso ... Warwick, RI
Marotti, Regina M. ... New York, NY
Marotto, Melanie C. ... Buffalo, NY
Marotz, Robert G. ... Brookfield, WI
Marotz, Scott W. ... Idaho Falls, ID
Marouk, Edward V. ... Fresno, CA
Maroules, J. Christy ... Beaufort, NC
Maroules, Jerry ... Fairfield, NJ
Maroulis, James C. ... New York, NY
Maroulis, Victoria F. ... Palo Alto, CA
New York, NY
Maroun, Laurie Diann ... New York, NY
Maroun, Michel A. ... Bossier City, LA
Marous, James M. ... Columbus, OH
Marous, Kathryn Anne ... Boston, MA
Marousek, E. Jacqueline ... Belle Fourche, SD
Marousek, Kathy A. ... Fresno, CA
Marousek, Linda A. ... Seattle, WA
Marovich, George M. ... Chicago, IL
Marovich, Kelly A. ... St. Louis, MO
Marovich, Marsha E. ... San Francisco, CA
Marovich, Michael J. ... Orland Park, IL
Marovich, Milton J. ... Kalamazoo, MI

Marovich, Thomas M. ... Sonora, CA
Marovitch, Joseph A. ... Evergreen Park, IL
Marovitz, Abraham Lincoln ... Chicago, IL
Marovitz, Andrew S. ... Chicago, IL
Marovitz, James L. ... Chicago, IL
Marovitz, William A. ... Chicago, IL
Marowits, Jeffrey M. ... Los Angeles, CA
Marowitz, Albert W. ... Warren, OH
Marpe, William J., Jr. ... Houston, TX
Marpet, Jane R. ... Los Angeles, CA
Marpet, Stephen C. ... Santa Monica, CA
Marphatia, Raj ... Boston, MA
Marple, Anna E. ... Dallas, TX
Marple, Annette W. ... Lubbock, TX
Marple, Barbara J. ... Indianapolis, IN
Marple, David A. ... New York, NY
Marple, Harriet B. ... Detroit, MI
Marple, John D. ... Palo Alto, CA
Marple, John L. ... Holland, MI
Marple, Pamela J. ... Washington, DC
Marple, William E. ... Dallas, TX
Marqolies, Jacob ... New York, NY
Marquand, Brent R. ... Knoxville, TN
Marquard, David L. ... Duluth, MN
Marquard, Henry F. ... Muscatine, IA
Marquard, Henry J. ... Chicago, IL
Marquard, Robert Joseph ... Cleveland, OH
Marquard, Suzanne T. ... Newark, NJ
Marquardson, P. Warren ... Seattle, WA
Marquardt, Amy L. ... Milwaukee, WI
Marquardt, Barbara C. ... Austin, TX
Marquardt, Carl J. ... Seattle, WA
Marquardt, Carl R. ... Prairie Du Sac, WI
Marquardt, Carlson, Koeck, Kirk & Bruni, Ltd.
Mazomanie, WI
Prairie Du Sac, WI
Marquardt, Charles D. ... Upper Marlboro, MD
Marquardt, Cheryl A. ... Leavenworth, KS
Marquardt, Christel E. ... Topeka, KS
Marquardt, Christopher C. ... Atlanta, GA
Marquardt, Dennis M. ... Havelock, NC
Morehead City, NC
Marquardt, Donald E. ... Wilton, CT
Marquardt, E. Clifford ... Wheaton, IL
Marquardt, Emil C., Jr. ... Clearwater, FL
Marquardt, Gilbert H., Jr. ... Chicago, IL
Marquardt, H. Max ... Kalamazoo, MI
Marquardt, Hasenyager & Custen
Ogden, UT
Marquardt, Ilene B. ... Weehawken, NJ
Marquardt, James E. ... Phoenix, AZ
Marquardt, James M. ... Kalamazoo, MI
Marquardt, Jane A. ... Ogden, UT
Marquardt, Joan E. ... San Francisco, CA
Marquardt, Joan M. ... Los Angeles, CA
Marquardt, John Matthew
Clearwater, FL
Marquardt, Karl L. ... Florham Park, NJ
New York, NY
Marquardt, Karl W. ... Madison, WI
Marquardt, Lynda S. ... Aurora, IL
Marquardt, Matthew J. ... Seattle, WA
Marquardt, McGlynn & Teppert ... Chicago, IL
Marquardt, Merritt R. ... St. Paul, MN
Marquardt, Michele C. ... Kalamazoo, MI
Marquardt, Peter A. ... Detroit, MI
Marquardt, Robert R. ... Dallas, TX
Marquardt, Robt. F. ... Glen Ellyn, IL
Marquardt, Stephanie T. ... Clearwater, FL
Marquardt, William J. ... Syracuse, NY
Marquart, Ernest J. ... Tampa, FL
Marquart, Jaime W. ... Los Angeles, CA
Marquart, James T. ... Oshkosh, WI
Marquart, Jeffrey R. ... Santa Ana, CA
Marquart, Keith B. ... St. Joseph, MO
Marquart, Kurt D. ... Kansas City, MO
Marquart, Marti L.S. ... Milwaukee, WI
Marquart, Steven L. ... Moorhead, MN
Marquart, Waldo F. ... Minneapolis, MN
Marque, John A. ... New Orleans, LA
Marquer, Constant G., III
New Orleans, LA
Marquer, Constant G., Jr. ... New Orleans, LA
Marques, Christopher ... Fall River, MA
Marques, Javier E.
Advisory Council on Historic Preservation, GV
Marqués, Juan A. ... San Juan, PR
Marques, Leticia J. ... Orlando, FL
Marques, Rosa ... West Orange, NJ
Marquess, John J. ... Turnersville, NJ
Philadelphia, PA
Marquess, Lawrence W. ... Denver, CO
Marquess Morrison & Trimble, P.C.
Turnersville, NJ
Philadelphia, PA
Marquet, Edward J. ... Lafayette, LA
Marquet, Thomas M. ... Hoboken, NJ
Marquett, Gary L. ... Des Moines, IA
Marquette, David E. ... Baton Rouge, LA
Marquette, I. Edward ... Kansas City, MO
Marquette, Quinten B.
Bowling Green, KY
Marquette, Rebecca K. ... Houston, TX
Marquette, Richard Charles ... Orange, CT
Marquette, Robert C. ... Van Buren, AR
Marquette, Ronald M. ... Rocky Mount, NC
Houston, TX
Marquez, Alfred C. ... Chula Vista, CA
Marquez, Anthony P. ... Sacramento, CA
Marquez, Arturo A. ... Marysville, CA
Marquez & Associates, P.C. ... Pasadena, CA
Marquez, Awilda R.
Department of Commerce, GV
Marquez, Charlotte S. ... New Orleans, LA
Marquez, David W. ... Anchorage, AK
Marquez, Edward S. ... El Paso, TX
Marquez, Elena M. ... Miami, FL

Márquez, Ernest F. ... Salida, CO
Marquez, Ernest R. ... Manchester, CT
Márquez, Francisco X. ... San Francisco, CA
Marquez, George P., Jr ... Los Lunas, NM
Marquez, Jim J. ... Washington, DC
McLean, VA
Marquez, Joaquin A. ... Washington, DC
Marquez, John R. ... White Plains, NY
Marquez, John T., Jr
Department of Transportation, Maritime Administration, GV
Marquez, Jose D. L. ... Denver, CO
Marquez, Juan Carlos A.
Falls Church, VA
Marquez, Karen ... Miami, FL
Marquez, Lydia ... Los Angeles, CA
Marquez, Melissa F. ... Alexandria, VA
Marquez, Michael ... Burlingame, CA
Marquez, Monica ... Los Angeles, CA
Marquez, Monica C.
Cardiff-By-The-Sea, CA
Marquez, Monica M. ... Englewood, CO
Marquez, Myriam ... Annapolis, MD
Marquez, O. G. ... Tucson, AZ
Marquez, Philip A. ... El Segundo, CA
Marquez, R. David ... Bronx, NY
Marquez, Raymond J. ... Trenton, NJ
Márquez, Rebecca A. ... Houston, TX
Marquez, Richard A. ... Albuquerque, NM
Marquez, Richard L. ... Garden City, KS
Marquez, Richard T. ... Los Angeles, CA
Marquez, Robert B. ... Pasadena, CA
Marquez, Roberto ... Marysville, CA
Marquez, Sergio ... Bronx, NY
Marquez, Victor M. ... San Francisco, CA
Márquez-Sánchez, Roberto ... San Juan, PR
Marquez-Sterling, Alfredo ... Miami, FL
Marquis, A. Danielle ... Gastonia, NC
Marquis, Albert G. ... Las Vegas, NV
Marquis & Aurbach, A Professional Corporation ... Las Vegas, NV
Marquis, Catherine Bjork ... Park Ridge, IL
Marquis, Charles K. ... New York, NY
Marquis, David W. ... Dayton, OH
Marquis, G. Trent ... Rock Island, IL
Marquis, George C. ... Rock Island, IL
Marquis, Harold L. ... Atlanta, GA
Marquis, Harry Paul ... Las Vegas, NV
Marquis, Harry Paul, Chartered
Las Vegas, NV
Marquis, John E. ... Philadelphia, PA
Marquis, John R. ... Holland, MI
Marquis, Joshua K. ... Astoria, OR
Marquis, Julie A. ... San Francisco, CA
Marquis, Kathy A. ... Laramie, WY
Marquis, Keith E. ... Hartford, CT
Marquis, Laurie L. ... Sacramento, CA
Marquis, Lisa ... Plano, TX
Marquis, Lisa R. ... Monterey, CA
Marquis, Matthew E. ... Palo Alto, CA
Marquis, Milton A. ... Department of Justice, Antitrust Division, GV
Marquis, Oscar ... Chicago, IL
Marquis, Randall L. ... Yakima, WA
Marquis, Renée ... Fort Pierce, FL
Marquis, Robert E. ... Pennington, NJ
Marquis, Robert H. ... Knoxville, TN
Marquis, Robert S. ... Knoxville, TN
Marquis, Scott A. ... Las Vegas, NV
Marquis, Stephen B. ... Farmington Hills, MI
Marquis, William ... Milwaukee, WI
Marquis, William A. ... Newport Beach, CA
Tustin, CA
Marquis, William E. ... Pittsburgh, PA
Marquit, Michele E. ... Houston, TX
Marquith, Susan ... New City, NY
Marquitz, Kevin J. ... St. Louis, MO
Marquiz, Craig A. ... Phoenix, AZ
Marquoit, James T. ... Portland, OR
Marr, Barry W. ... Honolulu, HI
Marr, Bruce B. ... Chicago, IL
Marr, Charles K. ... Sunnyvale, CA
Marr, Charles M. ... Morenci, MI
Marr, David E. ... Natick, MA
Marr, David J. ... Chicago, IL
Marr, Elizabeth A. ... Kansas City, MO
Marr, Frederick Irvin ... Los Angeles, CA
Marr, Freeman Anthony ... Nashville, TN
Marr, Freeman C. ... Bartlett, TN
Marr & Friedlander ... Mobile, AL
Marr, Gloria Rice ... Dallas, TX
Marr Hipp Jones & Pepper ... Honolulu, HI
Marr, J. Daniel ... Nashua, NH
Marr, Jack W. ... Victoria, TX
Marr, James Anderson ... Oklahoma City, OK
Marr, Jeff D. ... Oklahoma City, OK
Marr, Judith A. ... Campbell, CA
Marr, Kathleen A. ... Dayton, OH
Marr, Kathleen R. ... Albuquerque, NM
Marr Law Offices ... Natick, MA
Marr & Malone ... Bartlett, TN
Marr, Margaret H. ... Santa Cruz, CA
Marr, Meier & Hartman ... Victoria, TX
Marr, Melissa M. ... Lancaster, NY
Marr, Michael S. ... Charlotte, NC
Marr, Michael T. ... Charlotte, NC
Marr, Nancy J. ... Portland, ME
Marr, Paul Reece ... Atlanta, GA
Marr, Paul Reece, P.C. ... Atlanta, GA
Marr, Susan K. ... Chicago, IL
Marr, Thomas L. ... Atlanta, GA
Marr, Thomas M. ... Mobile, AL
Marr, William A., Jr. ... Fairfax, VA
Marra, A. Scott ... Boston, MA
Marra, Alessandro F. ... Brooklyn, NY
Marra, Alfred A. ... Manhasset, NY
Marra, Allen C. ... Montclair, NJ
Marra, Anthony F. ... Washington, DC

Marra, Anthony F. ... New York, NY
Marra, Anthony J. ... Glen Cove, NY
Marra, Anthony J., Jr. ... Edison, NJ
Marra, Antonia Prudich ... Great Falls, MT
Marra, Catherine E. ... Buffalo, NY
Marra, Daniel R. ... Jeffersonville, IN
Marra, Gerstein & Richman ... Edison, NJ
Marra, John ... Boston, MA
Marra, Joseph A. ... Bronx, NY
Somers, NY
Yonkers, NY
Marra, Joseph G. ... Seattle, WA
Marra, Joseph R. ... Great Falls, MT
Marra, Kathryn A. ... Detroit, MI
Marra, Kenneth A. ... West Palm Beach, FL
Marra, Michael A. ... Lexington, KY
Marra, Michael R. ... New York, NY
Marra, Peter A. ... Morristown, NJ
Marra, Ralph J., Jr. ... Newark, NJ
Marra, Ralph Peter ... Staten Island, NY
Marra, Susan M. ... Hackensack, NJ
Marra, Teresa A. ... Sarasota, FL
Marra, Thomas A. ... Great Falls, MT
Marra, Virginia M. ... Fairfax, VA
Marra, Wenz & Johnson, P.C.
Great Falls, MT
Marraccini, Bruno D. ... Sacramento, CA
Marraccini, Philip A. ... Harrison, NY
Marraccini, Rodney A. ... Walnut Creek, CA
Marraccini, Silvio P. ... Staten Island, NY
Marrack, Alexander C. ... Honolulu, HI
Marrack, Peter J. ... Honolulu, HI
Marrah, Michael T. ... St. Louis, MO
Marrah, Scott L. ... Atlanta, GA
Marrama, Anthony R. ... Leominster, MA
Marran, Joseph E., III ... Pawtucket, RI
Marran, Joseph E., Jr. ... Pawtucket, RI
Marran, Laura F. ... San Diego, CA
Marran, Lori A. ... Grand Blanc, MI
Marran, Michael K. ... Providence, RI
Marrapese, Arthur A., III ... Rochester, NY
Marrapese, Martha E. ... Washington, DC
Marraro, Christopher H.
Washington, DC
Marrazzo, Dante ... North Olmsted, OH
Marrazzo, Gregg ... Neenah, WI
Marrazzo, Joseph A., Jr. ... Pennsauken, NJ
Marrazzo, Kevin ... Melville, NY
Marrazzo, Orlando, Jr. ... Staten Island, NY
Marre, Daniel G.M. ... Chicago, IL
Marre, Jennifer ... New York, NY
Marré, Lisa L. ... Chicago, IL
Marrella, Amey W.
Environmental Protection Agency, Office of the General Counsel, GV
Marrella, John A. ... Department of Justice, Tax Division, GV
Marren, Bernard D., Jr. ... Rye, NY
Marren, Daniel F. ... Chicago, IL
Marren, Daniel J. ... Buffalo, NY
Marren, Elizabeth T. ... Greenwich, CT
Marren, Janet L. ... Chicago, IL
Marren, Joan Murtagh ... Harrison, NY
Marren, Joanne T. ... New York, NY
Marren, John P. ... Chicago, IL
Marren, Thomas J. ... Stockton, CA
Marrer, Steven A. ... Cleveland, OH
Marrero, Amanda ... Hawthorne, NY
Marrero, Angel Rafael ... San Juan, PR
Marrero, Ernesto, Jr.
Commodity Futures Trading Commission, Division of Enforcement, GV
Marrero & Gibbs, P.A. ... Orlando, FL
Marrero, Guillermo ... San Diego, CA
Marrero, Ivan G. ... San Juan, PR
Marrero, Janine M. ... San Juan, PR
Marrero, Jerry Lucas ... San Juan, PR
Marrero, Julio C. ... Coral Gables, FL
Marrero, Kathleen D. ... Los Angeles, CA
Marrero, Louis J. ... Brooklyn, NY
Marrero, Mary Searcy ... Austin, TX
Marrero, Michael A. ... Cincinnati, OH
Marrero, Oscar E. ... Miami, FL
Marrero, Robert L. ... Gretna, LA
Marrero, Teodoro, Jr. ... Orlando, FL
Marrero, Teresa ... Staten Island, NY
Marrero, Victor ... New York, NY
Marrero, Yery ... Miami, FL
Marrero, Yery, P.A. ... Miami, FL
Marrero Melecio, Waleska ... San Juan, PR
Marrero-Priegues, Inés ... Miami, FL
Marrero Ruiz, Julio ... San Juan, PR
Marrese, Michael D. ... Chicago, IL
Marrese, Thomas J. ... Colorado Springs, CO
Marria, Suzanne P.
South San Francisco, CA
Marrie, Kirk E. ... Highland, IN
Marrin, James M. ... Albany, NY
Marrin, Michael J. ... Islandia, NY
Marrin, Phebe Thorne ... New York, NY
Marrin, Richard B. ... New York, NY
Marrin, Richard B. ... New York, NY
Marrinan, Kevin ... New York, NY
Marrinan, Margaret M. ... St. Paul, MN
Marrinan, Michael R. ... San Diego, CA
Marrinan, Susan F. ... Kenosha, WI
Marrinan, Timothy D. ... Minneapolis, MN
Marriner, Alan A. ... Wenatchee, WA
Marriner, Jones & Fitch ... Washington, PA
Marriner, Stephen D., Jr. ... Washington, PA
Marriner, Thomas C. ... Annapolis, MD
Baltimore, MD
Marrinson, Thomas A. ... Chicago, IL
Marrion, Catherine A. ... New York, NY
Marrion, Robert W. ... New London, CT
Old Lyme, CT
Marrion, Thomas S. ... Hartford, CT
Marriott, Albert G. ... Export, PA

Marriott, Brian M. ... Lansdale, PA
Marriott, Carmen A. ... Tucson, AZ
Marriott Casagrande Callahan & Blair, A Professional Corporation ... Cherry Hill, NJ
Marriott Casagrande Callahan Blair & Greer, A Professional Corporation
Spring Lake Heights, NJ
Marriott, Catherine A. ... Philadelphia, PA
Marriott, Catherine M. ... Richmond, VA
Marriott, Frank, Jr. ... Daytona Beach, FL
Marriott, Frank S. ... Washington, DC
Marriott, John F., Sr. ... Wallingford, CT
Marriott, Robert S. ... Cincinnati, OH
Marriott, Vincent J., III ... Philadelphia, PA
Marriott, William G.
Spring Lake Heights, NJ
Marriotto, Donald L. ... Los Angeles, CA
Marris, Alice E. ... Denver, CO
Marris & Bartholomae ... Syracuse, NY
Marris, Joseph M. ... Buffalo, NY
Marris, Karin Huntley ... Syracuse, NY
Marris, Margaret A. ... Syracuse, NY
Marris, Richard F. ... Syracuse, NY
Marris, Susan B. ... Syracuse, NY
Marrison, Dale F. ... Pittsburgh, PA
Marrison, James W., Jr. ... Nashville, TN
Marrison, M. Patricia ... Colorado Springs, CO
Marritz, Robert O. ... Seattle, WA
Marrkand, Kim V. ... Boston, MA
Marro, Charles J. ... Rutland, VT
Marro, Frank ... Alpharetta, GA
Marro, Fredric ... Bridgewater, NJ
Haddonfield, NJ
Marro, Joseph P. ... New York, NY
Marro, Nicole M. ... Rochester, NY
Marrocco, Drew W. ... Washington, DC
Marrocco, Victor G. ... Dearborn, MI
Marrocco, William T., Jr. ... Garden City, MI
Marroletti, Alfred, and Associates
Philadelphia, PA
Marron, Amy M. ... San Diego, CA
Marron, Brian R. ... Richmond, VA
Marron, Dana S. ... Alamo, CA
San Francisco, CA
Marron, Donna C. ... Indianapolis, IN
Marron, Edward A. ... New York, NY
Marron, George E., III ... Highland, IL
Marron, John B. ... Phoenix, AZ
Marron, Kathleen A. ... Minneapolis, MN
Marron, McKinnon & Ewing
Albuquerque, NM
Marron, Michael R., (P.C.)
San Francisco, CA
Marron, Michelle R. ... Denver, CO
Marron, Paul J. ... Long Beach, CA
Marron, Philip ... Minneapolis, MN
Marron, Russell C., Jr. ... Rochester, NY
Marron, Timothy W. ... Council Bluffs, IA
Marrone, Anthony E. ... Lemoyne, PA
Marrone, David A. ... Memphis, TN
Marrone, Deborah A. ... New York, NY
Marrone, Dominic T. ... West Chester, PA
Marrone, Jane L. ... Minneapolis, MN
Marrone, Jeffrey V. ... Los Angeles, CA
Marrone, Matthew Steven ... Philadelphia, PA
Marrone, Mitchell J. ... Oyster Bay, NY
Marrone, Paul R. ... Bronx, NY
Marrone, Phillip R. ... Burbank, CA
Marrone Robinson Frederick & Foster
Los Angeles, CA
Burbank, CA
Glendale, CA
Pasadena, CA
Marrone, Ryan A. ... New Brunswick, NJ
Marrone, Thomas More ... Philadelphia, PA
Marroney, Gerald A. ... Pueblo, CO
Marroni, Kimberly B. ... Boston, MA
Marroni, Lisa J. ... New York, NY
Marroquin, Victor M. ... Chicago, IL
Marroso, Edmund R. ... Flint, MI
Marroso, Peter A. ... Lansing, MI
Marrow, Arnold M. ... Danvers, MA
Marrow, James C. ... Houston, TX
Marrow, James C., Jr. ... Tarboro, NC
Marrow, Joseph C. ... Boston, MA
Marrow, Paul B. ... Chappaqua, NY
Marrow, Robert V. ... New York, NY
Marrs, Alison Dean ... Glenwood Springs, CO
Marrs, Bradley P. ... Richmond, VA
Marrs, Clinton W. ... Albuquerque, NM
Marrs, Flaherty ... Valencia, CA
Marrs, Freddie Lee ... Wichita, KS
Marrs, Jerald N. ... Denver, CO
Marrs, Judith L. ... Chicago, IL
Marrs, Melanie Sublett ... Lexington, KY
Marrs, Michael D. ... St. Joseph, MI
Marrs, Michael D., A Professional Corporation ... St. Joseph, MI
Marrs, Nathaniel M. ... Chicago, IL
Marrs, Perry T., Jr. ... Oklahoma City, OK
Marrs, Peter B. ... Stamford, CT
Marrs, Richard D. ... Tulsa, OK
Marrs, Robert Lee ... Port Charlotte, FL
Marrs, Scott D. ... Houston, TX
Marrs, William S. ... Valencia, CA
Marrus, Alan D. ... Bronx, NY
Marrus, Christopher R. ... Austin, TX
Marry, Philip E. ... Kenosha, WI
Marryatt-Romaniello, Glorie ... Waterbury, CT
Marryott, Thomas D. ... Punta Gorda, FL
Mars, Burton H. ... Fort Lauderdale, FL
Mars, Daniel F. ... Philadelphia, MS
Mars, Frederick M. ... Hauppauge, NY
Mars, Gary M. ... Miami, FL
Mars, James M., II ... Philadelphia, MS
Mars, Lori R. ... Los Angeles, CA
Mars, Mars & Mars, P.A. ... Philadelphia, MS
Mars, Richard D. ... Bartow, FL

Mars, Richard D., P.A. .... Bartow, FL
Mars, Robert .... Laguna Niguel, CA
Mars, Sara .... Los Angeles, CA
Mars, Sloane & Conlon .... Hauppauge, NY
Mars, Thomas A. .... Fayetteville, AR
Mars, William M. .... Philadelphia, MS
Marsa, Lee .... Sarasota, FL
Marsa, Myrlene R. .... Chattanooga, TN
Marsac, Robert A. .... Detroit, MI
Marsack, Gary A. .... Milwaukee, WI
Marsaglia, Robert C. .... Morris, IL
Marsal, Jill D. .... Palo Alto, CA
Marsal, Louis A. .... Mobile, AL
Marsala, Anthony .... Lansing, MI
Marsala, Christopher .... Staten Island, NY
Marsala, James A. .... Sacramento, CA
Marsala, James W. .... Camarillo, CA
Marsala, William Edward
White Plains, NY
Marsalek, Diann K. .... Chicago, IL
Marsalek, Frank W. .... Baltimore, MD
Marsalek, Stephen F. .... Towson, MD
Marsalis, Steven W .... Spokane, WA
Marsalka, Joseph P. .... Dublin, OH
Marsalli, Daniel V. .... Chicago, IL
Marsan, David E. .... Easton, MA
Marsan, Donald E. .... Worcester, MA
Marsan, Gerard S. .... Easton, MA
Marsan & Marsan .... Easton, MA
Marsan, William P. .... Washington, DC
Marsano, Francis C. .... Belfast, ME
Marsaw, Terry L. .... Dallas, TX
Marsch, Susan M. .... Los Angeles, CA
Marschall, Robert P.
Palm Beach Gardens, FL
Marschang, Diane L. .... Minneapolis, MN
Marschang, Linda M. .... Bakersfield, CA
Marschean, Amy .... Alexandria, VA
Marscher, Anne C.
Hilton Head Island, SC
Marscher, William F., III .... Bluffton, SC
Marschewski, James R. .... Fort Smith, AR
Marsching, Ronald .... Woodbury, CT
Marschinke Bish, Helen A. .... Toledo, OH
Marschner, Edward C. .... New York, NY
Marschner, Jeffrey B. .... Yreka, CA
Marsden, Brian M. .... Roseville, MN
Marsden, Cahoon, Gottfredson & Bell, LLC
Salt Lake City, UT
Marsden, Duane C. .... Detroit, MI
Marsden, Elliott Jay .... Baltimore, MD
Marsden, Erica Weiss .... Lansing, MI
Marsden, Mary E. .... Manasquan, NJ
Marsden, McKay .... Salt Lake City, UT
Marsden, Milo S., Jr. .... Salt Lake City, UT
Marsden, Milo Steven .... Salt Lake City, UT
Marsden, Robert W. .... Tacoma, WA
Marsden, Sullivan (Lee) F. .... Nashville, TN
Marsden, Warren P. .... Carmel, CA
Marsden, William G. .... Salt Lake City, UT
Marsden, William J., Jr. .... Wilmington, DE
Marsee, H. Gray .... Huntsville, AL
Marsee, Howard R. .... Orlando, FL
Marsee, J. Daniel .... Lake City, FL
Marseglia, Everard A., Jr. .... Houston, TX
Marsel, Diane R. .... Los Angeles, CA
Marsella, Eve A. .... Torrance, CA
Marsella, Gregory E. .... Costa Mesa, CA
Marsella, Paul D .... Wenham, MA
Marsella, Samuel A. .... Springfield, MA
Marsella, Vincent W. .... San Francisco, CA
Marselli, Monica S. .... Tampa, FL
Marsey, Steven .... Virginia Beach, VA
Marsey, Steven J. .... Chesapeake, VA
Marsh, Aberdeen W. .... Chicago, IL
Marsh, Adrienne J. .... Scarsdale, NY
Marsh, Alan B. .... Earlville, IL
Ottawa, IL
Marsh, Andrew C. .... Alexandria, IN
Marsh, Angela .... Park Ridge, IL
Marsh, Ann V. .... Pasadena, CA
Marsh, Anthony E., (L.C.) .... San Jose, CA
Marsh & Associates, P.C. .... Albany, NY
Marsh, B. Richard .... Los Angeles, CA
Marsh, Barry C. .... Saratoga, CA
Marsh, Benjamin F. .... Maumee, OH
Marsh, Berridge R. .... San Francisco, CA
Marsh, Bettie J., (Ms.) .... Newkirk, OK
Marsh, Bobbie L. .... Canton, OH
Marsh & Bouregy, LLC .... Deep River, CT
Marsh, C. Bradford .... Atlanta, GA
Marsh, C. Duke .... Irving, TX
Marsh, C. Richard .... Bowling Green, OH
Grand Rapids, OH
Marsh, C. Stephan .... Rock Island, IL
Marsh, Carrie G. .... Mankato, MN
Marsh, Charlene F. .... Little Rock, AR
Marsh, Cheryl L. .... Beverly Hills, CA
Marsh, Christopher C. .... Springfield, MO
Marsh, Clayton K. .... New York, NY
Marsh, Clayton Knight .... New York, NY
Marsh, Clayton S. .... Boston, MA
Marsh, Curtis L. .... Dallas, TX
Marsh, D. Diane Hooks
West Los Angeles, CA
Marsh, D. Steven .... Wichita, KS
Marsh, Daniel A., Jr. .... Chicago, IL
Marsh, Daniel G. .... Vancouver, WA
Marsh, Darlene T. .... Nashville, TN
Marsh, David B. .... Houston, TX
Marsh, David D. .... Los Angeles, CA
Marsh, David D. .... Troy, MI
Marsh, David G. .... Albion, MI
Marsh, David H. .... Birmingham, AL
Marsh, David I. .... Denver, CO
Marsh, David J. .... St. Petersburg, FL
Marsh, David R. .... Washington, DC
Marsh, David S. .... Moorhead, MN
Marsh, David T. .... Tulsa, OK
Marsh, Donald R. .... Indiana, PA
Marsh, Douglas B. .... Mill Creek, WA
Marsh, Earl Holman .... Knoxville, TN
Marsh, Edward E., Jr. .... El Cajon, CA
Marsh, Edward M., Jr. .... Charlotte, NC
Marsh, Edward W. .... Pittsburgh, PA
Marsh, Eileen M. .... River Edge, NJ
Marsh, Elizabeth A. .... Annandale, VA
Marsh, Elizabeth M. .... Austin, TX
Beaumont, TX
Marsh, Elizabeth Phillips .... Hamden, CT
Marsh, Evelyn L. .... Chicago, IL
Marsh Fleischer & Quiggle, Chartered
Washington, DC
Bethesda, MD
Rockville, MD
Marsh, Frances Kate .... Houston, TX
Marsh, Frank D. .... Montgomery, AL
Marsh, Fred W., Jr. .... Dallas, TX
Marsh, Freddie Dean .... Denton, TX
Marsh & Gaffner, P.C. .... Great Neck, NY
Marsh, Gary W. .... Atlanta, GA
Marsh, Gene A. .... Tuscaloosa, AL
Marsh, Geoffrey D. .... Prestonsburg, KY
Marsh, Georganne E. .... Chicago, IL
Marsh, George B. .... Aberdeen, WA
Marsh, Gina W. .... Louisville, KY
Marsh, Gordon H. .... New York, NY
Marsh, Greg W. .... Las Vegas, NV
Marsh, Greg W., Chartered, A Prof. Corp., Law Offices of .... Las Vegas, NV
Marsh, Guy Y. .... Costa Mesa, CA
Marsh, Gwendolyn Wendy O'Brien
Amarillo, TX
Marsh, Harold, Jr. .... Tyler, TX
Marsh, Harold M. .... Richmond, VA
Marsh, Helen E.
National Labor Relations Board, Office of the General Counsel, GV
Marsh, Helen L. .... San Francisco, CA
Marsh, Henry G. .... Saginaw, MI
Marsh, Henry L., III .... Richmond, VA
Marsh, Herbert E., Jr. .... El Paso, TX
Marsh & Higgins .... Stevenson, WA
Vancouver, WA
Marsh, Howard J. .... Salt Lake City, UT
Marsh, Jack A. .... Monrovia, CA
Marsh, James A. .... Randolph, MA
Marsh, James E. .... Pierre, SD
Marsh, James E., Jr. .... Erie, PA
Marsh, James F. .... Stroudsburg, PA
Marsh, James G. .... Garden City, NY
Marsh, James H., Jr. .... Kansas City, MO
Marsh, James Marlin .... Houston, TX
Marsh, James O. .... Portland, OR
Marsh, James P. .... Downers Grove, IL
Marsh, James R. .... Washington, DC
Marsh, James R. .... Stroudsburg, PA
Marsh, Jane R. .... Deep River, CT
Marsh, Jeffrey H. .... Houston, TX
Marsh, Jenelle Mims .... Tuscaloosa, AL
Marsh, Jennifer McGehee .... Frankfort, KY
Marsh, Jeremiah, (P.C.) .... Chicago, IL
Marsh, Jerrold V. .... St. Clair Shores, MI
Marsh, Jo Bennett .... Baltimore, MD
Marsh, Joan .... Washington, DC
Chicago, IL
Marsh, Joel C. .... Birmingham, AL
Marsh, Joel E. .... Oakland, CA
Marsh, Joel W.
Charlotte Amalie, St. Thomas, VI
Marsh, John .... Lexington, NE
Marsh, John F. .... Columbus, OH
Marsh, John H. .... Kearney, NE
Marsh, John H. .... Portland, OR
Marsh, John O., Jr. .... Winchester, VA
Marsh, John S. .... Brookline, MA
Marsh, Jonathan E. .... New York, NY
Marsh, Joseph H. .... North Canton, OH
Marsh, Judith Wilson .... Oakland, CA
Marsh, Karyl L. .... Sacramento, CA
Marsh, Kenneth E. .... Baltimore, MD
Marsh, Kermit D. .... Santa Ana, CA
Marsh, Kerry D. .... Albany, NY
Marsh, Kevin B. .... Chicago, IL
Marsh, Kimberley .... Chicago, IL
Marsh, Kimberly Lisette .... Atlanta, GA
Marsh, Kirke .... New York, NY
Marsh, Lanette Susan .... Newton, MA
Marsh, Larry D. .... Daytona Beach, FL
Marsh, Laura Taulbee .... Statesboro, GA
Marsh, Laurie S. .... New York, NY
Marsh Law Firm, PLLC .... Charlotte, NC
Marsh, Leonard R. .... Watertown, NY
Marsh, Lila Clark .... Dallas, TX
Marsh, Linda J. .... Buffalo, NY
Marsh, Linda Sue .... Northfield, OH
Marsh, Lindell L. .... Irvine, CA
Marsh, Lisa .... Olympia, WA
Marsh, Loren .... Muncie, IN
Marsh, Lucille .... Scranton, PA
Marsh, Luke B. .... Department of Justice, Civil Division, GV
Marsh, M. Dale .... Enterprise, AL
Marsh, Malcolm F. .... Portland, OR
Marsh, Mark A. .... Carson City, NV
Marsh and Marsh .... Durham, NC
Marsh & Marsh .... Bowling Green, OH
Grand Rapids, OH
Marsh and Marsh, P.C.
Oklahoma City, OK
Tulsa, OK
Marsh, Mary Y., (Mrs.) .... Indianapolis, IN
Marsh & McAdams .... Maumee, OH
Marsh, Melissa C. .... Los Angeles, CA
Marsh, Melissa C. .... North Hollywood, CA
Marsh, Merton St. C. .... Atlanta, GA
Marsh, Michael C. .... Miami, FL
Marsh, Michael E. .... Naperville, IL
Marsh, Michael G. .... Seattle, WA
Marsh, Michael H. .... Boston, MA
Marsh, Michael J. .... Bowling Green, OH
Marsh, Michael K. .... Corpus Christi, TX
Marsh, Michael L. .... Marietta, GA
Marsh, Michael L. .... Rochester, NY
Marsh, Michael R. .... Honolulu, HI
Marsh, Michael V. .... Chicago, IL
Marsh, Michele .... Los Angeles, CA
Marsh, Michelle Bellamy .... Nashville, TN
Marsh, Minzing and Metzner
Delphos, OH
Marsh, Moriarty, Ontell & Dacey, P.C.
Boston, MA
Marsh Mundorf Pratt & Sullivan, A Professional Service Corporation
Mill Creek, WA
Marsh, Nicole R. .... New Orleans, LA
Marsh, Nora H. .... Chicago, IL
Hinsdale, IL
Marsh, Norman J., Jr. .... Nashua, NH
Marsh, Pamela B. .... Barnstable, MA
Yarmouth Port, MA
Marsh, Patricia J. .... Great Neck, NY
Marsh & Perna .... Oakland, CA
Marsh, Peter K. .... New Haven, CT
Marsh, Peter K. .... Concord, NH
Marsh, Peter L. .... Albany, NY
Marsh, R. Blake .... Houston, TX
Marsh, Rabe F., III .... Greensburg, PA
Marsh, Ralph J. .... Salt Lake City, UT
Marsh, Randolph Lee .... Houston, TX
Marsh, Ray T. .... Ashland, OR
Marsh, Raymond L. .... Oakland, CA
Marsh, Richard A. .... Denver, CO
Frederick, CO
Frederick, CO
Marsh, Richard C. .... Detroit, MI
Marsh, Richard E., Jr. .... Washington, DC
Charlotte, NC
Marsh, Richard M. .... Phoenix, AZ
Marsh, Richard M. .... Murray, UT
Marsh, Richard M., Jr. .... Houston, TX
Marsh, Richard P. .... Rochester, NH
Marsh, Richard S. T. .... Washington, DC
Marsh, Rick E. .... Columbus, OH
Marsh, Rickard & Bryan, P.C.
Birmingham, AL
Marsh, Ricky A. .... Hobart, OK
Marsh, Riley B. .... San Francisco, CA
Marsh, Ritchie T. .... Erie, PA
Marsh, Robert E. .... Kansas City, MO
Marsh, Robert E., Jr. .... Wilkes-Barre, PA
Marsh, Robert L. .... Oakbrook Terrace, IL
Marsh, Roger A. .... Urbana, IL
Marsh, Rolfe C. .... Media, PA
Marsh, Ronald L. .... Clinton Township, MI
Marsh, Ronald S. .... Detroit, MI
Marsh, Samuel J. .... Columbus, KS
Marsh, Samuel S. D. .... Bethesda, MD
Marsh, Sandra M. .... New York, NY
Marsh, Sharon R. .... Department of Commerce, Patent and Trademark Office, GV
Marsh, Sheila C. .... Lake Forest, IL
Marsh, Spaeder, Baur, Spaeder & Schaaf, LLP .... Erie, PA
Marsh, Stephanie J. .... Philadelphia, PA
Marsh, Stephen L. .... San Diego, CA
Marsh, Stephen R. .... Dallas, TX
Marsh, Steven E. .... Springfield, MO
Marsh, Sunia Yvette .... Orlando, FL
Marsh, Suzanne S. .... Plano, TX
Marsh, Theron L., II .... Chesterfield, VA
Marsh, Thomas .... Oakland, CA
Marsh, Thomas G. .... Tulsa, OK
Marsh, Thomas R. .... Denver, CO
Marsh, Troy .... Statesboro, GA
Marsh, Troy, P.C. .... Statesboro, GA
Marsh & Valentine LLP .... New York, NY
Marsh, Victor R. .... Canton, OH
Marsh, Virgil H. .... Washington, DC
Marsh, Wayne C. .... Memphis, TN
Marsh, Wayne P. .... Sun City, AZ
Sun City West, AZ
Marsh, Wendy A. .... Syracuse, NY
Marsh, Wendy K. .... Des Moines, IA
Omaha, NE
Marsh, Weston W. .... Chicago, IL
Marsh, William A., Jr. .... Durham, NC
Marsh, William Andrew, III .... Durham, NC
Marsh, William C. .... Monterey, CA
Marsh, William D. .... Lafayette, CA
Marsh, William D. .... Houston, TX
Marsh, William E. .... Indianapolis, IN
Marsh, William F. .... Allentown, PA
Marsh, William R. .... Denver, CO
Marsh, William T. .... Butler, PA
Marsh, Wm. Douglas .... Pensacola, FL
Marsh & Yanik .... Pocono, PA
Scranton, PA
Wilkes-Barre, PA
Marshack, Howard H. .... Vancouver, WA
Marshack, Morton J. .... New York, NY
Marshack, Richard A. .... Irvine, CA
Marshack Shulman & Hodges LLP
Irvine, CA
Marshak, Michael .... San Diego, CA
Marshak, Morton .... Monroe, NY
Marshak, Ned H. .... New York, NY
Marshall, A. Carter .... Richmond, VA
Marshall, Abigail Story .... Bryn Mawr, PA
Marshall, Abigail V. .... Beaverton, OR
Marshall, Abike .... Chicago, IL
Marshall, Akawie & LaPietra, Professional Corporation .... Oakland, CA
Walnut Creek, CA
Marshall, Alan L. .... North Vernon, IN
Marshall, Albert B., Jr. .... Clearwater, FL
Marshall, Alexander J., III
Birmingham, AL
Marshall, Alexandra L. .... New York, NY
Marshall, Alfred T. .... San Gabriel, CA
Marshall, Alice B. .... Tustin, CA
Marshall, Alison B. .... Washington, DC
Marshall, Alvin B. .... Pottsville, PA
Marshall, Andrew F. .... Phoenix, AZ
Marshall, Andrew H. .... Athens, GA
Marshall, Andrew L. .... Minneapolis, MN
Marshall, Angela D. .... North Wilkesboro, NC
Marshall, Angela Jolene
United States Senate, Senatorial Assistants, GV
Marshall, Ann Dudley .... Oklahoma City, OK
Marshall, Ann Dunagan .... Birmingham, AL
Marshall, Ann T. .... Seattle, WA
Marshall, Anne Bradley .... Sheridan, WY
Marshall, Anne E. .... Hayward, CA
Marshall, Anne Marie .... Corpus Christi, TX
Marshall, Anthony G. .... North Miami, FL
Marshall, Anthony P. .... New York, NY
Marshall, Anthony P. .... Syracuse, NY
Marshall, Arthur K. .... Los Angeles, CA
Marshall, Arthur M. .... Springfield, MA
Marshall Batt & Fisher LLP .... Boise, ID
Caldwell, ID
Marshall & Bellard .... Garden City, NY
Marshall, Ben, Jr. .... Shreveport, LA
Marshall, Ben P. .... Phoenix, AZ
Marshall, Benjamin F., IV .... Monroe, LA
Marshall, Benson C. .... San Bernardino, CA
San Diego, CA
Marshall, Bernard S., Jr .... Lebanon, OH
Marshall, Bert E. .... Oklahoma City, OK
Marshall, Beth Ann .... Philadelphia, PA
Marshall, Bethany N. .... San Jose, CA
Marshall, Bettie Baker .... Campbell, CA
Marshall, Betty .... Fort Worth, TX
Marshall, Bradley R. .... Seattle, WA
Tacoma, WA
Marshall, Brent E. .... Department of Justice, Antitrust Division, GV
Marshall, Brooks P. .... Los Angeles, CA
Marshall, Bruce A. .... Phillips, WI
Marshall, Bruce M. .... Richmond, VA
Marshall, B. R. W. .... Gloucester, VA
Marshall, Bryant .... Jonesboro, AR
Marshall, Burke .... New Haven, CT
Marshall, Byrd F., Jr. .... Orlando, FL
Marshall, C. Lance, Jr. .... Cranbury, NJ
Marshall, C. Richard .... Columbus, IN
Marshall, Cameron Lee
North Charleston, SC
Marshall, Carl J. .... Paducah, KY
Marshall, Carol J. .... San Francisco, CA
Marshall, Carol Mayer .... San Francisco, CA
Marshall, Carol R. .... Calabasas, CA
Marshall, Cassandra L. .... Bloomington, IN
Marshall, Catherine D. ....
Department of State, GV
Marshall, Catherine E. .... Washington, DC
Marshall, Catherine Lynn .... Philadelphia, PA
Marshall, Charles B. .... Evanston, IL
Marshall, Charles C. .... Rutherford, NJ
Marshall, Charles D. .... Chicago, IL
Marshall, Charles D., Jr. (P.C.)
New Orleans, LA
Marshall, Charles E. .... Phoenix, AZ
Marshall, Charles E. .... Somonauk, IL
Marshall, Charles F., III
Department of Justice, Office of the Attorney General, GV
Marshall, Charles M. .... Beaver, PA
Marshall, Charles O. .... Nashville, TN
Marshall, Charles R. .... Ashland, KY
Marshall, Charles T. .... Dallas, TX
Marshall, Charles V. .... St. Louis, MO
Marshall, Christina M. .... New York, NY
Marshall, Christine C.
Fort Lauderdale, FL
Marshall, Christopher B.
Los Angeles, CA
Riverside, CA
Marshall, Christopher J. .... Portland, OR
Marshall, Clara A. .... Pelham, NY
Marshall, Clifford C., Jr. .... Asheville, NC
Marshall, Clyde M. .... Fort Worth, TX
Marshall, Colin S. .... Boston, MA
Marshall, Conrad J. .... McLean, VA
Marshall, Consuelo B. .... Los Angeles, CA
Marshall Conway & Wright, P.C.
Jersey City, NJ
New York, NY
Marshall, Conway & Wright, P.C.
White Plains, NY
Marshall, Courtney W. .... Toulon, IL
Marshall, Craig M. .... Riverside, CA
Marshall, Craig S. .... Akron, OH
Marshall, Curt D. .... New York, NY
Marshall, D. Price, Jr. .... Jonesboro, AR
Marshall, Dan .... Des Moines, IA
Marshall, Dan A. .... Parkersburg, WV
Marshall, Daniel .... Cleveland, OH
Marshall, Daniel Parr, III .... San Francisco, CA
Marshall, Daniel T. .... Commerce, CA
Marshall, Dave B. .... Dallas, TX
Marshall, David B. .... Sarasota, FL
Marshall, David C. .... Atlanta, GA
Marshall, David C. .... Waldorf, MD
Marshall, David C. .... Harrisburg, PA
Marshall, David D. .... Redwood City, CA
Marshall, David J. .... Washington, DC
Marshall, David J. .... Plattsburgh, NY
Marshall, David L. .... Washington, DC
Marshall, David L. .... Doylestown, PA

Marshall, David M. ...San Diego, CA
Marshall, David R. ...Lodi, CA
Marshall, David R. ...Minneapolis, MN
Marshall, David R. ...New York, NY
Marshall, David Rollins ...Lexington, KY
Marshall, David Russell ...Nicholasville, KY
Marshall, David S. ...Seattle, WA
Marshall, David V. ...Bellevue, WA
Marshall, David W. ...Concord, NH
Marshall, David W. ...San Antonio, TX
Marshall, David W., PLLC
San Antonio, TX
Marshall, Dawn ...Miami, FL
Marshall, D. B. ...Charlottesville, VA
Marshall, Deana K. ...Riverview, FL
Marshall, Deborah A. ...Palo Alto, CA
Marshall, Delius and Taylor, P.A.
Sevierville, TN
Marshall, Delsia G. ...Yonkers, NY
Marshall, Dennehey, Warner, Coleman and Goggin ...Wilmington, DE
Cherry Hill, NJ
Livingston, NJ
Steubenville, OH
Bethlehem, PA
Doylestown, PA
Erie, PA
Harrisburg, PA
Lancaster, PA
Newtown Square, PA
Norristown, PA
Philadelphia, PA
Pittsburgh, PA
Scranton, PA
Williamsport, PA
Weirton, WV
Marshall, Dennis E. ...Huntsville, AL
Marshall, Dennis R. ...Morristown, NJ
Marshall, Diana E. ...Houston, TX
Marshall, Diana S. ...Allentown, PA
Marshall, Diane O. ...Universal City, CA
Marshall, Dirk H. ...Oregon City, OR
Marshall, Don F. ...Newtown, PA
Marshall, Don L. ...Torrance, CA
Marshall, Donald A. ...Philadelphia, PA
Marshall, Donald B. ...San Antonio, TX
Marshall, Donald G. ...Minneapolis, MN
Marshall, Donald W., Jr. ...Brighton, CO
Marshall, Donna ...Deerfield, MA
Marshall, Douglas A. ...San Francisco, CA
Marshall, Douglas B. ...Blue Bell, PA
Marshall, Douglas D.
Rehoboth Beach, DE
Marshall, Douglas E. ...Irvine, CA
Marshall, Douglas E. ...Santa Cruz, CA
Marshall, Douglas H. ...Stamford, CT
Marshall, Douglas M. ...Honolulu, HI
Marshall, Douglas Wendell ...Bozeman, MT
Marshall, Douglass A. ...Peoria, IL
Marshall, Dwight A. ...Worthington, OH
Marshall, E. Bonnie ...Glendale, CA
Marshall, E. David ...Lexington, KY
Marshall, E. Pierce, Jr. ...Dallas, TX
Marshall, Edith S. ...Washington, DC
Marshall, Edw. S. ...Lake Success, NY
Marshall, Edward G. ...Las Vegas, NV
Marshall, Edward T. ...Oakland, CA
Marshall, Eileen ...Palo Alto, CA
Marshall, Elaine E. ...Roseville, MI
Marshall, Elaine F. ...Raleigh, NC
Marshall, Elizabeth A. ...Washington, DC
Marshall, Elizabeth C. ...Sarasota, FL
Marshall, Elizabeth J. ...Dearborn, MI
Marshall, Elizabeth P. ...Frankfort, KY
Marshall, Ellen C. ...Newark, NJ
Marshall, Ellen C. ...West Orange, NJ
Marshall, Ellen R. ...Irvine, CA
Marshall, Ellis Hayes, Jr. ...Hermitage, TN
Marshall, Elmer Paul ...Chicago, IL
Marshall, Emmett J. ...Chicago, IL
Marshall, Eric C. ...Chicago, IL
Marshall, Eric W. ...Greensburg, KS
Marshall, Evans H. ...Montgomery, AL
Marshall, F. John ...Grand Forks, ND
Marshall, Foster Fitzgerald ...Birmingham, AL
Marshall, Foster, Jr. ...Chicago, IL
Marshall, Frances E. ...Department of Justice, Antitrust Division, GV
Marshall, Francis E. ...Philadelphia, PA
Marshall, Francis E., Jr. ...Camp Hill, PA
Marshall, Francis N. ...San Francisco, CA
Marshall, Frank C., Jr. ...Woodland Hills, CA
Marshall, Franklin, IV ...Sikeston, MO
Marshall, Franz R. ...Department of Justice, Civil Rights Division, GV
Marshall, Frederick M. ...East Aurora, NY
Marshall, G. Timothy ...Cleveland, OH
Marshall, Gail A.
Securities and Exchange Commission, Division of Market Regulation, GV
Marshall, Gail Starling ...Rapidan, VA
Marshall, Gary K. ...Seattle, WA
Marshall, Gary S. ...Uniondale, NY
Marshall, Gary S. ...Richmond, VA
Marshall, G. E., IV ...Palo Alto, CA
Marshall, Geoffrey D. ...Troy, MI
Marshall, George A. ...Marshall, MN
Marshall, George D. ...Pleasanton, CA
Marshall, Gina C. ...Atlanta, GA
Marshall, Glenn R. ...New York, NY
Marshall, Gordon ...New York, NY
Marshall, Gregory J. ...West Chester, PA
Marshall, Gregory R. ...Palo Cedro, CA
Marshall, Gregory S. ...Seattle, WA
Marshall, Gretchen A. ...Alexandria, VA
Marshall, Guinise Marie
Oklahoma City, OK
Marshall, H. Gayle ...Lake Charles, LA
Marshall, H. Gayle, A Prof. Law Corp.
Lake Charles, LA
Marshall, Hal, P.C. ...Dallas, TX
Marshall, Harold F. "Hal" ...Dallas, TX
Marshall, Harrison L., Jr. ...Charlotte, NC
Marshall, Harry R., Jr.
Department of Justice, Criminal Division, GV
Marshall, Harry T. ...Charlottesville, VA
Marshall, Heman A., III ...Roanoke, VA
Marshall, Henry C. ...Williamsburg, VA
Marshall, Herbert A. ...Topeka, KS
Marshall Hill Cassas & de Lipkau
Carson City, NV
Elko, NV
Gardnerville, NV
Incline Village, NV
Las Vegas, NV
Minden, NV
Reno, NV
Marshall, Holcombe T. ...Decatur, GA
Marshall, Holly L. ...Phoenix, AZ
Marshall, Howard ...Somonauk, IL
Marshall, Hubert Lincoln ...Brooklyn, NY
Marshall, Huey B. ...Concord, NC
Marshall, Hugh L. ...Jefferson City, MO
Marshall, Hugh L. ...San Antonio, TX
Marshall, Hugh R. ...Harper Woods, MI
Marshall, Ira B. ...Matawan, NJ
Marshall, J. Howard, Jr. ...New York, NY
Marshall, J. Paull ...Bethesda, MD
Marshall, J. Richard ...Muncie, IN
Marshall, J. Scott ...Washington, DC
Marshall, J. Stephen ...Grand Rapids, MI
Marshall, J. A. ...Bacliff, TX
Marshall, Jack A. ...Arlington, MA
Marshall, Jacob B. ...Dallas, TX
Marshall, Jacqueline ...Tucson, AZ
Marshall, James ...East Lansing, MI
Marshall, James A. ...Albany, OR
Marshall, James A., P.C. ...Albany, OR
Marshall, James B., Jr. ...Austin, TX
Marshall, James D. ...Springfield, OH
Marshall, James F. ...Santa Monica, CA
Marshall, James H. ...Chicago, IL
Marshall, James J., Jr. ...New York, NY
Marshall, James, Jr. ...St. Petersburg, FL
Marshall, James K. ...Sycamore, IL
Marshall, James M. ...Napa, CA
Marshall, James Markham ...Seattle, WA
Marshall, James R. ...Shawnee, OK
Marshall, Janet Wessler ...New Orleans, LA
Marshall, Janice K. ...Breckenridge, CO
Marshall, Janiece S. ...Las Vegas, NV
Marshall, Jason C. ...Dallas, TX
Marshall, Jason P. ...Encino, CA
Marshall, Jason P. ...Providence, RI
Marshall, Jay G. ...Hackensack, NJ
Marshall, J. B., Jr. ...Portsmouth, OH
Marshall, Jeanne-Marie ...Elk Rapids, MI
Marshall, Jeannette ...Medford, OR
Marshall, Jeffrey A. ...New York, NY
Marshall, Jeffrey A. ...Jersey Shore, PA
Williamsport, PA
Marshall, Jeffrey C. ...York, PA
Marshall, Jeffrey E. ...Raleigh, NC
Marshall, Jeffrey O. ...Dallas, TX
Marshall, Jerry B. ...Macon, GA
Marshall, Jimmie D. ...Jackson, MS
Marshall, Joan E. ...Washington, DC
Marshall, Joan E. ...Dallas, TX
Marshall, Joe E. ...Dallas, TX
Marshall, John ...Rockville, MD
Marshall, John ...Plainview, NY
Marshall, John A., (P.C.) ...Los Angeles, CA
Marshall, John B. ...Encino, CA
Marshall, John B. ...Nashville, TN
Marshall, John C., III ...Houston, TX
Marshall, John D. ...Atlanta, GA
Marshall, John D. ...Honolulu, HI
Marshall, John D. ...Chicago, IL
Marshall, John D., Jr. ...Atlanta, GA
Marshall, John Dean, Jr. ...Atlanta, GA
Marshall, John F. ...San Jose, CA
Marshall, John G. ...Salt Lake City, UT
Marshall, John H. ...St. Louis, MO
Marshall, John H. ...Butler, PA
Marshall, John H. ...Houston, TX
Marshall, John H. ...St. Johnsbury, VT
Marshall, John J. ...Philadelphia, PA
Marshall, John L., III ...Jacksonville, FL
Marshall, John L., Jr. ...Richmond, VA
Marshall, John M. ...Boise, ID
Marshall, John McClellan ...Dallas, TX
Marshall, John P. ...Kinston, NC
Marshall, John S. ...Columbus, OH
Marshall, John T. ...Tampa, FL
Marshall, John T. ...Atlanta, GA
Marshall, John W. ...Glendale, CA
Marshall, John W. ...Riverside, CA
Marshall, John W. ...Watertown, MA
Marshall, John W., P.C. ...Watertown, MA
Marshall, Jonathan A. ...New York, NY
Marshall, Jonathan W. ...Columbus, OH
Marshall, Joseph ...Lincolnwood, IL
Marshall, Joseph B. ...Circle Pines, MN
Marshall, Joseph C., III ...Detroit, MI
Marshall, Joseph L. ...San Diego, CA
Marshall, Joseph W., III ...Philadelphia, PA
Marshall, Joseph W., Jr. ...Philadelphia, PA
Marshall, Juli Wilson ...Chicago, IL
Marshall, Julia J. ...Carmel, IN
Marshall, Julie Ann ...Pittsburgh, PA
Marshall, Julie G. ...Canon City, CO
Marshall, Karl N. ...Washington, DC
Marshall, Katherine A. ...Chicago, IL
Northbrook, IL
Marshall, Katherine M. ...Potomac, MD
Marshall, Kathleen M. ...Reno, NV
Marshall, Kathryn S. ...Anacortes, WA
Marshall, Keith W. ...Richardson, TX
Marshall, Kenneth N. ...Chicago, IL
Marshall, Kent Hamlin ...Portland, OR
Marshall, Kent, Jr. ...Cleveland, OH
Marshall, Keri J. ...East Kingston, NH
Marshall, Kevin W. ...Hammond, IN
Marshall, Kimber Reid ...Alvin, TX
Marshall, Kimberly D. ...Waldorf, MD
Marshall, Kimberly L. ...Washington, DC
Marshall, Larry H. ...Frankfort, KY
Marshall, Larry L. ...San Diego, CA
Marshall, Lauren Goldman ...Seattle, WA
Marshall Law Firm ...New York, NY
Marshall Law Group, The ...Atlanta, GA
Marshall Law Offices, P.A.
Minnetonka, MN
Marshall, Lawrence C ...Chicago, IL
Marshall, Lawrence E., II ...Richmond, VA
Marshall, Lee ...Santa Monica, CA
Marshall, Lenora E. ...Montclair, NJ
Marshall, Leslie A. ...New York, NY
Marshall, Lester D. ...Glendale, CA
Marshall, Lila Craddock ...Dallas, TX
Marshall, Linda G. ...Houston, TX
Marshall, Linda K. ...New Orleans, LA
Marshall, Linda L., P.C. ...Lake Oswego, OR
Marshall, Linda S. F. ...Treasury Department, Internal Revenue Service, GV
Marshall, Lorraine ...White Plains, NY
Marshall, Lucinda K. ...Houston, TX
Marshall, Lyle A. ...Indian Wells, CA
Marshall, Lyle Norman ...Lansing, MI
Marshall, Lynda K. ...Washington, DC
Marshall, Lynda L. ...New Orleans, LA
Marshall, M. Joyce ...Columbia, SC
Marshall, M. Keith ...Dania, FL
Marshall, M. Stephen ...St. Louis, MO
Marshall, Malcolm Y. ...Louisville, KY
Marshall, Marcia K. ...New York, NY
Marshall, Margaret H. ...Cambridge, MA
Marshall, Margaret R. ...Atlanta, GA
Marshall, Mariam ...San Francisco, CA
Marshall, Mariam S. ...Oakland, CA
Marshall, Marianne Lipscombe
Swanton, VT
Marshall, Marilee ...Pasadena, CA
Marshall, Marilu ...Miami, FL
Marshall, Marilyn J. ...Tallahassee, FL
Marshall, Marita K., Law Offices of
San Francisco, CA
Marshall, Mark F., P.C. ...Sioux Falls, SD
Marshall, Mark H. ...Austin, TX
Marshall, Marlys ...Los Lunas, NM
Marshall & Marshall ...Lodi, CA
Marshall & Marshall ...Swanton, VT
Marshall & Marshall, Ltd. ...Somonauk, IL
Marshall & Marshall, P.C.
Charlottesville, VA
Marshall, Martha L. ...Oklahoma City, OK
Marshall, Marvin P. ...Shelbyville, TN
Marshall, Mary A. ...Gainesville, FL
Marshall, Mary Beth ...Dallas, TX
Marshall, Mary L., & Associates
Wellesley, MA
Marshall, Mary T. ...Boston, MA
Marshall, Matthew F.
Cranberry Township, PA
Marshall, Matthew L. ...Los Angeles, CA
Marshall, McAlister C., II ...Richmond, VA
Marshall & McCracken, P.C.
Houston, TX
Marshall & McEvoy ...New York, NY
Marshall & Melhorn ...Toledo, OH
Marshall, Melissa Page
Environmental Protection Agency, Office of Enforcement and Compliance Assurance, GV
Marshall, Michael J. ...St. Louis, MO
Marshall, Michael L. ...Baltimore, MD
Marshall, Michael L. ...Woodbine, MD
Marshall, Michael P. ...Norristown, PA
Marshall, Michael P., Jr. ...Atlanta, GA
Marshall, Michael R. ...Memphis, TN
Marshall, Michael S. ...Clearfield, PA
Marshall, Michael T. ...Greensboro, NC
Marshall, Michelle G. ...Phoenix, AZ
Marshall, Mira Nan
Federal Deposit Insurance Corporation, GV
Marshall, Mishka L. ...Phoenix, AZ
Marshall, Monte ...Salem, OR
Marshall, Monte K. ...Sarasota, FL
Marshall, Nancy ...Montauk, NY
Marshall, Nancy Ann ...St. Louis, MO
Marshall, Nancy J. ...New Orleans, LA
Marshall, Natalie J. ...Fishkill, NY
Marshall, Newton C., II ...Chicago, IL
Marshall, Nicholas N. ...Springfield, MA
Marshall, Nicole W. ...New York, NY
Marshall, Norma S. ...San Diego, CA
Marshall, Norman S. ...Pasadena, CA
Marshall, O'Toole, Gerstein, Murray & Borun ...Chicago, IL
Marshall and Owens, P.A. ...Jonesboro, AR
Marshall, Patricia A. ...St. Louis, MO
Marshall, Patricia Ann ...Irvine, CA
Marshall, Patrick C. ...San Francisco, CA
Marshall, Patrick E. ...Hollister, CA
Marshall, Paul G. ...New York, NY
Marshall, Paul K. ...Kingfield, ME
Marshall, Paul L. ...Troy, MI
Marshall, Paulette A. ...Fullerton, CA
Marshall, Penny ...Washington, DC
Marshall, Peter C. K. ...Boise, ID
Marshall, Peter F. ...Daytona Beach, FL
Marshall, Peter W. ...Stamford, CT
Marshall, Philip M. ...Buffalo, NY
Marshall, Phillip G. "Casey"
Vancouver, WA
Marshall, Phyllis Ann ...Sacramento, CA
Marshall, Polly V. ...San Francisco, CA
Marshall, Prentice H. ...Ponce Inlet, FL
Chicago, IL
Markesan, WI
Marshall, Prentice H., Jr. ...Chicago, IL
Marshall, Quin E. ...Walnut Creek, CA
Marshall, R. Bryant ...Jonesboro, AR
Marshall, R. Lindsay ...Atlanta, GA
Marshall, R. Stephen ...Salt Lake City, UT
Marshall, Rachel E. ...Seattle, WA
Marshall, Raeburn A. ...Houston, TX
Marshall, Randall C. ...Fort Lauderdale, FL
Pittsburgh, PA
Marshall, Randall J. ...Orange City, FL
Marshall, Raymond Charles
San Francisco, CA
Marshall, Raymond H. ...El Paso, TX
Marshall, Raymond O. ...Lake Elmo, MN
Marshall, Rebecca Osborn ...Nashville, TN
Marshall, Reginald S. ...Garden City, NY
Marshall, Richard A. ...Beverly Hills, CA
Marshall, Richard A. ...Honolulu, HI
Marshall, Richard A., Jr. ...Williston, FL
Marshall, Richard D. ...New York, NY
Marshall, Richard E. ...New York, NY
Marshall, Richard L. ...Coeur d'Alene, ID
Marshall, Richard M. ...St. Louis, MO
Marshall, Richard M. ...New York, NY
Marshall, Richard P. ...Dallas, TX
Marshall, Richard P., Jr. ...Austin, TX
Marshall, Richard S. ...San Francisco, CA
Marshall, Richard S. ...Washington, DC
Marshall, Richard T. ...El Paso, TX
Marshall, Richard T., P.C., The Law Offices of ...El Paso, TX
Marshall, Richard Todd ...Houston, TX
Marshall, Robert ...Burlington, MA
Marshall, Robert ...Detroit, MI
Marshall, Robert A. ...Louisville, KY
Marshall, Robert A. ...Trenton, NJ
Marshall, Robert B. ...Charlotte, NC
Marshall, Robert B., Jr. ...West Point, MS
Marshall, Robert B., Jr. ...Beaufort, SC
Marshall, Robert C. ...Atlanta, GA
Marshall, Robert C. ...Minnetonka, MN
Marshall, Robert D. ...Sacramento, CA
Marshall, Robert D. ...Atlanta, GA
Marshall, Robert D. ...Salem, NH
Marshall, Robert D., Jr. ...Dallas, TX
Marshall, Robert E. ...Shelbyville, IN
Marshall, Robert F. ...Los Angeles, CA
Marshall, Robert G., II
San Francisco, CA
Marshall, Robert J. ...Palmetto, FL
Marshall, Robert J. ...Chicago, IL
Marshall, Robert L. ...Chico, CA
Marshall, Robert M. ...Secaucus, NJ
Marshall, Robert R. ...Hattiesburg, MS
Marshall, Robert R., Jr. ...Denver, CO
Marshall, Robert S. Bretz
Silver Spring, MD
Marshall, Robert W. ...Reno, NV
Marshall, Roderick Scott ...Huntington, WV
Marshall, Roger V. ...Chico, CA
Marshall, Rolf ...Washington, DC
Marshall, Ronald J. ...Bethesda, MD
Marshall, Ronald S. ...Kelso, WA
Marshall, S. Pitkin ...New York, NY
Marshall, Sally J. ...Chapel Hill, NC
Marshall, Sandra D. ...Clarksdale, MS
Marshall, Sandra L. ...Irvine, CA
Marshall, Schuyler B., IV ...Dallas, TX
Marshall, Scott E. ...Visalia, CA
Marshall, Scott O. ...St. Louis, MO
Marshall, Seth, III ...Marietta, GA
Marshall, Sharon A. ...San Diego, CA
Marshall, Sharon G. ...Anderson, SC
Marshall, Shauna I. ...Palo Alto, CA
Marshall, Sheila Ann ...Indianapolis, IN
Marshall, Sheila H., (P.C.) ...New York, NY
Marshall, Sherman J. ...Mission, SD
Marshall, Shirley Moana ...Alexandria, VA
Marshall, Sidney R., Jr. ...Lexington, KY
Marshall, Siri S. ...Minneapolis, MN
Marshall & Smith ...Bozeman, MT
Marshall, Smith & Haddick, A Professional Corporation ...Camp Hill, PA
Carlisle, PA
Harrisburg, PA
Marshall, Snyder & Crane ...Burlington, MA
Marshall, Stanley J. ...Ackley, IA
Marshall, Stephan E. ...Fort Worth, TX
Marshall, Stephen ...Cherry Hill, NJ
Blue Bell, PA
Marshall, Stephen A. ...New York, NY
Marshall, Stephen E. ...Baltimore, MD
Marshall, Stephen J. ...South Plainfield, NJ
Marshall, Stephen R. ...New York, NY
Marshall, Steven C., (P.S.) ...Bellevue, WA
Marshall, Steven D. ...Swanton, VT
Marshall, Steven E. ...Sevierville, TN
Marshall, Steven P. ...Woodbridge, NJ
Marshall, Steven T. ...Guntersville, AL
Marshall, Stewart Andrew, III
Orlando, FL
Marshall, Susan ...Lincoln, KS
Marshall, Susan A. ...Washington, DC
Arlington, VA
Marshall, Susan A. ...New York, NY
Marshall, Susan E. ...Concord, NH
Marshall, T. Keith, III ...Charleston, SC
Marshall, T. Thaddeus ...Philadelphia, PA
Marshall, Teresa McCraig ...Paris, TN
Marshall, Teri S. ...Honolulu, HI
Marshall, Terrell ...North Little Rock, AR

Marshall, Thomas ... Omaha, NE
Marshall, Thomas A. ... Frankfort, KY
Marshall, Thomas A., Jr. ... Chicago, IL
Marshall, Thomas C. ... New Britain, CT
Marshall, Thomas C. ... Williamsport, PA
Marshall, Thomas C. ... Vienna, VA
Marshall, Thomas E. ... Bel Air, MD
Marshall, Thomas E. ... Troy, MI
Marshall, Thomas E. ... Minneapolis, MN
Marshall, Thomas F. ... Rushville, IN
Marshall, Thomas F. ... Mount Holly, NJ
Marshall, Thomas H. ... Kansas City, KS
Marshall, Thomas J. ... Moberly, MO
Marshall, Thomas L. ... San Diego, CA
Marshall, Thomas O., Jr. ... Atlanta, GA
Marshall, Thurgood, Jr. ...
Executive Office Of The President, GV
Marshall, Timon Lee ... Atlanta, GA
Marshall, Todd E. ... El Paso, TX
Marshall, Tom
Environmental Protection Agency, Office of the General Counsel, GV
Marshall, Torsten M. ... New York, NY
Marshall, Townsell G., Jr. ... Atlanta, GA
Marshall, Tracy Ann ... Orlando, FL
Marshall, Tyler E. ... Portland, OR
Marshall, Valerie A. ... Orlando, FL
Marshall, Valerie A., L.L.C. ... Orlando, FL
Marshall, Victor R. ... Albuquerque, NM
Marshall, Victor R., & Associates, P.C.
Albuquerque, NM
Marshall, Virginia L. ... Frackville, PA
Marshall, Walter C. ... Lynbrook, NY
Marshall, Walter L., Jr. ... Woodbury, NJ
Marshall, Ward D. ... Salem, OR
Marshall, Watson C. ... Pittsburgh, PA
Marshall, Watson M. ... Richmond, VA
Marshall, Wayna M., P.C.
Colorado Springs, CO
Marshall, Wayne S. ... Encino, CA
Marshall, Wayne S., A Professional Law Corporation ... Encino, CA
Marshall, Wentworth J., Jr.
Cleveland, OH
Marshall, Wesley G. ... Fredericksburg, VA
Marshall, Wesley J., Jr. ... Boston, MA
Marshall Wheeler Zaug LaBorde, PLLC
Seattle, WA
Tacoma, WA
Marshall, William A. ... Roseburg, OR
Marshall, William A. ... Houston, TX
Marshall, William A. ... Salt Lake City, UT
Marshall, William B., Jr. ... Denver, CO
Marshall, William D., Jr. ... Memphis, TN
Marshall, William E., Jr., (P.A.)
Raleigh, NC
Marshall, William F. ... Columbus, IN
Marshall, William F., Jr. ... Danbury, NC
Marshall, William J. ... Princeton, IN
Marshall, William J., Jr. ... Wilmette, IL
Marshall, William M. ... Charlottesville, VA
Marshall, William M., Jr. ... Youngstown, OH
Marshall, William N., III ... Grandview, MO
Marshall, William P. ... Philadelphia, PA
Marshall, William Porter ... Cleveland, OH
Marshall, William R., Jr. ... Richmond, VA
Marshall, William S. ... Miami, FL
Marshall, William S., Jr.
New Orleans, LA
Marshall, William T. ... Little Rock, AR
Marshall, William T. ... Portsmouth, OH
Marshall, William T., Jr.
Green Village, NJ
New York, NY
Marshall, William W., III ... Grand Island, NE
Marshall, Williams & Gorham, L.L.P.
Wilmington, NC
Marshall & Willis ... Salt Lake City, UT
Marshall, Wm. Bynum ... Sparta, NC
Marshall, Wyre J. ... San Antonio, TX
Marshall, Zofia Kessler ... Chicago, IL
Marshall-Morley, Mary Ann ... Newark, NJ
Marshall-Needleman, Brenda ... Dallas, TX
Marshall-Walker, Robert W.
San Francisco, CA
Marshbanks, M. Lynn ... Raleigh, NC
Marshburn, Christopher S. ... Memphis, TN
Marshburn, G. Wriston, Jr
Winston-Salem, NC
Marshek, Ronald S. ... Beachwood, OH
Marshek, Ronald S., Co. L.P.A.
Beachwood, OH
Cleveland, OH
Marshik, Lisa J. ... Sioux Falls, SD
Marshman, Homer H., Jr., Law Offices of
Palm Beach, FL
Marsh-Raetz, Linda ... Traverse City, MI
Marsh Stormer, Elinore ... Akron, OH
Marsi, Fredk. V. ... Vestal, NY
Marsich, Veronica A. ... East Lansing, MI
Marsick, Philip J. ... Cincinnati, OH
Marsico, Anthony J. ... New York, NY
Marsico, Douglas K. ... Harrisburg, PA
Marsico, Frank J. ... Chicago, IL
Marsico, Karen J. ... New York, NY
Marsico, Leonard J. ... Pittsburgh, PA
Marsico, Nick ... Chicago, IL
Marsico, Richard ... New York, NY
Marsico, Richard D., Jr. ... Bronx, NY
Marsico, Robert A. ... Newark, NJ
Marsicovetere, Sharetha S. ... Montpelier, VT
Marsiglia, Gregory S. ... New Orleans, LA
Marsiglia, John V. ... New Orleans, LA
Marsiglia, Victor A., Jr. ... Metairie, LA
Marsigliano, John L. ... Baldwin, NY
Marsik, J. Scott ... Westmont, IL
Marsili, Anthony G. ... Greensburg, PA
Marsili, Maria ... Scranton, PA
Marsili, Yolanda ... San Bernardino, CA
Marsilio, Tommie J. ... Columbus, OH
Marsillo, Lino A. ... Missoula, MT
Marsillo, Susan ... Miami, FL
Marsillo, Tornabene, Schuyler & McKenna
Missoula, MT
Marsillo, William ... Armonk, NY
Marske, Larry K. ... Kansas City, MO
Marske, William N. ... Michigan City, IN
Marsland, Ana Maria ... Austin, TX
Marsland, Charles F., Jr. ... Honolulu, HI
Marsnik, Susan J. ... Minneapolis, MN
Marso, Lisa Hansen ... Sioux Falls, SD
Marso, Paul F. ... Minneapolis, MN
Marso, Therese Marie ... Minneapolis, MN
St. Paul, MN
Marso, Virginia A. ... St. Cloud, MN
Marsocci, Jeffrey ... Raleigh, NC
Marsolais, Elaine M. ... Montgomery, TX
Marson, Allan K. A. ... New York, NY
Marson, Charles C. ... San Francisco, CA
Marson, Deborah ... Boston, MA
Marson, Jay ... White Plains, NY
Marson, Ralph E. ... New York, NY
Marstad, Betsy L. ... Minneapolis, MN
Marsteller, Derek W. ... Huntington, WV
Marsteller & Hayes ... Ironton, OH
Huntington, WV
Marsteller, Marcia E. ... Cleveland, OH
Marsteller, Thomas F., Jr. ... Dallas, TX
Marsten, David ... Calistoga, CA
Marsten, Michelle Robinson ... San Jose, CA
Marstiller, James A. ... Clarksburg, WV
Marstiller, Philip S. ... Richmond, VA
Marstiller, Philip S., P.C. ... Richmond, VA
Marstin, Ronald ... Louisville, KY
Marston, Andrea L. ... Manchester, NH
Marston, Blythe W. ... Anchorage, AK
Marston, Brett ... Roanoke, VA
Marston, C. Henry ... Birmingham, AL
Marston & Cole, P.C. ... Anchorage, AK
Marston, David W. ... Philadelphia, PA
Marston, Donald E. ... Wilmington, DE
Marston, Douglas J. ... Fort Morgan, CO
Marston, Edgar J., III ... Houston, TX
Marston, Eileen A. ... Rockville, MD
Marston, Elizabeth J. ... Miami, FL
Marston, Erin B. ... Anchorage, AK
Marston, Frank J. ... Tallahassee, FL
Marston, Glenn Alan ... Reston, VA
Marston, Hall R. ... Los Angeles, CA
Marston & Heffernan, PLLC
Bellevue, WA
Marston, James D. ... Austin, TX
Marston, James T. ... Monroe, WA
Marston, Jeffrey P. ... Rockville, MD
Marston, Jerrilyn G. ... Philadelphia, PA
Marston, John C. ... Doylestown, PA
Marston, Joseph G. L., III ... Montgomery, AL
Marston, Karen S. ... Charlotte, NC
Marston, Lester J. ... Ukiah, CA
Marston, Margaret S. ... Birmingham, AL
Marston, Michael V. ... Detroit, MI
Marston, Philip M. ... Washington, DC
Marston, Robert E. ... Sherwood, AR
Marston, Sarah E. ... Boston, MA
Marston, Terry R., II ... Bellevue, WA
Marston, W. Emmett ... Memphis, TN
Marston, W. Wesley ... Gainesville, FL
Marston, Walter A., Jr. ... Richmond, VA
Marston-Moore, Elizabeth ... Germantown, TN
Marszal, Lisa A. ... Chicago, IL
Marszalek, James J. ... Chicago, IL
Marszalek, John E. ... Chicago, IL
Marszalek, Joseph D. ... Palos Heights, IL
Marszalek & Marszalek ... Chicago, IL
Marszalkowski, Michael E. ... Buffalo, NY
Mart & deVries ... Sacramento, CA
Mart, H. Kevin
Charlotte Amalie, St. Thomas, VI
Mart, James D. ... Sacramento, CA
Mart, Susan Nevelow ... Berkeley, CA
Marta, Martin P. ... Chicago, IL
Marta, Wayne P. ... Cleveland, OH
Marta, Wayne P., Co., L.P.A. ... Cleveland, OH
Martabano, Charles V. ... Mount Kisco, NY
Martahus, Craig R. ... Cleveland, OH
Martaus, Cecilia M. ... Cleveland, OH
Marte, Charles O., Jr. ... Langhorne, PA
Marte, Keith, Falkenstein, Sullivan, Meggers & Paul, P.C. ... Manchester, CT
Marte, Paul R. ... Manchester, CT
Marte and Toadvine ... Langhorne, PA
Marteeny, Kathryn & Associates
Houston, TX
Marteeny, Kathryn P. ... Houston, TX
Marte-Indzonka, Michele Mary ... Bronx, NY
Martel, Charles F. ... Washington, DC
Martel, Charles R. ... San Francisco, CA
Martel, David J. ... Springfield, MA
Martel, Elaine A. ... Bedford, MA
Martel, Eleanor L. ... Atlanta, GA
Martel, Jane G. ... Springfield, MA
Martel, Jeffrey A. ... New York, NY
Martel, John G. ... Portland, OR
Martel, John S. ... San Francisco, CA
Martel, Jonathan S. ... Washington, DC
Martel, Kathryn E. ... Okemos, MI
Martel, Lauren L. ... Hilton Head Island, SC
Martel, Louis V. ... Glendale, CA
Martel, Mark W. ... Palo Alto, CA
Martel, Matthew A. ... Boston, MA
Martel, Nina H. ... Sturgeon Bay, WI
Martel, Richard I., Jr. ... Baltimore, MD
Martelino, JoséA.G., Jr. ... Richmond, VA
Martell, Alice Fried ... New York, NY
Martell & Associates ... Washington, DC
Martell, Blake W. ... San Francisco, CA
Martell, Charles E., P.C. ... Kalamazoo, MI
Martell, Dale F. ...
Department of Justice, GV
Martell, Donald H. ... Kent, OH
Martell, Donald M. ... Sonora, CA
Martell, Donnelly, Grimaldi & Gallagher, P.A. ... Washington, DC
Rockville, MD
Fairfax, VA
Martell, Frank J. ... Washington, DC
Rockville, MD
Martell, James A. ... Fort Collins, CO
Martell, James L. ... Melville, NY
Martell, Javier F. ... San Rafael, CA
Martell, Joseph E. ... Ashland, WI
Martell, Karen S. ... Saratoga Springs, NY
Martell, Leslie G. ... Charlotte, NC
Martell, Linda S. ... Honolulu, HI
Martell, Martha ... West Des Moines, IA
Martell, Mary ... Washington, DC
Martell, Mary Anne ... Fort Collins, CO
Martell, Matthew Z. ... Fort Lauderdale, FL
Martell, Michael L. ... New York, NY
Martell, Michele J. ... Los Angeles, CA
Martell, Patrick J. ... Emeryville, CA
Martell, Pedro F. ... Coral Gables, FL
Martell, Pedro F., P.A. ... Coral Gables, FL
Martell, Réné A. ... Wolf Point, MT
Martell, Richard B. ... Tallahassee, FL
Martell, Ronald E. ... Minneapolis, MN
Martell, Saundra A. ... Bloomington, MN
Martell, Thomas J. ... Shawano, WI
Martell, Wayne R. ... Elmsford, NY
Martella & Corrado ... Bloomfield, NJ
Martella, David L. ... Worcester, MA
Martella, Jennifer E. ... Washington, DC
Martella, Mario A. ... Culver City, CA
Martella, Mark ... Bloomfield, NJ
Martella, Roger R., Jr. ... Department of Justice, Environment and Natural Resources Division, GV
Martelle Law Offices, P.A. ... Boise, ID
Martelle, Martin J. ... Boise, ID
Martelle, Robert Kenneth
Rutherfordton, NC
Martelli, Cynthia C. ... Philadelphia, PA
Martelli, Monica L. ... Costa Mesa, CA
Martelli, Paul L. ... Modesto, CA
Martellino, Paul ... Newport, RI
Martell-Jovet, Marcelle D. ... San Juan, PR
Martello, James P. ... Cleveland, OH
Martello, Michael D. ... Mountain View, CA
Martello, Patric ... Jamaica, NY
Martello, Suzanne Elswick ... Columbus, OH
Martello, Thomas F., Jr. ... Columbus, OH
Martelon, George F., Jr. ... Milford, CT
Martemucci, James F. ... Portland, ME
Marten, Bradley M. ... Seattle, WA
Marten & Brown LLP ... Olympia, WA
Seattle, WA
Marten, Catherine ... New York, NY
Marten, J. Thomas ... Wichita, KS
Marten, Judd R. ... Seattle, WA
Marten, Kenneth L. ... Mineola, NY
Marten, Ramona J ... St Louis, MO
Martenet, David L. ... Indianapolis, IN
Marteney, Cheryl A. ... New Bern, NC
Marteney, M. Paul ... Charleston, WV
Martens, Adrian J. ... Mount Pocono, PA
Martens, Brian R. ... Minneapolis, MN
Martens, Christopher W. ... Middletown, NY
Martens, Dan E. ... Addison, TX
Martens, Daniel L. ... Los Angeles, CA
Martens, Don W., (P.C.)
Newport Beach, CA
Martens Dunaj Marlowe Davis & Marlowe
Fort Lauderdale, FL
Miami, FL
New Port Richey, FL
Martens, Erin E. ... Los Angeles, CA
Martens, Franklin A. ... Columbus, OH
Martens, George F. ... Denver, CO
Martens, Harlan Craig ... Houston, TX
Martens, Ice, Geary, Klass, Legghio, Israel & Gorchow, P.C. ... Southfield, MI
Martens, James Frederick ... Austin, TX
Martens, Jeffrey D. ... Moline, IL
Martens, John G. ... Estherville, IA
Martens, John J. ...
Department of Defense, GV
Martens, Kenneth R. ... Marengo, IA
Victor, IA
Martens, Kim R. ... Wichita, KS
Martens Law Office ... Marengo, IA
Victor, IA
Martens, Lisa M. ... Menlo Park, CA
Martens, Lonnie K. (Browne)
West Palm Beach, FL
Martens, Mark P. ... Englewood, CO
Martens, Mary ... Monroe, LA
Martens, Matthew T. ... Newark, NJ
Martens, Michael John ... Boston, MA
Martens, Norma B. ... Phoenix, AZ
Martens, Richard G. ... Ruby, NY
Martens, Richard L. ... Seattle, WA
Martens, Richard L., (P.A.)
West Palm Beach, FL
Martens, Robert B., Jr. ... Bradford, MA
Martens, Sharon W. ... Grafton, ND
Martens, Steven P. ... Denver, CO
Martens, Steven R. ... Austin, TX
Martens, Tara ... Twin Falls, ID
Martens, Timothy J. ... Chandler, AZ
Martens, W. Keith ... Rock Hill, SC
Martens, William C., Jr. ... Fishers, IN
Martens, William L. ... Southfield, MI
Martensen, Andrew & Niemann ... Paxton, IL
Martensen, Finn ... Sacramento, CA
Martensen, Robert E. ... Paxton, IL
Martenson, David L. ... Rockford, IL
Martenson, Eugene D. ... Birmingham, AL
Martenson, Greenlee & Kreitlow, P.C.
Rockford, IL
Martenson, Marty N. ... Atlanta, GA
Marter, Andrew J. ... Rockville, MD
Marter, Cyrus D., IV ... Houston, TX
Marth, Letitia D. ... Toledo, OH
Marth, Paul E. ... Greensboro, NC
Marth, Wm. J. ... West Bend, WI
Martha, J. Paul ... Pittsburgh, PA
Marthage, Brian K. ... Poultney, VT
Marthaler, Annette Lynn ... Rockville, MD
Marthaler, Jamie Sue ... Baltimore, MD
Marthaler, Kathleen A. ... Bethesda, MD
Marthaller, Chris R. ... McMinnville, OR
Marthinsen, Hugh H. ... Phoenix, AZ
Marti, Alicia L. ... Washington, DC
Marti, Daniel H. ... Miami, FL
Marti, Douglas ... Greenville, IL
Marti, Jon P. ... Warren, PA
Marti, Lydia S. ... Chicago, IL
Marti, Maria E. ... Brooklyn, NY
Marticelli, Joseph J. ... Pittsford, NY
Martick, Alexander R. ... Baltimore, MD
Marti-Colon, Noelia ... Glendale, CA
Marticorena, Lynda E. ... Laguna Hills, CA
Marticorena, William M. ... Costa Mesa, CA
Martie, Lee R. ... Monticello, MN
Martielli, Marina M ... Patchogue, NY
Martien, Charles P. ... Boulder, CO
Martier, Robert L. ... Chicago, IL
Martiesian, Terrance S. ... Providence, RI
Martignetti, Joseph A. ... Boston, MA
Martignetti, Ronald F. ... Coral Springs, FL
Martillotta, Samuel R. ... Cleveland, OH
Martillotti, Gerard J. ... Philadelphia, PA
Martillotti, Jay A. ... Scranton, PA
Martillotti, Mary Ann
Plymouth Meeting, PA
Martin, A.J., Esquire, P.C. ... Monroeville, PA
Martin, A. Keith ... Eugene, OR
Martin, A. Lee, Jr. ... Birmingham, AL
Martin, A. Manuel ... San Juan, PR
Martin, A. René ... Boise, ID
Martin, Aaron D. ... Kennett Square, PA
Martin, Abby L. ... Atlanta, GA
Martin, Ade, Birchfield & Mickler, P.A.
Fernandina Beach, FL
Jacksonville, FL
Jacksonville Beach, FL
Lake City, FL
Ocala, FL
St. Augustine, FL
Martin, A. J. ... Monroeville, PA
Martin, Alan ... Department of Transportation, Federal Aviation Administration, GV
Martin, Alan Braddy ... Lexington, NC
Martin, Alan H. ... Costa Mesa, CA
Martin, Alan J. ... Chicago, IL
Martin, Albert E., III ... Atlanta, GA
Martin, Albert K. ... San Mateo, CA
Martin, Alethia A. ... Houston, TX
Martin, Alice Howze ... Florence, AL
Martin, Alice O. ... Chicago, IL
Martin, Alison L. ... Butler, PA
Martin, Allan A. ... New York, NY
Martin, Allan L. ... Treasury Department, U.S. Customs Service, GV
Martin, Allen ... Burlington, VT
Martin, Alson R. ... Overland Park, KS
Martin, Alton A. ... Richmond, VA
Martin, Alton L., Jr. ... Greenville, SC
Martin, Alvin C. ... Florham Park, NJ
New York, NY
Martin, Amanda A. ... Houston, TX
Martin, Amy C. ... Nashville, TN
Martin, Amy D. ... Oakland, CA
Martin, Amy Jo ... Clearwater, FL
Martin, Andrea E. ... Clarence, NY
Martin, Andrew S. ... Raleigh, NC
Martin, Andrew W. ... Cedar Rapids, IA
Martin, Angela F. ... Cumming, GA
Martin, Angela L. ... Phoenix, AZ
Martin, Anna Maria ... San Francisco, CA
San Francisco, CA
Martin, Anne C. ... Rockville, MD
Martin, Anne Clayton ... Nashville, TN
Martin, Annette F. ... Cedar Rapids, IA
Martin, Anthony D. ... Boston, MA
Martin, Anthony J. ... Monroeville, PA
Martin, Anthony L. ... St. Louis, MO
Martin, Anthony P. ... Los Angeles, CA
Martin, Antonia E. ... San Diego, CA
Martin, Areva Bell ... Los Angeles, CA
Martin, Aric D. ... Cleveland, OH
Martin, Arif & Petrovich ... Springfield, VA
Martin, Arlene E. ... Chicago, IL
Martin, Armen S. ... Palo Alto, CA
Martin, Arthur B. ... Miles City, MT
Martin, Arthur B. L. ... Atlanta, GA
Martin, Arthur J. ... St. Louis, MO
Martin, Arthur J. ... Fayetteville, NY
Martin, Arthur J., Jr. ... Caldwell, NJ
Martin, Arthur L. ... Los Angeles, CA
Martin, Arthur L. ... Los Angeles, CA
Martin, Arthur Mead ... Chicago, IL
Martin & Associates ... Tulsa, OK
Martin & Associates, A Professional Corporation ... Austin, TX
Martin & Associates, L.L.C. ... Phoenix, AZ
Martin & Associates, LLC ... Carthage, MO
Martin & Associates, LLC ... New York, NY
Martin & Associates, P.A.
Minneapolis, MN
Martin & Associates, P.C. ... Joplin, MO
Springfield, MO

Martin & Associés, LLC ... **New York, NY**
Martin, Atea ... **New York, NY**
Martin, Aubrey D., Jr. ... Houston, TX
Martin, Augustus C. ... **Allentown, PA**
Martin, B. Douglas ... Greensboro, NC
Martin, B. Franklin, III, (P.C.)
New Orleans, LA
Martin, B. G. ... Winston-Salem, NC
Martin, B. Keith ... **Santa Barbara, CA**
Martin, B. M., & Associates, P.C.
Jasper, GA
Martin, B. Morris ... **Jasper, GA**
Martin, Bacon & Martin, P.C.
Detroit, MI
Mount Clemens, MI
Pontiac, MI
Martin, Bailey & MacDonald
Cincinnati, OH
Martin, Banks, Pond, Lehocky & Wilson
Philadelphia, PA
Martin, Barbara A. ... **Detroit, MI**
Martin, Barbara G. ... **Danville, PA**
Martin, Barbara H. ... **Marietta, GA**
Martin, Barbara J. ... Huntington Woods, MI
Martin, Barbara J. ... Jackson, MO
Martin, Baron H. ... Boston, MA
Martin, Barry D. ... **Overland Park, KS**
Martin, Barry S. ... Sacramento, CA
Martin, Beaumont ... Bellaire, TX
Martin, Ben C. ... **Dallas, TX**
Martin, Benjamin G., III ... Sarasota, FL
Martin, Benjamin R. ... **Los Angeles, CA**
Martin & Bennis, P.A. ... Fort Lauderdale, FL
Martin, Bentford E. ... **Charlotte, NC**
Martin, Bernard J. ... Winter Park, FL
Martin, Bernard J., P.E. ... Winter Park, FL
Martin, Bernard T., Jr. ... La Grange, IL
Martin, Beverly B. ... Macon, GA
Martin, Bill A., Sr. ... Newton, TX
Martin, Bill R. ... Lexington, TN
Martin, Billy L. ... Okmulgee, OK
Martin, Billy R. ... Longview, TX
Martin, Bischoff, Templeton, Langslet & Hoffman, LLP ... **Anchorage, AK**
Portland, OR
Martin, Blake A. ... Conway, SC
Martin, Blake E. ... Chambersburg, PA
Martin, Bobby F., Jr. ... **Memphis, TN**
Martin, Bobby G. ... Winston-Salem, NC
Martin, Boe W. ... **Dallas, TX**
Martin & Bonnett, P.L.L.C. ... Phoenix, AZ
Martin, Bonnie L. ... **Muncie, IN**
Martin, Bonnie Lee ... Los Angeles, CA
Martin, Bonnie Mahon ... **Bradenton, FL**
Martin, Boyce F., III ... **Louisville, KY**
Martin, Boyce F., Jr. ... Louisville, KY
Martin & Brackin ... Dothan, AL
Martin, Brad ... New York, NY
Martin, Bradford Neal ... **Greenville, SC**
Martin, Bradford R., Jr. ... **Springfield, MA**
Martin, Bradley J. ... Chicago, IL
Martin, Bradley J. ... Findlay, OH
Martin, Brandon C. ... Richmond, VA
Martin, Brandon L. ... Freehold, NJ
New Brunswick, NJ
Somerville, NJ
Martin, Brandye Caroline ... Columbia, SC
Martin, Brant C. ... **Dallas, TX**
Martin, Brecount & Rush, P.L.L.
Springfield, OH
Martin, Bredt D. ... **Los Angeles, CA**
Martin, Breen & Merrick ... **Chicago, IL**
Oak Park, IL
Martin, Brenda K. ... **Phoenix, AZ**
Martin, Brent L. ... **St. Peters, MO**
Martin, Brent M. ... **Denver, CO**
Martin, Brent W. ... Blytheville, AR
Martin, Brett W. ... **Denver, CO**
Martin, Brett W., P.C. ... **Denver, CO**
Martin, Brian ... **Houston, TX**
Martin, Brian D. ... **San Diego, CA**
Martin, Brian D. ... **Kansas City, MO**
Martin, Brian E. ... **Chicago, IL**
Martin, Brian J. ... **New York, NY**
Martin, Brian James ... Birmingham, AL
Martin, Brian P. ... Sterling, IL
Martin, Brian S. ... **Houston, TX**
Martin Brothers, P.C. ... Atlanta, GA
Martin, Brown & Sullivan, Ltd.
Chicago, IL
Martin, Browne, Hull & Harper, P.L.L.
London, OH
Springfield, OH
Urbana, OH
Xenia, OH
Yellow Springs, OH
Martin, Bruce A. ... Wichita Falls, TX
Martin, Bruce E. ... **Phoenix, AZ**
Martin, Bruce G. ... Bremerton, WA
Martin, Bruce W. ... Tucson, AZ
Martin, Bruce W. ... Kalamazoo, MI
Martin & Brunavs ... Atlanta, GA
Martin, Bryan E. ... Blue Springs, MO
Martin, Bryan G. ... Fresno, CA
Martin, Bryce N. ... Santa Rosa, CA
Martin, Burchard S. ... **Westmont, NJ**
Martin, Burchard V. ... **Westmont, NJ**
Martin, Burke ... Houston, TX
Martin, Burt M. ... Houston, TX
Martin, C. Amanda ... **Raleigh, NC**
Martin, C. Gerald ... Winchester, KY
Martin, C. Keith ... Natchez, MS
Martin, C. Rabon ... Tulsa, OK
Martin, C. Richard ... **Milford, OH**
Martin, C. Richard ... Austin, TX
Martin, C. Truitt, Jr. ... Dawson, GA
Martin, C. Wendell ... Indianapolis, IN
Martin, C. Wesley ... Fairfield, CT
Martin, Caleb B., Jr. ... Detroit, MI
Martin, Cara L. ... Santa Ana, CA
Martin, Carl J. ... Garrison, ND
Martin, Carl N., II ... Philadelphia, PA
Martin, Carla Alexandria Young
St. Louis, MO
Martin, Carla J.
Department of Transportation, Federal Aviation Administration, GV
Martin, Carla L. ... Houston, TX
Martin, Carmel, Jr. ... **Monterey, CA**
Martin, Carmen S. ... Ojai, CA
Martin, Carol A. ... Chicago, IL
Martin, Carol A. ... Cincinnati, OH
Martin, Carol F. ... Amarillo, TX
Martin, Carol L. ... **Palo Alto, CA**
Martin, Carol L. ... Pueblo, CO
Martin, Carol L. K. ... Western Springs, IL
Martin, Carolyn Jean ... Long Beach, CA
Martin, Carolyn Wimbly ... **Arlington, VA**
Martin, Carroll Greer ... **Austin, TX**
Martin, Catherine G. ... Bangor, ME
Martin, Catherine Jurgensmeyer
Washington, DC
Martin, Cathleen A. ... **Jefferson City, MO**
Martin, C. D. ... **Midland, TX**
Martin, Cecil E., III ... **Baltimore, MD**
Martin, Cecilia Ackels ... Dallas, TX
Martin, C. G. Gordon ... Pasadena, CA
Martin, Chanley M. ... Louisville, KY
Martin, Channing J. ... **Richmond, VA**
Martin, Charlene M. ... Atlanta, GA
Martin, Charles Blake ... **Chicago, IL**
Martin, Charles C., Jr. ... Nashville, TN
Martin, Charles D. ... Gadsden, AL
Martin, Charles Dudley ... Springfield, MO
Martin, Charles E. ... Houston, TX
Martin, Charles E., Sr. ... Springfield, VA
Martin, Charles H. ... **Reston, VA**
Martin, Charles L. ... **Decatur, GA**
Martin, Charles L. ... Boonville, IN
Martin, Charles L., Jr. ... Bonifay, FL
Martin, Charles L., Law Offices of
Decatur, GA
Martin, Charles R. ... **Kingsport, TN**
Martin, Charles R. ... Springfield, VA
Martin, Charles S. ... Barre, VT
Martin, Charles T. ... **Chicago, IL**
Martin, Chas. C. ... Tybee Island, GA
Martin, Chas. R. ... San Marino, CA
Martin, Cheryl A. ... **Denver, CO**
Martin, Chris A. ... Lancaster, OH
Martin, Christine F. ... **Chicago, IL**
Martin, Christine R. ... Staten Island, NY
Martin, Christopher E. ... **Phoenix, AZ**
Martin, Christopher E. ... **Parsippany, NJ**
Martin, Christopher E. ... Portland, OR
Martin, Christopher G. ... **Stamford, CT**
New York, NY
Martin, Christopher J. ... **Palo Alto, CA**
Martin, Christopher J. ... Evergreen, CO
Martin, Christopher L. ... Houston, TX
Martin, Christopher M. ... **Chicago, IL**
Martin, Christopher M. ... **Philadelphia, PA**
Martin, Christopher P. ... **Tawas City, MI**
Martin, Christopher W. ... **Knoxville, TN**
Martin, Christopher W. ... **Houston, TX**
Martin, Chrys A. ... **Portland, OR**
Martin, Churchill, Blair, Hill, Cole & Hollander, Chartered ... **Wichita, KS**
Martin, Cindy Galpin ... **New Orleans, LA**
Martin, Clara Ruyan ... **Los Angeles, CA**
Martin, Clarence A., III ... **Monroe, LA**
Martin, Clarence E., III ... Hagerstown, MD
Martinsburg, WV
Martin, Claudia J. ... **Novato, CA**
Martin, Clay ... **Huntsville, AL**
Martin, Clearwater & Bell ... **New York, NY**
Martin, Clifford ... Baltimore, MD
Martin, Clive D. ... **Boston, MA**
Martin, Clive Standlee, Jr. ... Long Beach, CA
Martin, Colin G. ... **Dallas, TX**
Martin, Colleen J. ... Wilmington, DE
Martin, Colleen Mahoney ... Dallas, TX
Martin, Conn Lee ... Garrett Park, MD
Martin, Connie R. ... **Las Cruces, NM**
Martin, Connie Sue Manos ... **Seattle, WA**
Martin, Cory M. ... Oakland, CA
Martin, Costello, Leiter, Downey & Steiger, P.C. ... **Springfield, MA**
Martin, Coy M. ... **Wichita, KS**
Martin, Craig A. ... Florence, AZ
Martin, Craig C. ... **Chicago, IL**
Martin, Craig, Chester & Sonnenschein
Chicago, IL
Oak Brook, IL
Martin, Craig J. ... **Falmouth, MA**
Taunton, MA
Martin, Craig T. ... Summit, IL
Martin, Crystal Wise ... **Jackson, MS**
Martin, Cuauhtemoc V. ... Montebello, CA
Martin, Curtis C. ... North Canton, OH
Martin, Curtis Joe ... Kansas City, MO
Martin, Curtis W. ... **Atlanta, GA**
Martin, Curtis W. ... **Mount Vernon, IL**
Martin, Cynthia A. ... **Birmingham, AL**
Martin, Cynthia Anita-Reddick
House of Representatives, Congressional Assistants, GV
Martin, Cynthia Castle ... Redding, CA
Martin, Cynthia Marie ... **Santa Cruz, CA**
Martin, Cynthia Newberry ... Columbus, GA
Martin, D. Craig ... **Kalamazoo, MI**
Martin, D. Neal ... Shawnee, OK
Martin, D. Quinn ... Waterloo, IA
Martin, D. Ross ... **Boston, MA**
Martin, Dale P. ... **Morgan City, LA**
Martin, Dale R. ... Romulus, MI
Martin, Dale R. ... **Seattle, WA**
Martin, Dallas R. ... Englewood, CO
Martin, Damien J. ... Springfield, MA
Martin, Dan ... Lima, OH
Martin, Dana J. ... Washington, DC
Martin, Dana K. ... **Houston, TX**
Martin, Dana Lynn ... Richmond, VA
Martin, Dana R. ... United States Senate, Committee Legal Personnel, GV
Martin, Daniel ... Cheboygan, MI
Martin, Daniel ... Huntington, NY
Martin, Daniel A. ... Hindman, KY
Martin, Daniel A. ... Fremont, NE
Martin, Daniel D. ... West Chester, PA
Martin, Daniel E. ... Charleston, SC
Martin, Daniel G. ... **Phoenix, AZ**
Martin, Daniel G. ... Chicago, IL
Martin, Daniel J. ... San Diego, CA
Martin, Daniel L. ... Montclair, NJ
Martin, Daniel R. ... **Grand Haven, MI**
Martin, Daniel W. ... Malibu, CA
Martin, Darrell C., II ... Martinez, CA
Martin, Darrow & O'Bryan ... Cabot, AR
Martin, Daryl E. ... **Las Vegas, NV**
Martin, Daryll W. ... Memphis, TN
Martin, David A. ... **Chicago, IL**
Martin, David A. ... **Trenton, NJ**
Martin, David A. ... Charlottesville, VA
Martin, David B. H. ... Barnstable, MA
Martin, David B. H., Jr. ... **Washington, DC**
Martin, David C., Jr. ... Pittsburgh, PA
Martin, David E. ... St. Louis, MO
Martin, David E. ... New York, NY
Martin, David E. ... **Myrtle Beach, SC**
Martin, David G. ... **Minneapolis, MN**
Martin, David G. ... **Raleigh, NC**
Martin, David H. ... **Los Angeles, CA**
Martin, David H. ... Taylorville, IL
Martin, David H. ... **Waco, TX**
Martin, David J. ... Lakeside, AZ
Martin, David J. ... Phoenix, AZ
Martin, David J. ... Berkeley, CA
Martin, David J. ... **Riverdale, MD**
Martin, David J. ... New York, NY
Martin, David J. ... Haverford, PA
Martin, David K. ... **Overland Park, KS**
Martin, David K. ... **Wichita, KS**
Martin, David L. ... San Mateo, CA
Martin, David L. ... **Washington, DC**
Martin, David L. ... **Jackson, MS**
Martin, David L. ... Sylvania, OH
Martin, David L. ... Toledo, OH
Martin, David L. ... **Seattle, WA**
Martin, David L., III ... **Moulton, AL**
Martin, David M. ... **Washington, DC**
Martin, David M. ... **Springfield, OH**
Martin, David N. ... Okemah, OK
Martin, David P. ... **Tuscaloosa, AL**
Martin, David P. ... **Little Rock, AR**
Martin, David P.
National Labor Relations Board, Office of Board Members, GV
Martin, David P. ... Franklin, KY
Martin, David P. ... **Syracuse, NY**
Martin, David S. ... **Chicago, IL**
Martin, David W. ... Rancho Cucamonga, CA
Martin, David W. ... **Covington, KY**
Martin, David W. ... Shelby Township, MI
Martin, David W. ... New York, NY
Martin, David W. ... **Houston, TX**
Martin, David W., P.C.
Shelby Township, MI
Martin, Davida W. ... Winston-Salem, NC
Martin, Dawn ... Washington, DC
Martin, Dawn Kimberly
Federal Energy Regulatory Commission, Office of the General Counsel, GV
Martin, Dean ... Sherman, TX
Martin, Dean Eric ... Seattle, WA
Martin, Deborah ... **Seattle, WA**
Martin, Deborah L. ... **Santa Barbara, CA**
Martin, Debra A. ... Rochester, NY
Martin, Debra A. ... Snohomish, WA
Martin, Delbert Eugene ... Las Vegas, NV
Martin, Denise ... **Palos Verdes Estates, CA**
Martin, Denise L. ... **New Orleans, LA**
Martin, Dennis A. ... Bala Cynwyd, PA
Martin, Dennis Duane ... Olympia, WA
Martin, Dennis E. ... Omaha, NE
Martin, Dennis G. ... **Los Angeles, CA**
Martin, Dennis G. ... Jonesville, NC
Martin, Dennis R. ... San Antonio, TX
Martin, Denny R., P.C. ... **Garland, TX**
Martin, Derek P. ... Carthage, MO
Martin, Deric ... Seattle, WA
Martin, Dewey Rick ... **Livonia, MI**
Martin, Dexter E. ... **Portland, OR**
Martin, Diana ... **Los Angeles, CA**
Martin, Diana L. ... Flint, MI
Martin, Diane Y. ... Atlanta, GA
Martin, Dolores ... Charleston, WV
Martin, Don G. ... Beaumont, TX
Martin, Don P. ... **Phoenix, AZ**
Martin, Donald ... Chicago, IL
Martin, Donald B. ... **Denver, CO**
Littleton, CO
Martin, Donald C. ... **Princeton, IL**
Martin, Donald C. ... Houston, TX
Martin, Donald D. ... Michigan City, IN
Martin, Donald E. ... **Lansing, MI**
Martin, Donald F. ... **Overland Park, KS**
Martin, Donald G. ... **Las Vegas, NV**
Reno, NV
Martin, Donald J. ... **Syracuse, NY**
Martin, Donald J. ... **Norristown, PA**
Martin, Donald K. ... Grand Junction, CO
Martin, Donald K. ... Hilo, HI
Martin, Donald L. ... Ellis, KS
Martin, Donald L. ... Twinsburg, OH
Martin, Donald L. ... Houston, TX
Martin, Donald R. ... Pittsburgh, PA
Martin, Donald R., Jr.
Oklahoma City, OK
Martin, Donna L. ... Suffern, NY
Martin, Donnie E. ... **Lexington, KY**
Martin, Doris L. ... **Great Neck, NY**
Martin, Dorsey C., III ... Baton Rouge, LA
Martin, Douglas ... **Indian Wells, CA**
Martin, Douglas, A Law Corporation
Indian Wells, CA
Palm Springs, CA
Martin, Douglas B., Jr. ... San Francisco, CA
Martin, Douglas E. ... **Mount Olive, NJ**
Martin, Douglas G. ... **Phoenix, AZ**
Martin, Douglas M. ... **Charlotte, NC**
Martin, Douglas M. ... Madison, WI
Martin, Douglas P. ... **Phoenix, AZ**
Martin, Douglas R. ... Bayou La Batre, AL
Martin, Drought & Torres, Inc.
McAllen, TX
San Antonio, TX
Martin, Duane ... Manteca, CA
Martin, Duane A. ... **Liberty, MO**
Martin, Duane C. ... Indianapolis, IN
Martin, E. Franklin ... Waynesboro, PA
Martin, E. Gregory ... **Boulder, CO**
Martin, E. Snow ... **Lakeland, FL**
Martin, E. Snow, Jr. ... **Lakeland, FL**
Martin, Earle P., III ... Houston, TX
Martin, E. B., Jr. ... Jackson, MS
Martin, Eddy Dale ... Dallas, TX
Martin, Edgar H. ... Washington, DC
Martin, Edward C. ... Birmingham, AL
Martin, Edward C. ... **Charleston, WV**
Martin, Edward F. ... **New Orleans, LA**
Martin, Edward H. ... **New York, NY**
Martin, Edward J. ... Lockport, NY
Martin, Edward J., III ... **New York, NY**
Martin, Edward R. ... **Boston, MA**
Martin, Edward R. ... Whitehouse, NJ
Martin, Edward S. ... Washington, PA
Martin, Edward W. ... **Wayne, NJ**
Martin & Edwards ... Honesdale, PA
Martin, Edwin A. ... Waterbury, CT
Martin, Edwin E. ... Toledo, OH
Martin, Edwin M., Jr. ... **Washington, DC**
Martin, Edwin P., Jr. ... **Columbia, SC**
Martin, Edwina F. ... New York, NY
Martin, E. F., Jr. ... Hartford, KY
Martin, Eileen ... **Buffalo, NY**
Martin, Elaine M. ... Omaha, NE
Martin, ElChino M. ... Washington, DC
Martin, Eleanor Frances ... Brockton, MA
Martin, Elizabeth A. ... Lake City, FL
Martin, Elizabeth A. ... Cincinnati, OH
Martin, Elizabeth A. H. K. Pa ... Honolulu, HI
Martin, Elizabeth H. ... St. Paul, MN
Martin, Elizabeth P.
United States Postal Service, Law Department, GV
Martin, Elizabeth Palmer ... **New York, NY**
Martin, Elizabeth Pike ... **Seattle, WA**
Tacoma, WA
Martin, Elizabeth W. ... Charlotte, NC
Martin, Ella S. ... Los Angeles, CA
Martin, Ellen M. ... **New York, NY**
Martin, Ellen Sullivan ... Kansas City, MO
Martin, Elmer Dean, III ... **Irvine, CA**
Martin, Elton F. ... Menlo Park, CA
Martin, Elveta M. ... Kensington, MD
Martin, Enrique J. ... **Miami, FL**
Martin, Eric A. ... Jefferson City, MO
Martin, Eric D. ... **St. Louis, MO**
Martin, Eric D. ... **Zanesville, OH**
Martin, Eric L. ... Atlanta, GA
Martin, Erica Kelly ... Los Angeles, CA
Martin, Ernest A., Jr. ... Gladewater, TX
Martin, Ernest G., Jr. ... Gulfport, MS
Martin, Ernest, Jr. ... **Dallas, TX**
Martin, Eugene L. ... Huron, SD
Martin, Eunice Lorraine
North Miami Beach, FL
Martin, Everett A., Jr. ... Norfolk, VA
Martin, Everette L. ... **Little Rock, AR**
Martin, E. X., III ... **Dallas, TX**
Martin, Faith ... **Morristown, NJ**
Martin & Farley, L.L.P. ... Houston, TX
Martin, Farr, Miller & Price, LLP
Dallas, TX
Houston, TX
Martin, Farris J., III ... **Miami, FL**
Martin, Faye Sanders ... Statesboro, GA
Martin, Felix M. ... **Los Angeles, CA**
Martin, Fenton L. ... **Baltimore, MD**
Martin, Fest & Jessel, LLC ... **Boulder, CO**
Martin Firm, The ... **Columbus, GA**
Martin, Flory L. ... **Vancouver, WA**
Martin, Fontaine ... New Orleans, LA
Martin, Frances H. ... **Milwaukee, WI**
Martin, Frances L. ... Torrance, CA
Martin, Francis X. ... Sandwich, MA
Martin, Francisco A. ... Sacramento, CA
Martin, Frank, Jr. ... Department of Agriculture, Office of the General Counsel, GV
Martin, Frank K. ... **Columbus, GA**
Martin, Frank M. ... Spokane, WA
Martin, Frank R. ... **Chicago, IL**
Martin, Franklin E. ... **Wilmington, NC**
Martin, Fred, Jr. ... Saginaw, MI
Martin, Frederick E. ... Williamsport, PA
Martin, Frederick H. ... Pennsauken, NJ
Martin, Frederick J. ... Monroe, CT
Martin, Frederick J. ... **White Plains, NY**
Martin, Frederick W., III ... West Plains, MO
Martin, Fredrick Joseph, III
White Plains, NY

Martin, Kathleen G. ....Caldwell, NJ
Martin, Kathleen M. ....Minneapolis, MN
Martin, Kathleen O. ....Department of Energy, Office of the General Counsel, GV
Martin, Kathryn E. ....Irvine, CA
Martin, Kathryn R. ....Everett, WA
Martin, Kathy J. ....Fayetteville, NC
Martin, Kathy King ....Charlotte, NC
Martin, Keith ....Washington, DC
Martin, Keith ....Overland Park, KS
Martin, Keith B. ....Largo, FL
Martin, Keith C. ....Arlington, VA
Martin, Keith D. ....Buffalo, NY
Martin, Keith E. ....Wichita, KS
Martin, Keith W. ....Neptune, NJ
Martin, Kelly ....Los Angeles, CA
Martin, Kelly Lynn ....Chicago, IL
Martin, Kenneth A. ....Washington, DC
Martin, Kenneth Bruce ....Pompano Beach, FL
Martin, Kenneth C. ....Charlotte, NC
Martin, Kenneth D. ....Rockford, IL
Martin, Kenneth D. ....Lewisville, TX
Martin, Kenneth D., & Associates, P.C.
Lewisville, TX
Martin, Kenneth F. ....Roseville, MI
Martin, Kenneth J. ....Boston, MA
Martin, Kenneth R. ....Goshen, IN
Martin, Kent A. ....Hales Corners, WI
Martin, Kerri L. ....New York, NY
Martin, Kevin B. ....Los Angeles, CA
Martin, Kevin G. ....Utica, NY
Martin, Kevin Jeffrey
Federal Communications Commission, Office of the Commissioners, GV
Martin, Kevin Richard ....San Jose, CA
Martin, Kevin T. ....Chicago, IL
Martin & Kieklak ....Fayetteville, AR
Martin, Kimberly B. ....Huntsville, AL
Martin, Kimberly D. ....Fort Wayne, IN
Martin, Kimberly N. ....Atlanta, GA
Martin, Kirk D. ....Weatherford, TX
Martin, Kirk E. ....Beaumont, TX
Martin, Krista K. ....Pine City, MN
Martin, Kristen H. ....Albany, NY
Martin, Kristin M. ....Fort Worth, TX
Martin, Kristine M.J. ....Department of Justice, Federal Bureau of Investigation, GV
Martin, Kyle D. ....Dayton, OH
Martin, Kyle L. ....Houston, TX
Martin, L. Don ....San Diego, CA
Martin, L. James ....Kent, OH
Martin, L. Morgan ....Conway, SC
Myrtle Beach, SC
Martin, Lance C. ....San Francisco, CA
Martin, Lance S. ....Lincolnwood, IL
Martin, Laree ....United States Postal Service, Mid-Atlantic Office, GV
Martin, Larnzell, Jr. ....Upper Marlboro, MD
Martin, Larry C. ....Seattle, WA
Martin, Larry D. ....Minneapolis, MN
Martin, Larry J. ....Milwaukee, WI
Martin, Larry L. ....Dallas, TX
Martin, Larry W. ....Chicago, IL
Martin, Latia W. ....Bronx, NY
Martin, Laura Enright ....Greenville, SC
Martin, Laura Grether ....Kansas City, MO
Martin, Laura H. ....Cincinnati, OH
Martin, Laura Jean ....San Antonio, TX
Martin, Laura Keidan ....Chicago, IL
Martin, Laura L. ....Upper Marlboro, MD
Martin, Laura S. ....Austin, TX
Martin, Laureen L. ....Wailuku, HI
Martin, Lauren B. ....Columbus, OH
Martin, Laurence H. ....Modesto, CA
Martin, Laurence R. ....Billings, MT
Martin, Lauri Kritt ....Los Angeles, CA
Martin Law Firm, P.A. ....Jasper, AR
Martin Law Firm, The ....Chicago, IL
Martin Law Office ....Oklahoma City, OK
Martin, Lawrence A. ....Hampton, VA
Martin, Lawrence A., P.C. ....Hampton, VA
Newport News, VA
Martin, Lawrence D. ....Colorado Springs, CO
Martin, Lawrence D. ....Naples, FL
Martin, Lawrence E. ....Yakima, WA
Martin, Lawrence H. ....Boston, MA
Martin, Lawrence M. ....New York, NY
Martin, Lawrence N., Jr. ....White Plains, NY
Martin, Leah A. ....Hartford, CT
Martin, Leanne B. ....Tempe, AZ
Martin, Leigh & Laws, P.C.
Kansas City, MO
Martin, Leo P. ....Council Bluffs, IA
Martin, Leonard C. ....Jackson, MS
Martin, Leonard E. ....Milwaukee, WI
Martin, Leonard N. ....Houston, TX
Martin, Leonard W. ....Charlotte, TN
Martin, LeRoy K ....Chicago, IL
Martin, Les A. ....Belle Chasse, LA
Martin, Leslie ....Garden City, NY
Martin, Leslie G. ....Dallas, TX
Martin, Leslie Jones ....Natchez, MS
Martin, Lester P., Jr. ....Mocksville, NC
Martin & Levasseur ....Towson, MD
Martin, Lewe B. ....Washington, DC
Martin, Lewis A., III ....Charlottesville, VA
Martin, Lewis A., Jr. ....Charlottesville, VA
Martin, Lewis W. ....Richmond, VA
Martin, Lillian Ros ....Miami, FL
Martin, Linda B. ....Santa Ana, CA
Martin, Linda C. ....Tulsa, OK
Martin, Linda H. ....New York, NY
Martin, Linda M. ....Philadelphia, PA
Martin, Linda M. ....Nashville, TN
Martin, Lindsey E. ....Oklahoma City, OK
Martin, Linzy E. ....Strawberry Point, IA
Martin, Lipsky, Kaufman & Weinstein, P.A.
Fort Lauderdale, FL
Miami, FL
Miami Lakes, FL
Martin, Lisa Anne ....Chicago, IL
Martin, Lisa Demet ....St. Louis, MO
Martin, Lisa Jennifer ....Los Angeles, CA
Martin, Lisa M. ....Fresno, CA
Martin, Lisa M. ....Orange, CA
Martin, Lisa Yoke ....Treasury Department, Bureau of the Public Debt, GV
Parkersburg, WV
Martin, Lizabeth A. ....Buffalo, NY
Martin, Lloyd A., II ....Alexandria, VA
Martin, Lloyd C. ....Huntsville, TX
Martin, Lloyd N. ....Lewiston, ME
Martin, Lois & Gasparrini, LLC
Stamford, CT
New York, NY
Martin, Lois J. ....Brookline, MA
Martin, Lord & Osman, P.A.
Concord, NH
Dover, NH
Laconia, NH
Lancaster, NH
Lebanon, NH
Wolfeboro, NH
Martin, Loren D. ....Salt Lake City, UT
Martin, Loren D., P.C. ....Salt Lake City, UT
Martin, Lori ....Dallas, TX
Martin, Louis ....Baltimore, MD
Martin, Louis R. ....Harrisburg, PA
Martin, Louis R. ....Harrisburg, PA
Martin, Lowell F. ....Washington, DC
Martin, Loyal R. ....Cherokee, IA
Martin, Ludger D. ....Gadsden, AL
Martin, Lutz, Roggow & Brower, P.C.
Las Cruces, NM
Martin, Lynn ....Conroe, TX
Martin, Lynn E. ....Paola, KS
Martin, M. Fleming, III ....Brunswick, GA
Martin, M. Jack, III ....Austin, TX
Martin, M. Kay ....Los Angeles, CA
San Francisco, CA
Martin, M. Linda ....Katonah, NY
Martin, M. Paul ....San Antonio, TX
Martin, M. Shannon ....Dayton, OH
Martin, M. Stanley ....Warner Robins, GA
Martin, Mack K. ....Oklahoma City, OK
Martin, Magnuson, McCarthy & Kenney
Boston, MA
Martin, Malcolm E. ....New York, NY
Martin, Malcolm W. ....St. Louis, MO
Martin, Maralene ....Houston, TX
Martin, Marc S. ....Washington, DC
Martin, Marc W. ....Chicago, IL
Martin, Marcia C. ....Parsippany, NJ
Martin, Marcus A. ....Chicago, IL
Martin, Margaret Ann ....Treasury Department, Internal Revenue Service, GV
Martin, Margaret Laughlin ....San Mateo, CA
Martin, Margaret R. ....Atlanta, GA
Martin, Margaret Rand ....Raleigh, NC
Martin, Marguerite Regan ....Kansas City, MO
Martin, Maria V. ....Montvale, NJ
Martin, Marie F ....St. Paul, MN
Martin, Marilyn Barker ....Georgetown, DE
Martin, Marilyn Herod ....New York, NY
Martin, Marilyn J. ....Chicago, IL
Martin, Marion Handley ....Atlanta, GA
Martin, Marjorie ....Houston, TX
Martin, Mark A. ....Chicago, IL
Martin, Mark B. ....Baltimore, MD
Martin, Mark C. ....Asheville, NC
Martin, Mark D. ....Raleigh, NC
Martin, Mark E. ....Washington, DC
Martin, Mark L. ....Fayetteville, AR
Martin, Mark R. ....Cincinnati, OH
Martin, Marlene M. ....San Antonio, TX
Martin, Marlene M. ....San Antonio, TX
Martin, Marsha B. (Higbee)
New Orleans, LA
Martin, Marsha L. ....Seattle, WA
Martin, Marshall A. ....Scottsdale, AZ
Martin, Marshall B. ....Norfolk, VA
Martin, Marshall G. ....Albuquerque, NM
Martin, Martha L. ....Oklahoma City, OK
Martin & Martin ....Berkeley, CA
Martin and Martin ....Merrillville, IN
Martin & Martin ....Saginaw, MI
Martin & Martin ....Comanche, OK
Martin and Martin, A Professional Corporation
Monroeville, PA
Martin & Martin, P.A. ....Lakeland, FL
Tampa, FL
Martin & Martin, P.A. A Professional Association ....Hillsborough, NC
Martin & Martin, P.C. ....Omaha, NE
Martin and Martin, P.C. ....Philadelphia, PA
Martin, Martin & Woodard, LLP
Syracuse, NY
Martin, Marty ....Raleigh, NC
Martin, Marvin B. ....Bryan, TX
Martin, Marvin J. ....Wichita, KS
Martin, Marvin L. ....Newport, KY
Martin, Mary ....Honolulu, HI
Martin, Mary A. ....Chicago, IL
Martin, Mary Ann
Department of Commerce, GV
Martin, Mary Anne O'Connor
Hoffman Estates, IL
Martin, Mary Beth ....Albany, NY
Martin, Mary E. ....San Diego, CA
Martin, Mary K. ....St. Paul, MN
Martin, Mary Kennedy ....East Aurora, NY
Martin, Mary Lou ....Joplin, MO
Martin, Mary Lou, P.C. ....Joplin, MO
Martin, Mary Messner ....New York, NY
Martin, Maryellen Sheehan ....Harrisburg, PA
Martin, Mason ....Conroe, TX
Martin, Matthew Alan ....Pontiac, MI
Martin, Matthew Charles ....Dallas, TX
Martin, Matthew Eric ....New York, NY
Martin, Matthew F.G. ....Columbus, OH
Martin, Matthew J. ....New York, NY
Martin, Matthew Scott ....Pueblo, CO
Martin, Maureen ....Chicago, IL
Martin, Maureen A. ....Hartland, VT
Martin, Maurice L. ....Saratoga, CA
Martin, Max A. ....Comanche, OK
Martin, McCarty, Richman & Wright Co., L.P.A. ....Fairborn, OH
Martin & McCormick ....Newport Beach, CA
Martin, McKinley C., Jr. ....Memphis, TN
Martin & Mehaffy, LLC ....Boulder, CO
Denver, CO
Martin, Melinda J. ....Tulsa, OK
Martin, Melissa A. ....Lebanon, NH
Martin, Merle M. ....Montclair, NJ
Martin, Mia M. ....Dallas, TX
Martin, Micaela H. ....San Diego, CA
Martin, Michael A. ....Rockville, MD
Martin, Michael A. ....Fishkill, NY
Martin, Michael A. ....Pittsburgh, PA
Martin, Michael B. ....San Diego, CA
Martin, Michael B. ....Naperville, IL
Martin, Michael B., P.C. ....Houston, TX
Martin, Michael D. ....Denver, CO
Martin, Michael D.
Department Of Veterans Affairs, Board of Veterans Appeals, GV
Martin, Michael D. ....Lakeland, FL
Martin, Michael D. ....Stephenville, TX
Martin, Michael D. ....Bellevue, WA
Martin, Michael E. ....New York, NY
Martin, Michael G. ....Denver, CO
Martin, Michael G. ....Seattle, WA
Martin, Michael Guy ....Montclair, CA
Martin, Michael H. ....Fort Worth, TX
Martin, Michael Hal ....Galliano, LA
Martin, Michael J. ....Chicago, IL
Martin, Michael J. ....Joliet, IL
Martin, Michael K. ....Department of Justice, Environment and Natural Resources Division, GV
Martin, Michael K. ....Portland, ME
Martin, Michael L.
Department of Transportation, Surface Transportation Board, GV
Martin, Michael L. ....Belle Chasse, LA
Martin, Michael Lawrence
San Francisco, CA
Martin, Michael M. ....New York, NY
Martin, Michael M. ....Lampasas, TX
Martin, Michael P. ....Atlanta, GA
Martin, Michael P. ....New York, NY
Martin, Michael Perry ....Pittsburgh, PA
Martin, Michael R. ....Enid, OK
Martin, Michael W. ....New York, NY
Martin, Michele E. ....Philadelphia, PA
Martin, Michelle F. ....Waukesha, WI
Martin, Middleton A. ....Washington, DC
Martin, Mike D. ....Norman, OK
Martin, Mildred D. ....Santa Ana, CA
Martin and Miller ....Houston, TX
Martin & Millican ....Lampasas, TX
Martin, Mireya Castillo ....Phoenix, AZ
Martin, Mitzi Harris ....Indianapolis, IN
Martin & Molinari, LLP ....Freeport, NY
Martin, Molly ....Del City, OK
Martin, Molly K. ....Milwaukee, WI
Martin, Mont L. ....Milwaukee, WI
Martin, Morrisann ....Baltimore, MD
Martin, Myron A. ....Oakland, CA
Martin, N. Keith ....Lee's Summit, MO
Martin, Nancy ....Comanche, OK
Martin, Nancy A. ....Sallisaw, OK
Martin, Nancy A. ....Houston, TX
Martin, Nancy E. ....San Francisco, CA
Martin, Nancy Eckert ....Springfield, IL
Martin, Nancy F. ....Houston, TX
Martin, Nancy L. ....Houston, TX
Martin, Nancy Lake ....Mount Olive, NJ
Martin, Nancy Sue Lebrecht ....St. Joseph, MO
Martin, Natasha T. ....Atlanta, GA
Martin, Nathalie ....Philadelphia, PA
Martin, Naurice Grant C. ....Houston, TX
Martin, Neil ....Houston, TX
Martin, Neil A. ....Worcester, MA
Martin, Neil B. ....Beverly Hills, CA
Martin, Neil D., (P.C.) ....Los Angeles, CA
Martin, Neil F. ....San Diego, CA
Martin, Nelson, Glasrud & Klopfleisch, P.A.
Morris, MN
Martin, Nelson and Glasrud, P.A.
Wheaton, MN
Martin, Nicole Duarte ....New Orleans, LA
Martin, Nicolle H. ....Denver, CO
Martin & Norman ....Prattville, AL
Martin, Norman J. ....Baldwinsville, NY
Martin, Norman Lee ....Tacoma, WA
Martin, Nutting, Miller, Pedersen, Pieters & Kelsen ....Waterloo, IA
Martin, O. Doyle ....Greenville, SC
Martin, Ockerman & Brabant
Lexington, KY
Martin, Olga L. ....Coral Gables, FL
Martin, P. Stephen ....Overland Park, KS
Martin, Paige A. ....Phoenix, AZ
Martin, Paige A. ....Columbus, OH
Martin, Paige A. Co., L.P.A. ....Columbus, OH
Martin, Pamela A. ....Bradenton, FL
Martin, Pamela A., P.A. ....Bradenton, FL
Martin, Pamela M. ....Lakewood, CO
Martin, Pamela Murch ....Washington, DC
Martin & Paolini, P.C. ....Barre, VT
Martin, Patricia A. ....Phoenix, AZ
Martin, Patricia A., P.C. ....Phoenix, AZ
Martin, Patricia Ann ....Pottstown, PA
Martin, Patricia J. ....Newton, IA
Martin, Patricia L. ....Washington, DC
Martin, Patricia L. ....Asbury, MO
Martin, Patricia L. ....Kansas City, MO
Martin, Patricia Manila ....Bridgeview, IL
Martin, Patricia Speake ....Hackensack, NJ
Martin, Patricia W. ....Versailles, KY
Martin, Patrick D. ....Rochester, NY
Martin, Patrick E. ....Buffalo, NY
Martin, Patrick E. ....North Syracuse, NY
Martin, Patrick F. ....Washington, DC
Martin, Patrick F. ....Atlantic City, NJ
Pleasantville, NJ
Martin, Patrick F. ....Jackson, TN
Martin, Patrick G. ....Denver, CO
Martin, Patrick H. ....Baton Rouge, LA
Martin, Patrick H., V ....Baton Rouge, LA
Martin, Patrick James ....Reno, NV
Martin, Patrick R. ....Minneapolis, MN
Martin, Patrick S. ....Gulf Breeze, FL
Martin, Patrick V. ....Jersey City, NJ
New York, NY
Martin, Patrick W. ....San Diego, CA
Martin, Patrick W. ....Chicago, IL
Martin, Patt, (Ms.) ....Tucson, AZ
Monroeville, PA
Martin, Paul ....Huntington Woods, MI
Martin, Paul A. ....Overland Park, KS
Martin, Paul A. ....Dallas, TX
Martin, Paul E. ....St. Louis, MO
Martin, Paul E. ....Houston, TX
Martin, Paul H. ....Neshanic Station, NJ
Martin, Paul J. ....Tallahassee, FL
Martin, Paul L. ....Mason City, IA
Martin, Paul N. ....Baldwinsville, NY
Martin, Paul R. ....Berkeley, CA
Martin, Paul R. ....Berkeley, CA
Martin, Paul S. ....Fort Lauderdale, FL
Martin, Paul S. ....Flushing, NY
Martin, Paul S. ....Ponca City, OK
Martin, Paul T. ....Los Angeles, CA
Martin, Paul T. ....Memphis, TN
Martin, Paul V. ....Ottawa, IL
Martin, Paul W. ....Rochester, NY
Martin, Paul W. ....Dayton, OH
Martin, Paula A. ....Philadelphia, PA
Martin, Paula B. ....Lawrence, KS
Martin, Paula J. ....Denver, CO
Martin, Pedro A. ....Miami, FL
Martin, Penny M. ....Fort Lauderdale, FL
Martin, Perry N. ....Birmingham, AL
Martin, Perry W. ....Ahoskie, NC
Martin, Peter A. ....Irvine, CA
Martin, Peter A. ....Redstone, CO
Martin, Peter A. ....Washington, DC
Martin, Peter A. ....Madison, WI
Martin, Peter A., P.C. ....Redstone, CO
Martin, Peter Andrew ....Commerce, CA
Martin, Peter F. ....Staten Island, NY
Martin, Peter J. ....Boston, MA
Martin, Peter J. ....Buffalo, NY
Martin, Peter J.R., P.C. ....St. Albans, VT
Martin, Peter J. R. ....St. Albans, VT
Martin, Peter M. D. ....Baltimore, MD
Martin, Peter R. ....Albany, NY
Martin, Peter T. ....Aberdeen, MS
Martin, Peter T. ....Dallas, TX
Martin, Peter W. ....Sarasota, FL
Martin, Peter W. ....Ithaca, NY
Martin & Pfluger ....Huntington, NY
Martin, Philip H. ....Chicago, IL
Martin, Philip L. ....Atlanta, GA
Martin, Phillip B. ....Minneapolis, MN
Martin, Phillip H., (P.A.)
Minneapolis, MN
Martin, Phlete A., III ....Corpus Christi, TX
Martin, Porter J. ....Madison, WI
Martin, Pringle, Oliver, Wallace & Swartz, L.L.P. ....Overland Park, KS
Wichita, KS
Kansas City, MO
Martin, Quinn W. ....Milwaukee, WI
Martin, R. Christopher ....New Orleans, LA
Martin, R. Douglas ....Lexington, KY
Martin, R. Eden ....Chicago, IL
Martin, R. Kimber ....Port Charlotte, FL
Martin, R. Lee ....Nashville, TN
Martin, R. Matthew ....Atlanta, GA
Martin, R. Michael ....Saco, ME
Martin, R. Wilson ....Las Cruces, NM
Martin, Rachael ....Austin, TX
Martin, Rae E. ....Terre Haute, IN
Martin, Ralph C., II ....Boston, MA
Martin, Ralph Drury ....Washington, DC
Martin, Ralph E. ....Indianapolis, IN
Martin, Ralph H. ....Jacksonville, FL
Martin, Ralph L. ....Kansas City, MO
Martin, Ralph M. (Rick) ....Longmont, CO
Martin, Ralph V. ....Wayne, NJ
Martin, Randall A. ....St. Louis, MO
Martin, Randy R. ....Wichita Falls, TX
Martin, Rawson & Woosley, P.C.
Birmingham, AL
Martin, Ray J. ....Wichita Falls, TX
Martin, Ray O. ....Indianapolis, IN
Martin, Raymond J., Jr. ....Dallas, TX
Martin, Raymond Scott ....Atlanta, GA
Martin, Raymond W. ....Denver, CO
Martin, Raymond W. ....Cheyenne, WY
Martin & Raynor, P.C.
Charlottesville, VA
Martin, Rebecca ....New York, NY
Martin, Rebecca D. ....Kansas City, MO
Martin, Rebecca J. ....Salt Point, NY
Martin, Reed ....Galveston, TX

Martin, William R. ......Washington, DC
Martin, William R. ......Worthington, KY
Martin, William S. ......Denver, CO
Martin, William S. ......Pratt, KS
Martin, William T. ......Las Vegas, NV
Martin, Wilson & MacDowell, A Professional Corporation ......Santa Ana, CA
Martin, Winfield T. ......Greenville, SC
Martin, W. L. ......Shreveport, LA
Martin, Wm. H. ......Roanoke, VA
Martin, Wm. H., Jr. ......Richmond, VA
Martin, W. T., Jr. ......Carlsbad, NM
Martin, Wyatt T. ......Arden, NC
Martin & Zerilla ......Memphis, TN
Martina, Carlo J. ......Southfield, MI
Martina, Carlo J., P.C., Law Offices
Southfield, MI
Martina, John F. ......Buffalo, NY
Martina, Robert M. ......Lafayette, LA
Martinak, Delano F. ......Victoria, TX
Martin-Anderson, Vicki ......Midland, MI
Martin-Boyan, Annemarie ......Philadelphia, PA
Martincavage, Allen W., Sr.
Boynton Beach, FL
Martinchek, Thomas G.
San Francisco, CA
Martin-Cross, Denise L. ......Dayton, OH
Martindale, Ann ......New Milford, CT
Martindale, Brzytwa & Quick LLC
Cleveland, OH
Martindale, Daniel ......Hudson Falls, NY
Martindale, David L. ......Laurel, MS
Martindale, Dorothy M. ......Portland, OR
Martindale, Edward ......Jackson, TN
Martindale, Everett O. ......Little Rock, AR
Martindale & Faveluke ......Portland, OR
Martindale, J. Bruce, III ......Dallas, TX
Martindale, J. A. "Gene" ......Pampa, TX
Martindale, Janis Brady ......Covina, CA
Martindale, John E. ......Cleveland, OH
Martindale, Lanny R. ......College Station, TX
Martindale, Lowell C., Jr.
Newport Beach, CA
San Francisco, CA
Martindale, Nancy D. ......Palo Alto, CA
Martindale, Nancy L.
Department of Justice,
Criminal Division, GV
Martindale, Nicola J. ......New York, NY
Martindale, Richard D. ......Fairfax, VA
Martindale, Rick L. ......Orlando, FL
Martindale, Robin C. ......Scottsdale, AZ
Martindell, Robert C. ......Hutchinson, KS
Martindell, Roger C. ......Princeton, NJ
Martindell, Stan A. ......Sparks, MD
Martindell, Swearer & Shaffer, LLP
Hutchinson, KS
Kingman, KS
Martindill, Michael J. ......La Mesa, CA
Martine, Anthony D. ......New York, NY
Martine, Colleen J. ......Madison, WI
Martine, Louis J. ......New York, NY
Martineau, Anthony R. ......Salt Lake City, UT
Martineau, Catherine B. ......Toledo, OH
Martineau, Daniel J. ......Aspen, CO
Martineau, Dennis M. ......Santa Ana, CA
Martineau, Elizabeth A. ......Charlotte, NC
Martineau, Elizabeth Ada
Department of Transportation,
Federal Transit Administration, GV
Martineau, Eric D. ......Worthington, OH
Martineau, Fernand A. ......Portland, ME
Martineau, J. Stanley ......Mesa, AZ
Martineau, J. Stanley, P.C. ......Mesa, AZ
Martineau, James E., Jr. ......Plattsburgh, NY
Martineau, John R. ......San Marino, CA
Martineau, Joseph E. ......St. Louis, MO
Martineau & Knudson ......Los Angeles, CA
San Marino, CA
Santa Monica, CA
Martineau, Michael J.
Department of Justice, Tax Division, GV
Martineau, Paul A. ......Pleasantville, NY
Martineau, Paul W., Jr. ......Clifton Park, NY
Martineau, Perry H. ......Dallas, TX
Martineau, Ray G. ......Salt Lake City, UT
Martineau, Ray G., A Professional Corporation
Salt Lake City, UT
Martineau, Reed L. ......Salt Lake City, UT
Martineau, Rene Gerard ......New Haven, CT
Martineau, Robert J., Jr. ......Nashville, TN
Martineau, Stephanie Jones ......Marietta, GA
Martineau, Steven W.
Mount Pleasant, MI
Martineau, Susan Linsley ......Denver, CO
Martineau, Theodore J. ......Oak Brook, IL
Martinec, Joseph D. ......San Antonio, TX
Martinek, David E. ......Eureka, CA
Martinek & Francis Co., L.P.A. ......Lorain, OH
Martinek, James H. ......Iowa City, IA
Martinek, Paul J. ......Boston, MA
Martinek, Randolph J. ......Port Huron, MI
Martinek, Ron D. ......Topeka, KS
Martinek, Steven ......Lorain, OH
Martinell, Robert G. ......Chicago, IL
Martinell, Tracy L. ......Tampa, FL
Martinelli, Alyse F. ......Troy, MI
Martinelli, Carol Ann ......Troy, MI
Martinelli, E. Jane ......Raleigh, NC
Martinelli, Gary E. ......Springfield, MA
Martinelli, Gary E., & Associates, P.C.
Springfield, MA
Martinelli, Gregory S. ......Vineland, NJ
Martinelli, Krista J. ......Palo Alto, CA
Martinelli, Laurie ......Lincoln, MA
Martinelli, Leslie M. ......Cherry Hill, NJ
Martinelli, Lisa ......Los Angeles, CA
Martinelli, Mary J. ......Sacramento, CA
Martinelli, Michael A. ......Yonkers, NY
Martinelli, Patricia ......Springfield, MA
Martinelli, Patricia ......Albany, NY
Martinelli, Peter J. ......Fresno, CA
Martinelli, Robert F. ......Yonkers, NY
Martinelli, S. Thomas ......Springfield, MA
Martines, Barry ......Fort Worth, TX
Martines, Mark J. ......Boston, MA
Martines, Sue B. ......Ruidoso, NM
Martinet, Leonard J. ......Los Angeles, CA
Novato, CA
Martinetti, Philip ......Naples, FL
Martinez, Abel ......San Antonio, TX
Martinez, Adrian R. ......McAllen, TX
Martinez, Aida ......Miami, FL
Martinez, Alberto C., Jr. ......Milledgeville, GA
Martinez, Aldo J. ......New York, NY
Martinez, Alex Joseph ......Denver, CO
Martinez, Alma Maria Benavides
Laredo, TX
Martinez, Amelia M. ......Miami, FL
Martinez, Amie C. ......Lincoln, NE
Martinez, Ana Cristina ......Tallahassee, FL
Martinez, Ana Maria ......Miami, FL
Martinez, Andrew T. ......New Orleans, LA
Martinez, Angela L. ......Bala Cynwyd, PA
Martinez, Angela M. ......Albuquerque, NM
Martinez, Anna G. ......Albuquerque, NM
Martinez, Anthony L. ......Salida, CO
Martinez, Antonio ......Trenton, NJ
Martinez, Antonio C., Law Offices of
New York, NY
Martinez, Antonio, Jr. ......El Paso, TX
Martinez, Antonio, Jr., (P.A.) ......Miami, FL
Martinez, Arthur ......Santa Ana, CA
Martinez & Barrera, L.L.P.
Brownsville, TX
Martinez, Benjamin A. ......Eagle Pass, TX
Martinez, Bernie ......Houston, TX
San Antonio, TX
Martinez, Bonnie A. ......Chicago, IL
Martinez, C. David ......Phoenix, AZ
Martinez, C. Olivia ......Chicago, IL
Martínez, Carlos E. ......New York, NY
Martinez, Carlos E. ......Round Rock, TX
Martinez, Carlos Edward ......Austin, TX
Martinez, Carlos G. ......Albuquerque, NM
Martinez, Catherine S. ......Denver, CO
Martinez, Cathrin J. ......San Antonio, TX
Martinez, Chad A. ......Stroudsburg, PA
Martinez, Charles ......Baltimore, MD
Martinez, Charles E. ......Phoenix, AZ
Martinez, Charles, III ......Bay City, TX
Martinez, Charlotte P. ......Millbrae, CA
Martinez, Christina Lee ......San Antonio, TX
Martinez, Christine ......Fort Worth, TX
Martinez, Cira A. ......Bronx, NY
Martinez & Coombs ......Phoenix, AZ
Martinez & Curtis, A Prof. Corp.
Phoenix, AZ
Martinez, Cynthia ......Los Angeles, CA
Martinez, Cynthia I. ......Belle Chasse, LA
Martinez & Dalton ......Orlando, FL
Martinez, Damian ......Los Angeles, CA
Martinez, Daniel ......San Mateo, CA
Martinez, Daniel A. ......St. Petersburg, FL
Martinez, Daniel V. ......Yuba City, CA
Martinez, Darren R. ......Los Angeles, CA
Martinez, David ......Los Angeles, CA
Martinez, David ......New York, NY
Martinez, David ......Lubbock, TX
Martinez, David A. ......Gretna, LA
Martinez, David Arnold ......Denver, CO
Martinez, David B. ......Albuquerque, NM
Martinez, David J. ......Waldorf, MD
Martinez, David R. ......Atlanta, GA
Martinez, David R., LLC ......Atlanta, GA
Martinez, Deanna L. ......Hanford, CA
Martinez, Deborah M. ......St. Louis, MO
Martinez, Delia E. ......San Antonio, TX
Martinez, Diana L. ......Newport Beach, CA
Martinez, Donald A. ......Las Vegas, NM
Martinez, Donald E. ......Albuquerque, NM
Martinez, Edelmiro, Jr. ......Springfield, MA
Martinez, Eduardo ......Atlanta, GA
Martinez, Eduardo V. ......Madison, MS
Martinez, Edward P. ......Aurora, CO
Martinez, Elena ......Las Vegas, NV
Martinez, Elio F., Jr. ......Miami, FL
Martinez, Elisa M. ......Burbank, CA
Martinez, Ella J. ......Dallas, TX
Martinez, Elvin L. ......Tampa, FL
Martinez, Emilio ......Laredo, TX
Martinez, Ernest R. ......Brea, CA
Martinez, Ernest R. ......Redding, CA
Martinez, Esther D. ......San Mateo, CA
Martinez, Eugene G. ......St. Paul, MN
Martinez, Eugene J. ......Lompoc, CA
Martinez, Eva ......New York, NY
Martinez, Francesca E. ......Jersey City, NJ
Martinez, Francis M. ......Rockford, IL
Martinez, Francisco C. ......Washington, DC
Martinez, Francisco E.T. ......Alamosa, CO
Martinez, Francisco J. ......Houston, TX
Martinez, Frank F. ......New York, NY
Martinez, Frank J. ......Mora, NM
Martinez, Frank J. ......Mineola, NY
Martinez, Frank R., III ......Crown Point, IN
Martinez, Frank S. ......Morrison, IL
Martinez, Fred C. ......Albuquerque, NM
Martínez, Fred H. ......San Juan, PR
Martinez, Freddie L. ......Martinez, CA
Martinez, Fredrick T. ......Denver, CO
Martinez, Gabriel A. ......Las Vegas, NV
Martinez, George C. ......Belvedere-Tiburon, CA
Martinez, George O. ......Columbus, OH
Martinez, Gilbert ......Austin, TX
Martinez, G.J. ......Chino, CA
Martinez, Glenda E. ......Los Angeles, CA
Martinez, Graciela ......Los Angeles, CA
Martinez, Guillermo F. ......Chicago, IL
Martinez, Guillermo F., & Assocs., A Prof. Corp. ......Chicago, IL
Martinez, Gustavo L. ......Redding, CA
Martinez & Gutierrez ......Miami, FL
Martinez, Hector A., Jr.
Jackson Heights, NY
Martinez, Hector G., Jr. ......Cleveland, OH
Martinez, Henry J., Jr. ......Minneapolis, MN
Martinez, J. Michael ......Norcross, GA
Martinez, Jacqueline L.
Office Of Special Counsel,
San Francisco Field Office, GV
Martinez, James A. ......El Paso, TX
Martinez, Janet E. ......Daytona Beach, FL
Martinez, Janette Marie
Department of Justice,
Immigration and Naturalization Service, GV
Martinez, Jason L. ......Raleigh, NC
Martinez, Javier S. ......Houston, TX
Martinez, Jay M. ......Phoenix, AZ
Martinez, Jehan'ad G. ......Hagåtña, GU
Martinez, Jennifer ......Tampa, FL
Martinez & Jennings ......West Trenton, NJ
Martinez, Jenny Lanell ......Dallas, TX
Martinez, Jess, Jr. ......Waukesha, WI
Martinez, Jesus P. ......Santa Maria, CA
Martinez, Jill Sandhaas ......Melville, NY
Martinez, Joaquin E. ......Atlanta, GA
Martinez, Joe Leland, Jr. ......Denver, CO
Martinez, Joel O. ......Pomona, CA
Martinez, John B. ......Corpus Christi, TX
Martinez, John L. ......Bartow, FL
Martinez, Jorge A. ......Riverside, CA
Martinez, Jorge L. ......San Juan, PR
Martinez, Jose E., (P.A.) ......Miami, FL
Martinez, Jose L. ......Albuquerque, NM
Martinez, Jose L. ......Irving, TX
Martinez, Jose R. ......Bronx, NY
Martinez, Jose V. ......Brookfield, CT
Martinez, Josefina M. ......Boston, MA
Martinez, Joseph A. ......Santa Barbara, CA
Martinez, Joseph G. ......San Diego, CA
Martinez, Joseph P., II
San Francisco, CA
Martinez, Joseph R. ......Los Angeles, CA
Martinez, Joseph R. ......Boston, MA
Martinez, Josue ......San Antonio, TX
Martinez, Juan C. ......Coral Gables, FL
Martinez, Juan J. ......St. Paul, MN
Martinez, Judy Perry ......New Orleans, LA
Martinez, Julio C., Jr. ......Kissimmee, FL
Orlando, FL
Martinez, Julio Ricardo ......New York, NY
Martinez & Kaloyanides
Newport Beach, CA
Martinez, Karen D. ......Atlanta, GA
Martinez, Karen L. ......Salt Lake City, UT
Martinez, Karen Lynn ......Costa Mesa, CA
Martinez, Katherine ......Tampa, FL
Martinez, Katherine Hall ......New York, NY
Martinez, Kay ......San Antonio, TX
Martinez, Kay, P.C., Law Offices of
San Antonio, TX
Martinez, Kenneth A. ......San Francisco, CA
Martinez, Kenneth H. ......Albuquerque, NM
Martinez, Kenneth H., P.A.
Albuquerque, NM
Martinez, Kimberly Alyson
Research Triangle Park, NC
Martinez, Kristina ......Denver, CO
Martinez, Lance A. ......Los Angeles, CA
Martinez, Larry R. ......Denver, CO
Martinez Law Firm, The ......Kansas City, MO
Martinez, Leonard M. ......Austin, TX
Martinez, Lili Denise ......San Antonio, TX
Martinez, Lisa M. ......St. Louis, MO
Martinez, Lisa ......Milwaukee, WI
Martinez, Loretta P. ......Denver, CO
Martínez, Louis R. ......New York, NY
Martinez, Lourdes ......Great Neck, NY
Martinez, Luis ......Fort Lee, NJ
Martinez, Luis A. ......Victoria, TX
Martinez, Luis Manuel ......New York, NY
Martinez, Lupe ......Oakland, CA
Martinez, Manglardi & Diez-Arguelles
Kissimmee, FL
Orlando, FL
Martinez, Manny C. ......Los Angeles, CA
Martinez, Manuel A. ......San Francisco, CA
Martinez, Manuel J. ......Maywood, CA
Martinez, Manuel L. ......Denver, CO
Martinez, Manuel R., Jr. ......Lancaster, CA
Martinez, Manuel S. ......New York, NY
Martinez, Marco A. ......Riverside, CA
Martinez, Margarita M. ......Fresno, CA
Martinez, Maria Antonieta ......Miami, FL
Martinez, Maria E. ......New York, NY
Martinez, Marilyn Kading
Monterey Park, CA
Martinez, Mario A. ......Galveston, TX
Martinez, Mario J. ......El Paso, TX
Martinez, Mario J., A Professional Law Corporation ......El Paso, TX
Martinez, Marla A. ......Burbank, CA
Martinez, Martin M. ......Espanola, NM
Martinez & Martinez ......San Mateo, CA
Martinez, Marvin A. ......Newport Beach, CA
Martinez, Meghan W. ......Denver, CO
Martinez, Mel R. ......Orlando, FL
Martinez, Melissa C. ......Middletown, OH
Martinez, Melvin H. ......San Antonio, TX
Martinez, Michael ......Newark, NJ
Martinez, Michael C. ......Santa Monica, CA
Martinez, Michael C. ......Brooklyn, NY
Martinez, Michael D. ......San Bernardino, CA
Martínez, Michael E. ......Minneapolis, MN
Martinez, Michael L. ......Washington, DC
Martinez, Michael L. ......Golden Valley, MN
Martinez, Michelle A. ......Albuquerque, NM
Martinez, Mike ......Woodland Hills, CA
Martinez, Milena ......Flushing, NY
Martinez, Mirna E. ......New York, NY
Martinez, Misha M. ......Newport Beach, CA
Martinez Molina, P.A. ......Miami, FL
Martinez, Octavio L. ......Miami, FL
Martínez Odell & Calabria ......San Juan, PR
Martinez & O'Neil ......Springfield, MA
Martinez, Osmundo O. ......Coral Gables, FL
Martinez, Patrick G. ......Baltimore, MD
Martinez, Patrick J. ......Albuquerque, NM
Martinez, Patrick M. ......Corpus Christi, TX
Martinez, Paul H. ......Norwalk, CT
Martinez, Peter L. ......Glendale, CA
Martinez, Peter R. ......San Diego, CA
Martinez, Peter W. ......Costa Mesa, CA
Martinez, Philip R. ......El Paso, TX
Martinez, Phillip A. ......Albuquerque, NM
Martinez, Preciliano ......Modesto, CA
Martinez, Rafael ......New York, NY
Martinez, Rafael E. "Ralph" ......Orlando, FL
Martinez, Rafael Fuster ......Ponce, PR
Martinez, Ramiro B. ......McAllen, TX
Martinez, Ramon, Jr. ......Oak Brook, IL
Martinez, Ramona ......Dallas, TX
Martinez, Raul E. ......Rochester, NY
Martinez, Raul L., (P.C.) ......Los Angeles, CA
Martinez, Raymond A.
Department of Transportation,
Federal Aviation Administration, GV
Martinez, Rene M. ......Tucson, AZ
Martinez, Reynold M. ......San Francisco, CA
Martinez, Ricardo A. ......Walnut Creek, CA
Martinez, Ricardo S. ......New York, NY
Martinez, Ricardo S. ......Seattle, WA
Martinez, Richard D. ......Cleveland, OH
Martinez, Richard G. ......Seattle, WA
Martinez, Richard M. ......Minneapolis, MN
Martinez, Richard R., Jr.
Department Of The Interior,
Minerals Management Service, GV
Martinez, Richard W., (A Professional Law Corp.) ......Metairie, LA
New Orleans, LA
Martinez & Ritorto, P.C. ......New York, NY
Martinez, Robert B. ......Albuquerque, NM
Martinez, Robert B., Law Office of, P.A.
Albuquerque, NM
Martinez, Robert C. ......Oakland, CA
Martinez, Robert C. ......San Diego, CA
Martinez, Robert D. ......Fort Worth, TX
Martinez, Robert J. ......Washington, DC
Martinez, Robert P. ......West Trenton, NJ
Martinez, Robert S. ......Albuquerque, NM
Martinez, Robert V. (Vince) ......Lubbock, TX
Martinez, Roberto ......Miami, FL
Martínez, Roberto J.
Merit Systems Protection Board,
Office of Appeals Counsel, GV
Martinez, Robin S. ......Kansas City, MO
Martínez, Rodolfo ......Edinburg, TX
Martinez, Roland J. ......Coral Gables, FL
Martinez, Rosemarie L. ......Las Vegas, NV
Martinez, Roxane E. ......Houston, TX
Martinez, Roy R., Jr ......Fairfax, VA
Martinez, Ruth M. ......West Palm Beach, FL
Martinez, Ruth M., P.A.
West Palm Beach, FL
Martinez, Shannon Sullivan
Los Angeles, CA
Martinez, Sonia G. ......Trenton, NJ
Martinez, Stacey A. ......Austin, TX
Martinez, Stefanie A. ......Omaha, NE
Martinez, Steven ......Houston, TX
Martinez, Susana ......Las Cruces, NM
Martinez, Susanne ......United States Senate,
Committee Legal Personnel, GV
Martinez, Thelma E. ......Milltown, NJ
Martinez, Timothy J. ......Baton Rouge, LA
Martínez, Tomás M. Acevedo
San Juan, PR
Martinez, Tony ......Brownsville, TX
Martinez, Tricia A. ......New Orleans, LA
Martinez, Tyrone R. ......Santa Monica, CA
Martinez, Victor D. ......Tampa, FL
Martinez, Victor D., P.A. ......Tampa, FL
Martinez, Victor J. ......Tampa, FL
Martinez, Victor J., P.A. ......Tampa, FL
Martinez, Vidal G. ......Houston, TX
Martinez, Vilma S. ......Los Angeles, CA
Martinez, Vincent T. ......Santa Maria, CA
Martinez, Vicente L. ......Washington, DC
Martinez, Virginia ......Chicago, IL
Martinez, Vivian T., Jr., (P.C.) ......Denver, CO
Martinez, W. Ken ......Grants, NM
Martinez, Walfrido J. ......Miami, FL
Martinez, Walter S., Jr. ......Upland, CA
Martinez, Wilfredo ......Orlando, FL
Martinez, William A. ......Alamosa, CO
Martinez, William A., P.C. ......Alamosa, CO
Martinez, William J. ......Denver, CO
Martínez, Xavier ......Miami, FL
Martinez, Z. Ileana ......Atlanta, GA
Martinez-Alonso, Osvaldo C. ......Miami, FL
Martinez-Alvarez, Alfredo ......San Juan, PR
Martínez-Alvarez, Francisco J.
Arlington, VA
Martínez-Alvarez, Menéndez Cortada & Lefranc Romero, PSC ......San Juan, PR
Martinez Alvarez, Rafael, III ......San Juan, PR
Martinez-Baca, Horacio J.
San Francisco, CA
Martinez-Cancel, Angel A. ......San Juan, PR
Martínez Cazón, Silvia N. ......Richmond, VA

Marvin, Charles, III, A Professional Corporation ... Encinitas, CA
Idyllwild, CA
Marvin, Charles R. "Rod", Jr.
Washington, DC
Marvin, Chorzempa & Associates, P.C.
Portland, OR
Marvin, David E. S. ... Lansing, MI
Marvin, Douglas R. ... Fairfax, VA
Marvin, Douglas R., P.C. ... Washington, DC
Fairfax, VA
Marvin, Elliot R. ... New York, NY
Marvin, Eric W. ... Eugene, OR
Marvin and Ferro ... New Canaan, CT
Marvin, Frank R. ... Herndon, VA
Marvin, Guy, III ... Jacksonville, FL
Marvin, H. Bruce ... Seattle, WA
Marvin, Herbert Zachary ... Miami, FL
Marvin, Jack C. ... Wichita, KS
Marvin, James H. ... Portland, OR
Marvin, James L. ... Chicago, IL
Marvin, Janet L. ... Park Falls, WI
Marvin, Jerry A. ... Sarasota, FL
Marvin, Joanne R. ... Fairfax, VA
Marvin, John F. ... Kansas City, MO
Marvin, John R. ... Bayside, NY
Marvin, John R. ... Rhinebeck, NY
Marvin, John Schuyler ... Minden, LA
Marvin, Jonathan P. ... Emeryville, CA
Marvin, Kristine Elizabeth ... Boston, MA
Marvin and Marvin ... Rhinebeck, NY
Marvin, Mary C. ... Bronxville, NY
Marvin, Michael B. ... Miami, FL
Marvin, Monica L. Wolf ... St. Helena, CA
Marvin, Morton E. ... New Canaan, CT
Marvin, Peter F. ... Philadelphia, PA
Marvin, Philip P. ... Sarasota, FL
Marvin, Richard A. ... Grand Rapids, MI
Marvin, Robert J., Jr. ... Pawling, NY
Marvin, Robert J., Sr. ... Rhinebeck, NY
Marvin, Ronald S. ... Farmington Hills, MI
Marvin, Seth L. ... Brooklyn, NY
Marvin, Sheri L. ... Irvine, CA
Marvin, Stephen W. ... Yakima, WA
Marvin, Terry ... Tucson, AZ
Marvin, Thomas C.
Environmental Protection Agency, Program Office Attorneys, GV
Marvin, Thomas R. ... Oakland, CA
Marvin, Valerie ... New Suffolk, NY
Marvin, Walter ... New Brunswick, NJ
Marvin, Wendy Byers ... Kansas City, MO
Marvin, William A. ... Roswell, GA
Marvin, William D. ... Philadelphia, PA
Marvine, Charles D. ... Kansas City, MO
Marvine, Charles F., Jr.
Overland Park, KS
Kansas City, MO
Marvinney, Craig A. ... Cleveland, OH
Marvinney, Michelle Powe ... Cleveland, OH
Marwedel, Minichello & Reeb, P.C.
Chicago, IL
Marwedel, Warren J. ... Chicago, IL
Marwell, Emily ... Treasury Department, Office of the Comptroller of the Currency, GV
Marwell, John S. ... Mount Kisco, NY
Marwil, Jeff J. ... Chicago, IL
Marx, Alan L. ... Nashville, TN
Marx, Brendan R. ... New York, NY
Marx, Bruce R. ... Miami, FL
Marx, Carol Seubert ... Lancaster, OH
Marx, Charles A. ... Jackson, MS
Marx, Charles M. ... San Carlos, CA
Marx, Christine A. ... Boston, MA
Marx, Christine M. ... Short Hills, NJ
Marx, David, Jr. ... Chicago, IL
Marx, David K., Jr. ... Denville, NJ
Marx, Deborah J. ... Oakland, CA
Marx, Dianne F. ... Dayton, OH
Marx, Douglas Todd ... Fort Lauderdale, FL
Marx & Duffy, LLP ... San Francisco, CA
Marx, Eric C.
National Labor Relations Board, Office of the General Counsel, GV
Marx, Ernest L. ... Santa Barbara, CA
Marx, Frederic J. ... Boston, MA
Marx, Fredrick M. ... Washington, DC
Marx, G. Paul ... Lafayette, LA
Marx, Gary Samuel ... Washington, DC
Marx, Gregg ... Lancaster, OH
Marx, Gretchen Kah ... San Francisco, CA
Marx, Howard J. ... Norfolk, VA
Marx, Ian S. ... New York, NY
Marx, James A. ... Cincinnati, OH
Marx, James A. ... Cleveland, OH
Marx, Jan Howell ... San Luis Obispo, CA
Marx, Jane ... Albuquerque, NM
Marx, Jason E. ... Morristown, NJ
Marx, Jean Simonoff ... Atlanta, GA
Marx, Joseph W. ... New York, NY
Marx, Julia S. ... New York, NY
Marx, Kathleen E. ... Browning, MT
Marx, Kenneth Andrew ... New York, NY
Marx, Leona ... Nashville, TN
Marx, Marvin C. ... Fair Oaks, CA
Marx & Marx ... Atlanta, GA
New York, NY
Marx and Marx ... Lancaster, OH
Marx, Max C. ... New York, NY
Marx, Melvin D. ... Chatham, NJ
Marx, Michael L. ... San Francisco, CA
Marx, Michael S. ... Los Angeles, CA
Marx, Nancy P. ... Stamford, CT
Marx, Owen C. ... New York, NY
Marx, Pamela A. ... Los Angeles, CA
Marx, Paul Frederic ... Costa Mesa, CA
Marx, Paul Gerard ... Leawood, KS
Marx, Paul I. ... New York, NY
White Plains, NY
Marx, Paula Corley ... Crowley, LA
Marx, Peter A. ... Boston, MA
Marx, Peter A. ... Wellesley, MA
Marx, Peter J. ... Los Angeles, CA
Marx, Peter L. ... Chicago, IL
Marx, Philip R. ... Philadelphia, PA
Marx, Randy P. ... Dallas, TX
Marx, Richard B., & Associates, Law Offices of ... Miami, FL
Marx, Richard M. ... San Francisco, CA
Marx, Richard S. ... St. Louis, MO
Marx, Richard S. ... Richmond Hill, NY
Marx, Robert ... New York, NY
Marx, Robert N. ... Atlanta, GA
New York, NY
Marx, Robert P. ... Hilo, HI
Marx, Stephen D. ... Metairie, LA
Marx, Timothy E. ... St. Paul, MN
Marx, William E. ... West Covina, CA
Marx, William F. ... Indianapolis, IN
Marxer, John A., (P.C.) ... Troy, MI
Marxer, Joseph H. ... Indianapolis, IN
Marxkors, Marianne ... Florissant, MO
Marxuach, Sergio M. ... New York, NY
Marxuach-Torrós, Gilberto J.
San Juan, PR
Mary, Brandon E. ... New Orleans, LA
Mary, Cameron M. ... New Orleans, LA
Mary, Lara Burns ... New Orleans, LA
Maryan, Norman E., Jr. ... Fairfax, VA
Maryan, Robert M. ... Houston, TX
Maryanski, Bernard J. ... San Francisco, CA
Maryanski, Donna M. ... Orange, CA
Marye, David A. ... Lexington, KY
Marye, Edward A., Jr. ... Mount Sterling, KY
Marylander, Grant ... Denver, CO
Maryles, David M. ... New York, NY
Marymor, Julius ... Charlottesville, VA
Maryn, Michael R. ... Washington, DC
Marynell, John E. ... Downers Grove, IL
Maryott, Michele L. ... Irvine, CA
Maryscuk, Lori A. ... Suwanee, GA
Marz, Matthew ... Indianapolis, IN
Marzal, V. Andrew ... Chicago, IL
Marzan, Jacqueline C. ... New York, NY
Marzan, James M. ... Walnut Creek, CA
Marzan, Shirley A. ... Tulsa, OK
Marzano, Maryann R. ... Santa Monica, CA
Marzano, Robert A. ... Detroit, MI
Marzano-Doty, Denise ... Melville, NY
Marzano-Lesnevich, Madeline ... Tenafly, NJ
Marzec, Edwin K. ... Los Angeles, CA
Marzec, Philip ... San Antonio, TX
Marzek, Alex A. ... Wildwood, FL
Marzella, Neil ... Harbor Springs, MI
Marzella, R.J., & Associates, P.C.
Harrisburg, PA
Marzella, Robin J. ... Harrisburg, PA
Marzelli, Robert L. ... Marshfield, MA
Marzen, Stephen James ... Washington, DC
Marzen, Thomas J. ... Terre Haute, IN
Marzetta, Susan M. ... Baltimore, MD
Marzetti, Alfred P. ... King Of Prussia, PA
Marzetti, Christopher L. ... Seattle, WA
Marzetti, Lawrence A. ... Oxon Hill, MD
Marzetti, Philip J. ... Atlanta, GA
Marziale, Arthur J., Jr. ... Columbus, OH
Marziani, Gini S. ... Chicago, IL
Marziani, Rula ... Northbrook, IL
Marzik, Robert K. ... Stratford, CT
New York, NY
Marzik, Robert K., P.C., Law Offices of
Stratford, CT
New York, NY
Marzilli, Frederic A. ... East Providence, RI
Marzilli, Joseph ... Gardner, MA
Mar-Zimmer, Robin ... Seattle, WA
Marzina, Barbara F. ... Pittsburgh, PA
Marziotti, Catherine B. ... Houston, TX
Marziotti, John D. ... Houston, TX
Marzloff, George E. ... Stafford, VA
Marzloff, George E., P.C.
Spotsylvania, VA
Stafford, VA
Marzluf, Eric S. ... Philadelphia, PA
Marzocchi, Marco J. ... Syracuse, NY
Marzocchi, Zita P. ... Rochester, NY
Marzolf, Kristine T. ... Boston, MA
Marzolla, Mary Elizabeth ... Nyack, NY
Marzouk & Parry ... Washington, DC
Marzouk, Tobey B. ... Washington, DC
Marzuk, George C. ... New York, NY
Marzulla, Nancie G. ... Washington, DC
Marzulla, Roger J. ... Washington, DC
Marzulli, John A. ... Montclair, NJ
Marzulli, John A., Jr. ... New York, NY
Marzullo, Christopher D. ... Baltimore, MD
Marzullo, Henry A., Jr. ... Scarsdale, NY
Marzullo, Jo-Ann M. ... Boston, MA
Marzullo, John A. ... New Orleans, LA
Marzullo, Ronald J. ... St. Petersburg, FL
Marzullo, Steven ... Las Vegas, NV
Marzullo, Thomas G. ... Bronxville, NY
Marzzacco, Christopher J. ... Dillsburg, PA
Mas, Carlos ... Miami, FL
Mas, Edward A., II ... Chicago, IL
Mas, Joseph L. ... Pataskala, OH
Masada, Linda Scasserra
Marina Del Rey, CA
Masago, Tohru ... Los Angeles, CA
Masaitis, Peter E. ... Los Angeles, CA
Masalla, Robert Marshall Paul
Columbia, SC
Masana, Henry A. ... Hamilton, OH
Masana, Michael P. ... Hamilton, OH
Masano, Heidi B. ... Reading, PA
Masanoff, Michael D. ... Parkland, FL
Masanotti, Peter Louis ... Stamford, CT
Masar, Dennis ... Scotch Plains, NJ
Masar, James J. ... Missoula, MT
Masarachia, Sarah R. ... Chicago, IL
Masarweh, Tony E. ... Santa Rosa, CA
Masatsugu, Jeffrey S. ... Honolulu, HI
Masback, Craig Alford ... Washington, DC
Masback, Harold E., III ... Washington, DC
Mascagni, Frank, III ... Louisville, KY
Mascagni, Kenneth ... Shreveport, LA
Mascal, Christine ... Portland, OR
Mascali, Arnold F. ... Roseland, NJ
Mascali, Robert P. ... Albany, NY
Mascara, Ernest L. ... St. Petersburg, FL
Mascara, Mark E. ... Washington, PA
Mascarello, John A. ... Bronx, NY
Mascarenas, Cresencio L. ... Bayside, NY
Mascarenas, Fred L., Jr.
Department of Defense, Defense Legal Services Agency, GV
Mascarenhas, Liscombe
Rockville Centre, NY
Mascari, John C. ... White Plains, NY
Mascari, Pamela Roman
Baton Rouge, LA
Mascaro, Daniel P. ... Cleveland, OH
Mascaro, Guillermo F., Law Offices of
Coral Gables, FL
Mascaro, Isa M. ... Miami, FL
Mascaro, Joseph R. ... Utica, NY
Mascaro, Rocco S. ... Utica, NY
Mascelli, John C. ... Scranton, PA
Mascelli & Paterson ... Scranton, PA
Mascenik, Robert J. ... Iselin, NJ
Mascera, Gregory ... Verona, NJ
Masch, Clifford C. ... Cleveland, OH
Masch, James R. ... Manahawkin, NJ
Masch, Julia Louise ... Upper Nyack, NY
Masch, Visotsky & Cerefice
Manahawkin, NJ
Maschal, Craig R. ... Morristown, NJ
Maschal, William E. ... Round Rock, TX
Maschari, Ann B. ... Sandusky, OH
Maschek, Linda J. ... Chicago, IL
Mascher, Gilbert E. ... Indianapolis, IN
Mascherin, Terri L. ... Chicago, IL
Mascherino, Stephen J. ... Downingtown, PA
Masching, Irvin L. ... Dwight, IL
Maschio, Michael F. ... New York, NY
Maschka, Gerald L. ... Mankato, MN
Maschler, Brian P. ... San Francisco, CA
Maschler, Matthew H. ... New York, NY
Maschman, Curtis L. ... Falls City, NE
Maschmann, Jason Edward
St. Louis, MO
Maschmeyer, Kimberly A. ... St. Louis, MO
Maschmeyer, Michael M. ... Jeffersonville, IN
Maschmeyer, Paul Brinton
Philadelphia, PA
Maschmeyer, Thomas L., Jr. ... Memphis, TN
Maschmeyer, William A. ... Indianapolis, IN
Maschoff, Eric L. ... Salt Lake City, UT
Maschoff, James D. ... St. Louis, MO
Masci, David F. ... Rockville, MD
Masci, David R. ... Thousand Oaks, CA
Masci, Felix G. ... Thousand Oaks, CA
Masci & Masci, Law Offices of
Thousand Oaks, CA
Mascia, Emil G. ... Verona, NJ
Mascia, Joseph A. ... New York, NY
Mascia, Louis A. ... North Providence, RI
Mascia, Michael C. ... Greensboro, NC
Mascia, Patrick E. ... Minnetonka, MN
Masciantonio, Domenic M., Jr.
Philadelphia, PA
Masciarella, Raymond M., II
North Palm Beach, FL
Masciarella, Raymond M., II, P.A.
North Palm Beach, FL
Masciarelli, Marilyn S. ... San Jose, CA
Mascio, John J. ... Steubenville, OH
Mascio, John J. ... Steubenville, OH
Masciocchi, Francis J. ... Philadelphia, PA
Masciocchi, Francis J., P.C.
Philadelphia, PA
Masciocchi, Stephen ... Denver, CO
Masciocchi, Thomas G. ... Haddonfield, NJ
Masciola, Peter R. ... Washington, DC
Mascioli, Frank X. ... Jericho, NY
Mascioli, Robert A. ... Berwyn, PA
Mascioli, William G.
National Labor Relations Board, Office of the General Counsel, GV
Masciopinto, Julie D. ... Chicago, IL
Masciopinto, Victoria L. ... Chicago, IL
Masciopinto, Vito M. ... Chicago, IL
Mascis, Michael J. ... Worcester, MA
Mascitti, Gregory J. ... Rochester, NY
Mascola, Robert E. ... Washington, DC
Mascola, Thomas M. ... Nanuet, NY
Mascolino, Thomas A. ... Department of Labor, Office of the Solicitor, GV
Mascoll, Carson D. ... Hempstead, NY
Mascolo, Anna Marie ... Garden City, NY
Mascolo, Anthony A. ... Staten Island, NY
Mascolo, Anthony L. ... Kew Gardens, NY
Mascolo, Frederic E. ... Waterbury, CT
Mascolo, Neil C., Jr. ... Mineola, NY
New York, NY
White Plains, NY
Mascolo, Nino J. ... Rosemead, CA
Mascot, Paul J. ... Austin, TX
Mascotte, John P. ... New York, NY
Mascotte, Mark F. ... Oakland, CA
Mascotti, Silvio L. ... Decatur, GA
Mascovich, Joseph P. ... Oakland, CA
Masden, Robert L. ... Midlothian, VA
Masdon & Masdon ... Haleyville, AL
Masdon, Samuel A. ... Haleyville, AL
Masdon, Samuel L. ... Haleyville, AL
Mase, Curtis J. ... Miami, FL
Mase & Gassenheimer, P.A.
Fort Lauderdale, FL
Miami, FL
Mase, Gregory A. ... Berkeley, CA
Mase, John A. ... Los Angeles, CA
Mase, Lawrence L., II ... Lorain, OH
Maseberg, Barbara J. ... Houston, TX
Maseda, Stephen B. ... Pasadena, CA
Masek, Edward J. ... Dallas, TX
Masek, Elizabeth ... Dearborn, MI
Masek, James E. ... Arlington, TX
Masek, James E. ... Grand Prairie, TX
Masek, Raymond J. ... Warren, OH
Masek, Richard E. ... Columbus, OH
Masel, C. Scott ... Myrtle Beach, SC
Masel, Richard P. ... Newton, NJ
Maselan, James P. ... Boston, MA
Maselan Jones & Stanzler, P.C.
Boston, MA
Maselek, Robert J. ... Boston, MA
Maseles, Danita J. M. ... San Jose, CA
Masella, James V., III ... New York, NY
Masella, Joseph ... Syracuse, NY
Masella Law Firm, The, P.A.
Columbia, SC
Masella, Robert F. ... New York, NY
Masella, Robert M.P. ... Columbia, SC
Maselli, David M. ... Philadelphia, PA
Maselli, Jani J. ... Austin, TX
Maselli, Joseph F. ... New York, NY
Maselli, Joseph, Jr. ... New Orleans, LA
Maselli, Michael C. ... Greensburg, PA
Maselli, Nicholas C., Jr. ... White Plains, NY
Maselli, Paul J. ... Princeton, NJ
Maselli, Richard Scott ... St. Petersburg, FL
Maselli, Warren & Lanciano, P.C.
Princeton, NJ
Maselli, William D. ... Andover, ME
Masenga, Robert V. ... El Segundo, CA
Masenga, Thomas J. ... Los Angeles, CA
Masengale, Roy L. ... Tacoma, WA
Masengill, Addison C.
Department Of Health And Human Services, Social Security Administration, GV
Masenheimer, David L. ... Palmerton, PA
Maser & Amundson, P.A. ... Minneapolis, MN
Maser, Charles R. ... Grand Island, NE
Maser, Clark W. ... Ross, CA
Maser, David J. ... Sutton, NE
Maser, Debra H. ... Philadelphia, PA
Maser, Douglas J. ... Columbus, OH
Maser, Henry ... Columbus, OH
Maser, Joel D. ... Orlando, FL
Maser, John K., III ... Washington, DC
Maser, Kris L. ... Minneapolis, MN
Maser, Marc S. ... Radnor, PA
Maser, Matthew D. ... Omaha, NE
Maser, Scott M. ... Hamden, CT
Maser, Thomas F. ... Palo Alto, CA
Maser, Thomas O. ... Department of Defense, Defense Legal Services Agency, GV
Maseredjian, David G. ... Los Angeles, CA
Maseritz, Guy B. ... Columbia, MD
Maserjian, Leslie D. ... Poughkeepsie, NY
Masessa & Cluff ... Butler, NJ
Masessa, Robert C. ... Butler, NJ
Maseth, Michael W. ... Columbus, OH
Maseth, William E., Jr. ... Towson, MD
Masetti, James J. ... Palo Alto, CA
Masferrer, Marta D. ... San Juan, PR
Masfield, Meredith ... Houston, TX
Mash, Gordon S. ... Bridgeview, IL
Mash, Laura B. ... Dallas, TX
Mash, Robert A. ... Honolulu, HI
Mash, Toby L. ... Ennis, TX
Mashaal, David R. ... New York, NY
Mashariki, Zola B. ... New York, NY
Mashaw, Jerry L. ... New Haven, CT
Mashayekh, Kayvan ... Houston, TX
Mashayekhi, Ali Kirk ... Orlando, FL
Mashberg, Gregg M. ... New York, NY
Mashburn, Amy R. ... Gainesville, FL
Mashburn, Charles E. ... Marshall, NC
Mashburn, Eric S. ... Winter Garden, FL
Mashburn, John B. ... Groveport, OH
Mashburn, John D. ... Oklahoma City, OK
Pauls Valley, OK
Mashburn, Mayo L. ... Cleveland, TN
Mashburn, Michael H. ... Fayetteville, AR
Mashburn, Peri Elisabeth ... Houston, TX
Mashburn, Randal S. ... Nashville, TN
Mashburn, Richard A. ... Cincinnati, OH
Mashburn, Robert T., Jr. ... Houston, TX
Mashburn, T. Matthew, (P.C.)
Atlanta, GA
Mashburn & Taylor ... Bentonville, AR
Fayetteville, AR
Mashburn, Timothy ... Austin, TX
Mashburn, Wes ... Salt Lake City, UT
Masheb, Craig A. ... New York, NY
Mashel, Stephan T. ... Clifton, NJ
Mashhour, Mouhsin ... Dearborn, MI
Mashian, Bryan ... Los Angeles, CA
Mashian, Fred F. ... Santa Monica, CA
Mashiba, Chris S. ... Honolulu, HI
Mashin, Alison R. ... Los Angeles, CA
Mashita, Lloyd I. ... Kolonia, TT
Mashney, Stephen B. ... Anaheim, CA
Masho, Paul N. ... King Of Prussia, PA
Masi, Carmela M. ... Boston, MA
Masi, Gary R. ... Lynbrook, NY
Masi, J. Roger ... Hackensack, NJ
Masi, James ... Ravenna, OH
Masi, Jeffrey R. ... Seattle, WA

Masi, Joseph J., III .... Vero Beach, FL
Masia, Adam H. .... Chicago, IL
Masia, Howard I. .... Freehold, NJ
Masia, Jacqueline Rothbart .... Northbrook, IL
Masic, Biserka .... New York, NY
Masica, Eugene M. .... Somerset, TX
Masica, Mark Alexis .... St. Louis Park, MN
Masick, Thomas M. .... Marlton, NJ
Masid, Mariam J. .... Fort Collins, CO
Masiello, Anthony R. .... Washington, DC
Masiello, Dominick J. .... Ridgewood, NY
Masiello, Melissa .... Chicago, IL
Masiello, Richard J. .... Philadelphia, PA
Masiello, Stephanie Sadwin
Lexington, MA
Masiello, Steven M. .... Denver, CO
Masiello, Thomas P., Jr. .... Canton, MA
Masih, Aruna A. .... Portland, OR
Masih, Jéneen .... New York, NY
Masilamani, Radha .... Oklahoma City, OK
Masin, Jeff S. .... Trenton, NJ
Masin, Linda Alba .... West Islip, NY
Masin, Michael T. .... New York, NY
Masin, Richard M. .... Laguna Beach, CA
Masingill, James Byron .... San Diego, CA
Masingill, R. Brad .... Weiser, ID
Masington, Nicholas J., Jr.
Philadelphia, PA
Masington, Richard S. .... Miami, FL
Sarasota, FL
Masini, Jon B. .... Chicago, IL
Masini, Robert J. .... Waukegan, IL
Masini-Soler, Jose A. .... San Juan, PR
Masino, Alfred A., Jr. .... Great Neck, NY
Masino, Dennis .... Farmingville, NY
Masino, Dennis, P.C. .... Farmingville, NY
Masino, Gina Joanne .... Red Bank, NJ
Masino, Michael J. .... Rochester, NY
Masinter, E. Michael .... Atlanta, GA
Masinter, Edgar M., (P.C.) .... New York, NY
Masinter, Eve B. .... New Orleans, LA
Masinter, Maria Kayanan .... Miami, FL
Masinter, Michael R. .... Fort Lauderdale, FL
Masinter, Paul J. .... New Orleans, LA
Masinter, Renee Williams .... New Orleans, LA
Masio, Carol A. .... Bradenton, FL
Masiowski, Michele A. .... Santa Fe, NM
Mask, J. Chadwick .... Jackson, MS
Tupelo, MS
Mask, Jacqueline Estes .... Tupelo, MS
Mask, Jody Ray .... Houston, TX
Mask, John Carlin, Jr. .... Bolivar, TN
Mask, Johnnie W., Jr. .... Newark, NJ
Mask, Michael Glenn .... Jacksboro, TX
Maska, Anthony S. .... New Orleans, LA
Maska, John L. .... Colorado Springs, CO
Maska, Mark M. .... Cherry Hill, NJ
Maskaleris & Associates .... Morristown, NJ
Maskaleris, Stephen N. .... Morristown, NJ
Maskantz, Sheree L. .... Trenton, NJ
Maskas, George P. .... Columbus, OH
Maske, Edward C. .... Sparta, NJ
Maskell, Arthur M. .... Springfield, MA
Maskell, Jack H. .... Library of Congress, Congressional Research Service, GV
Maskell, Patricia L. .... Chantilly, VA
Maskery, Robert A. .... West Bloomfield, MI
Masket, Edward S. .... Universal City, CA
Maskiewicz, Steven .... San Diego, CA
Maskin, Arvin .... New York, NY
Maskin, Douglas J. .... Sterling Heights, MI
Maskin, Leslie A. .... Los Angeles, CA
Maskol, Cynthia L. .... Towson, MD
Maskovyak, Joseph V. .... Columbus, OH
Maskrey, Robert M., Jr. .... Stroudsburg, PA
Maslach, Michael J. .... San Francisco, CA
Maslan, Gary R. .... Baltimore, MD
Maslan, M. Michael .... Baltimore, MD
Maslan, Maslan, Rothwell & O'Brien, P.A.
Baltimore, MD
Maslan, Michael .... Seattle, WA
Maslan, Robert F., Jr. .... Darien, CT
Maslan, Robert G. .... Seattle, WA
Masland, Albert H. .... Carlisle, PA
Masland, Thomas N. .... Concord, NH
Maslaniak, Kimberly A. .... San Jose, CA
Maslanik, Austin H. .... Bartow, FL
Maslanik, Michael B. .... Denver, CO
Maslanka, Michael J. .... Chicago, IL
Maslanka, Michael P. .... Dallas, TX
Maslansky, Michael F. .... New York, NY
Maslauski, Steven M. .... Los Angeles, CA
Maslen, David .... Arkansas City, KS
Maslen, David P. .... Newburyport, MA
Masler, Gregory S. .... Santa Ana, CA
Masler, Mark G. .... Ithaca, NY
Masler, Ross P. .... New York, NY
Masley, Andrea .... New York, NY
Masley, Mark A. .... Philadelphia, PA
Maslia, David J. .... Atlanta, GA
Masliah, Noemi E. .... New York, NY
Masliansky, Nechama .... New York, NY
Maslime, Gary William .... Rensselaer, NY
Maslin, Jonathan N. .... New York, NY
Masline, Gary W. .... Rensselaer, NY
Masling, Mark .... Department of Justice, Civil Rights Division, GV
Maslo & Sica .... Union City, NJ
Maslo, Steven R. .... Union City, NJ
Maslon Edelman Borman & Brand
Minneapolis, MN
Maslov, Edward I. .... South Barrington, IL
Maslow, Aaron D. .... New York, NY
Maslow, Andrew D. .... New York, NY
Maslow, Lisa Spann .... Mill Valley, CA
Maslow, Robert W. .... Port Washington, NY
Maslow, Susan A. .... Doylestown, PA
Maslow, Will .... New York, NY

Maslowe, Richard H. .... Glen Ellyn, IL
Maslowski, John .... Staten Island, NY
Maslowski, Julie M. .... Milwaukee, WI
Maslowsky, Len .... Chicago, IL
Maslyn, James E. .... Rochester, NY
Maslyn, Patrick J. .... Washington, DC
Maslyn, Robert A. .... Schenectady, NY
Maslynsky, Jill A. .... Philadelphia, PA
Masner, Charles M. .... Washington, DC
Masnica, Michael J. .... Burlington, WI
Kenosha, WI
Masnik, George L. .... Treasury Department, Internal Revenue Service, GV
Masnik, Peter L. .... Haddonfield, NJ
Masnik, Robert H.
Treasury Department, GV
Masnikoff, Lyle B. .... West Palm Beach, FL
Masnyj, Zenon B. .... New York, NY
Maso, Jeffrey B. .... San Francisco, CA
Masog, John A. .... Park Rapids, MN
Masom, Jeffrey Scott .... Wilmington, DE
Mason, A. Craig, Jr. .... Lincoln, NE
Mason, A. George, Jr. .... Kingsport, TN
Mason, A. Richard .... Rocky Hill, CT
Mason, Albert R. .... Chicopee, MA
Mason, Andrew D., Jr.
Linthicum Heights, MD
Mason, Andrew S. .... New York, NY
Mason, Angela J. .... Dothan, AL
Mason, Anita B. .... Washington, DC
Mason, Anna M. .... Monterey Park, CA
Mason, Anne S. .... Clearwater, FL
Mason, Anthony H. .... Phoenix, AZ
Mason & April, LLC .... Garden City, NY
Mason, Arthur K. .... Washington, DC
Mason, Arthur M. .... Natick, MA
Mason, Arthur M. .... New York, NY
Mason, Arthur P. .... La Verne, CA
Mason, Asa D. .... Newport Beach, CA
Mason & Associates .... Tampa, FL
Clearwater, FL
Mason, Barbara .... Westwood, MA
Mason, Barbara A. .... Philadelphia, PA
Mason, Barbara E. .... Oxnard, CA
Mason, Barbara, Law Offices of
Westwood, MA
Mason, Barney Jay .... Seattle, WA
Mason, Barry S. .... Upland, CA
Mason, Belle C. .... Los Angeles, CA
Mason, Benjamin M. .... Newport News, VA
Mason, Bertrand A. .... Arnold, MD
Mason, Beth .... Beaverton, OR
Mason & Breitenecker, LLP
New York, NY
Mason, Brian W. .... Fairfield, NJ
Mason, Bruce A. .... Wilmington, NC
Mason, Bryan St. Clair .... Little Rock, AR
Mason, Byron K. .... Indianapolis, IN
Mason, C. Steven .... Raleigh, NC
Mason, C. Vernon .... New York, NY
Mason, Carl R.
Department Of Health And Human Services, Social Security Administration, GV
Mason, Carolyn M. .... Los Angeles, CA
Mason, Chandler W. .... Atlanta, GA
Mason, Charles A. .... Larchmont, NY
Mason, Charles C., Jr. .... Latrobe, PA
Mason, Charles C., Jr. .... Houston, TX
Mason, Charles J., Jr. .... Fort Worth, TX
Mason, Charles N., Jr. .... Washington, DC
Mason, Charles R. .... Plainville, MA
Mason, Cheryl White .... Los Angeles, CA
San Francisco, CA
Mason, Chris Schiller .... Salisbury, MD
Mason, Christina M. .... New York, NY
Mason, Christopher M. .... New York, NY
Mason, Christopher R. .... Syracuse, NY
Mason, Clark W. .... Little Rock, AR
Mason, Claude D. .... Duluth, GA
Mason, Corinne A. .... Dallas, TX
Mason, Courtney H., & Associates, P.C.
Birmingham, AL
Mason, Courtney H., Jr. .... Birmingham, AL
Mason, Crissy .... Mount Olive, NC
Mason, Curtis C. .... Huntsville, TX
Mason, Cynthia Aleksa .... Brook Park, OH
Mason, D. Lenore .... New York, NY
Mason, DaCosta R. .... Washington, DC
Mason, Dana L. .... Natick, MA
Mason, Daniel D. .... Lorain, OH
Mason, Daniel H. .... Morehead, KY
Mason, Daniel S. .... San Francisco, CA
Mason, David A. .... Paw Paw, MI
Mason, David A., Jr. .... Detroit, MI
Mason, David C. .... St. Louis, MO
Mason, David C. .... Upper Sandusky, OH
Mason, David C. .... Philipsburg, PA
Mason, David E. .... Des Plaines, IL
Mason, David G. .... Shelbyville, KY
Mason, David H. .... Minneapolis, MN
Mason, David J. .... Waterloo, IA
Mason, David M. .... Chicago, IL
Mason, David P. .... New York, NY
Mason, David R. .... Cedar Falls, IA
Mason, David V. .... Annandale, VA
Mason, Deborah L. .... Atlantic City, NJ
Mason, Deborah M. .... Storrs, CT
Mason, Derrel M. .... Wilton, CT
New York, NY
Mason, Desrie L. .... Woodbridge, NJ
Mason, Diane J. .... San Francisco, CA
Mason, Dolores H. .... Chula Vista, CA
Mason, Donald Edward
Fort Lauderdale, FL
Miami, FL
Mason, Donald F., Jr. .... Kingsport, TN
Mason, Donald H. .... Barnstable, MA
Mason, Donald L. .... Chicago, IL

Mason, Donald R. .... Chicago, IL
Mason, Donald R. .... Morgantown, WV
Mason, Donna M. .... Annandale, VA
Mason, Dwayne L. .... Houston, TX
Mason, E. Palmer .... Tallahassee, FL
Mason, Earl S. .... Grand Forks, ND
Mason, Edgar A. .... Dallas, TX
Mason, Edith W. .... Morehead City, NC
Mason, Edward T. .... Lakeland, FL
Mason, Edwin D. .... Chicago, IL
Mason, Edwin L. .... Tallahassee, FL
Mason, Edwyn E. .... Delhi, NY
Mason, Elise J. .... Baltimore, MD
Mason, Elizabeth .... Albuquerque, NM
Mason, Elizabeth A. .... New York, NY
Mason, Elizabeth Lipscomb .... Beaufort, SC
Mason, Ellen E. .... Detroit, MI
Mason, Ellen Rhodes .... Newton, MA
Mason, Emma N. .... Lorain, OH
Mason, Eric J. .... Dallas, TX
Mason, F. Morris .... Tyler, TX
Mason, Falton O., Jr. .... Oxford, MS
Mason, Frank M. .... Longview, TX
Mason, Frederick T. .... Fullerton, CA
Mason, Frederick T., Inc. .... Fullerton, CA
Mason, G. Chadd .... Fayetteville, AR
Mason, Gail D. .... Department of Defense, Defense Legal Services Agency, GV
Mason, Gary E. .... Washington, DC
Mason, Gary L. .... Marlboro, NJ
Mason, Gary T. .... Mission Viejo, CA
Mason, Gayla D. .... Fort Scott, KS
Mason, Geoffrey C. .... Fairfax, VA
Mason, Geoffrey Colbourne
Washington, DC
Mason, George E. .... Lansing, MI
Mason, George, III .... Colonial Beach, VA
Mason, George J. .... Los Angeles, CA
Mason, George, Jr. .... Colonial Beach, VA
Mason, George L. .... Bridgewater, VA
Mason, Gerald .... Morro Bay, CA
Mason, Gerald .... Menominee, MI
Stephenson, MI
Mason, Gerald R. .... Pinedale, WY
Mason, G. J., III .... Plano, TX
Mason, Grant A. .... Millersburg, OH
Mason, Greg J. .... Edina, MN
Mason, Gregory J. .... Mineola, NY
Mason, Gregory S. .... Fresno, CA
Mason & Griffin .... Anchorage, AK
Mason, Griffin & Pierson, A Professional Corporation .... Princeton, NJ
Mason, Guy A. .... Chicago, IL
Mason, H. Denning .... Bellefonte, PA
Mason, Heather Eden .... New York, NY
Mason, Heather M. .... Los Angeles, CA
Mason, Heide E. .... Brooklyn, NY
Mason, Heidi Akins .... Dallas, TX
Mason, Henry L., III .... Chicago, IL
Mason, Howard H. .... San Diego, CA
Mason, Irvin L. .... Durango, CO
Mason, Isaacson & Macik, P.A., Law Offices of .... Gallup, NM
Grants, NM
Mason, J. Cheney .... Orlando, FL
Mason, J. Cheney, P.A. .... Orlando, FL
Mason, J. Derek .... Arlington, VA
Mason, J. Parker .... Seattle, WA
Mason, J. Thomas .... Columbus, OH
Mason, J. Thomas .... Tulsa, OK
Mason, J. William L. .... Portsmouth, NH
Mason, Jackie S. .... Denver, CO
Mason, Jackson H., Jr. .... Campbell, CA
El Dorado Hills, CA
Mason, James A. .... Hood River, OR
Mason, James B. .... Westport, CT
Mason, James C. .... La Jolla, CA
Mason, James D. .... Mankato, MN
Mason, James Demere .... Jacksonville, FL
Mason, James E. .... Westminster, CA
Mason, James E. .... Sioux Falls, SD
Mason, James J. .... Tacoma, WA
Mason, James Jay .... Gallup, NM
Mason, James L., Jr. .... Charlotte, NC
Mason, James M. .... West Haven, CT
Mason, James M. .... Portland, OR
Mason, James Patrick
South Lake Tahoe, CA
Mason, James R. .... Palatine, IL
Mason, James R., III .... Terre Haute, IN
Mason, James R., Jr. .... Decatur, AL
Mason, James W. .... New York, NY
Mason, James W. .... Laurinburg, NC
Mason, James W. .... Columbus, OH
Mason, Jan Stanley .... Pasadena, CA
Mason, Janet Sue .... Las Vegas, NV
Mason, Jeffery A. .... Goodland, KS
Mason, Jeffrey C. .... Hackensack, NJ
Mason, Jeffrey N. .... Arlington, VA
Mason, Jerry A. .... Chicago, IL
Mason, Jerry D. .... Coeur d'Alene, ID
Mason, Jerry D. .... Dallas, TX
Mason, Jerry G. .... Meridian, MS
Mason, Jess W. .... Houston, TX
Mason, Joan D. .... Meadville, PA
Mason, John A. .... Sacramento, CA
Mason, John B. .... Odessa, TX
Mason, John B. .... Salt Lake City, UT
Mason, John B. .... Redmond, WA
Mason, John C. .... Estes Park, CO
Mason, John E. .... Stateline, NV
Nashville, TN
Mason, John H. .... Boston, MA
Mason, John H. .... Wichita Falls, TX
Mason, John, Jr. .... Denver, CO
Mason, John L. .... Cincinnati, OH
Mason, John L., Jr. .... Belmont, MA
Mason, John M. .... Fayetteville, NY

Mason, John M. (Jack) .... St. Paul, MN
Mason, John P. .... Philadelphia, PA
Mason, John, Partners, Ltd. .... Stateline, NV
Nashville, TN
Mason, John R. .... Department of Education, Office of the General Counsel, GV
Mason, John R., Jr. .... Greenfield, MA
Mason, John S. .... Pittsburgh, PA
Mason, John W. .... Dearborn, MI
Mason, John W. .... Asheville, NC
Mason, John W., Law Offices, P.C.
Dearborn, MI
Mason, Johnny W., Jr. .... Atlanta, GA
Mason, Jon G. .... Kenosha, WI
Mason, Jon G., S.C. .... Kenosha, WI
Mason, Jonathan A. .... Covington, KY
Cincinnati, OH
Columbus, OH
Dayton, OH
Lima, OH
Mason, Jonathan B. .... Atlanta, GA
Mason, Joni F. .... Newark, NJ
Mason, Joseph C., Jr. .... Clearwater, FL
Mason, Joseph G. .... San Jose, CA
Mason, Joseph M., Jr. .... Brooksville, FL
Spring Hill, FL
Mason, Josiah L. .... Ashland, OH
Mason, Joyce J. .... Mamaroneck, NY
Mason, Judy K. .... Little Rock, AR
Mason, Julian L., III .... Anchorage, AK
Mason, Julien J. .... Bowling Green, VA
Mason, Karen E. .... Washington, DC
Mason, Karen E. .... Belleville, IL
St. Louis, MO
Mason, Karol V. .... Atlanta, GA
Mason, Kathleen C. .... Baton Rouge, LA
Mason, Keith B. .... Washington, NC
Mason, Keith R. .... Pittsburgh, PA
Mason, Keith W. .... Atlanta, GA
Mason, Kelly Taylor .... Kansas City, MO
Mason, Kenneth A. .... Overland Park, KS
Mason, Kenneth B. .... Jacksonville Beach, FL
Mason, Kenneth G. .... Chicago, IL
Mason, Kent A. .... Washington, DC
Mason, Ketterman & Morgan, A Professional Association .... Annapolis, MD
Baltimore, MD
Hunt Valley, MD
Mason, Ketterman, Morgan & Shelsby
Newark, DE
Wilmington, DE
Mason, Kevin E. .... Katy, TX
Mason, Kevin L. .... Newington, CT
Mason, Kevin M. .... Fairfield, CT
Locust Valley, NY
Mason, Kimball W. .... Idaho Falls, ID
Mason, Kirby Gould .... Savannah, GA
Mason, Kolehmainen, Rathburn & Wyss
Chicago, IL
Mason and Krieg .... Morton, IL
Mason, L. Patten .... Morehead City, NC
Mason, Larry G. .... Southfield, MI
Mason, Larry K. .... Berkeley, CA
Mason, Laura .... Albuquerque, NM
Mason, Laura D.
Grosse Pointe Woods, MI
Troy, MI
Mason, Laura D., P.C.
Grosse Pointe Woods, MI
Mason, Laurence E. .... Seattle, WA
Mason Law Firm, P.L.C. .... Fayetteville, AR
Mason Law Firm, The, P.A.
Mount Pleasant, SC
Mason, Lawrence D. .... Chicago, IL
Mason, Leah M. .... Kansas City, MO
Mason, Len R. .... San Diego, CA
Mason, Leonard .... Chicago, IL
Mason, Leslie L., Jr. .... Powhatan, VA
Mason, Lillian Linz .... Rockville, MD
Mason, Lisa A. .... Chicago, IL
Mason, Lloyd W. .... Chicago, IL
Mason, Lori J. .... Pittsburgh, PA
Mason, Lorraine H. .... Wilmington, NC
Mason, Lucy E. .... San Francisco, CA
Mason, M. Dan .... Meadville, PA
Mason, Madeline J. .... Boulder, CO
Mason, Madelynn R. .... Garden City, NY
Mason, Malcolm .... New York, NY
Mason, Marc S. .... New York, NY
Mason, Marcia .... Des Moines, IA
Mason, Margaret P. .... New Haven, CT
Mason, Mark A. .... Mount Pleasant, SC
Mason, Mark D. .... Springfield, MA
Mason, Mark E. .... Annapolis, MD
Mason, Marshall "Allen", III
Durham, NC
Mason, Martha Jones .... Raleigh, NC
Mason & Martin .... Boston, MA
Mason, Mary Anne .... Washington, DC
Mason, Mary Anne .... Chicago, IL
Mason, Mary H. .... Department of Justice, Civil Division, GV
Mason, Mary L. .... Grand Rapids, MI
Mason & Mason .... Meadville, PA
Colonial Beach, VA
Mason & Mason, P.A.
Morehead City, NC
Mason & Mason, P.C. .... Newport News, VA
Mason, Mason, Sullivan & Mason
Ashland, OH
Mason, Matthew C. .... Wilton, CT
New York, NY
Mason, Matthew C. .... Rosemont, IL
Mason, Matthew D. .... Novi, MI
Mason, Matthew J. .... Detroit, MI
Mason, Matthew L. .... Greensboro, NC
Mason, Maurice .... Sarasota, FL
Mason, Maurice P., Jr. .... Lowell, MA

Mason, Max ... Suffern, NY
Mason, Meridith F. ... Princeton, NJ
Mason, Merrill McCall ... Raleigh, NC
Mason, Michael A. ... Flint, MI
Mason, Michael C. ... Burbank, CA
Mason, Michael D. ... San Francisco, CA
Mason, Michael D. ... Rockville, MD
Mason, Michael David ... Augusta, KY
Mason, Michael F. ... Washington, DC
Mason, Michael G. ... Cincinnati, OH
Mason, Michael J. ... Livonia, MI
Mason, Michael L. ... Merced, CA
Mason, Michael L. ... Atlanta, GA
Mason, Michael R. ... Bethesda, MD
Mason, Michael T. ... Chicago, IL
Mason, Michele D. ... Houston, TX
Mason, Mike R. ... Jefferson, TX
Mason, Miles S. ... Washington, DC
Mason, Milo C.
Department Of The Interior, Office of the Solicitor, GV
Mason, Miriam E. ... Tampa, FL
Mason, Molly C. ... Chicago, IL
Mason, Monica Bridgeford ... Tampa, FL
Mason, Monica Lee ... Little Rock, AR
Mason & Musella ... Hasbrouck Heights, NJ
Mason, Nancy O. ... Garner, NC
Mason, Nicole B. ... Los Gatos, CA
Mason, Nicole C. ... Washington, DC
Mason, Orvel B. ... Arkansas City, KS
Mason, Orvel, P.A., Law Offices of
Arkansas City, KS
Mason, Patricia ... Kalamazoo, MI
Mason, Patrick B. ... Memphis, TN
Mason, Patrick S. ... Neptune, NJ
Mason, Patrick W. ... Seattle, WA
Mason, Paul A. R. ... Cottage Grove, MN
Mason, Paul G. ... Fairbury, IL
Mason, Paul H. W. ... Brooklyn, NY
Mason, Paul J. ... San Jose, CA
Mason, Paul J. ...
Department of Defense, GV
Mason, Peter C., Jr. ... Lansing, MI
Mason, Peter H. ... Los Angeles, CA
Mason, Peter I. ... Chicago, IL
Mason, Peter K. ... Searsport, ME
Mason, Peter R. ... Los Angeles, CA
Mason, Peter W. ... Los Angeles, CA
Mason, Peter W. ... Department of State, Office of the Legal Adviser, GV
Mason, Philip A. ... Boston, MA
Mason, Phillip E. ... Thomasville, AL
Mason, R. Miles ... Memphis, TN
Somerville, TN
Mason, Ralph S., III ... Princeton, NJ
Mason, Ramon H. ... Morton, IL
Mason, Randal T. ... San Diego, CA
Mason, Randall L. ... San Diego, CA
Mason, Reese ... New York, NY
Mason, Renee Bryant ... Salem, OR
Mason, Richard C. ... Philadelphia, PA
Mason, Richard G. ... New York, NY
Mason, Richard J. ... Chicago, IL
Mason, Richard K. ... Los Angeles, CA
Mason, Rick A. ... Joliet, IL
Mason, Robbins, Gnass & Browning
Merced, CA
Mason, Robert ... Dallas, TX
Mason, Robert A. ... Statesboro, GA
Mason, Robert B. ... Anchorage, AK
Mason, Robert C. ... New York, NY
Mason, Robert E. ... Holland, MI
Mason, Robert M., III ... Los Angeles, CA
Mason, Robert P. ... San Francisco, CA
Mason, Robert W. ... Jacksonville, FL
Mason, Robert W. ... Dallas, TX
Mason, Robt. D. ... Waterloo, IA
Mason, Rodney C. ... Asheboro, NC
Mason, Rodney J. ... St. Paul, MN
Mason, Roger M. ... Los Gatos, CA
Mason, Ronald A. ... Knox, NY
Mason, Ronald A. ... Milford, OH
Mason, Ronald C. ... Dodge City, KS
Mason, Ronald E. ... Adel, IA
Mason, Ronald, Jr. ... New Orleans, LA
Mason, Ronald L. ... Columbus, OH
Mason, Rothwell B. ... Port Townsend, WA
Mason, Roy L. ... Newark, DE
Annapolis, MD
Baltimore, MD
Hunt Valley, MD
Mason, S. Michael ... Marseilles, IL
Mason, Sally Q. ... New York, NY
Mason, Sam W. ... Bennington, VT
Mason, Samuel ... Philadelphia, PA
Mason, Sandra G.A. ... Norcross, GA
Mason, Sarah ... San Diego, CA
Mason, Scott C. ... Olathe, KS
Mason, Shannon M. ... Los Angeles, CA
Mason, Shannon T., Jr. ... Newport News, VA
Mason, Sharon Lynn ... Pasadena, CA
Mason, Shawn M. ... Mountain View, CA
Mason, Slovin & Schilling Co., L.P.A.
Covington, KY
Florence, KY
Cincinnati, OH
Columbus, OH
Dayton, OH
Lima, OH
Mason & Snodgrass, A Professional Corporation ... Wichita Falls, TX
Mason, Stefan M. ... Los Angeles, CA
Mason, Stefan M., A Law Corporation
Los Angeles, CA
Mason Steinhardt Jacobs Perlman & Pesick, Professional Corporation ... Detroit, MI
Southfield, MI
Mason, Stephen A. ... Sacramento, CA
Mason, Stephen G. ... Irvine, CA
Westlake Village, CA
Mason, Stephen L. ... New York, NY
Mason, Stephen M., (P.C.) ... Houston, TX
Mason, Sterlon ... Washington, DC
Mason, Steven A. ... Hollywood, FL
Mason, Steven A., P.A. ... Hollywood, FL
Mason, Steven C. ... Chicago, IL
Mason, Steven G. ... Orlando, FL
Mason, Steven G., P.A., Law Offices of
Orlando, FL
Mason, Steven J. ... La Vergne, TN
Mason, Steven M. ... Tyler, TX
Mason, Susan E. ... Detroit, MI
Mason, Susan L. ... San Diego, CA
Mason, Susan M. ... Irvine, CA
Mason, Susan McMillion ... Midlothian, TX
Mason, Susan Valerie ... Pittsburgh, PA
Mason, Susan Wright ... Anchorage, AK
Mason, Suzanne G. ... Atlanta, GA
Mason, T. Lee
Charlotte Amalie, St. Thomas, VI
Mason, Tara L. ... New Orleans, LA
Mason, Taylor & Colicchio
New Brunswick, NJ
Princeton, NJ
Trenton, NJ
Mason, Terrel J. ... San Rafael, CA
Mason, Theodore W. ... Philadelphia, PA
Mason & Thomas ... Sacramento, CA
Mason, Thomas A. ... Cleveland, OH
Mason, Thomas B. ... Washington, DC
Mason, Thomas B. ... Roanoke, VA
Mason, Thomas E., Jr.
Hasbrouck Heights, NJ
Mason, Thomas G. ... Austin, TX
Mason, Thomas J. ... Mineola, NY
Mason, Thomas L. ... Ashland, OH
Mason, Thomas O. ... Boston, MA
Mason, Thomas O. ... McLean, VA
Mason, Thomas P. ... Houston, TX
Mason, Thomasine G. ... Columbia, SC
Mason, Thos. ... Oracle, AZ
Mason, Thos. J. ... Richmond, VA
Mason & Tini ... Mineola, NY
Mason, Todd E. ... New York, NY
Mason, Todd J. ... Cresskill, NJ
Mason, Tom R. ... University, MS
Mason, Tracey D. ... Lawrenceville, GA
Mason, Valerie S. ... New York, NY
Mason, Verice M. ... Lawrenceville, NJ
Mason, W. Brett ... Baton Rouge, LA
Mason, W. Scott ... Spokane, WA
Mason, Walter B., Jr. ... Southfield, MI
Mason, Walter Scott, III ... Cordell, OK
Mason, Walter W. ... Seattle, WA
Mason, Wayne B. ... Dallas, TX
Mason, Wesley R., III ... San Diego, CA
Mason, W. F., Jr., Law Office of
Roanoke, VA
Mason & Wheatley, P.C. ... Annandale, VA
Mason, William A., IV ... Burlington, VT
Mason, William B. ... Arlington, VA
Mason, William B., Jr. ... Annandale, VA
Mason, William D. ... Parma, OH
Mason, William E. ... Knoxville, TN
Mason, William E. ... Knoxville, TN
Mason, William E., P.C., Law Offices of
Knoxville, TN
Mason, William G. ... Cleburne, TX
Mason, William J. ... Wilmington, NC
Mason, William L. ... Wadesboro, NC
Mason, William M. ... Garden City, NY
Mason, William Norton ... Wilmington, NC
Mason, William P. ... Atlanta, GA
Mason, William S. (Bill) ... Ozona, TX
Mason, William T., Jr. ... Norfolk, VA
Mason, Winton J. ... Grand Rapids, MN
Mason, Wm. E. ... Minneapolis, MN
Masoncup, Stephan C. ... Indianapolis, IN
Masone, Leonard ... Maspeth, NY
Masone, Linda A. ... Central Islip, NY
Masone, White & Penkava ... Maspeth, NY
Masoner, Barbara J. ... Denver, CO
Masoner, Christopher J. ... Lawrence, KS
Masoner, Leslie A. ... Long Beach, CA
Masonis, Robert J. ... Philadelphia, PA
Mason-Miller, Alicia ... Santa Fe, NM
Masonson, Nina ... Bronx, NY
Mason-Williams, Tamara
San Francisco, CA
Masotti, Alexander V. ... Bronx, NY
Masotti, Kenneth A. ... San Francisco, CA
Masotti, Marco ... New York, NY
Masotto, Laurie F. ... Encinitas, CA
Masoudi, Gerald F. ... Washington, DC
Masouredis, Linus S. ... Oakland, CA
Masover, Jos. ... Chicago, IL
Maspons, Miguel A. ... Miami, FL
Masquelette, Philip A. ... Houston, TX
Masquelette, Philip E. ... Franklin, MA
Masri, Laila ... Cincinnati, OH
Masri, Michael H. ... Mineola, NY
Masri, Rabih Chakib ... McLean, VA
Masri, Rob C. ... Reston, VA
Masri, Selwa ... Washington, DC
Masry, Edward L. ... Westlake Village, CA
Masry & Vititoe ... Westlake Village, CA
Mass, Alan H. ... New York, NY
Mass, Alvin ... New York, NY
Mass, Amy ... Columbus, OH
Mass, Arthur L. ... New York, NY
Mass, Christopher L. ... Long Beach, CA
Mass, Clifford J. ... New York, NY
Mass, Julia Harumi ... Pasadena, CA
Mass, Kathleen S. ... West Haven, CT
Mass, Laurence D. ... St. Louis, MO
Mass, Marian ... New York, NY
Mass, Michael A. ... Alexandria, VA
Mass, Mitchell R. ... New York, NY
Mass, Norman S. ... Union, NJ
Mass, Paul J. ... Birmingham, AL
Mass, Robert ... St. Louis, MO
Mass, Robin D. ... New York, NY
Mass, Stuart ... New York, NY
Massa, Amel R. ... Commack, NY
Massa, Cliff ... Washington, DC
Massa, David J. ... St. Louis, MO
Massa, Dominic E. ... Boston, MA
Massa, Donna Simpson ... Cookeville, TN
Massa, Frank B. ... Houston, TX
Massa, Heidi ... Chicago, IL
Massa, Jean M. ... Winner, SD
Massa, Joseph A., Jr. ... Warren, PA
Massa, Joseph J. ... Cherry Hill, NJ
Massa, Mark S. ... Indianapolis, IN
Massa & Massa ... New Rochelle, NY
Massa, Maureen ... New York, NY
Massa, Michael J. ... Merrillville, IN
Massa, Patrick C. ... North Palm Beach, FL
Massa, Patrick C., P.A., Law Offices of
North Palm Beach, FL
Massa, Philip J. ... West Palm Beach, FL
Massa, Raymond G. ... New Rochelle, NY
Massa, Richard J. ... Lakeport, CA
Massa, Robert E. ... Tulsa, OK
Massa, Salvatore ... Department of Justice, Antitrust Division, GV
Massa, Susan ... Miamisburg, OH
Massa, Teresa A. ... Valparaiso, IN
Massa, Todd A. ... St. Louis, MO
Massa, Vincent J., III ... Hackensack, NJ
Massa, William A. ... Jersey City, NJ
Massa, William Gregory ... Pequannock, NJ
Massa, William Stanton, III ... Morristown, TN
Massad, Anthony M. ... Frederick, OK
Massad, Evans & Kent, Inc. A Professional Corporation ... Frederick, OK
Massad, Gail P. ... Livonia, MI
Massad, Kelly M. ... Dallas, TX
Massad, Marcus J. ... Arlington, TX
Massad, Michael J. ... Oklahoma City, OK
Massad, Michael P., Jr. ... Dallas, TX
Massad, Pamela A. ... Worcester, MA
Massad, Stan F. ... Glendale, AZ
Massad, Stephen A. ... Houston, TX
Massa Diaz, Juan ... San Juan, PR
Massafra, G. E. ... Atlanta, GA
Massagee, B. B., III ... Hendersonville, NC
Massagee, Boyd B., Jr.
Hendersonville, NC
Massahos, Debera L. ... Palo Alto, CA
Massalon, John A. ... Charleston, SC
Massameno, John M. ... Rocky Hill, CT
Massamillo, Eugene F. ... New York, NY
Massamore, David G. ... Madisonville, KY
Massamore & Senter, P.S.C.
Madisonville, KY
Massaquoi, Hans J., Jr. ... Detroit, MI
Massar, Johannes Bernardus ... Dallas, TX
Massar, Nedda G. ... Trenton, NJ
Massar, Sheppard B. ... East Windsor, NJ
Massar, Sheppard, P.A. ... East Windsor, NJ
Massar, William ... West Palm Beach, FL
Massar, William T. ... Houston, TX
Massara, Mark A. ... San Francisco, CA
Massarano, David Ledyard ... Houston, TX
Massare, Edward J. ... Rochester, NY
Massari, Domenic L., III ... Tampa, FL
Massari, Jeffrey T. ... Chicago, IL
Massari, Kerry M. ... Lafayette, LA
Massari Law Group ... Tampa, FL
Massari, Michael V. ... Fort Lauderdale, FL
Massari, Michael V. ... Miami, FL
Massari, Patrick J. ... Washington, DC
Massarini, Dale J. ... Chalmette, LA
Massaro, Angelo ... Niagara Falls, NY
Massaro, Carl A., Jr. ... Bridgeport, CT
Massaro, Carlo ... Washington, DC
Massaro, Dante A. ... Syracuse, NY
Massaro, Jane A. ... New York, NY
Massaro, Jason M. ... Munster, IN
Massaro, John C. ... Washington, DC
Massaro, John J. ... Plantation, FL
Massaro Keating & Cosgriff ... Buffalo, NY
Massaro, Kevin C. ... Denver, CO
Massaro, Lorraine ... New York, NY
Massaro, Louis P., Jr. ... Stoneham, MA
Massaro, Louis P., Jr., P.C. ... Stoneham, MA
Massaro, Mary ... Iselin, NJ
Massaro, Patti L. ... Houston, TX
Massaro, Paul A ... Montclair, NJ
Massaro, Peter T. ... Cleveland, OH
Massaro Keating, Lisa ... Buffalo, NY
Massaroni, Christopher ... Albany, NY
Massaroni, John R. ... Schenectady, NY
Massaroni, Kenneth Michael
Norcross, GA
Massarsky, Irving E. ... Fort Lee, NJ
Massarsky, Reuben W. ... Hoboken, NJ
Massarweh, William A.
Walnut Creek, CA
Massco, Francis P. ... Wheeling, WV
Massé, Drew R. ... Toledo, OH
Masse, Frank W. ... San Pedro, CA
Masse, Jeannie E. ... San Francisco, CA
Masse, Scott L. ... Peabody, MA
Masse, Simone Diana ... Dover, NH
Masse, Steven J. ... Hyde Park, MA
Massee & Leonard ... East Grand Forks, MN
Massee, Michael J. ... Tucson, AZ
Massel, Elihu S. ... New York, NY
Massel, Mark S. ... Carmel, CA
Massel, Susan J. ... Highland Park, IL
Massel, Suzanne J. ... Chicago, IL
Masselam, Amanda P. ... Boston, MA
Massell, Gerald J. ... Middletown, NJ
Massell, Jerry J. ... Middletown, NJ
Massell, Massell & Vincent ... Middletown, NJ
Massella, Ines M. ... Erie, PA
Masselli, David C. ... Arlington, VA
Masselli & Lane, P.C. ... Arlington, VA
McLean, VA
Massen, Nina ... New York, NY
Massenburg, Edgar A. ... Hampton, VA
Massengale Debruhl, L.L.C.
New Orleans, LA
Massengale, Frank E. ... New Orleans, LA
Massengale, Marcy V. ... New Orleans, LA
Massengale, Michael C. ... Houston, TX
Massengale & Ozer ... Chapel Hill, NC
Massengale, Roger L., Law Offices of
Paintsville, KY
Massengale, Roger L., Law Offices of
Pikeville, KY
Massengale, William F.W. ... Chapel Hill, NC
Massengill, Alan D. ... Gaithersburg, MD
Massengill, Brian J. ... Chicago, IL
Massengill, Caldwell & Hyder, P.C.
Bristol, TN
Massengill, Clint E. ... Rocky Mount, NC
Massengill, David E. ... New York, NY
Massengill, J. Ross ... Ennis, TX
Massengill, Kimm A. ... Worthington, OH
Massengill, Linda Burdt
Saddle Brook, NJ
Massengill, Myers N. ... Bristol, TN
Massengill, Nona K. ... Richmond, VA
Massengill, Roy H. ... Alexandria, VA
Masser, Annaliese P. ... Greensburg, PA
Masser, Paul G. ... Timonium, MD
Masserman, Dean ... Beverly Hills, CA
Masserman, Terri Lynn ... Sherman Oaks, CA
Massery, Gillis & Guiney ... Boston, MA
Massery, Louis N. ... Boston, MA
Massery, R. David ... Little Rock, AR
Massett, Marguarite ... Syracuse, NY
Massetti, Regina M. ... Cleveland, OH
Massey, A. Blanton ... Fredericksburg, VA
Massey, A. Blanton, & Associates, P.C.
Fredericksburg, VA
Massey, A. Moses ... Danbury, NC
Massey, Abit ... Gainesville, GA
Massey, Albert P., III ... Fort Lauderdale, FL
Massey, Albert P., Jr. ... Kennett Square, PA
Malvern, PA
Massey, Allan S. ... Fort Collins, CO
Massey, Allen C. ... Sacramento, CA
Massey, Balentine, Edwards & Psencik, P.C.
Eden, TX
San Angelo, TX
Massey, Barbara J. ... San Francisco, CA
Massey, Bert V., II ... Brownwood, TX
Massey, C. Warren ... Winder, GA
Massey, Calvin R. ... San Francisco, CA
Massey, Cannon & Smith, P.L.L.C.
Statesville, NC
Massey, Carl B., Jr. ... Winston-Salem, NC
Massey, Charles E. ... Covington, KY
Massey, Coican & Schuster
Fort Lauderdale, FL
Massey, Daniel J. ... Columbus, OH
Massey, Daniel P. ... Phoenix, AZ
Massey, Daniel T. ... Rawlins, WY
Massey, David A. ... Washington, DC
Massey, David B. ... New York, NY
Massey, David E. ... Columbia, SC
Massey, David Lee ... Decatur, IL
Massey, David Sanders ... Raleigh, NC
Massey, Dean R. ... Denver, CO
Massey, Dean T. ... Madison, WI
Massey, Desmond ... Los Angeles, CA
Roseland, NJ
New York, NY
Massey, Diane Dunham ... Houston, TX
Massey, Donald B. ... Grand Junction, CO
Massey, Donald C. ... New Orleans, LA
Massey, Donald L. ... San Jose, CA
Massey, Donald T. ... Yarmouth, ME
Massey, Donald T., P.A. ... Yarmouth, ME
Massey, Donna Harris ... Chicago, IL
Massey, Dwaine M. ... Houston, TX
Massey, Edmund M. ... Morrilton, AR
Massey, Eugene A. ... Washington, DC
Massey, Evan M., Jr. ... Richmond, VA
Massey, Fred H., Jr.
Export-Import Bank of The United States, Office of the General Counsel, GV
Massey, Frederick V. ... Dublin, GA
Winder, GA
Massey & Frizzell, LLC ... Albuquerque, NM
Massey, G. Michael ... Jackson, MS
Massey, Gaines Michael ... Jackson, MS
Massey, Gary E. ... Altamonte Springs, FL
Massey, Gary E., P.A.
Altamonte Springs, FL
Orlando, FL
Massey, Gary M., Jr. ... Chattanooga, TN
Massey, Harmon O., Jr.
Fort Walton Beach, FL
Massey, Harold ... Camden, NY
Massey, Henry Nelson ... Morristown, NJ
New York, NY
Massey, Henry P., Jr. ... Palo Alto, CA
Massey & Higginbotham, P.A. ... Jackson, MS
Massey, Ivor, Jr. ... Richmond, VA
Massey, J. Christopher ... San Francisco, CA
Massey, J. Gary ... Jackson, MS
Massey, Jack T. ... Oklahoma City, OK
Massey, Jackson R. ... Augusta, GA
Massey, Jackson R., & Associates, P.C.
Augusta, GA
Massey, James B., III ... Roanoke, VA
Massey, James E. ... Atlanta, GA

Massey, James T. .... Sisters, OR
Massey, James W. .... Chattanooga, TN
Massey, Janine Keck .... San Francisco, CA
Massey, Jefferson H. .... Zanesville, OH
Massey, Jeffery W. .... Oklahoma City, OK
Massey, Jeffery W. .... Oklahoma City, OK
Massey, Jill A. .... Bethesda, MD
Massey, Joel T. .... Chandler, OK
Massey, John M. .... Statesville, NC
Massey, John P. .... Albuquerque, NM
Massey, Jon G. .... New Orleans, LA
Massey, Jonathan S. .... New York, NY
Massey, Joyce A. Naumann .... Manassas, VA
Massey, Karen A. .... Augusta, ME
Massey, Karen L. .... Jefferson City, MO
Massey, Kathleen M. .... Schaumburg, IL
Massey, Kathleen Nicholson .... New York, NY
Massey, Lori A. .... Columbus, OH
Massey, M. Elaina .... Waycross, GA
Massey, M. Minnette .... Coral Gables, FL
Massey, Marilyn E. .... Winston-Salem, NC
Massey, Marion L. .... Fort Worth, TX
Massey, Mark A. .... Ocala, FL
Massey, Marsha C. .... Indianapolis, IN
Massey, Martha Hoppe .... Lincoln, NE
Massey, Mary E. .... West Chester, PA
Massey, Mary O'Keefe .... Ocean Township, NJ
Massey, Mel John, Jr. .... Indianapolis, IN
Massey, Michael .... Fort Lauderdale, FL
Massey, Michael B. .... Houston, TX
Massey, Michael B. .... Roanoke, VA
Massey, Michael G. .... Denver, CO
Massey, Michael J. .... Topeka, KS
Massey, Morris R. .... Casper, WY
Massey, Preston L. .... Austin, TX
Massey & Putnam .... Lakeland, FL
Massey, R. David, (P.A.) .... Greenville, SC
Massey, R. Edward, Jr. .... Mobile, AL
Massey, Randy G. .... Fairview Heights, IL
Massey, Raymond L. .... St. Louis, MO
Massey, Richard N. .... Little Rock, AR
Massey, Robert D. .... Columbia, TN; Fayetteville, TN; Lewisburg, TN
Massey, Robert D. .... Pulaski, TN
Massey, Robert H. .... Franklin, TN
Massey, Robert R. .... Bloomington, CA
Massey, Robert V., Jr. .... Philadelphia, PA
Massey, Russsell S. .... Philadelphia, PA
Massey, Ryan W. .... Troy, MI
Massey, Sandra L. .... Bellevue, WA; Seattle, WA
Massey Semenoff Stern & Schwarz, P.C. .... Denver, CO
Massey, Shalem A. .... Los Angeles, CA
Massey, Sharon T. .... Clarksville, TN
Massey, Shaw & West .... Abilene, TX; Brownwood, TX
Massey, Shirley S. .... Ellicott City, MD
Massey Showalter & Marsh, P.C. .... Denver, CO
Massey, Stephanie H. .... Boston, MA
Massey, Stephen .... Miami, FL
Massey, Steven Jay .... West Palm Beach, FL
Massey and Stotser .... Birmingham, AL
Massey, Susan .... Cleveland, OH
Massey, Tammie B. .... Palm Beach, FL
Massey, Terry N. .... Conyers, GA
Massey, Thomas .... Lincoln, NE
Massey, Thomas A. .... Evansville, IN
Massey, Thomas J., Jr. .... Lake Arrowhead, CA
Massey, Timothy A. .... Birmingham, AL
Massey, Tom C. .... San Angelo, TX
Massey, Valgene L. .... Brownsville, TX
Massey, Vincent F. .... Boston, MA
Massey, Virginia L. .... Redondo Beach, CA
Massey, W. Troy .... Montgomery, AL
Massey, William D., & Associates .... Memphis, TN
Massey, William E. .... Great Neck, NY
Massey, William L. .... Federal Energy Regulatory Commission, Office of the Commissioners, GV
Massey, William R. .... New York, NY
Massey, William W., III .... Jacksonville, FL
Massey, Wm. Ray .... Aiken, SC
Massey, Wynetta P. .... Colorado Springs, CO
Massey-Jones, Vera .... Detroit, MI
Massi, Albert D., Ltd. .... Las Vegas, NV
Massi, Anthony M. .... Trenton, NJ
Massi, Giulio .... Palm Springs, CA
Massi, Giulio, Law Offices of .... Palm Springs, CA
Massi, Robert A. .... Las Vegas, NV
Massi, Robert A., Ltd. .... Las Vegas, NV
Massicot, John Paul .... New Orleans, LA
Massie, Allen B. .... Midwest City, OK
Massie, Ann MacLean .... Lexington, VA
Massie, C. Scott .... Wayzata, MN
Massie, Debra L. .... Beaufort, NC
Massie, E. Rodney, Jr. .... Daytona Beach, FL
Massie, Henry M., Jr. .... Norfolk, VA
Massie, Inger, Boyd & Iden, P.C. .... Winchester, VA
Massie, James C. .... Tallahassee, FL
Massie, James H., III .... Madison Heights, VA
Massie, James P. .... Little Rock, AR
Massie, Jason M. .... Memphis, TN
Massie, Joel L. .... Bessemer, MI
Massie, Joseph A., Jr. .... Winchester, VA
Massie, Kent B. .... Lexington, VA
Massie, Lynel E. .... Jackson, MS
Massie, Marshall J. .... Xenia, OH
Massie, Michael E. .... Galva, IL
Massie, Nancy Helen .... Mansfield, OH
Massie, Noel D. .... Birmingham, MI; Detroit, MI
Massie, Richard A. .... Forsyth, MO
Massie, Robert J. .... New York, NY
Massie, Robert L. .... Charleston, WV; Huntington, WV
Massie, Sam F., Jr. .... Grand Rapids, MI
Massie & Scott .... Tallahassee, FL
Massie & Singleton .... Madison Heights, VA
Massie, Wade W. .... Abingdon, VA
Massieon, Richard J. .... Seneca, KS
Massih, Mehran .... New York, NY
Massih, Melody D. .... Rifle, CO
Massih, Pauline .... Los Angeles, CA
Massimiano, Anthony G. .... Pittsfield, MA
Massimino, Elisa Christine .... Washington, DC
Massimo, Thomas Gilbert .... Boston, MA
Massin, Kimberlee .... Chicago, IL
Massina, Barbra Ann .... Melville, NY
Massina, Glenn M. .... Philadelphia, PA
Massing, Bertram K. .... Beverly Hills, CA
Massing, Beverly M. .... Madison, WI
Massing, Gregory I. .... Boston, MA
Massingale, Cheryl S. .... Knoxville, TN
Massingale, Kyle Dennis .... Wetumpka, AL
Massinger, Douglas Wm. .... Media, PA
Massinger Law Office .... Media, PA
Massingill, Ron .... Dallas, TX
Massingill, Ron, P.C. .... Dallas, TX
Massini, Susan B. .... Ukiah, CA
Massino, Michael H. .... Morris, IL
Massler, Howard A. .... Hackensack, NJ
Massman, Hubert J. .... Helena, MT
Massman, Jennifer L. .... Great Falls, MT
Massman, Joseph R. .... Helena, MT
Massman, Kenneth R. .... Department of Housing and Urban Development, Office of General Counsel, GV
Massman Law Firm .... Helena, MT
Massman, Richard A. .... Dallas, TX
Massmann, Andrew P. .... Chicago, IL
Masso, Nancy Lynn .... Brownsville, TX
Massock, Elaine .... Urbana, IL
Massod, David J. .... Stockton, CA
Massoff, Melinda J. .... New York, NY
Massoglia, Dennis J. .... Stevens Point, WI
Masson, Erin M. .... Jacksonville, FL
Masson, George T., Jr. .... Washington, DC
Masson, Grace M. .... Milwaukee, WI
Masson, Robert H. .... Brockton, MA
Masson, Robin Abrahamson .... Ithaca, NY
Masson, Susan M. .... Irvine, CA
Massong, Judy I. .... Seattle, WA
Massong & Knopp, P.S. .... Seattle, WA
Massoni, J. Steven .... Wichita, KS
Massonne, Karen M. .... Spokane, WA
Massony, Richard P. .... New Orleans, LA
Massood & Covello .... Wayne, NJ
Massood, Joseph A. .... Wayne, NJ
Massopust, John Buck .... Minneapolis, MN
Massopust, Richard H., Jr. .... Minneapolis, MN
Massoth, Elisa G. .... Boise, ID
Massoud, Ahmed Aly .... New York, NY
Massoud, George J. .... Utica, NY
Massoud & Pashkoff, P.C. .... New York, NY
Massoud, Zeinab A. .... New York, NY
Massoumi, Mandana .... Menlo Park, CA
Massry, Norman C. .... Newtonville, NY
Massucci, Lauren M. .... Pittsburgh, PA
Massucci, Peter J. .... Bryn Mawr, PA
Massucci, Raymond R. .... Arlington Heights, IL
Massucci, Thomas V. .... Brooklyn, NY
Massucco, L. Raymond .... Bellows Falls, VT
Massuch, Richard D. .... New Hudson, MI
Massuda, Cindy A. .... Upper Marlboro, MD
Massullo, Anne Christine .... San Francisco, CA
Massumi, Ronald R. .... Washington, DC
Massung, Howard G. .... Elyria, OH
Mast, Andrea .... Los Angeles, CA
Mast, Bernadette Mihalic .... Cleveland, OH
Mast, Charles D. .... Smithfield, NC
Mast, Christine Lupo .... Atlanta, GA
Mast, Christopher E. .... Naples, FL
Mast, Christopher E., P.A. .... Naples, FL
Mast, D. Chet .... Loveland, CO
Mast, Daniel D. .... Delaware, OH
Mast, David P., Jr. .... Winston-Salem, NC
Mast, Diane Stromme .... Millersburg, OH
Mast, Everett L. .... Sugar Grove, NC
Mast, Frank .... Pittsburgh, PA
Mast, George B. .... Smithfield, NC
Mast, Gregory L. .... Phoenix, AZ
Mast, Hans A. .... Park Ridge, IL
Mast, J. Timothy .... Atlanta, GA
Mast, James W. .... Dallas, TX
Mast, John Allen, Jr. .... Spartanburg, SC
Mast, Joseph .... St. Paul, MN
Mast, Kent E. .... Atlanta, GA
Mast, Louis L. .... Brooklyn, NY
Mast, Sandra .... Northridge, CA
Mast, Schulz, Mast, Mills & Stem, P.A. .... Garner, NC; Smithfield, NC
Mast, Theodore L. .... Lanham, MD
Mast, Timothy W. .... Birmingham, MI
Mastache, Jorge .... Modesto, CA
Mastaglio, Peter J. .... Garden City, NY
Mastagni, David P. .... Sacramento, CA
Mastagni, Holstedt & Chiurazzi, A Professional Corporation .... Sacramento, CA
Mastaitis, Stephen J., Jr. .... Saratoga Springs, NY
Mastalir, Dawn E. .... Sioux City, IA
Mastalir, Milton J., Jr. .... Englewood, CO
Mastalli, Grace L. .... Department of Justice, Office of Policy Development, GV
Mastan, David F. .... Los Angeles, CA
Mastan, Peter J. .... Los Angeles, CA
Mastando, Dennis A., Jr. .... Federal Communications Commission, Common Carrier Bureau, GV
Mastando, John P., III .... New York, NY
Mastandrea, Jamie A. .... Burke, VA
Mastandrea, John .... New York, NY
Mastandrea, Joseph M. .... Cleveland Heights, OH
Mastandrea, Linda L. .... Chicago, IL
Mastandrea, Rod R. .... Cleveland Heights, OH
Mastantuono, Craig A. .... Waukesha, WI
Mastaw, Richard A. .... Detroit, MI
Mastbaum, Steven .... New York, NY
Masteller, John Q. .... Oxnard, CA
Masten, Donald J. .... Orlando, FL
Masten, Donald L. .... Pennsville, NJ
Masten, Jeffrey P. .... Sioux Falls, SD
Masten, John E. .... Rye, NY
Masten, Linda .... Stockton, CA
Masten, Mary .... Rapid City, SD
Masten, Patricia Kurp .... Greensburg, PA
Masten & Ray .... Pennsville, NJ
Masten, Stephen B. .... St. Paul, MN
Master, Anne Marie .... San Francisco, CA
Master, Barry L. .... Asheville, NC
Master, Geofrey L. .... Plano, TX
Master, Jeffrey M. .... Parsippany, NJ
Master, John E. .... Lewis Center, OH
Master, John J., III .... New York, NY
Master, John J., Jr. .... Haddonfield, NJ
Master, Joseph J. .... Blackwood, NJ
Master, Maureen .... New York, NY
Master, Michael J. .... Pottsville, PA
Master, Todd H. .... Redwood City, CA
Master, Weinstein, Schnoll & Dodig, P.C. .... Haddonfield, NJ; **Philadelphia, PA**; Pottsville, PA
Master, William E. .... Portland, ME
Masterly, John G. .... Chicago, IL
Masterman, Beth J. .... Boston, MA
Masterman, Culbert & Tully, LLP .... Atlanta, GA; Boston, MA
Masterman, David D. .... Vienna, VA
Masterman, Edward I. .... Boston, MA
Masterman, James D. .... Boston, MA
Masterman, John Richard .... Folsom, CA
Masternak, Brian J. .... Grand Rapids, MI
Masternick, John .... Girard, OH; Youngstown, OH
Masternick, John J. .... Girard, OH
Masterpole, Kathleen .... Des Moines, IA
Masters, Alfred O., Jr. .... Newport News, VA
Masters, Allan W., (Ltd.) .... Chicago, IL
Masters, Amanda .... New York, NY
Masters, Anna Segobia .... Los Angeles, CA
Masters, Arlie G. .... Tacoma, WA
Masters & Associates, A Legal Professional Association .... Cleveland, OH
Masters, Barbara J. .... Norwich, CT
Masters, Bernard H. .... Dallas, TX
Masters, C. Richard .... Oklahoma City, OK
Masters, Carole A. .... Hartford, CT
Masters, Catherine M. .... Chicago, IL
Masters, Charles J. .... Chicago, IL
Masters, Christine .... Santa Monica, CA
Masters, Claude B. .... Houston, TX
Masters & Co., L.P.A. .... Cincinnati, OH
Masters, Cynthia E. .... Houston, TX
Masters, Cynthia L. .... Santa Monica, CA
Masters, Daryl L. .... Montgomery, AL
Masters, David A. .... Macon, MO
Masters, David L. .... Montrose, CO
Masters, Dianne Gruler .... Minneapolis, MN
Masters, Douglas N. .... Chicago, IL
Masters, Edward F. .... Joliet, IL
Masters, Ellen Sly .... Lakeland, FL
Masters, Frank M. .... Jefferson City, MO
Masters, Frederick H. .... Fort Washington, PA
Masters, G. Stanton .... Kansas City, MO
Masters, G. Thomas, (P.S.) .... Bellevue, WA
Masters, Gaylerd B. .... Tacoma, WA
Masters, Gaylerd B., P.S.C. .... Tacoma, WA
Masters, Gregory L. .... Washington, DC
Masters, J. William, II .... Orlando, FL
Masters, James A. .... South Bend, IN
Masters, Janet .... Department of Energy, Office of the General Counsel, GV
Masters, Janet Gerwig .... Charleston, WV
Masters, Jeffrey D. .... Los Angeles, CA
Masters, Joan E. .... Washington, DC
Masters, John E. .... Cheyenne, WY
Masters, John M. .... Cleveland, OH
Masters, John W. .... Atlanta, GA
Masters, Jon Marshall .... Oklahoma City, OK
Masters, Jonathan S. .... Clarksdale, MS
Masters, Joseph .... San Francisco, CA
Masters, Kenneth H. .... Catonsville, MD
Masters, Kenneth W. .... Bainbridge Island, WA
Masters, Lorelie S. .... Washington, DC
Masters, Lynne G. .... Seattle, WA
Masters, Marc E. .... Los Angeles, CA
Masters, Mark D. .... Elizabeth, CO
Masters, Mark F. .... Farmington Hills, MI
Masters, Mark W. .... New York, NY
Masters, Marvin W. .... Charleston, WV
Masters, Mullins & Arrington .... Clarksville, IN; Louisville, KY
Masters, Pamela Rogers .... Atlanta, GA
Masters, Paul Holmes .... Chicago, IL
Masters, R. Gibson .... Chicago, IL
Masters, Ralph T., Jr. .... Garden City, NY
Masters, Randy K. .... Richmond, VA
Masters & Ribakoff .... Los Angeles, CA; Santa Monica, CA
Masters, Richard L., (P.S.C.) .... Louisville, KY
Masters, Robert .... Port Washington, NY
Masters, Robert F., II .... Charleston, SC
Masters, Robert L. .... Cincinnati, OH
Masters, Robert M. .... Washington, DC
Masters, Robt. J. .... Beaver Falls, PA
Masters, Ruth F. .... Chicago, IL
Masters, Sam N. .... Daytona Beach, FL
Masters, Sharon S. .... West Chester, PA
Masters, Stephen, & Associates .... Joliet, IL
Masters, Stephen M., Sr. .... Joliet, IL
Masters & Taylor, L.C. .... Charleston, WV
Masters, Tracy Dean .... Lawrenceville, GA
Masters, Valerie Susan .... West Palm Beach, FL
Masters, W. Alfred .... Midland, TX
Masters, William A. .... Portland, OR
Masters, William B. .... New Orleans, LA
Masters, William J. .... Tigard, OR
Masters, William N. .... Cleveland, OH
Masterson, Barbara A. .... Los Angeles, CA
Masterson • Braunfeld .... Norristown, PA
Masterson, Bret J. .... Tulsa, OK
Masterson, C. Parke, Jr. .... Hollywood, FL
Masterson, Charles V., III .... West Mifflin, PA
Masterson, Cynthia A. .... St. Louis, MO
Masterson, D. Elizabeth .... Dallas, TX
Masterson, David .... Peoria, IL
Masterson, David N. .... Phoenix, AZ
Masterson, Deborah C. .... Randolph, MA
Masterson, Donna P. .... Medfield, MA
Masterson, Edward H. .... Quincy, MA
Masterson, Eshelle M. .... Needham, MA
Masterson, George H. .... Nashville, TN
Masterson, Gina B. .... Denver, CO
Masterson, J. Bruce .... Framingham, MA
Masterson, James C. .... Englewood, CO
Masterson, James P. .... New York, NY
Masterson, John A. .... Casper, WY
Masterson, John H. .... Mansfield, MA
Masterson, John T. .... Phoenix, AZ
Masterson, John T., Jr. .... Department of Commerce, Office of the General Counsel, GV
Masterson, Joseph D. .... Milwaukee, WI
Masterson, Karen L. .... Milpitas, CA
Masterson, Kathleen E. .... Wappingers Falls, NY
Masterson, Kenneth R. .... Memphis, TN
Masterson, Kevin F. .... Mobile, AL; Pensacola, FL
Masterson, Mary Ann .... Department of Energy, Office of the General Counsel, GV
Masterson, Michael E. .... Milford, OH
Masterson, Michael J. .... Tulsa, OK
Masterson, Michael J., Sr. .... Springfield, IL
Masterson, Paul J. .... Tampa, FL
Masterson, Philip T. .... New York, NY
Masterson, Richard K. .... Norristown, PA
Masterson, Robert J. .... San Jose, CA
Masterson, Rogers, Masterson & Lopez .... St. Petersburg, FL
Masterson, Stephen M. .... Tallahassee, FL
Masterson, Stephen V. .... Los Angeles, CA
Masterson, T. Michael .... New Orleans, LA
Masterson, Thomas A. .... Norristown, PA
Masterson, Thomas A., & Associates, P.C. .... Norristown, PA; Philadelphia, PA
Masterson, Thomas A., Jr. .... Philadelphia, PA
Masterson, Thomas D. .... St. Petersburg, FL
Masterson, Thomas J. .... Dallas, TX
Masterson, Thomas M. .... Montvale, NJ
Masterson, Timothy K. .... St. Paul, MN
Masterson, William A. .... Los Angeles, CA
Masterson, Wilmer D., III .... Dallas, TX
Masterton, Lucinda C. .... Lexington, KY
Masterton, Reynold Peter .... Storrs, CT
Mastey, Leslie C. .... Milwaukee, WI
Mastics, George E. .... Palm Beach, FL
Mastin, Andrew D. .... San Francisco, CA
Mastin, Deborah Bovarnick .... Miami, FL
Mastin, Dorothy Jo .... Cynthiana, KY
Mastin, Gary E. .... Springfield, MA
Mastin, J. David .... Walla Walla, WA
Mastin, John N. .... San Antonio, TX
Mastin, Karen L. .... Montgomery, AL
Mastin, Mary M. .... Cookeville, TN
Mastin, Scott J. .... New Philadelphia, OH
Mastin, Thomas F., IV .... Fort Worth, TX
Mastin, Tony L. .... Oklahoma City, OK
Mast Murray, Susanne .... New York, NY
Maston, Bruce M. .... Great Neck, NY
Maston, Karen Kay .... Houston, TX
Maston, William G. .... Savannah, GA
Maston, William H. .... Pittsburgh, PA
Mastondrea, Christian R. .... Hackettstown, NJ; Morristown, NJ; Trenton, NJ
Mastor, George C. .... Litchfield Park, AZ
Mastorakos, Homer N. .... Chesterfield, MO
Mastorakos Law Offices .... Chesterfield, MO
Mastores, Kent N. .... San Francisco, CA
Mastoris, Kathy .... Northbrook, IL
Mastos, Theodore G. .... Miami, FL
Mastovich, George B. .... Pittsburgh, PA
Mastracchio, James N. .... Cleveland, OH
Mastracci, A. Gus .... Glen Burnie, MD
Mastracco, Marcus J. .... Albany, NY
Mastracco, Vincent J., Jr. .... Norfolk, VA
Mastran, Christine E .... Akron, OH
Mastrangel, Paul J. .... Troy, MI

Mastrangelo, Angelo A. ..... Roseland, NJ
Mastrangelo, Christopher ..... Boston, MA
Mastrangelo, Dean Shaun ..... Farmingville, NY
Mastrangelo, Edward M. ..... Lafayette, CA
Mastrangelo, Edward M., A Prof. Corp., Law Offices of ..... Lafayette, CA
Mastrangelo, E. W. ..... Willoughby, OH
Mastrangelo, Jonathan M.
Washington, DC
Mastrangelo, Joseph N. ..... New York, NY
Mastrangelo, Michael J. ..... Hackensack, NJ
Mastrangelo, Nicholas ..... Lafayette, CA
Mastrangelo, Nikolas L. ..... Las Vegas, NV
Mastrangelo, Nikolas L., Esq. Ltd
Las Vegas, NV
Mastrangelo, Raymond S. ..... New York, NY
Mastrangelo, Rebecca L. ..... Las Vegas, NV
Mastrangelo, S. John ..... Houston, TX
Mastrangelo & Sattely ..... Hackensack, NJ
Mastrangelo, Vito A. ..... Mount Vernon, IL
Mastrantonio, Robert ..... Hauppauge, NY
Mastrantonio, Steven W. ..... Akron, OH
Mastras, George, Jr. ..... Burbank, CA
Mastrati, Frank, Jr. ..... Cranston, RI
Mastrella, Daniel J. ..... Rochester, NY
Mastrella, Liza J. ..... Ventura, CA
Mastrella, Victor J. ..... Woodland Hills, CA
Mastrian, Debra A. ..... Indianapolis, IN
Mastrian, Patrick F., III ..... Indianapolis, IN
Mastriana & Christiansen, Professional Association ..... Fort Lauderdale, FL
Mastriana, F. Ronald
Fort Lauderdale, FL
Mastriana, Richard J. ..... Boardman, OH
Mastriani, James J. ..... New York, NY
Mastriani, Louis S. ..... Washington, DC
Mastrianni, Michael W. ..... Plainville, CT
Mastrianni & Seguljic, LLC ..... Plainville, CT
Mastro, Arkley L., Jr. ..... Latham, NY
Mastro, Francis A. ..... Liberty Corner, NJ
Mastro, Frank J. ..... Baltimore, MD
Mastro, J. Albert ..... Bernardsville, NJ
Mastro, Jeffrey J. ..... Phoenix, AZ
Mastro, Randy Michael ..... New York, NY
Mastro, William F. ..... Staten Island, NY
Mastrobattista, Amy J. ..... Boston, MA
Mastrobattista, Mary P. ..... Palo Alto, CA
Mastrobattisto, Joseph F. ..... Las Vegas, NV
Mastroberti, Brian T. ..... Garden City, NY
Mastrocola, Dimitri G. ..... New York, NY
Mastrocola, Paul R. ..... Boston, MA
Mastrocola, Richard A. ..... New York, NY
Mastroddi, Travis M. ..... Baltimore, MD
Mastrodomenico, Donald ..... Forest Hills, NY
Mastrodomenico, Emil F. ..... Forest Hills, NY
Mastrodonato, Anthony J. ..... Rochester, NY
Mastrodonato, George C. ..... Olympia, WA
Mastrodonato, Michael A. ..... Rochester, NY
Mastroeni, Anthony J. ..... Valhalla, NY
Mastrogiacomo, William ..... New York, NY
Mastrogiannis, Anastasia ..... Northport, NY
Mastrogiovanni, Dena B. ..... Dallas, TX
Mastrogiovanni, Joseph J. ..... Dallas, TX
Mastrogiovanni Schorsch Mersky & Zagar, P.C.
Dallas, TX
Mastroianni, A. Douglas ..... Los Angeles, CA
Mastroianni, Francis N. ..... Boston, MA
Mastroianni, Joseph J., Jr. ..... Clinton, NY
Mastroianni, Peggy R.
Equal Employment Opportunity Commission, Office of Legal Counsel, GV
Mastroianni, Raymond M. ..... Milford, MA
Mastroianni, Ronald M.
San Francisco, CA
Mastroleo, William F. ..... Buffalo, NY
Mastromarco, Victor J., Jr. ..... Saginaw, MI
Mastromarino, Anthony R. ..... Brockton, MA
Mastromonaco, Leonard P.
San Francisco, CA
Mastromonaco, Leonard P.
San Francisco, CA
Mastromonaco, Peter A.
San Francisco, CA
Mastronardi, Corinne M
Fort Lauderdale, FL
Mastronardi, Gary A. ..... Bridgeport, CT
Mastronardi, John J. ..... Cherry Hill, NJ
Mastroni, Angela V. ..... Solana Beach, CA
Mastroni, Kenneth J. ..... New Haven, CT
Mastroni, Nick V. ..... Mission Viejo, CA
Mastropaolo, Mary M. ..... New York, NY
Mastropietro, John P. ..... Clifton, NJ
Albany, NY
New York, NY
Mastrosimone, Joseph P. ..... Washington, DC
Mastrosimone, Salvatore J.
New York, NY
Mastrostefano, Sherry Booth
Washington, DC
Mastrovito, Marie Anne ..... New York, NY
Mastrucci, Jane Thornton ..... Miami, FL
Mastruserio, Dominic ..... Cincinnati, OH
Mastruserio, Karen L, L.P.A.
Cincinnati, OH
Mastry, Johnny ..... Maitland, FL
Mastry, R. Donald ..... St. Petersburg, FL
Masty, Jay S. ..... Goose Creek, SC
Masucci, Deborah ..... New York, NY
Masucci, Gerald ..... New York, NY
Masucci, Louis M., Jr. ..... Montclair, NJ
Masucci, Michele A. ..... New York, NY
Masud, David John ..... Saginaw, MI
Masud, Gilbert & Patterson, P.C.
Bay City, MI
Flint, MI
Midland, MI
Saginaw, MI

Masud, Robert ..... Boston, MA
Masuda, Beverly N. ..... Chicago, IL
Masuda & Ejiri ..... New York, NY
New York, NY
Masuda, Funai, Eifert & Mitchell, Ltd.
Chicago, IL
Rolling Meadows, IL
Cincinnati, OH
Masuda, Junji ..... New York, NY
Masuda, Kevin S. ..... Los Angeles, CA
Masuda, Michael P. ..... Monterey, CA
Salinas, CA
Masuda, Robert ..... Sacramento, CA
Masuda, Roger K. ..... Turlock, CA
Masui, Stanford H. ..... Honolulu, HI
Masumoto, Harold S. ..... Honolulu, HI
Masunaga, Bruce A. ..... Honolulu, HI
Masunaga, Laura Jean ..... Yreka, CA
Masunaga, Margaret Kuroda ..... Kealakekua, HI
Masuoka, George M. ..... Lihue, HI
Masur, Daniel A. ..... Washington, DC
Masur, James D., II ..... Indianapolis, IN
Masur, Joshua M. ..... Palo Alto, CA
Masur, Samuel E. ..... Lafayette, LA
Masur, Steven R. ..... New York, NY
Masur, Wolodymyr M. ..... Aurora, IL
Masurovsky, Laura P. ..... Washington, DC
Masutani, David J. ..... Los Angeles, CA
Masyr, Jesse ..... New York, NY
Mata, Art G. ..... Lawton, OK
Mata, Elizabeth W. ..... Lexington, MA
Mata, Jaime ..... Bellaire, TX
Mata, Jill Long ..... San Antonio, TX
Mata, Leticia Garcia ..... Laredo, TX
Mata, Luis ..... Lenexa, KS
Shawnee, KS
Mata, Mario A. ..... Austin, TX
Mata, Rodolfo ..... El Paso, TX
Mata, Todd E. ..... Chicago, IL
Matacio, Timothy P. ..... Glen Ellyn, IL
Mataconis, Douglas ..... Fairfax Station, VA
Mata De La Garza, Marina ..... El Paso, TX
Matal, Joseph D. ..... Washington, DC
Matalon, Howard A. ..... Princeton, NJ
Matalon, Jack ..... Hackensack, NJ
Matalon, Ralph A. ..... New York, NY
Matalon, Renee R. ..... Washington, DC
Matalon & Schachter ..... New York, NY
Matalone, Steve Anthony, II
Kansas City, MO
Matalonis, Paul ..... Murphysboro, IL
Matamoros, Ronald A.
Winston-Salem, NC
Matan, Eugene L. ..... Columbus, OH
Matan, Geer & Wright ..... Columbus, OH
Matan, Maria K. ..... San Francisco, CA
Matan, Schlenger & Weaver
San Francisco, CA
Matanky, James E. ..... Chicago, IL
Matanky, Robert W. ..... Chicago, IL
Matanle, Richard K., II ..... Roseland, NJ
Matano, Gary R. ..... Passaic, NJ
Matanovic, Stephan ..... Philadelphia, PA
Matar, Norman J. ..... Milwaukee, WI
Mataranglas, Dennis S. ..... New York, NY
Mataranglas, Nicholas R. ..... Seattle, WA
Mataraso, Matthew H. ..... Albany, NY
New York, NY
Matarazzi, William H. ..... Topeka, KS
Matarazzo, Barbara A. ..... New York, NY
Matarazzo Blumberg & Associates, P.C.
New York, NY
Matarazzo, Harris S. ..... Portland, OR
Matarazzo, Harris S. ..... Salem, OR
Matarazzo, Judith Hudson ..... Portland, OR
Matarazzo, Mark E. ..... Oyster Bay, NY
Matarazzo, Sara H. ..... Portland, OR
Matarazzo, Stephen M. ..... Northfield, NJ
Matarese, A. L. ..... Bethlehem, CT
Matarese, Antonio A., Jr. ..... Framingham, MA
Matarese, Barry & Pendergast
Framingham, MA
Matarese, Christopher J.
Newport Beach, CA
Matarese, James A. ..... Boston, MA
Matarese, Linda Bauman ..... Reston, VA
Matarrese, Pamela Lee ..... Somerville, NJ
Matarrese, Patrick R. ..... Atlanta, GA
Matas, Bruce A. ..... Lakewood, CO
Matas, Raquel M. ..... Miami, FL
Matas, Vytas R. ..... Pepper Pike, OH
Matasar, Lawrence ..... Portland, OR
Matasar, Lawrence, P.C. ..... Portland, OR
Matasar, Richard A. ..... Chicago, IL
Matasar, Scott C. ..... Cleveland, OH
Matasavage, Mark ..... Waterbury, CT
Matasavage & Matasavage ..... Waterbury, CT
Matasavage, Paul ..... Waterbury, CT
Matasavage, Vincent P. ..... Waterbury, CT
Matasich, Stephen E. ..... Canton, OH
Matassa, Anthony V. ..... Brooklyn, NY
Matassa, Michael S. ..... Wheat Ridge, CO
Matassini, Nicholas M. ..... Tampa, FL
Matathia, Sanford M. ..... Boston, MA
Matatia, Jos. V. ..... New York, NY
Matava, George G. ..... Denver, CO
Matavich, Alan J. ..... Youngstown, OH
Mataya, Charles J. ..... Nashville, TN
Mataya, James M. ..... Washington, DC
Matayoshi, Coralie Chun ..... Honolulu, HI
Matayoshi, Jerold T., (A Law Corporation)
Honolulu, HI
Matayoshi, Kathryn S. ..... Honolulu, HI
Matays, Charles ..... New York, NY
Matays & Kretschmann ..... New York, NY
Matcham, Susan J. ..... Salinas, CA
Matchefts, James L. ..... Jefferson City, MO
Matchett, Arnold & Palmer ..... Shelbyville, IN

Matchett, Carol L. ..... San Mateo, CA
Matchett, Christopher D.
Baton Rouge, LA
Matchett, Edward W. ..... Bisbee, AZ
Matchett Law Offices ..... Bisbee, AZ
Matchett, Samuel M. ..... Atlanta, GA
Matchett, Scott D. ..... Richmond, VA
Matchett, Susan M. ..... Virginia Beach, VA
Matchett, Theresa G. ..... Baton Rouge, LA
Matchett, Theresa Rooney ..... Jacksonville, FL
Matchett, Verbois, Futrell and Henchy, A Professional Law Corporation
Baton Rouge, LA
Matchinga, Walter R. ..... Cleveland, OH
Matchinski, Elizabeth M.
Department of Defense, Defense Legal Services Agency, GV
Matchinski, Jayme R. ..... Rockford, IL
Matchneer, William W., III
Occupational Safety and Health Review Commission, Office of a Commissioner, GV
Matchulat, John J. ..... Nashville, TN
Matchulet, Anne ..... Exton, PA
Matchus, Nancy K. ..... Austin, TX
Mate, Jonathan L. ..... Oradell, NJ
Brooklyn, NY
Garden City, NY
Mate, Laura E. ..... Seattle, WA
Mateas, Kenneth E. ..... Aurora, IL
Matechak, Jason P. ..... Washington, DC
Matecheck, Vincent G. ..... Massillon, OH
Matecki, Paul L. ..... St. Petersburg, FL
Matecki, Thomas A. ..... Williamsville, NY
Matecko, Claire W. ..... San Antonio, TX
Matecun, Glenn R. ..... Howell, MI
Matedero, Jerome F. ..... Westbury, NY
Mateen, Fatimah A. ..... Department of Justice, Executive Office for Immigration Review, GV
Mateer, Alan ..... Vacaville, CA
Mateer & Associates ..... Rockford, IL
Mateer, Carol Anne ..... West Harrison, NY
Mateer, Don M. ..... Rockford, IL
Mateer & Harbert, P.A. ..... Kissimmee, FL
Orlando, FL
Sanford, FL
Mateer, Jeffrey C. ..... Dallas, TX
Mateer, Karen L. ..... Pasadena, CA
Mateer, Richard B. ..... Boca Raton, FL
Mateer, Richard B., P.A. ..... Boca Raton, FL
Mateer, William G. ..... Orlando, FL
Mateikis, William J. ..... Minneapolis, MN
Mateja, William B. ..... Lubbock, TX
Matejcak, Susan I. ..... Chicago, IL
Matejczyk, David M. ..... Cleveland, OH
Matejek, Michael M. ..... Princeton, NJ
Matejka, Dennis A. ..... Cleveland, OH
Matejka, Lauren E. ..... Great Neck, NY
Matejka, Marcella M. ..... Cleveland, OH
Matejka, Michael D. ..... Omaha, NE
Matejka, Regina A. ..... New York, NY
Matejka, Rick L. ..... St. Louis, MO
Matejkovic, John E. ..... Akron, OH
Matejkovic, Joseph R. ..... Middletown, OH
Matel, Didier A. ..... Hampton, NH
Matelis, Joseph James, II ..... Washington, DC
Matelski, Wayne H. ..... Washington, DC
Matelson, Bennett J. ..... Washington, DC
Mateo, Daniel ..... Princeton, NJ
Mateo, Juan A., Jr. ..... Detroit, MI
Mateo, Rene D. ..... Miami, FL
Mateo, Scott A. ..... Livingston, NJ
Mateo-Santos, Lillian ..... San Juan, PR
Mater, Maud ..... McLean, VA
Matera, Anthony L. ..... Quincy, MA
Matera, Barbara F. ..... Pittsburgh, PA
Matera, Fred J., Jr. ..... Boston, MA
Matera, Glenn J. ..... Mineola, NY
Matera, Lia ..... Santa Cruz, CA
Matera, Marguerite M. ..... Gloucester, MA
Matera, Rico ..... Quincy, MA
Matera, Rosemarie E. ..... Spring Valley, NY
Matera, Vopat, Matera & Johnson, P.C.
Quincy, MA
Materazzo, Jane A. ..... Sherborn, MA
Matergia & Dunn ..... Stroudsburg, PA
Matergia, Ralph Anthony ..... Stroudsburg, PA
Materka, Robert J. ..... Ann Arbor, MI
Materna, Joseph A. ..... New York, NY
Materniak, Terrance A. ..... Severna Park, MD
Maternowski, Joseph G.
Minneapolis, MN
Materre, Gloria L. ..... Chicago, IL
Maters, Bruce R. ..... Detroit, MI
Mates, Carol M. ..... Washington, DC
Mates, Christopher I. ..... Chicago, IL
Mates, Donald E. ..... Fort Lauderdale, FL
Mates, Jacob W. ..... San Francisco, CA
Mates, Lucille M. ..... San Francisco, CA
Mates, Paul S. ..... New York, NY
Mates, Robert E. ..... Minneapolis, MN
Mates, Stephen L. ..... Brooklyn, NY
Matetsky, Ira B. ..... New York, NY
Matevich, William J. ..... Chicago, IL
Matey, Edward J., Jr. ..... Philadelphia, PA
Mateyak, John A. ..... Lancaster, PA
Mateyka, William J. ..... Granite City, IL
Matez, Bruce P. ..... Haddonfield, NJ
Math, Leonard N. ..... Montgomery, AL
Math, Melissa G. ..... Montgomery, AL
Math, Stephan ..... Thousand Oaks, CA
Mathai & Thorson, P.C. ..... Chicago, IL
Mathai, Tom V. ..... Chicago, IL
Mathaler, Bill ..... Tuscumbia, AL
Mathas, William D. ..... DeLand, FL
Mathay, Charles E. ..... Coshocton, OH

Mathay, Charles E., Co., L.P.A.
Coshocton, OH
Mathe, Jennifer K. ..... Cleveland, OH
Matheeussen, Ellen C ..... Chicago, IL
Mathein, Veronica B. ..... Chicago, IL
Matheis, Carol Meilman
Mission Viejo, CA
Matheis, Charles W., Jr. ..... Santa Ana, CA
Matheis, Donna L. ..... Louisville, KY
Matheis, Kenneth S. ..... Louisville, KY
Matheke, Cynthia A. ..... Roseland, NJ
Matheke, Otto G., III
Department of Transportation, National Highway Traffic Safety Administration, GV
Mathen, Kuruvilla ..... Berkeley, CA
Mathena, Larry ..... Newport Beach, CA
Matheney, Lawrence L. ..... Ventura, CA
Matheny, Anthony F. ..... Houston, TX
Matheny, Edward T., Jr.
Kansas City, MO
Matheny, Gary G. ..... Farmington, MO
Matheny, Gordon W. ..... Hammond, LA
Matheny, Joe D. ..... Titusville, FL
Matheny, John B. ..... Sacramento, CA
Matheny, John R. ..... Oceanside, CA
Matheny, Kathryn Richmond ..... Frankfort, KY
Matheny, Marc ..... Indianapolis, IN
Matheny, Mary Jane ..... Sebring, FL
Matheny, Mary Jane, P.A. ..... Sebring, FL
Matheny, Michael D. ..... Beaumont, TX
Matheny, Michael, Hahn & Bailey
Huntington, IN
Matheny, Paul M. ..... Baltimore, MD
Matheny, Randolph Y. ..... Longwood, FL
Matheny, Richard E. ..... Baton Rouge, LA
Matheny, Ronald S. ..... Phoenix, AZ
Matheny Sears Linkert & Long, LLP
Sacramento, CA
Matheny, Stanley H. ..... Huntington, IN
Matheny, Tom ..... Hammond, LA
Matheny, Tom, & Associates, LLC
Hammond, LA
Mather, Barbara W. ..... Philadelphia, PA
Mather, Bettina M. ..... Brockton, MA
Mather, Charles E., III ..... Philadelphia, PA
Mather, Donald E. ..... Mount Clemens, MI
Mather, F. Hubert ..... L'Anse, MI
Mather, Frederick G. ..... Baldwin, MI
Mather, H. Melissa ..... Austin, TX
Mather, James A. ..... Tucson, AZ
Mather, James S. ..... Maywood, IL
Mather, John G. ..... Monclova, OH
Mather, John R. ..... Atlanta, GA
Mather, Judith A. ..... Washington, DC
Mather, Kenneth G. M. ..... Tulsa, OK
Mather, Lance R. ..... Grand Rapids, MI
Mather, Maria W. ..... Cupertino, CA
Mather, R. Russell ..... Bismarck, ND
Mather, Richard Edward ..... Mobile, AL
Mather, Richard P. ..... Harrisburg, PA
Mather, Richard W. ..... Hartford, CT
Mather, Robert J. ..... Department of Justice, Civil Rights Division, GV
Mather, Robert J. ..... Middleboro, MA
Mather, Russell R. ..... Bismarck, ND
Mather, Stephanie J. ..... Oklahoma City, OK
Mather, Steven R. ..... Beverly Hills, CA
Mather, Victoria M. ..... San Antonio, TX
Mather, Walter S. ..... Glastonbury, CT
Matherly, Jeffrey K. ..... Charleston, WV
Matherne, Cindy T. ..... New Orleans, LA
Matherne, Debra A. ..... Frackville, PA
Matherne, Erin E. ..... Austin, TX
Matherne, J. Graham ..... Nashville, TN
Matherne, L. Kirby ..... Brownsville, TN
Matherne, Valerie Van ..... Monroe, LA
Mathers, Allen S. ..... Long Island City, NY
Mathers, Carla M. ..... College Park, MD
Mathers, Carolyn Palley ..... Salisbury, MD
Mathers, Christopher C. ..... Brockton, MA
Mathers, Daniel K. ..... Williamsport, PA
Mathers, Douglas J. ..... New York, NY
Mathers, Elizabeth Gage ..... Phoenix, AZ
Mathers, Kim M. ..... Chicago, IL
Mathers, Martin H. ..... Phoenix, AZ
Mathers, Max E. ..... Knoxville, IL
Mathers, Peter R. ..... Washington, DC
Mathers, Richard J. ..... Washington, DC
Mathers, Stephen C. ..... Galesburg, IL
Mathers, Todd W. ..... Culver City, CA
Mathers, William E. ..... Asheboro, NC
Mathers, William H. ..... New York, NY
Mathes, Anne B. ..... Memphis, TN
Mathes, Carleton K. ..... Woodbury, CT
Mathes, D. Michael ..... Middlebury, VT
Mathes, Gail O. ..... Memphis, TN
Mathes, George B. ..... Spencer, IN
Mathes, Karen L. ..... San Francisco, CA
Mathes, Linda A. ..... Sacramento, CA
Mathes, Patricia A. ..... Chalmette, LA
Mathes, Peggy D. ..... Nashville, TN
Mathes, Stephen J. ..... Philadelphia, PA
Mathesius, Bill ..... Hopewell, NJ
Matheson, Alan A. ..... Phoenix, AZ
Matheson, Alan A. ..... Tempe, AZ
Matheson, Anna A. ..... Washington, DC
Matheson, Cameron S. ..... Boston, MA
Matheson, Charles E. ..... Denver, CO
Matheson, Christopher A. ..... Boston, MA
Matheson, Craig ..... Everett, WA
Matheson, Craig J. ..... Kennewick, WA
Matheson, Daniel N., III ..... Austin, TX
Matheson, David P. ..... Phoenix, AZ
Matheson, David S. ..... Portland, OR
Matheson, Douglas P. ..... Rocky Mount, NC
Matheson, Edward G. ..... Vero Beach, FL
Matheson, Eric J. ..... Palm Beach, FL

Matheson, Eric J., P.A. .... **Boca Raton, FL**
Palm Beach, FL
Matheson, Jane A. .... **Austin, TX**
Matheson, Janeal .... Liberty, MO
Matheson, John H. .... **Minneapolis, MN**
Matheson, John M. .... **Tulsa, OK**
Matheson, Julia Anne .... **Washington, DC**
Matheson, Kenneth .... Grand Rapids, MI
Matheson, Mark Darin .... Atoka, OK
Matheson, Mark E. .... **Santa Ana, CA**
Matheson, Matt David .... **Tulsa, OK**
Matheson, Maureen M. .... Melbourne, FL
Matheson, Michael C. .... **Denver, CO**
Matheson, Michael F. .... **Okemos, MI**
Matheson, Michael J. .... Department of State, Office of the Legal Adviser, GV
Matheson, Monique S. .... Portland, OR
Matheson, Nicole S. .... **Boston, MA**
Matheson Ormsby Prentice ..... **Palo Alto, CA**
Matheson, Parr, Schuler, Ewald & Jolly, L.L.P. .... **Troy, MI**
Matheson, Peter A. .... South Natick, MA
Matheson, Ralph G. .... Department of Defense, Defense Commissary Agency, GV
Matheson, Richard T. .... Liberty, MO
Matheson, Robert C. .... Sandy, UT
Matheson, Robert H., Jr. .... Stuart, FL
Matheson, Rodney M. .... Mesa, AZ
Matheson, Ronald G. .... Colton, CA
Matheson, Scott H. .... **Dallas, TX**
Matheson, Stuart T. .... Salt Lake City, UT
Matheson, Timothy J. .... Johnson City, TN
Matheson, W. Yale .... Palm Beach, FL
Matheson, William C. .... San Francisco, CA
Matheu, Kathleen E. .... Humble, TX
Matheussen, John J. .... **Turnersville, NJ**
Philadelphia, PA
Mathew, Asha A. .... **Washington, DC**
Mathew, Francis J. .... **Santa Fe, NM**
Mathew, Ivan K. .... **Phoenix, AZ**
Mathew & Mathew, P.C. .... **Phoenix, AZ**
Mathew, N. Ajoy .... **Washington, DC**
Mathew, Shannon G.
San Luis Obispo, CA
Mathew, Susan T. .... **Phoenix, AZ**
Mathew, Vadakeparambil M. .... Portland, OR
Mathews, Abigail A. .... **Dallas, TX**
Mathews, Alison Michele .... Raleigh, NC
Mathews, Alison S. .... **Long Beach, CA**
Mathews, Alvin E., Jr. .... **Columbus, OH**
Mathews, Annemarie B. .... **Columbia, SC**
Mathews, Barbara A. .... Tallahassee, FL
Mathews, Barbara B. .... Lakeland, FL
Mathews, Barbara E. .... **Rosemead, CA**
Mathews, Barbara Mance
San Francisco, CA
Mathews Bergen & Grier .... San Diego, CA
Mathews, Bernard Lilse, III .... Spring, TX
Mathews, Byron B., Jr. .... **Tallahassee, FL**
Mathews, C. Larry, Jr. .... San Antonio, TX
Mathews, C. Richard, Jr. .... **New York, NY**
Mathews, Carolyn A. .... **Los Angeles, CA**
Mathews, Carolyn E. .... Columbia, MO
Mathews, Charles Theodore "Ted"
Pasadena, CA
Mathews, Christopher .... **Oakland, CA**
Mathews, Christopher A.
Los Angeles, CA
Mathews, Christopher E. .... Seattle, WA
Mathews, Claire Anne .... Greenwich, CT
Mathews, Colin A. .... **Columbus, OH**
Mathews, Collins, Shepherd & Gould, A Professional Corporation
Morristown, NJ
Parsippany, NJ
Princeton, NJ
Trenton, NJ
Mathews, Craig .... **Washington, DC**
Mathews, Daniel .... **New York, NY**
Mathews, Daniel F., III .... Syracuse, NY
Mathews, Daniel F., Jr. .... Syracuse, NY
Mathews, David J. .... Chicago, IL
Mathews, David L. .... **Albuquerque, NM**
Mathews, David P.
Securities and Exchange Commission, Division of Investment Management, GV
Mathews, Deborah Topping
North Miami Beach, FL
Mathews, Denise .... Ambridge, PA
Mathews, E. Lewis, Jr. .... **New York, NY**
Mathews, Edward D., Jr .... Bartow, FL
Mathews, Eileen T. .... **Cleveland, OH**
Mathews, Elizabeth A. .... Eagan, MN
Mathews, Emet C. .... Berkeley, CA
Mathews, Ernest L., Jr. .... New York, NY
Mathews, Eugene Edward, III
Richmond, VA
Mathews, Eugene H. .... Oklahoma City, OK
Mathews, Ferrin Y. .... Roswell, GA
Mathews, Floyd .... Santa Monica, CA
Mathews, Francis B. .... Eureka, CA
Mathews & Freeland, L.L.P. .... **Austin, TX**
Mathews Garlington-Mathews & Chesnin
Seattle, WA
Mathews, Gary D. .... Houston, TX
Mathews, Gary Robert .... Overland Park, KS
Mathews, George H. B. .... Montgomery, AL
Mathews, George W., III
Boynton Beach, FL
Mathews, Gerald J. .... **Syracuse, NY**
Mathews, Gilbert Lang .... **San Antonio, TX**
Mathews, Gregory B. .... Westerville, OH
Mathews, Gregory H. .... **Philadelphia, PA**
Mathews, Gregory K. .... Beaumont, TX
Mathews, Gregory S. .... **Chicago, IL**
Mathews, Gregory S. .... **Houston, TX**
Mathews & Hall .... Syracuse, NY
Mathews, Harlan .... **Nashville, TN**
Mathews, Holly S. .... Jackson, MS
Mathews, J. Kevin .... Louisville, KY
Mathews, J. Llewellyn .... **Cherry Hill, NJ**
Mathews & Jakabcin .... **Boynton Beach, FL**
Mathews, Jake B., Jr. .... Anniston, AL
Mathews, James F. .... **Canton, OH**
Mathews, James S. .... **Norfolk, VA**
Mathews, Jane Y. C. .... **Nutley, NJ**
Mathews, Jeanne M. .... **Fairfield, CT**
Mathews, Jennifer J. .... **New York, NY**
Mathews, Jimmie D. .... **Austin, TX**
Mathews, John C. .... Yorktown, VA
Mathews, John E., III .... Jacksonville, FL
Mathews, John M. .... **Oxnard, CA**
Mathews, John R. .... **Northbrook, IL**
Mathews, Joseph C. .... **Dallas, TX**
Mathews, Joseph O. .... Greenlawn, NY
Mathews, Joseph P., Jr. .... Arlington, WA
Mathews, Joseph R. .... Syracuse, NY
Mathews, Joseph W., Jr. .... **Birmingham, AL**
Mathews, Karen L. .... Buffalo, NY
Mathews & Keller, L.L.P. .... Houston, TX
Mathews, Kenneth M. .... Columbia, SC
Mathews, Kenneth R. .... Fort Myers, FL
Mathews, Kevin D. .... Milwaukee, WI
Mathews, Kimberly A. .... **Springfield, MA**
Mathews, Kristen J. .... **New York, NY**
Mathews, Laurie Uustal .... **Miami, FL**
Mathews, Leavy, III .... **Washington, DC**
Mathews, Lon E. .... Clayton, MO
Mathews, M. Lauren .... **Dallas, TX**
Mathews, Margaret D. .... **Tampa, FL**
Mathews, Marion P. .... Winfield, KS
Mathews, Mark A. .... **Houston, TX**
Mathews, Mark J. .... **Denver, CO**
Mathews, Matt .... **Tallahassee, FL**
Mathews, Matt, P.A. .... **Tallahassee, FL**
Mathews, Matthew R. .... Pittsburgh, PA
Mathews, Melinda McEachern
Birmingham, AL
Mathews, Meridee J. .... Tacoma, WA
Mathews, Michael A. .... **Morristown, NJ**
Mathews, Michael P. .... Big Rapids, MI
Mathews, Nell E. .... **Minneapolis, MN**
Mathews, Nelson E. .... San Francisco, CA
Mathews, Nikiforos .... **New York, NY**
Mathews, Pamela Viney .... Lake Charles, LA
Mathews, Paul D. .... Gardiner, ME
Mathews, R. Glenn, Jr. .... **Lansing, MI**
Mathews Railey & DeCubellis, P.A.
Orlando, FL
Mathews, Robert E. .... Anaheim, CA
Mathews, Robert E., Jr. .... Belle Glade, FL
Mathews, Roberta I. .... Washington, DC
Mathews, Roderick B. .... **Richmond, VA**
Mathews, S. Paul .... Cincinnati, OH
Mathews, Sarah D. .... **Kansas City, MO**
Mathews, Stanley A. .... Cincinnati, OH
Mathews, Stanton T. .... **Laguna Hills, CA**
Mathews, Stanton T., & Associates, A Law Corp. .... **Laguna Hills, CA**
Mathews, Susan Cregor .... **Houston, TX**
Mathews, Susan M. .... **Washington, DC**
Mathews, Taylor & Krusor, L.L.P.
Winfield, KS
Mathews, Terry L. .... **Little Rock, AR**
Russellville, AR
Mathews, Thomas A. .... Marion, OH
Mathews, Thomas E. .... **St. Cloud, MN**
Mathews, Thomas F. .... Marysville, CA
Mathews, Tyler L. .... **Cleveland, OH**
Mathews, Van B. .... New Orleans, LA
Shreveport, LA
Mathews, Walter, IV .... **Orlando, FL**
Mathews, Walter J. .... **Miami, FL**
Mathews, Ward Os .... Rialto, CA
Mathews, Wayne R. .... Brockton, MA
Mathews, Wesley H. .... San Diego, CA
Mathews, Wesley M., Jr. .... Atlanta, GA
Mathews, William B. .... **Denver, CO**
Mathews, William C. .... San Diego, CA
Mathews, William E. .... Birmingham, AL
Mathews, William Lee .... Vicksburg, MS
Mathews, William S. .... Cincinnati, OH
Mathews, William W. .... **Indianapolis, IN**
Mathews, Wm. Stewart, II .... Cincinnati, OH
Mathewson, Alfred D. .... Albuquerque, NM
Mathewson, Edward P., (A P.C.)
San Jose, CA
Mathewson, George A. .... Syracuse, NY
Mathewson, George A., P.C. .... Syracuse, NY
Mathewson, Gwen C. .... San Francisco, CA
Mathewson, Henry C. .... Oshkosh, WI
Mathewson, J. Kent .... **Chicago, IL**
Mathewson, Kathleen D. .... **Chicago, IL**
Mathewson, Laurie M. .... Washington, DC
Mathewson, Lisa A. .... **Philadelphia, PA**
Mathewson, Margaret P. .... Wichita, KS
Mathewson, Mark S. .... Springfield, IL
Mathewson, Richard D. .... Rochester, NY
Mathewson, Thomas G. .... Dayton, OH
Mathewson, Wilbur F. .... San Rafael, CA
Mathewson, William C. .... Ann Arbor, MI
Mathey, Barbara J. .... York, PA
Mathey, Mary Beth .... Wampsville, NY
Mathey, Richard J. .... Green River, WY
Mathias, Allison Kim .... Sherman Oaks, CA
Mathias, Ann G. .... Pittsburgh, PA
Mathias, Charles McCurdy, Jr.
Washington, DC
Mathias, D. Stephen .... Department of State, Office of the Legal Adviser, GV
Mathias, David C. .... **Visalia, CA**
Mathias, David E. .... Melbourne, FL
Mathias, F. Gregory .... El Dorado, KS
Mathias, James D. .... **Baltimore, MD**
Mathias, Jeffrey P. .... Ames, IA
Mathias, John H., Jr. .... **Chicago, IL**
Mathias, John R. .... **St. Petersburg, FL**
Mathias, John S. .... Frederick, MD
Mathias, Karen E. .... Pittsburgh, PA
Mathias, Lynn Goldman .... Baltimore, MD
Mathias, Mark N. .... Chicago, IL
Mathias, Marla J. .... Summit, NJ
Mathias, Paul D. .... Fort Wayne, IN
Mathias, Richard D. .... **Washington, DC**
Mathias, Richard J. .... Los Angeles, CA
Mathias, Robert J. .... **Baltimore, MD**
Mathias, Scott L. .... **Mineola, NY**
Mathias, Sidney H. .... Arlington Heights, IL
Mathias, Sidney H., P.C., Law Offices of
Arlington Heights, IL
Mathias, Stephen McDowell
Martinsburg, WV
Mathias, Susan J. .... Baltimore, MD
Mathias, Susan M. .... Department of Justice, Immigration and Naturalization Service, GV
Mathias, William E., II .... **Buffalo, NY**
Mathias, William T. .... **Baltimore, MD**
Mathias, Wilson S. .... Queensbury, NY
Mathiascheck, Susan .... **Washington, DC**
Mathiasen, Karen .... **Boston, MA**
Mathiason, Garry G. .... **San Francisco, CA**
Mathiason, Julie Ann .... **Houston, TX**
Mathiason, Marion P. .... **Tampa, FL**
Mathie, Daniel L. .... **Millersburg, OH**
Mathie, Gloria Urbanik .... Pittsburgh, PA
Mathie, James J. .... **Brookfield, WI**
Mathie, Mark L. .... **Dallas, TX**
Mathies, Blair, Jr. .... Lindenhurst, NY
Mathies, Lisa T. .... Fort Smith, AR
Mathiesen, Mark C. .... San Diego, CA
Mathiesen, Mark J. .... United States Senate, Office of the Legislative Counsel, GV
Mathiesen, Pamela C. .... Santa Cruz, CA
Mathieson, Randall C. .... Farmington, CT
Mathieu, Dickens .... Washington, DC
Mathieu, Elizabeth L. .... New York, NY
Mathieu, Gail D. T. .... Department of State, Foreign Service Institute, GV
Mathieu & Gummer .... Philadelphia, PA
Mathieu, James .... **New York, NY**
Mathieu, James H. .... Midland, MI
Mathieu, James V. .... Philadelphia, PA
Mathieu, Joan .... Clearwater, FL
Mathieu, John P. .... **New Bedford, MA**
Mathieu, John R. .... Glenwood, IL
Mathieu, Joseph B. .... **Hartford, CT**
Mathieu, Kelli R. .... Metairie, LA
Mathieu & Lee .... Midland, MI
Mathieu & Mathieu .... **New Bedford, MA**
Mathieu, Maurice P. .... Houma, LA
Mathieu, Michael E. .... Houma, LA
Mathieu, Michael E., A Professional Law Corporation .... Houma, LA
Mathieu, Michelle E.
Farmington Hills, MI
Mathieu, Paul J. .... **New Bedford, MA**
Mathieu, Peter F. .... **Providence, RI**
Mathieu, Pierre J. C. .... Somersworth, NH
Mathieu, Richard .... Yakima, WA
Mathieu, Robert J. .... Hartford, CT
Mathieu, Stephen J. .... Portland, OR
Mathieu, Thomas J. .... **New Bedford, MA**
Mathieu, William H. .... **Atlanta, GA**
Mathioudakis, Nicholas E.
Indianapolis, IN
Mathiowetz, Duane H. .... **San Francisco, CA**
Mathis, Angeline Fleeman .... Atlanta, GA
Mathis, Annalee .... Houston, TX
Mathis, Barbara L. .... Albuquerque, NM
Mathis, Benton J., Jr. .... **Atlanta, GA**
Mathis, B. G. .... Detroit, MI
Mathis, Billy C., Jr. .... Albany, GA
Mathis, C. James .... **Anchorage, AK**
Mathis, C. Lewis, Jr. .... **Shelbyville, KY**
Mathis, Cecil S. .... **Dallas, TX**
Mathis, Cecil Shelton, A Professional Corporation .... **Dallas, TX**
Mathis, Charles A., Jr. (P.C.) .... **Atlanta, GA**
Mathis, Craig S. .... Albany, GA
Mathis, Dallas K. .... **Arlington, VA**
Mathis, David J. .... Hartford, CT
Mathis & DeJanes .... **Arkadelphia, AR**
Kansas City, MO
Mathis, Dena L. .... **Dallas, TX**
Mathis, Douglas J. .... Rome, GA
Mathis, Erskine R. .... Birmingham, AL
Mathis, Eugenio S. .... Las Vegas, NM
Mathis, Frances R. .... Atlanta, GA
Mathis, Gary D. .... New Braunfels, TX
Mathis, Gregory C. .... **Austin, TX**
Mathis, Gregory W. .... **Palo Alto, CA**
Mathis, J. Michael .... **Peoria, IL**
Mathis, Jacinta M. .... Orlando, FL
Mathis, James H. .... La Crosse, WI
Mathis, James M. .... **Gering, NE**
Mathis, James S. .... Brentwood, TN
Mathis, James Weldon .... **St. Louis, MO**
Mathis, Janice S. .... Margate City, NJ
Mathis, Jennifer .... **Irvine, CA**
Mathis, Jennifer L. .... **Austin, TX**
Mathis, John P. .... **Washington, DC**
Mathis, Joseph L. .... Gaffney, SC
Mathis, Joseph Michael, Jr. .... **Peoria, IL**
Mathis, Judith L. .... **Arlington, VA**
Mathis, Karen J. .... **Denver, CO**
Mathis, Kelly B. .... **Jacksonville, FL**
Mathis, Kenneth G. .... Pasadena, TX
Mathis, Kimberley Smith .... **St. Louis, MO**
Mathis, Kirk .... **Lufkin, TX**
Mathis Law Firm, The .... **Peoria, IL**
Mathis Law Offices, L.L.P. .... Albany, GA
Mathis, Lee R. .... Dana Point, CA
Mathis, Leslie B. .... Butler, PA
Mathis, Linda Jew .... Memphis, TN
Mathis, Lisa G. .... Little Rock, AR
Mathis & Long, Professional Corporation
St. Louis, MO
Mathis, Louis F. .... Port Arthur, TX
Mathis, Lynda V. .... Baltimore, MD
Mathis, Lynda V., P.A. .... Baltimore, MD
Mathis, Marifian, Richter & Grandy, Ltd.
Belleville, IL
St. Louis, MO
Mathis, Mark R. .... Bardstown, KY
Mathis & Masters, L.L.C. .... **Montrose, CO**
Mathis & Mathis, P.C. .... **Arlington, VA**
Mathis, Michael C. .... **Las Vegas, NV**
Mathis, Michael H. .... Tuckerton, NJ
Mathis, Nancy L. .... **San Jose, CA**
Mathis, Njeri I. .... **Houston, TX**
Mathis, Patrick B. .... **Belleville, IL**
Mathis, Paul C., III .... Arlington, VA
Mathis, Paul, Jr. .... **Greenville, MS**
Mathis, Rachel Carver .... **Tulsa, OK**
Mathis, Randal G. .... **Dallas, TX**
Mathis, Reginald A. .... **Miami, FL**
Mathis, Riggs & Prather, P.S.C.
Shelbyville, KY
Mathis, Robert A. .... **Metairie, LA**
Mathis, Robert J. .... Silver Spring, MD
Mathis, Robert K. .... St. Augustine, FL
Mathis, Robin Goddard .... **McLean, VA**
Oakton, VA
Mathis, Rodney L. .... Calhoun, GA
Mathis, Rollin D. .... Atlanta, GA
Mathis, Samuel M. .... Auburn, ME
Mathis, Sandra J. .... **Jacksonville, FL**
Mathis, Shirley Hale .... **Laredo, TX**
Mathis, Shirley Hale, P.C. .... **Laredo, TX**
Mathis, Stephen M. .... **Montrose, CO**
Mathis, Suzanne Patten .... Lakeland, GA
Mathis, Thane R. .... Anchorage, AK
Mathis, Tracy .... **St. Louis, MO**
Mathis, Vincent W.
Securities and Exchange Commission, Executive Staff, GV
Mathis, Virginia A. .... Phoenix, AZ
Mathis, Wayne E. .... Morrison, CO
Mathis, William H. .... St. Louis, MO
Mathis, William L. .... Baltimore, MD
Mathis, William L. .... **Alexandria, VA**
Mathis, Willie, Jr., (P.S.C.) .... Florence, KY
Walton, KY
Mathis, Winston Clinton
Arkadelphia, AR
Mathis-Dorline, Cecile Denise .... Buffalo, NY
Mathisen, Amy E. .... **Charleston, SC**
Mathisen, Dennis M. .... Minneapolis, MN
Mathisen, Eric P. .... **South Bend, IN**
Mathisen, Michael E. .... Philadelphia, PA
Mathisen, Raymond H.
Palm Beach Gardens, FL
Mathisen, Richard A. .... Ambler, PA
Mathisen, Richard G. .... Spokane, WA
Mathison, Carl M., Jr.
Palm Beach Gardens, FL
West Palm Beach, FL
Mathison, Donald J. .... Detroit, MI
Mathison, Eric N. .... **Milwaukee, WI**
Mathison, Harry L., Jr. .... **Henderson, KY**
Mathison, James D. .... Solana Beach, CA
Mathison, Jane Melson .... Ames, IA
Mathison, Kerry F.
Hilton Head Island, SC
Mathison, Leigh Deveny .... Bloomington, MN
Mathison, Mark S. .... **Minneapolis, MN**
Mathison & Mathison
Palm Beach Gardens, FL
Mathison & Mathison
Hilton Head Island, SC
Mathison, Penny L. .... Santa Barbara, CA
Mathison, Robert V., Jr.
Hilton Head Island, SC
Mathison, Stephen S.
Palm Beach Gardens, FL
Mathison, Stephen S., P.A.
Palm Beach Gardens, FL
Mathison, Tara M. .... **Milwaukee, WI**
Mathison, Timothy .... New Orleans, LA
Mathius, Frank J. .... New Orleans, LA
Mathless, Daniel S. .... Chicago, IL
Mathless, Scott L. .... New York, NY
Mathless, Steven .... Columbus, OH
Mathon, Benjamin D. .... Beverly Hills, CA
Mathon, Lauren R., (Ms.) .... Falls Church, VA
Mathon & Rosensweig, A Law Corporation
Beverly Hills, CA
Mathues, Stephen S. .... Tallahassee, FL
Mathur, Arvind N. .... **New York, NY**
Mathur Law Offices, P.C. .... **Dallas, TX**
Mathur, Prad B. .... Mount Pleasant, MI
Mathur, Sanjay S. .... **Dallas, TX**
Mathura, Rani Newman .... **Vero Beach, FL**
Mathurin, Richard A. .... **Los Angeles, CA**
Mathus, David L. .... **New York, NY**
Mathy, Jos. C. .... Milwaukee, WI
Mathy, Pamela A. .... San Antonio, TX
Matia, David T. .... Cleveland, OH
Matia, David T., Jr. .... Cleveland, OH
Matia, Paul R. .... Cleveland, OH
Matia, Robert L. .... **Phoenix, AZ**
Matias, Joaquin .... Boston, MA
Matias, Maria C. .... Miami, FL
Matias, Robert W. .... Cedar Rapids, IA
Matias, Thomas R. .... Albany, NY
Matiasek, Melanie J. .... La Grange, IL
Matiasevich, Matthew P.
San Francisco, CA
Matiatos, Peter A. .... Tucson, AZ
Matiauda, Andrea Setran
Los Angeles, CA
Matichak, Jill H. .... **San Francisco, CA**

Matics, MarkA. ....Winchester, KY
Matik, Paul, Jr. ....Glenview, IL
Matika, Joseph Jude ....Lehighton, PA
Matin, Arthur ....San Rafael, CA
Matinho, Paul J. ....Newark, NJ
Matinog, Alfonso C. ....Los Angeles, CA
Matis, Erin M. ....St. Louis, MO
Matis, Greg J. ....Salt Lake City, UT
Matis, Jeffery S. ....Farmington Hills, MI
Matis, Nina B., (P.C.) ....Chicago, IL
Matis, Thomas A. ....Pittsburgh, PA
Matisak, Kelly A. ....Philadelphia, PA
Matise, Geraldine A.
Federal Communications Commission,
Office of Engineering & Technology, GV
Matise, RoxeAnne B. ....Alamogordo, NM
Matise, Salvatore A. ....Columbus, GA
Matish, George G. ....Detroit, MI
Matish, James A. ....Clarksburg, WV
Matisik, Edward N. ....Washington, DC
Matiski, Michelle M. ....Phoenix, AZ
Matisoff, Edward S. ....Westlake Village, CA
Matisoff, Robert ....Washington, DC
Matison, Charles A. ....Northfield, NJ
Matison, Charles A., P.C., The Law Offices of ....Northfield, NJ
Matison, Dave A., III ....Tacoma, WA
Matison, Jason ....Santa Monica, CA
Matison, Katie Smith ....Seattle, WA
Matityahu, Lynn S. ....San Francisco, CA
Matkin, C. Michael ....Houston, TX
Matkin, Hollowick & Barfield ....Houston, TX
Matkin, Jennifer L. ....San Francisco, CA
Matkin, Karen C. ....Waco, TX
Matkin, Mark S. ....Spokane, WA
Matkins, Jerome D. ....Albuquerque, NM
Matkins, Michael L. ....Los Angeles, CA
Matko, Christopher B. ....Martinsburg, WV
Matko, Edmund J. ....Clarksburg, WV
Matkoff, Louis ....Philadelphia, PA
Matkoff & Shengold ....Philadelphia, PA
Matkom, Edward B. ....Milwaukee, WI
Matkov, George J., Jr. ....Chicago, IL
Matkov, Salzman, Madoff & Gunn
Chicago, IL
Matkov, Thomas J. ....Miami, FL
Matkovich, John A. ....Indian Head Park, IL
Matkovich, Mark Welling ....Beckley, WV
Matl, Lois T. ....Lexington, KY
Matl, Lois T., & Associates, P.S.C.
Lexington, KY
Matl, Victor George ....Sacramento, CA
Matlack, Don ....Clearwater, KS
Matlack, Joan ....Chicago, IL
Matlack, Linda S. ....Washington, DC
Matlack, Terry C. ....Lee's Summit, MO
Matlack, William T. ....Boston, MA
Matlago, John T. ....Culver City, CA
Matland, Kim Quincy ....Sharon, MA
Matland, Marc A. ....Vienna, VA
Matlaw, Leslie V. ....New Orleans, LA
Matlawski, Anne DeLuca ....Broomall, PA
Matlawski, J. Adam ....Media, PA
Matles, Marc D. ....Brooklyn, NY
Matlin, Dana ....New York, NY
Matlin, David S. ....Princeton, NJ
Matlin, Gerald W. ....Mount Kisco, NY
Matlin, Janice A. ....Glendale, CA
Matlin, Laura P. ....Jersey City, NJ
Matlin, Robert ....Chicago, IL
Matlin, Robert S. ....New York, NY
Matlin, Robin B. ....Philadelphia, PA
Matlin, Sam ....Freehold, NJ
Matlin, Shoshannah L. ....San Francisco, CA
Matlin & Siegel ....Freehold, NJ
Matlin, Steven B. ....Oakland, CA
Matlin, Steven J. ....New York, NY
Matlin, Susanne Summer ....Chicago, IL
Matlin, William Scott ....Mineola, NY
Matlock, Bruce ....Highland, CA
Matlock, Darell R., Jr. ....Tulsa, OK
Matlock, David N. ....Shreveport, LA
Matlock, George V. ....Tallahassee, FL
Matlock, James A., Jr. ....Knoxville, TN
Matlock, John W. ....Mesa, AZ
Matlock, Judith M. ....Denver, CO
Matlock Law Firm, A Professional Corporation
Oklahoma City, OK
Matlock, Malinda S. ....Tulsa, OK
Matlock, Marc D. ....Lansing, MI
Matlock, Michael E. ....Upland, CA
Matlock, Norman G. ....Philadelphia, PA
Matlock, Norman G., P.C. ....Philadelphia, PA
Matlock, Raymond H. ....Cincinnati, OH
Matlock, Richard S. ....Knoxville, TN
Matlock, Robert J. ....Dallas, TX
Matlock, Ronald L. ....Oklahoma City, OK
Matlock, Tom ....McAllen, TX
Matlof, David J. ....Los Angeles, CA
Matloff, Howard B. ....San Diego, CA
Matloff, Randee M. ....Livingston, NJ
Matlow, Laura ....New York, NY
Matlow, Susan K. ....Fairfax, VA
Matluck, Susan Rose ....New York, NY
Matney & Associates, P.A. ....Asheville, NC
Matney, David F., III ....Asheville, NC
Matney, Edward A. ....Grundy, VA
Matney, Edwin V. ....Phoenix, AZ
Matney, Gregory S. ....Tazewell, VA
Matney, John R., Jr. ....Dallas, TX
Matney, Mark R. ....Arlington, VA
Matney, Scott H. ....Farmington, CT
Matney, William Jackson, Jr.
Washington, DC
Mato, Ana Maria ....Miami, FL
Matoesian, A. Andreas ....Edwardsville, IL
Matoesian, M. Jane ....St. Louis, MO
Matoesian, Vahog ....Granite City, IL

Maton, Larry L. ....Colorado Springs, CO
Maton, Paul J. ....Skokie, IL
Maton, Paul J., P.C. ....Skokie, IL
Matonich, Edward J. ....Hibbing, MN
Matonich & Persson, Chartered
Hibbing, MN
Matorin, Carol M. ....Brooklyn, NY
Matorin, Mitchell J. ....Washington, DC
Matorin, Peter S. ....New York, NY
Matorin, Sidney R. ....Calabasas, CA
Matos, Arturo W. ....New York, NY
Matos, Carmen T. ....Chicago, IL
Matos, Carmen T. ....Chicago, IL
Matos Colon & Matos Rodriguez
San Juan, PR
Matos, Daniel S. ....Hartford, CT
Matos, Karin L. ....Miami, FL
Matos, Myriam ....San Juan, PR
Matos, Paula C. ....Laguna Hills, CA
Orange, CA
Matos, Peter A. ....Fort Lauderdale, FL
Miami, FL
Matos, Raul ....Ponce, PR
Matos, Roberto ....Stone Mountain, GA
Matos-Bonet, Juan F. ....San Juan, PR
Matos Colon, Miguel ....San Juan, PR
Matosich, Andrew J. ....Santa Monica, CA
Matosky, John E. ....Boston, MA
Matos Rodriguez, Miguel M. ....San Juan, PR
Matossian, Rosemary ....Walnut Creek, CA
Matour, James M. ....Philadelphia, PA
Matousek, Joanne J. ....Chicago, IL
Matousek, Paul F. ....Chicago, IL
Matoush, Carol S. ....Colorado Springs, CO
Matoush, Robert W. ....Salem, IL
Matoush, William R. ....Colorado Springs, CO
Matovcik, Lana S. ....Baltimore, MD
Matovich, Carey E. ....Billings, MT
Matovich and Keller, P.C. ....Billings, MT
Matowik, Ellen ....Kew Gardens, NY
Matra, John A. ....Culver City, CA
Matraia, Michael T. ....Boston, MA
Matranga, Dominick J. ....Mobile, AL
Matranga, Henry L. ....Utica, MI
Matranga, Joseph M. ....Mobile, AL
Matranga, Mark P. ....Chicago, IL
Matranga, Richard D. ....Sonora, CA
Matre, James A. ....Cincinnati, OH
Matri, Henry M. ....Hackensack, NJ
Matricardi, Edmund A., Jr.
Springfield, VA
Matricardi & Moylan, LLP
Springfield, VA
Matricardi, Philip J. ....Seattle, WA
Matricciani, Albert J., Jr. ....Baltimore, MD
Matricciani, Christopher P. ....Miami, FL
Matricciani, Roseanne M. ....Baltimore, MD
Matrician, William F. ....Morristown, NJ
Matrick, J. Morton ....Jackson, MS
Matrisch, Steve ....Springfield, IL
Matsa, Aristotle R. ....Columbus, OH
Matsakis, Elias N. ....Chicago, IL
Matsas, Constantine Dean ....Chicago, IL
Matsch, Richd. P. ....Denver, CO
Matsche, Diane L. ....Green Bay, WI
Matschke, Sara Schepps
White Plains, NY
Matschullat, Dale L. ....Rockford, IL
Matsen, Jeffrey R., & Associates
Newport Beach, CA
Matsen, Joseph R. ....Bellevue, WA
Matsen, S. Suzanne ....Bellevue, WA
Matsey, David Paul ....Knox, IN
Matsik, Bradley W. ....Charlotte, NC
Matsikoudis, Philip John ....Jersey City, NJ
Matsikoudis, William ....Woodbridge, NJ
Matsil, Ira S. ....Dallas, TX
Matsil, Melvin I. ....Brooklyn, NY
Matsinger, Diane M. ....Santa Barbara, CA
Matsis, Demetra K. ....Chicago, IL
Matsis, Elena E. ....San Francisco, CA
Matsko, Gary S. ....Boston, MA
Matsler, Michael J. ....Newburgh, NY
Matsno, Dawn M. ....Los Angeles, CA
Matson, Bruce H. ....Richmond, VA
Matson, Candace L. ....Los Angeles, CA
Matson, Christine B. ....Saipan, TT
Matson, D. Douglas ....Seattle, WA
Matson, Daniel C. ....DeWitt, MI
Matson, David G. ....Brookville, PA
Matson, David W. ....Kansas City, MO
Matson, Diana B. ....Fort Lauderdale, FL
Matson, Gregg A. ....Santa Monica, CA
Matson, James J. ....Danville, CA
Matson, Janice M. ....Tampa, FL
Matson, Jennifer H. ....York, PA
Matson, JoAnne Liebman ....Little Rock, AR
Matson, John ....New York, NY
Matson, John C. ....Chicago, IL
Matson, John E. ....New York, NY
Matson, John J. L. ....Westborough, MA
Matson, John R., III ....Washington, DC
Matson, Lisa Lazarus-Black
Philadelphia, PA
Matson, Lynne S. ....Jacksonville, FL
Matson, Marcy R. ....Lansing, MI
Matson, Mark D. ....San Angelo, TX
Matson, Morgan M. ....Austin, TX
Matson, Peter L. ....Lewisburg, PA
Matson, Peter L., P.C. ....Lewisburg, PA
Matson, Richard G. ....Vancouver, WA
Matson, Richard S. ....Chico, CA
Matson, Robert I. ....White Plains, NY
Matson, Roland F. ....Atlanta, GA
Matson, Russell J. ....Brockton, MA
Matson, Stephen K. ....Pasadena, CA
Matson, Timothy C. ....Minneapolis, MN
Matson, William L. ....McLean, VA

Matsoukas, Peter N. ....New York, NY
Matsubara, Benjamin M. ....Honolulu, HI
Matsubara, Kerne H. ....San Francisco, CA
Matsubara, Lee & Kotake, Attorneys at Law, A Law Corporation ....Honolulu, HI
Matsubayashi, Hugh H. ....San Jose, CA
Matsuda, Kent M. ....San Francisco, CA
Matsuda, Mari J. ....Honolulu, HI
Matsuda, Masaru ....Los Angeles, CA
Matsuda, Thomas J. ....Portland, OR
Matsui, Bruce Y. ....Honolulu, HI
Matsui, Clyde Wm. ....Honolulu, HI
Matsui, Douglas G. ....Santa Ana, CA
Matsui, Melanie S. ....Honolulu, HI
Matsui, Robert T. ....Sacramento, CA
Matsui, Susan S. ....Costa Mesa, CA
Matsuk, Leonard A. ....Long Beach, CA
Matsuk and Orr ....Long Beach, CA
Matsukage, Fay M. ....Denver, CO
Matsukas, Garimarie A. ....Glendale, CA
Matsukawa, Michael J. ....Kailua-Kona, HI
Matsumori, Douglas ....Salt Lake City, UT
Matsumoto, Barry D. ....Iowa City, IA
Matsumoto, Colbert M. ....Honolulu, HI
Matsumoto, Ellen Mariko ....Gardena, CA
Matsumoto, Kent ....Fort Lee, NJ
Matsumoto, Kiyo A. ....Brooklyn, NY
Matsumoto, Russell ....Coalinga, CA
Matsumura, Michele M. ....Pleasanton, CA
Matsumura, Sharon K. ....Palmdale, CA
Matsumura, William E. ....Los Angeles, CA
Matsunaga, Emma S. ....Honolulu, HI
Matsunaga, Geoffrey D. ....Torrance, CA
Matsunaga, Gerald S. ....Lihue, HI
Matsunaga, Kim ....Chicago, IL
Matsunaga, Len ....New York, NY
Matsunaga, Matthew M. ....Honolulu, HI
Matsunaga, Mitsuo ....New York, NY
Matsunaka, Stanley T. ....Loveland, CO
Matsunaka, Stanley T., P.C. ....Loveland, CO
Matsuo, Gene Yukio ....New York, NY
Matsuo, Michele Y. ....Honolulu, HI
Matsuoka, Keith A. ....Honolulu, HI
Matsushige, Cary S. ....Honolulu, HI
Matsushima, Alicia M. ....Corpus Christi, TX
Matsushima, David T. ....Basking Ridge, NJ
Matsutani, Sadaaki ....Sierra Madre, CA
Matsuura, Albert ....Pocatello, ID
Matsuura, Jeffrey H. ....Clarksburg, MD
Matsuura, Jeffrey H. ....McLean, VA
Matsuura, Wayne A. ....Honolulu, HI
Matsuyama, W. Brian ....Seattle, WA
Matt, David L. ....Santa Rosa, CA
Matt, Diane L. ....Stamford, CT
Matt, Erika B. ....Greenville, SC
Matt, Francis X., III ....Pittsburgh, PA
Matt, Miles A. ....Lafayette, LA
Matt, Nicholas J. ....Grand Forks, ND
Matt, Pamela Germain ....Pittsburgh, PA
Matt, Peter K. ....Washington, DC
Matt, Sean R. ....Seattle, WA
Matt, Theo. F. ....Oconomowoc, WI
Matt, Walter J., Jr. ....Buffalo, NY
Matta, Aline ....New York, NY
Matta, Antonio Fiol ....San Juan, PR
Matta, Antonio R. ....Ponce, PR
Matta, Carla G. ....Santa Monica, CA
Matta, Derek ....Austin, TX
Matta, Joseph C. ....Houston, TX
Matta & Matta ....Ponce, PR
Matta, Richard K. ....Washington, DC
Matta, Robert E. ....Minersville, PA
Matta, Steven A. ....Troy, MI
Mattachione, Steven E. ....Los Angeles, CA
Mattaini, Paul G. ....Hanover, PA
Lancaster, PA
Reading, PA
Mattaini, Steven F. ....St. Paul, MN
Mattair, Mary L. ....Pensacola, FL
Mattair, Mary L., P.A. ....Pensacola, FL
Mattan, Claire R. ....Kansas City, MO
Mattar, Brenda A. ....Buffalo, NY
Mattar & D'Agostino, LLP ....Buffalo, NY
Mattar, Lawrence J. ....Buffalo, NY
Mattar, Norman J. ....Williamsville, NY
Mattar, Richard E. ....Blowing Rock, NC
Mattar, William K. ....Williamsville, NY
Mattarella, Joseph G. ....Atlanta, GA
Mattas, Steven T. ....San Leandro, CA
Mattaway, L. Richard ....Miami, FL
Mattax, David C. ....Austin, TX
Mattchen, Michael K. ....Boston, MA
Matte, James L. ....Atlanta, GA
Matte, Jeanine L. ....Washington, DC
Matte, Jeffrey C. ....Glens Falls, NY
Matte, Virginia S. ....Phoenix, AZ
Mattei, Andrew ....New York, NY
Mattei, Barbara M. ....Baraboo, WI
Mattei, Ernest J. ....Hartford, CT
Mattei, Grace V. ....Staten Island, NY
Mattei, Ivan E. ....New York, NY
Mattei, Lyn O. ....Portland, OR
Mattei, Mario Francis ....Staten Island, NY
Mattei, Suzanne Yvonne ....New York, NY
Matteis, August J., Jr. ....Washington, DC
Mattel, Harvey K. ....Fort Lauderdale, FL
Matteliano, Joseph A. ....Buffalo, NY
Matten, Bradley K. ....Newport Beach, CA
Matten, Byron L. ....Oakbrook Terrace, IL
Mattenson, Charles R. ....Deerfield, IL
Mattenson, David M. ....Chicago, IL
Mattenson, Laurie S.
Prospect Heights, IL
Mattenson, Myles M. ....Los Angeles, CA
Matteo, Belko, Baker & Hinlicky
Moorestown, NJ
Matteo, Carole L. ....Plainville, CT

Matteo, Connie A. ....Morristown, NJ
New York, NY
Matteo, George W., Jr. ....Moorestown, NJ
Matteo, Jeffrey V. ....Norristown, PA
Matteo, John J. ....Washington, DC
Baltimore, MD
Rockville, MD
Vienna, VA
Matteo, Melissa A. ....Mamaroneck, NY
Matteo, Michael D. ....Cherry Hill, NJ
Matteoni, Bradley M. ....San Jose, CA
Matteoni, Norman E. ....San Jose, CA
Matteoni, Paul A. ....Reno, NV
Matteoni, Saxe & O'Laughlin
San Jose, CA
Matteosian, Gregory M. ....Belmont, MA
Matter, Bruce E. ....Bethesda, MD
Mattera, Alex F. ....Boston, MA
Mattera, Catherine Romania
Hackensack, NJ
Mattera, Frank ....Mineola, NY
Mattera, John J. ....New York, NY
Mattera, Joseph P. ....Hartsdale, NY
Mattera, Laura M. ....New York, NY
Mattera, Nicholas A. ....Hackensack, NJ
Mattera, Paul ....Boston, MA
Mattera, Richard J. ....Cleveland, OH
Matterer, Mary B. ....Wilmington, DE
Matterfis, Heidi C. ....New York, NY
Mattern, David D. ....St. Louis, MO
Mattern, Harry P. ....Kingston, PA
Mattern, James E. ....East Lyme, CT
Mattern, John A. ....San Jose, CA
Mattern, Kenneth G. ....Boston, MA
Mattern, Mark D. ....Minot, ND
Mattern, Mathias M. ....Chicago, IL
Mattern, Michael G. ....Irvine, CA
Mattern, Patricia A. ....Philadelphia, PA
Mattern, Phil ....Seattle, WA
Mattern, Roy E., Jr. ....Bellevue, WA
Mattern, Thomas J. ....Wabash, IN
Matters, James R. ....Stevensville, MD
Matters, Michael A. ....Miami, FL
Mattes, Barry A. ....Chicago, IL
Mattes, Bradford E. ....Los Angeles, CA
Mattes, David D. ....Springfield, OH
Mattes, David J. ....West Homestead, PA
Mattes, Edward C., Jr. ....New York, NY
Mattes, Julie F. ....Sedgwick, ME
Mattes, Martin A. ....San Francisco, CA
Mattes, Martin J. ....Southfield, MI
Mattes, Martin J., P.C. ....Southfield, MI
Mattes & Mattes, P.C. ....Scranton, PA
Mattes, Robert Emmett, III ....Cherry Hill, NJ
Mattes, Roger ....Scranton, PA
Mattes, Roger, Jr. ....Scranton, PA
Mattes, Troy J. ....Lancaster, PA
Mattes, William M. ....Columbus, OH
Mattesich, James M. ....Sacramento, CA
Mattesky, Stephen E. ....New Orleans, LA
Matteson, Andrew C. ....Nashville, TN
Matteson, Andrew R. ....Roseville, CA
Matteson, C. Diane Williams
Wichita Falls, TX
Matteson, Darrel L. ....Littleton, CO
Matteson, David K. ....Kansas City, MO
Matteson, David M. ....Chicago, IL
Matteson, Duncan L., Jr. ....Redwood City, CA
Matteson, Holly J. ....Brooklyn, NY
Matteson, Ilana Eden
Commodity Futures Trading Commission,
Division of Enforcement, GV
Matteson, Karen Lynn ....Los Angeles, CA
Matteson, Lance ....Mercer Island, WA
Matteson, Shannon ....Lafayette, CA
Matteson, Thomas R. ....Los Angeles, CA
Matteson, Timothy J. ....Newark, NJ
Matteson, William B. ....New York, NY
Mattessich, Danielle I. ....Arlington, VA
Mattessich, Kevin M. ....New York, NY
Mattessich, Richard S. ....Princeton, NJ
New York, NY
Mattessich, Tara D. ....St. Paul, MN
Matteucci, Arthur G. ....Great Falls, MT
Matteucci, Edward L. ....Albuquerque, NM
Matteucci, Falcon & Lester, P.C.
Great Falls, MT
Matteucci, Linda M. ....Albuquerque, NM
Matteucci, M. Gene ....Las Vegas, NV
Matteucci, Michael J. ....Stockton, CA
Matteucci, Paul J. ....Albuquerque, NM
Matteucci, Sherry Scheel ....Billings, MT
Matteucci, Stephen J. ....Newport News, VA
Matteuzzi, Michael D. ....Kansas City, MO
Mattey, Carol E.
Federal Communications Commission,
Common Carrier Bureau, GV
Mattey, John D. ....Wilmington, DE
Mattey, John J. ....Englewood, CO
Mattfeld, Kenneth F. ....San Francisco, CA
Matthai, Edith R. ....Los Angeles, CA
Matthei, Kimberly A. ....Chicago, IL
Mattheis, Peter J. ....Washington, DC
Matthes, F. Stephenson ....Harrisburg, PA
Matthes, Ian Neil ....Atlanta, GA
Matthes, Julie ....Roslyn, NY
Matthes, Mark ....Houston, TX
Matthes, Mark A. ....Goshen, IN
Matthes, Paul C. ....New York, NY
Mattheson, Margaret Cornillon ....Chalfont, PA
Matthew, Amy ....Walnut Creek, CA
Matthew, Dayna Bowen ....Louisville, KY
Matthew, Lawrence S. ....Phoenix, AZ
Matthew, Millard E., Jr. ....Houston, TX
Matthew, Norman L. ....Niles, IL
Matthew, Robin J. ....Washington, DC
Matthew, Sandra Medway ....Agoura Hills, CA
Matthew, Sidney Lewis ....Tallahassee, FL

Matthew, Susan J. .... Boston, MA
Matthewman, William D. .... Boca Raton, FL
Miami, FL
West Palm Beach, FL
Matthews, A. Douglas .... Cambridge, MA
Matthews, A. Lamar, Jr. .... Sarasota, FL
Matthews, A. Llewellyn .... Bellevue, WA
Matthews, A. Robert .... Mansfield, OH
Matthews, Acie W. .... Sioux Falls, SD
Matthews, Albert R. .... Muskogee, OK
Matthews, Alexandra Julia .... Harrisburg, PA
Matthews, Alicia Caterino .... Boston, MA
Matthews, Amos T., Jr.
Department of Commerce, Patent and Trademark Office, GV
Matthews, Amy Jo .... Boston, MA
Matthews, Andrew .... Los Angeles, CA
Matthews, Andrew A., Jr. .... Pittsfield, MA
Matthews, Ann Kimberly
Federal Communications Commission, Mass Media Bureau, GV
Matthews, Antonio L. .... Chattanooga, TN
Matthews, Arturo E., Jr. .... Irvine, CA
Matthews & Associates .... Houston, TX
Matthews, Barbara .... New York, NY
Matthews, Barbara A. .... Department of Labor, Office of the Solicitor, GV
Matthews, Barbara C. .... Washington, DC
Matthews, Barbara J.
Department of Labor, GV
Matthews, Barrett G. .... Corpus Christi, TX
Matthews, Ben G. .... Shelbyville, KY
Matthews, Benjamin R. .... Florence, SC
Matthews, Bernard P., Jr.
Greensburg, PA
Matthews, Blakeley D. .... Nashville, TN
Matthews & Branscomb, A Professional Corporation .... Carrizo Springs, TX
Corpus Christi, TX
Eagle Pass, TX
San Antonio, TX
Uvalde, TX
Matthews, Brian C. .... Roseland, NJ
Matthews, Bruce O.
Spring Lake Heights, NJ
Matthews, Byron .... Fort Worth, TX
Matthews, Campbell, Rhoads, McClure & Thompson .... Bentonville, AR
Rogers, AR
Matthews, Careton R. .... Stone Mountain, GA
Matthews, Carl T., Jr. .... Tulsa, OK
Matthews, Carla S. .... Vero Beach, FL
Matthews, Carlton, Stein, Shiels, Pearce, Dunn & Knott, L.L.P. .... Dallas, TX
Matthews, Carol L. B. .... Washington, DC
Matthews, Carol W. .... Washington, DC
Matthews, Caroline B. .... Montgomery, AL
Matthews, Carolyn Cason .... Columbia, SC
Matthews, Carolyn Ratti .... Phoenix, AZ
Matthews, Catherine E. .... Tulsa, OK
Matthews, Charles D., Jr. .... Chico, CA
Matthews, Charles D., V .... Alton, IL
Matthews, Charles E., Jr. .... Stamford, CT
Matthews, Charles T. .... Huntington, NY
Matthews, Charles W., Jr. .... Irving, TX
Matthews, Charles W., Jr. (P.A.) .... Tampa, FL
Matthews, Cheryl A. .... Pontiac, MI
Matthews, Christian F., III, P.C.
Mount Clemens, MI
Matthews, Christian F., III, P.C.
Mount Clemens, MI
Matthews, Christopher T. .... Portland, OR
Matthews, Clark J., II .... Dallas, TX
Matthews, Claude L., Jr. .... Washington, DC
Matthews, Claude L., Jr. .... Houston, TX
Matthews, Coke S., III .... Birmingham, AL
Matthews, Craig T. .... Yellow Springs, OH
Matthews, Craig T., and Associates, LPA
Yellow Springs, OH
Matthews, Cynthia A. .... Brooklyn, NY
Matthews, Cynthia Clark
Equal Employment Opportunity Commission, GV
Matthews, Cynthia M. .... Washington, DC
Matthews, D. Lane .... Charlotte, NC
Matthews, D. Turner .... Bradenton, FL
Matthews, Dan G. .... San Antonio, TX
Matthews, Dana C. .... Destin, FL
Matthews, Dana P. .... Hollister, CA
Matthews, Daniel P. .... Needham, MA
Matthews, David A. .... Sacramento, CA
Matthews, David G.
Research Triangle Park, NC
Matthews, David Ian .... Marietta, GA
Matthews, David L. .... Wapello, IA
Matthews, David P. .... Houston, TX
Matthews, David R. .... Rogers, AR
Matthews, David W. .... Cincinnati, OH
Matthews, Dean .... Washington, MO
Matthews, Deborah G. .... Fairfax, VA
Matthews, Deborah P. .... Miami, FL
Matthews, Diane Lloyd .... New Orleans, LA
Matthews, Donald G. .... Butler, NJ
Wayne, NJ
Matthews, Donald R. .... Missoula, MT
Matthews, Donald W. .... Jacksonville, FL
Matthews, Donna .... Fairfax, VA
Matthews, Doris M. .... Madisonville, TN
Matthews, Dorothy Gibson .... Chicago, IL
Matthews, Douglas A. .... Olathe, KS
Matthews, Douglas E. .... Crystal Lake, IL
Matthews, Douglas P. .... New Orleans, LA
Matthews, Douglas R. .... Columbus, OH
Matthews, E. Vince, III .... Houston, TX
Matthews, E. Warren .... Bracey, VA
Matthews, Ean .... Stamford, CT
Matthews, Earl G. .... Philadelphia, PA
Matthews, Edsel "Eddie" F., Jr., P.A.
Milton, FL
Pensacola, FL
Matthews, Edsel "Eddie" F., Jr.
Pensacola, FL
Matthews, Edwin R. .... Short Hills, NJ
Matthews, Edwin R., P.C.
Morristown, NJ
Newark, NJ
Short Hills, NJ
Summit, NJ
Matthews, Edwin Spencer, Jr.
New York, NY
Matthews, Eileen P. .... New York, NY
Matthews, Elaine Moore
Grand Junction, CO
Matthews, Elizabeth A. .... Washington, DC
Matthews, Elizabeth L. .... Birmingham, MI
Matthews, Elizabeth M. .... New York, NY
Matthews, Ellen .... Berkeley, CA
Matthews, Ellison M. .... Boise, ID
Matthews, Elmer M. .... Trenton, NJ
Matthews, Eugene A., Jr.
Hot Springs National Park, AR
Matthews, Eugene H. .... Winston-Salem, NC
Matthews, Eulanda Lynn
Los Angeles, CA
Matthews, F. Marianne .... Dallas, TX
Matthews, F. Patrick .... Milwaukee, WI
Matthews & Filmore, L.L.C.
Daleville, AL
Dothan, AL
Ozark, AL
Matthews Firm, The .... Austin, TX
Houston, TX
Matthews, Floyd L., Jr. .... Jacksonville, FL
Matthews, Francis P. .... Elkhorn, NE
Matthews, Frank E. .... Tallahassee, FL
Matthews, Fred B. .... Montgomery, AL
Matthews, Frederic E. .... Bowling Green, OH
Matthews & Freeland .... Somerville, TN
Matthews, Freeman R. .... Metairie, LA
Matthews, Fuqua, Riley & Davis .... Chico, CA
Matthews, Gabriela J. .... Durham, NC
Matthews, Gabriela J., & Associates, P.A.
Durham, NC
Matthews, Gail A. .... Brooklyn, NY
Matthews, Gail O., (Mr.) .... Little Rock, AR
Matthews, Gale F. .... Parsippany, NJ
Matthews, Gary K. .... Hammond, IN
Matthews, Gary R. .... Lexington, KY
Matthews, Gayle B. .... Falls Church, VA
Matthews, Gene W. .... Atlanta, GA
Matthews, George E. .... Prior Lake, MN
Matthews, Gloria J. .... Washington, DC
Matthews, Gregory Kirk .... Portsmouth, VA
Matthews, Guy E. .... Houston, TX
Matthews, Guy F. .... Media, PA
Matthews, H. Seth, III .... San Andreas, CA
Matthews & Ham .... Southampton, NY
Matthews, Harold T. .... Glasgow, KY
Matthews & Hawkins, P.A. .... Destin, FL
Matthews, Herbert S.
South San Francisco, CA
Matthews, Hugh T. .... Gilmer, TX
Matthews, Hutton & Eastmoore
Sarasota, FL
Matthews, J. Aubrey .... Marion, VA
Matthews, J. Michael .... San Francisco, CA
Matthews, J. Michael
Altamonte Springs, FL
Matthews, J. Michael, P.A.
Altamonte Springs, FL
Matthews, Jacqueline J. .... Uniondale, NY
Matthews, James A., III .... Philadelphia, PA
Matthews, James B., III .... Atlanta, GA
Matthews, James D. .... Indianapolis, IN
Matthews, James D. .... Austin, TX
Fort Worth, TX
Houston, TX
Matthews, James F. .... San Jose, CA
Matthews, James F. .... Indianapolis, IN
Matthews, James F. .... Summit, NJ
Matthews, James F. .... Huntington, NY
Matthews, James G. .... Winston-Salem, NC
Matthews, James J., Jr. .... Arlington, VA
Matthews, James M. .... South Bend, IN
Matthews, James M. .... Kansas City, MO
Matthews, James R. .... Cincinnati, OH
Matthews, James S. .... Minneapolis, MN
Matthews, James S. .... Dallas, TX
Matthews, James S., Jr. .... Oklahoma City, OK
Matthews, James W. .... Boston, MA
Matthews, Jane .... Barnwell, SC
Matthews, Jeffery J. .... Eugene, OR
Matthews, Jeffrey R. .... Houston, TX
Matthews, Jeffrey S. .... Portland, OR
Matthews, Jenell M. .... Minneapolis, MN
Matthews, Jennifer E. .... Huntsville, AL
Matthews, Jerome E. .... Oakland, CA
Matthews, Jerry L. .... Pine Ridge, SD
Matthews, Joe W. .... Dallas, TX
Matthews, John A., III .... Trenton, NJ
Matthews, John A., Jr. .... Roseland, NJ
Matthews, John A., Jr.
Rockville Centre, NY
Matthews, John C. .... Atlantic City, NJ
Matthews, John D. .... Washington, DC
Matthews, John D. .... Seattle, WA
Matthews, John E. .... Washington, DC
Matthews, John E. .... Albany, NY
Matthews, John J. .... Tallahassee, FL
Matthews, John P. .... Atlanta, GA
Matthews, John R., Jr. .... Montgomery, AL
Matthews, John V. .... Fayetteville, TN
Matthews, John V., III .... Fayetteville, TN
Matthews, John V., Jr. .... Hertford, NC
Matthews, John W. .... Philadelphia, PA
Matthews, John W. .... Fairfax, VA
Matthews, Johnnie L. .... Baton Rouge, LA
Matthews, Jolly W., III .... Hattiesburg, MS
Matthews & Jorgensen .... Sioux Falls, SD
Matthews, Joseph A., Jr. .... Roanoke, VA
Matthews, Joseph M. .... Miami, FL
Matthews, J. P. .... Somerville, TN
Matthews, J. P. (Jack) .... New York, NY
Matthews, Juliane R. B. .... Seattle, WA
Matthews, K. Kyle .... Pleasanton, CA
Matthews, Karl B. .... Eugene, OR
Matthews, Katharine I. .... Washington, DC
Matthews, Kathleen G. .... Boston, MA
Matthews, Kathy .... Kansas City, MO
Matthews, Kay L. .... Little Rock, AR
Matthews, Keith A.
Environmental Protection Agency, Office of the General Counsel, GV
Matthews, Keith G. .... New York, NY
Matthews, Kelly A. .... Austin, TX
Matthews, Kendra M. .... Salem, OR
Matthews, Kendra Marie .... Portland, OR
Matthews, Kenneth .... New York, NY
Matthews, Kenneth A. .... Denver, CO
Matthews, Keri N. .... New York, NY
Matthews, Kevin G. .... Cincinnati, OH
Matthews, Kim .... Portland, ME
Matthews, Kimberly Grigsby
Jacksonville, FL
Matthews, Kimberly R. .... Charlotte, NC
Matthews, Kurt E. .... Los Angeles, CA
Matthews, L. Charlene .... Flagler Beach, FL
Matthews, Lane K. .... Boynton Beach, FL
Matthews, Larry A.
Fort Walton Beach, FL
Panama City, FL
Pensacola, FL
Matthews, Laurel Ann .... Cleveland, OH
Matthews, Laurie Droughton
Morristown, NJ
Matthews Law Firm .... Washington, MO
Matthews Law Firm .... Houston, TX
Matthews Law Offices .... Boise, ID
Matthews Law Offices, S.C.
Milwaukee, WI
Matthews, Lee A. .... Houston, TX
Matthews, Lisa Carol .... New Orleans, LA
Matthews, Lynn A. .... Dunn, NC
Matthews, M. Grace .... Schenectady, NY
Matthews, Mara Medvin .... Miami, FL
Matthews, Marcella .... Middletown, NY
Matthews, Margie Bright .... Walterboro, SC
Matthews, Maria Gutierrez .... Birmingham, AL
Matthews, Maria I. .... Tallahassee, FL
Matthews, Mark A. .... Westerville, OH
Matthews, Mark E. .... Washington, DC
Matthews, Mark R. .... Fountain Valley, CA
Matthews, Mark S. .... Stuart, FL
Matthews, Marsha .... Stamford, CT
Matthews, Marsha Dula .... Washington, DC
Matthews, Mart C. .... Denver, CO
Matthews, Martha A. .... San Francisco, CA
Matthews, Martha A. .... Washington, DC
Matthews, Marty L., Law Office of
Dallas, TX
Matthews, Mary Elizabeth .... Rogers, AR
Matthews, Mary F. .... Palm Springs, CA
Matthews, Mary Helen .... Denver, CO
Matthews, Mary Jean .... Fort Lauderdale, FL
Matthews, Mary S. .... Park Ridge, IL
Matthews, Mercia C. .... New York, NY
Matthews, Michael D. .... Beaumont, TX
Matthews, Michael G. .... Rock Hill, SC
Matthews, Michael P. .... Denver, CO
Matthews, Michael P. .... Washington, DC
Matthews, Michael V. .... Charlotte, NC
Matthews, Michael V., P.C., Law Offices of
Charlotte, NC
Matthews, Miesha L. .... White Plains, NY
Matthews, Milburn A.
San Juan Capistrano, CA
Matthews, Monica S. .... Tampa, FL
Matthews & Myles .... Shelbyville, KY
Matthews, Nancy P. .... Lancaster, PA
Matthews, Nona C. .... Irving, TX
Matthews, P. Joan .... Irvine, CA
Matthews, Pamela G. .... San Antonio, TX
Matthews, Pamela J. .... Bannockburn, IL
Matthews, Pamela Lord .... Santa Fe, NM
Matthews, Patricia A. .... Santa Fe, NM
Matthews, Patricia C. .... Oak Brook, IL
Matthews, Patricia L. .... Rockville Centre, NY
Matthews, Patrick T. .... Fall River, MA
Matthews, Paul A. .... Memphis, TN
Matthews, Paul H. .... Salt Lake City, UT
Matthews, Paul J., II .... Decatur, AL
Matthews, Paul R. .... Boston, MA
Matthews, Philip R. .... San Francisco, CA
Matthews, Philip Wilson .... Dearborn, MI
Matthews, R. Ellen .... Madison, MS
Matthews, R. Hardin .... Boston, MA
Matthews, Ralph B. .... Lithonia, GA
Matthews, Ray .... Houston, TX
Matthews, Raymond T. .... Houston, TX
Matthews, Rebecca S. .... Houston, TX
Matthews, Regina O. .... New Orleans, LA
Matthews, Reginald S. .... Jamaica, NY
Matthews, Richard H. .... Virginia Beach, VA
Matthews, Richard J. .... Elko, NV
Matthews, Richard J. .... Jamaica, NY
Matthews, Richard M. .... Detroit, MI
Matthews, Richard P. .... Seattle, WA
Matthews, Richard Thomas .... Columbia, TN
Matthews & Rigsby PLLC
Lexington, KY
Matthews, Robert .... Emporia, KS
Matthews, Robert A. .... Washington, DC
Matthews, Robert A., Jr. .... Washington, DC
Matthews, Robert Donald
El Segundo, CA
Matthews, Robert E. .... Marietta, GA
Matthews, Robert E. .... Seattle, WA
Matthews, Robert F. .... Louisville, KY
Matthews, Robert H. .... Covington, LA
New Orleans, LA
Matthews, Robert J. .... Newport Beach, CA
Matthews, Robert J., Associates
Philadelphia, PA
Southampton, PA
Matthews, Robert L. .... Boulder, CO
Matthews, Robert T. .... Huntington Beach, CA
Matthews, Roderick J. .... Madison, WI
Matthews, Roger D. .... Boston, MA
Matthews, Roger S. .... Pittsburgh, PA
Matthews, S. James .... Kingston, NY
Matthews, Sam S. .... Paramus, NJ
Matthews, Sanders & Sayes
Little Rock, AR
Matthews, Sarah .... Edgartown, MA
Matthews, Scott A. .... Hickory, NC
Pittsburgh, PA
Matthews, Scott D. .... Indianapolis, IN
Matthews, Scott R. .... Lodi, CA
Matthews, Seth G. .... Quincy, MA
Matthews, Snider & Williams .... Fairfax, VA
Matthews, Stafford .... San Francisco, CA
Matthews & Steel .... Atlanta, GA
Matthews, Stephanie L. .... Chicago, IL
Matthews, Stephen A. .... Pine Bluff, AR
Matthews, Stephen C. .... Newark, NJ
Matthews, Stephen F. .... Columbia, MO
Matthews, Stephen R. .... St. Louis, MO
Matthews, Stephen R. .... Spokane, WA
Matthews, Steve A. .... Columbia, SC
Matthews, Steve T. .... Austin, TX
Matthews, Steven R. .... Boise, ID
Matthews, Stroud & Ratliff, Professional Association .... Hattiesburg, MS
Jackson, MS
Matthews, Suzanne B. .... Boston, MA
Matthews, T. Randall .... Dallas, TX
Matthews, Terri C. .... New York, NY
Matthews, Thomas A. .... Anchorage, AK
Matthews, Thomas A. .... Brighton, MI
Matthews, Thomas F. .... Solana Beach, CA
Matthews, Thomas M. .... Orlando, FL
Matthews, Thomas M., Jr. .... Wiggins, MS
Matthews, Thomas P. .... San Diego, CA
Matthews, Thomas W. .... Roseland, NJ
Matthews, Timothy B. .... Cincinnati, OH
Matthews, Timothy P. .... Washington, DC
Matthews, Tisher & Free .... Columbia, TN
Matthews, Tom D., Jr. .... Dallas, TX
Matthews, Tom H. .... Rocky Mount, NC
Matthews, Tomi Rachel .... Huntsville, TX
Matthews, V. Joyce .... Baton Rouge, LA
Matthews, Victor B. .... Denville, NJ
Matthews, W. Douglas .... Houston, TX
Matthews, Walter J. .... Rome, GA
Matthews, Wanda Wardlaw .... Jamaica, NY
Matthews & Ward .... Madisonville, TN
Matthews, Warren C. .... Birmingham, AL
Matthews, Warren W. .... Anchorage, AK
Matthews, William .... Philadelphia, PA
Matthews, William A. .... Washington, DC
Matthews, William B., Jr. .... Ozark, AL
Matthews, William B., Jr. .... Houston, TX
Matthews, William B., Sr. .... Ozark, AL
Matthews, William C., II .... Reading, PA
Matthews, William C., Jr. .... Raleigh, NC
Matthews, William D. .... Atlanta, GA
Matthews, William D. .... Oneida, NY
Matthews, William E. .... Houston, TX
Matthews, William L. .... Wapello, IA
Matthews, William M. .... Atlanta, GA
Matthews, William N. .... Huntington, WV
Matthews, William P. .... Wichita, KS
Matthews, William P. .... Newton, MA
Matthews, William R. .... Boston, MA
Matthews, William T. .... Port Washington, NY
Matthews, William W., III
Philadelphia, PA
Matthews, Wilson M. .... Alexandria, VA
Matthews and Wines, P.C. .... Elko, NV
Matthews & Zahare, P.C. .... Anchorage, AK
Matthews-Pennanen, Michael .... Berkley, MI
Matthey, Denise .... Rancho Cucamonga, CA
Matthias, Alison M. .... Nashville, TN
Matthias & Berg LLP .... Los Angeles, CA
Matthias, Brent E. .... Chicago, IL
Matthias, Campbell, Tyler, Nuzum, Greta & Rickers .... Monroe, IA
Newton, IA
Sully, IA
Matthias, Elizabeth M. .... Rosemead, CA
Matthias, Frederic .... Newton, IA
Matthias, Mary K. .... Madison, WI
Matthias & Matthias .... Orlando, FL
Matthias, Michael R. .... Los Angeles, CA
Matthias, Robert C. .... Orlando, FL
Matthias, Ronald S. .... San Francisco, CA
Matthias, Russell H., Jr. .... Park Ridge, IL
Matthies & deBoisblanc, P.A. .... Ocala, FL
Matthies, Eric F. .... Ocala, FL
Matthies Law Firm, A Professional Corporation .... Tulsa, OK
Matthies, Mary Constance T., (Ms.)
Tulsa, OK
Matthies, Roland C. .... Springfield, OH
Matthiesen, Bradley W. .... Hartford, WI
Matthiesen, Chase & Erwin, L.L.P.
Houston, TX
Matthiesen, David G. .... Houston, TX
Matthiesen, JoAnn .... Houston, TX
Matthiessen, C. J. .... Monticello, IA
Matthis, John R. B. .... Raleigh, NC

Matthys, Larry A. ... Corpus Christi, TX
Matthys, Shelly ... Portland, OR
Matti, Michelle E. ... Glendale, CA
Mattia, M. Steven ... Flagstaff, AZ
Mattia, Mark ... Bedminster, NJ
Mattia, Philip F., & Associates ... Wayne, NJ
Mattia, Robert A. ... Newton, NJ
Mattiaccio, Richard L. ... New York, NY
Mattiace, Joanne E., Law Offices of ... McLean, VA
Mattice, Alice ... Department of Justice, Environment and Natural Resources Division, GV
Mattice, Dale K. ... Honolulu, HI
Mattice, Harry S. (Sandy), Jr. ... Chattanooga, TN
Mattice, Michael C. ... Fairfield, CA
Mattick, Janet E. ... New York, NY
Matticks, Kenneth R. ... Dallas, TX
Mattie, Christian T., III ... Bradford, PA
Mattie, Tonda L., (P.A.) ... Minneapolis, MN
Mattiello, Donna M. ... Hartford, CT
Mattier, Russell J., (Inc.) ... West Covina, CA
Matties, Donna M. ... Sacramento, CA
Matties, Herbert M. ... Binghamton, NY
Matties, Richard N. ... Binghamton, NY
Mattil, Arthur G. ... Hackensack, NJ
Mattimoe, James M. ... Columbus, OH
Mattimoe, John G. ... Toledo, OH
Mattimoe, John I. ... Toledo, OH
Mattimoe, Margaret A. ... Toledo, OH
Mattimoe, Patrick C. ... Pinedale, WY
Mattimoe, Thomas E. ... Atlanta, GA
Mattimoe, Thomas E., LLC ... Atlanta, GA
Mattimore, Mary Elizabeth ... Buffalo, NY
Mattimore, Michael ... Tallahassee, FL
Mattimore, Timothy J. ... East Islip, NY
Mattimore, Timothy J., Jr. ... New York, NY
Mattina, Jacqueline C. ... Buffalo, NY
Mattina, Joseph S. ... Buffalo, NY
Mattina, Philip J. ... Staten Island, NY
Mattina, Sam J. ... Houston, TX
Mattingley, Gregory A. ... Decatur, IL
Mattingley, Michael B. ... Santa Ana, CA
Mattingly, Alfred Shane ... Leonardtown, MD
Mattingly, Alix L. ... Santa Clara, CA
Springfield, VA
Mattingly, Amy J. ... Columbus, OH
Mattingly & Bowling ... Blanchester, OH
Sabina, OH
Wilmington, OH
Mattingly, Bryan K. ... Lexington, KY
Mattingly, Charles C., III ... Hardinsburg, KY
Mattingly, Christopher S. ... Buffalo, NY
Mattingly, David B. ... Lexington, KY
Mattingly, David J., Law Office of ... San Francisco, CA
Mattingly, David J., Law Office of ... Sausalito, CA
Mattingly, David M. ... Indianapolis, IN
Mattingly, Dennis L. ... Louisville, KY
Mattingly, Dennis W. ... Sabina, OH
Wilmington, OH
Mattingly, Edward A. ... Houston, TX
Mattingly, Edward L. ... Louisville, KY
Mattingly, Elizabeth B. ... Cincinnati, OH
Mattingly, Ellen ... Brockton, MA
Mattingly, George A. ... Atlanta, GA
Mattingly, Harry A. ... Coral Gables, FL
Mattingly, Jack A. ... Seminole, OK
Mattingly, Jack A., Jr. ... Seminole, OK
Mattingly, Jack F. ... Lexington, KY
Mattingly, Jack L. ... Van Nuys, CA
Mattingly, James L. ... Springfield, KY
Mattingly, James M. ... St. Louis, MO
Mattingly, James V., Jr. ... Board of Governors Of The Federal Reserve System, Office of the General Counsel, GV
Mattingly, Jennifer J. ... Austin, TX
Mattingly, John Michael ... Portland, OR
Mattingly, John R. ... Alexandria, VA
Mattingly, Jonathan D. ... Indianapolis, IN
Mattingly, Jos. A. ... Leonardtown, MD
Mattingly, Joseph A. ... Bethesda, MD
Mattingly, Joseph H., III ... Lebanon, KY
Mattingly, Joseph H., III, P.S.C., Law Offices of ... Lebanon, KY
Mattingly, Joseph M. ... Arlington, VA
Mattingly, Kelly J. ... Janesville, WI
Mattingly, Lesly W. ... Shreveport, LA
Mattingly & Marsh, L.L.P. ... Houston, TX
Mattingly, Melissa S. ... Indianapolis, IN
Mattingly, Michael A. ... Morris, IL
Mattingly, Patrick W. ... Louisville, KY
Mattingly, Paul P. ... Atlanta, GA
Mattingly, Paul R. ... Cincinnati, OH
Mattingly, Phyllis Lee Sharp ... Versailles, KY
Mattingly, Robert D., Jr. ... Benton, KY
Mattingly, Rudolph, Fine & Porter, LLP ... Evansville, IN
Mattingly, Sharon A. ... Louisville, KY
Mattingly, Simms & Cocanougher ... Springfield, KY
Mattingly & Snow, P.C. ... Seminole, OK
Mattingly, Todd D. ... Dallas, TX
Houston, TX
Mattingly & Weiskopf, CHTD. ... California, MD
Mattingly, William E., (P.C.) ... Chicago, IL
Mattingly, William H. ... Pawhuska, OK
Mattingly, William S. ... Morgantown, WV
Mattio, John J. ... Niagara Falls, NY
Mattioli, Carlos A. ... Houston, TX
Mattioli, Clarence J. ... Hammonton, NJ
Mattioli, Clarence, Jr. ... Hammonton, NJ
Mattioli, Edward A. ... Akron, NY
Mattioli, Eli R. ... New York, NY
Mattioli, Gloria ... Redwood City, CA
Mattioli, Mark L. ... Philadelphia, PA
Mattioni, Alan ... Westmont, NJ
Philadelphia, PA
Mattioni, Blasco ... Westmont, NJ
Philadelphia, PA
Mattioni, Dante ... Westmont, NJ
Philadelphia, PA
Mattioni, Elizabeth S. ... Philadelphia, PA
Mattioni, Eugene ... Westmont, NJ
Philadelphia, PA
Mattioni, Faustino ... Westmont, NJ
Philadelphia, PA
Mattioni, John ... Westmont, NJ
Philadelphia, PA
Mattioni, LLP ... Westmont, NJ
Conshohocken, PA
Philadelphia, PA
Mattioni, Michael ... Westmont, NJ
Philadelphia, PA
Mattis, Brian E. ... Carbondale, IL
Mattis, Caran Cress ... Shamokin, PA
Mattis, H. Robert, Jr. ... Shamokin, PA
Mattis, James M. ... Portland, OR
Mattis, Lawrence ... New York, NY
Mattis, Marileni ... San Francisco, CA
Mattis, Marileni (Mia) ... San Francisco, CA
Mattis & Mattis ... Shamokin, PA
Mattis, Theodore P. ... Columbus, OH
Mattise & Kelly ... Scranton, PA
Mattise, Nicholas S. ... Scranton, PA
Mattisinko, Susan ... New York, NY
Mattison, Beatrice M. ... Washington, DC
Mattison, Charles E. ... New York, NY
Mattison, Chris A. ... Denver, CO
Mattison, Christine D. ... San Jose, CA
Mattison, Deborah A. ... Birmingham, AL
Mattison, Eric J. ... Owatonna, MN
Mattison, Eugene D. ... Crofton, MD
Mattison, Glenn D. ... Rochester, NY
Mattison, Jack L. ... Eugene, OR
Mattison, James R. ... Milwaukee, WI
Mattison, James R., Jr. ... Dallas, TX
Mattison, Kenneth A. ... Winder, GA
Mattison, Kenneth M. ... Anderson, SC
Mattison, Priscilla J. ... Philadelphia, PA
Mattison, Raymond E. ... San Luis Obispo, CA
Mattison, Robert M. ... Minneapolis, MN
Mattison, Tamara Gail ... Dallas, TX
Mattison, Timothy K. ... Elmira, NY
Mattison, Victoria ... Washington, DC
Mattisson, Peter L. ... Westminster, CO
Mattivi, Anthony W. ... Topeka, KS
Mattix, C. Michael ... Overland Park, KS
Mattix, Carla C. ... Department Of The Interior, Office of the Solicitor, GV
Mattix, Thomas L. ... Indianapolis, IN
Mattix, William J. ... Billings, MT
Mattka, David C. ... Dallas, TX
Mattka & Ohm ... Ettrick, WI
Galesville, WI
Whitehall, WI
Mattka, William A. ... Whitehall, WI
Mattke, Paul E. ... Circle Pines, MN
Mattlage, Karl P. ... Austin, TX
Mattleman, Gwen Hollis ... Treasury Department, United States Mint, GV
Mattleman, Weinroth & Miller ... Wilmington, DE
Cherry Hill, NJ
Clifton, NJ
Mattler, Michael J. ... Department of State, Office of the Legal Adviser, GV
Mattlin, Fred W. ... Boca Raton, FL
Mattlin & McClosky ... Boca Raton, FL
Mattly, Will B. ... Reno, NV
Mattmiller, Mark Scott ... Lexington, KY
Mattner, Richard A. ... New York, NY
Matto, Edward A. ... Columbus, OH
Mattoch, Ian L., Law Offices of ... Hilo, HI
Honolulu, HI
Kailua-Kona, HI
Kaneohe, HI
Wailuku, HI
Waimea, HI
Mattoch, Ian L., Law Offices of ... Honolulu, HI
Lihue, HI
Mattock, Bruce E. ... Greensburg, PA
Mattocks, Clarence V. ... High Point, NC
Mattocks, James ... High Point, NC
Mattocks & Mattocks ... High Point, NC
Mattocks, N. Randolph, Jr. ... Winston-Salem, NC
Matton, Melissa Ross ... Research Triangle Park, NC
Matton, W. Christopher ... Raleigh, NC
Mattone, Irene M. ... College Point, NY
Mattone, Joseph M. ... College Point, NY
Mattone, Joseph M., Jr. ... College Point, NY
Mattone, Michael X. ... College Point, NY
Mattone, Teresa A. ... College Point, NY
Mattoni, Marc A. ... Troy, MI
Mattoon, Frederick N. ... Pueblo, CO
Mattoon, Jill ... Pueblo, CO
Mattoon Law Offices ... Norman, OK
Mattoon, Peter M. ... Philadelphia, PA
Mattoon, Richard O., II ... Gillette, NJ
Mattoon, Steven F. ... Sidney, NE
Mattoon, William F. ... Pueblo, CO
Mattoon, William H. ... Norman, OK
Mattos, Abel J. ... Administrative Office Of The United States Courts, GV
Mattos, Joe A. ... San Jose, CA
Mattos, Weldon J., Jr. ... Merced, CA
Mattos Neto, Sebastiao de Souza ... Chicago, IL
Mattox, Barbara Groves ... Washington, DC
Mattox, Christopher R. ... Media, PA
Mattox, Conard B., III ... Richmond, VA
Mattox, Conard B., Jr. ... Richmond, VA
Mattox, Davis & Barnhill, P.A. ... Greenville, NC
Mattox, Dawn Snow ... Fort Wayne, IN
Mattox, Fred T. ... Greenville, NC
Mattox, George F. ... Office of Personnel Management, Personnel in Non-Legal Positions, GV
Mattox, Isabel Worthy ... Raleigh, NC
Mattox, J. Pressly ... Statesville, NC
Mattox, Janice L. ... Dallas, TX
Mattox, John H. ... Sacramento, CA
Mattox, Judith Ward ... Colorado Springs, CO
Mattox, Kendrick W., Jr. ... La Grange, GA
Mattox, Linda A. ... New Albany, IN
Mattox, Mallory and Associates, L.L.P. ... Statesville, NC
Mattox, Matthew H. ... Oregon City, OR
Mattox & Mattox ... Clarksville, IN
Corydon, IN
Jeffersonville, IN
Madison, IN
New Albany, IN
Salem, IN
Scottsburg, IN
Louisville, KY
Mattox, Michael W. ... Atlanta, GA
Mattox, Phillip R. ... Brooklyn, NY
Mattox, Ray ... Winter Haven, FL
Mattox, Richard D. ... Portsmouth, VA
Mattox, Richard L. ... New Albany, IN
Mattox, Rick E. ... Apple Valley, MN
Mattox, S. Frank ... New Albany, IN
Mattox, Sharon M. ... Houston, TX
Mattox, V. Leigh ... Birmingham, AL
Mattras, John J., Jr. ... New York, NY
Mattrella, Linda Anne ... New York, NY
Mattrey, William H. ... Buffalo, NY
Matts, Joseph Jay ... University Heights, OH
Matts, Noreen R. ... Tucson, AZ
Mattsen, Richard A. ... Seattle, WA
Mattson, Allen C. ... Hartford City, IN
Mattson & Associates, P.A. ... Clearwater, FL
New Port Richey, FL
St. Petersburg, FL
Mattson, Brian M. ... Chicago, IL
Mattson, Carter Alan ... Calera, OK
Mattson, Catherine E. ... Rapid City, SD
Mattson, Charles E. ... Vista, CA
Mattson, Charles W. ... St. Paul, MN
Mattson, Cheryl L. ... Corte Madera, CA
Mattson, Christopher W. ... Chambersburg, PA
Lancaster, PA
York, PA
Mattson, Claire Ann ... Atlanta, GA
Mattson, Cynthia J. ... Treasury Department, Internal Revenue Service, GV
Mattson, Demal I., Jr. ... Mount Pleasant, SC
Mattson, Douglas L. ... Minot, ND
Mattson, Elvin J. ... Citrus Heights, CA
Mattson, Eric S. ... Chicago, IL
Mattson, Fred W., Jr. ... Englewood, CO
Mattson, Gary G. ... West Des Moines, IA
Mattson, George T. ... Seattle, WA
Mattson, Gerald A., Jr. ... Auburn, AL
Mattson, Howard H. ... Pleasantville, NY
Mattson, James S. ... Key Largo, FL
Naples, FL
Mattson, Jeffrey S. ... Salem, OR
Mattson, Jon W. ... Deadwood, SD
Mattson, Joseph T. ... Havertown, PA
Mattson, Joshua ... Burnsville, MN
Mattson, Katherine M. ... Minneapolis, MN
Mattson, Kenneth M. ... Southfield, MI
Mattson, Kent D. ... Fergus Falls, MN
Mattson, Kurt R. ... Eagan, MN
Mattson, Le Roy H. ... Newark, NJ
Mattson, Lee A. ... San Diego, CA
Mattson, Lee W. ... Gilford, NH
Mattson, Luke A. ... New Port Richey, FL
Mattson, Lynn Paul ... Tulsa, OK
Mattson & Madden ... Newark, NJ
Mattson, Mark D. ... Minneapolis, MN
Mattson, Michael C. ... Fort Lauderdale, FL
Mattson, Nancy J. ... Duluth, MN
Mattson, Richard W. ... Nashville, TN
Mattson, Rick A. ... St. Petersburg, FL
Mattson, Ricketts, Davies, Stewart & Calkins
Adams, NE
Hickman, NE
Lincoln, NE
Waverly, NE
Mattson, Robert M., Jr. ... Irvine, CA
Mattson, Robert N. ... Armonk, NY
Mattson, Roger C. ... Woodbury, NJ
Mattson, Ronald C. ... Renton, WA
Mattson, Stephen J. ... Chicago, IL
Mattson, Susan Cummings ... Whitehouse Station, NJ
Mattson, Thomas G. ... Chicago, IL
Mattson, Thomas R. ... Boulder, CO
Mattson, Timothy J. ... Minneapolis, MN
Mattson & Tobin ... Key Largo, FL
Naples, FL
Mattson, Walter R. ... Lakeland, FL
Mattson-Cotter, Faye Lynette ... Kent, WA
Mattson Markell, Patricia ... Fresno, CA
Mattuch, Kathryn Offer ... Atlanta, GA
Matturri, Alexander J., Jr. ... New York, NY
Matturro, Anthony, (P.C.) ... Carle Place, NY
Matturro, Dominick E. ... Tallahassee, FL
Matty, David J. ... Cleveland, OH
Matty, Jack E. ... Philadelphia, PA
Matty, Peter A. ... Silverdale, WA
Matty, Robert J. ... Landover, MD
Matty, Rosaria C. ... Woodbury, NY
Matty & Templeton ... Silverdale, WA
Matug, Alexander P. ... Palos Heights, IL
Matug, Alexander P., P.C. ... Palos Heights, IL
Matuga, Edward A. ... Westchester, IL
Matuga, Edward A., Ltd. ... Westchester, IL
Matuga, Jos. B. ... Highland, IN
Matuga, Richard J. ... Lansing, IL
Matuga, Richard J., Ltd. ... Lansing, IL
Matuk, Alejandro ... San Diego, CA
Matukaitis, Paul D. ... Rahway, NJ
Matukewicz, Michael J. ... Breckenridge, CO
Matula, Brian Richard ... Oklahoma City, OK
Matula, Carol E. ... Newark, NJ
Matula, Daniel J. ... Kansas City, MO
Matula, Mark C. ... Fort Worth, TX
Matula, Michael L. ... Kansas City, MO
Matula, Susan M. ... Brooklyn, NY
Matula, Theodore D. ... Denver, CO
Matule, Matthew J. ... Boston, MA
Matule, Robert C. ... Hoboken, NJ
Matulewicz, Anthony ... McAllen, TX
Matulewicz, Dennis M. ... Detroit, MI
Matulich, Barry K., Law Office of ... Sacramento, CA
Matulich, Keith M. ... Baton Rouge, LA
Matulionis, Margis J. ... Glendale, CA
Matulis & Associates ... San Francisco, CA
Matulis, James M. ... Tampa, FL
Matulis, John C., Jr. ... New Britain, CT
Matulis, Steven M. ... San Francisco, CA
Matulka, Meghan A. ... Fairfax, VA
Matuna, Curtis K. ... Denver, CO
Matune, Frank J. ... Youngstown, OH
Matune, Timothy J. ... Youngstown, OH
Maturen, Howard A., Jr. ... Saginaw, MI
Maturi, Jon A. ... Grand Rapids, MN
Maturin, Brenda Brown ... Lafayette, LA
Matus, Christine L. ... Atlantic City, NJ
Northfield, NJ
Matus, Mark W. ... Lansing, MI
Matus, Seth D. ... Santa Fe, NM
Matus, T. Patrick, II ... Charlotte, NC
Matus, Wayne C. ... New York, NY
Matusak, John J. ... Chicago, IL
Matus-Argüello, Roberto ... Miami, FL
Matuschak, Mark G. ... Boston, MA
Matuschka, Thomas H. ... Baton Rouge, LA
Matusek, Ivan ... St. Petersburg, FL
Matusek, McKnight, Poluse & Cangro, P.A. ... St. Petersburg, FL
Matushek, Edward J., III, Law Offices of ... Chicago, IL
Matusiak, James J. ... Manhasset, NY
Matusiak, Patricia S. McKay ... Milwaukee, WI
Matusick, Mitchell ... Buffalo, NY
Matusick, Spadafora & Verrastro ... Buffalo, NY
Matusinka, Jean E. ... Torrance, CA
Matuska, Michael C. ... Columbus, OH
Matuska, Michael L. ... Minden, NV
Matusky, Patrick ... Camden, NJ
Matusoff, Robert B. ... Dayton, OH
Matusow, Donald E. ... Philadelphia, PA
Matusow, Naomi C. ... Mount Kisco, NY
Matusz, Arnold J. ... Southfield, MI
Matusz, Stanley J. ... Rochester, NY
Matuszak, Lynne Marie ... Dearborn, MI
Matuszak, Olivia S. ... Fort Lauderdale, FL
Matuszak, Russell J. ... Buffalo, NY
Matuszeski, John ... Westport, CT
Matuszewich, Lewis F. ... Chicago, IL
Matuszewski, David M. ... Washington, DC
Matuszewski, Mary Ann ... Wilmington, DE
Matuzak, Joyce A. ... Chicago, IL
Matuzak, Michael J. ... West Branch, MI
Matuzek, Marina R. ... Worcester, MA
Matwiczyk, Peter ... West Palm Beach, FL
Matyas, David A. ... Washington, DC
Matyas, David J. ... De Pere, WI
Matyas, Harlene G. ... Chicago, IL
Matyas, Thomas I. ... Chicago, IL
Matychowiak, Thomas C. ... Fresno, CA
Matye, Joseph G. ... Kansas City, MO
Matyi, James E. ... Redondo Beach, CA
Matyi, Phyllis A. ... Larkspur, CA
Matyjasik, Robert E. ... Cleveland, OH
Matyjaszek, Robert ... Jackson, MI
Matykiewicz, Richard L. ... St. Paul, MN
Matyola, Daniel J. ... Bridgewater, NJ
Matyskiela, Joseph A. ... Martinsburg, WV
Wheeling, WV
Matz, A. Howard ... Los Angeles, CA
Matz, Andrew L. ... Brookline, MA
Matz, Bethany E. ... Washington, DC
Matz, Edward I. ... DeLand, FL
Matz, Edward W. ... Newport News, VA
Matz, Gary R. ... Stamford, CT
Matz, Harry J. ... Department of Justice, Criminal Division, GV
Matz, Herbert ... Baltimore, MD
Matz, Jacob, (P.A.) ... Baltimore, MD
Matz, Jay B. ... Danbury, CT
Matz, Jeffrey A., Law Offices of
Scottsdale, AZ
Los Angeles, CA
Matz, Jennifer E. ... San Francisco, CA
Matz, Joseph L. ... Chicago, IL
Matz, Kevin D. ... Lyons, IL

Mauthe, Daniel .... Stockton, CA
Mauti, Antonio .... Detroit, MI
Mautino, John Lawrence .... Jackson, MO
Mautino, Kathrin S. .... San Diego, CA
Mautino, Philip K. .... Bellflower, CA
Mautino, Robert A. .... San Diego, CA
Mautner, Gail E. .... Seattle, WA
Mautner, Kathie P. .... Carmel, IN
Mautner, Michael E. .... Napa, CA
Mautner, Paul F. .... Portland, OR
Mautner, Paul J. .... Boca Raton, FL
Mautner, Robert S. .... Phoenix, AZ
Mautner, Scott A. .... New York, NY
Mautone, Anthony R. .... West Orange, NJ
Mautone, Dennis M. .... Belleville, NJ
Mautz Baum & O'Hanlon, LLP
La Grande, OR
Pendleton, OR
Mautz, Kathryn Ann .... Spokane, WA
Mautz, Robert T. .... Pendleton, OR
Mauzaka, Judith A. .... Bridgeport, CT
Mauzé, George W., II .... San Antonio, TX
Mauzé, George W., II., P.C., Law Offices of
San Antonio, TX
Mauzé, James F. .... St. Louis, MO
Mauzy, Aglaia D. .... Dallas, TX
Grand Prairie, TX
Mauzy, Catherine A. .... Austin, TX
Mauzy, Charles P. .... Louisville, KY
Mauzy, K. Renée .... Austin, TX
Mauzy Law Firm .... Minneapolis, MN
Mauzy, Oscar H. .... Houston, TX
Mauzy, William J. .... Minneapolis, MN
Mavar, Gerald M. .... Highlands, NC
Mavar, Nick A., Jr. .... Highlands, NC
Maveety, Fredrica S. .... San Diego, CA
Maveety, L. J. .... Los Alamos, NM
Maver, Thomas B., Jr. .... Peoria, IL
Maverick, Albert, III .... Houston, TX
Maverick, Angela R. .... Dallas, TX
Maverick, Chilton, (Inc.) .... San Antonio, TX
Maverick, Maury, Jr. .... San Antonio, TX
Maviglia, Beatrice .... New York, NY
Maville, John H. .... Belvidere, IL
Maville & Loos .... Belvidere, IL
Mavis, Darrell .... Los Angeles, CA
Mavis, John L. .... Dearborn, MI
Mavity & Associates .... Minneapolis, MN
Red Wing, MN
Mavity, Chad L. .... Houston, TX
Mavity, Gary N. .... Walnut Creek, CA
Mavity, Howard A. .... Atlanta, GA
Mavity, William J. .... Minneapolis, MN
Red Wing, MN
Mavligit, Shirat .... Houston, TX
Mavrakakis, Thomas C. .... Palo Alto, CA
Mavredakis, Joyce L. .... Pasadena, CA
Mavrelis, William N. .... Long Island City, NY
Mavretic, Laura K. .... Raleigh, NC
Mavrias, James G. .... Chicago, IL
Mavrick, Peter T. .... Fort Lauderdale, FL
Mavrick, Peter T., P.A.
Fort Lauderdale, FL
Mavrick, Theodore P. .... St. Petersburg, FL
Mavricos, John A. .... Worcester, MA
Mavricos, Patrice Jordan .... Worcester, MA
Mavrides, Michael Fotios .... New York, NY
Mavridis, James .... Encino, CA
Mavridis, James C. .... Los Angeles, CA
Mavrin, Robert J. .... Joliet, IL
Mavrinac, Anthony J. .... Detroit, MI
Mavrinac, Susan E. .... Middleton, MA
Mavris, George M. .... Crescent City, CA
Mavronicolas, Anthony J. .... New York, NY
Mavros, Eli G. .... Lynn, MA
Mavros & Fitzgerald .... Boston, MA
Lynn, MA
Mavroudis, John M. .... Oradell, NJ
Mavroudis & Rizzo .... Oradell, NJ
Mavroyannis, Irene .... New York, NY
Maw, Barbara L. .... Salt Lake City, UT
Maw, Barbara L., P.C., Law Offices of
Salt Lake City, UT
Mawdsley, Richard A., Jr.
Oklahoma City, OK
Mawdsley, Russell J. .... Holyoke, MA
Mawe, Kevin F. .... Boston, MA
Mawer, Muriel .... Seattle, WA
Mawer, William T., II .... Camden, OH
Eaton, OH
Mawhinney, Daniel R. .... Portland, ME
Mawhinney, Donald M., Jr. .... Syracuse, NY
Mawhinney, Fara Schneider .... Denver, CO
Mawhinney, Joseph P. .... Lakeland, FL
Mawhinney, Kent D. .... Bloomfield, CT
Mawhinney, Robert J. .... San Diego, CA
MaWhinney, Ronald L. .... Los Angeles, CA
Mawhinney, Suzanne K. .... San Rafael, CA
Mawhorr, Douglas K. .... Muncie, IN
Mawicke, Jeffrey J. .... Milwaukee, WI
Mawla, Hany A. .... Roseland, NJ
Mawla, L. Ted .... Los Gatos, CA
Mawla, Tina Mitzi .... San Jose, CA
Mawn, David G. .... Barbourville, KY
Mawn-Mahlau, Sam A. .... Boston, MA
Mawson, Margaret M. Softcheck
Bellingham, WA
Mawson & Mawson .... Bellingham, WA
Mawson, Morris M. .... Santa Rosa, CA
Mawson, Richard S. .... Bellingham, WA
Mawyer, Karen S. .... Charlottesville, VA
Max, Aaron M. .... Owings Mills, MD
Max, Aaron M., P.A. .... Owings Mills, MD
Max, Alan S. .... Phoenix, AZ
Max, Arthur L. .... Mountain Lakes, NJ
Max, Daniel .... McLean, VA
Max, Eric R. .... Trenton, NJ
Max, Henry L. .... Huntington, WV

Max, Herbert B. .... New York, NY
Max, Kenneth A. .... Bethesda, MD
Max, Rodney A. .... Birmingham, AL
Max, Theodore C. .... New York, NY
Maxa, Bradley A. .... Tacoma, WA
Maxa, John G. .... New Bremen, OH
Maxant, William H. .... Sun City, AZ
Maxcey, Timothy D. .... McAlester, OK
Maxeiner, C. William .... Pebble Beach, CA
Maxeiner, James R. .... Murray Hill, NJ
Maxeiner, Mary Katherine .... Santa Rosa, CA
Maxey, Bevan J. .... Spokane, WA
Maxey, David S. .... Birmingham, AL
Maxey, David W. .... Philadelphia, PA
Maxey, Gary Lee .... Enid, OK
Maxey, Herbert E., Jr. .... Buckingham, VA
Maxey, Herbert E., Jr., P.C., A Prof. Law Corp. .... Buckingham, VA
Maxey, Jo Ann C. .... Little Rock, AR
Maxey, Joe W. .... Edmond, OK
Maxey, John D. .... Roseville, CA
Maxey, John P. .... Huron, OH
Maxey Law Offices, P.S. .... Spokane, WA
Maxey, Michael M. .... Quincy, MA
Maxey, Neil R. .... Mount Sterling, KY
Maxey, Phillip A. .... Ashland City, TN
Maxey, Rebecca A. .... Coral Gables, FL
Maxey, Tom .... Coral Gables, FL
Maxey, Wann, Begley & Fyke, PLLC
Jackson, MS
Maxey, Wayne E. .... Pekin, IL
Maxey, William C. .... Spokane, WA
Maxey, Wirt T. .... Coral Gables, FL
Maxfield, Charles J. .... Fairfax, VA
Maxfield, David Andrew .... Columbia, SC
Maxfield, Donald E. .... Waxahachie, TX
Maxfield, Elizabeth F. .... Washington, DC
Maxfield, Eric G. .... Phoenix, AZ
Maxfield, Gary W. .... Dallas, TX
Maxfield, Grace R. .... Highland, MI
Maxfield, Guy B. .... New York, NY
Maxfield, Harold O., Jr. .... Cleveland, OH
Maxfield, James W. .... El Paso, TX
Maxfield, Jane Uhlman .... Columbus, OH
Maxfield, John R. .... Denver, CO
Maxfield, Kenneth W. .... Fort Wayne, IN
Maxfield, Marietta M. .... Houston, TX
Maxfield, Michael L. .... Columbus, OH
Maxfield, Peter C. .... Laramie, WY
Maxfield, Richard L. .... Orem, UT
Maxfield, Robert F. .... Garland, TX
Maxfield, Sean H. .... Columbus, OH
Maxfield, Sheryl L. .... Columbus, OH
Maxfield, Thomas H. .... Denver, CO
Maxfield, Wendy J. .... Davison, MI
Maxham, Lawrence A. .... San Diego, CA
Maxie Rheinheimer Stephens & Vrevich, LLP .... Los Angeles, CA
Newport Beach, CA
Sacramento, CA
San Diego, CA
Maxie, Robert C. .... San Diego, CA
Maxim, Cheryl E. .... Livingston Manor, NY
Maxim, John A., Jr. .... Washington, DC
Maxim, Kevin A. .... Atlanta, GA
Maximiuk, Gary A. .... Grand Rapids, MI
Maximoff, J. Timothy .... San Jose, CA
Maximov, Bruce .... San Francisco, CA
Maxin, John Lawrence .... Richardson, TX
Maxin, Joseph J. .... Youngstown, OH
Maxin, Joseph W. .... Youngstown, OH
Maxin and Maxin .... Youngstown, OH
Maxino, Marcelino .... San Jose, CA
Maxion, Richard W. .... Redding, CA
Maxman, Joel .... New York, NY
Maxman, Melissa H. .... Philadelphia, PA
Maxon, Ilene R. .... Rye Brook, NY
Maxon, Jodi M. .... Stamford, CT
Maxon, Robin G. .... Topeka, KS
Maxse, Paul J.
General Services Administration, Office of Regional Counsel, GV
Maxson, Bruce .... Cooperstown, NY
Maxson, Catherine E. .... Seattle, WA
Maxson, F. Gordon .... Washington, DC
Maxson, Finley Peter .... Chicago, IL
Maxson, James W. .... Atlanta, GA
Maxson, Lane T. .... Melville, NY
Maxson, M. Finley .... Chicago, IL
Maxson, R. James .... Minot, ND
Maxson, Robert H. .... Fairlawn, OH
Maxson, Susan C. .... Washington, DC
Maxson, Thomas D. .... Pittsburgh, PA
Maxton, Bonnie L. .... Columbus, OH
Maxton, Reginald .... Cleveland, OH
Maxtutis, Lisa A. .... Tucson, AZ
Maxwell, Alan M. .... Atlanta, GA
Maxwell, Amanda .... Miami, FL
Maxwell & Anderson .... Aiken, SC
North Augusta, SC
Maxwell, Andrew J. .... Chicago, IL
Maxwell, Anna Maria .... Greenville, SC
Maxwell, Anne S. .... Philadelphia, PA
Maxwell, Anne S., P.C. .... Norristown, PA
Philadelphia, PA
Maxwell, Anthony C. .... Cookeville, TN
Maxwell, Augusto .... Miami, FL
Maxwell Baker & McFatridge, P.C.
Galveston, TX
Houston, TX
League City, TX
Maxwell, Barbara L. .... Pasadena, CA
Maxwell, Barbara T. .... Mansfield, MA
Maxwell, Barry Douglas
West Palm Beach, FL
Maxwell, Barry K. .... Knoxville, TN
Maxwell, Beth Lynn .... Austin, TX
Maxwell, Brenda J. .... Detroit, MI

Maxwell, Brian A. .... Phoenix, AZ
Maxwell, Bruce A. .... Atlanta, GA
Maxwell, C. Douglas, Jr. .... Fayetteville, NC
Maxwell, Charles E. .... Mesa, AZ
Maxwell, Charles E., P.C., Law Offices of
Mesa, AZ
Maxwell, Charles F., III .... Omaha, NE
Maxwell, Chas. P. .... North Boston, NY
Maxwell, Cherie L. .... Newark, NJ
Maxwell, Christopher Eric .... Dallas, TX
Maxwell, Clyde R. .... Irvine, CA
Maxwell, Cory H. .... West Valley City, UT
Maxwell, Craig T. .... Green Bay, WI
Maxwell, Cynthia E. .... Oakland, CA
Maxwell, Darold .... Galveston, TX
League City, TX
Maxwell, David J. .... Minnetonka, MN
Maxwell, David M. .... Atlanta, GA
Maxwell, David S. .... Canoga Park, CA
Maxwell, Dawn M. .... Chicago, IL
Maxwell, Donald .... Scottsdale, AZ
Maxwell, Donald E. .... Kansas City, MO
Maxwell, Douglas R. .... Jacksonville, FL
Maxwell, E. David .... Orlando, FL
Maxwell, E. Gilmore .... McDonough, GA
Maxwell, E. Thomas, Jr. .... Glen Burnie, MD
Maxwell, Edmund F. .... Buffalo, NY
Maxwell, Edward B., 2nd
Wilmington, DE
Maxwell, Edward S. .... Stockton, CA
Maxwell, Emily .... San Diego, CA
Maxwell, Eric .... Boston, MA
Maxwell, Eric K. .... Fayetteville, GA
Maxwell, Eric K., P.C. Law Offices of
Fayetteville, GA
Maxwell, Eugenia B. .... Manhattan Beach, CA
Maxwell, Francis E. .... Nashville, IL
Maxwell, Freeman & Bowman, P.A.
Durham, NC
Maxwell, Gary R. .... Dothan, AL
Maxwell, George M., Jr. .... Atlanta, GA
Maxwell, George W., III .... Melbourne, FL
Maxwell, Georges A. .... Los Alamitos, CA
Maxwell, Gilbert C. .... Boulder, CO
Maxwell, Gregg S. .... Buffalo, NY
Maxwell, Gregory H. .... Jacksonville, FL
Maxwell, H. James .... Kansas City, MO
Maxwell, Hugh D., III
Department of Agriculture, Forest Service, GV
Maxwell, J. Barton .... Denver, CO
Maxwell, J. Robert .... San Francisco, CA
Maxwell, J. Robert .... Pittsburgh, PA
Maxwell, J. Scott .... Lansdale, PA
Maxwell, James B. .... Durham, NC
Maxwell, James D. .... Kenner, LA
Maxwell, James Jeffrey .... Wilmington, DE
Maxwell, James, Jr. .... Columbus, OH
Maxwell, James L. .... Tacoma, WA
Maxwell, James P. .... Syracuse, NY
Maxwell, James S. .... New York, NY
Maxwell, James S. .... Dallas, TX
Maxwell, Jan Haley .... Topeka, KS
Maxwell, Jane B. .... Washington, DC
Maxwell, Jason Edward .... Liberal, KS
Maxwell, Jason P. .... Dallas, TX
Maxwell, Jeanne Nielsen .... Jefferson, GA
Maxwell, Jerry R. .... Dyer, TN
Maxwell, Joanne M. .... Newark, NJ
Maxwell, Joel Edward .... Miami, FL
Maxwell, John A. .... Marble Falls, TX
Maxwell, John A., Jr. .... Yakima, WA
Maxwell, John B., Jr. .... Memphis, TN
Maxwell, John C. .... St. Charles, MO
Maxwell, John D. .... Hartford, CT
Maxwell, John D. .... Memphis, TN
Maxwell, John E. .... Auburn, CA
Maxwell, John E. .... Grandview, WA
Maxwell, John F. .... Buffalo, NY
Maxwell, John F. .... Delmar, NY
Maxwell, John M. .... Long Beach, CA
Maxwell, John P. .... New Philadelphia, OH
Maxwell, John T. .... San Jose, CA
Maxwell, Jonathan V. .... Greensboro, NC
Maxwell, Joseph E. .... Mexico, MO
Maxwell, Joyce L. .... Houston, TX
Maxwell, Judith R. .... Delaware, OH
Maxwell, Kathryn E. .... Phoenix, AZ
Maxwell, K.C. .... Albuquerque, NM
Maxwell, Kenneth L., Jr. .... Sweetwater, TX
Maxwell, Kenneth W. .... Phoenix, AZ
Maxwell, Kimberly L. .... Los Angeles, CA
Maxwell, Kristin White .... Sacramento, CA
Maxwell, Larry A. "Max" .... Sunnyvale, TX
Maxwell Law Firm, The .... Lafayette, LA
Maxwell Law Offices .... Greencastle, PA
Waynesboro, PA
Maxwell, Lawrence C. .... Nashville, TN
Maxwell, Lawrence D. .... San Diego, CA
Maxwell, Lawrence R., Jr. .... Dallas, TX
Maxwell, LeRoy S. .... Greencastle, PA
Waynesboro, PA
Maxwell, LeRoy S., Jr. .... Greencastle, PA
Waynesboro, PA
Maxwell, Lisa Nelson .... San Francisco, CA
Maxwell, Lon J. .... Coon Rapids, MN
Maxwell, Lylton E. .... Winston-Salem, NC
Maxwell, M. Clifton .... Fort Worth, TX
Maxwell, M. Craig .... Lafayette, LA
Maxwell, Madalyn .... Springfield, IL
Maxwell, Manuel .... New York, NY
Maxwell, Margaret L. .... Tucson, AZ
Maxwell, Margo J. .... Knoxville, TN
Maxwell, Mark H. .... Nashville, TN
Maxwell, Mark S. .... Indianapolis, IN
Maxwell, Martin J. .... Kansas City, MO
Maxwell, Melanie A. .... Seattle, WA
Maxwell, Melissa E. .... Houston, TX

Maxwell & Melvin .... Fayetteville, NC
Spring Lake, NC
Maxwell, Melvin Larry .... Lafayette, LA
Maxwell, Michael A. .... Fort Collins, CO
Maxwell, Michael A. .... Fayetteville, GA
Maxwell, Michael A. .... Seattle, WA
Maxwell, Michael D. .... Des Moines, IA
Maxwell, Michael E. .... Buffalo, NY
Maxwell, Michael P., Jr. .... Indianapolis, IN
Maxwell, Miriam Park .... San Francisco, CA
Maxwell, Nancy G. .... Topeka, KS
Maxwell, Neil H. .... Youngstown, OH
Maxwell, Odin .... Spokane, WA
Maxwell, Palmer P. .... Talladega, AL
Maxwell, Patricia A. .... North Boston, NY
Maxwell, Patrick J. .... Hamburg, NY
Maxwell, Pauline Scheinberg
Los Angeles, CA
Maxwell, Philip K. .... Austin, TX
Maxwell, Phillip B. .... Troy, MI
Maxwell & Power, P.C. .... Dallas, TX
Maxwell, R. Blinn .... Oxnard, CA
Maxwell, R. Bruce .... Washington, DC
Maxwell, R. Patrick .... Minneapolis, MN
Maxwell, R. C. .... Durham, NC
Maxwell, Rebecca .... Rolling Meadows, IL
Maxwell, Regnald, Jr. .... Augusta, GA
Maxwell, Richard C. .... Charlottesville, VA
Maxwell, Richard L. .... Chesterfield, MO
Maxwell, Richard T. .... Santa Fe, NM
Maxwell, Robert A. .... Bloomfield Hills, MI
Maxwell, Robert B., II .... Ventura, CA
Maxwell, Robert E. .... Elkins, WV
Maxwell, Robert F. .... Rosemont, PA
Maxwell, Robert G. .... Sanibel, FL
Maxwell, Robert H. .... Atmore, AL
Maxwell, Robert H., P.C. .... Atmore, AL
Maxwell, Robert MacFarland .... Lansdale, PA
Maxwell, Robert N. .... Fargo, ND
Maxwell, Robert R. .... Bingham Farms, MI
Maxwell, Robert S. .... Topeka, KS
Maxwell, Robert W. .... Covington, LA
Maxwell, Robert W., II .... Cincinnati, OH
Maxwell, Robin J. H. .... New York, NY
Maxwell, Roger L. .... Dallas, TX
Maxwell, Ronald A. .... Aiken, SC
North Augusta, SC
Maxwell, Ronald W. .... Jacksonville, FL
Maxwell, Rosemary .... Washington, DC
Maxwell, S. Strom .... Tallahassee, FL
Maxwell, Saranne K .... Denver, CO
Maxwell, Sharon .... Tucson, AZ
Maxwell, Sheila Ann .... Dodge City, KS
Maxwell, Sheila M. .... Minneapolis, MN
Maxwell, Shirley A. .... Minneapolis, MN
Maxwell, Silas J. .... Austin, TX
Maxwell, Stephen C. .... Arlington, TX
Maxwell, Stephen D. .... Topeka, KS
Maxwell, Stephen L. .... St. Paul, MN
Maxwell, Susannah I. .... Towson, MD
Maxwell, Suzanne M. .... Buffalo, NY
Maxwell, Thomas E. .... Birmingham, AL
Maxwell, Thomas F., Jr. .... Bridgeport, CT
Maxwell, Thomas K. .... Marinette, WI
Maxwell, Thomas M. .... Indianapolis, IN
Maxwell, Timothy .... Philadelphia, PA
Maxwell, Timothy G. .... St. Louis, MO
Maxwell & Van Ryn .... Albany, NY
Delmar, NY
Maxwell, Verne H. .... Dallas, TX
Maxwell, W. Stirling .... Brookings, OR
Maxwell, Walter G. .... Pasadena, CA
Maxwell, Walter M. .... Rochester, NY
Maxwell, William B. .... Enid, OK
Maxwell, William B., III .... Charleston, WV
Maxwell, William C. .... Roanoke, VA
Salem, VA
Maxwell, William E. .... Southfield, MI
Maxwell, William Earl, Jr. .... Houston, TX
Maxwell, William T., Jr. .... Memphis, TN
Maxwell-Hoffman, Ellen .... Charleston, WV
Maxwell-Wickett, Janet K. .... Woodstock, IL
Maxymuik, Nicholas .... Philadelphia, PA
May, A. Cinclair .... Hernando, MS
May, A. Jack .... Richmond, KY
May, A. John .... Philadelphia, PA
May, A. John, III .... Berwyn, PA
May, A. Michelle .... Belton, TX
May, Adam, Gerdes & Thompson, L.L.P.
Pierre, SD
May, Alan A. .... Southfield, MI
May, Albert E. .... Washington, DC
May, Alexander John .... Annapolis, MD
May, Allan W. .... Woodside, CA
May, Allen W., Jr. .... Tuscaloosa, AL
May, Andrea L. .... Atlanta, GA
May, Anne Klayman .... Manhasset Hills, NY
May, Arnold P. .... Boston, MA
May, Arthur A. .... South Bend, IN
May, Arthur William (Bill) .... Jackson, MS
May, Barbara J. .... Arden Hills, MN
May, Belinda Bush .... St. Louis, MO
May, Benjamin M. .... Texarkana, TX
May, Brian H. .... St. Louis, MO
May, Brian J. .... South Bend, IN
May, Brian T. .... Los Angeles, CA
May, Bruce B. .... Phoenix, AZ
May, Bruce D. .... Newport Beach, CA
May, Bruce J. .... Barberton, OH
May & Buege .... Waukegan, IL
May, C. Kent .... Pittsburgh, PA
May, Carol Lynn .... Framingham, MA
May, Carol S. .... Santa Monica, CA
May, Caroline F. .... Department of Justice, Tax Division, GV
May, Charles D. .... Los Angeles, CA
Oxnard, CA
May, Charles H., II .... Chicago, IL

Mayer, Gregory P. ... Charlotte, NC
Mayer, H. Robert ... United States Court Of Appeals For The Federal Circuit, GV
Mayer, Harold B., Jr. ... Smithtown, NY
Mayer, Harry R. ... Drexel Hill, PA
Mayer, Herbert F., Jr. ... Grand Island, NE
Mayer, Irving B. ... Chicago, IL
Mayer, J. Harold, Jr. ... Walterboro, SC
Mayer, J. Michael ... Des Moines, IA
Mayer, J. Russell ... Chamblee, GA
Mayer, J. William ... Montgomery, AL
Mayer, James ... Westwood, NJ
Mayer, James A. ... San Antonio, TX
Mayer, James H. ... San Diego, CA
Mayer, James H. ... Latrobe, PA
Mayer, James J. ... Cincinnati, OH
Mayer, James, Jr. ... Mansfield, OH
Mayer, James L. ... Columbia, MD
Mayer, James L., P.A. ... Columbia, MD
Mayer, James R. ... Kenmore, NY
Mayer, James T. ... Chicago, IL
Mayer, Jeffrey J. ... Southfield, MI
Mayer, Jerome A. ... Danbury, CT
Mayer, Jessica R. ... Woodbridge, NJ
Mayer, Joel B. ... New York, NY
Mayer, John ... Houston, TX
Mayer, John F. ... Bloomfield Hills, MI
Mayer, John F. ... Manitowoc, WI
Mayer, John G. ... Santa Monica, CA
Mayer, John M., Jr. ... Clarksville, IN
Mayer, John P. ... Detroit, MI
Mayer, John R. ... San Diego, CA
Mayer, John R. ... Boston, MA
Mayer, John R. ... Highlands, NC
Mayer, Joseph L. ... Washington, DC
Mayer, Joseph N., III ... New Orleans, LA
Mayer, Jules F. ... Dallas, TX
Mayer, Julie A. ... Chicago, IL
Mayer, Julie Chenot ... Southfield, MI
Mayer, Karen L. ... Roseland, NJ
Mayer, Karen R. ... New York, NY
Mayer, Karl S. ... San Francisco, CA
Mayer, Kathryn W. ... Allentown, PA
Mayer, Kennedy & Randolph
West Palm Beach, FL
Mayer, Kenneth Franklin ... Salem, OR
Mayer, Kevin C. ... Los Angeles, CA
Mayer, Kimberly ... San Jose, CA
Mayer, Kimberly Anderson ... Dallas, TX
Mayer, Kristan S. ... San Francisco, CA
Mayer, Kristen L. ... Cleveland, OH
Mayer, Larry J. ... Denver, CO
Mayer, Laura B. ... Houston, TX
Mayer, Laurel Ann ... San Francisco, CA
Mayer Law Offices ... Nashua, NH
Mayer, Lee R. ... Rockford, IL
Mayer, Leon, (A L.C.) ... Glendale, CA
Mayer & Leshy ... Columbus, OH
Mayer, Linda A. ... Washington, DC
Mayer, Linda G. ... Monroe, WI
Mayer, Lisa A. ... Fenton, MO
Mayer, Lisa E. ... Lafayette, LA
Mayer, Lisa Kavajecz ... Oshkosh, WI
Mayer, Lloyd H. ... Washington, DC
Mayer, Lori Ilene ... Livingston, NJ
Mayer, Marc E. ... Los Angeles, CA
Mayer, Marc R. ... Palo Alto, CA
Mayer, Maria Chang ... Miami, FL
Mayer, Mark A. ... Houston, TX
Mayer, Marshall S. ... Paradise, CA
Mayer, Martin J. ... Long Beach, CA
Mayer, Marvin D. ... Orange, CA
Mayer, Matt A. ... Denver, CO
Mayer, Matthew S. ... West Bend, WI
Mayer, Matthew W. ... New York, NY
Mayer, Mayer, Lonergan & Rolfes
Clinton, IA
Mayer, Michael A. ... Fairborn, OH
Mayer, Michael F. ... Scarsdale, NY
Mayer, Michael J. ... Eagan, MN
Mayer, Michael L. ... Woodland Hills, CA
Mayer, Michael P. ... Rocky River, OH
Mayer, Michael S. ... Washington, DC
Mayer, Minton P. ... Memphis, TN
Mayer, Monroe E. ... New City, NY
Mayer, Murray ... New York, NY
Mayer, Myron S. ... New York, NY
Mayer, Neal Michael ... Washington, DC
Mayer, Pamela Jane ... Johnstown, PA
Mayer, Patricia F. ... Santa Monica, CA
Mayer, Patricia V. ... Santa Monica, CA
Mayer, Patrick W. ... Los Angeles, CA
Mayer, Paul E. ... Hyannis, MA
Mayer, Paul G., Jr. ... Pittsburgh, PA
Mayer, Paul R. ... Shreveport, LA
Mayer, Paul R., Jr. ... Shreveport, LA
Mayer, Peter H. ... Hauppauge, NY
Mayer, Peter M. ... Clayton, MO
Mayer, Peter R. ... Lakeland, FL
Mayer, Peter R. ... Sheboygan, WI
Mayer, Peter R., P.A. ... Lakeland, FL
Mayer, Philip Alan B. ... Mansfield, OH
Mayer, Phillip H. ... Chicago, IL
Mayer, Randolph A. ... Atlanta, GA
Mayer, Randolph J. ... New York, NY
Mayer, Raymond C. ... Smyrna, GA
Mayer, Richard A. ... Peoria, IL
Mayer, Richard A. ... Merrillville, IN
Mayer, Richard D. ... Sacramento, CA
Mayer, Richard L. ... Merrillville, IN
Mayer, Richard L. ... New York, NY
Mayer, Richard M. ... Columbus, OH
Mayer, Richard M. ... Knoxville, TN
Mayer, Rick A. ... Houston, TX
Mayer & Riser, PLLC ... Highlands, NC
Mayer, Robbie J. ... Tucson, AZ
Mayer, Robert ... Coral Gables, FL
Mayer, Robert C. ... Washington, DC
Mayer, Robert D., (P.C.) ... Los Angeles, CA
Mayer, Robert E. ... Pierre, SD
Mayer, Robert G. ... Fairfax, VA
Mayer, Robert G., P.C. ... Fairfax, VA
Mayer, Robert J. ... Commack, NY
Mayer, Robert K. ... Chicago, IL
Mayer, Robert M. ... Miami, FL
Mayer, Robert S. ... White Plains, NY
Mayer, Robert T. ... Tarrytown, NY
Mayer, Robin Goff ... Newnan, GA
Mayer, Rodney J. ... Louisville, KY
Mayer, Ronald A. ... Chicago, IL
Mayer, Ronald C. ... New York, NY
Mayer, Rosanne ... Ithaca, NY
Mayer, Samuel B. ... New York, NY
Mayer, Sarah B. ... West Palm Beach, FL
Mayer, Scott A. ... North Chicago, IL
Mayer, Scott A. ... Philadelphia, PA
Mayer, Scott D. ... Los Angeles, CA
Mayer, Smith & Roberts, L.L.P.
Bossier City, LA
Shreveport, LA
Mayer, Stanley J. ... Pompano Beach, FL
Mayer, Steven C. ... Angola, IN
Mayer, Steven D. ... Milwaukee, WI
Mayer, Steven E. ... Clinton, IA
Mayer, Steven L. ... San Francisco, CA
Mayer, Steven M. ... Los Angeles, CA
Mayer, Steven M. ... Richmond, VA
Mayer, Susan A. ... Soquel, CA
Mayer, Theodore V. H. ... New York, NY
Mayer, Thomas A. ... Bismarck, ND
Mayer, Thomas C. ... Peoria, IL
Mayer, Thomas C. ... Detroit, MI
Mayer, Thomas Moers ... New York, NY
Mayer, Thomas P. ... Pierre, SD
Mayer, Tomea C. ... St. Louis, MO
Mayer, Valerie T. ... Louisville, KY
Mayer, Velia Ann ... Jackson, MS
Mayer, Vogt, Smith & Palmquist
Clarksville, IN
Jeffersonville, IN
New Albany, IN
Louisville, KY
Mayer, W. Frederick, Jr. ... Towson, MD
Mayer, W. James, Jr. ... Lakewood, OH
Mayer, William A. ... Kansas City, MO
Mayer, William A. ... West Bend, WI
Mayer, William E. ... San Diego, CA
Mayer, William G. ... King Ferry, NY
Mayer, William H. ... Framingham, MA
Mayer, William P. ... Boston, MA
Mayer, William R. ... Trenton, NJ
Mayer, Yvonne Mena ... Ann Arbor, MI
Mayer, Zach T. ... Dallas, TX
Mayerfeld, Ernest ... Bethesda, MD
Mayerfeld, J. Michael ... New York, NY
Mayeri, David A. ... New York, NY
Mayeri, Israella F. ... Jamaica, NY
Mayerle, Thomas M. ... Minneapolis, MN
Mayernick-Lezinski, Christine S.
Scranton, PA
Mayernik, David J. ... Pittsburgh, PA
Mayernik, Thomas J. ... Cleveland, OH
Mayeron, Candace N. ... Playa Del Rey, CA
Mayeron, Janie S. ... Minneapolis, MN
Mayeron, Steven B. ... Minneapolis, MN
Mayers, Abraham J. ... Boston, MA
Mayers, Barbara W. ... Chicago, IL
Mayers & Bouchner, L.L.C. ... Lafayette, LA
Mayers, Charles C. ... Augusta, GA
Mayers, Daniel K. ... Washington, DC
Mayers, Gregory J. ... Denver, CO
Mayers, John A. ... San Diego, CA
Mayers, Joseph B. ... Blue Bell, PA
Mayers, Joyce E. ... Washington, DC
Mayers, Kenneth J. ... South Orange, NJ
Mayers, Kenneth P. ... Lafayette, LA
Mayers, Lisa K. ... Denver, CO
Mayers, Mennies & Sherr LLP
Blue Bell, PA
Norristown, PA
Philadelphia, PA
Mayers, Oscar S., Jr. ... Washington, DC
Mayers, Richd. L. ... Sacramento, CA
Mayers, Russell S. ... Arlington, VA
Mayers, Steven W. ... Pittsburgh, PA
Mayerschoff, Glenn E.
Department of Commerce, Patent and Trademark Office, GV
Mayersohn, Arnold L., Jr.
Los Angeles, CA
Mayersohn, Joel D. ... Fort Lauderdale, FL
Mayersohn, Paul F. ... Los Angeles, CA
Mayerson, Anne Ronnel ... Washington, DC
Mayerson, Don A. ... North Miami, FL
Mayerson, Frederic H. ... Cincinnati, OH
Mayerson, Gary S. ... New York, NY
Mayerson, Harold A. ... New York, NY
Mayerson, Hy ... Trappe, PA
Mayerson, Lynn ... Dayton, OH
Mayerson, Marc S. ... Washington, DC
Mayerson, Michael A. ... Los Angeles, CA
Mayerson, Rachel F. ... New York, NY
Mayerson, Sandra E. ... New York, NY
Mayerson Stutman, LLP ... New York, NY
Mayes, André F. ... Troy, MI
Mayes, Basil L. ... San Diego, CA
Mayes, Bob I. ... Fayetteville, AR
Mayes, Catherine D. ... Reston, VA
Mayes, Derrick P. ... Ferndale, MI
Mayes, Dibrel C. ... Dinwiddie, VA
Mayes, Donald E. ... San Diego, CA
Mayes, Frederick W. ... Lewisville, TX
Mayes, Gary ... St. Louis, MO
Mayes, Gregory T. ... Philadelphia, PA
Mayes, Howard L., Jr. ... Titusville, FL
Mayes, James P. ... Greensboro, NC
Mayes, Jeff S. ... Houston, TX
Mayes, Jeffrey C. ... Los Angeles, CA
Mayes, Jeffrey W. ... Washington, DC
Mayes, John B. ... Blytheville, AR
Mayes, Jonathan O. ... Pleasanton, CA
Mayes, Jonathan Robert ... Tampa, FL
Mayes, Joseph R. ... Virginia Beach, VA
Mayes, K. Michael, Law Offices of, P.C.
Conroe, TX
Mayes, Michael D. ... Springfield, MO
Mayes, Michele Coleman ... New York, NY
Mayes, Phyllis L. ... St. Louis, MO
Mayes, Robert J. ... Gulf Breeze, FL
Mayes, Robert J. ... Pensacola, FL
Mayes, S. Hubert, Jr. ... Little Rock, AR
Mayes, Sandra Lee ... Worcester, MA
Mayes, Suzanne Serianni
Philadelphia, PA
Mayes, Taylor B. ... Nashville, TN
Mayes, Thompson M. ... Washington, DC
Mayes, W. Daniel ... Aiken, SC
Mayesh, Jay P. ... New York, NY
Mayet-Astorga, Juan Antonio
Washington, DC
Mayette, Anastasia M. ... Mishawaka, IN
Mayette, Eileen M. ... Norfolk, VA
Mayette, Patrick M. ... Norfolk, VA
Mayette, Wilfred J. ... Mishawaka, IN
Mayeux, Donald L. ... Eunice, LA
Mayeux, Donald L., A P.L.C. ... Eunice, LA
Mayeux, Mitzi A. ... Lafayette, LA
Mayew, Donald E. ... Kenosha, WI
Mayfield, Alan M. ... Waco, TX
Mayfield, Andrew B. ... St. Louis, MO
Mayfield & Associates ... Solana Beach, CA
Mayfield, Barbara Lovingfoss ... Austin, TX
Mayfield, Beth McRae ... Atlanta, GA
Mayfield, Bobby M. ... Las Cruces, NM
Mayfield, Bobby M., P.A. ... Las Cruces, NM
Mayfield, Bonnie L. ... Detroit, MI
Mayfield and Brooks ... Lafayette, IN
Mayfield, Bruce ... Newport Beach, CA
Mayfield, Bruce D. ... Overland Park, KS
Mayfield, C. David ... Park Ridge, IL
Mayfield, Carey T. ... Atlanta, GA
Mayfield, Catherine A. ... Troy, MI
Mayfield, Charles N. ... Columbia, SC
Mayfield, Charles R., Jr. ... Jackson, MS
Mayfield, Clayton E. ... Beaumont, TX
Mayfield, Clell I. ... Birmingham, AL
Mayfield, Craig C. ... Woodland, CA
Mayfield, Dan E. ... Waco, TX
Mayfield, Dan W. ... Lawrenceville, GA
Mayfield, Daniel M. ... San Jose, CA
Mayfield, David E. ... Rockford, IL
Mayfield, David M. ... Cherry Hill, NJ
Mayfield, Debra K. ... Boston, MA
Mayfield, Debra W. ... Chattanooga, TN
Mayfield, Denise L. ... Dallas, TX
Mayfield, Dianne C. ... Alexandria, VA
Mayfield, Earl N., III ... Washington, DC
Mayfield, Edward ... Stamford, CT
Mayfield, Eli ... Palacios, TX
Mayfield, Ellis O. ... El Paso, TX
Mayfield, Franki J. ... Boise, ID
Mayfield, Gayle J. ... Solana Beach, CA
Mayfield, Gene ... Hilton Head Island, SC
Mayfield, Gerald K. ... Philadelphia, PA
Mayfield, Gregory N. ... Atlanta, GA
Mayfield, Jack H., III ... Houston, TX
Mayfield, Jack L. ... Johnson City, TN
Mayfield, John R. ... Phoenix, AZ
Mayfield, Kathryn Jean Williams ... Ozona, TX
Mayfield, Kenneth ... Tupelo, MS
Mayfield, Kenneth A. ... Dallas, TX
Mayfield, Kenneth G. ... Oklahoma City, OK
Mayfield, Kent T. ... Palacios, TX
Mayfield, Krista Kay
West Palm Beach, FL
Mayfield, Lakeisha R. ... Chicago, IL
Mayfield, Larry Wayne ... Morgantown, WV
Mayfield & Lester ... Chattanooga, TN
Mayfield, Lisa A. ... Bloomington, IN
Mayfield, Lori R. ... Fresno, CA
Mayfield, M Christopher ... Nashville, TN
Mayfield, Marc C. ... Houston, TX
Mayfield, Mark A. ... Austin, TX
Mayfield, Mark Alan ... Jonesboro, AR
Mayfield, Mark J. ... Chattanooga, TN
Mayfield, Mark S.
Department of State, GV
Mayfield, Mark S. ... Jackson, MS
Mayfield & Mayfield ... Jackson, MS
Mayfield & Mayfield ... Palacios, TX
Mayfield, Melvin E. ... Little Rock, AR
Mayfield, Michael D. ... Salt Lake City, UT
Mayfield, Michelle R. ... Reading, PA
Mayfield & Milling, L.L.C. ... Atlanta, GA
Mayfield, Mitzi S. ... Dallas, TX
Mayfield, Paul ... Burlingame, CA
Mayfield & Perrenot, P.C. ... El Paso, TX
Mayfield, Reid K. ... Atoka, OK
Mayfield, Richard H. ... Washington, DC
Mayfield, Robert B. ... Fort Worth, TX
Mayfield, Robert U. ... Austin, TX
Mayfield, Robin Dietz ... St. Paul, MN
Mayfield, Stanley F. ... Salem, OR
Mayfield, Tod ... Amarillo, TX
Mayfield, Trey N. ... Washington, DC
Mayfield, Vernon C. ... Fort Worth, TX
Mayfield, W. Glenn ... Ormond Beach, FL
Mayfield, W. Scott ... Atlanta, GA
Mayfield, William ... Dothan, AL
Mayfield, William J. R. ... Atlanta, GA
Mayhall, Danna Kirk ... Athens, TX
Mayhall, Donald G. ... Atlanta, GA
Mayhall, Jair Edgar ... Kansas City, MO
Mayhall, Jay R., (A Professional Corporation)
San Francisco, CA
Mayhall, Kim G. ... Baton Rouge, LA
Lafayette, LA
Mayhall & Ling ... Memphis, TN
Mayhall, Michael A. ... New Orleans, LA
Mayhall, Michael A., A Professional Law Corporation ... New Orleans, LA
Mayhall, Michael C. ... Lawton, OK
Mayhall, Millard N. ... Marshall, MI
Mayhall, R.A., Jr. ... Memphis, TN
Mayhall, Richard E. ... Springfield, OH
Mayhall, Robert F. ... El Paso, TX
Mayhall, Van R., Jr. ... Baton Rouge, LA
New Orleans, LA
Mayhan, David G.
Greenwood Village, CO
Mayhart, Scott G. ... West Chester, PA
Mayher, Donna M. ... Cleveland, OH
Mayhew, Bradley C. ... Birmingham, AL
Mayhew, Elaine ... Mt. Vernon, OH
Mayhew, Everett Allen, Jr. ... Albany, NY
Mayhew, Fred E. ... Mt. Vernon, OH
Mayhew, Gerald J. ... Milwaukee, WI
Mayhew, Jeffrey C. ... Orange, CA
Mayhew, Kristen B. ... Philadelphia, PA
Mayhew, Mary Ann ... Rockville, MD
Mayhew, Michael Alan ... Anaheim, CA
Mayhew, Paul McLane
Upper Marlboro, MD
Mayhew, Randall F. ... Woodstock, VT
Mayhew, Sharon L. ... Bethesda, MD
Mayhew, Stanley J. ... Fairplay, CO
Mayhew, Thomas ... San Francisco, CA
Mayhew, William A. ... Modesto, CA
Mayhoffer, David ... Kremmling, CO
Mayhook, J. Jeffrey ... Vancouver, WA
Mayhorne, Eugene W. ... Baltimore, MD
Mayhue, Charles D. ... Ada, OK
Mayhue, Francis E.
Department Of Health And Human Services, Social Security Administration, GV
Mayhue, G. C., Jr. ... Ada, OK
Mayhue, Sue C. ... Tulsa, OK
Mayhugh, David L. ... Park Hills, MO
Mayhugh, George M. ... Warrenton, VA
Mayian, Stephen M. ... Escondido, CA
Mayk, Joseph E. ... Philadelphia, PA
Mayka, Stephen P. ... Rochester, NY
Maykel, Marla A. ... Worcester, MA
Maykut, Elizabeth J. ... Tallahassee, FL
Maylack, Jean H. ... St. Louis, MO
Mayland, Donald K., Jr. ... New York, NY
Mayland, Gail B. ... Cleveland, OH
Maylath, Sharon R. ... St. Paul, MN
Mayle, David R. ... McKinney, TX
Mayle, Ronald J. ... Fremont, OH
Mayle, Virginia K. ... Columbus, OH
Maylen, Charles E., III ... Modesto, CA
Maylie & Grayson ... Portland, OR
Maylie, Joseph W. ... Portland, OR
Maylin, Kathleen G. ... Encino, CA
Walnut Creek, CA
Maylott, Ralph M. ... Knoxville, TN
Mayman, Georgia McCullough
Santa Ana, CA
Mayman, Linda Goldenberg
Los Angeles, CA
Mayman, Rina M. ... Boston, MA
Mayman, Robert M. ... Los Angeles, CA
Mayman, Todd A. ... Arlington, VA
Maymí, Gilberto ... Guaynabo, PR
Maymir, Javier A. ... Treasury Department, Office of the Comptroller of the Currency, GV
Maymudes, Carol Sue ... Plainview, NY
Maymudes, Rena ... Los Angeles, CA
Maynard, A. L., P.C. ... Virginia Beach, VA
Maynard, Alan I. ... Elizabethtown, NC
Maynard, Alison ... Denver, CO
Maynard, Allison L. ... Virginia Beach, VA
Maynard, Angela L. ... Cleveland, OH
Maynard, April D. ... Auburn, CA
Maynard, Ava R. ... New York, NY
Maynard, Betty W. ... Clarksdale, MS
Maynard, C. Douglas, Jr.
Winston-Salem, NC
Maynard, Cary ... New York, NY
Maynard, Charles D., Jr. ... Houston, TX
Maynard, Christopher
Department Of Veterans Affairs, Board of Veterans Appeals, GV
Maynard, Cooper & Gale, P.C.
Birmingham, AL
Montgomery, AL
Maynard, Creighton C., Jr. ... Fort Worth, TX
Maynard, Cynthia L. ... Tampa, FL
Maynard, Daniel D. ... Phoenix, AZ
Maynard, David L. ... High Point, NC
Maynard, Deanne E. ... Washington, DC
Maynard, Douglas Scott ... Campbell, CA
Maynard, Douglass B. ... New York, NY
Maynard, Durward W. ... Louisville, KY
Maynard, Edwin S. ... New York, NY
Maynard, Eleanor A. ... St. Louis, MO
Maynard, Elliott E. ... Williamson, WV
Maynard, George F. ... Birmingham, AL
Maynard, George F. ... Atlanta, GA
Maynard, Glen B. ... Golden, CO
Maynard, Glen B., P.C. ... Golden, CO
Maynard, Glen C. ... Oklahoma City, OK
Maynard, Gregg R. ... Houston, TX
Maynard, Hugh M. ... Minneapolis, MN
Maynard, James H. ... Morristown, NJ
Maynard, James L. ... Everett, WA
Maynard, Jeffrey A. ... Virginia Beach, VA
Maynard, Jerome I. ... Chicago, IL
Maynard, Jerry L. ... Middleburg Heights, OH

Maynard, Jerry L., II ... Nashville, TN
Maynard, Jo-Ann Horn ... Los Angeles, CA
Maynard, Joe C., Jr. ... Billings, MT
Maynard, John ... New York, NY
Maynard, John B. ... Boston, MA
Maynard, John G. ... Tampa, FL
Maynard, John H. ... Lewiston, ID
Maynard, John H. ... Helena, MT
Maynard, John P. ... Lowell, MA
Maynard, John R. ... Milwaukee, WI
Maynard, Katherine Terrell ... Atlanta, GA
Maynard, Kelly C. ... Washington, DC
Maynard, Kennis ... Inez, KY
Maynard, Kent, Jr. ... Chicago, IL
Maynard, Kevin C. ... Springfield, MA
Maynard, Kevin J. ... Washington, DC
Maynard, Kimberly A. ... Los Angeles, CA
Maynard Law Offices ... Campbell, CA
Los Gatos, CA
San Jose, CA
Maynard, Leila L. ... Bow, NH
Maynard, Lynn M. ... Centralia, WA
Maynard, Mallam J. ... Wilmington, NC
Maynard, Mark A. ... Sarasota, FL
Maynard, Mark D. ... Anderson, IN
Maynard, Mark S. ... Worcester, MA
Maynard, Michelle M. ... Houston, TX
Maynard Murray Cronin & O'Sullivan, P.L.C.
Phoenix, AZ
Maynard, Natasha C. ... New York, NY
Maynard, Noelle Y. ... Fairfax, VA
Maynard, O'Connor, Smith & Catalinotto, LLP ... Albany, NY
Saugerties, NY
Maynard, Otis V. ... Philadelphia, PA
Maynard, Patricia F. ... Medina, OH
Maynard, Philip C. ... Irvine, CA
Maynard, Richard H. ... Belchertown, MA
Maynard, Robert A. ... Boise, ID
Maynard, Robert C. ... Largo, MD
Maynard, Robert C. ... Warren, OH
Maynard, Robert H. ... Columbus, OH
Maynard, Robert R. ... Bristol, CT
Maynard, Robert W. ... Minneapolis, MN
Maynard, Sara ... Tyler, TX
Maynard, Sharon ... Portland, OR
Maynard, Steven A. ... Chicago, IL
Maynard, Therese H. ... Los Angeles, CA
Maynard, Wayne R. ... Merchantville, NJ
Philadelphia, PA
Maynard, William ... El Paso, TX
Maynard, William J. ... Marquette, MI
Maynard, William J. ... San Antonio, TX
Maynard, William L. ... Houston, TX
Maynard, Zollie M., Jr.
Fort Lauderdale, FL
Tallahassee, FL
Maynard-Elliott, Nichelle ... Stamford, CT
Mayne, Amy G. ... Memphis, TN
Mayne, Florence Pfullmann ... Austin, TX
Mayne, John D. ... Sioux City, IA
Mayne, Kevin E. ... Woodburn, OR
Mayne, Lisa Ann ... Fairfax, VA
Mayne, Martin D. ... Houston, TX
Mayne & Mayne ... Sioux City, IA
Mayne, Stephen S. ... San Francisco, CA
Mayne, Troy A. ... Madison, WI
Mayne, Wiley ... Sioux City, IA
Mayne, Wiley E., Jr. ... Denver, CO
Mayner, Crystal G. ... New York, NY
Maynes, Bradford, Shipps & Sheftel LLP
Bayfield, CO
Durango, CO
Maynes, Frank E. (Sam) ... Durango, CO
Maynes, Joe L. ... Aberdeen, SD
Maynes, John L. ... Sioux Falls, SD
Maynes, Judith A. ... Basking Ridge, NJ
Maynes, Mark E. ... Seattle, WA
Maynes, Paula G. ... Santa Fe, NM
Maynes, Robert A. ... Basking Ridge, NJ
Maynes, Sam W. ... Durango, CO
Maynes, Todd F. ... Chicago, IL
Maynez, Robert Anthony ... Boston, MA
Maynor, Donald H. ... Atherton, CA
Maynor, Donald H., A Professional Law Corporation ... Atherton, CA
Maynor, Harry D. ... Buffalo, NY
Maynor, J. Mark ... West Palm Beach, FL
Maynor, Walter H. ... Mount Vernon, IL
Maynor, Willie D. ... Baton Rouge, LA
Maynord, Harris A. ... St. Louis, MO
Mayo, A. Kent ... Department of Justice, Environment and Natural Resources Division, GV
Mayo, A. T., Legal Services, P.C.
Chesapeake, VA
Mayo, A. Todd ... East Brunswick, NJ
Mayo, Alex T., Jr. ... Chesapeake, VA
Mayo, Amy B. ... San Antonio, TX
Mayo, Anita D. ... San Francisco, CA
Mayo, Beatrice ... Kittery, ME
Mayo, Brigitte M. ... Sacramento, CA
Mayo, Christopher P. ... San Antonio, TX
Mayo, Clayton F. ... Jackson, TN
Mayo, Dana Wilt ... New Brunswick, NJ
Mayo, Daniel ... New York, NY
Mayo, David R. ... Cleveland, OH
Mayo, David W. ... New York, NY
Mayo, Deborah R. ... Miami, FL
Mayo, Diane Vodrey ... Sacramento, CA
Mayo, Dianne Marie ... Jonesville, LA
Mayo, Douglas Petty ... Indianapolis, IN
Mayo, Elizabeth B. ... Bluffton, SC
Hilton Head Island, SC
Mayo, Ernest G. ... Warren, RI
Mayo, Francis T. ... Salem, MA
Mayo, George W., Jr. ... Washington, DC
Mayo, Gerda Ladd ... Knoxville, TN
Mayo, Gilligan & Zito, LLP
Glastonbury, CT
Hartford, CT
Middletown, CT
Newington, CT
Rocky Hill, CT
Wethersfield, CT
Mayo, Gordon R. ... East Greenbush, NY
Mayo, Hiram J., Jr. ... New Bern, NC
Mayo, J. Cal, Jr. ... Oxford, MS
Mayo, J. Keith ... Dallas, TX
Tyler, TX
Mayo, James C. ... Louisville, MS
Mayo, James P. ... Sacramento, CA
Mayo, James R. ... Ukiah, CA
Mayo, Jeanne L. ... Houston, TX
Mayo, Jeffrey ... Tulsa, OK
Mayo, Jennifer L. ... Wilmington, DE
Mayo, Jerry D. ... Nashville, TN
Mayo, Joel A. ... Denver, CO
Mayo, John R. ... Charlotte, NC
Mayo, John T. ... Goshen, NY
Mayo, Judy Zecchin ... Charlotte, NC
Mayo, Kenneth Reed ... Norfolk, VA
Mayo, Kevin L. ... Riverhead, NY
Mayo, Larry L. ... Houston, TX
Mayo, Linda N. Marini ... Waterbury, CT
Mayo, Louis H. ... Clifton, VA
Mayo, Marc M. ... Jacksonville, FL
Mayo, Margaret H. ... New York, NY
Mayo, Mark H. ... Carthage, MO
Joplin, MO
Mayo, Martin L. ... Houston, TX
Mayo, Mary Anne ... New York, NY
Mayo, Mary Beth ... San Francisco, CA
Mayo, Mary Kay ... Warren, RI
Mayo & Mayo ... Washington, NC
Mayo & Mayo ... Colonial Beach, VA
Mayo McDavid, PLLC ... Oxford, MS
Mayo Mendolia & Schultz ... Dallas, TX
Tyler, TX
Mayo, Michael C. ... Fort Worth, TX
Mayo, Michael C. ... Colonial Beach, VA
Mayo, Norris, Johns & Carpenter
Nashville, TN
Mayo, Ofelia M. ... Houston, TX
Mayo, Ollie K. ... San Antonio, TX
Mayo & Pickering ... Fort Worth, TX
Mayo, Pi-Yi ... Baytown, TX
Mayo, R. Cody, Jr. ... Shreveport, LA
Mayo, R. Scott ... Lubbock, TX
Mayo, Ralph ... New Brunswick, NJ
Mayo, Ralph E. ... Bakersfield, CA
Mayo, Richard C. ... West Islip, NY
Mayo, Robert K. ... Shreveport, LA
Mayo, Sonia M. ... Austin, TX
Mayo, Stanley O. ... Dallas, TX
Mayo, Stephen A. ... Charlotte, NC
Mayo, Ted, III ... Fort Worth, TX
Mayo, Terri A. ... Albany, OR
Mayo, Thomas Wm. ... Dallas, TX
Mayo, Timothy L. ... Madison, WV
Mayo, Todd ... Nashua, NH
Mayo, Valerie J. ... Colonial Beach, VA
Mayo, Virgil Q. ... Blountstown, FL
Mayo, Virginia S. ... Brentwood, TN
Mayo, Walker P. ... Lexington, KY
Mayo, Walter H. ... Wethersfield, CT
Mayo, Walter H., III ... Boston, MA
Mayo, Wilka V. ... Dallas, TX
Mayo, William P. ... Washington, NC
Mayo, William P., Jr. ... Washington, NC
Mayo, William R. ... Fayetteville, AR
Mayock, James R. ... San Francisco, CA
Mayock, W. Michael ... Los Angeles, CA
Mayock, W. Michael ... Pasadena, CA
Mayol & Barringer ... Modesto, CA
Mayol, James D. ... Modesto, CA
Mayol, Juan J., Jr. ... Miami, FL
Mayol, Linda C. ... Miami, FL
Mayol-Bianchi, Jaime ... Guaynabo, PR
Mayol-Bianchi P.S.C. Law Office
Guaynabo, PR
Mayopoulos, Timothy J. ... New York, NY
Mayor, Bruce
Merit Systems Protection Board, Policy and Evaluation, GV
Mayor, Day, Caldwell & Keeton, L.L.P.
Austin, TX
Houston, TX
Mayor, Ernesto, Jr. ... Tampa, FL
Mayor, Heidi H. ... Washington, DC
Mayor & Horner, Ltd. ... Las Vegas, NV
Mayor, James H. ... Houston, TX
Mayor, Kim R. ... San Francisco, CA
Mayor, Richard B. ... Houston, TX
Mayor, Richard H. ... Portland, OR
Mayor, Sherman B. ... Las Vegas, NV
Mayora, Margaret ... New York, NY
Mayoral, Paul G. ... New Orleans, LA
Mayoral-Megwinoff, Ernesto N.
San Juan, PR
Mayoral-Morales, Rafael ... San Juan, PR
Mayorga, David C. ... San Antonio, TX
Mayorga, Judith ... Salt Lake City, UT
Mayorga, Lorie Ann ... Chicago, IL
Mayorga, Scott L. ... Beverly Hills, CA
Mayorkas, Helena C. ... Los Angeles, CA
Mayorowski, Gale T. ... Avoca, PA
Mayo-Tall, Karen L.
Department of Education, Office of the General Counsel, GV
Mayotte, Debra L. ... Manchester, NH
Mayotte, James A. ... Detroit, MI
Mayotte, Maureen C. ... Newton, MA
Mayou, Catherine I. ... Newport Beach, CA
Mayoue, Ellen M. ... Brunswick, GA
Mayoue, John C. ... Atlanta, GA
Mayper, Matthew B. ... Sarasota, FL
Mayr, Edward G. ... Kew Gardens, NY
Mayr, Vincent R. ... Mesa, AZ
Mayrides, Mark T. ... Skillman, NJ
Mayro, Kurt V. ... Brigantine, NJ
Mayro, Michael ... Philadelphia, PA
Reading, PA
Mayro, Tina C. ... Brigantine, NJ
Mayron, Michael ... San Jose, CA
Mayrosh, George F. ... Vero Beach, FL
May-Rucker, Rhonda ... Monterey Park, CA
Mays, A. Earl ... Lancaster, PA
Mays, Allison M. ... Tuscaloosa, AL
Mays, André F. ... Detroit, MI
Mays, Andrea L. ... Albuquerque, NM
Mays, A. R. (Bud) ... Cleveland, OH
Mays, C. Parkhill, Jr. ... Lakeland, FL
Orlando, FL
Mays, Charles A. ... Minneapolis, MN
Mays, Charles D. ... Atlanta, GA
Mays, Charles, Jr. ... Fort Worth, TX
Mays, Charlita ... New York, NY
Mays, Dale D ... Bend, OR
Mays, Derek Charles ... Kansas City, MO
Mays, Douglas A. ... Charlotte, NC
Mays, Edwin D. ... Dallas, TX
Mays, Foster, Booth & Gunter, L.L.P.
Columbia, SC
Mays, Glynn L.
Commodity Futures Trading Commission, Office of the General Counsel, GV
Mays, Gregory T. ... Dallas, TX
Mays, Howard W., Jr. ... Houston, TX
Mays, James C. ... Chesterfield, MO
Mays, James W., Jr. ... Dallas, TX
Mays, Janice ... House of Representatives, Committee on Ways & Means, GV
Mays, Jeff W. ... Atlanta, TX
Mays, Jimanne Harris
Oklahoma City, OK
Mays, John E. ... Decatur, AL
Mays, John H. ... Chicago, IL
Mays, John W. ... Sausalito, CA
Mays, Joseph B., Jr. ... Birmingham, AL
Mays, Karberg & Wachter
Cleveland, OH
Mays, Karen Gayle ... Eugene, OR
Mays, Kimberly K. ... Mission Viejo, CA
Mays, Lisa Pierobon ... Madison, WI
Mays, Matthew C. ... Virginia, IL
Mays, Meredith E. ... Atlanta, GA
Mays, Michael A. ... Fairfax, VA
Mays, Michael J. ... Marietta, GA
Mays, Michael Phillip ... Jamaica, NY
Mays, Natalie D. ... Atlanta, GA
Mays, P. Douglas ... Little Rock, AR
Mays, Paula B. ... Department of Commerce, Patent and Trademark Office, GV
Mays, Phyllis E. ... Jackson, MS
Mays, Richard D. ... Maumee, OH
Mays, Richard D. ... Dallas, TX
Mays, Richard H. ... Little Rock, AR
Mays, Richard L. ... Little Rock, AR
Mays, Robert C., III ... Columbia, SC
Mays, Robin J. ... Little Rock, AR
Mays, Samuel H., Jr. ... Nashville, TN
Mays, Sandra H. ... Tallahassee, FL
Mays, Shirley L. ... Columbus, OH
Mays, Stephen Eric ... Madison, WI
Mays, Thomas D. ... Washington, DC
Mays, Thomas L. ... Fordyce, AR
Mays, Tom J. ... Atlanta, TX
Mays & Valentine, L.L.P. ... Norfolk, VA
Richmond, VA
Tysons Corner, VA
Virginia Beach, VA
Mays, Walden & Anastas ... Quincy, IL
Mays, William G., II ... Columbia, MO
Fulton, MO
Holts Summit, MO
Mays, William H. ... Tacoma, WA
Mays, William J. ... Washington, DC
Mays, William O., Jr. ... Quincy, IL
Mays, William T., Jr. ... Memphis, TN
Mays, Wm. Owen ... Quincy, IL
Maysack, Robert G. ... Manassas, VA
Mayse, Mallory V. ... Columbia, MO
Maysel, Kyle W. ... San Marcos, TX
Maysilles, D. Duncan ... Atlanta, GA
May-Skinner, Nancy E. ... Albany, NY
Mayson, Ann W. ... Greensboro, NC
Mayson, J. D. ... Vero Beach, FL
Mayson, Preston B., Jr. ... Roanoke, VA
Mayson, Preston B., Jr., P.C. ... Roanoke, VA
Mayson, William A. ... Minneapolis, MN
Maysonett, James A. ... Washington, DC
Mayster, Bryan S. ... Chicago, IL
Mayster, Jerrold H. ... Chicago, IL
Mayster, Jerrold H., Ltd. ... Chicago, IL
Mayton, Dana Bynum ... Frankfort, KY
Mayton, Gary W. ... San Antonio, TX
Mayton, Kathleen M. ... Atlanta, GA
Mayton, Keith A. ... Columbus, OH
Mayton, Michael R. ... Little Rock, AR
West Memphis, AR
Mayton, William T. ... Atlanta, GA
Mayuga, Sandor X. ... Los Angeles, CA
Mayus, Catherine A. ... Yonkers, NY
Maywald, Tammy J., (Miss) ... Phoenix, AZ
Maywalt, Roxane E. ... Washington, DC
Maywhort, William W.
Greenwood Village, CO
Mayzel, Isabella ... East Brunswick, NJ
Fair Lawn, NJ
Marlboro, NJ
Mayzel, Isabella ... Union, NJ
Maza, Alan S. ... Livingston, NJ
New York, NY
Maza, Carl ... Westbury, NY
Maza, James W. ... Souderton, PA
Maza, Miguel A., & Associates
San Juan, PR
Maza, Susan A. ... Wilkes-Barre, PA
Mazacoufa, Demetrius ... Atlanta, GA
Mazadoorian, Harry N. ... Bloomfield, CT
Mazaheri, Harry A. ... Lancaster, PA
Mazaheri, Tina ... Lambertville, NJ
Doylestown, PA
Mazak, Edward P., Jr. ... Akron, OH
Mazakas, Pamela J.
Environmental Protection Agency, Program Office Attorneys, GV
Mazal, Michael R. ... Santa Ana, CA
Mazan, Kate Duffy ... Washington, DC
Mazanec, David T. ... Cleveland, OH
Mazanec, Kamilla M.
Highland Heights, KY
Mazanec, Raskin & Ryder Co., L.P.A.
Cleveland, OH
Columbus, OH
Solon, OH
Mazanec, Richard O. ... Cleveland, OH
Mazanec, Rosaleen K. ... Fairview Park, OH
Mazanec, Thomas S. ... Cleveland, OH
Mazanec, William F., III ... Greenfield, MA
Mazar, Adrian E. ... Chicago, IL
Mazareas, Cynthia T. ... Boston, MA
Mazarei, Rayehe ... Irvine, CA
Mazarei, Rayehe, Law Offices of ... Irvine, CA
Mazaroff, Bert S. ... Baltimore, MD
Mazaroff, Stanley, (P.C.) ... Baltimore, MD
Mazart, Gary ... Morristown, NJ
Mazawey, Louis T. ... Washington, DC
Mazawey, Richard S. ... Clifton, NJ
Mazda, Mark N. ... Irvine, CA
Maze, Carl David ... Costa Mesa, CA
Maze, Donald A. ... Owingsville, KY
Maze, Gary R. ... Houston, TX
Maze, Irvin G. ... Louisville, KY
Maze, Susan A. ... Brookline, MA
Mazeau, Annette Lampe ... Malibu, CA
Mazeau, Richard K. ... Longboat Key, FL
Mazeau, Robert G. ... Hackensack, NJ
Mazeika, Tomas V. ... Irvine, CA
San Diego, CA
Mazek, Susan Chapman ... Garden City, NY
Mazel, Arnold I. ... New York, NY
Mazel, Geoffrey R. ... New York, NY
Mazel, Joel M. ... Pickerington, OH
Mazel, Joseph W. ... New York, NY
Mazel, Laura J. ... Portland, OR
Mazel, Miriam S. ... Denver, CO
Mazel, William ... Norfolk, VA
Mazelis, Noreen B. ... Davis, CA
Mazelis, Noreen B. ... Sacramento, CA
Mazelis, Stuart Y. ... Baltimore, MD
Mazella, A. John ... Lisbon, NH
Mazella, Daniel J. ... Treasury Department, Financial Management Service, GV
Mazen, Brian K. ... Los Angeles, CA
Mazen, Samuel M. ... New York, NY
Mazer, Barry J. ... Venice, FL
Mazer, Edward H. ... Kenilworth, NJ
Mazer, Ira L. ... Voorhees, NJ
Philadelphia, PA
Mazer, Ira R. ... Monroeville, PA
Mazer, Irving L. ... Conshohocken, PA
Mazer, Jason S. ... Miami, FL
Mazer, Jeffrey A. ... Northbrook, IL
Mazer, Jennifer H. ... Atlanta, GA
Mazer, Jerald D. ... Owings Mills, MD
Mazer, Joel O. ... Chelsea, MA
Mazer, John ... Grosse Pointe, MI
Mazer, Jonathan ... New York, NY
Mazer, Lawrence F. ... Raleigh, NC
Mazer, Leo B. ... Oradell, NJ
Mazer, Marc S. ... San Francisco, CA
Mazer, Marcia L. ... Cherry Hill, NJ
Mazer, Michael E. ... Washington, DC
Mazer, Ned M. ... Somerdale, NJ
Mazer, Peter M. ... East Meadow, NY
Mazer, Ralph S. ... Newtown, PA
Mazer, Robert A. ... Washington, DC
Mazer, Robert E. ... Baltimore, MD
Mazer, Roslyn A. ... Department of Justice, Criminal Division, GV
Mazer, Steve H. ... Albuquerque, NM
Mazer, Steve H., P.A. ... Albuquerque, NM
Mazer, Steven H. ... Jericho, NY
Mazer-Marino, Jil ... New York, NY
Mazero, Joyce G. ... Dallas, TX
Mazerolle & Frasca ... Nashua, NH
Mazerolle, Jeffrey H. ... Nashua, NH
Mazeski, Edw. J., Jr. ... Pittsburgh, PA
Mazeski, Mark J. ... Stevenson, WA
Mazeski, Paul S. ... Pittsburgh, PA
Mazey, John E. ... Cleveland, OH
Mazey, Larry W. ... Southfield, MI
Mazey, William M. ... Southfield, MI
Mazgaj, Frank G. ... Akron, OH
Mazgani, Pedram F. ... Los Angeles, CA
Mazhari, Niloufar ... San Francisco, CA
Mazia, Judith A. ... San Francisco, CA
Mazia, Judith A., A Professional Law Corporation ... San Francisco, CA
Mazian, Gary J. ... Orland Park, IL
Maziarz, John E. ... Trenton, NJ
Maziarz, Peri ... Santa Barbara, CA
Mazie, Beth ... Richmond, CA
Mazie, David A. ... Livingston, NJ
Mazie, Eric A. ... Wilmington, DE
Mazie, Mark Todd ... Beverly Hills, CA
Mazie, Marvin E. ... Des Moines, IA
Mazier, Vivian J. ... Boston, MA
Mazin, Benjamin ... Louisville, KY
Mazin, Caryn ... New York, NY

Mazin, Donald S. ... Larchmont, NY
Mazin, George J. ... Roseland, NJ
Mazin, Nancy R. ... Ventnor City, NJ
Mazin, Steve ... Agoura Hills, CA
Mazique, Robert J. ... Palo Alto, CA
Mazirow, Arthur ... Los Angeles, CA
Mazirow, Harold ... San Diego, CA
Mazlen, Emiliano ... New York, NY
Mazliah, Sandra ... Washington, DC
Mazlin, Margaret ... Brooklyn, NY
Mazloff, Howard W. ... Miami, FL
Mazloom, Maziar ... Atlanta, GA
Mazloom III, Albert S. ... Washington, DC
Mazo, Daniel P. ... Philadelphia, PA
Mazo, Judith F. ... New York, NY
Mazo, Mark E. ... Washington, DC
Mazola, Peter J., Jr. ... Manhasset, NY
Mazon, Michael E. ... Seattle, WA
Mazor, Arnold L. ... Baltimore, MD
Mazor, Donald P. ... Baltimore, MD
Mazor, Lester J. ... Amherst, MA
Mazorol, Patrick A. ... Minneapolis, MN
Mazorow, Marc A. ... Torrance, CA
Mazour, A. Mari ... San Francisco, CA
Mazour, Denise C. ... Des Moines, IA
Omaha, NE
Mazow, Barnett ... Boston, MA
Mazow & Mazow ... Boston, MA
Mazow, Richard K. ... Boston, MA
Mazow, Robert E. ... Boston, MA
Mazquiaran, Michael F. ... Miami, FL
Mazrum, James L. ... Alpena, MI
Mazuca, James V. ... San Antonio, TX
Mazuco, Gayl R. ... Trenton, NJ
Mazullo, Anthony J., Jr. ... Wyncote, PA
Mazullo, Christopher ... Wyncote, PA
Mazumdar, Amitava (Jay) ... Arlington, VA
Mazumdar, Anandashankar
Washington, DC
Mazur, Alois C. ... Buffalo, NY
Mazur, Carp & Rubin, P.C.
New York, NY
Mazur, Christopher M. ... Niagara Falls, NY
Mazur, Cynthia Stelle
Federal Emergency Management Agency, Office of the General Counsel, GV
Mazur, Danielle G. ... New York, NY
Mazur, Davia Odell ... Hollywood, FL
Mazur, David L. ... Mount Clemens, MI
Mazur, Francois-Ihor ... New York, NY
Mazur, Genevieve A. ... Troy, MI
Mazur, Gerald ... New York, NY
Mazur, James A. ... Lakeside, OH
Mazur, Janice R. ... El Cajon, CA
Mazur, Joan B. ... New York, NY
Mazur, John M. ... Pittsburgh, PA
Mazur, John R. ... Saginaw, MI
Mazur, Jos. ... New York, NY
Mazur, Lawrence J. ... La Porte, IN
Mazur, Lee J. ... Pittsburgh, PA
Mazur, Linda Wight ... Beverly Hills, CA
Mazur, Lloyd D. ... Cleveland, OH
Mazur, Lori A. ... Roseland, NJ
Mazur, Louis ... New York, NY
Mazur, Louise Michelle ... Akron, OH
Mazur, Maria L. ... Boston, MA
Mazur, Marilyn C. ... New York, NY
Mazur, Mary-Jane ... New York, NY
Mazur, Matyjaszek & Brandt, P.C.
Jackson, MI
Mazur, Michael D. ... Newport Beach, CA
Mazur, Michael D., And Associates
Newport Beach, CA
Mazur, Michael S. ... Detroit, MI
Mazur, Patricia A. ... Wakefield, MA
Mazur, R. Darryl ... Jackson, MI
Mazur, Robert B. ... New York, NY
Mazur, Robyn C. ... Baltimore, MD
Mazur, Sayward ... New York, NY
Mazur, Sigmund V. ... Brewster, NY
Mazur, Stephen H. ... Los Angeles, CA
Mazur, Terri A. ... Chicago, IL
Mazur, William A., Jr. ... Grand Prairie, TX
Mazura, Adrianne C. ... Chicago, IL
Mazura, Terrence A. ... Santa Ana, CA
Mazurak, Stephen A. ... Detroit, MI
Mazuran & Hayes, A Prof. Corp.
Salt Lake City, UT
Mazuran, Michael J. ... Salt Lake City, UT
Mazurczak, Michael J. ... Boston, MA
Mazure, David E. ... New York, NY
Mazure, Kathleen L. ... Washington, DC
Mazure, Lisa ... Briarcliff Manor, NY
Mazurek, Brian E. ... Washington, DC
Mazurek, Cheryl L. ... Brockton, MA
Mazurek, Edward S. ... Philadelphia, PA
Mazurek, Henry E., Jr. ... New York, NY
Mazurek, Janet L. ... Deerfield, IL
Mazurek, Jo ... Department of Justice, Criminal Division, GV
Mazurek, John G. ... Pittsburg, KS
Mazurek, Joseph M. ... Hudsonville, MI
Mazurek, LeRoy F. ... Arlington Heights, IL
Mazurek, Mike ... Anaheim, CA
Mazurek, Nathan J. ... New York, NY
Mazurek, Ralph R. ... Newport Beach, CA
Mazurek, Thaddeus A., Jr. ... Aurora, CO
Mazur-Hart, Helen L. ... Salem, OR
Mazurkevich, Dorian S. ... Philadelphia, PA
Mazurkiewcz, Janice L. ... Cleveland, OH
Mazurowski, Suellen (Miller) ... Sidney, OH
Mazursky, Charles J. ... Los Angeles, CA
Mazursky, Don A. ... Atlanta, GA
Mazursky & Dunaway, LLP ... Atlanta, GA
Mazursky, Morris D. ... Sumter, SC
Mazursky, Schwartz & Angelo
Los Angeles, CA
Mazuy, Jon C. ... Boston, MA
Mazza, Angelo E. P. ... New York, NY
Mazza, Anthony ... West Orange, NJ
Mazza, Bruno A., Jr. ... Ithaca, NY
Mazza, Carolann ... Houston, TX
Mazza, David J. ... Winston-Salem, NC
Mazza, Domenic A. ... Syracuse, NY
Mazza, Edward A. ... Ithaca, NY
Mazza, Gary E.
Office of Personnel Management, GV
Mazza, George J. ... Washington, DC
Mazza, George J. ... Department of Justice, Office of Justice Programs, GV
Mazza, Gregory M. ... Simi Valley, CA
Mazza, John P. ... Columbus, OH
Mazza, Julie S. ... Wilmington, DE
Mazza, Kevin M. ... Springfield, NJ
Mazza, Leslie M. ... New York, NY
Mazza, Margaret M. ... Cleveland, OH
Mazza, Marie G. ... Springfield, MA
Mazza and Mazza ... Ithaca, NY
Mazza, Michael J. ... Oakland, CA
Mazza, Michael J. ... Milwaukee, WI
Mazza, Michael P. ... Chicago, IL
Mazza, Pamela J. ... Washington, DC
New York, NY
Mazza, Patrick, & Associates ... Chicago, IL
Mazza, Peter D. ... West Springfield, MA
Mazza, Ralph F. ... Boston, MA
Mazza, Richard J. ... Thousand Oaks, CA
Mazza, S. Paul ... State College, PA
Mazza, Schneider, Arbuckle & Bascom
Bellefonte, PA
State College, PA
Mazza, Sisto J. ... Trinidad, CO
Mazza, Susan K. ... San Diego, CA
Mazza, Thomas C. ... New York, NY
Mazza, Thomas J. ... New York, NY
Mazza, Tina L. ... Tarrytown, NY
Mazza, Vito ... Trumbull, CT
Mazzaccaro, Joseph A. ... Southington, CT
Mazzafro, Kathleen B. ... Philadelphia, PA
Mazzagatti, Linda M. ... Bellaire, TX
Mazza-Martinez, Tania A. ... Miami, FL
Mazza-Martinez, Tania A., P.A. ... Miami, FL
Mazzant, Amos L., III ... Sherman, TX
Mazzanti, Diane M. ... Scarsdale, NY
Mazzanti, Eugene J. ... Little Rock, AR
Mazzanti, Gino V. ... San Diego, CA
Mazzanti, Jerry E. ... Lake Village, AR
Mazzanti, Joseph P., III ... Lake Village, AR
Mazzanti, Mark L. ... Paoli, PA
Mazzanti, Maron & Bauman, LLP
New York, NY
Scarsdale, NY
White Plains, NY
Mazzara, Jack J. ... Troy, MI
Mazzarantani, George H. ... Sarasota, FL
Mazzarella, Daral B., (P.C.)
San Diego, CA
Mazzarella, Dunwoody & Caldarelli LLP
San Diego, CA
Mazzarella, Frank ... Leominster, MA
Mazzarella, James J. ... Westbury, NY
Mazzarella, Joseph R. ... Wallingford, CT
Mazzarella, Mark C. ... San Diego, CA
Mazzarese, Joseph M. ... Parsippany, NJ
Mazzarese, Neysa Nelms ... Miami, FL
Mazzarese, Robert A. ... Boston, MA
Mazzariello, Arcangela M. ... Gastonia, NC
Mazzariello, Michael ... Brooklyn, NY
Mazzarisi, Leonard J., Jr. ... Brooklyn, NY
Mazzarisi, Leonard J., Sr. ... Brooklyn, NY
Mazzarisi & Mazzarisi ... Brooklyn, NY
Mazzarisi, Thomas J. ... New York, NY
Mazzei, Adolph Domenic ... Suisun, CA
Mazzei and Broshot ... Steelville, MO
Mazzei, Franco ... Westmont, NJ
Philadelphia, PA
Mazzei, Gina E. ... Charleston, WV
Mazzei, Mark E. ... Pittsburgh, PA
Mazzei, Mark J. ... Boston, MA
Mazzei, Martin ... Steelville, MO
Mazzei, Patrick Joseph ... San Diego, CA
Mazzei, Richard R. ... Beachwood, NJ
Mazzei, Rocco E. ... Clarksburg, WV
Mazzei, Stephen S. ... Cincinnati, OH
Mazzei, Timothy P. ... Hauppauge, NY
Mazzela, Timothy W. ... Fresno, CA
Mazzella, Christopher R.
North Miami Beach, FL
Mazzella, Daniel T. ... San Diego, CA
Mazzella, Jennifer R. ... Stamford, CT
Mazzella, Joseph F. ... Boston, MA
Mazzella, Lauron Weilburg ... Boston, MA
Mazzella, Nancy A. ... Brooklyn, NY
Mazzeo, Anthony J. ... Virginia Beach, VA
Mazzeo, Frank A. ... Doylestown, PA
Mazzeo, James J. ... San Diego, CA
Mazzeo, Maria B. ... Honolulu, HI
Mazzeo, Mark W. ... Venice, FL
Mazzeo, Ralph R. ... Philadelphia, PA
Mazzeo, Rik ... Farmington Hills, MI
Mazzeo, Robert L. ... New York, NY
Mazzeo, Rosa ... Boston, MA
Mazzera, Snyder & De Martini
Stockton, CA
Mazzera, Thomas W. ... Stockton, CA
Mazzera, Wm. J. ... Stockton, CA
Mazzetta, Tito ... Miami, FL
Atlanta, GA
Mazzetta, Tito, & Associates, P.C.
Miami, FL
Atlanta, GA
Mazzetti, Peter P., Jr. ... White Plains, NY
Mazzia, Alexander L. ... Torrance, CA
Mazzia, Alexander L., Jr. ... Torrance, CA
Las Vegas, NV
Mazzia, Christopher M. ... Santa Rosa, CA
Mazzia, Valentino D. B. ... New York, NY
Mazzie, Carl ... Totowa, NJ
Mazzie, Joseph W., Jr. ... Springfield, MA
Mazzilli, Karen ... San Jose, CA
Mazzini, Michelle H. ... Richardson, TX
Mazzio, Mary C. ... Boston, MA
Mazzio, Philip G. ... Bloomingdale, IL
Mazziotti, Joseph R. ... Portland, ME
Mazziotti, Mary L. ... Toledo, OH
Mazziotti, Thomas J. ... Atlanta, GA
Mazzitelli and Associates, P.A.
Minneapolis, MN
Mazzitelli, John P. ... Minneapolis, MN
Mazzocca, Richard P. ... Boston, MA
Mazzochi, Deanne M. ... Chicago, IL
Mazzocone, Michael A.
San Francisco, CA
Mazzola, Francis ... Philadelphia, PA
Mazzola, John W. ... New York, NY
Mazzola, Louis E. ... Central Islip, NY
Mazzola, Russell J. ... Yakima, WA
Mazzola, Simon A. ... Redwood City, CA
Mazzola, Todd A. ... Columbus, OH
Mazzola, William J. ... Philadelphia, PA
Mazzoli, Christopher P. ... Troy, MI
Mazzoli, Henri R. ... Greensboro, NC
Mazzoli, Julio C. ... Dearborn, MI
Mazzoli, Michael R. ... Louisville, KY
Mazzoli, Romano L. ... Louisville, KY
Louisville, KY
Mazzone, A. David ... Boston, MA
Mazzone, Annemarie J. ... New York, NY
Mazzone, Dominic ... Atlanta, GA
Mazzone, James P. ... Weirton, WV
Mazzone, John Anthony ... Chicago, IL
Mazzone, Joseph R. ... Joliet, IL
Mazzone, Lewis A ... Mineola, NY
Mazzone, Lucy F. ... New York, NY
Mazzone, Margaret C. ... Brentwood, TN
Mazzone, Martha Ann ... Washington, DC
Mazzone, Michael J. ... Houston, TX
Mazzoni, James R., Jr. ... Healdsburg, CA
Mazzoni & Karam ... Scranton, PA
Mazzoni, Meghan ... San Francisco, CA
Mazzoni, Paul R. ... Scranton, PA
Mazzoni, Robert A. ... Scranton, PA
Mazzotta, D. S. ... Pittsburgh, PA
Mazzotta, James A. ... Pittsburgh, PA
Mazzotta Law Offices ... Pittsburgh, PA
Mazzotta, Salvatore A. ... Norwich, CT
Mazzotta, Thomas G. ... Albany, NY
Mazzotti, Joan C. ... Philadelphia, PA
Mazzotti, Victor L. ... Albany, NY
Mazzu, Anne Marie ... Florham Park, NJ
Mazzu, Joanne ... Marina Del Rey, CA
Mazzucchelli, Michael G.
Department Of Veterans Affairs, Board of Veterans Appeals, GV
Mazzucco, David ... New York, NY
Mazzucco, Ronald J. ... Staten Island, NY
Mazzucco, Ward J. ... Danbury, CT
Mazzuchelli, David T. ... Revere, MA
Mazzuchi, Michael A. ... Washington, DC
Mazzullo, Donald S. ... Albany, NY
Rochester, NY
Mazzullo, Michael J. ... Rochester, NY
Mba, Frank A. ... Houston, TX
Mbabazi, Deborah L. ... Brooklyn, NY
Mba-Jonas, Victor ... Hyattsville, MD
Mbamah, Donald E. ... Farmington Hills, MI
McAbee, Deborah F. ... Houston, TX
McAbee, F. Timothy ... Birmingham, AL
McAbee, Myra Wilson ... Birmingham, AL
McAchran, Kathleen L. ... Los Angeles, CA
McAdam, Barbara R. ... Indianapolis, IN
McAdam & Fallon, P.C. ... Walden, NY
McAdam, Gregory ... Walden, NY
Mc Adam, Patrick M. ... Los Angeles, CA
McAdam, Paul J. ... Roseland, NJ
McAdam, Robert M. ... Roanoke, VA
McAdam, Samuel T. ... Sacramento, CA
McAdam, Thomas A., III ... Louisville, KY
McAdam, Timothy S. ... Walden, NY
McAdams, Amanda ... Logan, UT
McAdams, Anne P. ... Houston, TX
McAdams, Barbara S. ... Memphis, TN
McAdams, Clifton J. ... Houston, TX
McAdams, David K. ... Portland, OR
McAdams, H. Hall, III ... Little Rock, AR
McAdams, Herbert H., II ... Little Rock, AR
McAdams, James M. ... Los Angeles, CA
McAdams, James R. ... Jefferson City, MO
McAdams, Jeffrey ... Brooklyn, NY
McAdams, John B. ... Fort Worth, TX
McAdams, John M., Jr.
Department of Justice, Civil Division, GV
McAdams, John P. ... Tampa, FL
McAdams, Kandi A. ... Austin, TX
McAdams, Kathleen M. ... Philadelphia, PA
McAdams, Kristin ... Raleigh, NC
McAdams, M. Mark ... Florence, SC
McAdams & Mitchell, Co., L.P.A.
Columbus, OH
McAdams, Natalie A. ... San Diego, CA
McAdams, Ponti & Wernette, P.S.
Walla Walla, WA
McAdams, Richard ... Santa Cruz, CA
McAdams, Richard H. ... Chicago, IL
McAdams, Robert W., Jr. ... Columbus, OH
McAdams, Ronald K. ... Walla Walla, WA
McAdams, Russell W.
Hot Springs National Park, AR
McAdams, Sheilah H. ... Maumee, OH
McAdams, Thomas J. ... Milwaukee, WI
McAdams, Thomas N. ... Knoxville, TN
McAdams, Thomas O. ... Winfield, IL
McAdams, Thomas O., P.C. ... Winfield, IL
McAdams, William L. ... Huntsville, TX
McAdoo, Barbara J. ... St. Paul, MN
McAdoo, Everett S., Jr. ... San Diego, CA
McAdoo, Garland H., Jr. ... Pittsburgh, PA
McAdoo, McKinley C. ... Radnor, PA
McAdoo, Michael R. ... Washington, DC
Gaithersburg, MD
Arlington, VA
McAdoo, Nina E. ... New York, NY
McAdoo, William A., Jr. ... Boston, MA
McAdoo-Brobson, Leslie S.
Washington, DC
McAdorey, Hugh ... Baltimore, MD
McAdory, Bradley D. ... Memphis, TN
McAdory, Elizabeth Cowart ... Opelika, AL
McAdory, Elizabeth Cowart, P.C.
Opelika, AL
McAdow, Jerry E. ... Madison, WI
McAdow, Sam J. ... Dublin, OH
McAfee, Anne W. ... Shepherdsville, KY
McAfee, Chesney Falk ... Memphis, TN
McAfee, Cindy Leigh ... Savannah, GA
McAfee, Eldon L. ... Des Moines, IA
McAfee, Helen Wagner
West Palm Beach, FL
McAfee, J. Kent ... Fort Worth, TX
McAfee, J. Kent, P.C., Law Offices of
Fort Worth, TX
McAfee, James ... Richmond, VA
McAfee, James E., Jr. ... Fort Lauderdale, FL
McAfee, Joe M. ... Knoxville, TN
McAfee, John D. ... Tazewell, TN
McAfee, Laura K. ... Colorado Springs, CO
McAfee, Matthew Stuart ... Jacksonville, FL
McAfee, Melinda R. ... Columbus, OH
McAfee, Richard J. ... Chattanooga, TN
McAfee, Robert John ... New Bern, NC
McAfee, Ron W. ... Memphis, TN
McAfee, Stanley R. ... Kansas City, KS
McAfee & Taft, A Professional Corporation
Oklahoma City, OK
McAfee, William J. ... West Palm Beach, FL
McAffee, Thomas B. ... Carbondale, IL
McAlarney, Julie D. ... Worcester, MA
McAlary, Frederick B., Jr. ... Andover, MA
McAlary, John J. ... Albany, NY
McAlduff, Thomas P. ... Dix Hills, NY
McAlear, Allen L. ... Bozeman, MT
McAlearney, John D., Jr. ... Redlands, CA
McAleavey, Tom ... Orlando, FL
McAlee, Joseph J. ... Philadelphia, PA
McAlee, Lawrence E. ... Philadelphia, PA
McAlee, Richard G. ... Crofton, MD
McAlee, Richard G., P.A. ... Crofton, MD
McAleenan, A. Frank ... Chicago, IL
McAleenan, Brian A. ... Chicago, IL
McAleenan, Donald F. ... Toledo, OH
McAleenan, G. Mark, Jr.
Grand Rapids, MI
McAleenan, Kevin K. ... Los Angeles, CA
McAleenan, Sharon P. ... Glendale, CA
McAleer, Charles F. B., Jr.
Washington, DC
McAleer, Daniel J. ... Philadelphia, PA
McAleer, Dennis P. ... Redding, CA
McAleer, Francis J., Jr. ... Denver, CO
McAleer, Gaskin & Johnson ... Savannah, GA
McAleer, James Edward, Jr. ... Savannah, GA
McAleer, James Farrell ... Providence, RI
McAleer, James P.
Department of Housing and Urban Development, Office of General Counsel, GV
McAleer, Joseph ... Allentown, PA
McAleer, Kathryn ... Columbia, MD
McAleer, Michael M. ... Bangor, ME
McAleese & Associates, P.C.
Washington, DC
McLean, VA
McAleese, James, Jr. ... McLean, VA
McAleese, John J., III ... Philadelphia, PA
McAleese, John J., Jr.
King Of Prussia, PA
McAleese, McGoldrick & Susanin, P.C.
King Of Prussia, PA
McAlenney, Paul F. ... Hartford, CT
Mc Alerney, Matthew J. ... McArthur, CA
McAlester, J. Mark ... Norman, OK
McAlevey, John F. ... Tallman, NY
McAlevy, Dennis D. S. ... Union City, NJ
McAlevy, Mary Grace Manion
Department of the Navy, Office of the Judge Advocate General, GV
McAlevy, Vincent W. ... Arlington, VA
McAlexander, Thomas ... Jackson, TN
Mcalhany, Gina Jolly ... Summerville, SC
McAlhany, Toni A. ... Angola, IN
Coldwater, MI
McAliley, Chris M. ... Miami, FL
McAliley, Eric L. ... Jacksonville, FL
McAliley, Gary L. ... Enterprise, AL
McAliley, Robert D. ... Fort Pierce, FL
McAliley, Stephen C.
West Palm Beach, FL
McAlilly, Stephen ... Tupelo, MS
McAlindin, Brian W. ... Newark, NJ
McAliney, Kevin P. ... Pittston, PA
McAliney & McAliney, P.C. ... Pittston, PA
Scranton, PA
Wilkes-Barre, PA
McAliney, Myles P. ... Pittston, PA
McAlister, Albert D. ... Laurens, SC
McAlister, Alister ... Wilton, CA
McAlister, Bruce K. ... Topeka, KS
McAlister, Cathy L. ... Houston, TX
Mcalister, Cynthia V. ... Raleigh, NC
McAlister, Dalton C. ... Fort Wayne, IN
McAlister, Daniel K. ... Greensboro, NC
McAlister, David B. ... Atlanta, GA

McAlister, David L. .... **Birmingham, AL**
McAlister, Don E. .... Alliance, OH
McAlister, Donald R. .... **Greenville, SC**
McAlister, Edmund S. .... Chicago, IL
McAlister, James D. .... Albuquerque, NM
McAlister, James H. .... **San Francisco, CA**
McAlister, Jamie .... Phoenix, AZ
McAlister, Joyce P. .... New York, NY
McAlister, Karla .... **Edmond, OK**
McAlister, Kenneth L. .... **Fort Worth, TX**
McAlister, Kevin S. .... New York, NY
McAlister, Kristine N. .... **Atlanta, GA**
McAlister, Lloyd G. .... **Edmond, OK**
McAlister, Martha Jett .... **Little Rock, AR**
McAlister, Mary E. .... **San Luis Obispo, CA**
McAlister, Mary E. .... **Jackson, MS**
McAlister, McAlister & Burnett, P.C.
Edmond, OK
Oklahoma City, OK
McAlister & McAlister, P.A. .... **Laurens, SC**
McAlister, Michael E. .... Little Rock, AR
McAlister, Minard A. .... Anderson, SC
McAlister, Paul W. .... **Laurens, SC**
McAlister, Robert B. .... **Columbus, OH**
McAlister, Susan Gilman
Birmingham, AL
McAlister, Thomas P. .... **New Orleans, LA**
McAlister, Vance Bryan .... **El Centro, CA**
Palm Springs, CA
San Diego, CA
McAlister, Victoria Ivy .... St. Louis, MO
McAlister, Vincent .... **Tuscumbia, AL**
McAlister, William Bruce .... Bothell, WA
McAlister, William C. .... Oklahoma City, OK
McAllen, Alfred B. .... Houston, TX
McAllen, Daniel W., III .... Dallas, TX
McAllen, Henry R. H. .... Fort Lauderdale, FL
McAllen, Peter G. .... **Los Angeles, CA**
McAllester, Allen E. .... Canton, NY
McAllester, Chamberlain .... Chattanooga, TN
McAllester & McAllester .... Chattanooga, TN
McAllester, Robert M. .... Chattanooga, TN
McAllester, Sam J., III .... **Nashville, TN**
McAllester, Sam J., Jr. .... Brentwood, TN
McAllister & Abromovitz .... **Phoenix, AZ**
Tucson, AZ
McAllister, A. D., Jr. .... Fayetteville, AR
McAllister, Alan V. .... San Jose, CA
McAllister, Amy L. .... **Phoenix, AZ**
McAllister, Bowdre Mays
Hendersonville, NC
McAllister, Brian .... Indianapolis, IN
McAllister, Brian B.A. .... New York, NY
McAllister, Bruce A.
West Palm Beach, FL
McAllister, Bruce D. .... Los Angeles, CA
McAllister, Bruce R. .... **Boise, ID**
Mcallister, Coleman J. .... **Dallas, TX**
McAllister, Conway C. .... Portland, OR
McAllister, Dale E. .... Kansas City, MO
McAllister, David E. .... **El Cajon, CA**
McAllister, David J. .... **Pittsburgh, PA**
McAllister, Douglas C. .... Washington, DC
McAllister, Douglas F. .... New York, NY
McAllister, Douglas M. .... **New Haven, CT**
McAllister, E. Craig .... Provo, UT
McAllister, Elizabeth A. .... Monticello, NY
McAllister, G. Robert .... Cazenovia, NY
McAllister, Glenn Rowe .... Ramona, CA
McAllister, Gordon D., Jr. .... Tulsa, OK
McAllister, Harl L., Jr. .... Northbrook, IL
McAllister, Hyberg & White
Atlantic City, NJ
Northfield, NJ
McAllister, J. Robert, III .... **McLean, VA**
McAllister, Jane B. .... **Des Moines, IA**
McAllister, Jane E. .... **Modesto, CA**
McAllister, Jeanann R. .... Pittsburgh, PA
McAllister, Jeffrey T. .... **Great Falls, MT**
McAllister, Jennifer L. .... Houston, TX
McAllister, John .... Salt Lake City, UT
McAllister, John D., Jr. .... King Of Prussia, PA
McAllister, John M. .... Philadelphia, PA
McAllister, John M. "Bo" .... Little Rock, AR
McAllister, John M., P.A. .... Little Rock, AR
McAllister, John P. .... **Washington, DC**
McAllister, Kathleen S. .... **Pittsburgh, PA**
McAllister, Kenneth K.
Belvedere-Tiburon, CA
McAllister, Kenneth W. .... **Columbia, SC**
McAllister, Kent W. .... Washington, DC
McAllister, Kevin J. .... **Providence, RI**
McAllister, Kirk W. .... **Modesto, CA**
McAllister Law Office .... **Mt. Pleasant, IA**
McAllister, Lawana M. .... Newell, NC
McAllister, Lorna J. .... **Bronx, NY**
McAllister, Lucie M. .... **Miami, FL**
McAllister, Lucy S. .... San Jose, CA
McAllister, Marcia .... Palatine, IL
McAllister, Margaret A. .... **Moorestown, NJ**
Philadelphia, PA
McAllister, Marlis .... San Jose, CA
McAllister & McAllister .... **Modesto, CA**
McAllister & McCarthy .... San Jose, CA
McAllister, Michael D. .... New York, NY
McAllister, Michael J. .... **New York, NY**
McAllister, Michael L. .... **Phoenix, AZ**
McAllister & Murphy, P.C. .... **Denver, CO**
McAllister, Nancy E. .... **Orange, CA**
McAllister, Neil R., Jr. .... Sacramento, CA
McAllister, Newman E.
Colorado Springs, CO
McAllister, Patrick D. .... **Aspen, CO**
McAllister, Patrick D., P.C. .... **Aspen, CO**
McAllister, Patrick F. .... **Jackson, MS**
McAllister, Paul J. .... New York, NY
McAllister, R. Conner .... **Jackson, MS**
McAllister, Ralph A. .... Cleveland, OH
McAllister, Rande A. .... **Mt. Pleasant, IA**
McAllister, Ray E. .... Lake San Marcos, CA
McAllister, Richard G. .... Boston, MA
McAllister, Robert A., Jr. .... Houston, TX
McAllister, Robert D. .... Chesterfield, MO
McAllister, Robert H. .... Menasha, WI
McAllister, Robert L. .... Wayland, NY
McAllister, Robert N. .... **Northfield, NJ**
McAllister, Robert T. .... **Denver, CO**
McAllister, Robert W. .... Northfield, IL
McAllister, Robert W., Ltd. .... Northfield, IL
McAllister, Scott A. .... Essex Junction, VT
McAllister, Sherrie Thompson
Claremore, OK
Tulsa, OK
McAllister, Singleton B.
Agency for International Development,
Office of the General Counsel, GV
McAllister, Stephen P. .... **Atlanta, GA**
McAllister, Stephen R. .... Lawrence, KS
McAllister, Susan Pannell .... **Raleigh, NC**
McAllister, Terrence J. .... **Stamford, CT**
McAllister, Thomas L. .... **Las Vegas, NV**
McAllister & Wade, P.L.C. .... Fayetteville, AR
McAllister, William C. .... Billings, MT
McAllister, William J. .... Seattle, WA
McAllister, William M. .... **Portland, OR**
McAllister, William W., Jr.
Cambridge, MD
McAlmon, George A. .... El Paso, TX
McAlonan, Francis R. .... Philadelphia, PA
McAlonan, John P. .... **Murray Hill, NJ**
McAlonan, Kevin J. .... Phoenix, AZ
McAlonan, Raymond E. .... Lake Success, NY
McAloon & Friedman, P.C.
Palisades Park, NJ
New York, NY
McAloon, George P. .... Alexandria Bay, NY
McAloon, Leo R., III .... **New Orleans, LA**
McAloon, Michelle .... **Los Angeles, CA**
McAloon, Paul F. .... New York, NY
McAloon, Paul F., P.C. .... New York, NY
McAloon, Timothy P. .... **Boston, MA**
McAlpin, America L. .... **Highland, IN**
McAlpin & Brais, P.A. .... **Miami, FL**
McAlpin, Dolton W. .... **Starkville, MS**
McAlpin, Dolton W., P.A. .... **Starkville, MS**
McAlpin & Henson, A Professional Corporation
Atlanta, GA
McAlpin, James J., Jr. .... **Atlanta, GA**
McAlpin, Kirk M. .... Savannah, GA
McAlpin, Kirk M., Jr. .... Atlanta, GA
McAlpin & Northwood, A Professional Corporation .... **Covina, CA**
Pomona, CA
McAlpin, Richard J. .... **Miami, FL**
McAlpin, V. J. .... **Covina, CA**
McAlpine, Anne Saad .... **Detroit, MI**
McAlpine, Cheree L. .... Palo Alto, CA
McAlpine, Douglas J. .... **Atlanta, GA**
McAlpine, Eric P. .... **Chicago, IL**
McAlpine, Frank D. .... Lansing, MI
McAlpine, Fraser A. .... **Houston, TX**
McAlpine, Kenneth R. .... St. Clair Shores, MI
McAlpine, Linda S. .... Bloomfield Hills, MI
McAlpine, Mark L. .... Bloomfield Hills, MI
McAlpine & McAlpine, P.C.
Bloomfield Hills, MI
McAlpine, Michael J. .... Sparta, WI
McAlpine, Michael L. .... **New Orleans, LA**
McAlpine, Peuler & Cozad, A Professional Law Corporation .... **New Orleans, LA**
Houston, TX
McAlpine, Stephen A. .... Anchorage, AK
McAlpine, Suzanne L. .... **New Haven, CT**
McAlpine, Thomas R. .... **Mobile, AL**
McAlpin-Grant, Lola M. .... Inglewood, CA
McAlvanah, Thomas P. .... **Dade City, FL**
McAlvanah, Thomas P. .... **Zephyrhills, FL**
McAlvanah, William E. .... Clifton, NJ
McAmis, Agnes W. .... Greeneville, TN
McAmis, Donald M.
Department of Agriculture,
Office of the General Counsel, GV
McAmis, Edwin E. .... Miami, FL
McAmis, Elizabeth Lee .... **Tacoma, WA**
McAnallen, Jeffery O. .... **Aurora, CO**
McAnalley, Lynley Killough .... Plano, TX
McAnally, Carolyn S. .... Bradbury, CA
McAnally, Daniel P. .... Chicago, IL
McAnally, Patricia E. .... Franklin, TN
McAnally, Perry A. .... Edmond, OK
McAnally, Richard L. .... **Tucson, AZ**
McAnaney & Associates .... **Boise, ID**
McAnaney, Brian T. .... **Stamford, CT**
McAnaney, David P. .... **Boise, ID**
McAnaney, Edward G. .... New York, NY
McAnaney, Frank, Jr. .... **New York, NY**
Mcananey, Joseph E. .... Suffield, CT
McAnaney, Kevin G. .... Washington, DC
McAnanly, Robert F., Jr. .... Hackensack, NJ
McAnany, Christopher G.
Grand Junction, CO
McAnany, Lisa D. .... **Pittsburgh, PA**
McAnany, Patrick Bevan .... Olathe, KS
McAnany, Patrick D. .... Chicago, IL
McAnany, Patrick D. .... Lenexa, KS
McAnany, Van Cleave & Phillips, P.A.
Kansas City, KS
Lenexa, KS
St. Louis, MO
McAndrew, Amy G. .... **Berwyn, PA**
McAndrew, Catherine D. .... Sacramento, CA
McAndrew, Conboy & Prisco
Mineola, NY
New York, NY
Riverhead, NY
Woodbury, NY
McAndrew, Dennis C. .... Wayne, PA
McAndrew, Edward J. .... **Washington, DC**
McAndrew, Eileen T. .... Oakland, CA
McAndrew, Gregory M. .... **New York, NY**
McAndrew, John K. .... **Rochester, NY**
McAndrew, Karen .... **Burlington, VT**
McAndrew, Kevin B. .... **Woodbury, NY**
McAndrew, Kimberly A. .... Philadelphia, PA
McAndrew, Mark .... **Lake Success, NY**
McAndrew, Mark J. .... **Downers Grove, IL**
McAndrew, Melissa A. .... **New York, NY**
McAndrew, Michael R. .... Oswego, NY
McAndrew, Patrick F. .... Medford, NJ
McAndrew, Patrick J. .... Beltsville, MD
McAndrew, Paul J., Jr. .... **Iowa City, IA**
McAndrew, Robert .... Columbus, OH
McAndrew, Robert H. .... Hoboken, NJ
McAndrew, Robert W. .... New Brunswick, NJ
McAndrew, Sara
Nuclear Regulatory Commission,
Office of the General Counsel, GV
McAndrew, Stephen F. .... Woodland Hills, CA
McAndrew, Susan D. .... Washington, DC
McAndrew, Thomas J. .... **Providence, RI**
McAndrew, Thomas J., Esq., Ltd.
Providence, RI
McAndrew, Thomas P. .... Pontiac, MI
McAndrew, Thomas X., Jr. .... **Exton, PA**
McAndrew, W. Scott .... **Madison, WI**
McAndrews, Alicia Taylor .... **Torrance, CA**
McAndrews, Anne Hewitt .... Larchmont, NY
McAndrews, Colleen C. .... Santa Monica, CA
McAndrews & Cunabaugh, P.C.
McHenry, IL
McAndrews, Dennis C. .... Wayne, PA
McAndrews, George .... Alexandria, VA
McAndrews, George P. .... **Chicago, IL**
McAndrews, Held & Malloy, Ltd.
Chicago, IL
McAndrews, James P. .... Attleboro, MA
McAndrews, James P. .... Cleveland, OH
McAndrews, James P., III .... **McLean, VA**
McAndrews, John G. .... **New York, NY**
McAndrews, John M. .... **Chicago, IL**
Des Plaines, IL
McAndrews, Lauren S. .... **Pittsburgh, PA**
McAndrews, Matthew G. .... **Chicago, IL**
McAndrews, Michael A. .... **Los Angeles, CA**
McAndrews, Patrick J. .... McHenry, IL
McAndrews, Peter F. .... Santa Monica, CA
McAndrews, Peter J. .... **Chicago, IL**
McAndrews, R. Barry .... Doylestown, PA
McAndrews, Roland George, Jr.
Washington, DC
McAndrews, Thomas F.
Manhattan Beach, CA
McAndrews, William J. .... **New York, NY**
McAnelly, David F. .... Liberty, KY
McAnelly, Elaine S. .... **Houston, TX**
McAnelly, Eric B. .... Houston, TX
McAnelly, Robert V. .... Baton Rouge, LA
McAnelly, Robert V. .... Houston, TX
McAnelly, W. James .... **Houston, TX**
McAnelly, W. James, Jr. .... **Houston, TX**
McAneney, Andrew M. .... **Doylestown, PA**
Philadelphia, PA
Mc Aneney, John J. .... **Fort Washington, PA**
McAneny, Eileen S. .... Philadelphia, PA
McAneny, James L. .... Harrisburg, PA
McAneny, Redmond "Pete"
Newport Beach, CA
McAnerney, Robert M. .... **Stamford, CT**
McAnespie, Thomas P. .... Dracut, MA
McAngus, Goudelock & Courie, L.L.C.
Charlotte, NC
Columbia, SC
McAngus, W. Hugh .... **Columbia, SC**
McAniff, Edward J. .... **Los Angeles, CA**
San Francisco, CA
McAniff, Peter J. .... New York, NY
McAninch, Barbara .... Dallas, TX
McAninch, Douglas A. .... **Houston, TX**
McAninch, Edwin Lee .... **Houston, TX**
McAninch, William S. .... Columbia, SC
McAnnally, L. Thomas
Green Cove Springs, FL
McAnnally, Robert S. .... **Decatur, AL**
McAnney, Christine M. .... **McLean, VA**
McAnney, Jonathan S. .... **Pittsburgh, PA**
McAnulty, Dorothea .... Springfield, IL
McAnulty, Francis J. .... **Rochester, MN**
McAnulty, Mark A. .... **Evansville, IN**
McAnulty, Vera Sanchas .... Pittsburgh, PA
McAnulty, William E., Jr. .... Louisville, KY
McAra, Bernard L. .... **Flint, MI**
McAra, Michael D. .... Flint, MI
McAravy, Patrick A. .... Sacramento, CA
McArdle, Andrea L. .... New York, NY
McArdle, Anne M. .... Pittsburgh, PA
McArdle, Bernard T. .... Greensburg, PA
McArdle, Brian D. .... Randolph, NJ
McArdle, Bruce A. .... Kingsport, TN
McArdle, David A. .... St. Charles, IL
McArdle, David W. .... **Crystal Lake, IL**
McArdle, Edward F. .... Syracuse, NY
McArdle, Elaine .... Boston, MA
McArdle & Fahy .... New Orleans, LA
McArdle, J. Patrick .... Wilber, NE
McArdle, James J. .... Seattle, WA
McArdle, John A., III .... Portland, ME
McArdle, John J. .... Boston, MA
McArdle, John J., Jr. .... Lexington, KY
McArdle, Joyce L. .... St. Charles, IL
McArdle, J. W. "Bill" .... Yakima, WA
McArdle, Kevin M. .... Lowville, NY
McArdle, Kevin S. .... Hackensack, NJ
McArdle, Laura Ann .... Chicago, IL
McArdle, Lisa M. .... **Santa Ana, CA**
McArdle, Margaret L. .... Sarasota, FL
McArdle, Maureen .... **Newton, MA**
McArdle, Michael J. .... Chicago, IL
McArdle, Michael M. .... Marblehead, MA
McArdle, Michael W. .... **Naples, FL**
McArdle, Patrick D. .... New Orleans, LA
McArdle, Patrick F. .... Port Charlotte, FL
Sarasota, FL
McArdle, Paul J. .... Pittsburgh, PA
McArdle, Paul J. .... Pittsburgh, PA
McArdle, Peter E. .... Charlotte, NC
McArdle, Richard P. .... **Chicago, IL**
McArdle, Robert P. .... **Bloomfield Hills, MI**
McArdle & Schmoyer .... Port Charlotte, FL
Sarasota, FL
McArdle, Scott A. .... Edmond, OK
McArdle, Scott T. .... **Montgomery, AL**
McArdle, Steven J. .... Crystal Lake, IL
McArdle, Thomas F. .... San Diego, CA
McArdle, Thomas J. .... Toledo, OH
McArdle, Tim .... Sacramento, CA
McArdle, Timothy I. .... Chicago, IL
McArdle, Vincent J., Jr. .... Albany, NY
McArdle, W. Elgine Heceta
Wheeling, WV
McArdle, Walter F. .... **Birmingham, AL**
McAree, Timothy M. .... **Grand Rapids, MI**
McArn, Heather D. .... **New York, NY**
McArthur, A. James .... Lincoln, NE
McArthur, Alan D. .... United States Senate,
Senatorial Assistants, GV
McArthur, B. Palmer, Jr. .... **Charlotte, NC**
McArthur, Bruce C. F. .... **Walnut Creek, CA**
McArthur, C. Douglas
General Accounting Office,
Office of the General Counsel, GV
McArthur, Caleb J. .... Cleveland, OH
McArthur, Cathy Felty .... Dallas, TX
McArthur, Clovis W., Jr. .... **El Paso, TX**
McArthur, Connolly Clark .... **Tampa, FL**
McArthur, Craig W. .... West Jordan, UT
McArthur, Dana G. .... **Dallas, TX**
McArthur, Donna L. .... Seattle, WA
McArthur, Dorothy W. .... **Memphis, TN**
McArthur, Douglas .... Lincoln, NE
McArthur, E. Pamela .... Bel Air, MD
McArthur, E.J. (Mac), Jr. .... Montgomery, AL
McArthur, Elizabeth Waas
Tallahassee, FL
McArthur, Francis R. .... Northridge, CA
McArthur, George W. .... Purchase, NY
McArthur, James R. .... Wickenburg, AZ
McArthur, John A. .... Fenton, MO
McArthur, John B. .... **Columbia, SC**
McArthur, John Jay .... **Athens, GA**
McArthur, John R. .... Raleigh, NC
McArthur, John T. .... **Maryville, TN**
McArthur, K. Scott .... Monmouth, OR
McArthur, Karen E. .... **Stamford, CT**
McArthur, Katherine L. .... **Atlanta, GA**
Macon, GA
McArthur, Kenneth D., Jr. .... **Richmond, VA**
McArthur, K. Scott, P.C. .... Monmouth, OR
McArthur, Lisa C. .... **Los Angeles, CA**
McArthur, Malcolm C. .... **Athens, GA**
McArthur, Mark A. .... Anchorage, AK
McArthur, Matthew R. .... Olympia Fields, IL
McArthur & McArthur, P.A. .... **Athens, GA**
McArthur & McGuire .... Wickenburg, AZ
McArthur, M.R., & Associates, Ltd.
Olympia Fields, IL
McArthur, Neill W., Jr. .... Jacksonville, FL
McArthur, Peter V. .... Pompton Plains, NJ
McArthur, R. Lee .... Panama City, FL
McArthur, Robert .... **Los Angeles, CA**
McArthur, Sara Miller .... **Athens, GA**
McArthur, Todd Y. .... **Washington, DC**
McArthur, Virginia A., Law Office of
Washington, DC
McArthur, Walter L. .... Visalia, CA
McArthur-Phillips, Mike ("McP")
Portland, OR
McArtney, Barbara .... Grand Island, NY
McArtor, Keith Overton .... Tulsa, OK
McArtor, Tanya L. .... Grant, NE
McArty, Robert L. .... Jackson, MS
McArver, R. Dennis .... **McLean, VA**
McAsey, Christine .... **Joliet, IL**
McAshan, Karen D. .... Houston, TX
McAskin, Thomas R. .... Royal Oak, MI
McAtee, David R. .... **Dallas, TX**
McAtee, David R., II .... **Dallas, TX**
McAtee, Fred S. .... Bakersfield, CA
McAtee, Greg A. .... San Diego, CA
McAtee, Gregory B. .... Mobile, AL
McAtee, Gregory B., P.C. .... Mobile, AL
McAtee, J. Stuart .... **Birmingham, AL**
McAtee, Jane A. .... Chicago, IL
McAtee, Linda K. .... Sacramento, CA
McAtee, M. Anne .... Davenport, IA
McAtee, Michael G. .... Oklahoma City, OK
McAtee, Miles F. .... Seattle, WA
McAtee, R. Jay .... **Tulsa, OK**
McAtee, Richard S. .... **Pittsburgh, PA**
McAtee, Sparrell H. .... Houston, TX
McAteer, Christopher E. .... San Diego, CA
McAteer, Daniel J. .... Troy, MO
McAteer, Dennis .... **San Francisco, CA**
McAteer, J. Davitt .... Department of Labor,
Office of the Solicitor, GV
McAteer, James F. .... **Seattle, WA**
McAteer, James H. .... Baltimore, MD
McAteer, James H., P.A. .... Baltimore, MD
McAteer, Melanie .... West Chester, PA
McAteer, Michael M. .... Providence, RI
McAteer, Sheilagh A. .... Colorado Springs, CO
McAteer, Theresa Castagneto
San Diego, CA

McAughan, Robert J., Jr. ... Houston, TX
McAulay, F. Lawrence, Jr. ... Lenexa, KS
McAulay, Lloyd ... New York, NY
McAulay Nissen Goldberg Kiel & Hand, LLP ... New York, NY
McAuley, Bernard J. ... Pittsburgh, PA
Mcauley, Daniel G., Jr. ... Medford, MA
McAuley, Donan B. ... Rock Island, IL
McAuley, Gordon D. ... San Francisco, CA
McAuley, James ... Tallahassee, FL
McAuley, John G. ... Chicago, IL
McAuley, Malcolm D., III ... Pontotoc, MS
McAuley, Meagan ... Lafayette, IN
McAuley, Michael J. ... Chicago, IL
McAuley, Michael P. ... Boston, MA
McAuley, Patrick J. ... Roseland, NJ
McAuley, Steven Anthony
Minneapolis, MN
McAuley, Sula S. ... Memphis, TN
McAuley, Thomas ... New York, NY
McAuley, Thomas J. ... Howell, NJ
Mcauley, Timothy J. ... Norwalk, CT
McAuliff, David J. ... Oakland, CA
McAuliff, James A. ... Tulsa, OK
McAuliff, James L., Jr. ... Chicago, IL
McAuliffe, Barbara A. ... Fresno, CA
McAuliffe, Brian J. ... Albuquerque, NM
McAuliffe, Brian Shawn ... Houston, TX
McAuliffe, Cathe Donham ... Hackensack, NJ
McAuliffe, Charles H. ... Livingston, NJ
McAuliffe, Christopher J. ... Morristown, NJ
McAuliffe, Conor ... Chicago, IL
McAuliffe, Daneil M. ... Tampa, FL
McAuliffe, Daniel C. ... Denver, CO
McAuliffe, Daniel J. ... Phoenix, AZ
McAuliffe, Daniel J. ... St. Louis, MO
McAuliffe, Don S. ... Canal Winchester, OH
McAuliffe, E. Timothy ... New York, NY
McAuliffe, Edward Timothy, Jr.
New York, NY
McAuliffe, Gerard S. ... Quincy, MA
McAuliffe, Gervais Ward, III ... Spokane, WA
McAuliffe, Hinson ... Atlanta, GA
McAuliffe, J. Gary ... San Francisco, CA
McAuliffe, J. Gerard, Jr. ... Mayfield, NY
McAuliffe, J. Gregory ... Denver, CO
McAuliffe, J. Stephen, III ... Rockville, MD
McAuliffe, Jack I. ... Reno, NV
McAuliffe, Jack I., Chtd. ... Reno, NV
McAuliffe, James S., Jr. ... Potomac, MD
McAuliffe, Jennifer Toolin ... Boston, MA
McAuliffe, Jeremiah D. ... Chicago, IL
McAuliffe, John E., Jr. ... Metairie, LA
McAuliffe, John F. ... Rockville, MD
McAuliffe, John J., Jr. ... Philadelphia, PA
McAuliffe, John Michael ... Boston, MA
McAuliffe, John P. ... Chicago, IL
McAuliffe, Jon A. ... Tampa, FL
McAuliffe, Joseph S. ... Wayne, NJ
McAuliffe, Kathleen M.
House of Representatives, Congressional Assistants, GV
McAuliffe, Kevin J.
St. Petersburg Beach, FL
McAuliffe, Kevin R. ... Syracuse, NY
McAuliffe Law Firm, The, L.L.P.
St. Louis, MO
McAuliffe, Lawrence F. ... Pepperell, MA
McAuliffe, Leo ... Quincy, MA
McAuliffe, Lester E. ... Chicago, IL
McAuliffe, Martin G. ... Tempe, AZ
Las Vegas, NV
McAuliffe, Mary M. ... Brockton, MA
McAuliffe & McAuliffe ... Wakefield, MA
McAuliffe, Michael F. ... Palm Beach, FL
McAuliffe, Michael G. ... Westbury, NY
McAuliffe, Michael J. ... Glastonbury, CT
McAuliffe, Michael J. ... Washington, DC
Frederick, MD
Rockville, MD
McAuliffe, Michael Thomas ... Reno, NV
McAuliffe, Patricia ... Southfield, MI
McAuliffe, Philip L., Jr. ... Wakefield, MA
McAuliffe, R. Emmett ... St. Louis, MO
McAuliffe, Robert E. ... Oak Park, IL
McAuliffe, Robert J. ... Department of Justice, Civil Division, GV
Mcauliffe, Rosemary ... Boston, MA
McAuliffe, Sharon A. ... Syracuse, NY
McAuliffe, Stephanie Cutting
Cambridge, MA
McAuliffe, Steven J. ... Concord, NH
McAuliffe, Susan ... Houston, TX
McAuliffe, Susan Kozinn
General Accounting Office, Office of the General Counsel, GV
McAuliffe, Susan Rotatori
Washington, DC
McAuliffe, Terence R. ... Washington, DC
McAuliffe, Terry ... Los Angeles, CA
Mc Ausland, K. Iain ... Palo Alto, CA
McAusland, L. Iana ... Menlo Park, CA
McAvey, Joanne Schlenk ... Deer Park, NY
McAviney, Donald ... Wilmington, DE
McAvoy, Bahn & Tolin ... Fenton, MO
McAvoy, Brian V. ... Fort Myers, FL
Naples, FL
McAvoy, Colleen E. ... San Mateo, CA
McAvoy, David Robert ... Indianapolis, IN
McAvoy, Garrett J. ... Charlotte, NC
McAvoy, Gerald F. ... Providence, RI
Mcavoy, James A., Jr ... Melrose, MA
McAvoy, John J. ... San Diego, CA
McAvoy, John J. ... Washington, DC
McAvoy, John S. ... Clearwater, FL
McAvoy, Katherine A. ... Chicago, IL
McAvoy, Laura K. ... Oxnard, CA
McAvoy, Michael J. ... Fenton, MO
McAvoy, Peter M. ... South Hadley, MA
McAvoy, Sean M. ... Cleveland, OH
McAvoy, Stephen H. ... San Diego, CA
McAvoy, Terrence P. ... Chicago, IL
McAvoy, Thomas J. ... Binghamton, NY
McAvoy, Timothy R. ... Flossmoor, IL
McAvoy, William M. ... Boston, MA
McAweeney, Peter F. ... San Francisco, CA
McBain, James K. ... Seattle, WA
McBain, Nola Mae ... Palo Alto, CA
McBain, Robert P. ... Grand Rapids, MI
McBain, Scott A. ... Cleveland, OH
McBain, Wm. H. ... Duxbury, MA
McBaine, John N. ... San Francisco, CA
McBaine, Turner H. ... San Francisco, CA
McBaine-Cook, Diana D. ... New York, NY
McBane, Louis R., (P.A.)
West Palm Beach, FL
McBarnette, Andrea ... New York, NY
McBarnette, Bruce O. ... Sterling, VA
McBarron, James P. ... Roseland, NJ
McBath, Donald Linus, Jr ... Tampa, FL
McBath & Godsey ... Tampa, FL
McBath, Jennifer Margot ... Atlanta, GA
McBath, Tom R. ... Corpus Christi, TX
McBay, William R. ... Santa Clara, CA
McBeath, Gretchen A. ... Columbus, OH
McBeath, Marc D. ... Lubbock, TX
McBeath, Michael K. ... Las Vegas, NV
McBeath, Michael K., Ltd., Law Offices of
Las Vegas, NV
McBeath, Robert English ... Frankfort, KY
McBee, Anne P. ... Florence, KY
McBee, Barry R. ... Dallas, TX
McBee, Benson & Benson, A Professional Corporation ... Frederick, OK
McBee, Clint M. ... Toledo, OH
McBee, Dalton, Jr. ... Jackson, MS
McBee, Donald L. ... Grand Junction, CO
McBee & Ford ... Winchester, TN
McBee, George H. ... Poteau, OK
McBee, Howard M. ... Frederick, OK
McBee, L. L. "Mick", Jr. ... Dallas, TX
McBee, Michael ... Baltimore, MD
McBee, Mick, P.C., Law Offices of
Dallas, TX
McBee, Robert F. ... Houston, TX
McBee, Scott A. ... Houston, TX
McBee, Thomas C. ... Winchester, TN
McBee, William A. ... Hobbs, NM
McBennett, Cindy Marisa ... New York, NY
McBennett, Larry D. ... Raleigh, NC
McBeth, Anthony T. ... Harrisburg, PA
McBeth, Charles R. ... Richardson, TX
McBeth, Dan C. ... Trenton, TN
McBeth, Gerald D. ... Nevada, MO
McBeth, Robert ... Renton, WA
Mcbeth, Robert F. ... Livonia, MI
McBeth, Ronald W. ... Wahpeton, ND
McBeth, Steven J. ... Cincinnati, OH
McBirney, Bruce H. ... Los Angeles, CA
McBirney & Chuck, P.C.
Los Angeles, CA
Mcbirnie, Carol M. ... Arroyo Grande, CA
McBirnie, Thomas J., Jr. ... San Francisco, CA
McBlain, John P. ... Media, PA
McBlief, William ... Winston-Salem, NC
Mcbrady, James A. ... Portland, ME
McBratney, Dorothea A. ... Annapolis, MD
McBratney, James T., Jr. ... Florence, SC
McBratnie, Michael C. ... Exton, PA
McBrayer, Annette Kerlin ... Atlanta, GA
McBrayer, Arthur ... Phoenix, AZ
McBrayer, John A. ... Pelham, AL
McBrayer, Karen L. ... Marietta, GA
McBrayer, McGinnis, Leslie & Kirkland
Frankfort, KY
Greenup, KY
Lexington, KY
McBrayer, Sharon L. ... Atlanta, GA
McBrayer, W. Neal ... Nashville, TN
McBrayer, W. Terry ... Frankfort, KY
Greenup, KY
Lexington, KY
McBrearty, Brian K. ... St. Louis, MO
McBrearty & Huck ... St. Louis, MO
McBrearty, John ... Long Beach, CA
McBrearty, Mary Ella ... San Antonio, TX
McBrearty, Susan Lynch ... Chicago, IL
McBrearty, William R., Jr.
Grosse Pointe Park, MI
McBreen, Hugh G. ... Chicago, IL
McBreen & Kopko ... Irvine, CA
Chicago, IL
Montvale, NJ
Philadelphia, PA
McBreen, Maura Ann ... Chicago, IL
McBreen, Michele Tate ... Chicago, IL
McBreen, Paul J. ... Chicago, IL
McBreen, Peter James ... Los Angeles, CA
McBreen & Senior ... Los Angeles, CA
McBreen, Siobhan E. ... Chicago, IL
McBride, Albert, Jr. ... Pittsburgh, PA
McBride, Andrew F., III
Liberty Corner, NJ
McBride, Andrew G. ... Washington, DC
McBride, AndrewR. ... Norcross, GA
McBride & Associates, P.C.
Oklahoma City, OK
McBride, B. Gary ... Toledo, OH
McBride, B. Scott ... Houston, TX
McBride Baker & Coles ... Chicago, IL
Oakbrook Terrace, IL
McBride, Barbara A. ... Department of Defense, Office of the General Counsel, GV
McBride, Barry ... Santa Rosa, CA
McBride, Bemon G., III ... Columbus, GA
McBride, Beverly J. ... Maumee, OH
McBride, Bill ... Tampa, FL
McBride, Brenda K. ... Grove City, PA
McBride, Brendan K. ... San Antonio, TX
McBride, Brian A. ... Cleveland, OH
McBride, C. Donald ... San Jose, CA
McBride, C. Gordon ... Hartsville, SC
McBride, C. Kathleen ... Butte, MT
McBride, Charles L. ... Stillwater, OK
McBride, Charles L., Jr. ... Jackson, MS
McBride, Cheryl L. ... Harrisburg, PA
McBride, Christine A. ... Denver, CO
McBride, Clifford C. ... Florence, SC
McBride & Collier ... Alexandria, LA
McBride, Curtis W. ... Pittsburgh, PA
McBride, D. Michael, III ... Tulsa, OK
McBride, Dale ... Morgantown, WV
McBride, Dale R. ... Covina, CA
McBride, Dana Farrell ... Atlanta, GA
McBride, Daniel G. ... San Francisco, CA
Chicago, IL
McBride, Danny R. ... Chicago, IL
McBride, Darren G. ... Chattanooga, TN
McBride, David C. ... Wilmington, DE
McBride, David C. ... Danvers, MA
McBride, David F. ... Hackensack, NJ
McBride, David N. ... Chicago, IL
McBride, Denis P. ... Cherry Hill, NJ
Philadelphia, PA
McBride, Dennis M. ... Odessa, DE
Wilmington, DE
McBride, Dennis M. ... Cleveland, OH
McBride, Dennis R. ... Milwaukee, WI
McBride, Derek G. ... Detroit, MI
McBride, Donna E. ... Rockville, MD
McBride, Douglas J. ... New York, NY
McBride, Edward ... Naples, FL
McBride, Edward J. ... Pullman, WA
McBride, Edward J., Jr. ... Cherry Hill, NJ
Philadelphia, PA
McBride, Edward W. ... Salt Lake City, UT
McBride, Eileen L. ... Omaha, NE
McBride, Elizabeth Aulik
Palos Verdes Estates, CA
McBride, Elizabeth M. ... Spokane, WA
McBride, Elizabeth Threatt ... Miami, FL
McBride, Elizabeth W. ... Columbus, GA
McBride, Floyd ... St. Louis, MO
McBride, Foret, Rozas & Leonard, A Law Corporation ... Lafayette, LA
McBride, Francis G. ... Fairfax, VA
McBride, Frederick L. ... Santa Ana, CA
McBride, G. Scott ... Bucyrus, OH
McBride, Galen (Allen) W. ... Alexandria, LA
McBride, Gerald ... Fort Myers, FL
McBride, Gregory B.
Department of Transportation, Federal Transit Administration, GV
McBride, H. Colin ... New York, NY
McBride, Hesser G., Jr. ... Woodbridge, NJ
McBride, Hubert A. ... Memphis, TN
McBride, Inez M. ... San Antonio, TX
McBride, J. Calvin ... Decatur, AL
McBride, J. Kevin ... McHenry, IL
McBride, J. Lawrence ... Pittsburgh, PA
McBride, J. Michael ... Fort Worth, TX
McBride, J. Michael, P.C.
Fort Worth, TX
McBride, James DeWitt ... Redmond, WA
Seattle, WA
McBride, James E. ... Pittsburgh, PA
McBride, James F. ... Woodbury, NJ
Philadelphia, PA
McBride, James J. ... Redwood City, CA
San Francisco, CA
McBride, James L. ... Ventura, CA
McBride, James P. ... Hayward, CA
McBride, James R. ... Chicago, IL
McBride, James T. ... The Woodlands, TX
McBride, James W. ... Long Beach, CA
McBride, James W. ... Washington, DC
McBride, Jerry P. ... Atlanta, GA
McBride, Jerry R. ... Batavia, OH
McBride, John ... San Jose, CA
McBride, John B. ... Albany, NY
McBride, John C., Law Offices of
Boston, MA
McBride, John D. ... Wichita, KS
McBride, John F. ... Denver, CO
McBride, John K. ... Lafayette, IN
McBride, John L. ... Leesburg, VA
McBride, John P. ... Cheyenne, WY
McBride, John R. ... Minneapolis, MN
McBride, Joseph A. ... Norwich, NY
McBride, Joseph F., P.A. ... Silver Spring, MD
McBride, Joseph M. ... New York, NY
McBride, Joseph V. ... New York, NY
McBride, Judith Bliss ... Brecksville, OH
McBride, Justin H. ... Foley, MN
McBride, Karen L. ... Bismarck, ND
McBride, Karyn D. ... Austin, MN
McBride, Katherine A. ... Minneapolis, MN
McBride, Keith W. ... Sacramento, CA
McBride, Kenneth E. ... Oklahoma City, OK
McBride, Kerri L. ... Chicago, IL
McBride, Kerry L. ... Corona, CA
McBride, Kevin G. ... Los Angeles, CA
McBride, Kevin P. ... Salt Lake City, UT
McBride, Kim E. ... Redwood City, CA
McBride, Kurt R. ... Cozad, NE
McBride, L. David ... Oklahoma City, OK
McBride, Larry ... San Diego, CA
McBride, Laurie J. ... Chicago, IL
McBride, Lawrence G. ... Washington, DC
McBride, Leonard H. ... Norco, CA
McBride, Lois A. Fenner ... Baltimore, MD
Mcbride, Marc D. ... Rialto, CA
McBride, Margaret Stanton
Rolling Meadows, IL
McBride, Mark R. ... Cincinnati, OH
Toledo, OH
McBride, Matthew ... Minneapolis, MN
McBride, Matthew S. ... St. Louis, MO
McBride, Maureen ... Detroit, MI
McBride, Maureen Murphy
West Chester, PA
McBride, Maurice H. ... Washington, DC
McBride and McBride, P.C.
Grove City, PA
McBride, Michael D. ... Waterford, MI
McBride, Michael F. ... Washington, DC
McBride, Michael F. ... Seattle, WA
McBride, Michael L. ... Cincinnati, OH
McBride, Michael R. ... Idaho Falls, ID
McBride, Michael S. ... New York, NY
McBride, Michael X. ... Roseland, NJ
McBride, Milford L., III ... Grove City, PA
McBride, Milford L., Jr. ... Grove City, PA
McBride, Molly T. ... Buffalo, NY
McBride and Murphy ... Horsham, PA
Newtown, PA
McBride, Owen B. ... St. James, NY
McBride, Patricia A. ... Los Angeles, CA
McBride, Patricia A. ... Mercer, PA
McBride, Patrick ... Salt Lake City, UT
McBride, Patrick E. ... Seattle, WA
McBride, Patrick G. ... Milwaukee, WI
McBride, Patrick Seamus ... Denver, CO
McBride, Paul P., II ... Santa Ana, CA
McBride, Paul T. ... Irvine, CA
McBride, Peter ... Chesapeake, VA
Mcbride, Peter James ... Norwich, NY
McBride, R. Michael ... San Diego, CA
McBride, Rachelle R. ... Boca Raton, FL
McBride, Ralph C. ... Marietta, GA
McBride, Ralph D. ... Houston, TX
McBride, Ralph, Jr. ... Shelbyville, TN
McBride, Rebekah A. ... Craig, CO
McBride, Richard P. ... Horsham, PA
Newtown, PA
Mc Bride, Robert C. ... Irvine, CA
McBride, Robert C. ... Elmhurst, IL
McBride, Robert D. ... Wooster, OH
McBride, Robert E. ... Erie, PA
McBride, Robert H. ... Albuquerque, NM
McBride, Robert J. ... Canton, OH
McBride, Robert K. ... Covington, KY
McBride, Robert L. ... Dayton, OH
McBride, Robert M. ... Peoria, IL
McBride, Robert R. ... Lafayette, LA
McBride, Robert T. ... Southfield, MI
McBride, Rosemary L. ... Groton, CT
McBride, Scott P. ... Chicago, IL
McBride, Scott P. ... Melville, NY
McBride, Sean H. ... Maitland, FL
McBride, Stephen A. ... Milford, PA
McBride, Steven E. ... Englewood, CO
McBride, Steven P. ... Memphis, TN
McBride, Ted L. ... Rapid City, SD
Mc Bride, Thomas ... Alexandria, LA
McBride, Thomas F. ... Palo Alto, CA
McBride, Thomas J. ... Albuquerque, NM
McBride, Thomas J. ... Philadelphia, PA
McBride, Thomas K. ... Des Plaines, IL
McBride, Thomas M. ... Seattle, WA
McBride, Thomas O. ... Denver, CO
McBride, Thomas P. ... St. Louis, MO
McBride, Timothy B. ... Washington, DC
McBride, Tom ... St. Joseph, MO
McBride, Valeri J. ... Memphis, TN
McBride, Victor G. ... Selmer, TN
McBride, Vivian Maris ... St. Louis, MO
McBride, W. Scott ... St. Louis, MO
McBride, W. Thomas ... Cherry Hill, NJ
Philadelphia, PA
McBride, Warren L. ... Houston, TX
Mc Bride, Wayne M. ... Troy, MI
McBride, William A. ... New York, NY
McBride, William H. ... Raleigh, NC
McBride-Mouton, Peggy L. ... Lafayette, LA
McBrien, Frederick W., III ... Norristown, PA
McBrien, John J. ... Farmington, MN
McBrien, John R. ... Treasury Department, Departmental Offices, GV
McBrien, Mary ... Staten Island, NY
McBrien, Montalto & Jennings
Norristown, PA
McBrien, Morris J. ... Chattanooga, TN
McBrien, Neil ... Staten Island, NY
McBrien, Peter J. ... Sacramento, CA
McBrien, Rose M. ... New York, NY
McBrien, Shawn J. ... Lebanon, TN
McBrier, Charles R., Jr. ... Washington, DC
McBroom, Christine L. ... Cincinnati, OH
McBroom, Douglas D. ... Seattle, WA
McBroom, E. G. ... Drake, CO
McBroom, James C. ... Nashville, TN
McBroom, Maurin K. ... Seattle, WA
McBroom, Thomas W. ... Atlanta, GA
McBroom, Victoria M. ... Indianapolis, IN
McBroom-Redwine, Katherine A.
Milwaukee, WI
McBryan, Louis G. ... Atlanta, GA
McBryar, Roy E. ... Montgomery, AL
McBryde, John H. ... Fort Worth, TX
McBryde, Neill G. ... Charlotte, NC
McBurnett, Laura Gray ... Houston, TX
McBurney, Bryan A. ... Newport Beach, CA
McBurney, Charles W., Jr.
Jacksonville, FL
McBurney, Christian M. ... Washington, DC
McBurney, Cristine L. ... Pawtucket, RI
McBurney, H. Edward, Jr.
North Conway, NH
McBurney, John F. ... Pawtucket, RI
McBurney, John F., III ... Pawtucket, RI
McBurney Law Services, Inc. ... Pawtucket, RI

McBurney, Lucinda J. ... Anchorage, AK
McBurney, Mark E. ... Austin, TX
McBurnie, Richard G. ... Bakersfield, CA
McBurrows, Theodius ... Department of Justice, Justice Management Division, GV
McCaa, James C., III ... Norfolk, VA
McCaa, Janet C. ... Portland, ME
McCabe, Agnes T. ... Tampa, FL
McCabe, Alicia M. ... Irvine, CA
McCabe, Amy L. ... Indianapolis, IN
McCabe, Arthur J., II ... Andover, MA
McCabe, Barry ... Los Angeles, CA
McCabe, Bernard J. ... Clearwater, FL
McCabe, Brian D. ... Boston, MA
McCabe, Brian L. ... Merced, CA
McCabe, Brian P. S. ... Parsippany, NJ
McCabe Brown Tipton & Davis, A Professional Corporation ... Boston, MA
McCabe, C. Kevin ... Chicago, IL
McCabe, Carol Fitzpatrick ... Bala Cynwyd, PA
McCabe, Carroll L. ... Annapolis, MD
McCabe, Catherine H. ... Chicago, IL
McCabe, Catherine R. ... Department of Justice, Environment and Natural Resources Division, GV
McCabe, Chad R. ... Bismarck, ND
McCabe, Christopher I. ... Philadelphia, PA
McCabe, Christopher P. ... New York, NY
McCabe, Collins, McGeough & Fowler, LLP ... Mineola, NY
New York, NY
McCabe, Craig M. ... San Francisco, CA
McCabe, Daniel C. ... Wheaton, IL
McCabe, Daniel J. ... Poughkeepsie, NY
McCabe, Daniel M. ... Stamford, CT
McCabe, Daniel M. ... Cleveland, OH
McCabe, Daniel R. ... Fort Worth, TX
McCabe, David J. ... New York, NY
McCabe and Delyani, P.C. ... Andover, MA
McCabe, Diane Doubleday ... San Francisco, CA
McCabe, Donald C. ... Daleville, AL
McCabe, Donald F. ... Pension Benefit Guaranty Corporation, Office of the General Counsel, GV
McCabe, Donald G. ... New York, NY
McCabe, Dorothy E. ... New York, NY
McCabe, Duane J. ... Bend, OR
McCabe, Edward A. ... Washington, DC
McCabe, Edward G. ... East Meadow, NY
McCabe, Edward G. ... Mineola, NY
McCabe, Edward J. ... Bay City, MI
McCabe, Edwin A. ... Boston, MA
McCabe, Eileen J. ... Jamaica, NY
McCabe, Eileen T. ... New York, NY
McCabe, Erin ... Woodbury, NY
McCabe & Flynn ... New York, NY
McCabe, Francis X. ... Rochester, NY
McCabe, Gavin Geraghty ... San Francisco, CA
McCabe, George N. ... Great Falls, MT
McCabe, Gerard M. ... Philadelphia, PA
McCabe, Gisela C. ... Farmington Hills, MI
McCabe, Hugh A. ... San Diego, CA
McCabe, J. Frank ... San Francisco, CA
McCabe, James B. ... Seattle, WA
McCabe, James E. ... Williamsport, IN
McCabe, James E. ... Omaha, NE
McCabe, James F. ... San Francisco, CA
McCabe, James J. ... Philadelphia, PA
McCabe, James K. ... Brookfield, IL
McCabe, James L. ... Arlington Heights, IL
McCabe, James M. ... San Diego, CA
McCabe, James N. ... Long Beach, CA
McCabe, James P. ... New York, NY
McCabe, James T. ... Exeter, NE
McCabe, Jeffrey S. ... Pleasanton, CA
McCabe, Jennifer H. ... Fairfax, VA
McCabe, John B. ... Chicago, IL
McCabe, John Edward ... Wellesley, MA
McCabe, John F. ... Washington, DC
McCabe, John F. ... Des Plaines, IL
McCabe, John F. ... Annapolis, MD
McCabe, John F. ... Boston, MA
McCabe, John F., Jr. ... Rockville, MD
McCabe, John H. ... Hastings-On-Hudson, NY
McCabe, John J., Jr. ... La Jolla, CA
McCabe, John L. ... Denver, CO
McCabe, John M. ... Chicago, IL
McCabe, John M. ... Okemos, MI
McCabe, John P. ... Chicago, IL
McCabe, John Q. ... Midland, TX
McCabe, Jos. P. ... Philadelphia, PA
McCabe, Joseph I. ... Phoenix, AZ
McCabe, Joseph V. ... Irvine, CA
McCabe, Judith T. ... Seattle, WA
McCabe, Julianne ... Boulder, CO
McCabe, Kat ... Palo Alto, CA
McCabe, Kathleen L. ... Brookfield, IL
McCabe, Kathleen M. ... Chicago, IL
McCabe, Keith S. ... Hartford, CT
McCabe, Kelly R. ... Cortez, CO
McCabe, Kevin William ... Washington, DC
McCabe, Kirk J. ... Kansas City, MO
McCabe, Kurt W. ... Lancaster, PA
McCabe, Lawrence D. ... New York, NY
McCabe, Lawrence J. ... Pittsburgh, PA
McCabe, Lee Ann ... Woodbridge, NJ
McCabe, Leo P. ... Holden, MA
McCabe, Loretta Leone ... Hingham, MA
McCabe, Louise M. ... San Francisco, CA
McCabe, Lucy Kelly ... San Francisco, CA
McCabe, Lynn Diringer ... San Francisco, CA
McCabe & Mack LLP ... Carmel, NY
Goshen, NY
Hudson, NY
Kingston, NY
Newburgh, NY
Poughkeepsie, NY
McCabe, Mark C. ... Fenton, MI
McCabe, Martha ... Lubbock, TX
McCabe, Mary Frances ... Lawrence, MA
McCabe, Mary M. ... Rochester, NY
McCabe, MaryBeth ... Doylestown, PA
Mccabe, Matthew Clark ... Jordan, NY
McCabe, Matthew E. ... New York, NY
McCabe, Maureen A. ... Waltham, MA
McCabe, Maureen M. ... Morristown, NJ
McCabe & McCabe ... Brookfield, IL
Seattle, WA
McCabe, Merrily ... Salem, OR
McCabe, Michael ... Concord, CA
McCabe, Michael ... San Francisco, CA
McCabe, Michael ... Santa Rosa, CA
McCabe, Michael A. ... Dallas, TX
McCabe, Michael E. ... Los Angeles, CA
McCabe, Michael E., Jr. ... Arlington, VA
McCabe, Michael F. ... San Francisco, CA
McCabe, Michael G. ... Pittsburgh, PA
McCabe, Michael H. ... Lombard, IL
McCabe, Michael J. ... San Diego, CA
McCabe, Michael J. ... East Hampton, CT
McCabe, Michael J. ... Northbrook, IL
McCabe, Michael J., II ... Atlanta, GA
McCabe, Michael R. ... El Cajon, CA
McCabe, Michael R. ... Redding, CA
McCabe, Michael T. ... Helena, MT
McCabe, Monica P. ... New York, NY
McCabe, Nancy Kessler ... New York, NY
McCabe, Neil Colman ... Houston, TX
McCabe, Neil H. ... Oroville, CA
McCabe O'Donnell, A Professional Association ... Phoenix, AZ
McCabe, P. Christopher ... Gunnison, CO
McCabe, Pamela J. ... Mason, MI
McCabe, Patricia L. ... Sherman Oaks, CA
McCabe, Patrick ... Pomeroy, WA
McCabe, Patrick J ... Anchorage, AK
McCabe, Patrick J. ... Gretna, LA
McCabe, Patrick L. ... Lincoln, NE
McCabe, Patrick R. ... San Francisco, CA
McCabe, Paul D. ... Coeur d'Alene, ID
McCabe, Pegi Money ... Tampa, FL
McCabe, Peter A., Jr. ... Brooklyn, NY
McCabe, Peter C., III ... Chicago, IL
McCabe, Peter D. ... San Francisco, CA
McCabe, Peter G. ... Administrative Office Of The United States Courts, GV
McCabe, Peter J. ... Cleveland, OH
Mccabe, Peter M. ... New York, NY
McCabe, Philip J. ... San Jose, CA
McCabe, Raymond N. ... Buffalo, NY
McCabe, Rebecca Gunn ... Atlanta, GA
McCabe, Regina K. ... Chicago, IL
McCabe, Robert C. ... Houston, TX
McCabe, Robert D. ... New York, NY
McCabe, Robert F., Jr. ... Pittsburgh, PA
McCabe, Robert L. ... Aurora, CO
McCabe, Robert O. ... New York, NY
McCabe, Robin ... New York, NY
McCabe, Roger S. ... Beaumont, TX
McCabe, Sally J. ... Department of the Navy, GV
McCabe, Scott A. ... Towson, MD
McCabe, Sean P. ... Phoenix, AZ
McCabe, Shirley A. ... Fullerton, CA
McCabe, Stephen M. ... Mineola, NY
McCabe, Susan Holt ... Houston, TX
McCabe, Terrence D. ... Chicago, IL
McCabe, Terrence J. ... Philadelphia, PA
McCabe, Terrence M. ... Bronx, NY
White Plains, NY
McCabe, Theodore A. ... Los Angeles, CA
McCabe, Thomas E. ... Vienna, VA
McCabe, Thomas J. ... Boise, ID
McCabe, Thomas J. ... Boston, MA
McCabe, Thomas J. ... New York, NY
McCabe, Thomas J., Jr. ... Hartford, CT
McCabe, Thomas J., Jr. ... Durham, NC
McCabe, Thomas P. ... Bergenfield, NJ
McCabe, Tracy ... New York, NY
McCabe, Walter R., III ... Boston, MA
McCabe, Wayne L. ... Bonsall, CA
McCabe, Weisberg and Conway, P.C. ... New York, NY
Philadelphia, PA
McCabe, William J. ... Longwood, FL
McCabe, William J. ... New York, NY
McCabe, William J. ... Greensburg, PA
McCabe, William James ... New York, NY
McCabria, James R. ... Coffeyville, KS
McCachran, Marshall T. ... Cincinnati, OH
McCachren, James R., III ... Jacksonville, FL
McCachren, James R., Jr., P.A. ... Tallahassee, FL
McCachren, Jon H. ... Charlotte, NC
McCadams, Hansel J. ... Paris, TN
McCadden, Jim ... Towson, MD
McCadden, Michael J. ... Philadelphia, PA
McCade, Kathleen M. ... Sacramento, CA
McCafferty, Brian P. ... Washington, DC
Norristown, PA
McCafferty, Bridget M. ... Cleveland, OH
McCafferty, Christine F. ... Voorhees, NJ
Philadelphia, PA
McCafferty, Dennis C. ... La Grange, TX
McCafferty, Edward J. ... Department Of Veterans Affairs, Board of Veterans Appeals, GV
McCafferty, E. L., III ... Mobile, AL
McCafferty, Gary E. ... Westmont, NJ
Philadelphia, PA
McCafferty, Gerald D., Law Office of ... Flagstaff, AZ
McCafferty, Geraldine ... Denver, CO
McCafferty, James T. ... Jackson, MS
McCafferty, John T. ... Dallas, TX
McCafferty, Joseph P. ... Cleveland, OH
McCafferty, Karen M. ... Buffalo, NY
McCafferty, Mary Gill ... Miami, FL
McCafferty, Mary-Janet ... Portland, ME
McCafferty, Michael L. ... Wichita, KS
McCafferty, Michael P. ... Runnemede, NJ
McCafferty, Owen J. ... Cleveland, OH
McCafferty & Perelman ... Cleveland, OH
McCafferty, Sarah ... Baltimore, MD
McCafferty, William ... Middle Village, NY
McCafferty and Williams ... Cleveland, OH
McCafferty-Valenti, Vlinda ... Livonia, MI
McCaffery, Coleen J. ... Warren, NJ
McCaffery, Daniel D. ... Elkins Park, PA
McCaffery, John C. ... Atlanta, GA
McCaffery, Josephine ... New York, NY
McCaffery, Maura ... Boston, MA
McCaffery, Michael J. ... Chicago, IL
McCaffery, Robert M. ... Scotch Plains, NJ
McCaffery, Seamus P. ... Philadelphia, PA
McCaffery, Thomas F., III ... Wayne, PA
McCaffery, Timothy J. ... Oakland, CA
McCaffery, William T. ... New York, NY
McCaffity, Sean J. ... Dallas, TX
McCaffree, Landoll & Slaby ... Nevada, MO
McCaffree, Sheridan A. ... Oklahoma City, OK
McCaffree, William G. ... Nevada, MO
McCaffrey, Angela ... St. Paul, MN
McCaffrey, Brian ... New York, NY
McCaffrey, Brian F. ... Exeter, NH
McCaffrey, Brian J. ... San Francisco, CA
McCaffrey, Carlyn S. ... New York, NY
McCaffrey, Christopher ... Dallas, TX
McCaffrey, Christopher ... Plano, TX
McCaffrey, Dennis ... Gaithersburg, MD
McCaffrey, Eugene J., Jr. ... Woodbury, NJ
McCaffrey, Eugene J., Jr. ... Warwick, RI
McCaffrey, Frances ... Woodcliff Lake, NJ
McCaffrey, Francis B. ... Rutland, VT
McCaffrey, Francis J. ... Shelter Island Heights, NY
McCaffrey, Francis J., Jr. ... Bronx, NY
McCaffrey, George J. ... Oklahoma City, OK
McCaffrey, James A. ... Oklahoma City, OK
McCaffrey, James F. ... San Ysidro, CA
McCaffrey, James J. ... Boston, MA
McCaffrey, John ... New York, NY
McCaffrey, John E. ... Washington, DC
McCaffrey, John F. ... Cleveland, OH
McCaffrey, John S. ... Ithaca, NY
McCaffrey, John T. ... Warwick, RI
McCaffrey, John W. ... Chicago, IL
McCaffrey, Joseph F. ... Wilmington, DE
McCaffrey, Judith E. ... Naples, FL
Sarasota, FL
Mc Caffrey, Kathleen M. ... Salem, MA
McCaffrey, Kevin J. ... New York, NY
Mccaffrey, Margo H. ... Quincy, MA
McCaffrey, Mary Elizabeth ... Warwick, RI
McCaffrey, Mary Lynn ... Hillsdale, NJ
New City, NY
McCaffrey & McCaffrey ... Warwick, RI
McCaffrey, Michael D. ... Irvine, CA
McCaffrey, Michael J. ... Bedminster, NJ
McCaffrey, Michael J. ... Warwick, RI
McCaffrey, Patrick Joseph ... New York, NY
McCaffrey, Patrick, Jr. ... Columbus, OH
McCaffrey, Philip T. ... General Accounting Office, Office of the General Counsel, GV
McCaffrey Professional Association ... Exeter, NH
Portsmouth, NH
McCaffrey & Raimi, P.A. ... Naples, FL
Sarasota, FL
McCaffrey, Read Kemp ... Washington, DC
McCaffrey, Richard P. ... Concord, NH
McCaffrey, Roger ... Anaheim, CA
McCaffrey, Shaun Matthew ... Fort Smith, AR
McCaffrey, Stephen C. ... Sacramento, CA
McCaffrey, Stephen W. ... Hicksville, NY
McCaffrey & Tawwater ... Oklahoma City, OK
McCaffrey, Thomas A. ... Pittsburgh, PA
McCaffrey, Thomas J. ... Houston, TX
McCaffrey, Thomas M. ... Denver, CO
McCaffrey, Thomas M. ... New York, NY
McCaffrey, Thomas P. ... New York, NY
McCaffrey, Timothy B., Jr. ... Los Angeles, CA
McCaffrey, Timothy J. ... Chicago, IL
McCaffrey, Timothy T. ... Stamford, CT
McCaffrey-Dombroski, Laura B. ... New York, NY
McCaghey, Charles M. ... Stamford, CT
New York, NY
McCaghren, C. Brent ... Winter Park, FL
McCague, J. Michael, Jr. ... Pittsburgh, PA
McCague, John J., III ... Pittsburgh, PA
McCague, William L., II ... Morristown, NJ
McCahan, Nancy S. ... St. Louis, MO
McCahey, John P. ... New York, NY
McCahey, Stephen J. ... New York, NY
McCahill, Burke F. ... Leesburg, VA
McCahill, Francis X., Jr. ... Melbourne, FL
McCahill, Jane K. ... Chicago, IL
McCahill, Jane O. ... Philadelphia, PA
McCahill, John A. ... Washington, DC
McCahill, John A. ... Alexandria, VA
McCahill, John William, II ... Denver, CO
McCahill, Woods ... Albany, NY
McCahon, Sam Woodburn ... Jefferson City, MO
McCahren, Lee C. (Kit) ... Pierre, SD
McCahren, Lee M. ... Vermillion, SD
McCaig, Albert M., Jr. ... Waller, TX
McCaig, Robert M. ... Salisbury, MD
McCain, Carter B. ... Tampa, FL
McCain, Catherine A. ... Chicago, IL
McCain, Charles F. ... Boston, MA
McCain, Charles F., II ... Boston, MA
McCain, Charles P. ... Brownwood, TX
McCain, David B. ... Miami, FL
McCain, David B. ... Lake Charles, LA
McCain, David H. ... La Porte, IN
McCain, Gary R. ... Atlanta, GA
McCain, George A., Jr. ... Galveston, TX
McCain, Gordon W., Jr. ... Ozark, AR
McCain, Greg "Scooter" ... Dothan, AL
McCain, Grover C., Jr. ... Chapel Hill, NC
McCain, James R., Jr. ... Jacksonville, FL
McCain, Jennifer R. ... Birmingham, AL
McCain, John E. ... Fairfield, CT
McCain, Joseph J., Jr. ... Tulsa, OK
McCain, Kathleen Mary ... Los Angeles, CA
McCain, Leonard H. ... Brighton, CO
McCain, Linn H., III ... Nashville, TN
McCain, Lynn ... Gadsden, AL
McCain, Marc D. ... Phoenix, AZ
McCain, Michelle Noble ... Salinas, CA
McCain, Ogletree, Sasser and Ozmint, P.C. ... Gadsden, AL
McCain, Rebecca R. ... Kokomo, IN
McCain, Richard E. ... Santa Ana, CA
McCain, Richard J. ... Portland, OR
McCain, Robert C. ... Lakewood, CO
McCain, Robert G., III ... Dallas, TX
McCain, Shellie G., Jr. ... Memphis, TN
McCain, Steven E. ... Houston, TX
McCain, Steven R. ... Fort Pierce, FL
McCain, Talbot O. ... Greenwood, MS
McCain, Taryn Marie ... Seattle, WA
McCain Parson, Linda Faye ... Washington, DC
McCaleb, Alfred F., III ... Baton Rouge, LA
McCaleb, E. Howard, III ... Metairie, LA
McCaleb, Joe W. ... Hendersonville, TN
McCaleb, John A. ... Oklahoma City, OK
McCaleb, Jolene L. ... Albuquerque, NM
McCaleb, Kelly S. ... Fayette, AL
McCaleb, Lucas & Brugman ... Oakbrook Terrace, IL
McCaleb, Malcolm ... Dillon, CO
McCaleb, Malcolm, Jr. ... Chicago, IL
McCaleb, Marlin R. ... Mechanicsburg, PA
McCaleb, Nicky W. ... Memphis, TN
McCaleb, Philip A. ... Sacramento, CA
McCaleb, Robert H. ... Huntsville, AL
McCaleb, Scott M. ... Washington, DC
McCalister, Philip V. ... New Kensington, PA
McCall, Albert B., II ... Carthage, TN
McCall, Ambrose V. ... New Orleans, LA
Mccall, Angela Marie ... Spartanburg, SC
McCall, Barbara Blazek ... Lincoln, NE
McCall, Betsy Birns ... Atlanta, GA
McCall, Bradley ... Grinnell, IA
Newton, IA
Sully, IA
McCall, C. Allen, Jr. ... Lawton, OK
McCall, C. Robert ... Pittsburgh, PA
McCall, Candace ... Fairfax, VA
McCall, Charles J. ... Midlothian, VA
McCall, Charles S. ... Jacksonville, FL
McCall, Cheryl ... Nevada City, CA
McCall, Christopher C. ... Lake Charles, LA
McCall, Clifton H. ... Gering, NE
McCall, Colleen J. ... San Francisco, CA
McCall, Colleen McMillin ... Dallas, TX
McCall, Craig T. ... Durham, NC
McCall, Dan T., Jr. ... Mobile, AL
McCall, Daniel K. ... Marietta, GA
Mccall, Daniel L. ... Katy, TX
McCall, David B. ... Austin, TX
McCall, David B., III ... Plano, TX
McCall, David T. ... Greeley, CO
McCall, Donn J. ... Casper, WY
McCall, Doreen A. ... Harrisburg, PA
McCall, Doughton & Blancato, P.L.L.C. ... Winston-Salem, NC
McCall, Douglas Mark ... Washington, DC
McCall, Doy Leale, III ... Montgomery, AL
McCall, Duke K., III ... Washington, DC
McCall, Duke K., Jr. ... Greenville, SC
McCall, Elizabeth S. ... Lake Charles, LA
McCall, Eugene C., Jr. ... Greenville, SC
McCall & Finney, P.C. ... Albany, GA
McCall, Frederick C., Jr. ... Buffalo, NY
McCall, G. Emmett ... Winston-Salem, NC
McCall, George Steven, (P.C.) ... Irving, TX
McCall, Gregory K. ... Seattle, WA
McCall, Guyton B. ... Atlanta, GA
McCall, H. Alan ... Lake Charles, LA
McCall, Harry, Jr. ... New Orleans, LA
McCall, Henry C. ... Brentwood, TN
McCall, Hillary A. ... Tampa, FL
McCall, J. Kevin ... Chicago, IL
McCall, Jack H. ... Knoxville, TN
McCall, James A. ... Bethesda, MD
Mccall, James E. ... Boston, MA
McCall, James R. ... San Francisco, CA
McCall, Jeffrey L. ... Knoxville, TN
McCall, Jesse A., Jr. ... Greenville, SC
McCall, John C. ... Los Angeles, CA
McCall, John P. ... San Rafael, CA
McCall, John R. ... Louisville, KY
McCall, John S., Jr. ... Canton, OH
McCall, John Tim ... Louisville, KY
McCall, Jonathan C. ... New Orleans, LA

McCall, Joseph P. ....New York, NY
Mc Call, Kathryn ....San Diego, CA
McCall, Kathryn L. ....San Francisco, CA
McCall, Kevin M. ....Los Angeles, CA
McCall, Kim L. ....Jacksonville, FL
McCall, Laura Ann ....Okeechobee, FL
Mccall, Laurie H. ....Indianapolis, IN
McCall, Lee Ann Anderson
Washington, DC
McCall, Linda L. ....San Francisco, CA
McCall, Mariam E.
Department of Commerce,
National Oceanic and Atmospheric
Administration, GV
McCall, Michael Craig ....San Juan, PR
McCall, Michael T. ....Orange, CA
McCall, Michael W. ....Sacramento, CA
McCall, Mike W. ....Metairie, LA
McCall, Molly A. ....Washington, DC
McCall, Nella ....Franklin, TN
McCall, Parkhurst & Horton L.L.P.
Austin, TX
Dallas, TX
San Antonio, TX
McCall, Patricia H. ....Santa Clara, CA
McCall, Patrick A. ....Orange, CA
McCall, Peter J. ....St. Paul, MN
McCall, Peter L. ....Cleveland, OH
McCall, Rachel W. ....Seattle, WA
McCall, Randolph D. ....Dallas, TX
McCall, Raymond D. ....Denver, CO
McCall, Rex C., Jr. ....Springfield, MO
McCall, Richard H., Jr. ....Houston, TX
McCall, Richard V. ....Waco, TX
McCall & Ritchie, LLP ....Austin, TX
McCall, Robert A. ....Boston, MA
McCall, Robert A. ....Boston, MA
McCall, Robert C. ....Lake Charles, LA
McCall, Robert J.
General Services Administration,
Office of Regional Counsel, GV
McCall, Ronald ....Tampa, FL
McCall, Ronald H. ....Hampton, VA
McCall, Ronald P. ....Sharon, PA
McCall, Ronald, P.A. ....Port Richey, FL
Tampa, FL
Mccall, Rosemary Grace ....Conifer, CO
McCall, Sean M. ....Arlington, VA
McCall, Shane T. ....Smith Center, KS
McCall, Sheree Lynn, (P.C.) ....Dallas, TX
McCall, Teri Dyan ....Phoenix, AZ
McCall, Terry A. ....New Orleans, LA
McCall, Tom C. ....Austin, TX
McCall, W. Earl ....Albany, GA
McCall, Wallace B., Law Office of
Jupiter, FL
McCall, Walter L. ....Los Angeles, CA
McCall, Wayne C. ....Ocala, FL
McCall, William G. ....Charlotte, NC
McCall, William J. ....Wilkes-Barre, PA
McCall, William T. ....Lake Charles, LA
McCall, Winston B. ....Mountain Brook, AL
McCall, Winston B., Jr. ....Birmingham, AL
McCall, Wm. Rogers, P.C. ....Bristol, TN
McCall, W. R. ....Bristol, TN
McCalla, Carl W., III ....Atlanta, GA
McCalla, Dudley D. ....Austin, TX
McCalla, J. Douglas ....Salt Lake City, UT
Jackson, WY
McCalla, Jon P. ....Memphis, TN
McCalla Law Firm, The ....Atlanta, GA
McCalla, Patrick D. ....Costa Mesa, CA
McCalla, Randolph G. ......San Francisco, CA
McCalla, Randy R., (P.A.) ....Olathe, KS
McCalla, Raymer, Padrick, Cobb, Nichols &
Clark, LLC ....Atlanta, GA
Dallas, GA
Lilburn, GA
Marietta, GA
Norcross, GA
Roswell, GA
Woodstock, GA
McCalla, Richard C. ....Brewster, NY
McCalla, Robert K., (P.C.)
New Orleans, LA
Gulfport, MS
McCalla, Sheryl ....Atlanta, GA
McCalla, Stanley H., Sr. ....Atlanta, GA
Memphis, TN
Nashville, TN
McCalla, Stephen R. ....Chickasha, OK
Oklahoma City, OK
McCalla, Thompson, Pyburn, Hymowitz &
Shapiro ....New Orleans, LA
Gulfport, MS
McCallan, John B. ....San Diego, CA
McCallar and Associates ....Brunswick, GA
Savannah, GA
McCallar, C. James, Jr. ....Savannah, GA
McCall-Austin, Maureen ....El Cajon, CA
McCallen, Grace C. ....Mineola, NY
New York, NY
White Plains, NY
McCallen, Robert R. ....Wabash, IN
Mccallen, Thomas J. ....New York, NY
McCalley, Gorham & Bowman
Richmond, MO
McCalley, William C. ....Moultrie, GA
McCalley, William C., P.C. ....Moultrie, GA
McCallie, Allen L. ....Chattanooga, TN
McCallie, S. Wyatt ....Englewood, CO
McCallie, Thomas Hooke, III
Chattanooga, TN
McCallin, Alfred D. ....Canton, OH
McCallion, Donald G. ....Garden City, NY
McCallion, Donald G., Jr. ....White Plains, NY
McCallion, Gail K. ....New York, NY
McCallion, James ....Ontario, CA
McCallion, Kenneth F. ....New York, NY
McCallion, Sandra C. ....New York, NY
McCallister, Bobby D. ....Benton, AR
McCallister, Brian F. ....Kansas City, MO
McCallister, David Rhodes
Wesley Chapel, FL
McCallister, Fred D. ....Irving, TX
McCallister, Gary D. ....Chicago, IL
Topeka, KS
McCallister, Gary D., & Associates, Ltd.
Chicago, IL
McCallister, Ian N. ....Lexington, MA
McCallister, Ian W. ....Los Angeles, CA
McCallister, J. Wilson ....Moline, IL
McCallister, Joan E. ....Bethesda, MD
McCallister & Jones ....Benton, AR
McCallister Law Firm, The, P.C.
Kansas City, MO
McCallister, Mark A. ....Arlington, VA
McCallister, Orville C. ....Placitas, NM
McCallister, Steven K. ....Greensboro, NC
McCallister, Thomas M.
San Francisco, CA
McCallister, Wayne A. ....Niles, IL
McCallister, William K., Jr.
Los Angeles, CA
McCallum, Albert D. ....Springport, MI
McCallum, Barbara Eiland
Sacramento, CA
McCallum, Barbara I. ......San Luis Obispo, CA
McCallum, Catherine ....Fullerton, CA
McCallum, Charles A., III
Birmingham, AL
McCallum, Charles E. ......Grand Rapids, MI
McCallum, Darryl G. ....Washington, DC
McCallum, Deborah K.
Department Of Veterans Affairs,
VA Regional Counsel Office, Washington,
D.C., GV
McCallum and De Goede ....Fresno, CA
McCallum, Donald G. ....Sacramento, CA
McCallum, Donald R. ....Stoughton, WI
McCallum, Duncan E., II ....Chesapeake, VA
McCallum, Edward S., III ....Greenwood, SC
McCallum, Elizabeth B. ....Washington, DC
McCallum, Franklin H. ....Midland, TX
McCallum, George B., III
Charlottesville, VA
McCallum, Gretchen ....Renton, WA
McCallum, Harold L. ....South Gate, CA
McCallum, John M. ....Portland, ME
McCallum, Kelley Laughlin
Birmingham, AL
McCallum & Kudravetz, P.C.
Charlottesville, VA
McCallum, Laurie R. ....Madison, WI
McCallum, Lenell Topol ....Belmont, CA
McCallum, Leslie D. ....Hartford, CT
McCallum, Linda F. ....Jacksonville, FL
McCallum, Lisa A. ....Indianapolis, IN
McCallum, Mark H. ....Alexandria, VA
McCallum, Mary M. ....Milton, MA
McCallum & McCallum ......Sacramento, CA
McCallum, Michael N. ....Carmichael, CA
McCallum, Pamela A. ....Pittsburgh, PA
McCallum, Patric P. ....Marshall, TX
McCallum, Philip ....Williamsburg, VA
McCallum, Phillip W. ....Birmingham, AL
McCallum, Robert D., Jr. ....Atlanta, GA
McCallum, Robert E. ....Arkadelphia, AR
McCallum, Robert L. ....Dallas, TX
McCallum, Robert M. ....Seattle, WA
McCallum, Ronald L.
Environmental Protection Agency,
Environmental Appeals Board, GV
McCallum, Scott N. ....Fresno, CA
McCallum, Steven C. ....Richmond, VA
Mccallum, Wendy Lynn ....Brighton, CO
McCally, Daniel W. ....Melville, NY
McCally, Sharon S. ....Houston, TX
McCally, Thomas L. ....Washington, DC
McCalman, Patrick S. ....Andalusia, AL
McCalmon, Brian K. ....Washington, DC
McCalmon, Julia M. ....Washington, DC
McCalmont, Lisa S. ....Houston, TX
McCalpin, F. Wm. ....St. Louis, MO
McCamant, Mary Ann ....San Bruno, CA
McCambley, Maris E. ....Charleston, WV
McCambridge, Deixler & Marmaro, LLP
Los Angeles, CA
McCambridge, Edward J. ....Chicago, IL
Ann Arbor, MI
McCambridge, George R. ....Los Angeles, CA
McCambridge, Gregory P. ......Los Angeles, CA
McCambridge, James E., III
North Attleboro, MA
McCambridge, John R. ....Chicago, IL
McCambridge, Michael J. ....Chicago, IL
McCambridge, Siobhan ....Chicago, IL
McCament, Warren H. ....San Fernando, CA
McCamey, Randal E. ....Pittsburgh, PA
McCamic, Jay T. ....Wheeling, WV
McCamic, Jeffrey W. ....Wheeling, WV
McCamic, Jeremy C. ....Wheeling, WV
McCamic, Jolyon W. ....Wheeling, WV
McCamic & McCamic ....Wheeling, WV
McCamish, John N., Jr. ....San Antonio, TX
McCamish, Larry O. ....La Habra, CA
McCamish, M. Warren ....Kansas City, KS
McCamish, Marion E.
Department of Commerce,
Patent and Trademark Office, GV
Mc Camish, Nancy B. ....San Antonio, TX
McCamish & Socks, A Professional
Corporation ....San Antonio, TX
McCamley, Janet ....Beachwood, OH
McCamley, John E. ....Rutland, VT
McCamman, Kurt P. ....Kalamazoo, MI
McCammon, Catherine G.
Santa Barbara, CA
McCammon, Jennifer A.
Birmingham, AL
McCammon, John B. ....Richmond, VA
McCammon, Phillip R. ....San Antonio, TX
McCamont, Christine J. ....Detroit, MI
McCampbell, Daniel J. ....Chico, CA
McCampbell, J. Brad ....Greenville, TX
McCampbell, Peggy J. ....Jourdanton, TX
McCampbell, Robert G.
Oklahoma City, OK
Mc Campbell, Roy F. ....Schiller Park, IL
McCampbell, Thomas ....Chico, CA
McCampbell & Walthall, P.C.
Washington, DC
McCampbell, William A., III
Washington, DC
McCampbell, William R. ....San Antonio, TX
McCampbell & Young, A Professional
Corporation ....Knoxville, TN
McCamy, Phillips, Tuggle & Fordham, LLP
Calhoun, GA
Chatsworth, GA
Dalton, GA
Ellijay, GA
La Fayette, GA
McCandless & Associates ....Coatesville, PA
Latrobe, PA
Philadelphia, PA
McCandless, Edward L. ....Coatesville, PA
Philadelphia, PA
McCandless, Elizabeth A. ....Austin, TX
McCandless, Elizabeth T. ....Portland, ME
McCandless Epstein & O'Donovan L.L.P.
Kennebunk, ME
Portland, ME
McCandless, Erin E. ....Omaha, NE
McCandless, J. Scott ....Kansas City, MO
McCandless, Jett A. ....Menlo Park, CA
McCandless, John R. ....Oklahoma City, OK
McCandless, John W. ....Erie, PA
McCandless, Michael R. ....Troy, MI
McCandless, O. Carlysle ....Lexington, KY
McCandless, Patricia Fuller ....Austin, TX
McCandless, Richard L. ....Butler, PA
McCandless, Robert C. ....Washington, DC
McCandless, Roy S. ....Concord, NH
McCandless, Sandra R.
San Francisco, CA
McCandless, Victoria M. ....Milwaukee, WI
McCandless, William ....Detroit, MI
McCandlis, Paula L. ....Bellingham, WA
McCandlish, Charles S. ....Winchester, VA
McCandlish, Fairfax Sheild ....McLean, VA
McCandlish, James E. ....Portland, OR
McCandlish & Lillard, A Professional
Corporation ....Alexandria, VA
Fairfax, VA
Leesburg, VA
McCandlish, Thomas W. ....Richmond, VA
McCandliss, Glenn A. ....Center Line, MI
McCane, Kevin F. ....Albany, NY
McCaney, Michael J., Jr. ....Blue Bell, PA
McCanless, R. William ....Salisbury, NC
McCanliss & Early L.L.P. ....New York, NY
McCann, Alexander F. ....Portland, ME
McCann, Bernard T. ....Queensbury, NY
McCann, Bradley S. ....Chicago, IL
McCann, Brian J. ....Schenectady, NY
McCann, Bruce W. ....Santa Rosa, CA
McCann, Carolyn M. ....St. Paul, MN
McCann & Carroll ....Carlsbad, CA
McCann, Catherine Anne ....New York, NY
McCann, Charles D. ....Rockford, IL
McCann, Christine A. ....New York, NY
McCann, Christine H. ....Raleigh, NC
McCann, Clifton E. ....Washington, DC
McCann, D. Michael ....Birmingham, MI
McCann, Daniel F. ....Los Angeles, CA
McCann, David ....Charleston, SC
McCann, David F. ....Council Bluffs, IA
McCann, David J. ....Council Bluffs, IA
McCann, David T. ....Los Angeles, CA
McCann, Dean M. ....Irvine, CA
McCann, Dennis J. ....Columbus, OH
Mc Cann, Dennise L. ....Chicago, IL
McCann, Donald B. ....Cleveland, OH
McCann, Donald W. ....Salem, OR
McCann, Douglas A. ....Paducah, KY
McCann, E. Michael ....Milwaukee, WI
McCann, Edmund V. ....Ridgefield Park, NJ
McCann, Eileen M. ....St. Louis, MO
McCann, Elizabeth H. ....Denver, CO
McCann, Elizabeth I. ....New York, NY
McCann, Ellen M. Foley ....Philadelphia, PA
McCann, Eric J. ....Birmingham, MI
McCann, Eric J., P.C. ....Birmingham, MI
McCann FitzGerald ....New York, NY
McCann, Francis X., P.A. ....Charleston, SC
McCann, Gail E. ....Providence, RI
McCann, Garland, Ridall & Burke
Latrobe, PA
Pittsburgh, PA
McCann, George R. ....Columbus, OH
McCann, Gina S. ....Lexington, KY
McCann, Glenn E. ....Kansas City, MO
McCann, Gregory L. ....Dayton, OH
McCann, Heather R. ....Charlotte, NC
McCann, Holly E. ....San Jose, CA
McCann, Holly S. ....Pittsburgh, PA
McCann, Jack Maynard ....Columbus, OH
McCann, James ....Avon, NY
McCann, James A. ....Wolf Point, MT
McCann, James C. ....Jersey City, NJ
McCann, James F. ....Wallingford, CT
McCann, James M., Jr.
West Palm Beach, FL
McCann, James P. ....Spring, TX
McCann, James Patrick ....Tulsa, OK
McCann, James R. ....Chicago, IL
McCann, James W. ....Stuart, FL
McCann, James W., P.A. ....Stuart, FL
McCann, Jas. R. ....Livonia, MI
McCann, Jeffrey Allen ....Pensacola, FL
McCann, Jeffrey Allen, P.A. ....Pensacola, FL
McCann, John D. ....Lexington, KY
McCann, John E. ....Baltimore, MD
McCann, John E., III ....Cranston, RI
McCann, John E., Jr. ....Baltimore, MD
McCann, John F., Jr. ....Indianapolis, IN
McCann, John G. ....New York, NY
McCann, John H., III ....Pawtucket, RI
McCann, John J. ....Farmington, CT
McCann, John J. ....Wheaton, IL
McCann, John P. ....Fresno, CA
McCann, John R. ....Los Angeles, CA
McCann, John S. ....Westborough, MA
McCann, John T. ....Syracuse, NY
McCann, John T. ....Milwaukee, WI
McCann, John V. ....New York, NY
McCann, John W. ....Boston, MA
McCann, Joseph ....Bryn Mawr, PA
Mc Cann, Joseph D. ....Rockville Centre, NY
McCann, Joseph E.
Office of Personnel Management,
Merit Systems Division, GV
McCann, Joseph J., Jr. ....Los Angeles, CA
McCann, Joseph L.
General Services Administration,
Office of the General Counsel, GV
McCann, Kathleen Duckett ....Baltimore, MD
McCann, Kathleen J. ....Livonia, MI
McCann, Kathleen Marliss ....Vancouver, WA
McCann, Kenneth K. ....Hermitage, PA
McCann, Kenneth R. ....Valencia, CA
McCann, Kerry R. ....Pittsburgh, PA
McCann, Kevin ....Hartford, CT
McCann, Kevin C. ....San Francisco, CA
McCann, Kevin E. ....Carlsbad, CA
McCann, Kevin P. ....Bridgeton, NJ
McCann, Kimberly M. ....Burlington, MA
McCann, Kimberly Scott ....Ashland, KY
Ironton, OH
Mccann, Laura A. ....Orangeburg, SC
McCann, Leslie M. ....Danville, VA
McCann, Linda R. ....Stuart, FL
McCann, Mailey & Geschke, P.C.
Philadelphia, PA
McCann, Margaret ....Philadelphia, PA
McCann, Marie L. ....Elmsford, NY
McCann, Mark A. ....Kokomo, IN
McCann, Martin L. ....Bridgeport, CT
McCann, Mary Naughton
Philadelphia, PA
McCann, Matthew ....Amarillo, TX
McCann, Matthew J. ....Silver Spring, MD
McCann, Matthew R. ....Worcester, MA
McCann, Maurice J. ....Murphysboro, IL
McCann and McCann ....Ridgefield Park, NJ
McCann, Melissa C. ....New York, NY
McCann, Michael C. ....Rosemount, MN
McCann, Michael C. ....Richmond, VA
McCann, Michael E. ....Chicago, IL
McCann, Michael E. ....Brookings, SD
McCann, Michael F. ....Boston, MA
McCann, Michael L. ....Kansas City, MO
McCann, Michael M. ....Golden, CO
McCann, Michael P. ....Monterey, CA
McCann, Michael P. ....Palisades Park, NJ
McCann, Michael R. ....Baltimore, MD
McCann, Michael R. ....Madison, WI
McCann, Michael W. ....Santa Barbara, CA
Mccann, Michaelene O'Neill ....Salem, MA
McCann, Michele R. ....Rock Island, IL
McCann, P. Shawn ....Omaha, NE
McCann, Patrick M. ....Benton, IL
Mc Cann, Paul A. ....Missoula, MT
McCann, Paul J. ....Great Falls, MT
McCann, Paul L. ....Boston, MA
McCann, Paula J. ....Denver, CO
McCann, Philip P. ....Charlotte, NC
McCann, Randal P. ....Lafayette, LA
McCann, Raymond C. ....Fullerton, CA
McCann & Ribstein, P.C. ....Brookings, SD
McCann, Richard E. ....Seattle, WA
McCann, Richard S. ....Newark, DE
McCann, Robert A. ....Tinley Park, IL
McCann, Robert C. ....Danvers, MA
McCann, Robert C., Jr. ....Albany, OR
McCann, Robert E. ....Bala Cynwyd, PA
McCann, Robert W. ....Washington, DC
McCann, Robert W. ....Hawthorne, NJ
McCann, Ronald M. ....Fayetteville, AR
McCann, Ronald Z. ....Hamlin, WV
McCann, Russell J. ....Franklin, TN
McCann, Scott Earle ....El Reno, OK
McCann, Scott J. ....Flint, MI
Mc Cann, Sheila M. ....San Luis Obispo, CA
McCann, Stephen D. ....Naples, FL
McCann, Stephen D., P.A. ....Naples, FL
McCann, Stephen R. ....Zanesville, OH
McCann, Steven ....Washington, DC
McCann, Suzanne ....Phoenix, AZ
McCann, Thomas H. ....Malone, NY
McCann, Thomas P. ....Monterey, CA
McCann, Thomas P. ....Washington, DC
McCann, Thomas W. ....Phoenix, AZ
McCann, Timothy C. ....Detroit, MI
McCann, Timothy I. ....Philadelphia, PA
McCann, Timothy M. ....New York, NY
McCann, Timothy S. ....San Francisco, CA
McCann, Timothy W.
East Grand Forks, MN
McCann, Todd C. ....Salem, OR
McCann, Todd C., P.C. ....Salem, OR

McCann, Tristan .... Boston, MA
McCann, Vonya B. .... Department of State, Bureau of Economic and Business Affairs, GV
McCann, W. Nevins .... Roseland, NJ
McCann, Wilford D. (Will) .... Austin, TX
McCann, William D. .... Danville, CA
McCann, William F. .... Fort Worth, TX
McCann, William H. .... Lexington, KY
McCann, William John, Jr. .... New City, NY
McCann, William M. .... San Jose, CA
McCann, William R. .... Sedro Woolley, WA
McCann, William Vern, Jr. .... Lewiston, ID
McCanna, James P. .... Auburn, IN
McCanna, Konz, Dudas, Kewley & Papendorf, S.C. .... Appleton, WI
McCanna, Michael R. .... Appleton, WI
McCanney, David M. .... Reading, PA
McCann Ezring, Bernadette
New York, NY
McCann O'Connor, Julie
Bloomfield Hills, MI
McCannon, John G. .... Wichita, KS
McCannon, John R. .... Forest Park, GA
McCannon, Marjorie G. .... Augusta, WV
McCanse, Thad C. .... Carthage, MO
McCants & Associates, LLC
Silver Spring, MD
McCants, Clarke W., III .... Aiken, SC
McCants, Clarke W., Jr. .... Columbia, SC
Mccants, Ericka L. .... Georgetown, SC
McCants, J. Lynn .... Mount Pleasant, SC
McCants, John L. .... Columbia, SC
McCants, Jonathan T. .... Jackson, MS
McCants, Leonard Lewis .... Silver Spring, MD
McCants, William R. .... Jacksonville, FL
McCarberg, Peggy J. .... Escondido, CA
McCard, R. Harold, Jr. .... Smyrna, GA
McCardell, Edward .... New York, NY
McCardell, Steven J. .... Salt Lake City, UT
McCardell, Vivian S. .... Philadelphia, PA
McCardell, William E. .... Madison, WI
McCardle, Arthur A. .... El Monte, CA
McCardle, Edward C. .... Allentown, PA
McCardle, Janet Lynn .... Allentown, PA
McCardle, John H. .... Sacramento, CA
McCardle, John R. .... Hayward, CA
McCardle, K. Leigh .... Allentown, PA
McCardwell, Kenneth L. .... Louisville, KY
McCareins, R. Mark .... Chicago, IL
McCarey, Wilma R. .... Oakton, VA
McCargar, George L., III
Grand Rapids, MI
McCargar, George L., Jr. .... Lansing, MI
McCargar, Ian D. .... Fort Collins, CO
McCargo, Samuel E. .... Detroit, MI
McCarl & Harris .... Montgomery, NY
McCarl, James R. .... Montgomery, NY
McCarl, Lucy R. .... Lenoir, NC
McCarley, DeWitt F. .... Charlotte, NC
McCarley, Harold B., Jr. .... Ridgeland, MS
McCarley, Harold B., Jr., PLLC
Jackson, MS
Ridgeland, MS
McCarnan, John R. .... New Castle, DE
McCarney, James G. .... New York, NY
McCarr, Henry W. .... Minneapolis, MN
McCarragher, James D. .... Iowa City, IA
McCarragher, Molly J. .... Madison, WI
McCarrel, Daniel J. .... City of Industry, CA
McCarren, Edward J. .... New York, NY
McCarren, Maureen .... Valley Stream, NY
McCarren, V. Louise .... Burlington, VT
McCarren, William J. .... Denver, CO
Longmont, CO
McCarrey, James L., III .... Anchorage, AK
McCarrey & McCarrey, Inc., A Prof. Corp.
Anchorage, AK
McCarrick, James M. .... New York, NY
McCarrick, John E. .... Washington, DC
McCarrick, John F. .... New York, NY
McCarrick, John J.
Department of Justice, GV
McCarrick & Mayer, P.C. .... New York, NY
McCarrie, Michael J. .... Newtown, PA
McCarroll, E. Allison .... Jamesburg, NJ
McCarroll, Elaine .... Independence, OH
McCarroll, Francis A.
Grosse Pointe Park, MI
McCarroll, J. Patrick .... Torrance, CA
McCarroll, James C.
Pension Benefit Guaranty Corporation, Office of the General Counsel, GV
McCarroll, Jean M. .... New York, NY
Mc Carroll, John J. .... Medina, OH
McCarroll, John K. .... New York, NY
McCarroll, John R., Jr. .... Memphis, TN
McCarroll, John Ramsey, III
Southaven, MS
McCarroll, Joseph Patrick .... Detroit, MI
McCarroll, M. Kathryn .... Derry, NH
McCarroll, Mary H. .... South Laguna, CA
McCarroll, Neil G. .... South Laguna, CA
McCarroll, Neil, II .... Mammoth Lakes, CA
McCarroll, Nunley & Hartz
Owensboro, KY
McCarroll, Orville W.
Manhattan Beach, CA
McCarroll, Patricia .... New York, NY
McCarroll, Patrick J. .... Detroit, MI
McCarroll, Richard T. .... Austin, TX
McCarroll, Scott Thomas .... Austin, TX
McCarroll, Walter J. .... Brooklyn, NY
McCarron, Adrian G. .... Portland, ME
McCarron, Andrew .... Santa Ana, CA
McCarron & Associates .... Washington, DC
McCarron, Catherine F. .... Boston, MA
McCarron, Claudia Drennen
Willow Grove, PA
McCarron, David C.
Grosse Pointe Woods, MI
McCarron, Diane M. .... Boston, MA
McCarron, Elizabeth M. .... Boston, MA
McCarron, James R. .... Englewood, CO
McCarron, Jeffrey B. .... Philadelphia, PA
McCarron, John C. .... Anchorage, AK
McCarron, John T. .... New York, NY
McCarron, Joseph A. .... Bloomington, IL
McCarron, Kerry E. .... Winchester, MA
McCarron, Kevin P. .... Pleasant Ridge, MI
McCarron, Leslie Anne .... Kew Gardens, NY
McCarron, Michael P. .... Danvers, MA
McCarron, Neil F., Jr. .... Bedford, MA
McCarron, Oliver J. .... Philadelphia, PA
McCarron, Philip F. .... Rockaway Park, NY
McCarron, Richard J. .... Edgartown, MA
McCarron, Robert M. .... Edgartown, MA
McCarron, Stephen P. .... Washington, DC
McCarron, Thomas P. .... Upper Marlboro, MD
McCarron, Thomas V. .... Baltimore, MD
McCarron, William, Jr. .... Alexandria, VA
McCart, Alice M. .... Savage, MD
McCart, Donald K., Jr. .... Indianapolis, IN
McCart, Harold F., Jr. .... Jacksonville, FL
McCart, Jason G. .... Covington, GA
Mccart, Linda Fay .... Columbus, OH
McCartan, Bernard T. .... Madison, WI
McCartan, Edw. F. .... Lee's Summit, MO
McCartan, Gary R. .... Ladysmith, WI
McCartan Law Firm, S.C. .... Ladysmith, WI
McCartan, Patrick F. .... Cleveland, OH
McCartan, William T. .... Cedar Rapids, IA
McCarten, Dennis J. .... Providence, RI
McCarten, James M. .... Knoxville, TN
McCarten, Paul V. .... Alexandria, MN
McCarter, C. Thomas .... Toledo, OH
McCarter, Charles C. .... St. Louis, MO
McCarter, David W. .... Stoughton, MA
McCarter, Dorothy B. .... Helena, MT
McCarter, Elizabeth Dunlop .... St. Louis, MO
McCarter, Elizabeth P. .... Nashville, TN
McCarter & English, LLP
Wilmington, DE
Boca Raton, FL
Camden, NJ
Cherry Hill, NJ
Elizabeth, NJ
Hackensack, NJ
Morristown, NJ
Newark, NJ
New Brunswick, NJ
Princeton, NJ
Princeton, NJ
Roseland, NJ
Trenton, NJ
Trenton, NJ
New York, NY
Philadelphia, PA
McCarter, George W. C. .... Shrewsbury, NJ
McCarter & Greenley .... St. Louis, MO
McCarter, Herbert L. .... Hackensack, NJ
McCarter & Higgins .... Shrewsbury, NJ
McCarter, James V. .... Chicago, IL
McCarter, Jerry H. .... Gatlinburg, TN
McCarter, John M. .... Atlanta, GA
McCarter, Kimberly M. .... Chicago, IL
McCarter, Louis E. .... Houston, TX
McCarter, Michael .... Helena, MT
McCarter, Robert A., III .... Washington, DC
McCarter, Sean A., The Law Office of
Columbus, OH
McCarter, Susan A. .... New York, NY
McCarter, Thomas E. .... Atlanta, GA
McCarter, Thomas E., Law Offices of
Atlanta, GA
McCarter, W. Dudley .... St. Louis, MO
McCarter, William K. .... Mentor, OH
McCartha, Jason Paul .... Montgomery, AL
McCartha & Snowden, L.L.C.
Montgomery, AL
McCarthy, A. Justin .... Westford, MA
McCarthy, A. Justin .... Westford, MA
McCarthy, Agnes L. .... Rockland, MA
McCarthy, Alice M. .... Atlanta, GA
McCarthy, Alicia C. .... New York, NY
Mccarthy, Allen J. .... Lowell, MA
McCarthy, Amelia L. .... Milwaukee, WI
McCarthy, Amy .... Detroit, MI
McCarthy, Amy S. .... Cincinnati, OH
McCarthy, Andrea Wenz
Department of Justice, Civil Division, GV
McCarthy, Andrew F. .... Worcester, MA
McCarthy, Anewalt & Alpert, L.L.P.
Allentown, PA
McCarthy, Ann Bridget .... Los Angeles, CA
McCarthy, Ann Price .... Reno, NV
McCarthy, Anne M. .... Allen Park, MI
McCarthy, Anthony J. .... San Jose, CA
McCarthy and Associates .... Chicago, IL
McCarthy, Audrey Hilda .... Danbury, CT
McCarthy, Barry F. .... San Jose, CA
McCarthy, Becky R. .... Ventura, CA
McCarthy, Bernard W. .... New York, NY
McCarthy, Betsy A. .... Philadelphia, PA
McCarthy, Bill D. .... Oklahoma City, OK
McCarthy, Blane Gerard .... Jacksonville, FL
McCarthy, Bob J. .... Lewiston, ID
McCarthy, Bouley & Barry, P.C.
Cambridge, MA
McCarthy, Brendan J. .... Atlanta, GA
McCarthy, Brian .... San Diego, CA
McCarthy, Brian J. .... Los Angeles, CA
McCarthy, Brian J. .... Chicago, IL
McCarthy, Brian J. .... Butler, NJ
McCarthy, Brian J. .... New York, NY
McCarthy, Brian M. .... Dublin, CA
McCarthy, Brian P. .... Mobile, AL
McCarthy, Brian P. .... Chicago, IL
McCarthy, Brian R. .... Duluth, MN
McCarthy, Brian Thomas .... Belleville, IL
McCarthy, Bridget .... San Francisco, CA
McCarthy, Bryan R. .... San Rafael, CA
McCarthy, C. Kevin .... Juneau, AK
McCarthy, Callas, Fuhr & Ellison, P.C.
Moline, IL
Rock Island, IL
Davenport, IA
McCarthy, Carlotta E. .... Boston, MA
McCarthy, Carol A. .... Everett, MA
McCarthy, Carol A. .... Hicksville, NY
McCarthy, Carol M. .... Baltimore, MD
McCarthy, Carol S. Mills .... Pittsburgh, PA
McCarthy, Caroline C. .... Mobile, AL
McCarthy, Catherine F. .... Pelham, NY
McCarthy, Catherine P. .... Washington, DC
McCarthy, Celeste M. .... San Francisco, CA
McCarthy, Charles F., Jr. .... Springfield, MA
McCarthy, Charles J.
Cleveland Heights, OH
McCarthy, Charles J. .... Providence, RI
McCarthy, Charles J., (Ltd.) .... Chicago, IL
McCarthy, Charles R., Jr.
Washington, DC
McCarthy, Christine .... Palo Alto, CA
McCarthy, Christopher .... Morristown, NJ
McCarthy, Christopher J. .... Hartford, CT
McCarthy, Christopher J. .... Clayton, MO
McCarthy, Christopher J. .... Somerville, NJ
McCarthy, Christopher J. .... Bridgeport, WV
McCarthy, Coleen M. .... New Haven, CT
McCarthy, Colin G. .... San Jose, CA
McCarthy, Colleen A. .... Albany, NY
McCarthy, Colleen C. .... Erie, PA
McCarthy, Conna M. .... San Francisco, CA
McCarthy, Corin M. .... Atlanta, GA
McCarthy, Cornelius P. .... New York, NY
McCarthy & Costello, L.L.P.
Lanham, MD
Upper Marlboro, MD
McCarthy, Craig A. .... Phoenix, AZ
McCarthy, Craig A. .... Tallahassee, FL
McCarthy, Craig M. .... Akron, OH
McCarthy, D. Douglas .... Decatur, IL
McCarthy, Daniel A. .... New York, NY
McCarthy, Daniel B. .... San Diego, CA
McCarthy, Daniel F. .... Melrose, MA
McCarthy, Daniel F. .... New York, NY
McCarthy, Daniel J. .... San Francisco, CA
McCarthy, Daniel J. .... Troy, MI
McCarthy, Daniel J. .... Cranford, NJ
McCarthy, Daniel J. .... Philadelphia, PA
McCarthy, Daniel J., (P.C.)
Los Angeles, CA
McCarthy, Daniel K. .... Allentown, PA
McCarthy, Daniel L. .... Bridgeport, WV
McCarthy, Daniel M. .... Chicago, IL
McCarthy, Daniel M. .... Boston, MA
McCarthy, Daniel P. .... Hempstead, NY
McCarthy, Daniel P. .... San Antonio, TX
McCarthy, Daniel P. .... Salt Lake City, UT
McCarthy, Daniel R. .... Cleveland, OH
McCarthy, Daniel T. .... Highland Park, IL
McCarthy, Daniel T. .... Brooklyn, NY
McCarthy, Daniel W. .... Phoenix, AZ
McCarthy, Darren L. .... Dallas, TX
McCarthy, David F. .... Binghamton, NY
McCarthy, David H. .... Peoria, IL
McCarthy, David H., III .... Naperville, IL
McCarthy, David J. .... Washington, DC
McCarthy, David J. .... New York, NY
McCarthy, David J. .... Green Bay, WI
McCarthy, David J., Jr. .... Washington, DC
McCarthy, David W. .... Deer Park, NY
McCarthy, Dawn L. .... Department of Justice, Federal Bureau of Investigation, GV
McCarthy, Deborah A. .... San Diego, CA
McCarthy, Deborah Beckerich
Columbus, OH
McCarthy, Deborah H. .... Hindman, KY
McCarthy, Deborah Yurchuk
White Plains, NY
McCarthy, Denis J. .... San Francisco, CA
McCarthy, Denis J. .... Lapeer, MI
McCarthy, Denis J. .... New York, NY
McCarthy, Denis J. .... Blackstone, VA
McCarthy, Denis J., P.C. .... Lapeer, MI
McCarthy, Denise .... Bloomfield, CT
McCarthy, Dennis F. .... Hartford, CT
McCarthy, Dennis G. .... Monterey, CA
McCarthy, Dennis M. .... Columbus, OH
McCarthy, Dennis M. .... Allentown, PA
McCarthy, Dennis P. .... Globe, AZ
McCarthy, Diana E. .... Philadelphia, PA
McCarthy, Diane M. .... Burlington, VT
McCarthy, Dianna D. .... New York, NY
McCarthy, Dianne .... Boston, MA
McCarthy, Donal F. .... Manhasset, NY
McCarthy, Donald F. .... Hempstead, NY
McCarthy, Donald J., Jr. .... Hartford, CT
McCarthy, Donald J., Jr. .... Albany, NY
McCarthy, Donald P. .... Syracuse, NY
McCarthy, Douglas .... San Bernardino, CA
McCarthy, Duffy, Neidhart & Snakard
Chicago, IL
Skokie, IL
Mc Carthy, E. Thomas, Jr.
Grand Rapids, MI
McCarthy, Edmond R., Jr. .... Austin, TX
McCarthy, Edward A. .... Chicago, IL
McCarthy, Edward C. .... East Chicago, IN
McCarthy, Edward D. .... Cambridge, MA
McCarthy, Edward, III .... Jacksonville, FL
McCarthy, Edward J. .... Omaha, NE
McCarthy, Edward J. .... Voorhees, NJ
Philadelphia, PA
McCarthy, Edward, Jr. .... Jacksonville, FL
McCarthy, Edward, Jr., P.A.
Jacksonville, FL
McCarthy, Edward L. .... Sacramento, CA
McCarthy, Edward P. .... Wellesley, MA
McCarthy, Edward Quentin .... Boston, MA
McCarthy, Edward T. .... Edwardsville, IL
McCarthy, Eileen M. .... Department of Labor, Office of the Solicitor, GV
McCarthy, Eileen P. .... New York, NY
McCarthy, Eileen Songer
New Rochelle, NY
McCarthy, Elisabeth M. .... New York, NY
McCarthy, Elisabeth St. Blaise
New York, NY
McCarthy, Elizabeth K. .... Sebastopol, CA
McCarthy, Ellen M. .... Cleveland, OH
McCarthy, Ellen R. .... New York, NY
McCarthy, Eric J. .... Washington, DC
McCarthy, Eric P. .... Key West, FL
McCarthy, Eugene B. .... New Haven, CT
McCarthy, Fingar, Donovan, Drazen & Smith, L.L.P. .... New York, NY
White Plains, NY
McCarthy & Fish .... Olean, NY
McCarthy, Francis B. .... Pittsburgh, PA
McCarthy, Francis J. .... New Britain, CT
McCarthy, Frank A., Jr. .... St. Paul, MN
McCarthy, Frank D. .... Oceanside, CA
McCarthy, Frank E. .... McLean, VA
McCarthy, Frank H. .... Tulsa, OK
McCarthy, Frederica H. .... Springfield, MA
McCarthy, G. Daniel .... Woodbridge, NJ
McCarthy, G. Milton, Jr. .... Jasper, AL
McCarthy, G. William, Jr. .... Columbia, SC
McCarthy, Gail K. .... Milwaukee, WI
McCarthy, Gale & Moore
North Platte, NE
McCarthy, Gary J. .... Haddonfield, NJ
Philadelphia, PA
McCarthy, George C., (A Professional Corporation) .... Santa Monica, CA
McCarthy, George D. .... Wichita, KS
McCarthy, George E. .... Rockledge, FL
McCarthy, George E., Jr.
Framingham, MA
Mccarthy, George P. .... Athens, OH
McCarthy, Gerald E. .... San Diego, CA
McCarthy, Gerald T. .... New York, NY
McCarthy, Gertrude L. .... Chicago, IL
McCarthy, Gianna M. .... New York, NY
McCarthy, Glenn C. .... Great Neck, NY
Philadelphia, PA
McCarthy, Greg .... Dallas, TX
McCarthy, Gregory A. .... Los Angeles, CA
McCarthy, Gregory C. .... Doylestown, PA
McCarthy, Gyemant & Babbits, A Professional Law Corporation .... Pasadena, CA
San Francisco, CA
McCarthy, Harry J. .... Seattle, WA
McCarthy, Helen M. .... Washington, DC
McCarthy, Helen Waldbillig .... Butte, MT
McCarthy, Henry R. .... Syracuse, NY
McCarthy & Hogan, A Professional Service Corporation .... Puyallup, WA
McCarthy, Hugh J. .... Chicago, IL
McCarthy, Hugh J., & Associates, Ltd.
Chicago, IL
McCarthy, Hugh J., Jr. .... Chicago, IL
McCarthy, Hugh T. .... Upper Saddle River, NJ
McCarthy, Irene .... Morristown, NJ
McCarthy, J. Brian .... New York, NY
McCarthy, J. Donald .... Los Angeles, CA
McCarthy, J. Kevin .... New York, NY
McCarthy, J. Mark .... Syracuse, NY
McCarthy, J. Michael .... Lakeland, FL
McCarthy, J. Patrick .... Sacramento, CA
McCarthy, J. Thomas .... San Francisco, CA
McCarthy, Jack .... Whitehall, MT
McCarthy, James A. P. .... Albany, NY
McCarthy, James B. .... Stratford, CT
McCarthy, James D. .... Mineola, NY
McCarthy, James D. .... Dallas, TX
McCarthy, James E. .... West Des Moines, IA
McCarthy, James E. .... Plymouth, MI
McCarthy, James F. .... Clayton, MO
McCarthy, James F. .... Woodbridge, VA
McCarthy, James F., III .... Cincinnati, OH
McCarthy, James G. .... Chicago, IL
McCarthy, James H. .... Dover, NJ
McCarthy, James J. .... Los Angeles, CA
McCarthy, James L. .... Anderson, SC
McCarthy, James M. .... Chicago, IL
McCarthy, James M. .... Gulfport, MS
McCarthy, James M. .... Rutherford, NJ
McCarthy, James P. .... Chicago, IL
St. Louis, MO
McCarthy, James P. .... Chicago, IL
McCarthy, James P. .... Minneapolis, MN
McCarthy, James P. .... Melville, NY
McCarthy, James P. .... New York, NY
McCarthy, James P., Law Offices of
Boston, MA
McCarthy, James P., P.C. .... New York, NY
McCarthy, James Patrick .... Chicago, IL
McCarthy, James Patrick .... Mineola, NY
McCarthy, James S. .... Elmhurst, NY
McCarthy, James Steven .... Menlo Park, CA
San Francisco, CA
McCarthy, James T. .... Fairfield, CT
McCarthy, James W. .... Fort Dodge, IA
McCarthy, James W. .... Carnegie, PA
McCarthy, James W., II .... Brookline, MA
McCarthy, Jeannette A. .... Waltham, MA
McCarthy & Jennerich .... Rutherford, NJ

McCarthy, Jennifer L. Desmond
Washington, DC
McCarthy, Jeremiah J. ....Buffalo, NY
McCarthy, Jerome F. ....Tacoma, WA
McCarthy, Joan A.
Securities and Exchange Commission, Office of the General Counsel, GV
McCarthy, Joan H. ....Tarrytown, NY
McCarthy, Joanna E. ....New York, NY
McCarthy, Joanne M. ....Chicopee, MA
McCarthy, Joanne N. ....Walnut Creek, CA
McCarthy, John A.
Securities and Exchange Commission, Office of Compliance Inspections and Examinations, GV
McCarthy, John A. ....Atlanta, GA
Mccarthy, John A. ....New York, NY
McCarthy, John A. ....Tacoma, WA
McCarthy, John B., Jr. ....Madison, WI
McCarthy, John C. ....Claremont, CA
McCarthy, John C. ....Los Angeles, CA
San Francisco, CA
McCarthy, John C. ....Rockford, IL
McCarthy, John C. ....Shreveport, LA
McCarthy, John D. ....Denver, CO
McCarthy, John E. ....Southgate, MI
McCarthy, John E., Jr. ....Washington, DC
McCarthy, John F. ....Toledo, OH
McCarthy, John F., III ....Princeton, NJ
McCarthy, John F., Jr. ....Princeton, NJ
McCarthy, John F., Jr. ....Santa Fe, NM
McCarthy, John F., Jr. ....Dallas, TX
McCarthy, John G. ....Stamford, CT
New York, NY
McCarthy, John G. ....Huntington Station, NY
McCarthy, John H. ....Philadelphia, PA
McCarthy, John J. ....Canton, IL
McCarthy, John J. ....Louisville, KY
McCarthy, John J. ....Rockville, MD
McCarthy, John J. ....Boston, MA
McCarthy, John J. ....Wellesley Hills, MA
McCarthy, John J. ....Omaha, NE
McCarthy, John J. ....Brooklyn, NY
McCarthy, John J. ....Cleveland, OH
McCarthy, John J., III ....New York, NY
McCarthy, John J., Jr. ....Wellesley, MA
McCarthy, John J., Jr. ....New York, NY
McCarthy, John J., Jr. ....New York, NY
McCarthy, John James ....Springfield, MA
McCarthy, John Justin ....Norristown, PA
McCarthy, John K. ....Bath, NY
McCarthy, John L. ....East Islip, NY
McCarthy, John M. ....Hancock, MI
McCarthy, John M. ....Richmond, VA
McCarthy, John P. ....Sacramento, CA
McCarthy, John P. ....Fairfield, CT
McCarthy, John P. ....Philadelphia, PA
McCarthy, John R. ....Waterbury, CT
McCarthy, John T. ....Chicago, IL
McCarthy, John T. ....Boston, MA
McCarthy, John V. ....Tallahassee, FL
McCarthy, John W. ....Bangor, ME
McCarthy, Johnson & Miller
San Francisco, CA
McCarthy, Jolianne ....Yonkers, NY
McCarthy, Joseph A. ....Milwaukee, WI
McCarthy, Joseph F. ....Southfield, MI
McCarthy, Joseph G. ....Costa Mesa, CA
McCarthy, Joseph J. ....Portland, OR
McCarthy, Joseph J. ....Alexandria, VA
McCarthy, Joseph M. ....Bartow, FL
McCarthy, Joseph P. ....Buffalo, NY
McCarthy, Joseph P. ....New York, NY
McCarthy, Joseph P. ....Seattle, WA
McCarthy, Joseph V. ....Buffalo, NY
McCarthy, Joseph V. ....Jericho, NY
McCarthy, Judith C. ....New York, NY
McCarthy, Julie Collins ....Boston, MA
McCarthy, Justin G. ....Plymouth Meeting, PA
McCarthy, Justin H., II ....York, PA
McCarthy, Justin J. ....Exton, PA
McCarthy, Justin K. ....Bethlehem, PA
McCarthy, Justin M. ....Riverside, CA
McCarthy, Justin P. ....New York, NY
McCarthy, Karen A. ....Springfield, MA
McCarthy, Karen D. ....New Orleans, LA
McCarthy, Karen M. ....South Sioux City, NE
McCarthy, Karen M. ....New York, NY
McCarthy, Karen R. ....St. Louis, MO
McCarthy, Karin M. ....Uniondale, NY
McCarthy, Kathleen A.
San Francisco, CA
McCarthy, Kathleen A. ....Wheaton, IL
McCarthy, Kathleen Alistair ....Tucson, AZ
McCarthy, Kathleen E. ....New York, NY
McCarthy, Kathleen M. ....Newton, MA
McCarthy, Kathleen M. ....New York, NY
McCarthy, Kathleen M. ....Irving, TX
McCarthy, Kathleen T.
San Francisco, CA
McCarthy, Kathleen V. ....Tallahassee, FL
McCarthy, Kathleen Z.
West Palm Beach, FL
McCarthy, Kathryn A. ....New York, NY
McCarthy, Kathryn A. ....Findlay, OH
McCarthy, Kay H. ....Excelsior, MN
McCarthy, Kay L. ....Kansas City, MO
McCarthy, Kaye L. ....Tempe, AZ
McCarthy, Kelly A. ....Springfield, MA
McCarthy, Kelly A. ....Rochester, NY
McCarthy, Kenneth J. ....Oakland, CA
McCarthy, Kenneth W., Jr. ....Puyallup, WA
McCarthy, Kevin ....Melville, NY
McCarthy, Kevin D. ....Buffalo, NY
McCarthy, Kevin E. ....Newark, NJ
McCarthy, Kevin J. ....Santa Rosa, CA
McCarthy, Kevin J.
West Palm Beach, FL
McCarthy, Kevin J. ....Chicago, IL
McCarthy, Kevin J. ....Portland, ME
McCarthy, Kevin J. ....Lanham, MD
McCarthy, Kevin M. ....Kalamazoo, MI
McCarthy, Kevin M. ....Mineola, NY
McCarthy, Kevin P. ....Newport Beach, CA
San Francisco, CA
McCarthy, Kevin R. ....Santa Ana, CA
McCarthy, Kevin R. ....Washington, DC
McCarthy, Kevin R. ....Cohasset, MA
McCarthy, Kimberly I. ....Providence, RI
McCarthy & Kroes ....San Luis Obispo, CA
Santa Barbara, CA
Santa Maria, CA
Ventura, CA
McCarthy, Lammers & Hines ....Clinton, IA
Davenport, IA
Muscatine, IA
McCarthy, Lara Orsi ....San Francisco, CA
McCarthy Law Firm, The ....New York, NY
McCarthy, Lawrence K. ....Boston, MA
McCarthy, Lawrence P., III
Providence, RI
McCarthy, Lebit, Crystal & Haiman Co., L.P.A. ....Cleveland, OH
McCarthy, Leigh Stephens ....Bangor, ME
McCarthy, Leo A. ....Dubuque, IA
McCarthy, Leo. T. ....Sacramento, CA
McCarthy and Leonard ....Dublin, CA
McCarthy, Leonard, Kaemmerer, Owen, Lamkin & McGovern, L.C.
Chesterfield, MO
St. Louis, MO
McCarthy and Levin ....Chicago, IL
McCarthy, Linda K. ....Danville, CA
McCarthy, Linda T. Pellegrino ....Roseland, NJ
McCarthy, Linda Williams ....Irvington, NY
McCarthy, Lorraine E. ....Coraopolis, PA
McCarthy, Louise M. ....Boston, MA
McCarthy, Luke V. ....Pasadena, CA
McCarthy, M. Charles ....North Platte, NE
McCarthy, Mallary K. ....San Diego, CA
McCarthy, Marcia K. ....Arlington, VA
McCarthy, Margaret ....Brooklyn, NY
McCarthy, Margaret Evans ....Pittsburgh, PA
McCarthy, Maria Christine ....Chicago, IL
McCarthy, Marianne ....Garden City, NY
McCarthy, Marijo ....Newton, MA
McCarthy, Mark F. ....Cleveland, OH
McCarthy, Mark J. ....Albany, NY
McCarthy, Mark Kevin ....Owings Mills, MD
McCarthy, Mark M. ....Cleveland, OH
McCarthy, Mark W. ....Boston, MA
McCarthy, Martin L. ....Kansas City, MO
McCarthy, Martone & Peasley ....Erie, PA
McCarthy, Mary Ann ....Milwaukee, WI
McCarthy, Mary Beth ....Pittsburgh, PA
McCarthy, Mary E. ....King Of Prussia, PA
McCarthy, Mary Ellen ....Carson City, NV
McCarthy, Mary Margaret ....Chicago, IL
McCarthy, Mary R. ....Wakefield, MA
McCarthy, Maryann K. ....Albany, NY
McCarthy & Massey, P.C. ....Fairfax, VA
Manassas, VA
McCarthy, Matthew M. ....St. Louis, MO
Mc Carthy, Maureen ....Toms River, NJ
McCarthy, Maureen W. ....New York, NY
McCarthy, Maurice ....Auburn, MA
McCarthy, Maurice J. ....Chicago, IL
McCarthy & McCarthy ....Wakefield, MA
McCarthy, McDonald, Schulberg & Joy
Pittsburgh, PA
McCarthy, Meredith Lynn ....Larkspur, CA
McCarthy, Michael ....Los Angeles, CA
McCarthy, Michael A. ....San Francisco, CA
McCarthy, Michael C. ....Minneapolis, MN
McCarthy, Michael C. ....Hampton, NH
McCarthy, Michael E. ....Huntington, NY
McCarthy, Michael E.S. ....Los Angeles, CA
McCarthy, Michael F. ....Atlanta, GA
McCarthy, Michael F. ....Honolulu, HI
McCarthy, Michael F. ....Twin Falls, ID
McCarthy, Michael Francis ....Malvern, PA
McCarthy, Michael J. ....Hotchkiss, CO
McCarthy, Michael J. ....Davenport, IA
McCarthy, Michael J. ....Bowie, MD
McCarthy, Michael J. ....Pittsfield, MA
McCarthy, Michael J. ....North Platte, NE
McCarthy, Michael J. ....Omaha, NE
McCarthy, Michael J. ....Powell, OH
McCarthy, Michael J. ....Dallas, TX
McCarthy, Michael L. ....Buffalo, NY
McCarthy, Michael O., III ....Washington, DC
McCarthy, Michael P. ....Wakefield, MA
McCarthy, Michael P. ....Rochester, NY
McCarthy, Michael P. ....Syracuse, NY
McCarthy, Michael P. ....Portland, OR
McCarthy, Michael R. ....Spotsylvania, VA
McCarthy, Michael R. ....Seattle, WA
McCarthy, Michael Robert ....Dalton, GA
McCarthy, Michael S. ....Denver, CO
McCarthy, Michael S. ....Park Ridge, IL
McCarthy, Michael T. ....Chicago, IL
McCarthy, Michael W. ....Phoenix, AZ
McCarthy, Michael W. ....New York, NY
McCarthy, Michele Meyer ....Louisville, KY
McCarthy, Milby Amott ....Richmond, VA
McCarthy, Mitchell K.
Oklahoma City, OK
McCarthy, M. J. ....West Haven, CT
McCarthy and Modelewski ....Huntington, NY
McCarthy, Monika L. ....Los Angeles, CA
McCarthy & Murray ....Medford, MA
McCarthy, Nancy Ellen ....Detroit, MI
McCarthy, Nancy K. ....Brant Rock, MA
McCarthy, Nancy K., P.C. ....Brant Rock, MA
McCarthy, Nancy P. ....San Rafael, CA
McCarthy, Nanette A. ....Chicago, IL
McCarthy, Neil D. ....Beverly Hills, CA
McCarthy, Neil M. ....Washington, DC
McCarthy, Niall P. ....Burlingame, CA
McCarthy, Nora ....New York, NY
McCarthy, Nora A. ....Chattanooga, TN
McCarthy, Noreen E. ....Department of Justice, Environment and Natural Resources Division, GV
McCarthy, Palmer, Volkema & Thomas, A Legal Professional Association
Columbus, OH
McCarthy, Patrice Ann ....Wethersfield, CT
McCarthy, Patricia A. ....Kirkland, WA
McCarthy, Patricia A. B. ....Tampa, FL
McCarthy, Patricia Lynn ....Chicago, IL
McCarthy, Patricia M.
Department of Justice, Civil Division, GV
McCarthy, Patrick ....Santa Barbara, CA
McCarthy, Patrick F. ....Warren, OH
McCarthy, Patrick H. ....Philadelphia, PA
McCarthy, Patrick J. ....St. Louis, MO
McCarthy, Patrick J. ....Morristown, NJ
McCarthy, Patrick J. ....Cleveland, OH
McCarthy, Patrick K. ....Columbia, SC
McCarthy, Patrick M.
Bloomfield Hills, MI
McCarthy, Paul ....Chicago, IL
McCarthy, Paul ....Seattle, WA
McCarthy, Paul A. ....Grand Rapids, MI
McCarthy, Paul B. ....Chicago, IL
McCarthy, Paul F. ....Buffalo, NY
McCarthy, Paul K. ....Vienna, VA
McCarthy, Paul N. ....Philadelphia, PA
McCarthy, Peter J. ....White Plains, NY
McCarthy, Peter L. ....Minneapolis, MN
McCarthy, Peter M. ....New York, NY
McCarthy, Philip E., II ....New York, NY
McCarthy, Philip J. ....Boston, MA
McCarthy, Philip (Jay), Jr. ....Flagstaff, AZ
McCarthy, Randall K.
Oklahoma City, OK
McCarthy, Randolph, Jr. ....Kalamazoo, MI
McCarthy, Richard ....Fairfield, CT
McCarthy, Richard ....Princeton, NJ
McCarthy, Richard C. ....Dundee, IL
McCarthy, Richard C. ....Millville, NJ
McCarthy, Richard E. ....San Diego, CA
McCarthy, Richard F. ....Boston, MA
McCarthy, Richard J.
Department of Transportation, Federal Aviation Administration, GV
McCarthy, Richard J. ....Boston, MA
McCarthy, Richard J. ....Albany, NY
McCarthy, Richard J. ....McLean, VA
McCarthy, Richard T. ....Basking Ridge, NJ
McCarthy, Richard W. ....Rock Island, IL
McCarthy, Richard W., Jr. ....Pittsfield, ME
McCarthy, Rita J. ....River Forest, IL
McCarthy, Robert A. ....Troy, OH
McCarthy, Robert B. ....St. Paul, MN
McCarthy, Robert E. ....Red Bluff, CA
McCarthy, Robert E. ....East Lansing, MI
McCarthy, Robert E. ....New York, NY
McCarthy, Robert E. ....New York, NY
McCarthy, Robert F. ....Albany, NY
McCarthy, Robert F. ....East Meadow, NY
McCarthy, Robert I. ....San Rafael, CA
McCarthy, Robert J. ....San Francisco, CA
McCarthy, Robert J. ....Framingham, MA
McCarthy, Robert J., Jr. ....Saugus, MA
McCarthy, Robert M. ....Bethesda, MD
McCarthy, Robert M. ....Butte, MT
McCarthy, Robert P. ....Williamsville, NY
McCarthy, Robert W. ....Decatur, IL
McCarthy, Robert W. ....Harwich, MA
McCarthy, Robert Weller ....Atlanta, GA
McCarthy, Robin A. ....Philadelphia, PA
McCarthy, Rosemary Conlon
Houston, TX
McCarthy, Rosemary L. ....San Jose, CA
McCarthy, Rowden & Faber ....Decatur, IL
McCarthy, Roy M., Jr. ....Dallas, TX
McCarthy & Rubright, LLP
Red Bluff, CA
McCarthy, Sabrina A. ....Notre Dame, IN
McCarthy & Sadler, L.C.
Salt Lake City, UT
McCarthy and Schatzman, P.A.
Princeton, NJ
McCarthy, Schuman & Coombes
Hartford, CT
McCarthy & Schwartz
San Francisco, CA
McCarthy, Scott K. ....Milton, WI
McCarthy, Scott R. ....New Milford, CT
McCarthy, Sean E. ....Sacramento, CA
McCarthy, Sean Michael ....Arvada, CO
McCarthy, Sean Ryan ....Cass Lake, MN
McCarthy, Shannon
Merit Systems Protection Board, Clerk of the Board, GV
McCarthy, Shannon K. ....Hartford, CT
McCarthy, Shawn P. ....Brick, NJ
McCarthy, Sheila M. ....Cleveland, OH
McCarthy, Sheilah F. ....Wellesley, MA
McCarthy, Sheron D. ....Arnold, CA
McCarthy Small & Associates, P.C.
New York, NY
White Plains, NY
McCarthy, Stephen A. ....Houston, TX
McCarthy, Stephen Gordon, Jr.
Brooklyn, NY
McCarthy, Stephen P. ....Portland, OR
McCarthy, Stephen P. ....Houston, TX
McCarthy, Stephen R. ....Portland, OR
McCarthy, Steven B. ....Red Bluff, CA
McCarthy, Steven D. A. ....Dayton, OH
McCarthy, Steven M. ....Oakland, CA
McCarthy & Sullivan ....Bowie, MD
McCarthy, Summers, Bobko, McKey, Wood & Sawyer, P.A. ....Fort Pierce, FL
Okeechobee, FL
Port St. Lucie, FL
Stuart, FL
Vero Beach, FL
McCarthy, Susan B. ....Cupertino, CA
McCarthy, Susan Chan ....Hillsborough, CA
McCarthy, Susan L. ....Ventura, CA
McCarthy, Susan Mulcahy
Basking Ridge, NJ
McCarthy, Suzanne ....New York, NY
McCarthy, Suzanne E. ....White Plains, NY
McCarthy, Sweeney & Harkaway, P.C.
Washington, DC
McCarthy, T. Carroll, Jr. ....Wheeling, WV
McCarthy, Tara M. ....Manassas, VA
McCarthy, Terence P. ....Stuart, FL
McCarthy, Theresa L. ....San Diego, CA
McCarthy, Thomas A., Jr. ....Glendale, AZ
McCarthy, Thomas C. ....Bellevue, WA
McCarthy, Thomas E. ....Denver, CO
McCarthy, Thomas F. ....New York, NY
McCarthy, Thomas G. ....Gaylord, MN
McCarthy, Thomas H., Jr. ....Denver, CO
McCarthy, Thomas J. ....Wilmington, DE
McCarthy, Thomas J. ....Washington, DC
McCarthy, Thomas J. ....Chicago, IL
McCarthy, Thomas J. ....Chicago, IL
Oak Brook, IL
McCarthy, Thomas J.
Bloomfield Hills, MI
McCarthy, Thomas J. ....Erie, PA
McCarthy, Thomas J., Jr. ....Blacksburg, VA
Pulaski, VA
McCarthy, Thomas, Jr.
Sherwood Forest, MD
McCarthy, Thomas M. ....New York, NY
McCarthy, Thomas O. ....St. Louis, MO
McCarthy, Thomas P. ....Louisville, KY
McCarthy, Thomas P. ....Baltimore, MD
McCarthy, Thomas R. ....Woodbury, NY
McCarthy, Thomas, Sr.
Sherwood Forest, MD
McCarthy, Thomas, Sr., LLP
Sherwood Forest, MD
McCarthy, Thomas W., III ....St. Louis, MO
McCarthy, Timothy ....Des Moines, IA
McCarthy, Timothy ....Louisville, KY
McCarthy, Timothy C. ....Toledo, OH
McCarthy, Timothy H. ....Salinas, CA
McCarthy, Timothy, II
West Des Moines, IA
McCarthy, Timothy J. ....Miami, FL
New York, NY
McCarthy, Timothy J. ....Medford, MA
McCarthy, Timothy M. ....Chicago, IL
McCarthy, Timothy P. ....Delray Beach, FL
McCarthy, Timothy P. ....Kansas City, KS
McCarthy, Timothy P. ....Minneapolis, MN
McCarthy, Tracey Buell ....Syracuse, NY
McCarthy, Vicki K. ....Duncanville, TX
McCarthy, Vincent P. ....Boston, MA
McCarthy, Vincent Patrick ....New Milford, CT
McCarthy, Vincent R. ....Kansas City, MO
McCarthy, Vincent T. ....Flushing, NY
McCarthy, Virginia A. ....Beverly, MA
McCarthy, W. Donn ....Buffalo, NY
McCarthy, W. James ....Tulsa, OK
McCarthy, Warren L. ....Phoenix, AZ
McCarthy & Wayland ....Newton, MA
McCarthy, William ....Boca Raton, FL
McCarthy, William A. ....Thousand Oaks, CA
McCarthy, William A. ....Boston, MA
McCarthy, William B. ....Sunrise, FL
McCarthy, William E. ....Albany, NY
McCarthy, William F. ....Boston, MA
McCarthy, William F. ....Lockport, NY
McCarthy, William H. ....Bakersfield, CA
McCarthy, William H., Jr. ....Boston, MA
McCarthy, William J. ....Clinton, NJ
McCarthy, William J. ....Edinburg, TX
McCarthy, William J., III ....Hellertown, PA
McCarthy, William J., Jr. ....Marlborough, MA
McCarthy, William J., (P.C.)
Baltimore, MD
McCarthy, William M., Law Offices of
Albany, NY
McCarthy, Wilson ....Loomis, CA
McCarthy, Wilson & Ethridge
Washington, DC
Rockville, MD
McCarthy Charney, Bonnie L.
Spokane, WA
McCarthy-Drew, Anita J. ....Osterville, MA
McCarthy-Riegel, Patricia Ann ....Bowie, MD
McCartie, Joseph B. ....Memphis, TN
McCartin, Charles L. ....Lutherville, MD
McCartin, Donald A. ....Santa Ana, CA
McCartin, Edward J., III ....Omaha, NE
McCartin, Gerald P. ....Washington, DC
McCartin, Michael S. ....Westminster, CA
McCartin, Muftiah M.
House of Representatives, Office of Parliamentarian, GV
McCartin, Robert M. ....New York, NY
McCartin, Stephen A. ....Dallas, TX
McCartin, Terrence J.
Department of Commerce, Office of the General Counsel, GV
McCartin, Thomas M., Law Offices of
Rockville, MD
McCartin, William F. ....New York, NY
McCartney, Alan N. ....Library, PA
McCartney, Brian P. ....Schenectady, NY
McCartney, Brian T. ....Jefferson City, MO
McCartney, Carol A. ....Houston, TX

McCartney, Charles E., Jr. .... Shelby, NC
McCartney, David H. .... Philadelphia, PA
McCartney, Donald J. .... Baltimore, MD
McCartney, Donald J. .... Columbia, MD
McCartney, Donald R. .... Kansas City, MO
McCartney, Frank H. .... Flemingsburg, KY
McCartney, James E. .... Hempstead, NY
McCartney, James J. .... Hanford, CA
McCartney, James W. .... San Juan, PR
McCartney, James W. .... Houston, TX
McCartney, James W., Jr. .... St. Louis, MO
McCartney, John H. .... Inkster, MI
McCartney, Joseph P. .... East Hills, NY
McCartney, Julia Helen .... Philadelphia, PA
McCartney, Kathleen M.
General Services Administration, Office of Regional Counsel, GV
McCartney, Ken .... Cheyenne, WY
McCartney, Kendra L. .... Albany, NY
McCartney Law Office, P.C. .... Cheyenne, WY
McCartney, M. Suzanne .... Pittsburgh, PA
McCartney, Marsha McNeill
Flemingsburg, KY
McCartney, Melvin G. .... Madison, WI
McCartney, Michael D. .... Bath, NY
McCartney, Michael J. .... Breckenridge, MN
McCartney, Michael P. .... St. Louis, MO
McCartney, Michelle A. .... East St. Louis, IL
McCartney, N. Thomas .... Bakersfield, CA
McCartney, Noble .... Washington, DC
McCartney, P. Abbott
Federal Trade Commission, Bureau of Competition, GV
McCartney, Patrick A. .... New York, NY
McCartney, Paul W. .... Cincinnati, OH
McCartney, R. Allen .... Louisville, KY
McCartney, Ralph F. .... Charles City, IA
McCartney, Randy L. .... Erie, PA
McCartney, Robert C. .... Pittsburgh, PA
McCartney, Robert M.
Saint Simons Island, GA
McCartney, Shari L. .... Fort Lauderdale, FL
McCartney, Sheila J. .... Purchase, NY
McCartney, Terrence E. .... New York, NY
McCartney, William C. .... New York, NY
McCartney, William H. .... San Antonio, TX
McCartney, William W., Jr. .... Augusta, GA
McCartney-Smith, Enger
Philadelphia, PA
McCartt, James T. .... Houston, TX
McCartt, Roberta L. .... Phoenix, AZ
McCarty, Alison Elizabeth .... Akron, OH
McCarty, Allan P. .... Buffalo, NY
McCarty, Amelia A. .... Covington, KY
McCarty, Barbara J. .... Sacramento, CA
McCarty, Benjamin S. .... Boston, MA
McCarty, Blakemore .... Colorado Springs, CO
McCarty, Bryan K. .... Nashville, TN
McCarty, Charles Barry
Securities and Exchange Commission, Division of Corporation Finance, GV
McCarty, Charles E. .... Spencer, WV
McCarty, Chester E. .... Portland, OR
McCarty, Christopher J. .... Providence, RI
McCarty, Christopher K. .... Southampton, MA
McCarty, Colette L. .... Arthur, IL
McCarty Curry Wydeven Peeters & Haak, LLP .... Appleton, WI
Chilton, WI
Green Bay, WI
Kaukauna, WI
Oshkosh, WI
McCarty, Daniel E. .... Houston, TX
McCarty, Danny J. .... Houston, TX
McCarty, Darren Lee .... Orangeburg, SC
McCarty, David J. .... Los Angeles, CA
McCarty, David M. .... Columbus, OH
McCarty, Deborah O. .... Atlanta, GA
McCarty, Dennis L. .... Ketchikan, AK
McCarty, Devan .... Palo Alto, CA
McCarty, Donald L. .... Julian, CA
McCarty, Edward W., III .... Mineola, NY
McCarty, F. William .... Kalamazoo, MI
McCarty, Franklin B., Jr. .... Winnetka, IL
McCarty, Gary K. .... Liberty, IN
McCarty, Glenn P. .... Santa Fe, NM
McCarty, Holly Garrett .... Birmingham, AL
McCarty, I. Keith .... Charleston, SC
McCarty, J. Laurence .... Washington, DC
McCarty, J. Patrick .... Fort Smith, AR
McCarty, Jack De .... Newkirk, OK
McCarty, Jack M. .... Charleston, WV
McCarty, James A. .... Reno, NV
McCarty, James E. .... Denver, CO
McCarty, James H. .... Gainesville, FL
McCarty, James H., Jr. .... Gainesville, FL
Jacksonville, FL
Ocala, FL
McCarty, James Richard .... Casper, WY
McCarty, James Richard, P.C. .... Casper, WY
McCarty, Jane Ellen .... Wichita, KS
McCarty, Jarrie Davis .... Houston, TX
McCarty, Jeremy R. .... Oakland, CA
McCarty, Jerry F. .... Ennis, TX
McCarty, Joel B., Jr. .... High Point, NC
McCarty, John C. .... Newport Beach, CA
McCarty, John F. .... North Eastham, MA
McCarty, John F., Jr. .... Brockton, MA
McCarty, John J. .... Philadelphia, PA
McCarty, John M. .... Hawesville, KY
McCarty, John V. .... Baltimore, MD
McCarty, Jon Paul .... El Paso, TX
McCarty, Jon S. .... Great Falls, MT
McCarty, Joseph C. .... Memphis, TN
McCarty, Joyce E. .... Washington, DC
McCarty, Julia Stern .... Seattle, WA
McCarty, Karen A.
Jacksonville Beach, FL
Otsego, MI
McCarty, Kevin E. .... Oklahoma City, OK
McCarty, Kevin J. .... Bend, OR
McCarty, Kevin M. .... West Dundee, IL
McCarty, Kevin P. .... Haddonfield, NJ
McCarty, Kimberly A. .... Dublin, OH
McCarty Law Offices, P.C.
Brattleboro, VT
Newfane, VT
McCarty, Lenz, Doyle & Tolkan, S.C.
Milwaukee, WI
McCarty & Lieberman .... Oakland, CA
McCarty, Linda L. .... Chicago, IL
McCarty, Lisbeth L. .... Norman, OK
McCarty, Marcus C. .... Kansas City, MO
McCarty, Mark A. .... Atlanta, GA
McCarty, Mark L. .... Salt Lake City, UT
McCarty, Mark S. .... Seattle, WA
McCarty, Mark Thomas .... Little Rock, AR
McCarty, Matthew Gavin .... Chicago, IL
McCarty & McCarty .... Baltimore, MD
Houston, TX
McCarty, Michael D. .... St. Paul, MN
McCarty, Michael E. .... Cincinnati, OH
McCarty, Michael G. .... San Diego, CA
McCarty, Michael H. .... Cody, WY
McCarty, Michael L. .... Little Rock, AR
McCarty, Michael N. .... Washington, DC
McCarty, Michael R. .... Philadelphia, PA
McCarty, Naomi J. .... Catoosa, OK
McCarty, Neil J. .... Kaukauna, WI
McCarty, P. Gayle .... Memphis, TN
McCarty, Patrick J.
Federal Deposit Insurance Corporation, Regulation and Legislation Section, GV
McCarty, Patrick L. .... Indianapolis, IN
McCarty & Pearcy LLP .... Riverside, CA
McCarty, Philip A. .... Washington, DC
McCarty & Reed .... Cody, WY
McCarty, Richard G. .... Stamford, CT
McCarty, Robert A. .... Riverside, CA
McCarty, Robert A. .... Akron, OH
McCarty, Robert A., Jr. .... Riverside, CA
McCarty, Robert S. .... Chicago, IL
McCarty, Royce A., Jr. .... Hamilton, MT
McCarty & Salerno .... Las Vegas, NV
Reno, NV
McCarty, Shirley .... Birmingham, AL
McCarty, Steven M. .... Columbus, OH
Mccarty, Terence .... Rochester, NY
McCarty, Thomas B. .... Baltimore, MD
McCarty, Thomas E. .... Denver, CO
McCarty, Tonya M. .... Chicago, IL
McCarty, Virginia Dill .... Indianapolis, IN
McCarty, William Blake .... Atlanta, GA
McCarty, William C. .... Lancaster, PA
McCarty, William D. .... Anderson, IN
McCarty, William E. .... Milwaukee, WI
McCarty, William H., Jr. .... Princeton, NJ
McCarty, William L. .... Birmingham, AL
McCarty, William M. .... Brattleboro, VT
McCarty, William M., A Professional Corporation .... San Diego, CA
McCarty, William R. .... Fairborn, OH
McCarty, Wilson & Mash, P.C. .... Ennis, TX
McCarty-Jones, Brendolyn R.
Washington, DC
McCarvel, Francis J. .... Glasgow, MT
McCarvel, John M. .... Great Falls, MT
McCarver, Douglas .... Nacogdoches, TX
McCarver, Leslie Moran .... Scottsdale, AZ
McCarver, Shawn R. .... Farmington, MO
McCarville, Brian Shevlin
San Bernardino, CA
McCarville, Cooper & Vasquez, P.C.
Casa Grande, AZ
Florence, AZ
Phoenix, AZ
Tucson, AZ
McCarville, Joseph B. .... Fort Dodge, IA
McCarville, Joseph L., III .... Hutchinson, KS
McCarville, Kirk A. .... Phoenix, AZ
McCarville, Kirk A., P.C. .... Phoenix, AZ
McCarville, Stephen F. .... Casa Grande, AZ
McCarville, Thomas A. .... Casa Grande, AZ
McCary, Dennis M. .... Albuquerque, NM
McCary & Huff, LLP .... Scotia, NY
McCary, Kathryn .... Scotia, NY
McCary, Paul R. .... Hartford, CT
McCary, Wilson & Pryor
Albuquerque, NM
McCasey, Michael P. .... Grand Rapids, MI
McCash, Sally Presler .... Greenbelt, MD
McCash, Thomas M. .... Dublin, OH
McCashin & Associates, A Professional Corporation .... Pacific Palisades, CA
McCashin, DeAnna M. .... Appleton, MN
McCashin, James P., II
Pacific Palisades, CA
McCaskey, Anthony S. .... Newark, NJ
McCaskey, David I. .... Staunton, VA
McCaskey, Donald L. .... Pittsburgh, PA
McCaskey, Kenneth .... Anchorage, AK
McCaskill, Austin, Sr. .... Little Rock, AR
McCaskill, Claire C. .... Kansas City, MO
McCaskill, D. Paul .... Orlando, FL
McCaskill, Jeffrey S. .... Southaven, MS
McCaskill, Johnathan T. .... Madison, WI
McCaskill, Shawn M. .... Dallas, TX
McCaskill, William G., Jr. .... Nashville, TN
McCasland, Cassandra M. .... Denver, CO
McCasland, Kenneth D. .... Knoxville, TN
McCasland, Kristi I. .... Texarkana, TX
McCasland, Laura L.
Oklahoma City, OK
McCasland, Linda K. .... Purcell, OK
McCaslin, Candace .... Lihue, HI
McCaslin, Collin Bruce .... Torrance, CA
McCaslin, David .... Yuba City, CA
McCaslin, Imbus & McCaslin, A Legal Professional Association .... Cincinnati, OH
McCaslin, James L. .... Elkhart, IN
McCaslin, Leon .... Yuba City, CA
McCaslin & McCaslin .... Elkhart, IN
McCaslin & McCaslin, LLP
Yuba City, CA
McCaslin, Michael C. .... Portland, OR
McCaslin, Nancy A. .... Elkhart, IN
McCaslin, Sharon .... Los Angeles, CA
McCaslin, William G. .... Princeton, KY
McCastlain, Cal .... Little Rock, AR
McCathern, Levi G., II .... Dallas, TX
McCathern • Wadlington • Mooty, L.L.P.
Dallas, TX
McCathren, Randall R. .... Nashville, TN
McCatty, David J. .... Bloomfield Hills, MI
McCaughan, Janice E. .... Fort Lee, NJ
McCaughan, Lorie L. .... Westerville, OH
McCaughan, Nancy Ann .... Detroit, MI
McCaughan, Ralph Lee .... Durham, NC
Durham, NC
McCaughan, Russell .... Fort Lauderdale, FL
McCaughan, William P., Law Office of
Miami, FL
McCaughey, Anne F. .... New York, NY
McCaughey, Constance J. .... Dunedin, FL
McCaughey, Julie A. .... Des Moines, IA
McCaughey, Matthew .... Las Vegas, NV
McCaughey, Maura A. .... Twinsburg, OH
McCaughey & Metos .... Salt Lake City, UT
McCaughey, Stephen R.
Salt Lake City, UT
McCaughey, Timothy J. .... San Jose, CA
McCaughey, Vincent J. .... Warren, MA
McCaul, Eugene W. .... Mechanicsville, VA
McCaul, Martin, Evans & Cook
Mechanicsville, VA
McCaul, Michael T. .... Department of Justice, Criminal Division, GV
McCaul, Paul F. .... Manhattan Beach, CA
McCaul, Shaun P. .... Brockton, MA
McCaulay, J. Timothy .... Fort Wayne, IN
McCauley, Andrea S. .... Fredericksburg, VA
McCauley, Ann .... Framingham, MA
McCauley & Associates ALC
Newport Beach, CA
McCauley, Barbara C. .... Miami, FL
McCauley, Barbara C., P.A. .... Miami, FL
McCauley, Brian C. .... Trenton, NJ
McCauley, Brian T. .... Thornton, CO
McCauley, Carroll L. .... Panama City, FL
McCauley, Carroll L., III .... Panama City, FL
McCauley, Christopher J. .... Parma, OH
McCauley, Clarice K. M. .... Chicago, IL
McCauley, Cleyburn L. .... Wilmington, NC
McCauley, Curtis W. .... Indianapolis, IN
McCauley, Daniel J. .... Darien, CT
McCauley, Daniel P. .... Trenton, NJ
Mccauley, David E. .... Cambridge, MA
McCauley, David M. .... Cedar Rapids, IA
McCauley, David P. .... Honolulu, HI
McCauley, David W. .... Buckhannon, WV
McCauley, Deanne B. .... Lafayette, LA
McCauley, Edward P. .... Chicago, IL
McCauley, Ellen F. .... Boston, MA
McCauley, F. Mark .... Montesano, WA
McCauley, Gentry E., Jr. .... Versailles, KY
McCauley, Gregory M. .... Chadds Ford, PA
McCauley, J. Brian .... San Francisco, CA
McCauley, J. Brian, A Prof. Corp., Law Offices of .... San Francisco, CA
McCauley, James A. .... Fort Lauderdale, FL
McCauley, James A. .... Richmond, VA
McCauley, James Brenton .... Chicago, IL
McCauley, James H. .... Belpre, OH
Marietta, OH
McCauley, James M. .... Richmond, VA
McCauley, James N. .... Ithaca, NY
McCauley, James P. .... Houston, TX
McCauley, John A. .... Baltimore, MD
McCauley, John B. .... Ontario, CA
McCauley, John B. .... Chicago, IL
McCauley, John E. .... Norwalk, CT
McCauley, John F. .... Indianapolis, IN
McCauley, John J. .... Newport Beach, CA
McCauley, John J. .... Lexington, SC
McCauley, John W. .... Los Angeles, CA
McCauley, John W. .... Queensbury, NY
McCauley, Joseph C. .... Lake Delton, WI
Mc Cauley, Joseph G. .... Louisville, KY
McCauley, Judith L. .... Waterville, WA
McCauley, Kathleen M. .... Glen Allen, VA
McCauley, Kathryn A. .... Atlanta, GA
McCauley, Kathryn M. .... Dallas, TX
McCauley, Kevin J. .... New York, NY
McCauley, Linda .... Newport Beach, CA
McCauley, Macdonald, Devin & Huddleston, P.C. .... Dallas, TX
McCauley, Mary Anne .... Santa Ana, CA
McCauley, Mary D. .... Summerville, SC
McCauley, Matthew P. .... St. Louis, MO
McCauley, Matthew R. .... Medford, OR
McCauley & Mattingly .... Versailles, KY
McCauley, Michael B. .... Wilmington, DE
Camden, NJ
New York, NY
Philadelphia, PA
McCauley, Michael Lee .... Bentonville, AR
McCauley, Michael S. .... Los Angeles, CA
McCauley, Michael S. .... Dubuque, IA
McCauley, Michael S. .... Milwaukee, WI
McCauley, Nancy J. .... Harrisburg, PA
Philadelphia, PA
McCauley, Patricia A. .... Baltimore, MD
McCauley, Patrick B. .... Southfield, MI
McCauley, Patrick H. .... Kalamazoo, MI
McCauley & Peters .... Panama City, FL
McCauley, R. Michael .... Dallas, TX
McCauley, R. Michael, Jr. .... Lubbock, TX
McCauley, R. Williford .... Fayetteville, NC
McCauley, Richard G. .... Columbia, MD
McCauley, Richd. R. .... Atlanta, GA
McCauley, Robert F. .... San Jose, CA
McCauley, Robert G. .... Atlanta, GA
McCauley, Robert J. .... Lexington, MA
McCauley, Rosemary .... Bellevue, WA
McCauley, Sharon .... Lake Charles, LA
McCauley, Stephen L. .... Cleveland, OH
McCauley, Steven M. .... Lexington, KY
McCauley, Terrence M. .... Cashmere, WA
McCauley, Thomas Edward, Jr. .... Mesa, AZ
McCauley, Thomas V. .... Chicago, IL
McCauley, Todd M. .... Lake Success, NY
McCauley, Victoria M.
Federal Communications Commission, Mass Media Bureau, GV
McCauley, Vincent P. .... Columbus, GA
McCauley, Webster & Emrick
Belpre, OH
Marietta, OH
McCauley & Weir .... Harvard, IL
McCauley-Libert, Catherine
Monterey, CA
McCauley-Myers, Janie P. .... Middletown, OH
McCaulie, W. Gregg .... Jacksonville, FL
McCauliff, Catherine M. A. .... Newark, NJ
McCaull, John .... Sacramento, CA
McCaulley, Matthew S. .... Sioux Falls, SD
McCaulley, Melissa M. .... Chicago, IL
McCaulley, Richard T., Jr. .... Chicago, IL
McCausland, Cheryl A. .... Roscoe, NY
McCausland, Keen & Buckman, A Professional Corporation
Philadelphia, PA
Radnor, PA
McCausland, Kimberly Barrett .... Boston, MA
McCausland, Margaret A.
Philadelphia, PA
McCausland, Michael E. .... Overland Park, KS
Kansas City, MO
McCausland, Paul S. .... Wichita, KS
McCausland, Peter .... Radnor, PA
McCausland, Robert Bruce
Fort Lauderdale, FL
McCausland, Thomas G. .... Monkton, MD
McCausland, Thomas J.
Fort Lauderdale, FL
McCausland, Timothy J. .... Malibu, CA
McCausland, Timothy J. .... Lakeland, FL
McCausland, Zilda Santos .... Santa Rosa, CA
McCauslin, Anne S. .... Mount Clemens, MI
McCauslin, John E. .... Southfield, MI
McCavitt, Mary Jane
Department of Agriculture, Office of the General Counsel, GV
McCaw & Barnum .... San Francisco, CA
McCaw, Donald B. .... San Francisco, CA
McCaw, Fred H. .... Dubuque, IA
McCaw, Kenneth M., Jr. .... Portland, OR
McCaw, Kirsten L. .... Springfield, NJ
McCaw, Michael E. .... Cincinnati, OH
McCaw, N. Elizabeth .... Seattle, WA
McCaw, Robert B. .... Washington, DC
McCawley, A. Mills .... Evergreen, CO
McCawley, Daniel D. .... Washington, DC
McCawley, Harrison B. .... Washington, DC
McCawley, John M. .... Los Angeles, CA
Mccawley, Matthew C. .... San Diego, CA
McCawley, Paul B. .... Fort Lauderdale, FL
McCawley, Paul J. .... New Bedford, MA
McCawley & Zovich .... Los Angeles, CA
McCay, D. Caffery .... Metairie, LA
McCay, David L. .... Baton Rouge, LA
McCay, Frank .... New York, NY
McCay, James K., II .... Baton Rouge, LA
McCay, Jean A. .... Springfield, IL
McCay, John A. .... Knoxville, TN
McCay, John F. .... Brea, CA
Mc Cay, R. Scott .... Houston, TX
McCeney, Natalie D. .... Glencoe, MD
McChain, Scot Fitzgerald
Christiansted, St. Croix, VI
McCharen, Lealand L. .... Tallahassee, FL
McCharen, Silas W. .... Jackson, MS
McChesney, Amy Hembree .... Marietta, GA
McChesney & Dale, P.C. .... Washington, DC
Bowie, MD
Alexandria, VA
McChesney, Evelyn C. .... Seattle, WA
McChesney, Frances L. .... Sacramento, CA
McChesney, Fred S. .... Atlanta, GA
McChesney, H. L. .... Missoula, MT
McChesney, H. V., Jr. .... Frankfort, KY
McChesney, K. Craig .... Philadelphia, PA
McChesney, Kathleen M. .... Dallas, TX
McChesney, Kathleen Marie
Washington, DC
McChesney & Kinker .... Frankfort, KY
McChesney, Paul S., Jr. .... Spartanburg, SC
McChesney, Paul T. .... Spartanburg, SC
McChesney, Richard .... Los Angeles, CA
McChesney, Robert W., Jr.
Washington, DC
Bowie, MD
McChesney, S. Elaine .... Boston, MA
McChord, John H., Jr. .... New York, NY
McChristian, John W., Jr. .... El Paso, TX
McChristian, Steven C. .... St. Cloud, MN
McChrystal, Michael K. .... Boston, MA
McClafferty, Charles C. .... Jackson, MI
McClafferty, Charles C., P.C. .... Jackson, MI
McClafferty, Charles E. .... Philadelphia, PA

McClafferty, Eric R. ....Washington, DC
McClafferty, Lawrence J. ....Fairfax, VA
Leesburg, VA
McClain, Albert C. ....Bella Vista, AR
McClain, Alfonso & Hernandez, P.A.
Dade City, FL
Zephyrhills, FL
McClain, Allan ....Martinsville, VA
McClain, Andrew Bradley ....Akron, OH
McClain, Anne J. ....Chicago, IL
McClain, Ashley Bates ....Dallas, TX
McClain & Associates, P.A. ....Tampa, FL
McClain, Barat S. ....Chicago, IL
McClain, Brian K. ....Orlando, FL
McClain, C. Dale ....Haverford, PA
McClain, C. Sidney ....Dallas, TX
McClain, Carolyn Briggs ....Harrisburg, PA
McClain, Charles J. ....Berkeley, CA
McClain, Dan D. ....Tampa, FL
McClain, Daniel D. ....Philadelphia, PA
McClain, Daniel L. ....Kansas City, MO
McClain, David H. ....Tampa, FL
McClain, David H. ....Pittsburgh, PA
McClain, David M. ....Oakland, CA
McClain, David M. ....Oroville, CA
McClain, Deborah A. ....Winnetka, IL
McClain, Deborah L. ....Arcadia, CA
McClain, Donald C. ....Portland, OR
McClain, Drexler & Matthews, LLC
Denver, CO
McClain, Edward J. ....Beaver Falls, PA
McClain, Elizabeth Flando
Highland Park, IL
McClain, Ellen Y. ....Treasury Department,
U.S. Customs Service, GV
McClain, Gary Carl ....Memphis, TN
McClain, Gwendolyn Kay
Oklahoma City, OK
McClain & Harrell ....Conroe, TX
McClain, Howard E. ....Adel, GA
McClain, J. Franklin ....Anderson, SC
McClain, J. Gary ....Milwaukie, OR
McClain, J. Kyle ....Houston, TX
McClain, J. Scott ....Atlanta, GA
McClain, James E. ....Dallas, TX
McClain, James M. ....Atlantic City, NJ
McClain, James M. ....Elyria, OH
McClain, James O. ....Memphis, TN
McClain, James W. ....San Diego, CA
McClain, James W., Jr. ....Roxbury, MA
McClain, Janet Treichel ....Indianapolis, IN
McClain, Jeffrey S. ....Cherry Hill, NJ
McClain, Jeffrie M. ....Chattanooga, TN
McClain, Jerry R. ....The Colony, TX
McClain, Joe A. ....Dade City, FL
McClain, John C. ....Grand Rapids, MI
McClain, John C. ....Fort Worth, TX
McClain, John L. ....Olathe, KS
McClain, John N., Jr. ....Raleigh, NC
McClain, Kenneth B. ....Independence, MO
McClain, Kevin T. ....Springfield, IL
McClain, Larry ....Olathe, KS
McClain, Laurene Wu ....San Francisco, CA
McClain, Lee B. ....Chicago, IL
McClain, Linda Christine ....Hempstead, NY
McClain, Linda S. ....Springfield, IL
McClain, Lisa M. ....Houston, TX
McClain, Lucy Pepe ....Philadelphia, PA
McClain, Lyle ....Fort Washington, MD
McClain, Mark A. ....Cleveland, OH
McClain, Martin J. ....Dayton, OH
McClain, Maureen E. ....San Francisco, CA
McClain, Michael F. ....Quincy, IL
McClain, Michael F. ....Albany, OR
McClain & Morgan, A Professional Law
Corporation ....Lake Charles, LA
McClain, Neil L. ....Denver, CO
McClain, Oren W. ....Daytona Beach, FL
Mcclain, Pamela M. ....Richmond, VA
McClain, R. Scott ....Lake Charles, LA
McClain, Ray P. ....Charleston, SC
McClain, Ray P., Attorney, P.A.
Charleston, SC
McClain, Richard A. ....West Palm Beach, FL
McClain, Richard B. ....Pauls Valley, OK
McClain, Richard D. ....Lincoln, NE
McClain, Richard Douglas, P.C.
Lincoln, NE
McClain, Robert Charles ....Melbourne, FL
McClain, Robyn S. ....San Diego, CA
McClain, Ronald R. ....Oakland, CA
McClain, Russell A. ....Los Angeles, CA
McClain, Scott K. ....Hackensack, NJ
McClain, Stephen H. ....Los Angeles, CA
McClain, Stephen W. ....Conroe, TX
McClain, Thomas B. ....Tyler, TX
McClain, Thomas J. ....Pittsburgh, PA
McClain, Tim S. ....La Jolla, CA
Mc Clain, Timothy J. ....Atlanta, GA
McClain, Vaughn L. ....Canon City, CO
McClain, W. Benjamin, Jr. .....Greenville, SC
McClain, W. Benjamin, Jr., P.A.
Greenville, SC
McClain, William A. ....Cincinnati, OH
McClain, William C. ....West Terre Haute, IN
McClain, William H. ....Douglasville, GA
McClain, William, Jr. ....San Diego, CA
McClain, William L. ....Houston, TX
McClain, William T. ....Washington, DC
McClain, William T. ....Dallas, TX
McClain & Young ....Beaver Falls, PA
McClaine, April L. ....Harrisburg, PA
McClaine, Douglas K. ....Pittsburgh, PA
McClain-Sewer, Frank ....New York, NY
McClallen, Robert P. ....Rutland, VT
McClallen Ruggiero, P.C. ....Rutland, VT
McClamma, Charles F. ....Tallahassee, FL
McClamma, T. Edward ....Jacksonville, FL
McClammy, Erika ....Baltimore, MD
McClammy, Melissa Rose ....New York, NY
McClammy, Robert K. ....Montgomery, TX
McClamroch, Michael T. ....Knoxville, TN
McClamroch, W. Tobin ....Indianapolis, IN
McClamroch, William E., III
Knoxville, TN
McClamrock, Grady L., Jr. ....Mocksville, NC
McClanahan, A. A., Jr. ....Sanford, FL
McClanahan, Byron E. ....Shelton, WA
McClanahan, Christopher W.
Denville, NJ
McClanahan & Clearman, L.L.P.
Houston, TX
McClanahan, Elizabeth A. ....Abingdon, VA
McClanahan, Frank C., III ......Greensboro, NC
McClanahan, Gary E. ....Atlanta, GA
McClanahan, Hal H. H., III ....Columbus, MS
McClanahan, J. Michael ....Tucson, AZ
McClanahan, John Baker, Jr.
Richmond, VA
McClanahan, Kay M. ....Washington, DC
McClanahan, L. Scott ....Palm Desert, CA
Rancho Mirage, CA
McClanahan, Marion (Roy)
San Antonio, TX
McClanahan, Mark C. ....Portland, OR
McClanahan, Max L. ....Fremont, CA
McClanahan, Patricia ....Arlington, VA
McClanahan, Randall D.
Birmingham, AL
McClanahan, Randy J. ....Houston, TX
McClanahan, Robert D. ....Durham, NC
McClanahan, Wesley R. ....Enid, OK
McClanan, Glenn B. ....Virginia Beach, VA
McClanathan, Mark P. ....Irvine, CA
McClancy, Christopher P. ....Darien, CT
McClancy, John W., Jr. ....Woodside, NY
McClane, Clarence J. ....Indianapolis, IN
McClane, Dennis R. ....Knoxville, TN
McClane, J. Brock ....Orlando, FL
McClane, John B. ....Fort Worth, TX
McClane, Kim Robert ....Vacaville, CA
McClane Professional Association
Orlando, FL
McClannahan, Cindy A.
Kansas City, MO
McClaran, Joe ....Eureka, CA
McClaran, Pamela ....Seattle, WA
McClaran, Patricia L. ....San Francisco, CA
McClaran, Reid A. ....San Francisco, CA
McClard, Gina Sophia ....Portland, OR
McClard, Jack E. ....Richmond, VA
McClard, Peggy S. ....Houston, TX
McClaren, Michael P. ....Buffalo, NY
Mcclaren, Robert J. ....Mt. Vernon, OH
McClaren, Robert S. ....Houston, TX
McClaren, Samuel L., (P.C.) ....Denver, CO
McClaren, Steven A. ....Harrisburg, PA
McClaren, Susan Moslander
Williamsville, NY
McClarey, Donald R. ....Dwight, IL
McClarkin, Richard B. ....Albuquerque, NM
McClarkin, Richard B., P.C.
Albuquerque, NM
McClarnon, Carol T. ....Washington, DC
McClarty, Homer W. ....Southfield, MI
McClarty, John W. ....Chattanooga, TN
McClary, Andrew F. ....Fort Morgan, CO
McClary, Cheryl L. ....Asheville, NC
McClary, Donald F. ....Fort Morgan, CO
McClary, Glen A. ....Jacksonville, FL
McClary, Patricia A. ....Ithaca, NY
McClary, Paul D., Jr. ....Newport Beach, CA
McClary, Ronald A. ....Kansas City, MO
McClaskey, James A. ....Vancouver, WA
McClaskey, Lori A. ....Irvine, CA
McClaskey, Norman D. ....Rochester, NY
McClaskey, Wayne I. ....Orange, CA
McClaskey, William H. ....Louisville, KY
McClatchey, Christopher J.
Cleveland, OH
McClatchey, Devereaux F. ....Atlanta, GA
McClatchey, Devereaux F., IV ....Atlanta, GA
McClatchey, John F. ....Cleveland, OH
McClatchey, Larry J. ....Columbus, OH
McClatchey, Mary S. ....Denver, CO
McClatchey, Ted P. ....Columbus, OH
McClatchy, Marianne Rice ....Media, PA
McClatchy, Walter A., Jr. ....Upper Darby, PA
McClaugherty & Associates ....Brea, CA
Irvine, CA
Los Angeles, CA
Ontario, CA
Palm Desert, CA
Pasadena, CA
McClaugherty, Jay S. ....Brea, CA
Ontario, CA
Palm Desert, CA
Pasadena, CA
McClaugherty, Joe L. ....Santa Fe, NM
McClaugherty, John L. ....Charleston, WV
McClaugherty, Silver & Downes
Santa Fe, NM
McClaughry, David A. ....Troy, MI
McClave, Christine A. ....Boston, MA
McClave, David R. A. ....Boston, MA
McClave, Wilkes, III ....Stamford, CT
McClay - Alton, P.L.L.P. ....St. Paul, MN
McClay, Brian C. ....Sacramento, CA
McClay, Robert M. ....St. Paul, MN
McClay, Susan D. ....Toledo, OH
McClay, Tyler S. ....Orlando, FL
McClean, Alicia J. ....Valparaiso, IN
McClean & Feinstein ....Media, PA
Philadelphia, PA
Spring City, PA
West Chester, PA
McClean, Geo. W. ....Towson, MD
McClean, James Allen, Jr.
Philadelphia, PA
Spring City, PA
McClean, John Richard, Jr. ....Rock Island, IL
McClean, Robert S. ....Kailua-Kona, HI
Mcclean, Sarah ....Boston, MA
McClean, Steven John ....Baltimore, MD
McClean, Steven M. ....Fresno, CA
McClean, Wayne ....Woodland Hills, CA
McClear, Kevin R. ....Chicago, IL
McClear, Michael J. ....Troy, MI
Mc Clear, Nicholas W., Law Offices of
Montclair, NJ
McClear, Rebecca Chapman ....Owosso, MI
McClear, Richard J. ....Detroit, MI
McClear, Thomas E. ....Lansing, MI
McClearen, R. Edwin ....Raleigh, NC
McClearn, Brenda S. ....Greensboro, NC
McClearn, Hugh J. ....Denver, CO
McClearn, William C. ....Denver, CO
McCleary, Barry W. ....Pensacola, FL
McCleary, Charles A. ....Hartford, CT
McCleary, Dale A. ....El Paso, TX
McCleary, Helen Hendel ....New York, NY
McCleary, Henry G., Jr. ....Lacey, WA
McCleary, James ....Washington, DC
McCleary, Kevin D. ....Baton Rouge, LA
McCleary, M. Aubrey, Jr.
Baton Rouge, LA
McCleary, Mary H. ....Fort Lauderdale, FL
McCleary, Meredith A.
Fort Lauderdale, FL
McCleary, Paul C., Jr. ....York, PA
McCleary, Roger L. ....Houston, TX
McCleary, Scott T. ....Newark, NJ
McCleary, Siobhan ....New York, NY
McCleary, Standish, III ....Portland, OR
McCleary, Thomas A. ....Alta Loma, CA
McCleave, Daniel L. ....Mobile, AL
McCleave, Earl E. ....Kansas City, MO
McCleave, Robert W. ....Rock Hill, SC
McCleave, Roberts, Shields & Green, P.C.
Mobile, AL
McCleerey, Terrance K. ....Monterey, CA
McCleery, Kendall D. ....Ventura, CA
McCleery, P. Scott ....Eugene, OR
McCleery, Philip E. ....Waco, TX
McCleery, Stephen E. ....Houston, TX
McCleery, Stephen L. ....Austin, TX
McCleery, William M., Jr. ....Quincy, IL
McClees, Charles J. ....Houston, TX
McClees, J. Rushton ....Birmingham, AL
McClees, Susan H. ....New Bern, NC
McCleese, Gary D. ....Akron, OH
McClellan, Aaron Karl
San Francisco, CA
McClellan, Ann Brittian ....Gastonia, NC
McClellan, Anne V. ....Bellevue, WA
McClellan, Arthur E. ....Gallatin, TN
McClellan, B. Edward ....Laurel, MD
McClellan, Brian R. ....Walnut Creek, CA
McClellan & Brown, A Professional
Corporation ....San Diego, CA
McClellan, Bryan Lyn ....Spring, TX
McClellan, Carl F. ....Richardson, TX
McClellan, Catherine ....Atlanta, GA
McClellan, Cecil D., III ....Jackson, MS
McClellan, Charles E. ....Oak Brook, IL
McClellan, Christopher A. ....Austin, TX
McClellan, Clark A. ....Roosevelt, UT
Vernal, UT
McClellan, Craig R. ....San Diego, CA
McClellan, Donald K. ....Muncie, IN
McClellan, Dudley ....Austin, TX
McClellan, Edson K. ....Los Angeles, CA
McClellan, Edward T. ....Columbus, OH
McClellan, Fonda V. ....La Grange, KY
McClellan, Frank M. ....Philadelphia, PA
McClellan, Frederick ....Upland, CA
McClellan, Gerald
Department of Defense, GV
McClellan, Gero G. ....Red Bank, NJ
Houston, TX
McClellan, Gregory H. ....Clarksdale, MS
McClellan, Gregory H., P.A.
Clarksdale, MS
McClellan, H. Hentz ....Blountstown, FL
McClellan, Hal D. ....Issaquah, WA
McClellan, Hollis McCray, (Ms.)
Los Angeles, CA
McClellan, Holly Klus ....Chicago, IL
McClellan & House, P.A. ....Blountstown, FL
Marianna, FL
McClellan, J. Stephen ....Tulsa, OK
McClellan, James M. ....Sikeston, MO
McClellan, Jeffrey B. ....Atlanta, GA
McClellan, Jennifer L. ....Richmond, VA
McClellan, John B. ....Baltimore, MD
McClellan, John F., Jr. ....Rome, GA
McClellan, Joseph M. ....Greenwood, SC
McClellan, Julie D. ....Richmond, VA
McClellan, L. Edward, Jr. ....Ocala, FL
McClellan, Larry L. ....San Diego, CA
McClellan, Laura L. ....Dallas, TX
McClellan, Laurel D. ....Kingman, KS
McClellan, Leonard ....Oxford, MS
McClellan, Linda J. ....Pittsburgh, PA
McClellan, Lyle ....Dallas, TX
McClellan, Madison B. ....Stuart, FL
McClellan, Margaret M. ....Denver, CO
McClellan, Mark R. ....Monroe, MI
McClellan, Martha W.
Federal Deposit Insurance Corporation, GV
McClellan, Matthew W. ....Portland, OR
McClellan, McClellan & Arnold ....Muncie, IN
McClellan, Michael B. ....Santa Ana, CA
McClellan, Michael B. ....Champaign, IL
McClellan, Michael D. ....Omaha, NE
McClellan, Nancy F. ....Cullman, AL
McClellan, Powers, Ehmling & Dix, P.C.
Gallatin, TN
Murfreesboro, TN
McClellan, Reagan F. ....Atlanta, GA
McClellan, Renie ....Dallas, TX
McClellan, Richard Paul, III
Honolulu, HI
McClellan, Robert J., Jr. ....Warren, MI
McClellan, Robert L. ....Greensboro, NC
McClellan, Robert M. ....Newport Beach, CA
McClellan, Roger E. ....Wichita, KS
McClellan, Stephen L. ....Ponca City, OK
McClellan, Thomas C. ....Dallas, TX
McClellan, Thomas E.
Arlington Heights, IL
McClellan, Thomas G. ....Mt. Vernon, IN
McClellan, Thomas K. ....Asheville, NC
McClellan, Thomas R. ....Alexandria, VA
McClellan, Timothy J. ....Overland Park, KS
McClellan, Van F. ....Johnson City, TN
McClellan, Vostrejs & Batsel, P.A.
Ocala, FL
Mcclellan, Wendy E. ....Boston, MA
McClellan, Wendy L. ....San Antonio, TX
McClellan, William R. ....Boston, MA
McClellan & Wilson ....Banning, CA
Yucaipa, CA
McClelland & Anderson, L.L.P.
Lansing, MI
McClelland, Anne H. ....New York, NY
McClelland, B. Colt ....Kansas City, MO
McClelland, Bruce ....Oklahoma City, OK
McClelland, C. Irvin ....Arlington, VA
McClelland, Clifton A., Jr.
Melbourne, FL
McClelland, David H. ....Bloomfield Hills, MI
McClelland, Denise H. ....Lexington, KY
McClelland, Denise M. ....Katy, TX
McClelland, Dennis M. ....Tampa, FL
McClelland, Dianne J. ....Pittsburgh, PA
McClelland, Donald C., Jr. ....Sarasota, FL
McClelland, Douglas E. ....Bozeman, MT
McClelland, Frederick R. ....San Diego, CA
McClelland, Gerald R. ....Largo, FL
McClelland, Gregory L. ....Lansing, MI
McClelland, Helvi ....Rochester, NY
McClelland, J. Ralph, III ....Marietta, GA
McClelland, Jack J. ....Zanesville, OH
McClelland, James R. ....Franklin, LA
Morgan City, LA
McClelland, Jas. S. ....Cleveland, OH
McClelland, Jeffrey L. ....Columbus, OH
McClelland, Jill Kleppe ....Washington, DC
McClelland, John W. ....Kansas City, MO
McClelland, Julie M. ....Chicago, IL
McClelland, Keith T. ....Seattle, WA
McClelland, Kelly L. ....Liberty, MO
McClelland, Kem E. ....Austin, TX
McClelland Law Firm, P.C. ....Liberty, MO
McClelland, Lee W. ....Mt. Gilead, OH
McClelland, Lisa K. ....New York, NY
McClelland, Marion G., (Ms.) ....Chicago, IL
McClelland & McClelland ....Marietta, GA
McClelland, Michael A. ....Dallas, TX
McClelland, Michael P. ....Deerfield, IL
McClelland, Michelle Olivia
Department of Commerce,
Office of the General Counsel, GV
McClelland, Muriel ....Albuquerque, NM
McClelland, Nancy P. ....Los Angeles, CA
McClelland, Neal P. ....Canandaigua, NY
McClelland, Philip F. ....Harrisburg, PA
McClelland, Regis M. ....Pittsburgh, PA
McClelland, Robert C. ....Cleveland, OH
McClelland, Robert L. ....Lexington, KY
McClelland, Robert M.
Department of Commerce, GV
McClelland, Robert W. ....Broomfield, CO
McClelland, Roger ....Mystic, CT
McClelland, T. Russell, III ....Roswell, GA
McClelland, Todd S. ....Atlanta, GA
McClelland, Walter B. ....Atlanta, GA
McClellan-Leavitt, Julia ....Indianapolis, IN
McClellian, Michael M. ....Locust Valley, NY
McClellion, W. Richard, Jr. ....Anderson, SC
McClements, Susan K. ....Lexington, MA
McClenaghan, Charles Halle
Coral Springs, FL
McClenaghan, Shannon V.
San Francisco, CA
McClenahan, Barry A. ....San Antonio, TX
McClenahan, David L. ....Pittsburgh, PA
McClenahan, Dianne C. ....Bloomington, MN
McClenahan, George R. ....San Diego, CA
McClenahan, Gregory A.
Minneapolis, MN
McClenahan, Keenan E. ....Santa Ana, CA
McClenahan, William S. ....Madison, WI
McClenan, Jennifer P. ....Washington, DC
McClenathan, Mark J. ....Rockford, IL
McClenathen, Chad M. ....Sarasota, FL
McClendon, Albert Majors ....Dallas, TX
McClendon, Amanda J. ....Nashville, TN
McClendon & Anderson, Inc. ....Eureka, CA
McClendon, B. B., Jr. ....Jackson, MS
McClendon, Ernest L., Jr. ....Livingston, TX
McClendon, Frank L., Jr. ....Henderson, NV
McClendon, Frank O., III ....Tyler, TX
McClendon, Glen P. ....Portland, OR
McClendon, J. Kevin ....Austin, TX
McClendon, J. Stewart ....New York, NY
McClendon, Jack ....Lubbock, TX
McClendon, James C., II ....St. Petersburg, FL
McClendon, James K. ....Austin, TX
McClendon, James L., Jr ....Dallas, TX

McClendon, Jim ... Broken Bow, OK
Idabel, OK
McClendon, Jim, - Lawyer, P.C.
Broken Bow, OK
Idabel, OK
McClendon, John G. ... Orange, CA
McClendon, Kellen ... Pittsburgh, PA
McClendon Law Firm ... Lubbock, TX
McClendon, Leslie B. ... Alexandria, VA
McClendon, Mark A. ... Shakopee, MN
McClendon and McClendon ... Jackson, MS
McClendon, Mont ... Lubbock, TX
McClendon, Regina J. ... San Francisco, CA
McClendon, Rodney P. ... College Station, TX
McClendon, Samuel ... Washington, DC
McClendon, Shannon K.
Dripping Springs, TX
McClendon, Sidney S., III ... Houston, TX
McClendon, Stuart A. ... Metairie, LA
McClendon, William H., III
Baton Rouge, LA
McClendon, William R., III ... Eureka, CA
McClennahan, Kelly D. ... Georgetown, TX
McClennahan, Kelly D., P.C.
Georgetown, TX
McClennen, Crane ... Phoenix, AZ
McClennen, Persis, (Ms.) ... Waltham, MA
Mc Clenney, William, Jr. ... Louisa, VA
McClenny, Carl O. ... Houston, TX
McClenny, Carl O., P.C. ... Houston, TX
McClenny, William M. ... Amherst, VA
Mcclenon, Stephen W. ... Boston, MA
McClerin, Richard Leon ... Charlotte, NC
McClerkin, Hayes C. ... Texarkana, AR
McClernonijk, Francis H. ... Springfield, MO
McCleskey, George H. ... Lubbock, TX
McCleskey, Harriger, Brazill & Graf, L.L.P.
Lubbock, TX
McCleskey, Robert P., Jr.
New Orleans, LA
McCleskey, Steven H. ... Memphis, TN
McCleve, Darren J. ... Mesa, AZ
McCleve, Sheila K. ... Salt Lake City, UT
McCliman, Michelle M. ... San Jose, CA
McClimans, Christine M.
Edwardsville, IL
McClimon, Timothy J. ... New York, NY
McClinchie, Malcolm U., III
San Antonio, TX
McClintic, Denise A. ... Newport, NH
McClintic, Elaine Ferris ... Walnut Creek, CA
McClintic, J. G. ... Mount Pleasant, MI
McClintic, John S. ... Walnut Creek, CA
McClintic, Kelly Jeanne ... Chicago, IL
McClintic, Nancy ... Orlando, FL
McClintic, Nancy, P.A. ... Orlando, FL
McClintock, A. G. ... Cheyenne, WY
McClintock, Amanda L. ... Los Angeles, CA
McClintock, Andrew D. ... Atlanta, GA
McClintock, Burton
Indian Rocks Beach, FL
McClintock, Darren John ... St. Petersburg, FL
McClintock, Donald W., III
Anchorage, AK
McClintock, Douglas J. ... New York, NY
McClintock, Douglas R. ... Plano, TX
McClintock, E. L., Jr. ... Sanibel, FL
McClintock, Elizabeth Ann ... Pueblo, CO
McClintock, Gary F. ... Independence, IA
McClintock, George D. ... Minneapolis, MN
McClintock, Gordon E. ... Palo Alto, CA
McClintock, Gregory R. ... Los Angeles, CA
McClintock, Ingrid Olson ... Charlotte, NC
McClintock, J. Wesley, III ... Tazewell, VA
McClintock, Janet M. ... Augusta, ME
McClintock, John A. ... Des Moines, IA
McClintock, John C., Jr. ... Rugby, ND
McClintock, John R. D.
North Andover, MA
McClintock, John W., Jr. ... Tazewell, VA
McClintock, Keith E. ... New York, NY
McClintock, Kenneth W. ... Council Grove, KS
McClintock, Linda B. ... Pittsburgh, PA
McClintock, Lissa Lieberman ... Pittsburgh, PA
McClintock, Lon T. ... Bennington, VT
McClintock, Marley C. ... Denver, CO
McClintock & McClintock ... Tazewell, VA
McClintock, Michael C. ... Spokane, WA
McClintock, Morris K. ... Sherborn, MA
McClintock, Nathan B. ... Coos Bay, OR
McClintock, Patrick R. ... Tazewell, VA
McClintock, Robert G. ... St. Louis, MO
McClintock, Roberta G. ... New York, NY
McClintock, Rocky L. ... Georgetown, KY
McClintock, Shawn L., (Ms.) ... Horsham, PA
McClintock, Stephen H.
Corona Del Mar, CA
McClintock, Steven D. ... Kingsport, TN
McClintock, Thomas L. ... La Salle, IL
McClinton, Ben ... San Francisco, CA
McClinton, Gregory L. ... Culver City, CA
McClinton, Matthew C. ... Waco, TX
McClinton, Michael C. ... Salem, OR
McClinton, Rex J. ... Dawsonville, GA
Mc Clinton, Robert L. ... Detroit, MI
Mcclinton, Tamara Lee Pierce ... Boston, MA
McClish, John N. ... Austin, TX
McClister, Chase G. ... Kittanning, PA
McClister, James D. ... Kittanning, PA
McCloat, Karen G. ... New York, NY
McClorey, David M. ... Berkley, MI
McClory, Michael G. ... Portland, OR
McClory, Michael J. ... Detroit, MI
McClory, Thomas I. ... Phoenix, AZ
McClory, Toni S. ... Phoenix, AZ
McCloskey, Andrew R. ... San Diego, CA
McCloskey, Ann E. ... Rego Park, NY
McCloskey, Carol J. ... Detroit, MI
McCloskey, Charles F., Jr. ... Denver, CO
McCloskey, Daniel T. ... San Francisco, CA
McCloskey, David M. ... Pittsburgh, PA
McCloskey, David M., P.C.
Pittsburgh, PA
McCloskey, Dennery, Page & Hennesy
New Orleans, LA
McCloskey, Douglas O. ... Kirkwood, MO
McCloskey, Edward J. ... New Orleans, LA
McCloskey, Frank ... Bloomington, IN
McCloskey & Fritsch, P.C. ... Washington, PA
McCloskey, Gregory R. ... Moorestown, NJ
McCloskey, H. Sloan ... New Orleans, LA
McCloskey, Heather L. ... Los Angeles, CA
McCloskey, Holland Denton
San Diego, CA
McCloskey, Jane ... Schenectady, NY
McCloskey, John V., Jr. ... Wakefield, RI
McCloskey, Julie A. ... Orange, CA
McCloskey, Kelly A. ... Chicago, IL
McCloskey, Kevin J. ... Covina, CA
McCloskey, Langenstein & Stoller, L.L.P.
Metairie, LA
New Orleans, LA
McCloskey, Marilyn R. ... Sacramento, CA
McCloskey, Mark T. ... St. Louis, MO
McCloskey, Mark T., P.C. ... St. Louis, MO
McCloskey, Maureen A. ... Washington, DC
McCloskey, Michael P. ... San Diego, CA
McCloskey, Patricia N. ... St. Louis, MO
McCloskey, Patrick L. ... Mineola, NY
McCloskey, Paul (Pete) N., Jr.
Redwood City, CA
McCloskey, Peter F. ... Arlington, VA
McCloskey, Richard J.
Department Of Health And Human Services, GV
McCloskey, Robert D. ... Walnut Creek, CA
McCloskey, Robert L. ... Washington, DC
McCloskey, Sarah ... Deer Isle, ME
McCloskey, Sean Francis ... Santa Rosa, CA
McCloskey, Sharon A. ... New York, NY
McCloskey, Stephen P. ... Washington, PA
McCloskey, Stephen S. ... Baltimore, MD
McCloskey, Terence J. ... New Brighton, MN
McCloskey, Thomas D. ... Holmdel, NJ
McCloskey, Thomas P. ... Ozone Park, NY
McCloskey, Timothy ... Houston, TX
McCloskey, William F., Jr.
New Brunswick, NJ
McCloskey, Wynn B., III ... Houston, TX
McClosky, Donald C.
Fort Lauderdale, FL
McClosky, E. Jacob ... Chicago, IL
McClosky, Gregg W. ... Boca Raton, FL
McClosky, Marcus Ryan ... Los Angeles, CA
McClosky, Reed B. ... Fort Lauderdale, FL
McCloud, Barbara L ... Lawrence, KS
McCloud & Boedigheimer, P.L.L.P.
Minneapolis, MN
Shakopee, MN
McCloud, Duke ... Rockville, MD
McCloud, George E. ... Clayton, MO
McCloud, Howard D. ... Tulsa, OK
McCloud, Janet S. ... Los Angeles, CA
McCloud, Karen D. ... Dallas, TX
McCloud, Kelly W. ... San Francisco, CA
McCloud, Linda K. ... Houston, TX
McCloud, Michael J., Jr. ... Dallas, TX
McCloud, Peter L. ... Charlottesville, VA
McCloud, Robert O., Jr. ... Atlanta, GA
McCloud, Samuel A. ... Minneapolis, MN
McCloud, Sharon L. ... Gainesville, FL
McCloud, Steven B. ... Nashville, TN
McCloud, Tyler S. ... Baton Rouge, LA
McClow, John H. ... Gunnison, CO
McClow, Roger J. ... Southfield, MI
McClow, Thomas A. ... Geneva, IL
McClow, Thomas A., Ltd. ... Geneva, IL
McCloy, Clifford E., Jr. ... Little Rock, AR
McCloy, D. Ross, Jr. ... Panama City, FL
McCloy, Elizabeth K. ... Chicago, IL
McCloy, Robert J., III ... Parkersburg, WV
McCloy, Rosemarie R. ... New York, NY
McCloy, Stuart ... Nashville, TN
McCluan, William T. ... Melbourne, FL
McClue, Sidney G., Jr. ... La Jolla, CA
McCluen, J. Scott ... Harriman, TN
McCluer, Etelka ... San Antonio, TX
McCluer, Richmond H., Jr. ... Rochester, MN
McCluggage, Michael L. ... Chicago, IL
McClune, Gregory W. ... San Francisco, CA
McClune, John D. ... Broomfield, CO
Troy, MI
McClune, Pamela ... Denver, CO
McClung, A. Keith, Jr. ... Baltimore, MD
McClung, Barbara G. ... Emeryville, CA
McClung, Charles D. ... Portland, OR
McClung, Charles E., (A Professional Corporation) ... Laguna Beach, CA
McClung, Charles E., Jr.
Laguna Beach, CA
McClung, Christopher C. ... Winfield, WV
McClung, Craig T. ... Miami, FL
McClung, Daniel C. ... Blackwell, OK
McClung & Davis ... Laguna Beach, CA
McClung, Deborah ... Horseshoe Bay, TX
McClung, Donald R. ... Hollywood, FL
McClung, Frank A. ... Brooksville, FL
McClung, Jack C. ... Charleston, WV
McClung, John B. ... St. Paul, MN
McClung, John L. ... San Antonio, TX
McClung, L. Thomas ... Metairie, LA
McClung, Larry S. ... Denver, CO
McClung, Megan Healy ... Chicago, IL
McClung, Melinda E. ... Birmingham, AL
McClung, Merle S. ... Littleton, CO
McClung, Pat ... McKinney, TX
McClung, Paul J. ... Fort Worth, TX
McClung, Peters and Simon ... Albany, NY
McClung, William B. ... Lexington, VA
McClung, William B., & Assocs., P.C.
Lexington, VA
McClure, Alexandra ... Menlo Park, CA
McClure, Alfred E. ... Lafayette, IN
McClure, Allen W. ... Dallas, TX
McClure, Ann ... Bloomfield, CT
McClure, Ann C. ... El Paso, TX
McClure, Ann L. ... Hays, KS
McClure, Anne E. Warner ... Alvarado, TX
McClure, Benjamin M. ... Fort Worth, TX
McClure, Benton J. ... St. Petersburg, FL
McClure, Brannan & Hardwick
Beardstown, IL
Virginia, IL
McClure, Bruce L. ... Covington, KY
McClure, C. Micheal ... Monterey, CA
McClure, Callaghan & Atkins
Charlottesville, VA
McClure, Carol Bingham ... Houston, TX
McClure & Carter ... Santa Ana, CA
McClure, Catherine Carson ... Boston, MA
McClure, Charles A. ... Tampa, FL
McClure, Charles D. ... Tallahassee, FL
McClure, Charles I. ... Olympia, WA
McClure, Charles J. ... Tigard, OR
McClure, Christa ... Library of Congress, Office of the General Counsel, GV
McClure, Christine Hall ... Erie, PA
McClure, Christopher L. ... Miami, FL
McClure, Daniel M. ... Houston, TX
McClure, Daniel R. ... Atlanta, GA
McClure, David ... San Diego, CA
McClure, David E. ... Indianapolis, IN
McClure, David E. ... Winchester, VA
McClure, David J. ... Alexandria, VA
McClure, David R. ... Wichita, KS
McClure, David R. ... El Paso, TX
McClure, David W. ... Lawrence, KS
McClure, Deborah S. ... Amarillo, TX
McClure, D. L. ... Houston, TX
McClure, Don E. ... Houston, TX
McClure, Douglas C. ... Walnut Creek, CA
McClure, Douglas G. ... Ann Arbor, MI
McClure, Douglas L. ... Visalia, CA
McClure, Edith F. ... Hartford, CT
McClure, Edward M. ... Vienna, VA
McClure, Edwin N. ... Rogers, AR
McClure & Eggleston, A Prtn. incl. Prof. Corps. ... Monte Vista, CO
Denver, CO
McClure, Elizabeth S. ... Towson, MD
McClure, F. Steven ... Burleson, TX
McClure, Frank A. ... Cambridge, OH
McClure, Frederick P. ... Boston, MA
Providence, RI
McClure, Fredrick H. L. ... Tampa, FL
McClure, Gene B. ... Atlanta, GA
McClure, Gene B., P.C. ... Atlanta, GA
McClure, George L., Jr. ... Malvern, AR
McClure, George M. ... St. Augustine, FL
McClure, George M., III ... Danville, KY
McClure, George S ... Beardstown, IL
Virginia, IL
McClure, George W. ... Martinez, CA
McClure, George W., Jr. ... Ukiah, CA
McClure, Harvey D. ... Erie, PA
McClure, Heather P. ... Dallas, TX
McClure, Helen P. ... Washington, DC
McClure, Howard J. ... Moorpark, CA
McClure, Hugh ... Seattle, WA
McClure, J. David ... Lebanon, IN
Zionsville, IN
McClure, J. Justin ... Washington, DC
McClure, J. Michael ... Santa Ana, CA
McClure, James A. ... Boise, ID
McClure, James A., Jr. ... St. Petersburg, FL
McClure, James E. ... Plantation, FL
McClure, James E., Jr. ... Irving, TX
McClure, James F., Jr. ... Williamsport, PA
McClure, James H. ... Atlanta, GA
McClure, James, III ... Sardis, MS
McClure, James J., Jr. ... Chicago, IL
McClure, James, Jr. ... Sardis, MS
McClure, James M. ... Huntingdon, PA
McClure, James R. ... Muskogee, OK
McClure, James T. ... Wheeling, WV
McClure, Jay Y. ... Atlanta, GA
McClure, Jeanah Pearson ... Nashville, TN
McClure, Jeffrey B. ... Houston, TX
McClure, Jeffrey G. ... Walnut Creek, CA
McClure, Jennifer Riel ... Irvine, CA
McClure, Jesse Foster, III ... Austin, TX
McClure, John ... Miami, FL
McClure, John C. ... Columbus, NE
McClure, John C., (P.C.) ... Denver, CO
Monte Vista, CO
McClure, John D. ... Cincinnati, OH
McClure, John F. ... Chicago, IL
McClure, John K. ... Lake Placid, FL
Sebring, FL
McClure, Jon W. ... Valdosta, GA
McClure, Julia L. ... New Brunswick, NJ
McClure, Julian H. ... Tucson, AZ
McClure, Karen Orr ... Lafayette, IN
McClure, Katherine ... Quincy, MA
McClure, Kathie Gunter ... Atlanta, GA
McClure, Kathleen Fehr ... Cincinnati, OH
McClure, Kathy L. ... Department of Justice, Criminal Division, GV
McClure, Kelly Gaffney ... Dallas, TX
McClure, Kelly J. ... Stamford, CT
McClure, Kenneth R. ... Boise, ID
McClure, Kent D. ... Dallas, TX
McClure, L. Milton ... Beardstown, IL
Virginia, IL
Mc Clure, L. Shannon ... Memphis, TN
McClure, Lamont G. ... Lancaster, PA
McClure, Larry J. ... Newton, NJ
McClure Law Offices, S.C. ... Delafield, WI
McClure, Lawrence J. ... Pasadena, CA
McClure, Lawrence R. ... Marshall, MO
McClure, Lorie A. ... Chicago, IL
McClure, L. R. ... Louisville, KY
McClure, Luci Jankowski ... Philadelphia, PA
McClure, M. Clifton ... Charlottesville, VA
McClure, M. Tom ... St. Petersburg, FL
McClure, Marcia B. ... Bingham Farms, MI
McClure, Margaret Maxwell
Houston, TX
McClure, McClure & Kammen
Indianapolis, IN
McClure & McClure, L.L.C. ... Atlanta, GA
McClure, Melanie A. ... Sacramento, CA
Mcclure, Melanie J. ... Little Rock, AR
McClure, Melvin, Jr. ... Senatobia, MS
McClure, Meredith Ann ... Washington, DC
McClure, Michelle A. ... Chicago, IL
McClure, Michelle DeVondria ... Charlotte, NC
McClure, Michelle K. ... Portland, OR
McClure, Mike ... Fort Worth, TX
McClure & Miller ... Erie, PA
McClure, Milton ... Beardstown, IL
McClure, Mindy ... Colleyville, TX
Mc Clure, Monique A. ... New York, NY
McClure, Nancy Arneson ... St. Paul, MN
McClure, Neal E. ... Glendale, CA
McClure, Paul J., Jr. ... Memphis, TN
McClure, Ramsay & Dickerson, LLP
Clayton, GA
Toccoa, GA
McClure, Raymond ... Sacramento, CA
McClure, Rebecca S. ... Indianapolis, IN
McClure, Rebecca S. ... York, PA
McClure, Richard D. ... Avon Lake, OH
McClure, Richard P. ... Belleville, MI
McClure, Rick H. ... Tallahassee, FL
McClure, Robert A. ... Topeka, KS
McClure, Robert A., II ... San Antonio, TX
McClure, Robert D. ... Louisville, KY
McClure, Robert F. ... Trenton, GA
McClure, Robert W. ... Naples, FL
McClure, Robt. C. ... Minneapolis, MN
McClure, Roger ... Alexandria, VA
McClure, Sarah B. ... Washington, DC
McClure, Scott D. ... Washington, DC
McClure, Scott P. ... Washington, DC
McClure, Searcy D. ... Albany, GA
McClure & Shuler ... Sardis, MS
McClure, Stephanie ... Fort Worth, TX
McClure, Steven W. ... Gila Bend, AZ
McClure, Teri Plummer ... Atlanta, GA
McClure, Terry N. ... Fort Worth, TX
McClure, Thomas E. ... Bourbonnais, IL
McClure, Thomas J. ... Delafield, WI
McClure, Wade L. ... Dallas, TX
McClure & Weatherby, LLC
Bloomfield, CT
McClure, William C. ... Pittsburgh, PA
McClure, William F., Jr. ... Danbury, CT
McClure, William L. ... Menlo Park, CA
McClure, William P. ... Washington, DC
McClure, William R. ... Hackensack, NJ
McClurg, Andrew J. ... Little Rock, AR
McClurg, David A. ... Milwaukee, WI
McClurg, Douglas P. ... Tampa, FL
McClurg, E.V. ... Lakeland, FL
McClurg, James W. ... Portland, OR
McClurg, Marcia M. ... Lincoln, NE
McClurg, Mark A. ... Des Moines, IA
McClurg, Michael D. ... Greenville, OH
Versailles, OH
McCluskey and Associates ... Austin, TX
McCluskey, Christine Crockett
Jackson, MS
McCluskey, David ... San Francisco, CA
McCluskey, Gerald E. ... Santa Monica, CA
McCluskey, Glen R. ... Edina, MN
McCluskey, Holly Lee ... Lima, OH
McCluskey, J. Joseph ... Stroudsburg, PA
McCluskey, James B. ... Wheeling, WV
McCluskey, James F. ... Downers Grove, IL
McCluskey, Jeff ... Huntsville, AL
McCluskey, John E. ... Brockton, MA
McCluskey, John E. ... Lynnwood, WA
McCluskey, John J., Jr.
Downers Grove, IL
McCluskey, Joseph A. ... Fort Pierce, FL
McCluskey, Joseph D. ... Richmond, VA
McCluskey, Joseph P. ... York, NE
McCluskey, Kevin G. ... Santa Monica, CA
McCluskey, Laurie A. ... Portland, OR
McCluskey, Michael J. ... Stuart, FL
McCluskey, Murray P. ... Sylacauga, AL
McCluskey, Phillips Kimberly
Wheeling, WV
McCluskey, Robert E. ... Federal Way, WA
McCluskey, Ronald P. ... Austin, TX
McCluskey, Ruth L. ... Modesto, CA
McCluskey, Susan D.
Federal Labor Relations Authority, Authority Member Staff, GV
McCluskey, William J. ... Key Largo, FL
McCluskey-Schink, Danielle ... Flint, MI
McClusky, James P. ... Adams, NY
McClusky, John P. ... Birmingham, AL
McClusky, John P., P.C. ... Birmingham, AL
McClusky, Timothy M. ... Adams, NY
McClusky, William J. ... Adams, NY
McClutchey, Elizabeth L. ... San Diego, CA
McClutchy, James T., Jr. ... Milwaukee, WI
McClymond, J. L., Jr. ... Breckenridge, TX
Mcclymonds, James Taylor ... Albany, NY
McClymonds, Robert C. ... Miami, FL

McClymonds, Susan E. ... Los Angeles, CA
McClymont, James R. ... North Platte, NE
McClymont, John F. ... Norton, KS
McCoach, Howard J. ... Stratford, NJ
McCobb, James E. ... Portland, OR
McCobb, John B., Jr. ... Armonk, NY
McCobb, Thomas ... Syracuse, NY
McCoid, David L. ... Mt. Pleasant, IA
McCoid, Jennifer A. ... Atlanta, GA
McCoid, John C., II ... Charlottesville, VA
McCoid & McCoid ... Mt. Pleasant, IA
McCoid, Nancy K. ... Seattle, WA
McCoid, Robert G. ... Wheeling, WV
McCoin, Ann Yarbro ... Cleveland, TN
McCoin, George N. ... Cleveland, TN
McCoin, Michael A.
Federal Communications Commission, International Bureau, GV
McCole, Timothy S. ... Jackson, MS
Mccolery, Gary Ray ... Athens, GA
McColgan, Arthur J., II ... Chicago, IL
Mccolgan, Daniel J. ... New Bedford, MA
McColgan, Hugh E. ... Pasadena, CA
McColgan, James T., III ... Memphis, TN
McColgan, John A., Jr. ... Saginaw, MI
Mccolgan, Lisa M. ... Andover, MA
McColgan, Susan Magee ... Chicago, IL
McColgan and Vanni ... Pasadena, CA
McColgin, David L. ... Philadelphia, PA
McColgin, Quentin P. ... Chicago, IL
McColl, Alexander M. S. ... Boulder, CO
McColl, Ann W. ... Raleigh, NC
McColl, Archibald C., III ... Dallas, TX
McColl, Brian F. ... Boise, ID
McColl, Diane Barber ... Washington, DC
McColl, Jennifer Duncan Collier
Washington, DC
McColl, John C. ... Fort Gratiot, MI
McColl, Mark A. ... St. Louis, MO
McColl & McColloch ... Dallas, TX
McColl, Michael H. ... Chicago, IL
McColl, William Duncan D, II
Arlington, VA
McCollam, Andrew, III ... Houston, TX
McCollam, Brian J. ... Chicago, IL
McCollam, Edmund ... Houma, LA
McCollam & Glassco, P.A. ... Tulsa, OK
McCollam, John M., (A P.L.C.)
New Orleans, LA
McCollam, M. E. (Malcolm) ... Tulsa, OK
McCollem, Mark R. ... Fort Lauderdale, FL
McCollem, Mark R., P.A., Law Offices of
Fort Lauderdale, FL
McCollester, Lauren E. ... New York, NY
McColley, Dawn M. ... Tacoma, WA
McColley, Denise Herman ... Napoleon, OH
McColley, John C. ... Indianapolis, IN
McCollister, H. R., P.C. ... Denver, CO
McCollister, H. Richard ... Denver, CO
McCollister & McCleary, A Professional Law Corporation ... Baton Rouge, LA
McCollister, Rolfe H. ... Baton Rouge, LA
McCollister, Scott Andrew ... Cleveland, OH
McCollister, Sharon F. Kopp
Westerville, OH
McCollister, Stephen G. ... Baton Rouge, LA
McColloch, Andrew H. ... St. Charles, MO
McColloch & Burns ... Greybull, WY
McColloch & Campitiello ... Carlsbad, CA
San Diego, CA
McColloch, Janet Baldwin ... Dallas, TX
McColloch, M. Scott ... Greybull, WY
Lovell, WY
McColloch, Michael T. ... Carlsbad, CA
McColloch, Murray M. ... Plano, TX
McColloch, Rodney R. ... Marietta, GA
McColloch, S. Michael ... Dallas, TX
McCollom, Alan T. ... Portland, OR
McCollom, Charles R., III ... Henderson, KY
McCollom, Daniel P. ... Wilmington, DE
McCollom, James P., Jr. ... Corpus Christi, TX
McCollom, Lara L. ... West Des Moines, IA
McCollom, Leslie L. ... Austin, TX
McCollom, Marjorie E. ... Chicago, IL
McCollester, Lee S. ... Harahan, LA
McCollough & Associates, P.C.
Austin, TX
McCollough, Celeste ... Atlanta, GA
McCollough, J. Parker ... Austin, TX
McCollough, John S. ... St. Louis, MO
McCollough, Katherine A. ... Houston, TX
McCollough & McCollough ... Houston, TX
McCollough, Milton B. ... Houston, TX
McCollough, Pamela J. ... Houston, TX
McCollough, Patrick H. ... Lansing, MI
McCollough, Terry L. ... Orlando, FL
McCollough, Terry L., P.A. ... Orlando, FL
McCollough, W. Bennett ... Kingstree, SC
McCollough, W. Scott ... Austin, TX
McCollow, Laura Anne ... Minneapolis, MN
McCollum, Alice O. ... Dayton, OH
McCollum, Bayer and Bunch, P.C.
Encino, CA
Fresno, CA
San Jose, CA
McCollum, Carolyn B.
National Labor Relations Board, Office of the General Counsel, GV
McCollum, Craig R.
San Luis Obispo, CA
McCollum, Crowley, Vehanen, Moschet & Miller, Ltd. ... Bloomington, MN
Minneapolis, MN
Rice Lake, WI
McCollum, Cynthia L. ... Minneapolis, MN
McCollum, Donna J. ... Youngstown, OH
McCollum, Douglass J. ... Arlington, VA
McCollum, Duane L. ... Riverside, CA
McCollum, Elliott P., Jr. ... Macon, GA
McCollum, Frank B. W.
Kansas City, MO
McCollum, Gail Smith ... Opelika, AL
McCollum, Ira W. (Bill), Jr. ... Orlando, FL
McCollum, James E. ... Columbus, OH
McCollum, James E., Jr.
College Park, MD
McCollum, James E., Jr., & Associates, P.C.
College Park, MD
McCollum, James F. ... Sebring, FL
McCollum, James F., P.A., Law Office of
Sebring, FL
McCollum, James H. ... Anchorage, AK
McCollum, James K., Jr. ... Scottsboro, AL
McCollum, Jeffrey K. ... Medford, OR
McCollum, Joe P., Jr. ... Monroe, NC
McCollum, John E. ... Alexandria, VA
McCollum, John Wesley, Jr. ... Auburn, AL
McCollum, Johnny R. ... Marshall, TX
McCollum, Johnny R., P.C. ... Marshall, TX
McCollum, Jordan ... Los Angeles, CA
McCollum, Joseph D., Jr. ... Boise, ID
McCollum & Klobnak ... Flora, IL
McCollum, Laura J. ... Boston, MA
McCollum, Lawrence K. ... Shreveport, LA
McCollum, Lawrence K., A Professional Law Corporation ... Shreveport, LA
McCollum, M. Gregory ... Myrtle Beach, SC
McCollum, Margaret Halnon
Middletown, OH
McCollum, Mary Lynn ... Storm Lake, IA
McCollum, Michael D. ... Minneapolis, MN
McCollum, Michael T. ... Clinton, MS
McCollum, Mike ... Dallas, TX
McCollum, Molly L. ... Macon, GA
McCollum, Molly L., P.C. ... Macon, GA
McCollum, Parks & Wilson, L.C.
Kansas City, MO
McCollum, Paul J. ... Thomasville, GA
McCollum, Perry J. ... Houston, TX
McCollum, Rathuel L. ... Cleveland, OH
McCollum & Rawlins ... Thomasville, GA
McCollum, Robert L. ... Minneapolis, MN
McCollum, Sam, III ... Brady, TX
McCollum, Schacht V., II ... Houston, TX
McCollum, Sidney H. ... Bentonville, AR
Fort Smith, AR
Little Rock, AR
McCollum, Steven P. ... Waukegan, IL
McCollum, Susan H. ... Santa Barbara, CA
McCollum, Timothy D., (A.P.C.)
Encino, CA
Fresno, CA
San Jose, CA
McCollum, Timothy P. ... Atlanta, GA
McCollum, William D., Jr. ... Baltimore, MD
McColly, Amy L. ... Indianapolis, IN
McColough, Wendy M.
Department of Labor, Pension and Welfare Benefits, GV
Mccolough, William F. ... Boston, MA
McColpin, Andrew K. ... Rowayton, CT
McColpin, Glenn T. ... Chattanooga, TN
McComas, Albert L. ... Baltimore, MD
McComas, Beverly A. ... Fort Lauderdale, FL
McComas, Debra J. ... Dallas, TX
McComas, Edwin ... Elk City, OK
McComas, Eva P. ... San Francisco, CA
McComas, Harrold J. ... Milwaukee, WI
McComas, J. Scott, (P.C.) ... Boulder, CO
McComas, James H. ... Anchorage, AK
McComas, Jennifer T. ... Dublin, GA
Vidalia, GA
McComas, Lauren Evers ... Baltimore, MD
McComas, Susan K. Cosgriff ... Bel Air, MD
McComas, Susan K., P.A. ... Bel Air, MD
McComas, William A. ... Baltimore, MD
McComas, Willis F. ... Walnut Creek, CA
McComb, April Denice ... Tacoma, WA
McComb, Brian R. ... Miami, FL
McComb, Brian R., P.A. ... Miami, FL
McComb, Daniel R. ... Batavia, NY
McComb, David F. ... Camden, NJ
McComb, David L. ... New Orleans, LA
McComb, Donovan O. ... Laurel, MS
McComb, JoEllen S. ... Lexington, KY
McComb, John A. ... Stevens Point, WI
McComb, Shirley ... Atlanta, GA
McComb, Susan S. ... Springfield, IL
McComb, Thomas J. ... Fort Collins, CO
McComber, James A. ... Apple Valley, MN
McCombs, Allan M. ... Houston, TX
McCombs, David L. ... Andover, OH
McCombs, David L. ... Dallas, TX
McCombs, Harold K., Jr.
Washington, DC
McCombs, Hugh R. ... Chicago, IL
McCombs, Jerry L. ... Idabel, OK
McCombs & Kotila ... Andover, OH
McCombs, Mark J. ... Chicago, IL
McCombs, Peter W. ... Milwaukee, WI
McCombs, Rufe E. ... Columbus, GA
McCombs, Steven B. ... Versailles, IN
McCombs, Thomas R. ... Flint, MI
McCombs, Van Kirk, II ... Birmingham, AL
Jacksonville, FL
Atlanta, GA
McComic, Robert B. ... San Diego, CA
McComiskey, Mark A., Jr. ... Andover, MA
McComiskey, Mark Adrian
New York, NY
McComiskey, Robert ... Metairie, LA
McCommas, Christine Schubert
Department of the Army, U.S. Army Legal Services Agency, GV
McCommon, Paul C., III ... Macon, GA
McCommons, Alicia J. ... Lakewood, CO
McConachie, Charles R. ... Dallas, TX
McConaghy, Dennis A. ... Riverside, CA
Mcconaghy, Elizabeth Ann ... Melville, NY
McConaghy, John D., (A Professional Corporation) ... Los Angeles, CA
McConaghy, T.A. ... Southfield, MI
McConaghy, Timothy K.
Birmingham, MI
McConaghy-Roel, Elizabeth A.
Melville, NY
McConaha, Jacqueline M. ... Mobile, AL
McConahay, Charles L., Jr. ... Hesperia, CA
McConahy, Julie A. ... Camp Hill, PA
McConahy, Michael P. ... Fairbanks, AK
McConahy, Zimmerman & Wallace
Fairbanks, AK
McConathy, Evelyn H. ... Washington, DC
McConathy, Lucinda O. ... Washington, DC
McConathy, Lucinda O. ... New York, NY
McConaty, Brian G. ... Glendale, CO
McConaughey, Dan E. ... Decatur, GA
McConaughey & Goff ... Atlanta, GA
Decatur, GA
Lawrenceville, GA
Marietta, GA
McConaughy, Bennet A. ... Seattle, WA
McConaughy, David H.
Glenwood Springs, CO
McConaughy, Mary Ann ... Seattle, WA
McConaughy, Robert T. ... Cincinnati, OH
McConaughy, Stewart H. ... Burlington, VT
McConchie, Scott L. ... Boston, MA
McCone, Cody ... New York, NY
McCone, James G. ... Orange, CA
McCone, Susan Jonal ... New York, NY
McConeghy, Gerald J. ... Philadelphia, PA
McConeghy, Mary Anne ... Cliffside Park, NJ
McConica, John R., II ... Santa Paula, CA
McConihe, Michael H. ... Washington, DC
McConkey, Billie S. ... Phoenix, AZ
McConkey, Diane E.
Environmental Protection Agency, Office of the General Counsel, GV
McConkey, Elmer L. ... Arbutus, MD
McConkey, James W. ... Chicago, IL
McConkey, Matthew J. ... Washington, DC
McConkey, Nathan R. ... Des Moines, IA
McConkey, Robert C., III ... Memphis, TN
McConkey, Samuel A. ... Phoenix, AZ
McConkey, Samuel A., Jr. ... Havelock, NC
Morehead City, NC
McConkie, Daniel S. ... Salt Lake City, UT
McConkie, David M. ... Salt Lake City, UT
McConkie, Kathleen ... Salt Lake City, UT
McConkie, Oscar W., III
Salt Lake City, UT
McConkie, Oscar W., Jr.
Salt Lake City, UT
McConkie, Pace J. ... Baltimore, MD
McConkie, Roger J. ... Salt Lake City, UT
McConkie, William R. ... Salt Lake City, UT
McConn & Cutrell ... Georgetown, OH
McConn, James J., Jr. ... Houston, TX
McConn, John Luke ... Houston, TX
McConn, Robert G., Jr. ... Houston, TX
McConn, Robert L. ... Grand Forks, ND
McConn & Williams, L.L.P. ... Houston, TX
McConnaghay, Thomas A. ... Peoria, IL
McConnaughey, George C. ... Columbus, OH
McConnaughey, Jan R. ... Rochester, NY
McConnaughey, Jefferson C. ... Atlanta, GA
McConnaughey, Robert S.
Chevy Chase, MD
McConnaughey, Sally P. ... Amelia, VA
McConnaughhay, Duffy, Coonrod, Pope & Weaver, P.A. ... Gainesville, FL
Jacksonville, FL
Ocala, FL
Panama City, FL
Pensacola, FL
Sarasota, FL
Tallahassee, FL
McConnaughhay, James N. ... Pensacola, FL
Tallahassee, FL
McConnaughhay, Jana E. ... Tallahassee, FL
McConnaughton, Mary C. ... Boston, MA
McConnel, W. Bruce, III ... Philadelphia, PA
McConnell, Alan H. ... Raleigh, NC
McConnell, Andrew S. ... Milwaukee, WI
McConnell, Anthony ... Ozark, MO
McConnell & Associates, P.C.
Berwyn, PA
West Chester, PA
McConnell, Barbara A. W.
Department of Labor, Office of the Solicitor, GV
McConnell, Beverly J. ... Phoenix, AZ
McConnell, Bill ... Arlington, TX
McConnell, Bradley K. ... Washington, DC
McConnell, C. Allen ... Toledo, OH
McConnell, C. Stokes, Jr.
Baton Rouge, LA
McConnell, Carl L. ... San Jose, CA
McConnell, Catherine D. ... Morgantown, WV
McConnell, Charles C. ... Louisville, KY
McConnell, Charles E. ... Springhill, LA
McConnell, Daniel D. ... Columbus, GA
McConnell, Daniel E. ... Raleigh, NC
McConnell, David B. ... Portland, ME
McConnell, David C. ... Kansas City, MO
McConnell, David M.
Department of Justice, Civil Division, GV
McConnell, David M. ... Charlotte, NC
McConnell, David W.
Fort Myers Beach, FL
McConnell, Dawn T. ... White Plains, NY
McConnell, Dean A. ... Denver, CO
McConnell, Dean E. ... Indianapolis, IN
McConnell, Dennis P. ... New York, NY
McConnell, Dennis R. ... Stanhope, NJ
McConnell, Diane Willis ... Oldwick, NJ
McConnell, Donald J. ... Cleveland, OH
McConnell, Donald K. ... Garland, TX
McConnell, Donald L. ... Bloomington, MN
McConnell, Donald R. ... Santa Ana, CA
McConnell, E. John ... Wailuku, HI
McConnell, Ed ... Amarillo, TX
McConnell, Edward B. ... Williamsburg, VA
McConnell, Edward N. ... Des Moines, IA
McConnell, Elizabeth L. ... Kingsport, TN
McConnell and Finnerty
North Vernon, IN
Vernon, IN
McConnell, Floyd T. ... Mobile, AL
McConnell, Forrest Talma, III
Montgomery, AL
McConnell, Francis J. ... Chicago, IL
McConnell, Gaelle D. ... Albuquerque, NM
McConnell, Gary D. ... Elkhart, IN
McConnell, Gary L. ... Angleton, TX
McConnell, Geoffrey J. ... Boise, ID
McConnell, George ... Sugar Land, TX
McConnell & Goodrich ... Dallas, TX
Fort Worth, TX
McConnell, Gregory M. ... Savannah, GA
McConnell, Gregory S. ... Dallas, TX
McConnell, Guy P. ... Tampa, FL
Mc Connell, H. Hugh ... Miami, FL
McConnell, Harley W. ... Houston, TX
McConnell, Harold H. ... North Vernon, IN
McConnell, Harry G. ... Daytona Beach, FL
McConnell, Heather A. ... Los Angeles, CA
McConnell, J. Patrick ... Fairfax, VA
McConnell, James D. ... Shelbina, MO
McConnell, James F., Jr. ... Washington, DC
McConnell, James G. ... Chicago, IL
McConnell, James J. ... Brooklyn, NY
McConnell, James J. ... Allentown, PA
McConnell, James L. ... Somerville, NJ
McConnell, Jamie M. ... Glendale, CA
McConnell, Jeffrey M. ... Irvine, CA
McConnell, J. H. Tyler ... Wilmington, DE
McConnell, Joel C., Jr. ... United States Senate, Senatorial Assistants, GV
McConnell, John A. ... Studio City, CA
McConnell, John Hay ... New York, NY
McConnell, John J., Jr. ... Providence, RI
McConnell, John P. ... New York, NY
McConnell, John P. ... New York, NY
McConnell, John R. ... Gladwyne, PA
McConnell, John W. ... New York, NY
McConnell, John W., III ... Los Angeles, CA
McConnell, John W., Jr. ... Washington, DC
McConnell, Joseph B. ... Atlanta, GA
McConnell, Joseph H. ... Brevard, NC
McConnell, Joseph L. ... Washington, IA
McConnell, Joseph P. ... Boston, MA
McConnell, Judith ... San Diego, CA
McConnell, Julie K.
Federal Trade Commission, GV
McConnell, Karen Ciupak ... Phoenix, AZ
McConnell, Karen Hennon
Pittsburgh, PA
McConnell, Karen Kirkland ... Houston, TX
McConnell, Karl N. ... Philadelphia, PA
McConnell, Karyn R. ... Toledo, OH
Mcconnell, Kathleen C. ... Raleigh, NC
McConnell, Kelly Greene ... Boise, ID
McConnell, Kenneth B.
Bloomfield Hills, MI
McConnell, Kevin ... Jacksonville, NC
McConnell, Kevin R. ... New York, NY
McConnell, Kirk D. ... Atlanta, GA
McConnell & Klement, P.C. ... Angleton, TX
McConnell, L. A., Jr. ... Perry, GA
McConnell, Laura Haag
Oklahoma City, OK
McConnell, Lloyd L. ... Cayucos, CA
McConnell, Lyman F. ... Fallon, NV
McConnell, Malcolm P., III
Richmond, VA
McConnell, Margaret E. ... Phoenix, AZ
McConnell, Mark R. ... Jasper, IN
McConnell, Mark S. ... Washington, DC
McConnell, Mary Ann K. ... Mercer, PA
McConnell, Matthew S. ... McLean, VA
McConnell & McMahon ... Lenexa, KS
McConnell & Mendelson ... Chicago, IL
McConnell, Merle J. ... Colorado Springs, CO
McConnell, Michael A. ... Fort Worth, TX
McConnell, Michael E. ... Chicago, IL
McConnell, Michael Joseph ... Atlanta, GA
McConnell, Michael T. ... Denver, CO
McConnell, Michael W. ... Chicago, IL
McConnell, Nicholas S. ... Washington, DC
Baltimore, MD
Rockville, MD
Vienna, VA
McConnell & Norton ... Stanhope, NJ
McConnell, Nuala ... Washington, DC
McConnell, Patricia ... Mineola, NY
McConnell, Paul J., III ... Houston, TX
McConnell, Paul S. ... Seattle, WA
McConnell, R. Perry ... The Woodlands, TX
McConnell, R. Perry, P.C.
The Woodlands, TX
McConnell, Randall J., Jr. ... Erie, PA
McConnell, Richard H. ... San Francisco, CA
McConnell, Richard L. ... Washington, DC
McConnell, Richard S., Jr. ... Atlanta, GA
McConnell, R. J. ... Indianapolis, IN
McConnell, Robert A. ... Washington, DC
McConnell, Robert A. ... Salt Lake City, UT
McConnell, Robert A. ... Seattle, WA
McConnell, Robert B. ... Waltham, MA
McConnell, Robert D. C. ... Baton Rouge, LA

McConnell, Robert Hale ....Vallejo, CA
McConnell, Robert J. ....Providence, RI
McConnell, Robert M.
Colorado Springs, CO
McConnell, Robert P. ....Houston, TX
McConnell, Robin M. ....Santa Monica, CA
McConnell, Robt. B., Sr. ....Madison, WI
McConnell, Rosemarie ....Atlanta, GA
McConnell, Sarah Hlavinka ....Houston, TX
McConnell, Scott E. ....Laguna Niguel, CA
McConnell, Sharon Moylan ....Raleigh, NC
McConnell, Sheryl S. ....Eugene, OR
Florence, OR
McConnell, Shivaun M. ....Morristown, NJ
McConnell & Slattery, A Professional Law Corporation ....Springhill, LA
McConnell, Stacey W. ....Berwyn, PA
McConnell, Stephen J. ....Philadelphia, PA
McConnell, Steven L. ....Raton, NM
McConnell, Steven R. ....Lenexa, KS
McConnell, T. Allen ....Dallas, TX
McConnell, T. Stephen ....Atlanta, GA
McConnell & Taylor ....Toledo, OH
McConnell, Theodore A. ....Pittsburgh, PA
McConnell, Thomas A. ....Lexington, KY
McConnell, Thomas R. ....Fowler, IN
McConnell, Thomas S. ......Walnut Creek, CA
McConnell, Timothy B. ....Kingsport, TN
McConnell Valdés ....San Juan, PR
McConnell, Vic L. ....Nashville, TN
McConnell, Vincent M. ....Philadelphia, PA
McConnell, Virginia E. ....Richmond, VA
McConnell, W. Ross ....Athens, GA
McConnell, Walter G. ....San Juan, PR
McConnell, William G. ....Hermitage, PA
New Wilmington, PA
Sharon, PA
McConnell, William G., Jr. ......Hermitage, PA
New Wilmington, PA
Sharon, PA
McConnell, William J. ....Fort Myers, FL
McConnell, William S.
Charlotte Amalie, St. Thomas, VI
McConnell, Woodrow H.
Oklahoma City, OK
McConney, Jean Marie ....New York, NY
McConnico, Kate Hilton ....Houston, TX
McConnico, Kenneth D. ....Houston, TX
McConnico, Stephen E. ....Austin, TX
McConnie, Julian O., Jr. ....San Juan, PR
McConnin, John E. ....Fairfax, VA
McConnon, Edward S. ....Acworth, GA
McConnon, James C. ....Philadelphia, PA
McConnon, Linda J. ....Broomfield, CO
McConn-Pirman, Julie A.
Georgetown, OH
McConologue, Susan L. ....Andover, MA
McConomy, Gerald J. ....Exton, PA
McConomy, James H. ....Pittsburgh, PA
McConomy, John W. ....Memphis, TN
McConoughey, David M. ....New York, NY
McConvery, Sharon ....Woodbridge, NJ
Staten Island, NY
McConville, Bernard R. ....Douglaston, NY
McConville, Celestine Richards
Cleveland, OH
McConville, Considine, Cooman & Morin, P.C. ....Rochester, NY
McConville, Daniel ....Pasadena, CA
McConville, Edward P. ......East Greenbush, NY
McConville, Frederick J. .....Washington, DC
McConville, Henry B. ....Wakefield, MA
McConville, James ....Annandale, VA
McConville, Kevin J. .... Los Angeles, CA
San Diego, CA
Santa Ana, CA
McConville, Luke F. ....Cleveland, OH
McConville, Mary Cook ....Cleveland, OH
McConville, Michael F. ....Rochester, NY
McConville, Paul D. ....New York, NY
McConville, Philip R. ....Eugene, OR
McConville, Richard O.
West Des Moines, IA
McConville, Stephanie L. ....Milwaukee, WI
McConville, Terence N. ....Mission Hills, CA
McConville, Theresa L. ....Camarillo, CA
McConville, Timothy M. ....Norfolk, VA
McConwell, Edward A. ....Mission, KS
McConwell, Edward A., Jr. ....Mission, KS
McConwell, Laura L. ....Mission, KS
McConwell Law Offices, A Professional Association ....Mission, KS
Kansas City, MO
McCooe, Dennis P. ....Philadelphia, PA
McCooe, William P. ....New York, NY
McCoog, Arlene ....Baltimore, MD
McCoog, Carol J. ....Portland, OR
McCook, Brian J. ....Springfield, MA
McCook, Charles T., Jr. ....Clark, NJ
McCool, Christopher J.
North Charleston, SC
McCool, Clinton T. ....Los Angeles, CA
McCool, David P. ....Clayton, MO
McCool, Deirdre Shelton ....Charleston, SC
McCool, Dennis M. ....Dunn, NC
McCool, Douglas L. ....Eugene, OR
McCool, Douglas L., P.C. ....Eugene, OR
McCool, Findlay M. ....Elkton, MD
McCool, G. Walter ....Austin, TX
Dallas, TX
McCool, George T., Jr.
Mount Ephraim, NJ
Conshohocken, PA
Philadelphia, PA
McCool, Gordon ....Gilmer, TX
McCool, Janice R. ....Cedar Rapids, IA
McCool, Jennifer A. ....New York, NY
McCool, Philip L. ....Indianapolis, IN
McCool, Robert E. ....Baird, TX
McCool, Rosemary ....Denver, CO
McCool, Thomas S. ....San Juan, PR
McCool, Timothy Benson ....Nashville, TN
McCool, William D. ....Walla Walla, WA
McCoombs, Jennifer E. ....Syracuse, NY
McCoppin, Dorothy Lancaster
Houston, TX
McCoppin, John T., III ....Houston, TX
McCoppin, Richard Andrew ....Durham, NC
McCoppin, Scott David ....Pueblo, CO
McCord, Bubsey, Ketchum & Donohue, LLP
Monticello, FL
Tallahassee, FL
New Orleans, LA
McCord & Burns Law Firm ....Lincoln, NE
McCord, Charles B. ....Portland, OR
McCord, Charles B., III ....Cincinnati, OH
McCord, Cheryl L. ....Lake Oswego, OR
McCord, Clint ....Los Angeles, CA
McCord, Dan L. ....Lincoln, NE
McCord, David ....Des Moines, IA
Mccord, David L. ....Knoxville, TN
McCord, Dean M. ....Raleigh, NC
McCord, Donald S., Jr. ....Morristown, NJ
McCord, Edward L. ....Pittsburgh, PA
McCord, Edward M., P.C.
Colorado Springs, CO
Denver, CO
McCord, Elizabeth A. ....Cincinnati, OH
McCord, Elizabeth Anne, Law Office of
Kenai, AK
McCord, Fiona G. ....Dallas, TX
McCord, George E. ....Dallas, TX
McCord, Guyte P., III ....Tallahassee, FL
McCord, Guyte P., Jr. ....Tallahassee, FL
McCord, James D. ....Indian Shores, FL
McCord, James N. ....Fayetteville, AR
McCord, James W. ....Los Angeles, CA
McCord, John C. ....Louisville, KY
McCord, John D. ....Gadsden, AL
McCord, John H. ....Champaign, IL
McCord, John L. ....Knoxville, TN
McCord, Larry L., Jr. ....Kansas City, MO
McCord, Larry R. ....Fort Smith, AR
McCord, M. Faye ....Cartersville, GA
McCord & Martin ....Gadsden, AL
Mc Cord, Michael A. ....Washington, DC
McCord, Michael B. ....Cleveland, OH
McCord, Michael B. ....Bend, OR
McCord, Paul J. ....Fort Walton Beach, FL
McCord, Paul V. ....Bloomington, IL
McCord, Peter A. ....Elizabeth, NJ
McCord, Peter C. ....Portland, OR
McCord, R. Mansell, Jr. ....Atlanta, GA
McCord, Raymond V. ....Los Angeles, CA
McCord, Richard J. ....East Meadow, NY
McCord, Robert A. ....Peoria, IL
McCord, Robert B., Jr. ....Hapeville, GA
McCord, Robert D. ....Indianapolis, IN
McCord, Robert L., Jr. ....Ventura, CA
McCord, Ronald G. ....Tampa, FL
McCord, Roy O. ....Gadsden, AL
McCord, Samuel R. ....Birmingham, AL
McCord, Samuel R., P.C.
Birmingham, AL
McCord, Steven G. ....Batesville, MS
McCord, Thomas J. ....Boston, MA
McCord, Troutman & Irwin, P.C.
Knoxville, TN
McCord, W. Keith ....Knoxville, TN
McCord, W. Kirk ....Richardson, TX
McCord, Walter C., Jr. ....Baltimore, MD
McCorkel, Janice H. ....Dallas, TX
McCorkell, Don, Jr. ....Oklahoma City, OK
McCorkell, Peter L. ....San Rafael, CA
McCorkhill, C. Grant ....Chicago, IL
McCorkindale, D. Kevin ....Dallas, TX
McCorkindale, Douglas H. ....Arlington, VA
McCorkindale, Robert W., II ....Harrison, AR
McCorkle, Angela C. ....Louisville, KY
McCorkle, Dorothy Martin ....Roanoke, VA
McCorkle, Ed. W. ....Arkadelphia, AR
McCorkle, Elizabeth Sue ....Bandon, OR
McCorkle, Holly J. ....Jacksonville, FL
McCorkle, James ....Columbus, OH
McCorkle, Kimberly Rae ....Honolulu, HI
McCorkle, Leon M., Jr. ....Dublin, OH
McCorkle, Pedigo & Johnson, LLP
Savannah, GA
Statesboro, GA
McCorkle, Phillip R. ....Savannah, GA
McCorkle, Pope (Mac), III ....Durham, NC
McCorkle, Robert G. ....Albuquerque, NM
McCorkle, T. Lamar, Jr. ....Houston, TX
McCorkle, Tom S. ....Dallas, TX
McCorkle, W. Joseph, Jr.
Montgomery, AL
McCorkle Westerburg & Thornton, P.C.
Dallas, TX
Mc Cormac, Douglas W. ....New Bedford, MA
McCormac, John W. ....Columbus, OH
McCormac, Kathleen A. ....San Francisco, CA
McCormac, Mary C. ....Clemson, SC
McCormac, Orville Theodore
Cleveland, OH
McCormack, Aidan M. ....Newark, NJ
New York, NY
McCormack, Brian C. ....Dallas, TX
McCormack, Brian J. ....Miami, FL
McCormack, Brian J. ....Las Vegas, NV
McCormack, Brian M. ....Fairfax, VA
McCormack, Bryan J. ....San Bruno, CA
McCormack, Carla M. ....Fresno, CA
McCormack, Cecilia M. ....Milwaukee, WI
McCormack, Chris ....Midland, TX
McCormack, Christopher P.
New Haven, CT
McCormack, Clay M. ....Jackson, TN
McCormack, Damiani, Lowe & Mellion
New City, NY
McCormack, Daniel ....Westmont, NJ
McCormack, Daniel J. ....Houston, TX
McCormack, David B. ....Charleston, SC
McCormack, David C. ....Brookfield, WI
McCormack, David R. ....Houston, TX
McCormack, Dennis A. ....Windsor, CT
McCormack, Donnell J., Jr. ....Atlanta, GA
McCormack, Douglas E. ....New York, NY
McCormack, Douglas J.
Englewood Cliffs, NJ
McCormack, Edward F. ....Chicago, IL
McCormack, Edward J., III ....Wellesley, MA
McCormack, Edward T. ....Garrison, NY
McCormack & Epstein ....Boston, MA
New York, NY
McCormack, Fay I. ....Atlanta, GA
McCormack, Francis X. ....Arcadia, CA
McCormack, Fred A. ....Tallahassee, FL
McCormack, Garry P. .... Princeton, NJ
New York, NY
McCormack, George J. ....New York, NY
McCormack, Greg D. ....Virginia Beach, VA
McCormack, Greg D., P.C.
Virginia Beach, VA
McCormack, Howard M. ....New York, NY
McCormack, J. Parrish ....Charlotte, NC
McCormack, J. Robert ....Clearwater, FL
McCormack, J. Robert, P.A.
Clearwater, FL
Tampa, FL
McCormack, J. Stephen ....Lexington, SC
McCormack, James A. ....Portland, ME
McCormack, James F. ....New Britain, CT
McCormack, James K. ....Waterbury, CT
McCormack, James K., and Matthew D. McCormack ....Waterbury, CT
McCormack, James M. ....Austin, TX
McCormack, James P. ....Garden City, NY
McCormack, Jeffrey P. ....Baltimore, MD
McCormack, Jerry D. ....Antigo, WI
McCormack, Joanne M. ....Rockford, IL
McCormack, John ....Boston, MA
McCormack, John ....Dallas, TX
McCormack, John J. ....Los Angeles, CA
McCormack, John J. ....Ashland, NH
McCormack, John J. ....Oswego, NY
McCormack, John L. ....Chicago, IL
McCormack, John L. ....Seattle, WA
McCormack, John M. ....Palo Alto, CA
Portland, OR
McCormack, John R. ....Omaha, NE
McCormack, Joseph D. ....Jackson, MI
McCormack, Joseph D.
Port Washington, WI
Mccormack, Kara ....Georgetown, MA
McCormack, Karen A. ....Fairfield, CT
McCormack, Kathleen M. ......New York, NY
McCormack, Kevin E. ....Syracuse, NY
McCormack & Knoblock, P.A. ....Miami, FL
Ocala, FL
McCormack, Larry W. ....Aiken, SC
McCormack, Leo M. ....Scranton, PA
McCormack, Marcia ....Farmington, CT
McCormack, Marcia ....Concord, NH
McCormack, Marie Judith ....Cranford, NJ
McCormack, Mark A. ....Quincy, MA
McCormack, Martha Carlson ....Billings, MT
McCormack, Matthew D. ....Waterbury, CT
McCormack & Matthews, P.C. .....Roseland, NJ
McCormack, Michael ....Lincoln, NE
McCormack, Michael ....Seattle, WA
McCormack, Michael ....Seattle, WA
McCormack, Michael A. ....New York, NY
McCormack, Michael J. ....Boston, MA
McCormack, Michael T. ....Hartford, CT
McCormack, Myra H. ....Summit, NJ
McCormack, Nancy R. ....Pembroke Pines, FL
McCormack, Pamela L. ....New York, NY
McCormack, Patricia ....Omaha, NE
McCormack, Patrick F. ....Jacksonville, FL
McCormack, Patrick M. ....Boston, MA
McCormack, Peter R. ....Houston, TX
McCormack & Phillips ....Nyack, NY
McCormack, R. Christopher, Jr. ......Albany, NY
McCormack, R. Thad ....Gainesville, GA
McCormack, Rachel M. ....Canton, MI
McCormack, Richard E.
New Orleans, LA
McCormack, Richard R. ....Miami, FL
Ocala, FL
McCormack, Robert E., III ....Atlanta, GA
McCormack, Robert J. ....Chicago, IL
McCormack, Robt. B. ....Hingham, MA
McCormack, Ronald G. ....Nyack, NY
McCormack, Sandra Kuhn, Law Office of
Bakersfield, CA
McCormack, Scott B. ....Cleveland, OH
McCormack, Stephen Allan ....Columbia, TN
McCormack, Susan M. .....Albuquerque, NM
McCormack, Sybil Bates ....Atlanta, GA
McCormack, Teresa Roos ......Harrisburg, PA
McCormack, Thomas A. ....Cleveland, OH
McCormack, Thomas A. ......Philadelphia, PA
McCormack, Thomas J. ....New York, NY
McCormack, Thomas L. ....Baldwin, WI
McCormack, Thomas M. ....Roseland, NJ
McCormack, Tim ....Cleveland, OH
McCormack, Timothy B. ....Seattle, WA
McCormack, Timothy F. ....Baltimore, MD
Mccormack, Timothy N. ....Sheridan, WY
McCormack, Tracy Walters ....Austin, TX
McCormack, Wayne ....Salt Lake City, UT
McCormack, William A. ....Boston, MA
McCormack, William A. ....Dallas, TX
McCormack, William F. ....New York, NY
McCormack, William O. ....Marshall, MN
McCormack, William U. ....Rutland, VT
McCormack & Wolgamuth Company, L.P.A
Cleveland, OH
McCormack-Healy, Virginia C.
San Rafael, CA
McCormally, Brian C. ......Treasury Department, Office of the Comptroller of the Currency, GV
McCormally, Timothy J. ....Washington, DC
McCormic, Daniel C. ....Wildwood, FL
McCormick, Adam & Long
Overland Park, KS
Kansas City, MO
McCormick, Allen K. ....Orlando, FL
McCormick, Andrea Lynn ....Philadelphia, PA
McCormick, Andrew G. ....New York, NY
McCormick, Andrew P. ....Houston, TX
McCormick, Ann C. ....Redmond, WA
McCormick, Ann Schnepp ....Rochester, NY
McCormick, Anne M.
Department of Justice, Civil Division, GV
McCormick, Arthur E. ....Albany, NY
McCormick, Arthur F. ....South Miami, FL
McCormick, B. Michael ....Terre Haute, IN
McCormick, Barbara A.
New Brunswick, NJ
McCormick, Barry W.
Overland Park, KS
McCormick, Barstow, Sheppard, Wayte & Carruth LLP ....Fresno, CA
Modesto, CA
McCormick, Brad J. ....Miami, FL
McCormick, Brenda L. ....Ventura, CA
McCormick, Brian ....Torrington, CT
McCormick, Brian J., Jr. ....Blue Bell, PA
McCormick & Cannon, Law Offices of
San Diego, CA
McCormick, Caraway, Tabor and Madrid, L.L.P. ....Carlsbad, NM
McCormick, Carl ....Chicago, IL
McCormick, Carmen M. Mosier
San Diego, CA
McCormick, Catherine M. ....Memphis, TN
McCormick, Charles D. ....Wilkes-Barre, PA
McCormick, Charles E. ....Los Angeles, CA
McCormick, Charles F. ....New York, NY
McCormick, Charles L., III ....Halifax, VA
McCormick, Chas. B., Jr. ....Chicago, IL
McCormick, Christina A. .....San Francisco, CA
McCormick and Christoph, P.C.
Boulder, CO
McCormick, Christopher H.
Securities and Exchange Commission, Office of the General Counsel, GV
McCormick, Clarisse R. ....Scottsdale, AZ
McCormick, Clyde R. "Skip", II
San Antonio, TX
McCormick, Curtis G. .....West Des Moines, IA
McCormick, Daniel E. ....Houston, TX
McCormick, David A.
Department of the Army, U.S. Army Legal Services Agency, GV
McCormick, David C. .....West Des Moines, IA
McCormick, David H. ....Russellville, AR
McCormick, David J. ....Milwaukee, WI
McCormick, David M. ....Philadelphia, PA
McCormick, David O. ....Pascagoula, MS
McCormick and Davies ....Monroe, MI
McCormick, Deane E., Jr.
Woodland Hills, CA
McCormick, Debra W.
Oklahoma City, OK
McCormick, Donald C. ....Miami, FL
McCormick, Donald G. ....Houston, TX
McCormick, Donald J. ....Pittsburgh, PA
McCormick, Donald W. ....Glendale, CA
McCormick, Douglas F. ....Costa Mesa, CA
McCormick, Drury & Scaff ....Jasper, FL
McCormick, Dunn & Black, A Professional Service Corporation ....Coeur d'Alene, ID
Spokane, WA
McCormick Dunne & Foley
New York, NY
McCormick, Edward G.
Great Barrington, MA
McCormick, Edward H. ....Lillington, NC
McCormick, Edward J. ....Miami, FL
McCormick, Edward J. ....New York, NY
McCormick, Edward J., III ....Norfolk, MA
McCormick, Edward J., Jr. ....Toledo, OH
McCormick, Edward R., Jr. ....Homewood, IL
McCormick, E. J., Jr. ....Monroe, MI
McCormick, Elizabeth Botticelli
Ossining, NY
McCormick, Eric T. ....Flint, MI
Mccormick, Ferris E. ....Manassas, VA
McCormick & Field, P.L.L.C. ....Tulsa, OK
McCormick, Fitzpatrick, Kasper & Burchard, P.C. ....Burlington, VT
McCormick, Francis X. ....Westfield, NJ
McCormick, Frank T. ....Richmond, VA
McCormick, Fred M. ....Selma, AL
McCormick, G. Paul ....Boulder, CO
McCormick, George L. ....Covina, CA
McCormick, Gerald F. ....West Chester, PA
McCormick, Gregory A. ....Chicago, IL
McCormick, Gregory H. ....Oakland, CA
McCormick, Heather ....San Francisco, CA
McCormick, Hoffman, Rees, Faubion, Van Buskirk, Johnson & Schumock, P.S.
Federal Way, WA
Lakewood, WA
McCormick, Homer L. (Mike), Jr., (P.C.)
Costa Mesa, CA
McCormick, Hugh B., III
Newport News, VA
Richmond, VA

McCormick, Hugh T. .... **New York, NY**
McCormick, J. Burke .... **Richmond, VA**
McCormick, Jack E. .... Columbus, OH
McCormick, James E. .... Atlanta, MI
McCormick, James E., III
Newport Beach, CA
McCormick, James F. .... Pittsburgh, PA
McCormick, James G. .... **New York, NY**
McCormick, James H. .... Bloomfield Hills, MI
McCormick, James J. .... San Diego, CA
McCormick, James (Kimo) E., III
Newport Beach, CA
McCormick, James L.
Manhattan Beach, CA
McCormick, James R. .... Traverse City, MI
McCormick, James T. .... **Providence, RI**
McCormick, Jan D. .... **Jacksonville, FL**
McCormick, Janet Gray .... Sacramento, CA
McCormick, Jean K. .... Beaufort, SC
McCormick, Jeffrey L. .... **Springfield, MA**
McCormick, Jeffrey M. .... **Stamford, CT**
McCormick, Jeffrey V. .... Rocky Hill, CT
McCormick, Jeremiah F. .... Charleston, WV
McCormick, Jeremiah M. .... Seattle, WA
McCormick, Jerrilann Spence .... **Troy, MI**
McCormick, Joan A. .... Westerly, RI
McCormick, Jody M. .... **Spokane, WA**
McCormick, Joel C., III .... Spokane, WA
McCormick, John D. .... Ann Arbor, MI
McCormick, John E. .... **Portland, OR**
McCormick, John E. .... **Herndon, VA**
McCormick, John F. .... Austin, TX
McCormick, John F., Jr. .... **Tulsa, OK**
McCormick, John G. .... **Philadelphia, PA**
McCormick, John H. .... Jasper, FL
McCormick, John K. .... **Buffalo, NY**
McCormick, John M. .... Orlando, FL
McCormick, John M. .... Oklahoma City, OK
McCormick, John M., P.A. .... Orlando, FL
McCormick, John Michael, Jr.
Los Angeles, CA
McCormick, John P. .... **San Diego, CA**
McCormick, John P. .... Orleans, MA
McCormick, John P. .... White Plains, NY
McCormick, John Roderick .... Fallon, NV
McCormick, Jon A. .... **Bedford, TX**
McCormick, Jonathan F. .... Albuquerque, NM
McCormick, Joseph A. .... **Tulsa, OK**
McCormick, Joseph A., Jr.
Haddonfield, NJ
McCormick, Joseph C. .... McLean, VA
McCormick, Joseph C. .... Oconto, WI
Mccormick, Julie A. .... Santa Monica, CA
McCormick Kabot Foley Jenner & Watson, PC
Visalia, CA
McCormick, Karen E. .... Charleston, SC
McCormick, Kate .... **Houston, TX**
McCormick, Kathleen .... **San Diego, CA**
McCormick, Kathleen .... **Richmond, VA**
McCormick, Kathleen .... Shelton, WA
McCormick, Kathy J. .... Newport Beach, CA
McCormick, Keith .... Morehead, KY
McCormick, Keith L. .... North Olmsted, OH
McCormick, Kelly A. .... Washington, DC
McCormick, Kenneth T., Jr. .... **Madison, WI**
McCormick, Kenneth W. .... Martinez, CA
McCormick, Kevin C. .... **Baltimore, MD**
McCormick, Kevin F. .... Pearl River, NY
McCormick, Kevin M. .... Glendale, CA
Ventura, CA
McCormick, Kevin M. .... **Kansas City, MO**
McCormick, Kidman & Behrens, LLP
Costa Mesa, CA
McCormick Kidman & Behrens, LLP
Sacramento, CA
McCormick, Kimberly M. .... **San Diego, CA**
McCormick, Kirk R.
Colorado Springs, CO
McCormick & Koretzky .... Miami, FL
McCormick Law Firm .... **Williamsport, PA**
McCormick Law Firm, P.A.
Dardanelle, AR
Russellville, AR
McCormick, Lawrence W. .... Sioux City, IA
McCormick, Leo H., Jr. .... South Bend, IN
McCormick, Leslie A. .... **Miami, FL**
McCormick, Linda C.
National Labor Relations Board,
Office of the General Counsel, GV
McCormick, Linda Claire .... Chicago, IL
McCormick, Lisette M. .... **Pittsburgh, PA**
McCormick, Loyd W. .... San Francisco, CA
McCormick & Maitland .... **Norfolk, MA**
Mccormick, Marcia Mydra .... Reno, NV
McCormick, Margaret H. .... **Chicago, IL**
McCormick, Margo J. .... Albuquerque, NM
McCormick, Mark .... **Des Moines, IA**
McCormick, Mark .... Philadelphia, PA
McCormick, Mark D. .... Hanford, CA
McCormick, Marnie A. .... **Austin, TX**
McCormick, Marshall S. .... Hilliard, OH
McCormick, Mary Beth .... Rockville, MD
McCormick, Mary Elizabeth
Minneapolis, MN
McCormick, Mary K. .... Eagan, MN
McCormick, Mary M. .... Rothschild, WI
McCormick, Mary Ramsay
Kansas City, MO
McCormick, Matthew H.
Washington, DC
McCormick, Matthew J. .... Santa Ana, CA
McCormick, Maurice G. .... **Fargo, ND**
McCormick & McCormick
Raymondville, TX
McCormick, Melissa R.
Newport Beach, CA
McCormick, Michael C. .... Lee's Summit, MO
McCormick, Michael D. .... **Chicago, IL**
McCormick, Michael D. .... Indianapolis, IN
McCormick, Michael D. .... Keeseville, NY
McCormick, Michael F. .... McAllen, TX
McCormick, Michael H. .... Beverly Hills, MI
McCormick, Michael J. .... Orland Park, IL
McCormick, Michael J. .... Ypsilanti, MI
McCormick, Michael J. .... Austin, TX
McCormick, Michael John .... Biloxi, MS
McCormick, Michael P.
St. Clairsville, OH
McCormick, Michael T. .... Chicago, IL
McCormick, Michael T. .... **Minneapolis, MN**
McCormick, Michael Y. .... **Houston, TX**
McCormick, Michele V. .... Boston, MA
McCormick, Mike, and Associates
Vienna, IL
McCormick, Mike W. .... Birmingham, AL
McCormick & Mitchell, A Professional Corporation .... **San Diego, CA**
McCormick & Murphy, P.C.
Colorado Springs, CO
McCormick, Murtagh, Marcus & Smith
Great Barrington, MA
Pittsfield, MA
McCormick, Nancy C. .... Columbia, SC
McCormick and O'Dell .... Charleston, SC
McCormick, Patricia A. .... San Francisco, CA
McCormick, Patricia A. .... Toledo, OH
McCormick, Patrick .... **East Meadow, NY**
McCormick, Patrick A., Jr. .... San Diego, CA
McCormick, Patrick C. .... Sioux City, IA
McCormick, Patrick J., III
Washington, DC
McCormick, Paul L. .... **Hartford, CT**
'McCormick, Paul V., & Associates
Rockville, MD
McCormick, Paulding & Huber, LLP
Hartford, CT
New Haven, CT
Waterbury, CT
Pittsfield, MA
Springfield, MA
Worcester, MA
McCormick, Peter .... **Pittsburgh, PA**
McCormick, Peter S. .... **Seattle, WA**
McCormick & Priore, P.C. .... **Marlton, NJ**
Philadelphia, PA
McCormick, R. Dillon .... **Muskegon, MI**
McCormick, R. Saul .... Glen Burnie, MD
McCormick, Reed .... **State College, PA**
McCormick, Richard .... **New York, NY**
McCormick, Richard E., Jr. .... Greensburg, PA
McCormick, Richard J. .... **Kenosha, WI**
McCormick, Rick J. .... Albany, OR
McCormick, Robert .... **Dallas, TX**
McCormick, Robert E. .... Wiggins, MS
McCormick, Robert G. .... **New York, NY**
McCormick, Robert J. .... **Denver, CO**
McCormick, Robert J. .... Grand Tower, IL
McCormick, Robert J. .... Holdrege, NE
McCormick, Robert M. .... **Sacramento, CA**
McCormick, Robert M. .... Madison, WI
McCormick, Robert M. .... West Allis, WI
McCormick, Robert S. .... Washington, DC
McCormick, Robert S. .... Fort Lauderdale, FL
McCormick, Robert S. .... Vincennes, IN
McCormick, Robin M. .... **Burlington, VT**
McCormick, Ronald M.
San Bernardino, CA
McCormick, Ronald O. .... Westerville, OH
McCormick & Russell .... Selma, AL
McCormick, Samuel C. .... Randolph, NJ
McCormick, Sarah A. .... Bay Springs, MS
McCormick, Schoenenberger & Robertson, A Professional Association
Oklahoma City, OK
Tulsa, OK
McCormick, Shawn C. .... Covington, KY
McCormick, Shawn F.S., P.C. .... Boston, MA
McCormick, Shawn F.S. .... Boston, MA
McCormick, Sheryl A. .... **Atlanta, GA**
McCormick & Silver .... Columbus, OH
McCormick, Stanley E., Jr.
San Antonio, TX
McCormick, Steven D. .... **Chicago, IL**
McCormick, Steven J. .... San Francisco, CA
McCormick, Teresa M. .... Chatham, MA
McCormick, Theodora .... **Princeton, NJ**
McCormick, Thomas .... Atlantic City, NJ
McCormick, Thomas A. .... Montpelier, VT
McCormick, Thomas D. .... Minneapolis, MN
McCormick, Thomas D.
Oklahoma City, OK
McCormick, Thomas E. .... **Burlington, VT**
McCormick, Thomas H. .... **Washington, DC**
McCormick, Thomas J.
Northampton, MA
McCormick, Thomas J. .... Trenton, NJ
McCormick, Thomas L. .... Menlo Park, CA
McCormick, Thomas R. .... Seattle, WA
McCormick, Thomas R. .... Midland, MI
McCormick, Thomas T. .... Orinda, CA
McCormick, Timothy B. .... Walnut Creek, CA
McCormick, Timothy E.
Oklahoma City, OK
Tulsa, OK
McCormick, Timothy J. .... Greensburg, PA
McCormick, Timothy P. .... Ozark, MO
McCormick, Timothy P. .... Cleveland, OH
McCormick, Timothy R. .... **Dallas, TX**
McCormick, Tristan A. .... **Columbus, OH**
McCormick & von Mehren, P.C.
Atlanta, GA
McCormick, W. A. .... Little Rock, AR
McCormick, Walter K. .... Visalia, CA
Mccormick, Warren Austin .... Little Rock, AR
McCormick, William A. .... Santa Ana, CA
McCormick, William A. .... **Cincinnati, OH**
McCormick, William A. .... Raymondville, TX
McCormick, William A. .... Prosser, WA
McCormick, William G. .... **Sarasota, FL**
McCormick, William J. .... **Pittsburgh, PA**
McCormick, William P. .... Pittsburgh, PA
McCormick, William T. .... Downers Grove, IL
McCormick, William T., Jr. .... Chicago, IL
McCormick & Zerante .... Homewood, IL
McCormies, Walter .... Tucson, AZ
Mccormish, Kristin M. .... **Pittsburgh, PA**
McCormley, J. Lawrence .... **Phoenix, AZ**
McCormmach, Jane M. .... Seattle, WA
McCormmach, Maureen .... Pendleton, OR
McCornack, Hannah S. .... United States Senate,
Senatorial Assistants, GV
McCorquodale, Donald F., Jr. .... Raleigh, NC
McCorquodale, Douglas R., (A Professional Corporation) .... San Diego, CA
McCorquodale, Gaines C. .... **Jackson, AL**
McCorquodale, James A., (P.C.)
Dallas, TX
McCorquodale, Joseph C., III
Jackson, AL
McCorquodale & McCorquodale
Jackson, AL
McCorriston Miho Miller Mukai
Honolulu, HI
McCorriston, Thomas P., Jr.
Philadelphia, PA
McCorriston, William C. .... **Honolulu, HI**
McCorry & Gannon .... Pawtucket, RI
McCorry, Mary .... Brooklyn, NY
McCorry, Robert E., Jr. .... Pawtucket, RI
McCorry, Theresa N. C. .... **Syracuse, NY**
McCorry, Thomas J. .... Garden City, NY
McCort, Wayne Allan .... **Long Beach, CA**
McCortney, Carroll A. .... Glendale, CA
McCortney, Ryan D. .... **Costa Mesa, CA**
McCortney, Susan Freeman
Los Angeles, CA
McCorvey, Gary C. .... Tifton, GA
McCorvey, John H., Jr., Law Office of
Jacksonville, FL
McCorvey, William R., Jr. .... Richmond, VA
McCoskey, Daniel T. .... Los Angeles, CA
McCoskey, Gregory M. .... **Tampa, FL**
McCoskey, Julie Smith .... **Birmingham, MI**
McCoski, Kelli P. .... Amsterdam, NY
McCoskrie, Carol W. .... Arlington, VA
McCostis, Richard M. .... Ludlow, VT
McCotter, Charles K., Jr. .... **New Bern, NC**
McCotter, DeWitt C., III .... **Raleigh, NC**
McCotter, James R. .... **El Paso, TX**
McCotter, James V. .... Jamaica, NY
McCotter, McAfee & Ashton, PLLC
New Bern, NC
McCotter, Patricia I. .... Tacoma, WA
McCotter, Verjeana Carol
Upper Marlboro, MD
McCoubrey, Wm. K. .... Chicopee, MA
McCoun, Thomas B., III .... Tampa, FL
McCourt, Catherine L. .... Glenview, IL
McCourt, Elizabeth C. .... Albuquerque, NM
McCourt, Frank J. .... Baltimore, MD
McCourt, James P. .... Evanston, IL
McCourt, John .... Beaverton, OR
McCourt, John F., Jr. .... Detroit, MI
McCourt, John J. .... Marlboro, NY
McCourt, Joyce E. .... Boston, MA
McCourt, Patricia .... Ventura, CA
McCourt, Patricia Ann .... Orlando, FL
McCourt, Philip B., Jr. .... Waltham, MA
McCourt, Ronald V. .... Toledo, OH
McCourt, Terence P. .... **Boston, MA**
McCourt, Timothy J. .... **New York, NY**
McCourt, William J. .... Santa Ana, CA
McCowan, Charles S., III
Baton Rouge, LA
McCowan, Charles S., Jr.
Baton Rouge, LA
McCowan, Horace D., Jr. .... Richmond, VA
McCowan, Jack B., Jr. .... **San Francisco, CA**
Mccowan, Philip Edward
Oklahoma City, OK
McCowan, Philip R. .... **San Jose, CA**
McCowan, Philip R., A Professional Corporation .... **San Jose, CA**
McCowan, Thomas R. .... Prescott, AZ
McCowen, Cecily E. .... Martinez, CA
McCowen, Hale, Jr. .... Ukiah, CA
McCowen, Lisa C. .... Lafayette, LA
McCowin, Steven E. .... Salt Lake City, UT
McCown, Barry L. .... Bakersfield, CA
McCown, Brigham A.
West Palm Beach, FL
McCown, David H. .... Ironton, OH
McCown, Davis G. .... Fort Worth, TX
McCown, F. Scott .... Austin, TX
McCown, Frank D. .... Fort Worth, TX
McCown, Frank J. .... Ironton, OH
McCown, Gary W. .... Boerne, TX
McCown, Hale .... Lincoln, NE
McCown, Harrison J. .... Chicago, IL
McCown, Harrison J. .... **Tuscola, IL**
McCown, James M. .... **Dallas, TX**
McCown, Jay F. .... Oklahoma City, OK
McCown, Jean K. .... **Palo Alto, CA**
McCown, John R. .... **Dalton, GA**
McCown, Josh .... Wharton, TX
McCown, Keith H. .... **Boston, MA**
Mccown, Kelly M. .... San Francisco, CA
McCown, L. Kenneth, Jr. .... Memphis, TN
McCown, Linda H. .... Manteo, NC
McCown & McCown .... Manteo, NC
McCown, Steven R. .... **Dallas, TX**
McCown, Sue Vick .... Manteo, NC
McCown, Susan E. .... Nashville, TN
Mccown, Susan Elizabeth .... Nashville, TN
McCown, W. Vance .... Tryon, NC
McCown, Wallace H. .... Manteo, NC
McCown, William L. .... **Milwaukee, WI**
McCoy, Albert L. .... Alabaster, AL
McCoy, Anne M. .... Chicago, IL
McCoy & Associates, P.C.
Mount Laurel, NJ
Philadelphia, PA
McCoy, B. Scott .... Louisville, KY
McCoy, Barney C. .... Kansas City, MO
McCoy, Barney L. .... Houston, TX
McCoy, Benjamin D. .... **Columbia, SC**
McCoy, Bert, Jr. .... Eugene, OR
McCoy, Bill .... Odessa, TX
McCoy, Bob F. .... Tulsa, OK
McCoy & Bode .... Pekin, IL
McCoy, Brian C. .... Monterey, CA
McCoy, Bruce W., Jr. .... **Westfield, NJ**
McCoy, Bryan S., Jr. .... Louisville, KY
McCoy, Candace G. .... West Chester, PA
McCoy, Carl E., Jr. .... Newark, OH
McCoy, Carol
Department Of The Interior, GV
McCoy, Carol Ann .... **Birmingham, AL**
McCoy, Carol L. .... Nashville, TN
McCoy, Caroline Jeanne .... Englewood, FL
McCoy, Challen P. .... Bardstown, KY
McCoy, Charles F. .... **Greensboro, NC**
McCoy, Charles R. .... Tallahassee, FL
McCoy, Charles W., Jr. .... Pomona, CA
McCoy, Christi R. .... **Booneville, MS**
McCoy, Clark H., Jr. .... **Sherman, TX**
McCoy, Claud (Skip) E., Jr. .... **Lanett, AL**
McCoy, Cynthia Y. .... **Phoenix, AZ**
McCoy, Dale E. .... Phoenix, AZ
McCoy, Daniel G. .... **Sacramento, CA**
McCoy, Daniel J. .... **Spokane, WA**
McCoy, Darlene Evans .... **Cleveland, OH**
McCoy, David .... Raleigh, NC
McCoy, David M. .... **Florham Park, NJ**
McCoy, David M. .... Childress, TX
McCoy, Deborah .... Fair Oaks, CA
McCoy, Dennis F. .... Newport, RI
McCoy, Dennis R. .... Washington, DC
McCoy, Dennis R. .... **Buffalo, NY**
McCoy, Diane S. .... Flagstaff, AZ
McCoy, Dionne Carroll .... **Indianapolis, IN**
McCoy, Donald B. .... Southampton, PA
McCoy, Douglas L. .... **Mobile, AL**
McCoy, Douglas M. .... Bloomington, IN
McCoy, Dustan Chad .... **Lexington, KY**
McCoy, Dustan E. .... Greenwich, CT
McCoy, Earl Edward, III .... Lafayette, IN
McCoy, Earl W. .... Silver Spring, MD
McCoy, Edwin F. .... **Philadelphia, PA**
McCoy, Elizabeth A. .... New York, NY
McCoy, Ellison F. .... **Greenville, SC**
McCoy, Erin L. .... **Chicago, IL**
McCoy, Ernest H. .... Oakland, CA
McCoy, Faulkner & Broerman
Oskaloosa, IA
McCoy, Frank J. .... Vernon, CT
McCoy, Frank T., Jr. .... Nashville, TN
McCoy, Fred A. .... Wilbraham, MA
McCoy, Gary A. .... Houston, TX
McCoy, Gene L. .... Dallas, TX
McCoy, Gloyd L. .... **Oklahoma City, OK**
McCoy, Gregory J. .... **Holland, MI**
McCoy, Gregory L. .... **Danville, CA**
McCoy, Harold V. .... Garden City, NY
McCoy, Harold V., Jr. .... White Plains, NY
McCoy, Harry E. .... Norfolk, VA
McCoy, Harry E., II .... **Salt Lake City, UT**
McCoy, Henry D., II .... Peterstown, WV
McCoy, Holly .... Kansas City, MO
McCoy, H. P., Jr. .... Halifax, NC
McCoy, Hugh B. .... Oskaloosa, IA
McCoy, J. Michael .... **Oklahoma City, OK**
McCoy, J. Tully .... Oklahoma City, OK
McCoy, Jackson F. .... **Miami, FL**
McCoy, Jacqueline J. .... **Kansas City, MO**
McCoy, James .... Streamwood, IL
McCoy, James F. .... Pawtucket, RI
McCoy, James J. .... Madison, WI
McCoy, James M. .... Jefferson City, MO
McCoy, James M. .... **Dallas, TX**
McCoy, James M. .... Longview, TX
McCoy, James R., Jr. .... **Irvine, CA**
McCoy, J.B. Todd .... **Philadelphia, PA**
McCoy, Jean M. .... **Vancouver, WA**
McCoy, Jennifer Hamilton
Kansas City, MO
McCoy, Jerry J. .... **Washington, DC**
McCoy, John C., Jr. .... **Washington, DC**
McCoy, John D. .... Boston, MA
McCoy, John J. .... **Cincinnati, OH**
McCoy, John L. .... Salt Lake City, UT
McCoy, John Milton, III .... **Los Angeles, CA**
McCoy, John P. .... **Providence, RI**
McCoy, John R. .... Holbrook, MA
McCoy, John T. .... **Waterloo, IA**
McCoy, John V. .... **Waukesha, WI**
McCoy, Jonathan K. .... Independence, MO
McCoy, Jonathan T. .... Olympia, WA
McCoy, Joseph L. .... **Jackson, MS**
McCoy, Joseph M. .... **Albany, NY**
McCoy, Joy Reynolds .... **Williamsport, PA**
McCoy, Joyce A. .... **San Diego, CA**
McCoy, K. Byron .... Houston, TX
McCoy, Karen A. .... **Detroit, MI**
McCoy, Kathleen A. .... **Denver, CO**
McCoy, Kelly J. .... Taunton, MA
McCoy, Kenneth C. .... Oklahoma City, OK
McCoy, Kenneth D., Jr. .... **Natchitoches, LA**
McCoy, Kevin F. .... Anchorage, AK
McCoy, Kevin J. .... Omaha, NE
McCoy & Kula .... Chicago, IL
McCoy, Lance T. .... Marietta, GA

McCoy, Laura Clark ... Richmond, VA
McCoy, Lee A. ... Santa Barbara, CA
McCoy, Leigh A. ... Raleigh, NC
McCoy, Leonard H. ... Charlotte, NC
McCoy, Lilys Doris ... San Diego, CA
McCoy, Lisa ... Indianapolis, IN
McCoy, Lisa ... Lancaster, PA
McCoy, Lisa D. ... Chicago, IL
McCoy, M. Scott ... Chicago, IL
McCoy, Margarita Candace ... Seattle, WA
McCoy, Marjorie S. ... Albany, NY
McCoy, Mark B. ... Washington, DC
McCoy, Marvin G. ... Hagåtña, GU
McCoy, Matthew J. ... United States Senate, Committee Legal Personnel, GV
McCoy, Matthew K. ... New York, NY
McCoy, Melody L. ... Boulder, CO
McCoy, Michael D. ... Charlotte, NC
McCoy, Michael K. ... Mount Clemens, MI
McCoy, Michael S. ... Houston, TX
McCoy, Michael T. ... Murray, UT
McCoy, Michael W. ... Broken Arrow, OK
McCoy, Michael W. ... Houston, TX
McCoy, Moni Bertrand ... Lafayette, LA
McCoy, Monica M. ... Indianapolis, IN
McCoy, Nancy H. ... Riverside, CA
Mccoy, Nancy K. ... Charleston, WV
McCoy, Neal S. ... Washington, DC
McCoy, Newton G. ... St. Louis, MO
McCoy, Nicholas F. ... Baltimore, MD
McCoy, Nolan M. ... Meadville, MS
McCoy, Norah Ann ... Carson City, NV
McCoy, Patricia A. ... Cleveland, OH
McCoy, Patrick D. ... Saginaw, MI
McCoy, Patrick D. ... St. Paul, MN
McCoy, Patrick J. ... Boise, ID
McCoy Peterson Jorstad Brabbit, Ltd. ... Minneapolis, MN
McCoy, Phillip S. ... Boston, MA
McCoy, Phyllis R. ... Poultney, VT
McCoy, R. Burl, Jr. ... Lexington, KY
McCoy, Reagan S. ... San Antonio, TX
McCoy, Richard D. ... Pekin, IL
McCoy, Richard L. ... Mechanicsburg, PA
McCoy, Richard T., III ... Los Angeles, CA
McCoy, Robert ... Fort Worth, TX
McCoy, Robert C. ... Norwich, CT
McCoy, Robert D. ... Wickenburg, AZ
McCoy, Robert E. ... Los Angeles, CA
McCoy, Robert G., Jr. ... Modesto, CA
McCoy, Robert I. ... Ann Arbor, MI
McCoy, Robert J. ... San Francisco, CA
McCoy, Robert J. ... Metairie, LA
McCoy, Robert W. ... Albuquerque, NM
McCoy Roberts Begnaud & Friedman, A Law Corporation ... Natchitoches, LA
McCoy, Roche S. ... Chatsworth, CA
McCoy, Ruth E. Goldwater ... Chicago, IL
McCoy, Sandra Smith ... Cupertino, CA
McCoy, Scott E. ... Houston, TX
McCoy, Shelia Yvonne ... Marshall, TX
McCoy, Stanford Kenneth ... Washington, DC
McCoy, Stephan A. ... Covington, KY
McCoy, Stephen C. ... Richmond, VA
McCoy, Stephen J. ... Norwell, MA
McCoy, Steven J. ... Chicago, IL
McCoy, Steven J. ... Columbus, OH
McCoy, Susan ... Paterson, NJ
McCoy, Tene LaVi ... Chicago, IL
McCoy, Terrence L. ... Louisville, KY
McCoy, Thomas C. ... Manahawkin, NJ
McCoy, Thomas M. ... Sunnyvale, CA
McCoy, Thomas Raymond ... Nashville, TN
McCoy, Thomas T. ... Englewood, CO
McCoy, Thomas V. ... Georgetown, DE
McCoy, Timothy D. ... Charleston, SC
McCoy, Timothy E. ... Tulsa, OK
McCoy, Timothy J. ... Minneapolis, MN
McCoy, Timothy J. ... Appleton, WI
Green Bay, WI
McCoy, Toby Dale ... Department of the Army, U.S. Army Legal Services Agency, GV
McCoy, Vera ... Wenonah, NJ
McCoy, Victor A. ... Southfield, MI
McCoy, Walter V. ... New Rochelle, NY
McCoy, Watson A. ... Columbus, OH
McCoy, Wayne A. ... Chicago, IL
McCoy, Weaver, Wiggins, Cleveland & Raper, PLLC ... Fayetteville, NC
McCoy & West ... Lexington, KY
McCoy, Wilkins, Stephens & Tipton, P.A. ... Jackson, MS
McCoy, William B. ... Berkeley, CA
McCoy, William C. ... Cleveland, OH
McCoy, William C. ... Durant, OK
McCoy, William E. ... Uncasville, CT
McCoy, William F. ... New York, NY
McCoy, Wm., Jr. ... Franklin, WV
McCoyd, Edward A. ... Garden City, NY
McCoyd, Edward A., P.C. ... Garden City, NY
McCoyd, Edward M. ... Garden City, NY
McCoyd, Matthew J. ... Atlanta, GA
McCoyd, Patrick K. ... Philadelphia, PA
McCoy-Evans, Melisa ... San Jose, CA
McCoy-Pfau, Rhonda L. ... Bloomfield Hills, MI
McCracken, Alan P. ... Buffalo, NY
McCracken, Amy E. ... Detroit, MI
McCracken & Byers ... Burlingame, CA
McCracken, Carol W. ... Bloomingdale, NJ
McCracken, Christopher C. ... Cleveland, OH
McCracken, Christopher F. ... Portland, OR
McCracken, Craig W. ... New York, NY
McCracken, Cresap S. ... Great Falls, MT
McCracken, David E., III ... Chicago, IL

McCracken, David G. ... Dallas, TX
McCracken, Ellis W., Jr. ... Chesterfield, MO
McCracken, Eugene ... Savannah, GA
McCracken, Eugene W. ... Graham, TX
McCracken, Glenn, Jr. ... New Castle, PA
McCracken, Gregory E. ... Oklahoma City, OK
McCracken, H. Richd. ... Sun City West, AZ
McCracken, Harrold J. ... Fallon, NV
McCracken, J. Barry ... Norfolk, VA
McCracken, J. Matthew ... Department of Labor, Office of the Solicitor, GV
McCracken, J. Van ... Little Rock, AR
McCracken, J. Van, P.A. ... Little Rock, AR
McCracken, Jack J. ... Findlay, OH
McCracken, Jill A. ... Chambersburg, PA
McCracken, Jill C. ... Los Angeles, CA
McCracken, JoAnne ... San Jose, CA
McCracken, John Blair ... West Palm Beach, FL
McCracken, John E. ... New York, NY
McCracken, John H. ... Bowling Green, KY
McCracken, John W. ... Edwardsville, IL
McCracken, Karen E. ... Covington, KY
McCracken, Kate L. ... Wheaton, IL
McCracken, Ken ... Geneva, IL
Mc Cracken, Kenneth William ... Newton, KS
McCracken, M. Michelle P. ... Virginia Beach, VA
McCracken, Marisa L. ... Indianapolis, IN
McCracken, Martin T. ... Charlotte, NC
McCracken, Mary Frances ... Grand Junction, CO
McCracken, Matthew T. ... Houston, TX
McCracken & McCracken, P.C. ... Chicago, IL
McCracken, Michael D. ... Burlingame, CA
McCracken, Peggy A. ... Downers Grove, IL
McCracken, Richard G. ... Las Vegas, NV
McCracken, Richard John ... Lancaster, PA
McCracken, Robert C. ... St. Louis, MO
McCracken, Robert D., (P.C.) ... Phoenix, AZ
McCracken, Robert L. ... Manitowoc, WI
McCracken, Ronald J. ... Easley, SC
McCracken, Samuel R., Jr. ... Franklin, KY
Mc Cracken, Sheri Peterson ... Olathe, KS
McCracken, Sherrie L. ... Antioch, CA
McCracken, Stemerman, Bowen and Holsberry ... Las Vegas, NV
McCracken, Steven C. ... Carlsbad, CA
McCracken, Tamara ... Bremerton, WA
McCracken Taylor & Nelson, P.C. ... Carrollton, TX
McCracken, Terri L. ... Fresno, CA
McCracken, Thomas G. ... Batavia, IL
McCracken, Thomas J. ... Chicago, IL
McCracken, Thomas J., Jr. ... Chicago, IL
Mccracken, Thomas L. ... Fort Worth, TX
McCracken, Thomas P.G. ... Fremont, CA
McCracken, W. Brewster ... Austin, TX
McCracken, Walsh, DeLavan & Hetler ... Chicago, IL
McCracken, Wendy Reuter ... Cincinnati, OH
McCracken, William B. ... Sun Lakes, AZ
McCracken, William D. ... Wilmington, OH
McCracken, William E. ... Chicago, IL
McCracken, William J. ... Hawthorne, CA
McCracken, William L. ... Phoenix, AZ
McCracken, William R. ... Augusta, GA
McCrackin, Ann M. ... Minneapolis, MN
McCrackin, Barnett, Richardson & Clemmons, LLP ... Myrtle Beach, SC
McCrackin, E. Windell ... Myrtle Beach, SC
McCrackin, James F. ... Myrtle Beach, SC
McCrackin, Sidney M. ... Fort Walton Beach, FL
Panama City, FL
Pensacola, FL
McCrady, Allen D. ... Idaho Falls, ID
McCrady, William F., Jr. ... Pittsburgh, PA
McCrae, James M. ... Orlando, FL
McCrae, Sally Staples ... Longwood, FL
McCrae, Stephen R., Jr. ... Rock Hill, SC
McCrae, William ... San Antonio, TX
McCraley, Gavin T. ... Los Angeles, CA
McCrandall, Susan A. ... Grand Blanc, MI
McCraney, Mack H. ... Hammond, LA
McCraney, Percy P. ... Baton Rouge, LA
McCraney, W. Thomas, III ... Jackson, MS
McCranie, Burgess E., Jr. ... Metairie, LA
McCranie, Charles E. ... Atlanta, GA
Jonesboro, GA
McCranie, Clauye C. ... Ocilla, GA
McCranie, D. Mitchell ... Gulfport, MS
McCranie, Daniel I. ... Fernandina Beach, FL
McCranie, Daniel I., P.A. ... Fernandina Beach, FL
McCranie, David A. ... Jacksonville, FL
McCranie, Weyman W., Jr. ... Mobile, AL
McCrann, Michael Johnathan ... Aberdeen, NC
McCrary, Barry N. ... Talladega, AL
McCrary, Charles D. ... Birmingham, AL
McCrary, Christy B. ... Austin, TX
McCrary, Dan H. ... Birmingham, AL
McCrary, Darold G. ... Ventura, CA
McCrary & Dove ... Miami, FL
Ocala, FL
McCrary, Duane M. ... Madison, WI
McCrary, George D., III ... Bartlett, TN
McCrary, J. Patrick ... Atlanta, GA
McCrary, Jesse J., Jr. ... Miami, FL
Ocala, FL
McCrary, John M. ... Palo Alto, CA
McCrary Law Offices ... Casper, WY
McCrary, Michael S. ... Hot Springs National Park, AR
McCrary, Peter K. ... Manassas, VA
McCrary, Robert H. ... Casper, WY

McCrary, Roderick D. ... Atlanta, GA
McCrary, S. Denise, Law Offices of ... Memphis, TN
Mccrary, Sammy M. ... Lamesa, TX
McCrary, Susan Denise ... Memphis, TN
McCrary, Timothy J. ... Baton Rouge, LA
McCrary, Toni M. ... West Des Moines, IA
McCrary, William A. ... Montgomery, AL
McCravey, Mary A. ... Portland, OR
McCravy, Angela Denise ... Tampa, FL
McCravy, Dewey H., III ... Dallas, TX
McCravy, John R., III ... Greenwood, SC
McCravy Law Firm, The, P.A. ... Greenwood, SC
McCravy, S. Tucker ... Columbia, SC
McCravy, Sheila E. ... Needham, MA
McCraw, Dan ... Hot Springs National Park, AR
McCraw, David E. ... New York, NY
McCraw, Douglas C. ... Glendale, CA
McCraw, John L., Jr. ... McKinney, TX
McCraw, John L. (Lin), III ... McKinney, TX
McCraw, Katherine M. ... Wendell, NC
McCraw, Marcus "Mark" Hamilton ... McKinney, TX
McCraw & McCraw ... McKinney, TX
McCraw, Scott H. ... San Bernardino, CA
McCraw, Thomas K., Jr. ... Rockville, MD
McCray, Alfred L. ... Dayton, OH
McCray, Becky S. ... Springfield, IL
McCray, Cheryl A. ... Morgantown, WV
McCray, David Harvey ... Arlington, VA
McCray, Deanna E. ... Los Angeles, CA
McCray, George F. ... Treasury Department, Office of Regulations and Rulings, GV
McCray, J. William ... Elyria, OH
McCray, Jeffrey W. ... Department of the Navy, Office of the Judge Advocate General, GV
McCray, Joe R. ... San Francisco, CA
McCray, Joe R., P.C., Law Offices of ... San Francisco, CA
McCray, Joel M. ... Richmond, VA
McCray, Johnny L., Jr. ... Pompano Beach, FL
McCray, Jonas D.L. ... Trumbull, CT
McCray, Kevin B. ... Richmond, VA
McCray, Larry L. ... Pueblo, CO
McCray and McCray ... Dayton, OH
McCray, Michael ... Evansville, IN
McCray, Muzilla, Smith & Meyers Co., L.P.A. ... Cleveland, OH
Elyria, OH
McCray, Renee D. ... Washington, DC
McCray, Risa C. ... Dayton, OH
McCray, Ronald D. ... Neenah, WI
McCray, Samuel A. ... Dayton, OH
McCray, Scott R. ... Raleigh, NC
McCray, Stephen S. ... San Jose, CA
McCrea, A. Grant ... New York, NY
McCrea, Bruce B. ... Denver, CO
McCrea, Charles H., Jr. ... Las Vegas, NV
McCrea, Charles H., Sr. ... Las Vegas, NV
McCrea, Claire D. ... Southampton, NY
McCrea, David B., (P.A.) ... Miami, FL
McCrea, David S. ... Bloomington, IN
McCrea, Edward F. ... Bloomington, IN
McCrea, George E. ... San Angelo, TX
McCrea, John A. ... Louisville, KY
McCrea, Keck & Buck, L.L.C. ... Denver, CO
McCrea, Keith R. ... Washington, DC
McCrea, Lisa ... Washington, DC
McCrea & McCrea ... Bloomington, IN
McCrea, P.C. ... Eugene, OR
McCrea, Richard C., Jr. ... Tampa, FL
McCrea, Robert J. ... Eugene, OR
McCrea, Shaun S. ... Eugene, OR
McCrea, Stephen B. ... Coeur d'Alene, ID
McCrea, Susan B. ... Somerville, NJ
McCrea, Thomas G. ... Everett, WA
McCrea, Victor C., Jr. ... Dallas, TX
McCrea, Victoria H. ... Durham, NC
McCreadie, David W. ... Cape Canaveral, FL
Tampa, FL
McCreadie, Robert B., (P.C.) ... San Rafael, CA
McCready, Andrew W. ... Department of Commerce, Office of the General Counsel, GV
McCready, Donna J. ... Anchorage, AK
McCready, Doris ... Dixon, CA
McCready, James E. ... San Francisco, CA
McCready, James W., III ... Miami, FL
McCready, Kent J. ... Charlotte, NC
McCready, Kevin J. ... Albuquerque, NM
McCready, L. Stephen ... Northborough, MA
McCready, Maureen A. ... Buffalo, NY
Mccready, Michael P. ... Chicago Heights, IL
McCready, Richard F., Jr. ... Winchester, KY
Mc Cready, Roger Lawrence ... Brooklyn, NY
McCready, Steven J. ... Springfield, OH
McCready, Susan E. ... Securities and Exchange Commission, Division of Enforcement, GV
McCready, Thomas S. ... Lansford, PA
McCready, Travis A. ... Minneapolis, MN
McCready, William H. ... Tawas City, MI
McCready, William S. ... Toledo, OH
McCreary, Ann M. ... New York, NY
McCreary & Associates ... Dallas, TX
Frisco, TX
The Colony, TX
McCreary, Charles H., III ... Columbus, OH
McCreary, David M. ... Columbus, OH

McCreary, David S. ... Dallas, TX
Frisco, TX
The Colony, TX
McCreary, Erin L. ... San Diego, CA
McCreary, Evelyn J. ... Louisville, KY
McCreary, Frank E., III ... Houston, TX
McCreary, Frank R., III ... Long Beach, MS
McCreary, J. Franklin ... Memphis, TN
Nashville, TN
McCreary, Jack H. ... Austin, TX
McCreary, Jacqueline M. ... Houston, TX
McCreary, Jean H. ... Rochester, NY
McCreary, John A., Jr. ... Pittsburgh, PA
McCreary, John R. ... Latrobe, PA
McCreary, Josh A. ... Murfreesboro, TN
McCreary, Kathleen S. ... New York, NY
McCreary, Lynn S. ... Overland Park, KS
McCreary, Marcee C. ... Columbus, OH
McCreary, Margaret Jane ... Durham, NC
McCreary, Michael E. ... Westlake Village, CA
McCreary, Pierce N. ... Larchmont, NY
McCreary, Robert G., III ... Cleveland, OH
McCreary, Robert V. ... Houston, TX
McCreary, Scott D. ... Oklahoma City, OK
McCreary, Stephen D. ... Department of State, Office of the Legal Adviser, GV
McCreary, Timothy A. ... Villa Rica, GA
McCreary, Veselka, Bragg & Allen, P.C. ... Austin, TX
McCreary, Wm. F. ... Tujunga, CA
McCredie, Timothy S. ... Kirkland, WA
McCree, Wade Harper ... Detroit, MI
McCreedy and Cox ... Cranford, NJ
Elizabeth, NJ
Newark, NJ
McCreedy, Edwin J. ... Cranford, NJ
Mccreedy, James M. ... Morristown, NJ
McCreedy, John C. ... Boise, ID
McCreedy, W. Greer, II ... Norfolk, VA
McCreery, Charles N., II ... Charleston, WV
McCreery, Edward P., III ... Bridgeport, CT
Hartford, CT
McCreery, Lawrence D., A Law Corp. ... Kapaa, HI
McCreery, Robert D. ... Brecksville, OH
McCreery, William G. ... New York, NY
McCreery, William M. ... Mason City, IL
McCreesh, John J., III ... Upper Darby, PA
McCreesh, John J., IV ... Upper Darby, PA
McCreesh & McCreesh ... Upper Darby, PA
McCreesh, Patrick J. ... New York, NY
McCreight, Allen H. ... Tampa, FL
McCreight, Curtis W. ... Houston, TX
McCreight, Gerard J. ... Garden City, NY
McCreight, Henry H., Jr. ... Houston, TX
McCreight, Henry H., Jr., A Professional Corporation ... Houston, TX
McCreight, James C. ... Washington, PA
McCreight, James M. ... Boston, MA
McCreight, John W. ... Washington, PA
McCreight, Kimberly E. ... New York, NY
McCrery, David N., III ... Galesburg, IL
McCrery, James O., III ... Shreveport, LA
McCrery, Michael Joseph ... Burr Ridge, IL
McCrevan, William J., Jr. ... Boston, MA
McCright, Jon M. ... Cedar Rapids, IA
McCright, Joseph E. ... Cincinnati, OH
McCrimlisk, Mary A. ... New York, NY
McCrimmon, Edward W. ... Atlanta, GA
McCrimmon, Lisa L. ... Atlanta, GA
McCrimmon, Mark ... Austin, TX
McCrimmon & McCrimmon ... Atlanta, GA
McCrindle, C. Kevin, Law Offices of ... Hudson, IA
Waterloo, IA
McCrink, Christine ... New York, NY
McCrink, Matthew R. ... West Berlin, NJ
McCrink, Nelson & Kehler ... West Berlin, NJ
McCririe, William D., Jr. ... Brighton, MI
McCrocklin, James P. ... Louisville, KY
McCrocklin, Sophia M. ... Environmental Protection Agency, Office of Congressional and Legislative Affairs, GV
McCrohan, Elizabeth ... Jacksonville, FL
McCrohan, Erinn ... Atlanta, GA
McCrohon, Craig ... Chicago, IL
McCrone, Kathleen A. ... Fairview Park, OH
McCrone, Willard P. ... Monterey, CA
McCroom, E. Winther ... Youngstown, OH
McCrorey, James K. ... Louisville, KY
McCrorey, Joseph D. ... Columbia, SC
McCrory, Anne O'Connor ... Bridgeport, CT
McCrory, Barbara W. ... Janesville, WI
McCrory, Bryan D. ... Dallas, TX
McCrory, Charles ... Mountain View, CA
McCrory, Charles K. ... Terre Haute, IN
McCrory & Clark Co., L.P.A. ... Toledo, OH
McCrory, Darrell P. ... Los Angeles, CA
Santa Ana, CA
McCrory, David ... Napa, CA
McCrory, Dorothy B. ... Toledo, OH
McCrory, Hugh G., Jr. ... New York, NY
McCrory, J. Walter ... Fort Lauderdale, FL
McCrory, James H. ... Livonia, MI
Mc Crory, James R. ... Albuquerque, NM
McCrory, Jill L. ... Indianapolis, IN
McCrory, John B. ... Rochester, NY
McCrory, John P. ... South Royalton, VT
McCrory & Kovsky, P.C. ... Livonia, MI
McCrory, Marc T. ... Janesville, WI
McCrory, Maris L. ... Baton Rouge, LA
McCrory, Mary J. ... Pittsburgh, PA
McCrory, Michael E. ... Houston, TX
McCrory, Michael K. ... Indianapolis, IN
McCrory, Patricia Polis ... Indianapolis, IN
McCrory, Paul A., Jr. ... Toledo, OH
McCrory, Richard J. ... St. Petersburg, FL

McCrory, Rosaleen T. ... New York, NY
McCrory, Susan I. ... Charlotte, NC
McCrory, Tom M., III ... Dallas, TX
McCroskey, Eddie A. ... Poteau, OK
McCroskey, Feldman, Cochrane & Brock, P.C. Muskegon, MI
McCroskey, Kevin J. ... Muskegon, MI
McCroskey, Thomas G. ... Maryville, TN
McCrossen, Anita S. ... Metairie, LA
McCrossen, Macon, (Mrs.) Albuquerque, NM
McCrossin, Edward J., III Jersey City, NJ
McCrossin, G. Michael ... Corpus Christi, TX
McCrosson, Dennis F. ... Indianapolis, IN
McCrosson, Dorothy F. ... Ocean City, NJ
McCrosson & Nerz ... Indianapolis, IN
McCrum, Bruce L. ... Newport, OR
McCrum, Everett S. ... Brownwood, TX
McCrum, John M. ... Hammond, IN
McCrum, Michael W. ... San Antonio, TX
McCrum, R. Timothy ... Washington, DC
McCrummen, Roger K. ... Kansas City, MO
McCrury, L. Douglass ... Toledo, OH
McCrury, Phillip W. ... Fort Worth, TX
McCrystal, Colleen B ... Washington, DC
McCrystal, Harry J. ... Massapequa, NY
McCrystal, James L. ... Sandusky, OH
McCrystal, James L., Jr. ... Cleveland, OH
McCrystal, Margaret A. ... Lansing, MI
McCrystal, Mark C. ... Boston, MA Providence, RI
McCrystal, Michael J. ... Dover, DE
McCrystal, Thomas W. ... Cleveland, OH
McCrystal, Timothy M. ... Boston, MA
McCuaig, Haeger, Bolz, McCarty & Baudin West Dundee, IL
McCuaig, Victor C., Jr. ... Melville, NY
McCubbin, D. James ... Kalispell, MT
McCubbin, Dennis T. ... St. Louis, MO
McCubbin, Donald J. ... San Francisco, CA
McCubbin, Garry ... St. Louis, MO
McCubbin, Harold T. ... Denver, CO
McCubbin, Patricia Ross Department of Justice, Environment and Natural Resources Division, GV
McCubbins, Benjamin D. ... Salisbury, NC
McCubbins, Robert R. ... Enid, OK
McCubbrey, J. Bruce ... San Francisco, CA
McCubbrey, Robert J. ... Southfield, MI
McCubrey, Timothy G. ... St. Paul, MN
McCue, Andrew H. ... Kansas City, MO
McCue, Arthur B. ... Somerville, MA
McCue & Bertocchi ... Kittanning, PA
McCue, Carl, Law Office of ... Hampden, ME
McCue, Carroll E. ... Roeland Park, KS
McCue, David C. ... Dallas, TX
Mccue, Debra Kelly ... Hampden, ME
McCue, Donald J. ... Connellsville, PA
McCue, Edward O., III ... Charlottesville, VA
McCue, Florence T. ... Elmsford, NY
McCue, George R., III ... Columbus, OH
McCue, Gregory S. ... Washington, DC
McCue, Harry R. ... San Diego, CA
McCue, Howard M., III ... Chicago, IL
McCue & Husband ... Connellsville, PA
McCue, James A. ... Shrewsbury, NJ
McCue, John B. ... Kittanning, PA
McCue, John F. ... Tampa, FL
McCue, John W. ... Atlanta, GA
McCue, John W., II ... Fairview, OK
McCue, Joseph S. ... Columbia, SC
McCue, Judith W. ... Chicago, IL
McCue, Kurt E. ... Newark, NJ
McCue, Lawrence J. ... Reading, MA
McCue & Lee, LLP ... Boston, MA
McCue & Lee, P.C. ... Dallas, TX
McCue, Leonard A. ... Bradenton, FL
McCue, Leonard J., (P.C.) ... Newburgh, NY
McCue, Margaret A. ... Atlanta, GA
McCue, Mark A. ... Boston, MA
McCue, Mark S. ... Concord, NH
McCue, Martin T. ... Rochester, NY
McCue, Mary E. ... Eden Prairie, MN
McCue, Matthew P. ... Worcester, MA
McCue & McCue ... Shrewsbury, NJ
McCue, Michael C. ... Chicago, IL
McCue, Michael E. ... Dallas, TX
McCue, Michael J. ... Las Vegas, NV
McCue, Michele M. ... Kansas City, MO
McCue, Paul J. ... Denver, CO
McCue, Peter J. ... Boston, MA
McCue, Richard E. ... Worcester, MA
McCue, Richard G. ... Cincinnati, OH
McCue, Richard G., Co., L.P.A. Cincinnati, OH
McCue, Richard J. ... Falls Church, VA
McCue, Robert T. ... Cheyenne, WY
McCue, Shannon V. ... Akron, OH
McCue, Stephen R. ... Helena, MT
McCue, Stephen V. ... San Diego, CA
McCue, Thomas F. ... Loudon, NH
McCue, Thomas P. ... Louisville, OH
McCue, Vincent J. ... Shrewsbury, NJ
McCue, William A. ... Portland, ME
McCue, William C. ... Fort Lauderdale, FL
McCuen, Charles M. ... Philadelphia, PA
McCuen, Douglas R. ... Albany, NY
McCuen, John F., Jr. ... Livonia, MI
McCuin, J. Scott ... Berlin, CT
McCuiston, W. Thomas ... Cary, NC
McCulla, Margaret C. ... Bethesda, MD
McCullagh, Eugene M. ... Dallas, TX
McCullagh, James ... Seattle, WA
McCullagh, Mary K. ... Bloomington, IL
McCullagh, Neil E. ... Richmond, VA
McCullagh, Samuel Boyd San Francisco, CA
McCullah, William F. ... Forsyth, MO
McCullar, Benjamin ... Norman, OK
McCullar, Janet ... Austin, TX
McCullar, Michael D. ... Memphis, TN
McCullar, Paul H. ... Safford, AZ
McCullaugh, James Louis Sherman Oaks, CA
McCullen, Dan ... Jackson, MS
McCullen, Owen B. ... Eugene, OR
McCullen, Richard J. ... Columbus, OH
McCullen, Robert J. ... Lansing, MI
McCuller, Alvin J. ... Douglasville, GA
McCuller, E. Owen, Jr. ... Jacksonville, FL
McCullers, C. Lanny ... Tampa, FL
McCullers, Robert D. ... Macon, GA
McCulley, Conrad L. ... Hurlock, MD
McCulley, Dan Mitchell Junction City, KS
McCulley, David C. ... Toledo, OH
McCulley, Hugh L. ... Houston, TX
McCulley, Marcine Gibson ... Flint, TX
McCulley, Mary Ann ... Houston, TX
McCulley, Melanie G. ... Greenville, SC
McCulley, Michael B. ... New Brunswick, NJ
McCulley, Michael D., Jr. ... New Bern, NC
McCulley, Michael D., Jr., P.A. New Bern, NC
McCulley, Susan N. ... Houston, TX
McCulley, Timothy S. ... Southampton, NY
McCulley, William L. ... Kansas City, MO
McCulloch, A. Kent ... Austin, TX
McCulloch, Andrew ... Dallas, TX
McCulloch, Andrew R. ... Dallas, TX
McCulloch, Anne Segrest Washington, DC
McCulloch, Bruce C. ... Washington, DC
McCulloch, Carol L. ... Sykesville, MD
McCulloch, Champe C. ... Arlington, VA
McCulloch, Colleen C. ... Beckley, WV
McCulloch, Debra M. ... Detroit, MI
McCulloch, Don L. ... Kelso, WA
McCulloch, Elizabeth ... Gainesville, FL
McCulloch, Felger, Fite & Gutmann Co., L.P.A. ... Dayton, OH Piqua, OH Sidney, OH Troy, OH
McCulloch, Frank H., II Pension Benefit Guaranty Corporation, Office of the General Counsel, GV
McCulloch, Gail Bowen ... Shreveport, LA
McCulloch, Gordon J. ... Albuquerque, NM
McCulloch, Hugh B. ... Evanston, IL
McCulloch, James E. ... Vermillion, SD
McCulloch, James L. ... Houston, TX
McCulloch, James R. ... Milwaukee, WI
McCulloch, Jere N. ... Lebanon, TN
McCulloch, John K. ... Saginaw, MI
McCulloch, John R., Jr. ... Portland, OR Salem, OR
McCulloch, Joseph M., Jr. ... Columbia, SC
McCulloch, Kari E. ... Salt Lake City, UT
McCulloch, Kathleen McCollum Odessa, TX
McCulloch, Kathryn V. ... New York, NY
McCulloch, Kenneth J. ... New York, NY
McCulloch, Kevin O. ... New York, NY
McCulloch, M. Jason ... Birmingham, AL
McCulloch, Marian P. ... Tampa, FL
McCulloch, Mark M. ... Portland, OR
McCulloch, Mary Catherine Albuquerque, NM
McCulloch & McCulloch ... Dallas, TX
McCulloch, Paula Dell ... Dallas, TX
McCulloch, R. Kenny ... Little Rock, AR
McCulloch, Raymond C. ... Waltham, MA
McCulloch, Robert A. ... Dallas, TX
McCulloch, Robert F. ... Washington, DC
McCulloch, Robert J. ... Encino, CA
McCulloch, Robert M., Jr. ... New York, NY
McCulloch, Robert P. ... Clayton, MO
McCulloch, Scott H. ... Beckley, WV
McCulloch, Sue-Del ... Portland, OR
McCulloch, Thomas M. ... Wheeling, WV
McCulloch, Thomas O. ... Aurora, IL
McCulloch, Thomas R. ... Lansing, MI
McCulloch, Tracy Beggs San Francisco, CA
McCulloch, W. Cameron ... Houston, TX
McCulloch, Wendell H. ... Long Beach, CA
McCulloch, William C. ... Houston, TX
McCulloch Burns, Michelle ... Greybull, WY
McCullogh, R. Patrick ... La Jolla, CA
McCulloh, Harry R. ... Petersburg, WV
McCulloh, John R. ... Chicago, IL
McCulloh, Neal ... Maitland, FL
McCullouch, John M. ... Jackson, MS
McCullough, Andrew Cuyugan San Rafael, CA
McCullough, Ann C. ... Denver, CO
Mccullough, Annelle ... Syracuse, NY
McCullough, Arthur Eugene Harlingen, TX
McCullough, Bernard L. ... Miami, FL
McCullough, Billi R. ... Denver, CO
McCullough, Bob J. ... Phoenix, AZ
McCullough, Brian J. Bloomfield Hills, MI
McCullough, Brian J. ... Doylestown, PA
McCullough, Bruce W. ... Wilmington, DE
McCullough, Burton V., Law Offices of Los Angeles, CA
McCullough, Calvin J. ... Memphis, TN
McCullough, Campbell & Lane Chicago, IL
McCullough, Carol B. ... Warminster, PA
McCullough, Charles J. ... Tacoma, WA
McCullough, Charles P. ... Pittsburgh, PA
McCullough, Cheryl R. ... Memphis, TN
McCullough, Chester C. ... River Forest, IL
McCullough, Christine M. ... Paoli, PA Philadelphia, PA
McCullough, Christopher R. ... Las Vegas, NV
McCullough, Clayton B. ... Columbia, SC
McCullough, Cody M. ... Sioux City, IA
McCullough, Colin J. ... Lake View, IA Sac City, IA
McCullough, Craig F. ... Salt Lake City, UT
McCullough, D. Patrick ... St. Paul, MN
McCullough, Darrin L. ... Savannah, GA
McCullough, David ... Oklahoma City, OK
McCullough, David A. ... Louisville, KY
McCullough, Debra D. ... New York, NY
McCullough, Don A. ... Denver, CO
McCullough, Douglas R. ... Houston, TX
McCullough, Edmund J. ... Hazleton, PA
McCullough, Edward A. ... Washington, DC
McCullough & Eisenberg, P.C. Warminster, PA
McCullough, Elizabeth Henderson Columbia, SC
McCullough, Erin Elizabeth ... Lake View, IA
McCullough, Eugene R. ... Knoxville, TN
McCullough, F. Witcher, III ... Austin, TX
McCullough, Francis X. ... McLean, VA
McCullough, Frank S., Jr. ... Harrison, NY White Plains, NY
McCullough, Gary C. ... Memphis, TN
McCullough, Geoffrey B. ... Boston, MA
McCullough, George E. ... Topeka, KS
McCullough, George V. ... Rocky River, OH
McCullough, Goldberger & Staudt Harrison, NY New York, NY White Plains, NY
McCullough, Graham ... Harlingen, TX
Mc Cullough, Gregory O. ... Sanford, ME
McCullough, Hugh J. ... Glennville, GA
McCullough, Hugh J., P.C., Law Offices of Glennville, GA
McCullough, Hugh R. ... Topeka, KS
McCullough, J. Bradford ... Bethesda, MD
McCullough, J. Douglas ... Raleigh, NC
McCullough, James A., II ... Jackson, MS
McCullough, James H. ... Hearne, TX
McCullough, James J. ... Washington, DC
McCullough, James M., III New York, NY
McCullough, Jane B. ... Chicago, IL
McCullough, Jeffrey C. ... Doylestown, PA
McCullough, Jill D. ... Baltimore, MD
McCullough, John A. ... Washington, DC
McCullough, John C. ... Boston, MA
McCullough, John C., Jr. ... Seattle, WA
McCullough, John E. ... Alexandria, VA
McCullough, John G. ... Atlanta, GA
McCullough, John J., III ... Montpelier, VT
McCullough, John J., Jr. ... Philadelphia, PA
McCullough, John P. ... Salem, OR
McCullough, John, P.L.C., Law Offices of Alexandria, VA
McCullough, John T. ... Lincoln, IL
McCullough, John T. ... Houston, TX
McCullough, John W. ... Birmingham, AL
McCullough, John W. ... Chicago, IL
McCullough, Jones & Ivins, L.L.C. Orem, UT
McCullough and Joseph ... Mount Laurel, NJ
McCullough, Joseph D. ... Charlotte, NC
McCullough, Joseph T., IV ... Chicago, IL
McCullough, Keith E., (P.C.) Costa Mesa, CA
McCullough, Kenneth R. ... Atlanta, GA
McCullough, Kevin C. ... Philadelphia, PA
McCullough, Kevin D. ... Dallas, TX
McCullough, Kevin J. ... Santa Rosa, CA
McCullough, Kim I. ... Denver, CO
McCullough, Kristyne H. ... Metairie, LA
McCullough, L. Ronald ... Mount Laurel, NJ
McCullough, Lee S., III Salt Lake City, UT
McCullough, Leland S. Salt Lake City, UT
McCullough, Leland S. ... Salt Lake City, UT
McCullough, Linda A. ... Boca Raton, FL
McCullough, M. Bruce ... Pittsburgh, PA
McCullough, Marjorie Oklahoma City, OK
McCullough, Mark C. ... Minneapolis, MN
McCullough, Mark E. ... Springfield, IL
McCullough, Marshall William West Fargo, ND
McCullough, Martin R. ... Arvada, CO
McCullough, Matthew W. ... Erie, PA
McCullough, Max D. ... Mount Clemens, MI
McCullough & McCullough ... Arvada, CO
McCullough & McCullough ... Memphis, TN
McCullough & McCullough Harlingen, TX
McCullough & McKenty, P.A. Wilmington, DE
McCullough, Michael A. ... Denver, CO
McCullough, Michael A. ... New York, NY
McCullough, Michael D. ... Chicago, IL
McCullough, Michael J. ... Richmond, VA
Mccullough, Michael Joseph ... New York, NY
McCullough, Michael L. ... Riverside, CA
McCullough, Michael P. ... Coshocton, OH
McCullough, Michael R. ... Jacksonville, FL
McCullough, Nancy ... Santa Monica, CA
McCullough, Nancy ... Arvada, CO
McCullough, P. Mike ... Dallas, TX
McCullough, Patrick B. ... Niles, MI
McCullough, Paul L. ... Stamford, CT
McCullough and Payne ... Atlanta, GA
McCullough, Ralph C., II ... Columbia, SC
McCullough, Ray T. ... Pasadena, CA
McCullough, Raymond L. ... Philadelphia, PA
McCullough & Ream, Ltd. ... Las Vegas, NV
McCullough, R. F. ... Carrollton, TX
McCullough, Rhonda Lea ... Jackson, MS
McCullough, Robert G. ... Washington, DC Knoxville, TN Nashville, TN
McCullough, Robert Spencer New Orleans, LA
McCullough, R. S. ... Little Rock, AR
McCullough, Scott T. ... Miami, FL
McCullough Sherrill, LLP ... Atlanta, GA
McCullough, Sherry F. ... Denver, CO
McCullough, Smith, Wright & Kempe, P.A. St. Paul, MN
McCullough, Steven E. ... West Fargo, ND
McCullough, Stievater & Polvere, LLP Boston, MA
McCullough, Teresa Ann ... Memphis, TN
McCullough, Theodore C. ... Seattle, WA
McCullough, Thomas B., Jr. Marina Del Rey, CA
McCullough, Thomas, Jr. Jackson Heights, NY
McCullough, Thomas L. ... Sac City, IA
McCullough, Travis C. ... Houston, TX
McCullough, W. Andrew ... Orem, UT
McCullough, Wareheim & LaBunker Topeka, KS
McCullough, William G. ... Miami, FL
McCullough, William H. ... Beverly Hills, CA
McCullough, William H. ... Seat Pleasant, MD
McCullough, William H. ... Raleigh, NC
McCullough, William J. ... Hartford, CT
McCullough, William T. ... Davenport, IA
McCullum, Elizabeth A. ... Augusta, ME
McCully, Barbara L. ... Los Angeles, CA
McCully & Beggs, P.C. ... Hagåtña, GU
McCully, Brian J. ... Fresno, CA
McCully, Bryan T. ... Maitland, FL
McCully, Duncan G. ... Hagåtña, GU
McCully, J. Thomas ... Seattle, WA
McCully, John T. ... Dallas, TX
McCully, Michael D. ... Salt Lake City, UT
McCully, R. Dyann ... Fort Worth, TX
McCully, Richard P. ... Atlanta, GA
McCully, Robert J. ... Wichita, KS
McCully, Sharon P. ... Salt Lake City, UT
McCully, Thomas R. ... Lafayette, IN
McCumber, Andrew R. ... Tampa, FL
McCumber, David ... Roswell, NM
McCumber, Harry M. ... Jackson, MS
McCumber, Jerry D. ... Atlanta, GA
McCumber, Lloyd R. ... Rockford, IL
McCumber, Marilyn P. ... Glendale, CA
McCumber, Sean M. ... Chicago, IL
McCune, Andrew W. ... Chicago, IL
McCune, Barron P. ... Pittsburgh, PA
McCune, Candace ... Aurora, CO
McCune, C. M. ... Seattle, WA
McCune, D. Thomas ... San Francisco, CA
McCune, Dana J. ... Los Angeles, CA
McCune, Daniel L. ... Weirton, WV
McCune, Daniel R. ... Denver, CO
McCune, David S. ... Milford, OH
McCune, Dennis S., (P.C.) ... Kalamazoo, MI
McCune, Diana R. ... Dublin, OH
McCune, Francis P. ... Cincinnati, OH
McCune, George B. ... Anchorage, AK
McCune, George M. ... Salt Lake City, UT
McCune, Godfrey & Emerick, Inc., P.S. Seattle, WA
McCune, James H. ... Charleroi, PA Washington, PA
McCune, James N. ... Fairfax, VA
McCune, James P., III ... Pittsburgh, PA
McCune, Jeffrey D. ... Las Vegas, NV
McCune, John G. ... San Antonio, TX
McCune, John J. ... Reno, NV
McCune, John N. ... Front Royal, VA
McCune, Kevin J. ... Portland, OR
McCune, Malcolm L. ... Nashville, TN
McCune, Mitchell M. ... Tulsa, OK
McCune, Philip S. ... Seattle, WA
McCune, Phyllis L. ... Tulsa, OK
McCune, Richard D., Jr. ... Redlands, CA
McCune, Richard E. ... North Canton, OH
McCune, Robert J. ... Atlanta, GA
McCune, Robert James, Jr. ... Ocala, FL
McCune, Robin Marie ... Falls Church, VA
McCune, Timothy F. ... Butler, PA
McCune, Wm. Richard, Jr. Martinsburg, WV
McCune, Wm. Richard, Jr., P.L.L.C. Martinsburg, WV
McCunn, Drummond F. ... Menlo Park, CA
McCurdy, Barbara Clarke Washington, DC
McCurdy, Bethany C. ... Milwaukee, WI
McCurdy & Candler, L.L.C. ... Decatur, GA
McCurdy, Charles E. ... Long Beach, CA
McCurdy, Christopher John ... Wichita, KS
McCurdy, Claire K. ... Kansas City, MO
McCurdy, David D. ... Sierra Madre, CA
McCurdy, David K. ... Norman, OK
McCurdy, David S. ... Cadillac, MI
McCurdy, Donald M. ... Media, PA
McCurdy, Gary D. ... El Reno, OK
McCurdy, Gary E. ... Sacramento, CA
McCurdy, Gay Lynn ... Dublin, OH
McCurdy, Gregor B. ... Washington, DC
Mccurdy, Jack D., II ... Yukon, OK
McCurdy, Janet I. ... Frederick, MD
McCurdy, Kay W. ... Chicago, IL
McCurdy, Keith W. ... Polson, MT

McCurdy, Kevin G. ......Redwood City, CA
McCurdy Law Firm ......Polson, MT
McCurdy, Leonard L., Jr. ......Chattanooga, TN
McCurdy, Mark D. ......Ellicott City, MD
McCurdy, Mary Kyle ......Portland, OR
McCurdy, Mary P. ......Redwood City, CA
McCurdy, Michael R. ......Denver, CO
McCurdy, Mollie A. ......Camp Hill, PA
McCurdy, Paul F. ......Stamford, CT
McCurdy, Robert Kurt ......Portsmouth, OH
McCurdy, Ronald R. ......Boulder, CO
McCurdy, Sean M. ......Englewood, CO
McCurdy & Stone ......Norcross, GA
McCurdy, T. Wray ......Baltimore, MD
McCurdy, Valjean H. ......Arvada, CO
McCurdy, W. Phillip ......Norcross, GA
McCurdy, Walter P., Jr. ......Stone Mountain, GA
McCurdy, William A. ......Boise, ID
McCurdy, William A., Jr.
Wilmington, DE
McCurdy, William C. ......Woodstock, GA
McCurdy & Wotila, P.C. ......Cadillac, MI
McCurine, William, Jr. ......San Diego, CA
McCurley, D. Wayne ......Marietta, GA
McCurley, Janette M. ......St. Petersburg, FL
McCurley, Kelly A-R ......Monument, CO
McCurley, Kinser, McCurley & Nelson, L.L.P. ......Dallas, TX
McCurley, Mary Johanna ......Dallas, TX
McCurley, Mike ......Dallas, TX
McCurley, Robert L., Jr. ......Tuscaloosa, AL
McCurley, William M. ......Belvidere, NJ
McCurn, Neal P. ......Syracuse, NY
McCurn, Neal P., Jr. ......Syracuse, NY
McCurnin, Thomas E. ......Los Angeles, CA
McCurrach, Duncan C. ......New York, NY
McCurrie, Lester D. ......Bridgeview, IL
McCurrie McCurrie & McCurrie
Kearny, NJ
Newark, NJ
McCurrie, Paul J. ......Kearny, NJ
McCurrie, Stephen J. ......Kearny, NJ
McCurrie, Susan A. ......Kearny, NJ
McCurry, Amy Beth ......Kansas City, MO
McCurry, Bruce ......Springfield, MO
McCurry, C. LeeAnn ......Atlanta, GA
McCurry, Edgar W., Jr. ......Jacksonville, FL
McCurry, FredRicco ......Van Nuys, CA
McCurry, Jayne A. ......Lufkin, TX
McCurry, Kenneth T. ......Chicago, IL
McCurry, Liane ......Sarasota, FL
McCurry, Robert F., Jr. ......Orangeburg, SC
McCurry, Robert G. ......Dalton, GA
McCurry, Todd E. ......Durham, NC
McCurry, William S., Jr. ......Savannah, GA
McCusker, Anselmi, Rosen, Carvelli & Walsh, A Professional Corporation
Chatham, NJ
Morristown, NJ
Newark, NJ
Toms River, NJ
New York, NY
McCusker, Anthony J. ......Menlo Park, CA
McCusker, Claire E. ......Philadelphia, PA
McCusker, Daniel J. ......Media, PA
McCusker, Denis P. ......St. Louis, MO
McCusker, James J. ......Boston, MA
McCusker, Jerome A. ......Boston, MA
McCusker, John B. ......Chatham, NJ
Toms River, NJ
McCusker, Joseph H., III ......New Orleans, LA
McCusker, Leo X. ......Bristol, RI
McCusker, Michael J. ......Jamaica Plain, MA
McCusker, Michelle A. ......Boston, MA
McCusker, Paul D. ......New York, NY
McCusker, Paul G. ......Chatham, NJ
Toms River, NJ
McCusker, Philip T. ......Pikesville, MD
McCusker, Stephen M. ......Savannah, GA
McCusker, Theresa Smith ......Cordova, TN
McCusker, Thomas J. ......Omaha, NE
McCusker, Timothy K. ......Rochester, NY
McCusker, William L., Law Offices
Madison, WI
McCuskey, David L. ......Minneapolis, MN
McCuskey, John F. ......Charleston, WV
McCuskey, Lowell ......Linn, MO
McCuskey, Mary Browne
Hendersonville, TN
McCuskey, Michael P. ......Urbana, IL
McCuskey, Thomas G. ......Cedar Rapids, IA
McCusty, M. Kevin ......Tysons Corner, VA
McCutchan, B. Edward, Jr. ......Santa Rosa, CA
McCutchan, Charles L. ......Ventura, CA
McCutchan, Gordon E. ......Columbus, OH
McCutchan, Jeffrey S. ......Elgin, IL
McCutchan, R. Lindsey ......Columbus, OH
McCutchan, Robert D., III ......Dallas, TX
McCutchan, Susan Wells ......Dallas, TX
McCutchen, Blanton, Rhodes & Johnson, L.L.P. ......Columbia, SC
Winnsboro, SC
McCutchen, Clark L. ......Denver, CO
McCutchen, Doyle, Brown & Enersen, LLP
Los Angeles, CA
Palo Alto, CA
San Francisco, CA
Walnut Creek, CA
McCutchen, Larry M. ......Dallas, TX
McCutchen, Luther O., III
Myrtle Beach, SC
McCutchen, Matthew B. ......Seattle, WA
McCutchen, Maureen Kuzik
Galveston, TX
McCutchen, Mumford & Vaught, P.A.
Myrtle Beach, SC
McCutchen, Peter B. ......Chicago, IL
McCutchen, P. T., Jr. ......Atlanta, GA
McCutchen, Royce C. ......Bethany, OK
McCutchen, T. English, III ......Columbia, SC
McCutchen, Thomas E. ......Columbia, SC
McCutchen, William W., III ......New York, NY
McCutchen, Wilmot Hill ......Orinda, CA
McCutcheon, Aubrey V., Jr. ......Ypsilanti, MI
McCutcheon, Aubrey V., Jr., P.C.
Ypsilanti, MI
McCutcheon, Beverly Ann ......Detroit, MI
McCutcheon, Charles T., Jr. ......Detroit, MI
McCutcheon, Deborah L. ......Cambridge, MA
McCutcheon, James E., III
San Antonio, TX
Bellevue, WA
Redmond, WA
McCutcheon, James E., III, P.C., Law Offices of ......Redmond, WA
Mccutcheon, James K. ......New York, NY
McCutcheon, John Betts, Jr. ......Conway, SC
McCutcheon, Karen L. ......Midland, MI
McCutcheon, Kenneth O., Jr. ......Versailles, MO
McCutcheon, Mary E. ......San Francisco, CA
McCutcheon, McCutcheon & Baxter, P.A.
Conway, SC
McCutcheon, Melody B. ......Seattle, WA
McCutcheon, Nathan W. ......Washington, DC
McCutcheon, R. Scott ......Charlotte, NC
McCutcheon, Robert B. ......Batavia, NY
McCutcheon, Robert D.
Oklahoma City, OK
McCutcheon, Robert D. ......Carrollton, TX
McCutcheon & Rowan ......St. Petersburg, FL
McCutcheon, Roy I. ......Canton, MI
McCutcheon, Sue G. ......Boise, ID
McCutcheon, Thomas W. ......Florence, AL
McCutcheon, Timothy ......Englewood, CO
McCutchin, Jack, Jr. ......Lubbock, TX
McCutchon, Frederick J.
Corpus Christi, TX
McDade, Carlos Lewis ......Oklahoma City, OK
Mc Dade, Darold J. ......Provo, UT
McDade, Fogler, Maines & Lohse, L.L.P.
Houston, TX
McDade, J. Michael ......San Diego, CA
McDade, J. Victor ......Anderson, SC
Mc Dade, James D. ......Austin, TX
McDade, James David ......Douglasville, GA
McDade, James R. ......Modesto, CA
McDade, Joe Billy ......Peoria, IL
McDade, Joseph M., Jr.
Department of the Air Force, Office of the General Counsel, GV
McDade, Lawrence G.
Department of Justice, Civil Division, GV
McDade, Mary W. ......Peoria, IL
McDade, Nancy E. ......Tucson, AZ
McDade, Patricia Ann ......Franklin, TN
McDade, Rebecca J. ......Chicago, IL
McDade, Robert J. ......Collingswood, NJ
Philadelphia, PA
McDade, Sandy D. ......Tacoma, WA
McDade, Thomas R. ......Houston, TX
McDade Warran & Zimmerman
Washington, DC
McDaid, Edward B. ......Philadelphia, PA
McDanel, John W. ......Berwick, PA
McDanel, Mike ......Norman, OK
McDaniel, A. Scott ......Tulsa, OK
McDaniel, A. Stephen ......Memphis, TN
McDaniel & Allen, A Professional Corporation ......Houston, TX
McDaniel, Alsee ......Indianola, MS
McDaniel, Alysa M.
Joint Committees And Commissions, GV
McDaniel, Amyli A. ......Washington, DC
McDaniel, Anderson & Stephenson, L.L.P.
Raleigh, NC
McDaniel, Andrew H. ......Raleigh, NC
McDaniel, Arthur J. ......Los Angeles, CA
McDaniel & Associates ......Tulsa, OK
McDaniel & Associates, P.C. ......Austin, TX
McDaniel, Bains & Norris, P.C.
Birmingham, AL
McDaniel & Ball, P.A. ......Sarasota, FL
McDaniel, Baty, Miller & Robbins, L.L.C.
Durango, CO
McDaniel, Bert T. ......Houston, TX
McDaniel, Beth A. ......Seattle, WA
McDaniel, Bobby R. ......Jonesboro, AR
McDaniel, Bonnie Bayes ......Bremerton, WA
McDaniel, Brian ......Palo Alto, CA
McDaniel, Brian Allen ......Moultrie, GA
McDaniel, Brian R. ......Edina, MN
McDaniel, Bruce I. ......Rochester, NY
McDaniel, C. Ray ......Bartow, FL
McDaniel, C. Ray, P.A. ......Bartow, FL
McDaniel, C. Steven ......Austin, TX
McDaniel, C. William ......Atlanta, GA
McDaniel, Charles D. ......Little Rock, AR
McDaniel, Charles M., Jr. ......Atlanta, GA
McDaniel, Chris J. ......Weslaco, TX
McDaniel, Christine L. ......Kansas City, MO
McDaniel, Christopher B. ......Hattiesburg, MS
McDaniel & Connor ......Uniontown, PA
McDaniel, Dale F. ......Tulsa, OK
McDaniel, Dan M., Jr. ......Jackson, MS
McDaniel, Dana D. ......Richmond, VA
McDaniel, Daniel A. ......Stockton, CA
McDaniel, David R. ......Metairie, LA
McDaniel, David S. ......Detroit, MI
McDaniel, Demetrius ......Austin, TX
Mcdaniel, Derrick Young ......New York, NY
McDaniel, Diane L. ......Pullman, WA
McDaniel, Don S. ......Arlington, TX
McDaniel, Don S. ......Fort Worth, TX
McDaniel, Donald C. ......Santa Monica, CA
Westlake Village, CA
McDaniel, Donald H. ......New Orleans, LA
McDaniel, Donna J. ......Pittsburgh, PA
McDaniel, Duke A. ......Petersburg, WV
McDaniel, Dwight P. ......Hemphill, TX
McDaniel, Ed Neal ......Selmer, TN
McDaniel, Erika P. ......New York, NY
McDaniel, F. Douglas ......Riverside, CA
McDaniel, Floyd, II ......Saginaw, MI
McDaniel, Francis E. ......Atlanta, GA
McDaniel, Francis S. ......Dayton, OH
McDaniel, Gene A. ......Kansas City, MO
McDaniel, George O., III ......Houston, TX
McDaniel, Gerald B. ......Durango, CO
McDaniel, Gerald F. ......Louisville, KY
McDaniel, Glen ......Los Angeles, CA
McDaniel, H. Francis, Jr. ......Norwalk, OH
McDaniel, Henri Butler ......Huntsville, AL
McDaniel, J. Douglas ......St. Louis, MO
McDaniel, James A., (P.C.) ......Boston, MA
McDaniel, James B. ......Washington, DC
McDaniel, James D., Jr. ......Boston, MA
McDaniel, James E. ......St. Louis, MO
McDaniel, James F. ......Cincinnati, OH
McDaniel, James Larry ......Decatur, GA
McDaniel, James M. ......Cleveland, GA
McDaniel, James R. ......Los Angeles, CA
McDaniel, James R. ......Chicago, IL
McDaniel, James R. ......Schenectady, NY
McDaniel, Janet L. ......Denver, CO
McDaniel, Jarrel D. ......Houston, TX
McDaniel, Jason Brett ......Valdosta, GA
McDaniel, Jay R. ......Morristown, NJ
New York, NY
McDaniel, Jeff A. ......Austin, TX
McDaniel, Jeffrey C. ......Rock Island, IL
McDaniel, Jerry "Jay" L., III ......Tampa, FL
McDaniel, Jesse W. ......Houston, TX
McDaniel, Joe, Jr. ......Pleasanton, CA
McDaniel, John F. ......Birmingham, AL
McDaniel, John, Jr. ......Washington, DC
McDaniel, John M. ......Fresno, CA
McDaniel, John S. ......Wilmington, DE
McDaniel, Joseph C. ......Phoenix, AZ
McDaniel, Joseph O. ......Elko, NV
McDaniel, Karen D. ......Minneapolis, MN
McDaniel, Katherine L. ......Los Angeles, CA
McDaniel, K. C. ......New York, NY
McDaniel, Keith W. ......New Orleans, LA
McDaniel, Kelli F. ......Montgomery, AL
McDaniel, Kent ......Brandon, MS
McDaniel, Kim R. ......Santa Barbara, CA
McDaniel, Kimberly ......Pittsburgh, PA
McDaniel, L. Bruce ......Raleigh, NC
McDaniel, Lane ......Dallas, TX
McDaniel, Lane, P.C., Law Offices of
Dallas, TX
McDaniel, Lucinda ......Jonesboro, AR
McDaniel, L.W. ......Durango, CO
Mcdaniel, Lynda B. ......Dayton, TN
McDaniel, M. Elizabeth
San Francisco, CA
McDaniel, Marcus A. ......Los Angeles, CA
McDaniel, Marion E., Jr. ......Houston, TX
McDaniel, Mark ......Huntsville, AL
McDaniel, Mark B. ......Oklahoma City, OK
McDaniel, Mark B., P.C.
Oklahoma City, OK
McDaniel, Mark S. ......Memphis, TN
McDaniel & Marsh ......Baltimore, MD
McDaniel, Marshall L. ......El Segundo, CA
McDaniel, Mary Anne ......Knoxville, TN
McDaniel, Mary E. ......Coeur d'Alene, ID
McDaniel, Mary Frances
Winston-Salem, NC
McDaniel, Mary L. ......Racine, WI
McDaniel, Mary M. ......Tavares, FL
McDaniel, Mary M., & Associates, A Prof. Assn. ......Tavares, FL
McDaniel and McDaniel ......Huntsville, AL
McDaniel & McDaniel ......El Segundo, CA
McDaniel, Melvin L. ......Oklahoma City, OK
McDaniel, Michael C. ......Lansing, MI
McDaniel, Michael E. ......Raleigh, NC
McDaniel, Michael J. ......New Albany, IN
McDaniel, Michael Patrick ......Bartow, FL
McDaniel, Michael S. ......Los Angeles, CA
McDaniel, Micki Woodward
Lexington, KY
McDaniel, Morey W. ......New Canaan, CT
McDaniel, Myra A. ......Austin, TX
McDaniel, Nancy Krolikowski
Raleigh, NC
McDaniel, Patrick C. ......Mena, AR
McDaniel, Patrick C. ......Uniontown, PA
McDaniel, Perry D. ......Charleston, WV
McDaniel, Philip L. ......Midlothian, VA
McDaniel, Rankin H., III ......Fallbrook, CA
McDaniel, Rebecca J. ......Minneapolis, MN
McDaniel, Robert C. ......Norwalk, CA
McDaniel, Robert P. ......Manchester, NH
McDaniel, Robert R. ......Pensacola, FL
McDaniel, Robert S., Jr. ......Sarasota, FL
Mc Daniel, Roger B. ......Carbondale, KS
McDaniel, Ronald A. ......Atlanta, GA
McDaniel, Roy Thornton, Jr. ......Key Largo, FL
McDaniel, S. Randall ......Portsmouth, VA
McDaniel, S. Tovan ......Seattle, WA
McDaniel, Samuel D. ......Austin, TX
McDaniel, Scott F. ......Cincinnati, OH
McDaniel, Shannon Kay ......Chicago, IL
McDaniel, Shelley Wells ......Kansas City, MO
McDaniel, Sondra K. ......Birmingham, AL
McDaniel, Stacy Cole ......Oklahoma City, OK
McDaniel, Stacy W. ......Mission Viejo, CA
McDaniel, Stephen J. ......Naperville, IL
McDaniel, Stephen W. ......Longview, TX
McDaniel, Susan J. ......Wilmington, NC
McDaniel, Terry B. ......Charleston, SC
McDaniel, Terry R. ......Boise, ID
McDaniel, Thomas W. ......Memphis, TN
McDaniel, Timothy E. ......Ann Arbor, MI
McDaniel, Timothy M. ......Houston, TX
McDaniel, Tom J. ......Oklahoma City, OK
McDaniel, Tovan ......Washington, DC
McDaniel, Truly W. ......Shreveport, LA
McDaniel, Valerie A. ......Detroit, MI
McDaniel, Vernon W. ......Cincinnati, OH
McDaniel, Vickie R. M. ......Lometa, TX
McDaniel, W. Shawn ......Charlottesville, VA
Norton, VA
McDaniel & Wells, P.A. ......Blytheville, AR
Jonesboro, AR
McDaniel, William A. ......Coos Bay, OR
McDaniel, William Alden, Jr.
Baltimore, MD
McDaniel, William C. ......Kingsville, TX
McDaniel, William E., II ......Dumfries, VA
McDaniel, William Griffin ......Atlanta, GA
McDaniel, William J. ......Birmingham, AL
McDaniel, William K. ......Darlington, WI
McDaniel, Wm. H. ......Charleston, SC
McDaniel, Yonne P. ......Mangum, OK
McDaniels, Clara ......Bloomington, IL
McDaniels, Keith A. ......San Francisco, CA
McDaniels, Kenneth L. ......Philadelphia, PA
McDaniels, William E. ......Washington, DC
McDannel, Marcelle ......Anchorage, AK
Mc Dannel, Michael W. ......Lincoln, NE
McDannell, Jennifer K. ......Washington, DC
McDarris, Charles F. ......Raleigh, NC
McDarris, Dori Casey ......Raleigh, NC
McDavid, Amy K. ......Madison, WI
McDavid, Ashley S. ......London, KY
McDavid, Christopher B.
Los Angeles, CA
McDavid, Diana L. ......Charleston, WV
McDavid, George E. ......Princeton, NJ
McDavid, J. Gary ......Washington, DC
McDavid, Jack W. ......Ocean Springs, MS
McDavid, Jan P. ......Atlanta, GA
McDavid, Janet L. ......Washington, DC
McDavid, John K. ......Indianapolis, IN
McDavid, John Land ......Jackson, MS
McDavid, John Sanford ......Jackson, MS
McDavid, Marion Foy ......Harriman, TN
McDavid, Noblin & West PLLC
Jackson, MS
McDavid, R. M. ......Pensacola, FL
McDavid, Sarah Ann (Sally) ......Jackson, MS
McDavid, Saundra Terry ......Chesterfield, MO
McDavid, Stephan L. ......Oxford, MS
McDavid, Sylvia S. ......Jackson, MS
McDavid, Terry ......Lake City, FL
McDavid, William H. ......New York, NY
McDavid, William R. ......Charleston, WV
McDavitt, Dale H. ......Mc Comb, MS
McDavitt, J. Patrick ......Minneapolis, MN
McDavitt, James Thaddeus ......Cambridge, MA
McDay, Temple ......Farmingville, NY
McDearman, J. Scott ......Chattanooga, TN
McDearman, Ronald G. ......Dallas, TX
McDemus, Christopher D.
Philadelphia, PA
McDermed, Clark E. ......Orange, CA
McDermed, Marguerite F. ......Chicago, IL
McDermett, Don J., Jr. ......Dallas, TX
McDermid, Harold E. ......Woodside, CA
McDermid, John F. ......Washington, DC
McDermid, Nancy G. ......San Francisco, CA
McDermitt, Donald R. ......Plano, TX
McDermitt, Norbert J. (Jim) ......Waco, TX
McDermond, Maurice L., Jr.
Sandusky, OH
McDermott, Albert L. ......United States Senate, Committee Legal Personnel, GV
McDermott, Anthony X. ......Malibu, CA
McDermott, Arthur T. ......Carlisle, PA
McDermott, Barbara A. ......Philadelphia, PA
McDermott, Bernard V. ......Dallas, TX
McDermott & Bonenberger, P.L.L.C.
St. Clairsville, OH
Martinsburg, WV
Wheeling, WV
McDermott, Brian E. ......Wareham, MA
McDermott, Brian L. ......Indianapolis, IN
McDermott, Brian M. ......Washington, DC
McDermott, Bronwyn McNeill
New York, NY
McDermott, Bruce A. ......Seattle, WA
McDermott, Bruce L. ......New Haven, CT
McDermott, C. David
Colorado Springs, CO
McDermott, Carol Anne ......Burbank, CA
McDermott, Christine M. ......Wilmington, DE
McDermott, Christine P ......Chester Springs, PA
McDermott, Christopher M.
Charlotte, NC
McDermott, Clark G. ......Des Moines, IA
McDermott, Craig Q. ......Omaha, NE
Mcdermott, Cynthia A. ......Olney, MD
McDermott, Cyril T. ......Putnam Valley, NY
McDermott, Daniel G. ......New York, NY
McDermott, Daniel J. ......Washington, DC
McDermott, Daniel L., (P.A.) ......DeLand, FL
McDermott, Daniel M. ......Cleveland, OH
McDermott, David G. ......Matteson, IL
McDermott, David H., Jr. ......New York, NY
McDermott, Deborah D. ......Matteson, IL
McDermott, Dennis K. ......Oneida, NY
McDermott, Derek ......Chilton, WI
New Holstein, WI
McDermott, Diane M. ......Boston, MA
McDermott & Doerr, P.C. ......Syracuse, NY
McDermott, Douglas J. ......New York, NY
McDermott, Douglas W. ......El Segundo, CA
McDermott, Edward A. ......Boca Raton, FL
McDermott, Edward A., Jr. ......New York, NY

McDermott, Edward B. ... Mobile, AL
McDermott, Edward F. ... Boston, MA
McDermott, Edward J. ... Hampton, NH
McDermott, Edward T. ... New York, NY
McDermott, Elizabeth ... Boston, MA
McDermott, Evelyn L. ... Wayne, NE
McDermott, Ferol Reed ... Middletown, NY
McDermott, Francis A. ... McLean, VA
McDermott, Francis H. ... New York, NY
McDermott, Francis O. ... Washington, DC
McDermott, Francis P. ... Milton, MA
McDermott, Francis P., P.C. ... Milton, MA
McDermott, Frank C. ... Brooklyn, NY
McDermott, Frank V., Jr. ... Boston, MA
McDermott, Frank W. ... St. Petersburg, FL
McDermott, Frank X. ... Liberty Corner, NJ
McDermott, Frederick M. ... Brockton, MA
McDermott, Frederick R. ... Oxon Hill, MD
McDermott, George M. ... Sanford, NC
McDermott, Gerald P. ... Denver, CO
McDermott and Hansen ... Denver, CO
McDermott, Harry E., III ... Fayetteville, AR
McDermott, Harry E., Jr. ... Little Rock, AR
McDermott, Heather K. ... Seattle, WA
McDermott, J. Thomas ... Oshkosh, WI
McDermott, James D. ... Wheeling, WV
McDermott, James E. ... Boston, MA
McDermott, James H. ... Madison, WI
McDermott, James K. ... Orange, CA
McDermott, James M. ... Dedham, MA
McDermott, James Q. ... Ventura, CA
McDermott, James T. ... Portland, OR
McDermott, James T. ... Philadelphia, PA
McDermott, Janice E. ... Fleetwood, PA
McDermott, Jeffrey C. ... Indianapolis, IN
McDermott, Jo E. ... Dayton, OH
McDermott, John A. ... Canon City, CO
McDermott, John A. ... Huntington, NY
McDermott, John A., II ... Newport Beach, CA
McDermott, John B. ... Grand Island, NE
McDermott, John C. ... Murphysboro, IL
McDermott, John E. ... Los Angeles, CA
McDermott, John Edward, Jr. New York, NY
McDermott, John F. ... Baton Rouge, LA
McDermott, John F., Jr. ... Oceanside, NY
McDermott, John H. ... Chicago, IL
McDermott, John J. ... Washington, DC
Vienna, VA
McDermott, John J. ... New York, NY
McDermott, John J. ... Alexandria, VA
McDermott, John J., III ... Wall Township, NJ
McDermott, John L. ... Honolulu, HI
McDermott, John L. ... Millburn, NJ
McDermott, John L., Jr. ... Millburn, NJ
McDermott, John M. ... New York, NY
McDermott, John M. ... Rocky River, OH
McDermott, John R., Jr. ... Syracuse, NY
McDermott, John T. ... Los Angeles, CA
McDermott, John V. ... Denver, CO
McDermott, John V., Jr. ... Vernon, NJ
McDermott, John Vincent ... Detroit, MI
McDermott, Joseph A., III ... Houston, TX
McDermott, Joseph F. ... St. Petersburg, FL
McDermott, Joseph M. ... Pittsburgh, PA
McDermott, Joseph W. ... Cambridge, MA
McDermott, Judith A. ... Bethesda, MD
McDermott, Kathleen ... Baltimore, MD
McDermott, Kathleen A. ... Lynnfield, MA
McDermott, Kathleen E. ... Salt Lake City, UT
McDermott, Kathleen M. ... McLean, VA
McDermott, Kathryn J. ... Harrisburg, PA
McDermott, Kevin B. ... Tustin, CA
McDermott, Kevin E. ... Syosset, NY
McDermott, Kevin E. ... Cleveland, OH
McDermott, Kevin M. ... Garden City, NY
McDermott, Kevin N. ... Rochester, IL
McDermott, Kevin N. ... Springfield, IL
McDermott, Kevin R. ... Columbus, OH
McDermott, Kevin T. ... Goshen, NY
McDermott, Laurie Dobkin
Wheeling, WV
McDermott, Laurie Tieder ... Goshen, NY
McDermott Law Firm ... Canon City, CO
Salida, CO
McDermott Law Firm, P.A.
St. Petersburg, FL
McDermott, Lawrence J., Jr.
East Hanover, NJ
McDermott, Leonard A. ... North Haven, CT
McDermott, M. Virginia
West Somerville, MA
McDermott, Mark A. ... Chicago, IL
McDermott, Mark T. ... Washington, DC
McDermott, Martin F. ... Department of Justice, Environment and Natural Resources Division, GV
McDermott, Mary ... Washington, DC
McDermott, Mary Lynne ... Florham Park, NJ
McDermott, Matthew J. ... New York, NY
McDermott & McDermott Co., L.P.A.
Rocky River, OH
McDermott & McDermott, Ltd.
Matteson, IL
McDermott & McGee ... Millburn, NJ
Newark, NJ
McDermott, Michael ... Daytona Beach, FL
Mc Dermott, Michael A.
Newport Beach, CA
McDermott, Michael B. ... Biloxi, MS
McDermott, Michael E. ... New York, NY
McDermott, Michael J. ... Parkville, MO
McDermott, Michael J. ... Fayetteville, NY
McDermott, Michael J., (P.A.) ... Brandon, FL
McDermott, Michael L., (P.C.)
Chicago, IL
McDermott, Michael O.
Cedar Rapids, IA

McDermott, Michael P. ... Albany, NY
Mcdermott, Michael P. ... Troy, NY
McDermott, Mickey J. G. ... Montgomery, AL
McDermott, Mikaela A. ... Washington, DC
McDermott, Noreen E.
San Francisco, CA
McDermott & O'Hanlon, P.C.
Putnam Valley, NY
McDermott, Patricia L. ... Pocatello, ID
McDermott, Patricia M.
United States Court Of Appeals For The Federal Circuit, GV
McDermott, Patricia M. ... Florence, SC
McDermott, Patrick B. ... Hampton, VA
Williamsburg, VA
McDermott, Patrick J. ... Wheeling, WV
McDermott, Paul M. ... Boston, MA
McDermott, Paul T. ... Middletown, NY
McDermott, Paula J. ... Harrisburg, PA
McDermott, Peter D. ... Pocatello, ID
McDermott, Peter D. ... Boston, MA
McDermott, Quilty & Miller ... Boston, MA
McDermott, R. Gregory ... Wheeling, WV
McDermott, Ralph T., Law Offices of
Ashland, KY
McDermott, Renee R. ... Tryon, NC
McDermott, Richard F., Jr. ... Bellevue, WA
McDermott, Richard F., Jr., P.S.
Bellevue, WA
McDermott, Richard H. ... Southfield, MI
McDermott, Richard M. ... Charlotte, NC
McDermott, Richard O. ... Chicago, IL
McDermott, Richard T. ... New York, NY
McDermott, Robert A. ... Millburn, NJ
McDermott, Robert B. ... Chicago, IL
McDermott, Robert F. ... Oneida, NY
McDermott, Robert F., Jr.
Washington, DC
McDermott, Robert J. ... Jacksonville, FL
McDermott, Robert J. ... Largo, FL
McDermott, Robert J. ... New York, NY
McDermott, Robert J., Jr. ... New York, NY
McDermott, Robert J., P.A. ... Largo, FL
McDermott, Robert T. ... Pittsburgh, PA
McDermott & Roe ... Hampton, VA
Newport News, VA
Williamsburg, VA
Yorktown, VA
McDermott, Ronald L. ... Covington, KY
McDermott, Rosemary A. ... Thurmont, MD
McDermott, Sam L. ... Costa Mesa, CA
McDermott, Scott F. ... Wellesley, MA
McDermott, Sean A. ... North Falmouth, MA
McDermott, Sean B. ... Farmington Hills, MI
McDermott, Shawn E. ... Denver, CO
McDermott, Stanley, III ... New York, NY
McDermott, Stanley, Jr., (A Prof. Law Corp.)
New Orleans, LA
McDermott, Susan E. ... Irvine, CA
McDermott, Susan M. ... Philadelphia, PA
McDermott, Terence P. ... Boston, MA
McDermott, Thomas A. ... Myrtle Beach, SC
McDermott, Thomas E. ... Portland, OR
McDermott, Thomas F., Jr. ... Litchfield, CT
Waterbury, CT
McDermott, Thomas J. ... Los Angeles, CA
McDermott, Thomas J., Jr.
Los Angeles, CA
McDermott, Thomas P. ... St. Louis, MO
McDermott, Thomas P. ... Pittsburgh, PA
McDermott, Thos. A. ... Rochester, NY
McDermott, Timothy G. ... Chicago, IL
McDermott, Timothy J. ... San Diego, CA
McDermott, Timothy J. ... Jacksonville, FL
McDermott & Trayner, Professional Law Corporation ... Newport Beach, CA
Pasadena, CA
McDermott, Wesley E. ... Ithaca, NY
McDermott, Will & Emery ... Irvine, CA
Los Angeles, CA
Menlo Park, CA
San Jose, CA
Washington, DC
Miami, FL
Chicago, IL
Boston, MA
New York, NY
McDermott, Willard H. ... Denver, CO
McDermott, William A., Jr. ... Boston, MA
McDermott, William F. ... Chicago, IL
McDermott, William J. ... Mount Prospect, IL
McDermott, William J. ... South Orange, NJ
McDermott, William J. ... Niagara Falls, NY
McDermott, William J., Jr.
Levittown, NY
McDermott, William J., L.L.P., Law Office of Garden City, NY
Levittown, NY
Mineola, NY
McDermott, William P. ... Boston, MA
McDermott, William T. ... Richmond, VA
McDermott, Wm. J. ... Fresno, CA
McDermott, Wm. Shaw ... Boston, MA
McDermott, Zollinger, Olley & Webber, Chartered ... Pocatello, ID
McDermott-Lundin, Shirley A.
Wilmington, DE
McDevitt, Brian ... Norristown, PA
McDevitt, Chas. F. ... Boise, ID
McDevitt, Dan S. ... Atlanta, GA
McDevitt, Daniel D. ... Chicago, IL
McDevitt, Daniel J. ... Media, PA
McDevitt, Daune M. ... Washington, DC
McDevitt, David A. ... Effingham, IL
McDevitt, Denis McCue ... San Diego, CA
McDevitt, Donna L. ... Chicago, IL
McDevitt, Edward D. ... Charleston, WV
McDevitt, Eileen A. ... Twin Falls, ID

McDevitt, Francis T. ... Cherry Hill, NJ
Media, PA
Philadelphia, PA
McDevitt, Frank D. ... Seminole, FL
McDevitt, Heather K. ... New York, NY
McDevitt, James A. ... Spokane, WA
McDevitt, Jerry S. ... Pittsburgh, PA
McDevitt, John F. ... Willoughby Hills, OH
McDevitt, John F., Jr. ... Wilmington, DE
McDevitt, John K. ... New Haven, CT
McDevitt, Joseph D. ... Milwaukee, WI
McDevitt, Joseph I.
West Conshohocken, PA
McDevitt, Kevin J. ... Evanston, IL
McDevitt, Larry S. ... Asheville, NC
McDevitt, Lynn G. ... Philadelphia, PA
McDevitt, Margaret A. ... Omaha, NE
McDevitt, Mary E. ... Roseville, MI
McDevitt, Mary-Lynn ... New York, NY
McDevitt, Mayhew & Malek, L.P.A.
Mt. Vernon, OH
McDevitt Mediation Services Inc.
Milwaukee, WI
McDevitt, Meyers & Thomsen ... Pocatello, ID
McDevitt & Miller, LLP ... Boise, ID
McDevitt, Noel B., Jr. ... Southern Pines, NC
McDevitt, Patricia M. ... Philadelphia, PA
McDevitt, Ray E. ... San Francisco, CA
McDevitt, Richard E. ... Malvern, PA
McDevitt, Richard F., Jr. ... Munster, IN
McDevitt, Robert J. ... Sarasota, FL
McDevitt, Sean P. ... Wilmington, DE
Berwyn, PA
McDevitt, Sheila M. ... Tampa, FL
McDevitt, Susan Schaefer ... Santa Fe, NM
McDevitt, Theresa A. ... Clifton Heights, PA
McDevitt, Thomas F. ... Philadelphia, PA
McDevitt, Thomas F., P.C. ... Philadelphia, PA
McDevitt, Tracey Marie ... Philadelphia, PA
McDevitt, William F. ... Philadelphia, PA
McDevitt, William G. ... San Francisco, CA
McDevitt, William J. ... Media, PA
McDiarmid, Bruce W. ... San Francisco, CA
McDiarmid, Katherine Bonan
Greensboro, NC
McDiarmid, Marjorie Anne
Morgantown, WV
McDiarmid, Robert C. ... Washington, DC
McDiarmid, William B. ... Boston, MA
McDill, Jessica M. ... Bay Minette, AL
McDivitt & Casey, A Professional Corporation ... Edmond, OK
McDivitt, John M. ... Palm Beach, FL
McDivitt Law Firm, P.C.
Colorado Springs, CO
McDivitt, Michael W. ... Colorado Springs, CO
McDivitt, Richard Frank ... Edmond, OK
McDivitt, Stewart E. ... Montour Falls, NY
McD.Kilborne, Francie ... Dallas, TX
McDole, Gregory J. ... Daytona Beach, FL
McDole, Jerry J. ... Red Cloud, NE
McDole, Keith C. ... Dallas, TX
McDole, Kelly L. ... Bend, OR
McDole, Sydney Bosworth ... Dallas, TX
McDonagh, Alan M. ... Grand Forks, ND
McDonagh, Harry F. ... San Francisco, CA
Mcdonagh, James P. ... Boston, MA
McDonagh, Janis Cowhey ... New York, NY
McDonagh, Janis Lynn ... New York, NY
McDonagh, John J. ... New Carlisle, IN
Mc Donagh, Maureen E. ... Boston, MA
McDonagh, Michael E. ... New York, NY
McDonagh, Michael J. ... Boise, ID
Milwaukee, WI
McDonagh, Patricia M. ... Livingston, NJ
McDonagh, Stephen B. ... San Francisco, CA
McDonagh, Thomas A. ... Braintree, MA
McDonald, A. Craig ... Yakima, WA
McDonald, A. Melvin, Jr. ... Phoenix, AZ
McDonald, Alan A. ... Yakima, WA
McDonald, Alan J. ... Newton, MA
McDonald, Alan R. ... Department of Justice, Federal Bureau of Investigation, GV
McDonald, Alex C. ... San Diego, CA
McDonald, Alexander B. ... Reno, NV
McDonald, Alexandra Varney ... Boston, MA
McDonald & Allen ... San Diego, CA
McDonald, Allison Carmine ... Orlando, FL
McDonald, Alvin L. ... Alamogordo, NM
McDonald, Amy L. ... Boston, MA
McDonald, Andrew G., Jr. ... Evanston, IL
McDonald, Andrew J. ... Stamford, CT
McDonald, Andrew M. ... Baltimore, MD
McDonald, Anne ... Minneapolis, MN
McDonald, Anne ... Seattle, WA
McDonald, Anne E. ... Acton, MA
McDonald, Arthur A., Jr. ... Durham, NC
McDonald Associates, PLLC ... Coppell, TX
McDonald, Barbara A. ... Chicago, IL
McDonald, Barbara E. ... Wilmington, DE
McDonald, Barbara G. ... Vista, CA
McDonald, Barry P. ... Reston, VA
McDonald, Ben F. ... Corpus Christi, TX
McDonald, Bonnie A. ... Walnut Creek, CA
McDonald, Bradley G. ... Washington, DC
McDonald, Brenda Nichols ... Coppell, TX
McDonald, Brian ... San Francisco, CA
McDonald, Brian M. ... Los Angeles, CA
McDonald, Brian M. ... Seattle, WA
McDonald, Brown & Fagen ... Adel, IA
Dallas Center, IA
Grimes, IA
McDonald, Bruce A. ... Washington, DC
McDonald, Bruce A., (P.A.) ... Pensacola, FL
McDonald, Bruce C. ... Keokuk, IA
McDonald, Bruce D. ... Evansville, IN
McDonald, Bruce L. ... Washington, DC
McDonald, Bruce S. ... Albuquerque, NM

McDonald, C. Brian ... Boston, MA
McDonald, C. Douglas, Jr. ... Tampa, FL
McDonald, C. R. (Pete), Jr. ... Fort Pierce, FL
McDonald, C. Richard ... Cleveland, OH
McDonald, C. Thomas, (A Professional Law Corporation) ... Santa Ana, CA
McDonald, Calonette M. ... Washington, DC
McDonald Carano Wilson McCune Bergin Frankovich & Hicks LLP
Las Vegas, NV
Reno, NV
McDonald, Carl P. ... Maryville, TN
McDonald, Carol T. ... Edna, TX
Mcdonald, Cary Jean Edwards ... Tulsa, OK
McDonald, Cassandra B. ... Stamford, CT
McDonald, Charles ... Austin, TX
McDonald, Charles E. ... Bangs, TX
McDonald, Charles E. ... El Paso, TX
McDonald, Charles E., III ... Greenville, SC
McDonald, Charles E., Jr. ... Greenville, SC
McDonald, Charles H. ... Columbia, SC
McDonald, Charles M. ... Waco, TX
McDonald, Charles R. ... Southfield, MI
McDonald, Charles W. ... Livonia, MI
McDonald, Charles W. ... Memphis, TN
McDonald, Charles W. ... Waco, TX
McDonald, Cheryl B. ... Los Angeles, CA
McDonald, Christopher J. ... New York, NY
McDonald, Christopher J. ... Suffern, NY
McDonald, Christopher John
Arlington, VA
McDonald, Christopher M.
Los Angeles, CA
McDonald, Christopher M.
Kansas City, MO
McDonald, Christopher W. ... Richmond, VA
McDonald, Christy E. ... Trenton, NJ
McDonald, Claiborne (Buddy), IV
Picayune, MS
McDonald, Claire H. ... Mount Laurel, NJ
McDonald, Clay, Crow & McGartland, L.L.P. ... Dallas, TX
Fort Worth, TX
McDonald & Cody ... Athens, GA
Cornelia, GA
Gainesville, GA
McDonald, Colin E. ... Jonesboro, GA
McDonald, Colleen Heather
San Francisco, CA
McDonald, C. R. (Pete), Jr. ... Fort Pierce, FL
McDonald, Craig S. ... Lynnwood, WA
McDonald, Crawford ... Memphis, TN
McDonald & Crawford, P.A.
Fort Lauderdale, FL
McDonald, D. Kyle ... Ruston, LA
McDonald, D. Richard
Bloomfield Hills, MI
McDonald, D. Scott ... Stockton, CA
McDonald, D. Terrence ... Austin, TX
McDonald, Dana E. ... Chamblee, GA
McDonald, Daniel E., Jr. ... Dallas, TX
McDonald, Daniel J. ... Huntington Beach, CA
McDonald, Daniel J. ... Salt Lake City, UT
McDonald, Daniel M. ... Windom, MN
McDonald, Daniel M., Law Offices of
Fall River, MA
McDonald, Daniel R. ... Rochester, NY
McDonald, Daniel S. ... Manhattan Beach, CA
McDonald, Daniel W. ... Minneapolis, MN
McDonald, Daniel W. ... Fort Worth, TX
Mcdonald, Danny R. ... San Marcos, CA
McDonald, Daryl P. ... Tecumseh, MI
McDonald, David ... Miami, FL
McDonald, David C. ... St. Paul, MN
McDonald, David E. ... Ironwood, MI
McDonald, David E. ... Houston, TX
McDonald, David E., Jr. ... Ironwood, MI
McDonald, David G. ... New York, NY
McDonald, David J. ... Fairfield, CT
McDonald, David M. ... Miami, FL
McDonald, David M. ... Miami, FL
McDonald, David M. ... New York, NY
McDonald, David P. ... St. Louis, MO
McDonald, David R. ... Galesburg, IL
McDonald, David S. ... Orlando, FL
McDonald, David T. ... Seattle, WA
McDonald, David Thomas ... Portland, OR
McDonald, David W. ... Greensboro, NC
McDonald, Davis ... Greensboro, NC
McDonald, Dawn I. ... Birmingham, AL
McDonald, Deanna D. ... San Diego, CA
McDonald, Deirdre Ann ... Dallas, TX
McDonald & DeMarco ... Monterey, CA
San Bernardino, CA
McDonald, Derek R. ... Austin, TX
McDonald, Diane K. ... Asheville, NC
McDonald, Donald ... Rosemont, PA
McDonald, Donald A. ... Providence, RI
McDonald, Douglas ... Davenport, IA
McDonald, Douglas B. ... McLean, VA
McDonald, Douglas J. ... Phoenix, AZ
McDonald, Douglas W. ... Cornelia, GA
McDonald, Doyle ... Galveston, TX
McDonald, Duard R., & Associates
Marietta, GA
McDonald, E. Crawford ... Dalton, GA
McDonald, E. Dandridge ... Charleston, WV
McDonald, Edward A. ... New York, NY
McDonald, Edward C., Jr. ... Los Gatos, CA
McDonald, Edward D. ... Braintree, MA
McDonald, Edward F. ... Denver, PA
McDonald, Edwin D. ... Fort Lauderdale, FL
McDonald, Elaine M. ... Des Moines, IA
McDonald, Elizabeth A. ... Boston, MA
McDonald, Elizabeth J. ... Webster, NY
McDonald, Elizabeth M. ... New York, NY
McDonald, Elizabeth Megan
Stockton, CA

McDonald, Tracy Carolyn ......Los Angeles, CA
McDonald, Travis LeRoy ....Huntsville, TX
McDonald, Valerie B. ....Columbia, SC
McDonald, Victor L. ....Carson City, NV
McDonald, W. Allen ....Knoxville, TN
McDonald, W. Grady ....Memphis, TN
McDonald, Wallace J. ....Syracuse, NY
McDonald, Ward F. ....Champaign, IL
McDonald, Wilburn O. (Bill), Jr.
Houston, TX
McDonald, Wilfred J. ....San Francisco, CA
McDonald, William ....Columbus, OH
McDonald, William B. ....Spencer, IA
McDonald, William C. ....Houston, TX
McDonald, William C., Jr.
Fort Stockton, TX
McDonald, William D. ....Milwaukie, OR
McDonald, William E. ....Minneapolis, MN
McDonald, William E. ....Lansford, PA
McDonald, William E. ....Houston, TX
McDonald, William E., Jr.
Grand Rapids, MI
McDonald, William F. ....Santa Ana, CA
McDonald, William F. ....Enfield, CT
McDonald, William F., Jr. ....Phoenix, AZ
McDonald, William G., Jr. ....Sacramento, CA
McDonald, William H. ....Springfield, MO
McDonald, William H., & Associates, P.C.
Springfield, MO
McDonald, William I. ....Marquette, MI
McDonald, William J. ....Boston, MA
McDonald, William J. ....Stillwater, MN
McDonald, William J. ....Geneva, NY
McDonald, William J. ....Lewiston, NY
McDonald, William J. ....Scarsdale, NY
McDonald, William J., Jr. ....Geneva, NY
McDonald, William M. ......Oklahoma City, OK
McDonald, William Marc
Fort Worth, TX
McDonald, William Norman ....Belen, NM
McDonald, William Norman, P.A.
Belen, NM
McDonald, William R. ....Denver, CO
McDonald, William R., P.C. ....Denver, CO
McDonald, William S. ....Milwaukie, OR
McDonald, Willis, IV ....New York, NY
McDonald & Wilson ....Richardson, TX
McDonald, Wilson W. ....Columbia, SC
McDonald, Ysleta W. ....Gainesville, FL
McDonald-Burkman, Judith E.
Louisville, KY
Mcdonald-Gallentine, Abby L. ....Fairfield, IA
Mcdonaugh, James Andrew ....Riverhead, NY
McDonell, Alexander A. ....New York, NY
McDonell, Celeste A. ....Seattle, WA
McDonell, Duncan A., II ....Orange Park, FL
McDonell, Jason S. ....Palo Alto, CA
McDonell, Jill P. ....Los Angeles, CA
McDonell, Kevin A. ....Millington, TN
McDonell, Leslie A. ....Washington, DC
McDonell, Neil E. ....New York, NY
McDonell, Thomas W. ....Sterling Heights, MI
McDonell, Wallace K. ....Whitewater, WI
McDonie, Marcia ....Tampa, FL
McDoniel, Michael R. ....Austin, TX
McDoniel, William P. .....Oklahoma City, OK
McDonnell, Adels & Goodstein
Lake Success, NY
McDonnell, Alfred T. ....Denver, CO
McDonnell, Anne ....Woodbury, NJ
McDonnell, Barry F. ....Michigan City, IN
McDonnell Boehnen Hulbert & Berghoff
Chicago, IL
McDonnell, Brendan R. ....Portland, OR
McDonnell, Brett M. ....San Francisco, CA
McDonnell, Brian ....Hempstead, NY
McDonnell, Brian J. ....New York, NY
McDonnell, Brian M. ....West Palm Beach, FL
McDonnell, Christine Tambakis
Savannah, GA
McDonnell, Conley, Arslanian & Neveux, LLP ....Bloomfield Hills, MI
Grosse Pointe Woods, MI
McDonnell, Dale Lindsay ....Roseville, MN
McDonnell, Daniel P. ....Cleveland, OH
McDonnell, David H. ......Treasury Department, Internal Revenue Service, GV
McDonnell, David J. ....Baltimore, MD
McDonnell, David K. ....Birmingham, MI
McDonnell, David K. ....Detroit, MI
McDonnell, Deirdre A. ....Washington, DC
McDonnell, E. F., Jr. ....Chicago, IL
McDonnell, Ellen K. ....Harrisburg, PA
McDonnell, Erin M.
Office Of Special Counsel, GV
McDonnell, Francis E. ....Bensalem, PA
McDonnell, Frank J. ....Scranton, PA
McDonnell, George T. ....Los Angeles, CA
McDonnell, Glen ....Atlanta, GA
McDonnell, Harriet E. ....Mineola, NY
McDonnell, J. Brian ....Worth, IL
McDonnell, J. Edwin ....Spartanburg, SC
McDonnell, James J. ....Cleveland, OH
McDonnell, James W., Jr. ....Memphis, TN
McDonnell, Jeffrey ....Philadelphia, PA
McDonnell, John F. ....Morristown, NJ
McDonnell, John J. ....Chicago, IL
McDonnell, John J., III ....Reston, VA
McDonnell, John L., Jr. ....Oakland, CA
McDonnell, John P. ....Los Altos, CA
McDonnell, John P. ....Newark, NJ
McDonnell, John S. ....East Meadow, NY
McDonnell, Joseph B. ....Belleville, IL
McDonnell, Joseph J. ....Detroit, MI
McDonnell, Joseph T. ....East Setauket, NY
McDonnell, Karen T. ....Chicago, IL
McDonnell, Kathryn E. ....Washington, DC
McDonnell, Keith B. ....Chicago, IL

McDonnell, Kenneth J. ....Essex, CT
McDonnell, Kenneth J. ....Waltham, MA
McDonnell & Kent, Inc., Law Offices of
La Habra, CA
Mc Donnell, Kimberly A. ....San Diego, CA
McDonnell, Laurence G. ....Hempstead, NY
McDonnell, Laurinda Lynne
Englewood, CO
McDonnell, Leo M. ....Duluth, MN
McDonnell, Leslianne ....Houston, TX
McDonnell, Loretta W.
San Francisco, CA
McDonnell, Mark G. ....Salem, OR
McDonnell, Martin P. ....Fort Lauderdale, FL
McDonnell, Mary C. ....Washington, DC
McDonnell, Matthew J. ....Quincy, MA
McDonnell & McDonnell, P.A.
Drexel Hill, PA
McDonnell, Michael ....Naples, FL
McDonnell, Michael B. ....La Jolla, CA
McDonnell, Michael B.
Colorado Springs, CO
McDonnell, Michael J. ....Minneapolis, MN
McDonnell, Michael J. ....St. Louis, MO
McDonnell, Michael L. ....Hartford, CT
McDonnell, Michael M. ....Brick, NJ
McDonnell, Michael R. ....La Habra, CA
McDonnell, Michael T., III .....Cherry Hill, NJ
Philadelphia, PA
McDonnell, Michael T., Jr. ....Drexel Hill, PA
McDonnell, Michele ....Philadelphia, PA
McDonnell, Miles C. ....Fern Park, FL
McDonnell, Patrick B. ....Milwaukee, WI
McDonnell, Patrick H. ....Omaha, NE
McDonnell, Patrick J. ....Lake Success, NY
McDonnell, Patrick J. ....Philadelphia, PA
McDonnell, Richard C. ....Ramsey, NJ
McDonnell, Richard L.
Bloomfield Hills, MI
McDonnell, Robert D. ....Charlotte, NC
McDonnell, Robert E. ....Boston, MA
McDonnell, Robert F. ....Virginia Beach, VA
McDonnell, Robert J. ....Newport Beach, CA
McDonnell, Robert J. ....Drexel Hill, PA
McDonnell, Ronald H., Jr. ....Dayton, OH
McDonnell, Sue K. ....Dayton, OH
McDonnell, Suzanne M. ....San Francisco, CA
McDonnell, Thomas A. ....Pittsburgh, PA
McDonnell, Thomas J. ....Sacramento, CA
McDonnell, Thomas J. ....Chicago, IL
McDonnell, Thomas R. ....St. Louis, MO
McDonnell, Timothy D. ....Chicago, IL
McDonnell Trial Lawyers ......Fort Myers, FL
Naples, FL
McDonnell, Tyrone M. ....Hackensack, NJ
McDonnell, Ursula M. ....Covington, KY
McDonnell, Vincent D. ....New York, NY
McDonnell & Weaver ....San Francisco, CA
McDonnell & Whitaker ....Ramsey, NJ
McDonnell, William E., Jr.
San Francisco, CA
McDonnell, William J. ....South Amboy, NJ
McDonnell, Xavier K.
Federal Election Commission, Office of the General Counsel, GV
McDonnold, Kyle H. ....Midland, TX
McDonnold, M., Jr. ....Midland, TX
McDonough, Andrew J. ....Chicago, IL
McDonough, Ann M. ....Dubuque, IA
McDonough, Anna ....McPherson, KS
McDonough, Anna Margaret
Philadelphia, PA
McDonough & Associates, P.C.
Houston, TX
McDonough, Barry R. ....Boston, MA
McDonough, Birch P. ....New Orleans, LA
McDonough, Brian E. ....Harrisburg, PA
McDonough, Brian F. ....Florham Park, NJ
New York, NY
McDonough, Brian J. ....Miami, FL
McDonough, Brian P. ....Boston, MA
McDonough, Brian T. ....Manchester, NH
McDonough, Cathleen G. ....Roseland, NJ
McDonough, Charles E.
Parkersburg, WV
McDonough, Darren A. ....Reidsville, NC
McDonough, David G. ....Manchester, NH
McDonough, David J. ....Fort Smith, AR
McDonough, Diana Brusca ....Melville, NY
McDonough, Diana Smith
San Rafael, CA
McDonough, Digby & Leiter ....Syracuse, NY
McDonough, Doris ....San Antonio, TX
McDonough, Douglas J. ....Little Falls, NJ
McDonough, Edward B., Jr. ....Mobile, AL
McDonough, Edward B., Jr. ....Houston, TX
McDonough, Edward B., Jr., P.C.
Mobile, AL
McDonough, Edward J. ....Toms River, NJ
McDonough, Edward J. ....Salt Lake City, UT
McDonough, Edward J., Jr.
Springfield, MA
McDonough, Eileen ....Department of Justice, Environment and Natural Resources Division, GV
McDonough, Elizabeth A. ....Upland, CA
McDonough, Elizabeth I.
Colorado Springs, CO
McDonough, Enid W. ....Bloomfield, NJ
McDonough, Fenton J. ....Scottsdale, AZ
McDonough, Francis J., Jr. ......Manchester, MA
McDonough, Francis X. ....Boston, MA
McDonough, Frank M. ....Red Bank, NJ
McDonough, Frederick J. ....Trenton, NJ
McDonough, Gail A. ....New Orleans, LA
Mc Donough, Gerald A. ....Boston, MA
McDonough, Guy M. ....Washington, DC

McDonough, Hacking & Neumeier
Boston, MA
McDonough, Harold B., Jr. ....Nashville, TN
McDonough, Helen Anne ....Bethesda, MD
McDonough, Helen L. ....Canton, CT
McDonough, Holland & Allen, A Professional Corporation ....Oakland, CA
Sacramento, CA
Yuba City, CA
McDonough, J. Edward ....Mineola, NY
New York, NY
White Plains, NY
McDonough, J. Martin, Jr. ....Baltimore, MD
McDonough, James C. ....San Antonio, TX
McDonough, James D. ....Chicago, IL
McDonough, James F.
Ocean Township, NJ
McDonough, James M. ....Louisville, KY
McDonough, James M. ....Boston, MA
McDonough, James M. ....San Antonio, TX
McDonough, James P. ....Santa Ana, CA
McDonough, James P. ....Westmont, NJ
McDonough, Janet H. ....San Diego, CA
McDonough, Janet M. ....Eau Claire, WI
McDonough, Jas. P. ....Cincinnati, OH
McDonough, Joan ....Brockton, MA
McDonough, John Christopher
Alexandria, VA
McDonough, John D. ....Chicago, IL
McDonough, John F. ....Syracuse, NY
McDonough, John F. ....Cranston, RI
McDonough, John F., Jr. ....Syracuse, NY
McDonough, John J. ....Boston, MA
McDonough, John J. ....St. Louis, MO
McDonough, John J., III ....New York, NY
McDonough, John L. ....Worcester, MA
McDonough, John M. ....Chicago, IL
McDonough, John P. ....Annapolis, MD
Greenbelt, MD
McDonough, John P. ....Springfield, OH
McDonough, John R. ....Los Angeles, CA
McDonough, John R. ....Sacramento, CA
McDonough, John R. ....Orlando, FL
McDonough, Joseph F. ....Pittsburgh, PA
McDonough, Joseph J. ....Oak Lawn, IL
McDonough, Joseph M., III
Manchester, NH
McDonough, Joseph P. ....San Diego, CA
McDonough, Joseph R. ....Morristown, NJ
McDonough, Judith A. ....San Diego, CA
McDonough, Julia A. ....Washington, DC
McDonough, Katherine A. ....Mineola, NY
Riverhead, NY
McDonough, Kathleen A.
Commodity Futures Trading Commission, Office of the General Counsel, GV
McDonough, Kathleen Furey
Wilmington, DE
McDonough, Kathleen M. ....Chicago, IL
McDonough, Kenneth E. ....Columbus, OH
McDonough, Kevin C. ....Clinton, CT
McDonough, Kevin C. ....Cincinnati, OH
McDonough, Kevin F. ....Binghamton, NY
McDonough, Kevin M. ....New York, NY
McDonough, Kevin M.
Salt Lake City, UT
McDonough, Kevin P. ......Rockville Centre, NY
McDonough, Korn & Eichhorn, A Professional Corporation ......Elizabeth, NJ
Morristown, NJ
Newark, NJ
Springfield, NJ
Westfield, NJ
McDonough, Kristin M. ....Boston, MA
McDonough, Lawrence ....Tucson, AZ
McDonough, Lawrence ....Washington, DC
McDonough & Lindh, P.A. ....Manchester, NH
McDonough, Lorraine M.
Redwood City, CA
McDonough, Louis E. ....Menlo Park, CA
McDonough, Louis E. ....Boca Raton, FL
McDonough, Lucille K. ....Chicago, IL
McDonough, M. Brigid ....St. Paul, MN
McDonough, M. Theresa
Upper Marlboro, MD
McDonough, Madeleine M.
Kansas City, MO
McDonough Marcus Cohn Tretter Heller & Kanca L.L.P. ....New York, NY
McDonough, Mark K ....Bangor, ME
McDonough, Mark T.
Department Of Veterans Affairs, Office of the General Counsel, GV
McDonough, Marsha L. ....St. Helens, OR
McDonough, Martin E. ....Markham, IL
McDonough, Mary ....Wilmington, DE
McDonough, Matthew J ....Boston, MA
McDonough, Matthew M. ....Garden City, NY
McDonough, Maureen A. ....Bolton, MA
McDonough & McDonough
New Orleans, LA
Bay City, MI
McDonough, Michael ....Cedar Rapids, IA
McDonough, Michael B. ....Lynnfield, MA
McDonough, Michael D. ....Wellington, FL
McDonough, Michael E. ....Hartford, CT
McDonough, Michael J. ....Washington, DC
McDonough, Michael M. ....Bay City, MI
McDonough, Michael S. ....Los Angeles, CA
McDonough, Myles W. ....Boston, MA
McDonough, Nancy N. ....Sacramento, CA
McDonough & O'Shaughnessy
Manchester, NH
McDonough, Patrick A., III ....Vidalia, LA
McDonough, Patrick J. ....Encino, CA
McDonough, Patrick J. ....Boston, MA
McDonough, Patrick John
Washington, DC

McDonough, Patrick M. ....Troy, MI
McDonough, Patrick M., P.C. ....Troy, MI
McDonough, Patrick W.
Treasury Department, Office of Director of Practice, GV
McDonough, Paul F., Jr. ....Boston, MA
McDonough, Paul M. ....Bethesda, MD
McDonough, Paul S. ....Richmond Hill, NY
McDonough, Peter G. ....Princeton, NJ
McDonough, Richard A. ....Ann Arbor, MI
Dallas, TX
McDonough, Richard C. ....Mantoloking, NJ
McDonough, Richard F. ....Williamsville, NY
McDonough, Robert ....Wheaton, IL
McDonough, Robert F. ....New York, NY
McDonough, Robert P. ....Springfield, NJ
McDonough, Robert S. ....Washington, DC
Alexandria, VA
McDonough, Robert T. ....Kalamazoo, MI
McDonough, Russell C. ....Helena, MT
McDonough, Sandra L. Williams
Los Angeles, CA
McDonough, Sandra M. ....Stratford, CT
McDonough, Sean C. E. ....Alexandria, VA
McDonough, Sean F. ....Boston, MA
McDonough, Sean M. ....Orlando, FL
McDonough, Sean P. ....Scranton, PA
McDonough, Shannon ....Minneapolis, MN
McDonough, Susan M. ....Mansfield, MA
McDonough, Suzanne ....Philadelphia, PA
McDonough, Suzanne C. M. ....Boston, MA
McDonough, T. James ....Des Moines, IA
McDonough, Therese S. ....Cincinnati, OH
McDonough, Thomas C. ....Chicago, IL
McDonough, Thomas D. ....New Albany, MS
McDonough, Thomas F. ....Towson, MD
McDonough, Thomas F. ....Seattle, WA
McDonough, Thomas Henry
Philadelphia, PA
McDonough, Thomas J. ....Glens Falls, NY
McDonough, Thomas K. ....Waterbury, CT
McDonough, Thomas M. ....Towson, MD
McDonough, Thomas P. .....White Plains, NY
Mc Donough, Thomas V. ....Wilmington, DE
McDonough, Timothy A. ....Pomona, CA
McDonough, Timothy R. ....Houston, TX
McDonough, Travis R. ....Chattanooga, TN
Mc Donough, Vincent R. ....Boston, MA
McDonough, W. Thomas, Jr. ....Montclair, NJ
McDonough, Walter K. ....Boston, MA
McDonough, Walter L. ....Philadelphia, PA
McDonough, Ward F., Jr. ....Kalamazoo, MI
McDonough & Wieland, P.A.
Orlando, FL
McDonough, William B. ....Holyoke, MA
McDonough, William F. ....Lakewood, OH
McDonough, William J. ....Philadelphia, PA
McDonough, William J., Jr.
San Antonio, TX
McDonough, William L., Jr.
Gulfport, MS
McDonough, William N. ....Boston, MA
McDonough, William P. ....Boston, MA
McDorman, Clarence L., Jr.
Birmingham, AL
McDorman & Hayden ....Versailles, MO
McDorman, Michael L. ....Versailles, MO
McDougal, Amy E. ....Towson, MD
McDougal and Associates ....San Diego, CA
McDougal, Cary L. ....Dallas, TX
Sherman, TX
McDougal, Craig Alan ....Dallas, TX
McDougal, Donald C., Jr. ....San Diego, CA
McDougal, Douglas S. ....Troy, MI
McDougal, Evans & Shelton, L.L.P.
Tulsa, OK
McDougal, Gregg E. ....Raleigh, NC
McDougal, J. Douglas ....Walpole, MA
McDougal, Jackie M., (Mr.) ....Bessemer, AL
McDougal, James F., III ....Austin, TX
McDougal, Jennifer E. ....Raleigh, NC
McDougal, John C. ....Richmond, VA
McDougal, John G. ....Chattanooga, TN
McDougal, Larry G. ....Cleveland, OH
McDougal, Larry P. ....Houston, TX
McDougal, Love, Eckis, Smith & Boehmer, A Professional Corporation ....El Cajon, CA
San Diego, CA
McDougal, Luther L., III ....New Orleans, LA
McDougal, Lynn R. ....El Cajon, CA
McDougal, Michael A. ....Conroe, TX
McDougal, M. M. ....Tulsa, OK
McDougal, Paul R. ....Garden City, NY
McDougal, Sarah H. ....Labadie, MO
McDougal, William Troy ....Collegedale, TN
McDougald, Cornelius, Jr. ....Somers, NY
McDougald, Heather A.
Salt Lake City, UT
McDougald, John G. ....Clarkton, NC
McDougald, Ronald J., (P.C.) ....Boston, MA
McDougald, Shannon L. ....Seattle, WA
McDougall, Dan C. ....Pocatello, ID
McDougall, Dennis S. ....Chula Vista, CA
McDougall, Donald T. ....Chicago, IL
McDougall, Dugald S. ....Haines City, FL
McDougall, Gerald D. ....Amarillo, TX
McDougall, G. S. ....Watsonville, CA
McDougall, Ian ....Columbus, OH
McDougall, Isaac ....Pocatello, ID
McDougall, J. Olin, II ....Beaufort, SC
McDougall, James E. ....Phoenix, AZ
McDougall, James R. ....Phoenix, AZ
McDougall, Jodi A. ....Seattle, WA
McDougall, John G. ....Media, PA
McDougall, John O. ....Columbia, SC
Sumter, SC
McDougall, John R. ....Berkeley, CA
McDougall, Jonathan D. ....Norristown, PA

McDougall, Joseph H. ....Los Angeles, CA
McDougall, Kent M. ....San Antonio, TX
McDougall, Kevin L. ....Durham, NC
McDougall, Laurel C. ....Federal Way, WA
McDougall, Lisa ....Buffalo, NY
McDougall, Lorne W. ....Boston, MA
Providence, RI
McDougall, Lynn B. ....Trenton, NJ
McDougall, Pauline T. ....Hartford, CT
McDougall, Peg L. ....Lansing, MI
McDougall, Raymond M. ....Lacombe, LA
McDougall, Robert D. ....New York, NY
McDougall, Roderick G. ....Phoenix, AZ
McDougall & Self, L.L.P. ....Columbia, SC
Sumter, SC
McDougall, Stephen Charles ......New York, NY
McDougall, Thomas E. ....Fallbrook, CA
McDougall, Wayne J. ....Chalmette, LA
McDougall, William Douglas ....Fairfax, VA
McDougall-Tural, Elizabeth ....Seattle, WA
McDougle, Charles H., Jr. ....Dothan, AL
McDougle, Ryan T. ....Mechanicsville, VA
McDow, Jeffery J. ....Santa Clara, CA
McDow, Joseph U. ....Atlanta, GA
Mcdow, Lisa T. ....Wilmington, NC
McDow, Lucy London ....Rock Hill, SC
McDow, Thomas F. ....Rock Hill, SC
McDow, W. Clarkson, Jr. ....Rock Hill, SC
McDow, William C. ....Columbia, SC
McDowall, Cotter, Dunn, Vale & Bracco, A Professional Corporation ....Palo Alto, CA
San Mateo, CA
McDowall, John R. ....Seattle, WA
McDowall & Lewis ....Asheville, NC
McDowall, Mackson P. ....Buffalo, NY
McDowall, Paul Haven ....Eden Prairie, MN
McDowall, Robert H. ....Cuyahoga Falls, OH
McDowall, William D. ....San Mateo, CA
McDowall, William D., Jr. ....Asheville, NC
McDowall-Nix, Marcia ....St. Paul, MN
McDow-Dunham, Kelly L. ....Cincinnati, OH
McDowell, Alfred J. ....Wolfeboro, NH
McDowell, Allen W. ....Chicago, IL
McDowell, Althea E. ....Wilmington, DE
McDowell, Amy S. ....Los Angeles, CA
McDowell, Andrew P. ....Reading, PA
McDowell, Anne Morgan ....Cleveland, OH
McDowell, A. V. ....Memphis, TN
McDowell, Barbara ....Department of Justice, Office of the Solicitor General, GV
McDowell, Barbara Ann ......Washington, DC
McDowell & Beason ....Russellville, AL
Tuscumbia, AL
McDowell, Boyd, II ....Elmira, NY
McDowell, Boyd, III ....Chicago, IL
McDowell, Brian A. ....Orlando, FL
McDowell & Butler, LLP ....Atlanta, GA
McDowell, Carol Duffy ....Topeka, KS
McDowell, Carter N., (P.A.) ....Miami, FL
McDowell, Charles E. ....Alexandria, VA
McDowell, Charles S. ....Wilmington, DE
McDowell, Christopher M. ....Dallas, TX
McDowell, Christopher Ray
Huntington, WV
McDowell, Cleve ....Drew, MS
McDowell & Colantoni, Ltd. ....Chicago, IL
McDowell, Cynthia T. ....Prattville, AL
McDowell, Dana Leahy ....Moraga, CA
McDowell, Daniel G. ....Russellville, AL
McDowell, David A. ....Prattville, AL
McDowell, David A. ....Laguna Hills, CA
McDowell, David A. ....Sacramento, CA
San Francisco, CA
Walnut Creek, CA
McDowell, David A., A Prof. Law Corp., Law Offices of ....Sacramento, CA
Walnut Creek, CA
San Francisco, CA
McDowell, David F., Jr. ....Los Angeles, CA
McDowell, David T. ....Houston, TX
McDowell, David Whittington
Birmingham, AL
McDowell, Dock, Jr. ....Merrillville, IN
McDowell, Donna S. ....Laytonsville, MD
McDowell & Edingfield, Chtd. ....Wichita, KS
McDowell, Edmund T. ....Copiague, NY
McDowell, Edward ....Tempe, AZ
McDowell, Elizabeth M. .....Minneapolis, MN
McDowell, Ellen M. ....Maple Shade, NJ
McDowell, Faulk & McDowell
Prattville, AL
McDowell, G. Simms, III ....Charleston, SC
McDowell, G. Simms, III
Moncks Corner, SC
Summerville, SC
McDowell, Gary D. ....Minneapolis, MN
McDowell, George E., Jr.
Myrtle Beach, SC
McDowell, Gerald E.
Department of Justice, Criminal Division, GV
McDowell & Gillman, P.C. ....Ogden, UT
Salt Lake City, UT
McDowell, Gregory W., P.S.C.
Florence, KY
McDowell, H. Woodward ....Bay Head, NJ
McDowell, Heather L. ....Washington, DC
McDowell, J. Joseph ....Daly City, CA
McDowell, James A. ....St. Louis, MO
McDowell, James B. ....Los Angeles, CA
McDowell, James F., III ....Clovis, NM
McDowell, James M. ....Cleveland, OH
McDowell, Jay H. ....New York, NY
McDowell, Jerrold R. ....Hackensack, NJ
McDowell, Jerry A. ....Mobile, AL
McDow, Jill K. ....Washington, DC
McDowell, John D. ....Thornton, CO
McDowell, John E. ....Cincinnati, OH
McDowell, John H. ....Hagerstown, MD
McDowell, John H., Jr. ....Dallas, TX
McDowell, John R. ....Sioux Falls, SD
McDowell, John T. ....Houston, TX
McDowell, Joseph F., III ....Manchester, NH
McDowell, Joseph F., III, P.A.
Manchester, NH
McDowell, Joseph W. ....Jackson, MS
McDowell, Karen A. ....Denver, CO
McDowell, Katherine A. ....Portland, OR
McDowell, Kathleen M. ....Los Angeles, CA
McDowell, Kevin C. ....Indianapolis, IN
McDowell, Kevin L. ....Boulder, CO
McDowell, Kevin P. ....Holland, MI
McDowell Knight Roedder & Sledge, L.L.C. Mobile, AL
McDowell, Larry R. ....Philadelphia, PA
McDowell, Laura S. ....Miami Beach, FL
McDowell Law Firm, The ......Merrillville, IN
McDowell Law Off., P.C. ....Holland, MI
McDowell, Lawrence A.
Thief River Falls, MN
McDowell, Lawrence R. ....Des Moines, IA
McDowell, Leah Draayer ....Jackson, MS
McDowell, Linda J. ....Hartford, CT
McDowell, Lonnie K. ....Prescott, AZ
McDowell, Lynn ....Indianapolis, IN
McDowell, M. Patrick ....Jackson, MS
McDowell, Madeline C. ....Sacramento, CA
McDowell, Marcus Edward ....Mobile, AL
McDowell, Margaret H. ....Brooklyn, NY
McDowell, Melvin ....Moorestown, NJ
McDowell, Michael D. ....Greensburg, PA
McDowell, Michael T. ....St. Louis, MO
McDowell, Michael-Shannon
Smith Center, KS
McDowell, Monique ....Atlanta, GA
McDowell, Pat ....Dallas, TX
McDowell, Paul H. ....New York, NY
McDowell, Paula Bohannon
Russellville, AL
McDowell, Peter T. ....Baltimore, MD
McDowell, Philip W. ....Independence, CA
McDowell, R. David ....Huntsville, AL
McDowell, R. Mont ....Salt Lake City, UT
McDowell, R. Scott ....Paris, TX
McDowell, Ralph E. ....Detroit, MI
McDowell, Ralph L. ....Dallas, TX
McDowell, Randal J. ....Jenkintown, PA
McDowell, Randall Gene ....Frankfort, KY
McDowell, Rice, Smith & Gaar, A Professional Corporation
Overland Park, KS
Kansas City, MO
McDowell, Richard R. ....Indianapolis, IN
McDowell, Robert G. ....Nashville, TN
McDowell, Robert L. ....Indianapolis, IN
McDowell, Robert U. ....St. Joseph, MI
McDowell, Robert U., A Professional Corporation ....St. Joseph, MI
McDowell, Rozetta Darby ....Pittsford, NY
McDowell, Sherwin T. ....Philadelphia, PA
McDowell, Stewart L. ....San Francisco, CA
McDowell, Sue B. ....Taos, NM
McDowell, Suzanne Ross .....Washington, DC
McDowell, T. Hughlon ....North Bend, WA
McDowell, Theodore N., Jr. ....Atlanta, GA
McDowell, Theron O., Jr. ....Prattville, AL
McDowell, Thomas C. ....Wichita, KS
McDowell, Thomas E. ....Huntingdon, PA
McDowell, Todd A. ....Cocoa, FL
McDowell, Valecia M. ....Charlotte, NC
Mcdowell, Wayne E. ....South Pasadena, CA
McDowell, Wick, Daly, Gallup, Hauser and Hartle ....Bradford, PA
McDowell, William A., Jr. ....St. Louis, MO
McDowell, William H.
Sulphur Springs, TX
McDowell, William J. ....Wenatchee, WA
McDowell, William, (P.C.)
Sulphur Springs, TX
McDowell, William S., Jr. ....Chicago, IL
McDuff, Douglas A. ....Coral Gables, FL
McDuff, J. Fred ....Birmingham, AL
McDuff, John ....Austin, TX
McDuff, John, P.C., A Professional Corporation ....Austin, TX
McDuff, Laurence J. ....Birmingham, AL
McDuff, Richard H. ....Fort Lauderdale, FL
McDuff, Robert B. ....Jackson, MS
McDuff, Robert E. ....Marietta, GA
McDuff, Wilbur S. ....Miami, FL
McDuffa, Stacey Lynn ....Birmingham, AL
McDuffee, David S. ....Caledonia, MI
McDuffee, Edward P. ....Hollis, NH
McDuffee, Paul G., II ....Tampa, FL
McDuffee, Renee R. ....Detroit, MI
McDuffey, Timothy M. ....Camdenton, MO
McDuffie, Brian K. ....Miami, FL
McDuffie, Colleen H. ....Washington, DC
McDuffie, David L. ....Ventura, CA
McDuffie, Elizabeth A. ....Milwaukee, WI
McDuffie, Kenneth P. ....Atlanta, GA
McDuffie, M. Allen ....Roswell, GA
McDuffie, Molly Manville ....Sumter, SC
McDugald, Barbara Hinske ....Phoenix, AZ
McDugald, Martha F. ....Houston, TX
McDugald, Richard W. ....Houston, TX
McDurmitt, Jon Jon ....Belton, TX
McDyer, Daniel P. ....Pittsburgh, PA
McEacharn, Joseph ....Portland, ME
McEachen, David T. ....Santa Ana, CA
McEachen, Edmund D. ....Omaha, NE
McEachen, J. Gary ....Kansas City, MO
McEachen, Richard E.
Overland Park, KS
McEachern, Alec L. ....Portsmouth, NH
McEachern, Bill B., Jr. ....Pensacola, FL
McEachern, Duncan A. ....Kittery, ME
McEachern, Edna Caroline ......Wilmington, NC
McEachern & FitzRoy, L.C.
St. Louis, MO
McEachern, Frank P. ....Dallas, TX
McEachern, G. Carson ....Naples, FL
McEachern, J. Richard ....St. Louis, MO
McEachern, Janet D. ....Seattle, WA
McEachern, John H. ....Portsmouth, NH
McEachern, Karen ....Hartland, VT
McEachern, Larry W. ....Lubbock, TX
McEachern, Marion K. ....Jonesboro, GA
McEachern, Paul ....Portsmouth, NH
McEachern, Peter ....Harrodsburg, KY
McEachern, Terry D. ....Plainview, TX
McEachern & Thornhill ....Kittery, ME
McEachern, William D. ....Palm Beach, FL
McEachern, William T. ....Sun City, AZ
McEachin, A. Donald ....Richmond, VA
McEachin, Dan M. ....Florence, SC
McEachin, Daniel Malloy, Jr. ....Florence, SC
McEachin, D. Malloy, Jr., P.A. ....Florence, SC
McEachin, Eugene M., Jr. ....Metairie, LA
McEachin & Gee, P.C. ....Richmond, VA
Mceachin, Scott William ....Tulsa, OK
McEachran, Daniel C. ....Chicago, IL
McEachran, David S. ....Bellingham, WA
McEachron, Brian L. ....Redmond, WA
McEachron, Thomas Scott ....St. Paul, MN
McEahern, Anthony K. ....Denver, CO
McEahern, Patricia A. ....Denver, CO
McEaneney, Shannon L. ....Cleveland, OH
McEdwards, Kitt N. ....San Francisco, CA
McElaney, Andrew J., Jr. ....Boston, MA
McElaney, Kevin D. ....Boston, MA
McElderry, Leslie ....West Des Moines, IA
McElderry, Marie Klimesz
Department of Justice, Civil Rights Division, GV
McElderry, Stanley R. ....Grinnell, IA
McEldowney, J. Gregory ....Houston, TX
McEldowney, John S. ....Galveston, TX
McEldowney, Todd R. ....Rhinelander, WI
McEldowney, Virginia C. ....Amherst, NY
McEldrew & Fullam, P.C.
Philadelphia, PA
McEldrew, James J., III ....New York, NY
Philadelphia, PA
McEldrew, James J., Jr. ....Philadelphia, PA
McEldrew & Ressler ....New York, NY
McElduff, Timothy P., Jr. ....New York, NY
McEleney, Dennis J. ....Chicago, IL
McEleney, John P. ....Woburn, MA
McEleney & McGrail ....Hartford, CT
McEleney, Stephen F. ....Hartford, CT
McElenney, Sean K. ....Phoenix, AZ
McElfatrick, Brian T. ....Tampa, FL
McElfish, James M. ....Pittsburgh, PA
McElfish, James M., Jr. ....Washington, DC
Mc Elfish, Raymond D. ....New York, NY
McElgunn, Christopher A. ....Wichita, KS
McElhaney, Christy L. ....New York, NY
McElhaney, James W. ....Cleveland, OH
McElhaney, Jeanette Ann ....Youngstown, OH
McElhaney, John C. ....Monroe, WI
McElhaney, John H. ....Dallas, TX
McElhaney, Karen Leah ....Fort Worth, TX
McElhaney, Leland P.
San Bernardino, CA
McElhaney, Michael J., Jr.
Pascagoula, MS
McElhaney, Renee ....San Antonio, TX
McElhaney, Scott M. ....Dallas, TX
McElhany, Harland H. "Chip"
Anchorage, AK
McElhany, Robert P. ....Auburn, CA
McElhattan, Howard B. ....San Francisco, CA
McElhatton, Daniel P. ....Philadelphia, PA
McElhatton, Michael J. ....Cherry Hill, NJ
McElhatton, Shaun C. ....Minneapolis, MN
McElhenney, Diane L. ....Lansdowne, PA
McElhenney, Hugh P. ....Clifton Heights, PA
McElhennon, Stephen H. ......Washington, DC
McElhenny, Brian W. ....Merrick, NY
McElheny, J. Terrell ....Birmingham, AL
McElheny, James P. ....Rochester, NY
McElheny, John D. ....Maitland, FL
McElhern, Diane E. ....Sacramento, CA
McElhern, Scott D. ....Sacramento, CA
McElhill, Frances A. ....Cherry Hill, NJ
Philadelphia, PA
McElhiney, John D. ....Woburn, MA
McElhiney, Matthew S. ....Englewood, CO
McElhinney, Colleen P. ....Boston, MA
McElhinney, David C. ....Reno, NV
McElhinney, Donna A. ....Kansas City, MO
McElhinney, James D. ....Fairplay, CO
McElhinney, Paul W. ....Sanford, ME
McElhinney, Stuart ....Los Osos, CA
McElhinney, Susan ....Los Osos, CA
McElhinny, Harold J. ....San Francisco, CA
McElhinny, Jeffrey M. ....Pittsburgh, PA
McElhinny, Karen M. ....Pittsburgh, PA
McElhinny, Patrick J. ....Pittsburgh, PA
McElhone, James E. ....Miller Place, NY
McElhone, Patrick S. ....Louisville, KY
McElhone, Patrick Shaheen, Jr.
Louisville, KY
McElhone, R. Bruce ....Baltimore, MD
McElligot, Ellen M. ....Treasury Department, Office of the Comptroller of the Currency, GV
McElligott, Denis J. ....Deer Park, NY
McElligott, Edmond J. ....Independence, MO
McElligott, F Brian ....Milwaukee, WI
McElligott, James P., Jr. ....Richmond, VA
McElligott, John A. ....Chicago, IL
McElligott, John E., Jr. ....Lafayette, LA
McElligott, John K. ....New York, NY
McElligott, Joseph P. ....Markham, IL
McElligott, Kujawski & Dellicarpini
Deer Park, NY
McElligott, Maurice T. ....Central Islip, NY
McElligott, Michael J. ....Hillsboro, OR
McElligott, Paul J. ....Washington, DC
McElligott, Thomas E. P. ....Houston, TX
McElligott, Thomas J., (P.C.)
Deer Park, NY
McElligott, Thomas P. ....Milwaukee, WI
McElligott, Thos. J. ....Chicago, IL
McElligott, William ....Pembroke, MA
McElligott, William P. ....Chicago, IL
McEllistrem, Michael J. .....Minneapolis, MN
McEllistrem, Paul Frederick
Minneapolis, MN
McEllistrem, Thomas E. ....St. Paul, MN
McEllroy, W. Edward ....Erie, PA
McElmeel, Thomas O. ....Seattle, WA
McElmurray, Ben Swain, Jr. ....Augusta, GA
McElmurray, Ben Swain, Jr., P.A.
Augusta, GA
McElmurry, Patrick ....Lansing, MI
McElnea, Brenda ....Verona, NJ
McElnea & WanderPolo ....Verona, NJ
McElrath, David L. ....Naples, FL
McElravey, Alison M. ....Los Gatos, CA
McElravey, C. Dirk ....Waukegan, IL
McElreath, Benjamin F. ....Augusta, GA
McElreath, George F. ....Dallas, TX
McElreath, Jane Stevens ....Cartersville, GA
McElreath, Mark F. ....Atlanta, GA
McElree, Mark C. ....Dallas, TX
McElree, Thomas J. ....Pittsburgh, PA
McElroen, Lawrence J. ....Mahopac, NY
McElroy, Allen A., Jr. ....Berwick, LA
McElroy, Amy ....Dallas, TX
McElroy, Andrew C. ....Roswell, GA
McElroy, Andrew H., III ....Birmingham, AL
McElroy, Angela Carter ....Augusta, GA
McElroy, B. Thomas ....Dallas, TX
McElroy, Barbara E. ....St. Louis, MO
McElroy, Brian ....Austin, TX
McElroy, C. Eugene ....Winston-Salem, NC
McElroy, Carolyn J. ....Baltimore, MD
McElroy, Charles W. ....Nashville, TN
McElroy, Christopher J. ....Chicago, IL
McElroy, Dana J. ....Miami, FL
McElroy, David W. ....Rockville, MD
McElroy, David W. ....Minneapolis, MN
McElroy, Dean J. ....Chicago, IL
McElroy, Deutsch and Mulvaney
Denver, CO
Morristown, NJ
Ridgewood, NJ
New York, NY
McElroy, Donna K. ....San Antonio, TX
McElroy, Edward M. ....Chicago, IL
McElroy, Edward T. ....Chicago, IL
McElroy, Eugene ....Troup, TX
McElroy, Eugene F. ....Rockville Centre, NY
McElroy, Frank L. ....Marblehead, MA
McElroy, Gavin D. ....New York, NY
McElroy, Gayle T., Law Office
Bellevue, WA
McElroy, Gayle T., Law Office
Mercer Island, WA
McElroy, Gayle T., Law Office
Seattle, WA
McElroy, George M. ....New York, NY
McElroy, Georgia A. ....Stockton, CA
McElroy, Gregory S. ....Seattle, WA
McElroy, Gregory S., P.L.L.C. ....Seattle, WA
McElroy, H. N. ....Spring, TX
McElroy, Howard C. ....Abingdon, VA
McElroy, Iwona ....New York, NY
McElroy, J. Daniel ....Dallas, TX
McElroy, J. Glenn ....Atlanta, GA
McElroy, J. Patrick ....Hernando, FL
McElroy, Jack C. ....Orlando, FL
McElroy, James B. ....Great Barrington, MA
McElroy, James E. ....San Diego, CA
McElroy, James E. ....Collierville, TN
McElroy, James L. ....Nashville, TN
McElroy, James P., Jr. ....Warwick, RI
McElroy, Jeff Foster ....Los Angeles, CA
McElroy, Jeffery W. ....El Paso, TX
McElroy, John M. ....Pittsburgh, PA
McElroy, John P. ....Cypress, CA
McElroy, John Peter ....Rockville Centre, NY
McElroy, Jonathan S. ....Asheville, NC
McElroy, Joseph, III ....Dallas, TX
McElroy, Joseph, Jr. ....Grand Prairie, TX
McElroy, Joseph M. ....Lufkin, TX
McElroy, Julie D. ....Sacramento, CA
McElroy, June S. ....Knoxville, TN
McElroy, Kathleen M. ....New York, NY
McElroy, Kathryn A. ....Boston, MA
McElroy, Kevin ....Garden City, NY
McElroy, Kyle R. ....Dallas, TX
McElroy, Laura ....Austin, TX
McElroy, Laura C. ....Booneville, MS
McElroy, Lisa T. ....Boston, MA
McElroy, Lori J. ....Harrisburg, PA
McElroy, Louis A., II ....Knoxville, TN
McElroy, Marian Frances ....North Chicago, IL
McElroy, Mary J. ....Templeton, CA
McElroy, Michael A. ....Islandia, NY
McElroy, Michael E. ....Austin, TX
McElroy, Michael J. ....Washington, DC
McElroy, Michael R. ....Providence, RI
McElroy, Michael W. ....Atlanta, GA
McElroy, Patrice E. ....San Francisco, CA
McElroy, Patricia A. ....Philadelphia, PA
McElroy, Paul J. ....Washington, DC
McElroy, Pender R. ....Charlotte, NC
McElroy, Peter M. ....Boston, MA

McElroy & Pheney ... Farmington Hills, MI
McElroy, Richard C., III ... Raleigh, NC
McElroy, Richard P. ... Philadelphia, PA
McElroy, Robert G. ... Richmond, VA
McElroy, Robert J. ... Wichita, KS
McElroy, Sara McDonald ... Beaumont, TX
McElroy, Scott B. ... Boulder, CO
McElroy, Scott E. ... Bastrop, LA
McElroy, Sherri K. ... San Francisco, CA
McElroy, Sullivan, Ryan & Miller, L.L.P. Austin, TX
McElroy, Terry L. ... Round Rock, TX
McElroy, Theodore R. ... Englewood, CO
McElroy, Thomas M. ... Tupelo, MS
McElroy, Thomas M., P.A. ... Tupelo, MS
McElroy, Thomas P. ... Grand Forks, ND
McElroy & Toole ... Augusta, GA
McElroy, V. M. ... Sun City Center, FL
McElroy, William Gerald, Jr. Waltham, MA
McElroy, William T. ... Morristown, NJ
McElroy, William Thomas, Jr. New Orleans, LA
McElvain, Carol K. ... Lisle, IL
McElvain, Mike ... Bloomington, IL
McElvain, Peter A. ... Chicago, IL
McElvain, Randy M. ... Los Angeles, CA
McElvaine, Bryan ... Philadelphia, PA
McElvane, Roxanne
Federal Communications Commission, International Bureau, GV
McElvaney, Deborah Heaton ... Houston, TX
McElvany, Jennifer M. ... San Francisco, CA
McElvany, Robert H. ... Arlington, VA
McElveen, Alvin L., Jr. ... Moncks Corner, SC
McElveen, G. Raymond, Jr. ... Columbia, SC
McElveen, George R., III ... Columbia, SC
McElveen, Joseph T., Jr. ... Sumter, SC
McElveen, Junius C., Jr. ... Washington, DC
McElveen & McElveen ... Columbia, SC
McElveen, William P., Jr. ... Columbia, SC
McElvein, Bruce B. ... Lexington, KY
McElvein, Denise Garrison ... Frankfort, KY
McElvein, Thomas I., Jr. ... Buffalo, NY
Mc Elvenny, Bruce R. ... Norwell, MA
McElvery, Richard M. ... Sudbury, MA
McElvy, Douglas ... Centreville, AL
Tuscaloosa, AL
McElvy & Ford, P.C. ... Centreville, AL
Tuscaloosa, AL
McElwain, Dennis M. ... Sioux City, IA
McElwain, Joseph A. ... Butte, MT
McElwain, Larry J. ... Charlottesville, VA
McElwain, Lester S. ... Castro Valley, CA
McElwain, Nancy E. ... Louisville, KY
McElwain, Warren ... Inverness, IL
McElwain, Warren L. ... Maysville, MO
McElwain, William G. ... Washington, DC
McElwaine, Felice Spatola West Chester, PA
McElwaine, James P., Jr. ... Greenbelt, MD
McElwaine, John Craig ... Columbia, SC
McElwee, Charles F. ... Harrisburg, PA
McElwee, Charles L. ... Albuquerque, NM
McElwee, Charles R. ... Charleston, WV
McElwee, Charles R., II ... Cleveland, OH
McElwee, Daniel Owen ... New York, NY
McElwee, Darcie N. ... Bangor, ME
McElwee, Dennis M. ... Houston, TX
McElwee, Donald L. ... Columbus, OH
McElwee, Douglas C. ... Charleston, WV
McElwee Firm, PLLC North Wilkesboro, NC
McElwee, James G., Jr. ... Phoenix, AZ
McElwee, John D. ... Caribou, ME
McElwee, Karen Inscore North Wilkesboro, NC
McElwee, Kenneth L. ... Short Hills, NJ
McElwee, L. A. ... Worthington, OH
McElwee, Michael S. ... Kalamazoo, MI
McElwee, Paul E. ... Milwaukee, WI
McElwee, Roma M. ... Oklahoma City, OK
McElwee, Stephen H. ... Athens, GA
McElwee, Therese R. ... Phoenix, AZ
McElwee, W. H., III North Wilkesboro, NC
McElya, Judith A. ... Houston, TX
McElya, Richard L. ... Angleton, TX
McElya, Richard L., P.C. ... Angleton, TX
McElyea, Charles E. ... Camdenton, MO
Osage Beach, MO
McElyea, James M. ... Downers Grove, IL
McElyea, John H. ... Maitland, FL
McElyea, John R. ... Chicago, IL
McElyea, Monica S. ... Frisco, CO
McElyea, Rienne H. ... Bozeman, MT
McElyea, Thomas E. ... Dallas, TX
McElyea, William D. ... New York, NY
McElyea, William R. ... Bozeman, MT
McEnally, Terence E., III ... Raleigh, NC
McEnaney, Francis A. ... San Francisco, CA
Mcenaney, James T. ... Smithtown, NY
McEnaney, Kelly A. ... Boston, MA
McEnaney, Kevin P. ... Houston, TX
Mcenaney, Thomas William ... Boston, MA
McEnanly, Bernard J., Jr. ... Grand Rapids, MI
Mceneaney, Janet ... New York, NY
McEneaney, Jennifer E. Walnut Creek, CA
McEneaney, Sean ... San Francisco, CA
McEnearney, Catherine J. ... Fairfax, VA
McEnelly, Kristen A. ... Braintree, MA
McEneney, Michael F. ... Washington, DC
McEneney, Michael F. ... Bronx, NY
McEneney, Victoria A. ... Washington, DC
McEnerney, Christina L. ... Los Angeles, CA
McEnerney, Michael T. ... Honolulu, HI
McEnerney, Thomas W. ... New York, NY
McEnery, C. J., Jr. ... Clayton, MO
McEnery, Cormac ... Bronx, NY
McEnery, Dennis J. ... New York, NY
McEnery, Gerard ... Bridgeport, CT
McEnery, Janet Goldberg ... Tampa, FL
McEnery, John E. ... Holmdel, NJ
McEnery, John F. ... Pittsburgh, PA
McEnery, Rosemary H. ... Washington, DC
McEniry, J. H., Jr. ... Bessemer, AL
McEniry, K. Lee ... Fayetteville, NC
McEniry, Matthew M. ... Des Moines, IA
McEniry, Murray W. ... Scarsdale, NY
McEniry, Thos R. ... Bessemer, AL
McEnroe, Carla M. ... Basking Ridge, NJ
McEnroe, Catherine A. ... Minneapolis, MN
McEnroe, Charles J. ... Somerset, KY
McEnroe, Diane C. ... New York, NY
McEnroe, Eugene F. ... Hazlet, NJ
McEnroe, Harry D. ... Florham Park, NJ
McEnroe, James J. ... New York, NY
McEnroe, John P. ... New York, NY
McEnroe, John T. ... Chicago, IL
McEnroe, Kathleen M. ... Commerce, CA
McEnroe, Mark T. ... New York, NY
McEnroe, McCarthy & Gotsdiner, P.C. Des Moines, IA
West Des Moines, IA
McEnroe, Megan E. ... Northbrook, IL
Mc Enroe, Michael A. ... Waterloo, IA
McEnroe, Michael L. West Des Moines, IA
McEnroe, William F. ... Hackensack, NJ
McEnrue, Michael A. ... Houston, TX
McEntarfer, James A. ... Tell City, IN
McEntee, Gary Thomas ... East Lansing, MI
McEntee, James J., III ... West Chester, PA
McEntee, Joan M. ... Washington, DC
McEntee, John P. ... Melville, NY
McEntee, John R. ... Flushing, NY
McEntee, Joseph L. ... Dallas, TX
McEntee, Martha E. ... New York, NY
McEntee, Matthew A. ... Houston, TX
McEntee, Michael J. ... Warwick, RI
McEntee, Michael R. ... Fort Wayne, IN
McEntee, Steve ... Lemont, IL
McEntee, Vera Marcus ... Oakland, CA
McEntire, Ann ... Arvada, CO
McEntire, James R. ... Topeka, KS
McEntire, J. M. ... Fort Worth, TX
McEntire, John B., III ... Park City, UT
McEntire, Michael J. ... Fort Worth, TX
McEntire, Mitchell M. ... Graham, NC
McEntire, Rex L. ... Fort Worth, TX
McEntire, Sawnie A. ... Houston, TX
McEntyre, Barbara R., Law Office of Corte Madera, CA
McEntyre, Barbara R., Law Office of San Rafael, CA
McEntyre, Joseph P. ... Plainfield, VT
McEntyre, Richard F. ... San Diego, CA
McEnulty, Ronald R. ... Wichita, KS
McEnulty, Sean C. ... Wichita, KS
McErlane, James E. ... West Chester, PA
McErlean, Carol A. ... Glencoe, IL
McErlean, Cathy A. ... Baltimore, MD
McErlean, Charles F., Jr. ... Chicago, IL
McErlean, Edward T. ... Media, PA
McErlean, Thomas P., Jr. ... Washington, DC
McErlean, William M. ... Chicago, IL
McEssey, Eugene ... Waupun, WI
McEttrick, Joseph P. ... Boston, MA
McEttrick, Marion V. ... Milton, MA
McEuen, Patrick B. ... Munster, IN
McEveny, Jack R. ... Omaha, NE
McEver, Mike ... Wagoner, OK
McEvers, David R. ... Leslie, MI
McEvers, Duff S. ... Newport Beach, CA
McEvers, Lisa K. ... Bismarck, ND
McEvilley, R. Michael ... Cincinnati, OH
McEvilly, Catherine M. ... Torrance, CA
McEvilly & Curley ... Leominster, MA
McEvilly, James P., III ... Philadelphia, PA
McEvilly, James P., Jr. ... Feasterville, PA
Lancaster, PA
McEvilly, Mark ... Carmichael, CA
McEvilly, Michael P. ... Leominster, MA
McEvilly, Robert ... Sacramento, CA
McEvilly, Thomas F. ... Leominster, MA
McEvilly, Walter P. ... Wilmington, DE
McEvilly, Walter P., Jr. ... Wilmington, DE
McEvily, Ann C. ... Armonk, NY
McEvily, Charles J. ... Garden City, NY
McEvily & Flowers ... Houston, TX
McEvily, Kevin J. ... Houston, TX
McEvily, Richard P. ... Park Ridge, NJ
McEvily, Stephanie ... Rockville Centre, NY
McEvily, Stephen P. ... Livingston, NJ
McEvoy, Andrew T., Jr. ... Albany, NY
McEvoy, Arthur ... Chicago, IL
McEvoy, Brian S. ... Baltimore, MD
McEvoy, Bruce ... Kalispell, MT
McEvoy, Carol G. ... New York, NY
McEvoy, Daniels, Darcy & Cheshire, P.C. Tucson, AZ
McEvoy, David A. ... Tucson, AZ
McEvoy, David L. ... Cambridge, MA
McEvoy, Dennis W. ... Hudson, NY
McEvoy, Douglas J. ... Birmingham, MI
McEvoy, Elizabeth C. ... Boston, MA
McEvoy, Gerald W. ... Blauvelt, NY
McEvoy, James F. ... Atlanta, GA
McEvoy, Jean C. ... Sacramento, CA
McEvoy, Jeffrey P. ... Frederick, MD
McEvoy, John E. ... Locust Valley, NY
McEvoy, John Patrick Santa Barbara, CA
McEvoy, John T. ... Washington, DC
McEvoy, John W. ... Belmont, MA
McEvoy, John W., Jr. ... Cambridge, MA
McEvoy, Josefina Fernandez Los Angeles, CA
McEvoy, Julia E. ... Washington, DC
McEvoy, Keith L. ... Muskegon, MI
McEvoy, Kenneth R. ... Ottawa, IL
McEvoy, Laurence J. ... San Jose, CA
McEvoy, Lawrence J., Jr. ... Atlanta, GA
McEvoy, Martha C. ... New York, NY
McEvoy, Maureen A. ... San Jose, CA
McEvoy & McEvoy ... Belmont, MA
McEvoy, Michael D. ... Santa Ana, CA
McEvoy, Michael J. ... Birmingham, MI
McEvoy, Michael R. ... Rochester, NY
Mc Evoy, Nion T. ... San Francisco, CA
McEvoy, Owen P. ... New York, NY
McEvoy, Patricia A. ... Hartford, CT
McEvoy, Patrick J. ... New York, NY
McEvoy, R. Sean ... Atlanta, GA
McEvoy, Rory J. ... New York, NY
McEvoy, Sharlene A. ... Derby, CT
McEvoy, Terrence E. ... Santa Ana, CA
McEvoy, Timothy J. ... Arlington, VA
McEwan, Andrew Scot ... Columbus, OH
McEwan, Bruce ... Orlando, FL
McEwan, Chris G. ... Bokeelia, FL
McEwan, Howard E. ... Sacramento, CA
McEwan, James A. ... Hampden, MA
McEwan, John J. ... Montvale, NJ
McEwan, John S., II ... Orlando, FL
McEwan, Kenneth S. ... Seattle, WA
McEwan, Leonard ... Story, WY
McEwan, Martinez, Luff, Dukes & Ruffier, P.A. ... Orlando, FL
McEwan, Robert S., Jr. ... Albany, NY
McEwan, Russell J. ... Roseland, NJ
New York, NY
McEwan, Shelley ... Sacramento, CA
McEwan, William H. ... Littleton, CO
McEwen, Carol Ann ... Scarsdale, NY
McEwen, Catherine Peek ... Tampa, FL
McEwen, Cathleen Anne ... Fort Collins, CO
McEwen, D. Neil ... Grove City, PA
McEwen, David B. ... St. Petersburg, FL
McEwen, David B., P.A. St. Petersburg, FL
McEwen, David R. ... Newport Beach, CA
McEwen, Dennis R. ... Pittsburgh, PA
McEwen, Donald W. ... Portland, OR
McEwen, Gisvold, Rankin, Carter & Streinz, LLP ... Portland, OR
McEwen, Homer E., Jr. ... Jonesboro, AR
McEwen, Jay W. ... Tucson, AZ
McEwen, Jean E. ... Newton, MA
McEwen, Kevin M. ... Union, NJ
McEwen, Lewis P. ... Grove City, PA
McEwen, Lillian A.
Securities and Exchange Commission, Office of Administrative Law Judges, GV
McEwen, Neil A. ... Thief River Falls, MN
McEwen, Paul C., Jr., Inc., A Professional Law Corp. ... San Diego, CA
McEwen, Randall H. ... Hutchinson, KS
McEwen, Robert C. ... Ogdensburg, NY
McEwen, Scott W. ... San Diego, CA
McEwen, Shannon O'Connell Newport News, VA
McEwen, Stephen J., Jr. ... Media, PA
McEwen, Steve ... Mountain City, TN
McEwen, Steven R. ... Columbus, MS
McEwen, Walter R., Jr.
Board of Governors Of The Federal Reserve System, Office of the General Counsel, GV
McEwen, Warren Martin, Jr. ... Orlando, FL
McEwen, Willard W., Jr. ... Santa Barbara, CA
McEwen, Willard W., Jr. ... Santa Barbara, CA
McEwen, William E. ... River Falls, WI
McEwing, David L. ... Houston, TX
McEwing, John R. ... St. Charles, IL
McFadden, Angus N. ... Birmingham, AL
McFadden, Anita Van ... Fairfax, VA
McFadden, Archibald G.W. ... Annapolis, MD
McFadden & Associates ... Palm Springs, CA
McFadden, Barry D. ... Canandaigua, NY
McFadden, Bernard J. ... Wilmington, DE
McFadden, Bradley J. ... West Covina, CA
McFadden, Brenda Lee ... West Chester, PA
McFadden, Candace R. ... Great Bend, KS
McFadden, Catherine M. Philadelphia, PA
McFadden, Christopher J. ... Decatur, GA
McFadden, Christopher J. ... Atlanta, GA
McFadden, Clark L. ... Livingston, NJ
McFadden, David R. ... San Francisco, CA
McFadden, David S. ... New Orleans, LA
McFadden & Dillon, A Professional Corporation ... Chicago, IL
McFadden, Donald D. ... Wilkes-Barre, PA
McFadden, Donald P. ... Cleveland, OH
McFadden, Douglas ... Belding, MI
McFadden, Douglas B. ... Washington, DC
McFadden, Edward A. ... Laguna Hills, CA
McFadden, Edward C. ... Tampa, FL
McFadden, Eric L. ... Chevy Chase, MD
McFadden, F. P. Kimberly ... Easton, PA
McFadden, Frank H. ... Montgomery, AL
McFadden, Frank Hampton, Jr. Birmingham, AL
McFadden, Gerald T. ... Solana Beach, CA
McFadden, Hallie Hochman Chattanooga, TN
McFadden, Howard L. ... Jefferson City, MO
McFadden, Hugh B., Jr. ... Laramie, WY
McFadden, James A., Jr. ... Naples, FL
McFadden, James F., Law Offices of San Francisco, CA
McFadden, Jamie Michael ... Allentown, PA
McFadden, Janet R. ... Washington, DC
McFadden, Jeffrey E. ... Washington, DC
McFadden, Jeffrey L. ... Houston, TX
McFadden, Jeffrey L., P.C. ... Houston, TX
McFadden, Jeffrey R. ... Greensboro, NC
McFadden, Jerome J. ... Princeton, WV
McFadden, John A. ... Carmichael, CA
McFadden, John C. ... Kansas City, KS
McFadden, John C. ... Media, PA
McFadden, John J. ... Boise, ID
McFadden, John J. ... Bryn Mawr, PA
McFadden, John J., Jr. ... Tucson, AZ
McFadden, Joseph R., Jr. ... Media, PA
McFadden, Joseph T., Jr. ... Norfolk, VA
McFadden, Kathleen M. ... Hartford, CT
McFadden, Kevin J. ... Springfield, IL
McFadden, Leona C. ... Mount Laurel, NJ
New York, NY
Philadelphia, PA
McFadden, Lisa R. ... Miami, FL
McFadden, Louis P. ... Atlantic City, NJ
McFadden, Louis P., Jr. ... Linwood, NJ
McFadden, Lyon & Rouse, L.L.C. Mobile, AL
McFadden, Marilyn M. ... Tallahassee, FL
McFadden, Mary J. ... Chicago, IL
McFadden, Mary Jane ... Columbus, OH
McFadden, Maureen S. San Francisco, CA
McFadden & McFadden ... South Bend, IN
McFadden, Michael F. ... Minneapolis, MN
McFadden, Michael K. ... Largo, FL
McFadden, Michael K. ... Camden, NJ
Linwood, NJ
McFadden, Michael von Leuchtenberg New York, NY
McFadden, Monte E. ... Sacramento, CA
McFadden, Nancy
Department of Transportation, Office of the General Counsel, GV
McFadden, Patrick M. ... Chicago, IL
McFadden, Patrick R. ... St. Maries, ID
McFadden, Patrick T. ... South Bend, IN
McFadden, Richard L. ... St. Maries, ID
McFadden, Robert E. ... Orlando, FL
McFadden, Robert J., Jr. ... Palm Springs, CA
McFadden, Robert L. ... Rock Hill, SC
McFadden, Roger J. ... Chicago, IL
McFadden, Roger R. ... Stockton, CA
McFadden, Samuel E. ... Pawleys Island, SC
McFadden, Sharon A. ... Chicago, IL
McFadden & Shoreman, P.C. Washington, DC
McFadden, Stova F. ... Mobile, AL
McFadden, Thomas J. ... Chicago, IL
McFadden, Timothy J. ... Issaquah, WA
McFadden, Timothy R. ... St. Louis, MO
McFadden, Vicki L. ... Austin, TX
McFadden, Victor L. ... South Bend, IN
McFadden, W. Clark, II ... Washington, DC
McFadden, Wayne A. ... San Mateo, CA
McFadden, William C., II
United States Senate, Committee Legal Personnel, GV
McFadden, William S. ... Mobile, AL
McFadden Winner and Savage Columbus, OH
McFadden-Elmore, Peggy
Department Of Health And Human Services, GV
McFaddin, Dwight E. ... Portland, OR
McFaddin, Edward C. ... Knoxville, TN
McFaddin, George M., Jr. ... Sumter, SC
McFaddin, Gustavus A. N. ... Beaumont, TX
McFaddin, Jane A. ... Charleston, SC
McFadin, Diane ... Brooklyn, NY
McFadin, Diane ... Brooklyn, NY
McFadin, Richard E. ... Gallatin, MO
McFadyen, Donald J. ... Fayetteville, NC
Mcfadyen, Douglas R. ... New York, NY
McFadyen, Duncan B., III ... Raeford, NC
McFadyen, F. M., (Mrs.) ... Anadarko, OK
McFadyen, Henry C., Jr. ... Dallas, TX
McFadyen, Jay D. ... Torrance, CA
McFadyen, John L. ... Morristown, TN
McFadyen, Mary E. "Beth" ... Little Rock, AR
McFadyen, Victoria A. ... Key West, FL
McFadyen, W. David, Jr. ... New Bern, NC
McFalda, Judy A. ... Rogers City, MI
McFall, Alan B. ... Bangor, PA
McFall, Allen R. ... Midland, TX
McFall, Brad J. ... Cedartown, GA
McFall, Bryant S. ... Dallas, TX
McFall, Burnett & Brinton ... Manteca, CA
McFall, D. Keith ... Oklahoma City, OK
McFall, Dennis ... Concordia, KS
McFall, Donald B. ... Houston, TX
McFall, Elizabeth A. ... Seattle, WA
McFall, George ... Southaven, MS
McFall, George R. ... Albuquerque, NM
McFall, James A. ... San Diego, CA
McFall, Jeffrey S. ... Fort Worth, TX
McFall, John E. ... Dallas, TX
McFall, John J. ... Manteca, CA
McFall, John R. ... Lubbock, TX
McFall, Leland V. ... Clintwood, VA
McFall, Leslie E. ... Birmingham, AL
McFall, Lisa G. ... Palo Alto, CA
McFall, Mark W. ... Naples, FL
McFall, Martha Louise ... Oklahoma City, OK
McFall, Michael M. ... Fort Lauderdale, FL
McFall, Patricia M. ... St. Louis, MO
McFall, Ronald D. ... Minneapolis, MN
Mcfall, Sara W. ... Norman, OK
McFall, Scott B. ... Los Angeles, CA
McFall, Sherwood & Sheehy, A Professional Corporation ... Houston, TX
McFalls, Maureen D. ... Pittsburgh, PA

McFalls, Michael S. Federal Trade Commission, Office of the Chairman, GV
McFalls, Patrick .... Pittsburgh, PA
McFalone, Raymond B. .... Pleasanton, CA
McFann & Beavers, P.A. Fort Lauderdale, FL
McFann, Robert J. .... Fort Lauderdale, FL
McFarlain, Richard C. .... Tallahassee, FL
McFarlain, Wiley, Cassedy & Jones, Professional Association .... Tallahassee, FL
McFarlan, Kenneth S., Jr. .... San Rafael, CA
McFarland, A. Keith .... Spring, TX
McFarland, Andrew J. .... Washington, DC
McFarland, Anne S. .... Akron, OH
McFarland, Anthony J. .... Nashville, TN
McFarland, Arthur C. .... Charleston, SC
McFarland, Barbara A. .... Cincinnati, OH
McFarland, Barbara P. .... Beaverton, OR
McFarland, Brian V. .... Catonsville, MD
McFarland, Burns H. .... Jackson, MS
McFarland, C. Victor .... Catonsville, MD
McFarland, Carl C. .... Norman, OK
McFarland, Carol Anne .... Oregon City, OR
McFarland, Cestjon L. .... Seattle, WA
McFarland, Charles B. .... Houston, TX
McFarland, Clifton J. .... Los Angeles, CA
McFarland, D. Mitchell .... Houston, TX
McFarland, David A. .... Dallas, TX
McFarland, David Christopher Adrian, MI
McFarland, Deborah N. .... New York, NY
McFarland, Dennis C. .... Sioux Falls, SD
McFarland, Donald O. .... Clearwater, FL
McFarland, Donald W. .... Salyersville, KY
McFarland, Doug .... Venice, CA
McFarland, Douglas D. .... St. Paul, MN
McFarland, Dylan J. .... Minneapolis, MN
McFarland, Edward A. .... Pittsburgh, PA
McFarland, Edward T. .... Lufkin, TX
McFarland, Elizabeth A. .... Washington, DC
McFarland, Eric A. .... Washington, DC
McFarland, George C., Jr. .... Norristown, PA
McFarland, Gould, Lyons & Sullivan, P.A. Clearwater, FL
McFarland, Grant T. .... San Antonio, TX
McFarland, Henry B. .... Jersey City, NJ
McFarland & Herman .... Chicago, IL
Mc Farland, J. Drew .... Granville, OH
McFarland, James D. .... San Diego, CA
McFarland, James E. .... Concord, CA
McFarland, James H. .... Helena, MT
McFarland, James L. .... Milwaukee, WI
McFarland, James T. .... Kenmore, NY
McFarland, James W. .... Phoenix, AZ
McFarland, Jeffrey D. .... Los Angeles, CA
McFarland, Jeffrey M. .... Jacksonville, FL
McFarland, John A. .... Columbia, MD
McFarland, John B. .... Austin, TX
McFarland, John H. .... Houston, TX
McFarland, John M. .... Kansas City, MO
McFarland, Johnny R. .... Memphis, TN
McFarland, Joseph B., P.A. .... Tampa, FL
McFarland, Joseph D. .... St. Petersburg, FL
Tampa, FL
McFarland, Joseph D., P.A. St. Petersburg, FL
McFarland, Kay .... Topeka, KS
McFarland, Larry W. .... Beverly Hills, CA
McFarland, Laura D. .... Alexandria, VA
McFarland, Leighton W., III Fayetteville, NC
McFarland, M. Gabriel .... Denver, CO
McFarland, Margaret H. Securities and Exchange Commission, Executive Staff, GV
McFarland, Mark E. .... Garden City, KS
McFarland & Masters .... Catonsville, MD
McFarland & McFarland .... Tryon, NC
McFarland, Mel A. .... Oklahoma City, OK
McFarland, Michael .... Adrian, MI
McFarland, Michael B. .... Coeur d'Alene, ID
McFarland, Michael E., Jr. .... Spokane, WA
McFarland, Pamela J. .... Fresno, CA
McFarland, Patricia J. .... Des Moines, IA
McFarland, Patrick Arthur .... Merrillville, IN
McFarland, Patrick E. .... Marietta, OH
McFarland, Patrick L. .... Sacramento, CA
McFarland, Philip J. .... Lynnfield, MA
McFarland, Regena R. .... San Antonio, TX
McFarland, Richard Weldon .... Tyler, TX
McFarland, Robert .... Arlington, TX
McFarland, Robert A. .... Santa Barbara, CA
McFarland, Robert A. .... Towson, MD
McFarland, Robert B. .... Camden, NJ
McFarland, Robert E. Farmington Hills, MI
McFarland, Robert P. .... Arcadia, MI
McFarland, Robert W. .... Norfolk, VA
McFarland, Sandra .... Austin, TX
McFarland, Scott E. .... Des Moines, IA
McFarland, Scotta E. .... Washington, DC
McFarland, Shannon R. .... Fresno, CA
McFarland, Sheila .... Chicago, IL
McFarland, Stanley A. .... Warren, MI
McFarland, Steven T. .... Annandale, VA
McFarland, Terri A. .... Sacramento, CA
McFarland, Theresa I. .... Los Angeles, CA
San Francisco, CA
McFarland, Thomas Bruce McDonough, GA
McFarland, Thomas D. .... Golden, CO
McFarland, Thomas F., Jr. .... Chicago, IL
McFarland, Timothy V. .... San Diego, CA
McFarland, Tina R. .... Henderson, KY
McFarland, Tom .... Kingston, TN
McFarland, Van, & Associates Houston, TX
McFarland, Wayne W., Jr. .... Morris, IL
McFarland & Weidenaar .... Sioux Falls, SD
McFarland, William A., Jr. .... Tryon, NC
McFarland, William D. .... Carefree, AZ
McFarland, William D. .... Coeur d'Alene, ID
McFarland, Wm. A. .... Tryon, NC
McFarland-Butler, Connie .... St. Louis, MO
McFarlane, Amy A. .... Anchorage, AK
McFarlane, Audrey G. .... Washington, DC
McFarlane, David E. .... Madison, WI
Sauk City, WI
McFarlane, Joe R., Jr. .... San Antonio, TX
McFarlane, John B. .... Oklahoma City, OK
McFarlane, Lauren L. .... Chicago, IL
McFarlane, Michael T. .... Fairfax, VA
McFarlane, Molly E. .... Grand Rapids, MI
McFarlane, Norman E., Jr. North Bellmore, NY
McFarlane, Paul D. .... Seattle, WA
McFarlane, Randall H. .... Washington, DC
McFarlane, Richard A. .... Orange, CA
McFarlane, Robert A. .... San Francisco, CA
McFarlane, Robert E. .... Anchorage, AK
McFarlane, Robert E., Jr. .... Kearney, MO
McFarlane, Sarah L. .... Chillicothe, OH
McFarlane, Stephen J. .... Phoenix, AZ
Mcfarlane, Steven H. .... Louisburg, NC
McFarlane, Theodore H. .... Lawrence, KS
McFarlane, Walter A. .... Richmond, VA
McFarlane, William D., Jr. West Palm Beach, FL
McFarlane, William J., III Fort Lauderdale, FL
McFarlane-Howard, Patricia Oak Brook, IL
McFarlen, Gerald D. .... San Antonio, TX
McFarlin & Anderson .... Lake Forest, CA
McFarlin, Ben H., Jr. .... Murfreesboro, TN
McFarlin, David R. .... Orlando, FL
McFarlin, George W. .... Lake Forest, CA
McFarlin, Janie Willbanks Little Rock, AR
McFarlin, Michael R. .... Pottstown, PA
McFarlin, Monica M. .... Lexington, KY
McFarlin, Patricia A. .... New York, NY
McFarlin, Sean .... Omaha, NE
McFarlin, Sheryl D. .... Tyler, TX
McFarlin, Susan J. .... Springfield, MA
McFarlin, Wm. F. .... Lake Forest, IL
McFarlin, Wynne Ellen .... Orlando, FL
McFarlind, Susie M. .... St. Louis, MO
McFarling, Muriel C. .... Dallas, TX
McFarling, Tom I. .... Austin, TX
McFarquhar, Erica .... Washington, DC
McFarquhar, Joan L. .... Mount Vernon, NY
McFarren, Gerald W. .... Kennett Square, PA
McFarren, John C. .... Austin, TX
McFarren, Todd D. .... Watsonville, CA
McFarron, Gary W. .... Chicago, IL
McFate, John E. .... Oil City, PA
McFate, McFate & McFate .... Oil City, PA
McFate, Robert W. .... Oil City, PA
McFate, Stephen P. .... Philadelphia, PA
McFate, William J. .... Oil City, PA
McFate, Yale .... Phoenix, AZ
McFatridge, Carolyn .... Dallas, TX
McFatridge, Keith W., Jr. .... Galveston, TX
League City, TX
McFatter, Herbert L., Jr. .... Tallahassee, FL
McFatter, Huey K. .... Lake Charles, LA
McFatter, Melvin H. .... Port Gibson, MS
McFatter, William D. .... Dothan, AL
McFaul, Charles D. .... New York, NY
McFaul, Duston K. .... Houston, TX
McFaul & Eisenhart .... Portland, ME
McFaul, James M. .... Carpinteria, CA
McFaul, John M. .... Mineola, NY
McFaul, Joseph R. .... Orange, CA
McFaul, Paula House .... Portland, ME
McFawn, Marili .... Palatine, IL
Mcfayden, Mary Elizabeth .... Little Rock, AR
McFeaters, Laura R. .... Los Angeles, CA
McFee, Linda C. .... Kansas City, MO
McFee, Robert D. .... Battle Creek, MI
McFee, Shannon H. .... Naples, FL
McFee, Susan N. .... Chicago, IL
McFee, William C., Jr. .... Decatur, GA
McFeeley, John, III .... Westmont, NJ
McFeeley, Mark B. .... Albuquerque, NM
McFeeley, Neil D. .... Boise, ID
McFeely, Brendan P. .... New York, NY
McFeely, Dennis D. .... Seattle, WA
McFeely, John R. .... New York, NY
McFeely, Joseph B. .... North Bergen, NJ
McFeely, Stephen A. .... Oakland, CA
McFeeters, John D., Jr. .... Glendale, CA
McFerren, Daphene R. Department of Justice, Civil Division, GV
McFerren and Fair .... Davenport, IA
Durant, IA
McFerren, J. David .... Davenport, IA
McFerren, Michael .... Detroit, MI
McFerrin, H. Edward .... Greenville, AL
McFerrin, James H. .... Homewood, AL
McFerrin, Lindsay K. .... Kansas City, MO
McFerrin, Philip N. .... Joliet, IL
McFerrin-Clancy, John J.D. New York, NY
McFerron, Jeana D. .... St. Louis, MO
McFetridge, James E. .... Sacramento, CA
McFetridge, Jane M. .... Chicago, IL
McFetridge, John D. .... Danville, IL
McField, Terri L. .... Washington, DC
McFlynn Pickett & Whitsitt, P.C. Aspen, CO
Carbondale, CO
Snowmass Village, CO
McFlynn, Timothy .... Aspen, CO
Snowmass Village, CO
McFrederick, Sam .... Miami Shores, FL
McGaan, Andrew R. .... Chicago, IL
McGaffey, Frederick C. .... New York, NY
McGaffey, J. A. .... Austin, TX
McGaffey, Jere D. .... Milwaukee, WI
McGaffey, Karen M. .... Seattle, WA
McGaffick, Gail Toraason .... Olympia, WA
McGaffick, Jeffrey M. .... Cleveland, OH
McGaffick, Timothy D. .... Columbus, OH
McGah, Edward R. .... Hillside, IL
McGah, Edward R., Jr. .... Los Angeles, CA
McGah, Joseph P., Jr. .... Hillside, IL
McGaha, Fred R. .... Monroe, LA
McGaha, Lesa Henderson .... Ruston, LA
McGaha, William W. .... Las Vegas, NV
McGahan, Charles A., Jr. .... Sutter Creek, CA
McGahan, Elizabeth A. .... Ardsley, NY
McGahan, James F. .... Ventura, CA
McGahan, James M. .... Jericho, NY
McGahan, Michael F. .... New York, NY
McGahan, Michael T. .... Attleboro, MA
McGahan, Robert J. .... Los Angeles, CA
McGahan, Theresa .... Grand Island, NE
McGahan, Timothy J. .... Attleboro, MA
McGahan, William J. .... Brisbane, CA
McGahan-Supple, Maureen .... Boston, MA
McGahee, Marvin W. .... Savannah, GA
McGahee, Pamela A. .... Martinez, GA
McGahee, Sharon K. .... New York, NY
McGahen, P. Kay .... Trenton, NJ
McGahey, Harry V., Jr. .... San Diego, CA
McGahey, Harry V., Jr., A P.C. San Diego, CA
McGahey, John P. .... Chicago, IL
McGahey, Philip C. .... Arlington, TX
McGahey, Philip C., P.C. .... Arlington, TX
McGahey, Robert L., Jr. .... Englewood, CO
McGahey, Shawn A. .... Los Angeles, CA
McGahn, Donald F., II .... Washington, DC
McGahn, Friss, Franks & Tripician Atlantic City, NJ
Longport, NJ
Northfield, NJ
McGahn, Patrick T., Jr. .... Atlantic City, NJ
Longport, NJ
McGahren, Eugene D., Jr. .... Yonkers, NY
McGahren, John .... Newark, NJ
McGahren, Matthew F. .... Norcross, GA
McGahren, Richard G. .... New York, NY
McGahren, Thomas J. .... New York, NY
McGair, James J. .... Providence, RI
McGair, Kenneth A. .... Portland, OR
McGair, Marilyn F. .... Portsmouth, NH
Mcgair, Marion J .... Cranston, RI
McGair and McGair .... Providence, RI
McGair, William J. .... Providence, RI
McGalliard & Brady .... Gainesville, FL
McGalliard, Rodney D. .... Gainesville, FL
McGann, Anita R. .... Arvada, CO
McGann, Bartlett & Brown .... Vernon, CT
McGann, Bryant C. .... Norfolk, VA
McGann, Curtis .... Southbury, CT
McGann, Diane M. .... St. Paul, MN
McGann, James J. .... Ocean Grove, NJ
McGann, Jeanne .... Department of the Navy, Office of the Judge Advocate General, GV
McGann, John L. .... Fairfax, VA
McGann, John P. .... Boston, MA
McGann, John P., Jr. .... Boston, MA
McGann, Kathleen .... Washington, DC
McGann, Kathleen M. .... New York, NY
McGann, Kevin D. .... Arlington, MA
McGann, Kevin X. .... New York, NY
McGann, Margaret Niver Salt Lake City, UT
McGann, Mark K. .... San Francisco, CA
McGann, Martin A., Jr. .... Red Bank, NJ
McGann, Michael E. .... Eatontown, NJ
McGann, Patrick J., Jr. .... Freehold, NJ
McGann, Regis E. .... Cleveland, OH
McGann, Robert D. .... Vernon, CT
McGann, Terrance B. .... Chicago, IL
McGann, Terrence J. .... College Park, MD
McGann, Thomas J., Jr. .... Mineola, NY
McGann, Timothy J. .... Atlanta, GA
McGann, W. Thomas .... Moorestown, NJ
McGann, William J. .... Lemont, IL
McGanney, Thomas .... New York, NY
McGannon, Christian M. .... Mineola, NY
McGannon, James J. .... Wichita, KS
McGannon, John L. .... Palo Alto, CA
McGannon, Mark J. .... Las Vegas, NV
McGannon, P. Casey .... Los Angeles, CA
McGannon, R. Eugene .... Kansas City, MO
McGannon, Susan Emery .... Murfreesboro, TN
McGann-Ryan, Maureen J. .... Chicago, IL
McGaraghan, Patrick J. .... Palo Alto, CA
McGarey, Jennifer C. .... Annandale, VA
McGargill, Jennifer A. .... Las Vegas, NV
McGarity & Associates .... Atlanta, GA
Gainesville, GA
Lawrenceville, GA
McGarity, Edward E. .... McDonough, GA
McGarity, J. Michael .... Lawrenceville, GA
McGarity, Margaret Dee .... Milwaukee, WI
McGarr, Cristina B. .... Austin, TX
McGarr, Frank J. .... Chicago, IL
McGarr, John G., Jr. .... Boerne, TX
McGarr, Marcus K. .... Greenville, SC
McGarr, Marcus K., P.A. .... Greenville, SC
McGarr, Maureen A. .... Arlington Heights, IL
McGarr, William G. .... Chicago, IL
McGarrah & Davenport .... Birmingham, AL
McGarrah, Donald R. .... Chicago, IL
McGarrah, Douglas M. .... Boston, MA
McGarrah, James R. .... Cambridge, MA
McGarrah, Robert E., Jr. .... Washington, DC
McGarrah, W. Scott, III .... Birmingham, AL
McGarrahan, John G. .... Cotuit, MA
McGarrell, Robert K. .... Boston, MA
McGarrell, Thomas P. .... Palm Bay, FL
McGarrh, James R., Jr. .... Memphis, TN
McGarrigle, Patrick C. .... Los Angeles, CA
McGarrigle, Philip L., Jr. Santa Clara, CA
McGarrigle, Thomas J. .... Philadelphia, PA
McGarrity, Edward J. .... Linthicum, MD
McGarrity, John P. .... Chicago, IL
McGarrity, Steven J. .... Canton, OH
McGarrity, Thomas .... White Plains, NY
McGarry, Alexander B. Bloomfield Hills, MI
McGarry, Amy L. .... Wadsworth, OH
McGarry, Ann .... Rye Brook, NY
McGarry, Annette M. .... Chicago, IL
McGarry, Arthur D. .... Seattle, WA
McGarry, Beth .... San Francisco, CA
McGarry, Brian C. .... Hope, NJ
McGarry, Brian P. .... Marion, IL
McGarry, Charles W. .... Dallas, TX
McGarry, Christopher M. Hackensack, NJ
McGarry, Daniel J. .... Minneapolis, MN
McGarry, Eugene .... Garden City, NY
McGarry, F. Joseph .... Denver, CO
McGarry, Francis P. .... Buffalo, NY
McGarry, H. Patrick, Sr. .... Los Angeles, CA
McGarry, J. Michael, III .... Washington, DC
McGarry, James .... New York, NY
McGarry, James J. .... Gardena, CA
McGarry, James J. .... Cleveland, OH
McGarry, James M. .... Ruby, NY
McGarry, James P. .... New York, NY
McGarry, James R. .... Martinsville, VA
Stuart, VA
McGarry, James W. .... Boston, MA
McGarry, Jennifer E. .... Arlington, VA
McGarry, John A. .... Waterford, CT
McGarry, John A., & Associates, P.C. Waterford, CT
McGarry, John E. .... Grand Rapids, MI
McGarry, John F. .... North Andover, MA
McGarry, John J. .... Joliet, IL
McGarry, John J., Jr. .... Glendale, CA
McGarry, John M. .... Chicago, IL
McGarry, John T. .... Chicago, IL
McGarry, John W. Federal Election Commission, Offices of the Commissioners, GV
McGarry, Joseph B. .... Sioux City, IA
McGarry, Joseph E. .... Phoenix, AZ
McGarry, Julieann .... Bozeman, MT
McGarry, Kathleen A. .... Columbus, OH
McGarry & Laufenberg .... Gardena, CA
Los Angeles, CA
Mc Garry, M. Eileen .... Los Angeles, CA
McGarry, Maria R. .... Philadelphia, PA
McGarry, Mark R. .... Clearwater, FL
McGarry, Mark R., Jr. .... St. Petersburg, FL
McGarry, Martha E. .... New York, NY
McGarry, Mary Elizabeth .... New York, NY
McGarry & McGarry .... Denver, CO
McGarry, Michael J. .... Port Charlotte, FL
McGarry, Michael S. .... New York, NY
McGarry, Michael T. .... Albany, NY
McGarry, Patricia A. .... St. Louis, MO
McGarry, Prince, McGarry, P.C. New London, CT
Old Lyme, CT
McGarry, Raymond .... Philadelphia, PA
McGarry, Robert E. .... Roseville, MN
McGarry, Robert E. .... St. Paul, MN
McGarry, Robert J. .... Providence, RI
McGarry, Shawn .... Salt Lake City, UT
McGarry, Sheridan L. .... Salt Lake City, UT
McGarry & Simon .... New York, NY
McGarry, Thomas F. .... New London, CT
McGarry, Thomas G. .... Washington, DC
McGarry, Thomas H. .... Denver, CO
McGarry, Thomas P. .... Chicago, IL
McGarry, Timothy J. .... Las Vegas, NV
McGarry, Timothy L. .... Cleveland, OH
McGarry, Timothy S. .... Seattle, WA
McGarry, William L., Jr. .... Syracuse, NY
McGartland, Michael P. .... Fort Worth, TX
McGarty, Patricia M. .... San Jose, CA
McGarvey, Allan M. .... Kalispell, MT
McGarvey, Casey K. .... Salt Lake City, UT
McGarvey, Charles A. .... Lake Success, NY
McGarvey, Dale L. .... Kalispell, MT
McGarvey, Diane R. .... North Andover, MA
McGarvey, Eugene J., Jr. .... Kokomo, IN
McGarvey, Genevieve Bacak Galveston, TX
McGarvey, Heberling, Sullivan & McGarvey, P.C. .... Kalispell, MT
McGarvey, Howard M., Jr. .... Exton, PA
McGarvey, Jack F. .... Owings Mills, MD
McGarvey, John F. .... Richmond, VA
McGarvey, John T. .... Lexington, KY
Louisville, KY
McGarvey, Paul J. .... Hyattsville, MD
McGarvey, William R. .... Dallas, TX
McGary, John A. .... Seattle, WA
McGary, Thomas H. .... Springfield, IL
McGaugh, James E. .... Boston, MA
McGaugh, Katherine M. .... Boston, MA
McGaugh, Kathleen J. .... Spokane, WA
McGaugh, Raymond S. .... Chicago, IL
McGaugh, Wm. Perry .... Jackson, MS
McGaughan, Brian J. .... Exton, PA
McGaughey, Ann-Marie M. .... Atlanta, GA
McGaughey, Frank S., III .... Atlanta, GA

McGaughey, George L., Jr. Cleveland, OH
McGaughey, Guy E., Jr. ....Lawrenceville, IL
McGaughey, James D. ....Hartford, CT
McGaughey, Lawrence H. ....New York, NY
McGaughey, M. Shaun ....Omaha, NE
McGaughey & McGaughey
Lawrenceville, IL
McGaughey, Michael J. ....Los Angeles, CA
McGaughey, Richard "Stoney"
Crawfordsville, IN
McGaughey, Robert J. ....Portland, OR
McGaughey, Shellie R. ....Bellevue, WA
McGaughey & Spirito ....Los Angeles, CA
Torrance, CA
McGaughey, Terence C. ....Torrance, CA
McGaughey, Terri Toth ....Raleigh, NC
McGaughey, Timothy J. ....Atlanta, GA
McGaughran, Michael ....Dallas, TX
McGaughran, Seth B. ....Orlando, FL
McGaughy, Sheri Gates ....Atlanta, GA
McGauley, Jennifer M. ....Vista, CA
McGavic, Derrick E. ....Eugene, OR
McGavick Graves, P.S. ....Tacoma, WA
McGavin, Annemarie ....Alexandria, VA
McGavin, Frederick G. ....Reading, PA
McGavin, Jeanne M. ....Hillsdale, NJ
McGavin, John D. ....Fairfax, VA
McGavin, Kim H. ....Towson, MD
McGavin, Kim H., P.C., Law Office of
Towson, MD
McGavin, Linda Peele ....Great Falls, VA
McGavin, Thomas A., Jr. ....New York, NY
McGavock, Richard M. ....Salem, OR
McGavran, Frank J.
Department of the Navy, GV
McGavran, Frederick J. ....Cincinnati, OH
McGavran, Jacqueline A. ....Urbana, IL
McGaw, D. Douglas ....Troy, MI
McGaw, John Scott ....Madisonville, KY
McGaw, K. Allison ....Seattle, WA
McGaw, Kenneth A., Jr. ....Houston, TX
McGaw, Peter W. ....Walnut Creek, CA
McGaw, Robert E. ....Cambridge, MA
McGaw, Ronald J. ....Poughkeepsie, NY
McGaw, Susan D. ....Jericho, NY
McGaw, Thomas ....New York, NY
McGaw, Wayne T. ....New Orleans, LA
McGeachy and Hudson ....Fayetteville, NC
McGeachy, N. Hector, Jr. ....Fayetteville, NC
McGeachy, Samuel P. ....San Francisco, CA
McGeady, M. Eamonn ....Baltimore, MD
McGeady, MaryAnn M. ....Denver, CO
McGeady, Paul J. ....New York, NY
McGeady, Richard H. ....Stamford, CT
McGeady, Roy F. ....Rochelle Park, NJ
McGeady Sisneros, P.C. ....Denver, CO
McGeady, Thomas J. ....Grove, OK
Vinita, OK
McGeagh, M. Tracy ....Los Angeles, CA
McGeary, Elizabeth Anne
Washington, DC
McGeary, Hunter A., Jr. ....Pittsburgh, PA
Wheeling, WV
McGeary, James E. ....Egg Harbor City, NJ
McGeary, Jeffrey O. ....Wheeling, WV
McGeary, Judith I. ....Austin, TX
McGeary, Raymond A. ....Carlisle, PA
McGeary, Robert P. ....Westfield, NJ
McGeary, Vincent E. ....Newark, NJ
McGeary, W. Scott ....Arlington, VA
McGee, Aaron Frank ....Opelousas, LA
McGee, Albert F., Jr. ....Atlantic City, NJ
McGee, Andrew B. ....Staten Island, NY
McGee, Ann ....Bloomington, MN
McGee, Ann, P.A. ....Bloomington, MN
McGee, Anne Maxwell ....Huntington, WV
McGee, Arthur J. ....Manhasset, NY
McGee & Associates ....Newport Beach, CA
Rancho Mirage, CA
McGee, Becky ....Dallas, TX
McGee, Bernard J. ....Rochester, NY
McGee, Bobby A. ....Linden, TN
McGee, Bobby R. ....Knoxville, TN
McGee & Bogen ....Greenville, MS
Leland, MS
McGee, Brant G. ....Anchorage, AK
McGee, Brendan Casey ....New York, NY
McGee, Brian E. ....Denver, CO
McGee, Bruce W. ....Fort Worth, TX
McGee, Burrell O. ....Leland, MS
McGee, C. Edward, Jr. ....Fort Lauderdale, FL
McGee, C. Stanley ....Boston, MA
McGee, C. William ....Greenville, SC
McGee, Carma Dennis ....Savannah, TN
McGee, Carol ....Washington, DC
McGee, Catherine Thomas ....High Point, NC
McGee, Charles A., Law Offices of
Fort Payne, AL
McGee, Charles M. ....Reno, NV
McGee, Christopher T. ....Richmond, VA
McGee, Daniel ....State College, PA
McGee, Daniel J. ....Wallace, ID
McGee, Daniel J. ....Mamou, LA
McGee, Daniel M. ....Los Angeles, CA
McGee, David A. ....Chardon, OH
McGee, David Howell ....Morganton, NC
McGee, David J. ....Minneapolis, MN
McGee, David L. ....Pensacola, FL
McGee, David L. ....Corpus Christi, TX
McGee, David L., Law Offices of, P.C.
Corpus Christi, TX
McGee, Delwin T. ....Dumas, TX
McGee, Denis T. ....Jericho, NY
McGee, Donald C. ....Mansfield, OH
McGee, Douglas P. ....Richmond, VA
McGee, Edward H. ....Allentown, PA
McGee, Elisabeth M. ....Little Rock, AR
McGee, Emmett F., Jr. ....Baltimore, MD
McGee, Erwin ....Austin, TX
McGee, Francis P. ....Butte, MT
McGee, Frank J. ....Marshfield, MA
McGee, Gainey & Huskey, P.A.
Fort Lauderdale, FL
McGee, Gary C. ....Charlottesville, VA
McGee & Gelman ....Buffalo, NY
McGee, Gerry W. ....Eureka, CA
McGee, Glen M. ....Glenwood, IA
McGee, Glenburn M.
Hilton Head Island, SC
McGee, H. Bartlett, Jr. ....Glens Falls, NY
McGee, Hankla, Backes & Dobrovolny, P.C.
Minot, ND
McGee, HeidiC. ....Bridgeport, CT
McGee, Helene K.
Securities and Exchange Commission,
Office of Compliance Inspections and
Examinations, GV
McGee, Henry L., Jr. ....Tyler, TX
McGee, Henry W., Jr. ....Tacoma, WA
McGee, Hommel & Starr, A Professional Corporation ....Tyler, TX
McGee, Hugh E., Jr. ....Houston, TX
McGee, Hugh P., Jr. ....Hartford, CT
McGee, J. Baker, Jr. ....Waycross, GA
McGee, James A. ....St. Petersburg, FL
McGee, James B., III ....Viera, FL
McGee, James B., III ....Waycross, GA
McGee, James F. ....Newport Beach, CA
Rancho Mirage, CA
McGee, James G., III ....Florence, SC
McGee, James H. ....Dayton, OH
McGee, James M. ....Atlanta, GA
McGee, James M. ....Dallas, TX
McGee, Janet E. ....Gloucester Pt., VA
McGee, John F. ....Wichita, KS
McGee, John L. ....Hammond, LA
McGee, John P. ....Millburn, NJ
McGee, John P. ....Hamburg, NY
McGee, John P., Jr. ....Portsmouth, NH
McGee, Jonathon L. ....Columbus, OH
McGee, Joseph A. ....Florence, KY
McGee, Joseph H. ....Charleston, SC
McGee, Joseph L. ....Seattle, WA
McGee, Joyce A. ....Washington, DC
McGee, Karen Fisher ....Staten Island, NY
McGee, Kevin C. ....Worcester, MA
McGee, Kevin J. ....Ventura, CA
McGee, Kevin John ....Millburn, NJ
McGee, L. Frank ....Miami Shores, FL
McGee Law Office ....Smithland, KY
McGee Law Offices, P.C. ....Clinton, IA
McGee, Lawrence U. ....Winston-Salem, NC
McGee, Leland S. ....Trenton, NJ
McGee, Leonard F., Jr. ....Glenview, IL
McGee, Linda Mace ....Boone, NC
McGee, Lonnie G. ....San Diego, CA
McGee, M. Gavin ....Houston, TX
McGee, Margaret C. ....Spartanburg, SC
McGee, Margaret H. ....Albany, CA
McGee, Martin B. ....Kannapolis, NC
McGee, Mary C. ....Lynn, MA
McGee, Mary Paxman ....Sandy, UT
McGee, Marybeth ....Department of Justice,
Antitrust Division, GV
McGee & Mason, P.A. ....Brooksville, FL
Spring Hill, FL
McGee, Maureen P. ....San Francisco, CA
McGee and McGee ....Waycross, GA
McGee, Melinda J. ....Whittier, CA
McGee, Melissa Arnold ....Orlando, FL
McGee, Michael G. ....Chicago, IL
McGee, Michael H. ....Charlotte, NC
McGee, Michael J. ....Chicago, IL
McGee, Michael P. ....Detroit, MI
McGee, Michael R. ....Buffalo, NY
McGee, O. Ronald ....Ponca City, OK
McGee, Otis, Jr. ....San Francisco, CA
McGee & Oxford ....Atlanta, GA
Jasper, GA
McGee, P. Joseph ....Atlanta, GA
McGee, P. Scott ....Norwich, VT
McGee, Palmer S., Jr. ....Hartford, CT
McGee, Park ....Olathe, KS
McGee, Park, Chartered ....Olathe, KS
McGee, Patricia ....Wilmington, DE
McGee, Patrick A. ....Orlando, FL
McGee, Patrick E. ....New York, NY
McGee, Paul H. ....Berkeley, CA
McGee, Peter ....Washington, DC
McGee, Peter M. ....Portland, ME
McGee & Powers, P.A. ....Orlando, FL
McGee, Preston W. ....Tyler, TX
McGee, Ramon ....Louisville, KY
McGee, Ramona L. ....Department of Justice,
Immigration and Naturalization Service, GV
McGee, Randall E. ....St. Matthews, SC
McGee, Rebecca Schmuck ....Houston, TX
McGee, Richard ....Nashville, TN
McGee, Richard E., Sr. ....Brooksville, FL
Spring Hill, FL
McGee, Richard G. ....Minneapolis, MN
McGee, Richard H., II ....Minot, ND
McGee, Richard Kelly ....Houston, TX
McGee, Robert J. ....Clinton, IA
McGee, Robert J. ....Boston, MA
McGee, Robert L., Jr. ....Denver, CO
McGee, Robert L., Jr. ....Dallas, TX
Mcgee, Robert William ....Dumont, NJ
McGee, Robt. P., (P.C.) ....Butte, MT
McGee, Sandra K. ....Phoenix, AZ
McGee, Sarah Perry ....Smithland, KY
McGee & Schiavoni ....Lynn, MA
McGee, Shane ....Columbus, OH
McLean, VA
McGee, Stanley G. ....Angleton, TX
McGee, Stephen J. ....Vernon, NJ
McGee, Stephen P., Law Office of
San Anselmo, CA
McGee, Steven D. ....Fresno, CA
McGee, Susan Mary ....Livingston, NJ
New York, NY
McGee, Suzanne ....Arnold, MD
McGee, Tekedra V. ....Washington, DC
McGee, Terence K. ....Seattle, WA
McGee, Teresa V. ....Tampa, FL
McGee, Thomas William, III
Columbia, SC
Mcgee, Thomas William, Jr. ....Merced, CA
McGee, Thos. P. ....River Ridge, LA
McGee, Timothy W. ....Worcester, MA
McGee, W. Farris ....Flagler Beach, FL
McGee, Walter H. ....Louisville, KY
McGee, Wayne ....Cynthiana, KY
McGee, William D. ....Nashville, TN
McGee, William F. ....Smithland, KY
McGee, William F., Jr. ....Smithland, KY
McGee, William J., Jr. ....Huntington, WV
McGee, William S. ....Vienna, VA
McGee, William T., Law Offices of
Fort Worth, TX
McGeehan, Ann Olivier ....Washington, DC
McGeehan, C. Kevin ....Los Angeles, CA
Mcgeehan, John J. ....Gaithersburg, MD
McGeehan, John P. ....Fairfax, VA
McGeehan, John R. ....New York, NY
McGeehan, Lisa M. ....St. Paul, MN
McGeehan, Patrick M. ....Atlanta, GA
McGeehee, Theresa ....Durant, OK
McGeehon, Michael B.
San Francisco, CA
McGeeney, John R. ....Louisville, KY
McGeeney, John S. ....Stamford, CT
McGeever, Eileen J. ....Rockford, IL
McGeever, Eileen L. ....Carlsbad, CA
McGeever, Elizabeth M. ....Wilmington, DE
McGeever, Kerry S. ....Rockville, MD
McGeever, Terrence P. ....Princeton, NJ
McGeever, Thomas D. ....Los Angeles, CA
McGehee, Boling, Whitmire, Olson & Pepping, Ltd. ....Silvis, IL
McGehee, Carl B. ....Roswell, GA
McGehee, Cary Stewart ....Royal Oak, MI
McGehee, Clark H. ....Atlanta, GA
McGehee, Daniel F. ....Knoxville, TN
McGehee, David E. ....Huntsville, AL
McGehee, Donald S. ....Lansing, MI
McGehee, Eddie G. ....Baton Rouge, LA
McGehee, Edward P., Jr. ....Richmond, VA
McGehee, Eugene W. ....Baton Rouge, LA
McGehee, H. B. Mayes ....Meadville, MS
McGehee, Helen E. ....Prescott, AZ
McGehee, Hollis ....Meadville, MS
McGehee, Jack E. ....Houston, TX
McGehee, James L. ....Stayton, OR
McGehee, John H. ....Cincinnati, OH
McGehee, John Layne ....Silvis, IL
McGehee, McGehee & Torrey
Meadville, MS
McGehee & McNair ....Jackson, MS
McGehee, Newton & Wykoff, P.C.
Knoxville, TN
McGehee, Noah L. ....Silvis, IL
McGehee, Peggy L. ....Portland, ME
McGehee & Pianelli, L.L.P. ....Houston, TX
McGehee, R. Ben, Jr. ....Jackson, MS
McGehee, Robert B. ....Raleigh, NC
McGehee, Robert N., Jr. ....Dallas, TX
Fort Worth, TX
McGehee, Teresa W. ....Meadville, MS
McGehee, W. Clay ....New Orleans, LA
McGehee, William C. ....Denver, CO
McGehee, William Carl, Jr. ....Natchez, MS
McGeoch, Alexander G. ....Dallas, TX
McGeoch, Barbara J. ....San Francisco, CA
McGeoghegan, Earl Leon ....Lewiston, ID
McGeorge, Randall C. ....Tampa, FL
McGeorge, Ray E. ....Topeka, KS
McGeorge, Robert L.
Department of Justice,
Antitrust Division, GV
McGeough, Brian J. ....Mineola, NY
McGeough, Robert S. ....Warren, OH
McGerity, Margaret ....New York, NY
McGetrick, Donald M. ....Sarasota, FL
McGetrick, Martin J. ....Charlottesville, VA
Fredericksburg, VA
Harrisonburg, VA
McGetrick, Michael S. ....Danbury, CT
McGettigan, E. Neal ....San Francisco, CA
McGettigan, Eileen M. ....Boston, MA
McGettigan, James W., Jr.
Washington, MO
McGettigan, John E. ....Houston, TX
McGettigan, Jos. E., Jr. ....Oakton, VA
Mc Gettigan, Justina A. ....Biddeford, ME
McGettigan, Manus J. ....Santa Ana, CA
McGettigan, Marianne ....Washington, DC
Portland, ME
McGettigan, Michael ....Alexandria, VA
McGettigan, Patrick J., Jr. ....Houston, TX
McGettigan, Steven V. ....Trenton, NJ
McGettigan, William J. ....Valley Forge, PA
McGettrick, Anthony C. ....Laredo, TX
McGevna, James P. ....Syracuse, NY
McGhee, Carl Andrew ....Pittsburgh, PA
McGhee, Charles W. ....Memphis, TN
McGhee, Connie Bentley ....Newark, NJ
McGhee & Dean, P.S.C. ....London, KY
McGhee, Glover ....Atlanta, GA
McGhee, James A. ....Pensacola, FL
McGhee, James E. ....Jefferson City, MO
McGhee, Jeffrey D. ....Phoenix, AZ
McGhee, John R. ....Bluefield, WV
McGhee, John R., Jr. ....Charleston, WV
McGhee, Kirkland A. ....Atlanta, GA
McGhee, L. Dale ....Bassett, VA
McGhee, Lynne P. ....Oakland, CA
McGhee, Marilyn Benge ....London, KY
McGhee, Matthew A. ....Moraga, CA
McGhee, Odell Gene ....Des Moines, IA
McGhee, Paul ....Dexter, MO
McGhee, Rayfield M. ....Miami, FL
McGhee, Victoria T. ....Woodland Hills, CA
McGhee, W. Thomas ....St. Louis, MO
McGhee, Walter C., Jr. ....El Paso, TX
McGhee, William J. ....Christiansburg, VA
McGhee, Zaida Angulo
Laguna Niguel, CA
McGhehey, Kathleen S. ....Denver, CO
McGhehey, Terry L. ....Chattanooga, TN
McGhie, Teresa L. ....New York, NY
McGhie-Lee, Monica L. ....Philadelphia, PA
McGibbon, James R. ....Atlanta, GA
McGie, Elizabeth ....Chico, CA
McGiff, James E. ....Patchogue, NY
McGiff, Stephen J. ....Woodbury, NY
McGiffert, David E. ....Washington, DC
McGiffert, Laurel F. ....Detroit, MI
McGiffert, Sarah ....Phoenix, AZ
McGiffert, Stephen D. ....Overland Park, KS
McGiffin, Donald N. ....Beaverton, OR
McGiffin, Thomas C. ....Liberty, MO
McGihon, Anne L. ....Denver, CO
McGihon & Leffert, P.C. ....Denver, CO
McGill, Alfred T. ....Portland, OR
Mcgill, Angela N. ....Los Angeles, CA
McGill, Arnold L. ....Aurora, IN
McGill, Billy R. ....Dallas, TX
McGill and Bogden ....Troy, MI
McGill, Brian Andrew ....Washington, DC
McGill, Brian E. ....Washington, DC
McGill, Cheryl A. ....Huntsville, AL
McGill, Daniel W. ....Indianapolis, IN
McGill, David C. ....Toledo, OH
McGill, David R. ....Uniondale, NY
McGill, Dennis L. ....Jersey City, NJ
McGill, Dennis W. ....Lubbock, TX
McGill, Diane E. ....Fort Myers, FL
McGill, Diane E., P.A. ....Fort Myers, FL
McGill, Donald W. ....Waterbury, CT
McGill, Douglas J. ....Florham Park, NJ
McGill, Edmond F. ....San Rafael, CA
McGill, Francis E., III ....Philadelphia, PA
McGill, George D. ....Belmar, NJ
McGill, George E. ....Cardiff-By-The-Sea, CA
McGill, Gerald A. ....Pensacola, FL
McGill, Gilbert W. ....Sea Cliff, NY
McGill, Gotsdiner, Workman & Lepp, P.C.
Omaha, NE
McGill, Gregory G. ....Scottsdale, AZ
McGill, Gregory G., P.C. ....Scottsdale, AZ
McGill Griffin ....Miami, FL
Orlando, FL
Pensacola, FL
McGill, J. Raymond, Jr. ....Philadelphia, PA
McGill, James W. ....Hackensack, MN
McGill, Joe K. ....Seminole, TX
McGill, Joe K., P.C. ....Seminole, TX
McGill, John F. K. ....Austin, TX
McGill, John G. ....Fernandina Beach, FL
Atlanta, GA
McGill, John Graham, Jr. ....Orange, CA
McGill, John K. ....Gastonia, NC
McGill, John L. ....Fulton, NY
McGill, John P. ....Oakland, CA
McGill, Joseph J. ....Philadelphia, PA
Mcgill, Joseph M. ....New York, NY
McGill, Joseph P. ....Detroit, MI
McGill, Kapranos & Wynn ....Portland, OR
McGill, Kathleen Amalia ....Charlotte, NC
McGill, Kerry L. ....Austin, TX
McGill, Kevin J. ....New York, NY
McGill, Larry D. ....La Mesa, CA
McGill, Leonard J. ....Irvine, CA
McGill, Linda D. ....Portland, ME
McGill, M. Lauren ....New York, NY
McGill, Martha L. ....San Diego, CA
McGill, Maureen E. ....Rock Valley, IA
McGill, Maureen L. ....Pensacola, FL
McGill & McGill ....Waterbury, CT
McGill & McGill ....Rock Valley, IA
McGill, Michael ....Omaha, NE
McGill, Michael E. ....Toledo, OH
McGill, Michael J. ....Beresford, SD
McGill, Michele L., Law Offices of, The
San Francisco, CA
McGill, Michele M. ....Rock Valley, IA
McGill, Norman L. ....Metropolis, IL
McGill, Olin R., Jr. ....Rutland, VT
McGill, Owen P. ....Tampa, FL
McGill, Patrick J. ....Phoenix, AZ
McGill, Patrick J. ....San Pedro, CA
McGill, Patrick R. ....Omaha, NE
McGill, Patrick R. ....Plattsburgh, NY
McGill, Paul L. ....Concord, MA
McGill, Paula J. ....Washington, DC
McGill Professional Law Corporation
Steamboat Springs, CO
McGill, Richard ....Newark, NJ
McGill, Richard H. ....Massapequa, NY
McGill, Richard M. ....Upper Marlboro, MD
McGill, Robert E., III ....Destin, FL
McGill, Robert E., III, P.A. ....Destin, FL
McGill, Robert J. ....Seattle, WA
McGill, Robert Jackaon, Law Offices of
Venice, FL
McGill, Robert Jackson, Law Offices of
Sarasota, FL
McGill, Roger D. ....Ebensburg, PA
Johnstown, PA

McGlothlin, John ..... San Diego, CA
McGlothlin, Joseph Allan ..... Tallahassee, FL
McGlothlin, Kathryn M. ..... Indianapolis, IN
McGlothlin, Larry J. ..... Fayetteville, NC
McGlothlin, Michael G. ..... Grundy, VA
McGlothlin, Sandra Keen ..... Grundy, VA
McGlothlin, Stanley E. ..... Carrollton, TX
McGlothlin, William C., Jr.
Colorado Springs, CO
McGlothren, Michael S. ..... Fairhope, AL
McGlothren, Michael S., P.C. ..... Daphne, AL
Fairhope, AL
Mobile, AL
McGlynn, Alan P. ..... Baton Rouge, LA
McGlynn, Allen ..... Bloomington, IL
McGlynn, Bradley M. ..... Woodside, NY
McGlynn, Brendan P. ..... Philadelphia, PA
McGlynn, D. Jerry ..... San Rafael, CA
McGlynn, Daniel J. ..... Baton Rouge, LA
McGlynn, Daniel J. ..... Bloomfield Hills, MI
McGlynn, Daniel R. ..... Bohemia, NY
McGlynn, E. Kevin ..... Wyckoff, NJ
McGlynn, Edmund R., Jr. ..... Chicago, IL
McGlynn, Edward R. ..... Roseland, NJ
McGlynn, Ernestine Rossi ..... Ann Arbor, MI
McGlynn, Frank R. ..... Woodside, NY
McGlynn, Gerald E., III ..... Troy, MI
McGlynn & Glisson, A Professional Law Corporation ..... Baton Rouge, LA
McGlynn, J. Casey ..... Palo Alto, CA
McGlynn, James ..... Belleville, IL
McGlynn, James A. ..... Webster City, IA
McGlynn, James J. ..... Stamford, CT
McGlynn, James R. ..... Coral Springs, FL
McGlynn, Jessica M. ..... Austin, TX
McGlynn, John E. ..... Philadelphia, PA
McGlynn, John F. ..... Mineola, NY
McGlynn, John P. ..... San Francisco, CA
McGlynn, Jos. L., Jr. ..... Philadelphia, PA
McGlynn, Joseph B., Jr. ..... St. Louis, MO
McGlynn, Joseph M. ..... Troy, MI
McGlynn, Justin P. ..... Philadelphia, PA
McGlynn, Lorraine B. ..... Philadelphia, PA
McGlynn, Louise A. ..... Westport, CT
McGlynn, Martin M. ..... New York, NY
McGlynn, Matthew C. ..... Red Bluff, CA
McGlynn, Maureen A. ..... St. Louis, MO
McGlynn, Maureen Dunn ..... Syracuse, NY
McGlynn & McGlynn ..... Red Bluff, CA
McGlynn & McGlynn ..... Belleville, IL
McGlynn & McGlynn ..... St. Louis, MO
McGlynn, McLorg & Ritchie
San Francisco, CA
McGlynn, Meghan A. ..... Port Huron, MI
McGlynn, Michael L. ..... Belleville, IL
McGlynn, Nancy J. ..... Washington, DC
McGlynn, Peter B. ..... Boston, MA
McGlynn, Phoebe Louise ..... Tucson, AZ
McGlynn, Richard B.
Harrington Park, NJ
McGlynn, Richard M. ..... Yonkers, NY
McGlynn, Robert E. ..... Belleville, IL
McGlynn, Roger H.
Mendham Township, NJ
McGlynn, Stephen P. ..... Belleville, IL
McGlynn, Terrence R. ..... Chicago, IL
McGlynn, Thomas J., (P.C.)
Red Bluff, CA
McGoey, Charles K. ..... New Rochelle, NY
Mcgoey, Gillian ..... Purchase, NY
McGoey, John J. ..... New Rochelle, NY
McGoey, Michael E. ..... Rolling Meadows, IL
McGoey, Robert J. ..... New Rochelle, NY
McGoey, Thomas J., II ..... New Orleans, LA
McGoey, William M. ..... New Orleans, LA
Mc Goff, James P. ..... Indianapolis, IN
McGoff, Kevin P. ..... Indianapolis, IN
McGoff, Michael C. ..... Atlanta, GA
McGoff, Peter M. ..... Palo Alto, CA
McGoff, Sharon L. ..... Indianapolis, IN
McGoffin, Gary ..... Lafayette, LA
McGoffin, Inc., Inc., P.S. ..... Burlington, WA
McGoffin, Keith D. ..... Burlington, WA
McGoffin, Kevin B. ..... Burlington, WA
McGogney, Glenn D. ..... Allentown, PA
McGoings, Michael C.
Department of Justice, Executive Office for Immigration Review, GV
McGoldrick, David ..... Tacoma, WA
McGoldrick, Dennis E. ..... Torrance, CA
McGoldrick, James G. ..... New York, NY
McGoldrick, James M. ..... Malibu, CA
McGoldrick, James P. ..... Westborough, MA
McGoldrick, Joanne ..... Columbus, OH
McGoldrick, John C. ..... La Grange Park, IL
McGoldrick, John G. ..... New York, NY
McGoldrick, John L. ..... New York, NY
McGoldrick, John T., Jr. ..... Macon, GA
McGoldrick, Joseph P., III ..... Macon, GA
McGoldrick, Lawrence S. ..... Atlanta, GA
McGoldrick, Margaret A.
Washington, DC
McGoldrick, Marilyn T. ..... Boston, MA
McGoldrick, Mary M. ..... Boston, MA
McGoldrick, Michael J. ..... Philadelphia, PA
McGoldrick, Michael P. ..... Hartford, CT
McGoldrick, Paul J. ..... Phoenix, AZ
McGoldrick, Robt. D. ..... Spokane, WA
McGoldrick, Thomas J.
King Of Prussia, PA
Mcgoldrick, Timothy J. ..... Watertown, MA
McGoldrick, William M. ..... Valley Stream, NY
McGolrick, J. Edward, Jr. ..... Manassas, VA
McGolrick, J. Edward, Jr., P.C.
Manassas, VA
McGolrick, Susan J. ..... Washington, DC

McGonagle, Erin N. ..... Washington, DC
Baltimore, MD
Rockville, MD
McGonagle, John P. ..... Rockland, MA
McGonagle, Mary Anne ..... Quincy, MA
McGonagle, Patrick J. ..... Newark, OH
McGonagle, Peter G. ..... Stamford, CT
McGonagle, Vincent A.
Commodity Futures Trading Commission, Division of Enforcement, GV
McGonagle, William S.
Bainbridge Island, WA
Poulsbo, WA
McGonegal, Terrance J.
New Philadelphia, OH
McGonegle, Timothy J. ..... Chicago, IL
McGonegle-Sievers, Barbara ..... Seattle, WA
McGonigal, Alan G. ..... Wheeling, WV
McGonigal, Jerry L. ..... Houston, TX
McGonigal, Joseph F. ..... Indianapolis, IN
McGonigal, Kyle A. ..... Washington, DC
McGonigal, Leo T. ..... Chicago, IL
McGonigal, Richard M. ..... New York, NY
McGonigle, Ann L. ..... Orlando, FL
Mcgonigle, Ann Therese ..... Boston, MA
Mcgonigle, Barry J ..... Braintree, MA
McGonigle, David F. ..... Pittsburgh, PA
McGonigle, Gerald D. ..... Boston, MA
McGonigle, Helen L. ..... Brookfield, CT
McGonigle, Helen L. ..... Danbury, CT
McGonigle, James J. ..... New York, NY
McGonigle, John W. ..... Pittsburgh, PA
McGonigle, Michael J. ..... Philadelphia, PA
McGonigle, Patricia P. ..... Wilmington, DE
McGonigle, Peter M. ..... Philadelphia, PA
McGonigle, Richard L. ..... Houston, TX
McGonigle, Richard T. ..... Tulsa, OK
McGonigle, Stephen M. ..... East Dennis, MA
McGonigle, Thomas J. ..... Washington, DC
McGonigle, Timothy D. ..... Los Angeles, CA
McGonnigal, Michael T. ..... Washington, DC
McGoogan, E. Graham, Jr. ..... Charlotte, NC
McGoogan, Elizabeth Dianne ..... Chicago, IL
McGookey, Dan L. ..... Sandusky, OH
McGookey, Doreen E. ..... Fort Worth, TX
McGookey, James E. ..... Sandusky, OH
McGookin, Ralph J. ..... Marina Del Rey, CA
McGoran, Joseph J. ..... Federal Way, WA
McGorisk, Brian T. ..... Flint, MI
McGorry, Brian M. ..... Brooklyn, NY
McGorry, Mark W. ..... New York, NY
McGorry, Michael P. J. ..... Buffalo, NY
McGorty, Glen G. ..... Department of Justice, Criminal Division, GV
McGory, Gregory S. ..... Sandusky, OH
McGory, Michael P. ..... Goleta, CA
McGory, Peter J. ..... Sandusky, OH
McGory, Starlene D. ..... Tampa, FL
McGougan, Wright, Worley and Harper, L.L.P. ..... Tabor City, NC
Whiteville, NC
McGough, Barry B. ..... Atlanta, GA
McGough, Brian E. ..... Chicago, IL
McGough, David W. ..... Boston, MA
Mcgough, Donald Edward
West Roxbury, MA
McGough Huddleston & Medori
Atlanta, GA
McGough, Hugh F. ..... Pittsburgh, PA
McGough, Hugh R. ..... Seattle, WA
McGough, James A. ..... Tarrytown, NY
McGough, James J. ..... Chicago, IL
McGough, James K. ..... Norfolk, NE
McGough, James V. ..... Altoona, PA
McGough, John T. ..... Columbus, OH
McGough, Jon P. ..... Wichita Falls, TX
McGough, Kevin J. ..... Rahway, NJ
McGough, Leo I. ..... Secaucus, NJ
McGough, Lynett ..... Elyria, OH
McGough, Phillip A. ..... North Little Rock, AR
McGough, Phillip A., P.A.
North Little Rock, AR
McGough, Stewart M. ..... Syracuse, NY
McGough, W. Thomas, Jr. ..... Pittsburgh, PA
McGoughran, Timothy F. ..... Oakhurst, NJ
McGourty, Edward F. ..... Boston, MA
McGourty, William M. ..... Worcester, MA
McGovern, A. Lane ..... Boston, MA
McGovern, Amanda M. ..... Miami, FL
McGovern, Amelia P. ..... New York, NY
McGovern & Associates ..... Greenwich, CT
Hartford, CT
Norwalk, CT
Stamford, CT
New York, NY
McGovern, Barbara A. ..... Fairlawn, OH
McGovern, Bernard F., Jr. ..... Hartford, CT
McGovern, Brian E. ..... St. Louis, MO
McGovern, Brian T. ..... New York, NY
New York, NY
McGovern, Brian Thomas ..... Benton, IL
Mount Vernon, IL
McGovern, Bruce A. ..... Houston, TX
McGovern, Catherine A. ..... Lima, OH
McGovern, Catherine P. ..... New York, NY
McGovern, Charles J. ..... Providence, RI
McGovern, Christopher W.
San Francisco, CA
McGovern, Clement J., III
Department of Justice, Criminal Division, GV
McGovern, Clement J., Jr. ..... Media, PA
McGovern, Connelly & Davidson
New Rochelle, NY
McGovern, Corinne Ligas ..... Jersey City, NJ
McGovern, Daniel A., III ..... New Orleans, LA
McGovern, Daniel W. ..... San Francisco, CA
McGovern, David C. ..... Santa Monica, CA

McGovern and Dawson ..... New York, NY
Scarsdale, NY
White Plains, NY
McGovern, Deborah L. ..... Jacksonville, FL
McGovern, Diana Powell ..... West Orange, NJ
McGovern, Eileen B. ..... Springfield, VA
McGovern, Elissa M. ..... Washington, DC
McGovern, Frances ..... Akron, OH
McGovern, Francis E., II ..... Tuscaloosa, AL
McGovern, Francis J. ..... Newton, NJ
McGovern, Francis J., Jr. ..... Princeton, NJ
McGovern, Gerald J. ..... San Francisco, CA
McGovern, Glenn C. ..... New Orleans, LA
McGovern, Harold T. ..... Newton, NJ
McGovern, Hug, Welch & Ganem, LLP
Boston, MA
McGovern, Hugh M. ..... New York, NY
McGovern, Imler and Rockwell
Tacoma, WA
McGovern, J. Thomas ..... Sterling Heights, MI
McGovern, James A. ..... Pittsburgh, PA
McGovern, James E. ..... Louisville, KY
McGovern, James F. ..... United States Senate, Committee Legal Personnel, GV
Mcgovern, James Gerard ..... New York, NY
McGovern, James J. ..... Paterson, NJ
McGovern, James J. ..... Blythewood, SC
McGovern, James J., III ..... Livingston, NJ
McGovern, James M. ..... New York, NY
McGovern, James M., Jr. ..... Freehold, NJ
McGovern, Janet G. ..... Treasury Department, Internal Revenue Service, GV
McGovern, Jennifer Hooker ..... Rochester, MN
Mcgovern, John B ..... Fair Lawn, NJ
McGovern, John E., Jr. ..... Chicago, IL
McGovern, John F., Jr. ..... Berkley, MI
McGovern, John H., Jr. ..... Brooklyn, NY
McGovern, John J., Jr. ..... Washington, DC
Mcgovern, John M. ..... New York, NY
McGovern, John N. ..... Evanston, IL
McGovern, John Patrick ..... Redwood City, CA
McGovern, Jonathan C. ..... Philadelphia, PA
McGovern, Joseph D. ..... Glennville, GA
McGovern, Joseph J. ..... Cherry Hill, NJ
Philadelphia, PA
McGovern, Joseph J. ..... Philadelphia, PA
McGovern, Joseph M. ..... Chicago, IL
McGovern, Joseph T. ..... Elmhurst, IL
McGovern, Joseph W. ..... White Plains, NY
McGovern, Julie S. ..... Washington, DC
McGovern, Katherine Savers ..... Dallas, TX
McGovern, Kathleen ..... Riverhead, NY
McGovern, Kathleen F. ..... Buffalo, NY
McGovern, Kevin M. ..... Greenwich, CT
McGovern, Kevin Patrick, Law Offices of
Bridgewater, NJ
Brooklyn, NY
McGovern, Kimberly S.
San Francisco, CA
McGovern, Kyle C. ..... White Plains, NY
McGovern, Lauren E. ..... Hackensack, NJ
McGovern, Laurie L. ..... Columbus, OH
McGovern, Lawrence F.
White Plains, NY
McGovern, Linda A. ..... Chicago, IL
McGovern, Lisa Stevenson ..... Cambridge, MA
McGovern, Lynn M. ..... Chicago, IL
McGovern, Margaret F. ..... Boston, MA
McGovern, Michael B. ..... Washington, DC
McGovern, Michael J. ..... Evesham, NJ
Philadelphia, PA
McGovern, Michael J. ..... Milwaukee, WI
McGovern, Michael M. ..... New York, NY
McGovern, Michael P. ..... Washington, DC
McGovern, Michael P. ..... Knoxville, TN
McGovern, Michelle A. ..... Des Moines, IA
McGovern, Noel & Benik, Inc.
Boston, MA
Millburn, NJ
Providence, RI
McGovern, Patricia ..... Boston, MA
McGovern, Patricia A. ..... New York, NY
McGovern, Patrick F. ..... Chicago, IL
McGovern, Patrick Michael
Los Angeles, CA
Denver, CO
Chicago, IL
Boston, MA
Philadelphia, PA
McGovern, Patrick S. ..... East Lansing, MI
McGovern, Patrick W. ..... Morristown, NJ
McGovern, Peter J.
Federal Energy Regulatory Commission, Office of Hydro Power Licensing, GV
McGovern, Peter J. ..... Chicago, IL
McGovern, Philip C. ..... White Plains, NY
McGovern, Philip F. ..... Danbury, CT
McGovern, Philip F., Jr. ..... Roseland, NJ
McGovern, Philip R. ..... Greenwood, IN
McGovern, Raymond E., Jr. ..... New York, NY
McGovern, Richard A. ..... Boston, MA
McGovern, Richard W. ..... Fairview Heights, IL
McGovern, Robert B. ..... Montvale, NJ
McGovern, Robert P. ..... Newark, NJ
McGovern, Robert T. ..... White Plains, NY
McGovern and Roseman, P.A. ..... Newton, NJ
McGovern, Sheila E. ..... Cambridge, MA
McGovern, Stephen J. ..... Hartford, CT
McGovern, Steven E. ..... Tacoma, WA
Mcgovern, Theresa Marie ..... New York, NY
McGovern, Thomas E. ..... Richmond, MI
McGovern, Thomas L., III
Washington, DC
McGovern, Thomas P. ..... Phoenix, AZ
McGovern, Tracy M. ..... Medford, OR
McGovern, Walter T. ..... Seattle, WA
McGovern, William ..... Encino, CA
McGovern, William C. ..... Philadelphia, PA

McGovern, William J. ..... Newton, NJ
McGovern, William J., III ..... Newton, NJ
McGovern, William P., III ..... Troy, NY
McGovern, William P., Jr.
New Orleans, LA
McGovern, Yvonne Q. ..... San Francisco, CA
McGow, Patrick F. ..... Detroit, MI
McGowan, Adrian A. ..... Houston, TX
McGowan, Andrew J. ..... Peoria, IL
McGowan, Anne D. ..... Carmel, CA
McGowan, Arthur P., Jr. ..... Hartford, CT
McGowan, Bernard J. ..... Pittsburgh, PA
McGowan, Bill ..... Brownfield, TX
McGowan, Brian M. ..... Erie, PA
McGowan and Brownell ..... Geneva, NY
McGowan, Candis A. ..... Birmingham, AL
McGowan, Carol M. ..... Annapolis, MD
McGowan, Chad A. ..... Atlanta, GA
Anderson, SC
McGowan, Charles M. ..... Boston, MA
McGowan, Clarence R. ..... San Antonio, TX
McGowan & Cousins, P.C. ..... Stamford, CT
Wilton, CT
White Plains, NY
McGowan, Daniel A. ..... Pottsville, PA
McGowan, Daniel P. ..... St. Paul, MN
McGowan, David A. ..... Pittsburgh, PA
McGowan, David K. ..... Jackson, MS
McGowan, Debra S. ..... Harrisburg, IL
McGowan, Eaton, Stewart, Hiller & McLaurin, P.A. ..... Florence, SC
McGowan, Edgar L. ..... Columbia, SC
McGowan, Edward B., II
San Francisco, CA
McGowan, Edward J. ..... Holmdel, NJ
McGowan, Edward J. ..... Massapequa, NY
McGowan, Edward M. ..... Maspeth, NY
McGowan, Edward M. ..... Mineola, NY
McGowan, Engel, Tucker, Garrett & Schultz, P.A. ..... Boston, MA
McGowan Firm ..... Atlanta, GA
Anderson, SC
McGowan, Frank A., Jr. ..... Stamford, CT
Wilton, CT
White Plains, NY
McGowan, G. Rico ..... Washington, DC
McGowan, Gary V. ..... Houston, TX
McGowan, Gerald S. ..... Washington, DC
McGowan, Gerard J., Jr. ..... Edgewater, NJ
McGowan, Gertrude C. ..... Wilkes-Barre, PA
McGowan, Harvey J. ..... Cleveland, OH
McGowan, Hope P. ..... Department of Justice, Office of the Pardon Attorney, GV
McGowan, J. Joseph ..... Poughkeepsie, NY
McGowan, J. Phil, Jr. ..... Houston, TX
McGowan, Jack C., & Associates
Hamilton, OH
McGowan, Jacqueline F. ..... Morristown, NJ
McGowan, James F., III ..... Fairfax, VA
McGowan, James H., III ..... Syracuse, NY
McGowan, James J. ..... Bronx, NY
McGowan, James J., Jr. ..... Houston, TX
McGowan, James P. ..... Seattle, WA
McGowan, James P., Jr. ..... La Jolla, CA
McGowan, James W. ..... Sitka, AK
McGowan, Jas. J. ..... Bronx, NY
McGowan, Jennifer M. ..... Columbus, OH
Columbus, OH
McGowan, John B. ..... Santa Clara, CA
McGowan, John F. ..... Washington, DC
McGowan, John G. ..... Oswego, NY
Syracuse, NY
McGowan, John J., Jr. ..... Cleveland, OH
McGowan, John L. ..... Florence, SC
McGowan, John M. ..... Orlando, FL
McGowan, John M. ..... New York, NY
McGowan, John M., II ..... Phoenix, AZ
McGowan, John S. ..... Roseland, NJ
McGowan, John T. ..... East Hampton, NY
McGowan, John W., III ..... Warren, NJ
McGowan, Joseph A. ..... Blue Ridge, GA
McGowan, Joseph C. ..... Irvine, CA
McGowan, Joseph F., Jr. ..... Cherry Hill, NJ
McGowan, Joseph P. ..... Scranton, PA
McGowan, Joseph W., III ..... Laurens, SC
McGowan, Karen D. ..... Sarasota, FL
McGowan, Kevin M. ..... Chesterfield, VA
McGowan, Krista A. ..... Frederick, MD
McGowan, Laurie L. ..... Camp Hill, PA
McGowan, Leticia D. ..... Austin, TX
McGowan, Linda Cole ..... Tulsa, OK
McGowan, Lynne G. ..... Littleton, CO
McGowan, Malcolm K. ..... Alexandria, VA
McGowan, Margaret E. ..... New York, NY
McGowan, Marianna M. ..... Dallas, TX
McGowan, Marie C. ..... Houston, TX
McGowan, Mark ..... Bloomfield Hills, MI
McGowan, Mark J. ..... Sierra Vista, AZ
McGowan, Mark L. ..... Chicago, IL
McGowan, Mark S. ..... Jacksonville, FL
McGowan, Mary E. ..... Oswego, NY
McGowan, Mary E. ..... Fairfax, VA
McGowan, Mary V. ..... New York, NY
McGowan, Matthew J. ..... Providence, RI
McGowan, Maureen C. ..... San Francisco, CA
McGowan & McGowan ..... Omaha, NE
McGowan & McGowan, P.C.
Brownfield, TX
McGowan, Melvin J. ..... Waukegan, IL
McGowan, Michael ..... Lanham, MD
McGowan, Michael ..... Dulles, VA
McGowan, Michael F. ..... New York, NY
McGowan, Michael H.
West Sacramento, CA
McGowan, Michael J. ..... Chicago, IL
McGowan, Michael L. ..... Akron, OH
McGowan, Michael P. ..... Washington, DC
McGowan, Michael S. ..... Toledo, OH

McGraw, Martin & Heyn, P.C.
Saginaw, MI
Tawas City, MI
McGraw & McGraw ... Thomasville, GA
McGraw, Michael J. ... Louisville, KY
McGraw & Miles ... Syracuse, NY
McGraw, Patricia D. ... Charlottesville, VA
McGraw, Patrick A. ... Cleveland, OH
McGraw, Patrick J. ... Saginaw, MI
Tawas City, MI
McGraw, Peggy Stevens ... Kansas City, MO
McGraw, Phillip R. ... Newport Beach, CA
McGraw, R.J., P.A. ... Hutchinson, MN
McGraw, Regina S. ... Philadelphia, PA
McGraw, Richard J. ... Cleveland, OH
Mcgraw, Richard W. ... St. Petersburg, FL
McGraw, Richard W. ... Bloomington, IL
McGraw, Richard Withrow ... Bexley, OH
McGraw, Robert E. ... Cleveland, OH
McGraw, Ronald J. ... Hutchinson, MN
McGraw, Royal A. ... Thomasville, GA
McGraw, Sandra E.D.
Plymouth Meeting, PA
McGraw, Scott W. ... Salem, OR
McGraw, Shawn M. ... Cleveland, OH
McGraw, Sonya Campbell ... Gastonia, NC
McGraw, Stacey L. ... Washington, DC
McGraw, Stephen D. ... Detroit, MI
McGraw, Terence Sean ... Norristown, PA
McGraw, Thomas C. ... Dallas, TX
McGraw, Thomas F., III ... Overland Park, KS
McGraw, Thomas F., III, Chartered
Overland Park, KS
McGraw, Thomas J. ... Detroit, MI
McGraw, Thomas J. ... Detroit, MI
McGraw, Thomas Scott ... McLean, VA
McGraw, Timothy J. ... Dearborn, MI
McGraw, Vincent J. ... Fresno, CA
McGraw, Warren R. ... Pineville, WV
McGraw, Wendy C. ... Washington, DC
McGraw, Willard G., Jr. ... Boston, MA
McGraw, William F. ... Front Royal, VA
McGraw, William J., III ... Troy, OH
McGraw, William Kenneth ... Seattle, WA
McGreal, Austin J. ... Philadelphia, PA
McGreal, Eugene P. ... Plano, TX
McGreal, Jerry D. ... Rockledge, FL
McGreal, Margaret A. ... Chicago, IL
McGreal, Michael ... Pittsburgh, PA
McGreal, Michael J. ... Piscataway, NJ
McGreal, Patrick I. ... Sacramento, CA
McGreal, Thomas M. ... Pomona, CA
McGree, Timothy V. ... Chicago, IL
McGreen, John V. ... Cranston, RI
McGreevey, James E. ... Carteret, NJ
McGreevey, Robert M. ... Chicago, IL
McGreevey, William K. ... Atlanta, GA
McGreevy, Cynthia Ann
Treasury Department,
Internal Revenue Service, GV
McGreevy, Georganne DeLaughter
Daytona Beach, FL
McGreevy, James F. ... Sun City, AZ
McGreevy, Joanne M. ... Harrisburg, PA
McGreevy, John J. ... New York, NY
McGreevy, Johnson & Williams, P.C.
Rockford, IL
McGreevy, Kevin Michael ... Denver, CO
McGreevy, Martin J. ... Asbury Park, NJ
McGreevy, Paul F. ... Chula Vista, CA
McGreevy, Peter R. ... Woodbury, NY
McGreevy, Richard E. ... Mission Viejo, CA
San Francisco, CA
McGreevy, Robert P. ... New York, NY
McGreevy, Stephen J. ... Santa Ana, CA
McGreevy, Susan Linden
Kansas City, MO
McGreevy, Terrence G. ... Houston, TX
McGregor & Associates, P.C. ... Boston, MA
McGregor, Beth ... Houston, TX
McGregor, Bruce B. ... Torrance, CA
McGregor, Bruce C. ... Schenevus, NY
McGregor, Dahl, Sullivan & Klug
Fresno, CA
McGregor, Daniel B. ... Helena, MT
McGregor, Deborah B. ... Indianapolis, IN
McGregor, Deborah Thompson ... Waco, TX
McGregor, Dick ... Corpus Christi, TX
McGregor, Donald G. ... North Miami, FL
McGregor, Emanuel H. ... Chardon, OH
McGregor, Erica E. ... Cleveland, OH
McGregor, Frank B. (Bob), Jr.
Hillsboro, TX
McGregor, Frank Bobbitt ... Hillsboro, TX
McGregor, Frank H., III
Oklahoma City, OK
McGregor, Frank H., III, P.C.
Oklahoma City, OK
McGregor & Garrie, LLP ... San Diego, CA
McGregor, Gary C. ... Hartford, WI
McGregor, Grant K. ... Prescott, AZ
McGregor, Gregor I. ... Boston, MA
McGregor, Holly H. ... Laguna Hills, CA
McGregor, J. Keith
La Canada Flintridge, CA
McGregor, J. Russell, Jr. ... Pittsburgh, PA
McGregor, Jack E. ... Bridgeport, CT
Stamford, CT
McGregor, James E., Jr. ... Waco, TX
McGregor, James R. ... Pittsburgh, PA
McGregor, James R. ... McMinnville, TN
McGregor, Jane C. ... Cincinnati, OH
McGregor, Jason Floyd ... Louisville, KY
McGregor, John F. ... Santa Maria, CA
McGregor, John J. ... Fresno, CA
McGregor, John W. ... Ballinger, TX
McGregor, Kent D. ... Los Angeles, CA
McGregor, Laura D. ... Summerville, SC

McGregor, Lauren L. ... Farmington, CT
McGregor, Loren G. ... Princeton, IN
McGregor, Malcolm ... El Paso, TX
McGregor, Malcolm, Inc., A Prof. Corp., Law
Offices of ... El Paso, TX
McGregor, Marc M. ... Coeur d'Alene, ID
McGregor, Martha L. ... Hillsboro, TX
McGregor, Martin L., Jr. ... Dallas, TX
McGregor, Mary L. ... Portland, ME
McGregor, McGregor & Carmichael, Inc. P.C.
Hillsboro, TX
McGregor, Michael E.
Department of the Navy, GV
McGregor & Patterson ... Pittsburgh, PA
McGregor, Prudence M. ... Taunton, MA
McGregor, Robert A. ... San Diego, CA
McGregor, Robert L.
Department of Labor, GV
McGregor, Ruth V. ... Phoenix, AZ
McGregor, Scott D. ... Rapid City, SD
McGregor, Stephen E. ... Washington, DC
McGregor, Stuart J. ... Miami, FL
McGregor, Suzanne ... New York, NY
McGregor, Tanya B. ... Palo Alto, CA
McGregor, Theodore S. ... Spokane, WA
McGregor, Thomas C. ... Montgomery, AL
Mcgregor, Thomas C. ... New York, NY
McGregor, Veronica K.
San Francisco, CA
McGregory, Deborah L., Law Office of
Sherman, TX
McGrevey, Dan T. ... Fort Dodge, IA
McGrevey Law Office ... Fort Dodge, IA
McGrevey, Sean T. ... Overland Park, KS
McGrew, Buck & Associates
Oklahoma City, OK
McGrew, Cynthia Brack ... San Diego, CA
McGrew, Dan ... Denver, CO
McGrew, Douglas A. ... Imperial Beach, CA
McGrew, Dwight W. ... Watseka, IL
McGrew, Gale I. ... Grandview, MO
McGrew, George R., (Of Counsel)
Kansas City, MO
McGrew, James H. ... Washington, DC
McGrew, James M., (P.C.)
New Orleans, LA
McGrew, Janet Daly ... New Orleans, LA
McGrew, John L. ... Washington, DC
McGrew, Michael D. ... Oklahoma City, OK
McGrew, Patrick F. ... Baton Rouge, LA
McGrew, R. Scott ... Portland, OR
McGrew, Raymond D. ... Houston, TX
McGrew, Robin D. ... Ventura, CA
McGrew, Spencer P. ... Modesto, CA
McGrew, T. Michelle ... San Diego, CA
McGrew, Theresa M. ... Chicago, IL
McGrew, Wayne D., III ... Atlanta, GA
McGrew, William E. ... Fort Myers, FL
McGrievy, Mark P. ... Cleveland, OH
McGriff, Alison J. ... Washington, DC
Baltimore, MD
McGriff, Barbara B. ... Jacksonville, FL
McGriff, Carol Reilly ... Atlanta, GA
McGriff, Cecil L. ... San Francisco, CA
McGriff, Karen L. ... Clarksville, TN
McGriff, Kelly A. ... Foley, AL
McGriff, Laurie T. ... Birmingham, AL
McGriff-Smith, Shannon M.
San Francisco, CA
McGrimley, Thomas J. ... Boston, MA
McGrinder, Rose M. ... Westfield, NJ
New York, NY
McGroarty, Edward P.
Department Of Health And Human Services,
Social Security Administration, GV
McGroarty, J. Michael ... Las Vegas, NV
McGroarty, J. Robert ... Atlantic City, NJ
Deptford, NJ
McGroarty, John ... Washington, DC
McGroarty, Joseph P. ... Linwood, NJ
McGroarty & Lane, Chtd. ... Las Vegas, NV
McGroarty, Michael P. ... Shelton, CT
McGroarty, Patrick T. ... Treasury Department,
Internal Revenue Service, GV
McGroarty, William V. ... Philadelphia, PA
McGroddy, Charles B. ... Katonah, NY
McGroder, Lori C. ... Kansas City, MO
McGroder, Patrick J., III ... Phoenix, AZ
McGroerty, Michael F. ... Seaford, DE
McGroerty, Michael F., P.A. ... Seaford, DE
McGrogan, Frances ... Hackensack, NJ
McGrory, Daniel T. ... King Of Prussia, PA
McGrory, Frank "Francis" H.
Cambridge, MA
McGrory, John ... La Jolla, CA
McGrory, John F., Jr. ... Portland, OR
McGrory, Joseph J., Jr. ... Limerick, PA
Norristown, PA
McGrory, Mark W. ... Kansas City, MO
McGrory, Matthew ... Des Moines, IA
McGrory, Michael D.
Executive Office Of The President,
Office of National Drug Control Policy, GV
McGrory, Philip L., Jr. ... New York, NY
McGrory, R. Kevin ... Trenton, NJ
McGrory, Richard F. ... Hagerstown, MD
McGrory and Schaefer ... Hagerstown, MD
McGrory, Timothy P. ... Chicago, IL
McGrory, Wentz, Fernandez & O'Hara, L.L.P. ... Limerick, PA
Norristown, PA
McGrotty, Amy C., P.A.
North Miami Beach, FL
McGrotty, Amy C., P.A.
North Miami Beach, FL
McGrotty, Heather C. ... Atlanta, GA
McGrotty, Patrick ... Lantana, FL

McGrouther, Robert, Jr.
San Francisco, CA
McGruder, Elaine T. ... Atlanta, GA
Jonesboro, GA
McGruder, Paul J. ... Cumming, GA
McGruder, Shawn Shyrlena
Falls Church, VA
McGruther, Randall B. ... Fort Myers, FL
McGuan, Kathleen H. ... Washington, DC
McGuan, Patrick J. ... Hawthorn Woods, IL
McGuane, Allan ... Greenfield, MA
McGuane, Frank L., Jr. ... Aspen, CO
Denver, CO
McGuane and Hogan LLP ... Aspen, CO
Denver, CO
McGuane, Michael W. ... Wheeling, WV
McGuane, Thomas F. ... Newark, NJ
McGucken, John T. ... Cockeysville, MD
McGucken, Kay J. ... Tampa, FL
McGucken, Kay J., P.A. ... Tampa, FL
McGuckian, Paul A. ... Rockville, MD
McGuckian, Rachel T. ... Rockville, MD
McGuckin, Gregory P. ... Forked River, NJ
McGuckin, Janice L. ... New York, NY
McGuckin, John H., Jr. ... San Francisco, CA
McGuckin, John J., Jr. ... Franklinton, LA
McGuckin, Michael W. ... Philadelphia, PA
McGuckin, Richard B. ... Akron, OH
McGuckin, Ronald V. ... Lumberville, PA
McGue, Clinton Dale ... Cabot, AR
McGue, Frank J. ... Phoenix, AZ
McGue, Joan ... Phoenix, AZ
Mc Guff, Jack D., III ... Pearland, TX
Mcguffage, William M. ... Chicago, IL
McGuffee, Neil P. ... Oklahoma City, OK
McGuffey, C. Wade, Jr. ... Atlanta, GA
McGuffey, Catherine P. ... Washington, DC
McGuffey & Clare, P.L.C. ... Louisville, KY
McGuffey, David LeBron ... Dalton, GA
McGuffey, Gaye L. ... Louisville, KY
McGuffey, Joseph Paul ... Amarillo, TX
McGuffey, Kristen ... Atlanta, GA
McGuffey, Paul, L.L.P. ... Amarillo, TX
McGuffie, Ginger ... Vienna, VA
McGuffin, Brian T. ... Warminster, PA
McGuffin, John G. ... Las Vegas, NV
McGuffin, Stanley H. ... Columbia, SC
McGuffog, Howard E. ... Melville, NY
McGuffog, Norman M. ... Atlanta, GA
McGugin, George B. ... Nashville, TN
McGuigan, A. Ryan ... Hartford, CT
McGuigan, Ann B. ... Burlington, MA
McGuigan, Austin J. ... Hartford, CT
McGuigan, Bruce F. ... Oklahoma City, OK
Mc Guigan, Charles D. ... Pierre, SD
McGuigan, Chris Ann ... Muskegon, MI
McGuigan, Donald G., II ... Southfield, MI
McGuigan, Epiphany ... Atlantic City, NJ
McGuigan & Holly, P.L.C. ... St. Paul, MN
McGuigan, J. April ... Washington, DC
McGuigan, James L. ... Murrysville, PA
McGuigan, John H. ... St. Paul, MN
McGuigan, John M. ... Portland, OR
McGuigan, John V. ... Princeton, NJ
McGuigan, Kathleen Cosgrove
Cherry Hill, NJ
McGuigan, Michael J. ... Honolulu, HI
McGuigan, Patrick J. ... St. Paul, MN
McGuigan, Philip P. ... Chicago, IL
Mcguigan, Susan E. ... Costa Mesa, CA
McGuigan, Thomas R., (P.A.) ... Miami, FL
McGuigan, Timothy P. ... Seattle, WA
McGuigan, William M. ... Chula Vista, CA
McGuill, Robert P. ... Refugio, TX
McGuiness, Jeffrey C. ... Washington, DC
McGuiness, John F., Jr. ... Philadelphia, PA
McGuiness, Kevin S. ... United States Senate,
Committee Legal Personnel, GV
McGuiness Norris & Williams, LLP
Washington, DC
Reston, VA
McGuiness, Robert D. ... Oakland, CA
McGuiness, William R. ... Sacramento, CA
McGuiness-Moody, Maureen M.
Gloucester, MA
McGuinn, Hillsman & Palefsky, A Professional Corporation
San Francisco, CA
McGuinn, John A. ... San Francisco, CA
McGuinn, John A. ... Washington, DC
McGuinn, Kerry C., Jr. ... Tampa, FL
McGuinn, Kerry G. ... Portland, OR
McGuinn, Martin G. ... Pittsburgh, PA
McGuinn, Martin T. ... San Diego, CA
McGuinn, Matthew J. ... Washington, DC
McGuinn, William F. ... Chicago, IL
McGuinn, Wm. Patrick ... Dayton, OH
McGuinness, Andrew J. ... Ann Arbor, MI
McGuinness, Brady K. ... Fresno, CA
McGuinness, Charles E. ... Southampton, NY
McGuinness, Christine A. ... New York, NY
McGuinness, Denis E. ... Newburgh, NY
McGuinness, Eugene J. ... White Plains, NY
McGuinness, J. Michael ... Washington, DC
Boston, MA
Elizabethtown, NC
McGuinness, John J., Jr. ... Bridgeport, CT
McGuinness, Karen A. ... Camden, NJ
Westmont, NJ
McGuinness, Kathleen G. ... Los Angeles, CA
McGuinness, Lynette Ebeoglu ... Miami, FL
McGuinness, Maria Charles ... Miami, FL
McGuinness and McNamara, P.C.
Mountain Lakes, NJ
New York, NY
McGuinness, Michael G. ... Los Angeles, CA
McGuinness, Michael L. ... Huntington, NY
McGuinness, Michael R. ... San Diego, CA

McGuinness, Neil F. ... Miami, FL
McGuinness, Patrick C. ... New York, NY
McGuinness, Peter J. ... Shelton, CT
McGuinness, Peter J. ... New York, NY
McGuinness, Richard
Mountain Lakes, NJ
McGuinness, Robert B. ... Towanda, PA
McGuinness, Sean P. ... Washington, DC
McGuinness, Tara ... Torrance, CA
McGuinness, Thomas P. ... Palos Heights, IL
McGuinness, Vincent R., Jr. ... Westmont, NJ
Philadelphia, PA
McGuinness, William G. ... New York, NY
McGuinn-Ringe, Patricia ... Philadelphia, PA
McGuire, Andre L. ... Millburn, NJ
McGuire, Andrew J. ... Phoenix, AZ
McGuire, Andrew P. ... Washington, DC
McGuire, Ann L. ... Seattle, WA
McGuire, Arthur H. ... New York, NY
McGuire, Bartlett H. ... New York, NY
McGuire, Bernadine Feller ... Rock Island, IL
McGuire, Bernard J. ... Provo, UT
McGuire, Bernard M. ... San Francisco, CA
McGuire, Beryl E. ... Cape Coral, FL
Mc Guire, Bruce E. ... Louisiana, MO
McGuire, Carol A. ... Chicago, IL
McGuire, Catherine
Securities and Exchange Commission,
Division of Market Regulation, GV
McGuire, Catherine A. ... Waynesboro, VA
McGuire, Catherine Kiley ... Great Neck, NY
McGuire, Charles J. ... Dallas, TX
McGuire, Charles Lewis Winston
Liberty, TX
McGuire, Charles S. ... Syracuse, NY
McGuire, Charles W. ... Baltimore, MD
McGuire, Christine A. ... Dallas, TX
McGuire, Christopher ... Washington, DC
McGuire, Christopher D. ... Tallahassee, FL
McGuire, Claire L.
Federal Deposit Insurance Corporation,
Appellate Litigation Section, GV
McGuire, Claire R. ... Boston, MA
McGuire, Clint E. ... Houston, TX
McGuire, Clinton C. ... Louisville, KY
McGuire, Constance Smith ... Waxahachie, TX
McGuire & Cox ... Gulfport, MS
McGuire, Craddock, Strother & Hale, P.C.
Dallas, TX
McGuire, Craig Eugene ... Polo, IL
McGuire, Cristie C. ... San Diego, CA
McGuire, Daniel Clay ... Las Vegas, NV
McGuire, Daniel J. ... Chicago, IL
McGuire, Daniel J. ... Cleveland, OH
McGuire, Daniel R. L. ... Duncannon, PA
McGuire, David A. ... Chicago, IL
McGuire, David F. ... Anaheim, CA
McGuire, David F. ... Cedar Rapids, IA
McGuire, Debra A. ... Washington, DC
McGuire, Dennis L. ... Seattle, WA
McGuire, Dennis M. ... Columbus, OH
McGuire, Derril W. ... Ardmore, OK
McGuire, Diane M. ... Key Largo, FL
McGuire, Douglas F. ... Richfield, MN
McGuire, E. James ... Oakland, CA
McGuire, E. Patrick ... Provo, UT
McGuire, E. Warren ... Kentfield, CA
McGuire, Earl M. ... Prestonsburg, KY
McGuire, Edward D., Jr. ... Rockville, MD
Annandale, VA
McGuire, Edward D., Jr. ... Alexandria, VA
Arlington, VA
Fairfax, VA
McGuire, Edward J., Jr. ... New York, NY
McGuire, Eileen M. ... Wickenburg, AZ
McGuire, Elyse K. ... San Rafael, CA
McGuire, Eugene F. ... Denver, CO
McGuire, Eugene G. ... New York, NY
McGuire, Felicia M. ... Riverside, CA
McGuire, Francis J. ... Woodland, CA
McGuire, Frank L., III ... Andalusia, AL
McGuire, Frank T. ... Bangor, ME
McGuire, George R. ... Syracuse, NY
McGuire, Glenda M. ... Houston, TX
McGuire, Grant W. ... Newark, NJ
McGuire, Gregory P. ... Raleigh, NC
McGuire, H. Joseph ... Orlando, FL
McGuire, H. Lee, Jr. ... Leavenworth, KS
McGuire, Harold F., Jr. ... New York, NY
McGuire, Hines, Steigerwald & Hawk
Dayton, OH
McGuire, Hugh A., III ... Jersey City, NJ
McGuire, Hugh E., Jr. ... Bradenton, FL
McGuire, Hugh J. ... Troy, MI
McGuire, J. Grant ... Ashland, KY
Huntington, WV
McGuire, J. Kent ... Waxahachie, TX
McGuire, J. Michael ... Baltimore, MD
McGuire, James A. ... Annapolis, MD
McGuire, James A. ... Edgewater, MD
McGuire, James A. ... New York, NY
McGuire, James C. ... Joshua Tree, CA
McGuire, James C. ... New London, CT
McGuire, James C. ... Frankfort, KY
McGuire, James C. ... Dayton, OH
McGuire, James D. ... Atlanta, GA
McGuire, James E. ... Atlanta, GA
McGuire, James E. ... Boston, MA
McGuire, James E. ... Princeton, NJ
McGuire, James F. ... Atlanta, GA
McGuire, James H. ... Los Angeles, CA
McGuire, James J. ... Tampa, FL
McGuire, James J. ... Edgewater, MD
McGuire, James J. ... New York, NY
McGuire, James J. ... Woodbury, NY
McGuire, James J. ... Cleveland, OH
McGuire, James J. ... Winchester, VA
McGuire, James J., Jr. ... Tinton Falls, NJ

McHugh, Lynn D. ....Murdock, NE
McHugh, M. Colleen ....Corpus Christi, TX
McHugh, M. Maureen ....Detroit, MI
McHugh and Macri ....East Hanover, NJ
McHugh, Margaret C. ......San Francisco, CA
McHugh, Marianna Bush
Charleston, WV
McHugh, Martin J. ....Trenton, NJ
McHugh, Martin S. ....Chico, CA
McHugh, Mary ....Upper Marlboro, MD
McHugh, Mary ....New York, NY
Mc Hugh, Mary Frances ....Yreka, CA
McHugh, Matthew F. ....Washington, DC
McHugh, Michael C., II
Wilkes-Barre, PA
McHugh, Michael Francis ....Philadelphia, PA
McHugh, Michael J. ....Boston, MA
McHugh, Patricia A. ....Helena, MT
McHugh, Patrick C. ....Manchester, NH
McHugh, Patrick J. ....Stamford, CT
McHugh, Patrick J. ....Cambridge, MA
Springfield, MA
McHugh, Patrick J. ....Missoula, MT
McHugh, Patrick M. ....Philadelphia, PA
McHugh, Patrick N. ....St. Louis, MO
McHugh, Paul H.
Department of the Air Force, Office of the General Counsel, GV
McHugh, Peter B. ....Schenectady, NY
McHugh, Peter Gerard ....Washington, DC
McHugh, Peter J. ....Denver, CO
McHugh, Peter J. ....Washington, DC
Newark, NJ
New York, NY
McHugh, Peter M. ....Wentworth, NC
McHugh, Randall S. ....Farmington, CT
McHugh, Raymond F. ....Feasterville, PA
McHugh, Richard C. ....Pittsburgh, PA
McHugh, Richard P. ....Washington, DC
McHugh, Richard W. ....Ann Arbor, MI
McHugh, Robert C. ....Colorado Springs, CO
McHugh, Robert D. ....Chicago, IL
McHugh, Robin A. ....Helena, MT
McHugh, Russell T. ....Mineola, NY
McHugh, Sarah A. ....Toledo, OH
McHugh & Sherman ....New York, NY
McHugh, Stefanie T. ....Atlanta, GA
Peachtree City, GA
McHugh, Stephen M. ....Dayton, OH
McHugh, Stephen V. ....Cherry Hill, NJ
Philadelphia, PA
McHugh, Steven J. ....South Lake Tahoe, CA
McHugh, Susan Papanek ....Boston, MA
McHugh, Thomas D., IV ......West Hartford, CT
McHugh, Thomas E. ....Charleston, WV
McHugh, Thomas G. ....St. Martinville, LA
McHugh, Thomas G. ....Mount Clemens, MI
McHugh, Thomas J. ....San Francisco, CA
McHugh, Thomas P. ....Williamstown, MA
McHugh, Thomas P. ....Florham Park, NJ
McHugh, Timothy C. ....Tampa, FL
McHugh, Timothy J. ....New York, NY
Mchugh, Timothy K. ....Williamstown, NJ
McHugh, Timothy P. ....Elmhurst, IL
McHugh, Timothy P., Ltd. ....Elmhurst, IL
McHugh, Timothy R., (P.C.) ....Boston, MA
McHugh, Wetzel, Caverly & Phillips
Shickshinny, PA
Wilkes-Barre, PA
McHugh, William D. ....San Jose, CA
McHugh, William F. ....Tallahassee, FL
McHugh, William J., Sr. ....St. Louis, MO
McHugh, William M. ....Atlanta, GA
Peachtree City, GA
McHugh, Wm. Thomas ....Nashville, TN
McHughes, Josh E. ....Little Rock, AR
McIlhany, Grainger W. ....Wheeler, TX
McIlhany, Thomas G. ....Abilene, TX
McIlhany, William R. ....Austin, TX
McIlhargie, Cyril J. ....Chicago, IL
McIlhenny, Deborah B. ....Wichita, KS
McIlhenny, John K., Jr. ....Portland, OR
McIlmail, Timothy P.
Department of Justice, Civil Division, GV
McIlnay, Bruce A. ....Grafton, WI
Milwaukee, WI
McIlnay, Sharon A. ....Dearborn, MI
McIlquham, Sharon Gibbs
Eau Claire, WI
McIlrath, James W. ....Tampa, FL
McIlrath, Paul E. ....Port Townsend, WA
McIlroy, Daniel F. ....Phoenix, AZ
McIlroy, John B. ....Los Angeles, CA
McIlroy, John M., Jr. ....Bowling Green, MO
McIlroy, John M., Sr. ....Bowling Green, MO
McIlroy & Millan ....Bowling Green, MO
Vandalia, MO
McIlroy, Robert D. ....Quincy, CA
McIlroy, Robert N. ....Norman, OK
McIlroy, Terry A. ....Chicago, IL
McIlroy, William C. ....Bowling Green, MO
Vandalia, MO
McIlvain, Alan M. ....Oklahoma City, OK
McIlvain, Grace ....Tucson, AZ
McIlvain, J. Bradford ....Cherry Hill, NJ
Philadelphia, PA
McIlvain, Joseph C., Jr. ....Memphis, TN
McIlvain, Karen Kubovec ....Madison, KS
McIlvain & McIlvain ....Madison, KS
McIlvain, Ross R. ....Madison, KS
McIlvaine, Andrew S. ....Wadsworth, OH
McIlvaine, James R. ....Wadsworth, OH
McIlvaine, John W. ....Washington, PA
McIlvaine, John W., III ....Pittsburgh, PA
McIlvaine, Kerrin E. ....Washington, PA
McIlvaine, Stephen B. ....Wadsworth, OH
McIlvery, John J. ....Los Angeles, CA
McIlwain, Carol Newell ....Cincinnati, OH
McIlwain, Christopher L. ....Tuscaloosa, AL
McIlwain, David L. ....Department of Justice, Environment and Natural Resources Division, GV
McIlwain, Desmond Terrell
Baltimore, MD
McIlwain, Douglas W. ....Cincinnati, OH
McIlwain, Harry H. ....Cincinnati, OH
McIlwain, Harry H., Jr. ....Cincinnati, OH
McIlwain, James R. ....Baton Rouge, LA
McIlwain, Jeaneen J. ....Canton, OH
McIlwain & McIlwain ....Cincinnati, OH
McIlwain, Merrell S., II ....Charleston, WV
McIlwain, Russell L. ....Chicago, IL
McIlwain, Samuel D. ....Richmond, VA
McIlwain, Stephen E. ....Albuquerque, NM
McIlwain, Timothy J. ....El Segundo, CA
McIlwain, Willard L. ....Greenville, MS
McIlwain, Willard L., Jr. ....Greenville, MS
McIlwain, William C., III ....Laurinburg, NC
McIlwaine, Robert D., III ....Petersburg, VA
McIlwrath, Rolleen Kent ....Stockton, CA
McIlyar, W. Kent, III ....Dallas, TX
McInally, Fiona A. ....Austin, TX
McInally, LeRoy B.
Grosse Pointe Farms, MI
McInaney, Michele Glavinovich
San Jose, CA
McIndoe, David T. ....Richmond, VA
McInerney, Alice ....New York, NY
McInerney Baker ....Seattle, WA
McInerney, Barrett W. ....Santa Clarita, CA
McInerney, Brendan ....New York, NY
McInerney, Christine ....Mineola, NY
McInerney, Daniel J., Jr.
Minneapolis, MN
McInerney, Danl. J. ....St. Paul, MN
McInerney, Denis ....New York, NY
McInerney, Denis J. ....New York, NY
McInerney, Diana D. ....Providence, RI
McInerney & Dillon, Professional Corporation ....Oakland, CA
McInerney, Donald B. ....Chicago, IL
McInerney, Francis M., Jr. ....Patchogue, NY
McInerney, Francis M., Jr., P.C.
Patchogue, NY
McInerney, Gary J. ....Grand Rapids, MI
McInerney, Gary J., P.C. ....Grand Rapids, MI
McInerney, George F.X. ....Bayport, NY
McInerney, J. Bernard ....Detroit, MI
McInerney, James L. ....Pinehurst, NC
McInerney, John D.
Department of Commerce, Office of the General Counsel, GV
McInerney, John E., III
San Francisco, CA
McInerney, John J. ....East Islip, NY
McInerney, John J., Jr. ....Chicago, IL
McInerney, John K. ....Redwood City, CA
McInerney, John L. ....New York, NY
McInerney, John Peter ....Campbelltown, PA
McInerney, Joseph ....Auburn, CA
McInerney, Kerry Patrick
Birmingham, AL
McInerney, Kevin J. ....San Diego, CA
McInerney, Kirk M. ....Chicago, IL
McInerney, Mark W. ....Detroit, MI
McInerney, Mary Elizabeth
Long Beach, CA
McInerney, Mary M. ....Chicago, IL
McInerney, Maura I. ....Philadelphia, PA
McInerney, Michael E.
Sterling Heights, MI
McInerney & Mulvaney ....Far Rockaway, NY
McInerney, Roberta K. .....Treasury Department, Office of the General Counsel, GV
McInerney, Susan Barbara ....Chicago, IL
McInerney, Thomas F., III ....New York, NY
McInerney, Thomas F., Jr. ....Hershey, PA
McInerney, Thomas J. ....Yonkers, NY
McInerney, Thomas M.
San Francisco, CA
McInerney, Timothy L. ....Oakland, CA
McInerney, William H. ....Oakland, CA
McInerney, William H., Jr. ....Oakland, CA
McInerney, William K., Jr. ....Seattle, WA
McInerney, William P. ....New York, NY
McInerny, Daniel C. ....Minnetonka, MN
McInerny, Daniel C., P.A.
Minnetonka, MN
McInerny, Daniel P. ....Indianapolis, IN
McInerny, Francis W. ....Washington, DC
McInerny, George F. ....Dedham, MA
McInerny, James P. ....Houston, TX
McInerny, John S. ....San Jose, CA
McInerny & Jordan ....Washington, DC
McInerny, Julia Wernett ....Washington, DC
McInerny, Justin Francis ....Rockville, MD
McInerny, Kia W. ....Los Angeles, CA
McInerny, Mary M. ....Los Alamos, NM
McInerny, Michael T. ....Boston, MA
McIninch, Douglas A. ....Manchester, NH
McInish, H. Dwight ....Dothan, AL
McInish, Peter A. ....Dothan, AL
McInnes, Alan D. ....Asheville, NC
McInnes, David G. ....Sacramento, CA
McInnes, Donald K. ....Cambridge, MA
McInnis, A. Kell, III ....Baton Rouge, LA
McInnis, Brian M. ....St. Louis, MO
McInnis, C. Jeffrey
Fort Walton Beach, FL
McInnis, Daniel F. ....Washington, DC
McInnis, Daniel S. ....Boston, MA
McInnis, David F. ....Sumter, SC
McInnis, E. Winton, III ....Little Rock, AR
McInnis, Emmett E., Jr. ....Seattle, WA
McInnis, Gavin H. ....Houston, TX
McInnis, George E. ....Salinas, CA
McInnis, Gerard A. ....Chicago, IL
McInnis, James C. ....Lake Charles, LA
McInnis, James J., P.C. ....North Andover, MA
McInnis, John ....Miami, FL
McInnis, John D., Jr. ....Dillon, SC
McInnis, John R. ....Missoula, MT
McInnis, John S. ....Brandon, MS
McInnis, Jonathan L. ....Laurinburg, NC
McInnis, Judith L. ....Columbia, SC
McInnis, Kirk ....Palo Alto, CA
McInnis, Lou Anne D. ....New York, NY
McInnis, Malcolm C., Jr. ....Knoxville, TN
McInnis, Mary E. ....St. Louis, MO
Mcinnis, Marybeth ....North Andover, MA
McInnis, Michael L. ....Fairfax, VA
McInnis, Michaela Shea ....Jamestown, RI
McInnis, Neil E., & Associates
Hattiesburg, MS
McInnis, Richard Kevin ....Houston, TX
McInnis, Robert M.
North Myrtle Beach, SC
McInnis, Scott S. ....Glenwood Springs, CO
McInnis, Steven M. ....Newport, RI
McInnis, Steven M. ....Providence, RI
McInnis, Terrence R. ....Irvine, CA
San Diego, CA
McInnis, Timothy J., Law Office of
New York, NY
McInnis, Treva Lowery ....Jackson, MS
McInnis, Vernon A. ....Philadelphia, PA
McInnish, C. Michael ....Montgomery, AL
Mcinnis-Nixon, R. Amanda
Oklahoma City, OK
McInroy, Cheryl A. ....San Francisco, CA
McInroy, Kevin D. ....Arlington, VA
McInroy & Rigby, L.L.P. ....Alexandria, VA
Arlington, VA
McInroy, Valarie L. ....Palo Alto, CA
McIntee, James M. ....McHenry, IL
McIntee Law Firm ....Bottineau, ND
Towner, ND
McIntee, Michael R. ....Williston, ND
McIntee, Michael S. ....Towner, ND
McIntee, Shawn R. ....Minneapolis, MN
Mc Inteer, Carlotta R. ....Los Alamos, NM
McInteer, Jack Scott ....Wichita, KS
McIntire, Christopher D.
Big Bear Lake, CA
McIntire, Diane L. ....Bethesda, MD
McIntire, Edward A. ....Kankakee, IL
McIntire, Everette L. ....Atlanta, GA
McIntire, Gerald L. ....Noblesville, IN
McIntire, John M. ....Washington, DC
McIntire, John P. ....Menlo Park, CA
McIntire, Johnson, Levin & Webb, LLC
Westminster, MD
McIntire Law Corporation
Big Bear Lake, CA
McIntire, Lee S. ....Oklahoma City, OK
McIntire, Linda Parker ....Montpelier, VT
Mc Intire, Margaret A. ....Wichita, KS
McIntire, Mark A. ....Las Vegas, NV
McIntire, Mary K. ....Mackinac Island, MI
McIntire, Michael H. ....Hammond, LA
McIntire, Michael V. ....Big Bear Lake, CA
McIntire, Neil Martin ....Nashville, TN
McIntire, Patrick B. ....Lafayette, LA
McIntire, Philip C. ....Glens Falls, NY
McIntire, Robert A. ....Baltimore, MD
Mcintire, Robert E. ....Danville, IL
McIntire, Robert P. ....Lubbock, TX
McIntire, Ronald A. ....Santa Monica, CA
McIntire, T. Bryan, Jr. ....Westminster, MD
McIntire, Thomas E. ....Wheeling, WV
McIntire, Thomas E., & Associates, L.C.
Wheeling, WV
McIntire, Thomas O. ....Antioch, TN
McIntire, Yvonne D. ....Treasury Department, Office of the Comptroller of the Currency, GV
McIntosh, Alexandra R. ....Solana Beach, CA
McIntosh, Andrea K. ....Los Angeles, CA
McIntosh, Andrew C. ....Minneapolis, MN
McIntosh, Andrew L. ....Tampa, FL
McIntosh, Audrey Hanson
Jefferson City, MO
McIntosh, Barbara G. ....Seattle, WA
McIntosh, Brett Donald ....Sarasota, FL
McIntosh, Bruce A. ....Oakland, CA
McIntosh, Bruce B. ....Cincinnati, OH
McIntosh, Bruce T. ....Los Angeles, CA
McIntosh, C. Arthur ....Oxford, MS
McIntosh, Cal ....Palm Desert, CA
McIntosh, Chad B. ....Parkersburg, WV
McIntosh, Colleen M. ....New York, NY
McIntosh, Craig G. ....Sacramento, CA
McIntosh, D. Laurence ....Florence, SC
McIntosh, Dan A., III ....Collins, MS
McIntosh, Daniel F. ....Orlando, FL
McIntosh, Daniel G. ....Los Angeles, CA
McIntosh, David F. ....Miami, FL
McIntosh, David M. ....Boston, MA
McIntosh, Deborah R. ....Lewiston, ID
McIntosh, Denise Marie ....Nashville, TN
McIntosh, Dennis E. ....Farmington, MO
McIntosh & Dockery, LLC ....Englewood, CO
McIntosh, Donna M. ....Manassas, VA
McIntosh, Douglas F. ....Wilmington, NC
McIntosh, Douglas M.
Fort Lauderdale, FL
McIntosh, Duncan S. ....Columbia, SC
McIntosh, Ed ....Wichita Falls, TX
McIntosh, Edna E. ....Waycross, GA
McIntosh, Edwin N. ....Des Moines, IA
McIntosh, Eric S. ....Orange, CA
McIntosh, Ernest W., Jr. ....Washington, DC
McIntosh, Erskine D. ....Bridgeport, CT
New Haven, CT
McIntosh, Fox & Lancaster
Lake Providence, LA
Oak Grove, LA
McIntosh, Frank J. ....Groton, CT
McIntosh, Gail H. ....Newport Beach, CA
McIntosh, George E. ....Mount Vernon, WA
McIntosh, H. Thomas, Jr. ....Charleston, SC
McIntosh, H. William, (P.C.)
Kansas City, MO
McIntosh, Heidi J. ....Salt Lake City, UT
McIntosh, Howard A. ....Monterey Park, CA
McIntosh, Hugh M. ....Washington, DC
McIntosh, Ian C ....Billings, MT
McIntosh, Jack F. ....Anderson, SC
McIntosh, James A. ....Knoxville, TN
McIntosh, James Elliot ....Santa Ana, CA
McIntosh, James L. ....Napa, CA
McIntosh, James O. ....Orlando, FL
McIntosh, James R. ....Hartford, CT
McIntosh, Jerry L. ....Fort Wayne, IN
McIntosh, Jill Valiton ....Toledo, OH
McIntosh, Joanna K.
Executive Office Of The President, Office of the U.S. Trade Representative, GV
Mcintosh, Joanne P. ....New York, NY
McIntosh, Jock G. ....Portland, OR
McIntosh, John C. ....Flint, MI
Lansing, MI
Pontiac, MI
McIntosh, John C. ....Buffalo, MN
McIntosh, John E., Jr. ....Fairfax, VA
McIntosh, John V. ....Charlotte, NC
McIntosh, John W. ....Columbia, SC
McIntosh, Joseph A. ....Seattle, WA
McIntosh, Joseph Thomas ....Chicago, IL
McIntosh, Kenneth W. ....Sanford, FL
McIntosh, Kevin C. ....Hickory, NC
McIntosh, Knepper, Hobson & Healy, A Professional Association .....Kansas City, MO
McIntosh, Lauri S. ....Irvine, CA
McIntosh Law Firm, The, P.C.
Charlotte, NC
Concord, NC
Davidson, NC
Mooresville, NC
McIntosh & Lee ....Darlington, SC
Florence, SC
McIntosh, Lesa Renee ......Point Richmond, CA
McIntosh, Lynn S. ....Washington, DC
McIntosh, Mark A. ....Huntington, IN
McIntosh, Mark F. ....Atlanta, GA
McIntosh, Martha H. ....Orlando, FL
McIntosh, Mary Going ....Columbia, SC
McIntosh, Mary H. ....Mount Vernon, WA
McIntosh, Maxwell D.
Christiansted, St. Croix, VI
McIntosh, McColl, Carson, McNamee & Strickler ....Fort Gratiot, MI
McIntosh, McIntosh & Knabe, A Legal Professional Association .....Cincinnati, OH
McIntosh, Michael ....Springfield, IL
McIntosh, Michael ....New York, NY
McIntosh, Michael C. ....Independence, MO
McIntosh, Michael D. ....Englewood, CO
McIntosh, Michael Todd ....Cincinnati, OH
McIntosh, Molly B. ....Albuquerque, NM
McIntosh, Owen L. ....Hacienda Heights, CA
McIntosh, Peter ....Charlottesville, VA
McIntosh, Phillip L. ....Jackson, MS
McIntosh, Rivers Lawton ....Anderson, SC
McIntosh, Robert D. .....Fort Lauderdale, FL
McIntosh, Robert G. ....Davidson, NC
McIntosh, Robert H. ....Malibu, CA
McIntosh, Robert J. ....Washington, DC
Fort Gratiot, MI
McIntosh, Robert K. ....Sanford, FL
McIntosh, Robert K. ....Berlin, MD
McIntosh, Robert M. ....Olympia, WA
McIntosh, Robert W. ....Rochester, MN
McIntosh, Sandra R. ....San Jose, CA
McIntosh, Sarah Barber ....Charleston, SC
McIntosh, Sawran, Peltz & Cartaya, P.A.
Fort Lauderdale, FL
Miami, FL
West Palm Beach, FL
McIntosh & Schanno, P.A. ....Berlin, MD
Ocean City, MD
McIntosh, Scott A. ....Washington, DC
McIntosh, Sherrard & Sullivan
Anderson, SC
McIntosh, Sherman C., Jr. ....Palm Desert, CA
McIntosh, Stephen L. ....Columbus, OH
McIntosh, Stuart A. ....San Francisco, CA
McIntosh, Susan K. ....Seattle, WA
McIntosh, Susan L. ....Ouray, CO
McIntosh, Susan L. ....New York, NY
McIntosh, Terrie T. ....Salt Lake City, UT
McIntosh, Thomas B., Jr. ....Jefferson, LA
McIntosh, Thomas J. ....Lafayette, CA
McIntosh, Thomas Maxwell ....Santa Ana, CA
McIntosh, Thomas S. ....Bakersfield, CA
McIntosh, W. Charles ....Lansing, MI
McIntosh, William E. ....Charleston, SC
McIntosh, William M. ....Moultrie, GA
McInturf, Timothy T. ....Houston, TX
McInturff, Burkett C. ....Kingsport, TN
McInturff, Carl ....Johnson City, TN
McInturff, George R. ....Chattanooga, TN
McInturff, J. Ben. ....Spokane, WA
McInturff, Judith M. ....Columbus, OH
McInturff, Patrick S. ....Hanford, CA
McInturff, Russell N. ....Odessa, TX
McIntyre, Alexander M., Jr.
New Orleans, LA
McIntyre, Amelia J. ....Topeka, KS
McIntyre, Amy Fortenberry
Birmingham, AL
McIntyre, Andrea J. ....Chicago, IL

McKean, Gary O. ....Farmington, UT
McKean, George H. ....Mobile, AL
McKean, Gordon A. ....Ossining, NY
McKean, Gordon W. ....Delray Beach, FL
McKean, Grover L. ....Los Angeles, CA
McKean, James Daniel ....Ames, IA
McKean, Jeffrey L. ....Indianapolis, IN
McKean, John P. ....Topeka, KS
Mckean, Laura J. ....St. Louis, MO
McKean, Mattson and Latici
Laconia, NH
Gilford, NH
McKean, Pamela A. ....Oak Harbor, OH
McKean, Paul A. ....Acton, MA
McKean, Paul L. ....Sarasota, FL
McKean, Quincy A. S., Jr. ....Rumson, NJ
McKean, Robert J., Jr. ....Reston, VA
McKean, Thomas A. ....Atlanta, GA
McKean, William J. ....Reno, NV
McKeand, Jeri R. ....Santa Ana, CA
McKeaney, Frank J., Jr. ....Philadelphia, PA
McKearin, George S. ....Plano, TX
McKearin, George S. ....Richardson, TX
McKearin, Robert R. ....Burlington, VT
McKearney, Diana ....Burlington, MA
McKeating, Michael P. ....Buffalo, NY
McKeating, Sean P. ....Gonzales, TX
McKechnie, C. Logan ....Merced, CA
Mckechnie, Jon A. ....Pittsburgh, PA
McKechnie, Joseph R., Jr. ....New York, NY
McKechnie, William Elliott
Grand Forks, ND
McKee, Albert Wesley ....Livingston, NJ
McKee, Alison Mitchell ....Norfolk, VA
McKee, Angela D. ....Dallas, TX
McKee, Archie C. ....Amsterdam, NY
McKee, Barbara J. ....San Francisco, CA
McKee, Barnet M. ....St. Louis, MO
McKee, Barry W. ....Stillwater, MN
McKee, Bill ....San Antonio, TX
McKee & Bowker, P.C. ....Tulsa, OK
McKee, Bruce B. ....San Francisco, CA
McKee, Bruce J. ....Birmingham, AL
McKee, Bruce W. ....Des Moines, IA
Omaha, NE
McKee and Butler ....Winchester, VA
McKee, Carolyn A. ....Chicago, IL
McKee, Catherine L. ....San Antonio, TX
McKee, Charles C., Sr. ....Santa Ana, CA
McKee, Charles E. ....Westlake Village, CA
McKee, Charles E. ....Havertown, PA
McKee, Charles H. ....Tulsa, OK
McKee, Charles Joseph ....San Rafael, CA
McKee, Charles W. ....Kansas City, MO
McKee, Christina M. ....Indianapolis, IN
McKee, Christine M. ....Kansas City, MO
McKee, Christopher J. ....Roswell, GA
McKee, Christopher L. ....Washington, DC
McKee, Craig M. ....Terre Haute, IN
Mckee, Cynthia N. ....Newark, NJ
McKee, D. Duff ....Boise, ID
McKee, Dana Whitehead ....Baltimore, MD
McKee, Darwin ....Austin, TX
McKee, David C. ....Deerfield, IL
McKee, David J. ....Billings, MT
McKee, Delores P. ....Bullhead City, AZ
McKee, Dennis H. ....San Diego, CA
McKee, Donald B. ....Miami, FL
Mckee, Donald L. ....Indiana, PA
McKee, Dorris, Peltz & Barnes ....Jericho, NY
McKee, Douglas R. ....Lansing, MI
McKee, Dovette ....Chicago, IL
McKee, Duncan O. ....Levittown, PA
McKee, Evelyn Palfrey ....Austin, TX
McKee, F. William ....Grand Rapids, MI
McKee, F. William ....Grand Rapids, MI
McKee, Forrest W. ....Golden, CO
McKee, Gary S. ....Columbia, TN
McKee, George C. ....Mississippi State, MS
McKee, George C., P.A.
Mississippi State, MS
McKee, George W. ....Newtown, PA
McKee, Giuliani & Cleveland, A Professional Corporation ....Montpelier, VT
McKee, Graydon S., III
Upper Marlboro, MD
McKee, Gregory J. ....Belleville, IL
McKee, Gregory Samuel ....Washington, DC
McKee, H. Anne ....Chicago, IL
McKee, Harold E. ....Chicago, IL
McKee, Harry W. ....Tyler, TX
McKee, Heather Anne ....Oakland, CA
McKee, Howard A. ....Chicago, IL
McKee, Ira Keith ....Acworth, GA
Mckee, Ira Keith, P.C. ....Acworth, GA
McKee, James E. ....Tallahassee, FL
McKee, James E. ....Rye, NY
McKee, James W. ....Cleveland, OH
McKee, Jean ....Grand Rapids, MI
McKee, Jennifer D. ....Los Angeles, CA
McKee, Jennifer K.
Federal Communications Commission, Common Carrier Bureau, GV
McKee, John C., Jr. ....Wayzata, MN
McKee, John E. ....Memphis, TN
McKee, John M. ....Buffalo, NY
McKee, John R. ....Oklahoma City, OK
McKee, Jonathan D. ....St. Louis, MO
McKee, Joseph R. ....Richmond, VA
McKee, Judith E. ....Harrisonburg, VA
McKee, Judy H. ....Yorba Linda, CA
McKee, Julia Riggle ....Kansas City, MO
McKee, K. Roxanne ....Austin, TX
McKee, Kate C. ....Nashville, TN
McKee, Kathleen D. ....Seattle, WA
McKee, Kathleen J. ....San Diego, CA
McKee, Kathleen J. ....Chicago, IL
McKee, Laurel J. ....Morristown, NJ

McKee, M. Curtiss ....Jackson, MS
McKee, Margaret M. ....Towson, MD
McKee, Martha ....Durham, NC
McKee, Mary B. ....Oberlin, OH
McKee, Mary Porter ....Lexington, KY
McKee, Mary Victoria Mullen ....Clayton, MO
Mckee, Matthew S. ....Philadelphia, PA
McKee & McKee, P.C. ....Austin, TX
McKee, Michael E. ....Knoxville, TN
McKee, Michael R. ....Norman, OK
McKee, Miles F. ....Detroit, MI
McKee, Mitchell E. ....Houston, TX
McKee and Moore ....Amsterdam, NY
McKee, Pamela ....Annapolis, MD
McKee, Patricia ....Exeter, NH
McKee, Patrick W. ....Atlanta, GA
Newnan, GA
McKee, Patrick W. ....Newnan, GA
McKee, Peter H. D. ....Seattle, WA
McKee, Peter K., Jr. ....Dallas, TX
McKee, Phelps & Bowman ....Buffalo, NY
McKee, Ralph R. ....Detroit, MI
McKee, Raymond W. ....San Francisco, CA
McKee, Rebecca I. ....Oakland, CA
McKee, Richard W. ....Tucson, AZ
McKee, Robert C. ....Birmingham, AL
McKee, Robert E., Jr. ....Honolulu, HI
McKee, Robert E., Jr. ....Elizabeth, PA
Pittsburgh, PA
McKee, Robert F. ....Tampa, FL
McKee, Robert J. ....Fort Lauderdale, FL
McKee, Robert J., Jr. ....Basking Ridge, NJ
McKee, Sally J. ....Belleville, IL
McKee, Sarah ....Department of Justice, Criminal Division, GV
McKee, Scott Cummings ....San Diego, CA
McKee, Sean H. ....Tulsa, OK
McKee, Sharon F. ....Cherry Hill, NJ
Philadelphia, PA
McKee, Stephen F. ....Anchorage, AK
McKee, Susan Ellen ....Columbus, OH
McKee, T. Braxton ....Norfolk, VA
McKee, Teresa M. ....Lander, WY
McKee, Theodore A. ....Philadelphia, PA
McKee, Thomas C. ....Denver, CO
McKee, Thomas C. ....Johnson City, TN
McKee, Thomas F. ....Cleveland, OH
McKee, Thomas J. ....Greenwich, CT
McKee, Timothy C. ....Norfolk, VA
McKee, Timothy E. ....Wichita, KS
McKee, Todd C. ....Nashville, TN
McKee, W. Mark ....West Monroe, LA
McKee, Walter F. ....Augusta, ME
McKee, Wayne T.
Federal Communications Commission, Cable Services Bureau, GV
McKee, Wesley J. ....Monroe, MI
McKee, William A. ....Columbus, OH
McKee, William F. ....Savannah, GA
McKee, William N. ....Jericho, NY
McKee, William R. ....Pittsburgh, PA
McKee, William S. ....Washington, DC
McKee, William Todd ....Tulsa, OK
McKee, Wm. Miles ....Ann Arbor, MI
Findlay, OH
Toledo, OH
McKeeby, Paulo B. ....Dallas, TX
McKeefe, John P. ....Patterson, NY
McKeegan, Bruce J. ....Delhi, NY
McKeegan, George P. ....New York, NY
McKeegan, John N. ....Scottsdale, AZ
McKeegan, Kevin F. ....Pittsburgh, PA
McKeegan & McKeegan ....Delhi, NY
McKeegan, McShane & Drager
New York, NY
McKeegan, Robert J. ....Delhi, NY
McKeehan, Cynthia Nichols ....Odessa, TX
McKeehan, Danice L. ....Dallas, TX
McKeehan, Emby A. ....Williamsburg, KY
McKeehan, James W. ....Pleasanton, CA
McKeehan, Judy Campos ....Sacramento, CA
McKeehan, Stewart ....Odessa, TX
McKeehan, William J. ....Coral Gables, FL
McKeehen, Monte C. ....Seattle, WA
McKeel, Agather Celeste ....Little Rock, AR
McKeel, J. Thomas ....Jacksonville, FL
McKeel, Richard P. ....Odessa, TX
McKeeman, Christine E. ....Austin, TX
McKeeman, Larry E. ....Everett, WA
McKeeman, Leland P. ....Austin, TX
McKeeman, Michael T.
San Francisco, CA
McKeeman & Tuttle ....Austin, TX
McKeen, Mark E. ....San Francisco, CA
McKeen, Mary Alice ....Juneau, AK
McKeen, P. Douglas ....St. Paul, MN
McKeen, Sam A. ....Sun Valley, NV
McKeen, Steven D. ....Sacramento, CA
McKeever, Benjamin
Department of Housing and Urban Development, Office of General Counsel, GV
McKeever, Brian ....Los Angeles, CA
McKeever and Chappell PC
Albuquerque, NM
McKeever, Clark ....Enid, OK
McKeever, Cynthia G. ....Philadelphia, PA
McKeever, Daniel A., Jr. ....Auburn, AL
McKeever, Don, (P.A.) ....Winter Park, FL
McKeever, Edward D. (IBA) ....Warren, NJ
McKeever, Edwards, Davis & Hays, P.A.
Bryson City, NC
Hayesville, NC
Murphy, NC
McKeever, Elizabeth A. ....Littleton, CO
McKeever, Harold R., Jr. ....Dallas, TX
McKeever, Heather M. ....Lexington, KY
McKeever, J. Nicholas, Jr. ....Denver, CO

McKeever, James ....New York, NY
McKeever, Jeffrey A. ....Birmingham, MI
McKeever, Joe G. ....Salem, OR
McKeever, John E. ....Philadelphia, PA
McKeever, John H. ....Allentown, PA
McKeever, John P. ....Ocala, FL
McKeever, Joseph D. ....Winter Park, FL
McKeever, Joseph E. ....Newport Beach, CA
McKeever, Joseph F., III ....Washington, DC
McKeever, Joyce ....Harrisburg, PA
McKeever, Kenneth M., (P.C.) ....Niantic, CT
McKeever, Kristin ....Santa Fe, NM
McKeever, Lester H. ....Chicago, IL
McKeever, Lynn ....Albuquerque, NM
McKeever, Martin L. ....Milford, CT
McKeever, Michael ....Chicago, IL
McKeever, Michael T. ....Westmont, NJ
Philadelphia, PA
McKeever, Patrick C. ....Rockville, MD
McKeever, Patrick J. ....Pierre, SD
McKeever, Roberta Sessa ....Chicago, IL
McKeever, Stuart A. ....Westport, CT
McKeever, Susan L. ....Chicago, IL
McKeever, Thomas J., Jr.
Department Of Veterans Affairs, Office of the General Counsel, GV
McKeever, Timothy A. ....Anchorage, AK
McKeever, William H. ....Murphy, NC
McKegney, Elizabeth B. ....Bronx, NY
McKeige, Douglas M. ....New York, NY
McKeighan, Jace D. ....Phoenix, AZ
McKeil, John T. ....Miami, FL
McKeirnan, Ross ....Warren, PA
McKeirnan, Thomas L. ....Spokane, WA
McKeith, Malissa Hathaway
Los Angeles, CA
McKeithan, William P. ....Arlington, VA
McKeithen, A. Ward ....Charlotte, NC
McKeithen, Anita Dorman ....Shreveport, LA
McKeithen, Bruce B. ....Monroe, LA
McKeithen, Daniel R. ....Atlanta, GA
McKeithen, Donald D., Jr. ....Columbia, LA
McKeithen, Gregory ....Atlanta, GA
McKeithen, Lee S. ....Greenwich, CT
McKeithen, Marjorie A.
Baton Rouge, LA
McKeithen & McKeithen ....Monroe, LA
McKeithen, McKeithen & Bohman
Baton Rouge, LA
McKeithen, R. Malloy ....Charlotte, NC
McKeithen, R. L. Smith ....San Jose, CA
McKeithen & Ryland ....Columbia, LA
Mckeithen, Sheila R. ....Fort Lauderdale, FL
McKeithen, Sheila Rena
Fort Lauderdale, FL
McKeldin, Theodore R., Jr. ....Baltimore, MD
McKell, Brian M. ....Miami, FL
McKellar, Andrea Taylor ....Nashville, TN
McKellar, Clinton, Jr. ....Atlanta, GA
McKellar, Colleen L. ....Portland, OR
McKellar, Edwin I., Jr. ....Houston, TX
McKellar, James W. ....Dallas, TX
McKellar, John F. ....Jackson, NC
McKellar, Julie Fulmer ....Lakeland, FL
McKellar, L. Henry ....Columbia, SC
McKellar, Michele King ....Cheyenne, WY
McKellar, Robert L. ....Midland, MI
McKellar & Vick ....Jackson, NC
McKellar, William M. ....Cheyenne, WY
McKelley, Jane Dement ....Nashville, TN
McKelligott, John P. ....Doylestown, PA
McKellips, G. Wayne, Jr. ....Phoenix, AZ
McKellips, John L. ....Houston, TX
McKellogg, R. Keith ....La Jolla, CA
McKelvey & Calhoun, P.C. ....Americus, GA
McKelvey, Charles J. ....Williamsport, PA
McKelvey, Connie Elkins ....Portland, OR
McKelvey, Daniel E., Jr. ....Spokane, WA
McKelvey, Daniel E., Jr., P.S. ....Spokane, WA
McKelvey, Donald D. ....Portland, OR
McKelvey, Elizabeth S. ....Denver, CO
McKelvey & Hayers ....Electra, TX
McKelvey, Howard S., Jr. ....Americus, GA
McKelvey, James A. ....Fresno, CA
McKelvey, Jeanne W. ....Johnstown, PA
Mc Connellsburg, PA
McKelvey, John C. ....Tuscumbia, AL
McKelvey, John E. ....Electra, TX
McKelvey, Judith G. ....San Francisco, CA
McKelvey, Judy L. ....Los Angeles, CA
McKelvey, Maura K. ....Boston, MA
McKelvey, M. R. (Yogi) ....San Antonio, TX
McKelvey, Ronald ....Yuma, AZ
McKelvey, Ross J., Jr.
Pompano Beach, FL
McKelvey, Ross J., Jr., P.A.
Pompano Beach, FL
Mckelvey, Sean Michael ....McAlester, OK
McKelvey, Steven A., Jr. ....Columbia, SC
McKelvey, Terrence D. ....Buffalo, NY
McKelvey, Thomas H. ....Silver Creek, NY
McKelvey, W. Gordon, Jr. ....Franklin, TN
McKelvie, Allan Douglas ....Washington, DC
McKelvie, Charles L. ....Troy, MI
McKelvie, Dennis E. ....Tempe, AZ
McKelvie, Roderick R. ....Wilmington, DE
McKelvy, Carol L. ....Los Angeles, CA
McKelvy, Deborah H. ....Birmingham, MI
McKelvy, Ian Douglas ....Roswell, NM
McKelvy, Tina Eubanks ....Memphis, TN
McKelway, John M., Jr. ....Boston, MA
McKendall, Miriam J. ....Boston, MA
McKendree, Elizabeth G. ....Denver, CO
McKendree, John W., Law Offices of
Denver, CO
Mckendrick, Courtney A.
San Antonio, TX
McKendrick, Robert V. ....Encino, CA

McKendry, Bruce D. ....Omaha, NE
McKendry, Erwin W. ....Chicago, IL
McKendry, John H., Jr. ....Muskegon, MI
McKendry, Kevin P. ....New York, NY
McKenery, Deborah L. ....Harrison, OH
McKenna, Alice Hannelore
Department of Commerce, Office of the General Counsel, GV
McKenna, Allen J. ....Cocoa, FL
Orlando, FL
McKenna, Alvin J. ....Columbus, OH
McKenna, Andrew Francis ....Palo Alto, CA
McKenna, Anita F. ....New York, NY
McKenna, Anne Toomey ....Baltimore, MD
McKenna, Brian A. ....Detroit, MI
McKenna, Brian E. ....East Rockaway, NY
McKenna, Brian F. ....Keswick, VA
McKenna, Bruce A. ....Tulsa, OK
McKenna, Bryan A. ....New York, NY
McKenna, Carol A. ....Rochester, NY
McKenna, Charles A., Jr. ....Irvine, CA
McKenna, Charles C. ....Whittier, CA
Mckenna, Charles R. ....Modesto, CA
McKenna, Christopher ....Somerville, NJ
McKenna, Christopher B. ....Bethesda, MD
McKenna, Claudia M. ....Lake Worth, FL
McKenna & Cuneo, L.L.P.
Los Angeles, CA
San Diego, CA
San Francisco, CA
Denver, CO
Washington, DC
Dallas, TX
McKenna, David H. ....Hillsboro, OH
McKenna, David I. ....Providence, RI
McKenna, David L. ....San Bernardino, CA
McKenna, David W. ....Minneapolis, MN
McKenna, Denis D. ....Washington, DC
Fairfax, VA
McKenna, Denise T. ....Phoenix, AZ
McKenna, Dennis E. ....Boston, MA
McKenna, Dennis P. ....Mobile, AL
McKenna, Don ....Birmingham, AL
McKenna, Donald F. ....Buffalo, NY
McKenna, Donald R. ....Houston, TX
McKenna, Douglas C. ....Kansas City, MO
McKenna, D. W. ....Hamilton, MT
McKenna, Edmund J. ....Tampa, FL
McKenna, Edward J. ....Cherry Hill, NJ
Jersey City, NJ
Philadelphia, PA
McKenna, Edward J., Jr. ....Red Bank, NJ
McKenna, Edward R. ....Chevy Chase, MD
McKenna, Edward S. ....Pittsburgh, PA
McKenna, Elizabeth ....Philadelphia, PA
McKenna, Elizabeth A.
Environmental Protection Agency, Office of Congressional and Legislative Affairs, GV
McKenna, Elizabeth Norma ....Plymouth, MI
McKenna, F. Gregory ....Denver, CO
Washington, DC
McKenna, Francis G., P.C. ....Alexandria, VA
McKenna, Gary E. ....Eastport, MI
McKenna, Gene H. ....Akron, OH
McKenna, George H., Jr. ....Somerville, MA
McKenna, J. Andrew ....Salinas, CA
McKenna, J. Frank, III ....Pittsburgh, PA
McKenna, J. Glennon ....St. Louis, MO
McKenna, J. James ....Rockville, MD
McKenna, James ....Boston, MA
McKenna, James A. ....Chicago, IL
McKenna, James A., III ....Augusta, ME
McKenna, James D. ....North Attleboro, MA
McKenna, James D. ....Bozeman, MT
McKenna, James F. ....Hartford, CT
McKenna, James J. ....Providence, RI
McKenna, James L. ....Cherry Hill, NJ
Wynnewood, PA
McKenna, James L., P.C. ....Cherry Hill, NJ
Wynnewood, PA
McKenna, James M. ....Morristown, NJ
McKenna, James M. ....Toms River, NJ
McKenna, James P. ....Chico, CA
McKenna, James P. ....Worcester, MA
McKenna, James P., Jr. ....Pittsburgh, PA
McKenna, James R. ....Steubenville, OH
McKenna, Jan ....Fort Worth, TX
McKenna, Jane G. ....Reno, NV
McKenna, Jeffery J. ....St. George, UT
McKenna, Jeremiah B. ....Staten Island, NY
McKenna, John D. ....Garden City, NY
McKenna, John F. ....West Hartford, CT
McKenna, John F. ....Boston, MA
McKenna, John F. ....West Chester, PA
McKenna, John F., Jr. ....Pasadena, CA
McKenna, John J. ....Tucson, AZ
McKenna, John J. ....Laurel, MD
McKenna, John J. ....Boston, MA
McKenna, John J. ....Somerville, MA
McKenna, John J., II ....Middletown, NY
McKenna, John M. ....Orange, CA
McKenna, John M. ....San Mateo, CA
McKenna, John M. ....Florham Park, NJ
McKenna, John N. ....Los Angeles, CA
McKenna, John P. ....Washington, DC
McKenna, John P. ....Houston, TX
McKenna, John P., Jr. ....Greenbelt, MD
McKenna, John T. ....Palo Alto, CA
McKenna, Joseph A. ....Pottsville, PA
McKenna, Joseph P., Jr. ....Boston, MA
McKenna, Judith A.
Federal Judicial Center, GV
McKenna, Julie ....Salina, KS
McKenna, Juliet J. ....Washington, DC
Mc Kenna, Karen D. ....Pittsburgh, PA
McKenna, Karen L. ....Rochester, NY
Mckenna, Kathleen M. ....Los Angeles, CA

McKenna, Kathleen M. ....Newark, NJ
New York, NY
McKenna, Kathleen P.M. ....Wayland, MA
McKenna, Keith ....New York, NY
McKenna, Keith A. ....Bloomfield, NJ
McKenna, Kenneth G. ....Los Angeles, CA
McKenna, Kenneth J. ....Orlando, FL
McKenna, Keven A. ....Providence, RI
McKenna, Keven A., P.C. ....Providence, RI
McKenna, Kevin J. ....Newark, NJ
McKenna, Kevin M. ....Boston, MA
McKenna, Kevin M. ....Mount Laurel, NJ
Harrisburg, PA
Malvern, PA
McKenna, Kevin R. ....Cincinnati, OH
McKenna & Kostantinous ....Williamsburg, VA
Mc Kenna, Laura ....Islip, NY
McKenna, Lauren P. ....Philadelphia, PA
McKenna, Lawrence F. ....San Rafael, CA
McKenna, Lawrence M. ....New York, NY
McKenna, Leone, DuPont & Higgins, A Professional Corporation ....Red Bank, NJ
McKenna, M. Catherine ....San Francisco, CA
Mckenna & Marconi ....Cherry Hill, NJ
McKenna, Margaret A. ....Cambridge, MA
McKenna, Maria Germaine ....Holland, MI
McKenna, Mark F. ....Pittsburgh, PA
McKenna, Martha D. ....San Francisco, CA
McKenna, Mary ....New York, NY
McKenna, Mary Jane ....Boston, MA
McKenna, Mary P. ....Cleveland, OH
McKenna, Matthew M. ....Purchase, NY
McKenna, Maureen E. ....Pittsburgh, PA
McKenna & McCormick ....Providence, RI
McKenna, Michael F. ....Tallahassee, FL
Saddle River, NJ
New York, NY
McKenna, Michael G. ....San Mateo, CA
McKenna, Michael J.
National Credit Union Administration, Office of General Counsel, GV
McKenna, Michael J. ....Cherry Hill, NJ
McKenna, Michael J. ....Friendship, WI
McKenna, Michael P. ....Philadelphia, PA
McKenna, Michael R. ....Kailua-Kona, HI
Chicago, IL
Northbrook, IL
McKenna, Michael S. ....Kent, CT
New Milford, CT
McKenna and Miller, P.L.C. ....Plymouth, MI
McKenna & Modugno ....Akron, OH
McKenna & Morris ....Irvine, CA
McKenna, Noreen M. ....Melrose, MA
McKenna and Obront ....Miami, FL
McKenna, Patrice R. ....New York, NY
McKenna, Patrick J. ....Atlanta, GA
McKenna, Patrick J. ....Albany, NY
McKenna, Patrick J. ....Virginia Beach, VA
McKenna, Patrick M. ....Valley Stream, NY
McKenna, Paul A. ....Miami, FL
McKenna, Peter A. ....Washington, DC
McKenna, Peter D. ....New York, NY
McKenna, Peter J. ....New York, NY
McKenna, R. Colette
General Services Administration, Office of the General Counsel, GV
McKenna, R. Tim ....Colorado Springs, CO
McKenna, Ralph J. ....Billerica, MA
McKenna, Raymond J.
House of Representatives, Congressional Assistants, GV
McKenna, Richard ....Irving, TX
McKenna, Richard J. ....Itasca, IL
McKenna, Richard J. ....Milwaukee, WI
McKenna, Richard P. ....Jacksonville, FL
McKenna, Robert B. ....Denver, CO
McKenna, Robert F. ....Staten Island, NY
McKenna, Robert J. ....Morristown, NJ
McKenna, Robert J., Jr. ....Boston, MA
McKenna, Robert L., III ....Long Beach, CA
McKenna, Robert M. ....Columbus, GA
McKenna, Roger W. ....Kewaskum, WI
McKenna, Sabrina Shizue ....Honolulu, HI
McKenna & Schneier ....Valley Stream, NY
McKenna, Sean ....New York, NY
McKenna, Sean R. ....Dallas, TX
McKenna, Shannon D. ....Chicago, IL
McKenna, Siracusano, Fehringer & Chianese
East Rockaway, NY
McKenna, Stephen C. ....Denver, CO
McKenna, Stephen J. ....Bethesda, MD
McKenna, Storer, Rowe, White & Farrug
Chicago, IL
Waukegan, IL
Woodstock, IL
McKenna, Susan K. ....Cocoa, FL
Orlando, FL
McKenna, Sydney E. ....Missoula, MT
McKenna, Terrence J. ....Marengo, IL
McKenna, Terry P. ....Covington, GA
McKenna, Thomas ....Boston, MA
McKenna, Thomas A. ....McLean, VA
McKenna, Thomas F. ....Walnut Creek, CA
McKenna, Thomas F., Sr. ....Albuquerque, NM
McKenna, Thomas G. ....Delcambre, LA
McKenna, Thomas H. ....Ossining, NY
McKenna, Thomas J. ....Southfield, MI
McKenna, Thomas J. ....New York, NY
McKenna, Thomas P. ....Columbus, GA
McKenna, Timothy E. ....Houston, TX
McKenna, Timothy J. ....Woodsville, NH
McKenna, Todd J. ....Cleveland, OH
McKenna, Trenton T. ....Houston, TX
McKenna, Wendy Feiss ....Collegeville, PA
McKenna, Willafay H. ....Williamsburg, VA
McKenna, William A., Jr. ....Lincoln Park, NJ
McKenna, William F. ....Los Angeles, CA
McKenna, William F. ....Silver Spring, MD
McKenna, William H. ....White Plains, NY
McKenna, William J., Jr. ....Chicago, IL
McKennan, John T. ....New Hartford, NY
McKennan, Marian ....Centreville, MD
Easton, MD
McKennedy, Nikki S. ....San Francisco, CA
McKennett, Richard A. ....Williston, ND
McKennett Stenehjem Reierson Forsberg & Chapman, P.C. ....Watford City, ND
Williston, ND
McKenney, A. Chad ....Minneapolis, MN
McKenney, Andrew C. ....Maple Grove, MN
McKenney, Carolyn ....Washington, DC
McKenney, Charles ....Pasadena, CA
McKenney, Charles E. ....New York, NY
McKenney, Chris L. ....Ann Arbor, MI
McKenney, Deborah L.
Winston-Salem, NC
McKenney, Drake D. ....New York, NY
McKenney, Edward J., Jr. ....Memphis, TN
McKenney, Frank M. ....Macon, GA
McKenney, Frederick L. ....Brockton, MA
McKenney & Froelich ....Atlanta, GA
McKenney, Harold C. ....Crystal Lake, IL
McKenney, Hubert F., Jr.
Virginia Beach, VA
McKenney, Hugh L. ....Houston, TX
McKenney, James B. ....Novato, CA
McKenney, Jeffrey & Quigley
Providence, RI
Mckenney, Jerry R. ....Houston, TX
McKenney & Jesse, P.C. ....Houston, TX
McKenney, John W., Jr. ....Sarasota, FL
McKenney, Jordan & Carey ....Macon, GA
McKenney, Kathleen K. ....Nashville, TN
McKenney, Kevin E. ....San Jose, CA
McKenney, Larry B. ....Aliso Viejo, CA
McKenney, Mark P. ....Providence, RI
McKenney, Patti L. ....Grand Rapids, MI
McKenney, Paul L. B. ....Southfield, MI
McKenney and Perreault, P.C.
Amherst, NH
McKenney, Philip M. ....San Diego, CA
McKenney, Robert A. ....Boston, MA
McKenney, Robert A. ....Holly, MI
McKenney, Robert V. ....Amherst, NH
Mckenney, Rudge S. ....Roxbury, MA
McKenney, Samuel S., III ....Pittsburgh, PA
McKenney, Steven D. ....Seattle, WA
McKenney, Thomas P.
Farmington Hills, MI
McKenney, Thomas P. ....Omaha, NE
McKenney, Todd M. ....Akron, OH
McKenney, W. Gibbs ....Lutherville, MD
McKenney, Warren P. ....San Antonio, TX
McKenney, William J. ....Atlanta, GA
McKenney, William P. ....Treasury Department, Departmental Offices, GV
McKennon, Elizabeth A. ....Baltimore, MD
McKennon, Janice Crosby
Round Rock, TX
McKennon, Richard O. ....Dallas, TX
Frisco, TX
McKennon, Richard O., P.C. ....Dallas, TX
Frisco, TX
McKennon, Robert J.
Newport Beach, CA
Mckenny, Betsy B. ....New York, NY
McKenrick, Bruce F. ....Ebensburg, PA
McKenrick, Fremont J. ....Ebensburg, PA
McKenrick, Gary D. ....Davenport, IA
McKenrick & McKenrick ....Ebensburg, PA
McKenry, Carl E. B., Jr. ....Coral Gables, FL
McKenry, James R. ....Norfolk, VA
McKenty, Daniel L. ....Wilmington, DE
McKenty, Deborah A. ....West Chester, PA
McKenzie, A. Bruce ....Seattle, WA
McKenzie, A. Donald ....Elizabeth, NJ
McKenzie, A. Gregory ....West Linn, OR
McKenzie, A. Gregory, & Associates
West Linn, OR
McKenzie, A. Kirk ....San Francisco, CA
McKenzie, Alex W. ....Sacramento, CA
McKenzie, Alfred B. ....Fair Oaks, CA
McKenzie, Ann C. ....Chicago, IL
McKenzie, Ann L. ....Baltimore, MD
McKenzie & Associates ....Miami, FL
McKenzie and Baer ....Dallas, TX
McKenzie, Bettyann K. ....Dedham, MA
McKenzie, Brent L. ....Toledo, OH
McKenzie, C. Marshall ....Shreveport, LA
McKenzie, Charles H. ....Kansas City, MO
McKenzie, Christopher J. ....New York, NY
McKenzie, Christopher K. ....Topeka, KS
McKenzie, Claire R. ....Chicago, IL
McKenzie, Claude Fleet ....Baltimore, MD
McKenzie, Clyde W. ....Warren, MI
McKenzie, Coy H. ....Noble, OK
McKenzie, Curtis D. ....Boise, ID
McKenzie & Dalby ....Fair Oaks, CA
McKenzie, Dale W. ....San Francisco, CA
McKenzie, Daphne D. ....New York, NY
McKenzie, Darla Grinstead ....Atlanta, GA
McKenzie, Darren L. ....Seattle, WA
McKenzie, David L. ....Haines, AK
McKenzie, Denise L. ....Los Angeles, CA
McKenzie, Denzil D. ....Boston, MA
McKenzie, Dewey Ray, Jr.
La Grange, GA
McKenzie, Diana J.P. ....Chicago, IL
McKenzie, Donald C. ....Carmichael, CA
McKenzie, Donald I. N. ....Nashville, TN
McKenzie, Donald W. ....Rosemont, IL
McKenzie, Douglas G. ....Kentwood, MI
McKenzie, Dwayne P. ....Los Angeles, CA
McKenzie, Edward P. ....Morristown, NJ
McKenzie & Edwards, P.C. ....Boston, MA
McKenzie, Elizabeth M. ....Boston, MA
McKenzie, Frank G. ....Dearborn, MI
McKenzie, Frank William ....Troy, MI
McKenzie, Franklin C., Jr. ....Laurel, MS
McKenzie, Gale ....Atlanta, GA
McKenzie, Gary K. ....Baton Rouge, LA
McKenzie, Gene A., Jr. ....Orange, CA
McKenzie, George K. ....Phillips, ME
McKenzie, Gerald ....Pensacola, FL
McKenzie, Gregory M. ....New York, NY
McKenzie, Gregory P. ....Ozark, AR
McKenzie, Harold C., Jr. ....Atlanta, GA
McKenzie, Henry ....New York, NY
McKenzie, James D. ....Bessemer, MI
McKenzie, James D., III
Briarcliff Manor, NY
McKenzie, James F. ....Pensacola, FL
McKenzie, James F. ....Hattiesburg, MS
McKenzie, James H. ....Hope, AR
Prescott, AR
McKenzie, James J. ....Medfield, MA
McKenzie, James W. ....Dayton, TN
McKenzie, James W., Jr. ....Duluth, GA
McKenzie, James W., Jr. ....Philadelphia, PA
McKenzie, James W., Jr., P.C.
Atlanta, GA
Duluth, GA
McKenzie, Jane Ann ....Seattle, WA
McKenzie, Jay R. ....Preston, ID
McKenzie, Jeffrey A. ....Louisville, KY
Cincinnati, OH
McKenzie, Jeffrey Thomas
House of Representatives, Congressional Assistants, GV
McKenzie, Joan Elaine ....Waldorf, MD
McKenzie, Joe Mac ....San Diego, CA
McKenzie, John D. ....North St. Paul, MN
McKenzie, John F. ....San Francisco, CA
McKenzie, John G., Jr. ....Santa Fe, NM
McKenzie, John J. ....Albany, NY
McKenzie, John L. ....St. Paul, MN
McKenzie, John M. ....Minneapolis, MN
McKenzie, John W. ....Akron, OH
McKenzie, K. Kelley ....Fremont, CA
McKenzie, Kenneth B. ....Walnut Creek, CA
McKenzie, Kevin A. ....Hemet, CA
Sun City, CA
McKenzie, Kirk R. ....Seattle, WA
McKenzie, Kyle B. ....Cincinnati, OH
McKenzie, Larry F. ....Henderson, TN
McKenzie, Larry W. ....Memphis, TN
McKenzie, Leeanna ....Houston, TX
McKenzie, Linda Byars ....Greenville, SC
McKenzie, Linda "Fritz" Campbell
Mililani Town, HI
McKenzie, Lisa B. ....Knoxville, TN
McKenzie, Lorna M. ....New York, NY
McKenzie, Marianne ....Sea Bright, NJ
McKenzie, Mark Jonathan ....Houston, TX
McKenzie, Martin G. ....Santa Barbara, CA
McKenzie, Martin J. ....Chicago, IL
McKenzie, Mary C.
House of Representatives, Congressional Assistants, GV
McKenzie, Mary F. ....San Francisco, CA
McKenzie, Mary Minehan
Philadelphia, PA
McKenzie & McKenzie, P.C. ....Chicago, IL
McKenzie, McRae, Vasser & Barber, PLLC
Hope, AR
Prescott, AR
McKenzie, Melanie ....Houston, TX
McKenzie, Meredith M. ....Menlo Park, CA
McKenzie, Michael A. ....Washington, DC
McKenzie, Michael A. ....Atlanta, GA
McKenzie, Michael B. ....Miami, FL
McKenzie, Michael E. ....Arlington, VA
McKenzie, Michelle Burke ....Modesto, CA
McKenzie, Milton D. ....Tulsa, OK
McKenzie, Monica M. ....Carlsbad, CA
McKenzie, Nan K.
United States Postal Service, Law Department, GV
Mckenzie, Nancy Brouillard
Department Of Health And Human Services, Social Security Administration, GV
McKenzie, Patricia A. ....Damascus, MD
McKenzie, Patricia G. ....Atlanta, GA
McKenzie, Patrick K. ....Mill Creek, WA
McKenzie, Patrick R. ....Laguna Hills, CA
McKenzie, Philip D. ....Grayson, KY
McKenzie, Philip D., P.S.C. ....Grayson, KY
McKenzie, Phyllis M. ....Little Rock, AR
McKenzie, Richard W. ....Hattiesburg, MS
McKenzie, Richardson B., III
Montgomery, AL
McKenzie, Richd. R. ....Madison, WI
McKenzie, Robert ....Pittsburgh, PA
McKenzie, Robert A. ....Columbia, SC
McKenzie, Robert E. ....Chicago, IL
McKenzie, Robert H. ....Florence, AL
McKenzie, Robert K., Jr. ....Brighton, MI
McKenzie, Ronald E. ....Portsmouth, OH
McKenzie, Ronald R. ....Hannibal, MO
McKenzie, S. Lynn Marie ....Cullman, AL
Mckenzie, Sandra Craig ....Lawrence, KS
McKenzie, Sandra L. ....Victoria, TX
McKenzie, Sarah ....Minneapolis, MN
McKenzie, Scott C. ....Belvedere-Tiburon, CA
McKenzie, Scott D. ....Topeka, KS
Mc Kenzie, Sherea ....Houston, TX
McKenzie, Sonja S. ....Denver, CO
McKenzie, Steven Q. ....Cleveland, OH
McKenzie, Steven S. ....Manning, SC
McKenzie, Stuart A.
Huntington Beach, CA
McKenzie, Susan Beth ....Covington, KY
Huntington, WV
McKenzie, Susan Steinle ....Canton, OH
McKenzie, Tara L. ....Ann Arbor, MI
McKenzie & Taylor, P.A. ....Pensacola, FL
McKenzie, Terri Frantz ....Virginia Beach, VA
McKenzie, Terri L ....Baltimore, MD
McKenzie, Terry Alan ....Atlanta, GA
McKenzie, Thomas B. ....Appleton, WI
McKenzie, Thomas J. ....Pittsburgh, PA
McKenzie, Thomas W. ....Euless, TX
McKenzie, Thomas W. ....San Antonio, TX
McKenzie, Timothy Cass
San Francisco, CA
McKenzie, W. Guy, Jr. ....Tallahassee, FL
McKenzie, W. Locke, Jr. ....Columbus, OH
Mckenzie, Wayne Seretse ....Brooklyn, NY
McKenzie, William A. ....Dallas, TX
McKenzie, William B. ....Decatur, TN
McKenzie, William H.
San Luis Obispo, CA
McKenzie, William H., III ....Batesville, MS
McKenzie, William M., Jr. ....San Diego, CA
McKenzie, William Shelby
Baton Rouge, LA
McKenzie, William Sherman ....Columbia, MO
McKenzie, William T. ....Atlanta, GA
McKenzie, Wm. Robert, A Professional Law Corporation ....Shreveport, LA
McKenzie, Woolery, Emrick & Webb, P.S.C.
Ashland, KY
McKenzie, W. R. ....Modesto, CA
McKeogh, Patricia L. ....New York, NY
McKeon, Agnes C. ....New York, NY
McKeon & Anderson, P.C. ....Butte, MT
McKeon, Ann ....Springfield, NJ
McKeon, Arthur J., III ....Los Angeles, CA
McKeon, Charles E. ....Tampa, FL
McKeon, Charles M. ....Kansas City, MO
McKeon, Christopher M. ....New Haven, CT
McKeon, Douglas E. ....New York, NY
McKeon, Eileen E. ....San Francisco, CA
McKeon, G. Dale ....Upland, CA
McKeon, George A. ....Hartford, CT
McKeon, Graceann ....New York, NY
McKeon, James E. ....Englishtown, NJ
McKeon, James L., III ....Riverdale, NJ
McKeon, Jami Wintz ....Philadelphia, PA
McKeon, John C. ....Malta, MT
McKeon, John F. ....Springfield, NJ
McKeon, John H., Jr. ....Mount Laurel, NJ
Philadelphia, PA
McKeon, John L. ....Anaconda, MT
McKeon, John P. ....Manchester, CT
McKeon, Jonathan Edward ....Elmira, NY
McKeon, Joseph F., Jr. ....Westport, CT
McKeon, Joseph F., Jr., P.C. ....Westport, CT
McKeon, Kevin J. ....Harrisburg, PA
McKeon, Kevin J. ....Pittsburgh, PA
McKeon, Kevin M. ....Cherry Hill, NJ
McKeon, Maria F. ....Hartford, CT
McKeon, Marianne ....New York, NY
McKeon, Mark G. ....Cold Spring, MN
McKeon, Mark J. ....Sacramento, CA
McKeon, Merritt L. ....Laguna Beach, CA
McKeon, Michael F. ....Auburn, NY
McKeon, Michael J. ....Washington, DC
McKeon, Michael J. ....Butte, MT
McKeon, Michael Peter ....Hartford, CT
McKeon, Patricia A. ....New York, NY
McKeon, Peter T. ....New York, NY
McKeon, Robert M. ....Toms River, NJ
McKeon, Robert W., Jr., P.C.
Washington, DC
McKeon, Robert William, Jr.
Washington, DC
McKeon, Sheila A. ....Cleveland, OH
McKeon, Shelly D. ....Bethesda, MD
McKeon, Susan E. ....Kansas City, MO
McKeon, Thomas ....Baltimore, MD
McKeon, Thomas D. ....Kearny, NJ
McKeon, Thomas G. ....Omaha, NE
McKeon, Thomas G. ....Brewster, NY
McKeon, Thomas J. ....Indianapolis, IN
McKeon, Thomas P. ....North Haven, CT
McKeon, Thomas R. ....Portland, ME
McKeon, Timothy W. ....Missoula, MT
McKeon, Tina W. ....Atlanta, GA
McKeon, William E., Jr. ....Fall River, MA
McKeon, William H. ....Auburn, NY
McKeon, William M. ....Wailuku, HI
McKeon, Willis M. ....Malta, MT
Mckeone, Deborah Jean ....Omaha, NE
McKeone, Keri M. ....Troy, MI
McKeone, Mark R. ....Cozad, NE
McKeone, Tod A. ....Lexington, NE
McKeough, Brendan J.
Hoffman Estates, IL
McKeown & Brindle, P.C. ....Beaverton, OR
Portland, OR
McKeown, Clifford W. ....Middletown, PA
McKeown, Craig W. ....Secaucus, NJ
McKeown, Daniel B. ....Trenton, NJ
McKeown, Denis J. ....Waukegan, IL
McKeown, Douglas J. ....Joliet, IL
McKeown, Edwin S. ....Pleasanton, CA
McKeown, Fitzgerald, Zollner, Buck, Hutchison & Ruttle ....Frankfort, IL
Joliet, IL
Shorewood, IL
McKeown, Francis M. ....San Francisco, CA
McKeown, Frank J., Jr.
West Palm Beach, FL
McKeown, Frank J., Jr., P.A.
West Palm Beach, FL
McKeown, Glenn E. ....Hoffman Estates, IL
McKeown, H. Mary ....St. Petersburg, FL
McKeown, James F. ....Washington, DC
McKeown, James T. ....Milwaukee, WI
McKeown, Laurie A. ....Boston, MA

McKeown Law Firm .... **Clover, SC**
Rock Hill, SC
York, SC
McKeown, M. Margaret .... Seattle, WA
McKeown, Martin J. .... Eugene, OR
McKeown, Martin J., P.C. .... Eugene, OR
McKeown, Mary Adele .... White Plains, NY
McKeown, Melvin B., Jr. .... **York, SC**
McKeown, Noel K. .... **Xenia, OH**
McKeown Price, LLP .... **San Francisco, CA**
McKeown & Rosengren .... Los Angeles, CA
McKeown, Scott A. .... Portland, OR
McKeown, Scott A. .... **Philadelphia, PA**
McKeown, Sheila M. .... Los Angeles, CA
McKeown, Tamara D. .... **Miami, FL**
McKeown, Thomas F. .... Pittsburgh, PA
McKeown, Timothy P. .... **Somerville, NJ**
McKeown, W. B. .... Bronx, NY
McKeown, William D. .... Cedarburg, WI
McKerall, Keith Michael .... Birmingham, AL
McKerall, Samuel G. .... Gulf Shores, AL
McKercher, Timothy M. .... **Clawson, MI**
Plymouth, MI
McKerley, Michael L. .... **Birmingham, AL**
McKernan, Betsy .... Modesto, CA
McKernan, Diane .... Mount Freedom, NJ
McKernan and Gatins .... Staten Island, NY
McKernan, Gordon J. .... **Baton Rouge, LA**
McKernan, James P. .... Hebron, NE
McKernan, Joseph J. (Jerry), P.C.
Baton Rouge, LA
Houston, TX
McKernan, Joseph T. .... **New York, NY**
McKernan, Kevin P. .... Staten Island, NY
McKernan, Lanam, Bakke, Benson & Bodney .... **Chico, CA**
Paradise, CA
McKernan Law Firm, A Professional Corporation .... **Baton Rouge, LA**
McKernan Law Office .... Hebron, NE
McKernan, Lynn Y. .... **San Jose, CA**
McKernan, Martin F. .... **Camden, NJ**
McKernan, Martin F., Jr. .... **Camden, NJ**
McKernan, Mary Borden .... Hartford, CT
McKernan, McKernan & Godino
Camden, NJ
McKernan, Michael A. .... Collingswood, NJ
Woodlyn, PA
McKernan, Patricia R. .... Palo Alto, CA
McKernan, Roy .... **Chico, CA**
Paradise, CA
McKernan, Thomas J. .... Tigard, OR
Mckernan, Wendy Joan .... Aurora, CO
McKernon & Rand .... Rockville, MD
McKerns, Charles J. .... **Heathsville, VA**
McKerns, Charles J., Jr. .... **Heathsville, VA**
McKerns & McKerns .... **Heathsville, VA**
McKerricher, John A. .... Chehalis, WA
McKerroll, Margaret G. .... Fremont, CA
McKerrow, Nancy A. .... Columbia, MO
McKesson, Anthony B. .... Oklahoma City, OK
McKesson, Winston K. .... Beverly Hills, CA
McKessy, Ana-Maria .... **Washington, DC**
McKessy, Scott S. .... **New York, NY**
McKetta, John J., III .... **Austin, TX**
McKeveny, Robert .... Farmingdale, NY
McKeveny, Wm. Colm .... **New York, NY**
McKevitt, James D. "Mike"
Washington, DC
McKevitt, Jane A. .... Los Angeles, CA
McKevitt, Martin O., Jr. .... Chicago, IL
McKevitt, Robert P. .... West Long Branch, NJ
McKevitt, Thomas .... Hempstead, NY
McKew, John J., Jr. .... New York, NY
McKew, Robert E., Jr. .... Washington, DC
McKew, Walter M. .... Cleveland, OH
McKewen, Curt W. .... Jackson, MS
McKewin, E. Mildred, (Miss) .... Lowell, MA
McKey, Arthur D. .... **Washington, DC**
McKey, Bracken Duane .... Hillsboro, OR
McKey, John D., Jr. .... **Stuart, FL**
McKey, Ray E. .... Portland, OR
McKey, S. Patrick .... **Chicago, IL**
McKibben, Dale H. .... **Jackson, MS**
McKibben, Frank C. .... Englewood, CO
McKibben, Howard D. .... Reno, NV
McKibben, James F., Jr.
Corpus Christi, TX
McKibben, James H. .... **Redwood City, CA**
McKibben, Jeff J. .... Wauchula, FL
McKibben, Larry E. .... **Marshalltown, IA**
McKibben, Leonard O., Jr. .... Cedartown, GA
McKibben, Lizabeth A. .... Saipan, TT
McKibben, Michael D. .... **Birmingham, AL**
McKibben, R. Bruce, Jr. .... Tallahassee, FL
McKibben, R. Bruce, P.A. .... Tallahassee, FL
McKibben, Tracy B. .... **Washington, DC**
McKibbin, Colin John .... Seal Beach, CA
McKibbin, David, III .... Malibu, CA
McKibbin, Michael D. .... San Diego, CA
McKibbin, Michael K. .... San Bernardino, CA
McKibbin, Noel .... West Des Moines, IA
McKibbin, Robyn M. .... San Francisco, CA
McKibbon, Wm. Ross, Jr. .... **Greenville, SC**
McKible, Gary H. .... Concord, NH
McKible, Gary H., Law Office of, PC
Concord, NH
McKichan, Mac A., Jr. .... **Platteville, WI**
McKie, Edward F., Jr. .... **Washington, DC**
McKie, Glen J. .... Englewood, CO
McKie, John E. .... **Chicago, IL**
McKiernan, Daniel P. .... **Providence, RI**
McKiernan, Dennis M. .... Louisville, KY
McKiernan, Donald E. .... Providence, RI
McKiernan, Holiday Hart .... Indianapolis, IN
McKiernan, James J., Jr. .... Hamden, CT
McKiernan, Michael J. .... Houston, TX
McKiernan, Peter G. .... White Plains, NY

McKiernan, Philip B. .... **Indianapolis, IN**
McKiernan, Stanley W. .... Los Angeles, CA
McKiernan, Thomas Edward
St. Clair Shores, MI
McKiever, Colli C. .... **Fayetteville, AR**
McKilligan, Richard .... **New York, NY**
McKillip, Brian R. .... Wheaton, IL
McKillip, Leslie Jo .... **Waukesha, WI**
McKillop, Alexander .... Fairfax, VA
McKillop, Christopher .... Portland, OR
McKillop, Donald R., Sr. .... **Los Angeles, CA**
San Diego, CA
Santa Ana, CA
McKillop, Donna M. .... **Doylestown, PA**
McKillop, Eileen I. .... **Seattle, WA**
Mckillop, Steven A. .... **Winter Park, FL**
McKim, Amee R. .... Fort Wayne, IN
McKim, Andrew S. .... Seattle, WA
McKim, Bradley S. .... **Denver, CO**
McKim, David M. .... Burlingame, CA
McKim, Gerald K. .... **West Palm Beach, FL**
McKim, Joanna .... San Diego, CA
McKim, Kay R. .... Golden, CO
McKim, Ray L. .... Midland, TX
McKim, Samuel J., III, (P.C.) .... **Detroit, MI**
McKim, Thomas F. .... **Winston-Salem, NC**
McKim, William J. .... Pittsburgh, PA
McKimm, William H. .... Mount Ida, AR
McKimmey, Joseph E. .... Shawnee, OK
McKimmey Law Office, P.C. .... Shawnee, OK
McKimmey, Stephen D. .... **Dallas, TX**
McKindles, John M. .... Mesa, AZ
McKinlay, Amy M. .... **Columbus, OH**
McKinlay, Donald C. .... Denver, CO
McKinlay, Edward H. .... Pasco, WA
McKinlay, Hultgrenn & VanderSchoor
Pasco, WA
McKinlay, James T.
West Palm Beach, FL
McKinlay, Scott D. .... San Francisco, CA
McKinlay, Shira .... San Francisco, CA
McKinlay, Stuart W. .... Colorado Springs, CO
McKinley, Arthur B. .... **Sublette, KS**
McKinley and Associates, P.L.C.
Muscatine, IA
McKinley & Bornmann, P.L.C.
Alexandria, VA
McKinley, Bowman & Bowman
Pittsburgh, PA
Mc Kinley, Bridget Barbara .... Jupiter, FL
McKinley, Bruce T. .... Cocoa, FL
McKinley, Bryan H. .... Osage, IA
McKinley, C. Clinton .... **Lexington, KY**
McKinley & Capeloto .... **Los Angeles, CA**
Pasadena, CA
McKinley, Colleen .... Louisville, KY
McKinley & Crates .... Kenton, OH
McKinley, David A. .... Boulder, CO
McKinley, Donald B. .... Dallas, TX
McKinley, Douglas E. .... **Alexandria, VA**
McKinley, Douglas R. .... Crystal Springs, MS
McKinley, Edmon H. .... Thomasville, AL
McKinley, Erin E. .... **Ithaca, NY**
McKinley, Gail G. .... Orinda, CA
McKinley, Gary F. .... Marysville, OH
McKinley, George T. .... **Jim Thorpe, PA**
McKinley, Hall F., III .... **Atlanta, GA**
McKinley, J. Mel .... Brandon, FL
McKinley, Jack .... **Houston, TX**
McKinley, Jack, & Associates, P.C.
Houston, TX
McKinley, Jack B. .... Decatur, IL
McKinley, James C. .... Indianapolis, IN
McKinley, John B. .... Monroe, LA
McKinley, John C. .... **Cheyenne, WY**
Sheridan, WY
McKinley, John H. .... **Stockton, CA**
McKinley, John L. .... **Atlanta, GA**
McKinley, Jon .... El Cajon, CA
McKinley, Joseph A. .... Berkeley, CA
McKinley, Joseph H., Jr. .... Owensboro, KY
McKinley, Kathleen A. .... **San Francisco, CA**
McKinley, Kathryn R. .... **Spokane, WA**
McKinley, Keith A. .... **Osage, IA**
McKinley, Kevin F. .... Oak Ridge, TN
McKinley, Kristen E. .... Columbus, OH
McKinley Law Firm .... Seattle, WA
McKinley, Leroy T. .... Columbus, OH
McKinley, Leslie R. .... Independence, MO
McKinley, Lester A. .... De Witt, AR
McKinley, Loralyn .... Philadelphia, PA
McKinley, Marcia J. .... Fairfax, VA
McKinley, Michael D. .... **Dallas, TX**
McKinley, Michael F. .... Des Plaines, IL
McKinley, Michael P. .... Albany, NY
McKinley, Michael R. .... **Port Charlotte, FL**
McKinley, Michael S. .... **Peoria, IL**
McKinley, Nancy T. .... Seattle, WA
McKinley, Patrick J. .... Santa Barbara, CA
McKinley, Paul N., Jr. .... Kenton, OH
McKinley, Richard A., Law Offices of
Bartow, FL
McKinley, Richard B. .... Chicago, IL
McKinley, Robert A. .... **Philadelphia, PA**
McKinley, Robert B. .... Pittsburgh, PA
McKinley, Robert D. .... **Pasadena, CA**
McKinley, Robert W. .... **Kansas City, MO**
McKinley, Robert W. .... Chippewa Falls, WI
McKinley & Smith, A Professional Corporation .... **Sacramento, CA**
McKinley, Stacey L. .... **Cleveland, OH**
McKinley, Stannard & Carter, L.L.P.
Cedar Rapids, IA
Coralville, IA
Iowa City, IA
Waterloo, IA
McKinley, Steven A. .... **San Diego, CA**
McKinley, Steven M. .... **Walnut Creek, CA**

McKinley, Terry L. .... **Covington, KY**
McKinley, Timothy B. .... Dodgeville, WI
McKinley, Vernon A. .... **Coralville, IA**
Muscatine, IA
McKinley, William C. .... **Sacramento, CA**
McKinley, William D. .... Seattle, WA
McKinley, William E. .... Portland, ME
McKinley, William K. .... **Portland, ME**
McKinley, William W., Jr. .... **Jackson, MS**
McKinley and Zebert .... Pearl, MS
McKinley & Zeiger, L.L.P. .... **Dallas, TX**
McKinnell, Alison .... **New York, NY**
McKinney, Adam E. .... **Dallas, TX**
McKinney, Aften P. .... **Kansas City, MO**
McKinney, Andrew T. .... Houston, TX
McKinney, Andrew T., IV .... **Houston, TX**
McKinney, Angela D. .... **Nashville, TN**
McKinney, Anne M. .... **Knoxville, TN**
McKinney, Anne M., P.C. .... **Knoxville, TN**
McKinney, B. Blair .... San Marcos, CA
McKinney, Barbara E. .... Bloomington, IN
McKinney, Bryan Thomas .... Arkadelphia, AR
McKinney, Buck .... Austin, TX
McKinney, Cameron .... Tyler, TX
McKinney, Camilla Carolyn
Washington, DC
McKinney, Carie G. .... **Austin, TX**
McKinney, Carolyn J. .... **Houston, TX**
McKinney, Carroll V. .... Hillsboro, OH
McKinney, Caryn R. .... Atlanta, GA
McKinney, Charles A. .... Dayton, OH
McKinney, Charles W. .... Gordonsville, TN
McKinney, Christopher J.
San Antonio, TX
McKinney, Craig R. .... Topeka, KS
McKinney, Cullen B. .... **Detroit, MI**
McKinney, Dagnee Bavier .... Houston, TX
McKinney, Dan G. .... **Riverside, CA**
McKinney, Dan G. .... Greenville, SC
McKinney, Daniel H. .... **Cincinnati, OH**
McKinney, Dara L. .... Los Alamos, NM
McKinney, David B. .... South Bend, IN
McKinney, David B. .... **Tulsa, OK**
McKinney, David R. .... **Sandy, UT**
McKinney, Debbie Cannon
Oklahoma City, OK
McKinney, Dee (Delores) Bruening
Wentzville, MO
McKinney, Dennis K. .... Zionsville, IN
McKinney, Dennis M. .... **Longview, TX**
McKinney, Don S. .... **Little Rock, AR**
McKinney, Donald A. .... Wichita, KS
McKinney, Donna H. .... **Corpus Christi, TX**
McKinney, E. Gene .... Topeka, KS
McKinney, E. Melville .... Mendocino, CA
McKinney, Elizabeth Blair .... **Wilson, NC**
McKinney, Elizabeth J.
Bowling Green, KY
McKinney, Gerald R. .... **Newland, NC**
McKinney, Gerald R., P.A. .... **Newland, NC**
McKinney, Givens & Associates, PLLC
Fort Mill, SC
Rock Hill, SC
York, SC
McKinney, Harley J. .... Rock Springs, WY
McKinney, Ivy Thomas .... **Stamford, CT**
McKinney, J. Andrew, Jr. .... **Rockville, MD**
McKinney, J. Bruce .... Asheville, NC
McKinney, J. Randle .... Gulf Shores, AL
McKinney, J. Robin, Jr. .... **Nashville, TN**
McKinney, James C. .... Elkton, MD
McKinney, James D. .... Brentwood, TN
McKinney, James D., Jr. .... **Washington, DC**
McKinney, James H. .... Greensboro, NC
McKinney, James R. .... Tulsa, OK
McKinney, James V. .... Waukee, IA
McKinney, Jamie-Lou .... Oswego, NY
McKinney, Jas. D., Jr. .... Greenville, SC
McKinney, Jeffery W. .... **Huntsville, AL**
McKinney, Jeffrey A. .... **San Francisco, CA**
McKinney, Jessica D. .... **Atlanta, GA**
McKinney, John A., Jr. .... **Newark, NJ**
McKinney, John F., Jr. .... **Des Moines, IA**
McKinney, John, III .... Grinnell, IA
McKinney, John L. .... Ames, IA
McKinney, John P. .... **Detroit, MI**
McKinney, John P. .... **New Boston, MI**
McKinney, John S. .... Salmon, ID
McKinney, John T., Jr. .... Ventura, CA
McKinney, Joseph E. .... **Topeka, KS**
McKinney, Julia C. .... **Newport Beach, CA**
McKinney, Karin Haas .... Brunswick, OH
McKinney, Kathleen Crum
Greenville, SC
McKinney, Kathryn Marie
Department of Justice, Civil Division, GV
McKinney, Kenneth N.
Oklahoma City, OK
McKinney, Kirk A. .... San Francisco, CA
McKinney, Kristi Diane .... **Knoxville, TN**
McKinney, L. Cregg .... Clearwater, FL
McKinney, Lance M. .... Fort Myers, FL
McKinney, Langston C. .... Syracuse, NY
McKinney, Larry J. .... Indianapolis, IN
McKinney Law Offices, P.C. .... Waukee, IA
McKinney, Linda Otani .... Washington, DC
McKinney, Linda T. .... Juneau, AK
McKinney, Louise E. W. .... Cleveland, OH
McKinney, Luther C. .... Chicago, IL
McKinney, Lynn E. .... Spokane, WA
McKinney, Margaret M. .... Indianapolis, IN
McKinney, Mark E. .... Pittsburgh, PA
McKinney, Mark R. .... Muncie, IN
McKinney, Martin E. .... Denver, CO
McKinney & McKinney .... Topeka, KS
McKinney & McKinney .... Tiffin, OH
Fairfield, TX
McKinney, Michael B. .... **Midland, TX**

McKinney, Michael M. .... **Kingsport, TN**
McKinney, Michael T. .... Burlington, KY
McKinney, Mitchell Matthew
Columbus, GA
McKinney & Moore, P.C. .... Abingdon, VA
McKinney & Namei Co., L.P.A.
Cincinnati, OH
McKinney, Natalie J. .... **Durham, NC**
McKinney & Nazareth, P.C. .... Wakefield, RI
McKinney, Pamela .... Albany, NY
McKinney, Patrice .... **Houston, TX**
McKinney, Patricia A. .... Philadelphia, PA
McKinney, Patrick L. .... Wakefield, RI
McKinney, Patrick L. .... Knoxville, TN
McKinney, Patrick Lynn .... Canton, OH
McKinney, Paul .... Shawnee, OK
McKinney, Phillip A. .... **Corpus Christi, TX**
McKinney, Phillip S. .... **Atlanta, GA**
McKinney, Rebecca Graham
Indianapolis, IN
McKinney, Richard A. .... Dallas, TX
McKinney, Ricky J. .... **Birmingham, AL**
McKinney, Rita M. .... Columbia, SC
McKinney, R. L. Pete .... **Houston, TX**
McKinney, Robert B. .... Charlottesville, VA
McKinney, Robert C. .... **Nashville, TN**
McKinney, Robert E. .... Waukee, IA
McKinney, Robert H. .... **Indianapolis, IN**
McKinney, Robert L. .... Miami, FL
McKinney, Robert Lee, II
Charleston, WV
McKinney, Robert P. .... Glen Allen, VA
McKinney, Ronald W. .... Greer, SC
McKinney, Rozanne Moore .... Fairfield, TX
McKinney, Rufus W. .... Bethesda, MD
McKinney, Russell R. .... **Dinuba, CA**
Visalia, CA
McKinney, Ruth A. .... Pittsboro, NC
McKinney, Samuel, III .... Fairfield, TX
McKinney, Samuel R. .... Tiffin, OH
McKinney, Samuel R., Jr. .... Tiffin, OH
McKinney, Sarah Jane .... **Tulsa, OK**
McKinney, Scott D. .... **Washington, DC**
McKinney, Scott F. .... **Oklahoma City, OK**
McKinney, Scott T. .... Madison, WI
McKinney, Stephanie Popivchak
Pittsburgh, PA
McKinney, Stephen F. .... **Columbia, SC**
McKinney, Steven G. .... **Birmingham, AL**
McKinney, Steven K. .... **Oklahoma City, OK**
McKinney & Stringer, A Professional Corporation .... **Oklahoma City, OK**
Tulsa, OK
McKinney, T.A. .... **New York, NY**
McKinney & Tallant .... **Robbinsville, NC**
McKinney, Theos D., III .... Westborough, MA
McKinney, Thomas A. .... Hawthorne, NJ
McKinney, Thomas A. .... **Rock Hill, SC**
McKinney, Timothy J., Jr.
Department Of Veterans Affairs, Office of the General Counsel, GV
McKinney, V. Blake .... Abingdon, VA
McKinney, Wainwright & Saul-Olson
Dinuba, CA
Visalia, CA
McKinney, Wayne H. Jr. .... Waukee, IA
McKinney, William C. .... Salem, OR
McKinney, William F. .... Fort Worth, TX
McKinney, William L. .... Los Angeles, CA
McKinney, William R. .... Oklahoma City, OK
McKinney, William R., Jr. .... Amarillo, TX
McKinney, Zeyland G., Jr.
Robbinsville, NC
McKinney-Foster, Rozia Marie
Oklahoma City, OK
McKinney-Lins, Patricia .... **Madison, WI**
McKinnie, Dennis .... Cary, NC
McKinnie, Karen .... San Francisco, CA
McKinnie, Patricia M. .... San Jose, CA
McKinnie, T. Holland .... Bolivar, TN
McKinnis, Doris C. .... Minneapolis, MN
McKinnis, George C. .... **Shelton, CT**
Bronxville, NY
New York, NY
McKinnis, John D. .... Kingsport, TN
McKinnis, Kelly K. .... McAllen, TX
McKinnis, Linda J. .... Dallas, TX
McKinnis, Michael B. .... **St. Louis, MO**
McKinnis & Scott .... Kingsport, TN
McKinnis, Todd A. .... **Edmond, OK**
McKinniss, Ted M. .... **Marion, OH**
McKinnon, Arnold B. .... Norfolk, VA
McKinnon & Associates, P.C.
Sterling Heights, MI
McKinnon, Charles M. .... Albuquerque, NM
McKinnon, Charles R. .... **Vero Beach, FL**
McKinnon, Charles W. .... **Vero Beach, FL**
McKinnon, Dan A., III .... Albuquerque, NM
McKinnon, Donald J. .... Eufaula, AL
McKinnon, Douglas G. .... Littleton, CO
Mc Kinnon, Douglas H., Jr.
Albuquerque, NM
McKinnon, Fowler, Fox & Taylor
Johnson City, TN
McKinnon, Frederick J., Jr. .... Bothell, WA
McKinnon, Graham, IV .... **Gainesville, GA**
McKinnon, Henry A., Jr. .... Lumberton, NC
McKinnon, J. Hugh, Jr. .... Detroit, MI
McKinnon, James E. .... Richmond, VA
McKinnon, John B., III .... **Johnson City, TN**
McKinnon, John P. .... Alexandria, VA
McKinnon, Joseph H. .... Anchorage, AK
McKinnon, Laura J. .... **Fayetteville, AR**
Russellville, AR
McKinnon, Laurie A. .... Topeka, KS
McKinnon Law Firm .... **Fayetteville, AR**
Russellville, AR
McKinnon, Linda M. .... Orlando, FL

McKinnon, Lynn G. ....Portola Valley, CA
McKinnon, M. Craig ....Santa Ana, CA
McKinnon, Malcolm L. ....Holland, MI
Williamston, MI
McKinnon, Malcolm R., (P.C.) ....Holland, MI
McKinnon, Mark E. ....Washington, DC
Mckinnon, Marva L. ....Statesville, NC
McKinnon, Mary Ann ....Detroit, MI
McKinnon, Matthew C. ....East Lansing, MI
McKinnon and McKinnon ....Holland, MI
Williamston, MI
McKinnon & McKinnon, Chartered
Vero Beach, FL
McKinnon, Michael C. ....Troy, MI
McKinnon, Michael G. ....Costa Mesa, CA
McKinnon, Michele A. W. ....Richmond, VA
McKinnon, Neil J. ....Buffalo, NY
McKinnon, Noah C., Jr.
Daytona Beach, FL
Ormond Beach, FL
McKinnon, R. Anthony ....Dallas, TX
McKinnon, Randall R. ....Sacramento, CA
Las Vegas, NV
McKinnon, Sheila ....Seattle, WA
McKinnon, Thomas C. ....Seattle, WA
McKinnon, William A. ....Glen Ellen, CA
McKinnon, William H. ....Lavallette, NJ
McKinnon, William L., Jr. ....Atlanta, GA
McKinsey, Brian A. ....St. Louis, MO
McKinsey, John ....Sacramento, CA
McKinsey, Judy Ann ....St. Louis, MO
McKinsey, Paul F. ....Lancaster, PA
McKinster, Art W. ....Riverside, CA
McKinstry, Charles L. ....Riverside, CA
McKinstry, John O. ....Versailles, KY
McKinstry, John R. ....Swarthmore, PA
McKinstry, Larry A. ....Juneau, AK
McKinstry, Michael M. ....Denver, CO
McKinstry, Michael R. ....Seattle, WA
McKinstry, Robert B., Jr.
Philadelphia, PA
McKinstry, Ronald E. ....Seattle, WA
McKinstry, Taft A. ....Lexington, KY
McKinstry, Toby M. ....Oklahoma City, OK
McKinstry, W. Earl ....Dallas, TX
McKinzie, C. Wayne ....Charlotte, NC
McKinzie, Carl W. ....Los Angeles, CA
McKinzie, J. Mark ....Indianapolis, IN
Mckinzie, L. Rachel ....Chicago, IL
McKinzie, Mark W. ....Overland Park, KS
McKinzie, Steve M. ....Amarillo, TX
McKirahan, Jay ....Columbus, OH
McKirdy, Charles R. ....Chicago, IL
McKirdy, Edward D. ....Morristown, NJ
McKirdy and Riskin, A Professional Corporation ....Morristown, NJ
McKirgan, Robert H. ....Phoenix, AZ
McKirnan, Kevin M. ....Celina, OH
McKissick, B. Alan ....Reno, NV
McKissick, Bill D., Jr. ......Lexington Park, MD
McKissick, Floyd B., Jr. ....Durham, NC
Mckissick, Robert David ....Florence, SC
McKissick, Van Walraven & Harris, Chtd.
Reno, NV
McKissock, Chas. E. ....Pittsburgh, PA
McKissock, Ellen ....San Jose, CA
McKissock & Hoffman, P.C.
Westmont, NJ
Doylestown, PA
Harrisburg, PA
Philadelphia, PA
West Chester, PA
McKissock, J. Bruce ....Doylestown, PA
Philadelphia, PA
McKissock, Keith E. ....Pittsburgh, PA
McKissock, Timothy M. ....Columbia, SC
McKisson, Mary Ann ....San Francisco, CA
McKisson, Robert W., Jr. ....Seattle, WA
McKisson & Sargent, Inc., P.S. ....Seattle, WA
McKitrick, Michael J. ....St. Louis, MO
McKitterick, Gary S. ....Irvine, CA
McKittrick, Ann-Marie ....Seattle, WA
McKittrick, Christe L. ....Madison, WI
McKittrick, D. Patrick ....Great Falls, MT
McKittrick, Deborah K. ....Ankeny, IA
McKittrick, Helen M.Bresnahan
North Hampton, NH
McKittrick, J. Joseph ....North Hampton, NH
McKittrick, James R. ....Eureka, CA
McKittrick Law Firm, P.C. ....Great Falls, MT
McKittrick, Murray & Parr ....St. Albans, WV
McKittrick, Neil V. ....Boston, MA
McKittrick, Parrish, Law Offices of
St. Albans, WV
McKittrick, Peter C. ....Portland, OR
McKittrick, Richard A. ....Camden, ME
McKittrick, Timothy J. ....Great Falls, MT
McKittrick & Warren, P.A. ....Camden, ME
McKittrick, William W. ....Kenilworth, IL
McKitty, Tricia ....New York, NY
McKleroy, John P., Jr. ....Birmingham, AL
Mckleroy, Michael J., Jr. ....Dallas, TX
McKloskey, Neil R. ....Green Bay, WI
McKlveen, William J. ....Boise, ID
McKneely, Roland V., Jr. ....Bossier City, LA
McKneely, Steven L. ....Hammond, LA
McKnew, Della Karpeles ....Pasadena, MD
McKnew, Leslie ....San Francisco, CA
McKnew, Louise Bouscaren ....Rockville, MD
McKnew, Natalma M. ....Greenville, SC
McKnew, Thomas I., Jr. ....Norwalk, CA
McKnight, Albert W. ....San Antonio, TX
McKnight, Benton F. ....Bakersfield, CA
McKnight, Betsy D. ....Washington, PA
McKnight, Beverly A. ....Washington, DC
McKnight, Bill M. ....Dallas, TX
McKnight, Charles E. ....Cambridge, OH
McKnight, Charles K., Jr. ....Atlanta, GA
McKnight, Charles N. ....Mobile, AL
McKnight, Cherre M. ....Long Beach, CA
McKnight, Cleve ....Bakersfield, CA
McKnight, Cornelius E. ....Chicago, IL
McKnight, Cynthia G. ....Bethesda, MD
McKnight, Cynthia M. ....Washington, DC
McKnight, Daniel H. ....Dayton, OH
McKnight, Deborah K. ....St. Paul, MN
McKnight DeHart & Crockett, P.C.
Fort Worth, TX
McKnight, DeLoss ....Hickory Ridge, AR
McKnight, DeLoss, III ....Kansas City, MO
McKnight, Douglas G. ....Everett, WA
McKnight, Edwin H., Jr. ....Santa Ana, CA
McKnight, Elaine ....New York, NY
McKnight, Eugene W. ....Bakersfield, CA
McKnight, F. Douglas ....Orlando, FL
McKnight, F. Rush ....Cleveland, OH
McKnight & Fouts ....Dallas, TX
McKnight, Frederick L. ....Los Angeles, CA
McKnight, Gary L. ....McAlester, OK
McKnight, Gary L., Inc. ....McAlester, OK
McKnight & Gasaway ....Medford, OK
Cherokee, OK
Enid, OK
Fairview, OK
Kingfisher, OK
McKnight, H. Brent ....Charlotte, NC
McKnight, H. Gail ....Westland, MI
McKnight, H. James ....Coraopolis, PA
McKnight, H. Turney ....Baltimore, MD
McKnight, H. Vincent, Jr.
Washington, DC
McKnight & Hendrix, P.C. ....Las Vegas, NV
McKnight Hudson/ Ford & Harrison LLP
Memphis, TN
McKnight, J. Clay ....Georgetown, KY
McKnight, J. Wallace ....Calimesa, CA
McKnight, James D. ....Chelsea, VT
McKnight, James D., Jr. ....Aurora, CO
McKnight, James L. ....Chicago, IL
McKnight, James M. ....New York, NY
McKnight, Jane Osborne ....Burlington, VT
McKnight, Jeanne S. ....Boston, MA
McKnight, Jeffrey G. ....Atlanta, GA
McKnight, Jody V. ....North Charleston, SC
McKnight, John B. ....Dallas, TX
McKnight, John F. ....Houston, TX
McKnight, John T. ....Brunswick, GA
McKnight, Joseph W. ....Dallas, TX
McKnight, Katherine Louise
Benton Harbor, MI
McKnight, Kathleen A. ....Irvine, CA
McKnight, Kathleen Mary
San Francisco, CA
McKnight, Kathy J. ....Washington, DC
McKnight, Kevin L. ....Pittsburgh, PA
McKnight, Kristin ....Avon, CO
McKnight, Laura J. ....Minneapolis, MN
McKnight, Laura W. ....Overland Park, KS
McKnight, Lisa B. ....Richmond, VA
McKnight, Lisa M. ....Phoenix, AZ
McKnight, Marcus A., III ....Carlisle, PA
McKnight, Mark D. ....Birmingham, AL
McKnight, Mark D., P.C. ....Birmingham, AL
McKnight, Mark W. ....Charleston, SC
McKnight, Mary D. ....Dallas, TX
McKnight, Mary M. ....Idaho Falls, ID
McKnight, Maxwell S. ....Washington, DC
McKnight & McKnight ....Dallas, TX
McKnight, McKnight, McKnight & McKnight
Bakersfield, CA
McKnight, Merritt E. ....Lock Haven, PA
McKnight, Michael S. ....Sioux Falls, SD
McKnight, P. Michael ....Chandler, AZ
McKnight, Patrick E. ....Hamilton, OH
McKnight, Patrick K. ....Las Vegas, NV
McKnight, Philip C. ....Kansas City, MO
McKnight, Philip R. ....Greenwich, CT
McKnight, R. Leanne ....Jacksonville, FL
McKnight, Ralph L. ....Bakersfield, CA
McKnight, Ralph L., Jr. ....Bakersfield, CA
McKnight & Reese ....Mobile, AL
McKnight, Reggie E. ....Creedmoor, NC
Durham, NC
Greensboro, NC
Raleigh, NC
McKnight, Richard ....Las Vegas, NV
McKnight, Richard L. ....Enid, OK
McKnight, Riche T. ....Atlanta, GA
McKnight, Robert A. ....Milwaukee, WI
McKnight, Robert H., Jr. ....Atlanta, GA
McKnight, Rufus N., Jr. ....Dallas, TX
McKnight, Scott B. ....Fort Worth, TX
McKnight, Scott C. ....Oakland, CA
McKnight, Steven G. ....Merrifield, VA
McKnight, Stewart D., III
Birmingham, AL
McKnight, Susan C. ....Kansas City, MO
McKnight, Susan F. ....Albuquerque, NM
McKnight, T. Michael ....St. Petersburg, FL
McKnight, Thomas R. ....Dallas, TX
McKnight, Timothy J. ....Fort Collins, CO
McKnight, Tina D. ....Chatsworth, CA
McKnight, William G. ....Montgomery, AL
McKnight, William H. ....Tampa, FL
McKnight, Woodrow B. ....Little Rock, AR
McKnight-Chavers, Ginger
New York, NY
McKoan, Joseph H., III ....Algonac, MI
McKoan, Joseph H., IV ....Algonac, MI
McKoan & McKoan ....Algonac, MI
Mc Koin, Wanda C. ....Clinton, MO
McKone, Charles R. ....Flint, MI
McKone, David C. ....Milwaukee, WI
McKone, Frederick W. ....Rockville, CT
McKone, Michael M. ....Sacramento, CA
McKone, Michael M. ....Sacramento, CA
McKone, Michael P. ....Junction City, KS
McKone, Unruh & Graham, Chartered
Junction City, KS
McKonly, G. Steven ....Hanover, PA
McKonly, G. Steven, P.C. ....Hanover, PA
McKool, Mike, Jr. ....Dallas, TX
McKool Smith, A Professional Corporation
Dallas, TX
Marshall, TX
McKoon, Billings, Gold & Presley, P.C.
Chattanooga, TN
McKoon, James R. ....Chattanooga, TN
McKoon, James R., Jr. ....Phenix City, AL
McKoon, Thomas & Gray ....Phenix City, AL
McKoski, Raymond J. ....Waukegan, IL
McKosky, Paul M. ....Lake Havasu City, AZ
McKowen, James A. ....Charleston, WV
McKowen, Laurie Garrigan
Charleston, WV
McKowen, Thomas C., IV
Baton Rouge, LA
Lafayette, LA
McKown, Ann E. ....Durham, NC
McKown, Bryan Sean ......San Francisco, CA
McKown, Daniel C. ....Morro Bay, CA
McKown, Euell E. ....Sacramento, CA
McKown, James R. ....Kansas City, MO
McKown, Jeremy K. ....Washington, DC
McKown, Joan E.
Securities and Exchange Commission,
Division of Enforcement, GV
McKown, Jonathan Z. ....Gaffney, SC
McKown & Mckown ....Shelby, OH
McKown, Mia L. ....Lakeland, FL
McKown, Mike ....Hartford, KY
McKown, Neil A. ....Shelby, OH
McKown, Robt. A. ....Shelby, OH
McKown, Stephen B. ....Allegan, MI
McKoy, Katherine B. ....Atlanta, GA
McKoy, Linda C. ....Washington, DC
McKray, George A. ....San Francisco, CA
McKugh, Michael T. ....Fort Myers, FL
McKuin, Joel ....Beverly Hills, CA
McKuin, Michael A. ....Lake Arrowhead, CA
McKulla, Lawrence Robert ....Orinda, CA
McKune, Kathleen O. ....Louisville, KY
McKusick, Vincent L. ....Portland, ME
McKyton, Richard J. ....St. Petersburg, FL
McLachlan, Amy N.
Rancho Palos Verdes, CA
McLachlan, Bryan K. ....St. Petersburg, FL
McLachlan, George ....Lamar, CO
McLachlan, John D. ....Redwood City, CA
McLachlan, Michael D. ....Los Angeles, CA
McLachlan, Michael E. ....Denver, CO
McLachlan, Niall T. ....Miami, FL
McLachlan, Rissman & Doll ....Chicago, IL
McLachlan, W. Ian ....Stamford, CT
McLachlen, Thomas H. ......Mount Lebanon, PA
McLachlin, Harry Day ....New York, NY
McLafferty, Bernard J. ....Erdenheim, PA
McLafferty, David P. ....Conshohocken, PA
McLafferty, Irene M. ....Philadelphia, PA
McLafferty, J. William ....Santa Barbara, CA
McLafferty, John P. ....Boston, MA
McLafferty & Krohberger, P.C.
Erdenheim, PA
Norristown, PA
McLagan, Clinton R. ......Mendota Heights, MN
McLagan & Lerman, P.A.
Mendota Heights, MN
McLain, A. Lee ....Houston, TX
McLain, Addison T., Jr. ....Milwaukee, WI
McLain, Brenda S. ....Shelby, NC
McLain, C. Alleen ....Jackson, MS
Mclain, Christopher Charles ....Visalia, CA
McLain, Christopher M. ....Oakland, CA
McLain, D. Scott ....Huntsville, AL
McLain, David F. ....Warren, OH
McLain, David H. ....Warren, OH
McLain, David H. ....Philadelphia, PA
Philadelphia, PA
McLain, David M. ....Denver, CO
McLain, David R. ....Overland Park, KS
McLain, Dennis O. ....Ypsilanti, MI
McLain, Donna Dee ....Oklahoma City, OK
McLain, Frank E. ....Dallas, TX
McLain, George R. ....Sarasota, FL
McLain, George R., Chartered ....Sarasota, FL
McLain, J. Scott ....Edinburg, TX
McLain, James A. ....Montgomery, AL
McLain, James A. ....Houston, TX
McLain, James P. ....Atlanta, GA
McLain, Janice M. ....Chicago, IL
McLain, John E., III ....Orlando, FL
McLain, John L. ....Fort Worth, TX
McLain, John R. ....Des Plaines, IL
McLain, Kerry David ....Arlington, TX
McLain, Kevin G. ....Charlotte, NC
McLain, Kline, & Associates, L.L.P.
Dallas, TX
McLain Law Firm ....Houston, TX
McLain, Linda Meekins ....Bryan, TX
McLain, Lynn ....Baltimore, MD
McLain, M.C. "Mac" ....Dallas, TX
McLain & Merritt, P.C. ....Atlanta, GA
McLain, Patrick ....Detroit, MI
McLain, Peter R. ....Houston, TX
McLain, Richard S. ....Oklahoma City, OK
McLain, Richard W. ....Burbank, CA
McLain, Ronald T. ....Dallas, TX
McLain, Silvia M. ....Altamonte Springs, FL
McLain, Thomas E. ....Los Angeles, CA
McLain, Thomas H., Jr.
St. Petersburg, FL
McLain, Thomas L. ....Atlanta, GA
McLain, Warren W. ....Fairfax, VA
McLain, William A., P.C. ....Denver, CO
McLain, William C. ....Tallahassee, FL
McLain, William I. ....Milan, TN
McLain, William P. ....Warren, OH
McLain, William Thomas ....Dallas, TX
McLain & Winters ....Ypsilanti, MI
McLam, Fredrick C. ....Decatur, GA
McLamb, Catherine C. ....Raleigh, NC
McLamb, Dan J. ....Raleigh, NC
McLamb, Jack E. ....Raleigh, NC
McLamb, Janet H. ....Chapel Hill, NC
McLamb, Sheila K. ....Shallotte, NC
McLamore, Rebecca M. (Elliott) ......Austin, TX
McLanahan, Bruce ....New Canaan, CT
McLanahan & Comolli ....Athens, GA
McLanahan, John D. ....Atlanta, GA
McLanahan, John D., Jr. ....Athens, GA
McLanahan, Jon W. ....Oklahoma City, OK
McLandrich, Andrew J. ....Cleveland, OH
McLandrich, John T. ....Cleveland, OH
McLane, Alicen ....Tampa, FL
McLane, Ben C. ....Encino, CA
McLane, Bruce E. ....Marion, IN
McLane, Charles A., II ....Roswell, GA
McLane, D. Scott ....Largo, FL
McLane, Daniel B. ....Pittsburgh, PA
McLane, David G. ....Dallas, TX
McLane, David L. ....Pittsburg, KS
McLane, David Lawrence ....San Antonio, TX
McLane, David S. ....Los Angeles, CA
McLane, Francis A. ....Omaha, NE
McLane, Frank O. ....Marion, IN
McLane, Frederick B. ....Los Angeles, CA
McLane, Graf, Raulerson & Middleton, Professional Association ....Concord, NH
Manchester, NH
Nashua, NH
Portsmouth, NH
McLane, H. Arthur ....Valdosta, GA
McLane, James P. ....Fort Lauderdale, FL
McLane, Jodi-Ann ....Providence, RI
McLane, John P. ....Auburn, NY
McLane, John R., Jr. ....Manchester, NH
McLane, John T. ....Scranton, PA
McLane, L. Thos. ....West Point, GA
McLane, Larry ....Oklahoma City, OK
McLane, Malcolm ....Concord, NH
McLane, Mark W. ....Utica, NY
McLane, Mary Anne ....Wilmington, DE
McLane, Matthew R. ....Kansas City, MO
McLane & McLane ....Phoenix, AZ
McLane & McLane ....Marion, IN
McLane, Michael J. ....Wakefield, MA
McLane, Michael J. ....Columbus, OH
McLane, Michael R. ....Portland, OR
McLane, Nola ....Phoenix, AZ
McLane, Patrick L. ....Honolulu, HI
McLane Smith & Lascurettes, L.L.P.
Utica, NY
McLane, Theodore F. ....Largo, FL
McLane, Thomas W. ....Spokane, WA
McLane, William G. ....New Philadelphia, OH
McLane, William Lee ....Phoenix, AZ
McLane, William P. ....Newark, NJ
McLaney, C. Knox, III ....Montgomery, AL
McLaren, Bonnie J. ....Denver, CO
McLaren, Bruce W. ....Muncie, IN
McLaren, Douglas E. ....Washington, DC
McLaren, Gary R. ....Lubbock, TX
McLaren, James B., Jr. ....Memphis, TN
McLaren, James T. ....Columbia, SC
McLaren, John R. ....Hamden, CT
McLaren, Kenneth M., Jr. ....Gray, TN
McLaren & Lee ....Columbia, SC
McLaren, Linda J. ....Riverside, CA
McLaren, Michael G. ....Memphis, TN
McLaren, Richard K. ....New York, NY
McLaren, Richard W., Jr. ....Chicago, IL
McLaren, Roderic J. ....Cambridge, MA
McLaren, Sarah A. ....Bloomfield Hills, MI
McLaren, Scott A. ....Atlanta, GA
McLaren, Teresa Greco
Lake Arrowhead, CA
McLaren, William P. ....Westwood, MA
McLario, Helm & Bertling, S.C.
Menomonee Falls, WI
Milwaukee, WI
McLario, John J. ....Menomonee Falls, WI
McLarnan, Hannaher, Vaa & Skatvold, P.L.L.P. ....Barnesville, MN
Hawley, MN
Moorhead, MN
McLarnan, Roderick B. ....Moorhead, MN
McLarnan, Timothy J. ....Moorhead, MN
McLarney, James H. ....Overland Park, KS
Kansas City, MO
McLarney, Patrick ....Kansas City, MO
McLarnon, James P., Jr. ....Worcester, MA
McLarnon, Thomas P. ....Los Angeles, CA
McLarty, Bruce B. ....Denver, CO
McLarty, Edward L. ....Woodland Hills, CA
McLarty, James A., III ....Newport, AR
McLarty, M. Michael ....Arlington, TX
McLarty, Marlene Y. ....New York, NY
McLarty, Mary Alice ....Dallas, TX
McLarty, M. Michael, P.C. ....Arlington, TX
McLarty, Paul M., Jr. ....Decatur, GA
McLarty, Robert A., Jr. ....Trenton, NJ
McLarty, Robinson & Van Voorhies, LLP
Atlanta, GA
Decatur, GA
Greensboro, GA
McLarty, William Jackson, Jr.
Falls Church, VA
McLary, Steve M. ....Atlanta, GA
McLatchey, Russell F. ....Longwood, FL
McLatchy, M. Gene ....Helena, MT
McLauchlan, David C. ....Chicago, IL
McLauchlan, Karen ....Broadview, IL

McLauchlan, Peter A. ... Houston, TX
McLauchlin, Eric E. ... Bel Air, MD
McLauchlin, John W. ... Arlington, VA
McLauchlin, P. B., Jr. ... Ozark, AL
McLauchlin, Tracey J. ... Baltimore, MD
McLaughlin, Alan L. ... Indianapolis, IN
Mclaughlin, Alan Manus ... Staten Island, NY
McLaughlin, Amber ... Enid, OK
McLaughlin, Anne D. ... Lakeland, FL
McLaughlin, Anne M. ... Livonia, MI
McLaughlin, Annie M. ... Irvine, CA
McLaughlin, Barbara A. ... Albany, NY
McLaughlin, Barbara M. ... Red Wing, MN
McLaughlin, Bennett, Gelson & Cramer, A Professional Corporation ... Neptune, NJ
McLaughlin, Beth D. ... Cambridge, MA
McLaughlin, Bonnie A. ... Buffalo, NY
McLaughlin, Brian E. ... Napa, CA
McLaughlin, Brian J. ... Sacramento, CA
McLaughlin, Brian J. ... Bethany Beach, DE
Wilmington, DE
McLaughlin, Brian T. ... Midland, TX
McLaughlin Brothers, The ... Boston, MA
McLaughlin, Bruce ... Miami, FL
McLaughlin, Bruce D. ... Portland, OR
McLaughlin, Carol A. ... Cleveland, OH
McLaughlin, Cathleen E. ... New York, NY
McLaughlin, Cathleen Nelson
Anchorage, AK
McLaughlin, Charles H.
Department of Transportation, Federal Highway Administration, GV
McLaughlin, Charles H., IV ... Portland, ME
McLaughlin, Charles M. ... Troy, MI
McLaughlin, Chester R. ... Brockton, MA
McLaughlin, Christine E. ... Wilkes-Barre, PA
McLaughlin, Christine L. ... Cedar Rapids, IA
McLaughlin, Christine Malia
Portland, OR
McLaughlin, Christopher A.
New York, NY
McLaughlin, Christopher B.
Portland, ME
McLaughlin, Christopher J.
Minneapolis, MN
McLaughlin, Colleen M. ... Chicago, IL
McLaughlin & Cooper, A Professional Corporation ... Trenton, NJ
McLaughlin, Craig ... Seal Beach, CA
McLaughlin and Curry ... Fairmont, WV
Morgantown, WV
McLaughlin, Dale B. ... Louisville, KY
McLaughlin, Daniel A. ... New York, NY
McLaughlin, Daniel D. ... Brooklyn, NY
McLaughlin, Daniel F. ... Philadelphia, PA
McLaughlin, Darren L. ... Alexandria, VA
McLaughlin, David A. ... New Bedford, MA
McLaughlin, David A. ... Memphis, TN
McLaughlin, David C. ... Ortonville, MN
Mclaughlin, David John ... Boston, MA
McLaughlin, David M.
Redwood City, CA
McLaughlin, David S. ... Philadelphia, PA
Mclaughlin, Dawn R. ... San Antonio, TX
McLaughlin, Debra M. ... Portland, IN
McLaughlin, Debra MH ... York, PA
McLaughlin, Delbert L. ... Odessa, FL
McLaughlin, Denis F. ... Newark, NJ
McLaughlin, Denise Harvey
Lake George, NY
McLaughlin, Dennis, & Associates, P.S.
Spokane, WA
McLaughlin, Dennis J. ... Fremont, CA
McLaughlin, Dennis M. ... Spokane, WA
McLaughlin, Devin ... Middlebury, VT
McLaughlin, Dolphy T. ... Chicago, IL
McLaughlin, Donald C. ... Denver, CO
McLaughlin, Donald P. ... Greenbelt, MD
McLaughlin, Donald W., Jr.
Washington, DC
McLaughlin, Donn C. ... Des Moines, IA
McLaughlin, Douglas B. ... Boston, MA
McLaughlin, Douglas R. ... Casper, WY
McLaughlin, Duane ... New York, NY
McLaughlin, Edgar J. ... St. Louis, MO
McLaughlin, Edward F. ... Boston, MA
McLaughlin, Edward F. ... Armonk, NY
McLaughlin, Edward F., Jr. ... Hyannis, MA
McLaughlin, Edward J. ... New York, NY
McLaughlin, Elizabeth A.
Washington, DC
McLaughlin, Elizabeth B. ... Boston, MA
McLaughlin, Elizabeth B. ... Grand Rapids, MI
McLaughlin, Elizabeth K. ... Hartford, CT
Mclaughlin, Elizabeth P. ... Raleigh, NC
McLaughlin, Ellen E. ... Chicago, IL
McLaughlin, Ellen M. ... Yakima, WA
McLaughlin, Eric Marcel
Menlo Park, CA
McLaughlin, Eugene F., Jr. ... Greenwich, CT
McLaughlin, F. Moore, IV ... Providence, RI
McLaughlin, F. William ... Chicago, IL
McLaughlin and Florini, Ltd. ... Sullivan, IL
McLaughlin, Folan & McGlone, P.C.
New Bedford, MA
McLaughlin, Frank C., Jr. ... New York, NY
McLaughlin, G. William ... Boston, MA
McLaughlin, George A., III ... Boston, MA
McLaughlin, George A., Jr. ... Boston, MA
McLaughlin, George E. ... Wheeling, WV
McLaughlin, George J., Jr. ... New York, NY
McLaughlin, George W. ... Boston, MA
McLaughlin & Glazer ... Easton, PA
McLaughlin, Gordon L. ... Wilmington, DE
McLaughlin, Greg S. ... Atlanta, GA
McLaughlin, Gregg M. ... Arlington, TX
McLaughlin, Gregory A.
Fort Lauderdale, FL

McLaughlin, H. Vincent ... Sacramento, CA
McLaughlin, Harold B. ... Brooklyn, NY
McLaughlin, Harry L. ... Miami, FL
McLaughlin, Heather ... Shelbyville, IN
McLaughlin, Hemeon & Lahey, P.A.
Laconia, NH
McLaughlin, Hendon and Miller
Atlanta, GA
McLaughlin, Henry W., III ... Richmond, VA
McLaughlin, Hutchison & Hunt
Paris, TX
McLaughlin, Ian E. ... San Francisco, CA
McLaughlin, Irene ... Pittsburgh, PA
McLaughlin and Irvin ... Granada Hills, CA
McLaughlin, J. Kevin ... Southold, NY
McLaughlin, J. Mark ... San Angelo, TX
McLaughlin, J. Patrick ... Maryville, MO
McLaughlin, J. Patrick ... Dallas, TX
McLaughlin, J. Patrick, P.C. ... Dallas, TX
McLaughlin, J. Sherman ... Pittsburgh, PA
McLaughlin, J. Stewart ... Bay Shore, NY
McLaughlin, Jack M. ... Decatur, GA
McLaughlin, James A.
Department Of Health And Human Services, Social Security Administration, GV
McLaughlin, James A. ... South Natick, MA
McLaughlin, James A. ... Charlottesville, VA
McLaughlin, James A. ... Fairmont, WV
McLaughlin, James B., Jr. ... Buies Creek, NC
McLaughlin, James C. ... Atlanta, GA
McLaughlin, James C. ... Lennon, MI
McLaughlin, James C. ... Spooner, WI
McLaughlin, James D. ... Auburn, AL
McLaughlin, James D. ... St. Davids, PA
McLaughlin, James F. ... Windsor, CT
McLaughlin, James F. ... Brockton, MA
McLaughlin, James J. ... Richton Park, IL
McLaughlin, James J. ... Trenton, NJ
McLaughlin, James J. ... Portland, OR
McLaughlin, James M. ... Sullivan, IL
McLaughlin, James M., Jr.
New York, NY
McLaughlin, James P. ... San Mateo, CA
McLaughlin, James T. ... Clinton, MA
McLaughlin, Jane F. ... Milton, MA
McLaughlin, Jane M. ... Medford, NY
McLaughlin, Janice ... Laconia, NH
McLaughlin, Jaye P. ... Kenilworth, NJ
McLaughlin, J. D. ... Paris, TX
McLaughlin, Jeffrey R. ... Guntersville, AL
McLaughlin, Jerome M. ... San Francisco, CA
McLaughlin, Jerry D. ... Amarillo, TX
McLaughlin, Jim G. ... Birmingham, AL
McLaughlin, John A. ... Northbrook, IL
McLaughlin, John A. ... Jersey City, NJ
McLaughlin, John A., Jr.
Colorado Springs, CO
Denver, CO
McLaughlin, John B. ... Cleveland, OH
McLaughlin, John D., Jr. ... Philadelphia, PA
McLaughlin, John F. ... Red Bank, NJ
McLaughlin, John F. ... Cincinnati, OH
McLaughlin, John F., Jr. ... Pittsfield, MA
McLaughlin, John J. ... Tampa, FL
McLaughlin, John J. ... Des Moines, IA
McLaughlin, John J. ... Louisville, KY
McLaughlin, John J. ... Boston, MA
McLaughlin, John J. ... Hackettstown, NJ
McLaughlin, John J. ... Morrisville, PA
McLaughlin, John L. ... Danville, PA
McLaughlin, John M. ... Northampton, MA
McLaughlin, John M. ... Erie, PA
McLaughlin, John M., Jr. ... Jackson, MI
McLaughlin, John P. ... Philadelphia, PA
McLaughlin, John Raymond ... Seattle, WA
McLaughlin, John T. ... Huntington, NY
McLaughlin, Joseph ... New York, NY
McLaughlin, Joseph M. ... Granada Hills, CA
McLaughlin, Joseph M. ... Lawrenceville, GA
McLaughlin, Joseph M. ... New York, NY
McLaughlin, Joseph M. ... New York, NY
McLaughlin, Joseph P. ... Des Moines, IA
McLaughlin, Joseph T. ... New York, NY
McLaughlin, Julia C. ... Chicago, IL
McLaughlin, Karen B. ... Boston, MA
McLaughlin, Karen M. ... Cincinnati, OH
McLaughlin, Kathryn A. ... New York, NY
McLaughlin, Kelly L. ... Akron, OH
McLaughlin, Ken M. ... Pinedale, WY
McLaughlin, Ken M., P.C. ... Pinedale, WY
McLaughlin, Kenneth ... Houston, TX
McLaughlin, Kenneth C. ... Columbus, OH
McLaughlin, Kenneth F. ... Nashua, NH
McLaughlin, Kenneth L. ... Columbus, OH
McLaughlin, Kenneth S., Jr. ... Lisle, IL
McLaughlin, Kevin A. ... Sparta, NJ
McLaughlin, Kevin E. ... Blue Bell, PA
McLaughlin, Kevin M. ... Tampa, FL
McLaughlin, Kevin T. ... St. Louis, MO
McLaughlin, Laurel A. ... Ventura, CA
McLaughlin, Lauren A. ... Denver, CO
McLaughlin, Laurie ... New York, NY
McLaughlin, Lawrence D. ... Detroit, MI
McLaughlin, Lawrence J.
Granada Hills, CA
McLaughlin, Lawrence W. ... Santa Rosa, CA
McLaughlin, Leigh A. ... Boston, MA
McLaughlin, Leo A. ... San Mateo, CA
McLaughlin, Leslie G. ... Midland, TX
McLaughlin, Linda Hodge ... Santa Ana, CA
McLaughlin, Lisa Cresci ... Wilmington, DE
McLaughlin, Lisa Dale ... St. Louis, MO
McLaughlin, Lori ... Philadelphia, PA
McLaughlin, Luke F., III ... Norristown, PA
McLaughlin, Lynn A. ... Cleveland, OH
McLaughlin, Madeline G.
Walnut Creek, CA

McLaughlin, Margaret Kramer
Chicago, IL
Mclaughlin, Maria C. ... Worcester, MA
McLaughlin, Marianne G.
Philadelphia, PA
McLaughlin, Marianne M. ... Boston, MA
McLaughlin, Mark D. ... Redwood City, CA
McLaughlin, Mark E. ... Tampa, FL
McLaughlin, Mark R. ... Moline, IL
McLaughlin & Marshall, LLC
Guntersville, AL
McLaughlin, Martin A. ... Milwaukee, WI
McLaughlin, Martin D. ... Warsaw, MO
McLaughlin, Martin J. ... Milwaukee, WI
McLaughlin, Martina Walsh
Philadelphia, PA
McLaughlin, Martricia ... Easton, PA
McLaughlin, Mary A. ... Philadelphia, PA
McLaughlin, Mary Alice S.
New Bedford, MA
McLaughlin, Mary K. ... St. Paul, MN
McLaughlin, Matthew A. ... Pittsburgh, PA
McLaughlin, Matthew G. ... Irvine, CA
McLaughlin, Matthew J. ... Erie, PA
McLaughlin, Matthew T. ... New York, NY
McLaughlin, Maura D. ... Boston, MA
McLaughlin, Maurice W.
Saddle Brook, NJ
McLaughlin & McCaffrey, LLP
Cleveland, OH
McLaughlin & McLaughlin ... Lennon, MI
McLaughlin and McNally
Youngstown, OH
McLaughlin, Michael ... Nashua, NH
McLaughlin, Michael ... Somerville, NJ
McLaughlin, Michael C. ... Boston, MA
McLaughlin, Michael E. ... Atlanta, GA
McLaughlin, Michael J.
South Lake Tahoe, CA
McLaughlin, Michael J. ... Greenwich, CT
McLaughlin, Michael J. ... New York, NY
McLaughlin, Michael J. ... Philadelphia, PA
McLaughlin, Michael K.
Oklahoma City, OK
McLaughlin, Michael R.
Mountain Home, ID
McLaughlin, Michael R. ... Terre Haute, IN
McLaughlin, Michael Stephan
Anchorage, AK
McLaughlin, Michael T.
Newport Beach, CA
McLaughlin, Michael V. ... Buffalo, NY
McLaughlin, Michael W. ... Reston, VA
McLaughlin, Minerva ... Amarillo, TX
McLaughlin, Monique D. ... San Juan, PR
Charlotte Amalie, St. Thomas, VI
McLaughlin, Nancy A. ... Charlottesville, VA
McLaughlin, Neil ... Boston, MA
Mclaughlin, Patricia L. ... West Hartford, CT
McLaughlin, Patricia L. ... Nashua, NH
McLaughlin, Patricia O'Leary ... Hartford, CT
McLaughlin, Patrick E. ... Redwood City, CA
McLaughlin, Patrick F. ... Olney, IL
McLaughlin, Patrick J. ... Minneapolis, MN
McLaughlin, Patrick John ... Chicago, IL
McLaughlin, Patrick M. ... Cleveland, OH
McLaughlin, Patrick W. ... Los Angeles, CA
McLaughlin, Paul E. ... Kansas City, MO
McLaughlin, Paul R. ... Boston, MA
McLaughlin, Paul V. ... Irvine, CA
Mclaughlin, Peter C. ... Andover, MA
McLaughlin, Peter F. (IBA) ... New York, NY
McLaughlin, Philip T. ... Concord, NH
McLaughlin, R. Brian ... Teaneck, NJ
McLaughlin, R. Craig ... Cincinnati, OH
McLaughlin, R. Thomas ... Philadelphia, PA
McLaughlin, Raymond L. ... Moline, IL
McLaughlin, Richard B. ... Salinas, CA
McLaughlin, Richard B. ... Madison, WI
McLaughlin, Richard D.
Englewood Cliffs, NJ
McLaughlin, Richard E. ... Weatherford, TX
McLaughlin, Richard J. ... University, MS
McLaughlin, Richard L. ... Wagoner, OK
McLaughlin, Richard P. ... Youngstown, OH
McLaughlin, Richard S. ... Boston, MA
McLaughlin, Robert ... Orange, CA
McLaughlin, Robert A., Jr. ... San Diego, CA
McLaughlin, Robert B.W. ... Mobile, AL
McLaughlin, Robert E. ... Washington, DC
McLaughlin, Robert E. ... Atlanta, GA
McLaughlin, Robert E. ... Galesburg, IL
McLaughlin, Robert E. ... Boston, MA
McLaughlin, Robert E., Jr. ... Boston, MA
McLaughlin, Robert F.
San Francisco, CA
McLaughlin, Robert F. ... Damariscotta, ME
McLaughlin, Robert F. ... Salisbury, NC
McLaughlin, Robert Hugh ... Chicago, IL
McLaughlin, Robert J. ... New Hyde Park, NY
McLaughlin, Robert J. ... Tacoma, WA
McLaughlin, Robert L. ... Indianapolis, IN
McLaughlin, Robert L. ... Ashland, PA
McLaughlin, Robert M. ... New York, NY
McLaughlin, Robert S. ... Syracuse, NY
McLaughlin, Robin A. ... Los Angeles, CA
McLaughlin, Robt. V. ... Fayetteville, NY
McLaughlin, Roger J. ... Neptune, NJ
McLaughlin, Ronald D. ... Bentonville, AR
McLaughlin, Ronald K. ... Tallahassee, FL
McLaughlin, Ronald L. ... Lakewood, OH
McLaughlin, Ronée C. ... Washington, DC
McLaughlin, Roy Lee, III ... Selma, AL
McLaughlin & Russell, P.C. ... Clinton, MA
McLaughlin, Russell T. ... Avon, OH
McLaughlin, Ruth A. ... West Yarmouth, MA
McLaughlin, S. Douglas ... Vail, CO
Mc Laughlin, Sandra J. ... Boston, MA

Mclaughlin, Sarah Elizabeth ... Boston, MA
McLaughlin, Schuyler J. ... New York, NY
McLaughlin, Scott L.B., III ... San Jose, CA
McLaughlin, Scott R. ... Houston, TX
McLaughlin, Sean J. ... Erie, PA
McLaughlin, Seth J. ... Annapolis, MD
Greenbelt, MD
McLaughlin, Shane A. ... Nashua, NH
Mclaughlin, Sharon E. ... San Diego, CA
Mclaughlin, Shawn P. ... York, PA
McLaughlin, Sheila F. ... Philadelphia, PA
McLaughlin, Sheila J. ... Olney, MD
McLaughlin, Sheilah R. ... Portland, ME
McLaughlin, Slade H. ... Philadelphia, PA
McLaughlin, Stephen A.
United States International Trade Commission, Office of Administration, GV
McLaughlin, Stephen J. ... Braintree, MA
McLaughlin, Stephen P. ... New York, NY
McLaughlin & Stern, LLP ... New York, NY
McLaughlin, Steven J. ... Ames, IA
McLaughlin, Susan ... Cherry Hill, NJ
New York, NY
Philadelphia, PA
McLaughlin, Susan Kipp ... Fairmont, WV
McLaughlin, T. Mark ... Chicago, IL
McLaughlin, Terence K. ... New York, NY
McLaughlin, Teresa E.
Department of Justice, Tax Division, GV
McLaughlin, Teresa F. ... New York, NY
McLaughlin, Theresa M.
Fort Lauderdale, FL
McLaughlin, Thomas A.
Department Of Veterans Affairs, Office of the General Counsel, GV
McLaughlin, Thomas G. ... Antioch, CA
McLaughlin, Thomas J. ... Phoenix, AZ
McLaughlin, Thomas J. ... West Roxbury, MA
McLaughlin, Thomas J. ... Seattle, WA
McLaughlin, Thomas Joseph ... Bel Air, MD
McLaughlin, Thomas L. ... Athol, MA
McLaughlin, Thomas L. ... Milford, MA
McLaughlin, Thomas O. ... Seattle, WA
McLaughlin, Thomas P. ... Hoffman Estates, IL
McLaughlin, Thomas P. ... Somerville, NJ
McLaughlin, Thomas P., Jr. ... Harrison, MI
McLaughlin, Thomas W. ... Washington, DC
Mclaughlin, Timothy M. ... Knoxville, TN
McLaughlin, Timothy P. ... South Bend, IN
McLaughlin, Valerie L. ... San Diego, CA
McLaughlin, Veronica D.
Washington, DC
McLaughlin, Vincent A. ... Portland, OR
McLaughlin, W. Kevin, Jr. ... Asheville, NC
McLaughlin, Walter H., Jr. ... Boston, MA
McLaughlin, William F. ... Buffalo, NY
McLaughlin, William L., Jr. ... Paoli, PA
McLaughlin, William T., II ... Fresno, CA
McLaughlin, Wilmer L. ... Goshen, IN
McLaurin, Anselm J. ... Brandon, MS
McLaurin, C. Stevens ... Florence, SC
McLaurin, Claire W. ... Lufkin, TX
McLaurin, David B. ... Tupelo, MS
McLaurin, G. Gordon, Jr. ... Dillon, SC
McLaurin, John C. ... Brandon, MS
McLaurin, John C., Jr. ... Brandon, MS
McLaurin, John P., III
Department of the Army, Office of the Assistant Secretary of the Army (Manpower & Reserve Affairs), GV
McLaurin, Kathleen Ryan ... Dallas, TX
McLaurin Law Firm ... Oxford, MS
Tupelo, MS
McLaurin & McLaurin ... Brandon, MS
McLaurin & McLaurin ... Dillon, SC
McLaurin, R. Edward, Jr. ... Pittsboro, NC
McLaurin, Robert L. ... Cincinnati, OH
McLaury, Shane ... Snyder, OK
McLawhorn, Charles L., Jr. ... Greenville, NC
McLawhorn, Daniel F. ... Raleigh, NC
McLawhorn, Donald E. ... Tampa, FL
Mclawhorn, Melissa Dail ... Norman, OK
McLawhorn, Richard E. ... Columbia, SC
McLawhorn, Todd L. ... Chicago, IL
McLaws, John Larry ... Mesa, AZ
McLaws, John Larry, P.C. ... Mesa, AZ
McLay, Elgin A., (Ms.) ... Spokane, WA
McLay, Robert S. ... Sacramento, CA
McLeaish, Donald C. ... Duncanville, TX
McLeaish, Laurel Theresa
Department of Defense, GV
McLeaish Law Office, A Professional Corporation ... Duncanville, TX
McLeaish, Michael ... Odessa, TX
McLeaish, Robert B., Jr. ... McAllen, TX
McLean, Alan H. ... Stamford, CT
New York, NY
McLean, Albert G. ... Memphis, TN
McLean, Amy Clayborne ... Atlanta, GA
McLean, Andrew ... New York, NY
Mclean, Andrew H. ... Boston, MA
McLean, Anna S. ... San Francisco, CA
McLean, Arthur Frazier, III
Greenville, SC
McLean, Barbara ... Kew Gardens, NY
McLean, Bruce C. ... Utica, NY
McLean, Carley B., Jr. ... Raleigh, NC
McLean, Catrina ... Houston, TX
McLean, Charles G. ... Lumberton, NC
McLean, Christine L. ... Washington, DC
McLean, Christopher A.
United States Senate, Senatorial Assistants, GV
McLean, Clifford M. ... Longview, WA
McLean, D. Bruce ... Enterprise, AL
McLean, Daniel N. ... Helena, MT
McLean, David A. ... Madison, WI

McLean, David J. ....Los Angeles, CA
McLean, David L. ....New York, NY
McLean, David M. ....Anaconda, MT
McLean, David M. ....Missoula, MT
McLean, David P. ....Dallas, TX
McLean, Dennis E. ....Seattle, WA
McLean, Dickson, Jr. ....Lumberton, NC
McLean, Donald C. ....Washington, DC
McLean, Donald F., Jr. ....El Cajon, CA
McLean, Donald M. ....Kansas City, KS
McLean, Douglas L. ....Madison, WI
McLean, Edward C., Jr. ....New York, NY
McLean, Edward D. ....Mankato, MN
McLean, Edward P. ....Missoula, MT
McLean, Ernest C., III ....Atlanta, GA
McLean, Fred N. ....Paris, TN
McLean, G. Hite ....Greenwood, MS
McLean, G. Hite, Jr. ....Memphis, TN
McLean, Gary P. ....Freehold, NJ
McLean, George A., Jr. ....Roanoke, VA
McLean, George W., Jr. ....Seattle, WA
McLean, Gloria Scheid ....El Cajon, CA
McLean, H. Randolph ....Charlotte, NC
McLean, Hae Kyung
Federal Communications Commission,
Mass Media Bureau, GV
McLean, Harold A. ....Tallahassee, FL
McLean, Holly R. ....Portland, OR
McLean, Hugh K., Jr. ....Paris, TN
McLean, Hunter T. ....Fort Worth, TX
McLean, J. Dickson ....Wilmington, NC
McLean, J. Gerald ....Romeo, MI
McLean, Jack L., Jr. ....Boca Raton, FL
Atlanta, GA
McLean, James A. ....Bozeman, MT
McLean, James E., Jr. ....Cincinnati, OH
McLean, James G. ....Pittsburgh, PA
McLean, James H. ....Pittsburgh, PA
McLean, James Lankford ....Northridge, CA
McLean, James M. ....Jacksonville, FL
McLean, James M. ....Missoula, MT
McLean, James S. ....Spokane, WA
McLean, Janice Murray ....Tallahassee, FL
McLean, John E. ....New York, NY
McLean, John F. ....Tiburon, CA
McLean, John J., Jr. ....Pittsburgh, PA
McLean, John L. G. ....New York, NY
McLean, John T. ....Charlotte, NC
McLean, John T. ....Bellevue, WA
McLean, Joseph A. ....Juneau, AK
McLean, Joseph P. ....Florence, SC
McLean, Joseph S. ....Burlington, VT
McLean, Juanita E. ....Los Angeles, CA
McLean, Julianne B. ....Boston, MA
McLean, Julie Johnson ....Des Moines, IA
McLean, Kerry J. ....San Francisco, CA
McLean, Kevin A. ....Tampa, FL
McLean, Kevin C. ....San Diego, CA
McLean, Kevin G. ....New York, NY
McLean, Kevin R. ....San Francisco, CA
McLean, Kevin W.
Environmental Protection Agency,
Office of the General Counsel, GV
McLean, Kirsten Pyle ....Houston, TX
McLean, Kris A. ....Helena, MT
McLean, Lauchlin H. ....Hartford, CT
McLean, Lauri Konishi ....Los Angeles, CA
McLean, Lisa S. ....Cambridge, MA
McLean, L. M., Jr. ....Birmingham, AL
McLean, Louis A. ....Evanston, IL
McLean, Louisa Belle ....Los Angeles, CA
McLean, Lynn M. ....San Francisco, CA
McLean, Majorie W. ....Denver, CO
McLean, Maple A. ....Forest Hills, NY
McLean, Marci M. ....Dallas, TX
McLean, Margaret B. ....Englewood, CO
McLean, Margaret C. ....Port Orchard, WA
McLean, Margaret N. ....Jackson, MS
McLean, Margaret Smith ....Worcester, MA
McLean, Marian E. ....San Francisco, CA
McLean, Marilyn ....Bellingham, WA
McLean, Marilyn R. ....Gainesville, FL
McLean, Mark A. ....Woodland Hills, CA
McLean, Mark G. ....St. Louis, MO
McLean, Mary Ann F. ....Palatine, IL
McLean, Mary Park ....Fairfax, VA
McLean, Matthew F. ....Billings, MT
McLean & McLean ....El Cajon, CA
McLean & McLean ....Kansas City, KS
McLean & McLean ....Worcester, MA
McLean and McLean, P.C. ....Paris, TN
McLean, Mendelssohn V.
Florham Park, NJ
McLean, Meredith L.
Environmental Protection Agency,
Program Office Attorneys, GV
McLean, Michael ....Chicago, IL
McLean, Michael C. ....Pittsburgh, PA
McLean, Michael D. ....Anaconda, MT
McLean, Michael G. ....El Paso, TX
McLean, Mijak & Clark, P.C. ....Romeo, MI
McLean, Mitchell L. ....North Wilkesboro, NC
McLean, Mitchell S. ....Ahoskie, NC
McLean, Nancy M. ....Plymouth, MA
McLean, Nancy Washburn
Eden Prairie, MN
McLean, Neil A. ....Grand Ledge, MI
Lansing, MI
McLean, Pamela L. ....Schaumburg, IL
McLean, Patricia A. ....Tampa, FL
McLean, Patricia J. ....Butler, PA
McLean, Peter, III ....Charlotte, NC
McLean, R. Bruce ....Washington, DC
McLean, R. Davidson ....Tampa, FL
McLean, R. Taylor ....Towson, MD
Mc Lean, Raymond L. ....Lakeside, CA
McLean, Rhonda J. ....New York, NY
McLean, Richard C. ....Boulder, CO
McLean, Richard D. ....Romeo, MI
McLean, Robbie Louise ....Chattanooga, TN
McLean, Robert A. ....Memphis, TN
McLean, Robert D.
Federal Energy Regulatory Commission,
Office of the General Counsel, GV
McLean, Robert D. ....Tampa, FL
McLean, Robert F. ....Rochester, NY
McLean, Robert H. ....Ocala, FL
McLean, Robert J. ....Birmingham, AL
McLean, Robert S. ....Charlotte, NC
McLean, Robt. G. ....Alamo, TN
McLean, Roger W. ....Kansas City, KS
McLean, Ronald G. ....Indianapolis, IN
McLean, Ronald H. ....Fargo, ND
McLean, Roseanne ....Hollister, CA
McLean, Russell L., III ....Waynesville, NC
McLean, S. David, Jr. ....Atlanta, GA
McLean, Sandra M. ....Stamford, CT
McLean, Sara ....Department of Justice,
Civil Division, GV
McLean, Sarah E. ....Houston, TX
McLean, Sheila Avrin ....New York, NY
McLean, Stacy, McLean, McIntyre, Ramsaur & Murray, Professional Association
Lumberton, NC
McLean, Stephen G. ....Sheboygan, WI
McLean, Stephen M. ....Oakes, ND
McLean, Susan Ralston ....Dallas, TX
McLean, Terence J. ....Worcester, MA
McLean, Theresa ....Greenbrae, CA
McLean, Thomas P. ....Burbank, CA
McLean, Thurman T., Jr. ....Madison, TN
McLean, Timothy M. ....Wheaton, IL
Mclean, Tracey A. ....Syracuse, NY
McLean & Trichak ....Seattle, WA
McLean, W. Campbell ....Tampa, FL
McLean, Warner H. ....Beverly Hills, CA
McLean, Wendy W. ....Malvern, PA
McLean, William A. ....Little Rock, AR
McLean, William C., Jr. ....Tampa, FL
McLean, William C., Jr., P.A. ....Tampa, FL
McLean, William H. ....Phoenix, AZ
McLean, William J., III ....Palo Alto, CA
McLean, William M. ....Charleston, SC
Mclean, William P. ....Austin, TX
McLean, William S. ....Lumberton, NC
McLean-Utley, Marsha ....Los Angeles, CA
McLearn, Michael B. ....New York, NY
McLeary, Everett C. ....Chicago, IL
McLeary, Harold W., Jr. ....Memphis, TN
McLeay, Bartholomew L. ....Omaha, NE
McLeay, Thomas ....Chicago, IL
McLee, Edward G. ....Arcadia, CA
McLees, John A. ....Chicago, IL
McLees, John H., Jr. ....Richmond, VA
McLees, Matthew J. ....Philadelphia, PA
McLees, William W. ....Watford City, ND
McLeese, Karen R. ....Kansas City, MO
McLeese, Richard H. ....Chicago, IL
McLeester, William H. ....Englewood, NJ
McLeigh, Charles J. ....Pittsburgh, PA
McLeish, Steven ....Woburn, MA
McLeland, Joseph C. ....Munroe Falls, OH
McLeland, Le-Nhung ....Washington, DC
McLellan, Amy S. ....San Jose, CA
McLellan, Beth ....Santa Clara, CA
McLellan & Bialkowski ....Hackensack, NJ
McLellan, Bruce G. ....Lakewood, CO
Mclellan, Bruce G., P.C. ....Lakewood, CO
McLellan, Bruce L. ....Minneapolis, MN
McLellan, D. Daniel ....Lansing, MI
McLellan, Dale J. ....Southfield, MI
McLellan, David L. ....Andover, MA
McLellan, Donald F. ....Schaumburg, IL
McLellan, Gerald D. ....Boston, MA
McLellan, Harry E., III ....Hackensack, NJ
McLellan, Jeffrey C. ....Washington, GA
McLellan, John S., III ....Kingsport, TN
McLellan, Joseph F. ....San Diego, CA
McLellan, Julia P. ....New Orleans, LA
McLellan, Lawrence P. ....Des Moines, IA
McLellan, Malcolm C. ....Wenatchee, WA
McLellan, Peter E. ....Syracuse, NY
McLellan, Richard D. ....Lansing, MI
McLellan, Robert D. ....Florham Park, NJ
McLellan, Scott D. ....West Springfield, MA
McLellan, Scott W. ....Breinigsville, PA
McLellan, Thomas W. ....Phoenix, AZ
McLellan, W. Scott ....Houston, TX
McLellan, Walter J.
Department of Commerce,
Office of the General Counsel, GV
McLellan, William T. ....Highland Park, MI
McLellan & Zack ....Boston, MA
McLelland, D. Marsh ....Burlington, NC
McLelland, Krista L.
Department of Transportation,
Federal Aviation Administration, GV
McLellon, Richard S. ....Portsmouth, VA
McLemore, Alan D. ....Kirbyville, TX
McLemore, B. Michael ....St. Petersburg, FL
McLemore, Barbara Romberger
Harrisburg, PA
McLemore, Claiborne K., III ....Nashville, TN
McLemore, Collins & Toschi
Oakland, CA
Santa Rosa, CA
McLemore, Don Lee ....Jackson, MS
McLemore, Doyal E., Jr. ....Fort Wayne, IN
McLemore, Eugene L. ....Jackson, MS
McLemore Firm, The ....Fort Wayne, IN
McLemore, George D. ....Oakland, CA
Santa Rosa, CA
McLemore, Gerald R. ....Corinth, MS
McLemore, Gilbert C., Jr.
Brunswick, GA
McLemore, Heather C. ....Houston, TX
Mclemore, Heidi Baier ....Mangum, OK
McLemore, Jack H., Jr. ....Vidalia, LA
McLemore, James G., Jr. ....Carthage, MS
McLemore, James H. ....Montgomery, AL
McLemore, James L., III ....Suffolk, VA
McLemore, Jay R. ....Jackson, MS
McLemore, J. L., Jr. ....Suffolk, VA
McLemore, John C. ....Nashville, TN
McLemore, John C. ....Portsmouth, VA
McLemore, John C., P.C. ....Portsmouth, VA
McLemore, Kent P. ....Fayetteville, AR
McLemore, Lucie Underwood
Montgomery, AL
McLemore, Mary Megan ....Seattle, WA
McLemore, Michael T. ....Rockport, TX
McLemore, Mignon
Securities and Exchange Commission,
Division of Market Regulation, GV
McLemore, Paul D., Sr. ....Trenton, NJ
McLemore, R. Burke, Jr. ....Bethlehem, PA
Harrisburg, PA
Mclemore, Scott H. ....Houston, TX
McLemore, Timothy M. ....Knoxville, TN
McLendon, Bernard S. ....Atlanta, GA
McLendon, C. Keith ....Chevy Chase, MD
McLendon, Cecil G. ....Marietta, GA
McLendon, Christopher B. ....Washington, NC
McLendon, Christopher B., P.A.
Washington, NC
McLendon, Dana C., III ....Franklin, TN
McLendon, Dana Crosland, III
Nashville, TN
McLendon, Jacqueline K. ....Atlanta, GA
McLendon, Joan C. ....Conway, AR
McLendon, John A., Jr. ....Greensboro, NC
McLendon, Kathrine A. ....New York, NY
McLendon, Kennerly M. ....Columbia, SC
McLendon, Lennox P., Jr.
Greensboro, NC
Raleigh, NC
McLendon, Marna Lynn ....Ellicott City, MD
McLendon, Martin L. ....Atlanta, GA
McLendon, Melburne D. ....Atlanta, GA
McLendon, Moran D., Jr. ....Wadesboro, NC
McLendon, Robert R., IV ....Blakely, GA
McLendon, Sally B. ....Waterloo, IA
McLendon, Susan M. ....New York, NY
McLennan, Bruce A. ....Columbus, OH
McLennan, Donald J. ....Rogers City, MI
McLennan, Eric Robert ....Dyersburg, TN
McLennan, Janet ....Portland, OR
McLennan, Keith B. ....Norristown, PA
McLennan, Laura C. ....Glendale, CA
McLennan, Mary L. ....Wheaton, IL
McLennan, Michael E. ....Portland, OR
McLennan, Richard L. ....Chesterfield, MO
St. Louis, MO
McLennan, Richard L. ....Marlow, OK
McLennan, Robert B. ....San Francisco, CA
McLennan, Robert G. ....Elk Grove Village, IL
McLennan, Thomas D.
Bloomfield Hills, MI
McLennan, William L., Jr. ....Medford, MA
McLennan, William S. ....Portland, OR
McLennon, Daniel F. ....San Francisco, CA
McLennon, Mark J. ....Milwaukee, WI
McLennon, Paul A., Jr. ....Chicago, IL
McLennon, Thomas P. ....Englewood, FL
Port Charlotte, FL
Mcleod, Alastair N. ....La Jolla, CA
McLeod, Alec J. ....Detroit, MI
McLeod, Alexander, Powel & Apffel
Houston, TX
Galveston, TX
McLeod, Andrew F. ....Cheraw, SC
McLeod, Anne W. ....Austin, TX
McLeod & Associates, P.C. ....Boston, MA
McLeod, Barbara E. ....Detroit, MI
McLeod, Benton, Begnaud & Marshall, L.L.P. ....Athens, GA
Monroe, GA
McLeod, Blanchard L., Jr. ....Selma, AL
McLeod, Brian K. ....Wichita, KS
McLeod, Brigette R. ....New York, NY
McLeod, Bruce E. ....Oakland, CA
McLeod, Camille Reid ....Dallas, TX
McLeod & Canan, P.A. ....St. Augustine, FL
McLeod, Chanse L. ....Houston, TX
McLeod, Chas. C. ....Oakland, CA
McLeod, Cheri D. ....Atlanta, GA
McLeod, Cheryl A. ....Rockville, MD
McLeod, Chester ....Miramar, FL
McLeod, Christine A. ....Sitka, AK
McLeod, Christine Q. ....Gainesville, FL
McLeod, Christopher R. ....Tacoma, WA
McLeod, Clarence E.
Cleveland Heights, OH
McLeod, Daniel D. ....Marina, CA
McLeod, Daniel R., Jr. ....Greenville, SC
McLeod, David ....Gainesville, GA
McLeod, David K. ....Detroit, MI
McLeod, David S. ....Los Angeles, CA
McLeod, Donald M. ....Camden, AL
McLeod, Donald N. ....White Plains, NY
McLeod, Douglas P. ....Kansas City, MO
McLeod, Duncan A., Jr. ....Palo Alto, CA
McLeod, Duncan E. ....Fitchburg, MA
McLeod, E. Douglas ....Galveston, TX
McLeod, Edward A. ....Chesterland, OH
McLeod, Elizabeth A., (P.C.)
Augusta, GA
McLeod, Eric M. ....Madison, WI
Mcleod, Evans Martin ....New Orleans, LA
McLeod, Fraser & Cone ....Edisto Island, SC
Walterboro, SC
McLeod, Fred D.
Office of Personnel Management,
Personnel in Non-Legal Positions, GV
McLeod, George M. ....Oakland, CA
McLeod, Gina G. ....Los Angeles, CA
McLeod, Gregory S. ....Greensboro, NC
McLeod, Grover S. ....Birmingham, AL
McLeod, Gwendolen C. Lesh
Rockville, MD
McLeod, H. Jeff ....Anderson, SC
McLeod, Harold G. ....Knoxville, TN
McLeod & Harrop ....Dunn, NC
Mcleod, Heidi ....San Antonio, TX
McLeod, Henry M., III ....Charleston, WV
McLeod, Ian C. ....Okemos, MI
McLeod, Ingram B., Jr. ....San Antonio, TX
McLeod, J. Michael ....Dunn, NC
McLeod, James A. W. ....Buffalo, NY
McLeod, James C., Jr. ....Florence, SC
McLeod, James E. ....Washington, DC
McLeod, James F. ....Springfield, MO
McLeod, Janice Galli ....Department of Justice,
Office of Information and Privacy, GV
McLeod, Jeffrey R. ....Detroit, MI
McLeod, Jennifer ....Douglasville, GA
McLeod, Jennifer Byers ....Huntsville, AL
McLeod, Jennifer J. ....Hutchinson, KS
McLeod, Jody M. ....Pontiac, MI
McLeod, Joe ....Fayetteville, NC
McLeod, Johanna Elizabeth Tice
San Antonio, TX
McLeod, John B. ....Newtown Square, PA
McLeod, John B. ....Greenville, SC
McLeod, John D. ....Winnsboro, SC
McLeod, John Donald
Bloomfield Hills, MI
McLeod, John H. ....Waco, TX
McLeod, John J. ....San Diego, CA
McLeod, John M. ....New York, NY
McLeod, John M. G. ....Columbia, SC
McLeod, John W. ....San Antonio, TX
McLeod, Johnie A. ....Apopka, FL
McLeod, Katharine ....Carthage, NC
Pinehurst, NC
McLeod, Kathleen A. ....New York, NY
McLeod, Keith J. ....Warren, MI
McLeod, Larry V. ....Athens, GA
McLeod Law Firm, The, P.A.
Fayetteville, NC
McLeod Law Firm, The, P.C.
Kansas City, MO
McLeod, Leslie, Jr. ....Tallahassee, FL
McLeod, Linda ....Department of Commerce,
Patent and Trademark Office, GV
McLeod, Malcolm S., Inc. P.S. ....Seattle, WA
McLeod, Mark A. ....Columbus, OH
McLeod, Mary ....Wakefield, RI
McLeod, Mary Beth ....Spokane, WA
McLeod, Mary E. ....Department of State,
Office of the Legal Adviser, GV
McLeod, Maryellen ....Southfield, MI
McLeod, Marymichael ....Riverside, CA
McLeod, McLeod & McLeod, P.A.
Apopka, FL
McLeod, Michael R. ....Washington, DC
McLeod, Michael W. ....Fort Lauderdale, FL
McLeod, Michelle A. ....Miami, FL
McLeod & Moyne, P.C. ....Lansing, MI
Okemos, MI
McLeod, Peden B. ....Edisto Island, SC
Walterboro, SC
McLeod, Philip ....San Francisco, CA
McLeod, Philip A. ....St. Petersburg, FL
McLeod, Philip A., P.A. ....St. Petersburg, FL
McLeod, R. Jeffrey ....Golden Valley, MN
McLeod, Raymond A. ....Apopka, FL
McLeod, Richard E. ....Kansas City, MO
McLeod, Richard M. ....Quincy, MA
McLeod, Richard W. ....Boston, MA
McLeod, Robert A. ....St. Paul, MN
McLeod, Robert L. (Mac), II
St. Augustine, FL
McLeod, Robert M. ....San Diego, CA
McLeod, Robert P., (P.L.C.) ....Monroe, LA
McLeod, Roderick A. ....San Francisco, CA
McLeod, Rosland Fisher ....Dallas, TX
McLeod, Ryan Alexander ....Sumter, SC
McLeod, Sara M. ....New York, NY
McLeod, Scott E. ....Cedar Rapids, IA
McLeod, Skye ....New Orleans, LA
McLeod, Stanley E., (P.A.) ....Greenville, SC
McLeod, Stephen R. ....Sherman Oaks, CA
McLeod, Susan M. ....Cartersville, GA
McLeod, T. Michael
Fort Walton Beach, FL
Panama City, FL
Pensacola, FL
Mcleod, Thomas J. ....St. Paul, MN
McLeod, Thomas S. ....Canton, MI
McLeod, Tyler P. ....Topeka, KS
McLeod Verlander ....Monroe, LA
McLeod, Vivian W. ....Kansas City, MO
McLeod, Vonda S. ....Montgomery, AL
McLeod, W. Edward (Ned)
Winter Park, FL
McLeod, W. Edward, P.A. ....Orlando, FL
Winter Park, FL
McLeod, W. Mullins ....Walterboro, SC
McLeod, Walton J, III ....Columbia, SC
McLeod, Watkinson & Miller
Washington, DC
McLeod, Wilkins & McLeod ....Reidsville, NC
McLeod, Will E. ....Treasury Department,
Internal Revenue Service, GV
McLeod, William E. ....Jackson, MS
McLeod, William F. ....Reidsville, NC
McLeod, William F., Jr. ....Reidsville, NC
McLeod, William J. ....Apopka, FL
McLeod, William J. ....Boston, MA
McLeod, William J. ....Dillon, SC
McLeod, William L., Jr. ....Lake Charles, LA

McLeod, William Mullins, Jr.
Charleston, SC
McLeod, W. J., Jr. ... Clearwater, FL
McLeod, Yancey A., Jr. ... Columbia, SC
McLeod-Cain, Margaret L.
Charlottesville, VA
McLeran, Shawn M. ... Phoenix, AZ
McLeran, William T., Jr. ... Dayton, OH
Mcleron, Timothy William ... Albany, NY
McLeroy, Alberts & Benjamin, P.C.
Austin, TX
McLeroy, D. Todd ... Cullman, AL
McLeroy, Frederick G. ... Austin, TX
McLeroy, Jamie ... Austin, TX
Mcleroy, Jenny L. ... Decatur, AL
McLeroy, Jim D. ... Sulphur Springs, TX
McLeroy, Kathleen S. ... Tampa, FL
McLeRoy, Laurie J. ... Milwaukee, WI
McLeroy, Leah E. ... Dallas, TX
McLeroy, Litzler & Rutherford, P.C.
Greenville, TX
Paris, TX
Sulphur Springs, TX
McLeroy, Reuben J.
Department Of Health And Human Services,
Public Health Service, GV
McLeroy, Thomas R., Jr. ... Center, TX
Mclerran, Bradley Dwayne ... Norman, OK
McLerran, Ira G. ... Kansas City, MO
McLeskey, Waymon B., II ... Columbus, OH
McLester, Laura Lencses ... Newark, NJ
McLester, Scott G. ... Newark, NJ
McLetchie, Erland C. L. ... Ossipee, NH
McLetchie, Sherrie B. ... San Francisco, CA
McLevey, Alesia Holliday ... Pensacola, FL
McLewee, Robert W. ... Baltimore, MD
McLey, Stacey Lynn ... Kansas City, MO
McLin, Burnsed, Morrison, Johnson,
Newman & Roy, P.A. ... Lady Lake, FL
Leesburg, FL
McLin, Ian M. ... San Antonio, TX
McLin, Walter S., III ... Leesburg, FL
McLin, William C. ... Indianapolis, IN
McLinden, Daniel H. ... Santa Ana, CA
McLinden, Peter M. ... Worthington, OH
McLindon, John S. ... Baton Rouge, LA
McLinn, Jerry E. ... Carpinteria, CA
McLish, Thomas P. ... Washington, DC
McLister, Patrick F. ... Frederick, MD
McLocklin, Wayne D. ... Winder, GA
McLoon, Christopher S. ... Portland, ME
McLoon, Daniel J. ... Los Angeles, CA
McLoon, David T. ... Ipswich, MA
McLoone, John H., IV ... Waseca, MN
Mcloone, John J., Jr. ... Scottsdale, AZ
McLoone, John J., Jr. ... Mineola, NY
Mcloone, Kevin D. ... Scarsdale, NY
McLorg, Malcolm E. ... San Francisco, CA
McLorg, Vincent B. ... San Francisco, CA
McLoughlin, C. Glenn ... Oklahoma City, OK
McLoughlin, Charles M.
Oklahoma City, OK
McLoughlin, Christopher G.
Oklahoma City, OK
McLoughlin, Dennis J. ... Winchester, VA
McLoughlin, Frederick J., Jr.
New Bedford, MA
McLoughlin, Gerard P. ... Garden City, NY
McLoughlin, James J. ... Buffalo, NY
McLoughlin, James P., Jr. ... Charlotte, NC
McLoughlin, Jean M. ... New York, NY
McLoughlin, John E. ... Mineola, NY
McLoughlin, John J., Jr. ... Brick, NJ
McLoughlin, John M. ... Providence, RI
McLoughlin, John P. ... Los Angeles, CA
McLoughlin, John T. ... New York, NY
McLoughlin, Karenann ... Providence, RI
McLoughlin & LaMonica, P.C. ... Brick, NJ
McLoughlin, Laura A. ... Boca Raton, FL
McLoughlin, Linda G. ... Miami, FL
McLoughlin, Mark P. ... Detroit, MI
McLoughlin, Martin P. ... Oak Ridge, NJ
McLoughlin, Mary Elizabeth
Treasury Department,
Office of Regulations and Rulings, GV
McLoughlin, Maura A. ... Brooklyn, NY
McLoughlin, Maureen ... Roseland, NJ
McLoughlin, Maurice E., Jr. ... Boston, MA
McLoughlin, Megan Anne ... Fairfield, CT
McLoughlin, Michael T. ... Cassopolis, MI
McLoughlin, Neil Patrick ... Cape Coral, FL
McLoughlin, Thomas J. ... Bronx, NY
McLoughlin, William J. ... Columbus, OH
McLoughlin, William P. ... Princeton, NJ
New York, NY
McLoy, Kara Moheban ... Boston, MA
McLravy, R. Charles ... East Lansing, MI
McLucas, Don H. ... Lake Forest, IL
McLucas, Jeffrey C. ... Boston, MA
McLucas, Nancy Zytkewick
West Hartford, CT
McLucas, William R. ... Washington, DC
McLure, John G. ... Alexandria, LA
McLure, Joseph H., Jr. ... Atlanta, GA
McLure and Pickels ... Alexandria, LA
McLurkin, Elise B. ... Mooresville, NC
Statesville, NC
McLurkin, Reed Leonard ... Los Angeles, CA
McLurkin, Thomas C., Jr. ... Los Angeles, CA
McLurkin, Wayne B. ... Washington, DC
McLuskey, John W. ... Miami, FL
McLuskey McDonald & Payne, P.A.
Miami, FL
McLusky, Robert G. ... Charleston, WV
McLymont, Virginia B. ... Columbus, OH
McMachan, William D. ... Birmingham, MI
McMackin, David W. ... Brentwood, TN
McMackin, F. Joseph, III ... Naples, FL
McMackin, John J., Jr. ... Washington, DC
McMackin, John W. ... Fort Worth, TX
McMackin, Thomas K. ... Fairfield, OH
McMahan & Associates ... Chattanooga, TN
McMahan, Brian Edward
Oklahoma City, OK
McMahan, Brian L. ... McCall, ID
McMahan, Carl A., Law Offices of
Carlsbad, CA
McMahan, Carl A., Law Offices of
Los Angeles, CA
McMahan, Carol I. ... Columbia, SC
McMahan, Carol Sharpe ... Chicago, IL
McMahan & Cavenagh, Ltd. ... Chicago, IL
McMahan, Charles ... Chicago, IL
McMahan, Daniel E. ... Altus, OK
McMahan, Donald ... Littleton, CO
McMahan, Elizabeth Ann
Birmingham, AL
McMahan, J. Kenneth ... Charlotte, NC
McMahan, James M. ... Allentown, PA
McMahan, Janette A. ... Chicago, IL
McMahan, Jeffrey J. ... Burlington, VT
McMahan, John A. ... Claremore, OK
Tulsa, OK
McMahan, John D. ... Chattanooga, TN
McMahan, Kent H. ... Houston, TX
McMahan, Linda A. ... Colorado Springs, CO
McMahan, Lynne M. ... Indianapolis, IN
McMahan, Marcia C. ... Hattiesburg, MS
McMahan, McMahan & Brinkley, PLLC
Hattiesburg, MS
McMahan, Michael A. ... Chattanooga, TN
McMahan, Michael B. ... Hattiesburg, MS
Mcmahan, Michael Davis
Oklahoma City, OK
McMahan, Michael L. ... Carmel, CA
McMahan, Parker F., Jr. ... Chicago, IL
McMahan, Robert Allen ... Altus, OK
McMahan, Robert D. ... Terre Haute, IN
McMahan, Robert F., Jr. ... Columbia, SC
McMahan, R. R. ... Chicago, IL
McMahan, Terry P. ... Naples, FL
McMahan, Thomas V. ... Houston, TX
McMahan, Thomas Vance, Jr. ... Houston, TX
McMahan, Troy D. ... San Francisco, CA
McMahan, Trude I. ... Las Vegas, NV
McMahan, Van Douglas ... Birmingham, AL
McMahill, J. Brian ... Fort Collins, CO
McMahon, Alexander J. ... Santa Rosa, CA
McMahon, Allen R. ... Santa Ana, CA
McMahon, Alphonse ... Mt. Vernon, IN
McMahon, Amy Danise ... Dallas, TX
McMahon, Anthony J. ... Bethesda, MD
McMahon, Arthur F., III ... New York, NY
McMahon, Arthur F., Jr. ... New York, NY
McMahon, Arthur J. ... Charlotte, NC
McMahon, Berger, Hanna, Linihan, Cody &
McCarthy, A Professional Corporation
Clayton, MO
St. Louis, MO
McMahon, Beth Linn ... Roseville, MN
McMahon, Beth V. ... Norfolk, VA
McMahon, Blaine G. ... Marrero, LA
McMahon, Brian A. ... Cleveland, OH
McMahon, Brian D. ... Los Angeles, CA
McMahon, Brian J. ... Detroit, MI
McMahon, Brian J. ... Newark, NJ
McMahon, Brian K. ... Boca Raton, FL
McMahon, Brian M. ... Reno, NV
McMahon, Brian N. ... Toledo, OH
McMahon, Brian P. ... St. Joseph, MI
McMahon, Brian W. ... Saipan, TT
McMahon, Brien F. ... Santa Rosa, CA
McMahon, Bruce K. ... Encino, CA
McMahon, Carl G. ... Cleveland, OH
McMahon, Catherine D. ... Houston, TX
McMahon, Catherine H. ... Basalt, CO
McMahon, Christopher B. ... Southfield, MI
McMahon, Colleen ... New York, NY
McMahon & Coseo ... Saratoga Springs, NY
McMahon, Craig R. ... Bethel, AK
McMahon, Daniel A. ... Syracuse, NY
McMahon, Daniel B. ... Farmington Hills, MI
McMahon, Daniel G. ... Syracuse, NY
McMahon, Daniel J. ... Chicago, IL
McMahon, David H. ... Lynchburg, VA
McMahon, David J. ... San Francisco, CA
McMahon, David J. ... Metairie, LA
McMahon, David P. ... Stamford, CT
McMahon, DeGulis, Hoffmann &
Blumenthal L.L.P. ... Cleveland, OH
McMahon, Dennis A. ... River Grove, IL
McMahon, Dennis C. ... Glendale, NY
McMahon, Dennis C. ... New York, NY
McMahon, Dennis E. ... Cambridge, MA
McMahon, Dennis P. ... Manchester, CT
McMahon, Diane J. ... Buffalo, NY
McMahon, Earl F. ... Hartford, CT
McMahon, Earl J. ... Portage, WI
McMahon, Edward A. ... Albany, NY
McMahon, Edward J. ... Northampton, MA
McMahon, Edward J. ... Saratoga Springs, NY
McMahon, Edward R. ... Roseland, NJ
McMahon, Edward T. ... Arlington, VA
McMahon, Elizabeth Lorion ... Branford, CT
McMahon & Elliott ... Park Ridge, IL
McMahon, Emily S. ... New York, NY
McMahon, Emmett J. ... Minneapolis, MN
McMahon, Erin Brisbay ... Lexington, KY
McMahon, Eugene Francis ... Chicago, IL
McMahon, Eugene J. ... St. Louis, MO
McMahon, Fredk. E., Jr. ... Eugene, OR
McMahon, G. Douglas ... Chicago, IL
McMahon, George C. ... North Quincy, MA
McMahon, Gerald J. ... New York, NY
McMahon, Gerald L. ... San Diego, CA
McMahon, Gilbert K. ... Mahopac, NY
McMahon, Gregory D. ... Rochester, MI
McMahon, Gregory P.
Fort Lauderdale, FL
McMahon, Grow & Getty ... Rome, NY
McMahon, Howard G. ... Eau Claire, WI
McMahon, J. Alexander ... Durham, NC
McMahon, J. Patrick ... McLean, VA
McMahon, J. Robert ... Philadelphia, PA
McMahon, Jack ... Abilene, TX
McMahon, Jacqueline A. ... Biloxi, MS
McMahon, James A. ... Valley Stream, NY
McMahon, James B. ... Washington, DC
McMahon, James C., Jr. ... New York, NY
McMahon, James E. ... Oak Park, IL
McMahon, James E. ... Sioux Falls, SD
McMahon, James F. ... Algona, IA
McMahon, James F. ... Lenexa, KS
McMahon, James G. ... St. Clair Shores, MI
McMahon, James J. ... Marietta, GA
McMahon, James J., Jr. ... Phoenix, AZ
McMahon, James J., Law Offices of
Memphis, TN
McMahon, James Kane ... Brooklyn, NY
McMahon, James M. ... Buffalo, NY
McMahon, James P. ... Brockton, MA
McMahon, James P. ... Brooklyn, NY
McMahon, James S., Jr. ... New York, NY
McMahon, James Scott ... Chicago, IL
McMahon, James V. ... Phoenix, AZ
McMahon, Jane R. ... St. Paul, MN
McMahon, Jeanmarie ... Colts Neck, NJ
McMahon, Joanne Lendway ... Chicago, IL
McMahon, John B. ... Culver City, CA
McMahon, John C. ... Kansas City, MO
McMahon, John D. ... New York, NY
McMahon, John E. ... Portsmouth, NH
McMahon, John F. ... Newark, NJ
McMahon, John F., Jr. ... Boston, MA
McMahon, John J. ... Boise, ID
McMahon, John J. ... Champaign, IL
McMahon, John J. ... White Plains, NY
McMahon, John J. ... Solon, OH
McMahon, John J. ... Providence, RI
McMahon, John J., Jr. ... Birmingham, AL
McMahon, John James ... Honolulu, HI
McMahon, John K. ... Cleveland, OH
McMahon, John L. ... Saratoga Springs, NY
McMahon, John P. ... Columbus, OH
McMahon, John P. ... Vienna, VA
McMahon, John T. ... Chevy Chase, MD
McMahon, Joseph H. ... Wheaton, IL
McMahon, Joseph P. ... Laurel, MD
McMahon, Joseph P., Jr. ... Denver, CO
McMahon, Joseph R., III ... Covington, LA
Metairie, LA
McMahon, Joseph R., Jr. ... Metairie, LA
McMahon, Judith A. ... Brooklyn, NY
McMahon, Judith D. ... Anaheim, CA
McMahon, Julie K. ... Tulsa, OK
McMahon, Karen M. ... Rochester, NY
McMahon, Katherine E. ... Worcester, MA
McMahon, Kathleen A. ... Palos Heights, IL
McMahon, Kathleen A. ... Burlington, VT
McMahon, Kathryn J. ... Los Angeles, CA
McMahon, Kerry Marc ... Houston, TX
McMahon, Kevin ... New York, NY
McMahon, Kevin P. ... Jackson, TN
McMahon, Kimberly J. ... Argonne, IL
McMahon, Kristin Dodge ... Chicago, IL
McMahon, Kristine Connolly ... Boston, MA
McMahon, Kublick, McGinty & Smith, P.C.
Syracuse, NY
McMahon, Laura J. ... Houston, TX
McMahon, Lawrence D., Jr.
Morganton, NC
McMahon, Lawrence P., (P.C.) ... Tulsa, OK
McMahon, Leah A. ... Red Bank, NJ
McMahon, Lewis A. ... Keene, NH
Mc Mahon, Linda ... New York, NY
McMahon, Linda M. ... Washington, DC
McMahon & Losi ... Buffalo, NY
McMahon, Louis L. ... Cleveland, OH
McMahon, M. Brian ... Los Angeles, CA
McMahon, M. Suzanne ... Binghamton, NY
McMahon, Margie ... Jackson, NJ
McMahon, Maribeth S. ... Kansas City, MO
McMahon, Mark G. ... Clayton, MO
McMahon, Mark P. ... Longview, TX
McMahon, Marshal I., Jr. ... Park Ridge, IL
McMahon, Martha J. ... Boston, MA
McMahon, Martin F., & Associates
Washington, DC
McMahon, Martin J., Jr. ... Lexington, KY
McMahon, Martine & Gallagher
New York, NY
McMahon, Mary F. ... Providence, RI
McMahon, Mary Margaret ... Roseville, MN
McMahon, Mary P. ... Cincinnati, OH
McMahon & McCollam ... Houma, LA
McMahon & McMahon ... Laguna Beach, CA
McMahon & McMahon ... Providence, RI
McMahon, Melissa ... New York, NY
McMahon, Michael E. ... Wichita, KS
McMahon, Michael E. ... Lynn, MA
McMahon, Michael E. ... Staten Island, NY
McMahon, Michael F. ... Helena, MT
McMahon, Michael J. ... Coeur d'Alene, ID
Spokane, WA
McMahon, Michael J. ... Indianapolis, IN
McMahon, Michael Mark
Santa Monica, CA
McMahon, Michael P. ... Orlando, FL
McMahon, Michael R. ... Louisville, KY
McMahon, Michael S. ... Cleveland, OH
McMahon, Michael W. ... New Orleans, LA
McMahon, Nancy K. ... San Ramon, CA
McMahon, Nancy Owens ... Wethersfield, CT
McMahon, Neal M. ... Buffalo, NY
McMahon, Paige J. ... Chillicothe, OH
McMahon, Patricia A. ... San Jose, CA
McMahon, Patricia D. ... Milwaukee, WI
McMahon, Patricia Mastrianni
Glenmont, NY
McMahon, Patrick ... Wenatchee, WA
McMahon, Patrick B. ... Lovington, NM
McMahon, Patrick C. ... Littleton, CO
McMahon, Patrick F. ... Atlanta, GA
McMahon, Patrick J. ... Danville, CA
McMahon, Patrick J. ... Fort Lauderdale, FL
McMahon, Patrick, Law Office of
San Francisco, CA
McMahon, Patrick M.
Arlington Heights, IL
McMahon, Patrick R. ... San Jose, CA
McMahon, Patrick R., A Prof. Corp., Law
Offices of ... San Jose, CA
McMahon, Patrick T. ... Milwaukee, WI
McMahon, Paul B. ... Pawtucket, RI
McMahon, Paul J., III ... Lafayette, LA
McMahon, Paul J., (P.C.) ... Danbury, CT
McMahon, Paul Joseph ... Miami, FL
McMahon, Paul Joseph, P.A. ... Miami, FL
McMahon, Paul P. ... Fort Pierce, FL
Stuart, FL
McMahon, Peter C. ... Laguna Beach, CA
McMahon, Peter C. ... Menlo Park, CA
McMahon, Philip J. ... Houma, LA
Mc Mahon, Raymond J. ... Santa Ana, CA
McMahon, Raymond J., Jr. ... Providence, RI
McMahon, Richard E. ... Marco Island, FL
McMahon, Richard H. ... Rome, NY
McMahon, Richard H., Jr. ... Rome, NY
McMahon, Richard J. ... Grayslake, IL
McMahon, Richard J. ... Philadelphia, PA
McMahon, Richard L. ... Wilmington, DE
McMahon, Richard M., Sr. ... Upperco, MD
McMahon, Richard P. ... Providence, RI
McMahon, Robert A. ... Cincinnati, OH
McMahon, Robert A., Jr. ... Metairie, LA
McMahon, Robert F. ... Uncasville, CT
McMahon, Robert V. ... Laguna Beach, CA
McMahon, Robert W. ... Quincy, MA
McMahon, Ruth E. ... West Palm Beach, FL
McMahon, Shawn G. ... Pittsburgh, PA
McMahon & Spiegel ... Los Angeles, CA
McMahon, Stanton D. ... Jamesburg, NJ
McMahon, Stephen T. ... Syracuse, NY
McMahon, Steven J. ... St. Louis, MO
McMahon, Sue ... Amarillo, TX
McMahon, Surovik, Suttle, Buhrmann, Hicks
& Gill, A Professional Corporation
Abilene, TX
McMahon, Susan B. ... Elmhurst, IL
McMahon, Susan M., P.C.
Mount Pleasant, MI
McMahon, T. James, Jr. ... Pass Christian, MS
McMahon, Terence R. ... Shawnee, KS
McMahon, Teri Lynn ... Atlanta, GA
McMahon, Terrance Christopher
Bakersfield, CA
McMahon, Terrence P. ... Menlo Park, CA
McMahon, Thomas C., (P.C.) ... Houston, TX
McMahon, Thomas E. ... Chicago, IL
McMahon, Thomas G. ... Princeton, NJ
McMahon, Thomas J. ... Kansas City, MO
McMahon, Thomas M. ... Los Angeles, CA
McMahon, Thomas M. ... Chicago, IL
McMahon, Thomas M. ... Utica, MI
McMahon, Thomas M. ... Eugene, OR
McMahon, Thomas P. ... Denver, CO
McMahon, Thomas P. ... Washington, DC
McMahon, Thomas P. ... Buffalo, NY
McMahon, Thomas R. ... Chicago, IL
McMahon, Thomas V. ... Riverhead, NY
McMahon, Tidwell, Hansen, Atkins &
Peacock, P.C. ... Midland, TX
Odessa, TX
McMahon, Timothy D. ... San Jose, CA
McMahon, Timothy D. ... Chicago, IL
McMahon, Timothy F. ... Santa Ynez, CA
McMahon, Timothy J. ... Syracuse, NY
McMahon, Timothy J. ... Harrisburg, PA
McMahon, Timothy L. ... Raleigh, NC
McMahon, Timothy M. ... Ontario, CA
Walnut Creek, CA
McMahon, Timothy O. ... Royal Oak, MI
McMahon, V. Lee ... St. Louis, MO
McMahon, Vincent J. ... Coronado, CA
McMahon, Vincent J. ... Columbia, NJ
McMahon, William F. ... Providence, RI
McMahon, William J., Jr. ... Toms River, NJ
McMahon-Boies, Carole ... Lincoln, NE
McMahon-Lohrer, Kathryn
Washington, DC
McMahon-Stoll, Kathleen E. ... Buffalo, NY
McMain, Keith A. ... Florence, KY
McMain, Michael J. ... Florence, KY
McMains, Andrew T. ... Baton Rouge, LA
McMains, F. Charles, Jr. ... Baton Rouge, LA
McMains, Goodin & Orzeske, P.C.
Indianapolis, IN
McMains, Jay G. ... Baton Rouge, LA
McMains, Jeanne Lee ... Indianapolis, IN
McMains, Larry Jay ... Seminole, OK
McMains, Lisa J. ... Santa Ana, CA
McMains, Michael B. ... Indianapolis, IN
McMains, Randall A. ... Arkansas City, KS
McMains, Russell H., Law Offices of
Corpus Christi, TX
Houston, TX
McMaken, Lynda H. ... Bainbridge Island, WA
McMaken, Michael E. ... Mobile, AL
McMakin, J. Gary, P.A. ... Tampa, FL
McMakin, Susan Wolff, (P.C.)
Richmond, VA
McManama, Patrick J. ... Crown Point, IN

McManaman, Kenneth C.
Cape Girardeau, MO
McManaman, Kevin R. ... Omaha, NE
McManamon, Joseph F. ... Cleveland, OH
McManamon, Mary Brigid ... Wilmington, DE
Mc Manamon, Peter M. ... Huntingdon, PA
McManamon, Thomas V. ... Spokane, WA
McManamon, William T. ... Altadena, CA
McManamy, Douglas P. ... Savannah, GA
McManemin, Joseph P. ... Wyckoff, NJ
McManemin, Patrick F. ... Dallas, TX
McManemin & Smith, A Professional Corporation ... Dallas, TX
McManes, A. Spencer, Jr. ... Atlanta, GA
Roswell, GA
McManes, A. Spencer, Jr., P.C. ... Roswell, GA
McManes, Alison Ann ... Oklahoma City, OK
McManigal, Charles W. ... Mason City, IA
McManigal, James K., Jr. ... Sacramento, CA
McManigal, Mark L. ... Newport Beach, CA
McManigal, Robert M. ... South Pasadena, CA
McManimon, Doreen E. ... Tenafly, NJ
McManimon, Edward J., III ... Newark, NJ
McManimon, F. Patrick ... Trenton, NJ
McManimon & Scotland, L.L.C.
Newark, NJ
McManis, Charles R. ... St. Louis, MO
McManis, Faulkner & Morgan
San Jose, CA
McManis, James ... San Jose, CA
McManmon, James ... Riverhead, NY
McMann, James P. ... Washington, DC
McMann, Vincent J., Jr. ... Livingston, NJ
McMannis, Donald L. ... Pullman, WA
McMannis, James D. ... Pullman, WA
McMannon, Steven R. ... Chicago, IL
McManus, Alan C. ... Bloomfield Hills, MI
McManus, Anthony A., P.A. ... Dover, NH
McManus, Brandon Galloway
Gulfport, MS
McManus, Brian J. ... Washington, DC
McManus, Brian J. ... Chicago, IL
McManus, Brian J., & Associates, Ltd.
Chicago, IL
McManus, Brian P. ... Orange, CT
McManus, Brian T. ... Seattle, WA
McManus, Charles E., III ... Rancocas, NJ
McManus, Christine ... Boston, MA
McManus, Clarence E. ... Gretna, LA
Mcmanus, Colleen E. ... Chicago, IL
McManus, Constance ... Marietta, GA
McManus & Crane, L.L.P. ... Victoria, TX
McManus, Daniel E., Jr. ... New York, NY
Mcmanus, Daniel P. ... Houston, TX
McManus, Darcy E. ... Port Washington, WI
McManus, David A. ... New York, NY
McManus, David J., Jr. ... Baltimore, MD
McManus, David P. ... Cedar Rapids, IA
McManus, Dennis M. ... Windsor Locks, CT
Mcmanus, Dennis P. ... Worcester, MA
McManus, Diane M. ... Houston, TX
McManus, Edward J. ... Cedar Rapids, IA
McManus, Eugenie Marie
Small Business Administration, Office of the General Counsel, GV
McManus, F. Shields ... Stuart, FL
McManus, George G., Jr. ... Madison, CT
McManus, George W., Jr. ... Baltimore, MD
McManus, George W., Jr. ... Towson, MD
McManus, Heather Ribar ... New York, NY
McManus, Hugh S. ... Milwaukee, WI
McManus, J. Douglas, Jr. ... Schenectady, NY
McManus, J. Terence
North Palm Beach, FL
McManus, Jack ... Oregon, WI
McManus, Jacqueline P. ... Monterey, CA
McManus, James D. ... Duluth, MN
McManus, James J. ... Chicago, IL
McManus, James M. ... Red Springs, NC
McManus, James R., III ... Lancaster, PA
McManus, James T. ... Washington, DC
McManus, James T. ... Lafayette, LA
McManus, James V. ... Chestnut Hill, MA
McManus, James W. ... Kansas City, MO
McManus, Jeanne Ann ... Montville, NJ
McManus, Jeffrey J. ... Traverse City, MI
McManus, Jennifer L. ... Chicago, IL
Mcmanus, Jerome T. ... Lynn, MA
McManus, Jill ... New York, NY
McManus, John A. ... East Hartford, CT
McManus, John A. ... New York, NY
McManus, John C., (P.C.) ... Atlanta, GA
McManus, John E. ... Memphis, TN
McManus, John F. ... Fredericksburg, VA
Richmond, VA
McManus, John J. ... Rockville, MD
McManus, John K. ... Columbus, OH
McManus, John L. ... Fort Lauderdale, FL
McManus, John M. ... Birmingham, MI
Columbus, OH
McManus, John M. ... Las Vegas, NV
McManus, John O. ... Morristown, NJ
Newark, NJ
New York, NY
McManus, John T. ... Far Rockaway, NY
McManus, John T. ... New York, NY
McManus, John U. ... Red Springs, NC
McManus, Joseph A., Jr. ... Washington, DC
McManus, Joseph M. ... Washington, DC
McManus, Katherine D. ... Washington, DC
McManus, Katherine Sherwood
New York, NY
Mc Manus, Kathleen H. ... Milwaukee, WI
McManus, Kathleen M. ... Minneapolis, MN
Mcmanus, Keith A. ... Hyannis, MA
McManus, Kerry A. ... Hauppauge, NY
McManus, Kevin P. ... New York, NY
McManus, Krista B. ... New York, NY
McManus, Margaret ... New York, NY
McManus, Marilyn C. ... Portland, OR
McManus, Mark B., Sr. ... Roswell, GA
McManus, Mark B., Sr., P.C.
Roswell, GA
McManus, Marsha R. ... North Andover, MA
McManus, Mary C. ... Milwaukee, WI
McManus, Mary L. ... Largo, FL
McManus & McManus ... Red Springs, NC
Largo, FL
McManus, Michael A. ... Denver, CO
McManus, Michael G. ... Treasury Department, Office of Regulations and Rulings, GV
McManus, Michael J. ... Washington, DC
McManus, Michael J.
Palm Beach Gardens, FL
McManus, Michael J. ... Milford, MA
McManus, Michael J., P.A.
Palm Beach Gardens, FL
McManus, Michael S. ... Modesto, CA
McManus, Michael T. ... Detroit, MI
McManus & O'Byrne ... Port Washington, WI
McManus, Pamela Harrison ... Columbus, OH
McManus, Paula ... Everett, WA
McManus, Philip J. ... Albertson, NY
New York, NY
McManus, Randolph Quaile
Washington, DC
McManus, Regina D. ... Reisterstown, MD
McManus, Richard G. (MAC), Jr., Law Offices of ... Denver, CO
McManus, Richard J. ... Trenton, NJ
McManus, Richard Karl
Treasury Department, U.S. Customs Service, GV
McManus, Robert Bruce ... Largo, FL
McManus, Robert D. ... New York, NY
McManus, Robert E. ... Anchorage, AK
McManus, Robert E. ... Owings Mills, MD
McManus, Robert F. ... Warwick, NY
McManus, Robert J. ... Washington, DC
McManus, Robert Joseph
Washington, DC
McManus, Robert P. ... Cleveland, OH
McManus, Roberta L. ... Garden City, NY
McManus, Roger L. ... Osprey, FL
McManus, Sandra J. ... San Jose, CA
McManus, Schor, Asmar & Darden, L.L.P.
Washington, DC
McManus, Stephen ... Bloomington, IL
McManus, Stephen A. ... St. Louis, MO
McManus, Stephen M. ... Los Angeles, CA
McManus, Stephen M. ... Marlton, NJ
Philadelphia, PA
McManus, Steve Q. ... Victoria, TX
McManus, Thomas A.
Upper Marlboro, MD
McManus, Thomas N. ... New York, NY
McManus, Thomas P. ... Minneapolis, MN
McManus, Timothy J. ... Minneapolis, MN
McManus, Timothy J. ... Stroudsburg, PA
McManus, Vincent T., Jr. ... Wallingford, CT
McManus, Vincent T., Jr., Professional Corporation ... Wallingford, CT
McManus, Walter R., Jr. ... Des Moines, IA
McManus, Warren E. ... Lakehurst, NJ
McManus, William B. ... Phoenix, AZ
McManus, William J., II ... Worcester, MA
McManus, William L. ... Centreville, MI
McManus, William Q. ... Victoria, TX
McManus, Wilson P. ... Lutherville, MD
McManus, Wilson P., P.A. ... Lutherville, MD
McManus & Zacharisen ... Morristown, NJ
Newark, NJ
New York, NY
McMartin, Edwin K. ... Pueblo, CO
McMartin, W. Richard ... Englewood, CO
McMaster, Alan B. ... Novi, MI
McMaster, Boyd M. ... Cheyenne, WY
McMaster, Bridgette J. ... Providence, RI
McMaster, Clifford F. ... Fort Worth, TX
McMaster, D. Lee ... Wichita, KS
McMaster, Frank Barnwell ... Columbia, SC
McMaster, Frank C. ... Wichita, KS
McMaster, George Hunter ... Columbia, SC
McMaster, Gina Rossi ... Greenville, SC
McMaster, Heather M. ... New York, NY
McMaster, Henry Dargan ... Columbia, SC
McMaster, James D. ... Miami, FL
McMaster, James M. ... Newtown, PA
McMaster, James R. ... Denver, CO
McMaster, Jean ... El Toro, CA
McMaster, Jodi G ... San Antonio, TX
McMaster, Joe B. ... Georgetown, TX
McMaster, Joe B., A Professional Corporation
Georgetown, TX
McMaster, John B. ... Georgetown, TX
McMaster, John Gregg ... Columbia, SC
McMaster, John J. ... Northborough, MA
McMaster, Joseph D. ... Columbia, SC
McMaster, Joseph S. ... Pittsburgh, PA
McMaster, Kevin M. ... Wichita, KS
McMaster, Loren E. ... Sacramento, CA
McMaster, L. R. ... Williamsburg, VA
McMaster, Maureen T. ...
Department Of Health And Human Services, GV
McMaster & McMaster ... Wichita, KS
McMaster, Russell J. ... Paulding, OH
McMaster, Sarah Jane ... Wichita, KS
McMaster, Steven T. ... Logan, UT
McMaster, William G., Jr. ... Chicago, IL
McMaster, William Spencer
Columbia, SC
McMaster & Wommack ... Sandersville, GA
McMasters, Beth H. ... Louisville, KY
McMasters, David D. ... Seattle, WA
McMasters, James W. ... Chicago, IL
McMasters, John S. ... Seattle, WA
McMasters, Linda Gray ... Avon, CT
McMasters, Thomas L. ... Minneapolis, MN
McMath, Dale B. ... Houston, TX
McMath, James Bruce ... Little Rock, AR
McMath, John F. ... Miami, FL
McMath, Kimberly D. ... Houston, TX
McMath, Mary S. ... St. Louis, MO
McMath, Phillip H. ... Little Rock, AR
McMath, Sandy S. ... Little Rock, AR
McMath, Sandy S., & Associates, P.A.
Little Rock, AR
McMath, Sidney S. ... Little Rock, AR
McMath, Tonya Jill ... Phoenix, AZ
McMath, Vehik, Drummond, Harrison & Ledbetter, P.A. ... Little Rock, AR
McMeans, Cynthia Cargile ... Daphne, AL
McMeans, Cynthia Cargile, P.C.
Daphne, AL
Mc Means, Jeffrey A. ... Richmond, TX
McMeans, Paul E. ... Encinitas, CA
McMeans, Walter S. ... Richmond, TX
McMearty, Edward J. ... Newtown Square, PA
McMechan, Richard L. ... Mariposa, CA
McMeekan, Dee B. ... Boston, MA
McMeekin, Daniel G. ... Covina, CA
McMeekin, John Christie, II
Philadelphia, PA
McMeekin, Kelly A. ... Novato, CA
McMeen, E. Ellsworth, III ... New York, NY
McMeen, Herbert E. ... Murphysboro, IL
McMeen, L. C. ... Marengo, IA
McMeen, Tim D. ... Marengo, IA
McMehan, Grady E. ... Rock Hill, SC
McMeley, Christin S. ... Washington, DC
McMenaman, Paul X. ... Wintersville, OH
McMenamin, Cara M. ... Norristown, PA
McMenamin, Eugene F. ... Cerritos, CA
McMenamin, Hugh J. ... Richmond, VA
McMenamin, J. Robert ... Chicago, IL
McMenamin, John A.
Department Of Health And Human Services, Social Security Administration, GV
McMenamin, Joseph A. ... Vero Beach, FL
McMenamin, Joseph E. ... Springfield, IL
McMenamin, Joseph P. ... Richmond, VA
McMenamin, Laurel F., A Prof. Corp., Law Offices ... San Diego, CA
McMenamin, Laurel M. ... San Diego, CA
McMenamin, Michael A.
Tompkins Cove, NY
McMenamin, Michael T. ... Cleveland, OH
McMenamin, Patrick J., Jr.
Montgomeryville, PA
McMenamin, Patrick M. ... Seattle, WA
McMenamin, Paul J. ... Santa Barbara, CA
McMenamin, Paul R. ... New York, NY
McMenamin, Paula Hunt ... Chicago, IL
McMenamin, Richard F. ... Philadelphia, PA
McMenamin, Robert W. ... Beaverton, OR
McMenamin, Sean Patrick ... Raleigh, NC
McMenamin & Taylor ... Beaverton, OR
McMenamin, Thomas P. ... Chicago, IL
McMenamin, William G. ... Joliet, IL
McMenamy, Gregory B., Jr. ... Atlanta, GA
McMenamy, Mark T. ... Florham Park, NJ
McMenamy, William B. ... Jacksonville, FL
McMenimen, Brian J. ... Boston, MA
McMenimen, Dennis J. ... Cedar Rapids, IA
McMennamin, M. Breeze ... New York, NY
McMenomy, Edward B. ... Rosemount, MN
McMenomy, Hansen & McCann, P.A.
Rosemount, MN
McMenomy, Shawn E. ... Claremont, CA
McMerty, Edward A., III ... Harrisburg, PA
McMican, Christopher A.
Birmingham, MI
McMichael, Alan E. ... Daytona Beach, FL
Gainesville, FL
Maitland, FL
McMichael, Daniel J. ... Chesterfield, MO
McMichael, Donald E. ... Denver, CO
McMichael, Gregory L. ... Clarkston, MI
McMichael, Guy H., III
Department Of Veterans Affairs, Board of Contract Appeals, GV
McMichael, J. Richard ... Palo Alto, CA
McMichael, James C., Jr. ... Shreveport, LA
McMichael, James D. ... Washington, DC
McMichael, Karin U. ... Bellingham, WA
McMichael, Kristen L. ... Los Angeles, CA
McMichael, Lawrence G.
Philadelphia, PA
McMichael, Medlin & Weir, L.L.C.
Shreveport, LA
McMichael, Miriam K. ... New Orleans, LA
McMichael, Paige ... Longboat Key, FL
McMichael, R. Neale, III ... Troy, MI
McMichael, R. Samuel ... Oxford, PA
McMichael, Scott A. ... Wichita Falls, TX
McMichael, Sell & Agresti, L.L.P.
Denver, CO
McMichael, Tom ... Angleton, TX
McMichael, Virginia Hinrichs
Philadelphia, PA
McMichael, Walton H., (P.A.) ... Tampa, FL
McMichen, Dorothy J. ... Orlando, FL
McMickens, Jacqueline ... Brooklyn, NY
McMickle, Scott W. ... Atlanta, GA
McMilan, Hollis K. ... Wilsonville, OR
McMillan, Andrea D.
West Palm Beach, FL
McMillan, Ann C. ... Washington, DC
McMillan, Brian J. ... Greensboro, NC
McMillan, Brian T. ... San Jose, CA
McMillan, Calvin L. ... Wichita, KS
McMillan, Charles M. ... Oakland, CA
McMillan, Christine T. ... Pittsburgh, PA
McMillan Constabile, LLP
Larchmont, NY
White Plains, NY
McMillan, Cyrus J. ... Burlingame, CA
McMillan, D. Mark ... Chicago, IL
McMillan, Daniel D. ... Los Angeles, CA
McMillan, David J. ... Duluth, MN
Mcmillan, Denise Deal ... Crossett, AR
McMillan, Donald R. ... Detroit, MI
McMillan, Donald T. ... Santa Rosa, CA
McMillan, Donna M. ... Rockville, MD
McMillan, Dougald D. ... Dallas, TX
McMillan, Douglas ... Chicago, IL
McMillan, Duncan ... Dallas, TX
McMillan, Duncan A. ... Grand Rapids, MI
McMillan, Duncan A. ... Raleigh, NC
McMillan, Earl I., Jr. ... Baltimore, MD
McMillan, E. G., III ... Seguin, TX
McMillan, Elizabeth M. ... Greenville, SC
McMillan, Frank ... Winter Park, FL
McMillan, George D. H., Jr.
Birmingham, AL
McMillan, Gerald M. ... Mc Comb, MS
McMillan, Gregory S. ... Knoxville, TN
McMillan, H. Knox ... Boise, ID
McMillan, Harold B., Jr.
Oklahoma City, OK
McMillan, Harry M. ... Bristow, OK
McMillan, Herbert V., III ... Orlando, FL
McMillan & Herrell ... Beverly Hills, CA
McMillan, Hilary Merkel ... Rochester, NY
McMillan, Ian ... Oakbrook Terrace, IL
McMillan, Ian R. ... Trumbull, CT
McMillan, J. Murphy, III ... Birmingham, AL
McMillan, James B., Jr. ... Thomasville, NC
McMillan, James F. ... San Francisco, CA
McMillan, James G. ... Washington, DC
McMillan, James T. ... Long Beach, CA
McMillan, Jamie M. ... Santa Maria, CA
McMillan, Jan Rewers ... Southfield, MI
McMillan, Jane S. ... Middletown, CT
McMillan, Jane W. ... Miami, FL
McMillan, Jane-Ashley ... Plano, TX
McMillan, Janet E. ... Springfield, MA
McMillan & Jennings, LLP
Santa Ana, CA
McMillan, J. I. ... San Diego, CA
McMillan, John B. ... Raleigh, NC
McMillan, John D. ... Macomb, IL
McMillan, John E. ... Temple Terrace, FL
McMillan, John R. ... Las Vegas, NV
McMillan, Joseph C. ... Kansas City, MO
McMillan, Joseph Michael ... Seattle, WA
McMillan, Karen Hess ... Washington, DC
McMillan, Kate ... Tucson, AZ
McMillan, Keith J. ... Larchmont, NY
McMillan, Kim A. ... Clarksville, TN
McMillan, Kristin B. ... Las Vegas, NV
McMillan, L. Londell ... New York, NY
McMillan, L. Richards, II
New Orleans, LA
McMillan, Laura J. ... Mesa, AZ
McMillan, Laurence M., Jr. ... Clarksville, TN
McMillan, Laurence, (P.C.)
White Plains, NY
McMillan, Leslie E. ... Los Angeles, CA
McMillan, Linda Lee ... Pueblo, CO
McMillan, Linda P. ... New York, NY
McMillan, Lisa Schloss ... Fort Lauderdale, FL
McMillan, L. Londell, P.C. ... New York, NY
McMillan, M. Sean, (A Professional Corporation) ... Santa Monica, CA
McMillan, Marie A. ... Fairfield, NJ
McMillan, Marvin E., Jr. ... Sumter, SC
McMillan, Matthew E. ... Bradenton, FL
McMillan, Melissa M. ... Miami, FL
Mc Millan, Michael W. ... Corunna, MI
McMillan, Murray L. ... Rockport, TX
McMillan, Oscar J., Jr. ... Covington, LA
McMillan, R. Michael ... Clearwater, FL
McMillan, R. Wayne ... Pasadena, CA
McMillan & Rabinow ... Trumbull, CT
McMillan, Ralph R. ... Charlotte, NC
McMillan, Rather, Bennett & Rigano, P.C.
Garden City, NY
Melville, NY
Smithtown, NY
McMillan, Richard, Jr. ... Washington, DC
McMillan, Richard L. ... Pittsburgh, PA
McMillan, Richard T. ... Midland, TX
McMillan, Robert A. ... Sanford, FL
McMillan, Robert C. ... Oxnard, CA
McMillan, Robert H. ... Santa Ana, CA
McMillan, Robert L. ... Raleigh, NC
McMillan, Robert R. ... Melville, NY
McMillan, Samuel M. ... Mobile, AL
McMillan, Sandra Ramsey ... Houston, TX
McMillan, Scott M. ... Dallas, TX
McMillan, Sheila D. ... Columbia, SC
McMillan, Shelby M. ... Dayton, OH
McMillan, Shelly D. ... Beverly Hills, CA
McMillan, Smith & Plyler ... Raleigh, NC
McMillan, Stewart J. ... Larchmont, NY
McMillan, Stuart A. ... Charleston, WV
McMillan, Surles & Terry, P.A.
Charlotte, NC
McMillan, Susan A. ... Boise, ID
McMillan, Taylor ... Raleigh, NC
McMillan, Terry R., P.C.
Oklahoma City, OK
McMillan, Thomas R. ... Grafton, VT
McMillan, Tina M. ... Fairfax, VA
McMillan, Toney D. ... Arkadelphia, AR
McMillan, Tracey J. ... Knoxville, TN
McMillan, Turner, McCorkle & Curry
Arkadelphia, AR
McMillan, Tuwana J. ... Orlando, FL
McMillan, Veronica A. ... Poughkeepsie, NY

McMillan, W. Robert ... **Monroeville, AL**
McMillan, Walter C., Jr. ... Sandersville, GA
McMillan, William H. ... **Statesville, NC**
McMillan, William M. ... Sacramento, CA
McMillan, William N., III
Los Angeles, CA
McMillan, William N., III ... **Pasadena, CA**
McMillan, William P. ... **Charlotte, NC**
McMillan-McCartney, Elizabeth A.
Highland Heights, KY
McMillan-Rose, LaJuene ... Memphis, TN
Mc Millen, Alesia A. ... Rushville, IL
McMillen, Anne B. ... New York, NY
McMillen, Cynthia J. ... Largo, FL
McMillen, David Todd ... Boulder, CO
McMillen, Elissa L. ... **Boston, MA**
McMillen, James T. ... Corpus Christi, TX
McMillen, Jeffrey B. ... Laguna Hills, CA
McMillen, John A. ... **Winston-Salem, NC**
Mc Millen, Joseph A. ... Prairie Village, KS
McMillen, Joseph S. ... **Santa Ana, CA**
McMillen, Joy D. ... **Chesterfield, MO**
McMillen, Julia ... **Washington, DC**
McMillen, Katherine R. ... **Fairfax, VA**
McMillen, Keith R. ... Aliquippa, PA
McMillen, Leonard R. ... Fort Myers, FL
McMillen, Linda L. ... Arlington, TX
McMillen, Martha K. ... Wethersfield, CT
McMillen, Nancy H. ... Department of Justice, Antitrust Division, GV
McMillen, Patricia R. ... Chicago, IL
McMillen, Phyllis C. ... Waterford, MI
McMillen, R. Scott ... San Francisco, CA
McMillen, Reinhart & Voght, P.A.
Orlando, FL
McMillen, Robert S. ... **Glens Falls, NY**
McMillen, Sarah M. ... Salem, OR
McMillen, Scott R. ... **Orlando, FL**
McMillen, Stephen ... **Dallas, TX**
McMillen, Thomas Hayes ... Westminster, CO
McMillen, Thomas R. ... Winnetka, IL
McMillen, Urick, Tocci & Fouse
Aliquippa, PA
McMillian, Alfonso, Jr. ... **Chicago, IL**
McMillian, Amanda M. ... **Dallas, TX**
McMillian, Hayden D. ... Richmond, VA
McMillian, Lance P. ... **Atlanta, GA**
McMillian, Roger L. ... Stillwater, OK
McMillian, Theo. ... St. Louis, MO
McMillin, Anne Milton ... **Louisville, KY**
McMillin, Blair S. ... **Pittsburgh, PA**
McMillin, Brian J. ... **Boston, MA**
McMillin, David C. ... **Monroe, LA**
McMillin, Earl R. ... Port Canaveral, FL
McMillin, F. Lovell ... **Ardmore, OK**
McMillin, James ... Santa Cruz, CA
McMillin, James C. ... **Oklahoma City, OK**
McMillin, Jane ... Roseburg, OR
McMillin, Joe B. ... **Palm Desert, CA**
McMillin, Joe B. ... **Palm Springs, CA**
McMillin, Larry H. ... Cincinnati, OH
McMillin, Lowell C. ... Brookville, IN
McMillin, Mark M. ... Norfolk, VA
McMillin, Markus W. ... **San Francisco, CA**
McMillin, Martha Pitts ... Atlanta, GA
McMillin, Michael S. ... **Oklahoma City, OK**
McMillin, Raymond C. ... Salem, OR
McMillin, Richard S., (P.C.) ... **Omaha, NE**
McMillin, Robert A. ... Houston, TX
McMillin, Roger H., Jr. ... Jackson, MS
McMillin, Ronald R. ... **Jefferson City, MO**
McMillin, Ronnie O. ... Ferriday, LA
McMillin, Ryan J. ... Liberty, MO
McMillin, Scott ... **Chicago, IL**
McMillin, Terrence W. ... **Chicago, IL**
McMillion, Benjamin R. ... Princeton, WV
McMillion, Donald C. ... Greensboro, NC
McMillion, James A. ... Charleston, WV
McMillion, Keith W. ... Summersville, WV
Mcmillion, Renea ... **Texarkana, TX**
McMillon, L. Mark ... **McKinney, TX**
McMillon, Wendy A. ... **McKinney, TX**
McMinimee, Gary L. ... Carroll, IA
McMinimee, Marcie R. ... Salem, OR
McMinimee, Sally Buck
Salt Lake City, UT
McMinn, Benjamin C., (P.A.)
Little Rock, AR
McMinn, Bryan K. ... **Orlando, FL**
McMinn, Donald R. ... **Washington, DC**
McMinn, Eileen M. ... **Asheville, NC**
McMinn, Glenn S. ... **Phoenix, AZ**
McMinn, J. S. ... Hamilton, TX
McMinn, Richard W. ... **Indianapolis, IN**
McMinn, Robert S. ... Huntingdon, PA
McMinn, Wilbur C. ... San Francisco, CA
McMonagle & Associates, P.S. ... Seattle, WA
McMonagle, Brian J. ... Sacramento, CA
McMonagle, Brian J. ... Philadelphia, PA
McMonagle, Christine T. ... Cleveland, OH
McMonagle, Daniel S., Jr. ... Seattle, WA
McMonagle, James J. ... Cleveland, OH
McMonagle, James L., Jr. ... Wilkes-Barre, PA
McMonagle, Mary C. ... Bala Cynwyd, PA
McMonagle, Richard J. ... Cleveland, OH
McMonagle, Robert Blake ... **Davenport, IA**
McMonagle, Timothy E. ... Cleveland, OH
McMonagle-Glass, Diane ... **Woonsocket, RI**
McMonies, Walter W., Jr. ... **Portland, OR**
McMonigal, William M. ... Green Lake, WI
McMonigle, Bernard ... Sacramento, CA
McMonigle, Joseph P. ... **San Francisco, CA**
McMonigle, Joseph P. ... United States Senate, Senatorial Assistants, GV
McMonigle, Patrick K. ... **Kansas City, MO**
McMonigle, Richard L. ... **Philadelphia, PA**
McMonigle, Robert E. ... Pittsburgh, PA
McMonigle, Vesely & Perego, P.C.
Pittsburgh, PA
McMoran & Associates, P.C. ... **Iselin, NJ**
Morristown, NJ
Newark, NJ
McMoran, Bruce P. ... **Iselin, NJ**
McMoran, Kelly A. ... Auburn, ME
McMorrin, Delores ... South Orange, NJ
McMorris, David J. ... **Boston, MA**
McMorris, Fred R. ... **Joliet, IL**
Lisle, IL
McMorris, Jeffrey E. ... Fort Edward, NY
McMorris, Ron D. ... Kansas City, MO
McMorris, William J. ... New York, NY
McMorris, William J., Jr. ... Lake Success, NY
McMorrough, Edmond L. ... Hollywood, FL
McMorrow, Daniel B. ... New York, NY
McMorrow, David W. ... Kalamazoo, MI
McMorrow, Doris Schumacher ... Chicago, IL
McMorrow, Doris Schumacher
Chicago, IL
McMorrow, Elizabeth A. B. ... **Atlanta, GA**
McMorrow, Gerald P. ... Westbury, NY
McMorrow, John B. ... Fremont, CA
McMorrow, John P. ... Chicago, IL
McMorrow, Josh M. ... **Houston, TX**
McMorrow, Judith A. ... Newton, MA
McMorrow, Kevin G. ... **Albertson, NY**
McMorrow, Kimberly Martin ... Palo Alto, CA
McMorrow, Margaret L. ... **Naples, FL**
McMorrow, Michael E. ... Mequon, WI
McMorrow, Michael J.
Department of Transportation, Maritime Administration, GV
McMorrow, Robert G., Jr.
Wilmington, DE
McMorrow, Robert G., (P.C.)
Washington, DC
McMorrow, Scholz & Hasson ... Fremont, CA
McMorrow, Thomas F. ... **Jacksonville, FL**
McMorrow, Thomas F., P.A.
Jacksonville, FL
McMorrow, Thomas R. ... **Sacramento, CA**
McMorrow, Timothy K. ... Grand Rapids, MI
McMorrow, William J. ... Scottsdale, AZ
McMorrow-Love, Margaret
Oklahoma City, OK
McMullan, Alasdair James ... New York, NY
McMullan, C. Grice, Jr. ... **Richmond, VA**
McMullan, Cheryl Lynn ... San Antonio, TX
McMullan, David M. ... Jackson, MS
McMullan, David M., Jr. ... **Jackson, MS**
McMullan, James B. ... Washington, NC
McMullan, James B., Jr. ... Washington, NC
McMullan, James F., Jr. ... Milton, VT
McMullan, John T. ... Kennett, MO
McMullan Law Firm ... **Little Rock, AR**
McMullan, Marian Major
Little Rock, AR
McMullan & McMullan ... Washington, NC
McMullan, William R. ... New York, NY
McMullen, Albert R., Jr. ... Newport, OR
McMullen, Alexander R., III ... Towson, MD
McMullen, Andrew J. ... Kearney, NE
McMullen, Andrew L. ... **Kansas City, MO**
McMullen, Andy J. ... Hamilton, TX
McMullen, Betty Jo ... Murrieta, CA
McMullen, Bruce A. ... **Memphis, TN**
McMullen, Carolyn V. ... Tampa, FL
McMullen, Catherine A.
Office Of Special Counsel, GV
McMullen, Charles H. ... **Milwaukee, WI**
McMullen, Cynthia E. ... Spokane, WA
McMullen, Daniel F., Jr. ... Cumberland, MD
McMullen, Daniel J. ... **Cleveland, OH**
McMullen, Darin John ... **Philadelphia, PA**
McMullen, David B. ... **Chicago, IL**
McMullen, Frederick E. ... Rochester, NY
McMullen, Greerson G. ... **Melbourne, FL**
McMullen, Hugh A. ... **Cumberland, MD**
McMullen, Hugh S. ... Culver City, CA
McMullen, Jack K. ... **Orlando, FL**
McMullen, James A., III, Law Offices of
Fort Worth, TX
McMullen, James D. ... **Lawrence, KS**
Kansas City, MO
McMullen, James E.
Department of Labor, GV
McMullen, James J., Jr. ... **San Diego, CA**
McMullen, James P., Jr. ... Wellsburg, WV
McMullen, Joan Kay ... Eagle, CO
McMullen, John A. ... Cambridge, MA
McMullen, John J., Jr. ... **Cumberland, MD**
McMullen, John N. ... Denver, CO
McMullen, John W. ... **Omaha, NE**
McMullen, Jon J. ... **Vancouver, WA**
McMullen, Judith Gorske ... Milwaukee, WI
McMullen, Kevin L. ... **Peoria, IL**
McMullen, Kevin P. ... Northport, NY
McMullen, Larry E. ... **Seattle, WA**
McMullen, Larry L. ... **Kansas City, MO**
McMullen Law Firm ... **Fort Worth, TX**
McMullen, Linda ... Jackson, MS
McMullen, Lori A. ... **Sheridan, WY**
McMullen, Marshall A., Jr. ... Charleston, WV
McMullen, Mary Anne Sherman
Tallahassee, FL
McMullen, Michael C. ... **Kansas City, MO**
McMullen, Michael D. ... **Columbia, SC**
McMullen, Nathan J., Jr. ... Clarksdale, MS
McMullen, Patrick R. ... Bellingham, WA
McMullen, Richard F. ... **Addison, TX**
McMullen, Richard F., P.C. ... **Addison, TX**
McMullen, Robert B., Jr. ... Hillsboro, OH
McMullen, Robert J. ... Philadelphia, PA
McMullen, Samuel P. ... **Reno, NV**
McMullen, Scott L. ... **West Palm Beach, FL**
McMullen, Stephanie C. ... Waco, TX
McMullen, Stephen J., P.C. ... Chicago, IL
McMullen, Stephen J., P.C. ... Chicago, IL
McMullen, Steven K. ... East Brunswick, NJ
McMullen, Wade H. ... **Fort Worth, TX**
McMullen, William H., Jr. ... Charlotte, NC
McMullin, Charles J. ... St. Louis, MO
McMullin, Colin W. ... Missoula, MT
McMullin, Collin W. ... Salt Lake City, UT
McMullin, James F. ... St. Louis, MO
McMullin, James L. ... Kansas City, MO
McMullin, John L., III ... **Belleville, IL**
St. Louis, MO
McMullin, Joseph B. ... Altadena, CA
McMullin, Karen Watson ... Sebastopol, CA
McMullin, Kimball R. ... **St. Louis, MO**
McMullin, Leslie K. ... Tempe, AZ
McMullin, Thomas R. ... Stamford, CT
McMunigal, Elizabethanne D.
Reading, PA
McMunigal, Harry D. ... **Reading, PA**
McMunigal, Kevin C. ... Cleveland, OH
McMunigal, Philip A., Jr. ... Media, PA
McMunigal, Rosemary C. ... Media, PA
McMunn, C. David ... **Clarksburg, WV**
McMunn, D. Andrew ... **Clarksburg, WV**
McMunn, John Scott ... San Bruno, CA
Mc Murchie, Boyd L. ... Mitchell, SD
McMurchie, Charles J. ... **Portland, OR**
McMurchie, David W. ... Sacramento, CA
McMurchie, Donald W. ... Sacramento, CA
McMurchie, Foley, Brandenburger, Weill & Lenahan ... Fresno, CA
Sacramento, CA
McMurdie, J. Neil ... **Hartford, CT**
McMurdie, Paul J. ... Phoenix, AZ
McMurdo, Matthew C. ... **New York, NY**
McMurdy, Keith R. ... **Akron, OH**
McMurphy, Mattew A. ... **Dallas, TX**
McMurphy, Michael A. ... Bethesda, MD
McMurray, Charles H.
Dearborn Heights, MI
McMurray, Claudia Anne
United States Senate, Senatorial Assistants, GV
McMurray, David L. ... **Kansas City, MO**
McMurray, David L. ... **Greenville, SC**
McMurray, David L., P.A. ... **Greenville, SC**
McMurray, Don T. ... Lenoir City, TN
McMurray, Edmund D. ... Sacramento, CA
McMurray, Graham G. ... Atlanta, GA
McMurray, James K. ... **Wichita, KS**
McMurray, John W. ... Northfield, IL
McMurray, Julie L. ... **Nutley, NJ**
McMurray, Kerry D. ... Burley, ID
McMurray, Kevin N. ... **Cincinnati, OH**
McMurray, Kevin S. ... San Diego, CA
Salt Lake City, UT
McMurray, Kurston P. ... **Tulsa, OK**
McMurray Law Office, PLLC
Cleveland, TN
McMurray, Lee Clayton ... **St. Louis, MO**
McMurray, Leslie G. ... **Los Angeles, CA**
McMurray, Locke R. ... New York, NY
McMurray, Louise H. ... Miami, FL
McMurray, Lynn C. ... **Salt Lake City, UT**
McMurray, M. Carl ... **Keokuk, IA**
McMurray, M. Shawn ... Little Rock, AR
McMurray, Macoy A. ... **Salt Lake City, UT**
McMurray, Marcia M. ... **Cleveland, TN**
McMurray, Margaret ... Madison, WI
McMurray, Maurice E. ... Detroit, MI
McMurray, McMurray & Alexander
Morganton, NC
McMurray, McMurray, Dale & Parkinson, P.C. ... **Salt Lake City, UT**
McMurray & Monfort ... Newport, KY
McMurray, Patricia B. ... **Baton Rouge, LA**
McMurray, Paul T. ... Yakima, WA
McMurray, Randy H. ... **Los Angeles, CA**
McMurray, Robert L. ... **Cleveland, TN**
McMurray, Sara J. ... Whitehall, MI
McMurray, Sara J., Attorney at Law P.C.
Whitehall, MI
McMurray, Scott D. ... Newport, KY
McMurray, Steven R. ... **Salt Lake City, UT**
McMurray, Thomas H. ... Coralville, IA
McMurray, William L., JR. ... Atlanta, GA
McMurray-Russ, Martha L. ... Morganton, NC
McMurrer, Edward J. ... **New York, NY**
McMurrer, Nancy ... Seattle, WA
McMurrey, Allen L., Jr. ... Bastrop, TX
McMurrey, Jim, III ... Dallas, TX
McMurry, C. Steven ... Phoenix, AZ
McMurry, Charles A. ... Tallahassee, FL
McMurry, Garry P. ... Portland, OR
McMurry, Gayle M. ... Chicago, IL
McMurry, John C. ... **Oklahoma City, OK**
McMurry, Karen ... **Boulder, CO**
McMurry, Karen W. ... San Antonio, TX
McMurry, Kyndle ... Cincinnati, OH
McMurry & Livingston ... **Paducah, KY**
McMurry, Mark B. ... East Hartford, CT
McMurry, Michael Baird ... **Chicago, IL**
McMurry, Michael S. ... Ankeny, IA
McMurry, Ralph L. ... Basking Ridge, NJ
McMurry, Robert I. ... **Irvine, CA**
McMurry, Stan ... **Dallas, TX**
McMurry & Talbott ... **Louisville, KY**
McMurry, W. Pelham ... **Paducah, KY**
McMurry, William F. ... **Louisville, KY**
McMurtray, Janet D. ... **Jackson, MS**
McMurtray, Noel ... Mill Creek, WA
McMurtray, Patrick D. ... Jackson, MS
McMurtray, Gene R. ... Bakersfield, CA
McMurtrey & Hartsock, A Professional Corporation ... Bakersfield, CA
McMurtrey, Matthew W.
Los Angeles, CA
McMurtrie, Alexander B., Jr. ... Richmond, VA
McMurtrie, Edward C. ... Las Vegas, NV
McMurtrie, Grubbs & Associates
Richmond, VA
McMurtrie, L. Thompson ... Huntsville, AL
McMurtrie, Shaen M. ... Tonkawa, OK
McMurtrie, Timothy D.
Corpus Christi, TX
McMurtrie, William G. ... Fairfax, VA
McMurtry, Barbara J. ... Jackson, MS
McMurtry, David W. ... Sacramento, CA
McMurtry, Dorothy L. ... St. Louis, MO
McMurtry, Elizabeth K. ... Henderson, KY
McMurtry, Ewald & Blackwelder, P.C.
Austin, TX
McMurtry, James L. ... Austin, TX
McMurtry, L. Lee, III ... **Houston, TX**
McMurtry, Larry N. ... Jackson, MS
McMurtry, Rick D. ... **Atlanta, GA**
McMurtry, Sarannah L. ... **Philadelphia, PA**
McMurtry, Sean D. ... Whitehouse Station, NJ
McMurtry, Stephen T. ... Covington, KY
McMurtry, Vanda B. ... **Hartford, CT**
McNab, Cecil R. ... Los Angeles, CA
McNab, F. Mitch ... **Dothan, AL**
McNab, James, III ... Santa Rosa, CA
McNab, Molly Beth ... Newtown, PA
McNab, S. Kay ... **Chicago, IL**
McNab, Stewart ... Denver, CO
McNabb, Carolyn A. ... Houma, LA
McNabb, Carolyn A., A Prof. Law Corp.
Houma, LA
McNabb, Charles F. ... El Paso, TX
McNabb, Deborah Lynn ... Grand Rapids, MI
McNabb, Douglas C. ... **Austin, TX**
Dallas, TX
McNabb, Douglas C. ... **Houston, TX**
McNabb, Douglas C. ... **San Antonio, TX**
McNabb, Frederick W., Jr. ... New York, NY
McNabb, H. H., Jr. ... Butler, MO
McNabb, Holley & Waldrop, PLLC
Hernando, MS
Oxford, MS
Tupelo, MS
Jackson, TN
Memphis, TN
McNabb, J. Alan ... **Atlanta, GA**
McNabb, James A., Jr. ... Maitland, FL
McNabb, John K. ... Boston, MA
McNabb, Joseph V. ... **Tampa, FL**
McNabb, Leland M. ... **Memphis, TN**
McNabb, LuAnn Maciulla ... Centreville, VA
McNabb, Michael W. ... Burnsville, MN
McNabb, Pursley & Karr ... Butler, MO
McNabb, Sandra J. ... **Orinda, CA**
McNabb, Stephen M. ... **Washington, DC**
McNabb, T. Joseph, Jr. ... **Boston, MA**
McNabb, Tabitha Francisco ... **Memphis, TN**
McNabb, Terrance E. ... **Nashville, TN**
McNabnay, Neil J. ... **Dallas, TX**
McNabney, Ronald L. ... Anderson, IN
McNaboe, James F. ... Rutherford, NJ
McNabola, Edward W. ... **Chicago, IL**
McNabola, Mark E. ... **Chicago, IL**
McNaghten, Robert H. ... Columbus, OH
McNagny, Charles W. ... **Fort Wayne, IN**
McNagny, Marcia A. ... Columbia City, IN
McNagny, Patricia Gates ... Columbia City, IN
McNagny, William F. ... **Fort Wayne, IN**
McNail, Teresa A. ... **St. Louis, MO**
McNair & Bobulsky, Co., L.P.A.
Jefferson, OH
McNair, Brian E. ... **Fairfield, OH**
McNair, Brian Scott ... **Baltimore, MD**
McNair, Charles M. ... **Medford, OR**
McNair, D. Malcolm, Jr. ... Fayetteville, AR
McNair, Dan B. ... Columbus, NE
McNair, Eben O., IV ... **Cleveland, OH**
McNair, Gregory L. ... Los Angeles, CA
McNair, James E., III ... **Vienna, VA**
McNair, Jeanne F. ... **Ventura, CA**
McNair, Jennifer D. ... **Indianapolis, IN**
McNair, Jimmie ... Jackson, MS
McNair, John W. ... **Ann Arbor, MI**
McNair, Karen ... **Liberty, TX**
McNair, L. Avery ... Washington, DC
McNair, Larson & Carlson, Ltd. ... Fargo, ND
McNair Law Firm, P.A. ... **Charlotte, NC**
Anderson, SC
Charleston, SC
Columbia, SC
Georgetown, SC
Greenville, SC
Hilton Head Island, SC
Myrtle Beach, SC
Spartanburg, SC
McNair, Michael D. ... Fargo, ND
McNair, Michael S. ... **Mobile, AL**
McNair, Pamela J. ... Rego Park, NY
McNair, R. Nancy ... Tulsa, OK
McNair, Robert E. ... **Columbia, SC**
Myrtle Beach, SC
McNair, Robert J. ... **Orinda, CA**
McNair, Robert M. ... Jefferson, OH
McNair, Robert M., Jr. ... **Philadelphia, PA**
McNair, Russell A., Jr. ... **Detroit, MI**
McNair, Timothy D., Law Offices of
Erie, PA
McNair, Trudy E. ... Winter Park, FL
McNair, Vicki Joiner ... Concord, CA
Edison, GA
McNair, William H. ... **Charlotte, NC**
McNairy & Baker ... Santa Monica, CA
McNairy, Frederic M. ... Santa Monica, CA
McNairy, John O. ... Kinston, NC
McNairy, R. Walton ... Greensboro, NC
McNairy, William G. ... **Greensboro, NC**
Raleigh, NC

McNalis, Daniel M. ... Lake Worth, FL
McNall & Associates, P.C. ... Anchorage, AK
McNall, Carole B. ... Olean, NY
McNall, William L. ... Anchorage, AK
McNally, Brenda J. ... Raynham, MA
McNally, Brian F. ... Charlotte, NC
McNally, Carrie C. ... Chicago, IL
McNally, Christina M. ... Cherry Hill, NJ
McNally, Daniel J. ... Milwaukee, WI
McNally, Danny D. ... Greenville, NC
McNally, Daren S. ... Roseland, NJ
McNally, Dennis F. ... Schoolcraft, MI
McNally, Dennis J. ... Milwaukee, WI
Mc Nally, Douglas K. ... Northport, NY
McNally, Edward E. ... Washington, DC
Chicago, IL
McNally, Edward M. ... Wilmington, DE
McNally, Edward T. ... Cambridge, MA
McNally, Edwards, Bailey & Lander
Decatur, GA
McNally, Fox & Cameron, P.C.
Fayetteville, GA
McNally, Francis W. ... Mariposa, CA
McNally, Frank J. ... Rocky River, OH
McNally, Garrett T. ... Marcellus, MI
McNally & George ... Le Mars, IA
McNally, George F. ... Carson City, NV
McNally, Gerald, Jr. ... La Crescenta, CA
McNally, H. Vincent ... Los Angeles, CA
McNally, Harry D. ... Akron, OH
McNally, James ... Boston, MA
McNally, James ... Pittsburgh, PA
McNally, James F., Jr. ... Austin, TX
McNally, James J. ... Miami, FL
McNally, James J. ... Bartlett, NE
Neligh, NE
McNally, James M. ... Youngstown, OH
McNally, James N., IV ... Harper Woods, MI
McNally, James P. ... Jenkintown, PA
McNally, James P. ... Ione, WA
Newport, WA
McNally, James T. ... Sacramento, CA
McNally, Jennifer F. ... Boston, MA
McNally, Jerry B. ... Atlanta, GA
McNally, John A. ... Columbus, OH
McNally, John A., III ... Youngstown, OH
McNally, John B. ... Jenkintown, PA
McNally, John D. ... Springfield, MA
McNally, John F. ... Boulder, CO
McNally, John F. ... Milwaukee, WI
McNally, John G. ... Trenton, MI
McNally, John J. ... Miami, FL
McNally, John J. ... New York, NY
McNally, John J., III ... Hershey, PA
McNally, John M. ... Washington, DC
McNally, John M., Jr. ... Rydal, PA
McNally, John Wm., Jr. ... Cincinnati, OH
McNally, Joseph A. ... Berwyn, PA
McNally, Joseph J. ... San Diego, CA
McNally, Joy Gobos ... Pittsburgh, PA
McNally, Kendra S. ... Los Angeles, CA
McNally, Kevin M. ... Frankfort, KY
McNally, Kim E. ... Glendale, CA
McNally, Kipley J. ... Louisville, KY
McNally, Laura K. ... Washington, DC
McNally Law Firm, The, Ltd.
Carson City, NV
Reno, NV
McNally, Lawrence J., Jr. ... Boston, MA
McNally, Leilan K. ... Chicago, IL
McNally, Lydia T. ... Bridgewater, NJ
McNally, Maloney & Peterson, S.C.
Milwaukee, WI
Waukesha, WI
McNally, Margaret H. ... St. Louis, MO
McNally, Mariann ... Livonia, MI
McNally, Maribeth ... Milwaukee, WI
McNally, Mark J. ... North Andover, MA
McNally, Martin J. ... Markham, IL
McNally, Maureen K. ... Worcester, MA
McNally, Melinda ... Atlanta, GA
McNally, Michael J. ... Englewood, CO
McNally, Michael J. ... Tyler, TX
McNally, Michael J.T. ... Boston, MA
McNally, Michael K. ... Trenton, MI
McNally, M. K. ... Pittsburgh, PA
McNally, Nancy Maule ... Rockland, MA
McNally, Neil E. ... Roanoke, VA
McNally, Norman E. ... Louisville, KY
McNally, Patrick J. ... Ipswich, MA
McNally, Patrick J., Jr. ... Des Plaines, IL
McNally & Patrick, L.L.P. ... Tyler, TX
McNally, Patrick T. ... Nashville, TN
Mcnally, Paul David ... Boston, MA
McNally, Philip F. ... Morris Plains, NJ
McNally, R. Ryan ... Kalamazoo, MI
McNally, R. Stephen ... Austin, TX
McNally, Raymond F., Jr. ... St. Louis, MO
McNally, Regis J. ... Pittsburgh, PA
McNally, Richard D. ... Rockville, MD
McNally, Richard F., Jr., (P.C.) ... Flint, MI
McNally, Richard J., Jr. ... Troy, NY
McNally, Robert C. ... Hartford, CT
McNally, Robert P. ... Glens Falls, NY
McNally, Robert T. ... Morristown, NJ
McNally and Robinson ... Frankfort, KY
McNally, Sean P. ... San Bernardino, CA
McNally, Sheila F. ... Grand Haven, MI
McNally, Stephen ... Newark, NJ
McNally, Stephen ... Princeton, NJ
McNally, Susan E. ... Warner Robins, GA
McNally, Susan Fowler
Santa Monica, CA
McNally, Susan V.
Department Of Health And Human Services, GV
McNally, Teresa C. ... Seattle, WA
McNally, Thomas C., III
San Francisco, CA
McNally, Thomas F., Jr. ... Decatur, GA
McNally, Thomas J. ... Detroit, MI
McNally, Thomas J. ... Richmond, VA
McNally, Thomas J. ... Necedah, WI
McNally, Thomas P. ... Omaha, NE
McNally, Timothy W. ... Thompson, CT
McNally & Walker ... Miami, FL
McNally, William E. ... Davenport, IA
McNally, William F. ... Muskegon, MI
McNally, William J. ... Boston, MA
McNally, William R. ... Fayetteville, GA
McNally, Yone C. ... Portland, OR
McNamar, David F. ... Indianapolis, IN
McNamar, Fearnow & McSharar, P.C.
Indianapolis, IN
McNamar, Mary Ann
Federal Deposit Insurance Corporation, GV
McNamara, Adrienne O'Connell
Denver, CO
McNamara, A. J. ... New Orleans, LA
McNamara, Ana M. ... Chicago, IL
McNamara, Ann C. ... New York, NY
McNamara, Ann M. ... Boston, MA
McNamara, Anne B. ... Escanaba, MI
McNamara, Anne H. ... Dallas, TX
Dallas, TX
McNamara, B. Joy ... Waco, TX
McNamara, Bailey & Kelly ... Jackson, MS
McNamara & Bolla ... Doylestown, PA
McNamara, Brendon M. ... New York, NY
McNamara, Brian F. ... Wayne, PA
McNamara, Brian J. ... Washington, DC
Annapolis, MD
McNamara, Brian J. ... Kingwood, TX
McNamara, Brian Jay ... Towson, MD
McNamara, Bruce M. ... Palo Alto, CA
McNamara, Carol A. ... Orlando, FL
McNamara, Charles W., II ... Jersey City, NJ
McNamara, Daniel G. ... Naperville, IL
McNamara, Daniel G. ... Fort Wayne, IN
McNamara, Daniel Gerard ... Lombard, IL
McNamara, Daniel J. ... Walnut Creek, CA
McNamara, Daniel J. ... Chicago, IL
McNamara, Daniel J. ... New York, NY
McNamara, Daniel J. ... New York, NY
McNamara, Daniel L. ... Denver, CO
McNamara, David J. ... Buffalo, NY
McNamara, David R. ... Fresno, CA
McNamara, David V. ... Melrose Park, IL
McNamara, Dawn ... New York, NY
McNamara, Deena R. ... West Palm Beach, FL
McNamara, Dennis W. ... Columbus, OH
McNamara, Diane C.H. ... Manassas, VA
McNamara, Donald S. ... Columbus, OH
McNamara, Donna K. ... Denver, CO
McNamara, Donna Reilly ... Seattle, WA
McNamara, Douglas J. ... New York, NY
McNamara, Dwight L. ... Metairie, LA
McNamara, Edw. G., Jr. ... St. Ignace, MI
McNamara, Edward D., Jr.
Edwardsville, IL
Springfield, IL
McNamara, Edward J. ... Rockford, IL
McNamara, Edward J., III
West Hartford, CT
McNamara, Edward M. ... Greenville, MI
McNamara, Edward R. ... Dover, DE
McNamara, Eileen ... Orange, CA
McNamara, Elizabeth ... New York, NY
McNamara, Elizabeth Collins
East Aurora, NY
McNamara, Ellen M. ... Washington, DC
McNamara, Emmett F.
New Smyrna Beach, FL
McNamara, Erin M. ... Boston, MA
McNamara & Evans ... Edwardsville, IL
Springfield, IL
McNamara, F. Timothy ... Hartford, CT
McNamara, F. Timothy, P.C.
Hartford, CT
McNamara Firm, The, PLLC ... Austin, TX
McNamara & Fizer ... Baltimore, MD
McNamara & Flynn, P.A. ... Boston, MA
McNamara, Francis B., Jr. ... Boston, MA
McNamara, Francis H. ... New York, NY
McNamara, Francis J., III ... Boston, MA
McNamara, Francis J., III ... Mineola, NY
McNamara, Francis J., Jr. ... Stamford, CT
McNamara, Francis V., III ... Berwyn, PA
Mcnamara, Frank L., Jr. ... Marlborough, MA
McNamara & Freeman Co., L.P.A.
Uniontown, OH
McNamara, George J. ... Venice, FL
McNamara, George M. ... Denver, CO
McNamara, Glenn F. ... Hartford, CT
McNamara & Goldsmith, P.C.
Nogales, AZ
Tucson, AZ
McNamara & Goodman ... New Haven, CT
McNamara, Harlow J. ... Idaho Falls, ID
McNamara, Henry D., Jr., (P.L.C.)
Metairie, LA
McNamara, Houston, Dodge, McClure & Ney ... Fairfield, CA
Oakland, CA
Walnut Creek, CA
McNamara, J. Burk ... Marengo, IL
McNamara, J. Scott ... San Francisco, CA
McNamara, Jacqueline Mohyla
Washington, DC
McNamara, James E. ... Moorpark, CA
McNamara, James J. ... Burlington, VT
McNamara, James J. ... Bremerton, WA
McNamara, James K. ... Erie, PA
McNamara, James M. ... Doylestown, PA
McNamara, Jane M. ... Glendale, CA
McNamara, Jeffrey A. ... Niantic, CT
McNamara, JoAnna E. ... Lake Oswego, OR
McNamara, John ... Washington, DC
McNamara, John A. ... Santa Rosa, CA
McNamara, John A. ... Brighton, CO
McNamara, John B. ... Waco, TX
McNamara, John B., III ... Waco, TX
McNamara, John C. ... South Laguna, CA
McNamara, John C. ... Philadelphia, PA
McNamara, John F. ... Rockford, IL
McNamara, John F. ... Austin, TX
McNamara, John J. ... Ventura, CA
McNamara, John J. ... Boston, MA
McNamara, John J. (Jack) ... Agoura Hills, CA
McNamara, John J., Jr. ... Indialantic, FL
McNamara, John J., Jr. ... Mountain Lakes, NJ
McNamara, John K., Jr.
Mountain Lakes, NJ
New York, NY
McNamara, John L. ... Ionia, MI
McNamara, John N., Jr. ... Denver, CO
McNamara, John P. ... Lancaster, WI
McNamara, John Price ... Metairie, LA
McNamara, John R. ... Acton, MA
Mc Namara, John T. ... New York, NY
McNamara, John W. ... San Francisco, CA
McNamara, John W. ... Atlanta, GA
McNamara & Jones ... Frankfort, KY
McNamara, Joseph P. ... Wellesley, MA
McNamara, Joseph W., Jr. ... Omaha, NE
McNamara, Kate ... Philadelphia, PA
McNamara, Kathleen A.
New London, CT
McNamara, Kathleen A. ... Kansas City, MO
McNamara, Keith ... Columbus, OH
McNamara and Kenney ... Fairfield, CT
McNamara, Kevin C. ... Harrisburg, PA
McNamara, Kevin C. ... Bethlehem, PA
McNamara, Kevin P. ... Los Angeles, CA
McNamara, Kevin R. ... Wellesley, MA
McNamara, Kevin T. ... Woodbridge, NJ
McNamara, LaNelle L. ... Waco, TX
McNamara Law Firm, P.C. ... Denver, CO
McNamara, Lawr. J. ... Oak Lawn, IL
McNamara, Lawrence J. ... Dallas, TX
McNamara, Lawrence L.
New Orleans, LA
McNamara, Leo F. ... Canoga Park, CA
McNamara, Leo J. ... Niantic, CT
McNamara, Leo S. ... Boston, MA
McNamara, Lisa Miles ... Boston, MA
McNamara, Lucci, Hanrahan & Loxterman
Mentor, OH
McNamara, Marilyn Billings
Amherst, NH
Lebanon, NH
McNamara, Maris J. ... Cleveland, OH
McNamara, Mark L. ... New Orleans, LA
McNamara, Mark R. ... Buffalo, NY
McNamara, Martin B. ... Dallas, TX
McNamara, Martin J., III ... Ellicott City, MD
McNamara, Martin J., Jr. ... Kensington, MD
McNamara, Mary Alice ... Baltimore, MD
McNamara, Mary Beth ... Baltimore, MD
McNamara, Mary G. ... San Francisco, CA
McNamara, Matthew F. ... Chicago, IL
McNamara, Matthew J. ... Osterville, MA
Mcnamara, Maureen ... New City, NY
McNamara & McNamara ... Jersey City, NJ
McNamara and McNamara
Columbus, OH
McNamara & McNamara ... Waco, TX
McNamara & McNamara, P.C. ... Niantic, CT
McNamara, Meggin R. ... Fond du Lac, WI
McNamara, Michael F. ... Nogales, AZ
Tucson, AZ
McNamara, Michael G. ... Toms River, NJ
McNamara, Michael J. ... Minneapolis, MN
McNamara, Michael J. ... New York, NY
McNamara, Michael J.
South Padre Island, TX
McNamara, Michael James
Rancho Palos Verdes, CA
McNamara, Michael M. ... Northville, MI
McNamara, Michael P., Jr.
Cleveland, OH
McNamara, Michael Patrick
Santa Monica, CA
McNamara, Michael T. ... Washington, DC
McNamara, Michael W. ... Scottsdale, AZ
McNamara, Michele E. ... Pittsburgh, PA
McNamara, Molly M. ... Grand Rapids, MI
McNamara, Neal J. ... Providence, RI
McNamara & Newman ... Amherst, NH
Lebanon, NH
McNamara, Nicholas J. ... Madison, WI
McNamara, O'Keeffe & Sykes
Belding, MI
Ionia, MI
McNamara, Owen G. ... Florissant, MO
McNamara, Paddy Harris ... Chicago, IL
McNamara, Paola C. ... Oakland, CA
McNamara, Patricia B. ... Portland, ME
McNamara, Patrick ... New York, NY
McNamara, Patrick J. ... San Francisco, CA
McNamara, Patrick J. ... Tampa, FL
McNamara, Patrick J. ... Joliet, IL
McNamara, Patrick J. ... Secaucus, NJ
McNamara, Patrick R. ... Tucson, AZ
McNamara, Paul F. ... Mount Clemens, MI
McNamara, Paul G. ... Los Angeles, CA
McNamara, Paul J. ... Boston, MA
McNamara, Paul S. ... Ridgefield, CT
McNamara, Peter J. ... Baltimore, MD
McNamara, Peter J. ... Philadelphia, PA
McNamara, Peter P. ... Uniondale, NY
McNamara, Richard B. ... Manchester, NH
McNamara, Richard J. ... Southport, CT
McNamara, Robert A. ... Milwaukee, WI
McNamara, Robert F. ... Uniontown, OH
McNamara, Robert J. ... Houston, TX
McNamara, Robert M., Jr.
Central Intelligence Agency, Office of the General Counsel, GV
McNamara, Robert R. ... Chicago, IL
McNamara, Rosalee Miller
Kansas City, MO
McNamara, Rosemary B.
New Rochelle, NY
McNamara, Sam G. ... Frankfort, KY
McNamara, Scott D. ... Utica, NY
McNamara & Smith, P.L.L.C.
Jacksonville, NC
McNamara & Spira ... Los Angeles, CA
Santa Monica, CA
McNamara, Stephanie L. ... Cleveland, OH
Mcnamara, Stephen F., IV ... Fall River, MA
McNamara, Stephen H. ... Washington, DC
McNamara, Stephen M. ... Orange, CA
McNamara, Stephen P. ... Stamford, CT
McNamara, Stephen R. (IBA) **... Tulsa, OK**
McNamara, Steven J. ... Houston, TX
McNamara, Steven Patrick ... Orange, CA
McNamara, Suzanne H.
Federal Energy Regulatory Commission, Office of the General Counsel, GV
McNamara, Suzanne Muslin
Clarendon Hills, IL
McNamara, T. Neal ... San Francisco, CA
McNamara, Terence J. ... Belleville, MI
McNamara, Theresa A. ... Lancaster, PA
McNamara, Thomas B. ... Denver, CO
McNamara, Thomas D. ... Jacksonville, NC
McNamara, Thomas J. ... Savannah, GA
McNamara, Thomas J. ... Baltimore, MD
McNamara, Thomas J. ... East Meadow, NY
McNamara, Thomas J. ... Milwaukee, WI
McNamara, Thomas J., P.C. ... Savannah, GA
McNamara, Thomas M. ... New Haven, CT
McNamara, Thomas M. ... Lafayette, LA
McNamara, Thomas P. ... Tampa, FL
McNamara, Thomas P. ... Raleigh, NC
McNamara, Thomas P., P.A. ... Tampa, FL
McNamara, Thomas R. ... Cleveland, OH
McNamara, Thomas R. ... Norfolk, VA
McNamara, Thomas S. ... Philadelphia, PA
McNamara, Thomas W. ... Chicago, IL
McNamara, Timothy G. ... Suffern, NY
McNamara, Timothy J. ... Lafayette, LA
Mc Namara, Timothy J. ... Princeton, NJ
McNamara, Timothy K. ... Kansas City, MO
McNamara, Timothy W. ... Wantagh, NY
McNamara, Todd J. ... Denver, CO
McNamara, Todd J., P.C. ... Denver, CO
McNamara, Tracy L. ... Harrisburg, PA
McNamara, Valerie L. ... Orange, CA
McNamara, Walter J., III ... Mentor, OH
McNamara, Walter L. ... Cedar Rapids, IA
McNamara, Wesley F. ... Portland, OR
McNamara, William B. ... Danville, IL
McNamara, William F. ... Springfield, MA
McNamara, William J. ... Grand Rapids, MI
McNamara, William J. ... St. Louis, MO
McNamara, William J.
Yorktown Heights, NY
McNamara, William J., Jr. ... Danbury, CT
McNamara, William Zoller ... Cicero, IL
McNamara, Wm. J. ... Staten Island, NY
McNamee, Robert C. ... Boston, MA
McNamee, Alfred A. ... Okeechobee, FL
McNamee, Bernard J. ... Dallas, TX
McNamee, Bernard L., II ... Charlotte, NC
McNamee, Cynthia P. ... Dayton, OH
McNamee, David A. ... Greenbelt, MD
McNamee, Dennis Patrick ... Nashville, TN
McNamee, Donald E. ... Boston, MA
McNamee, G. Allen, III ... Los Angeles, CA
McNamee, Gwen Hoerr ... Park Ridge, IL
McNamee, Harry K. ... Butler, PA
McNamee, Hosea, Jernigan & Kim, P.A.
Washington, DC
Annapolis, MD
Greenbelt, MD
Falls Church, VA
McNamee, James J. ... Lansdale, PA
McNamee, James M., Jr. ... Nashua, NH
McNamee, John B. ... Fort Gratiot, MI
McNamee, Joseph W. ... Las Vegas, NV
McNamee, L. J. ... Cleveland, OH
McNamee, Lochner, Titus & Williams, P.C.
Albany, NY
McNamee, Marc T. ... Nashville, TN
McNamee, Matthew W. ... Boston, MA
McNamee, Michael ... Port Huron, MI
McNamee, Michael P. ... Minneapolis, MN
McNamee, Michael P. ... Dayton, OH
McNamee, Owen F. ... Fort Lauderdale, FL
McNamee, Peter F. ... Bloomington, IL
McNamee, Shelley A. ... Boston, MA
McNamee, Stafford F., Jr. ... Brentwood, TN
Mcnamee, Susan Olson ... Columbia, SC
McNamee, Thomas ... Columbus, OH
McNamer, Amy M. ... San Francisco, CA
McNamer Thompson Law Firm, P.C. A Professional Corporation ... Billings, MT
McNamer, William R. ... Billings, MT
McNames, Dennis W. ... Winston-Salem, NC
McNames, William P. ... Laguna Niguel, CA
McNaney, Robert T. ... Lake Forest, IL
McNarie, Susan Decker ... Jefferson City, MO
McNarny, Patrick E. ... Logansport, IN
McNary, Bernard L. ... Omaha, NE
McNary, Carolyn L. ... Los Angeles, CA
McNary, Gene ... Washington, DC
St. Louis, MO
McNary, George William ... Omaha, NE

McNary, J. Kevin ... Covington, LA
McNary, James T. ... Red Wing, MN
McNary, Morris & Smalley
Washington, DC
Greenbelt, MD
St. Louis, MO
McNary, Scott R. ... Miami, FL
McNary & Shohat, P.A. ... Miami, FL
McNary, Susan A. ... St. Louis, MO
McNasby, James J. ... New York, NY
McNasby, Jennifer D. ... Washington, DC
McNatt, Bobby W. ... Stockton, CA
McNatt, Christopher C., Jr.
Los Angeles, CA
McNatt, Greene & Thompson ... Vidalia, GA
McNatt, Hugh B. ... Vidalia, GA
McNatt, Isaac G. ... Teaneck, NJ
McNatt, J. Daniel ... Columbia, SC
McNatt, Joel H. ... Oklahoma City, OK
McNatt, John M., Jr. ... Jacksonville, FL
McNatt, Jud E. ... Atlanta, GA
McNatt, Marvin A. ... Pasadena, CA
McNatt, Michael W. ... Orlando, FL
McNatt, Robert R. ... Rusk, TX
McNaught, Jeannine R. ... Stoneham, MA
McNaught, Jeffery J. ... St. Paul, MN
McNaught, John J., Jr. ... Melrose, MA
McNaught, Joseph T. ... Salem, OR
McNaught, Karen L. ... Springfield, IL
Mcnaught, Mary C. ... Pinnacle, NC
McNaught & Moriarty, P.C. ... Boston, MA
Melrose, MA
McNaught, Stephen R. ... Melrose, MA
McNaughton, Alexander B. ... Enid, OK
McNaughton, Earlford Foy ... Richmond, IN
McNaughton, Edward J. ... Atlanta, GA
McNaughton, Janet Keating ... Phoenix, AZ
McNaughton, John S. ... Independence, MO
McNaughton, Kevin J. ... Los Angeles, CA
McNaughton Law Office, P.C.
Independence, MO
McNaughton, Michael B.
San Francisco, CA
McNaughton, Paul P. ... Swampscott, MA
McNaughton, Susan M. ... Enid, OK
McNaughton, Thomas J.
San Francisco, CA
McNaul Ebel Nawrot Helgren & Vance P.L.L.C. ... Seattle, WA
McNaul, Jerry R. ... Seattle, WA
McNaull, Tara G. ... Alpharetta, GA
McNaull, W. D., Jr. ... Charlotte, NC
McNay, Brita J. ... Sacramento, CA
McNay, Heather E. ... Norcross, GA
Mc Nay, James William ... Athens, GA
McNeace, Lewis B., Jr. ... Richlands, VA
McNeal, Angela M. ... Louisville, KY
McNeal & Clark ... Columbus, OH
McNeal, Clark E. ... Iowa Falls, IA
McNeal, Dan L. ... Lansing, MI
McNeal, Earl Darren ... Columbus, OH
McNeal, Harry L., Jr. ... York, PA
McNeal, Jacqueline A. ... Redwood City, CA
McNeal, James ... Indianapolis, IN
McNeal, Jan C. ... Ada, OH
McNeal, Kathleen Keller ... Columbus, OH
McNeal, Mary Helen ... Missoula, MT
McNeal, Mitchell A. ... Lowell, MI
McNeal, Raymond T. ... Ocala, FL
McNeal, Robert B. ... New Orleans, LA
McNeal, Schick, Archibald & Biro Co., L.P.A. ... Cleveland, OH
McNeal, Shannon ... Columbus, MS
McNeal, Sherae M. ... Columbia, MD
McNeal, Steven L. ... Sacramento, CA
McNeal, William S. ... Morrison, IL
McNeal, W. W. ... Lockhart, TX
McNealey, Anne G. ... Columbus, OH
McNealey, J. Jeffrey ... Columbus, OH
McNealey, Katherine A., R.N.
Baltimore, MD
McNealis, Mark P. ... Sweet Valley, PA
McNealy, Connie Skinner ... Troy, MI
McNear, Mary Grace ... Phoenix, AZ
McNear, Sara A. ... Chicago, IL
McNearney, John P. ... St. Louis, MO
McNearney, Robert O. ... St. Louis, MO
McNearney, Timothy A. ... Overland Park, KS
Kansas City, MO
McNeary & Anderson ... Aberdeen, SD
McNeary, Jerald M. ... Aberdeen, SD
McNee, Frederick L., II ... Wayzata, MN
McNee, John R. ... Jacksonville, AR
McNee, Michael W. ... Minneapolis, MN
McNee, R.P. Andrew ... New Hyde Park, NY
McNeece, John B., III ... San Diego, CA
McNeel, Albert M., Jr. ... San Antonio, TX
McNeel & Ballard ... Louisville, MS
McNeel, J. Niles ... Louisville, MS
McNeel, James Maverick ... Miami, FL
McNeel, Wm. D. ... San Antonio, TX
McNeela, Andrew ... New York, NY
McNeela, Edward P. ... Chicago, IL
McNeeley, Patrick H. ... Cleveland, OH
McNeeley, Charles E. ... Jacksonville, IL
McNeely, Christopher E.
Rochester Hills, MI
McNeely, Cynthia A. ... Tallahassee, FL
McNeely, Cynthia Lynn "Cindy" ... Tulsa, OK
McNeely, Cynthia V. ... Charlotte, NC
McNeely, Dennis L. ... Huntington, IN
Warren, IN
McNeely & Hefferon ... Charlotte, NC
McNeely, J. Lee ... Shelbyville, IN
McNeely, John J. ... St. Paul, MN
McNeely, Kenneth P. ... Atlanta, GA
McNeely, Kevin A. ... Southfield, MI
McNeely, Kevin J. ... Providence, RI

McNeely, Mark W. ... Shelbyville, IN
McNeely, Martha H.
Securities and Exchange Commission, Office of the General Counsel, GV
McNeely, Michael D.
Federal Trade Commission, Bureau of Competition, GV
McNeely, Milinda L. ... Los Angeles, CA
McNeely, O. Murray ... Lubbock, TX
McNeely, Patrick M. ... Charlotte, NC
McNeely, Richard M. ... Walnut Creek, CA
McNeely, Richard M. ... Swainsboro, GA
McNeely, Robert A. ... Tallahassee, FL
McNeely, Sanders, Stephenson & Thopy
Shelbyville, IN
McNeely, Thomas A. ... Charlotte, NC
McNeely, Thomas M., Jr. ... Natchez, MS
McNeely, Timothy A. ... Charleston, WV
McNeely-Johnson, Kathy A. ... Rockford, IL
McNeer, Alice L. ... Raleigh, NC
McNeer, Highland, McMunn and Varner, L.C. ... Clarksburg, WV
Martinsburg, WV
Parkersburg, WV
McNeer, James E. ... Clarksburg, WV
McNeer, Richard Gregory
Huntington, WV
McNeer, Richard Gregory, Jr. ... Norfolk, VA
McNeer, Selden S., Jr. ... Huntington, WV
McNees, Autenreith, Rackley, Walker & Carr ... Beaver, PA
McNees, David N. ... Sherman, TX
McNees, E. Donald ... Dallas, TX
McNees, Richard B. ... Seattle, WA
McNees, Robert A. ... Carol Stream, IL
McNees, Robert A., III ... Knoxville, TN
McNees, Robert A., III ... Oak Ridge, TN
McNees, Ruth Ann ... Palo Alto, CA
McNees, W. Scott ... Newark, NJ
McNees, Wallace & Nurick
Washington, DC
Columbus, OH
Harrisburg, PA
Hazleton, PA
McNees, William H., Jr. ... Beaver, PA
McNeese, A. John ... Portland, OR
McNeese, A. G., Jr. ... Houston, TX
McNeese & Arthur, PLLC ... Memphis, TN
McNeese & Hahn, PLLC ... Columbia, MS
McNeese, John C. ... New Orleans, LA
McNeese, Lynn Smith ... Jonesboro, GA
McNeese, Richard S. ... Memphis, TN
McNeese, Thomas D. ... Columbia, MS
McNeff, Donald E. ... Ypsilanti, MI
McNeff, Joseph D. ... Plano, TX
Mcneff, Michael E. ... Okanogan, WA
McNeice, Carolyn M. ... Wilmington, DE
McNeil, Alexander M. ... Boston, MA
McNeil, Alvin D. ... San Francisco, CA
McNeil, Andre E. ... Conway, AR
McNeil, Andrea J. ... Sacramento, CA
McNeil, Andrew M. ... Indianapolis, IN
McNeil, Artemeus Elton ... Bartow, FL
McNeil, Barry F. ... Dallas, TX
McNeil, Bonnie Kay ... Fresno, CA
McNeil, Bruce J. ... Minneapolis, MN
McNeil, Buck W. ... Lubbock, TX
McNeil, C. B. ... Polson, MT
McNeil, Charles E. ... Missoula, MT
McNeil, Charles L. ... Mason City, IL
McNeil, Chris E., Jr. ... Washington, DC
McNeil, Christopher B. ... Worthington, OH
McNeil, Constance J. ... Oakland, CA
McNeil, Daniel F. ... Portland, OR
McNeil, Daniel James ... Washington, DC
McNeil, Darrell O. ... Topeka, KS
McNeil, David W. F. ... Portland, OR
McNeil, DeMont W. ... Tulsa, OK
Mcneil, Dona F. ... Brooklyn, NY
McNeil, Donald J. ... Chicago, IL
McNeil, Donald R., Jr. ... Minneapolis, MN
McNeil, Doris E. ... New Brunswick, NJ
McNeil, Douglas J. ... Grand Haven, MI
McNeil, Edd R. ... Davis, OK
Sulphur, OK
McNeil, Edward J. ... Newark, NJ
McNeil, Eric W. ... Dallas, TX
McNeil, Gary W. ... Austin, TX
McNeil & Gilbert ... Jacksonville, TX
McNeil Grafton ... Grand Haven, MI
McNeil, Jack B. ... Atlanta, GA
McNeil, James H. ... Fort Myers, FL
McNeil, James H., Jr. ... Orlando, FL
McNeil, J. E. ... Washington, DC
McNeil, John M. ... Salem, VA
McNeil, John N. ... Iron Mountain, MI
McNeil, John T. ... Boston, MA
McNeil, John T. ... Paw Paw, MI
McNeil, John W. ... Atascadero, CA
McNeil, John W. ... Grand Rapids, MI
McNeil, Joseph D. ... Santa Ana, CA
McNeil, Joseph E. ... Burlington, VT
McNeil, Judy P. ... Little Rock, AR
McNeil, Kathleen G. ... Madison, WI
Mcneil, Kathleen M. ... Arlington, MA
McNeil, Keith P. ... Akron, OH
McNeil, Kenneth E. ... Houston, TX
McNeil, Kenneth W. ... Beaverton, OR
McNeil, Kevin Michael ... Laurel, MD
McNeil, Laura Ruth ... Atlanta, GA
McNeil, Lawrence ... Boston, MA
McNeil, Leddy & Sheahan, A Professional Corporation ... Burlington, VT
McNeil, Malcolm S. ... Los Angeles, CA
McNeil, Marion D. ... Dobson, NC
McNeil, Mark S. ... Minneapolis, MN
McNeil, Mary A. ... Atlanta, GA
McNeil, Mary F. ... Fallbrook, CA

McNeil, Melanie S. ... Marietta, GA
McNeil, Michael B. ... Bloomington, IN
McNeil, Michael D. ... Cincinnati, OH
McNeil, Michael J. ... Albany, NY
McNeil, Patrick J., (A Professional Corporation) ... San Rafael, CA
McNeil, Patrick T. ... Chicago, IL
McNeil, R. Donald ... San Jose, CA
McNeil, Regina ... Whippany, NJ
McNeil, Richard D. ... Minneapolis, MN
McNeil, Richard J. ... Newport Beach, CA
McNeil, Richard T. ... Jacksonville, NC
McNeil & Ricks, P.C. ... Washington, DC
McNeil, Ronald G. ... Philadelphia, PA
McNeil, Ronald M. ... Department of Justice, Criminal Division, GV
McNeil, Silveira & Rice ... San Rafael, CA
McNeil & Sunleaf ... Montezuma, IA
McNeil, Susson, Parrett & Tropp, A Professional Corporation ... Santa Ana, CA
McNeil, Thomas Eamon ... San Jose, CA
McNeil & Torreano, P.C. ... Iron Mountain, MI
McNeil, Wanda S. ... New York, NY
McNeil, Wayne K. ... New Orleans, LA
McNeil, William B. ... Piqua, OH
McNeil, William H. ... Reno, NV
McNeil, W. T. ... Edna, TX
McNeil, Yass ... Santa Ana, CA
McNeilage, Carol A. ... Southfield, MI
McNeile, James M. ... Leawood, KS
Kansas City, MO
McNeill, Aileen S. ... Jackson, MS
McNeill, Alan ... Beaumont, TX
McNeill, Andrea Lynn ... Marion, IL
McNeill & Associates ... Bloomfield, CT
McNeill, Barry S. ... Raleigh, NC
McNeill, Bobby Burns ... Raeford, NC
McNeill, Bruce G. ... Boston, MA
McNeill, Carolyn J. ... Boulder, CO
McNeill, Caryn Coppedge ... Raleigh, NC
McNeill, Cynthia Ann ... Baltimore, MD
McNeill, David A. ... West Des Moines, IA
McNeill, David E., Jr. ... Houston, TX
McNeill, David, Jr. ... Las Cruces, NM
McNeill, Donald W. ... Bartlesville, OK
McNeill, Elizabeth A. ... Memphis, TN
Mc Neill, Frederick A. ... Minneapolis, MN
McNeill, H. Gregory ... Orlando, FL
McNeill, Harold L. ... Sarasota, FL
McNeill, Heather D. ... Los Angeles, CA
McNeill, J. David, III ... Baton Rouge, LA
McNeill, J. Layne ... Wilmington, NC
McNeill, J. Mark, The Law Offices of
San Diego, CA
McNeill, James B., Jr. ... Selma, AL
Mcneill, James E. ... Boston, MA
McNeill, James P., III ... Spokane, WA
McNeill, James S. ... San Diego, CA
McNeill, Jennifer Quesinberry
Orlando, FL
McNeill, Jenny L. ... Muskegon, MI
McNeill, John F. ... Onancock, VA
McNeill, John Garry ... Lexington, KY
McNeill, John H. ... Secaucus, NJ
McNeill, John P. ... Washington, DC
McNeill, John R. ... Tempe, AZ
McNeill, John T., III ... Runnemede, NJ
McNeill, John W., III ... Maysville, KY
McNeill, Joyce D. ... Peabody, MA
McNeill, Larry ... Austin, TX
McNeill Law Offices ... Beaumont, TX
McNeill, Lawrence ... Lakeland, FL
McNeill, Malcolm R., Jr. ... Dover, NH
McNeill, Mary B. ... Berkeley, CA
McNeill, Neal E. ... Tulsa, OK
McNeill, Omar Y. ... Wilmington, DE
McNeill, Paschall Hancock ... Chapel Hill, NC
McNeill, Paul D. ... Jonesboro, AR
McNeill, Polly L. ... Seattle, WA
McNeill, Rebecca ... Washington, DC
McNeill, Richard C., Jr. ... Philadelphia, PA
McNeill, Robert A. ... Edina, MN
McNeill, Robert B. ... Charlotte, NC
McNeill, Robert H., II ... Morehead City, NC
McNeill, Robert H., Jr. ... Los Angeles, CA
McNeill, Robert P. ... Albuquerque, NM
McNeill, S. David ... Troy, MI
McNeill & Schumacher ... Maysville, KY
McNeill, Sheila Frances ... Tampa, FL
McNeill, Stephen H. ... Winter Park, FL
McNeill, Steven G. ... Montesano, WA
McNeill, Suzanne B. ... San Diego, CA
McNeill & Taylor, Professional Association
Dover, NH
McNeill, Thomas C., Jr. ... Bloomfield, CT
McNeill, Thomas E. ... Charlotte, NC
McNeill, Thomas G. ... Detroit, MI
McNeill, Thomas H. ... Minneapolis, MN
McNeill, Thomas R. ... Atlanta, GA
McNeill, Wallis D., Jr. ... Alice, TX
McNeill, Walter G. ... New York, NY
McNeill, Walter P. ... Redding, CA
McNeill, William C., III ... San Francisco, CA
McNeilly, A. Kathleen ... DeLand, FL
McNeilly, A. Kathleen, and Associates, P.A.
DeLand, FL
McNeilly, James W., Jr. ... La Crosse, WI
McNeilly, John J. ... Georgetown, DE
McNeilly, R. Scott ... Washington, DC
McNeilly, W. Warner, III ... Nashville, TN
McNeilly, W. Warner, Jr. ... Nashville, TN
McNeily, Curtlan R., (P.C.) ... Washington, DC
McNeily, Robert M. ... Houston, TX
McNeily & Rosenfeld ... Washington, DC
New York, NY
McNeish, Charles S. ... Washington, DC
McNeish, Gilbert F. ... Denver, CO
McNeive, Gerald T., Jr. ... St. Louis, MO

McNeive, Lynda A. ... Denver, CO
McNelis, Charles A. ... Bethesda, MD
McNelis, Darice ... Pittsburgh, PA
McNelis, Edward J., III ... Richmond, VA
McNelis, Edward P. ... Hazleton, PA
McNelis, Frank L. ... Utica, MI
McNelis, George Barnett ... Philadelphia, PA
McNelis, John T. ... Palo Alto, CA
McNelis, Julia Kelly
Farmington Hills, MI
McNelis, Lisa A. ... Fort Lauderdale, FL
McNelis, Michael T. ... Indianapolis, IN
Mcnelis, Patrick James ... Houston, TX
McNelis, Philip K. ... Birmingham, MI
McNelis, Richard P. ... Tallahassee, FL
McNelis, Sean B. ... San Antonio, TX
McNelley, Donald B. ... Indian Wells, CA
McNelley, Donald B. ... Palm Springs, CA
McNelley, Edward J. ... Everett, MA
McNellie, Elizabeth A. ... Columbus, OH
McNellie, Richard L. ... Cleveland, OH
McNellis, Lucille I. ... Bethlehem, PA
McNellis, Paul B. ... Fort Wayne, IN
McNellis, Susan K. ... Shakopee, MN
McNemar, Georgia ... Washington, DC
McNemar Law Offices, P.C. ... Phoenix, AZ
McNemar, T. Troy ... Phoenix, AZ
McNemar, W. V., Jr. ... Richmond, VA
McNenly, Peter F. ... Southfield, MI
McNenney, Edward J. ... Bronxville, NY
McNenny, James H. ... Westerville, OH
McNerney, Daniel Barrett ... Santa Ana, CA
McNerney, Daniel P. ... Hackensack, NJ
McNerney, Dennis M. ... Santa Ana, CA
McNerney, Gerald M. ... Butler, IN
McNerney, James E. ... Houston, TX
Mcnerney, Jane E. ... Media, PA
McNerney, John P. ... Washington, DC
McNerney, Joseph J. ... Chicago, IL
McNerney, Lauren L. ... Long Beach, CA
McNerney, Martin M. ... Washington, DC
McNerney, Michael J.
Fort Lauderdale, FL
McNerney, Michael J. ... Woodstock, IL
McNerney, Page, Vanderlin & Hall
Muncy, PA
Williamsport, PA
McNerney, Patricia ... United States Senate, Committee Legal Personnel, GV
McNerney, Patrick J. ... Chicago, IL
McNerney, Stephen A. ... Worcester, MA
McNerney, Tiernan & Burns
New Haven, CT
McNerny, Judith C. ... Denver, CO
McNerthney, Lawrence B. ... Tacoma, WA
McNertney, H. J. ... Bancroft, IA
McNertney, William John ... Atherton, CA
McNery, Dan R. ... Round Rock, TX
McNery & Voelker ... Round Rock, TX
McNett, Douglas W. ... Larned, KS
McNett, John C. ... Indianapolis, IN
McNett, Margaret R. ... Santa Fe, NM
McNett, Mary Ann ... Jackson, CA
McNevin, Christopher J. ... Los Angeles, CA
Mcnevin, Valerie J. ... Glastonbury, CT
McNevin, William J. ... Pomona, CA
McNew, Barbara Scherer ... Nocona, TX
McNew, C. Sanders ... New York, NY
McNew, Edward H., Jr. ... Portsmouth, VA
McNew, Hugh D. ... North Miami Beach, FL
McNew, James W. ... Greenfield, IN
McNew, Jeb ... Nocona, TX
McNew & McNew ... Nocona, TX
McNew, R. Bruce ... Wilmington, DE
Kennett Square, PA
McNew, William T. ... Monroe, LA
McNichol, Christopher M. ... Phoenix, AZ
McNichol, Joan E. ... Smithtown, NY
McNichol, John A. ... Riverhead, NY
McNichol, Michele L. ... Miami, FL
McNichol, Paul D. ... Media, PA
McNichol, William J. ... Trenton, NJ
McNichol, William J., Jr.
Philadelphia, PA
McNicholas, Anthony J., III
West Palm Beach, FL
McNicholas, Bernadette ... Chicago, IL
McNicholas, Christine M. ... New York, NY
McNicholas, Cynthia A. ... Media, PA
McNicholas, Dennis J. ... Lombard, IL
McNicholas, Dennis J., Ltd. ... Lombard, IL
McNicholas, Edward R. ... Washington, DC
McNicholas, James D. ... Beaumont, TX
McNicholas, Janet M. ... Chicago, IL
McNicholas, John J. ... Medfield, MA
McNicholas, John P. ... Los Angeles, CA
McNicholas, John P. ... New York, NY
McNicholas, Leeann G. ... Las Vegas, NV
McNicholas, Matthew S. ... Los Angeles, CA
McNicholas & McNicholas, LLP
Los Angeles, CA
McNicholas, Patrick ... Los Angeles, CA
McNicholas, Patrick J. ... Concord, NH
McNicholas & Viles ... Concord, NH
McNicholas, Walter J. ... Kearny, NJ
McNicholl, M. A. Damian ... Mineola, NY
McNichols, David J. ... Columbus, OH
McNichols, Edwin J. ... Schaumburg, IL
McNichols, Elizabeth A. ... Mashpee, MA
McNichols, Gerald F. ... Wheaton, IL
McNichols, James F. ... St. Louis, MO
McNichols, John E. ... Boston, MA
McNichols, John F. ... Clearwater, FL
McNichols, Mary J. ... Chicago, IL
McNichols, Melinda L. ... Miami Springs, FL
McNichols, Michael D. ... Canby, OR
McNichols, Michael E. ... Lewiston, ID
McNichols, Robert J. ... Spokane, WA

McNichols, Stephen L. R. ....Englewood, CO
McNichols, Stephen L. R., Jr.
Pleasanton, CA
McNichols, Steven ....San Francisco, CA
McNichols, Thomas R. II ....New Castle, IN
McNichols, William J. ....Norman, OK
McNickle & Bonner ....Grove City, PA
McNickle, Timothy L. ....Grove City, PA
McNicol, Donald E. ....New York, NY
McNicol, Paul M. ....Parsippany, NJ
McNicol, Randolph D. ....San Diego, CA
McNicol, Timothy J. ....Lisbon, OH
McNicol, Ulric ....Bethpage, NY
McNicoll, Elizabeth Carmen ....Burbank, CA
McNider, James S., III ....Hampton, VA
McNider, James S., III, P.L.C.
Hampton, VA
Newport News, VA
McNiece, James T. ....Merrillville, IN
McNiece, Laraine ....Oregon City, OR
McNiece, Maureen Flaherty
San Antonio, TX
McNiece, Neil G. ....Santa Monica, CA
McNiece, Sidney L., Jr. ....Bellaire, TX
McNiel, D. Ferguson, III ....Houston, TX
McNiel, Dale E. ....Washington, DC
McNierney, Tamara A. ....Fort Lauderdale, FL
McNiff, Frank L., Jr. ....Corpus Christi, TX
McNiff, James F., II ....Boston, MA
McNiff, John A. ....Peabody, MA
McNiff, Lisa A. ....Marshall, MI
McNiff, Peter J. ....Cheyenne, WY
Mc Niff, Terry ....Los Angeles, CA
McNiff, Thomas J. ....New York, NY
McNinch, Deborah L. ....Cleveland, OH
McNinch, Sandra Jones ....Richmond, VA
McNish, Douglas S. ....Wailuku, HI
McNish, J. H. ....Lawrence, KS
McNish, John ....Topeka, KS
McNish, Karen A. ....Saginaw, MI
McNish, Knabe and Kroning ....Chicago, IL
McNish, Robert J., Jr. ....Chicago, IL
McNish, Sharon Darmetko ....Rutherford, NJ
McNish, Susan K. ....Detroit, MI
McNish, Thomas ....Jackson, MI
McNitt, David G. ....Thornton, PA
McNitt, David G., P.C. ....Thornton, PA
McNitt, Douglas W. ....Dulles, VA
McNitt, George A. ....Berkeley, CA
McNitt, Jan M. ....Stephenville, TX
McNitt, Julie Jinkens ....Osage Beach, MO
McNitt, R. Lee, Jr. ....Whittier, CA
McNitt, Robert C., Jr. ....Los Angeles, CA
McNitt, Robert M. ....Columbus, OH
McNitt, Roger L. ....San Diego, CA
Mc Nitt, Theodore R., Jr. ....Golden, CO
McNitzky, Richard ....San Antonio, TX
McNiven, Carolyn F. ....Chicago, IL
McNiven, Melissa Heitmann
Washington, DC
McNown, Lynne E. ....Chicago, IL
McNulty, Aimeé Hueston
Florham Park, NJ
Toms River, NJ
McNulty, Anthony J. ....New York, NY
McNulty, Anthony J. ....Media, PA
McNulty, Anthony J., P.C. & Associates
Media, PA
McNulty, Barbara Downs ....Old Bridge, NJ
McNulty, Bernard J., Jr. ....Norristown, PA
McNulty, Brian J. ....Florham Park, NJ
Toms River, NJ
McNulty, C. Howard ....Winter Park, FL
McNulty, Charles M. ....Phoenix, AZ
McNulty, Charles S., III ....Harrisonburg, VA
McNulty, Christopher M.
Washington, DC
New York, NY
McNulty, Christopher S. ....Seattle, WA
McNulty, Daniel A. ....Sunnyvale, CA
McNulty, Daniel E. Orren ....New York, NY
McNulty, Daniel J. ....Pittsburgh, PA
McNulty, Daniel J. ....Lumberton, TX
Mcnulty, David John ....New York, NY
McNulty, David W. ....Springfield, PA
McNulty, Deborah Ashby ....Wailuku, HI
McNulty, Dennis P. ....Oxnard, CA
McNulty, Edward M. ....Lawrenceville, NJ
McNulty, Eleanor P. ....Wexford, PA
McNulty, Elizabeth B. ....Essex, NY
McNulty, Francis A. ....Rosemead, CA
McNulty, Gregory F., Jr. ....North Canton, OH
McNulty, Holly A. ....Pasadena, CA
McNulty, Hugh W. ....Denver, CO
McNulty, Hugh W., Professional Corporation
Denver, CO
McNulty, J. Gordon ....El Monte, CA
McNulty, J. William ....Reno, NV
McNulty, Jack A. ....Pine Bluff, AR
McNulty, Jack L., Jr. ....Tulsa, OK
McNulty, Jacquelyn A. ....Cherry Hill, NJ
McNulty, James ....Los Angeles, CA
McNulty, James F., Jr. ....Tucson, AZ
McNulty, James F. M. ....Washington, DC
McNulty, James H., Jr. ....Boston, MA
McNulty, James J. ....Boston, MA
Lynn, MA
McNulty, John C. ....Minneapolis, MN
St. Paul, MN
McNulty, John F. ....Philadelphia, PA
McNulty, John J. ....Marlborough, MA
McNulty, John K. ....Berkeley, CA
McNulty, John R. ....Riverhead, NY
McNulty, John W. ....Chicago, IL
McNulty, Joseph F., Jr. ....Greensboro, NC
McNulty, Joseph F., Jr. ....Allentown, PA
Philadelphia, PA
McNulty, Joseph P. ....Clearwater, FL
McNulty, Joseph P., Jr. ....Gladstone, NJ
New York, NY
McNulty, J. P. ....Fort Collins, CO
McNulty, Kevin ....Newark, NJ
McNulty, Kevin A. ....Clarkston, MI
McNulty, Kevin R. ....Philadelphia, PA
McNulty, Lauren K. ....Chicago, IL
McNulty, Linda C. ....Tucson, AZ
McNulty, M. Sean ....Toledo, OH
McNulty, Margaret A. ....El Segundo, CA
McNulty, Marsha ....Franklin, LA
McNulty, Mary A. ....Dallas, TX
McNulty, Mary F. ....Canton, OH
McNulty, Matthew F., III
Salt Lake City, UT
McNulty, Maura S. ....Washington, DC
McNulty, Maureen H. ....Greenlawn, NY
McNulty, Michael A., Jr. ....New Orleans, LA
McNulty, Michael F. ....Tucson, AZ
McNulty, Michael J. ....Department of Justice, Environment and Natural Resources Division, GV
McNulty, Michael J. ....New York, NY
McNulty, Michael J. ....Barberton, OH
McNulty, Michael J., III
Lake Charles, LA
McNulty, Michael J., Jr. ....Franklin, LA
McNulty, Michael, P.C. ....Oklahoma City, OK
McNulty, Michelle Allaire ....Braintree, MA
McNulty, Norman R., Jr. ....Spokane, WA
McNulty, Patricia A. ....New York, NY
McNulty, Patrick J. ....Des Moines, IA
McNulty, Paul E. ....Washington, DC
McNulty, Paul Francis ....Dallas, TX
McNulty, Paul G. ....Northfield, IL
McNulty, Paul J. ....Washington, DC
McNulty, Peter J. ....Gilroy, CA
Los Angeles, CA
McNulty, Peter J. ....Chicago, IL
McNulty, Priscilla ....Duluth, MN
McNulty, R. James, Jr. ....Minneapolis, MN
McNulty, Raymond J. ....Swampscott, MA
McNulty, Richard D ....Lansing, MI
McNulty, Robert E., (P.C.) ....Torrance, CA
Walnut Creek, CA
McNulty, Robert H. ....Washington, DC
McNulty, Robt. G. ....Largo, FL
McNulty & Saacke ....Torrance, CA
Walnut Creek, CA
McNulty, Samuel J. ....Florham Park, NJ
Toms River, NJ
Mcnulty, Sharon L. ....Albany, NY
McNulty, Sibyl S. ....Pittsburgh, PA
McNulty - Spiess ....Riverhead, NY
McNulty, Suzanne Naatz ....Los Angeles, CA
McNulty, Tamara Lynn ....Tustin, CA
McNulty, Tamara M. ....Washington, DC
McNulty, Thomas J. ....Chicago, IL
McNulty, Thomas J., Jr. ....Barnstable, MA
McNulty, Thomas J., Jr. ....Hyannis, MA
McNulty, Thomas P. ....Chicago, IL
McNulty, Timothy G.
Cardiff-By-The-Sea, CA
McNulty, Timothy P., Law Office of
Kihei, HI
McNulty, Truman O. ....Milwaukee, WI
McNulty, Ulrich Roy ....Indio, CA
McNulty, William J., Jr. ....Dedham, MA
McNulty, William T., Jr. ....Hayward, CA
McNulty-Jagel, Molly ....Rochester, NY
McNutt, Briar L. ....New York, NY
McNutt, Charles P. ....Bakersfield, CA
McNutt, Daphne ....New Orleans, LA
McNutt, Douglas P. ....Concord, NH
McNutt, F. L. ....Houston, TX
McNutt, Gaye L. ....Redmond, WA
McNutt, James T., Jr. ....El Paso, TX
McNutt, Jan S. ....Westport, CT
McNutt, Jason E. ....Merrifield, VA
McNutt, John P. ....Miami, FL
McNutt, Kristen W. ....New York, NY
McNutt, Lynne W. ....Coos Bay, OR
McNutt, Marcy L. ....Houston, TX
McNutt, Matthew B. ....Austin, TX
McNutt, Mona J. ....Conway, AR
McNutt, Patricia L. ....Oak Ridge, TN
McNutt, Paul, Jr. ....Dallas, TX
McNutt, Philip J. ....Rockville, MD
McNutt, Robert N. ....Tupelo, MS
McNutt, Ronald W. ....Nashville, TN
McNutt, Scott H. ....San Francisco, CA
McNutt, Scott M. ....Coos Bay, OR
McNutt, Stephanie Berrington
Los Angeles, CA
McNutt, Thomas B. ....Los Angeles, CA
McNutt, William A. ....Decatur, IL
McOmber, Adrienne Haroutunian
Red Bank, NJ
McOmber, F. Bryant, Jr. ....San Ramon, CA
Mc Omber, Martin G. ....Santa Rosa, CA
McOmber & McOmber, P.C. ....Red Bank, NJ
McOmber, Richard D. ....Red Bank, NJ
McOmber, Richard L. ....Indianapolis, IN
McOmber, Robert A. ....Bowling Green, OH
M'Cormick, Robert Stuart ....Fort Collins, CO
McOscar, Gerald K. ....West Chester, PA
McOsker, David J. ....Providence, RI
McOsker, Gerald P. ....Providence, RI
McOsker, John Erin ....Los Angeles, CA
McOsker, Joseph A., III ....Boston, MA
McOsker, Michael A. ....Boston, MA
McOsker, Timothy B. ....Los Angeles, CA
McOwen, John W. ....Fullerton, CA
McOwen, Mark W. ....Charleston, WV
McPadden, Leslie Gold ....Waterbury, CT
McParland, James E. ....Chicago, IL
McParland, Joseph P.
Fort Lauderdale, FL
McParland, Kevin B. ....Bethesda, MD
McParland, Paul F. ....Cleveland, OH
McPartlan, Kerry A. ....Brooklyn, NY
McPartland, Anne T. ....Bronx, NY
McPartland, Donald ....Waterbury, CT
McPartland, Donald C. ....Waterbury, CT
McPartland, Donna E.M. ....McLean, VA
McPartland, Elizabeth J. Calianese
Parsippany, NJ
McPartland, Michael B. ....Palm Desert, CA
McPartland, Patrick J. ....Minneapolis, MN
McPartland, Sean W. ....Cedar Rapids, IA
McPartland-Good, Sarah J. ....Bangor, ME
McPartlin, Dennis W. ....St. Paul, MN
McPartlin, Edward P. ....Boston, MA
McPartlin, Margaret E.
National Credit Union Administration, Office of General Counsel, GV
McPartlin & McPartlin ....La Grange, IL
McPartlin, Michael A. ....La Grange, IL
McPartlin, Peter J. ....Los Angeles, CA
McPayah-Obiamalu, Vivian
West Covina, CA
McPeak, Charles J. ....Port Washington, NY
McPeak, Jack F. ....Jackson, MS
McPeak, James E. ....Marengo, IL
McPeak, Jennifer L. ....Pittsburgh, PA
McPeak, Troy A. ....Radcliff, KY
McPeck, Mitzi Lynn ....Grand Rapids, MI
McPeek, Alexandra M.H. ....Boston, MA
McPeek, Anna Lee ....Dayton, OH
McPeek, Michael G. ....Boise, ID
McPeek, Scott K. ....West Palm Beach, FL
McPeek, Wesley L. ....Kalamazoo, MI
McPencow, Dennis P. ....Sonoma, CA
McPeters McAlearney Shimoff & Hatt, A Professional Corporation ....Redlands, CA
San Bernardino, CA
McPeters, Ray W. ....Mount Clemens, MI
McPeters, Roberta ....San Bernardino, CA
McPeters, Thomas H. ....Redlands, CA
McPhail, Brian R. ....Osage, IA
McPhail, David K. ....Oklahoma City, OK
McPhail, Donald R. ....Washington, DC
McPhail, Douglas H. ....Muskegon, MI
McPhail, Douglas H., P.C. ....Muskegon, MI
McPhail, E. Fred, Jr. ....Charlotte, NC
McPhail, Heather E. ....Los Angeles, CA
McPhail, Ian D. ....Monterey, CA
Santa Cruz, CA
McPhail, James H. ....Irvine, CA
McPhail, John R. ....Columbus, NE
McPhail, John W. ....Enid, OK
McPhail, Jon B. ....Atlanta, GA
McPhail, Kendall R. ....Springfield, MO
McPhail, Kent D. ....Mobile, AL
McPhail, Mark ....Conroe, TX
McPhail, Mark R. ....Oklahoma City, OK
McPhail & Marmur, P.C. ....Atlanta, GA
McPhail, Michael W. ....Hattiesburg, MS
McPhail, R. Louis, Jr. ....Fargo, ND
McPhail, Raymond E. ....Hillsboro, IL
McPhail, Sharon ....Detroit, MI
McPhail, W. Rex ....Oklahoma City, OK
McPharlin, Eldon V. ....Los Angeles, CA
McPharlin, Linda Hendrix ....San Jose, CA
McPharlin, Sprinkles & Thomas, LLP
San Jose, CA
McPhaul, Thomas F. ....Norfolk, VA
McPhearson, J. Lee ....Butler, AL
McPhedran, Charles ....Philadelphia, PA
McPhedran, James A. ....Peru, IL
McPhedran, Michelle L. ....Ottawa, IL
McPhee & Aiman-Smith
San Francisco, CA
McPhee, Charles A., Jr. ....Alameda, CA
McPhee, Charles A., Jr., Law Offices of
Alameda, CA
McPhee, Dean W. ....San Francisco, CA
McPhee, Deborah M. ....Wheatfield, IN
McPhee, Donald P. ....Buffalo, NY
McPhee, Edward C. ....Bayonet Point, FL
McPhee, Elizabeth J. ....Reading, PA
McPhee, Gillian ....Washington, DC
McPhee, Henry Roemer ....Washington, DC
McPhee, Jerold D. ....Salt Lake City, UT
McPhee, Joan ....Providence, RI
McPhee, Joe G. ....Telluride, CO
McPhee, John Scott ....Miami, FL
McPhee, Martha A. ....Minneapolis, MN
McPhee, Michael J. ....La Jolla, CA
McPhee, Rodney E. ....Rutland, VT
McPhee, Sandra Ferguson ....Wilmette, IL
McPhee, Scott A. ....Los Angeles, CA
McPhee, W. Allan ....Torrance, CA
McPhee, Wm. Thomas ....Olympia, WA
McPheeters, Bruce B. ....Minneapolis, MN
McPheeters, Charles J.
Jefferson City, MO
McPheeters, Howard F. ....Honolulu, HI
McPheeters, Hugh ....St. Louis, MO
McPheeters, Hugh, Jr. ....Sarasota, FL
McPheeters, Nancy L. ....Malden, MA
McPheeters, Steven L. ....Birmingham, AL
McPheeters, William G. ....Dayton, TN
McPheron, Alan B. ....Durant, OK
McPheron, Ian J. ....Chicago, IL
McPherson, Amanda C. ....Santa Barbara, CA
McPherson & Associates, P.C. ....Plano, TX
McPherson, Barbara A. D.
St. Petersburg, FL
McPherson, Becky ....Floydada, TX
Mc Pherson, Bernadette Prendergast
Rutherford, NJ
McPherson, Billy J. ....Oneonta, AL
McPherson, Boyd R. ....Wichita, KS
Mcpherson, Brian H. ....Beverly Hills, CA
McPherson, Brock R. ....Great Bend, KS
McPherson, Carl W. ....Bremen, GA
McPherson, Catherine Mary
Minneapolis, MN
McPherson, Charles O. ....Memphis, TN
McPherson, Chester A. ....Washington, DC
McPherson, Dale T.
Grosse Pointe Farms, MI
McPherson, Daniel N. ....Jefferson City, MO
McPherson, Darryl N. ....Buffalo, NY
McPherson, David A. ....Secaucus, NJ
McPherson, David F. ....Irvine, CA
McPherson, David J. ....Washington, DC
McPherson, David J. ....Cincinnati, OH
McPherson, David M. ....Washington, DC
McPherson, Dennis P. ....Sacramento, CA
McPherson, Dennis P. ....Columbus, GA
McPherson, Donald P., III ....Baltimore, MD
McPherson, Douglas M. ....Pasadena, CA
McPherson, Duncan R. ....Stockton, CA
McPherson, Edwin F. ....Los Angeles, CA
McPherson, Erin L. ....Los Angeles, CA
McPherson, G. Thomas ....Memphis, TN
McPherson, Gary L. ....Aurora, CO
McPherson, George K., Jr. ....Atlanta, GA
McPherson, Harry ....Washington, DC
McPherson, Heather ....Indianapolis, IN
McPherson, Howard G. ....Honolulu, HI
McPherson & Hull, P.C. ....Aurora, CO
McPherson, J. Mark ....Plano, TX
McPherson, Jack B. ....New Port Richey, FL
McPherson, Jack H., Jr. ....Kingston, TN
McPherson, Jacqueline ....New Orleans, LA
McPherson, James A. ....New Orleans, LA
McPherson, James R. ....Sanford, NC
McPherson, James S. ....San Francisco, CA
McPherson, Jamieson G. ....Louisville, KY
McPherson, Jeanette E. ....Las Vegas, NV
McPherson, Jeffery T. ....St. Louis, MO
McPherson, Jeffery Thomas
Jefferson City, MO
McPherson, Joan H. ....Coupeville, WA
McPherson, Jody L. ....Mount Carmel, IL
McPherson, Joel S. ....Springfield, OH
McPherson, John E. ....Los Angeles, CA
McPherson, John K. ....Gainesville, FL
McPherson, Jos. D. ....Decatur, AL
McPherson, Joseph ....Canton, OH
McPherson, Joseph W., Jr.
Silver Spring, MD
McPherson, Juddson H. ....Joplin, MO
McPherson, J. W., Jr. ....Hartville, OH
McPherson & Kalmansohn
Los Angeles, CA
McPherson, Kathleen Z. ....La Jolla, CA
McPherson, Keith Martin
Little Rock, AR
McPherson, Kenneth D. ....Secaucus, NJ
Trenton, NJ
McPherson, Kenneth D., Jr. ....Secaucus, NJ
McPherson, Kenneth E. ....Riverdale, MD
McPherson, King G. ....Nevada City, CA
McPherson, L. Lisa ....Lexington, SC
McPherson, Larry G., Jr. ....Tallahassee, FL
McPherson, Laurie J. ....New York, NY
McPherson Law Offices, Chtd.
Great Bend, KS
McPherson, Lawrence G. ....Washington, DC
McPherson, Lisa Adrian ....Wichita, KS
McPherson, Lori Marie ....Fredericksburg, VA
Mc Pherson, Malcolm A. ....San Antonio, TX
McPherson, Malcolm C. ....Freeport, IL
McPherson, Malcolm J., Jr. ....Lyndhurst, NJ
McPherson, Marena L. ....Chicago, IL
McPherson, Mark C. ....Seattle, WA
McPherson, Mark D. ....New York, NY
McPherson, Mark J. ....Secaucus, NJ
McPherson, Mary E. ....Los Angeles, CA
McPherson, Mary Jane ....Brooklyn, NY
McPherson, McPherson & Beam, P.A.
Clearwater, FL
New Port Richey, FL
McPherson & McPherson, P.L.L.P.
Coupeville, WA
McPherson, Michael L. ....Great Falls, MT
McPherson, Michael L., P.C.
Great Falls, MT
McPherson, Michelle Bagley ....Raleigh, NC
McPherson, Molly M. ....Coupeville, WA
McPherson & Monk, L.L.P., Law Offices of
Port Arthur, TX
McPherson, Nancy A. ....Walnut Creek, CA
McPherson, Nancy A. ....Tacoma, WA
McPherson, Patrick Dennis
Alexandria, VA
McPherson, Perry R. ....Port Arthur, TX
McPherson, Richard F. ....Staunton, VA
McPherson, Rick ....Carthage, TX
McPherson, Robert B. ....Evergreen, CO
McPherson, Robert D. ....Galveston, TX
McPherson, Robert D. ....Pampa, TX
McPherson, Robert Wayne ....Memphis, TN
McPherson & Rocamora, PLLC
Durham, NC
McPherson, Sandra L. ....Rancho Santa Fe, CA
McPherson & Schillesci ....New Orleans, LA
McPherson, Scott M.
New Port Richey, FL
McPherson, Sean K. ....Houston, TX
McPherson, Steven S. ....Glendive, MT
McPherson, Sybil Anne ....Albany, NY
McPherson, Theresa J. ....San Francisco, CA
McPherson, Thomas J. ....Philadelphia, PA
McPherson, Thomas P. ....Staunton, VA
McPherson, Thomas W. ....Minnetonka, MN
McPherson, Thomas W. ....Portland, OR
McPherson, Timothy C. ....Williamsburg, VA
McPherson, Tommy E. ....Pensacola, FL
McPherson, Vanzetta P. ....Montgomery, AL

McPherson, William B., III .... **Peoria, IL**
McPherson, William H. .... **Fairfield, CA**
McPherson, William H. .... Mission, TX
McPherson, William V., Jr. .... **Durham, NC**
McPheters, Brian L. .... **Champaign, IL**
McPheters & Dankin, P.C. .... **New York, NY**
McPheters, R. Douglas .... **New York, NY**
Mcphetres, Jaydee Bachman .... Golden, CO
McPhie, David A. .... Salt Lake City, UT
McPhie, Neil A. G. .... Richmond, VA
McPhilamy, W. Patrick, III
Beverly Hills, CA
McPhilliamy, John A. .... **Albertson, NY**
McPhillips, Bernard F. .... **Glens Falls, NY**
McPhillips, Charles V. .... **Norfolk, VA**
McPhillips, Fitzgerald & Cullum, L.L.P.
Glens Falls, NY
Saratoga Springs, NY
McPhillips, Frank D. .... **Birmingham, AL**
McPhillips, Frank L., Jr. .... **New York, NY**
McPhillips, Joseph W. .... **Glens Falls, NY**
McPhillips, Joseph W.
South Glens Falls, NY
McPhillips, Julian L., Jr.
Montgomery, AL
McPhillips, Lissette P. .... **New York, NY**
McPhillips, Michael D. .... Cleveland, OH
McPhillips, Michael J. .... Hastings, MI
McPhillips, Ronald D. .... Shelby, MT
McPhillips, Rose A. .... Mobile, AL
McPhillips, Sean Angus .... **Detroit, MI**
McPhillips, Shinbaum & Gill LLP
Hayneville, AL
Montgomery, AL
Prattville, AL
Tuskegee, AL
Wetumpka, AL
McPhillips, Susan D. .... **Englewood, CO**
McPhillips, Toni Marie .... **Hackensack, NJ**
McPike, Cynthia L. .... Charleston, IL
McPike, H. Roger .... Las Vegas, NV
McPike, H. Roger, Ltd., A Prof. Corp.
Las Vegas, NV
McPike, Joseph D., II .... **Indianapolis, IN**
McPike, Linda S. .... Milwaukee, WI
McPike, Richard H. .... **Plano, TX**
McPike, Timothy K. .... Evanston, IL
McPike, William R. .... Fresno, CA
McPoland, Paula A. .... Washington, DC
McPolin, James J. .... Bloomingdale, IL
McPolin, James J., Ltd. .... Bloomingdale, IL
McProud, Clarence H. .... **Nevada City, CA**
McQuade, Carolyn .... **New York, NY**
Mcquade, Christopher .... Framingham, MA
McQuade, Colin J. .... **Swanton, OH**
Whitehouse, OH
McQuade, Daniel P. .... Archbold, OH
Swanton, OH
Whitehouse, OH
McQuade, Francis J. .... Derby, CT
McQuade, Francis P. .... Newark, NJ
Mcquade, Francis Xavier .... Long Beach, NY
McQuade & Hite .... **Washington, DC**
Alexandria, VA
McQuade, James .... **New York, NY**
McQuade, James E. .... Department of Labor, Office of the Solicitor, GV
McQuade, John J., Jr. .... Boston, MA
McQuade, John P. .... Department of Commerce, Patent and Trademark Office, GV
McQuade, Joseph A. .... **Chicago, IL**
McQuade, Joseph L. .... Framingham, MA
McQuade, Joseph W. .... **Hartford, CT**
McQuade, Lawrence C. .... Boca Raton, FL
McQuade, Louise K. .... Carmel, NY
McQuade, Martha JP .... **Alexandria, VA**
McQuade, Michael .... Clifton, NJ
McQuade, Paul F. .... **Washington, DC**
McQuade, Rachel .... **Cleveland, OH**
McQuade, Richard B., Jr. .... Swanton, OH
McQuade, Ruth A. .... Department of Justice, Environment and Natural Resources Division, GV
McQuade, Terrence .... **Atlanta, GA**
McQuade, Thomas G. .... Omaha, NE
Mc Quade, Thomas Patrick .... Albany, NY
McQuade-Grisham, Sharon L. .... Boise, ID
McQuades, The, Co., L.P.A. .... Archbold, OH
Swanton, OH
Toledo, OH
Wauseon, OH
Whitehouse, OH
McQuaid, Douglas W. .... Seattle, WA
McQuaid, J. Dennis .... **San Francisco, CA**
McQuaid, Janet L. .... **Austin, TX**
McQuaid, John G. .... **White Plains, NY**
McQuaid, Metzler, Bedford & Van Zandt, L.L.P. .... **San Francisco, CA**
McQuaid, Michael J. .... **Burlingame, CA**
San Francisco, CA
McQuaid, Robert A., Jr. .... Reno, NV
McQuaide, Blasko, Schwartz, Fleming & Faulkner, Inc. .... Harrisburg, PA
State College, PA
McQuaide, Earl Graham .... San Diego, CA
McQuaide, John J., Jr. .... San Diego, CA
McQuaide, Rex William .... Johnstown, PA
McQuaide, Robert L. .... **Gettysburg, PA**
McQuaig, David H. .... Jacksonville, FL
McQuaig, Scott W. .... **Metairie, LA**
McQuaig & Stelly, A Professional Law Corporation .... **Metairie, LA**
New Orleans, LA
McQuain, Block, DeHardt & Rosenbloom, P.C.
Overland Park, KS
Kansas City, MO
McQuain, Mary .... **Charleston, WV**
McQuain, Robert R. .... Kansas City, MO

McQuality, Mark S. .... Dallas, TX
McQuarrie, Claude M., III .... **Houston, TX**
McQuarrie, Jennifer L. .... **Sacramento, CA**
McQuarrie, John D., Jr. .... **Princeton, NJ**
McQuarrie, Neil A. .... Bingham Farms, MI
McQuarrie, Patricia S. .... Kingwood, TX
McQuary, Ray J. .... Houston, TX
McQuary, Ray J., P.C. .... Houston, TX
McQuat, Edward J. .... Syracuse, NY
McQuater, Patricia A. .... **San Diego, CA**
McQuay, Sandra Sue .... **Boston, MA**
McQuay, William E. .... Fairfax, VA
McQueary, Mark L. .... **Springfield, MO**
McQueary & Powell .... Osawatomie, KS
McQueary, Willis H. .... Osawatomie, KS
McQueen, Aaron E. .... **Canton, OH**
McQueen, Albert B., Jr. .... **Lexington, KY**
McQueen, Andrew A. .... Beckley, WV
McQueen, Arthur H., Jr. .... Spartanburg, SC
McQueen, C. Richard .... **Atlanta, GA**
McQueen, Carolyn Taylor
Los Angeles, CA
McQueen, Edgar G., Jr.
Oklahoma City, OK
McQueen, Erin Marie .... Indianapolis, IN
McQueen, Geoffrey P. .... Pleasant Hill, CA
McQueen, Glen H., Jr. .... Decatur, GA
McQueen Harmon & Potter, A Legal Corporation .... **Charleston, WV**
McQueen, James A. .... **Costa Mesa, CA**
McQueen, James A., P.L.C.
Costa Mesa, CA
McQueen, James D., Jr. .... **Charleston, WV**
McQueen, Joetta Irene .... Thomasville, NC
McQueen, John J. .... Tulsa, OK
McQueen, John R. .... **Rochester, NY**
McQueen, Karen Soehnlen .... **Canton, OH**
Salem, OH
McQueen, Kathryn E. .... **San Francisco, CA**
McQueen, Kelly Murphy .... **Little Rock, AR**
McQueen, Kerry E. .... **Liberal, KS**
McQueen, L. Dru .... Tulsa, OK
McQueen Law Firm, P.C. .... Spartanburg, SC
McQueen, Mark E. .... **Omaha, NE**
McQueen, Martha E. .... **Franklin, IN**
McQueen, Mary L. .... Shelbyville, IN
McQueen, Matthew .... **Santa Fe, NM**
McQueen, Matthew G. .... **Chicago, IL**
McQueen, Michael D. .... **El Paso, TX**
McQueen, Michael L. .... Camarillo, CA
McQueen, Mindy H. .... **Los Angeles, CA**
McQueen, Robert K. .... Waukegan, IL
McQueen, Shirla R. .... **Liberal, KS**
McQueen, Tabitha D. .... Portsmouth, VA
McQueen, Thomas K. .... **Chicago, IL**
McQueen, William B. .... St. Petersburg, FL
McQueeney, James M. .... Malverne, NY
McQueeney, Jane Rye .... **Houston, TX**
McQueeney, John A. .... **Providence, RI**
McQueeney, John A., Sr. .... Riverside, RI
McQueeney, Kathleen .... Los Angeles, CA
McQueeney, Margaret .... New Rochelle, NY
McQueeney, Marijane .... Merrick, NY
McQueeney, Mary .... **West Hartford, CT**
McQueeney, Michael G. .... Houston, TX
McQueeney, Ryan J. .... Chicago, IL
McQueeney, William A. .... Wethersfield, CT
McQueeney-Lally, Mary Ellen
Providence, RI
McQueeny, Kathleen A. .... **Chicago, IL**
McQuerter, Kent L. .... San Diego, CA
McQuesten, Gary D. .... **Barre, VT**
McQueston, James K. .... Montpelier, VT
McQuiddy, Kirk D. .... **Richmond, VA**
McQuiddy, MerryM. .... Sylvan Lake, MI
McQuiddy, Richard Kirkland
Surfside Beach, SC
McQuide, Stephen .... Delmar, NY
McQuie, Walter D., III .... Cambridge, MD
McQuie, Walter D., Jr.
Montgomery City, MO
McQuigg, Jacqueline .... Westlake Village, CA
McQuigg, John .... **Tampa, FL**
McQuigg, John P. .... **Brunswick, GA**
McQuilkin, Francis D. .... Houston, TX
McQuilkin, Gail A. .... **Miami, FL**
McQuilkin, Scott A. .... **Boston, MA**
McQuillan, Arthur T. .... Garden City, NY
McQuillan, Arthur T. .... Johnstown, PA
McQuillan, Elizabeth A. .... **New York, NY**
McQuillan, Elizabeth M.
San Francisco, CA
McQuillan, J. Joseph .... **Omaha, NE**
McQuillan, James B. .... **St. Joseph, MI**
McQuillan, James D. .... **Merrillville, IN**
McQuillan, James M. .... **Ogallala, NE**
McQuillan, Jean M. .... Cleveland, OH
McQuillan, John F. .... Treasury Department, Internal Revenue Service, GV
McQuillan, John J. .... **Bay City, MI**
McQuillan, John P. .... **Merrillville, IN**
McQuillan, John Q. .... **New York, NY**
McQuillan, Kevin K. .... **Chicago, IL**
McQuillan, Martin .... **New Britain, CT**
McQuillan, Michael .... Black River Falls, WI
McQuillan, Michael J. .... **Ogallala, NE**
McQuillan, Michele .... **New York, NY**
McQuillan, Paul J. .... **New Britain, CT**
McQuillan, Peter J. .... Lawrence, MA
McQuillan, Phillip .... Springfield, IL
McQuillan, Raymond E. .... **Jackson, MI**
McQuillan, Richard C. .... Jackson, MI
McQuillan, Robert E. .... Parsippany, NJ
McQuillan, Robert F. .... Succasunna, NJ
McQuillan, Steenburg & McQuillan, P.C.
Ogallala, NE
McQuillan, Steven M. .... **Fresno, CA**
McQuillan, Thomas Higgins .... Alexandria, VA

McQuillan, William R. .... Troy, KS
McQuillen, Brian P. .... **Seattle, WA**
McQuillen, David K. .... Hudson, WI
McQuillen, Gordon E. .... Madison, WI
McQuillen, Mark S. .... Boston, MA
McQuillen, Mary .... **South Portland, ME**
McQuillen, Matthew G. .... Anamosa, IA
McQuillen, Michael G. .... **Chicago, IL**
McQuillen, Michael P. .... Gaithersburg, MD
McQuillen, Michael T. .... San Diego, CA
McQuillen, Patricia Adams
Washington, DC
McQuillen, William F.
Avon-By-The-Sea, NJ
McQuiller, Michael J. .... **San Francisco, CA**
McQuilling, Lenore E. .... **New York, NY**
McQuin, R. Scott .... Wellington, KS
McQuin, Randall L. .... Manhattan, KS
McQuinn, John C. .... Lincoln, NE
McQuinn, Rand .... **Washington, DC**
McQuinn, Urenthea .... Washington, DC
McQuiston, Cathie J. .... Washington, DC
McQuiston, David M. .... **Pittsburgh, PA**
McQuiston, Douglas I. .... Aurora, CO
McQuiston, Glenn R., Jr. .... Seattle, WA
McQuiston, Jeffrey R. .... Dayton, OH
McQuiston, John W., II .... **Memphis, TN**
McQuiston, Julian A. .... **New York, NY**
McQuiston, Raymer W. .... **New York, NY**
McQuiston, Robert E. .... **Philadelphia, PA**
Mcquiston, Todd R. .... **Chicago, IL**
McQuitty, Alissa A. .... **San Francisco, CA**
McQuitty, Jack H., Jr. .... **Denver, CO**
McQuoid, Ronald R. .... Coronado, CA
McQuoid, Thomas F. .... Clinton, MA
McQuown, H. Phillip .... Arroyo Grande, CA
McQuown, Richard C. .... **Columbus, OH**
McQuown, Russell P. .... Orange, CA
McRackan, Deena Smith .... Charleston, SC
McRae, Albert T. .... **Memphis, TN**
McRae, Ann Dalton .... San Antonio, TX
McRae, Anna M. .... **Delray Beach, FL**
McRae, Arnetta .... Wilmington, DE
McRae & Bisbee, LLP .... **Atlanta, GA**
McRae, Bonnie L. .... New Orleans, LA
McRae, Christopher T. .... **Tallahassee, FL**
McRae, Colin D. .... San Francisco, CA
McRae, Cori Fisher .... **Newark, NJ**
McRae, C. R. .... Jackson, MS
McRae, Dana M. .... Santa Cruz, CA
McRae, Daniel M. .... **Atlanta, GA**
McRae, David F. .... **Lillington, NC**
McRae, David K. .... **Washington, DC**
McRae, Don J. .... **Kewanee, IL**
McRae, Don J., and Associates
Kewanee, IL
McRae, Duncan L. .... Hope, AR
Prescott, AR
McRae, Earl M., Jr. .... Douglas, GA
McRae, Ernest .... Wichita, KS
McRae, F. E., III .... **West Point, MS**
McRae, Ferrill D. .... Mobile, AL
McRae, Ginger S. .... **Atlanta, GA**
McRae, Hamilton E., III .... Phoenix, AZ
McRae, James B. .... Department of Energy, Office of the General Counsel, GV
McRae, James O. .... Houston, TX
McRae, James W. .... **Atlanta, GA**
McRae, Jennifer Herndon .... Orlando, FL
McRae, John .... Spokane, WA
McRae, John A., Jr. .... Kinston, NC
McRae, Joseph P. .... **Syracuse, NY**
McRae, Karen E. .... **Garland, TX**
McRae, Karen E., P.C. .... **Garland, TX**
McRae, Karen S. .... Kalispell, MT
McRae, Kenneth M. .... Lawrence, KS
McRae, Lauren Blair .... **Morristown, NJ**
McRae, Leander E. .... Pittsburgh, PA
McRae, Loretta M. .... San Francisco, CA
McRae, Mara .... **Atlanta, GA**
McRae, Marcellus Antonio
Los Angeles, CA
McRae, Margie .... Oakland, CA
McRae & McRae, P.A. .... Bemidji, MN
McRae & Metcalf, P.A. .... **Tallahassee, FL**
McRae, Michael D. .... **Cedartown, GA**
McRae, Mitchell T. .... **Delray Beach, FL**
McRae, Mitchell T., P.A. .... **Boca Raton, FL**
Delray Beach, FL
McRae, Nora F. Stone .... Jackson, MS
McRae, Sheldon D., Jr. .... Bemidji, MN
McRae, Stephanie A. .... **Phoenix, AZ**
McRae, Terry S. .... Cairo, GA
McRae, Thomas A. T. .... **San Antonio, TX**
McRae, W. Philip .... Laurinburg, NC
McRae, William .... **New York, NY**
McRae, William Bowen, Jr.
Baton Rouge, LA
McRae, William H. .... Dallas, TX
McRae, William H., P.C. .... Dallas, TX
McRaith, Michael T. .... **Chicago, IL**
McRaney, Trace D. .... **Gulfport, MS**
McRaven, J. Dixson .... **Macomb, IL**
McRay, Charles E. .... Fort Smith, AR
McRay, Gary J. .... **Lansing, MI**
McRay, Jack L. .... **Orlando, FL**
McRay, K. Heather .... **New York, NY**
McRea, Terrence C. .... **Dallas, TX**
McReddie, Maria I. Boyesen .... **Miami, FL**
McRee, George W. .... Bristol, TN
McRee, J. David .... Milledgeville, GA
McRee, Ronald A. .... Haileyville, OK
McReynolds, Bernice
Bingham Farms, MI
McReynolds, Charles L. .... Dallas, TX
McReynolds, Don M. .... Rosanky, TX
McReynolds, Gregg C. .... **Denver, CO**
McReynolds, Gregg C., P.C. .... **Denver, CO**

McReynolds, H. Lewis .... **Houston, TX**
McReynolds, Holly L. .... **Philadelphia, PA**
McReynolds, John A., Jr. .... **Knoxville, TN**
McReynolds, John W. .... New York, NY
McReynolds, John W. .... **Dallas, TX**
McReynolds, Joseph B. .... Austin, TX
McReynolds, Joseph L. .... **New Orleans, LA**
McReynolds, Kevin S.
San Luis Obispo, CA
McReynolds, Larry S. .... **Atlanta, GA**
McReynolds, Lelan D. .... Brookston, IN
McReynolds, Linda K. .... Tempe, AZ
McReynolds, Mary A. .... **Washington, DC**
McReynolds, Mary A., P.C.
Washington, DC
McReynolds, Michael L. .... **San Antonio, TX**
McReynolds, Michael M. .... Dallas, TX
McReynolds, Michael P. .... **Minneapolis, MN**
McReynolds, Richard W. .... Oxnard, CA
McReynolds, Roland G. .... Durham, NC
McReynolds, S. Victoria .... Southaven, MS
McReynolds, Sherry C. .... **Wilmington, DE**
McReynolds, Timothy J. .... Omaha, NE
McRight, Edward L., Jr. .... Birmingham, AL
McRight, Frank .... **Huntsville, AL**
Mobile, AL
McRight, Jackson, Myrick & Moore, L.L.C.
Mobile, AL
McRill, Emery B. .... **Baltimore, MD**
McRobbie, Michael D. .... **Kansas City, MO**
McRoberts, Aleathea H.
West Palm Beach, FL
McRoberts & Associates, P.C.
Kansas City, MO
McRoberts, C. Eugene, Jr. .... **Jackson, MS**
McRoberts, Glenn S. .... San Diego, CA
McRoberts, James W. .... Belleville, IL
McRoberts, M. Randall .... **Boston, MA**
Kansas City, MO
McRoberts, Paul D. .... Minneapolis, MN
McRoberts, Robert F., Jr. .... Stuart, FL
McRoberts, Robert H., Jr. .... **St. Louis, MO**
McRoberts & Roberts, L.L.P. .... **Boston, MA**
McRoberts, Roger L., Jr. .... Lubbock, TX
McRoberts, Teresa K. .... Richmond, VA
McRobie, Henry L. .... Baltimore, MD
McRoble, Fred S. .... Purchase, NY
McRorey, Robert E. .... Olathe, KS
McRorie, Raymond C. .... Fayetteville, NC
McRorie, William E. .... **Lynchburg, VA**
McRory, Rick .... **Houston, TX**
McRoskey, Barbara L. .... Encinitas, CA
McRoss, Loren H. .... **San Francisco, CA**
McRostie, James J. .... Portland, OR
McRoy, Bruce W. .... **Santa Barbara, CA**
McRoy, Kevin P. .... **Raynham, MA**
McSally, Mark A. .... **Providence, RI**
McSally, Mary Kaitlin .... **Washington, DC**
McSeveney, Robert B. C. .... Bellevue, WA
McShan, J. Tyler, IV .... McShan, AL
McShan, Richard D. .... Amite, LA
McShane, Antony J. .... **Chicago, IL**
McShane & Bowie, P.L.C.
Grand Rapids, MI
McShane, Brandy M. .... **Springfield, MO**
McShane, Breitfeller & Witten
Columbus, OH
McShane, Brian J. .... San Jose, CA
McShane, Bruce W. .... **New York, NY**
McShane, Chad M. .... Sioux City, IA
McShane, Christopher M.
Jacksonville, FL
McShane, Davis & Hance, L.L.P.
Dallas, TX
McShane, Edward J., Jr. .... Kansas City, MO
McShane, Eugene F. .... **Columbus, OH**
McShane, Francis X. .... Summit, NJ
McShane, James A. .... **Wilmington, DE**
McShane, James E. .... Edison, NJ
McShane, James F. .... **Los Angeles, CA**
McShane, James F. .... New York, NY
McShane, Joanne T. .... Folsom, CA
McShane, John B. .... New York, NY
McShane, John David .... Berwyn, IL
McShane, John Q. .... Minneapolis, MN
McShane, John V. .... **Dallas, TX**
McShane, Joseph Patrick, III
Cherry Hill, NJ
McShane, Kathleen T. .... El Cerrito, CA
McShane, Kevin .... Indianapolis, IN
McShane, Kevin J. .... Los Angeles, CA
McShane, Leo .... Miami, FL
McShane, Leslie J. .... Los Angeles, CA
McShane, Mary .... **New York, NY**
McShane, Maura B. .... St. Louis, MO
McShane, Michael .... **San Jose, CA**
McShane, Michael .... Portland, OR
McShane, Michael B.
Department of the Air Force, Office of the Judge Advocate General, GV
McShane, Michael J. .... Downingtown, PA
McShane, Michael O. .... Montpelier, VT
McShane, Michael Patrick .... San Diego, CA
McShane, Michele L. .... **El Segundo, CA**
McShane, Neal T. .... Orlando, FL
McShane, Neal T., P.A. .... Orlando, FL
McShane, Patrick J. .... **New Orleans, LA**
McShane, Raymond D. .... Dallas, TX
McShane, Schnack & Cheitlin, Professional Corporation .... Walnut Creek, CA
McShane, Shawn M. .... Van Nuys, CA
McShane, Stephanie G. .... **New Orleans, LA**
McShane, Terrence M. .... **Washington, DC**
McShane, Thomas A. .... New York, NY
McShane, William E. .... **Wilmington, DE**
McSharar, Janet A. .... **Indianapolis, IN**
McSharry, James M. .... San Leandro, CA
McShea, David F. .... **Seattle, WA**

McWilliams Law Firm, The, P.C.
Marietta, GA
McWilliams, Leslie B. ....Chattanooga, TN
Mc Williams, Lisa R. ....Kansas City, MO
McWilliams, Marilee M.
Hendersonville, TN
McWilliams, Marilyn W. ....Denver, CO
McWilliams, Marion L. ....Oakland, CA
McWilliams, Martin C., Jr. ......Columbia, SC
McWilliams, Mary Martha ......Birmingham, AL
McWilliams & McWilliams ....Indianola, MS
McWilliams Mediation Group Ltd.
Denver, CO
McWilliams, Melvin S. ....Lansing, MI
McWilliams, Melvin S., P.C. ....Lansing, MI
McWilliams, Michael E. ....Jackson, MS
McWilliams, Mike C. ....Dallas, TX
McWilliams, O'Kelly E., III
Washington, DC
McWilliams, Paul A. ....Palatine, IL
McWilliams, Paul R. ....Beaumont, TX
McWilliams, Richard D. ....Spokane, WA
McWilliams, Robert A. ....Chicago, IL
McWilliams, Robert E., Jr. ....St. Louis, MO
McWilliams, Robert H. ....Denver, CO
McWilliams, Robert H., Jr. ....Wheeling, WV
McWilliams, Robert P. ....Philadelphia, PA
McWilliams, Robert R. ....Rockford, IL
McWilliams, Sarah M. ....Washington, DC
McWilliams, Sharon L. ....Sacramento, CA
McWilliams, Stanley R. ....McKinney, TX
McWilliams, Susan Pedrick
Columbia, SC
McWilliams & Thompson, A Professional Corporation ....McKinney, TX
McWilliams, Timothy ....Los Angeles, CA
McWilliams, Valerie Dykstra .....Champaign, IL
McWilliams, W. Kelly ....Media, PA
McWilliams, W.James ....Annapolis, MD
McWilson, Frank Boyd ....West Mifflin, PA
McWinn, Jere D. ....Ocala, FL
McZier, Ruby B. ....Washington, DC
McZinc, Kenneth ....New York, NY
M De La Cerna, Patricia ....Chicago, IL
Meabe, Gary J. ....Portland, OR
Meacham, Barbara J. ......Department of Justice, Civil Rights Division, GV
Meacham, Betsy ....Little Rock, AR
Meacham, Catherine M. ....Dallas, TX
Meacham, Chad E. ....Lockhart, TX
Meacham, Charles Edward ....Houston, TX
Meacham, Christopher L. ......Columbus, GA
Meacham, Clifford L. ....Chicago, IL
Meacham, Colquitt L. ....Somerville, MA
Meacham, Darren J. ....Boise, ID
Meacham & Decker, PLLC
Idaho Falls, ID
Meacham, Denver W., II ....Clinton, OK
Meacham, Donald D. ....Voorheesville, NY
Meacham, Earley & Jones, P.C.
Phenix City, AL
Columbus, GA
Hamilton, GA
Meacham, Eddie H. ....Carthage, NC
Pinehurst, NC
Meacham, Ellis K. ....Chattanooga, TN
Meacham, Gregory P. ....Idaho Falls, ID
Meacham, Holland ....Elk City, OK
Meacham, Jeannette C. ....Washington, DC
Meacham, John R. ....Kansas City, MO
Meacham, Keith G. ....Greenville, SC
Meacham, Madeline J. ....Boulder, CO
Meacham, Malenda Harris ....Hernando, MS
Meacham, Margie W. ....Rawlins, WY
Meacham, Marianne ....Boston, MA
Meacham & Meacham, A Professional Corporation ....Clinton, OK
Meacham, Michael R. ....Coventry, CT
Wichita, KS
Meacham, Nancy K. ....Wichita, KS
Meacham, Norma ....Albany, NY
Meacham, Owen Thomas ......Charlestown, MA
Meacham, Patrick M. ....Raleigh, NC
Meacham, Randolph S. ....Clinton, OK
Meacham, Randolph S., P.C. ....Clinton, OK
Meacham, Robert C.
Fort Lauderdale, FL
Meacham, Robert E. ....Kansas City, MO
Meacham, Ruth A. ....Toledo, OH
Meacham, Scott A. ....Elk City, OK
Meacham, Shelley R. ....Los Angeles, CA
Meacham, Steve D. ....Seattle, WA
Meacham, Thomas E. ....Anchorage, AK
Meacham, Thornton J., Jr. ....St. Albans, NY
Meacham, Timothy E. ....Florence, SC
Meacham, William J. ....Edwardsville, IL
Meachum, Bruce J. ....Danville, IL
Meachum, Clyde ....Danville, IL
Meachum, Daniel R. ....Media, PA
Meachum, Debra J. ....Denver, CO
Meachum, H. Wayne ....Dallas, TX
Meachum, Hubert J. ....Batesville, AR
Meachum, John W. ....Oak Brook, IL
Meachum, Lauren K. ....Chicago, IL
Meachum & Meachum ....Danville, IL
Meachum, Robert Francis ....Juneau, AK
Meachum, Thomas M. ....Columbia, MD
Mead, Albert E., Jr. ....Pasadena, CA
Mead, Alice N. ....Irvine, CA
Mead, Alice P. ....San Francisco, CA
Mead, Andrew M. ....Bangor, ME
Mead, Andrew T. ....San Francisco, CA
Mead & Associates ....Glendale, AZ
Peoria, AZ
Mead & Bane ....Yardley, PA
Mead, Brian S. ....Quinebaug, CT
Mead, Bromley & Bishop ....Stamford, CT
Mead, Caroline H. ....San Francisco, CA
Mead, Charles B. ....Chelmsford, MA
Mead, Christopher B. ....Washington, DC
Mead, Christopher J. ....San Francisco, CA
Mead, Dale C. ....San Jose, CA
Mead, Daniel D. ....Frisco, CO
Mead, David A. ....Washington, DC
Mead, David E. ....Los Angeles, CA
Mead, Earl A. ....Yardley, PA
Mead, Edward Scott ....New York, NY
Mead, Elaine Lytle ....Harrisburg, PA
Mead, Eleanor T. ....Goodlettsville, TN
Mead, Ellen P. ....Sherman Oaks, CA
Mead, Frank F., III ....Irvine, CA
Mead, George E., III ....Watertown, NY
Mead, George R., II ....Pensacola, FL
Mead, George W. ....Portland, OR
Mead, Gilbert D. ....Washington, DC
Mead, H. Lawson ....Laguna Beach, CA
Mead, Harold F. ....Boston, MA
Mead, Harry L., Jr. ....Tampa, FL
Mead, Hecht, Conklin & Gallagher
New York, NY
White Plains, NY
Mead, Howard N. ....Atlanta, GA
Mead, Hudson ....Grosse Pointe Park, MI
Mead, Hudson A. ....Birmingham, MI
Mead, John H. ....Cape May, NJ
Mead, John H., A Professional Corporation
Cape May, NJ
Mead, John J. ....Erie, PA
Mead, John Michael ....Fort Wayne, IN
Indianapolis, IN
Mead, John P. ....New York, NY
Mead, John T. ....Chicago, IL
Mead, John W. ....Salem, IN
Mead, Kathy L. ....Glendale, MO
Mead, Kenneth M.
Department of Transportation, GV
Mead, Kristen K. ....Boston, MA
Mead, Kyle J. ....Topeka, KS
Mead, La Rue T. ....Ferndale, MI
Mead, Leon F., II ....Los Angeles, CA
Mead, Leslie S. ....Arlington, VA
Mead, Linda J. ....West Hartford, CT
Mead, Lisa ....Woodland Hills, CA
Mead, Lisa Louise ....Boston, MA
Mead, Malcolm S. ....Denver, CO
Mead, Martin Blase ....Grand Rapids, MI
Mead, Martin C. ....Los Angeles, CA
Mead, Mary Sherrill ....Piedmont, CA
Mead, Matthew R. ....Albany, NY
Mead, Maxine M. ....Baltimore, MD
Mead and Mead ....Irvine, CA
Mead, Mead & Clark, P.C. ....Salem, IN
Mead, Michael Wm ....Fort Walton Beach, FL
Mead, Michael Wm, P.A.
Fort Walton Beach, FL
Mead, Norman W. ....Brant Lake, NY
Mead, Penfield C. ....New Canaan, CT
Mead, Perry B. ....Omaha, NE
Mead, Randall A. ....Springfield, IL
Mead, Robert J. ....Milford, CT
Mead, Robert W., Jr. ....Orlando, FL
Mead, Roger B. ....Los Angeles, CA
San Francisco, CA
Mead, Rosanne M. ....Des Moines, IA
Mead, Russell B. ....St. Louis, MO
Mead, Russell B., P.C. ....St. Louis, MO
Mead, Sean M. ....Salem, IN
Mead, Slade ....McLean, VA
Mead, Stephen B. ....Chicago, IL
Mead, Susan ....Dallas, TX
Mead, Susanah M. ....Indianapolis, IN
Mead, Terrance C. ....Glendale, AZ
Mead, Terry M. ....San Francisco, CA
Mead, Victor O. ....Winter Park, FL
Mead, Wayland M. ....New York, NY
Mead, Wendy M. ....Sutton, MA
Mead, William C., Jr. ....Cherry Hill, NJ
Mead, William G. ....New York, NY
Meade, Albert ....Los Angeles, CA
Meade, Alissa A. ....New York, NY
Meade, Barry ....Newark, NJ
New York, NY
Meade, Brodovsky, Aiken, Jacobsen & Hine, A Limited Liability Partnership
Sacramento, CA
Meade, Charles A. ....Portsmouth, NH
Meade, Christopher J. ....New York, NY
Meade, Colleen A. ....Hicksville, NY
Meade, David E. ....House of Representatives, Office of Legislative Counsel, GV
Meade, David L. ....Charleston, WV
Meade, Dawn R. ....Houston, TX
Meade, Don C. ....Louisville, KY
Meade, Donald F. ......Whitehouse Station, NJ
Meade, Evan, & Associates
Johnson City, TN
Meade, G. Kirk ....Scottsbluff, NE
Meade, Gary N., Jr. ....Nashville, TN
Meade, Gary S. ....Harrisburg, PA
Meade, J. Michael ....Ann Arbor, MI
Meade, James B. ....Tacoma, WA
Meade, James D. ....New York, NY
Meade, James F. ....Santa Ana, CA
Meade, James G. ....Great Neck, NY
Meade, James M. ....West Des Moines, IA
Meade, James P., Jr. ....Chicago, IL
Meade, Jerome J. ....Port Washington, NY
Meade, John C. ....Indianapolis, IN
Meade, John P. ....Washington, DC
Meade, Karen Ellen ....Denver, CO
Meade, Karen Kaye ....Cleveland, OH
Meade, Keith W. ....Salt Lake City, UT
Meade, Kenneth R. ....Washington, DC
Meade, Kevin T. ....Irvine, CA
Meade, Kris David ....Washington, DC
Meade, K. T., Jr. ....Oklahoma City, OK
Meade, Les A. ....Lafayette, IN
Meade, Lesley A. ....Lafayette, IN
Meade, Marcia M. ....Spokane, WA
Meade, Marguerite E. ....El Cerrito, CA
Meade, Mary S. ....Vienna, VA
Meade, Matthew H. ....Pittsburgh, PA
Meade, Michael M. ....Sacramento, CA
Meade, Nancy Beth ....Berkeley, CA
Meade, Nikelle Susanne ....Austin, TX
Meade, Norma J. ....Marshalltown, IA
Meade, Paul D. ....Hartford, CT
Meade, Philip R. ....Seattle, WA
Meade, Richard E. ....Newark, NJ
Meade, Robert D. ....White Plains, NY
Meade, Roger D. ....Baltimore, MD
Meade, Russell A. ....Venice, FL
Meade, Ryan D. ....Chicago, IL
Meade, Steven A. ....Newport News, VA
Meade, Tammy H. ....Nashville, TN
Meade, Teri L. ....Chicago, IL
Des Plaines, IL
Meade, Theodore C., III ....Midland, TX
Meade, Thomas P. ....Palmyra, MO
Meade, Timothy ....Orland Park, IL
Meade, Timothy Ireland
Fort Walton Beach, FL
Meade, Tyler Roberts ....San Francisco, CA
Meade, Victoria L. ....Des Moines, IA
Meade, W. Paul ....Amherst, MA
Meade, William J. ....Boston, MA
Meade-Hood, Kimberly E.
New Windsor, NY
Meaden, John A., III ....Concord, CA
Meaden, Laura A. ....Pittsburgh, PA
Meaden, Mary B. ....Boston, MA
Meader, Arthur L., III ....San Francisco, CA
Meader, George W. ....Sun City, AZ
Meader, Jean H. ....Pearl River, NY
Meader, John D. ....Albany, NY
Meader, John L. ....Vancouver, WA
Meader, Raymond E. ....Joliet, IL
Meader, Robert E. ....Ann Arbor, MI
Meaders, Donald W. ....Los Angeles, CA
Meaders, Duckworth & Moore
New York, NY
Meaders, Gerald, Jr. ....Tampa, FL
Meaders, Kim M. ....Dallas, TX
Meaders, Kurt W. ....Dallas, TX
Meaders, Leigh M. ....New York, NY
Meaders, Trent S. ....Fort Worth, TX
Meaders, William A., Jr.
Salt Lake City, UT
Meadlock, William A., (P.C.) ......Eastpointe, MI
Meadoff, Harold L. ....Denver, CO
Meadoff, Marilyn T. ....Denver, CO
Meador, Carl E. ....Akron, OH
Meador, Charles R., Jr.
Fort Myers Beach, FL
Meador, Christina S. ....Atlanta, GA
Meador, Chrys ....Plano, TX
Meador, Cindy A. ....Galveston, TX
Meador & Crump ....Cleveland, MS
Rosedale, MS
Meador, Dan M. ....Austin, TX
Meador, Daniel J. ....Charlottesville, VA
Meador, Daniel J., Jr. ....Charlottesville, VA
Meador, Edwin L. ....Dallas, TX
Meador, H. B., Jr. ....Martinsville, VA
Meador, Joe ....San Antonio, TX
Meador, Joe, Inc., Law Offices of
San Antonio, TX
Meador, Lindsey C. ....Cleveland, MS
Meador & Lowrey ....Akron, OH
Meador, Mark D. ....Atlanta, GA
Meador, Melinda ....Knoxville, TN
Meador, Nita ....Brownwood, TX
Meador, Patricia T.
Research Triangle Park, NC
Meador, Paul M. ....Las Vegas, NV
Meador, Robert B., II ....Miami, FL
Meador, Ross D. ....San Francisco, CA
Meador, Saml. J. ....Houston, TX
Meador, Shawn B ....Reno, NV
Meador, Stephen L. ....El Paso, TX
Meador, Terrance A. ....San Diego, CA
Meador, Vernon T., III ....Los Angeles, CA
Meadors, Allen ....Atlanta, GA
Meadors, Alyce T. ....Columbus, IN
Meadors, David C. ....Greenwood, MS
Meadors, E. Drexel ....West Point, GA
Meadors, Gayle M. ....Chicago, IL
Meadors, George H. ....Homer, LA
Meadors, Karen M. ....McKinney, TX
Meadough, Erica ....Houston, TX
Meadow, Alvin H. ....Mamaroneck, NY
Meadow, Barry L. ....Miami, FL
Meadow, Cary M. ....Malibu, CA
Meadow, Claire S. ....Larchmont, NY
Meadow, Frank S. ....Waterbury, CT
Meadow, Judith L. ....Los Angeles, CA
Meadow, Landon W. ....Clarksville, TN
Meadow, Myron J. ....New York, NY
Meadow, Peter B. ....Teaneck, NJ
Woodbourne, NY
Meadow, Robin ....Beverly Hills, CA
Meadow, Sam ....Rockville, MD
Meadow, Stephen T. ....Phoenix, AZ
Meadow, Stephen T., P.C. ....Phoenix, AZ
Meadowbrook, Paul B. ....Salem, OR
Meadowcraft, Francis X. ....Bel Air, MD
Meadowcroft, Reynar, Jr. ....Naperville, IL
Meadows, Ann M. ....Jacksonville, FL
Meadows, Arthur Lee, Jr. ....Atlanta, GA
Meadows, Arthur Lee, Jr., P.C. ....Atlanta, GA
Meadows, Benjamin J., III
United States Postal Service, Law Department, GV
Meadows, Brian M. ....Los Angeles, CA
Santa Ana, CA
Meadows, Bruce R. ....Helena, MT
Meadows, Charles D. ....Pleasant Ridge, MI
Meadows, Charles M., Jr. ....Dallas, TX
Meadows, Craig L. ....Boise, ID
Meadows, Curtis W., Jr. ....Dallas, TX
Meadows, Daniel N. ....Cocoa, FL
Meadows, David J. ....Oakland, CA
Meadows, David M. ....Baltimore, MD
Meadows, David W. ....Los Angeles, CA
Meadows, Debra J. ....Edwardsville, IL
Meadows, E. Richard, Jr. ....Ottumwa, IA
Meadows, Elizabeth K. B. ....Knoxville, TN
Meadows, Elmer O. ....Birmingham, AL
Meadows, Frank P., Jr.
Rocky Mount, NC
Meadows & Futch, P.C. ....Jonesboro, GA
Stockbridge, GA
Meadows, Gary A. ....Edwardsville, IL
Meadows, Gregory D. ....Knoxville, TN
Meadows, Ichter & Trigg, P.C. A Professional Corporation ....Atlanta, GA
Meadows, James Dartlin (Dart)
Atlanta, GA
Meadows, James E. ....Atlanta, GA
Meadows, James H. ....Washington, DC
Meadows, Jan ....Norman, OK
Meadows, Jed ....Branson, MO
Springfield, MO
Meadows, Jerry A. ....Dayton, OH
Meadows, Joe N. ....Midland, TX
Meadows, John A. ....Winston-Salem, NC
Meadows, John A., P.A.
Winston-Salem, NC
Meadows, John B. ....Austin, TX
Meadows, John F. ....San Francisco, CA
Meadows, John Lyons ....Memphis, TN
Meadows, Joseph R. ....Gulfport, MS
Meadows, Kathryn B.
Hermosa Beach, CA
Meadows, Kenneth D. ....Phoenix, AZ
Meadows, Laura Lou ....New York, NY
Meadows, Lee ....Key West, FL
Tallahassee, FL
Meadows, Mark S. ....Lansing, MI
Meadows, Mary E. ....Dayton, OH
Meadows, Mary T. ....Oberlin, OH
Meadows, Michael D. ....Walnut Creek, CA
Meadows, Owens, Collier, Reed, Cousins & Blau, L.L.P. ....Dallas, TX
Meadows, Patricia F. ....Fort Worth, TX
Meadows, Peter J.
Department Of Veterans Affairs, Office of the General Counsel, GV
Winter Park, FL
Meadows, Philip A. ....Boyd, WI
Meadows, Philip E. ....Harrison, AR
Meadows, Richard N. ....Montgomery, AL
Meadows Riley Law Firm
Bay St. Louis, MS
Biloxi, MS
Gulfport, MS
Hattiesburg, MS
Jackson, MS
Pascagoula, MS
Meadows, Robert E. ....Houston, TX
Meadows, Robert L. ....Bakersfield, CA
Meadows, Robert T., III ....Opelika, AL
Meadows, Robyn L. ....Wilmington, DE
Meadows, Rod G. ....Stockbridge, GA
Meadows, Roger R. ....Pomona, CA
Meadows, Ronald C. ....Lubbock, TX
Meadows, Sheree ....Buffalo, NY
Meadows, Sidney R. ....McAllen, TX
Meadows, Stanley H. ....Chicago, IL
Meadows, Steven F. ....Houston, TX
Meadows, Susan K. ....San Francisco, CA
Meadows, Ted G. ....Birmingham, AL
Meadows, Victoria ....Shelton, WA
Meadows, Virgil D., (P.C.)
Colorado Springs, CO
Meadows & Welch ....Austin, TX
Meadows, William A. ....Cleveland, OH
Meadows, William A., Jr. ....Miami, FL
Meadows, William C. ....Sentinel, OK
Meadows, William C., Inc. ....Sentinel, OK
Meadows, William H., III ....Lexington, KY
Meads, Margaret Bunn ....Little Rock, AR
Meads & Sampson ....San Diego, CA
Meads, Stephen G. ....Farmington Hills, MI
Meads, Thomas W. ....San Diego, CA
Meadville, Steven A. ....Encino, CA
Meadvin, Michael M. ....Harrison, NY
Meadway, Jay K. ....Philadelphia, PA
Meagher, Andrew C. J. ....Worcester, MA
Meagher, Anne LaLonde ....Portland, OR
Meagher, Anthony L. ....Baltimore, MD
Meagher, Bruce J. ....Iola, WI
Meagher, Cynthia K. ....Southfield, MI
Meagher, Daniel J., Jr. ....San Francisco, CA
Meagher, Denise L. ....Worcester, MA
Meagher, Dermot ....Boston, MA
Meagher, Edward C. ....Uniondale, NY
Meagher, Ellen M. ....Boston, MA
Meagher, Erin D. ....Tinton Falls, NJ
Meagher, Francis J. ....Baltimore, MD
Meagher, Frederick J. ....Binghamton, NY
Meagher, Frederick J., Jr. ....Binghamton, NY
Montrose, PA
Meagher & Geer, P.L.L.P.
Minneapolis, MN
Meagher, Georgia H. ....San Francisco, CA
Meagher, J. Bradley ....Everett, WA
Meagher, J. Christopher ....New York, NY
Meagher, J. Kenneth ....Cincinnati, OH
Meagher, J. Patrick ....Washington, DC
Meagher, John E. ....Miami, FL

Meagher, John H. ... Worcester, MA
Meagher, John M. ... Dayton, OH
Meagher, Joseph ... Everett, WA
Meagher, Joseph B. ... Endicott, NY
Meagher, Kathleen A. ... Clearwater, FL
Meagher, Kathleen M. ... San Francisco, CA
Meagher, Kenneth P. ... New York, NY
Meagher, Kieran B. ... Boston, MA
Meagher, Laura C. ... Cleveland, OH
Meagher, Linda Vogt ... Milwaukee, WI
Meagher, Mark J. ... Denver, CO
Meagher & Meagher ... Binghamton, NY
Montrose, PA
Meagher, Michael J. ... Boston, MA
Meagher, Michael J. ... Stockbridge, MA
Meagher, Niall P. ... Washington, DC
Meagher, Patricia A. ... San Francisco, CA
Meagher, Robert F. ... Somerville, MA
Meagher, Robert J. ... Manchester, NH
Meagher, Roger K. ... Plano, TX
Meagher, Stephen L. ... San Francisco, CA
Meagher, Stephen W. ... Columbus, OH
Meagher, Teresa Marie ... Olathe, KS
Meagher, Thomas F. ... Bronxville, NY
Meagher, Thomas F. ... New York, NY
Meagher, Thomas R. ... Lansing, MI
Meagher, Thomas W. ... Somerset, NJ
Meagher, Timothy J. ... Lexington, MA
Meagher, Virginia ... Jackson, KY
Meagher, Walter L., Jr. ... Syracuse, NY
Meagher, William D. ... Bingham Farms, MI
Meagher, William H. ... Princeton, NJ
Meagher-Leonard, Rosemary Jane
San Diego, CA
Meagher-Walker, Cynthia S.
Los Angeles, CA
Meagle, Shay E. ... Albuquerque, NM
Meagley, James G. ... Buffalo, NY
Meaglia, Richard ... Monrovia, CA
Meaher, Augustine, III ... Mobile, AL
Meaher, Augustine, III, P.C. ... Mobile, AL
Meaker, Dennis J. ... Nashville, TN
Meakim, Dennis R. ... Abington, PA
Meakin, Christopher H. ... Houston, TX
Meal, Douglas H. ... Boston, MA
Meale, Robert E. ... Tallahassee, FL
Mealer, Jere E. ... Fresno, CA
Mealey, Catherine ... Laramie, WY
Mealey, Ronald P. ... Totowa, NJ
Mealey, Thomas F. ... Evanston, WY
Mealey-Lohmann, Linda M.
Minneapolis, MN
Mealman, William E. ... Kansas City, MO
Mealor, Ronald E. ... Sacramento, CA
Meals, Bryan K. ... Norfolk, VA
Meals, Cameron S. ... Norfolk, VA
Meals, Robert N. ... Langley, WA
Seattle, WA
Meals, Robert N., P.L.L.C. ... Langley, WA
Seattle, WA
Mealy, Chris A. ... Georgetown, TX
Mealy & Kelly, S.C. ... Whitewater, WI
Mealy, Melanie L. ... Alexandria, VA
Mealy, Michael J. ... Whitewater, WI
Mealy, Terrence L. ... Muscatine, IA
Meamber, Richard B. ... Palo Alto, CA
Chicago, IL
Meana, Ricardo ... Tampa, FL
Meana, Ricardo ... Wimauma, FL
Meanes, Pamela J. ... St. Louis, MO
Meaney, Daniel J., Jr. ... Santa Barbara, CA
Meaney, Donald C. ... Redding, CA
Meaney, Donald C. ... Washington, DC
Meaney, Francis X. ... Washington, DC
Boston, MA
Meaney, James A.
Christiansted, St. Croix, VI
Meaney, James A., III ... Chattanooga, TN
Meaney, John C. ... Portland, OR
Meaney, Jon C. ... Portland, OR
Meaney, Joseph R. ... Phoenix, AZ
Meaney, Joseph V., Jr. ... Hartford, CT
Meaney, Kathleen W. ... Boston, MA
Meaney, Martin Daniel ... Mineola, NY
Meaney, Maryellen ... Minneapolis, MN
Meaney, Michael J. ... Cleveland, OH
Meaney, Susan C. ... Bronxville, NY
Meaney, Suzanne W. ... Ludlow, VT
Meaney, Thomas J. ... Dallas, TX
Meaney, Thomas P., Jr. ... Cleveland, OH
Meaney, William M. ... San Diego, CA
Meaney, William M. ... Jeffersontown, KY
Meanix, Richard E. ... West Chester, PA
Meanix, William H., Jr. ... Tryon, NC
Meanor, H. Curtis ... Newark, NJ
Means, Bichimer, Burkholder & Baker Co., L.P.A. ... Cleveland, OH
Columbus, OH
Means, Brenda ... Bothell, WA
Means, Brian R. ... Sacramento, CA
Means, Charles M. ... Pittsburgh, PA
Means, David B., III ... Mansfield, LA
Means, Deborah Glover ... Dallas, TX
Means, Donald S. ... Seattle, WA
Means, E. L. ... Woodland, CA
Means, Eldon L. ... Houston, TX
Means, Ernest E. ... Tallahassee, FL
Means, George M. ... Los Angeles, CA
Means, James E. ... Bridgeville, PA
Means, Jesse L., Jr. ... St. Francisville, LA
Means, JoAnn H. ... Fort Worth, TX
Means, John M. ... Pittsburgh, PA
Means, Johnston H. ... Columbus, OH
Means, Judith F. ... Department of Commerce, Office of the General Counsel, GV
Means, Karl W. ... Rockville, MD
Means, Margaret O. C. ... Tujunga, CA
Means, Margaret W. ... Jacksonville, FL
Means, Milton T. ... Detroit, MI
Means, Paul N., Jr. ... Little Rock, AR
Means, Rebecca M. ... Chicago, IL
Means, Steven P. ... Madison, WI
Means, T. Sam, Jr. ... Spartanburg, SC
Means, Thomas C. ... Washington, DC
Means, Thomas H. ... Provo, UT
Means, Tyrone C. ... Montgomery, AL
Means, William T. ... South Bend, IN
Means, William W. ... Tulsa, OK
Meany, Carol A. ... Boston, MA
Meany, David G. ... Reno, NV
Meany, David V. ... Milwaukee, WI
Meany, Dennis M. ... Montvale, NJ
Meany, Edward A. ... Lansing, MI
Meany, John Stewart, Jr. ... Chicago, IL
Meany, Julie G. ... Minneapolis, MN
Meany, Terence L. ... Austin, MN
Meany, Thomas F. ... Minneapolis, MN
Meara, Andrew J. ... Glen Rock, NJ
Meara, Daniel F. ... Fort Scott, KS
Meara, Edward C. ... San Diego, CA
Meara, J. William ... Orlando, FL
Meara, Michael J. ... Springfield, MA
Meara, William F., Jr.
South Weymouth, MA
Mearan, Michael H. ... Ironton, OH
Portsmouth, OH
Meardon, Charles A. ... Iowa City, IA
Meardon, Sueppel, Downer & Hayes P.L.C.
Iowa City, IA
Meares, Beth Kelly ... Raleigh, NC
Meares, Frank ... Omaha, NE
Meares, Martha J. ... Maryville, TN
Meares, Michael H. ... Maryville, TN
Meares, Patricia Ewing ... Maryville, TN
Meares, Rom ... Maryville, TN
Meares-Morton Law Offices ... Maryville, TN
Mearn, Kathleen M. ... Boston, MA
Mearns, Edward A., Jr. ... Cleveland, OH
Mearns, Geoffrey S. ... Cleveland, OH
Mearns, Sherri M. ... Norfolk, VA
Mears, Beverly J. ... Altoona, PA
Mears, C. Lane ... Austin, TX
Mears, Christopher B. ... Irvine, CA
Mears, Christopher B., A P.C. ... Irvine, CA
Mears, Darlene W. ... Crown Point, IN
Mears, David E. ... Highland, IN
Mears, Edward I. ... Redwood City, CA
Mears, Gordon C. ... Santa Monica, CA
Mears, James F., Jr. ... Peabody, MA
Mears, John H., III ... Woodstock, VT
Mears, John S. ... Chicago, IL
Mears, Judith M. ... Oakland, CA
Mears, Julia ... Iowa City, IA
Mears, Kay Carolyn ... Redwood City, CA
Mears, Larry R. ... Atchison, KS
Mears, Larry R., Chartered ... Atchison, KS
Troy, KS
Mears, Mark A. ... Los Angeles, CA
Mears, Mercea P., (Mrs.) ... Doylestown, PA
Mears, Michael ... Atlanta, GA
Mears, Michael A. ... Grandview, WA
Mears, Michael E. ... Dallas, TX
Mears, Michael P. ... Bakersfield, CA
Mears, Patrick E. ... Grand Rapids, MI
Mears, Philip B. ... Iowa City, IA
Mears, Rona R. ... Dallas, TX
Mears, Sandra A. ... Jefferson City, MO
Mears, Scott O. ... Greensburg, PA
Mears, Scott O., Jr. ... Greensburg, PA
Mears and Smith, P.C. ... Greensburg, PA
Mears, Stephen D. ... Indianapolis, IN
Mears, Stephen T. ... Boston, MA
Mears, William H., Jr. ... New York, NY
Mears, Wm. J. ... Richmond, VA
Mease, Laura J. ... Kansas City, MO
Mease, Roy D. ... Pasadena, TX
Mease-White, Alexandra D. ... Hartford, CT
Measley, Harold F., Jr. ... Greenville, DE
Measley, Harold F., Jr., P.A.
Greenville, DE
Measom, Bruce A. ... Troy, MI
Measure, Ambrose G., Law Office of
Kalispell, MT
Measure, Bruce A. ... Kalispell, MT
Meath, Anne G. ... Tacoma, WA
Meath, Brian P. ... Canandaigua, NY
Meath, Donald G. ... Tacoma, WA
Meath, Gregory T. ... Stockton, CA
Meath, James V. ... Richmond, VA
Meath, Richard V. ... Queensbury, NY
Meatto, Christopher F. ... Tarrytown, NY
Meaux, Antone M. ... Washington, DC
Meaux, Jean Morgan ... Metairie, LA
Meaux, Richard C., Jr. ... Lafayette, LA
Meaux, Richard C., Sr. ... Lafayette, LA
Mebane, Adrienne D. ... Chicago, IL
Mebane, David A. ... Livingston, NJ
Mebane, David C. ... Madison, WI
Mebane, Julie S. ... San Diego, CA
Mebane, Robert L. ... Rutherfordton, NC
Mebane, Scott P. ... Raleigh, NC
Mebel, Ellen B. ... Dedham, MA
Mebel, Roger L. ... Boston, MA
Mebruer, Nicholas E. ... Springfield, MO
Mebs, Frederick W. ... Cincinnati, OH
Mebtahi, Elena ... Los Angeles, CA
Mebus, Robert G. ... Dallas, TX
Mecadon, Girard J. ... Pittston, PA
Mecartney, Mary ... Keene, CA
Mecca, Andrew A. ... Syracuse, NY
Mecca, Christopher D. ... Grants Pass, OR
Mecca, Daniel P. ... Hackensack, NJ
Mecca, Joseph A. ... Totowa, NJ
Mecca, Joseph L., Jr. ... Paramus, NJ
Meccariello, Bryan F. ... Southington, CT
Mecchella, John N. ... Bardonia, NY
Mech, Ann B. ... Dayton, MD
Mech, David A. ... Springfield, MA
Mech, Raymond R. ... Chicago, IL
Mechahonis, Anthony
West Palm Beach, FL
Mecham, Alan F. ... Salt Lake City, UT
Salt Lake City, UT
Mecham, Allan E. ... Salt Lake City, UT
Mecham, Garth D. ... Magna, UT
Mecham, Glenn J. ... Ogden, UT
Mecham, L. Ralph
Administrative Office Of The United States Courts, GV
Mecham, M. Kent ... Phoenix, AZ
Mecham, Thomas A. ... Salt Lake City, UT
Mechanic, Gene B. ... Portland, OR
Mechanic & Goldstein ... Miami, FL
Mechanic, Harvey ... Los Angeles, CA
Mechanic, Jonathan L. ... New York, NY
Mechanic, Samuel R. ... Montclair, NJ
Mechanic, Stephen I. ... Miami, FL
Mechanic, Steven L. ... Florham Park, NJ
Mechanick, Maury J. ... Clarksburg, MD
Mechanik, David M. ... Tampa, FL
Mechanik Nuccio Bentley Williams & Hearne, A Professional Association
Tampa, FL
Mechas, Patrick L. ... Pittsburgh, PA
Mechcatie, Anthony P. ... New York, NY
Meche, Timothy Allison ... New Orleans, LA
Mechem, Charles S., Jr. ... Cincinnati, OH
Mechem, E. L. ... Albuquerque, NM
Mechem, Everett H. ... Kingsport, TN
Mecherikunnel, Thomas Paul
Equal Employment Opportunity Commission,
Office of Federal Operations, GV
Mecherle, Gregg R. ... Bloomington, IL
Mecherle, Richard W. ... Wayne, NJ
Mechler, James Richard
Overland Park, KS
Mechler, Kevin L. ... Carbondale, IL
Mechley, Albert, Jr. (Co., L.P.A.)
Cincinnati, OH
Mechley, Braden A. ... Cincinnati, OH
Mechlin, David R. ... Calumet, MI
Houghton, MI
Mechling, Curtis C. ... New York, NY
Mechling, Roger T. ... Kittanning, PA
Mechling, William C. ... Columbus, OH
Mechnig, Stephan A. ... Atlanta, GA
Mechur, Robert F. ... Rochester, NY
Mecia, Joseph A. ... San Francisco, CA
Mecia, Taryn Gordon ... Charlotte, NC
Meck, Brian L. ... Spokane, WA
Meck, Brian L., P.S. ... Spokane, WA
Meck, John F. ... Denver, CO
Meck, John F. ... Pittsburgh, PA
Meck, John P. ... Los Angeles, CA
Meck, Steven E. ... Irvine, CA
Meck, William L., II ... Tucker, GA
Mecka, Melanie L. ... Morristown, NJ
Meckel, Theresa ... Irving, TX
Meckert, G. William, III ... Essex Junction, VT
Meckes, Joseph ... San Francisco, CA
Meckfessel, Fred J. ... Willows, CA
Meckfessel, Hopkins & Byrd ... Willows, CA
Meckle, Edward J. ... South Pasadena, CA
Mecklenberg, Lisa ... Helena, MT
Mecklenborg, Daniel P. ... Nashville, TN
Mecklenborg, Robert P. ... Cincinnati, OH
Mecklenburg, Randy ... Kingfisher, OK
Oklahoma City, OK
Meckler, Bruce R. ... Chicago, IL
Meckler, David C. ... Costa Mesa, CA
Meckler, Janine L. ... Baltimore, MD
Meckler, Lawrence M. ... Buffalo, NY
Meckler, Marsha C. ... Honolulu, HI
Meckler, Ronald S. ... San Jose, CA
Meckler, Sandra J. ... New York, NY
Meckler, Stephen G. ... Elyria, OH
Meckler, Steven A. ... Charlotte, NC
Meckler, Theodore E. ... Cleveland, OH
Meckley, Eric ... San Francisco, CA
Meckley, John E., III ... Washington, DC
Meckley, Neill Irene, (Ms.) ... Voorhees, NJ
Mecklin, C. David, Jr. ... Carrollton, GA
Mecklosky, Laura Lee ... Mineola, NY
Meckstroth, Alan F. ... Dayton, OH
Meckstroth, James J. ... Cincinnati, OH
Meckstroth, John R., Jr. ... Cincinnati, OH
Meckstroth, Karen ... Los Angeles, CA
Meckstroth, Kurt S. ... Milwaukee, WI
Meckus, Kevin F. ... Department of Agriculture, Office of the General Counsel, GV
Mecky, Irene Ute ... Clifton, NJ
Mecoli, Gino P. ... Philadelphia, PA
Mecoli Kamp, Carla ... Detroit, MI
Mecom, William H. ... Los Angeles, CA
Meconi & Jackson ... Canon City, CO
Meconi, Louis P. ... Plattsburgh, NY
Meconi & Meconi ... Plattsburgh, NY
Meconi, Rocco F. ... Canon City, CO
Meconi, William T. ... Plattsburgh, NY
Mecsas, Michael E. ... Boston, MA
Mecum, Samuel M. ... Ephrata, PA
Lancaster, PA
Lititz, PA
Meda, Alan A. ... Scottsdale, AZ
Meda, Barry ... Warren, MI
Medacier, Adenet ... Miami, FL
Medack, David W. ... Houston, TX
Medaglia, Anthony J., Jr. (P.C.)
Boston, MA
Medaglia, M. Elizabeth ... Washington, DC
Baltimore, MD
Rockville, MD
Vienna, VA
Medaglio, Ellen L. ... Parkersburg, WV
Medairy, Bernard J., Jr. ... Towson, MD
Medairy, John W. T. ... Houston, TX
Medak, Walter H. ... Orinda, CA
Medalie, Donald B. ... Fort Lauderdale, FL
Medalie, Greg ... Fort Lauderdale, FL
Medalie, Randolph M. ... Bay Shore, NY
Medalie, Richard J. ... Washington, DC
New York, NY
Medalie, Susan D. ... Washington, DC
Medansky, Earl T. ... Chicago, IL
Medansky, Keith W. ... Chicago, IL
Medaris, Carol W. ... Madison, WI
Medaris, Frank C., Jr. ... Hazard, KY
Medaris, J. Bruce, Jr. ... Huntington, NY
Medaris, John E. ... Pelham, AL
Medawar, Jeanne S. ... Sarasota, FL
Medawar, Jill E. ... Compton, CA
Medcalf, Mark E. ... Salt Lake City, UT
Medcalf, Robert G. ... New York, NY
Medcoff, Timothy ... Phoenix, AZ
Medcraf, James H. ... Syracuse, NY
Medd, Joel D. ... Grand Forks, ND
Meddaugh, Mark M. ... Monticello, NY
Medders, Joe P. ... Carmichael, CA
Meddis, Eileen Joyce ... Pittsburgh, PA
Meddock, Adrienne Lea ... Durham, NC
Mede, William F. ... Anchorage, AK
Medearis, Charles A. ... St. Petersburg, FL
Medearis, Charles A., P.A.
St. Petersburg, FL
Medearis, Frank M. ... Tahlequah, OK
Medearis & Grimm ... Los Angeles, CA
Medearis, Mark A. ... Menlo Park, CA
Medearis, Miller ... Los Angeles, CA
Medearis, Robert Park, Jr. ... Tahlequah, OK
Medeiros, A. David ... Hanford, CA
Medeiros, Alan B. ... Taunton, MA
Medeiros, Anthony F. ... Santa Fe, NM
Medeiros and Associates ... Victorville, CA
Medeiros, Bruce K. ... Spokane, WA
Medeiros, Christina L. ... Wichita, KS
Medeiros, Donald Michael ... Victorville, CA
Medeiros, Dyan M. ... Honolulu, HI
Medeiros, George M. ... Billerica, MA
Medeiros, Gil ... Walnut Creek, CA
Medeiros, Jeanne Marie ... Boston, MA
Medeiros, Jeffrey Joseph ... Hartford, CT
Medeiros, Jeffrey P. ... Fall River, MA
Medeiros, Joan M. ... Sacramento, CA
Medeiros Law Firm ... Hanford, CA
Medeiros, Leonel D. ... Crockett, CA
Medeiros, Lisa Bianca ... Dorchester, MA
Medeiros, Manuel M. ... Sacramento, CA
Medeiros, Matthew F. ... Providence, RI
Medeiros, Michael ... New Bedford, MA
Medeiros, Philip J., Jr. ... Springfield, MA
Medeiros + Sanford Inc. ... Providence, RI
Medeiros, Sheryl C. ... San Francisco, CA
Medeiros, Steven R. ... Carver, MA
Medel, Arthur V. ... Washington, DC
Medel, Ivy V. ... New York, NY
Medel, Kenneth J. ... San Diego, CA
Medel, Maria Eugenia ... Miami, FL
Medel & Rawers ... San Diego, CA
Medema, Alexa M ... Boise, ID
Medema, Mary Ann Fenner
Baltimore, MD
Medema, Richard A. ... Department of Justice, Drug Enforcement Administration, GV
Meder, Julie W. ... Pittsburgh, PA
Meder, Martin G. ... Plymouth Meeting, PA
Medero, Frederick R. ... United States Senate, Senatorial Assistants, GV
Medero, Joanne T. ... San Francisco, CA
Mederos, Dennis A. ... Tulare, CA
Mederos, Julie A. ... Dallas, TX
Mederos, Paul G. ... New York, NY
Mederos-Jacobs, Connie ... Bradenton, FL
Sarasota, FL
Mederos-Jacobs, Connie, P.A.
Bradenton, FL
Sarasota, FL
Mederrick, Charles T. ... New York, NY
Mederrick, Michael E. ... New York, NY
Medetsky, Jeffrey A. ... Brooklyn, NY
Medford, Cecil L. ... Bedford Heights, OH
Medford, James A. ... Greensboro, NC
Medford, Leanne Capps ... Dallas, TX
Medford, Michael T. ... Raleigh, NC
Medford, Thomas A., Jr. ... Lanham, MD
Medford, William L. ... Dallas, TX
Medford-Rosow, Traci J. ... New York, NY
Medgyesy, Laura L. ... Los Angeles, CA
Medi, Srini R. ... Houston, TX
Mediation Consultants ... Pensacola, FL
Medice, Mark L. ... Cincinnati, OH
Medich, Julie Oswald ... Charleston, SC
Medici, Albert E., Jr. ... Providence, RI
Medici, Andrea E.
Environmental Protection Agency, Office of the General Counsel, GV
Medicis, Joseph G., Jr. ... Syracuse, NY
Medico, Anthony J. ... New York, NY
Medige, Patricia Louise ... Denver, CO
Medill, Colleen E. ... Knoxville, TN
Medill, Daniel K. ... York, PA
Medill, Thomas L., Jr. ... Seneca, KS
Medin, Fran E. ... Encino, CA
Medin, Ronald K. ... Jefferson City, MO
Medina, Agustin, Jr. ... Los Angeles, CA
Medina, Alma Rosa ... Arlington, VA
Medina, Anthony M. ... Seattle, WA
Medina, Arnoldo, Jr. ... Austin, TX
Medina, Daniel ... Lakeland, FL
Medina, David ... Bridgeport, CT
Medina, David Rafael ... Greeley, CO
Medina, Diane W. ... Carson, CA

Medina, Donna Marie ....Bingham Farms, MI
Medina, Erin Nemirovsky
Universal City, CA
Medina, Ernesto S. ....Miami, FL
Medina, Ernesto S., P.A. ....Miami, FL
Medina, Francisco ....Washington, DC
Medina, Frank ....Madison, WI
Medina, Gustavo ....Brooklyn, NY
Medina, J. Michael ....Tulsa, OK
Medina, J. J. ....San Antonio, TX
Medina, John A. ....Atlanta, GA
Medina, Jose ....Torrance, CA
Medina, Laura B. ....Houston, TX
Medina, Laura Majerfeld ....Boulder, CO
Denver, CO
Medina, Lee A. ....Pueblo, CO
Medina, Liza Hirsch ....Los Angeles, CA
Medina, Loretta F. ....Albuquerque, NM
Medina, Luis A. ....Hawthorne, NY
Medina, M. Isabel ....New Orleans, LA
Medina, Marian Hamilton ....Covina, CA
Medina, Maribel S. ....Los Angeles, CA
Medina, Mark E. ....Denver, CO
Medina, Mary Helen ....Bethesda, MD
Medina, Maximino, Jr. ....Bridgeport, CT
Medina, Michael E., Jr. ....Tucson, AZ
Medina, Monica ....Miami, FL
Medina, Monica P. ....Washington, DC
Medina & Mundy, P.A. ....Lakeland, FL
Medina, Nuria ....Miami, FL
Medina & O'Brien, P.C. ....Hawthorne, NY
Medina, Olga S. ....West Palm Beach, FL
Medina, Omar F. ....Tampa, FL
Medina, Omar F., P.A., Law Offices of
Brooksville, FL
Clearwater, FL
St. Petersburg, FL
Spring Hill, FL
Tampa, FL
Medina, Patricia J. ....San Francisco, CA
Medina, Rafael ....Oak Brook, IL
Medina, Randy W. ....Los Angeles, CA
Medina, Renato L. ....Pasadena, CA
Medina, Richard A. ....New York, NY
Medina, Samuel A. ....Lubbock, TX
Medina, Sandra E. ....Mammoth Lakes, CA
Medina, Sergio V. ....Miami, FL
Medina, Standish F. ....Green Village, NJ
New York, NY
Medina, Standish Forde, Jr. ....New York, NY
Medina, Steven ....Garden City, NY
Medina, Steven A. ....Tallahassee, FL
Medina, Steven J. ....San Antonio, TX
Medina, Tomas E. ....New York, NY
Medina, Veronica R. ....Albuquerque, NM
Medina, Virginia ....New York, NY
Medina-Lugo, Rubén M. ....San Juan, PR
Medina-Richman, Leticia ....Worcester, MA
Medina-Rivera, Jose David ....San Juan, PR
Medina-Shore, Sylvia ......West Palm Beach, FL
Medina Torres, Juan E. ....Ponce, PR
Medina-Zurinaga, Norberto ....San Juan, PR
Medine, David ....Federal Trade Commission,
Bureau of Consumer Protection, GV
Medinets, Lee David ....Lakewood, NJ
Meding, Paul A. ....Columbia, SC
Meding, Paul A. ....Columbia, SC
Medintz, Barry I. ....Atlanta, GA
Medla, Linda G. ....North Salem, NY
Medland, Michael F. ....Madison, WI
Medlar, Deborah L. ....Bothell, WA
Medlen & Carroll, LLP
Redwood City, CA
San Francisco, CA
Cambridge, MA
Madison, WI
Medlen, Virginia Shaw
San Francisco, CA
Medlen, William P. ....Calabasas, CA
Medler, Gary E. ....Chicago, IL
Medler, Jeffrey Paul ....St. Louis, MO
Medler, John F., Jr. ....St. Louis, MO
Medler, Robert J. ....Roanoke, VA
Medler, Teresa Uliva ....Washington, DC
Medley, Arthur R. ....Dothan, AL
Medley, Barbara ....Fort Worth, TX
Medley, Barbara Gillespie ....Lewisburg, TN
Medley, Barry H. ....McMinnville, TN
Medley, Beverly M. ....Nashville, TN
Medley, Carole Faye Coil ....Huntsville, AL
Medley, Charles W. ....Farmington, MO
Medley, Diane F. ....West Palm Beach, FL
Medley, Donald W. ....Hattiesburg, MS
Medley, Gregory L. ....Dallas, TX
Medley, Jason M. ....Houston, TX
Medley, Leroy D. ....Indianapolis, IN
Medley, Mark L. ....San Antonio, TX
Medley, Mark L., P.C. ....San Antonio, TX
Medley, Martha White ....Danville, VA
South Boston, VA
Medley, Mary Lou ....Rochester, NY
Medley, Richard A. ....Coffeyville, KS
Medley, Steven P.
Yosemite National Park, CA
Medley, Terry L. ....Department of Agriculture,
Animal and Plant Health Inspection Service,
GV
Medley, Thomas P. ....White Plains, NY
Medley, William C., IV
Oklahoma City, OK
Medlin, William S. ....Gallipolis, OH
Medlin, Charles K., Jr. ....Jacksonville, NC
Medlin, Charles M. ....Atlanta, GA
Medlin, Don A. ....Seattle, WA
Medlin, Dwain D. ....Lafayette, LA
Medlin, Elmer J. ....Carbondale, IL
Medlin, Frederick L. ....Dallas, TX
Medlin, Gary L. ....Fort Worth, TX

Medlin, James S. ....Carbondale, IL
Medlin, John D. ....Columbia, SC
Medlin, Kay Cowden ....Shreveport, LA
Medlin Law Office ....Eden, NC
Medlin, Mark S. ....Paducah, KY
Medlin & Medlin ....Carbondale, IL
Concord, NC
Medlin, R. Ward ....Albemarle, NC
Medlin, Rachel N. ....Bartow, FL
Medlin, Raymond P., Jr. ....Albion, NE
Medlin, Steven L. ....Concord, NC
Medlin, Theodore W. ....Germantown, TN
Medlin, Thomas E., Jr. ....Eden, NC
Medlin, Virgil D. ....Oklahoma City, OK
Medlin, W. Deryl ....Shreveport, LA
Medlin, Webster S. ....Concord, NC
Medlinsky, Earl G. ....Philadelphia, PA
Medlinsky, Mark A. ....Marblehead, MA
Medlock, Donald L. ....New York, NY
Medlock, Jonathan B. ....Huntsville, AL
Medlock, Larry W. ....Salem, IN
Medlock, Michael J. ....Van Buren, AR
Medlock, Nina L. ....Washington, DC
Medlock, Ricky R. ....Arkadelphia, AR
Medlock, T. Travis ....Columbia, SC
Medlock, V. Bryan, Jr. ....Dallas, TX
Mednick, Allen D. ....Diamond Bar, CA
Mednick, Arnold W. ....Beverly Hills, CA
Mednick, Glenn M. ....Boca Raton, FL
Mednick, Herbert S. ....Philadelphia, PA
Mednick, I. Robert ....San Jose, CA
Mednick, Kevin S. ....Atlanta, GA
Schenectady, NY
Mednick, Michael Brett ....Monticello, NY
Mednick, Norman ....New York, NY
Mednick, Richard ....Los Angeles, CA
Mednick, Richard D. ....Seattle, WA
Mednick, Richard M. ....Buffalo Grove, IL
Mednick, Steven B. ....Santa Ana, CA
Mednick, Steven G. ....New Haven, CT
Medo, Anne E. ....New Orleans, LA
Medo, Steven O., Jr. ....New Orleans, LA
Medo & Tête ....New Orleans, LA
Medof, Carol J. ....Encino, CA
Medof, Robert G. ....Arroyo Grande, CA
Medoff, Bernard ....Port Washington, NY
Medoff, Irving I. ....Natick, MA
Medoff, Jan I. ....Pittsburgh, PA
Medoff, M. Craig ....Fallbrook, CA
Medoff, Marshall ....Brookline, MA
Medoff, Roger H. ....Lutherville, MD
Medonich, Brant M. ....Bend, OR
Medonis, Linda M. ....Boston, MA
Medonis, Robert X. ....Pittsburgh, PA
Medor, Alan R. ....Rutland, VT
Medor, McCamley & Doherty, P.C.
Rutland, VT
Medori, Eugene A., Jr. ....Atlanta, GA
Decatur, GA
Medoro-Whited, Janean
Colorado Springs, CO
Medosch, John E., Jr. ....Philadelphia, PA
Medow, Arthur ....Chicago, IL
Medow, Jonathan C. ....Chicago, IL
Medowar, Jerome S. ....Westbury, NY
Medoway, Ellis I. ....Haddonfield, NJ
Medrano, Manuel A. ....Burbank, CA
Medrano, Melissa B. ....Miami, FL
Medrano, Patricia M. ....Dallas, TX
Medrano, Tom Robert ....Pasadena, CA
Medrea, Daniel A. ....Merrillville, IN
Medsger, William R.
Department of the Army,
Army Materiel Command, GV
Medsker, Donald F. ....Englewood, CO
Medsker, Richard R. ....Ogden, UT
Medsker, Stanley R. ....Littleton, CO
Medura, Wendy ....Las Vegas, NV
Meduski, Michael ....Quincy, MA
Medve, Marianna ....New York, NY
Medveckus, Michael J. ....Philadelphia, PA
Medvecky, Robert S. ....Fort Myers, FL
Medvecky, Thomas E. ....Bethel, CT
Medved, George M. ....Pittsburgh, PA
Medved, Joseph W. ....Kansas City, MO
Medved, Keith F. ....Crown Point, IN
Medved, Michael P. ....Lakewood, CO
Medved, Paul S. ....Milwaukee, WI
Medved, William J. ....Kirtland, OH
Medvedoff, David L. ....San Luis Obispo, CA
Medvei, Adrien ....Los Angeles, CA
Medvene, Edward M. ....Los Angeles, CA
Medverd, Richard L. ....Boston, MA
Medverd & Simmons, P.C. ....Boston, MA
Medvesky, Mark M. ....Allentown, PA
Easton, PA
Lehighton, PA
Reading, PA
Medvetz, Thea M. ....Norfolk, VA
Medvigy, Gary A. ....Santa Rosa, CA
Medvin, Alan Y. ....Newark, NJ
Medvin & Elberg ....Newark, NJ
Medvin, Joel D. ....Patchogue, NY
Medvin, Joshua D. ....Miami, FL
Medvin, Mark S. ....Woburn, MA
Medvin, Philip D. ....Coral Gables, FL
Medvin, Tropp, & Associates ....Miami, FL
Medvinsky, Larry P. ....New York, NY
Medway, Leah E. ....Washington, DC
Medway, Richard A. ....Washington, DC
Medwed, Howard D. ....Boston, MA
Medwick, Craig S. ....New York, NY
Medwick, George M. ....Wilmington, DE
Medwid, Joanne H. ....Sacramento, CA
Medwied, Susan R. ....Laguna Hills, CA
Medzhibovsky, Leon ....New York, NY
Medzie, Kenneth S. ....Wallingford, PA
Medzonsky, Faina ....Palo Alto, CA

Mee, Anne Toland ....Portland, OR
Mee, C. David ....Houston, TX
Mee, Caroline Mapuana ....Honolulu, HI
Mee, Glenn R. ....Fort Lauderdale, FL
Mee & Goodwin LLP ....Oklahoma City, OK
Mee, James K., (A Law Corporation)
Honolulu, HI
Mee, John F. ....Newton, MA
Mee, John M. ....Oklahoma City, OK
Mee, John W., III ....Oklahoma City, OK
Mee, John W., Jr. ....Oklahoma City, OK
Mee, Mary J. ....Sacramento, CA
Mee, Mee & Hoge ....Oklahoma City, OK
Mee, Michael J. ....Walnut Creek, CA
Mee, Patrick H. ....Oklahoma City, OK
Mee, Siobhan Elizabeth ....Boston, MA
Mee, William H. ....Santa Fe, NM
Meece, C. Patrick ....Bryan, TX
Meece, Darin P. ....Durham, NC
Meece, David G. ....Fort Worth, TX
Meece, E. Ted ....Portland, OR
Meece, Gregory S. ....Houston, TX
Meece & Kohn ....Bryan, TX
Meece, Michael E. ....Washington, DC
Meece, Robert Scott ....Duluth, GA
Meece, Timothy C. ....Chicago, IL
Meech, Constance M. ....Auburn Hills, MI
Meeder, Clinton C. ....Sherman, NY
Meeder, Curt N. ....Elmira, NY
Meeder, Gregory R. ....Chicago, IL
Meeder, James L. ....San Francisco, CA
Meeder, Theodore H., Jr. ....Ventura, CA
Meedon, Carol L. ....Orange, CA
Meeds, Lloyd ....Washington, DC
Meeds-Williams, Pamela ....Moraga, CA
Meegan, Brian D. ....Denver, CO
Meegan, Cathleen E. ....Chicago, IL
Meegan, David M. ....Sacramento, CA
Meegan, David R. ....Providence, RI
Meegan, Hanschu & Kassenbrock
Sacramento, CA
Meegan, Mary T. ....Chicago, IL
Megan & Meegan ....Chicago, IL
Meegan, Molly A. ....Washington, DC
Meegan, Owen D. ....River Forest, IL
Meegan, Owen J. ....Salem, MA
Meeh, Judy Harris ....Houston, TX
Meehan, A. Duer
Securities and Exchange Commission,
Office of Compliance Inspections and
Examinations, GV
Meehan, Aileen C. ....New York, NY
Meehan, Andrew C. ....Washington, DC
Meehan & Associates, Law Offices of
Tucson, AZ
Meehan, Boyle & Cohen, P.C.
Boston, MA
Meehan, Brian P. ....Philadelphia, PA
Meehan, Charles M. ....Washington, DC
Meehan, Coleen M. ....Philadelphia, PA
Meehan, Daniel J. ....Convent Station, NJ
Meehan, Daniel P. ....Denver, CO
Meehan, David T. ....Chicago, IL
Meehan, Deidre H. ....New York, NY
Meehan, Dorothy K. ....Arlington, MA
Meehan, Edward J. ....Washington, DC
Meehan, Edward J., Jr. ....Philadelphia, PA
Meehan, Ellen K. ....Cleveland, OH
Meehan & Foley ....Palm Beach Gardens, FL
Meehan, Frances ....Chicago, IL
Meehan, Francis P., Jr. ....South Orange, NJ
Meehan, Francis X. ....Philadelphia, PA
Meehan, George E., Jr.
Spring Lake Heights, NJ
Meehan, Gerald J. ....Rock Island, IL
Meehan, Gerard M. ....Buffalo, NY
Meehan, Gregory F. ....Hawthorne, NY
Meehan, Gwen ....Louisville, KY
Meehan, J. Justin ....St. Louis, MO
Meehan, James C. ....Dakota Dunes, SD
Meehan, James F. ....Boston, MA
Meehan, James K. ....Taunton, MA
Meehan, James P.
Department of the Navy, GV
Meehan, James P. ....Westborough, MA
Meehan, James Patrick ....Oakland, CA
Meehan, Jeffrey A. ....Vancouver, WA
Meehan, John Dwyer ....Orlando, FL
Meehan, John F. ....Goshen, NY
Meehan, John F., III ....Los Alamos, NM
Meehan, John J. ....Chicago, IL
Meehan, John J. ....Brooklyn, NY
Meehan, John P. ....Short Hills, NJ
Meehan, Joseph ....Long Branch, NJ
Meehan, Joseph, P.A. ....Long Branch, NJ
Meehan, K. Patrick ....Tampa, FL
Meehan, Karen Osiecki ....Chicago, IL
Meehan, Katherine H. ....Media, PA
Meehan, Kathleen A. ....Fresno, CA
Meehan, Kevin L. ....Rowayton, CT
Meehan, L. Jeffrey ....Springfield, MA
Meehan, Laura J. ....Goshen, NY
Meehan, Laurie ....Federal Trade Commission,
Bureau of Consumer Protection, GV
Meehan, Lawrence F., Jr. ....Philadelphia, PA
Meehan, Lori L. ....Chicago, IL
Meehan, Mark R. ....Arlington, MA
Meehan, Martin T. ....Lowell, MA
Meehan & Meehan ....Bridgeport, CT
Stamford, CT
Meehan, Michael A. ....Danbury, CT
Meehan, Michael A. ....Philadelphia, PA
Meehan, Michael J. ....Tucson, AZ
Meehan, Michael J. ....Edwardsville, IL
Meehan, Michael J. ....Cleveland, OH
Meehan, Michael P. ....Philadelphia, PA
Meehan, Michael T. ....Bridgeport, CT
Meehan, Patrick M. ....Oakland, CA

Meehan, Richard Dan, Jr. ....Bonham, TX
Meehan, Richard J. ....Los Angeles, CA
Meehan, Richard J.
Palm Beach Gardens, FL
Meehan, Richard T., Jr. ....Bridgeport, CT
Meehan, Richard T., Sr. ....Bridgeport, CT
Meehan, Robert F. ....Hawthorne, NY
Meehan, Robert F. ....Plainview, NY
Meehan, Robert P. ....Pittsburgh, PA
Meehan, Robert R. ....New City, NY
Meehan, Scott A. ....Malibu, CA
Meehan, Sean Brosnahan
San Francisco, CA
Meehan, Sheila ....McLean, VA
Meehan, Stephen Z. ....Baltimore, MD
Chestertown, MD
Meehan, Thomas ....Tucson, AZ
Meehan, Thomas A. ....Troy, MI
Toledo, OH
Meehan, Thomas P. ....Washington, DC
Meehan, Timothy M. ....New York, NY
Meehan, Timothy S. ....Minneapolis, MN
Meehan, Valentine A. ....Seaford, NY
Meehan, Wayne D. ....New York, NY
Meehan, William A. ....New York, NY
Meehan, William Austin, Jr.
Philadelphia, PA
Meehan, William C. ....Hackensack, NJ
Meehan, William F. ....Carbondale, IL
Meehan, William F. ....Boston, MA
Meehan, William K. ....St. Louis, MO
Meehan, William P. ....Cape Coral, FL
Meehan, William P. ....Fort Myers, FL
Meehan, William P. ....Long Grove, IL
Meehl, Daniel B. ....Twin Falls, ID
Meehling & Bernardoni ....Marshall, IL
Meehling, William F. ....Marshall, IL
Meek, Adam M. ....Chicago, IL
Meek, Alan S. ....Lexington, KY
Meek, Barry T. ....Richmond, VA
Meek, Brian R. ....Santa Ana, CA
Meek, Cecil D., Jr. ....Knoxville, TN
Meek, Chad L. ....Lancaster, CA
Minneapolis, MN
Meek, Christopher Young
Baxter Springs, KS
Meek, Clara L. ....Houston, TX
Meek, Clay L. ....Daytona Beach, FL
Meek, Danny E. ....Indianapolis, IN
Meek, Dustin Elizabeth ....Louisville, KY
Meek, E. Robert ....Jacksonville, FL
Meek, Fredric W. ....Oak Park, IL
Meek, Gary ....Oklahoma City, OK
Meek, Gerald F. (Jerry) ....Dallas, TX
Meek, Jason C. ....Miami, FL
Meek, Jeffery D., & Associates
Livonia, MI
Meek, Jeffery D., & Associates
Plymouth, MI
Meek, Jennifer Burkett ....Jacksonville, FL
Meek, Joseph William ....Ada, OH
Meek, Kevin C. ....Great Falls, MT
Meek, Kevin J. ....Dallas, TX
Meek, Mary Theresa ....Delray Beach, FL
Meek & Meek ....Eupora, MS
Meek, Patricia S. ....Cincinnati, OH
Meek, Philip A.
Department of the Air Force,
Office of the General Counsel, GV
Meek, Richard T. ....Charlotte, NC
Meek, Robert M. ....Boise, ID
Meek, Ronald B. ....Waco, TX
Meek, Stuart F., Jr. ....St. Joseph, MI
Meek and Swartz, A Law Corporation
Redding, CA
Meek, Thomas J. ....Wichita, KS
Meek, Timothy A. ....Midland, TX
Meek, W. Buchanan ....Eupora, MS
Meek, W. Buchanan, Jr. ....Eupora, MS
Meek, William L. ....Redding, CA
Meeker, Benjamin L. ....Temecula, CA
Meeker, Brian A. ....Cleveland, OH
Meeker, Charles A. ....Novato, CA
Meeker, Charles C. ....Raleigh, NC
Meeker, David R. ....Sacramento, CA
Meeker, Donald W. ....Mission, KS
Meeker, Everett ....Washington, IA
Meeker, Frederic M. ....Washington, DC
Meeker, Frederick W. ....Hampton Bays, NY
New York, NY
Meeker, Gregory J. ....Madison, WI
Meeker, Heather ....Palo Alto, CA
Meeker, Herbert S. ....New York, NY
Meeker, J. Gordon ....Portland, IN
Meeker, Jade ....Austin, TX
Meeker, James W. ....Amherst, NY
Meeker, Keith L. ....La Mesa, CA
Meeker, Kenneth C. ....Indianapolis, IN
Meeker, Larry K. ....Wichita, KS
Meeker, Laura Kuitunen
Department of the Army,
Office, Chief of Engineers/Headquarters,
U.S. Army Corps of Engineers, GV
Meeker, Leonard C. ....Washington, DC
Meeker, Lori B. ....Bloomfield, CT
Meeker, Michael D. ....Greensboro, NC
Meeker, Mona ....McLean, VA
Meeker, Murray M.
Office of Personnel Management,
Compensation Division, GV
Meeker, Peter R. ....Austin, TX
Meeker, Robert C. ....Akron, OH
Meeker, Roger V. ....Kamuela, HI
Meeker, Suzanne E. ....Portland, ME
Meeker, Tara D.
Federal Election Commission,
Office of the General Counsel, GV
Meeker, Theodore G. ....Honolulu, HI

Meeker, Theodore P., III ....**Newnan, GA**
Meeker, Thomas H. ....Louisville, KY
Meekins, C. Martin ....**Houston, TX**
Meekins, Frank W. ....Markham, IL
Meekins, Fred C., Jr. ....Whiteville, NC
Meekins, Frederick C. ....Charlotte, NC
Meekins, John M. ....Albany, NY
Meekins, Marsha Smith ....**Burlington, VT**
Meekins, Pamela D. ....**Boston, MA**
Meekins, Samuel W., Jr.
Virginia Beach, VA
Meekins, Susan L. ....New York, NY
Meekison, David ....Napoleon, OH
Meekison, David F. ....Napoleon, OH
Meekison Law Firm ....Napoleon, OH
Meeks, Alan W. ....Lubbock, TX
Meeks, Bruce R. ....Tallahassee, FL
Meeks, Cordell D., Jr. ....Kansas City, KS
Meeks, David Everett ....Warwick, NY
Meeks, Geron W., Jr. ....Houston, TX
Meeks, Gregory A. ....Baton Rouge, LA
Meeks, Gregory W. ....Far Rockaway, NY
Meeks, Heber S., Law Office of ....Covina, CA
Meeks, J. Byron ....Kinsley, KS
Meeks, James E. ....Columbus, OH
Meeks, Jeffrey A. ....**New York, NY**
Meeks, Jennifer J. ....**Charleston, WV**
Meeks & Jernigan, P.A. ....Little Rock, AR
meeks, jessica lynn ....**Oakland, CA**
Meeks, Jo Lanier ....**Atlanta, GA**
Meeks, John R. ....Tallahassee, FL
Meeks, Karen I. ....**Lakeland, FL**
Meeks, Larry M. ....**Los Angeles, CA**
Meeks, Lisa ....Cincinnati, OH
Meeks, Malcolm T. ....**Washington, DC**
Meeks, Marjorie A. ....**Evansville, IN**
Meeks, Mark D. ....**Toledo, OH**
Meeks, Mary B. ....**Orlando, FL**
Meeks, Michael L. ....**Los Angeles, CA**
Meeks, Montie S. ....Virginia Beach, VA
Meeks Morgan Bauer ....Olympia, WA
Meeks, Nicole Marie ....Winston-Salem, NC
Meeks, Patti A. ....**Miami, FL**
Meeks, Perker L., Jr. ....San Francisco, CA
Meeks, R. Harold, Jr. ....**Atlanta, GA**
Meeks, R. William ....**Columbus, OH**
Meeks, Robert M. ....**Raleigh, NC**
Meeks, Ronald L. ....Conroe, TX
Meeks, Rowdy B. ....**Kansas City, MO**
Meeks, S. Daniel ....**Metairie, LA**
Meeks & Sheppard ....**New York, NY**
Meeks, Stephen T. ....Fort Worth, TX
Meeks, Steven R. ....Olympia, WA
Meeks, Sydney Nolen ....Charleston, SC
Meeks, Tamara I. ....Kansas City, MO
Meeks, Thomas J. ....**Miami, FL**
Meeks, Thomas R. ....Clarksville, TN
Meeks, Virginia D. ....**Beaufort, SC**
Meeks, W. Edward, III ....Amherst, VA
Meeks, W. Edward, Jr. ....**Albany, GA**
Meeks, W. Russell, III ....Little Rock, AR
Meeks, William H. ....**Fort Lauderdale, FL**
Meeks, William H., Jr. ....Bradenton, FL
Meeks, William S. ....**Crossett, AR**
Meeley, Walter D. ....Upper Darby, PA
Meelheim, Christa H. ....**Birmingham, AL**
Meelheim, Helen Diane ....Raleigh, NC
Meelheim, Richard A. ....**Birmingham, AL**
Meelheim, Wilkinson & Meelheim, P.C.
Birmingham, AL
Meell, Gregory J. ....**Phoenix, AZ**
Meena, Caroline George ....**Louisville, KY**
Meena, James W. ....Columbus, OH
Meena, Richard, Jr. ....Louisville, KY
Meenagh, John P., Jr. ....**Poughkeepsie, NY**
Meenaghan, Brian J. ....**Seattle, WA**
Meenaghan, James ....**Burbank, CA**
Meenan, Colleen M. ....New York, NY
Meenan, Daniel C., Jr. ....Chicago, IL
Meenan, James F. ....Cheshire, CT
Meenan, John M. ....**Washington, DC**
Meenan, Karen F ....Framingham, MA
Meenan, Kevin ....**Pasadena, CA**
Meenan, Kevin P. ....Casper, WY
Meenan & Lariviere ....**Los Angeles, CA**
Pasadena, CA
Meenan, Stephen R. ....**Norfolk, VA**
Meenan, Timothy J. ....**Tallahassee, FL**
Meengs, Lisa A. ....**Washington, DC**
Meengs, Philip G. ....San Marcos, CA
Meengs-Bakker, Marcia Ann ....Riverhead, NY
Meepos, Penny Kelen ....Los Angeles, CA
Meer, Brian ....West Bloomfield, MI
Meer, Cary J. ....**Washington, DC**
Meer, E. Harvey ....North Bergen, NJ
Meer, Jon D. ....**Los Angeles, CA**
Meer, Jonah M. ....Brooklyn, NY
Meer, Julian M. ....Dallas, TX
Meer, Julius ....Denver, CO
Meer & Meer, P.C. ....**Denver, CO**
Meer, Melvyn L. ....Bayside, NY
Meer, Robert D. ....Canton, MI
Meer, Robert S. ....**Denver, CO**
Meer, Sheila H. ....**Denver, CO**
Meerbaum, Joseph ....Cherry Hill, NJ
Meerbergen, John E. ....**Greenwich, CT**
Meerchaum, John E. ....**Redwood City, CA**
Meerkreebs, Samuel ....Chevy Chase, MD
Meermans, Mary K. ....**Haverford, PA**
Meermans, Robert S. ....Warren, OH
Meermans, Zimmer & Cauffield
Warren, OH
Meeropol, Robert H. ....Springfield, MA
Meerovitch, Shelly ....**New York, NY**
Meers, Amanda S. ....Laredo, TX
Meers, Arthur J. ....St. Joseph, MO
Meers, Charles R. ....Louisville, KY
Meers, Elizabeth A. ....Cleveland, OH
Meers, Madeline M. ....Munster, IN
Meers, Tommy C., Sr. ....Jacksonville, FL
Meers, Tommy C., Sr., P.A. ....Jacksonville, FL
Meerse, Sara A. ....Presque Isle, ME
Meersman, F. Michael ....Rock Island, IL
Meersman, H. Moss ....Moline, IL
Meersman, Kathleen T. ....Mount Prospect, IL
Meersman, Maureen P.
Mount Prospect, IL
Meersman & Meersman ....Mount Prospect, IL
Meersman, Robert F. ....Mount Prospect, IL
Meertens, Michelle A. ....**New York, NY**
Meese, Alan J. ....Washington, DC
Meese, Gregory D. ....**Woodcliff Lake, NJ**
Meese, Jan Leslie ....**Rice Lake, WI**
Meese, Leigh Ammons ....Myrtle Beach, SC
Meese, William F. ....Scottsville, VA
Meeske, William J. ....**Los Angeles, CA**
Meess, Diane C. ....**Memphis, TN**
Meessen, Frederick S. ....Lafayette, IN
Meetin, Ronald J. ....**San Jose, CA**
Meetre, Steven ....**New York, NY**
Meetze, Walter S. ....Augusta, GA
Meeusen, Michael J. ....**Sterling Heights, MI**
Meezan, David M. ....**Atlanta, GA**
Mefferd, Frank H. ....College Station, TX
Mefferd, James B., Jr. ....Chariton, IA
Mefferd, James, P.C. ....Chariton, IA
Meffert, J. Christian ....Salt Springs, FL
Meffert, Wellington H., II ....Tallahassee, FL
Mefford, Allison E. ....Louisville, KY
Mefford and Carpenter, P.C. ....**Auburn, IN**
Mefford, Donald T. ....**Auburn, IN**
Mefford, Harold D. ....Hayward, CA
Mefford, Marty R. ....Franklin, KY
Mefford, R. Douglas ....Nashville, TN
Mefford, Timothy D. ....Franklin, KY
Meftah, Diane M. ....Columbus, OH
Mega, Gerald E. ....Palmer, MA
Mega, Robert A. ....East Providence, RI
Mega, Robert J. ....Clark, NJ
Megaard, Michael M. ....**Spokane, WA**
Megaffin, Brown & McCall ....Pratt, KS
Megahan, John B. ....Houston, TX
Megan, David C. ....**Boston, MA**
Meganck, Allan G. ....**Detroit, MI**
Meganck, Allan G.
Grosse Pointe Park, MI
Megara, John M. ....**New York, NY**
Megard, Bruce W., Jr. ....**Seattle, WA**
Megargel, Ralph C. ....Walton Hills, OH
Megargle, Thomas C. ....Bronson, MI
Megaro, Kim M. ....Chicago, IL
Megarry, Carole M. ....Minneapolis, MN
Megary, Bryan Scott ....**Harrisburg, PA**
Megas, Carol Bladyka ....Santa Clara, CA
Megaw, Mark T. ....Philadelphia, PA
Megay, David A. ....**Pottstown, PA**
Megdal, Ira G. ....**Cherry Hill, NJ**
Megdell, David I. ....Flint, MI
Mege, Alan R. ....Allentown, PA
Megee, Ann H. ....**San Antonio, TX**
Megehee, Carl A. ....**Pascagoula, MS**
Megel, J. Timothy ....Troy, MI
Megel, Roberta Jean Penning
Council Bluffs, IA
Megel, W. David ....Suitland, MD
Megerian, Aram P. ....**Miami, FL**
Megerian, Jonathan L. ....**Asheboro, NC**
Megerian & Wells ....**Asheboro, NC**
Megery, Laurie Burstein ....**Burbank, CA**
Megevick, William F., Jr. ....**New York, NY**
Meggelin, Maryann S. ....Los Angeles, CA
Meggesin, Laurie J. ....**Dallas, TX**
Meggesto, James A. ....Syracuse, NY
Meggesto, James T. ....**Washington, DC**
Meggett, Paul A. ....Durham, NC
Megginson, Elizabeth R.
House of Representatives,
Committee on Resources, GV
Meggs, Charles W. ....San Jose, CA
Meggs, James S. ....Columbia, SC
Meggs, Lisa L. ....Oxford, MS
Meggs, Sally Reed ....**San Jose, CA**
Meggs, Scott W. ....San Jose, CA
Meggs, Trisha E. ....Tallahassee, FL
Meggs, William N. ....Tallahassee, FL
Meghjee, Munir R. ....**Denver, CO**
Meghnot, Hedye ....Saginaw, MI
Meghrigian, Astrid ....San Francisco, CA
Meghrouni, Alexis D. ....**Newport Beach, CA**
Meghrouni, Michelle A., (P.C.)
Los Angeles, CA
Megias, Carlos M. ....West Palm Beach, FL
Megibben, Hart T. ....Shelbyville, KY
Megibow & Edwards, P.S.C. ....Paducah, KY
Megibow, Tod D. ....Paducah, KY
Megill, Andrew M. ....Toms River, NJ
Megill, Edward C. ....Wall Township, NJ
Meginnes, Brian J. ....**Peoria, IL**
Meginniss, David H. ....**Huntsville, AL**
Meginniss, Walter M. ....Tallahassee, FL
Meginniss, Walter M., Jr. ....New York, NY
Megley, Richard B. ....**Chicago, IL**
Megley, Richard Burns, Jr. ....**Chicago, IL**
Meglic, Mark Stan ....Greenville, SC
Meglic, Wilkes & DelCampo ....Greenville, SC
Meglow, William ....Elizabeth, NJ
Megna, Christine M. ....**New York, NY**
Megna, Philip W. ....College Point, NY
Megna, Ronald J. ....Chicago, IL
Megna, Vincent P. ....Waukesha, WI
Megna, William F.R. ....**Trenton, NJ**
Mego, Diane M.
United States Postal Service,
Judicial Officer, GV
Mego, Kelly W. ....Houston, TX
Megregian, Scott S. ....**Washington, DC**
Megret, Catherine F. ....**New York, NY**
Meguerian, Garen ....**Philadelphia, PA**
Meguerian, James K. ....Chicago, IL
Meguire, Jacques K. ....**Chicago, IL**
Megyesy, Eugene F., Jr. ....**Denver, CO**
Mehaffey, Steven A. ....Manakin-Sabot, VA
Mehaffy, James W. ....Beaumont, TX
Mehaffy, John R. ....**Boulder, CO**
Mehaffy & Weber, A Professional
Corporation ....**Beaumont, TX**
Houston, TX
Orange, TX
Mehalchick, George E. ....**Scranton, PA**
Mehalic, Jeffrey V. ....Charleston, WV
Mehalick, David M. ....Rochester, NY
Mehalick, James B. ....San Diego, CA
Mehalko, Megan Lum ....**Cleveland, OH**
Mehall, Michael J. ....**Torrance, CA**
Mehall, Philip S. ....Portsmouth, NH
Mehall, Robert J. ....**San Diego, CA**
Mehan, Donald J., Jr. ....**St. Louis, MO**
Mehan, George T., Jr. ....St. Louis, MO
Mehan, Marian V. ....**St. Louis, MO**
Mehan, Patrick Niall ....**Chesterfield, MO**
Mehan, Richard J., Sr. ....**St. Louis, MO**
Mehan, Thomas J. ....St. Louis, MO
Meharry, John R. ....Kansas City, MO
Mehary, Michael G. ....Merrick, NY
Mehas, Andrew G. ....Cincinnati, OH
Mehas, Michael W. ....**Ventura, CA**
Mehdi, Azra Z. ....**New York, NY**
Mehdy, Mitchell J. ....San Diego, CA
Meheen, M. Michael ....Oakland, CA
Mehesan, Thomas C. ....Las Vegas, NV
Meheula, William K. ....**Kailua, HI**
Mehfoud, Kathleen S. ....**Richmond, VA**
Mehigan, Patrick B. ....Milwaukee, WI
Mehigan, Richard M. ....Sacramento, CA
Mehigan, Richard M., A Professional
Corporation ....Sacramento, CA
Mehl, Cheryl Tremaine ....**Austin, TX**
Mehl, Frederick ....New York, NY
Mehl, J David ....Goshen, IN
Mehl, Jacob M. ....New York, NY
Mehl, Jeffrey E. ....Brooklyn, NY
Mehl, Karen A. ....Washington, DC
Mehl & Mehl ....Goshen, IN
Mehl, Richard L. ....Goshen, IN
Mehl, Shirley F. ....Woodmere, NY
Mehl, Spence Jonathan ....East Rutherford, NJ
Mehl, Williams, Cummings & Groce, P.C.
Fort Worth, TX
Mehlburger, Max C. ....Little Rock, AR
Mehlburger, Ragenea Thompson
Little Rock, AR
Mehle, Roger W. ....Washington, DC
Mehler, Charles V., III ....**Roanoke, VA**
Mehler, Evelyn L. ....**St. Louis, MO**
Mehler, Fern R. ....**New York, NY**
Mehler, Gordon ....Brooklyn, NY
Mehler, Irving M. ....Denver, CO
Mehler, John J. ....**Erie, PA**
Mehler, Nicholas G. ....**New York, NY**
Mehler, Randal A. ....Louisville, KY
Mehler, Raymond M. ....**Chicago, IL**
Mehler, William F. ....New Carrollton, MD
Mehlhaff, William N. ....**Portland, OR**
Mehlhaff and Hay ....Tracy, CA
Mehlhaff, Robert ....Tracy, CA
Mehlhop, Bart L. ....Sacramento, CA
Mehlick, John A. ....Springfield, IL
Mehlig, John Louis ....Montrose, CO
Mehling, Christopher J. ....**Covington, KY**
Mehling, Ronald B. ....Wheaton, IL
Mehlinger, Dianne Y. ....Falls Church, VA
Mehlinger, M. James ....Arlington, VA
Mehlman, Avery S. ....Brooklyn, NY
Mehlman, Barry T. ....**New York, NY**
Mehlman, Benjamin Wm. ....New York, NY
Mehlman, Bruce P. ....Potomac, MD
Mehlman, Edward B. ....Wilmette, IL
Mehlman, Frederick G. ....Columbia, MD
Mehlman, Frederick K. ....New York, NY
Mehlman, George B. ....Palm Beach, FL
Mehlman, Gerald J. ....**Los Angeles, CA**
Mehlman, Gerson B. ....**Baltimore, MD**
Mehlman & Greenblatt, LLC
Baltimore, MD
Pikesville, MD
Mehlman, Hope D. ....Princeton, NJ
Mehlman, Kenneth B. ....Washington, DC
Mehlman, Lester ....Morton Grove, IL
Mehlman, Madelyn B. ....New York, NY
Mehlman, Mark F. ....**Chicago, IL**
Mehlman, Maxwell J. ....Cleveland, OH
Mehlman, Peter W. ....Dobbs Ferry, NY
Mehlman, Rhonda H. ....**Los Angeles, CA**
Mehlman, Steven Jeffrey ....Walnut Creek, CA
Mehlsack, Barbara S. ....**New York, NY**
Mehltretter, Kathleen Mary ....Buffalo, NY
Mehn, Keith A. ....Kewaunee, WI
Mehne, Christopher G. ....**Worcester, MA**
Mehner, Roger ....**Summit, NJ**
Mehnert, Cynthia M. ....Augusta, ME
Boston, MA
Mehnert, Eric M. ....Augusta, ME
Boston, MA
Mehnert, Kristl L. ....Philadelphia, PA
Mehnert, Paul J. ....San Diego, CA
Mehnert, Thomas P. ....Cincinnati, OH
Mehochko, Kenneth E. ....Carlyle, IL
Mehok, Frank P., Jr. ....Delray Beach, FL
Mehok, Frank P., Jr., P.A. ....Delray Beach, FL
Mehok, George K. ....Cleveland, OH
Mehok, Scott R. ....**Harrisburg, PA**
Mehr, Adam R. ....Los Angeles, CA
Mehr, Erik W. ....Freehold, NJ
Mehr, Ethan ....Crescent City, CA
Mehr & LaFrance ....**Freehold, NJ**
Mehr, M. Austin ....Lexington, KY
Mehr, Matthew ....**Phoenix, AZ**
Mehr, Michael J. ....**Detroit, MI**
Mehr, Michael J. ....**Secaucus, NJ**
Mehr, Paul F. ....Milltown, NJ
Mehr, Robert W. ....**Novato, CA**
Mehr, Ryna E. ....**Boca Raton, FL**
Mehr, Tedd A. ....Colusa, CA
Mehr, William J. ....**Freehold, NJ**
Mehra, Ajay
Securities and Exchange Commission,
Division of Investment Management, GV
Mehra, Salil ....**New York, NY**
Mehra, Sarah ....**New York, NY**
Mehra, Shailesh ....**Palo Alto, CA**
Mehrara, Sasan ....**Mineola, NY**
New York, NY
Mehrbach, Tara L. ....**Washington, DC**
Mehrberg, Peter B. ....Emeryville, CA
Mehrberg, Randall E. ....**Chicago, IL**
Mehregan, Susan J. ....Monroe, MI
Mehrens, Craig ....**Phoenix, AZ**
Mehrens, Duane L. ....Lincoln, NE
Mehrens, Patrick W. ....Billings, MT
Mehrens and Wilemon, P.A. ....**Phoenix, AZ**
Mehrer, Owen ....Dickinson, ND
Mehrespand, Mehrdad ....**Washington, DC**
Mehrez, Alan ....Los Angeles, CA
Mehrhof, Richard R., Jr. ....**Augusta, GA**
Mehrhoff, Patricia A. ....Tucson, AZ
Mehri, Cyrus ....**Washington, DC**
Mehri, Malkin & Ross, PLLC
Washington, DC
Mehring, Christopher S. ....**Chicago, IL**
Mehring, Melissa A.
Office Of Special Counsel, GV
Mehring, Michael E. ....Baltimore, MD
Mehring, Samuel S., Jr., Law Offices of
Tampa, FL
Mehringer, Rebecca Pihl ....Corpus Christi, TX
Mehringer, Susan E. ....**Indianapolis, IN**
Mehringer, Theresa M. ....**Denver, CO**
Mehrkens, Wayne L. ....**Rochester, MN**
Mehrle, Joseph P. ....Liberty Township, OH
Mehrman, Leanne C. ....**Atlanta, GA**
Mehrman, Michael John ....**Atlanta, GA**
Mehrmann, Michael S. ....Kingston, MA
Mehrotra, Ajay ....**Chicago, IL**
Mehrtens, Thomas E. ....**New York, NY**
Mehrtens, Timothy R. J. ....**Denver, CO**
Mehta, Amit P. ....**Washington, DC**
Mehta, Cyrus D. ....**New York, NY**
Mehta, Dipali B. ....**Washington, DC**
Mehta, Eileen Ball, (P.A.) ....**Miami, FL**
Mehta, Irene K. ....New York, NY
Mehta, Khurshid K. ....Knoxville, TN
Mehta, Kiku N. ....Philadelphia, PA
Mehta, Kiran H. ....**Charlotte, NC**
Mehta, Mukund G. ....White Plains, NY
Mehta, Payal ....**Kansas City, MO**
Mehta, Pinak A. ....Washington, DC
Mehta, Prakash H. ....**Washington, DC**
Mehta, Raj ....Middletown, NY
Mehta, Ravi ....**Sacramento, CA**
Mehta, Ravinder ....Sacramento, CA
Mehta, Samita ....Houston, TX
Mehta, Sandhya ....**New York, NY**
Mehta, Sonal J. ....**Washington, DC**
Mehta, Steven G. ....**Los Angeles, CA**
Mehta, Sujal D. ....**Marlton, NJ**
Mehta, Tejal
Federal Communications Commission,
Common Carrier Bureau, GV
Mehta, Utpal P. ....Houston, TX
Mei, Eugene T. ....**San Francisco, CA**
Mei, Frederick E. ....Oyster Bay, NY
Mei, James M. ....**Portland, OR**
Mei, Peter C. ....**San Jose, CA**
Mei, Tom Y. K. ....**Santa Ana, CA**
Mei, Vesper ....Chicago, IL
Meibach, Ina Lea ....**New York, NY**
Meibaum, Diane M. ....Boston, MA
Meibeyer, Charles W. ....**Napa, CA**
Meiburger & Associates, P.C.
McLean, VA
Meiburger, George J. ....**Washington, DC**
Meiburger, Janet M. ....**McLean, VA**
Meiburger, Mary Alexis
United States Tax Court, GV
Meidam, Lynn M. ....Milwaukee, WI
Meide, Cheryl Dawn ....**Jacksonville, FL**
Meide, Moses, Jr. ....Jacksonville, FL
Meidenbauer, Randall C. ....Varysburg, NY
Meidinger, Dawn G. ....Phoenix, AZ
Meidinger, Floyd E. ....Leola, SD
Meidl, Christopher D. A. ....Pleasanton, CA
Meier, Aimee M. ....Cincinnati, OH
Meier, Albert J. ....Hanover, PA
Meier, Barbara J. ....**Indianapolis, IN**
Meier, Bradley J. ....**New York, NY**
Meier, Carl Lore ....Cincinnati, OH
Meier, Carol Stanton ....Trenton, NJ
Meier, Carolyn B. ....Charlottesville, VA
Meier, Charles D. ....**Wilmington, NC**
Meier, Cheryl L. ....**Chicago, IL**
Meier, Christina E. ....Virginia Beach, VA
Meier, Christine Chalk ....**Elmira, NY**
Meier, Christopher Thomas ....Acton, MA
Meier, Cole & O'Dell, P.A. ....**Tulsa, OK**
Meier, Dana G. ....**Indianapolis, IN**
Meier, David E. ....Cambridge, MA
Meier, David W. ....**Moline, IL**
Meier, Debra S. ....**Bloomfield Hills, MI**
Detroit, MI
Meier, Dennis C. ....Lusk, WY
Meier, Derek I. ....**Detroit, MI**
Meier, Diana E. ....**Dallas, TX**

Meier, Donna L. ....Greeley, CO
Meier, Donna L. ....St. Paul, MN
Meier, Dwight D. ....Washington, DC
Meier, Edward K. ....Vero Beach, FL
Meier, Fred J. ....Dallas, TX
Meier, Frederick L., II ....Paola, KS
Meier, George A., III ....Orlando, FL
Meier, Gerry H., (Ms.) ....Dallas, TX
Meier, Glenn F. ....Las Vegas, NV
Meier, Gregory G. ....Tulsa, OK
Meier, Gregory P. ....Madison, WI
Meier, Gregory W. ....Orlando, FL
Meier, Harold C. ....Columbus, OH
Meier, Harold E. ....Dallas, TX
Meier, Henry N., Jr. ....Oakbrook Terrace, IL
Meier, James A. ....Janesville, WI
Meier, James L. ....Santa Ana, CA
Meier, Jean A. ....Long Grove, IL
Meier, Jeanne M. ....Madison, WI
Meier, Jeremy A. ....San Francisco, CA
Meier, Jerome D. ....Pasadena, CA
Meier, Joan S. ....Washington, DC
Meier, John A. ....Overland Park, KS
Meier, John A., II ....Albany, GA
Meier, John G. ....Ishpeming, MI
Meier, John Otto ....Birmingham, AL
Meier, Jonathan P. ....Seattle, WA
Meier, Joseph M. ....Boise, ID
Meier, Karla M. ....Palm Springs, CA
Meier, Kathryn ....San Jose, CA
Meier, Keith A. ....Newburgh, IN
Meier, Kennedy & Quinn ....St. Paul, MN
Meier, Lawrence H. ....Burlington, VT
Meier, Lengauer, Bonner, Muszynski & Doyle, P.A. ....Daytona Beach, FL
Melbourne, FL
Ocala, FL
Orlando, FL
Sanford, FL
Tavares, FL
Meier, Leo J. ....Dubuque, IA
Meier, Linda Blair ....Madison, WI
Meier, Linda K. ....Greenwood, IN
Meier, Mark A. ....Sacramento, CA
Meier, Markus H. ....Washington, DC
Meier, Marvin O. ....Deerfield, IL
Meier, Matthew H. ....Wellesley, MA
Meier & Meier ....Cincinnati, OH
Meier, Michael ....Victoria, TX
Meier, Nancy ....Houston, TX
Meier, Paul ....Newark, NJ
Meier, Paul H. ....Los Angeles, CA
Meier, Peter C. ....San Francisco, CA
Meier, Peter E. ....Bethesda, MD
Meier, Raymond A. ....Rome, NY
Utica, NY
Meier, Richard A. ....Detroit, MI
Meier, Richard A. ....Farmington Hills, MI
Meier, Richard A. ....Plymouth, MI
Meier, Richard W. ....Oakland, CA
Meier, Rick B. ....Madison, WI
Meier, Robert A., Jr. ....Damascus, MD
Meier, Robert C. ....Creve Coeur, MO
Meier, Robert C. ....Cincinnati, OH
Meier, Roger A. ....Chicago, IL
Meier, Scott W. ....Cheyenne, WY
Meier, Sharon K. ....Dickinson, TX
Meier, Steven D. ....San Francisco, CA
Meier, Steven K. ....New York, NY
Meier, Steven P. ....Denver, CO
Meier, Steven R. ....New York, NY
Meier, Thomas J. ....Chicago, IL
Meier, Todd C. ....Dallas, TX
Meier, Tonya L. ....Dallas, TX
Meier, W. Kurt ....Chicago, IL
Meier, Wickhem, Lyons & Schulz, S.C.
Janesville, WI
Meier, William A. ....Columbus, OH
Meier, William C., Law Office of
Bedford, TX
Meier, William G. ....Flushing, NY
Meier, William J. ....Muskegon, MI
Meier, William W., III ....Dallas, TX
Meieran, Sharon E. ....San Francisco, CA
Meierding, Nina R. ....Ventura, CA
Meierhenry, Mark V. ....Sioux Falls, SD
Meierhenry, Sabrina ....Sioux Falls, SD
Meierhenry, Todd V. ....Sioux Falls, SD
Meierhofer, George F. ....New York, NY
Meierhoff, Gayle P. ....Topeka, KS
Meiering, Mark C. ....Albuquerque, NM
Meierkord, Brian G. ....Lacon, IL
Meierotto, Theodore M. ....Kansas City, MO
Meiers, Barbara A. ....Los Angeles, CA
Meiers, Donald H. ....Washington, DC
Meiers, Erwin F., III ....Flint, MI
Meiers, Steven Alan ....Los Angeles, CA
Meigel, Robin L. ....Washington, DC
Meighan, Burton C. ....Mamaroneck, NY
Meighan, Cecilia ....Wilkes-Barre, PA
Meighan, Hunter ....Mamaroneck, NY
Meighan, Jefferson D. ....Mamaroneck, NY
Meighan, John M., Jr. ....Annapolis, MD
Meighan, Katherine Wells
Washington, DC
Meighan & Necarsulmer ....Mamaroneck, NY
Meighen, G. Allen, Jr. ....Birmingham, AL
Meigher, Eugene J. ....Washington, DC
Meigher, Eva L. ....Washington, DC
Meigs, Arthur V. ....Washington, DC
Meigs, Eldon L. ....Pratt, KS
Meigs, Henry, II ....Louisville, KY
Meigs, J. Timothy ....Raleigh, NC
Meigs, Jack W. ....Centreville, AL
Meigs, John ....Inglewood, CA
Meigs, John F. ....Philadelphia, PA
Meigs, John V., Jr. ....Los Angeles, CA
Meigs, Randyl S. ....Fort Worth, TX

Meigs, Richard L. ....Olympia, WA
Meigs, Walter R. ....Mobile, AL
Meihn, G. Michael ....Bloomfield Hills, MI
Meihofer, Kurt C. ....Chicago, IL
Meihsner, Larry S. ....Milwaukee, WI
Meija, Janis ....Lansing, MI
Meikle, Andrew D. ....Falls Church, VA
Meikle, Brian L. ....Tacoma, WA
Meikle, Christopher G. ....Chatham, NJ
Meikle, Gary Lane ....Idaho Falls, ID
Meikle, Kristin L. ....Washington, DC
Meikle, Ted S. ....Minneapolis, MN
Meikle, Tesno & Luth ....Celina, OH
Meikle, William ....Celina, OH
Meiklejohn, Alexander M. ....Hamden, CT
Meiklejohn, Alvin J., Jr. ....Denver, CO
Meiklejohn, Anita L. ....Boston, MA
Meiklejohn, D. Stuart ....New York, NY
Meiklejohn, Douglas ....Santa Fe, NM
Meiklejohn, Joyce E. ....Boston, MA
Meiklejohn, Paul T. ....Seattle, WA
Meiklejohn, Rebecca ....New York, NY
Meiklejohn, Scott A. ....Denver, CO
Meiklejohn, Thomas W. ....Hartford, CT
Meilen, Gerhard ....New York, NY
Meili, Barbara C. ....New York, NY
Meili, Brett R. ....Milwaukee, WI
Meili, Stephen E. ....Madison, WI
Meilinger, Rex F. ....Sycamore, IL
Meilke & Holladay, LLP ....New York, NY
Meilman, Edward A. ....New York, NY
Meilman, Roy K. ....New York, NY
Meilman, Stephanie K. ....Newton, MA
Meilman, Stephanie K., P.C., Law Offices of
Newton, MA
Meils, Rick D. ....Indianapolis, IN
Meils, Thompson & Dietz
Indianapolis, IN
Meilton, Roger B. ....Mechanicsburg, PA
Meilton, Sandra L. ....Harrisburg, PA
Meilus, Ann E. ....Barre, MA
Meily, William D. ....Dayton, OH
Meiman, Gregory J. ....Louisville, KY
Meimaris, Emmanuel V. ....Belmont, MA
Meimaris, James George ....Cleveland, OH
Mein, Joseph I. ....Coeur d'Alene, ID
Mein, Kevin G. ....Alameda, CA
Meinardus, Karen H. ....El Campo, TX
Meinck, Doreen A. ....Chicago, IL
Meincke, D. Jennings ....Irvine, CA
Meincke, Randall A. ....Cumming, GA
Meinders, Hildred McCants
Pauls Valley, OK
Meinders, John R. ....Woodward, OK
Meindertsma, Donn C. ....Washington, DC
Meindl, J. Nicholson ....Dallas, TX
Meindl, John M. ....Newport Beach, CA
Meinecke, Joel W. ....Topeka, KS
Meinel, Max ....Monroe, LA
Meiner, Charles E. ....Orlando, FL
Meiner, Grant S. ....Port Angeles, WA
Meiner, Sam C. ....Orlando, FL
Meiner, Steven Jay ....New York, NY
Meiners, Carla ....West Des Moines, IA
Meiners, Denise F.
National Labor Relations Board,
Office of the General Counsel, GV
Meiners, Eckart ....Piscataway, NJ
Meiners, Everett F. ....Los Angeles, CA
Meiners, Louis M., Jr. ....Carmel, IN
Meiners, Louis P. ....Covington, KY
Cincinnati, OH
Meiners, Luke Emmanuel ....St. Louis, MO
Meiners, Michael J. ....Greenwood, IN
Meiners, Michele Claire ....Vienna, VA
Meiners, Robert G. ....San Diego, CA
Meiners, Roger S. ....Milford, MI
Meiners, Sharman R. ....Stayton, OR
Meiners, Valerie Seal ....Baton Rouge, LA
Meinert, James M. ....Pittsburgh, PA
Meinert, Scott D. ....Fresno, CA
Meinert, Timothy A. ....Eagle, CO
Meinerts, Merlyn L. ....Lakeville, MN
Meinertzhagen, Stephen R. ....Chicago, IL
Meingossner, Robert P. ....Blue Bell, PA
Meinhard, David G. ....Teterboro, NJ
Meinhardt, Howard J. ....Pittsburgh, PA
Meinhardt, Paul W. ....Mount Prospect, IL
Meinhardt, Robyn A. ....Los Angeles, CA
Denver, CO
Meinhart, Carol B. ....Radcliff, KY
Meinhart, Chris ....Louisville, KY
Meinhold, Don H. ....Colorado Springs, CO
Meinhold, William T. ....Redwood City, CA
Meinig, Robert R. ....Seattle, WA
Meininger, Carl R. ....Chevy Chase, MD
Meininger, Leigh R. ....Orlando, FL
Meininger, Mark M. ....Portland, OR
Meininger & Meininger, P.A. ....Orlando, FL
Meinken, Gary S. ....Peachtree City, GA
Meinrath, John C. ....Washington, DC
Meinrath, Steven ....Sacramento, CA
Meinster, Ann Gail ....Conifer, CO
Meinster, Barry ....Denver, CO
Meinster and Francy, Attorneys at Law, P.C.
Denver, CO
Meints, Paul A. ....Bloomington, IL
Meints, Steven Lester ....Omaha, NE
Meinwald, Barbara J. ....New York, NY
Meinwald, Harlan Mark ....Solon, OH
Meinz, George E. ....St. Cloud, MN
Meinz, Thomas J. ....Princeton, MN
Meinz, Verlin R. ....Ottawa, IL
Meinzer, Christopher H. ....Pennsburg, PA
Meinzer, Karen E. ....Buffalo, NY
Meinzer Law Offices ....Pennsburg, PA
Meinzer, Neal ....Austin, TX
Meinzer, Robert L., Jr. ....St. John, IN

Meinzer, Staci L. ....Los Angeles, CA
Meir, Dennis S. ....Atlanta, GA
Meir, Rakel M. ....Boston, MA
Meire, Patti G. ....Richmond, VA
Meiring, Ronald C. ....Prudenville, MI
Meirose & Friscia, P.A. ....Clearwater, FL
St. Petersburg, FL
Tampa, FL
Meirose, Leo H., Jr. ....Tampa, FL
Meirowitz, Clifford A. ....New York, NY
Meirowitz, Joel B. ....Glen Cove, NY
Meirowitz, Mark ....New York, NY
Meirowitz, Richard W. ....New York, NY
Meis, Alexander & Dean
San Francisco, CA
Meis, Fred G. ....San Francisco, CA
Meis, Lucille Charlotte ....Seattle, WA
Meis, Lucille Gonzales ....Denver, CO
Meis, Robert F. ....Sioux City, IA
Meis, Steven J. ....West Hartford, CT
Meisburg, John Marshall, Jr. ....Atlanta, GA
Meisburg, Robt. L. ....Louisville, KY
Meisburg, Ronald E. ....Washington, DC
Meisch, Peter J. ....Osseo, MN
Meise, Ashley Anne ....Washington, DC
Meise, Clyde G. ....Kansas City, MO
Meise, Coen & McMorris ....Kansas City, MO
Meise, Gary John ....Nashville, TN
Meise, William H. ....Bethesda, MD
Meisel, Alan ....Pittsburgh, PA
Meisel, Andrew H. ....San Francisco, CA
Meisel, Arthur ....Princeton, NJ
Meisel, Brian Paul ....Los Angeles, CA
Meisel, Bruce M. ....Westwood, NJ
Meisel, Einat ....San Francisco, CA
Meisel, Elliott ....New York, NY
Meisel, Gary J. ....Burbank, CA
Meisel, George I. ....Palm City, FL
Meisel, George V. ....St. Louis, MO
Meisel, Gerald S. ....Westwood, NJ
Meisel, Keith W. ....North Palm Beach, FL
Meisel, Keith W., P.A.
North Palm Beach, FL
Meisel, L. J. ....Huntington, WV
Meisel, Lois F. ....Glen Rock, NJ
Meisel, Marvin ....Palo Alto, CA
Meisel, Michael S. ....Hackensack, NJ
Meisel, Robert H. ....Saginaw, MI
Meisel, Robert P. ....New York, NY
Meisel, Robin L. ....San Francisco, CA
Meisel, Stacey L. ....Millburn, NJ
Meisel, Susan A. ....New York, NY
Meisel, Tobie G. ....Hackensack, NJ
Meiselas, Kenneth ....Great Neck, NY
Meiseles, Rochelle C. ....Newark, NJ
Meiselman, Abby S. ....New York, NY
Meiselman, Alyson ....North Potomac, MD
Meiselman, Boland, Reilly & Fugazzi
Mineola, NY
Meiselman, David J. ....White Plains, NY
Meiselman, Farber, Packman & Eberz, P.C.
Mount Kisco, NY
White Plains, NY
Meiselman & Gordon ....New York, NY
Meiselman, Irwin G. ....Rockville, MD
Meiselman, Michael L. ....New York, NY
Meiselman, Neal J. ....Rockville, MD
Meiselman & Salzer, P.C. ....Rockville, MD
Meiselman, Sanford H. ....Wilmette, IL
Meisels, David M. ....New York, NY
Meisels, David M. ....Portland, OR
Meisels, Ellen K. ....Charleston, WV
Meisels, Grant M. ....New York, NY
Meisels, Hillary S. ....Redondo Beach, CA
Meisels, Naomi P. ....New York, NY
Meisels, Peter A. ....White Plains, NY
Meisenbach, Earl E. ....Grand Rapids, MI
Meisenbacher, Raymond F. ....Bridgewater, NJ
Meisenbacher, Thomas M. ....Bridgewater, NJ
Meisenberg, Jay F., (P.A.) ....Fort Myers, FL
Meisenheimer, Francis E. ....Kingman, KS
Meisenheimer Herron & Steele, A Professional Corporation ....San Diego, CA
Meisenheimer, James W. ....San Diego, CA
Meisenheimer, Keith E. ....Portland, OR
Meisenheimer, Patricia M. ....Islandia, NY
Meisenhelder, John F. ....Cincinnati, OH
Meisenhelder, Robert J., II ....Kalamazoo, MI
Meisenhelder, Samuel F. ....York, PA
Meisenholder, Lynda ....Manhattan Beach, CA
Meisenzahl, Stuart B. ....Rochester, NY
Meiser, C. Keith ....Jacksonville, FL
Meiser, Frederick A., Jr. ....San Diego, CA
Meiser, Kenneth E. ....Princeton, NJ
Meiser, Margaret A. ....Window Rock, AZ
Meiser, Maria Cristina ....New York, NY
Meiser, Rita A. ....Phoenix, AZ
Meiser, Robert N. ....Washington, DC
Meises, Michele J. ....New York, NY
Meisgeier, Nathan J. ....Kansas City, MO
Meisgeier, Steven C. ....Houston, TX
Meisinger, David A.
Glenwood Springs, CO
Meisinger, Deana K. ....Omaha, NE
Meisinger, Edmund C. ....West St. Paul, MN
Meisinger & Filewicz ....Omaha, NE
Meisinger, Kirk L., (P.C.) ....Omaha, NE
Meisinger, Louis M. ....Burbank, CA
Meisinger & Meisinger ....West St. Paul, MN
Meisinger, Stephen ....West St. Paul, MN
Meisinger, Susan R. ....Alexandria, VA
Meislahn, Harry P. ....Albany, NY
Meisler, Arthur P. ....Vernon, CT
Meisler, Joanne F. ....Roseland, NJ
Meisler, Marc A. ....Baltimore, MD
Meisler, Sharon R. ....Norristown, PA
Meislik, Ira ....Montclair, NJ
Meislik, Karen ....West Orange, NJ

Meislik & Levavy ....Montclair, NJ
Meislik, Stuart R. ....Phoenix, AZ
Meismer, Paul C. ....Missoula, MT
Meismer, Alfred ....Bethesda, MD
Meisner & Associates, P.C.
Bingham Farms, MI
Detroit, MI
Meisner, Daniel ....Newark, NJ
Meisner, Derek M. ....Washington, DC
Meisner, Gordon R. ....West Bloomfield, MI
Meisner, Ivo ....Edgartown, MA
Meisner, Jerome L. ....Sarasota, FL
Meisner, Julie C. ....Tampa, FL
Meisner, Kevin W. ....Uncasville, CT
Meisner, Lara Strayer ....Washington, DC
Meisner, Mary M. ....Pittsburgh, PA
Meisner, Matthew
Federal Trade Commission,
Bureau of Competition, GV
Meisner, Mitchell R. ....Detroit, MI
Meisner, Peter M., (P.C.)
New Orleans, LA
Meisner, Richard S. ....Parsippany, NJ
Meisner, Robert M. ....Bingham Farms, MI
Meisner, Roland D. ....Alexandria, VA
Meisner, William S. ....Eugene, OR
Meiss, Richard L. ....San Francisco, CA
Meiss, Thomas M. ....Atlanta, GA
Meissel, Richard A. ....Irvine, CA
Meissner, Carl L. ....Marshfield, WI
Meissner, Corinna E. ....San Francisco, CA
Meissner, George S. ....New York, NY
Meissner, Gregory C. ....Bradenton, FL
Meissner, John J., Jr. ....Sacramento, CA
Meissner, Joseph P. ....Cleveland, OH
Meissner, Ken ....Falls Church, VA
Meissner, Kleinberg & Finkel
New York, NY
Meissner, Michael G. ....Cleveland, OH
Meissner, Paul A., Jr. ....Clearwater, FL
Meissner, Paul F. ....Milwaukee, WI
Meissner, Philip M. ....New York, NY
Meissner, Robert L. ....Fair Oaks, CA
Meissner, Stuart ....New York, NY
Meissner, Thomas P. ....Lewistown, MT
Meissner Tierney Fisher & Nichols S.C.
Milwaukee, WI
Meissner, Wayne D. ....Austin, TX
Meissner, Wendell E. ....Omaha, NE
Meissner, Werner R. ....San Pedro, CA
Meissner, Werner R., Law Office of, A Prof. Law Corp. ....San Pedro, CA
Meissner-Cutler, Susanna L.
Castle Rock, CO
Meister & Ayers Company, LPA ....Toledo, OH
Meister, Barry P. ....Northbrook, IL
Meister, Brenda G. ....Washington, DC
Meister, Brian H. ....Cleveland, OH
Meister, Christopher B. ....Chicago, IL
Meister, Cynthia A. ....Chicago, IL
Meister, David ....New York, NY
Meister, David Lee ....Pittsburgh, PA
Meister, Douglas C. ....Riverdale, MD
Meister, Frederick ....Columbus, OH
Meister, Frederick W. ....Phoenix, AZ
Meister, Harry R. ....Scottsbluff, NE
Meister, Jacob J. ....Chicago, IL
Meister, James M.
Department of Commerce,
Patent and Trademark Office, GV
Meister, James M. ....St. Louis, MO
Meister, Jill M. ....Minneapolis, MN
Meister, Joan B. ....Delta, OH
Meister, Jonathan A. ....Jersey City, NJ
New York, NY
Meister, Julia B. ....Cincinnati, OH
Meister, Kenneth E. ....New York, NY
Meister, Lawrence M. ....Baltimore, MD
Meister, Lotte Anderson ....New York, NY
Meister, Marc J. ....Toledo, OH
Meister, Margaret L. ....Albuquerque, NM
Meister & Meister ....Delta, OH
Meister, Michael W. ....Scottsbluff, NE
Meister, Paul A. ....Chicago, IL
Meister, Philip K. ....Hartford, CT
Meister, Robert A. ....New York, NY
Meister, Ronald W. ....New York, NY
Meister Seelig & Fein LLP ....New York, NY
Meister & Segrist ....Scottsbluff, NE
Meister, Sheldon C. ....Delta, OH
Meister, Stephani Amelia ....Mineola, NY
Meister, Stephen B. ....New York, NY
Meister, Stuart G. ....Chantilly, VA
Meister, Thomas E. ....Cincinnati, OH
Meister, Thomas F. ....York, PA
Meister, William A. ....Rockford, IL
Meistrell, Gerard M. ....New York, NY
Meistrich, Benn William ....Iselin, NJ
Meistrich, Herbert A. ....San Diego, CA
Meiswinkle, David ....Belle Mead, NJ
Meites, Frackman, Mulder & Burger
Chicago, IL
Meites, Jerome B. ....Chicago, IL
Meites, Thomas R. ....Chicago, IL
Meith, Jeffrey A. ....Oroville, CA
Meith, Melissa M. ....Sacramento, CA
Meitlis, Erit S. ....New York, NY
Meitner, Alfred Victor, Jr. ....Broad Axe, PA
Meitner, Pamela ....Wilmington, DE
Meitz, Curt R. ....Waukesha, WI
Meitz, Ronald M. ....Phoenix, AZ
Meitzen, William A. ....Richmond, TX
Meives, Joseph R. ....St. Louis, MO
Meives, Mary Jo ....Fort Lauderdale, FL
Meives, Richard L. ....St. Louis, MO
Meixsell, Raymond K., Jr. ....Wilmington, DE
Meizler & Benowitz, P.C. ....Boston, MA
Meizler, Harold ....Boston, MA

Mellette, Peter M. ....Richmond, VA
Melletz, Paul R., (P.A.) ....Cherry Hill, NJ
Mellevold, Christopher G. ....New York, NY
Melley, Anne Sara ....Philadelphia, PA
Melley, Maura L. ....West Hartford, CT
Melley, Steven M. ....Rhinebeck, NY
Melley, William J., III ....Hartford, CT
Mellgard, David M. ....New York, NY
Melli, Andrew Shea ....Paramus, NJ
Melli, Charles R., Jr. ....Paramus, NJ
Melli, Guerin & Melli, A Professional Corporation ....Hackensack, NJ
Paramus, NJ
Madison, WI
Melli, Joseph A. ....Madison, WI
Melli, Mark A. ....Paramus, NJ
Melli, Marygold S. ....Madison, WI
Melli, Walker, Pease & Ruhly, S.C.
Madison, WI
Mellichamp, Joseph C., III ....Tallahassee, FL
Mellick, Edward G. ....New Canaan, CT
Mellick, James U. ....Waukon, IA
Mellick & Sexton, P.C. ....New Canaan, CT
Mellicker, Joseph B. ....New York, NY
Melliere, Michael J. ....Columbus, OH
Mellies, Charles B. ....Falls Church, VA
Mellin, Cecil R. ....Cleveland, OH
Mellin, Daniel J. ....Annapolis, MD
Mellin, Matthew P. ....Baltimore, MD
Mellina, David M. ....Fort Worth, TX
Mellina & Larson, P.C. ....Fort Worth, TX
Melling, Blair N. ....Bedford, OH
Melling, Brian J. ....Bedford, OH
Melling, George D., Jr.
Salt Lake City, UT
Melling, Louise F. ....New York, NY
Melling, Melling & Bell ....Bedford, OH
Melling, Thomas G. ....Seattle, WA
Mellinger, Jacob ....Morris Plains, NJ
Mellinger, John W. ....Milwaukee, WI
Mellinger, Joyce Hall ....Baltimore, MD
Mellinger, Lawrence P.
Department Of The Interior, Office of the Solicitor, GV
Mellinger, Lee F. ....Elkhart, IN
Mellinger, Louis ....Morris Plains, NJ
Mellinger, Michelle K. ....Chicago, IL
Mellinger, Robert L. ....Miami, FL
Mellinger, S. Richard ....Lawrence, KS
Mellinger & Sanders, P.C. ......Morris Plains, NJ
Mellinger, Victor M. ....Lubbock, TX
Mellini, Susan E. ....St. Petersburg, FL
Mellinkoff, David ....Los Angeles, CA
Mellinkoff, Debra Lea ....Sausalito, CA
Mellino, Christopher M. ....Cleveland, OH
Mellino, Gaynel F., (Ms.) ....Cleveland, OH
Mellion, James H. ....New City, NY
Mellion, Michael B. ....Smithfield, RI
Mellis, Joel P. ....Stamford, CT
Mellis, Jon Andrew ....Stamford, CT
Mellis, Michael J. ....New York, NY
Mellits, Bart I. ....Camden, NJ
Philadelphia, PA
Mellitz, Jacob ....Fairfield, CT
Mellitz, Jeremy A. ....New Haven, CT
Mellitz, John L. ....St. Louis, MO
Mellitz, Jonathan A. ....Hartford, CT
Mellk, Arnold M. ....Princeton, NJ
Mellk, Wendy J. ....Woodbury, NY
Mellman, Bernard J. ....St. Louis, MO
Mellman, Richard B.
Department of Education, Office of the General Counsel, GV
Mello, Anthony V. ....Ault, CO
Mello, Barbara ....Baltimore, MD
Mello, David M. ....Boston, MA
Mello, Ellen M. ....White Plains, NY
Mello, H. Joseph ....New York, NY
Mello, James E. ....St. Louis, MO
Mello, Jane M. ....New Bedford, MA
Mello, Kenneth M. ....Modesto, CA
Mello, Kenneth S., Law Offices of
Fall River, MA
Mello, Laura S. ....Newark, NJ
Mello, Lori R.P. ....Sacramento, CA
Mello, Melissa Lee ....Los Angeles, CA
Mello, Michael A. ....South Royalton, VT
Mello, Patricia J. ....Mashpee, MA
Mello, Paul Brian ....San Francisco, CA
Mello, Ralph W. ....Brentwood, TN
Mello, Robert A. ....Burlington, VT
Mello, Robert A. ....South Burlington, VT
Mello, Susan H. ....Clayton, MO
Mello, Susan M. ....Newark, NJ
Mello, Wayne L. ....Morristown, NJ
Mellody, Jerome M.
Department of Transportation, Federal Aviation Administration, GV
Mellody, Joseph P., Jr. ....Sayre, PA
Mellody, Katherine A. ....Treasury Department, Internal Revenue Service, GV
Mellody, Patrick J. ....Scranton, PA
Melloh, David R. ....Minneapolis, MN
Mellom, Peter ....Alexandria, MN
Mellom, Ralph M. ....Greenville, SC
Mellon, Amy A. ....New York, NY
Mellon, Francis X. ....McLean, VA
Mellon, Howard J. ....Columbus, OH
Mellon, James T. ....Troy, MI
Mellon, Jane M. ....Northbrook, IL
Mellon, John E. ....Ogdensburg, NY
Mellon, John W., Jr. ....Oreland, PA
Mellon, Joseph J. ....Denver, CO
Mellon, Kathleen G. ....Troy, MI
Mellon Law Firm, The ....Denver, CO
Mellon, Leonard M. ....Easton, PA
Mellon, M. Richard ....Pittsburgh, PA
Mellon, Mary F. ....Denver, CO
Mellon, McCarthy & Van Dusen, P.C.
Detroit, MI
Troy, MI
Mellon, Raymond T. ....New York, NY
Mellon, Richard C., Jr. ....Boise, ID
Mellon, Robert E. ....Waterbury, CT
Mellon, Robert J. ....Doylestown, PA
Mellon, Robert S. ....Denham Springs, LA
Mellon, Sharon A. ....Iowa City, IA
Mellon & Spies ....Iowa City, IA
Mellon, Thomas E., Jr. ....Doylestown, PA
Mellon, Thomas S. ....Glenside, PA
Mellon, Victor H. ....Los Angeles, CA
Mellon, Webster & Mellon, A Prof. Corp., The Law Offices of ....Doylestown, PA
Mellone, Carl J. ....Hackensack, NJ
Melloni, Thomas R. ....Burlington, VT
Mellon-Werch, Michelle D. ....Houston, TX
Mellor, Brian A. ....Sacramento, CA
Mellor, Charles Jervis ....Petaluma, CA
Mellor, Cord C. ....North Port, FL
Mellor, Elizabeth ....Kansas City, KS
Mellor, James R., Jr. ....Irvine, CA
Mellor, K. Bradley ....Pittsburgh, PA
Mellor, Mark A. ....Riverside, CA
Mellor, Mark L. ....Wichita, KS
Mellor, Merwin A. ....La Crosse, WI
Mellor and Miller, P.A. ....Wichita, KS
Mellor, Patricia K. ....Nashua, NH
Mellor, Phillip ....Wichita, KS
Mellor, Robert E. ....San Francisco, CA
Mellor, Thomas Christopher
New York, NY
Mellott, Christopher R. ....Baltimore, MD
Mellott, Cloyd R. ....Pittsburgh, PA
Mellott, David W. ....Cleveland, OH
Mellott, Earl W., II ....Boston, MA
Mellott, John T. ....Newark, OH
Mellott & Joyce, P.C. ....Sterling, IL
Mellott, Michael A. ....Sterling, IL
Mellott, Timothy R. ....Malvern, PA
Mellotte, Bradley Alan ....Yakima, WA
Mellow, Juliet ....Washington, DC
Mellow, Karen R. ....Chicago, IL
Mellow, Mary Anne ....Belleville, IL
St. Louis, MO
Mellow, Richard W. ....St. Louis, MO
Mellow, William G. ....Juneau, AK
Melloway, D. David ....St. Louis, MO
Mellowitz, James A. ....Indianapolis, IN
Melloy, Michael J. ....Cedar Rapids, IA
Melloy, Thomas P. ....St. Cloud, MN
Mells, Alexandra Kathryn ....Van Nuys, CA
Mellstrom, Brian H. ....New York, NY
Melluish, Ronald L. ....Elk Grove, CA
Mellum, Gale R. ....Minneapolis, MN
Mellum, Wendy J. ....Minneapolis, MN
Mellups, Ivars V. ....Oakton, VA
Mellusi, Caroline A. ....New York, NY
Mellusi, Ralph J. ....New York, NY
Melly, Francis P. ....Flushing, NY
Mellyn, John E., Jr. ....Cleveland, OH
Melman, David A. ....Lafayette, LA
Melman, David G. ....New York, NY
Melman, Gil M. ....Houston, TX
Melman, Helen W. ....Los Angeles, CA
Melman, James A. ....Los Angeles, CA
Melman, Leslie Rice
Federal Trade Commission, Office of the General Counsel, GV
Melman, Marla J. ....Allentown, PA
Melman, Michael P. ....San Diego, CA
Melmed, Jonathan M.A. ....New York, NY
Melmed, Julian K. ....Stamford, CT
Melmed, Lynden ....Dallas, TX
Melmed & Trombly ....Stamford, CT
Melmet, Steven J. ....Santa Ana, CA
Melmet, Steven J., Inc., Law Offices of
Santa Ana, CA
Melnbrencis, Velta A.
Department of Justice, Civil Division, GV
Melner, Amy R. ....Los Angeles, CA
Melner, Michael L. ....Reno, NV
Melnick, Andrew B. ....New York, NY
Melnick, Andrew J. ....Weehawken, NJ
Melnick, Arseny A. ....Youngstown, OH
Melnick, Arseny A., & Robert R. Melnick
Youngstown, OH
Melnick, Carol A. ....Garden City, NY
Melnick, Cliff ....Novato, CA
Melnick, David A. ....Milwaukee, WI
Melnick, David H. ....San Francisco, CA
Melnick, David M. ....Rockville, MD
Melnick, Deborah Lynn ....Bartow, FL
Melnick, Diane B.
Department of Commerce, Patent and Trademark Office, GV
Melnick, Gregory E., Jr. ....Orlando, FL
Melnick, Irving H. ....Chicago, IL
Melnick, Jeffry A. ....Chicago, IL
Melnick, John L. ....Falls Church, VA
Melnick, Kim ....Litchfield, CT
Melnick, Larry M. ....Jonesboro, GA
Melnick, Larry M., P.C. ....Jonesboro, GA
Melnick, Laura ....St. Paul, MN
Melnick, Lawrence J. ....Hallandale Beach, FL
Melnick, Lisa A. ....Boston, MA
Melnick, Lou M. ....Denver, CO
Melnick, Mark ....Stamford, CT
Melnick, Mark A. ....Department of Justice, Civil Division, GV
Melnick & Melnick ....Arlington, VA
Falls Church, VA
Melnick, Mitchell J. ....New Milford, CT
Melnick, Paul H. ....Falls Church, VA
Melnick, Phyllis ....Shaker Heights, OH
Melnick, Richard A. ....Vancouver, WA
Melnick, Richard H. ....Rockville, MD
Melnick, Richard J. ....Rockville, MD
Melnick, Robert Russell ....Youngstown, OH
Melnick, Robert S. ....New York, NY
Melnick, Robt. J. ....Old Orchard Beach, ME
Melnick, Roy E. ....Londonderry, NH
Melnick, Sam S. ....Chicago, IL
Melnick, Stephen Alan ....Boca Raton, FL
Melnick, Stephen Alan, P.A.
Boca Raton, FL
Melnick, Stuart L. ....New York, NY
Melnicke, Briendy ....Brooklyn, NY
Melnicoe, Alan H. ....San Jose, CA
Melnicoe, Peter ....Sacramento, CA
Melnicoff, Joel N. ....Syracuse, NY
Melnicove, Howard D. ....Bridgeton, NJ
Melnik, Karen L. ....Washington, DC
Melnik, Karen S. ....Chicago, IL
Melnik, Patrick J. ....Northampton, MA
Melnik, Roman ....Los Angeles, CA
Melnik, Selinda A. ....New York, NY
Melnik, Todd L. ....Encino, CA
Melnik, W. Joseph ....Cleveland, OH
Melniker, Benj. ....New York, NY
Melnikoff, Marcy J. ....New York, NY
Melnikoff, Ruth M. ....Harrison, NY
Melnitsky, Sheldon S. ....Maplewood, NJ
Melnychuk, Theodore S. ....Media, PA
Melnyk, Markian M. ....Washington, DC
Melnyk, Michael ....Greenwich, CT
Melnyk, Peter T. ....Florham Park, NJ
Melo, David J. ....Jackson Heights, NY
Melo, Mark Igmedio ....Torrance, CA
Melo, Thomas M. ....Houston, TX
Melo, Tina Lundy ....Houston, TX
Meloan, Paul ....Montgomery Village, MD
Meloan, Paul A., P.C.
Montgomery Village, MD
Meloch, Mary T. ....Santa Ana, CA
Meloch, Sally Lynn ....Los Angeles, CA
Meloche, Ann Hunt ....Pontiac, MI
Meloche, Ann Hunt, P.C. ....Pontiac, MI
Meloche, Charles H., Jr. ....Spencer, MA
Meloche, Donald L. ....San Diego, CA
Meloche, James P. ....Birmingham, MI
Meloche, Michael C. ....Spencer, MA
Melodia, Mark S. ....Princeton, NJ
Melodia, Paul V. ....San Francisco, CA
Melody, Christine Saryn
General Accounting Office, Office of the General Counsel, GV
Melody, Eugene J. ....Red Bank, NJ
Melody, John M. ......General Accounting Office, Office of the General Counsel, GV
Melody, Michael J., Jr. ....West Chester, PA
Melody, Robert C. ....Keyser, WV
Melody, Thomas A. ....Irving, TX
Melody, Thomas M. ....Chicago, IL
Melofchik, Dennis J. ....Ocean Township, NJ
Meloff, Bruce J. ....Blue Bell, PA
Melograne, Jules C. ....Pittsburgh, PA
Meloling, Albert W. ....Oakland, CA
Melom, Gail B. ....Arcadia, CA
Melom, Halvor S. ....Los Angeles, CA
Melonakis, Anthony ....Denver, CO
Melonas, Jacqueline M. ....Vienna, VA
Melone, Carl J. ....Newtown Square, PA
Melone, David R. ....San Francisco, CA
Melone, James A. ....Youngstown, OH
Melone, Jerry M. ....Tulsa, OK
Melone, Joan Ellen ....Upper Saddle River, NJ
Melone, Joseph ....Waltham, MA
Melone, Matt Allan ....Tulsa, OK
Melone & Melone ....Tulsa, OK
Melone, Michael E. ....Treasury Department, Internal Revenue Service, GV
Melone, Robert F. ....Tampa, FL
Melone, Robert J. ....Barrington, IL
Melone, Thomas M. ....New York, NY
Melone, Wendy M. ....Chicago, IL
Meloni, Edoardo ....Boca Raton, FL
Meloni, Louis R. ....Haddonfield, NJ
Meloni, Robert S. ....New York, NY
Meloni, William N. ....Boston, MA
Melore, Stephen F. ....Uniondale, NY
Meloro, Bobbi-Lee ....Miami, FL
Meloro, Francis Anthony ....Las Vegas, NV
Meloro, Thomas J. ....New York, NY
Melotik, Lorraine S. ....Dearborn, MI
Melott, Robert A. ....Raleigh, NC
Meloun, Matthew J. ....Birmingham, AL
Melowski, Dennis M. ....Elkhart Lake, WI
Meloy, Ada ....New York, NY
Meloy, Brian M. ....St. Paul, MN
Meloy, Colleen L. ....Madison, WI
Meloy, Daniel A. ....Cherokee, IA
Meloy, David J. ....Davenport, IA
Muscatine, IA
Meloy, Gary E. ....Marshall, WI
Meloy, Loretta ....Shelbyville, IN
Meloy, Michael J. ....Davenport, IA
Meloy, Michael M. ....Bala Cynwyd, PA
Meloy & Morrison ....Helena, MT
Meloy, Nancy ....Wilmette, IL
Meloy, Peter M. (Mike) ....Helena, MT
Meloy, Sybil ....Washington, DC
Jacksonville, FL
Orlando, FL
Tampa, FL
West Palm Beach, FL
Meloy, Thomas C. ....Columbus, OH
Meloy, Timothy J. ....Helena, MT
Melrod, Abram I. ....Millburn, NJ
Melrod, Daniel ....Washington, DC
Melrod, Leonard S. ....Washington, DC
Melrose, Mark R. ....Sylva, NC
Melrose, Mary Jane ....Longwood, FL
Melrose, Paul ....Boston, MA
Melrose, Seago & Lay, P.A.
Bryson City, NC
Franklin, NC
Sylva, NC
Waynesville, NC
Melroy, Robert L. ....Oak Brook, IL
Melroy, Theresa A. ....Lake Forest, IL
Melser, Allen S. ....Washington, DC
Melsha, Christopher J. ....Minneapolis, MN
Melsheimer, Thomas M., (P.C.)
Dallas, TX
Melsher, Alice Rosen ....Cleveland, OH
Melsher, Gary W. ....Cleveland, OH
Melson, David E. ....Richmond, VA
Melson, Earl Jerome ....Knoxville, TN
Melson, Gordon R. ....Wewoka, OK
Melson, James B. ....Anderson, IN
Melson, Lynn A. ....Lincoln, NE
Melson, Mark D. ....New York, NY
Melson, Ramona E.
Federal Communications Commission, Wireless Telecommunications Bureau, GV
Melson, Richard D. ....Tallahassee, FL
Melson, Theresa M. ....Los Angeles, CA
Meltaus, John A. ....Boston, MA
Meltebeke, Brenda L. ....Portland, OR
Melton, Angela M. ....Butler, PA
Melton, Barry ....Woodland, CA
Melton, Brian D. ....Dallas, TX
Melton, Bruce W. ....Chicago, IL
Melton, Buckner F. ....Macon, GA
Melton, C. Robert ....Forsyth, GA
Melton, Carl D. ....Henderson, KY
Melton, Carol A. ....Washington, DC
Melton, Charisse C. ....Los Angeles, CA
Melton, Charles D. ....Bakersfield, CA
Melton, Christopher M. ....Littleton, CO
Melton, Crawford S. ....Opelika, AL
Melton, David A. ....Sacramento, CA
Melton, David R. ....Chicago, IL
Melton, David Ray ....Charlottesville, VA
Melton, Douglas J. ....San Francisco, CA
Melton, Elizabeth Marie ....St. Paul, MN
Melton, Emory ....Cassville, MO
Melton, Espy, Williams & Hayes, P.C.
Montgomery, AL
Melton, F. Gregory ....Dalton, GA
Melton, Floyd M., III ....Greenwood, MS
Melton, Floyd M., Jr. ....Greenwood, MS
Melton, Frank E. ....Los Angeles, CA
Melton, Gail ....Sterling, VA
Melton, Gunter & Melton ....Opelika, AL
Melton, Harold D. ....Atlanta, GA
Melton, H. D., III ....Waco, TX
Melton, Herbert S., Jr. ....Paducah, KY
Melton, Howell W. ....Jacksonville, FL
Melton, Howell W., Jr. ....Orlando, FL
Melton, J. Barrett, Jr. ....Woodbury, TN
Melton, J. Carroll, II ....Norfolk, VA
Melton, J. Scott ....Spartanburg, SC
Melton, Janna Howard ....Austin, TX
Melton, Jared ....Plainview, TX
Melton, Jennifer ....Beverly Hills, CA
Melton, Jennifer L. ....Calabasas, CA
Melton, Jerry W. ....Dallas, TX
Melton, John B., III ....Murfreesboro, TN
Melton, John F. ....Austin, TX
Melton, John R. ....Charleston, WV
Melton, Judy P. ....New Orleans, LA
Melton, Katherine J. ....Indianapolis, IN
Melton, Kirsta Leeburg ....Washington, DC
Melton, L. Joseph, III ....New Orleans, LA
Melton, Lawrence C. ....Washington, DC
Melton, Leroy J., Jr. ....New Orleans, LA
Melton, Lori S. ....Atlanta, GA
Melton, M. LeAnn ....Charlotte, NC
Melton, M. Tod ....Morrison, IL
Melton, Melissa ....Rock Island, IL
Melton & Melton ....New Orleans, LA
Melton & Melton, P.C. ....Dallas, TX
Melton, Michael J. ....Pasadena, CA
Melton, Michael W. ....Boston, MA
Melton, Nancy J. ....Independence, MO
Melton, Oakley, Jr. ....Montgomery, AL
Melton, Pamela Rogers ....United States Senate, Committee Legal Personnel, GV
Melton, Raymond Andrew ....Denver, CO
Melton, Rebecca E. ....Austin, TX
Melton, Rebecca L. ....Covington, KY
Huntington, WV
Melton, Richard ....West Chicago, IL
Melton, Richard D. ....Houston, TX
Melton, Robert D. ....Orlando, FL
Melton, Robert D., P.A. ....Orlando, FL
Melton, Robert E. ....Albuquerque, NM
Melton, Robt. A. ....Macomb, IL
Melton, Roger W. ....Falls Church, VA
Melton, Ruby H. ....Wilton, CT
Melton, Russell D. ....Minneapolis, MN
Melton, Scott L. ....Conway, PA
Melton, Scott R. ....Grand Rapids, MI
Melton, Stephen A. ....Warner Robins, GA
Melton, Stuart L. ....Pittsford, NY
Melton, Susan D. ....San Diego, CA
Melton, Teresa Bryant ....Hermitage, TN
Melton, Teselyn Afrique ....Jackson, MS
Melton, Thomas H. ....Denver, CO
Melton, Thomas P., IV ....Birmingham, AL
Melton, Thomas S. ....Opelika, AL
Melton, Timothy J. ....Chicago, IL
Melton, Timothy M. ....Oklahoma City, OK
Melton, Todd H. ....Lake Charles, LA
Melton, V. A. (Bo), Jr. ....Nashville, TN
Melton, Wayne A. ....Dallas, TX
Melton, William D. ....Evergreen, AL
Melton, William D. ....Monroeville, AL
Melton, William R. ....Overland Park, KS
Meltontree, Beverly ....Houston, TX

Mendelson, David L. ... Memphis, TN
Mendelson, David Scott ... Birmingham, MI
Mendelson, Ellen ... San Francisco, CA
Mendelson, Eric C. ... New York, NY
Mendelson, George J. ... Rockville, MD
Mendelson, Gilbert Alan ... Pittsburgh, PA
Mendelson, Howard S. ... Cherry Hill, NJ
Mendelson, Hyman J. ... Brooklyn, NY
Mendelson, James S. ... Santa Ana, CA
Mendelson, Jason A. ... Palo Alto, CA
Mendelson, Jedd E. ... Los Angeles, CA
Roseland, NJ
New York, NY
Mendelson, Joan R. ... Tucson, AZ
Mendelson, Joseph, III ... Washington, DC
Mendelson, Karen T. ... Ann Arbor, MI
Mendelson, Keith J. ... Vienna, VA
Mendelson Law Firm ... Memphis, TN
Mendelson, Lee Jeffrey ... Great Neck, NY
Mendelson, Lee M. ... Memphis, TN
Mendelson, Leonard M. ... Pittsburgh, PA
Mendelson & Mendelson ... Brooklyn, NY
Mendelson, Michael B., (P.C.) ... Portland, OR
Mendelson, Michael J. ... Washington, DC
Mendelson, Morley G. ... Los Angeles, CA
Mendelson, Nina A. ... Department of Justice, Environment and Natural Resources Division, GV
Mendelson, Norman M. ... Great Neck, NY
Mendelson, Paul ... Miami, FL
Mendelson, Paul I. ... Memphis, TN
Mendelson, Pinchas ... New York, NY
Mendelson, Richard C. ... Los Angeles, CA
Mendelson, Richard D
Palm Beach Gardens, FL
Mendelson, Richard P. ... Napa, CA
Mendelson, Richard S. ... Alexandria, VA
Mendelson, Robert A. ... Oakland, CA
Mendelson, Robert C. ... New York, NY
Mendelson, Robert D. ... Tallahassee, FL
Mendelson, Sanford H. ... Los Angeles, CA
Mendelson, Shirley Young ... Austin, TX
Mendelson, Steven E. ... Oakland, CA
Mendelson, Tilden ... Indianapolis, IN
Mendelson, Tobias M. ... Louisville, KY
Mendelson, Tom ... St. Louis, MO
Mendelson, Victor Howard ... Miami, FL
Mendelson-Steigerwald, Anne
Bloomington, IN
Menden, Craig A. ... Palo Alto, CA
Menden & Freiman, LLP ... Atlanta, GA
Menden, George D. ... Atlanta, GA
Mendenhall, Audrey ... Richmond Heights, OH
Mendenhall, Bernd ... San Diego, CA
Mendenhall, Cynthia Kaufman
McMinnville, OR
Mendenhall, Douglas R. ... Alton, IL
Mendenhall, Greggory B.
Washington, DC
New York, NY
Mendenhall, H. Barton, II ... La Junta, CO
Rocky Ford, CO
Mendenhall, James E. ... Washington, DC
Mendenhall, Jerry E. ... Dallas, TX
Mendenhall, John M. ... Cleveland, OH
Mendenhall, Karen S. ... Albuquerque, NM
Mendenhall, Kiefer ... Aspen, CO
Mendenhall, Kristin L. ... Los Angeles, CA
Mendenhall, Larry ... San Francisco, CA
Mendenhall & Malouff ... La Junta, CO
Rocky Ford, CO
Mendenhall, Mark R. ... San Francisco, CA
Mendenhall, Paul S. ... Richmond, IN
Mendenhall, Robert D. ... Evergreen, CO
Mendenhall, Robert J. ... Cincinnati, OH
Mendenhall, Robert L. ... Charlotte, NC
Mendenhall, Roberta K. ... Cupertino, CA
Mendenhall, Samuel ... Chicago, IL
Mendenhall, Steven C. ... Old Greenwich, CT
Mendenhall, Thaddeus E., III
Richmond, VA
Mendenhall, Thomas A. ... Rochester, NY
Mendenhall, W. Carl ... Missoula, MT
Mendenhall, Warner D., III ... Akron, OH
Mendenhall, William S. ... Jackson, MS
Mender, Wigberto Lugo ... San Juan, PR
Menders, Robert S. ... Livonia, MI
Mendes & Gonzales, PLLC ... Nashville, TN
Mendes, Jeffrey W. ... Indianapolis, IN
Mendes, Key Alexandra ... New York, NY
Mendes, Meredith Wise ... Mundelein, IL
Mendes & Mount, LLP ... Los Angeles, CA
Newark, NJ
New York, NY
Mendes, Patrick J. ... San Diego, CA
Mendes, Robert J. ... Nashville, TN
Mendes, Ronald A. ... San Diego, CA
Mendes, Scott Michael ... Cleveland, OH
Mendez, Alfonse ... Dallas, TX
Mendez, Alfredo F. ... New York, NY
Mendez, Ana Maria ... Los Angeles, CA
Mendez, Andrew D. ... Kansas City, MO
Méndez, Armando ... Modesto, CA
Mendez, Belinda ... Laredo, TX
Mendez, Carole McFee ... Beltsville, MD
Mendez, Celia M. ... Maitland, FL
Mendez, David ... Austin, TX
Mendez, Diane K. ... Uniondale, NY
Mendez, Eduardo ... Miami, FL
Mendez, Francis X. ... Maitland, FL
Mendez, Frank M. ... Miami, FL
Mendez, H. E. ... San Antonio, TX
Mendez, Jaime R. ... St. Louis, MO
Mendez, Joaquin ... Coral Gables, FL
Mendez, John A. ... Sacramento, CA
Mendez, John D. ... Pompano Beach, FL
Mendez, John E. ... Los Angeles, CA
Mendez, Jose R. ... Brooklyn, NY
Mendez, Jose R., The Law Firm of
Brooklyn, NY
Mendez, Joseph R. ... Portland, OR
Mendez, Juan F. ... New York, NY
Mendez, Juan M. ... Chicago, IL
Mendez, Juan M., Law Offices of
Chicago, IL
Mendez, Julio L. ... Vineland, NJ
Mendez, Luis F. ... Miami, FL
Mendez, Manuel Jacobo ... New York, NY
Mendez, Manuel O. ... Austin, TX
Mendez & Mendez, P.A. ... Miami, FL
Mendez, Michelle A. ... Dallas, TX
Mendez, Miguel A. ... Palo Alto, CA
Mendez, Miguel A. ... West Palm Beach, FL
Mendez, Miguel A., P.A.
West Palm Beach, FL
Mendez, Nelson A. ... Oxnard, CA
Méndez, Omara ... San Juan, PR
Mendez, Pepe J. ... Denver, CO
Mendez, Pepe J., & Associates, P.C.
Denver, CO
Mendez, Robert G. ... Los Angeles, CA
Mendez, Roberto ... Hollywood, FL
Mendez, Sergio L. ... Miami, FL
Mendez, William, Jr. ... New York, NY
Mendez-Bernard, Omara ... San Juan, PR
Mendez Dawahare, Sandra
Lexington, KY
Mendez-Fontanez, Miguel A.
San Juan, PR
Méndez-Gómez, Néstor M. ... San Juan, PR
Mendez-Loucil, Hector ... Ponce, PR
Méndez-Ondina, Diana ... San Juan, PR
Mendez-Pagan, Wilma G. ... San Juan, PR
Mendez-Peñate, Carlos E. ... New York, NY
Méndez-Santoni, Rosa M. ... San Juan, PR
Mendez Solis, Juan M. ... San Juan, PR
Mendez-Vilella, Gretchen M.
San Juan, PR
Mendheim, Brad E. ... Dothan, AL
Mendheim, Jack J. ... Folsom, LA
Mendia, Henry E. ... Miami, FL
Mendicino, Derek A. ... Atlanta, GA
Mendicino, Fred A. ... McLean, VA
Mendicino, Lori D. ... Pittsburgh, PA
Mendicino, Thomas R. ... Radnor, PA
Mendick, Diane O'Hara ... Pittsford, NY
Mendiguren, Phillip A. ... La Grande, OR
Mendiguren, Phillip A., P.C. ... La Grande, OR
Mendik, Bernard H. ... New York, NY
Mendik, Kevin Russell ... Newton, MA
Mendillo, Abby M. ... St. Louis, MO
Mendillo, James R. ... Belleville, IL
Mendillo, Robert M. ... Boston, MA
Mendillo & Ross LLP ... Boston, MA
Mendín, Jorge L. ... San Juan, PR
Mendini, G. Jon ... Charlotte, NC
Mendini, Mary Guy ... Durham, NC
Mendiola, Elia R. ... Hackettstown, NJ
Mendiola, Lino ... Austin, TX
Mendiquitia, Fernando C. ... Miami, FL
Menditto, John E. ... Washington, DC
Mendizabal, Lorenzo ... Windsor, CT
Mendler, Edward C. ... Boston, MA
Mendler, Joel A. ... New Orleans, LA
Mendler, Scott M. ... Los Angeles, CA
Mendles, Richard L. ... New York, NY
Mendleson, Ira, III ... Albany, NY
Mendlin, Andrew S. ... Modesto, CA
Mendlin, Joyce S., Law Offices of
Los Angeles, CA
Mendlovitz, Saul ... New York, NY
Mendlovitz, Sidney ... Lakewood, CA
Mendlow, Wm. H. ... Pittsburgh, PA
Mendola, Gina L. ... Chatham, NJ
Mendola, Joseph A. ... New York, NY
Mendola, Joseph Vincent
West Hempstead, NY
Mendola, Michael R. ... Rochester, NY
Mendola, Sally ... New York, NY
Mendola, Tracy A. ... Las Vegas, NV
Mendolia, Lonnie M. ... Brooklyn, NY
Mendolia, Timothy J. ... Dallas, TX
Mendonca, Jeannette Hane ... Damascus, MD
Mendonca, Louis P. ... Hilo, HI
Mendonca, Louis P., A Law Corporation
Hilo, HI
Mendonca, Patrick A. ... Damascus, MD
Mendonca, Sonia ... Washington, DC
Mendonides, Diamond ... Chicago, IL
Mendonsa, John A. ... Los Angeles, CA
Mendonsa, Paul A. ... Lake Oswego, OR
Mendoza, Adrian ... Chicago, IL
Mendoza, Al J. ... Harvey, LA
Mendoza, Alex, Jr. ... Santa Ana, CA
Mendoza, Anthony S. ... Minneapolis, MN
Mendoza, Antonio ... Malibu, CA
Mendoza, Arlene ... San Francisco, CA
Mendoza & Bacó ... San Juan, PR
Mendoza, Callas & Schilling
Palm Beach, FL
Mendoza, Cristina Lagueruela
Coral Gables, FL
Mendoza, Cristina M. ... Washington, DC
Mendoza, Cynthia J. ... Granada Hills, CA
Mendoza, Dalia ... Tampa, FL
Mendoza, Edward A. ... Los Angeles, CA
Mendoza, Emirene ... Detroit, MI
Mendoza, Enid Duany ... Miami, FL
Mendoza, Eve Dery ... Simi Valley, CA
Mendoza, Frederick ... Kent, WA
Mendoza, Gary S. ... Los Angeles, CA
Mendoza, Gianna M. ... Albuquerque, NM
Mendoza, Javier G. ... Philadelphia, PA
Mendoza, Jerilyn López ... Los Angeles, CA
Mendoza, Joanna R. ... Sacramento, CA
Mendoza, John A. ... Santa Ana, CA
Mendoza, Jose ... Los Angeles, CA
Mendoza, Julie C. ... Washington, DC
Mendoza, Julio E., Jr. ... Columbia, SC
Mendoza, Kevin L. ... Newport Beach, CA
Mendoza, Lucy G. ... Burbank, CA
Mendoza, Lynette ... Hartford, CT
Mendoza, Marcos A. ... Beaumont, TX
Mendoza, Maria C. ... Rockville, MD
Mendoza, Maria R. ... Oakland, CA
Mendoza, Mario D. ... Madison, WI
Mendoza, Mario G. de, III ... Palm Beach, FL
Mendoza, Martin J. ... Los Angeles, CA
Mendoza, Mary Simmons ... Austin, TX
Mendoza, Matthew M. ... Columbus, OH
Mendoza, Miguel A. ... Houston, TX
Mendoza, Moses M. ... Fresno, CA
Mendoza, Natalie C. ... Boise, ID
Mendoza, Raymundo G.S. ... San Jose, CA
Mendoza, Renee C. ... Mountain View, CA
Mendoza, Robert Gary ... Costa Mesa, CA
Mendoza, Robert I. ... Los Angeles, CA
Mendoza, Romona Forbes ... Bellflower, CA
Mendoza, Ronald E. ... San Antonio, TX
Mendoza, Ronald J. ... Los Angeles, CA
Mendoza, Roy A. ... Florence, AZ
Mendoza, Salvador, Jr. ... Yakima, WA
Mendoza, Victor G., III ... Miami, FL
Mendoza, Victoria S. ... Reno, NV
Mendoza Adleman, Maria Lourdes C.
Chicago, IL
Mendoza Mendez, Enrique J.
San Juan, PR
Mendoza-Vidal, Carlos A. ... Bayamon, PR
Mendoza Vidal, Jose E. ... San Juan, PR
Mendoza-Waterhouse, Angelita ... Austin, TX
Mendrala, Edmund J. ... New York, NY
Mendrick, Ronald J. ... Rochester, NY
Mendrzycki, Edward C. ... New York, NY
Mendrzycki, William J.
Florham Park, NJ
Menduiña, Cristiana F. ... New York, NY
Mendy, Edward B. ... New Orleans, LA
Mendy & McElroy, LLC ... New Orleans, LA
Mendyk, Ruth E. ... Fresno, CA
Mendyk, Stephen A. ... Fresno, CA
Menear, Barbara Ann ... Flint, MI
Menebroker, Wayne L. ... Carmichael, CA
Menechino, John E., Jr. ... Atlanta, GA
Meneely, Bruce K. ... Oklahoma City, OK
Meneely, Henry T., Jr. ... Annapolis, MD
Meneely, Sandi L. ... San Francisco, CA
San Jose, CA
Menees, Hardy C. ... St. Louis, MO
Menees, Whitney & Burnet
St. Louis, MO
Menefee, B. K. (Pete) ... Jacksonville, TX
Menefee, Bruce T. ... El Dorado, AR
Menefee, Charles C. ... Alpena, MI
Menefee, Constance M. ... San Francisco, CA
Menefee, Curtis H.-P. ... Lakewood, CO
Menefee, David K. ... Fort Worth, TX
Menefee, Gregory C. ... Louisville, KY
Okolona, KY
Shively, KY
Menefee, Irving C. ... Fairfax, VA
Menefee, James F. ... Forney, TX
Menefee, James F., P.C. ... Forney, TX
Menefee, John F. ... Louisville, KY
Menefee, Larry T. ... Montgomery, AL
Menefee, Lisa V.L. ... Winston-Salem, NC
Menefee, Lynn Michele ... Altadena, CA
Menefee, Mark ...
Department of Commerce, GV
Menefee, Samuel P. ... New Orleans, LA
Menefee, Terry R. ... Lancaster, CA
Menefee, Wm. D. ... Louisville, KY
Menegakis, Byron S. ... New York, NY
Menegakis, Jason C. ... Philadelphia, PA
Menegat, Norman D.
United States Postal Service, Judicial Officer, GV
Menegaz, Gregory S. ... Washington, DC
Meneghello, Kirsten Cook ... Portland, OR
Meneghello, Richard R. ... Portland, OR
Meneilly, J. Kevin ... Westbury, NY
Menell, Gregg A. ... New York, NY
Menell, Howard A. ... Washington, DC
Menello, Joseph P. ... Orlando, FL
Menelly, Lisa Ann ... Boston, MA
Menelly, Richard A. ... Windsor, CT
Menely, Michelle ... Seattle, WA
Menendez, Alicia M. ... Miami, FL
Menendez, Antonio R. ... Miami, FL
Menendez, Arlene ... North Miami, FL
Menendez, Bernard ... Somerville, MA
Menendez, Francisco J. ... Miami, FL
Menendez, George ... Detroit, MI
Menendez, Harold ... Madison, WI
Menendez, Jose M. ... Miami, FL
Menendez, Kenneth G. ... Atlanta, GA
Menendez, Kirk Reagan ... Miami, FL
Menendez, Louis James ... Juneau, AK
Menendez, Manuel, Jr. ... Tampa, FL
Menendez, Silvia M. ... Morristown, NJ
Menendez Cambo, Patricia ... Miami, FL
Menéndez Cortada, José A. ... San Juan, PR
Menéndez-Valentín, Nydia ... Tallahassee, FL
Meneo & Goldfield, L.L.C. ... New Haven, CT
Meneo, Ronald Michael ... New Haven, CT
Mener, Leon Z. ... New York, NY
Menes, Barry A. ... Los Angeles, CA
Menes, Caroline K. ... New York, NY
Menes Law Corporation ... Los Angeles, CA
Menes, N. Jude ... Dallas, TX
Menes, Paul I. ... Los Angeles, CA
Meneses, E. Val ... San Diego, CA
Meneses, G. Arthur ... Los Angeles, CA
Menet, David ... Alachua, FL
Menet, David E. ... Gainesville, FL
Menezes, Darrin M. ... Sacramento, CA
Menezes, Marco S. ... Cadillac, MI
Menezes, Mark W. ... Dallas, TX
Menezes, Mitchell H. ... Denver, CO
Menezes, Stephen J. ... Hilo, HI
Menezes, Tsukazaki, Yeh & Moore ... Hilo, HI
Meng, Catherine Ryan ... Louisville, KY
Meng, George E. ... Upper Marlboro, MD
Meng, Joseph ... Cambridge, MA
Meng, Linda J. ... Portland, OR
Meng, M. Kathryn ... Uniondale, NY
Meng, Martha E. ... New Haven, CT
Meng, Michael R. ... Boca Raton, FL
Meng, Thomas E. ... Lexington, KY
Meng & Urey ... Upper Marlboro, MD
Mengacci, Joseph A. ... Waterbury, CT
Mengarelli, Martin J. ... Granite City, IL
Mengden, Walter H., Jr. ... Houston, TX
Menge, Delvin C. ... Humble, TX
Menge, Eric E. ... Washington, DC
Menge, Jerry S. ... Chicago, IL
Menge, M. J. ... Pensacola, FL
Mengedoth, Paul B. ... Phoenix, AZ
Mengel, Allen S. ... Harrisburg, PA
Mengel, Christopher E. ... Detroit, MI
Mengel, Edward C., Jr. ... Philadelphia, PA
Mengel, Marie W. ... Elkhart, IN
Mengel, Paul T. ... Bloomfield Hills, MI
Mengel, Paul W., III ... Alexandria, VA
Mengelberg, Mark R. ... San Francisco, CA
Mengeling, Daniel A. ... Woodstock, IL
Mengelkamp, John M. ... Cincinnati, OH
Mengers, David Gerhardt ... Ocala, FL
Menges, Charles L. ... Richmond, VA
Menges, Charles P. ... Chicago, IL
Menges, Eugene C. ... Belleville, IL
Menges, Gent & McLaughlin, LLP
York, PA
Menges, J. Kenneth, Jr., (P.C.) ... Dallas, TX
Menges, Mikus & Molzahn ... Chicago, IL
Menges, N. Christopher ... York, PA
Menges, Tracy S. ... St. Louis, MO
Menges, William C., Jr. ... Kokomo, IN
Menges, William H. ... Moorestown, NJ
Menghetti, Linda C. ... Washington, DC
Menghini, C. A. ... Pittsburg, KS
Menghini, Charles ... Pittsburg, KS
Menghini, David F. ... Kansas City, KS
Menghini, Donna L. ... New York, NY
Menghini, Frank D. ... Kansas City, KS
Menghini, Henry C. ... Pittsburg, KS
Menghini, Henry D. ... St. Louis, MO
Menghini, Mark A. ... St. Louis, MO
Menghini, Matthew D. ... St. Louis, MO
Menghini & Menghini, L.L.C.
Pittsburg, KS
Menghini, Scott J. ... San Diego, CA
Mengine, Anthony C. ... Pittsburgh, PA
Mengis, Joseph W. ... Baton Rouge, LA
Mengis, Michael W. ... Houston, TX
Mengis, Warren L. ... Baton Rouge, LA
Mengle, John S. ... Lebanon, OH
Mengle, John, The Law Office of
Lebanon, OH
Mengler, Richd. ... Corvallis, OR
Mengler, Thomas M. ... Champaign, IL
Mengo, Gail Marie ... Richton Park, IL
Mengo, Sally Yule ... Kenosha, WI
Mengo, Sally Yule, S.C. ... Kenosha, WI
Mengoli, Jeffrey L. ... Palo Alto, CA
Mengshol, John G. ... Fresno, CA
Menhall, Dalton W. ... Bonita, CA
Meni, Reynold
Environmental Protection Agency, Office of Congressional and Legislative Affairs, GV
Menicos, Patrick L. ... Uniontown, OH
Menicucci, Jeffrey D. ... Reno, NV
Menicucci, Margaret M. ... Austin, TX
Menicucci, Michael F. ... Albuquerque, NM
Menicucci, Michael J. ... Anaheim, CA
Menikoff, Carrie ... Cleveland, OH
Menillo, Gregory P. ... Hartsdale, NY
Menillo, Michael A. ... New York, NY
Menin, Geoffrey D. ... New York, NY
Menin, Henry L.
Charlotte Amalie, St. Thomas, VI
Menin, Lisa S. ... Mechanicsville, VA
Menin, Samuel D. ... Denver, CO
Menis, Meyer ... San Juan, PR
Menjivar, Ana M. ... Novato, CA
Menjou, Christopher J. ... Los Angeles, CA
Menk, Bruce A. ... Denver, CO
Menk, John C. ... Winnetka, IL
Menk, Peter D. ... Charlottesville, VA
Menk, Tandy M., (P.C.) ... Augusta, GA
Menk, Wolfgang M. ... San Diego, CA
Henderson, NV
Menke, Annelie ... Houston, TX
Menke, Anthony F. ... Yakima, WA
Menke, Bernard W. ... Las Vegas, NV
Menke, Bruce R. ... Long Beach, CA
Menke, Charles A. ... Chicago, IL
Menke, David J. ... Binghamton, NY
Menke, David J. ... Cincinnati, OH
Menke, Dennis V. ... Costa Mesa, CA
Menke, Fahrney & Carroll, A Professional Corporation ... Costa Mesa, CA
Menke Jackson Beyer & Elofson, LLP
Yakima, WA
Menke, John A.
Pension Benefit Guaranty Corporation, Office of the General Counsel, GV
Menke, John D. ... San Francisco, CA
Menke, John W. ... Houston, TX
Menke, Michon K. ... Solana Beach, CA
Menke, R. Bruce ... Humble, TX

Menke, Richard J. ... Shakopee, MN
Menke, Teri L. ... Baltimore, MD
Menke, William C. ... New Richmond, OH
Menkel, Melissa L. ... Baltimore, MD
Menkel-Meadow, Carrie J. ... Washington, DC
Menken, Bruce E. ... New York, NY
Menken, Bruce S. ... West Bloomfield, MI
Menken, David A. ... Mount Kisco, NY
New York, NY
Menken, John F. ... Carmel, CA
Menken, Steven A. ... West Bloomfield, MI
Menker, James R. ... Charlotte, NC
Menkes, Brian J. ... Washington, DC
Menkes, Bruce N. ... Chicago, IL
Menkes, Eric G. ... New York, NY
Menkes, Lauren Dale ... Los Angeles, CA
Menkes, Lawrence S. ... New York, NY
Menkes, Michael E. ... Gaylord, MI
Menkes, Roslyn ... Newport Beach, CA
Menkes, Sheryl R. ... New York, NY
Menkes, Susan W. ... Irvine, CA
Menkin, Edward Z. ... Syracuse, NY
Menkin, Edward Z., P.C. ... Syracuse, NY
Menkin, Jeffrey L. ... Department of Justice, Criminal Division, GV
Menkin, Lita S. ... Atlanta, GA
Menking, Bonner ... Fairfax, VA
Menkins, Deborah S.
Colorado Springs, CO
Menkowitz, Michael G. ... Philadelphia, PA
Menkveld, Paul G. ... Tucson, AZ
Menlow, Elaine P. ... Westfield, NJ
Menmuir, Zimmerman, Kuhn, Taylor and Quandt, PLC ... Beulah, MI
Leland, MI
Traverse City, MI
Menn, John B. ... Appleton, WI
Menn, Jonathan M. ... Appleton, WI
Menn, Nelson, Sharratt, Teetaert & Beisenstein, Ltd. ... Appleton, WI
Little Chute, WI
Menn, Stephen E. ... Houston, TX
Menna, Frank P. ... Department of Justice, Office of Information and Privacy, GV
Menna, Gilbert G., (P.C.) ... Boston, MA
Menna, Pasquale ... Red Bank, NJ
Menna, Philip F. ... Bronx, NY
Menna, Philip G. ... New York, NY
Menna, Ronald D. ... Oak Brook, IL
Mennel, Donald M. ... Fostoria, OH
Mennel, Eric E. ... Chicago, IL
Mennell, Ann I. ... Milwaukee, WI
Mennell, James A. ... Minneapolis, MN
Mennell, John C. ... Rochester, NY
Mennell, Robert L. ... Roseville, MN
Mennella, Anthony P. ... Brooklyn, NY
Mennella, Peter R. ... Chicago, IL
Mennella, Vincent ... Lansing, IL
Mennemeier, Glassman & Stroud LLP
Sacramento, CA
Mennemeier, Kenneth C. ... Sacramento, CA
Mennen, Christine Lynn ... Anoka, MN
Mennen, Sally S. ... Bronx, NY
Mennen, William G., IV
Basking Ridge, NJ
Mennenoh, John D. ... Morrison, IL
Mennes, Mark H. ... River Forest, IL
Mennie, John G. ... Ocean Township, NJ
Mennie, Vita S. ... Newark, NJ
Mennies, Richard J. ... Blue Bell, PA
Menninger, Carol ... Las Vegas, NV
Menninger, Henry E., Jr. ... Cincinnati, OH
Menninger, Karl A., II ... Springfield, IL
Menninger, Laura Anne ... New York, NY
Mennis, David L. ... Benson, MN
Mennite, Filomena M. ... Woodbury, NJ
Mennite, John A. ... Woodbury, NJ
Mennite, Joseph ... Woodbury, NJ
Mennite & Mennite ... Woodbury, NJ
Menniti, Daniel J. ... Shippensburg, PA
Mennitt, Gary J. ... New York, NY
Menno, James V. ... Walpole, MA
Mennucci, William L. ... Austin, TX
Meno, J. Richard ... Benld, IL
Carlinville, IL
Meno, Richard A. ... Stamford, CT
Menocal, Pedro, Jr. ... Miami, FL
Menogan, Annita M. ... Denver, CO
Menoken, Cassandra M.
Equal Employment Opportunity Commission, Office of Federal Operations, GV
Menon, Ashok ... New York, NY
Menon, Jody W. ... New Haven, CT
Menon, Kannan ... New York, NY
Menon, Leela V. ... Chelmsford, MA
Menon, Pia ... Chicago, IL
Menon, Ruby S. ... Indianapolis, IN
Menon, Shayam K. ... Washington, DC
Menor, Arthur J. ... West Palm Beach, FL
Menor, Judith A. ... Tempe, AZ
Menor, Ron ... Honolulu, HI
Menotti, David E. ... Washington, DC
Menoudakos, Peter ... Garden City, NY
Menowitz, Frederick A. ... Elmhurst, NY
Menowitz, Frederick A., P.C. ... Elmhurst, NY
Menoyo, Eric F. ... Boston, MA
Menozzi, Greg A. ... Geneva, IL
Mensack, Raymond W. ... New York, NY
Mensch, Andrew B. ... New York, NY
Mensch, Jeffrey L. ... Sunbury, PA
Mensch, Linda Susan ... Chicago, IL
Mensch, Linda Susan, P.C. ... Chicago, IL
Mensch, Martin ... New York, NY
Mensch, Rebecca Supple
Poughkeepsie, NY
Mensch, Susan E. ... Allentown, PA
Menscher, Mark B. ... Colorado Springs, CO

Menschik, Judith M. ... Hackensack, NJ
Blauvelt, NY
Menschik & Markstein ... Hackensack, NJ
Blauvelt, NY
Mensching, J. Patrick, Jr. ... Tulsa, OK
Mensching, Jack E. ... Itasca, IL
Mensching, John J. ... Toms River, NJ
Mense, Marilyn Suchecki
Washington, DC
Menser, Barton M. ... Charlotte, NC
Menser, Daniel J. ... Seattle, WA
Menser, Mark C. ... Tallahassee, FL
Menser, S. Tye ... Palo Alto, CA
Mensh, Keaton, Schuh, MacIntosh, Bursa & Kaplan ... St. Petersburg, FL
Mensh, Myron J., (P.A.)
St. Petersburg, FL
Mensh, Richard L. ... St. Petersburg, FL
Menshel, Denny ... Gowanda, NY
Mensher, Mark D. ... Garden City, NY
Mensher & Temsamani ... Garden City, NY
Mensi, Dennis W. ... New York, NY
Mensik, Michael S. ... Chicago, IL
Mensing, Harold F. ... Erie, MI
Mensing, Stephen A. ... Phoenix, AZ
Mensinger, Susan B. ... San Francisco, CA
Mensoian, Martha A.
Commodity Futures Trading Commission, Office of Proceedings, GV
Menson, Richard L. ... Chicago, IL
Mensore, John J. ... New Martinsville, WV
Mensore and Mensore
New Martinsville, WV
Mensore, Michelle Tulane ... Charleston, WV
Mensore, Tulane Bouch
New Martinsville, WV
Menszak, Charles P., Jr. ... Philadelphia, PA
Ment, Andrew W. ... New York, NY
Ment, Jeffrey L. ... Hartford, CT
Mentag, Robert G. ... Northville, MI
Mentel, Jeffery ... St. Louis, MO
Mentel, K. Lori ... Chicago, IL
Mentel, Michael C. ... Dublin, OH
Mentele, Peggy ... Anchorage, AK
Menter, Jeffery B. ... Littleton, CO
Menter, Joshua L. ... Washington, DC
Menter, Lawrence K. ... Atlanta, GA
Menter, Martin ... Chevy Chase, MD
Menter, Rudin & Trivelpiece, P.C.
Syracuse, NY
Watertown, NY
Menter, Timothy S. ... Newport Beach, CA
Mentesana, Regina W. ... Frisco, TX
Menthe, Darrel C. ... Los Angeles, CA
Menting, Anthony J. ... Oconomowoc, WI
Menting, Christopher J. ... Chicago, IL
Menting, Mark J. ... New York, NY
Menting, Peter (IBA) ... Hartford, CT
Mentkowski, Timothy F. ... Milwaukee, WI
Mentlik, William L. ... Westfield, NJ
Mento, Constance C. ... Houston, TX
Menton, Dennis J. ... Wilmington, DE
Menton, Francis J., Jr. ... New York, NY
Menton, J. Stephen ... Tallahassee, FL
Menton, James P., Jr. ... Los Angeles, CA
Menton, Robert F. ... Watertown, MA
Mentone, Ronald J. ... Melrose Park, IL
Mentor, Jennifer L. ... Seattle, WA
Mentor, Joseph P., Jr. ... Seattle, WA
Mentor, Serena M. ... New York, NY
Mentrek, Joseph Michael ... Cleveland, OH
Mentrup, Clifford ... Chicago, IL
Mentz, Arnold H. ... Daly City, CA
Mentz, Barbara A. ... New York, NY
Mentz, Henry A., Jr. ... New Orleans, LA
Mentz, J. Roger ... Washington, DC
Mentz, Jane Faia ... Metairie, LA
Mentz, Lawrence ... New York, NY
Mentz, Michael P. ... Metairie, LA
Mentzel, Michael J. ... Philadelphia, PA
Mentzer, Charles ... Baltimore, MD
Mentzer, Charles S. ... Baltimore, MD
Mentzer, Donald H. ... Reston, VA
Mentzer, Howard E. ... Akron, OH
Mentzer, Lawrence B. ... Dallas, TX
Mentzer, Leonard A. ... New York, NY
Mentzer, Linda B. ... Akron, OH
Mentzer & Mentzer ... Baltimore, MD
Mentzer, Susan L. ... Rockville, MD
Mentzer, Vuillemin and Mygrant Ltd.
Akron, OH
Canton, OH
Menu, Susan ... Riverhead, NY
Menucci, William R. ... Iron Mountain, MI
Menuck, Jill Mainster ... Detroit, MI
Menuck, Melvin R. ... Farmington Hills, MI
Menuet, Robert L. ... Napoleonville, LA
Menville, Ronald L. ... New Iberia, LA
Meny, Rachael E. ... San Francisco, CA
Menyhart, Andrew W. ... Merritt Island, FL
Menyhart, Andrew W., P.A.
Merritt Island, FL
Menyuk, Eric ... Los Angeles, CA
Menyuk, Gail L. ... Trenton, NJ
Menz, David F. ... Little Rock, AR
Menz, David F. ... Cleveland, OH
Menz, David P. ... Seattle, WA
Menz, Deborah K. ... Cape Girardeau, MO
Menz, John R. ... New York, NY
Menz and Luxenberg ... Kendall Park, NJ
Menz, Wayne J. ... Kendall Park, NJ
Menza, Alexander J. ... Elizabeth, NJ
Menzalora, William M. ... Cleveland, OH
Menzel, David L. ... Parsippany, NJ
Menzel, Gregory P. ... San Francisco, CA
Menzel, John ... Point Pleasant, NJ
Menzel, Linda K. ... Milwaukee, WI

Menzel, Nancy Roetman
Minneapolis, MN
Menzel, R. Blake ... Nashville, TN
Menzel, Robert C., Jr. ... New Bedford, MA
Menzer, James L. ... Blackwell, OK
Menzer, James L., P.C. ... Blackwell, OK
Menzer, Matthew N. ... Seattle, WA
Menzer, Mitchell B. ... Los Angeles, CA
Menzer, Susan B. ... Department of Justice, Tax Division, GV
Menzie, Daniel G. ... Wichita, KS
Springfield, MO
Menzie, Edward G. ... Columbia, SC
Menzie, Jennifer Karrels ... Nashville, TN
Menzie, John T. ... Fort Wayne, IN
Menzies, Charles L. ... Los Angeles, CA
Menzies, E. Bruce, Jr. ... San Diego, CA
Menzies, Janice G. ... Austin, TX
Menzies, Robert G. ... Naples, FL
Menzimer, Lisle W. ... Rockford, IL
Meo, Joseph A. ... Camden, NJ
Bala Cynwyd, PA
Meo, Matthew ... Encino, CA
Meo, R. Michael, Jr. ... Stamford, CT
Meo Reno & Associates, A Professional Corporation ... Bala Cynwyd, PA
Meo, Steven F. ... Hartford, CT
Meola, Anthony L., Jr. ... New York, NY
Meola, Deborah Marie ... Youngstown, OH
Meola, Jack F. ... Flemington, NJ
Meola, Janice G. ... Whippany, NJ
Meola, John F. ... Hawthorne, NJ
Meola, John F., P.A. ... Hawthorne, NJ
Meola, Richard ... Bayonne, NJ
Meola, Robert B. ... Short Hills, NJ
Meola, Rudolph J. ... Albany, NY
Meola, Sylvester J., Jr.
Mayfield Heights, OH
Meola, William Jack ... Warren, OH
Meola, William Jack, LLC ... Warren, OH
Meoli, Linda M. ... Oklahoma City, OK
Meoli, Marcia R. ... Holland, MI
Meosky, Paul D. ... Buffalo, NY
Meotti, Michael P. ... Hartford, CT
Mepham, David S. ... Portland, OR
Kirkland, WA
Meppen, Debra Ellwood ... Los Angeles, CA
Mequet, Sharon S. ... Los Angeles, CA
Mequi, Melissa ... Denver, CO
Mequio, James D. ... Kalamazoo, MI
Merachnik, Beth M. ... Cambridge, MA
Meraglio, Russell J., Jr. ... Cleveland, OH
Merani, Peter C. ... New York, NY
Merani, Peter J. ... Whitestone, NY
Merani, Peter P. T. ... Baltimore, MD
Merante, Mark A. ... Boston, MA
Merante, RoseMaria Plesh ... Rochester, NY
Merante, Vincent E. ... Rochester, NY
Meranto, Anthony P. ... Youngstown, OH
Meranus, Leonard S. ... Cincinnati, OH
Meranus, Norman ... Wellfleet, MA
Meranus, Philip ... New York, NY
Meranze and Katz ... Philadelphia, PA
Mera-Roure, Blanca I. ... San Juan, PR
Merati, Michael A. ... Torrington, CT
Merbaum, David J. ... Roswell, GA
Merber, Kenneth S. ... New York, NY
Merber, Selig S. ... Washington, DC
Merberg, Elinor L.
National Labor Relations Board, Office of the General Counsel, GV
Merberg, James M. ... Boston, MA
Merbeth, Russell C. ... Washington, DC
Mercadante, James A. ... New York, NY
Mercadante, John ... Red Bank, NJ
Whiting, NJ
Mercadante, Stephen ... Gainesville, FL
Mercado, Adrian ... San Juan, PR
Mercado, Alphonso A. ... East Meadow, NY
Mercado, Andrea M. ... New York, NY
Mercado, Arthur Wyler ... New York, NY
Mercado, David ... New York, NY
Mercado, Doreen M. ... Los Angeles, CA
Mercado, Ivan E. ... Jamaica Plain, MA
Mercado, Jaime ... New York, NY
Mercado, Josephine ... Bronx, NY
Mercado, Malu S. ... San Francisco, CA
Mercado, Paula J. ... Parsippany, NJ
Mercado, Raymond J. ... Chatsworth, CA
Mercado, Robert L. ... Troy, MI
Mercado, Sonia ... Los Angeles, CA
Mercado & Soto ... San Juan, PR
Mercado-Betancourt, Maria Alejandra
San Juan, PR
Mercado-Espinoza, Ramona
Hartford, CT
Mercado-Llorens, Segundo A. ... Bronx, NY
Mercado Vega, Cesar E. ... San Juan, PR
Mercado-Vizcarrondo, Teresita
San Juan, PR
Mercaldi, Vincent A. ... Houston, TX
Mercaldo, Marco B. ... San Diego, CA
Mercaldo, Ronald D. ... Tucson, AZ
Mercaldo, Ronald D., Ltd. ... Phoenix, AZ
Tucson, AZ
Mercant, Anthony J. ... San Jose, CA
Mercant, Jon ... Redondo Beach, CA
Mercant & O'Brien ... San Jose, CA
Mercante, James E. ... New York, NY
Mercante, Mark W. ... New Orleans, LA
Mercanti, Michael N. ... Princeton, NJ
Mercatelli, Dominick A. ... Staten Island, NY
Merce, Robert K. ... Honolulu, HI
Mercedes, Jeanette M. ... Brooklyn, NY
Mercep, Anthony W. ... Stony Brook, NY
Mercer, A. Bruce ... Bethesda, MD
Mercer, Alene M. ... Raleigh, NC
Mercer, Brian P. ... Rochester, NY

Mercer, Brian P., Law Office of
Rochester, NY
Mercer, Charles Eric ... Westlake Village, CA
Mercer, Charles H., Jr. ... Raleigh, NC
Mercer, Cindy M. ... Los Lunas, NM
Mercer, David A. ... Hollywood, FL
Mercer, David F. ... Ben Lomond, CA
Mercer, David G. ... Gainesville, GA
Mercer, David S. ... Tysons Corner, VA
Mercer, David T. ... Los Angeles, CA
Mercer, Dennis Scott ... Douglasville, GA
Mercer, Diana L. ... New Haven, CT
Mercer, Edwin Wayne ... Union City, CA
Mercer, Elizabeth J. ... Lansing, MI
Mercer, Ellen A. ... Columbia, SC
Mercer, Ellen P. ... Pittsburgh, PA
Mercer, Eric ... New York, NY
Mercer, Forrest C. ... Des Moines, IA
Mercer, Fritz Y., Jr. ... Charlotte, NC
Mercer, George D. ... Troy, MI
Mercer, Glen E. ... New Orleans, LA
Mercer, Grady, Jr. ... Jacksonville, NC
Mercer, H. Fred ... Pittsburgh, PA
Mercer, H. Fred, III ... Pittsburgh, PA
Mercer, H. Marvin, III ... Philadelphia, PA
Mercer, Harold A. ... Niagara Falls, NY
Mercer, Harry D. ... Cleveland, OH
Mercer, Helen R. ... Ventura, CA
Mercer, J. Joel, Jr. ... Atlanta, GA
Mercer, James R. ... Greeneville, TN
Mercer, James W. ... Los Angeles, CA
Mercer, Jean W. ... Memphis, TN
Mercer, Jerome P. ... Baraboo, WI
Mercer, John A. ... Polson, MT
Ronan, MT
Mercer, John A., Jr. ... Mount Laurel, NJ
Mercer, John C. ... Portland, OR
Mercer, John F. ... Washington, DC
Mercer, John L. ... Indianapolis, IN
Mercer, John M. ... Richmond, VA
Mercer, John R. ... Austin, TX
Mercer, John S. (Jay) ... Indianapolis, IN
Mercer, John T. W. ... Atlanta, GA
Mercer, Jon ... Houston, TX
Mercer, Jos. L., II ... Nashville, TN
Mercer, Joseph J., Jr. ... Oak Ridge, TN
Mercer, Joseph L., III ... Nashville, TN
Mercer, Joy M. ... Saddle Brook, NJ
Mercer, Karen A. ... Baraboo, WI
Mercer, Kari A. ... Atlanta, GA
Mercer, Kathryn Lynn ... Cleveland, OH
Mercer, Kell C. ... Austin, TX
Mercer, Kevin G. ... Orlando, FL
Mercer, Lawrence A. ... San Francisco, CA
Mercer, LeAnn ... Jackson, MS
Mercer, Lee W. ... United States Senate, Senatorial Assistants, GV
Mercer, Leroy A.
Charlotte Amalie, St. Thomas, VI
Mercer, M. Martin ... Littleton, CO
Mercer, Marty Hansen ... Jackson, MI
Mercer & Mercer ... Pittsburgh, PA
Mercer, Naomi S. ... Des Moines, IA
Mercer, Paul W. ... Atlanta, GA
Mercer, Paula H. ... Boston, MA
Mercer, Richard James ... Dover, MA
Mercer, Robert A. ... Miami, FL
Mercer, Robert A., P.A. ... Miami, FL
Mercer, Robert B. ... Rockleigh, NJ
Mercer, Robert M. ... Portland, OR
Mercer, Robert M. D. ... Birmingham, AL
Mercer, Sara A. ... Pittsburgh, PA
Mercer, Scott E. ... Baton Rouge, LA
Mercer, Scott O. ... Salt Lake City, UT
Mercer, S. H., IV ... Brooklyn, NY
Mercer, Shawn D. ... Raleigh, NC
Mercer, Shell L. ... Las Vegas, NV
Mercer, Stephanie A. ... Dallas, TX
Mercer, Stephen C. ... New York, NY
Mercer, Thomas C. ... Los Angeles, CA
Orange, CA
Walnut Creek, CA
Mercer, Tod S. ... Oklahoma City, OK
Mercer, Traylor T. ... Hagåtña, GU
Mercer, Tyler Gates ... San Antonio, TX
Mercer, Walter George, Jr. ... Dawson, GA
Mercer, William D., Jr ... Tampa, FL
Mercer, William W. ... Missoula, MT
Merceret, Elizabeth A. ... Hialeah, FL
Merceret, Francis J.
Kennedy Space Center, FL
Mercer-Falkoff, Robert D. ... North Haven, CT
Mercer-Klimowski, Jenifer L.
Des Moines, IA
Merchan, Juan M. ... New York, NY
Merchant, Alice D. ... Birmingham, AL
Merchant, Anne P. ... New York, NY
Merchant, Carolyn Nies
Albuquerque, NM
Merchant, Carolyn, P.C.
Albuquerque, NM
Merchant, Charles A. ... Pittsburgh, PA
Merchant, Charles E. ... Cleveland, OH
Merchant, David B. ... Olympia, WA
Merchant, David M. ... Little Compton, RI
Merchant, Evelyn M. ... Miami, FL
Merchant & Gould, Professional Corporation ... Denver, CO
Minneapolis, MN
Merchant, John C. ... Louisville, KY
Cincinnati, OH
Merchant, Kevin P. ... Lafayette, LA
Merchant, Margaret B. ... Pasadena, CA
Merchant, Mary Anthony ... Atlanta, GA
Merchant, Michael B. ... Portland, OR
Merchant, Pamela ... Department of Justice, Criminal Division, GV
Merchant, Paul Michael ... Oklahoma City, OK

Merchant, Randall C. ....Fort Worth, TX
Merchant, Shelly A. ....Pasadena, TX
Merchant, Thomas E. ....Philadelphia, PA
Merchant, Todd C. ....Santa Ana, CA
Merchant, William C. ....Cape Coral, FL
Merchant, William G. ....Pittsburgh, PA
Merchasin, Carol M. ....Chicago, IL
Merchasin, Robert K. ....Newton, MA
Merchat, Margaret Mari ....Santa Rosa, CA
Mercherson, Denise M. ....Chicago, IL
Merchlewitz, Ann E. ....Winona, MN
Merchlewitz, Mark A. ....Winona, MN
Mercieca, Mary Ann ....Northville, MI
Mercier, Beth ....Hartford, CT
Mercier, David B. ....Dudley, MA
Mercier, Douglas G. ....Ridgeland, MS
Mercier, Janet E. ....Natick, MA
Mercier, Judith M. ....Miami, FL
Mercier, Kent ....Lafayette, LA
Mercier, Kim W. ....Dallas, TX
Mercier, Lee F. ....Jacksonville, FL
Mercier, Lynn Snopek ....Springfield, MA
Mercier, Marc P. ....Manchester, CT
Mercier, Marie Frances ....Boston, MA
Mercier, Rebecca J. ....Tallahassee, FL
Mercier, Thomas H., Jr. ....Detroit, MI
Merck, Antony M. ....Charleston, SC
Merck & Co., Inc. ....Rahway, NJ
Merck, Hal B. ....Chicago, IL
Merck, Larry S. ....Department of the Army,
U.S. Army Court of Criminal Appeals, GV
Merck, Norbert J. ....Blauvelt, NY
Merck, Ralph E. ....Decatur, GA
Merck, Robert M. ....Norwalk, CT
Merck, Weston Trey ....Piedmont, SC
Mercker, George E. ....Louisville, KY
Mercogliano, Guy ....Philadelphia, PA
Mercogliano, Theresa L. ....Boston, MA
Mercolini, James A. ....Pittsburgh, PA
Mercorella, Anthony J. ....New York, NY
Mercun, John J. ....Trenton, NJ
Mercure, Lynne ....North Miami Beach, FL
Mercure, Steven J. ....Tecumseh, NE
Mercure, Susan A. ....San Diego, CA
Mercure, Thomas E. ....Fort Edward, NY
Mercure, Thomas M. ....Buffalo, NY
Mercuri, John J. ....Moscow, PA
Mercurio, Brenda M. ....Boston, MA
Mercurio, Frederick P. ....Sarasota, FL
Mercurio, Frederick P., P.A., Law Office of
Sarasota, FL
Mercurio, James P. ....Washington, DC
Mercurio, John A. ....Melville, NY
Mercurio, Joseph R. ....Islip, NY
Mercurio, Lisa Gillispie ....Sacramento, CA
Mercurio, Lucia M. ....New London, CT
Mercurio, Michael N. ....Washington, DC
Mercurio, Michael P. ....North Babylon, NY
Mercurio, Pat R. ....Rockville Centre, NY
Mercurio, Robert D. ....New York, NY
Mercurio, Sal L. ....Cincinnati, OH
Mercurio, Thomas D. ....Burlington, VT
Mercurio, Vincent M. ....Cincinnati, OH
Mercuris, Bret L. ....Melville, NY
Mercury, Albert M. ....Rochester, NY
Mercury, John M. ....New York, NY
Mercy, John R. ....Texarkana, TX
Mercy, Michael I.D. ....Lancaster, CA
Merdek, Andrew A. ....Atlanta, GA
Merdes, Mark E. ....Fairbanks, AK
Merdes & Merdes, P.C. ....Fairbanks, AK
Merdes, Ward M. ....Fairbanks, AK
Merdian, Monica Jane ....Tulsa, OK
Merdinger, Mindy B. ....New York, NY
Mere, Yvonne R. ....San Francisco, CA
Meredith, Arthur S. ....Flemington, NJ
Meredith, Benjamin E. ....Dothan, AL
Meredith, Bruce ....Madison, WI
Meredith, Byron K. ....Caldwell, ID
Meredith, C. Locke, Jr. ....Baton Rouge, LA
Meredith, Charles T. ....Carson City, NV
Meredith Cohen Greenfogel & Skirnick, P.C.
New York, NY
Philadelphia, PA
Meredith, Colleen ....North Olmsted, OH
Meredith, Connie G. W. ....Honolulu, HI
Meredith, Craig S. ....Larkspur, CA
Meredith, Daphne G. ....Wellesley, MA
Meredith, David ....New York, NY
Meredith, David E. ....Carrollton, TX
Meredith, Donna K. ....Chicago, IL
Meredith, Donnell & Abernethy
Houston, TX
McAllen, TX
Corpus Christi, TX
Meredith, Dwight A. ....Atlanta, GA
Meredith, Edward B. ....Princeton, NJ
Trenton, NJ
Meredith, Francis, Jr. ....Columbia, SC
Meredith, Gregory A. ....Sacramento, CA
Meredith, Gregory G. ....Hutchinson, KS
Meredith, Gregory S. ....New York, NY
Meredith, Hugh S. ....Norfolk, VA
Meredith, J. Keith ....Fairfield, TX
Meredith, James E. ....Lima, OH
Meredith, James M. ....Vinita, OK
Meredith, James R. ....Tulsa, OK
Meredith, Janet M. ....Sacramento, CA
Meredith, Jason D. ....Amarillo, TX
Meredith, Jennings B. ....Clinton, TN
Meredith, Joel C. ....New York, NY
Philadelphia, PA
Meredith, John T. ....Cleveland, OH
Meredith, Jon A. ....Helena, MT
Meredith & Jones, A P.L.C.
Baton Rouge, LA
Meredith, Karen B. ....New York, NY

Meredith, Kathleen Howard
Baltimore, MD
Meredith, Kenneth A., II
Bowling Green, KY
Meredith, Kristin E. ....Los Angeles, CA
Meredith, Kristine Keala ....Danville, CA
Meredith, Larry D. ....Erie, PA
Meredith, Les W. ....Fort Wayne, IN
Meredith, Lynne R. ....Modesto, CA
Meredith, Mark D. ....Boston, MA
Meredith, Mark F. ....San Francisco, CA
Meredith, Matthew C. ....Panama City, FL
Meredith, Meredith & Chase
Princeton, NJ
Trenton, NJ
Meredith, Michael D. ....Amarillo, TX
Meredith, Miller Wm., Jr.
Corpus Christi, TX
Meredith, Nicole L. ....San Francisco, CA
Meredith, O. Byron, III ....Atlanta, GA
Meredith, O. Robert ....Salt Lake City, UT
Meredith, Olen W. ....St. Augustine, FL
Meredith, Pamela L. ....Washington, DC
Meredith, Paul M. ....Palatka, FL
Meredith, Peter J. ....Birmingham, AL
Meredith, Regina Haig ....Princeton, NJ
Trenton, NJ
Meredith, Richard A. ....Tustin, CA
Meredith, Richard D. ....Omaha, NE
Meredith, Robert D. ....Leitchfield, KY
Meredith, Robert J. ....Lima, OH
Meredith, Roger L. ....San Francisco, CA
Meredith, Roger L. ....Denver, CO
Meredith, Rose M. ....Pittsburgh, PA
Meredith, Ross ....Elgin, TX
Meredith, Samuel E. ....San Francisco, CA
Meredith, Shirley S. ....Houston, TX
Meredith, Stephen O. ....Boston, MA
Meredith, Susan A. ....Pittsburgh, PA
Meredith, Susan R. ....New Haven, CT
Meredith, Timothy E. ....Severna Park, MD
Meredith, Timothy P. ....Crofton, MD
Meredith, W. Clark ....Oak Ridge, TN
Meredith, Weinstein & Numbers
Larkspur, CA
Meredith, William R. ....Harrodsburg, KY
Merek, James J. ....Alexandria, VA
Merek & Voorhees ....Alexandria, VA
Merel, Gail ....Houston, TX
Merel, Richard A. ....Chicago, IL
Merelman, Jack M. ....Washington, DC
Merenbach, Alice T. ....Bakersfield, CA
Merenbach, Dennis G. ....Santa Barbara, CA
Merenbach, Richard Newburgh
Los Angeles, CA
Merene, Deon C. ....Sacramento, CA
Mereness, Everett D. ....Phoenix, AZ
Mereness, John M. ....Cincinnati, OH
Merenich, Molly Todd ....Linwood, NJ
Merenich, Robert P. ....Vineland, NJ
Merens, Henry B. ....Chicago, IL
Merenstein, Bruce P. ....Philadelphia, PA
Mereson, Julie S. ....Albany, NY
Meretsky, Jonathan A. ....Los Angeles, CA
Meretta, David J. ....Lansing, MI
Meretta, James L. ....Ann Arbor, MI
Merewether, Diana ....Arlington, MA
Merewitz, Seth ....Sacramento, CA
Merewitz, Susan Greene ....Rockville, MD
Merg & Anderson, S.C. ....Madison, WI
Merg, Dona J. ....Madison, WI
Mergel, Alan J. ....New York, NY
Mergel, Tubman & Grossman
New York, NY
Mergele, Carl E. ....Great Falls, VA
Mergele, Cary W. ....Washington, DC
Mergen, Andrew C. ....Department of Justice,
Environment and Natural Resources
Division, GV
Mergen, Michael P. ....Springfield, MO
Mergener, Tracey L. ....Galesburg, IL
Mergens, Cyril J. ....Warroad, MN
Mergenthal, Kenneth P.
Fredericksburg, VA
Mergenthal, Kenneth P., P.C.
Fredericksburg, VA
Mergenthaler, Michael ....Los Angeles, CA
Mergenthaler, Scott R. ....Columbus, OH
Merges, Robert P. ....Boston, MA
Mergler, Edward F. ....Bolivar, NY
Mergler & Pignone ....Manassas, VA
Mergler, Rod K. ....Manassas, VA
Mergner, William H., Jr.
Cedar Knolls, NJ
Mergus, Athan Michael ....Cliffside Park, NJ
Mergus, Athan M., Law Offices of, P.A.
Cliffside Park, NJ
Merhige, Anthony J. ....Philadelphia, PA
Merhige, Louis B. ....Metairie, LA
Merhige, Louis B. ....New Orleans, LA
Merhige, Robert R., IV ....Charlotte, NC
Merhige, Robert R., Jr. ....Richmond, VA
Merholtz, William R. ....Marinette, WI
Meriam, Harold A., III ....New York, NY
Meriam, Thomas C. ....New York, NY
Merica, Jo Ann ....Austin, TX
Merica, Kent J. ....Lewiston, ID
Merican, Linda S. ....Providence, RI
Merican, Steven R. ....Naperville, IL
Merican, Steven R., P.C. ....Chicago, IL
Naperville, IL
Mericle, Denise A. ....Cleveland, OH
Mericle, John L. ....Seattle, WA
Mericle, Linda S. ....Greenbelt, MD
Mericli, Kemal Alexander ....Pittsburgh, PA
Merideth, Angela R. ....Memphis, TN
Merideth, Angela R. ....Memphis, TN
Merideth, David L. ....Ridgeland, MS

Merideth, David L., P.L.L.C.
Ridgeland, MS
Merideth, Elinor T. ....San Diego, CA
Merideth, Frank E., Jr.
Santa Monica, CA
Merideth, H. L., Jr. ....Greenville, MS
Merideth, Paul L. ....Clarkston, MI
Meridian Law Group, L.L.P.
Los Angeles, CA
Meridith, Dennis D. ....Columbus, NE
Merigan, Gary D. ....Royal Oak, MI
Merigan, Gary D., P.C., Law Offices of
Royal Oak, MI
Merikas, Demetra ....Chicago, IL
Merila, Edith F. ....Madison, WI
Merillat, Robert N. ....Peoria, AZ
Merin, Kenneth D. ....Bedminster, NJ
Merin, Mark E. ....Sacramento, CA
Merinar, John R., Jr. ....Clarksburg, WV
Mering, Donald R. ....Baltimore, MD
Mering, Peter N. ....Sacramento, CA
Mering, Philip C. ....Sacramento, CA
Mering, Timothy E. ....Baltimore, MD
Meringer, Donald S. ....Hartford, CT
Meringer, Gary ....Erie, PA
Meringer, Patricia Carteaux
New Orleans, LA
Meringolo, John A. ....Commack, NY
Meringolo, Louis M. ....New York, NY
Meringolo, Peter P. ....San Francisco, CA
Merino, Dawn A. ....Glen Burnie, MD
Merino, Jeanne E. ....Menlo Park, CA
Merino, Monica ....Chicago, IL
Merino, R. Robert ....Niagara Falls, NY
Merino, Robert Paul ....Niagara Falls, NY
Merinoff, Hermen I. ....Astoria, NY
Merithew, Stephanie L. ....Fort Worth, TX
Merithew, Tracey L. ....Detroit, MI
Meritz, Judith K. ....Dix Hills, NY
Meritz, Maxine L. ....Newark, DE
Meriwether, Catherine S. ....Columbia, SC
Meriwether, Charlotte G. ....Los Angeles, CA
Meriwether, Ellen ....Philadelphia, PA
Meriwether, Hunter M. ....Grand Rapids, MI
Meriwether, James R. ....Chickasaw, AL
Meriwether, Porter L. ....Chicago, IL
Meriwether, Robert O. ....Columbia, SC
Meriwether, Thomas J. ....Vista, CA
Merjian, Mardi ....New York, NY
Merk, Howard S. ....North Haven, CT
Merk, Melinda S. ....Washington, DC
Merkadeau, Lisa A. ....El Segundo, CA
Merkadeau, Stuart L. ....Los Angeles, CA
Merkatz, Stephen Z. ....Los Angeles, CA
Merkel, Albert B. ....Jackson, TN
Merkel & Associates, Inc. ....San Diego, CA
Merkel, Barbara Lynn ....San Diego, CA
Merkel, Cecil E. ....Wichita, KS
Merkel, Charles M. ....Clarksdale, MS
Merkel, Charles M., III ....Jackson, MS
Merkel Chartered ....Wichita, KS
Merkel & Cocke, A Professional Association
Clarksdale, MS
Merkel, David A. ....Rochester, NY
Merkel, David R. ....Tempe, AZ
Merkel, Diana ....Norfolk, NE
Merkel, Edward W. ....Cincinnati, OH
Merkel, Edwin V. ....Rochester, NY
Merkel, Joel V. ....Fairview Heights, IL
Merkel, Kellyanne ....Parsippany, NJ
Merkel and Merkel ....Rochester, NY
Merkel, Neal P. ....New York, NY
Merkel, Philip L. ....Savannah, GA
Merkel, Raymond W. ....Cicero, IL
Merkel, Richard L. ....Phoenix, AZ
Merkel, Robert G. ....West Palm Beach, FL
Merkel, Roland P. ....Frankfort, KY
Lexington, KY
Merkel & Spang ....Reading, PA
Merkel, Stephanie L. ....Dallas, TX
Merkel, Stephen M. ....New York, NY
Merkel & Tabor ....Jackson, TN
Merkel, Thomas G. ....Elgin, IL
Merkel, Thomas Richard ....Topeka, KS
Merkel, William G. ....Washington, DC
Merkel, William K. ....Chicago, IL
Merkelbach, Donald W. ....Newark, NJ
Merkelson, Wayne P. ....Summit, NJ
Merken, Andrew J. ....Boston, MA
Merken, Leo ....New York, NY
Merker, Evelyn K. ....Boca Raton, FL
Merker, George E. ....Seattle, WA
Merker, Howard B. ....Towson, MD
Merker, Neal E. ....Fort Lee, NJ
Merker, Peter L. ....New York, NY
Merker, Richard T. ....Overland Park, KS
Merker, Steven J. ....Denver, CO
Merker, Steven L. ....San Diego, CA
Merker, Timothy G. ....Chicago, IL
Merkin, Alan G. ....New City, NY
Merkin, David C. ....Rockville, MD
Merkin, Donald ....La Jolla, CA
Merkin, Elizabeth G.
San Bernardino, CA
Merkin, Frederick N. ....Los Angeles, CA
Merkin, J. Ezra ....New York, NY
Merkin, Stacey M. ....Philadelphia, PA
Merkin, Stewart A., Law Office of
Miami, FL
Merkl, Kathleen A. ....Brooklyn, NY
Merkl, Neil ....New York, NY
Merkl, Neil M. ....New York, NY
Merkle, Alan R. ....Seattle, WA
Merkle, Craig B. ....Baltimore, MD
Merkle, Daniel R. ....Seattle, WA
Merkle, Emil A. ....Akron, OH
Merkle, Gary L. ....Woodland Hills, CA
Merkle, Gregory O. ....Wichita Falls, TX

Merkle, H. Tim ....Columbus, OH
Merkle, John H. ....Minneapolis, MN
Merkle, John W. ....San Francisco, CA
Merkle, LeRoy H., Jr. ....Tampa, FL
Merkle, LeRoy H., Jr., P.A. ....Tampa, FL
Merkle & Magri, P.A., Law Offices of
Clearwater, FL
Tampa, FL
Merkle, Mark J. R. ....Indianapolis, IN
Merkle, Mark K., Jr. ....Columbus, OH
Merkle, Mary L. ....New York, NY
Merkle, Pamela N. ....Wayzata, MN
Merkle, Patrick G. ....Washington, DC
Merkle, Patrick G., PLLC
Washington, DC
Merkle, Paul C., Jr. ....Janesville, WI
Merkle, Paula Krahn ....Baltimore, MD
Merkle, Phillip Kent ....Department of Justice,
Office of Justice Programs, GV
Merkle, Robert W. ....Tampa, FL
Merkle Siegel & Friedrichsen, P.C.
Seattle, WA
Merkle, Thomas A. ....Milwaukee, WI
Merkle, Walter F., Jr. ....San Francisco, CA
Merkle, William R. ....Boynton Beach, FL
Merkle, William R., P.A.
Boynton Beach, FL
Merklen, Kenneth E. ....Coral Springs, FL
Merkley, David L. ....Beaumont, TX
Merkley, Douglas K. ....Pocatello, ID
Merkley, Leslie D. ....Jeffersonville, IN
Merklin, Jeffrey A. ....Marysville, OH
Merklin, Marc B. ....Akron, OH
Merklinger, James Anthony
Washington, DC
Merklinger, M. Richard
Florham Park, NJ
Merkow, Erica D. ....Pittsburgh, PA
Merkow, Harold J. ....Phoenix, AZ
Merksamer, Steven A. ....Sacramento, CA
San Francisco, CA
Merkt, Julia E. ....El Paso, TX
Merkt, Richard A. ....Trenton, NJ
Merkur, Rhona L. ....New York, NY
Merl, Burstyn & Associates, P.A.
Miami, FL
Merl, Daryl L. ....Miami, FL
Merl, Eric L. ....Miami, FL
Merlanti, Denise K. ....Ann Arbor, MI
Merlanti, Mark ....Southfield, MI
Merlau, John S. ....New Palestine, IN
Merle, Hugh M. ....New York, NY
Westhampton Beach, NY
Merle, Pierre F. V., (P.C.) ....New York, NY
Merlen, Deena R. ....New York, NY
Merley, Dennis J. ....Minneapolis, MN
Merley, Mark R. ....Washington, DC
Merli, John Edward ....Houston, TX
Merli, Joseph T. ....Charleston, SC
Merlie, Barbara R. ....New Britain, PA
Merlie, Donald L. ....Danville, IL
Merlie & Merlie ....Danville, IL
Merlie, Michael F. ....Exton, PA
Merlie, Michael J. ....Danville, IL
Merlin, Debrah S. ....Pittsburgh, PA
Merlin, H. Stephen ....Atlanta, GA
Merlin & Hertz, P.A. ....Coral Gables, FL
Merlin, Joseph B. ....Miami, FL
Merlin, Kimbel L., (P.A.) ....Jacksonville, FL
Tampa, FL
Winter Park, FL
Merlin Law Group, The, P.A.
St. Petersburg, FL
Tampa, FL
Merlin, Lawrence E. ....West Hartford, CT
Merlin, Lawrence M. ....Atlanta, GA
Merlin, Paul
Federal Mine Safety and Health Review
Commission,
Office of the Administrative Law Judges, GV
Merlin, Peter H. ....Chicago, IL
Merlin, Robert J. ....Coral Gables, FL
Merlin, William F., Jr. ....Tampa, FL
Merline, David A. ....Greenville, SC
Merline, David A., Jr. ....Greenville, SC
Merline, Michael John ....Newport Beach, CA
Merline & Thomas, P.A. ....Anderson, SC
Greenville, SC
Spartanburg, SC
Merling, Gayle M. ....Winchester, MA
Merling, Joseph C. ....Cincinnati, OH
Merlino, Frank G. ....Dallas, TX
Merlino, John R., Jr. ....Staten Island, NY
Merlino, Joseph P. ....Trenton, NJ
Merlino, Kenneth J. ....Chicago, IL
Merlino, Maria B. ....New York, NY
Merlino, Michael R., II ....Atlanta, GA
Merlino, Nancie S. ....Toledo, OH
Merlino, Patrick A. ....Greensburg, PA
Merlino, Paul R. ....Providence, RI
Merlino, Silvana M. ....New York, NY
Merlis, Albert L. ....New York, NY
Merlis, Charles Isaac ....Yonkers, NY
Merlis, Erika Suzanne ....Chicago, IL
Merliss, Joshua M. ....Los Angeles, CA
Merlitti, James A. ....Akron, OH
Merlo, A. John ....Chico, CA
Merlo, Andrew ....Boca Raton, FL
Merlo & Bell ....Indiana, PA
Merlo, Charles M. ....Eastpointe, MI
Merlo, Grace S. ....Cortez, CO
Merlo, John P. ....Indiana, PA
Merlo, Kanofsky & Brinkmeier, Ltd.
Chicago, IL
Merlo, Maryesther S. ....Allentown, PA
Merlo, Michael G. ....Chicago, IL
Merlo, Michael J. ....Chicago, IL
Merlo, Perry D. ....Harrisburg, PA

Merlo, Samuel J. ....Cortez, CO
Merlo, Samuel P. ....Rochester, NY
Merlo, Theodore C. ....Wellesley, MA
Merly, Lawrence J. ....Bridgeport, CT
Mermall, Meribeth ....Chicago, IL
Mermall, Michael E. ....Chicago, IL
Mermall, Neal ....Skokie, IL
Merman, Mary M. ....Pittsburgh, PA
Merman, Steven H. ....Cranford, NJ
Mermel, Mark D. ....Great Neck, NY
Mermel, Michael G. ....Park Ridge, IL
Mermell, Clifford R. ....Miami, FL
Mermell, Mac ....Miami, FL
Mermelstein, Bernard H. ....Great Neck, NY
Mermelstein, Beth ....Brooklyn, NY
Mermelstein, Bruce ....Reisterstown, MD
Mermelstein, Edward A. ....New York, NY
Mermelstein, Elliott J. ....Jamaica, NY
Mermelstein, Evan R. ....Atlanta, GA
Mermelstein, Irvin A. ....Concord, NH
Mermelstein, Joshua ....New York, NY
Mermelstein, Jules J. ....Glenside, PA
Mermelstein, Laurie E. ....Brooklyn, NY
Mermelstein, Lee ....New York, NY
Mermelstein, Mark ....New York, NY
Mermelstein, Merle ....Pittsburgh, PA
Mermelstein, Richard T. ....New York, NY
Mermelstein, Robert J. ....Raleigh, NC
Mermelstein, Stephen Edward ....Boston, MA
Mermelstein, Stuart S. ....Miami, FL
Mermigousis, Mathew ....New York, NY
Mermin, Samuel ....Madison, WI
Mermin, Seth E. ....San Francisco, CA
Mermis, Greg J. ....Kansas City, MO
Mermis, Jos. A., Jr. ....Great Bend, KS
Merna, James F. ....Atlanta, GA
Merna, Jan E. ....San Diego, CA
Merner, R. William ....Cedar Falls, IA
Mernick, George H., III ....Washington, DC
Mernick, Paul M. ....Woodmere, NY
Mernin, Corinne D. ....Boston, MA
Mernin, Michael J. ....Montclair, NJ
Mernitz, David W. ....Westcliffe, CO
Mero, Steven C. ....New York, NY
Meroe, Masao ....Greenville, NC
Meroe, Masao, P.A. ....Greenville, NC
Merola, Andrew R. ....New York, NY
Merola, Frank A. ....Los Angeles, CA
Merola, James R. ....Palm Beach Gardens, FL
Merola, Jerry A. ....New York, NY
Merola, Mary Jane ....West Palm Beach, FL
Merola, Michael J. ....New York, NY
Merola, Michelle ....Washington, DC
Merola, Richard A. ....Providence, RI
Merolla, Amedeo C. ....Providence, RI
Merolla, Katherine A. ....Providence, RI
Merolla, Paul A. ....New York, NY
Merolla, Steven B. ....Providence, RI
Merolli, Mark A. ....Chicago, IL
Meron, Daniel ....Washington, DC
Meron, Jennifer R. ....Washington, DC
Meron, Terry M. ....Plattsburgh, NY
Merone, William M. ....Washington, DC
Meronek, Gregory D. ....San Francisco, CA
Meroney, Bernard F. ....Baton Rouge, LA
Meroney, Millicent S. ....Austin, TX
Meroney, Ranelle M ....Austin, TX
Meroney, Robert A. ....Port Arthur, TX
Meroney, Robert A., P.C. ....Port Arthur, TX
Meroni, Charles F., Jr. ....Barrington, IL
Meroni & Meroni ....Barrington, IL
Meroni, Thomas J. ....Miami, FL
Meronoff, Patricia E. ....Bryan, TX
Meros, Alicia A. ....Washington, DC
Meros, Dede ....Clearwater, FL
Meros, George N., Jr. ....Tallahassee, FL
Meros, John C. ....Cleveland, OH
Meros, Peter N. ....St. Petersburg, FL
Meros, Smith & Olney, P.A.
St. Petersburg, FL
Merouse, Steven L. ....Chicago, IL
Merow, James F.
United States Court of Federal Claims, GV
Merow, Joel H. ....Reading, PA
Merow, John E. ....New York, NY
Merra, Kanakis, Creme & Mellor, P.C.
Nashua, NH
Merra, Michael F. ....Nashua, NH
Merran, Harold ....Hartsdale, NY
Merrell, Bruce R. ....Elyria, OH
Merrell, Bryan S. ....Anchorage, AK
Merrell, Charles C. ....Lowville, NY
Merrell, Clyde Nelson ....Westerville, OH
Merrell, Edgar S. K., 3rd ....Lowville, NY
Merrell, Huette M. ....Austin, TX
Merrell, J. Scott
Research Triangle Park, NC
Merrell & Jahn, P.A. ....Clemson, SC
Seneca, SC
Merrell, James B. ....Houston, TX
Merrell, Jeffrey M. ....Forsyth, MO
Merrell, Jerry M. ....Poplar Bluff, MO
Merrell, John R. ....Delaware, OH
Merrell, John Y. ....McLean, VA
Merrell, John Y., Jr. ....McLean, VA
Merrell, Matthew B. ....Cornelius, NC
Merrell & Merrell ....Lowville, NY
Merrell & Merrell, P.C. ....McLean, VA
Merrell, Michael E. ....Forsyth, MO
Merrell, Nathaniel B. ....Lowville, NY
Merrell, Pamela K. ....Butte, MT
Merrell, Robert A., III
Daytona Beach, FL
Merrell, Sally C. ....Milwaukee, WI
Merrell, Timothy C. ....Seneca, SC
Merrell, William W. ....Houston, TX
Merrelli, Robert G. ....Mount Clemens, MI
Merren, Luis A., Jr. ....Dallas, TX
Merrett, André H. ....Phoenix, AZ
Merrett, John M. ....Jacksonville, FL
Merrett, N. Rhys ....Dallas, TX
Merriam, Christopher S. ....Washington, DC
Merriam, Daniel B. ....Ladysmith, WI
Merriam, Deborah J. ....Moorestown, NJ
Merriam, Dennis C. ....Charlotte, NC
Merriam, Dwight H. ....Hartford, CT
Merriam, J. Tom ....West Bend, WI
Merriam, Jeffrey A. ....Greenville, SC
Greer, SC
Merriam, Jessica Lee ....Newton, MA
Merriam, John G. ....Minneapolis, MN
Merriam, Lauren E., III ....Ocala, FL
Merriam, Martin M. ....New Haven, CT
Merriam, Michael James ....Worcester, MA
Merriam, Michael W. ....Topeka, KS
Merriam, Roger D. ....Tallahassee, FL
Merriam, Stephen C. ....Cleveland, OH
Merriam, Susan S. ....Hartford, CT
Merriam, Terri A. ....Seattle, WA
Merriam, Theodore H., (P.C.) ....Denver, CO
Merric, Mark Earl ....Denver, CO
Merrick, Andrew D. ....Buffalo, NY
Merrick, Baker, Hufft & Strauss, P.C.
Mission, KS
Overland Park, KS
Kansas City, MO
Merrick, Doris M. ....Short Hills, NJ
Merrick, Frank E. ....Oviedo, FL
Merrick, Gale M. ....Boise, ID
Merrick, Glenn W. ....Denver, CO
Merrick, H. J. ....Seattle, WA
Merrick, Hofstedt & Lindsey, P.S.
Seattle, WA
Merrick, Jack C. ....Los Angeles, CA
Merrick, James J. ....Willington, CT
Merrick, Jeffrey J. ....San Diego, CA
Merrick, Jeffrey S. ....Portland, OR
Merrick, John J. ....Malibu, CA
Merrick, John J. ....Chicago, IL
Merrick, John R. ....Kennett Square, PA
Merrick & Klimek, P.C. ....Chicago, IL
Merrick, Lori A. ....Bellevue, WA
Merrick & Louison ....Boston, MA
Merrick, Marc L. ....Long Beach, CA
Merrick & Merrick ....Dixon, IL
Merrick, Michael J. ....Chicago, IL
Merrick, N. Munro ....Del Mar, CA
Merrick, Nancy ....Boston, MA
Merrick & Olver, P.S. ....Seattle, WA
Merrick, Robert A., Jr. ....Chicago, IL
Oak Park, IL
Merrick, Robert T. ....Sunland, CA
Merrick, Ruth L., (Mrs.) ....Dixon, IL
Merrick, Samuel V.
Joint Committees And Commissions, GV
Merrick, Stephen M. ....Chicago, IL
Chicago, IL
Merrick, Suzanne Bernard
Pittsburgh, PA
Merrick, Terence C. ....Lansing, MI
Merrick, Thomas E. ....Fargo, ND
Merrick, Thomas F. ....Pittsburgh, PA
Merrick, Thomas R. ....San Diego, CA
Merrick, Thomas R. ....Seattle, WA
Merrick, Toni D. ....Chicago, IL
Merricks, Julia Wesley
Research Triangle Park, NC
Merriell, Howard S., Jr. ....Dallas, TX
Merrifield, Gregory C. ....Marion, MI
Merrifield, Leroy S. ....Alexandria, VA
Merrifield, Lewis B., III
Beverly Hills, CA
Merrifield, Lewis B. III ....Los Angeles, CA
Merrifield, Pamela G.
Occupational Safety and Health Review Commission, GV
Merrifield, Rodney B. ....Fairmont, WV
Merrifield, William P. ....Sacramento, CA
Merrigan, Claire M. ....Jacksonville, FL
Merrigan, David J. ....Braintree, MA
Merrigan, Edward H., Jr. ....Jacksonville, FL
Merrigan, Edward L. ....Washington, DC
Merrigan, Francis G. ....Braintree, MA
Merrigan, Joanne ....Boston, MA
Merrigan, John A. ....Washington, DC
Merrigan, L. T. (Mike) ....Hopkins, MN
Merrigan, Michael, Jr. ....Springfield, MO
Merrigan, Michael W. ....Los Angeles, CA
Merrigan, Quayle, Brandt & Ostenso
Hopkins, MN
Merrigan, Thomas E. ....Commerce City, CO
Merrigan, Thomas T. ....Orange, MA
Merrigan, Thomas W. ....Greenfield, MA
Merrigan, William F. ....Braintree, MA
Merrihew, Noel H. ....San Francisco, CA
Merrihugh, David R.
Westlake Village, CA
Merriken, Robert J. ....Easton, MD
Merrikin, Karen J. ....Seattle, WA
Merril, Steven A. ....Fairfax, VA
Merrilees, Alison York ....Auburn, CA
Merrilees, Edward J. ....Santa Ana, CA
Merrill, Abel J. ....Annapolis, MD
Merrill, Abel J., P.A. ....Annapolis, MD
Merrill, Adam P. ....Chicago, IL
Merrill, Allen H. ....Oyster Bay, NY
Merrill, Anderson, King & Harris, LLC
Colorado Springs, CO
Merrill, Andrew A. ....Manchester, NH
Merrill, Arnone & Jones, LLP
Santa Rosa, CA
Merrill & Associates ....Worcester, MA
Merrill & Ball ....Forest Hills, NY
Merrill, Barbara E. ....Augusta, ME
Merrill, Barton C. ....Ventura, CA
Merrill, Bradley W. ....Salt Lake City, UT
Merrill, Bruce M. ....Portland, ME
Merrill, Burton ....Marina Del Rey, CA
Merrill, Carl H. ....Heflin, AL
Merrill, Charles E. ....San Ramon, CA
Merrill, Charles E. ....St. Louis, MO
Merrill, Charles R. ....Newark, NJ
Merrill, Chas. Brett, Jr. ....Augusta, GA
Statesboro, GA
Swainsboro, GA
Merrill, Craig A. ....Columbia Heights, MN
Merrill, Dale Marie ....Cambridge, MA
Merrill, David D. ....Boston, MA
Merrill, David J. ....Las Vegas, NV
Merrill, David L. ....Port St. Lucie, FL
Merrill, David R.
Commodity Futures Trading Commission, Office of the General Counsel, GV
Merrill, Denise W. ....Vershire, VT
Merrill, E. Chouteau ....Boston, MA
Merrill, Edward L. ....Rancho Mirage, CA
Merrill, Edward S. ....Palo Alto, CA
San Francisco, CA
Merrill, Elizabeth Hoskins ....Tampa, FL
Merrill, Elizabeth L. ....Sacramento, CA
Merrill, Erich W. ....Memphis, TN
Merrill, Erich W., Jr., P.C. ....Portland, OR
Merrill, Esther S. ....Loxahatchee, FL
Merrill, Forrest G. ....Ramsey, NJ
Merrill, Frank L. ....Columbus, OH
Merrill, Freeman G. ....Sheldon, IA
Merrill, George V. ....New York, NY
Merrill, Gilbert L. ....Worcester, MA
Merrill, Gitta Maria ....Clovis, CA
Merrill, Gretchen Gunn ....Salem, OR
Merrill Harrison & Adams, P.C.
Abbeville, AL
Dothan, AL
Ozark, AL
Merrill, Heather G. ....Boston, MA
Merrill, Heloise C. ....Charlotte, NC
Merrill, Hugh D., Jr. ....Anniston, AL
Merrill, Hyde, Fortier & Youney, P.A.
Skowhegan, ME
Merrill, Irma W. ....Memphis, TN
Merrill, Jack, Jr. ....Natick, MA
Merrill, James L. ....Colorado Springs, CO
Merrill, Jane B. ....Indianapolis, IN
Merrill, Janice L. ....Orlando, FL
Merrill, Jeffrey R. ....Syracuse, NY
Merrill, Jo Lynne H. ....Dallas, TX
Merrill, John A. ....Ramsey, NJ
Merrill, John A. ....Buffalo, NY
Merrill, John D. ....Steamboat Springs, CO
Merrill, John L. ....Skowhegan, ME
Merrill, Judith ....Hartford, CT
Merrill, Kathleen M. ....Chicago, IL
Merrill, Keith J. ....Coral Gables, FL
Merrill, Kenneth B. ....Long Beach, CA
Merrill, Kevin E. ....Jacksonville, FL
Merrill, Lawrence E. ....Bangor, ME
Merrill, Leesa B. ....Frankfort, KY
Merrill, Lisa C. ....San Diego, CA
Merrill, Lois B. ....Waltham, MA
Merrill, Marion B. ....Houston, TX
Merrill, Mark J. ....Clarksburg, WV
Merrill, Mark W. ....Sarasota, FL
Merrill, Marsha Lynn ....San Antonio, TX
Merrill, Martha D. ....Union, ME
Merrill, Max ....Bend, OR
Merrill & Merrill, Chartered
Blackfoot, ID
Idaho Falls, ID
Pocatello, ID
Soda Springs, ID
Merrill, Merrill, Mathews & Allen
Anniston, AL
Merrill, Michael E. ....San Diego, CA
Merrill, Michael P. ....Santa Rosa, CA
Merrill, Milford S. ....Boise, ID
Merrill, Mullins & Spears, A Professional Association ....Memphis, TN
Merrill, Nancy B. ....Louisville, CO
Merrill O'Sullivan, LLP ....Bend, OR
Merrill, Pamela Kurvink ....League City, TX
Merrill, Patricia ....Richmond, VA
Merrill, Phyllis Garbe ....Houston, TX
Merrill, Randy E. ....Naples, FL
Merrill, Raymond K. ....Elgin, IL
Merrill, Richard A. ....Washington, DC
Merrill, Richard A. ....Minneapolis, MN
Merrill, Richard L. ....Houston, TX
Merrill, Richard V. ....Naperville, IL
Merrill, Richard Walter, Jr. ....Deerfield, IL
Merrill, Rick H. ....Everett, WA
Mount Vernon, WA
Merrill, Robert L. ....New York, NY
Merrill, Robert T. ....Littleton, CO
Merrill, Robert W. ....San Francisco, CA
Merrill, Robin ....Forest Hills, NY
Merrill, Roger L. ....Houston, TX
Merrill, Ronald B. ....Denver, CO
Merrill, Roy L. ....Los Fresnos, TX
Merrill, Roy L., Jr. ....Dallas, TX
Merrill, S. Todd ....Tampa, FL
Merrill, Sandra Lynn ....Canton, OH
Merrill, Schultz & Wolds, Limited
San Diego, CA
Merrill, Scott C ....Boston, MA
Merrill, Scott R. ....Sacramento, CA
Merrill, Stephen G. ....Norfolk, VA
Merrill, Stone & Hamilton, LLC
Statesboro, GA
Swainsboro, GA
Merrill, Stone & Parks ....Augusta, GA
Merrill, Susan L. ....New York, NY
Merrill, Susan T. ....Louisville, KY
Merrill, T. Randolph ....Atlanta, GA
Merrill & Tatham ....Birmingham, MI
Merrill, Thomas B. ....Louisville, KY
Merrill, Thomas W. ....Chicago, IL
Merrill, Thomas W. ....Boston, MA
Merrill, Victor S. ....Salt Lake City, UT
Merrill, Walter J. ....Anniston, AL
Merrill, Walter T. ....Ogden, UT
Merrill, Wendy L. ....Bellingham, WA
Merrill, Wesley F. ....Pocatello, ID
Merrill, William H., Jr. ....Indianapolis, IN
Merrill, William R.H. ....Houston, TX
Merrill, William W. ....San Diego, CA
Merrill, William W. ....Sarasota, FL
Merrill, William W., III ....Sarasota, FL
Merrill-Hall, Martha ....Breckenridge, CO
Englewood, CO
Merrill-Long, Michelle A. ....San Diego, CA
Merrills, Andrew W. ....Raleigh, NC
Merriman, Aimee L. ....Chicago, IL
Merriman, Christine O. ....New York, NY
Merriman, Donald L. ....Timonium, MD
Merriman, E. Lawrence, (P.C.)
Longview, TX
Merriman, E. Porter ....Redwood City, CA
Merriman, Jack C. ....Baltimore, MD
Merriman, James E. ....Scottsdale, AZ
Merriman, James J. ....San Francisco, CA
Merriman, James J. ....Chicago, IL
Merriman, John A. ....Des Moines, IA
Merriman, Kenneth E. ....Florence, SC
Merriman, Kevin T. ....Buffalo, NY
Merriman, Pat J. ....St. Joseph, MO
Merriman, Patricia A. ....Chicago, IL
Merriman, Patterson & Allison, L.L.P.
Longview, TX
Merriman, R. Marshall, Jr. ....Richmond, VA
Merriman, Richard M. ....Washington, DC
Merriman, Robert B. ....Port Deposit, MD
Merriman, Robert D. ....Kennewick, WA
Merriman, Russell W. ....Tampa, FL
Merriman, Sharon R. ....Indianapolis, IN
Merriman, Thomas Conley ....Cleveland, OH
Merriman, Thorpe ....Madison, WI
Merriman, Troy D. ....Los Angeles, CA
Merriman, Vicki J. ....Indianapolis, IN
Merriman, William O., Jr.
Parkersburg, WV
Ripley, WV
Merriman, William R. ....Towson, MD
Merriman, William W., III ....Raleigh, NC
Merrin, Richard C. ....San Diego, CA
Merriner, Charles M. ....Anchorage, AK
Merrinette, Jenifer ....Chicago, IL
Merring, Robert A. ....Irvine, CA
Merriott, Neal ....Atoka, OK
Merris, Donna R. ....New York, NY
Merrit, Manes M. ....New York, NY
Merritt & Albert ....Rock Falls, IL
Merritt, Andrea ....Lavonia, GA
Merritt, Andrew L. ....Champaign, IL
Merritt, Angelia M. ....Largo, MD
Merritt & Associates, P.C.
Oklahoma City, OK
Merritt, Barbara Anne ....Oklahoma City, OK
Merritt, Billie J. ....De Funiak Springs, FL
Seagrove Beach, FL
Merritt, Billie J., P.A.
De Funiak Springs, FL
Seagrove Beach, FL
Merritt, Brent S. ....Beverly Hills, CA
Merritt, Bruce G. ....New York, NY
Merritt, C. Nathaniel ....Hinesville, GA
Merritt, Cama C. ....Mount Airy, NC
Merritt, Carolyn L. ....Oklahoma City, OK
Merritt, Cecil P. ....Goldsboro, NC
Merritt, Charles G. ....New Orleans, LA
Merritt, Charles W. ....Keystone Heights, FL
Merritt, Charles W., Jr. ....Madison, GA
Merritt, C. J., Jr. ....Olympia, WA
Merritt, Clyde D. ....New Orleans, LA
Merritt, Colin D. ....High Point, NC
Merritt, Craig T. ....Richmond, VA
Merritt, D. Donovan ....Raleigh, NC
Merritt, Daniel B., Jr. ....Brooksville, FL
Merritt, Daniel B., Sr. ....Brooksville, FL
Merritt, David D. ....Hoffman Estates, IL
Merritt, Dianne L. Y. ....Honolulu, HI
Merritt, Edward L. ....Longview, TX
Merritt, Elizabeth Sherrill ....Washington, DC
Merritt, Ellis, Jr. ....Denver, CO
Merritt, Floyd I. ....Los Angeles, CA
Merritt, Frances M. ....Princeton, NJ
Merritt, Frances M. H. ....Llano, TX
Merritt, Frank S. ....Toledo, OH
Merritt, G. Edward ....New Orleans, LA
Merritt, Garry A. ....Houston, TX
Merritt, Gary M. ....San Mateo, CA
Merritt, Gilbert S., Jr. ....Nashville, TN
Merritt, Glenn C. ....Secaucus, NJ
Merritt, Grant J. ....Minneapolis, MN
Merritt, Gregory T. ....London, OH
Mechanicsburg, OH
Merritt, H. Kenneth, Jr. ....Burlington, VT
Merritt, H. Lee, Jr. ....Mount Airy, NC
Merritt & Hagen ....Los Angeles, CA
Woodland Hills, CA
Merritt, Harley A. ....Chico, CA
Merritt, J. Scott, Jr. ....Kansas City, MO
Merritt, Jack W. ....Punta Gorda, FL
Baltimore, MD
Merritt, James A., Jr. ....Columbia, SC
Merritt, James E. ....San Francisco, CA
Merritt, James E., Jr. ....Vicksburg, MS
Merritt, Jas. R. ....Louisville, KY
Merritt, Jeralyn E. ....Denver, CO
Merritt, John B. ....Washington, DC
Merritt, John I. ....Eustis, FL
Merritt, John J. ....Grass Valley, CA
Merritt, John M. ....Oklahoma City, OK

Merritt, John W. .... Fresno, CA
Merritt, Johnny K. .... Amarillo, TX
Merritt, Joyce Ann .... Lexington, KY
Merritt, Karen Palecek .... Scottsdale, AZ
Merritt, Keith J. .... Charlotte, NC
Merritt & Keller .... Brooksville, FL
Merritt, Kenneth C. .... Southfield, MI
Merritt, Kenni B. .... Oklahoma City, OK
Merritt, Kevin R. .... Phoenix, AZ
Merritt, Laura M. .... Austin, TX
Merritt, Laurence D. .... Woodland Hills, CA
Merritt, Linda M. .... Dallas, TX
Merritt, Lorenzo C. .... Statesboro, GA
Merritt, Lorenzo C., P.C. .... Statesboro, GA
Merritt, M. David .... Atlanta, GA
Merritt, Marianne R. .... Alexandria, VA
Merritt, Mark .... Lawrenceville, GA
Merritt, Mark H. .... Rock Falls, IL
Merritt, Mark, P.C. .... Lawrenceville, GA
Merritt, Mark W. .... Charlotte, NC
Merritt, Martin Randal .... Dallas, TX
Merritt, Maurice A. .... Royal Oak, MI
Merritt & Merritt .... Dallas, TX
Merritt & Merritt .... Burlington, VT
Merritt, Michael F. .... Howell, MI
Merritt, Michael F. .... St. Louis, MO
Merritt, Nancy Kistler .... Toledo, OH
Merritt, Nancy-Jo .... Phoenix, AZ
Merritt, Nelson B. .... Richmond, VA
Merritt, Normarene C. .... Kennesaw, GA
Merritt, Paul D., Jr. .... Lincoln, NE
Merritt, Randy L. .... Sarasota, FL
Merritt, Randy R. .... Los Angeles, CA
Merritt and Ratchford .... Pensacola, FL
Merritt, Ray B. .... Lafayette, IN
Merritt, Raymond W. .... New York, NY
Merritt, Reid .... Lawrenceville, GA
Merritt, Richard A. .... Tucson, AZ
Merritt, Robert E. .... Walnut Creek, CA
Merritt, Robert E. .... Columbia, SC
Merritt, Robert G. .... San Francisco, CA
Merritt, Robert H., Jr. .... Raleigh, NC
Merritt, Robert M. .... Sacramento, CA
Merritt, Robert N. .... Hartford, CT
Merritt, Robin C. .... Duluth, MN
Merritt, Roger J. .... Miami Beach, FL
Merritt, Ronald W. .... Chapel Hill, NC
Merritt, Sharon J. .... Burlington, VT
Merritt & Sikes, P.A. .... Miami, FL
Merritt, Sydney La Branche
Los Angeles, CA
Merritt, Tahira Khan .... Dallas, TX
Merritt & Tenney LLP .... Atlanta, GA
Merritt, Terrence A. .... Apple Valley, MN
Merritt, Thomas B. .... Hollis, NH
Merritt, Thomas M. .... Hauppauge, NY
Merritt, Tom O. .... Dayton, OH
Merritt & Troemel .... Indianapolis, IN
Kokomo, IN
Lafayette, IN
Merritt, Valerie J. .... Pasadena, CA
Merritt, Walter Gregory .... New Bern, NC
Merritt and Watson, P.A. .... Eustis, FL
Merritt, Weldon L. .... Santa Fe, NM
Merritt, William .... San Diego, CA
Merritt, William A., Jr. .... New York, NY
Merritt, William C. .... Miami, FL
Merritt, William D. .... Dallas, TX
Merritt, William E. .... Dallas, TX
Merritt, William Gregory
New Orleans, LA
Merritt, William J. .... Rosemont, IL
Merritt, William J. W., (P.C.)
Atlanta, GA
Merritt, Wm. Lee .... Lincoln, NE
Merritt, Wooten & Janvier, P.A.
Raleigh, NC
Merritt, Yuka Ohashi .... Great Falls, VA
Merritt-Epps, Gina M. .... Atlantic City, NJ
Merritt-Glenny, Susan .... Hyannis, MA
Merritt-Poree, Tsan .... San Francisco, CA
Merritts, Jack M. .... Denver, CO
Merritts, Melissa A. .... Allentown, PA
Merriweather, Marc D. .... New York, NY
Merriwether, Keith M., III .... Mineola, NY
Merrow, Donald L. .... Tallmadge, OH
Merrow, Douglas A. .... Detroit, MI
Merrow, L. Ross .... Westborough, MA
Merry, Ann .... Southfield, MI
Merry, Cynthia E. .... St. Clair Shores, MI
Merry, Farnen & Ryan, A Professional Corporation .... Detroit, MI
Mount Clemens, MI
Pontiac, MI
St. Clair Shores, MI
Merry, Joanne M. .... Davis, CA
Merry, Joseph W. .... Zanesville, OH
Merry, Max T. .... Dell Rapids, SD
Merry, Paul Henry .... Boston, MA
Merry, Peter R. .... Salem, MA
Merry, Susan M. .... Lebanon, TN
Merry, Tony C. .... Columbus, OH
Merryday, Lew A., Jr. .... Palatka, FL
Merryday, Steven D. .... Tampa, FL
Merryfield, Ann E. .... Seattle, WA
Merryman, Bryan A. .... Los Angeles, CA
Merryman, Charles B., Jr. .... Davidson, NC
Merryman, Dani Jo .... San Dimas, CA
Merryman and DeArmon .... Davidson, NC
Merryman, Emory H., Jr. .... Philadelphia, PA
Merryman, Gregory K. .... Detroit, MI
Merryman, Jack E., Jr. .... Cleveland, OH
Merryman, Lavaughn A. .... Medford, OR
Merryman, Lewis B., Jr. .... Elizabethton, TN
Merryman, Robert J. .... Liberty Corner, NJ
Merryman, Robin K. .... Sacramento, CA
Merryman, William R. .... Kansas City, MO
Merryman, William R., P.C.
Kansas City, MO
Merryweather, E. Thomas
Cambridge, MD
Merryweather, Marjolane
Cambridge, MD
Mers, Scott J. .... Atlanta, GA
Mersch, Angela .... Chicago, IL
Mersch, Julie A. .... Las Vegas, NV
Mersch, Thomas F. .... Fort Lauderdale, FL
Mersch, William L. .... Aurora, NE
Merschman, Kurt D. .... Phoenix, AZ
Mersel, H. Mark .... Irvine, CA
Mersel, Marjorie P. .... Sherman Oaks, CA
Mersereau, Adam G. .... Atlanta, GA
Mersereau, Adam S. .... Duluth, GA
Mersereau, Charles G. .... Minneapolis, MN
Mersereau, David H. .... Anchorage, AK
Mersereau, Jon A. .... Charleston, SC
Mersereau, Kristen P. .... Atlanta, GA
Mersereau, Lori M. .... Treasury Department, Internal Revenue Service, GV
Mersereau, Paul E. .... Avon, CT
Mersereau, Peter R. .... Portland, OR
Mersereau & Shannon LLP .... Portland, OR
Mershon, Craig N. .... Cedar Falls, IA
Mershon, Creighton E., Sr. .... Louisville, KY
Mershon, Jerry L. .... Manhattan, KS
Mershon, John Hays .... Atlanta, GA
Mershon Law Firm .... Cedar Falls, IA
Mershon, Mark E. .... Cedar Falls, IA
Mershon, Sawyer, Johnston, Dunwody & Cole
Miami, FL
Mershon, Steven W. .... Granville, OH
Mersky, Charles .... Dallas, TX
Mersky, David W. .... Lancaster, PA
Mersky, Michael S. .... West Palm Beach, FL
Mersky, Rachel B. .... Bethany Beach, DE
Wilmington, DE
Mersky, Robert G. .... New York, NY
Mersky, Roy M. .... Austin, TX
Mersman, Richard K., III .... St. Louis, MO
Mersol, Gregory V. .... Cleveland, OH
Merson, David S. .... Barnstable, MA
Merson, Harry .... Oklahoma City, OK
Merson, Harry, P.C. .... Oklahoma City, OK
Merson, Herman .... Oklahoma City, OK
Merson, Jacqueline M. .... Basking Ridge, NJ
Merson, Loren .... Haddonfield, NJ
Merson, Tamara Clark .... Woodland Hills, CA
Mersten, Christine B. .... Oakland, CA
Mersten, David R. .... Santa Clara, CA
Mertel, Charles W. .... Seattle, WA
Mertel, Geo. C. .... Baltimore, MD
Mertel, Rita Kennedy .... Ottawa, IL
Merten, Charles J. .... Beaverton, OR
Merten, Dean Joseph .... Fort Pierce, FL
Merten, Howard A., Jr. .... Providence, RI
Merten, Laura Keller .... Deerfield, IL
Merten, Maurice K. .... Eugene, OR
Merten, W. Glenn .... Washington, DC
Merten, Walter L. .... Milwaukee, WI
Merten, William W. .... Chicago, IL
Mertens, Anton F. .... Atlanta, GA
Mertens, Bruce L. .... Richmond, VA
Mertens, Carl G. .... Oklahoma City, OK
Mertens, Christopher J. .... Richland, WA
Mertens, Cynthia A. .... Santa Clara, CA
Mertens, George L. .... Lincoln, CA
Mertens, Glen H. .... Los Angeles, CA
Mertens, John .... St. Louis, MO
Mertens, Mitchel G. .... Treasury Department, Office of the Comptroller of the Currency, GV
Mertens, Richard W. .... Binghamton, NY
Mertens, Susan D. .... San Jose, CA
Mertens, William J. .... Clayton, CA
Mertens, William J. .... Washington, DC
Mertensotto, Charles E. .... St. Paul, MN
Mertes, Arthur E. .... Chicago, IL
Mertes, Daniel J. .... Milwaukee, WI
Mertes, Drake D. .... Des Plaines, IL
Mertes, Lawrence S. .... Boulder, CO
Mertes, Lawrence S., P.C. .... Boulder, CO
Mertes, Martin W. .... San Jose, CA
Merting, John W. .... Pensacola, FL
Merting, John W., P.A. .... Pensacola, FL
Mertins, William F., Jr. .... Springdale, AR
Mertler, Amy .... Charlotte, NC
Merton, Jennifer Field Gibbs
East Longmeadow, MA
Merton, Vanessa H. .... White Plains, NY
Mertsching, Charles T. .... Longview, WA
Mertus, Julie A. .... New York, NY
Mertz, Andrew R. .... Lawrenceville, GA
Mertz, Barry Philip .... Cherry Hill, NJ
Mertz, Catherine W. .... Boston, MA
Mertz, Craig M. .... Minneapolis, MN
Mertz, Dennis B. .... St. Louis, MO
Mertz, Douglas K. .... Juneau, AK
Mertz, Eric A. .... Defiance, OH
Mertz, Francis J. .... Teaneck, NJ
Mertz, Gregory J.
Environmental Protection Agency, Office of Enforcement and Compliance Assurance, GV
Mertz, Gregory S., Law Offices of
Burlington, VT
Mertz, Jennifer Horton .... Indianapolis, IN
Mertz, John C. .... Punta Gorda, FL
Mertz, John D. .... Detroit, MI
Mertz, Martha L. .... Knoxville, IA
Mertz, Michael T .... Chicago, IL
Mertz, Monty G. .... Fargo, ND
Mertz, Neil P. .... Socorro, NM
Mertz, Peter A. .... New York, NY
Mertz, Richard A. .... Oak Park, IL
Mertz, Richard A. .... Saginaw, MI
Mertz, Robert Arthur .... Saginaw, MI
Mertz, Robert E. .... Pittsburgh, PA
Mertz, Robert J. .... Lodi, CA
Mertz, Roger S. .... San Francisco, CA
Mertz, Stephen M. .... Minneapolis, MN
Mertz, William L. .... Clearwater, FL
Mertzel, Nancy J. .... New York, NY
Meruelo, Raul P. .... New York, NY
Merullo, Reister & Swinford Co., L.P.A.
Columbus, OH
Merullo, Roland A. .... Revere, MA
Merullo, Victor Davis .... Columbus, OH
Merutka, Craig E. .... Manhattan, KS
Merva, John R. .... Wyomissing, PA
Merva, Mark A. .... Washington, DC
Mervan, Lorraine W. .... Pittsburgh, PA
Mervan & Mervan .... Pittsburgh, PA
Mervan, Stephen C. .... Pittsburgh, PA
Merves, Edward H. .... Philadelphia, PA
Merves, Lauren H. .... New York, NY
Mervine, Calderwood & Mervine
Warren, PA
Mervine, Edward A. .... Oswego, NY
Mervine, William R. .... Warren, PA
Mervis, Charles L. .... Northbrook, IL
Mervis, Clark D. .... Miami, FL
Mervis, Harvey D. .... Binghamton, NY
Mervis, Jeffrey M. .... Bethesda, MD
Mervis, Lisa L. .... Owings Mills, MD
Mervis, Michael T. .... New York, NY
Mervis, Roger .... Boston, MA
Mervis, Stanley H. .... Newton, MA
Mervish, Amy B. .... New York, NY
Merwald, Jerome A. .... Omaha, NE
Merwin, Bruce W. .... Houston, TX
Merwin, Earl N. .... Columbus, OH
Merwin, Jack .... Florence, CO
Merwin, Jay G., Jr. .... Towson, MD
Merwin, Paul .... St. Paul, MN
Merwin, Rodney .... Houston, TX
Merwin, Walter S. .... Clarence Center, NY
Merwine, Connie J. .... Effort, PA
Merwise, Stephen D. .... Chicago, IL
Merwise, Tracey K. .... San Francisco, CA
Mery, Bruce J. .... San Antonio, TX
Mery, James Q. .... Fairbanks, AK
Mery, Michael E. .... Austin, TX
Meryhew, Brad A. .... Seattle, WA
Merz, Charles F. .... Louisville, KY
Merz, Charles L. .... St. Louis, MO
Merz, Deborah L. .... Fairfax, VA
Merz, Douglas E. .... Falls City, NE
Merz, Gregory .... Boston, MA
Merz, Gregory R. .... Minneapolis, MN
Merz, Mary Catherine .... Oak Park, IL
Merz, Michael R. .... Dayton, OH
Merz, Richard H. .... New York, NY
Merz, Stuart O. H. .... Cleveland, OH
Merzbach, Ralph K. .... Rochester, NY
Merzbach, Ralph, P.C. .... Rochester, NY
Merzenich, Daniel P. .... San Diego, CA
Merzig, David S. .... Oneonta, NY
Merzoian, Teresa A. .... Hanford, CA
Merzon, James B. .... Morro Bay, CA
San Luis Obispo, CA
Merzon, Melvin S. .... Chicago, IL
Mesa, Blanca .... Key Biscayne, FL
Mesa, Carlos .... Coral Gables, FL
Mesa, Caron D. .... Santa Rosa, CA
Mesa, Christina M. .... Tampa, FL
Mesa, Gabriel J. .... New York, NY
Mesa, Ingrid M. .... New York, NY
Mesa, Richard P. .... El Paso, TX
Mesard, Michael D. .... New York, NY
Mesaros, David P. .... Dayton, OH
Mesaros, John G. .... Redwood City, CA
Mesaros, Steven G. .... Phoenix, AZ
Mesberg, Christine .... Waccabuc, NY
Mescall, Dennis P. .... Buffalo, NY
Mescall, James C. .... Florham Park, NJ
Mescall, Thomas J. .... Albuquerque, NM
Mesce, Linda M. .... Hackensack, NJ
Mesch, Clark & Rothschild, P.C.
Tucson, AZ
Mesch, John K. .... Tucson, AZ
Mesch, Lester D. .... Cleveland, OH
Meschan, David F. .... Greensboro, NC
Meschansky, Anna F. .... Boston, MA
Mescher, Carl J. .... Kettering, OH
Mescher, Gregory A. .... Washington, IL
Mescher, Kelly K. .... Columbia, MO
Mescher, Richard M. .... Cleveland, OH
Mesches, Larry M. .... West Palm Beach, FL
Meschewski, James A. .... New York, NY
Meschino, Michael A. .... Des Plaines, IL
Meschke, Herbert L. .... Bismarck, ND
Meschke, John A. .... San Francisco, CA
Meschkow, Gerald .... Hollywood, FL
Meschkow & Gresham, P.L.C.
Phoenix, AZ
Meschkow, Jordan M. .... Phoenix, AZ
Mescia, Nicholas A. .... Staten Island, NY
Mescobi, A. Allen .... Los Angeles, CA
Mescolotto, Lee D. .... Pottstown, PA
Wescosville, PA
Mescon, Debbie L. .... Atlanta, GA
Mescon, Richard A. .... New York, NY
Mese, Mark D. .... Baton Rouge, LA
Mesecher, L. G. .... Santa Maria, CA
Mesel, Kathleen L. .... Cleveland, OH
Mesenbrink, Drake D. .... Silverdale, WA
Mesereau, Thomas A., Jr. (A Professional Corporation) .... Los Angeles, CA
Meserole, William H. .... Arlington, VA
Meserve, Alice M. .... Woodland, CA
Meserve, Barbara K. .... San Diego, CA
Meserve, Christina A. .... Olympia, WA
Meserve, Donald O. .... Albany, NY
Meserve, James A. .... Rochester, NY
Meserve, Judith A. .... St. Petersburg, FL
Meserve, Leslie M. .... Portland, OR
Meserve, Mumper & Hughes LLP
Irvine, CA
Los Angeles, CA
San Diego, CA
Meserve, Richard A. .... Washington, DC
Meserve, William G. .... Boston, MA
Meservey, F. William .... Huntington, NY
Meservy, James C. .... Jerome, ID
Meservy, Jay A. .... Centerville, UT
Mesevage, Thomas E. .... Tarrytown, NY
Mesh, Dana J. .... New York, NY
Mesh, Gene, & Associates .... Cincinnati, OH
Mesh, Theodore E. .... Indianapolis, IN
Meshack, Betty L. .... Los Angeles, CA
Meshad, John W. .... Sarasota, FL
Meshak, Sarah E. .... Boulder, CO
Meshako, Katherine Elizabeth .... Hartford, CT
Meshberger, Ryan W. .... Baton Rouge, LA
Meshbesher & Associates
Minneapolis, MN
Meshbesher, Kenneth .... Minneapolis, MN
Meshbesher Law Office .... Minnetonka, MN
Meshbesher, Richard M. .... Minnetonka, MN
Meshbesher, Ronald I. .... Minneapolis, MN
Meshbesher & Spence .... Maplewood, MN
Minneapolis, MN
St. Louis Park, MN
Woodbury, MN
Rochester, MN
St. Cloud, MN
Meshbesher, Steven J. .... Minneapolis, MN
Meshbesher, Thomas M. .... Wilmington, DE
Meshek, Paul J. .... Culver City, CA
Meshel, Adam R. .... New York, NY
Meshel, Milton .... Brooklyn, NY
Meshel, Robert E. .... San Francisco, CA
Meshenberg, Milana .... Hollywood, FL
Mesher, Barry N. .... Seattle, WA
Mesher, John R. .... Valley Forge, PA
Meshke, Michelle M. .... Juneau, AK
Meshki, Cyrus .... Beverly Hills, CA
Meshnick, Howard R. .... Boston, MA
Meshnick, Stacey J. .... Great Neck, NY
Mesholam, Deborah R.
Securities and Exchange Commission, Division of Enforcement, GV
Meshon, Brener, Gordon & Ladov, P.C.
Philadelphia, PA
Meshon, Max .... Philadelphia, PA
Meshorer, Hank .... Department of Justice, Environment and Natural Resources Division, GV
Meshorer, Judith M. .... Cleveland, OH
Meshot, Charles R. .... Santa Barbara, CA
Meshot, Mark A. .... Santa Barbara, CA
Meshot, Peter A. .... Sacramento, CA
Meshreky, Usi N. .... Riverside, CA
Meshulam, David J. .... Florham Park, NJ
Meshulam, Deborah R. .... Washington, DC
Mesi, Douglas P. .... Cleveland, OH
Mesi, Stephen A. .... Los Angeles, CA
Mesiano, Ben V. .... Coral Gables, FL
Mesibov, Brian D. .... Charlotte, NC
Mesic, Robert E. .... Chicago, IL
Mesich, James J. .... Rock Island, IL
Mesics, Joseph C. .... Lebanon, PA
Mesigh, Herbert J. .... Oklahoma City, OK
Mesina, Barto, Hughes & Messina
Granbury, TX
Mesina, Dennis G. .... San Francisco, CA
Mesinger, Maria Galvagna .... Boston, MA
Mesirov Gelman Jaffe Cramer & Jamieson, LLP .... Cherry Hill, NJ
Philadelphia, PA
Mesirow & Associates Co., L.P.A.
Columbus, OH
Dublin, OH
Mesirow, Charles M. .... San Jose, CA
Mesirow, Fink, Rosenblatt & Dawson
San Jose, CA
Mesirow, Harold E. .... Washington, DC
Mesirow, John Blanken .... Washington, DC
Mesirow, Keith S. .... Dublin, OH
Mesirow, Michael A. .... Milwaukee, WI
Mesis, Vincent, Jr. .... Hennessey, OK
Mesisca, Patrick A., Jr. .... Los Angeles, CA
Mesiti, Nicholas .... Albany, NY
Meske, Gordon E. .... San Diego, CA
Meske, Michele C. .... Bellevue, WA
Meskill, John B .... Kensington, CT
Meskill, Michael .... Dallas, TX
Meskill, Thomas J. .... New Britain, CT
Meskimen, Connie M. .... Little Rock, AR
Meskin, Eisenberg & Wayne
Los Angeles, CA
Meskin, Joel W. .... Los Angeles, CA
Meskin, Kenneth D. .... Somerville, NJ
Meskin, Sanford A. .... Hillside, NJ
Mesle, Ann .... Kansas City, MO
Mesler, Betty Ora Grace .... Pittsburgh, PA
Mesler, Linda Love .... Andover, MA
Mesler, Mark S. .... Atlanta, GA
Mesler, Neil V. .... Canton, GA
Meslow, Douglas B. .... St. Paul, MN
Mesman, Douglas L. .... Grand Haven, MI
Mesmer, Ann E. .... Englewood, CO
Mesmer, Frank B., Jr. .... Manchester, NH
Mesmer Law Offices, P.A. .... Manchester, NH
Mesna, Gary P. .... Minneapolis, MN
Mesnard, James M. .... Washington, DC
Mesnekoff, David .... Miami, FL
Mesnekoff, Faith .... Miami, FL
Mesner, Clifford F. .... Central City, NE
Mesner, Kathryn L. .... Central City, NE
Mesner & Mesner .... Central City, NE

Mesner, Susan Marie ....Toledo, OH
Mesnick, Darla K. Jaben ....Atlanta, GA
Mesnick, Samuel B. ....Medford, MA
Mesnick, Wendy M. ....Los Angeles, CA
Mesnier, James E. ....Sacramento, CA
Mesnikoff, Norman H. ....Long Branch, NJ
Mesrey, George M. ....Detroit, MI
Mesritz, Ann E. ....Alexandria, VA
Mesritz, George D. ....Detroit, MI
Mesrobian, Camelia H. ....Joshua Tree, CA
Mesrobian, John L. ....Princeton, NJ
Mesrop, Alden ....Pelham, NY
Mesrop, Robert B., Jr. ....Los Angeles, CA
Mess, Michael A. ....Powell, OH
Mess, Thomas J. ....Cincinnati, OH
Messa, Joseph L., Jr. ....Marlton, NJ
Philadelphia, PA
Messaglia, Michael J. ....Indianapolis, IN
Messamore, Kristen N. ....Joliet, IL
Messana, Frank S. ....Rochester, MI
Messana, Robert P. ....Fort Collins, CO
Messana, Thomas M. ....Miami, FL
Messana-Morrow, Carolyn ....Buffalo, NY
Messano, Carmen ....Jersey City, NJ
Messano, Paul J. ....Bloomfield Hills, MI
Messaris, Brian E. ....Baltimore, MD
Messarra, Alan ....South Pasadena, CA
Messegee, Orvin H. ....Seattle, WA
Messemer, Cynthia K. ....White Plains, NY
Messemer, Glenn M. ....Bloomfield, CT
Messenbaugh, Mark W. ....New York, NY
Messenbrink, Judy N. ....Pine, CO
Messenger & Callahan, P.A.
Beltsville, MD
Ellicott City, MD
Messenger, Derinda L. ....Salinas, CA
Messenger, Donald B. W. ....Beltsville, MD
Ellicott City, MD
Messenger, Ernamarie ....Provo, UT
Messenger, Harold W. ....Washington, DC
Messenger, Herbert E. ....Waltham, MA
Messenger, James H., Jr. ....Syracuse, NY
Messenger, James L. ....Boston, MA
Messenger, James L. ....Youngstown, OH
Wexford, PA
Messenger, Jessie A. ....Lakewood, CO
Messenger, John B. ....Boston, MA
Messenger, John R. ....Anchorage, AK
Messenger & Jurovich ....Cody, WY
Thermopolis, WY
Worland, WY
Messenger, Michael S. ....Toledo, OH
Messenger, Michael S. ....Thermopolis, WY
Messer, Allen Lucas ....Wichita, KS
Messer, Bernard W. ....Denver, CO
Messer, Caparello & Self, A Professional Association ....Tallahassee, FL
Messer, Carol ....Houston, TX
Messer, Charles R. ....Los Angeles, CA
Messer, Christine G. ....Boston, MA
Messer, David S. ....West Long Branch, NJ
Messer, Diane M. ....Knoxville, TN
Messer, Earl K. ....Cincinnati, OH
Messer, Gregory ....Brooklyn, NY
Messer, Howard F. ....Pittsburgh, PA
Messer, Howard F., P.C. ....Pittsburgh, PA
Messer, J. Kaye ....Memphis, TX
Messer, James Elliott ....Tallahassee, FL
Messer, James Michael ....Pensacola, FL
Messer, John ....Madison, WI
Messer, John B. ....Belton, TX
Messer, Kelley Kemper ....Amarillo, TX
Messer, Kristy Banks ....Denver, CO
Messer, Lynn Margaret ....Houston, TX
Messer, Michael C. ....Chicago, IL
Messer, Michael L. ....Hackensack, NJ
Messer, Peter M. ....New York, NY
Messer, Potts and Messer, Inc., P.C.
Belton, TX
Messer & Ray ....Port St. Lucie, FL
Messer, Richard J. ....San Diego, CA
Messer, Roger N. ....Port St. Lucie, FL
Messer, S. Charles ....Los Angeles, CA
Messer, Stuart M. ....Memphis, TX
Messer, Susan J. ....Pittsburgh, PA
Messer, W. A. "Bill", III ....Belton, TX
Messer, William Andrew ....Dallas, TX
Messer, William Z. ....Montgomery, AL
Messerich, Jeffrey J. ....West St. Paul, MN
Messerich, Kathryn H. Davis
Minnetonka, MN
Messerli & Kramer, P.A.
Minneapolis, MN
St. Paul, MN
Messerli, William F. ....Minneapolis, MN
Messerlian, Vahe K. ....Sherman Oaks, CA
Messer-Liebrock, Joli A. ....Denver, CO
Messerly, Chris A. ....Minneapolis, MN
Messerly, Edwin C. ....Canton, OH
Messerly, Robert F. ....Chicago, IL
Messerly, Ronald W. ....Portland, OR
Messerman, Gale S. ....Cleveland, OH
Messerman, Gerald A. ....Cleveland, OH
Messerman & Messerman Co., L.P.A.
Cleveland, OH
Messerschmidt, Fred A. ....Elmhurst, IL
Messerschmidt, Michael G. ......Portland, ME
Messersmith, Cynthia E. ....Dallas, TX
Messersmith, Gary A., (P.C.)
Houston, TX
Messersmith, Jennifer T. ....San Diego, CA
Messersmith, John K., IV ....Richmond, VA
Messersmith, Julia B. ....Richmond, VA
Messersmith, Lanny D., (P.A.)
Albuquerque, NM
Messersmith, William W., III, (P.L.C.)
New Orleans, LA
Messervy, James H. ....Summerville, SC

Messham, Robert E., Jr. ....Miamisburg, OH
Messi, Michael ....New York, NY
Messiana, Laura ....Brooklyn, NY
Messick, Bill Clayton ....Mobile, AL
Messick, D. Jeanne ....Middletown, CT
Old Saybrook, CT
Messick, Guy A. ....Media, PA
Messick Law Firm, LLC ....Annapolis, MD
Messick, Lloyd L. ....Kansas City, MO
Messick, Messick & Messick
Burlington, NC
Messick, Paul S., Jr. ....Pittsboro, NC
Messick, Robert E. ....Sarasota, FL
Messick, Robert L. ....Haddonfield, NJ
Messick, Robert M., Jr. ....Annapolis, MD
Messick, Sandra E. ....Newark, DE
Messick, Steven H. ....Burlington, NC
Messick, T. Paul ....Burlington, NC
Messick, T. Paul, Jr. ....Burlington, NC
Messick, Terry T. ....Anthony, KS
Messick, Walter H. ....Washington, DC
Boca Raton, FL
Fairfax, VA
Messick, Wiley S. ....Atlanta, GA
Messier, Alan R. ....New London, CT
Messier, Chad C.
Charlotte Amalie, St. Thomas, VI
Messier, Dawn M.
Environmental Protection Agency,
Office of the General Counsel, GV
Messiha, Dominic J. ....Los Angeles, CA
Messina, A. Russell ....Troy, MI
Messina, Alice Lyons ....Rochester, NY
Messina, Andrew G., Jr. ....Windsor, CT
Messina, Anthony John ....Greenwich, CT
Katonah, NY
Messina, Anthony R. ....Gretna, LA
Messina, Ben N. ....St. Louis, MO
Messina, Bonnie L. ....Baltimore, MD
Messina Bulzomi ....Tacoma, WA
Messina & Cahill ....Slingerlands, NY
Messina, Carey J. ....Baton Rouge, LA
Messina, Cherisse M. ....Chicago, IL
Messina, Christopher ....Miami, FL
Messina, Crucian S. ....Buffalo, NY
Messina, Daniel J. ....Danvers, MA
Lowell, MA
Messina, David J. ....New Orleans, LA
Messina & DeWeese LLP ....Covina, CA
Messina, Edith L. ....Kansas City, MO
Messina, Ellen Lacy ....Albany, NY
Messina, Frank G. ....Elmhurst, NY
Messina, Gerard A. ....New York, NY
Messina, Gil Douglas ....Holmdel, NJ
Messina, Harry P., Jr. ....Rochester, NY
Messina, J. Anthony ....Philadelphia, PA
Messina, Joel R. ....Houston, TX
Messina, John ....West Orange, NJ
Messina, John A., Jr. ....Covina, CA
Messina, John J. ....Kenner, LA
Messina, John L. ....Tacoma, WA
Messina, Joseph ....New York, NY
Messina, Joseph A. ....Brooklyn, NY
Messina, Joseph C. ....New Brunswick, NJ
Messina, Joseph C. ....Mamaroneck, NY
Messina, Joseph D. ....Johnstown, PA
Messina, Joseph F. ....Philadelphia, PA
Messina, Joseph M. ....New Orleans, LA
Messina, Joseph P. ....Boston, MA
Messina, Joseph R. ....Slingerlands, NY
Messina, Joseph T. ....Erie, PA
Messina & Kane, P.C. ....Greenwich, CT
Katonah, NY
Messina, Lalafarian, Manning, Mendel & Ryan ....Glendale, CA
Los Angeles, CA
Messina, Laura L. ....Austin, TX
Messina, Lynne A. ....Dallas, TX
Messina, Michael A. ....Washington, DC
Messina, Michael H. ....Rochester, NY
Messina, Michael J. ....San Diego, CA
Messina, Michael J. ....Kansas City, MO
Messina, Michael P. ....Burbank, CA
Messina, Natale A. ....Farmington, CT
Messina, Nina R. ....Glendale, CA
Messina, Raymond A. ....Washington, DC
Messina, Raymond J. ....New York, NY
Messina, Robert M. ....Long Valley, NJ
Messina, Roy ....Newark, NJ
Messina, Steven M. ....New York, NY
Messina, Toni M. ....New York, NY
Messina, Vincent J., Jr. ....Hauppauge, NY
Messineo, Alessandra M. ....New York, NY
Messineo, Arthur J., III ....Paramus, NJ
Messineo, Arthur J., Jr. ....Ridgewood, NJ
Messineo, Carl L. ....Washington, DC
Messineo, Leslie J. ....Pittsburgh, PA
Messineo, Marc M. ....Los Angeles, CA
Messineo, Robert L. ....New York, NY
Messineo, William M. ....Fair Lawn, NJ
Messinetti, John E. ....Shirley, NY
Messing, Arnold P., (P.C.) ....Boston, MA
Messing, Carol ....Department of Commerce,
National Oceanic and Atmospheric
Administration, GV
Messing, Edward F. ....North Tonawanda, NY
Messing, Edward V., Jr. ....Sandusky, MI
Messing, Elias ....Coconut Creek, FL
Messing, Ellen J. ....Boston, MA
Messing, Gary M. ....Sacramento, CA
Messing, Harvey J. ....Lansing, MI
Messing, Howard R. ....Fort Lauderdale, FL
Messing, Jeff E. ....Baltimore, MD
Messing, Jeffrey ....Phoenix, AZ
Messing, John H., (P.C.) ....Tucson, AZ
Messing, Mark M. ....Traverse City, MI
Messing, Palmer & Waibel, P.C. ....Taylor, MI
Traverse City, MI

Messing, Paul M. ....Philadelphia, PA
Messing, Paul T. ....Athens, GA
Messing & Rudavsky, P.C. ....Boston, MA
Messing, Scott Jeffrey ....Harrisburg, PA
Messing, William L. ....New York, NY
Messinger, Arlene Paula
Small Business Administration,
Office of the General Counsel, GV
Messinger, Barry William ....New York, NY
Messinger, Brett L. ....Wayne, PA
Messinger, David A. ....Miami, FL
Messinger, Donald H. ....Cleveland, OH
Messinger, Flaster & Levitz, P.C.
New York, NY
Messinger, Gloria ....New York, NY
Messinger, J. Henry, (P.C.)
Albuquerque, NM
Messinger, Jules G. ....Brooklyn, NY
Messinger, Leonard A. ....New York, NY
Messinger, Leonard D. ....Los Angeles, CA
Messinger, Martin P. ....New York, NY
Messinger, Michael V. ....Washington, DC
Messinger, Ojile & Pierce .....Minneapolis, MN
Messinger, Robert F. ....Irvine, CA
Messinger, Scott ....Garden City, NY
Messinger, Sheldon A. ....New Haven, CT
Messinger, Stanley ....White Plains, NY
Messinger, Stephen E. ....New York, NY
Messinger, Steven J. ....Sylvania, GA
Messinger, William F. ....Minneapolis, MN
Messite, Andrew B. ....New York, NY
Messite & Davidson ....New York, NY
Messite, Herbert J. ....New York, NY
Messito, Carol ....Washington, DC
Messitt, Peter R. ....Harrisonburg, VA
Messitte, Michael F.
National Labor Relations Board,
Office of the General Counsel, GV
Messitte, Peter J. ....Greenbelt, MD
Messler, J. Peter ....Tulsa, OK
Messmaker, Garrett E. ....Chicago, IL
Messman, C. Daniel ....Bloomington, IL
Messman, Max G. ....Majuro, TT
Messmann, Douglas J. ....Green Bay, WI
Kewaunee, WI
Messmer, Dean A. ....Seattle, WA
Messmer, Gail Elizabeth ....Powell, OH
Messmer, Jane S. ....Cleveland, OH
Messmer, Robert W. ....Lutherville, MD
Messmore, Hiram A. ....Houston, TX
Messner, Bryant S. ....Denver, CO
Messner, Ernest L. ....Pasadena, CA
Messner, Harold D. ....Vallejo, CA
Messner, James A. ....Columbus, GA
Messner, Megan A. ....Charlotte, NC
Messner, Randel L. ....Pittsburg, KS
Messner & Reeves, LLC ....Denver, CO
Evergreen, CO
Messner, Robert F. ....New York, NY
Messner, Robert T. ....Pittsburgh, PA
Messner, Steven ....Wilmette, IL
Messner, Terri Marie ....Harrisburg, PA
Messner, William M. ....Torrance, CA
Messock, Jeffrey J. ....Houston, TX
Messonnier, Terrence M. ....Sedalia, MO
Messore, Constance I. ....Providence, RI
Messore, Gregory J. ....Jacksonville, FL
Messore, Michael B., Jr. ....Barrington, RI
Messplay, Gary C. ....Indianapolis, IN
Messrobian, Peter J. ....San Francisco, CA
Messuri, Nicholas J. ....Boston, MA
Messutta, Stephen S. ....Chicago, IL
Mestad, John B. ....North Hollywood, CA
Mestas, David A. ....Denver, CO
Mestas, Dennis M. ....Anchorage, AK
Mestas, Dennis M., A Prof. Corp., Law Offices of ....Anchorage, AK
Mestayer & Associates, P.A.
Pascagoula, MS
Mestayer, Elliot G. ....Pascagoula, MS
Mestayer, Matthew G. ....Biloxi, MS
Mestayer and Mestayer, (A Law Corporation)
New Iberia, LA
Mestayer, Michael J., (P.C.)
New Iberia, LA
New Orleans, LA
Mestayer, Roland J., Jr. ....Pascagoula, MS
Mestayer, Stephen F. ....New Iberia, LA
Mestaz, Daniel B. ....Los Angeles, CA
Mestecky, Jiri M. ....Chicago, IL
Mestel, Lynn ....New York, NY
Mestel, Mariella ....Canton, OH
Mestel, Mark D. ....Everett, WA
Mestel, Mark D., Inc., P.S. ....Everett, WA
Mestelle Law Office, P.C. ....Sturgis, MI
Mestelle, Michael A. ....Sturgis, MI
Mestemaker, Albert J. ....Cincinnati, OH
Mestep, Antoinette H. ....Greenbelt, MD
Mester, Anne K. ....San Francisco, CA
Mester, Charles L. ....New York, NY
Mester, Christian C. ....Rockville, MD
Mester, Denise L. ....Costa Mesa, CA
Mester, Elizabeth Denney ....San Mateo, CA
Mester, Fred M. ....Pontiac, MI
Mester, John S.
Department of Defense, GV
Mester, Jonathan D. ....Cleveland, OH
Mester, Joshua M. ....Los Angeles, CA
Mester, Laurence A. ....Philadelphia, PA
Mester, Mark S. ....Chicago, IL
Mester, Peter C. ....Wilmington, DE
Mester, Thomas ....Cleveland, OH
Mester & Wiss ....New York, NY
Mesterman, Dan ....New York, NY
Mestler, Gilbert E. ....New York, NY
Mestman, Adrienne ....San Diego, CA
Meston, Mary Elizabeth ....Kansas City, MO
Mestre, Alvaro J. ....Washington, DC

Mestre, Cathleen M ....Orlando, FL
Mestre, Ceasar, Jr. ....Hialeah, FL
Mestre, Eduardo G. ....New York, NY
Mestre, Iolanda R. ....Stoneham, MA
Mestre, Jorge A. ....Miami, FL
Mestre, Louis J. ....Milwaukee, WI
Mestre-Perez, Cesar ....Hialeah, FL
Mestres, Ricardo A., Jr. ....New York, NY
Mesuk, Lynn B. ....New York, NY
Mesun, Kim Buechel ....St. Paul, MN
Mesuraca, Melania ....Plymouth Meeting, PA
Meszaros, James A. ....Roseland, NJ
Meszaros, Judith L. ....Edison, NJ
Meszaros, Liora ....Los Angeles, CA
Meszaros, Magdalene H. ....Cleveland, OH
Meszaros, Michael ....Department of State,
Bureau of Consular Affairs, GV
Meszaros, Patrick A. ....Joliet, IL
Meszaros, Terry D. ....Cleveland, OH
Meszner-Eltrich, A. Suzanne
Boxborough, MA
Meszoly, Peter T. ....Washington, DC
Metal, Renée A. ....Pittsburgh, PA
Metalios, Menelaos E. ....Jackson Heights, NY
Metalitz, Steven J. ....Washington, DC
Metallo, Samuel J. ....New Brunswick, NJ
Metallo, Virginia R. ....Washington, DC
Metaxas, Anthony M. ....Haverhill, MA
Salem, MA
Metaxas, John C. ....New York, NY
Metaxas, Norman & Pidgeon
Haverhill, MA
Salem, MA
Metayer, Ann M. ....White River Junction, VT
Metcalf, Aaron ....Jacksonville, FL
Metcalf, Alan W. ....Fullerton, CA
Metcalf, Andrew B. ....Vero Beach, FL
Metcalf, Andrew Millar ....New York, NY
Metcalf, Andrew O. ....Department of the Navy,
Office of the Judge Advocate General, GV
Metcalf, Brian D. ....San Antonio, TX
Metcalf, Bryan W. ....Nashville, TN
Metcalf, Cameron A. ....Dothan, AL
Metcalf, Caywood ....Lancaster, KY
Metcalf, Charles W. ....Lexington, KY
Metcalf, Conlon, Siering & Poock, P.L.C.
Muscatine, IA
Metcalf, D. Douglas ....Tucson, AZ
Metcalf, David G. ....Everett, WA
Metcalf, David J. ....Tallahassee, FL
Metcalf, David L. ....Boise, ID
Metcalf, Diana H. ....Bethesda, MD
Rockville, MD
Metcalf, Earl E. ....Providence, RI
Metcalf, Everett H., Jr.
Fort Lauderdale, FL
Metcalf, Frank B. ....Orange Park, FL
Metcalf, Fred H. ....Overland Park, KS
Metcalf, Glenn A. ....Kingsley, IA
Moville, IA
Metcalf, J. Conard ....Boulder, CO
Metcalf, J. Michael ....Muscatine, IA
Metcalf, J. Todd ....Washington, DC
Metcalf, James G. ....Monticello, MN
Metcalf, James M. ....Reinbeck, IA
Metcalf, James M. ....Oswego, NY
Metcalf, Janet A. ....Salem, OR
Metcalf, Janet H. ....Yuma, AZ
Metcalf, Janine Cone ....Atlanta, GA
Metcalf, Jerry L. ....Houston, TX
Metcalf, Jill T. ....Boston, MA
Metcalf, Jodie ....Anoka, MN
Metcalf, John C. ....Madison, WI
Metcalf, John G. ....Jacksonville, FL
Metcalf, Joyce Ferris ....San Jose, CA
Metcalf, Judy A.S. ....Brunswick, ME
Metcalf, L. Craig ....Salt Lake City, UT
Metcalf, L. Drew ....Phoenix, AZ
Metcalf, Larson & Muth, P.A.
Monticello, MN
Metcalf, Lili C. ....Orlando, FL
Metcalf, Lori A. ....Phoenix, AZ
Metcalf, M. Barbara ....San Clemente, CA
Metcalf, Mark A. ....Los Angeles, CA
Boston, MA
Metcalf, Mark Hammonds ....Lancaster, KY
Metcalf, Matthew H. ....Chicago, IL
Metcalf & McKenzie
Huntington Beach, CA
Metcalf & Metcalf ....Lancaster, KY
Metcalf, Michael P. ....Dallas, TX
Metcalf, Michael P., P.C., The Law Offices of
Dallas, TX
Metcalf, Michael T. ....Kansas City, MO
Metcalf, Morgan ....El Dorado, KS
Metcalf, M. P. ....Ocala, FL
Metcalf, Natasha K. ....Nashville, TN
Metcalf, Norval G. ....Richmond, VA
Metcalf, Paula J. ....Lincoln, NE
Metcalf, Richard B. ....Columbus, OH
Metcalf, Richard I. ....Dallas, TX
Metcalf, Robert D. ....Minneapolis, MN
Metcalf, Robert S. ....Minneapolis, MN
Metcalf, Rockell C. ....Minneapolis, MN
Metcalf, Ronald W. ....Fort Smith, AR
Metcalf, Ronald W., P.A. ....Fort Smith, AR
Van Buren, AR
Metcalf, Sara ....Fort Lauderdale, FL
Metcalf, Sharon S. ....Seattle, WA
Metcalf, Slade R. ....New York, NY
Metcalf, Steven K. ....Tulsa, OK
Metcalf, Teresa ....Dallas, TX
Metcalf, Thomas W. ....Fort Collins, CO
Metcalf, Thompson & Phipps
Kingsley, IA
Moville, IA
Remsen, IA

Metcalf, Timothy E. Huntington Beach, CA
Metcalf, W. Carleton .... **Asheville, NC**
Metcalf, W. Eugene .... Winston-Salem, NC
Metcalf, Walker .... **Lubbock, TX**
Metcalf, Wayne C., III .... Hilo, HI
Metcalf, William A. .... Wisconsin Rapids, WI
Metcalf, William E. .... Topeka, KS
Metcalf, William J. .... **Florham Park, NJ**
Metcalfe, Charles Harold .... Elmira, NY
Metcalfe, Chas. R. .... Long Beach, CA
Metcalfe, Daniel J. .... Department of Justice, Office of Information and Privacy, GV
Metcalfe, David T. .... **Brooklyn, NY**
Metcalfe, Don .... Dallas, TX
Metcalfe, Elliott, Jr. .... Sarasota, FL
Metcalfe, George L. .... Coral Gables, FL
Metcalfe, James A. .... Norfolk, VA
Metcalfe, James K. "Jake" .... Anchorage, AK
Metcalfe, Joseph C. .... Washington, DC
Metcalfe Law Office .... Elmira, NY
Metcalfe, Michele H. .... **Richmond, VA**
Metcalfe, Sally S. .... **Austin, TX**
Metcalfe, Steven C. .... **Austin, TX**
Metcalfe, Walter L., Jr. .... **St. Louis, MO**
Metchik, Mortimer J. .... Long Beach, NY
Metchik, Paul G. .... Avila Beach, CA
Metchnek, James .... St. Louis Park, MN
Metchnek, Wendy E. .... **Minneapolis, MN**
Metelmann, Thomas K. .... Cavalier, ND
Metelski, John .... Boca Raton, FL
Metelski, Marion Peter .... **New York, NY**
Meter, Gregory E. .... **Bay City, MI**
Meter, James J. .... Litchfield, CT
Meter, Nicolas F. .... Pottstown, PA
Meter, Patrick M. .... Saginaw, MI
Metevier, Thomas E. .... Fort Lauderdale, FL
Metge, Marvin F. .... **Chicago, IL**
Metge, Spitzer & Kreid .... **Chicago, IL**
Meth, David .... Staten Island, NY
Meth, Edward B. .... **Southfield, MI**
Meth, Eric L. .... **Cherry Hill, NJ**
Meth, Karl T. .... Westfield, NJ
Meth, Michael David .... **Chester, NY**
Meth, Richard M. .... **Princeton, NJ**; **New York, NY**
Meth, Stephanie K. .... **New York, NY**
Meth, Theodore Sager .... Westfield, NJ
Meth, Warren E. .... Monroe, NY
Methe, Daniel C. .... West Palm Beach, FL
Methe, James E. .... Springfield, MA
Methelis, Alan D. .... Fort Lauderdale, FL
Metheney, Wesley W. .... Morgantown, WV
Methenitis, William M. .... **Dallas, TX**
Metheny, Fred R., Jr. .... Palm Springs, CA
Metheny, Kristin Bryance **Birmingham, AL**
Metheny, Steven P. .... Oklahoma City, OK
Methfessel, Harley A. J. .... Manassas Park, VA
Methfessel, John D. .... Rahway, NJ
Methfessel, John, Jr. .... Rahway, NJ
Methfessel & Werbel, P.C. .... Rahway, NJ
Methven & Associates .... Berkeley, CA
Methven, Bruce E. .... Berkeley, CA
Methvin, De Witt T., Jr. .... **Alexandria, LA**
Methvin, Jason O. .... **Natchitoches, LA**
Methvin, Lexi S. .... **Denver, CO**
Methvin, Mildred E. .... Lafayette, LA
Methvin, Myron .... Dallas, TX
Methvin, Robert Gordon, Jr. Birmingham, AL
Methvin, Thomas J. .... **Montgomery, AL**
Metier, Ardeth Ted .... Fort Collins, CO
Metier, T. Thomas .... **Fort Collins, CO**
Metier, T. Thomas, LLC .... **Fort Collins, CO**
Metis, Peter .... **White Plains, NY**
Metjian, Charles, Jr. .... Boston, MA
Metka, James F. .... Philadelphia, PA
Metli, Richard .... Smithtown, NY
Metli, Robert J. .... Scottsdale, AZ
Metlin, Elaine .... **Washington, DC**
Metni, N. Alan .... Phoenix, AZ
Metnick, Cherry & Frazier .... **Decatur, IL**; **Springfield, IL**
Metnick, Dennis .... Margaretville, NY
Metnick, Kenneth N. .... Delray Beach, FL
Metnick, Michael B. .... **Springfield, IL**
Metnick, Seymour H. .... **Garden City, NY**
Metos, G. Fred .... **Salt Lake City, UT**
Metos, Tom .... Salt Lake City, UT
Metosky, Sandra R. .... Pittsburgh, PA
Metoyer, Carl B. .... Oakland, CA
Metoyer, Helene Garduno .... Albuquerque, NM
Metoyer, Jessica N. .... **San Francisco, CA**
Metoyer, Michael A .... Chicago, IL
Metoyer, Stephen A. Department of Transportation, Office of the General Counsel, GV
Metrailer, Albert C. .... Plano, TX
Metrailer, Rosemary .... Sacramento, CA
Metrick, Allan S. .... **New York, NY**
Metrick, Deborah S. .... New York, NY
Metrick, Kimberly Grossman .... Deerfield, IL
Metrinko, Peter P. .... Postal Rate Commission, Offices of the Commissioners, GV
Metro, A. Howard .... **Rockville, MD**
Metro, Gary .... San Jose, CA
Metro, Joseph W. .... **Washington, DC**
Metro, Michael E. .... Pittsburgh, PA
Metropoulos, Demetrios G. .... **Chicago, IL**
Metropoulos, Jon .... **Helena, MT**
Metropulos, Mitchell J. .... Appleton, WI
Metros, William .... Bath, MI
Metry, Dean C. .... Detroit, MI; Mount Clemens, MI
Metry, Frederick E. .... Detroit, MI; Mount Clemens, MI
Metry, Gilbert E. .... Detroit, MI; Mount Clemens, MI
Metry, Mark S. .... Mount Clemens, MI
Metry, Metry & Sanom .... Detroit, MI; Mount Clemens, MI
Metry, Robert A. .... Stuart, FL
Mets, Denis E. .... New York, NY
Mets, James M. .... Kenilworth, NJ
Metsch, Burton .... Boynton Beach, FL
Metsch, Christine F. .... **New York, NY**
Metsch, Paul S. .... **San Diego, CA**
Metsch, Richard H. .... **New York, NY**
Metsch, Seth .... New York, NY
Metsch, Susan .... San Diego, CA
Metsch, Victor M. .... **New York, NY**
Metsch-Ampel, Glenn R. .... New York, NY
Metscher, Joseph G. .... Malibu, CA
Metschl, Daniel R. .... Buffalo, NY
Metselaar, Paul A. .... New York, NY
Metsger, Kurt A. .... Denver, CO
Metsika, Valerie A. .... Columbus, OH
Metskas, Thomas S. .... Chicago, IL
Metsker-Handegan, Nancy A. .... Decatur, IL
Metta, Michael S. .... **Boca Raton, FL**
Mettalia, Robert J. .... **Garden City, NY**
Mettauer, Matthew D. .... **Houston, TX**; **Nacogdoches, TX**
Mette, Daniel J. .... **New York, NY**
Mette, Evans & Woodside, A Professional Corporation .... **Harrisburg, PA**
Mette, Howell C. .... **Harrisburg, PA**
Mette, Jacqueline Paradee .... Wilmington, DE
Mette, Luke W. .... Wilmington, DE
Mette, Roderick A. Federal Communications Commission, Wireless Telecommunications Bureau, GV
Metteauer, Michael S. .... **Austin, TX**
Mettee, Bradley T. J., Jr. .... Baltimore, MD
Mettee, Thomas J. .... Philadelphia, PA
Metteer, Sally .... **Seattle, WA**
Metter, Devera .... Los Angeles, CA
Metter, Joel J. .... Fort Lauderdale, FL
Metters, Peter A. .... Taylor, MI
Mettes, Linda D. .... **New York, NY**
Metthe, Francis D. .... New Bedford, MA
Metthe, Joyce Lacourse .... New Bedford, MA
Metthe & Metthe .... New Bedford, MA
Mettica, Bonnie L. .... **Pittsburgh, PA**
Mettler, Annetta Kay National Labor Relations Board, Office of the General Counsel, GV
Mettler, Earl R. .... Shiprock, NM
Mettler, Greg L. .... Gresham, OR
Mettler, Greg L., P.C. .... Gresham, OR
Mettler, Helen .... New York, NY
Mettler, Jeanne E. .... White Plains, NY
Mettler, Peter W. .... **Palm Beach, FL**
Mettler, Sharon Wallis .... Bakersfield, CA
Mettler, Thomas M. .... **Palm Beach, FL**
Mettler, William R., Jr. .... Phoenix, AZ
Mettley, Jason .... Pittsburgh, PA
Mettner, John R., Jr. .... Topeka, KS
Mettner, Joseph P. .... Madison, WI
Metts, Elizabeth B. .... Williamsburg, VA
Metts, Harold L. .... **Houston, TX**
Metts, J. Mark .... Houston, TX
Metts, James Clayton, III .... Savannah, GA
Metts, Lisa Quick .... **Houston, TX**
Metts, Robert J. .... **Geneva, IL**
Metusalem, Mark J. .... Toledo, OH
Metz, Abby L. .... **Seattle, WA**
Metz, Albert A. .... Denver, CO
Metz, Alfred N. .... **Mamaroneck, NY**; **New York, NY**
Metz, Amy E. .... **Detroit, MI**
Metz, Andrew Harold Department of Commerce, Patent and Trademark Office, GV
Metz, Anthony J., III .... Indianapolis, IN
Metz and Bailey .... **Columbus, OH**
Metz, Bonnie L. .... **Dover, DE**; **Wilmington, DE**
Metz, Bruce N. .... Raleigh, NC
Metz, Carl E., II .... **Chicago, IL**
Metz, Cary Alan .... Camden, NJ
Metz, Charles J. .... New Brunswick, NJ
Metz, Corinna L. .... Farmington Hills, MI
Metz & Crangle, Chtd. .... **Lincoln, KS**
Metz, Daniel D. .... **Lincoln, KS**
Metz, David E. .... **Chicago, IL**
Metz, Deborah Gayl .... Minnetonka, MN
Metz, Donald B. .... Augusta, GA
Metz, Donald P. .... Tulsa, OK
Metz, Donald R. .... North Manchester, IN; Wabash, IN
Metz, Douglas E. .... **Toledo, OH**
Metz, Edward R. .... Santa Ana, CA
Metz, Eric B. .... **Wichita, KS**
Metz, Gregory Randolph .... Santa Monica, CA
Metz, Hauser & Husband, A Professional Association .... **Tallahassee, FL**
Metz, Howard L. .... **Rockville, MD**
Metz, James T. .... **Grenada, MS**; **Jackson, MS**; **Oxford, MS**
Metz, James W. .... Detroit, MI
Metz, James W., II .... Brighton, MI
Metz, Jeffrey R. .... **New York, NY**
Metz, Jeremy M. .... New York, NY
Metz, Jerome J., Jr. .... **Cincinnati, OH**
Metz, Jill .... Chicago, IL
Metz, John G., Jr. .... Department of Defense, Defense Legal Services Agency, GV
Metz, John H. .... San Diego, CA
Metz, John H. .... Indianapolis, IN
Metz, John H. .... Cincinnati, OH
Metz, John R. .... **Bethesda, MD**
Metz, Jordon .... Encino, CA
Metz, Joseph G. .... **New York, NY**
Metz, Joseph Uhl .... Harrisburg, PA
Metz, Kenneth B. .... Westfield, NJ
Metz, Kenneth W. .... Charles Town, WV
Metz, Larry E. .... **Orlando, FL**
Metz, Lawrence A. .... Salt Lake City, UT
Metz, Lawrence F. .... **New York, NY**
Metz, LeRoy L., II .... **Pittsburgh, PA**
Metz, Lisa F. .... Southport, CT
Metz, Lori R. .... **Portland, OR**
Metz, Mark A. .... **Detroit, MI**
Metz, Mark K. .... Charlotte, NC
Metz, Mark L. .... **Milwaukee, WI**
Metz, Marsha Clare .... San Antonio, TX
Metz, Marsha Clare, P.C., Law Offices of San Antonio, TX
Metz, Marsha E. .... Los Angeles, CA
Metz, Martin M. .... Elmhurst, NY
Metz, Mary Elizabeth .... **Kansas City, MO**
Metz, Matthew N. .... Santa Monica, CA
Metz, Michael .... Fort Lauderdale, FL
Metz, Michael A. .... Elkhart, IN
Metz, Michael M. .... Tallahassee, FL
Metz, Michael M. .... **Bloomfield Hills, MI**
Metz, Michael, P.A., Law Offices of Fort Lauderdale, FL
Metz, Nancy D. .... Fairfield, ME
Metz, Nathaniel .... **Philadelphia, PA**
Metz, Nelson F., Jr. .... Alton, IL
Metz, Oscar K. .... Santa Monica, CA
Metz, Peter A. .... Madison, CT
Metz, Regina M. National Credit Union Administration, Office of General Counsel, GV
Metz, Richard A. .... St. Petersburg, FL
Metz, Richard B. .... Pleasanton, CA
Metz, Richard C. .... Savannah, GA
Metz, Richard H. .... Bowie, MD
Metz, Richard M. .... Wilsonville, OR
Metz, Richard W. .... St. Louis, MO
Metz, Robert H. .... **Silver Spring, MD**
Metz, Roger E. .... Spokane, WA
Metz, Roger K. .... Chicago, IL
Metz, Roy E. .... **Columbus, OH**
Metz, Russell A. .... Seattle, WA
Metz, Sandra J. .... Longmeadow, MA
Metz, Scott D. .... Appleton, WI
Metz, Stephen A. .... **Greenbelt, MD**
Metz, Stephen W. .... **Tallahassee, FL**
Metz, Steven J. .... River Vale, NJ
Metz, Tiffany L. .... Detroit, MI
Metz, Timothy L. .... **Lawrence, KS**
Metz, Todd R. .... **McLean, VA**
Metz, Virginia F. .... **Bingham Farms, MI**
Metz, Walter R., Jr. .... Omaha, NE
Metz, William T. .... **Burlington, IA**
Metzbower, S. David, Jr. Department of Transportation, Federal Aviation Administration, GV
Metzcher-Carr, Deirdre Lee San Antonio, TX
Metze, Patrick S. .... Levelland, TX
Metzel, Suzanne M. .... **Chicago, IL**
Metzen, Joseph H. .... Fergus Falls, MN
Metzen, Leslie May .... Hastings, MN
Metzenbaum, Howard M. .... Cleveland, OH
Metzendorf, Lauren A. .... Bridgewater, NJ
Metzenthin, George A. .... **Washington, DC**
Metzer, Greg A. .... Edmond, OK
Metzer, James F. .... Houston, TX
Metzer, Patricia Ann, (Miss) .... **Boston, MA**
Metzer, Robert W. .... Sidney, OH
Metzgar, Bernard P. .... Albuquerque, NM
Metzgar, Curtis L. .... Rancho Cucamonga, CA
Metzgar, Matthew R. .... Alcester, SD
Metzger, Alan G. .... Wichita, KS
Metzger, Alfred W., Jr. Colorado Springs, CO
Metzger, Allen M. .... Philadelphia, PA
Metzger & Associates, Ltd. .... **Chicago, IL**
Metzger, Barry (IBA) .... **New York, NY**
Metzger, Bruce D. .... Richmond, IN
Metzger, Burton F. .... Savannah, GA
Metzger, Carl E. .... **Boston, MA**
Metzger, Christine L. .... Campbell, CA
Metzger, Christopher D. .... **Fitchburg, MA**
Metzger, Christopher G. .... Eureka, CA
Metzger, Clyde M., III .... **Ann Arbor, MI**
Metzger, David L. .... **Hartford, CT**
Metzger, David L. .... **New York, NY**
Metzger, David P. .... **Washington, DC**
Metzger, David R. .... **Chicago, IL**
Metzger, Dirk T. .... **San Diego, CA**
Metzger, Dirk T., A Professional Corporation **San Diego, CA**
Metzger, Donald L. .... **Edwardsville, IL**
Metzger, Donald L. F. .... **Chicago, IL**
Metzger, Edward R. .... Belleville, IL
Metzger, Elisa D. .... **Washington, DC**
Metzger, Elizabeth A. .... **Stuart, FL**; **West Palm Beach, FL**
Metzger, Ellen .... New York, NY
Metzger, Emanuel I. .... Union, NJ
Metzger, Emily B. .... Wichita, KS
Metzger, Frank E. .... Manchester, MO
Metzger, Gerard G. .... New Orleans, LA
Metzger, Gerard G., P.C. .... New Orleans, LA
Metzger, Gregg H. .... **Miami, FL**
Metzger, Gregory S. .... Louisville, KY
Metzger, Hollis, Gordon & Alprin Washington, DC
Metzger, Jay P. .... Ashdown, AR
Metzger, Jeffrey C. .... Laguna Hills, CA
Metzger, Jeffrey P. .... **McLean, VA**
Metzger, John M. .... Trenton, NJ
Metzger, John N. .... **Newark, NJ**
Metzger, John S. .... **St. Louis, MO**
Metzger, John T. .... **West Palm Beach, FL**
Metzger, John W. .... Lancaster, PA
Metzger, Jordan J. .... New York, NY
Metzger, Joseph T. .... **Tampa, FL**
Metzger, Julia M. .... **Torrance, CA**
Metzger, Juliette Anita .... New York, NY
Metzger, Karen Sue .... Fostoria, OH
Metzger, Kari A. .... Tampa, FL
Metzger, Kathleen A. .... Decatur, GA
Metzger, Kathy A. .... Stuart, FL
Metzger, Kenneth J. .... **Tallahassee, FL**
Metzger, Kimberly C. .... **South Bend, IN**
Metzger, Kristofer M. .... Allentown, PA
Metzger, Lawrence G. .... Philadelphia, PA
Metzger, Margaret Ann .... Waltham, MA
Metzger, Margot J. .... **New York, NY**
Metzger, Mark A. .... **Indianapolis, IN**
Metzger, Mark C. .... **Chicago, IL**
Metzger, Mark F. .... Minneapolis, MN
Metzger, Mark J. .... **Poughkeepsie, NY**
Metzger, Mary D. .... Arlington, VA
Metzger, Melissa R. .... **Louisville, KY**
Metzger, Melvin .... Flushing, NY
Metzger, Michael J. .... **Washington, DC**
Metzger, Michael L. .... **Benton Harbor, MI**
Metzger, Michelle Pepin .... **Columbus, OH**
Metzger, Moira K. .... **Chicago, IL**
Metzger, Myra G. .... Rochelle Park, NJ
Metzger, Nathan T. .... **Phoenix, AZ**
Metzger, Oliver .... **New York, NY**
Metzger, Pamela R. .... New York, NY
Metzger, Paul .... Culver City, CA
Metzger, Paul .... Glenwood Springs, CO
Metzger, Paul T. .... **Chicago, IL**
Metzger, Peter M. .... **Brooklyn, NY**
Metzger, R. William, Jr. .... **Columbia, SC**
Metzger, Ralph, III .... Highland Beach, FL
Metzger, Raphael .... Long Beach, CA
Metzger, Raphael .... Washington, DC
Metzger, Raymond S., Jr. .... Toledo, OH
Metzger, Richard .... **Atlanta, GA**
Metzger, Richard J. .... Detroit, MI
Metzger & Richters LLP .... **Hartford, CT**
Metzger, Robert L. .... **Cleveland, OH**
Metzger, Robert S. .... **Los Angeles, CA**
Metzger, Ronni P. .... **White Plains, NY**
Metzger, Rosalyn A. .... Somerville, NJ
Metzger, Sania Andrea .... Bronx, NY
Metzger, Scott L. .... **San Diego, CA**
Metzger & Shilling .... Ozark, MO
Metzger, Sol A. .... Trenton, NJ
Metzger, Steven C. .... **Dallas, TX**
Metzger, Susan S. .... Ozark, MO
Metzger, Theodore G. .... West Palm Beach, FL
Metzger, Theodore J. .... **New York, NY**
Metzger, Thomas A. .... Newport, WA
Metzger, Thomas M. L. .... **Columbus, OH**
Metzger, Timothy M. .... **Chicago, IL**
Metzger, Ursula .... Miami, FL
Metzger, Ward Lee .... Jacksonville, FL
Metzger, Wendy .... **New York, NY**
Metzger, Wickersham, Knauss & Erb, P.C. **Harrisburg, PA**
Metzger, William D. .... Springfield, MA
Metzger, William Todd .... **Indianapolis, IN**
Metzger, Yale H. .... Anchorage, AK
Metzger, Yvonne M. .... San Rafael, CA
Metzinger, Bruce A. .... **Dallas, TX**
Metzinger, Margaret M. .... **Cleveland, OH**
Metzinger, Paul H. .... Denver, CO
Metzinger, Philip J. .... Cypress, CA
Metzinger, Ronald M. .... Sacramento, CA
Metzinger, Timothy E. **Santa Barbara, CA**
Metzke, John J. .... **Cheyenne, WY**
Metzler, Alison D. .... **New York, NY**
Metzler, Amy J. .... **Cupertino, CA**
Metzler, Catherine C. .... **Kalamazoo, MI**
Metzler, Claude G. .... Evanston, IL
Metzler, Cynthia A. .... **Washington, DC**; **Philadelphia, PA**
Metzler, David J. K. .... **Dallas, TX**
Metzler, David L. .... Batavia, NY
Metzler, Debra M. .... Tampa, FL
Metzler, Dennis K. .... Del Rey, CA
Metzler, Donna K. .... **Aurora, IL**
Metzler, Eric John .... Rochester, NY
Metzler and Hager, S.C. .... Green Bay, WI
Metzler, Holly .... Santa Barbara, CA
Metzler, James E. .... **Rochester, NY**
Metzler, Kimberly I. .... Xenia, OH
Metzler, Laurent W. .... Haddonfield, NJ
Metzler, Malcolm M. .... **Muncie, IN**
Metzler, Monica M. .... Chicago, IL
Metzler, Robert E. .... St. Louis, MO
Metzler, Robert J., II .... **Hartford, CT**
Metzler, Robert L. .... Pekin, IL
Metzler, Robert W. .... Department of Justice, Tax Division, GV
Metzler, Roger J. .... **San Francisco, CA**
Metzler, Ronald F. .... Green Bay, WI
Metzloff, Thomas B. .... Durham, NC
Metzmeier, Jeffrey Thomas .... Morehead, KY
Metzner, Carroll E. .... Madison, WI
Metzner, Charles M. .... Woodstock, NY
Metzner, Christine M. .... **Pittsburgh, PA**
Metzner, Henry J. .... Glens Falls, NY
Metzner, John A., Jr. .... **Delphos, OH**
Metzner, Kenneth L. .... **New York, NY**
Metzner, Lewis C. .... Hagerstown, MD
Metzner, Margot A. .... **Los Angeles, CA**
Metzner, Richard J. .... Chicago, IL
Metzner, William R., Sr. .... Wheeling, WV
Meub, William H., III .... **Rutland, VT**
Meuers, Christine L. .... Minneapolis, MN
Meuers, Dressler & Kerr, LLP Columbia, MD
Meuers, John J. .... **St. Cloud, MN**

Meuers Law Firm, LLP ... Irvine, CA
Naples, FL
Meuers, Lawrence H. ... Naples, FL
Meulbroek, Thomas ... Indianapolis, IN
Meuleman, Daniel E. ... St. Louis, MO
Meuleman & Miller, L.L.P. ... Boise, ID
Meuleman, Wayne V. ... Boise, ID
Meuleman, William L., III
East Lansing, MI
Flint, MI
Meulemans, Catherine S.
San Francisco, CA
Meuly, Caroline L. ... New Brunswick, NJ
Meunier, Andrew T. ... Charlotte, NC
Meunier, Gerald E. ... New Orleans, LA
Meunier, James W. ... Minneapolis, MN
Meunier, Jeffrey O. ... Indianapolis, IN
Meunier, Michael M. ... New Orleans, LA
Meunier, Paul D. ... Orlando, FL
Meunier, Richard E. ... Denver, CO
Meunier, William A. ... Chicago, IL
Meunkle, John L. ... Garden City, NY
Meunkle, Karen S. ... Amityville, NY
Meurer, Argentina Cronfel ... Laredo, TX
Meurer, George R. ... Laredo, TX
Meurer, Gregory J. ... Batavia, OH
Meurer Law Office ... Elkhorn, WI
Meurer, Michael James ... Durham, NC
Meurer, Michael T. ... Elkhorn, WI
Meurer, Robert F. ... Searcy, AR
Meurlin, Craig N. ... Ada, MI
Meurling, John E. ... Houston, TX
Meuse, Charles K. ... Rutherford, NJ
Meuse, Kevin M. ... Boston, MA
Meuser, Craig S. ... Hartford, CT
Meuser, Eckenrode & Hayes ... Milford, CT
Meuser, Joseph E. ... Bridgeport, CT
Meuser Law Offices, P.A. ... Minneapolis, MN
Meuser, Michael D. ... Lexington, KY
Meuser, Rick ... Huntington Station, NY
Meuser, Robert L. ... Washington, DC
Meuser, Ronald F., Jr. ... Minneapolis, MN
Meuser, William J. ... Milford, CT
Meusey, Joseph K. ... Omaha, NE
Meuter, Michael L. ... Salinas, CA
Meuter, Walter F. ... Louisville, KY
Meuth, Donna M. ... Alexandria, VA
Meuth, Patterson Carl ... Libertyville, IL
Meuwissen & Kieffer, P.A.
Minnetonka, MN
Meuwissen, Lawrence E.
Minnetonka, MN
Meux, Joseph Clay ... Jacksonville, FL
Meux, Peter C. ... Fresno, CA
Mevec, Danny Louis ... Syracuse, NY
Mevi, Edward ... San Francisco, CA
Mevis, Willis H. ... Los Angeles, CA
Mevorach, Jack ... Cedarhurst, NY
Mevorah, Steven H., & Associates
Lombard, IL
Mew, Alicia D. ... Washington, DC
Mewaldt, Jennifer R. ... Minneapolis, MN
Mewborn, James F. ... Minneapolis, MN
Mewhinney, Douglas V. ... San Andreas, CA
Mewhinney, Kate ... Winston-Salem, NC
Mewhinney, Larsh B. ... Cold Spring, NY
Mewhinney, Len E. ... Temple, TX
Mewhinney, Richard L. ... Temple, TX
Mewhort, Donald M., Jr. ... Toledo, OH
Mewis, Paul ... Houston, TX
Mewton, William D. ... Montgomery, AL
Mexic, Darryl, (P.C.) ... Washington, DC
Mexic, Scott B. ...
Department of Housing and Urban Development, GV
Mey, Michael R. ... Scranton, PA
Meyberg, Leonard J., Jr. ... Los Angeles, CA
Meyberg, Leonard J., Jr., The Law Office of
Los Angeles, CA
Meyen, Blake A. ... Fresno, CA
Meyen, Bradley E. ... Anchorage, AK
Meyenberg, Werner D. ("Randy"), III
Monterey, CA
Salinas, CA
Meyenschein, Heiko P. ... New York, NY
Meyer, A. David ... Fishers, IN
Indianapolis, IN
Meyer, Adrian L. ... Doylestown, PA
Meyer, Aileen ... Washington, DC
Meyer, Alan J. ... Brooklyn, NY
Meyer, Albert J. ... New York, NY
Meyer, Albert R. ... Tampa, FL
Meyer, Alfred W. ... Valparaiso, IN
Meyer, Alice ... Tenafly, NJ
Meyer, Allan F. ... Fort Lauderdale, FL
Meyer, Allen ... New York, NY
Meyer, Allen A. ... Scarsdale, NY
Meyer, Allen H. ... Chicago, IL
Meyer, Allen J. ... Sea Girt, NJ
Meyer, Alvin R. ... Shorewood, WI
Meyer, A.M. (Russ), Jr. ... Dallas, TX
Meyer, Andrea R. ... Portland, OR
Meyer, Andrew C. ... Cleveland, OH
Meyer, Andrew C., Jr. ... Boston, MA
Meyer, Andrew Gill ... Boston, MA
Meyer, Andrew Hays ... Atlanta, GA
Meyer, Andrew S. ... St. Louis, MO
Meyer, Ann Holman ... Lincoln, NE
Meyer, Ann M. ... Minneapolis, MN
Meyer, Anne H. ... Boston, MA
Meyer, Anne W. ... San Francisco, CA
Meyer, Anthony C. ... Lawrenceburg, IN
Meyer, Arnold R. ... Cleveland, OH
Meyer, Arthur G. ... Dayton, OH
Meyer, Arthur L. ... Chesterfield, MO
Meyer, Arthur L., P.C. ... Chesterfield, MO
Meyer & Associates, A Professional Law Corporation ... Costa Mesa, CA
Meyer & Associates, P.A. ... Minneapolis, MN
Meyer, August C. ... San Diego, CA
Meyer, August C., Jr. ... Champaign, IL
Meyer, August R. ... Boston, MA
Meyer, Austin & Romano, P.C.
Taylorville, IL
Meyer, Barry A. ... Fairfield, OH
Meyer, Barry K. ... Minneapolis, MN
Meyer, Barry W. ... Santa Rosa, CA
Meyer, Becky ... Decatur, AL
Meyer, Bernadine ... Pittsburgh, PA
Meyer, Bernard G., Jr. ... Richmond, VA
Meyer, Bernard K. ... Smithtown, NY
Meyer, Bernard S. ... Mineola, NY
Meyer, Beverly A. ... Dayton, OH
Meyer, Brenda G. ... Toledo, OH
Meyer, Brett J. ... New York, NY
Meyer, Brian A. ... New York, NY
Meyer, Brian B. ... Pierre, SD
Meyer, Brian S. ... Boston, MA
Meyer and Brooks, P.A. ... Tallahassee, FL
Meyer, Bruce D. ... Los Angeles, CA
Meyer, Bruce J. ... Alamosa, CO
Meyer, Bruce L. ... Bemidji, MN
Meyer, Bruce S. ... New York, NY
Meyer, Bruce V. ... Cleveland, OH
Memphis, TN
Meyer, Bruce W. J. ... South Sioux City, NE
Meyer, C. Lawrence ... Atlanta, GA
Meyer, Capel, Hirschfeld, Muncy, Jahn & Aldeen, P.C. ... Champaign, IL
Monticello, IL
Rantoul, IL
Tuscola, IL
Meyer, Carey Sirota ... Minneapolis, MN
Meyer, Carl B. ... Las Vegas, NV
Meyer, Carl F. ... Pittsburgh, PA
Meyer, Carl F., Jr. ... Department of Defense, Defense Legal Services Agency, GV
Meyer, Carl J. ... Columbus, OH
Meyer, Carl R. ... Redford, MI
Meyer, Cassie L. ... Orlando, FL
Meyer, Catherine D. ... Los Angeles, CA
Meyer, Charles A. ... Memphis, TN
Meyer, Charles B. ... Cleveland, OH
Meyer, Charles B. ... Houston, TX
Meyer, Charles D. ... Los Angeles, CA
Meyer, Charles F. ... Inglewood, CA
Meyer, Charles G., III ... Richmond, VA
Meyer, Charles H. ... Stamford, CT
Meyer, Charles J. ... Van Nuys, CA
Meyer, Charles J. ... Indianapolis, IN
Meyer, Charles J. ... Bala Cynwyd, PA
Meyer, Charles L. ... Seattle, WA
Meyer, Charles M. ... Carter Lake, IA
Meyer, Charles M. ... Cincinnati, OH
Meyer, Charlotte M. ... Houston, TX
Meyer, Cheryl A. ... Covington, KY
Meyer, Cheryl Ann ... Flushing, NY
Meyer, Christian E. ... Grand Rapids, MI
Meyer, Christopher Allen ... Richmond, VA
Meyer, Christopher H. ... Boise, ID
Meyer, Christopher J. ... Denver, CO
Meyer, Christopher P. ... Danville, IL
Meyer, Christopher Paul ... Cohoes, NY
Meyer, Christopher R. ... Newark, OH
Meyer, Christopher W. ... Washington, DC
Meyer, Clarence C. ... Houston, TX
Meyer, Clifford John ... Irvine, CA
Meyer, Clifford Scott ... Cherry Hill, NJ
Philadelphia, PA
Meyer, Clyde B. ... Houston, TX
Meyer, Colette K. ... Jupiter, FL
Meyer, Colette K., P.A. ... Jupiter, FL
Meyer, Connolly, Sloman & Macdonald LLP
Boston, MA
Meyer, Conrad, III ... New Orleans, LA
Meyer, Conrad, IV ... New Orleans, LA
Meyer, Cora ... Carthage, TX
Meyer, Cora L. ... Carthage, TX
Meyer, Craig R. ... Avon, CT
Meyer, Cynthia K.C. ... Salt Lake City, UT
Meyer, Cynthia L. ... Philadelphia, PA
Meyer, Dale C. ... Cockeysville, MD
Meyer, Dana M. ... Kankakee, IL
Meyer, Daniel B. ... Chicago, IL
Meyer, Daniel J. ... Dallas, TX
Meyer, Daniel N. ... Atlanta, GA
Meyer, Daniel R. ... Louisville, KY
Meyer • Darragh • Buckler • Bebenek & Eck, P.L.L.C. ... Altoona, PA
Greensburg, PA
Pittsburgh, PA
Meyer, Darrell D. ... Emporia, KS
Meyer, Darrin F. ... Los Angeles, CA
Meyer, David A. ... St. Paul, MN
Meyer, David B. ... Frankenmuth, MI
Saginaw, MI
Meyer, David C. ... Los Angeles, CA
Meyer, David D. ... Champaign, IL
Meyer, David D. ... Minneapolis, MN
Meyer, David G. ... Los Angeles, CA
Meyer, David J. ... Los Angeles, CA
Meyer, David J. ... Spokane, WA
Meyer, David L. ... Treasury Department, Internal Revenue Service, GV
Meyer, David Lawrence ... Washington, DC
Meyer, David M. ... Vista, CA
Meyer, David N. ... New York, NY
Meyer, David P. ... Columbus, OH
Meyer, David P. ... Portland, OR
Meyer, David S. ... Los Angeles, CA
Meyer, Deborah N. ... Raleigh, NC
Meyer, Dena ... Newark, DE
Meyer, Denise L. ... New York, NY
Meyer, Dennis I. ... Washington, DC
Meyer, Derek J. ... Chicago, IL
Meyer, Dianne A. ... Philadelphia, PA
Meyer & Diesenhouse ... Middletown, NY
Meyer, Donald Bancroft ... Charleston, SC
Meyer, Donald C. ... Palo Alto, CA
Meyer, Donald E. ... Atlanta, GA
Meyer, Donald E. ... Louisville, KY
Meyer, Donald E. ... Springfield, MO
Meyer, Donald J. ... Clayton, MO
Meyer, Donald M. ... Indianapolis, IN
Meyer, Donna J. ... Cleveland, OH
Meyer, Donna R. ... Portland, OR
Meyer, Dorothy Dick ... Bakersfield, CA
Meyer, Douglas A. ... Chattanooga, TN
Meyer, Douglas C. ... Cedar Rapids, IA
Central City, IA
Meyer, Douglas O. ... North Hollywood, CA
Meyer, Douglas R. ... Lafayette, IN
Meyer, Douglas W. ... Brownsburg, IN
Meyer, Dwaine F. ... Pella, IA
Meyer, Edward A. ... Greensboro, NC
Meyer, Edward B., Jr. ... Wheaton, IL
Meyer, Edward Henry ... Bronx, NY
Meyer, Edward J. ... Middletown, NY
Meyer, Edward S. ... St. Louis, MO
Meyer, Edwin L., Jr. ... Woodbury, NJ
Meyer, Eileen M. ... Hoffman Estates, IL
Meyer, Elitza M. ... Nutley, NJ
Meyer, Elizabeth ... Boulder, CO
Meyer, Elizabeth F.
Securities and Exchange Commission, Division of Enforcement, GV
Meyer, Elizabeth L. ... Lincoln, NE
Meyer, Ellen C. ... Chicago, IL
Meyer, Ellen Shaffer ... Wilmington, DE
Meyer, Elzinga, Gannett & Stone, P.C.
Portland, OR
Meyer, Eric E. ... St. Louis, MO
Portland, OR
Meyer, Ernest L. ... Olympia, WA
Meyer & Erskine, P.A. ... Big Pine Key, FL
Key West, FL
Sugarloaf Key, FL
Summerland Key, FL
Meyer, Ferd. C., Jr. ... Dallas, TX
Meyer, Filomena E. ... Santa Monica, CA
Meyer, Fluegge and Tenney, P.S.
Yakima, WA
Meyer & Ford ... Charleston, WV
Meyer, Frank C., IV ... Sacramento, CA
Meyer, Frank E. ... Sedalia, MO
Meyer, Frank R., Jr. ... Edison, NJ
Meyer, Franklin N. ... New York, NY
Meyer, Fred C. ... Toledo, OH
Meyer, Fred J. ... Portland, ME
Meyer, Fred P. ... Lawrenceville, GA
Meyer, Frederick C. ... Hampton Bays, NY
Meyer, Frederick G. ... Denver, CO
Meyer, Frederick R. ... Stamford, CT
Meyer & Friedman ... Dallas, TX
Meyer, G. Christopher ... Cleveland, OH
Meyer, Gary A. ... Los Angeles, CA
Meyer, Gary E. ... Salinas, CA
Meyer, Gary J. ... Buffalo, MN
Meyer, Gary L. ... Minneapolis, MN
Meyer, Gary Robert ... Philadelphia, PA
Meyer, Geoffrey E. ... Wilmington, DE
Meyer, George F., Jr. ... St. Louis, MO
Meyer, George H. ... Bloomfield Hills, MI
Detroit, MI
Meyer, George J. ... Tampa, FL
Meyer, George, Law Office of ... Denver, CO
Meyer, Gerald ... New York, NY
Meyer, Gerald D. ... Tiffin, OH
Meyer, Gerald L. ... New Orleans, LA
Meyer, Glen F. ... Rockford, MN
Meyer, Goergen & Marrs, P.C.
Richmond, VA
Meyer, Gordon D. ... Franklin Lakes, NJ
Meyer, Gordon G. ... Escondido, CA
Meyer, Grace T. ... River Vale, NJ
Meyer, Gracia-Jean ... Indianapolis, IN
Meyer, Gracia-Jean, P.C. ... Indianapolis, IN
Meyer Greenawalt Taub & Wild, LLP
New York, NY
Meyer, Gregor F. ... Pittsburgh, PA
Meyer, Gregory ... Madison, WI
Meyer, Gregory A. ... Corinth, MS
Meyer, Gregory G. ... Evansville, IN
Meyer, Gregory R. ... Armonk, NY
Meyer & Guerrero ... McAllen, TX
Meyer, H. Theodore ... Columbus, OH
Meyer, Harry A., II ... Bloomfield Hills, MI
Meyer, Harry E. ... Hartford, CT
Meyer, Harry G. ... Buffalo, NY
Meyer, Harry Lee ... Louisville, KY
Meyer, Harvey B. ... Creve Coeur, MO
Meyer, Heidi K. ... Terre Haute, IN
Meyer, Helen M. ... Minneapolis, MN
Meyer, Hendricks & Bivens, P.A.
Flagstaff, AZ
Phoenix, AZ
Tucson, AZ
Meyer, Henry A., III ... Oklahoma City, OK
Meyer, Henry J. ... Auburn, ME
Meyer, Henry S. ... Hondo, TX
Meyer, Henry T., III ... Melville, NY
Meyer, Herbert I. ... New York, NY
Meyer, Herman J. ... Ridgewood, NY
Meyer, Holley C. ... Boston, MA
Meyer, Holly Lodge ... Little Rock, AR
Meyer, Howard J., Jr. ... Anchorage, AK
Meyer, Howard L. ... Buffalo, NY
Meyer, Howard N. ... New York, NY
Meyer, Hugh H. ... Hondo, TX
Meyer, Ira H. ... Berkeley, CA
Meyer, Irving ... Los Angeles, CA
Meyer, Irwin S. ... Pearl River, NY
Meyer, Isadore ... Decorah, IA
Meyer, J. Andrew ... St. Petersburg, FL
Meyer, J. Carter ... Dallas, TX
Meyer, J. David ... Mays Landing, NJ
Meyer, J. Edward ... New York, NY
Meyer, J. Patrick, Jr. ... Macon, GA
Meyer, J. Robert ... Hinsdale, IL
Meyer, J. Theodore ... Chicago, IL
Meyer, Jack ... Madison, WI
Meyer, Jacqueline I. ... New York, NY
Meyer, James A. ... White Bear Lake, MN
Meyer, James A. ... St. Marys, PA
Meyer, James B. ... Mishawaka, IN
Meyer, James C. ... Morristown, NJ
Meyer, James C. ... Nashville, TN
Meyer, James D. ... Chariton, IA
Meyer, James, Jr. ... Mishawaka, IN
Meyer, James L. ... Detroit, MI
Meyer, James L. ... Tyler, TX
Meyer, James M. ... Miami, FL
Meyer, James P. ... Covington, LA
Meyer, James R. ... Bartow, FL
Meyer, James R. ... Frankenmuth, MI
Saginaw, MI
Meyer, James R. ... Philadelphia, PA
Meyer, James S. ... Oak Park, IL
Meyer, James S. ... Dallas, TX
Meyer, James T. ... Harrison, NY
Meyer, Jane A. ... New York, NY
Meyer, Jane E. ... Harrisburg, PA
Meyer, Jane L. ... Omaha, NE
Meyer, Janis M. ... New York, NY
Meyer, Jared H. ... Pittsburgh, PA
Meyer, Jason F. ... San Diego, CA
Meyer, Jay C. ... Newton, NC
Meyer, Jaye Powell ... Raleigh, NC
Meyer, Jayma M. ... New York, NY
Meyer, Jeannie J. ... Foster City, CA
Meyer, Jeffrey A. ... New Haven, CT
Meyer, Jeffrey Blake ... Big Pine Key, FL
Meyer, Jeffrey D. ... Bexley, OH
Meyer, Jeffrey D. ... Houston, TX
Meyer, Jeffrey R. ... Department of Justice, Tax Division, GV
Meyer, Jeffrey S. ... Hamburg, NY
Meyer, Jeffrey Scott ... St. Francis, WI
Meyer, Jennifer A. ... New York, NY
Meyer, Jerald L. ... Washington, DC
Meyer, Jim ... Waco, TX
Meyer, Jim, & Associates, P.C. ... Waco, TX
Meyer, Joan Freedman ... Atlantic City, NJ
Northfield, NJ
Meyer, Joel R. ... Portland, OR
Meyer, John ... Des Moines, IA
Meyer, John A. ... Chicago, IL
Meyer, John B. ... Kansas City, MO
Meyer, John C. ... Sterling, IL
Meyer, John F. ... Metairie, LA
Meyer, John G. ... Union, MO
Meyer, John H. ... Aberdeen, SD
Meyer, John Hewitt ... Jacksonville Beach, FL
Meyer, John J. ... Washington, DC
Meyer, John K. ... Houston, TX
Meyer, John P. ... Danville, IL
Meyer, John R. ... Flora, IL
Meyer, John R. ... Cadillac, MI
Meyer, John S. ... Vista, CA
Meyer, John Strauch, Jr. ... St. Louis, MO
Meyer, John W. ... Sauk Centre, MN
Meyer, John W. ... Houston, TX
Meyer, Johnathan L. ... Overland Park, KS
Kansas City, MO
Meyer, Jon ... Manchester, NH
Meyer, Jonas J., III ... Bridgeport, CT
Meyer, Jonathan E. ... Washington, DC
Meyer, Joseph B. ... Cheyenne, WY
Meyer, Joseph E., III ... Denver, CO
Meyer, Joseph, Jr. ... New Orleans, LA
Meyer, Joseph T. ... Miami, FL
Meyer, Joseph U. ... Covington, KY
Meyer, Joshua A. ... Los Angeles, CA
Meyer, Joshua J. ... Yuma, AZ
Meyer, Joyce L. ... Chicago, IL
Meyer, Judith A. ... Houston, TX
Meyer, Judith, Associates
Philadelphia, PA
Meyer, Judith D., Law Office of ... Avon, CT
Meyer, Judith D., Law Office of
Hartford, CT
Meyer, Julie E. ... Rochester, NY
Meyer, Julie Neale ... San Jose, CA
Meyer, Karen ... Boise, ID
Meyer, Karen P. ... Cincinnati, OH
Meyer, Karl A., Jr. ... Milwaukee, WI
Meyer, Karl V. ... Aurora, IL
Meyer, Kathryn C. ... New York, NY
Meyer, Keith ... Costa Mesa, CA
Meyer, Keith A. ... Santa Monica, CA
Meyer, Keith D. ... Cincinnati, OH
Meyer, Keith G. ... Lawrence, KS
Meyer, Kendall R. ... Chicago, IL
Meyer, Kenneth ... Los Angeles, CA
Meyer, Kenneth H. ... Los Angeles, CA
Meyer, Kenneth H. ... Purvis, MS
Meyer, Kenneth M. ... Hollywood, FL
Meyer, Kenneth M. ... Alexandria, VA
Meyer, Kenneth R. ... Morristown, NJ
New York, NY
Meyer, Kent C. ... Seattle, WA
Meyer, Kevin L. ... Lansing, MI
Meyer, Kim G. ... Atlanta, GA
Meyer, Kimberly ... Lafayette, IN
Meyer, Kimberly Howland
Marina Del Rey, CA
Meyer, Kirk, Snyder & Safford, PLLC
Bloomfield Hills, MI
Detroit, MI
Meyer, K. L., Jr. ... Muskogee, OK
Meyer & Klipper, PLLC ... Washington, DC
Meyer, Kurt G. ... Worth, IL

Meyer, Lamar & Haynes, LLP
Owensboro, KY
Meyer, Larry E. .... **Houston, TX**
Meyer, Larry J. .... Chicago, IL
Meyer, Larry K. .... **Clearwater, FL**
Meyer, Larry K., P.A. .... **Clearwater, FL**
Meyer, Larry P. .... **Toledo, OH**
Meyer, Larry W. .... Aurora, MO
Meyer, Laura G. .... **Scottsdale, AZ**
Meyer, Laura K. .... **Oakland, CA**
Meyer, Laurence E. .... Hanford, CA
Meyer, Laurence P. .... Hauppauge, NY
Meyer, Laurie E. .... **Milwaukee, WI**
Meyer, Laurie W. .... Minneapolis, MN
Meyer Law Firm .... Chariton, IA
Meyer Law Firm, P.C. .... Portland, OR
Meyer Law Office .... **Olympia, WA**
Meyer, Lawrence F. .... **Glendale, CA**
Meyer, Lawrence G. .... **Washington, DC**
Meyer, Lawrence J. .... Hollywood, FL
Meyer, Lawrence J., P.A. .... Hollywood, FL
Meyer, Lee .... **Fairfield, CT**
Meyer, Lee G. .... **Denver, CO**
Meyer, Leon S. .... Chicago, IL
Meyer, Leonard J. .... **Houston, TX**
Meyer, Leonard L. .... Independence, MO
Meyer, Lesley A. .... Denver, CO
Meyer, Lewis .... Tulsa, OK
Meyer, Linda R. .... Hamden, CT
Meyer, Linda S. .... **San Francisco, CA**
Meyer, Lindsay Beardsworth
Washington, DC
Meyer, Lionel D. .... Hilo, HI
Meyer, Lisa Helfend .... **Los Angeles, CA**
Meyer, Lisa M. .... **Omaha, NE**
Meyer, Lisa S. .... **Chicago, IL**
Meyer, Lorentzen & Nelson .... Calmar, IA
Decorah, IA
Meyer, Louis B. .... Raleigh, NC
Meyer, Louis B., III .... **Raleigh, NC**
Meyer, Louis C., Jr. .... Paramus, NJ
Meyer, Lydia S. .... Loves Park, IL
Meyer, Lyles & Godshack, P.C. .... Gary, IN
Meyer, Lynn Moran .... **St. Paul, MN**
Meyer, Lynn Nix .... Lakewood, CO
Meyer, M. Holt .... Staten Island, NY
Meyer, M. Michael .... **Houston, TX**
Meyer, Malcolm A. .... **New Orleans, LA**
Meyer & Maliszewski .... Oak Park, IL
Meyer, Marcellus B. .... Michigan City, IN
Meyer, Marcy R. .... Lansing, MI
Meyer, Marilyn S. .... Flint, MI
Meyer, Mark A. .... **Denver, CO**
Meyer, Mark A. .... **New York, NY**
Meyer, Mark A. .... Wahpeton, ND
Meyer, Mark C. .... Phoenix, AZ
Meyer, Mark C. .... Wheaton, IL
Meyer, Mark C. .... Cedar Rapids, IA
Iowa City, IA
Meyer, Mark C. .... **Johnstown, PA**
Pittsburgh, PA
Meyer, Mark D. .... **Minneapolis, MN**
Meyer, Mark H. .... Melrose, MN
Meyer, Mark W. .... Atlanta, GA
Meyer, Marlane A. .... **McAllen, TX**
Meyer, Marsha R. .... **Cincinnati, OH**
Meyer, Marshall .... Waukegan, IL
Meyer, Martha Payne .... Columbus, OH
Meyer, Martin A. .... Glens Falls, NY
Meyer, Martin A., Jr. .... Jupiter, FL
Meyer, Martin D. .... **Olympia, WA**
Meyer, Martin J. .... **Wilkes-Barre, PA**
Meyer, Martin W. .... **Milwaukee, WI**
Meyer, Marvin B. .... **Beverly Hills, CA**
Meyer, Marvin W. .... Topeka, KS
Meyer, Mary Angela .... **Houston, TX**
Meyer, Mary Ann .... New Orleans, LA
Meyer, Mary Beth .... **New Orleans, LA**
Meyer, Mary D. .... Stamford, CT
Meyer, Mary L. .... **New Orleans, LA**
Meyer, Mathew M. .... **Minneapolis, MN**
Meyer, Matthew J. .... **Tampa, FL**
Meyer, Matthew J. .... New York, NY
Meyer, Matthew L. .... **Grand Rapids, MI**
Meyer, Maureen A. .... Washington, DC
Meyer, Maureen M. .... West Bend, WI
Meyer, Maurice S. .... Potomac, MD
Meyer, Max E. .... Chicago, IL
Meyer, Melvin P. .... **New York, NY**
Meyer, Mercedes K. .... **Alexandria, VA**
Meyer and Meyer .... Bartow, FL
Meyer & Meyer .... Flora, IL
Meyer & Meyer .... Greenville, IL
Meyer & Meyer .... Houston, TX
Meyer, Meyer & Metli Esqs., LLP
Smithtown, NY
Meyer, Meyer and Pottratz .... Melrose, MN
Meyer, Michael A. .... **Washington, DC**
Meyer, Michael A. .... Franklin, TN
Meyer, Michael A. .... San Antonio, TX
Meyer, Michael B. .... **Boston, MA**
Meyer, Michael C. .... Marion, WI
Meyer, Michael D. .... New Orleans, LA
Meyer, Michael D., Law Corporation
New Orleans, LA
Meyer, Michael E. .... **Los Angeles, CA**
Meyer, Michael J. .... **Chicago, IL**
Meyer, Michael J., Law Offices of
Effingham, IL
Meyer, Michael L. .... **Chicago, IL**
Meyer, Michael L. .... **Minneapolis, MN**
Meyer, Michael W. .... **Houston, TX**
Meyer, Michele .... Treasury Department, Office of the Comptroller of the Currency, GV
Meyer, Milton E., Jr. .... Englewood, CO
Meyer, Morton H. .... Lincolnwood, IL
Meyer, Morton H. .... New York, NY

Meyer, Murray .... Los Angeles, CA
Meyer, Myrl A. .... Palo Alto, CA
Meyer, Neil E. .... Beverly Hills, CA
Meyer, Neil H. .... Philadelphia, PA
Meyer, Neil M. .... **Minneapolis, MN**
Meyer, Nicole M. .... **Washington, DC**
Meyer & Njus, P.A. .... Chicago, IL
Southfield, MI
Minneapolis, MN
Stillwater, MN
Meyer Orlando & Evans, A Professional Corporation .... **Houston, TX**
Meyer, P. Richard .... Phoenix, AZ
Jackson, WY
Meyer, Pamela G. .... **Los Angeles, CA**
Meyer, Patricia A. .... San Diego, CA
Meyer, Patrick W. .... **Omaha, NE**
Meyer, Paul .... Sacramento, CA
Meyer, Paul .... **Chicago, IL**
Meyer, Paul A. .... Bethesda, MD
Meyer, Paul A. .... Raleigh, NC
Meyer, Paul C. .... **New York, NY**
Meyer, Paul Douglas .... **Savannah, GA**
Meyer, Paul E. .... Rochester, NY
Meyer, Paul E. .... Bath, OH
Meyer, Paul E. .... Prosser, WA
Meyer, Paul H. .... **Olympia, WA**
Meyer, Paul I. .... **San Diego, CA**
Meyer, Paul J. .... **Phoenix, AZ**
Meyer, Paul R. .... Portland, OR
Meyer, Paul S. .... **Costa Mesa, CA**
Meyer, Paul S. .... **Atlanta, GA**
Meyer, Paul T. .... Minneapolis, MN
Meyer, Paul W. .... Sharon Center, OH
Meyer, Paul W., Jr. .... Yonkers, NY
Meyer, Paula E. .... **Tustin, CA**
Meyer, Paula Jean .... Hermann, MO
Meyer, Peter Alexander .... **Concord, NH**
Meyer, Peter J. .... **Chicago, IL**
Meyer, Philip A. .... San Antonio, TX
Meyer, Philip G. .... **West Bloomfield, MI**
Meyer, Philip N. .... Boynton Beach, FL
Meyer, Philip, P.C., Law Office of
San Antonio, TX
Meyer, Phillip J. .... **Philadelphia, PA**
Meyer, Phyllis Ann .... Spokane, WA
Meyer, R. Kenyon .... **Louisville, KY**
Meyer, Ralph F. .... **Corpus Christi, TX**
Meyer, Randall J. .... New Orleans, LA
Meyer, Randolph A. .... Geneseo, NY
Meyer, Rauer L. .... **San Francisco, CA**
Meyer, Raymond C. .... Chariton, IA
Meyer, Raymond G., II
Port Washington, WI
Meyer, Raymond J. .... Chicago, IL
Meyer, Raymond, Jr. .... **Orange, CA**
Meyer, Raymond M. .... St. Louis, MO
Meyer, Reynold D. .... Tallahassee, FL
Meyer, Rhonda L. .... Great Neck, NY
Meyer, Richard .... **Estherville, IA**
Meyer, Richard .... **Arlington, VA**
Meyer, Richard A. .... Southfield, MI
Meyer, Richard A. .... Urbana, OH
Meyer, Richard A., Jr. .... Toledo, OH
Meyer, Richard B. .... **Lake Placid, NY**
Meyer, Richard C.
Agency for International Development, Other Offices of A.I.D., GV
Meyer, Richard D. .... South Lake Tahoe, CA
Meyer, Richard E. .... **Irvine, CA**
Meyer, Richard E. .... Yonkers, NY
Meyer, Richard E. .... Cincinnati, OH
Meyer, Richard F. .... Boston, MA
Meyer, Richard F. .... **Columbus, OH**
Meyer, Richard G. .... **Covington, KY**
Meyer, Richard L. .... Concordville, PA
Meyer, Richard M. .... **New York, NY**
Meyer, Richard P. .... **Rockville, MD**
Meyer, Richard S. .... **Washington, DC**
Meyer, Richard S. .... **Philadelphia, PA**
Meyer, Richard W. .... Austin, TX
Meyer, Robert .... **Wilmington, DE**
Meyer, Robert .... **New York, NY**
Meyer, Robert A. .... **Los Angeles, CA**
Meyer, Robert A. .... Fort Wayne, IN
Meyer, Robert A. .... West End, NC
Meyer, Robert A., Jr. .... Dublin, OH
Meyer, Robert B. .... **Charlotte, NC**
Meyer, Robert C. .... **Miami, FL**
Meyer, Robert C. .... Davenport, IA
Meyer, Robert C. .... **Canton, OH**
Meyer, Robert C., P.A. .... **Miami, FL**
Meyer, Robert E. .... Glendora, CA
Meyer, Robert E. .... East Orleans, MA
Meyer, Robert G. .... Fortuna, CA
Meyer, Robert H. .... Estes Park, CO
Meyer, Robert Harry .... Dallas, TX
Meyer, Robert J. .... Department of Justice, Criminal Division, GV
Meyer, Robert J. .... **Chicago, IL**
Meyer, Robert J. .... Albany, NY
Meyer, Robert L. .... Marshall, MI
Meyer, Robert L. .... St. Louis, MO
Meyer, Robert O. .... Morristown, NJ
Meyer, Robert (Tito) .... Las Cruces, NM
Meyer, Roberta B. .... Washington, DC
Meyer, Robin .... Oklahoma City, OK
Meyer, Robin B. .... Austin, TX
Meyer, Roger Edward .... Minneapolis, MN
Meyer, Roger L. .... **Portland, OR**
Meyer & Rogers .... Pierre, SD
Meyer, Ronald A. .... **Cincinnati, OH**
Meyer, Ronald G. .... Tallahassee, FL
Meyer, Ronald K. .... **Los Angeles, CA**
Meyer, Ronald W. .... **Phoenix, AZ**
Meyer, Roy C. .... Newtown Square, PA
Meyer, S. Russell .... Alton, IL
Meyer, Samuel G. .... **Olympia, WA**

Meyer, Saul M. .... Dallas, TX
Meyer, Scott A. .... **Miami, FL**
Meyer, Scott B. .... Belleville, IL
Meyer, Scott D. .... **Spokane, WA**
Meyer, Scott J. .... **Portland, OR**
Meyer, Scott L. .... St. Louis, MO
Meyer, Scott, Law Office of .... Tucson, AZ
Meyer, Scott Randall .... Tucson, AZ
Meyer, Sheldon R. .... **San Francisco, CA**
Meyer, Sidney L. .... New York, NY
Meyer, Stanley M. .... Merrick, NY
Meyer, Stephany A. .... Denver, CO
Meyer, Stephen D. .... Beloit, WI
Meyer, Stephen F. .... Troy, MO
Meyer, Stephen H.
Board of Governors Of The Federal Reserve System, Office of the General Counsel, GV
Meyer, Stephen J. .... **Sacramento, CA**
Meyer, Stephen J. .... Madison, WI
Meyer, Stephen P. .... Charleston, WV
Meyer, Steven A. .... **Boston, MA**
Meyer, Steven E. .... **Los Angeles, CA**
Meyer, Steven F. .... **New York, NY**
Meyer, Steven H. .... Boca Raton, FL
Meyer, Steven H. .... **Philadelphia, PA**
Meyer, Steven P. .... Kokomo, IN
Lafayette, IN
Meyer, Steven W. .... **Minneapolis, MN**
Meyer, Stuart F. .... St. Louis, MO
Meyer, Stuart P. .... **Palo Alto, CA**
Meyer, Sue Figert .... **Indianapolis, IN**
Meyer, Suozzi, English & Klein, P.C.
Washington, DC
Albany, NY
Mineola, NY
New York, NY
Meyer, Susan Campbell .... **Richmond, VA**
Meyer, Susan K. .... Palo Alto, CA
Meyer, Susan L. .... **Palo Alto, CA**
Meyer, Susan, Law Offices of
Morton Grove, IL
Meyer, Susan M. .... Horsham, PA
Meyer and Swatkoski Associates, A Professional Corporation
Wilkes-Barre, PA
Meyer, Tammy J. .... **Indianapolis, IN**
Meyer, Terence X. .... Smithtown, NY
Meyer, Terrence L. .... Fair Oaks, CA
Meyer, Theodore D. .... **Houston, TX**
Meyer, Thomas .... Greenville, IL
Meyer, Thomas A. .... **Woodstock, IL**
Meyer, Thomas B. .... Danville, IL
Meyer, Thomas F. .... Delray Beach, FL
Meyer, Thomas F. .... Elkhorn, WI
Meyer, Thomas J. .... Fort Atkinson, WI
Meyer, Thomas Joseph .... **Owensboro, KY**
Meyer, Thomas L. .... **Cleveland, OH**
Meyer, Thomas L. .... **Olympia, WA**
Meyer, Thomas M. .... Oakland, CA
Meyer, Thomas O. .... Rockford, IL
Meyer, Thomas P. .... Roseville, CA
Stockton, CA
Meyer, Timothy C. .... Kansas City, KS
Meyer, Todd J. .... **Lebanon, IN**
Meyer, Tracy Anette .... **Arlington, VA**
Meyer, Tracy L. .... Boynton Beach, FL
Meyer, Unkovic & Scott LLP
Pittsburgh, PA
Meyer, Virginia H. .... Sausalito, CA
Meyer & Vucichevich, P.C. .... Phoenix, AZ
Meyer, W. Christian .... Lafayette, IN
Meyer & Wagner .... St. Marys, PA
Meyer, Walter G. .... **Yakima, WA**
Meyer & Watts .... Clearwater, FL
Meyer, Wayne A. .... Chicago, IL
Meyer, Werner J. .... **Phoenix, AZ**
Meyer, Willets S. .... **Uniondale, NY**
Meyer, William A. .... West Palm Beach, FL
Meyer, William A. .... Pittsburgh, PA
Meyer, William A., Jr. .... **Pittsburgh, PA**
Meyer, William Aring .... Portland, OR
Meyer, William C. "Bill" .... Houston, TX
Meyer, William Craig, II .... Princeton, WV
Meyer, William D. .... **Boulder, CO**
Meyer, William D. .... Cincinnati, OH
Meyer, William E. .... **La Crosse, WI**
Meyer, William E., Jr. .... **Chicago, IL**
Meyer, William F. .... Melbourne, FL
Meyer, William F. .... Cincinnati, OH
Meyer, William G. .... Melrose, MN
Meyer, William G. .... **Toledo, OH**
Meyer, William G., III .... **Honolulu, HI**
Meyer, William H. .... Ann Arbor, MI
Meyer, William H. .... **Kansas City, MO**
Meyer, William J., Jr. .... **Taylorville, IL**
Meyer, William Joseph .... **Pittsburgh, PA**
Meyer, William L. (IBA) .... **Atlanta, GA**
Meyer, William R. .... Portland, OR
Meyer, William R. .... **Nashville, TN**
Meyer, William Scott .... Vero Beach, FL
Meyer and Williams, Attorneys at Law, P.C.
Jackson, WY
Meyer & Wyse, LLP .... **Portland, OR**
Meyerand, James S. .... Mount Clemens, MI
Meyer-Betts, Vivian P. .... Waterloo, IA
Meyercord, Andrew N. .... **Dallas, TX**
Meyercord, David K., (P.C.) .... **Dallas, TX**
Meyere, Marina .... Hayward, CA
Meyere-Fong, Ming-Yuen
Department of Justice, Civil Division, GV
Meyerherm, Charles H. .... Fairfield, CA
Meyerhoefer, Paul F. .... **Norwalk, OH**
Meyerhoeffer, Christopher L. .... Twin Falls, ID
Meyerhofer, William P. .... **New York, NY**
Meyerhoff, Albert H., Jr. .... **Los Angeles, CA**
Meyerhoff, Gary .... **New York, NY**
Meyerhoff, Kent A. .... **Wichita, KS**

Meyerhoff, Lisa H. .... **Houston, TX**
Meyerhoff, Neil A. .... Baltimore, MD
Meyerhoff, Peter S. .... Castro Valley, CA
Meyerhoff, Samuel .... Los Angeles, CA
Meyerhoff, Sayra Wells .... Baltimore, MD
Meyerhoff, Scott A. .... **Newport Beach, CA**
Meyerhoff, Terrence A. .... **Los Angeles, CA**
Meyerholz, John P. .... New York, NY
Meyering, Clinton .... Taylor, MI
Meyering, Jules V., Jr. .... Wheaton, IL
Meyering, Patrick .... Cupertino, CA
Meyerkord, Stephen F. .... St. Louis, MO
Meyerle, Hilary A. .... Bothell, WA
Meyerle, Kathleen A. .... **Rochester, MN**
Meyer-Leon, Leslie .... **Boston, MA**
Meyeroff, Robert M .... Milwaukee, WI
Meyerowitz, Adam S. .... **Atlanta, GA**
Meyerowitz, Eric P. .... **New York, NY**
Meyerowitz, Ira Scot .... **New York, NY**
Meyerowitz, Jean F. .... New York, NY
Meyerowitz, Steven A. .... Northport, NY
Meyers, A. Elizabeth "Liza" .... Denver, CO
Meyers, Addison J. .... **Miami, FL**
Meyers, Alan H. .... **Midland, TX**
Meyers, Alaya B. .... **Los Angeles, CA**
Meyers, Alfred .... New York, NY
Meyers, Allan S. .... New York, NY
Meyers, Allen M. .... **Troy, MI**
Meyers & Alterman .... Washington, DC
Meyers, Alvin D. .... Chicago, IL
Meyers, Amos I. .... Baltimore, MD
Meyers, Amy J. .... **Raleigh, NC**
Meyers, Andrew H. .... **Lafayette, LA**
Meyers, Andrew J. .... Delray Beach, FL
Meyers, Andrew R. .... Kew Gardens, NY
Meyers, Anne L. .... **Cleveland, OH**
Meyers, Arthur S., Jr. .... **Boston, MA**
Meyers, Barry M. .... Los Angeles, CA
Meyers, Barry M. .... Bellingham, WA
Meyers, Bernard H. .... San Francisco, CA
Meyers, Bertram D. .... Chicago, IL
Meyers, Beth R. .... **New York, NY**
Meyers, Beverley R. .... San Francisco, CA
Meyers, Beverly T. .... St. Paul, MN
Meyers, Billingsley, Rodbell & Rosenbaum, P.A. .... **Annapolis, MD**
Riverdale, MD
Meyers Breiner & Neufeld, L.L.P.
Fairfield, CT
Meyers, Brian .... Philadelphia, PA
Meyers, Bruce F. .... Issaquah, WA
Meyers, Burton .... Los Angeles, CA
Meyers, Carl A. .... Cincinnati, OH
Meyers, Carl G. .... Dearborn, MI
Meyers, Carla J. .... Alpharetta, GA
Meyers, Charles A. .... Stillwater, OK
Meyers, Charles J. .... Lufkin, TX
Meyers, Cheryl .... Buffalo, NY
Williamsville, NY
Meyers, Christine .... **New York, NY**
Meyers, Christopher W. .... Buchanan, NY
Meyers, Conor A. .... San Jose, CA
Meyers, D. Kent .... **Oklahoma City, OK**
Meyers, Daniel D. .... **Palo Alto, CA**
Meyers, Daniel L. .... New York, NY
Meyers, Daniel L. .... Lake Oswego, OR
Meyers, Darryl L. .... Minneapolis, MN
Meyers, David I. .... **Richmond, VA**
Meyers, David J. .... **St. Cloud, MN**
Meyers, David S. .... Great Neck, NY
Meyers, David W. .... **Napa, CA**
Meyers, David W. .... Albany, NY
Meyers, Dawn M. .... **Fort Lauderdale, FL**
Meyers, Desfor, Saltzgiver & Boyle
Harrisburg, PA
Meyers, Diane .... **New York, NY**
Meyers, Diane R. .... **Pittsburgh, PA**
Meyers, Donald D. .... **Phoenix, AZ**
Meyers, Donald J. .... Keene, NH
Meyers, Donald L. .... **Phoenix, AZ**
Meyers, Donald L. .... Plymouth, MI
Meyers, Donna M. .... **Anchorage, AK**
Meyers, Dorothy D. .... Paradise Valley, AZ
Meyers, E. Stuart .... Banning, CA
Meyers, Edw. J. .... Columbia City, IN
Meyers, Edward .... **Washington, DC**
Meyers, Edward F., Jr. .... **Cleveland, OH**
Meyers, Eliot N. .... **Cincinnati, OH**
Meyers, Erik J. .... **Washington, DC**
Meyers, Felicia R. .... Santa Monica, CA
Meyers, Felicia R. .... **Santa Monica, CA**
Meyers, Frederick M. .... **Seattle, WA**
Meyers, Frederick W. .... **Chicago, IL**
Meyers, G. Martin .... **Denville, NJ**
Meyers, G. Martin, P.C., Law Offices of
Denville, NJ
Meyers, Gail E. .... Kenilworth, IL
Meyers, George W. .... Cincinnati, OH
Meyers, Gerson E. .... Glenview, IL
Meyers, Gregg .... **Charleston, SC**
Meyers, Gregory E. .... Findlay, OH
Meyers, Hannes, Jr. .... Holland, MI
Meyers, Harvey A. .... **Marengo, IL**
Meyers & Heim, LLP .... **New York, NY**
Meyers, Helen G. .... Hartsdale, NY
Meyers, Hentemann & Rea Co., L.P.A.
Cleveland, OH
Elyria, OH
Meyers, Howard C. .... **Phoenix, AZ**
Meyers, Howard D. .... Santa Monica, CA
Meyers, Howard G., Jr. .... New York, NY
Meyers, Howard L. .... **Philadelphia, PA**
Meyers, Howard M. .... Pasadena, MD
Meyers, Howard S. .... **New York, NY**
Meyers, Irvin A. .... **Orlando, FL**
Meyers, Irving .... Chicago, IL
Meyers, Irwin .... Brooklyn, NY

Meyers, Ishmael A. Charlotte Amalie, St. Thomas, VI
Meyers, Ishmael A., Jr. Charlotte Amalie, St. Thomas, VI
Meyers, James A. Washington, DC
Meyers, James E. Washington, DC
Meyers, James J., Jr., Law Offices of San Francisco, CA
Meyers, James R. Austin, TX
Meyers, James T. Provo, UT
Meyers, Janet Marie David Denver, CO
Meyers, Jason D. Santa Monica, CA
Meyers, Jay Philadelphia, PA
Meyers, Jeffrey Philadelphia, PA
Meyers, Jeffrey A. Los Angeles, CA
Meyers, Jeffrey A. Portland, ME
Meyers, Jeffrey G. Los Angeles, CA
New York, NY
Meyers, Jeffrey T. Detroit, MI
Meyers, Jeffrey W. Omaha, NE
Meyers, Jeffrey W. New York, NY
Meyers, Jerome M. Pittsburgh, PA
Meyers, Jerrold I. Seattle, WA
Meyers, Jerry I. Pittsburgh, PA
Meyers, Jerry R. Salmon, ID
Meyers, Joan M. Chicago, IL
Meyers, JoAnne Chelmsford, MA
Meyers, Joel G. Chicago, IL
Meyers, John A. Beverly Hills, CA
Meyers, John D. Lexington, KY
Meyers, John D., Jr. Lexington, KY
Meyers, John E. Los Angeles, CA
Meyers, John E. Bellevue, OH
Meyers, John F. Atlanta, GA
Meyers, John H. Houston, TX
Meyers, John H., IV Lafayette, IN
Meyers, John O., III Los Angeles, CA
Meyers, John P. Philadelphia, PA
Meyers, John W. Englewood, NJ
Meyers, Jonathan C. Allentown, PA
Meyers, Jonathan P. Pearl River, NY
Meyers, Joseph C., Jr. New Orleans, LA
Meyers, Joseph L. New York, NY
Meyers, Joseph P. San Francisco, CA
Meyers, Joseph V. Hackensack, NJ
Meyers, Joyce S. Philadelphia, PA
Meyers, Judy Boston, MA
Meyers, Julie P. Philadelphia, PA
Meyers, Justine San Francisco, CA
Meyers & Kages Chicago, IL
Meyers, Karen A. Boston, MA
Meyers, Karen J. Albuquerque, NM
Meyers, Karen T. Irvine, CA
Meyers, Kenneth J. East St. Louis, IL
Meyers, Kenneth John Washington, DC
Meyers, Kenneth R. New York, NY
Meyers, Kenneth S. Los Angeles, CA
Meyers, Kenneth S. Warren, NJ
Meyers & Keyser Pittsburgh, PA
Meyers, Kim R. Elyria, OH
Meyers, Kimberly M. Seattle, WA
Meyers, Kipp E. Lanark, IL
Meyers, Lamanna & Roman, A Legal Prof. Association Cleveland, OH
Meyers, Larry E. Anchorage, AK
Meyers, Laura San Francisco, CA
Meyers, Laurie B. Omaha, NE
Meyers, Laurie E. New York, NY
Meyers Law Firm, The Kansas City, MO
Meyers, Lawrence E. Austin, TX
Meyers, Lawrence Paul, Jr. Stockton, CA
Meyers, Leonard I. Fresno, CA
Meyers, Lesa M. Los Angeles, CA
Meyers, Lincoln Narberth, PA
Meyers, Lincoln & Associates, P.C. Narberth, PA
Meyers, Linda B. Avon, CT
East Hartford, CT
Meyers, Lisa P. Buffalo, NY
Meyers, Lori M. New York, NY
Meyers, Lynn F. Hagerstown, MD
Meyers, M. Evan Riverdale, MD
Meyers, M. Jay Pocatello, ID
Meyers, M. Richard Greenwich, CT
Meyers & Maistrow New York, NY
Meyers, Marcia San Jose, CA
Meyers, Margaret A. Lansing, MI
Meyers, Maria Robles Oklahoma City, OK
Meyers, Marjorie A. Houston, TX
Meyers, Mark B. Houston, TX
Meyers, Mark J. Huntington Beach, CA
Meyers, Mark J. Chicago, IL
Meyers, Marta T. Madison, WI
Meyers, Martin M. Kansas City, MO
Meyers, Martin P. Portland, OR
Meyers, Mary Frances Orlando, FL
Meyers, Maurice D. Beverly Hills, CA
Meyers & McConnell, A Professional Corporation Los Angeles, CA
New York, NY
Meyers, Melanie E. New York, NY
Meyers, Melissa C. New York, NY
Meyers, Melissa R. San Francisco, CA
Meyers, Merle C. San Francisco, CA
Meyers & Meyers Chicago, IL
Meyers & Meyers Albany, NY
Meyers, Michael A. Fairfield, CT
Meyers, Michael A. New York, NY
Meyers, Michael L. San Francisco, CA
Meyers, Michael R. New York, NY
Meyers, Mitchell A. Miami, FL
Meyers, Mooney, Stanley & Hollingsworth Jacksonville, FL
Orlando, FL
Meyers, Morton I. Baltimore, MD
Meyers, M.R., & Associates, P.C. Oklahoma City, OK

Meyers, Myron, (P.C.) Los Angeles, CA
Meyers, N. Marshall Washington, DC
Meyers, Nancy R. Greensboro, NC
Meyers, Naomi San Francisco, CA
Meyers, Nave, Riback, Silver & Wilson San Leandro, CA
Santa Rosa, CA
Stockton, CA
Meyers, Neal Solana Beach, CA
Meyers, Neil L. Seattle, WA
Meyers, O. Christopher Lawton, OK
Meyers, O. Christopher, Inc. Lawton, OK
Meyers, Patricia A. Rapid City, SD
Meyers, Patricia C. Wayne, PA
Meyers, Patrick E. Denver, CO
Meyers, Patrick T. Los Angeles, CA
Meyers, Paul W. Cincinnati, OH
Meyers, Peter R. Chicago, IL
Meyers, Philip G. Dallas, TX
Meyers, Philip G. Port Edwards, WI
Meyers, Radler, Replogle & Bohy Lake Oswego, OR
Meyers, Reid E. San Antonio, TX
Meyers, Richard St. Paul, MN
Meyers, Richard A. Woodland Hills, CA
Meyers, Richard B. Chesapeake, OH
Meyers, Richard E. Milwaukee, WI
Meyers, Richard F. Tampa, FL
Meyers, Richard J. Detroit, MI
Meyers, Richard M. Albany, NY
Meyers, Robert New York, NY
Meyers, Robert Seattle, WA
Meyers, Robert A. Kansas City, MO
Meyers, Robert A. Mahwah, NJ
Meyers, Robert D. Ventura, CA
Meyers, Robert D., Sr. Lafayette, LA
Meyers, Robert David Memphis, TN
Meyers, Robert F. Hudson, NY
Meyers, Robert G. Tacoma, WA
Meyers, Robert J. House of Representatives, Committee Legal Personnel, GV
Meyers, Robert J. Cincinnati, OH
Meyers, Robert L. Waco, TX
Meyers, Robert L., III Dallas, TX
Meyers, Robert M. East Hartford, CT
Meyers, Robert S., Law Offices of Bayside, NY
Meyers, Robert W. St. Louis, MO
Meyers, Ron, & Associates Brookline, MA
Meyers, Rosemary Casey St. Louis, MO
Meyers, Rufus Waldo, Jr. McLean, VA
Meyers, Sandra M. Berkeley, CA
Meyers, Sara Johnson Weston, MA
Meyers, Schuster & Pitcher, P.C. Elgin, IL
Meyers, Scott A. Chicago, IL
Meyers, Shawn D. Mercersburg, PA
Meyers, Stacey A. St. Louis, MO
Meyers, Stephanie S. Mineola, NY
Meyers, Stephen J. Philadelphia, PA
Meyers, Stephen M. Frederick, MD
Meyers, Stephen Z. New York, NY
Meyers, Steven D. New Haven, CT
Meyers, Steven M. Miami, FL
Meyers, Steven M., P.A. Miami, FL
Meyers, Steven R. San Leandro, CA
Stockton, CA
Meyers, Stuart Atlanta, GA
Meyers, Stuart D. Los Angeles, CA
Meyers, Stuart D. Longmeadow, MA
Meyers, Susan Gell Grand Rapids, MI
Meyers, Suzanne Loseke Kansas City, MO
Meyers & Taber, P.C. Phoenix, AZ
Meyers, Ted August Elgin, IL
Meyers, Tedson J. Washington, DC
Meyers, Terri Miami, FL
Meyers Tersigni Feldman & Gray New York, NY
Meyers, Thomas A., III Denver, CO
Meyers, Thomas C. Boston, MA
Meyers, Thomas E. Tampa, FL
Meyers, Todd C. Atlanta, GA
Meyers, Valerie L. Mountainside, NJ
Meyers, Valerie L. New York, NY
Meyers, Veryl N. Grand Rapids, MI
Meyers, Victor M. Hudson, NY
Poughkeepsie, NY
Meyers & Wallingford Bellevue, OH
Meyers, Walter D. Southfield, MI
Meyers, Warrin C. Plymouth Meeting, PA
Meyers, William Buddy Chicago, IL
Meyers, William Buddy, & Associates, Ltd. Chicago, IL
Meyers, William C. Chicago, IL
Meyers, William J. Sedona, AZ
Meyers, William M. New Orleans, LA
Meyers, William S. McLean, VA
Meyers, William V. Annapolis, MD
Riverdale, MD
Meyers, Young, Grove & Thomas, P.A. Hagerstown, MD
Meyer-Scirri, Pamela Buffalo, NY
Meyers-Harvey, Nancy J. San Antonio, TX
Meyer-Shipp, Michele C. Somerset, NJ
Meyerson, Alfred M. Houston, TX
Meyerson, Amy Lin Atlanta, GA
Meyerson, Arthur G. Coral Springs, FL
Meyerson, Bruce E. Phoenix, AZ
Meyerson, Bruce P. New York, NY
Meyerson, Craig A. Albany, NY
Meyerson, David Cleveland, OH
Meyerson, David L. Cleveland, OH
Meyerson, Edward P. Birmingham, AL
Meyerson, Elizabeth M. New York, NY
Meyerson & Fishbein Cherry Hill, NJ
Philadelphia, PA

Meyerson, Gerald L. Charleston, SC
Meyerson, Harold New York, NY
Meyerson, Harold I. New York, NY
Meyerson, Hilary Seattle, WA
Meyerson, Howard L. New York, NY
Meyerson, Ivan D. San Francisco, CA
Meyerson, Jack A. Philadelphia, PA
Meyerson, Laura A. Los Angeles, CA
Meyerson, Laurence Miami, FL
Meyerson Law Office Omaha, NE
Meyerson, Lawrence A. Detroit, MI
Meyerson, Lawrence C. Los Angeles, CA
Meyerson, Lawrence N. Oakland, NJ
Meyerson, Lee New York, NY
Meyerson, Leonard Jersey City, NJ
Millburn, NJ
Meyerson, Mark Eric Beverly Hills, CA
Meyerson, Marvin I. Franklin Square, NY
Meyerson, Michael I. Albany, NY
Meyerson, Murray S. Miami, FL
Meyerson, Pamela McLean Oak Park, IL
Meyerson & Ramos New York, NY
Meyerson, Richard A. Bronx, NY
Meyerson, Robert A. Rockville Centre, NY
Meyerson, Roberta A. Delray Beach, FL
Meyerson, Scott A. Omaha, NE
Meyerson, Stanley P. Atlanta, GA
Meyerson, Tami, Law Office of Garden City, NY
Meyerson, Tami, Law Office of New York, NY
Meyertons, Eric B. Austin, TX
Meyertons, Karl R. South River, NJ
Meyer Vollman, Jill Cincinnati, OH
Meyer von Bremen, Michael S. Albany, GA
Meyhardie, E. Jane Washington, DC
Meyka, Judith I. Englewood, CO
Meylan, Robert L. Santa Monica, CA
Meyland, A. L. Greensboro, NC
Meyland, Sarah J. Massapequa, NY
Meyler, John J. New York, NY
Meyler, Ruth P. San Francisco, CA
Meymarian, Sharon L. Santa Monica, CA
Meynardie, Jane Wallace Jackson, MS
Meynardie, John A. Jackson, MS
Meynardie, Robert A. Charlotte, NC
Raleigh, NC
Meyner and Landis Jersey City, NJ
Newark, NJ
Paterson, NJ
Meynier, Maurice J., IV Houston, TX
Meyr, Gerald L. Jefferson City, MO
Meyrelles, Joseph A., III Glendale, CA
Meyrich, Steven Boulder, CO
Meyrich, Steven Denver, CO
Meyrowitz, David H. New York, NY
Meyrowitz, Elliott L. Philadelphia, PA
Meyrowitz, Elliott L., P.C. Philadelphia, PA
Meyrowitz, Martin L., (P.C.) Washington, DC
Meyrowitz, Paul New York, NY
Meysenburg, Corinne M. Philadelphia, PA
Meysing, Leo S., (P.C.) Portland, OR
Meystre, Douglas Q. Worcester, MA
Meythaler, Luther Charles Houston, TX
Meythaler, Ward A. Tampa, FL
Meytina, Anna New York, NY
Meza, Amalia L. San Diego, CA
Meza, Daniel Garcia La Puente, CA
Meza, Florence A. San Francisco, CA
Meza, James, III New Orleans, LA
Meza, Matthew S. Los Angeles, CA
New York, NY
Meza, Michael S. Santa Ana, CA
Meza, Peter J. Colorado Springs, CO
Meza, Ricardo Chicago, IL
Meza, Robert E. Chicago, IL
Meza, Scott Reston, VA
Mezacapa & O'Brien, The Law Firm of Cleveland, OH
Mezacapa, Victor A. Cleveland, OH
Meza-Dombkowski, Elvira D. Department of the Army, Army Materiel Command, GV
Mezan, Richard S. New York, NY
Mezan, Stolzberg and Schwartzman, P.C. New York, NY
Mezer, Harry C. Boston, MA
Mezer, Harry C., P.C. Boston, MA
Mezer, Steven H. Clearwater, FL
Mezer, Steven H., P.A. Clearwater, FL
Mezetti, Robert L., II San Jose, CA
Mezey, Frederick C. Freehold, NJ
Mezey, Jacqueline A. Princeton, NJ
Mezey, Laura Kenilworth, NJ
Mezey & Mezey, A Professional Corporation Freehold, NJ
New Brunswick, NJ
Mezey, Naomi Jewel Washington, DC
Mezger, Muly & Yateman Glen Burnie, MD
Mezger-Lashly, Gabriele Ventura, CA
Mezher, Kathleen, & Associates Cincinnati, OH
Mezias, Donna M. San Francisco, CA
Mezibov, Marc D. Cincinnati, OH
Mezines, Basil J. Washington, DC
Mezines, Joan D. Washington, DC
Mezny, Alexander J. Rockford, IL
Mezoff, Arieh Albany, NY
Mezrahi, Joseph I. Brooklyn, NY
Mezrano, Louis A. Birmingham, AL
Mezrich, Jonathan Lee Boston, MA
Mezrow, Steven M. Haddonfield, NJ
Philadelphia, PA

Mezrow, Steven M., & Associates, P.C. Haddonfield, NJ
Philadelphia, PA
Mezvinsky, Edward M. Narberth, PA
Mezvinsky, Edward M. Philadelphia, PA
Mezvinsky, James A. Davenport, IA
Mezyk, Jill R. Philadelphia, PA
Mezzacappa, Ann L. Santa Ana, CA
Mezzacappa, John C. New York, NY
Mezzacappa, Joseph A. Morristown, NJ
Mezzacappa, Michael M. New York, NY
Mezzacappa, Michael P. White Plains, NY
Mezzacca, Joseph, Jr. Madison, NJ
Mezzanotte, Albert J., Jr. Baltimore, MD
Columbia, MD
Mezzanotte, James A. Charlotte, NC
Mezzanotte, John C. Milwaukee, WI
Mezzanotte, John F. Wallingford, CT
Mezzanotte, John J. Orange, CT
Mezzanotte, John J., Jr. Media, PA
Mezzanotte, Joseph J. Baltimore, MD
Mezzanotte, Katherine M. Philadelphia, PA
Mezzanotte, Mary Love Timonium, MD
Mezzaroba, Albert A. Philadelphia, PA
Mezzetta, Marc D. Sonoma, CA
Mezzetti, Leon J., Jr. Fremont, CA
Mezzetti, Lisa M. Washington, DC
Mezzetti, Robert L. San Jose, CA
Mezzina, Mary Jean Long Island City, NY
Mezzomo, William S. Springfield, NJ
Mezzullo, Louis A. Richmond, VA
Mezzullo & McCandlish, A Professional Corporation Washington, DC
Raleigh, NC
Norfolk, VA
Richmond, VA
Mezzy, Gary Jenkintown, PA
Mezzy, Randi Faith Waterbury, CT
Mgbeke, Ikechukwu S. Beverly Hills, CA
M'Guinness, Thomas A. San Francisco, CA
Mhoon, Ezekiel O. Chicago, IL
Mhoon, Michelle M. Little Rock, AR
Mian, Lubna A. New York, NY
Miani, Nicole Eugene, OR
Miano, Andrea S. Washington, DC
Miano, Anne M. Washington, DC
Miano, Bert J. Birmingham, AL
Miano, Frederick J. Westbrook, CT
Miano, Paula L. Houston, TX
Miano, Rosemary Milton Piscataway, NJ
Miano, Steven T. Bala Cynwyd, PA
Miano, Thomas P. Hartford, CT
Miao, Emily Chicago, IL
Miao, Kenneth New York, NY
Miarecki, Edmund A. Department of Defense, Defense Legal Services Agency, GV
Miarecki, Greg J. Chicago, IL
Miars, Mark J. Wilmington, OH
Miaskoff, Carol R. Equal Employment Opportunity Commission, Office of Legal Counsel, GV
Miazga, Mark J. Fagan, MN
Micale, Anthony E. Dearborn, MI
Micale, Frank J. Port St. Lucie, FL
Micale, Frederick J. Syracuse, NY
Micale & Rivera, LLP Syracuse, NY
Micali, James M. Greenville, SC
Micali, Thomas A. Winnetka, IL
Micalizio, Gina Atlanta, GA
Micallef, Joseph A. Washington, DC
Micallef, Joseph S. St. Paul, MN
Micallef, Joseph S., P.A. St. Paul, MN
Micallef, Lisa R. St. Paul, MN
Micallef, Margaret A. New York, NY
Mican, Stephen George Chicago, IL
Micare, Joseph J. Mobile, AL
Micarelli, Carl J. New York, NY
Micas, Steven L. Chesterfield, VA
Micca, Louis J. Rochester, NY
Micchia, Cristina G. Boston, MA
Micci, Eugene D. Derby, CT
Micci, Robert J. Chelmsford, MA
Micciche, Daniel J., (P.C.) Dallas, TX
Miccio, G. Kristian Bronx, NY
Miccio, Ralph P. Latham, NY
Miccioli, Mark Brentwood, TN
Micek, Andrew M. New Rochelle, NY
Micek, Patricia G. White Plains, NY
Micek, Terrance D. Golden, CO
Miceli, David F. Carrollton, GA
Miceli, Donald F. Roseland, NJ
Miceli, Frank S. Lock Haven, PA
Miceli, Frederick D. Caldwell, NJ
Miceli, Jeffrey B. Marlton, NJ
Philadelphia, PA
Miceli, Joline Tampa, FL
Miceli, Lawrence G. Pompano Beach, FL
Miceli, Lawrence R., Jr. Wilmington, MA
Miceli, Roberto S. Chicago, IL
Miceli, Samuel A., Jr. New Orleans, LA
Miceli, Suzanne J. Carrollton, GA
Miceli, Victor L. Riverside, CA
Miceli, William A. Chicago, IL
Micevski, Gordana Rochester, NY
Mich, Robert A., Jr. Madison, WI
Micha, Emil T., III New York, NY
Michael, Amy Philadelphia, PA
Michael, Ann Los Angeles, CA
Michael, Bayard H. Milwaukee, WI
Michael, Bernard J. New York, NY
Michael, Bess Johnson Treasury Department, Financial Crimes Enforcement Network, GV
Michael Best & Friedrich (Illinois) Chicago, IL

Michael Best & Friedrich LLP
Madison, WI
Manitowoc, WI
Milwaukee, WI
Michael & Cammack .... Stockton, CA
Michael, Chad R. .... Chicago, IL
Michael, Charles J. .... Houston, TX
Michael, Charles J., P.C. .... Houston, TX
Michael, Charles K. .... Logansport, IN
Michael, Christina Katris .... Novato, CA
Michael, Curtis L. .... Secaucus, NJ
Michael, Dale R. .... Culver City, CA
Michael, David L. .... Denver, CO
Michael, David N. .... Chicago, IL
Michael, Deidre E. .... New York, NY
Michael, Dinah J. .... Murfreesboro, TN
Michael, Douglas C. .... Lexington, KY
Michael, Edward L. .... North Chicago, IL
Michael, Elaine S. .... League City, TX
Michael, Floyd D. .... Portage, IN
Michael, G. Gregory .... Oregon, OH
Michael, G. Wythe, Jr. .... Richmond, VA
Michael, Gary G. .... Hackensack, NJ
Michael, Gary R. .... Danbury, CT
Michael, Geoffrey P. .... Redondo Beach, CA
Michael, Gregg D. .... Pittsburgh, PA
Michael, Gregory E. .... Merrimack, NH
Michael, Gregory E., Professional Association .... Merrimack, NH
Michael, Guy S. .... Atlantic City, NJ
Michael, H. Perry .... Atlanta, GA
Michael, Helen Katherine
Washington, DC
Michael, Howard S. .... Chicago, IL
Michael, Issa J. .... San Francisco, CA
Michael, Ivan A. .... New York, NY
Michael, J. Anthony, III .... Fort Worth, TX
Michael, James .... San Francisco, CA
Michael, James A. .... Salinas, CA
Michael, James David .... Decatur, GA
Michael, James E. .... Oxford, OH
Michael, James H., Jr. .... Roanoke, VA
Michael, James R. .... Mount Pleasant, PA
Michael, Jas. H. .... Minneapolis, MN
Michael, Jay E. .... Columbus, OH
Michael, Jeanette Ann .... Washington, DC
Michael, Jeffrey A. .... Indianapolis, IN
Michael, Jeffrey D. .... Badin, NC
Michael, Jeffrey E. .... Chicago, IL
Michael, Jeffrey L. .... Bel Air, MD
Michael, Joel T. .... St. Paul, MN
Michael, John .... Altamonte Springs, FL
Michael, John G. .... Fresno, CA
Michael, John J. .... Pittsburgh, PA
Michael, John R. .... Charlevoix, MI
Michael, John W. .... Enid, OK
Michael, Jonathan W. .... Chicago, IL
Michael, Jordan Bradley .... Waltham, MA
Michael, Joseph D. .... Lodi, CA
Michael, Joseph E., Jr. .... Durham, NH
Michael, Joseph S. .... Boonsboro, MD
Michael, Kathryn Ann .... Akron, OH
Michael, Kemp A. .... Mount Holly, NC
Michael, Kenneth .... Treasury Department, Internal Revenue Service, GV
Michael, Kenneth R. .... Winston-Salem, NC
Michael & Kupec .... Clarksburg, WV
Michael, LeRoy, Jr. .... Phoenix, AZ
Michael, Leslie, & Associates .... Chicago, IL
Michael, Leslie W. .... Chicago, IL
Michael, Lewis R. .... Melrose, FL
Michael, Lisa Goodwin .... Los Angeles, CA
Michael, M. Blane .... Charleston, WV
Michael, M. Kim .... Athens, GA
Michael, M. Sue .... Indianapolis, IN
Michael, Marc N. .... Fall River, MA
Michael, Marc Zaki .... Washington, DC
Michael, Mark A. .... Charlotte, NC
Michael, Mark D. .... Santa Clara, CA
Michael, Martin H. .... La Verne, CA
Michael, Martin P. .... New York, NY
Michael, Mervyn D. .... Decatur, AL
Michael & Michael .... Sweetwater, TN
Michael, Michael L. .... Boston, MA
Michael, Musette A., (Ms.) .... Lansing, MI
Michael, Nelson M. .... Keyser, WV
Michael, Nicholas G. .... Newtown, PA
Michael, Nicholas J. .... Stewart Manor, NY
Michael, Patrick .... Louisville, KY
Michael, Patrick T. .... San Francisco, CA
Michael, Paul T. .... Department of Energy, Office of the General Counsel, GV
Michael, Peter K. .... Cheyenne, WY
Michael, Peter Z. .... San Francisco, CA
Michael, Philip R. .... Bronx, NY
Michael, Rebecca .... San Diego, CA
Michael, Rebecca J. .... Washington, DC
Michael, Richard A. .... Chicago, IL
Michael, Richard D. .... Harrisburg, PA
Michael, Robert Anthony .... Dallas, TX
Michael, Robert E. .... New York, NY
Michael, Robert F., Jr. .... St. Petersburg, FL
Michael, Robert J. .... Rochester, NY
Michael, Robert R. .... Rockville, MD
Michael, Robert S. .... Iowa City, IA
Michael, Robin .... Department of Justice, Environment and Natural Resources Division, GV
Michael, Ronald D. .... Booneville, MS
Michael, Sally E. .... Boston, MA
Michael, Sara C. .... Jefferson City, MO
Michael, Stanley J., III .... Oakland, CA
Michael, Stephen J. .... Huntington, IN
Michael & Stephenson .... Logansport, IN
Michael, Steven A. .... Vienna, VA
Michael, Steven D. .... Kitty Hawk, NC
Michael, Steven P. .... Everett, WA
Michael, Suzanne Kelly .... Seattle, WA
Michael, Terrence L. .... Tulsa, OK
Michael, Thomas J. .... Pittsburgh, PA
Michael, Thomas P. .... Columbus, OH
Michael, Thomas R. .... Clarksburg, WV
Michael, Thomas W. .... Marion, IN
Michael, Toby .... Milan, NM
Michael, Van R. .... Sweetwater, TN
Michael, W. Smith, Jr. .... Tucson, AZ
Michael, Wendy C. .... New York, NY
Michael, William H. .... Modesto, CA
Michaeles, Michael James .... Worcester, MA
Michaelides, Denise .... Las Vegas, NV
Michaelides, Phillip G. .... Fresno, CA
Michaelis, Brian L. .... Boston, MA
Michaelis, Cheri E. .... San Francisco, CA
Michaelis, Gunther R. .... Metairie, LA
Michaelis, James I. .... Westlake Village, CA
Michaelis, Julie Ann .... San Diego, CA
Michaelis, Julie L. .... Indianapolis, IN
Michaelis, Kathryn .... Chicago, IL
Michaelis, Matthew J. .... Passaic, NJ
Michaelis, Montanari & Johnson, A Professional Law Corporation
Los Angeles, CA
Westlake Village, CA
Michaelis, Robert C. .... Baldwin, NY
Michaelis, William M.
Huntingdon Valley, PA
Michaelree, Jack M. .... Effingham, IL
Michaels, Adam B. .... Boston, MA
Michaels, Alan T. .... Providence, RI
Michaels, Andrew J. .... Akron, OH
Michaels, Andrew J. .... Wadsworth, OH
Michaels, Anthony .... New York, NY
Michaels, Barbara A. .... Waukesha, WI
Michaels, Beverly A. .... Syracuse, NY
Michaels & Bonner, P.C. .... Washington, DC
Michaels, Brian E. .... San Diego, CA
Michaels, Burton M. .... Tallahassee, FL
Michaels, C. William .... Baltimore, MD
Michaels, Carol A. .... Orlando, FL
Michaels, Charles G. .... Denver, CO
Michaels, Charles G., P.C. .... Denver, CO
Michaels, Christian C. .... Little Rock, AR
Michaels, Christopher A. .... Ithaca, NY
Michaels, Connie L. .... Los Angeles, CA
Michaels, Daniel T. .... Fort Collins, CO
Michaels, David K. .... Palo Alto, CA
Michaels, David Seth .... Spencertown, NY
Michaels, Deborah D. .... Gillette, WY
Michaels, Dennis D. .... Nyack, NY
Michaels, Edward A. .... Syracuse, NY
Michaels, Elizabeth A. .... Tulsa, OK
Michaels, Ellen R. .... San Diego, CA
Michaels, Eric Andrew
Bloomfield Hills, MI
Michaels, Eric J. .... Florham Park, NJ
Michaels, Erica .... Reno, NV
Michaels, Franklin .... Rochester, MN
Michaels, Franklin, Jr., Law Offices of
Los Angeles, CA
Michaels, Gary D.
Federal Communications Commission, Wireless Telecommunications Bureau, GV
Michaels, George .... Boston, MA
Michaels, George M. .... Auburn, NY
Michaels, Gloria L. .... San Diego, CA
Michaels, Harold .... New York, NY
Michaels, Harry Lewis .... Tallahassee, FL
Michaels, J. David .... Birmingham, AL
Michaels, James A.
Board of Governors Of The Federal Reserve System, Division of Consumer and Community Affairs, GV
Michaels, Jan M. .... Chicago, IL
Michaels, Jane .... Denver, CO
Michaels, Janice M. .... Los Angeles, CA
Las Vegas, NV
Michaels, Jennifer .... Highland Park, NJ
Michaels, Jeremy D. .... Gillette, WY
Michaels, Joel L. .... Washington, DC
Michaels, John A. .... Raleigh, NC
Michaels, John F. .... Overland Park, KS
Michaels, Jonathan Ambrose .... Irvine, CA
Michaels, Jonathan M. .... Seattle, WA
Michaels, Jones, Martin, Parris & Tessener Law Offices, PLLC .... Cary, NC
Chapel Hill, NC
Charlotte, NC
Durham, NC
Raleigh, NC
Research Triangle Park, NC
Wilmington, NC
Michaels, Joseph D. .... Wyandotte, MI
Michaels, Joseph, IV .... New York, NY
Michaels, Kristin Edell .... Chicago, IL
Michaels, Laura Freeman .... Denver, CO
Michaels, Lawrence A., (A Professional Corporation) .... Los Angeles, CA
Michaels, Lee S. .... Auburn, NY
Michaels, Linda M. .... Tampa, FL
Michaels, Louis P. .... Washington, DC
Michaels, Marcia M. .... Trenton, NJ
Michaels, Margaret .... Albany, CA
Michaels, Mark Alpiner
Yorktown Heights, NY
Michaels, Marnin J. .... Buffalo, NY
Michaels, Martha A. .... St. Louis, MO
Michaels, Martin M. .... Syracuse, NY
Michaels, Marvin D. .... Miami, FL
Michaels and Michaels .... Syracuse, NY
Michaels & Michaels, A Partnership Randall T. Cox, P.C. .... Gillette, WY
Michaels, Michelle S. L. .... Los Angeles, CA
Michaels, Norman C. .... Springfield, MA
Michaels, Pamela A. .... Spring House, PA
Michaels, Patricia A. .... Wayne, NJ
Michaels, Patrick G. .... Fort Wayne, IN
Michaels, Patrick J. .... Gaylord, MI
Michaels, Paul J. .... Raleigh, NC
Michaels, Pete S. .... Boston, MA
Michaels, Peter W. .... San Francisco, CA
Michaels, Philip J. .... New York, NY
Michaels, Regina Victoria .... Bethesda, MD
Michaels, Richard B. .... Chicago, IL
Michaels, Richard E. .... Chicago, IL
Michaels, Robert A. .... Des Moines, IA
Michaels, Robert L. .... Tacoma, WA
Michaels, Robert S. .... Chicago, IL
Michaels, Robert Seth .... New York, NY
Michaels, Rudolf H. .... Sacramento, CA
Michaels, Sandra Louise .... Atlanta, GA
Michaels, Sharon L. .... Houston, TX
Michaels, Sheldon .... San Francisco, CA
Michaels, Sheri .... Fort Lee, NJ
Michaels & Smolak, P.C. .... Auburn, NY
Michaels, Stanley .... Treasury Department, Internal Revenue Service, GV
Michaels, Stephen G. .... West Roxbury, MA
Michaels, Steven S. .... New York, NY
Michaels, Steven Scott .... Honolulu, HI
Michaels, Theodore P. .... Phoenixville, PA
Michaels, Thomas O. .... Dunedin, FL
Michaels, Thomas P. .... Chicago, IL
Michaels, Wayne H. .... Rolling Meadows, IL
Michaels, William P. .... Akron, OH
Michaelsen, Alfred L. .... Corning, NY
Michaelsen, Howard C., Jr. .... Chicago, IL
Michaelsen, Howard K. .... Spokane, WA
Michaelsen, Mix & Rodrigues, L.L.C.
Spokane, WA
Michaelson, Alvin S., Law Offices of
Los Angeles, CA
Michaelson, Arthur M. .... New York, NY
Michaelson, Barry S. .... Santa Ana, CA
Michaelson, Benjamin, Jr. .... Annapolis, MD
Michaelson, Benjamin, Jr., P.A.
Annapolis, MD
Michaelson, Brian L. .... Sioux City, IA
Michaelson, David J. .... Los Angeles, CA
Michaelson, David M. .... Highland Park, IL
Michaelson, Franklyn S. .... Santa Barbara, CA
Michaelson, Grant P. .... Los Angeles, CA
Michaelson, Jay L. .... Santa Barbara, CA
Michaelson, Jay Matthew .... New York, NY
Michaelson, Jeffrey S. .... Providence, RI
Michaelson, Jennifer J. .... Kew Gardens, NY
Michaelson, John O. .... East Greenbush, NY
Michaelson, Jon .... San Jose, CA
Michaelson, Julius C. .... Providence, RI
Michaelson, Kenneth S. .... New York, NY
Michaelson, Leonard .... Providence, RI
Michaelson, Linda Giunta
Los Angeles, CA
Michaelson, Lloyd J. .... Westlake Village, CA
Michaelson, Martin .... Washington, DC
Michaelson, Melvin .... New York, NY
Michaelson, Michael Gary
Washington, DC
Michaelson, Michaelson & Zurier
Providence, RI
Michaelson, Paul R. .... Las Vegas, NV
Michaelson, Peter F. .... Westcliffe, CO
Michaelson, Peter L. .... Red Bank, NJ
Michaelson, Richard F. .... Philadelphia, PA
Michaelson, Richard M. .... New York, NY
Michaelson, Robert L. .... Beacon, NY
Michaelson, Robert N. .... New York, NY
Michaelson, Ronald M. .... Minneapolis, MN
Michaelson, Sherryl Elise
Los Angeles, CA
Michaelson, Shirley M. .... Chicago, IL
Michaelson, Steven .... Fort Lauderdale, FL
Michaelson, Susi & Michaelson
Santa Barbara, CA
Michaelson, Terry .... Nampa, ID
Michaelson & Wallace .... Ventura, CA
Red Bank, NJ
Michaelson, Walter .... Harrison, NJ
Michael-Ziereis, Donna M.
Atlantic City, NJ
Michail, Maureen M. .... Los Angeles, CA
Michailoff, Christopher J. .... Weehawken, NJ
Michak, George A. .... Harrisburg, PA
Michal, James R. .... Washington, DC
Baltimore, MD
Rockville, MD
Michal, Jon A. .... Chicago, IL
Michal, Karen A. .... Rockville Centre, NY
Michal, Mary H. .... Madison, WI
Michal, Richard W. .... Chicago, IL
Michal, Richard W., P.C. .... Chicago, IL
Michalak, Donald H. .... Fredonia, NY
Michalak, Edmund C. .... Montvale, NJ
Michalak, Edward F. .... Chicago, IL
Michalak, James L. .... Houston, TX
Michalak, LaVerne F. .... Independence, WI
Michalak, Richd. F. .... Toledo, OH
Michalak, Robert A. .... Chicago, IL
Michalak, Robert W. .... Buffalo, NY
Michalak, William S. .... Tulsa, OK
Michalczyk, Mildred J. .... Farmingdale, NY
Michalczyk, Richard M. .... Metairie, LA
Michalec, Daniel J. .... Cleveland, OH
Michalec, Ronald J. .... Albany, NY
Michalec, Scott L. .... Peoria, IL
Michalek, Charles A. .... Las Vegas, NV
Michalek, Jane L. .... Lackawanna, NY
Michalek, Paul M. .... Lackawanna, NY
Michalek, Schnippert & Associates
Pittsburgh, PA
Michalek, Steven A. .... Denver, CO
Michalek, Thomas G. .... Pittsburgh, PA
Michales, Marilyn J. .... Minneapolis, MN
Michaletz, Russell V. .... Minneapolis, MN
Michalik, James E. .... Berlin, NH
Michalik, Michelle A. .... Chicago, IL
Michalik, Paul A. .... Chicago, IL
Michalik, Robert A. .... New Britain, CT
Michalk, Beatty & Alcozer, PLLC
Killeen, TX
Michalk, Craig S. .... Fort Worth, TX
Michalk, Glenn W. .... Killeen, TX
Michalopoulos, Pantelis .... Washington, DC
Michalos, Peter C. .... New York, NY
Orangeburg, NY
Michalove, Scott H. .... Atlanta, GA
Michalovsky, Joel .... Maspeth, NY
Michalowski, Joseph J. .... Parsippany, NJ
Michalowski, Mark C. .... Boston, MA
Michals, Lauren M. .... San Francisco, CA
Michals, Thomas I. .... Cleveland, OH
Michals, Wahl, Silver & Leitner
Elizabeth, NJ
New Brunswick, NJ
Trenton, NJ
Jersey City, NJ
Newark, NJ
Woodbridge, NJ
Michals, William P. .... Woodbridge, NJ
Michalske, Michael A. .... Irvine, CA
Michalski, Brian F. .... Rochester, NY
Michalski, Daniel J.
National Labor Relations Board, Office of the General Counsel, GV
Michalski, David J. .... Cleveland, OH
Michalski, James W. .... Los Angeles, CA
Michalski, Jan K.
Department Of Health And Human Services, Social Security Administration, GV
Michalski, John L. .... West Seneca, NY
Michalski, Joseph B. .... Madison, WI
Michalski, Michael J. .... St. Cloud, MN
Michalski, Peter A. .... Anchorage, AK
Michalski, Raymond R. .... Lancaster, OH
Michalski, Rick .... Milwaukee, WI
Michalski, Robert E. .... Santa Rosa, CA
Michalski, Sharon A. .... Belle Mead, NJ
Michalski, Thomas R. .... Toledo, OH
Michalsky, Melissa Feldman .... Wayne, NJ
Michal-Smith, Susan
General Accounting Office, Office of the General Counsel, GV
Michalson, George D. .... Kansas City, MO
Michau, David R. .... Indianapolis, IN
Michaud, Bryan J. .... Peru, IN
Michaud, Buschmann, Fox, Ferrara & Mittelmark, P.A. .... Boca Raton, FL
Michaud, David C. .... Burlington, NJ
Michaud, David E. .... Spokane, WA
Michaud, Douglas W. .... Chicago, IL
Michaud, Elaine M. .... Manchester, NH
Michaud, Frederick C. .... San Jose, CA
Michaud, Frederick G., Jr.
Alexandria, VA
Michaud, Gerald L. .... Derby, KS
Michaud, Hillary J. .... Baltimore, MD
Michaud & Hoshiyama .... San Francisco, CA
Michaud, James R. .... Sandpoint, ID
Michaud, John R.
Environmental Protection Agency, Office of the General Counsel, GV
Michaud, Joseph L. .... New Bedford, MA
Michaud, Kimberly Ruth .... Bedford, VA
Michaud, Laurie Ashley .... Davis, CA
Michaud, Leo C. .... Seagoville, TX
Michaud, Lewellyn R. .... Bangor, ME
Michaud, Lori A., Law Offices of
West Orange, NJ
New York, NY
New York, NY
Michaud, Lucy .... Farmington, CT
Michaud, Matthew H. .... Atlanta, GA
Michaud, Michael C. .... Baltimore, MD
Michaud, Michel P. .... Dallas, TX
Michaud, Michelle Marie .... Portland, OR
Michaud, Nancy Heckard .... Miamisburg, OH
Michaud, Paul W. .... Denver, CO
Michaud, Peter P. .... Portland, ME
Michaud, Peter V. .... Minneapolis, MN
Michaud, Richard B. .... Boston, MA
Michaud, Richard R. .... Hartford, CT
Michaud, Robert R. .... Fort Kent, ME
Michaud, Robert R., P.A. .... Fort Kent, ME
Michaud, Saralee Smith .... Mount Holly, NJ
Michaud, Scott H. .... Boca Raton, FL
Michaud & Solari, LLC .... Farmington, CT
Michaud, Steven .... New York, NY
Michaud, Suzanne R. .... Boston, MA
Michaud, Thomas C. .... Detroit, MI
Michaud, Wilfrid J., Jr. .... Boston, MA
Michaud, William F. .... San Francisco, CA
Michaux, Denise A. .... Brooklyn, NY
Michaux, Eric C. .... Durham, NC
Michaux, H. M., Jr. .... Durham, NC
Michaux, Jill A. .... Topeka, KS
Michaux, Lisa D. .... Houston, TX
Michaux, Michael D. .... Minneapolis, MN
Michaux, Roy H., Jr. .... Charlotte, NC
Micheaels, John A. .... Phoenix, AZ
Micheau, Jack B. .... Aberdeen, WA
Micheel, Douglas E. .... Jefferson City, MO
Micheel, Stephanie M. .... Memphis, TN
Micheels, Barbara Ann .... Springfield, IL
Michel, Aaron E. .... Charlotte, NC
Michel, Alix C. .... Miami, FL
Michel, Allen L. .... Los Angeles, CA
Michel, Anthony R. .... Shaker Heights, OH
Michel, Antje .... San Francisco, CA
Michel, Arturo G. .... Houston, TX
Michel, Benjamin P. .... Morristown, NJ
Michel, Betsy S. .... Gladstone, NJ
Michel, Carol Loupe .... New Orleans, LA

Middlebrook, Kaiser & Popka, A Professional Corporation—Continued
Riverside, CA
San Bernardino, CA
Victorville, CA
Middlebrook, Krista Marie ....Portland, OR
Middlebrook, Mark T. ....Bal Harbour, FL
Middlebrook, Richard O. ....Bakersfield, CA
Middlebrook, S. Ancial ....San Angelo, TX
Middlebrook, Stephen B. ....Hartford, CT
Middlebrook, Stephen T.
Treasury Department, Financial Management Service, GV
Middlebrooks, Theresa W. ....Pasadena, CA
Middlebrooks, David J. ....Birmingham, AL
Middlebrooks, Donald M.
West Palm Beach, FL
Middlebrooks, Ed ....Fort Lauderdale, FL
Middlebrooks & Gray, P.A. ....Jackson, TN
Middlebrooks, J. Hugh ....Sarasota, FL
Middlebrooks, James C. ....Seattle, WA
Middlebrooks, James G. ....Charlotte, NC
Middlebrooks, Kimberly A.
Albuquerque, NM
Middlebrooks, Lilli Beiduk ....Media, PA
Middlebrooks, Mary Jo ....Jackson, TN
Middlebrooks, Melinda Dee
Parsippany, NJ
Middlebrooks & Middlebrooks, P.A.
Fort Lauderdale, FL
Middlebrooks & Shapiro, P.C.
Morristown, NJ
Parsippany, NJ
Middlebrooks, Sherwood C., III
Mobile, AL
Middlebrooks, Todd ......Fort Lauderdale, FL
Middleditch, Leigh B., Jr.
Charlottesville, VA
Middlehurst, Carl R. ....Palo Alto, CA
Middlekauff, Charles R.
San Francisco, CA
Middlekauff, Robt. M. ......West Bloomfield, MI
Middleman & Matour, A Professional Corporation ....Philadelphia, PA
Middleman, Maureen C. ....Pittsburgh, PA
Middleman, Ray F. ....Wexford, PA
Middleman, Sanford A. ....Pittsburgh, PA
Middleman, Stewart M. ....Philadelphia, PA
Middlemas, Davis Lawson ....Gadsden, AL
Middlemiss, John F., Jr. ....Bay Shore, NY
Middlemiss, Paul ....New York, NY
Middlen, Mark Henrik ....Worcester, MA
Middler, David M. ....Mountain View, CA
Sunnyvale, CA
Middlesworth, Charles, Jr. ....Linwood, NJ
Middleton, Alan S. ....Seattle, WA
Middleton, Bard G. ....Billings, MT
Middleton, Berry W. ....McGehee, AR
Middleton, Beth ....Columbia, SC
Middleton, Brett M. ....Los Angeles, CA
Middleton, Charles G., III ....Louisville, KY
Middleton, Charles I. ....Atlanta, GA
Middleton, Charles J. ....Santa Ana, CA
Middleton, Cheryl Huntz ....Seattle, WA
Middleton & Craver ....Rantoul, IL
Urbana, IL
Middleton, D. Tara ....Northport, AL
Middleton, David E. ....Lexington, KY
Middleton, David H. ....Federal Way, WA
Middleton, David H., & Associates, P.S.
Federal Way, WA
Middleton, Diane L. ....San Pedro, CA
Middleton, Donald R. ....Fountain Hills, AZ
Middleton, Douglas D. ....Marietta, GA
Middleton, Douglas D., P.C. ....Marietta, GA
Middleton, Edith A.
National Labor Relations Board, Office of Board Members, GV
Middleton, Elizabeth W. ....Alexandria, LA
Middleton, F. Faison, IV ....Atlanta, GA
Middleton, Grace ....Houston, TX
Middleton, H. Frank ....Rantoul, IL
Urbana, IL
Middleton, Harlow C. ....Mount Dora, FL
Middleton, J. Howard, Jr.
Falls Church, VA
Middleton, J. Lane, III ....Miami, FL
Middleton, Jack B. ....Manchester, NH
Middleton, Jacqueline L. ....Hoboken, NJ
Middleton, James B. ....Decatur, GA
Middleton, James Ogden, II
Alexandria, LA
Middleton, James W. .....Fort Walton Beach, FL
Middleton, James W. ....Jacksonville, FL
Middleton, James W., P.A.
Fort Walton Beach, FL
Middleton, Jayne L. ....Baton Rouge, LA
Middleton, Jeffrey Allen ....Alexandria, VA
Middleton, Jeffrey C. ....Centreville, MI
Middleton, Jennifer M. ....New York, NY
Middleton, John C. ....Covington, KY
Cincinnati, OH
Middleton, John D. ....Melrose, FL
Middleton, John H. ....Washington, DC
Middleton, John Howard, II
Washington, DC
Middleton, John J. ....Harrisburg, PA
Middleton, John R., Jr. ....New York, NY
Middleton, Keith B. ....Houston, TX
Middleton, Kennie Earl ....Fayette, MS
Middleton, Kerry L. ....Minneapolis, MN
Middleton, Laurie ....Louisville, KY
Middleton, Lawrence W. ....Nashville, TN
Middleton, Lelan S. ....Bowling Green, OH
Middleton, Linda G. ....Plano, TX
Middleton, Lorraine A. ....Los Angeles, CA
Middleton, Lyle D. ....Des Moines, IA
Middleton, M. Gail ....Lansing, MI

Middleton, Margaret E.K.
Washington, DC
Middleton, Margaret R., (Mrs.) ....Aurora, IL
Middleton, Mark M. ....Norcross, GA
Middleton, Mark M., P.C. ....Atlanta, GA
Norcross, GA
Middleton, Martha ....Oak Park, IL
Middleton, Mathis, Adams & Tate, P.C.
Atlanta, GA
Milledgeville, GA
Savannah, GA
Middleton, Maureen M. ....Atlanta, GA
Middleton, Michael A. ....Columbia, MO
Middleton, Michael T. ....Tempe, AZ
Middleton, Michael W. ....Bryan, TX
Middleton, Michael W., P.C. ....Bryan, TX
Middleton, Middleton & Dueringer
Gibson City, IL
Middleton, Patrick G. ....Seattle, WA
Middleton, Paul B. ....Oklahoma City, OK
Middleton, Peter C. ....Chicago, IL
Middleton, Peter T. ....Burlington, MA
Middleton, Philip A. ....Charleston, SC
Middleton, Phillip A. ....San Antonio, TX
Middleton & Prugh, P.A. ....Melrose, FL
Middleton, R. Collin ....Anchorage, AK
Middleton & Reutlinger, P.S.C.
Jeffersonville, IN
Louisville, KY
Middleton, Richard ....Detroit, MI
Middleton, Richard H., Jr. ....Atlanta, GA
Savannah, GA
Middleton, Rick L. ....Paw Paw, MI
Middleton, Robert E. ....Minneapolis, MN
Middleton, Robert F., (P.C.) ....Dallas, TX
Middleton, Robert J., Jr. ....Atlanta, GA
Middleton, Robert James (Jim)
Beaumont, TX
Middleton, Robert O. ....Chicago, IL
Middleton Roebke & Woessner
Bowling Green, OH
Middleton, Ronald N. ....Philadelphia, PA
Middleton, Rore M. ....Houston, TX
Middleton, Sabrina M. ....Brunswick, GA
Middleton, Sarah Collins ....Clinton, NJ
Middleton, Scott D. ....Bohemia, NY
Middleton & Shrull ....Burlington, MA
Middleton, Staten T. ....Bowling Green, OH
Middleton, Stephanie A. ....Philadelphia, PA
Middleton, Susan A. ....Costa Mesa, CA
Middleton, Thomas S. ....Bowling Green, OH
Middleton, Thomas T., Jr. ....Seattle, WA
Middleton & Timme, P.C. ......Anchorage, AK
Middleton, Timothy G. ....Anchorage, AK
Middleton, Tom W. ....Ephrata, WA
Middleton, Vernon P. ....Baton Rouge, LA
Middleton, Virginia Y. ....Fayetteville, AR
Middleton, W. B., Jr. ....Plaquemine, LA
Middleton, William J. ....Los Angeles, CA
Middleton, William J. ....Salt Lake City, UT
Middleton, William L., III ....Decatur, AL
Midei, Matt C. ....Cincinnati, OH
Midelis, James W. ....Fort Pierce, FL
Midey, Nicholas V. ....Seneca Falls, NY
Midey, Nicholas V., Jr. ....Seneca Falls, NY
Midey & Swinehart ....Seneca Falls, NY
Midgen, Philip M. ....Los Angeles, CA
Midgett, David F. ....Ocala, FL
Midgett, James C., Jr. ....Nashville, TN
Midgett, John T. ....Chicago, IL
Midgett, John T. ....Norfolk, VA
Midgett, John T. ....Virginia Beach, VA
Midgett, Raymond W., Jr.
Philadelphia, PA
Midgett, Roslyn ....New York, NY
Midgette, Nonnie F. ....Raleigh, NC
Midgley, David B. ....Chicago, IL
Midgley, Douglas M. ....Fort Myers, FL
Midgley, James W. ....El Monte, CA
Midgley, John B. ....Tacoma, WA
Midgley, Scott K. ....Phoenix, AZ
Midgley, Scott K., P.C. ....Phoenix, AZ
Midgley, Steve ....Mansfield, MA
Midgley, Steven B. ....Fort Worth, TX
Midgley, Timothy J. ....Los Angeles, CA
Midis, Panos S. ....Atlanta, GA
Midkiff, Charles F. ....Richmond, VA
Midkiff, David W. ....Quakertown, PA
Midkiff, Dawn ....Minneapolis, MN
Midkiff & Hiner, P.C. ....Chesterfield, VA
Richmond, VA
Midkiff, Ralph A. ....Houston, TX
Midkiff, Sandra C. ....Kansas City, MO
Midkiff, W Mark ....Fort Worth, TX
Midlam, Kevin W. ....San Diego, CA
Midlarsky, Jacalyn L. ......West Palm Beach, FL
Midlen, John H., Jr. ....Washington, DC
Midlen Law Center ....Washington, DC
Midler, Joseph M. ....White Plains, NY
Midler, Laurence H. ....Norwalk, CT
Midler, Reuben S. ....Norwalk, CT
Midler, Robert A. ....Washington, DC
Midlige, Michael F. ....Lebanon, NJ
Midlige, Suzanne Cocco ....Morristown, NJ
Midlo, Bennett A. ....Houston, TX
Midness, Sjur ....Minneapolis, MN
Midonick, Millard L. ....New York, NY
Midtbo, Barbara A. ....Vancouver, WA
Midtgard, Jon M. ....Bloomfield Hills, MI
Midthun, Morgan L. ....Wisconsin Rapids, WI
Midulla, Robin Greiwe ....Tampa, FL
Midura, Janna Miller ....Chicago, IL
Midura, Timothy S. ....Chicago, IL
Midvidy, David H. ....New York, NY
Midwall, Jonathan Mare ....Miami, FL
Midyett, Michael L. ....Keytesville, MO
Midyett, Susan ....Houston, TX
Midyett, Thomas E., Jr. ....Knoxville, TN

Midyette, William M., III ....Lakeland, FL
Miears, Steven R. ....Frisco, TX
Miech, Robert J. ....South Milwaukee, WI
Mieczkowski, Francis E., Jr.
Wilmington, DE
Mieczynski, T. Gregory
Oakbrook Terrace, IL
Miedaner, Randall M. ....Sheboygan, WI
Miede, Debbie L. ....Irvine, CA
Miede, Norman ....Fullerton, CA
Miedema, Karen S. ....Grand Haven, MI
Miedzianogora, Yves ....New York, NY
Miehe, Patrick K. ....Boston, MA
Miehls, Donald E. ....Medina, OH
Miel, C. Homer ....Stanton, MI
Miel, Charles H. ....Stanton, MI
Miel Miel & Perry ....Stanton, MI
Miela, Deborah L. ....Troy, MI
Mielak, Jason D. ....Columbus, NE
Miele, Angela Gottsche ....Atlanta, GA
Miele, Anthony D. ....Williamsport, PA
Miele, Anthony L. ....Washington, DC
Miele, Anthony M. ....New York, NY
Miele & Callahan ....Williamsport, PA
Miele, Charles D. ....Brooklyn, NY
Miele, Christina R. ....West Keansburg, NJ
Miele, Cooper, Spinrad & Kronberg
Millburn, NJ
Miele, David T. ....Providence, RI
Miele, Frank J. ....Parsippany, NJ
Miele, James M. ....Cheshire, CT
Miele, John A., III ....West Keansburg, NJ
Miele, John A., Jr. ....West Keansburg, NJ
Miele, John S. ....Cambridge, MA
Miele, Joseph P. ....Millburn, NJ
Miele, Joseph R. ....St. Petersburg, FL
Miele, Mark A. ....Westbury, NY
Miele & Miele ....West Keansburg, NJ
Miele, Philip R. ....Warren, OH
Miele, Robert M. ....Suffern, NY
Miele, Robert V.
United States Court Of Appeals For The Armed Forces, GV
Miele, Ronald W. ....Burbank, CA
Miele, Stefano M. ....Atlanta, GA
Miele, Wendy L. R. ....Huntington Beach, CA
Miele, William J. ....Harrisonburg, VA
Mielech, Anne Marie ....Covington, KY
Mielenhausen, Thomas C.
Minneapolis, MN
Mieling, Michael J. ....Lake Forest, IL
Mieliulis, Benjamin ....Appleton, WI
Mielke, Craig S. ....Aurora, IL
Mielke, David C. ....Albuquerque, NM
Mielke, Frederick C. ....Waukesha, WI
Mielke, Gregg ....Houston, TX
Mielke, Kenneth D. ....Knoxville, TN
Mielke, Lynn Leonhardt ....Easton, MD
Mielke, Steven P. ....Celina, OH
Mielke, Thomas J. ....Neenah, WI
Mielke, Wayne R. ....Wellsburg, WV
Miello, Dawn A. ....Wilmington, DE
Mielnicki, Daniel D. ....Miami, FL
West Palm Beach, FL
Mielnikowski, Susan A. ....Springfield, MA
Mielo, Patrick S. ....Farmingdale, NY
Mielock, Douglas A. ....Lansing, MI
Mielock, Gary K. ....Lansing, MI
Miely, Gregory J. ....Champaign, IL
Mielziner, Bruce L. ....Beachwood, OH
Miener, Barbara W. ....Seattle, WA
Miener, Roger J. ....Tacoma, WA
Mienk, Roy G. ....Gladwin, MI
Mier, Beth A. ....Detroit, MI
Mier, Greg R. ....Lafayette, LA
Mier, Leonard W. ....Livonia, MI
Mier, Roy S. ....Webster, MA
Miera, Alberto O., Jr. ....St. Paul, MN
Miera, Anthony M. ....Los Angeles, CA
Miercort, David B. ....Beverly Hills, CA
Mierendorf, David A. ....Escanaba, MI
Mierjeski, Edward ....Bend, OR
Mierke, Harvey O., Jr. ....Cleveland, OH
Mierl, Steven L. ....Austin, TX
Mierop, Stephen D. ....Houston, TX
Miers, Charles T. ....Houston, TX
Miers, Donna Lyn ....Snowflake, AZ
Miers, Gail E. ....New York, NY
Miers, Harriet E. ....Dallas, TX
Miers, James W. ....Englewood, CO
Miers, Sheppard F., Jr. ....Tulsa, OK
Miersma, Eric J. ....San Diego, CA
Miersma, James K. ....Seattle, WA
Mierswa, Thomas M., Jr. ....New York, NY
Miertschin, J. Robert, Jr. ....Hollywood, FL
Mierzejewski, Joseph S.
Bloomfield Hills, MI
Mierzewski, Michael B. ....Washington, DC
Mierzwa, Craig T. ....New York, NY
Mierzwa, Frederick S. ....Harvey, IL
Mierzwa, Kevin G. ....Southfield, MI
Mierzwa, Matthew J., Jr. ....Lake Worth, FL
Mierzwa, Michelle A. ....El Cajon, CA
Mierzwa, Nancy J. ....Utica, NY
Mierzwinski, Gregory E. ....Tampa, FL
Mies & Associates, P.C. ....Livonia, MI
Mies, James E. ....Livonia, MI
Mies, Lorene Lynn ....Santa Ana, CA
Mies, Thomas G. ....Livonia, MI
Miesen, Jonathan C. ....Minneapolis, MN
Miesfeld, Bart J. ....Chula Vista, CA
Miesfeld, Corinne Chase ....San Diego, CA
Mieske, Ernest S. ....Chico, CA
Mieskoski, Dennis J., Jr. ....San Diego, CA
Miesle, Gary E. ....Toledo, OH
Miesner, John Thomas ....Charleston, WV
Miesnieks, Andre K. ....Red Bank, NJ
Miesowitz, John J. ....Summit, NJ

Miessau, James A. ....Branford, CT
Miesse, Mark B. ....Memphis, TN
Miesse, Timothy S. ....Berea, OH
Miessner, Leslie G. ....Fresno, CA
Miester, Alvin C., III ....New Orleans, LA
Miester, Donald J., Jr. ....New Orleans, LA
Mieszala, Michael ....Albuquerque, NM
Mieszkuc, Daughtry & Scott, P.C.
Houston, TX
Mieszkuc, Marilyn ....Houston, TX
Mieth, Kurt A. ....Buffalo, NY
Miethke, Eric J. ....Sacramento, CA
San Francisco, CA
Mietlicki, James F. ....Buffalo, NY
Mietlicki, Vincent A. ....Wichita, KS
Miettinen, Richard M. ....Detroit, MI
Mietty, David R. ....Cleveland, OH
Mietus, Edmund R. ....Los Angeles, CA
Mietus, John R., Jr. ....Washington, DC
Mietus, Norbert J. ....Sacramento, CA
Mietzel, Ann M. ....El Cajon, CA
Mietzel, James J. ....El Cajon, CA
Mifflin, R. Mark ....Springfield, IL
Mifka, John F. ....Mount Laurel, NJ
Mifsud, James C. ....Fort Worth, TX
Mifsud, Kenneth ....Oakland, CA
Mifsud, Paul V. ....Elmsford, NY
Mifsud, Paul V., Jr. ....New York, NY
Migan, Michael James ....Anaheim, CA
Migas, Joseph J. ....Washington, DC
Migatz, Anne P. ....Media, PA
Migatz, Bruce W. ....Manhasset, NY
Migausky, Stephen J. ....Boston, MA
Migchelbrink, Paul D. ....Portland, OR
Migdail, Evan M. ....Washington, DC
Migdal, David ....New York, NY
Migdal, Ellen Barbara ....Fort Lauderdale, FL
Migdal, Harvey Jay ....Honolulu, HI
Migdal, Jean M. ....New York, NY
Migdal, Karen B. ....Kew Gardens, NY
Migdal, Lester C. ....New York, NY
Migdal, Michelle ....Boynton Beach, FL
Migdal & Migdal, P.A. ....Boynton Beach, FL
Migdal, Nelson F. ....Washington, DC
Migdal, Paul L. ....Los Angeles, CA
Migdal, Phillip M. ....Chicago, IL
Migdal, Pollack, Rosenkrantz & Migdal LLP
New York, NY
Migdal, Sheldon P. ....Chicago, IL
Migdal, Stanley B. ....Akron, OH
Migdal, Steven R. ....Annapolis, MD
Migdall, Allan M. ....Fort Lauderdale, FL
Migdal-Mack, Judith B. ....Boynton Beach, FL
Migdalof, Jessica K.
North Miami Beach, FL
Migdol, Jonathan L. ....Needham, MA
Migdon, Andrew H. ....New York, NY
Migdon, Michelle R. ....New York, NY
Migdon, Sidney A. ....New York, NY
Miggins, James E. ....Boca Raton, FL
Miggins, Janet L. ....Twinsburg, OH
Mighdoll, Preston ....West Palm Beach, FL
Mighell, Kenneth J. ....Dallas, TX
Mighell, Thomas L. ....Dallas, TX
Migit, Jeff D. ....Houston, TX
Miglani, Shabnam B. ....Des Moines, IA
Migliaccio, Anthony J., Jr. ....Purchase, NY
Migliaccio, Davide C.
Colorado Springs, CO
Migliaccio, Domenic J. ....Buffalo, NY
Migliaccio, Mark ....Philadelphia, PA
Migliaccio, Michael ....Philadelphia, PA
Migliaccio, Nick ....Bronx, NY
Migliaccio, Nicola ....Irvine, CA
Migliaccio, Richard C. ....Winter Park, FL
Migliaccio, Richard C., P.A.
Winter Park, FL
Migliaccio, Richard J. ....Purchase, NY
Migliaccio, Robert A. ....Providence, RI
Miglian, Robert M. ....San Jose, CA
Migliara, Alex J. ....Memphis, TN
Migliaro, Joanne ....Harvard, MA
Migliazza, Mary Rose ....Kenilworth, NJ
Miglicco, Anthony ....Houston, TX
Miglietta, Margaret R. ....Irvine, CA
Miglino, Michael P. ....New York, NY
Miglino, Nicholas J. ....New York, NY
Miglio, Terrence J. ....Detroit, MI
Miglionico, John H. ....Birmingham, AL
Miglionico, Nina ....Birmingham, AL
Miglionico & Rumore ....Birmingham, AL
Migliore, Alfonso J. ....Anaheim, CA
Migliore, Benjamin J. ....Scotia, NY
Migliore & Infranco ....Commack, NY
Migliore, John A. ....San Diego, CA
Migliore, Joseph M., Jr. ....Birmingham, MI
Migliore, Marcus C. ....Washington, DC
Migliore, Rudolph F. X. ....Commack, NY
Migliori, Donald A. ....Providence, RI
Migliori, Michael J. ....Haverhill, MA
Migliorino, Frank ....Little Ferry, NJ
Migliozzi, Joseph Andrew
Virginia Beach, VA
Miglore, Salvatore C. ....Wheaton, IL
Mignanelli, Anthony R. ....Providence, RI
Mignanelli & Associates, Ltd.
Providence, RI
Mignanelli, Robert Andrew
Chevy Chase, MD
Mignano, Stephen John ....Tarrytown, NY
Migneault, David J. ....Punta Gorda, FL
Mignella, Anthony J. ....Somerville, NJ
Mignella, Mark R. ....Phoenix, AZ
Mignella, Mark R., P.C. ....Phoenix, AZ
Mignella, Michael ....Phoenix, AZ
Mignella, Robert C. ....Roseland, NJ
Migner, J. Channing ....Marlborough, MA
Worcester, MA

Milberg Weiss Bershad Hynes & Lerach LLP—Continued

Boca Raton, FL
New York, NY
Milberger, Arthur J. ..... Bay City, TX
Milbery, Jack E. ..... Plantation, FL
Milbourn, Don L. ..... Mount Clemens, MI
Milbourn, Douglas R. ..... Columbus, NE
Milbourn, Elizabeth J. ..... Baltimore, MD
Milbourn, Fehringer, Kessler & Peetz, P.C.
Columbus, NE
Humphrey, NE
Newman Grove, NE
Milbourn, J. Brett ..... Kansas City, MO
Milbourne, Bernard B. ..... Accomac, VA
Milbourne, Walter R. ..... Philadelphia, PA
Milbrand, Dayna ..... Mount Clemens, MI
Milbrand, Dayna, Professional Corporation
Mount Clemens, MI
Milbrand, James P. ..... Buffalo, NY
Milbranth, Russell ..... Valparaiso, IN
Milbrath, Dennis H. ..... Cedarburg, WI
Milbrath, Elizabeth ..... Washington, DC
Milbrath, Stephen D. ..... Orlando, FL
Milbrodt, Jeremy David ..... Long Beach, CA
Milburn, Calvin V. ..... Odessa, TX
Milburn, Claude L. ..... Midland, TX
Milburn, Cullom F. ..... Odessa, TX
Milburn, Devereux ..... New York, NY
Milburn, DiLissa G. ..... Hopkinsville, KY
Milburn, Elisabeth F. ..... San Diego, CA
Milburn, Fabian F., Jr. ..... Washington, DC
Milburn, H. Ted ..... Signal Mountain, TN
Milburn, Joe R. ..... Lincolnwood, IL
Milburn, Kermit M. ..... Shawnee, OK
Milburn, Laird T. ..... Grand Junction, CO
Milburn, Monica A. ..... Tulsa, OK
Milburn, Nancy G. ..... New York, NY
Milburn, Nolen P., Jr. ..... Palmdale, CA
Milburn & Peterson, P.C. ..... Odessa, TX
Milburn, Sara E. ..... San Juan Capistrano, CA
Milbury, Lesley G. ..... Waukegan, IL
Milby, Dana Manweiler ..... Wichita, KS
Milby, Eric C. ..... Narberth, PA
Milby, Michael W. ..... Bardstown, KY
Milby, Mitchell S. ..... Dallas, TX
Milby, Robert L. ..... London, KY
Milby, Rosemary Taft ..... Cleveland, OH
Milby, Steven R. ..... Dayton, OH
Milcetic, Paul B. ..... Philadelphia, PA
Milch, Angela Lurie ..... New York, NY
Milch, Arthur H. ..... Cinnaminson, NJ
Milch, Charles E. ..... Buffalo, NY
Milch, James S., (A P.C.) ..... San Diego, CA
Milch, Leslie P. Michel ..... Woodmere, NY
Milch, Myron D. ..... Hackensack, NJ
Milch, Myron D., P.C. ..... Hackensack, NJ
Jersey City, NJ
Newark, NJ
Milch, Philip A. ..... Tonawanda, NY
Milch, Philip E. ..... Pittsburgh, PA
Milch, Randal S. ..... New York, NY
Milch, Steven Robert ..... Billings, MT
Milch, Stewart G. ..... Mineola, NY
New York, NY
Milch, Susan N. ..... Wayne, NJ
Milch, Thomas H. ..... Washington, DC
Milch & Wolfsheimer ..... San Diego, CA
Milchak, Joseph A. ..... Huntington Beach, CA
Milchan, Michael ..... New York, NY
Milchen, Joseph ..... San Diego, CA
Milchman, Howard J. ..... Coral Springs, FL
Milchman, Howard J., P.A.
Coral Springs, FL
Milchman, Scot Jay ..... St. Paul, MN
Milcic, Ellen P. ..... Pittsburgh, PA
Milcowitz, Leonard ..... Clearwater, FL
Milcsik, Laura L. ..... West Orange, NJ
Mild, William H., III ..... Trenton, NJ
Milde, Breck E. ..... Burlingame, CA
San Jose, CA
Milde, Hoffberg & Macklin, LLP
New York, NY
White Plains, NY
Milde, Karl F., Jr. ..... New York, NY
White Plains, NY
Mildenberg, Erich ..... Milwaukee, WI
Mildenberger, Kristin Marie ..... Lakewood, CO
Mildenberger, Mark B. ..... Seattle, WA
Milden-Haas, Margo ..... Ventura, CA
Milder, Alice R. ..... Omaha, NE
Milder, Alvin S. ..... Los Angeles, CA
Milder, Brian L. ..... Granada Hills, CA
Milder, Forrest David ..... Boston, MA
Milder, Laurie Beth ..... New York, NY
Milder, Merle ..... Edison, NJ
Milder, Richard J. ..... Secaucus, NJ
Mildfelt, Robert J. ..... Oklahoma City, OK
Mildner, Esther E. ..... Ardsley, NY
Mildner, Roy T. ..... Port St. Lucie, FL
Mildren, Richard A. ..... Oklahoma City, OK
Mildworm, Saul ..... New York, NY
Mildwurm, Alan W. ..... Fremont, CA
Mileaf, Howard A ..... New York, NY
Mileff, Jean M. ..... San Francisco, CA
Milefsky, Norman R. ..... Hartsdale, NY
Milek, John J. ..... Owatonna, MN
Milella, Angela F. ..... Chicago, IL
Milelli, Antonietta L. ..... Morristown, NJ
Milem, Anne L. ..... Washington, DC
Milenkovich, Melinda M.
Board of Governors Of The Federal Reserve System,
Office of the General Counsel, GV
Milenkovich, Milosh D. ..... Cleveland, OH
Mileo, Janice ..... Minneapolis, MN
Miler, Todd A. ..... Greenfield, IA

Miles, Alan J. ..... Raleigh, NC
Miles, Alan L. ..... Bainbridge Island, WA
Miles, Albert S. ..... Tuscaloosa, AL
Miles, Allan C. ..... Walnut Creek, CA
Miles, Andrew, III ..... Commack, NY
Miles, Anne ..... New York, NY
Miles, Anne-Marie M. ..... Richmond, VA
Miles, Anthony R. ..... Seattle, WA
Miles & Baker ..... Baxley, GA
Miles, Bradley C. ..... San Angelo, TX
Miles, Brian J. ..... Mount Clemens, MI
Miles & Brummitt ..... Walnut Creek, CA
Miles, C. Todd ..... New York, NY
Miles, Carolyn J. ..... Hanford, CA
Miles, Carrie J. ..... Franklin, IN
Miles, Charles H., Jr. ..... Las Vegas, NV
Miles, Chipman ..... Walnut Creek, CA
Miles, Christopher E. ..... Washington, PA
Miles, Coe F. ..... Houston, TX
Miles, Cordelia ..... Hillsboro, OR
Miles, Craig ..... Fort Collins, CO
Miles, Craig S. ..... Houston, TX
Miles, C. W., III ..... Union City, TN
Miles, Dana B. ..... Atlanta, GA
Miles, Dana E. ..... Milpitas, CA
Miles, David H. ..... Kew Gardens, NY
Miles, David L. ..... Moundsville, WV
Miles, David Michael ..... Washington, DC
Miles, David R.
Federal Maritime Commission,
Office of the General Counsel, GV
Miles, David R. ..... Fairborn, OH
Miles, Debra M. ..... Rock Island, IL
Miles, Don ..... Olympia, WA
Miles, Donald F. ..... San Francisco, CA
Miles, Donald W. ..... Bethlehem, PA
Miles, Douglas C. ..... Salt Lake City, UT
Miles, Douglas E. ..... Santa Ana, CA
Miles, Dudley D. ..... United States Senate,
Senatorial Assistants, GV
Miles, Eugene L., III ..... Havre de Grace, MD
Towson, MD
Miles, Forest J. ..... Chicago, IL
Skokie, IL
Miles, Frank ..... Bloomington, IL
Miles, Frankland W. L., Jr. ..... Duxbury, MA
Plymouth, MA
Miles, Franklin A., Jr. ..... Harrisburg, PA
Miles, Frederick ..... Denver, CO
Miles, Garry M. ..... Dallas, TX
Miles, Gary W. ..... Syracuse, NY
Miles, Gavin Wentworth ..... Brooklyn, NY
Miles, Gene D. ..... Houston, TX
Miles, George M. ..... Tulsa, OK
Miles, Gerard F. ..... Towson, MD
Miles & Gillard ..... Commack, NY
Miles, Gregory A. ..... Las Vegas, NV
Miles, Gregory L. ..... Mesa, AZ
Miles, Gregory Palmer ..... Winter Park, FL
Miles, H. Michael ..... Palm Springs, CA
Miles, Harry L. ..... Northampton, MA
Miles, Hubert D. ..... Albany, NY
Miles, J. Benjamin ..... Greensboro, NC
Miles, J. Michael ..... Roseville, MN
Miles, Jacob J. ..... New York, NY
Miles, Jacques B. ..... Boston, MA
Miles, James B. ..... Little Rock, AR
Miles, James E. ..... San Leandro, CA
Miles, James E. M. ..... Elm City, NC
Miles, James F. ..... Denver, CO
Miles, James M. ..... Columbia, SC
Miles, James R. ..... Columbus, OH
Miles, James S. ..... Taylor, TX
Miles, James Tod ..... Chicago, IL
Miles, James W., Jr. ..... Greensboro, NC
Miles, Jerry K., Jr. ..... Milwaukee, WI
Miles, Joan ..... New York, NY
Miles, Jodi A. ..... Jacksonville, FL
Miles, Jodi A., P.A. ..... Jacksonville, FL
Miles, John B. ..... Irvine, CA
Miles, John C. ..... Lincoln, NE
Omaha, NE
Miles, John E. ..... Sumter, SC
Miles, John Grother ..... Duxbury, MA
Plymouth, MA
Miles, John J. ..... Orange, CA
Ventura, CA
Miles, John J. ..... Washington, DC
Miles, John K., Jr. ..... Atlanta, GA
Miles, John L. ..... St. Louis, MO
Miles, John L. ..... St. George, UT
Miles, John M. ..... Houston, TX
Miles, John R. ..... Washington, DC
Miles, John R. ..... Nashville, TN
Miles, John Randolph ..... Greenbelt, MD
Miles, John S. ..... Washington, DC
McLean, VA
Miles, Jonathan Eric ..... Birmingham, AL
Miles, Jonathan S. ..... San Antonio, TX
Miles, Joseph A. ..... Miami, FL
Miles, Judith C. ..... San Francisco, CA
Miles, Judith E. ..... Springfield, MA
Miles, K. Scott ..... Charlottesville, VA
Miles, Kathleen ..... Washington, DC
Miles, Keith D. ..... Lincoln, NE
Miles, Kelly Anne ..... Gainesville, GA
Miles, Kelly B. ..... Ogden, UT
Miles, Kenneth A. ..... Monroe, NY
Miles, Kenneth F. ..... Elgin, IL
Miles, Kirk M. ..... Parsippany, NJ
Miles Law Firm ..... Corydon, IA
Miles Law Firm, The ..... Sacramento, CA
Miles, Lawrence W., Jr. ..... Sacramento, CA
Miles, Leslie K. ..... United States Senate,
Senatorial Assistants, GV
Miles, Linda A. ..... Greensboro, NC
Miles, Linda H. ..... Mesa, AZ
Miles, Lisa M. ..... Durham, NC

Miles, M. Virginia ..... Annapolis, MD
Miles, Manderson L. ..... Lewiston, ID
Miles, MarCine Miller ..... Vancouver, WA
Miles, Margaret T. ..... Palo Alto, CA
Miles, Marilyn B. ..... Eureka, CA
Miles, M.C. Cottingham ..... Amarillo, TX
Miles, McLaren & Peters, P.C.
Denver, CO
Miles, Melissa A. ..... Dallas, TX
Miles, Michael R. ..... Washington, DC
Miles, Michael S. ..... Hartford, CT
Miles, Michele G. ..... Fort Lauderdale, FL
Miles, Mildred L. ..... Buffalo, OK
Miles & Miles ..... Union City, TN
Miles and Miles, A Professional Association
Duxbury, MA
Plymouth, MA
Miles & Miles, P.S. ..... Vancouver, WA
Miles, Nelson A. ..... Grayling, MI
Miles, Nicole M. ..... Cherry Hill, NJ
Miles, Oliver H. ..... Los Alamos, NM
Miles, Pamela L. ..... Washington, DC
Miles, Patricia A. ..... Mechanicsburg, PA
Miles, Patrick A., Jr. ..... Grand Rapids, MI
Miles, Paul A. ..... Cherry Hill, NJ
Miles, Paul I. ..... Medina, NY
Miles, Perry W., IV ..... Richmond, VA
Miles, Peyton ..... Baxley, GA
Miles, Philip E. ..... Gadsden, AL
Miles, R. Matthews, Jr. ..... Daytona Beach, FL
Miles, R. Stephen, Jr. ..... Kissimmee, FL
Miles, Rachelle ..... Costa Mesa, CA
Miles, Ralph ..... New York, NY
Miles, Ralph F. ..... Hialeah, FL
Miles, Raymond T. ..... Tonawanda, NY
Miles, Raymond T., III ..... Tonawanda, NY
Miles & Reese, LLC ..... Atlanta, GA
Cumming, GA
Decatur, GA
Miles, Richard E. ..... Fort Worth, TX
Miles, Richard J. ..... Danville, IL
Miles, Richard L.
Federal Energy Regulatory Commission,
Office of the General Counsel, GV
Miles, Robert A. ..... Tampa, FL
Miles, Robert D. ..... Saint Simons Island, GA
Miles, Robert D., P.C.
Saint Simons Island, GA
Miles, Robert E. ..... Phoenix, AZ
Miles, Robin J. ..... Houston, TX
Miles, Roger Kent, The Law Offices of
Reno, NV
Miles, Ronald J ..... Lansing, MI
Miles, Roy A., Jr. ..... Nashville, TN
Miles, Scott ..... Charlottesville, VA
Miles, Sears & Eanni, A Professional Corporation ..... Fresno, CA
Miles, Stephen D. ..... Dayton, OH
Miles, Stephen L. ..... Baltimore, MD
Miles, Steven R. ..... Washington, DC
Miles & Stockbridge, P.C.
Washington, DC
Baltimore, MD
Cambridge, MD
Columbia, MD
Easton, MD
Frederick, MD
Rockville, MD
Towson, MD
McLean, VA
Miles, Susan P. ..... Washington, DC
Miles, Susan P. ..... Treasury Department,
Office of Thrift Supervision, GV
Miles, Teri Craig ..... Richmond, VA
Miles, Teri L. ..... Stroudsburg, PA
Miles, Terrence ..... Danville, IL
Miles, Terri M. ..... Metairie, LA
Miles, Theodore A.
National Science Foundation,
Office of the General Counsel, GV
Miles, Thomas V. ..... Fresno, CA
Miles, Toni Charice ..... Dallas, TX
Miles, Tony B. ..... Ogden, UT
Miles, Victoria Smith ..... Department of Justice,
Drug Enforcement Administration, GV
Miles, W. Daniel "Dee", III
Montgomery, AL
Miles, Way & Coyne ..... Olympia, WA
Miles, Wendell A. ..... Grand Rapids, MI
Miles, William H. ..... Jacksonville, FL
Miles, William H. ..... Corydon, IA
Miles, William L. ..... Vancouver, WA
Miles, William M. ..... New York, NY
Miles Fugazi, Lisa Marie ..... Stockton, CA
Milesky, Richard L., Jr. ..... Wexford, PA
Milesky, Richard Stephen ..... Burlington, MA
Milestone, Dale Lynn ..... New York, NY
Milestone, Jan ..... Hallandale Beach, FL
Milestone, Joseph ..... Philadelphia, PA
Milestone, Neil Alan ..... Hallandale Beach, FL
Mileti, Charlene R. ..... Cleveland, OH
Miletich, Amy L. ..... Denver, CO
Miletich, James Michael ..... Denver, CO
Miletsky, Robert J. ..... New York, NY
Milett, Mark E.
Department Of Health And Human Services,
Social Security Administration, GV
Mileur, Alfred Donald ..... Rush Springs, OK
Milew, Rosemary G. ..... Chicago, IL
Milewich, Daniel A. ..... Bedford, MA
Milewski, Michael J. ..... Denville, NJ
Milewski, Taryn N. ..... Dallas, TX
Miley, Anthony E. ..... Gettysburg, PA
Miley & Brown, P.C. ..... Dallas, TX
Miley, Claire F. ..... Nashville, TN
Miley, Craig E. ..... Dallas, TX
Miley, Edward R. ..... Las Vegas, NV
Miley, Kathryn M. ..... Cleveland, OH

Miley, Kelly G. ..... Hartford, CT
Miley, Michael F. ..... Lafayette, LA
Miley, Norman L., Jr. ..... Walnut Creek, CA
Miley, Phil E. ..... Baton Rouge, LA
Miley, Richard E. ..... Augusta, GA
North Augusta, SC
Miley, Richard E., Attorney at Law, P.A.
North Augusta, SC
Miley, Robert A. ..... Boston, MA
Miley, Samuel A. ..... Nashville, TN
Miley, Stefany Tewell ..... Las Vegas, NV
Miley, Timothy R. ..... Clarksburg, WV
Milford, C. Patrick ..... Carnesville, GA
Milford, Charles P., Jr.
Jacksonville Beach, FL
Milford, Douglas J. ..... St. Louis, MO
Milford & Drook ..... Marion, IN
Milford, John B. ..... Marion, IN
Milford, Lewis M. ..... Montpelier, VT
Milford, Lynch & Shannon ..... Skaneateles, NY
Milford, M. Calvin, Jr. ..... Lafayette, AL
Milford & Milford ..... Carnesville, GA
Milford, R. Keith ..... Carnesville, GA
Milford, Robert J. ..... Indianapolis, IN
Milford, Robt. Lindley ..... Marion, IN
Milfred, Linda L. ..... Atlanta, GA
Milgate, John, Law Office of ..... Antioch, CA
Milgate, John, Law Office of
Pleasant Hill, CA
Milgate, John, Law Office of
Walnut Creek, CA
Milgram, Marla R. ..... Blue Bell, PA
Milgram, Patricia Weeks
Treasury Department,
Bureau of Alcohol, Tobacco and Firearms, GV
Milgram, Sydney S. ..... Boston, MA
Milgraum, Glenn P. ..... New York, NY
Milgrim, Edward G.
Lake Buena Vista, FL
Milgrim, Herb M. ..... North Miami Beach, FL
Milgrim, Laurie Engelberg
Hollywood, FL
Milgrim, Pamela L. ..... New York, NY
Milgrim, Randi ..... Mineola, NY
Milgrim, Roger M. ..... New York, NY
Milgrom, Barry ..... San Francisco, CA
San Jose, CA
Milgrom, Brent M., Jr. ..... Charlotte, NC
Columbia, SC
Spartanburg, SC
Milgrom, Daniel R. ..... Los Angeles, CA
Milgrom, Mary K. ..... Englewood, CO
Milgrom, Michael ..... Cleveland, OH
Milgrom, Miriam R. ..... Garden City, NY
Milgrom, Steve ..... West Bloomfield, MI
Milgrom, Susan Jody
Bloomfield Township, MI
Milgrom, Valery ..... New York, NY
Milgroom, Charles E. ..... Littleton, MA
Milgrub, Richard H. ..... Clearfield, PA
Du Bois, PA
Milham, Deborah Ann ..... Albany, NY
Milham, Julee L. ..... St. Petersburg Beach, FL
Milham, Richard J. ..... Gig Harbor, WA
Milhaupt, Curtis J. ..... New York, NY
Milhaupt, Thomas J. ..... Thousand Oaks, CA
Milhem, Robert C. ..... Spokane, WA
Milholland, Ellen R. ..... Roswell, GA
Milholland, Valerie Ueckert ..... Houston, TX
Milhollin, Gary ..... Madison, WI
Milhollin, Karen Klaas ..... Houston, TX
Milhomme, Tanya Marie ..... Miami, FL
Milhoua, Karen C. ..... New York, NY
Milhouse, Donna Rose ..... Dearborn, MI
Milia, Robert P. ..... Troy, MI
Milian, David P. ..... Miami, FL
Milian, Mary Hoerber ..... Miami, FL
Milian, Richard N., (P.A.) ..... Orlando, FL
Milianta, Dorothy J. ..... White Plains, NY
Milianti, Peter A. ..... Chicago, IL
Miliauskas, Bradley R. ..... Washington, DC
Miliband, Joel S. ..... Irvine, CA
Milich, Lee ..... North Miami, FL
Milich, Lee, P.A. ..... North Miami, FL
Milich, Marvin F. ..... Islandia, NY
Milich, Milton V. ..... Fort Lauderdale, FL
Milich, Paul S. ..... Atlanta, GA
Milich, Robert P. ..... Youngstown, OH
Milici, John A. ..... Norwalk, CT
Milicic, Heidi J. ..... Cleveland, OH
Milicich, Louis ..... Chicago, IL
Milides, Beth Ann ..... Waretown, NJ
Milides, Gus ..... Easton, PA
Milie, Robert J. ..... Greensburg, PA
Milik, Wanda M. ..... Concord, MA
Milikovsky, Dmitry ..... San Francisco, CA
Milillo, Antonio ..... Troy, NY
Miliman, David J. ..... Baltimore, MD
Miliman, Howard A. ..... Baltimore, MD
Miliman, Jacob Y. ..... Baltimore, MD
Milin, Richard Kolb ..... New York, NY
Milione, Victor G. ..... Boston, MA
Miliotis, Mark G. ..... Boston, MA
Miliotis, Mark G. ..... Boston, MA
Milis, Robert J. ..... St. Paul, MN
Milita, Martin J., Jr. ..... Newark, NJ
Milita, Vincent James, II ..... Marmora, NJ
Militana, John ..... Miami, FL
Militana, Militana & Militana, P.A.
Miami, FL
Militana, Richard ..... Miami, FL
Militano, Mary Cosgrove ..... Scotia, NY
Militano, Thomas F. ..... Moorestown, NJ
Militello, James G. ..... Crystal Lake, IL
Militello, James G., III ..... Crystal Lake, IL
Militello, Janet E. ..... Houston, TX
Militello, Joseph M., Jr. ..... Beaver Dam, WI

Militello Law Office, The, P.C.
Watertown, NY
Militello, Paul L. ....**Crystal River, FL**
Militello, Ric A. ....La Jolla, CA
Militello, Samuel B. ....New York, NY
Militello, Samuel P. ....**Watertown, NY**
Militello, Zanck & Coen, P.C.
Crystal Lake, IL
Huntley, IL
Woodstock, IL
Militi, Joseph M. ....Syracuse, NY
Milito, Joseph Frank ....Chicago, IL
Milito, Michael V. ....Providence, RI
Militzok, Matthew ....Miami Beach, FL
Militzok, Nathan ....Hallandale Beach, FL
Militzok, Steven ....**Irvine, CA**
Milius, Pauline H. ....Department of Justice, Environment and Natural Resources Division, GV
Milizio, Joseph G. ....Lake Success, NY
New York, NY
Miljak, Manuela Saric ....Eastlake, OH
Miljanic, Kathy Marlo ....**Washington, DC**
Milken, Lowell J. ....Los Angeles, CA
Milkes, A. Ron ....**Los Angeles, CA**
Milkes, Elisa ....Boston, MA
Milkes, Jay G. ....**New York, NY**
Milkes, Milton ....San Diego, CA
Milkes, Samuel W. ....Carlisle, PA
Milkey, James R. ....Boston, MA
Milkie, William S. ....Dallas, TX
Milkis, Jack E. ....Somerdale, NJ
Milkis, Jack E., P.C. ....Somerdale, NJ
Milkman, Louise F. ....Department of Justice, Environment and Natural Resources Division, GV
Milkman, Murray ....Allentown, PA
Milko, James ....Greenbelt, MD
Milkovich, John C. ....Shreveport, LA
Milkowski, Louis.....................Los Angeles, CA
Milks, Bryan R. ....Delevan, NY
Milks, Joyce Stewart ....Santa Rosa, CA
Milks, Marie N. ....Honolulu, HI
Milks, Norman S. ....**Seattle, WA**
Milks, William C., III ....**Palo Alto, CA**
Milks, William E. ....Newark, NJ
Milks, William W. ....Honolulu, HI
Mill, John W. ....**Denver, CO**
Mill Law Corporation ....Pasadena, CA
Milla, Steve G. ....Rockville, MD
Millage, David A. ....**Davenport, IA**
Millan, Felipe De Jesus ....El Paso, TX
Millán, Juan A. ....**Washington, DC**
Millan, Rebecca A. ....Hillsboro, MO
Millan, Stanley A. ....**New Orleans, LA**
Millan, Stephen T. ....**Miami, FL**
Millan, Stephen T., P.A. ....**Miami, FL**
Millan, Theodore H. ....**Seattle, WA**
Milland, Charles F. ....Towson, MD
Millane, James H. ....**Orange, CA**
Millane, Kathy ....Sugar Land, TX
Millar, Albert S. C., Jr. ....Atlantic Beach, FL
Millar, Alexander C. ....**Princeton, NJ**
New York, NY
Millar & Ambrette ....**Darien, CT**
Millar, Barbara B. ....Mont Vernon, NH
Millar, David G. ....**St. Louis, MO**
Millar, Diane L. ....**New York, NY**
Millar, Emily C. ....**Danville, CA**
Millar, Eric S. ....Los Altos, CA
Millar, Fredrick L. ....Sacramento, CA
Millar, G. Michael ....**Searcy, AR**
Millar, G. Michael, P.A. ....**Searcy, AR**
Millar, Glenn L., Jr. ....Memphis, TN
Millar, Hodges & Bemis
Newport Beach, CA
Millar, Jacqueline M. ....Boston, MA
Millar, James H. ....**New York, NY**
Millar, James M. ....San Francisco, CA
Millar, Joel W. L. ....**New York, NY**
Millar, John W. ....**San Diego, CA**
Millar, Michael T. ....Somers Point, NJ
Millar, Murray J. ....Wayne, MI
Millar, Patrick D. ....**Waco, TX**
Millar, R.A. "Andy", P.C.
Milton-Freewater, OR
Millar, R.A. "Andy" ....Milton-Freewater, OR
Millar, Richard W., Jr.
Newport Beach, CA
Millar, Robert G. ....Dyersburg, TN
Millar, Robert L. ....Chico, CA
Millar, Samuel D. B., Jr. ....**Darien, CT**
Millar, Sanford I. ....**Los Angeles, CA**
Millar, Schaefer, Hoffmann & Robertson
St. Louis, MO
Millar, Sheila A. ....**Washington, DC**
Millar, Susan B. ....Portland, OR
Millar, Terry B. ....Rock Hill, SC
Millar, Terry B., L.L.C. ....Rock Hill, SC
Millar, Todd W. ....**Traverse City, MI**
Millar, Weinberg, Necker, Johnson and Ryan
Plymouth, MI
Wayne, MI
Millar, W. J., Jr. ....Hyattsville, MD
Millar, Wm. I. ....Waynesville, NC
Millar, Wm. I., P.A. ....Waynesville, NC
Millard, Amy E. ....**New York, NY**
Millard, Arthur F. ....Atlanta, GA
Millard, Castle & Monarch
Santa Ana, CA
Millard, Christen M. ....**Reynoldsburg, OH**
Millard, David B. ....**Indianapolis, IN**
Millard, David V. ....**Denver, CO**
Millard, Dianne H. ....Chicago, IL
Millard, Douglas ....Seattle, WA
Millard, D. R. (Duke), III ....Dallas, TX
Millard, Elizabeth R. ....**Hackensack, NJ**
Millard, Elizabeth W. ....**New York, NY**
Millard, F. Earl, Jr. ....St. Louis, MO
Millard, Frank H., Jr. ....Pontiac, MI
Millard, Gerald ....Rancho Santa Fe, CA
Millard, Greene & Udell ....New York, NY
Millard & Hunter, P.C. ....**Englewood, CO**
Millard, John A. ....**New York, NY**
Millard, John R. ....**Houston, TX**
Millard, John R., P.L.L.C., Law Office of
Houston, TX
Millard, Joseph ....Riverside, CA
Millard, Kendall ....**Washington, DC**
Millard, Kevin D. ....**Englewood, CO**
Millard, Kristine Snow ....Yarmouth, ME
Millard, L. Raymond, (P.C.)
Los Angeles, CA
Millard, Lisa A. ....Houston, TX
Millard, Malcolm S. ....Carmel, CA
Millard, Mark Evans ....**Los Angeles, CA**
Millard, Mark S. ....**Santa Ana, CA**
Millard, Michael Kimball ....Bel Air, MD
Millard, Neal S. ....**Los Angeles, CA**
Millard, Olivia P. ....Santa Fe, NM
Millard, Pilchowski, Holweger & Child
Los Angeles, CA
Millard, Randy G. ....Minneapolis, MN
Millard, Richard H. ....Los Angeles, CA
Millard, Richard S. ....**Menlo Park, CA**
Millard, Robert L. ....Garrett Park, MD
Millard, Rochelle ....Palm Springs, CA
Millard, S. Brook ....Salt Lake City, UT
Millard, Theodore E. ....Orange, CA
Millard, Thomas M. ....San Diego, CA
Millard, William H., Jr. ....**Dallas, TX**
Millard, William L. ....Akron, OH
Millard, William L. ....Columbus, OH
Millas, Stephen ....**New York, NY**
Millauer, Birgit ....**Palo Alto, CA**
Millberg & Gordon, P.L.L.C. ......**Raleigh, NC**
Research Triangle Park, NC
Millberg, John C. ....**Raleigh, NC**
Mille, Dennis G. ....Middleburg Heights, OH
Mille, Jean-Marie Edouard ....Columbia, SC
Millea, Christopher T. ......North Providence, RI
Millea, Daniel J. ....**Minneapolis, MN**
Millea, James F., Jr. ....**Boston, MA**
Millea, James S., Jr. ....Rensselaer, NY
Millea, Matthew P. ....Phoenix, AZ
Millea & Robichaud ....Rensselaer, NY
Milledge, Allan ....**Miami, FL**
Milledge & Iden ....**Miami, FL**
Milledge, John M. ....**Fort Lauderdale, FL**
Milledge, John M., P.A.
Fort Lauderdale, FL
Milledge, Lewis D., Jr. ....Miami, FL
Milledge, Samuel L. ....Houston, TX
Millemann, Audrey A. ....**Sacramento, CA**
Millemann, Michael ....Baltimore, MD
Millemann & Pittenger ....McCall, ID
Millemann, Steven J. ....McCall, ID
Millen, David L. ....Indianapolis, IN
Millen, Douglas A. ....**Chicago, IL**
Millen, F. Newton ....Austin, TX
Millen, Helen M. ....Palo Alto, CA
Millen, I. William ....**Arlington, VA**
Millen, Mathew L. ....Los Angeles, CA
Millen, Matt M. ....Pewaukee, WI
Millen, Michael D. ....San Jose, CA
Millen, Pressly M. ....**Raleigh, NC**
Millen, Richard H. ....Sherman Oaks, CA
Millen, Robert W. ....**Dallas, TX**
Millen, Robin Ashton
Department of Justice, Antitrust Division, GV
Millen, White, Zelano & Branigan, P.C.
Washington, DC
Arlington, VA
Richmond, VA
Millenacker, Mark A. ....Santa Cruz, CA
Millenbach, Lew A. ....Albany, NY
Millenbach, Paul J. ....**Farmington Hills, MI**
Millender, Beatrice K. Pennir ....Detroit, MI
Millender, Franchelle Cole ....**Columbia, SC**
Millender, Ivan A. ....Atlanta, GA
Millender, Kimberly Ann ....Westminster, MD
Millender, Roy J., III ....Escondido, CA
Millender, Roy J., Jr. ....**Santa Barbara, CA**
Millenky, Robert G. ....Camden, NJ
Millenson, Debra A. ....Department of Labor, Office of the Solicitor, GV
Miller, A. Dennis ....Cincinnati, OH
Miller, A. Fred ....Ketchikan, AK
Miller, A. Fred, A Professional Corporation
Ketchikan, AK
Miller, A. Matthew ....**Hollywood, FL**
Miller, A. Montague ....**Augusta, GA**
Miller, Abbe A. ....Philadelphia, PA
Miller, Abner ....Miami Beach, FL
Miller, Adam Clay ....Columbus, OH
Miller, Adam D. ....**Los Angeles, CA**
Miller, Adam E. ....**St. Louis, MO**
Miller, Adam M. ....**New York, NY**
Miller, Adam T. ....Decatur, IN
Miller, Adelaide M. ....Washington, DC
Miller, Adrienne E. ....San Lorenzo, CA
Miller, Adrienne Lea ....New Holland, PA
Miller, Aileen ....Havre, MT
Miller, Alan B. ....**New York, NY**
Miller, Alan Benjamin ....**Chicago, IL**
Miller, Alan Benjamin ....**Highland Park, IL**
Miller, Alan C. ....**Detroit, MI**
Miller, Alan D. ....Hayward, CA
Miller, Alan G. ....**Boston, MA**
Miller, Alan J. ....Jupiter, FL
Miller, Alan J. ....Troy, MI
Toledo, OH
Miller, Alan L. ....Cleveland, OH
Miller, Alan P. ....**Chicago, IL**
Miller, Alan R. ....Anderson, IN
Miller, Alan R. ....New Albany, IN
Miller, Alan R. ....**Boston, MA**
Miller, Alan R. ....**Birmingham, MI**
Miller, Alan R., Professional Corporation
Birmingham, MI
Detroit, MI
Miller, Alan S. ....**Boston, MA**
Miller, Alan S. ....**Pittsburgh, PA**
Miller, Alan S. ....**Dallas, TX**
Miller, Alan Scott ....**New Port Richey, FL**
Miller, Albert A. ....**Detroit, MI**
Miller, Albert C. ....Keizer, OR
Miller, Albert C., P.C. ....Keizer, OR
Miller, Albert J. ....Westport, CA
Miller, Albert M.
Department of Housing and Urban Development, GV
Miller, Albert M. ....Baltimore, MD
Miller, Albert Wesley, III ....Clearwater, FL
Miller, Alex E. ....**San Francisco, CA**
Miller, Alex J. ....**West Bloomfield, MI**
Miller, Alex M. ....**San Antonio, TX**
Miller, Alex W. ....**Chicago, IL**
Miller, Alfano & Raspanti
Haddonfield, NJ
Philadelphia, PA
Miller, Alfred ....**New York, NY**
Miller, Alfred E. ....Greenwich, CT
Miller, Alfred Louis ....Miami, FL
Miller, Alice E. ....Dayton, OH
Miller, Alison W. ....**Miami, FL**
Miller, Allan ....Irvine, CA
Miller, Allan C. ....Berkeley, CA
Miller, Allan C. ....Tawas City, MI
Miller, Allan L. ....Columbus, OH
Miller, Allen Robert ....Cincinnati, OH
Miller, Allen T., Jr. ....**Olympia, WA**
Miller, Allison ....New York, NY
Miller & Ament ....Pittsburgh, PA
Miller, Amy L. ....**Washington, DC**
Miller, Amy S. ....Westbury, NY
Miller, Amy T. ....Washington, DC
Miller, Andrea L. ....Mount Holly, NC
Miller, Andrea M. ....**Sacramento, CA**
Miller, Andrew ....**Rogers, AR**
Miller, Andrew ....Washington, DC
Miller, Andrew
Board of Governors Of The Federal Reserve System, Office of the General Counsel, GV
Miller, Andrew ....Portland, OR
Miller, Andrew B. ....**Logansport, IN**
Miller, Andrew Carter ....Trenton, NJ
Miller, Andrew E. ....**New York, NY**
Miller, Andrew G. ....Phoenix, AZ
Miller, Andrew H. ....Las Vegas, NV
Miller, Andrew H. ....Huntington, WV
Miller, Andrew J. ....**Short Hills, NJ**
Miller, Andrew K. ....Kennewick, WA
Miller, Andrew L. ....Northfield, NJ
Miller, Andrew L. ....Bala Cynwyd, PA
Miller, Andrew M. ....Peoria, AZ
Miller, Andrew M. ....Farrell, PA
Miller, Andrew P. ....**Washington, DC**
Miller, Andrew R.
National Aeronautics And Space Administration, Goddard Space Flight Center, GV
Miller, Andrew S. ....**Danville, CA**
Miller, Andrew S. ....**Philadelphia, PA**
Miller, Andrew S. ....**Austin, TX**
Miller, Andrew W. ....**Houston, TX**
Miller, Angela Rushton ....**Greenville, SC**
Miller & Angstadt, A Professional Corporation ....**Oakland, CA**
San Francisco, CA
Walnut Creek, CA
Miller, Anita C. ....**Rochester, NY**
Miller, Anita L. ....Houston, TX
Miller, Anita P. ....Albuquerque, NM
Miller, Ann ....**Philadelphia, PA**
Miller, Ann B. ....**Cincinnati, OH**
Miller, Ann E. ....Dallas, TX
Miller, Ann Elizabeth ....Hannibal, MO
Miller, Ann Fox ....Salisbury, MD
Miller, Ann Gray ....**San Francisco, CA**
Miller, Ann L. ....**Troy, MI**
Miller, Anne Burke ....**Manhattan, KS**
Miller, Anne Harmon ....Glenview, IL
Miller, Anne K. ....Rockville, MD
Miller, Anne Marie ....Cleveland, OH
Miller, Anne W. ....**Louisville, KY**
Miller, Anthony E. ....Akron, OH
Miller, Anthony J. ....New York, NY
Miller, Anthony S. ....**Dallas, TX**
Miller, April D. ....Phoenix, AZ
Miller, Arden P. ....Wichita, KS
Miller, Arleen L. ....Huntington Woods, MI
Miller, Arlene Cohen ....**Longmont, CO**
Miller, Arlyn G. ....**Deerfield, IL**
Miller, Arnold ....Chatham, NJ
Miller, Arnold N. ....Amarillo, TX
Miller, Arnold N., & Associates
Amarillo, TX
Miller, Arthur D. ....Vancouver, WA
Miller, Arthur E. ....Canoga Park, CA
Miller, Arthur E. ....Norwalk, CT
Miller, Arthur H. ....**Worcester, MA**
Miller, Arthur H. ....**New Brunswick, NJ**
Miller, Arthur H. ....Philadelphia, PA
Miller, Arthur L. ....Rego Park, NY
Miller, Arthur M. ....New York, NY
Miller, Arthur R. ....Chicago, IL
Miller, Arthur R. ....Cambridge, MA
Miller, Arthur W. ....**Long Beach, CA**
Miller, Arthur W. ....**Detroit, MI**
Miller, Arthur W., P.C. ....**Detroit, MI**
Miller, Asher H. ....**New York, NY**
Miller, Ashton C., Jr. ....Virginia Beach, VA
Miller & Associates ....Newport Beach, CA
Miller & Associates ....**Destin, FL**
Fort Walton Beach, FL
Shalimar, FL
Miller & Associates ....Chicago, IL
Southfield, MI
Worthington, OH
Santa Monica, CA
Miller & Associates, P.C., Law Offices of
Harrisburg, PA
Lemoyne, PA
Miller, Austin R. ....**Philadelphia, PA**
Miller, Aviva L. ....Great Neck, NY
Miller, Balis & O'Neil, P.C.
Washington, DC
Miller, Barbara ....Chicago, IL
Miller, Barbara A. ....Ponca City, OK
Miller, Barbara Anne ....Bethesda, MD
Miller, Barbara J. ....**Irvine, CA**
Miller, Barbara J. ....Oakland, CA
Miller, Barbara J. ....Boise, ID
Miller, Barbara K. ....Hudson, WI
Miller, Barbara Kaye ....Toledo, OH
Miller, Barbara L. ....Dover, DE
Miller, Barbara Matusik ....Hinsdale, IL
Miller, Barbara R. ....**Washington, DC**
Miller, Barbara S. ....**Southport, CT**
Miller, Barbara Sadow ....**Deerfield, IL**
Miller, Barbara W. ....Chester Springs, PA
Miller, Bardell D. ....Everett, WA
Miller, Barkley T. ....**Dallas, TX**
Miller, Barnes and Christian ....Lancaster, OH
Miller, Barry A. ....**Chicago, IL**
Miller, Barry D.
Securities and Exchange Commission, Division of Investment Management, GV
Miller, Barry J. ....**Cleveland, OH**
Miller, Barry K. ....Lynbrook, NY
Miller, Barry L. ....Orlando, FL
Miller, Barry M. ....**Lexington, KY**
Miller, Barry M. ....Norristown, PA
Miller, Barry P. ....**Rockville, MD**
McLean, VA
Miller, Barry R. ....**Houston, TX**
Miller, Barry S. ....North Plainfield, NJ
Miller, Barry Todd .....San Juan Capistrano, CA
Miller, Barry W. ....Baton Rouge, LA
Miller, Barry W., PLC ....Baton Rouge, LA
Miller, Bart W. ....Denver, CO
Miller, Bartlett P.
Department Of The Interior, Office of the Solicitor, GV
Miller, Bartley C. ....Miami, FL
Miller, Bayard J. ....Lafayette, CA
Miller and Beck ....Corte Madera, CA
San Francisco, CA
Miller, Behn ....General Accounting Office, Office of the General Counsel, GV
Miller, Belinda Hoffman ....Tallahassee, FL
Miller, Ben J. ....Griffin, GA
Miller, Ben J., Jr. ....**Thomaston, GA**
Miller, Ben N., III ....**Columbia, SC**
Miller, Ben R., Jr. ....**Baton Rouge, LA**
Miller, Benj. G. ....Baltimore, MD
Miller, Benjamin A. ....New York, NY
Miller, Benjamin F. ....Sacramento, CA
Miller, Benjamin K. ....Springfield, IL
Miller, Bennet M. ....Toledo, OH
Miller, Bernard ....Portsmouth, VA
Miller, Bernard Prince, Jr. ....Cleveland, TN
Miller, Bernice G. ....Seven Hills, OH
Miller, Bert G. ....San Antonio, TX
Miller, Beth A. ....**Tulsa, OK**
Miller, Beth Amy ....Weston, FL
Miller, Beth Anne ....**Detroit, MI**
Miller, Beth Buzzell ....**Dover, DE**
Miller, Beth E. ....**Cleveland, OH**
Miller, Beth W. ....Orlando, FL
Miller, Beth W., P.A. ....Orlando, FL
Miller, Betsy Ann ....Ionia, MI
Miller, Betsy Benjamin ....Bow, NH
Miller, Betty A. ....Westlake Village, CA
Miller, Betty A. ....Union, SC
Miller, Beverly G. ....**New York, NY**
Miller, Billie Jean ....**East Meadow, NY**
Miller, Binny ....Washington, DC
Miller, Blake D. ....**Salt Lake City, UT**
Miller, Blanche Rose ....**Atlanta, GA**
Miller, Blazkovec & Evans ....Algoma, WI
Miller, Bobby R., Jr. ....**Paducah, KY**
Miller & Bondurant, Ltd. ....Portsmouth, VA
Miller, Bonnie J. ....Howell, MI
Miller, Bonnie J. ....St. Louis, MO
Miller, Bonnie L. ....San Carlos, CA
Miller, Bonnie Weaver ....Columbus, OH
Miller, Boyko and Bell, A Professional Corporation ....**San Diego, CA**
Miller, Brad J. ....**St. Paul, MN**
Miller, Brad P. ....**Boise, ID**
Miller, Bradford F. ....Seneca Falls, NY
Miller, Bradford F. ....San Antonio, TX
Miller, Bradford H., (A Professional Corporation) ....**Irvine, CA**
Miller, Bradley Davis ....Wyomissing, PA
Miller, Bradley J. ....**Atlanta, GA**
Miller, Bradley K. ....Portland, OR
Miller, Bradley P. ....**Tucson, AZ**
Miller, Bradley S. ....**Portland, OR**
Miller, Bradley Scott ....**Los Angeles, CA**
Miller, Bradstreet, Jr. ....Santa Monica, CA
Miller, Brant T. ....**Canton, OH**
Miller, Brenda J. ....Middletown, NY
Miller, Brenda M. ....Detroit, MI
Miller, Brendon D. ....Jackson, KY
Miller, Brent Ashley
Hot Springs National Park, AR
Miller, Brent Charles ....Winter Park, FL

Miller, Brent D. ... **Brick, NJ**
Toms River, NJ
Miller, Brent S. ... Madison, MS
Miller, Brett H. ... **New York, NY**
Miller, Brett I. ... **Washington, DC**
Miller, Brett James ... **Indianapolis, IN**
Miller, Brett K. ... **Milwaukee, WI**
Miller, Brett L. ... **Columbus, OH**
Miller, Brian A. ... **New York, NY**
Miller, Brian C. ... **Phoenix, AZ**
Miller, Brian C. ... **Corpus Christi, TX**
Miller, Brian D. ... **San Diego, CA**
Miller, Brian G. ... **Columbus, OH**
Miller, Brian H. ... St. Paul, MN
Miller, Brian H. ... Moses Lake, WA
Othello, WA
Ritzville, WA
Miller, Brian K. ... Richmond, VA
Miller, Brian M. ... **Fairfax, VA**
Miller, Brian P. ... **Miami, FL**
Miller, Brian P. ... **Salt Lake City, UT**
Miller, Brian S. ... **Memphis, TN**
Miller, Brian W. ... **Mobile, AL**
Miller, Brian Y. ... Sarasota, FL
Miller, Brian Y., P.A. ... Sarasota, FL
Miller, Brigid T. ... **Nashville, TN**
Miller, Bronwyn C. ... Miami, FL
Miller, Brooks C. ... **Miami, FL**
Miller, Brooks C., P.A. ... **Miami, FL**
Miller Brown & Dannis, A Professional Corporation ... **Palos Verdes Estates, CA**
San Francisco, CA
Miller, Bruce ... Department of Agriculture, Rural Utilities Service, GV
Miller, Bruce A. ... **Metairie, LA**
Miller, Bruce A. ... **New Orleans, LA**
Miller, Bruce A. ... Detroit, MI
Miller, Bruce E. ... Brea, CA
Miller, Bruce E. ... Topeka, KS
Miller, Bruce E. ... **Charleston, SC**
Miller, Bruce I. ... Boston, MA
Miller, Bruce Joel ... Los Angeles, CA
Miller, Bruce K. ... Springfield, MA
Miller, Bruce M. ... San Antonio, TX
Miller, Bruce N. ... Los Angeles, CA
Miller, Bruce P. ... Princeton, NJ
Miller, Bruce R. ... Baltimore, MD
Miller, Bruce S. ... **Hazleton, PA**
Miller, Bruce V. ... **New York, NY**
Miller, Bruce W. ... Philadelphia, PA
Miller, Bryan B. ... **Encino, CA**
Miller, Bryan E. ... **Buffalo, NY**
Miller & Buchenberger ... Wantagh, NY
Miller, Buck C. ... Houston, TX
Miller, Burke ... Lincoln, IL
Miller, Burnett, III ... Richmond, VA
Miller, Burton S. ... Santa Monica, CA
Miller, Byron N. ... **Louisville, KY**
Miller, Byron S. ... **Chicago, IL**
Miller, C. David, II ... **Detroit, MI**
Miller, C. Douglas ... Gainesville, FL
Miller, C. Joseph ... **Indianapolis, IN**
Miller, C. Kevin ... **Spartanburg, SC**
Miller, C. Kevin, P.A. ... **Spartanburg, SC**
Miller, C. Phillip ... Boulder, CO
Miller, C. Steven ... **Allentown, PA**
Miller, C. Terrell ... **Bowling Green, KY**
Miller, C. Theodore ... Frankfort, KY
Miller, C. Thomas ... **Louisville, KY**
Miller, C. William, II ... Columbus, OH
Miller, C. A., Jr. ... Lake Charles, LA
Miller & Caine, L.L.P. ... **Providence, RI**
Miller, Calvert S. ... **Fort Wayne, IN**
Miller, Cameron ... Redwood City, CA
Miller, Camille M. ... **Philadelphia, PA**
Miller, Camille Stearns ... **Detroit, MI**
Miller & Candon ... **Hanover, NH**
Norwich, VT
Miller, Canfield, Paddock, Stone and Lott, P.A. ... **Pensacola, FL**
Miller, Canfield, Paddock and Stone, P.L.C.
Washington, DC
Ann Arbor, MI
Bloomfield Hills, MI
Detroit, MI
Grand Rapids, MI
Howell, MI
Kalamazoo, MI
Lansing, MI
Monroe, MI
Troy, MI
New York, NY
Miller, Cara D. ... **Los Angeles, CA**
Miller, Carey Balog ... **Pittsburgh, PA**
Miller, Carl J. ... Clearwater, FL
Miller, Carl K. E., Jr. ... Trenton, NJ
Miller, Carl M. ... **New Haven, IN**
Miller, Carl S. ... Columbia, MD
Miller, Carl T., Jr. ... Pullman, WA
Miller, Carla ... Jacksonville, FL
Miller, Carla M. ... **New York, NY**
Miller, Carlyle ... Sun City, AZ
Miller, Carmen A. ... Corning, NY
Miller, Carol ... New York, NY
Miller, Carol G. ... Los Angeles, CA
Miller, Carol J. ... Jefferson City, MO
Miller, Carol Vincent ... **Burlington, NC**
Miller, Carole G. ... **Birmingham, AL**
Miller, Carolyn A.
Securities and Exchange Commission, Division of Corporation Finance, GV
Miller, Carolyn A. ... Ponca City, OK
Miller, Carolyn M. ... Louisville, KY
Miller, Carolyn S. ... Columbus, OH
Miller, Carolyn W. ... **Portland, OR**
Miller, Carrie Bowers ... **Dallas, TX**

Miller Carson Boxberger & Murphy, LLP **Bloomington, IN**
Fort Wayne, IN
Miller, Cary ... **Kansas City, MO**
Miller, Cary W. ... **San Diego, CA**
Miller, Caryn A. ... New York, NY
Miller, Cassidy, Larroca & Lewin, L.L.P. **Washington, DC**
Miller & Castner ... South Berwick, ME
Miller, Catherine A. ... **Dulles, VA**
Miller, Catherine C. ... **Portland, ME**
Miller, Catherine Jolliffe ... **Troy, MI**
Miller, Catherine M. ... Austin, TX
Miller, Catherine V. P. ... Fredericksburg, VA
Miller, Cathleen Shortsleeve ... Wellesley, MA
Miller, Cathy S. ... **Santa Monica, CA**
Miller, Celeste ... Boise, ID
Miller, Chad W. ... **Irvine, CA**
Miller, Charles ... **Washington, DC**
Miller, Charles A. ... **Denver, CO**
Miller, Charles A. ... **Washington, DC**
Miller, Charles B. ... La Mesa, CA
Miller, Charles C., III ... Atlanta, GA
Miller, Charles D. ... Lincolnwood, IL
Miller, Charles D. ... Hudson, OH
Miller, Charles E. ... Fort Myers, FL
Miller, Charles E. ... Largo, FL
Miller, Charles E. ... Winter Springs, FL
Miller, Charles E. ... **Rock Island, IL**
Davenport, IA
Miller, Charles E. ... Atlantic, IA
Miller, Charles E. ... **Portland, ME**
Miller, Charles E. ... Mc Comb, MS
Miller, Charles E. ... **New York, NY**
Miller, Charles E., Jr. ... Mesquite, TX
Miller, Charles E., Jr., P.C. ... Mesquite, TX
Miller, Charles F. ... **Kansas City, MO**
Miller, Charles F., III ... **Pittsburgh, PA**
Miller, Charles F., Jr. ... Indianapolis, IN
Miller, Charles Fox ... **Hollywood, FL**
Miller, Charles G. ... **San Francisco, CA**
Miller, Charles G. ... **Houston, TX**
Miller, Charles H. ... **New York, NY**
Miller, Charles H., III ... Rochester, NY
Miller, Charles H., Jr. ... Rochester, NY
Miller, Charles I. ... West Hartford, CT
Miller, Charles J. ... Sacramento, CA
Miller, Charles J. ... Baltimore, MD
Miller, Charles J. ... Silver Spring, MD
Miller, Charles J. ... Camillus, NY
Miller, Charles L. ... Baker, LA
Miller, Charles L., Jr. ... **Mobile, AL**
Miller, Charles L., Jr. ... **Washington, DC**
Miller, Charles M. ... **Studio City, CA**
Miller, Charles M. ... **New York, NY**
Miller, Charles M. ... Frackville, PA
Miller, Charles Michael ... Columbus, OH
Miller, Charles N. ... Livingston, NJ
Miller, Charles N., Jr. ... New Orleans, LA
Miller, Charles P. ... Montgomery, AL
Miller, Charles P. ... Aiea, HI
Miller, Charles P. ... **Dallas, TX**
Miller, Charles R. ... St. Louis, MO
Miller, Charles S., Jr. ... **Bismarck, ND**
Miller, Charles T. ... Milan, IL
Miller, Charles T. ... Charleston, WV
Miller, Charles W. ... **Columbus, GA**
Miller, Charles W., III ... **Somerville, NJ**
Miller, Charles Wade ... **Amarillo, TX**
Miller, Charles Wayne ... **Louisville, KY**
Miller, Charlotte L. ... Salt Lake City, UT
Miller, Chas. H. ... Knoxville, TN
Miller, Chas. R. ... Cleveland, OH
Miller & Chernoff ... Woodland Hills, CA
Miller, Cherrie N. ... Chagrin Falls, OH
Miller & Chevalier, Chartered
Washington, DC
Miller, Chris ... Lawrence, KS
Miller, Christian B. ... Houston, TX
Miller, Christin Sandahl ... San Jose, CA
Miller, Christina E. ... Boston, MA
Miller, Christina Inge ... **Park City, UT**
Miller, Christina J. ... Merrillville, IN
Miller, Christina V. ... **Denver, CO**
Miller, Christine A. ... **Newport Beach, CA**
Miller, Christine A. ... **Chicago, IL**
Miller, Christine B. ... **Portland, OR**
Miller, Christine E. ... **St. Louis, MO**
Miller, Christine F. ... **Austin, TX**
Miller, Christine H. ... **New York, NY**
Miller, Christine L. ... New York, NY
Miller, Christine M. ... **Boston, MA**
Miller, Christine O'Dell Cook ...
United States Court of Federal Claims, GV
Miller, Christopher D. ... Oakland, CA
Miller, Christopher D. ... **Lexington, KY**
Miller, Christopher G. ... Washington, DC
Miller, Christopher G. ... Clearwater, FL
Miller, Christopher J. ... Santa Ana, CA
Miller, Christopher J. ... **Doniphan, MO**
Miller, Christopher K. ... **Denver, CO**
Miller, Christopher L. ... **Columbus, OH**
Miller, Christopher M. ... **Baltimore, MD**
Miller, Christopher M. ... **Pittsburgh, PA**
Miller, Christopher Ralph
Santa Rosa, CA
Miller, Christopher S. ... **Atlanta, GA**
Miller, Christopher S. ... **Berwyn, PA**
Miller, Christopher W. ... **Sacramento, CA**
Miller & Chudzik ... East Brunswick, NJ
Miller, Cindy K. ... Newark, NJ
Miller, Cindy L. ... **Bryan, TX**
Miller, Claire Cody ... Staten Island, NY
Miller, Clare K. ... **Garden City, NY**
Miller, Clarence A. ... Sylvester, GA
Miller, Clark A. ... Salinas, CA
Miller, Clark, Calvert and Raimondi
Berkeley, CA

Miller, Claude Henry ... Detroit, MI
Miller, Claudette P. ... **Chicago, IL**
Miller, Claudia D. ... Lakewood, CO
Miller, Claudia D., P.C. ... Lakewood, CO
Miller, Clay ... Dallas, TX
Miller, Clayton R. ... Gunnison, CO
Miller & Clearwaters ... Los Angeles, CA
Miller, Cleaveland D. ... **Baltimore, MD**
Miller, Clement ... Spokane, WA
Miller, Clifford J. ... **Honolulu, HI**
Miller, Clifford M. ... Fort Lauderdale, FL
Miller, Clifton N. ... **Tullahoma, TN**
Miller, Clinton F. ... Wilmington, DE
Miller, Clinton J., III ... Cleveland, OH
Miller, Cloud H., III ... Atlanta, GA
Miller, Clyde ... Houston, TX
Miller & Cohen, P.C. ... **Longmont, CO**
Miller, Colleen M. ... Garden City, KS
Miller & Company P.C. ... **Washington, DC**
Kansas City, MO
Miller, Connie Fern ... Watkins Glen, NY
Miller, Connie J. ... Charlotte, NC
Miller, Conrad J., III ... **Lansdale, PA**
Miller, Constance J. ... Austin, TX
Miller, Conway D. ... Arlington, VA
Miller, Corinne A. ... Casper, WY
Miller, Cory J. ... Stanley, WI
Miller, Courtlandt G. ... New York, NY
Miller, Craig ... Montgomery, AL
Miller, Craig ... Lock Haven, PA
Miller, Craig ... **Seattle, WA**
Miller, Craig A. ... **San Diego, CA**
Miller, Craig A. ... **Kalamazoo, MI**
Miller, Craig D. ... **Los Angeles, CA**
Miller, Craig D. ... **Atlanta, GA**
Miller, Craig E. ... **Akron, OH**
Miller, Craig F. ... **New York, NY**
Miller, Craig J. ... Pasadena, CA
Miller, Craig L. ... **Buffalo, NY**
Miller, Craig L. ... Port Angeles, WA
Miller, Craig P. ... **Minneapolis, MN**
Miller, Craig S. ... San Francisco, CA
Miller, Craig S. ... **Cleveland, OH**
Miller, Craig W. ... **Hackensack, NJ**
Miller, Creighton E. ... Cleveland, OH
Miller, Crosby & Miller, P.A.
Lakeland, FL
Miller, Curtis W. ... Lithonia, GA
Miller, Cylenthia LaToye ... **Detroit, MI**
Miller, Cynthia B. ... Tallahassee, FL
Miller, Cynthia C. ... Los Angeles, CA
Miller, Cynthia Hall ... Trenton, NJ
Miller, Cynthia L. ... **Moscow, ID**
Miller, Cynthia R. ... **New York, NY**
Miller, D. Byron, Jr. ... Palo Alto, CA
Miller, D. Gregory ... Rayville, LA
Miller, D. Michael ... **Columbus, OH**
Miller, D. Sigsbee ... Raleigh, NC
Miller, Dale A. ... Martinez, CA
Miller, Dale E. ... Lakewood, CO
Miller, Dale K. ... Savannah, MO
Miller, Dale T. ... **Chicago, IL**
Miller, Dale W. ... Philadelphia, PA
Miller, Dale Wood ... Jefferson City, MO
Miller, Damon C. ... Department of Justice, Civil Division, GV
Miller, Dan ... **New York, NY**
Miller, Dan ... **Austin, TX**
Miller, Dan B. ... **Chicago, IL**
Miller, Dan M.
Department of State, GV
Miller, Dana S. ... **Santa Rosa, CA**
Miller, Dane C. ... Warrensburg, MO
Miller, Dane Lee ... **Honolulu, HI**
Miller, Danette E. ... Corning, NY
Miller, Dani M. ... **San Francisco, CA**
Miller, Danieal H. ... **Columbia, MO**
Miller, Danieal H., P.C. ... **Columbia, MO**
Miller, Daniel ... Haverstraw, NY
Miller, Daniel ... Virginia Beach, VA
Miller, Daniel A. ... **Boise, ID**
Miller, Daniel E. ... Montville, NJ
Miller, Daniel F. ... **Milwaukee, WI**
Miller, Daniel H. ... Lexington, KY
Miller, Daniel Lincoln ... Rochester, NY
Miller, Daniel L. R. ... **Erie, PA**
Miller, Daniel M. ... **White Plains, NY**
Miller, Daniel M. ... **Erie, PA**
Miller, Daniel M. ... **Pittsburgh, PA**
Miller, Daniel P. J. ... **Phoenix, AZ**
Miller, Daniel R. ... **Walnut Creek, CA**
Miller, Daniel R. ... Indianapolis, IN
Miller, Daniel S. ... Richfield, MN
Miller, Daniel S. ... Murray Hill, NJ
Miller, Danielle E. ... **Los Angeles, CA**
Miller, Danny ... Mena, AR
Miller, Darrell C. ... **Denver, CO**
Miller, Darrell D. ... Santa Monica, CA
Miller, Darrell E. ... Mankato, KS
Miller, Darrell J. ... Newport News, VA
Miller, Darren B. ... **Irvine, CA**
Miller, Darren D. ... Batavia, OH
Miller, Darren T. ... Ballston Spa, NY
Miller, Daryl Anne ... Washington, DC
Miller, Daryl J. ... Newport Beach, CA
Miller, David ... **Oakland, CA**
Walnut Creek, CA
Miller, David ... Chicago, IL
Miller, David ... Opelousas, LA
Miller, David ... New York, NY
Miller, David A. ... El Segundo, CA
Miller, David A. ... Indianapolis, IN
Miller, David A. ... Boston, MA
Miller, David A. ... **Boston, MA**
Miller, David A. ... South River, NJ
Miller, David A. ... **Elizabeth City, NC**
Miller, David A. ... Donora, PA
Miller, David A. ... **Pottstown, PA**

Miller, David A. ... **Dallas, TX**
Palmer, TX
Miller, David A. ... Dallas, TX
Miller, David A., Jr. ... Virginia Beach, VA
Miller, David A., Jr., P.C.
Virginia Beach, VA
Miller, David Alan ... **New York, NY**
Miller, David B. ... **Minneapolis, MN**
Miller, David B. ... **Scranton, PA**
Miller, David B. ... **Myrtle Beach, SC**
Miller, David Blair ... West Chester, PA
Miller, David C. ... **Miami, FL**
Miller, David C. ... **Miami, FL**
Miller, David C. ... Hawthorn Woods, IL
Miller, David C. ... **St. Louis, MO**
Miller, David C. ... New York, NY
Miller, David C., Jr. ... Harrisburg, PA
Miller, David D. ... **San Diego, CA**
Miller, David D. ... Kansas City, MO
Miller, David E. ... Melbourne, AR
Miller, David E. ... San Francisco, CA
Miller, David E. ... **Washington, DC**
Miller, David E. ... Lynnfield, MA
Miller, David E., Jr. ... Birmingham, AL
Miller, David G. ... **Palos Verdes Estates, CA**
Miller, David G. ... **New York, NY**
Miller, David G. ... **St. Albans, VT**
Miller, David H. ... **Los Angeles, CA**
Miller, David H. ... **Denver, CO**
Miller, David H. ... Washington, DC
Miller, David H. ... Fort Wayne, IN
Miller, David H. ... Bloomfield Hills, MI
Miller, David H. ... Chillicothe, MO
Miller, David H. ... Cleveland, OH
Miller, David H. ... Easton, PA
Miller, David J. ... Sacramento, CA
Miller, David J. ... **San Francisco, CA**
Miller, David J. ... **Walnut Creek, CA**
Miller, David J. ... Denver, CO
Miller, David K. ... **Portland, OR**
Miller, David K., (P.A.) ... **Tallahassee, FL**
Miller, David L. ... **Denver, CO**
Miller, David L. ... **Washington, DC**
Miller, David L. ... **Atlanta, GA**
Miller, David L. ... **Chicago, IL**
Miller, David L. ... **Greenville, IL**
Vandalia, IL
Miller, David L. ... Vincennes, IN
Miller, David L. ... Paola, KS
Miller, David L. ... Topeka, KS
Miller, David L. ... Columbus, OH
Miller, David L. ... Medford, OR
Miller, David L. ... Houston, TX
Miller, David L., (P.C.) ... **McLean, VA**
Miller, David M. ... **Oakland, CA**
Miller, David M. ... **Denver, CO**
Miller, David M. ... **Southfield, MI**
Miller, David M. ... Chatham, NJ
Miller, David N. ... Ronkonkoma, NY
Miller, David P. ... Davenport, IA
Miller, David P. ... Libertyville, IA
Miller, David P. ... Lancaster, PA
Miller, David P., II ... **Portland, OR**
Miller, David R. ... Los Angeles, CA
Miller, David R. ... Oceanside, CA
Miller, David R. ... Springfield, IL
Miller, David R. ... **Houston, TX**
Miller, David Ross ... Montvale, NJ
Miller, David S. ... Chicago, IL
Miller, David S. ... Minneapolis, MN
Miller, David S. ... **New York, NY**
Miller, David S. ... Wilkesboro, NC
Miller, David T. ... Lexington, KY
Miller, David V. ... **Evansville, IN**
Miller, David W. ... Sacramento, CA
Miller, David W. ... Denver, CO
Miller, David W. ... **Indianapolis, IN**
Miller, David W. ... New York, NY
Miller, David W. ... Springfield, VA
Miller, David Warren ... Lakewood, CO
Miller, Davidson C. ... Arlington, VA
Miller & Davison ... Bethlehem, PA
Miller, Dawn ... Austin, TX
Miller, Day ... Maysville, MO
Miller, Dean C. ... **Denver, CO**
Miller, Dean E. ... **Aliso Viejo, CA**
Miller, Dean E. ... **Washington, DC**
Miller, Dean G. ... San Leandro, CA
Miller, Dean J. ... **Bakersfield, CA**
Miller, Dean J. ... **Boise, ID**
Miller, Deanne L. Chun ... **Los Angeles, CA**
Miller, Deborah ... Santa Clara, CA
Miller, Deborah ... Dallas, TX
Miller, Deborah B. ... Philadelphia, PA
Miller, Deborah E. ... **New York, NY**
Miller, Deborah J. ... **Miami, FL**
Miller, Deborah K. ... **San Francisco, CA**
Miller, Deborah Kay ... Montgomery, AL
Miller, Deborah Kay, L.L.C.
Montgomery, AL
Miller, Deborah L. ... San Jose, CA
Miller, Deborah L. ... **San Antonio, TX**
Miller, Deborah L. ... Morgantown, WV
Miller, Deborah P. ... **Atlanta, GA**
Miller, Deborah W. ... **Scottsdale, AZ**
Miller, Deborah Wolf ... New Berlin, NY
Miller, Debra A. ... Scarsdale, NY
Miller, Debra Gail ... Harahan, LA
Miller, Debra H. ... Northbrook, IL
Miller, Debra Hanley ... **Indianapolis, IN**
Miller, Debra J. ... **Oakland, CA**
Miller, Debra L. ... **Elkhart, IN**
Miller, Debra L. ... New York, NY
Miller, Decatur H. ... **Baltimore, MD**
Miller, Dee ... Amarillo, TX
Miller, Dee ... Dallas, TX
Miller, Deena Charisse ... **Cleveland, OH**
Miller, Del W. ... Stanton, KY

Miller, Denise Arenth ... **Atlanta, GA**
Miller, Denise Hansen ... Palos Verdes Estates, CA
Miller, Dennis D. ... **San Francisco, CA**
Miller, Dennis H. ... Taylor, MI
Miller, Dennis H., P.C. ... Taylor, MI
Miller, Dennis M. ... Westminster, CO
Miller, Dennis M. ... Sugar Land, TX
Miller, Dennis W. ... **Jackson, MS**
Miller, Desirée V. ... **New York, NY**
Miller, Devlin & McLean, P.S. ... **Spokane, WA**
Miller, Devon Lee ... **Washington, DC**
Miller, Dewey B. ... Pearl, MS
Miller, Diana Frazier ... Library of Congress, Law Library, GV
Miller, Diana R. ... San Mateo, CA
Miller, Diane C. ... Pleasanton, CA
Miller, Diane H. ... **New York, NY**
Miller, Diane L. ... Minneapolis, MN
Miller, Diane M. ... Phoenix, AZ
Miller, Diane M. ... Morristown, NJ
Miller, Dianne D. ... **Greenwood Village, CO**
Miller & Diepenbrock, P.A. ... **Liberal, KS**
Miller, Dina Talmor ... Merrick, NY
Miller, Dixon F. ... **Naples, FL**
Columbus, OH
Miller Dollarhide, A Professional Corporation ... **Oklahoma City, OK**
Miller, Don B. ... Boulder, CO
Miller, Don G. ... Archdale, NC
Miller, Don R. ... Akron, OH
Miller, Donald ... **Washington, DC**
Miller, Donald ... Tampa, FL
Miller, Donald ... New York, NY
Miller, Donald A. ... Detroit, MI
Miller, Donald B. ... **Detroit, MI**
Miller, Donald C. ... **Los Angeles, CA**
Miller, Donald D. ... Green Bay, WI
Miller, Donald E. ... Phoenix, AZ
Miller, Donald E. ... Germantown, TN
Miller, Donald E. ... **Dulles, VA**
Miller, Donald E. ... **Cheyenne, WY**
Miller, Donald G. ... Suches, GA
Miller, Donald J. ... Forreston, IL
Miller, Donald J. ... **Detroit, MI**
Miller, Donald L. ... Baltimore, MD
Miller, Donald L., II ... **Louisville, KY**
Miller, Donald M. ... Canton, OH
Miller, Donald P. ... Los Angeles, CA
Miller, Donald R. ... Shreveport, LA
Miller, Donald R. ... Columbus, OH
Miller, Donald R., A Prof. Law Corp. ... Shreveport, LA
Miller, Donald W. ... Palm Beach Gardens, FL
Miller, Donn B. ... Los Angeles, CA
Miller, Donna ... Chattanooga, TN
Miller, Donna Lynn ... Pittsburgh, PA
Miller, Donna M. ... **Allentown, PA**
Miller, Donna R. ... **Des Moines, IA**
Miller, Donna R. ... Flemington, NJ
Miller, Donna Rae ... Tavares, FL
Miller, Donovan C. ... Austin, TX
Miller, Donovan, P.C. ... Austin, TX
Miller, Dora A. ... **Atlanta, GA**
Miller, Doris F. ... Oroville, CA
Miller, Douglas ... Charleston, WV
Miller, Douglas A. ... **Chicago, IL**
Miller, Douglas A., Jr. ... Westport, CT
Miller, Douglas B. ... New York, NY
Miller, Douglas C. ... Long Beach, CA
Miller, Douglas C. ... Westwood, KS
Miller, Douglas D. ... Webb City, MO
Miller, Douglas E. ... Fort Wayne, IN
Miller, Douglas E. ... Purvis, MS
Miller, Douglas E. ... **Newport News, VA**
Miller, Douglas F. ... **Pensacola, FL**
Miller, Douglas G. ... Baldwin Park, CA
Miller, Douglas H. ... Towson, MD
Miller, Douglas J. ... **Concord, NH**
Miller, Douglas K. ... Phoenix, AZ
Miller, Douglas L. ... San Diego, CA
Miller, Douglas L. ... Kansas City, MO
Miller, Douglas L. ... Neenah, WI
Miller, Douglas P. ... Indio, CA
Miller, Douglas R ... Shorewood, MN
Miller, Douglas S. ... Houston, TX
Miller, Doyle ... Kingfisher, OK
Miller, Duane C. ... Sacramento, CA
Miller, Duane H. ... Yukon, OK
Miller, Duane S. ... **Concord, NC**
Miller, Duane S. ... **Kannapolis, NC**
Miller, Dudley E. ... Escondido, CA
Miller, Dwight L. ... **Indianapolis, IN**
Miller, Dwight L. ... Topeka, KS
Miller, Dwight W. ... St. Louis, MO
Miller, E. Alan ... **Atlanta, GA**
Miller, E. Douglas ... **Cynthiana, KY**
Miller, E. Glenn ... Hartford, KY
Miller, E. Lawrence ... Boston, MA
Miller, E. Powell ... **Troy, MI**
Miller, E. Robert, Jr. ... **Tampa, FL**
Miller, E. Spencer ... South Portland, ME
Miller, E. Suzan ... Westminster, MD
Miller, Earl R. ... Salem, OH
Miller, Earle D. ... **Los Angeles, CA**
Miller, Edgar ... Coral Gables, FL
Miller, Edgar D., III ... Dallas, TX
Miller, Edgar L. ... Bellefontaine, OH
Miller, Edith L. ... New York, NY
Miller, Edmond "Buddy" James, Jr. ... **Reno, NV**
Miller, Edw. A. ... Youngstown, OH
Miller, Edward ... Department of Justice, Civil Rights Division, GV
Miller, Edward ... **Texarkana, TX**
Miller, Edward A. ... Los Angeles, CA
Miller, Edward A. ... Okeechobee, FL
Miller, Edward A. ... New York, NY
Miller, Edward A. ... **Pittsburgh, PA**
Miller, Edward A., Jr. ... **Northfield, VT**
Miller, Edward B. ... Chicago, IL
Miller, Edward B. ... **Chicago, IL**
Miller, Edward B. ... Rockland, ME
Miller, Edward Bradford ... **Tampa, FL**
Miller, Edward C. ... Birmingham, AL
Miller, Edward C. ... Dandridge, TN
Miller, Edward F. ... Palatine, IL
Miller, Edward G. ... New York, NY
Miller, Edward H. ... Rye Brook, NY
Miller, Edward H. ... **Lebanon, PA**
Miller, Edward J. ... Falls City, NE
Miller, Edward J. ... Mineola, NY
Miller, Edward J., Jr. ... **St. Louis, MO**
Miller, Edward L. ... **Whittier, CA**
Miller, Edward L. ... **Lancaster, PA**
Miller, Edward M. ... **Farmington Hills, MI**
Miller, Edward M. ... White Plains, NY
Miller, Edward M., P.C. ... **Farmington Hills, MI**
Miller, Edward Michael ... Westminster, MD
Miller, Edward O. ... Gulfport, MS
Miller, Edward P. ... Havana, IL
Miller, Edward R. ... Naples, FL
Miller, Edward R. ... White Plains, NY
Miller, Edward S. ... Millville, NJ
Miller, Edward S. ... Valley Stream, NY
Miller, Edward Terhune ... Department of Labor, Office of Secretary, GV
Miller, Edward V. ... Columbus, OH
Miller, Edward V., Co., A Legal Professional Association ... Columbus, OH
Miller, Edward W. ... New York, NY
Miller, Edward W. ... **Greenville, SC**
Miller, Edwin ... Smithtown, NY
Miller, Edwin H. ... **Hagerstown, MD**
Miller, Edwin L., Jr. ... La Jolla, CA
Miller, Edwin L., Jr. ... **Boston, MA**
Miller, Edwin M. ... Rockville, MD
Miller, Edwina E. ... Tuscaloosa, AL
Miller, Edythe A. ... Mount Holly, NJ
Miller, Eggleston & Cramer, Ltd. ... **Burlington, VT**
Miller, Eileen Hamamura ... Treasury Department, Financial Crimes Enforcement Network, GV
Miller, Eileen N. ... Chicago, IL
Miller, Eileen P. ... Waukesha, WI
Miller, E. L. ... **Coeur d'Alene, ID**
Miller, Elaine F. ... Jupiter, FL
Miller, Eleanor ... Los Angeles, CA
Miller, Eleanor L. ... **Phoenix, AZ**
Miller, Eleanor R. ... Trenton, NJ
Miller, Eleanor R. ... Brookfield, VT
Miller, Elijah L., Jr. ... Elizabeth, NJ
Miller, Elise C. ... San Jose, CA
Miller, Elissa D. ... **Los Angeles, CA**
Miller, Elissa M. ... Department of Labor, GV
Miller, Elizabeth A. ... Sacramento, CA
Miller, Elizabeth A. ... **Boston, MA**
Miller, Elizabeth A. ... **Dallas, TX**
Miller, Elizabeth Ann Hollingsworth ... Waco, TX
Miller, Elizabeth B. ... Houston, TX
Miller, Elizabeth D. ... Fort Wayne, IN
Miller, Elizabeth Gaglione ... Newark, OH
Miller, Elizabeth H. ... **Burlington, VT**
Miller, Elizabeth J. ... Los Angeles, CA
Miller, Elizabeth L. ... Nashville, TN
Miller, Elizabeth M. ... **New York, NY**
Miller, Elizabeth N. ... **Austin, TX**
Miller, Elizabeth S. ... Waco, TX
Miller, Elizabeth T. ... **Rutherfordton, NC**
Miller, Ellen Lesley ... **Nicholasville, KY**
Miller, Elliot I. ... **Southport, CT**
Miller, Elliott C. ... Hartford, CT
Miller & Ellison ... Hazel Crest, IL
Miller, Elsa ... Carol Stream, IL
Miller, Elwynn J. ... East Sandwich, MA
Miller, Elyse Caraco ... Newport Beach, CA
Miller, Emanuel ... Boynton Beach, FL
Miller, Emily A. ... **Washington, DC**
Miller, Emily B. ... Torrance, CA
Miller, Emmett H. ... **Washington, DC**
Miller & Engel ... **Madison, NJ**
Miller & Entwisle ... Pittsburgh, PA
Miller, E. R. (Boots), Jr. ... Ely, NV
Miller, Eric ... **Palo Alto, CA**
Miller, Eric B. ... **Baltimore, MD**
Miller, Eric D. ... San Francisco, CA
Miller, Eric D. ... **Atlanta, GA**
Miller, Eric E. ... Philadelphia, PA
Miller, Eric H. ... Miami, FL
Miller, Eric I. ... Indianapolis, IN
Miller, Eric L. ... General Services Administration, Office of Inspector General, GV
Miller, Eric N. ... **Overland Park, KS**
Miller, Eric R. ... Waterloo, IA
Miller, Eric R. ... **Baton Rouge, LA**
Miller, Eric R. ... Lake Oswego, OR
Miller, Eric S. ... **Mansfield, OH**
Miller, Eric S. ... **Burlington, VT**
Miller, Erika E. ... **Cherry Hill, NJ**
Philadelphia, PA
Miller, Erin ... Phoenix, AZ
Miller, Erin S. ... Camden, NJ
Miller, Ernest ... Brooklyn, NY
Miller, Ernest J. ... Brooklyn, NY
Miller, Ernest L. ... San Jose, CA
Miller, Ernest L., Jr. ... Fredericksburg, TX
Miller, Errol S. ... **Pittsburgh, PA**
Miller, Erwin ... Philadelphia, PA
Miller, Erwin H. ... **Worcester, MA**
Miller, Esson M., Jr. ... Richmond, VA
Miller, Esther D. ... **New York, NY**
Miller, Esti ... **Los Angeles, CA**
Miller, Ethan A. ... **San Francisco, CA**
Miller, Ethan A. ... Charlottesville, VA
Miller, Eugene ... Seaside, CA
Miller, Eugene C. ... McLean, VA
Miller, Eugene C., Jr. ... Indianapolis, IN
Miller, Eugene H. ... **Walnut Creek, CA**
Miller, Eugene P. ... **Washington, DC**
Miller, Eugene V. ... Stark City, MO
Miller, Eugene W. ... St. Paul, MN
Miller, Eva C. ... **Phoenix, AZ**
Miller, Evan ... **Washington, DC**
Miller, Evangelin M. ... Wilton, CA
Miller, Eve L. ... Lake Oswego, OR
Miller, F. Chester, III, (P.C.) ... Farmington, NM
Miller Faignant & Behrens, P.C. ... **Rutland, VT**
Miller & Fanwick, LLP ... **Palo Alto, CA**
Miller & Fasse ... Riverton, WY
Miller Faucher Cafferty and Wexler LLP ... **Chicago, IL**
Ann Arbor, MI
Philadelphia, PA
Miller, Faust & Bekhor, P.C. ... Covina, CA
Miller & Fegen Co., L.P.A. ... Norwalk, OH
Miller, Felicia R. ... New York, NY
Miller, Felicia Styler ... Milwaukee, WI
Miller & Ferguson ... Chicago, IL
Miller, Fern B. ... **Chicago, IL**
Miller, Finney, Clark, McKeown & Baker ... **Xenia, OH**
Miller, Floranna S. ... New York, NY
Miller, Florence E. ... Chicago, IL
Miller, Floyd B. ... Cincinnati, OH
Miller, Floyd J., Jr. ... Department of Justice, Tax Division, GV
Miller, Floyd, Jr. ... Madill, OK
Miller, Floyd V. ... Richfield, MN
Miller & Folse ... Thousand Oaks, CA
Miller, Forest and Downing, Ltd. ... Glenview, IL
Miller & Foulk ... Wilmington, DE
Miller, Fowlkes & Farrior, P.L.L.C. ... **Biloxi, MS**
Miller, Frances H. ... **Boston, MA**
Miller, Frances J. ... **Washington, DC**
Miller, Francine ... **New York, NY**
Miller, Francis Anthony ... **Brooksville, FL**
Tampa, FL
Miller, Francis J. ... Sicklerville, NJ
Miller, Francis L., Jr. ... Highland Park, MI
Miller, Francis X. "Butch" ... St. Louis, MO
Miller, Frank B., III ... **Richmond, VA**
Miller, Frank C. ... Roswell, NM
Miller, Frank C., III ... **Lake Charles, LA**
Miller, Frank Estes ... **Jacksonville, FL**
Miller, Frank J. ... Wilmington, DE
Miller, Frank J. ... **New York, NY**
Miller, Frank, Jr. ... **Louisville, KY**
Miller, Frank L. ... Kailua-Kona, HI
Miller, Frank P. ... Bristol, TN
Miller, Frank W. ... Olivette, MO
Miller, Frank W. ... **Syracuse, NY**
Miller, Franklin ... New York, NY
Miller, Franz E. ... Santa Ana, CA
Miller, Fred B. ... **Portland, OR**
Miller, Fred B. ... Tyrone, PA
Miller, Fred H. ... Oklahoma City, OK
Miller, Fred L. ... **Dallas, TX**
Miller, Fred R. ... West Covina, CA
Miller, Fred S. ... Hamilton, OH
Miller, Fred S., Co., L.P.A. ... Hamilton, OH
Miller, Fred W. ... Norristown, PA
Miller, Frederic L. ... **Shreveport, LA**
Miller, Frederica L. ... **New York, NY**
Miller, Frederick ... Albany, NY
Miller, Frederick A. ... Pittsburgh, PA
Miller, Frederick A., & Associates ... **Metairie, LA**
Miller, Frederick A., & Associates ... **New Orleans, LA**
Miller, Frederick G. ... Hudson, MA
Miller, Frederick J. ... Sunnyvale, CA
Miller, Frederick L. ... New York, NY
Miller, Frederick L., Jr. ... **Washington, DC**
Miller, Frederick W. ... Baltimore, MD
Miller, Fredrick I. ... **Great Neck, NY**
Miller, Fredrick M. ... **Detroit, MI**
Miller, Fredrika V. ... New York, NY
Miller, G. Daniel ... **Washington, DC**
Miller, G. David, Jr. ... **Colorado Springs, CO**
Miller, G. Franklin ... **Cincinnati, OH**
Miller, G. Hobart ... Department of Justice, Tax Division, GV
Miller, G. Kenneth ... Richmond, VA
Miller, G. Michael ... Sacramento, CA
Miller, G. Michael ... Rochester, NY
Miller, G. Ray, Jr. ... **Corpus Christi, TX**
Miller, G. Scott ... Del Mar, CA
Miller, G. Spencer ... **Gladstone, MO**
Miller, G. Spencer, L.L.C., Law Offices of ... **Gladstone, MO**
Miller, G. Thomas ... **Harrisburg, PA**
Miller, G. Thompson ... **Lexington, NC**
Miller, G. William ... **Indianapolis, IN**
Miller, Gabriel ... Boston, MA
Miller, Gabrielle ... New York, NY
Miller, Gail F. ... Jenkintown, PA
Miller, Gail Harrington ... Richmond, VA
Miller, Gail Prentiss ... **Manassas, VA**
Miller, Gail Suzanne ... Washington, DC
Miller & Gaines, P.C. ... Atlanta, GA
Decatur, GA
Miller & Galdieri ... Jersey City, NJ
Miller, Gale T. ... **Denver, CO**
Miller, Gardner B. ... St. Helena Island, SC
Miller, Garfield A. ... **Boston, MA**
Miller, Garfield H. ... **Norwich, VT**
Miller, Garner R. ... Shreveport, LA
Miller, Gary A. ... Hollywood, FL
Miller, Gary A. ... **Philadelphia, PA**
Miller, Gary A. ... Madison, WI
Miller, Gary Alan ... **Detroit, MI**
Miller, Gary C. ... **Houston, TX**
Miller, Gary D. ... Golden, CO
Miller, Gary D. ... **Kingsport, TN**
Miller, Gary E. ... Staten Island, NY
Miller, Gary G. ... Topeka, KS
Miller, Gary H. ... **New Orleans, LA**
Miller, Gary L. ... Tampa, FL
Miller, Gary L. ... Indianapolis, IN
Miller, Gary L. ... **Toledo, OH**
Miller, Gary M. ... **Fort Lauderdale, FL**
Miller, Gary M. ... **Chicago, IL**
Miller, Gary M. ... Bethlehem, PA
Miller, Gary N. ... Los Angeles, CA
Miller, Gary R. ... New York, NY
Miller, Gary T. ... Murphysboro, IL
Miller, Gary W. ... **Houston, TX**
Miller & Gaudio, P.C. ... Red Bank, NJ
Miller, Gayle L. ... Rolling Meadows, IL
Miller, Gayle P. ... Department of Justice, Tax Division, GV
Miller, Geo. H. ... Riverside, CA
Miller, Geoffrey P. ... Chicago, IL
Miller, George ... **Oklahoma City, OK**
Miller, George A. ... Pittsburgh, PA
Miller, George D., Jr. ... **Detroit, MI**
Miller, George David, Jr. ... Omaha, NE
Miller, George E. ... Eau Claire, WI
Miller, George F. ... Algoma, WI
Miller, George H. ... Waco, TX
Miller, George H., Jr. ... Department of Commerce, Patent and Trademark Office, GV
Miller, George, III ... Antioch, CA
Miller, George J. ... **Lexington, KY**
Miller, George J. ... Eureka, MO
Miller, George J. ... **Charlotte, NC**
Miller, George J. ... Philadelphia, PA
Miller, George J. ... Pittsburgh, PA
Miller, George K., Jr. ... Atlantic City, NJ
Miller, George Keith (IBA) ... **New York, NY**
Miller, George L. ... Memphis, TN
Miller, George M. ... Tallmadge, OH
Miller, George Marshall ... Charlotte Amalie, St. Thomas, VI
Miller, George N. ... **Charlotte, NC**
Miller, George P. ... New York, NY
Miller, George Ralph ... **De Funiak Springs, FL**
Miller, George S. ... Urbana, IL
Miller, George W. ... **Washington, DC**
Miller, George W., III ... **Durham, NC**
Miller, George W., Jr. ... **Durham, NC**
Miller, George W., Jr. ... Stillwater, OK
Miller, George William ... New York, NY
Miller, Georgette M. ... New York, NY
Miller, Gerald ... New York, NY
Miller, Gerald A. ... Minneapolis, MN
Miller, Gerald C. ... Department of Justice, Tax Division, GV
Miller, Gerald D. ... Lansing, MI
Miller, Gerald D. ... **Jersey City, NJ**
Millburn, NJ
Miller, Gerald F. ... Northridge, CA
Miller, Gerald Foster ... Vancouver, WA
Miller, Gerald J. ... **Los Angeles, CA**
Miller, Gerald L. ... **Birmingham, AL**
Miller, Gerald M. ... Chicago, IL
Miller, Geraldene Y. ... Galena, KS
Ponca City, OK
Miller, Gerhard A. ... **Raleigh, NC**
Miller, Gerry ... Corpus Christi, TX
Miller, Gerry M. ... Green Bay, WI
Milwaukee, WI
Waukesha, WI
Miller & Giannini ... San Jose, CA
Miller, Gilbert C. ... **Washington, DC**
Miller, Gilbert G. ... **Somerville, NJ**
Miller, Gilman T. ... **San Francisco, CA**
Miller, Gina ... Birmingham, AL
Miller, Gina L. ... **Houston, TX**
Miller, Girard P. ... **Minneapolis, MN**
Miller, Glen B., Jr. ... Princeton, NJ
Miller, Glenda F. ... Richardson, TX
Miller, Glenn D. ... Brooklyn, NY
Miller, Glenn M. ... West Palm Beach, FL
Miller, Glenn M. ... Sewickley, PA
Miller, Glenn Martin ... New York, NY
Miller, Glenn S. ... **Washington, DC**
Miller & Goldman ... **Hamden, CT**
Miller, Gordon ... Board of Governors Of The Federal Reserve System, Office of the General Counsel, GV
Miller, Gordon A. ... Winston-Salem, NC
Miller, Gordon C. ... **Kalamazoo, MI**
Miller, Gordon D. ... New York, NY
Miller, Gordon H. ... Atlanta, GA
Miller, Gordon K. ... **Milwaukee, WI**
Miller, Gordon R. ... Meadville, PA
Miller, G.R. "Bob" ... **Durango, CO**
Miller, Graham C. ... Coral Gables, FL
Miller, Grant H., Jr. ... West Hartford, CT
Miller, Gray H. ... **Houston, TX**
Miller, Greg R. ... **Los Angeles, CA**
Miller, Gregg ... **New York, NY**
Miller, Gregg R. ... San Antonio, TX
Miller, Gregory A. ... **Anchorage, AK**
Miller, Gregory A. ... **Pittsburgh, PA**
Miller, Gregory B. ... Lima, OH

Miller, Gregory D. ... Newark, NJ
Miller, Gregory D. ... Albuquerque, NM
Miller, Gregory E.
Christiansted, St. Croix, VI
Miller, Gregory H. ... Crawfordsville, IN
Miller, Gregory J. ... San Jose, CA
Miller, Gregory J. ... West Redding, CT
Miller, Gregory J. ... Baton Rouge, LA
Miller, Gregory K. ... San Francisco, CA
Miller, Gregory K. ... Jacksboro, TN
Miller, Gregory K. ... Big Bend, WI
Miller, Gregory L. ... Dallas, TX
Miller, Gregory M. ... Baltimore, MD
Miller, Gregory M. ... Seattle, WA
Miller, Gregory P. ... Haddonfield, NJ
Philadelphia, PA
Miller, Gregory P. ... Buffalo, NY
Miller, Gregory R. ... Tallahassee, FL
Miller, Gregory R. ... Atlanta, GA
Miller, Gregory S. ... Encino, CA
Miller, Gregory T. ... Buffalo, NY
Miller, Gregory T. ... Fort Worth, TX
Miller, Gregory V. ... Chicago, IL
Miller, Gretchen E. ... Shorewood, WI
Miller, Gretchen L. ... Eugene, OR
Miller, Griffin & Marks, P.S.C.
Lexington, KY
Miller, Gunnar ... Jacksonville, FL
Miller, Guy F. ... Charlottesville, VA
Miller, Guy M.
National Aeronautics And Space Administration, Goddard Space Flight Center, GV
Miller, Guy M. ... New York, NY
Miller, H. Anthony ... Malibu, CA
Miller, H. Craig ... Sacramento, CA
Miller, H. Crane
Federal Emergency Management Agency, Office of the General Counsel, GV
Miller, H. Jack ... Coral Gables, FL
Miller, H. Jack ... Jacksonville, FL
Miller, H. Keith ... Troy, MI
Miller, H. Lawrence ... St. Louis, MO
Miller, H. Lockwood, III
Florham Park, NJ
Miller, H. Michael ... Denver, CO
Miller, H. Todd ... Washington, DC
Miller, Hadley B. ... Waldoboro, ME
Miller, Hainon A. ... Greenville, MS
Miller & Hall, P.A. ... Charlotte, NC
Miller, Hall & Triggs ... Peoria, IL
Miller, Halvor T., Jr. ... Los Angeles, CA
Miller, Hamilton, Snider, Odom & Bridgeman, L.L.C. ... Washington, DC
Miller, Hamilton, Snider & Odom, L.L.C.
Mobile, AL
Montgomery, AL
Miller, Harbaugh ... Pittsburgh, PA
Miller, Harlan S., III ... Atlanta, GA
Miller, Harland L., III ... Burlington, VT
Miller, Harlene ... Santa Ana, CA
Miller, Harold A. ... Champaign, IL
Miller, Harold A. ... Perth Amboy, NJ
Miller, Harold A., P.A. ... Perth Amboy, NJ
Miller, Harold D., Jr. ... Jackson, MS
Miller, Harold F., Jr. ... Birmingham, AL
Miller, Harold I. ... Stockton, CA
Miller, Harold L. ... Pearl, MS
Miller, Harold N. ... Fredericksburg, TX
Miller, Harriet H. ... Jersey City, NJ
Miller, Harris M., II ... Los Angeles, CA
Miller and Harrison, LLC ... Boulder, CO
Miller, Harry ... Tucson, AZ
Miller, Harry B., Jr. ... Lexington, KY
Miller, Harry C. ... Calistoga, CA
Miller, Harry D. ... Walnut Creek, CA
Miller, Harry S. ... Chicago, IL
Miller, Harry S. ... Boston, MA
Miller, Harry V. B. ... Albany, NY
Miller, Harry Willis, III ... Nashville, TN
Miller, Harvey A. ... Hackensack, NJ
Miller, Harvey A., Jr. ... Pittsburgh, PA
Miller, Harvey F. ... Akron, OH
Miller, Harvey R., (P.C.) ... New York, NY
Miller, Harvey S. ... Lancaster, PA
Miller, Harvey S. Shipley ... New York, NY
Miller, Heath A. ... Dallas, TX
Miller, Heather Leigh ... Washington, DC
Miller, Helen P. ... Fort Washington, MD
Miller & Hendren ... Champaign, IL
Miller, Henry B. ... Washington, DC
Miller, Henry B. ... Jefferson, WI
Miller, Henry F. ... Philadelphia, PA
Miller, Henry G. ... White Plains, NY
Miller, Henry, III ... Pittsburgh, PA
Miller, Henry J. ... Atlanta, GA
Miller, Henry L. ... Pittsburgh, PA
Miller, Henry S., Jr. ... Groton, MA
Miller, Henry Stuckert ... Jenkintown, PA
Miller, Henry T. ... Department of Justice, Civil Division, GV
Miller, Henry T. V. ... Memphis, TN
Miller, Henry Warren, III ... Memphis, TN
Miller, Herbert A., Jr. ... Lexington, KY
Miller, Herbert D., Jr. ... Washington, DC
Miller, Herbert H. ... Towson, MD
Miller, Herbert H., P.A. ... Towson, MD
Miller, Herbert J., Jr. ... Washington, DC
Miller, Herbert S. ... Reston, VA
Miller, Herman B. ... Frederick, MD
Miller, Hilary B. ... Greenwich, CT
Miller, Hilary B., (Mr.) ... Greenwich, CT
Miller & Hill ... Riverside, CA
Miller, Homer K. ... Pompano Beach, FL
Miller, Howard B. ... El Segundo, CA
Miller, Howard B. ... Baltimore, MD
Miller, Howard J. ... Wheat Ridge, CO
Miller, Howard M. ... Boston, MA
Miller, Howard M. ... Mineola, NY
New York, NY
Miller, Howard M. ... Hilton Head Island, SC
Miller, Howard M. ... Norfolk, VA
Miller, Howard N. ... Highland Beach, FL
Miller, Howard P. ... Columbia, MD
Miller, Howard S. ... Cooper City, FL
Miller, Howard S. ... St. Petersburg, FL
Miller, Howard S. ... Elgin, IL
Miller, Howard S., and Associates, P.C.
Elgin, IL
Miller, Howard S., P.A. ... Cooper City, FL
Miller, Hugh, III ... Boston, MA
Miller, Hugh M. ... Galveston, TX
Miller & Hutson ... Lebanon, MO
Miller, I. Clinton ... Woodstock, VA
Miller, Ian H. ... Atlanta, GA
Miller & Im, P.A. ... New Port Richey, FL
Miller, Ira C. ... Princeton, NJ
Miller, Ira J. ... Los Angeles, CA
Miller, Irving E. ... Miami, FL
Miller, Irving I. ... Westbury, NY
Miller, Irving M. ... Miami, FL
Miller, Irwin D. ... New York, NY
Miller, Irwin M., (P.C.) ... Carle Place, NY
Miller, Irwin R. (Rob) ... Encino, CA
Ventura, CA
Miller, Irwin R. (Rob) ... Oxnard, CA
Miller, Ivan L. ... Cleveland, OH
Miller, J. Allen ... New York, NY
Miller, J. Anthony ... Tulsa, OK
Miller, J. Bruce ... Louisville, KY
Miller, J. Bruce, Law Group
Louisville, KY
Miller, J. Christian ... Monticello, IL
Miller, J. Clark ... Los Angeles, CA
Miller, J. David ... Kingsport, TN
Miller, J. Douglas ... Liberal, KS
Miller, J. Dupre ... Bennettsville, SC
Miller, J. Gary ... Winter Park, FL
Miller, J. Greg ... New Philadelphia, OH
Miller, J. Gregg ... Philadelphia, PA
Miller, J. Gregg, Jr. ... Palo Alto, CA
Miller, J. Jefferson, II ... Ruxton, MD
Miller, J. Jerome ... Destin, FL
Miller, J. Kent ... Denver, CO
Miller, J. Kirkland ... Troy, MI
Miller, J. Lee ... Pittsburgh, PA
Miller, J. Lynn ... Arco, ID
Miller, J. Mark ... Natchitoches, LA
Miller, J. Marshall ... New Orleans, LA
Miller, J. Matthew ... Clarksville, TN
Miller, J. Maurice, Jr. ... Richmond, VA
Miller, J. Mitchell ... Dallas, TX
Miller, J. Patrick ... Houston, TX
Miller, J. Peter ... Indianapolis, IN
Miller, J. Randal ... Golden, CO
Miller, J. Randall ... Tulsa, OK
Miller, J. Randolph ... Knoxville, TN
Miller, J. Robert ... Huntsville, AL
Miller, J. Russell ... Washington, DC
Miller, J. Scott ... Spokane, WA
Miller, Jack ... Newark, OH
Miller, Jack B. ... Jamestown, KY
Miller, Jack D. ... Hartford, CT
Miller, Jack Derrick ... Crowley, LA
Miller, Jack G. ... Clarksville, TN
Miller, Jack J. ... Irvine, CA
Miller, Jack L. ... Lexington, KY
Miller, Jack L. ... Lebanon, MO
Miller, Jack L. ... Washington, WV
Miller, Jack M. ... La Habra, CA
Miller, Jack R. ... Plainview, TX
Miller, Jackson D., III ... Bradenton, FL
Miller, Jacob ... Ridge, NY
Miller, Jacob H. ... Seattle, WA
Miller, Jacob S. ... Indianapolis, IN
Miller, Jacqueline ... Eden Prairie, MN
Miller, Jacqueline A. ... Cambridge, MA
Miller, Jacqueline S. ... Palm Beach, FL
Miller & James ... San Diego, CA
Miller, James A. ... Lakewood, CO
Miller, James A. ... Agawam, MA
Miller, James A. ... Springfield, MO
Miller, James A. ... Harrisburg, PA
Miller, James A. ... Pittsburgh, PA
Miller, James A. ... Seattle, WA
Miller, James A., A Professional Corporation
Springfield, MO
Miller, James A., Jr. ... Fairfield, CT
Miller, James B. ... Omaha, NE
Miller, James B. ... Fairfax, VA
Miller, James C. ... Campbellsville, KY
Miller, James C. ... White Plains, NY
Miller, James D. ... Burlingame, CA
Miller, James D. ... San Diego, CA
Miller, James D. ... Santa Ana, CA
Miller, James D. ... Washington, DC
Miller, James D. ... Des Moines, IA
Miller, James D. ... Bloomington, MN
Miller, James D. ... New York, NY
Miller, James D. ... Columbus, OH
Miller, James D. ... Dallas, TX
Miller, James E. ... San Francisco, CA
Miller, James E. ... Springfield, MO
Miller, James E. ... Haddonfield, NJ
Philadelphia, PA
Miller, James E. ... Houston, TX
Miller, James E. ... San Antonio, TX
Miller, James E., P.C. ... Springfield, MO
Miller, James F. ... Pasadena, CA
Miller, James F. ... West Palm Beach, FL
Miller, James F. ... Lexington, KY
Miller, James F. ... Canandaigua, NY
Miller, James F., Jr. ... Madison, WI
Miller, James Forrest ... Washington, DC
Miller, James Fox ... Hollywood, FL
Miller, James G. ... Cupertino, CA
Miller, James H. ... Enka, NC
Miller, James H. ... Houston, TX
Miller, James H. ... Seattle, WA
Miller, James H., III ... Birmingham, AL
Miller, James H., P.C. ... Houston, TX
Miller, James Ian ... Phoenix, AZ
Miller, James J., Jr ... Alpine, TX
Miller, James Joseph ... Carbondale, IL
Miller, James Joseph ... Las Vegas, NV
Miller, James L. ... San Francisco, CA
Miller, James L. ... San Francisco, CA
Miller, James L. ... McHenry, IL
Miller, James L. ... Winston-Salem, NC
Miller, James L. ... Cleveland, OH
Miller, James L. ... Norfolk, VA
Miller, James L.I. ... Newport Beach, CA
Miller, James M. ... Altamonte Springs, FL
Miller, James M. ... Miami, FL
Miller, James M. ... Atlanta, GA
Miller, James M. ... Owensboro, KY
Miller, James M. ... Oak Grove, LA
Miller, James M. ... Cassopolis, MI
Miller, James M. ... Fairmont, MN
Miller, James M., Jr. ... Rayne, LA
Miller, James, Miller, Wyly & Hornsby, L.L.P. ... Texarkana, TX
Miller, James N. ... Forrest City, AR
Miller, James O. ... Long Beach, CA
Miller, James O. ... Portage, WI
Miller, James P. ... Corning, NY
Miller, James P. ... Wilmington, OH
Miller, James P. ... Smethport, PA
Miller, James R. ... Burbank, CA
Miller, James R. ... Louisville, KY
Miller, James R. ... Detroit, MI
Miller, James R. ... Wyoming, MI
Miller, James R. ... Pittsburgh, PA
Miller, James R. ... Dallas, TX
Miller, James R., Jr. ... Rockville, MD
Miller, James R., P.C. ... Wyoming, MI
Miller, James Robert ... Washington, DC
Rockville, MD
Rockville, MD
Miller, James Rollin, Jr. ... Denver, CO
Miller, James T. ... Jacksonville, FL
Miller, James T. ... Louisville, KY
Miller, James T. ... Romeo, MI
Miller, James W. ... Los Angeles, CA
Miller, James W. ... Burlington, IA
Miller, James W. ... Minneapolis, MN
Miller, James W. ... Lancaster, OH
Miller, Jamie G. ... Atlanta, GA
Miller, Jamie G., P.C. ... Atlanta, GA
Miller, Jan Paul ... Baltimore, MD
Miller, Jan W.
Agency for International Development, Office of the General Counsel, GV
Miller, Jana ... Russell, KY
Miller, Jana R. ... Palo Alto, CA
Miller, Jane Brindle ... Palo Alto, CA
Miller, Jane E. ... Grafton, WI
Miller, Jane E. L. ... Beverly, MA
Miller, Jane H. ... Columbus, OH
Miller, Jane S. ... Detroit, MI
Miller, Jane Sweeney ... Salisbury, MD
Miller, Jane W. ... South Bend, IN
Miller, Janeen R. ... Charlotte, NC
Miller, Janet ... Novato, CA
Miller, Janet Brownlee ... Mount Holly, NJ
Miller, Janet Clare ... San Diego, CA
Miller, Janet D. ... New York, NY
Miller, Janet L. ... Cleveland, OH
Miller, Janet L. ... Harrisburg, PA
Miller, Janice Davis ... Red Bank, NJ
Miller, Janice Lee ... Universal City, CA
Miller, Janice R. ... Chicago, IL
Miller, Janise L. ... Atlanta, GA
Miller, Jason E. ... Los Angeles, CA
Miller, Jason H. ... Chicago, IL
Miller, Jason J. ... Hackensack, NJ
Miller, Jason S. ... Miami, FL
Miller, Jason S ... Dayton, OH
Miller, Jason T. ... Los Angeles, CA
Miller, Jaxon E. ... Riverside, CA
Miller, Jay C. ... Malibu, CA
Miller, Jay D. ... Baltimore, MD
Miller, Jay G. ... Bayside, NY
Miller, Jay J. ... New York, NY
Miller, Jay L. ... Barrington, IL
Miller, Jay M.
Commodity Futures Trading Commission, Division of Enforcement, GV
Miller, Jay W. ... Milwaukee, WI
Miller, J. D. ... Wheeling, WV
Miller, Jean E. ... Atlanta, GA
Miller, Jean S. ... Seattle, WA
Miller, Jeanie Owen ... Owensboro, KY
Miller, Jeanmarie ... Flint, MI
Miller, Jeanne C. ... New York, NY
Miller, Jeanne M. ... Jacksonville, FL
Miller, Jeanne M. ... Chicago, IL
Miller, Jeanne M. ... St. Louis, MO
Miller, Jeanne S. ... New Haven, IN
Miller, Jeannine L. ... Denver, CO
Miller, Jeff C. ... Omaha, NE
Miller, Jeffords D. ... Orlando, FL
Miller, Jeffrey ... Phoenix, AZ
Miller, Jeffrey ... Jersey City, NJ
New York, NY
Miller, Jeffrey A. ... Los Angeles, CA
Miller, Jeffrey A. ... Orinda, CA
Miller, Jeffrey A. ... San Jose, CA
Miller, Jeffrey A. ... Boca Raton, FL
Miller, Jeffrey A. ... Orlando, FL
Miller, Jeffrey A. ... Baltimore, MD
Miller, Jeffrey A. ... Garden City, NY
Miller, Jeffrey A. ... Cincinnati, OH
Miller, Jeffrey A., P.A. ... Baltimore, MD
Miller, Jeffrey Andrew ... Cleveland, TN
Miller, Jeffrey B. ... Frederick, MD
Miller, Jeffrey B., (P.C.) ... Phoenix, AZ
Miller, Jeffrey C. ... Palo Alto, CA
Miller, Jeffrey C. ... Santa Ana, CA
Miller, Jeffrey C. ... Berlin, CT
Miller, Jeffrey C. ... Cleveland, OH
Miller, Jeffrey Craig ... New York, NY
Miller, Jeffrey D. ... Raleigh, NC
Miller, Jeffrey David ... Austin, TX
Miller, Jeffrey G. ... Washington, DC
Miller, Jeffrey H. ... New York, NY
Miller, Jeffrey H. ... Toledo, OH
Miller, Jeffrey J. ... Phoenix, AZ
Miller, Jeffrey J. ... Stamford, CT
Miller, Jeffrey J. ... Charleston, WV
Miller, Jeffrey L. ... Los Angeles, CA
Miller, Jeffrey L. ... Merced, CA
Miller, Jeffrey L. ... Greenville, NC
Miller, Jeffrey L. ... Redmond, WA
Miller, Jeffrey M. ... Department of Justice, Executive Office for United States Trustees, GV
Miller, Jeffrey M. ... Chicago, IL
Miller, Jeffrey N. ... Schenectady, NY
Miller, Jeffrey P. ... San Francisco, CA
Miller, Jeffrey R. ... Ellicott City, MD
Miller, Jeffrey R. ... New York, NY
Miller, Jeffrey R. ... Wheeling, WV
Miller, Jeffrey S. ... Shepherdsville, KY
Miller, Jeffrey S. ... Portsmouth, VA
Miller, Jeffrey S. ... Seattle, WA
Miller, Jeffrey T. ... San Diego, CA
Miller, Jeffrey T. ... New York, NY
Miller, Jeffrey W. ... Tulsa, OK
Miller, Jeffry A. ... San Diego, CA
Miller, Jennifer B. ... Washington, DC
Miller, Jennifer G. ... Chicago, IL
Miller, Jennifer J. ... Santa Ana, CA
Miller, Jennifer J. ... Greenville, SC
Miller, Jennifer L. ... New York, NY
Miller, Jennifer L. ... Philadelphia, PA
Miller, Jennifer T. ... Franklin, MA
Miller, Jerald L. ... Indianapolis, IN
Miller, Jeremiah S. ... New Canaan, CT
Miller, Jeremy B. ... Washington, DC
Miller, Jeremy N. ... Los Angeles, CA
Miller, Jerome ... Jericho, NY
Miller, Jerome R. ... Boca Raton, FL
Millburn, NJ
Miller, Jerome R., P.A. ... Boca Raton, FL
Miller, Jerre A. ... Hopkins, MN
Miller, Jerri ... Cleveland, OH
Miller, Jerrold D. ... Washington, DC
Miller, Jerry ... Beverly Hills, CA
Miller, Jerry ... Fairview Heights, IL
Miller, Jerry D. ... Olney, IL
Miller, Jerry D ... Greenbelt, MD
Miller, Jerry J. ... Amarillo, TX
Miller, Jerry L. ... Kalamazoo, MI
Miller, Jerry M., Jr. ... Charlotte, NC
Miller, Jerry W. ... New Castle, IN
Miller, Jerry W. ... Asheville, NC
Miller, Jesse D. ... Los Angeles, CA
Miller, Jesse L. ... San Francisco, CA
Miller, Jesse W. ... Miami, FL
Miller, Jessica Davidson ... Washington, DC
Miller Jester & Kearney L.L.C.
Denver, CO
Miller, Jill, & Associates ... Scranton, PA
Miller, Jill D. ... Bellevue, WA
Miller, Jill Hilary ... Scranton, PA
Miller, Jill K. ... Chicago, IL
Miller, Jill L. ... New York, NY
Miller, Jill S. ... Chicago, IL
Miller, Jim ... Toledo, OH
Miller, Jim B. ... McAlester, OK
Miller, Jimmie Carpenter
Johnson City, TN
Kingsport, TN
Miller, Jimmy L. ... Marks, MS
Miller, J. L. (Skip) ... St. Petersburg, FL
Miller, Joan L. ... Shakopee, MN
Miller, Joan R. ... Whittier, CA
Miller, Joanna F. ... Houston, TX
Miller, Joanne ... Los Angeles, CA
Miller, Jody ... Summit, NJ
Miller, Joe C., II ... St. Augustine, FL
Miller, Joel ... Treasury Department, Office of the Comptroller of the Currency, GV
Miller, Joel ...
Treasury Department, GV
Miller, Joel ... Fort Lauderdale, FL
Miller, Joel ... West Orange, NJ
Miller, Joel B. ... Great Neck, NY
Miller, Joel B. ... New York, NY
Miller, Joel Bron ... Department of Justice, Tax Division, GV
Miller, Joel D. ... Department of the Army, U.S. Army Legal Services Agency, GV
Miller, Joel E. ... Flushing, NY
Miller, Joel L. ... Chicago, IL
Miller, Joel M. ... Cherry Hill, NJ
Miller, Joel M. ... New York, NY
Miller, Joel S. ... Lake Zurich, IL
Miller, John ... Russellville, KY
Miller, John ... Boston, MA
Miller, John A. ... Phoenix, AZ
Miller, John A. ... Berkeley, CA
Miller, John A. ... Fort Lauderdale, FL
Miller, John A. ... North Miami Beach, FL
Miller, John A. ... Tallahassee, FL
Miller, John A. ... Detroit, MI
Miller, John A. ... Troy, MI
Miller, John A. ... Minneapolis, MN
Miller, John A. ... Beaver, PA
Miller, John A. ... Fircrest, WA

Miller, Lisa J. P. .... Washington, DC
Miller, Lisa K. .... Washington, DC
Miller, Lisa M.
Federal Deposit Insurance Corporation, Trial Litigation Section, GV
Miller, Lisa M. R. .... Washington, DC
Miller, Lisa Okolish .... Barberton, OH
Miller, Lloyd Benton .... Anchorage, AK
Miller, Lohra L. .... West Jordan, UT
Miller & Loosemore .... Evansville, IN
Miller, LoRang and Jordening .... Nevada, IA
Miller, Loren B. .... White Plains, NY
Miller, Loren, Jr. .... Los Angeles, CA
Miller, Lorena Haumann .... Princeton, NJ
Miller, Lori J. .... Blue Bell, PA
Miller, Lori K. .... Chicago, IL
Miller, Lori R. .... Scottsdale, AZ
Miller, Lorraine D. .... New York, NY
Miller, Louis C., (P.C.) .... Boston, MA
Miller, Louis E. .... Pekin, IL
Miller, Louis H. .... Flemington, NJ
Miller, Louis J. .... Memphis, TN
Miller, Louis R., III .... Los Angeles, CA
Miller, Louise K. .... Austin, TX
Miller, Lowell B. .... Basking Ridge, NJ
Miller, Lowell S. .... Whitehouse, NJ
Miller, Lowry J. .... Fairfax, VA
Miller, Lucia E. .... Cambridge, MA
Miller & Ludwig .... Beloit, KS
Mankato, KS
Miller & Luring Co., L.P.A. .... Troy, OH
Miller, Luther W. .... Rochester, NY
Miller, Lynda M. .... Moorestown, NJ
Philadelphia, PA
Miller, Lynn A. .... St. Louis, MO
Miller, Lynn C. .... Mobile, AL
Miller, Lynn F. .... New Brunswick, NJ
Miller, Lynn I. .... Washington, DC
Miller, Lynn L. .... Palo Alto, CA
Miller, Lynn M. .... Elkhart, IN
Miller, Lynne D. .... Philadelphia, PA
Miller, Lynne M. .... Cleveland, OH
Miller, M. Ann .... Lansing, MI
Miller, M. Dale .... Knoxville, TN
Miller, M. Kathleen .... Mobile, AL
Miller, M. Larry .... Louisville, KY
Miller, M. Val .... Las Vegas, NV
Miller, M. Wallace .... Aurelia, IA
Cherokee, IA
Miller, Machale A. .... New Orleans, LA
Miller, Makkai & Dowdle .... Westminster, CO
Miller, Malcolm L. .... Columbus, OH
Miller, Malinda A. .... Jersey City, NJ
Miller, Mallory L., Jr. .... San Antonio, TX
Miller, Mamie R.
Environmental Protection Agency, Program Office Attorneys, GV
Miller, Mandy E. .... Fort Lauderdale, FL
Miller, Mannix & Pratt, P.C.
Glens Falls, NY
Lake George, NY
Saratoga Springs, NY
Miller, Manuel H. .... Woodland Hills, CA
Miller, Marc E. .... Washington, DC
Miller, Marc Eric .... Washington, DC
Miller, Marc J. .... Boston, MA
Miller, Marc L. .... Atlanta, GA
Miller, Marc R. .... Champaign, IL
Miller, Marc W., & Associates
Kingston, NY
Miller, Marci L. .... Somerset, PA
Miller, Marci Lerner .... Costa Mesa, CA
Miller, Marcia Ann .... Morristown, NJ
Miller, Marcia F. .... West Trenton, NJ
Miller, Marcia Groves .... Scottsdale, AZ
Miller, Marcus Jay .... Tacoma, WA
Miller, Marcy B. .... Chicago, IL
Miller, Margaret A. .... Novato, CA
Miller, Margaret A. .... Lexington, KY
Miller, Margaret Apel .... Portsmouth, OH
Miller, Margaret Bannon .... Indianapolis, IN
Miller, Margaret L. .... Washington, DC
Miller, Margaret P. .... Towaco, NJ
Miller, Margaret R. .... Towson, MD
Miller, Margery K. .... Philadelphia, PA
Miller, Margie Rigsby .... Murfreesboro, TN
Miller, Mari L. .... Salem, OR
Miller, Maria D. .... Newark, NJ
Miller, Marian C. .... Philadelphia, PA
Miller, Marie E. .... Detroit, MI
Miller, Marie K. .... San Antonio, CA
Miller, Marie L. .... Washington, DC
Miller, Marie-Bernarde .... Little Rock, AR
Miller, Mari-Eleanor .... Austin, TX
Miller, Marilyn G. .... Portland, OR
Miller, Marilyn W. .... Cape Coral, FL
Miller, Marion C., (Mr.)
Hilton Head Island, SC
Miller, Marjorie .... Rocklin, CA
Miller, Marjorie .... Portland, OR
Miller, Marjorie A. .... New York, NY
Miller, Mark A. .... Santa Rosa, CA
Miller, Mark A. .... Santa Rosa, CA
Miller, Mark A. .... Hollywood, FL
Miller, Mark A. .... Mount Clemens, MI
Miller, Mark A. .... St. Joseph, MI
Miller, Mark A. .... Manitowoc, WI
Miller, Mark D. .... Fresno, CA
Miller, Mark D. .... Roseland, NJ
Miller, Mark E. .... San Francisco, CA
Miller, Mark E. .... Tampa, FL
Miller, Mark E. .... Evansville, IN
Miller, Mark E. .... Bozeman, MT
Miller, Mark Edwin .... Washington, DC
Miller, Mark F. .... Agoura Hills, CA
Miller, Mark F. .... Chicago, IL
Miller, Mark F. .... Detroit, MI
Miller, Mark H. .... San Antonio, TX

Miller, Mark H. .... Richmond, VA
Miller, Mark H., Law Offices of
Brookfield, WI
Miller, Mark Howard .... Cedarhurst, NY
Miller, Mark J. .... Department of Justice, Justice Management Division, GV
Miller, Mark J. .... Cleveland, OH
Miller, Mark J .... Milwaukee, WI
Miller, Mark L. .... Louisville, KY
Miller, Mark L. .... Louisville, KY
Miller, Mark L. .... Columbia, MD
Miller, Mark L. .... Appleton, WI
Miller, Mark M. .... Bellevue, WA
Miller, Mark Montgomery .... Austin, TX
Miller, Mark N. .... Lakeland, FL
Miller, Mark P. .... Chicago, IL
Miller, Mark P. .... White Plains, NY
Miller, Mark R. .... Jacksonville, FL
Miller, Mark R. .... Minneapolis, MN
Miller, Mark S. .... Healdsburg, CA
Miller, Mark S. .... Atlanta, GA
Miller, Mark S. .... Boston, MA
Miller, Mark S. .... New York, NY
Miller, Mark S. .... Columbus, OH
Miller, Mark S. .... Norristown, PA
Miller, Mark Stephen .... Houston, TX
Miller, Mark W. .... Nashville, TN
Miller, Mark W. .... Houston, TX
Miller, Mark Williams .... Winston-Salem, NC
Miller & Markle, L.L.P. .... Atlanta, GA
Miller, Marla J. .... San Francisco, CA
Miller, Marleen B. .... Baltimore, MD
Miller, Marna F. .... Los Angeles, CA
Miller, Marsden W., Jr. .... Lafayette, LA
Miller, Marshall B., Jr. .... San Antonio, TX
Miller, Marshall Lee .... Washington, DC
Miller, Marshall V. .... Washington, DC
Kansas City, MO
Miller, Marteen J. .... Santa Rosa, CA
Miller, Martha Ann .... Montgomery, AL
Miller, Martha Ann .... Lakeville, CT
Miller, Martha Gaumer .... Columbus, OH
Miller, Martha L. .... Erie, PA
Miller, Martha Walker Albrecht
Greenville, SC
Miller, Martin .... Miami Beach, FL
Miller & Martin .... Frankfort, IN
Miller, Martin .... York, PA
Miller, Martin B. .... New York, NY
Miller, Martin J. .... Cincinnati, OH
Miller, Martin J. .... Alexandria, VA
Miller, Martin K. .... Burlington, VT
Miller, Martin L. .... Glenview, IL
Miller, Martin L. .... Lawrence, KS
Miller, Martin, Law Offices of .... York, PA
Miller & Martin LLP .... Atlanta, GA
Chattanooga, TN
Miller, Martin M. .... Detroit, MI
Miller, Martin P. .... Littleton, CO
Miller, Martin R. .... New York, NY
Miller, Martin S. .... Jeffersonville, NY
Monticello, NY
Miller, Martin & Trabue .... Nashville, TN
Miller, Marvin .... San Antonio, TX
Miller, Marvin A. .... Chicago, IL
Miller, Marvin A. .... Cincinnati, OH
Miller, Marvin B. .... Upper Marlboro, MD
Miller, Marvin C. .... Sunbury, OH
Miller, Marvin D. .... Alexandria, VA
Miller, Marvin G. .... Centralia, IL
Miller, Marvin W. .... Cherokee, IA
Miller, Mary A. .... Fairbanks, AK
Miller, Mary A. .... Norcross, GA
Miller, Mary C.
Joint Committees And Commissions, GV
Miller, Mary Catherine .... Charlotte, NC
Miller, Mary Claire .... Jacksonville, FL
Miller, Mary Dillard .... Knoxville, TN
Miller, Mary E. .... Malibu, CA
Miller, Mary Ellen .... United States Senate, Committee Legal Personnel, GV
Miller, Mary Erin Wilcox .... Dallas, TX
Miller, Mary Helen .... Boulder, CO
Miller, Mary J. .... Columbus, OH
Miller, Mary J. .... Sugar Land, TX
Miller, Mary Jane .... Santa Barbara, CA
Miller, Mary Jane .... Minneapolis, MN
Miller, Mary K. .... Mill Creek, WA
Miller, Mary K. Baty .... San Francisco, CA
Miller, Mary L. .... Phoenix, AZ
Miller, Mary L. .... Atlanta, GA
Miller, Mary Louise .... Asbury Park, NJ
Miller, Mary Sieger, P.A. .... Jacksonville, FL
Miller, Mary-Anne Meyers .... Las Vegas, NV
Miller, Maryn L. .... Vernon, CA
Miller, Mason C. .... Newark, NJ
Miller & Mast, Ltd. .... Millersburg, OH
Miller, Matthew .... New York, NY
Miller, Matthew A. .... New York, NY
Miller, Matthew C. .... Overland Park, KS
Miller, Matthew D. .... Gulfport, MS
Miller, Matthew G. .... Chicago, IL
Miller, Matthew G. .... Omaha, NE
Miller, Matthew G. .... Paramus, NJ
Miller, Matthew J. .... New York, NY
Miller, Matthew M. .... Slidell, LA
Miller, Matthew R. .... San Diego, CA
Miller, Matthew R. .... New York, NY
Seattle, WA
Miller, Matthew S. .... Chicago, IL
Miller, Matthew W. .... Fort Lauderdale, FL
Miller, Maureen A. .... Chicago, IL
Miller, Maureen Shellooe .... El Cajon, CA
Miller, Maurice A. .... Columbus, OH
Miller, Maurice E. .... San Francisco, CA
Miller, Maurice J. .... Chicago, IL
Miller, Maurice L. .... New York, NY
Miller, Max A. .... Millersburg, OH

Miller, Max Dunham, Jr. .... Bel Air, MD
Miller, Max Dunham, Jr., P.A., Law Offices of .... Bel Air, MD
Elkton, MD
Miller, Max E. .... Washington, DC
Miller, Max F. .... Pittsburgh, PA
Miller, Max M., Jr. .... Portland, OR
Miller, Max R. .... Cedar Rapids, IA
Miller, Maxwell A. .... Salt Lake City, UT
Miller, Maxwell M. .... Chicago, IL
Miller, Maynard R., Jr. .... Hartford, CT
Miller, Mayne .... New York, NY
Miller & McCarren, P.C. .... Denver, CO
Miller & Meade, P.S.C. .... Louisville, KY
Miller, Megan E. .... Tucson, AZ
Miller, Melanie A. .... Philadelphia, PA
Miller, Melissa .... Los Angeles, CA
Miller, Melissa A.
Equal Employment Opportunity Commission, Office of Federal Operations, GV
Miller, Melissa A. .... Upper Saddle River, NJ
Miller, Melissa Ann .... Chicago, IL
Miller, Melissa C. .... Palatka, FL
Miller, Melissa Elaine .... Denver, CO
Miller, Melissa F. .... Oak Park, MI
Miller, Melissa Ferverda .... Indianapolis, IN
Miller, Melissa R. .... Tampa, FL
Miller, Melville D., Jr. .... Edison, NJ
Miller, Melvin B. .... Bala Cynwyd, PA
Miller, Melvin B., Ltd. .... Bala Cynwyd, PA
Philadelphia, PA
Miller, Melvin E. .... Silver Spring, MD
Miller, Melvin H. .... New York, NY
Miller, Melvin W. .... Beverly Hills, CA
Miller & Menaker .... Jersey City, NJ
Miller & Meola, A Professional Corporation
Albany, NY
Miller, Merlin L. .... Walnut Creek, CA
Miller, Merry .... Houston, TX
Miller, Mertens & Spanner
Kennewick, WA
Pasco, WA
Richland, WA
Miller, Merwyn J. .... Encinitas, CA
Miller, Meyerson, Schwartz & Corbo
Jersey City, NJ
Millburn, NJ
Newark, NJ
Paterson, NJ
Miller, Michael .... Santa Monica, CA
Miller, Michael .... Nashville, TN
Miller, Michael A. .... Orlando, FL
Miller, Michael A. .... Newton, MA
Miller, Michael A. .... Columbia, SC
Miller, Michael A. .... Dallas, TX
Miller, Michael Alden .... Woodland Hills, CA
Miller, Michael B. .... Beverly Hills, CA
Miller, Michael Britt .... Prattville, AL
Miller, Michael C. .... Los Angeles, CA
Miller, Michael C. .... San Francisco, CA
Miller, Michael C.
Pension Benefit Guaranty Corporation, Office of the General Counsel, GV
Miller, Michael C. .... New York, NY
Miller, Michael C. .... Asheboro, NC
Miller, Michael D. .... Tucson, AZ
Miller, Michael D. .... Los Angeles, CA
Miller, Michael D. .... Royal Palm Beach, FL
Miller, Michael D. .... Tampa, FL
Miller, Michael D. .... Minneapolis, MN
Miller, Michael D. .... West Collingswood, NJ
Miller, Michael D. .... Houston, TX
Miller, Michael D., Jr., P.C. .... Chandler, AZ
Miller, Michael E. .... Chicago, IL
Miller, Michael E. .... Lanham, MD
Miller, Michael E. .... Austin, TX
Miller, Michael Elliot .... Brooklyn, NY
Miller, Michael F. .... Jersey City, NJ
Miller, Michael G. .... Santa Rosa, CA
Miller, Michael G. .... Chicago, IL
Miller, Michael H. .... Arcadia, CA
Miller, Michael H. .... Marina Del Rey, CA
Miller, Michael H. .... Topeka, KS
Miller, Michael I. .... Chicago, IL
Miller, Michael J. .... South Gate, CA
Miller, Michael J. .... Fairmount, IN
Miller, Michael J. .... Des Moines, IA
Miller, Michael J. .... Kalamazoo, MI
Miller, Michael J. .... Excelsior, MN
Miller, Michael J. .... New York, NY
Miller, Michael J. .... Riverhead, NY
Miller, Michael J. .... Rochester, NY
Miller, Michael J. .... Charlotte, NC
Miller, Michael J. .... Lawton, OK
Miller, Michael J. .... Malvern, PA
Miller, Michael K. .... Fayetteville, AR
Miller, Michael K. .... Palm Beach, FL
Miller, Michael L. .... St. Paul, MN
Miller, Michael L. .... Bozeman, MT
Miller, Michael L. .... Asheville, NC
Miller, Michael L. .... Cleveland, OH
Miller, Michael L., P.A. .... Asheville, NC
Miller, Michael, Law Offices of
New York, NY
Miller, Michael Lewis .... Atlanta, GA
Miller, Michael McAuliffe .... Pittsburgh, PA
Miller, Michael Owen .... Tucson, AZ
Miller, Michael P. .... Littleton, CO
Miller, Michael Patiky .... Palo Alto, CA
Miller, Michael R. .... Denver, CO
Miller, Michael R. .... Washington, DC
Miller, Michael R. .... Fort Myers, FL
Sarasota, FL
Tampa, FL
Miller, Michael R. .... North Miami Beach, FL
Miller, Michael R. .... Minneapolis, MN
Miller, Michael R. .... New York, NY

Miller, Michael R. .... Cincinnati, OH
Miller, Michael R. .... Belton, TX
Miller, Michael R., P.C., Attorney at Law
Belton, TX
Miller, Michael Reed .... Washington, DC
Miller, Michael S. .... San Jose, CA
Miller, Michael S. .... Indianapolis, IN
Miller, Michael S. .... Chatham, NJ
Miller, Michael S. .... Newark, NJ
Miller, Michael S. .... New York, NY
Miller, Michael S. .... Columbus, OH
Miller, Michael S. .... San Antonio, TX
Miller, Michael T. .... North Wilkesboro, NC
Miller, Michael Thomas .... Minneapolis, MN
Miller, Michael V. .... Fort Smith, AR
Miller, Michael W. .... Newport, RI
Miller, Michael W. .... Memphis, TN
Miller, Michele Ballard .... Larkspur, CA
Miller, Michele O. .... Houston, TX
Miller, Michelle B. .... Omaha, NE
Miller, Michelle Bass .... Little Rock, AR
Miller, Michelle C. .... Philadelphia, PA
Miller, Michelle D. .... Boston, MA
Miller, Michelle Marie .... Towson, MD
Miller, Michelle S. .... Minneapolis, MN
Miller, Michelle S. .... Houston, TX
Miller, Mickey M. .... Fort Wayne, IN
Miller, Mike .... Fargo, ND
Miller, Mike C. .... Marshall, TX
Miller, Mike C., P.C. .... Marshall, TX
Miller, Mikel R. .... Bend, OR
Miller, Milford M., Jr. .... Fort Wayne, IN
Miller & Miller .... Los Angeles, CA
Miller and Miller .... Lincoln, IL
Miller & Miller .... Anderson, IN
Miller and Miller .... Elkhart, IN
Miller & Miller .... Lexington, KY
Miller and Miller .... Louisville, KY
Miller & Miller .... Baltimore, MD
Pearl, MS
Miller and Miller .... Chatham, NJ
Miller & Miller .... New Berlin, NY
Miller & Miller .... Seneca Falls, NY
Cleveland, OH
Miller and Miller .... Harrisburg, PA
Miller & Miller .... Indiana, PA
Miller & Miller .... Pittsburgh, PA
Miller & Miller .... San Antonio, TX
Miller and Miller .... Portage, WI
Miller, Miller & Canby, Chartered
Rockville, MD
Miller & Miller Firm, The, PLLC
Dallas, TX
Miller, Miller, Kearney & Geschickter, L.L.P.
Alexandria, VA
Arlington, VA
Fairfax, VA
Miller & Miller, LLP .... Westminster, MD
Miller, Miller, Miller, P.C. .... Aurelia, IA
Cherokee, IA
Miller, Miller & Miller, PLC
Campbellsville, KY
Miller & Miller, P.A. .... New Brunswick, NJ
Miller & Miller, P.C. .... Washington, DC
Miller & Miller, P.C. .... Haverstraw, NY
Miller, Milo G. .... Bargaintown, NJ
Miller Milove & Kob, P.C. .... San Diego, CA
Miller, Milton .... Coral Gables, FL
Miller, Milton A. .... Los Angeles, CA
Miller, Milton B. .... Woodland Hills, CA
Miller, Milton J. .... Detroit, MI
Miller, Milton Louis .... Los Angeles, CA
Miller, Milton P. .... Richmond, VA
Miller, Minos D., Jr. .... Jennings, LA
Miller, Miriam McD. .... Department of Labor, Office of the Solicitor, GV
Miller, Mishelle C. .... Washington, DC
Miller, Mitchell H. .... Chicago, IL
Miller, Mitchell P. .... Palo Alto, CA
Miller & Mitchell, P.C. .... Princeton, NJ
Miller, Mitchell R. .... Beverly Hills, CA
Miller, Mitchell W. .... Norristown, PA
Miller, Mitchell W. .... Philadelphia, PA
Miller, Mollie Lax .... Boston, MA
Miller, Mona D. .... Los Angeles, CA
Miller, Monica J. .... Jacksonville, FL
Miller, Monson, Peshel & Polacek
San Diego, CA
Miller, Monte L. .... Emporia, KS
Miller, Monte M. .... Minneapolis, MN
Miller, Montserrat C. .... Washington, DC
Miller, Morris A. .... San Antonio, TX
Miller, Morris G. (Skip)
Palm Beach Gardens, FL
Miller, Morris H. .... Tallahassee, FL
Miller, Morriss & Pappas
East Lansing, MI
Miller, Morton, Caillat & Nevis
San Jose, CA
Miller Muller Mendelson & Kennedy
Indianapolis, IN
Miller, Murl E. .... Yankton, SD
Miller, Murphy C. .... Young Harris, GA
Miller, Murray, & Associates .... Phoenix, AZ
Miller and Murray, LLP .... Reading, PA
Miller, Myron M. .... Denver, CO
Miller, N. Barr .... Washington, DC
Miller, Nan A. .... Minneapolis, MN
Miller, Nan D. .... San Diego, CA
Miller, Nancy .... Oxnard, CA
Miller, Nancy .... Tenafly, NJ
Miller, Nancy A. .... Baltimore, MD
Miller, Nancy A. .... Seattle, WA
Miller, Nancy C. .... Sacramento, CA
Miller, Nancy Chase .... Chicago, IL
Miller, Nancy Costello .... Newark, NJ
Miller, Nancy D. .... Denver, CO

Miller, Nancy D., P.C., Law Offices of ... Denver, CO
Miller, Nancy E. ... Pasadena, CA
Miller, Nancy G. ... Administrative Office Of The United States Courts, GV
Miller, Nancy Herbst ... Cleveland, OH
Miller, Nancy J. ... Santa Monica, CA
Miller, Nancy J. ... Minneapolis, MN
Miller, Nancy J. ... Columbus, OH
Miller, Nancy L. ... Clinton, MD
Miller, Nancy L. ... New York, NY
Miller, Nancy S. ... Chicago, IL
Miller, Nancy W. ... Pittsburgh, PA
Miller Nash LLP ... Portland, OR
Seattle, WA
Vancouver, WA
Miller, Nathan H. ... Harrisonburg, VA
Miller, Nathan R. ... Peoria, IL
Miller, Neal E. ... Nashville, TN
Miller, Ned P. ... West Des Moines, IA
Miller, Ned P., Law Office
West Des Moines, IA
Miller, Neil A. ... Troy, MI
Miller, Neil A. ... Garden City, NY
Miller, Neil A. ... Mineola, NY
Miller, Neil A., Professional Corporation
Troy, MI
Miller, Neil H. ... St. Louis, MO
Miller, Neil P. ... Department of Justice, Executive Office for Immigration Review, GV
Miller, Neil S. ... New York, NY
Miller, Neil T. ... East Meadow, NY
Miller, Nelson P. ... Ann Arbor, MI
Grand Haven, MI
Miller, Nicholas A. ... Houston, TX
Miller, Nicholas G. ... Boise, ID
Miller, Nicholas M. ... Cleveland, OH
Miller, Nicholas P. ... Washington, DC
Miller, Nicholas P. ... Washington, DC
Miller, Nick J. ... Charlotte, NC
Matthews, NC
Miller, Nicolas H. ... Calabasas, CA
Miller, Nicole E. ... New York, NY
Miller, Nicolette K. ... Eureka, MO
Miller, Nodine ... Columbus, OH
Miller & Nogaro, L.L.P. ... New York, NY
Miller & Nolan, Incorporated
Los Angeles, CA
Miller, Nora J. ... Boydton, VA
Miller, Norma C. ... Louisville, KY
Miller, Norman ... Atlanta, GA
Miller, Norman ... New York, NY
Miller, Norman & Associates, Ltd.
Moorhead, MN
Miller, Norman F. ... Marietta, GA
Miller, Norman F. ... Columbus, OH
Miller, Norman L. ... Phoenix, AZ
Miller, Norman R. ... Dallas, TX
Miller, Norman S. ... Southfield, MI
Miller, Nory ... Washington, DC
Miller, Obediah R. ... White Plains, NY
Miller • O'Brien • Bloom, P.L.L.P.
Minneapolis, MN
Miller & Ogorchock, S.C. ... Milwaukee, WI
Miller, Oliver, Baker, Moylan & Stone, A Professional Corporation
Hagerstown, MD
Miller, O'Malley M. ... Los Angeles, CA
Miller, Ophelia L. ... Key West, FL
Miller, Orville J. ... Cincinnati, OH
Miller, Oscar J. ... East Orange, NJ
Miller, Oth ... Amarillo, TX
Miller, Ovvie ... Beverly Hills, CA
Miller, P. Galt ... Louisville, KY
Miller, P. Michael ... Fort Wayne, IN
Miller, Paige R. ... Seattle, WA
Miller, Pamela A. ... New York, NY
Miller, Pamela E. ... United States Senate, Senatorial Assistants, GV
Miller, Pamela E. ... Indiana, PA
Miller, Pamela J. ... New Castle, PA
Miller, Pamela M. ... Minneapolis, MN
Miller, Pamela R. ... New York, NY
Miller, Pamela T. ... Newark, NJ
Miller & Partridge ... Lafayette, CA
Miller & Paschal ... Greenville, SC
Miller, Patience A. ... Southfield, MI
Miller, Patricia A.
Securities and Exchange Commission, Division of Corporation Finance, GV
Miller, Patricia B. ... Baltimore, MD
Miller, Patricia B. ... New York, NY
Miller, Patricia C. ... Philadelphia, PA
Miller, Patricia G. ... Pittsburgh, PA
Miller, Patricia Husted ... Lakewood, CO
Miller, Patricia J. ... DeWitt, MI
Miller, Patricia M. ... San Diego, CA
Miller, Patricia Y. ... Los Angeles, CA
Miller, Patrick C. ... Milwaukee, WI
Miller, Patrick E. ... Coeur d'Alene, ID
Miller, Patrick J. ... Boise, ID
Miller, Patrick L. ... Indianapolis, IN
Miller, Patrick L. ... Baton Rouge, LA
Miller, Patrick O'Neal ... Phenix City, AL
Miller, Patrick Ross ... Overland Park, KS
Miller, Paul ... Universal City, CA
Miller, Paul ... Texarkana, TX
Miller, Paul A. ... Birmingham, AL
Miller, Paul A. ... Oxnard, CA
Miller, Paul A. ... Orlando, FL
Miller, Paul A. ... Millersburg, OH
Miller, Paul B., Jr. ... Houston, TX
Miller, Paul D. ... Iowa City, IA
Miller, Paul D. ... Hardinsburg, KY
Miller, Paul D. ... Billings, MT
Miller, Paul D. ... Galveston, TX
Miller, Paul E. ... Manhattan, KS
Miller, Paul E., Jr. ... Boone, NC
Miller, Paul G. ... Goshen, NY
Miller, Paul H. ... Downey, CA
Miller, Paul H. ... Santa Fe Springs, CA
Miller, Paul H. ... Whittier, CA
Miller, Paul I. ... San Diego, CA
Miller, Paul J. ... Washington, DC
Miller, Paul J. ... Chicago, IL
Miller, Paul J. ... Seattle, WA
Miller, Paul J., Jr. ... Phenix City, AL
Miller, Paul L. ... Baltimore, MD
Miller, Paul M. ... Washington, DC
Miller, Paul O., III ... Jackson, MS
Miller, Paul R. ... New York, NY
Miller, Paul R. ... Tarrytown, NY
Miller, Paul R. ... Houston, TX
Miller, Paul S. ... Troy, MI
Miller, Paul S. ... New York, NY
Miller, Paul Steven
Equal Employment Opportunity Commission, Office of the Commissioners, GV
Miller, Paul W., Jr. ... Wantagh, NY
Miller, Paul William ... Columbus, OH
Miller, Paula ... Colorado Springs, CO
Miller, Paula A. ... Stony Brook, NY
Miller, Paula Jean ... Dallas, TX
Miller, Paula Rafferty ... Atlanta, GA
Miller, Paula Sullivan ... Brockton, MA
Miller, Pauline A. ... Department of Justice, Civil Rights Division, GV
Miller, Pearson, Gloe, Burns, Beatty & Cowie, P.C. ... Decorah, IA
Miller, Peggy A. ... Largo, MD
Miller, Peggy A. ... New York, NY
Miller, Peggy Jo Pentecost ... Anniston, AL
Miller, Peggy L. ... Lansing, MI
Miller, Penny L. ... Bismarck, ND
Miller, Percy S. ... New York, NY
Miller, Peter ... New York, NY
Miller, Peter ... Portland, OR
Miller, Peter A. ... Little Rock, AR
Miller, Peter A. ... Miami, FL
Miller, Peter A. ... New York, NY
Miller, Peter, A Professional Corporation
Portland, OR
Miller, Peter B. ... Department of Justice, Civil Division, GV
Miller, Peter B. ... New York, NY
Miller, Peter C. ... Chicago, IL
Miller, Peter C., Inc. ... Hanalei, HI
Miller, Peter D. ... Shaker Heights, OH
Miller, Peter D., (P.C.) ... Indianapolis, IN
Miller, Peter H. ... Leesburg, VA
Miller, Peter J. ... Chicago, IL
Miller, Peter J. ... Albany, NY
Miller, Peter J. ... Greensboro, NC
Miller, Peter M. ... Boston, MA
Miller, Peter M. ... Salisbury, VT
Miller, Peter P. ... Fairfax, VA
Miller, Peter S. ... Philadelphia, PA
Miller, Peter T. ... Palatka, FL
Miller, Peter W. ... San Juan, PR
Miller, Phebe C. ... New York, NY
Miller, Phillip C. ... Albany, NY
Miller, Philip E. ... Old Bridge, NJ
Miller, Philip F. ... West Des Moines, IA
Miller, Philip G. ... North Hollywood, CA
Miller, Philip H. ... Los Angeles, CA
Miller, Philip H. ... Staunton, VA
Miller, Philip J. ... Milwaukee, WI
Miller, Philip M. ... San Francisco, CA
Miller, Philip R. ... Mountain Home, ID
Miller, Philip R. ... Chevy Chase, MD
Miller, Philip R., III ... Raleigh, NC
Miller, Philip S. ... Los Angeles, CA
Miller, Phillip A. ... Kansas City, MO
Miller, Phillip H. ... Nashville, TN
Miller, Phillip L. ... Goshen, IN
Miller, Phillip N. ... Chicago, IL
Miller, Phillip R. ... Wichita, KS
Miller, Phillip S. ... Danville, IL
Miller, Phillip S. ... Seattle, WA
Miller, Phyllis D. ... Jamaica, NY
Miller, Phyllis H. ... Blountville, TN
Miller, Pierre V., II ... New Orleans, LA
Miller & Pincus, P.A. ... Livingston, NJ
Miller, Pitt & McAnally, P.C. ... Tucson, AZ
Miller & Podell ... Miami Beach, FL
Miller & Ponn, P.A. ... Coral Gables, FL
Miller, Poole & Lord, LLP ... York, PA
Miller, Porter & Muller, P.C.
Princeton, NJ
Trenton, NJ
Miller, Powell W. ... New Orleans, LA
Miller, R. Boyd ... Mobile, AL
Miller, R. Brad ... Oklahoma City, OK
Miller, R. Brad ... Midland, TX
Miller, R. Bradley ... Raleigh, NC
Miller, R. Bruce ... Atlanta, GA
Miller, R. (Chix) ... Macon, GA
Miller, R. Craig, Jr. ... Charlotte, NC
Miller, R. Douglas ... Cincinnati, OH
Miller, R. Gordon ... Scottsdale, AZ
Miller, R. James ... Sacramento, CA
Miller, R. James ... Ithaca, NY
Miller, R. Joseph, Jr. ... Beaverton, OR
Miller, R. Leroy ... Trenton, MO
Miller, R. Michael ... Kansas City, MO
Miller, R. Terry ... Dallas, TX
Miller, R. Wayne ... Tampa, FL
Miller, Rachel A. ... New York, NY
Miller, Rachel M. ... Newport Beach, CA
San Francisco, CA
Miller, Ralph A. ... Cleveland, OH
Miller, Ralph E. ... Montrose, CO
Miller, Ralph F. ... Ashland, KY
Miller, Ralph Gano ... San Diego, CA
Miller, Ralph H. ... Salt Lake City, UT
Miller, Ralph I. ... Dallas, TX
Miller, Ralph Kenneth, Jr. ... Houston, TX
Miller, Ralph W., Jr. ... Oak Brook, IL
Miller, Ralston & Earle
Harrisonburg, VA
Miller, Randal J. ... Joliet, IL
Miller, Randall ... Elizabethtown, PA
Miller, Randall A. ... Los Angeles, CA
Miller, Randall B. ... Long Beach, CA
Miller, Randall B. ... Baton Rouge, LA
Miller, Randall C. ... Cary, NC
Miller, Randall H. ... Chicago, IL
Miller, Randall K. ... Washington, DC
Miller, Randall L. ... Bristol, PA
Langhorne, PA
Miller, Randall S. ... Detroit, MI
Southfield, MI
Miller, Randel K. ... Jonesboro, AR
Miller, Randell ... Sun City Center, FL
Tampa, FL
Miller, Randi S. ... New York, NY
Miller, Randy ... Wall, NJ
Miller, Randy E. ... Washington, DC
Miller, Randy K. ... Elkins, WV
Miller, Ranne B. ... Albuquerque, NM
Miller, Raphael J. ... Gaylord, MN
Gibbon, MN
Le Sueur, MN
Miller, Ray ... Indianapolis, IN
Miller, Ray G. ... Zanesville, OH
Miller, Raymond A. ... Pittsburgh, PA
Miller, Raymond C. ... Fort Lauderdale, FL
Miller, Raymond E. ... Venice, FL
Miller, Raymond F. ... Hartford, CT
Miller, Raymond L. ... Tempe, AZ
Miller, Raymond P. ... Rochester, NY
Miller, Raymond Shawn ... Pleasantville, NY
Miller, Raymond V., Jr. ... Miami, FL
Miller, Rea P., Jr. ... Pittsburgh, PA
Miller, Rebecca E. ... Topeka, KS
Miller, Rebecca Hopkins ... Las Vegas, NV
Miller, Rebecca J. ... Atlanta, GA
Miller, Rebecca M. ... Miami, FL
Miller, Reed ... Washington, DC
Miller, Reeder C. ... Decatur, IL
Miller, Reese ... Denver, CO
Miller, Regan A. ... Charlotte, NC
Miller, Relma M. ... Morganfield, KY
Miller, Rena Ashauer ... Salt Lake City, UT
Miller, Retta A. ... Dallas, TX
Miller, Reuben ... Chicago, IL
Miller, Reuben ... Union, NJ
Miller, Rex W. ... Canton, OH
Miller, Rhonda A. ... Orange, CA
Miller, Rhonda L. ... Charleston, WV
Miller, Richard ... San Antonio, TX
Miller, Richard A. ... Department of Justice, Civil Division, GV
Miller, Richard A. ... St. Petersburg, FL
Miller, Richard A. ... Sarasota, FL
Miller, Richard A. ... Evanston, IL
Miller, Richard A. ... Merrillville, IN
Miller, Richard A. ... Detroit, MI
Miller, Richard A. ... Minneapolis, MN
Miller, Richard A. ... Brooklyn, NY
Miller, Richard A. ... Islandia, NY
Miller, Richard A. ... New York, NY
Miller, Richard A. ... Rochester, NY
Miller, Richard A. ... Aurora, OH
Miller, Richard A. ... Madill, OK
Miller, Richard A. ... Fairfax, VA
Miller, Richard A., Jr. ... West Simsbury, CT
Miller, Richard A., Sr. ... Hartford, CT
Miller, Richard Alan ... Lakeland, FL
Miller, Richard Allen ... New York, NY
Miller, Richard, & Associates
Portland, OR
Miller, Richard B. ... Honolulu, HI
Miller, Richard B. ... Houston, TX
Miller, Richard C. ... Kansas City, MO
Springfield, MO
Miller, Richard C. ... Rochester, NY
Miller, Richard Charles ... Washington, DC
Miller, Richard D. ... St. Joseph, MI
Miller, Richard D. ... Pittsburgh, PA
Miller, Richard E. ... Montchanin, DE
Miller, Richard E. ... New York, NY
Miller, Richard E. ... West Islip, NY
Miller, Richard E. ... Philadelphia, PA
Miller, Richard F. ... Pasadena, CA
Miller, Richard F. ... Nantucket, MA
Miller, Richard F., A Professional Corporation ... Los Angeles, CA
Pasadena, CA
Miller, Richard G. ... Oklahoma City, OK
Miller, Richard G. ... Dallas, TX
Alexandria, VA
Miller, Richard G. ... Casper, WY
Miller, Richard G., Jr. ... Washington, PA
Miller, Richard G., P.C. ... Casper, WY
Miller, Richard Glenn ... Searcy, AR
Miller, Richard H. ... Santa Fe, NM
Miller, Richard H. ... Milwaukee, WI
Miller, Richard I. ... Greenbelt, MD
Miller, Richard I. ... Boston, MA
Miller, Richard I. ... Clifton, NJ
Miller, Richard I. ... Jersey City, NJ
Miller, Richard I. ... Pittsburgh, PA
Miller, Richard J. ... Palm Beach, FL
Miller, Richard J. ... Eldersburg, MD
Miller, Richard J. ... Albany, NY
Miller, Richard Joseph, Jr. ... Albany, NY
Miller, Richard K. ... Phoenix, AZ
Miller, Richard L. ... Fayetteville, AR
Miller, Richard L. ... Santa Monica, CA
Miller, Richard L. ... Sarasota, FL
Miller, Richard L. ... Columbia, MD
Miller, Richard L. ... Columbus, OH
Miller, Richard L., II ... Urbana, IL
Miller, Richard L., III ... Boston, MA
Miller, Richard M. ... Bloomington, IL
Miller, Richard M. ... Princeton, NJ
Miller, Richard N. ... Bloomfield, NJ
Miller, Richard P. ... San Diego, CA
Miller, Richard P. ... Drayton Plains, MI
Miller, Richard S. ... Encino, CA
Miller, Richard S. ... San Francisco, CA
Miller, Richard S. ... Honolulu, HI
Miller, Richard S. ... Wayne, NJ
Miller, Richard S. ... New York, NY
Miller, Richard S. ... Lynchburg, VA
Miller, Richard T. ... Los Angeles, CA
Miller, Richard T. ... Washington, DC
Miller, Richard T. ... Chicago, IL
Miller, Richard T. ... Columbus, OH
Miller, Richard T. ... San Saba, TX
Miller, Richard W. ... Irvine, CA
Miller, Richard W. ... Kansas City, MO
Miller, Richard W. ... East Islip, NY
Miller, Richard W. ... Ritzville, WA
Miller, Richard W., Jr. ... Washington, DC
Miller, Richd. H. ... Cleveland, OH
Miller, Rick ... Atlanta, GA
Miller, Rick S. ... Wilmington, DE
Miller, Rita Fribush ... Edmonds, WA
Miller, Rita J. ... Los Angeles, CA
Miller, Rita J. ... Larchmont, NY
Miller, Robert ... Danville, CA
Miller, Robert ... Buffalo, NY
Miller, Robert A. ... Prescott, AZ
Miller, Robert A. ... Treasury Department, Internal Revenue Service, GV
Miller, Robert A. ... Louisville, KY
Miller, Robert A. ... Auburn Hills, MI
Miller, Robert A. ... Jackson, MS
Miller, Robert A. ... St. Louis, MO
Miller, Robert A. ... Cleveland, OH
Miller, Robert A. ... Toledo, OH
Miller, Robert A. ... Xenia, OH
Miller, Robert A. ... Oklahoma City, OK
Miller, Robert A. ... Eugene, OR
Miller, Robert A. ... Pierre, SD
Miller, Robert A. ... Dallas, TX
Miller, Robert A. ... Alexandria, VA
Miller, Robert A. ... Milwaukee, WI
Miller, Robert A., Jr. ... Los Angeles, CA
Miller, Robert A., Jr. ... St. Johnsbury, VT
Miller, Robert Anthony ... New York, NY
Miller, Robert B. ... Los Angeles, CA
Miller, Robert B. ... Aventura, FL
Miller, Robert B. ... Tampa, FL
Miller, Robert B. ... New York, NY
Miller, Robert B. ... Portland, OR
Miller, Robert B., Jr. ... Stroudsburg, PA
Miller, Robert Browning ... Sacramento, CA
Miller, Robert Bruce ... Irvine, CA
Miller, Robert Bruce ... Boulder, CO
Miller, Robert C. ... Kansas City, KS
Miller, Robert C. ... Saginaw, MI
Miller, Robert C. ... Clifton Park, NY
Miller, Robert C. ... New York, NY
Miller, Robert C. ... Nashville, TN
Miller, Robert C. ... Norfolk, VA
Miller, Robert D. ... West Palm Beach, FL
Miller, Robert D. ... Davidsonville, MD
Miller, Robert D. ... Minneapolis, MN
Miller, Robert D. ... Big Spring, TX
Marfa, TX
Miller, Robert D. ... Houston, TX
Miller, Robert D., Jr. ... Spokane, WA
Miller, Robert E. ... Menlo Park, CA
Miller, Robert E. ... Old Town, ME
Miller, Robert E., Inc., A Professional Corporation ... Menlo Park, CA
Miller, Robert F. ... Tucson, AZ
Miller, Robert F. ... Honolulu, HI
Miller, Robert F. ... Chicago, IL
Miller, Robert F. ... Memphis, TN
Miller, Robert F., Jr. ... Brea, CA
Miller, Robert Fraser ... Cherry Hill, NJ
Miller, Robert G. ... Sacramento, CA
Miller, Robert G. ... San Francisco, CA
Miller, Robert G. ... San Francisco, CA
Miller, Robert G. ... Muncie, IN
Miller, Robert G. ... Cleveland, OH
Miller, Robert G. ... Houston, TX
Miller, Robert G., Jr. ... Paintsville, KY
Miller, Robert G., Jr. ... New Orleans, LA
Miller, Robert H. ... Palo Alto, CA
Miller, Robert H. ... San Francisco, CA
Miller, Robert H. ... Department of Justice, Environment and Natural Resources Division, GV
Miller, Robert H. ... Topeka, KS
Miller, Robert H., II ... Bluefield, WV
Miller, Robert H. "Rick" ... Denver, CO
Miller, Robert Hollis ... Peoria, IL
Miller, Robert Ira ... Forest Hills, NY
Miller, Robert Irving ... Poughkeepsie, NY
Miller, Robert J. ... Phoenix, AZ
Miller, Robert J. ... Greenwich, CT
Stamford, CT
Miller, Robert J. ... Towson, MD
Miller, Robert J. ... New Hope, MN
Miller, Robert J. ... Las Vegas, NV
Miller, Robert J. ... New York, NY
Miller, Robert J. ... Raleigh, NC
Miller, Robert J. ... Dallas, TX
Miller, Robert J., Sr. ... Beaverton, OR
Miller, Robert Joel ... Chicago, IL
Miller, Robert K. ... Torrance, CA
Miller, Robert K. ... Marathon, FL
Miller, Robert L. ... Los Angeles, CA
Miller, Robert L. ... San Diego, CA

Miller, Robert L. .... San Francisco, CA
Miller, Robert L. .... Washington, DC
Miller, Robert L. .... Boise, ID
Miller, Robert L. .... Benton, IL
Miller, Robert L. .... Boston, MA
Miller, Robert L. .... Waverly, NY
Miller, Robert L. .... Cleveland, OH
Miller, Robert L., Jr. .... South Bend, IN
Miller, Robert L., Jr. .... Bel Air, MD
Miller, Robert L., Law Offices of
Santa Ana, CA
Miller, Robert L., Sr. .... South Bend, IN
Miller, Robert M. .... San Diego, CA
Miller, Robert M. .... Fairfield, CT
Miller, Robert M. .... Miami, FL
Miller, Robert M. .... New York, NY
Miller, Robert M. .... New York, NY
Miller, Robert M. .... Warrenton, VA
Miller, Robert M., Jr. .... Harrisburg, PA
Miller, Robert Matthew
St. Clair Shores, MI
Miller, Robert N. .... Denver, CO
Miller, Robert N. .... Jacksonville, FL
Ponte Vedra Beach, FL
Miller, Robert Neal .... Jacksonville, FL
Miller, Robert O. .... Los Alamitos, CA
Miller, Robert O. .... Murray, KY
Miller, Robert P. .... Daytona Beach, FL
Maitland, FL
Miller, Robert R. .... Denver, CO
Miller, Robert R. .... Wellston, OH
Miller, Robert R. .... Corpus Christi, TX
Miller, Robert S. .... Fort Lauderdale, FL
Miller, Robert S. .... Lexington, KY
Miller, Robert S. .... Nesconset, NY
Miller, Robert S. .... Philadelphia, PA
Miller, Robert S., P.A. .... Fort Lauderdale, FL
Miller, Robert Scott .... Northfield, MN
Miller, Robert Stephen .... Los Angeles, CA
Miller, Robert Stevens, III .... Bandon, OR
Miller, Robert T. .... Lakeland, FL
Miller, Robert T. .... Bloomington, IN
Miller, Robert T. .... New York, NY
Miller, Robert T., Jr. .... Perrysburg, OH
Miller, Robert T., Jr. .... Bedford, TX
Miller, Robert W. .... Anderson, IN
Miller, Robert W. .... Elkhart, IN
Miller, Robert W. .... Grayson, KY
Miller, Robert W. .... St. Louis, MO
Miller, Robertson and Rodgers, P.C.
Somerville, NJ
Miller, Robin .... Fayetteville, AR
Miller, Robin .... Colorado Springs, CO
Miller, Robin Davis .... New York, NY
Miller, Robin L. .... Washington, DC
Miller, Robin L. .... Minneapolis, MN
Miller, Robin L. .... Chattanooga, TN
Miller, Robin R. .... Wheaton, IL
Miller, Robin S. .... New York, NY
Miller & Robinson .... Gonzales, TX
Miller, Robyn E. .... Lexington, KY
Miller, Robyn L. .... Los Angeles, CA
Miller, Rochelle C., Law Offices of
Chicago, IL
Miller, Rod D. .... New York, NY
Miller, Rod, P.C., Law Offices of
Cleveland, TN
Miller, Roderick L. .... Lafayette, LA
Miller, Rodman B. .... Seattle, WA
Miller, Rodney A. .... Fulton, KY
Miller, Rodney Craig .... Cleveland, TN
Miller, Rodney R. .... Dallas, TX
Miller, Rodney W. .... Salem, OR
Miller, Roger .... Fort Wayne, IN
Miller, Roger C. .... South St. Paul, MN
Miller, Roger H. .... Boca Raton, FL
Miller, Roger J. .... Omaha, NE
Miller, Roger L. .... Frankfort, IN
Miller, Roger L. .... Findlay, OH
Miller, Roger M. .... Sacramento, CA
Miller, Roger W. .... Phoenix, AZ
Miller, Roger W. .... Greenville, KY
Miller, Roland B., III .... Kansas City, MO
Miller, Ron R. .... Stamford, CT
Miller, Ronald .... St. Petersburg, FL
Miller, Ronald A. .... San Bernardino, CA
Miller, Ronald A., P.L.C.
San Bernardino, CA
Miller, Ronald C. .... St. Louis, MO
Miller, Ronald D. .... Santa Monica, CA
Chicago, IL
Southfield, MI
Worthington, OH
Miller, Ronald D. .... Roswell, GA
Miller, Ronald E. .... Nashville, TN
Miller, Ronald H. .... Wapakoneta, OH
Miller, Ronald J. .... Las Vegas, NV
Miller, Ronald K. .... Chamberlain, SD
Miller, Ronald L. .... Lakewood, CO
Miller, Ronald L. .... Hollywood, FL
Miller, Ronald L. .... Long Beach, WA
Miller, Ronald M. .... Upper Marlboro, MD
Miller, Ronald P. .... Richardson, TX
Miller, Ronald S. .... Chicago, IL
Miller, Ronald V., Jr. .... Towson, MD
Miller, Ronda L. .... Rapid City, SD
Miller and Roney .... Murfreesboro, TN
Miller, Rosa Copeland .... Pittsburgh, PA
Miller, Rosalind .... Indio, CA
Miller, Rosanne .... Newark, DE
Miller, Rosnick & D'Amico, P.C.
Bridgeport, CT
Miller, Ross A. .... Arlington Heights, IL
Miller, Ross A. .... Everett, WA
Miller, Ross D. .... Philadelphia, PA
Miller, Roswitha .... New Haven, CT
Miller, Roy .... Bend, OR
Miller, Roy D. .... Los Angeles, CA

Miller, Roy E., Jr. .... Lakeport, CA
Miller, Roy P. .... New York, NY
Miller, Roy Wesley .... Huntsville, AL
Miller, Royal M. .... Springfield, MO
Miller, Rubin H. .... New York, NY
Miller and Russell .... Coral Gables, FL
Miller, Russell Ben .... San Diego, CA
Miller, Russell C. .... Allison Park, PA
Miller, Russell G. .... Chicago, IL
Northbrook, IL
Miller, Russell H. .... Burlingame, CA
Miller, Russell H., Law Office of
Burlingame, CA
Miller, Russell K. .... New York, NY
Miller, Russell L. .... Encinitas, CA
Miller, Russell Lloyd .... Annapolis, MD
Miller, Russell R. .... Toledo, OH
Miller, Russell W. .... Houston, TX
Miller, Ruth
Charlotte Amalie, St. Thomas, VI
Miller, Ruth L. .... Jennings, LA
Miller, S. Dennis .... Oregon City, OR
Miller, S. Ira .... Chicago, IL
Miller, S. Lee .... Hanover, MA
Miller, S. Marie .... Fort Wayne, IN
Miller, S. Michael .... Columbus, OH
Miller, S. Michael .... Fairfax, VA
Miller, S. Michael, P.C. .... Fairfax, VA
Miller, S. Patrick .... San Francisco, CA
Miller, S. Stanton, Jr. .... Media, PA
Miller, S. Tara .... Boston, MA
Miller, Sally A. .... Imlay City, MI
Miller, Sally Takacs .... Houston, TX
Miller, Sam L. .... Chicago, IL
Des Plaines, IL
Miller, Sam Scott .... New York, NY
Miller, Samantha L. .... Philadelphia, PA
Miller, Samuel .... Miami Beach, FL
Miller, Samuel A. .... Atlanta, GA
Miller, Samuel A. .... Providence, RI
Miller, Samuel B. .... Johnson City, TN
Miller, Samuel C., III .... Alexandria, VA
Miller, Samuel H. .... Houston, TX
Miller, Samuel J. .... Houston, TX
Miller, Samuel J., Jr. .... Baltimore, MD
Miller, Samuel R. .... Los Angeles, CA
San Francisco, CA
Miller, Samuel R. .... San Francisco, CA
Miller, Samuel S. .... Chicago, IL
Miller, Samuel T. .... Highland, IN
Miller, Samuel W. .... Lynbrook, NY
Miller, Sandford J. .... St. Louis, MO
Miller, Sandra .... Sacramento, CA
Miller, Sandra F. .... New York, NY
Miller, Sandra H. .... Indianapolis, IN
Miller, Sandra L. .... Seal Beach, CA
Miller, Sandra L. W. .... Greenville, SC
Miller & Sanford, A Professional Corporation .... Springfield, MO
Miller, Sara Dodman .... New York, NY
Miller, Sara E. .... Norfolk, NE
Miller, Sara J. .... Columbia, MO
Miller, Sara K. .... Milwaukee, WI
Miller, Sarah J. .... Cincinnati, OH
Miller, Sarah Susannah .... Springfield, OR
Miller, Sascha Fischer .... Denver, CO
Miller, Schwartz and Miller, P.A.
Hollywood, FL
Miller, Scott .... New Port Richey, FL
Miller, Scott A. .... Newport Beach, CA
Miller, Scott A. .... Atlanta, GA
Miller, Scott A. .... Brooklyn, NY
Miller, Scott A. .... Bismarck, ND
Miller, Scott Alan .... Ithaca, NY
Miller, Scott B. .... Orlando, FL
Miller, Scott C. .... Encino, CA
Miller, Scott Carpenter .... Aspen, CO
Miller, Scott D. .... Encino, CA
Miller, Scott D. .... Frederick, MD
Miller, Scott D. .... St. Louis, MO
Miller, Scott D. .... Buffalo, NY
Miller, Scott D. .... Cleveland, OH
Miller, Scott E. .... Edina, MN
Miller, Scott E. .... New York, NY
Miller, Scott E. .... Erie, PA
Miller, Scott G. .... Orlando, FL
Miller, Scott H. .... San Francisco, CA
Miller, Scott H. .... Santa Clara, CA
Miller, Scott & Holbrook .... Newport, RI
Miller, Scott Joseph .... Houston, TX
Miller, Scott K.
Department Of The Interior, Office of the Solicitor, GV
Miller, Scott M. .... Apopka, FL
Oak Park, IL
Miller, Scott M. .... Louisville, KY
Miller, Scott M. .... New York, NY
New York, NY
Miller, Scott P. .... Champlin, MN
Miller, Scott P. .... New York, NY
Miller, Scott R. .... Costa Mesa, CA
Miller, Scott R. .... Los Angeles, CA
Miller, Scott R. .... New Brunswick, NJ
Miller, Scott R. .... Canton, OH
Salem, OH
Miller, Scott R. .... Cleveland, OH
Miller, Scott T. .... Corydon, IN
Miller, Scott W. .... Newark, NJ
Miller, Scott W. .... Beachwood, OH
Miller, Searl & Fitch, A Legal Professional Association .... Portsmouth, OH
Miller, Seidel, Havens and Adkins, LLP
Trenton, MO
Miller, Seth A. .... Los Angeles, CA
Miller, Severn ES .... Baltimore, MD
Miller, Seymour .... New York, NY
Miller, Seymour W. .... New York, NY

Miller, Shakman, Hamilton, Kurtzon & Schlifke .... Chicago, IL
Miller, Shannon E. .... Louisville, KY
Miller, Sharon G. .... Voorheesville, NY
Miller, Sharon L. .... Long Beach, CA
Miller, Sharon L. .... Cleveland, OH
Miller, Sharon L. R. .... Dublin, OH
Miller, Sharon P. .... Fort Lauderdale, FL
Miller, Sharon S. .... Detroit, MI
Miller, Sharon Z. .... New York, NY
Miller, Shawn R. .... Irvine, CA
Los Angeles, CA
Miller, Sheila R. .... Camden, NJ
Miller, Sheldon E., (P.C.) .... Beverly Hills, CA
Miller, Sheldon J. .... Memphis, TN
Miller, Sheldon L. .... Detroit, MI
Miller, Sheldon L. .... Southfield, MI
Miller, Sheldon P. .... Chicago, IL
Miller, Shelley K. .... Birmingham, MI
Miller, Shelly Merritt .... Denver, CO
Miller, Shelly S. .... Campbellsville, KY
Miller, Shelmerdeane A. .... Chicago, IL
Miller, Sher & Sawyer .... Sacramento, CA
Miller, Sherri K. .... Indianapolis, IN
Miller, Sherrie L. .... Memphis, TN
Miller, Sherry E. .... Fayetteville, NC
Miller, Sheryl Rosensky .... Washington, DC
Miller, Shine & Bryan, P.A.
St. Augustine, FL
Miller, Shpiece & Andrews, P.C.
Southfield, MI
Miller, Shrader R. .... Cedar Key, FL
Miller & Shultis .... Hanover, PA
Miller, Sid M. .... Hamden, CT
Miller, Simon A. .... Atlanta, GA
Miller, Simon J.K. .... New York, NY
Miller, Simon, McGinn & Clark S.C.
Milwaukee, WI
Miller & Skubik .... Islandia, NY
Miller & Smith .... Gulfport, MS
Miller Smith, LLP .... Tucson, AZ
Miller & Smith, P.L.L.P.
Minneapolis, MN
Miller & Snyder .... Charleston, WV
Miller, Solomon I. .... Huntsville, AL
Miller, Sondra M. .... White Plains, NY
Miller, Sonny F. .... Minneapolis, MN
Miller, South & Di Masi, P.A.
Orlando, FL
Winter Park, FL
Miller, Spencer N. .... Jersey City, NJ
Miller, Stacey A. .... Los Angeles, CA
Miller, Stacey D. .... New York, NY
Miller, Stacey R. .... Melville, NY
Miller, Stacy L. .... Boston, MA
Miller, Stacy L. .... Nashville, TN
Miller, Stacy P. .... Morgantown, WV
Miller, Stanley A. .... La Conner, WA
Miller, Stanley A. .... Milwaukee, WI
Miller, Stanley D.
Hot Springs National Park, AR
Little Rock, AR
Miller, Stanley N. .... Lafayette, IN
Miller, Stanley R. .... Cleveland, OH
Miller, Stanton B. .... Chicago, IL
Miller, Stanton R. .... West Chester, OH
Miller, Starr & Regalia, A Professional Law Corporation .... Menlo Park, CA
Oakland, CA
Sacramento, CA
San Francisco, CA
San Jose, CA
Walnut Creek, CA
Miller and Steeno, P.C. .... St. Louis, MO
Miller, Stefan Ress .... Torrance, CA
Miller & Steiert, P.C. .... Denver, CO
Englewood, CO
Littleton, CO
Miller, Stephan K. .... Seattle, WA
Miller, Stephanie B. .... Chicago, IL
Miller, Stephanie Gale .... Washington, DC
Miller, Stephanie R. .... Louisville, KY
Miller, Stephen .... San Bernardino, CA
Miller, Stephen .... Chicago, IL
Miller, Stephen A. .... Harrisburg, PA
Miller, Stephen B. .... Battle Creek, MI
Miller, Stephen B. .... Chapel Hill, NC
Miller, Stephen C. .... Rock Island, IL
Miller, Stephen C. .... Seven Hills, OH
Miller, Stephen C., P.C. .... Boulder, CO
Miller, Stephen D. .... Los Angeles, CA
Miller, Stephen D. .... Delevan, NY
Miller, Stephen G. .... Bloomington, IN
Miller, Stephen H. .... Louisville, KY
Miller, Stephen H. .... Reedsport, OR
Miller, Stephen H. .... Lancaster, PA
Miller, Stephen H. .... Denton, TX
Miller, Stephen H. .... Plano, TX
Miller, Stephen I. .... Iselin, NJ
Miller, Stephen J. .... Springdale, AR
Miller, Stephen J. .... Hartford, CT
Miller, Stephen J. .... Orland Park, IL
Miller, Stephen K. .... Los Angeles, CA
Miller, Stephen K. .... Martinez, CA
Miller, Stephen K. .... Gainesville, FL
Miller, Stephen K. .... Indianapolis, IN
Miller, Stephen K., P.C. .... Los Angeles, CA
Miller, Stephen L. .... La Mesa, CA
Miller, Stephen L. .... Lincoln, IL
Miller, Stephen L. .... Lexington, KY
Miller, Stephen M. .... Wilmington, DE
Miller, Stephen M. .... Treasury Department, Internal Revenue Service, GV
Miller, Stephen Mark .... Nashville, TN
Miller, Stephen P. .... Indianapolis, IN
Miller, Stephen P. .... Memphis, TN
Miller, Stephen R. .... La Jolla, CA
Miller, Stephen R. .... Chicago, IL

Miller, Stephen R. .... Chicago, IL
Miller, Stephen R. .... Chicago, IL
Miller, Stephen R. .... Kansas City, MO
Miller, Stephen R. .... Missoula, MT
Miller, Stephen T. .... Houston, TX
Miller, Stephen V. .... Boston, MA
Miller, Stephen W. .... Philadelphia, PA
Miller, Stephen W. .... Richmond, VA
Miller, Stevan A. .... Atlanta, GA
Miller, Steve A. .... Denver, CO
Miller, Steve A., P.C. .... Denver, CO
Miller, Steve Allen .... Chicago, IL
Miller, Steven .... Encino, CA
Miller, Steven .... Englewood, CO
Miller, Steven .... Roslyn Heights, NY
Miller, Steven A. .... Chicago, IL
Miller, Steven C. .... Costa Mesa, CA
Miller, Steven C. .... Minneapolis, MN
Miller, Steven C. .... Cheney, WA
Miller, Steven D. .... Denver, CO
Miller, Steven E. .... Tampa, FL
Miller, Steven E. .... Columbus, OH
Miller, Steven G. .... Boca Raton, FL
Miller, Steven J. .... Santa Monica, CA
Miller, Steven J. .... Gulfport, MS
Miller, Steven J. .... Cleveland, OH
Miller, Steven Joseph .... Stamford, CT
Miller, Steven L. .... Los Angeles, CA
Miller, Steven L. .... Washington, DC
Miller, Steven L. .... Department of the Navy, Office of the Judge Advocate General, GV
Miller, Steven L. .... Somerset, PA
Miller, Steven L. .... Cross Lanes, WV
Miller, Steven L., Jr. .... Dallas, TX
Miller, Steven M. .... Philadelphia, PA
Miller, Steven M. .... Charlottesville, VA
Miller, Steven R. .... Chicago, IL
Miller, Steven R. .... Hazel Crest, IL
Miller, Steven R. .... New York, NY
Miller, Steven R. .... Columbus, OH
Miller, Steven Richard
Department of Energy, Office of the General Counsel, GV
Miller, Steven S. .... New York, NY
Miller, Steven W. .... Cincinnati, OH
Miller, Stewart R. .... Dallas, TX
Miller, Stillman & Bartel .... Cleveland, OH
Miller and Stone .... Hagerstown, MD
Miller, Stratvert & Torgerson, P.A.
Albuquerque, NM
Farmington, NM
Las Cruces, NM
Santa Fe, NM
Miller, Stuart Farrell .... New York, NY
Miller, Stuart J. .... New York, NY
Miller, Stuart O. .... Seneca Falls, NY
Miller, Stuart P. .... Little Rock, AR
Miller, Stuart W. .... San Francisco, CA
Miller & Sur .... Honolulu, HI
Miller, Susan A. .... St. Paul, MN
Miller, Susan B. .... Minneapolis, MN
Miller, Susan Brownlee .... Houston, TX
Miller, Susan C. .... Anchorage, AK
Miller, Susan Dietz .... Spokane, WA
Miller, Susan E. .... Tucson, AZ
Miller, Susan E. .... Columbus, OH
Miller, Susan G. .... Paoli, PA
Miller, Susan J. .... Hartford, CT
Miller, Susan J. .... New York, NY
Miller, Susan Jean .... Freeport, TX
Miller, Susan K. .... Boston, MA
Miller, Susan L. .... Hartford, CT
Miller, Susan M. .... South Bend, IN
Miller, Susan M. .... Boston, MA
Miller, Susan Morrow .... San Marcos, TX
Miller, Susan S. .... Lexington, KY
Miller, Susan S. .... Baltimore, MD
Miller, Susan S. .... Quincy, MA
Miller, Susannah E. .... San Francisco, CA
Miller, Suzan A. .... Santa Clara, CA
Miller, Suzanne E. .... Philadelphia, PA
Miller, Suzanne Ray .... Palo Alto, CA
Miller, Sydney .... Valley Stream, NY
Miller, T. Kurt .... Birmingham, AL
Miller, T. Matthew .... Birmingham, AL
Miller, Talbott .... Stamford, CT
Parsippany, NJ
New York, NY
Miller, Tamara A. .... Chicago, IL
Miller, Tamara L. .... Department of Justice, Civil Rights Division, GV
Miller, Tanya B. .... Buffalo, NY
Miller, Taunja Willis .... Charleston, WV
Miller, Taylor O. .... Sacramento, CA
Miller, Ted G. .... Erie, PA
Miller, Ted M. .... Portland, OR
Miller, Ted S. .... Fort Wayne, IN
Miller & Tennant .... Archdale, NC
Miller, Teresa A. .... Media, PA
Miller, Teresa Rothi .... Gardnerville, NV
Miller, Terrance M. .... Columbus, OH
Miller, Terri Senesac .... Studio City, CA
Miller, Terry E. .... Kennewick, WA
Miller, Terry L. .... Mission Viejo, CA
Miller, Terry L. .... Dalton, GA
Miller, Terry M. .... Columbus, OH
Miller, Thajauna D.
Federal Energy Regulatory Commission, Office of the General Counsel, GV
Miller, Theo. A. .... Providence, RI
Miller, Theo. H. .... West Des Moines, IA
Miller, Theodore .... Englewood, CO
Miller, Theodore J. .... Port Angeles, WA
Miller, Theodore N. .... Los Angeles, CA
Miller, Theodore S. .... Baltimore, MD
Miller, Thomas .... Brighton, MA
Miller, Thomas A. .... Costa Mesa, CA
Miller, Thomas A. .... Boise, ID

Miller, Thomas A. ... Chicago, IL
Miller, Thomas A. ... Cypress, TX
Miller, Thomas A. ... Houston, TX
Miller, Thomas A. ... Richardson, TX
Miller, Thomas A. ... Milwaukee, WI
Miller, Thomas B. ... Wheeling, WV
Miller, Thomas Brown ... Birmingham, AL
West Palm Beach, FL
Miller, Thomas C. ... Birmingham, MI
Miller, Thomas C. ... Somerville, NJ
Miller, Thomas D. ... Cohasset, MA
Miller, Thomas E. ... Los Angeles, CA
Miller, Thomas E. ... Newport Beach, CA
San Francisco, CA
Miller, Thomas E. ... San Francisco, CA
Miller, Thomas E. ... Bay Village, OH
Miller, Thomas E. ... Sugarcreek, OH
Miller, Thomas E. ... Hanover, PA
Miller, Thomas F. ... Minneapolis, MN
Miller, Thomas F. ... Wyoming, MN
Miller, Thomas F. ... Olympia, WA
Miller, Thomas H. ... Des Moines, IA
Miller, Thomas H. ... Roanoke, VA
Miller, Thomas H., Jr. ... Harrisonburg, VA
Miller, Thomas Hobson ... New Berlin, NY
Miller, Thomas J. ... Covina, CA
Miller, Thomas J.
Treasury Department, GV
Miller, Thomas J. ... Des Moines, IA
Miller, Thomas J. ... Metairie, LA
Miller, Thomas J. ... Minneapolis, MN
Miller, Thomas J. ... New York, NY
Miller, Thomas J. ... Syracuse, NY
Miller, Thomas J. ... Warwick, NY
Miller, Thomas J. ... Oklahoma City, OK
Miller, Thomas J. ... Pittsburgh, PA
Miller, Thomas L. ... Riverside, CA
Miller, Thomas L. ... Milwaukee, WI
Miller, Thomas L., A Professional Law Corporation ... Riverside, CA
Miller, Thomas M. ... Atlanta, GA
Miller, Thomas M. ... Grand Rapids, MI
Miller, Thomas P. ... Washington, DC
Miller, Thomas R. ... Oakland, CA
Miller, Thomas R. ... Monticello, IL
Miller, Thomas R. ... Harrisburg, PA
Miller, Thomas R., A Professional Law Corporation ... Oakland, CA
Miller, Thomas S. ... St. Petersburg, FL
Miller, Thomas V. ... Chicago, IL
Miller, Thomas V. Mike, Jr. ... Clinton, MD
Miller, Thomas W. ... Lexington, KY
Miller, Thomas W. ... Cincinnati, OH
Miller, Thormund A. ... Atherton, CA
Miller, Thos. A., Sr. ... Tampa, FL
Miller, Thos. O. ... Columbus, OH
Miller, Timm A. ... White Plains, NY
Miller, Timmie Maine ... Concord, NH
Miller, Timothy A. ... San Francisco, CA
Miller, Timothy A. ... St. Petersburg, FL
Miller, Timothy A. ... Rockford, IL
Miller, Timothy Bryan ... Cleveland, OH
Miller, Timothy C. ... Gaithersburg, MD
Miller, Timothy E. ... Columbus, OH
Miller, Timothy E. ... Lake Oswego, OR
Miller, Timothy J. ... Chicago, IL
Miller, Timothy Jay ... Temecula, CA
Miller, Timothy L. ... Carbondale, IL
Miller, Timothy M. ... Charleston, WV
Miller, Timothy P. ... Riverside, CA
Miller, Timothy T. ... Columbus, OH
Miller, Timothy W. ... Fort Wayne, IN
Miller, Timothy W. ... Casper, WY
Miller, Tina ... West Redding, CT
Miller, Tobin L. ... Lansing, MI
Miller, Todd A. ... Detroit, MI
Miller, Todd C. ... Beresford, SD
Sioux Falls, SD
Miller, Todd G. ... La Jolla, CA
Miller, Todd R. ... Los Angeles, CA
Miller, Todd S., & Associates
Allentown, PA
Miller, Todd T. ... Toledo, OH
Miller, Todd W. ... Greenwood Village, CO
Miller, Tolbert, Muehlhausen, Muehlhausen, Groff & Damm, P.C. ... Logansport, IN
Miller, Tommy E. ... Norfolk, VA
Miller & Tonelli ... Randolph, VT
Miller, Tony G. ... Birmingham, AL
Miller, Torrey J. ... Palo Alto, CA
Miller & Towson ... Macon, GA
Miller, Tracey J. ... New York, NY
Miller, Tracy A. ... Phoenix, AZ
Miller, Tracy, Braun, Funk & Paisley, Ltd.
Monticello, IL
Miller, Tracy E. ... New York, NY
Miller, Tracy M. ... Seattle, WA
Miller, Tracye T. ... Atlanta, GA
Miller, Travis L. ... Tallahassee, FL
Miller, Trent Dale ... West Palm Beach, FL
Miller, Turetsky, Rule & McLennan, A Professional Corporation
Collegeville, PA
Norristown, PA
Miller, Val R. ... Oklahoma City, OK
Miller, Valerie ... Chico, CA
Miller, Vance D. ... St. Louis, MO
Miller & Van Eaton, L.L.P.
San Francisco, CA
Washington, DC
Miller, Verdelski V. ... Evansville, IN
Miller, Verna A. ... San Francisco, CA
Miller, Vernon C., Jr. ... Greenwich, CT
Miller, Victor J. ... Washington, DC
Miller, Victor Lawrence, Jr.
Birmingham, AL
Miller, Victor Lee ... Las Vegas, NV
Miller, Victor W. ... Topeka, KS
Miller, Victoria L. ... Stamford, CT
Miller, Viginia Kay ... Jefferson, OH
Miller, Vincent ... Fort Pierce, FL
Stuart, FL
Miller, Virginia J. ... Department of Labor, Pension and Welfare Benefits, GV
Miller, Vivian ... Fort Lauderdale, FL
Miller, W. Andrew ... San Francisco, CA
Miller, W. Brady ... Louisville, KY
Miller, W. Kent ... Des Moines, IA
Miller, W. Lane ... East Brunswick, NJ
Miller, W. McCook, Jr. ... Pittsburgh, PA
Miller, W. McNab, III ... Houston, TX
Miller, W. Michael ... Orlando, FL
Miller, W. Orrin ... Dallas, TX
Miller, W. Rowland ... Scarsdale, NY
Miller, W. Scott, Jr. ... Louisville, KY
Miller, W. Stacy, II ... Raleigh, NC
Miller, W. Thaddeus ... New York, NY
Miller, W. Timothy ... Cincinnati, OH
Miller, W. Todd ... Washington, DC
Miller, W. Walters ... Ritzville, WA
Miller, Walker ... Denver, CO
Miller, Wallace, III ... Macon, GA
Miller, Wallace, Jr. ... Macon, GA
Miller, Walter A. ... Brooklyn, NY
Miller, Walter C. ... Plankinton, SD
Miller, Walter Duval ... Dallas, TX
Miller, Walter W. ... Eugene, OR
Miller, Walter W., Jr. ... Boston, MA
Miller, Ward K. ... San Francisco, CA
Miller, Ward M., III ... New York, NY
Miller, Ward M., Jr. ... New York, NY
Miller, Ward W. ... Fort Wayne, IN
Miller, Warner J. ... Woodinville, WA
Miller, Warren ... New London, CT
Miller, Warren ... Memphis, TN
Miller, Warren B. ... Dixon, KY
Miller, Warren G. ... Boston, MA
Miller, Warren K. ... Los Angeles, CA
Miller, Warren L. ... Washington, DC
Miller, Warren L., P.C. ... Washington, DC
Miller, Waters, Martin & Hall
Indianapolis, IN
Miller, Wayne H. ... Boston, MA
Miller, Wayne H. ... Minneapolis, MN
Miller, Wayne J. ... Los Angeles, CA
Miller, Wayne J. ... Southfield, MI
Miller, Wayne M. ... Key West, FL
Miller, Wayne R. ... Dallas, TX
Miller, Wayne W.
Federal Energy Regulatory Commission, Office of the General Counsel, GV
Miller & Webster, P.A. ... Clinton, MD
Miller & Welch, L.L.C. ... Boulder, CO
Denver, CO
Englewood, CO
Miller, Wendell R. ... Jennings, LA
Miller, Wendy Ann
Environmental Protection Agency, Program Office Attorneys, GV
Miller, Wendy E. ... New York, NY
Miller, Wendy J.
Environmental Protection Agency, Program Office Attorneys, GV
Miller, Wendy Kaplan ... Boston, MA
Miller, Wendy L. ... Morristown, NJ
Miller, Wesley ... Tahlequah, OK
Miller, Wesley A. ... Denver, CO
Miller, Weston C. ... Palo Alto, CA
Miller & Whitmore ... Gibbon, MN
Le Sueur, MN
Gaylord, MN
Miller, Whitney F. ... Kansas City, MO
Miller & Wilets ... Northridge, CA
Miller, Wilford R. ... New Philadelphia, OH
Miller, Wilhelmina Dingemans
St. Johnsbury, VT
Miller, William ... Philadelphia, PA
Miller, William ... San Antonio, TX
Miller, William A. ... Phoenix, AZ
Miller, William A. ... San Diego, CA
Miller, William A. ... Department of Justice, Federal Bureau of Investigation, GV
Miller, William A. ... Ocala, FL
Miller, William A. ... Chicago, IL
Miller, William A. ... Louisville, KY
Miller, William A., Jr. ... Atlanta, GA
Decatur, GA
Miller, William A., Jr. ... Louisville, KY
Miller, William B. ... Midland, MI
Miller, William B. ... Kansas City, MO
Miller, William B., III ... Atlanta, GA
Miller, William B., Jr. ... Middlebury, VT
Miller, William C. ... Palo Alto, CA
Miller, William C. ... San Francisco, CA
Miller, William C. ... Rockville, MD
Miller, William C. ... Philadelphia, PA
Miller, William C., II ... Charleston, WV
Miller, William Carl ... Biloxi, MS
Miller, William D. ... St. Paul, MN
Miller, William D. ... Freeport, TX
Miller, William E. ... Memphis, TN
Miller, William E., III ... Alton, IL
Miller, William E., Jr. ... Lemoyne, PA
Miller, William E., Jr. ... Pittsburgh, PA
Miller, William E., Jr. ... Bellaire, TX
Miller, William F. ... Boston, MA
Miller, William F. ... Colonial Beach, VA
Miller, William F. ... Williamsburg, VA
Miller, William F., P.C. ... Williamsburg, VA
Miller, William G. ... Washington, DC
Miller, William G., Jr. ... Fort Lauderdale, FL
Miller, William H. ... Denver, CO
Miller, William H. ... Landover, MD
Miller, William H. ... Batavia, NY
Miller, William H., Jr. ... Darien, CT
New York, NY
Miller, William H., Jr. ... New York, NY
Miller, William I. ... Ann Arbor, MI
Miller, William J. ... Anniston, AL
Miller, William J. ... Longwood, FL
Miller, William J. ... Columbus, OH
Miller, William J. ... Ponca City, OK
Miller, William J., Jr. ... Tallahassee, FL
Miller, William J., Jr. ... Monongahela, PA
Miller, William John ... Pittsburgh, PA
Miller, William, Jr. ... Bruceton Mills, WV
Miller, William L. ... Washington, DC
Miller, William L. ... Philipsburg, PA
Miller, William L. ... Riverton, WY
Miller, William L., Jr. ... St. Louis, MO
Miller, William M. ... Parsons, WV
Miller, William McD., III
Los Angeles, CA
Miller, William O. ... Atlanta, GA
Miller, William P. ... New York, NY
Miller, William P. ... High Point, NC
Miller, William R. ... Edwardsville, IL
Miller, William R. ... Minneapolis, MN
Miller, William R. ... Irvington, NJ
Miller, William R., Jr. ... Portland, OR
Miller, William R., P.A. ... Minneapolis, MN
Miller, William Read ... Beaverdam, VA
Miller, William S. ... Oakland, CA
Miller, William S. ... Honolulu, HI
Miller, William S. ... Toledo, OH
Miller, William S., Jr. ... Little Rock, AR
Miller, William S., Jr. ... Arlington, VA
Miller, William T. ... Washington, DC
Miller, William T. ... Gonzales, TX
Miller, William T. ... Houston, TX
Miller, William T., Jr. ... Anahuac, TX
Miller, William W., Jr.
Treasury Department, GV
Miller, William W., Jr. ... Texarkana, TX
Miller & Williamson, LLC
New Orleans, LA
Miller, Willie J., Jr. ... Chicago, IL
Miller, Willis L., III ... Valdosta, GA
Miller, Wilma Kerner ... Huntington, NY
Miller, Wilmot J. ... Spokane, WA
Miller, Wilmot J., Jr. ... Spokane, WA
Miller, Wilton R. ... Tallahassee, FL
Miller, Winlock W. ... Riverside, CA
Miller, Winston E. ... Louisville, KY
Miller, Winston E. ... East Lansing, MI
Miller, Wm. Alan ... Baton Rouge, LA
Miller, Wm. H. ... Evansville, IN
Miller, Woddell & Baker, A Professional Corporation ... Indianapolis, IN
Miller & Woods, P.A. ... West Palm Beach, FL
Miller & Wrubel P.C. ... New York, NY
Miller, Yoram J. ... New York, NY
Miller, Yvette ... New York, NY
Miller, Yvonne V. ... Macon, GA
Miller, Zach C. ... Denver, CO
Miller/Salsbury Law Firm, The ... Eureka, MO
Miller-Cohn, Joan ... Rye, NY
Miller DeWalt, Sherri Lynn ... Hastings, MN
Miller-Dolan, Cary E. ... St. Paul, MN
Miller Gordon, Beth ... Los Angeles, CA
Miller-Hall, Elizabeth A. ... Newark, NJ
Miller-Herron, Nancy ... Dresden, TN
Millerick, Michael F. ... San Diego, CA
Millerick, Richard S. ... McLean, VA
Miller-Lerman, Lindsey ... Omaha, NE
Miller-Meyer, Trista J. ... Riverside, CA
Miller Mickel, Marilyn D. ... Toledo, OH
Miller Rigney, Christine ... New York, NY
Miller-Roche, Lisa S. ... Las Vegas, NV
Miller-Romero, Jeanne ... Costa Mesa, CA
Miller-Rostant, Donna ... Reston, VA
Millers, David T. ... San Jose, CA
Millers, John E. ... Fullerton, CA
Miller-Schaufelberger-Bauer Law Offices, The, Ltd. ... Edwardsville, IL
Effingham, IL
Greenville, IL
Vandalia, IL
Millert, Gregory T. ... Morristown, NJ
Millert, Neal E. ... Kansas City, MO
Miller-Todd, Kathrine S. ... Des Moines, IA
Miller-Tshudy, Denise Lynne ... Harrisburg, PA
Miller-Van Oort, Sonia ... Minneapolis, MN
Miller-Wachtel, Ellen ... New York, NY
Milles, James G. ... Cleveland, OH
Milless, Charles K. ... Columbus, OH
Millet, Alan E. ... Sequim, WA
Millet, Craig H. ... Irvine, CA
Millet & Hermes ... Somerset, NJ
Millet, John P. ... San Antonio, TX
Millet, Leandre M. ... La Place, LA
Millet, Marcus J. ... Westfield, NJ
Millet, Michael A. ... Brooklyn, NY
Millet, Paul L. ... Cleveland, OH
Millet, Paul L., and Associates, A Legal Prof. Assn. ... Cleveland, OH
Millet, Richard D. ... Somerset, NJ
Millet, Richard M. ... La Place, LA
Millet, Ronald ... New York, NY
Millet & Snowdy ... La Place, LA
Millet, Stephanie J. ... Palo Alto, CA
Millet, Thomas W. ... Department of Justice, Civil Division, GV
Millett, Derrill ... Salinas, CA
Millett, Douglas R. ... San Jose, CA
Millett, Eileen Daphne ... Brooklyn, NY
Millett, Francis N., Jr. ... Tallahassee, FL
Millett, George J. ... Laramie, WY
Millett, James E. ... Westbrook, ME
Millett, James S. ... Hamilton, MO
Millett, Joan L. ... Treasury Department, Internal Revenue Service, GV
Millett, Katherine T. ... Deerfield, IL
Millett, Patricia A. ... Los Angeles, CA
Millett, Patricia A. ... Department of Justice, Office of the Solicitor General, GV
Millett, Richard L., Jr. ... Broomfield, CO
Millett, Thomas D., P.C. ... Boston, MA
Millett, Thomas David ... Boston, MA
Millett, Timothy W. ... United States Senate, Office of Senate Chief Counsel for Employment, GV
Millette, Janice I. ... Chicago, IL
Millette, Samuel M. ... Charlotte, NC
Millette, Samuel M., Jr. ... Pascagoula, MS
Milleville, Annette L. ... Joliet, IL
Millgate, John D. ... Holyoke, MA
Millham, Anne K. ... Branford, CT
Millham, Peter V. ... Laconia, NH
Millhauser, Lisa Novick ... Miami, FL
Millhauser, Marguerite S. ... Washington, DC
Millheiser, David John ... Miami, FL
Millhiser, Frederick R. ... Takoma Park, MD
Millhiser, Thomas McNally
Richmond, VA
Millhoff, Patricia A. ... Akron, OH
Millhollin, Jeffrey B. ... Corning, IA
Millhollin Law Office ... Corning, IA
Millhone & Anderson ... Clarinda, IA
Millhone, James N. ... Clarinda, IA
Millhorn, Michael D. ... Summerfield, FL
Millhouse, G. Stefan, III ... Houston, TX
Millhouse, Jeanne M. ... Lancaster, PA
Millhouse, Keith F. ... Westlake Village, CA
Millhouse, Scott A. ... Pittsburgh, PA
Millian, John C. ... Washington, DC
Millian, Kathleen L. ... Washington, DC
Millian, Marc T. ... Boca Raton, FL
Millian, Richard C. ... Clearwater, FL
Millians, Michael W. ... Augusta, GA
Millians, Sharon S. ... Fort Worth, TX
Milliard, Daniel R. ... Coudersport, PA
Millibergity, Lenore K. ... St. Paul, MN
Millican, Adrienne F. ... Seattle, WA
Millican, Cassidy & Riley ... Jennings, LA
Millican, Clarence N. ... Seabrook, TX
Millican, J. Michael ... Baton Rouge, LA
Millican, James T., II ... Cleveland, OH
Millican, Joshua A. ... Atlanta, GA
Millican, Kenneth H. ... Hamilton, AL
Millican, Patrick R. ... Sylvania, OH
Millican, Paul H. ... San Angelo, TX
Millican & Ryland ... Baton Rouge, LA
Millican, Sherman P. ... Lampasas, TX
Millican, W. A. ... Gadsden, AL
Millichap, Paul A. ... Chicago, IL
Millie, Carol Webster ... Los Altos, CA
Millien, Jennifer C. ... Xenia, OH
Millien, Raymond ... Washington, DC
Milligan, Alicia Murphy ... Providence, RI
Milligan, Barry, Hensley & Evans
Chattanooga, TN
Milligan and Beswick ... San Bernardino, CA
Milligan, Betty Ann ... Memphis, TN
Milligan, Brian D. ... Denver, CO
Milligan, C. Patrick ... San Bernardino, CA
Milligan, Charles ... Key West, FL
Milligan & Coleman ... Greeneville, TN
Milligan, Cynthia H. ... Lincoln, NE
Milligan, Daniel A. ... Oklahoma City, OK
Milligan, Daniel L. ... Springfield, IL
Milligan, David R. ... West Des Moines, IA
Milligan, David T. ... Westerville, OH
Milligan, Donald R. ... Loveland, CO
Milligan, Edward J., Jr. ... Lafayette, LA
Milligan, Edward J., Jr., Ltd. ... Lafayette, LA
Milligan, F. Scott ... Knoxville, TN
Milligan, Fred J., Jr. ... Westerville, OH
Milligan, Fred J., Jr., Co., L.P.A.
Westerville, OH
Milligan, James L., Jr. ... Knoxville, TN
Milligan, James M., Jr. ... Quincy, MA
Milligan, Jo Ann ... Kalamazoo, MI
Milligan, John P., Jr. ... Fort Myers, FL
Milligan, John R. ... North Canton, OH
Milligan, Joseph A. ... Babylon, NY
Milligan, Joseph F. ... St. Petersburg, FL
Milligan, Kelly ... San Francisco, CA
Milligan, Kelly W. ... Dallas, TX
Milligan Law Offices ... Fort Smith, AR
Milligan, Mark L.
Christiansted, St. Croix, VI
Milligan, Mark L., P.C.
Christiansted, St. Croix, VI
Milligan, Maureen ... Scottsdale, AZ
Milligan, Michael J. ... Oklahoma City, OK
Milligan, Michael Patrick
San Bernardino, CA
Milligan, Michael R. "Mickey" ... El Paso, TX
Milligan, Michael T. ... St. Cloud, MN
Milligan, Mike ... El Paso, TX
Milligan, Paul T. ... Boston, MA
Milligan, Phillip J. ... Fort Smith, AR
Milligan, Richard A. ... Kalamazoo, MI
Milligan, Richard S. ... Canton, OH
Milligan, Robert J. ... Phoenix, AZ
Milligan, Robert S. ... Lincoln, NE
Milligan, Samuel J. ... Tustin, CA
Milligan, Sandra A. ... Newport Beach, CA
Milligan & Signorella ... Fort Myers, FL
Milligan, Suanne C. ... Crawfordsville, IN
Milligan, Susan ... Washington, DC
Milligan, Thomas H. ... Charleston, SC
Milligan, Thomas K. ... Crawfordsville, IN
Milligan, Thomas S. ... Richmond, IN
Milligan, William D. ... San Diego, CA
Milligan, William W. ... Columbus, OH
Milligan-Harmon, Tamara L. ... Wilton, CA
Milligram, Steven I. ... Newburgh, NY
Millikan, Catharine Karl ... Pasadena, CA
Millikan, Gregory F. ... Pasadena, CA
Millikan, Ian G. ... Marysville, WA

Millikan, James E. .... **New Castle, IN**
Millikan, Jess B. .... **San Francisco, CA**
Millikan, Kathleen M. .... Durham, NC
Millikan, Kent B. .... **Everett, WA**
Millikan, Michael E. .... **Indianapolis, IN**
Millikan, Robert C. .... Roseburg, OR
Millikan & Stamper .... **New Castle, IN**
Millikan & Swanson .... Marysville, WA
Millikan, Troy R. .... **Gainesville, GA**
Milliken, Charles B. .... **Hartford, CT**
Milliken, Charles B. .... **Fort Worth, TX**
Milliken, Darren J. .... **Sunnyvale, CA**
Milliken, Emery E. .... **Charlotte, NC**
Milliken, James B. .... Chapel Hill, NC
Milliken, James M. .... Bird City, KS
St. Francis, KS
Milliken, James M., Chartered
St. Francis, KS
Milliken, James R. .... San Diego, CA
Milliken, James T. .... Phoenix, AZ
Milliken, James T. .... **Johnson City, TN**
Milliken, Jerry S. .... Los Angeles, CA
Milliken, Jerry S., A Professional Corp.
Los Angeles, CA
Milliken, John C. .... **Bryan, OH**
Milliken, John G. .... **McLean, VA**
Milliken, John M. .... Bowling Green, KY
Milliken, John R. .... Monroe, NC
Milliken, Jon C. .... San Diego, CA
Milliken, Kari .... St. Francis, KS
Milliken, Kevin F. .... Madison, WI
Milliken, Laura .... Claremont, NH
Milliken Law Firm .... **Bowling Green, KY**
Milliken, Lloyd H., Jr. .... **Indianapolis, IN**
Milliken, Magee & Yuille .... Burton, MI
Milliken, Margie S. .... San Diego, CA
Milliken, Michael J. .... Superior, WI
Milliken, Paul E. .... Massillon, OH
Milliken, Paul S. .... Randolph, MA
Milliken, Rankin A. .... Walnut Creek, CA
Milliken, Sarah C. .... Los Angeles, CA
Milliken, Seth M., Jr. .... West Southport, ME
Milliken, Stephen .... Washington, DC
Milliken, W. Currie .... **Bowling Green, KY**
Milliken, W. Dickerson .... Los Angeles, CA
Milliken, Wesley V. .... **Bowling Green, KY**
Milliken, William Barry
Cape Canaveral, FL
Miami, FL
Tampa, FL
Millikin & Fitton Law Firm, A Legal Professional Association .... **Fairfield, OH**
Hamilton, OH
Oxford, OH
Millikin, J. Richard, Jr. .... Longview, TX
Millikin, Margaret S. .... **Oklahoma City, OK**
Millikin, Michael P. .... **Detroit, MI**
Millikin, Stephen Perry .... **Greensboro, NC**
Millikin, Thomas J. .... Hamilton, OH
Milliman, James E. .... **Louisville, KY**
Milliman, Lou Anne .... **New Orleans, LA**
Milliman, Rebecca A. .... **Chicago, IL**
Millimet, Erwin .... **New York, NY**
Millimet, Joseph A. .... **Manchester, NH**
Millimet, Robert M. .... **St. Louis, MO**
Dallas, TX
Millin, F. Russell .... **Kansas City, MO**
Millin, Jeffrey K. .... **Meadville, PA**
Millin, Paul H. .... Tionesta, PA
Warren, PA
Millin, Stephen B., Jr. .... **Kansas City, MO**
Milling Benson Woodward L.L.P.
Lafayette, LA
Mandeville, LA
New Orleans, LA
Milling, Bert W., Jr. .... Mobile, AL
Milling, Brooks P. .... **Mobile, AL**
Milling, John L. .... Edgewater, NJ
Milling, John M. .... Darlington, SC
Milling, John M., Jr. .... **Montgomery, AL**
Milling, King .... **New York, NY**
Milling Law Firm, P.A. .... Darlington, SC
Milling, Lawrence B. .... New York, NY
Milling, Leonard F. .... Atlanta, GA
Milling, R. Clay .... **Atlanta, GA**
Milling, R. King .... New Orleans, LA
Milling, R. King, Jr. .... New Orleans, LA
Millinger, Donald M. .... **Philadelphia, PA**
Millinger, Irwin J. .... East Brunswick, NJ
Millington, Brian K. .... Warren, MI
Millington, Jan Y. .... **Springfield, MO**
Millington, Jennifer Brown .... Denver, CO
Millington, June H. .... **Trenton, NJ**
Millington, Kimberly A. .... **Los Angeles, CA**
Millington, Michael William .... Denver, CO
Millington & Millington .... Gridley, CA
Millington, Robert .... Gridley, CA
Millington, Scott T. .... Los Angeles, CA
Millington, Susan E. .... Shedd, OR
Millington, Thomas W. .... Springfield, MO
Millington, William W. .... Lake George, NY
Million, Carol B. .... Denver, CO
Million, Gary E. .... Irvine, CA
Million, James T. .... Kansas City, MO
Million, John T. .... Monticello, IN
Million, Lulit
Charlotte Amalie, St. Thomas, VI
Million, W. Dean .... Poplar Bluff, MO
Millious, Joseph M. .... **Columbus, OH**
Millirons, Paul L. .... **Huntsville, AL**
Millirons, Timothy J. .... **Chattanooga, TN**
Millis, A. Edward .... Salem, OR
Millis, Benton R. .... Greensburg, IN
Millis, Bert J. .... **Jacksonville, FL**
Millis, Edward A. .... **Ormond Beach, FL**
Millis, Edward A., P.A.
Daytona Beach, FL
Ormond Beach, FL

Millis, Jennifer Kolinski .... Jacksonville, FL
Millis, Susan K. .... **Dallas, TX**
Millison, Gayle S. .... **Tampa, FL**
Millison & Millison, P.A. .... **Tampa, FL**
Millison, Theodore S. .... **Tampa, FL**
Millisor, Kenneth R. .... **Cleveland, OH**
Millisor & Nobil, A Legal Professional Association .... **Cleveland, OH**
Dublin, OH
North Canton, OH
Millisor, Richard A. .... **Cleveland, OH**
Millisor, William P. .... Norcross, GA
Millkey & Associates, P.C. .... Atlanta, GA
Millkey, John M. .... Atlanta, GA
Millkey, Mark T. .... Staten Island, NY
Millman, Arthur .... Westport, CT
Millman, Bruce R. .... **Mineola, NY**
New York, NY
Millman, Charles J. .... Harrisburg, PA
Millman, Claude .... New York, NY
Millman, Craig .... Chicago, IL
Millman, Daniel L. .... Hempstead, NY
Millman, Dennis G. .... Pittsburgh, PA
Millman, Debra J. .... **New York, NY**
Millman, Diane S. .... **Washington, DC**
Millman, Jay O. .... **Richmond, VA**
Millman, Jode Susan .... Poughkeepsie, NY
Millman, Judith A. .... Westfield, NJ
Millman, Kenneth .... **Wyomissing, PA**
Millman, Kenneth M. .... Georgetown, DE
Millman, Laura Diane
United States Court of Federal Claims, Office of Special Masters, GV
Millman, Linda J. .... St. Louis, MO
Millman, Linda R. .... Nashua, NH
Millman, Mary D. .... Berkeley, CA
Millman, Michael G. .... San Francisco, CA
Millman, Neil H. .... Great Neck, NY
Millman, Paul M. .... White Plains, NY
Millman, Robert A. .... Colorado Springs, CO
Millman, Robert A. .... Cambridge, MA
Millman, Robert A., P.C.
Colorado Springs, CO
Millman, Robert B. .... Redmond, WA
Millman, Robert B., Jr. .... Richmond, VA
Millman, Robert F. .... **Los Angeles, CA**
Millman, Robert N. .... West Orange, NJ
Millman, Robyn B. .... New York, NY
Millman, Samuel .... Garden City, NY
Millman, Sherry J. .... **New York, NY**
Millman, Stephen L. .... **New York, NY**
Millman, Timothy S. .... **Kansas City, MO**
Millman, Valerie .... **New York, NY**
Millman, Wendy B. .... **New York, NY**
Millman, William G., Jr. .... **New Haven, CT**
Millner, A. David .... Roseland, NJ
Millner, Ari A. .... Fairfax, VA
Millner, B. M. .... **Newport News, VA**
Millner, Christopher B. .... **Atlanta, GA**
Millner, Dawn I. Giebler .... **Orlando, FL**
Millner, H. Victor, Jr. .... **Chatham, VA**
Millner, H. Victor, Jr., P.C. .... **Chatham, VA**
Millner, James W. .... New Brunswick, NJ
Millner, Jeffrey B., P.C. .... **Portland, OR**
Millner, Jennifer Weisberg
Lawrenceville, NJ
Millner, Robert B. .... **Chicago, IL**
Millner, Stephen J. .... Yardley, PA
Millo, Frank R. .... New York, NY
Millock, Peter J. .... **Albany, NY**
Millon, David .... Lexington, VA
Millon, James W. .... **Maumee, OH**
Millon, James W., Co., L.P.A.
Maumee, OH
Toledo, OH
Millon, Kevin H. .... Wheaton, IL
Millon, Steven E. .... **Bronx, NY**
Millones, Peter J., Jr. .... **New York, NY**
Millonig, Arthur F., Jr. .... Dayton, OH
Millonig, Arthur F., Jr., Co., L.P.A.
Dayton, OH
Millonig, Michael J. .... Dayton, OH
Millonig, Robert C. .... **Washington, DC**
Millora, Salina L. .... Plymouth, NH
Millot, Marc Dean .... Alexandria, VA
Millott, Massad & Misilo, P.C.
Worcester, MA
Millott, Thomas P. .... Worcester, MA
Milloy, Marianne M. .... Brainerd, MN
Milloy, Maryrose .... Houston, TX
Millrood, Tobias L. .... **Philadelphia, PA**
Mills, A. Carter, IV .... **New Orleans, LA**
Mills, A. J., Jr., P.C. .... Boulder, CO
Mills, A. J., Jr. .... Boulder, CO
Mills, Alan .... Chicago, IL
Mills, Alan K. .... **Indianapolis, IN**
Mills, Albert A. .... Cherry Hill, NJ
Mills, Amy B. .... Nashua, NH
Mills, Amy J. .... Des Moines, IA
Mills, Amy M. .... Tyler, TX
Mills, Andrew Don .... El Paso, TX
Mills, Anna S. .... **Nashville, TN**
Mills, Anthony B. .... Danville, CA
Mills, Antoinette Gary .... **San Jose, CA**
Mills, Aubrey W. .... Montgomery, AL
Mills, Barry .... **New York, NY**
Mills, Barry K. .... **Ellsworth, ME**
Mills, Ben B., Jr. .... **Fitzgerald, GA**
Mills, Beth Bechard .... **Gainesville, FL**
Mills, Beth S. .... **Pittsburgh, PA**
Mills, Beverly .... Torrance, CA
Mills, Billy D. .... Fort Worth, TX
Mills, Bobby D. .... **Raleigh, NC**
Mills, Brady W. .... **Washington, DC**
Mills, Brent L. .... Norman, OK
Mills, Brian A. .... **Beaumont, TX**
Mills, Bruce C. .... Walnut Creek, CA
Mills, Bruce Frank .... **Milwaukee, WI**

Mills, Bryan L. .... **Montpelier, VT**
Mills, Bryson E. .... Wichita, KS
Mills & Butler .... Lakewood, CO
Mills, Byron L. .... **Las Vegas, NV**
Mills, Carleton S. .... Santa Ana, CA
Mills, Carol D. .... Fresno, CA
Mills, Caroline A. .... Madisonville, KY
Mills, Carolyn B. .... Jackson, MS
Mills, Carson L. .... Rockville, MD
Mills, Casey W. .... Fort Lauderdale, FL
Mills, Casey W., P.A. .... Fort Lauderdale, FL
Mills, Catherine F. .... Tierra Verde, FL
Mills, Cathlyn J., (P.C.) .... **Tulsa, OK**
Mills, Cathy .... Oakland, CA
Mills, Cecil J. .... Torrance, CA
Mills, Chad .... **Houston, TX**
Mills, Chadwick L. .... **Irvine, CA**
Mills, Charles B., Jr. .... **Columbus, OH**
Mills, Charles E. .... Rocky River, OH
Mills, Charles F. .... Little Rock, AR
Mills, Charles G. .... **Glen Cove, NY**
Mills, Charles K. .... **Irvine, CA**
Mills, Charles R. .... **Washington, DC**
Mills, Charlton .... Sandpoint, ID
Mills & Chasteen, P.C. .... **Douglas, GA**
Fitzgerald, GA
Mills, Cheryl D.
Executive Office Of The President, GV
Mills, Cheryl Rae .... **Walnut Creek, CA**
Mills, Christa R. .... Houston, TX
Mills, Christopher A. .... **Washington, DC**
Mills, Christopher H. .... **Somerset, NJ**
Mills, Colen A. .... Costa Mesa, CA
Mills, Craig D. .... **Philadelphia, PA**
Mills, Craig D., (P.C.) .... **Boston, MA**
Mills, Creighton D. .... **Irvine, CA**
Mills, Cynthia A. .... **Greenville, NC**
Mills, D. Michael .... Salem, OR
Mills, Daniel B. .... **Chicago, IL**
Mills, Daniel C. .... **Chicago, IL**
Mills, Daniel C., Jr. .... **Bethlehem, PA**
Mills, Daniel H. .... Austin, TX
Mills, Daniel M. .... Bloomington, IN
Mills, Daniel M. .... Canton, OH
Mills, David A. .... **Boston, MA**
Danvers, MA
Provincetown, MA
Mills, David A. .... **York, PA**
Mills, David B. .... Eugene, OR
Mills, David B. .... Madison, WI
Mills, David E. .... **Washington, DC**
Mills, David E. .... Naples, FL
Mills, David F. .... **Smithfield, NC**
Mills, David G. .... **Memphis, TN**
Mills, David J. .... **Georgetown, SC**
Myrtle Beach, SC
Mills, David L. .... **Rolla, MO**
Mills, David M. .... Cleveland, OH
Mills, David M. .... Ponca City, OK
Mills, David N. .... **Detroit, MI**
Mills, David W. .... Treasury Department, Office of Foreign Assets Control, GV
Mills, David W. .... Roseland, NJ
Mills, Demetra J. .... **Arlington, VA**
Mills, Denise K. .... **Denver, CO**
Mills, Don B. .... Barbourville, KY
Mills, Don C.
Charlotte Amalie, St. Thomas, VI
Mills, Don Harper .... Long Beach, CA
Mills, Don Harper, A Professional Corporation
Long Beach, CA
Mills, Don M. .... Dallas, TX
Mills, Donald B. .... Cynthiana, KY
Mills, Donald J. .... Baton Rouge, LA
Mills, Donald W. .... Dallas, TX
Mills, Donna Marie .... Brooklyn, NY
Mills, Douglas .... Huntington, WV
Mills, Douglas C. .... Saratoga Springs, NY
Mills, E. Ronald .... Metairie, LA
Mills, E. A. "Seth", Jr. .... **Tampa, FL**
Mills, Earl D. .... **Oklahoma City, OK**
Mills, Edward E. .... White Plains, NY
Mills, Edward F. .... Milpitas, CA
Mills, Edward J. .... Pittsburgh, PA
Mills, Edward V. .... San Francisco, CA
Mills, Elaine Black .... **Dearborn, MI**
Mills, Elaine P. .... New York, NY
Mills, Elizabeth M. .... **Chicago, IL**
Mills, Emily Carolyn .... Martinsville, IN
Mills, F. Fetzer .... Wadesboro, NC
Mills, Flaire Hope .... New York, NY
Mills, Frank C., III .... Canton, GA
Mills, Franklin Darryl .... **Wilmington, NC**
Mills, Frederick E. .... Columbus, OH
Mills, Frederick J. .... **Tampa, FL**
Mills, Gail Livingston .... **Birmingham, AL**
Mills, Gary Andrew .... **Newport News, VA**
Mills, Gary M. .... Deerfield Beach, FL
Mills, Gary S. .... **Durham, NC**
Mills, George A., III .... Huntington, WV
Mills, George H., Jr. .... **Shreveport, LA**
Mills, George P. .... **Carlsbad, CA**
Mills, George R., Jr. .... Scotia, NY
Mills, George W. .... **Lexington, KY**
Mills, Gerald L. .... Toledo, OH
Mills, Golden .... Pride, LA
Mills, Gregory S. .... **Clifton Park, NY**
Mills and Hauser, L.L.P. .... **Thomasville, NC**
Mills & Henry .... **Pittsburgh, PA**
Mills, Hugh C. .... **Mount Airy, NC**
Mills, J. Christopher .... **Columbia, SC**
Mills, J. Edwin .... Orlando, FL
Mills, J. Kevin .... **Washington, DC**
Mills, J. Michael .... **New Bern, NC**
Mills, J. Rodney .... **Fort Smith, AR**
Mills, Jack W. .... Houston, TX
Mills, Jacqueline W. .... Galveston, TX
Mills, James A. .... Los Angeles, CA

Mills, James A. .... **Cincinnati, OH**
Mills, James A., Jr. .... Chandler, TX
Mills, James D. .... Princeton, NJ
Mills, James D. .... Arlington, TX
Mills, James David .... Mobile, AL
Mills, James G. .... Federal Trade Commission, Bureau of Consumer Protection, GV
Mills, James M .... New York, NY
Mills, James T. .... New York, NY
Mills, James W., III .... Dallas, TX
Mills, James W., III .... Dallas, TX
Mills, Jane Kent .... **Southfield, MI**
Mills, Janet T. .... **Skowhegan, ME**
Mills, Janice L. .... Durham, NC
Mills, Janice M. .... Brighton, MI
Mills, Jeffrey A. .... **Lancaster, PA**
Mills, Jeffrey A. .... **Pittsburgh, PA**
Mills, Jeffrey D. .... **Chicago, IL**
Mills, Jennifer A. .... **Cleveland, OH**
Mills, Jennifer T. .... **Columbus, OH**
Mills, Jerry L. .... Jackson, MS
Mills, Jerry W. .... **Dallas, TX**
Mills, Jim D. .... Garden City, KS
Mills, Jimmie D. .... Lakewood, CO
Mills, John Carl .... **Newark, NJ**
Mills, John Casey, P.C. .... **Portland, OR**
Mills, John D. .... Fort Myers, FL
Mills, John F. .... **Phoenix, AZ**
Mills, John F. .... **Birmingham, MI**
Bloomfield Hills, MI
Mills, John F. .... **Garden City, NY**
Mills, John G. .... **Greenville, NC**
Wake Forest, NC
Mills, John Knox .... Barbourville, KY
Mills, John L. .... Washington, DC
Mills, John M., III .... Morristown, NJ
Mills, John R. .... **Rochester, MN**
Mills, John S. .... **Palo Alto, CA**
Wilmington, DE
Mills, John S. .... **Jacksonville, FL**
Mills, John T., Jr. .... Houston, TX
Mills, John W. .... Los Angeles, CA
Mills, John W. .... **Bridgeport, CT**
Mills, John W. .... Lincolnshire, IL
Mills, John W., III .... **Los Angeles, CA**
Mills, JoJene E. .... **Tucson, AZ**
Mills, Jon A. .... Warwick, RI
Mills, Jon L. .... Gainesville, FL
Mills, Jonathan B. .... **Greenwich, CT**
Mills, Jonathan L. .... **Chicago, IL**
Mills, Joshua A. .... **San Francisco, CA**
Mills, Julie A. .... Los Altos, CA
Mills, K. Dane .... **Virginia Beach, VA**
Mills, Karen A. .... Federal Trade Commission, Bureau of Competition, GV
Mills, Karen N. .... Sacramento, CA
Mills, Kathleen M. .... **Bethlehem, PA**
Mills, Kendall .... Waukegan, IL
Mills, Kenneth W. .... Austin, TX
Mills, Kevin A. .... San Francisco, CA
Mills, Kevin D. .... Martinsburg, WV
Mills, Lamond R. .... **Las Vegas, NV**
Mills, Lamond R., & Associates, L.L.C.
Las Vegas, NV
Mills & Larson .... **Walnut Creek, CA**
Mills, Laura A. .... Evanston, IL
Mills, Laurence A. .... Needham Heights, MA
Mills, Laurin H. .... **Washington, DC**
Mills Law Firm, PLLC .... **Greenville, NC**
Raleigh, NC
Wake Forest, NC
Mills Law Firm, The .... **Greenbrae, CA**
San Francisco, CA
Mills Law Firm, The .... **Clifton Park, NY**
Mills Law Firm, The .... **Concord, NC**
Mills Law Firm, The, P.C. .... **Edmond, OK**
El Reno, OK
Norman, OK
Oklahoma City, OK
Shawnee, OK
Mills Law Office .... **Tulsa, OK**
Mills, Lawrence .... Woods Cross, UT
Mills, Lawrence R. .... **Seattle, WA**
Mills, Lee A. .... Miami, FL
Mills, Lee A. .... **Medford, OR**
Mills, Leon J. .... **Indianapolis, IN**
Mills, Lewis R. .... **St. Louis, MO**
Mills, Linda A. .... Santa Monica, CA
Mills, Linda B.R. .... Department of the Army, Army Materiel Command, GV
Mills, Linda G. .... Los Angeles, CA
Mills, Lionel .... Houston, TX
Mills, Lori A. .... **Princeton, NJ**
Mills, M. Dale, Jr. .... El Cajon, CA
Mills, M. A., Jr. .... Osceola, NE
Mills, Marcia J. .... Gaithersburg, MD
Mills, Mark Edward .... **Seattle, WA**
Mills, Marsha V. .... Harrisburg, PA
Mills, Martha Torr .... Anchorage, AK
Mills, Mary H. .... Schenectady, NY
Mills, Mary K. .... St. Paul, MN
Mills, Mary L. .... **Chicago, IL**
Mills, Mary Louise .... Largo, FL
Mills, Maury, The Law Office of
Los Angeles, CA
Riverside, CA
San Diego, CA
San Luis Obispo, CA
Santa Ana, CA
Santa Barbara, CA
Mills, Maury, The Law Office of
Ventura, CA
Mills & McMillin .... Salem, OR
Mills, Melanie Dummer .... Denver, CO
Mills, Melbourne, Jr. .... Versailles, KY
Mills, Melody Tadlock .... Fort Worth, TX
Mills, Melvin E. .... Austin, TX
Mills, Meredith .... Houston, TX

Milstein, Craig Richard ... Lancaster, PA
Milstein, Daniel R. ... Garden City, NY
Milstein, David E. ... Niskayuna, NY
Milstein, Edward P. ... New York, NY
Milstein, Elise Natalie ... Vienna, VA
Milstein, Elliott S. ... Washington, DC
Milstein, Fredric M. ... Neptune, NJ
Milstein, Harold J. ... Palo Alto, CA
Milstein, Herbert E. ... Washington, DC
Milstein, James P. ... Albany, NY
Milstein, Jonathan W. ... Olympia, WA
Milstein, Joshua David ... San Francisco, CA
Milstein, Leonard R.
San Luis Obispo, CA
Milstein, Louis N. ... Vista, CA
Milstein, Mark ... Los Angeles, CA
Milstein, Michael G. ... Denver, CO
Milstein & Milstein ... Albany, NY
Milstein, Nathan L. ... Detroit, MI
Milstein, Rachelle H. ... Florham Park, NJ
Milstein, Richard C. ... Miami, FL
Milstein, Richard S. ... Springfield, MA
Milstein, Ronald S. ... Greensboro, NC
Milstein, Stanley I. ... Staten Island, NY
Milstein, Susan Buff ... Albany, NY
Milsten, Craig R. ... York, PA
Milsten, Nancy E. ... Moorestown, NJ
Milsten, Robert B. ... Oklahoma City, OK
Milsten, Scott K. ... San Francisco, CA
Milster, Richard O. ... Bay City, MI
Milstone, James H. ... South Bend, IN
Milstone, Jason M. ... Holland, MI
Miltenberg, Andrew T. ... New York, NY
Miltenberg, Ned I. ... Washington, DC
Miltenberger, Barbara L.
Jefferson City, MO
Miltenberger, Christopher R. ... Dallas, TX
Miltenberger, Henry J., Jr. ... Covington, LA
Miltenberger, Robert H., II
Fort Lauderdale, FL
Miltenberger, Timothy D.
New Haven, CT
Miltiades, Shari Sigman ... Savannah, GA
Miltko, Susan Moriarity ... Missoula, MT
Miltner, Lawrence J. ... Columbus, OH
Miltner, William L. ... San Diego, CA
Milton, Audrey S. ... Fort Myers, FL
Milton, Chad E. ... Kansas City, MO
Milton, Cheryl L. ... Perry, GA
Milton, Christine Rieger ... Jacksonville, FL
Milton, Christopher H. ... Boston, MA
Milton, David R. ... Middleburg, VA
Milton, David Sherman ... Los Angeles, CA
Milton, Denise B. ... San Francisco, CA
Milton, Dennis E. ... New York, NY
Milton, Dennis P. ... Elizabeth, NJ
Milton, Donn R. ... Lanham, MD
Milton, Frederick A. ... Kalamazoo, MI
Milton, Gabriel B. ... West Orange, NJ
Milton, Harold W., Jr.
Bloomfield Hills, MI
Milton, James C. ... Tulsa, OK
Milton, Jeral A. ... Baltimore, MD
Milton, John D., Jr. ... Jacksonville, FL
Milton, John F., Jr. ... Holliston, MA
Milton, John T. ... Palm Beach, FL
Milton, Joseph P. ... Jacksonville, FL
Milton, Kathleen M. ... Department of State, Office of the Legal Adviser, GV
Milton, Laurence & Dixon
Worcester, MA
Milton, Leach & D'Andrea, P.A.
Jacksonville, FL
Milton, Lisa T. ... Troy, MI
Milton, Marvin ... Boston, MA
Milton, Michael J. ... Washington, DC
Milton, Michael P. ... Jacksonville, FL
Milton, Naomi H. ... Department of Justice, Civil Rights Division, GV
Milton, Rodney F. ... Overland Park, KS
Milton, Steve W. ... Fort Worth, TX
Milton, Tamson W. ... Washington, DC
Milton, Thomas P. ... New York, NY
Milton, William A., III ... Tavares, FL
Miltz, Arthur Ian, Esq. ... Livingston, NJ
Miltz, Arthur Ian, Esq., P.A. ... Livingston, NJ
Miluski, Mary K. ... Philadelphia, PA
Milutin, John ... Sugar Land, TX
Milutin & Richard ... Houston, TX
Sugar Land, TX
Milvain, Lori T. ... Orlando, FL
Milvenan, Richard D. ... Austin, TX
Milward, Michael W. ... Petaluma, CA
Milwe, Jeffrey M. ... Stratford, CT
Milwe and Loew ... Stratford, CT
Milwee, Fran Kilpatrick ... Guntersville, AL
Milwid, Peter A. ... Denver, CO
Milwid & Schlosser, P.C. ... Denver, CO
Milz, Michael E. ... Chicago, IL
Mimbu, Robert T. ... Seattle, WA
Mimlitz, John E. ... St. Louis, MO
Mimlitz, Katherine H. ... St. Louis, MO
Mimmo, Michael F. ... Concord, NH
Mimms, Malcolm L., Jr. ... Nashville, TN
Mimna, Roy A. ... Hubbard, OH
Mims, Bobby D. ... Tyler, TX
Mims, Brian Lee ... Houston, TX
Mims, Carnegie H., Jr. ... Houston, TX
Mims, Christopher W. ... Dallas, TX
Mims, David A., Jr. ... Roanoke, TX
Mims, Dawn Hendrix ... Rayville, LA
Mims, Gary B. ... Fairfax, VA
Mims, Henry J. ... Greer, SC
Mims, Jerry L. ... Washington, DC
Mims, Joseph C. ... New York, NY
Mims, L. Daniel ... Mobile, AL
Mims, Larry B. ... Tifton, GA
Mims Law Firm, The ... Greer, SC

Mims, L. Daniel, P.C. ... Mobile, AL
Mims, Lisabeth Ann ... Dallas, TX
Mims, Mary M. ... Grand Haven, MI
Holland, MI
Mims, Natalie S. ... Fort Lauderdale, FL
Mims, Peter E. ... Houston, TX
Mims, Rhonda R. ... Department of Justice, Environment and Natural Resources Division, GV
Mims, Robin A. ... Los Angeles, CA
Mims & Rochelle, L.L.P. ... Dallas, TX
Mims, Roy L. ... Leesburg, FL
Mims, S. M. ... Dallas, TX
Mims, Stephen S. ... Houston, TX
Mims, Stewart S. ... Los Angeles, CA
Mims, William C. ... Leesburg, VA
Mims, William Jemison, Jr. ... Pensacola, FL
Mims, William L. ... Orlando, FL
Mims, William L., Jr. ... Orlando, FL
Mims, William L., Jr., P.A. ... Orlando, FL
Mims-Sandidge, Marise ... Clanton, AL
Mimura, Susan L. ... Boise, ID
Min, April ... Morgantown, WV
Min, Byung Joon ... Washington, DC
Min, Catharina Yoosun
San Francisco, CA
Min, Dae-Ki ... New York, NY
Min, Esther Kyong ... New York, NY
Min, Janet S. ... Santa Monica, CA
Columbus, OH
Min, Kelly L. ... Honolulu, HI
Min, Kollin ... Seattle, WA
Min, Sophia ShangKuan ... Lawrenceville, NJ
Min, Steve T. ... New York, NY
Min, Sueyoung ... Boston, MA
Min, William E. ... Stamford, CT
Min, YeWon ... Boston, MA
Mina, F. V., (P.C.) ... New York, NY
Mina, Jennifer Lynn ... Boston, MA
Mina, Thimi R. ... Portland, ME
Minaberrigarai, Amelia T. ... Bakersfield, CA
Minaberrigarai, Dominique
Bakersfield, CA
Minacci, David K. ... Tallahassee, FL
Minadeo, Joseph M. ... Montpelier, VT
Minaga-Miya, Karie ... West Valley City, UT
Minagil, Stephen R. ... Las Vegas, NV
Minaglia, Madeleine M.V. Young
Beverly Hills, CA
Honolulu, HI
Minahan, Daniel F. ... Southport, CT
Minahan, Daniel F., Jr. ... Lakewood, CO
Minahan, Daniel J. ... Menomonee Falls, WI
Minahan, Donald P. ... Pittsburgh, PA
Minahan, John C., Jr. ... Lincoln, NE
Minahan, Kathleen M. ... Cleveland, OH
Minahan & Shapiro, P.C. ... Lakewood, CO
Minahan, W. Thomas ... Bellefontaine, OH
Minaldi, Thad D. ... Sulphur, LA
Minalga, Maryanne ... San Francisco, CA
Minami, Dale ... San Francisco, CA
Minami, Eri ... New York, NY
Minami, Ken R. ... Glendale, CA
Minami, Lew & Tamaki, LLP
San Francisco, CA
Minan, John H. ... San Diego, CA
Minana, Gregory J. ... St. Louis, MO
Minano, J. Gregory ... Atlanta, GA
Minarcik, Thomas J. ... Erie, PA
Minard, Cameron C. ... Columbia, LA
Minard and Evans ... Columbia, LA
Minardi, Andrew J. ... Clayton, MO
Minardi, Ann S. ... Treasury Department, Office of Regulations and Rulings, GV
Minardi, Joseph P. ... Northampton, MA
Springfield, MA
Minardi, Richard A., Jr. ... Richmond, VA
Minardi, Richard C. ... Tampa, FL
Minarick, Jean E.
Securities and Exchange Commission, Office of Compliance Inspections and Examinations, GV
Minarik, Bernard J., II ... Sierra Vista, AZ
Minarik, Irwin J. ... Lake Zurich, IL
Minary, John S. ... New York, NY
Minas, Jacob A. ... New York, NY
Minasi, Joseph P. ... Northport, NY
Minasian, Armen Don ... Chatsworth, CA
Minasian, David ... Oroville, CA
Minasian, Haig J. ... Lawrence, MA
Minasian, Jane E. ... Arlington, MA
Minasian, Lawrence D.
West Caldwell, NJ
Minasian, Paul R. ... Oroville, CA
Minasian, Spruance, Baber, Meith, Soares & Sexton, LLP ... Oroville, CA
Minasian, Susan ... Oroville, CA
Minassian, Apik ... Los Angeles, CA
Minassian, Arthur ... Sherman Oaks, CA
Minassian, Donald L. ... River Edge, NJ
Minassian, Edvin E. ... Glendale, CA
Minassian, Karineh J. ... Los Angeles, CA
Minassian, Richard Z. ... Stoughton, MA
Minato, Alan M. ... Vineland, NJ
Minato, Susan M. ... Los Angeles, CA
Minatoya, Richard K. ... Lihue, HI
Minatra, Terri J. ... Johnson City, TN
Minault, Paul M., Law Offices of
San Francisco, CA
Minc, David C. ... New York, NY
Minc, Gabriel J. ... Chicago, IL
Mincarelli, Frank P. ... Lancaster, PA
Mincavage, Karen M. ... Washington, DC
Mincberg, David M. ... Bellaire, TX
Mincberg, Elliot M. ... Washington, DC
Mince, Loretta G. ... New Orleans, LA
Mince, V. Aubrey, Jr. ... Miami, FL
Mincer, David J. ... Charleston, WV

Mincer, Deborah Ford ... Cheyenne, WY
Mincer, Lawrence M.
Glenwood Springs, CO
Mincer, Richard A. ... Cheyenne, WY
Mincer, Thomas Earl ... Milford, PA
Mincey, David L. ... Macon, GA
Mincey, David L., Jr. ... Roberta, GA
Mincey & Green ... Roberta, GA
Mincey, James M., Jr. ... Dallas, TX
Minch, Janet A. ... Nevada City, CA
Minch, Lawrence N. ... Department of Justice, Civil Division, GV
Minch, Roger J. ... Fargo, ND
Minchak, JoEllen M. ... Cleveland, OH
Minchella, Anthony R. ... Bridgeport, CT
Minchella, Claudine ... San Francisco, CA
Minchella, Erica Crohn ... Schaumburg, IL
Minchella, Erica Crohn, P.C.
Schaumburg, IL
Minchella, Michael F., (P.C.)
Los Angeles, CA
Minchenberg, Alfred ... New York, NY
Minchenberg & Wallace, P.C.
New York, NY
Minches, Leonard H. ... Palm Beach, FL
Minchew, Delman L. ... Waycross, GA
Minchew, J. Randall ... Leesburg, VA
Minchew, Jamie Marie ... Staten Island, NY
Minciell, Jonathan P. ... New York, NY
Mincin, David ... Las Vegas, NV
Minck, Linda R. ... Columbus, OH
Minckley, Carla B. ... Denver, CO
Mincks, Jeffrey L. ... Chesterfield, VA
Mincone, John V. ... Huntington Station, NY
Mincone, Joseph ... Huntington Station, NY
Mincone, Mincone & Tanen, L.L.C.
Huntington Station, NY
Minczeski, Edward V. ... South Bend, IN
Minda, Gary ... Brooklyn, NY
Mindas, Patrick R. ... Springfield, NJ
Mindel & Faermark ... Itasca, IL
Mindel, Nancy J. ... Los Angeles, CA
Mindel, Norbert M. ... Itasca, IL
Mindel, Steven A. ... Los Angeles, CA
Mindell, Bernard ... Southfield, MI
Mindell, Doris F. ... Tucson, AZ
Mindell, Gerald D. ... Chicago, IL
Mindell, James Jordan ... Bronx, NY
Mindell, Jeffrey ... Southfield, MI
Mindell, Panzer, Malin, Kutinsky & Benson
Detroit, MI
Flint, MI
Southfield, MI
Sterling Heights, MI
Westland, MI
Mindell, Stephen E. ... New York, NY
Mindell, Susan ... New York, NY
Mindeman, Roxanne Baumer
Apple Valley, MN
Minden, Scott D. ... Palo Alto, CA
Minder, Carolyn M. ... Boise, ID
Minder, Debbie V. ... Medford, OR
Minder, Gordon L. ... Orinda, CA
Minder & Muro ... Sacramento, CA
Minder, Thomas G. ... Sacramento, CA
Minder, Walter R. ... Marshfield, WI
Mindes, Sarah ... Miami, FL
Mindess, Robert G. ... Paramount, CA
Mindich, Bernard ... Goldens Bridge, NY
Mindle, Adam H. ... Los Angeles, CA
Mindlin, Bradley Hunter
Sherman Oaks, CA
Mindlin, Charles R. ... North Miami, FL
Mindlin, David M. ... Chelsea, MA
Mindlin, Frederic R. ... New York, NY
Mindlin, Jill R. ... New York, NY
Mindlin, Morris ... Bethlehem, PA
Mindlin, Philip ... New York, NY
Mindlin, Steven T., (P.A.) ... Tallahassee, FL
Mindnich, Jodi F. ... Princeton, NJ
Mindrup, Nancy H. ... Rockford, IL
Mindrup-Ivie, Anita M. ... Henderson, KY
Mine, Andrew S. ... Chicago, IL
Minear, Barry N. ... Des Moines, IA
Minear, Jeffrey P. ... Department of Justice, Office of the Solicitor General, GV
Minear, Nathan E. ... Atlanta, GA
Minear, Nicholas R. ... Chicago, IL
Mineart, Carrie A. ... Fort Collins, CO
Mineau, Louis X. ... Beloit, WI
Mineaux, John R. ... Albany, NY
Mineer, James ... Springfield, NJ
Mineff, George, Jr. ... Cleveland, OH
Minegar, Craig A. ... Orlando, FL
Minehan, John H. ... New York, NY
Minehan, Karen E. ... Lancaster, PA
Minehan, McFaul & McLinn, LLP
Carpinteria, CA
Santa Barbara, CA
Ventura, CA
Minehan, Thomas P. ... Carpinteria, CA
Minehart, Jeffrey P. ... Philadelphia, PA
Minella, Adam A. ... Smithtown, NY
Minella, Alexander, (P.C.) ... Bronx, NY
Minella, Louis A. ... Wilmington, DE
Minella, Mary R. ... Chicago, IL
Minella, Shirley C. ... Dayton, OH
Minelli, Matthew ... Washington, DC
Minely, Ivy Starr ... Hopewell, NJ
Minenko, Eugene ... Minneapolis, MN
Minenko, Mary Ellyn ... Minneapolis, MN
Minenko, Michael J. ... Minneapolis, MN
Mineo, Athena R. ... Raleigh, NC
Mineo, David Christopher ... Buffalo, NY
Mineo, John ... Buffalo, NY
Mineo, L. Kevin, (A Professional Law Corporation) ... San Diego, CA

Mineo, Peter R. ... Melville, NY
Mineola, NY
Mineo, Raymond F. ... Valley Stream, NY
Mineo, Raymond F., P.C.
Valley Stream, NY
Mineo, Robert A. ... Raleigh, NC
Mineo, Wayne C. ... Philadelphia, PA
Mineo & Whittaker ... Charlotte, NC
Raleigh, NC
Miner, Alison ... Chicago, IL
Miner, Amy L. ... Chicago, IL
Miner, Andrew P. ... Santa Rosa, CA
Miner, Ann S. ... Easley, SC
Miner, Arly ... Boulder, CO
Miner, Audrey F. ... Harrisburg, PA
Miner, B. Hal ... Amarillo, TX
Miner, Barnhill & Galland, P.C.
Visalia, CA
Chicago, IL
Madison, WI
Miner, Brian C. ... Philadelphia, PA
Miner, Celia ... Yankton, SD
Miner, Charles D. ... Orlando, FL
Miner, Charles E., Jr. ... Tallahassee, FL
Miner, Charles H., Jr. ... Wilkes-Barre, PA
Miner, Christopher R. ... Orleans, MA
Miner, Clinton E. ... Boise, ID
Miner, David W. ... Bradenton, FL
Miner, Don J. ... Phoenix, AZ
Miner, Edgar M. ... Quantico, VA
Miner, Edward L. ... Anchorage, AK
Miner, F. William ... El Cerrito, CA
Miner, Frederick C. ... Phoenix, AZ
Miner, Henry C., III ... Brooklyn, NY
Miner, Hugh A. ... St. Joseph, MO
Miner, James R. ... Richmond, VA
Miner, James S., II ... Bay City, MI
Miner, Jason D. ... Portland, OR
Miner, Jay C. ... Eureka Springs, AR
Miner, Jeffrey C. ... Salt Lake City, UT
Miner, Jeffrey R. ... Hallandale Beach, FL
Miner, Joanne M. ... Ithaca, NY
Miner, Jodie L. ... Indianapolis, IN
Miner, Joseph B. ... Oklahoma City, OK
Miner, Judson H. ... Chicago, IL
Miner, Julia S. ... San Francisco, CA
Miner, Juliet F. ... Castle Rock, CO
Miner, Kevin W. ... Nashua, NH
Miner, Lance R. ... Hudson, NY
Miner, Larry J. ... Jacksonville, NC
Miner, Lorrie A. ... Mitchell, SD
Miner, Loyal A. ... Citrus Heights, CA
Miner, M. Bruce ... Naples, FL
Miner, Marc H. ... New York, NY
Miner, Martin P. ... New York, NY
Miner, Maryellen Chaban ... Hudson, NY
Miner, Matthew S. ... Philadelphia, PA
Miner, Michael E. ... Boulder, CO
Miner, Michael L. ... Warsaw, IN
Miner, Michael M. ... Arlington, TX
Miner, Michael R. ... Washington, DC
Miner & Miner ... Fenton, MI
Miner & Miner ... Hudson, NY
Miner, Natalie B. ... Homer, NY
Miner, R. Charles ... Buffalo, NY
Miner, R. Michael ... Indianapolis, IN
Miner, Robert B. ... St. Joseph, MO
Miner, Robert G. ... Woodland Hills, CA
Miner, Roger J. ... Albany, NY
Miner, Sharon K. S. ... Fenton, MI
Miner, Stanley C. ... Wichita, KS
Miner, Stanton A. ... Fenton, MI
Miner, Stephen M. ... Marlton, NJ
Miner, Steven A. ... Palatine, IL
Miner, Steven P. ... Harrisburg, PA
Miner, Susan D. ... Boise, ID
Miner, Thomas A. ... Belmont, NY
Miner, Thomas J. ... McMinnville, TN
Miner, Thos. H. ... Chicago, IL
Miner, Timothy I. ... Grand Rapids, MI
Miner, Todd K. ... Orlando, FL
Miner, Tracy A. ... Boston, MA
Miner, William A. ... Annandale, VA
Miner, William W. ... New London, CT
Minerbi, Laurie Burg ... Bethesda, MD
Minerich, Paul T. ... Santa Ana, CA
Minerley, Kenneth L. ... Boca Raton, FL
Minerman, Charles M. ... Madison, WI
Minerof, Candice Beth ... Chicago, IL
Miners, Jon ... St. Paul, MN
Minerva & D'Agostino, P.C.
Valley Stream, NY
Minerva, Dana D. ... Tallahassee, FL
Minerva, Dominick M. ... Valley Stream, NY
Minerva, Michael J. ... Tallahassee, FL
Minerva, Michael J., Jr. ... Salisbury, MD
Minerva, Steven W. ... Commack, NY
Minervini, Francine A. ... Montclair, NJ
Minervino, Rocco ... Mount Holly, NJ
Mines, Amand K. ... Los Angeles, CA
Mines, Carlen Magad ... Clearwater, FL
Mines, Michael ... Seattle, WA
Mines, Robert G. ... Smithwick, SD
Mines, Stacy Roberts ... Rosemead, CA
Mines, Timothy ... New Orleans, LA
Minesinger, Kenneth ... Yorba Linda, CA
Minesinger, Kenneth M. ... Washington, DC
Miness, Irwin ... New York, NY
Mineta, Elisabeth K. ... Salinas, CA
Minetree, Thomas A. ... New Orleans, LA
Minett, Thomas W. ... Ellwood City, PA
Minette, Henri G. ... Minneapolis, MN
Minetto, Pamela Joan ... Jersey City, NJ
New York, NY
Minetto, Steven L. ... Portland, OR
Minetz, Robert S. ... Chicago, IL
Mineweaser, Jo-Anne M. ... Pittsburgh, PA

Ming, Charles
Department of Housing and Urban Development, GV
Ming, Chin See ... Portland, OR
Ming, Marian S. K. ... Chicago, IL
Ming, Mary Egan ... Columbus, OH
Ming, Robert D. ... Los Angeles, CA
Mingace, Christopher H.
Framingham, MA
Mingace & Heineman ... Boston, MA
Framingham, MA
Mingarelli, Henry V. ... Pearland, TX
Minge, David R. ... Montevideo, MN
Minge, James ... New Orleans, LA
Minge, Jerry L. ... Rome, GA
Minge, John C. ... Perham, MN
Minge, Lisa J. ... Burbank, CA
Mingee, James C. ... Madison, MS
Minger, Douglas E. ... Eugene, OR
Minger, John S. ... Portland, OR
Minger, Marilyn E. ... Oakland, CA
Minges, A. Jacqueline ... New Bern, NC
Minges, John ... Philadelphia, PA
Mingione, Dominick J. ... New York, NY
Mingione, Phyllis M. ... New York, NY
Mingle, James J. ... Ithaca, NY
Mingle, John O. ... Laramie, WY
Mingledorff, Ann F. ... Atlanta, GA
Mingledorff, Judy P. ... Houston, TX
Mingledorff, Kenneth P. ... Houston, TX
Mingledorff, W. Lee ... Falls Church, VA
Mingleton, Count D. ... Bakersfield, CA
Minglin, Michael Alan ... Indianapolis, IN
Mingo, Kim M. ... Vancouver, WA
Mingo, Mark J. ... Milwaukee, WI
Mingo & Yankala, S.C. ... Milwaukee, WI
Mingolelli, Gerald J., Jr. ... Syracuse, NY
Mingolelli, Ralph Albert ... Uniontown, MD
Mingolla, Joseph J., II, Law Offices of
Charlotte Amalie, St. Thomas, VI
Mingolla, Joseph P. ... Boston, MA
Mingolla, Lisa Nalchajian ... Boston, MA
Mings, John M. ... Houston, TX
Mingus, John S. ... Ravenna, NE
Mingus & Mingus ... Ravenna, NE
Mingus, Odis Simpson, II
Christiansted, St. Croix, VI
Mingus, Ronald A. ... Cleveland, OH
Mingus, Thomas M., Jr. ... Columbia, MO
Minhas, Kam S. ... Mendham, NJ
Minhas, Sandip S. ... Milwaukee, WI
Miniaci, Dominick ... Fort Lauderdale, FL
Miniard, Chris ... Corbin, KY
Miniard, James B. ... Lexington, KY
Miniard, Vernon, Jr. ... Monticello, KY
Miniat, Kevin E. ... Tucson, AZ
Miniat, Kevin E., P.C. ... Tucson, AZ
Miniccucci, Jill Hanau ... Norwalk, CT
Minich, Mark A. ... Colorado Springs, CO
Minich, Stephen H. ... West Hartford, CT
Minichello, Dennis ... Chicago, IL
Minichiello, Alfred C. ... Cleveland, OH
Minichiello, Jane H. ... Newark, NJ
Minichiello, Thomas J., Jr. ... Raynham, MA
Minichillo, Lora E. ... Chicago, IL
Minick, Carolyn ... Garden City, NY
Minick, Cheyenne ... Fort Worth, TX
Minick, Robin K. ... Addison, TX
Minick, W. Ted ... Houston, TX
Minick, Wendy Sue ... Washington, DC
Miniclier, Joseph E., (P.A.) ... Cocoa, FL
Miniclier, Paul C. ... New Orleans, LA
Minicozzi, Florence M. ... Scarsdale, NY
Minicozzi, Louis M., III, Law Offices of
Las Vegas, NV
Pahrump, NV
Minicucci, Elena Rose ... Fort Lauderdale, FL
Minicucci, Richard F. ... Garden City, NY
Minicus, John F. ... Katonah, NY
Minier, Alan B. ... Cheyenne, WY
Minier, Andrew L. ... Lincoln, NE
Minier, Christopher A. ... Irvine, CA
Minier, David D. ... Madera, CA
Minier, Jeffrie ... Albuquerque, NM
Minier, John W. ... Raleigh, NC
Minier, Robert L. ... Hot Springs Village, AR
Minier, Stanley, Inc., Law Offices of
Santa Ana, CA
Minier, Stanley W. ... Santa Ana, CA
Minieri, Michael A. ... Washington, DC
Philadelphia, PA
McLean, VA
Miniex, Rickey W. ... Lafayette, LA
Minifie, Margaret C. ... Washington, DC
Minifie, Sarah H. ... New York, NY
Minihan, Anne E. ... White Plains, NY
Minihan, John E. ... Horsham, PA
Minihane, Derek E. ... San Jose, CA
Minikes, Jon C. ... New York, NY
Minikes, Jonathan Z. ... New York, NY
Minikes, Morton ... Los Angeles, CA
Minikes, Morton, A Law Corporation
Los Angeles, CA
Minikes, Nancy Gail ... Haworth, NJ
Minikes, Ronald L. ... New York, NY
Minikes, Stephan M. ... Washington, DC
Minikon, Patricia B. ... St. Charles, MO
Miniman, Arnold H. ... Riverdale, NJ
Mininall, Jeanne M. ... New York, NY
Mininberg, Irwin ... McLean, VA
Mininberg, Mark ... Killingworth, CT
Mininno, John R. ... Haddonfield, NJ
Mininsohn, Gary S. ... Rockville, MD
Mininsohn, H. William ... Santa Ana, CA
Mininsohn, Peter J. ... Long Beach, CA
Minion, Joseph W. R. ... Mantoloking, NJ
Minion, Robert C. ... Williston Park, NY
Minion, Robert G. ... Roseland, NJ
Minion, Zachary S. ... West Orange, NJ
Minion, Zachary S., P.C. ... West Orange, NJ
Minior, David ... Somerset, MA
Minisandram, Raghunath S.
Scotts Valley, CA
Minish, George J. ... Roseland, NJ
Minish, Joseph N. ... Roseland, NJ
Minish, Robert A. ... Minneapolis, MN
Minisi, Anthony S. ... Philadelphia, PA
Minisi, Joseph J. ... Harrisburg, PA
Minisman, B. G., Jr. ... Birmingham, AL
Minissale, Dana Lynn ... Dallas, TX
Minister, Margaret K. ... Portland, ME
Minister, Mark ... Santa Monica, CA
Minister, Michael E. ... Columbus, OH
Miniter and Associates ... Hartford, CT
Miniter, Francis A. ... Hartford, CT
Miniter, Margaret E. ... New York, NY
Miniutti, Krista ... New York, NY
Minix, James A. ... Bradenton, FL
Minix, James A., P.A. ... Bradenton, FL
Minjares, Victor M. ... Los Angeles, CA
Mink, Allen ... Torrance, CA
Mink & Blair ... Lawrenceburg, TN
Nashville, TN
Smithville, TN
Mink, Duane E. ... Radford, VA
Mink, Jennifer J. ... Washington, DC
Mink, Lyle R., Law Offices of
Los Angeles, CA
Mink & Meislik ... West Orange, NJ
Mink, Michael S. ... Encino, CA
Mink and Molloy, A Professional Corporation
Torrance, CA
Mink, Patsy T. ... Honolulu, HI
Mink, Robert L. ... Benton Harbor, MI
Mink, Ronda K. ... Flower Mound, TX
Mink, Rosalind ... West Orange, NJ
Mink, Thomas F., II ... Lawrenceburg, TN
Nashville, TN
Minka, Imants M. ... Pontiac, MI
Minkel, William J. ... Albany, NY
Minker, Allen G. ... Clifton, AZ
Minker, S. Jeffrey ... Tucson, AZ
Minkin, David J. ... Honolulu, HI
Minkin, David N. ... Atlanta, GA
Minkin, George ... New York, NY
Minkin, Helen ... New York, NY
Minkin, Irving E. ... New York, NY
Minkin, Jason P. ... Chicago, IL
Minkin, Keith M. ... Cleveland, OH
Minkin, Michael ... Miami, FL
Minkin & Snyder, A Professional
Corporation ... Atlanta, GA
Minkin, Thomas ... Baltimore, MD
Minkin, William G. ... Baltimore, MD
Minklei, Lisa A. ... Granville, OH
Minkler, Daniel A. ... Canton, OH
Minkler, Debra J. ... Urbandale, IA
Minkler, Harvey E. ... Phoenix, AZ
Minkler, Patricia P. ... North Canton, OH
Minkley, William E. ... Dallas, TX
Minkner, William H. ... Santa Cruz, CA
Minkoff, Barbara B. ... Woodland Hills, CA
Minkoff, Barry A. ... Bethesda, MD
Minkoff, Bruce ... Lake Worth, FL
Minkoff, Bruce ... White Plains, NY
Minkoff, Bruce J. ... Gaithersburg, MD
Minkoff, Deborah Melamut ... Westmont, NJ
Philadelphia, PA
Minkoff, Elizabeth B. ... Brentwood, TN
Minkoff, Jared M. ... St. Louis, MO
Minkoff, Jon F. ... Nashville, TN
Minkoff, Linda Swain ... Boston, MA
Minkoff, Lisa E. ... Dallas, TX
Minkoff, Paul N. ... Philadelphia, PA
Minkoff, Richard M. ... San Mateo, CA
Minkoff, Robert K. ... Hackensack, NJ
Minkoff, Ronald C. ... New York, NY
Minkoff, Sanford A. ... Tavares, FL
Minkoff, Thomas H. ... Gulfport, FL
Minkove, Marc D. ... Baltimore, MD
Minkow, Gregg I. ... Totowa, NJ
Minkow, Peter J. ... Meredith, NH
Minkow, Sander L. ... West Palm Beach, FL
Minkowitz, Martin ... New York, NY
Minks, Christopher H. ... Hackensack, NJ
Minks, Merle E. ... South Laguna, CA
Minkus, April A. ... Northbrook, IL
Minkus, Daniel H. ... Birmingham, MI
Minkus, Leslie A. ... San Francisco, CA
Minkus, Mark ... Ramsey, NJ
Minkus, Mayton ... Palo Alto, CA
Minkus, Robert J. ... Chicago, IL
Minn, Reginald P. ... Honolulu, HI
Minna, Dennis F. ... Santa Ana, CA
Minna, Lynn ... Dallas, TX
Minnard, Carla Vanessa
Walnut Creek, CA
Minnard, Lawrence R. ... Lima, OH
Minnefor, Eileen ... New York, NY
Minnella, Martin J. ... Waterbury, CT
Minnen, Jonathan M. ... Atlanta, GA
Minner, Julia A. ... Frederick, MD
Minner, Matthew C. ... Birmingham, AL
Minner, Toni J. ... Pittsburgh, PA
Minnerop, Henry F. ... New York, NY
Minnes, Frederick D. ... San Francisco, CA
Minnetian, Christopher P. ... Newark, NJ
Minnett, Constance B. ... Burbank, CA
Minnette, James Kent ... Chicago, IL
Minney, Andrew Gordon
Walnut Creek, CA
Minney, Michael J. ... Lancaster, PA
Minney, Paul C. ... Walnut Creek, CA
Minney, R. Brent ... Akron, OH
Minni, Dennis E., Law Office of
Strongsville, OH
Minni, Joseph F.
Department of Justice, GV
Minnich, Jeffrey R. ... Carroll, IA
Minnich, Joseph P., Jr. ... Binghamton, NY
Minnich, Michael G. ... Bellefontaine, OH
Minnich, Michelle M. ... Winston-Salem, NC
Minnich, Paul W. ... York, PA
Minnich, Richard J. ... Cleveland, OH
Minnich, Sheila E. ... Lima, OH
Minnich, Stephen C. ... Winston-Salem, NC
Minnich, Steven L. ... Lock Haven, PA
Minnich, William A. ... Westlake, OH
Minnick, Bruce Alexander
Tallahassee, FL
Minnick, Bruce Alexander, P.A.
Tallahassee, FL
Minnick, Craig A. ... Chicago, IL
Minnick, Daniel R. ... Cleveland, OH
Minnick, David M. ... Kansas City, MO
Minnick • Hayner, A Professional Service
Corporation ... Walla Walla, WA
Minnick, John B. ... Fredericksburg, VA
Minnick, John D. ... Topeka, KS
Minnick, M. David ... San Francisco, CA
Minnick, Walter C. ... Boise, ID
Minniear, Michael ... Milford, OH
Minniece, John G., III ... Marfa, TX
Minnig, Ellen Marie ... Denver, CO
Minnig, Max A., Jr. ... Denver, CO
Minnig, Max, Jr. & Associates, LLC
Denver, CO
Minnigerode, Martin R. ... St. Louis, MO
Minnihan, John K. ... Beverly Hills, CA
Minnillo, Christopher J. ... Columbus, OH
Minnillo, Mary T. ... Cincinnati, OH
Minnis, Daniel L. ... Browning, MT
Minnis, Deborah Stephens
Tallahassee, FL
Minnis, Elaine ... Bonita Springs, FL
Minnis, Frederick G., Jr.
Federal Energy Regulatory Commission, Office of the General Counsel, GV
Minnis, Herschel C. ... Tallahassee, FL
Minnis, James C. ... Wilmington, DE
Minnis, Jennifer Roberts ... Houston, TX
Minnis, Martha Anne ... Houston, TX
Minnis, Michael ... Oklahoma City, OK
Minnis, Michael, & Associates, P.C.
Oklahoma City, OK
Minnis, Robin Van Dien ... Oregon, IL
Minnis, Stephen D. ... Overland Park, KS
Minniti, Joseph A. ... Mamaroneck, NY
Minniti, Joseph A., P.C. ... Mamaroneck, NY
Minniti, Kathleen S. ... New York, NY
Minnix, Larry A. ... Indianapolis, IN
Minno, Frances P. F. ... Pittsburgh, PA
Minno Law Firm, The, P.A.
Tallahassee, FL
Minno, Matthew F. ... Tallahassee, FL
Minnock, Joseph E. ... Salt Lake City, UT
Minnott, John M. ... San Clemente, CA
Minnotte, Elizabeth J. Surgent
Pittsburgh, PA
Minns, Emily A. ... Bloomfield Hills, MI
Minns, Michael H. ... Phillipsburg, NJ
Minns, Michael L. ... Houston, TX
Minns, Michael L., P.L.C. ... Houston, TX
Mino, Greg T. ... Sacramento, CA
Mino, John M. ... Cleveland, OH
Minock, John R. ... Ann Arbor, MI
Minoff, Jack ... New York, NY
Minoff, Keith A. ... Springfield, MA
Minoff, Paul H. ... Fort Lauderdale, FL
Minogue, James S., III ... Bethesda, MD
Minogue, Michael D. ... Shreveport, LA
Minogue, Richard B. ... New Roads, LA
Minogue, Roderick J. ... Floral Park, NY
Minogue, Thomas E., Jr. ... Southport, CT
Minogue, Thomas J. ... St. Louis, MO
Minogue-Garrity, Colleen M.
Downers Grove, IL
Minola, Patricia J. ... Mercer Island, WA
Minoletti, John ... Redding, CA
Minoletti, Paul G. ... San Jose, CA
San Mateo, CA
Minoofar, Pedram ... Pasadena, CA
Minor, Anna R. ... Birmingham, AL
Minor, Anne E. ... Westerville, OH
Minor, Annette Williams ... Minneapolis, MN
Minor and Associates ... Biloxi, MS
Gulfport, MS
Hattiesburg, MS
Jackson, MS
Mc Comb, MS
Pascagoula, MS
Minor, Bell & Neal, P.C. ... Dalton, GA
Minor & Boone, P.C. ... Newport, OR
Minor & Brown, P.C. ... Denver, CO
Minor, C. Jeff ... El Paso, TX
Minor, Charles D. ... Columbus, OH
Minor, Claudeidra M. ... Baton Rouge, LA
Minor, Cynthia A. ... Merrillville, IN
Minor, Daniel B. ... Kingsport, TN
Minor, Daniel J. ... Columbus, OH
Minor, David W., Law Office of
Statesville, NC
Minor, Deane W. ... Everett, WA
Minor, Denise ... Chicago, IL
Minor, Donald R. ... Shreveport, LA
Minor, Edward C. ... Franklin, VA
Minor, Edward T. ... Washington, DC
Minor, Emilie A. ... Roswell, GA
Minor, Gary B. ... Franklin, TN
Minor, Gary L. ... Kirkland, WA
Minor, George, Jr. ... Portsmouth, VA
Minor, H. Dean ... Atlanta, GA
Minor, H. Franklin ... Richmond, VA
Minor, Haight & Arundell, P.C.
Hilton Head Island, SC
Minor, J. Christopher ... Newport, OR
Minor, J. Douglas, Jr. ... Jackson, MS
Minor, J. Floyd ... Montgomery, AL
Minor, Jacqueline P. ... San Francisco, CA
Minor, James B. ... Terra Alta, WV
Minor, James D. ... Oxford, MS
Minor, James M., Jr. ... Richmond, VA
Minor, James V. ... Wilton, CT
Minor, Janlaw G. ... Evanston, IL
Minor & Jester ... Denton, TX
Minor, John A., III ... Los Angeles, CA
Minor, John T., III ... Dalton, GA
Minor, John T., IV ... Dalton, GA
Minor, John W., Jr.
Hilton Head Island, SC
Minor, Joseph B. ... Miami Shores, FL
Minor, Joseph H. ... Culver City, CA
Minor, Laird ... Pittsburgh, PA
Minor, Lancelot L., III ... Memphis, TN
Minor, Laura C.
Administrative Office Of The United States Courts, GV
Minor, Maria J. ... Chicago, IL
Minor, Marti Anne ... Savannah, GA
Minor, Matthew ... Chicago, IL
Minor, Michael ... Kaufman, TX
Minor, Michelle V. ... Anchorage, AK
Minor, Ned A. ... Denver, CO
Minor, Norman R. ... Worcester, MA
Minor & Olszewski, L.L.C.
Montgomery, AL
Minor, Paul S., (P.A.) ... Biloxi, MS
Minor, Richard H. ... Jacksonville, FL
Minor, Robert A. ... Columbus, OH
Minor, Robert E. ... Birmingham, AL
Minor, Robert L. ... Pell City, AL
Minor, Robert W. ... Columbus, OH
Minor, Roger L. ... Torrance, CA
Minor, Roger T. ... Fort Myers, FL
Minor, Sterling A. ... Houston, TX
Minor, Steven R. ... Bristol, VA
Minor, Steven T. ... Carrollton, GA
Minor, Teresa G. ... Birmingham, AL
Minor, Timothy J. ... Salinas, CA
Minor, Virgil A. ... Memphis, TN
Minor, William H. ... Washington, DC
Minor, William O. ... Oakdale, CA
Minor, Wilsie Y.
Corporation for National and Community Service, Office of the General Counsel, GV
Minora, Amil M. ... Scranton, PA
Minora, Carmen D., (Mr.) ... Scranton, PA
Minora, Minora, Colbassani & Ratchford
Scranton, PA
Minorchio, James W. ... Seattle, WA
Minore, Dominic J.
Securities and Exchange Commission, Division of Corporation Finance, GV
Minorini, Paul A. ... Washington, DC
Minorini, Theodore J. ... Highwood, IL
Minors, Timothy S. ... Marietta, GA
Minot, Fannie I. ... Boston, MA
Minot, Jeffrey R. ... New York, NY
Minot, John ... Cocoa, FL
Minot, Martha Tinsley ... Durango, CO
Minot, Michael S. ... Cocoa, FL
Minot, Winthrop G. ... Boston, MA
Minott, Darrell J. ... Dover, DE
Minott, Debra F. ... Fort Wayne, IN
Minott, Geoffrey D. ... Philadelphia, PA
Minott, Joseph Otis ... Philadelphia, PA
Minott, Laurence Patten, Jr.
North Windham, ME
Minotti & DeEsch ... Easton, PA
Minotti, Louis S., Jr. ... Easton, PA
Minotti, Mark L. ... Easton, PA
Minotti, Martha L. ... Cambridge, MA
Minow, Newton N. ... Chicago, IL
Minsberg, Susan Dickel ... Minneapolis, MN
Minshall, Kent R. ... Cleveland, OH
Minshall, Kent R., Jr. ... Cleveland, OH
Minshall, Richard E. ... Tulsa, OK
Minshew, Lisa S. ... Pensacola, FL
Minshew, Robert W. ... Sherman, TX
Minshew, Terri D. ... Dallas, TX
Minsk, Alan D. ... San Francisco, CA
Minsk, Alan G. ... Atlanta, GA
Minsk, Laurie H. ... Seattle, WA
Minsk, Ronald E.
Executive Office Of The President, GV
Minsk, Stephen L. ... Marietta, GA
Minsker, Helen Hill ... Washington, DC
Minsker, Joel N., (P.A.) ... Miami, FL
Minsker, Jonathan E. ... New York, NY
Minsker, Martin D. ... Washington, DC
Minski, George A. ... Hollywood, FL
Minski, Leonard J. ... Brooklyn, NY
Minsky, Bernard W. ... Los Angeles, CA
Minsky, Bruce W. ... New York, NY
Minsky, Eleanor ... San Diego, CA
Minsky, Ellen ... New York, NY
Minsky, Howard A. ... East Meadow, NY
Minsky, Howard A. ... Pittsburgh, PA
Minsky, Kevin D. ... Washington, DC
Minsky, Larry ... Long Beach, CA
Minsky, Lew I. ... Atlanta, GA
Minsky, Mark J. ... Nashville, TN
Minsky, Martin ... New York, NY
Minsky, McCormick & Hallagan, P.C.
Chicago, IL
Minsky, Melvyn N. ... New York, NY
Minsky, Norman ... Bangor, ME
Minsley, Morton S. ... Hackensack, NJ
Minsley, Morton S. ... New York, NY
Minsloff, Jon C. ... Santa Cruz, CA

Minson, Douglas L. ....Hillsboro, OR
Minster, Carl John, III ....Philadelphia, PA
Minteer, Daniel C. ....San Diego, CA
Minteer, Richard P. ....Delran, NJ
Mintel, Judith K. ....Bloomington, IL
Mintel, William A.
Department of Commerce, Patent and Trademark Office, GV
Minten, K. Henry ....San Antonio, TX
Mintener, Linda M. ....Madison, WI
Minter, Alan H. ....Austin, TX
Minter, Albert H. ....San Ramon, CA
Minter, Carolyn V. ....Ossining, NY
Minter, Claude J. ....Secaucus, NJ
Minter, Darrell D. ....Dallas, TX
Minter, Fred W. ....Decatur, GA
Minter, Gregory B. ....Omaha, NE
Minter, James R. ....Phoenix, AZ
Minter, Jim ....Fort Worth, TX
Minter, Joseph O., V ....Madill, OK
Minter, Joseph & Thornhill, P.C.
Austin, TX
Minter, Kendall A. ....New York, NY
Minter Law Firm ....Wichita, KS
Minter, Lewis S. ....Richmond, VA
Minter, Lloyd G. ....Tulsa, OK
Minter, Philip D. ....Santa Rosa, CA
Minter, Rachel J. ....Milford, CT
Minter, Rex H. ....Santa Monica, CA
Minter, Richard C. ....Eastman, GA
Minter, Richard L. ....Kalamazoo, MI
Minter, Robert ....Wichita, KS
Minter, Sam S. ....Houston, TX
Minter, Scott C. ....Madison, WI
Mintie, Nancy J. ....Los Angeles, CA
Mintmire & Associates ....Palm Beach, FL
West Palm Beach, FL
Mintmire, Donald F. ....Palm Beach, FL
Minto, Eileen L. ....Louisville, KY
Minto, John R. ....Lake Ronkonkoma, NY
Minto, Ralph, Jr. ....Pittsburgh, PA
Minto, Robert W., Jr. ....Missoula, MT
Minton, Amy M. ....Department of Justice, Executive Office for Immigration Review, GV
Minton, Andrea S. ....Aurora, OH
Minton, Bernard L. ....McLeansboro, IL
Minton, Blan V. ....Chapel Hill, NC
Minton, Burton, Foster & Collins, A Professional Corporation ....Austin, TX
Minton, Carl ....Los Angeles, CA
Minton, Darrell M. ....Beaumont, TX
Minton, David ....Washington, DC
Minton, David F. ....Austin, TX
Minton, David S. ....San Diego, CA
Minton, Don W. ....El Paso, TX
Minton, Eddie J. ....Harrisburg, IL
Minton, Edward ....New York, NY
Minton Firm, The ....Chicago, IL
Rolling Meadows, IL
Minton, Garry D. ....Jacksonville, TX
Minton, Gregory Eugene ....Littleton, CO
Minton, Gregory W. ....Belle Chasse, LA
Minton, Harvey S., & Associates
Columbus, OH
Minton, James Bruce ....Victorville, CA
Minton, Jeffrey J.
Securities and Exchange Commission, Division of Corporation Finance, GV
Minton, John D., Jr. ....Bowling Green, KY
Minton, John H. ....Tyler, TX
Minton, Joseph J., Jr. ....Fort Worth, TX
Minton, Karen E. ....Tampa, FL
Minton, Karen E. ....Independence, MO
Minton, Kelly C. ....Scottsburg, IN
Minton, Kent ....Independence, MO
Minton, Larry B. ....Alexandria, LA
Minton, Larry C. ....Biwabik, MN
Hibbing, MN
Minton, Larry C., Ltd., Law Offices of
Biwabik, MN
Hibbing, MN
Minton, Marcus D. ....Petersburg, VA
Minton, Mark V. ....Dallas, TX
Minton, Melissa Stewart ....Tulsa, OK
Minton, Michael B. ....St. Louis, MO
Minton, Michael D. ....Fort Pierce, FL
Minton, Michael Harry ....Chicago, IL
Rolling Meadows, IL
Minton, Michael W. ....Fort Worth, TX
Minton, Minton and Rand LLP
Los Angeles, CA
Minton, M.L., III ....Weatherford, OK
Minton, Paul H. ....Pittsburgh, PA
Minton, Phillip H. ....Indianapolis, IN
Minton, Richard ....Mineola, NY
Minton, Richard E. ....Stratford, CT
Minton, Robert Barry ....Lexington, KY
Minton, Robert M. ....Henderson, TX
Minton, Roy Q. ....Austin, TX
Minton, Sandra B. ....Towson, MD
Minton, Shira Pavis
Federal Trade Commission, Office of the General Counsel, GV
Minton, Thomas J. ....Baltimore, MD
Minton, Walter J. ....Ponte Vedra Beach, FL
Minton, Wm. F. ....San Francisco, CA
Mints, Sheila ....Morristown, NJ
Minturn, James B. ....Prineville, OR
Minturn, Robert B., Jr. ....Boston, MA
Minturn, Scott J. ....Temecula, CA
Mintz, Alan L. ....Washington, DC
Mintz, Alan M. ....New York, NY
Mintz, Albert, (A Professional Law Corporation) ....New Orleans, LA
Mintz, Arthur M. ....Woodside, CA
Mintz, Barbara ....Department of Commerce, Office of the General Counsel, GV

Mintz, Benjamin ....New York, NY
Mintz, Bernard D. ....Metairie, LA
Mintz, Bernard H. ....Rockville Centre, NY
Mintz, Bernard S. ....Newark, NJ
Mintz, Bruce McKamy ....Monroe, LA
Mintz, Carl A. ....Beachwood, OH
Mintz and Colangelo ....Norwalk, CT
Mintz, David ....Los Angeles, CA
Mintz, David B. ....Washington, DC
Mintz, David F. ....Far Rockaway, NY
Mintz, David G. ....Hadley, MA
Mintz, David J. ....Denver, CO
Mintz, Donald H. ....East Orange, NJ
Mintz, Douglas C. ....Stamford, CT
Mintz, Evvajean Malter ....Boston, MA
Mintz & Fraade, P.C. ....New York, NY
Mintz, Francis ....Los Angeles, CA
Mintz, Frederick M. ....New York, NY
Mintz, Gary M. ....New York, NY
Mintz, Geoffrey Belford ....Burlington, MA
Mintz, Giller & Mintz, A Law Corporation
Oakland, CA
Mintz & Gold LLP ....New York, NY
Mintz, Herbert H. ....Washington, DC
Mintz, Herbert W. ....New York, NY
Mintz, Ira W. ....Trenton, NJ
Mintz, Jaclyn L. ....New York, NY
Mintz, Jacqueline Wei ....Baltimore, MD
Mintz, Janice Mitchell ....Philadelphia, PA
Mintz, Jeffrey ....New York, NY
Mintz, Jeffrey M. ....Atlanta, GA
Mintz, Jeffry S. ....Iselin, NJ
Mintz, Jeffry A., Law Offices of
Mount Holly, NJ
Mintz, Jennifer N. ....Monterey Park, CA
Mintz, Joel ....Carle Place, NY
Mintz, Joel A. ....Fort Lauderdale, FL
Mintz, Jonathan Alan ....Denver, CO
Mintz, Joseph D. ....Buffalo, NY
Mintz, Joshua J. ....Chicago, IL
Mintz, Kevin R. ....Oakland, CA
Mintz, Laurie J. ....San Francisco, CA
Mintz, Lawrence A. ....Atlantic City, NJ
Mintz, Leslie S. ....Santa Monica, CA
Mintz, Levin, Cohn, Ferris, Glovsky and Popeo, P.C. ....Washington, DC
Boston, MA
Reston, VA
Mintz, Lincoln N. ....Oakland, CA
Mintz, Linda Schwartzman
New York, NY
Mintz, Marcie S. ....New York, NY
Mintz, Mark A. ....New York, NY
Mintz, Mark J. ....Miami, FL
Mintz, Marshall G. ....Los Angeles, CA
Mintz, Michael J. ....Vienna, VA
Mintz, Michele ....McLean, VA
Mintz, Mindy S. ....Baltimore, MD
Mintz, M. J. ....Washington, DC
Mintz, Perry L. ....New York, NY
Mintz, Philip W. ....Conroe, TX
Mintz, Richard A. ....Houston, TX
Mintz, Richard D. ....Royal Oak, MI
Mintz, Richard D., P.C. ....Royal Oak, MI
Mintz, Richard G. ....Boston, MA
Mintz, Richard L. ....Norwalk, CT
Mintz, Richard L. ....South Bend, IN
Mintz, Robert ....Denver, CO
Mintz, Robert A. ....Anchorage, AK
Mintz, Robert A. ....Overland Park, KS
Mintz, Robert A. ....Newark, NJ
Mintz, Robert D. ....Haddonfield, NJ
Mintz, Robert E. ....Anchorage, AK
Mintz, Robert J. ....Mesa, AZ
Mintz, Robert J. ....Del Mar, CA
Mintz, Robert M. ....Chicago, IL
Mintz, Ronald Steven ....Los Angeles, CA
Mintz & Schaffer ....Freeport, NY
Mintz, Seymour D. ....New York, NY
Mintz, Seymour S. ....Washington, DC
Mintz, Shana Torem ....Los Angeles, CA
Mintz, Shelley E. ....Baltimore, MD
Mintz, Sol ....New York, NY
Mintz, Stein & Sternbach
Rockville Centre, NY
Mintz, Stephen A. ....New York, NY
Mintz, Steven C. ....Richmond, VA
Mintz, Steven G. ....New York, NY
Mintz, Steven J. ....Washington, DC
Mintz, Stuart A. ....Cleveland, OH
Mintz, Susan G. ....New York, NY
Mintz, Thomas ....Santa Monica, CA
Mintz, Truppman Clein & Higer, P.A.
Miami, FL
Mintz, Victor K. ....New York, NY
Mintzer, Barry L. ....Boston, MA
Mintzer, Edward C., Jr. ....Philadelphia, PA
Mintzer, Glenn E. ....Baltimore, MD
Mintzer, Jay E. ....Philadelphia, PA
Mintzer, Joel A. ....Minneapolis, MN
Mintzer, Jonathan C. ....New York, NY
Mintzer, Kevin ....New York, NY
Mintzer, Laurie S. ....Washington, DC
Mintzer, Marjorie Heyman ....New York, NY
Mintzer, Michael A. ....New York, NY
Mintzer, Pamela Schock ....Oakland, CA
Mintzer, Patrick S. ....Philadelphia, PA
Mintzer, Peter J. ....Seattle, WA
Mintzer, Sarowitz, Zeris & Ledva
Cherry Hill, NJ
New York, NY
Philadelphia, PA
Mintzer, Stewart A. ....Los Angeles, CA
Mintzer, Sydney H. ....Washington, DC
Mintzer, Zabicki, Powell & Mintzer, P.C.
Philadelphia, PA
Mintzes, Alvin S. ....Baltimore, MD
Mintzes, David M. ....Dobbs Ferry, NY

Minus, Joseph J., Jr. ....Mobile, AL
Minuse, Catherine J. ....New York, NY
Minuskin, Heidi S. ....Morristown, NJ
Minuth, Ana M. V. ....El Paso, TX
Minuti, Mark ....Wilmington, DE
Minutillo, Daniel C. ....San Jose, CA
Minutillo, Daniel C., A Professional Corporation ....San Jose, CA
Minuto, James T. ....Calabasas, CA
Minutola, Lisa A. ....Wilmington, DE
Minutoli, Gianni ....Washington, DC
Minutolo, James P. ....Cincinnati, OH
Minvielle, Leon J., III ....New Iberia, LA
Minvielle, Scott T. ....Metairie, LA
Minx, Brook F. ....Houston, TX
Minx-Bays, Lisa Gayle ....Oklahoma City, OK
Minyard, Charles R. ....Lafayette, LA
Minyard, David ....Visalia, CA
Minyard, Handsel B. ....Philadelphia, PA
Minyard, Harold G. ....Orange, CA
Minyard, M. Scott ....Jackson, MS
Minyard, Mark E. ....Orange, CA
Minyard and Morris, LLP ....Orange, CA
Minyard, Robert J. ....Fairfax, VA
Minzer, Daniel M. ....Denver, CO
Minzer, Irwin K. ....Melville, NY
Minzer, Marilyn ....New York, NY
Minzing, Paula ....Delphos, OH
Minzner, Pamela B. ....Santa Fe, NM
Minzner, Richard C. ....Albuquerque, NM
Miodus, Mitchell J. ....Miami, FL
Mioduszewski, Mark E. ....Erie, PA
Miofsky, Andrew J. ....Granite City, IL
Miolla, Raymond L., Jr. ....Miami, FL
Mion, John H., (P.C.) ....Washington, DC
Miorelli, Arthur F. ....St. Louis, MO
Miosi, Dianna K. ....Treasury Department, Internal Revenue Service, GV
Miossi, William G. ....Washington, DC
Chicago, IL
Miotke, Gary T. ....Inkster, MI
Miotke, Thomas E. ....New York, NY
Miovski, Lourene Marija
Department of Justice, Executive Office for Immigration Review, GV
Mir, Hector J. ....Coral Gables, FL
Mir, John ....Erie, PA
Mir Law Associates, LLC ....Rockville, MD
Mira, Charles J. ....Toledo, OH
Mira, Joseph L. ....Dallas, TX
Mira, Kris R. ....Houston, TX
Mira, Lawrence J. ....Malibu, CA
Mira, Thomas C. ....Washington, DC
Mirabal, Carlos W. ....San Juan, PR
Mirabal, Jeannette ....Miami, FL
Mirabal, Josefa Sicard ....New York, NY
Mirabal, Margaret Garner ....Houston, TX
Mirabal-Conde, Rafael A. ....Caguas, PR
Mirabel, Catherine A. ....East Meadow, NY
Mirabel, Christine E. ....South Gate, CA
Mirabell, James K. ....Sacramento, CA
Mirabella, John ....Philadelphia, PA
Mirabella, Joseph F., Jr. ....Wheaton, IL
Mirabella & Kincaid, P.C. ....Wheaton, IL
Mirabella, Laurel A. ....Chicago, IL
Mirabella, Lynn M. ....Wheaton, IL
Mirabella, Michael J. ....Denver, CO
Mirabelli, Dominick A. ....Hazlet, NJ
Mirabelli, Enrico J. ....Chicago, IL
Mirabelli, Mario V. ....Washington, DC
Mirabello, Francis J. ....Philadelphia, PA
Mirabile, Carolyn R. ....Norristown, PA
Mirabile, Christopher M. ....Cambridge, MA
Mirabile, Elizabeth Madden ....Boston, MA
Mirabile, John L. ....Spring Valley, NY
Mirabile, Lori Ann ....Ansonia, CT
Mirabile, Marzia P. Tongiani
Phoenixville, PA
Mirabile, Matthew V. ....Poughkeepsie, NY
Mirabile, Paul J. ....New Orleans, LA
Mirabile, Russell M. ....New York, NY
Mirabile, Thomas J. ....Garden City, NY
Mirabile, Thomas K. ....Chicago, IL
Mirabito, A. Jason ....Boston, MA
Mirabito, Andrew J. ....Miami, FL
Mirabito, Diane ....Westbury, NY
Miracchi, Silvano ....San Jose, CA
Miracle, Charles E. ....Boston, MA
Miracle, Dale N. ....Elm Grove, WI
Miracle, Douglas T. ....Jackson, MS
Miracle, Garry W. ....Brandon, FL
Miracle, Katherine Kolenberg ....Dallas, TX
Miracle, Pruzan, Pruzan & Baker
Seattle, WA
Miracle, Trent B. ....San Antonio, TX
Mirage, James A. ....Philadelphia, PA
Mirageas, Peter M. ....Framingham, MA
Miraglia, Amy Anderson ....Philadelphia, PA
Miraglia, Bettina M. ....New York, NY
Miraglia, Carmela M. ....Portland, ME
Miraglia, Cynthia S. ....Landover, MD
Miraglia, Thomas J. ....Philadelphia, PA
Miraglia, Vincent J. ....Atlanta, GA
Miragliotta, Angela M. ....Boston, MA
Miragliotta, Anthony ....Trenton, NJ
Miragliotta, Camille D. ....Lawrence, MA
Miragliotta, Constance Marie
Lawrence, MA
Miragliotta, James V. ....Lawrence, MA
Miragliotta, Jos. A. ....Lawrence, MA
Miragliotta, Joseph A., P.C. ....Lawrence, MA
Mirahmadi, Hedieh ....Los Angeles, CA
Mirakian, Peter, III ....Kansas City, MO
Mirakian, Stephen G. ....Kansas City, MO
Miraldi & Barrett Co. ....Lorain, OH
Miraldi, David P. ....Lorain, OH
Miraldi, James L. ....Lorain, OH

Miraldi, John R. ....Lorain, OH
Miraldi, Leslee W. ....Cleveland, OH
Miram, George A. ....Redwood City, CA
Miran, Claudia B. ....Madison, WI
Miranda, Albert C. ....Metairie, LA
New Orleans, LA
Miranda, Ana T. ....New York, NY
Miranda, Anthony M. ....Fairfield, CA
Miranda, Anthony M. ....Buffalo, NY
Miranda, Armando ....Dallas, TX
Miranda, Armando, Law Offices, P.C.
Dallas, TX
Miranda & Boyaki ....El Paso, TX
Miranda Cardenas & Cordova
San Juan, PR
Miranda, Carlos A., III ....El Paso, TX
Miranda, Carlos Ortiz ....Washington, DC
Miranda, Christopher A. ....Denver, CO
Miranda, Daniel F. ....Chicago, IL
Miranda, Daniel R. ....Brookfield, IL
Miranda, David P. ....Albany, NY
Miranda, Eduardo ....El Paso, TX
Miranda, Georgiana O. ....Montpelier, VT
Miranda, Helen Leen ....Miami, FL
Miranda, Jason A. ....Studio City, CA
Miranda, Joey Lee ....Hartford, CT
Miranda, John A. ....Department of Agriculture, Foreign Agricultural Service, GV
Miranda, Jorge A. ....San Juan, PR
Miranda, Laura M. ....New York, NY
Miranda, Lillian ....Northampton, MA
Miranda, Luis Domingo ....San Juan, PR
Miranda, Mary A. ....San Antonio, TX
Miranda, Michael ....Denver, CO
Miranda, Michael A. ....New York, NY
Miranda, Michael J. ....Kingston, NY
Miranda, Neal J. ....New York, NY
Miranda, Pedro L. ....Frankfort, KY
Miranda, Peter ....Wakefield, MA
Miranda, Ralph G. ....El Paso, TX
Miranda, Raul A. ....Tucson, AZ
Miranda, Roland ....Los Angeles, CA
Miranda, Silvestre M. ....San Juan, PR
Miranda & Sokoloff, LLP ....New York, NY
Miranda, Thomas A. ....Northampton, MA
Miranda, Thomas B. ....United States Senate, Committee Legal Personnel, GV
Miranda, Veronica I.
Small Business Administration, Office of the General Counsel, GV
Miranda-Cardenas, Alfonso ....San Juan, PR
Miranda-Daleccio, Jose A. ....San Juan, PR
Miranda Díaz, Juan Ramón ....Manati, PR
Miranda-Kirschner, Iris I. ....Belleville, IL
Miranda-Mazzucca, Isabel ....New York, NY
Miranda-Schmidt, Gail ....New York, NY
Miranda-Watkins, Frances ....Durham, NC
Mirande, Michael P. ....Seattle, WA
Mirandes-Ramirez, Enrique A.
San Juan, PR
Mirando, Carol ....Jacksonville, FL
Miranne, Joseph J., III ....Port Washington, NY
Miranne, Michael O. ....Covington, LA
Mirano, Marilyn Watson ....Laguna Beach, CA
Mirano, Miguel David ....Laguna Beach, CA
Miranowski, Jerome A. ....Minneapolis, MN
Mirante, Rand A. ....Princeton, NJ
Mirarchi, Charles P., III ....Philadelphia, PA
Mirarchi, Charles P., III, A Professional Corporation ....Philadelphia, PA
Mirarchi, Charles P., Jr. ....Philadelphia, PA
Mirarchi, Michael J. ....West Long Branch, NJ
Mirarchi, Philip J. ....Quantico, VA
Mirarchi, Ralph E. ....Wayne, PA
Mirarchi, Ralph E., Law Associates, P.C.
Wayne, PA
Mirasol, Manuel E. ....New York, NY
Mirasola, Vito J. ....St. Clair Shores, MI
Mirassou, Jean B. ....Redondo Beach, CA
Mirate, Galen A., Ms. ....Valdosta, GA
Mirau, Edwards, Cannon, Harter & Lewin, A Professional Corporation
Redlands, CA
San Bernardino, CA
Temecula, CA
Mirau, John K. ....Redlands, CA
San Bernardino, CA
Miravich, John J. ....Reading, PA
Mirbagheri, Ladan ....Washington, DC
Mirch, Kevin ....Reno, NV
Mirchandani, Harish C. ....McLean, VA
Mirchin, David M. ....Norwood, MA
Mircoff, Frederick H. ....Irvington, NJ
Mire, Cynthia L. ....San Francisco, CA
Mire, Francis E. ....Houston, TX
Mire, J. Matthew ....Denver, CO
Mire, Michael N. ....New Orleans, LA
Mire, Pegram J., Jr. ....Gonzales, LA
Mire, Stephanie Pearl ....Los Angeles, CA
Mire, Terrence A. ....Cincinnati, OH
Mire, Wm. N. ....Cincinnati, OH
Mirecki, Kevin J. ....Santa Ana, CA
Mirecki, Philip ....Los Angeles, CA
Miree, Kathryn Waller ....Birmingham, AL
Miree, Vanessa A. ....Birmingham, MI
Mirel and Alegi ....Washington, DC
Lanham, MD
Mirel, Lawrence H. ....Washington, DC
Mirel, S. Louis ....Long Beach, NY
Mireles, Ernest ....Eagle Pass, TX
Mireles, Mike ....Sacramento, CA
Mireles, Patricia ....Ontario, CA
Mireles, Paul Andrew ....San Antonio, TX
Mirell, Douglas E. ....Los Angeles, CA
Mirenda, Anthony D. ....Boston, MA
Mirengoff, Paul E. ....Washington, DC
Mires & Bierce ....San Francisco, CA
Mires, Douglas W. ....Rochester Hills, MI

Mistretta, Martha Jacoff ... Great Barrington, MA
Mistretta, Rosanne ... Wilkes-Barre, PA
Mistretta, Susan E. ... Binghamton, NY
Mistrioty, George D. ... Elkhorn, WI
Mistrot, Brenda L. ... Lafayette, LA
Mistrot, John L. ... Houston, TX
Misturak-Gingrich, Kathleen ... Harrisburg, PA
Philadelphia, PA
Misuraca, Frank A. ... Ann Arbor, MI
Misuraca, Malcolm A., Law Offices of ... San Francisco, CA
Misuraca, Samuel P. ... Royal Oak, MI
Misuraca, Thomas L. ... Detroit, MI
Misuraca, Tracey M. ... Wilmington, MA
Misurek, Mary Christine ... Hastings, MN
Mita, Roy G. ... Madison, WI
Mitar, George J. ... Fort Myers, FL
Mitau, Lee R. ... Minneapolis, MN
Mitby, John C. ... Madison, WI
Mitby, Julie K. ... Madison, WI
Mitch, William E. ... Birmingham, AL
Mitcham, B. Anderson ... Tampa, FL
Mitcham, Claira E. ... Ludowici, GA
Mitcham, John Preston ... Anniston, AL
Mitchard, Leonard C. ... Arlington, VA
Mitchel, Alan M. ... Miami, FL
Mitchel, Alvin ... Bronx, NY
Mitchel, Andrea K. ... Pittsburgh, PA
Mitchel, Arthur B. ... Pewaukee, WI
Mitchel & Associates, P.A. ... Miami, FL
Mitchel, Elizabeth A. ... West Bend, WI
Mitchel, Gary L. ... Woodward, OK
Mitchel, Gaston & Mitchel, A Professional Corporation ... Woodward, OK
Mitchel, George C. ... Los Angeles, CA
Mitchel, John J. ... Gunnison, CO
Mitchel, John J. ... Montrose, CO
Mitchel, John J. ... Telluride, CO
Mitchel, Michael M. ... Chicago, IL
Mitchel, Michael W. ... Woodward, OK
Mitchel, R. Stanley ... Pittsburgh, PA
Mitchel, Steven J. ... Miami, FL
Mitchel, Steven M. ... Costa Mesa, CA
Los Angeles, CA
Mitchell, A. Alan ... Columbus, OH
Mitchell, A. Ben ... Mount Vernon, IL
Mitchell, Aaron L. ... Dallas, TX
Mitchell, Alan L. ... Duluth, MN
Mitchell, Alan L. ... Tigard, OR
Mitchell, Alan R. ... St. Paul, MN
Mitchell, Alan V. ... Highland Park, IL
Mitchell, Albert A. ... Atlanta, GA
Mitchell, Albert J., Jr. ... Tucumcari, NM
Mitchell, Albert J., Jr., P.A. ... Tucumcari, NM
Mitchell, Albert T. ... Woodstock, VA
Mitchell, Alexander B., II ... Wichita, KS
Mitchell, Alice S. ... Oklahoma City, OK
Mitchell, Alison M. ... Chicago, IL
Mitchell, Allan E. ... Cherokee, OK
Mitchell & Allen ... Chicago, IL
Mitchell, Allen B., A Professional Corporation ... Sapulpa, OK
Mitchell, Allen, Catalano & Boda, Co., L.P.A. ... Columbus, OH
Mitchell, Allen J., II ... Lake Charles, LA
Mitchell, Allison ... Washington, DC
Mitchell, Americus ... Kilmarnock, VA
Mitchell, Amy C. ... Minneapolis, MN
Mitchell, Amy C. ... Cincinnati, OH
Mitchell, Amy Maislin ... Austin, TX
Mitchell, Andrew C., Jr. ... Salisbury, MD
Mitchell, Anis ... Scottsdale, AZ
Mitchell, Ann Marie P. ... New York, NY
Mitchell, Anne E. ... Poughkeepsie, NY
Mitchell, Anne M. ... Washington, DC
Mitchell, Anne Patricia ... Santa Clara, CA
Mitchell, Anne T. ... Boston, MA
Mitchell, Anne W. ... Birmingham, AL
Mitchell, Annina Marie ... Salt Lake City, UT
Mitchell, Anshu Vats ... Houston, TX
Mitchell, Anthony G. ... Hobart, OK
Mitchell, A. R. M. ... Tyler, TX
Mitchell, Arthur ... Bastrop, TX
Dallas, TX
Mitchell, Arthur, & Associates, Ltd. ... Bastrop, TX
Mitchell, Arthur J. ... St. Louis, MO
Mitchell, Arthur Kennedy ... Oakland, CA
Mitchell, Arthur M., III ... New York, NY
Mitchell, Arthur P. ... New Orleans, LA
Mitchell & Associates ... Oregon City, OR
Mitchell & Associates, A Professional Corporation ... Atlanta, GA
Mitchell & Associates, P.A. ... Miami, FL
Mitchell & Associates, P.A. ... Winter Park, FL
Mitchell, Auburn L. ... Austin, TX
Mitchell, Augustus J., Jr. ... New York, NY
Mitchell, Austin L. ... Salem, MO
Mitchell, Barbara H. ... Boston, MA
Mitchell, Barrett D. ... Pittsburgh, PA
Mitchell, Bartly L ... New York, NY
Mitchell, Belinda Bell ... Consumer Product Safety Commission, Office of Compliance, GV
Mitchell, Benjamin M. ... Grenada, MS
Mitchell, Bert O. ... Las Vegas, NV
Mitchell, Beth H. ... Boston, MA
Mitchell, Beth Loren ... Austin, TX
Mitchell, Beverly Lebowitz ... Dallas, TX
Mitchell, Beverly R. ... Winston-Salem, NC
Mitchell, Beverly Sumner ... Atlanta, GA
Mitchell, Billy F. ... Birmingham, AL
Mitchell, Blackstock, Barnes, Wagoner & Ivers ... Little Rock, AR
Mitchell, Blackwell & Mitchell, P.A. ... Valdese, NC
Mitchell, Bobby B. ... Leslie, GA
Mitchell, Bouton, Yokel & Childs ... Greenville, SC
Mitchell, Brad J. ... Boston, MA
Mitchell, Bradley L. ... Princeton, NJ
Mitchell, Brendan P. ... Boston, MA
Mitchell, Brent A. ... Wichita, KS
Mitchell, Brian ... Oklahoma City, OK
Mitchell, Brian C. ... San Diego, CA
Mitchell, Brian E. ... San Jose, CA
Mitchell, Briane Nelson ... Santa Monica, CA
Mitchell, Bridget Anne ... Chicago, IL
Mitchell, Brisso, Delaney & Vrieze ... Crescent City, CA
Eureka, CA
Weaverville, CA
Mitchell, Bruce A. ... Melbourne, FL
Mitchell, Bruce E. ... Los Angeles, CA
Mitchell, Bruce E. ... Atlanta, GA
Mitchell, Bruce M. ... New York, NY
Mitchell, Bruce M. ... San Antonio, TX
Mitchell, Bruce T. ... San Francisco, CA
Mitchell, Bruce W. ... Marion, IL
Mitchell, Burley B., Jr. ... Raleigh, NC
Mitchell, Burrow, Gingerich & Loquaci, A Professional Corporation ... San Jose, CA
Mitchell, Burton A., (P.C.) ... Los Angeles, CA
Mitchell, Byron J. ... Rockville, MD
Mitchell, C. Edward S. ... Williamsport, PA
Mitchell, C. Gary ... Shreveport, LA
Mitchell, C. Geoffrey ... Los Angeles, CA
Mitchell, C. MacNeil ... New York, NY
Mitchell, Carl B. ... San Jose, CA
Mitchell, Carla D. ... Memphis, TN
Mitchell, Carmen Jones ... Chicago, IL
Mitchell, Carmen S. ... Dallas, TX
Mitchell, Carol A. ... Washington, DC
Mitchell, Carol A. ... Missoula, MT
Mitchell, Carol C. ... Tacoma, WA
Mitchell, Carol L. ... Portland, ME
Mitchell, Carole A. ... Columbus, OH
Mitchell, Caroline ... North Miami Beach, FL
Mitchell, Caroline ... Pittsburgh, PA
Mitchell, Caroline Emerson ... Oklahoma City, OK
Mitchell, Caroline N. ... San Francisco, CA
Mitchell, Carolyn ... Fort Worth, TX
Mitchell, Carolyn M. ... Worcester, MA
Mitchell, Carrie R. ... Dallas, TX
Mitchell, Caryn R. ... Boston, MA
Mitchell, Catherine P. ... Asheville, NC
Mitchell, Cathryn A. ... Princeton, NJ
Mitchell, Ceasar C., II. ... Atlanta, GA
Mitchell, Charlene Padovani ... San Francisco, CA
Mitchell, Charles B., Jr. ... Dallas, TX
Mitchell, Charles D. ... Vicksburg, MS
Mitchell, Charles D., Jr. ... Phoenix, AZ
Mitchell, Charles E. ... Wilmington, DE
Mitchell, Charles E. ... Cincinnati, OH
Mitchell, Charles F. ... Oregon City, OR
Mitchell, Charles F. ... Kirbyville, TX
Mitchell, Charles K. ... Marina Del Rey, CA
Mitchell, Charles L. ... King Of Prussia, PA
Mitchell, Charles McKim ... New Bedford, MA
Mitchell, Charles O., Jr. ... Jacksonville, FL
Mitchell, Charles P. ... Washington, DC
Mitchell, Charles P. ... Orlando, FL
Mitchell, Charles Philip ... Peoria, IL
Mitchell, Charles R. ... San Augustine, TX
Mitchell, Charles S. ... Fairfax, VA
Mitchell, Charles T. ... Denver, CO
Mitchell, Charlotte M. ... Hartford, CT
Mitchell, Cheryl A. ... New York, NY
Mitchell, Cheryl C. ... Spokane, WA
Mitchell, Chris ... Birmingham, AL
Mitchell, Christine L.H. ... Atlanta, GA
Mitchell, Christopher A. ... Troy, MI
Mitchell, Christopher D. ... Palo Alto, CA
Mitchell, Christopher H. ... Washington, DC
Mitchell, Clarence B. ... Kansas City, MO
Mitchell, Clark A. ... Washington, PA
Mitchell, Clay J. ... Wauconda, IL
Mitchell, Clayton R. ... Exeter, NH
Mitchell, Clifford B. ... Eureka, CA
Mitchell, Clifton J. ... Peoria, IL
Mitchell, Clyde ... New York, NY
Mitchell, Clyde ... New York, NY
Mitchell, C. M. ... Jackson, MS
Mitchell, Colmon S. ... Batesville, MS
Mitchell & Condon, P.A. ... Pensacola, FL
Mitchell, Connie M. ... Texarkana, TX
Mitchell & Courts ... Oakland, CA
Mitchell, Craig A. ... Newport Beach, CA
Mitchell, Craig B. ... New Orleans, LA
Mitchell, Craig C. ... Fort Myers, FL
Mitchell, Cynthia ... Palo Alto, CA
Fort Collins, CO
Mitchell, Cynthia A. ... Broomfield, CO
Mitchell, Cynthia I. ... Clarksdale, MS
Mitchell, Cynthia L. ... San Francisco, CA
Mitchell, D. Rebecca ... Chicago, IL
Northbrook, IL
Mitchell, Dale B. ... Somerset, KY
Mitchell, Dana ... New York, NY
Mitchell, Dana C., III ... Greenville, SC
Mitchell, Daneene B. ... Redwood City, CA
Mitchell, Daniel ... Boston, MA
Mitchell, Daniel J. ... Portland, ME
Mitchell, Daniel L. ... Oakland, CA
Mitchell, Daniel L. ... Topeka, KS
Mitchell, Daniel M., Jr. ... Quitman, GA
Mitchell, Daniel P. ... Tampa, FL
Mitchell, Daniel Prescott ... Mobile, AL
Mitchell, Daphna H. ... New York, NY
Mitchell, Darel C. ... Lawrenceville, GA
Mitchell, Darryl ... Cincinnati, OH
Mitchell, Darryl ... Cincinnati, OH
Mitchell, David B. ... Coral Gables, FL
Mitchell, David B. ... Baltimore, MD
Mitchell, David B. ... Kansas City, MO
Mitchell, David B., P.A. ... Coral Gables, FL
Mitchell, David C. ... Fremont, NE
Mitchell, David C. ... Everett, WA
Mitchell, David Cary ... Washington, DC
Mitchell, David D. ... Cedar Rapids, IA
Mitchell, David H., III ... Bronx, NY
Mitchell, David J. ... New Orleans, LA
Mitchell, David John ... Calais, ME
Mitchell, David L. ... Fort Collins, CO
Mitchell, David L. ... Waltham, MA
Mitchell, David L. ... Minneapolis, MN
Mitchell, David M. ... Sarasota, FL
Mitchell, David P. ... Charlotte, NC
Mitchell, David R. ... Blue Springs, MO
Mitchell, David S. ... Little Rock, AR
Mitchell, David S. ... New York, NY
Mitchell, David W. ... San Jose, CA
Mitchell, Deborah ... Sedalia, MO
Mitchell, Debra Faye ... Chicago, IL
Mitchell & DeClerck, P.L.L.C. ... Enid, OK
Mitchell, Delmer R., Jr. ... Quincy, IL
Mitchell, Dennis ... Los Angeles, CA
Mitchell, Dennis E. ... Kansas City, KS
Mitchell, Dennis E. ... Baltimore, MD
Mitchell, Derenda J. ... Topeka, KS
Mitchell, Derrick ... Houston, TX
Mitchell, Dianna L. ... Chicago, IL
Mitchell, Don ... Anchorage, AK
Mitchell, Don W. ... Encinitas, CA
Mitchell, Donald ... Boise, ID
Mitchell, Donald A. ... Danbury, CT
Mitchell, Donald B. ... Atlanta, GA
Mitchell, Donald B., Jr. ... Washington, DC
Mitchell, Donald C., II ... Cincinnati, OH
Mitchell, Donald E. ... Portsmouth, NH
Mitchell, Donald F. ... Venice, FL
Mitchell, Donald J. ... Williamsville, NY
Mitchell, Donald L. ... Oakland, CA
Mitchell, Donald R. ... Carterville, IL
Mitchell, Donald V., (P.C.) ... Sacramento, CA
Mitchell, Donna ... New York, NY
Mitchell, Donna Mendoza ... Las Vegas, NV
Mitchell & Doran ... Houston, TX
Mitchell, Dorothy C. ... New York, NY
Mitchell, Dorothy J. ... Zion, IL
Mitchell, Douglas B. ... Washington, DC
Mitchell, Douglas F. ... Washington, DC
Mitchell, Douglas F. ... Palm Harbor, FL
Mitchell, Douglas J. ... Denver, CO
Mitchell, Douglas P. ... Tucson, AZ
Mitchell, Douglas S. ... Eugene, OR
Mitchell, Douglass A. ... Las Vegas, NV
Mitchell and Dunn ... Washington, DC
Mitchell, E. Marlee ... Nashville, TN
Mitchell, E. A. Burke ... San Jose, CA
Mitchell, Earl B., Jr. ... Enid, OK
Mitchell, Eddie C. ... Winston-Salem, NC
Mitchell, Eddie C., P.A. ... Winston-Salem, NC
Mitchell, Edward B. ... Cincinnati, OH
Mitchell, Edward F. ... San Francisco, CA
Mitchell, Edward J. ... Lanark, IL
Mitchell, Edwin L. ... Alton, IA
Mitchell, Edwin L. ... Marion, OH
Mitchell, Eileen M. ... Morrisville, PA
Mitchell, E. J. (Bilbo) ... Meridian, MS
Mitchell, Elisa ... Oakbrook Terrace, IL
Mitchell, Elise ... Dallas, TX
Mitchell, Elizabeth A. ... Denver, CO
Mitchell, Elizabeth M. ... Boston, MA
Mitchell, Elizabeth S. ... Jackson, MS
Mitchell, Ellen B. ... San Antonio, TX
Mitchell, Ellen H. ... Salina, KS
Mitchell and Ellinger, P.A. ... La Plata, MD
Mitchell, Emery D. ... San Francisco, CA
Mitchell, Eric D. ... Chevy Chase, MD
Mitchell, Erwin ... Dalton, GA
Mitchell, Ethel Carr Hunter ... Charlotte Amalie, St. Thomas, VI
Mitchell, Ethel Carr Hunter, P.C. ... Charlotte Amalie, St. Thomas, VI
Mitchell, Eugene A. ... Minneapolis, MN
Mitchell, Eugene E. ... Fort Collins, CO
Mitchell, Eugenie Denise ... Sacramento, CA
Mitchell, Evelyn P. ... Jacksonville, FL
Mitchell, F. King ... Vancouver, WA
Mitchell, F. Lon ... Helena, MT
Mitchell, Frances (Bumsted) ... Scottsdale, AZ
Mitchell, Frank W., P.C. ... Houston, TX
Mitchell, Franklin J., Jr. ... Vista, CA
Mitchell, Gail Esther ... Emeryville, CA
Mitchell, Gail Jean Hann ... Union, NJ
Mitchell, Gail Y. ... Buffalo, NY
Mitchell, Gary B. ... San Jose, CA
Mitchell, Gary C. ... Ruidoso, NM
Mitchell, Gary J. ... Kingsport, TN
Mitchell, Gary R. ... Long Beach, CA
Mitchell, Gene Edward ... Pensacola, FL
Mitchell, Geo. H. ... Keyser, WV
Mitchell, Geoffrey S. ... Washington, DC
Mitchell, George E. ... Spartanburg, SC
Mitchell, George H. ... Phoenix, AZ
Mitchell, George H. ... Knob Noster, MO
Mitchell, George J. ... Washington, DC
Portland, ME
Mitchell, George M., Jr. ... Eupora, MS
Mitchell, George O. ... Miami, FL
Mitchell, George W. ... Washington, DC
Mitchell, Georgia Anna ... Columbia, SC
Mitchell, Gerald L. ... Washington, DC
Mitchell, Gerard E. ... Washington, DC
Mitchell, Gillian K. ... Piscataway, NJ
Mitchell, Glen T. ... Millbrae, CA
Mitchell, Glenn A. ... Washington, DC
Mitchell, Glenn H. ... West Palm Beach, FL
Mitchell, Glenn M. ... New York, NY
Mitchell, Goff & Mitchell, LLP ... Dallas, TX
Mitchell, Gordon Robert ... Birmingham, AL
Mitchell Graham & Stroud, P.C. ... Decatur, GA
Mitchell, Grainne ... Columbia, SC
Mitchell, Grant E. ... Washington, DC
Mitchell, Greg ... Oklahoma City, OK
Mitchell, Greg E. ... Lexington, KY
Mitchell, Gregory ... Nashville, TN
Mitchell, Gregory A. ... Chicago, IL
Mitchell, Gregory C. ... Washington, DC
Mitchell, Gregory C. ... Jefferson City, MO
Mitchell, Gregory J. ... Department of Justice, Drug Enforcement Administration, GV
Mitchell, Gregory Lee ... Magnolia, AR
Mitchell, Gregory R. ... Columbus, OH
Mitchell, Gregory Scott ... Denver, CO
Mitchell, Guy H. ... Bronx, NY
Mitchell, Guy O. ... Ville Platte, LA
Mitchell, Guy O., P.L.C. ... Ville Platte, LA
Mitchell, Guy W., III ... Columbus, MS
Oxford, MS
Tupelo, MS
Mitchell, Gwendolyn V. ... San Mateo, CA
Mitchell, Gwendolyn V., A Professional Corp. ... San Mateo, CA
Mitchell, H. Clay ... Pensacola, FL
Mitchell, H. Maurice ... Little Rock, AR
Mitchell, H. Thomas ... Eden Prairie, MN
Mitchell, Hans A. ... Ontario, OR
Mitchell, Harold H., Jr. ... Greenville, MS
Mitchell, Harry H. ... La Canada Flintridge, CA
Mitchell, Harry H. ... Tallahassee, FL
Mitchell, Harry J. ... Palmyra, MO
Mitchell, Heather Johnson ... Oklahoma City, OK
Mitchell & Henry ... Hutchinson, KS
Sterling, KS
Mitchell, Henry A., III ... Durham, NC
Mitchell, Henry A., Jr. ... Raleigh, NC
Mitchell, Henry Ray, III ... Ocean Springs, MS
Mitchell, Herbert G., Jr. ... Hiller, PA
Mitchell & Herzog ... Palo Alto, CA
Mitchell, Holly T. ... New York, NY
Mitchell, Horace A. ... Lubbock, TX
Mitchell, Horace A., P.C. ... Lubbock, TX
Mitchell, Huey P. ... Fort Worth, TX
Mitchell, Hugh A. ("Jay"), Jr. ... Baltimore, MD
Mitchell Hurst Jacobs & Dick ... Indianapolis, IN
Mitchell & Ison ... Sacramento, CA
Mitchell, Ivar W. ... Vero Beach, FL
Mitchell, J. Chad ... Chicago, IL
Mitchell, J. Douglas ... Salt Lake City, UT
Mitchell, J. Mart ... Houston, TX
Mitchell, J. Oscar ... Lithonia, GA
Mitchell, J. Tracy ... Baton Rouge, LA
Mitchell, J. Tucker ... Jackson, MS
Mitchell, J. Wilson ... Florence, AL
Mitchell, Jack ... Auburn, CA
Mitchell, Jack E. ... North Muskegon, MI
Mitchell, Jack H., III ... Greenville, SC
Mitchell, Jacquelyn ... Newport News, VA
Mitchell, Jama Dee ... Wichita, KS
Mitchell, James ... Stockton, CA
Mitchell, James A. ... Washington, DC
Mitchell, James A. ... Waterville, ME
Mitchell, James A. ... Grand Rapids, MI
Mitchell, James A. ... New York, NY
Mitchell, James B. ... Walla Walla, WA
Mitchell, James C. ... Tucson, AZ
Mitchell, James D. ... Austell, GA
Mitchell, James D. ... Seattle, WA
Mitchell, James E. ... Chicago, IL
Mitchell, James E. ... Boston, MA
Mitchell, James E. ... Los Alamos, NM
Mitchell, James E. ... Youngstown, OH
Mitchell, James F., Inc. ... Lafayette, CA
Mitchell, James H. ... Boston, MA
Mitchell, James K. ... Washington, DC
Mitchell, James K. ... Bingham Farms, MI
Mitchell, James K. ... Dallas, TX
Mitchell, James L., Jr. ... Dallas, TX
Mitchell, James M. ... Scottsdale, AZ
Mitchell, James P. ... San Francisco, CA
Mitchell, James Paul ... Melrose, MA
Mitchell, James R. ... Orlando, FL
Mitchell, James R. ... Tampa, FL
Mitchell, James R. ... Leesville, LA
Mitchell, James R. ... Bethesda, MD
Mitchell, James R. ... Interlaken, NJ
Mitchell, James R. ... Dayton, OH
Mitchell, James S. ... Omaha, NE
Mitchell, James T. ... Hagåtña, GU
Mitchell, James T. ... Louisville, KY
Mitchell, James W. ... Fairfield, CT
Mitchell, Jan E. ... Albuquerque, NM
Mitchell, Janet Vining ... Santa Barbara, CA
Mitchell, Janyce R. ... Palo Alto, CA
Mitchell, Jas. R. ... Madison, WI
Mitchell, Jason A. ... Wheeling, WV
Mitchell, Jay A. ... Palo Alto, CA
Mitchell, Jay B. ... Monroe, LA
Mitchell, Jay D. ... Nashville, TN
Mitchell, Jayne ... Conrad, MT
Mitchell, J. C. ... Marion, IL
Mitchell, Jeanine M. ... New York, NY
Mitchell, Jefferson L. ... Cleveland, OH
Mitchell, Jeffery G. ... Treasury Department, Internal Revenue Service, GV

Mitchell, Stephen A. .... Austin, TX
Mitchell, Stephen B. .... Salt Lake City, UT
Mitchell, Stephen Carrington .... Columbia, SC
Mitchell, Stephen D. .... Columbus, OH
Mitchell, Stephen E. .... Tallahassee, FL
Mitchell, Stephen G. .... Kansas City, MO
Mitchell, Stephen J. .... Tampa, FL
Mitchell, Stephen L. .... Revere, MA
Mitchell, Stephen L. .... El Paso, TX; Van Horn, TX
Mitchell, Stephen R. .... Bloomfield, MO
Mitchell, Stephen S. .... Chicago, IL
Mitchell, Stephen S. .... Alexandria, VA
Mitchell, Stephen W. .... Hurst, TX
Mitchell, Stevan D. .... Department of Justice, Criminal Division, GV
Mitchell, Steve D. .... Somerset, NJ
Mitchell, Steven A. .... East Lansing, MI
Mitchell, Steven B. .... St. Louis, MO
Mitchell, Steven C. .... Phoenix, AZ
Mitchell, Steven C. .... Santa Rosa, CA
Mitchell, Steven M. .... Independence, MO
Mitchell, Steven R. .... Dallas, TX
Mitchell, Steven S. .... Santa Ana, CA
Mitchell, Stewart L. .... Plano, TX
Mitchell, Stuart B. .... Alexandria, VA
Mitchell, Stuart M. .... Nyack, NY
Mitchell, Sumner C., Jr. .... Santa Rosa, CA
Mitchell, Susan A. .... Los Angeles, CA
Mitchell, Susan A. .... Norwalk, CA
Mitchell, Susan J. .... Chicago, IL
Mitchell, Susan L. .... Manassas, VA
Mitchell, Susannah M. .... Walnut Creek, CA
Mitchell, Suzanna J. .... Providence, RI
Mitchell, Suzanne .... Oklahoma City, OK
Mitchell, Suzanne Harmatz .... Santa Monica, CA
Mitchell, Suzanne M. .... Danville, PA
Mitchell, Suzanne M. .... Philadelphia, PA
Mitchell, T. David .... Cleveland, OH
Mitchell, T. Eugene .... Spindale, NC
Mitchell, T. Gary .... Princeton, NJ
Mitchell, Tamara O. .... Birmingham, AL
Mitchell, Tamra L. .... Cedar Rapids, IA
Mitchell, Tangerla D. .... Elizabeth, NJ
Mitchell, Ted F. .... Asheville, NC
Mitchell, Ted H., II .... Dallas, TX
Mitchell, Ted M. .... Metairie, LA
Mitchell, Terrance .... Park Forest, IL
Mitchell, Terry E. .... Austin, TX
Mitchell, Terry L. .... New Brighton, MN
Mitchell, Theo. W. .... Greenville, SC
Mitchell, Theodore A. .... Zion, IL
Mitchell, Theodore R. .... Saipan, TT
Mitchell, Theresa Eileen .... Los Angeles, CA
Mitchell, Thomas A. .... Honolulu, HI
Mitchell, Thomas A. .... Coeur d'Alene, ID
Mitchell, Thomas A. .... Madisonville, KY
Mitchell, Thomas A. .... Merchantville, NJ
Mitchell, Thomas A. .... Albany, NY
Mitchell, Thomas B. .... Hartford, CT
Mitchell, Thomas C. .... San Francisco, CA
Mitchell, Thomas E. .... Albertville, AL
Mitchell, Thomas J. .... Laurel, MD
Mitchell, Thomas J. .... New York, NY
Mitchell, Thomas J. .... Houston, TX
Mitchell, Thomas J. .... Richmond, VA
Mitchell, Thomas J., III .... Austin, TX
Mitchell, Thomas L. .... Charlotte, NC
Mitchell, Thomas M. .... Buford, GA
Mitchell, Thomas R. .... San Diego, CA
Mitchell, Thomas W. .... Washington, DC
Mitchell, Thomas W., Jr. .... New Port Richey, FL
Mitchell, Timothy A. .... Edmond, OK
Mitchell, Timothy B. .... Columbus, OH
Mitchell, Timothy S. .... Greenbelt, MD
Mitchell, Timothy T. .... Dallas, TX
Mitchell, T. L. .... Washington, DC
Mitchell, Todd .... San Francisco, CA
Mitchell, Todd A. .... Vancouver, WA
Mitchell, Todd J. .... Milwaukee, WI
Mitchell, Tom P. .... Memphis, TN
Mitchell, Tracy .... Elbow Lake, MN
Mitchell, Tracy L. .... Olympia, WA
Mitchell, Traynham E., Jr. .... Securities and Exchange Commission, Division of Enforcement, GV
Mitchell, Trent .... St. Louis, MO
Mitchell, T. W. .... Jackson, OH
Mitchell, Valerie Elaine .... New York, NY
Mitchell, Veena A. .... Santa Rosa, CA
Mitchell, Vincent J. .... Providence, RI
Mitchell, Virginia G. .... Beaverton, OR
Mitchell, Voge, Corban and Morris .... Tupelo, MS
Mitchell, W. Clay, Jr. .... Orlando, FL
Mitchell, W. Eason .... Tuscaloosa, AL
Mitchell, W. Harold .... Valdese, NC
Mitchell, W. Scott .... Billings, MT
Mitchell, W. Seth .... Salisbury, MD
Mitchell, W. Wright .... Atlanta, GA
Mitchell, Wade A. .... Cleveland, OH
Mitchell, Wallace L., II .... Newport Beach, CA
Mitchell, Walter L., III .... Laconia, NH
Mitchell, Walter R. .... Los Angeles, CA
Mitchell, Walter W. .... Atlanta, GA
Mitchell & Walwyn .... San Jose, CA
Mitchell, Wandra G. .... Fairfax, VA
Mitchell, Wayne E. .... Seattle, WA
Mitchell, Wayne H. .... Tallahassee, FL
Mitchell, Wendall A. .... Oakland, CA
Mitchell, Wendell W. .... Luverne, AL
Mitchell, Wendy Aline .... Orange, CA
Mitchell, W. H. .... Florence, AL
Mitchell, Wiley F., Jr. .... Norfolk, VA
Mitchell, William .... Cleveland, OH
Mitchell, William A. .... Owensboro, KY
Mitchell, William A. .... Washington, PA
Mitchell, William A., Jr. .... Boston, MA
Mitchell, William C. .... Tulsa, OK
Mitchell, William C., A Professional Corporation .... Tulsa, OK
Mitchell, William C., Jr. .... Annapolis, MD
Mitchell, William D. .... Tampa, FL
Mitchell, William D. .... Philadelphia, PA
Mitchell, William D. .... Sparta, TN
Mitchell, William E. .... Dixon, KY
Mitchell, William F. .... Eureka, CA
Mitchell, William F. .... Atlanta, GA
Mitchell, William G. .... Colton, CA
Mitchell, William G. .... Fort Lauderdale, FL
Mitchell, William G. .... Orlando, FL
Mitchell, William G.C., Jr. .... Charlotte, NC
Mitchell, William H. .... Portland, OR
Mitchell, William H. .... Sparta, TN
Mitchell, William, III .... Detroit, MI; Troy, MI
Mitchell, William J. .... Schaumburg, IL
Mitchell, William J. .... Cincinnati, OH
Mitchell, William J., II .... Baton Rouge, LA
Mitchell, William L. .... Woodland Park, CO
Mitchell, William L., II .... Baltimore, MD
Mitchell, William L., (P.A.) .... Hutchinson, KS; Sterling, KS
Mitchell, William M. .... Linthicum, MD
Mitchell, William R. .... Modesto, CA
Mitchell, William R. .... Newport Beach, CA
Mitchell, William R. .... Pensacola, FL
Mitchell, William T. .... Atlanta, GA
Mitchell, William W. .... Bay Harbor Islands, FL
Mitchell, Williams, Selig, Gates & Woodyard, P.L.L.C. .... Bentonville, AR; Little Rock, AR
Mitchell, Willis Wilson, II .... Dallas, TX
Mitchell, Wilmer H. .... Pensacola, FL
Mitchell, Wm. Glenn, Jr. .... Orlando, FL
Mitchell, W. P. .... Tupelo, MS
Mitchell, Zenford A. .... Aliquippa, PA
Mitchell-Bittorf, Tammy A. .... Martinsburg, WV
Mitchell-Davis, Judy I. .... Chicago, IL
Mitchell-Dix, Janet E. .... Leo, IN
Mitchell Graham, Tanya .... Decatur, GA
Mitchell-Guttman, Christie B. .... Rancho Cordova, CA
Mitchell-Lizars, Jane P. .... Eugene, OR
Mitchell-Rankin, Zinora .... Washington, DC
Mitchells, Rebecca A. .... Palo Alto, CA
Mitchell-Wallace, Keeley P. .... Miami, FL
MitchellWeiler, J. Dana .... Corona, CA
Mitchelson, Fred .... Pittsburg, KS
Mitchelson, Jennifer Smith .... Boston, MA
Mitchelson, John H. .... Pittsburg, KS
Mitchelson, Kevin F. .... Pittsburg, KS
Mitchelson, Mary .... Office of Personnel Management, Office of the General Counsel, GV
Mitchelson, Michael .... Oklahoma City, OK
Mitchelson & Mitchelson .... Mission, KS
Mitchelson, Thomas P. .... Mission, KS
Mitchelson, Timothy M. .... Boston, MA
Mitchelson, William R., Jr. .... Atlanta, GA
Mitchem, Allen P. .... Denver, CO
Mitchem & Flanigan .... Denver, CO
Mitchem, James E. .... Denver, CO
Mitchem, M. Todd .... Atlanta, GA
Mitchem, Russell L. .... Chicago, IL
Mitchem, W. Spencer .... Pensacola, FL
Mitchem, Wade W. .... Gastonia, NC
Mitchener, Frierson W. .... Clarksdale, MS
Mitchenor, Dennis C. .... Grosse Pointe Farms, MI
Mitchiner, Joseph H. .... Raleigh, NC
Mitchiner, Stephanie L. .... Clayton, NC
Mitchner, Kent D. .... Brandenburg, KY
Mitchnick, Jamie Persky .... New York, NY
Mitchum, Jo Claudia .... Montgomery, AL
Mitchum, Robert W. .... Lawrenceville, GA
Mitchusson, Gary J. .... Forrest City, AR
Mitea, Victor T. .... Taylor, MI
Miteff & Finney .... Fort Worth, TX
Miteff, Meto .... Fort Worth, TX
Mitek, Mark M. .... Washington, DC
Mitelman, Rimma .... Edgewater, NJ
Mitgang, Iris, Law Office of .... Walnut Creek, CA
Mithal, Maneesha .... Federal Trade Commission, Bureau of Consumer Protection, GV
Mithalal, Kerry H. .... New York, NY
Mithani, Sonal H. .... Washington, DC
Mithoff & Jacks, L.L.P. .... Austin, TX; Houston, TX
Mithoff, Richard Warren .... Austin, TX; Houston, TX
Mithun, Howard .... Minneapolis, MN
Mitidiere, Barry T., (A Professional Corporation) .... Los Angeles, CA
Mitinger, Alice B. .... Pittsburgh, PA
Mitinger, Robert B., Jr. .... State College, PA
Mitka, Gloria R. .... Chicago, IL
Mitkoff, Marci .... New York, NY
Mitlak, Stefany L. .... Indianapolis, IN
Mitler, Laura S. .... West Haven, CT
Mitlitzky, Steven R. .... New York, NY
Mitman, William H. .... West Chester, PA
Mitman, William H., Jr. .... West Chester, PA
Mitnick, Amy H. .... Decatur, GA
Mitnick, Amy H., P.C. .... Decatur, GA
Mitnick, Andrew K. .... Philadelphia, PA
Mitnick, Audy L. .... Wilmington, DE
Mitnick, Cara E. .... New York, NY
Mitnick, Eric Alan .... Torrance, CA
Mitnick, Harvey D. .... Wayne, NJ
Mitnick, Harvey M. .... Haddonfield, NJ
Mitnick, Howard S. .... Morristown, NJ
Mitnick, Jack .... Garden City, NY
Mitnick, Janice S. .... Securities and Exchange Commission, Division of Market Regulation, GV
Mitnick, Jeffrey L. .... New York, NY
Mitnick, Joel M. .... New York, NY
Mitnick, John H. .... Baltimore, MD
Mitnick, John M. .... Atlanta, GA
Mitnick, Judith A. .... Falls Church, VA
Mitnick, Marcia R. .... Washington, DC
Mitnick, Martin A. .... Baltimore, MD
Mitnick & Mitnick .... Baltimore, MD
Mitnick, Mona K. .... Small Business Administration, Office of Hearings and Appeals, GV
Mitnick, Scott J. .... Atlantic City, NJ
Mitnick, Searle E. .... Baltimore, MD
Mitnick, Stephen L. .... Ventura, CA
Mitnick, Steven .... Frenchtown, NJ
Mitnick, Vogelson, Josselson & DePersia .... Haddonfield, NJ
Mitnik, Daniel W. .... White Plains, NY
Mitnik, Diane S. .... New Orleans, LA
Mitnik, Keith R. .... Orlando, FL
Mitofsky, Joel A. .... New York, NY
Mitofsky & Shapiro .... New York, NY
Mitola, Daniel Marc .... Hauppauge, NY
Mitola, John R. .... Southport, CT
Mitola, Thomas F. .... Shelton, CT
Mitra, Joydeep .... New York, NY
Mitra, Keesha-Lu M. .... Bloomington, IL
Mitrakas, Greg .... Marlborough, MA
Mitrakos, Iris Sockel .... San Francisco, CA
Mitrani, Ada L. .... Bartlesville, OK
Mitrani, Eduardo .... Houston, TX
Mitrani, Isaac J. .... Miami, FL
Mitrani, Morris K. .... New York, NY
Mitrani, Rynor, Adamsky, Macaulay & Zorrilla, P.A. .... Fort Lauderdale, FL; **Miami, FL**
Mitrani, Silversmith & Veraja .... New York, NY
Mitrano, Catherine C. .... Burlington, MA
Mitrano, Gerard A. .... Webster, NY
Mitrano, Peter Paul .... Etna, NH
Mitrano, Thomas J. .... Honolulu, HI
Mitrano, Vincent P. .... Rochester, NY
Mitrany, Leon D. .... Long Beach, NY
Mitre, Ann Marie .... Denver, CO
Mitri, Michael F. .... Stamford, CT
Mitri, Salvatore C. .... Staten Island, NY
Mitrione, Michael V. .... West Palm Beach, FL
Mitrius, Janice V. .... Chicago, IL
Mitroff, George B. .... Hayward, CA; San Francisco, CA
Mitrokostas, Paul .... New York, NY
Mitropoulos-Gonzalez, Maria C. .... North Miami Beach, FL
Mitroussia, Antonia .... Cincinnati, OH
Mitrovich, Julie E. .... Painesville, OH
Mitrovich, Milica .... Emeryville, CA
Mitrovich, Paul H. .... Painesville, OH
Mitrovich, Robert P. .... Los Angeles, CA
Mitsch, Rupert M. .... Department of Justice, Civil Division, GV
Mitschke, Marla Yvonne .... Houston, TX
Mitseff, Bradley S. .... Detroit, MI
Mitseff, C. Randall .... Detroit, MI
Mitseff, Carl .... Detroit, MI
Mitsopoulos, Sophie .... Akron, OH
Mitsos, Chris J. .... New Castle, PA
Mitsuhata, Grace N. .... Santa Monica, CA
Mitsumori, Jas. K. .... Los Angeles, CA
Mitsunaga, Darrell S. .... Seattle, WA
Mitsunaga, Jimi .... Salt Lake City, UT
Mitsuoka, Steven K. .... San Francisco, CA
Mittel, Asen, Hunter & Cary, LLC .... Portland, ME
Mittel, Robert E. .... Portland, ME
Mittelberg, Barry S. .... Coral Springs, FL
Mittelberger, Ralph A. .... Washington, DC
Mittelhauser, Jeff .... Sedalia, MO
Mittelholzer & Ferrini .... Dover, NH
Mittelholzer, George E. .... New Orleans, LA
Mittelholzer, Lisel M. .... Boston, MA
Mittelholzer, Robert T. .... Dover, NH
Mittelman, Alan Harvey .... Los Angeles, CA
Mittelman, Alan J. .... Philadelphia, PA
Mittelman, Deborah E. .... Phoenix, AZ
Mittelman, Helen M. .... New York, NY
Mittelman, Irwin D. .... Middletown, CT
Mittelman, Jenny K. .... Atlanta, GA
Mittelman, Mark R. .... Walnut Creek, CA
Mittelman, Mark R., P.C., Law Offices of .... Walnut Creek, CA
Mittelman, Neil .... Abington, PA; Philadelphia, PA
Mittelman, Richard S. .... Lake Zurich, IL
Mittelmark, Michael K. .... Boca Raton, FL
Mittelstadt, David J. .... Stamford, CT
Mittelstadt, Eric .... Salt Lake City, UT
Mittelstadt, Homer C. .... Cable, WI
Mittelstadt, Louis R. .... Long Beach, CA
Mittelstadt, Miles S. .... Green Bay, WI
Mittelstadt, Monica G. .... New York, NY
Mittelstadt and Moreno .... Long Beach, CA
Mittelstadt, Russell J. .... Monona, WI
Mittelstaedt, David J. .... Toledo, OH
Mittelstaedt, Earl A. .... Toledo, OH
Mittelstaedt, Henry J., III .... Rochester Hills, MI
Mittelstaedt, Robert A. .... San Francisco, CA
Mitten, Anthony D. .... Phoenix, AZ
Mitten, Bruce R. .... Onalaska, WI
Mitten, Holly .... Half Moon Bay, CA
Mitten, L. Russell .... Stamford, CT
Mitten, Nelson L. .... St. Louis, MO
Mitten, Raymond E., Jr. .... Department of Labor, GV
Mitten, Roger C. .... Phoenix, AZ; Tucson, AZ
Mittendorf, John H. .... Springfield, MO
Mittendorf, Larry G. .... Union, MO
Mittendorf, Richard K. .... Terrace Park, OH
Mittendorf, William J. .... Westlake, OH
Mittendorff, Robert E. .... Washington, DC
Mittenthal, Barry S. .... Atlanta, GA
Mittenthal, Freeman L. .... Dallas, TX
Mittenthal, Herbert B. .... Baltimore, MD
Mittenthal, James Peter .... Boston, MA
Mittenthal, Joshua M. .... Boca Raton, FL
Mittenthal, Peter A. .... Encino, CA
Mittenthal, Richard .... Bingham Farms, MI
Mitterhoff, Daniel J. .... Washington, DC
Mitterhoff Henrichsen & Stewart, P.L.L.C. .... Washington, DC; West Palm Beach, FL
Mitterhoff, Mary Louise .... Administrative Office Of The United States Courts, GV
Mitterhoff, Stephanie Ann .... Scotch Plains, NJ
Mitterling, Allen R. .... Modesto, CA
Mitterling, Sandra W. .... Raleigh, NC
Mittermaier, Ingrid P. .... San Francisco, CA
Mittermiller, James J. .... San Diego, CA
Mittin, Lawrence Elliot .... Las Vegas, NV
Mittin, Neil I. .... Philadelphia, PA
Mittledorf, Kenneth J. .... Nashville, TN
Mittleman, David M. .... Los Angeles, CA
Mittleman, David S. .... Lansing, MI
Mittleman, Elaine J. .... Falls Church, VA
Mittleman, Harry A. .... Los Angeles, CA
Mittleman, Irwin J. .... Maplewood, NJ
Mittleman, Jeffrey W. .... Waltham, MA
Mittleman, Lester S. .... Rochester, NY
Mittleman, Linda R. .... Cleveland, OH
Mittleman, Mark D. .... St. Louis, MO
Mittleman, Philip A. .... Bronx, NY
Mittleman & Pritel .... Sonoma, CA
Mittleman, Richard S. .... Providence, RI
Mittleman, Ronald A. .... Rochester, NY
Mittleman, Sheldon M. .... Universal City, CA
Mittleman, Steve Richard .... Sonoma, CA
Mittleman, Vivian W. .... National Transportation Safety Board, Office of the General Counsel, GV
Mittler, Austin S. .... Washington, DC
Mittler, Harvey D. .... Daly City, CA
Mittlesteadt, Carol L. .... Redwood City, CA
Mittman, Alan L. .... Mineola, NY
Mittman, Barbara Ruth .... New York, NY
Mittman, Benjamin .... New York, NY
Mittman, Dan A. .... New York, NY
Mittman, Ellyn Roth .... New York, NY
Mittman, Lawrence .... New York, NY
Mittman, Lee C. .... Columbus, OH
Mittman, Lee C., & Associates Co., L.P.A. .... Columbus, OH
Mittman & Liebman Associates .... Montgomeryville, PA
Mittman, Norman .... Montgomeryville, PA
Mittman, Robert J. .... New York, NY
Mittman, Scott A. .... Columbus, OH
Mitton, Andrew C. .... Anchorage, AK
Mitton & Burningham .... Newport Beach, CA; San Francisco, CA; Dallas, TX; **Salt Lake City, UT**
Mitton, Cyndi Jo .... San Diego, CA
Mitton, Jay W. .... Newport Beach, CA; San Francisco, CA; Dallas, TX; **Salt Lake City, UT**
Mittry, Andreas .... Redding, CA
Mitts, Eric .... Oklahoma City, OK
Mitts, F.W., III .... Meridian, MS
Mitts, Grace W. .... Meridian, MS
Mitts, Gregory H. .... Bakersfield, CA
Mitts, Harold W., Jr. .... Kansas City, MO
Mitts, Maurice R. .... Cherry Hill, NJ; Philadelphia, PA
Mittwede, Harry L. .... Nashville, TN
Mittweg, Christian H. .... New York, NY
Mitty, Samantha .... San Francisco, CA
Mitvalsky, Frank S. .... Cedar Rapids, IA
Mitvalsky, Franklin S. .... Moline, IL
Mitvalsky, Richard F. .... Cedar Rapids, IA
Mitwell, Milton .... Freeport, NY
Mitz, Daniel R. .... Palo Alto, CA
Mitz, Howard B. .... Mequon, WI
Mitz, Howard B., S.C. .... Mequon, WI
Mitz, Lisolette E. .... National Labor Relations Board, Office of the General Counsel, GV
Mitzel, Dennis M. .... Birmingham, MI; Detroit, MI
Mitzel, John W. .... Tampa, FL
Mitzel, Mitzel & Gray, P.A. .... Tampa, FL
Mitzel, Richard M. .... Tampa, FL
Mitzel, S. Monica .... Baltimore, MD
Mitzelfeld, James A. .... Department of Justice, Civil Division, GV
Mitzenmacher, Allen .... Chicago, IL
Mitzenmacher, Deborah .... Los Angeles, CA
Mitzman, Myra .... Oakland, CA
Mitzner, Adam D. .... New York, NY
Mitzner & Associates .... Edmond, OK
Mitzner, Bonnie M. .... Monticello, NY
Mitzner, David T. .... Denver, CO

Mock, Diana D. ...... Andalusia, AL
Mock, Donald J. ...... Chicago, IL
Mock, Douglas E. ...... Houston, TX
Mock, Eric V. ...... New York, NY
Mock, Frank M. ...... Orlando, FL
Mock, Frederic C. ...... Boston, MA
Mock, H. Byron ...... Salt Lake City, UT
Mock, James F. ...... Lexington, NC
Mock, James J. ...... St. Paul, MN
Mock, Janice Vaughn ...... Menlo Park, CA
Mock, John Franklin ...... Columbia, SC
Mock, Karen E. ...... Chicago, IL
Mock, Kathleen Daily ...... Philadelphia, PA
Mock, L. Patricia ...... Clarksville, TN
Mock, Linda S. ...... Atchison, KS
Mock, Mary Beth ...... Madison, IN
Mock, Michael L. ...... Des Moines, IA
Mock, R. John ...... Youngstown, OH
Mock, Randall D. ...... Oklahoma City, OK
Mock, Richard D. ...... Burnet, TX
Mock, Robert W., Sr. ...... Lawrenceville, GA
Mock, Ronald L. ...... Newberg, OR
Mock, Russell J., II ...... Cincinnati, OH
Mock, Sally ...... Oklahoma City, OK
Mock, Sandra Ford ...... Danville, CA
Mock, Schwabe, Waldo, Elder, Reeves & Bryant, A Prof. Limited Liability Co.
Oklahoma City, OK
Mock, Stephen L. ...... Woodland, CA
Mock, Steven P. ...... Houston, TX
Mock, T. Ryan, Jr. ...... Atlanta, GA
Mock, Terry L. ...... Tuscumbia, AL
Mock, Thomas B. ...... Dallas, TX
Mock, Valerie Henning
St. Clair Shores, MI
Mock, Walter E. ...... Wilmington, DE
Mock, William B.T., Jr. ...... Chicago, IL
Mockbee, Charles D., III ...... Danville, IL
Mockbee, David W. ...... Jackson, MS
Mockbee Hall & Drake, A Professional Association ...... Jackson, MS
Mockford, Phil ...... Austin, TX
Mockford, Philip D. ...... Austin, TX
Mockler, Dewey ...... Fort Myers, FL
Mockler, Dominic
Charlotte Amalie, St. Thomas, VI
Mockler, Frank C. ...... Boston, MA
Mockler, John T. ...... Dallas, TX
Mockler, Terri A. ...... Martinez, CA
Mockus, Joseph E. ...... Hayward, CA
Mocniak, Michael J. ...... North Chicago, IL
Moculeski, Karen C. ...... St. Louis, MO
Moczula, Boris ...... Paterson, NJ
Moczynski, Richard J. ...... Metuchen, NJ
Modabber, Zia F. ...... Los Angeles, CA
Modad & Miller ...... Houston, TX
Modad, Ralph A. ...... Houston, TX
Modafferi, Anthony K., III ...... Jersey City, NJ
Modafferi, Anthony K., III, P.C., & Assoc.
Jersey City, NJ
Modafferi, Silvio F. ...... Philadelphia, PA
Modafferi, Silvio F., P.C. ...... Philadelphia, PA
Modahl, William B. ...... Maynard, MA
Modak-Truran, Anita ...... Jackson, MS
Modansky, Michael C. ...... New York, NY
Modarelli, Jas. M., Jr. ...... Canfield, OH
Modarelli, Nicholas E. ...... Youngstown, OH
Modarelli, Paul J. ...... Hackensack, NJ
Moday, Juliana M. ...... New York, NY
Modder, J. Joseph ...... Los Angeles, CA
Moddes, Roger ...... Kenosha, WI
Mode, Gregory J. ...... Fort Atkinson, WI
Mode, Paul J., Jr. ...... Washington, DC
Modecker, Lisa A. Martinez ...... Boston, MA
Modecki, Carl A. ...... Arlington, VA
Modeer, Robert M. ...... Kansas City, MO
Model, Alan Ira ...... Roseland, NJ
Model, Alan L. ...... White Plains, NY
Model, Eric L. ...... Livingston, NJ
Model, Paul ...... New York, NY
Model, Rosanne ...... White Plains, NY
Modelewski, Christopher ...... Huntington, NY
Modell, Charles S. ...... Minneapolis, MN
Modell, David P. ...... Bethesda, MD
Modell, Edward G. ...... Washington, DC
Modell, Gerald P. ...... New York, NY
Modell, Jeffrey D. ...... Bingham Farms, MI
Modell, Jennifer ...... Brooklyn, NY
Modell, Karen L. ...... Rockville, MD
Modell, Michael S. ...... Long Island City, NY
Modell, Shira D. ...... Federal Trade Commission, Bureau of Consumer Protection, GV
Modelski, Alexander R. ...... Bellevue, WA
Modena, Daniel ...... South San Francisco, CA
Modena, Robert S. ...... Bayside, NY
Moder, William ...... Hermitage, PA
Moderi, William E. ...... Boston, MA
Moderow, Joseph R. ...... Atlanta, GA
Moderow, Richard C. ...... Franklin Lakes, NJ
Modersbach, Roger J. ...... Berkeley, CA
Moderson, Martin J. ...... Kansas City, MO
Modesett, Jack, III, Law Offices of
Corpus Christi, TX
Modesitt, Bough & Kelly ...... Terre Haute, IN
Modesitt, Fritz D. ...... Brazil, IN
Modesitt, Katherine L. ...... Indianapolis, IN
Modesitt, Leland E. ...... Littleton, CO
Modesitt, Nancy M. ...... McLean, VA
Modesitt, Raymond H. ...... Terre Haute, IN
Modesitt, Terry R. ...... Terre Haute, IN
Modesti, Claudius B. ...... Department of Justice, Criminal Division, GV
Modesti, Julian B. ...... Syracuse, NY
Modesti, Maryann Q. ...... Lafayette Hill, PA
Modestow, Lawrence E. ...... Boston, MA
Modgling, Maida Corder ...... Hondo, TX
Modgling, Maida Corder, P.C. ...... Hondo, TX
Modhera, Gazal G.
Equal Employment Opportunity Commission, Office of the General Counsel, GV
Modi, David T. ...... Washington, DC
Modi, Sarah ...... Phoenix, AZ
Modic, Victor M. ...... Charlottesville, VA
Modica, Andrew F. ...... Croton-On-Hudson, NY
Modica, Diane J. ...... Boston, MA
Modica, Donald A. ...... Lyndhurst, OH
Modica and Dowden ...... Baton Rouge, LA
Modica, Guy A., Sr. ...... Baton Rouge, LA
Modica, Michael W. ...... Odessa, DE
Wilmington, DE
Modica & Schmidt ...... Bay Shore, NY
Modica, Steven V. ...... Rochester, NY
Modica-Snow, Maria
Croton-On-Hudson, NY
Modig, Alan P. ...... Santa Ana, CA
Modigliani, Marta ...... Concord, NH
Modin, Richard F. ...... Kansas City, MO
Modine, Morgan M. ...... Missoula, MT
Modine & Thompson ...... Missoula, MT
Modisette, James P. ...... Los Angeles, CA
Ellsworth, ME
Modisette, Ruth ...... San Francisco, CA
Modisher, Christine ...... Nashville, TN
Modiste, Edward I. ...... Stoughton, MA
Modiste, Jacqueline ...... Quincy, MA
Modjeska, Lee ...... Raleigh, NC
Modjeski, Dennis C. ...... San Marino, CA
Modl, Michael J. ...... Madison, WI
Modla, Jacob J. ...... Charlotte, NC
Modla, Jane Pittman ...... Rock Hill, SC
Modlin, Charles M. ...... New York, NY
Modlin, Claire A. ...... Raleigh, NC
Modlin, Claudia R. ...... Sherman Oaks, CA
Modlin, Craig E. ...... San Francisco, CA
Modlin, Elihu H. ...... New York, NY
Modlin Haftel & Nathan LLP
New York, NY
Modlin, Howard S. ...... New York, NY
Modlin, James M. ...... New York, NY
Modlin, L. Ronald ...... Naples, FL
Modlin, Peter S. ...... San Francisco, CA
Modlin, Philip H. ...... Alexandria, VA
Modlin, Reginald R. ...... Trenton, MI
Modlin, Scott E. ...... Miami, FL
Modlin, Stacy M. ...... New York, NY
Modlin, Wendy Kreinen ...... New York, NY
Modney, Taras ...... Cleveland, OH
Modrall, James R., III ...... Traverse City, MI
Modrall, Sperling, Roehl, Harris & Sisk, P.A. ...... Alamogordo, NM
Albuquerque, NM
Las Cruces, NM
Roswell, NM
Santa Fe, NM
Modrcin, William M. ...... Kansas City, MO
Modry, Reneé ...... New York, NY
Modrzejewski, John ...... Rochester, MI
Modugno, Agatha M. ...... New York, NY
Modugno, Dominick ...... Stamford, CT
Modugno, Frank ...... Norwalk, CT
Modugno, Louis A. ...... Morristown, NJ
Modugno, Vincent R. ...... Akron, OH
Mody, Rajanikant C. ...... Jersey City, NJ
Mody, Renu N. ...... Miami, FL
Modzelewski, Dennis C. ...... Southfield, MI
Modzelewski, Ernest F. ...... Denver, CO
Modzelewski, James F. ...... Philadelphia, PA
Modzelewski, Patricia H.
New London, CT
Moe, Barbara J. ...... Corsicana, TX
Moe, Christine-Ann ...... Waukegan, IL
Moe, Dale J. ...... Minneapolis, MN
Moe, David L. ...... Maple Valley, WA
Moe, Debra K. ...... San Jose, CA
Moe, Dixie ...... North Hollywood, CA
Moe, James D. ...... Minneapolis, MN
Moe, Jerome R. ...... San Diego, CA
Moe, Jessica C. ...... Charleston, SC
Moe, John Arthur, II ...... Los Angeles, CA
Moe, Leroy H. ...... Fort Lauderdale, FL
Moe, Margaret J. ...... Los Angeles, CA
Moe, Martin T. ...... Washington, DC
Moe, Michael A. ...... Marina Del Rey, CA
Moe, Nancy K. ...... Missoula, MT
Moe, P. Arthur ...... Brooklyn Center, MN
Moe, Paul G. ...... Hartville, OH
Moe, Paul S. ...... Minneapolis, MN
Moe, Richard ...... New York, NY
Moe, Richard ...... Sioux Falls, SD
Moe, Ronald E. ...... Dixon, CA
Moe, Royce H. ...... Spokane, WA
Moe, Thomas O. ...... Portland, OR
Moe, Thomas O., (P.A.) ...... Minneapolis, MN
Moe, Thomas O., P.C. ...... Portland, OR
Moe, Thomas R. ...... Mayville, ND
Moe, Thomas S., Jr. ...... Denver, CO
Moe & York, PLLC ...... Corsicana, TX
Moebes, M. Anne ...... Santa Monica, CA
Moebius, Michelle L. ...... Los Angeles, CA
Moeckel, Jennifer Shea ...... Manchester, NH
Moeckler, Debbie L. ...... Chicago, IL
Moed, Louise A. ...... New York, NY
Moed, Peniel ...... Department of Defense, Armed Services Board of Contract Appeals, GV
Moede, Carole D. ...... Greenville, SC
Moede, G. Hans, III ...... Milwaukee, WI
Moeder, Randy E. ...... Oklahoma City, OK
Moedritzer, Mark ...... Kansas City, MO
Moegenburg, Frederick A. ...... Milwaukee, WI
Moegerle, Heidi L. ...... Indianapolis, IN
Moehle, Carm R. ...... Phoenix, AZ
Moehle, Carm R., P.C. ...... Phoenix, AZ
Moehle, Edward C. ...... Pekin, IL
Moehle, Melvin O. ...... Washington, IL
Moehle, Robert C. ...... Oregon, IL
Moehle, Smith, Nieman, Hanson & Hahn, P.C. ...... Byron, IL
Mount Morris, IL
Oregon, IL
Moehle, Swearingen & Umholtz, Ltd.
Pekin, IL
Washington, IL
Moehle, Walter E. ...... Okawville, IL
Moehle, William W. ...... Rochester, NY
Moehling, James A. ...... Chicago, IL
Moehlman, Albert E. ...... Bloomfield Hills, MI
Moehlman, Denise B. ...... Los Angeles, CA
Moehlman, Herman ...... Northville, MI
Moehlman, Michael S. (IBA) ...... **Houston, TX**
Moehlman, Theresa A. ...... New York, NY
Moehlmann, Holly E.
Department Of Veterans Affairs, Board of Veterans Appeals, GV
Moehlmann, Robbie A. ...... Houston, TX
Moehl-McClelland, Denise
San Francisco, CA
Moehring, Boyd ...... Columbus, OH
Moehring, Cynthia P. ...... Phoenix, AZ
Moehring, Galyn W. ...... Rockford, IL
Moehringer, John T. ...... New York, NY
Moehrke, Anton T. ...... Boston, MA
Moehrke, Mackie & Shea, P.C.
Boston, MA
Moehrke, Scott A. ...... Milwaukee, WI
Moel, Marc D. ...... New York, NY
Moeling, Walter G., IV ...... Atlanta, GA
Moelis, Herbert ...... New York, NY
Moelis, Laurence S. ...... New York, NY
Moelk, James F. ...... Fairfield, CA
Moellenberg, Charles H., Jr.
Pittsburgh, PA
Moellenberg, Dalva L. ...... Phoenix, AZ
Moellenberg, Jon ...... Denver, CO
Moellenberg, Karen N. (Gittler)
Upper St. Clair, PA
Moeller, Armand D. ...... Minneapolis, MN
Moeller, Armin J., Jr. ...... Jackson, MS
Moeller, Chad W. ...... Chicago, IL
Moeller, C.J. ...... Joplin, MO
Moeller, David R. ...... St. Paul, MN
Moeller, Deborah A. ...... Kansas City, MO
Moeller, Donald R. ...... Newberg, OR
Moeller, Elizabeth C. ...... Los Angeles, CA
Moeller, Emily M. ...... Portland, OR
Moeller, Erick F. ...... Roanoke, VA
Moeller, F. Douglas ...... Farmington, NM
Moeller, Galen A. ...... San Angelo, TX
Moeller, George F. ...... Cincinnati, OH
Moeller, Gregory W. ...... Rexburg, ID
Moeller, Harold C. ...... New York, NY
Moeller, Ingrid A. ...... Denver, CO
Moeller, J. Michael ...... Tucson, AZ
Moeller, James ...... Phoenix, AZ
Moeller, James C.A. ...... Joppa, MD
Moeller, James L. ...... Kansas City, MO
Moeller, James W. ...... Washington, DC
Moeller, Jeffrey E. ...... Washington, DC
Moeller, Jeffrey S. ...... Anchorage, AK
Moeller, Joanne Lee ...... Des Moines, IA
Moeller, John E., Jr. ...... Dallas, TX
Moeller, John O. ...... Davenport, IA
Moeller, John R., Jr. ...... Wall Township, NJ
Moeller, John S. ...... Sioux City, IA
Moeller, Karl H. ...... Austin, TX
Moeller, Kenneth R. ...... Tucson, AZ
Moeller, Lesley E. ...... New York, NY
Moeller, Linda D. ...... Baltimore, MD
Moeller, Lon D. ...... Madison, WI
Moeller, M. Ted ...... Tucson, AZ
Moeller, Marguerite M. ...... Madison, WI
Moeller, Mark R. ...... Newark, NJ
Moeller, Michael D. ...... Kansas City, MO
Moeller, Patrick G. ...... Hamilton, OH
Moeller, Paul H. ...... Los Angeles, CA
Moeller, Raymond H. ...... Willowbrook, IL
Moeller, Regis J. ...... Pittsburgh, PA
Moeller, Renée E. ...... Houston, TX
Moeller, Renée E., & Associates
Houston, TX
Moeller, Richard H. ...... Sioux City, IA
Moeller, Robert A. ...... West Seneca, NY
Moeller, Robert B., (P.A.) ...... Cross City, FL
Moeller, Sheila AnnMarie ...... New York, NY
Moeller, Stephen F. ...... Los Angeles, CA
Moeller, Susan J. ...... Cincinnati, OH
Moeller, Thomas R. ...... Evergreen, CO
Moeller, Walter S. ...... Dayton, NV
Moeller, William A. ...... New Ulm, MN
Moeller, William D. ...... Tulsa, OK
Moeller, William F. ...... Victoria, TX
Moellering, John J. ...... St. Louis, MO
Moellering, Michael C. ...... Fort Wayne, IN
Moelling, Kay D. ...... Fort Worth, TX
Moelling, Kirt E. ...... Amarillo, TX
Moellring, Marcia L. ...... Hannibal, MO
Moelmann, Lawrence R. ...... Chicago, IL
Moelter, Kristina ...... Bismarck, ND
Moen, Bruce R. ...... Seattle, WA
Moen, Cain & O'Brien ...... Houston, TX
Moen, Chad L. ...... Columbia, MO
Moen, Christopher M. ...... Los Angeles, CA
Moen, Christopher P. ...... Williamsville, NY
Moen, Daniel R. ...... Aberdeen, SD
Moen, David J. ...... Jefferson City, MO
Moen, Eugene M. ...... Seattle, WA
Moen, Guy T. ...... Wailuku, HI
Moen, Jacqueline M. ...... Minneapolis, MN
Moen, James W. ...... Minneapolis, MN
Moen, Joyce L. ...... Seattle, WA
Moen, Kenneth R. ...... Rochester, MN
Moen, Marc B. ...... Iowa City, IA
Moen, Mary Ann D. ...... Cumberland, MD
Moen, Michael S. ...... La Crosse, WI
Moen, Monica ...... Boise, ID
Moen, Richard J.
General Services Administration, Office of Regional Counsel, GV
Moen, Richard S. ...... La Crosse, WI
Moen, Robert A. ...... Houston, TX
Moen, Scott P. ...... St. Paul, MN
Moen, Sheehan, Meyer, Ltd.
La Crosse, WI
Moen, Steve Paul ...... Seattle, WA
Moen & Sullivan ...... Williamsville, NY
Moench, Dale W. ...... Bismarck, ND
Moench, Douglas J., Jr. ...... Cheyenne, WY
Moench, Malin G. ...... Postal Rate Commission, Office of the General Counsel, GV
Moench, Mark C. ...... Salt Lake City, UT
Moench, William E. ...... St. Louis, MO
Moench, William G., Jr. ...... Fabius, NY
Lafayette, NY
Moenckmeier, Jeanene ...... Irvine, CA
Moening, Ronald S. ...... Toledo, OH
Moennich, James W. ...... Lorain, OH
Moenning, Elizabeth P. ...... Merrillville, IN
Moenning, Richard C. ...... Chicago, IL
Moens, Thomas O. ...... Moline, IL
Moenssens, Susan G. ...... Kilmarnock, VA
Moentmann, Werner A. ...... Richmond, MO
Moerbeek, Stanley L. ...... Fullerton, CA
Moerdler, Charles G. ...... New York, NY
Moerdler, Jeffrey A. ...... New York, NY
Moerdyke, Carl B., & Associates
Palo Alto, CA
Moerer, Brent C. ...... Oskaloosa, KS
Moerer & Burton, L.L.P. ...... Houston, TX
Moerer, Carl H., Jr. ...... Houston, TX
Moerke, Ewald L., Jr.
Menomonee Falls, WI
Moerlein Law Offices ...... Knox, IN
South Bend, IN
Moerlein, Steven J. ...... Knox, IN
South Bend, IN
Moerman, Filip ...... New York, NY
Moerman, Samuel H. ...... Washington, DC
Moermond, Jack E. ...... Midland, MI
Moermond, James O., III ...... Wausau, WI
Moermond, Kim I. ...... Madison, WI
Moers, Andrew N. ...... New York, NY
Moers, Stacy L. ...... Philadelphia, PA
Moersch, Nancy L. ...... St. Paul, MN
Moersch, Ronald L. ...... Northfield, MN
Moerschbaecher, Lynda S.
San Francisco, CA
Moerschel, Rollin J. ...... St. Louis, MO
Moersfelder, Edward M. ...... Mankato, MN
Moersfelder, Karel L. M. ...... Minneapolis, MN
Moershel, Diane C. ...... Oklahoma City, OK
Moershel, Diane C., P.C.
Oklahoma City, OK
Moertl, Jack D. ...... Milwaukee, WI
Moertl, Katie A. ...... Oak Brook, IL
Moertl, Wilkins & Campbell, S.C.
Milwaukee, WI
Moes, Brian ...... Orlando, FL
Moes, Harvey W. ...... Hillsdale, MI
Moes, Jacqueline A. ...... Oak Park, IL
Moes, Kenneth L. ...... Santa Barbara, CA
Moes, Lacy N. ...... Santa Barbara, CA
Moeschl, Deborah M. ...... Hopkins, MN
Moeschl, Dennis L. ...... Indianapolis, IN
Moesel, Frederick C., Jr. ...... Rosemont, PA
Moesel, Peter A. ...... Bronxville, NY
Moeser, Erica ...... Madison, WI
Moeser, Lillian R. ...... Bremen, GA
Moeser, William O. ...... Springfield, VT
Moeslinger, Otto ...... Little Neck, NY
Moesser, Dean M. ...... Houston, TX
Moest, Robert C. ...... Redondo Beach, CA
Moetell, Michael C. ...... Washington, DC
Moettus, Alda L. ...... Albuquerque, NM
Moeves, Patrick E. ...... Covington, KY
Moewe, Parke W. ...... Rancho Palos Verdes, CA
Moewes, Denice E. ...... Seattle, WA
Moezie, Minna F. ...... Department of Commerce, Patent and Trademark Office, GV
Mofenson, David J. ...... Newton, MA
Mofenson & Nicoletti ...... Boston, MA
Newton, MA
Moffa, Donna Siegel ...... Cherry Hill, NJ
Moffa, John S. ...... Hyannis, MA
Moffa, Joseph C. ...... Fort Lauderdale, FL
Moffa, Louis R., Jr. ...... Cherry Hill, NJ
Moffa & Mulligan ...... Hyannis, MA
Moffat, Diana L. ...... Salem, OR
Moffat & Dicharry ...... Albuquerque, NM
Moffat, Donald ...... Wilbraham, MA
Moffat, Edward P., II ...... Madera, CA
Moffat, Gerald ...... Marietta, GA
Moffat, Henry M. ...... Pacific Palisades, CA
Moffat, J. Kelly ...... Los Angeles, CA
Moffat, Jeffrey C. ...... Los Angeles, CA
Moffat, John R. ...... Mount Vernon, WA
Moffat, Keith M. ...... New York, NY
Moffat, Kenneth M. ...... Lincoln, RI
Moffat, Laura Yoshino ...... Honolulu, HI
Moffat, Marian M. (Mimi)
Kansas City, MO
Moffat, Mark R. ...... Salt Lake City, UT
Moffat, Michele J. ...... Wilson, WY
Moffat, Robert C. L. ...... Gainesville, FL
Moffat, Stephen A. ...... Albuquerque, NM
Moffat, Travis W., P.C. ...... Lander, WY
Moffatt, Brett P. ...... San Francisco, CA
Moffatt, Brian T. ...... Houston, TX
Moffatt, Charles K. ...... Erie, PA
Moffatt, Charles L. ...... Bristol, TN
Moffatt, D. Kevin ...... Charleston, WV

Moffatt, J. Curtis ... Washington, DC
Moffatt, James D. ... Athens, AL
Moffatt, James R. ... Mineola, NY
Moffatt, Jonathan A. ... Knoxville, TN
Moffatt, Keith E. ... Charleston, WV
Moffatt, Kevin L. ... Mount Clemens, MI
Moffatt, Lora A. ... New York, NY
Moffatt, Maura Griffith ... Boston, MA
Moffatt, Michael A. ... Indianapolis, IN
Moffatt, Michael J. ... Irvine, CA
Moffatt, Nancy Norman ... Indianapolis, IN
Moffatt, Robert B. ... Pine City, MN
Moffatt, Robert J. ... Shreveport, LA
Moffatt Thomas Barrett Rock & Fields, Chartered ... Boise, ID
Idaho Falls, ID
Pocatello, ID
Moffatt, Thomas S. ... Woonsocket, RI
Moffatt, Timothy J. ... Fort Lauderdale, FL
Moffatt, William D. ... Vilas, NC
Moffeit, Michael P. ... El Paso, TX
Moffeit, Michael P., A Professional Corporation ... El Paso, TX
Moffet & Alexander, P.A. West Palm Beach, FL
Moffet, Beverly L. ... Cleveland, OH
Moffet, Brian L. ... Baltimore, MD
Moffet, Diane J. ... Roslyn, NY
Moffet, John A., Jr. ... Fairfax, VA
Moffet, Kenneth W. ... West Palm Beach, FL
Moffet, Michael C. ... United States Senate, Senatorial Assistants, GV
Moffet, Stacey A. ... Baltimore, MD
Moffet, Susan C. ... Portland, OR
Moffet, Victoria K. ... Enterprise, OR
Moffet, William M. ... Abingdon, VA
Moffett, Amy E. ... Los Angeles, CA
Moffett & Associates, P.C. ... Tulsa, OK
Moffett, Christine M. ... New York, NY
Moffett, David B. ... Orlando, FL
Moffett & Dillon, A Professional Corporation Birmingham, MI
Detroit, MI
Columbus, OH
Moffett, F. Glenn, Jr. ... Atlanta, GA
Moffett, Glen D. ... York, PA
Moffett, Gregory A. ... Concord, NH
Moffett, Harry McClellan, IV Monroe, LA
Moffett, Howard M. ... Concord, NH
Moffett, J. Denny ... Tulsa, OK
Moffett, John C. ... Rockville, MD
Moffett, Joseph B. ... Fayette, MS
Moffett, Kenneth E., Jr. ... New York, NY
Moffett, Larry D. ... Oxford, MS
Moffett Law Firm, P.C. ... Atlanta, GA
Moffett, M. Ellen ... Philadelphia, PA
Moffett, Matthew G. ... Atlanta, GA
Moffett, Michael J. ... Atlanta, GA
Moffett, Robert K. ... New Orleans, LA
Moffett, Robert T. ... Houston, TX
Moffett, Samuel L. ... Tucson, AZ
Moffett, Stephen T. ... Birmingham, MI
Columbus, OH
Moffett, Susan F. ... Leesburg, VA
Moffett, T.K. ... Tupelo, MS
Moffett, Todd A. ... Newark, NJ
Moffett, Vickie N. ... Chicago, IL
Moffett, Wm. S., Jr. ... Staunton, VA
Moffic-Silver, Joanne ... Chicago, IL
Moffitt, Brenda A. ... Boston, MA
Moffitt, Brian Edward ... Morristown, NJ
Moffitt, Christopher S., P.C. Alexandria, VA
Moffitt, Christopher S. ... Alexandria, VA
Moffitt, David James ... Boston, MA
Moffitt, David L. ... Bingham Farms, MI
Moffitt, David R. ... Aurora, CO
Moffitt, David R. ... Philadelphia, PA
Moffitt, Donna Dutty ... Raleigh, NC
Moffitt, Earle W. ... Tampa, FL
Moffitt, Earle W., P.A. ... Tampa, FL
Moffitt, Franklin G. ... Dallas, TX
Moffitt, Frederick V. ... Austin, TX
Moffitt, H. Lee ... Tallahassee, FL
Tampa, FL
Moffitt, H. Lee, P.A. ... Tallahassee, FL
Tampa, FL
Moffitt, J. Walter ... Nashville, TN
Moffitt, Jack A., Jr. ... Dallas, TX
Moffitt, Jack & Associates, P.C. ... Dallas, TX
Moffitt, James E. ... Nashville, TN
Moffitt, Jane A. ... Redwood City, CA
Moffitt, John P. ... Los Angeles, CA
Moffitt, John R. ... Prescott, AZ
Moffitt, Marilyn A. ... Oakland, CA
Moffitt, Richard L. ... Marblehead, MA
Moffitt, Robert E. ... Fort Mitchell, KY
Moffitt, Ronald G. ... Salt Lake City, UT
Moffitt, Terrence F. ... St. Louis, MO
Moffitt, Thomas D., III ... Treasury Department, Internal Revenue Service, GV
Moffitt, Thomas F. ... Raleigh, NC
Moffitt, Thomas G. ... Chicago, IL
Moffitt, Verden Mardell ... Whittier, CA
Moffitt, Weagant & Loo LLP Los Angeles, CA
Moffitt, William A., Jr. ... Creve Coeur, MO
Moffitt, William B. ... Washington, DC
Moffitt, William R. ... Redlands, CA
Mog, Cynthia C. ... Cleveland, OH
Mog, Willis L. ... Lebanon, IL
Moga, Thomas Traian ... Troy, MI
Moga, Thomas W. ... Rancho Cucamonga, CA
Mogab, Charles A. ... St. Louis, MO
Mogab, Gerard C. ... Denver, CO
Mogab & Hughes, P.C. ... St. Louis, MO
Mogab, Nancy R. ... St. Louis, MO
Mogabgab, Stephen A. ... Covington, LA
New Orleans, LA
Mogan, Angela C. ... Houston, TX
Mogan, James F., III ... Atlantic City, NJ
Mogan, James F., III ... Philadelphia, PA
Mogan, Michael F. ... Seattle, WA
Mogan-Kulinski, M. Patricia ... Cordova, TN
Mogannam, Jamal F. ... San Francisco, CA
Mogavero, Albert J. ... Buffalo, NY
Mogavero, Bruce K. ... Yonkers, NY
Mogavero, Leona ... Philadelphia, PA
Mogavero, Robert F. ... St. Petersburg, FL
Mogck, Steven A. ... Minneapolis, MN
Mogel, David L. ... Atlanta, GA
New York, NY
Mogel, Frederick R. ... Reading, PA
Mogel, Greg C. ... Hartford, CT
Mogel, Jason ... New York, NY
Mogel, Murray ... New York, NY
Mogel, Ronald D. ... Houston, TX
Mogel, Speidel, Bobb & Kershner, A Professional Corporation ... Reading, PA
Mogel, William A. ... Washington, DC
Mogen, Philip C. ... Albuquerque, NM
Mogensen, Andrea M. ... St. Charles, IL
Mogensen, Eric ... Campbell, CA
Mogensen, Lauren A. ... Boston, MA
Mogensen, Orville L. ... Bethlehem, PA
Moger, Daniel W., Jr. ... Greenwich, CT
Moger, John A. ... Sacramento, CA
Moger, Peggy Ann ... West Sacramento, CA
Mogerman, Cary J. ... St. Louis, MO
Mogford, John L., Jr. (P.C.) San Antonio, TX
Moghadam, Sara Z. ... Washington, DC
Moghadassi, Ramyar ... New York, NY
Moghaddam, B. Alexander Long Beach, CA
Moghimi, Golnar Yazdi ... Menlo Park, CA
Moghrabi & Larkin ... New York, NY
Moghrabi, Zuhayr A. ... New York, NY
Moghtader, Karen Jill ... Concord, CA
Mogielnicki, Marion S. ... Westfield, NJ
Mogil, B. Marc ... Mineola, NY
Mogil, David ... St. Charles, MO
Mogil, Gary M. ... San Mateo, CA
Mogil, Lisa C. ... Austin, TX
Mogilka, Henry J. ... Edmond, OK
Mogill, Kenneth M. ... Detroit, MI
Mogill, Posner & Cohen ... Detroit, MI
Mogilnicki, Eric J. ... Washington, DC
Mogin, Angela M. ... San Diego, CA
Mogin, Daniel J. ... San Diego, CA
Mogin, Joshua ... New York, NY
Mogin Law Firm, The, P.C. San Diego, CA
Mogin, Paul ... Washington, DC
Mogk, John E. ... Detroit, MI
Moglen, Eben ... New York, NY
Moglen, Leland ... Auburn, CA
Moglia, Alejandro D. ... Schaumburg, IL
Moglin, Neal J. ... Chicago, IL
Moglovkin, Thomas C. ... Malibu, CA
Moglowsky, Arthur M. ... Milwaukee, WI
Moglowsky, Steven W. ... Milwaukee, WI
Mogol, Alan J. ... Baltimore, MD
Mogor, Cornelia ... Albany, NY
Mograss, Melissa A. ... Boulder, CO
Mogren, Linda G. ... Sycamore, IL
Mogren, Peter W. ... Renton, WA
Mogul, David ... Boca Raton, FL
Mogul, Edward ... Chicago, IL
Mogul, James B. ... Bensalem, PA
Mogul, Martin H. ... Woodland Hills, CA
Mogul & Mogul ... Chicago, IL
Mogul, S. Stacy ... Philadelphia, PA
Mogul, Steven J. ... Bangor, ME
Mogulescu, Miles V. ... Los Angeles, CA
Mogulescu, Sara ... New York, NY
Moh, Sangwook ... New York, NY
Mohajery, Barbara Ann ... Pittsburgh, PA
Mohamed, Aneezal H. ... Dearborn, MI
Mohammad, Christina A. ... Harrisburg, PA
Mohammadbhoy, Adam ... Bradenton, FL
Mohammed, Philip F. ... Tacoma, WA
Mohammed, Sandra Anne ... New York, NY
Mohammed-Derzaph, Wendy Los Angeles, CA
Mohan, Alewelt, Prillaman & Adami Springfield, IL
Mohan, Anne M. ... Parsippany, NJ
Mohan, Anthony J. ... Crownsville, MD
Mohan, Catherine Ann ... Hartford, CT
Mohan, Daniel J. ... Atlanta, GA
Mohan, Daniel J. ... Chicago, IL
Mohan, J. Patrick ... Decatur, IL
Mohan, James T. ... Springfield, IL
Mohan, John C. ... Pittsburgh, PA
Mohan, John J. ... Streator, IL
Mohan, John J. ... St. Louis, MO
Mohan, John & Richard ... Streator, IL
Mohan, Richd. A. ... Streator, IL
Mohan, Rose E. ... Fresno, CA
Mohan, Sheila R. ... Sacramento, CA
Mohan, Theresa K. ... Armonk, NY
Mohan, Thomas J. ... Detroit, MI
Mohan, Timothy P. ... Chicago, IL
Mohanty, Nihar R. ... Washington, DC
Mohanty & Rothmel, LLC ... Voorhees, NJ
Mohanty, Sujeet K. ... Voorhees, NJ
Mohanty, Yasodhara ... Oklahoma City, OK
Mohapatra, Lok ... Harrisburg, PA
Philadelphia, PA
Mohar, Gregory ... Cincinnati, OH
Mohar, Melanie W. ... Cleveland, OH
Moharram, Shereef ... Los Angeles, CA
Mohbat, Joseph E. ... Brooklyn, NY
Moheban, Keith S. ... St. Paul, MN
Moheban, Steven M. ... Boston, MA
Mohel, S. Karl ... Toms River, NJ
Moheno, Victor B. ... Visalia, CA
Moher & Cannello, P.C. ... Newberry, MI
Sault Ste. Marie, MI
Moher, James M. ... Glastonbury, CT
Hartford, CT
Moher, James P. ... San Francisco, CA
Moher, Thomas C. ... Dover, NH
Moher, Thomas G. ... Newberry, MI
Sault Ste. Marie, MI
Moher, Timothy S. ... Newberry, MI
Sault Ste. Marie, MI
Mohi, Gary ... Los Angeles, CA
Mohill, Alan L. ... Temecula, CA
Mohin, Brian J. ... Collingswood, NJ
Philadelphia, PA
Mohindra, Gitanjali ... Burlingame, CA
Mohip, Aminie ... Tampa, FL
Mohiuddin, Cynthia Ingrid Lake Oswego, OR
Mohiuddin, Maria ... San Francisco, CA
Mohl, Bruce E. ... Concord, NH
Mohl, Douglas C. ... Cincinnati, OH
Mohl, Lary W. ... St. Louis, MO
Mohl, Marvin ... Issaquah, WA
Mohlar, Philip G. ... Norridgewock, ME
Möhle, Lindsey A. ... New York, NY
Mohlenhoff, Dale G. ... Indianapolis, IN
Mohlenhoff, Edward C. ... Garden City, NY
Mohler, Bradley K. ... Frankfort, IN
Mohler, Dan ... Colorado Springs, CO
Mohler, Dan, P.C. ... Colorado Springs, CO
Mohler, David A. ... Charleston, WV
Mohler, Dina M. ... Charleston, WV
Mohler, Harold Roderick ... Union, WV
Mohler, Jean Smith ... Washington, DC
Mohler, Jeanie J. ... Spokane, WA
Mohler, Jeffrey D. ... Lancaster, PA
Mohler Law Office ... Toledo, OH
Mohler, Mark R. ... Orlando, FL
Mohler, Martin E. ... Toledo, OH
Mohler, Nancy LeCroy ... Raleigh, NC
Mohler, Nancy Rizzo ... Washington, DC
Mohler, Paul B. Federal Energy Regulatory Commission, Office of the General Counsel, GV
Mohler, Richard H. ... Harveyville, KS
Mohler, Richard M. ... Lewistown, PA
Mohler, Robert E. ... Akron, OH
Mohler, Sandra Schuffert Hattiesburg, MS
Mohler, Shaun C. ... Washington, DC
Mohler, Susan J. ... Lexington, KY
Mohler, William E. ... Charleston, WV
Mohler, William E., III ... Charleston, WV
Mohling, T. Andrew ... Tucson, AZ
Mohlman, Don T. ... Seattle, WA
Mohlman, Frank T. ... Tooele, UT
Mohlman, Jay R. ... Salt Lake City, UT
Mohlman, Michael J. ... Kansas City, MO
Mohlman & Young ... Tooele, UT
Mohmand, Sheri Renee' ... South Haven, MI
Mohn, J. Peter ... Seal Beach, CA
Mohn and Kauer ... Estherville, IA
Mohn, Marvin D. ... Los Angeles, CA
Mohn, Maynard M. ... Estherville, IA
Mohn, Nell J. ... Buffalo, NY
Mohn, W. Scott ... Columbia, MD
Mohnacs, John P. ... Sharon Hill, PA
Mohney, C. Blair ... Grand Rapids, MI
Mohney, Christopher E. ... Du Bois, PA
Mohney, D. Scott ... Newport Beach, CA
Mohney, Douglas D. ... Cape Coral, FL
Mohney, Mark W. ... Pittsburgh, PA
Mohney, Marvin R. ... Dallas, TX
Mohnkern, Ann H. ... Portland, ME
Mohnsam, Lisa Ellis ... Cincinnati, OH
Mohoney, James A. ... Woodbridge, NJ
Mohorek, Ronald E. ... Milwaukee, WI
Mohoroski, John E. ... Corona, CA
Mohr, Aline L. ... Mequon, WI
Mohr & Anderson, S.C. ... Hartford, WI
Mohr, Andrew J. ... Washington, DC
Mohr, Anthony J. ... Van Nuys, CA
Mohr & Associates, P.C. ... Houston, TX
Mohr, Bradley ... Albany, NY
Mohr, Brian C. ... Washington, DC
Mohr, Carolyn Nicander ... Plainsboro, NJ
Mohr, Christopher A. ... Washington, DC
Mohr, David M. ... Toledo, OH
Mohr, Derek J. ... Buffalo, NY
Mohr, Elaine G. ... Skokie, IL
Mohr, Frederick J. ... Green Bay, WI
Mohr, Frederick J., S.C. ... Green Bay, WI
Mohr, Gordon A. ... Phoenix, AZ
Mohr, Gordon G. (Jeff) ... Bloomington, MN
Mohr, Hackett, Pederson, Blakley & Randolph, P.C. ... Phoenix, AZ
Mohr, J. Gary ... Oceanport, NJ
Mohr, Jacqueline M. ... Phoenix, AZ
Mohr, James W., Jr. ... Hartford, WI
Mohr, Jeffrey T. ... Sheboygan, WI
Mohr, Jeremy G., Esq. ... Beverly Hills, CA
Mohr, John E. S. ... Maumee, OH
Mohr, John L. ... Laurel, MT
Mohr, John P. ... Arlington, VA
Mohr, John R. ... Dayton, OH
Mohr, Joseph A. ... Houston, TX
Mohr, Kathryn M. ... Adrian, MI
Toledo, OH
Mohr, Kevin D. ... Corpus Christi, TX
Mohr, Kevin E. ... Fullerton, CA
Mohr, Larraine ... Rye, NY
Mohr, Lee R. ... Indian Wells, CA
Mohr, Lee R., A Prof. Corp., Law Offices of Indian Wells, CA
Palm Desert, CA
Palm Springs, CA
Mohr, Lenore Kramer ... Union, NJ
Mohr, Mark ... Union, NJ
Mohr, Michael ... Ada, MI
Mohr, Nancy A. ... Redondo Beach, CA
Mohr, Onita ... Des Moines, IA
Mohr, Pamela K. ... Seattle, WA
Mohr, Paul J. ... Wichita, KS
Mohr, Philip J. ... Winston-Salem, NC
Mohr, Polly Stephenson ... Kokomo, IN
Mohr, Reinhard ... Honolulu, HI
Mohr, Robert H. ... Sun City Center, FL
Mohr, Samuel A. ... Cleveland, OH
Mohr, Stephen F. ... Princeton, NJ
Mohr, Terry R. ... McHenry, IL
Mohr, Thomas P. ... West Chester, PA
Mohr, Tina L. ... Rochester, MN
Mohr, Tom, Law Office, P.C. West Chester, PA
Mohr, William H. ... New York, NY
Mohr, William W. ... Naperville, IL
Mohrbacher, Jean M. ... South Pasadena, CA
Mohre, Elizabeth Howard ... New Orleans, LA
Mohrer, Katrina Borchers ... Laredo, TX
Mohrfeld, Eileen M. ... Philadelphia, PA
Mohrfeld, Jan M. ... Des Moines, IA
Mohrfeld, John H., III ... Cherry Hill, NJ
Mohrhauser, Jeffrey R. ... Sioux City, IA
Mohrhauser, Thomas R. ... Mapleton, IA
Mohring, Andrew H. ... Minneapolis, MN
Mohrman, Christopher C. Milwaukee, WI
Mohrman, Henry J. ... St. Louis, MO
Mohrman, Henry J. (Joe), Jr. St. Louis, MO
Mohrman, Joel W. ... Houston, TX
Mohrman, Michael K. ... Salt Lake City, UT
Mohrman-Gillis, Marilyn ... Washington, DC
Mohr-Ramirez, Karen ... New York, NY
Mohs, Daniel L. ... St. Louis, MO
St. Louis, MO
Mohs, Doreen A. ... Minneapolis, MN
Mohs, Frederic E. ... Madison, WI
Mohs, MacDonald, Widder & Paradise Madison, WI
Mohsen, Arya A. ... Washington, DC
Mohsenzadeh, Jafar ... Los Angeles, CA
Mohsin, Mobina F. ... Boston, MA
Mohtadi, Negin ... Washington, DC
Mohtares, Paul A. ... Dallas, TX
Mohun, Fred J. ... Santa Ana, CA
Mohun, Gerald Fitzgibbon, Jr. Mammoth Lakes, CA
Mohun, Paul R. ... San Francisco, CA
Mohundro, Charles W. ... Texarkana, TX
Mohylsky, Katherine A. ... Cincinnati, OH
Moidel, Shari L. ... New York, NY
Moilanen, Jason T. ... Omaha, NE
Moilanen, Philip M. ... Jackson, MI
Moilanen, Robert C. ... Minneapolis, MN
Moin, Cheryl R. Eisberg ... New York, NY
Moin, Linda J. ... Redwood City, CA
Moine, Pamela A. ... Pensacola, FL
Moinester & Hafner ... Lynbrook, NY
Moinester, Robert ... Lynbrook, NY
Moir, Bradford B. ... Westfield, MA
Moir, Brian R. ... Washington, DC
Moir & Brodich, P.A. ... Concord, NH
Moir, Bruce D. ... Portland, ME
Moir & Hardman ... Washington, DC
Moir, James H. ... Concord, NH
Moir, Katharine P. ... New York, NY
Moir, Keith E. ... Dearborn Heights, MI
Moir, Keith E. ... Detroit, MI
Moir, Linda Tucker ... Sandusky, OH
Moir, Maria I. ... Huntington, NY
Moir, Peter A. ... Dallas, TX
Moir, Peter J., Jr. ... Ypsilanti, MI
Moir, Robert G. ... Union Lake, MI
Moir, Robert J. ... Dundee, MI
Moir, Robert K. ... Alexandria, VA
Moir & Ross ... Westfield, MA
Moir & Saltz, LLP ... Huntington, NY
Moir, Vickie L. ... Raleigh, NC
Moir, William W., III ... Sheboygan, WI
Moirano, Michael H. ... Chicago, IL
Moisa, Alex M. ... Whittier, CA
Moisa, Irma Rodriguez ... Los Angeles, CA
Moisan, Cynthia M. ... Des Moines, IA
Moise & Co. ... Albuquerque, NM
Moise, E. Warren ... Charleston, SC
Moïse, Elizabeth Scott ... Columbia, SC
Moise, F. Marion, III ... Charleston, SC
Moise, Guy R. ... North Miami, FL
Moise, Harold A., Jr. ... Metairie, LA
Moïse, Philip H. ... Atlanta, GA
Moise, Steven K. ... Albuquerque, NM
Moise, William Gowan ... Tucker, GA
Moiseeff, Gregory ... Burbank, CA
Moiseev, Susan M. ... Southfield, MI
Moiseyev, Michael R. Federal Trade Commission, Bureau of Competition, GV
Moisio, Mary V. ... Tucson, AZ
Moison, Peter R. ... Denver, CO
Moister, Roger W., Jr. ... Atlanta, GA
Moister, Roger W., Jr., P.C. ... Atlanta, GA
Mojares-Moore, Maricel San Francisco, CA
Chicago, IL
Mojcher, J. Jeffrey ... San Francisco, CA
Mojdehi, Ali M. M. ... San Diego, CA
Mojibi, Kathy ... Pasadena, CA
Mojiri-Azad, R. Lisa ... Washington, DC
Mojock, David T. ... New Castle, PA

Mok, Arthur C. ....**Washington, DC**
Mok, Linda Barr ....Los Angeles, CA
Mok, Louis A. ....**Los Angeles, CA**
Mokarram, Ali ....Houston, TX
Mokarram & Associates ....Houston, TX
Mokarry, Virginia G. ....New York, NY
Moke, Paul ....Wilmington, OH
Moke, Randall H. ....Denver, CO
Moken, George L. ....**Clinton, NJ**
Moker, Russell R. ....**Sedona, AZ**
Moker, Russell R., A Professional Law Corporation ....**Sedona, AZ**
Mokhiber, Albert, Law Offices of, P.C.
Alexandria, VA
Mokhiber, Albert P. ....Alexandria, VA
Mokhtarzadeh, Shahrokh
Los Angeles, CA
Mokhtarzadeh, Shahrokh, PLC
Los Angeles, CA
Mokodean, Michael J., Jr. ....Canton, OH
Mokoid, Jacqueline A. ....**Westmont, NJ**
Mokos, Deirdre M. ....Tucson, AZ
Mokosaik, Michael J. ....Wheaton, IL
Mokosh, Trisha C. ....Cleveland, OH
Mokotoff, Alexis ....**Boston, MA**
New York, NY
Mokotoff, David ....Highland Park, IL
Mokotoff, Harold S. ....Sagaponack, NY
Mokotoff, Jeffrey D. ....**Atlanta, GA**
Mokotoff, Milton M. ....Garden City, NY
Mokotoff, Shirley H. ....Garden City, NY
Mokri, Namvar Amir ....**Irvine, CA**
Mokris, Paul J. ....Orlando, FL
Mokriski, Diane C. ....**Hartford, CT**
Mokriski, J. Charles ....**Boston, MA**
Mokrzecki, Philip S. ....Hadley, MA
Moks, Robert L. ....Westport, CT
Moktarian, Mark ....Los Angeles, CA
Mok-Wang, Frannie S. ....San Francisco, CA
Mol, Robert L. ....Lansing, MI
Mola, Elena C. ....Washington, DC
Molaison, Colvin, Greenberg, Zelenka, Morris & Loeb, LLP ....**Gretna, LA**
Metairie, LA
New Orleans, LA
Molaison, Harold E., PLC ....**Gretna, LA**
Molamphy, Dennis J. ....Wichita, KS
Molan, Richard E. ....**Concord, NH**
Molan, Robert A. ....**Arlington, VA**
Moland, Bruce U. ....Minneapolis, MN
Moland, William W. ....Centerville, OH
Molander, Garth Alfred ....New York, NY
Molander, Julia A. ....**San Francisco, CA**
Molano, Anita T. ....**Chicago, IL**
Molano, Michael A. ....San Francisco, CA
Molanphy, Jane M. ....Corona, NY
Molans, James A. ....Miami, FL
Molar, Barry L.
Department of Transportation,
Federal Aviation Administration, GV
Molaro, Robert S. ....Chicago, IL
Molash, R. Matthew ....**Dallas, TX**
Molasky, Joseph W. ....Chalfont, PA
Molatore, Jerry ....Klamath Falls, OR
Molavi, Kamyar ....**Atlanta, GA**
Molay, Hilary S. ....**Plano, TX**
Molay, Seth R., (P.C.) ....**Dallas, TX**
Molbegott, Elinor D. ....East Williston, NY
Molberg, Eric P. ....Reedsburg, WI
Molberg, Kenneth H. ....Dallas, TX
Molberger, Neil S. ....**New York, NY**
Molbert, Andrew Mason ....New York, NY
Molbert, Herbin J. ....Port Arthur, TX
Molbert, Lauris N. ....**Fargo, ND**
Molbert, Ralph ....Steele, ND
Molchan, John A. ....San Antonio, TX
Molchan, Richard N. ....**Peoria, IL**
Molchan, Thomas M. ....Frazer, PA
Molchen, William E., II ....West Chester, PA
Molchin, Cathy A. ....**Mapleton, IL**
Molchin, Cathy A., P.C. ....**Mapleton, IL**
Molchior, Carol J. ....Seattle, WA
Molczan, William T. ....**Pittsburgh, PA**
Moldane, Milton I. ....Creve Coeur, MO
Moldauer, Ralph W. ....Bellevue, WA
Moldave, Peter M. ....**Boston, MA**
Moldawer, Alan B. ....**Rockville, MD**
Moldawer & Marshall, P.C.
Rockville, MD
Molde & Black, P.C. ....Johnson, VT
Molde, Douglas L. ....Johnson, VT
Moldenhauer, David T. ....**New York, NY**
Moldenhauer, James G. ....Eau Claire, WI
Moldenhauer, Lenn A. ....**Denver, CO**
Moldenhauer, Paul M. ....Superior, WI
Molder, Leslie Bornstein ....**Philadelphia, PA**
Molder, Michael J. ....**Philadelphia, PA**
Moldermaker, Wilfred A., P.C.
Paradise Valley, AZ
Moldes, Juan A. ....San Juan, PR
Moldo, Byron Z. ....**Los Angeles, CA**
Moldof, Hilliard E. ....**Fort Lauderdale, FL**
Moldof, Hilliard E., P.A.
Fort Lauderdale, FL
Moldof, Stephen B. ....**New York, NY**
Moldoff, Alan I. ....**Philadelphia, PA**
Moldoff, William M. ....Nassau, NY
Moldovan, Bert M. ....Mc Keesport, PA
Moldovan, Florina A. ....**Morristown, NJ**
Moldovan, Joseph T. ....**New York, NY**
Moldovan, Kristopher E. ....Chicago, IL
Dallas, TX
Moldovan, Neil ....Carle Place, NY
Moldovan, Susan A. ....**New York, NY**
Moldovan, Victor L., (P.C.) ....**Norcross, GA**
Moldovanyi, Jay F. ....**Cleveland, OH**
Moldover, Edward D. ....**New York, NY**
Moldover Hertz & Gidaly ....**New York, NY**
Moldover, Judith A. ....**New York, NY**
Moldovsky, Ari S. ....Philadelphia, PA
Moldovsky, Brem M. ....Philadelphia, PA
Moldovsky, Joel S. ....Philadelphia, PA
Moldovsky & Moldovsky ....Philadelphia, PA
Moldow, Bruce J. ....**Fort Lauderdale, FL**
Moldowan, Laura G. ....**Washington, DC**
Mole, Joseph N. ....**New Orleans, LA**
Molé, Matthew C. ....New York, NY
Molé, Michael G. ....Clark, NJ
Molé, Ronald B. ....**New York, NY**
Molea, Anthony A. ....White Plains, NY
Molea, Richard A. ....White Plains, NY
Molee, Lenore M. ....Rockaway, NJ
Molek, David W. ....Yeagertown, PA
Molen, Chris D. ....**Atlanta, GA**
Molen, Donald S. ....Denver, CO
Molen, John K. ....**Birmingham, AL**
Molenaar, Dennis L. ....Coeur d'Alene, ID
Molenaar, James E. ....Lansing, IL
Molenari, Lizabeth Ann
Huntingdon Valley, PA
Molenda, Carrie J. ....**Seattle, WA**
Molenda, Jeffrey W. ....**Charleston, WV**
Molenda, Mary Louise ....**Anchorage, AK**
Molenda, Michael E. ....**Apple Valley, MN**
Molenda, Michael J. ....Miami, FL
Molenda, Paul B. ....**Southfield, MI**
Molenda, Paul B., P.C.
Mount Clemens, MI
Southfield, MI
Molenkamp, Jack A. ....**McLean, VA**
Molepske, Louis J. ....Stevens Point, WI
Moler, Andrew C., Law Offices of
Orlando, FL
Moler, D. Grove ....Mullens, WV
Moler, Donald L., Jr. ....Topeka, KS
Moler, Edward H. ....**Oklahoma City, OK**
Moler, Elizabeth Anne ....**Washington, DC**
Moler, Staton, Staton & Houck
Mullens, WV
Moles, Charles F. ....**Chicago, IL**
Moles, Nicholas F. ....Atlantic City, NJ
Molesky, James E. ....Berkeley, CA
San Francisco, CA
Molesky, Michael J. ....**Alma, MI**
Moless, Joseph H., Jr. ....Santa Clara, CA
Molesso, Jason C. ....**Dallas, TX**
Molestina, Antonio ....New York, NY
Molesworth, Rita M. ....**New York, NY**
Moletteire, Robert M. ....**Melbourne, FL**
Vero Beach, FL
Moletteri, Andrea F. ....Brooklyn, NY
Molever, Cathy Feinstein ....Minnetonka, MN
Molever, Loren ....**Phoenix, AZ**
Molfetta & Associates ....Glendale, CA
Molfetta, Michael A. ....Tustin, CA
Molfetta, William M. ....Glendale, CA
Molgaard, Anne Cecile ....Ukiah, CA
Molgaard, David D. ....Charleston, WV
Molgaard, Janine ....Stockton, CA
Molgaard, Peter B. ....**San Francisco, CA**
Molgard & Hunsaker ....Brigham City, UT
Molgard, Jack H. ....Brigham City, UT
Molhem, David W. ....**Tampa, FL**
Molho, Robin S. ....New York, NY
Molho, Ross I. ....**Chicago, IL**
Molho, Sonya Bekoff ....Los Angeles, CA
Molhoek, Daniel C. ....**Grand Rapids, MI**
Molica, Frank H. ....Merritt Island, FL
Molica, Frank Henry, P.A.
Merritt Island, FL
Molick, Tracy Jo ....Fargo, ND
Molidor, Mary Clare ....Los Angeles, CA
Moliere, Donna R. ....Lafayette, LA
Molieri, Joseph T., Jr. ....Philadelphia, PA
Molik, David ....Albany, NY
Molik, Edward J. ....Alden, NY
Molik, Steven ....Buffalo, NY
Moliken, Cheryl S. ....North Bay Village, FL
Moliken, Gary H. ....**Fairfax, VA**
Molin, Franklin B. ....**Pittsburgh, PA**
Molin, Michelle M. ....**Indianapolis, IN**
Molin, Nicole M. ....**Wilmington, NC**
Molin, Richard J. ....**Chico, CA**
Molina, Adolph U. ....Santa Ana, CA
Molina, Alan ....Union City, NJ
Molina, Alexander A. ....**Universal City, CA**
Molina, Ana L. ....**New York, NY**
Molina, Arlette M. ....Houston, TX
Molina, Barbara L. ....Lockhart, TX
Molina, Carlos D. ....San Diego, CA
Molina, Ernesto Horacio, Jr.
Department of Justice,
Civil Division, GV
Molina, Humberto, Jr. ....Houston, TX
Molina, J. C. ....Houston, TX
Molina, Joseph C. ....Washington, DC
Molina, Juan R. ....Weslaco, TX
Molina, Luis G ....San Francisco, CA
Molina, Luz M., Ms. ....New Orleans, LA
Molina, Manuel A. ....**New York, NY**
Molina, Marco A. ....**Dallas, TX**
Molina, Mark S. ....Melbourne, FL
Molina, Pablo E. ....Los Angeles, CA
Molina, Robert Patrick ....**Las Vegas, NV**
Molina, Robert S. ....Plano, TX
Molina, Romero ....Rio Grande City, TX
Molina, Vibiana ....**Los Angeles, CA**
Molina Lopez, Daniel ....**San Juan, PR**
Molinares, Ivette Patricia ....Garden City, NY
Molinari, Brian M. ....New London, CT
New York, NY
Molinari, David G. ....**San Diego, CA**
Molinari, Ernest V. ....Newark, NJ
Molinari, Gino J. ....San Francisco, CA
Molinari, Guy N. ....**New York, NY**
Molinari, Guy V. ....Staten Island, NY
Molinari, James R. ....Philadelphia, PA
Molinari, John E. ....**Chatham, NJ**
Jersey City, NJ
North Bergen, NJ
Molinari, John E. ....**Freeport, NY**
Molinari, Laura ....**New York, NY**
Molinari, Laurie K. ....**Hartford, CT**
Molinari, Lisa S. ....Indiana, PA
Molinari, Louis J. ....Weymouth, MA
Molinari, Ralph J. ....Staten Island, NY
Molinari, Rosanna ....**Miami, FL**
Molinari, Samuel L. ....**Hartford, CT**
Molinari, Stephen P.
Department Of Health And Human Services,
Food & Drug Administration, GV
Molinaro, Carmine V., Jr. ....Connellsville, PA
Molinaro, Frank S. ....**Des Plaines, IL**
Molinaro, Joseph A. ....**Morristown, NJ**
Molinaro, Mary C. ....**Sacramento, CA**
Molinaro, Mary Robin ....Waterloo, IA
Molinaro, Michael K. ....Broomall, PA
Molinaro, Michael L. ....**Chicago, IL**
Molinaro, Michael M. ....Santa Monica, CA
Molinaro, Michael S. ....**Columbia, MD**
Molinaro, Michael V. ....Santa Clara, CA
Molinaro, Peter J. ....Albany, NY
Molinaro, Peter, Jr. ....Pittsburgh, PA
Molinaro, Terri D. ....**San Francisco, CA**
San Jose, CA
Molinaro, Thomas J. ....Wausau, WI
Molinaro, Thomas J., S.C. ....Wausau, WI
Molinaro, Valerie A. ....**New York, NY**
Molinaro, Yvette, (A Professional Corporation) ....**Los Angeles, CA**
Molinary, Jo D. ....**Abingdon, VA**
Molinary De La Cruz, Aida N.
Humacao, PR
Molina-Serrano, Ismael ....San Juan, PR
Moline, Brian J. ....Topeka, KS
Moline, Denise B. ....**Sterling, VA**
Moline, Denise B., P.C. ....**Sterling, VA**
Moline, Harry O. ....**St. Louis, MO**
Moline, Michael C. ....**Irving, TX**
Moline, Michael R. ....Minneapolis, MN
Moline, Shostak, Strand & Mehan, L.L.C.
Clayton, MO
St. Louis, MO
Moline, Stephen H. ....Des Moines, IA
Molineaux, Charles B. ....**Vienna, VA**
Molineaux, Jeanne E. ....Ojai, CA
Molinelli, Eugene J. ....**Washington, DC**
Molinelli, James P., Jr. ....Berkeley, CA
Molinelli, John L. ....**Hackensack, NJ**
Molinengo, Henry R., II
Department of the Navy,
Office of the Judge Advocate General, GV
Molinet, Joaquin "King" ....**Houston, TX**
Molinet, Robert T. ....**Atlanta, GA**
Molineux, Karl ....**San Ramon, CA**
Molineux, Stephen Dean ....Collingdale, PA
Molino, Anthony A. ....Los Angeles, CA
Molino, Mildred A. ....Easton, PA
Molino, Paul J. ....**Chicago, IL**
Molino, Ronald A. ....New York, NY
Molino, Virginia L. ....**New York, NY**
Molinoff, Daniel D. ....Larchmont, NY
Molins, Arthur J. ....East Meadow, NY
Molins, Marcel J. ....**Chicago, IL**
Molins, Thomas N. ....**Chicago, IL**
Molinsek, Stephen L. ....Delmar, NY
Molinski, William A. ....**Los Angeles, CA**
Molinsky, Barbara Cushman ....Ardmore, PA
Molinsky, George D. ....**Cincinnati, OH**
Molinsky, Kathleen McAnaney
Cincinnati, OH
Molinsky, William J., Jr.
Oklahoma City, OK
Molique, Richard A. ....Logansport, IN
Molish, Richard J. ....**Elkins Park, PA**
Moliterno, Joseph V. ....Eastchester, NY
Moliterno, Louis R. ....**Twinsburg, OH**
Molitierno, Thomas ....Fayette, OH
Molitor, Ann M. ....Seattle, WA
Molitor, Karen Ann ....Hartford, CT
Molitor, Michael K. ....**Grand Rapids, MI**
Molitor, Richard E. ....Mount Clemens, MI
Molitor, Steven J. ....**Philadelphia, PA**
Molitor, Thomas R. ....Evanston, IL
Molitoris, Theodore M. ....Winston-Salem, NC
Molitz, Deborah ....Troy, MI
Molitz, Michael K. ....**San Francisco, CA**
Molk, Alan G. ....**Denver, CO**
Molk, David ....Ridgefield Park, NJ
Molk, Elliot I. ....**Chicago, IL**
Molk, Laura D. ....Chicago, IL
Molkenbuhr, Edward, Jr. ....San Francisco, CA
Molko, Joseph R. ....**New York, NY**
Molko, Robert ....Santa Ana, CA
Moll, A. J. ....Salt Lake City, UT
Moll, Brian K. ....Scottsdale, AZ
Moll, Charles J., III ....**San Francisco, CA**
Moll, Debra C. ....Newton, MA
Moll, Eric W. ....Department of Commerce,
Office of the General Counsel, GV
Moll, James W. ....Brookfield, WI
Moll, Jeanette M. ....Cambridge, OH
Moll, John R. ....Los Angeles, CA
Moll, Jon H. ....**Muncie, IN**
Moll, Jonathan L. ....**Boston, MA**
Moll, Julia A. ....San Francisco, CA
Moll, Kathryn A. ....**Indianapolis, IN**
Moll, Kelli L. ....**New York, NY**
Moll, Kenneth B. ....Chicago, IL
Moll, Kenneth B. & Associates, Ltd.
Chicago, IL
Moll, Kurt A. ....Irvine, CA
Moll, Lawrence E. ....Oakland, CA
Moll, Loren W. ....**Overland Park, KS**
Moll, Mark A. ....**Fort Smith, AR**
Moll, Melissa ....**Ellsworth, ME**
Moll, Peter E. ....**Washington, DC**
Moll, Rhonda J. ....New York, NY
Moll, Robert G. ....Los Altos, CA
Moll, Robert G. ....**Houston, TX**
Moll, Robert H.
Department Of The Interior,
Office of the Solicitor, GV
Moll, Robert M. ....New York, NY
Moll, Ronald B. ....Hermann, MO
Moll, Stefanie R. ....**Houston, TX**
Moll, Stephen L. ....**Houston, TX**
Moll, Steven A. ....**Stamford, CT**
Moll, Thomas M. ....**Buffalo, NY**
Moll, Timothy L. ....**Lincoln, NE**
Moll, William L., Jr. ....**Houston, TX**
Molla, Negatu ....**Tucson, AZ**
Molla, William W. ....Newton, MA
Molland, Michael E. ....**San Francisco, CA**
Mollath, Stephen C. ....Las Vegas, NV
Reno, NV
Molldrem, Bernhard P., Jr. ....**Syracuse, NY**
Mollé, A. Paul ....**Clearwater, FL**
Molle, Edward G. ....Wilmington, CA
Molle, John E. ....Marshall, MN
Molle, Paul ....Boca Raton, FL
Mollen, Milton ....**New York, NY**
Mollen, Neal D. ....**Washington, DC**
Mollen, Scott E. ....**New York, NY**
Mollengarden, Peter C.
West Palm Beach, FL
Mollenkamp, Alan L. ....Toledo, OH
Mollenkamp, James J. ....**Kansas City, MO**
Mollenkopf, Kristine L. ....**Los Angeles, CA**
Moller, Allan S., Law Offices of
New York, NY
White Plains, NY
Moller, Arthur C., III ....**Miami, FL**
Moller, Arthur C., P.A. ....**Miami, FL**
Moller, Arthur L. ....Houston, TX
Moller, Ashley E. ....**Denver, CO**
Moller, Barry S. ....**Litchfield, CT**
Moller, Carolyn E. ....Columbus, GA
Moller, Charles E., Jr. ....Wethersfield, CT
Moller, Christian ....**Seattle, WA**
Moller, Daniel K. ....**Reston, VA**
Moller, David C. ....Columbus, OH
Moller, Erik K. ....**Menlo Park, CA**
Moller, James W. ....Wilsonville, OR
Moller, Jay ....Redway, CA
Moller, Jeffrey S. ....**Philadelphia, PA**
Moller, Johann ....Birmingham, AL
Moller, Kelly O'Neill ....St. Paul, MN
Moller, Lawrence E. ....Mount Vernon, WA
Moller, Marc J. ....Colts Neck, NJ
Moller, Marc S. ....**New York, NY**
Moller, Peck and O'Brien, LLC
Hartford, CT
Moller, Scott A. ....Rhinelander, WI
Moller, Shelah S. ....New York, NY
Moller, Sid L. ....Jackson, MS
Moller, Stephen Fairbanks ....Alexandria, VA
Moller, William R. ....**Hartford, CT**
Mollere, Flanagan & Landry, L.L.C.
Metairie, LA
New Orleans, LA
Mollerup, Richard W. ....**Boise, ID**
Mollerus, Michael J., Ltd. ....Minneapolis, MN
Mollerus, Michael T. ....**New York, NY**
Molleston, J. G. ....Magnolia, AR
Fort Worth, TX
Mollet, Jeffrey A. ....Edwardsville, IL
Mollet, Laura K. ....Minneapolis, MN
Mollett, Darrin J. ....**Phoenix, AZ**
Mollett, Gregory C. ....**St. Louis, MO**
Molleur, Denis R. ....New York, NY
Molleur, James F. ....Biddeford, ME
Molleur, John T. ....**Charleston, WV**
Molleur, R. Jay ....South Windsor, CT
Molleur, Richard R. ....**Los Angeles, CA**
Mollhagen, Robert D.
Bloomfield Hills, MI
Lansing, MI
Mollica, Andrew J. ....**Athens, OH**
Mollica, Anthony C. ....Athens, OH
Mollica, Gall, Sloan & Sillery Co., L.P.A.
Athens, OH
Mollica, Gerald A. ....**Athens, OH**
Mollica, James A., Jr. ....**Pittsburgh, PA**
Mollica, Joseph G. ....Dayton, OH
Mollica, Kenneth S. ....Sudbury, MA
Mollica, Kim T. ....Boca Raton, FL
Mollica, Kim T., P.A. ....Boca Raton, FL
Mollica & Murray ....**Pittsburgh, PA**
Mollica, Salvatore D. ....Gainesville, FL
Mollica, Terry J. ....**San Francisco, CA**
Mollick, Constance ....**New York, NY**
Mollick, Don R. ....Bellevue, WA
Mollick, Georgina Marie ....Raleigh, NC
Mollick & Moravan ....Bellevue, WA
Mollicone, David A. ....**Troy, MI**
Molligan, Cox & Moyer, A Professional Corporation ....**San Francisco, CA**
Molligan, Peter N. ....**San Francisco, CA**
Molligan, Rene J. ....Los Angeles, CA
Mollin, Alfred ....Department of Justice,
Civil Division, GV
Mollin, Daniel Z. ....**New York, NY**
Mollin, Richard C. ....Downers Grove, IL
Molling, Charles F., Law Office of
Denver, CO
Mollino, Joseph A., Jr. ....Memphis, TN
Mollis, Charles A. ....**Irvine, CA**
Mollis, Ronald A. ....**Irvine, CA**
Mollison, Andrew R. ....Niles, MI
Mollison, C. Suzanne ....Altus, OK
Mollison, James Anthony ....Niles, MI

Mollison, James J. ... Niles, MI
Mollison Law Offices, P.C. ... Niles, MI
Mollison, Marcus A. ... Minneapolis, MN
Mollison, Richard M. ... Washington, DC
Mollman, Michael L. ... Cedar Rapids, IA
Mollman Elliott, Sharon ... Madison, WI
Mollnow, Kristen E. ... Rochester, NY
Mollo, Heather M. ... Nashville, IN
Mollo, Peter Joseph ... Brooklyn, NY
Mollod, Jonathan ... New York, NY
Mollod, Michael A. ... New York, NY
Mollón, David E. ... New York, NY
Mollon, Mark L. ... Dearborn, MI
Molloy, Ann K. ... Worcester, MA
Molloy, Ann Kenney ... Kansas City, MO
Molloy, Anne M. ... Riverhead, NY
Molloy & Associates, Professional Corporation ... Milford, MA
Molloy, Bartholomew P. ... Milford, MA
Molloy, Brian J. ... Woodbridge, NJ
Molloy, Brian P. ... Orono, ME
Molloy, C. Terrence ... Torrance, CA
Molloy, Christopher H. ... Fort Worth, TX
Molloy, Cindy E. ... New York, NY
Molloy, Cora Cisneros ... Fort Myers, FL
Molloy, Daniel L. ... Tampa, FL
Molloy, Donald E. ... Santa Monica, CA
Molloy, Donald E. ... Florissant, MO
Molloy, Donald W. ... Missoula, MT
Molloy, Edwin A. ... Massapequa, NY
Molloy, Elizabeth M.
Federal Energy Regulatory Commission, Office of the General Counsel, GV
Molloy, Gerald Peter, Jr.
Farmington Hills, MI
Molloy, J. Brian ... Washington, DC
Molloy, James Dennis ... Washington, DC
Molloy, James P. ... Helena, MT
Molloy, Jean D. ... Glastonbury, CT
Molloy, Joan C. ... Wallingford, CT
Molloy, John C. ... Boston, MA
Molloy, John F. ... Tucson, AZ
Molloy, John J., III ... Los Angeles, CA
Molloy, John L., Jr. ... Westbury, NY
Molloy, Joseph F. ... Dickinson, TX
Molloy, Joseph K. ... New York, NY
Molloy, Julie C. ... Boston, MA
Molloy, Kathleen A. ... Wilson, NY
Molloy, Kenneth J. ... East Islip, NY
Molloy, Kevin R. ... Shreveport, LA
Molloy, Kyran P. ... Troy, NY
Molloy & Landry ... Kenai, AK
Molloy, Laura A. ... Fishers, IN
Molloy, Laurence B., III ... Morristown, NJ
Molloy, Mark A. ... Buffalo, NY
Molloy, Mary Kathleen ... Covington, KY
Molloy, Maureen K. ... Shelburne, VT
Molloy, Michael A. ... Boston, MA
Molloy, Michael J. ... Riverside, CA
Molloy, Michael J. ... St. Louis, MO
Molloy, Monica S. ... Rockville, MD
Molloy, Neal D. ... Maringouin, LA
Molloy, Paul J. ... Somerville, MA
Molloy, Peter, P.C. ... Farmington Hills, MI
Molloy, Richard J. ... Dearborn, MI
Molloy, Robert J. ... Kenai, AK
Molloy, Robert S. ... Boston, MA
Molloy, Robert T. ... Vienna, VA
Molloy, Russ ... Trenton, NJ
Molloy, Sam C. ... Memphis, TN
Molloy & Stanfield, P.C. ... Vienna, VA
Molloy, Thomas P. ... Seattle, WA
Mollozzi, John D. ... Elizabeth, NJ
Molluso, A. Jay ... Pittsburgh, PA
Mollway, Daniel J. ... Honolulu, HI
Mollway, Susan Oki ... Honolulu, HI
Mollway, William D. ... Madison, WI
Molly, Kenneth R. ... Eugene, OR
Mollycheck, Debbie S. ... Rock Hill, SC
Molmen, Steven M. ... Honolulu, HI
Molmen, William P. ... San Francisco, CA
Molnar, Allen E. ... New York, NY
Molnar, Christian Stephen
Los Angeles, CA
Molnar, Edward S. ... Cleveland, OH
Molnar, F. Scott ... Syracuse, NY
Molnar, Gary R. ... New York, NY
Molnar, Gerald J. ... Freehold, NJ
Molnar, Jacqueline D. ... Palo Alto, CA
Molnar, Jason ... Columbus, OH
Molnar, John ... Wind Gap, PA
Molnar, John A., Jr. ... Cleveland, OH
Molnar, John B. ... Toledo, OH
Molnar, Kenneth J. ... Galena, OH
Molnar Law Offices, The ... Bangor, PA
Wind Gap, PA
Molnar, Lawrence ... New York, NY
Molnar, Marie Elena ... Irvine, CA
Molnar, Michael P. ... Mount Laurel, NJ
Molnar, Rhonda K. ... Lima, OH
Molnar, Robert Saul ... Wayne, NJ
Molnar-Boncela, Catherine L. ... Griffith, IN
Molner, Brenda S. ... Seattle, WA
Molner, Leo J. ... Palm Harbor, FL
Molner, Thomas E. ... New York, NY
Molner, William E. ... Lansing, MI
Molner, William F. ... Phoenix, AZ
Molo, Steven F. ... Chicago, IL
Molock, Dennis R. ... Stuttgart, AR
Molock, Guy, Jr. ...
Administrative Office Of The United States Courts, GV
Molock Law Firm, P.A. ... Stuttgart, AR
Molod, Alan H. ... Philadelphia, PA
Molod, Frederick M. ... New York, NY
Molod, Irene ... New York, NY
Molod, Julie E. ... New York, NY
Molod Spitz DeSantis & Stark, P.C.
New York, NY
Molodanof, Jack T. ... Sacramento, CA
Molodec, Lisa S. ... Boston, MA
Molodovsky, Elizabeth ... Boston, MA
Molof, Lee S., Law Offices of ... Reno, NV
Molofsky, Robert A. ... Washington, DC
Molohon, Patrick J. ... Palatine, IL
Moloney & Anker ... Valhalla, NY
Moloney, Donald P., II ... Lexington, KY
Moloney, Edward J. ... Lowell, MA
Moloney, Edward J., Jr. ... Lowell, MA
Moloney, James ... New York, NY
Moloney, James B. ... McLean, VA
Moloney, James J.
Securities and Exchange Commission, Division of Corporation Finance, GV
Moloney, Joanne M. ... Princeton, NJ
Moloney, Joseph A. ... Louisville, KY
Moloney, Kelley ... Simsbury, CT
Moloney, Kevin D. ... Valhalla, NY
Moloney, Kevin F. ... Boston, MA
Moloney, Laureen A. ... Wayne, NJ
Moloney, Lawrence A. ... Minneapolis, MN
Moloney, Mary Gumbert ... Lexington, KY
Moloney, Michael P. ... Dayton, OH
Moloney, Michael R. ... Lexington, KY
Moloney & Moloney ... Lowell, MA
Moloney, Monica A. ... Columbus, OH
Moloney, Nancy P. ... Los Angeles, CA
Moloney, Patrick K. ... San Francisco, CA
Moloney, Phillip M. ... Lexington, KY
Moloney, Stephen J. ... Austin, TX
Moloney, Stephen M. ... Los Angeles, CA
Moloney, Thomas E. ... Columbus, OH
Moloney, Thomas J. ... New York, NY
Moloney, Thos. ... Orange, NJ
Molony, Daniel F. ... Tampa, FL
Molony, Douglas A. ... New Orleans, LA
Molony, Lawrence J. ... New Orleans, LA
Molony, Maureen A. ... Madison, WI
Molony, Michael A. ... Charleston, SC
Molony, Michael J., Jr. (P.C.)
New Orleans, LA
Molony, Thomas J. ... Charlotte, NC
Molony, Winifred D. ... Chicago, IL
Moloshok, Matthew E. ... Newark, NJ
Moloshok, Norman ... New York, NY
Molosky, Donald J. ... Clinton Township, MI
Petoskey, MI
Molosky, Donald J., P.C.
Clinton Township, MI
Petoskey, MI
Molot, David S. ... Washington, DC
Molot, Richard M. ... Brooklyn, NY
Molot, Valery L. ... New York, NY
Molotsky, Alan E. ... Chicago, IL
Molotsky, Allan C. ... Philadelphia, PA
Molotsky, Brad A. ... Newtown Square, PA
Molotsky, Drew A. ... Haddonfield, NJ
Molotsky, Harold S. ... Camden, NJ
Molotsky & Schwartz, A Professional Corporation ... Camden, NJ
Moloughney, James J. ... Warren, NJ
Moloughney, Kevin P. ... Southfield, MI
Moloughney, Terence Michael ... Detroit, MI
Moloughney, Walter J. ... Valley Stream, NY
Moloy, James P. ... Indianapolis, IN
Moloznik, David J. ... Philadelphia, PA
Moloznik, Joseph S. ... Philadelphia, PA
Molseed, Michael C. ... Newport Beach, CA
Molstad, Donald H. ... Sioux City, IA
Molstad, Robert J. ... Stillwater, MN
Molstad, Russell C., Jr. ... Huron, SD
Molster, Charles B., III ... Washington, DC
Molt, Michael J. ... Fairfield, IL
Molta, Catherine Fitzgerald ... Springfield, MA
Molta, Thomas J. ... San Diego, CA
Moltar, Norman M., Jr. ... Los Angeles, CA
Molta-Tetrault, Linda A. ... Springfield, MA
Moltenbrey, Mary Jean
Department of Justice, Antitrust Division, GV
Molteni, Claudio E. ... Kansas City, MO
Molter, Daniel J. ... Kentland, IN
Molter, David J. ... Milwaukee, WI
Molter, Donald S., Jr. ... Waukesha, WI
Molter, Edward H. ... Austin, TX
Molter, Ronald A. ... Detroit, MI
Molter, Samuel E. ... Kentland, IN
Molter, Timothy I. ... Oakland, CA
Molthrop, Morgan McCall ... New York, NY
Moltner, Kenneth M. ... New York, NY
Moltner, Steven ... New York, NY
Molton, David J. ... Upper Montclair, NJ
New York, NY
Molton, Lawrence S. ... Emeryville, CA
San Francisco, CA
Molton & Meekins ... Upper Montclair, NJ
New York, NY
Moltz, Bernard W. ... Chicago, IL
Moltz, Ira A. ... Chicago, IL
Moltz, Marshall J. ... Chicago, IL
Moltz, Marshall J., P.C. ... Chicago, IL
Moltz, Martin P. ... Elgin, IL
Moltz, William J. ... Austin, TX
Moltzen, Allan R. ... Belvedere-Tiburon, CA
Moltzen, Allan R., Jr. ... Palo Alto, CA
Moltzen, David W. ... San Mateo, CA
Moltzen, Edward W. ... Chicago, IL
Joliet, IL
Moltzen, Mary Jo ... Department of Justice, Civil Division, GV
Molumby, Ronan J. ... New York, NY
Molumphy, John T., III ... Roanoke, VA
Molumphy, Linda J. ... Boston, MA
Molumphy, Mark C. ... Burlingame, CA
Molyet, Jeffrey ... Mansfield, OH
Molyneaux, Christopher J. ... Ridgefield, CT
Molyneaux, Edward L., III ... Fremont, CA
Molyneaux, Jay W. ... Juno Beach, FL
Molyneaux, John E. ... Davenport, IA
Molyneux, Gregory A. ... Bedminster, NJ
Molyneux, Sharisse E. ... Long Beach, CA
Molyneux, Timothy P. ... Franklin, TN
Molz, Mark J. ... Hainesport, NJ
Molz, Todd E. ... Los Angeles, CA
Molz, Wendi B. ... Mobile, AL
Molzahn, Lyndon C. ... Chicago, IL
Molzen, Christine ... Topeka, KS
Molzen, Christopher J. ... Kansas City, MO
Molzen, Karen B. ... Las Cruces, NM
Molzon, Justina A. ... Chicago, IL
Mombach, Boyle & Hardin, P.A.
Fort Lauderdale, FL
Mombach, Geoffrey S.
Fort Lauderdale, FL
Momborquette, David K. ... New York, NY
Mombrun, Reginald ... Treasury Department, Internal Revenue Service, GV
Momeyer, Douglas H. ... Chicago, IL
Momin, Karim N. ... New York, NY
Momjian, Albert ... Norristown, PA
Philadelphia, PA
Momjian, Arthur J. ... Cherry Hill, NJ
Momjian, Carol Esther ... Philadelphia, PA
Momjian, Mark A. ... Philadelphia, PA
Momjian, Thomas J. ... Paoli, PA
Momkus, Edward J. ... Downers Grove, IL
Momkus Ozog & McCluskey LLC
Chicago, IL
Downers Grove, IL
Wheaton, IL
Mommaerts, Quentin F. ... Campbell, CA
Mommaerts, Robert W. A. ... Los Angeles, CA
Mommaerts & Rutledge ... Los Angeles, CA
Mommer, Anthony W. ... Indianapolis, IN
Momo, Jane Tobey ... New York, NY
Momot, John J., Jr. ... Las Vegas, NV
Momot & Tidwell ... Las Vegas, NV
Momotiuk, Sandra J. ... Studio City, CA
Momsen, Brian S. ... Ukiah, CA
Momsen, Leo J. ... San Diego, CA
Mon, Donald D. ... Pasadena, CA
Mona, Joseph M. ... Irvine, CA
Monac, Clifford A. ... Walpole, MA
Monacell, James P. ... Atlanta, GA
Monacell, Louis R. ... Richmond, VA
Monacelli, Walter J. ... St. Petersburg, FL
Monach, Andrew E. ... San Francisco, CA
Monachino, Benedict A. ... Boston, MA
Providence, RI
Monachino, Benedict J., Law Offices of
Brooklyn, NY
Monachino, David M. ... New York, NY
Monachino, Mark M. ... Irvine, CA
Monachino, Sam P. ... Binghamton, NY
Monack, Mark P. ... New York, NY
Monaco, Albert M., Jr. ... Lakeview, OR
Monaco, Anthony ... Rochester, NY
Monaco, Anthony J. ... Freehold, NJ
Monaco, Antonietta Maria ... New York, NY
Monaco, Antonio, Jr. ... New York, NY
Monaco, Armando O., II
East Greenwich, RI
Monaco, Carol C. ... Andover, MA
Monaco, Cynthia M. ... Washington, DC
Monaco, Cynthia S. ... Beverly Hills, CA
Monaco, Daniel A. ... Philadelphia, PA
Monaco, Daniel J. ... San Mateo, CA
Monaco, Daniel R. ... Naples, FL
Monaco, David A. ... Daytona Beach, FL
Monaco, Francis A., Jr.
Bethany Beach, DE
Wilmington, DE
Monaco, Francis R. ... New York, NY
Monaco, Gail J. ... East Meadow, NY
Monaco, George M. ... La Grange, IL
Monaco, Helen L. ... New York, NY
Monaco, Joseph A. ... Philadelphia, PA
Monaco, Joseph D., III ... New York, NY
Monaco, Lisa O. ... Department of Justice, Office of the Attorney General, GV
Monaco, Lynn Erickson ... Gainesville, FL
Monaco, Lynne A. ... Rochester, NY
Monaco, Margaret M. ... New York, NY
Monaco, Mario A. ... Warren, NJ
Monaco, Mark C. ... Geneva, IL
Monaco, Martin L., Jr. ... Trenton, NJ
Monaco, Mary Wilson ... Fort Lauderdale, FL
Monaco, Meredith A. ... Chicago, IL
Monaco, Michael P. ... Seattle, WA
Monaco & Monaco ... New York, NY
Monaco, Monaco & Birder
Gainesville, FL
Monaco, Nicholas M. ... Jefferson City, MO
Lake Ozark, MO
Monaco, Ralph A., II ... Kansas City, MO
Monaco, Ralph J. ... New London, CT
Monaco, Roger ... Oxford, NY
Monaco, Roy E. ... Floral Park, NY
Monaco, Russell G. ... Elmsford, NY
Monaco, Stephanie ... Newark, NJ
Monaco, Stephanie M. ... Washington, DC
Monaco, Stephen C. ... White Plains, NY
Monaco, Stephen C. ... Yonkers, NY
Monaco, Susan ... Dallas, TX
Monaco, Toby S. ... Gainesville, FL
Monaco, William J. ... Hauppauge, NY
Monafo, James F. ... St. Louis, MO
Monagan, Joanne P. ... Troy, NY
Monagan, John S. ... Washington, DC
Monagan and Niesobecki ... Waterbury, CT
Monagan, Philip H. ... Waterbury, CT
Monagan, Walter E., Jr. ... Shelburne, VT
Monaghan, Ann G. ... Hartford, CT
Monaghan, Ann M. ... Butte, MT
Monaghan, Barney Andrew ... Foley, AL
Monaghan, Brian D. ... San Diego, CA
Monaghan, Bryan L. ... Birmingham, MI
Detroit, MI
Monaghan & Conger ... San Diego, CA
Monaghan, Dennis J. ... Bethlehem, PA
Monaghan, Dennis P. ... Morristown, NJ
Monaghan, Douglas J. ... Groton, CT
Monaghan, Edward P. ... Bethlehem, PA
Monaghan, Erin K.
Federal Election Commission, Office of the General Counsel, GV
Monaghan, Gerald E. ... Ridgefield, NJ
Monaghan & Gold, P.C. ... Elkins Park, PA
Philadelphia, PA
Monaghan, Henry P. ... New York, NY
Monaghan, Imelda ... Boston, MA
Monaghan, Jeffrey S. ... Woodbridge, NJ
Monaghan, John D. ... Port Huron, MI
Monaghan, John F. X., Jr.
Elkins Park, PA
Monaghan, John J. ... Boston, MA
Monaghan, John P. ... Springfield, NJ
Monaghan, John P. ... Blue Bell, PA
Monaghan, John R. ... Port Huron, MI
Monaghan, John R., Jr. ... Farmingdale, NY
Monaghan, Jos. F. ... Watervliet, NY
Monaghan, Joseph F. ... Watervliet, NY
Monaghan, Joseph G. ... Hackensack, NJ
Monaghan, Justin M. ... Florham Park, NJ
Monaghan, Kelly F. ... Tulsa, OK
Monaghan, Kevin P. ... San Diego, CA
Monaghan, L. Edward ... Canandaigua, NY
Monaghan, Leahy, Hochadel & Libby, LLP
Portland, ME
Monaghan, LoPrete, McDonald, Yakima & Grenke, A Professional Corporation
Bloomfield Hills, MI
Monaghan, Louise Dixon ... Uniontown, PA
Monaghan, Matthew J. ... Cocoa, FL
Monaghan, Matthew J. ... Portland, ME
Monaghan, Maxine ... San Francisco, CA
Monaghan, Michael J. ... Paradise Valley, AZ
Monaghan, Michael J. ... Bronx, NY
Monaghan, Michael P. ... Southfield, MI
Monaghan, Patricia M. ... Albuquerque, NM
Monaghan, Patrick J., Jr. ... Hackensack, NJ
Monaghan, Paul E., Jr. ... New Haven, CT
Monaghan, Peter G. ... Mineola, NY
New York, NY
White Plains, NY
Monaghan, Rem & Zeller, A Professional Corporation ... Hackensack, NJ
Monaghan, Richard A. ... Vancouver, WA
Monaghan, Richard F. ... New York, NY
Monaghan, Richard W. ... Concord, MA
Monaghan, Robert E. ... Livingston, NJ
Monaghan, Robert F. ... Chicago, IL
Monaghan, Robert W. ... Boston, MA
Monaghan, Sean ... Florham Park, NJ
Monaghan, Sean T. ... San Francisco, CA
Monaghan, Terrence E. ... Birmingham, MI
Detroit, MI
Monaghan, Thomas F. ... Portland, ME
Monaghan, Thomas J. ... Omaha, NE
Monaghan, Thomas Patrick ... New Hope, KY
Monaghan, Timothy E. ... Delray Beach, FL
Fort Lauderdale, FL
Monaghan, Timothy P.
United States International Trade Commission, Office of the General Counsel, GV
Monaghan, Walter E. ... Summit, NJ
Monaghan, William A., III ... Hawthorne, NJ
Monaghan, William F., II ... Baltimore, MD
Monaghen, Patricia D. ... Houston, TX
Monagle, Daniel Edward
Philadelphia, PA
Monagle, Lawrence ... Princeton, NJ
Monagle, William Christopher ... Paramus, NJ
Monago, Frank A. ... Houston, TX
Monahan, Allison L. ... New Orleans, LA
Monahan, Ann K. ... Seattle, WA
Monahan & Associates, P.C. ... Boston, MA
Monahan, Barbara S. ... Fort Lauderdale, FL
Monahan, Beatrice Peca ... Williamsburg, VA
Monahan & Biagi, P.L.L.C. ... Seattle, WA
Monahan, Brendan Victor ... Yakima, WA
Monahan, Brian M. ... Easton, PA
Monahan, Brian T. ... Waltham, MA
Monahan, Charles J. ... Treasury Department, Internal Revenue Service, GV
Monahan, Christopher G.
San Francisco, CA
Monahan, Courtney Wilson
New York, NY
Scarsdale, NY
Monahan, Daniel F. ... Exton, PA
Monahan, Daniel L. ... Lake Worth, FL
Monahan, David E. ... San Diego, CA
Monahan, David W. ... New York, NY
Monahan, Diane M. ... St. Louis, MO
Monahan, Edward C. ... Frankfort, KY
Monahan, Eugene J. ... Stratford, CT
Monahan, Gabriela I. ... Chicago, IL
Monahan, Gary L. ... Le Sueur, MN
Monahan, Grove, Tucker & Wallace LLP
Milton-Freewater, OR
Monahan, Helena ... San Antonio, TX
Monahan, Henry J. ... Rockville, MD
Monahan, J. Dominic ... Eugene, OR
Monahan, J. Michael, II
New Orleans, LA
Monahan, J. Stephen ... Montpelier, VT
Monahan, James F. ... Boston, MA
Monahan, James H. ... Omaha, NE
Monahan, James S. ... Columbus, OH

Monahan, James T. ....Seattle, WA
Monahan, Jane T. ....Wilmington, DE
Monahan, Jay ....San Jose, CA
Monahan, Joan E. ....New York, NY
Monahan, Joanne ....Jersey City, NJ
Monahan, John ....United States Senate, Committee Legal Personnel, GV
Monahan, John B., Jr. ....Burbank, CA
Monahan, John C. ....Rockville, MD
Monahan, John D., Jr. ....Burlington, VT
Monahan, John E. ....South Bend, IN
Monahan, John H. ....Boston, MA
Monahan, John M. ....New Haven, CT
Monahan, John M. ....Seattle, WA
Monahan, John T. ....Chicago, IL
Monahan, Joseph C. ....Portland, OR
Monahan, Joseph M. ....Arcola, IL
Monahan, Joseph W., III ....Cambridge, MA
Monahan, Joy M. ....San Francisco, CA
Monahan, Julie A. ....Lynnfield, MA
Monahan, Katherine Beaver ....Atlanta, GA
Monahan, Katherine E. ....Los Angeles, CA
Monahan, Kevin J. ....New York, NY
Monahan, Kevin Patrick ....Baton Rouge, LA
Monahan, Kevin R. ....Palatka, FL
Monahan, Lesleigh Wiggs ....Lakewood, CO
Monahan, Linda C. ....Charlottesville, VA
Monahan, Lora Tarle ....Jacksonville, FL
Monahan, M. Michael ....St. Paul, MN
Monahan, Marie T. ....Newton, MA
Monahan, Marilyn A. ....Los Angeles, CA
Monahan, Mark F. ....Woodbridge, VA
Monahan, Mary E. ....Washington, DC
Monahan, Mary K. Office Of Special Counsel, GV
Monahan, Michael A. ....Los Angeles, CA
Monahan, Michael A. ....Newark, NJ
Monahan, Michael J. ....Chelsea, MA
Monahan, Michael J. ....Brooklyn, NY
Monahan, Michael L. ....Tifton, GA
Monahan, Michael M. ....Santa Fe, NM
Monahan, Michael R. ....New York, NY
Monahan & Padellaro, Law Offices of Cambridge, MA
Monahan, Pamela ....Huntington Station, NY
Monahan, Patricia A. ....Pittsburgh, PA
Monahan, Patrick J., II ....Hartford, CT
Monahan, Patrick J., Jr. ....Trenton, NJ
Monahan, Peter A. ....Chicago, IL
Monahan, Peter R. ....Chicago, IL
Monahan, Priscilla A. ....Cambridge, MA
Monahan, Richard A. ....Charleston, WV
Monahan, Richard F. (Dick) Walla Walla, WA
Monahan, Richard J. ....Waltham, MA
Monahan, Richard V. ....Bakersfield, CA
Monahan, Robert J. ....Dudley, MA
Monahan, Russell T. ....Louisville, KY
Monahan, Sharon O'Malley Washington, DC
Monahan, Terrence T. ....Beloit, WI
Monahan, Thomas ....Brooklyn, NY
Monahan, Thomas E. ....Toms River, NJ
Monahan, Thomas M. ....Joliet, IL
Monahan, Thomas P., Jr. ....Hackensack, NJ
Monahan, Thomas V. ....Leesburg, VA
Winchester, VA
Monahan, Thomas V., Jr. ....Baltimore, MD
Monahan, Timothy J. ....Detroit, MI
Monahan, Timothy Jerome ....Spartanburg, SC
Monahan, Timothy M. ....Rockville, MD
Monahan, William G. P. Department of State, Office of the Legal Adviser, GV
Monahan, William J. ....Phoenix, AZ
Monahan, William J. ....Mountain View, CA
Monahan, William J., P.C. ....Phoenix, AZ
Monahan, William L. ....Omaha, NE
Monahan, William O. ....Boston, MA
Monahan, William P. ....Boston, MA
Monahan, J. Grant ....Boston, MA
Monaldo, Tino M. ....Hutchinson, KS
Monaldo, Tino M., Chartered Hutchinson, KS
Monarch, Charles Edward ....Louisville, KY
Monarch, Joel R. ....Chicago, IL
Monarch, Kammie ....Oklahoma City, OK
Monarch, Michael J. ....Santa Ana, CA
Monarch, Nancy E. ....Department of Labor, Office of the Solicitor, GV
Monarch, Robert D. ....Santa Ana, CA
Monarch, Sam H. ....Hardinsburg, KY
Monarch, Selwyn J. ....Studio City, CA
Monard, Larry R. ....Oklahoma City, OK
Monard, Ronald E. ....Mission Viejo, CA
Monari, Francis J. ....Camden, NJ
Monarski, Francis K. ....Lowell, MA
Monas, Edmund M. ....Denver, CO
Monas, Robert G. ....Coral Springs, FL
Monasebian, Nazanien E. ....New York, NY
Monash, Richard ....Detroit, MI
Monasmith, Patrick A. ....Chewelah, WA
Monast, Charles H. ....Fort Lauderdale, FL
Monast, James P. ....Columbus, OH
Monastersky, David S. ....Hartford, CT
Monastra, Andrew J. ....Pottstown, PA
Monastra, Carl C. ....Cleveland, OH
Monat, Helene K. ....Arlington, VA
Monat, Lawrence M. ....Hauppauge, NY
Monath, Robert A. ....Chapel Hill, NC
Monborne, Mark Allen ....Treasury Department, Office of Foreign Assets Control, GV
Moncada, Bonnie J. ....Miami, FL
Moncada, Kirsten J. ....Department of Justice, Office of Information and Privacy, GV
Monce, Michael ....Florence, KY
MonCeret, A. Thomas ....Knoxville, TN
MonCeret & Johnson ....Knoxville, TN

Monchak, Sam ....Clifton, NJ
Moncharsh, Leila H., (P.C.) ....Oakland, CA
Moncharsh, Philip I. ....Santa Barbara, CA
Moncher, Lawrence G. ....Trenton, NJ
Monchick, Michael J. ....West Palm Beach, FL
Monchick, Randolph B. ....Raleigh, NC
Moncier, Herbert S. ....Knoxville, TN
Monckton, John V. ....New York, NY
Moncla, Dan Paul ....Mobile, AL
Moncla, Gayla M. ....Baton Rouge, LA
Moncla, Jean ....Beaumont, TX
Monclova, Irma J. ....Lexington, KY
Monco, Dean A. ....Chicago, IL
Monco, Walter J. ....Chicago, IL
Moncol, Jan K. ....Clearwater, FL
Moncreiff, Robert P. ....Boston, MA
Moncrief, Andrew M. ....Houston, TX
Moncrief, Brad ....Hastings, NE
Moncrief, John L. ....New York, NY
Moncrief, Lawrence E. ....Pittsburgh, PA
Moncrief, Lee E. ....Pensacola, FL
Moncrief and Moncrief ....Stuttgart, AR
Moncrief, Monty B. ....Fort Worth, TX
Moncrief, S. Kirby ....Sanford, FL
Moncrief, Virgil R. ....Stuttgart, AR
Moncrief, William A. ....Atlanta, GA
Moncrieff, Charles W., III ....Costa Mesa, CA
Moncure, Albert F., Jr. ....New York, NY
Moncure & Barnicle ....Brunswick, ME
Moncure, Henry, III ....Wilmington, DE
Moncure, John ....Brunswick, ME
Moncure, John L. ....Houston, TX
Moncure, Margaret Ann Dean Charlotte Court House, VA
Moncure, William I. ....Blackstone, VA
Moncus, Catherine ....Alexander City, AL
Moncus, Claude McCain Birmingham, AL
Moncus, James R., Jr. ....Birmingham, AL
Mond, Florence ....Canoga Park, CA
Mond, Jerry ....New York, NY
Mond, Joshua ....Dallas, TX
Mond, Richard H. ....Stamford, CT
Mond, Steven D. ....Carson City, NV
Mondale, Walter F. ....Minneapolis, MN
Mondale, William H. ....St. Paul, MN
Mondani, James F. ....Charlotte, NC
Mondano, Frank ....Chelsea, MA
Mondaro, Paul V. ....East Orange, NJ
Monday, Doyle R. ....Brentwood, TN
Monday, Eric H. ....Stuart, VA
Monday, Frances Helms ....Martinsville, VA
Monday, Franklin T. ....Dayton, OH
Monday, Gregory F. ....Madison, WI
Monday, J. Grady ....Martinsville, VA
Monday, Jennifer L. ....Houston, TX
Monday, Michael G. ....Los Angeles, CA
Monday & Monday ....Martinsville, VA
Monday Rodeheffer Jones & Albright Indianapolis, IN
Monday, Terry L. ....Indianapolis, IN
Monde, David M. ....Atlanta, GA
Mondell, Catherine A. ....Boston, MA
Mondell, Denise ....Hartford, CT
Mondell, Scott R. ....Wilmington, DE
Mondelli, Frank E. ....Nashville, TN
Mondelli, Greg ....New York, NY
Mondelli, James V. ....Brentwood, TN
Mondelli, Leslie L. ....Nashville, TN
Mondelli, Michael F. ....Nashville, TN
Mondelli, Victoria A. ....Morristown, NJ
Mondello, Anthony L. ....Bethesda, MD
Mondello, Anthony P. ....Medford, MA
Mondello, Joseph N. ....East Meadow, NY
Mondello, Joseph T. ....Cleveland, OH
Mondello, Philip J. ....Irvington, NY
Monden, Linda N. ....Wailuku, HI
Monderer, Howard ....Washington, DC
Mondesir, Alix ....New York, NY
Mondhink, Harry R. ....Jerseyville, IL
Mondi, James R. ....Los Angeles, CA
Mondike, Roy L. ....San Diego, CA
Mondjack, Gregory F., Sr. ....Perkasie, PA
Mondl, James K. ....St. Louis, MO
Mondlak, John S. ....Philadelphia, PA
Mondlick, Martin I. ....Albuquerque, NM
Mondlin, Sozeen J. ....McLean, VA
Mondo, Glenn ....Irvine, CA
Mondo, Joseph ....Batavia, NY
Mondoil, Harry T. ....Philadelphia, PA
Mondoil, Harry T., P.C., Law Offices of Philadelphia, PA
Mondolino, Dennis J. ....New York, NY
Mondon, Dana S. ....Columbus, OH
Mondor, Paul A. ....Washington, DC
Mondorf, Alfred W. ....Redding, CA
Mondori, Lisa A. ....Sacramento, CA
Mondou, Darla J. ....Upton, MA
Mondou, Martha J. ....Indianapolis, IN
Mondragon, Lawrence A. ....White Plains, NY
Mondre, Richard D., (P.A.) ....Miami, FL
Mondress, M. Ellen ....Seattle, WA
Mondro, James Michael ....Detroit, MI
Mondros, Herbert W. ....Wilmington, DE
Mondrowski, Laura A. ....Chicago, IL
Mondrut, Sharon ....Orlando, FL
Mondry, Jay D. ....Park Rapids, MN
Mondry, Jill M. ....San Mateo, CA
Mondry, Karen M. ....Chicago, IL
Mondry, Karen M., P.C., Law Offices of Chicago, IL
Mondry, Mark B. ....Santa Clara, CA
Mondry, Paul M. ....Ludlow, MA
Monds, Douglas A. ....Detroit, MI
Mondschean, Caroline A. ....Chicago, IL
Mondschein Associates ....Allentown, PA
Mondschein, Brad N. ....Cheshire, CT
Mondschein, John R. ....Allentown, PA

Mondschein, Leonard E. ....Miami, FL
Mondschein, Michael Joel ....Brooklyn, NY
Mondschein & Mondschein, P.A. ....Miami, FL
Mondschein, Morris A. ....New York, NY
White Plains, NY
White Plains, NY
Mondschein, Philip H. ....Miami, FL
Mondschein, Stacey B. ....New York, NY
Mondschein, Stuart G. ....Madison, WI
Mondschein, Warren ....Chicago, IL
Mondshein, Lee J. ....Woodbury, NY
Mondt, Denice Y. ....West Des Moines, IA
Mondul, Donald D. Research Triangle Park, NC
Mondus, Dawn Marie ....St. Paul, MN
Mondville, Jeffrey J. ....Toledo, OH
Mone, Brian J. ....Brockton, MA
Mone, Carol S. ....Wellesley Hills, MA
Mone, Charles K. ....Portland, ME
Boston, MA
Mone, D. Joseph ....Bridgewater, NJ
Mone, D'Ambrose & Hanyen, P.C. Brockton, MA
Mone, Jennifer M. ....Uniondale, NY
Mone, Maria L. ....Columbus, OH
Mone, Mary C. ....New York, NY
Mone, Mathias E. ....New York, NY
Mone, Michael A. ....Frankfort, KY
Mone, Michael Christopher Belleair Beach, FL
Mone, Michael E. ....Boston, MA
Mone, Peter J. ....Chicago, IL
Mone, Robert P. ....Columbus, OH
Mone, Ronald J. ....Brockton, MA
Mone, Sheila E. ....Boston, MA
Mone, William D. ....Wellesley, MA
Moneer, James J. ....San Diego, CA
Monefeldt, Lois A. ....Brookfield, WI
Monegan, Theodora M. ....Akron, OH
Monell, James L. ....Newburgh, NY
Monen, Craig W. ....Rogue River, OR
Monen, Daniel J., Jr. ....Omaha, NE
Monen & Whitmore ....Omaha, NE
Monera, Lanae L. ....Grand Rapids, MI
Troy, MI
Mones, Paul A. ....Santa Monica, CA
Mones, Steven F. ....Wilmington, DE
Monesmith, Heath B. ....Pittsburgh, PA
Monet, Philippe J. ....Carlsbad, CA
Monetta, David L. ....San Francisco, CA
Monette, Douglas R. ....Omaha, NE
Monette, John P. ....Newport, VT
Monette, Michael D. ....Omaha, NE
Monette, Steven L. ....Burbank, CA
Money, Charles S. ....Birmingham, AL
Money, Christopher C. ....Las Vegas, NV
Money, Christy Preston ....Louisville, KY
Money, David R. ....Englewood, CO
Money, J. Michael ....Douglasville, GA
Money, Kenneth F., Jr. ....Portsmouth, NH
Money Law Offices, P.L.L.C. Portsmouth, NH
Money, Richard A. ....Marion, VA
Money, Samuel C. ....Abbeville, AL
Moneyham, John P. ....Panama City, FL
Moneyham, John P., P.A. ....Panama City, FL
Moneyhun, Harold V. ....Sheridan, WY
Moneymaker, Elizabeth Dianne ....Lawton, OK
Moneymaker, Richard M. Los Angeles, CA
Moneymaker, Richard M., The Law Firm of Los Angeles, CA
Moneymaker, Vincent B. ....Los Angeles, CA
Monfils, Owen F. ....Green Bay, WI
Monfils, Scott P. ....Portland, OR
Monfort, Mark E. ....Oklahoma City, OK
Monfort, Myra H. ....Greeley, CO
Monfort, Renee L. ....Champaign, IL
Monfort, Robert D. ....Newport, KY
Monfred, Jerome B. ....Baltimore, MD
Monfredo, Frank R. ....Pittsford, NY
Monfredo, Shawn W. ....Rochester, NY
Monfried, Thomas S. ....New York, NY
Monfross, Bruce A. ....Sacramento, CA
Mong, Frederick ....Logan, OH
Mong, James F. ....Worthington, OH
Mong, Keith A. ....Washington, DC
Mong, Melissa L. ....Denver, CO
Mongan, A. David ....San Diego, CA
Mongan, Daniel T. ....Hoffman Estates, IL
Mongan, Deborah M. ....San Francisco, CA
Mongan, Edgar J., Jr. ....Folsom, CA
Mongan, Thomas E. ....Tucson, AZ
Mongan, Thos. H. ....Cincinnati, OH
Mongan, Tod V. ....Dallas, TX
Monge, Gregory Lee ....Ashland, KY
Monge, Jay Parry ....New York, NY
Monge, Jose F. ....Columbia, SC
Monge, Joseph P. ....Rancho Santa Fe, CA
Monge, Richard H. ....Fresno, CA
Monge, Roberto Schmidt ....San Juan, PR
Mongeau, Lawrence P. ....Newport, RI
Mongeau, Todd A. ....Cumberland, RI
Mongelli, Gerald J. ....St. Davids, PA
Mongelli, Jeffrey ....Brooklyn, NY
Mongelli, Joseph T. ....Hackensack, NJ
Mongelli, Michael F., II ....Flushing, NY
Mongelli, Thomas ....Mineola, NY
New York, NY
Mongello, Marshall & Scialabba, P.A. South Plainfield, NJ
Mongello, Nicolas F. ....South Plainfield, NJ
Mongelluzzo, Brian J. ....Atlanta, GA
Mongelluzzo, John A. ....Milford, OH
Mongeluzzi, Robert J. ....Philadelphia, PA
Mongeon, Leonard F., Jr. ....Rockville, MD
Mongeon, Nichole ....Orange, CA
Monger, Daniel L. ....Denver, CO

Monger, Michelle McCoy ....Dallas, TX
Mongia, Nisha ....Washington, DC
Mongiardo, Bruno ....Ridgewood, NJ
Mongiardo, Dante P. ....Paterson, NJ
Mongiardo, James F. ....West Paterson, NJ
Mongiardo, Vincent A., II ....Frankfort, KY
Lexington, KY
Mongil-Casasnovas, Luis J. ....San Juan, PR
Mongillo, Carmen J. ....Derby, CT
Mongillo, Frank J., Jr. ....New Haven, CT
Mongillo & Insler ....New Haven, CT
Mongillo, James A. ....New Haven, CT
Mongillo, Susan M. ....Chicago, IL
Mongini, Michael E.J. ....Flagstaff, AZ
Mongiovi, John ....Lancaster, PA
Mongno, Genienne Anne ....Keene, NH
Mongogna, John J. ....Carrollton, TX
Mongolis, Gregory P. ....Chicago, IL
Mongoven, James Federal Trade Commission, Bureau of Competition, GV
Mongoven, William J. ....Chipley, FL
Mongrue, Roy A., Jr. ....Baton Rouge, LA
Mongue, David B. ....Adams, MA
Mongue, Robert E. ....Kennebunk, ME
Monguia, Anna Rose ....Escondido, CA
Monguia, Manuel ....Escondido, CA
Monguia & Monguia ....Escondido, CA
Monhait, Norman M. ....Wilmington, DE
Monhart, Jeffrey A. ....Department of Labor, Pension and Welfare Benefits, GV
Monheim, Thomas A. ....Washington, DC
Monheimer and Associates, A Professional Association ....Wellesley, MA
Monheimer, Marc H. Overseas Private Investment Corporation, GV
Monheimer, Melville ....Seattle, WA
Monheimer, Robert H. ....Wellesley, MA
Monheit, Barbara A. ....New York, NY
Monheit, Deborah R. ....East Setauket, NY
Monheit, Herbert ....Philadelphia, PA
Monheit, Michael H. ....Philadelphia, PA
Monheit Monheit Silverman & Fodera, A Professional Corporation ....Philadelphia, PA
Monheit, Robert S. ....Uniondale, NY
Monhollon & Kelley, P.S.C. Madisonville, KY
Monhollon, Lake Pylant, (Ms.) ....Abilene, TX
Monhollon, Leland ....Madisonville, KY
Moniak, Raymond I. ....Torrance, CA
Moniak, Stephen ....Harrisburg, PA
Monica, Ann Christine ....New Brunswick, NJ
Monica, Christopher T. ....Treasury Department, Internal Revenue Service, GV
Monica, John C. ....Kansas City, MO
Monica, John C., Jr. ....Washington, DC
Monica, John F. ....Orange, NJ
Monica, Linda A. ....Portland, ME
Monica, Woodrow S., Jr. ....Houston, TX
Monical, Christine E. ....Carmel, IN
Monical, John S. ....Chicago, IL
Monicatti, Paul F. ....Troy, MI
Monick, Maria C. ....Willimantic, CT
Monick, Stephen B. ....New York, NY
Monico, Michael D. ....Chicago, IL
Monico, Pavich & Spevack ....Chicago, IL
Monico, Ralph M. ....Hollidaysburg, PA
Monier, Philip, III ....New York, NY
Monighan, James J. ....Salamanca, NY
Monihan, M. Elizabeth ....Cleveland, OH
Monikowski, Richard A. Department of Justice, Environment and Natural Resources Division, GV
Monin, Lawrence O. ....San Francisco, CA
Monioudis, Anthony H. ....Danville, VA
Monioudis, Perry D. West Palm Beach, FL
Monippallil, Matthew M. ....Mattoon, IL
Monistere, Michael J. ....New Orleans, LA
Monitz, Jay L. ....New York, NY
Monitz, Ronald M. ....Burbank, CA
Moniz, Donna M. ....Seattle, WA
Moniz, Henry T. A. ....Boston, MA
Moniz, J. Webb ....New York, NY
Moniz, Joseph A. ....Hartford, CT
Moniz, Lawrence ....Taunton, MA
Moniz, Stacy ....Honolulu, HI
Moniz, Susan A. ....Boston, MA
Monjarez, Kirk R. ....Omaha, NE
Monje & Gordon ....Bakersfield, CA
Monje, Richard A. ....Bakersfield, CA
Monjot, James A. ....Rocky River, OH
Monju, Paul A. ....Lafayette, LA
Monk, Alonzo ....Marina Del Rey, CA
Monk, Anne Marie ....Dallas, TX
Monk, Bob K. ....Port Arthur, TX
Monk, C. Wade ....Rome, GA
Monk, Carl C. ....Topeka, KS
Monk, Charles O., II ....Baltimore, MD
Monk, David G. ....Dallas, TX
Monk, George A. ....Anniston, AL
Monk, Gerald R. ....Grundy Center, IA
Monk, Gerald W. ....Littleton, CO
Monk, Glenn A. ....White Plains, NY
Monk, Hal ....Bedford, TX
Monk, James C. ....Carrollton, KY
Monk, James R. ....Indianapolis, IN
Monk & Knudson, P.C. ....Bedford, TX
Monk Law Office ....Grundy Center, IA
Monk, Marie A. ....Jamaica Plain, MA
Monk, Michael W. ....Los Angeles, CA
Monk, Richard C. ....Santa Barbara, CA
Monk, Richard H., III ....Birmingham, AL
Monk, Richard H., Jr. ....Sylacauga, AL
Monk, Robert A. ....Chicago, IL
Monk, Robert L. ....Santa Barbara, CA

Montanari, R. Ernest, III ... Fresno, CA
Montanaro, Jocelyn E. ... Santa Barbara, CA
Montandon, Arther R. ... Santa Maria, CA
Montaner-Sevillano, Anita ... San Juan, PR
Montanez, Steven ... Tustin, CA
Montanez, Zulma Y ... Bronx, NY
Montanez-Santiago, Angelina
Hammonton, NJ
Montanez-Santiago, Teofilo ... Hammonton, NJ
Montanez-Torres, Angel L. ... Bayamon, PR
Montange, Charles H. ... Seattle, WA
Montani-Beavers, Maria Claudia
El Paso, TX
Montanile, Joseph A. ... New York, NY
Montano, Albert N. ... Roseland, NJ
Montaño, Alfonso J. ... Portland, OR
Montano, Ana Margarita ... San Francisco, CA
Montano, Anton Pal ... Midland, TX
Montano, Arthur ... Audubon, NJ
Cherry Hill, NJ
Montano, Donna Marie ... Nutley, NJ
Montano, Duane ... Denver, CO
Montano, Eltia I. ... New York, NY
Montano, Francine E. ... Florence, AZ
Montano, James S. ... Livingston, NJ
Montano, John Carlos ... Tustin, CA
Montano, Joseph M. ... Denver, CO
Montano, Kevin E. ... Washington, DC
Montano, Mark J. ... Washington, DC
Montaño, Peggy E. ... Denver, CO
Montano, Ricardo ... Central Islip, NY
Montano, Summers, Mullen, Manuel and Owens, A Professional Corporation
Cherry Hill, NJ
Montano, Thomas B. ... Salt Lake City, UT
Montante, Carl J. ... Tonawanda, NY
Montante, Claudia W. ... Emeryville, CA
Montante, James ... Detroit, MI
Montante, Philip J., Jr. ... Miami, FL
Montanus, Caroline ... Orlando, FL
Montanye, George A. ... Alexandria, VA
Montanye, Larry L. ... Bartlesville, OK
Montapert, William D. ... Palm Springs, CA
Montaquila, Arnold N. ... Providence, RI
Montaquila & Summer, P.C. ... Providence, RI
Montaquila, Susan R. ... Winston-Salem, NC
Montarbo & Hansen ... Redding, CA
Montarbo, Richard L. ... Redding, CA
Montare, Ariadne S. ... New York, NY
Montauk, Lance E. ... Berkeley, CA
Montavon, Michael C. ... Fairfax, VA
Montavon, Michael C., P.C. ... Fairfax, VA
Montazzoli, John E. ... Edmond, OK
Montbach, Francis A. ... New York, NY
Montbertrand, Lois Shiner ... Madison, WI
Montbriand, Michael P. ... Sacramento, CA
Montclair, Roy L., III ... Salt Lake City, UT
Montclare, Paul D. ... New York, NY
Montclare & Wachtler ... New York, NY
Monte, Daniel J. ... Santa Fe, NM
Monte, Daniel T. ... Barre, VT
Monte, Donald W. ... Eugene, OR
Florence, OR
Monte, Ines M. ... Chicago, IL
Monte, Jacqueline F.
Fort Lauderdale, FL
Monte, John D. ... Los Angeles, CA
Monte, José M. ... Barre, VT
Monte, Joseph L., Jr. ... Media, PA
Monte, Laura A. ... Buffalo, NY
Monte, Michelle A. ... Sea Girt, NJ
Monte & Monte ... Barre, VT
Monte, Paul G. ... New York, NY
Monte, Peter J. ... Northfield, VT
Monte, Philip F., Jr. ... Atlanta, GA
Monte, Rebecca E. ... Buffalo, NY
Cheektowaga, NY
Monte, Sachs & Borowsky, Counsellors At Law, P.A. ... Sea Girt, NJ
Monte, Thomas D., Jr. ... Sea Girt, NJ
Monteau, Harold A. ... Washington, DC
Omaha, NE
Monteau, Peebles & Marks, L.L.P.
Washington, DC
Omaha, NE
Monteavaro, Joanne ... New York, NY
Montebello, Mary A. ... Washington, DC
Montecallo, Robert ... Hackensack, NJ
Montecalvo, Frank ... Albany, NY
Montecalvo, Michael ... Winston-Salem, NC
Montecalvo, Vincent J. ... Warwick, RI
Montecinos, Flavio ... Denver, CO
Montecucco, William S. ... Vancouver, WA
Montecuollo, John A. ... New Milford, NJ
Montedonico, Edward L. ... Memphis, TN
Montedonico, Hamilton & Altman, P.C.
Washington, DC
Chevy Chase, MD
Frederick, MD
Fairfax, VA
Montedonico, John S. ... Memphis, TN
Montedonico, Joseph ... Chevy Chase, MD
Montefinise, Michael R. ... Garden City, NY
Monteforte, Joseph A., Jr. ... Saugus, MA
Monteforte, Nickolas F. ... Trenton, NJ
Monteforte, Steven ... New York, NY
Montefusco, John J. ... Parsippany, NJ
Montefusco, Joseph L. ... Keansburg, NJ
Montefusco & Kesselman, P.A.
Parsippany, NJ
Montefusco, Marie P. ... Salt Lake City, UT
Montegna, Anthony Roy ... Chula Vista, CA
Montegna, Gregory Alan ... Chula Vista, CA
Montegna, Joseph A. ... Chula Vista, CA
Montegna, Joseph A. ... Westchester, IL
Montegut, Christian E. ... Kirkland, WA
Montei, Lawrence J. ... Kalamazoo, MI
Monteiro, Catherine A. ... Columbus, OH
Monteiro, Kenneth T. ... New York, NY
Monteiro, Nelson C. ... Elizabeth, NJ
Monteith, Charles E. ... Cary, NC
Monteith, David Yates, III ... Columbia, SC
Monteith, Dennis P. ... Rochester, NY
Monteith, Dorrance W. ... Houston, TX
Monteith, Edgar W. ... Houston, TX
Monteith, Edmund H. ... Columbia, SC
Monteith & Harding ... Norfolk, VA
Monteith, J. Derel, Jr. ... Charlotte, NC
Monteith, James D. ... Charlotte, NC
Monteith, James F. ... Philadelphia, PA
Monteith, Kris Anne
Federal Communications Commission, Common Carrier Bureau, GV
Monteith, Mary Austin ... Hernando, MS
Southaven, MS
Monteith & Monteith ... Houston, TX
Monteith, Richard A. ... Norfolk, VA
Monteith, Robert A. ... Rawlins, WY
Monteith, T. Weldon, Jr. ... Trappe, MD
Monteith, Thomas J. ... Omaha, NE
Monteith, Walter S. ... Waynesboro, GA
Montejo, Felipe ... New York, NY
Montel, Joseph J. ... Indianapolis, IN
Monteleone, Anthony J. ... Mount Kisco, NY
Monteleone, Danil J. ... Los Angeles, CA
Monteleone, David F. ... Rockford, IL
Monteleone, Gregory A. ... Thiells, NY
Monteleone, J. Michael ... Cleveland, OH
Monteleone, Jason R.N. ... Boise, ID
Monteleone, John A. ... Brooklyn, NY
Monteleone, Joseph P. ... Warren, NJ
Monteleone, Joseph P. ... New York, NY
Monteleone, Marc A. ... Charleston, WV
Monteleone, Marlene ... New York, NY
Monteleone & McCrory, LLP
Los Angeles, CA
Santa Ana, CA
Monteleone & Monteleone
Mount Kisco, NY
Peekskill, NY
White Plains, NY
Monteleone, Nicholas J. ... Cumberland, MD
Monteleone, Robert A., Jr.
North Adams, MA
Pittsfield, MA
Monteleone, Sally Ann ... New York, NY
Monteleone, Tara Koenig
Mount Kisco, NY
Montelepre, Philip ... New Orleans, LA
Montelione & Associates, P.C.
New York, NY
Montelione, Louis ... Hempstead, NY
Montelione, Richard J. ... New York, NY
Montell, Edward C. ... Long Island City, NY
Montell & Marciano ... Long Island City, NY
Montell, R. Scott ... Houston, TX
Montell, Vincent J. ... Phoenix, AZ
Montella, Gerald C. ... Media, PA
Montella, Mary R. ... San Francisco, CA
Montellaro, Randell ... New York, NY
Montello, John J. ... Pepper Pike, OH
Montello & Kenney, P.A. ... Miami, FL
Montello, Louis R ... Miami, FL
Montello, Madeline ... Kansas City, MO
Montello, Mardi J. ... Clayton, MO
Montelongo, Alfred ... Corpus Christi, TX
Montelongo, Debra S. ... Corpus Christi, TX
Montelongo & Montelongo
Corpus Christi, TX
Montemaggi, Lewis F. ... Rochester, NY
Montemagni, Thomas J. ... West Dover, VT
Montemalo, Frank G. ... Rochester, NY
Montemayor, Alfonso F. ... San Antonio, TX
Montemayor, Charles ... Dallas, TX
Montemayor, Joseph ... Dallas, TX
Montemayor, Linda F. ... Valley Forge, PA
Montemayor & Montemayor ... Dallas, TX
Montemayor, Myrna G. ... Laredo, TX
Montemayor, Oscar J. ... Harlingen, TX
Montemayor, Ruben R., (Law Offices of, P.C.)
San Antonio, TX
Montemore, Martin M. ... Kansas City, MO
Montemorra, Donald R. ... Boston, MA
Montemuro, Paul R. ... Salisbury, MD
Montemurro, John P. ... Haddonfield, NJ
Montemurro, Michael J.
Treasury Department, Internal Revenue Service, GV
Montenaro, Daniel L. ... Cleveland, OH
Montenegro, Carlos M. ... Oakton, VA
Montenegro, Carlos M., P.C. ... Oakton, VA
Montenegro, David L. ... Chicago, IL
Montenegro, Maria C.
Fort Lauderdale, FL
Montenegro, Nicholas C. ... Brick, NJ
Montepelier & Young ... Knoxville, TN
Monter, John C. ... Yakima, WA
Monter, Marilyn B. ... Westbury, NY
Montera, David J. ... West Bloomfield, MI
Montera, David J., P.C.
West Bloomfield, MI
Monterisi, John, Jr. ... Brookline, MA
Montero Finizio Velasquez Weissing and Reyes, P.A. ... Boca Raton, FL
Fort Lauderdale, FL
Miami, FL
Montero, Francisco R. ... Washington, DC
Montero, Hiram M. ... Boca Raton, FL
Fort Lauderdale, FL
Miami, FL
Montero, Joan Blanchard ... Metairie, LA
Montero, Julian F. ... Miami, FL
Montero, Kenneth B. E. ... Richmond, VA
Montero, M. Suzanne ... New Orleans, LA
Montero, Michael C. ... Roslindale, MA
Montero, Michael R. ... Reno, NV
Montero, Vania ... Chicago, IL
Monteros, Janet I. ... Austin, TX
Monteros, Roland ... El Paso, TX
Monterosso, Christine C. ... New York, NY
Monterosso, John M. ... Riverside, CA
Monterosso, Ronald L. ... Edgartown, MA
Monterosso, Vincent J. ... Staten Island, NY
Montes, Armando M. ... San Diego, CA
Montes, Frank S., Jr. ... Redwood City, CA
Montes, John J. ... Bronx, NY
Montes, Jose, Jr. ... El Paso, TX
Montes, Joseph M. ... Los Angeles, CA
Montes, Joyce A. ... Las Cruces, NM
Montes, Pat S. ... Fort Worth, TX
Montes, Patricia S. ... Arlington, TX
Montes & Potack ... Bronx, NY
Montes, Rachel E. ... Arlington, TX
Montes, Rachel E., And Associates
Arlington, TX
Montes, Raul M. ... Glendale, CA
Montes, Raul R. ... Houston, TX
Montes, Robert, Jr. ... Long Beach, CA
Montes, Thomas M. ... Stockton, CA
Montes, Yelva ... Miami Shores, FL
Montesano, Carmela T. ... Washington, DC
Montesano, Michael A. ... Glen Cove, NY
Montesano, Michael J., Jr. ... Buffalo, NY
Montesano, Michael Joseph ... Hamburg, NY
Montesano, Randy ... San Francisco, CA
Monte-Sano, Vincent ... New York, NY
Montesi, Michael F. ... Memphis, TN
Montesi, Thomas J. ... Boston, MA
Montesino, Braulio ... Los Angeles, CA
Montet, N. Forrest ... Atlanta, GA
Monteverde, McAlee, FitzPatrick, Tanker & Hurd, A Professional Corporation
Evesham, NJ
Philadelphia, PA
Monteverde, Tom P. ... Philadelphia, PA
Montevideo, John A. ... Santa Ana, CA
Montevideo, Richard ... Costa Mesa, CA
Montez, Abel P. ... New York, NY
Montez, Angela C. ... Washington, DC
Montez, John A. ... Waco, TX
Montez, Lisa ... Chicago, IL
Montez, Manuel ... San Antonio, TX
Montez, Ralph M. ... Santa Fe, NM
Montez, Williams & Baird, P.C.
Waco, TX
Montford, John T. ... Lubbock, TX
Montfort, Donald G. ... Cincinnati, OH
Montfort, Fredric C. ... Garden City, NY
Montfort, Fredric H. ... Garden City, NY
Montfort, Healy, McGuire & Salley
Garden City, NY
Mineola, NY
New York, NY
Riverhead, NY
Montgomerie, Bruce M. ... New York, NY
Montgomery, Adams & Wyatt, PLC
Little Rock, AR
Montgomery, Adele ... McMechen, WV
Montgomery, Alan L. ... Seattle, WA
Montgomery, Allen K., Jr. ... Louisville, KY
Montgomery, Alpha L. ... San Diego, CA
Montgomery, Andrew S. ... Santa Fe, NM
Montgomery & Andrews, Professional Association ... Santa Fe, NM
Montgomery, Angela K. ... Jacksonville, FL
Montgomery, Ann D. ... Minneapolis, MN
Montgomery, Anthony F. ... Houston, TX
Montgomery, Anthony F., P.C., A Professional Corporation ... Houston, TX
Montgomery, April C. ... Houston, TX
Montgomery, Archibald R., IV ... Newport, RI
Montgomery, Aylmer E., Jr. ... Monroe, LA
Montgomery, B. Keefe ... Louisville, KY
Montgomery & Barker ... Hobart, OK
Montgomery, Barnett, Brown, Read, Hammond & Mintz ... New Orleans, LA
Montgomery, Barry & Bovee ... Spencer, IA
Montgomery, Betsy Lou ... Chatom, AL
Montgomery, Betty D. ... Columbus, OH
Montgomery, Bradley S. ... Saginaw, MI
Montgomery, Brian M. ... Chicago, IL
Montgomery, Bridget E. ... Harrisburg, PA
Montgomery, Bronte I.
Department of the Army, Office of the Assistant Secretary of the Army (Manpower & Reserve Affairs), GV
Montgomery, Bruce Gartner ... Chicago, IL
Montgomery, Bruce L. ... Washington, DC
Montgomery, C. Barry ... Chicago, IL
Montgomery, C. Michael ... Denver, CO
Montgomery, C. Michael
San Antonio, TX
Montgomery, C. Robert ... Chatom, AL
Montgomery, Carl R. ... Canton, MS
Jackson, MS
Montgomery, Carl V. (Vince)
Clarksdale, MS
Montgomery, Carroll & Gales ... Spokane, WA
Montgomery, Charles H., Law Offices of
Cary, NC
Montgomery, Charles H., Law Offices of
Raleigh, NC
Montgomery, Charles R. ... Washington, DC
Montgomery, Charles R. ... Des Moines, IA
Montgomery, Charles S. ... Mount Olive, NJ
Montgomery, Cheryl ... Sacramento, CA
Montgomery, Chris A. ... Colville, WA
Montgomery, Christina M.
White Plains, NY
Montgomery, Claude D. ... New York, NY
Montgomery, Clinton H. ... Waco, TX
Montgomery, Connie F. ... Springfield, MO
Montgomery, Connie S. ... Kenner, LA
Montgomery, Connie Sue ... New Orleans, LA
Montgomery, Cranston P. ... Pasadena, CA
Montgomery, Cromwell R.
Los Angeles, CA
Montgomery, Cynthia L. ... Atlanta, GA
Montgomery, D. Randall ... Dallas, TX
Montgomery, Dan W., Law Office of
Tucson, AZ
Montgomery, Daniel G. ... Oroville, CA
Montgomery, David ... Cincinnati, OH
Montgomery, David ... Houston, TX
Montgomery, David B. ... Chicago, IL
Montgomery, David E. ... New York, NY
Montgomery, David H. ... Dayton, OH
Montgomery, David J. ... Pittsburgh, PA
Montgomery, David K. ... Cincinnati, OH
Montgomery, David L. ... Butler, PA
Montgomery, David P. ... Bradenton, FL
Montgomery, David P. ... Boston, MA
Montgomery, David R. ... Athens, GA
Montgomery, David Robert ... Eugene, OR
Montgomery, Dennis M. ... Denver, CO
Montgomery, Derek T. ... Detroit, MI
Montgomery, Diana G. ... Globe, AZ
Montgomery, Diane U. ... Richmond, VA
Montgomery, Dick H. ... Spencer, IA
Montgomery, Don ... Detroit, MI
Montgomery, Don D. ... Dallas, TX
Montgomery, Donald E. ... Duluth, GA
Montgomery, Donita F. ... Indianapolis, IN
Montgomery, Douglas W.
San Francisco, CA
Montgomery, Duane M.
Santa Monica, CA
Montgomery, Duncan E. ... Los Angeles, CA
Montgomery, Dwight M. ... Riverside, CA
Montgomery, Earline Smith
Stone Mountain, GA
Montgomery, Edward R. P. ... Pasadena, CA
Montgomery, Elsner & Pardieck
Seymour, IN
Montgomery, Elton M., Law Offices of
Graham, TX
Montgomery, Eric A. ... Columbia, SC
Montgomery, Eve ... Philadelphia, PA
Montgomery, Francis G. ... New York, NY
Montgomery, Frank M. ... Salisbury, NC
Montgomery, Frank R. ... Winnetka, IL
Montgomery, Franklin W. ... New York, NY
Montgomery, Fred H. ... Chicago, IL
Montgomery, Frederick W.
Santa Barbara, CA
Montgomery, Gail F. ... San Bernardino, CA
Montgomery, Gary L. ... Boise, ID
Montgomery, Gary T. ... Riverside, CA
Montgomery, Gaye C. ... New York, NY
Montgomery, George ... Indianapolis, IN
Montgomery, George Cranwell
Washington, DC
Montgomery, George E.
Mount Clemens, MI
Montgomery, George F., II
San Francisco, CA
Montgomery, George P. ... Batavia, OH
Montgomery, Gerald E. ... Lake Oswego, OR
Montgomery, Gina S. ... New Orleans, LA
Montgomery, Glenn A., Sr. ... Bedminster, NJ
Montgomery, Gordon H. ... Dallas, TX
Montgomery, Greg ... Seattle, WA
Montgomery, Gregory B. ... Lawnside, NJ
Montgomery, Guy S. ... Newport, AR
Montgomery, H. Paul ... Wilsonville, OR
Montgomery, H. Ronnie ... Jonesville, VA
Montgomery, Haley Haynes ... Asheville, NC
Montgomery, Harrison K. ... Wilmington, DE
Montgomery, Harry ... Moulton, AL
Montgomery, Harry M., Jr. ... Pittsburgh, PA
Montgomery, Heather Love ... Riverwoods, IL
Montgomery, Henry P., IV
Columbus, OH
Montgomery Hines & Fugate, PLC
Jonesville, VA
Montgomery, H. S., Jr. ... South Hill, VA
Montgomery, Hugh C., Jr. ... Jackson, MS
Montgomery, Ilene Nowicki
Farmington Hills, MI
Montgomery, J. Marshall ... Lafayette, LA
Montgomery, J. Tucker ... Knoxville, TN
Montgomery, Jack Bertram ... Santa Rosa, CA
Montgomery, James D. ... Chicago, IL
Montgomery, James D., & Associates, Ltd.
Chicago, IL
Montgomery, James E., Jr.
San Antonio, TX
Montgomery, James L., Jr.
Los Angeles, CA
Montgomery, James J. ... Cincinnati, OH
Montgomery, James L. ... New York, NY
Montgomery, James L. ... Austin, TX
Montgomery, James M. ... New York, NY
Montgomery, James N., Jr. ... Talladega, AL
Montgomery, James R. ... Sacramento, CA
Montgomery, James R. ... Boulder, CO
Montgomery, James R. ... Blacksburg, VA
Montgomery, James T. ... Wichita Falls, TX
Montgomery, James T., Jr.
Washington, DC
Montgomery, James T. M.
Oklahoma City, OK
Montgomery, Jan E. ... Denver, CO
Montgomery, Jane Ellen ... Chicago, IL
Montgomery, Jane Lowell ... Denver, CO
Montgomery, Janet Rae ... La Grange, IL
Montgomery, Jayne N. ... Purcell, OK
Montgomery, Jeffrey F. ... Atlanta, GA
Montgomery, Jerome A. ... Los Angeles, CA
Montgomery, Jerry F. ... Akron, OH
Montgomery, Jerry Joe ... Buffalo, MO
Montgomery, Jill K. H. ... Greeley, CO

Moody, Edward O. ....Little Rock, AR
Moody, Fred H., Jr. ....Bryson City, NC
Moody, G. Randall ....Atlanta, GA
Moody, Gary Allan ....Lansing, MI
Moody, Gerald M. ....Danvers, MA
Moody, Gerald W. ....West Chicago, IL
Moody, Graham B. ....Mill Valley, CA
Moody, Gregory J. ....Darien, IL
Moody, H. Rex ....Memphis, TN
Moody, Harold F., Jr. ....Boston, MA
Moody & Hays, L.L.P. ....Lubbock, TX
Moody, Herbert L., Jr.
Department of Justice, Tax Division, GV
Moody & Hill ....San Francisco, CA
Moody, Holly Eakin ....Fort Lauderdale, FL
Moody, Holly Eakin, P.A.
Fort Lauderdale, FL
Moody, J. Whitfield ....Liberty, MO
Moody, Jack A. ....Siler City, NC
Moody, Jack H., Jr. ....Lumberton, NC
Moody, James E.
Department of the Air Force, Office of the Judge Advocate General, GV
Moody, James G.
Federal Energy Regulatory Commission, Office of the General Counsel, GV
Moody, James H. ....West Long Branch, NJ
Moody, James Hamilton, III ....Dallas, TX
Moody, James M. ....Little Rock, AR
Moody, James M., Jr. ....Little Rock, AR
Moody, James S. ....Plant City, FL
Moody, James S., Jr. ....Tampa, FL
Moody, James T. ....Hammond, IN
Moody, Joe E. ....Gaithersburg, MD
Moody, John Anthony ....College Park, MD
Moody, John D. ....Sacramento, CA
Moody, John G. ....Mansfield, MO
Moody, John P. ....Ramona, CA
San Diego, CA
Moody, John S., Jr. ....Houston, TX
Moody, John Stephen ....New York, NY
Moody, John W. ....Phoenix, AZ
Moody & Jones, P.A. ....Plantation, FL
Moody, Julie S. ....Andalusia, AL
Moody, Karl L. ....Moorpark, CA
Moody, Keane Joseph ....Highland, IN
Moody, Kevin J. ....Lansing, MI
Moody, Kevin J. ....Harrisburg, PA
Moody, Kristi ....Little Rock, AR
Moody, Lawrence G. ....San Dimas, CA
Moody, Leah Bess ....Columbia, SC
Moody, Lee R. ....Walterboro, SC
Moody, Leonard D. ....Vancouver, WA
Moody, Lizabeth A. ....Cleveland, OH
Moody, Louan M. ....Denver, CO
Moody, LoVeen J. ....Pittsburgh, PA
Moody, M. Bradford ....Houston, TX
Moody, Martha A. ....Vero Beach, FL
Moody, Marvin ....Chicago, IL
Moody, Mary Blinn ....Frederick, MD
Moody, Mary G. ....Nashville, TN
Moody, Maurice Marnea ....Baltimore, MD
Moody & Meyers ....Provo, UT
Moody, Michael C. ....Chicago, IL
Moody, Michael J. ....Cleveland, OH
Moody, Michael S. ....Atlanta, GA
Moody, Michelle L. ....Chesapeake, VA
Moody, Nancy D. ....Toledo, OH
Moody, Pamela S. ....Lake Worth, FL
Moody, Patrick S. ....Fresno, CA
Moody, Quinn Adele ....San Francisco, CA
Moody, Randall J. ....Lincoln, NE
Moody, Rebecca Cates ....Warner Robins, GA
Moody, Richard S. ....Henniker, NH
Moody, Robert C. ....Boise, ID
Moody, Robert L. ....Provo, UT
Moody, Rochelle D. ....Gary, IN
Moody, Ronald H. ....Waco, TX
Moody & Salzman, P.A. ....Gainesville, FL
Moody, Sandra L. ....Boston, MA
Moody, S. E., III ....Macon, GA
Moody, Sheryl Leicht ....Old Westbury, NY
Moody, Simon K. ....Auburn, NY
Moody, Steve E. ....Plantation, FL
Moody, Steve L. ....Temple, TX
Moody, Strople & Kloeppel, Inc.
Tampa, FL
Portsmouth, VA
Moody, Susan B. ....Detroit, MI
Moody, Susan C. ....Philadelphia, PA
Moody, T. Rush, Jr. ....Washington, DC
Moody, Thomas C., III ....Hagåtña, GU
Moody, Thomas H. ....Burlington, VT
Moody, Thomas W. ....Atlanta, GA
Moody, Todd J. ....Knoxville, TN
Moody, Todd L. ....Las Vegas, NV
Moody, Trisha L. ....Oklahoma City, OK
Moody, W. Michael ....Anchorage, AK
Moody, W. A. ....Nashville, TN
Moody, Wallace M. ....El Dorado, AR
Moody, Walter D., Jr. ....Tallahassee, FL
Moody, Whitfield & Castellarin, P.C.
Nashville, TN
Moody, Willard J., Jr. ....Tampa, FL
Portsmouth, VA
Moody, Willard J., Sr. ....Portsmouth, VA
Moody, William B., III ....Breckenridge, CO
Moody, William C. ....Nashville, TN
Moody, William E. ....El Paso, TX
Moody, William R., Jr. ....Jonesboro, GA
Moody, William S. ....New York, NY
Moody, William T. ....Myrtle Beach, SC
Moody, Williams & Roper ....Siler City, NC
Moody, Willis E., Jr. ....Buford, GA
Moody-O'Grady, Kristin ....Denver, CO
Mooers, Daniel W. ....Portland, ME
Mooers, Daniel W., & Associate, LLC
Portland, ME
Mooers, Edwin A., Jr. ....Washington, DC
Mooers, John W. ....Jacksonville, FL
Mooers, Thomas R., & Associates
Washington, DC
Moog, Mary Ann ....Havre, MT
Moog, Robert S. ....Raleigh, NC
Moog, Velda J. ....Los Angeles, CA
Mooi, Leslie A. ....Redwood City, CA
Mook, Amanda Bartlett
Jefferson City, MO
Mook, Darrell ....Boston, MA
Mook, H. Telfer ....Beulah, MI
Mook, Jonathan R. ....Alexandria, VA
Mook, Robert W. ....Columbiana, OH
Mook, Ronald H. ....Tulsa, OK
Mookerjee, Leela ....New York, NY
Mool, Deanna Seward ....Chicago, IL
Mool, Robert G. ....Springfield, IL
Moomau, Richard L. ....Oxnard, CA
Moomau, William D. ....Moorefield, WV
Moomaw, James A. ....Dallas, TX
Moomaw, Larry D. ....Beaverton, OR
Moomaw, Miller & Hildebrand, L.L.P.
Beaverton, OR
Moomey, Travis Scott ....New York, NY
Moomjian, Cary A., Jr. ....Dallas, TX
Moomjian, Edward, II ....Tucson, AZ
Moomjian, Gary T. ....Uniondale, NY
Moon, Albert E. ....Fort Myers, FL
Moon, Albert I., Jr. ....Los Angeles, CA
Moon, Alexander P. ....New York, NY
Moon, Alvin ....New Orleans, LA
Moon, Barbara G. ....Jonesboro, GA
Moon, Caitlin Noe ....Franklin, TN
Moon, Carolyn D. ....Bridgewater, NJ
Moon, Catherine Raymond ....Fort Worth, TX
Moon, Charles R. ....Detroit, MI
Moon, Chas. M., Jr. ....Atlanta, GA
Moon, Dallas G. ....Birmingham, MI
Moon, Daniel B. ....Department of Commerce, Patent and Trademark Office, GV
Moon, Daniel D. S. ....Honolulu, HI
Moon, Darrell Dean ....Monterey, CA
Moon, David ....West Des Moines, IA
Moon, David B., Jr. ....Vista, CA
Moon, David C. ....St. Louis, MO
Moon, David C. ....Eugene, OR
Moon, David W. ....Los Angeles, CA
Moon, Deborah A. ....Chickasha, OK
Moon, Donald A. ....Brighton, MI
Moon, Dorothy Suzanne ....Conyers, GA
Moon, Floyd B. ....Valdosta, GA
Moon, Fred C., (P.C.) ....Springfield, MO
Moon, Hee-Jung Shin ....New York, NY
Moon, Horace, Jr. ....Mobile, AL
Moon & Ikeda, A Professional Corporation
New York, NY
Moon, Ilryong ....Annandale, VA
Moon, J. Robert, Jr. ....Baker City, OR
Ontario, OR
Moon, Ja K. ....Palo Alto, CA
Moon, James M. ....San Francisco, CA
Moon, James P. ....Fort Worth, TX
Moon, J. D. ....Fayetteville, AR
Moon, Je ....New York, NY
Moon, Jeffrey A. ....Largo, FL
Moon, Jeffrey Hunter ....Washington, DC
Moon, John ....Kahoka, MO
Moon, John W. ....Duluth, MN
Moon, Kenneth L. ....Cedar Rapids, IA
Moon, Larry Horton ....Oklahoma City, OK
Moon, Laurence M. ....Whitefish Bay, WI
Moon, Linda Sapiro ....Huntington Beach, CA
Moon, Lorie A. ....Sunnyvale, CA
Moon, Lynn A. ....Marquette, MI
Moon, Michael D., Jr. ....Indianapolis, IN
Moon, Michael J. ....Marshalltown, IA
Moon, Michael T. ....Los Angeles, CA
Moon, Mickey Steven ....Tulsa, OK
Moon and Moon ....Chickasha, OK
Moon, Moss, McGill, Hayes & Shapiro, P.A.
Portland, ME
Moon, Myungsoo ....San Francisco, CA
Moon, Nicholas J. ....Old Brookville, NY
Moon, Norman K. ....Lynchburg, VA
Moon, Parker F. ....Springfield, MO
Moon, Patricia Ann ....Seal Beach, CA
Moon, Paul C. ....Port Clinton, OH
Moon, R. Bruce ....Fort Worth, TX
Moon, Ralph E., Jr. ....Palm Harbor, FL
Moon, Randall J. ....Richmond, VA
Moon, Randall W. ....Plainsboro, NJ
Moon, Rebecca L. ....San Jose, CA
Moon, Richard B. ....Dallas, TX
Fort Worth, TX
Moon, Richard G. ....Portland, ME
Moon, Robert L. ....San Francisco, CA
Moon, Robert L., Jr. ....Chattanooga, TN
Moon, Robert R. ....Kingman, AZ
Moon, Ronald T. Y. ....Honolulu, HI
Moon, Sharon Maitland ....Richmond, VA
Moon, Stephen M. ....Port Canaveral, FL
Moon, Stephen M., P.A. ....Melbourne, FL
Port Canaveral, FL
Moon, Steven Todd ....Columbia, SC
Moon, Sun J. ....Lake Forest, IL
Moon, Susan C. ....New York, NY
Moon, Tara L. ....San Diego, CA
Moon, Terry D. ....Brenham, TX
Moon, Thomas W. ....Franklin, TN
Moon, Tina Kyunghi ....New York, NY
Moon, Tracy L., Jr. ....Atlanta, GA
Moon, Travis W. ....Charlotte, NC
Moon, Walter R. ....Orlando, FL
Moon, Walter R., P.A. ....Orlando, FL
Moon, William A. ....Springfield, MO
Moon, William D. ....Dallas, TX
Moon, William D., Jr. ....Chattanooga, TN
Moon, W. R., Sr. ....Chickasha, OK
Moon, Young D. ....Los Angeles, CA
Moonan, Jeffrey P. ....Brookfield, CT
Moonan, John R. ....Mankato, MN
Moonan, Melisa ....Washington, DC
Moonan, Thomas P. ....Rochester, NY
Moonay, Daniel A. ....Plainsboro, NJ
Moonay, Hillary J. ....Philadelphia, PA
Moone, Merrill K. ....Westerly, RI
Moonen, Donald F. ....Epworth, IA
Mooney, Alba N. ....Lynn, MA
Mooney, Ann M. ....San Francisco, CA
Mooney, Arline R. ....Granby, CT
Mooney, Aubrey R. ....Dixon, KY
Mooney, Brian G. ....Tampa, FL
Mooney, Brian J. ....San Francisco, CA
Mooney, C. Duane ....Los Angeles, CA
Mooney, C. William ....Nashville, TN
Mooney, Carol A. ....Notre Dame, IN
Mooney, Charles Andrew
Oklahoma City, OK
Mooney, Charles D. ....New York, NY
Mooney, Charles M. ....Jonesboro, AR
Mooney, Charles M (Skip), Jr.
Jonesboro, AR
Mooney, Charles W., Jr. ....Philadelphia, PA
Mooney & Condino, P.C. ....Detroit, MI
Southfield, MI
Mooney, Cynthia C. ....Chicago, IL
Mooney, Daniel C. ....Mattituck, NY
Mooney, David J. ....Rochester, NY
Mooney, David O. ....Baton Rouge, LA
Mooney, David Patrick Joseph ....Exeter, NH
Mooney, Diane L. ....Newark, NJ
Mooney, Donald B. ....Sacramento, CA
Mooney, Donald F. ....New York, NY
Mooney, Donald J., Jr. ....Cincinnati, OH
Mooney, Douglas G. ....Seattle, WA
Mooney, Edward J. ....New York, NY
Mooney, Elvis A. ....Bloomfield, MO
Mooney, Elvis A., Jr. ....Bloomfield, MO
Mooney, Eric G. ....Georgetown, DE
Mooney, Eugene F. ....Lexington, KY
Mooney, F. Bentley, Jr.
North Hollywood, CA
Mooney, F. Bentley, Jr., A Law Corportaion
Los Angeles, CA
North Hollywood, CA
Mooney, Francis J. ....New York, NY
Mooney, Green, Gleason, Baker, Gibson and Saindon, P.C. ....Washington, DC
Mooney, Harry F. ....Buffalo, NY
Mooney, J. Gregory ....Covington, VA
Mooney, James B. ....Cleveland, OH
Mooney, James M. ....Lexington, KY
Mooney, James P. ....Fairfield, CT
Mooney, James R. ....Woodland Hills, CA
Mooney, Jerome H. ....Hollywood, CA
Salt Lake City, UT
Mooney, Joan A. ....Morgantown, WV
Mooney, John C. ....Chattanooga, TN
Mooney, John E. ....Chicago, IL
Mooney, John G. ....Detroit, MI
Southfield, MI
Mooney, John J. ....Merrick, NY
Mooney, John J., III ....Hanover, PA
Mooney, John M. ....San Francisco, CA
Mooney, John M. ....Bloomfield Hills, MI
Mooney, John R. ....Washington, DC
Mooney, John T., Jr. ....Philadelphia, PA
Mooney, Jon R. ....Philadelphia, PA
Mooney, Jos. C. ....Brookfield, IL
Mooney, Joseph C. ....Boston, MA
Mooney, Joseph E. ....Detroit, MI
Mooney, Joseph L. ....Buffalo, NY
Mooney, Joseph W. ....St. Louis, MO
Mooney, Josephine H. ....Eugene, OR
Mooney, Kathleen A. ....Albany, NY
Mooney, Kelly Ann ....Binghamton, NY
Mooney, Kenneth L. ....Atlanta, GA
Mooney, Kevin E. ....Virginia Beach, VA
Mooney, Kevin James
Woodland Hills, CA
Mooney, L. Wayne ....Van Nuys, CA
Mooney, Laura Muggeo ....Naugatuck, CT
Mooney Law Firm ....Jonesboro, AR
Mooney, Lawrence E. ....Clayton, MO
Mooney, Lawrence M. ....Palmyra, NY
Mooney, Lori-Anne M. ....Kennewick, WA
Mooney, Lynda ....Boston, MA
Mooney, Margaret E. ....Baltimore, MD
Mooney, Margaret M. ....St. Louis, MO
Mooney, Marilyn ....Washington, DC
Mooney, Mark F. ....Tampa, FL
Mooney, Mark F., P.A., Law Offices of
Tampa, FL
Mooney, Martin Ahearn ....Albany, NY
Mooney, Martin C., Sr. ....Mount Holly, NJ
Mooney, Martin E. ....Cincinnati, OH
Mooney, Mary A. ....New York, NY
Mooney, Michael A. ....San Mateo, CA
Mooney, Michael E. ....Boston, MA
Mooney, Michael J. ....Omaha, NE
Mooney, Michael J. ....Omaha, NE
Mooney, Michael R. ....Boulder Creek, CA
Mooney, Monique M. ....Philadelphia, PA
Mooney & Mooney ....Bloomfield, MO
Mooney, Mooney & Mooney
Lexington, KY
Mooney, Naomi L. ....Concord, NH
Mooney, Nicholas F. ....Tampa, FL
Mooney, Nichole M. ....Orlando, FL
Mooney, Patrick B. ....Denver, CO
Mooney, Patrick M. ....Reno, NV
Mooney, Paul J. ....Phoenix, AZ
Mooney, Peter J. ....Philadelphia, PA
Mooney, Peter T. ....Flint, MI
Mooney, Philip D. ....Morgantown, WV
Mooney, Phyllis Ann ....New York, NY
Mooney, R. Kevin ....Fort Worth, TX
Mooney, Richard C. ....Concord, NH
Mooney, Richard C. ....Garden City, NY
Mooney, Richard J. ....San Francisco, CA
Mooney, Richard J., III ....Rochester, NY
Mooney, Robert A. ....Omaha, NE
Mooney, Robert F. ....Nantucket, MA
Mooney, Robert J. ....Syracuse, NY
Mooney, Robert J. T. ....Williamsburg, VA
Mooney, Robert P. ....Castro Valley, CA
Mooney, Robert T. ....Richmond, VA
Mooney, Stephen W. ....Atlanta, GA
Mooney, Susan M. ....Stoneham, MA
Mooney, T. Kevin ....Conyers, GA
Mooney, T. Kevin, P.C. ....Conyers, GA
Mooney, Thomas B. ....Hartford, CT
Mooney, Thomas E. ....Orlando, FL
Mooney, Thomas J. ....Silver Spring, MD
Mooney, Thomas J. ....Edison, NJ
Mooney, Thomas J. ....New York, NY
Mooney, Thomas M. ....St. Paul, MN
Mooney, Thomas R. ....Orlando, FL
Mooney, Timothy C. ....St. Louis, MO
Mooney, W. Terrence ....Houston, TX
Mooney, William A. ....Rockville, MD
Mooney, William D. ....Cleveland, OH
Mooney, William E., Jr. ....Omaha, NE
Mooney, William H. ....Louisville, KY
Mooney, William J. ....Columbus, OH
Mooneyham, John A.
De Funiak Springs, FL
Mooneyham, Joseph A. ....Greenville, SC
Mooneyham, Sarah Booth ....Elmore, AL
Mooneyham, Sonya C. ....Clinton, OK
Mooney II, Nicholas P. ....Charleston, WV
Moonie, Gregory J. ....Scarsdale, NY
Moonly, Stephen K. ....Jacksonville, FL
Moons, Monica Demko ....Birmingham, MI
Moonves, Jonathan D. ....Los Angeles, CA
Moor, Carl H. ....Los Angeles, CA
Moor, Edward R. ....Chicago, IL
Moor, Judith B. ....Brick, NJ
Moor, Karl R. ....Washington, DC
Moor, Wayne T. ....Dallas, TX
Moor, William L. ....Tallahassee, FL
Moorad, Calvin ....Modesto, CA
Moorad, Clark & Gleason ....Modesto, CA
Moorad, Jeffrey S. ....Newport Beach, CA
Mooradian, Arthur ....Morton Grove, IL
Mooradian, Ashod ....Montebello, CA
Mooradian, George T. ....Long Beach, CA
Mooradian, M. George ....Philadelphia, PA
Mooradian, Michael ....Haverhill, MA
Mooradian, Zorik ....Glendale, CA
Moore, A. Jerome ....Trenton, NJ
Moore, A. Patricia ....Kew Gardens, NY
Moore, Aaron J. ....New York, NY
Moore, Aaron W. ....Boston, MA
Moore, A. D. ....Springfield, MO
Moore, Adam ....Dallas, TX
Moore, Adam ....Yakima, WA
Moore, Adriana C. ....Redwood City, CA
Moore, Aidan J. ....Greenland, NH
Moore, A.J. Bosman ....Rome, NY
Moore, Al J. ....Kingwood, TX
Moore, Alan L. ....Jackson, MS
Moore, Alan Powers ....Dallas, TX
Moore, Albert A. ....Boston, MA
Moore, Albert C. ....Georgetown, SC
Moore, Albert F. ....Nashville, TN
Moore, Albert G., Jr. ....Atlanta, GA
Moore, Albert J. ....Los Angeles, CA
Moore, Albert W. L., Jr. ....Independence, MO
Moore, Alexander Rolph ....Oakland, CA
Moore, Alexander T. ....Chicago, IL
Moore, Alexander W. ....Boston, MA
Moore, Alfred ....Hattiesburg, MS
Moore, Alfred D. ....San Francisco, CA
Moore, Alice Keith ....Charlotte, NC
Moore, Alice R. ....Santa Fe, NM
Moore, Alice S. ....Columbia, SC
Moore, Alison H. ....Dallas, TX
Moore, Allan C. ....Danville, CA
Moore, Alyce T. ....Waltham, MA
Moore, Amanda Booker
Parkersburg, WV
Moore, Amanda L. ....New York, NY
Moore, Amber S. ....Aurora, IL
Moore, Amory O. ....Brookfield, WI
Moore, Amy E. ....Oklahoma City, OK
Moore, Amy N. ....Washington, DC
Moore, Andrea McKinney ....Granbury, TX
Moore, Andrea N. ....Houston, TX
Moore, Andrew B. ....Seattle, WA
Moore, Andrew F. ....Berkley, MI
Moore, Andrew G. T., II ....New York, NY
Moore, Andrew P. ....Doylestown, PA
Moore, Angela Gaddis ....Alexandria, VA
Moore, Angela M. ....Washington, DC
Moore, Ann ....Houston, TX
Moore, Ann Turner ....Jackson, TN
Moore, Ann Y. ....San Diego, CA
Moore, Annalisa ....Tucson, AZ
Moore, Anne R. ....Statesboro, GA
Moore, Anthony R. ....Cleveland, OH
Moore, Ardon "Ace" ....Tyler, TX
Moore, Arlie ....Colorado Springs, CO
Moore, Arnold C. ....Atlanta, GA
Moore, Arnold C., Jr. ....Richmond, VA
Moore, Arthur B. ....Pasadena, CA
Moore, Ayrie ....Chicago, IL
Moore, B. Richard, Jr. ....New Orleans, LA
Moore and Bailey ....La Mesa, CA
Moore, Barbara A. ....Cranbury, NJ
Moore, Barbara A. ....Armonk, NY
Moore, Barbara D. ....Sacramento, CA

Moore, Barbara E. Glover ... Plant City, FL
Moore, Barbara L. ... Boston, MA
Moore, Barry D. ... La Grange, KY
Moore, Barry D. ... New Braunfels, TX
Moore, Bart O. ... Niceville, FL
Moore, Basil E., Jr. ... Annapolis, MD
Moore, Baskin & Parker ... Boise, ID
Idaho Falls, ID
Lewiston, ID
Moore, Becky J. ... Alexandria, VA
Moore, Ben C. ... Pascagoula, MS
Moore, Ben F., P.C. ... Troy, MI
Moore & Benham ... Phoenix, AZ
Moore, Benjamin Allston, Jr.
Charleston, SC
Moore, Benjamin D. ... Florence, SC
Moore & Berkowitz ... Philadelphia, PA
Southampton, PA
Moore, Bernard A. ... Norristown, PA
Moore, Bernard S. ... Medford, OR
Moore, Bert E. ... Niceville, FL
Moore, Betsy J. ... Doylestown, PA
Moore, Bettina E. ... San Francisco, CA
Moore, Betty ... Attalla, AL
Moore, Beverly C. ... Greensboro, NC
Moore, Beverly C., Jr., P.C.
Washington, DC
Moore, Beverly Campbell
Winston-Salem, NC
Moore, B. G. ... Castro Valley, CA
Moore, Bill ... Atoka, OK
Moore, Bill ... Cleburne, TX
Moore, Billy D. ... Farmers Branch, TX
Moore, Billy E. ... Atlanta, GA
Moore, Billy J. ... Ennis, TX
Moore, Blaine A. ... New Orleans, LA
Moore, Bob G. ... Amarillo, TX
Moore, Bobbie A. ... Oklahoma City, OK
Moore & Bogosian ... Providence, RI
Moore, Boler & McDermott, P.C.
Omaha, NE
Moore, Bonnie L. ... Honolulu, HI
Moore, Boyce F. ... Little Rock, AR
Moore, Brad J. ... Seattle, WA
Moore, Bradene L. ... Toledo, OH
Moore, Bradford G. ... La Conner, WA
Seattle, WA
Moore, Bradford L. ... Brownfield, TX
Moore, Bradly Edward ... London, KY
Moore, Brenton B. ... Tulsa, OK
Moore, Bret A. ... Niceville, FL
Moore, Brewer & Burbott, A Professional Corporation ... La Jolla, CA
San Dimas, CA
Austin, TX
Moore, Brian D. ... Hoffman Estates, IL
Moore, Brian E. ... Raleigh, NC
Moore, Brian Fintan ... Roseland, NJ
Moore, Brian G. ... Minneapolis, MN
Moore, Brian J. ... Wilmington, NC
Moore, Brian J. ... Akron, OH
Moore, Brian M. ... Calabasas, CA
Moore, Brian Michael
Farmington Hills, MI
Moore, Brian S. ... Monroe, LA
Moore, Brian T. ... Denver, CO
Moore, Brian W. ... Montgomery, AL
Moore, Brian W. ... Morristown, NJ
Moore, Brooks W. ... West Palm Beach, FL
Moore & Brown ... Upland, CA
Moore & Brown ... Washington, DC
Greensboro, NC
High Point, NC
Lexington, NC
Winston-Salem, NC
Moore & Browning ... San Francisco, CA
Moore, Bruce A. ... Santa Ana, CA
Moore, Bruce C. ... Eugene, OR
Moore, Bruce E. ... Englewood, CO
Moore, Bruce E. ... Salina, KS
Moore, Bruce L., P.C. ... Arlington Heights, IL
Moore & Bruce, LLP ... Washington, DC
Moore, Brucie Waggener ... Morganfield, KY
Moore, Bryan ... New York, NY
Moore, Bryan & Schroff, A Law Corporation
Torrance, CA
Moore, Bryce B. ... Overland Park, KS
Moore, C. Grady, III ... Birmingham, AL
Moore, C. Grady, Jr. ... Nashville, TN
Moore, C. Richard, Jr. ... Clanton, AL
Moore, C. Steven ... Brentwood, TN
Moore, Candada J. ... Columbus, OH
Moore, Carl E. ... Chicago, IL
Moore, Carl F. ... Minneapolis, MN
Moore, Carl Jackson ... Palatka, FL
Moore, Carl N. ... Erie, PA
Moore, Carla D. ... Akron, OH
Moore, Carlton H., Jr. ... San Diego, CA
Moore, Carney, Ryan & Lattanzi
Baltimore, MD
Moore, Carol J. ... Huntington Beach, CA
Moore, Carol L. ... Central Islip, NY
Moore, Caroline C. ... Ridgeland, MS
Moore, Caroline Kelley
Santa Monica, CA
Moore, Caroline R. ... Greenwood, MS
Moore, Carolyn E. ... Belleville, IL
Moore, Carolyn F. ... Lubbock, TX
Moore, Carter Hays ... Houston, TX
Moore, Catherine ... Menlo Park, CA
Moore, Catherine E. ... Mission, KS
Moore, Cathy ... Charlotte, NC
Moore, Cathy E. ... Philadelphia, PA
Moore, Cecelia M. ... Bartow, FL
Moore, Cecil G., Law Offices of
Newport News, VA
Moore, Celia Delano ... Boston, MA
Moore, C. F., Jr. ... Beeville, TX
Moore, Chandra ... Santa Monica, CA
Moore, Chantel D. ... Los Angeles, CA
Moore, Charla F. ... Arlington, TX
Moore, Charles A. ... Detroit, MI
Moore, Charles A. ... Ahoskie, NC
Moore, Charles A. ... Gladstone, OR
Moore, Charles A., III ... Tampa, FL
Moore, Charles A., (P.C.) ... Houston, TX
Moore, Charles A. B. ... Atlanta, GA
Moore, Charles C. ... San Francisco, CA
Moore, Charles C. ... Washington, DC
Moore, Charles C. ... Washington, DC
Moore, Charles Cline, A Prof. Corp.
San Francisco, CA
Moore, Charles D., Jr. ... Frankfort, KY
Moore, Charles E. ... San Diego, CA
Moore, Charles E. ... Milledgeville, GA
Moore, Charles E. ... Owensboro, KY
Moore, Charles E., Jr. ... Atlanta, GA
Moore, Charles F. ... Cambridge, MA
Moore, Charles Foster ... Wilsonville, OR
Moore, Charles J. ... Los Angeles, CA
Moore, Charles J. ... Providence, RI
Moore, Charles L. ... Pacific Grove, CA
Moore, Charles L. ... Albuquerque, NM
Moore, Charles L. ... Gastonia, NC
Moore, Charles L., Jr.
Research Triangle Park, NC
Moore, Charles M. ... Dallas, TX
Moore, Charles O. ... Ridgeland, MS
Moore, Charles R. ... Baton Rouge, LA
Moore, Charles R., Jr. ... Hartford, CT
Moore, Charles T. ... Tampa, FL
Moore, Charles T. ... Burlington, KY
Moore, Charles T. ... Nashville, TN
Moore, Charles T., (P.A.)
Daytona Beach, FL
South Daytona, FL
Moore, Charles V. ... Kneeland, CA
Moore, Charles V., Jr. ... Dyersburg, TN
Moore, Charlotte Ann ... Arkadelphia, AR
Moore, Charmaine Y. ... Baton Rouge, LA
Moore, Chas. E. ... Baton Rouge, LA
Moore, Cheryl Jerome ... Dallas, TX
Moore, Chester G., III ... Burlingame, CA
Moore, Chris A. ... Fort Smith, AR
Moore, Christian L. ... Reno, NV
Moore, Christiana Talbird ... Tallahassee, FL
Moore, Christie A. ... Louisville, KY
Moore, Christine ... New York, NY
Moore, Christine G. ... Morristown, NJ
Moore, Christopher D. ... Washington, DC
Moore, Christopher D. ... Boston, MA
Moore, Christopher D. ... Eugene, OR
Moore, Christopher E. ... New Orleans, LA
Moore, Christopher H. ... Seguin, TX
Moore, Christopher J. ... Lewiston, ID
Moore, Christopher J. ... New York, NY
Moore, Christopher L. ... Cincinnati, OH
Moore, Christopher L. ... Seattle, WA
Moore, Christopher M. ... Torrance, CA
Moore, Christopher R. ... San Francisco, CA
Moore, Christopher S. ... Chicago, IL
Moore, Clarence W. ... Washington, DC
Moore, Clarke, DuVall & Rodgers, P.C.
Albany, GA
Moore, Claudia M. ... Manassas, VA
Moore, Clay R. ... Minneapolis, MN
Moore, Clayton W., III ... Atlanta, GA
Moore, Cliff G. ... Milpitas, CA
Moore, Clifton L., Jr. ... Burgaw, NC
Moore, Cole, Nunley & Whittaker
San Jose, CA
Moore, Colleen J. ... Anchorage, AK
Moore, Conrad L., P.C. ... Portland, OR
Moore, Constance ... Hesperia, CA
Moore, Cora L. ... Mineral Wells, TX
Moore, Corinne Katz ... Cleveland, OH
Moore, Cornell L. ... Minneapolis, MN
Moore, Corzine & Bunch Co., L.P.A.
Chillicothe, OH
Moore, Costello & Hart, P.L.L.P.
Minneapolis, MN
St. Paul, MN
Moore, Craig L. ... Cleveland, OH
Moore, Craig N. ... Providence, RI
Moore, Curtis A. ... McLean, VA
Moore, C. W. ... Anaheim, CA
Moore, Cynthia ... New York, NY
Moore, Cynthia A. ... Bloomfield Hills, MI
Moore, Cynthia L. ... Tampa, FL
Moore, Cynthia M. ... Orlando, FL
Armonk, NY
Moore, D. Franklin, Jr. ... Atlanta, GA
Moore, D. Milton, III ... Monroe, LA
Moore, D. Rook, III ... Holly Springs, MS
Moore, D. Scott ... Raleigh, NC
Moore, D. Wayne ... Newport News, VA
Moore, Dale Louise ... Albany, NY
Moore, Dan ... Athens, TX
Moore, Dan A. ... Sioux City, IA
Moore, Dana C., Jr. ... Cleveland, OH
Moore, Daniel A., Jr. ... Anchorage, AK
Wilsonville, OR
Moore, Daniel E. ... Jeffersonville, IN
Moore, Daniel J. ... Towson, MD
Moore, Daniel J. ... Rochester, NY
Moore, Daniel J. ... Knoxville, TN
Moore, Daniel K. ... Atherton, CA
Moore, Daniel L. ... Indianapolis, IN
Moore, Daniel M. ... Detroit, MI
Moore, Daniel M., Jr. ... Decatur, IL
Moore, Daniel T. ... Poplar Bluff, MO
Moore, Danny L. ... Sacramento, CA
Moore, Daphne d'Avbigny
San Francisco, CA
Moore, Daphne G. ... Hartford, CT
Moore, Darlene ... Harrellsville, NC
Moore, Darrell K. ... Palm Springs, CA
Moore, Darrell W. ... Abilene, TX
Moore, Daryl L. ... Houston, TX
Moore, David B. ... Des Moines, IA
Moore, David C. ... Los Angeles, CA
Moore, David C. ... Gladewater, TX
Moore, David C. ... Janesville, WI
Moore, David G. ... Riverside, CA
Moore, David G. ... Watsonville, CA
Moore, David G. ... Shreveport, LA
Moore, David G. ... Albion, MI
Moore, David G. ... Flint, MI
Moore, David G. ... Dallas, TX
Moore, David H. ... Department of Justice, Civil Division, GV
Moore, David K. ... Ripley, WV
Moore, David L. ... Fort Smith, AR
Moore, David L. ... Baltimore, MD
Moore, David L., Jr. ... Greenville, SC
Moore, David L., P.A. ... Baltimore, MD
Moore, David Lee ... Oak View, CA
Moore, David M.
Department of Justice, GV
Moore, David M. ... Bloomington, IL
Moore, David M. ... Crown Point, IN
Moore, David M. ... Worcester, MA
Moore, David M. ... Marietta, OH
Moore, David M. ... Austin, TX
Moore, David M., II ... Greensboro, NC
Moore, David P. ... Cincinnati, OH
Moore, David R. ... Carlsbad, CA
Moore, David R. ... Jonesboro, GA
Moore, David R. ... Urbana, IL
Moore, David Reid ... Baltimore, MD
Moore, David Venable ... Charleston, WV
Moore, David W. ... Salisbury, MD
Moore, David W. ... Troy, MI
Moore, David W., & Associates, P.C.
Troy, MI
Moore, Davis W., Jr. ... Sedalia, CO
Moore, Dawn D. ... Columbia, TN
Moore, Debora R. ... Boca Raton, FL
Moore, Deborah E. ... Syracuse, NY
Moore, Deborah Lynn Baldwin
Cockeysville, MD
Moore, Debra L. ... Overland Park, KS
Moore, Deirdre E. ... Morristown, NJ
Moore, Denise C. ... Lexington, MA
Moore, Denise Donalda ... Los Angeles, CA
Moore, Dennis L. ... Edmore, MI
Moore, Dennis M. ... Washington, DC
Moore, Dennis W., Jr. ... Austin, TX
Moore, Dewey, Jr. ... Little Rock, AR
Moore, Diana M. ... Akron, OH
Moore, Diane Balchak ... Cleveland, OH
Moore, Diane E. ... St. Louis, MO
Moore, Diane Marger ... Indianapolis, IN
Moore, Diane Preston ... Washington, DC
Moore, Dickson & Maxwell, P.L.L.C.
Sweetwater, TX
Moore, Diedrick, Carlisle & Hester
Rocky Mount, NC
Moore, Dion W. ... Bridgeport, CT
Moore & Dodgen ... Columbus, GA
Moore & Dodson
Charlotte Amalie, St. Thomas, VI
Moore, Don ... Chattanooga, TN
Moore, Don A. ... Homewood, IL
Moore, Don, P.C. ... Miami, FL
Moore, Donald C. ... Cincinnati, OH
Moore, Donald C., Jr. ... Cincinnati, OH
Moore, Donald C., Jr., L.P.A., & Co.
Cincinnati, OH
Moore, Donald F. ... New York, NY
Moore, Donald G. ... Denver, CO
Moore, Donald Hugh ... Marina Del Rey, CA
Moore, Donald K. ... Somerville, NJ
Moore, Donald L. ... Warren, AR
Moore, Donald L. ... Rockford, IL
Moore, Donald L. ... Hampton, VA
Moore, Donald P. ... Miami, FL
Moore, Donald P. ... Gulfport, MS
Moore, Donald R. ... Washington, DC
Moore, Donald R. ... Blue Springs, MO
Moore, Donald T. ... Akron, OH
Moore, Donald W. ... Clarkston, WA
Moore, Donna L. ... Colorado Springs, CO
Moore, Donna L. ... Indianapolis, IN
Moore, Donna Ryan ... Boston, MA
Moore, Dorothea O. ... Vero Beach, FL
Moore, Dorothy H. ... Silver Spring, MD
Moore, Douglas E. ... Jersey City, NJ
Moore, Douglas H. ... Ironwood, MI
Moore, Douglas H., Jr. ... Kensington, MD
Moore, Douglas K. ... New York, NY
Moore, Douglas R. ... Paducah, KY
Moore, Douglas S. ... Old Saybrook, CT
Moore, Douglas Thomas ... Honolulu, HI
Moore, Dov ... Bowling Green, KY
Moore, Drew ... Grand Junction, CO
Moore, Durward D. ... Dallas, TX
Moore, Durwood G. ... Charlotte, TN
Moore, Dwight A. ... Tonganoxie, KS
Moore, Dwight B. ... Santa Ana, CA
Moore, Dwight J. ... Omaha, NE
Moore, Dwight W. ... San Bernardino, CA
Moore, Dympna Margaret ... Plymouth, MA
Moore, E. Blake, Jr. ... San Diego, CA
Moore, E. Holt, III ... Wilmington, NC
Moore, E. James ... North Wilkesboro, NC
Moore, E. Kent ... Lafayette, IN
Moore, E. Murray, Jr. ... Tallahassee, FL
Moore, E. Raymond, III ... Columbia, SC
Moore, Earle K. ... New York, NY
Moore, Eddie D., Jr. ... Jacksonville, TX
Moore, Edgar M. ... Tallahassee, FL
Moore, Edgar M., Jr. ... Canton, OH
Moore, Edgar Murray, Jr. ... Tallahassee, FL
Moore, Edward Blake ... Chattanooga, TN
Moore, Edward E. ... Raytown, MO
Moore, Edward F.
Department Of Health And Human Services, Social Security Administration, GV
Moore, Edward H., Jr. ... Dallas, TX
Moore, Edward T. ... La Porte, TX
Moore, Edward W. ... Cleveland, OH
Moore, Edward W. ... Dallas, TX
Moore, Edwin H. ... Nacogdoches, TX
Moore, Edwin M. ... Santa Barbara, CA
Moore, Edwin M. ... Pryor, OK
Moore, Edwin S., III ... Philadelphia, PA
Moore, Elaine Ghrist ... Houston, TX
Moore, Elaine M. ... Albuquerque, NM
Moore, Eli M. ... Bronx, NY
Moore, Elisabeth R. ... Boston, MA
Moore, Elizabeth Berner ... Columbus, OH
Moore, Elizabeth D. ... New York, NY
Moore, Elizabeth E. ... Nashville, TN
Moore, Elizabeth Felton ... Toccoa, GA
Moore, Elizabeth L. ... Charlotte, NC
Moore, Elizabeth M. ... Foster City, CA
Moore, Elizabeth R. ... Treasury Department, Office of Thrift Supervision, GV
Moore, Ellen S. ... Department of Justice, Office of Intelligence Policy and Review, GV
Moore, Elliott ... Oriental, NC
Moore, Emanuel A. ... Jamaica, NY
Moore, Emerson L. ... Tuscola, IL
Moore, Emily ... Tallahassee, FL
Moore, Emily C. ... Louisville, KY
Moore, Emmett ... Houston, TX
Moore, Emmit D. ... Eastpointe, MI
Moore, Eric Michael ... St. Petersburg, FL
Moore, Erik S. ... San Diego, CA
Moore, Erika ... Denver, CO
Moore, Ernest C., III ... Honolulu, HI
Moore, Escum L., Jr. ... Lexington, KY
Moore, E. T., Jr. ... Barnwell, SC
Moore, Eugene Authur ... Pontiac, MI
Moore, Eugene F. ... Los Angeles, CA
Moore, Everett C. ... Los Angeles, CA
Moore, Everett D. ... Maumee, OH
Moore, Faye Bornstein ... Charlotte, NC
Moore, Foard & Dias ... Gloucester, VA
Moore & Fogle., P.S.C. ... Mount Sterling, KY
Moore, Frances ... Houston, TX
Moore, Francis K. ... Buffalo, NY
Moore, Francis M., Jr. ... Pittsburgh, PA
Moore, Francis X. ... Atlanta, GA
Moore, Francis X. ... Red Bank, NJ
Woodbridge, NJ
Moore, Frank D. ... Cooper, TX
Moore, Frank D., Jr. ... New York, NY
Moore, Frank H. ... Dallas, TX
Moore, Frank Hampton, Jr.
Bowling Green, KY
Moore, Frank R. ... Palm Desert, CA
Moore, Frank S. ... San Francisco, CA
Moore, Frank T., Jr. ... Jackson, MS
Moore, Frankie J. ... North Platte, NE
Moore, Franklin ... Fort Worth, TX
Moore, Franklin H., Jr. ... St. Clair, MI
Moore, Franklin H., Jr. ... New York, NY
Moore, Franklin, Jr. ... Neenah, WI
Moore, Fred A. ... Lockhart, TX
Moore, Fred B. ... Bloomington, IL
Moore, Fred D. ... Dallas, TX
Moore, Fred Henry ... Chattanooga, TN
Moore, Fred J. ... Seguin, TX
Moore, Fred S., Jr. ... Birmingham, AL
Moore, Frederick C. ... Irvine, CA
Moore, Frederick C. ... Portland, ME
Moore, Frederick V. ... Storm Lake, IA
Moore, Fredericka Lynne ... Sacramento, CA
Moore, G. Hugh ... Sanford, NC
Moore, G. Robert ... Washington, PA
Moore, G. Stanley ... Lebanon, MO
Moore, G. Timothy ... Mount Clemens, MI
Moore, Gail Degenhart ... Columbia, SC
Moore, Gale H. ... Largo, FL
Moore, Gale H., P.A. ... Largo, FL
Moore, Garrett M. ... Cheshire, CT
Moore, Garry Robert ... Clearwater, FL
Moore, Gary ... Hackensack, NJ
Moore, Gary A. ... Mobile, AL
Moore, Gary Alan ... Kalamazoo, MI
Moore, Gary H. ... Palo Alto, CA
San Francisco, CA
Moore, Gary K. ... Chicago, IL
Moore, Gary L. ... San Clemente, CA
Moore, Gary M. ... Naperville, IL
Moore, Gary R. ... Fort Worth, TX
Moore, Gary R. N., A Prof. Corp.
Saratoga, CA
Moore, Gary R. N. ... Saratoga, CA
Moore, G. B., III ... Gray, GA
Moore, Gene ... Boynton Beach, FL
Moore, Gene ... The Woodlands, TX
Moore, Genevieve M. ... San Francisco, CA
Moore, Geoffrey M. ... Newport Beach, CA
Moore, Geoffrey T. ... Irvine, CA
Moore, George A. ... Huntsville, AL
Moore, George C. ... Arlington, VA
Moore, George C. J.
West Palm Beach, FL
Moore, George Cline ... Perry, FL
Moore, George E. ... Pasadena, CA
Moore, George E. ... Philadelphia, PA
Moore, George E., A Professional Law Corporation ... Los Angeles, CA
Pasadena, CA
Moore, George J. ... Mobile, AL
Moore, George M. ... San Francisco, CA
Moore, George Moore ... Albuquerque, NM
Moore, George P. ... Worcester, MA

Moore, George R. ... **Manchester, NH**
Moore, George W. ... Mount Sterling, KY
Moore, George W. ... Highland Park, MI
Moore, George W. ... **Asheville, NC**
Moore, George W. ... Cleveland, OH
Moore, George W. ... **Philadelphia, PA**
Moore, George W. ... Richmond, VA
Moore, George W., III ... Bloomfield Hills, MI
Moore, Gerald A. ... Marion, OH
Moore, Gerald F. ... Lowell, MA
Moore, Gerald F., (P.C.) ... Phoenix, AZ
Moore, Gerald R. ... Billings, MT
Moore, Gerald W., (P.A.) ... Miami, FL
Moore, Ginevera K. ... **Kansas City, MO**
Moore, Glen J. ... **Greenwich, CT**
New York, NY
Moore, Glen R. ... Fayetteville, TN
Moore, Glenn R. ... **Richmond, VA**
Moore, Gloria J. ... **Las Vegas, NV**
Moore, Gloria J. ... **Oklahoma City, OK**
Moore, Gloria S. ... Knoxville, TN
Moore & Golden, P.A. ... **Santa Fe, NM**
Moore, Gordon F., II ... **Haddonfield, NJ**
Moore, Gordon Lynn, III ... Worthington, MN
Moore, Gregory A. ... Miami Lakes, FL
Moore, Gregory A. ... St. Augustine, FL
Moore, Gregory B. ... Berkeley, CA
Moore, Gregory C. ... Davis, CA
Moore, Gregory E. ... **Boston, MA**
Moore, Gregory F. ... Washington, DC
Moore, Gregory G. ... Portland, OR
Moore, Gregory L. ... Detroit, MI
Moore, Gregory Scott ... Monroe, LA
Moore, Gregory W. ... **Indianapolis, IN**
Moore & Groseclose ... Pulaski, VA
Moore, Gunter & Bruneman ... Dallas, TX
Moore, H. Clay ... Houston, TX
Moore, H. David ... Warner Robins, GA
Moore, H. Edward, Jr. ... **Pensacola, FL**
Moore, H. Keith ... **Vinton, VA**
Moore, H. Kirk, Jr. ... Senatobia, MS
Moore, H. Lowell ... Colorado Springs, CO
Moore, H. Mathew ... **San Francisco, CA**
Moore, H.A., III ... **Hattiesburg, MS**
Moore, Halsey & Eskola ... Fridley, MN
Moore, Hamilton D., Law Offices of
Las Vegas, NV
Moore & Hansen ... **Minneapolis, MN**
Moore, Hardy Goodner ... **Paris, TX**
Moore, Harold C. ... **Indianapolis, IN**
Moore, Harold E. ... Arlington, TX
Moore, Harold F. ... **New York, NY**
Moore, Harold T. ... **Santa Fe, NM**
Moore, Harry A. ... Madison, NE
Moore, Harry F. ... Kansas City, MO
Moore, Harry R. ... Moneta, VA
Moore, Harry Truman ... **Paragould, AR**
Moore, Harvey M. ... **Newport Beach, CA**
Moore, Heather D. ... **Yuma, AZ**
Moore, Heather Stuart ... **Seattle, WA**
Moore & Hedges ... Tullahoma, TN
Moore, Helen J.
Securities and Exchange Commission, Office of Compliance Inspections and Examinations, GV
Moore Hennessy & Freeman, P.C.
Kansas City, MO
Moore, Henry ... **Hillsboro, TX**
Moore, Henry M. ... **Reston, VA**
Moore, Henry T., Jr. ... Santa Ana, CA
Moore, Herbert F. ... **Princeton, NJ**
Moore, Herbert P., Jr. ... Orinda, CA
Moore, Hill, Westmoreland, Hook & Bolton, P.A. ... **Pensacola, FL**
Moore, Hillar C., III, Law Offices of
Baton Rouge, LA
Moore, Hollis I., Jr. ... Nashville, TN
Moore, Holly Toye ... Department of State, Office of the Legal Adviser, GV
Moore, Howard, Jr. ... Oakland, CA
Moore, Howard L. ... Dallas, TX
Moore & Howell ... Morristown, NJ
Moore, Hugh D. ... Owensboro, KY
Moore, Hugh J., Jr. ... **Chattanooga, TN**
Moore, Hugh L. ... **Chicago, IL**
Moore, Hugh L., Jr. ... **Providence, RI**
Moore, Hullihen Williams ... Richmond, VA
Moore Ingram Johnson & Steele, LLP
Atlanta, GA
Marietta, GA
Moore International Law Offices
San Francisco, CA
Moore, Irving, Jr. ... Wharton, TX
Moore, J. Ashley ... **Baton Rouge, LA**
Moore, J. Benton, III ... **San Diego, CA**
Moore, J. David ... **Birmingham, AL**
Moore, J. David ... Port Arthur, TX
Moore, J. Dennis ... Dallas, TX
Moore, J. Derek ... **Bryan, TX**
Moore, J. Donel ... Albion, MI
Moore, J. Edgar ... Rocky Mount, NC
Moore, J. Everett, Jr. ... **Georgetown, DE**
Milford, DE
Moore, J. Gregory ... Erie, PA
Moore, J. Kevin ... **Oakland, CA**
Moore, J. Kevin ... **Marietta, GA**
Moore, J. Mark ... **Los Angeles, CA**
Moore, J. Marks, III ... **Baltimore, MD**
Moore, J. Michael, The Law Office of
McAllen, TX
Moore, J. Peyton ... Shreveport, LA
Moore, J. Ralph ... Pryor, OK
Moore, J. Ralph, P.C. ... Pryor, OK
Moore, J. Reneé ... Oxford, MS
Moore, J. Richard ... **Jacksonville, FL**
Moore, J. Richard ... **Indianapolis, IN**
Moore, J. Richard, III ... Bel Air, MD
Moore, J. Richard III, P.A. ... Bel Air, MD
Moore, J. Richard, Jr ... **Jacksonville, FL**
Moore, J. Sam, Jr. ... El Paso, TX
Moore, J. Tatum, III ... Austin, TX
Moore, J. William ... Phoenix, AZ
Moore, Jack C. ... Tulsa, OK
Moore, Jack D. ... **St. Paul, MN**
Moore, Jack H. ... Richmond, TX
Moore, Jack M. ... Silver Spring, MD
Moore, Jack M. ... **Temple, TX**
Moore, Jackson, Ralston & Crist
Harrisonburg, VA
Moore, Jackson W. ... Cordova, TN
Moore, Jackson W. ... **Houston, TX**
Moore, Jacqueline A. ... Bel Air, MD
Moore, Jacqueline E. ... **St. Louis, MO**
Moore, Jacqueline J. ... Washington, DC
Moore, Jacqueline Rich ... **Sacramento, CA**
Moore, Jadie ... Detroit, MI
Moore, James A. ... Boston, MA
Moore, James A. ... Kansas City, MO
Moore, James A. ... **Pittsburgh, PA**
Moore, James A. ... Houston, TX
Moore, James A. ... Suffolk, VA
Moore, James B. ... Chicago, IL
Moore, James B. ... New London, NH
Moore, James B., Jr. ... **Georgetown, SC**
Myrtle Beach, SC
Moore, James C. ... **Rochester, NY**
Moore, James C. ... Houston, TX
Moore, James C., II ... Santa Fe, NM
Moore, James D. ... El Centro, CA
Moore, James D. ... **Frankfort, IN**
Moore, James D. ... Lynn, MA
Moore, James D. ... Tulsa, OK
Moore, James D., Law Office of
Kalispell, MT
Moore, James E. ... Mobile, AL
Moore, James E. ... Niceville, FL
Moore, James E. ... Baton Rouge, LA
Moore, James E. ... Greenwood, SC
Moore, James E. ... **Sioux Falls, SD**
Moore, James E. ... **Sioux Falls, SD**
Moore, James E. ... **Richmond, VA**
Moore, James E., III ... **Punta Gorda, FL**
Moore, James E., III ... Sikeston, MO
Moore, James E., Jr. ... **Baton Rouge, LA**
Moore, James Edward ... Merritt Island, FL
Moore, James F. ... Farmington Hills, MI
Moore, James F., II ... Lubbock, TX
Moore, James H., III ... **Albany, GA**
Moore, James H., III ... **Ashland, KY**
Moore, James H., Jr. ... Waynesville, NC
Moore, James I. ... New York, NY
Moore, James J., Jr. ... Houston, TX
Moore, James L. ... **Houston, TX**
Moore, James L., Jr. ... Jacksonville, NC
Moore, James L., Jr. ... **Philadelphia, PA**
Moore, James L. (Lee), III ... **Pine Bluff, AR**
Moore, James M. ... Detroit, MI
Moore, James M. ... **Cincinnati, OH**
Moore, James M. ... **Cleveland, OH**
Moore, James M., Jr. ... Knoxville, TN
Moore, James R. ... **Sacramento, CA**
Moore, James R. ... Carterville, IL
Moore, James R. ... **Marshalltown, IA**
Moore, James R. ... Lebanon, MO
Moore, James R. ... Oklahoma City, OK
Moore, James R. ... **Portland, OR**
Moore, James R. ... Knoxville, TN
Moore, James R. ... **Salt Lake City, UT**
Moore, James R., & Associates, P.C.
Oklahoma City, OK
Moore, James R., Jr. ... **Jackson, MS**
Moore, James R., Jr. ... Altus, OK
Hollis, OK
Moore, James R., (P.C.) ... **Costa Mesa, CA**
Moore, James S. ... Buffalo, NY
Moore, James S. ... Wolfforth, TX
Moore, James T. ... Apple Valley, CA
Moore, James T. ... Plantation, FL
Moore, James T. ... Richmond, VA
Moore, James Verner ... Cambridge, MA
Moore, James W. ... **Little Rock, AR**
Moore, James W. ... Lilburn, GA
Moore, James W. ... Weston, MA
Moore, James W., (P.A.) ... Miami, FL
Moore, Jamie M. ... Olympia, WA
Moore, Jane A. ... Chicago, IL
Moore, Jane Bond ... Oakland, CA
Moore, Janet ... Osceola, AR
Moore, Janet ... **Houston, TX**
Moore, Janet I. ... Blue Bell, PA
Moore, Janet S. ... Los Angeles, CA
Moore, Janet Wilson ... **Worcester, MA**
Moore, Janice ... Mount Vernon, WA
Moore, Janice E.
Nuclear Regulatory Commission, Office of the General Counsel, GV
Moore, Janice H. ... **Phoenix, AZ**
Moore, Janice R. ... **Houston, TX**
Moore, Jay R. ... Vineland, NJ
Moore, J.D. ... **Kansas City, MO**
Moore, Jean Bante ... Katy, TX
Moore, Jean S. ... **Washington, DC**
Moore, Jeffrey C. ... **Schaumburg, IL**
Moore, Jeffrey C. ... Willow Grove, PA
Moore, Jeffrey G. ... **Salem, OR**
Moore, Jeffrey H. ... **Chattanooga, TN**
Moore, Jeffrey H., (P.A.) ... **Little Rock, AR**
Moore, Jeffrey M. ... San Jose, CA
Moore, Jeffrey S. ... **Tupelo, MS**
Moore, Jennifer A. ... **San Francisco, CA**
Louisville, KY
Moore, Jennifer Brown ... **Atlanta, GA**
Moore, Jennifer E. ... **Atlanta, GA**
Moore, Jennifer M. ... New York, NY
Moore, Jennifer Sigafoos ... **Los Angeles, CA**
Moore, Jennifer Wayland ... **Asheville, NC**
Moore, Jerome Anderson ... San Francisco, CA
Moore, Jerre De Spain ... St. Joseph, MO
Moore, Jerry A., III ... **Washington, DC**
Moore, Jerry D. ... North Wilkesboro, NC
Moore, Jerry D. ... **Franklin, WV**
Moore, Jerry F. ... Downey, CA
Moore, Jerry L. ... Bowling Green, KY
Moore, Jerry S. ... Tahlequah, OK
Moore, Jim ... Dallas, TX
Moore, Jo Gruidl ... Wilmette, IL
Moore, Joan Marie Roake ... Newark, NJ
Moore, Joan R. ... Vienna, VA
Moore, Joanna L. ... **Chicago, IL**
Moore, Joanne A. ... Willits, CA
Moore, Jody C. ... **Ventura, CA**
Moore, Joe A. ... Pascagoula, MS
Moore, Joe K. ... Jacksonville, FL
Moore, Joel B. ... **Harbor Springs, MI**
Moore, Joey P. ... **Tustin, CA**
Moore, John ... Austin, TX
Moore, John A. ... El Dorado, AR
Moore, John A. ... **Miami, FL**
Moore, John A., Jr. ... Oakland, CA
Moore, John A., Jr. ... Lansdowne, PA
Moore, John B. ... Louisville, KY
Moore, John B., Jr. ... Clarendon, AR
Moore, John Bruce ... Dallas, TX
Moore, John C. ... Ocala, FL
Moore, John C. ... Lake Oswego, OR
Moore, John C. ... Memphis, TN
Moore, John C. ... **Richmond, VA**
Moore, John C. ... Springfield, VA
Moore, John C. ... **Tacoma, WA**
Moore, John C. ... Milwaukee, WI
Moore, John C., & Associates, P.C.
Lake Oswego, OR
Moore, John C., III ... New York, NY
Moore, John D. ... Jackson, MS
Moore, John D., A Prof. Corp.
Mineral Wells, TX
Moore, John Daniel ... **Kansas City, MO**
Moore, John David ... **Nashville, TN**
Moore, John Douglas ... San Francisco, CA
San Rafael, CA
Moore, John E. ... **Little Rock, AR**
Moore, John E., III ... **Vero Beach, FL**
Moore, John E., Jr. ... Little Rock, AR
Moore, John G. ... Napa, CA
Moore, John G. ... **Chicago, IL**
Moore, John G. ... **Carthage, MO**
Moore, John H. ... Boynton Beach, FL
Moore, John H. ... **Marietta, GA**
Moore, John H. ... Chicago, IL
Moore, John H. ... Rockville, MD
Moore, John H. ... Erie, PA
Moore, John H., II ... Jacksonville, FL
Moore, John J. ... **Indianapolis, IN**
Moore, John J. ... **New York, NY**
White Plains, NY
Moore, John K. ... Virginia Beach, VA
Moore, John L. ... Mobile, AL
Moore, John L. ... **Sarasota, FL**
Moore, John L. ... Oregon, IL
Moore, John L. ... Morristown, NJ
Moore, John L. ... Houston, TX
Moore, John L., IV ... Mobile, AL
Moore, John L., Jr. ... **Washington, DC**
Moore, John M. ... Rancho Palos Verdes, CA
Moore, John M. ... Sacramento, CA
Moore, John M. ... **Denver, CO**
Moore, John M. ... Memphis, TN
Moore, John M. ... **Madison, WI**
Moore, John N. ... Washington, DC
Moore, John N., III ... **Key West, FL**
Moore, John Norton ... Charlottesville, VA
Moore, John O., Jr. ... **Little Rock, AR**
Moore, John P. ... **Phoenix, AZ**
Moore, John P. ... Fresno, CA
Moore, John P. ... **Cut Bank, MT**
Moore, John P. ... Eau Claire, WI
Moore, John P., Jr. ... **Fort Lauderdale, FL**
Moore, John Paul ... Winchester, KY
Moore, John Paul ... Starkville, MS
Moore, John R. ... **Palo Alto, CA**
Moore, John R. ... Department of Justice, Civil Rights Division, GV
Moore, John R. ... **Selinsgrove, PA**
Moore, John S. ... **Batavia, OH**
Moore, John S. ... Bellingham, WA
Moore, John S. ... **Yakima, WA**
Moore, John S. ... **Charleston, WV**
Moore, John T. ... Apple Valley, MN
Moore, John T. ... **Columbia, SC**
Moore, John T. ... Richardson, TX
Moore, John Terry ... **Wichita, KS**
Moore, John Thaddeus ... **Brewton, AL**
Moore, John V. ... **Elmira, NY**
Moore, John W. ... **Atlanta, GA**
Moore, John W. ... Chicago, IL
Moore, John W. ... **Dallas, TX**
Moore, John W., Jr. ... Farmington, CT
Moore, Jonathan A. ... Forest Hills, NY
Moore, Jonathan Clifford ... New York, NY
Moore, Jonathon R. ... **Washington, DC**
Moore and Jones ... Hattiesburg, MS
Moore, Joseph B. ... St. Louis, MO
Moore, Joseph C., II ... Scottsdale, AZ
Moore, Joseph C., III ... **Raleigh, NC**
Moore, Joseph E. ... **Berlin, MD**
Ocean City, MD
Moore, Joseph F. ... Pasadena, CA
Moore, Joseph F. ... **San Francisco, CA**
Moore, Joseph F. ... **Jackson, WY**
Moore, Joseph G. ... New Haven, CT
Moore, Joseph H. ... **Kansas City, MO**
Moore, Joseph K.
United States Postal Service, Law Department, GV
Moore, Joseph L. ... San Jose, CA
Moore, Joseph M. ... Juneau, WI
Moore, Joseph P. ... Dayton, OH
Moore, Joseph R.
Department Of Veterans Affairs, Board of Veterans Appeals, GV
Moore, Joseph T. ... **Boston, MA**
Moore, Joy T. ... **Tallahassee, FL**
Moore, Joy Topazian ... Milford, CT
Moore, Joyce W. ... **San Antonio, TX**
Moore, Judy C. ... **Carthage, MO**
Moore, Judy K. ... Albuquerque, NM
Moore, Julia M. ... **Washington, DC**
Moore, Julia M. ... Hackensack, NJ
New York, NY
Moore, Juliana S. ... **Akron, OH**
Moore, Julie A. ... Minneapolis, MN
Moore, Julie E. ... Colorado Springs, CO
Moore, K. Michael ... Miami, FL
Moore, K. Randy ... San Jose, CA
Moore, K. (Teya) ... **Bethesda, MD**
Moore & Kandaras, A Professional Law Corporation ... Rapid City, SD
Moore, Karen H. ... Chicago, IL
Moore, Karen Keiger ... Greensboro, NC
Moore, Karen L. ... Bedford, MA
Moore, Karen Mueller ... **Columbus, OH**
Moore, Karen Nelson ... Cleveland, OH
Moore, Karen S. ... Lexington, KY
Moore, Karen W. ... **Milwaukee, WI**
Moore, Kathe R. ... Los Angeles, CA
Moore, Katherine S. ... Clayton, CA
Moore, Kathleen E. ... Tallahassee, FL
Moore, Kathleen Kelly ... Portland, OR
Moore, Kathleen M. ... Colorado Springs, CO
Moore, Kathleen McDonnell
Bridgewater, MA
Moore, Kathleen S. ... **Boston, MA**
Moore, Kathy L. ... Cleveland, OH
Moore, Keith Douglas ... Cincinnati, OH
Moore, Keith L. ... **Chicago, IL**
Moore, Keith Lawson ... Ewing, NJ
Moore, Keith V. ... Memphis, TN
Moore, Kelly ... Brooklyn, NY
Moore, Kelly A. ... **St. Louis, MO**
Moore, Kelly G. ... Brownfield, TX
Moore, Kelly J. ... San Jose, CA
Moore, Kelly L. ... Cedar Rapids, IA
Moore, Kellye C. ... **Perry, GA**
Moore, Kendale A. ... Tucker, GA
Moore, Kenneth C. ... Cupertino, CA
Moore, Kenneth C. ... **Cleveland, OH**
Moore, Kenneth I. ... **New York, NY**
Moore, Kenneth R. ... Morning Sun, IA
Moore, Kent R. ... Chattanooga, TN
Moore, Kenton E. ... **Los Angeles, CA**
Moore, Kermit J. ... **Bluefield, WV**
Moore, Kerry B. ... Phoenix, AZ
Moore, Kessler & Moore ... Niceville, FL
Moore, Kevin A. ... Chicago, IL
Moore, Kevin A. ... **Wyomissing, PA**
Moore, Kevin E. ... **Honolulu, HI**
Moore, Kevin J. ... Pasadena, CA
Moore, Kevin J. ... **Chicago, IL**
Moore, Kevin J. ... **Princeton, NJ**
Moore, Kevin J. ... Spencerport, NY
Moore, Kevin M. ... Syracuse, NY
Moore, Kevin T. ... Atlanta, GA
Moore, Kieren M. ... Meriden, CT
Moore, Kim E. ... **New Orleans, LA**
Moore, Kim R. ... Perryville, MO
Moore, Kimberlee L. ... Platte City, MO
Moore, Kimberly Hope ... Moorestown, NJ
Moore, Kimberly L. ... **Reno, NV**
Moore, Kimberly S. ... **Dallas, TX**
Moore, Kirby R. ... **Macon, GA**
Warner Robins, GA
Moore, Kirk A. ... **Houston, TX**
Moore, Kirk D. ... San Bernardino, CA
Moore, Kirkmichael T. ... Houston, TX
Moore, Klio Arvanitidis ... **Seattle, WA**
Moore, Kyle E. ... **Dallas, TX**
Moore, L. Dean ... **Cookeville, TN**
Moore, L. Hutch ... **Atlanta, GA**
Moore, Landrey, L.L.P. ... **Beaumont, TX**
Moore, Larry ... Bridgewater, NJ
Moore, Larry ... Memphis, TN
Moore, Larry B. ... **Florence, AL**
Moore, Larry B. ... Springfield, MO
Moore, Larry Dean ... Muskogee, OK
Moore, Larry G. ... **Provo, UT**
Salt Lake City, UT
Moore, Larry I., III ... **Greensboro, NC**
Moore, Larry M. ... Fort Worth, TX
Moore, Larry S. ... Wilkesboro, NC
Moore, Larry W. ... Kettering, OH
Moore, Latonya S. ... **Atlanta, GA**
Moore, Laur. S. ... Pasco, WA
Moore, Laura S. ... **Boulder, CO**
Moore, Laurentia Duff ... Austin, TX
Moore, Laurie ... San Francisco, CA
Moore Law Firm ... **Barnwell, SC**
Moore Law Firm, The, L.L.P. ... **Paris, TX**
Moore, Lawrence C., III ... **Charlotte, NC**
Moore, Lawrence E., Jr. ... **Latrobe, PA**
Moore, Lawrence J. ... Horseshoe Bay, TX
Moore, Lawrence R. ... Fair Oaks, CA
Moore, Lawrence W. ... New Orleans, LA
Moore, LeAnne ... Dresden, TN
Moore & Lee ... Burgaw, NC
Moore, Lee Alan ... Independence, MO
Moore & Lee, LLP ... **Vienna, VA**
Moore, Leigh A. ... Decatur, GA
Moore, Leigh Ann ... Abilene, TX
Moore, Leland C. ... **Baltimore, MD**
Moore, Leo G., Jr. ... Scotland, SD
Moore, Leon W. ... **Chicago, IL**
Moore, Leonard M. ... Dearborn, MI

Moore, Rutter & Evans—Continued
Newport Beach, CA
Moore, S. Clark ... Monrovia, CA
Moore, S. Jahue (Jake)
West Columbia, SC
Moore, Sally Young ... Cincinnati, OH
Moore, Sam ... Abilene, TX
Moore, Samuel A. ... Brooklyn, NY
Moore, Samuel A. ... Bethel Park, PA
Pittsburgh, PA
Moore, Samuel E. ... Tulsa, OK
Moore, Samuel M., III ... Houston, TX
Moore, Samuel N. ... Annandale, VA
Moore, Samuel W., II ... Greensburg, KY
Moore, Sandra M. ... St. Louis, MO
Moore, Sandra Sue ... El Paso, TX
Moore, Sanford E. ... New York, NY
Moore, Sara F. ... Lubbock, TX
Moore, Sara Mason ... Lexington, KY
Moore & Saunders, L.L.C. ... Suffolk, VA
Moore, Schuyler M. ... Los Angeles, CA
Moore, Scott ... Austin, TX
Moore, Scott A. ... Austin, TX
Moore, Scott D. ... Elmira, NY
Moore, Scott D. ... Fort Worth, TX
Moore, Scott J. ... Los Angeles, CA
Moore, Scott J. ... Parsippany, NJ
Moore, Scott Michael ... San Francisco, CA
Moore, Scott Parrish ... Department of Justice,
Civil Rights Division, GV
Moore, Scott S. ... Omaha, NE
Moore, S. D. Roberts ... Roanoke, VA
Moore, Sean D. ... New Orleans, LA
Moore, Sean L. ... Fort Lauderdale, FL
Moore, Sean P. ... Des Moines, IA
Moore & Serio ... Clarendon, AR
Moore, Sharon H. ... Clinton, NJ
Moore, Shaun ... San Jose, CA
Moore, Shawn C. ... Sacramento, CA
Moore, Shelby H., Jr. ... Thousand Oaks, CA
Moore, Sheri E. ... Houston, TX
Moore, Sherrie L. ... Oxford, MS
Tupelo, MS
Moore, Sherry M. ... Bismarck, ND
Moore, Sheryl A. ... Mercer Island, WA
Moore, Sheryl Ann ... Charleston, SC
Moore, Sidaya ... San Francisco, CA
Moore, Sizoo & Nieman
Walnut Creek, CA
Moore and Skiljan ... Carlsbad, CA
Moore, Smith & Moore, P.A.
Jacksonville, FL
Moore and Smith, P.C. ... Knoxville, TN
Moore, Sophia Leigh ... Dallas, TX
Moore, Stacy L., Jr. ... Marlton, NJ
Moore, Stanley C., III ... Bloomfield Hills, MI
Moore, Stanley D. ... Coeur d'Alene, ID
Spokane, WA
Moore, Stanley J. ... Pleasanton, CA
Moore, Stanley R. ... Dallas, TX
Moore, Stanley William, (P.A.) ... Miami, FL
Sarasota, FL
Winter Park, FL
Moore, Stephan M. ... Santa Clara, CA
Moore, Stephanie ... Memphis, TN
Moore, Stephanie Y.
Commission on Civil Rights,
Office of the General Counsel, GV
Moore, Stephen A. ... Winchester, MA
Moore, Stephen A. ... Harrisburg, PA
Moore, Stephen C. ... Los Angeles, CA
Moore, Stephen C., P.C. ... Mobile, AL
Moore, Stephen Craig ... Nashville, TN
Moore, Stephen D.
Cape May Court House, NJ
Moore, Stephen D., Jr. ... Jacksonville, FL
Moore, Stephen E. ... Boston, MA
Moore, Stephen E. ... Mount Laurel, NJ
Philadelphia, PA
Moore, Stephen E. ... Bothell, WA
Moore, Stephen F. ... Harrisburg, PA
Moore, Stephen J. ... Carlsbad, CA
Moore, Stephen J. ... New Orleans, LA
Moore, Stephen J., (P.C.)
Kansas City, MO
Moore, Stephen M. ... Danbury, CT
Moore, Stephen P. ... Carmel, NY
Moore, Stephen P. ... Cleveland, OH
Moore, Stephen R. ... Portland, OR
Moore, Stephen T. ... Rockford, IL
Moore, Stephen W. ... Homewood, IL
Moore, Stephen Ward ... Long Beach, CA
Moore, Steven A. ... Portland, OR
Moore, Steven B. ... Kansas City, MO
Moore, Steven C. ... Boulder, CO
Moore, Steven C. ... Morning Sun, IA
Moore, Steven C. ... Waltham, MA
Moore, Steven D. ... Atlanta, GA
Moore, Steven D. ... Cedar Falls, IA
Moore, Steven D. ... Austin, TX
Moore, Steven E. ... Oklahoma City, OK
Moore, Steven G. ... Fort Oglethorpe, GA
Moore, Steven J. ... Stamford, CT
Moore, Steven J. ... Baton Rouge, LA
Moore, Steven M., & Associates
Nashville, TN
Moore, Steven W. ... Yuma, AZ
Moore, Steven W. ... Denver, CO
Moore, Stevens E. ... New Orleans, LA
Moore, Stoddard, Stoddard & Wood
Spartanburg, SC
Moore, Stout, Waddell & Ledford, P.C.
Kingsport, TN
Moore & Studstill, P.C. ... Nashville, GA
Moore, Sue Helen ... Livingston, TX
Moore, Sully Wade
Rancho Cucamonga, CA
Moore, Susan A. ... Washington, DC

Moore, Susan E. ... Chicago, IL
Moore, Susan Finch ... Washington, DC
Moore, Susan L. ... Fresno, CA
Moore, Susan L. ... Austin, TX
Moore, Susan M. ... Long Beach, CA
Moore, Susie H. ... Henderson, KY
Moore, Susler, McNutt, Wrigley & Root
Decatur, IL
Moore, Suzan E. ... Lebanon, VA
Moore, Suzanne L. ... San Diego, CA
Moore, Suzanne L. ... Waterbury, VT
Moore, Suzy C. ... San Diego, CA
Moore, T. Darrah ... Ludlow, VT
Moore, T. Deven ... Bay Minette, AL
Daphne, AL
Foley, AL
Moore, T. Douglas ... St. Louis, MO
Moore, T. Jeff ... Clarkesville, GA
Moore, T. Justin, III ... Richmond, VA
Moore, Tamara A. ... Indianapolis, IN
Moore, Tamara A. ... Versailles, KY
Moore, Tammie Y. ... Arlington, TX
Moore, Tebbs S. ... Harrodsburg, KY
Moore, Terence L. ... Newport, KY
Moore, Terence S. ... Tampa, FL
Moore, Teresa J. ... West Palm Beach, FL
Moore, Teresa L. ... Newark, NJ
Moore, Terrence Jay ... Dana Point, CA
Moore, Terri B. ... Dallas, TX
Moore, Terry A. ... Mobile, AL
Moore, Terry A. ... Jacksonville, FL
Moore, Terry A. ... Canton, OH
Salem, OH
Moore, Terry E. ... Cincinnati, OH
Moore, Terry L. ... Eau Claire, WI
Moore, Terry Mason ... Minneapolis, MN
Moore, Theresa M. ... Denver, CO
Moore, Thomas A. ... San Francisco, CA
Moore, Thomas A. ... Orlando, FL
Moore, Thomas A. ... Palos Hills, IL
Moore, Thomas A. ... New York, NY
Moore, Thomas A. ... Columbus, OH
Moore, Thomas A. ... Williamsburg, VA
Moore, Thomas C. ... New York, NY
Moore, Thomas C. ... Dumas, TX
Moore, Thomas C., III ... Indianapolis, IN
Moore, Thomas D., Jr. ... Denton, TX
Moore, Thomas E. ... Xenia, OH
Moore, Thomas E., III ... Palo Alto, CA
Moore, Thomas F., Jr. ... Matthews, NC
Moore, Thomas H. ... Fort Collins, CO
Moore, Thomas H.
Consumer Product Safety Commission,
Commissioners Office, GV
Moore, Thomas H. ... Albuquerque, NM
Moore, Thomas Henry ... Durham, NC
Moore, Thomas J. ... Denver, CO
Moore, Thomas J. ... Niwot, CO
Moore, Thomas J. ... Hillsboro, OR
Moore, Thomas J. ... Philadelphia, PA
Moore, Thomas J. ... Alexandria, VA
Moore, Thomas J. ... Richmond, VA
Moore, Thomas J., II ... Rocky Mount, NC
Moore, Thomas Jon ... Reading, PA
Moore, Thomas K. ... New York, NY
Moore, Thomas K.
Charlotte Amalie, St. Thomas, VI
Moore, Thomas Kendall ... Wentworth, NC
Moore, Thomas L. ... Traverse City, MI
Moore, Thomas L., Jr. ... Dresden, TN
Moore, Thomas M. ... Capitola, CA
Moore, Thomas M. ... Santa Monica, CA
Moore, Thomas M. ... Sherman Oaks, CA
Moore, Thomas M. ... Kansas City, MO
Moore, Thomas M. ... Newark, NJ
Moore, Thomas M. ... Nashville, TN
Moore, Thomas N., III ... Chicago, IL
Moore, Thomas O., III ... Houston, TX
Moore, Thomas O., Jr. ... Kernersville, NC
Moore, Thomas P. ... San Antonio, TX
Moore, Thomas P. ... Madison, WI
Moore, Thomas R. ... Tallahassee, FL
Moore, Thomas R. ... Pittsburgh, PA
Moore, Thomas R., Law Offices of
New York, NY
Moore, Thomas S.
Nuclear Regulatory Commission,
Atomic Safety and Licensing Board Panel,
GV
Moore, Thomas S. ... Portland, OR
Moore, Thomas S., P.C. ... Portland, OR
Moore, Thomas T. ... Columbia, SC
Moore, Thomas V. ... Riverdale, MD
Moore, Thomas W. ... Birmingham, AL
Moore, Thomas W. ... Stafford, TX
Moore, Thomas W., III
West Caldwell, NJ
New York, NY
Moore, Thomas W., Jr. ... Winston-Salem, NC
Moore, Thomas Wilson, Jr. ... Tuscaloosa, AL
Moore, Thomasina F. ... Orlando, FL
Moore, Thomasine E., and Associates
Jacksonville, NC
Moore, Thos. E. ... Okmulgee, OK
Moore, Thurman W., III ... Albuquerque, NM
Moore, Thurston R. ... Richmond, VA
Moore, Tim ... Redondo Beach, CA
Moore, Tim ... Fort Worth, TX
Moore, Tim ... Houston, TX
Moore, Tim J. ... Wichita, KS
Moore, Timothy A. ... Syracuse, NY
Moore, Timothy D. ... Jackson, MS
Moore, Timothy G. ... Longview, TX
Moore, Timothy G. ... Richmond, VA
Moore, Timothy J. ... Palo Alto, CA
Moore, Timothy J. ... Green Bay, WI
Moore, Timothy K. ... Shelby, NC
Moore, Timothy R. ... Charlotte, NC

Moore, Todd L. ... Troy, MI
Moore, Todd R. ... Pasadena, CA
Moore, Todd R. ... Houston, TX
Moore, Tom, Jr. ... Waco, TX
Moore, Tom L. ... Tacoma, WA
Moore, Tom M. ... Oklahoma City, OK
Moore, Tom W., Jr. ... Columbia, TN
Moore, Tommy L. ... Fincastle, VA
Moore, Toni Anderson ... Philadelphia, PA
Moore, Traci Ann ... Shreveport, LA
Moore, Tracy W. ... Columbia, TN
Moore, Travis Warren ... Greenwood, SC
Moore, Tresi L. ... Arlington, TX
Moore, Treston E.
Charlotte Amalie, St. Thomas, VI
Moore & Trousdale, P.C. ... Athens, AL
Florence, AL
Moulton, AL
Tuscumbia, AL
Moore, Troy L. ... Northwood, OH
Toledo, OH
Moore, Tyler M. ... Roanoke, VA
Moore, Tyndall and Castellow ... Moultrie, GA
Moore, Valerie A. ... Santa Monica, CA
Moore & Van Allen, PLLC ... Charlotte, NC
Durham, NC
Raleigh, NC
Research Triangle Park, NC
Research Triangle Park, NC
Charleston, SC
Moore, Vanessa M. ... Pembroke Pines, FL
Moore, Verlinda P. ... Manchester, MA
Moore, Verne, Jr. ... Omaha, NE
Moore, Vernon A. ... Oakland, CA
Moore, Vestrand and Pozehl, P.C.
Southfield, MI
Moore, Vicki L.
Agency for International Development,
Legal Advisers-Overseas, GV
Moore, Vincent J. ... Buffalo, NY
Moore, Virgadamo & Lynch, Ltd.
Newport, RI
Moore, Virgil, P.C. ... Des Moines, IA
Moore, Virginia A. ... Dallas, TX
Moore, Virginia Lee ... Myrtle Beach, SC
Surfside Beach, SC
Moore, Virginia Maddux ... Cookeville, TN
Moore & Vrana ... Dallas, TX
Moore, W. Andrew ... Costa Mesa, CA
Moore, W. Carl, Jr. ... Houston, TX
Moore, W. Cliff, III ... Columbia, SC
Moore, W. David ... Boerne, TX
Moore, W. David ... San Antonio, TX
Moore, W. David ... San Antonio, TX
Moore, W. Dean ... Stuart, IA
Moore, W. Gary ... Lawrenceville, GA
Moore, W. Joseph, Jr. ... Columbia, SC
Moore, W. Lee, Jr. ... Dallas, TX
Moore, W. Michael ... Charleston, WV
Moore, W. Newton ... Atlanta, GA
Moore, W. Richard ... Raleigh, NC
Moore, W. Rudy, Jr. ... Fayetteville, AR
Moore, W. Stephen ... Hampton, VA
Moore, W. Tyler, Jr. ... Bryan, TX
Moore, W. Tyler, Jr., P.C. ... Bryan, TX
Moore and Waksler ... Port Charlotte, FL
Punta Gorda, FL
Moore, Walter D. ... Marion, OH
Moore, Walter T. ... Menlo Park, CA
Moore, Walter T. ... Redlands, CA
Yucaipa, CA
Moore, Walter W. ... Marina Del Rey, CA
Moore, Walters & Thompson, A Professional Corporation ... Baton Rouge, LA
Moore, Wanda Holly
Charlotte Amalie, St. Thomas, VI
Moore, Warfield, Jr. ... Detroit, MI
Moore, Warner ... Wichita, KS
Moore, Wayne D. ... Blacksburg, VA
Moore, Weldon L., III ... Dallas, TX
Moore, Weldon W. ... Rolla, MO
Moore, Wendy L. ... Menlo Park, CA
Moore, Weston Reed ... Overland Park, KS
Moore, Wilbur N., Jr. ... Columbia, SC
Moore, Wilburn Davis, Jr. ... Philadelphia, MS
Moore, Wilburn L. ... Vienna, VA
Moore, Willard S. ... New York, NY
Moore, William A. ... Detroit, MI
Moore, William A. ... New York, NY
Moore, William A. ... Dallas, TX
Moore, William A., Jr. ... Los Angeles, CA
Moore, William B. ... Champaign, IL
Moore, William B. ... Rolling Meadows, IL
Moore, William B. ... Independence, MO
Moore, William B. ... Chillicothe, OH
Moore, William B. ... Cochranton, PA
Meadville, PA
Moore, William B. ... Fairfax, VA
Moore, William B., Jr. ... Montgomery, AL
Moore, William C. ... Columbus, GA
Moore, William C. ... Indianapolis, IN
Moore, William C. ... Asheville, NC
Moore, William C. ... Cary, NC
Moore, William C. ... Houston, TX
Moore, William D. ... Southold, NY
Moore, William D. ... Cleveland, OH
Moore, William D., Jr. ... Rockford, IL
Moore, William E. ... Amsterdam, NY
Moore, William E. ... Lansdale, PA
Moore, William E. ... Gloucester, VA
Moore, William E., Jr. ... Valdosta, GA
Moore, William E., Jr. ... Gastonia, NC
Moore, William E., Jr., A Professional
Corporation ... Valdosta, GA
Moore, William G. ... Fridley, MN
Moore, William Grayson, III ... Houston, TX
Moore, William H., Jr. ... Charlotte, NC
Moore, William J. ... New York, NY

Moore, William J., Jr.
Consumer Product Safety Commission,
Office of Compliance, GV
Moore, William Jeffrey ... Columbus, OH
Moore, William K. ... Versailles, KY
Moore, William K., Jr. ... Frankfort, KY
Moore, William L., Jr. ... Gallatin, TN
Moore, William M. ... Mobile, AL
Moore, William M. ... San Diego, CA
Moore, William M. ... Sherman Oaks, CA
Moore, William R. ... Calabasas, CA
Moore, William R. ... Houston, TX
Moore, William R., Jr. ... Isle of Wight, VA
Moore, William S. ... Washington, DC
Moore, William S., Jr. ... Portsmouth, VA
Moore, William Sebastian ... Jackson, MS
Moore, William T. ... Daytona Beach, FL
Moore, William T. ... Tallahassee, FL
Moore, William T. ... Cuyahoga Falls, OH
Moore, William T. ... Bryan, TX
Moore, William T., Jr. ... Savannah, GA
Moore, William V.W. ... Stockton, CA
Moore, William W., 3rd
Department of Commerce,
Patent and Trademark Office, GV
Moore, William X., Jr. ... Wilmington, DE
Moore, Willis C. ... New York, NY
Moore, Willson C., Jr. ... Honolulu, HI
Moore, Winston C. ... Chicago, IL
Moore, Winston S. ... Arlington, VA
Moore, Winter, Skebba & McLennan, LLP
Glendale, CA
San Bernardino, CA
Moore, Wm. S. ... St. Petersburg, FL
Moore, Wm. V. ... Billings, MT
Moore & Wolfe, A Ptrshp. of Prof Corps.
Mobile, AL
Moore, Y. Albert, III ... Huntsville, AL
Moore, Yaklevich & Mauger ... Columbus, OH
Moore, Yolanda L. ... Indianapolis, IN
Moore, Yvonne B. ... Burnsville, MN
Moore, Zoe Ann ... Cleveland, OH
Moore-Beckert, Karin ... Boonville, NY
Moore-Driggers, Zanetta N.
Philadelphia, PA
Moore-Duncan, Dorothy L. ... Philadelphia, PA
Moorefield, Carlton S. ... Springfield, VA
Moorefield, G. Crawford ... Houston, TX
Moorefield, Harold D., Jr. ... Miami, FL
Moorefield, Rickey L. ... Graham, NC
Moore Hamrick, Mary ... Washington, DC
Moorehead, Carey B. ... Los Angeles, CA
Moorehead, Donald V. ... Washington, DC
Moorehead, Douglas A. ... Zanesville, OH
Moorehead, John S. ... Englewood, FL
Moorehead, John T. ... San Diego, CA
Moorehead, Lisa L. ... Chicago, IL
Moorehead, Robert E ... Jackson, MS
Moorehead, Robert S., Jr. ... Cambridge, OH
Moorehead, Rochelle M.
Charlotte Amalie, St. Thomas, VI
Moorehead, Sandra Stayer ... Sacramento, CA
Moorehead, Susan Bruch
Charlotte Amalie, St. Thomas, VI
Moorehead, Susan Foley ... Decatur, IL
Moorehead, Timothy L. ... Chicago, IL
Moore-Henson, Julie ... Guthrie, OK
Moore-Hewitt, Sheilarayne ... Cleveland, OH
Moore-Hunley, Camille ... Rosemead, CA
Moore-Jason, Linda ... Auburn Hills, MI
Mooreland-Rucker, Diana Lynn ... Dallas, TX
Mooreman, Robert G. ... Phoenix, AZ
Moore-McSpedon, Sheila A. ... New York, NY
Moorer, John D. ... Orangeburg, SC
Moorer, Mac M. ... Birmingham, AL
Moorer, Mark S. ... Moscow, ID
Moorer, Robert E. ... Birmingham, AL
Moores, E. Patrick ... Lexington, KY
Moores, Edward H. ... Allison Park, PA
Moores, Ian W. ... Salem, MA
Moores, John B. ... West Palm Beach, FL
Moores, Jon H. ... Decatur, AL
Moores, Lorri M. ... West Palm Beach, FL
Moores, Marilyn Ann ... Indianapolis, IN
Moores, Merrill ... Indianapolis, IN
Moores, Patricia A. ... New York, NY
Moores, Roland F. ... Sun City, AZ
Moores, Steven B. ... Santa Fe, NM
Mooresmith, John T. ... Birmingham, AL
Moorey, Scott Thomas ... Fort Myers, FL
Moorey, Thomas E. ... Fort Myers, FL
Moorey, Thomas E. ... Sanibel, FL
Moorhead, Amer C. ... Santa Clara, CA
Moorhead, Bridget Klein ... San Diego, CA
Moorhead, Bruce W., Jr. ... Atlanta, GA
Moorhead, Carlos J. ... Glendale, CA
Moorhead, Cora ... Department of Commerce,
Patent and Trademark Office, GV
Moorhead, Derek R. ... Overland Park, KS
Moorhead, Dixon D. ... Los Angeles, CA
Moorhead, Donald R. ... Greenville, SC
Moorhead, Donald R., P.A.
Greenville, SC
Moorhead, Gary L. ... Laguna Hills, CA
Moorhead, J. Kirkman ... Anderson, SC
Moorhead, J. Phillip ... Redondo Beach, CA
Moorhead, James B. ... Washington, DC
Moorhead, James Dan ... Arlington, TX
Moorhead, Jeffrey B. C.
Christiansted, St. Croix, VI
Moorhead, Joanna L. ... Washington, DC
Moorhead, Joe M. ... Findlay, OH
Moorhead, John B. ... Denver, CO
Moorhead, Kathleen J. ... San Mateo, CA
Moorhead, Kerry L. ... San Mateo, CA
Moorhead, M. Jennifer
Daytona Beach, FL

Moran, John Thomas ..... Chicago, IL
Moran, John V. ..... Grosse Pointe Farms, MI
Moran, John W. ..... Milford, CT
Moran, Joseph L. ..... Cincinnati, OH
Moran, Joseph M. ..... Anchorage, AK
Moran, Joseph M. ..... Wilmington, DE
Moran, Joseph S. ..... Waukegan, IL
Moran, Joseph T. ..... Pittsburgh, PA
Moran, Joseph T., Jr. ..... Baltimore, MD
Moran, Joyce E. ..... Hoffman Estates, IL
Moran, Judith B. D. ..... Baltimore, MD
Moran, Julie Taylor ..... Boston, MA
Moran, Justine Clare ..... New York, NY
Moran, Kara B. ..... Honolulu, HI
Moran, Karen M. ..... Washington, DC
Moran, Karen Michaud ..... Damariscotta, ME
Moran, Kathleen F. ..... East Hanover, NJ
Moran, Kathleen M. ..... Oak Brook, IL
Moran, Kathleen P. ..... Trenton, IL
Moran, Kathryn A. ..... Boulder, CO
Moran, Kathryn Montgomery
Chicago, IL
Moran, Kenneth J. ..... Richmond, VA
Moran, Kenneth S. ..... Metairie, LA
Moran, Kevin J. ..... Norcross, GA
Moran, Kevin J. ..... New York, NY
Moran, Kevin P. ..... Silverdale, WA
Moran, Kevin P. ..... Milwaukee, WI
Moran, Kristie Macchio ..... Oyster Bay, NY
Moran, Kyle Anne ..... New York, NY
Moran, Kyle Stuart ..... Gulfport, MS
Moran, Larry W. ..... Bozeman, MT
Moran, Lauretta J. ..... Chicago, IL
Moran Law Office, Ltd. ..... Minneapolis, MN
Moran, Lawrence J. ..... Scranton, PA
Moran, Leroy ..... Roanoke, VA
Moran, Leroy, & Associates, P.C.
Roanoke, VA
Moran, Liam J. ..... Anchorage, AK
Moran, Linda M. ..... Sebastopol, CA
Moran, Linda M. ..... Olympia, WA
Moran, Lisa L. ..... Tulsa, OK
Moran, Lisa M. ..... Houston, TX
Moran, Lisa V. ..... New York, NY
Moran, Lynn A. ..... Custer, SD
Moran, M. Katherine ..... Aurora, IL
Moran, Marcia Hennelly ..... Concord, NH
Moran, Margaret-Ann ..... Hillsborough, NH
Moran, Maria R. ..... Omaha, NE
Moran, Marianna P. ..... Indianapolis, IN
Moran, Mark A. ..... Washington, DC
Moran, Mark B. ..... St. Louis, MO
Moran, Mark E. ..... New York, NY
Moran, Mark R. ..... Flagstaff, AZ
Moran, Mark W. ..... Dallas, TX
Moran, Marnie M. ..... Minnetonka, MN
Moran, Mary Ann ..... San Francisco, CA
Moran, Mary Ansbro ..... Cleveland, OH
Moran, Mary Beth ..... Toledo, OH
Moran, Mary Jane ..... La Jolla, CA
Moran, Mary Lou Michels ..... Hagåtña, GU
Moran, Mary Louise ..... Milton, MA
Moran, Mary Theresa ..... Boston, MA
Moran, Mary-Louise ..... St. Louis, MO
Moran, Matthew S. ..... Deerfield, IL
Moran, Matthew T. ..... Chicago, IL
Moran, Matthew W. ..... Dallas, TX
Moran, Maura K. ..... Sudbury, MA
Moran, Maureen ..... New York, NY
Moran, Michael ..... Chico, CA
Moran, Michael ..... Sarasota, FL
Moran, Michael ..... Atlanta, GA
Moran, Michael C. ..... Ann Arbor, MI
Moran, Michael D. ..... Englewood, CO
Moran, Michael J.
Department of Housing and Urban Development,
Office of General Counsel, GV
Moran, Michael J. ..... Arlington Heights, IL
Moran, Michael J. ..... Chicago, IL
Moran, Michael J. ..... Metairie, LA
Moran, Michael J. ..... Boston, MA
Moran, Michael J. ..... Cuyahoga Falls, OH
Moran, Michael J. ..... Dallas, TX
Moran, Michael O. ..... Portland, OR
Moran, Michael P. ..... Department of Justice,
Executive Office for United States Attorneys,
GV
Moran, Michael P. ..... Houston, TX
Moran, Michael R. ..... Downers Grove, IL
Moran, Michael R. ..... Columbus, OH
Moran, Michael W. ..... Dallas, TX
Moran, Michelle F. ..... Minneapolis, MN
Moran, Miller F. ..... Carthage, NY
Moran, M. J. ..... Pittsburgh, PA
Moran, Molly J. ..... Chicago, IL
Moran & Montgomery, Ltd. ..... Columbus, OH
Moran, Montgomery F. ..... Denver, CO
Moran & Moran ..... Toledo, OH
Moran, Morehouse and Bruno ..... Erie, PA
Moran, Myra N. ..... Waycross, GA
Moran, Nancy Lee ..... Washington, DC
Moran, Nancy M. ..... Oklahoma City, OK
Moran, Neil J. ..... San Rafael, CA
Moran & Ozbirn, P.C. ..... Dallas, TX
Moran, P. Thomas ..... Silver Spring, MD
Moran, Pat ..... Rogers, AR
Moran, Patricia A. ..... New York, NY
Moran, Patricia C. ..... Norwalk, CT
Moran, Patrick A. ..... Detroit, MI
Moran, Patrick D. ..... Los Angeles, CA
Moran, Patrick G. ..... Chicago, IL
Moran, Patrick J. ..... Washington, DC
Houston, TX
Moran, Patrick J. ..... Westchester, IL
Moran, Patrick J. ..... Blue Bell, PA
Moran, Patrick J., P.C., A Professional Corporation ..... Houston, TX

Moran, Patrick M. ..... Bellevue, WA
Moran & Patrick, P.A. ..... Murrells Inlet, SC
Moran, Paul A., (P.A.) ..... Sarasota, FL
Moran, Paul E. ..... New York, NY
Moran, Paul R. ..... Cincinnati, OH
Moran, Paul X. ..... Aurora, CO
Moran, Paula G. ..... Canandaigua, NY
Moran, Peter ..... New York, NY
Moran, Peter L. ..... Toledo, OH
Moran, Philip D. ..... Boston, MA
Salem, MA
Salem, MA
Moran, Philip D., P.C. ..... Salem, MA
Moran, R. Emmett ..... Cleveland, OH
Moran, R. Scott ..... Dallas, TX
Moran, Richard A. ..... Las Vegas, NV
Moran, Richard J. ..... St. Louis, MO
Moran, Richard T. ..... Saratoga Springs, NY
Moran, Robert A. ..... Garden City, NY
Moran, Robert C. ..... Winchester, MA
Moran, Robert E. ..... Boston, MA
Moran, Robert E. ..... Boston, MA
Moran, Robert J. ..... Chicago, IL
Moran, Robert J. ..... Palmer, MA
Moran, Robert J., Jr. ..... Murrells Inlet, SC
Moran, Robert L. ..... Houston, TX
Moran, Robert Patrick ..... Utica, NY
Moran, Robert R. ..... Alliance, NE
Moran, Robert R., Jr. ..... Avon, CT
Moran, Robert S., Jr. ..... Montvale, NJ
Moran, Ronald P. ..... Vandalia, OH
Moran, Rosa ..... Oakland, CA
Moran, Russell F. ..... East Islip, NY
Moran & Sarafin, A Professional Corporation ..... Anchorage, AK
Moran, Scott E. ..... Atlanta, GA
Moran, Sean ..... New York, NY
Moran, Sean W. ..... Pittsburgh, PA
Moran & Shams, P.A. ..... Orlando, FL
Moran, Sharon M. ..... Vineland, NJ
Moran, Sharon T. ..... Rockford, IL
Moran, Shawn M. ..... Chicago, IL
Moran, Shuster, Carignan & Knierim
Avon, CT
Moran, Siobhan E. ..... New York, NY
Moran, Stephen M. ..... Irvine, CA
Moran, Stephen V. ..... New Haven, CT
Moran, Stephen W. ..... Lakeland, FL
Moran, Susan J. ..... Chicago, IL
Moran, Susan J. ..... Cleveland, OH
Moran, Susan P. ..... Oklahoma City, OK
Moran, Suzanna Kay ..... Denver, CO
Moran and Sweeney ..... Boston, MA
Lynn, MA
Moran, Tara A. ..... Chicago, IL
Moran, Terence J. ..... Chicago, IL
Moran, Teresa A. ..... San Bruno, CA
Moran, Terrence J. ..... Stafford, NY
Moran, Theresa G. ..... San Francisco, CA
Moran, Thomas ..... Saratoga, CA
Moran, Thomas C. ..... Boston, MA
Moran, Thomas E. ..... Chicago, IL
Moran, Thomas E. ..... Geneseo, NY
Moran, Thomas F. ..... New York, NY
Moran, Thomas F. ..... Myrtle Beach, SC
Moran, Thomas J., Jr. ..... Fitchburg, MA
Moran, Thomas James ..... Chicago, IL
Moran, Thomas P. ..... Orlando, FL
Moran, Thomas Paul ..... Washington, DC
Moran, Thomas R. ..... Atlanta, GA
Moran, Tim ..... Tampa, FL
Moran, Timothy E. ..... New Haven, CT
Moran, Timothy F. ..... Attica, NY
Moran, Timothy J. ..... Washington, DC
Moran, Timothy J. ..... Department of Justice,
Civil Rights Division, GV
Moran, Timothy J. ..... Beavercreek, OH
Moran, Timothy P. ..... Chicago, IL
Moran, Tom M. ..... Palo Alto, CA
Moran, Vincent L. ..... Philadelphia, PA
Moran, William B.
Department Of Health And Human Services,
Social Security Administration, GV
Moran, William C. ..... Williamsville, NY
Moran, William C., & Associates, P.C.
Williamsville, NY
Moran, William C., Jr. ..... Cranbury, NJ
Moran, William F. ..... Bethlehem, PA
Moran, William F., III ..... Springfield, IL
Moran, William J. ..... Anchorage, AK
Moran, William J. ..... Costa Mesa, CA
Moran, William J. ..... San Francisco, CA
Moran, William J. ..... Bensenville, IL
Moran, William J. ..... Highland, IN
Moran, William J., Jr. ..... Cincinnati, OH
Hamilton, OH
Moran, William L. ..... St. Paul, MN
Moran, William M. ..... Mission Hills, CA
Moran, William R. ..... New York, NY
Moran-Barry, Susan ..... Framingham, MA
Morancy, George ..... Boston, MA
Morand, Leo D. ..... Vero Beach, FL
Morand, Robert F. ..... Cincinnati, OH
Morandi, Dominic P. ..... New York, NY
Morando, James W. ..... San Francisco, CA
Morando, Marta L. ..... Palo Alto, CA
Moran-Eriksen, Vivian A. ..... San Diego, CA
Morang, Charles H. ..... Keene, NH
Moranis, Cynthia Dixon ..... Tallahassee, FL
Morán-Loubriel, Ramón ..... San Juan, PR
Morano, Anthony A. ..... Toledo, OH
Morano, Carl J. ..... McLean, VA
Morano, Charles A. ..... Barnstable, MA
Edgartown, MA
Nantucket, MA
Morano, Christopher J.
Hasbrouck Heights, NJ
Morano, Christopher L. ..... Essex, CT

Morano, Colan and Butler ..... Richmond, VA
Morano, Donald V. ..... Chicago, IL
Morano, James F., Jr. ..... Richmond, VA
Morano, John A., Jr. ..... Scranton, PA
Morano, Joseph Richard
Florham Park, NJ
Morano, Linda T. ..... Miami, FL
Morano, Mark R. ..... Greenville, NC
Morano, Michael ..... Danvers, MA
Morano, Michael F. ..... New York, NY
Morano, Norman ..... Ocean Township, NJ
Morano, Regina Gabrielle ..... Albany, NY
Moran-Pennington, Sharon ..... Atlantic City, NJ
Morant, Johnny ..... Georgetown, SC
Morant, Louis R. ..... Georgetown, SC
Morante, Kathy M. ..... Nashville, TN
Morante, Paolo ..... Washington, DC
Morante, Thomas F. ..... Miami, FL
Moranville, Barry ..... West Des Moines, IA
Moranz, Elaine N. ..... Philadelphia, PA
Morar, Sandra D. ..... Omaha, NE
Morasch, Mark A. ..... Joplin, MO
Morasch, Marsha M. ..... Portland, OR
Morasch, Steve C. ..... Portland, OR
Morascyzk, Edward C. M. ..... Washington, PA
Morask, Dean C. ..... Chicago, IL
Moraska, Kathleen Jane ..... Charleston, SC
Moraski, Christina Potter ..... Rochester, NY
Morasse, Steven R. ..... Newport Beach, CA
Morassi, Richard C. ..... Feeding Hills, MA
Morasutti, Bruno R. ..... Meriden, CT
Moratzka, Timothy D. ..... Minneapolis, MN
Morauski, Karen A. ..... Gahanna, OH
Morava, Carol ..... Los Angeles, CA
Morava, Mark W. ..... Moon Township, PA
Moravan, Gregory W. ..... Bellevue, WA
Moravcik, Alan G. ..... Midland, TX
Moravcik, George C. ..... St. Charles, IL
Moravec, Henry J., III ..... Los Angeles, CA
Moravec, Linda K. ..... Pasadena, CA
Moravec, Michael R. ..... Buffalo, NY
Moravek, A. James ..... Alliance, NE
Moravick, Robert J. ..... Cleveland, OH
Moravsik, Robert J. ..... Somerville, NJ
Morawetz, James ..... Atlanta, GA
Morawiec, Eli ..... New York, NY
Morawski, Sigmund G. ..... Abington, PA
Moray, Dean ..... Glendale, CA
Moray and Vallette ..... Glendale, CA
Moraytis, Louis J. ..... Pittsburgh, PA
Moraz, Michaeleen ..... Monterey, CA
Morazzi, Deborah F. ..... Manchester, NH
Morbach, Nicole R. ..... Denver, CO
Morbey, Alison J. ..... San Francisco, CA
Morburger, Arthur J. ..... Miami, FL
Morchel, Mark E. ..... Jersey City, NJ
Morchower, Adrian L. ..... Washington, DC
Morchower, Luxton and Whaley
Chesterfield, VA
Richmond, VA
Morchower, Michael ..... Richmond, VA
Morck & Berenfeld ..... San Mateo, CA
Morck, Wendy A. ..... San Mateo, CA
Morcroft, C. Randal ..... Deerfield Beach, FL
Morcroft, Heather ..... Orlando, FL
Mord, Conrad ..... Tylertown, MS
Morda, Sebastiano N. ..... Atlantic City, NJ
Mordan, William R. ..... Cincinnati, OH
Mordarski, Daniel R. ..... Columbus, OH
Mordarski, Paul R. ..... Boston, MA
Mordas, Christopher D. ..... Canton, MA
Mordas, Greg G. ..... Perrineville, NJ
Mordaunt, Kristina ..... Houston, TX
Mordaunt, Michael R. ..... Sonora, CA
Stockton, CA
Mordaunt, Timothy J. ..... Grand Island, NY
Mordecai, John S., Sr. ..... Jacksonville, FL
Mordente, Anthony R. ..... Kew Gardens, NY
Mordente, Anthony R., P.C.
Kew Gardens, NY
Mordfin, Gerald Y. ..... Great Neck, NY
Mordhorst, Robert A. ..... Fairfax, VA
Mordhorst & Taweel ..... Fairfax, VA
Mordi, Francisca N. ..... Washington, DC
Mordini, Mark A. ..... Chicago, IL
Mordini, Rebecca Ann ..... Ames, IA
Mordini & Schwartz ..... Chicago, IL
Mordino, Joseph M. ..... Depew, NY
Mordkin, Arnold P. ..... Fountain Valley, CA
Mordkoff, Allan R. ..... Roseland, NJ
Mordkofsky, Harold ..... Washington, DC
Mordock, Craig S. ..... Irvine, CA
Mordock, Gary E. ..... Fullerton, CA
Mordoff, John R. ..... West Covina, CA
Mordoh, Craig ..... Santa Monica, CA
Mordowitz, Abraham M. ..... New York, NY
Morduch, Ruth N. ..... Washington, DC
Mordue, Norman A. ..... Syracuse, NY
Mordy, Burke ..... Ardmore, OK
Mordy, David G. ..... Ardmore, OK
Mordy, James C. ..... Kansas City, MO
Mordy Law Offices ..... Ardmore, OK
Mordy, Michael C. ..... Ardmore, OK
Mordy, Paul F. ..... San Bernardino, CA
More, Angus S., Jr. ..... Rockford, IL
More, Daniel A. ..... Upper Arlington, OH
More, Donna B. ..... Chicago, IL
More, Donna M. ..... Orlando, FL
More, Douglas M. ..... Greenwich, CT
Moré, Hector A. ..... Orlando, FL
More, James L. ..... Bronxville, NY
More, James M. ..... Fort Wayne, IN
More, John H. ..... Washington, DC
More, John R. ..... San Francisco, CA
More, Keith P. ..... Santa Ana, CA
More Phillips & Duncan, P.C.
Greenwich, CT
Stamford, CT

More, R. Jeffrey ..... New York, NY
More, Robert S.
Department Of The Interior,
Office of the Solicitor, GV
More, Robert S. ..... South Euclid, OH
More, Robin L. ..... Newport Beach, CA
More, Timothy T. ..... Providence, RI
More, William J. ..... New Orleans, LA
Morea, Anne ..... Beverly Hills, CA
Morea, Grace L. ..... Hempstead, NY
Morea, Michael N. ..... Ridgefield Park, NJ
Morea, Russell C. ..... Kew Gardens, NY
Morean, Gary A. ..... Aberdeen, WA
Moreau, Alex ..... Roseland, NJ
Moreau, Alfred E. ..... Department of the Army,
Office of the Judge Advocate General, GV
Moreau, Angelique Bradley ..... Lafayette, LA
Moreau, Arthur S., III ..... Los Angeles, CA
San Diego, CA
Moreau, Charles A. ..... Danville, VA
Moreau, D. William, Jr. ..... Indianapolis, IN
Moreau, David S. ..... Cary, NC
Moreau, Doug ..... Baton Rouge, LA
Moreau, Karen B. ..... Slingerlands, NY
Moreau, Lucien E. ..... Washington, DC
Moreau, Mark ..... New Orleans, LA
Moreau & Marks ..... Charlotte, NC
Moreau, Melissa ..... Florence, AL
Moreau, Melissa Washispack ..... Houma, LA
Moreau, Pamela A. ..... Department of Justice,
Environment and Natural Resources
Division, GV
Moreau, Sheryl L. ..... Jefferson City, MO
Moreau, Stacey Williams ..... Danville, VA
Moreau, Terry J. "Teska" ..... Houston, TX
Moreau, W. Timothy ..... Charlotte, NC
Morecock, Robert G. ..... Virginia Beach, VA
Moreda, Manuel A. ..... San Juan, PR
Moreda-Toledo, Manuel ..... San Juan, PR
Moredock, Charles M. ..... Charleston, WV
Moree, Anthony I. ..... Mundelein, IL
Moreen, Verl David ..... Farmington Hills, MI
Morefield, James D. ..... Abingdon, VA
Morefield, Kendrick, Hess & Largen, P.C.
Abingdon, VA
Morefield, Mark ..... Liberty, TX
Morefield, Richard W., Jr.
Kansas City, MO
Morehart, Don ..... Austin, TX
Morehart, Douglas M. ..... Cincinnati, OH
Morehart, Paul D. ..... Lancaster, OH
Morehead, Arthur E., III ..... Florence, SC
Morehead, Arthur E., IV ..... Columbia, SC
Morehead, Charles A., III
Fort Lauderdale, FL
Morehead, David S. ..... New London, CT
Morehead, Dwight H. ..... Toledo, OH
Morehead & Flynn ..... Chicago, IL
Morehead, G. Philip ..... Abilene, TX
Morehead, J. Lyon ..... Tulsa, OK
Morehead, Jere W. ..... Athens, GA
Morehead, John C. ..... Edenton, NC
Morehead, John F. ..... Austin, TX
Morehead, John H. ..... Falls City, NE
Morehead, Jordan & Carmona, A Professional Corporation ..... Austin, TX
Morehead, Joseph C. ..... San Francisco, CA
Morehead, Keith E. ..... Chicago, IL
Morehead, Kelly Ames ..... Palo Alto, CA
Morehead, Lucian ..... Plainview, TX
Morehead, Michael D. ..... Palo Alto, CA
Morehead, Michael D. ..... Norman, OK
Morehead, Robert F. ..... Pine Bluff, AR
Morehead, Sandra L. ..... Houston, TX
Morehead, Sarah Kanwit ..... Seattle, WA
Morehead & Sweeting, P.A.
Fort Lauderdale, FL
Morehead, Terra D. ..... Kansas City, KS
Morehead & Tisdel ..... Plainview, TX
Morehous, David L. ..... Knoxville, TN
Morehous, Dean A., Jr.
San Francisco, CA
Morehous, Lynn G. ..... Knoxville, TN
Morehouse, Carol ..... Erie, PA
Morehouse, David M. ..... Minneapolis, MN
Morehouse, Edward J. ..... White Plains, NY
Morehouse, Eric D. ..... Alexandria, VA
Morehouse, Harlow & Weldy
Fairfield, CT
Morehouse, Jeff ..... San Antonio, TX
Morehouse, Larry N. ..... Phoenix, AZ
Morehouse, Michael L. ..... Medford, OR
Morehouse, Philip A. ..... Darien, CT
Morehouse, Scott A. ..... Washington, DC
Morehouse, Susan Currie ..... Larchmont, NY
Morehouse, Thomas J. ..... Hamburg, NY
Morehouse, Val S. ..... St. Paul, MN
Morehouse, W. Bradley ..... Fairfield, CT
Morehouse, Walter H. ..... Cerritos, CA
Morehouse, William J. ..... Philadelphia, PA
Moreinis, Susan L. ..... Collingswood, NJ
Moreira, Ana C. ..... Jersey City, NJ
Moreira, Barbara Lyne ..... Manchester, NH
Moreira, George Monteiro
Waterbury, CT
Moreira, Jacqueline M. ..... Santa Rosa, CA
Moreira, Jose P. ..... Hudson, MA
Moreira-Brown, Herbert ..... Bronx, NY
Morejon, Julio C. ..... Union City, NJ
Morejon, Maria E. Lasso ..... Tampa, FL
Morejon & Puñales ..... Union City, NJ
Morel, Aaron ..... Waltham, MA
Morel, Alan P. ..... Ruidoso, NM
Morel, Alan P., P.A. ..... Ruidoso, NM
Morel, Deborah A. ..... East Hanover, NJ
Morel, Gerald L. ..... Chicago, IL
Morel, Harry J., Jr. ..... Boutte, LA

Morel, Harry J., Jr., A Law Corp. Boutte, LA
Morel, John L. ... Bloomington, IL
Morel, John L., P.C. ... Bloomington, IL
Morel, Thuynhi D. ... Houston, TX
Morel, William R. ... Washington, DC
Moreland, Allen D. ... New York, NY
Moreland, Carey L. ... Maitland, FL
Moreland, Carl C. ... Steubenville, OH
Moreland, Cason E. ... Old Hickory, TN
Moreland, Cathe L. ... Romney, WV
Moreland, Charles P. ... Boulder, CO
Moreland, Charles T. ... Willis, TX
Moreland, Christopher J. Minneapolis, MN
Moreland, Cynthia J. ... Northbrook, IL
Moreland, Daniel C. ... New York, NY
Moreland, Debra J. ... Trainer, PA
Moreland, Denise ... Newport Beach, CA
Moreland, Douglas H. ... Seattle, WA
Moreland, Earl W., Jr. ... Sarasota, FL
Moreland, Edmond S. ... Dallas, TX
Moreland, Everett R. ... Eugene, OR
Moreland, Gail A. ... Marengo, IL
Wonder Lake, IL
Moreland, Gary A. ... Tallmadge, OH
Moreland, Gordon R. ... Waldorf, MD
Moreland, Hallie A. ... Baltimore, MD
Moreland, Hulon L. ... Levelland, TX
Moreland, James A., (P.A.) ... Orlando, FL
Moreland, Jay W. ... New Port Richey, FL
Moreland, Jay W., P.A. New Port Richey, FL
Moreland, Jeffrey R. ... Schaumburg, IL
Fort Worth, TX
Moreland, Jennafer W. ... Department of Justice, GV
Moreland, John N. ... Ottumwa, IA
Moreland, Joseph A. ... Washington, DC
Moreland, Joseph T. ... Iowa City, IA
Moreland, Joseph W. ... Kansas City, KS
Moreland, Judith A. Federal Trade Commission, Bureau of Competition, GV
Moreland, Lori Abbott ... Sacramento, CA
Moreland, Maret R. ... Minneapolis, MN
Moreland, Mark E. ... St. Louis, MO
Moreland, Mary L. ... Houston, TX
Moreland, Matthew B. ... New Orleans, LA
Moreland & Mendez, P.A. ... Maitland, FL
Moreland, Michael J. ... Ottumwa, IA
Moreland, Michael S. ... Fort Myers, FL
Moreland, Michele E. ... Palo Alto, CA
Moreland and Moreland ... Romney, WV
Moreland, Olga Budor ... New York, NY
Moreland, Robert ... Austin, TX
Moreland, Robert D. ... Fort Wayne, IN
Moreland, Robert E. ... Norfolk, VA
Moreland, Robert H. ... Waldorf, MD
Moreland, Ruth ... Toledo, OH
Moreland, Sherman, III ... Elmira, NY
Moreland, Sidney S. ... Baton Rouge, LA
Moreland, Stephen W. ... Romney, WV
Moreland, Su-Jim Lee ... Palo Alto, CA
Moreland, Thomas H. ... New York, NY
Moreland, Vickie G. ... Hamilton, OH
Moreland, Vincent S. ... Houston, TX
Morell, Avram Eric ... Roseland, NJ
Morell, Dan A., Jr. ... Cleveland, OH
Morell, Frank T. ... Chula Vista, CA
Morell, Gary D. ... Palmyra, NY
Morell, James Brian ... Santa Monica, CA
Morell, Jerauld F. ... San Antonio, TX
Morell, Karl ... Washington, DC
Morell, Konstant W. ... Norwich, CT
Morell, Michael A. ... San Antonio, TX
Morell, MichaelWm. ... West Palm Beach, FL
Morell, Philip Mark ... White Plains, NY
Morell, Randy J. ... Virginia Beach, VA
Morell, Thomas D. ... Palo Alto, CA
Morell, Timothy J. ... Palm Beach, FL
Morella, Anthony C. ... Washington, DC
Morella & Associates ... Pittsburgh, PA
Morella, Jeffrey J. ... Pittsburgh, PA
Morella, Joseph P. ... Patterson, LA
Morella, Timothy M. ... Evanston, IL
Morelle, Fredric T. ... Latham, NY
Morelli, Alan E. ... Los Angeles, CA
Morelli, Arnold ... Cincinnati, OH
Morelli, Barbara J. ... Plantsville, CT
Morelli, Benedict P. ... New York, NY
Morelli, Benedict P., & Associates, P.C. New York, NY
Morelli, Brad ... Edmond, OK
Morelli, Carl J. ... New York, NY
Morelli, Carmen ... Windsor, CT
Morelli, Denise ... Department of Education, Office of the General Counsel, GV
Morelli, Douglas A. ... La Jolla, CA
Morelli, Edward ... Hartford, CT
Morelli, Frank Mario ... San Francisco, CA
Morelli, Fred M., Jr. ... Aurora, IL
Morelli, Genevieve ... Washington, DC
Morelli & Gold, LLP ... New York, NY
Morelli, Janis A. ... Neshanic Station, NJ
Morelli, John ... Cherry Hill, NJ
Morelli, Joseph C. ... Hartford, CT
Morelli, Kenneth P. ... New York, NY
Morelli, Lisa Ann ... Washington, DC
Morelli, Lisa J. ... Morristown, NJ
Morelli, Louis ... Los Angeles, CA
Morelli, Lynn ... Concord, MA
Morelli, Matthew J. ... Cincinnati, OH
Morelli, Richard A. ... Windsor, CT
Morelli, Ronald D. ... Pittsburgh, PA
Morelli, Rosary A. ... New York, NY
Morelli, Stephen M. ... Hartford, CT
Morelli, Steven A. ... Carle Place, NY
Morelli, Theresa E. ... Warren, OH
Morelli, William P. ... Nashville, TN
Morell Losada, Pedro ... San Juan, PR
Morello, Arthur P. ... Huntington Beach, CA
Morello, Arthur P., Jr. ... Costa Mesa, CA
Morello, Frederick C. ... Daytona Beach, FL
Morello, Frederick C., P.A., Law Office of Daytona Beach, FL
Morello, Gerald M., Jr. ... Southfield, MI
Morello, Gianluca ... New York, NY
Morello, Marsha A. ... Boston, MA
Morello, Michael Dennis, II ... Nashville, TN
Morello, Paul A., Jr. ... Cromwell, CT
Meriden, CT
Morello, Richard A ... Brooklyn, NY
Morello, Sally A. ... Palo Alto, CA
Morello, Steven J. ... Southgate, MI
Morelly, Michael D. ... Plantation, FL
Morelock, Fred M. ... Raleigh, NC
Morelock, Gregg H. ... Greenfield, IN
Indianapolis, IN
Morelock, Scott A. ... Brownwood, TX
Morely, John A. ... San Jose, CA
Morem, Neil R. ... Le Sueur, MN
Moren, Charles V. ... Sequim, WA
Moren, Conrad L. ... Houston, TX
Moren, James R. ... Oakland, CA
Moren, Matthew D. ... New York, NY
Moren, Patrick D. ... Roseau, MN
Morena, Jos. A. ... Media, PA
Morency, Michel ... Boston, MA
Morency, Paula J. ... Chicago, IL
Moreno, Albert F. ... San Francisco, CA
Moreno, Alejandro ... New York, NY
Moreno, Andres ... Chula Vista, CA
Moreno, Anthony J ... Orlando, FL
Moreno, Barbara Kumm ... High Point, NC
Moreno, Becerra & Guerrero Montebello, CA
Moreno, C. Miguel ... Los Angeles, CA
Moreno, Carlos A ... Kew Gardens, NY
Moreno, Carlos R. ... Los Angeles, CA
Moreno, Christopher P. ... Chicago, IL
Moreno, Daniel C. ... Minneapolis, MN
Moreno, Douglas F. ... Sacramento, CA
Moreno, Elizabeth A. ... Los Angeles, CA
Moreno, Enrique, Law Offices of El Paso, TX
Moreno, Esther L. ... Miami, FL
Moreno, Evelyn Venables ... Boston, MA
Moreno, Federico A. ... Miami, FL
Moreno & Fry ... El Paso, TX
Moreno, Gregory W. ... Montebello, CA
Moreno, Hermez ... Marina Del Rey, CA
Moreno, Hilario (Larry), Jr Harlingen, TX
McAllen, TX
Moreno, Ignacia S. ... Department of Justice, Environment and Natural Resources Division, GV
Moreno, Jeffrey O. ... Washington, DC
Moreno, Joelle Anne ... Boston, MA
Moreno, John J. ... Sacramento, CA
Moreno, Jose A. ... Laredo, TX
Moreno, Jose H. ... San Jose, CA
Moreno, Joseph G. ... Buffalo, NY
Moreno, Joseph Mario, (Ltd.) ... Chicago, IL
Moreno, Kathleen ... Long Beach, CA
Moreno, Kenneth H. ... San Diego, CA
Moreno, Kevin S. ... Downingtown, PA
Moreno, Krista Mosier ... Redlands, CA
Moreno, Larry ... McAllen, TX
Moreno, Leticia T. ... Los Angeles, CA
Moreno, Lisa Elin ... Springfield, IL
Moreno, Louis N. ... Houston, TX
Moreno, Luis ... Los Angeles, CA
Moreno, Luis ... San Antonio, TX
Moreno, M. Cristina ... Miami, FL
Moreno, Marilyn E. ... San Jose, CA
Moreno, Mario F. ... Patterson, NY
Moreno, Mark A. ... Oak Brook, IL
Moreno, Mark A. ... Pierre, SD
Moreno, Myriam ... Hempstead, NY
Moreno, Patricia Lee Kraus ... New York, NY
Moreno, Paul C. ... El Paso, TX
Moreno, Rafael G. ... Miami, FL
Moreno, Ralph J. ... San Diego, CA
Santa Ana, CA
Moreno, Ricardo A. ... Columbia, SC
Moreno, Richard C. ... Los Angeles, CA
Moreno, Richard D. ... Lake Charles, LA
Moreno & Rivera ... Elk Grove, CA
Roseville, CA
Sacramento, CA
Moreno, Sandra C. ... Santa Monica, CA
Moreno, Sheri L. ... Albany, NY
Moreno, Victor C. ... Cincinnati, OH
Moreno, Walter R. ... Santa Rosa, CA
Moreno, William F. ... Salinas, CA
Moreno, Yolanda ... New York, NY
Moreno, Zenas A. ... Visalia, CA
Moreno-Sneed, M. Cristina ... Scottsdale, AZ
Morenstein, Donald S. ... New York, NY
Morenus, Eugene O., Jr. ... Garden City, NY
Moreo, Thomas J. ... Las Vegas, NV
Morera-Ledón, Lourdes I. ... San Juan, PR
Moreschi, Paul P. ... Oakbrook Terrace, IL
Moresco, Judith F. ... Staten Island, NY
Moreshead, Charles E. ... Augusta, ME
Moreshead, Elizabeth Twoney New London, CT
Moreshead & Moreshead ... New London, CT
Moresi, Alfonso J. ... San Francisco, CA
Moresi & Moresi ... Abbeville, LA
Moresi, Paul G., III ... Abbeville, LA
Moresi, Paul G., Jr. ... Abbeville, LA
Moresi, Vicki J. ... West Berlin, NJ
Moret, David Jonathan ... Miami, FL
Moret, Gilbert A. ... Los Angeles, CA
Moret, Glenn C. ... Monterey Park, CA
Moret, Laura M. ... Minneapolis, MN
Moret, Marisa A. ... San Francisco, CA
Moret, Pamela J. ... Minneapolis, MN
Moreton, Alfred E., III ... Oxford, MS
Moreton, Catherine L. ... Hartford, CT
Moreton, Keith W. ... Encino, CA
Moretsky, Lesa D. ... Warren, MI
Moretti, August J. ... Menlo Park, CA
Moretti, Beth Marie ... Elmsford, NY
Moretti, Daniel S. ... New York, NY
Moretti, David C. ... Cranston, RI
Moretti, Jay D. ... Cross Plains, WI
Moretti, Lynn A. ... Boston, MA
Moretti, Mark J. ... Rochester, NY
Moretti, Olga ... Encino, CA
Moretti, Paul M. ... Boston, MA
Moretti and Perlow Law Offices Cranston, RI
Moretti, Steven A. ... Providence, RI
Moretti, Valentine J. ... New York, NY
Moretz, J. Douglas ... Sanford, NC
Moretz, J. Douglas, P.A. ... Sanford, NC
Moretz, M. Denise ... Knoxville, TN
Moretz, Zachary M. ... Burlington, NC
Moretz-Edmisten, Jane ... Washington, DC
Moretz-Edmisten, Jane, P.A., & Associates Washington, DC
Morewitz, Burt M. ... Newport News, VA
Morey, Blondell L. ... Detroit, MI
Morey, Carole A. ... Chicago, IL
Morey, Carter ... Tucson, AZ
Morey, Carter, P.C. ... Tucson, AZ
Morey, Charles E. ... Boise, ID
Morey, Christopher J. ... Long Beach, CA
Morey, Clifford G. ... Tacoma, WA
Morey, Craig R. ... San Leandro, CA
Morey, Dane F. ... Durand, WI
Morey, David Barnett ... New Orleans, LA
Morey, Donald F. ... Sacramento, CA
Morey, James F. ... East Bridgewater, MA
Morey, Joseph H., Jr. ... Buffalo, NY
Morey, Kimberly A. ... Dallas, TX
Morey, Marcia H. ... Durham, NC
Morey, Michael S. ... Lake Oswego, OR
Morey & Nicholas ... San Leandro, CA
Morey, Phyllis Golden ... Detroit, MI
Morey, Randall E. ... Mondovi, WI
Morey, Richard ... Chicago, IL
Morey, Richard S. ... Washington, DC
Morey, Robin Wilson ... New York, NY
Morey & Shade, An Association of Sole Practioners ... Decatur, IL
Morey, Thomas C. ... Washington, DC
Morey, Timothy J. ... North Adams, MA
Morey, Walter T. ... Decatur, IL
Morey Caldwell, Jennifer ... Bedford, TX
Morezzi, Eugenia J. ... Wantagh, NY
Morf, Darrel A. ... Cedar Rapids, IA
Morf, Jenny M. ... Portland, OR
Morf, Paul P. ... Cedar Rapids, IA
Morfas, Craig C. ... Indianapolis, IN
Morfe, Claudio ... Sunrise, FL
Morfeld, Martin R. ... Seattle, WA
Morfesis, Stephanie ... New York, NY
Morfey, Michael D. ... Houston, TX
Morfitt, James C. ... Caldwell, ID
Morfitt, Michael G. ... Boise, ID
Morfopoulos, Mark ... New York, NY
Morford and Benson ... Alva, OK
Morford, Douglas H. ... Jacksonville, FL
Morford, J Mark ... Portland, OR
Morford, Joseph J. ... Cleveland, OH
Morford, Kevin M. ... Anchorage, AK
Morford, Richard G. ... Melrose Park, IL
Morford, Steven D. ... Scottsdale, AZ
Morford, Tom H. ... Alva, OK
Morford, Warren N., Jr. ... Chesapeake, OH
Morford & Whitefield, P.A. Jacksonville, FL
Morga, Maria J. ... San Francisco, CA
Morga, W. E., P.C. ... Scottsdale, AZ
Morga, William E. (Gene) ... Scottsdale, AZ
Morgado, Mary E. ... Somerset, MA
Morgado, Mildred ... Miami, FL
Morgan, Adam J. ... Boca Raton, FL
Morgan, Alan J. ... Chicago, IL
Morgan, Albert ... Phoenix, AZ
Morgan, Alexander E. ... Fairfax, VA
Morgan, Alfred J., Jr. ... New York, NY
Morgan, Alfred, Jr. ... Anaheim, CA
Morgan, Allen L. ... Menlo Park, CA
Morgan, Amy E. ... Santa Ana, CA
Morgan, Andrew H. ... Milwaukee, WI
Morgan, Andrew W. ... New York, NY
Morgan, Angela L. ... Southaven, MS
Morgan, Ann ... Las Vegas, NV
Reno, NV
Morgan, Ann M. ... Cincinnati, OH
Morgan, Anne L. ... Austin, TX
Morgan, Anne M. ... St. Louis, MO
Morgan, Anne Whitehead Salt Lake City, UT
Morgan, Annette ... Manchester, KY
Morgan, Annette, Law Office Manchester, KY
Morgan, Arthur J. ... Oklahoma City, OK
Morgan, Arthur L., Jr. ... Redding, CA
Morgan & Associates ... Oklahoma City, OK
Morgan & Associates, Professional Corporation ... Ann Arbor, MI
Birmingham, MI
Bloomfield Hills, MI
Detroit, MI
Southfield, MI
Morgan, B. Gayle ... Richmond, VA
Morgan, B. Monte ... Scottsdale, AZ
Morgan, B. Monte, P.C. ... Scottsdale, AZ
Morgan, Bagg & Persons ... Eastchester, NY
Morgan, Barbara J. ... Princeton, NJ
Morgan, Barbara Kramer Washington, DC
Morgan, Barry L. ... San Bernardino, CA
Morgan & Bartholomew ... Olympia, WA
Morgan, Betsy Stelle ... Chicago, IL
Morgan, Bornstein & Morgan Cherry Hill, NJ
Morgan, Brewster Q. ... Sacramento, CA
Morgan, Brian D. ... Lorain, OH
Morgan, Brian J. ... Barstow, CA
Morgan, Brian W. ... Salt Lake City, UT
Morgan, Brown & Joy, LLP ... Boston, MA
Morgan, Bruce ... Riverside, CA
Morgan, Bryan Earl ... Montgomery, AL
Morgan, C. Cloud ... Macon, GA
Morgan, C. Dennis ... Foster City, CA
Morgan, C. Forrest, III ... Denver, CO
Morgan, C. Richard ... Miami, FL
Morgan, Cameron A. ... Scottsdale, AZ
Morgan & Cameron, P.C. ... Bozeman, MT
Morgan, Candy ... Des Moines, IA
Morgan, Caren M. ... Gretna, LA
Morgan, Carl W. ... Dallas, TX
Morgan, Carolyn F. ... Birmingham, AL
Morgan, Carolyn Y. ... Los Angeles, CA
Morgan, Carratt and O'Connor, P.A. Fort Lauderdale, FL
Morgan, Cathleen M. ... Boise, ID
Morgan, Charles ... New York, NY
Morgan, Charles A. ... Texarkana, AR
Morgan, Charles A., Jr. ... Canton, OH
Morgan, Charles C. ... Florham Park, NJ
Morgan, Charles E. ... Tuscaloosa, AL
Morgan, Charles F. ... Towson, MD
Morgan, Charles H. ... Atlanta, GA
Morgan, Charles, Jr. ... Birmingham, AL
Morgan, Charles L., Jr. ... Huntsville, TX
Morgan, Charles L., Jr., Law Offices of Charlotte, NC
Morgan, Charles O., Jr. ... San Francisco, CA
Morgan, Charles O., Jr. ... Miami, FL
Morgan, Charles O., Jr., P.A. ... Miami, FL
Morgan, Charles R. ... Fort Lauderdale, FL
Morgan, Charles R. ... Atlanta, GA
Morgan, Chase ... Seal Beach, CA
Morgan, Cheryl D. ... Lexington, KY
Morgan, Cheryle L. ... Herndon, VA
Morgan, Christie C. ... Birmingham, AL
Morgan, Christine Connolly ... Acton, MA
Morgan, Christine M. ... Oakland, CA
Morgan, Christine M. ... Atlanta, GA
Morgan, Christine Owens New Haven, CT
Morgan, Christopher H. ... Cleveland, OH
Morgan, Christopher L. ... Kansas City, MO
Morgan, Clarence E. (Cem), III Kosciusko, MS
Morgan, Clarold F. ... Denver, CO
Morgan, Claude D. ... Amarillo, TX
Morgan, Clay D. ... Melbourne, FL
Morgan, Clay D., P.A. ... Melbourne, FL
Morgan, Clinton J. ... Nashville, TN
Morgan, Clive N. ... Jacksonville, FL
Morgan, Clive N., P.A. ... Jacksonville, FL
Morgan, Colby S., Jr. ... Memphis, TN
Morgan Colling & Gilbert, A Professional Association ... Orlando, FL
Tampa, FL
Morgan & Cooper, P.C. ... Yuma, AZ
Morgan, Courtney E., Jr. ... Detroit, MI
Morgan, Craig A. ... Austin, TX
Morgan, C.W. Bill ... Anadarko, OK
Morgan, Cynthia M. ... Tacoma, WA
Morgan, D. Bruce ... Newcastle, WA
Morgan, D. James ... Salt Lake City, UT
Morgan, D. Russell, Jr. ... Montpelier, VT
Morgan, D. Scott ... Washington, DC
Morgan, Dale J., Jr. ... North Little Rock, AR
Morgan, Dale O. ... Orlando, FL
Morgan, Damon B., Jr. Point Pleasant, WV
Morgan, Dana Lynn ... Sherman, TX
Morgan, Daniel ... Scranton, PA
Morgan, Daniel B. ... East Lansing, MI
Morgan, Daniel J. ... Oklahoma City, OK
Morgan, Daniel L. ... Palm Desert, CA
Morgan, Daniel L. ... Washington, DC
Morgan, Daniel Luke ... Lexington, KY
Morgan, Daniel S. ... Missoula, MT
Morgan, Darin Ross ... Philadelphia, PA
Morgan, Darlynn Campbell Costa Mesa, CA
Morgan, David ... Greeley, CO
Morgan, David A. ... House of Representatives, Office of Legislative Counsel, GV
Morgan, David C. ... Fort Pierce, FL
Morgan, David D. ... Oklahoma City, OK
Morgan, David E., III ... Abbeville, GA
Morgan, David F. ... Los Angeles, CA
Morgan, David J. ... Wichita, KS
Morgan, David Jay ... San Mateo, CA
Morgan, David Jay, A Professional Corporation ... San Mateo, CA
Morgan, David K. ... Houston, TX
Morgan, David L., Jr. ... Mandeville, LA
Morgan, David N. ... St. Louis, MO
Morgan, David R. ... Baltimore, MD
Morgan, David R. ... Harrisburg, PA
Morgan, David S. ... Daytona Beach, FL
Morgan, David W. ... Princeton, NJ
Morgan, Dawn H. ... Winston-Salem, NC
Morgan, Deborah E. ... St. Louis, MO
Morgan, Deborah L. ... Marietta, GA
Morgan, Deborah Paris ... Columbia, SC
Morgan, Deborah R. ... Oklahoma City, OK

Morgan, Dee Anne ....Okemos, MI
Morgan, Dee Gayle ....Cheyenne, WY
Morgan, Denise C. ....New York, NY
Morgan, Dennis K. (IBA) ....**Austin, TX**
Morgan, Dennis L., II ....Cleveland, OH
Morgan, Dennis R. ....Columbus, OH
Morgan, Dennis W. ....Ritzville, WA
Morgan, DeWitt Michael
Albuquerque, NM
Morgan, Dia M. ....Chicago, IL
Morgan, Dianne F. ....Metairie, LA
Morgan, Don B. ....Austin, TX
Morgan, Donald C. ....Plymouth, MI
Morgan, Donald J. ....Portland, OR
Morgan, Donald L. ....Washington, DC
Morgan, Donelle ....San Jose, CA
Morgan, Donna Evensen ....Chicago, IL
Morgan, Dorothy D. ....Erie, PA
Morgan, Dothan E., Jr. ....Chickasaw, AL
Morgan, Doug ....Dallas, TX
Morgan, Douglas A. ....Boston, MA
Morgan, Douglas H. ....Oklahoma City, OK
Morgan, Douglas J., (L.C.) ....San Jose, CA
Morgan, Douglas S. ....Columbus, OH
Morgan, Dwight D. ....Medina, OH
Morgan, E. Lee ....Florence, SC
Morgan, Earl E. ....North Platte, NE
Morgan, Earl H., Jr. ....Lapeer, MI
Morgan, Edward A. ....New York, NY
Morgan, Edward F. ....Tuscaloosa, AL
Morgan, Edward Thomas ....Annapolis, MD
Morgan, Edward W. ....Columbus, OH
Morgan, Elford H. ....Spartanburg, SC
Morgan, Elinore C. ....El Cerrito, CA
Morgan, Elizabeth Ann ....Miami, FL
Morgan, Elizabeth Stacy ....Columbus, GA
Morgan, Ellen E. ....St. Louis, MO
Morgan, Ellen J. ....Chicago, IL
Morgan, Elmer E. ....Louisville, KY
Morgan, Eloise L. ....Bronxville, NY
Morgan, Emory E. ....Columbia, MS
Morgan, Eric K. ....San Bernardino, CA
Morgan, Ethel L.
Federal Energy Regulatory Commission, Office of the General Counsel, GV
Morgan, F. Beth ....San Antonio, TX
Morgan & Finnegan, L.L.P.
Washington, DC
New York, NY
Morgan & Flannelly ....York, PA
Morgan, Franich, Fredkin & Marsh
San Jose, CA
Morgan, Frank C. ....Oxford, MA
Morgan, Frank E., II ....New York, NY
Morgan, Frank H. ....New York, NY
Morgan, Frank H., Jr. ....Wynnewood, PA
Morgan, Frank J., Jr. ....Troy, NY
Morgan, Frank W. ....The Woodlands, TX
Morgan, Frank W., & Associates, P.C., The Law Offices of ....The Woodlands, TX
Morgan, Fred S. ....Oklahoma City, OK
Morgan, Frederick A., Law Offices of
San Francisco, CA
Morgan, Frederick M., Jr.
Cincinnati, OH
Morgan, Frieda Goldman ....Toledo, OH
Morgan, G. Brian ....Poughkeepsie, NY
Morgan, G. Terrell ....Mc Comb, MS
Morgan, Garfield R. ....Lynn, MA
Morgan, Gary C. ....Dallas, TX
Morgan, Gary K. ....St. Louis, MO
Morgan, Gary L., P.A. ....Caldwell, ID
Morgan, Gary W. ....Tyler, TX
Morgan, G. D., Jr. ....Columbia, SC
Morgan, Geoffrey R. ....Milwaukee, WI
Morgan, George J. ....Lancaster, PA
Morgan, George S. ....Chevy Chase, MD
Morgan, George T. ....Chicago, IL
Morgan, Gerald D., Jr. ....Washington, DC
Morgan, Gerald G., Jr., (P.C.) ....Amarillo, TX
Morgan, Gerard T. ....Baton Rouge, LA
Morgan, Glen B. ....Akron, OH
Morgan, Glen D. ....Hartford, CT
Morgan, Glen W. ....Beaumont, TX
Morgan, Glenn L. ....New Orleans, LA
Morgan, Glenn S. ....Rutland, VT
Morgan, Glyn D. ....Monterey Park, CA
Morgan and Gotcher ....Greenville, TX
Rockwall, TX
Morgan, Grady Bryan ....Denver, CO
Morgan, Gregory A. ....Clarksburg, WV
Morgan, Gregory K. ....Atlanta, GA
Morgan, Gregory K., Law Offices of
Auburn, AL
Morgan, Gregory K., Law Offices of
Opelika, AL
Morgan, Gregory O. ....Bozeman, MT
Morgan, Gregory W. ....Kankakee, IL
Morgan, Hal B. ....St. Louis, MO
Morgan & Hall ....Pontiac, MI
Morgan, Hallgren, Crosswell & Kane, P.C.
Lancaster, PA
Morgan, Harold D. ....Santa Ana, CA
Morgan, Harold Van, Jr. ....Florence, AL
Morgan, Helen D. ....Raleigh, NC
Morgan, Helen E. ....Denver, CO
Morgan, Helen L. ....Washington, DC
Morgan & Hendrick ....Key West, FL
Morgan, Henry C., Jr. ....Norfolk, VA
Morgan, Henry G. ....Livingston, NJ
Morgan, Henry M., Jr. ....Lakeland, FL
Morgan, Henry Sayler ....Savannah, GA
Morgan, Herbert D. ....Seneca, SC
Morgan, Herbert N. ....Fairfax, VA
Morgan, Herring, Morgan, Green, Rosenblutt & Gill, LLP ....Asheboro, NC
Greensboro, NC
High Point, NC
Lexington, NC
Winston-Salem, NC
Morgan, Hicks B. ....Garland, TX
Morgan, Hope Guiver ....Santa Ana, CA
Morgan, Hugh J. ....Key West, FL
Morgan, Hugh J. ....Cleveland, OH
Morgan, Hugh W. ....Knoxville, TN
Morgan, J. Bert, III ....Walnut Creek, CA
Morgan, J. Daniel ....Tulsa, OK
Morgan, J. Dean ....Tacoma, WA
Morgan, J. Donald ....Baton Rouge, LA
Morgan, J. Griffin ....Winston-Salem, NC
Morgan, J. Harris ....Greenville, TX
Morgan, J. Keith ....Waukesha, WI
Morgan, J. Mac, Law Office of
New Orleans, LA
Morgan, J. Michael ....Denver, CO
Morgan, J. Michael ....Tulsa, OK
Morgan, J. Michael ....Nashville, TN
Morgan, J. Michael ....Olympia, WA
Morgan, J. Miles ....Charleston, WV
Morgan, J. Perry ....Birmingham, AL
Morgan, J. Reid ....Winston-Salem, NC
Morgan, J. Robert ....Saint Marys, GA
Morgan, J. Sue ....Seattle, WA
Morgan, J. Tom ....Decatur, GA
Morgan, Jack C., III ....Fort Myers, FL
Morgan, Jack Cochran ....Kaufman, TX
Morgan, Jack M., Jr. ....Salt Lake City, UT
Morgan, Jack W. ....Mobile, AL
Morgan, Jack W. ....Compton, CA
Morgan, Jacqueline Mairs ....Kansas City, MO
Morgan, James A. ....Wooster, OH
Morgan, James B. ....Hurst, TX
Morgan, James B., Jr. ....Wilmington, NC
Morgan, James D. ....Pawcatuck, CT
Morgan, James D. ....New Orleans, LA
Morgan, James E. ....Washington, DC
Morgan, James E. ....Delmar, NY
Morgan, James E. ....Columbus, OH
Morgan, James E. ....Toledo, OH
Morgan, James E. ....Comanche, TX
Morgan, James E., III, (P.A.) ....Miami, FL
Morgan, James F. ....High Point, NC
Morgan, James F., Jr.
Department of the Navy, GV
Morgan, James G., Jr. ....Harrisburg, PA
Morgan, James H., Jr. ....Atlanta, GA
Morgan, James H., Sr. ....Lilburn, GA
Morgan, James K. ....Longview, WA
Morgan, James L. ....Searcy, AR
Morgan, James L. ....Springfield, IL
Morgan, James L., (P.C.) ....Reno, NV
Morgan, James M. ....Anchorage, AK
Morgan, James M. ....Lighthouse Point, FL
Morgan, James M. ....Lincoln, NE
Morgan, James Norman
Newport Beach, CA
Morgan, James P. ....Oak Brook, IL
Morgan, James R. ....Walnut Creek, CA
Morgan, James R., Jr.
Winston-Salem, NC
Morgan, James W. ....Utica, NY
Morgan, James W., Jr. ....Newport, KY
Morgan, Jane B. ....Jackson, MS
Morgan, Janet ....San Francisco, CA
Morgan, Janice R. ....Washington, DC
Morgan, Jas. R. ....Madison, WI
Morgan, Jason W. ....Boston, MA
Morgan, Jean Ann ....Chaska, MN
Morgan, Jeffrey C. ....Boston, MA
Morgan, Jeffrey J. ....San Antonio, TX
Morgan, Jeffrey J. ....Milwaukee, WI
Morgan, Jeffrey R. ....Hazard, KY
Morgan, Jeffrey S. ....St. Louis, MO
Morgan, Jennifer S.
San Juan Capistrano, CA
Morgan, Jeremy R. ....Hazard, KY
Morgan, Jewell ....Norton, VA
Morgan, Joan Ellerbusch ....Detroit, MI
Morgan, Joan L.G. ....Seattle, WA
Morgan, Joann K. Miller ....Albuquerque, NM
Morgan, John A. ....Springfield, VA
Morgan, John B. ....Orlando, FL
Tampa, FL
Morgan, John B. ....New York, NY
Morgan, John C. ....Kansas City, MO
Morgan, John Carter, Jr. ....Warrenton, VA
Morgan, John D. ....Rockville Centre, NY
Morgan, John D. ....Silverdale, WA
Morgan, John G. ....Camarillo, CA
Morgan, John G., A Professional Corporation
Camarillo, CA
Morgan, John H. ....Fort Myers Beach, FL
Morgan, John Hunt ....Hoskinston, KY
Morgan, John J. ....Stamford, CT
Morgan, John J. ....Butler, PA
Morgan, John J. ....Pittsburgh, PA
Morgan, John L. ....Huron, SD
Mitchell, SD
Morgan, John M. ....Lehigh Acres, FL
Morgan, John M. ....Irving, TX
Morgan, John N. ....Gadsden, AL
Morgan, John O., Jr. ....Lexington, KY
Morgan, John O., Jr., P.S.C. ....Lexington, KY
Morgan, John P. ....Oklahoma City, OK
Morgan, John P. ....Seattle, WA
Morgan, John Philip ....Bedford, MA
Morgan, John R. ....Hindman, KY
Morgan, John R. ....Greensboro, NC
Morgan, John R. ....Tunkhannock, PA
Morgan, John R. ....Chattanooga, TN
Morgan, John S. ....Beaumont, TX
Morgan, John S., Jr. ....Marco, FL
Morgan, John Story ....Marietta, GA
Morgan, John T. ....Hamden, CT
Morgan, John T. ....Salt Lake City, UT
Morgan, John V. ....Fullerton, NE
Morgan, John W. ....Wilmington, DE
Morgan, John W. ....Lexington, KY
Morgan & Johnson, P.A. ....Orlando, FL
Tavares, FL
Morgan, Jon B. ....Kissimmee, FL
Morgan, Jonathan Brian ....Austin, TX
Morgan, Jonathan P. ....Rockville, MD
Morgan, Joseph A. ....El Paso, TX
Morgan, Joseph Michael ....Riverside, CA
Morgan, J. P. ....Jefferson City, MO
Morgan, J. T. ....Odessa, TX
Morgan, Judith A. ....Oklahoma City, OK
Morgan, Julia M. ....Honolulu, HI
Morgan, Julian H., Jr. ....Spartanburg, SC
Morgan, Julie A. ....Bridgeport, CT
Morgan, Justin R. ....Lexington, KY
Morgan, J. W. ....Milledgeville, GA
Morgan, Karen A. ....Chicago, IL
Morgan, Karen D. ....Annapolis, MD
Morgan, Karen E. ....Melville, NY
Morgan, Karen L. ....Portland, ME
Morgan, Karin Wyman ....Boulder, CO
Morgan, Katherine C. ....Chicago, IL
Morgan, Katherine Cook ....Cincinnati, OH
Morgan, Katherine D. ....Worcester, MA
Morgan, Kathleen P. ....Jackson, MS
Morgan, Kathryn L. ....Los Angeles, CA
Morgan, Kathryn Letter Boe ....Arlington, VA
Morgan, Kay K. (Daniel) ....Houston, TX
Morgan, Kayo E. ....Fort Lauderdale, FL
Morgan, Keith B. ....Cherry Hill, NJ
Morgan, Keith V. ....Silver Spring, MD
Morgan, Kelly Ann ....Houston, TX
Morgan, Kelly M. ....Columbus, OH
Morgan, Kenneth B. ....Birmingham, MI
Morgan, Kenneth C. ....Somerset, NJ
Morgan, Kenneth W., Jr.
Fort Lauderdale, FL
Tampa, FL
West Palm Beach, FL
Morgan, Kent D. ....Tucson, AZ
Morgan, Kermit J. ....Santa Monica, CA
Morgan, Kerry J. ....Trenton, NJ
Morgan, Kerry L. ....Taylor, MI
Morgan, Kerry Sigler ....Bowling Green, KY
Morgan, Kevan L. ....Seattle, WA
Morgan, Kevin P. ....Mount Holly, NJ
Morgan, Kimberly A. ....Carson City, NV
Morgan, L. Linton ....Covington, LA
Morgan, Lance G. ....Minneapolis, MN
Morgan, Lanoff, Denniston & Madigan, Ltd.
Chicago, IL
Morgan, Larry ....Huntsville, AL
Morgan, Larry A. ....Oklahoma City, OK
Morgan, Larry, Attorney at Law, P.C.
Huntsville, AL
Morgan, Laura F. ....Plantation, FL
Morgan Law Firm ....Seneca, SC
Morgan Law Offices ....San Jose, CA
Morgan, Lawrence I. ....Seaford, NY
Morgan, Lawrence J. ....Austin, TX
Morgan, Lawrence S. ....Fort Smith, AR
Morgan, Lawrence W. ....Lansing, MI
Morgan, Lee P. ....Athens, GA
Morgan, Leeton & Meyers, A Professional Corporation ....Midland, TX
Morgan, Leslie J. ....Walnut Creek, CA
Morgan, Lewis & Bockius LLP
Los Angeles, CA
Washington, DC
Miami, FL
Princeton, NJ
New York, NY
Harrisburg, PA
Philadelphia, PA
Pittsburgh, PA
Morgan, Lewis R. ....Atlanta, GA
Morgan, Lillian M. ....York, PA
Morgan, Linda J.
Department of Transportation, Surface Transportation Board, GV
Morgan, Linda R.
Christiansted, St. Croix, VI
Morgan, Lisa Kelly ....Hartford, CT
Morgan, Lisa Mumma ....Harrisburg, PA
Morgan, Lois A. ....New York, NY
Morgan, Lori Bryant ....Nashville, TN
Morgan, Lorie Ann
Research Triangle Park, NC
Morgan, Louise B. ....San Diego, CA
Morgan, Lynelle Detzler ....Ann Arbor, MI
Morgan, Lynn M. ....Clearwater, FL
Morgan, Lynne B. ....Portland, OR
Morgan, M. Brent ....Pocatello, ID
Morgan, M. Byron ....Jonesboro, GA
Morgan, M. Edward ....Clinton, AR
Morgan, M. Michael ....San Diego, CA
Morgan, Mack J., III
Oklahoma City, OK
Morgan, Marcie ....Cherry Hill, NJ
Morgan, Margaret ....Raleigh, NC
Morgan, Mariann ....Winston-Salem, NC
Morgan, Marilyn ....San Jose, CA
Morgan, Mark C. ....Gretna, LA
Morgan, Mark G., M.D. ....Tampa, FL
Morgan, Mark L. ....Campbellsville, KY
Morgan, Mark L. ....Lebanon, KY
Morgan, Mark S. ....Washington, DC
Morgan, Marni M. ....Tampa, FL
Morgan, Marshal David ....San Juan, PR
Morgan, Martha Steiner ....Baton Rouge, LA
Morgan, Martin L. ....Covington, LA
Morgan, Mary Ann ....Orlando, FL
Morgan, Mary Nelson ....Jacksonville, FL
Morgan, Mary W. ....Mandeville, LA
Columbus, OH
Morgan, Matthew C. ....Warrensburg, MO
Morgan, Maura Kathleen Lutz
Chicago, IL
Morgan & McDonald, P.S. ....Newcastle, WA
Morgan, Melanie J. ....Oakland, CA
Morgan, Melanie K. ....Dallas, TX
Morgan, Melanie S. ....Kansas City, KS
Morgan, Melhuish, Monaghan, Arvidson, Abrutyn & Lisowski ....Livingston, NJ
New York, NY
Morgan, Melinda ....Florence, AL
Morgan, Melinda A. ....Salt Lake City, UT
Morgan, Melinda P. ....Atlanta, GA
Morgan, Melvin D. ....Dallas, TX
Houston, TX
Morgan, Melvin H. ....San Francisco, CA
Morgan, Melvin S. ....Alexandria, VA
Morgan, Melzer A. (Pat), Jr. ....Wentworth, NC
Morgan, Meyer & Rice, L.C.
Salt Lake City, UT
Morgan, Michael C. ....Sykesville, MD
Morgan, Michael D. ....Montgomery, AL
Morgan, Michael D. ....Albany, NY
Morgan, Michael E. ....Seattle, WA
Morgan, Michael G. ....Los Angeles, CA
Morgan, Michael H. ....Wichita, KS
Morgan, Michael L. ....Sarasota, FL
Morgan, Michael L. ....Atlanta, GA
Morgan, Michael M., (P.C.) ....Portland, OR
Morgan, Michael R. ....Mountain View, CA
Morgan, Michael S. ....New York, NY
Morgan, Michael S. ....Stillwater, OK
Morgan, Michael T. ....Midland, TX
Morgan, Michael Trevor ....Silverdale, WA
Morgan, Michael V. ....Troy, MI
Morgan, Michelle A. ....Dallas, TX
Morgan, Michelle A. ....Dallas, TX
Morgan, Michelle M. ....Cleveland, OH
Morgan, Michelle M. ....Toledo, OH
Morgan, Micol L.
Charlotte Amalie, St. Thomas, VI
Morgan, Miller & Blair, Professional Corporation ....Walnut Creek, CA
Morgan, Mina J. ....Tampa, FL
Morgan, Minor L. ....Dallas, TX
Morgan, Mitchell L. ....Bryn Mawr, PA
Morgan & Mittelman, Ltd. ....Lake Zurich, IL
Morgan & Morgan ....Fullerton, NE
Rockville Centre, NY
Morgan, Morgan & Furr ....Watonga, OK
Morgan and Morgan, Inc.
Oklahoma City, OK
Morgan & Morgan, P.C. ....Denver, CO
Morgan & Morgan, P.C. ....Harrisburg, PA
Morgan & Mosley, P.C. ....Kaufman, TX
Morgan & Mullin, LLP ....Columbus, GA
Morgan, Nancy G. ....Chevy Chase, MD
Morgan & Newman ....Victorville, CA
Morgan, Nicolas ....Los Angeles, CA
Morgan, Noel M. ....Cincinnati, OH
Morgan, O. Forrest, Jr. ....Richmond, VA
Morgan, Olsen & Olsen
Fort Lauderdale, FL
Morgan, Padgett & Mierzwinski, P.A.
Tampa, FL
Morgan, Page P. ....Oklahoma City, OK
Morgan, Pamela ....Kansas City, KS
Morgan, Patricia B. ....Spokane, WA
Morgan, Patricia L. ....Olympia, WA
Morgan, Patricia T. ....Atlanta, GA
Morgan, Patrick E. ....Louisville, KY
Morgan, Patrick J. ....New Canaan, CT
Morgan, Patrick J. ....New York, NY
Morgan, Patrick J. ....Cleveland, OH
Morgan, Patrick J. ....Norman, OK
Morgan, Patsy S. ....Raleigh, NC
Morgan, Paul C. ....Wellesley Hills, MA
Morgan, Paul F. ....Rochester, NY
Morgan, Paul J. ....Winter Park, FL
Morgan, Paul Michael ....Kalamazoo, MI
Morgan, Paul V. ....Albany, NY
Morgan, Paul V., Jr. ....Albany, NY
Morgan, Paula Keve ....Walnut Creek, CA
Morgan, Pauline K. ....Wilmington, DE
Morgan, Penelope W. ....Ossining, NY
Morgan, Peter E. ....Denver, CO
Morgan, Peter F. ....Salisbury, NC
Morgan, Peter I. ....Greenville, TX
Morgan, Peter J. ....Denver, CO
Morgan, Peter J., III ....San Francisco, CA
Morgan, Peter S. ....New York, NY
Morgan, Peter W. ....Washington, DC
Morgan & Petrucci ....Columbus, OH
Grove City, OH
Hilliard, OH
Morgan, Philip C. ....San Francisco, CA
Morgan, Philip D. ....Newark, NJ
Morgan, Philip J. ....Fort Lauderdale, FL
Morgan, Philip J. ....Camdenton, MO
Morgan, Philip R. ....San Francisco, CA
Morgan, Philip T. ....Fullerton, NE
Morgan, Philip W. ....Britton, SD
Morgan, Phillip R. ....Monticello, KY
Morgan, Phillis R. ....Phoenix, AZ
Morgan, Porter H., III
Oklahoma City, OK
Morgan & Posilippo ....Mountain View, CA
Morgan & Pottinger, P.S.C.
New Albany, IN
Lexington, KY
Louisville, KY
Shelbyville, KY
Morgan, R. Barry ....Orlando, FL
Morgan, R. Barry, P.A., Law Office of
Orlando, FL
Morgan, R. Glen ....Chesterfield, VA
Morgan, R. Gregory ....Los Angeles, CA
Morgan, R. Scott ....Pine Bluff, AR
Morgan, R. Todd ....Raleigh, NC

Moriarty, Joan E.
Department Of Veterans Affairs, Office of the General Counsel, GV
Moriarty, Joan L. .... St. Louis, MO
Moriarty, John B. .... Parsippany, NJ
Moriarty, John B., Jr. .... Washington, DC
Moriarty, John D. .... Indianapolis, IN
Moriarty, John F. .... Boston, MA
Moriarty, John F., Jr. .... Holyoke, MA
Moriarty, John P. .... Treasury Department, Internal Revenue Service, GV
Moriarty, John T. .... Springfield, MA
Moriarty, John T., II .... Springfield, MA
Moriarty, John V. .... Indianapolis, IN
Moriarty, Joseph L. .... Quincy, MA
Moriarty, Joseph T. .... Chicago, IL
Moriarty, Joseph T. .... Leominster, MA
Moriarty, Kate E. .... Cincinnati, OH
Moriarty, Katherine S. .... Idaho Falls, ID
Moriarty, Kathleen H. .... New York, NY
Moriarty, Kevin J .... Moline, IL
Moriarty, Kevin P. .... Burlington, VT
Moriarty Law Firm .... San Francisco, CA
Moriarty, Leo J., Jr. .... Garden Grove, CA
Moriarty, Lisa J. .... Roeland Park, KS
Moriarty, Louis J. .... Minneapolis, MN
Moriarty, Madigan and Wallis
Houston, TX
Moriarty, Marilyn R. .... San Diego, CA
Moriarty, Matthew P. .... Cleveland, OH
Moriarty, Matthew P., Co., L.P.A.
Cleveland, OH
Moriarty, Michael A. .... Houston, TX
Moriarty, Michael D. .... Indianapolis, IN
Moriarty, Michael F. .... Newark, NJ
Moriarty, Michael J. .... Holyoke, MA
Moriarty, Michael J. .... New York, NY
Moriarty, Michael James .... San Rafael, CA
Moriarty, Michael M. .... New York, NY
Moriarty, Nancy J. .... Portland, OR
Moriarty, Neil J., Jr. .... Holyoke, MA
Moriarty, Patrick J. .... New Ulm, MN
Moriarty, Patrick J. .... New York, NY
Moriarty, Patrick M. .... Everett, WA
Moriarty, Paul F. X. .... Brockton, MA
Moriarty, Paul J. .... Norwell, MA
Moriarty, Regina S. .... Department of Justice, Tax Division, GV
Moriarty, Richard Briles .... Madison, WI
Moriarty, Richard J. .... Cleveland, OH
Moriarty, Robert B. .... Buffalo, NY
Moriarty, Robert B. .... Cleveland, OH
Moriarty, Robert F. .... Summit, NJ
Moriarty, Robert J., Jr. .... Boston, MA
Moriarty, Sean P. .... San Francisco, CA
Moriarty, Stephanie E. .... Albany, NY
Moriarty, Stephen C. .... Port Angeles, WA
Moriarty, Stephen Harris, II .... Fairfax, VA
Moriarty, Stephen J. .... Oklahoma City, OK
Moriarty, Stephen M. .... Seattle, WA
Moriarty, Stephen W. .... Portland, ME
Moriarty & Swanz .... Franklinville, NY
Moriarty, Thomas .... Hollywood, FL
Moriarty, Thomas F. .... Longmeadow, MA
Moriarty, Thomas J. .... Easthampton, MA
Moriarty, Thomas M. .... West Point, PA
Moriarty, Thomas O. .... Braintree, MA
Moriarty, Thomas P. .... Manchester, CT
Moriarty, Timothy J. .... Jersey City, NJ
Moriarty, W. Herbert .... Fort Lauderdale, FL
Moriarty, Wade D. .... Houston, TX
Moriarty, Wahl .... Treasury Department, Internal Revenue Service, GV
Moriarty, William R. .... Boston, MA
Moriarty-Schlick, Mark C. .... Miami, FL
Moriber, Andrew H. .... Miami Beach, FL
Moriber, Joseph .... Lauderhill, FL
Moriber, Samuel Asa .... New York, NY
Moriber, Sara Dreiling .... Miami Beach, FL
Moribondo, Thomas P. .... Philadelphia, PA
Morical, Alice McKenzie .... Indianapolis, IN
Morical, Gregory J. .... Indianapolis, IN
Morice, Craig J. .... Cleveland, OH
Morice, David T. .... Dallas, TX
Morice, Mark E. .... Gretna, LA
Morici, Alfred G. .... West Palm Beach, FL
Morici, Katherine D. .... New York, NY
Morici, Michael D. .... Brooklyn, NY
Garden City, NY
Morici & Morici .... Brooklyn, NY
Garden City, NY
Morici, Robert .... Brooklyn, NY
Garden City, NY
Morico, Paul R. .... Houston, TX
Moricoli, Harris & Cottingham, A Professional Corporation
Oklahoma City, OK
Moricoli, John C., Jr.
Oklahoma City, OK
Morie, Angelia D. .... Maryville, TN
Morie, G. Glen .... Bellevue, WA
Morie, Roger P.
Federal Energy Regulatory Commission, Office of the General Counsel, GV
Moriearty, Scott Carson .... Boston, MA
Moriello, Joseph M. .... Highland, NY
Moriguchi, Eugene T. .... Fair Oaks, CA
Morihara, Kent D. .... Honolulu, HI
Morikawa, Dennis J. .... Philadelphia, PA
Morikawa, Duane .... New York, NY
Morikawa, Randall I. .... Honolulu, HI
Morikubo, Yukio .... Bellevue, WA
Morillo, Juan P. .... Washington, DC
Morimoto, Jan C. .... San Francisco, CA
Morimoto, Mary Ann .... Long Beach, CA
Morimoto, Neil S. .... Mountain View, CA
Morimoto, Peter M. .... Kapaa, HI
Morimoto, Robert T. .... Los Angeles, CA
Morimoto, Teresa R. .... San Francisco, CA
Morin, Alfred L. .... Lake Worth, FL
Morin, Andrew M. .... Nashville, TN
Morin, Angela .... League City, TX
Morin, Angela M. .... Livonia, MI
Morin & Barkley .... Charlottesville, VA
Morin, Barry E. .... Boston, MA
Morin, Bobette J. .... Syracuse, NY
Morin, Charles H. .... Washington, DC
Morin, Charles H., Jr. .... Boston, MA
Morin, Charles L. .... San Francisco, CA
Morin, Christine A. .... Manchester, NH
Morin, Christine E. .... Boston, MA
Morin, Christopher S. .... Tampa, FL
Morin, Danny T. .... Los Angeles, CA
Morin, David M. .... Sherman Oaks, CA
Morin, Diane J. N. .... Palo Alto, CA
Morin, Donald R. .... Charlottesville, VA
Morin, Elizabeth C. .... Oakland, MD
Morin, Geo. C. .... Cambridge, MA
Morin, George P.
Department of Labor, GV
Morin, Heather .... Washington, DC
Morin, James B. .... Gilmer, TX
Marshall, TX
Morin, James C. .... Washington, DC
Morin, John A. .... Boston, MA
Morin, John T. .... New York, NY
Morin, Joyce A. .... Carmel, NY
Morin, Karin V. .... Needham, MA
Morin & Krasny, LLP .... San Francisco, CA
Morin, Laurence P. .... Lynchburg, VA
Morin, Linda P. .... New Orleans, LA
Morin, Lucien A., II .... Rochester, NY
Morin, Mark W. .... Department of Labor, Office of the Solicitor, GV
Morin, Mary M. .... Minneapolis, MN
Morin, Michael A. .... Washington, DC
Morin, Michael D. .... Los Angeles, CA
Morin, Michael D. .... Spartanburg, SC
Morin, Michael L. .... St. Paul, MN
Morin, Nancy L. .... Brunswick, ME
Morin, Peter B. .... Boston, MA
Morin, Philip E., (P.C.) .... Lakeland, FL
Morin, Philip J., III .... Newark, NJ
Morin, Pierre J. .... Berlin, NH
Morin, Pilar .... Los Angeles, CA
Morin, Rachel Ann .... Chelmsford, MA
Morin, Robert A.
Export-Import Bank of The United States, Office of the General Counsel, GV
Morin, Robert E. .... Potomac, MD
Morin, Ronald A. .... East Providence, RI
Morin, Sharon Baker .... Boston, MA
Morin, Tina L. .... Butte, MT
Morin, Tracey Lin .... Missoula, MT
Morin, Volney F. .... Green Valley, AZ
Morin, William J. .... Pittsburg, KS
Morina, J. Thomas .... New York, NY
Morinaka, Barry S. .... Los Angeles, CA
Morinelli, Elaine L. .... Oakland, CA
Morinelli, Karen M. .... Sarasota, FL
Morinello, Angelo J. .... Buffalo, NY
Morinello, Carmen A. .... Irvine, CA
Moriner, Robert H. .... Atlanta, GA
Moring, Carleton L. .... Coolidge, AZ
Moring, David G. .... Magnolia, TX
Moring, David L. .... Los Angeles, CA
Moring, Douglas T. .... Chicago, IL
Moring, Dwayne K. .... San Diego, CA
Moring, Ellen R. .... New York, NY
Moring, F. Delores .... Magnolia, TX
Moring, Frederick .... Washington, DC
Moring, Jack A. .... Crystal River, FL
Moring, Martha A. .... McLean, VA
Moring, Platte B., III .... Allentown, PA
Moringello, Thomas G. .... Brooklyn, NY
Moringlane de Vargas, Aida .... Humacao, PR
Morinigo, Maria Jose .... Philadelphia, PA
Morio, John D. .... New York, NY
Morio, Winifred D. .... New York, NY
Morioka, Leslie .... New York, NY
Moris, Alberto N. .... Darien, CT
Moris, Halim .... Boston, MA
Morisaki, David .... Los Angeles, CA
Morisaki-Price, Maxine M.
Santa Ana, CA
Morishige, Stanley M. .... Honolulu, HI
Morishita, Robert Ryan .... Las Vegas, NV
Morisi, Andrea .... Washington, DC
Morisi, Mark G. .... Springfield, MA
Morisi, Michael V. .... Quincy, MA
Morisi, O'Connell & Brighenti
Springfield, MA
Morisky, Richard J. .... San Francisco, CA
Morison, D. Lynn .... Lansing, MI
Morison, Francis J. .... New York, NY
Morison, Frank H. .... Denver, CO
Morison, Melinda Chalich .... Burlingame, CA
Morison, Samuel T. .... Department of Justice, Office of the Pardon Attorney, GV
Morison, Sarah Meals .... Boston, MA
Morison-Knox Holden Melendez & Prough, LLP .... San Francisco, CA
San Jose, CA
Walnut Creek, CA
Morison-Knox, William C.
Walnut Creek, CA
Morisse, Carl F. .... Hartford, CT
Morisseau, Fay E. .... Irvine, CA
Morisset, Mason D. .... Seattle, WA
Morissette, Daniel J., P.C. .... Manassas, VA
Morissette, Laurie .... Manassas, VA
Morissette, Sherri .... Chicago, IL
Morita, Carol Hiromi .... Northbrook, IL
Morita, Carole Sei .... Los Angeles, CA
Morita, Dennis H. .... El Centro, CA
Morita, James M. .... Honolulu, HI
Morita, Joyce H. .... Glendale, CA
Morita, Mark K. .... Honolulu, HI
Morita, Mark K. .... Honolulu, HI
Morita, Susan T. .... Washington, DC
Moritis, Valdis .... Lakewood, CO
Moritt, Hock & Hamroff, LLP
Garden City, NY
Hempstead, NY
Mineola, NY
Moritt, Neil J. .... Garden City, NY
Moritz, Andrew W. .... Los Angeles, CA
Moritz, Bernard .... Williamsburg, VA
Moritz, Cary E. .... Philadelphia, PA
Moritz, Claire L. .... Raleigh, NC
Moritz, Dawn Clenney .... Detroit, MI
Moritz, Deborah C. .... Madison, WI
Moritz, Donald I. .... Pittsburgh, PA
Moritz, E. Stewart .... San Francisco, CA
Moritz, Edward A. .... Huntington, NY
Moritz, Eloise L. .... Palm Harbor, FL
Moritz, Francis .... Philadelphia, PA
Moritz, Jeremy C. .... Chicago, IL
Moritz, Joel A. .... Denver, CO
Moritz, John D. .... Springfield, MN
Moritz, Joseph John, Jr. .... Phoenix, AZ
Moritz, Larry G. .... Lima, OH
Moritz, Louis P. .... Chicago, IL
Moritz, Luc .... Los Angeles, CA
Moritz, Margaret E. .... New York, NY
Moritz, Michael E. .... Columbus, OH
Moritz, Michelle K. .... Chicago, IL
Moritz, Natalie Chetlin .... Pittsburgh, PA
Moritz, Preston W. .... Nazareth, PA
Moritz, Richard D. .... Grand Rapids, MI
Moritz, Stephen D. .... Pittsburgh, PA
Moritz, Terry F. .... Chicago, IL
Moritz, V. William .... Colorado Springs, CO
Moritz, Victor R. .... New York, NY
Moritz, William C. .... Ventura, CA
Moriwaki, Gary S. .... New York, NY
Moriyama, Rachel Shimazu .... Honolulu, HI
Morizio, Gabriella .... New York, NY
Morizio, Lawrence F. .... New Haven, CT
Morizio, Michael P. .... Boston, MA
Morje, Robert J. .... Columbus, OH
Mork, H. Darling, Hagemann & Kohler
Worthington, MN
Mork, James L. .... Rochester, MN
Mork, Lindsay S. .... Pittsburgh, PA
Mork, Norman A. .... Scarsdale, NY
Mork, Peter .... Miami, FL
Mork, Raymond E. .... Worthington, MN
Mork, Robert G. .... Indianapolis, IN
Morkan, John F., III .... Baltimore, MD
Morkan, Linda L. .... Hartford, CT
Morken, John F. .... San Francisco, CA
Morken, John R. .... Uniondale, NY
Morken, John S. .... Martinez, CA
Morken, Michael E. .... Indianapolis, IN
Morkin, Michael L. .... Chicago, IL
Morkunas, Frank G. .... San Diego, CA
Morlan, Alfred K. .... Tulsa, OK
Morlan & Associates, P.C. .... Tulsa, OK
Morlan, Garold L. .... Tierra Verde, FL
Morlan, Harold E., II .... Orlando, FL
Morlan, Michael N. .... Canoga Park, CA
Morlan & Stovash, P.A. .... Orlando, FL
Morland, Dennis W. .... Norfolk, NE
Morland, John .... Arlington, VA
Morland, Linda J. .... Englewood, FL
Morland, Steven H., Jr. .... Lambertville, NJ
Morlang, Craig T. .... Cobleskill, NY
Morlang, Erik .... Denver, CO
Morlang, Merton .... Cobleskill, NY
Morlang & Morlang .... Cobleskill, NY
Morledge, W. Frank .... Forrest City, AR
Morledge, W. Frank, P.A.
Forrest City, AR
Morley, Arden J. .... Bellaire, TX
Morley & Associates, P.C. .... Bellaire, TX
Morley, C. Val .... Pleasant Grove, UT
Morley, Carroll A. .... Woodbridge, NJ
Morley Caskin .... Washington, DC
Morley, Daniel M. .... Escanaba, MI
Morley, Dean R. .... Little Rock, AR
Morley, Dean R., III .... Atlanta, GA
Morley, Dean R., IV .... Washington, DC
Morley, Edward B. .... Monroe, CT
Morley, E.K. .... Hendersonville, NC
Morley, Elaine V. .... Bellaire, TX
Morley & Farber .... Philadelphia, PA
Morley, Guy A. .... Washington, DC
Morley, Harold, Jr. .... North Andover, MA
Morley, Jacqueline M. .... Feasterville, PA
Morley, James J. .... Trenton, NJ
Morley, Jeremy D. .... New York, NY
Morley, John C. .... Campbell, CA
Morley, John F. X., Jr. .... Prospect Park, PA
Morley, John S. .... Norwood, MA
Morley, Karen D.
Environmental Protection Agency, Program Office Attorneys, GV
Morley, Kevin .... Ketchikan, AK
Morley, Kimberlin L. .... Emeryville, CA
Morley, Laurence .... Lebanon, OR
Morley Law Firm, Ltd. .... Fargo, ND
Grand Forks, ND
Morley, Leonard F., Jr. .... Portland, ME
Morley, Linda .... Springfield, MA
Morley, Mariam M. .... San Francisco, CA
Morley, Mark E. .... Farmington Hills, MI
Morley, Matt T. .... Washington, DC
Morley, Michael .... Boardman, OH
Morley, Michael E. .... New York, NY
Morley, Michael J. .... Grand Forks, ND
Morley, Michael P. .... Akron, OH
Morley, Michele H. .... Cheshire, CT
Morley, Michelle T. .... Tavares, FL
Morley, Patrick .... Cape May, NJ
Morley, Patrick R. .... Grand Forks, ND
Morley, Paul M. .... San Diego, CA
Morley, Randal D. .... Tulsa, OK
Morley, Raymond J., Jr. .... Woodbridge, VA
Morley, Richard K. .... Chicago, IL
Morley, Robert E. .... Wentzville, MO
Morley, Sam R. .... Los Altos, CA
Morley, Samuel J. .... Tallahassee, FL
Morley, Sean E. .... Palo Alto, CA
Morley, Steven A. .... Philadelphia, PA
Morley, Susan Davis .... Tallahassee, FL
Morley, Thomas & McHill .... Lebanon, OR
Morley & Trager .... New York, NY
Morley, William E.
Securities and Exchange Commission, Division of Corporation Finance, GV
Morley, William F. .... Cranford, NJ
Morley, William H., Jr. .... New York, NY
Morlitz, Gerald .... New York, NY
Morman, Carla J. .... Dayton, OH
Morman, Dale L. .... Sturgis, SD
Morman Law Firm .... Sturgis, SD
Morman, Stephanie N. .... Montgomery, AL
Morman, William .... Dearborn, MI
Mormando, Mark A. .... San Diego, CA
Mormann, Marlon D. .... Dakota City, NE
Mormile, Robert J. .... Springfield, NJ
Mormino, Anthony J. .... Washington, DC
Mormino, Raymond R. .... Waco, TX
Mormino, Samuel A, Jr .... Alton, IL
Mormorunni, Carlo C.
San Francisco, CA
Mornarich, Jeffrey A. .... Roseburg, OR
Morneau, Daniel William .... San Diego, CA
Morneau & Murphy .... Jamestown, RI
Providence, RI
Morneau, Richard N. .... Providence, RI
Morneau, Roland E., Jr.
Londonderry, NH
Morneau, Thomas Michael .... Houston, TX
Morneault, Michael D. .... Pittsburgh, PA
Morneault, Monique Ann .... Chicago, IL
Morner-Ritt, Mara .... Los Angeles, CA
Morning, Ingrid E. .... New York, NY
Morning, John F. .... Los Angeles, CA
Morning, Leigh S. .... Rushville, IN
Morningstar, Deborah E. .... New York, NY
Morningstar, Janet R., (P.C.)
Costa Mesa, CA
Sacramento, CA
Morningstar, M. Albert .... Cascade, MD
Morningstar, W. W. .... Newport Beach, CA
Moro, Diana L. .... Philadelphia, PA
Moro, Gregory T. .... Bloomsburg, PA
Moro, Hope R. .... Bloomsburg, PA
Moro, Joseph A. .... Youngstown, OH
Moro, Michele A. .... Dracut, MA
Moro & Moro .... Bloomsburg, PA
Morocco, Maria Luisa .... Washington, DC
Morocco, Morocco & Specht, P.C.
Trafford, PA
Morocco, Rachel E. .... Greensburg, PA
Morocco, Richard A. .... Worcester, MA
Morocco, Richard A., P.C. .... Worcester, MA
Morocco, Vincent J. .... Trafford, PA
Morocco-O'Connell, Kara E.
San Diego, CA
Morochnik, Paul J. .... Norcross, GA
Moroco, Richard F. .... Sharon, PA
Morodomi, Mark Takeshi .... Sacramento, CA
Morof, Jeffrey W. .... Santa Monica, CA
Morof, Lee Howard .... Southfield, MI
Moroff, Shelley S. .... New York, NY
Morofsky, Allan M. .... Bronx, NY
Morofsky, Paul B. .... Norwalk, CT
Morog, Christopher W. .... Boston, MA
Providence, RI
Morog, Tamie Jo .... Indianapolis, IN
Moro-Grossman, Dolores .... New York, NY
Moroh, Peter K. .... Bakersfield, CA
Moroknek, Harold L. .... White Plains, NY
Moroknek, Mark S. .... Syosset, NY
Morokoff, Carol G. .... New York, NY
Morone, Pamela A. .... Philadelphia, PA
Moroney, Adele E. .... North Grafton, MA
Moroney, Brett T. .... Redwood City, CA
Moroney, Carl J. .... Menlo Park, CA
Sacramento, CA
San Francisco, CA
Moroney, Carl V. .... Los Angeles, CA
Moroney, Carole Jo Hanzes .... Aurora, OH
Moroney, Dennis P. .... Milwaukee, WI
Moroney, E. Thomas, Jr. .... Torrance, CA
Moroney, Francis X. .... Carle Place, NY
Moroney, James V. .... Cleveland, OH
Moroney, John J. .... Simsbury, CT
Moroney, John J., IV .... Chicago, IL
Moroney, John P. .... Mineola, NY
Moroney, Kathleen L. .... Notre Dame, IN
Moroney, Linda L. S. .... Houston, TX
Moroney, Linda Sauser .... Milwaukee, WI
Moroney, Michael A. .... Morristown, NJ
Moroney, Michael G. .... Kansas City, KS
Moroney, Michael J. .... Honolulu, HI
Moroney, Paul R. .... Arlington, MA
Moroney, William T. .... Phoenix, AZ
Moroni & Handley .... Carol Stream, IL
Moroni, James J. .... Carol Stream, IL
Moroni, Michael A. .... Bloomfield, MO
Morony, Jean .... Chico, CA
Moropoulos, Christopher M.
Santa Clara, CA
Moroscak, Richard J. .... Cleveland, OH
Morosco, B. Anthony .... White Plains, NY
Morosi, John M. .... Bay City, MI
Moroski, Martin P. .... Paso Robles, CA
Moros-Nahim, Jorge .... New York, NY

Morosoff, Nicholas V. ... San Marino, CA
Morosoli, Eugene B., Jr. ... Palo Alto, CA
Moross, Jeffrey A. ... New York, NY
Moroux, Marc D. ... Lafayette, LA
New Orleans, LA
Morow, Jewell J. ... Indianapolis, IN
Morow, Michael R. ... Indianapolis, IN
Morowitz, David ... Providence, RI
Morowitz, David, Inc. ... Providence, RI
Morowitz, Deborah A. ... New York, NY
Morowitz, Donald H., (Ltd.) ... Chicago, IL
Morowitz, Lisa ... Somerset, NJ
Moroz, Eugene ... New York, NY
Moroz, Harold Ronald ... Saint Marys, GA
Moroz, Nicholas M. ... Cleveland, OH
Moroz, Robin L. ... Braintree, MA
Morozin, Christopher B. ... Fox Lake, IL
Morozuk, John Jay ... Oklahoma City, OK
Morozumi, Damien ... San Francisco, CA
Morphew, Danielle ... West Columbia, TX
Morphew, Donna E. ... Indianapolis, IN
Morphew, James M. ... Springfield, IL
Morphew, Joe ... Little Rock, AR
Morphew, Michael C. ... Boulder, CO
Morphew-Wittman, Stacie ... Topeka, KS
Morphis, Gerald A. ... Jackson, MS
Morphis, Thomas C. ... Hickory, NC
Morphonios, Dean B. ... Tallahassee, FL
Morphonios, Ellen J. ... Miami, FL
Morphy, James C. ... New York, NY
Morphy, Paul, A Law Corporation
Metairie, LA
Morr, James E. ... Monroe, MI
Morr, Richard D. ... Chariton, IA
Morra, Joseph P. ... Rockville, MD
Morra, Linda Russano ... Los Angeles, CA
Morra, Maria G. ... Greenwich, CT
Morra, Michael A. ... Norcross, GA
Morra, Pietro ... Garden City, NY
Morrall, Matthew E.
Fort Lauderdale, FL
Morrall, Matthew E., P.A.
Fort Lauderdale, FL
Morran, Kay Reiter ... Los Angeles, CA
Morrato, James J. ... Denver, CO
Morreale, Frank E. ... New York, NY
Morreale, Gerald ... Scotch Plains, NJ
Morreale, John F. ... Glen Ellyn, IL
Morreale, Justin P. ... Boston, MA
Morreale, Leonard J., Jr. ... New York, NY
Morreale, Lynn Bavaro ... Philadelphia, PA
Morreale, Mack & Terry, P.C.
Chicago, IL
Glen Ellyn, IL
Morreale, Maria J. ... White Plains, NY
Morreale, Matthew G. ... New York, NY
Morreale, Peter C. ... Washington, DC
Morreau, James E., Jr. ... Louisville, KY
Morreim, Paul G. ... Burnsville, MN
Morrel, Reece B. ... Tulsa, OK
Morrel, Reece B., Jr. ... Tulsa, OK
Morrel, Ruth Yudenfriend ... Reston, VA
Morrel, West, Saffa, Craige & Hicks, Inc.
Tulsa, OK
Morrell, Barry ... Chicago, IL
Morrell, Carole L. ... San Francisco, CA
Morrell, Donald C. ... North Myrtle Beach, SC
Morrell, Eduardo F. ... Lakeland, FL
Morrell, Gary K. ... Bryant, AR
Memphis, TN
Morrell, Gene P. ... Houston, TX
Morrell, Gregory R. ... Newport Beach, CA
Morrell, J Gregory ... Greenwood Village, CO
Morrell, James G. ... New York, NY
Morrell, John C. ... Las Vegas, NV
Morrell, John L. ... San Diego, CA
Morrell, Joseph ... Orlando, FL
Morrell, Joseph, P.A. ... Orlando, FL
Morrell, Judith J. ... Davenport, IA
Morrell, Karin B. ... Miami, FL
Morrell, Kay Allan ... Washington, DC
Morrell, Linwood A. ... Fairfield, CT
Morrell, Malcolm E., Jr. ... Bangor, ME
Morrell, Marceil ... Tampa, FL
Morrell, Mark ... Portland, OR
Morrell, Martha A. ... Long Beach, CA
Morrell, Mindy A. ... Baltimore, MD
Morrell, Rivers J., III ... Irvine, CA
Morrell, Rivers J., III, A Prof. Corp.
Irvine, CA
Morrell, Scot D. ... Baltimore, MD
Morrell, Stephen G. ... Brunswick, ME
Morrell, Stephen P. ... Oakland, CA
Morrell, William C. ... Amityville, NY
Morren, Steven J. ... Grand Rapids, MI
Morrey, Joseph A. ... St. Joseph, MO
Morrical, Glenn E. ... Cleveland, OH
Morrical, Tisha S. ... Salina, KS
Morrice, Bradley A. ... Irvine, CA
Morrice, Donald E. ... Cedar Grove, NJ
Morrice, Donald E., P.A. ... Cedar Grove, NJ
Morrice, James D. ... Imlay City, MI
Morrice, John A. ... Charlotte, NC
Morrice, Lengemann & Zimmerman, P.C.
Imlay City, MI
Morrick, Clive I. ... New York, NY
Morriello, Henry G. ... New York, NY
Morrier, John T. ... Boston, MA
Morril, Mark C. ... New York, NY
Morrill, Aaron R. ... New York, NY
Morrill, Anne K. ... Billerica, MA
Morrill & Aronson, P.L.C. ... Phoenix, AZ
Morrill and Associates, P.C. ... Chicago, IL
Morrill, David E. ... Rapid City, SD
Morrill, Denis Roy ... Salt Lake City, UT
Morrill, Frank S. ... San Antonio, TX
Morrill, George P., II ... Beeville, TX
Morrill, Howard R. ... Seattle, WA
Morrill, Joseph M. ... San Jose, CA
Morrill, Julie S. ... Southbridge, MA
Morrill, K. Layne ... Phoenix, AZ
Morrill, Kendra L. ... Chicago, IL
Morrill & Lamarine, P.C. ... Southbridge, MA
Morrill, Leslie A. ... Snohomish, WA
Morrill, Michael J. ... Southbridge, MA
Morrill, Robert B. ... San Francisco, CA
San Jose, CA
Morrill, Robert E. K. ... Concord, NH
Morrill, Rodney T. ... Glendora, CA
Morrill, Stephen S. ... Chicago, IL
Morrill, Thomas L. ... Fairhope, AL
Morrill Thomas Nooney & Braun, LLP
Rapid City, SD
Morrill, William F. ... Lakeville, CT
Morrin, Daniel F. ... San Diego, CA
Morrin, Daniel M. ... Garden City, NY
Morrin, James R. ... Chicago, IL
Morrin, William B. ... Philadelphia, PA
Morring, Carl A., Jr. ... Huntsville, AL
Morring, Schrimsher & Riley
Huntsville, AL
Morris, A. Thomas ... Washington, DC
Morris, Aaron P. ... Irvine, CA
Morris, Abraham ... Yonkers, NY
Morris, Abraham L. ... Oakbrook Terrace, IL
Morris & Adelman, P.C. ... Philadelphia, PA
Morris, Aimee Robson ... San Diego, CA
Morris, Alan R. ... New York, NY
Morris, Alice J. ... Detroit, MI
Morris, Allen L. ... Jeffersonville, IN
Morris, Allison ... Daytona Beach, FL
Morris, Alvin C., Jr. ... Bronx, NY
Morris, Amy J. ... Punxsutawney, PA
Morris, Andrew J. ... Washington, DC
Morris, Andrew M. ... New Prague, MN
Morris, Andrew S., Jr. ... Richmond, CA
Morris, Angela ... Lake Jackson, TX
Morris, Anissa K. ... Covington, KY
Morris, Anthony ... West Chester, PA
Morris, Anthony Hal ... Asheboro, NC
Morris, Anthony W. ... Atlanta, GA
Morris, Archibald L. ... Savannah, GA
Morris, Arlene D. ... New York, NY
Morris, Arthur I. ... Chicago, IL
Morris, Arthur J. ... Atlanta, GA
Morris, Arthur O. ... Los Angeles, CA
Morris, Arthur W. ... Columbia, IL
Morris, Arval ... Seattle, WA
Morris & Associates ... Sherman Oaks, CA
Morris, Audrey M. ... Dallas, TX
Morris, B. Hume, II ... Louisville, KY
Morris, Bailey, Schem, & Associates
Midwest City, OK
Morris, Barbara A. ... New York, NY
Morris, Barbara Ann ... Lebanon, VA
Morris, Barry L. ... Hayward, CA
Morris, Barton W. ... Detroit, MI
Morris, Benjamin G. ... Tampa, FL
Morris, Benjamin H. ... Louisville, KY
Morris & Bernard ... Jacksonville, FL
Morris, Bernard ... Bellmore, NY
Morris, Betty H. ... Norcross, GA
Morris, Bradford E. ... Houston, TX
Morris, Bradley C. ... Indianapolis, IN
Morris, Bradley E. ... Provo, UT
Morris & Bray, P.C. ... Buffalo, NY
Morris, Brenton Kirk ... Birmingham, AL
Morris, Brett J. ... Sacramento, CA
Morris, Brian J. ... Moraga, CA
Morris, Brian J. ... New York, NY
Morris, Brian M. ... San Francisco, CA
Morris, Brian M. ... Bozeman, MT
Morris, Brian Michael ... Copperas Cove, TX
Morris, Brian T. ... Dallas, TX
Morris, Bruce C. ... Houston, TX
Morris, Bruce H. ... Atlanta, GA
Morris, Burton D. ... Harrisburg, PA
Morris, C. David ... Glen Burnie, MD
Morris, C. Donald ... Akron, OH
Morris, C. Glen ... Dallas, TX
Morris, C. Robert, Jr. ... Minneapolis, MN
Morris, C. Wayne ... Huntsville, AL
Morris & Campbell, A Professional Corporation ... Houston, TX
Morris, Cantor, Barnes, Goodman & Furlong ... Buffalo, NY
Cheektowaga, NY
Morris, Carl W. ... Oakland, CA
Morris, Carlson & Hoelscher, P.A.
Minneapolis, MN
Morris, Carol A. ... Livonia, MI
Morris, Carol Ann ... Issaquah, WA
Morris, Caroline ... Treasury Department, Office of Thrift Supervision, GV
Morris, Carolyn ... Berkeley, CA
Morris, Carolyn ... Washington, DC
Morris, Catherine C. ... West Bloomfield, MI
Morris, Catherine Cummings
Philadelphia, PA
Morris, Catherine N. ... Palo Alto, CA
Morris, Cecelia G. ... New York, NY
Morris, Cecil E., Jr. ... Denver, CO
Morris, Cecily L. ... Massena, NY
Morris, Charles ... Santa Ana, CA
Morris, Charles E., Jr. ... Cedartown, GA
Morris, Charles F. ... Trenton, MI
Morris, Charles H., III ... Selma, AL
Morris, Charles J. ... Waynesburg, PA
Morris, Charles J., Jr. ... Glendora, CA
Morris, Charles (Lefty) ... Austin, TX
Morris, Charles M. ... Austell, GA
Morris, Charles M., Jr. ... New Brunswick, NJ
Morris, Charles M., P.C. ... Atlanta, GA
Austell, GA
Morris, Charles N. ... Silver City, NM
Morris, Charles T. ... Andalusia, AL
Morris, Charles W. ... Dallas, TX
Morris, Charley G. ... College Park, GA
Morris, Chas. J. ... San Diego, CA
Morris, Cherie Danette ... Kansas City, MO
Morris, Cheryl A. ... San Francisco, CA
Morris, Chester ... Marysville, CA
Morris, Christina L. ... Kansas City, KS
Morris, Christopher D. ... Kalamazoo, MI
Morris, Christopher E. ... New Prague, MN
Morris, Christopher R. ... Minneapolis, MN
Morris, Christopher S. ... Williamsburg, MA
Morris & Church ... Olympia, WA
Morris, Cindi M. ... Fort Worth, TX
Morris, C. L. ... Richmond, CA
Morris, Clay A. ... Eastland, TX
Morris, Cloud and Conchin, P.C.
Huntsville, AL
Morris, Clyde Y., Jr. ... Alpharetta, GA
Morris, Colin M. ... Palo Alto, CA
Morris, Craig Bryant ... Mobile, AL
Morris, Craven & Sulak ... Austin, TX
Morris, Curtis J. ... Sonoma, CA
Morris, Curtis W. ... San Dimas, CA
Morris, Cynthia J. ... Washington, DC
Morris, D. Robert ... Sacramento, CA
Morris, D. Robert ... Bridgeport, CT
Stamford, CT
Morris, Dale M. ... Elizabethtown, KY
Morris, Dan R. ... Phoenix, AZ
Morris, Dana A. ... Camden, SC
Morris, Dana A. ... Houston, TX
Morris, Dana Earl ... Las Vegas, NV
Morris, Daniel Alan ... Omaha, NE
Morris, Daniel E. ... Anniston, AL
Morris, Daniel G. ... Pepper Pike, OH
Morris, Daniel M. ... Des Plaines, IL
Morris, Daniel P. ... Yorktown Heights, NY
Morris, Daniel R. ... Burlingame, CA
Morris, Daphne Ann ... La Plata, MD
Morris, Darrell M. ... Houston, TX
Morris & Davenport ... Belton, SC
Morris, David ... Fort Lauderdale, FL
Morris, David ... New York, NY
Morris, David A. ... Wichita, KS
Morris, David E. ... Fayetteville, AR
Morris, David F. ... St. Louis, MO
Morris, David F. ... Oklahoma City, OK
Morris, David F. ... Denton, TX
Morris, David H. ... San Marcos, TX
Morris, David J. ... Los Angeles, CA
Morris, David J. ... Chicago, IL
Morris, David L. ... Ada, OK
Morris, David M. ... Washington, DC
Greenbelt, MD
Morris, David M. ... Washington, DC
Morris, David M. ... Baltimore, MD
Morris, David M. ... New York, NY
Morris, David R. ... Topeka, KS
Morris, David R. ... Kansas City, MO
Morris, David R. ... Sunbury, OH
Morris, David S. ... Chicago, IL
Morris, David S. ... Cary, NC
Morris, David T. ... San Francisco, CA
Morris, David W. ... Saratoga Springs, NY
Morris, Dawn Marie ... Bensenville, IL
Morris, Deborah ... Chicago, IL
Morris, Deborah L. ... Atlanta, GA
Morris, Debra Dauzat ... Prairieville, LA
Morris, Delilah Baker ... Herndon, VA
Morris, Dennis ... Laguna Beach, CA
Morris, Dennis ... Ardmore, OK
Morris, Dennis J. ... San Francisco, CA
Morris, Dennis J. ... Watkins Glen, NY
Morris, Dewayne N. ... Birmingham, AL
Morris, Dewey B. ... Richmond, VA
Morris, Diallo Kobie ... Chesapeake, VA
Morris, Diana L. ... Baltimore, MD
Morris, Diane ... Owensboro, KY
Morris & Doherty, P.C. ... Birmingham, MI
Detroit, MI
Morris, Don H. ... Tequesta, FL
Morris, Dona B. ... New York, NY
Morris, Donald C. ... Chicago, IL
Morris, Donald C. ... Louisville, KY
Morris, Donald C. ... Bridgehampton, NY
Morris, Donald E. ... Islip, NY
Morris, Donald Wayne ... McLeansboro, IL
Morris, Donna Decker ... New Haven, CT
Morris, Donna Roberts
Flower Mound, TX
Morris, Donna T. ... Midland, MI
Morris, Dorinda K. ... Fairview, OK
Morris, Douglas A. ... Anchorage, AK
Morris, Douglas D. ... Portland, OR
Morris, Douglas G. ... Brooklyn, NY
Morris, Douglas H. ... Fort Lauderdale, FL
Morris, Douglas H., II ... Louisville, KY
Morris, Douglas Wayne ... Washington, DC
Morris, Downing & Sherred ... Newton, NJ
Morris, Duane ... Akron, OH
Morris, Duffy, Alonso & Faley, LLP
New York, NY
Morris, Dwayne A. ... Chicago, IL
Morris, E. Gerry ... Austin, TX
Morris, E. Lee, III ... Atlanta, GA
Morris, E. Michael ... Birmingham, MI
Morris, E. Patrick ... Santa Barbara, CA
Morris, Edith H. ... New Orleans, LA
Morris, Edward A. ... Los Angeles, CA
Morris, Edward A. ... San Francisco, CA
Morris, Edward J. ... Mechanicsburg, PA
Morris, Edward J. ... Philadelphia, PA
Morris, Edward J., P.C. ... Philadelphia, PA
Morris, Edward L. ... Amarillo, TX
Morris, Edward Lee ... Dallas, TX
Morris, Edward M. ... New Orleans, LA
Morris, Edward N. ... Fullerton, CA
Morris, Edward W. ... Hoboken, NJ
Morris, Edwin ... Lebanon, NJ
Morris, Eileen M. ... Oklahoma City, OK
Morris & Eisenberg ... Bellmore, NY
Morris, Elaine S. ... Fort Worth, TX
Morris, Ellen ... West Palm Beach, FL
Morris, Ellen C. ... York, PA
Morris, Elsa L. ... San Marcos, CA
Morris, Elwood N. ... Lillington, NC
Morris, Emma W. ... Seneca, SC
Morris, Eugene J. ... New York, NY
Morris, Evan W. ... Alliance, OH
Morris, Evan W. ... Canton, OH
Morris, Eveline R. ... San Diego, CA
Morris, F. Marvin, III ... Hattiesburg, MS
Morris, F. L. ... Slidell, LA
Morris & Florey, L.L.P. ... Austin, TX
Georgetown, TX
Morris, Forrest M., Jr. ... Hattiesburg, MS
Morris, Frances M. ... Tampa, FL
Morris, Frances M. ... Gaithersburg, MD
Morris, Francine J. ... New York, NY
Morris, Francis E. ... New York, NY
Morris, Frank C., Jr. ... Washington, DC
Alexandria, VA
Morris, Frank E. ... Olympia, WA
Morris, Frank L., Jr. ... Boston, MA
Morris, Frank R., Jr. ... Columbus, OH
Morris, Franklin D. ... Pittsburgh, PA
Morris, Fred L. ... Des Moines, IA
Morris, Frederic A. ... Seattle, WA
Morris, Frederick D. ... New York, NY
Morris, Frederick W. ... Minneapolis, MN
Morris, Fulvia A. ... Coral Gables, FL
Morris, Fulvia A., P.A. ... Coral Gables, FL
Morris, G. Clay ... Orlando, FL
Morris, G. Gus ... Detroit, MI
Morris, G. Robert ... Memphis, TN
Morris, Gael ... Chicago, IL
Morris, Gareth G.R. ... Chicago, IL
Morris, Garlove, Waterman & Johnson, PLLC ... Louisville, KY
Morris, Gary ... Midwest City, OK
Morris, Gary J., (L.C.) ... St. Louis, MO
Morris, Gary L. ... Peoria, IL
Morris, Gary S. ... Washington, DC
Morris, Gary Sven ... Graham, NC
Morris, Gary W. ... Pasadena, CA
Morris, Gary W. ... Columbia, SC
Morris, G. C. ... Austin, TX
Morris, Geo. W. ... Wilmington, DE
Morris, Geoffrey D. ... Venice, FL
Morris, Geoffrey P. ... Louisville, KY
Morris, Geoffrey S. ... Orange, CA
Morris, George C. ... Salt Lake City, UT
Morris, George C., III ... Houston, TX
Morris, George D. ... Pittsburgh, PA
Morris, George E. ... Alexandria, VA
Morris, George J. ... Charleston, SC
Morris, George L., Jr. ... Troy, MI
Morris, Gerald J. ... Silver Bay, MN
Morris, Gerald M. ... Fort Lauderdale, FL
Morris, Glen R. ... Philadelphia, PA
Morris, Glenn G. ... Baton Rouge, LA
Morris, Glenn W. ... Omaha, NE
Morris, Glenn W. ... Akron, OH
Morris, Gordon R. ... Houston, TX
Morris, Grant H. ... San Diego, CA
Morris, Granville R. ... Groton, CT
Morris, Gregg Lawrence ... Pittsburgh, PA
Morris, Gregory A. ... Dover, DE
Morris, Gregory J. ... Las Vegas, NV
Morris, Gregory Michael ... Springfield, OH
Morris, Gretchen R. ... Corvallis, OR
Morris, Gretchen R., P.C. ... Corvallis, OR
Morris, Guy E., Jr. ... Clarksburg, WV
Morris, G.W., II ... Weston, WV
Morris, H. Bradford, Jr. ... Gainesville, GA
Morris, Hal F. ... Austin, TX
Morris, Hal R. ... Chicago, IL
Morris, Harold G., Jr. ... Denver, CO
Morris, Harry A. ... Gloucester, VA
Morris, Harvey B., (P.C.) ... Huntsville, AL
Morris, Harvey Y. ... San Francisco, CA
Morris, Haynes & Hornsby
Alexander City, AL
Morris, Helen ... Washington, DC
Morris, Henry ... Syracuse, NY
Morris, Henry C. ... De Queen, AR
Morris, Henry, Jr. ... Washington, DC
Morris, Henry M. ... Chicago, IL
Morris, Herbert ... Los Angeles, CA
Morris, Herbert E. ... Washington, DC
Morris, Herbert F. ... Quincy, MA
Morris, Herman I. ... Fort Worth, TX
Morris & Hlavinka ... Houston, TX
Morris, Howard L. ... Dallas, TX
Morris, Howard Patrick ... Chicago, IL
Morris, Howard S. ... Leola, PA
Morris, Ingraham & Hall, P.L.L.C.
Flagstaff, AZ
Mesa, AZ
Phoenix, AZ
Prescott, AZ
Tucson, AZ
Morris, Irving ... Wilmington, DE
Morris, Irving I. ... Short Hills, NJ
Morris, J. David ... Louisville, KY
Morris, J. Jeffrey ... Santa Monica, CA
Morris, J. Joseph ... Leawood, KS
Kansas City, MO
Morris, J. Malcolm ... New York, NY
Morris, J. Michael ... Wichita, KS
Morris, J. Patrick, Jr. ... New Orleans, LA
Morris, J. Robert ... Larchmont, NY
Morris, J. Scott ... Austin, TX
Morris, J. Scott, P.C. ... Austin, TX
Morris, J. Thomas ... Stuart, FL
Morris, J. Wil ... Miami, FL

Morris, J. Wil, P.A. .... Miami, FL
Morris, Jack A. .... Brentwood, TN
Morris, Jack E. .... Fort Wayne, IN
Morris, Jack Edward .... Gretna, LA
Morris, Jack H. .... Whitehall, MT
Morris, Jack I. .... Ormond Beach, FL
Morris, Jackson A., III .... Belmont, CA
Morris, Jackson L. .... Tampa, FL
Morris, James .... San Dimas, CA
Morris, James A., Jr. .... Beaumont, TX
Morris, James D. .... Philadelphia, PA
Morris, James E. .... Concord, NH
Morris, James E. .... Rochester, NY
Morris, James E. R. .... Buffalo, NY
Morris, James F. .... Marietta, GA
Morris, James G. .... Sherman Oaks, CA
Morris, James H. .... Boston, MA
Morris, James, Hitchens & Williams, LLP
Dover, DE
Newark, DE
Wilmington, DE
Morris, James J. .... Chicago, IL
Morris, James J. .... Merrick, NY
Morris, James L. .... Costa Mesa, CA
Morris, James L., Jr. .... Costa Mesa, CA
Morris, James M. .... Stockton, CA
Morris, James M.
Farm Credit Administration,
Legal Counsel Division, GV
Morris, James M. .... Lexington, KY
Morris, James M. .... Sherman, TX
Morris, James P. .... Riverside, CA
Morris, James P. .... Department of Justice,
Executive Office for Immigration Review,
GV
Morris, James R. .... Lake Charles, LA
Morris, James S. .... Daytona Beach, FL
Morris, James S. .... New York, NY
White Plains, NY
Morris, James T. .... Boston, MA
Morris, James W. .... Marion, IL
Morris, James W., III .... Richmond, VA
Morris, James W., Jr. .... Dallas, TX
Morris, Jan C. .... Louisville, KY
Morris, Jan Marie .... Seattle, WA
Morris, Jan Michael .... Boca Raton, FL
Morris, Jane .... Acton, MA
Morris, Janet .... Los Angeles, CA
Morris, Jason Barclay .... Phoenix, AZ
Morris, Jay B. .... Sacramento, CA
Morris, Jayne Allardyce .... Sacramento, CA
Morris, Jean .... Los Angeles, CA
Morris, Jeanne E. .... Minneapolis, MN
Morris, Jed W. .... Spokane, WA
Morris, Jeff A. .... Spokane, WA
Morris, Jeffery A. .... San Diego, CA
Morris, Jeffery B. .... Jacksonville, FL
Morris, Jeffrey .... Milwaukee, WI
Morris, Jeffrey B. .... New York, NY
Morris, Jeffrey D. .... Overland Park, KS
Morris, Jeffrey H. .... Victor, NY
Morris, Jeffrey M. .... Arlington Heights, IL
Morris, Jeffrey Michael, Ltd.
Arlington Heights, IL
Morris, Jeffrey P. .... Springfield, MA
Morris, Jeffrey P. .... Iselin, NJ
Morris, Jeffrey W. .... Dayton, OH
Morris, Jennifer A. .... Palo Alto, CA
Morris, Jennifer Evans .... Dallas, TX
Morris, Jennifer S. .... Fort Worth, TX
Morris, Jessie, Jr. .... Sacramento, CA
Morris, Jill A. .... Kansas City, MO
Morris, Jo Anne
Federal Deposit Insurance Corporation, GV
Morris, Joan E. Marshall .... Lexington, KY
Morris, Joan T. .... Newport News, VA
Morris, Joe C. .... Jackson, TN
Morris, Joe C., Jr. .... Ridgeland, MS
Morris, Joe H. .... Fayetteville, NC
Morris, Joel C. .... Jacksonville, FL
Morris, Joel J. .... Detroit, MI
Morris, John .... Sacramento, CA
Morris, John .... San Diego, CA
Morris, John A. .... Honolulu, HI
Morris, John A. .... New York, NY
Morris, John Alan .... Hattiesburg, MS
Morris, John Andrew .... New York, NY
Morris, John B., Jr. .... Washington, DC
Morris, John C. .... Pell City, AL
Morris, John C., III .... Monroe, LA
Morris, John D. .... Alliance, OH
Morris, John Dustin .... Salt Lake City, UT
Morris, John E. .... San Francisco, CA
Morris, John E. .... Oakland, NJ
Morris, John E., III .... Dallas, PA
Morris, John F. .... Hartford, CT
Morris, John F. .... Charlotte, NC
Morris, John F. .... Pittsburgh, PA
Morris, John G. .... Orlando, FL
Morris, John G. .... Atlanta, GA
Morris, John G., Jr. .... Tallahassee, FL
Morris, John H. .... Gainesville, TX
Morris, John H., IV .... Montrose, VA
Morris, John H., Jr. .... Baltimore, MD
Morris, John I. .... Riverside, CA
Morris, John M. .... Wichita, KS
Morris, John M., III .... Jefferson City, MO
Morris, John O. .... West Hartford, CT
Morris, John P. .... Bridgeton, NJ
Morris, John R. .... Los Angeles, CA
Morris, John R. .... Kansas City, MO
Morris, John R. .... Oklahoma City, OK
Morris, John R., Jr. .... Salt Lake City, UT
Morris, John S., III .... Richmond, VA
Morris, John T., Jr. .... Reston, VA
Morris, John T., Jr. .... Sterling, VA
Morris, John W. .... Morristown, NJ
Morris, John W. .... Smithfield, NC
Morris, John W. .... Philadelphia, PA
Morris, John W., Jr. .... Fresno, CA
Morris, Jomarie L. .... Rochester, MN
Morris, Jon Paul .... Washington, DC
Morris, Jonathan D. .... New York, NY
Morris, Jonathan Eugene .... Canton, OH
Morris, Jonathan R. .... Hartford, CT
Morris, Joseph A. .... Dothan, AL
Morris, Joseph A. .... Denver, CO
Morris, Joseph A. .... Chicago, IL
Morris, Joseph B. .... Dallas, TX
Morris, Joseph D. .... Brick, NJ
Morris, Joseph M. .... West Islip, NY
Morris, Joseph R. .... Plymouth, IN
Morris, Joseph R. .... Akron, OH
Morris, Joseph V. .... Akron, OH
Morris, Joseph W. .... Tulsa, OK
Morris, Judi E. .... Honolulu, HI
Morris, Judith K. .... Morganville, NJ
Morris, Judson W., Jr. .... Pasadena, CA
Morris, Jules J. .... Foxboro, MA
Morris, Juli A. .... Atlanta, GA
Morris, Julia B. .... Hartford, CT
Morris, Julia Caldwell .... Nashville, TN
Morris, Julius D. .... Farmington, CT
Morris, Karen Beth .... Kemah, TX
Morris, Karen L. .... Wilmington, DE
Morris, Karen L.
Pension Benefit Guaranty Corporation,
Office of the General Counsel, GV
Morris, Karen S. .... Phoenix, AZ
Morris, Karen Suizzo .... Northbrook, IL
Morris, Katherine M. .... Atlantic City, NJ
Morris, Kathleen B. .... Montgomery, AL
Morris, Kathleen G. .... Nashville, TN
Morris, Kathleen S. .... San Francisco, CA
Morris, Kathy .... Chicago, IL
Morris, Katrina Kimberlyn .... Oakland, CA
Morris, Keith M. .... Baxley, GA
Morris, Kellum .... Gastonia, NC
Morris, Kelly L. .... Albion, IN
Kendallville, IN
Morris, Kenneth D. .... Wilmington, DE
Morris, Kenneth D. .... Dallas, TX
Morris, Kenneth J. .... Livonia, MI
Morris, Kenneth L. .... Walnut, CA
Morris, Kenneth M. .... Houston, TX
Morris, Kenneth R. .... San Francisco, CA
Morris, Kerry J. .... Albuquerque, NM
Morris, Kevin D. .... San Luis Obispo, CA
Morris, Kevin J. .... Phoenix, AZ
Morris, Kevin J. .... Miami, FL
Morris, Kim L. .... Denver, CO
Morris, Kim L. .... Willowbrook, IL
Morris, Kimberly C. .... Dade City, FL
Morris, Kimbrel Bunn .... Charlotte, NC
Morris & Klippel .... St. Louis, MO
Morris, Kristen A. .... Philadelphia, PA
Morris, L. Daniel, Jr. .... Montgomery, AL
Morris, L. Keith .... Plano, TX
Morris, Laing, Evans, Brock & Kennedy, Chartered .... Topeka, KS
Wichita, KS
Morris, Lang & Associates, L.L.C.
Denver, CO
Morris, Larry B. .... Xenia, OH
Morris, Larry Creston .... Houston, TX
Morris, Larry W. .... Alexander City, AL
Morris, Laura Shaw .... Atlanta, GA
Morris, Laurence D. .... Long Beach, CA
Morris, Lauri D. .... Madison, WI
Morris & Lavette, P.C. .... Birmingham, AL
Morris Law Firm .... Tampa, FL
Morris Law Firm, (A Professional Corporation) .... Atlanta, GA
Morris Law Firm, P.A. .... Albuquerque, NM
Morris, Lawrence B. .... New York, NY
Morris, Lawrence B., Jr. .... Darien, CT
Morris, Leanna L.
Commodity Futures Trading Commission,
Division of Enforcement, GV
Morris, Lee Ann .... Durham, NC
Morris, Leigh B. .... Los Angeles, CA
Morris, Lendais, Hollrah & Snowden, A Professional Corporation .... Houston, TX
The Woodlands, TX
Morris, Leslie R. .... Houston, TX
Morris, Leslie W., II .... Lexington, KY
Morris, Lester J. .... Palm Beach, FL
Morris, Lewis D., Jr. .... Alexandria, VA
Morris, Lewis S., III .... Charlotte, NC
Morris, Leyser Q. .... Jackson, MS
Morris, Linda C. .... Horsham, PA
Morris, Linda L. .... Granville, OH
Morris, Lisa A. .... Moncks Corner, SC
Morris, Lisa Burgunder .... Rochester, NY
Morris, Lisa Sander .... Kansas City, MO
Morris, Lloyd D. .... Mason, MI
Morris, Loren J. .... Prospect Heights, IL
Morris, Lorraine M. .... New York, NY
Morris, Louis A. .... Dobbs Ferry, NY
Morris, Lucy E. .... Federal Trade Commission,
Bureau of Consumer Protection, GV
Morris, M. Camille .... Austin, TX
Morris, M. Christine .... Charleston, WV
Morris, M. Conway .... Anaheim, CA
Moreno Valley, CA
Morris, M. Jan .... Kansas City, MO
Morris, M. Robin .... Conway, SC
Morris, M. Scotland .... Baltimore, MD
Morris, M. Stephanie .... San Francisco, CA
Morris, M. Yvonne .... Carbondale, IL
Morris, Madelyn .... Boston, MA
Morris, Malcolm S. .... Houston, TX
Morris, Manning & Martin, LLP
Washington, DC
Atlanta, GA
Cumming, GA
Norcross, GA
Morris, Marc .... Pasadena, CA
Morris, Marcus R. .... Dalton, GA
Morris, Marcy S. .... Los Angeles, CA
Morris, Margaret J. .... Coronado, CA
Morris, Marian B. .... Jamaica, NY
Morris, Marie B. .... Library of Congress,
Congressional Research Service, GV
Morris, Marilyn .... Walnut Creek, CA
Morris, Marilyn K. .... Tallahassee, FL
Morris, Marjorie J. .... Deerfield Beach, FL
Morris, Mark .... Louisiana, MO
Morris, Mark .... Longview, TX
Morris, Mark D. .... Albany, NY
Morris, Mark D. .... Austin, TX
Morris, Mark K. .... Waco, TX
Morris, Mark L. .... Philadelphia, PA
Morris, Mark O. .... Salt Lake City, UT
Morris, Mark W. .... Durham, NC
Morris, Marlene Gale .... Oakland, CA
Morris, Martha A. .... Orlando, FL
Morris, Martin E. .... Brownsville, TX
McAllen, TX
Morris, Martin W. .... United States Senate,
Senatorial Assistants, GV
Morris, Marty A. .... Dallas, TX
Morris, Mary C. .... Skokie, IL
Morris, Mary E. .... Indianapolis, IN
Morris, Mary Ellen .... Nashville, TN
Morris, Mary J. .... Fairfield, CA
Morris, Mary Jane .... Morley, MI
Morris, Mary Lee .... Hewlett Bay Park, NY
Morris, Matt H. .... Palm Desert, CA
Morris, Matthew L. .... Chicago, IL
Morris, Matthew O. .... Kalamazoo, MI
Morris, Matthew S.
Securities and Exchange Commission,
Division of Market Regulation, GV
Morris, Max M. .... Lake Charles, LA
Morris & McDermott, L.L.C.
Montgomery, AL
Morris & McVeigh LLP .... New York, NY
Morris, Melanie R. B. .... Philadelphia, PA
Morris, Melissa A. .... Albuquerque, NM
Morris, Melissa A. .... Charleston, WV
Morris, Melissa C. .... Philadelphia, PA
Morris, Melody E. .... Dallas, TX
Morris, Melvin E. .... San Diego, CA
Morris, Merle E., Jr. .... Sacramento, CA
Morris, Merle Montgomery .... Houston, TX
Morris, Michael A. .... Los Angeles, CA
Morris, Michael A. .... Orange, CA
Morris, Michael A. .... Athens, GA
Morris, Michael C. .... Cherry Hill, NJ
Morris, Michael D. .... Beverly Hills, CA
Morris, Michael D. .... Louisville, KY
Morris, Michael E. .... Colorado Springs, CO
Morris, Michael G. .... Corpus Christi, TX
Morris, Michael J. .... San Luis Obispo, CA
Morris, Michael J. .... Savannah, GA
Morris, Michael J. .... St. Louis, MO
Morris, Michael J. .... Portland, OR
Morris, Michael J., Jr. .... Norristown, PA
Morris, Michael P. .... Summit, NJ
Morris, Michael P. .... Houston, TX
Morris, Michael R. .... Los Angeles, CA
Morris, Michael W. .... Andover, MA
Morris, Michele .... Akron, OH
Morris, Michele E. .... Charlotte, NC
Morris, Michelle M. .... Daytona Beach, FL
Morris, Mildred M. .... Jackson, MS
Morris, Milton .... Denver, CO
Morris, Mitchell S. .... Albany, NY
Morris, Monte J. .... Henderson, NV
Morris, Monte L. .... New York, NY
Morris and Morris .... Wilmington, DE
Morris and Morris .... Savannah, GA
Morris & Morris .... Rochester, NY
Morris & Morris .... Punxsutawney, PA
Morris and Morris, A Professional Corporation .... Chesterfield, VA
Richmond, VA
Morris & Morris, L.L.P. .... Denton, TX
Flower Mound, TX
Morris & Morris, P.S.C. .... Lexington, KY
Morris, Myra K. .... Corpus Christi, TX
Morris & Nakaue .... Stockton, CA
Morris, Nancy B. .... New City, NY
Morris, Nancy J. .... Fargo, ND
Morris, Nancy M. .... Baltimore, MD
Morris, Nancy T. .... Omaha, NE
Morris, Ned B. .... Houston, TX
Morris, Neil A. .... Philadelphia, PA
Morris, Neil A., Associates, P.C.
Marlton, NJ
Philadelphia, PA
Morris, Nellie T. .... Philadelphia, PA
Morris, Nichols, Arsht & Tunnell
Wilmington, DE
Morris, Nicole L. .... St. Louis, MO
Morris, Norman P. .... Encino, CA
Morris, O. Haynes, Jr. .... Dallas, TX
Morris, O. Machelle .... Odessa, TX
Morris, P. Kevin .... Santa Monica, CA
Morris, Pancho G. .... Charleston, WV
Morris, Parke S. .... Memphis, TN
Morris, Pat .... Corpus Christi, TX
Morris, Patricia A. .... Sellersville, PA
Morris, Patricia Anne .... Youngstown, OH
Morris, Patricia E. .... South Portland, ME
Morris, Patrick .... Cleveland, OH
Morris, Patrick F. .... Wilmington, DE
Morris, Patrick J. .... San Bernardino, CA
Morris, Patrick J. .... Chicago, IL
Morris, Patrick M. .... Sandwich, MA
Morris, Paul .... Miami, FL
Morris, Paul, Professional Association
Coral Gables, FL
Miami, FL
Morris, Paula D. .... Houston, TX
Morris, Pearl .... Los Angeles, CA
Morris, Penelope .... Markham, IL
Morris, Philip B. .... Richmond, VA
Morris, Philip M. .... Fontana, CA
Morris, Phillip E. .... Ellwood City, PA
Morris, Phillip L. .... Kansas City, MO
Morris, Polich & Purdy, LLP
Los Angeles, CA
Orange, CA
San Diego, CA
Morris & Pratt, LLP .... Aventura, FL
Boca Raton, FL
Fort Lauderdale, FL
West Palm Beach, FL
Morris, R. Bradley .... Hartford, CT
Morris, R. Cabell, Jr. .... Chicago, IL
Morris, R. Crawford .... Cleveland, OH
Morris, Ralph A. .... Chicago, IL
Morris, Ralph K. .... Minneapolis, MN
Morris, Ralph Larry .... Pensacola, FL
Morris, Randolph W. .... Minneapolis, MN
Morris, Rathnau & De La Rosa .... Chicago, IL
Morris, Raymond E. .... Rochester, NY
Morris, Rebecca R. .... Plano, TX
Morris, Reginald P., Jr.
Fort Lauderdale, FL
Morris, Richard .... Los Angeles, CA
Morris, Richard .... Oklahoma City, OK
Morris, Richard Alan .... Houston, TX
Morris, Richard B., Law Offices of
San Juan Bautista, CA
Morris, Richard C. .... Denver, CO
Morris, Richard D. .... Rochester, NY
Morris, Richard G., Law Offices of
Woodland Hills, CA
Morris, Richard H. .... Portage, MI
Morris, Richard L. .... Huntsville, AL
Morris, Richard L. .... Fresno, CA
Morris, Richard L. .... Minneapolis, MN
Morris, Richard M. .... New York, NY
Morris, Richard P. .... New York, NY
Morris, Richard R. .... Des Plaines, IL
Morris, Richard R. .... Waterloo, IA
Morris, Richard R. .... Philadelphia, PA
Morris, Richard S. .... Santa Fe, NM
Morris, Richard W. .... Sun City, AZ
Morris, Richard W. .... Fort Worth, TX
Morris, Richd. C. .... Los Altos, CA
Morris, Rick F. .... Washington, DC
Morris, Rick G. .... Evanston, IL
Morris, Ricky W, Jr .... Jonesboro, GA
Morris, Rita L. .... Gaithersburg, MD
Morris, Robbie S., (P.C.) .... Houston, TX
Morris, Robert Alexander .... Tallahassee, FL
Morris, Robert Allen, Jr. .... Brooksville, FL
Morris, Robert B. .... Washington, DC
Morris, Robert C. .... Glens Falls, NY
Morris, Robert C. .... Corpus Christi, TX
Morris, Robert E. .... Stamford, CT
Morris, Robert E. .... Tampa, FL
Morris, Robert F. .... Walnut Creek, CA
Morris, Robert F. .... Golden, CO
Morris, Robert F. .... Plymouth Meeting, PA
Morris, Robert G. .... Toledo, OH
Morris, Robert I. .... Philadelphia, PA
Morris, Robert J. .... Clarkston, MI
Morris, Robert Joseph .... Raleigh, NC
Morris, Robert K. .... Pittsburgh, PA
Morris, Robert L. .... Potomac, MD
Morris, Robert L. .... Greenville, OH
Morris, Robert L. .... Newark, OH
Morris, Robert L., II .... Belle Fourche, SD
Rapid City, SD
Morris, Robert Lane .... Los Angeles, CA
Morris, Robert M. .... Sanford, FL
Morris, Robert M. .... Brunswick, ME
Morris, Robert M. .... Philadelphia, PA
Morris, Robert M. .... Weston, WV
Morris, Robert P. .... Aspen, CO
Morris, Robert P. .... Boston, MA
Morris, Robert R., III .... Batesville, MS
Morris, Robert S. .... Coronado, CA
Morris, Robert S. .... Denton, TX
Morris, Robert T. .... Davis, CA
Morris, Robert T. .... Rochester, NY
Morris, Robert V., II .... Dublin, OH
Morris, Robert W. .... New York, NY
Morris, Robert W. .... Bismarck, ND
Morris, Robert W. .... Richmond, VA
Morris, Roberta J. .... Ann Arbor, MI
Morris, Robin A. .... New Orleans, LA
Morris, Robin Tatum .... Raleigh, NC
Morris, Roger M. .... Denver, CO
Morris, Roger N. .... Phoenix, AZ
Morris, Roland .... Philadelphia, PA
Morris, Ronald A. .... New York, NY
Morris, Ronald D. .... Yuma, AZ
Morris, Ronald L. .... Irvine, CA
Morris, Ronald L. .... Madison, VA
Stanardsville, VA
Morris, Ronald M. .... Casper, WY
Morris, Ronna B. .... Stockton, CA
Morris, Rossi & Hayes .... Andover, MA
Morris, Rowland, Prekel, Frederick, Lewis & Lewinski, P.L.C. .... Troy, MI
Morris, Roy G. .... Flower Mound, TX
Morris, Roy L. .... Cambridge, OH
Morris, Roy R. .... Washington, DC
Morris, Royce F. .... Atlanta, GA
Morris, Royce L. .... Harrisburg, PA
Morris, Russell F., Jr. .... Nashville, TN
Morris, S. Lee .... Portsmouth, VA
Morris, S. Tom .... Amarillo, TX
Morris & Sakalarios, P.A. .... Hattiesburg, MS

Morrison, Mahoney & Miller
Hartford, CT
Barnstable, MA
Boston, MA
Brockton, MA
Fall River, MA
Hyannis, MA
New Bedford, MA
Raynham, MA
Springfield, MA
Worcester, MA
Yarmouth Port, MA
Grand Rapids, MI
Southfield, MI
New York, NY
Providence, RI
Morrison, Mairi N. .... Miami, FL
Morrison, Margaret R. .... New York, NY
Morrison, Margaret Zonia .... Manchester, MO
Morrison, Marguerite E. H. .... New York, NY
Morrison, Maria J. .... West Palm Beach, FL
Morrison, Marifrances .... Raleigh, NC
Morrison, Marina M. .... Monrovia, CA
Morrison, Mark .... Woodsfield, OH
Morrison, Mark A. .... Corona Del Mar, CA
Morrison, Mark A. .... Durant, OK
Morrison, Mark D. .... Jackson, MS
Morrison, Mark E. .... Nashville, TN
Morrison, Mark F. .... Uniontown, PA
Morrison, Mark Lee .... Costa Mesa, CA
Morrison, Mark S. .... Warsaw, IN
Morrison, Marvin R. .... Oyster Bay, NY
Morrison, Mary Jane .... St. Paul, MN
Morrison, Mary Margaret B. .... Jackson, MS
Morrison, Matthew S. .... Rockford, IL
Morrison, Matthew W.
Department of Justice,
Environment and Natural Resources
Division, GV
Morrison, Maureen Carr .... Sacramento, CA
Morrison, Max M. .... Knoxville, TN
Morrison, Michael A. .... Burlington, MA
Morrison, Michael D. .... Waco, TX
Morrison, Michael G. .... Buffalo, NY
Morrison, Michael J. .... Reno, NV
Morrison, Michael J. T. .... New York, NY
Morrison, Michael P. .... Tucson, AZ
Morrison, Michael P. .... Chicago, IL
Morrison, Michael R. .... Rockford, IL
Morrison, Michael S. .... Wheaton, IL
Morrison, Michael W. .... Eureka, CA
Morrison, Michael W. .... Chicago, IL
Morrison, Michele .... Austin, TX
Morrison & Mills, P.A. .... Tampa, FL
Morrison & Mix .... Chicago, IL
Morrison & Morrison .... Scottsdale, AZ
Eureka, CA
Frankfort, IN
Fitchburg, MA
Morrison & Morrison, P.C. .... Waukegan, IL
Morrison, Myles C., III .... Morristown, NJ
Morrison, Nancy E. .... Columbus, OH
Morrison, Nancy G. .... Los Angeles, CA
Morrison, Nancy J. .... Hinsdale, IL
Morrison, Nancy Napier .... Waco, TX
Morrison, Neil R. .... New York, NY
Morrison, Norah M. .... Fountain Valley, CA
Morrison, Norman deVere .... Berryville, VA
Morrison, Norman E. .... Franklin Square, NY
Morrison, Patrice B. .... Rochester, NY
Morrison, Patricia A. .... Parkersburg, WV
Morrison, Patricia E. Martin .... Tulsa, OK
Morrison, Patricia W. .... Cincinnati, OH
Morrison, Paul A. .... Warrenton, VA
Morrison, Paul C. .... Cleveland, OH
Morrison, Paul J. .... Olathe, KS
Morrison, Paul V., II .... Clarksburg, WV
Morrison, Philip D. .... Washington, DC
Morrison, Philip W., II .... Charleston, WV
Morrison, Portia Owen .... Chicago, IL
Morrison, Preston A. .... Atlanta, GA
Morrison, R. Bruce .... Philadelphia, PA
Morrison, R. Bryan .... Tulsa, OK
Morrison, R. Clark .... Sacramento, CA
San Francisco, CA
Walnut Creek, CA
Morrison, R. Timothy .... Atlanta, GA
Columbus, GA
Morrison, Ralph R. .... Atlanta, GA
Morrison, Randal R. .... San Diego, CA
Morrison, Randall D. .... Oakland, CA
Morrison, Randall W. .... Tullahoma, TN
Morrison, Randi V. .... O'Fallon, MO
Morrison, Randy Sue .... Orange, CA
Morrison, Ray A. .... Austin, TX
Morrison, Rayna M. .... Los Angeles, CA
Morrison, Rees W. .... Newtown Square, PA
Morrison & Reynolds .... Washington, DC
Alexandria, VA
Morrison, Richard A. .... Miami, FL
Morrison, Richard C. .... Toms River, NJ
Morrison, Richard D. .... Montgomery, AL
Morrison, Richard J. .... Cambridge, MA
Morrison, Richard L. .... Austin, TX
Morrison, Richard N. .... Phoenix, AZ
Morrison, Richard Paul .... Willoughby, OH
Morrison, Richard, P.C., Law Office of
Kemah, TX
Morrison, Richard R., III .... Kemah, TX
Morrison, Richard S. .... Voorhees, NJ
Morrison, Richard T. .... Chicago, IL
Morrison, Richard W.
Fort Lauderdale, FL
Morrison, Richard W., P.C.
Smithtown, NY
Morrison & Robbins .... Frankfort, IN
Morrison, Robert .... Scottsdale, AZ
Morrison, Robert C. .... Stockton, CA
Morrison, Robert C. .... Houston, TX
Morrison, Robert Dale .... Albuquerque, NM
Morrison, Robert E. .... Dallas, TX
Morrison, Robert G. .... Ann Arbor, MI
Morrison, Robert H. .... Sun Valley, ID
Morrison, Robert H. .... Halifax, VA
Morrison, Robert H., III .... Amite, LA
Morrison, Robert I. .... Danbury, CT
Morrison, Robert J. .... Louisville, KY
Morrison, Robert L. .... Los Angeles, CA
Morrison, Robert L., Jr. .... Danville, VA
Morrison, Robert M. .... Dallas, TX
Morrison, Robert P. .... Seattle, WA
Morrison, Robert Torrence .... Boston, MA
Morrison, Robert W. .... San Francisco, CA
Morrison, Robert W. .... Orlando, FL
Morrison, Robert W. .... Mahomet, IL
Morrison, Roberta S. .... Miami Beach, FL
Morrison, Robt. L. .... El Reno, OK
Morrison, Roger A. .... Washington, DC
Morrison, Ron .... New York, NY
Morrison, Ronald G. .... Spokane, WA
Morrison, Ronald W. .... New Orleans, LA
Morrison, Ross .... New York, NY
Morrison, Russell J. .... Fort Lauderdale, FL
Morrison, Rusty E. .... Long Beach, CA
Morrison, S. Scott .... Washington, DC
Morrison & Saltz, P.C. .... Chicago, IL
Morrison, Samuel B. .... Toledo, OH
Morrison, Samuel M., Jr.
Washington, DC
Morrison, Sarah D .... Columbus, OH
Morrison, Sarah E. .... Los Angeles, CA
Morrison & Schlesinger .... Mount Carmel, PA
Shamokin, PA
Morrison, Scott .... Dallas, TX
Morrison, Scott A. .... Frederick, MD
Morrison, Scott A. .... Houston, TX
Morrison, Seth W. .... Seattle, WA
Morrison, Sharon M. .... Whitefish, MT
Morrison & Shelton, A Professional Corporation .... Wichita Falls, TX
Morrison, Sheryl G. .... Minneapolis, MN
Morrison, Sidney E. .... Chicago, IL
Morrison, Stephanie Kraus .... St. Louis, MO
Morrison, Stephanie W.
Mount Laurel, NJ
Morrison, Stephen D. .... Attica, IN
Morrison, Stephen D. .... Des Moines, IA
Morrison, Stephen D., Jr. .... Marietta, GA
Morrison, Stephen G. .... Columbia, SC
Morrison, Stephen M. .... Dover, NH
Morrison, Steven C. .... Irvine, CA
Morrison, Susan .... New York, NY
Morrison, Susan B. .... Tampa, FL
Morrison, Susan E. .... Bloomfield Hills, MI
Morrison, Susan G. .... Austin, TX
Morrison, Susan M. .... Boston, MA
Morrison, Susan Neel .... Swampscott, MA
Morrison, Susannah D. .... Jacksonville, FL
Morrison, Terri S. .... Denver, CO
Morrison, Theodore V., Jr. .... Richmond, VA
Morrison, Thomas B. .... Fairfax, VA
Morrison, Thomas C. .... Helena, MT
Morrison, Thomas C. .... New York, NY
Morrison, Thomas F. .... Sacramento, CA
Morrison, Thomas K. .... Tampa, FL
Morrison, Thomas Kent Ledyard
New Orleans, LA
Morrison, Thomas P. .... Charleston, SC
Morrison, Thomas R. .... Branford, CT
Mount Vernon, NY
Morrison, Timothy P. .... Albany, NY
Morrison, Todd A. .... Paramus, NJ
Morrison, Troy D. .... Holden, MA
Morrison, Truman A., III .... Washington, DC
Morrison, Tyree & Dunn, P.A.
Knoxville, TN
Morrison, Valerie P. .... Washington, DC
Alexandria, VA
Morrison, Victoria A. .... Morristown, NJ
Morrison, Vincent J. .... Turnersville, NJ
Philadelphia, PA
Morrison, W. Price, Jr. .... Memphis, TN
Morrison, Walter C., IV .... Jackson, MS
Morrison, Walter J. .... Houston, TX
Morrison, Walter M. .... Prague, OK
Morrison, Walton S. .... Big Spring, TX
Morrison, Wayne A. .... Atlanta, GA
Morrison & Webster .... Joplin, MO
Morrison, Wesley Ward, Jr. .... Seattle, WA
Morrison, Wiley W. .... Raytown, MO
Morrison, William A. .... Atlanta, GA
Morrison, William A. .... Batesville, IN
Morrison, William Brian .... Pittsford, NY
Morrison, William E. .... Tempe, AZ
Morrison, William F. .... Kalamazoo, MI
Morrison, William H. .... Fern Park, FL
Morrison, William J. .... St. Petersburg, FL
Morrison, William J. .... Fair Lawn, NJ
Morrison, William J., III .... San Diego, CA
Morrison, William L. .... Chicago, IL
Morrison, William S. .... Troy, MI
Morrison, William T. .... Mason City, IA
Morrison, Wm. Howell .... Charleston, SC
Morrison, Wm. McG., Jr. .... Charleston, SC
Morrison-Piñon, Gail R. .... Coral Gables, FL
Morrisons, McCarthy & Baraban
Claremont, CA
Whitefish, MT
Morrison-Taylor, Paul .... Buffalo, NY
Morrisroe, Daniel Edward
Bloomfield Hills, MI
Morrisroe, Donald P. .... Cincinnati, OH
Morrisroe, Garyowen P. .... New York, NY
Morrisroe, Kathleen M. .... Dallas, TX
Morrisroe, Michael J. .... Bloomingdale, IL
Morrisroe, Michael, Jr. .... Bloomingdale, IL
Morrisroe, Neil S. .... Atlanta, GA
Morrisroe, Richard F. .... Chicago, IL
Morrisroe, Sean W. .... Oakland, CA
Morriss, Andrew P. .... Cleveland, OH
Morriss Bateman O'Bryant & Compagni
Salt Lake City, UT
Morriss, Bruce F. .... Macon, GA
Morriss, C. Adam, III .... San Angelo, TX
Morriss, Dent .... Springfield, TN
Morriss, Edward T. .... Harrisburg, PA
Morriss, F. Chadwick .... Montgomery, AL
Morriss, Gordon S. .... Kerrville, TX
Morriss, Gordon S., P.C. .... Kerrville, TX
Morriss, J. Thomas .... Roswell, GA
Morriss, James C., III .... Austin, TX
Morriss, James R. .... Warwick, RI
Morriss, Josh R., III .... Texarkana, TX
Morriss, Julie K. .... Salt Lake City, UT
Morriss, Lober & Dobson .... Macon, GA
Morriss, Phyllis Dozier .... Springfield, TN
Morriss, Robert C. .... Syosset, NY
Morriss, William J. .... East Lansing, MI
Morriss & Witcher, P.A. .... Atlanta, GA
Morrissett, Steven H. .... Palo Alto, CA
Morrissette, George H. .... Manchester, NH
Morrissette, Henry T. .... Mobile, AL
Morrissette, Karen A.
Department of Justice,
Criminal Division, GV
Morrissette, Kenneth, Jr. .... Seattle, WA
Morrissette, Mark D. .... Manchester, NH
Morrissette, Peter J. .... St. Johnsbury, VT
Morrissey, Alan J.
Environmental Protection Agency,
Office of Enforcement and Compliance
Assurance, GV
Morrissey, Alice .... Philadelphia, PA
Morrissey, Amy N. .... Ann Arbor, MI
Morrissey, Andrew J. .... Chico, CA
Morrissey, Arthur J., Jr. .... Racine, WI
Morrissey, Barbara Z. .... New York, NY
Morrissey, Bove & Ebbott .... Flint, MI
Morrissey, Brian J. .... Atlanta, GA
Morrissey, Brian P. .... Garden City, NY
Morrissey Brothers, P.C. .... Washington, DC
Bowie, MD
Morrissey & Brown .... Fairfield, IA
Morrissey, Bruce C. .... Hackensack, NJ
Morrissey, Bruce W. .... Wilmington, DE
Morrissey, Caren E. .... Norristown, PA
Morrissey, Caroline Nolting .... Stratford, CT
Morrissey, Charlotte R. .... Phoenix, AZ
Morrissey, Cheryl .... Paramus, NJ
Morrissey, Clarence J. .... Glendale, CA
Morrissey, Corinne Seither .... Chicago, IL
Morrissey, Daniel C. .... Algonquin, IL
Morrissey, Daniel J. .... Miami, FL
Morrissey, David J. .... Naugatuck, CT
Morrissey, David J. .... Severna Park, MD
Morrissey, David John .... Englewood, CO
Morrissey, Diana Young .... Minneapolis, MN
Morrissey, Donald J., Jr. .... Palo Alto, CA
Morrissey, Edward P. .... Sandwich, IL
Morrissey, Ellen C. .... West Hartford, CT
Morrissey, Eugene .... New York, NY
Morrissey & Feil .... Racine, WI
Morrissey, Francis C. .... Boston, MA
Morrissey, Francis D. .... Chicago, IL
Morrissey, Francis P. .... Chicago, IL
Morrissey, Gail L. .... Dublin, OH
Morrissey, Gary L. .... Oklahoma City, OK
Morrissey, Hawkins & Lynch .... Boston, MA
Morrissey & Hershner .... Richmond, VA
Morrissey, J. Barry .... New London, NH
Morrissey, J. David, Jr. .... Farmington, CT
Morrissey, J. Richard .... Los Angeles, CA
Morrissey, J. Russell .... McLean, VA
Morrissey, James A. .... Princeton, NJ
Morrissey, James J., Jr. .... New York, NY
Morrissey, James Joseph, III .... New Paltz, NY
Morrissey, James M. .... Bowie, MD
Morrissey, James M. .... Buffalo, NY
Morrissey, James M. .... Woodside, NY
Morrissey, James T. .... Buffalo, NY
Morrissey, Jean G. .... Kansas City, MO
Morrissey, Jere .... San Bernardino, CA
Morrissey, John .... Treasury Department,
Internal Revenue Service, GV
Morrissey, John A. .... Fairfield, IA
Morrissey, John C. .... Los Angeles, CA
Morrissey, John C., Sr. .... San Francisco, CA
Morrissey, John E. .... Chicago, IL
Morrissey, John E., Jr. .... Syracuse, NY
Morrissey, John J. .... Boston, MA
Morrissey, John J. .... New York, NY
Morrissey, John P. .... Bowie, MD
Morrissey, John P. .... Bennington, VT
Morrissey, John Patrick
West Palm Beach, FL
Morrissey, Joseph A. .... Clearwater, FL
Morrissey, Joseph A. .... Rockford, IL
Morrissey, Joseph A. .... Branson, MO
Morrissey, Joseph D. .... Richmond, VA
Morrissey, Joseph M. .... Alexandria, VA
Morrissey, Joseph P. .... Boston, MA
Morrissey, Kathleen M. .... Boston, MA
Morrissey, Kathy S. .... Mount Holly, NJ
Morrissey, Kevin R. .... Brooklyn, NY
Morrissey, Kit Renae .... Fairview Heights, IL
Morrissey, Lauren Spector .... White Plains, NY
Morrissey, Lawrence E. .... Chicago, IL
Joliet, IL
Morrissey, Lawrence J. .... Rockford, IL
Morrissey, Leann D. .... Houston, TX
Morrissey, LLC, David J., Law Offices of
Naugatuck, CT
Morrissey, Margaret A. .... Union, NJ
Morrissey, Martin B. .... Toledo, OH
Morrissey, Martin K. .... Edwardsville, IL
Morrissey, Mary .... Clearwater, FL
Morrissey, Mary M. .... Chicago, IL
Morrissey, Matthew J. .... Chicago, IL
Morrissey, Matthew J., & Associates, Ltd.
Chicago, IL
Morrissey, Maureen M. .... Orlando, FL
Morrissey, Michael .... Austin, TX
Morrissey, Michael A. .... Menlo Park, CA
Morrissey, Michael A. .... Lafayette, IN
Morrissey, Michael F. .... Denver, CO
Morrissey, Michael J. .... Chicago, IL
Morrissey, Michael J. .... New York, NY
Morrissey, Michael J. .... Columbus, OH
Morrissey, Michael L. .... Angola, IN
Morrissey, Michael R .... Carle Place, NY
Morrissey, Michael W. .... Denver, CO
Morrissey, Michael W. .... Boston, MA
Morrissey & Morrissey .... Denver, CO
Morrissey, Morrissey & Dalluge
Tecumseh, NE
Morrissey & Morrissey, LLP
New York, NY
Morrissey, Patricia A. .... Stratford, CT
Morrissey, Patrick J. .... Okanogan, WA
Morrissey, Patrick T. .... Charleston, SC
Morrissey, Paul D. .... Washington, DC
Morrissey, Philip Patrick, Jr.
Stroudsburg, PA
Morrissey, Raymond A. .... Chicago, IL
Morrissey, Rebecca .... Chicago, IL
Morrissey, Richard C. .... Springfield, MA
Morrissey, Richard Thomas .... Troy, NY
Morrissey, Robert E. .... Chicago, IL
Morrissey, Robert J. .... Bowie, MD
Morrissey, Robert J. .... Boston, MA
Morrissey & Robinson .... Oak Brook, IL
Morrissey, Rose M. .... Bennington, VT
Morrissey, Rotolo & Di Donato
Hackensack, NJ
Morrissey, Sabrina E. .... New York, NY
Morrissey, Sara R. .... Corvallis, OR
Morrissey, Sharon A. .... San Francisco, CA
Morrissey, Stephen E. .... Los Angeles, CA
Morrissey, Stephen Joseph
Department of Transportation,
Office of the General Counsel, GV
Morrissey, Tami Zeisler .... St. Louis, MO
Morrissey, Thomas G. .... Chicago, IL
Morrissey, Thomas G., Ltd. .... Chicago, IL
Morrissey, Thomas L. .... Tecumseh, NE
Morrissey, Thomas L. .... Newark, NJ
Morrissey, Thomas V., Jr. .... Braintree, MA
Morrissey, Travis J. .... Little Rock, AR
Morrissey, Walter E. .... Bethlehem, PA
Morrissey, Walter W. .... Oak Brook, IL
Morrissey, William E., Jr. .... Merrick, NY
Morrissey, William G. .... Santa Ana, CA
Morrissey, William H. .... Flint, MI
Morrissey, William L., Jr.
Philadelphia, PA
Morrissey, Wm. F. .... Homewood, IL
Morrissey, Wm. J., Jr. .... Cincinnati, OH
Morrisson, Alan S. .... St. Louis, MO
Morrisson, Gildenita Breidenbach
Department Of Health And Human Services,
GV
Morrisson, John G. .... Elyria, OH
Lorain, OH
Morrisson, Scott S. .... Indianapolis, IN
Morrissy, Alice P. .... Elkhorn, WI
Morrissy, Bridget Elizabeth .... Detroit, MI
Morrissy, Dennis M. .... Chicago, IL
Lincolnwood, IL
Morrissy, Mary Caffrey
Downers Grove, IL
Morro, Frank, Jr. .... Hauppauge, NY
Morrocco, Alfred F., Jr. .... Bristol, CT
Morrocco, Alfred F., Jr. & Associates, Law Offices of .... Bristol, CT
Morrogh, Elizabeth Chichester
Fairfax, VA
Morron, Kelly L. .... New York, NY
Morrone, Ann M. .... Chicago, IL
Morrone, Anthony Francis
Santa Monica, CA
Morrone, Anthony J. .... Chicago, IL
Morrone, Charles L. .... San Jose, CA
Morrone, George B., III .... Kenova, WV
Morrone, James J. .... Palos Heights, IL
Morrone, John M. .... Palos Heights, IL
Morrone, John M., P.C. .... Palos Heights, IL
Morrone, Joseph A., Jr. .... Garden City, NY
Morrone, Kelley A. .... Pittsburgh, PA
Morrone, Mario O. .... New York, NY
Morrone, Michael .... Williamsport, PA
Morrone, Michael F. .... Washington, DC
Morrone, Michael M. .... Macon, GA
Morros, Mark A. .... Santa Ana, CA
Morrow, Albert .... Bainbridge Island, WA
Morrow, Alex H. .... Warner Robins, GA
Morrow Alexander Tash Long & Kurtz
Winston-Salem, NC
Morrow, Alice M. .... Corvallis, OR
Morrow, Allen L. .... Omaha, NE
Morrow, Andrew J., Jr. .... Portland, OR
Morrow, Andrew M., III .... Los Angeles, CA
Morrow, Ann Marie .... New York, NY
Morrow, Anthony G. .... Dearborn, MI
Morrow, Arthur E. .... Rochester, NY
Morrow, Arthur G. .... Warren, MI
Morrow, Barbara Corr .... Philadelphia, PA
Morrow, Beth Elise .... Washington, DC
Morrow, Brian T. .... Westmont, IL
Morrow, Bruce U. .... Detroit, MI
Morrow, C. Arthur .... Newark, OH

Morstein, Stanley I. ... Towson, MD
Morstein, William H. ... Ellicott City, MD
Mort, Geoffrey A. ... New York, NY
Mort, Kara Elizabeth ... St. Augustine, FL
Mort, Peter J. ... Los Angeles, CA
Mort, Susan A. ... Washington, DC
Mort, Terry J. ... St. Louis, MO
Mortara, Benjamin, Jr.
San Francisco, CA
Mortati, Julie S. ... Albany, NY
Mortati, Thomas J. ... Albany, NY
Mortazavi, Marjan ... San Diego, CA
Mortberg, Bern A. ... Addison, TX
Morte, Stephen G. ... Marlborough, MA
Mortell, Bennett B. ... Claremont, NH
Mortell, Edwin E. ... West Palm Beach, FL
Mortell, Edwin E., III ... Stuart, FL
West Palm Beach, FL
Mortell, Rebecca Walker ... Indianapolis, IN
Mortell, Richard W., Jr. ... Chicago, IL
Mortell, Thomas J. ... Pocatello, ID
Mortelliti, Stephen ... Media, PA
Morten, Larry W. ... Denton, NE
Morten, Robert F. ... Wilsonville, OR
Mortensen, Alan W. ... Bountiful, UT
Mortensen, Arvid L. ... St. Louis, MO
Mortensen, Bradley J. ... New York, NY
Philadelphia, PA
Mortensen, Craig C. ... Midvale, UT
Mortensen, Craig M. ... Fresno, CA
Mortensen, David J. ... Las Vegas, NV
Reno, NV
Mortensen, David Lynn
Salt Lake City, UT
Mortensen, David N. ... Provo, UT
Mortensen, David S. ... Boston, MA
Mortensen, Douglas G.
Salt Lake City, UT
Mortensen, Gene L. ... Tulsa, OK
Mortensen, Greg M. ... Newport Beach, CA
Mortensen, Heidi L. ... New York, NY
Mortensen, Irval L. ... Safford, AZ
Mortensen, Kenneth ... Berwyn, PA
Mortensen, Kirk I. ... Seattle, WA
Mortensen & Lunceford, PC
Bountiful, UT
Mortensen, Mimi B. ... Salt Lake City, UT
Mortensen, Philip S. ... New York, NY
Mortensen, Robert ... Madison, WI
Mortensen, Sherri Lee ... St. Paul, MN
Mortensen, Stan A. ... Newport Beach, CA
Mortensen, Susan E. ... Phoenix, AZ
Mortensen, Tom W. ... San Diego, CA
Mortensen, Walter G. ... Glendale, CA
Mortensen, Wayne B. ... Mesa, AZ
Mortensen, William C. ... Minneapolis, MN
Mortenson, Alexa J. ... Washington, DC
Mortenson, C. Walter ... Wilmington, DE
Mortenson, G. Russell ... Dallas, TX
Mortenson, Mark A. ... Minneapolis, MN
Mortenson, Mark G. ... Newark, DE
Mortenson, Peter B. ... Las Vegas, NV
Mortenson, Philip D. ... Seattle, WA
Mortenson and Pomeroy ... Elizabeth, NJ
Morristown, NJ
Newark, NJ
Springfield, NJ
Mortenson, R. Stan ... Washington, DC
Mortenson, Stanley N. ... St. Petersburg, FL
Mortenson, Stephen O. ... Springfield, NJ
Mortenson, Tracy Gaspardo ... Chicago, IL
Morter, Christopher S. ... Atlanta, GA
Morthland, Bolen & Morthland ... Decatur, IL
Morthland, David W. ... Portland, OR
Morthland, Donald ... Decatur, IL
Morthland, John B. ... Hannibal, MO
Morthland, Mark Stephen ... Decatur, IL
Morthland, Morthland & Kehoe ... Decatur, IL
Morthland, Richd. F. ... Decatur, IL
Morthole, Karl R. ... San Francisco, CA
Morthole & Zeppetello
San Francisco, CA
Morthorst, Michael E. ... Cincinnati, OH
Mortier, Jeffrey J. ... Indianapolis, IN
Mortier, Raymond David ... La Jolla, CA
Mortilla, Carolyn Hart ... Lauderhill, FL
Mortillaro, Duccio ... Los Angeles, CA
Mortillaro, Steve J. ... Metairie, LA
Mortimer, Anita L. ... Kansas City, MO
Mortimer, Ann Marie ... Los Angeles, CA
Mortimer, Charles E., Jr. ... Lakewood, CO
Mortimer and Elgin ... Madera, CA
Mortimer, George H. ... Salt Lake City, UT
Mortimer, Harold E. ... Washington, DC
Mortimer, Hope E. ... San Francisco, CA
Mortimer, J. Stirling, (Ltd.) ... Dolton, IL
Mortimer, James K. ... Glenview, IL
Mortimer, James R., Jr. ... Charlotte, NC
Mortimer, Jeannine ... Tucson, AZ
Mortimer, John E. ... Pasadena, CA
Mortimer, John J. ... Chicago, IL
Mortimer, John P. ... San Francisco, CA
Mortimer, John S. ... Chicago, IL
Mortimer, Michael E. ... San Francisco, CA
Mortimer, Michael R. ... Manchester, NH
Mortimer, Mindee K. ... Sacramento, CA
Mortimer, Pamela A. ... Columbus, OH
Mortimer, Patrick ... San Diego, CA
Mortimer, Peter M. ... New York, NY
Mortimer, Renee J. ... Munster, IN
Mortimer, Rory Dixon ... Summerville, SC
Mortimer & Rose, L.L.C. ... Summerville, SC
Mortimer, Scott ... Blue Bell, PA
Mortimer Sourwine & Sloane, Ltd.
Reno, NV
Mortimer, Stanley ... Shelton, CT
Mortimer, Stephen G. ... St. Petersburg, FL
Mortimer, Steven R. ... Madera, CA

Mortimer, Timothy R. ... Albuquerque, NM
Mortimer, Vicki Hunt ... Pittsburgh, PA
Mortimer, Wayne L. ... Reno, NV
Mortimore, P. Kent ... Eugene, OR
Mortinger, Alison D ... Hopewell Junction, NY
Mortinger, Christian ... New York, NY
Mortinger, Stephen A. ... Somers, NY
Mortis, Doris E. ... Brooklyn, NY
Mortl, Andrew T. ... Walnut Creek, CA
Mortland, J. William ... Garfield, WA
Mortland, Jean A. ... Columbus, OH
Mortman, Scott ... New York, NY
Mortman, Steven M. ... Oceanside, NY
Mortola, Richard D. ... San Mateo, CA
Morton, Aaron ... Philadelphia, PA
Morton, Adrienne Sanders ... Honolulu, HI
Morton, Alan L. ... Boise, ID
Morton, Allan ... Birmingham, AL
Morton, Allan S. ... Beverly Hills, CA
Morton, Amy F. ... Vallejo, CA
Morton, Andrew B. ... Akron, OH
Morton, B. Danforth ... Wilmington, NC
Morton, B. Lynn ... Clarksville, TN
Morton & Bach ... Henderson, KY
Morton, Belinda S. ... Fayetteville, WV
Morton, Betty J. ... Durham, NC
Morton, Bradley K. ... Charlotte, MI
Morton, Breakstone & Germany, PLLC
Memphis, TN
Morton, Bruce E. ... Department of Justice, Tax Division, GV
Morton, Bruce N. ... Huntington, NY
Morton, C. Brinkley ... Memphis, TN
Morton, C. Frank, III ... Richmond, VA
Morton, C. Read, Jr. ... Atlanta, GA
Morton, C. Richard ... West Chester, PA
Morton, Carolyn M. ... Bradford, MA
Morton, Cathy H. ... Maryville, TN
Morton, Charles B., Jr. ... Fort Lauderdale, FL
Morton, Charles E., IV ... Franklin, TN
Morton, Charles G., Jr. ... Bullard, TX
Morton, Charles J., Jr. ... Baltimore, MD
Morton, Chris R. ... Encino, CA
Morton, Clay L. ... Louisville, KY
Morton, Copeland, Jr. ... Baltimore, MD
Morton, Craig P. ... Elkton, MD
Morton, Craig P., P.A. ... Elkton, MD
Morton, Craig V. ... Memphis, TN
Morton, Crystal Lee ... Portland, OR
Morton, Cynthia D. ... Treasury Department, Internal Revenue Service, GV
Morton, Cyrus A. ... Minneapolis, MN
Morton, Daniel W. ... Columbus, OH
Morton, David A. ... Gahanna, OH
Morton, Deborah B. ... Fort Worth, TX
Morton, Dent M. ... Birmingham, AL
Morton, Don F. ... Indianapolis, IN
Morton, Donald E. ... Chattanooga, TN
Morton, Donald S. ... Philadelphia, PA
Morton, Donna T. ... Louisville, KY
Morton, Douglas B. ... Rochester, IN
Morton, Edward L. ... Kalispell, MT
Morton, Eric D. ... Oceanside, CA
Morton, Erin C. ... Austin, TX
Morton, Ernest H., Jr. ... Albemarle, NC
Morton, Ernest V., Jr. ... Webster Springs, WV
Morton, Ernest V., Jr., L.C.
Webster Springs, WV
Morton, Francis R. ... New Orleans, LA
Morton, Frank M., III ... Williamsburg, VA
Morton, Frank W. ... Indianapolis, IN
Morton, Fred J. ... El Paso, TX
Morton, Frederick A., Jr. ... New York, NY
Morton, G. Wright ... Walnut Creek, CA
Morton, Gail ... Santa Clara, CA
Morton, Garry H. ... Stamford, CT
Morton, George B. ... Fayetteville, AR
Morton, George B., P.A. ... Fayetteville, AR
Morton, Gerald A. ... Houston, TX
Morton, Glenn R. ... Batavia, NY
Le Roy, NY
Morton, Glenn W., Jr. ... Lincoln, NE
Morton, Grace M. ... San Francisco, CA
Morton, Gregory A. ... Greenville, SC
Morton, Grigg and Phillips, L.L.P.
Albemarle, NC
Morton, G. W., Jr. ... Knoxville, TN
Morton, Harvey L. ... Lubbock, TX
Slaton, TX
Morton, Herbert ... Glencoe, IL
Morton, J. Alex ... Beachwood, OH
Morton, J. Bruce ... Greensboro, NC
Morton, J. Craig ... Tulsa, OK
Morton, J. Kevin ... Winston-Salem, NC
Morton, J. Myers ... Knoxville, TN
Morton, James C. ... Atlanta, GA
Morton, James C., Jr. ... Greenville, SC
Morton, James D. ... Pittsburgh, PA
Morton, James E. ... Salt Lake City, UT
Morton, James F. ... Teaneck, NJ
Morton, James H. ... Charlotte, NC
Morton, James H. ... Tacoma, WA
Morton, James M. ... Rock Hill, SC
Morton, James M., Jr. ... Toledo, OH
Morton, James R. ... New Orleans, LA
Morton, James T. ... Burlingame, CA
Morton, Jennifer B. ... Knoxville, TN
Morton, John C. ... Henderson, KY
Morton, John E. ... Alexandria, LA
Morton, John H. ... Boston, MA
Morton, John J. ... St. Louis, MO
Morton, John R., Jr. ... Moorestown, NJ
Morton, John T. ... Department of Justice, Office of the Deputy Attorney General, GV
Morton, Jonathan B. ... Miami, FL
Morton, Joseph B., III ... Metairie, LA
Morton, Joseph W. ... Jacksonville, NC
Morton, Joshua J., Jr. ... Albemarle, NC

Morton, Joyce H. ... Webster Springs, WV
Morton, Julia A. ... Charleston, WV
Morton, Karen G. ... Washington, DC
Morton, Karen V. ... Boston, MA
Morton, Kari Ayers ... Cazenovia, NY
Morton, Kathryn R. ... Jay, OK
Morton, Kelly M. ... San Francisco, CA
Morton, Kent J. ... Meriden, CT
Morton, Kim Denise ... West Chester, PA
Morton, L. Clure ... Cookeville, TN
Morton Law Firm, PLLC ... Brandon, MS
Morton Law Offices, Chartered ... Boise, ID
Morton, Leonard ... New York, NY
Morton, Linda H. ... San Diego, CA
Morton, Lulofs & Wood, LLP
Oakland, CA
Morton, M. Rogan ... Buffalo, NY
Morton, Marcia R. ... Alexandria, VA
Morton, Margaret ... Birmingham, AL
Morton, Mark A. ... Wilmington, DE
Morton, Mary Beth ... Seattle, WA
Morton, Maurice G. ... Detroit, MI
Morton, Melinda ... New York, NY
Morton, Meredith ... Olympia, WA
Morton, Michael P. ... Wilmington, DE
Morton, Michael P., P.A. ... Wilmington, DE
Morton, Michael T. ... Whitefish, MT
Morton & Morton, PLLC ... Knoxville, TN
Morton, Nancy Weynand ... Houston, TX
Morton, Natasha J. ... Hardin, MT
Morton, Norman R. ... Mansfield, OH
Morton, Padraic McSherry
Baltimore, MD
Morton, Paul ... Great Neck, NY
Morton, Paul K. ... Chicago, IL
Morton, Perry W. ... Boston, MA
Morton, Peter G. ... Bayside, NY
Morton, R. Clark ... Wheeling, WV
Morton, R. Kemp ... Charleston, WV
Huntington, WV
Morton, R. Steven ... Austin, TX
Morton, Ramon E. ... Fort Wayne, IN
Morton, Reed & Counts, L.L.C.
St. Joseph, MO
Morton, Richard ... Miami, FL
Morton, Richard A. ... De Ridder, LA
Morton, Richard E. ... Bakersfield, CA
Morton, Richard E. ... Charlotte, NC
Morton, Richard H. ... West Chester, PA
Morton, Richard M. ... Farmington, ME
Morton, Robert B. ... Chicago, IL
Morton, Robert B. ... Wichita, KS
Morton, Robert C. ... Chicago, IL
Morton, Robert C. ... New York, NY
Morton, Robert C. ... Salt Lake City, UT
Morton, Robert G. ... Decatur, GA
Morton, Robert J. G. ... Columbus, OH
Morton, Robert L. ... Raleigh, NC
Morton, Roger L. ... Culpeper, VA
Morton, Ronald C. ... Brandon, MS
Morton, Rosalie L. ... Los Angeles, CA
Morton, Russell G. ... Little Rock, AR
Morton & Russo ... Vallejo, CA
Morton, S. Antoinette ... Norwalk, CT
Morton, Scott David ... North Andover, MA
Morton, Sheldon E. ... Tulsa, OK
Morton, Sheri L. ... Lake Buena Vista, FL
Morton, Stephen C. ... Dallas, TX
Morton, Stephen P., Jr. ... Florence, AL
Morton, Steven J. ... Chicago, IL
Morton, Susan H. ... New York, NY
Morton, Susan Thomas ... Austin, TX
Morton, Teresa E. ... Indianapolis, IN
Morton, Thomas D. ... Washington, DC
Morton, Thomas Edward, Jr. ... Dallas, TX
Morton, Thomas G., Jr. ... Pensacola, FL
Morton, Thomas H. ... Zebulon, GA
Morton, Thomas Jackson ... Austin, TX
Morton, Travis K. ... Raleigh, NC
Morton, W. Hugh M. ... Cambridge, MA
Morton, Walter P., Jr. ... Abilene, TX
Morton, Wendy Solomon ... Phoenix, AZ
Morton, William C. ... Madisonville, KY
Morton, William J. ... Canton, GA
Morton, William R. ... Oakland, CA
Morton, William T. ... Erie, PA
Morton, Wm. A. ... Charleston, WV
Morton, Wm. Stanley ... Cincinnati, OH
Mortrud, David L. ... Minneapolis, MN
Mortvedt, Ronald A. ... Santa Ana, CA
Mortyn, Russell M. ... San Diego, CA
Moruza, Christine Kasun ... Pleasanton, CA
Morvan, Tricia Y. ... Charlotte, NC
Morvant, Camille A., II ... Thibodaux, LA
Morvant & Cavell, A Professional Law Corporation ... Thibodaux, LA
Morvant, Kristine A. ... Thibodaux, LA
Morvant, Michel D., Jr. ... New Orleans, LA
Morvant, William A. ... Baton Rouge, LA
Morvay, Lilian ... White Plains, NY
Morvillo, Abramowitz, Grand, Iason & Silberberg, P.C. ... New York, NY
Morvillo, E. Scott ... New York, NY
Morvillo, Richard J. ... Washington, DC
Morvillo, Robert G. ... New York, NY
Morway, Debra S. ... New York, NY
Morwood, Nicholas A.
South Burlington, VT
Morwood, Paul R. ... South Burlington, VT
Mory, Claus Fritz ... Los Angeles, CA
Moryan, Jeffrey W. ... Roseland, NJ
Moryl, Mark J. ... Phoenix, AZ
Morytko, Jeremiah J. ... North Haven, CT
Mos, Richard H., Jr. ... Lathrop, MO
Mosakowski, Linda E.
Treasury Department, GV
Mosakowski, Robert A. ... Tampa, FL
Mosbacher, Bruce E. ... Chicago, IL

Mosbacher, Linda F. ... Gahanna, OH
Mosbacher, R. Bruce ... Menlo Park, CA
Mosbacher, Robert, Jr. ... Houston, TX
Mosbacher, Stuart W. ... Jamaica, NY
Mosbat, Azita ... Beverly Hills, CA
Mosberg, Michael A. ... New York, NY
Mosbey, James H., Jr. ... Watkinsville, GA
Mosburg, Ronald Dean ... Coweta, OK
Mosby, J. Leyburn, Jr. ... Lynchburg, VA
Mosby, J. Leyburn, Jr., P.C.
Lynchburg, VA
Mosby, John Edward ... Denver, CO
Mosby, Linda A. ... Kansas City, MO
Mosby, Lori Lanciani ... Chicago, IL
Mosby, Mark A. ... Downers Grove, IL
Mosby, Timmy D. ... Indianapolis, IN
Mosby-Scott, Michelle ... Bloomington, IL
Mosca, Angelo A., Jr. ... Providence, RI
Mosca, Domenic A., Jr.
North Kingstown, RI
Mosca, Edward C. ... Concord, NH
Mosca, Gerald A. ... Providence, RI
Mosca, Lynne Robinson ... New Orleans, LA
Mosca, MaryJo ... Miami, FL
Mosca, Michael R. ... Atlantic City, NJ
Mosca & Mosca ... New Orleans, LA
Mosca, Pasquale ... Edmond, OK
Mosca, Peter C. ... Trenton, NJ
Mosca, Provino C. ... New Orleans, LA
Mosca, Salvatore R. ... Westbury, NY
Mosca, Thomas J. ... Kingston, PA
Mosca and Volpe ... North Kingstown, RI
Mosca, William K., Jr. ... Basking Ridge, NJ
Mosca, Zammarelli & De Angelis Law Associates ... Providence, RI
Moscardelli, John M. ... Boston, MA
Moscardini, Frank A., Jr. ... Chicago, IL
Moscarelli, J. Beth ... Montgomery, AL
Moscaret, Kenneth M. ... Pasadena, CA
Moscariello, Joann C. ... Philadelphia, PA
Moscarino, George J. ... Cleveland, OH
Moscarino, George M. ... Cleveland, OH
Moscarino, John M. ... Santa Monica, CA
Moscarino & Treu, L.L.P. ... Cleveland, OH
Moscaritolo, S. Gregory ... Fairview, NJ
Moscatelli, Catherine M.
Federal Trade Commission, Bureau of Competition, GV
Moscatelli, Peter ... Ely, MN
Moscatello, Patrick ... Long Branch, NJ
Moscati, Anthony F. ... White Marsh, MD
Moscati, John A., Jr. ... Buffalo, NY
Moscati, Robert C. ... Buffalo, NY
Moscato, Anthony C. ... Department of Justice, Executive Office for Immigration Review, GV
Moscato, Frank A., (P.C.) ... Portland, OR
Moscato & Hallock ... Portland, OR
Moscato, John N. ... Denver, CO
Moscato, Michael J. ... New York, NY
Moscato, Stefano G. ... Los Angeles, CA
Moscatt, Salvatore A. ... New York, NY
Moschel, Michael S. ... Nashville, TN
Moschell & Moschell ... Miami, FL
Moschell, Robert S. ... Miami, FL
Moschell, William E. ... Miami, FL
Moschella, Alex L. ... Boston, MA
Moschella, Alex L. ... Somerville, MA
Moschella, Amy R. ... McLean, VA
Moschella, Emil P. ... Newark, NJ
Moschella, James M. ... New York, NY
Moschella, Kristine J. ... Atlanta, GA
Moschella, William A., III ... Colonie, NY
Moschella, William E.
House of Representatives, Committee on Rules, GV
Moschet, Robyn N. ... Minneapolis, MN
Moschetta, Anthony R. ... Short Hills, NJ
Moschetta, James A. ... Washington, PA
Moschetta, Jerry ... Washington, PA
Moschetta, John J., Jr. ... Fredericktown, PA
Moschetta, Joseph P., & Associates
Pittsburgh, PA
Moschetta, Joseph P., & Associates
Washington, PA
Moschetta, Michael ... Bronx, NY
Moschetta, RoseMarie Flocco ... Summit, NJ
Moschetta, Stephen P. ... Washington, PA
Moschetti, Gary C. ... Denver, CO
Moschetti, Guy A. ... New York, NY
Moschetti, Joseph V. ... Coal City, IL
Moschetti, Nick A., Jr. ... Reno, NV
Moschetti, Peter J., Jr. ... Troy, NY
Moschini, Stephen J. ... Vincentown, NJ
Moschos, Demitrios M. ... Worcester, MA
Moschos, Michael C. ... Worcester, MA
Mosco, Carole ... Yonkers, NY
Mosco, Michael A. ... Providence, RI
Moscon, D. Matthew ... Salt Lake City, UT
Moscona, Jodi Anthony ... Baton Rouge, LA
Moscone, Christopher ... San Francisco, CA
Moscone, Emblidge & Quadra, LLP
San Francisco, CA
Moscone, Philip J. ... San Francisco, CA
Mosconi, William ... Highwood, IL
Moscony, Charles E., Jr.
Huntingdon Valley, PA
Moscou, Joseph ... Rockville Centre, NY
Moscovitch, Ruth M. ... Chicago, IL
Moscow, Ann L. ... New York, NY
Moscow, Cyril ... Detroit, MI
Moscow, John W. ... New York, NY
Moscow, Karen Elizabeth ... Baltimore, MD
Moscow, Robert L. ... Cambridge, MA
Moscowitz, Alvin E. ... Woodstock, NY
Moscowitz, Barry A. ... Austin, TX
Moscowitz, Barry E. ... Bloomfield, NJ
Moscowitz, Grover M. ... Sunrise, FL

Moscowitz, Jane Wollner ....Miami, FL
Moscowitz, Jill F. ....West Orange, NJ
Moscowitz, Michael L. ....New Haven, CT
Moscowitz, Norman A. ....Miami, FL
Moscowitz Starkman & Magolnick
Miami, FL
Moscrip, Clark G. ....Oakland, CA
Moscrip, Douglas D. ....New Plymouth, ID
Mosé, Frederick P. ....Garden City, NY
Mosebach, Barry N. ....Lehigh Valley, PA
Mosebach, Carl V. ....Lancaster, PA
Mosee, George D., Jr. ....Philadelphia, PA
Moseley, Alice Neece ....Raleigh, NC
Moseley, Allen C. ....Boone, NC
Moseley, Anita Torti ....Englewood, CO
Moseley & Associates, A Professional Law
Corporation ....New Orleans, LA
Moseley, Bailey C. ....Marshall, TX
Moseley, Bernard R. ....Jacksonville, FL
Moseley, Cary P. ....Lynchburg, VA
Moseley, Charles V. ....San Francisco, CA
Moseley, Christine E. ....Dallas, TX
Moseley, Cynthia N. ....Salem, OR
Moseley, David B., Jr. ....Dallas, TX
Moseley, David H. ....Blakely, GA
Moseley, Douglas D. ....Bloomfield Hills, MI
Moseley, E. Clarke ....El Monte, CA
Moseley, Edw. D. ....Baton Rouge, LA
Moseley, Edw. E. ....Fort Worth, TX
Moseley, Elliott, Sholar & Dickens, L.L.P.
Roanoke Rapids, NC
Moseley, Frank S. ....New York, NY
Moseley, Gail P. ....Department of Labor,
Office of Secretary, GV
Moseley, Geo. T. ....Buffalo, NY
Moseley, George E. ....Spartanburg, SC
Moseley, George O. ....Friday Harbor, WA
Moseley, J. Wayne ....Warner Robins, GA
Moseley, James A. ....Dallas, TX
Moseley, James C., Jr. ....Simpsonville, SC
Moseley, James F. ....Jacksonville, FL
Moseley, James F., Jr. ....Jacksonville, FL
Moseley, Jeffrey D. ....Franklin, TN
Moseley, Joe L. ....Columbia, MO
Moseley, John D. ....Sherman, TX
Moseley, John R. ....Greenfield, MA
Moseley, Jon T. ....Long Beach, CA
Moseley, Kerry E. ....Fort Worth, TX
Moseley & Leech ....El Monte, CA
Moseley, Lehman A., Jr. ....Greenville, SC
Moseley, Madison C., (A Professional Law
Corp.) ....Metairie, LA
New Orleans, LA
Moseley, Marian Bentley ....Coppell, TX
Moseley, Mark L. ....Lexington, KY
Moseley, Mark W. ....Gainesville, FL
Moseley, Mary Lee ....San Francisco, CA
Moseley, Matthew Allen ....Athens, GA
Moseley, Melinda L. ....Atlanta, GA
Moseley, Melvin G., Jr.
Grand Rapids, MI
Moseley & Moseley ....Fort Worth, TX
Moseley, N. Bruce ....Mobile, AL
Moseley, Patricia Ann ....Lubbock, TX
Moseley, Ray H. ....Knoxville, TN
Moseley, Richard L. ....Houston, TX
Moseley, Robert D., Jr. ....Greenville, SC
Moseley, Rockne L. ....New Orleans, LA
Moseley, Roger S. ....Honolulu, HI
Moseley, Samuel R. ....Marshall, TX
Moseley & Standerfer, A Professional
Corporation ....Dallas, TX
Moseley, Stephen B. ....Rome, GA
Moseley, Stephen R. ....Knoxville, TN
Moseley, Susan D. ....Irwindale, CA
Moseley, Susan H. ....Nashville, TN
Moseley, Thomas A. ....Bradenton, FL
Moseley, Thomas A., Chartered
Bradenton, FL
Moseley, Thomas B., III ....San Antonio, TX
Moseley, Thomas E. ....Newark, NJ
Moseley, Thomas E. ....New York, NY
Moseley, Toni Charice ....Irving, TX
Moseley, Valerie J. ....Santa Monica, CA
Moseley, W. Phillip ....Burlington, NC
Moseley, Warren G. ....Tulsa, OK
Moseley, Warren, Prichard & Parrish, P.A.
Jacksonville, FL
Moseley, Wendell C. .....Roanoke Rapids, NC
Moseley, William Alexander ....Mobile, AL
Moseley, William E. ....Anchorage, AK
Moseley, William J., IV ....Long Beach, CA
Moseley, William O., Jr. ....Greensboro, NC
Moseley, William R., Jr. ....Houston, TX
Moseley, W. J., III ....Santa Ana, CA
Moseley, Zane R. ....Denver, CO
Moseley-Jones, Michele Coleen
Boston, MA
Moselle, Gary W. ....Carlsbad, CA
Moselle, Robert A. ....Monterey, CA
Moselle, Will ....Carlsbad, CA
Mosely, Kathryn S. M.
Sherman Oaks, CA
Mosely, Neal J. ....Tucson, AZ
Mose Mahrt, Geri ....Tucson, AZ
Moseman, James W. ....Remsen, NY
Moseman, John H. ....United States Senate,
Senatorial Assistants, GV
Moseng, Willard G. ....Haslett, MI
Mosenson, Steven H. ....New York, NY
Mosenthal, Katherine P. ....Rutland, VT
Mosentine, Perry T. ....St. Paul, MN
Mosentine, Perry T., P.A. ....St. Paul, MN
Moser, Alexander S. ....New York, NY
Philadelphia, PA
Moser, Arthur G. ....Phoenix, AZ
Moser, August C., III ....Dallas, TX
Moser, Barbara J. ....Cleveland, OH
Moser, Barbara W. ....San Francisco, CA
Moser, Bertrand C. ....Houston, TX
Moser, C. Thomas ....Mount Vernon, WA
Moser, Carol J. ....Des Moines, IA
Moser, Charles F. ....Oklahoma City, OK
Moser, Charles V. ....Laconia, NH
Moser, Christian A. ....Woodland Hills, CA
Moser, Christopher J. ....Dallas, TX
Moser, Cynthia C. ....Sioux City, IA
Moser, D. Wescott ....Asheboro, NC
Moser, David E. ....San Francisco, CA
Moser, Donald K. ....Fairfield, OH
Moser, Eric K. ....New York, NY
Moser, Gail C. ....Sunnyvale, CA
Moser, Gary L. ....Valdosta, GA
Moser, George P., Jr. ....Jersey City, NJ
Moser, Gregory V. ....San Diego, CA
Moser, H. Michael ....Wapakoneta, OH
Moser, James C. ....Poplar Bluff, MO
Moser, James C., Jr. ....Pine Bluff, AR
Moser, Janet E. ....San Diego, CA
Moser, Joel H. ....New York, NY
Philadelphia, PA
Moser, John W., III ....Valrico, FL
Moser, Joseph D. ....Belfast, ME
Moser, Keith ....Little Rock, AR
Moser, Kenneth A. ....Winston-Salem, NC
Moser, L. Gordon ....Chardon, OH
Moser, Larry Z. ....Anchorage, AK
Moser, Laura L. ....Chapel Hill, NC
Moser, Laurence E. ....Miami, FL
Moser, Leanne K. ....Canandaigua, NY
Moser, Lon ....Amarillo, TX
Moser, Lori P. ....New Orleans, LA
Moser, M. Peter ....Baltimore, MD
Moser and Mailloux, P.A. ....Belfast, ME
Moser, Margaret Broderick ....Cheshire, CT
Moser and Marsalek, P.C. ....Belleville, IL
Kansas City, MO
St. Louis, MO
Moser, Mary E. ....Denver, CO
Moser & McDaniel ....Valdosta, GA
Moser, Melvin L. ....Pittsburgh, PA
Moser, Michael A. ....New York, NY
Moser, Michael P. ....Salinas, CA
Moser, Michael R. ....Columbus, OH
Moser, Michèle A. ....New York, NY
Moser, Michele L. ....Norfolk, NE
Moser, Mitchell S. ....Milwaukee, WI
Moser & Moser ....Los Angeles, CA
Washington, DC
Albany, NY
Moser & Moser LLP ....New York, NY
Philadelphia, PA
Moser, Nathan F. ....New York, NY
Moser, Nicole E. ....New York, NY
Moser, Patricia M. ....Chicago, IL
Moser, Peter James ....Boston, MA
Moser, Peter K. ....Los Angeles, CA
Moser, Raymond R., Jr. ....San Jose, CA
Red Bank, NJ
Houston, TX
Moser, Richard J. ....Sacramento, CA
Moser, Richard L. ....Mariposa, CA
Moser, Robert J. ....Kalamazoo, MI
Moser, Roveto, McGough & von Schaumburg
Secaucus, NJ
Moser & Sanders ....Westlake Village, CA
Moser, Schmidly, Mason & Roose
Asheboro, NC
Moser, Stephen A. ....East Meadow, NY
Moser, Stephen V. ....Dayton, OH
Moser & Stubblefield ....Amarillo, TX
Moser, Susan P. ....Washington, PA
Moser, Theresia M. ....Atlanta, GA
Moser, Thomas L. ....Council Bluffs, IA
Moser, Timothy W. ....Phoenix, AZ
Moser, Tom, (A Law Corporation)
Westlake Village, CA
Moser, Wendy M. ....Denver, CO
Moser, William B., Jr. ....Beeville, TX
Moser, William F. ....Laurinburg, NC
Moser, William R. ....Department of Energy,
Office of the General Counsel, GV
Moses & Afonso, Ltd. ....Providence, RI
Moses & Aiken ....Washington, DC
Rockville, MD
Moses, Albert L. ....Columbia, SC
Moses, Alfred F. ....Pasadena, CA
Moses, Alfred H. ....Washington, DC
Moses, Alvin S. ....Jenkintown, PA
Moses, Ambrose, III ....Columbus, OH
Moses, Amos N., Jr. ....Norman, OK
Moses, Ann M. ....Lexington, MA
Moses, Anne R. ....Birmingham, AL
Moses, Anne R., P.C. ....Birmingham, AL
Moses, Ansley T. ....Chattanooga, TN
Moses, Barbara ....New York, NY
Moses, Barry W. ....Beachwood, OH
Moses, Bonnie Smith ....Jenkintown, PA
Media, PA
Philadelphia, PA
Moses, Brenda C. ....Rochester, NY
Moses, Carl M. ....Sharon, PA
Moses, Charles F. ....Billings, MT
Moses, Charles H., III ....Birmingham, AL
Moses, Charles H., Jr. ....Bessemer, AL
Moses, Charles T., III ....Department of Justice,
Office of Justice Programs, GV
Moses, Christine S. ....Santa Ana, CA
Moses, Dan W. ....Boca Raton, FL
Moses, Daniel ....Armonk, NY
Moses, Darby N. ....Denver, CO
Moses, David H. ....Wichita, KS
Moses, David J. ....Denver, CO
Moses, David L. ....Lake Success, NY
Moses, Debra G. ....Washington, DC
Moses, Dennis S. ....Largo, FL
Moses, Don R. ....Jellico, TN
Moses, Donald B. ....Albuquerque, NM
Moses, Donald E., A Professional Law
Corporation ....San Diego, CA
Moses, Donald T. ....Jacksonville, FL
Moses, Dori F. ....Austin, TX
Moses, Dunn, Farmer & Tuthill, P.C.
Albuquerque, NM
Moses, Easter Peter ....Roanoke, VA
Moses, Edward J. ....Syracuse, NY
Moses, Edward R. ....Sun City, AZ
Moses, Elizabeth Montgomery
Jacksonville, FL
Moses, Elliott S., Jr. ....San Diego, CA
Moses, Eric M. ....Los Angeles, CA
Moses, Erik A. ....Washington, DC
Moses, Eugene R. ....Bellingham, WA
Moses, Evan R. ....Los Angeles, CA
Moses, Garry O. ....Glendale, CA
Moses and Gelso, L.L.P. ....Wilkes-Barre, PA
Moses, Gena Cohen ....Concord, NH
Moses, Glenn D. ....Miami, FL
Moses, Hamilton, Jr. ....Bryn Mawr, PA
Moses, Harriet Liza ....New York, NY
Moses, Herman H. ....Chicago, IL
Moses, J. Barry ....Santa Ana, CA
Moses, James Barry ....Santa Ana, CA
Moses, James O. ....Sacramento, CA
Moses, James W. ....Gaithersburg, MD
Moses, Jamie Billotte ....Orlando, FL
Moses, Jerold A. ....Baltimore, MD
Moses, Joel O. ....Chicago, IL
Moses, John D. ....Peoria, IL
Moses, John D. ....New Bedford, MA
Moses, John M. ....Indianapolis, IN
Moses, John P. ....Wilkes-Barre, PA
Moses, John R. ....Arlington, VA
Moses, John R. ....Madison, WI
Moses, Jonathan M. ....New York, NY
Moses, Joseph J. ....Wheeling, WV
Moses, Judith A. ....Pittsburgh, PA
Moses, Karen T. ....Fort Wayne, IN
Moses, Keith O. D. ....Jersey City, NJ
Moses, Kevin E. ....San Francisco, CA
Moses, Kevin R. ....Atlantic City, NJ
Moses, Kim E. ....Baton Rouge, LA
Moses, Kimberly A. ....Orange, CA
Moses Law Firm, P.C. ....Billings, MT
Moses, Leann Opotowsky
New Orleans, LA
Moses, Lisa Fine ....Littleton, CO
Moses and Lockhart ....Beaumont, TX
Moses, Lucina Lea ....Anaheim, CA
Moses, Malcolm P. ....Merrick, NY
Moses, Margaret L. ....Maplewood, NJ
Moses, Marie Avery ....Lone Tree, CO
Moses, Marlene Eskind ....Nashville, TN
Moses, Maron, Jr. ....Rancho Santa Fe, CA
Moses, Marsha Belman ....Milford, CT
Moses, Martha D ....Berkeley, CA
Moses, Mary Helen ....Albany, NY
Moses, Matthew I. ....Canonsburg, PA
Moses, Matthew S. ....Syracuse, NY
Moses, Max G. ....Chicago, IL
Moses, McClellan & McDermott
Little Rock, AR
Moses, Michael A. ....Chicago, IL
Moses, Michael A. ....Columbus, OH
Moses, Michael F. ....Washington, DC
Moses, Michael G. ....Billings, MT
Moses, Michael J. "Mickey"
Louisville, GA
Moses, Paul A. ....Irvine, CA
Moses, Paul E. ....Pittsburgh, PA
Moses, Paul W., II ....Orlando, FL
Moses, Preston Donald ....Staunton, VA
Moses, Ralph J. ....Hardin, IL
Moses, Raphael J. ....Boulder, CO
Moses, Ray E. ....Houston, TX
Moses, Richard A. ....Pittsburgh, PA
Moses, Richard T. ....New Bedford, MA
Moses, Richd. S. ....Lincoln, NE
Moses, Robert D. ....West Palm Beach, FL
Moses, Robert E. ....Albany, NY
Syracuse, NY
Moses, Robert H. ....New York, NY
Moses, Robert P. ....Rockbridge, OH
Moses, Robert W. ....Rockville, MD
Moses, Robin ....Jersey City, NJ
Moses, Samuel Carl ....Columbia, SC
Moses, Sarah ....Coral Gables, FL
Moses, Shayne D. ....Fort Worth, TX
Moses, Sigmund ....New York, NY
Moses & Singer, LLP ....New York, NY
Moses, Stephen D. ....Los Angeles, CA
Moses, Stephen J. ....Newark, NJ
New York, NY
Moses, Susan L. ....Torrance, CA
Moses, Sybil R. ....Hackensack, NJ
Moses, Thomas J. ....Irving, TX
Moses, Thomas L., The Law Offices of
Columbia, SC
Moses, Thomas O. ....Beaumont, TX
Moses, Thomas V. ....Providence, RI
Moses, Timothy E. ....Augusta, GA
Aiken, SC
Moses, Victor I. ....Manchester, CT
Moses, Vijay ....Boston, MA
Moses, William L. ....Raeford, NC
Moses, William P. ....Menlo Park, CA
Moses, Wittemyer, Harrison and Woodruff,
P.C. ....Boulder, CO
Mosesi, Henrik M. ....Los Angeles, CA
Mosesian, Nicole M. ....Anchorage, AK
Moses-Rudorf, Judith ....Sonoma, CA
Mosesso, John A. ....Philippi, WV
Mosesso, Michael A. ....Tucson, AZ
Mosesson, Bernard, (Co., L.P.A.)
Cleveland, OH
Mosetick, Michael J. ....Pompano Beach, FL
Mosgrove, Thomas M. ....Bend, OR
Mosh, David Paul ....Kansas City, MO
Mosh, Maureen A. ....Chicago, IL
Moshaiv, Aksana ....Los Angeles, CA
Moshe, Elaine S. ....New York, NY
Moshein, Robert M. ....Austin, TX
Moshell & Moshell ....Garden City, NY
Moshell, Stuart R. ....Garden City, NY
Moshell, Susan Stein ....Garden City, NY
Moshenko, Terry M. ....Santa Ana, CA
Moshenko, Terry M., A Prof. Law Corp.
Santa Ana, CA
Mosher, Benjamin ....Great Neck, NY
Mosher, Bonita S. ....Torrance, CA
Mosher, Charles E. ....Greenwich, CT
Mosher, Christopher S. ....Boston, MA
Mosher, Ellsworth H. ....Washington, DC
Mosher, George M. ....Fort Worth, TX
Mosher, George R. ....Southfield, MI
Mosher, Harold I. ....Lincoln, NE
Mosher, James W. ....New York, NY
Mosher, Joel R. ....Kansas City, MO
Mosher, Jonathan C. ....Irvine, CA
Mosher, Laurance C., Jr. ....Houston, TX
Mosher, Lee W. ....Golden Valley, MN
Mosher, Louise H. ....Cleveland, OH
Mosher, Mia P. ....San Jose, CA
Mosher, Michael D., & Associates
Paris, TX
Mosher, Michael P. ....Chicago, IL
Mosher, Michael R. ....Worcester, MA
Mosher, Pamela Lewis ....Denver, CO
Mosher, Raymond J. ....Santa Ana, CA
Mosher, Raymond J., A Prof. Corp., Law
Offices of ....Santa Ana, CA
Mosher, Richard C. ....Newton, IA
Mosher, Richard Carter ....San Jose, CA
Mosher, Richard M. ....Dallas, TX
Mosher, Robert D. ....Los Angeles, CA
Mosher, Roger L. ....San Francisco, CA
Mosher, Ronald A. ....Los Angeles, CA
Mosher, Sanford D. ....Eastchester, NY
Mosher and Schneider, P.A.
West Palm Beach, FL
Mosher, Stephen S. ....Dallas, TX
Mosher, William J. ....Philadelphia, PA
Mosher-Beluris, Terese A.
Los Angeles, CA
Mosher-Canty, Jane M. ....Dedham, MA
Moshier, Becky A. ....St. Paul, MN
Moshier, David D. ....Salina, KS
Moshier, Douglas J. ....Wichita, KS
Moshier, Herbert F. ....El Paso, TX
Moshier, John T. ....Phoenix, AZ
Moshier, Thomas G. ....Phoenix, AZ
Moshkounian, Lusine ....Philadelphia, PA
Moshman, Jerome S. ....New York, NY
Mosholder, Brian T. ....Dothan, AL
Mosholder, Richard S. ....Columbus, OH
Mosholder, William ....Wilmington, DE
Moshos, Arthur L. ....Fairfax, VA
Moshos, Haden & De Deo, P.C. ....Fairfax, VA
Mosich, Nicholas J. ....Santa Ana, CA
Mosiello, Alfred R. ....Bronx, NY
Mosier, Andrew P. ....Baltimore, MD
Mosier, Bruce D. ....Houston, TX
Mosier, Carmen Marie ....San Diego, CA
Mosier, Charles B. ....Davison, MI
Mosier, Daniel T. ....Redding, CA
Mosier, David M. ....Erie, PA
Mosier, Eric H. ....Cleveland, OH
Mosier, Ginger L. ....Princeton, NJ
Mosier, James F. ....Reynoldsburg, OH
Mosier, Jerry M. ....Jackson, TN
Mosier, Joe D. ....Lansing, MI
Mosier, Margaret M. ....Sheffield Lake, OH
Mosier & McEnrue, P.C. ....Houston, TX
Mosier, Mickey W. ....Salina, KS
Mosier, R. Kimball ....Salt Lake City, UT
Mosier, Richard D. ....Claremore, OK
Mosier, Richard F. ....Port Huron, MI
Mosier, Robert A. ....Santa Ana, CA
Mosier, Scott D. ....St. Louis, MO
Mosier, Stephen B. ....Toledo, OH
Mosiman, Donald M. ....Mineral, VA
Mosimann, Lorraine G. ....Lee's Summit, MO
Mosinski, Jos. A. ....Cleveland, OH
Mosinski & Moss ....Cleveland, OH
Mosk, Richard M. ....Los Angeles, CA
Mosk, Stanley ....San Francisco, CA
Mosk, Susan H., Law Offices of
San Francisco, CA
Moskal, Agnieszka A. ....New York, NY
Moskal, Dennis Michael ....Pittsburgh, PA
Moskal, James ....Grand Rapids, MI
Moskal, Mary I. ....Oak Forest, IL
Moskal, Maureen ....Oak Forest, IL
Moskal, Melissa W. ....New York, NY
Moskal, Patricia Head ....Nashville, TN
Moskal, Stanley A., Jr. ....Buffalo, NY
Moskalenko, Tanya ....Los Angeles, CA
Moskalski, Elton A. ....Greeley, CO
Moskatel, Ira D. ....Los Angeles, CA
Moskatel Law Corporation .....Los Angeles, CA
Moskey, Eileen C. ....Hartford, CT
Moskin, Alan R. ....New York, NY
Moskin, Jonathan E. ....New York, NY
Moskin, Morton ....New York, NY
Moskitis, Richard L. ....San Diego, CA
Mosko, Leslie A. ....Los Angeles, CA
Mosko, Scott R. ....Palo Alto, CA
Moskoff, Arthur ....New City, NY
Moskoff, Miriam F. ....Pomona, NY
Moskoff, Saul ....Jamaica, NY
Moskol, Scott H. ....Washington, DC

Moskos, Costa Steven ......North Charleston, SC
Moskos, James, Jr. ....Baltimore, MD
Moskosky, James P. ....Miami, FL
Moskovic, Alex ....Arlington Heights, IL
Moskovic, Jeffrey ....Lawrence, NY
Moskovitz, Andrea M. ....Philadelphia, PA
Moskovitz, Gary N. ....Downingtown, PA
Moskovitz, Jeri Toporek ....Memphis, TN
Moskovitz, Michael ....Chicago, IL
Moskovitz, Mitchell David ....Memphis, TN
Moskovitz, Mitchell S. ....Smithville, NJ
Moskovitz, Myron ....San Francisco, CA
Moskovitz, Ronald B. ....San Francisco, CA
Moskovitz, Sidney B. ....Bergenfield, NJ
Moskow, Bencion M. ....Cambridge, MA
Moskow, Jean ....Tucson, AZ
Moskow, Neal L. ....Westport, CT
Moskow, Robert S., II
Overland Park, KS
Moskowitz, Adam L. ....Houston, TX
Moskowitz, Adam M. ....Miami, FL
Moskowitz, Albert ....Department of Justice, Civil Rights Division, GV
Moskowitz, Allan Gary ....Washington, DC
Moskowitz Altman & Hughes LLP
New York, NY
Moskowitz, Amy ....New York, NY
Moskowitz, Amy S. ....Baltimore, MD
Moskowitz, Andrew M. ....New York, NY
Moskowitz, Avraham C. ....New York, NY
Moskowitz, Barry Ted ....San Diego, CA
Moskowitz, Bernard ....East Meadow, NY
Moskowitz, Beth M. ....Miami, FL
Moskowitz & Book ....New York, NY
Moskowitz, Brestoff, Winston & Blinderman LLP ....Los Angeles, CA
Moskowitz, David H. ....Malvern, PA
Moskowitz, David J. ....Needham, MA
Moskowitz, David K. ....Littleton, CO
Moskowitz, Deborah L. ....Orlando, FL
Moskowitz, Dina J. ....New York, NY
Moskowitz, Ellen H. ....New York, NY
Moskowitz, Ellen M. ....New York, NY
Moskowitz, Emily J. ....West Hartford, CT
Moskowitz, Eric G.
National Labor Relations Board, Office of the General Counsel, GV
Moskowitz, Frank W. ....Phoenix, AZ
Moskowitz, Harold J. ....New York, NY
Moskowitz, Harold L. ....Chicago, IL
Moskowitz, Harold, Ltd., Law Offices of Chicago, IL
Moskowitz, Harry K. ....Newark, NJ
Moskowitz, Harvey D. ....New York, NY
Moskowitz, Harvey W. ....Atlanta, GA
Moskowitz, Howard D. ....Jersey City, NJ
Moskowitz, Ivan W. ....New York, NY
Moskowitz, Ivor R. ....Albany, NY
Moskowitz, James H. ....Cincinnati, OH
Moskowitz, James N. ....Washington, DC
Moskowitz, Jan S. ....Cleveland, OH
Moskowitz, Jay R. ....Miami, FL
Moskowitz, Jay Stuart ....New York, NY
Moskowitz, Jesse L. ....Trenton, NJ
Moskowitz, Jodi L. ....Newark, NJ
Moskowitz, Joel S. ....Los Angeles, CA
Moskowitz, Joel S. ....Cincinnati, OH
Moskowitz, Jules ....Kansas City, MO
Moskowitz, Karen ....Los Angeles, CA
Moskowitz, Karla ....New York, NY
Moskowitz, Keith ....Littleton, CO
Moskowitz, Keith ....New York, NY
Moskowitz, Kenneth L. ....Union, NJ
Moskowitz, Kenneth S. ....Maple Glen, PA
Moskowitz, Larry J. ....Washington, DC
Moskowitz, Lawrence A. ....Santa Rosa, CA
Moskowitz, Leah ....Cleveland, OH
Moskowitz, Mandell Salim & Simowitz, P.A.
Fort Lauderdale, FL
Miami, FL
West Palm Beach, FL
Moskowitz, Marc S. ....Washington, DC
Moskowitz, Mark R., (A Professional Corporation) ....Los Angeles, CA
Moskowitz, Marvin ....New York, NY
Moskowitz, Max ....New York, NY
Moskowitz, Michael A. ....Cincinnati, OH
Moskowitz, Michael J. ....Hollywood, FL
Moskowitz, Michael Lee ....New York, NY
Syosset, NY
Moskowitz, Michael W.
Fort Lauderdale, FL
Moskowitz & Moskowitz ....Cincinnati, OH
Moskowitz, Myron M. ....Shamokin, PA
Moskowitz, Neil A. ....Atlanta, GA
Moskowitz, Nelson
Department of Commerce, Patent and Trademark Office, GV
Moskowitz, Paul ....New York, NY
Moskowitz, Peter C. ....New York, NY
Moskowitz, Rachelle I. ....New York, NY
Moskowitz, Renée S. ....New York, NY
Moskowitz, Richard S. ....Washington, DC
Moskowitz, Rochelle N. ....Hackensack, NJ
Moskowitz, Ross F. ....New York, NY
Moskowitz, Roy P. ....New York, NY
Moskowitz, Samuel B. ....Boston, MA
Moskowitz, Sarah J. ....Boston, MA
Moskowitz, Saul L. ....Washington, DC
Moskowitz, Seth A. ....New York, NY
Moskowitz, Seymour ....Brooklyn, NY
Moskowitz, Sidney I.
Department of Commerce, Patent and Trademark Office, GV
Moskowitz, Sidney M. ....New York, NY
Moskowitz, Simor L. ....Washington, DC
Moskowitz, Stanley ....New York, NY
Moskowitz, Stephen M. ....San Francisco, CA

Moskowitz, Steven A. ....Portland, OR
Moskowitz, Steven P. ....New York, NY
Moskowitz, Stuart S. ....Armonk, NY
Moskowitz, Stuart W. ....Long Beach, NY
Moskowitz, Theodore D. ....Newark, NJ
Moskowitz & Thomas ....Portland, OR
Moskowitz, Wayne S. ....Minneapolis, MN
Moskowitz, Wendy finkel ....New York, NY
Moskus, Judith A. ....Ann Arbor, MI
Moskwa, Pamela A. ....Monroe, MI
Moslander, Carl E. ....Oklahoma City, OK
Mosle, Jennifer ....Plano, TX
Moslemi, Troy N. ....Miami, FL
Mosler, Damon Craig ....Newport Beach, CA
Mosler, Laurence A. ....Seattle, WA
Mosler Schermer Wallstrom Scruggs & Sieler ....Seattle, WA
Mosley, Audrey Byrd ....Washington, DC
Mosley, Beverly E. ....Los Angeles, CA
Mosley, Carolyn J. ....Tallahassee, FL
Mosley, Christopher R. ....Denver, CO
Mosley, Curtis R. ....Melbourne, FL
Mosley, Daniel L. ....New York, NY
Mosley, Daniel S. ....Las Vegas, NV
Mosley, Danielle Marie ....Annapolis, MD
Mosley, Dean F. ....Orlando, FL
Mosley, Deborah A. ....San Francisco, CA
Mosley, Donald M. ....Las Vegas, NV
Mosley, E. Jeffrey ....Louisville, KY
Mosley, Edmond ....La Jolla, CA
Mosley, Eugene L. ....Louisville, KY
Mosley, Ferne L. ....Department of Commerce, Office of the General Counsel, GV
Mosley, Gwendolyn T. ....Harrisburg, PA
Mosley, Henrietta E. ....Manhattan Beach, CA
Mosley, Iola, P.A. ....West Palm Beach, FL
Mosley, James C. ....Kew Gardens, NY
Mosley, James H. ....Wheat Ridge, CO
Mosley, James M. ....Midland, TX
Mosley, Jerald L. ....Pasadena, CA
Mosley, Jerre B. ....Chattanooga, TN
Mosley, John D. ....Kaufman, TX
Mosley, Kevin L. ....New York, NY
Mosley, Marian J. ....Fresno, CA
Mosley, Mark A. ....Akron, OH
Mosley, Mark L. ....Amarillo, TX
Mosley, Maurice B. ....Waterbury, CT
Mosley, Melody S. ....Irvine, CA
Mosley, Michael A. ....Dadeville, AL
Mosley & Mosley ....Kissimmee, FL
Orlando, FL
Mosley, Pamela C. ....Orlando, FL
Mosley, Patrick B. ....Amarillo, TX
Mosley, Paul B. ....Los Angeles, CA
Mosley, Paul E. ....Newport Beach, CA
Mosley, R. Sharon ....Sacramento, CA
Mosley & Sinclair ....Waterbury, CT
Mosley, Stephen ....Wichita, KS
Mosley, Susan T. ....Treasury Department, Internal Revenue Service, GV
Mosley & Wallis, P.A. ....Melbourne, FL
Mosley, Wells & McClain, LLC
Denver, CO
Mosley, William B. ....Fort Smith, AR
Mosley, William M., Jr. ....Houston, TX
Mosman, Craig W. ....Moscow, ID
Mosman, Michael W. ....Portland, OR
Mosman, Richard A. ....Minneapolis, MN
Mosman, Richard A., P.C. ....Minneapolis, MN
Mosman, Roy E. ....Moscow, ID
Mosman, Valerie A. ....Dallas, TX
Mosman, Wynn R. ....Moscow, ID
Mosmiller, Joseph W. ....Baltimore, MD
Mosner, Anita ....Washington, DC
Mosner, Matthew ....East Rutherford, NJ
Mosner, Zachary ....Seattle, WA
Mosoff, Serle Ian ....Port Chester, NY
Mosolino, William R. ....Orwigsburg, PA
Mosolygo, Carol ....Evanston, IL
Moson, Robert F. ....Newburgh, NY
Mosqueda, Roman P. ....Los Angeles, CA
Mosrie, Mary Margaret ....Knoxville, TN
Moss, A. Edward ....Akron, OH
Moss, A. Mundi ....Columbia, SC
Moss, Aaron J ....Los Angeles, CA
Moss, Aaron P. ....Van Nuys, CA
Moss, Abraham ....Corpus Christi, TX
Moss, Adrienne R. ....New York, NY
Moss, Alan M. ....New York, NY
Moss, Alan W. ....Langhorne, PA
Moss, Alfred G. ....Long Beach, CA
Moss, Allen J. ....Phoenix, AZ
Moss, Allen S. ....Beverly Hills, CA
Moss, Allison Effie ....Santa Clara, CA
Moss, Ambler H., Jr. ....Miami, FL
Moss, Andrea Carolyn ....Woodside, CA
Moss, Andrea E. ....Randallstown, MD
Moss, Andrew E. ....New York, NY
Moss, Andrew M. ....Miami, FL
Moss & Andrews ....Jacksonville, FL
Moss, Anne E. ....Washington, DC
Moss, Arthur H. ....Philadelphia, PA
Moss, Aubrey L. ....Bethesda, MD
Moss, Barbara J. ....Nashville, TN
Moss & Barnett, A Professional Association
Minneapolis, MN
Moss, Barry L. ....Bolingbrook, IL
Moss, Ben B. ....Winter Park, FL
Moss, Benedict S. ....New Haven, CT
Moss, Benton & Wallis, PLLC
Jackson, TN
Moss, Bill B. ....Cleveland, TN
Moss, Bill Ralph ....Austin, TX
Moss and Bloomberg, Ltd.
Bolingbrook, IL
Chicago, IL
Wheaton, IL
Moss & Boris, P.C. ....New York, NY

Moss & Bradley ....Lafayette, LA
Moss, Bradley K. ....Cherry Hill, NJ
Philadelphia, PA
Moss, Brent J. ....Rexburg, ID
Moss, Brent L. ....Little Rock, AR
Moss, Brian M. ....Houston, TX
Moss, Brian T. ....Irvine, CA
Moss, Bruce A. ....Los Angeles, CA
Moss, Bruce, Jr. ....Union City, TN
Moss, Bruce M. ....Alma, MI
Moss, Bruce N. ....Bloomfield Hills, MI
Moss, C. Arthur, Jr. ....Griffin, GA
Moss, C. Beth .....Christiansted, St. Croix, VI
Moss, Caine T. ....Palo Alto, CA
Moss, Calvin E. ....Webster City, IA
Moss, Carol Sperry ....Malibu, CA
Moss, Cas B. ....Columbia, LA
Moss, Chandra L. ....Corona, CA
Moss, Charles E. ....Amarillo, TX
Moss, Charles J. ....Birmingham, MI
Moss, Charles K. ....Leesburg, VA
Moss, Cheryl B. ....Las Vegas, NV
Moss, Christina D. ....Houston, TX
Moss and Cirillo ....New Haven, CT
Moss, C. K. ....Albuquerque, NM
Moss & Colella, P.C. ....Detroit, MI
Southfield, MI
Moss, D. Galton Cabot ....Harrisburg, PA
Moss, Daniel H., (P.C.)
Farmington Hills, MI
Moss, Daniel L. ....Philadelphia, PA
Moss, Darrel L. ....Denver, CO
Moss, David ....Southfield, MI
Moss, David L. ....Chattanooga, TN
Moss, David M. ....Clinton, IL
Moss, David M. ....New York, NY
Moss, David T. ....Canton, OH
Moss, Debbie L. ....Independence, OH
Moss, Debora S. ....Clearwater, FL
Moss, Deborah A. ....Washington, DC
Moss, Debra Cassens ....Chicago, IL
Moss, Dena Simone ....New York, NY
Moss, Dennis F. ....Glendale, CA
Moss, Dennis J. ....Olympia, WA
Moss, Devin E. ....New York, NY
Moss, Diane L. ....New York, NY
Moss, Donald C. ....New York, NY
Moss, Edgar E., II ....Moorestown, NJ
Moss, Edward A. ....Miami, FL
Moss, Edward A. ....Oxford, MS
Moss, Edward C. ....Denver, CO
Moss, Edward J. ....Highland Park, IL
Moss, Elaine M. ....St. Louis, MO
Moss, Ellen S. ....Marina Del Rey, CA
Moss & Enochian, A Law Corporation
Redding, CA
Moss, Everett W. ....El Paso, TX
Moss, Frances J. ....Green Cove Springs, FL
Moss, Francine H. ....Ronkonkoma, NY
Moss, Frank ....Costa Mesa, CA
Moss, Frank E. ....Salt Lake City, UT
Moss, Franklin K. ....New York, NY
Moss, Frederick ....New York, NY
Moss, Frederick C. ....Dallas, TX
Moss, Frederick Eugene ....Fort Worth, TX
Moss, Frederick S. ....New Haven, CT
Moss, Gabriel M. ....Philadelphia, PA
Moss, Gary C. ....Las Vegas, NV
Moss, Gary E. ....San Francisco, CA
Moss, Gary N. ....New York, NY
Moss, Gayla L. ....Chandler, AZ
Moss, Gene T. ....Jacksonville, FL
Moss, George E. ....Flushing, NY
Moss, George H., II ....Vero Beach, FL
Moss, Gerald ....New York, NY
Moss, Gerald L. ....Indianapolis, IN
Moss, Gerald R. ....El Cajon, CA
Moss, Glen L. ....Hayward, CA
Moss, Gordon W. ....Lexington, KY
Moss, Gordon W. ....Seattle, WA
Moss, Gregory H. ....Chicago, IL
Moss, Guy B. ....Boston, MA
Moss, H. Christopher ....Alexandria, VA
Moss, Harold P. ....Grand Junction, CO
Moss, Harris & Yates ....Fort Wayne, IN
Moss, Harvey K. ....La Mesa, CA
Moss, Heather R. ....Pasadena, CA
Moss, Heims & Casey ....Dyersville, IA
Moss, Henderson, Blanton & Lanier, P.A.
Vero Beach, FL
Moss, Herbert A. ....Santa Ana, CA
Moss & Hough ....San Francisco, CA
Moss, Hovden & Lindsay, A Professional Corporation ....Los Angeles, CA
Whittier, CA
Moss, Howard ....Sherman Oaks, CA
Moss Hurne Moss & Moss, LLC
Pueblo, CO
Moss, Hushel L. ....Raleigh, MS
Moss and Inglese ....Metuchen, NJ
Milltown, NJ
Moss, Irving M. ....New York, NY
Moss, Jack G. ....Raymond, MS
Moss, Jack W. ....San Francisco, CA
Moss, Jacqueline Alicia ....Spartanburg, SC
Moss, James A. ....Pasadena, CA
Moss, James A., (P.C.) ....Princeton, NJ
New York, NY
Moss, James E. ....Canton, OH
Moss, James H. ....Lakewood, CO
Moss, James H. ....Beaufort, SC
Moss, James Jeffrey ....St. Petersburg, FL
Moss, James R., Jr. ....Los Angeles, CA
Moss, James S. ....Bonham, TX
Moss, James W. ....Birmingham, AL
Moss, Jarod T. ....Dallas, TX
Moss, Jefferson J., Jr. ....Lafayette, LA
Moss, Jeffrey A. ....San Rafael, CA

Moss, Jeffrey Colson ....Lancaster, KY
Moss, Jeffrey D. ....Bloomfield Hills, MI
Moss, Jeffrey M. ....Boise, ID
Moss, Jeffrey W. ....Boston, MA
Moss, Jennifer Miller ....Sacramento, CA
Moss, Jerald Lee ....Cleveland, OH
Moss, Jerrold V. ....Bala Cynwyd, PA
Philadelphia, PA
Moss, Jessica K. ....Gainesville, GA
Moss, Jimmie L. ....Baton Rouge, LA
Moss, Joe B. ....Jackson, MS
Moss, Joe D. ....Bonham, TX
Moss, Joe G. ....Raymond, MS
Moss, Joe K. ....Point Blank, TX
Moss, Joel S. ....Melbourne, FL
Moss, Joel Y. ....Atlanta, GA
Moss, John A. ....Atlanta, GA
Moss, John A., Jr. ....Marcellus, NY
Moss, John B. ....Orange Park, FL
Moss, John D., Jr. ....Lake Forest, IL
Moss, John J. ....Cambridge, MA
Moss, John K. ....Garden City, NY
Moss, John O., III ....Indianapolis, IN
Moss, John P. ....Akron, OH
Moss, John P., Jr. ....Cambridge, MA
Moss, John R. ....Jackson, TN
Moss, John R., P.C. ....Jackson, TN
Moss, John W. ....Chicago, IL
Moss, Jon Roger ....Los Angeles, CA
Moss, Jonathan H. ....Laguna Niguel, CA
Moss, Jonathan Y. ....Naperville, IL
Moss, Joseph ....Chicago, IL
Moss, Joseph A. ....Kilmarnock, VA
Moss, Joseph R., Professional Association
Rockledge, FL
Moss, Joseph W. ....Greensboro, NC
Moss, Joseph W., Jr. ....Charlotte, NC
Moss, Josh J. ....Chicago, IL
Moss, Judith D. ....Columbus, OH
Moss, Julian M., Jr. ....Houston, TX
Moss, Julie G. ....Memphis, TN
Moss & Kalish ....New York, NY
Moss, Karen Gabriel ....Cleveland, OH
Moss, Karen J. ....Chicago, IL
Moss, Kenneth H. ....Los Angeles, CA
Moss, Kenneth L. ....Dyersville, IA
Moss, Kevin A. ....Altamont, NY
Moss, Kevin Michael ....New York, NY
Moss, Kirby G. ....Fort Wayne, IN
Moss & Kuhn, P.A. ....Beaufort, SC
Moss, Larry B. ....Redding, CA
Moss, Laurence M. ....New York, NY
Moss, Laurence S. ....Boston, MA
Moss, Laurie S. ....Fort Lauderdale, FL
Moss, Laurie S., P.A. ....Fort Lauderdale, FL
Moss, Lawrence C. ....New York, NY
Moss, Lawrence J. ....Los Angeles, CA
Moss, Lawrence J. ....Chicago, IL
Moss, Lawrence J., P.C. ....Los Angeles, CA
Moss, Leigh Dones ....West Bloomfield, MI
Moss, Leonard W. ....Runnemede, NJ
Moss, Levitt & Mandell, LLP
Los Angeles, CA
Moss, Linda A. ....Columbus, OH
Moss, Linda M. ....Orlando, FL
Moss, Lindy G. ....Fort Wayne, IN
Moss, Lisa ....Houston, TX
Moss, Logan V. ....Diboll, TX
Moss, M. Mitchell ....El Paso, TX
Moss & Mackrides, LLP ....Media, PA
Moss, Maggi ....Des Moines, IA
Moss, Margaret P. ....Augusta, ME
Moss, Marvin I. ....North Miami Beach, FL
Moss, Marvin I., P.A.
North Miami Beach, FL
Moss & Mason ....Greensboro, NC
Moss, Melanie A. ....Washington, DC
Moss, Melissa E. ....New York, NY
Moss, Meredith M. ....Santa Monica, CA
Moss, Michael B. ....New Haven, CT
Moss, Michael E. ....Fresno, CA
Moss, Michael E.C. ....Chicago, IL
Moss, Michael H. ....Chicago, IL
Moss, Michael J. ....Lenox, IA
Moss, Michael M. ....Point Richmond, CA
Moss, Michael R. ....Miamisburg, OH
Moss, Milton L. ....Pike Road, AL
Moss & Moss ....New York, NY
Moss & Murphy ....Hayward, CA
Moss, N. Dann ....New York, NY
Moss, Neil S. ....Bennington, VT
Moss, Nels C., Jr. ....St. Louis, MO
Moss, Nicole C. ....Austin, TX
Moss, Nicole S. ....Chillicothe, OH
Moss & O'Dell, P.C. ....Denver, CO
Moss, P. Quinn ....New York, NY
Moss, Parker L. ....Fort Wayne, IN
Moss, Patricia A. ....Worthington, OH
Moss, Patricia R. ....Fayetteville, NC
Moss, Patti W. ....Rochester, NY
Moss, Paul V. ....Pueblo, CO
Moss, Peter J. ....Fairfax, VA
Moss, Peter N. ....New York, NY
Moss, Peyton H. ....New York, NY
Moss, Philip J. ....Portland, ME
Moss Pite & Duncan, LLP ....El Cajon, CA
Moss & Popov ....Marcellus, NY
Moss, Ralph J. ....Cleveland, OH
Moss, Randolph D. ....Department of Justice, Office of Legal Counsel, GV
Moss, Ray ....Clinton, IL
Moss, Ray, and Associates, P.C.
Clinton, IL
Moss, Raymond L. ....Atlanta, GA
Moss, Rebecca S. ....Pueblo, CO
Moss, Reed L. ....Idaho Falls, ID
Moss, Richard A. ....Pasadena, CA
Moss, Richard A. ....Farmington Hills, MI

Moss, Richard D. ..... Joplin, MO
Moss, Richard F. ..... Santa Monica, CA
Moss, Richard H. ..... San Francisco, CA
Moss, Richard L. ..... New York, NY
Moss, Robert A. ..... Atlanta, GA
Moss, Robert D. ..... Akron, OH
Moss, Robert E. ..... Washington, DC
Moss, Robert F. ..... Metuchen, NJ
Moss, Robert G. ..... Farmington, NM
Moss, Robert G. ..... Dallas, TX
Moss, Robert J. ..... New York, NY
Moss, Robert J., (A Professional Corporation) ..... Santa Ana, CA
Moss, Robert James ..... Washington, DC
Moss, Robert M. ..... Santa Monica, CA
Moss, Robert M. ..... Beachwood, OH
Moss, Robyn F. ..... Houma, LA
Moss & Rocovich, Attorneys-at-Law, P.C. Roanoke, VA
Moss, Rod D., II ..... Orlando, FL
Moss, Rodney ..... Los Angeles, CA
Moss, Rodney E. ..... Whittier, CA
Moss, Rodney L. ..... Birmingham, AL
Moss, Roger A. ..... Honolulu, HI
Moss, Roger N. ..... Lufkin, TX
Moss, Ron H. ..... Austin, TX
Moss, Ronald J. ..... Quogue, NY
Moss, Ronald J. ..... Troy, NY
Moss, Ronald S. ..... San Mateo, CA
Moss, Roy O., Jr. ..... Orange, CA
Moss, Roy W. ..... Norwalk, CT
Moss, Sara E. ..... Stamford, CT
Moss, Saul J. ..... Chicago, IL
Moss, Scott ..... New York, NY
Moss, Scott A. ..... Highland Park, IL
Moss, Shelly ..... Birmingham, AL
Moss, Sherrill Duncan ..... Signal Mountain, TN
Moss, Stanley J. ..... New York, NY
Moss, Stephen B. ..... Fort Lauderdale, FL
Moss, Stephen C. ..... Reno, NV
Moss, Stephen C., A Prof. Corp., Law Office of ..... Reno, NV
Moss, Stephen E. ..... Bethesda, MD
Moss, Stephen Jon ..... Austin, TX
Moss, Steven B. ..... Media, PA
Moss, Steven C. ..... Bullhead City, AZ
Moss, Steven J. ..... Indianapolis, IN
Moss, Steven M. ..... Cleveland, OH
Moss, Stewart Michael ..... Dunedin, FL
Moss, Strickler & Sachitano, P.A. Bethesda, MD Rockville, MD
Moss, Susan ..... Newport Beach, CA
Moss, Susan M. ..... Jersey City, NJ New York, NY
Moss, Sylvion S. ..... Falls Church, VA
Moss, Theodore ..... Westfield, NJ
Moss, Thom W. ..... Decatur, IL
Moss, Thomas E. ..... Blackfoot, ID
Moss, Thomas E. ..... Hobart, IN
Moss, Thomas E., P.A. ..... Blackfoot, ID
Moss, Thomas P. ..... Orlando, FL
Moss, Thomas W., Jr. ..... Norfolk, VA
Moss, Tina Niehold ..... Roseland, NJ
Moss, Verne W. ..... Minneapolis, MN
Moss, Victor ..... Pueblo, CO
Moss, W. Anthony ..... Atlanta, GA
Moss, Wardell G. ..... Inglewood, CA
Moss, Wayne S. ..... Augusta, ME
Moss, Wendy ..... Sherman Oaks, CA
Moss, Wendy J. ..... Los Angeles, CA
Moss, William H. ..... Raleigh, NC
Moss, William J. ..... New York, NY
Moss, William M. ..... Detroit, MI
Moss, William R. ..... Tulsa, OK
Moss, William R. ..... Lubbock, TX
Moss, William S., III ..... Houston, TX
Moss, William S., Jr. ..... Houston, TX
Mossa, Vincent A. ..... Budd Lake, NJ
Mossaides, Maria Z. ..... Boston, MA
Mossberg, Christer L. ..... Washington, DC
Mossberg, John E. ..... Milwaukee, WI
Mossberg, Michael P. ..... New York, NY
Mossberg & Rappaport, P.C. ..... New York, NY
Mossberg, Sheldon A. ..... Willimantic, CT
Mossbrook, David W. ..... Frankfort, KY
Mossburg, Richard J. ..... Dearborn, MI
Mosse, Gail M.L. ..... San Francisco, CA
Mosse, Richard H. ..... New York, NY
Mosseau, Peter W. ..... Manchester, NH
Mosser, Edw. D. ..... Cadiz, OH
Mosser, Geoffrey B. ..... Cadiz, OH
Mosser, James C. ..... Dallas, TX
Mosser, James C., Inc. ..... Dallas, TX
Mosser, Terri Barziza ..... Houston, TX
Mosseri, Janet S. ..... Brooklyn, NY
Mossina, Charles L. ..... Richmond, CA
Mossing, Adria East ..... Chicago, IL
Mossinghoff, Gerald J. ..... Arlington, VA
Mossino, Ralph L. ..... Redwood City, CA
Mossler, Richelle Cohen ..... Indianapolis, IN
Mossman, Boyd P. ..... Wailuku, HI
Mossman, Burns ..... Des Moines, IA
Mossman, Cynthia L. ..... Cincinnati, OH
Mossman, Donald P. ..... Mahwah, NJ
Mossman, Donald W., II ..... Covington, KY
Mossman, Gianola & Ioakimedes Vallejo, CA
Mossman, Hugh V. ..... Boise, ID
Mossman, Keith D. ..... Vinton, IA
Mossman Law Office ..... Boise, ID
Mossman, Mark E. ..... Vinton, IA
Mossman, Michael I. ..... Nashville, TN
Mossman & Mossman, L.L.P. ..... Vinton, IA
Mossman, Romain S. ..... Woodward, OK
Mossman, Stephen D. ..... Lincoln, NE
Mossner, Alfred E., Jr. ..... La Grange, IL
Mossner, Eugene D. ..... Saginaw, MI

Mossop, Joseph C. ..... Pottsville, PA
Mossop, W. Brant ..... New York, NY
Mosston, Leora ..... Jersey City, NJ
Most, Carol W. ..... Mount Kisco, NY
Most, Eric D. ..... New York, NY
Most, Jack L. ..... New York, NY
Most, John S. ..... Department of Justice, Environment and Natural Resources Division, GV
Most, Jordan F. ..... New York, NY
Most, Lisa ..... Philadelphia, PA
Most, Peter J. ..... Los Angeles, CA
Most, Robert A. ..... San Luis Obispo, CA
Most, Robin Jane ..... Lawrenceville, NJ
Mostaghel, Deborah M. ..... Toledo, OH
Mostajo, Maria C. ..... Bronx, NY
Mostak, Richard L. ..... Merrillville, IN
Mostek, Michael S. ..... Omaha, NE
Mostek, Walter J., Jr. ..... Berwyn, PA
Mostel, Jon R. ..... New York, NY
Mosteller & Associates, P.C. ..... Oak Brook, IL
Mosteller, Brenda L. ..... Hudson, OH
Mosteller, David S. ..... Shohola, PA
Mosteller, James D., III ..... Oak Brook, IL
Mosteller, Robert P. ..... Durham, NC
Mosten, Forrest S. ..... Los Angeles, CA
Mosten & Tuffias ..... Beverly Hills, CA Los Angeles, CA Santa Monica, CA
Moster, Charles A. ..... Austin, TX
Moster, James M. ..... Indianapolis, IN
Moster, James T., Jr. ..... Chicago, IL
Moster, Todd N. ..... Playa Del Rey, CA
Moster & Wynne, A Professional Corporation ..... Los Angeles, CA **Austin, TX**
Mosterd, Edward H. ..... Chicago, IL
Mostert, Nick J. ..... Los Angeles, CA
Mosteshar, Sa'id ..... La Jolla, CA
Mostiler, Johnny B. ..... Griffin, GA
Mostkoff, Samuel ..... Monroe, MI
Mostman, Marc B. ..... Los Angeles, CA
Mostoff, Allan S. ..... Washington, DC
Mostofi, Mondonna ..... Martinez, CA
Mostofizadeh, Javad ..... San Francisco, CA
Mostofizaden, Kristine L. San Francisco, CA
Mostofsky, Steven Z. ..... Brooklyn, NY
Mostofsky, Steven Z., P.C. ..... Brooklyn, NY
Mostoller, Ann ..... Oak Ridge, TN
Mostoller, Sandra K. ..... Tacoma, WA
Mostoller, Stulberg & Whitfield Oak Ridge, TN
Moston, Kent V. ..... Hempstead, NY
Mostov, Charles H. ..... Los Angeles, CA
Mostovoi, Alexei ..... New York, NY
Mostovoy, Judith B. ..... Homewood, IL
Mostow, Gary S. ..... Chicago, IL
Mostow, Melissa B. ..... Boston, MA
Mostow, Michael S. ..... Chicago, IL
Mostow, Peter D. ..... Portland, OR
Mostul, Mark C. ..... Bellevue, WA
Mosty, Richard C. ..... Johnson City, TX
Mostyn, John Anthony ..... Millis, MA
Mostyn, William J., III ..... Boston, MA
Mostyn, William J., Jr. ..... North Eastham, MA
Mosunic, Monica C. ..... Danville, CA
Moszczynski, Antoni ..... Brooklyn, NY
Mota, Sue Ann ..... Bowling Green, OH
Motal, Rebecca S. ..... Austin, TX
Motamed, Nahal ..... New York, NY
Motchan, Brent L. ..... St. Louis, MO
Mote, Clyde A. ..... Bullard, TX
Mote, David B. ..... Springfield, IL
Mote, Gretchen Koehler ..... Columbus, OH
Mote, Jeffrey G. ..... Chicago, IL
Mote, Julie A. ..... Compton, CA
Mote, Scott R. ..... Columbus, OH
Mote, Thomas N. ..... Columbus, IN
Motejunas, Gerald W. ..... Boston, MA **Quincy, MA**
Motel, Andrew P. ..... West Chester, PA
Motel, Harold ..... Lincolnwood, IL
Motel, Robert A. ..... Lincolnwood, IL
Motelewski, Joseph R. ..... Jacksonville, NC
Motelson, Glenn E. ..... New York, NY
Motelson, Michael J. ..... New York, NY
Motelson, Stuart J. ..... New York, NY
Moten, MacArthur ..... St. Louis, MO
Motenko, Neil P. ..... Boston, MA
Motes, Alan K. ..... Dallas, TX
Motes, Carl D. ..... Orlando, FL
Motes, Carolyn Smith ..... McLean, VA
Motes, Carolyn Smith, P.C. ..... McLean, VA
Motes & Carr, P.A. ..... Orlando, FL
Motes, Cathy McCloud ..... Mobile, AL
Motes, Chad J. ..... Fort Myers, FL
Motes, David ..... Jefferson, GA
Motes, Joseph E ..... Chillicothe, OH
Motes, Joseph L., III ..... Dallas, TX
Motes, Nolie J. ..... Gainesville, GA
Motes, Robert M. ..... St. Louis, MO
Motes, T. Julian ..... Mobile, AL
Motheral, Linda ..... Houston, TX
Mothershead, James O. Department Of Health And Human Services, Social Security Administration, GV
Mothershead, Martha Fulford Grosse Pointe, MI
Motherway, Carmel A. ..... Providence, RI
Motherway, Glenn & Napleton Chicago, IL
Motherway, Nicholas J. ..... Chicago, IL
Motherway, Thomas J. ..... Santa Ana, CA
Moticka, John W. ..... St. Louis, MO
Motiey, Katayoun ..... Palo Alto, CA
Motil, Ronald S. ..... Edwardsville, IL
Motin Law Office, P.A. ..... Elk River, MN

Motin, Paul S. ..... Elk River, MN
Motiska, Robert J. ..... Brecksville, OH
Motiuk, I. Leo ..... Morristown, NJ
Motl, Jonathan R. ..... Helena, MT
Motl, Terri H. ..... San Angelo, TX
Motlagh, Cyrus K. ..... Franklin, MI
Motley, Chad W. ..... Jefferson City, MO
Motley, Cheryle D. ..... Dothan, AL
Motley, Christine E. ..... Redwood City, CA
Motley, Constance B. ..... New York, NY
Motley, Dale E. ..... Los Angeles, CA
Motley, David ..... Kerrville, TX
Motley, Erin C. Elliott ..... Jefferson City, MO
Motley, J. Lee ..... Dallas, TX
Motley, Joel W., III ..... United States Senate, Senatorial Assistants, GV
Motley, John B. ..... Salem, OR
Motley, John C. ..... Portland, OR
Motley, John H. ..... New York, NY
Motley, Jonathan E. ..... Nashville, TN
Motley, Kathrine G. ..... Trenton, NJ
Motley, Keith I. ..... San Diego, CA
Motley, Kristi Ulyn ..... Dallas, TX
Motley, Luke, IV ..... Sherman, TX
Motley, Marvin ..... Branson, MO
Motley, Mitch ..... Longview, TX
Motley & Motley ..... Dothan, AL
Motley & Motley ..... Branson, MO
Motley, Ronald L. ..... Charleston, SC
Motley, Susan D. ..... Dallas, TX
Motley, Susan Patrey Fort Lauderdale, FL
Motley, Thomas D. ..... Dothan, AL
Motley, Thomas David ..... Branson, MO
Motley, Thomas J. ..... Washington, DC
Motley, Thomas R. ..... Hannibal, MO
Motley, Victor A. ..... Richmond, VA
Motley, Victor A., Ltd. ..... Richmond, VA
Motley, Warren ..... New York, NY
Motley-Phillips, Kimberly ..... Pittsburgh, PA
Motloch, David L. ..... Dallas, TX
Motlong, Robert Edwin ..... Denver, CO
Motlow, William Dudley, Jr. Birmingham, AL
Motluck, Mark E. ..... Palos Heights, IL
Moto, Brian T. ..... Wailuku, HI
Motola, Antonia M. ..... Princeton, NJ
Motola, David H. ..... New York, NY
Motola Klar & Dinowitz, LLP Teaneck, NJ **New York, NY**
Motola, Niza Maria ..... Philadelphia, PA
Motola, Rene S. ..... White Plains, NY
Motola-Davis, Lauren ..... Providence, RI
Motomura, Hiroshi ..... Boulder, CO
Moton, Rodney E. ..... Houston, TX
Motooka, Marjorie E. ..... Los Angeles, CA
Motooka, Milton M. ..... Honolulu, HI
Motosko, Linda Anne ..... Youngstown, OH
Motosue, Stanley Y. ..... Honolulu, HI
Motowski, Michelle ..... Detroit, MI
Motozaki, S. Andrew ..... Santa Clara, CA
Motroni, Adrian R. ..... Granite Bay, CA
Motroni, Amelia R. ..... Santa Clara, CA
Motsch, Barry B. ..... Lorain, OH
Motschenbacher, Anthony J. Portland, OR
Motschiedler, J. Carl ..... Fresno, CA
Motschiedler, Michaelides & Wishon, LLP Fresno, CA
Motsenbocker, Gary L. ..... Fresno, CA
Motsenbocker, Marvin A. Washington, DC
Motsenbocker, Robert E. ..... Odessa, TX
Motsinger, C. Daniel ..... Indianapolis, IN
Motsinger, John, Jr. ..... Orlando, FL
Motsinger, John K. ..... Winston-Salem, NC
Motsinger, Mitzi ..... Orlando, FL
Motsko, Donald R. ..... New Haven, CT
Motsko, M. Lucinda ..... Columbia, MD
Motsko, Michell Mayer ..... Baltimore, MD
Mott, Amanda G. ..... Milwaukee, WI
Mott, Andrew H. ..... Washington, DC
Mott, Arthur S., Jr. ..... Hampton, NJ
Mott, Barbara K. ..... Norwalk, CT
Mott, Charles B., Jr. ..... Little Rock, AR
Mott, Daniel C. ..... Minneapolis, MN
Mott, David C. ..... Arlington, WA
Mott, Donald A. ..... St. Clair Shores, MI
Mott, Esta M. ..... Sylmar, CA
Mott, Geoffrey T. ..... Hempstead, NY
Mott, Geoffrey T., P.C. ..... Hempstead, NY
Mott, Gregory J. ..... Rochester, NY
Mott, H. Christopher ..... El Paso, TX
Mott, Hanno D. ..... New York, NY
Mott, J. Thomas ..... St. Paul, MN
Mott, Jefferson A. ..... Ocean City, NJ
Mott, Joanne C. ..... Towson, MD
Mott, Joel A., III ..... Ocean City, NJ
Mott, Joel A., Jr. ..... Ocean City, NJ
Mott, John C. ..... Denver, CO
Mott, John C. ..... Towanda, PA
Mott, John G. ..... Washington, DC
Mott, John M. ..... Department of Justice, Civil Rights Division, GV
Mott, Jonathan J. ..... Tustin, CA
Mott, Joseph M. ..... Rockville, MD
Mott, Joseph W. ..... Phoenix, AZ
Mott, Joseph W. H. ..... Roanoke, VA
Mott, Lovette M. ..... Gettysburg, PA
Mott, Mary Rose ..... Baptistown, NJ
Mott, Norman A., III ..... New Orleans, LA
Mott, Patricia D. Environmental Protection Agency, Office of Enforcement and Compliance Assurance, GV
Mott, Paula ..... New York, NY

Mott, Peter M. ..... Port Jefferson, NY Riverhead, NY
Mott, Peter T. ..... Southport, CT
Mott, Robert H. ..... San Luis Obispo, CA
Mott, Robert L., Jr. ..... Southfield, MI
Mott, Sarah D. ..... San Francisco, CA
Mott, Shelly J. ..... Kalispell, MT
Mott & Staniszewski, P.C. St. Clair Shores, MI
Mott, Stephanie L. ..... Milwaukee, WI
Mott, Stokes E., Jr. ..... Philadelphia, PA
Mott, Stokes E., Jr., P.C. ..... Philadelphia, PA
Mott, T. Allen ..... Baltimore, MD
Mott, Thomas R. ..... Daytona Beach, FL
Mott, Thomas Rafael, P.A. Daytona Beach, FL
Mott, Thomas W. ..... Newton, IA
Mott, Vernon and Mott ..... Ocean City, NJ
Mott, Vicki V. ..... Atlanta, GA
Mott, W. Gregory ..... Washington, DC
Motta, Anthony R. ..... New York, NY
Motta, Christine M. ..... New York, NY
Motta, Dawn Kawalek ..... Arlington, VA
Motta, John ..... Cranford, NJ
Motta, Joseph A. ..... Martinez, CA
Motta, Robert M. ..... Franklin Park, IL
Motta, Ronald J. ..... Arnold, CA
Motta, Thomas Gregory ..... Portsmouth, NH
Motta, Toni Ann ..... Boston, MA
Mottalini, John A. ..... Washington, DC
Mottaz, Mark C. ..... St. Louis, MO
Mottaz, Ronald C. ..... Alton, IL
Mottaz, Steven N. ..... Alton, IL
Mottaz, Thomas D. ..... Anoka, MN
Mottek, Jacqueline E. ..... San Francisco, CA
Motter, Anna Bryant ..... Tallahassee, FL
Motter, Dorothy Denise ..... Lompoc, CA
Motter, Neil E. ..... Culpeper, VA
Motter, Oliver W. ..... Chicago Heights, IL
Motter, Susan F. ..... Atlanta, GA
Motter, Thomas J. ..... Wilmington, DE
Mottern, Jeffrey M. ..... Hummelstown, PA
Mottes, Andrew J. ..... Philadelphia, PA
Mottesi, Marcelo A. ..... New York, NY
Mottet, Brian A. ..... Dallas, TX
Motti, Peter K. ..... Branford, CT
Mottier, Charles H. ..... Chicago, IL
Mottl, Charles T. ..... St. Paul, MN
Mottl, Ronald M. ..... Parma, OH
Mottley, J. Donald ..... Dayton, OH
Mottley, Kevin W. ..... Richmond, VA
Motto, Dominick ..... New Castle, PA
Motto, Joseph D. ..... Chicago, IL
Motto, Michael A. ..... West Palm Beach, FL
Motto, Michael J. ..... Davenport, IA
Motto, Patricia ..... Chicago, IL
Motto, Vincent J. ..... Davenport, IA
Motto, William P. ..... Chicago, IL
Mottola, Andrea Plavin ..... Islip Terrace, NY
Mottola, Charles Van S. ..... Newman, CA
Mottola, Gary F. ..... New York, NY
Mottola, Graham Daniel ..... Wailuku, HI
Mottola, Suzanne F. ..... Devon, PA
Mottolese, A. William ..... Stamford, CT
Mottolese, Maura C. ..... Schenectady, NY
Mottram, John F. ..... Portland, OR
Mott-Smith, Wiltrud R. ..... Concord, NH
Mottur, Alfred E. ..... Washington, DC
Mottweiler, Richard R. ..... Chicago, IL
Motulsky, John A. ..... New York, NY
Motwani, Ravi B. ..... New York, NY
Motycka, Jennifer L. ..... Longmont, CO
Motyczka, William J. ..... Miami, FL
Motyka, Gregory J. ..... Anchorage, AK
Motyka, Jane E. ..... Elmsford, NY
Motz, Anton ..... Oak Park, IL
Motz, Barbara Manheimer ..... Los Angeles, CA
Motz, Donald Forrest, Jr. ..... Wheaton, IL
Motz, J. Frederick ..... Baltimore, MD
Motz, Jeffrey A. ..... Scottsdale, AZ
Motz, Linda B. ..... Chicago, IL
Motz, Paul E. ..... Alamosa, CO
Motz, Paul E., LLC ..... Alamosa, CO
Motzenbecker, Amy P. K. ..... Morristown, NJ
Motzenbecker, Douglas E. ..... Newark, NJ
Motzer, Guy E., (P.A.) ..... Miami, FL
Motzkin, Randee Schuster ..... Los Angeles, CA
Motzkin, Richard L. ..... Los Angeles, CA
Motzny, Allan T. ..... Pontiac, MI
Moua, Mee ..... St. Paul, MN
Mouat, William G. ..... Billings, MT
Mouber, David S. ..... Kansas City, MO
Mouber, Michael L. ..... Mount Laurel, NJ
Mouch, Jeffrey J. ..... Tampa, FL
Mouchawar, Ellen S. ..... San Francisco, CA
Mouchet, Donald B. ..... Dearborn, MI
Mouchet, Donald B., P.C. ..... Dearborn, MI
Moudios, Nickolas W. ..... Worcester, MA
Moudrova, Kalinka H. ..... New York, NY
Moudry, Ladimir J. ..... Sycamore, IL
Moudy, Dan E. ..... Benton, AR
Moudy, Lou Ann ..... Henryetta, OK
Moudy, Ray P. ..... Midland, TX
Moudy, Ray P., Inc. ..... Midland, TX
Mouer, John Andrew ..... Houston, TX
Mouer, Meredith Steinfeld ..... Houston, TX
Mouer, Paul Vincent ..... Austin, TX
Mouer, Roy W. ..... Austin, TX
Mouganis, Joan ..... Garden City, NY
Moughan, James T. Plymouth Meeting, PA
Moughan, Peter R., Jr. ..... Albuquerque, NM
Moughon, Caitlin J. ..... Seattle, WA
Mougin, Robert ..... San Diego, CA
Mouhot, Andrew L., Jr. ..... Jackson, AL
Moukad, Joseph E. ..... New York, NY
Moukad, Rosemary A. ..... New York, NY
Moukawsher, Edward E. ..... Groton, CT

Moukawsher, Joseph E. ....**Groton, CT**
Hartford, CT
Moukawsher, Thomas G. ....**Groton, CT**
Hartford, CT
Moukawsher & Walsh LLC ....**Groton, CT**
Hartford, CT
Moukides, Maria ....**New York, NY**
Moul, Chas. E. ....St. Marys, OH
Moul, Geoffrey J. ....Columbus, OH
Moul, Jane M. ....St. Louis, MO
Moul, John F. ....Mendon, OH
St. Marys, OH
Moul, Robert G., II ....**Rockville, MD**
McLean, VA
Moul, Ursula P. ....Cheyenne, WY
Moul, Wardon H. ....Sacramento, CA
Moul, William C. ....**Columbus, OH**
Moulay-Rachid, Mostafa ....**Dearborn, MI**
Mould, Christopher M. ....Cushing, ME
Mould, George F. ....Syracuse, NY
Moulder, Carl W. ....Norcross, GA
Moulder, Heather E. ....**Dallas, TX**
Moulder, Todd ....Kansas City, MO
Moulder, William C. A., P.A.
Fernandina Beach, FL
Jacksonville, FL
Orange Park, FL
Moulder, William C. A. ....**Jacksonville, FL**
Moulds, David C. ....**Atlanta, GA**
Moulds, Gail F. ....**St. Petersburg, FL**
Moulds, Jeffery D. ....**Marietta, GA**
Moulds, John F. ....Sacramento, CA
Moule, David M. ....Eugene, OR
Moule & Frank ....Eugene, OR
Moulé, Mary K. ....Malone, NY
Moule, Reid S. ....Buffalo, NY
Moule, Rex E. ....**Melbourne, FL**
Moule, Rex E., P.A. ....**Melbourne, FL**
Mouledoux, André J. ....**New Orleans, LA**
Mouledoux, Bland, Legrand & Brackett, LLC ....**New Orleans, LA**
Mouledoux, George E. ....New Orleans, LA
Mouledoux, Rene J. ....**Houston, TX**
Mouledoux, Warren E., Jr. ....**Gretna, LA**
Mouledoux, Warren E., Jr., A Prof. Law Corp., Law Offices of ....**Gretna, LA**
Metairie, LA
New Orleans, LA
Moulin, A. Edward, III ....**New York, NY**
Moulin, Francis R. ....Kenmore, NY
Moulin, John M. ....Los Angeles, CA
Moulin, Linda Kathrine ....Roswell, GA
Moulinos, Peter ....**New York, NY**
Moulis, Raymond J. ....Milwaukee, WI
Moulliet, Sue Y. ....Dallas, TX
Mouloopoulos, Rena J. ....New York, NY
Moulos, Ernest H. ....Wichita, KS
Moulsdale, S. Keith ....**Baltimore, MD**
Moulthrop, Philip C. ....Atlanta, GA
Moulthrop, Roscoe E. ....Bethany, MO
Moulthrop, Samuel P. ....**Morristown, NJ**
Moulton, Arthur C. ....Madison, NJ
Moulton, Barbara ....Washington, DC
Moulton, Bellingham, Longo & Mather, P.C.
Billings, MT
Moulton, Bradley S. ....Ogunquit, ME
Moulton, C. Mike ....**Elizabethtown, KY**
Moulton, Claude R. ....Miami, FL
Moulton, Dan ....Rochester, MN
Moulton, David H. ....Bethesda, MD
Moulton, Debra J. ....**Albuquerque, NM**
Moulton, Francis S., Jr. ....**Boston, MA**
Moulton, Frederic R., P.C.
Watertown, SD
Moulton & Gans, LLP ....**Boston, MA**
Moulton, H. Geoffrey, Jr. ....Wilmington, DE
Moulton, Hugh G. ....Malvern, PA
Moulton, J. Kevin ....**Dothan, AL**
Moulton, J. Wayne ....**Conyers, GA**
Moulton, Janet Lee ....Metairie, LA
Moulton, Jeremy A. ....**Conyers, GA**
Moulton, Jonathan M. ....**Boston, MA**
Moulton Law Office ....**Watertown, SD**
Moulton Law Offices, P.S. ....Colfax, WA
Richland, WA
Spokane, WA
Yakima, WA
Moulton & Long, P.L.L.C
Elizabethtown, KY
Moulton, Marcia G. ....Cullman, AL
Moulton, Mary E. ....**Miami, FL**
Moulton & Massey, L.L.C. ....**Conyers, GA**
Moulton, Max ....Oklahoma City, OK
Moulton, Penn Starling ....Cambridge, MA
Moulton, Rial M. ....Colfax, WA
Richland, WA
Spokane, WA
Yakima, WA
Moulton, Robert E. ....**Eugene, OR**
Moulton, Robert T. ....Glendale, CA
Moulton, R.W. Eli, III ....**Burlington, VT**
Moulton, Stephen ....**Boston, MA**
Moulton, Stephen V. ....Louisville, KY
Moulton, Steven W. ....**Flint, MI**
Moulton, Steven W. ....Lake Oswego, OR
Moulton, Susanne Glen
Research Triangle Park, NC
Moulton, Thomas S. ....Gallipolis, OH
Moulton, Thomas S., Jr. ....Gallipolis, OH
Moulton, Tracy, Jr. ....Blakely, GA
Moulton, W. Thomas, Jr. ....**Boston, MA**
Moulton, Wright ....**Pensacola, FL**
Moultrie, Roy D. ....Sautee-Nacoochee, GA
Moultrie, Thomas L. ....Portland, OR
Moulun, Renee ....Portland, OR
Moum, Howard A. ....Little Rock, AR
Mounce, Green, Myers, Safi & Galatzan, A Professional Corporation ....**El Paso, TX**

Mounce, James L. ....Omaha, NE
Mounce, William J. ....**El Paso, TX**
Mouncer, Albert E. ....Richland, WA
Mound, Cotton & Wollan
San Francisco, CA
Newark, NJ
New York, NY
Mound, Hortense F. ....New York, NY
Moundas, Gregory J. ....New York, NY
Moundas, Harry J. ....**Bedford, NY**
Moundas, Harry J. ....**Eastchester, NY**
Moundas, Harry J. ....**Scarsdale, NY**
Mounedji, Selim ....**Costa Mesa, CA**
Mounger, Breed O., Jr. ....Tylertown, MS
Mounger, Chas. D., Jr. ....Knoxville, TN
Mounger, Dalton M. ....Columbia, TN
Mounger, Harvey T. ....Tallulah, LA
Mounger, Henry H. ....Jackson, MS
Mounger, Henry Price, III ....**Metairie, LA**
Mounger, J. Harbour ....Jackson, MS
Mounger, James A. ....New Orleans, LA
Mounger, Lon E., Jr. ....Bellaire, TX
Mounger, Rex C. ....Houston, TX
Mounger, Virginia Wilson ....Jackson, MS
Mounger, Whitman D. ....Greenwood, MS
Mounger, William H., Jr. ....Jackson, MS
Mounier, John F., Jr. ....Sacramento, CA
San Francisco, CA
Mounier Law Group, The, A Professional Corporation ....Sacramento, CA
San Francisco, CA
Mounsey, Peter R. ....Denver, CO
Mount, Barry M. ....**Portland, OR**
Mount, Benjamin W. ....**Lake Charles, LA**
Mount, Clifton Merritt ....**Washington, DC**
Mount, Daniel S. ....**San Jose, CA**
Mount, Dick W. ....Naples, FL
Mount, George B. ....Phoenix, AZ
Mount, Joe Horn ....Napanoch, NY
Mount, John H. ....San Francisco, CA
Mount, Kathleen Draper ....Westerville, OH
Mount, Kathy E. ....**San Leandro, CA**
Mount, Kelley L. ....**Charleston, WV**
Mount, Larry C. ....Irvine, CA
Mount, Lillard H. ....Chapel Hill, NC
Mount, Melissa K. ....**Atlanta, GA**
Mount, Michael P. ....**Palo Alto, CA**
Mount, Michele C. ....New Orleans, LA
Mount, Philip M. ....**Houston, TX**
Mount, Richard L. ....**Spokane, WA**
Mount, Stephen C. ....**San Antonio, TX**
Mount, Steven E. ....Woodland, CA
Mount, Steven F. ....**Columbus, OH**
Mount & Stoelker ....**San Jose, CA**
Mount, Todd A. ....**Madison, WV**
Mount, William D. ....Harlingen, TX
Mount, William D., Jr. ....**Brownsville, TX**
McAllen, TX
Mountain, Barbara W. ....Tuscaloosa, AL
Mountain, Bonnie Briggs ....South Orange, NJ
Mountain, C. Delaine ....Tuscaloosa, AL
Mountain, C. Delaine, & Associates, P.C.
Tuscaloosa, AL
Mountain, Dearborn & Whiting LLP
Worcester, MA
Mountain, James E., Jr. ....**Salem, OR**
Mountain, James W. ....Los Angeles, CA
Mountain, Maurice J., Jr. ....**McLean, VA**
Mountain, Robert E. ....Wayzata, MN
Mountain, Robert E., Jr. ....**Allegany, NY**
Mountain, Ronald H. ....Brooksville, FL
Mountain & Spears ....**Allegany, NY**
Mountain, Thomas R. ....**Worcester, MA**
Mountain, Will ....Olean, NY
Mountain, William H., III ....Olean, NY
Mountainspring, Stephen ....**Roseburg, OR**
Mountanos, Gus ....Northport, NY
Mountcastle, David G. ....Wheaton, IL
Mountcastle, George C.
Winston-Salem, NC
Mountcastle, Kelly & Dyer, P.C.
Chicago, IL
Wheaton, IL
Mountcastle, Rick A. ....Abingdon, VA
Mountcastle-Walsh, Harriet
Washington, DC
Mounteer, Carl A. ....Monterey, CA
Mounteer, Thomas R. ....**Washington, DC**
Mountford, Helen ....Kansas City, MO
Mountford, Janice H. ....Dallas, TX
Mountford, Joseph E. ....Quapaw, OK
Mountford, William E., Jr.
Mount Laurel, NJ
Mountin, Eric Kline ....Dallas, TX
Mountin, Thomas E. ....**Milwaukee, WI**
Mountjoy, Jesse T. ....**Owensboro, KY**
Mountjoy, S. Michael ....Beverly Hills, FL
Mounts, J. Everett ....Irvington, NJ
Mounts, James A., III ....**El Paso, TX**
Mounts, Kelly L. ....Kenton, OH
Mounts, Lynda S. ....Alexandria, VA
Mounts, Marvin U., Jr.
West Palm Beach, FL
Mounts, Mia M. ....**Cleveland, OH**
Mounts, R. Darrell ....**Washington, DC**
Mounts, Richard
Federal Deposit Insurance Corporation, GV
Mounts, Robert J. ....Phoenix, AZ
Mounts, Suzanne E. ....Oakland, CA
Mounts, Walter W. ....Oklahoma City, OK
Mountsier, Ronald L. ....**Des Moines, IA**
Mountz, David T. ....Columbia, PA
Mountz & Kreiser ....Columbia, PA
Mountz, Timothy W. ....**Dallas, TX**
Mountzoures, Louis W. ....Framingham, MA
Mour, David B. ....**Louisville, KY**
Moura, John J. ....**Los Angeles, CA**
Moura, Kathleen Marie ....Oakland, CA

Moura, Lisa Rosales ....Plymouth, MA
Moura, Richard J. ....**Dallas, TX**
Mourad, Roger P. ....St. Clair Shores, MI
Mouradian, George ....Boynton Beach, FL
Mouradian, Robert D. ....Farmington Hills, MI
Mouradian, Viken Samuel ....Pasadena, CA
Moure, Arthur A. ....Houston, TX
Moure, Elena ....Miami, FL
Moure, Helen Bergman ....**Seattle, WA**
Mourenza, Lydia Kraff ....Agoura Hills, CA
Mouret, Lauren D ....Opelousas, LA
Mourges, Melissa Ann ....New York, NY
Mourginis, Steven ....Worcester, MA
Mourglia, Richard H. ....**Houston, TX**
Mouritsen, Mark E. ....**Round Rock, TX**
Mouritsen, Robert K. ....Salt Lake City, UT
Mournian, Anthony F. ....**Chula Vista, CA**
Mourning, Donald B. ....Beulah, CO
Mourning, Paul W. ....**New York, NY**
Mourning, Robert H. ....Grand Rapids, MI
Moursund, A. W. ....Johnson City, TX
Llano, TX
Round Mountain, TX
Moursund, Ingrid W. ....Johnson City, TX
Llano, TX
Round Mountain, TX
Moursund, Kenneth C., Jr. ....**Houston, TX**
Moursund, Mary M. ....Johnson City, TX
Llano, TX
Round Mountain, TX
Moursund, Moursund, Moursund & Moursund
Johnson City, TX
Llano, TX
Round Mountain, TX
Moursund, Travis M. ....San Antonio, TX
Moursund, Will S. ....Johnson City, TX
Llano, TX
Round Mountain, TX
Mourton, Kenneth R. ....**Fayetteville, AR**
Mourtzanakis, Michael A. ....Rahway, NJ
Moury, Karen M. Oill ....Harrisburg, PA
Moury, Kevin A. ....Harrisburg, PA
Mousa, Easa R. ....Jacksonville, FL
Mousalam, Fadlo ....Burbank, CA
Mousaw, Delon F. ....Rochester, NY
Mouse, Boyd A. ....**Dallas, TX**
Mouse, Gary M. ....Independence, MO
Mousel, Craig L. ....Phoenix, AZ
Mousel, David L. ....**Reno, NV**
Mousel, Garner & Rasmussen
McCook, NE
Mousel, Lois M. ....San Diego, CA
Mousel, Ronald D. ....**McCook, NE**
Mousel, Stephen D. ....Bloomington, MN
Mouser, Deanna J. ....**Walnut Creek, CA**
Mouser, Denette A. ....**Dallas, TX**
Mouser, Edward M. ....Kinder, LA
Mouser, Frederick L. ....St. Petersburg, FL
Mouser, James W. ....Norman, OK
Mouser, Jennifer E. ....St. Petersburg, FL
Mouser, John E. ....Santa Ana, CA
Mouser, Julia A. ....**Irvine, CA**
Mouser, Julie M. ....**Walnut Creek, CA**
Mouser, Marlena J. ....**Los Angeles, CA**
Mouser, Paul W. ....Orinda, CA
Mouser, Rosalind M. ....**Pine Bluff, AR**
Mouser & Wells, P.A. ....St. Petersburg, FL
Mouser, William Kirby ....**Pine Bluff, AR**
Moushegian, James ....**San Francisco, CA**
Moushegian, Suzanne ....Virginia Beach, VA
Moushey, Michael L. ....Columbus, OH
Moushey, Thomas P. ....**Alliance, OH**
Moushon, Clayton W. ....Dunlap, IL
Mousin, Craig B. ....Chicago, IL
Mouslmoules, Byron G. ....**Irvine, CA**
Moussa, Rhanda ....**New York, NY**
Mousseau, Geoffrey C. ....Los Angeles, CA
Moussette, Kris A. ....**Boston, MA**
Moussouros, Elizabeth A.
Los Angeles, CA
Moussouttas, Joy ....New York, NY
Moustakas, George D. ....**Troy, MI**
Moustakas, John ....Washington, DC
Moustakis, Albert D. ....Eagle River, WI
Moutaw, Roy G. ....Valparaiso, IN
Moutes, Eugene A. ....Van Nuys, CA
Moutes-Lee, Celia D. ....**Los Angeles, CA**
Moutinho, Manuel A., III ....Ludlow, MA
Moutinho, Manuel, Jr. ....Ludlow, MA
Moutis, Daphne J. ....Springfield, MA
Mouton, Arthur D. ....Lafayette, LA
Mouton, Benjamin P. ....Baton Rouge, LA
Mouton, Charles A. ....**Lafayette, LA**
New Orleans, LA
Mouton, David B. ....Carthage, MO
Mouton, Drew ....**Big Spring, TX**
Mouton, Edgar G., Jr. ....Lafayette, LA
Mouton, F. Edward ....Shreveport, LA
Mouton, F. Fred ....Lafayette, LA
Mouton, Glynna Jones ....**Big Spring, TX**
Mouton, John A., III ....Lafayette, LA
Mouton, John R. ....Lafayette, LA
Mouton, Kent Y. ....**Los Angeles, CA**
Mouton & Mouton, A Professional Corporation ....**Big Spring, TX**
Mouton, Robert W. ....**New Orleans, LA**
Mouton, Welton P., Jr. ....Lafayette, LA
Mouton, William Hugh ....Lafayette, LA
Mouton, Wm H. ....Lafayette, LA
Mouton, Wm. H., A Prof. Law Corp., Law Offices of ....Lafayette, LA
Moutos, Lannette J. ....Salinas, CA
Moutoussamy, Penelope ....Chicago, IL
Moutoux, David T. ....**San Mateo, CA**
Moutrie, Beth L. ....Doniphan, MO
Moutrie, Marsha Jones ....Santa Monica, CA
Moutsatsos, Maria Politis ....**New York, NY**
Moutz, Thomas J. ....Destrehan, LA

Mouw, Allan R. ....**Los Angeles, CA**
Mouw & Celello, A Professional Corporation
Iron Mountain, MI
Mouw, Edward W. ....**Rhinelander, WI**
Mouw, John L. ....Iron Mountain, MI
Mouw, Saari, Krueger, Paulson & Smith, S.C. ....**Rhinelander, WI**
Mouyal, Marsha E. ....Department of Defense, Office of the General Counsel, GV
Mouysset, Isabelle ....Washington, DC
Mouzavires, William E., Law Offices of
Fairfax, VA
Mouzes, Thomas G. ....Woodbridge, CA
Mouzis, Gerald W. ....**Santa Ana, CA**
Mouzon, Daniel G. ....Kew Gardens, NY
Moverman, Judith E. ....Bridgewater, NJ
Moverman, Thomas J. ....**New York, NY**
Movish, Glenn Alan ....Rosemont, IL
Movitz, Louis ....Boston, MA
Movius, David T. ....**Cleveland, OH**
Movius, Lee West ....**Charlotte, NC**
Movius, Michael J. ....Glendale, CA
Movius, Robert T. ....**Santa Ana, CA**
Movroydis, John G. ....Milwaukee, WI
Movsesian, Anthony A. ....El Paso, TX
Movsesian, Mark L. ....Hempstead, NY
Movshin, Lawrence J. ....**Washington, DC**
Movsisian, Korean ....South Holland, IL
Movsovich, Michael ....**New York, NY**
Mow, Laura C. ....**Washington, DC**
Mow, Robert H., Jr. (P.C.) ....**Dallas, TX**
Mowad, George G., Jr. ....Waterbury, CT
Mowat, Donald W. ....Tarzana, CA
Mowatt, Cecillia A. ....Chicago, IL
Mowatt, Frederick W. ....Washington, DC
Mowatt, William E. ....Harrisburg, PA
Mowbray, Elinor H. ....Hartford, CT
Mowbray, James L. ....**Overland Park, KS**
Mowbray, James R. ....Lincoln, NE
Mowbray, Jerry H. ....**Reno, NV**
Mowbray, John C. ....Las Vegas, NV
Mowbray, John H. ....**Las Vegas, NV**
Mowbray, Rebecca Lack ....**San Diego, CA**
Mowday, David S. ....San Francisco, CA
Mowday, Jennifer L. ....Ebensburg, PA
Mowder, Gary L., (P.C.) ....**Chicago, IL**
Mowdood, Shirley Kirkland ....Florissant, MO
Mowdy, D. Clay ....Atoka, OK
Coalgate, OK
Mowdy, Robert F. ....Coalgate, OK
Mowe, Gregory Robert ....**Portland, OR**
Mowell, G. Mitchell ....**Chestertown, MD**
Mowell, Lawrence V., Jr. ....Hartford, CT
Mowen, James D. ....**Moline, IL**
Mower, Amy L. ....**Providence, RI**
Mower, Elizabeth J. ....**Denver, CO**
Mower, James P. ....Modesto, CA
Mower, Jon R. ....**Irvine, CA**
Mower, Karen M. ....**Atlanta, GA**
Mower, Koeller, Nebeker, Carlson & Haluck, LLP ....**Phoenix, AZ**
Yuma, AZ
Irvine, CA
San Bernardino, CA
San Diego, CA
Mower, Paul F. ....Chambersburg, PA
Mower, Robert S. ....**New York, NY**
Mower, Sheri Ann ....**Salt Lake City, UT**
Mower, William M. ....**Minneapolis, MN**
Mowers, Jeffrey A. ....**Miami, FL**
Mowers, Phillip K. ....**Grand Rapids, MI**
Mowery and Blume ....**Wheelersburg, OH**
Mowery, Bruce L. ....Salem, OR
Mowery, Carl R. ....Omaha, NE
Mowery, Charles F., Jr. ....Brandon, FL
Mowery, Gene F. ....Eufaula, OK
Mowery, James H., Jr. ....Alexandria, VA
Mowery, James S., Jr. ....**Dublin, OH**
Mowery, Joseph S. ....Fayetteville, AR
Little Rock, AR
Mowery, Karl D. ....Hemet, CA
Mowery, Lloyd R. ....Columbus, IN
Mowery, Michael W. ....**Walnut Creek, CA**
Mowery, Morris E., Jr. ....Charleston, WV
Mowery, Philip L. ....**Chicago, IL**
Mowery, Randal A. ....San Antonio, TX
Mowery, Steven L. ....**Wheelersburg, OH**
Mowery, W. Mark ....**Santa Fe, NM**
Mowery, Wayne L., Jr. ....**State College, PA**
Mowery, William Howard ....**Texarkana, TX**
Mowery & Youell ....**Dublin, OH**
Mowinckel, Larry E. ....Napa, CA
Mowles, Linda Jean Hamilton
Knoxville, TN
Mowls, Robert L. ....Cleveland, OH
Mowoe, Isaac J. ....Columbus, OH
Mowrer, Frederick M. ....Albuquerque, NM
Mowrer, Glen F. ....Santa Barbara, CA
Mowrer, J. Michael ....**Kennett, MO**
Mowrer, John C. ....Hattiesburg, MS
Mowrer, Jonathan Reid
Albuquerque, NM
Mowrey, David F. ....**Philadelphia, PA**
Mowrey, Douglass Lee ....**Newark, DE**
Mowrey, John R. ....Waldorf, MD
Mowrey, Michael L. ....San Jose, CA
Mowrey & Minacci, P.A.
Crawfordville, FL
Monticello, FL
Quincy, FL
Tallahassee, FL
Mowrey, Robert D. ....**Atlanta, GA**
Mowrey, Robert T. ....**Dallas, TX**
Mowrey, Ronald A. ....**Crawfordville, FL**
Tallahassee, FL
Mowrey, Stephen M. ....Easton, PA
Mowris, Gerald W. ....Madison, WI
Mowry, Anne M. ....Kelso, WA

Mowry, Christine B. ... New Brunswick, NJ
Mowry, Frank W. ... Woodburn, OR
Mowry, G. Barton ... Reno, NV
Mowry, Henry Pierce
Jacksonville Beach, FL
Mowry, Irvine, Giannetto & Moon
Marshalltown, IA
Mowry, Jas. W. ... Pittsburgh, PA
Mowry, John B. ... Mexico, NY
Mowry, John Michael ... Mexico, NY
Mowry, Kathy S. ... Bremen, OH
Mowry, Kristin H. ... Washington, DC
Mowry & Mowry ... Mexico, NY
Mowry, Oliver Warren, Jr. ... Greenville, SC
Mowry, Richard M., Jr., P.A.
Deerfield Beach, FL
Mowry, Ross E. ... Fort Lauderdale, FL
Mowry, Snowden S. ... Venice, FL
Mowry, Stephen L. ... Kansas City, MO
Mowson, Robt. L. ... Falls Church, VA
Moxham, Douglas G. ... Boston, MA
Moxham, Walter E., Jr. ... Lockport, NY
Wilson, NY
Moxley, Charles J., Jr. ... New York, NY
Moxley, Gregory D. ... Montrose, CO
Moxley, John ... Ocala, FL
Moxley, John Dean, Jr. ... Titusville, FL
Moxley, John, P.A. ... Ocala, FL
Moxley, Julie Anne ... Miami, FL
Moxley, Linda A. ... Hendersonville, NC
Moxley, Marcus L. ... Winston-Salem, NC
Moxley, Margaret (Peggi) ... Wenatchee, WA
Moxley, Paul T. ... Salt Lake City, UT
Moxley, Richard G., III ... Montgomery, AL
Moxley, Richard T. ... Baltimore, MD
Moxley, Robert T. ... Cheyenne, WY
Moxley, Stephen G. ... Baltimore, MD
Moxness, J. Michael ... Anchorage, AK
Moxness, Mark J. ... Minneapolis, MN
Moxon & Bartilson ... Los Angeles, CA
Moxon, George L. ... Fort Lauderdale, FL
Moxon, George W., II ... Brecksville, OH
Moxon, Jeffrey N. ... Newton, MA
Moxon, Keith E. ... Seattle, WA
Moxon, Kendrick L. ... Los Angeles, CA
Moxon, Linda Aileen ... Santa Monica, CA
Moxon, Shea Thomas ... Tampa, FL
Moy, Albert ... Orland Park, IL
Moy, Baldwin S. ... Madera, CA
Moy, Betty ... New York, NY
Moy, Cindy Jane ... Eagan, MN
Moy, Clarence J. ... San Francisco, CA
Moy, Clarence J., A Professional Corporation
San Francisco, CA
Moy, Curt W. ... Austin, TX
Moy, Dai Wah ... New York, NY
Moy, David G. ... Jamaica, NY
Moy, Donald R. ... Lake Success, NY
Moy, Edward J. ... Rye Brook, NY
Moy, Eric R. ... Indianapolis, IN
Moy, Frank ... Santa Ana, CA
Moy, Gwendolyn ... New York, NY
Moy, Henry H. ... Danbury, CT
Moy, Irene B. ... San Francisco, CA
Moy, Jeffrey ... Scottsdale, AZ
Carrollton, TX
Moy, John B. ... San Francisco, CA
Moy, John P. ... Washington, DC
Moy, Karen C. ... New York, NY
Moy, Kenneth ... Clarendon Hills, IL
Moy, Kenneth K. ... Oakland, CA
Moy, Laurence S. ... New York, NY
Moy, Lawrence Allan ... Torrance, CA
Moy, Lillian M. ... Macon, GA
Moy, Mary A. ... New York, NY
Moy, Ming Y. ... Sherman Oaks, CA
Moy, Nancy T. ... New York, NY
Moy, Pamela A. ... Moorestown, NJ
Moy, Patricia Dwyer ... Clarendon Hills, IL
Moy, Philip J., Jr. ... Cleveland, OH
Moy, R. Carl ... Minneapolis, MN
Moy, Robert B. ... New York, NY
Moy, Robert S. ... Department of Education, Office for Civil Rights, GV
Moy, Selma ... New York, NY
Moy, Susannah ... New York, NY
Moy, Wallace K. ... Chicago, IL
Moy, William Timothy ... New York, NY
Moya, Elizabeth M. ... Miami, FL
Moya, Evelyn L. ... Sarasota, FL
Moya, P. Robert ... Phoenix, AZ
Moya, R. Anthony ... San Diego, CA
Moya, Vestalia Aylsworth ... Miami, FL
Moya Huff, Francisco R. ... San Juan, PR
Moyal, Maurice S. ... Concord, CA
Moyal, Maurice S., A Professional Law Corporation ... Concord, CA
Moyano, Lucinda D. ... Salem, OR
Moyar, Bert W. ... Cleveland, OH
Moyar, Virginia E. ... Gainesville, FL
Moyce, David M. ... San Francisco, CA
Moyd, David Hewitt ... Hartsville, SC
Moyd, Olinda ... Washington, DC
Moye, Billy D. ... Mount Pleasant, TX
Moye, Charles A., Jr. ... Atlanta, GA
Moyé, David W. ... Tallahassee, FL
Moye, Donald B., Inc. ... Nederland, TX
Moye, E. Kristen ... McLean, VA
Moyé, Eric V., (P.C.) ... Dallas, TX
Moye, Giles, O'Keefe, Vermeire & Gorrell LLP ... Denver, CO
New York, NY
Moye, H. Allen ... Atlanta, GA
Moye, James Elton ... Orlando, FL
Atlanta, GA
Moye, James R. ... Columbus, GA
Moye, John E., (P.C.) ... Denver, CO
Moye, Maricia L. ... Durham, NC
Moye, Michael R. ... Atlanta, GA
Moye, O'Brien, O'Rourke, Hogan & Pickert
Orlando, FL
Atlanta, GA
Moye, Peter E. ... Spokane, WA
Moye, Robert J., III ... Atlanta, GA
Moye, Robert M. ... Chicago, IL
Moye, Tracy L. Peden ... Tallahassee, FL
Moyed, Richard M. ... Dallas, TX
Moyen, Christopher J. ... Atlanta, GA
Moyer, Allen D. ... Elizabethtown, PA
Moyer, Beal and Vranesic ... Lakewood, CO
Moyer & Bergman, P.L.C.
Cedar Rapids, IA
Moyer, Bradford S.
Grosse Pointe Woods, MI
Moyer, Bruce L. ... Alexandria, VA
Moyer, Charles R. ... Blue Bell, PA
Moyer, Charlie ... Harrison, AR
Moyer, Christopher T. ... Norristown, PA
Moyer, Clinton H. ... Aurora, CO
Moyer, Connie L. ... Hackensack, NJ
Moyer, Craig A. ... Los Angeles, CA
Moyer, Darlis E. ... Harrisonburg, VA
Moyer, Daryl F. ... Hamburg, PA
Moyer, David B. ... Palo Alto, CA
Moyer, David M. ... Cincinnati, OH
Moyer, David S. ... Birmingham, AL
Moyer, David W. ... San Francisco, CA
Moyer, David W. ... Cleveland, OH
Moyer, Dennis K. ... McLean, VA
Moyer, Donald W. ... Bowling Green, OH
Moyer, Gary T. ... San Diego, CA
Moyer, Gayle T. ... Franklin, TN
Moyer, George H., Jr. ... Madison, NE
Norfolk, NE
Moyer, George H., Jr. ... Norfolk, NE
Moyer, George S. ... Niagara Falls, NY
Moyer, H. Earl ... Lakewood, CO
Moyer, Hayne R., & Associates
Gold River, CA
Moyer, Hayne R., & Associates
Sacramento, CA
Moyer, Heather A. ... York, PA
Moyer, Heather H. ... Malvern, PA
Moyer, Heidi J. ... Kansas City, MO
Moyer & Holloran, P.C.
Harrisonburg, VA
Moyer, Homer E., Jr. ... Washington, DC
Moyer, James A. ... Flemington, NJ
East Meadow, NY
Moyer, James D. ... Louisville, KY
Moyer, Jeff A. ... Grand Rapids, MI
Moyer, Jeffrey G. ... New York, NY
Moyer, Jeffrey L. ... Wilmington, DE
Moyer, Joel C. ... Glassboro, NJ
Moyer, John F. ... Kenosha, WI
Moyer, John G., Jr. ... Tulsa, OK
Moyer, John T. ... Akron, OH
Moyer, John W. ... Baltimore, MD
Moyer, Joseph W. ... York, PA
Moyer, Kenneth E. ... Bullhead City, AZ
Moyer, Kerr L. ... Grand Rapids, MI
Moyer, Lane R. ... Chicago, IL
Moyer, Linton L. ... Pittsburgh, PA
Moyer, Louise E. ... Philadelphia, PA
Moyer, Lyman C. ... Schaumburg, IL
Moyer, Lynn E. ... Long Beach, CA
Moyer, Marc A. ... Harrisburg, PA
Moyer, Michael E. ... Allentown, PA
Moyer, Michael G. ... Valley Forge, PA
Moyer, Michelle M. ... Los Angeles, CA
Moyer, Moyer, Egley, Fullner & Warnemunde
Madison, NE
Norfolk, NE
Moyer, P. Glenn ... Souderton, PA
Moyer, Paul V. ... Altamonte Springs, FL
Moyer, Robert F., Jr. ... Chicago, IL
Moyer, Robert H. ... Clarksville, TN
Moyer, Samuel G. ... Philadelphia, PA
Sellersville, PA
Moyer, Sarah Diemer ... Anchorage, AK
Moyer, Sharon S. ... Scottsdale, AZ
Moyer, Sherill T. ... Harrisburg, PA
Moyer, Stephen A. ... Columbus, OH
Moyer, Stephen G. ... San Francisco, CA
Moyer, Steven E. ... Beverly Hills, CA
Moyer & Straus ... Altamonte Springs, FL
Moyer, Terry T. ... Spartanburg, SC
Moyer, Thomas F. ... Falls Church, VA
Moyer, Thomas J. ... Columbus, OH
Moyer, Vincent M. ... Rochester, NY
Moyer, William B. ... Doylestown, PA
Moyer, William C. ... New Albany, IN
Moyer, William D., Jr. ... Eagleville, PA
Moyerman, Ruth ... Scottsdale, AZ
Moyers, Hardy R. ... Nashville, TN
Moyers, James D. ... Knoxville, TN
Moyers, James W. ... Falls Church, VA
Moyers, Janet Selph ... Richmond, VA
Moyers, Jason ... Roanoke, VA
Moyers, Jon M. ... Billings, MT
Moyers, Martin, Santee, Imel & Tetrick
Bixby, OK
Tulsa, OK
Moyers, Michael C. ... Concord, NH
Moyers, Michael K. ... Cincinnati, OH
Moyers, Mitzi Sue ... Grand Island, NY
Moyers, Robert M. ... Colorado Springs, CO
Moyers, Stacy T. ... Saratoga, CA
Moyes, David H. ... Leesburg, VA
Moyes, Jay I. ... Phoenix, AZ
Moyes & Levay, P.L.L.C. ... Fairfax, VA
Leesburg, VA
Moyes Storey ... Phoenix, AZ
Moyes, Violet D. ... Quincy, MA
Moyik, Stephen A. ... Austin, TX
Moylan, Charles E., Jr. ... Baltimore, MD
Moylan, Christopher Ignatius
Baltimore, MD
Moylan, Christopher T.
East Hartford, CT
Moylan, Dana ... Hagerstown, MD
Moylan, Daniel P. ... Towson, MD
Moylan, Daniel W. ... Hagerstown, MD
Moylan, James H. ... Omaha, NE
Moylan, James J. ... Chicago, IL
Moylan, John C., III ... Columbia, SC
Moylan, John P. ... Chicopee, MA
Moylan, Joseph W. ... Omaha, NE
Moylan, Joyce A. ... Ellicott City, MD
Moylan, Kiernan P. ... Deerfield Beach, FL
Moylan, Lauri McEntire ... Towson, MD
Moylan, Lee Duck ... Philadelphia, PA
Moylan, Martin I. ... Baltimore, MD
Moylan, Mary-Beth ... Sacramento, CA
Moylan, Maurice E. ... Springfield, VA
Moylan, Richard J. ... Brooklyn, NY
Moylan, Richd. J. ... Baltimore, MD
Moylan, Robert J. ... New Canaan, CT
Moylan, Sean P. ... Hartford, CT
Moylan, Thomas J. ... Boston, MA
Providence, RI
Moylan, William S. ... Homewood, IL
Moyle, Bernard T. ... Fort Lauderdale, FL
Moyle, Daniel T., Jr. ... Wheat Ridge, CO
Moyle, Daniel T., Jr., P.C.
Wheat Ridge, CO
Moyle & Draper, P.C. ... Salt Lake City, UT
Moyle, Flanigan, Katz, Kolins, Raymond & Sheehan, P.A. ... Tallahassee, FL
West Palm Beach, FL
Moyle, James F. ... New York, NY
Moyle, Jon C. ... Tallahassee, FL
West Palm Beach, FL
Moyle, Jon C., Jr. ... Tallahassee, FL
Moyle, Kenneth J., Jr. ... Bellevue, WA
Moyle, Michael R. ... San Francisco, CA
Moyle, O. Wood, III ... Salt Lake City, UT
Moyle, Paul O., III ... West Palm Beach, FL
Moylen, Gary W. ... Hackettstown, NJ
Moyler, J. Edward, Jr. ... Franklin, VA
Moyler, Moyler, Rainey & Cobb, P.L.C.
Courtland, VA
Franklin, VA
Moyles, Daniel C. ... Gilroy, CA
Moyles, David P. ... San Jose, CA
Moyles, Lisa J. ... Wilmington, DE
Moyles, M. Sean ... Tampa, FL
Moyles, Philip V. ... New York, NY
Moyna, John J. ... Whitehouse Station, NJ
Moynagh, Ellen Bober ... Boston, MA
Moynahan, Bernard T., Jr.
Nicholasville, KY
Moynahan, Irvin & Smith ... Lexington, KY
Nicholasville, KY
Moynahan, John H., Jr. ... Merritt Island, FL
Moynahan, Kevin P. ... Trenton, NJ
Moynahan, Ronald F. ... Boston, MA
Moynahan, Ruskin, Mascolo & Minnella
Waterbury, CT
Moynahan, Timothy C. ... Waterbury, CT
Moyne, Mary M. ... Okemos, MI
Moynihan, Brian T. ... Providence, RI
Moynihan, Brooke Burroughs ... Flint, MI
Moynihan, Cornelius J., Jr., (P.C.)
Boston, MA
Moynihan, Daniel J., III ... Burlington, MA
Moynihan, Daniel Sanderson ... Albany, NY
Moynihan, Daniel W. ... San Francisco, CA
Moynihan, David K. ... Portsmouth, NH
Moynihan, Denise K. ... Reading, MA
Moynihan, Edward C., III ... Schenectady, NY
Moynihan, G. Thomas, Jr. ... Lake George, NY
Moynihan, Gregory J. ... West Falls, NY
Moynihan, H. C. ... Laurel, MS
Moynihan, J. Terrence ... Riverside, CA
Moynihan, Jack B. ... San Antonio, TX
Moynihan, James J. ... Glastonbury, CT
Moynihan, James P. ... Seattle, WA
Moynihan, John F. ... Northbrook, IL
Moynihan, John J. ... Holyoke, MA
Moynihan, John J. ... Worcester, MA
Moynihan, John R. ... Flint, MI
Moynihan, John W. ... Chicago, IL
Moynihan, Kathleen M. ... Chicago, IL
Moynihan, Kelly J. ... San Francisco, CA
Moynihan, Kenneth M. ... Syracuse, NY
Moynihan, Lara S. ... Chicago, IL
Moynihan, Lorraine ... Ithaca, NY
Moynihan, Maria C. ... Lynnfield, MA
Moynihan, Michael A. ... Chicago, IL
Moynihan & Michalik ... Berlin, NH
Moynihan, Neil W. ... Schenectady, NY
Moynihan, Patrick J. ... Boston, MA
Moynihan, Patrick J. ... New York, NY
Moynihan, Peter T. ... New York, NY
Moynihan, Philip M. ... Wakefield, MA
Moynihan, Scott J. ... Woodbridge, NJ
Moynihan, Sean A. ... New York, NY
Moynihan, Shawn M. ... Hastings, MN
Moynihan, Timothy F. ... Minneapolis, MN
Moynihan, Wayne T. ... Berlin, NH
Moynihan Conneely, Mary ... Boston, MA
Moyse, Elizabeth H. ... Baltimore, MD
Beltsville, MD
Moyse, Todd R. ... Arlington, VA
Moyson, Peter ... Denver, CO
Mozarsky, Peter ... New York, NY
Mozarsky, Scott M. ... New York, NY
Mozdzierz, Kimberly A. ... Chicago, IL
Mozée, Bradley R. ... Miami, FL
Mozena, Peter J. ... Portland, OR
Vancouver, WA
Mozenter, Joyce S. ... Haddonfield, NJ
Philadelphia, PA
Mozenter, Karen B. ... Columbus, OH
Mozenter & Mozenter ... Haddonfield, NJ
Philadelphia, PA
Mozenter, Robert B. ... Philadelphia, PA
Mozer, Robert J. ... New York, NY
Mozer, Stefan I. ... Chicago, IL
Mozes, Sanford K. ... Philadelphia, PA
Mozes, Ted T. ... New York, NY
Mozey, Ann M.I. ... Minneapolis, MN
Mozier, Edward J., Jr. ... New Orleans, LA
Mozingo, Anthony A. ... Hattiesburg, MS
Mozingo, Glen R. ... Newport Beach, CA
Sacramento, CA
Mozingo, J. Flynn ... Montgomery, AL
Mozingo, James R. ... Jackson, MS
Mozingo, Jennifer Walley
Hattiesburg, MS
Mozingo, L. Elaine ... Columbia, SC
Mozingo Law Offices ... Columbia, SC
Mozingo & Price ... Sacramento, CA
Newport Beach, CA
Mozingo, Robert H. ... Mount Pleasant, SC
Mozingo, Sandra P. ... Washington, DC
Mozingo, T. Aladdin ... Columbia, SC
Mozinski, Lorene M. ... Manitowoc, WI
Mozinski, Richard P. ... Manitowoc, WI
Mozley, Finlayson & Loggins LLP
Atlanta, GA
Mozley, J. Arthur ... Atlanta, GA
Mozley, Robert E. ... Decatur, GA
Mozola, John ... Amarillo, TX
Mozola, John M. ... Cleveland, OH
Mozqueda, Maricela S. ... Brea, CA
Mozulay, Edmund E. ... San Diego, CA
MPR Law Practice, P.C. ... New York, NY
Mrachek, Jacqueline A. ... Minneapolis, MN
Mrachek, L. Louis ... West Palm Beach, FL
Mrak, Christine M. ... Seattle, WA
Mrakich, Nick N. ... Pasadena, CA
Mrava, Susan Lynn S. ... Washington, DC
Mraz, Edward S. ... Roselle, IL
Mraz, Frank A. ... Chicago, IL
Mraz, J. Douglas ... Joliet, IL
Mraz, John A. ... Charlotte, NC
Mraz, John A., P.A. ... Charlotte, NC
Mraz, Mary J. ... Albany, NY
Mraz, Paul J. ... Elkton, MD
Mraz, Robert ... Oconto, WI
Mraz, Valerie ... Riverside, CA
Mrischin, Sandra L.
Administrative Office Of The United States Courts, GV
Mrizek, Jerry J. ... Willowbrook, IL
Mrizek, Richard J. ... Washington, DC
Chicago, IL
Mrizek, Robert J. ... Des Moines, IA
Mrkonich, Marko J. ... Minneapolis, MN
Mrkonich-Wilson, Kathryn
Minneapolis, MN
Mrksich, K. Shannon ... Chicago, IL
Mrochek, Keith A. ... Charlotte, NC
Mroczka, Frank D. ... Dunmore, PA
Mroczka, Richard ... Sterling Heights, MI
Mroczkowski, Stanislaus S. ... New York, NY
Mroczynski, Randall P. ... Costa Mesa, CA
Mrofka, Kristine E. ... Long Beach, CA
Mrofka, Robert J. ... Carson, CA
Mrohaly, Clayton J. ... Cleveland, OH
Mros, Don J. ... Washington, DC
Mrose, James E. ... Washington, DC
Mrosek, Elaine W. ... Columbia, CT
Mrosek, John W. ... Fayetteville, GA
Mrosek, John W., P.C. ... Fayetteville, GA
Mrosek, Wendy E. ... Armonk, NY
Mross, Ann Marie ... Cambridge, MN
Mross, Audrey E. ... Dallas, TX
Mross, William F. ... Racine, WI
Mrowca, Jerome ... Houston, TX
Mrowicki, James M. ... Schaumburg, IL
Mrowiec, John S. ... Chicago, IL
Mrowka, Molly J. ... Oakland, CA
Mroz, Denise Incorvaia ... Philadelphia, PA
Mroz, Francis E. ... Vienna, VA
Mroz, Kenneth S. ... Pittsburgh, PA
Mroz, Michael A. ... Wood River, IL
Mroz, Richard S. ... Trenton, NJ
Mroz, Robert J. ... Albuquerque, NM
Mroz, Rosa ... Phoenix, AZ
Mroz, Scott D. ... San Francisco, CA
Mroz, Terry J. ... Grand Rapids, MI
Mrozek, Donald L. ... Chicago, IL
Mrozek, Michelle ... Chicago, IL
Mrozek, Ronald A. ... Cincinnati, OH
Mrozek, Therese A. ... Palo Alto, CA
Mrozik, Jennifer G. ... St. Paul, MN
Mrozinski, Bradley G. ... Freeland, MI
Mrozinski, Martin M. ... Bel Air, MD
Mrozinski, Walter J. ... Barrington, IL
Mrozowicz, Jos. R. ... Garfield, NJ
Mrozowski, Gail E. ... Chicago, IL
Mrozowski, Ted ... Grosse Pointe Woods, MI
Mrsich, John M. ... New York, NY
Mruk, Kevin G. ... Chicago, IL
Mrzlak, James N. ... Monte Vista, CO
Mrzlak, James N., P.C. ... Monte Vista, CO
Msall, Anita M. ... Chicago, IL
Mshomba, Elaine O'Halloran
Philadelphia, PA
Mtima, Lateef ... Philadelphia, PA
Mu, Richard A. ... Elizabethtown, NC
Fayetteville, NC
Jacksonville, NC
New Bern, NC
Shallotte, NC
Wilmington, NC
Muallem, Daniel E. ... Sacramento, CA
Muawad, Brian Elias ... St. Clair Shores, MI
Mubarak & Radcliffe, S.C. ... Tomah, WI

Mubarak, Robert J. ... Tomah, WI
Mubashir, Sarah ... New York, NY
Mucchetti, Monica ... Palo Alto, CA
Mucchetti, Peter J. ... Washington, DC
Mucci, Elizabeth Fitzsimmons
Hartford, CT
Mucci, Gary L. ... Buffalo, NY
Mucci, Lisa R. ... Santa Monica, CA
Mucci, Mark L. ... Newark, NJ
Mucci, Mark S. ... Fort Lauderdale, FL
Mucci, Ralph S. ... St. Petersburg, FL
Mucci, Robert R. ... Winnetka, IL
Muccia, Joseph W. ... New York, NY
Muccifori, John C. ... Washington, DC
Muccifori, Thomas A. ... Haddonfield, NJ
Muccifori, Thomas J. ... Toms River, NJ
Muccigrosso, Mark Robert ... New York, NY
Muccilli, Robert A. ... Mount Laurel, NJ
Muccini, Edward J. ... New York, NY
Muccini, Lesa S. ... Boston, MA
Muccino, Richard R. ... Summit, NJ
Mucciolo, Francis C. ... Jacksonville, FL
Mucen, Erol, Law Offices of
New York, NY
Much, Andrew L. ... Alpharetta, GA
Much, Barry John, Sr. ... Media, PA
Much, Joe W. ... Salem, OR
Much, Mark P. ... Media, PA
Much, Morrie ... Chicago, IL
Much Shelist Freed Denenberg Ament & Rubenstein, P.C. ... Chicago, IL
Mucha, Donna L. ... Treasury Department, Internal Revenue Service, GV
Mucha, Jeff ... Chicago, IL
Mucha, John, III ... Bloomfield Hills, MI
Mucha, John R. ... Detroit, MI
Mucha, Robert A. ... Bloomfield Hills, MI
Mucha, Robert A., P.C.
Bloomfield Hills, MI
Mucha, Teresa Weinreber ... Buffalo, NY
Muchin, Allan B., (P.C.) ... Chicago, IL
Muchin, Andrea K. ... Chicago, IL
Muchin, Arden A. ... Manitowoc, WI
Muchin, Arthur B. ... Chicago, IL
Muchin, Marc L. ... Chicago, IL
Muchlinski, Robert J. ... St. Paul, MN
Muchmore, Charles J. ... Phoenix, AZ
Muchmore, Clyde A. ... Oklahoma City, OK
Muchmore, Iris E. ... Cedar Rapids, IA
Muchmore, Susan M. ... Washington, DC
Muchmore & Wallwork, A Professional Corporation ... Phoenix, AZ
Muchnic, Daphne Nan ... Kansas City, MO
Muchnick, Adam E. ... Irvine, CA
Muchnick, Golieb and Golieb, P.C.
New York, NY
Muchnick, Howard W. ... New York, NY
Muchnick, Michael E. ... Fort Lauderdale, FL
Muchnick, Michael E., P.A.
Fort Lauderdale, FL
Muchnick, Nicole E. ... New York, NY
Muchnick, Robert J. ... New York, NY
Muchnick, Sanford L. ... Hollywood, FL
Muchnick, Steven A. ... St. Louis, MO
Muchnick, Todd I. ... St. Louis, MO
Muchnick, Wasserman, Dolin & Levine
Fort Lauderdale, FL
Hollywood, FL
Miami, FL
Muchnikoff, Dave M., (P.C.)
Washington, DC
Muchnikoff, Lee D. ... Treasury Department, Internal Revenue Service, GV
Muchow, Daniel L. ... Phoenix, AZ
Muchow, David J. ... Arlington, VA
Muchow, Marie T. Maiolo ... Santa Rosa, CA
Muchow, Richard L. ... Pittsburgh, PA
Muchunas, Peter J. ... Chicago, IL
Muchunas, Peter J. ... Great Falls, VA
Muck, Bruce E. ... Dallas, TX
Muck, Curtis G. ... Redondo Beach, CA
Muck, Douglas A. ... Lincoln, IL
Muck, Kevin P. ... San Francisco, CA
Muck, Laurie E. ... Lincoln, IL
Muck, Susan S. ... San Francisco, CA
Muck, Thomas R. ... Minneapolis, MN
Muckelroy, J. Ken ... Center, TX
Muckenfuss, Cantwell Faulkner, III
Washington, DC
Muckenfuss, Robert A. ... Columbia, SC
Muckenthaler, George J. ... Dayton, OH
Mucker, Robert A. ... Lafayette, IN
Muckerman, Christopher A. ... Cocoa, FL
Muckerman, John F. ... Miami Beach, FL
Muckey, Cynthia L. ... San Diego, CA
Muckle, Melanie Julian ... Louisville, CO
Mucklestone, Jeannie P. ... Seattle, WA
Mucklestone, John P. ... Seattle, WA
Mucklestone, John Patrick ... Seattle, WA
Mucklestone & Mucklestone ... Seattle, WA
Mucklestone, Patricia J. ... Seattle, WA
Mucklestone, Peter J. ... Seattle, WA
Mucklewee, James M. ... Buffalo, NY
Mucklow, Thomas O. ... Wheeling, WV
Muczynski, Michael ... Chicago, IL
Mudano, Mara A. ... West Palm Beach, FL
Mudano, Matthew S. ... Tampa, FL
Mudd, Alfred E. ... La Plata, MD
Mudd, Anne Chestney ... Oak Brook, IL
Mudd, Brian R. ... Green Bay, WI
Mudd, Charles L., Jr. ... Indianapolis, IN
Mudd, Chris ... Oklahoma City, OK
Mudd, David J. ... New York, NY
Mudd, Harrison & Burch ... Baltimore, MD
Towson, MD
Mudd, Jack E. ... Louisville, KY
Mudd, Jill A. ... Waterloo, IA
Mudd, Jo Ellen ... Vincent, AL
Mudd, John E. ... Towson, MD
Mudd, John E. ... San Juan, PR
Mudd, John F. ... La Plata, MD
Mudd, John O. ... Missoula, MT
Mudd, John P. ... Miami, FL
Mudd, Joseph E. ... Irvine, CA
Mudd, Joseph E., P.L.C. ... Irvine, CA
Mudd, Joseph G. ... Great Falls, MT
Mudd, Ken J. ... Louisville, KY
Mudd, Lee S. ... Shreveport, LA
Mudd, Mudd & Fitzgerald, P.A.
La Plata, MD
Waldorf, MD
Mudd, Nathaniel D. ... Belleville, IL
Mudd, Paul R. ... Independence, MO
Mudd, Richard J. ... Washington, DC
Mudd, Robert H., Jr. ... Mobile, AL
Mudd, Thomas F. ... La Plata, MD
Mudd, Timothy J. ... Kansas City, MO
Mudd, William A. ... Birmingham, AL
Mudd, William D. ... San Diego, CA
Mudder, Steven J. ... Atlanta, GA
Mudford, Douglas ... Redding, CA
Mudge, Anne E. ... San Francisco, CA
Mudge, Arthur W., II ... Lyme, NH
Mudge, Brian S. ... Washington, DC
Mudge, Carter A. ... Irvine, CA
Mudge, Katherine K. ... Austin, TX
Mudge, Nathan ... Santa Ana, CA
Mudge, Porter, Lundeen & Seguin, S.C.
Hudson, WI
Mudge, Richard T. ... Laguna Hills, CA
Mudge, Robert P. ... Sarasota, FL
Mudge, Robert W. ... Hudson, WI
Mudge, Stephen C. ... Edwardsville, IL
Mudge, William A. ... Edwardsville, IL
Mudge, Wilson D. ... Washington, DC
Mudgett, James R. ... Baltimore, MD
Mudick, Stephanie B. ... New York, NY
Mudie, F. Patricia ... Los Angeles, CA
Mudie, F. Patricia, A Professional Corporation ... Los Angeles, CA
Mudie, Kent W. ... Caledonia, MI
Grand Rapids, MI
Mudrich, Paul S. ... Palo Alto, CA
Mudrick, Daniel P. ... Norristown, PA
Mudrick, David P. ... Topeka, KS
Mudrick, Mary ... Topeka, KS
Mudrick, Richard C. ... Charleroi, PA
Mudrick & Zucker, P.C. ... Norristown, PA
Mudroch Halaska & Weaver, S.C.
Elm Grove, WI
Mudroch, Rudolph J. ... Elm Grove, WI
Fredonia, WI
Mudrow, Michael T. ... Portland, OR
Mudry, Joey J. ... Brook Park, OH
Mudter, George E., Jr. ... Nashville, TN
Muecke, Carl A. ... Phoenix, AZ
Muecke, Natalie J. ... Waltham, MA
Mueckenheim, Robert C. ... Grosse Ile, MI
Muedeking, Mark ... Washington, DC
Baltimore, MD
Muegenburg, F. T., Jr. ... Ventura, CA
Muehe, Martin E. ... Canandaigua, NY
Muehe & Muehe ... Canandaigua, NY
Muehe, Robert E. ... Canandaigua, NY
Muehl, Edward S. ... San Diego, CA
Santa Ana, CA
Muehlbauer, James K. ... West Bend, WI
Muehlbauer, William G. ... Cheektowaga, NY
Muehlberg, Stephen L. ... Stillwater, MN
Muehlberger, James P. ... Kansas City, MO
Muehle, Maurice L. ... Los Angeles, CA
Muehle & Whitman ... Los Angeles, CA
Muehlebach, L. Matthew ... Tucson, AZ
Muehleck, Donna M. ... Portland, OR
Muehleck, Thomas C. ... Camden, SC
Muehleisen, H. Richard ... Oklahoma City, OK
Muehleisen, Robert Alan, Jr.
Cincinnati, OH
Muehlenkamp & Pankowski ... Dellwood, MO
Muehlenkamp, V. Jack ... Dellwood, MO
Muehlenweg, Robert J. ... Albuquerque, NM
Muehler, Paul A. ... Hankinson, ND
Muehler, Todd A. ... Wahpeton, ND
Muehlfeld, Keith P. ... Napoleon, OH
Muehlgay, Jeffrey L. ... New York, NY
Muehlhausen, James K. ... Logansport, IN
Muehlhausen, John C. ... Logansport, IN
Muehlhausen, Laurel A. ... Kailua-Kona, HI
Muehlhauser, Constance J. ... Sandusky, OH
Muehlhauser, Douglas G.
Newport Beach, CA
Muehlhauser, Eric M. ... Sandusky, OH
Muehlhauser, George M., III
Sandusky, OH
Muehlhauser & Moore ... Sandusky, OH
Muehlig, Ralph J.
Department of Labor, GV
Muehlstein, John H. ... Chicago, IL
Muehlstein, Mary C. ... Chicago, IL
Muehr, Nicolle Nanasy ... Austin, TX
Muela, Arthur L. ... Austin, TX
Muelhausen, James A. ... Chicago, IL
Muelken, Francis E. ... Prior Lake, MN
Muelker, Ruth A. ... Austin, TX
Muellenberg, Erin L. ... Riverside, CA
Muellenberg, Kurt W. ... Washington, DC
Mueller, Abby Lynn ... Kansas City, MO
Mueller, Allan L. ... Glendale, WI
Mueller, Allen C. ... Springfield, IL
Mueller, Andrew Arthur ... Montrose, CO
Ouray, CO
Mueller, Angelika E. ... South Bend, IN
Mueller, Anna M. ... San Diego, CA
Mueller, Anne L. ... Chicago, IL
Mueller, A. R. ... New Ulm, MN
Mueller, Barbara J. ... Denver, CO
Mueller, Barry S. ... Lansing, IA
Postville, IA
Mueller, Betty I. ... Jefferson City, MO
Mueller, Bradley A. ... Chicago, IL
Mueller, Brian K. ... Booneville, AR
Mueller, Brian M. ... Phoenix, AZ
Mueller, C. Lawrence ... St. Louis, MO
Mueller, Carl G., Jr. ... Houston, TX
Mueller, Carl G., Jr., P.C. ... Houston, TX
Mueller, Carol Ann ... Philadelphia, PA
Mueller, Carolyn L. ... Dayton, OH
Mueller, Catherine E. ... Waukegan, IL
Mueller, Charles E. ... Vero Beach, FL
Mueller, Charles G. ... Florham Park, NJ
Mueller, Christine Charysh ... Naperville, IL
Mueller, Clifford T. ... Lenexa, KS
Mueller, Craig A. ... Las Vegas, NV
Mueller, Curt H. ... San Francisco, CA
Mueller, Daniel ... Seattle, WA
Mueller, Daniel G. ... Honolulu, HI
Mueller, Daniel M. ... San Ramon, CA
Mueller, David B. ... Aspen, CO
Mueller, David B. ... Peoria, IL
Mueller, David G. ... Racine, WI
Mueller, Dawn M. ... Chicago, IL
Mueller, Deborah L. P. ... Honolulu, HI
Mueller, Denise B. ... New York, NY
Mueller, Diana E. ... Cranbury, NJ
Mueller, Diana G. ... Oklahoma City, OK
Mueller, Diane M. ... Albuquerque, NM
Mueller, Dirk R. ... San Francisco, CA
Mueller, Donald G., Jr. ... St. Louis, MO
Mueller, Donna M. ... Boston, MA
Mueller, Donna Thompson
New Orleans, LA
Mueller, Douglas P. ... Minneapolis, MN
Mueller, Edward B. (IBA) **... Chicago, IL**
Mueller, Edward L. ... Santa Rosa, CA
Woodinville, WA
Mueller, Edward L. ... Seattle, WA
Mueller, Egon W. ... Mariposa, CA
Mueller, Elisabeth J. ... New York, NY
Mueller, Eric Byron ... Santa Monica, CA
Mueller, Eric P. ... Garden City, NY
Mueller, Ernst D. ... Jacksonville, FL
Mueller, Eugene E. ... New York, NY
Mueller, Frank A. ... Indianapolis, IN
Mueller, Frederick E. ... Los Angeles, CA
Mueller, Frederick S. ... Chicago, IL
Mueller & Gallios, P.C. ... Phoenix, AZ
Mueller, Gary J. ... West Caldwell, NJ
New York, NY
Mueller, Gary S. ... Joliet, IL
Mueller, Gene A. ... Big Bear City, CA
Mueller, George ... Ottawa, IL
Mueller, George A. ... Crystal Lake, IL
Mueller, George W. ... Denver, CO
Mueller, Glenn B. ... San Diego, CA
Mueller, Goss & Possi, S.C.
Milwaukee, WI
Mueller, Grace E. ... Los Angeles, CA
Mueller, Gregory A. ... Denver, CO
Mueller, Gregory J.
Federal Election Commission, Office of the General Counsel, GV
Mueller, Gregory James ... Grand Junction, CO
Mueller, Gregory K. ... Tenafly, NJ
Mueller, Gregory T. ... St. Louis, MO
Mueller, Harold A. ... Fort Worth, TX
Mueller, Heidi ... Santa Ana, CA
Mueller, Helmut ... Osceola, IA
Mueller, Henry E. ... Skokie, IL
Mueller, Herbert J. ... Milwaukee, WI
Mueller, Howard R. ... La Mesa, CA
Mueller, J. Phil ... Sheboygan, WI
Mueller, James E. ... Tucson, AZ
Mueller, James F. ... Clayton, MO
Mueller, James L. ... Medford, OR
Mueller, James P. ... Scottsdale, AZ
Mueller, James R. ... Chicago, IL
Mueller, James R. ... Kansas City, MO
Mueller, James T. ... Chicago, IL
Mueller, James W. ... Phoenix, AZ
Mueller, Janet L.
Palos Verdes Estates, CA
Mueller, Janet Smith ... Phoenix, AZ
Mueller, Janice M. ... Boston, MA
Mueller, Jay ... Orlando, FL
Mueller, Jeffrey J. ... Brooklyn, NY
Mueller, Jerry K., Jr. ... Columbus, OH
Mueller, Jess L. ... Elsberry, MO
Troy, MO
Mueller, John A. ... Los Angeles, CA
Mueller, John C. ... Los Angeles, CA
Mueller, John C. ... New York, NY
Mueller, John E. ... Mill Valley, CA
Sacramento, CA
San Francisco, CA
Mueller, John H. ... Tampa, FL
Mueller, John, III ... Kansas City, MO
Mueller, John J. ... Cincinnati, OH
Mueller, John M. ... Dayton, OH
Mueller, John P. ... St. Louis, MO
Mueller, John W. ... Mankato, MN
Mueller, Jon A. ... Department of Justice, Environment and Natural Resources Division, GV
Mueller, Joseph A. ... Morris, IL
Mueller, Joseph F. ... St. Louis, MO
Mueller, Joseph H. ... Belleville, IL
Kansas City, MO
St. Louis, MO
Mueller, Joseph P. ... Springfield, IL
Mueller, Karen A. Pepper
Oklahoma City, OK
Mueller, Karl A. ... Phoenix, AZ
Mueller, Kathleen M. ... Pittsburgh, PA
Mueller, Kathleen T. ... St. Louis, MO
Mueller, Kenneth N. ... Los Angeles, CA
Mueller, Kim J. ... Sacramento, CA
Mueller, Kimberly Jo ... Sacramento, CA
Mueller, Kirstin Ames ... Washington, DC
Mueller, Kurt Michael ... Baltimore, MD
Mueller, L. Robert ... Springfield, IL
Mueller, Laura C. ... Kansas City, MO
Mueller, Len C. ... Raleigh, NC
Mueller, Leslye A. ... Chicago, IL
Mueller, Lisa Kramer ... St. Louis, MO
Mueller, Lisa von Bargen ... Chicago, IL
Mueller, Lori Leff ... Seattle, WA
Mueller, Lowther and Vickery
New Ulm, MN
Sleepy Eye, MN
Mueller, Lynne M. ... Milwaukee, WI
Mueller, M. Cody ... Charleston, WV
Mueller, Marcia L. ... Rockford, IL
Mueller, Mark ... Dallas, TX
Mueller, Mark D. ... Niles, MI
Mueller, Mark E. ... Troy, MI
Mueller, Mark R. ... Eastpointe, MI
Mueller, Martin A. ... Rancho Mirage, CA
Mueller, Mary Beth ... Columbia, MO
Mueller, Maryann C.
Department of State, GV
Mueller, Marybelle D. ... Jackson, MO
Mueller, Melissa A. ... United States Senate, Senatorial Assistants, GV
Mueller, Melvin T. ... Bakersfield, CA
Mueller, Michael A. ... San Diego, CA
Mueller, Michael C. ... Lincoln, NE
Omaha, NE
Mueller, Michael D. ... Richmond, VA
Mueller, Michael J. ... Washington, DC
Mueller, Michael J. ... Chicago, IL
Mueller, Michelle L. ... Sacramento, CA
Mueller, Nicole K ... Washington, DC
Mueller, Norman R. ... Denver, CO
Mueller, Patricia R., P.A. ... Tavares, FL
Mueller, Patricia Rethwill ... Tavares, FL
Mueller, Patrick E. ... Nacogdoches, TX
Mueller, Paul A. ... Chamberlain, SD
Mueller, Paul A., Jr. ... Lancaster, PA
Mueller, Paul L. ... Phoenix, AZ
Mueller, Paula J. ... New York, NY
Mueller, Paulette ... Dallas, TX
Mueller, Peter E. ... Hackensack, NJ
Mueller, Peter Jerome ... San Diego, CA
Mueller, Peter O. ... Seattle, WA
Mueller, Philip A. ... Washington, DC
Mueller, Philip W. ... Schenectady, NY
Mueller, R. Carl, Jr. ... Kansas City, MO
Mueller, R. Kirk ... Denver, CO
Mueller, R. Terence ... St. Louis, MO
Mueller, Randall P. ... Tampa, FL
Mueller, Raymond A. ... Chicago, IL
Mueller, Raymond C. ... Akron, OH
Mueller, Raymond U. ... Philadelphia, PA
Mueller, Rebecca Megna ... New York, NY
Mueller, Renee ... Berkeley, CA
Mueller, Renee Ann ... Brenham, TX
Mueller, Richard A. ... St. Louis, MO
Mueller, Richard E. ... Chicago, IL
Mueller, Richard N. ... Barrington, IL
Mueller, Richard P. ... Warren, MI
Mueller, Richard T. ... Milwaukee, WI
Mueller, Robert C.
United States Court Of Appeals For The Armed Forces, GV
Mueller, Robert C. ... Framingham, MA
Mueller, Robert J. ... Wichita, KS
Mueller, Robert L. ... Springfield, IL
Mueller, Robert L., Jr.
Corpus Christi, TX
Mueller, Robert M. ... Oroville, CA
Mueller, Robert S., III ... Washington, DC
Mueller, Robert W. ... Reston, VA
Mueller, Roger J. ... Dodgeville, WI
Mueller, Ronald J. ... Davenport, IA
Mueller, Ronald O. ... Washington, DC
Mueller, Roy D., Jr. ... St. Louis, MO
Mueller, Royce W. ... Denver, CO
Mueller, Rudolf V. ... Stanwood, WA
Mueller, Russ R. ... Milwaukee, WI
Mueller, Scott J. ... Boston, MA
Mueller, Shirley A. ... Louisville, KY
Mueller, Shirley A. ... New York, NY
Mueller and Smith, A Legal Professional Association ... Columbus, OH
Mueller, Stanley R. ... Bartlesville, OK
Mueller, Stephen K. ... Madison, WI
Mueller, Stephen N. ... Cypress, TX
Mueller, Steven F. ... Denver, CO
Mueller and Suddarth ... Elsberry, MO
Troy, MO
Mueller, Sue ... Springfield, IL
Mueller, Susan J. ... Salt Lake City, UT
Mueller, Tara L. ... Oakland, CA
Mueller, Teresa A. ... Madison, WI
Mueller, Thad J. ... New Albany, MS
Oxford, MS
Mueller, Thomas F. ... San Jose, CA
Mueller, Thomas F. ... Houston, TX
Mueller, Thomas F., A Professional Corporation ... San Jose, CA
Mueller, Thomas J. ... Milwaukee, WI
Mueller, Thomas M. ... New York, NY
Mueller, Thomas R. ... Los Angeles, CA
Mueller, V. Joseph ... St. Petersburg, FL
Mueller, Vacek & Kiecke, L.L.P.
Austin, TX
Mueller, Venus D. ... Crystal Lake, IL
Mueller, Virginia S. ... Sacramento, CA
Mueller, Wally ... Cleveland, OH
Mueller, Walter H. ... Los Angeles, CA
Mueller, Wayne A. ... Austin, TX
Mueller, Werner D. ... Cleveland, OH

Mueller, Wesley O. .... Chicago, IL
Mueller, William A., Jr. .... Bloomington, IL
Mueller, William F. .... Morristown, NJ
Mueller, William G., Jr. .... Danvers, MA
Mueller, William J. .... Lincoln, NE
Mueller, William K. .... Topeka, KS
Mueller, William L. .... Moorestown, NJ
Philadelphia, PA
Mueller, Wolfgang .... Detroit, MI
Muellerleile, Mary Alice .... Oakland, CA
Muellerleile, Michael J.
Newport Beach, CA
Muello, Anthony G. .... Boston, MA
Muello, Paul J. .... Boston, MA
Muench, Brian J. .... Omaha, NE
Muench, Jack R. .... Springfield, MO
Muench, James A. .... Tampa, FL
Muench, John E. .... Chicago, IL
Muench, John H. .... Florence, SC
Muench, Lisa .... Philadelphia, PA
Muench, Marilyn L. .... Treasury Department, Office of the General Counsel, GV
Muench, Nils L. .... Bloomfield Hills, MI
Muench, Richard A. .... Irvine, CA
Muench, Richard A., Jr. .... Laguna Hills, CA
Muench, Robert W. .... Philadelphia, PA
Muench, William B. .... Jacksonville, FL
Muenchau, Daryl D. .... San Diego, CA
Muenchen, Rebecca A. .... Santa Clara, CA
Muench-McElfresh, Jennifer R.
Cincinnati, OH
Muenich, Michael L. .... Highland, IN
Muenkel, Joseph P. .... Amherst, NY
Buffalo, NY
Muenker, James P. .... Dallas, TX
Muennink, Lloyd A. .... Austin, TX
Muenster, John R. .... Seattle, WA
Muenster and Koenig, Inc., P.S. .... Seattle, WA
Muenster, Mark W. .... Vancouver, WA
Muensterman, Peggy A. .... Chicago, IL
Muenter, Laura Ryan .... Santa Rosa, CA
Muentzer, Colleen M. .... Chicago, IL
Muentzer, Ralph .... Chicago, IL
Muenz, Donald P. .... Columbus, OH
Muenz, Lawrence A. .... Dix Hills, NY
Muenz & Meritz, P.C. .... Dix Hills, NY
Muenzberg, W. Randall .... Los Angeles, CA
Muenzer, Franklin B. .... Manhattan Beach, CA
Muer, Sandra E. .... Naperville, IL
Mues, Gregory R. .... Louisville, KY
Mues, Robert L. .... Dayton, OH
Mues, Wesley C. .... Kearney, NE
Muessel, Christopher A. .... Washington, DC
Muessig, Craig .... Baytown, TX
Mueth, James J. .... Lee's Summit, MO
Mueth, Joseph E. .... Pasadena, CA
Mueth, Joseph E., A Law Corporation
Los Angeles, CA
Pasadena, CA
Muething, John L. .... Cincinnati, OH
Muething, Mark F. .... Cincinnati, OH
Muething, Paul V. .... Cincinnati, OH
Muething, Robert J. .... Atlanta, GA
Mueting, Ann Marie .... Minneapolis, MN
Mueting, Donald J. .... St. Paul, MN
Mueting, Raasch & Gebhardt, P.A.
Minneapolis, MN
Mueting, Richard E. .... Norfolk, NE
Mueting & Stoffer .... Norfolk, NE
Muetterties, John Henry .... Las Cruces, NM
Muffett, William Carroll .... Washington, DC
Muffler, Robert J. .... St. Louis, MO
Muffley, Michael D. .... Jim Thorpe, PA
Muffly, Daniel C. .... Omaha, NE
Muffly, Robert C. .... New York, NY
Mufson, Ann .... West Orange, NJ
Mufson, Ellen Z. .... Columbus, IN
Mufson, John E. .... Pembroke Pines, FL
Mufson, John E., P.A.
Pembroke Pines, FL
Mufson, Stacey A. .... San Francisco, CA
Mug, Thomas H. .... St. Louis, MO
Muga, Richard D. .... Tampa, FL
Mugalian, Richard A. .... Palatine, IL
Mugan, John R. .... Sioux City, IA
Mugane, Bridget R. .... Columbia, MD
Mugavero, Patricia S. .... Washington, DC
Mugavero, Philip .... Miami, FL
Mugavero, Thomas C. .... Chevy Chase, MD
Mugdan, Walter E. .... New York, NY
Mugel, Albert R. .... Buffalo, NY
Mugel, Christopher J. .... Richmond, VA
Mugel, Jonathan A. .... Buffalo, NY
Mugel, Richard L. .... Buffalo, NY
Mugel, Sarah J. Moore .... Buffalo, NY
Mugerian, George .... Troy, MI
Mugerian, Marjorie Nanian
Farmington Hills, MI
Mugford, James E., Sr. .... Philadelphia, PA
Mugg & Harper, L.L.P.
San Bernardino, CA
Mugg, Michael W. .... San Bernardino, CA
Mugge, Sara .... San Francisco, CA
San Jose, CA
Muggeo, Louis J. .... Salem, MA
Muggia, Frank C. .... Tonawanda, NY
Mugglebee, Michael J. .... San Diego, CA
Mugglebee & Mugglebee .... San Diego, CA
Mugglebee, Stephen T. .... San Diego, CA
Mugglin, Carl J. .... Delhi, NY
Mugherini, Neal F. .... Reading, MA
Mugler, Frederick B. .... Oakland, CA
Mugler, Molly S. .... Boston, MA
Mugno, Cheryl A. .... Albany, NY
Mugno, John R. .... New York, NY
Mugno, Scott A. .... Memphis, TN
Mugridge, David R., Law Offices of
Fresno, CA

Muha, Ronald L. .... Whitaker, PA
Muhammad, Mustafa A. .... San Francisco, CA
Muhammad, Nadiyah .... Norcross, GA
Muhammad-Starling, Khadijah
Kew Gardens, NY
Muhar, John J. .... Grand Rapids, MN
Muhic, Peter A. .... Philadelphia, PA
Muhic, Theresa M. .... Dayton, OH
Muhich, Stephen S. .... Grand Rapids, MI
Muhl & Dixon, P.A. .... Catonsville, MD
Muhl, Howard L., Jr. .... Catonsville, MD
Muhl, Kristin Ann .... Santa Monica, CA
Muhl, Phillip E. .... Burbank, CA
Muhlanger, Gilda O. .... Blue Bell, PA
Muhlbach, James B. .... Atlanta, GA
Muhlbach, Robert A. .... Los Angeles, CA
Muhlbauer, Deborah J. .... Williamsville, NY
Muhlbaum, Joel D., Law Offices of
Stamford, CT
Muhlbeier, Barbara .... Knoxville, TN
Muhlenbeck, Sandra A. .... Chicago, IL
Muhlenbruch Law Office .... Ackley, IA
Muhlenbruch, Robert H. .... Ackley, IA
Muhlendorf, Kevin .... Norfolk, VA
Muhlenkamp, Priscilla H. .... Iselin, NJ
Muhlestein, Randolph G.
Los Angeles, CA
Muhletaler, Catherine .... Philadelphia, PA
Muhlfelder, Leslie F. .... Easton, PA
Muhlhauser, Milton .... Jamaica, NY
Muhlhauser, Tara Lea .... Grand Forks, ND
Muhlheim Palmer & Wade, A Professional Corporation .... Eugene, OR
Muhlheim, Wilson C. .... Eugene, OR
Muhlitner, David R. .... San Jose, CA
Muhlstock, Arthur C. .... New York, NY
Muhlstock, Gary P. .... Albertson, NY
Muhlstock, Steven A. .... Morristown, NJ
Muhlstock, Steven D. .... Fort Lee, NJ
Muhlstock, Todd David .... New York, NY
Muhly, Aaron M. .... Chicago, IL
Muhm, Harvard W. .... St. Louis, MO
Muhr, Robert A. .... Chicago, IL
Muhr, William D. .... Portsmouth, VA
Muhs, Peter L., (Professional Corporation)
San Francisco, CA
Muhs, Robert E. .... Garden City, NY
Mui, Bann Hiu-Fai .... Sacramento, CA
Mui, Thomas L. .... Honolulu, HI
Mui, Wanda .... Bradenton, FL
Muia, Joseph, Jr. .... Albany, NY
Muije, John W. .... Las Vegas, NV
Muije & Varricchio, A P.C.
Las Vegas, NV
Muilenberg, Chad O'Neal
San Francisco, CA
Muilenburg, Erin O'Neal
San Francisco, CA
Muilenburg, Melissa A. .... Elmwood Park, NJ
Muilenburg, Rafael F. .... San Diego, CA
Muilenburg, Robert W. .... Morristown, NJ
Muilenburg, Thomas H. .... Sioux Falls, SD
Muina, Margarita P. .... Miami, FL
Muir, Allan M. .... Portland, ME
Muir, Annette A. .... Syracuse, NY
Muir, Anthony Moyer .... Allentown, PA
Muir, Arthur B., (P.C.) .... Chicago, IL
Muir, Brenda C. .... Los Altos, CA
Muir, Brockett .... Kensington, MD
Muir, Bruce R. .... Denver, CO
Muir, Celeste Hardee .... Miami, FL
Muir, Costello & Carlson
Heron Lake, MN
Jackson, MN
Lakefield, MN
Muir, Dana M. .... Bloomfield Hills, MI
Muir, David J. .... Bristol, IN
Muir, David L. .... Pasadena, CA
Muir, Dennis J. .... Media, PA
Muir, Donald S. .... Paducah, KY
Muir, Donald W., Jr., Law Offices of
San Antonio, TX
Muir, Douglas A. .... Boston, MA
Muir, Gordon R. .... Reno, NV
Muir, Gregory A. .... Bakersfield, CA
Muir, Gregory R. .... Rockville, MD
Muir, Herman S., III .... Portland, OR
Muir, Hugh B. .... Albuquerque, NM
Muir, J. Dapray .... Washington, DC
Washington, DC
Muir, Jo-Ann McNally .... Alexandria, VA
Muir, John .... Houston, TX
Muir, John D., Jr. .... Washington, DC
Muir, John Edward .... Reading, PA
Muir, Karen G. .... State College, PA
Muir, Kenneth M. .... Harlingen, TX
Muir, Linda T. .... Atlanta, GA
Muir, Malcolm .... Williamsport, PA
Muir, Mary L. .... Los Angeles, CA
Muir, Maylon G. .... Punta Gorda, FL
Muir, Megan L. .... Kirkland, WA
Muir, Melinda N. .... Los Angeles, CA
Muir, Patrick D. .... Washington, DC
Muir, Phillip R. .... Portland, OR
Muir, R. Douglas .... Austin, TX
Muir, Richard B. .... Hilton, NY
Muir, Richard D. .... Vista, CA
Muir, Richard R. .... Ontario, CA
Muir, Robert A., Jr. .... Brooklyn, NY
Muir, Robert E. .... San Diego, CA
Muir, Robert F. .... Peoria, IL
Muir, Robert, III .... East Hanover, NJ
Muir, Robert S. .... Indiana, PA
Muir, Robert Warren .... Salem, OR
Muir, Ross M. .... Rochester, MN
Muir, Sally A. .... New York, NY
Muir, Samuel J. .... Pasadena, CA
Muir, Scott B. .... Boise, ID

Muir & Troutman .... Portland, OR
Muir, William T. .... Miami, FL
Muirden, Marjorie Anne .... Sharon Center, OH
Muirhead, Andrea .... Concord, NH
Muirhead, Christopher P.
Albuquerque, NM
Muirhead, Donald W. .... Boston, MA
Muirhead, Gaylor & Belle, P.A.
Sarasota, FL
Venice, FL
Venice, FL
Muirhead, James D. .... Hackensack, NJ
Muirhead, James R. .... Concord, NH
Muirhead, Mary Lou .... Braintree, MA
Muirhead, Michael L. .... Ventura, CA
Muirhead, William A. .... Sarasota, FL
Muise, Judith Ann .... Oklahoma City, OK
Muise, Patricia H., (P.C.) .... Duluth, GA
Mujica, John C. .... New York, NY
Mujica-Cotto, Esteban .... San Juan, PR
Mujtabaa, Khaled S. .... Honolulu, HI
Mukai, Dennis .... Los Angeles, CA
Mukai, Donald M. .... Bellevue, WA
Mukai, Francis K. .... Honolulu, HI
Mukai, Franklin K. .... Honolulu, HI
Mukai, John S. .... Honolulu, HI
Mukai, Mark K. .... Honolulu, HI
Mukai, Robert G. .... Alexandria, VA
Mukai, Robert L. .... Sacramento, CA
Mukai, Shaun M. .... Honolulu, HI
Mukai, Stanley Y. .... Honolulu, HI
Mukaida, Wayne H. .... Honolulu, HI
Mukamal, Betsy J. .... Chicago, IL
Mukamal, Steven S. .... New York, NY
Mukamal, Stuart S. .... Milwaukee, WI
Mukasey, Michael B. .... New York, NY
Mukatis, W. Alfred .... Corvallis, OR
Mukerji, Indranil "Indy" .... Boston, MA
Mukherjee, Misti .... Fairfax, VA
Mukherjee, Sanjoy .... Springfield, NJ
Mukherji, Mala .... Woodland Hills, CA
Mukhey, Ashok W. .... Los Angeles, CA
Mukhoty, Sumita
Federal Communications Commission, Common Carrier Bureau, GV
Muktarian, Edw. S. .... Sacramento, CA
Mukuna, Hazel A.W. .... New York, NY
Mulac, Carol A. .... Cleveland, OH
Mulach, Ronald W.
Department of Agriculture, Office of the General Counsel, GV
Mulack, Donald G. .... Chicago, IL
Mulae & Gelsomino .... Chicago, IL
Mulae, Paul A. .... Chicago, IL
Mulally, Edw. D. .... St. Paul, MN
Mulally, Thomas R. .... Sherman Oaks, CA
Mulanax, Virgil E. .... Bandera, TX
Mulaney, Charles W., Jr. .... Chicago, IL
Mulaney, Ellen Stanton .... Chicago, IL
Mular, Wayne L. .... St. Charles, IL
Mularadelis, Chris .... New York, NY
Mularski, Raymond J. .... Columbus, OH
Mularski, Raymond J. .... Gahanna, OH
Mulbarger, Matthew J. .... Worthington, OH
Mulbarger, Mitchell F. .... Santa Monica, CA
Mulcahey, Catherine Rotroff .... Lake Park, FL
Mulcahey, Danielle M. .... Scranton, PA
Mulcahey, Garie J. .... Bridgeport, CT
Mulcahey, John M. .... Scranton, PA
Mulcahey, Richard T. .... Scranton, PA
Mulcahey, Richard T., Jr.
Philadelphia, PA
Mulcahey-Hampson, Kathleen
Manchester, NH
Mulcahy, Benjamin R. .... Los Angeles, CA
Mulcahy, Brian J. .... Chicago, IL
Mulcahy, Brian J. .... Hicksville, NY
Mulcahy, Brian Thomas .... Boston, MA
Mulcahy, Casey & Mulcahy, P.C.
Detroit, MI
Southfield, MI
Mulcahy, Charles C. .... Milwaukee, WI
Mulcahy, Charles D. .... Raynham, MA
Mulcahy, Christine E. .... Long Beach, CA
Mulcahy, Daniel J. .... Washington, DC
Mulcahy, Daniel J. .... Chicago, IL
Mulcahy, Delaina .... Houston, TX
Mulcahy, Donna .... Austin, TX
Mulcahy, Edwin C., Jr. .... Washington, DC
Mulcahy, Elizabeth C. .... Northampton, MA
Mulcahy, Eugene J. .... Springfield, MA
Mulcahy, Francis J., Jr. .... Alpharetta, GA
Mulcahy, James H. .... Southfield, MI
Mulcahy, James M. .... Brea, CA
Mulcahy, Jane M.R. .... Milwaukee, WI
Mulcahy, John .... New York, NY
Mulcahy, John F., Jr. .... Hartford, CT
Mulcahy, John J., Jr. .... Ramsey, NJ
Mulcahy, Joseph F., Jr. .... Media, PA
Mulcahy, Kathleen A. .... Detroit, MI
Mulcahy, Kathleen A. .... Brooklyn, NY
Mulcahy, Kevin G. .... Brooklyn, NY
Mulcahy, Marcia A. .... Cape Girardeau, MO
Mulcahy, Maureen E. .... Woonsocket, RI
Mulcahy, Michael D. .... Bloomfield Hills, MI
Mulcahy, Michael E. .... Springfield, MA
Mulcahy, Michael J. .... Detroit, MI
Mulcahy, Michael J. .... Cranston, RI
Mulcahy, Michael J. .... West Bend, WI
Mulcahy, Michael R. .... Chicago, IL
Mulcahy, Michael T. .... Cleveland, OH
Mulcahy, Patrick F. .... Southfield, MI
Mulcahy, Peter H. .... Morristown, NJ
Mulcahy, Robert J. .... San Diego, CA
Mulcahy, Robert L. .... Seaford, NY
Mulcahy, Robert W. .... San Jose, CA
Red Bank, NJ
Mulcahy, Robert W. .... Milwaukee, WI

Mulcahy, Rodney Eric .... Charles City, IA
Mulcahy, Stephen F. .... Milton, MA
Mulcahy, Thomas L. .... Southfield, MI
Mulcahy, Thomas M. .... Bedminster, NJ
Mulcahy, Timothy .... Minneapolis, MN
Mulcahy, Timothy T. .... Kansas City, MO
Mulcahy, William D. .... Denver, CO
Mulcaire, George P. .... Irvine, CA
Mulcare, Michael F. .... Kenmore, WA
Mulcare, Ronald J. .... San Mateo, CA
Mulchay, Michael V. .... Phoenix, AZ
Mulchinock, David S. .... Princeton, NJ
Mulcrone, Jennifer Foley .... Atlanta, GA
Mulcrone, John W. .... Southfield, MI
Muldawer, Jeffrey A. .... Philadelphia, PA
Mulder, Andrew J. .... Holland, MI
Mulder, C. Christopher .... Santa Ana, CA
Mulder, Clara J. .... Tampa, FL
Mulder, Delwyn J. .... Glens Falls, NY
Mulder, Douglas D. .... Dallas, TX
Mulder, Gerald S. .... La Mesa, CA
Mulder, Jill S .... Grand Rapids, MI
Mulder, Kyndra L. .... Colorado Springs, CO
Mulder, Marc .... Waterford, MI
Mulder, Michael M. .... Chicago, IL
Mulder, Michelle .... Dallas, TX
Mulder, R. Troy .... Indianapolis, IN
Mulder, Russell E. .... Anchorage, AK
Mulder, Stephen J. .... Grand Rapids, MI
Mulder, Steven E. .... Anchorage, AK
Mulder, Theresa .... New York, NY
Mulder, Thomas J. .... Grand Rapids, MI
Mulderig, John J. .... New York, NY
Mulderig, Kevin M. .... Philadelphia, PA
Mulderig, Robert J. .... Carlisle, PA
Mulderink, Rudy Alan .... Palos Hills, IL
Mulderrig, Ann O. .... Stamford, CT
Mulderry, Francis P. .... Albany, NY
Mulderry, Maureen .... Westwood, MA
Muldoon, Brian .... Denver, CO
Muldoon, Bruce A. .... New City, NY
Muldoon, Catherine A. .... Westfield, NJ
Muldoon, Deborah L. .... Binghamton, NY
Muldoon, Edward T. .... Milton, MA
Muldoon, Francis H., Jr. .... Key West, FL
Muldoon, Freda Bein .... Boston, MA
Muldoon, Gary .... Rochester, NY
Muldoon, Horgan & Loughman
New Rochelle, NY
Muldoon, James B. .... Boston, MA
Muldoon, James R. .... Syracuse, NY
Muldoon, John E. .... Riverside, IL
Muldoon, John J. .... Chicago, IL
Muldoon, John J., III .... Chicago, IL
Muldoon, Joseph A., III .... Washington, DC
Muldoon, Joseph A., Jr. .... Washington, DC
Muldoon, Joseph L. .... St. Paul, MN
Muldoon, Joseph W. .... Glen Cove, NY
Muldoon, Joseph W., Jr. .... Glen Cove, NY
Muldoon, Margaret A. .... Boston, MA
Muldoon, Mark Edward .... Boston, MA
Muldoon, Marlow J., II .... Dallas, TX
Muldoon, Meghan E. .... Washington, DC
Muldoon, Michael K. .... Chicago, IL
Muldoon & Muldoon .... Glen Cove, NY
Muldoon, Murphy & Faucette
Washington, DC
Muldoon, Patrick M. .... Grand Rapids, MI
Muldoon, Robert J., Jr. .... Boston, MA
Muldoon, Sheila M. .... Irvine, CA
Muldoon, Thomas J. .... Chicago, IL
Muldoon, Thomas P., Jr. .... Philadelphia, PA
Muldoon, Thomas W. .... Boston, MA
Muldoon, William C., Jr. .... Binghamton, NY
Muldoon, William D. .... Red Lake Falls, MN
Muldoon, William P. .... Wilmington, CA
Muldowney, John J. .... Malone, NY
Muldowney, John J. .... Philadelphia, PA
Muldowney, Laura Carberry
Philadelphia, PA
Muldowney, Leslie B. .... Boston, MA
Muldowney, Patrick M. .... Orlando, FL
Muldowney, Patrick T. .... Chicago, IL
Muldowney, Shawn R. .... Youngstown, OH
Muldowney, Steven M. .... Irvine, CA
Muldowney, Timothy A. .... Overland Park, KS
Muldowney, Timothy J. .... Madison, WI
Muldrew, Michael .... Statesboro, GA
Muldrow, Cynthia E. .... Torrance, CA
Muldrow, Ken .... Brownfield, TX
Muldrow, Lee J. .... Little Rock, AR
Muldrow, Louis S. .... Waco, TX
Muldrow, W. Stephen .... San Juan, PR
Muldrow, Wayne S. .... Chicago, IL
Muldrow-Harris, Joy D. .... Columbus, OH
Mulé, Ann C. .... Philadelphia, PA
Mulé, Barbara .... Albany, NY
Mulé, David Brian .... Palm Springs, CA
Mule, Joseph A. .... Jericho, NY
Mulé, Joseph R. .... Commack, NY
Mule, Lawrence C. .... Glendale, NY
Mule, Linda Agnes .... Garden City, NY
Mule, Mary J. .... New York, NY
Mule, Michael A. .... Metairie, LA
Mulé, Michael C. .... Newark, NJ
New York, NY
Mule, Richard P. .... Trenton, NJ
Mulé, Robert M. .... Hartford, CT
Mule, Salvadore T. .... New Orleans, LA
Mulea, Annette M. .... Portland, OR
Mulera, Raymond R. .... Washington, DC
Mulert, Tara Gill
General Services Administration, Office of Regional Counsel, GV
Mulet, Joan .... San Juan, PR
Muley, Theresa N. .... Pleasanton, CA
Mulford, Anthony S. .... Chesapeake, VA
Mulford, David A. .... San Francisco, CA

Mulford, Elizabeth B. ....Cupertino, CA
Mulford, John G. ....Wilmington, DE
Cherry Hill, NJ
Mulford, Michael K. ....Kellogg, IA
Mulford, Michael K., PLC ....Kellogg, IA
Mulford, Michael W. ....Kirksville, MO
Mulford, Robert D. ....San Francisco, CA
Mulford, Ross Clayton ....Dallas, TX
Mulford, Sharon N. ....Hood River, OR
Mulford, William C., II ....Annapolis, MD
Mulgrew, D. Brent ....Columbus, OH
Mulgrew, James J. ....Santa Ana, CA
Mulgrew, John C., Jr. ....Peoria, IL
Mulgrew, John P. ....Washington, DC
Mulhall, Deborah Ross ....Weirton, WV
Mulhall, Edward, Jr.
Glenwood Springs, CO
Mulhall, Francis B. ....Metairie, LA
Mulhall, Francis B. ....New Orleans, LA
Mulhall, Frank J. ....Boca Raton, FL
Mulhall, Frank J., P.A. ....Boca Raton, FL
Mulhall, Gerard Lawrence ....Patchogue, NY
Mulhall, Jack ....Harrisburg, PA
Mulhall, James A., Jr. ....Naugatuck, CT
Mulhall, James J. A. ....Springfield, NJ
Mulhall, James T. ....Glendale, AZ
Mulhall, Jeffrey B. ....Garden City, NY
Mulhall, John T., III ....Boca Raton, FL
West Palm Beach, FL
Mulhall, Joseph Daniel ....Cambridge, MA
Mulhall, Lisa N. ....Delray Beach, FL
Mulhall, Thomas A. ....Louisville, KY
Mulhall, Turner, Hoffman & Coombs
Jeffersonville, IN
Louisville, KY
Mulhall, W. Thomas ....Louisville, KY
Mulhauser, Frederick R. ....Petoskey, MI
Mulhearn, Christopher M. ....Providence, RI
Mulhearn, John E., Jr. ....Natchez, MS
Mulhearn & Mulhearn ....Natchez, MS
Mulhearn, Richard A., & Associates, P.C.
Worcester, MA
Mulhearn, Richard A., Jr. ....Worcester, MA
Mulherin, Bernard J., Sr ....Augusta, GA
Mulherin, Brian G. ....Los Angeles, CA
Mulherin, John M. ....Wheaton, IL
Mulherin, Joseph A., III ....Savannah, GA
Mulherin, Joseph H. ....Flemington, NJ
Mulherin, Kelli Nabors ....Mobile, AL
Mulherin, Rehfeldt & Varchetto, P.C.
Geneva, IL
Wheaton, IL
Mulherin, W. Austin, III ....Mobile, AL
Mulhern, Brian J. ....Chicago, IL
Mulhern, David K. ....Concord, NH
Portsmouth, NH
Mulhern, Edwin J. ....Carle Place, NY
Mulhern, Edwin J. ....Mineola, NY
Mulhern, Edwin T. ....Carle Place, NY
Mulhern, Eugene E. ....Stamford, CT
Mulhern, Harriet Guber ....New York, NY
Mulhern, J. Barry ....Londonderry, NH
Mulhern, James F. ....Cleveland, OH
Mulhern, John E. ....Newton, NJ
Mulhern, John F. ....Boston, MA
Mulhern, John P. ....Newark, NJ
Mulhern, Jos. J., Jr. ....Boston, MA
Mulhern, Joseph J. ....Rockville, MD
Mulhern, Joseph P. ....Chicago, IL
Mulhern, Joseph P. ....Chicago, IL
Mulhern & Klein ....Wantagh, NY
Mulhern, Mathew F. ....Kansas City, MO
Mulhern, Michael L. ....Chicago, IL
Mulhern, Patrick J. ....New York, NY
Mulhern, Patrick J., Jr. ....Wantagh, NY
Mulhern and Patterson ....Rockville, MD
Mulhern, Paul C. ....Napa, CA
Mulhern, Pegeen ....Seattle, WA
Mulhern, Peter T.
Department Of Veterans Affairs,
Office of Management, GV
Mulhern, Richard W. ....Portland, ME
Mulhern, Robert B., Jr. ....Philadelphia, PA
Mulhern, Robert M., Jr. ....Berwyn, PA
Mulhern, Sally H. ....Concord, NH
Portsmouth, NH
Mulhern & Scott, Professional Association
Concord, NH
Portsmouth, NH
Mulhern, Thomas F. ....Des Plaines, IL
Mulhern, Timothy P. ....Springfield, MA
Mulhollan, Erin F. ....Philadelphia, PA
Mulhollan, John S. ....Columbus, OH
Mulhollan, Thurman L. ....Corpus Christi, TX
Mulholland, Angela Broadway
Mount Pleasant, SC
Mulholland, Brian B. ....Hauppauge, NY
Mulholland, Brian E. ....Haddonfield, NJ
Mulholland, Carrie L. ....St. Louis, MO
Mulholland, Catherine S. ....Dover, DE
Mulholland, Daniel J. ....Jackson, MS
Mulholland, Daniel M., III ....Pittsburgh, PA
Mulholland, David T. ....Seattle, WA
Mulholland, Donna A. ....Easton, PA
Mulholland, Edwin M. ....New York, NY
Mulholland, Ellin M. ....New York, NY
Mulholland, F. Edward, II ....Las Vegas, NV
Mulholland & Hickey ....Washington, DC
Mulholland, Howard F. ....Kew Gardens, NY
Mulholland, James C. ....Glastonbury, CT
Mulholland, Joe ....Philadelphia, MS
Mulholland, John F. ....Hicksville, NY
Mulholland, John H. ....Greenport, NY
Mulholland, Joyce Holtzman ....Miami, FL
Mulholland, Kathleen M. ....Westfield, NJ
New York, NY
Mulholland, Kelly C. ....Palo Alto, CA
Mulholland & Knapp ....New York, NY
Mulholland, Kristin A. ....Merrillville, IN
Mulholland, Linda F. ....Santa Clara, CA
Mulholland, Mark Steven ....Mineola, NY
Mulholland, Maryjane ....St. Paul, MN
Mulholland, Maryjane, P.C. ....St. Paul, MN
Mulholland, Maureen E. ....Rochester, NY
Mulholland, Minion & Roe
Williston Park, NY
Mulholland, Neven J. ....Fort Dodge, IA
Mulholland, Richard R. ....Tampa, FL
Mulholland, Robert E. ....Atlanta, GA
Mulholland, Roberta J. ....Wakefield, RI
Mulholland, Shane C. ....Fort Wayne, IN
Mulholland, Thad R. ....Columbia, MO
Mulholland, William F., II
Los Angeles, CA
Mulhollen, Roger D. ....Racine, WI
Mulichak, Hydee J. ....Los Angeles, CA
Orange, CA
Mulick, Mark ....Paterson, NJ
Mulick, Nicholas W. ....Islamorada, FL
Mulick, Nicholas W., P.A. ....Islamorada, FL
Mulieri, Vincent A. ....Glen Burnie, MD
Mulinex, Joy A. ....Washington, DC
Mulinix Ogden & Hall, P.A. ....Norman, OK
Oklahoma City, OK
Mulinix, Russell L. ....Norman, OK
Oklahoma City, OK
Mulitauaopele, Leiviifiloa S. ....Pago Pago, TT
Mulitz, Andrew G.
Federal Communications Commission,
Common Carrier Bureau, GV
Mulitz, Barbara C. ....Kensington, MD
Mulitz, Michael C. ....New York, NY
Mulkeen, James P. ....Los Angeles, CA
Mulkeen, John R. ....Jersey City, NJ
Mulkerin, John P. ....Edison, NJ
Mulkerin, Mark J. ....Los Angeles, CA
Mulkern, Joseph S. ....Boston, MA
Mulkern, Laureen A. ....Boston, MA
Mulkern, Paul V., Jr. ....Boston, MA
Mulkern, Robert V. ....Worcester, MA
Mulkey, Bruce L. ....Rogers, AR
Mulkey, Loyd H., Jr. ....Oroville, CA
Mulkey, Melissa M. ....Philadelphia, PA
Mulkey, Michael S. ....Newport News, VA
Mull, Allison B. ....McLean, VA
Mull, Archibald M., III, Law Office of
Sacramento, CA
Mull, Corinne M. ....Decatur, GA
Mull, Donald P., Co. (L.P.A.)
Cleveland, OH
Mull, Gale W. ....Atlanta, GA
Mull, Gale W., P.C. ....Atlanta, GA
Mull, George Warren ....Sacramento, CA
Mull, John C. ....Sun City, AZ
Sun City West, AZ
Mull, John G. ....Prescott, AZ
Mull, John R. ....Morganton, NC
Mull, Keith C. ....Front Royal, VA
Mull and Marsh, P.L.L.C. ....Sun City, AZ
Sun City West, AZ
Mull, Pamela A. ....Spokane, WA
Mull, Rex R. ....Bakersfield, CA
Mull, Rhoda J. ....Oklahoma City, OK
Mull, Richard E. ....Ames, IA
Mull, Richard L. ....Seattle, WA
Mull, Thomas W. ....Covington, LA
Mulla, James F., Jr. ....New Orleans, LA
Mullady, Christopher E. ....Boston, MA
Mullady, James M. ....Champaign, IL
Mullady, Raymond G., Jr. ....Baltimore, MD
Mullahy, James ....Boston, MA
Mullahy, John B. ....New York, NY
Mullahy, John M. ....Framingham, MA
Mullally, Claire M. ....Brooklyn, NY
Mullally, David S. ....Carmel Valley, CA
Mullally, Kathe Flinker ....Trenton, NJ
Mullally, Lawrence E. ....Oakland, CA
Mullally, Michael E. ....Jonesboro, AR
Mullally, Michael G. ....Seward, NE
Mullally, Neil G. ....Muskegon, MI
Mullally, Pierce H. ....Miami, FL
Mullally, Veronica ....New York, NY
Mullaly, Andrew P. ....El Cajon, CA
Mullaly & Diefenbach ....Pennington, NJ
Mullaly, E. James, III ....Pennington, NJ
Mullaly, Paula A. ....Pennington, NJ
Mullaly, Richard E. ....West Lebanon, NH
Mullaly, Rosemary E. ....Doylestown, PA
Mullan, Anne M. ....Cherry Hill, NJ
Mullan, Bob ....Denver, CO
Mullan, Jeffrey B. ....Boston, MA
Mullan, John Andrew ....New York, NY
Mullan, John Gibson ....Washington, DC
Mullan, John H. ....Los Angeles, CA
Mullan, John H. ....Chicago, IL
Mullan, Mary Jo ....New York, NY
Mullan, Richard G. ....New York, NY
Mullanax, M. Greg ....Fort Worth, TX
Mullane, Daniel C. ....Chelsea, MA
Mullane, E. Peter ....Vineyard Haven, MA
Mullane, Hugh G. ....Department of Justice,
Civil Division, GV
Mullane, John F. ....Solana Beach, CA
Mullane, John J., Jr. ....San Francisco, CA
Mullane, John J., Jr., Inc.
San Francisco, CA
Mullane, Maria C. ....Allentown, PA
Mullane, Michael W. ....Portland, ME
Mullane, Philip E. ....Chicago, IL
Mullane, Sheri L. ....Jacksonville, FL
Mullane, Sonja S. ....Falls Church, VA
Mullane, Terence M. ....Park City, UT
Mullaney, A. James, III ....Jacksonville, FL
Mullaney, Anne D. ....Pittsburgh, PA
Mullaney, Anne-Marie ....Kew Gardens, NY
Mullaney, Brian A. ....Jefferson, ME
Mullaney, Charles P. ....Danbury, CT
Mullaney, Christina H. ....Bronx, NY
Mullaney, Diane P. ....Treasury Department,
Bureau of Engraving and Printing, GV
Mullaney, Edward J. ....Kensington, MD
Mullaney, Eleanor K. ....Saratoga Springs, NY
Mullaney, Elizabeth A. ....Simsbury, CT
Mullaney, Gerald J., Sr. ....Red Hill, PA
Mullaney, Gerard J. ....Whitestone, NY
Mullaney, James Leo ....Kingsville, MD
Mullaney, John J. ....New York, NY
Mullaney, John T., Jr. ....Tinton Falls, NJ
Mullaney, Joseph E. ....Boston, MA
Mullaney, Joseph E., III ....Boston, MA
Mullaney, Joseph F. ....Flint, MI
Saginaw, MI
Mullaney, Joseph L. ....Scranton, PA
Mullaney, Joseph P. ....Whitestone, NY
Mullaney, Kenneth F., Jr. ....Montclair, NJ
Mullaney, Martin P. ....Skippack, PA
Mullaney, Mary Ann ....Philadelphia, PA
Mullaney, Matthew J. ....Clarksburg, WV
Mullaney, Michael J. ....Miami, FL
Mullaney, Michael P. ....Latham, NY
Mullaney, Patrick J. ....Seattle, WA
Mullaney, Paul V. ....Worcester, MA
Mullaney, Peter F. ....Milwaukee, WI
Mullaney, Richard A. ....Jacksonville, FL
Mullaney, Richard F. ....Saratoga Springs, NY
Mullaney, Richard R. ....Bloomfield Hills, MI
Mullaney & Richardson, A Prof. Assn.
Rochester, NH
Mullaney, Robert D. ....San Francisco, CA
Mullaney, Stanley J. ....Rochester, NH
Mullaney, Thomas F., Jr. ....New York, NY
Mullaney, Thomas J. ....Leominster, MA
Mullaney, Thomas J. ....New York, NY
Mullaney, Thomas M. ....New York, NY
Mullaney, Thomas P., III ....Glastonbury, CT
Mullaney, Timothy F. ....Warwick, RI
Mullaney-Westfall, Colleen C.
Lancaster, NY
Mullans & Piersel ....Pueblo, CO
Mullans, Thomas J. ....Pueblo, CO
Mullany, John T. ....Butte, MT
Mullany, Linda Hunt ....San Diego, CA
Mullany, Mary J. ....Philadelphia, PA
Mullany, Sean ....Albany, NY
Mullare, Amy E. ....Boston, MA
Mullare, T. Kenwood, Jr. ....Exeter, NH
Mullarkey, Catherine A. ....Melville, NY
Mullarkey, Daniel P. ....Department of Justice,
Tax Division, GV
Mullarkey, Edward J. ....Rocky Hill, CT
Mullarkey, Kathleen M. ....Jersey City, NJ
Mullarkey, Mary J. ....Denver, CO
Mullaugh, Elizabeth P. ....Harrisburg, PA
Mullaugh, Michael J. ....Pittsburgh, PA
Mullavey, Charles N. ....Seattle, WA
Mullavey, Prout, Grenley & Foe, LLP
Seattle, WA
Mulle, Richard C. ....East Setauket, NY
Mulle, Robert A. ....Harrisburg, PA
Mullee, Michelle A. ....Cincinnati, OH
Mullee, William A. ....Huntington Beach, CA
Mullen, Andrew J.
Department Of Veterans Affairs,
Office of the General Counsel, GV
Mullen, Beth ....Roseville, CA
Mullen, Brian B. ....Medford, OR
Mullen, Brian J. ....Phoenix, AZ
Mullen, Brian J. ....Red Bank, NJ
Mullen, Carole Pope ....Reno, NV
Mullen, Catherine A. ....New York, NY
Mullen, Cathleen Anne ....Rockville, MD
Mullen, C. H. ....Kalamazoo, MI
Mullen, Charles ....Cortland, NY
Mullen, Charles A. ....Iowa City, IA
Mullen, Charles S. ....Seattle, WA
Mullen, Chris A. ....Temecula, CA
Mullen, Christine ....Philadelphia, PA
Mullen, Christopher, (P.C.) ....Chicago, IL
Mullen, Clair X., Jr. ....Washington, DC
Mullen, Corinne M. ....Hoboken, NJ
Mullen, Corinne M. ....New York, NY
Mullen, Daniel A. ....New York, NY
Mullen, David Patrick ....Boston, MA
Mullen, David W. ....Christiansburg, VA
Mullen, Dennis M. ....Santa Monica, CA
Mullen, Douglas A. ....Troy, MI
Mullen, Edward B., III
San Francisco, CA
Mullen, Edward J. ....New York, NY
Mullen, Edward W. ....Florence, AL
Mullen, Emma A. Forry ....Englewood, FL
Mullen, Eugene (Jay) M., Jr. ....Boston, MA
Mullen & Felton ....Denver, CO
Mullen & Fernandez ....St. Louis, MO
Mullen & Filippi ....Bakersfield, CA
Fresno, CA
Oakland, CA
Redding, CA
Sacramento, CA
Salinas, CA
San Francisco, CA
San Jose, CA
Santa Rosa, CA
Stockton, CA
Mullen, Francis E. ....Smithtown, NY
Mullen, Frederick J., Jr. ....Hartford, CT
West Hartford, CT
Mullen, Gary S. ....Sacramento, CA
Mullen, George E.
Hilton Head Island, SC
Myrtle Beach, SC
Mullen, Gerald E. ....Manhattan Beach, CA
Mullen, Graham C. ....Charlotte, NC
Mullen, Grant R. ....Orange, CA
Zurich, KS
Mullen, Gregory H. ....Salem, OR
Mullen, H. Benjamin ....Pascagoula, MS
Mullen, Heather A. ....Norfolk, VA
Mullen & Henzell, L.L.P.
Santa Barbara, CA
Mullen, Herbert T., Jr. ....Elizabeth City, NC
Mullen, Howard M. ....Denver, CO
Mullen and Iannarone, P.C. ....Smithtown, NY
Mullen, J. Jeffrey ....New York, NY
Mullen, J. Patrick ....Omaha, NE
Mullen, J. Paul ....Baltimore, MD
Mullen, J. Robert ....Laguna Hills, CA
Mullen, J. Stephen ....Colorado Springs, CO
Mullen, J. Thomas ....Chicago, IL
Mullen, James A. ....Omaha, NE
Mullen, James A., Jr. ....Cherry Hill, NJ
Mullen, James F. ....Bridgeport, CT
New Haven, CT
Mullen, James F. ....New York, NY
Mullen, James J. ....Bristol, RI
Mullen, James J. ....Corpus Christi, TX
Mullen, James J., III ....San Diego, CA
Mullen, James N. ....West Chester, PA
Mullen, James N. ....Houston, TX
Mullen, James P. ....Florham Park, NJ
Mullen, Joanne Jirik ....St. Paul, MN
Mullen, John C., (Ltd.) ....Chicago, IL
Mullen, John F. ....Cherry Hill, NJ
Philadelphia, PA
Mullen, John Francis ....Philadelphia, PA
Mullen, John L. ....Kansas City, MO
Springfield, MO
Mullen, John M. ....Newton, MA
Mullen, John P. ....Omaha, NE
Mullen, John P. ....Sioux Falls, SD
Mullen, John P. ....Salt Lake City, UT
Mullen, John R. ....Walnut Creek, CA
Mullen, John R. ....New Brunswick, NJ
Mullen, John W. ....San Diego, CA
Mullen, Joseph J., Jr. ....Milton, MA
Mullen, Joseph P. ....Fort Lauderdale, FL
Mullen, Joseph T., Jr. ....New York, NY
Mullen, Judith H. ....Upper Marlboro, MD
Mullen, Julia A. ....Taos, NM
Mullen, Karl I. ....Portland, OR
Mullen, Kathleen S. ....Bronxville, NY
Mullen, Keith H. ....Dallas, TX
Mullen, Kenneth W. ....Fort Worth, TX
Mullen, Kevin B. ....Stockton, CA
Mullen, Kevin P. ....Washington, DC
Mullen, Kirby ....Bloomington, IN
Indianapolis, IN
Mullen Lackey & Atwood, L.L.P.
Austin, TX
Mullen, Lauren C. ....Washington, DC
Mullen, Laurie P. ....Fall River, MA
Mullen Law Firm ....Beaufort, SC
Hilton Head Island, SC
Myrtle Beach, SC
Mullen, Lawrence J. ....Boston, MA
Mullen, Lawrence R. ....Houston, TX
Mullen, Lloyd P. ....Merrillville, IN
Mullen, Margaret Jean ....Waukegan, IL
Mullen, Mark ....Morris Plains, NJ
Mullen, Mark M. ....Walnut Creek, CA
Mullen, Mark T. ....Philadelphia, PA
Mullen, Martin J. ....San Diego, CA
Mullen, Martin S. ....Wausau, WI
Mullen, Matthew P.
New Philadelphia, OH
Mullen & McGourty ....Boston, MA
Mullen, Michael ....St. Louis, MO
Mullen, Michael A. ....Miami, FL
Mullen, Michael G. ....Austin, TX
Mullen, Michael J. ....Chicago, IL
Mullen, Michael K. ....Morristown, NJ
Mullen, Michael P. ....Cherry Hill, NJ
Mullen, Michael P., (P.C.) ....Chicago, IL
Mullen, Michael S. ....Dallas, TX
Mullen, Michael Scott ....Fort Wayne, IN
Mullen & Minella ....Chicago, IL
Mullen, Mitchell L. ....Cherry Hill, NJ
Mullen, Molly Jo ....Portland, OR
Mullen, Norman J. ....Grand Junction, CO
Mullen, O. Michael ....Lincoln, NE
Mullen, Patrick W. ....Indianapolis, IN
Mullen, Paul Fabian ....Moon Township, PA
Mullen, Paul W. ....Hillsborough, NH
Mullen, Peter P. ....New York, NY
Mullen & Plummer, A Professional Corporation
San Diego, CA
Mullen, Raleigh, Cahill & Foster
Chicago, IL
Mullen, Ray T. ....Bakersfield, CA
Mullen, Regina M. ....Wilmington, DE
Mullen, Regis L. ....Dallas, TX
Mullen, Regis L., Inc., Law Offices of
Dallas, TX
Plano, TX
Mullen, Robert A. ....Des Moines, IA
Mullen, Robert G. ....Salem, OR
Mullen, Robert H. ....Lodi, CA
Mullen, Robert L. ....Casper, WY
Mullen, Robert W.
Department Of The Interior,
Office of Hearings & Appeals, GV
Mullen, Robert W. ....New York, NY
Mullen, Robert W., Jr. ....New York, NY
Mullen, Rochelle A. ....Lincoln, NE
Omaha, NE
Mullen, Sally A. ....St. Paul, MN
Mullen, Sean T. ....Omaha, NE
Mullen & Sproul LLP ....Walnut Creek, CA
Mullen, Sullivan & Newton LLP
Lodi, CA
Stockton, CA

Mullins, Harris & Jessee, A Professional Corporation—Continued
Wise, VA
Mullins, Homer S. ... **Atlanta, GA**
Mullins, J. Michael ... Santa Rosa, CA
Mullins, J. Ronald, Jr. ... **Columbus, GA**
Mullins, J. Sanford, III ... **Birmingham, AL**
Mullins, J. Scott ... **Cincinnati, OH**
Mullins, Jack A. ... Victoria, TX
Mullins, James A. ... Harrisburg, PA
Mullins, James C. ... Walnut Creek, CA
Mullins, James D. ... **Vancouver, WA**
Mullins, James Edward ... Alexandria, VA
Mullins, James L. ... Duluth, GA
Mullins, Jay G. ... Roseland, NJ
Reston, VA
Mullins, J.D. ... Detroit, MI
Mullins, Jeffrey A. ... **Kansas City, MO**
Mullins, Jeffrey A. ... **Dayton, OH**
Mullins, Jeffrey A. ... **Austin, TX**
Mullins, Jeffrey S. ... Cincinnati, OH
Mullins, Jerome P. ... San Jose, CA
Mullins, Joan E. ... **Oakbrook Terrace, IL**
Mullins, John J. ... **Denver, CO**
Mullins, Joseph D. ... Golden, CO
Mullins, Joseph J. ... **Albuquerque, NM**
Mullins, Joyce M. ... **La Jolla, CA**
Mullins, Karen T. ... Wise, VA
Mullins, Kathleen ... **Waltham, MA**
Mullins, Kayo ... Dallas, TX
Mullins, Keith ... Denver, CO
Mullins, Kelly Byrd ... Lexington, KY
Mullins, Kenton R. ... **Irvine, CA**
Mullins, Kevin R. ... Covington, KY
Mullins, Kimberly Hill ... **Houston, TX**
Mullins, Kimbrough Brown ... **Memphis, TN**
Mullins, Lance ... Amarillo, TX
Mullins, Laureen J. ... Fort Washington, MD
Mullins, Leslie Morris ... **Norton, VA**
Mullins, Linda Kay ... Lansing, MI
Mullins, Lisa ... **Miami, FL**
Mullins, Lisa A. ... Pikeville, KY
Mullins, Margaret Ann F. ... Paterson, NJ
Mullins, Mark D. ... Montgomery, AL
Mullins, Mark D. ... Port Angeles, WA
Mullins, Mark Lee ... Leesburg, VA
Mullins, Mark Richard
Oklahoma City, OK
Mullins, Martha Eveleth Norton
Van Wert, OH
Mullins, Mary Beth ... Larchmont, NY
Mullins, Mary Beth, P.C. ... Larchmont, NY
Mullins, Matt Allen ... **Washington, DC**
Mullins, Michael D. ... **Charleston, WV**
Mullins, Michael E. ... Detroit, MI
Mullins, Michael L. ... **Oklahoma City, OK**
Mullins, Michael L., P.C.
Oklahoma City, OK
Mullins, Michael M. ... **Los Angeles, CA**
Mullins, Michael R. ... **Washington, IA**
Mullins, Michael T. ... **Chicago, IL**
Mullins, Michelle D. ... **Las Vegas, NV**
Mullins, Morell E. ... Little Rock, AR
Mullins, Morell Eugene
North Little Rock, AR
Mullins, Morris T. ... Somers, NY
Mullins, Neil M., Jr. ... **Las Vegas, NV**
Mullins, Neil M., Jr., Ltd., A Prof. Corp.
Las Vegas, NV
Mullins, P. Todd ... **Washington, DC**
Mullins, Patrick M. ... **Providence, RI**
Mullins, Paul J ... Louisville, KY
Mullins, Philip A., IV ... **Wilmington, NC**
Mullins, Raymond G. ... Ypsilanti, MI
Mullins, Reginald E. ... San Antonio, TX
Mullins, Richard L. ... Griffin, GA
Mullins, Rima Youakim ... **Miami, FL**
Mullins, Robert ... Houston, TX
Mullins, Robert A. ... **Atlanta, GA**
Savannah, GA
Mullins, Robert H. ... **Fort Worth, TX**
Mullins, Robert Lee, Jr. ... Louisville, KY
Mullins, Roger W. ... **Tazewell, VA**
Mullins, Royal ... Greenville, TX
Mullins, Russell N. ... **Gunnison, CO**
Mullins, Scott W. ... Coeburn, VA
Mullins, Scott W., P.C. ... Coeburn, VA
Mullins, Sherri L. ... **Miami, FL**
Mullins, S. T. ... **Grundy, VA**
Mullins, Stacey D. ... Boca Raton, FL
Mullins, Stacey D., P.A. ... Boca Raton, FL
Mullins, Stephanie Carol ... Chicago, IL
Mullins, Stephanie L. ... Ocala, FL
Mullins, Stephen Wright
Ocean Springs, MS
Mullins, Steven K. ... Oklahoma City, OK
Mullins, Susan L. ... Norman, OK
Mullins, Tammy Renee ... Bentonville, AR
Mullins, Terrell S. ... Hallettsville, TX
Mullins, Thomas Earl ... San Diego, CA
Mullins, Thomas J. ... Crown Point, IN
Mullins, Thomas K. ... **Milwaukee, WI**
Mullins, Thomas P. ... **Jaffrey, NH**
Mullins, Timothy J. ... **Detroit, MI**
Mullins, Vincent J. ... San Francisco, CA
Mullins, Wayne E. ... **Fairfax, VA**
Mullins, Wendy Russell ... **Jackson, MS**
Mullins & Whalen ... Griffin, GA
Mullins, William A. ... **Washington, DC**
Mullins, William C. ... **Paintsville, KY**
Prestonsburg, KY
Mullins, William J. ... Broadview, IL
Mullins, William J., Jr. ... Overland Park, KS
Mullins, William R.
National Transportation Safety Board, Office of Administrative Law Judges, GV
Mullins, William R., III ... Baton Rouge, LA

Mullins, William S., III ... **Laurel, MS**
Mullins & Williams ... Tuscaloosa, AL
Mullins & Wise ... **San Francisco, CA**
Mullins, Wm. E. ... San Francisco, CA
Mullis, Bart, Law Offices of ... Pine Bluff, AR
Mullis & Barton ... Columbia, SC
Mullis, Carl W., III ... **Atlanta, GA**
Mullis, Claude L. ... Jacksonville, FL
Mullis, Danny H. ... **Charleston, SC**
Mullis, David E. ... **Valdosta, GA**
Mullis, Gerald S., (P.C.) ... Macon, GA
Mullis, H. Frederick, Jr. ... Hawkinsville, GA
Mullis, Harold W., Jr. ... **Tampa, FL**
Mullis, J. Marvin, Jr. ... Columbia, SC
Mullis, J. Thomas ... Arab, AL
Mullis, Marshall, Lindley & Powell, A Ptnrshp. incl. A Prof. Corp. ... Macon, GA
Mullis, Maryanne C. ... Santa Cruz, CA
Mullis, Pamela R. ... Columbia, SC
Mullis, Susan Cole ... Decatur, GA
Mullis, W. Dennis ... Cochran, GA
Mullis, William H. ... **Evansville, IN**
Mullison, George B. ... **Bay City, MI**
Mullkoff, Douglas R. ... Ann Arbor, MI
Mullman, Michael S. ... **New York, NY**
Mullman, Raymond Paul, Jr.
Spartanburg, SC
Mullman - Roberts, LLC ... **Atlanta, GA**
Silver Spring, MD
Mullman, Roy ... **Atlanta, GA**
Mullnix, Karen E. ... Livermore, CA
Mullooly, Jeffrey, Rooney & Flynn
Glen Cove, NY
Mullooly, Thomas McCann
Milwaukee, WI
Mullowney, Edward F. ... **Palo Alto, CA**
Mullowney, Henry G. ... Braintree, MA
Mullowney, William John ... Orlando, FL
Mulloy, B. Mark ... **Louisville, KY**
Mulloy, Eric E. ... **Seattle, WA**
Mulloy, Gardnar ... Miami, FL
Mulloy, Heather A. ... Rockville, MD
Mulloy, James N., Jr. ... Dublin, TX
Mulloy, Mary M. ... Overland Park, KS
Mulloy & Mulloy ... **Louisville, KY**
Mulloy, Nancy Evelyn ... Philadelphia, PA
Mulloy, Patrick A. ... United States Senate, Committee Legal Personnel, GV
Mulloy, Richard T. ... **San Diego, CA**
Mulloy, Robert E., Jr. ... **Kansas City, MO**
Mulloy, Sherry Yee ... **Boston, MA**
Mulloy, Timothy M. ... Louisville, KY
Mulloy, W. Patrick, II ... Louisville, KY
Mulloy, William P. ... **Louisville, KY**
Mulock, David G. ... **St. Petersburg, FL**
Mulock, Edwin T., (P.A.) ... **Bradenton, FL**
Mulock, Mary Hahalyak ... Pittsburgh, PA
Mulock, Thompson & Grieco, P.A.
Bradenton, FL
Mulopulos, Julie ... Chicago, IL
Mulpeter, Michael F. ... **Hartford, CT**
Mulqueen, Brian D. ... **Chicago, IL**
Mulqueen, Cliff S. ... Brooklyn, NY
Mulqueen, Jane E. ... Northampton, MA
Mulqueen, John P., Jr. ... New Haven, CT
Mulqueen, Kevin Riley ... Atlanta, GA
Mulqueen, Michael A. ... **New York, NY**
Mulquin, David G. ... **Rockville, MD**
Mulrain, C. Anthony ... **New York, NY**
Mulrain, John T. ... **Hartford, CT**
Mulrain, Lisa V.
Department of Housing and Urban Development, GV
Mulrain, Sandra Hall ... **Morristown, NJ**
Mulreany, Robert H. ... New York, NY
Mulreany, Timothy J. ... **Rockville, MD**
Mulrenin, Edward T.
Board of Governors Of The Federal Reserve System, Division of Information Resources Management, GV
Mulrenin & Hubbard, P.A.
Annapolis, MD
Mulrenin, Thomas J. ... **Annapolis, MD**
Mulrine, Thomas V. ... **Washington, DC**
Mulroney, Delaney & Scott ... Missoula, MT
Mulroney, Michael ... Villanova, PA
Mulroney, Michael J. ... **Helena, MT**
Mulroney, William F. ... **Baltimore, MD**
Mulrooney, Celeste M. ... Long Beach, CA
Mulrooney, Eugene H., Jr. ... Memphis, TN
Mulrooney, Garrett E. ... Eagan, MN
Mulrooney, John J. ... **Memphis, TN**
Mulrooney, Michele M. ... **Los Angeles, CA**
Mulrooney, Steven B. ... **Louisville, KY**
Mulrooney, Timothy Thomas ... St. Paul, MN
Mulroony, Kellyann ... Chattanooga, TN
Mulrow, Catherine D. ... **Islandia, NY**
Mulroy, Eileen P. ... **Hackensack, NJ**
Mulroy, J. Kevin ... Syracuse, NY
Mulroy, James E. ... **Cherry Hill, NJ**
Mulroy, James P. ... **Columbus, OH**
Mulroy, James R. ... **Memphis, TN**
Mulroy, Karen A. ... **St. Louis, MO**
Mulroy, Kathleen Marie ... New York, NY
Mulroy, Martha E. ... Brewerton, NY
Mulroy, Martin B. ... New York, NY
Mulroy, Matthew P. ... Nashville, TN
Mulroy, Michael J. ... La Crosse, WI
Mulroy, Richard E., Jr. ... New York, NY
Mulroy, Robert D. ... New York, NY
Mulroy, Steven J. ... Department of Justice, Civil Rights Division, GV
Mulroy, Thomas M. ... **Pittsburgh, PA**
Mulroy, Thomas R., III ... **Chicago, IL**
Mulroy, Thomas R., Jr. ... **Chicago, IL**
Mulry & Hernandez, P.L.L.C. ... **Dallas, TX**
Frisco, TX

Mulry, Patrick T. ... **Dallas, TX**
Mulry, Philip E. ... Tallahassee, FL
Mulry, Yvonne M. V. ... Forest Lake, MN
Mulryan, Lawrence E. ... Beverly Hills, CA
Mulshine, Dennis J. ... San Francisco, CA
Mulshine, Kevin
Architect of the Capitol, GV
Multani, Anju ... Downey, CA
Multer, Andrew J. ... New York, NY
Multer, Richard D. ... Bellingham, WA
Multhauf, John E. ... **Waukesha, WI**
Multhaup, Eric Stephen ... Mill Valley, CA
Multz, Carroll E., (P.C.)
Grand Junction, CO
Multz, Salmon & Lipton
Grand Junction, CO
Mulvahill, James P. ... Minnetonka, MN
Mulvahill, Maurice J., Jr.
The Woodlands, TX
Mulvahill, Peter J. ... Buhl, MN
Chisholm, MN
Hibbing, MN
Mulvahill, Thomas Francis ... Denver, CO
Mulvana, John C. ... **Santa Ana, CA**
Mulvaney & Associates, P.A. ... Charlotte, NC
Mulvaney, Barbara L. ... Dunsmuir, CA
Mulvaney, Bernard P., Sr. ... Palos Heights, IL
Mulvaney, Christopher J. ... **Cincinnati, OH**
Mulvaney, Coronato & Brady
Toms River, NJ
Mulvaney, Dennette A. ... **Pasadena, CA**
Mulvaney, Douglas A. ... **Elkhart, IN**
Mulvaney, Eugene M. ... Toms River, NJ
Mulvaney, J. Michael ... Charlotte, NC
Mulvaney, James E. ... Far Rockaway, NY
Mulvaney, James F. ... Los Angeles, CA
Orange, CA
San Diego, CA
Mulvaney, James M. ... **Morristown, NJ**
Mulvaney, James N. ... Chicago, IL
Mulvaney, John M. ... Charlotte, NC
Mulvaney, Kahan & Barry, A Professional Corporation ... **La Jolla, CA**
Los Angeles, CA
Orange, CA
San Diego, CA
Mulvaney, Karl L. ... **Indianapolis, IN**
Mulvaney, Marcella J. ... **Pittsburgh, PA**
Mulvaney, Michael D. ... **Birmingham, AL**
Mulvaney, Molly ... Portland, OR
Mulvaney, Peter J. ... Cheyenne, WY
Mulvaney, Priscilla C. ... **Cheshire, CT**
Mulvaney, Thomas F. ... Scotts Valley, CA
Mulvaney, Thomas F. ... Beaumont, TX
Mulvaney, Toni Pollock ... Beaumont, TX
Mulvania, Walter L. ... **Rock Port, MO**
Mulvanny, Daniel J. ... Oak Park, IL
Mulvehill, John H. ... St. James, NY
Mulvehill, John P. ... Norwood, MA
Mulvehill, Urban S. ... **New York, NY**
Mulvey, Bernard M. ... Los Angeles, CA
Mulvey, Deborah M. ... **Clark, NJ**
Mulvey, Elizabeth N. ... **Boston, MA**
Mulvey & Flanagan, P.C.
Philadelphia, PA
Mulvey, Harold M. ... New Haven, CT
Mulvey, Ingrid ... Albuquerque, NM
Mulvey, James Ryan ... **Danbury, CT**
Mulvey, John J. ... Cincinnati, OH
Mulvey, John P. ... **Boston, MA**
Mulvey, Joseph F. ... Norwalk, CT
Mulvey, Jude Brearton ... Troy, NY
Mulvey, Kathleen A. ... Morristown, NJ
Mulvey, Kenneth J., Jr. ... **New Haven, CT**
Mulvey & Korotash ... **Danbury, CT**
Mulvey Law Firm ... Ithaca, NY
Mulvey, Michael Bernard, Jr. ... Bronx, NY
Mulvey, Michael S. ... Dry Ridge, KY
Mulvey, Michelle ... Los Angeles, CA
Mulvey & Mulvey ... Los Angeles, CA
Mulvey, Oliver & Gould ... **New Haven, CT**
Mulvey, Philip F., III ... Wellesley Hills, MA
Mulvey, Professional Association
Portsmouth, NH
Mulvey, Richard I. ... Ithaca, NY
Mulvey, Robert C. ... Ithaca, NY
Mulvey, Robert J. ... Bethpage, NY
Mulvey, Robert P. ... **New York, NY**
Mulvey, Thomas J. ... Columbus, OH
Mulvey, Thomas P., Jr. ... Duxbury, MA
Mulvey, Timothy P. ... United States Senate, Senatorial Assistants, GV
Mulvey, Valerie W. ... Framingham, MA
Mulvey, W. Michael ... **Philadelphia, PA**
Mulvey, William A., Jr. ... Portsmouth, NH
Mulvey, William J. ... Cincinnati, OH
Mulvihill, Cheryl Torpey ... Parker, CO
Mulvihill, Cynthia Coulter ... Glendale, CA
Mulvihill, Dennis P. ... **Cleveland, OH**
Mulvihill, Dennis St. J. ... **Pittsburgh, PA**
Mulvihill, Donald J. ... **Washington, DC**
Mulvihill, Donna ... **New York, NY**
Mulvihill, Eamon Patrick ... **Louisville, KY**
Mulvihill, Grace C. ... Bethesda, MD
Mulvihill, Henry N. ... Denver, CO
Georgetown, CO
Mulvihill, Henry N., P.C. ... Denver, CO
Georgetown, CO
Mulvihill and Hunter ... Kansas City, MO
Mulvihill, John C. ... Englewood, CO
Mulvihill, John D. ... Bloomfield Hills, MI
Mulvihill, John F. ... Orange, CT
Mulvihill, John T. ... **South Bend, IN**
Mulvihill, Joseph J. ... Kansas City, MO
Mulvihill, Keithley D. ... **Pittsburgh, PA**
Mulvihill, Leonie H. ... Austin, TX
Mulvihill, Mead J., Jr. ... Pittsburgh, PA
Mulvihill, Michael D. ... Chicago, IL

Mulvihill, Michael F. ... Northbrook, IL
Mulvihill, Michael N. ... Lynnwood, WA
Mulvihill, P. Laurence ... **Grand Rapids, MI**
Mulvihill, Patrick M. ... Seattle, WA
Mulvihill, Robert A. ... Loveland, CO
Mulvihill, Robert J. ... **Santa Ana, CA**
Mulvihill, Robert J. ... Springfield, IL
Mulvihill, Roger ... **New York, NY**
Mulvihill, Thomas E. ... **San Francisco, CA**
Mulvihill, Thomas O. ... **Parsippany, NJ**
Mulvihill, William T. ... **Oakland, CA**
Mulville, Harold J. ... Covina, CA
Mulville, Kathleen T. ... **Washington, DC**
Mulville, Kurt T. ... **Irvine, CA**
Mulvoy, James E. ... **Bloomfield Hills, MI**
Pittsburgh, PA
Mulvoy, Kelly A. ... **New York, NY**
Muly, Carl Arnett ... Glen Burnie, MD
Mulzet, C. Kurt ... **Pittsburgh, PA**
Muma, Michael ... **Plymouth, MI**
Mumaugh, Brian M. ... **Denver, CO**
Mumaw, Daniel J. ... Youngstown, OH
Mumaw, James W. ... Youngstown, OH
Mumaw, Robert N. ... Silver Spring, MD
Mumaw, Thomas L. ... **Phoenix, AZ**
Mumbach, Michael W.
United States Postal Service, Law Department, GV
Mumbauer, William R. ... Brandon, FL
Mumbauer, William R., P.A. ... Brandon, FL
Mumby, Keith G. ... **Grand Junction, CO**
Mumby, Susan ... Grand Junction, CO
Mumey, Dana N. ... Eagle, CO
Mumey, Jane Johnston ... Houston, TX
Mumford, Brian F. ... **Albany, NY**
Mumford, C. "Lee" ... Boise, ID
Mumford, Christopher B. ... **Rochester, NY**
Mumford, Daniel R. ... Ocean City, MD
Mumford, Daryl J. ... **Battle Creek, MI**
Mumford, David M. ... Lorain, OH
Mumford, Deborah A. (Edmonds)
Houston, TX
Mumford, James R. ... Des Moines, IA
Mumford, Jay S. ... **Rochester, NY**
Mumford, John B., Jr. ... **Richmond, VA**
Mumford, John S. ... **Los Angeles, CA**
Mumford, Lauren M. ... **Syracuse, NY**
Mumford, Patrick Wayne
Myrtle Beach, SC
Mumford, Protsch & Pardy ... Howard, SD
Madison, SD
Woonsocket, SD
Mumford, Richard J. ... New York, NY
Mumford, Robert E. ... East Longmeadow, MA
Mumford, Robert F. ... Conyers, GA
Mumford, Roger E. ... New York, NY
Mumford, Ronald E. ... Lewiston, UT
Mumford, Schubel, Norlander, Macfarlane & Barnett, PLLC ... **Battle Creek, MI**
Mumford, Terry A. M. ... **Indianapolis, IN**
Mumford, William P. ... Eugene, OR
Mumgaard, Thomas O. ... Omaha, NE
Mumm, Christopher E. ... Sparks, NV
Mumm, Frederick F. ... **Los Angeles, CA**
Mumm, Jean D. ... **Virginia Beach, VA**
Mumm, John A. ... **Plano, TX**
Sherman, TX
Mumm, Lawrence W. ... **New York, NY**
Mumm, Noel K. ... Missouri Valley, IA
Mumm, Paula M. ... Folsom, CA
Mumma, Michael F. ... **Jefferson, IA**
Scranton, IA
Mumma & Pedersen ... **Jefferson, IA**
Scranton, IA
Mumma, Salmon B. ... Kansas City, MO
Mumme, Jules J., III ... New Orleans, LA
Mumme, Julie C. ... Sacramento, CA
Mumme, Mary Anne ... New Orleans, LA
Mummert, Catherine C. ... Bethel, CT
Mummert, Frederic H. ... Atlanta, GA
Mummert, Thomas C., III ... St. Louis, MO
Mummery, Daniel R. ... **New York, NY**
Mummolo, Dante G. ... Boston, MA
Mumper, John E. ... Tallmadge, OH
Mumphery, Elbert ... Richmond, VA
Mumphrey, J. Wayne ... Chalmette, LA
Mumuni, Nina ... South Plainfield, NJ
Mun, Andrew H. ... Bellevue, WA
Muna, Deena A. ... **Portland, OR**
Munaco, Salvatore ... Birmingham, MI
Munafo, Rachel R. ... Philadelphia, PA
Munak, James S. ... La Jolla, CA
Munak, Pearl M. ... Paso Robles, CA
Munayyer, Maha F. ... **Morristown, NJ**
Muncey, Kathleen P. ... **Plymouth, MA**
Muncey, Peter N., Jr. ... **Plymouth, MA**
Munch, Christopher H. ... **Denver, CO**
Munch, Christopher J. ... Golden, CO
Munch, Coleman L. ... Concord, CA
Munch, Jacob J. ... **Tampa, FL**
Munch, James C., III ... Bangor, ME
Munch, James C., Jr. ... Portland, ME
Munch, John A. ... Erie, PA
Munch, John C. ... **San Francisco, CA**
Munch, Kim W. ... **Tampa, FL**
Munch, Michael L. ... Papillion, NE
Munch and Munch, P.A. ... **Tampa, FL**
Munch, Shirley C. ... West Los Angeles, CA
Munchak, Jo-Elle ... Downers Grove, IL
Munchel, Patricia T. ... **Raleigh, NC**
Munchhof, Martha G. ... **Hartford, CT**
Muncie, Cynthia Smith ... Richmond, VA
Muncie, James G., Jr. ... **Richmond, VA**
Munck, Benson & Skinner ... Oakland, CA
Munck, William A. ... **Dallas, TX**
Muncy, Analeslie ... **Fort Worth, TX**
Muncy, Curtis L. ... Washington, DC
Muncy, Dennis K. ... **Champaign, IL**

Muncy, Elbert W., Jr. .... Barstow, CA
Muncy, Joe McKinney .... Falls Church, VA
Muncy, Judith K. .... Chicago, IL
Muncy, Kenneth S. .... Amarillo, TX
Muncy, Robt. C. .... Hyden, KY
Muncy, Thomas D. .... Inez, KY
Mund, Gary R. .... Brooklyn, NY
Mund, Geraldine .... Woodland Hills, CA
Mund, Mitchell .... Forest Hills, NY
Mund, Nathaniel B. .... Raleigh, NC
Mund, Ronald G. .... St. Paul, MN
Mundaca, Michael F. .... Treasury Department, Departmental Offices, GV
Mundahl, Larry L. .... Spokane, WA
Munday, John J. .... Chicago, IL
Munday, John L. .... Little Rock, AR
Munday, John S. .... Drexel Hill, PA
Munday, Leon M. .... Kansas City, MO
Munday, M. Madeleine .... Chicago, IL
Munday & Nathan, The Law Offices of Chicago, IL
Munday, Reuben A. .... Detroit, MI
Munday and Stanton .... Drexel Hill, PA
Munday, William P. .... Roseland, NJ
Mundell, Douglas Allen .... Pittsburgh, PA
Mundell, John A., Jr. .... Bloomfield Hills, MI
Mundell, Lee C. .... Savannah, GA
Mundell, Lynn A. .... Tulsa, OK
Mundell, Melissa Stebbins .... Savannah, GA
Mundell, Odlum & Haws, LLP San Bernardino, CA
Mundell, Thomas C. .... San Bernardino, CA
Mundell, William .... Chandler, AZ
Munden, C. E., III .... Lincoln, NE
Munden, J. Kathleen .... Tallahassee, FL
Fort Worth, TX
Munden, Jill M. .... Kansas City, MO
Munden, R. Michael .... Myrtle Beach, SC
Munden, R. Michael, P.A. Myrtle Beach, SC
Munden, Robert L. R. .... Austin, TX
Munden, Robin G. .... Des Plaines, IL
Munder, Terry C. .... Houston, TX
Mundheim, Marla M. .... Hurst, TX
Mundheim, Peter M. .... New York, NY
Mundheim, Robert H. .... New York, NY
Mundhenk, Thomas G. .... Portland, ME
Mundie, John G. .... El Paso, TX
Mundie, Paul J. .... San Francisco, CA
Munding, John D. .... Spokane, WA
Mundinger, Elizabeth O. .... Washington, DC
Mundinger, Paul C., II .... Stamford, CT
Mundkur, Rajat P. .... Chester, NY
Mundle, Winfred R. .... Washington, DC
Mundo, John P. .... Harvey, IL
Mundo, Vito V., (P.C.) .... New York, NY
Mundorf, Nancy Sellars .... Kernersville, NC
Mundorf, Terence L. .... Mill Creek, WA
Mundorff, Charles R. .... Eugene, OR
Mundorff, Gretchen A. .... Connellsville, PA
Mundorff, McClain & Kovac Milwaukie, OR
Mundorff, Roger P. .... Milwaukie, OR
Mundrake, Lisa .... Ventura, CA
Mundschau, Stephen H. .... San Francisco, CA
Mundstock, David .... Sacramento, CA
Mundstock, George .... Coral Gables, FL
Mundt, Daniel H. .... Duluth, MN
Mundt, David Michael .... Chicago, IL
Mundt, Franck & Schumacher Denison, IA
Mundt, George J., Jr. .... Newark Valley, NY
Mundt, Herman A. .... Denver, CO
Mundt, J. Carl .... Bainbridge Island, WA
Mundt, Jae L. .... Chicago, IL
Mundt, James A. .... Colorado Springs, CO
Mundt, James D. .... Indianapolis, IN
Mundt MacGregor L.L.P. .... Seattle, WA
Mundt, Michael R. .... Denison, IA
Mundt, Michelle Marie .... Washington, DC
Mundt, Paul E. .... Sioux Falls, SD
Mundt, Rick J. .... Madison, WI
Mundt, Steven C. .... St. Paul, MN
Mundt, Thomas G. .... Franklin Lakes, NJ
Mundt, William F. .... Madison, WI
Mundwiller, Orlando J. .... Hermann, MO
Mundy & Adkins .... Huntington, WV
Mundy, Claude .... Houston, TX
Mundy, Craig A. .... Lakeland, FL
Mundy, Douglas T., Jr. .... Toms River, NJ
Mundy, G. Marshall .... Roanoke, VA
Mundy & Gammage, P.C. Cedartown, GA Rome, GA
Mundy, Gardner M. .... New York, NY
Mundy, George E. .... Cedartown, GA
Mundy, George E., P.C. .... Cedartown, GA
Mundy, Hugh F. .... Wilkes-Barre, PA
Mundy, James F. .... Philadelphia, PA
Mundy, Jeffery .... Austin, TX
Mundy, John D. .... Hendersonville, NC
Mundy, Jonathan P. .... Metuchen, NJ
Mundy, Larry J. .... Grapevine, TX
Mundy, Maura .... Harrisburg, PA
Mundy & Mundy, P.A. .... Metuchen, NJ
Mundy, Nicholas H. .... Metuchen, NJ
Mundy, Patsy L. .... Richmond, VA
Mundy, R. Bernard .... Cincinnati, OH
Mundy, R. Garry .... Toms River, NJ
Mundy, Richard E. .... Cedar Rapids, IA
Iowa City, IA
Mundy, Richard H. .... Cocoa Beach, FL
Mundy, Robert E. .... Omaha, NE
Mundy, Rodney O. .... Birmingham, AL
Mundy, Rogers & Frith, LLP Roanoke, VA
Mundy, Sallie Updyke .... Philadelphia, PA

Mundy, Steven Eric Lake Havasu City, AZ
Mundy, Thomas William .... Silver Spring, MD
Mundy, Traci H. .... McLean, VA
Mundy, Ward .... Atlanta, GA
Mundy, William G. .... Irving, TX
Mundy, William J. .... Philadelphia, PA
Mundy, William L. .... Huntington, WV
Munemura, Marsha L. .... Northbrook, IL
Múnera-Pascual, María Victoria San Juan, PR
Munford, James B. .... Fort Worth, TX
Munford, Luther T. .... Jackson, MS
Munford, R. Donavon, Jr. .... Raleigh, NC
Munford, Virginia T. .... Jackson, MS
Mungall, Daniel, Jr. .... Philadelphia, PA
Mungello, Mark D. .... Blackwood, NJ
Mungen, Tessa L. .... New York, NY
Munger Chadwick, P.L.C. .... Phoenix, AZ Tucson, AZ
Munger, Charles T. .... Los Angeles, CA
Munger, Clark W. .... Tucson, AZ
Munger, Donald Ray .... Santa Rosa, CA
Munger, Gary E. .... Downey, CA
Munger, Harry L. .... Duluth, MN
Munger, John E. .... Racine, WI
Munger, John F. .... Phoenix, AZ Tucson, AZ
Munger, John Russell, Jr. .... Huntsville, AL
Munger, John Willard .... Robbinsdale, MN
Munger, Jon B. .... Troy, MI
Munger, Joseph A. .... Atlanta, GA
Munger, Judith K. .... Amherst, NY
Munger, Lisa Woods .... Honolulu, HI
Munger, Michael S. .... Norristown, PA
Munger, Molly .... Los Angeles, CA
Munger, Nicholas E. .... Crozet, VA
Munger, Paul C. .... Atlanta, GA
Munger, Peter C. .... Holland, OH
Munger, Peter F. .... Atlanta, GA
Munger & Reinschmidt .... Sioux City, IA
Munger, Sean .... Portland, OR
Munger, Stanley E. .... Sioux City, IA
Munger, Stephanie S. .... Chicago, IL
Munger, Stephen X. .... Atlanta, GA
Munger, Thomas J. .... Atlanta, GA
Munger, Tolles & Olson LLP Los Angeles, CA San Francisco, CA
Munger, Wendy .... South Pasadena, CA
Mungerson, Darren M. .... Chicago, IL
Mungia, Salvador A. .... Tacoma, WA
Mungle, James A. .... Albuquerque, NM
Mungle, James A., P.A. .... Albuquerque, NM
Mungo, David J. .... Denver, CO
Mungo, Derek A. .... Kankakee, IL
Mungo, Frank Middleton .... Covington, KY
Mungo, Leonard .... Detroit, MI
Mungo, Leonard, P.C. .... Detroit, MI
Mungovan, Timothy W. .... Boston, MA
Munguia, B. Kathleen .... Bronx, NY
Mungy, Virgil W. .... Chicago, IL
Munhall, Patricia K. .... Las Vegas, NV
Muni, Steven D. .... Jackson, CA
Muniak, Mark M. .... Charlevoix, MI
Muniak, William J. .... Cleveland, OH
Munic, Martin Daniel .... Minneapolis, MN
Munich, C. David .... Bridgeport, CT
Munich, John R. .... Atlanta, GA
Munich, Maritza .... San Juan, PR
Munier, Jonathan .... Houston, TX
Munier, William J. .... New Milford, NJ
Munin, Eugene L. .... Chicago, IL
Munion, Christine E. .... Bala Cynwyd, PA
Munir, Rahim A. .... Phillipsburg, NJ
Munisoglu, Elizabeth Mitchell Los Angeles, CA
Munisteri, Arthur A. .... New York, NY
Munisteri, James G. .... Houston, TX
Munisteri, Richard A. .... Houston, TX
Munisteri, Sprott, LeFevre & Rigby, P.C. Houston, TX
Munisteri, Stephen P. .... Houston, TX
Munitz, Gerald F. .... Chicago, IL
Munitz, Martin R. .... New York, NY
Muniz, Carlos A. .... Eagle Pass, TX
Muñiz, H. Michael .... Boca Raton, FL
Muniz, Inez .... Bronx, NY
Muniz, Juan M. .... Winter Park, FL
Muniz, Julie .... New York, NY
Muniz, Kristin P. .... Boston, MA
Muñiz, Michael .... Salem, OR
Muñiz, Nicolás José .... New York, NY
Muniz, Paul T. .... Danvers, MA
Muñiz, Peter J. .... Stamford, CT
Muñiz, Ricardo .... San Juan, PR
Muniz, Stephen M. .... Boston, MA
Muñiz, Yvonnilda G. .... Austin, TX
Munk, Barry .... New York, NY
Munk, Jeffrey W. .... Washington, DC
Munk, Joe B. .... Endicott, NY
Munk, LaRae G. .... Sanford, MI
Munk, La Rae G., P.C. .... Sanford, MI
Munk, Milton V., Jr. .... Mount Pleasant, PA
Munk, Rachel K. .... Sausalito, CA
Munk, Russell Lewis .... Treasury Department, Office of the General Counsel, GV
Munkacsi, Joyce E. .... New Brunswick, NJ
Munkacsy, John .... Lawton, OK
Munkelt, Stephen A. .... Nevada City, CA
Munker, Leonard D. .... Cheyenne, WY
Munkwitz, Kelly L. .... Albany, NY
Munley, Bernadine J. .... Philadelphia, PA
Munley, Daniel J. .... Wilmington, DE
Munley, Daniel W. .... Scranton, PA
Munley & Funda .... Buffalo, NY
Munley, James Christopher .... Scranton, PA
Wilkes-Barre, PA

Munley, James M. .... Scranton, PA
Munley, Julia K. .... Scranton, PA
Munley, Marion .... Scranton, PA
Munley, Meade, Nielsen & Ré Great Neck, NY
Munley, Michael L. .... Buffalo, NY
Munley, Munley & Cartwright, P.C. Allentown, PA Bloomsburg, PA Harrisburg, PA Scranton, PA Stroudsburg, PA
Wilkes-Barre, PA
Munley, Robert W. .... Scranton, PA
Munley, Robert W., III .... Scranton, PA
Munley, Thomas J. .... Scranton, PA
Munley, Thomas J., P.C. .... Scranton, PA
Munn, Cecil E. .... Fort Worth, TX
Munn, Charles A. .... Houston, TX
Munn, Charles H., Jr. .... Raleigh, NC
Munn, Christina L. .... Los Angeles, CA
Munn, David A. .... Pella, IA
Munn, Demetri E. (Rico) .... Denver, CO
Munn, Elise Berry .... Hazlehurst, MS
Munn & Flume .... San Antonio, TX
Munn, Ford Dent .... Palm Springs, CA
Munn, James M. .... Sand Springs, OK
Munn, James S. .... Seattle, WA
Munn, Janet T. .... Miami, FL
Munn, John D. .... Austin, TX
Munn, John L. .... Denver, CO
Munn, Justin B. .... Tulsa, OK
Munn, Michael J. .... Chicago, IL
Munn, O'Neal .... San Antonio, TX
Munn, Robert N. .... Redmond, WA
Munn, Robert S. .... Struthers, OH
Munn, Roger Roland, Jr .... Towson, MD
Munn, Timothy P. .... Boston, MA
Munn, William J. .... Aurora, CO
Munna, Raymond J. .... New Orleans, LA
Munneke, Gary A. .... White Plains, NY
Munnell, Elizabeth H. .... Boston, MA
Munnell, Jeffrey C. .... Mc Keesport, PA
Munnell, William A. .... Reno, NV
Munnelly, Margaret M. .... Houston, TX
Munnelly, Marlene A. .... Levittown, NY
Munnelly, Robert J., Jr. .... Boston, MA
Munnerlyn, Elizabeth R. .... Bennettsville, SC
Munnerlyn, Joseph F., Jr. .... Columbia, SC
Munnerlyn, Neely P. .... Dallas, TX
Munnerlyn, Sherri Lynn .... Los Angeles, CA
Munninghoff, Ann .... Rhinelander, WI
Munnis, James J. .... West Chester, PA
Munnis, Janis S. .... Wakefield, MA
Munno, M. William .... New York, NY
Munno, Thomas F. .... New York, NY
Munns, Christopher .... Dallas, TX
Munns, Earle D., Jr. .... Rockville, MD
Munns, Elizabeth A .... Portland, OR
Munns, Jay C. .... Santa Ana, CA
Munns, Jeffrey D. .... Oregon City, OR
Munns, Lawrence D. .... Topeka, KS
Munns, Michael D. .... Little Rock, AR
Munns, Michael J. .... Bronx, NY
Munns, Orlin C. .... Oakdale, CA
Munns, Ranier F. .... Deltona, FL Orlando, FL
Munns, Rulon D. .... Kissimmee, FL Orlando, FL
Munos, Jane Schulteis .... Evanston, IL
Muñoz, A. Patrick .... Costa Mesa, CA
Muñoz, Alberto A., II .... Edinburg, TX
Muñoz, Alberto A., II, P.C., Law Office of Edinburg, TX
Munoz, Alejandro E. .... Tucson, AZ
Muñoz, Alison M. .... Philadelphia, PA
Muñoz, Armando Del Valle .... San Juan, PR
Muñoz Boneta González Arbona Benitez & Peral .... San Juan, PR
Muñoz, Charles R. .... Findlay, OH
Muñoz, Dara Lystra .... Baltimore, MD
Muñoz, Edgardo .... San Juan, PR
Munoz, Ellis .... Conroe, TX
Muñoz, Enrique L. .... Los Angeles, CA
Munoz, Filbert .... Independence, MO
Munoz, Franco .... Washington, DC
Munoz, G. Mateo .... Sacramento, CA
Munoz, Gregory .... Santa Ana, CA
Munoz, Gustavo .... Chicago, IL
Munoz, Henrietta S. .... Dallas, TX
Munoz, Immaculada .... Washington, DC
Muñoz, J. David .... Los Angeles, CA
Muñoz, Jacobo G., P.C. Corpus Christi, TX
Mūnoz, Jeffrey Scott .... Houston, TX
Munoz, John G. .... New Orleans, LA
Munoz, Karen L. .... Springfield, IL
Munoz, Kenneth W. .... New York, NY
Munoz, Marilyn M. .... Palo Alto, CA
Muñoz, Milagros (Millie) G. Fort Lauderdale, FL
Muñoz, Monica DeSaix .... Albuquerque, NM
Muñoz, Nina C. .... Pomona, CA
Munoz, Patricia M. .... Los Angeles, CA
Muñoz, Peter S. .... San Francisco, CA
Munoz, Ralph A. .... Brooklyn, NY
Munoz, Robert F. .... Freehold, NJ
Munoz, Rodolfo R. .... San Antonio, TX
Muñoz, Rogelio, Jr. .... San Juan, PR
Munoz, Rosalio .... El Paso, TX
Muñoz, Shane T. .... Tampa, FL
Munoz, Vera E. .... Phoenix, AZ
Munoz, Verlyn A. .... Independence, MO
Muñoz, William Angelo .... Sacramento, CA
Munoz-Arill, Robert R. .... San Juan, PR
Munoz-Dones, Gerardo .... San Juan, PR
Munoz-Gandara, Cristina .... San Juan, PR
Munoz Maldonado, Edgardo .... San Juan, PR

Munoz-Muro, Patricia Segura Cathedral City, CA
Muñoz-Noya, Angel .... San Juan, PR
Muñoz Noya, Carmen I. .... San Juan, PR
Muñoz-Ocasio, David .... San Juan, PR
Munoz-Rauschenplat, Miguel A. Elizabeth, NJ
Munoz-Silva, Carmen .... Rosemead, CA
Munro, Alan B. .... Washington, DC
Munro, Alex W., Jr. .... Seattle, WA
Munro, Allan W. .... Seattle, WA
Munro, Andrew B. .... Los Angeles, CA
Munro, Andrew J. .... Troy, MI
Munro, Ann MacDonald .... San Jose, CA
Munro, Bruce H. .... Palo Alto, CA
Munro, Christine S. .... Reno, NV
Munro, Colin C. .... San Francisco, CA
Munro, David A. .... Albany, NY
Munro, David M., P.C. .... Portland, OR
Munro, Dawn A. .... Forest Hills, NY
Munro, Donald J. .... Washington, DC
Munro, Douglas J. .... San Diego, CA
Munro, Ellen Kane .... Chicago, IL
Munro, Gregory S. .... Missoula, MT
Munro, J. Danielle .... Baton Rouge, LA
Munro, James C., II .... Johnstown, PA
Munro, James S., Jr. .... Marblehead, MA
Munro, J. B., Jr. .... Westport, CT
Munro, John .... San Diego, CA
Munro, John R. .... Salem, OR
Munro, John W. .... Fayetteville, NY
Munro, Joyce Underwood .... Ypsilanti, MI
Munro, Kenneth R. .... Des Moines, IA
Munro, Lynda B. .... New Haven, CT
Munro, M. Vance .... Framingham, MA
Munro, Margaret .... Minneapolis, MN
Munro, Marilyn Fish .... Westport, CT
Munro, Mark S. .... New York, NY
Munro, Maureen A. .... Des Moines, IA
Munro, Michael D. .... Lincoln, NE
Munro, Michael P. .... Syosset, NY
Munro & Munro .... Westport, CT
Munro and Munro .... Detroit, MI Troy, MI
Munro & Munro, P.C. .... Kearney, NE
Munro, Nelson & Pearl .... San Diego, CA
San Francisco, CA
Munro, Robert A. .... Kearney, NE
Munro, Stevenson O. .... Washington, DC
Munro, Thomas D. .... Weatherby Lake, MO
Munro, Thomas F., II West Palm Beach, FL
Munro, W. Barton .... College Station, TX
Munro, Willard E. .... Troy, MI
Munroe, Andrew A. .... Montvale, NJ
Munroe, Barry Jacob .... Tallahassee, FL
Munroe, Carla E. .... Boston, MA
Munroe, David D. .... Treasury Department, Internal Revenue Service, GV
Munroe, David R. .... Bellaire, MI
Munroe, Earl D. .... Marblehead, MA
Munroe, Kathleen F. .... Hartford, CT
Munroe, Kirk W. .... Palm City, FL
Munroe, Mary K. .... St. Louis, MO
Munroe & McArdle .... Marblehead, MA
Munroe and Nobach, P.C. .... East Lansing, MI
Munroe, Peter .... East Lansing, MI
Munroe, Philip A. .... Neenah, WI
Munroe, Robert A. .... Sacramento, CA
Munroe, Robert A. .... Thousand Oaks, CA
Augusta, KS
Munroe, Robert A. .... Salem, MA
Munroe, Sally Gail .... Tallahassee, FL
Munroe, Stephanie G. .... New York, NY
Munroe, W. Bradley .... Tallahassee, FL
Munrow, Alfred E., III .... Stamford, CT
Muns, Edward C. .... San Diego, CA
Muns, Michele L. .... San Diego, CA
Muns, Wagner, Anastopulos & Lynn, A Professional Corporation .... San Diego, CA
Munsat, Susan Chertkof .... Washington, DC
Munsch Hardt Kopf & Harr, A Professional Corporation .... Austin, TX Dallas, TX
Munsch, John L. .... Greensburg, PA
Munsch, Martha Hartle .... Pittsburgh, PA
Munsch, Richard J. .... Pittsburgh, PA
Munsch, Russell L. .... Austin, TX Dallas, TX
Munsch, Thomas J., Jr. .... Pittsburgh, PA
Munsell, Alfred W. .... New Bedford, MA
Munsell, Clyde S. .... San Diego, CA
Munsell, Elizabeth Sanders New York, NY
Munsell, Elsie L. .... Department of the Navy, GV
Munsell, Glenn H. .... Ashland, OR
Munsell, James C. .... New York, NY
Munsell, James F. .... New York, NY
Munsell, Michael G. .... St. Louis, MO
Munsell, Raymond T. .... New York, NY
Munsell, Terri Roberts .... Kansas City, MO
Munsell, Theodore M. .... Columbus, OH
Munsell, Thomas Gregory Kansas City, MO
Munsey, David N. .... Beaverton, OR
Munsey, James M. .... West Palm Beach, FL
Munsey, Rodney R. .... Arlington, VA
Munsey, Stanley E. .... Tuscumbia, AL
Munsey, Stanley E., & Associates, P.C. Tuscumbia, AL
Munsey, William I., Jr. .... Tampa, FL
Munshani, Kalyani .... New York, NY
Munshi, Mihir A. .... Pittsburgh, PA
Munshi, Parth S. .... Wilmington, DE
Munshin, Sidney .... Los Angeles, CA
Munsiff, Virendra R. .... New York, NY
Munsill, John W. .... Sacramento, CA

Munsing, Peter N. ....Wyomissing, PA
Munsing, Peter N., Law Office, P.C. Wyomissing, PA
Munsinger, Harry L. ....San Antonio, TX
Munsinger, Stephen M. ....Denver, CO
Munson, Alex R. ....Saipan, TT
Munson, Allegra E. ....Boston, MA
Munson, Arnold ....Lake Forest, IL
Munson, Barbara A. ....Madison, WI
Munson, Bettina E. ....Freehold, NJ
Munson, Bruce E. ....Little Rock, AR
Munson, Bruce N. ....Muncie, IN
Munson, Carl A., Jr. ....Yakima, WA
Munson, Carl J., Jr. ....Purchase, NY
Munson, Charles E., Jr. ....Austin, TX
Munson, Charles J. ....Bettendorf, IA
Munson, Craig E. ....Los Angeles, CA
Munson, Deborah E. ....Biddeford, ME
Munson, Denise R. ....Walworth, NY
Munson, Douglas C. ....San Francisco, CA
Munson, Earl H. ....Madison, WI
Munson, Edward R. ....Salt Lake City, UT
Munson, Edwin P. ....Glen Allen, VA
Munson, Elizabeth P. ....New York, NY
Munson, Erin K. ....Minneapolis, MN
Munson, Gale ....Cambridge, MA
Munson, Gene M. ....Arlington, VA
Munson, Gregory W. ....Minneapolis, MN
Munson, Harrison W. ....Bloomfield Hills, MI
Munson, Harrison W., P.C. Bloomfield Hills, MI
Munson, Houston C., III ....Gonzales, TX
Munson, Houston C., Jr. ....Gonzales, TX
Munson, Howard G. ....Syracuse, NY
Munson, Howard Kent ....St. Louis, MO
Munson, J. Mark ....Pittsburgh, PA
Munson, James C., (P.C.) ....Chicago, IL
Munson, James S. ....Wharton, TX
Munson, Janice F. ....Gonzales, TX
Munson, J. D. ....Hermosa Beach, CA
Munson, Jill M. ....Milwaukee, WI
Munson, John B. ....Portland, OR
Munson, Joseph P. ....Indianapolis, IN
Munson, Joseph S. ....Boise, ID
Munson, Karen L. ....New Orleans, LA
Munson, Keith D. ....Greenville, SC
Munson, Kenneth ....Milwaukee, WI
Munson, Kimberly Janelle ....Dallas, TX
Munson Law Offices, P.C. ....Bettendorf, IA
Munson, Lee A. ....Little Rock, AR
Munson, M. A. ....Metuchen, NJ
Munson, Martin J. ....Torrance, CA
Munson, Mary M. ....Washington, DC
Munson, Melissa M. ....Austin, TX
Munson, Michael L. ....Hingham, MA
Munson, Munson, Pierce & Cardwell, A Professional Corporation ....Bonham, TX
Denison, TX
Frisco, TX
Pottsboro, TX
Sherman, TX
Whitesboro, TX
Munson, Myra M. ....Juneau, AK
Munson, Nancy K. ....Huntington, NY
Munson, Pamela A. ....Liverpool, NY
Munson, Patrick K ....New York, NY
Munson, Paul J., (S.C.) ....La Crosse, WI
Munson, Paula D. ....Columbia, PA
Lancaster, PA
Munson, Peter J. ....Lakeland, FL
Munson, Peter K. ....Carmel, IN
Sherman, TX
Munson, Peter R. ....La Jolla, CA
Munson, R. Greg ....Baton Rouge, LA
Munson, Ray E. ....Yakima, WA
Munson, Richard A. ....Denver, CO
Munson, Richard E., Jr. South Dartmouth, MA
Munson, Robt. J. ....Wayzata, MN
Munson, Sarah A. ....Columbia, SC
Munson, Stephen E. ....Modesto, CA
Munson, Steven G. ....Watertown, NY
Munson, Susan A. ....Morristown, NJ
Munson, Teresa Marie ....Sea Isle City, NJ
Munson, Thomas V. ....Boise, ID
Munson, Tim I. ....Omaha, NE
Munson, Valerie J. ....Philadelphia, PA
Munson, Walter N. ....Syracuse, NY
Munson, William B. ....Bonham, TX
Denison, TX
Pottsboro, TX
Sherman, TX
Whitesboro, TX
Munson, William T. ....Falmouth, MA
Munson, Winston E. ....Minneapolis, MN
Munson-Regala, Emmanuel T. St. Paul, MN
Munstenteiger & Schutter, P.A. ....Anoka, MN
Munstenteiger, Stephen H. ....Anoka, MN
Munster, Catherine D. ....Clarksburg, WV
Munster, Daniel Denzer ....Atlanta, GA
Munsterman, Charles H. ....Alexandria, LA
Munsterman, Herbert F. ....Des Plaines, IL
Munsterman, Jennifer A. ....Alexandria, LA
Munsterman, John W. ....Alexandria, LA
Munsterman Law Firm, The Alexandria, LA
Muntean, David A. ....Akron, OH
Muntean, Ronald ....Santa Monica, CA
Muntean, Susan M. ....Greenville, OH
Muntean, Teddy G. ....Atlanta, GA
Munteanu, Victor J. ....Denver, CO
Munter, Gavan R. ....Lakeport, CA
Munter, Godfrey L., Jr., Law Offices of San Francisco, CA
Munter, John E. ....San Francisco, CA
Munter, Karen ....San Francisco, CA
Munter, Katherine A. ....San Francisco, CA
Munter, William J. ....San Antonio, TX
Munther, Merrily ....Boise, ID
Munton, David R. ....Greenfield, MO
Muntwyler, Deborah E. ....Orlando, FL
Muntyan, Keith B. ....Boston, MA
Muntz, Jerry E. ....New York, NY
Muntz, John C. ....Hugo, OK
Muntz, Richard K. ....LaGrange, IN
Shipshewana, IN
Muntz, Richard K., P.C. ....LaGrange, IN
Shipshewana, IN
Muntzing, L. Manning ....Washington, DC
Muntzing, William H., II ....Kissimmee, FL
Munves, Russell D. ....New York, NY
Munyan, Franklin D. ....Richmond, VA
Munyan, Ralph Forrest ....Kansas City, MO
Munyan, Winthrop R. ....New York, NY
Munyon, Lisa D. ....New Orleans, LA
Munyon, Lisa T., Law Offices of Orlando, FL
Munyon, Wendy Nelson ....Grinnell, IA
Munz & Hannen ....Denver, CO
Munz, Karl F. ....Sacramento, CA
Münzberg, Nathalie ....New York, NY
Munzel, Jennifer A. ....San Antonio, TX
Munzel, John J. ....Riverhead, NY
Munzel & Napolitano, LLP ....Riverhead, NY
Munzen, Ernest Steven ....Forest Hills, NY
Munzer, Cynde Hirschtick ....Chicago, IL
Munzer & Saunders, LLP ....Fort Lee, NJ
New York, NY
Munzer, Stephen I. ....New York, NY
Munzing, Richard H. ....Brattleboro, VT
Munzinger, Richard G. ....El Paso, TX
Muoio, Ann WrayJohnson ....Washington, DC
Muoio, Elizabeth Maher ....Trenton, NJ
Muoio, Joseph ....Department of Justice, Antitrust Division, GV
Muoio, Ralph A. ....Washington, DC
Muoio, Ralph M. ....Washington, DC
Muolo, John E. ....Pittsburgh, PA
Muolo, Robert J. ....Sunbury, PA
Muoneke, Anthony Ugonna Los Angeles, CA
Muoneke, Christiana O. ....Redmond, WA
Muoneke and Ogan, A P.C. Los Angeles, CA
Mupo, Michael J. ....New York, NY
Mur & Associates, P.A. ....Miami, FL
Mur, Lazaro J. ....Miami, FL
Mur, Raphael ....Wantagh, NY
Mura, Anemarie Drees ....Kansas City, MO
Mura, Paul E. ....Rochester, NY
Mura, Roy A. ....Buffalo, NY
Mura, Steven J. ....Bellingham, WA
Murabayashi, Teryl ....Los Angeles, CA
Murabito, Anthony C. ....San Jose, CA
Murabito, Karin M. ....San Jose, CA
Murabito, Matthew J. ....New York, NY
Muraca, Felice J. ....Mineola, NY
Woodhaven, NY
Muraca, Gary ....Woodhaven, NY
Muraca & Kelly, L.L.P. ....Mineola, NY
Woodhaven, NY
Muracca, Francis A. ....Pittsburgh, PA
Muracca, Francis A., II ....Pittsburgh, PA
Murachanian, Edward ....Brick, NJ
Muraco, Marlene S. ....San Jose, CA
Murad, Anthony A. ....Utica, NY
Murad, Dale ....Department of the Air Force, Office of the Judge Advocate General, GV
Murad, David A. ....Utica, NY
Murad, Elizabeth J. ....Dallas, TX
Murad, Frederick W. ....Utica, NY
Murad, George C. ....Utica, NY
Murad, Gregory M. ....Washington, DC
Murad, James, (Professional Corporation) San Francisco, CA
Murad, Jerry, Jr. ....Fort Worth, TX
Murad, John L., Jr. ....Syracuse, NY
Murad, Leslie E., II ....San Bernardino, CA
Murad, Marcel J. ....Boston, MA
Murad & Murad ....Utica, NY
Murad & Murad ....Fort Worth, TX
Murad, Richard P. ....Boca Raton, FL
Murado, Sandra I. ....Miami, FL
Muraff, James P. ....Chicago, IL
Murai, Rene V. ....Miami, FL
Murai, Wald, Biondo & Moreno, P.A. Miami, FL
Muraidekh, Alan ....Newark, NJ
New York, NY
Murak, Paul F. ....Amherst, NY
Buffalo, NY
Murakami, Alan T. ....Honolulu, HI
Murakami, Alton A. ....Honolulu, HI
Murakami, Arthur T. ....Honolulu, HI
Murakami, Charla J.H. ....Honolulu, HI
Murakami, Glenn N. ....Pearl City, HI
Murakami, Judith Graumann ....Riverside, CA
Murakami, Mark K. ....Kapolei, HI
Murakami, Melanie S. ....Los Angeles, CA
Murakami, Paul T. ....Honolulu, HI
Murakami, Steven K. ....Rochester, MN
Mural, Walter V. ....Cleveland, OH
Muramatsu, Hisako ....Los Angeles, CA
Muramatsu, Yasuo ....Irvine, CA
Muramoto, Edward ....Los Angeles, CA
Muramoto, Edward T. ....Los Angeles, CA
Muramoto, Gene G. ....Sacramento, CA
Muranaka, Carol K. ....Honolulu, HI
Muranaka, Maureen M. Santa Monica, CA
Murane & Bostwick, L.L.C. ....Casper, WY
Cheyenne, WY
Murane, William E. ....Denver, CO
Murano, Donald K. ....Cleveland, OH
Murano, Frank William ....Susanville, CA
Reno, NV
Murano, Gabriel S. ....Novato, CA
Murano, John F. ....Oradell, NJ
Muransky, Heddy ....Hollywood, FL
Murante, David A. ....Rochester, NY
Muraoka, Dwight K. ....Wailuku, HI
Muraoka, Glenn K. ....San Jose, CA
Muraoka, Jerry J. ....Torrance, CA
Muraoka, Mamoru ....St. Paul, MN
Muraoka, Takenori ....San Diego, CA
Muraoka, Wayne H. ....Honolulu, HI
Muraoka, William K. ....Oakland, CA
Muraro, Robert E. ....Miami, FL
Murase, Jiro ....New York, NY
Murase, Satoru ....New York, NY
Murashige, Calvin K. ....Lihue, HI
Murashige, Kate H. ....San Diego, CA
Muraski, John A. ....Green Bay, WI
Muraskin, Ben E. ....Atlanta, GA
Muraskin, Joseph H. ....Hallandale Beach, FL
Muraskin, Matthew ....Hempstead, NY
Murasko, Joseph G. ....West Palm Beach, FL
Murasko, Joseph M. ....Fern Park, FL
Muratet, Elizabeth R. ....Tulsa, OK
Muratides, John N. ....Tampa, FL
Muratore, Anthony J. ....Flushing, NY
Muratore, Joseph F. ....New York, NY
Muratore, Joseph J., Jr. ....Racine, WI
Muratore, Joseph J., Law Offices, S.C. Racine, WI
Muratore, Joseph J., Sr. ....Racine, WI
Muratore, Joseph R., Jr. ....Warwick, RI
Muratore, Marjorie L. ....Stockton, CA
Muratori, Jack R. ....Flushing, NY
Muratori, Jill R. ....Glenmont, NY
Muratori & Meli ....Flushing, NY
Muratori, Raymond J. ....Springfield, MA
Muratori, Rosemary ....Westbury, NY
Muratsuchi, Albert Yasuro ......Los Angeles, CA
Muratta, Lori M. ....Houston, TX
Muravina, Elena ....Los Angeles, CA
Murawski, Benjamin J., Jr. ....Boston, MA
Murawski, Charles P. ....Orange, CA
Murawski & Grey, LLP ....Los Angeles, CA
Murawski, Kelly Maureen ....Chicago, IL
Murawski, Roberta L. ....Los Angeles, CA
Murawski, Steven J. ....Chicago, IL
Murawsky, Melissa Palat Philadelphia, PA
Murawsky, Nathan M. ....Philadelphia, PA
Murbach, Jacob F. ....Merrick, NY
Murburg, N. Michael, Jr. New Port Richey, FL
Murch, David R. ....Webster, NY
Murch, Donald H. ....Traverse City, MI
Murch, James L. ....Salem, OR
Murch, Kevin L. ....Columbus, OH
Murch, Nina P. ....Salinas, CA
Murch, Scott K. ....Long Beach, CA
Murch, Trent M. ....Chicago, IL
Murchison, Alton G., III ....Charlotte, NC
Murchison & Associates, P.A. Charlotte, NC
Matthews, NC
Murchison, Bradley D. ....Charlotte, NC
Murchison, Brian C. ....Lexington, VA
Murchison, Bruce K. ....Bakersfield, CA
Murchison & Cumming ....Los Angeles, CA
San Diego, CA
Santa Ana, CA
Murchison, Daniel T. ....Natchitoches, LA
Murchison, Daniel T., Jr. Natchitoches, LA
Murchison, David C. ....Washington, DC
Murchison, David R. ....Mobile, AL
Murchison, Frank B. ....Corsicana, TX
Murchison, Frank E. ....Lubbock, TX
Murchison, Franklin ....Jackson, TN
Murchison, Hund & Harriger, L.L.P. Lubbock, TX
Murchison, Jack M. ....Houston, TX
Murchison, James H. ....Portland, OR
Murchison, Jarrell L. ....Tallahassee, FL
Murchison, John L., Jr. ....Houston, TX
Murchison, John M., Jr. ....Charlotte, NC
Murchison, Karen L. ....Memphis, TN
Murchison, Kenneth M. ....Baton Rouge, LA
Murchison, Malcolm S. ....Shreveport, LA
Murchison, Mary E. ....Foley, AL
Murchison, Michael ....Wilmington, NC
Murchison and Murchison, L.L.C. Natchitoches, LA
Murchison, Pete M. ....Washington, DC
Murchison & Sutley, L.L.C. ....Foley, AL
Murchison, Taylor & Gibson, L.L.P. Wilmington, NC
Murchison, Wm. Vincent ....Dallas, TX
Murcia, Manuel T. ....East Greenbush, NY
Murcia, Svetlana ....Westlake, OH
Murck, William W. ....Washington, DC
Murcko, Matthew J. ....Washington, DC
Murcko, Thomas C. ....Pittsburgh, PA
Murdach, David W. ....Tacoma, WA
Murdach, David W., P.S. ....Tacoma, WA
Murdaugh, L. Lamar ....McRae, GA
Murdaugh, R. Alexander ....Hampton, SC
Murdaugh, Randolph, III ....Hampton, SC
Murdaugh, Randolph, IV ....Hampton, SC
Murdaugh, Randolph, Jr. ....Hampton, SC
Murdaugh, W. James, Jr. ....Houston, TX
Murday, Donald A. ....Chicago, IL
Murden, Wm. J. ....Peekskill, NY
Murdie, Laurel S. ....Topeka, KS
Murdo, Robert M. ....Helena, MT
Murdoch, Albert S. ....Albuquerque, NM
Murdoch, Bonnie J. ....Jacksonville, FL
Murdoch, Christopher J. ....Chicago, IL
Murdoch, Christopher John ....New York, NY
Murdoch, David Armor ....Pittsburgh, PA
Murdoch & Hughes ....Burlington, VT
Murdoch, James W. ....Burlington, VT
Murdoch, Karen L. ....Hartford, CT
Murdoch, Lauren K. S. ....El Paso, TX
Murdoch, Richard A. ....Boca Raton, FL
Murdoch, Robert Bruce ....Chesterland, OH
Murdoch, Robert E. ....Fort Lauderdale, FL
Murdoch, Robert W. ....Pittsburgh, PA
Murdoch, Timothy W. ....Russellville, AR
Murdoch-Kitt, Jonathan M. ....Richmond, VA
Murdock, Allison Marie .....Kansas City, MO
Murdock, B. Glenn ....Birmingham, AL
Murdock, Barbara W. ....Fort Worth, TX
Murdock, Ben L. ....Tulsa, OK
Murdock, Brenda D. ....Salinas, CA
Murdock, Bruce ....Santa Rosa, CA
Murdock, Carol A. ....Pasadena, CA
Murdock, Charles W. ....Chicago, IL
Murdock, Dan ....Oklahoma City, OK
Murdock, Daniel R. ....New York, NY
Murdock, Douglas C. ....La Jolla, CA
Murdock, Earl W. ....Wenatchee, WA
Murdock, Eric J. ....Washington, DC
Murdock, Frederick W., Jr. ....Salem, NH
Murdock, G. Steven ....Wheaton, IL
Murdock & Goldenberg, L.P.A. Cincinnati, OH
Murdock, Grady B., Jr. ....Chicago, IL
Murdock, Henry G. ....Markleeville, CA
Murdock, J. Nicholas ....Casper, WY
Murdock, Jack A. ....Cincinnati, OH
Murdock, J. E., III ....Washington, DC
Murdock, John B. ....Santa Monica, CA
Murdock, John C. ....Cincinnati, OH
Murdock, John E., III ....Nashville, TN
Murdock, John M. ....Washington, DC
Murdock, John R. ....Rockville, MD
Murdock, Joseph P. ....Indianapolis, IN
Murdock, Kathryn Wells ....Salem, OR
Murdock, Kent H. ....Salt Lake City, UT
Murdock, Lauretta E. ....New York, NY
Murdock, Leslie N. ....Santa Monica, CA
Murdock, M. Brooke ....Baltimore, MD
Murdock, Margaret Estelle ....Gulfport, MS
Murdock, Mark L. ....Austin, TX
Murdock, Mary G. ....Kansas City, MO
Murdock, Nanci E. ....Los Angeles, CA
Murdock, Norman A. ....Cincinnati, OH
Murdock & Palazzo, Chtd., A Prof. Law Corp. ....Las Vegas, NV
Murdock, Patricia Collins United States Senate, Senatorial Assistants, GV
Murdock, Randal D. ....New York, NY
Murdock, Robert B. ....Hagerstown, MD
Murdock, Robert B. ....Roanoke, VA
Murdock, Robert E. ....Las Vegas, NV
Murdock, Sharon R. ....Charlotte, NC
Murdock, Stephen T. ....Edmond, OK
Murdock, Susan E. ....Los Angeles, CA
Murdock, Ted C. ....Boise, ID
Murdock, Turalu Brady ....New Orleans, LA
Murdock, William L. ....Shreveport, LA
Murdock, Zachary ....Melville, NY
Murdock-Meggers, Robin S. Manchester, CT
Murdough, Sarah S. ....Concord, NH
Murdter, Charles P. ....San Francisco, CA
Murdy, M. Craig ....Phoenix, AZ
Murdy, Paul J. ....Garden City, NY
Murdy, Ralph M. ....Baltimore, MD
Murc, Joseph, Jr. ....Brooklyn, NY
Mureiko, William R. ....Dallas, TX
Muren, Robert W. ....Milwaukee, WI
Murena, Kenneth Dante Fort Lauderdale, FL
Murensky, Rudolph J., II ....Welch, WV
Murensky, Susan A. ....Charleston, WV
Murer, Matthew J. ....Chicago, IL
Murer, Michael A. ....Joliet, IL
Muret, Frank ....Stillwater, OK
Muret, W. Franklin, Jr. ....Stillwater, OK
Muret, William E. ....Winfield, KS
Murez, Libbe R. ....Marina Del Rey, CA
Murfey, George John ....La Jolla, CA
Murff, Lenox ....Ashland City, TN
Murfin, James I. ....Tucson, AZ
Murfitt, Flint ....Seattle, WA
Murfitt, Lucy C. ....Warren, PA
Murfitt, Walter S. ....Helena, MT
Murfree Cope Hudson & Scarlett Murfreesboro, TN
Smyrna, TN
Murfree, Matt B., III ....Murfreesboro, TN
Murgatroyd, Anthony J. ....Flemington, NJ
Murgatroyd, George W., III Los Angeles, CA
Murges, George J. ....Chicago, IL
Murgo, Rudolph M. ....Pendleton, OR
Murguia, Carlos ....Kansas City, KS
Murguia, David, Jr. ....San Antonio, TX
Murguia, Janet Executive Office Of The President, GV
Murguía, Ramón ....Kansas City, MO
Muri, Anthony F. ....Providence, RI
Muri, Laurence T., Law Offices of Stamford, CT
New York, NY
Muriana, Joseph Paul ....Bronx, NY
Muriceak, Jeffrey A. ....Hollidaysburg, PA
Muriel, Robert H. ....Chicago, IL
Muriella, Sam M. ....Mission Viejo, CA
Murillo, Janet S. ....Los Angeles, CA
Murillo, Jose Luis, Jr. ....New York, NY
Murillo, Rita C. ....Pittsburgh, PA
Murillo, Serena R. ....Los Angeles, CA

Muris, Timothy J. ... Arlington, VA
Murken, Douglas ... San Francisco, CA
Murkowski, David M. ... Grand Rapids, MI
Murkowski, Lisa A. ... Anchorage, AK
Murland, Alex J. ... Jenkintown, PA
Murland & Goldstein ... Jenkintown, PA
Murley, Alan J. ... Sarasota, FL
Murley, David ... Farmington Hills, MI
Murley, Elizabeth S. ... Waltham, MA
Murley, James F. ... Tallahassee, FL
Murley, Joanne K. ... Hartford, CT
Murley, Ray P. ... Sioux Falls, SD
Murley, Susan W. ... Boston, MA
Murley, Thomas S. ... Boston, MA
Murley, William C. ... Dallas, TX
Murman & Associates ... Cleveland, OH
Lakewood, OH
Murman, Ilyse D. ... Chicago, IL
Murman, James A. ... Tampa, FL
Murman, Michael E. ... Lakewood, OH
Murn, Donald J. ... Waukesha, WI
Murn Law Offices, S.C. ... Waukesha, WI
Murnaghan & Ferguson, P.A. ... Tampa, FL
Murnaghan, Francis D., Jr. ... Baltimore, MD
Murnaghan, Peter P. ... Tampa, FL
Murnahan, W. Shawn ... Atlanta, GA
Murnan, Robert J.
Charlotte Amalie, St. Thomas, VI
Murnane, Catherine W. ... Chicago, IL
Murnane, Colleen C. ... Cleveland, OH
Murnane, Conlin, White & Brandt, Professional Association ... St. Paul, MN
Murnane, Don P. ... Utica, NY
Murnane, Don P., Jr. ... New York, NY
Murnane, Harold B. ... Glen Burnie, MD
Murnane, Janet C. ... Burlington, VT
Murnane, Jean M. ... Baton Rouge, LA
Murnane, John D. ... New York, NY
Murnane, Larry N. ... San Diego, CA
Murnane, Linda Strite ... Cincinnati, OH
Murnane, Mark ... Chicago, IL
Murnane, Michael R. ... Tujunga, CA
Murnane & O'Neill ... Glen Burnie, MD
Murnane, Patricia A. Quinn ... New York, NY
Murnane, Patricia J. ... Paoli, PA
Murnane, Robert W. ... St. Paul, MN
Murnane, Thomas M. ... Plattsburgh, NY
Murnane, Timothy D. ... Davidsonville, MD
Murner, Daniel E. ... Lexington, KY
Murner, James J., Jr. ... Wayne, NJ
Murnighan, F. Kevin ... Chicago, IL
Murnighan, John B. ... Chicago, IL
Murnighan, Thomas J. ... Chicago, IL
Murnion, Nickolas C. ... Jordan, MT
Muro, Bradley J. ... New York, NY
Muro, Magdaleno C. ... Cathedral City, CA
Muro, Mark ... Sacramento, CA
Murock, Tamara W. ... Coeur d'Alene, ID
Spokane, WA
Muroff, Milestone & Milestone
Hallandale Beach, FL
Muroff, Mitchell B. ... Newton, MA
Murolo, Frederick L. ... Cheshire, CT
Muroski, Chester B. ... Wilkes-Barre, PA
Muroski, Cynthia A. ... Kingston, PA
Murov & Ades ... Lindenhurst, NY
Murov, Ellis B., (P.L.C.)
New Orleans, LA
Murov, Kenneth B. ... Newport News, VA
Murov, Mark G. ... New Orleans, LA
Murov, Ronald L. ... Oakland, CA
Murov & Ward, L.L.C. ... New Orleans, LA
Murov, Yale M. ... Lindenhurst, NY
Murph, Leonard R. ... Dallas, TX
Murphey, Arthur G., Jr. ... Little Rock, AR
Murphey, Bob ... Nacogdoches, TX
Murphey, Carole Estes ... University, MS
Murphey, Craig R. F. ... Erie, PA
Murphey, David P. ... Columbus, OH
Murphey, Deborah R. ... Atlanta, GA
Murphey, Dwight D. ... Wichita, KS
Murphey, Elmer, III ... Dallas, TX
Murphey, Elwood ... Lafayette, CA
Murphey, Heather L. ... Cleveland, OH
Murphey, James H. ... Minneapolis, MN
Murphey, James K., P.C. ... Dallas, TX
Murphey, John B. ... Chicago, IL
Murphey, John J. ... Carlsbad, CA
Murphey, Joseph M. ... Atlanta, GA
Murphey, Michael R. ... Washington, DC
Murphey, Murray C. ... Memphis, TN
Murphey, Patrick A. ... Peoria, IL
Murphey, Richard J. ... Corona, CA
Murphey, Richard R., Jr. ... Columbus, OH
Murphey, Smith, V ... Batesville, MS
Murphey, Smith, V ... Jackson, MS
Murphey, Susan Kastan ... Atlanta, GA
Murphey, Terrence P. ... Pleasanton, CA
Murphree & Avron, LLP ... Birmingham, AL
Murphree, Barney J., Jr. ... Hanover, MA
Murphree, Bill D. ... Fairbanks, AK
Murphree, Brad T. ... Wichita, KS
Murphree, Charles L. ... Decatur, AL
Murphree, Clyde E. ... Jacksonville, FL
Murphree, David H. ... Boston, MA
Murphree, David W. ... Birmingham, AL
Murphree, Gary L. ... Houston, TX
Murphree, Gary M. ... Miami, FL
Murphree, James R., Jr. ... Birmingham, AL
Murphree, Jerry D. ... Orange Beach, AL
Murphree, John D. ... Victoria, TX
Murphree, Larry W. ... San Marcos, TX
Murphree, Michele A. ... San Diego, CA
Murphree, R. Kent ... Toledo, OH
Murphree, Robert Smith ... Jackson, MS
Murphree, Sara J. ... Marietta, GA
Murphree, Walter L. ... Decatur, AL
Murphree, William C. ... Columbus, MS
Tupelo, MS
Murphrey, Jeff ... Houston, TX
Murphrey, John ... Houston, TX
Murphrey, Thomas J. ... Las Vegas, NV
Murphrey, W. Everette, IV
Winston-Salem, NC
Murphrey and Washburn ... Houston, TX
Murphrey, Willis E., III
Roanoke Rapids, NC
Murphy, A. John, Jr. ... San Francisco, CA
Murphy, A. Malcolm N. ... Lucedale, MS
Murphy, Aaron R. ... Osage, IA
Murphy, Alandra C. ... New York, NY
Murphy, Albert G. ... Hartford, CT
Murphy, Alexander B. ... Eugene, OR
Murphy, Alexander, Jr. ... West Chester, PA
Murphy, Alison L. ... Philadelphia, PA
Murphy, Alphonsus C. ... East Lansing, MI
Murphy, Ambrose J. G. ... Stamford, CT
Murphy, Ane R. ... San Jose, CA
Murphy, Ann ... Hayward, CA
Murphy, Ann M. ... Milwaukee, WI
Murphy, Ann Marie ... San Francisco, CA
Murphy, Anne M. ... Chicago, IL
Murphy, Anne M. ... Redmond, WA
Murphy, Anne McCully ... Washington, DC
Murphy, Anne T. ... San Mateo, CA
Murphy, Anne W. ... New York, NY
Murphy, Anthony J. ... Albany, NY
Murphy, Arthur A. ... Carlisle, PA
Murphy, Arthur J. ... Chicago, IL
Murphy, Arthur J., Jr. ... Pittsburgh, PA
Murphy, Arthur P. ... Quincy, MA
Murphy, Arthur W. ... New York, NY
Murphy, Arthur W. ... Newport, RI
Murphy Austin Adams Schoenfeld LLP
Sacramento, CA
Murphy, B. D., III, P.C. ... Fayetteville, GA
Murphy, Bantz & Bury ... Spokane, WA
Murphy, Barbara A. ... Washington, DC
Murphy, Barbara G. ... Los Angeles, CA
Murphy, Barbara G. ... Charlottesville, VA
Murphy, Barry A. ... San Anselmo, CA
Murphy, Barry D. ... Woodstock, VA
Murphy, Barry J. ... Stamford, CT
Murphy, Bart Thomas ... Chicago, IL
Murphy, Bartholomew ... San Francisco, CA
Murphy, Bartol & O'Brien, LLP
Mineola, NY
Murphy and Beane ... Culver City, CA
New London, CT
Boston, MA
Murphy & Beers LLP ... Oakland, CA
San Francisco, CA
Murphy, Benjamen W. ... Hammond, IN
Murphy & Bennett ... Newburgh, NY
Murphy, Bennett J. ... Los Angeles, CA
Murphy, Bernard F. ... Baltimore, MD
Murphy, Bernard J. ... Baltimore, MD
Murphy, Bertram S. ... Williamsport, PA
Murphy, Betty Southard ... Washington, DC
Murphy, Beverly P. ... New Orleans, LA
Murphy, Beverly S. ... Mocksville, NC
Murphy & Blanchar, P.A. ... Edina, MN
Murphy, Bobby Joe ... Boardman, OH
Murphy & Boyle, Chtd. ... Chicago, IL
Murphy, Brenda J. ... Chicago, IL
Murphy, Brenton & Spagnuolo, P.C.
East Lansing, MI
Lansing, MI
Murphy, Brian ... Chicago, IL
Murphy, Brian D. ... Tarrytown, NY
Murphy, Brian D. ... Richmond, VA
Murphy, Brian G. ... New York, NY
Murphy, Brian Gerald ... Englewood, CO
Murphy, Brian J. ... Manchester, CT
Murphy, Brian J. ... New Haven, CT
Murphy, Brian J. ... Baltimore, MD
Murphy, Brian J. ... Bethesda, MD
Murphy, Brian J. ... Towson, MD
Murphy, Brian J. ... Marshall, MN
Murphy, Brian Joseph ... Sterling Heights, MI
Murphy, Brian J. X. ... Boston, MA
Murphy, Brian K. ... Columbus, OH
Murphy, Brian M. ... Delmar, NY
Murphy, Brian P. ... Middletown, DE
Murphy, Brian P. ... Washington, DC
Murphy, Brian P. ... New York, NY
Murphy, Brian P. ... Greenville, SC
Murphy, Brian R. ... Lawrence, MA
Murphy, Brian R. ... Burlington, VT
Murphy, Brian T. ... Colorado Springs, CO
Murphy, Brick N. ... Green Bay, WI
Murphy, Bridget M. ... Springfield, MA
Murphy, Brock G. ... Birmingham, AL
Murphy, Brooke Smith
Oklahoma City, OK
Murphy, Bruce G. ... Vero Beach, FL
Murphy, Bruce G., P.C. ... Vero Beach, FL
Murphy, Bryan F. ... Phoenix, AZ
Murphy, Bryan P. ... Portland, OR
Murphy & Buchal, LLP ... Portland, OR
Murphy, Burkette D., III ... Fayetteville, GA
Murphy, Burns, Barber & Murphy, LLP
Albany, NY
Murphy, Butterfield & Holland, P.C.
Williamsport, PA
Murphy, Byran F ... Chicago, IL
Murphy, C. Nicole ... Sacramento, CA
Murphy, C. Theodore ... Block Island, RI
Murphy, C. Timothy, Jr. ... Chesterland, OH
Murphy, C. Westbrook ... Washington, DC
Murphy, Calvin E. ... Charlotte, NC
Murphy, Carey B. ... Anderson, SC
Murphy & Caris ... Fremont, MI
Murphy, Carl R. ... Mansfield, OH
Murphy & Carlisle ... Fayetteville, AR
Murphy & Carmen ... Media, PA
Murphy, Carol A. ... Fort Lauderdale, FL
Murphy, Carol Ann ... Philadelphia, PA
Murphy, Carol C. ... Lake Wales, FL
Murphy, Carol C., Law Office of
Lake Wales, FL
Murphy, Carolyn M. ... Phoenix, AZ
Murphy, Carolyn S. ... Cincinnati, OH
Murphy, Catherine A. ... New York, NY
Murphy, Catherine C. ... Fall River, MA
Murphy, Catherine H. ... Kansas City, MO
Murphy, Catherine M. ... Garden City, NY
Murphy, Celeste M. ... New York, NY
Murphy, Chapman & Miller, P.A.
Charlotte, NC
Murphy, Charles A. ... Burlington, MA
Murphy, Charles A. ... Waterford, MI
Murphy, Charles C., Jr., (P.C.)
Atlanta, GA
Murphy, Charles E. ... Southport, CT
New York, NY
Murphy, Charles E. ... Chicago, IL
Murphy, Charles E. ... Detroit, MI
Murphy, Charles E., Jr. ... New York, NY
Murphy, Charles Eugene, Jr. ... Atlanta, GA
Murphy, Charles F. ... Boston, MA
Murphy, Charles G. ... Chicago, IL
Murphy, Charles G. ... Boston, MA
Murphy, Charles J. ... Springfield, VA
Murphy, Charles M. ... Reno, NV
Murphy, Charles R. ... New Albany, IN
Murphy, Charles W. ... Tallahassee, FL
Murphy, Charles W. ... New York, NY
Murphy, Charlotte P. ... Bethesda, MD
Murphy, Cheryl C. ... Ontario, CA
Murphy, Cheryl O'Connor ... Los Angeles, CA
Murphy, Christina Butler
Florham Park, NJ
Murphy, Christine A. ... San Francisco, CA
Murphy, Christine A. ... Cleveland, OH
Murphy, Christine L. ... Denver, CO
Murphy, Christopher A. ... El Segundo, CA
Murphy, Christopher J.
Federal Communications Commission, GV
Murphy, Christopher J. ... Philadelphia, PA
Murphy, Christopher K. ... Washington, DC
Murphy, Christopher L. ... Charleston, SC
Murphy, Christopher M. ... Chicago, IL
Murphy, Christopher P. ... Los Angeles, CA
Murphy, Christopher P. ... Washington, DC
Murphy, Christopher W. ... Richmond, VA
Murphy, Cindy J. ... Harrisburg, PA
Murphy, Claire Perona ... Chicago, IL
Murphy & Clark ... Marquette, MI
Murphy, Clarke, Jr. ... Towson, MD
Murphy, Clifford J. ... Grand Rapids, MI
Murphy, Clyde E. ... Chicago, IL
Murphy, C. M. ... Memphis, TN
Murphy, Colin C. ... Mason City, IA
Murphy, Colleen ... Clarkston, MI
Murphy, Colleen A. ... Boston, MA
Murphy, Colleen A. ... New York, NY
Murphy, Colleen Dallavalle ... Austin, TX
Murphy, Colleen L. ... Chicago, IL
Murphy, Colleen M. ... Buffalo, NY
Murphy, Colleen P. ... Bristol, RI
Murphy & Collins, P.L.C. ... Le Mars, IA
Murphy, Connor ... New York, NY
Murphy, Constance K. ... Beverly Hills, CA
Murphy, Corinne Lee ... Sacramento, CA
Murphy, Cornelius A. ... Naples, FL
Murphy, Cornelius M. ... Chicago, IL
Murphy, Courtney E. ... New York, NY
Murphy and Coyne ... Lewiston, ME
Murphy, Craig C. ... Portland, OR
Murphy, Craig D. ... Northborough, MA
Murphy, Craig P. ... New Brunswick, NJ
New York, NY
Murphy, Cynthia L. ... Racine, WI
Murphy, Cynthia S. ... Port Charlotte, FL
Murphy, Cynthia S. ... Cleveland, OH
Murphy, D. Ray ... Dallas, TX
Murphy, D. Scott ... Springfield, IL
Murphy, D. Shane ... Kansas City, MO
Murphy, Dale E. ... York, PA
Murphy, Daniel ... Westminster, MD
Murphy, Daniel C. ... San Francisco, CA
Murphy, Daniel C. ... Buffalo, NY
Murphy, Daniel C. ... New York, NY
Murphy, Daniel E., II ... Washington, DC
Murphy, Daniel F. ... Omaha, NE
Murphy, Daniel F. ... Plainfield, NJ
Murphy, Daniel F., Jr. ... Iselin, NJ
New York, NY
Murphy, Daniel G. ... Los Angeles, CA
Murphy, Daniel H., II ... New York, NY
Pelham, NY
Murphy, Daniel I. ... Berwyn, PA
Murphy, Daniel J. ... Ventura, CA
Murphy, Daniel J. ... Boston, MA
Murphy, Daniel J. ... Boston, MA
Murphy, Daniel J. ... Somerville, MA
Murphy, Daniel J. ... Riverhead, NY
Murphy, Daniel J., III ... North Andover, MA
Murphy, Daniel L. ... Columbia, TN
Murphy, Daniel M. ... Princeton, NJ
Murphy, Daniel Michael ... Denver, CO
Murphy, Daniel P. ... Newport Beach, CA
Murphy, Daniel P. ... Denver, CO
Murphy, Daniel P. ... Atlanta, GA
Murphy, Daniel P. ... Winamac, IN
Murphy, Daniel P. ... Newton, MA
Murphy, Daniel R. ... Albany, OR
Murphy, Daniel Robert ... Albany, GA
Murphy, Daniel T. ... Kansas City, MO
Murphy, Daniel T. ... Richmond, VA
Murphy, Dannah R. ... Santa Ana, CA
Murphy, David ... Joliet, IL
Murphy, David ... Detroit, MI
Murphy, David B. ... Irvine, CA
Murphy, David H. ... Chicago, IL
Murphy, David J. ... San Jose, CA
Murphy, David J. ... Dade City, FL
Murphy, David J. ... Boston, MA
Murphy, David J. ... Media, PA
Murphy, David L. ... Denver, CO
Murphy, David L. ... Louisville, KY
Murphy, David L. ... Penfield, NY
Murphy, David L., Jr. ... Boston, MA
Murphy, David M. ... New York, NY
Murphy, David M. ... New York, NY
Murphy, David P. ... Greenfield, IN
Murphy, David P. ... Boston, MA
Murphy, David R. ... Washington, DC
Murphy, David R. ... Latham, NY
Murphy, David W. ... Pittsburgh, PA
Murphy, David W., Jr. ... Pittsfield, MA
Murphy, Dean F. ... Cary, NC
Murphy, Deborah C.
Pension Benefit Guaranty Corporation, Office of the General Counsel, GV
Murphy, Deborah J. ... Knoxville, TN
Murphy, Dena L. ... Long Beach, CA
Murphy, Denis G. ... Florham Park, NJ
Murphy, Denis J. ... Williston Park, NY
Murphy, Denis J. ... Columbus, OH
Murphy, Denise I. ... Boston, MA
Murphy, Denise N. ... Lakeland, FL
Murphy, Denise T ... San Jose, CA
Murphy, Dennis A. ... Jersey City, NJ
Murphy, Dennis D. ... Savannah, GA
Murphy, Dennis J. ... Glendale, CA
Murphy, Dennis J. ... Miami, FL
Murphy, Dennis J. ... Thief River Falls, MN
Murphy, Dennis J. (IBA) ... Cincinnati, OH
Murphy, Dennis L. ... Cleveland, OH
Murphy, Dennis M. ... Pasadena, CA
Murphy, Dennis M. ... Columbia, MO
Murphy, Dennis N. ... Martinez, CA
Murphy, Dennis P. ... Santa Fe, NM
Murphy, Dennis P. ... Bellingham, WA
Murphy, Dennis R. ... Tucson, AZ
Murphy, Dennis R. ... Sacramento, CA
Murphy, Derek D. ... Indianapolis, IN
Murphy & Desmond, S.C. ... Madison, WI
Murphy, Diana E. ... Minneapolis, MN
Murphy, Diane E. ... New Alexandria, PA
Murphy, Dianna D. ... Lexington, KY
Murphy, Donald H., P.C. ... Charlottesville, VA
Murphy, Donald J. ... Utica, NY
Murphy, Donald J. ... Harrisburg, PA
Murphy, Donald J. ... Monona, WI
Murphy, Donald L. ... Greensboro, NC
Murphy, Donald R. ... Madison, WI
Murphy, Donald X. ... Chicago, IL
Murphy, Donna M. ... Department of Justice, Civil Rights Division, GV
Murphy, Donna M. ... New York, NY
Murphy, Donna P. ... Hartford, CT
Murphy, Dorothy M. ... Mount Kisco, NY
Murphy, Douglas W. ... Berkeley Heights, NJ
Murphy, E. Michael ... Rocky Mount, NC
Murphy, E. Stanley ... Portsmouth, VA
Murphy, Earl D. ... Redding, CA
Murphy, Edmund P. ... New York, NY
Murphy, Edmund J. ... Manchester, NH
Murphy, Edmund J. ... Staten Island, NY
Murphy, Edmund M. ... Tacoma, WA
Murphy, Edward A. ... Missoula, MT
Murphy, Edward A., III
San Francisco, CA
Murphy, Edward B. ... Amherst, NY
Murphy, Edward D. ... Towson, MD
Murphy, Edward D. ... Brockton, MA
Murphy, Edward E. ... St. Louis, MO
Murphy, Edward F. ... Newtown, PA
Murphy, Edward J. ... Mission Viejo, CA
Murphy, Edward J. ... Milledgeville, GA
Murphy, Edward J. ... Chicago, IL
Joliet, IL
Murphy, Edward J. ... Covington, LA
Murphy, Edward J. ... Boston, MA
Murphy, Edward J. ... Houston, TX
Murphy, Edward J., III ... Buffalo, NY
Murphy, Edward J., Jr. ... Culver City, CA
New London, CT
Boston, MA
Murphy, Edward J., Jr. ... Hicksville, NY
Murphy, Edward J., Jr. ... Rainbow Lake, NY
Murphy, Edward L. ... Quincy, MA
Murphy, Edward L., Jr. ... Fort Wayne, IN
Murphy, Edward M. ... Bradenton, FL
Murphy, Edward P. ... Alameda, CA
Murphy, Edward P. ... Baltimore, MD
Murphy, Edward R. ... Haddonfield, NJ
Philadelphia, PA
Murphy, Edward T. ... Largo, FL
Murphy, Edward W. ... Malibu, CA
Murphy, Edward W. ... Boston, MA
Murphy, Edwin F. ... Naples, FL
Murphy, Edythe Clair ... Palm Desert, CA
Murphy, Eileen ... Northbrook, IL
Murphy, Eileen ... New York, NY
Murphy, Eileen M.
Department of the Navy, GV
Murphy, Eileen, P.C. ... Northbrook, IL
Murphy, Elaine A. ... Dallas, TX
Murphy, Elizabeth ... Department of Justice, Drug Enforcement Administration, GV
Murphy, Elizabeth A. ... St. Louis, MO
Murphy, Elizabeth Farley
Woodbridge, NJ
Murphy, Elizabeth Gow ... Dover, MA
Murphy, Elizabeth H. ... Los Angeles, CA
Murphy, Elizabeth K. ... Washington, DC

Murphy, Elizabeth M.
Securities and Exchange Commission, Division of Corporation Finance, GV
Murphy, Elizabeth O. ....Chicago, IL
Murphy, Elizabeth Stuckey
Charleston, SC
Murphy, Ellen K.V. ....Milwaukee, WI
Murphy, Ellen M. ....Chicago, IL
Murphy, Emalee G. ....Washington, DC
Murphy, Emi Anne ....Portland, OR
Murphy & Enlow ....Lexington, KY
Murphy, Ernest B. ....Boston, MA
Murphy, Eugene Donald ......Fairview Park, OH
Murphy, Eugene E. ....White Plains, NY
Murphy, Eugene E., Jr. ....Chicago, IL
Murphy, Eugene F. ....Jacksonville, FL
Murphy, Eugene F. ....Cincinnati, OH
Murphy, Eugene P. ....Anchorage, AK
Murphy, Eugene P. ....New York, NY
Murphy, Eugene P. ....Richmond, VA
Murphy, Eugene W., Jr., (P.A.)
Palm Beach, FL
Vero Beach, FL
Murphy, Ewell E., Jr. ....Houston, TX
Murphy, F. Gregory ....Marquette, MI
Murphy, F. B., Jr. ....Nashville, TN
Murphy, Floyd P., Jr. ....Houston, TX
Murphy, Francis G., Jr. ....Manchester, NH
Murphy, Francis J. ....Wilmington, DE
Murphy, Francis J. ....Asbury Park, NJ
Murphy, Francis J. ....Hamilton, NJ
Bryn Mawr, PA
Murphy, Francis J. ....New York, NY
Murphy, Francis J., III ....St. Louis, MO
Murphy, Francis P. ....Canton, IL
Murphy, Francis P. ....Wheaton, IL
Murphy, Francis Patrick ....Chicago, IL
Murphy, Francis T. ....New York, NY
Murphy, Francis W. ....Portage, WI
Murphy, Francis X. ....Buffalo, NY
Murphy, Frank G. ....Philadelphia, PA
Murphy, Frank J. ....Kansas City, MO
Murphy, Frank J., Jr. ....Charlotte, NC
Murphy, Frank, Jr. ....Sacramento, CA
Murphy, Frank M., III ....San Diego, CA
Murphy, Frank P. ....Norristown, PA
Murphy, Frank P., (P.A.) ....Naples, FL
Stuart, FL
Murphy, Frank W. ....Norwalk, CT
Murphy, Frank W. ....North Haledon, NJ
Murphy, Frederick F. ....Westchester, IL
Murphy, Frederick J., Jr. ....Bartow, FL
Murphy, G. Edward ....Peoria, IL
Murphy, G. Keith ....Moultrie, GA
Murphy, G. Patrick ....Marion, IL
Murphy, G. Wayne ....Los Angeles, CA
Murphy, Gary L. ....Millerton, NY
Murphy, Gary L. ....Charlotte, NC
Murphy, Gary W. ....Louisville, KY
Murphy, Gavin P. ....New York, NY
Murphy, Gayle T. ....Hamburg, NY
Murphy, Geo. H. ....Sacramento, CA
Murphy, George A. ....Mineola, NY
Murphy, George D., Jr. .....Bermuda Dunes, CA
Murphy, George E. ....Rancho Cordova, CA
Murphy, George F. ....Valparaiso, FL
Murphy, George F., Jr. ....Forked River, NJ
Murphy, George J. ....Paonia, CO
Murphy, George J. ....Philadelphia, PA
Murphy, George L., Jr. ....Atlanta, GA
Murphy, George M. ....New York, NY
Murphy, George R. ....Washington, DC
Murphy, George R. ....Benson, NC
Murphy, George Robertson, III
Houston, TX
Murphy, George S., Jr. ....Cisco, TX
Murphy, George W. ....Ocean Springs, MS
Murphy, George W., Jr. ....Washington, DC
Murphy, Gerald B. ....Billings, MT
Murphy, Gerald J. ....Euclid, OH
Murphy, Gerald J., Jr. ....Detroit, MI
Murphy, Gerald M. ....San Francisco, CA
Murphy, Gerald M., Jr. ......Falls Church, VA
Murphy, Gerald N. ....Rochester, NY
Murphy, Gerard E. ....Trumansburg, NY
Murphy, Gerard N. ....Rockville, MD
Murphy, Gillick, Wicht & Prachthauser
Brookfield, WI
Mequon, WI
Milwaukee, WI
Racine, WI
Murphy, Glen A. ....Charleston, WV
Murphy, Glenn A. ....Harrisburg, IL
Murphy, Glenn E. J.
Plymouth Meeting, PA
Murphy & Gold, A Professional Corporation
Calabasas, CA
Murphy & Grantland, P.A. .....Columbia, SC
Murphy, Gregory G. ....Billings, MT
Murphy, Gregory J. ....Charlotte, NC
Murphy, Gregory J. ....Tacoma, WA
Murphy, Gregory L. ....Alexandria, VA
Murphy, Gregory P. ....White Plains, NY
Murphy, Gretchen A. ....Charleston, WV
Murphy, Guy W., Jr. ....Springfield, MO
Murphy, Gwyneth MacKenzie
Brookline, MA
Murphy, Hardy Ray ....Los Angeles, CA
Murphy, Harlan E. ....Houston, TX
Murphy, Harold A. ....Westfield, MA
Murphy, Harold B. ....Boston, MA
Murphy, Harold L. ....Rome, GA
Murphy, Harriet L. ....Austin, TX
Murphy, Harris Patrick ....Baltimore, MD
Murphy and Hearn, P.C. ....Washington, DC
Murphy, Heather E. ....Atlanta, GA
Murphy, Helen D. ....New Haven, CT
Murphy, Henry L., Jr. ....Hyannis, MA

Murphy, Hesse, Toomey and Lehane
Boston, MA
Quincy, MA
Murphy and Higgins, LLP ......New York, NY
Murphy & Holden, P.A. ....St. Cloud, MN
Murphy, Howard F., IV ....Pittsburgh, PA
Murphy, Howard L. ....New Orleans, LA
Murphy, Howland D. ....New York, NY
Murphy, Hupp, Foote, Mielke and Kinnally
Aurora, IL
Geneva, IL
Sycamore, IL
Yorkville, IL
Murphy, Irving Olds ....Erie, PA
Murphy, J. Allen ....New Bern, NC
Murphy, J. Andrew ....New York, NY
Murphy, J. Douglas ....Hyannis, MA
Murphy, J. Emmett ....White Plains, NY
Murphy, J. Frasher ....Fort Worth, TX
Murphy, J. Frederick ....Pawtucket, RI
Murphy, J. James ....Tucson, AZ
Murphy, J. Justin ....Hammond, IN
Murphy, J. Lee ....Grand Rapids, MI
Murphy, J. Mark ....Andalusia, AL
Murphy, J. Michael ....Napa, CA
Murphy, J. Michael ....Liberty, MO
Murphy, J. Michael ....Memphis, TN
Murphy, J. Patrick ....Chattanooga, TN
Murphy, J. Read ....Hartford, CT
Murphy, J. Robert ....Aurora, IL
Murphy, J. Scott ....Orlando, FL
Murphy, Jack A. ....Baldwin City, KS
Murphy, Jack W. ....Washington, DC
Murphy & Jacobs, LLP ......Sacramento, CA
Murphy, Jacqueline A. ....Providence, RI
Murphy, James ....Detroit, MI
Murphy, James ....Cortland, NY
Murphy, James A. ....Sacramento, CA
San Francisco, CA
Murphy, James A. ....Chicago, IL
Murphy, James A. ....Richmond, VA
Murphy, James A. ....Seattle, WA
Murphy, James A., III ....Ballston Spa, NY
Murphy, James A., IV ....Irvine, CA
Murphy, James A., Jr. ....Middle Grove, NY
Murphy, James A., Jr. ....Virginia Beach, VA
Murphy, James B., Jr. ....Tampa, FL
Murphy, James C.
National Labor Relations Board, Office of Board Members, GV
Murphy, James C., Jr. ....New Orleans, LA
Murphy, James D., Jr. ....Chicago, IL
Murphy, James D., Jr. ....Pittsburgh, PA
Murphy, James D'Alton ....Stamford, CT
Murphy, James Duff ....Los Angeles, CA
Murphy, James E. ....Akron, OH
Murphy, James E. ....Providence, RI
Murphy, James E. ....Windsor, VT
Murphy, James E. ....Virginia Beach, VA
Murphy, James E. ....Marinette, WI
Murphy, James Edward ....Spring City, TN
Murphy, James F. ....Chicago, IL
Murphy, James G. ....Hartford, CT
Murphy, James G. ....Brooklyn, NY
Murphy, James G. ....New York, NY
Murphy, James G. ....Pen Argyl, PA
Murphy, James J. ....Los Angeles, CA
Murphy, James J. ....Colorado Springs, CO
Murphy, James J. ....Washington, DC
Murphy, James J. ....Washington, DC
Murphy, James J. ....Baltimore, MD
Murphy, James J. ....St. Louis, MO
Murphy, James J. ....Dallas, TX
Murphy, James J. ....Mequon, WI
Milwaukee, WI
Racine, WI
Murphy, James J., Jr. ....Norwich, CT
Murphy, James K. ....Douglasville, GA
Murphy, James K. ....Louisville, KY
Murphy, James L. ....Edina, MN
Murphy, James L., III ....Nashville, TN
Murphy, James Lee, III ....Austin, TX
Murphy, James M. ....Tucson, AZ
Murphy, James M. ....Los Angeles, CA
Murphy, James M. ....East Norwich, NY
Murphy, James M. ....New York, NY
Murphy, James M. ....Dallas, TX
Murphy, James M. ....Spokane, WA
Murphy, James M. A. ....Beverly Hills, CA
Murphy, James Michael ....Boston, MA
Murphy, James Michael ......Garden City, NY
Murphy, James O., Jr.
Fort Lauderdale, FL
Murphy, James P. ....Anaheim, CA
Murphy, James P. ....Washington, DC
Murphy, James P. ....Fort Lauderdale, FL
Murphy, James P. ....Chicago, IL
Murphy, James P. ....Detroit, MI
Murphy, James P. ....Billings, MT
Murphy, James P. ....New York, NY
Murphy, James P. ....Romulus, NY
Murphy, James P. ....Utica, NY
Murphy, James P. ....Camp Hill, PA
Murphy, James P. ....Pittsburgh, PA
Murphy, James P., Jr. ....Portland, OR
Murphy, James P., P.S. ....Portland, OR
Kirkland, WA
Murphy, James R. ....Hartford, CT
Murphy, James R.
National Labor Relations Board, Office of Board Members, GV
Murphy, James R. ....Aurora, IL
Murphy, James R. ....Detroit, MI
Murphy, James R. ....Trenton, NJ
Murphy, James R. ....Massapequa, NY
Murphy, James S. ....Livingston, NJ
Murphy, James Scott ....Orange, CA
Murphy, James T. ....Hackensack, NJ

Murphy, James T. ....Floral Park, NY
Murphy, James T. ....Staten Island, NY
Murphy, James T. ....Providence, RI
Murphy, James V., II ....Maywood, IL
Murphy, James W. ....Little Rock, AR
Murphy, James W. ....Boston, MA
Murphy, Jane C. ....Washington, DC
Murphy, Jane K. ....Chicago, IL
Murphy, Jane Sullivan ....New York, NY
Murphy, Janet E. ....Seattle, WA
Murphy, Janice Gail ....Newport News, VA
Murphy, Janine McPeters ....Chapel Hill, NC
Murphy, Jas. M. ....Omaha, NE
Murphy, Jas. P. ....New York, NY
Murphy, Jean ....Los Angeles, CA
Murphy, Jeanne Ann ....Largo, FL
Murphy, Jeanne Frick ....Clearwater, FL
Murphy, Jeanne M. ....Parsippany, NJ
Murphy, Jeffrey C. ....Okemos, MI
Murphy, Jeffrey D. ....Tampa, FL
Murphy, Jeffrey J. ....New York, NY
Murphy, Jeffrey J. ....Dallas, TX
Murphy, Jennifer L. ....Atlanta, GA
Murphy, Jennifer L. ....Manchester, NH
Murphy, Jennifer L. ....Harrisburg, PA
Murphy, Jennifer Pflug ....Milwaukee, WI
Murphy, Jeremiah D. ....Sioux Falls, SD
Murphy, Jeremiah E., Jr. ....Indianapolis, IN
Murphy, Jeremiah F. ....Tewksbury, MA
Murphy, Jeremy P. ....Lincoln, NE
Murphy, Jerold E. ....Fond du Lac, WI
Murphy, Jerome A. ....Washington, DC
Murphy, Jerome C. ....Baldwin, NY
Murphy, Jerome E. ....Kansas City, MO
Murphy, Jerome John ....Philadelphia, PA
Murphy, Jerome T. ....Chicago, IL
Murphy, Jerry G. ....Pleasanton, CA
Murphy, Jerry J., (P.C.) ....St. Louis, MO
Murphy, Jesse T., Jr. ....San Antonio, TX
Murphy, Jill Haley ....Newburyport, MA
Murphy, Jo Anne ....Irving, TX
Murphy, Joan L. ....Toms River, NJ
Murphy, Joan S. ....Albany, NY
Murphy, Joan W. ....Richmond, VA
Murphy, JoAnne ....Lancaster, PA
Murphy, Joanne M. ....Chicago, IL
Murphy, Joanne W. ....Columbus, OH
Murphy, Joel A. ....Morristown, NJ
Murphy, Joel K. ....Rock Springs, WY
Murphy, John A. ....Detroit, MI
Murphy, John A. ....Old Brookville, NY
Murphy, John A. ....Providence, RI
Murphy, John A., Jr. ....Phoenix, AZ
Murphy, John A., Jr. ....Canton, OH
Murphy, John A., Jr. ....Philadelphia, PA
Murphy, John Austin ....Jamestown, RI
Murphy, John B. ....Providence, RI
Murphy, John B. ....Sheboygan, WI
Murphy, John C. ....Irvine, CA
Murphy, John C. ....Melbourne, FL
Murphy, John C. ....Baltimore, MD
Murphy, John C. ....Madison, WI
Murphy, John C., Jr. ....Washington, DC
Murphy, John E. ....Brooklyn, NY
Murphy, John E., Jr. ....Boston, MA
Murphy, John F. ....Lawrence, KS
Murphy, John F. ....Worcester, MA
Murphy, John F. ....Hopkins, MN
Murphy, John F. ....Kansas City, MO
Murphy, John F. ....Eagle Bay, NY
Murphy, John F. ....Cleveland, OH
Murphy, John F. ....Wellsboro, PA
Murphy, John F. ....Elk Point, SD
Murphy, John F. ....Fort Worth, TX
Murphy, John F., & Associates, Law Offices of ....Orange, CA
Murphy, John F., Inc., L.P.A. ......Cleveland, OH
Murphy, John F., Jr. ....Florence, MA
Murphy, John F., The Law Office of
Hartford, CT
Murphy, John Francis ....Doylestown, PA
Murphy, John G. ....Chicago, IL
Murphy, John G., Jr. ....Washington, DC
Murphy, John G., Jr. ....Treasury Department, Office of the General Counsel, GV
Murphy, John H. ....Savannah, GA
Murphy, John H. ....Rochester, MI
Murphy, John J. ....Los Angeles, CA
Murphy, John J. ....Newport Beach, CA
Murphy, John J. ....San Francisco, CA
Murphy, John J. ....Hartford, CT
Murphy, John J. ....Wethersfield, CT
Murphy, John J.
Merit Systems Protection Board, Office of Appeals Counsel, GV
Murphy, John J. ....Fort Lauderdale, FL
Murphy, John J. ....Hollywood, FL
Murphy, John J. ....Ypsilanti, MI
Murphy, John J. ....New York, NY
Murphy, John J. ....Charleston, SC
Murphy, John J. ....Dallas, TX
Murphy, John J., III ....Cherry Hill, NJ
Murphy, John J., Jr. ....Calabasas, CA
Murphy, John J., Jr. ....Chicago, IL
Murphy, John J., Jr. ....New York, NY
Murphy, John L. ....Miami, FL
Murphy, John L., Jr. ....Boston, MA
Murphy, John M. ....Santa Monica, CA
Murphy, John M. ....Chicago, IL
Murphy, John M. ....Grand Rapids, MI
Murphy, John M. ....Scranton, PA
Murphy, John M., Jr. ....Staten Island, NY
Murphy, John Martin ....Cleveland, OH
Murphy, John M. G. ....Baltimore, MD
Murphy, John Michael ....Chicago, IL
Murphy, John P. ....Boston, MA
Murphy, John P. ....Ironwood, MI
Murphy, John P. ....North Platte, NE

Murphy, John P. ....New York, NY
Murphy, John P. ....Tacoma, WA
Murphy, John P., Jr. ....Wooster, OH
Murphy, John Patrick ....San Diego, CA
Murphy, John Patrick ....Fort Worth, TX
Murphy, John Patrick Michael
Colorado Springs, CO
Murphy, John R. ....Newton, MA
Murphy, John R. ....New York, NY
Murphy, John R. ....Columbia, SC
Murphy, John R. ....Rapid City, SD
Murphy, John R., III ....Louisville, GA
Murphy, John R., III ....Fairfax, VA
Murphy, John T. ....Modesto, CA
Murphy, John T. ....Melbourne, FL
Murphy, John T. ....Indianapolis, IN
Murphy, John T. ....North Easton, MA
Murphy, John T. ....Cleveland, OH
Murphy, John T., Jr. ....St. Louis, MO
Murphy, John V. ....Baltimore, MD
Murphy, John W. ....Sacramento, CA
Murphy, John W. ....Mount Vernon, WA
Murphy, John Wm. ....Fayetteville, AR
Murphy, Jon K. ....St. Paul, MN
Murphy, Jonathan ....New York, NY
Murphy, Jos. Dinsmore ....Washington, DC
Murphy, Joseph ....Tampa, FL
Murphy, Joseph A. ....St. Louis, MO
Murphy, Joseph A. ....Garden City, NY
Murphy, Joseph A. ....Scranton, PA
Murphy, Joseph A., III ....Stuart, FL
Murphy, Joseph A., Jr. ....Washington, DC
Murphy, Joseph B. ....Lexington, KY
Murphy, Joseph C. ....Somerville, NJ
Murphy, Joseph C. ....Toppenish, WA
Murphy, Joseph C., Jr. ....Memphis, TN
Murphy, Joseph D. ....Champaign, IL
Murphy, Joseph D. ....Seattle, WA
Murphy, Joseph E. ....Owego, NY
Murphy, Joseph F. ....Ridgefield, CT
Murphy, Joseph F. ....Rochester, NY
Murphy, Joseph F. ....Lancaster, PA
Murphy, Joseph F., Jr. ....Towson, MD
Murphy, Joseph F. X. ....San Francisco, CA
Murphy, Joseph G. ....Milton, MA
Murphy, Joseph I. ....St. Charles, MO
Murphy, Joseph J. ....Columbus, OH
Murphy, Joseph M. ....Washington, DC
Murphy, Joseph P. ....Cuba, NY
Olean, NY
Murphy, Joseph P., Jr. ....Santa Rosa, CA
Murphy, Joseph Patrick ....Philadelphia, PA
Murphy, Joseph T. ....Albany, NY
Murphy, Joseph T., Jr. ....Westmont, NJ
Allentown, PA
Philadelphia, PA
Murphy, Joseph W. ....Fort Wayne, IN
Indianapolis, IN
Murphy, Joseph W. ....Harrisburg, PA
Murphy, Joshua B. ....Chicago, IL
Murphy, Judith ....Los Angeles, CA
Murphy, Julia A. ....Bronxville, NY
Murphy, Julie A. ....Plainfield, NJ
Murphy, Julie C. ....Nashville, TN
Murphy, Justin ....Mechanicsburg, PA
Murphy, Justin R. ....Oneida, NY
Murphy, K. Kevin ....Harrisburg, PA
Murphy, Kara A.T. ....New Haven, CT
Murphy, Karen Ann ....St. Louis, MO
Murphy, Karen D. ....Baton Rouge, LA
Murphy, Karen E. ....Florham Park, NJ
Murphy, Karen Krajci ....Chapel Hill, NC
Murphy, Karen V. ....Lexington, KY
Murphy, Karen Veronica ....Mineola, NY
Murphy, Karleen M. ....San Francisco, CA
Murphy and Karpie, LLC
Bridgeport, CT
Danbury, CT
Murphy, Katherine L. ....Boston, MA
Murphy, Katherine L. ....Columbus, OH
Murphy, Kathleen ....Raleigh, NC
Murphy, Kathleen A. ....Hartford, CT
Murphy, Kathleen A.
Department of Defense, GV
Murphy, Kathleen A. ....Department of State, Office of the Legal Adviser, GV
Murphy, Kathleen A. ....Boston, MA
Murphy, Kathleen A. ....Las Vegas, NV
Murphy, Kathleen D. ....Miami Lakes, FL
Murphy, Kathleen K. ....New York, NY
Murphy, Kathleen M. ....Chicago, IL
Murphy, Kathleen M. ....Newtown Square, PA
Murphy, Kathleen S. ....Roseland, NJ
Murphy, Kathryn Cochrane ....Boston, MA
Murphy, Kathryn J. ....Dallas, TX
Plano, TX
Murphy, Kathryn M. ....San Francisco, CA
Murphy, Kathryn M. ....Quincy, MA
Murphy, Kathy Hoffmann ....Chicago, IL
Murphy, Keith J. ....Windsor, CT
Murphy, Keith R. ....New York, NY
Murphy, Keith T. ....Clarkston, MI
Murphy, Kellie M. ....Sacramento, CA
Murphy, Kenneth A. ....Philadelphia, PA
Murphy, Kenneth D. ....Portsmouth, NH
Murphy, Kenneth J. ....Los Angeles, CA
Murphy, Kenneth J. ....Little Silver, NJ
Murphy, Kenneth J. ....New City, NY
Murphy, Kent ....Atlanta, GA
Murphy, Kent D. ....King Of Prussia, PA
Murphy, Kenyon W. ....Atlanta, GA
Murphy, Kevin ....Rancho Cordova, CA
Murphy, Kevin ....Bronxville, NY
Murphy, Kevin C. ....Syracuse, NY
Murphy, Kevin F. ....Roseland, NJ
Murphy, Kevin F. ....Roseland, NJ
Murphy, Kevin F. ....Springfield, VA
Murphy, Kevin G. ....Springfield, MA

Murphy, Philip M. ... Bay Shore, NY
Murphy, Phillip J. ... Ridgewood, NJ
Nanuet, NY
Murphy, Piazza & Genello, P.C.
Lancaster, PA
Scranton, PA
Murphy, Pierre E., Law Offices of
Washington, DC
Murphy & Posner, L.L.P. ... Phoenix, AZ
Murphy, Post, Thompson, Arnold & Skinner
Batesville, AR
Jonesboro, AR
Murphy, R. Anthony ... Kansas City, MO
Murphy, R. Dan ... Los Angeles, CA
Murphy, R. Edward ... St. Joseph, MO
Murphy, R. Frank, II ... Winston-Salem, NC
Murphy, R. Napier ... Atlanta, GA
Macon, GA
Murphy, R. Patrick ... Washington, DC
Murphy, R. Vaughn ... Lexington, KY
Murphy, Rachel D. ... Palatka, FL
Murphy, Rae Ann ... Rye, NY
Murphy, Ralph C. ... Joliet, IL
Murphy, Randall R. ... Studio City, CA
Murphy, Randy P. ... Little Rock, AR
Murphy, Raphael R., Jr. ... Chappaqua, NY
Murphy, Raymond M. ... Boston, MA
Murphy, Raymond R., Jr.
Chattanooga, TN
Murphy, Raymond T. ... Northbrook, IL
Murphy, Raymond W. ... New York, NY
Murphy, Rebecca K. ... Galveston, TX
Murphy, Rebecca S. ... Cleveland, OH
Murphy, Reid, Pilotte, Ord & Austin
Palm Beach, FL
Vero Beach, FL
Murphy, Rena Carolyn ... Los Angeles, CA
Murphy, Richard B. ... Phoenix, AZ
Murphy, Richard C. ... Woodstock, GA
Murphy, Richard D., Jr. ... Chicago, IL
Murphy, Richard E. ... Stamford, CT
Murphy, Richard G., Jr. ... Atlanta, GA
Murphy, Richard H. ... Williamsville, NY
Murphy, Richard H., Jr. ... Boston, MA
Murphy, Richard J. ... Osceola, IA
Murphy, Richard J. ... Belmont, MA
Murphy, Richard J. ... Trenton, NJ
Murphy, Richard L. ... Chicago, IL
Murphy, Richard L. ... Cedar Rapids, IA
Murphy, Richard P. ... Denver, CO
Murphy, Richard S. ... Arlington, VA
Murphy, Richard V. ... Lexington, KY
Murphy, Richard W. ... Portland, ME
Murphy, Richard W. ... Braintree, MA
Murphy, Richard W. ... Minneapolis, MN
Murphy, Richd. C. ... Janesville, WI
Murphy, Rick F. ... Nashville, TN
Murphy, Rick J. ... San Francisco, CA
Murphy & Riley, P.C. ... Boston, MA
Murphy, Robert ... Chicago, IL
Murphy, Robert ... New York, NY
Murphy, Robert A. ... Boston, MA
Murphy, Robert A., Jr. ... Albany, NY
Murphy, Robert B. ... Washington, DC
Murphy, Robert B. L. ... Madison, WI
Murphy, Robert C. ... Annapolis, MD
Murphy, Robert C. ... Binghamton, NY
Murphy, Robert D., Jr. ... Richmond, VA
Murphy, Robert E. ... Sacramento, CA
San Francisco, CA
Murphy, Robert E. ... Woodland Hills, CA
Murphy, Robert E. ... Waterloo, IL
Murphy, Robert E. ... Springfield, MA
Murphy, Robert E. ... Detroit, MI
Murphy, Robert E., Jr. ... Manchester, NH
Murphy, Robert F. ... Woburn, MA
Murphy, Robert F., Jr. ... Lowell, MA
Murphy, Robert H. ... New Orleans, LA
Murphy, Robert J. ... Hartford, CT
Murphy, Robert J. ... Gary, IN
Murphy, Robert J. ... Independence, IA
Murphy, Robert J. ... Boston, MA
Murphy, Robert J. ... Boston, MA
Murphy, Robert J. ... Billings, MT
Murphy, Robert J. ... Wallington, NJ
Murphy, Robert J. ... Scranton, PA
Murphy, Robert J. ... Towanda, PA
Murphy, Robert J. ... Falls Church, VA
Murphy, Robert J. (Bob), Jr.
King Of Prussia, PA
Murphy, Robert J., III ... Portola Valley, CA
Murphy, Robert J., Jr ... Boston, MA
Murphy, Robert J., Jr. ... Milwaukee, WI
Murphy, Robert L. ... San Diego, CA
Murphy, Robert L. ... Pittsburgh, PA
Murphy, Robert L., Sr. ... Alexandria, VA
Murphy, Robert, Ltd. ... Chicago, IL
Murphy, Robert M. ... Gretna, LA
Murphy, Robert M. ... Youngstown, OH
Murphy, Robert M. ... Stillwater, OK
Murphy, Robert M., Jr. ... Stillwater, OK
Murphy, Robert Martin ... South Dennis, MA
Murphy, Robert P. ... Phoenix, AZ
Murphy, Robert P.
General Accounting Office,
Office of the General Counsel, GV
Murphy, Robert P. ... Pensacola, FL
Murphy, Robert Patrick ... Walnut Creek, CA
Murphy, Robert S. ... Phoenix, AZ
Murphy, Robert S. ... Mineola, NY
Murphy, Robert S., Jr. ... Springfield, MA
Murphy, Robert W. ... Hartford, CT
Murphy, Robert W. ... Fort Lauderdale, FL
Murphy, Robin D. ... Boston, MA
Murphy, Robinson, Heckathorn & Phillips, P.C.
Kalispell, MT
Murphy, Robt. J. ... Cleveland, OH
Murphy, Roger P. ... Waukesha, WI
Murphy, Roger S. ... Edwardsville, IL
Murphy, Roger T. ... Laguna Hills, CA
South Lake Tahoe, CA
Murphy, Roger T., A Professional Law
Corporation ... Laguna Hills, CA
Murphy, Rogers & Sloss ... Metairie, LA
New Orleans, LA
Murphy & Roig, P.A., Law Offices of
Fort Lauderdale, FL
Naples, FL
Murphy, Ron ... Hartford, CT
Murphy, Ronald D.
Federal Maritime Commission,
Other Offices of the Commission, GV
Murphy, Ronald J. ... Cold Spring, KY
Murphy, Ronald T. ... Lakeland, FL
Murphy, Rose M. ... Chicago, IL
Murphy, Roy, III ... Houston, TX
Murphy, Rudick J., II ... Brentwood, TN
Murphy, Russell G. ... Boston, MA
Murphy, Ruth November ... Glen Allen, VA
Murphy, Ruthanne Nash ... Little Rock, AR
Murphy, S. Sean ... Morgantown, WV
Murphy, S. Wayne ... New Orleans, LA
Murphy, Sally ... St. Louis, MO
Murphy, Sally A. ... Bronx, NY
Murphy, Samuel B., Jr. ... St. Louis, MO
Murphy, Sandi R. ... Cleveland, OH
Murphy, Sandra K. ... Denver, CO
Murphy, Sandra M. ... Charleston, WV
Murphy, Sandra R. ... Chicago, IL
Murphy, Sarah H. ... Fayetteville, GA
Murphy, Sarah H., P.C. ... Fayetteville, GA
Murphy, Scott H. ... Kansas City, MO
Murphy, Scott L. ... Hartford, CT
Murphy, Sean ... Washington, DC
Murphy, Sean ... Boston, MA
Murphy, Sean ... Highland, NY
Murphy, Sean B. ... Sacramento, CA
Murphy, Sean C. ... Hartford, CT
Murphy, Sean F. ... McLean, VA
Murphy, Sean J. ... Fairfield, CT
Murphy, Sean J. ... Woodbury, NJ
Murphy, Sean J.
Philadelphia, PA
Murphy, Sean K. ... Charlotte, NC
Murphy, Sean K. ... Milwaukee, WI
Murphy, Sean M. ... New York, NY
Murphy, Sean P. ... Boston, MA
Murphy, Sean Patrick ... Edison, NJ
Murphy & Shaffer ... Baltimore, MD
Murphy, Sharolyn L. ... Philadelphia, PA
Murphy, Sharon E. ... Los Angeles, CA
Murphy, Sharon Funcheon
Indianapolis, IN
Murphy, Sharon Grimes ... Denver, CO
Murphy, Sharon M. ... Washington, DC
Murphy, Shaun M. ... San Francisco, CA
Murphy, Shaun M.
Department of State, GV
Murphy, Shawn Michael ... Yakima, WA
Murphy, Shawn William ... Dearborn, MI
Murphy, Sheila A. ... Morristown, NJ
Murphy, Sheila Anne ... Keaau, HI
Murphy, Sheila M. ... Markham, IL
Murphy, Sheila M. ... New York, NY
Murphy, Sheila T. ... White Plains, NY
Murphy Sheneman Julian & Rogers, A
Professional Corporation
Los Angeles, CA
San Francisco, CA
Murphy & Shepard ... Lucedale, MS
Murphy, Sheri T. ... Albany, NY
Murphy, Shirley L. ... Hollister, CA
Murphy & Sibley, P.C. ... Atlanta, GA
Macon, GA
Murphy, Sidney L. ... Dallas, TX
Murphy, Sigurd E., Jr. ... Anchorage, AK
Murphy & Smith, Ltd. ... Chicago, IL
Murphy Spadaro & Landon
Wilmington, DE
Murphy, Stacey L. ... St. Louis, MO
Murphy, Stanley J. ... Tuscaloosa, AL
Murphy, Stanley J. ... Farmington, MO
Murphy, Starr L. ... Washington, DC
Murphy, Stephen ... Longwood, FL
Murphy, Stephen A. ... Chicago, IL
Murphy, Stephen C. ... St. Louis, MO
Murphy, Stephen D. ... Garden City, NY
Murphy, Stephen G. ... Wellesley, MA
Murphy, Stephen G., Jr. ... New Haven, CT
Murphy, Stephen J. ... St. Louis, MO
Murphy, Stephen J. ... Montpelier, VT
Murphy, Stephen J., III ... Detroit, MI
Murphy, Stephen M. ... San Francisco, CA
Murphy, Stephen P. ... Washington, DC
Murphy, Stephen P. ... Overland Park, KS
Murphy, Stephen R. ... San Diego, CA
Murphy, Stephen V. ... Mashpee, MA
Murphy, Steve H. ... Valencia, CA
Murphy, Steven D. ... Muncie, IN
Murphy, Steven Hugh ... Valencia, CA
Murphy, Steven J. ... Boston, MA
Murphy, Steven L. ... Brockton, MA
Murphy, Steven P. ... Berlin, MA
Murphy, Sue P. ... Dallas, TX
Murphy, Susan Bridenbaugh
Houston, TX
Murphy, Susan C. ... Boston, MA
Murphy, Susan E.
Equal Employment Opportunity
Commission,
Office of Legal Counsel, GV
Murphy, Susan F. ... Orlando, FL
Murphy, Susan K. ... San Antonio, TX
Murphy, Susan M. ... Haddonfield, NJ
Murphy, Susanne Kiester ... Columbia, SC
Murphy, Suzanne Curran
Philadelphia, PA
Murphy, T. Austin ... Baltimore, MD
Murphy, T. Jefferson ... Kalamazoo, MI
Murphy, T. N., Jr., P.A. ... Boca Raton, FL
Murphy, Tanya Y. ... Washington, DC
Murphy, Tara A. ... Morristown, NJ
Murphy, Tara L. ... San Francisco, CA
Murphy, Taylor & Trout, P.C. ... Erie, PA
Pittsburgh, PA
Murphy, Tecla A. ... Washington, DC
Murphy, Ted J. ... Washington, DC
Murphy, Terence ... Norfolk, VA
Murphy, Terence M. ... Concord, CA
Murphy, Terence M. ... Dallas, TX
Murphy, Terence P. ... Minneapolis, MN
Murphy, Terence Roche ... Washington, DC
Murphy, Terese Bartucci ... New City, NY
Murphy, Terrence H. ... Pittsburgh, PA
Murphy, Terrence J., Jr. ... Stamford, CT
Murphy, Terrence T. ... Birmingham, MI
Murphy, Theresa Brennan ... New York, NY
Murphy, Theresa Brodeur ... Peoria, IL
Murphy, Thomas ... Newton, MA
Murphy, Thomas A. ... Kingston, NY
Murphy, Thomas B. ... Bremen, GA
Murphy, Thomas B. ... Andover, MA
Murphy, Thomas C. ... New York, NY
Murphy, Thomas D. ... Los Angeles, CA
Murphy, Thomas D. ... Rockville, MD
Murphy, Thomas D., II ... Louisville, KY
Murphy, Thomas D., Jr. ... Chicopee, MA
Murphy, Thomas D., P.C. ... Rockville, MD
Murphy, Thomas E. ... Newtown, CT
Murphy, Thomas E. ... Sumner, IA
Murphy, Thomas E. ... South Dennis, MA
Murphy, Thomas E. ... Philadelphia, PA
Murphy, Thomas F. ... Burlington, MA
Murphy, Thomas F., Jr. ... Wellesley, MA
Murphy, Thomas G. ... Syracuse, NY
Murphy, Thomas H. ... Chicago, IL
Murphy, Thomas J. ... Coloma, CA
Murphy, Thomas J. ... Hartford, CT
Murphy, Thomas J. ... Roswell, GA
Murphy, Thomas J. ... Chicago, IL
Murphy, Thomas J. ... Chicago, IL
Murphy, Thomas J. ... Baltimore, MD
Murphy, Thomas J. ... Boston, MA
Murphy, Thomas J. ... Detroit, MI
Murphy, Thomas J. ... Marlton, NJ
Murphy, Thomas J. ... Newburgh, NY
Murphy, Thomas J. ... Syracuse, NY
Murphy, Thomas J. ... Cincinnati, OH
Murphy, Thomas J. ... Tigard, OR
Murphy, Thomas J. ... Dallas, TX
Murphy, Thomas J., Jr. ... Marlton, NJ
Murphy, Thomas J., P.C. ... Chicago, IL
Murphy, Thomas J., P.C. ... Marlton, NJ
Murphy, Thomas K. ... Albany, NY
Murphy, Thomas L. ... Atlanta, GA
Murphy, Thomas L. ... Orland Park, IL
Murphy, Thomas L. ... Albuquerque, NM
Murphy, Thomas M. ... Tucson, AZ
Murphy, Thomas M. ... Mission Viejo, CA
Murphy, Thomas M. ... Saginaw, MI
Murphy, Thomas M. ... Hastings, MN
Murphy, Thomas M. ... Virginia Beach, VA
Murphy, Thomas Neil, Jr.
Boca Raton, FL
Murphy, Thomas O. ... Cleveland, OH
Murphy, Thomas O. ... Manassas, VA
Murphy, Thomas P. ... San Jose, CA
Murphy, Thomas P. ... Chicago, IL
Murphy, Thomas P. ... Des Moines, IA
Murphy, Thomas P. ... North Augusta, SC
Murphy, Thomas P. ... McLean, VA
Murphy, Thomas R. ... El Cajon, CA
Murphy, Thomas R. ... Boston, MA
Murphy, Thomas Richard ... Osceola, IA
Murphy, Thomas W. ... Chicago, IL
Murphy, Thomas W. ... Thornton, PA
Murphy, Thos J. ... Syracuse, NY
Murphy, Timothy ... Saugerties, NY
Murphy, Timothy A. ... Caledonia, MN
La Crescent, MN
Murphy, Timothy C. ... New York, NY
Murphy, Timothy D. ... Severna Park, MD
Murphy, Timothy E. ... Columbus, OH
Murphy, Timothy H. ... New York, NY
Murphy, Timothy J. ... Arcadia, CA
Murphy, Timothy J. ... Oakland, CA
Murphy, Timothy J. ... Miami, FL
Murphy, Timothy J. ... Chicago, IL
Murphy, Timothy J ... Clinton, MD
Murphy, Timothy J. ... Kansas City, MO
Murphy, Timothy J. ... Williston Park, NY
Murphy, Timothy J. ... Portland, OR
Murphy, Timothy J. ... State College, PA
Murphy, Timothy J. ... Milwaukee, WI
Murphy, Timothy J. ... Milwaukee, WI
Murphy, Timothy M. ... Los Angeles, CA
Murphy, Timothy M. ... Washington, DC
Murphy, Timothy M. ... Boston, MA
Murphy, Timothy P. ... Sacramento, CA
Murphy, Timothy P. ... Walnut Creek, CA
Murphy, Timothy P. ... Lockport, NY
Murphy, Timothy P. ... Syracuse, NY
Murphy, Timothy R. ... Brainerd, MN
Murphy, Timothy R. ... Charleston, WV
Murphy, Timothy S. ... Saco, ME
Murphy, Timothy S. ... Minneapolis, MN
Murphy, Timothy S. ... St. Louis, MO
Murphy, Tobben & Wasinger, L.C.
St. Louis, MO
Murphy & Tobin ... Kansas City, MO
Murphy, Tolboe & Mabey
Salt Lake City, UT
Murphy, Tom J., Jr. ... Fort Worth, TX
Murphy, T. R., Jr. ... Eldorado, IL
Murphy, Travis M. ... Fernandina Beach, FL
Murphy, Tricia S. ... Dayton, OH
Murphy, Trish K. ... Seattle, WA
Murphy, Ty Michael ... Fresno, CA
Murphy, Valerie A. ... San Diego, CA
Murphy, Vanessa A. ... Atlanta, GA
Murphy, Veronica M. ... Toledo, OH
Murphy, Vincent ... Naples, FL
Murphy, Vincent F. ... New York, NY
Murphy & Vitch ... Niagara Falls, NY
Murphy, W. David, (P.C.) ... Denver, CO
Murphy, W. Dean, III ... Charleston, SC
Murphy, W. Elisa ... Dayton, OH
Murphy, W. Michael, Jr. ... Secaucus, NJ
Murphy, W. Scott ... Decatur, IL
Murphy, W. Spencer ... New Orleans, LA
Murphy, W. Tayloe, Jr. ... Warsaw, VA
Murphy, Walter D., Jr. ... Crownsville, MD
Murphy, Walter G. ... Boston, MA
Murphy, Walter J., Jr. ... Baltimore, MD
Murphy, Walter L. ... Concord, NH
Murphy, Warren D. ... Warsaw, IN
Murphy & Weber ... Washington, DC
Murphy, Wendy ... Boston, MA
Murphy, Wesley A. ... Chesapeake, VA
Murphy, Will ... Miami, FL
Murphy, William B. ... Grand Rapids, MI
Murphy, William C. ... Aurora, IL
Murphy, William C. ... Toppenish, WA
Murphy, William D. ... Concord, NH
Murphy, William D. ... Phoenixville, PA
Murphy, William David ... Buffalo, NY
Murphy, William E. ... Wellesley, MA
Murphy, William F. ... San Francisco, CA
Murphy, William F., III ... Miami, FL
Murphy, William G. ... New York, NY
Murphy, William H. ... Boston, MA
Murphy, William H., III ... Baltimore, MD
Murphy, William H., Jr. ... Baltimore, MD
Murphy, William H., Jr. & Associates, P.A.
Baltimore, MD
Murphy, William J. ... San Francisco, CA
Murphy, William J. ... Baltimore, MD
Murphy, William J. ... Albany, NY
Murphy, William J. ... Houston, TX
Murphy, William J. ... Houston, TX
Murphy, William J. ... Federal Way, WA
Murphy, William J. ... Seattle, WA
Murphy, William J. D. ... Central Islip, NY
Murphy, William K. ... Kalamazoo, MI
Murphy, William K. ... Easton, PA
Murphy, William King ... Hazel Crest, IL
Murphy, William L. ... Treasury Department,
Office of the General Counsel, GV
Murphy, William L. ... Staten Island, NY
Murphy, William L. ... Cleveland, OH
Murphy, William M. ... New York, NY
Murphy, William M. ... Fort Worth, TX
Murphy, William O. ... New York, NY
Murphy, William P. ... Tampa, FL
Murphy, William P. ... Chicago, IL
Murphy, William P. ... Quincy, MA
Murphy, William P. ... Point Pleasant, NJ
Murphy, William P. ... Chapel Hill, NC
Murphy, William P. ... Philadelphia, PA
Murphy, William R. ... New Haven, CT
Murphy, William R. ... Manassas, VA
Murphy, William S., Jr. ... Oklahoma City, OK
Murphy, William T. ... Missoula, MT
Murphy, William T. ... Providence, RI
Murphy, William T. ... Warwick, RI
Murphy, William T., Law Offices, Inc.
Providence, RI
Murphy, William W. ... Bridgewater, NJ
Murphy, William W. ... Oklahoma City, OK
Murphy, Williams S. ... Lucedale, MS
Murphy, Wm. M. ... Scranton, PA
Murphy, Wrennie I. ... Beverly Hills, CA
Murphy & Young ... Lewisville, MN
Madelia, MN
St. James, MN
Murphy, Yvette G. ... Coconut Grove, FL
Murphy & Zissu ... New York, NY
Murphy Kennedy, Sherri ... Cincinnati, OH
Murphy-Kinsler, Alison E. ... Chicago, IL
Murphy Markie, Kathleen
Columbia, MO
Murphy-Petros, Melissa A. ... Chicago, IL
Murphy-Robinson, Nancy
Bloomington, MN
Murphy-Robinson, Nancy E. ... Edina, MN
Murr, Austin ... Houston, TX
Murr, Compton, Claypoole & Macbeth
Dayton, OH
Murr, Edw. G. ... Houston, TX
Murr, Floyd K. ... Walsenburg, CO
Murr, George B. ... Houston, TX
Murr, Joseph A. ... Denver, CO
Murr, Marc D. ... Houston, TX
Murr, Ryan A. ... Irvine, CA
Murr, Susan J. ... Warren, NJ
Murr, Timothy L. ... Gulfport, MS
Murr, William ... Portland, OR
Murr, William H., P.C., Law Offices of
Portland, OR
Murrah, Alfred P., Jr.
Oklahoma City, OK
Murrah, C. Mark ... Houston, TX
Murrah, Doyle & Wigle, P.A.
Winter Park, FL
Murrah, Gilbert J. ... Bainbridge, GA
Murrah, John F. ... Memphis, TN
Murrah, Kenneth F. ... Winter Park, FL
Murrah, M. Lee ... Troy, MI
Murrah, Todd Britton ... Memphis, TN
Murrah, Watt ... Hondo, TX
Murrain, Godfrey H. ... New York, NY
Murrane, Mary Beth ... Boston, MA
Murray, Adam ... Los Angeles, CA

Murray, Adele Kittredge .... Melville, NY
Murray, A. G., Jr. .... Claremore, OK
Murray, Aisha Q. .... Washington, DC
Murray, Alan L. .... Dallas, TX
Murray, Albert R., Jr. .... East Stroudsburg, PA
Murray, Alfred B. .... Fairmont, WV
Murray, Alice Hale .... Niceville, FL
Murray, Allan J. .... Detroit, MI
Murray, Andrew J. .... Providence, RI
Murray, Andrew James .... Louisville, KY
Murray, Andrew K. .... Roseland, NJ
Murray, Ann E. .... Jacksonville, FL
Murray, Ann M. .... Sacramento, CA
Murray, Ann M. .... Bangor, ME
Murray, Anne M. .... Uniondale, NY
Murray, Anne M. .... Columbus, OH
Murray, Anthony, (A P.C.)
Los Angeles, CA
Murray, Anthony H., Jr. .... Philadelphia, PA
Murray, Anthony J., Jr. .... Chicago, IL
Murray, Archibald R. .... New York, NY
Murray & Bader .... Rockport, MA
Murray, Barbara A. .... Whitmore Lake, MI
Murray, Barbara Ann .... Briarcliff Manor, NY
Murray, Barbara Howe .... San Diego, CA
Murray, Barbara S. .... Florham Park, NJ
Murray, Bernard J. .... Chicago, IL
Murray, Bernard M. .... Gahanna, OH
Murray, Brenda P.
Securities and Exchange Commission,
Office of Administrative Law Judges, GV
Murray, Brian E. .... Garden City, NY
Murray, Brian L., Jr. .... Washington, DC
Murray, Brian P. .... Modesto, CA
Murray, Brian P. .... New York, NY
Murray, Brian T. .... Newark, DE
Murray, Brian T., P.A. .... Newark, DE
Murray, Brian W. .... Milford, MA
Murray, Bridget A. .... Pittsburgh, PA
Murray, Britton N. .... Washington, DC
Murray, Brownson .... West Bloomfield, MI
Murray, Bruce H .... Easton, MA
Murray, Bryan K. .... Pocatello, ID
Murray & Budzyn, A Law Corporation
Los Angeles, CA
Pasadena, CA
Murray, C. Joseph .... Metairie, LA
Murray, C. Perry .... Denver, CO
Murray, C. Robert, Jr. .... Miami, FL
Murray, Carlos W., Jr. .... Greenville, NC
Murray, Carol A. .... East Aurora, NY
Murray, Carolyn A. .... Newark, NJ
Murray, C. E. .... Nashville, TN
Murray, Cecily H. .... Oklahoma City, OK
Murray, Charles A. .... Tustin, CA
Murray, Charles A. .... Naples, FL
Murray, Charles A., P.A., Law Offices of
Naples, FL
Murray, Charles C. .... McAllen, TX
Murray, Charles E. .... Bakersfield, CA
Murray, Charles F. .... Denver, CO
Murray, Charles J. .... Boston, MA
Newton, MA
Murray, Charles J. .... Raleigh, NC
Murray, Charles L. .... Elkhart, IN
Murray, Charles M. .... Sandusky, OH
Murray, Charles O., III .... Blowing Rock, NC
Murray, Charles S., Jr. .... Atlanta, GA
Murray, Cheryl Tillberg .... Dallas, TX
Murray, Christina M. .... Boston, MA
Murray, Christopher .... New York, NY
Murray, Christopher A. .... Xenia, OH
Murray, Christopher C. .... Los Angeles, CA
Murray, Christopher J. .... Waterbury, CT
Murray, Christopher M. .... Detroit, MI
Murray, Christopher W. ..... Department of State,
Foreign Service Officers (Overseas), GV
Murray, Cindy Hastie .... Oklahoma City, OK
Murray, Clarence D. .... Crown Point, IN
Murray, Clark .... Floresville, TX
Murray, Clifford F. .... Dallas, TX
Murray, Colin H. .... San Diego, CA
Murray, Conal E. .... Tarrytown, NY
Murray, Cornelius D. .... Albany, NY
Murray, Cornelius J., III .... Boston, MA
Murray, Craig W. .... Houston, TX
Murray, Craven & Inman, L.L.P.
Fayetteville, NC
Murray & Cross .... Milwaukee, WI
Murray, Cutcliffe & Glavin
Providence, RI
Murray, Cynthia "Cindy" S.
Albuquerque, NM
Murray, D. Kim .... Mansfield, OH
Murray, D. Michael .... Chicago, IL
Murray, D. Michael, (P.C.) .... Batavia, NY
Murray, D. Scott .... Alpharetta, GA
Murray, Damian G. .... Toms River, NJ
Murray, Damian G., P.C. .... Toms River, NJ
Murray, Dan R. .... Sparta, NC
Murray, Dana Elizabeth .... Aurora, CO
Murray, Daniel A. .... Glenview, IL
Murray, Daniel C. .... Chicago, IL
Murray, Daniel E. .... Coral Gables, FL
Murray, Daniel E. .... Philadelphia, PA
Murray, Daniel F. .... Middleboro, MA
Murray, Daniel G. .... Princeton, NJ
Murray, Daniel H. .... Washington, DC
Murray, Daniel J. .... Westminster, CO
Murray, Daniel J. .... Providence, RI
Murray, Daniel P. .... South Glens Falls, NY
Murray, Daniel P. .... Waukesha, WI
Murray, Daniel Patrick .... River Falls, WI
Murray, Daniel R. .... Chicago, IL
Murray, Daniel T. .... Modesto, CA
Murray, Danielle S. .... San Diego, CA
Murray, Darnell & Associates, L.L.C.
New Orleans, LA
Murray, David D. .... Newport Beach, CA
Murray, David D. .... Detroit, MI
Toledo, OH
Murray, David E. .... Sterling, IL
Murray, David F. .... Denver, CO
Murray, David G. .... Fort Lauderdale, FL
Murray, David G., P.A.
Fort Lauderdale, FL
Murray, David J. .... Buffalo, NY
Murray, David J. .... Cleveland, OH
Murray, David L. .... Hunt Valley, MD
Murray, David P. .... Washington, DC
Murray, David S. .... Roseville, CA
Murray, David T. .... Washington, DC
Murray, Deborah .... Charlottesville, VA
Murray, Dennis E. .... Red Bluff, CA
Murray, Dennis E., Jr. .... Sandusky, OH
Murray, Dennis E., Sr. .... Sandusky, OH
Murray, Dennis P. .... Cleveland, OH
Murray, Desmond T. .... Fairport, NY
Murray, Don Anderson .... Kew Gardens, NY
Murray, Donald G. .... Baltimore, MD
Murray, Donald J. .... Miami, FL
Murray, Donald J. .... New York, NY
Murray, Donald R., Jr. .... Kalispell, MT
Murray, Donald W. .... Dedham, MA
Murray, Donald W. .... Rahway, NJ
Murray, Donald X. .... Chicago, IL
Murray, Donna A. .... Denver, CO
Murray, Donnie R. .... Atlanta, GA
Murray, Douglas .... Irvine, CA
Murray, Douglas D. .... Wayne, NE
Murray, Douglas F. .... Baltimore, MD
Murray, Douglas P. .... Lumberton, NC
Murray, Douglas R. .... Armonk, NY
Murray, Dunham & Murray .... Everett, WA
Seattle, WA
Murray, Dwayne R. .... Medford, OR
Murray, Dwight D. .... Washington, DC
Murray, Dylan L. .... Kansas City, MO
Murray, E. Christopher .... Garden City, NY
Murray, E. Patrick .... Troy, MI
Murray, E. Stephen .... Portland, ME
Murray, Edean .... Storm Lake, IA
Murray, Edw. E. .... Baltimore, MD
Murray, Edw. F., Jr. .... Cheyenne, WY
Murray, Edward D. .... Canton, OH
Salem, OH
Murray, Edward W. .... Rahway, NJ
Murray, Edwin R. .... New Orleans, LA
Murray, Eileen Hartney .... Cupertino, CA
Murray, Elizabeth A. .... Boston, MA
Murray, Elizabeth R. .... Cincinnati, OH
Murray, Elizabeth Robben, (P.A.)
Little Rock, AR
Murray, E.M. (Sandy) .... Gig Harbor, WA
Murray, Emmet V. .... Darien, CT
Murray, Erin .... Miamisburg, OH
Murray, Erin D. .... Philadelphia, PA
Murray, Ernie K. .... Ahoskie, NC
Rocky Mount, NC
Murray, Eugene R. .... Scottsdale, AZ
Murray, Felicia H. .... New York, NY
Murray, Florence K. .... Providence, RI
Murray, Francis J. .... Rockville Centre, NY
Murray, Francis J., Jr. .... Providence, RI
Murray, Francis T. .... Kingston, NY
Murray, Francis X. .... South Burlington, VT
Murray, Frank .... Santa Fe, NM
Murray, Frank L. .... Phoenix, AZ
Murray, Frank L. .... Miami, FL
Murray, Frank S. .... Washington, DC
Murray, Fred F. .... Washington, DC
Murray, Frederick (Rick) C.E.
Reidsville, NC
Murray, G. Richard .... San Francisco, CA
Murray, Gail N. .... Hibbing, MN
Murray, Garrett J. .... Elyria, OH
La Grange, OH
Murray, Garrett J., Co., L.P.A. .... Elyria, OH
Murray, George A. .... St. Louis, MO
Murray, George C., Jr. .... Vidalia, LA
Murray, George E. .... St. Louis, MO
Murray, George F. .... West Hartford, CT
Murray, George V. .... Roseville, MI
Murray, Georgia L. .... New York, NY
Murray, Gerald F. .... Chicago, IL
Murray, G. H. .... Sheldon, IA
Murray, Gilbert J. .... Plattsburgh, NY
Murray, Gilmur R. .... Greenbrae, CA
Murray, G. J. .... Mansfield, OH
Murray, Glen A. .... Grand Island, NE
Murray, Glenn E. .... Buffalo, NY
Murray, Gregory D. .... Madison, WI
Murray, Gregory S. .... Chicago, IL
Murray, Gregory V. .... Bingham Farms, MI
Murray & Griffin .... Texarkana, TX
Murray, Guy W. .... Nipomo, CA
Murray, Gwen E. .... Bethel, CT
Murray, Gwyn Firth .... Mountain View, CA
Murray, Harry J. .... Trenton, NJ
Murray, Heather L. .... Adams, MA
Murray, Helen G. .... Saratoga, CA
Murray, Helena C. .... St. Paul, MN
Murray, Henry C. .... Mackinac Island, MI
Murray, Herbert F. .... Baltimore, MD
Murray & Hollander LLP .... New York, NY
Murray, Hugh F., III .... Hartford, CT
Murray, Hulon .... Russellville, AL
Murray, Hyde H. .... Fort Washington, MD
Murray, Isobel M. .... Santa Barbara, CA
Murray, J. Edward .... Jupiter, FL
Murray, J. Manson .... Mobile, AL
Murray, J. Michael .... Cleveland, OH
Murray, J. Reese .... Birmingham, AL
Murray, J. Reese, III .... Birmingham, AL
Murray, Jack B., Jr. .... Houston, TX
Murray & Jacobs .... Alexandria, VA
Murray, Jacqueline B. .... Chicago, IL
Murray, Jacqueline Phillips .... Albany, NY
Murray, James .... Pawtucket, RI
Murray, James .... Madison, WI
Murray, James A. .... Santa Clara, CA
Murray, James A. .... Pueblo, CO
Murray, James B. .... Chicago, IL
Murray, James B., Jr. .... Charlottesville, VA
Murray, James C. .... Chicago, IL
Murray, James C., Jr. .... Chicago, IL
Murray, James D. .... Santa Monica, CA
Murray, James D., (P.A.) .... Lakeland, FL
Murray, James Donald .... Santa Monica, CA
Murray, James E. .... Washington, DC
Murray, James E. .... New York, NY
Murray, James E. .... White Plains, NY
Murray, James E. .... Mentor, OH
Murray, James F. .... Saugus, MA
Murray, James G. .... Long Beach, CA
Murray, James H. .... Birdsboro, PA
Morgantown, PA
Reading, PA
Murray, James H., Jr. .... Boynton Beach, FL
Murray, James H., Jr. .... Victoria, TX
Murray, James I. .... Lexington, KY
Murray, James J. .... Fremont, CA
Murray, James J. .... Petoskey, MI
Murray, James J. .... Accord, NY
Ellenville, NY
Murray, James J. .... New York, NY
Murray, James L. .... Berwyn, PA
Philadelphia, PA
Murray, James M. .... Rockledge, FL
Murray, James M. .... Arlington Heights, IL
Murray, James M. .... Spokane, WA
Murray, James P. .... Bethany Beach, DE
Murray, James P. .... Miami, FL
Murray, James P., III .... Ocean City, MD
Murray, James R. .... Pensacola, FL
Murray, James R. .... Chicago, IL
Murray, James R. .... Seattle, WA
Murray, James T. .... Evanston, IL
Murray, James T. .... Lutherville, MD
Murray, James T. .... Sandusky, OH
Murray, James T., Jr. .... Milwaukee, WI
Murray, James V. .... Stillwater, OK
Murray, James V., III .... Washington, DC
Murray, James W. .... Baton Rouge, LA
Murray, James W. .... Belleville, MI
Murray, James W., III
Oklahoma City, OK
Murray, Jan E. .... Cleveland, OH
Murray, Janalee M. .... Las Vegas, NV
Murray, Janice M. .... Palo Alto, CA
Murray, Jankins & Noble .... Des Moines, IA
Murray, Jason B. .... Mansfield, OH
Murray, Jason C. .... Los Angeles, CA
Murray, Jason M. .... Miami, FL
Murray, Jay J. .... Dallas, TX
Murray, Jean L. .... Worcester, MA
Murray, Jeanne M. .... Tallahassee, FL
Murray, Jeffrey H. .... Kalispell, MT
Murray, Jeneane Fountaine .... New York, NY
Murray, Jennifer Del .... Baton Rouge, LA
Murray, Jennifer S. .... Phoenix, AZ
Murray, Jeremiah P. .... Palos Hills, IL
Murray, Jerome .... New York, NY
Murray, Jerome C. .... Philadelphia, PA
Murray, Jerry B. .... Sandusky, OH
Murray, Jerry M. .... Rock Springs, WY
Murray, Jessica R. .... Rochester, NY
Murray, Jill E. .... Denver, CO
Murray, Jo Ann E. .... Tulsa, OK
Murray, Joanne M. .... Jenkintown, PA
Murray, Joel .... Chicago, IL
Murray, John .... Miami, FL
Murray, John A. .... Denver, CO
Murray, John A. .... Clearwater, FL
Murray, John A. .... Edina, MN
Murray, John A. .... St. Paul, MN
Murray, John A., & Associates, Ltd.
St. Paul, MN
Murray, John A., Jr. .... Houston, TX
Murray, John B. .... Roseland, NJ
Murray, John B.T., Jr.
West Palm Beach, FL
Murray, John C. .... Chicago, IL
Murray, John D. .... Cedar Knolls, NJ
Murray, John D. .... Appleton, WI
Murray, John E. .... Binghamton, NY
Murray, John E. .... Milwaukee, WI
Murray, John E., Jr. .... Pittsburgh, PA
Murray, John F. .... Washington, DC
Murray, John F. .... New York, NY
Murray, John G. .... Rio Rancho, NM
Murray, John H. .... Easton, MD
Murray, John J. .... San Francisco, CA
Murray, John J. .... San Francisco, CA
Murray, John J., Jr. .... Green Brook, NJ
Murray, John L. .... White Plains, NY
Murray, John M. .... Sacramento, CA
Murray, John M. .... Miami, FL
Murray, John M. .... Chicago, IL
Murray, John M. .... Storm Lake, IA
Murray, John M. .... New York, NY
Murray, John P. .... Coconut Grove, FL
Murray, John P. .... Chicago, IL
Murray, John P. .... Spokane, WA
Murray, John R. .... Morris Plains, NJ
Murray, John R. .... Oswego, NY
Murray, John S. .... Orange, CA
Murray, John S. .... Charlestown, MA
Murray, John S. .... Lubbock, TX
Murray, John T. .... Atlanta, GA
Murray, John T. .... Taunton, MA
Murray, John T. .... Albuquerque, NM
Murray, John T. .... Sandusky, OH
Murray, John V. A. .... Greenwich, CT
Stamford, CT
Murray, John Walshe .... Palo Alto, CA
Murray, Joseph C. .... Philadelphia, PA
Murray, Joseph E. .... Berkeley Heights, NJ
Murray, Joseph E., & Associates, P.A.
Berkeley Heights, NJ
Murray, Joseph F. .... Boston, MA
Murray, Joseph F. .... Columbus, OH
Murray, Joseph F. .... Warrington, PA
Murray, Joseph G. .... Saddle Brook, NJ
Staten Island, NY
Murray, Joseph G. .... Wilkes-Barre, PA
Murray, Joseph G., P.C., Law Offices of
Wilkes-Barre, PA
Murray, Joseph H. .... Deshler, NE
Hebron, NE
Murray, Joseph L., Jr. .... Oradell, NJ
Murray, Joseph M. .... Plymouth, MA
Murray, Joseph P. .... Belleville, IL
St. Louis, MO
Murray, Joseph P. .... Brigantine, NJ
Murray, Joseph T. .... New York, NY
Murray, Joseph W. .... Detroit, MI
Murray, Josiah S., III .... Durham, NC
Murray, Joy M. .... Phoenix, AZ
Murray, Julia E. .... Los Angeles, CA
Murray, Julia Heintz .... Houston, TX
Murray, Julia O. .... Pensacola, FL
Murray, Julian R., Jr. .... Metairie, LA
Murray, Julie A. .... Brielle, NJ
Murray, Karen M. .... Mount Laurel, NJ
Murray, Kathleen A. .... Novato, CA
Murray, Kathleen A. .... San Francisco, CA
Murray, Kathleen A. .... New York, NY
Murray, Kathleen Sullivan
Barrington, RI
Murray, Kay C. .... New York, NY
Murray, Kelly Duggan .... San Antonio, TX
Murray, Kelly J. .... Rapid City, SD
Murray, Kelly L. .... Chicago, IL
Murray, Ken .... Columbus, OH
Murray, Kenneth J. .... Milwaukee, WI
Murray, Kenneth L. .... Greensburg, PA
Murray, Kenneth T. .... Daytona Beach, FL
Murray, Kerry E. .... Washington, DC
Murray, Kevin .... Los Angeles, CA
Murray, Kevin .... Sac City, IA
Murray, Kevin Charles .... Indianapolis, IN
Murray, Kevin J. .... Miami, FL
Murray, Kevin J. .... Boston, MA
Murray, Kevin R. .... Salt Lake City, UT
Murray • Kittle, P.C. .... Denver, CO
Murray, Larry .... Baton Rouge, LA
Murray Law Firm .... West Helena, AR
Murray Law Firm .... New Orleans, LA
Murray Law Offices .... Atlanta, GA
Murray, Lawrence A. .... Dover, MA
Murray, Lawrence D. .... San Francisco, CA
Murray, Lawrence E. .... Old Bridge, NJ
Murray, Lawrence M. .... Winchester, MA
Murray, Lawrence P. .... Boston, MA
Murray, Lee Anne .... Nashville, TN
Murray, Leonard .... Chicago, IL
Murray, Leonard H. .... Edina, MN
Murray, Leslie C. .... New York, NY
Murray, Leslie G. .... Boise, ID
Murray, Lesly Gaynor .... Atlanta, GA
Murray, Lewis V., III .... Bogalusa, LA
Murray, Lisa A. .... Washington, DC
Murray, Lisa R. .... Burlingame, CA
Murray & Litteer .... Batavia, NY
Murray, Lloyd D. .... Pembroke, GA
Richmond Hill, GA
Murray & Lobb, L.L.P. .... Houston, TX
Murray, Lois A. .... Hudson, WI
Murray, Loretta H. .... Mill Neck, NY
Murray, Lori S. .... Columbia, SC
Murray, Lynn Hagman .... Chicago, IL
Murray, Lynn, (Ms.) .... Kokomo, IN
Murray, Malcolm M. .... Denver, CO
Murray, Malcolm S., P.C. .... Cumming, GA
Murray, Malcolm S., Sr., (P.C.)
Cumming, GA
Murray, Marcia S. .... Los Angeles, CA
Murray, Margaret E. .... San Francisco, CA
Murray, Margaret M. .... Brewster, NY
Murray, Margaret M. .... Sandusky, OH
Murray, Maria J. .... Denver, CO
Murray, Marianne F. .... Westport, CT
New York, NY
Murray, Marilyn F. .... Philadelphia, PA
Murray, Mark A. .... Hauppauge, NY
Murray, Mark E. .... Richmond, VA
Murray, Mark P. .... Worcester, MA
Murray, Mark R., Law Offices of
San Francisco, CA
Murray, Mark T. .... Houston, TX
Murray, Mark V. .... Dallas, TX
Murray, Marshall A. .... Houston, TX
Murray, Marshall H. .... Kalispell, MT
Murray, Martha .... New Haven, CT
Murray, Martin J. .... New York, NY
Murray, Martin T. .... Redwood City, CA
Murray, Mary Ann .... Chicago, IL
Murray, Mary J. .... Buffalo, NY
Murray, Matt .... Seattle, WA
Murray, Matthew B. .... Charlottesville, VA
Murray, Matthew J. .... New York, NY
Murray, Maureen Demarest
Greensboro, NC
Murray, Melinda G. .... Washington, DC
Murray, Menton, Jr. .... Brownsville, TX
Murray, Meta R. .... Albany, NY
Murray, Michael .... Lansing, MI
Murray, Michael A. .... Chicago, IL
Murray, Michael B. .... Worcester, MA
Murray, Michael B., Jr. .... Norristown, PA

Murray, Michael D. ..... Painesville, OH
Murray, Michael E. ..... St. Louis, MO
Murray, Michael F. ..... Alliance, OH
Murray, Michael H. ..... Houston, TX
Murray, Michael J. ..... Bridgeview, IL
Murray, Michael J. ..... Chicago, IL
Murray, Michael J. ..... Mount Clemens, MI
Murray, Michael J. ..... Providence, RI
Murray, Michael K. ..... Boston, MA
Murray, Michael K., P.S. ..... Seattle, WA
Murray, Michael L. ..... Jefferson City, MO
Murray, Michael L. ..... Arlington, VA
Murray, Michael M. ..... New York, NY
Murray, Michael P. ..... Stamford, CT
Murray, Michael Patrick ..... Fairfax, VA
Murray, Michael Q. ..... Louisville, KY
Murray, Michael Quinlan ..... Maumee, OH
Murray, Michael S. ..... Tampa, FL
Murray, Michael S. ..... Milwaukee, WI
Murray, Michael T. ..... Sandusky, OH
Murray, Michael W. ..... Green Valley, AZ
Tucson, AZ
Murray, Michelle Gill ..... St. Paul, MN
Murray, Milissa A. ..... Washington, DC
Murray, Misty A. ..... Los Angeles, CA
Murray, Muriel Johnson ..... Richmond, VA
Murray Murphy Moul & Basil, LLP
Columbus, OH
Murray & Murray ..... Boston, MA
Murray & Murray, A Professional Corporation ..... Palo Alto, CA
Murray & Murray Co., L.P.A.
Sandusky, OH
Murray, Murray and McManus ..... Milford, MA
Murray & Murray, P.L.C. ..... Storm Lake, IA
Murray, Nancee M. ..... Sacramento, CA
Murray, Nancy ..... Schaumburg, IL
Murray, Nancy A. ..... Washington, DC
Murray, Nancy B. ..... Portland, OR
Murray, Nancy L. ..... San Francisco, CA
Murray, Neal J. ..... Cherry Hill, NJ
Murray, Neil T. ..... Philadelphia, PA
Murray, Nicole Shurman ..... Boston, MA
Murray, Nita L. ..... Detroit, MI
Murray, Noel C. ..... Sacramento, CA
Murray, Noelle R. ..... Chillicothe, MO
Murray, Norman Douglas ..... Irvine, CA
Murray, O. Joseph ..... Ashland, OH
Murray, O. Russel ..... Denver, CO
Murray, Ocie F., Jr. ..... Fayetteville, NC
Murray, Olga D. ..... Sausalito, CA
Murray, Oliver C. (Tuffy), Jr. ..... Atlanta, GA
Murray, Owen J. ..... Chicago, IL
Murray, P. Bradley ..... Mobile, AL
Murray, P. Thomas, Jr. ..... Indianapolis, IN
Murray, Parker K. ..... New York, NY
Murray, Patricia A. ..... Detroit, MI
Murray, Patricia A. ..... Cranston, RI
Murray, Patricia C. ..... Hyattsville, MD
Upper Marlboro, MD
Murray, Patricia Gail ..... Wheaton, IL
Murray, Patricia I. ..... Fort Lauderdale, FL
Murray, Patricia L. ..... Albany, NY
Murray, Patricia M. ..... Fairfax, VA
Murray, Patrick ..... Minneapolis, MN
Murray, Patrick B. ..... House of Representatives, Committee Legal Personnel, GV
Murray, Patrick J.
Department of Transportation, U. S. Coast Guard, GV
Murray, Patrick J. ..... Cleveland, OH
Murray, Patrick O. ..... Springfield, MA
Murray, Paul B. ..... New Canaan, CT
Murray, Paul E. ..... New London, CT
Murray, Paul E. ..... Washington, DC
Murray, Paul S. ..... San Diego, CA
Murray, Paula M. ..... Atlanta, GA
Murray, Peter Allen ..... Lakewood, OH
Murray, Peter D. ..... Albany, NY
Murray, Peter D. ..... New York, NY
Murray, Peter F. ..... San Diego, CA
Murray, Peter J. ..... New Rochelle, NY
Murray, Peter L., Law Office of
Portland, ME
Murray, Philip E., Jr. ..... Boston, MA
Murray, Philip J., III ..... Pittsburgh, PA
Murray, Philip R. ..... Silver Spring, MD
Murray, Philip R. ..... Rensselaer, NY
Murray, Philip X. ..... Boston, MA
Murray, Plumb & Murray ..... Portland, ME
Murray & Quill ..... Winchester, MA
Murray, R. Andrew ..... Charlotte, NC
Murray, R. Michael ..... Syracuse, NY
Murray, Rachel E. ..... Towson, MD
Murray, Ralph C. ..... West Helena, AR
Murray, Raymond W., Jr. ..... Syracuse, NY
Murray, Rebecca Brake ..... Knoxville, TN
Murray and Reilly ..... Rensselaer, NY
Murray, Richard ..... Alexandria, VA
Murray, Richard A. ..... West Orange, NJ
Murray, Richard B. ..... Mt. Vernon, OH
Murray, Richard C. ..... Westminster, MD
Murray, Richard D., Jr. ..... Carbondale, IL
Murray, Richard H. ..... New York, NY
Murray, Richard H.B. ..... Lake Success, NY
Murray, Richard J. ..... Mendham, NJ
Murray, Richard J. ..... Somerville, NJ
Murray, Richard J. ..... Rapid City, SD
Murray, Richard J., Jr. ..... Plymouth, MA
Murray, Richard K. ..... Dalton, GA
Murray, Richard L., Jr. ..... Denver, CO
Murray, Richard P. ..... San Rafael, CA
Murray, Robert A. ..... Santa Rosa, CA
Murray, Robert A. ..... Boston, MA
Murray, Robert A. ..... Columbia, MO
Murray, Robert Alexander ..... Rockport, MA
Murray, Robert B. ..... Colorado Springs, CO
Murray, Robert B. ..... Washington, DC

Murray, Robert B., Jr. ..... Newtown, PA
Murray, Robert C. ..... Los Angeles, CA
Murray, Robert C. ..... Houston, TX
Murray, Robert D. ..... Cranston, RI
Murray, Robert E. ..... Oakton, VA
Murray, Robert E., Jr. ..... Stamford, CT
Murray, Robert E., Jr. ..... Bangor, ME
Murray, Robert F. ..... Brockton, MA
Murray, Robert F. ..... New Bedford, MA
Murray, Robert F. ..... St. Louis, MO
Murray, Robert J. ..... Meriden, CT
Murray, Robert J. ..... Omaha, NE
Murray, Robert L., Jr. ..... Philadelphia, PA
Murray, Robert Lee ..... Logansport, IN
Murray, Robert P. ..... Lakeland, FL
Murray, Robert P. ..... Leominster, MA
Murray, Robert R. ..... San Antonio, TX
Murray, Robert W. ..... Stamford, CT
Murray, Robert W. ..... Miami, FL
Murray, Robert W., Jr. ..... New York, NY
Murray, Robert Y. ..... Boston, MA
Murray, Robt. A. ..... Staten Island, NY
Murray, Roger Eugene ..... Atlanta, GA
Murray, Roger F., III ..... Wolfeboro, NH
Murray, Roger G., Jr. ..... Jackson, TN
Murray, Ronald A. ..... Houston, TX
Murray, Ronald D. ..... Portland, OR
Murray, Ronald D., P.C. ..... Portland, OR
Murray, Roy E., Jr. ..... Bigfork, MT
Murray, Russel, III ..... Denver, CO
Murray, Russel, III, P.C. ..... Aurora, CO
Denver, CO
Murray, Ruthanne ..... Brook Park, OH
Murray, S. Charles ..... Atlanta, GA
Murray, S. Mark ..... San Antonio, TX
Murray, Samuel A. ..... Griffin, GA
Murray, Samuel J. ..... Sarasota, FL
Murray, Samuel P. ..... Easton, PA
Murray, Sandra I. ..... Wilmette, IL
Murray, Sara ..... San Antonio, TX
Murray, Saranne P. ..... Hartford, CT
Murray, Scott B. ..... Washington, DC
Murray, Scott B. ..... Greensboro, NC
Murray, Scott C. ..... West Palm Beach, FL
Murray, Scott E. ..... Walnut Creek, CA
Murray, Scott M. ..... Chicago, IL
Murray, Sean A. ..... Cincinnati, OH
Murray, Sean T. ..... Kansas City, MO
Murray, Sherman Dee ..... Tecumseh, OK
Murray, Siobhan C. ..... Chicago, IL
Murray, Stephen B. ..... New Orleans, LA
Murray, Stephen B., Jr. ..... New Orleans, LA
Murray, Stephen D. ..... Studio City, CA
Murray, Stephen J. ..... Danbury, CT
Murray, Stephen M. ..... Chicago, IL
Murray, Stephen O. ..... Madison, WI
Murray, Stephen R. ..... Arlington Heights, IL
Murray, Stephen T. ..... Boston, MA
Murray, Steven L. ..... Denver, CO
Murray, Steven W. ..... Encino, CA
Murray, Susan A. ..... Philadelphia, PA
Murray, Susan C. ..... Woodbridge, NJ
Murray, Susan E. ..... Media, PA
Murray, Susan M. ..... Middlebury, VT
Murray, Susan M. ..... Charleston, WV
Murray, Tanya M. ..... Wilmington, DE
Murray, Teresa White ..... Washington, DC
Murray, Terrance C. ..... Lafayette, CA
Murray, Terrence J. ..... Boston, MA
Murray, Terrence P. ..... Evergreen, CO
Murray, Terrie Benson ..... Cheektowaga, NY
Murray, Thomas ..... Chicago, IL
Murray, Thomas A. ..... Hartford, CT
Murray, Thomas C., Jr. ..... New York, NY
Murray, Thomas D. ..... Chicago, IL
Murray, Thomas D. ..... Jackson, TN
Murray, Thomas G. ..... Boston, MA
Murray, Thomas J. ..... Farmington Hills, MI
Murray, Thomas J. ..... Sandusky, OH
Murray, Thomas J. ..... Charleston, WV
Huntington, WV
Murray, Thomas L. ..... Granger, IN
Murray, Thomas M. ..... San Diego, CA
Murray, Thomas M. ..... New York, NY
Murray, Thomas M., Jr. ..... Hackensack, NJ
Murray, Thomas P., Jr.
Grand Rapids, MI
Murray, Thomas V. ..... Lawrence, KS
Murray, Thomas W. ..... St. Paul, MN
Murray, Thora M. ..... New York, NY
Murray, Tillotson, Nelson and Wiley
Atchison, KS
Oskaloosa, KS
Leavenworth, KS
Murray, Timothy ..... Pittsburgh, PA
Murray, Timothy J. ..... Chicago, IL
Murray, Timothy John ..... Lakeland, FL
Murray, Todd A. ..... Sacramento, CA
Murray, Todd A. ..... Dallas, TX
Murray, Todd Hughes ..... West Helena, AR
Murray, Tyler L. ..... Dallas, TX
Murray, Vernon Edward ..... Pasadena, CA
Murray, Vida Sharpe ..... Frankfort, KY
Murray, Vikki S. ..... Rochester, MN
Murray, Vincent A., Jr. ..... Boston, MA
Murray, Virginia H. ..... Jefferson City, MO
Murray, W. Michael ..... Des Moines, IA
Murray, W. Michael ..... Austin, TX
Murray, W. Patrick ..... Sandusky, OH
Murray, Walter A. ..... Little Rock, AR
Murray, Walter A., Jr. ..... Union, MO
Murray, Walter A., Jr. ..... Casper, WY
Gillette, WY
Murray, Warren J. ..... New York, NY
Murray, Wayne ..... Seattle, WA
Murray, Wayne E. ..... New Castle, NH
Murray, Wayne E., P.A. ..... New Castle, NH
Murray, W. D., Jr. (P.C.) ..... Butte, MT

Murray & Whitehead ..... Nipomo, CA
San Luis Obispo, CA
Santa Maria, CA
Murray, William ..... Birmingham, MI
Murray, William ..... Schenectady, NY
Murray, William A., III ..... Westfield, MA
Murray, William A., Jr. ..... Milford, MA
Murray, William C. ..... Hartford, CT
Murray, William D. ..... Suisun City, CA
Murray, William D. ..... Riverside, IL
Murray, William E. ..... Hartford, CT
Murray, William E. ..... Missoula, MT
Murray, William E. ..... New York, NY
Murray, William E. ..... St. Albans, WV
Murray, William F., Jr. ..... Birmingham, AL
Murray, William G. ..... Goleta, CA
Murray, William G. ..... San Francisco, CA
Murray, William G. ..... Arlington, VA
Murray, William H. ..... Piscataway, NJ
Murray, William H. ..... Philadelphia, PA
Murray, William J. ..... Lafayette, CA
Murray, William J. ..... Stockton, CA
Murray, William J. ..... Stamford, CT
Murray, William J. ..... Warren, NJ
Murray, William J. ..... Pittsburgh, PA
Murray, William J., Jr ..... Philadelphia, PA
Murray, William J., Law Offices of
West Springfield, MA
Murray, William J., (P.C.) ..... Americus, GA
Murray, William K. ..... Birmingham, AL
Murray, William M. ..... Buffalo, NY
Murray, William P. ..... Southington, CT
Murray, William R. ..... Northport, AL
Murray, William R., Jr. ..... Washington, DC
Murray, William R., Jr. ..... Washington, DC
Murray & Williams ..... Batavia, NY
Murray, Wm. A. ..... Moline, IL
Murray, Wm. C., Jr. ..... Denver, CO
Murray-Gill Patton, Robin Catherine
Atlanta, GA
Murray-Kolb, Elizabeth ..... Seguin, TX
Murray-Lusby, Marsha ..... Portland, OR
Murray-Malysa, Theresa ..... Orland Park, IL
Murray-O'Toole, Maureen
Philadelphia, PA
Murrell & Brown ..... Washington, DC
Murrell, Catherine A. ..... New York, NY
Murrell, Cheri C. ..... Oakland, CA
Murrell, Dan S. ..... Memphis, TN
Murrell, David E. ..... Louisville, KY
Murrell, Dennis D. ..... Louisville, KY
Murrell, Frederick J. ..... Bradenton, FL
Murrell, Gregory L. ..... Encinitas, CA
Murrell, H. Guyton ..... Lexington, SC
Murrell, J. David ..... Anderson, SC
Murrell, Jack O. ..... McLean, VA
Murrell, Jean K. ..... Culver City, CA
Murrell, Jeffrey R. ..... Morristown, TN
Murrell, John M., Jr. ..... Miami, FL
Murrell, Lawrence R. ..... Kokomo, IN
Murrell, M. Troy ..... Dallas, TX
Murrell, Patricia L. ..... New York, NY
Murrell, Randolph P. ..... Tallahassee, FL
Murrell, Richard Marshall ..... Memphis, TN
Murrell, Robert E. ..... Naples, FL
Murrell, Robert G. ..... Orlando, FL
Murrell, Thomas W., III ..... Charlotte, NC
Murrell, Travis A. ..... Washington, DC
Murrell, Truman O. ..... Point Pleasant, NJ
Murrelle, Edward L. ..... Beaufort, NC
Murren & Homa ..... Fairfield, CT
Murren, Kathleen Buckley ..... Camp Hill, PA
Murren, Philip J. ..... Harrisburg, PA
Murren-Koether, Kathleen ..... New York, NY
Murrer, Gregory J. ..... Rochester, NY
Murrett, John C., Jr. ..... Buffalo, NY
Murrett, Kathleen Anne ..... Hartford, CT
Murrett, Peter J., III ..... Buffalo, NY
Murrett, Peter J., Jr. ..... Buffalo, NY
Murrey, Dudley W. ..... Dallas, TX
Murrey, John W., III ..... Chattanooga, TN
Murrey, Joseph H., Jr. ..... Jonesboro, AR
Murrey, Thomas W., Jr. ..... Jonesboro, AR
Murri, Evan L. ..... San Dimas, CA
Murrian, Robert P. ..... Knoxville, TN
Murrie, Richd. W. ..... New York, NY
Murrill, David W. ..... Kansas City, MO
Murrill, John P. ..... Baton Rouge, LA
Murrill, Mary I., P.A. ..... Monroe, NC
Murrill, Robert D., Jr. ..... Dallas, TX
Murrin, Charles P. ..... San Francisco, CA
Murrin & De Rose ..... Olean, NY
Murrin, John O., III ..... Minneapolis, MN
Murrin Law Firm ..... Minneapolis, MN
Murrin, Melissa ..... Nashua, NH
Murrin, Regis D. ..... Pittsburgh, PA
Murrin, Robert E. ..... Olean, NY
Murrin, Taylor & Flach ..... Butler, PA
Murrin, Thomas L.
La Canada Flintridge, CA
Murrman, Francis R. ..... Greensburg, PA
Murrow, Julia H. ..... Highlands Ranch, CO
Murrow, Rodney K. ..... Kansas City, MO
Murrow, Rodney K., P.A., Law Office of
Olathe, KS
Kansas City, MO
Murry, Anthony S. ..... Department of Justice, Office of the Deputy Attorney General, GV
Murry, C. Emerson ..... Bismarck, ND
Murry, Christine A. ..... Columbus, OH
Murry, Elizabeth P. ..... Springfield, LA
Murry, Harold A. ..... Alexandria, LA
Murry, Harold D., Jr. ..... Washington, DC
Murry, Ike ..... Little Rock, AR
Murry, Julie Cloud ..... Anaheim, CA
Murry, Kathleen L. ..... Petaluma, CA
Murry, Maureen A. ..... Dallas, TX
Murry, Michael K. ..... Dayton, OH

Murry, Monty G. ..... Texarkana, TX
Murry, Porter ..... Phoenix, AZ
Murry, Roy P. ..... Corpus Christi, TX
Murry, Thomas D. ..... Brandon, MS
Murstein, Isidore Leo ..... Reseda, CA
Murstein, Marjorie B. ..... Boca Raton, FL
Murszewski, Sue Dealy ..... Snyder, NY
Murtagh, Cohen & Byrne
Garden City, NY
Murtagh, Dean F. ..... Philadelphia, PA
Murtagh, Elizabeth P. ..... Lexington, VA
Murtagh, John M. ..... Anchorage, AK
Murtagh, John M., Jr. ..... White Plains, NY
Murtagh, John P. ..... Memphis, TN
Murtagh, John W., Jr. ..... Wexford, PA
Murtagh, Kathryn I. ..... Boston, MA
Murtagh, Kenneth P. ..... Durango, CO
Murtagh, Kevin M. ..... Boston, MA
Murtagh, Laura D. ..... Santa Monica, CA
Murtagh, Marisa A. ..... Boston, MA
Murtagh, Maurine M. ..... Palo Alto, CA
Murtagh, Paul G. ..... Los Angeles, CA
Murtagh, Thomas B. ..... Chicago, IL
Murtagh, Thomas R. ..... Boston, MA
Murtagh, William P.
Great Barrington, MA
Murtagh-Monks, Karen L. ..... Albany, NY
Murtaugh, Christopher D. ..... Chicago, IL
Murtaugh, Edward J. ..... Poughkeepsie, NY
Murtaugh, Genevieve ..... Cleveland, OH
Murtaugh, James O. ..... Chicago, IL
Murtaugh, John P. ..... Cleveland, OH
Murtaugh, Michael J., (A Professional Corporation) ..... Irvine, CA
Murtaugh Miller Meyer & Nelson LLP
Irvine, CA
Murtaugh, Timothy J., III ..... Chicago, IL
Murtha, Brian T. ..... Santa Cruz, CA
Murtha, Cullina, Richter and Pinney LLP
Hartford, CT
New Haven, CT
Murtha, Eugene A. ..... Mineola, NY
Murtha, Frank F. ..... Washington, DC
Murtha, Griffith L. ..... Melbourne, FL
Murtha, J. Garvan ..... Brattleboro, VT
Murtha, James J. ..... New York, NY
Murtha, James J. ..... New York, NY
Murtha, John F. ..... Reno, NV
Murtha, John M. ..... Worcester, MA
Murtha, John R. ..... Moraga, CA
Murtha, John S. ..... Hartford, CT
Murtha, Joseph ..... Baltimore, MD
Murtha, Kevin M. ..... Melbourne, FL
Murtha, Linda L. ..... Hyannis, MA
Murtha, Mark A. ..... Willow Grove, PA
Murtha & Murtha ..... Dickinson, ND
Murtha, Peter J. ..... Department of Justice, Environment and Natural Resources Division, GV
Murtha, Robert A., Jr. ..... New York, NY
Murtha, Selena K. ..... King Of Prussia, PA
Murtha, Sharon Cmar ..... Pittsburgh, PA
Murtha, T. Kevin ..... Westbury, NY
Murtha, T. Kevin, & Associates, P.C.
Westbury, NY
Murtha, Thomas D. ..... San Jose, CA
Murtha, Thomas F. ..... Dickinson, ND
Murtha, Thomas M. ..... Bridgeport, CT
Murtha, Thomas M. ..... Woodbury, NJ
Murtha, Todd C. ..... Palo Alto, CA
Murthy, Anu ..... Gastonia, NC
Murthy, Arun ..... Washington, DC
Murthy, Harsha ..... Stamford, CT
New York, NY
Murthy, Ramesh ..... Abingdon, VA
Murthy, Sheela, Law Office of
Baltimore, MD
Murthy, Sheela, Law Office of
Owings Mills, MD
Murto, Susan D. ..... Anchorage, AK
Murto, Thomas A. ..... Goshen, IN
Murto, Thomas V., III ..... Dallas, TX
Murtos, Alice ..... Atlanta, GA
Murty, Edward J., Jr. ..... Department of Labor, Office of Secretary, GV
Murty, Stephen G. ..... Ocala, FL
Murty, Timothy J. ..... Sanibel, FL
Murty, Timothy J., P.A. ..... Fort Myers, FL
Sanibel, FL
Murty & Tome, P.A. ..... Ocala, FL
Murvin, Leigh Ann ..... Orlando, FL
Murvin, Sandra W. ..... Birmingham, AL
Murway, Carl A. ..... Cleveland, OH
Murzyn, Brenda L. ..... Naperville, IL
Musacchia, Mary U. ..... Cary, NC
Musacchio, Anna L. ..... Morristown, NJ
Musacchio, Bruce W. ..... Gowanda, NY
Musacchio, Frederick L., Jr. ..... Richardson, TX
Musacchio, Joseph P. ..... Boston, MA
Musacchio & Pyle ..... Gowanda, NY
Musachio, Rosalie N. ..... Toledo, OH
Musante, Alan R. ..... Winter Park, FL
Musante, Allison Rose ..... Los Angeles, CA
Musante, James N. ..... New York, NY
Musante, Janis R. ..... Burlingame, CA
Musante, Robert ..... Walnut Creek, CA
Musante, Thomas A. ..... Los Angeles, CA
Musarra, Arthur F. ..... Buffalo, NY
Musarra, Claudette R. M. ..... Buffalo, NY
Musarra, Gerald ..... Arlington, VA
Musarra and Musarra, P.C. ..... Buffalo, NY
Musashe, Nicholas A. ..... Winter Park, FL
Musat, L. Richard ..... Denver, CO
Musbach, Randy Arden ..... Chelsea, MI
Musbach & Ritter ..... Chelsea, MI
Musburger, Todd W. ..... Chicago, IL
Musburger, Todd W., Ltd. ..... Chicago, IL
Musca, Anthony J. ..... Cleveland, OH

Muthig, Peter ... **Los Angeles, CA**
Muths, Sherman L., Jr. ... Gulfport, MS
Muti & Brennan ... Boonton, NJ
Muti, David A. ... Boonton, NJ
Muti, Richard S. ... Hackensack, NJ
Mutino, Paul A. ... Chantilly, VA
Mutino, Peter J. ... **White Plains, NY**
Mutkoski, John M. ... **Boston, MA**
Mutkoski, Stephen A. ... New York, NY
Mutnick, George G. ... Flushing, NY
Mutnick, Jeffrey S. ... **Portland, OR**
Mutnick, Mitchell I. ... Burke, VA
Mutnick, Mitchell I., P.C. ... Burke, VA
Muto, Andrea M. ... Ravenna, OH
Muto, Anthony J. ... **Cincinnati, OH**
Muto, Frederick T. ... **San Diego, CA**
Muto, Jennifer C. ... **Boston, MA**
Muto, Joseph S. ... **Long Beach, CA**
Mutope-Johnson, Ayesha G. ... Houston, TX
Mutrie, Alice G. ... Carlisle, MA
Mutryn, William J. ... **Washington, DC**
Mutsaers, Eveline ... **Palo Alto, CA**
Mutschelknaus, Brad E. ... **Washington, DC**
Mutschler, Christopher A. ... Fond du Lac, WI
Muttart, V. Michael ... **Beverly Hills, CA**
Mutter, Carol Anne ... Knoxville, TN
Mutter, H. B. ... Silver Spring, MD
Mutter, J. Mark ... Toms River, NJ
Mutter, John A. ... East Providence, RI
Mutter, Michael K. ... **Falls Church, VA**
Mutter, Shawn M. ... Medford, WI
Mutterperl, Barbara F.
Federal Deposit Insurance Corporation, Liquidation Branch, GV
Mutterperl, Mark N. ... **New York, NY**
Mutterperl, William C. ... Boston, MA
Mutty, Paul F. ... **Seattle, WA**
Mutua, Athena D. ... Cambridge, MA
Mutz, Gregory T. ... Chicago, IL
Mutz, J. Mark ... Indianapolis, IN
Mutz, Steven H. ... New York, NY
Mutzabaugh, Richard W. ... **Bradford, PA**
Mutzabaugh, Saunders, Hollenbeck & Clarke, L.L.P. ... **Bradford, PA**
Mutzebaugh, Richard F. ... Littleton, CO
Mutzel, Rodger L. ... **Media, PA**
Mutzel & Wesner, L.L.P. ... **Media, PA**
Philadelphia, PA
West Chester, PA
Mutzig, Allen J. ... West Chester, PA
Muuss, Emil C. A. ... Sheboygan, WI
Muxlow, Douglas B. ... Topeka, KS
Muxlow, Ralph W., II ... Richland, MO
Muys & Associates ... Washington, DC
Muys, Jerome C. ... Washington, DC
Muys, Jerome C., Jr. ... **Washington, DC**
Muyskens, Don ... **Des Moines, IA**
Muyskens, Nathan J.
Federal Trade Commission, Bureau of Competition, GV
Muyskens, Stephen G. ... St. Paul, MN
Muza, Daniel M. ... **Oshkosh, WI**
Muza, Donna J. ... Menomonie, WI
Muza, Robert F. ... Menomonie, WI
Muza, Stephen F. ... Menomonie, WI
Muza, Stephen R. ... Struthers, OH
Muzi, Andrew C. ... Costa Mesa, CA
Muzic, Joseph G. ... **Lancaster, PA**
Muzik, Susan M. ... Portland, OR
Muzik, Thelma J. ... Redondo Beach, CA
Muzilla, Raymond A. ... **Elyria, OH**
Muzilla, Thomas A. ... **Elyria, OH**
Muzingo, Gregory S. ... Highland Park, MI
Muzinich, Peter A. ... **Santa Barbara, CA**
Muzio, Joseph C. ... Garden City, NY
Muzyka, Thomas J. ... Boston, MA
Muzzall, Roger H. ... Grand Rapids, MI
Muzzin, Paulina Treiger ... Highland, MI
Muzzo, A. Lawrence ... Cincinnati, OH
Muzzo, Christopher L. ... **Cincinnati, OH**
Muzzy, Gray H. ... **Houston, TX**
Mwangi, Kambo F. ... **Boston, MA**
Myalls, Kathleen M. ... Chicago, IL
Myane, Dean C. ... Johnson City, TX
Myart, James W., Jr. & Associates
San Antonio, TX
Myaskovsky, Elena ... Los Angeles, CA
Myatt & Bell, P.C. ... Beaverton, OR
Myatt Brandes & Gast P.C.
Fort Collins, CO
Myatt, Christine L. ... **Greensboro, NC**
Myatt, David B., (P.C.) ... **Washington, DC**
Myatt, Dean J. ... **San Francisco, CA**
Myatt, J. Sue ... **Moline, IL**
Myatt, Janine M. ... Abingdon, VA
Myatt, Lewis E. ... Beaverton, OR
Myatt, Ramsey D. ... **Fort Collins, CO**
Myatt, René ... New York, NY
Myatt, Sandra E. ... Sevierville, TN
Myatt, Ted W. ... Houston, TX
Myatt, Tracy C. ... Raleigh, NC
Mybeck, Richard R. ... Scottsdale, AZ
Mycek, John J. ... **Amsterdam, NY**
Mycek Law Firm, The ... **Amsterdam, NY**
Mycek, William H. ... **Amsterdam, NY**
Mychajluk, Brian Michael
Bingham Farms, MI
Mychak, Michael F. ... Mount Carmel, PA
Mychak, Samuel, Jr. ... Philadelphia, PA
Mychalowych, Andrew W.
Farmington Hills, MI
Myck, Tonya J. ... Dallas, TX
Myckowiak Associates, A Professional Corporation ... **Detroit, MI**
Myckowiak, Michael E. ... **Detroit, MI**
Myckowiak, Vicki Sherman ... **Detroit, MI**
Mycock, Frederick C. ... Barnstable, MA
Mycock, Kilroy, Green & Ford, P.C.
Hyannis, MA
Mycock, Lisa E. ... Barnstable, MA
Mydans, Robert E. ... Denver, CO
Mydans, Shelley ... Sacramento, CA
Mydland, Gordon J. ... Lake Preston, SD
Myer, Audrey L. ... Santa Ana, CA
Myer, Clarence M., Jr. ... Akron, PA
Myer, Elspeth H., Mrs. ... La Jolla, CA
Myer, Jeffrey A. ... Phoenix, AZ
Myer, John A. ... **West Palm Beach, FL**
Myer, Kenneth L. ... **Seattle, WA**
Myer, Lawrence E. ... Barre, VT
Myer, Mari L. ... **Atlanta, GA**
Myer, Mary K. (Molly) ... Denver, CO
Myer, Paynter & Fock ... Santa Barbara, CA
Myer, Perry G., Jr. ... Alexander City, AL
Myer, Peter G. ... Department of Justice, Civil Division, GV
Myer, Philip ... Bronx, NY
Myer, Phillip ... **Pasadena, CA**
Myer, Raymond A. ... Santa Barbara, CA
Myer, Ruth E. ... **Indianapolis, IN**
Myer, Scott D. ... Los Angeles, CA
Myer, Swanson, Adams & Wolf, P.C.
Denver, CO
Myerberg, David Z., M.D.
Morgantown, WV
Myerberg, Henry J. ... Towson, MD
Myerberg, Neal P. ... New York, NY
Myerberg, Roger J. ... Lexington Park, MD
Myerchin, Gordon W. ... **Grand Forks, ND**
Myerly, Jim I. ... Santa Barbara, CA
Myerow, Dean Adam ... New York, NY
Myerow, Michael D. ... Franklin, MA
Myerow & Poirier ... Franklin, MA
Myers, A. Carl ... Salem, OR
Myers, A. C. ... Knoxville, TN
Myers, Alan C. ... **New York, NY**
Myers, Albert A., III ... Conyers, GA
Myers, Albert M., III ... **New York, NY**
Myers, Alden ... New York, NY
Myers, Alexander P. ... **Los Altos, CA**
Myers, Alexander "Sandy", (P.A.)
West Palm Beach, FL
Myers, Allen Murray ... New York, NY
Myers, Amy K. ... **Birmingham, AL**
Myers, Andrew D. ... Boston, MA
Myers, Andrew D. ... **Boston, MA**
Myers, Andrew S. ... Henderson, NV
Myers, Ann Catherine ... **New York, NY**
Myers, Anna H. ... Norfolk, VA
Myers, Anne R. ... **Dallas, TX**
Myers, Anne Smith ... **Denver, CO**
Myers, Arnold B. ... **Salinas, CA**
Myers, Arthur Lee, Jr. ... Atlanta, GA
Myers, Ashley McCorvey ... **Tampa, FL**
Myers & Associates ... Chicago, IL
Myers & Associates, Intellectual Property Law, P.C. ... **Atlanta, GA**
Marietta, GA
Powder Springs, GA
Myers & Associates PLLC ... **Hernando, MS**
Myers, Barry D. ... Colmar, PA
Myers, Barry Lee ... State College, PA
Myers, Barry W. ... Los Gatos, CA
Myers & Bell, P.C. ... **Newport, TN**
Myers, Benjamin ... Chicago, IL
Myers, Bern P. ... Santa Fe, NM
Myers, Beth A. ... **Cincinnati, OH**
Myers, Betty S. ... Memphis, TN
Myers, Beverly J. ... Gold River, CA
Myers Bigel Sibley & Sajovec, P.A.
Raleigh, NC
Research Triangle Park, NC
Myers, Bill ... Denver, CO
Myers, Bill, P.C. ... Denver, CO
Myers, Bline & Bettle, P.A. ... **Sarasota, FL**
Myers, Bobby D. ... **San Antonio, TX**
Myers, Bradley C. ... **Baton Rouge, LA**
Myers Bradley Devitt & Arp, P.C.
Golden, CO
Myers, Bradley K. ... **Portland, OR**
Myers, Brandon L. ... Topeka, KS
Myers, Brenda L. ... West Des Moines, IA
Myers, Brett ... Bakersfield, CA
Myers, Brett L. ... **Dallas, TX**
Myers, Brian B. ... **Kansas City, MO**
Myers, Brian D. ... **Phoenix, AZ**
Myers, Brian D. ... Sacramento, CA
Myers, Brian L. ... **Seattle, WA**
Myers, Brian S. ... **Valley Forge, PA**
Myers, Brier & Kelly, L.L.P.
Scranton, PA
Myers, Bruce A. ... **Fairfield, CA**
Napa, CA
Myers, Bruce E. ... Livingston, TN
Myers, Bryan ... **Broomfield, CO**
Myers, Byron L. ... **Indianapolis, IN**
Myers, C. Blaine ... **Parkersburg, WV**
Myers, C. Ray ... Orange, CA
Myers, C. Raymond, Jr. ... Brentwood, TN
Myers, Carol L. ... **Sarasota, FL**
Myers, Catherine E. ... Fort Worth, TX
Myers, Cathleen Curran ... **Harrisburg, PA**
Myers, Charles ... **Big Spring, TX**
Myers, Charles A. ... **Hammond, IN**
Myers, Charles E. (Ed) ... **Abilene, TX**
Myers, Charles F. ... Phoenix, AZ
Myers, Charles F. ... **Kansas City, MO**
Myers, Charles H. ... Denver, CO
Myers, Charles J. ... Kokomo, IN
Myers, Charles J. ... Bloomingdale, NJ
Myers, Charles P. ... Billings, MT
Myers, Charles R. ... Valparaiso, FL
Myers, Charlton ... Morral, OH
Myers, Cheryl D. ... Topeka, KS
Myers, Christina Frances ... Latham, NY
Myers, Christopher A. ... **Washington, DC**
Myers, Christopher C. ... Fort Wayne, IN
Myers, Colleen E. ... Kennebunk, ME
Myers, Corneal B. ... **Lakeland, FL**
Lake Wales, FL
Winter Haven, FL
Myers, Cornelius B., III ... Lakeland, FL
Myers, Courtenay U. ... **New York, NY**
Myers, Craig H. ... **Dallas, TX**
Myers, Craig S. ... Columbus, OH
Myers, Curt C. ... **New York, NY**
Myers, Cynthia Sue ... Santa Rosa, CA
Myers, Dale F. ... Los Angeles, CA
Myers, Dalhi N. ... Washington, DC
Myers, Dane J. ... Fayetteville, AR
Myers & D'Angelo ... **Los Angeles, CA**
Pasadena, CA
Myers, Daniel ... Celina, OH
Myers, Daniel B. ... **San Francisco, CA**
Myers, Daniel E. ... San Carlos, CA
Myers, Daniel E. ... **Tallahassee, FL**
Myers, Daniel N. ... Lisle, IL
Myers, Daniel O. ... **Charleston, SC**
Myers, Daniel P., II ... **Rehoboth Beach, DE**
Myers, Darin L. ... Laguna Beach, CA
Myers, Darsi Rae ... Escondido, CA
Myers, Daugherity, Berry, O'Conor & Kuzma, Ltd. ... **Morris, IL**
Ottawa, IL
Princeton, IL
Streator, IL
Myers, David A. ... Guadalupe, AZ
Myers, David A. ... **Los Angeles, CA**
Myers, David A. ... Elyria, OH
Myers, David C. ... Grand Rapids, MI
Myers, David C. ... **Dallas, TX**
Myers, David F. ... **Redwood City, CA**
Myers, David H. ... Department of the Navy, Office of the Judge Advocate General, GV
Myers, David J. ... Los Angeles, CA
Myers, David J. ... **Roswell, GA**
Myers, David L. ... **Kennett Square, PA**
Myers, Deanne Smith ... Torrance, CA
Myers, Debra L. ... Concord, CA
Myers, Denise ... **Grand Island, NE**
Myers, Denise Lombardo ... **Providence, RI**
Myers, Dennis L. ... Hoffman Estates, IL
Myers, Dennis M. ... **Chicago, IL**
Myers, Dennis P. ... Raleigh, NC
Myers, Diana L. ... Atlanta, GA
Myers, Donald A., Jr. ... **Maitland, FL**
Myers, Donald B. ... **Seattle, WA**
Myers, Donald Bruce, Jr.
Washington, DC
Myers, Donald J. ... **Washington, DC**
Myers, Donald M. ... Granada Hills, CA
Myers, Donald R. ... San Benito, TX
Myers, Donald V. ... Lexington, SC
Myers, Douglas K. ... Winston-Salem, NC
Myers, Douglas S. ... Virginia Beach, VA
Myers, Douglas W. ... Des Plaines, IL
Myers, E. John ... Los Angeles, CA
Myers, Earl R., Jr. ... Wahpeton, ND
Myers, Edmund G. ... Lemoyne, PA
Myers, Edward B. ... **Washington, DC**
Myers, Edward J. ... **St. Louis, MO**
Myers, Edward L., III ... Missoula, MT
Myers, Elizabeth Murdock ... **Boston, MA**
Providence, RI
Myers, Emily B. ... Washington, DC
Myers, Eric B. ... **Baltimore, MD**
Myers, Eric G., Jr. ... Jackson, MS
Myers, Eric R. ... Tampa, FL
Myers, Ernest J. ... **Orlando, FL**
Myers & Fleming, LLP
Newport Beach, CA
Myers, Forehand & Fuller, P.A.
Tallahassee, FL
Myers, Forest ... Shippensburg, PA
Myers, Frank B. ... **Newport Beach, CA**
Myers, Franklin ... **Houston, TX**
Myers & Frayne Co., L.P.A. ... **Dayton, OH**
Myers, Fred L., Jr. ... Newport, TN
Myers, Fred T. ... Geneva, IL
Myers, Frederick J. ... **Golden, CO**
Myers, Frederick M. ... **Pittsfield, MA**
Myers, Fredrick S. ... Longboat Key, FL
Myers, G. William ... Ebensburg, PA
Myers, Gail Alison ... Pittsburgh, PA
Myers, Gary ... University, MS
Myers, Gary A. ... Redlands, CA
Myers, Gary L. ... St. Joseph, MO
Myers, Gary L. ... **Las Vegas, NV**
Myers, Gary M. ... **Des Moines, IA**
Myers & Geisleman ... Fort Wayne, IN
Myers, Gene R. ... Burton, MI
Myers, Geoffrey R. ... **Potomac, MD**
Myers, George C., Jr. ... **Washington, DC**
Myers, George W., Jr. ... Gaylord, MI
Myers, Gerald E. ... Yorkville, IL
Myers, Gilbert F. ... Essex Junction, VT
Myers, Gilbert, P.C. ... Essex Junction, VT
Myers, Glenn W. ... **Jackson, WY**
Myers, Gloria J. ... Asheville, NC
Myers & Gomel ... **Las Vegas, NV**
Myers, Gordon I. ... Washington, DC
Myers, Gregory J. ... **Minneapolis, MN**
Myers, Gregory L. ... **Fresno, CA**
Myers, Gretchen, The Law Offices of
St. Louis, MO
Myers, Grover M. ... **Winston-Salem, NC**
Myers, H. Keith ... Edmond, OK
Myers, H. Keith ... **El Paso, TX**
Myers, Hardy ... Salem, OR
Myers, Harold W. ... Fort Wayne, IN
Myers, Hawley, Morley, Myers, & McDonnell ... **Los Altos, CA**
Myers, Helene Sfikas ... Canton, CT
Myers & Heyl ... Norwich, VT
Myers, Hockemeyer & McNagny
Columbia City, IN
Myers, Holly I. ... Chicago, IL
Myers & Hopson ... Ocala, FL
Myers, Howard B. ... **Concord, NH**
Lebanon, NH
Myers, Howard B. ... Dallas, TX
Myers, Howard D. ... **Los Angeles, CA**
Myers, Howard E. ... Webster City, IA
Myers, Howard N. ... Milwaukee, WI
Myers and Hulse ... Charlotte, NC
Myers, Ingrid A. ... **Los Angeles, CA**
Myers, J. Frank ... Americus, GA
Myers, J. Frank, III ... Columbus, GA
Myers, J. Kenneth ... Marshall, MN
Myers, J. Michael ... **San Antonio, TX**
Myers, J. Roger ... **Ventura, CA**
Myers, J. Scott ... Chicago, IL
Myers, J. William ... **Newport, TN**
Myers, Jack C. ... **Dallas, TX**
Myers, Jack L. ... Johnson City, TN
Myers, Jack M. ... Philadelphia, PA
Myers, Jacob A. ... **Dayton, OH**
Myers, James A. ... Fort Worth, TX
Myers, James B., Jr. ... Indianapolis, IN
Myers, James D. ... **Kansas City, MO**
Myers, James D. ... **Raleigh, NC**
Myers, James E. ... **Baltimore, MD**
Myers, James E. ... **Houston, TX**
Myers, James H. ... Culver City, CA
Myers, James I. ... **Buffalo, NY**
Myers, James J. ... **Boston, MA**
Myers, James L. ... Annapolis, MD
Myers, James L., Jr. ... Palm Beach, FL
Myers, James R. ... **Washington, DC**
Myers, James R. ... **Punta Gorda, FL**
Myers, James R. ... Vandalia, IL
Myers, James R. ... Woodstock, NY
Myers, James R. ... Sioux Falls, SD
Myers, James S. ... **Tampa, FL**
Myers, James T. ... Dodge City, KS
Myers, James Y. ... Cincinnati, OH
Myers, Jan Kevin ... **New York, NY**
Myers, Jane Barbara ... Portland, OR
Myers, Jane D. ... Santa Ana, CA
Myers, Jane L. ... Newark, NJ
Myers, Jane M. ... **Garden City, NY**
Myers, Jane Mainella ... Clarksburg, WV
Myers, Janel M. ... Canton, OH
Myers, Jay P. ... Tampa, FL
Myers, Jay W. ... Bloomsburg, PA
Myers, Jeffrey Cabot ... **Los Angeles, CA**
Myers, Jeffrey D. ... **Albuquerque, NM**
Myers, Jeffrey David ... Ravenna, OH
Myers, Jeffrey E. ... **Philadelphia, PA**
Myers, Jeffrey L. ... **St. Petersburg, FL**
Myers, Jeffrey L., P.A. ... **St. Petersburg, FL**
Myers, Jeffrey N. ... **Fort Worth, TX**
Myers, Jeffrey S. ... **Olympia, WA**
Myers, Jeffrey T. ... Sioux City, IA
Myers & Jenkins, A Professional Corporation ... **Phoenix, AZ**
Myers, Jennifer ... Washington, DC
Myers, Jennifer
Federal Communications Commission, Common Carrier Bureau, GV
Myers, Jennifer D. ... Bellevue, WA
Myers, Jennifer L. ... **Philadelphia, PA**
Myers, Jerry Mathias ... Tucson, AZ
Myers, Jerry T. ... **Raleigh, NC**
Myers, Jess J. ... Wichita, KS
Myers, Jill A. ... Beverly Hills, CA
Myers, Joan ... Bedford, TX
Myers, Joel D. ... **Atlanta, GA**
Powder Springs, GA
Myers, John A. ... **Albuquerque, NM**
Myers, John A., Jr., (Ltd.) ... Naperville, IL
Myers, John B. ... New York, NY
Myers, John Charles ... Cleveland, OH
Myers, John E. B. ... Sacramento, CA
Myers, John F. ... **Rockville, MD**
Myers, John F. ... Cleveland, OH
Myers, John Gregory ... Houston, TX
McAllen, TX
Myers, John H. ... Sarasota, FL
Myers, John J. ... Mc Keesport, PA
Myers, John J. ... **Pittsburgh, PA**
Myers, John M. ... Springfield, IL
Myers, John M. ... **Philadelphia, PA**
Myers, John Park ... Vicksburg, MS
Myers, John R. ... **Sacramento, CA**
Myers, John R. ... **Chicago, IL**
Myers, John R. ... **Murray Hill, NJ**
Myers, John Richard ... Little Rock, AR
Myers, John S. ... Saint Marys, GA
Myers, John S., P.C. ... Saint Marys, GA
Myers, John W. ... Beverly Hills, CA
Myers, John W., IV ... **Woodland Hills, CA**
Myers, Jon M. ... **Logansport, IN**
Myers, Jonathan E. ... **Philadelphia, PA**
Myers, Jonathan J. ... Columbia City, IN
Myers, Jonathan, (P.A.) ... Short Hills, NJ
Myers & Jones LLP ... Los Angeles, CA
Myers, Jos. N. ... Indianapolis, IN
Myers, Joseph B., Jr. ... **Louisville, KY**
Myers, Joseph F. ... Metairie, LA
Myers, Joseph M. ... Treasury Department, Financial Crimes Enforcement Network, GV
Myers, Joseph Peter ... **Del Mar, CA**
Myers, Joseph Peter ... **Riverside, CA**
Myers, Joseph V., III ... **Atlanta, GA**
Myers, Joseph V., Jr. ... **Atlanta, GA**
Myers, Joseph W. ... Norfolk, VA
Myers, Joyce J. ... **Houston, TX**
Myers, Julie Smith ... Tallahassee, FL
Myers, K. David ... Maynardville, TN
Myers, Karen J. ... Pittsburgh, PA

Myers, Kari A. ... Charleston, WV
Myers, Keith D. ... Wausau, WI
Myers Keller, Communications Law Group
Washington, DC
Myers, Kelly A. ... Lansing, MI
Myers, Kelly R. ... Corsicana, TX
Myers, Kenneth A. ... Canton, OH
Myers, Kenneth D. ... Cleveland, OH
Myers, Kenneth M. ... Miami, FL
Myers, Kenneth P. ... Colorado Springs, CO
Myers, Kenneth R. ... Philadelphia, PA
Myers, Kenneth Robert ... Las Vegas, NV
Myers, Kimberly A. ... Kansas City, MO
Myers, Kimberly L. ... Atlanta, GA
Myers, Kimberly S. ... St. Louis, MO
Myers, Kimberly Talbert ... California, MD
Myers & Kordenbrock, P.C. ... St. Louis, MO
Myers Krause & Stevens, Chartered
Naples, FL
Myers, Kristie J. ... Fort Lauderdale, FL
Myers, L. Agnew, Jr. ... Fort Washington, MD
Myers, Lance D. ... Brooklyn, NY
Myers, Larry G. ... Houston, TX
Myers, Larry L., (Atty. At Law, A Law Corp.) ... Honolulu, HI
Myers, Larry S. ... Eureka, CA
Myers, Larry W. ... Omaha, NE
Myers, Laura A. ... Newport Beach, CA
Myers Law Firm, The, LLP ... Oakland, CA
San Francisco, CA
Myers Law Offices, Chartered
Newton, KS
Myers, Lawrence E. ... Des Moines, IA
Myers, Lawrence J. ... Atlanta, GA
Myers, Lawrence R.
Department of Transportation,
Office of the General Counsel, GV
Myers, Lenore M.J. ... Norristown, PA
Myers, Leonard D., Jr. ... Gainesville, GA
Myers, Leonard J. D. ... Norristown, PA
Myers, Lewis, Jr. ... Chicago, IL
Myers, Lily Chang ... Dallas, TX
Myers, Linda A. ... New York, NY
Myers, Linda K. ... Chicago, IL
Myers, Linda L. ... Marshalltown, IA
Myers, Lindsay H. ... New York, NY
Myers, Lois A. ... Fair Lawn, NJ
Myers, Lonn W. ... Chicago, IL
Myers, Loring M., Jr. ... Manhattan Beach, CA
Myers, Louis Keith ... Wickliffe, KY
Myers, Louis R. ... Ravenna, OH
Myers, Lowell J. ... Chicago, IL
Myers, L. W. ... Lexington, KY
Myers, M. Thomas ... Towson, MD
Myers, M. Wayne ... Jacksonville, FL
Myers, Marc Douglas ... Houston, TX
Myers, Marc E. ... Dublin, OH
Myers, Marcia J. ... Cincinnati, OH
Myers, Margaret K. ... Oklahoma City, OK
Myers, Marion D. ... Sumter, SC
Myers, Mark A. ... New Orleans, LA
Myers, Mark C. ... Dallas, TX
Myers, Mark E. ... Monterey, CA
Myers, Mark E. ... Valencia, CA
Myers, Mark M. ... Seattle, WA
Myers, Mark McLucas
Colorado Springs, CO
Myers, Marlee S. ... Pittsburgh, PA
Myers, Martin H. ... Palo Alto, CA
Myers, Martin W. ... Evanston, IL
Myers, Mary Ellen ... Madison, NJ
Myers, Mary W. ... West Chester, PA
Myers, Mary Winkle ... Winter Haven, FL
Myers, Matthew L. ... Washington, DC
Myers, Max A. ... Fort Wayne, IN
Myers, Max C., Jr. ... Tulsa, OK
Myers, Melinda D. ... San Carlos, CA
Myers, Michael A. ... Springfield, IL
Myers, Michael A. ... Indianapolis, IN
Myers, Michael Alan ... Murfreesboro, TN
Myers, Michael B. ... Topeka, KS
Myers, Michael D. ... Houston, TX
Myers, Michael E. ... Sacramento, CA
Myers, Michael Edward ... St. Louis, MO
Myers, Michael F. ... Jackson, MS
Myers, Michael J. ... Los Angeles, CA
Myers, Michael J. ... Washington, DC
Myers, Michael J. ... New York, NY
Myers, Michael J. ... Spokane, WA
Myers, Michael P. ... Schaumburg, IL
Myers, Michael S. ... Las Vegas, NV
Myers, Michelle A. ... Brooklyn, NY
Myers, Michelle S. ... New York, NY
Myers, Mike ... Dallas, TX
Myers, Milfert W. ... Warren, OH
Myers, Minor ... Akron, OH
Myers, Mitchell ... Silver Spring, MD
Myers, Morey M. ... Scranton, PA
Myers & Moring, P.A. ... Crystal River, FL
Myers and Myers ... Topeka, KS
Myers & Myers ... Celina, OH
Myers & Myers ... Norristown, PA
Myers, Myers & Myers ... Norfolk, VA
Myers, Nancy L. ... Sacramento, CA
Myers, Nancy W. ... San Antonio, TX
Myers, Neil ... Euclid, OH
Myers Nelson Dillon & Shierk, PLLC
Bloomfield Hills, MI
Grand Rapids, MI
Myers, Noeline J. ... Corvallis, OR
Myers, Oliver & Price, P.C.
Albuquerque, NM
Santa Fe, NM
Myers, Otis W. ... Marshall, MI
Myers & Overstreet, A Professional Corporation ... Fresno, CA
Myers, Pamela Rossano ... Seattle, WA
Myers, Pamela Whitney ... Chicago, IL
Myers, Patricia M. ... Crystal River, FL
Myers, Patrick ... St. Louis, MO
Myers, Patrick A. ... Fort Worth, TX
Myers, Patsy Nanna ... Marina Del Rey, CA
Myers, Paul I. "Chico", III ... Los Altos, CA
Myers, Paul I., Jr. ... Los Altos, CA
Myers, Paul L. ... Dallas, TX
Myers, Paul L., Jr. ... Harrisburg, IL
Myers, Paul Louis ... Boston, MA
Myers, Paul McDonald ... Berkeley, CA
Myers, Paul V. ... Ringgold, LA
Myers, Paul V., A Professional Law Corporation ... Ringgold, LA
Myers, Peter C. ... Cleveland, OH
Myers, Peter C., Jr ... Carrollton, TX
Myers, Peter S. ... Oakland, CA
San Francisco, CA
Myers, Philip E. ... Santa Barbara, CA
Myers, Philip H. ... Pittsburgh, PA
Myers, Philip H. ... Norfolk, VA
Myers, Philip J. ... Minnetonka, MN
Myers, Phillip D. ... Monroe, LA
Myers and Pico ... Fair Lawn, NJ
Myers & Plough ... Ravenna, OH
Myers, Polly A. ... Washington, DC
Myers, Pottroff and Ball, A Professional Association ... Clay Center, KS
Junction City, KS
Manhattan, KS
Marysville, KS
Wamego, KS
Myers, Powell & Dunbar
Parkersburg, WV
Myers & Proctor, P.A., Law Offices of
Hagerstown, MD
Myers, R. Chandler, (P.C.) ... Pasadena, CA
Myers, R. Lee ... Charlotte, NC
Myers, R. Lynn ... Springfield, MO
Myers, R. Maureen ... Washington, PA
Myers, R. Rich ... Fresno, CA
Myers, Ralph, III ... McCrory, AR
Myers, Ralph M., Jr. ... Laguna Beach, CA
Myers, Randolph J.
Department Of The Interior,
Office of the Solicitor, GV
Myers, Randy ... Montgomery, AL
Myers, Rebecca L. ... Brooklyn, NY
Myers, Reneé C. ... Harrisburg, PA
Myers, Renee C.R. ... Newport Beach, CA
Myers, Rex T. ... Jackson, MS
Myers, Rhea A. ... Madison, WI
Myers, Richard A., Jr. ... Cleveland, OH
Myers, Richard D. ... Omaha, NE
Myers, Richard E. ... New Albany, IN
Myers, Richard E., II ... Los Angeles, CA
Myers, Richard Frank ... Tallahassee, FL
Myers, Richard J. ... Chicago, IL
Myers, Richard J. ... Memphis, TN
Myers, Richard L. ... Costa Mesa, CA
Myers, Richard P. ... Denver, CO
Myers, Richard R. ... Houston, TX
Myers, Richard S. ... Washington, DC
Myers, Richard S., Jr. ... Nashville, TN
Myers, Richard V. ... Banning, CA
Myers, Richard W. ... Las Vegas, NV
Myers, Rick M. ... Bluffton, IN
Markle, IN
Myers, Robert C. ... New York, NY
Myers, Robert D. ... Phoenix, AZ
Myers, Robert D. ... San Francisco, CA
Myers, Robert D. ... Newton, KS
Myers, Robert D. ... Harrisburg, PA
Myers, Robert E. ... Bala Cynwyd, PA
Myers, Robert E. ... New Cumberland, PA
Myers, Robert H., Jr. ... Washington, DC
Myers, Robert H., Jr. ... Painesville, OH
Myers, Robert J. ... Clearwater, FL
Myers, Robert J. ... San Antonio, TX
Myers, Robert J., & Associates
San Antonio, TX
Myers, Robert P., Jr. ... Gulfport, MS
Myers, Robert T. ... New Orleans, LA
Myers, Robert W. ... Columbus, OH
Myers, Robt. L. ... Portland, OR
Myers, Rodman N. ... Detroit, MI
Myers, Roger ... San Francisco, CA
Myers, Roger L. ... Birmingham, MI
Myers, Ron ... Arlington, VA
Myers, Ronald C. ... Eureka, KS
Myers, Ronald L. ... Opelika, AL
Myers, Rosalind E. ... San Ramon, CA
Myers, Rosemary Elizabeth ... Athens, GA
Myers, Ross S. ... Lenexa, KS
Myers, S. Kelly ... Washington, DC
Myers, S. Rebekah ... Atlanta, GA
Myers, Samuel D. ... Chicago, IL
Myers, Sandra Blackford ... Kansas City, MO
Myers, Sandra R. ... Sacramento, CA
Myers, Sara Steck ... San Francisco, CA
Myers, Scott E. ... Tucson, AZ
Myers, Scott P. ... Hartford, CT
Myers, Sharla H., (P.C.) ... Dallas, TX
Myers, Sharon E. ... East Berlin, PA
York, PA
Myers, Sheila C. ... New Orleans, LA
Myers, Sheldon D. ... Hartford, CT
Myers, Sherwood F. ... Miami, FL
Myers, Sidney ... Amherst, MA
Myers, Smithmoore P. ... Spokane, WA
Myers, Solomon M. ... Chicago, IL
Myers, Soultana S. ... Columbia City, IN
Myers, Stacey L. ... Orange Park, FL
Myers, Stanley J. ... Denver, CO
Myers, Stanley J., P.C. ... Denver, CO
Myers, Stanley L. ... Columbus, OH
Myers, Stephen A. ... Phoenix, AZ
Myers, Stephen C. ... Ottawa, IL
Streator, IL
Myers, Stephen H. ... Lafayette, LA
Myers, Stephen H., L.L.C. ... Lafayette, LA
Myers, Stephen R. ... Clinton, IL
Myers, Stephen W. ... Phoenix, AZ
Myers, Sterling E. ... Arcadia, CA
Myers, Steve C. ... Baton Rouge, LA
Myers, Steven D. ... Novi, MI
Myers, Steven L. ... Portland, OR
Myers, Steven L. ... Richmond, VA
Myers, Steven M. ... Santa Ana, CA
Myers, Steven T. ... Santa Ana, CA
Myers, Stewart S. ... Kansas City, MO
Myers & Stroberg, LLP ... Gainesville, GA
Myers, Stuart L. ... Glenmont, NY
Myers, Susan Baldwin ... Torrance, CA
Myers, Susan Leigh ... Princeton, NJ
Myers, Susan M. ... Santa Cruz, CA
Myers, Susan M. ... Revere, MA
Myers, Taylor and Whitworth, A Professional Corporation ... Joplin, MO
Webb City, MO
Myers, Teresa ... Denver, CO
Myers, Terry ... New York, NY
Myers, Terry A. ... Hagerstown, MD
Myers, Terry L. ... Boise, ID
Myers, Thad L. ... Columbia, SC
Myers, Thomas ... Los Angeles, CA
Myers, Thomas ... Washington, DC
Myers, Thomas A. ... Los Angeles, CA
Myers, Thomas A. ... Milwaukee, WI
Myers, Thomas E. ... New York, NY
Myers, Thomas E. ... Syracuse, NY
Myers, Thomas E. ... Fort Worth, TX
Myers, Thomas F. ... Detroit, MI
Myers, Thomas M. ... St. Clairsville, OH
Myers, Thomas R. ... Cincinnati, OH
Myers, Thomas S., Jr. ... Paoli, PA
Myers, Thomas V. ... Erie, PA
Myers, Thomas W. ... Cicero, NY
Myers, Thomas W. ... Houston, TX
Myers, Thomas Ward, Jr ... Bethesda, MD
Myers, Tim C., Sr. ... Omaha, NE
Myers, Timothy J. ... Fayetteville, AR
Myers, Timothy T. ... Blue Bell, PA
Myers, Timothy Todd ... Springfield, MO
Myers, Todd A. ... Denver, CO
Myers, Townsend & McKee, P.C.
Atlanta, GA
Roswell, GA
Myers, Troy H., Jr. ... Sarasota, FL
Myers, W. Allan ... Gainesville, GA
Myers, W. Dan ... Houston, TX
Myers, W. Douglas ... Hopkinsville, KY
Myers, W. Edward ... Duluth, MN
Myers, Wade ... Detroit, MI
Myers, Wallace H. ... Worcester, MA
Myers, Webster, Jr. ... Huntington, WV
Myers, Wendy ... Somers, NY
Myers, Wendy L. ... Powell, OH
Myers, Wesley T.D. ... Fort Worth, TX
Myers, Widders, Gibson & Long, L.L.P.
San Luis Obispo, CA
Santa Barbara, CA
Ventura, CA
Myers, William A. ... Graham, TX
Myers, William C. ... Winston-Salem, NC
Myers, William C., Jr. ... Knoxville, TN
Myers, William E. ... Syracuse, NY
Myers, William E. ... Parma, OH
Myers, William G. ... Fayetteville, AR
Myers, William G., III ... Boise, ID
Myers, William G., (P.C.) ... Chicago, IL
Myers, William H. ... Naples, FL
Myers, William H. ... Pascagoula, MS
Myers, William J. ... Huntingdon, PA
Myers, William Jeff ... Syracuse, NY
Myers, William L. ... Burlingame, CA
San Jose, CA
Myers, William L., Jr. ... Philadelphia, PA
Myers, William P. ... Hernando, MS
Myers, William R. ... Birmingham, AL
Myers, William S. ... Albany, NY
Myers, William S., Jr. ... Oklahoma City, OK
Myers, William Scott ... Columbus, OH
Myers, William Sneath ... Atlanta, GA
Myers, William T. ... Bloomfield Hills, MI
Myers, William T., Sr. ... Mineola, NY
Myers, Wilson ... Birmingham, AL
Myers & Wyche ... Johnson City, TN
Myerscough, Sue E. ... Springfield, IL
Myers-Kerbal, Elisabeth R.
Washington, DC
Myers-Newman, Jaymi L. ... Pittsburgh, PA
Myerson & Barton, P.C.
Kansas City, MO
Myerson, Bradley D.
Manchester Center, VT
Myerson, David J. ... New York, NY
Myerson, Gordon N. ... Kansas City, MO
Myerson, Jay B. ... Reston, VA
Myerson, Morton ... Hingham, MA
Myerson, Paul E. ... Washington, DC
Myerson, Peter P. ... Boston, MA
Myerson, Toby S. ... New York, NY
Myfelt, Dwight D. ... Cincinnati, OH
Mygatt, Ann B. ... Boulder, CO
Mygatt, Louisa S. ... Rosemont, PA
Mygatt, Samuel Gifford ... Concord, MA
Mygatt, Stephen B. ... Philadelphia, PA
West Chester, PA
Mygatt, Susan Hall ... Boston, MA
Mygrant, John W. ... Akron, OH
Myhra, Mark A. ... Minneapolis, MN
Myhre, Blain D. ... Denver, CO
Myhre, Deanna S. ... Vacaville, CA
Myhre, Deanna S., Law Offices Of
Vacaville, CA
Myhre, Earl J. ... Minneapolis, MN
Myhre, James V. ... Honolulu, HI
Myhre, Karen Sina ... Neenah, WI
Myhre, Steven J. ... Tampa, FL
Myhre, Steven W. ... Schaumburg, IL
Myhre, Valdemar H. ... Kailua, HI
Myhre, William N. ... Washington, DC
Myhrum, Christopher B. ... Springfield, MA
Myhrvold, Alton A. ... North Hollywood, CA
Myka, Jennifer L. ... Montpelier, VT
Myking, Stephen T. ... Chicago, IL
Myklebust, Kenneth B. ... Pullman, WA
Myklebust, Roger A. ... Seattle, WA
Mykolajtchuk, Jurij ... New York, NY
Mykulak, George W. ... Boston, MA
Mykyta, Alicia ... Phoenix, AZ
Mykytyn, Irene M. ... Burbank, CA
Mylan, John J. ... Dallas, TX
Mylan, Sheila Hughes ... Montclair, NJ
Myler, Charles J. ... Aurora, IL
Myler, David J. ... Aspen, CO
Myler, Glade A. ... Carson City, NV
Myler, Joel R. ... Traverse City, MI
Myler, Joel R., P.C. ... Traverse City, MI
Myler, John A.
Federal Energy Regulatory Commission,
Office of the General Counsel, GV
Myler, Robyn J. ... Carbondale, CO
Myler, Ruddy & Mc Tavish ... Aurora, IL
Myles, Allen J. ... Plaquemine, LA
Myles, Donald L., Jr. ... Phoenix, AZ
Myles, Elliott A. ... Pleasanton, CA
Myles, Gary M. ... Seattle, WA
Myles, Heather D. ... San Diego, CA
Myles, James L. ... Oklahoma City, OK
Myles, Jeffery T. ... Sanford, NC
Myles, John David ... Frankfort, KY
Myles, John E. ... Englewood, CO
Myles, John L. ... Oklahoma City, OK
Myles, Kenneth J. ... Tawas City, MI
Myles, Kevin M.
General Services Administration,
Office of Regional Counsel, GV
Myles, Kevin M. ... Portland, OR
Myles, Kristin Linsley ... San Francisco, CA
Myles, Linda M. ... New York, NY
Myles, Lonny A. ... Hammond, LA
Zachary, LA
Myles, Lora E. ... Reno, NV
Myles, Lucille R. ... Kansas City, MO
Myles and Martin, Law Offices of
East Tawas, MI
Oscoda, MI
Tawas City, MI
Myles, Mary Helen ... Louisville, KY
Myles & Myles ... Oklahoma City, OK
Myles & Myles ... Portland, OR
Myles & Myles, A Professional Law Corporation ... Plaquemine, LA
Myles, P. Russel ... Mobile, AL
Myles, Phylis C. ... Portland, OR
Myles, Raymond ... Chicago, IL
Myles, Robert W. ... Shelbyville, KY
Myles, Seth A. ... Brooklyn, NY
Myles, Thos. F. ... Wayland, MA
Myles, Tina L. ... Cleveland, OH
Myles, Travis Olen, Jr. ... Louisville, KY
Myles, Vale P. ... Upton, NY
Myles-Sanders, Leslie ... University Center, MI
Mylett, Robert E. ... Canton, OH
Mylles, James Mark ... Stockton, CA
Mylod, Philip G. ... Lavallette, NJ
Mylod, Philip J. ... Lavallette, NJ
Mylott, Andrew R. ... New York, NY
Mylott, Raymond L., Jr. ... Parsippany, NJ
Mylott, Thomas R., III ... Dallas, TX
Mylotte, David & Fitzpatrick
Voorhees, NJ
Hazleton, PA
Philadelphia, PA
Wilkes-Barre, PA
Mylrea, David R. ... Minneapolis, MN
Mylrea, Jane C. ... Dubuque, IA
Myman, Abell, Fineman & Greenspan, LLP
Los Angeles, CA
Myman, Martin L. ... San Rafael, CA
Myman, Robert H. ... New York, NY
Myman, Robert M. ... Los Angeles, CA
Mynard, Clayton J. ... Clearwater, FL
Mynatt, Gladys Smith ... Chattanooga, TN
Mynatt, James P., Jr. ... Knoxville, TN
Mynatt, Mary LeAnn ... Knoxville, TN
Mynatt, R. Neal ... Durango, CO
Mynatt, William A., Jr. ... Knoxville, TN
Mynick, Alison Wholey
Liberty Corner, NJ
Myntti-Groom, Andrea ... Mabank, TX
Myrabo, Lloyd K. ... Canton, SD
Myrabo, Vance S. ... Canton, SD
Myrbeck, Gunnar C. ... Augusta, ME
Myrdahl, Kim ... Eden Prairie, MN
Myrdal, John R. ... Honolulu, HI
Myre, Ann R. ... Paducah, KY
Myre, Bryan P. ... Yakima, WA
Myre, Catherine Miyoko Turner
Mercer Island, WA
Myre, D. Paul ... St. Louis, MO
Myre, David E., Jr. ... Seattle, WA
Myre, Theodore T., Jr. ... Louisville, KY
Myren, Matthew T. ... Hoffman Estates, IL
Myren, Scott P. ... Pierre, SD
Myres, James T. ... Phoenix, AZ
Myres, Susan ... Houston, TX
Myrick, Adelaide S. ... Charleston, SC
Myrick, Amber R. ... Boise, ID
Myrick, Davis & Brehany, P.A.
Pensacola, FL
Myrick, Donald F. ... Grants Pass, OR
Myrick, Edward D. ... Lake Charles, LA

Myrick, Edward L., Jr. ....Boca Raton, FL
Myrick, Elizabeth Rhoad
Summerville, SC
Myrick, Gary ....United States Senate, Senatorial Assistants, GV
Myrick, Gary F. ....Brighton, MA
Myrick, James D. ....Charleston, SC
Myrick, James J. ....Chicago, IL
Myrick, John L. ....Pensacola, FL
Myrick, Lynn Michael ....Grants Pass, OR
Myrick, Melanie K. ....Kansas City, MO
Myrick, Nolan A., Jr. ....Murfreesboro, TN
Myrick, Paul D. ....Mobile, AL
Myrick, Robert W. ....Durham, NC
Myrick, Ronald E. ....Fairfield, CT
Myrick, Seagraves, Adams & Davis
Grants Pass, OR
Myrick, Thomas D. ....Charlotte, NC
Myrick, W. Allen, Jr. ....Spartanburg, SC
Myrick, William E. ....Denver, CO
Myrick, William E., Jr. ....Allendale, SC
Myrick, William E., P.C. ....Denver, CO
Myricks, Randy J. ....Los Angeles, CA
Myrin, Marc A. ....Dallas, TX
Myron, Kari M. ....Newport Beach, CA
Myron, Robert E. ....Rancho Santa Fe, CA
Myrow, Stephen A. ....Washington, DC
Myrter, Ronald B. ....Philadelphia, PA
Myrtetus, E. Duffy ....Glen Allen, VA
Richmond, VA
Myrun, Maurice ....Wethersfield, CT
Myrus, Richard ....Boston, MA
Myse, Gordon G. ....Wausau, WI
Myser, Richard A. ....Bridgeport, OH
Myshin, Amil N. ....Boise, ID
Myshin, Daniel ....Monessen, PA
Myshin, Daniel M. ....Rochester, MN
Myshrall, George H., Jr. ....Atlanta, GA
Mysing, A. William, Jr. (A Prof. Law Corp.)
Covington, LA
Mysing, Peter F. ....Kenai, AK
Myska, Elizabeth L. ....Holden, MA
Myslis, Laura L. ....Minneapolis, MN
Mysliwiec, Aaron J. ....Minneapolis, MN
Mysliwiec, Michael C. ....Grand Rapids, MI
Mysliwiec, Regina C. ....New York, NY
Mysliwiec, Richard Allen ....Dallas, TX
Mysliwiec, Robert W. ....South Bend, IN
Mysliwiec, Ronald P., Law Offices of
New York, NY
Mysliwiec, Stephen R. ....Washington, DC
Mysliwy, Patrick ....Hammond, IN
Mysliwy, Teresa Muth ....Merrillville, IN
Mysock & Chevaillier ....Tulsa, OK
Mysock, Edward J., Jr. ....Tulsa, OK
Mysogland, Ernest C. ....Hartford, CT
Myster, Jay D. ....Fergus Falls, MN
Myster, Lloyd S. ....Northfield, MN
Myster, Susan E. ....San Francisco, CA
Myszka, Kenneth F. ....Williamsville, NY
Myszka-Ostberg, Karen A. ....Westfield, NJ
Myszkowski, Zenon M. ....Albuquerque, NM
Mytelka, Andrew J. ....Galveston, TX
Mytelka, Arnold K. ....Springfield, NJ
Mytelka, Craig L. ....Virginia Beach, VA
Mytich, Ketra A. ....Peoria, IL
Mytich, Ketra A., Ltd. ....Peoria, IL
Mytko, Sergei ....Chicago, IL
Mytnyk, Peter H., Jr. ....Mount Clemens, MI
Myzak, Ioan Terri ....Salem, OR
Myzel, Charles Joseph ....Lackawanna, NY
Myzer, John ....Topeka, KS
Mzhen, Vadim A. ....Owings Mills, MD

Naab, Donna J. ....Pittsburgh, PA
Naab, Geoffrey ....Manchester, CT
Naaf, Jenifer J. ....Kansas City, MO
Naal, Mary M. ....Joliet, IL
Naar, Alan S. ....Woodbridge, NJ
Naar, Sonya D. ....Chicago, IL
Naas, Barbara Lou ....Fort Collins, CO
Naas, Conrad John ....New York, NY
Naas, Lindsay R. ....Washington, DC
Naas, Lisa J. ....Norcross, GA
Naasko, Heidi A. ....Detroit, MI
Naatjes, Scott M. ....Minneapolis, MN
Naatz, Cecil E. ....Marshall, MN
Naatz, David A. ....Kansas City, MO
Naatz, Lisa K. ....Minneapolis, MN
Nabatoff, Ross A. ....Washington, DC
Nabavinejad, Negar ....New York, NY
Nabb, Edward H. ....Cambridge, MD
Nabb, Edward H., Jr. ....Cambridge, MD
Naber, Jennifer A. ....Chicago, IL
Naber, Joyner, Schardein & Jaffe
Clarksville, TN
Louisville, KY
Naber, Raymond J., Jr. ....Louisville, KY
Naber, Thomas C. ....Laguna Hills, CA
Nabers, Drayton, Jr. ....Birmingham, AL
Nabers, J. Lynn ....Austin, TX
Nabers, J. Scott ....Houston, TX
Nabers, Robert F. ....New York, NY
Nabers, Timothy Lynn ....Austin, TX
Nabers, Wallace J. ....Honolulu, HI
Nabeta, Nelson Y. ....Honolulu, HI
Nabhan, Colleen B. ....Dallas, TX
Nabhan, Douglas M. ....Richmond, VA
Nabhan, Harold G. ....Allentown, PA
Nabholz, W. James, III ....St. Louis, MO
Nabi, Durré ....New York, NY
Nabinger, Robert C. ....Boston, MA
Nable, Jeffrey L. ....Brooklyn, NY
Nabor, Adolfo ....Los Angeles, CA
Nabor, Joseph T. ....Chicago, IL
Naborowski, Clarence T. ....Chicago, IL
Nabors, G. Dennis ....Montgomery, AL
Nabors, Giblin & Nickerson, P.A.
Tallahassee, FL
Tampa, FL
Nabors, Jeffery R. ....Atlanta, GA
Nabors, Jeffery R., P.C. ....Atlanta, GA
Nabors, John C. ....Dallas, TX
Nabors, Mary Kay ....Durant, OK
Nabors, Ollie W. ....Gadsden, AL
Nabors, Robert L. ....Tallahassee, FL
Nabors, S. Jason ....Birmingham, AL
Nabors & Saliba, L.L.C. ....Montgomery, AL
Nabors, Scott R. ....Panama City, FL
Nabors, Theresa K. ....Washington, DC
Nabors, William B. ....Saipan, TT
Nabours, Gerald W. ....Flagstaff, AZ
Nabours, William W. ....Yuma, AZ
Nabozny, Ronald M. ....Southfield, MI
Nabozny-Younger, Sandra
Charlotte Amalie, St. Thomas, VI
Nabrit, H. Clarke ....Nashville, TN
Nabrit, James M., III ....New York, NY
Nabulsi, Basam E. ....Stamford, CT
Nacamuli, Ronald ....Winchester, MA
Naccarato, Dean M. ....Pittsburgh, PA
Naccarato, James J. ....Potomac, MD
Naccarato, Michael ....St. Louis, MO
Naccarato, Timothy E. ....Sacramento, CA
Naccarato, Vincent J. ....Westerly, RI
Naccarella, Theodore ....Philadelphia, PA
Naccari, Bradley P. ....Metairie, LA
Naccari, Bruce E. ....New Orleans, LA
Naccari, J. Bruce ....Metairie, LA
Naccasha, Ziyad I. ....Chicago, IL
Nacchio, Jean Flora ....Staten Island, NY
Nacchio, Richard F. ....Basking Ridge, NJ
Nace, Andrew B. ....Garland, TX
Nace, Barry J. ....Washington, DC
Martinsburg, WV
Nace, David L. ....Washington, DC
Nace, Eleanor ....Washington, DC
Nace, George M., III ....Allentown, PA
Nace, R. Bryan ....Akron, OH
Nace, Richard F., Jr. ....New Haven, CT
Nacev, Adrienne Noble ....Fort Thomas, KY
Nacev, Ljubomir ....Cincinnati, OH
Nacewicz, Richard S. ....Bowie, MD
Nach, Brian Michael ....Chicago, IL
Nachamie, Andrew S. ....Rockville Centre, NY
Nachamie, Barton (IBA) ....**New York, NY**
Nachamie, Bonnie S. ....Rockville Centre, NY
Nachand, Charles D., III ....Escondido, CA
Nachand, David D. ....Jeffersonville, IN
Nachand, Henry ....Jeffersonville, IN
Nachand & Nachand ....Jeffersonville, IN
Nachay, Joseph ....Bronx, NY
Nachazel, John ....Boston, MA
Nachbar, Ann D. ....McLean, VA
Nachbar, Karen L. ....New York, NY
Nachbar, Keith R. ....Casper, WY
Nachbar, Kenneth J. ....Wilmington, DE
Nachbar, Stuart M. ....Rahway, NJ
Nacheman, Jessica R. ....Florham Park, NJ
Nachi, Meena C. ....Los Angeles, CA
Nachison, Harold ....Staten Island, NY
Nachlas, R. I. ....Houston, TX
Nachlis, Debra E. Jacob ....New York, NY
Nachlis & Fink ....San Francisco, CA
Nachlis, Lorie S. ....San Francisco, CA
Nachlis, Warren L. ....New York, NY
Nachman, Allan ....Birmingham, MI
Nachman, Andrew H. ....Jacksonville, FL
Nachman, Anne M. ....Manahawkin, NJ
Nachman & Associates, P.C. ....Paramus, NJ
Nachman, Bernard ....Jacksonville, FL
Nachman, Bert A. ....Newport News, VA
Nachman, Carol P. ....Treasury Department, Internal Revenue Service, GV
Nachman, David E. ....New York, NY
Nachman, David H. ....Paramus, NJ
Nachman, David J. ....Thousand Oaks, CA
Nachman, David R. ....Kansas City, MO
Nachman, Eric P. ....Yonkers, NY
Nachman, Erwin B. ....Newport News, VA
Nachman, Fraidy ....Brooklyn, NY
Nachman, Franklin A. ....Denver, CO
Nachman, Gary S. ....Newport News, VA
Nachman, George J. ....Dallas, TX
Nachman, Guillemard & Rebollo
San Juan, PR
Nachman, Irvin W., (P.A.)
Fort Lauderdale, FL
Nachman, James L. ....Chicago, IL
Nachman, Leonard R., II
Baton Rouge, LA
Nachman, M. Roland, Jr.
Montgomery, AL
Nachman, Marc H. ....Towson, MD
Nachman, Martha S. ....Denver, CO
Nachman, Mary T. ....Torrance, CA
Nachman, Michael P. ....Philadelphia, PA
Nachman, Norman H. ....Chicago, IL
Nachman, Richard A. ....New York, NY
Nachman, Robert D. ....Chicago, IL
Nachman, Steven M. ....New York, NY
Nachman, Steven N. ....Garden City, NY
Nachman, Steven Z. ....New York, NY
Nachman, Stuart L. ....Norfolk, VA
Nachmann, John D. ....Washington, DC
Nachmanoff, Michael S. ....Alexandria, VA
Arlington, VA
Nachmias, Carolyn S. ....Philadelphia, PA
Nachmias, Mark D. ....Avenel, NJ
Nachowiak, Drew F. ....Dallas, TX
Nachshin, Robert J., (A Professional Corporation) ....Los Angeles, CA
Nachshin & Weston, LLP
Los Angeles, CA
Nachsin, Jonathan ....Chicago, IL
Nacht, David A. ....Ann Arbor, MI
Nacht, David A., P.C. ....Ann Arbor, MI
Nacht, Gary H. ....Seattle, WA
Nacht, Steven B. ....Setauket, NY
Nachtigal, Fred C. ....Hillsboro, OR
Nachtigal, Gayle A. ....Hillsboro, OR
Nachtigal, Kathleen B. ....Portland, OR
Nachtigal, Patricia ....Woodcliff Lake, NJ
Nachtigall, Ellen C. ....New York, NY
Nachtigall, George A. ....Houston, TX
Nachtrieb, Dennis Wayne ....Cary, NC
Nachtsheim, John J. ....Silver Spring, MD
Nachtwey, Paul D. ....Boston, MA
Nachwalter, George M. ....Miami, FL
Nachwalter, George M., P.A. ....Miami, FL
Nachwalter, Michael ....Miami, FL
Nack, Daniel E. ....St. Charles, MO
Nack, Emily Ann ....Fairfax, VA
Nack, Irwin ....New York, NY
Nack, James J. ....Galena, IL
Nack, Joseph E. ....Galena, IL
Nack, Louis A., Jr. ....Elizabeth, IL
Galena, IL
Nack, Michael R. ....St. Louis, MO
Nack, Richardson, Kelly & Kurt
Elizabeth, IL
Nack, Richardson & Kurt ....Galena, IL
Nacke, Mark A. ....Tavares, FL
Nacke, Philip A. ....Washington, DC
Nacker, Wayne E. ....Chicago, IL
Nackley, Jennifer J. ....Naples, FL
Nackson, Joseph Lewis ....Hackensack, NJ
Naclerio, Alphonse M. ....Elmsford, NY
Naclerio, Gregory J. ....Mineola, NY
Naclerio, Steven ....Coral Gables, FL
Nacol, Mae ....Houston, TX
Nacol, Mae, & Associates, Law Offices of, P.C.
Houston, TX
Nacol, Mark A. ....Richardson, TX
Nacol, Wortham and Associates, P.C.
Dallas, TX
Richardson, TX
Nacopoulos, Vasilios ....Erie, PA
Nacos, James J. ....Jericho, NY
Nacsin, Charles J. (Chuck)
San Bernardino, CA
Nacu, John ....Woonsocket, RI
Nacy, Joseph R.
Federal Energy Regulatory Commission, Office of the Administrative Law Judges, GV
Naczi, Anne L. ....Wilmington, DE
Nadai, Craig ....Santa Monica, CA
Nadal-Arcelay, Harry R. ....San Juan, PR
Nadal-Arcelay, Rafael A. ....San Juan, PR
Nadalin, Robert G. ....Houston, TX
Nadal-López, Néstor R. ....San Juan, PR
Nadamoto, Laurie Jayne ....Honolulu, HI
Nadan, Christian H. ....Palo Alto, CA
Nadan, Marshall ....Kingston, NY
Nadan, Michele Milnes ....Santa Clara, CA
Nadarajah, Bala ....Washington, DC
Nadarzanski, Jeannine A. ....Newburgh, NY
Nadas, John A., (P.C.) ....Boston, MA
Nadborne, Brad L. ....Chicago, IL
Nadborny, Daniel A. ....New York, NY
Nadborny, Jill S. ....Scarsdale, NY
Naddeo, James A. ....Clearfield, PA
Naddeo, James K. ....Flint, MI
Nadeau, Donna A.
Palm Beach Gardens, FL
Nadeau, Douglas A. ....Marblehead, MA
Nadeau, Edward L. ....Glens Falls, NY
Nadeau, Edwin T. ....Winchester, MA
Nadeau, James A. ....Nashua, NH
Nadeau, Joseph P. ....Concord, NH
Nadeau, Karen Piso ....Boston, MA
Nadeau, Mark A. ....Phoenix, AZ
Nadeau, Regina A. ....Laconia, NH
Nadeau, Richard, Jr. ....Providence, RI
Nadeau, Robert B., Jr. ....Orlando, FL
Nadeau, Robert P. ....Portland, ME
Nadeau & Simmons, P.C. ....Providence, RI
Nadeau, Steven C. ....Detroit, MI
Nadeau, Thomas L. ....Bridgeport, CT
Nadeau, Tina Louise ....Concord, NH
Nadel, Alan B. ....Ardsley, NY
Nadel, Alan S. ....Philadelphia, PA
Nadel, Andrea ....Rochester, NY
Nadel & Associates, P.C. ....Brooklyn, NY
New York, NY
Nadel, Darren E. ....Denver, CO
Nadel, David ....Brooklyn, NY
Nadel, Donna S. ....Torrance, CA
Nadel, Edward S. ....New York, NY
Nadel, Evan S. ....New York, NY
Nadel, Gilly ....Chicago, IL
Nadel Group, P.A. ....Palm Beach Gardens, FL
Nadel, Heidi A. ....Boston, MA
Nadel, Howard B. ....Fort Lauderdale, FL
Nadel, Irwin H. ....Westport, CT
Nadel, Jeffrey ....Silver Spring, MD
Nadel, Joseph ....San Francisco, CA
Nadel, Laurence P. ....New Haven, CT
Nadel, Laurence P., A Professional Corporation
New Haven, CT
Nadel, Lloyd J. ....Mineola, NY
Nadel, Lorraine ....Brooklyn, NY
New York, NY
Nadel, Marc D. ....New York, NY
Nadel, Marcia S. ....San Francisco, CA
Nadel, Mark S.
Federal Communications Commission, Common Carrier Bureau, GV
Nadel, Norbert A. ....Cincinnati, OH
Nadel, Norman ....New York, NY
Nadel, Norman Robert ....Los Angeles, CA
Nadel, Peter F. ....New York, NY
Nadel, Peter R. ....Denver, CO
Nadel, Richard D. ....Palm Beach Gardens, FL
Nadel, Robert ....Brooklyn, NY
Nadel, Robert B. ....Hartsdale, NY
Nadel, Robert M. ....Encino, CA
Nadel, Russell J. ....Westlake Village, CA
Nadel, S. Michael ....New York, NY
Nadel, Scott B. ....Binghamton, NY
Nadel, Steven B. ....New York, NY
Nadel, Steven Michael ....Des Moines, IA
Nadel, Victoria L. ....Boston, MA
Nadelbach, Jay ....Flushing, NY
Nadelhoffer, Carleton ....Naperville, IL
Nadelhoffer, Kuhn, Mitchell, Moss, Saloga, Kocsis & Lechowicz, P.C. ....Joliet, IL
Naperville, IL
Wheaton, IL
Nadelhoffer, Sarah ....Chicago, IL
Nadell, Bernhardt M. ....New York, NY
Nadell, Glenn A. ....Northbrook, IL
Nadell, Jeffrey A. ....Red Bank, NJ
Nadell, Joanne S. ....West Long Branch, NJ
Nadelman, Carol A.
Rancho Cucamonga, CA
Nadelman, Cary M. ....New York, NY
Nadelman, Jeffrey Dale
Rancho Cucamonga, CA
Nadelman & Nadelman
Rancho Cucamonga, CA
Nadelman, Richard ....New York, NY
Nadelmann, Deborah M. ....New York, NY
Nadelson, Eileen N. ....New York, NY
Nadelson, Elizabeth P. ....Irvine, CA
Nadelson, Stuart R., (P.C.) ....Great Neck, NY
Naden, Andrew W. ....Baldwin, MD
Naden, Andrew W., and Associates
Baldwin, MD
Naden, Marian Leslie ....Seattle, WA
Naden, Paul H. ....Lutherville, MD
Nader, Ann Marie Knops ....Raleigh, NC
Nader, Burl F. ....Libertyville, IL
Nader, George E. ....Tampa, FL
Nader, George Joseph ....Boston, MA
Nader, James P. ....New Orleans, LA
Nader, John M. ....Louisville, KY
Nader, Joyce A. ....Tampa, FL
Nader, Joyce E. ....Cleveland, OH
Nader, Michael J. ....Fort Wayne, IN
Nader, Michelle M. ....Elsmere, KY
Nader and Nader ....Middlefield, OH
Warren, OH
Youngstown, OH
Nader, Paul G. ....Warren, OH
Nader, Ralph ....Winsted, CT
Nader, Robert A. ....Warren, OH
Nader, Robert J. ....Tampa, FL
Nader, Thomas C. ....Middlefield, OH
Warren, OH
Nader, Victoria Scott
Chesapeake Beach, MD
Nader, William G. ....Shreveport, LA
Nader-Syiek, Cathy ....Pittsburgh, PA
Nadig, David G. ....Northbrook, IL
Nadile, Janet M. ....New York, NY
Nadile, Vincent S. ....Tarrytown, NY
Nadim, Mohammad ....Santa Monica, CA
Nading, Robert A., II ....Ankeny, IA
Nadir, Allan A. ....Van Nuys, CA
Nadis, Ronn S. ....Southfield, MI
Naditch, Ronald M. ....Annapolis, MD
Naditch, Ronald M., P.A.
Washington, DC
Annapolis, MD
Baltimore, MD
Nadjar, Mark E. ....Huntington, NY
Nadjari, Douglas M. ....New York, NY
Nadjari, Maurice ....Huntington, NY
Nadjmi, Mitra S. ....Boston, MA
Nadkarni, Girish V. ....Chatham, NJ
Nadkarni, Nancy J. ....East Brunswick, NJ
Nadle, Martin B. ....New York, NY
Nadler, Alfred J. ....Miami, FL
Nadler, Barry ....Ames, IA
Des Moines, IA
Nadler, Beskin & Scott ....Atlanta, GA
Nadler, Burton A. ....Boston, MA
Nadler, Carl S. ....Washington, DC
Nadler, Charles E. ....Minneapolis, MN
Nadler, Charles H. ....Cedar Rapids, IA
Iowa City, IA
Nadler, David ....Cedar Rapids, IA
Nadler, David ....New York, NY
Nadler, David M. ....Washington, DC
Nadler, Diane H. ....San Jose, CA
Nadler, Ellen R. ....New York, NY
Nadler, Floyd N. ....Chicago, IL
Nadler, Gary ....Petaluma, CA
Nadler, Gary M. ....Atlanta, GA
Nadler, H. S. ....New York, NY
Nadler, Jeffrey ....New York, NY
Nadler, Jonathan Jacob ....Washington, DC
Nadler, Jonathan R. ....Philadelphia, PA
Nadler, Joseph M. ....Miami, FL
Nadler, Judith L.
Treasury Department, GV
Nadler, Keith J. ....Birmingham, AL
Nadler, Lisa Reilly ....Chicago, IL
Nadler, Mark S. ....Seattle, WA
Nadler, Michael A. ....Stamford, CT
Nadler, Myron J. ....Youngstown, OH
Nadler, Myron R. ....New York, NY
Nadler Nadler & Burdman Co., L.P.A.
Lisbon, OH
Warren, OH
Youngstown, OH
Nadler, Nancy Kearns ....New York, NY
Nadler, Paul ....Garden City, NY
Nadler, Richard S. ....New York, NY
Nadler, Rita K. ....Hackensack, NJ

Nadler, Robert A. ... Los Angeles, CA
Nadler, Robert B. ... Nashville, TN
Nadler, Samuel James ... San Francisco, CA
Nadler, Simon M. ... Rockville, MD
Nadler & Weston ... Cedar Rapids, IA
Iowa City, IA
Nadlman, Jay Michael ... Kansas City, MO
Nadoff, David H. ... Chicago, IL
Nadol, Jos. B. ... Dedham, MA
Nadolenco, John ... Los Angeles, CA
Nadolink, Erik D. ... Richmond, VA
Nadolna, Andrew S. ... Chicago, IL
Nadolny, John R. ... North Billerica, MA
Nadolski, Cynthia J. ... Mount Holly, NJ
Nadolski, David L. ... Sioux Falls, SD
Nadolski, James Anthony ... St. Joseph, MO
Nadolski, Laura Sheridan ... Lexington, MA
Nadolski, Michael B. ... Hartford, CT
Nador, Joseph M. ... Hempstead, NY
Nadrich & Associates ... Los Angeles, CA
Nadrich, Jeffrey ... Los Angeles, CA
Nadworny, Eric J. ... Boston, MA
Nady, Xavier G. ... Salinas, CA
Nadzo, Nicholas S. ... Portland, ME
Naefach, Lynn D. ... Harrisburg, PA
Naegel, Mark R. ... Cincinnati, OH
Naegele, Charles J. ... San Jose, CA
Naegele, Jori Bloom ... Lorain, OH
Naegele, Joseph J. ... Cleveland, OH
Naegele, Joseph L. ... San Jose, CA
Naegele, Kurt D. ... Washington, DC
Naegele, Richard A. ... Lorain, OH
Naegele, Stephen H. ... East Tawas, MI
Naegele, Timothy D., & Associates
Los Angeles, CA
Washington, DC
Naegele, Tracy A. ... Canyon Country, CA
Naegeli, John H., II ... Taylor, PA
Naegely, Henry E., Jr. ... Stuart, FL
Naegle, George T. ... Salt Lake City, UT
Naegle, LaDawn ... Washington, DC
Naehu, Patrick ... Honolulu, HI
Naekel, Jane Elizabeth ... Sacramento, CA
Naekel & Phenix, LLP ... Sacramento, CA
Naeve, Clifford M. ... Washington, DC
Naeve, Robert A. ... Irvine, CA
Naeve, William D. ... Santa Ana, CA
Nafe, James D. ... South Bend, IN
Nafe, James D., Jr. ... South Bend, IN
Nafe & Nafe ... South Bend, IN
Nafe, Scott D. ... Winston-Salem, NC
Naff, Colleen B. ... Houston, TX
Naffah, Eli Thomas, (Co., L.P.A.)
Cleveland, OH
Naffky, Jeanne M. ... Rochester, NY
Naffziger, Anne E. ... Chicago, IL
Naficy, Liliana C. ... Novato, CA
Nafissian, Parviz ... New York, NY
Nafman, Charles P. ... New York, NY
Nafpliotis, Michael N. ... Atlanta, GA
Naftalin, Alan Y. ... Washington, DC
Naftalin, Charles R. ... Washington, DC
Naftalin, Ethan S. ... Raleigh, NC
Naftalis, Alan Robert ... New York, NY
Naftalis, Gary P. ... New York, NY
Naftalis, Tracy Lee ... Dallas, TX
Naftel, James Philip, II ... Birmingham, AL
Naftel, Jeremy T. ... Sacramento, CA
Naftel, Nancy M. ... Los Angeles, CA
Naftol, Jerome H. ... Bayside, NY
Naftolin, Michael E. ... New York, NY
Naftulin, Jeffrey L. ... Doylestown, PA
Naftulin, Ryan E. ... Menlo Park, CA
Naftz, Robert C. ... Pocatello, ID
Naftzger, J. Christopher ... Washington, DC
Naftzinger, David J. ... Cleveland, OH
Nafzger, Richard L. ... Silver Spring, MD
Nafziger, Gary L. ... Oskaloosa, KS
Nafziger, George H. ... Springfield, IL
Nafziger, James A. R. ... Salem, OR
Nafziger, Jamie N. ... Minneapolis, MN
Nafziger, Lois A. ... Norristown, PA
Nafziger, Verlin R. ... Detroit, MI
Nag, Rupak ... Berkeley, CA
Mountain View, CA
Nagae, Jerald E. ... Seattle, WA
Nagai, John T. ... Los Angeles, CA
Nagaj, Matthew J. ... St. Clair Shores, MI
Nagamine, Dean T. ... Honolulu, HI
Nagamine, Jill T. ... Honolulu, HI
Nagan, Jack ... San Francisco, CA
Nagan, Judith N. ... Gainesville, FL
Nagano, Joanne ... New York, NY
Nagao, Alvin T. ... United States Senate, Committee Legal Personnel, GV
Nagao, Clarence M. ... Honolulu, HI
Nagarajan, Kamesh ... Rochester, NY
Nagardeolekar, Lily S. ... New London, CT
Nagareda, Richard A. ... Athens, GA
Nagasako, Lynn T. ... Portland, OR
Nagasawa, Gary T. ... Folsom, CA
Nagata, Ernest A.
Federal Trade Commission, Bureau of Competition, GV
Nagata, Glenn M. ... Honolulu, HI
Nagata, Robert Y. ... Los Angeles, CA
Nagata, Russel S. ... Honolulu, HI
Nagata, Sheryl Lee A. ... Honolulu, HI
Nagata, Steven M. ... Honolulu, HI
Nagatani, Randal K. ... Honolulu, HI
Nagaue, Nelson T. ... Honolulu, HI
Nagby, Robert W. ... Riverside, CA
Nagby, Robert W., Law Office of
Riverside, CA
Nagda, A. Patrick ... Irvine, CA
Nagel, Andrew E. ... New York, NY
Nagel, Austin P. ... Pleasanton, CA
Nagel, Barbara J. ... New York, NY
Nagel, Beth A. ... Cleveland, OH
Nagel, Bruce H. ... Livingston, NJ
Nagel, Daniel S. ... Bridgeport, CT
Nagel, Dennis J. ... Des Moines, IA
Nagel, Doris K. ... North Chicago, IL
Nagel, Edw. M. ... Allentown, PA
Nagel, Ellen L. ... Cincinnati, OH
Nagel, Glen R. ... Jamestown, ND
Nagel & Goldstein ... Pittsburgh, PA
Nagel, Harold D. ... Stockton, IL
Nagel, Herbert ... Coeur d'Alene, ID
Nagel, Ira A. ... Boston, MA
Nagel, James Allan ... McLean, VA
Nagel, James E. ... Santa Rosa, CA
Nagel, Joan F. ... Boulder, CO
Nagel, Joan H. ... North Wales, PA
Nagel, Joel M. ... Pittsburgh, PA
Nagel, John A. ... Vallejo, CA
Nagel, John C. ... Washington, DC
Nagel, John T. ... Fresno, CA
Nagel, Karl E. ... Olympia, WA
Nagel, Kenneth C. ... Pleasanton, CA
Nagel, Kimberlee Ann ... Bartow, FL
Nagel, Lance Director ... San Francisco, CA
Nagel, Lisa Wootton ... American Fork, UT
Nagel, Marc ... Chicago, IL
Nagel, Martin I. ... New York, NY
Nagel, Mary T. ... Chicago, IL
Nagel, Merideth C. ... Tallahassee, FL
Nagel, Nancy L. ... Chicago, IL
Nagel, Patricia M., (P.C.) ... Denver, CO
Nagel, Peter B. ... Denver, CO
Nagel, Peter B., P.C. ... Denver, CO
Nagel Rice Dreifuss & Mazie, LLP
Livingston, NJ
Morristown, NJ
Newark, NJ
New York, NY
Nagel, Robert L. ... Denver, CO
Nagel, Roger D. ... Wauseon, OH
Nagel, Ronald G. ... Homewood, IL
Nagel, Sandra Bernardi ... Homewood, IL
Nagel, Scott S. ... Seattle, WA
Nagel, Sheila R. ... Houston, TX
Nagel, Stefan v. B. ... Boston, MA
Nagel, Stephanie L. ... Wilmington, DE
Nagel, Stuart ... Beverly Hills, CA
Ventura, CA
Nagel, Susan E. ... Pittsburgh, PA
Nagel, Terry S. ... Springfield, MA
Nagel, Thomas ... Atlanta, GA
Nagel, Tom H. ... Columbus, OH
Nagel, Trevor W. ... Washington, DC
Nagel, Walter ... Washington, DC
Nagel, William E. ... New York, NY
Nagel, Yvonne W. ... Laramie, WY
Nagela, Margaret A. ... Chicago, IL
Nagelberg, Allison L. ... East Brunswick, NJ
Nagelberg, Howard A. ... Chicago, IL
Nagelberg, Larry ... Los Angeles, CA
Nagelberg, Rhona G. ... Doylestown, PA
Nagelberg, Sheldon B. ... Chicago, IL
Nagele, Robin L. ... Philadelphia, PA
Nageley, Jack R. ... Miami Beach, FL
Nageley, Meredith & Miller, Inc.
Sacramento, CA
Nagey, Sam R. ... Sacramento, CA
Nagelhout, Mary ... Washington, DC
Nagely, Neal M. ... Dallas, TX
Nageotte, Frank X. ... San Diego, CA
Nageotte, Richard R., (Ltd.) ... Stafford, VA
Nageotte, Yvette Justine ... Stafford, VA
Nager, Barry R. ... Orlando, FL
Nager, Barry R., Chartered ... Orlando, FL
Nager, Benjamin L. ... New York, NY
Nager, C. Hampton ... Reston, VA
Nager, Charles J. ... Scarsdale, NY
Nager, David E. ... Cleveland, OH
Nager, Elizabeth Carr ... Raleigh, NC
Nager, George Norton ... Haddonfield, NJ
Nager, Glen D. ... Washington, DC
Nager, Jocelyn Ruth ... New York, NY
Nager, Peter ... New York, NY
Naggar, David ... San Francisco, CA
Naggar, Ziv ... Chicago, IL
Naggatz, Alan D. ... Merrillville, IN
Naggles, James E. ... Richmond, VA
Nagher, Frederick A. ... Dallas, TX
Naghi, Sheila E. ... San Pedro, CA
Naghshineh, Patricia J. ... Atlanta, GA
Nagi, Baxter & Seymour, P.C. ... Detroit, MI
Nagi, Leonard E. ... Detroit, MI
Nagib, Nadia A. ... Chicago, IL
Nagin, Benjamin R. ... New York, NY
Nagin Gallop Figueredo, P.A.
Fort Lauderdale, FL
Miami, FL
Nagin, Jeffrey L. ... Beverly Hills, CA
Nagin, Kenneth L. ... New York, NY
Nagin, Laurance W. ... New York, NY
Nagin & Nagin ... New York, NY
Nagin, Stephen E. ... Miami, FL
Nagl, Richard L. ... Colorado Springs, CO
Nagl, Susan ... Iowa City, IA
Naglak, Jeanne Rand ... Princeton, NJ
Nagle & Associates, P.C. ... Atlanta, GA
Nagle, Barbara A. ... Montclair, NJ
Nagle, Brian ... Yakima, WA
Nagle, Brien J. ... Naperville, IL
Nagle, Bustamante & O'Hara, A Professional Corporation ... San Jose, CA
Nagle, Carol Baldwin ... Kerrville, TX
Nagle, Charles O. ... Boise, ID
Nagle, Christine L. ... Baltimore, MD
Nagle, Claire W. ... Edison, NJ
Nagle, Dana ... Houston, TX
Nagle, Daniel A. ... Dayton, OH
Nagle, Daniel J. ... Brighton, MI
Nagle, David, & Assoc., P.C. ... Austin, TX
Nagle, David C. ... Chattanooga, TN
Nagle, David E. ... Richmond, VA
Nagle, David G. ... Brockton, MA
Nagle, David J. ... Boston, MA
Nagle, David J. ... Austin, TX
Nagle, David R. ... Waterloo, IA
Nagle, David W., Jr. ... Louisville, KY
Nagle, Dennis L. ... Pineville, KY
Nagle, Donald E. ... Houston, TX
Nagle, Donald P. ... Boston, MA
Nagle, Eric W. ... Portland, OR
Nagle, Frank T. ... Kerrville, TX
Nagle, Frederick L., Jr. ... Haverhill, MA
Nagle, Gary R. ... San Jose, CA
Nagle, George A., Jr. ... Garden City, NY
Nagle, George F. ... Philadelphia, PA
Nagle & Higgins, P.C. ... Naperville, IL
Nagle, James F. ... Honolulu, HI
Nagle, James F. ... Seattle, WA
Nagle, James L. ... Walla Walla, WA
Nagle, James P. ... Wheaton, IL
Nagle, James W. ... Boston, MA
Nagle, Jane E. ... Chicago, IL
Nagle, Jeffrey C. ... New York, NY
Nagle, Jennifer Fletcher ... Middlesboro, KY
Nagle, John Copeland ... Newark, NJ
Nagle, John E. ... Bettendorf, IA
Nagle, John J., III ... Towson, MD
Nagle, John T. ... San Francisco, CA
Nagle, Joseph J. ... Mount Prospect, IL
Nagle, Karen M. ... Nutley, NJ
Nagle, Keith A. ... Middlesboro, KY
Nagle, Kelly A. ... Pittsford, NY
Nagle, Kenneth R. ... Marietta, GA
Nagle, Laura J. ... Denver, CO
Nagle, M. Steve ... Dallas, TX
Nagle, Margaret A. ... Los Angeles, CA
Nagle, Mark Carpenter ... Pleasanton, CA
Nagle, Matthew J. ... Cedar Rapids, IA
Nagle, Michael D. ... San Diego, CA
Nagle, Michael J. ... Olympia, WA
Nagle & Nagle ... Kerrville, TX
Nagle, P. Michael ... Columbia, MD
Nagle, Perwin & Mills, PLLC ... Houston, TX
Nagle, Richard L. ... Chicago, IL
Nagle, Richard L. ... Fairfax, VA
Nagle, Richard L., Jr. ... Atlanta, GA
Nagle, Robert C. ... Philadelphia, PA
Nagle, Robert E. ... Calabasas, CA
Nagle, Robert H. ... Phoenix, AZ
Nagle, Robert H., P.C. ... Phoenix, AZ
Nagle, Robert O. ... San Francisco, CA
Nagle, Robert T. ... Boston, MA
Nagle, Ronald C. ... West Chester, PA
Nagle, Ronald T. ... Morristown, NJ
Nagle, Shannon Lowry ... Atlanta, GA
Nagle, Sharon M. ... Walnut Creek, CA
Nagle, Shawn Conrad ... Tampa, FL
Nagle, Stephen G. ... Austin, TX
Nagle, Stephen M. ... Albany, NY
Nagle, Theresa A. ... Los Angeles, CA
San Francisco, CA
Nagle, Theresa A. ... Dayton, OH
Nagle, Thomas C. ... Walnut Creek, CA
Nagle, Thomas C., A Prof. Corp., Law Offices of ... Walnut Creek, CA
Nagle, Thomas D. ... Yakima, WA
Nagle, Thomas P., Jr. ... Easthampton, MA
Nagle, Timothy J. ... Department of the Navy, Office of the Judge Advocate General, GV
Nagle, Vale, McDowall, Cotter & Dunn
San Mateo, CA
Nagle, William J., III ... Honolulu, HI
Nagle, William L. ... Burlingame, CA
Nagle, William P. ... Wausau, WI
Nagle, William T. ... San Francisco, CA
Nagle & Zaller, P.C. ... Columbia, MD
Nagler, Alan H.
Department of Transportation, Federal Railroad Administration, GV
Nagler, Anita M. ... Chicago, IL
Nagler, Arnold ... Chicago, IL
Nagler & Associates ... Los Angeles, CA
Nagler, Barry ... Stoughton, MA
Nagler, Christian O. ... New York, NY
Nagler, David L. ... New York, NY
Nagler, Ellen Roth ... Los Angeles, CA
Nagler, George I., Law Offices of
Beverly Hills, CA
Nagler, Gloria Z. ... Seattle, WA
Nagler, Jeffrey D. ... Burbank, CA
Nagler, Karen M. ... Coronado, CA
Nagler, Lawrence H. ... Los Angeles, CA
Nagler, Leon G. ... Wellesley Hills, MA
Nagler, Marvin I. ... New York, NY
Nagler, Robert H. ... Eugene, OR
Nagler, Samuel ... Boston, MA
Nagler, Stanley M. ... New York, NY
Nagler, Stephen M. ... New York, NY
Nagler, Steven B. ... Bannockburn, IL
Nagler, Thomas A. ... Dallas, TX
Nagler, Vincent A. ... New York, NY
Naglins, Lisa M. ... Portland, OR
Nagorka, Edward J. ... Schenectady, NY
Nagorka, Frank W. ... Chicago, IL
Nagorney, Frank P. ... Cleveland, OH
Nagorny, Edward J. ... Cleveland, OH
Nagorny, Wesley II ... Houston, TX
McAllen, TX
Nagorsky, Edward S. ... Hackettstown, NJ
Morristown, NJ
Trenton, NJ
Nagorsky, Mitchell R. ... Chicago, IL
Nagosky, David P. ... Erie, PA
Nagrich, Nicholas ... Springfield, MO
Nagrotsky, Sanford ... Great Neck, NY
Nagrotsky, Stephen A. ... Washington, DC
Nagubandi, Radhika S. ... New City, NY
Nagucki, Robert E. ... Toledo, OH
Nagumo, Mark ... Department of Commerce, Patent and Trademark Office, GV
Nagurney, John E. ... Buffalo, NY
Nagusky, Beth A. ... Augusta, ME
Nagy, Andre L. ... Southport, CT
Nagy, David S. ... Burbank, CA
Nagy, Elizabeth A. ... Department of Justice, Bureau of Prisons, GV
Nagy, Gregory E. ... Trenton, NJ
Nagy, Gretchen E. ... Atlanta, GA
Nagy, James J. ... Munster, IN
Nagy, Jill ... Troy, NY
Nagy, Joan U. ... Ann Arbor, MI
Nagy, Joe H. ... Lubbock, TX
Nagy, John D. ... Hempstead, NY
Nagy, John L. ... Plymouth, MI
Nagy, John S. ... Los Angeles, CA
Nagy, John S. ... Washington, DC
Nagy, Joseph J. ... Cleveland, OH
Nagy, Kimberly K. ... Atlanta, GA
Nagy, Larry ... Portage, WI
Nagy, Lawrence J. ... Somerville, NJ
Nagy, Louis ... Warren, NJ
Nagy, Mary Anne ... San Rafael, CA
Nagy, Mary Elizabeth ... Cherry Hill, NJ
Philadelphia, PA
Nagy, Michael R. ... St. Davids, PA
Nagy, Michael Stephen ... Largo, MD
Nagy, Paul G. ... Los Angeles, CA
Nagy, Raymond L. ... Trenton, NJ
Nagy, Robert A. ... Hartford, CT
Nagy, Robert A. ... Elyria, OH
Nagy, Robert J. ... Chicago, IL
Nagy, Stephen J. ... Glenview, IL
Nagy, Stephen R. ... Elyria, OH
Nagy, Steven J. ... Chicago, IL
Nagy, Tibor, Jr. ... Tucson, AZ
Nagy, Timothy P. ... Columbus, OH
Nagy & Trócsányi LLP ... New York, NY
Nah, Joseph T. ... Washington, DC
Nahabedian, Raffi A. ... Los Angeles, CA
Nahabedian, Richard F. ... Southfield, MI
Nahai, Behzad ... Los Angeles, CA
Nahai, Hamid David ... Los Angeles, CA
Nahai Law Corporation, A Professional Corporation ... Los Angeles, CA
Nahal, Ajeet S. ... Flushing, NY
Nahal, Henry J. ... Albany, NY
Naham, Andrea R. ... Cedarhurst, NY
Nahan, John B. ... Springfield, VA
Nahari, Mihal ... New York, NY
Nahas, Edmund A. ... New York, NY
Nahas, Elisa Anastasio ... Hartford, CT
Nahas, Kirsten Root ... Boston, MA
Nahas, Michael A. ... Pittsburgh, PA
Nahas, Stuart E. ... New York, NY
Nahat, Nicholas R. ... Southfield, MI
Nahey, Natalie J. ... Portland, OR
Nahhat, Edward M. ... Warren, MI
Nahhat & Nahhat, P.C. ... Warren, MI
Nahhat, Salem M. ... Warren, MI
Nahi, Sheila B. ... San Francisco, CA
Nahigian, Eliot S. ... Fresno, CA
Nahigian, Richard E. ... Pasadena, CA
Nahigian, Richard L. ... Boston, MA
Nahikian, D. James ... Chicago, IL
Nahikian, William Thomas
Bloomfield Hills, MI
Nahin, Bruce A. ... Los Angeles, CA
Valencia, CA
Nahin, Bruce A., A Professional Law Corporation ... Los Angeles, CA
Santa Clarita, CA
Valencia, CA
Nahin, Melville H. ... Los Angeles, CA
Nahins, Todd I. ... New York, NY
Nahirny, Janet L. ... Department of Justice, Antitrust Division, GV
Nahitchevansky, Georges ... New York, NY
Nahlen, Dana G. ... Plano, TX
Nahm, David S. ... Huntington Beach, CA
Nahm, Nathan I. ... New York, NY
Nahm, Rosemarie Y. ... Los Altos, CA
Nahm, Tae Hea ... Menlo Park, CA
Nahmani, Lynne N. ... Norristown, PA
Nahmias, Adam Michael ... Memphis, TN
Nahmias, Alan I. ... Encino, CA
Nahmias, Edward B. ... Los Angeles, CA
Nahmias, Evan ... Memphis, TN
Nahmias, Louis ... Jamesburg, NJ
Nahmias, Peter E. ... Roseland, NJ
Nahmod, Sheldon ... Chicago, IL
Nahmod, Sonia L. ... Wilmette, IL
Nahon, Marcus ... Memphis, TN
Nahon & Saharovich ... Memphis, TN
Nahorney, Cynthia A. ... Chesapeake, VA
Nahoum, Michael B. ... Newtown, CT
Nahra, Barbara H. ... Cleveland, OH
Nahra, John A. ... Davenport, IA
Nahra, John P. ... Santa Monica, CA
Nahra, Joseph J. ... Cleveland, OH
Nahra, Kirk J. ... Washington, DC
Nahra, Margit H. ... Washington, DC
Nahra, Paul Pearsons ... Venice, CA
Nahrstadt, Bradley C. ... Chicago, IL
Nahrstadt, Debra L. ... Chicago, IL
Nahrwold, Stacey M. ... New York, NY
Nahstoll, R. W. ... Portland, OR
Naibert, Robert W. ... Lombard, IL
Naiburg, Eric W. ... Hauppauge, NY
Naiburg, Jennifer Leslie ... Kew Gardens, NY
Naiburg & Rosenblum ... Hauppauge, NY
Naida, James D. ... Bingham Farms, MI
Naida & Pierce, P.C. ... Bingham Farms, MI

Naide, Laura A. ....
Overseas Private Investment Corporation, GV
Naidech, Alison .... New York, NY
Naideck, Andrew J. .... Nutley, NJ
Naides, Perrie H. .... Iowa City, IA
Naideth, Stephen Sam .... Pasadena, CA
Naidich, Richard S. .... Bellmore, NY
Naiditch, Barry S. .... San Diego, CA
Naiditch, Jack R. .... Wailuku, HI
Naidoff, Stephanie .... Philadelphia, PA
Naidoo, Kristen M. .... Brighton, MI
Naidoo, Nishani D. .... New York, NY
Naidu, Sree .... Schaumburg, IL
Naidus, Robert A. .... East Hanover, NJ
Naifeh & Associates, A Professional Corporation .... Norman, OK
Naifeh, Bill R. .... Dallas, TX
Naifeh, Clifton D. .... Norman, OK
Naifeh, Jack E. .... Tulsa, OK
Naifeh, Lawrence E. .... Norman, OK
Naifeh, Robert N. .... Norman, OK
Naifeh, Robert N., Jr.
Oklahoma City, OK
Naifeh, Sheila J. .... Tulsa, OK
Naik, Paul .... Palo Alto, CA
Nail, C. Richard .... Clearwater, FL
Nail, Charles L., Jr. .... Sioux Falls, SD
Nail, Daniel J. .... Napoleonville, LA
Nail, Douglas A. .... Atlanta, GA
Nail, Edwin S. .... Houston, TX
Nail, G. Douglas .... Maitland, FL
Nail, Lester C. .... Salisbury, NC
Nail, Mike .... Vallejo, CA
Nail, Pamela E. .... Cullman, AL
Nail, Roger Dean, Jr. .... St. Louis, MO
Nail, Steven E. .... Greenville, SC
Nail, Tommy .... Birmingham, AL
Naile, Peggy J. .... Indianapolis, IN
Nailen, Robert E. .... Milwaukee, WI
Nailling, Robert A. .... Boston, MA
Nailos, Heath B. .... Orlando, FL
Nailos, Kristin Cummins
Winter Park, FL
Nails, John W. .... Chester, PA
Nails, Kenneth H. .... Providence, RI
Nails, Patrick K. .... Long Grove, IL
Naim, Tahir J. .... Palo Alto, CA
Naim, Vivien G. .... New York, NY
Naima, Theodore A. .... Miami, FL
Naiman, Cara L. .... New York, NY
Naiman, David M. .... Denver, CO
Naiman and Diamond .... Denver, CO
Naiman, Eleanor C. .... Baltimore, MD
Naiman, Kara S. .... New York, NY
Naiman, Loren M. .... Los Angeles, CA
Naiman, Mayer .... New York, NY
Naiman, Randall D. .... San Diego, CA
Naiman, Randall D., A.P.C., Law Offices of
San Diego, CA
Naiman, Robert M., (Ltd.) .... Chicago, IL
Naiman-Kohn, Marilyn .... Birmingham, MI
Naimark, Sol .... New York, NY
Naimi, Haleh C. .... Encino, CA
Naimish, Mary J. .... San Diego, CA
Naimon, Alex .... Silver Spring, MD
Naimon, Jeffrey P. .... Washington, DC
Naini, Mariam J. .... Los Angeles, CA
Naioti, Stephen B. .... Branson, MO
Naipawer, Michele A. .... Cherry Hill, NJ
Nair, Gopalan .... Fremont, CA
Nair & Levin, P.C. .... Bloomfield, CT
Hartford, CT
Nair, Priya D. .... Dallas, TX
Nair, Steven G. .... Irvine, CA
Nairin, Brian N. .... Pasadena, CA
Nairn, John W. .... Washington, DC
Nairn, Regis C. .... Pittsburgh, PA
Nairn, William Paul .... Hagerstown, MD
Naisbitt, James W. .... Chicago, IL
Naiser, Lawrence E. .... El Campo, TX
Naish, John C. .... Oakland, CA
Naish, Shannon M. .... Lexington, KY
Naishtat, Elliott .... Austin, TX
Naishtut, Norman B. .... Greenwich, CT
Rye Brook, NY
Naito, Steven L. .... Portland, OR
Naito, Yukio .... Honolulu, HI
Naitove, Benjamin J. .... Philadelphia, PA
Naizby, John F. .... New Haven, CT
Najaiko, Edward G. .... El Paso, TX
Najam, Edward W., Jr. .... Indianapolis, IN
Najam, William J., Jr. .... Southwick, MA
Najar, Paul J. .... Poway, CA
Najarian, Ara .... Glendale, CA
Najarian, Carol E. .... Cranston, RI
Najarian, Carol E. .... Providence, RI
Najarian, Clinton J. .... Reading, PA
Najarian, David V. .... Wilmette, IL
Najarian, Edward P. .... Kempton, PA
Najarian, Haig .... New York, NY
Najarian, Jube J. .... Fresno, CA
Najarian, Mary B. .... Portland, ME
Najarian & Najarian .... Wilmette, IL
Najarian, Paul J. .... New York, NY
Najarian, Richard .... Shrewsbury, NJ
Najarian, Robert G., Jr. .... Hanover, MA
Najarian, Sean .... Los Angeles, CA
Najarian, Steven D. .... Washington, DC
Najder, Kenneth J. .... New Orleans, LA
Najdeski, Henry P. .... Fort Wayne, IN
Najdovski, Zoran .... New York, NY
Najdovski, Zoran, PLLC .... New York, NY
Najem, Lawrence J. .... Jacksonville, FL
Najemy, Jan L. .... Springfield, MA
Najera, Carlos J. .... Oxnard, CA
Najera, Carol Jane .... Los Angeles, CA
Najera, Roberto .... San Francisco, CA
Najewicz, Michael F. .... San Diego, CA
Najfabadi, Elahe .... Los Angeles, CA
Najib, Omar M. .... Oak Lawn, IL
Najim, Harry L. .... Wichita, KS
Najim Law Offices .... Wichita, KS
Najim, Samuel J. .... Atlanta, GA
Najjar, Alex A. .... San Francisco, CA
Najjar, Ameen R. .... Indianapolis, IN
Najjar, Carmine Bollella .... New York, NY
Najjar, Charles J. .... Birmingham, AL
Najjar, Daniel A. .... Santa Fe, NM
Najjar, David K. .... Noblesville, IN
Najjar, Debra Dyleski .... Boston, MA
Providence, RI
Najjar Denaburg, P.C. .... Birmingham, AL
Columbiana, AL
Jasper, AL
Montgomery, AL
Oneonta, AL
Tuscaloosa, AL
Najjar, Ewa Slobodow .... Spokane, WA
Najjar, George Richard .... San Diego, CA
Najjar, Michael .... Lowell, MA
Najjoum, Linda Lemmon .... McLean, VA
Najman, Leon .... Lake Forest, CA
Najmy, Joseph L. .... Bradenton, FL
Najmy, Louis Justin .... Tampa, FL
Najolia, Richard A. .... New Orleans, LA
Najpaver, Joseph C. .... Oakland, CA
Naka, David R. .... Baltimore, MD
Naka, Huttar & Oldhouser, LLP
Baltimore, MD
Nakachi, Mari .... New York, NY
Nakagawa, Ann M. .... Honolulu, HI
Nakagawa, Arthur K. .... Honolulu, HI
Nakagawa, Christine F. .... Palo Alto, CA
Nakagawa, Edwin S. .... Oakland, CA
Nakagawa, Lillian K. .... San Francisco, CA
Nakagawa, Mike K. .... Sacramento, CA
Nakagawa & Rico .... Sacramento, CA
Nakagawa, Robert Y. .... Los Angeles, CA
Nakagawa, Togo .... Honolulu, HI
Nakagiri, Neal E. .... Los Angeles, CA
Nakahara & Hinoki, Inc. .... San Jose, CA
Nakahara, Larry M. .... Torrance, CA
Nakahara, Peter M. .... San Jose, CA
Nakahara, Vicki Y. .... Portland, OR
Nakahiro, Fumio R. .... Pasadena, CA
Nakaki, Carolyn K. .... Los Angeles, CA
Nakakuki, Emma .... New York, NY
Nakama, Dorothy R.
Department of Transportation, National Highway Traffic Safety Administration, GV
Nakamachi, Akihito .... Palo Alto, CA
Nakamae, Robert A. .... San Jose, CA
Nakamichi, Mari .... New York, NY
Nakamoto, Craig K. .... Honolulu, HI
Nakamoto, Francis M. .... Honolulu, HI
Nakamoto, Henry T. .... Hilo, HI
Nakamoto, Lynn R. .... Portland, OR
Nakamoto, Robert Y., Jr. .... Honolulu, HI
Nakamoto, Roy K. .... Hilo, HI
Nakamoto, Stanford H. .... Honolulu, HI
Nakamoto, Yoshioka & Okamoto, Attorneys At Law, A Law Corporation .... Hilo, HI
Nakamura, Alyson J. .... Honolulu, HI
Nakamura, Bruce A. .... Honolulu, HI
Nakamura, Cheryl A. .... Honolulu, HI
Nakamura, Craig G. .... Wailuku, HI
Nakamura, Craig H. .... Honolulu, HI
Nakamura, Cynthia S. .... Honolulu, HI
Nakamura, David H. .... Wailuku, HI
Nakamura, Dean H. .... Washington, DC
Nakamura, Derek S. .... Honolulu, HI
Nakamura, Hope G. .... Washington, DC
Nakamura, Jackie N. .... Cupertino, CA
Nakamura, Johnnel L. .... Honolulu, HI
Nakamura, Jon Y. .... San Francisco, CA
Nakamura, Joyce H. .... Denver, CO
Nakamura, Kenneth H. .... Kaneohe, HI
Nakamura, Kent Y. .... Washington, DC
Nakamura, Kirk H. .... Santa Ana, CA
Nakamura, Lee T. .... Honolulu, HI
Nakamura, Mamoru .... Koror, TT
Nakamura, Michael V. .... Rockville, MD
Nakamura, Neil T. .... Honolulu, HI
Nakamura, Noriko K. .... Denver, CO
Nakamura, Patrick K. .... Birmingham, AL
Nakamura, Quinn & Walls, LLP
Birmingham, AL
Atlanta, GA
Nakamura, Reese R. .... Honolulu, HI
Nakamura, Reid A. .... Honolulu, HI
Nakamura, Richard F. .... Honolulu, HI
Nakamura, Richard H., Jr.
Los Angeles, CA
Nakamura, Tetsujiro .... Los Angeles, CA
Nakamura, Yoshiro .... Wahiawa, HI
Nakanishi, Craig I. .... Honolulu, HI
Nakano, Darren K. .... Los Angeles, CA
Nakano, Douglas K. .... San Francisco, CA
Nakano, Irene M. .... Honolulu, HI
Nakano, James A., (A Law Corporation)
Honolulu, HI
Nakano, Kelley G.A. .... Honolulu, HI
Nakano, Kunichika .... New York, NY
Nakano, Lawrence H. .... Honolulu, HI
Nakano, Michael .... Honolulu, HI
Nakano, Nana .... Santa Monica, CA
Nakao, Natalie H. .... Ventura, CA
Nakao, Shirley .... Oakland, CA
Nakao, Toshio .... Cincinnati, OH
Nakaoka, Tracy K. .... Los Angeles, CA
Nakarado, Gary L. .... Denver, CO
Nakasaka, Chananel H. .... Los Angeles, CA
Nakasato, Earl T. .... Hilo, HI
Nakashima & Boynton .... San Jose, CA
Nakashima, David A. .... Honolulu, HI
Nakashima, Jann M. .... San Jose, CA
Nakashima, John M. .... Newport Beach, CA
Nakashima, Richard A. .... Austin, TX
Nakashima, S. Stephen .... San Jose, CA
Nakashima, Steven M. .... Honolulu, HI
Nakashima, Sumio .... Kailua-Kona, HI
Nakasian, Samuel .... Greenwood, VA
Nakasian, Stacey P. .... Providence, RI
Nakasian, William E. .... Columbus, OH
Nakasone, Kenneth M. .... Honolulu, HI
Nakasu, Eric M. .... Costa Mesa, CA
Nakasuji, Lauren K. .... Gardena, CA
Nakata, Alicia Harumi .... Wenatchee, WA
Nakata, Carla M. .... Oakland, CA
Wailuku, HI
Nakata, Gary K. .... Honolulu, HI
Nakata, Ken S. .... Department of Justice, Civil Rights Division, GV
Nakata, Kenneth M. .... San Jose, CA
Nakata, Lisa .... Monterey, CA
Salinas, CA
Nakata, Michelle E. .... San Francisco, CA
Nakata, Nancy K. .... Portland, OR
Nakata, Robert H. .... Honolulu, HI
Nakata, Stephen .... Los Angeles, CA
Nakatani, Gail C. .... Honolulu, HI
Nakatani, Glenn M. .... Covina, CA
Nakatani, Robert N. .... Berkeley, CA
Nakatani, Warren Y. .... Chicago, IL
Nakatsu, Penny .... Hayward, CA
Nakaue, Paul G. .... Stockton, CA
Nakayama, Granta Y. .... Washington, DC
Nakayama, Kenichi .... Santa Clara, CA
Nakayama, Nancy L. .... Seattle, WA
Nakayama, Paula A. .... Honolulu, HI
Nakazato, Arthur .... Costa Mesa, CA
Nakazawa, Alan .... Long Beach, CA
Nakazawa, Lani D. H. .... Honolulu, HI
Nakazawa, Zenji
Federal Communications Commission, Wireless Telecommunications Bureau, GV
Nakea, Clifford L. .... Lihue, HI
Nakell, Barry .... Chapel Hill, NC
Nakfoor, Karen M. .... Houston, TX
Nakhleh, William .... Washington, DC
Nakian, Paul S. .... Stamford, CT
Nakken, Robert P. .... Woodland, CA
Nakles, Christopher D. .... Latrobe, PA
Nakles and Nakles .... Greensburg, PA
Latrobe, PA
Nakles, Ned J. .... Latrobe, PA
Nakles, Ned J., Jr. .... Latrobe, PA
Nakoa, Shawn M. .... Kailua-Kona, HI
Nakon, Matthew W. .... Lorain, OH
Nakon, Richard J. .... Wauconda, IL
Nakos, Alex E. .... Dallas, TX
Nakos, Nikos C. .... Fort Wayne, IN
Nakos, Telly C. .... Chicago, IL
Nakulak, George K. .... Rutherford, NJ
Nalagan, Ernest R., III .... Oklahoma City, OK
Nalazek, Barbara U. .... Columbus, OH
Nalbach, George J. .... San Clemente, CA
Nalbandian, Arthur M. .... Roseland, NJ
Nalbandian, John B. .... Washington, DC
Nalbandian, Martin A. .... Rochelle Park, NJ
Nalbandian, Roberta E. .... Fairfield, CA
Nalbone, Charles M. .... Atlanta, GA
Nalbone, Dean S. .... Trenton, NJ
Nalbor, Sally S. .... Crown Point, IN
Nalda, Carlos M. .... Washington, DC
Nalder, G. Lance .... Idaho Falls, ID
Nalducci, Walter .... Pittsburgh, PA
Nale, John E. .... Waterville, ME
Nale, Lucia .... Chicago, IL
Nale, Mark J. .... Waterville, ME
Nale & Nale .... Waterville, ME
Nale, Richard C. .... Waterville, ME
Nale, Thomas J. .... Waterville, ME
Nalean, Loren A. .... Boone, IA
Nalean & Nalean .... Boone, IA
Nalean, Steven K. .... Boone, IA
Nalefski, Andrew T. .... Fairview Heights, IL
Naleid, Thomas J., (S.C.) .... Park Falls, WI
Nalencz, Leonard P. .... Philadelphia, PA
Nalepka, Timothy J. .... Des Plaines, IL
Nales, Dennis J. .... Sarasota, FL
Nalibotsky, Albert S. .... Charlotte, NC
Nalitz, William R. .... Waynesburg, PA
Nall, David A. .... Washington, DC
Nall, Frank K. .... Pikeville, KY
Nall, John W. .... Tallahassee, FL
Nall, Kenneth M., Jr. .... Owensboro, KY
Nall, Miller, Owens, Hocutt & Howard, LLP
Atlanta, GA
Nall, Pelley and Wynne .... Bonham, TX
Gainesville, TX
Sherman, TX
Nall, R. Douglas, Jr. .... San Antonio, TX
Nall, Rayburn M. .... Sherman, TX
Nall, Rayburn M., Jr. .... Sherman, TX
Nall, Robert C. .... Vero Beach, FL
Nall, Robert C., P.A. .... Vero Beach, FL
Nall, Sarah E. .... Hobe Sound, FL
Nall, Theodore R., Jr. .... Los Angeles, CA
Nall, Thomas G. .... Mooresville, NC
Nallaseth, Cyrus .... New York, NY
Nalle, Karey A. .... Austin, TX
Nallengara, Lona S. .... New York, NY
Nalley, Christopher M. .... Louisville, KY
Nalley, Christopher P. .... Staten Island, NY
Nalley, David C. .... Cincinnati, OH
Nalley, Elliot T. .... Suwanee, GA
Nalley, George J., Jr. .... Metairie, LA
Nalley, John D. .... Benton, AR
Nalley, Suzanne K. .... Covina, CA
Nalli, Joseph A. .... Fort Plain, NY
Nalli, Siro .... Roseville, MI
Nalli & Soave, P.C. .... Roseville, MI
Nallin, James J. .... Lufkin, TX
Nallin, Judith A. .... Trenton, NJ
Nalls, Charles H. .... Washington, DC
Nalls, J. Willard, Jr. .... Bethesda, MD
Nalls, John G. .... Rockville, MD
Nalls, Michael T. .... Bethesda, MD
Nalls & Nalls, P.C. .... Bethesda, MD
Nalls, Thomas W. .... Leesburg, VA
Nally Haasis Jordan & Bauer, P.C.
Champaign, IL
Nally, James J. .... Norwell, MA
Nally, James P. .... Hempstead, NY
Nally, Patrick J. .... Miami, FL
Nally, R. Hite .... Lexington, KY
Louisville, KY
Nally, Thomas P. .... Tulsa, OK
Nally, Traci E. .... Champaign, IL
Nally-Martin, Lisa K. .... Lebanon, KY
Nalty, Paul A. .... New Orleans, LA
Nalty, Sean P. .... San Francisco, CA
Nalven, Joseph .... San Diego, CA
Nalven, Paul R. .... New York, NY
Nam & Basmadjian .... Glendale, CA
Nam, David W. .... Tallahassee, FL
Nam, Elizabeth E. .... Rochester, NY
Nam, Frances .... Department of Justice, Community Relations Service, GV
Nam, Harrison Tae-Hee
San Francisco, CA
Nam, Jennifer J. .... San Francisco, CA
Nam, Jeonghyan S. .... New York, NY
Nam, Jina A. .... Glendale, CA
Nam, Katherine H.
Environmental Protection Agency, Office of the General Counsel, GV
Nam, Ki W. .... Washington, DC
Nam, Mindy J. .... Chicago, IL
Nam, Sang-Jin .... Hayward, CA
Nam, Sue J. .... New York, NY
Nam, Sunwoo .... Silver Spring, MD
Nam, Suzanne .... Boston, MA
Nam, Tamara E. .... San Francisco, CA
Nama, Prakash .... Minneapolis, MN
Namack, Clark & Keeney .... Sarasota, FL
Namack, William H., III .... Sarasota, FL
Namaka, David K. .... Honolulu, HI
Naman, Edmond George .... Mobile, AL
Naman, Howell, Smith & Lee, A Professional Corporation .... Austin, TX
Fort Worth, TX
Temple, TX
Waco, TX
Naman, Paul E. .... Beaumont, TX
Namanny, Patrick Norman
Fountain Valley, CA
Namanworth & Bohlen Co., L.P.A.
Cincinnati, OH
Namanworth, Eli, Law Offices of
Cincinnati, OH
Namazi, Nooshin .... New York, NY
Namazie, Hamid R. .... Los Angeles, CA
Namba, Brian Jin .... Farmington, UT
Namba, Curtis R. .... Sacramento, CA
Namba, Hiroshi .... New York, NY
Namba, Jerry .... Santa Maria, CA
Namee, Eric S. .... Wichita, KS
Namei, Firooz T. .... Cincinnati, OH
Namenye, John J. .... Muskegon, MI
Nameroff, Larry L.
United States Tax Court, Special Trial Judges, GV
Nameroff, Neil M. .... Miami, FL
Nameroff, Neil M., Professional Association
Miami, FL
Names, Donald J.
Equal Employment Opportunity Commission, Office of Federal Operations, GV
Names, Edward J., (P.C.) .... Louisville, CO
Nameth, Frederick James, Law Offices of
Glendale, CA
Nametz, Michael A. .... Florham Park, NJ
Namey, Norman D. .... Kingston, PA
Namey-Richards, Sandra L.
Wilkes-Barre, PA
Namian, Michael D. .... Washington, DC
Namikas, Joseph A. .... Chicago, IL
Namm, Michele R. .... St. Louis, MO
Namm, Sheila J. .... Brooklyn, NY
Nammo, David S. .... Asheville, NC
Nammo, Laura Darien .... Enka, NC
Namnoum, Kenneth P., Jr. .... Hartford, CT
Namnum, Susana M. .... New York, NY
Namorato, Cono R. .... Washington, DC
Namovice, John A. .... Chicago, IL
Namrow, Eric S. .... Washington, DC
Baltimore, MD
Namrow, Morton .... Bethesda, MD
Nanasi, Mariel .... Chicago, IL
Nanavati, Mark C. .... Midlothian, VA
Nancarron, Matthew .... Bryan, TX
Nancarrow, James E. .... Ishpeming, MI
Marquette, MI
Nance, Allan T. .... New York, NY
New York, NY
Nance, Betty Purkey .... Sunnyvale, CA
Nance, Boone .... West Memphis, AR
Nance, Cacciatore and Hamilton
Melbourne, FL
Palm Bay, FL
Titusville, FL
Nance, Carol S. .... Richmond, VA
Nance & Caston .... Sherman, TX
Whitesboro, TX
Nance, Cecil B., Jr. .... West Memphis, AR
Nance, Charles H. .... Richmond, VA
Nance, Christopher J. .... Van Nuys, CA

Nance, Christopher Scott ... Newport, AR
Nance, D. Scott ... Washington, DC
Nance, Dale A. ... Chicago, IL
Nance, David W. ... Austin, TX
Nance, Deborah A. ... Charlotte, NC
Nance, Donald S. ... Cleveland, OH
Nance, Donald S., Co., L.P.A. Cleveland, OH
Nance, Donald W. ... Little Rock, AR
Nance, Donna J. ... Atlanta, GA
Nance, Elbert E., Jr. ... Detroit, MI
Nance, Frederick R. ... Cleveland, OH
Nance, Glynn D., Jr. ... Houston, TX
Nance, H. Hart ... Waco, TX
Nance, Howard C., Jr. ... Sunrise Beach, MO
Nance, J. Bradley ... Dallas, TX
Nance, James D. ... Aiken, SC
Nance, James H. ... Melbourne, FL
Nance, James K. ... Houston, TX
Nance, James N. ... Melbourne, FL
Nance, James R. ... Shelbyville, TN
Nance, James R., Jr. ... Fayetteville, NC
Nance, J. D. ... Tulsa, OK
Nance, John J. ... Tacoma, WA
Nance, John R. ... Concord, NC
Nance, Joseph Hanover ... Bryan, TX
Nance, Karen F. ... Richmond, CA
Nance, Larry H. ... Memphis, TN
Nance, Lars F. ... Raleigh, NC
Nance, Mark E. ... Atlanta, GA
Nance, Marshall E., III ... Fort Lauderdale, FL
Nance & McCants ... Aiken, SC
Nance, Melissa A. ... Houston, TX
Nance, Michael C. ... Seattle, WA
Nance, Murray H., Jr. ... Sherman, TX
Nance & Nance, P.A. ... West Memphis, AR
Nance, Patricia ... Fort Lauderdale, FL
Nance, Patrick H. ... Columbia, SC
Nance, R. Earl ... Richmond, VA
Nance, Robert A. ... Oklahoma City, OK
Nance, Russell E. ... New York, NY
Nance, Tamara R. ... Raleigh, NC
Wilmington, NC
Nance, Thomas C. ... Nashville, TN
Nance, Thomas G., II ... Charlotte, NC
Nance, W. Mitchell ... Glasgow, KY
Nance, William B. ... Dallas, TX
Nance, William M. ... San Francisco, CA
Nance, William M. ... Troy, MI
Nance, William S. ... Houston, TX
Nancoo-King, Alethia ... Washington, DC
Nanda, Deepak ... Los Angeles, CA
Nanda, Krishan Kumar Hans Department of State, GV
Nanda, Seema ... Seattle, WA
Nanda, Sushila R. Environmental Protection Agency, Office of Enforcement and Compliance Assurance, GV
Nandi, Melissa Jurecki ... Cleveland, OH
Nandi, Moona ... San Francisco, CA
Nandipati, Vinod "Bobby" Tilak Dallas, TX
Naness, Chaiet & Naness, LLC Jericho, NY
Naness, Jeffrey N. ... Jericho, NY
Naness, Richard M. ... Jericho, NY
Nanfeldt, Richard E. ... Piscataway, NJ
Nangano, Michael A. J. ... Los Angeles, CA
Nangia, Anshu ... New York, NY
Nangia, Shalini ... Bingham Farms, MI
Nangle, Cooper, Niemann & Bitting, L.L.C. St. Louis, MO
Nangle, E. Bruce ... St. Louis, MO
Nangle, James F., Jr. ... St. Louis, MO
Nangle, Jane Adams ... Savannah, GA
Nangle, Jennifer L. ... Boston, MA
Nangle, John C. ... Los Angeles, CA
Nangle, John F. ... Savannah, GA
Nangle & Nangle, P.C. ... St. Louis, MO
Nangle, Patricia ... Logan, OH
Nangle, Paul J., & Associates Anchorage, AK
Nangle, Richard P. ... St. Louis, MO
Nani, David T. ... Chicago, IL
Nania, Anthony J. ... Canaan, CT
Nania & Drury ... Canaan, CT
Nanis, William C. ... Astoria, NY
Nanji, Yogesh K. ... Meridian, MS
Fort Worth, TX
Nanjo, Henry D. ... Sacramento, CA
Nankin, Helene Schrier Federal Communications Commission, Common Carrier Bureau, GV
Nankin, Kenneth S. ... Washington, DC
Nankivell, Paul H., II ... Los Angeles, CA
Nanko, James R. ... Huntington Beach, CA
Nanna, Emmett H., Jr. ... Berlin, MD
Nanna, Thomas Anthony ... Titusville, FL
Nanna, Tofe ... New York, NY
Nannarone, Leonard J., Jr. ... Chicago, IL
Nanners, Steven B. ... Buckhannon, WV
Nannes, John M. ... Washington, DC
Nannes, Michael E. ... Washington, DC
Nanney, David P., Jr. ... Raleigh, NC
Nanney, Donald C. ... Los Angeles, CA
Nanney, Douglas P. ... Pelahatchie, MS
Nanney, Elaine R. ... Cary, NC
Nanney, J. Edward ... Chattanooga, TN
Nanney, John P., III ... Denver, CO
Nanney, Joseph H., Jr. ... Raleigh, NC
Nanney, Louis W., Jr. ... Rutherfordton, NC
Nanney, Philip Jeffery ... San Antonio, TX
Nanney, Thomas A. ... Fulton, KY
Nanni, Anthony V. ... Department of Justice, Antitrust Division, GV
Nanni, Rocco N. ... Dallas, TX
Nannicelli, Thomas E. ... Norwood, MA

Nannicelli & Woods ... Norwood, MA
Nannini, Eugene A. ... Westfield, MA
West Springfield, MA
Nannini, Kenneth J. ... Maywood, IL
Nanny, S. Matt ... Houston, TX
Nanos, Christopher W. ... Morristown, NJ
Nanos, John M. ... Long Beach, CA
Nanos, Nicholas P. ... Darien, CT
Nanos, Rania ... New York, NY
Nanovic, James R. ... Jim Thorpe, PA
Nanovic Law Offices ... Jim Thorpe, PA
Nanovic, Roger N. ... Jim Thorpe, PA
Nanovic, Roger N., II ... Jim Thorpe, PA
Nanovic, Susan J. ... Jim Thorpe, PA
Nanovic, Thomas S. ... Jim Thorpe, PA
Nansen, Earl K. ... Omak, WA
Nantell, Sharon C. ... Anaheim, CA
Nantker, Frederick W. ... Santa Barbara, CA
Nantkes, Donnell L. Environmental Protection Agency, Office of the General Counsel, GV
Nantois, Robert J. ... Oklahoma City, OK
Nantoski, Edw. J. ... Andover, MA
Nants, Bruce A. ... Orlando, FL
Nants, Jack A. ... Orlando, FL
Nantz, John ... Washington, DC
Nantz, Litowich, Smith & Girard, A Professional Corporation ... Grand Rapids, MI
Nantz, Philip W. ... Grand Rapids, MI
Nantz, William C. ... Houston, TX
Nanus, Arthur R. ... Wilmette, IL
Nanus, Joseph L. ... Austin, TX
Nanwani, Mahesh H. ... Miami, FL
Nanz, David G. ... New York, NY
Nanz, Theodore Roy ... Wauwatosa, WI
Naoum, Lynn Stevens Bingham Farms, MI
Napariu, Olivia A. ... Indianapolis, IN
Naparsteck, Noah G. ... Bloomsburg, PA
Naparty, Robert B. ... Brooklyn, NY
Napell, Bruce J. ... Sebastopol, CA
Napell, Sondra M. ... Piedmont, CA
Naper, Christine M. ... Chicago, IL
Naperstick, William ... Columbus, OH
Napheys, Ben, III ... Fort Collins, CO
Naphtali, Ashirah S., (Ms.) ... Laurelton, NY
Naphtali, Steven L. ... New York, NY
Napier, Catherine A. ... Oklahoma City, OK
Napier, Cindy Harrington ... Louisville, KY
Napier, Deborah L. ... Herndon, VA
Napier, Donald B. ... Brunswick, GA
Napier, Douglas H. ... Fort Madison, IA
Napier, Douglas W. ... Front Royal, VA
Napier, Elizabeth ... Chicago, IL
Napier Fitzgerald & Kirby ... Buffalo, NY
Napier, Gary L. ... Louisville, KY
Napier, Gary W. ... London, KY
Napier, Gene C. ... Kansas City, MO
Napier, George J. L. ... Macon, GA
Napier, James A. ... Des Moines, IA
Omaha, NE
Napier, James A., Jr. ... Largo, FL
Napier, John G. ... Denver, CO
Napier, John H. ... Buffalo, NY
Napier, John L. ... Washington, DC
Napier, Jon J. ... Portland, OR
Napier, Jonathan A. ... Indianapolis, IN
Napier, Judith M. ... Omaha, NE
Napier, Mark W. ... Cincinnati, OH
Napier, Michael P. ... Summit, NJ
Napier & Napier, P.C. ... Front Royal, VA
Napier & Napier, P.S.C. ... Louisville, KY
NaPier, Patricia Mathias ... Honolulu, HI
Napier Pond Athey & Athey, P.C. Front Royal, VA
Napier, Robert A. ... Rochester, NY
Napier, Robert T. ... Chicago, IL
Napier, Robert T., & Associates, P.C. Chicago, IL
Napier, Ronald L. ... Naples, FL
Napier, Ronald Lewis ... Front Royal, VA
Napier, Shirley Pardee ... Galveston, TX
Napier, Sonja F. ... State College, PA
Napier, Stephanie L. ... Washington, DC
Napier, Timothy H. ... Louisville, KY
Napier, William H. ... Fort Madison, IA
Napier, Wolf & Napier ... Fort Madison, IA
Napierala, Thomas R. ... West Allis, WI
Napieralski, William J. ... Grand Rapids, MI
Napier-Joyce, Joy M. ... Baltimore, MD
Napierski, Christine M. ... Albany, NY
Napierski, Eugene Daniel ... Albany, NY
Napierski, Eugene E. ... Albany, NY
Napiewocki, Laura M. ... Detroit, MI
Naples, Caesar J. ... Redondo Beach, CA
Naples, David M. ... Denver, CO
Naples, Gentile & Rosado ... Buffalo, NY
Naples, James P. ... Buffalo, NY
Naples, John J. ... Palm Springs, CA
Naples, Joseph John, III ... Houston, TX
Naples, Terrence P. ... Buffalo, NY
Naples, William N. ... Buffalo, NY
Napleton, Robert J. ... Chicago, IL
Napodano, Anthony J. ... Edison, NJ
Napodano & Raffo, P.A. ... Edison, NJ
Napoleon, Vincent J. ... New York, NY
Napoleone, Michael J. ... Boca Raton, FL
Napoles, Robert W. ... New York, NY
Napoletano, Domenick ... Brooklyn, NY
Napoli, Andrew F. ... Philadelphia, PA
Napoli, Anne Burke Federal Communications Commission, Wireless Telecommunications Bureau, GV
Napoli, Anthony M. ... White Plains, NY
Napoli, Elyse B. ... Columbia, MD
Napoli, James A. ... San Francisco, CA
Napoli, James C. ... New York, NY
Napoli, James J. ... Chicago, IL

Napoli, James R. ... Cleveland, OH
Napoli, Jequita Harmon ... Norman, OK
Napoli, John P. ... New York, NY
Napoli, John W. ... Hermosa Beach, CA
Napoli, Joseph A., Jr. ... Pittsburgh, PA
Napoli, Joseph R., Ltd. ... Peoria, IL
Napoli, Lisa ... New York, NY
Napoli, Lisa A. ... Las Vegas, NV
Napoli, Louis A. ... San Francisco, CA
Napoli, Michael D. ... Dallas, TX
Napoli, Michelle M. ... Stamford, CT
Napoli, Paul J. ... New York, NY
Napoli, Richard G. ... Chicago, IL
Napolitan, Gary S. ... Chattanooga, TN
Napolitan, Grace E. ... Windham, NH
Napolitana, LeeAnn B. San Francisco, CA
Napolitano, Andrea ... New York, NY
Napolitano, Andrew P. ... Newark, NJ
Napolitano, Anthony ... New York, NY
Napolitano, Daniel P. ... Bedford, MA
Napolitano, Eileen ... Basking Ridge, NJ
Napolitano, Frank J., Jr. East Stroudsburg, PA
Napolitano, George P. ... Boston, MA
Napolitano, James R. ... Ramsey, NJ
Teaneck, NJ
Napolitano, Janet A. ... Phoenix, AZ
Napolitano, Jeffrey C. ... Metairie, LA
Napolitano, John A. ... Saddle River, NJ
New York, NY
Napolitano, John E. ... Sarasota, FL
Napolitano, John J. ... Ozone Park, NY
Napolitano, John P., Jr. ... New Orleans, LA
Napolitano, Karen C. ... Riverhead, NY
Napolitano & Magnotti ... Staten Island, NY
Napolitano, Michael A. ... Albany, NY
Fishkill, NY
New York, NY
Napolitano, Michael T. ... Providence, RI
Napolitano, Michele Polito ... Deer Park, NY
Napolitano, Neil ... Bloomington, IL
Napolitano, Perry A. ... Pittsburgh, PA
Napolitano, Peter J. ... Staten Island, NY
Napolitano, Robert A. ... North Andover, MA
Napolitano, Robert M. ... Portland, ME
Napolitano, Roberta ... Bridgeport, CT
Napolitano, Steven F. ... New York, NY
Napolitano, Steven V. ... Chicago, IL
Napolitano, Thomas E. ... Ramsey, NJ
Teaneck, NJ
Napolitano, Vito A. ... Jamaica, NY
Napolski, Paul T. ... Naperville, IL
Naponick, Paul M., (P.A.) North Palm Beach, FL
Napp, Allan L. ... Alton, IL
Napp, Ilene D. ... Fort Lauderdale, FL
Napp, Joanna Kay ... Austin, TX
Napp, Thomas E. ... Denver, CO
Nappa, Joseph A. ... Huntington Beach, CA
Nappan, Alexander Z. ... Boston, MA
Nappan, Edw. ... Chelsea, MA
Nappan, Melissa K. ... Sacramento, CA
Nappen, Allen I. ... Montgomeryville, PA
Nappen, Evan F. ... Eatontown, NJ
Napper, James J. ... Lamesa, TX
Napper, Kevin Jon ... Tampa, FL
Napper, L. D. ... Ruston, LA
Napper, Marshall T. ... Monroe, LA
Napper, Steven ... Little Rock, AR
Napper, Steven E. ... Denver, CO
Napper, Steven, Ltd. ... Little Rock, AR
Napper, Waltman, Madden & Rogers Ruston, LA
Nappi, Douglas R. ... United States Senate, Committee Legal Personnel, GV
Nappi, John T. ... Huntington, NY
Nappi, Joseph, Jr. ... Spokane, WA
Nappi, Lawrence C. ... Holmes, NY
Nappi, Paul ... Cherry Hill, NJ
Paoli, PA
Philadelphia, PA
Nappi, Ralph A. ... Port Washington, NY
Nappi, Regina ... Windham, ME
Nappi, Sarah M. ... Washington, DC
Nappier, Betty A. ... Atlanta, GA
Nappier, Mark A. ... Calabash, NC
Myrtle Beach, SC
North Myrtle Beach, SC
Nappo, Philip G., III ... New York, NY
Naprstek, Kathleen Anne ... Newark, NJ
Napton, Thomas R. ... Cape Canaveral, FL
Naquin, Brad K. ... Thibodaux, LA
Naquin, C. John, Jr. ... Baton Rouge, LA
Naquin, Lester J., III ... Houma, LA
Naquin, Rodd A. ... Baton Rouge, LA
Naquin, Ronald L. ... New Orleans, LA
Naquin, Stephanie D. ... Metairie, LA
Naquin, Walter K., Jr. ... Thibodaux, LA
Nara, Fusae ... New York, NY
Naraghi, Hashem W. ... Modesto, CA
Naraghi, Wendell J. ... Escalon, CA
Naragon, Frederic E. ... Salem, OH
Naragon, Robert A. ... Doylestown, PA
Naramore, Ronald G. Hot Springs National Park, AR
Narancic, Perry J. ... Palo Alto, CA
Naranjo, Carolyn R. ... Baldwin, NY
Naranjo, Dan A. ... San Antonio, TX
Naranjo, Dan A., P.C. ... San Antonio, TX
Naranjo, Daniel ... Miami, FL
Naranjo, Lourdes A. ... Miami, FL
Naranjo, Orlinda L. ... Austin, TX
Naranjo, Richard E. ... Lancaster, CA
Naras, Edmund Joseph ... Boston, MA
Narasimhan, Subha ... New York, NY
Naratil, Stephen Paul ... San Diego, CA
Narayan, Beverly Elaine ... Burlingame, CA

Narayan Law Firm, The San Francisco, CA
Narayan, Maria G. ... San Francisco, CA
Narayan, Rajeev ... Raleigh, NC
Narayan, Sadhana (Sandy) D. San Francisco, CA
Narayan, Sanjay ... San Francisco, CA
Narayanan, Anant S. ... Washington, DC
Narayanan, Ash ... Los Angeles, CA
Narayanan, Tara ... Walnut Creek, CA
Narayanan, Usha ... Palo Alto, CA
Narbaitz, Dena L. ... San Francisco, CA
Narber, Gregg R. ... Des Moines, IA
Narbutas, Kes ... San Francisco, CA
Narby, Bonnie ... Oakland, CA
Narby, George W. ... Buffalo, NY
Narcisi, Geever & Coholan, P.C. Pittsburgh, PA
Narcisi, Lawrence A., III ... Philadelphia, PA
Narcisi, Patrick T. ... Pittsburgh, PA
Narciso, David Lee ... Cincinnati, OH
Narciso, David N. ... Englewood, NJ
Newark, NJ
Narciso, Joy Schmitt ... Plano, TX
Narcisse, Christine Griggs ... Worcester, MA
Narcisse, Claude ... Whippany, NJ
Narcisse, Robbie E. B. ... Stamford, CT
Nard, Dennis ... Fresno, CA
Nardachone, Emil W. ... Belleville, NJ
Nardell, J. Timothy ... San Francisco, CA
Nardella, Anthony J. ... Wayne, NJ
Nardella, Anthony M., Jr. Altamonte Springs, FL
Nardella, George C. ... Wayne, NJ
Nardella, Jerry A. ... Wayne, NJ
Nardella, Kathleen A. ... Germantown, MD
Nardella, Nancy S. ... Indianapolis, IN
Nardella & Nardella ... Wayne, NJ
Nardelli, Eugene ... New York, NY
Nardelli, James L. ... Pittsburgh, PA
Nardelli, James Louis, Jr. New Kensington, PA
Nardelli, James M. ... Red Bank, NJ
Nardelli Law Offices, P.C. New Kensington, PA
Nardelli, Michael D. ... New Kensington, PA
Nardi, Barbara A. ... Bloomington, IN
Nardi, Catherine D. ... Chicago, IL
Nardi, Denise A. ... Los Angeles, CA
Nardi, Donna Diamond ... Springfield, MA
Nardi, Frank M. ... Spencer, IN
Nardi, Frank Patrick ... Little Falls, NJ
Nardi, Joseph M, III ... Camden, NJ
Westmont, NJ
Nardi, Joseph M., Jr. ... Camden, NJ
Nardi, Karen J. ... San Francisco, CA
Nardi, Michael G. ... San Diego, CA
Nardi, Michel ... Clearwater, FL
Nardi, Michel, P.A. ... Clearwater, FL
Nardi, Ralph Anthony ... Miami, FL
Nardi, Richard A. ... New York, NY
Nardi, Robert R. ... Minneapolis, MN
Nardi, Stephen J. ... Kalispell, MT
Nardi, Vincent J. ... Manchester, NH
Nardicchio, Sam A., Jr. Bloomfield Hills, MI
Nardiello, Mary Anne ... Hamilton, OH
Nardine, Stephen J. ... Sacramento, CA
Nardini, Jay A. ... Cedar Falls, IA
Nardini, Lisa Malloy ... Washington, DC
Nardini, Lucas R. ... West Chester, PA
Nardini & Sheehan, P.C. West Chester, PA
Nardino, Marie D. ... Jersey City, NJ
Nardo, David D. ... Vernon Hills, IL
Nardo, Francis X. ... Wilmington, DE
Nardo, Raymond ... Huntington, NY
Nardolilli, Anthony ... Orlando, FL
Nardolilli, Pamela G. Board of Governors Of The Federal Reserve System, Office of the General Counsel, GV
Nardone, A. Joseph, Jr. ... Decatur, GA
Nardone, A. Joseph, Jr., P.C. ... Decatur, GA
Nardone, Andrew J. ... Pompton Lakes, NJ
Nardone, Charles A. ... Westerly, RI
Nardone, Diane C. ... Newark, NJ
Nardone, Enrico G. ... Kingston, PA
Nardone, Glenn A. ... Boston, MA
Nardone, John V. ... Ridgefield, NJ
Nardone, John V., P.A. ... Ridgefield, NJ
Nardone & Nardone ... Highland, NY
Nardone, Peter K. ... Tarrytown, NY
Nardone, Richard ... Highland, NY
Nardone, Robert G. ... Avondale Estates, GA
Nardone, S. Nicole ... San Francisco, CA
Nardone, Susan L. ... Newark, NJ
King Of Prussia, PA
Nardone, William A. ... Westerly, RI
Nardoni, Daniel A. ... Glendale, CA
Nardoni, Daniel A. ... Los Angeles, CA
Nardoni, Silvio ... Glendale, CA
Nardoni, Silvio ... Los Angeles, CA
Nardoni, Stanley C. ... Chicago, IL
Nardotti, Michael J., Jr. ... Washington, DC
Nardozzi, Salvatore J., Jr. ... Dunmore, PA
Nardozzi, Thomas C. ... New York, NY
Nardozzo, Thomas M., Jr. ... Cornelius, NC
Narducci, Christopher A. Fort Lauderdale, FL
Narducci, John ... New York, NY
Narducci, Leigh P. ... Blue Bell, PA
Narducci, Lucas J. ... Phoenix, AZ
Narducci, Moore & Fleisher ... Blue Bell, PA
Narducci, William A. ... Secaucus, NJ
Nardulli, Joseph J. ... Irvine, CA
Nardulli, Michael S. ... Chicago, IL
Narea, Amy Weiss ... Chicago, IL

Nareau, Joan G. .... San Diego, CA
Nareau, Robert J. .... Kealia, HI
Narefsky, David .... Chicago, IL
Narehood, Vivian B. .... Lancaster, PA
Narendran, Jothy .... East Meadow, NY
Narens, Mark E. .... Columbus, OH
Columbus, OH
Nares, Edward J. .... San Diego, CA
Nares, Gilbert .... San Diego, CA
Nares, Thomas D. .... Carlsbad, CA
Narey, Peter B. .... Spirit Lake, IA
Narges, Michael E. .... Toledo, OH
Nargizian, Sarkis .... Mission Viejo, CA
Narick, Emil E. .... Pittsburgh, PA
Narick, Steven D. .... Moundsville, WV
Narigon, David O. .... Des Moines, IA
Narikiyo, Chuck T. .... Honolulu, HI
Narikiyo, Lani, (Atty. at Law, A Law Corp.)
Honolulu, HI
Narimatsu, Susan M. .... Hoffman Estates, IL
Narine, Krishna B. .... New York, NY
Philadelphia, PA
Narine, Marcia L. .... Miami, FL
Narins, Charles S. .... Marblehead, MA
Narisi, S. Maria .... Houston, TX
Narita, Tomio B. .... San Francisco, CA
Narker, Steven R. .... New York, NY
Narkewicz, Susan M. .... Albany, NY
Narkier, Monchick & Pleasanton, P.A.
West Palm Beach, FL
Narkier, Stanley J. .... West Palm Beach, FL
Narkiewicz, David L.
Montgomeryville, PA
Narkiewicz Law Offices .... Lansdale, PA
Montgomeryville, PA
Narkin, Stephen J. .... Washington, DC
Narkis, Robert J. .... Waterbury, CT
Narko, Kevin J. .... Chicago, IL
Narko, Medard M. .... Oak Forest, IL
Narko, Medard M., Associates, P.C.
Oak Forest, IL
Narmore, Rebecca A. .... Muscle Shoals, AL
Naro, James G. .... Fort Lauderdale, FL
Naro, Melanie D. .... Pittsburgh, PA
Naro, Vincent F. .... Kew Gardens, NY
Naro, Wayne E. .... Omaha, NE
Narode, Dana M.
Department of Housing and Urban Development,
Office of General Counsel, GV
Narodick, Kit G. .... Seattle, WA
Naroian, Kachadoor .... Methuen, MA
Naroian, Nancy A. .... New York, NY
Narol, Mel .... Princeton, NJ
Naron, Gregory R. .... Chicago, IL
Naros, Kristen K. .... Minneapolis, MN
Narot, Adam J. .... Chicago, IL
Narotsky, Louis A. .... New York, NY
Narotzky, Philip L. .... New York, NY
Narregan, James W. .... Kalamazoo, MI
Narregan Law Offices, P.C. .... Kalamazoo, MI
Narrell-Mead, Lisa .... Birmingham, AL
Narron, Anglea R. .... Wake Forest, NC
Narron, Delbridge E. .... New York, NY
Narron & Holdford, P.A. .... Wilson, NC
Narron, James W. .... Smithfield, NC
Narron, John W. .... Raleigh, NC
Narron, Mary Anne .... Madison, MS
Narron, O'Hale & Whittington, P.A.
Benson, NC
Smithfield, NC
Narrow, David M.
Federal Trade Commission,
Bureau of Competition, GV
Narrow, S. Lee .... Washington, DC
Narsete, Michael S. .... Houston, TX
Narsh, Gregory S. .... Harrisburg, PA
Narsutis, John .... Denton, TX
Narucki, Robert J. .... Verona, NJ
Narum, Jeanne Devine .... Fargo, ND
Naruo, Richard T. .... Riverside, CA
Narup, Richard H. .... Springfield, IL
Narus, Edward R. .... Hartford, CT
Narus, Harold .... Reston, VA
Naruse, James K. .... Gardena, CA
Narusis, Bernard V. .... Cary, IL
Narusis & Narusis .... Cary, IL
Narusis, Regina G. F. .... Cary, IL
Narusis, Stanley W. .... Marion, IL
Narva, Adam S. .... Boston, MA
Narvaez, Henry F. .... Albuquerque, NM
Narvaez Law Firm, P.A.
Albuquerque, NM
Narvaez, Sarah .... New York, NY
Narvaez, Zandra Lee .... Corpus Christi, TX
Narvid, Doris B. .... Sherman Oaks, CA
Narvid, Michael J. .... Sherman Oaks, CA
Narvid, Scott, Schwartz & Frangie LLP
Los Angeles, CA
Sherman Oaks, CA
Narvil, Jeffrey C. .... Atlanta, GA
Narvin, Eileen Koepfer .... Pittsburgh, PA
Narvin, J. Richard .... Pittsburgh, PA
Narvol, Todd B. .... Bethlehem, PA
Harrisburg, PA
Narwold, Karen G. .... Nashville, TN
Narwold, William H. .... Hartford, CT
Stamford, CT
Nary, William L. M. .... Boise, ID
Nasal, Eugene J. .... Riverview, MI
Nasal, Gary A. .... Troy, OH
Nasarenko, Nicholas P. .... Garfield, NJ
Nasatir, David A. .... Philadelphia, PA
Nasatir, Hirsch & Podberesky
Los Angeles, CA
Santa Monica, CA
Nasatir, Iain A.W. .... Los Angeles, CA
Nasatir, Leonard D. .... Beverly Hills, CA
Nasatir, Michael D. .... Santa Monica, CA
Nasby, Howe E. .... Jackson, MN
Nasca, Joseph M. .... Buffalo, NY
Nasca, Kevin M. .... Boston, MA
Nasca, Sandra Ann .... Buffalo, NY
Nasci, John .... Clifton Park, NY
Nase, Jeffrey V. .... Department of Commerce,
Patent and Trademark Office, GV
Nase, Jonathan P. .... Harrisburg, PA
Nase, Ralph J. .... Auburn, CA
Naseem, Khalid .... Worcester, MA
Nasek, Ann Marie T. .... Stroudsburg, PA
Naselli, Carolyn .... Glenview, IL
Naselsky, Charles M. .... Philadelphia, PA
Naseman, David M. .... Washington, DC
Nasenbenny, Mary Blake .... Chicago, IL
Naser, Rebecca A. .... Washington, DC
Naser, William L. .... Pleasant Unity, PA
Nash, A. Heaton
Department of Housing and Urban Development,
Office of General Counsel, GV
Nash, Adrienne Elizabeth .... Los Angeles, CA
Nash, Allan F. .... Horseshoe Bend, AR
Nash, Andrea .... Washington, DC
Nash, Andrew H. .... Anaheim, CA
Nash, Ann O'Boyle .... Chicago, IL
Nash, Anne Bruner .... Moraga, CA
Nash & Associates, Attorneys, P.A.
Oneonta, AL
Nash, Bernard .... Washington, DC
Nash, Brian J. .... Annapolis, MD
Baltimore, MD
Nash, Brian Thomas .... Chicago, IL
Nash, C. Daniel .... Newport, KY
Nash, Cara N. .... Mamaroneck, NY
Nash, Carl .... Cleveland, OH
Nash, Cathy R. .... Atlanta, GA
Nash, Charles B. .... Canton, NY
Nash, Charles Ian .... Melbourne, FL
Nash, Christopher Charles .... Tampa, FL
Nash, Clare V. .... Dedham, MA
Nash, Clyde W. .... Howell, MI
Nash, Cohenour, Kelley & Hunt, P.C.
Oklahoma City, OK
Nash & Company, A Professional Corporation .... Pittsburgh, PA
Nash, Craig M. .... South Miami, FL
Nash, Dana A. .... Brooklyn, NY
Nash, Daniel L. .... Washington, DC
Nash, David A. .... Wilmington, NC
Nash, David E. .... Cleveland, OH
Nash, David M. ....
Department of the Navy, GV
Nash, Dean .... Kansas City, MO
Nash, Denise A. .... San Diego, CA
Nash, Donald A. .... Bozeman, MT
Nash, Donald F. .... Saginaw, MI
Nash, Douglas G. .... Portland, OR
Nash, Douglas J. .... Boston, MA
Nash, Douglas R. .... Boise, ID
Nash, D. P. .... Tipton, IN
Nash, E. Melvin, Law Office of
Boston, MA
Nash & Edgerton .... Hermosa Beach, CA
Los Angeles, CA
Pasadena, CA
Torrance, CA
Nash, Edith E. .... Department of Labor,
Office of the Solicitor, GV
Nash, Edwin L. .... Janesville, WI
Nash, Edythe A. .... Wheeling, WV
Nash, Eli, Jr.
Federal Labor Relations Authority,
Office of the Administrative Law Judges, GV
Nash, Elizabeth B. .... Oneonta, AL
Nash, Elmer L. .... Atlanta, GA
Nash, Ernest .... Seattle, WA
Nash, Foster P., III .... New Orleans, LA
Nash, Frank E. .... Portland, OR
Nash, G. Douglas .... New Haven, CT
Nash, Gary H. .... Erie, PA
Nash, George W. .... New York, NY
Nash, Glenn Gerard .... Palo Alto, CA
Nash, Gordon B. .... Chicago, IL
Nash, Gordon B., Jr. .... Chicago, IL
Nash, Harold .... Rancho Mirage, CA
Nash, Harold B. .... Dedham, MA
Nash, Horace L. .... Palo Alto, CA
Nash, James H. .... Geneseo, IL
Nash, James P. .... Washington, DC
Nash, James W., (P.C) .... Houston, TX
Nash, Jane Foley .... Tipton, IN
Nash, Janet A. .... Department of Justice,
Antitrust Division, GV
Nash, Janet A. .... Kansas City, MO
Nash, Jay W. .... Perth Amboy, NJ
Nash, Jean K. .... Cleveland, OH
Nash, Jeff D., Jr. .... San Antonio, TX
Nash, Jeffrey L. .... Philadelphia, PA
Nash, Jeffrey P. .... Mayfield Village, OH
Nash, Jim R. .... Little Rock, AR
Nash, Jodi G. .... Cherry Hill, NJ
Nash, Jodi Hitt .... Warrenton, VA
Nash, Joel A. .... Cleveland, OH
Nash, John A. .... Cedar Rapids, IA
Nash, John F. .... Mineola, NY
New York, NY
Nash, John F., Jr. .... Washington, DC
Nash, John J. .... Wilmette, IL
Nash, John S., Jr. .... Marysville, CA
Nash, Jonathan, Jr. .... Omaha, NE
Nash, Jonathan R. .... New York, NY
Nash, Jonathan S. .... Baltimore, MD
Nash, Judy R. .... Howell, MI
Nash, Kathy Contos
Farmington Hills, MI
Nash, Kendall E. M. .... Milwaukie, OR
Nash, Kenneth A. .... Oklahoma City, OK
Nash, Kenneth L. .... Houston, TX
Nash, Kevin C. .... Dallas, TX
Nash, Kevin J. .... New York, NY
Nash, Kimberly Y. .... Denver, CO
Nash, L. Chadwick .... Oak Brook, IL
Nash, Larry L. .... Northridge, CA
Nash, Laura C. .... Treasury Department,
Internal Revenue Service, GV
Nash, Laura H. .... Washington, DC
Nash, Laura P. .... Los Angeles, CA
Nash, Laura Smith .... Burbank, CA
Nash, Lawrence R. .... Wisconsin Rapids, WI
Nash & Lodge .... Anoka, MN
Nash, Marcus B. .... Seattle, WA
Nash, Margaret R. .... Boston, MA
Nash, Martin J. .... Miami, FL
Nash, Mary Beth .... Roanoke, VA
Nash, Mary Ellen .... Chicago, IL
Nash, Mary Paul .... Oakland, CA
Nash, MaryAnn E. .... Treasury Department,
Office of the Comptroller of the Currency,
GV
Nash, Megan Shemwell .... New Orleans, LA
Nash, Melvin S. .... Marietta, GA
Nash, Michael A. .... Menlo Park, CA
Nash, Michael A. .... St. Paul, MN
Nash, Michael B. .... Chicago, IL
Nash, Michael M. .... Anaconda, MT
Nash, Michael R. .... Greensboro, NC
Nash, Michael S. .... Alexandria, VA
Nash, Michele Y. .... Metuchen, NJ
Nash, Michelle T. .... Washington, DC
Nash & Monahan, P.C. .... Dedham, MA
Nash, Nan G. .... Albuquerque, NM
Nash, Nancy A. .... Dayton, OH
Nash, Nancy F. .... Conyers, GA
Nash & Nash .... Cleveland, OH
Nash, Nash, Bean & Ford .... Geneseo, IL
Nash, Nash & Stoess .... Louisville, KY
Nash, Norman W. .... Greeley, CO
Nash & Orlando, L.L.P. .... Houston, TX
Nash and Palm .... Canton, NY
Nash, Patrick F. .... Lexington, KY
Nash, Patrick J. .... Kansas City, MO
Nash, Patrick J., Jr. .... Chicago, IL
Nash, Patrick T. .... Chicago, IL
Nash, Paul F. .... Oldwick, NJ
Nash, Paul L. .... New York, NY
Nash, Paulette .... Wilmington, DE
Nash, Phil N., Law Office of .... Kenai, AK
Nash, Podvin, Tuchscherer, Huttenburg, Weymouth & Kryshak, S.C.
Wisconsin Rapids, WI
Nash, Ralph C., Jr. .... Washington, DC
Nash, Ralph W. .... Ithaca, NY
Nash, Randall E. .... Marshfield, MA
Nash, Randall L. .... Milwaukee, WI
Nash, Renee .... Granite Bay, CA
Nash, Richard A. .... Houston, TX
Nash, Richard D. .... Dryden, MI
Nash, Richard F. .... St. Louis, MO
Nash, Richard H., Jr. .... Louisville, KY
Nash, Richard H., Sr. .... Louisville, KY
Nash, Richard J. .... Bloomfield Hills, MI
Nash, Robert C. .... Sacramento, CA
Nash, Robert C. .... Chicago, IL
Nash, Robert L. .... Oxnard, CA
Nash, Robert L. .... Bend, OR
Nash, Robert M. .... Rapid City, SD
Nash, Robert N. .... Geneseo, IL
Nash, Robert P. .... Dallas, TX
Nash, Robert S. .... New York, NY
Nash, Robin S. .... Decatur, GA
Nash, Robyn Bandele .... Vineyard Haven, MA
Nash, Rollin, Jr. .... Oklahoma City, OK
Nash, Russell S., Jr. .... Reno, NV
Nash, Savery L. .... Hermosa Beach, CA
Torrance, CA
Nash, Sean .... Chicago, IL
Nash, Shannon King .... Washington, DC
Nash, Shannon T. .... Houston, TX
Nash, Shelley .... Hermosa Beach, CA
Torrance, CA
Nash, Spindler, Grimstad & McCracken
Manitowoc, WI
Nash, Stephen E. .... Pittsburgh, PA
Nash, Stephen J. .... Anoka, MN
Nash, Stephen P. .... Pittsburgh, PA
Nash, Steven M. .... Rockford, IL
Nash, Stuart C. .... Washington, DC
Nash, Stuart G. .... Washington, DC
Nash, Susan
Securities and Exchange Commission,
Division of Investment Management, GV
Nash, Susan M. .... Chicago, IL
Nash, Suzanne S. .... Bethesda, MD
Nash, Sylvester M., Jr. .... Cincinnati, OH
Nash, Thomas A., Jr. .... Savannah, GA
Nash, Thomas C., II .... Clearwater, FL
Nash, Thomas D., Jr. .... Chicago, IL
Nash, Thomas G., Jr. .... Dallas, TX
Nash, Thomas K. .... Portland, OR
Nash, Thomas L. .... Rockford, IL
Nash, Thomas P., IV .... Elizabeth City, NC
Nash, Thomas R. .... Chicago, IL
Nash, Thomas R., P.C. .... Chicago, IL
Nash, Timothy C. .... Phoenix, AZ
Portland, OR
Nash, Valerie .... Portland, OR
Nash, Vicki A. .... Newport Beach, CA
Nash, Wade L. .... Jefferson City, MO
Nash, Walter B., III .... Tucson, AZ
Nash, Walter B., III, P.C. .... Nogales, AZ
Phoenix, AZ
Tucson, AZ
Nash, Wanda A. .... Marshall, MI
Nash, Warren J. .... Washington, DC
Nash, Warren O., III .... Frankfort, KY
Nash, William .... Little Rock, AR
Nash, William B. .... San Antonio, TX
Nash, William R. .... Rockford, IL
Nash, Winifred M. .... Wynnewood, PA
Nash, Wm. Kelly .... Provo, UT
Nashak, George J., Jr. .... Glendale, NY
Nashak, Michael G. .... Hempstead, NY
Nashan, Melody L. .... Kansas City, MO
Nasharr, Anthony J., III .... Chicago, IL
Nashawaty, Keith C. .... Palo Alto, CA
Nashawaty, Nicholas T., Jr. .... Braintree, MA
Nashban, Ned R. .... West Palm Beach, FL
Nash-Caywood, Martha, Ms. .... Lexington, KY
Nashel, Howard M. .... Hackensack, NJ
Nashel Kates Nussman Rapone Ellis & Traum LLP .... Hackensack, NJ
Nashel and Nashel .... West New York, NJ
Nashel, Richard B. .... West New York, NJ
Nashel, Samuel .... West New York, NJ
Nashelsky, Larren M. .... New York, NY
Nasher, Nancy Arnole .... Dallas, TX
Nash-Goetz, Karen .... Baltimore, MD
Nashman, Alex E. .... New York, NY
Nasi, Michael J. .... Austin, TX
Nasiedlak, Lizzu C. .... Minneapolis, MN
Nasiedlak, Tyler L. .... Minneapolis, MN
Nasierowski, Edw. F. .... Lynbrook, NY
Nasif, Donald J. .... Cumberland, RI
Nasif, Kenneth P. .... Attleboro, MA
Nasir, Jamil E. .... Washington, DC
Nasis, Elbert F. .... Newark, NJ
Nasits, Alan .... El Paso, TX
Naski, Richard A. .... Farmington Hills, MI
Nasky, H. Gregory .... Las Vegas, NV
Naslund, Robert K. .... Eugene, OR
Nasmyth, Peter R. .... San Bernardino, CA
Naso, Francesca V. .... New York, NY
Naso, Michael A. .... Los Angeles, CA
Naso, Michael A. .... New York, NY
Naso, Paul W. .... Los Angeles, CA
Nasoff, Lisa M. .... Garden City, NY
Nason, Aimee L. Manocchio
Haddonfield, NJ
Nason, Andrew S. .... Charleston, WV
Nason, David G. .... Washington, DC
Nason, Deborah P. .... Princeton, NJ
Philadelphia, PA
Nason, G. Frank, IV .... Atlanta, GA
Nason, Gerald C. .... Biddeford, ME
Nason, Herbert .... New York, NY
Nason, John B., III .... Wayne, PA
Nason, John Charles .... Salisbury, MD
Nason, Jonathan Hastings .... Columbia, SC
Nason, Joseph G. .... Westborough, MA
Nason, Judith A. .... Trenton, NJ
Nason, Leigh M. .... Columbia, SC
Nason, Leonard Y. .... Lexington, MA
Nason, Nathan E. .... West Palm Beach, FL
Nason, Paul G. .... Dallas, TX
Nason, Stanley H. .... Brooklyn, NY
Nason, Tami Elizabeth .... Boston, MA
Nason, Wall & Wall, P.C. .... Lexington, MA
Nason, Yeager, Gerson, White & Lioce, P.A.
Palm Beach, FL
West Palm Beach, FL
Nasr, Ayman M. .... Troy, MI
Nasrah, Melissa M. .... Department of Justice,
Criminal Division, GV
Nasralla, Mohamed A. .... Daly City, CA
Nasrallah, Fuad B. .... Dayton, OH
Nasrallah, Mathew G. .... Marietta, GA
Nasrullah, Habib .... Denver, CO
Nasrullah, Irfan .... Hopkinton, MA
Nass & Brown, P.C. .... Houston, TX
Nass, Cory Brett .... Boca Raton, FL
Nass, Edward M. .... Philadelphia, PA
Nass, Eric M. .... New York, NY
Nass, Harry A., Jr. .... San Antonio, TX
Nass, Herbert E., & Associates
New York, NY
Nass, Jacob .... New York, NY
Nass, James W. .... Salem, OR
Nass, Joel A. .... Houston, TX
Nass, Joseph .... Roslyn, NY
Nass, Lowell E. .... Madison, WI
Nass, Marcia Thayer .... Kenilworth, NJ
Nass, Menasche M. .... Los Angeles, CA
Nass, Peter A. .... Gretna, LA
Nass, Rachael .... New York, NY
Nass, Scot D. .... Coeur d'Alene, ID
Nass, Terri L. .... Akron, OH
Nass, Theodore W. .... Gretna, LA
New Orleans, LA
Nass, Tiemann & Nass .... Gretna, LA
New Orleans, LA
Nassab, Rebecca .... Washington, DC
Nassan, Andrea V. .... Philadelphia, PA
Nassaney, George A., Jr. & Associates
Tuscaloosa, AL
Nassar, George J., Jr. .... Memphis, TN
Nassar, George M. .... Springfield, MA
Nassar, Joan Berry .... Melbourne, FL
Nassar, Micah George .... Springfield, MA
Nassar, Monique A. .... Memphis, TN
Nassar, Nicandra .... Boston, MA
Nassar, William M. .... Riverside, CA
Nassau, Aimee E. .... New York, NY
Nassau, Arthur M. .... Bloomfield, CT
Nassau, Benjamin .... New York, NY
Nassau, Borowy & French .... Newington, CT
Nassau, Henry N. .... Philadelphia, PA
Nassau, Isidore .... New York, NY
Nassau, Laura S. .... Mamaroneck, NY
Nassau, Louis E. .... Hartford, CT
Nassau, Michael J. .... New York, NY
Nassau, Randy Beth .... New York, NY
Nassau, Robert G. .... Rochester, NY

Naugle, Kip J. ....Department of the Navy, Office of the Judge Advocate General, GV
Naugle Law Offices ....Boise, ID
Naugle, Louis A. ....Pittsburgh, PA
Naugle, Page ....La Jolla, CA
Naugle, Todd E. ....Jonesboro, GA
Naugler, James ....La Crosse, WI
Nauheim, Stephen A., (P.C.)
Washington, DC
Nault, Andrew G. ....Cumberland, RI
Nault, Barbra Zan ....Juneau, AK
Nault, Casey M. ....Los Angeles, CA
Nault, J. Lloyd, II ....Atlanta, GA
Nault, Robert P. ....Boston, MA
Nault, Sharon B. ....Atlanta, GA
Naulty, Scaricamazza and McDevitt
Wilmington, DE
Cherry Hill, NJ
Media, PA
Philadelphia, PA
Naum, Taras K. ....Phoenix, AZ
Nauman, Daniel G. ....Sacramento, CA
Nauman, Joseph C. ....Minneapolis, MN
Nauman, Joseph G. ....Dayton, OH
Nauman, Kenneth C. ....Tampa, FL
Nauman, Smith, Shissler & Hall
Carlisle, PA
Harrisburg, PA
Lancaster, PA
York, PA
Nauman, Spencer G., Jr. ....Harrisburg, PA
Nauman, Timothy E. ....Cleveland, OH
Naumann, Catherine A. ....Pleasanton, CA
Naumann, Franklin F. ....Anaheim, CA
Naumann, Jenae R. ....Scottsdale, AZ
Naumann & Levine, LLP ....San Diego, CA
Naumann, Richard A. ....Hackensack, NJ
Naumann, Stephen L. ....Houston, TX
Naumann, Steven T. ....Chicago, IL
Naumann, William H. ....San Diego, CA
Naumer, Helen T. ....Murphysboro, IL
Naumer, Walter W., Jr. ....Du Quoin, IL
Naumes, Robert T. ....Boston, MA
Naumes, Susan F. ....Medford, OR
Naumoff, Mitchell A. ....Barberton, OH
Naun, John J. ....New York, NY
Naunton, Shawn P. ....New York, NY
Naurich, William P. ....Chicago, IL
Naus, Laura ....New York, NY
Naus, R. Joseph ....Shreveport, LA
Naus, Scott ....Bloomsburg, PA
Nauseef, Robert J., II ....Durham, NC
Nauss, Jennifer L. ....Kansas City, MO
Nauss, Loren R. ....The Woodlands, TX
Nauta Dutilh ....New York, NY
New York, NY
Nauta, Teresa L. ....Seattle, WA
Nauts, Charles W. ....Lincoln, IL
Nauts, David R. ....Detroit, MI
Nauyokas, Michael F. ....Honolulu, HI
Nava, César H. ....Irvine, CA
Nava, Ciro J. ....Edinburg, TX
Nava, Edward L. ....Tustin, CA
Nava, Elsa G. ....Fort Worth, TX
Nava, Francisco M. ....Miami Beach, FL
Nava, Hector O. ....Phoenix, AZ
Nava, Pedro I. ....Santa Barbara, CA
Nava, Robert ....Montebello, CA
Navagh, George J. ....Buffalo, NY
Navagh, Gerard A. ....Larchmont, NY
Navagh, James J. ....Akron, NY
Navaretta, Mary Jean ....Port St. Lucie, FL
Navaretta & Navaretta ....Port St. Lucie, FL
Navaretta, Stephen ....Port St. Lucie, FL
Navaro, A. Ralph, III ....Cincinnati, OH
Navaro, A. Ralph, Jr. ....Cincinnati, OH
Navaro, Ann D. ....Department of Justice, Environment and Natural Resources Division, GV
Navaro & Hopp, L.L.P. ....Englewood, CO
Navaro, Steven G. ....Englewood, CO
Navarra, Antoinette J. ....Cincinnati, OH
Navarra, Frank ....Newburgh, NY
Navarra, James K. ....Portland, OR
Navarra, John G. ....Howell, NJ
Navarra, Joseph J. ....Tampa, FL
Navarra, Sebastian J. ....New York, NY
Navarra, William ....Daytona Beach, FL
Navarre, David ....Farmington Hills, MI
Navarre, David R. ....Milwaukee, WI
Navarre, John P. ....Oberlin, LA
Navarre, Joseph A., III ....Jackson, MI
Navarre, Michael L. ....Austin, TX
Navarre & Navarre Lawyers, P.L.C.
Jackson, MI
Navarre, Stephen J. ....Chicago, IL
Navarre, William F. ....Brooklyn, MI
Navarre, William F., P.C. ....Brooklyn, MI
Navarrete, Andres L. ....Washington, DC
Navarrete, Jose M. ....Morristown, NJ
Navarrete, Libby Herrera ....Miami, FL
Navarrete, Yolanda ....Union City, NJ
Navarrette, Rick D. ....Los Angeles, CA
Navarro, Alicia M. ....Miami, FL
Navarro, Andy G. ....Tyler, TX
Navarro, Arthur I. ....Richardson, TX
Navarro & Barkley ....Aberdeen, MS
Navarro, Bruce C. ....Washington, DC
Navarro, Eduardo A. ....Boston, MA
Navarro, Gladys R. ....Miami, FL
Navarro, Jeffery M. ....Aberdeen, MS
Navarro, Jonathan C. ....Santa Ana, CA
Navarro, Kara S. ....San Francisco, CA
Navarro, Lawrence John
North Miami Beach, FL
Navarro, Lisa A. ....Los Angeles, CA
Navarro, Martin J. ....San Antonio, TX
Navarro, Meliza D. ....San Francisco, CA
Navarro, Monica Patricia ....Troy, MI
Navarro, Pablo A. ....San Diego, CA
Navarro, Paige Bickley ....Houston, TX
Navarro, Paul M. ....Charlotte, NC
Navarro, Pete P. ....Rosenberg, TX
Navarro, Ralph C. ....Los Angeles, CA
Navarro, Raymond J. ....San Diego, CA
Navarro, Rene ....San Jose, CA
Navarro, Rene ....Miami, FL
Navarro, Rene, P.A. ....Miami, FL
Navarro, Ricardo J. ....San Antonio, TX
Navarro, Rodolfo F. ....Los Angeles, CA
Navarro, Samuel A. ....Santa Fe, NM
Navarro, Stephen D. ....San Antonio, TX
Navarro, Steven A. ....New York, NY
Navarro, Thomas J., Jr. ....Buffalo, NY
Navarro, William A. ....Charlotte, NC
Navarro-Bowman, Chandri
Washington, DC
Navarro-Cabrer, Nilda M. ....San Juan, PR
Navarro-Pagán, Cynthia ....San Juan, PR
Navarro-Rivera, Margarita ....Philadelphia, PA
Navas, Bill A. ....Tampa, FL
Navas-Pavia, Manuel ....San Juan, PR
Navatsyk, Donald A. ....Chardon, OH
Navatta, Anna P. ....Hackensack, NJ
Nave, Bridget M. Monroig ....St. Louis, MO
Nave, Cecilia McGlew ....Nashville, TN
Nave, Dick D. ....Birmingham, AL
Nave, Edward ....Nashville, TN
Nave, Evan V. ....Austin, TX
Nave, Gregory A. ....Bloomfield Hills, MI
Nave, Irma Hampton ....Anderson, IN
Nave, James David ....Nashville, TN
Nave, James M. ....Indianapolis, IN
Nave, Jeffrey C. ....Spokane, WA
Nave, Leonard K. ....Versailles, KY
Nave, Lucibeth ....Nashville, TN
Nave, Michael K. ....Anchorage, AK
Nave, Michael R. ....San Leandro, CA
Stockton, CA
Nave, Scott C. ....Thousand Oaks, CA
Nave, Thomas G. ....Juneau, AK
Naveja, Christopher S. ....Chicago, IL
Naveja, Vicki A. ....Chicago, IL
Navelli, Julia M. ....Rome, NY
Naves, Larry J. ....Denver, CO
Naves, Ronald E., Jr. ....North Sioux City, SD
Navetta, David J. ....Chicago, IL
Navia, Talbert I. ....New York, NY
Naviasky, Laurence M. ....Schenectady, NY
Naviaux, William E. ....Omaha, NE
Navickas, Jo Ann M. ....Brooklyn, NY
Navid, Barry B. ....Chicago, IL
Navigato, Daniel J. ....San Diego, CA
Navigato, John E. ....Chicago, IL
Navigato, Michael T. ....Wheaton, IL
Naville, Herbert F. ....New Albany, IN
Naville, Michael G. ....New Albany, IN
Naville, Timothy J. ....New Albany, IN
Navin, John J. ....Short Hills, NJ
Navin, Joseph F. ....Columbus, OH
Navin, Mary Beth ....New York, NY
Navin, Patrick T. ....Chicago, IL
Navin, Paul J. ....Columbus, OH
Navin, Thomas J. ....Washington, DC
Navin, William H. ....Chicago, IL
Navins, Peter L. ....Wellesley, MA
Navins, Richard R. ....Wellesley, MA
Navis, Patricia M. ....Los Angeles, CA
Navis, William L. ....Belleville, KS
Navitsky, Michael J. ....Harrisburg, PA
Navolio, Stephen A. ....Elmhurst, IL
Navolio, William E. ....Oak Brook, IL
Navon, Gadi ....Cupertino, CA
Navon, Jeffrey M. ....New York, NY
Navon, Kopelman, O'Donnell & Lavin, P.A.
Boca Raton, FL
Fort Lauderdale, FL
Hollywood, FL
Navon, Peter S. ....Hackensack, NJ
Navon, Samuel D. ....Fort Lauderdale, FL
Navoni, Donald L., P.S. ....Seattle, WA
Navoy, John V. ....Woburn, MA
Navran, Susan H. ....Phoenix, AZ
Navrat, C. Todd ....Mission Woods, KS
Navratil, Boris F. ....Baton Rouge, LA
Navratil, Frankie J. ....North Kansas City, MO
Navratil, Gerald J. ....Glendive, MT
Navratil, Hardy & Bourgeois L.L.P.
Baton Rouge, LA
Nawa, Gary C. ....Pasadena, CA
Nawalanic, Frank J. ....Cleveland, OH
Nawalany, Thomas W. ....Portland, OR
Nawashiro, Aoi ....Washington, DC
Nawi, David ....Sacramento, CA
Nawi, Donald E. ....New Rochelle, NY
Naworski, David ....San Antonio, TX
Nawracaj, Richard E. ....Chicago, IL
Nawrath, W. Michael
Manchester Center, VT
Nawrocki, Bridget A. ....Blandon, PA
Nawrocki, Lawrence M. ....Minneapolis, MN
Nawrocki, Mary-Lynn ....Bristol, CT
Nawrocki, Nancy C. ....Brighton, MI
Nawrocki, Rooney & Sivertson, P.A.
Minneapolis, MN
Nawrocki-Verburgt, Marcia J. ....Naperville, IL
Nawrot, Louis F., Jr. ....Seattle, WA
Nay, Barbara L. ....Portland, OR
Nay, Don L. ....San Diego, CA
Nay, Elizabeth Drill ....Kansas City, MO
Nay, Sandra Y. ....New York, NY
Nay, William D. ....Tulsa, OK
Nayak, Avani S. ....Boston, MA
Nayak, Mahesh K. ....Bloomfield Hills, MI
Nayar, Kaladharan M. G. ....Berkeley, CA
Nayberg, Robert S. ....Carle Place, NY
Nayden, J. Frank ....Baltimore, MD
Nayden, James F. ....Chevy Chase, MD
Nayden, Matthew W. ....Baltimore, MD
Nayden, Robt. F. ....Baltimore, MD
Nayer, Arthur R. ....Chicago, IL
Nayer, Seymour M. ....Bloomfield Hills, MI
Nayer, Stanley M. ....Great Neck, NY
Nayes, Eric K. ....Spokane, WA
Naylon, Patrick B. ....Rochester, NY
Naylon, Patrick R. ....Westlake Village, CA
Naylor, Andrew S. ....San Diego, CA
Nashville, TN
Naylor, Beth Schneider ....Cincinnati, OH
Naylor, Brian T. ....Cupertino, CA
Naylor, C. Darlene ....Columbia City, IN
Naylor, Charles D. ....San Pedro, CA
Naylor, Charles R. ....Dubuque, IA
Naylor, Christine ....Cerritos, CA
Naylor, Colin T., III ....Binghamton, NY
Naylor, David ....Glens Falls, NY
Naylor, David E. ....Atlanta, GA
Naylor, Edwin A., (P.C.) ....Denver, CO
Naylor, Emory S., Jr. ....Chicago, IL
Naylor, Eugene R. ....Jackson, MS
Naylor & Geisel, P.C. ....Pueblo, CO
Naylor, Greg A. ....Des Moines, IA
Naylor, H.B. "Skip", III ....Houston, TX
Naylor, Henry E. ....Baton Rouge, LA
Naylor, Hoover, Peters & Blair, P.C.
Dubuque, IA
Naylor, Howard B., Jr. ....Norwalk, CT
Naylor, J. Edward ....Rocky Mount, NC
Naylor, Jacqueline ....Las Vegas, NV
Naylor, James B. ....Lyndhurst, OH
Naylor, John L., Jr. ....Cleveland, OH
Naylor, John M. ....Las Vegas, NV
Naylor, John R., II ....Pueblo, CO
Naylor, John T. ....Bloomington, IL
Naylor, Joseph David ....Houston, TX
Naylor, Julie D. ....Philadelphia, PA
Naylor, Karen Sue ....Santa Ana, CA
Naylor, Kathryn A.
Federal Labor Relations Authority, Authority Member Staff, GV
Naylor, Kimberly M. ....Fort Worth, TX
Naylor, Kirk E., Jr. ....Lincoln, NE
Naylor, Kirtlan G. ....Boise, ID
Naylor, Molly D. ....Houston, TX
Naylor, Mueller & Willard, P.C.
Bloomington, IL
Naylor, Patrick O. ....Irving, TX
Naylor, Paul B. ....Tulsa, OK
Naylor, Paul D. ....Cincinnati, OH
Naylor, R. Christopher ....Houston, TX
Naylor, Richard D. ....Austin, TX
Naylor, Robert E. ....Conneaut, OH
Naylor, Robert S. ....Columbus, OH
Naylor, Robert W. ....Sacramento, CA
San Francisco, CA
Naylor, Samuel, VI ....Carthage, IL
Naylor, Sandra F. ....Chester, PA
Naylor, Todd B. ....Cincinnati, OH
Naylor, Wanda M. ....Greenville, NC
Naylor, Wendy Hoge ....Chagrin Falls, OH
Naylor, Williams & Tracy, Inc. A Professional Corporation ....Tulsa, OK
Nayor, Charles F. ....Brookline, MA
Nayor, Michael A. ....Stamford, CT
Nayor, Michael A. ....Westport, CT
Nayowitz, Abr. ....New York, NY
Naythons, Edwin E. ....Philadelphia, PA
Nazaire, Jacques ....Brooklyn, NY
Nazar, Debra Monaghan (IBA)
Brooklyn, NY
Nazar, Edward J. ....Wichita, KS
Nazarenus, Brian M. ....Denver, CO
Nazareth, Annette L. ....New York, NY
Nazareth, Kelli ....South San Francisco, CA
Nazareth, Natasha M. ....Raleigh, NC
Nazareth, Nathaniel J., Jr. ....Wakefield, RI
Nazaretian, Peter N. ....New Port Richey, FL
Nazarian, Dalia ....Great Neck, NY
Nazarian, Douglas R. M. ....Baltimore, MD
Nazario, Esther Joan Cid ....Homeland, CA
Nazarov, Ari ....Department Of Veterans Affairs, Office of the General Counsel, GV
Nazaryk, Paul A. ....Denver, CO
Nazco, Lazaro ....Miami, FL
Naze, Peter J. ....Green Bay, WI
Nazerian, Lily R. ....Chicago, IL
Nazette, Marner, Wendt & Knoll
Cedar Rapids, IA
Nazette, Randall A. ....Cedar Rapids, IA
Nazette, Richard F. ....Cedar Rapids, IA
Nazro, Arthur Phillips ....Austin, TX
Nazzaro, John J. ....New London, CT
Nazzaro, Joseph C. ....Miami, FL
Nazzaro, Lillian ....Trenton, NJ
Ndenga, Peter A. ....New York, NY
Ndirika, Rita Grant ....Washington, DC
Nduka-Eze, Anthony Ngozi ....Oakland, CA
Ndukwu, Azuwuika H. ....Miami, FL
Nea, G. Andrew, Jr. ....Richmond, VA
Neace, Robert D. ....Florence, KY
Neach, Ronald R. ....Oakland, CA
Nead, John E. ....Washington, DC
Nead, Karey & Minton, LLP
Baltimore, MD
Towson, MD
Nead, Lena C. ....Washington, DC
Nead, Morris J. ....Albion, IL
Nead, Robert K. ....Towson, MD
Neafsey, William A. ....Ridgefield, CT
Neagele & Tyler ....East Tawas, MI
Neagle, Charlotte V. ....Boston, MA
Neagle, Christopher S. ....Portland, ME
Neagle, Cindy L. ....Kansas City, MO
Springfield, MO
Neagle, Damon A. ....Silver Spring, MD
Neagle, Rosanna Marrero
San Francisco, CA
Neagley, Clinton H. ....Oakland, CA
Neagli, Douglas B. ....Baytown, TX
Neaher, Edward R. ....Washington, DC
Neaher, Edward R., Jr. ....Washington, DC
Neal, A. Curtis ....Amarillo, TX
Neal, Albert M., Jr. ....Canton, NC
Neal, Alexander W., Jr. ....Richmond, VA
Neal, Alvin J. ....Irmo, SC
Neal, Andrew G. ....Chicago, IL
Neal, Angela ....New Orleans, LA
Neal, Anne C. ....Baltimore, MD
Neal, Anne deHayden ....Washington, DC
Neal, Anthony W. ....Boston, MA
Neal, A. R. ....Clearwater, FL
Neal, Arlene P. ....Washington, DC
Neal & Associates ....Oakland, CA
Neal, Austin B. ....Tallahassee, FL
Neal, Barry D. ....Fort Smith, AR
Neal, Bryan D. ....Oklahoma City, OK
Neal, Bryan P. ....Dallas, TX
Neal, Carla S. ....Grapevine, TX
Neal, Catherine S. ....Cincinnati, OH
Neal, Chad R. ....Amarillo, TX
Neal, Charles D. "Buddy", Jr.
McAlester, OK
Neal, Chellis E. ....Washington, DC
Neal, Cheryl S. ....Springfield, IL
Neal, Christopher A.
North Richland Hills, TX
Neal, Christopher L. ....Seattle, WA
Neal, Claren ....Helena, MT
Neal, Clyde W. ....Angleton, TX
Neal, Craven & Romer ....Jamestown, TN
Neal, Dale K. ....Los Angeles, CA
Neal, Dan E. ....Eugene, OR
Neal, Dana K. ....Red Oak, IA
Neal, David A. ....Los Angeles, CA
Neal, David E. ....Mill Valley, CA
Neal, David G. ....Eminence, MO
Neal, David H. ....Russellville, AL
Neal, David L. ....Department of Justice, Executive Office for Immigration Review, GV
Neal, David W. ....Joliet, IL
Neal & Davis ....Louisville, KY
Shelbyville, KY
Neal, Deborah A. ....Kansas City, MO
Neal, Douglas P. ....Louisville, KY
Neal, Earl L., & Associates, L.L.C.
Chicago, IL
Neal, Earl Langdon ....Chicago, IL
Neal, Earl-Ray ....Richmond, KY
Neal, Edmond A., III ....Southbridge, MA
Neal, Edward Garrison ....College Park, MD
Neal, Edward Squier ....Indianapolis, IN
Neal & Eng ....Eugene, OR
Neal, F. Bay, III ....Ponte Vedra Beach, FL
Neal, F. Brent ....Hamlet, NC
Rockingham, NC
Neal & Fox ....Los Angeles, CA
Neal, Fred R., III ....Portland, OR
Neal, Gary L. ....Boise, ID
Neal, Gary L. ....Tulsa, OK
Neal, Gary T. ....Muskegon, MI
Neal, George D. ....Dallas, TX
Neal, George M. (Jack), Jr.
Birmingham, AL
Neal, Gerald A. ....Louisville, KY
Neal, Gerald E. ....Winona, MN
Neal, Gerald F. ....Las Vegas, NV
Laughlin, NV
Neal, Gerald J. ....Chicago, IL
Neal, Gerber & Eisenberg ....Chicago, IL
Neal, Glen T. ....Madera, CA
Neal, Glenn R. ....Ripley, WV
Neal, Gregg Y. ....Shelbyville, KY
Neal, Guy S. ....Washington, DC
Neal & Harwell ....Nashville, TN
Neal, Henry G. ....Atlanta, GA
Neal, Hollis A. ....Jamestown, TN
Neal, Howard D. ....Oakland, CA
Neal, J. Archer ....Winston-Salem, NC
Neal, J. Barron ....Marshall, TX
Neal, J. Kennard ....Atlanta, GA
Neal, J. Robt., Jr. ....Saranac Lake, NY
Neal, J. W., P.C. ....Hobbs, NM
Neal, Jaay D. ....San Antonio, TX
Neal, Jack ....Flint, MI
Neal, James A. ....Minneapolis, MN
Neal, James E. ....Garden Grove, CA
Neal, James F. ....Nashville, TN
Neal, James M. ....Lawrenceville, IL
Neal, James O. ....Ephrata, WA
Neal, James R. ....Lansing, MI
Neal, Janet B. ....Modesto, CA
Neal, Janet M. ....Kenosha, WI
Neal, Jason C. ....Topeka, KS
Neal, Jeffery J. ....Highlands Ranch, CO
Neal, Jeffery S. ....Vincennes, IN
Neal, Jerry A., Sr. ....San Anselmo, CA
Neal, Jerry R. ....Spokane, WA
Neal, Joan E. ....Washington, DC
Neal, John A. ....Graham, TX
Neal, John A. ....Oshkosh, WI
Neal, John D. ....Madison, WI
Neal, John G. ....Columbus, OH
Neal, John M. ....Knoxville, TN
Neal, John P., III ....Dalton, GA
Neal, John S., Jr. ....Salem, SC
Neal, John T. ....Austin, TX
Neal, Joseph R. ....Augusta, GA
Neal, Joseph R., Jr. ....Augusta, GA
Neal, Judith Gayle ....Santa Paula, CA
Neal, Julia Turner ....Columbia, SC
Neal, J. W. ....Hobbs, NM

Needham, Thomas H. .... Providence, RI
Needham, Tom .... Dallas, TX
Needham, W. Paul, (P.C.) .... Boston, MA
Needham, W. Timothy .... Eureka, CA
Needham & Warren .... Boston, MA
Needle, Andrew .... Miami, FL
Needle, Barbara Wachter
Washington, DC
Needle, Charles M. .... Bridgeport, CT
Needle, Donald .... Columbia, MD
Needle, Emanuel .... Maplewood, NJ
Needle, Francine D. .... Los Angeles, CA
Needle Gallagher & Ellenberg, P.A.
Miami, FL
Needle, Gerald M. .... Redondo Beach, CA
Needle, Goldenziel and Pascale, P.C.
Scranton, PA
Needle, Howard J. .... Owings Mills, MD
Needle, Howard J., P.C. .... Owings Mills, MD
Needle, Joshua C. .... Santa Monica, CA
Needle, Leonard S. .... Fair Haven, NJ
Needle, Martin E. .... Treasury Department,
Internal Revenue Service, GV
Needle, Melissa J. .... Greenwich, CT
Needle, Michael R. .... Philadelphia, PA
Needle, Michael R., A Professional Corporation
Philadelphia, PA
Needle, Mylie A. .... Washington, DC
Needle, Robert .... Warminster, PA
Needle & Rosenberg, P.C. .... Atlanta, GA
Needle, Sol .... New York, NY
Needle, Steven D.
Department of Commerce, GV
Needle, William H. .... Atlanta, GA
Needle, William J. .... Novato, CA
Needleman, Abr. T. .... Philadelphia, PA
Needleman, Barry .... Concord, NH
Needleman, Brad Stephen .... New York, NY
Needleman, Bruce P. .... Woodland Hills, CA
Needleman, Daniel S. .... New York, NY
Needleman, David V. .... Brooklyn, NY
Needleman, Gary J. .... Montville, NJ
Needleman, Irving .... New York, NY
Needleman, Karen R. .... White Plains, NY
Needleman, Kathy E. .... Manchester, NH
Needleman, Mark S. .... Smithtown, NY
Needleman, Myra .... New York, NY
Needleman and Pisano .... Montville, NJ
Needleman, S. Allen .... Philadelphia, PA
Needleman, Saml. J. .... Philadelphia, PA
Needleman, Stanley H. .... Baltimore, MD
Needles, Carol Beckerle .... Linthicum, MD
Needles, Gene L. .... Des Moines, IA
Needles, Gregory L. .... Washington, DC
Needles, J. Stanley .... Findlay, OH
Needles, James L. .... Chicago, IL
Needles, Marc E. .... Philadelphia, PA
Needles, Nancy K. .... Chicago, IL
Needles, Stephen L. .... Newtown, PA
Needlman, Nancy A. .... Chicago, IL
Neef, Allan .... Detroit, MI
Neef, Allan .... Grosse Pointe Farms, MI
Neef, John W. .... Carneys Point, NJ
Neefe, Richard J. .... St. Petersburg, FL
Neefe, Richard J., P.A. .... St. Petersburg, FL
Neeff, Jerrold G. .... Boston, MA
Neel, Alan D. .... Arlington, TX
Neel, Angela L. .... New Orleans, LA
Neel, Benjamin K., Jr. .... Menard, TX
Neel, Bradley J. .... Los Angeles, CA
Neel, Bruce T. .... Phoenix, AZ
Neel, David S., Jr. .... Birmingham, AL
Neel, David W. .... Cleveland, OH
Neel, Edgar L. .... Denver, CO
Neel, Edwin R. .... Alpharetta, GA
Atlanta, GA
Duluth, GA
Marietta, GA
Neel, Glenn A. .... Fort Smith, AR
Neel, Heidi Lyn .... Salem, OR
Neel, Hooper & Kalmans, P.C.
Houston, TX
Neel, James A. .... Fort Myers, FL
Neel, James J. .... Fort Worth, TX
Neel, James M. .... Houston, TX
Neel, J. M., Jr. .... Cartersville, GA
Neel, John R. .... Austin, TX
Neel, Lynette K. .... Charlotte, NC
Neel, Mary Schaeffer .... Seattle, WA
Neel, Michael C. .... Houston, TX
Neel, Patricia .... Tulsa, OK
Neel, Paul J., Jr. .... Louisville, KY
Neel and Randall .... Mooresville, NC
Neel, Richard .... New York, NY
Neel, Richard F., Jr. .... Arlington, VA
Neel & Robinson, L.L.C. .... Alpharetta, GA
Atlanta, GA
Duluth, GA
Marietta, GA
Neel, Russell H., Jr. .... Houston, TX
Neel, Samuel E. .... McLean, VA
Neel, Samuel R., III .... Fort Lauderdale, FL
Tallahassee, FL
Neel, Scott A. .... Houston, TX
Neel & Smith .... Cartersville, GA
Neel, Stephen E. .... Cambridge, MA
Neel, William A., Jr. .... Cartersville, GA
Neel, William B.
United States Postal Service,
Mid-Atlantic Office, GV
Neel, William S. .... Mooresville, NC
Neel Wilson & Clem .... Henderson, KY
Neeld, James H., III .... Jackson, MS
Neeld, James H., IV .... Jackson, MS
Neeld, Renee R. .... Fort Wayne, IN
Neeleman, John R. .... Seattle, WA
Neeleman, Stanley D. .... Provo, UT
Neeleman, Thomas D. .... Salt Lake City, UT
Neeleman, Thomas D., L.C.
Salt Lake City, UT
Neeley, Alice J. .... Fort Wright, KY
Neeley & Anderson .... Honolulu, HI
Neeley, David H. .... Prestonsburg, KY
Neeley, Debra K. .... Houston, TX
Neeley, G. Steven .... Cresson, PA
Neeley, Glen W., P.C. .... Ogden, UT
Neeley, Gregory W. .... Longview, TX
Neeley, Jeffrey S. .... Washington, DC
Neeley, Joyce Y. .... Honolulu, HI
Neeley, Pamela Marie .... Broken Arrow, OK
Neeley, Richard L. .... Palo Alto, CA
Neeley, Robert L. .... Ogden, UT
Neeley, William Lee .... Grundy, VA
Neelley, Allen L. .... Glendale, CA
Neelley, Charles E., Jr. .... Taos, NM
Neelley, Laura M. .... Los Angeles, CA
Neelman, Beth H. .... New York, NY
Neelon, Daniel P. .... San Antonio, TX
Neelon, William R., III .... Quincy, MA
Neely, A. Locke .... Dallas, TX
Neely, Alfred S., IV .... Columbia, MO
Neely, Allen P. .... State College, PA
Neely, Andrew S. .... Knoxville, TN
Neely, Barbara P. .... Fort Worth, TX
Neely, Brian H. .... Tupelo, MS
Neely, Brian H., P.A. .... Tupelo, MS
Neely & Brien .... Mayfield, KY
Neely, Bruce W. .... Washington, DC
Neely, C. Richard .... Portland, OR
Neely, Carol C. .... Norwell, MA
Neely, Cassandra M. .... Clarion, PA
Neely, Charles B., Jr. .... Raleigh, NC
Neely, Christine T. .... Newark, NJ
Neely, Craig B. .... Allentown, PA
Neely, Cynthia Humbert .... Stockton, CA
Neely, David A. .... Pittsburgh, PA
Neely, David H. .... Palo Alto, CA
Neely, Demetries J. .... Columbus, OH
Neely, Edgar A., III .... Atlanta, GA
Neely, Elizabeth E., (Ms.) .... Atlanta, GA
Neely, Ellen J. .... Chicago, IL
Neely, Gerald J. .... Billings, MT
Neely, Green, Fargarson & Brooke
Brownsville, TN
Neely, Green, Fargarson, Brooke & Summers .... Memphis, TN
Neely, H. David, II .... Omaha, NE
Neely & Hunter .... Charleston, WV
Neely, John J., III .... Savannah, GA
Neely, John S. .... Washington, DC
Neely, John S., Jr. .... Tallahassee, FL
Neely, Joseph J. .... Metropolis, IL
Neely, Joyce Riddle .... Winston-Salem, NC
Neely, Kermit K. .... Brunswick, OH
Neely, Lucie MacKenzie
Alexander City, AL
Neely, Marion R. .... Iowa City, IA
Neely, Martha Z. .... Fairfax Station, VA
Neely and Martinek .... Iowa City, IA
Neely, Michael Graham .... Medina, WA
Neely, Michael L. .... Austin, TX
Neely and Neely .... Metropolis, IL
Neely, Patricia T. .... Sacramento, CA
Neely, R. Gregory .... New Albany, IN
Neely, Richard .... Charleston, WV
Neely, Richard E. .... Quincy, MA
Neely, Richard J. .... San Diego, CA
Neely, Richmond L. .... Albuquerque, NM
Neely, Robert J. .... Metropolis, IL
Vienna, IL
Neely, Robyn D. .... Orlando, FL
Neely, Roger T. .... Fort Worth, TX
Neely, S. Boyd, Jr. .... Mayfield, KY
Neely, Sally Schultz .... Los Angeles, CA
Neely, Sam Boyd .... Mayfield, KY
Neely, Sandra L. .... Columbus, OH
Neely, Stephanie Davis .... Charlotte, NC
Neely, Stephen D. .... Tucson, AZ
Neely, Stuart M. .... Philadelphia, PA
Neely, Thomas E. .... Boston, MA
Neely, Thomas W. .... Tulsa, OK
Neely, Tom .... Vernon, TX
Neely, W. Hamlin .... Allentown, PA
Neely, Walter E. .... Louisville, KY
Neely, William F. .... Spotsylvania, VA
Neely, William G. .... Austin, TX
Neely, William H. .... Nashville, TN
Neely, William M. .... Asheboro, NC
Neely, Wilson S. .... New York, NY
Neely, Wm. T. .... Jackson, MS
Neeman, Jeffrey .... New York, NY
Neemeyer, Vickie .... Santa Monica, CA
Neems, Harold J. .... San Jose, CA
Neenan, Gerald D. .... Nashville, TN
Neeper, Josiah L. .... San Francisco, CA
Neer, David Drew .... Irvine, CA
Neer, Lawrence A. .... Lake Oswego, OR
Neer, R. Jeffrey .... Santa Monica, CA
Neerbasch, Lenore M. .... Ithaca, NY
Neeriemer, Dean H. .... Washington, IN
Neering, Patrick D. .... Bay City, MI
Neerken, Julie P. .... Albuquerque, NM
Nees, C. Jon .... Spokane, WA
Nees, David K. .... Maumee, OH
Nees, H. H. .... Boulder, CO
Nees, William E. .... Los Angeles, CA
Neese, Beth K. .... Houston, TX
Neese, D. John, Jr. .... Houston, TX
Neese, Herron & Miller-Herron
Dresden, TN
Neese, Martha L. .... Phoenix, AZ
Neese, Michael T. .... Woodstock, IL
Neese, William R. .... Dresden, TN
Neesemann, Carroll E. .... New York, NY
Neeser, Darval, Nelson & Wermerskirchen, P.A. .... Willmar, MN
Neeser, Dennis J. .... St. Cloud, MN
Neeson, Peter J. .... Philadelphia, PA
Neet, James O., Jr. .... Kansas City, MO
Neetenbeek, Eric J. .... Duluth, MN
Neetenbeek, Janice B. .... Miami, FL
Neeter, Anne L. .... Mountain View, CA
Neeves, Kenneth Douglas
Richfield Springs, NY
Neff, A. Guy .... Orlando, FL
Neff, Alan H. .... Chicago, IL
Neff, Barbara C. .... Chicago, IL
Neff, Brian J. .... Hackensack, NJ
Neff, Carole Cukell .... New Orleans, LA
Neff, Carter .... Toledo, OH
Neff, Cathy A. .... Sacramento, CA
Neff, Caudell & Bedsaul .... Galax, VA
Neff, Charles Edward .... Houston, TX
Neff, Charles L. .... Williston, ND
Neff, Cheryl R. .... Paintsville, KY
Neff, Christina R. .... Jefferson City, MO
Neff, Christyne L. .... Washington, DC
Neff Cresap Eiken & Irigoin, P.C.
Sidney, MT
Williston, ND
Neff, Cynthia Spera .... Newark, NJ
Neff, D. Eric .... Crown Point, IN
Neff, Daniel A. .... New York, NY
Neff, David A. .... Grand Rapids, MI
Neff, David E. .... Salt Lake City, UT
Neff, David H. .... Syracuse, NY
Neff, David M. .... Chicago, IL
Neff, Deborah .... Jefferson City, MO
Neff, Deborah Jean .... Wilton, CT
Neff, D. Eric, P.C .... Crown Point, IN
Neff, Frank J. .... Columbus, OH
Neff, Gregor N. .... New York, NY
Neff, H. Alton .... Brick, NJ
Neff, James A. .... Cleveland, OH
Youngstown, OH
Neff, James M. .... Seattle, WA
Neff, James M., P.S. .... Seattle, WA
Neff, Janet T. .... Grand Rapids, MI
Neff, Jay W. .... Everett, WA
Neff, Jeffrey M. .... Tucson, AZ
Neff, John B., Jr. .... Collegeville, PA
Neff, John L. .... Spokane, WA
Neff, Jonathan C. .... Tulsa, OK
Neff, Kathleen .... Carbondale, KS
Topeka, KS
Neff, L. Harvey, Jr. .... Galax, VA
Neff & Lager .... Virginia, MN
Neff Law Firm, The, Ltd. .... Bucyrus, OH
Mansfield, OH
Neff Law Group, LLP .... Los Angeles, CA
Torrance, CA
Neff, Lily .... Poughkeepsie, NY
Neff, Lisa Parlato .... Buffalo, NY
Neff, Marc .... Philadelphia, PA
Neff, Mark .... Washington, PA
Neff, Mark E. .... Boonville, IN
Neff, Mary V., P.C. .... Chicago, IL
Neff, Michael A. .... New York, NY
Neff, Michael A., P.C. .... New York, NY
Neff, Michael G. .... Portland, OR
Neff, Michael L. .... Stronghurst, IL
Neff, Mike .... San Diego, CA
Neff, Owen A. .... New Orleans, LA
Neff, Owen C. .... Cleveland, OH
Neff, Paula E. .... Merrillville, IN
Neff, R. Bradley .... Sandy, UT
Neff, R. Bradley, P.C. .... Sandy, UT
Neff, R. Matthew .... Indianapolis, IN
Neff, Richard E. .... Los Angeles, CA
Torrance, CA
Neff, Richard L. .... Wexford, PA
Neff & Richardson, P.C. .... Jefferson City, MO
Neff, Robert C. .... Morristown, NJ
Neff, Robert Clark .... Bucyrus, OH
Neff, Robert Clark, Jr. .... Bucyrus, OH
Neff, Robert W. .... Cedar Rapids, IA
Neff, Ronda L. .... Austin, TX
Neff, Sara E. .... Chicago, IL
Neff, Scott C. .... Cook, MN
Virginia, MN
Neff, Thomas G. .... Overland Park, KS
Neff, Thomas R. .... Milford, MI
Neff, Vern C. .... Williston, ND
Neff, Virginia M. .... Indianapolis, IN
Neff, Wheeler K. .... Wilmington, DE
Neff, William H., Jr. .... York, PA
Neff, William J. .... San Francisco, CA
Neff, William L. .... Washington, DC
Neff, William M. .... Denver, CO
Neff-Brain, Jane S. .... Overland Park, KS
Neffner, Howard W. .... Bothell, WA
Nefouse, Amy G. .... San Diego, CA
Nefsky, Robert L. .... Lincoln, NE
Neft, Bryan S. .... Weirton, WV
Wheeling, WV
Neft, Rhoda Shear .... Pittsburgh, PA
Nefussy, Eli M. .... North Dartmouth, MA
Nefzger, John A. .... Frenchburg, KY
Nega, Joseph W.
Joint Committees And Commissions, GV
Nega, Marya .... Chicago, IL
Negaard, Donald A. .... Minot, ND
Negard, Jillisa L. .... Irvine, CA
Negele & Associates, A Law Corporation
Los Angeles, CA
Negele, Brian J. .... Detroit, MI
Negele, Hilary J. .... Round Lake, IL
Negele, James R. .... Los Angeles, CA
Negem Bickham & Clark .... Carthage, TX
Tyler, TX
Negem, Christopher H. .... San Antonio, TX
Negem, Jimmy M. .... Tyler, TX
Negen, Gary E. .... Wilburton, OK
Neger, Peter C. .... New York, NY
Negin, Alexandra P. .... Bethesda, MD
Negin, Arthur W. .... Mansfield, OH
Negin, Morton S. .... Mentor, OH
Negin, Richard A. .... Iselin, NJ
Negin, Ronald F. .... Norcross, GA
Negle, William L., Jr. .... Pittsburgh, PA
Negler, Helene E. .... Midlothian, VA
Negley, Charles .... San Francisco, CA
Negley, Christopher D. .... Charleston, WV
Negley, Robert W. .... Odessa, TX
Neglia, Patrick .... Brooklyn, NY
Negovan, Julie .... Philadelphia, PA
Negranti, Nina .... Paso Robles, CA
San Luis Obispo, CA
Negreira, Isabel V. .... Miami, FL
Negreira, Sergio Pedro, Jr. .... Miami, FL
Negrelli, William E. .... Cleveland, OH
Negrete & Battisti .... Bethlehem, PA
Negrete, Carlos F. .... San Juan Capistrano, CA
Negrete, Gilbert J., Jr. .... Bethlehem, PA
Negretti, Gino P. .... Miami, FL
Negri, Darrel C. .... Erie, PA
Negri, David .... Sacramento, CA
Negri, David L. .... Santa Fe, NM
Negri, Kathleen A. .... Denver, CO
Negri, Richard .... Lake Forest, CA
Negrin, Joel .... New York, NY
Negrin, Leo .... Coconut Creek, FL
Negrin, Robert L. .... Houston, TX
Negris, Karen A. .... River Edge, NJ
Negro, Harry John .... Princeton, NJ
Negro, Stephen J. .... Philadelphia, PA
Negron, Dennis .... Vernon, CA
Negron, Frank .... Fort Lauderdale, FL
Negron, Joseph, Jr. .... Stuart, FL
Negron, Luis Mariano .... San Juan, PR
Negron, Victor H., Jr. .... San Antonio, TX
Negrón Fernandez, José R. .... San Juan, PR
Negron-Fernandez, Luis .... San Juan, PR
Negroni, Andrea Lee .... Washington, DC
Negroni, Antonio J. .... Bayamon, PR
Negroni, Danielle W. .... San Diego, CA
Negroni & Kromer, P.L.L.C.
Washington, DC
Negroni & Winston, P.C. .... Rockville, MD
Negronida, Jane O'Brien .... Chicago, IL
Negrón-Monge, Sandra L. .... San Juan, PR
Negrón-Navas, Eduardo M. .... San Juan, PR
Negron Padilla, Victor M. .... San Juan, PR
Negron-Ramirez, Jeannette Marina
San Juan, PR
Negrón Rivera, Erick G. .... San Juan, PR
Negrón-Rodríguez, Eduardo .... San Juan, PR
Negrón-Soto, Ramón .... Guaynabo, PR
Negron-Vargas, Mariana .... San Juan, PR
Negrotto, Donna S. .... Biloxi, MS
Negrotto, Lewie G., IV, P.L.L.C
Gulfport, MS
Negrotto, Lewie G. "Skip", IV
Gulfport, MS
Negru, Robert R. .... Tustin, CA
Nehama, Serge D. .... New York, NY
Neher, James W. .... St. Paul, MN
Neher, John B. .... Higginsville, MO
Neher, Lawrence T. .... West Orange, NJ
Neher, R. E. .... Denver, CO
Neher, Robert A. .... Los Angeles, CA
Nehf, James P. .... Indianapolis, IN
Nehf, Laura C. .... Zionsville, IN
Nehil, Deborah Lee .... Saginaw, MI
Nehilla, Thomas J. .... Harrisburg, PA
Nehls, Harry L., Jr. .... Minneapolis, MN
Nehls, Richard C. .... Boulder, CO
Nehlsen, Bruce E. .... Pasadena, CA
Nehmad, Deborah Gottheil .... Honolulu, HI
Nehmad, Stephen R. .... Atlantic City, NJ
Nehmad, Todd A. .... Northfield, NJ
Nehmad, Tracey E. .... New York, NY
Nehoray, Siamak E. .... Sherman Oaks, CA
Nehr, Jeffrey D. .... Boulder, CO
Nehra, Gerald P. .... Muskegon, MI
Nehrbass, Douglas J. .... Lafayette, LA
Nehrbass, Jennifer Stuller .... Lafayette, LA
Nehrbass, Scott C. .... Overland Park, KS
Nehrbass, Seth M. .... Metairie, LA
Nehrenberg, Corinne L.
Santa Monica, CA
Nehrer, John A., (Co., L.P.A.)
Cuyahoga Falls, OH
Nehrig, Brian L. .... Fort Wayne, IN
Nehrig, Georgeanna .... Fort Wayne, IN
Nehring, Ilse .... Cambridge, MA
Nehring, Jeff .... Williston, ND
Nehring, Kay A. .... Mitchell, NE
Nehring, Michael Ellsworth
Hagerstown, MD
Nehring, Pamela .... Schaumburg, IL
Nehring, Roland G. .... Phoenix, AZ
Nehring, Ronald E. .... Salt Lake City, UT
Nehrke, Kristen D. .... New York, NY
Nehrkorn, William H., II .... Milwaukee, WI
Nehrt, Sachtleben, Fisher & Kerkhover
Chester, IL
Red Bud, IL
Nehs, De Wayne P. .... Milwaukee, WI
Nehs, W. Scott .... Chicago, IL
Neibart, Ralph .... West Orange, NJ
Neibauer, Douglas L. .... Modesto, CA
Neibel, John B. .... Houston, TX
Neibel, Oliver J., Jr. .... Omaha, NE
Neiberg, Mark H. .... Chicago, IL
Neiberg, Maurine J. .... Chicago, IL
Neiberg & Rojas .... Chicago, IL
Neibergs, Paul J. .... Emeryville, CA
Neibrief, Judith A.
Department of Agriculture,
Food Safety and Inspection Service, GV
Neiburger, Ben A. .... Chicago, IL

Neice, Richard A. .... Wichita, KS
Neice, William L. .... Downey, CA
Neichoy, Perry W. .... Beaumont, TX
Neichter, William Louis .... Louisville, KY
Neidell, Martin H. .... New York, NY
Neidell, Michael R. .... New York, NY
Neidenbach, Michael E. .... Gainesville, GA
Neidenberg, Adam S. .... Fort Lauderdale, FL
Neidenthal, K. Wallace .... Columbus, OH
Neidenthal, Randall C. .... Columbus, OH
Neider, Barbara A. .... Madison, WI
Neider & Boucher, S.C. .... Madison, WI
Neider, Charles E. .... Madison, WI
Neider, Le Roy J. .... Los Gatos, CA
Neider, Le Roy J., A Professional Law Corporation .... Los Gatos, CA
Neider, Michael A. .... Salt Lake City, UT
Neider, Mitchell .... Livingston, NJ
Neider, Neile A. .... Denver, CO
Neiderbach, Jonathan .... Des Moines, IA
Neiderhiser, Bryan S. .... Pittsburgh, PA
Neidert, Karl O. .... Washington, DC
Neidhardt, Donald J. .... Mineola, NY
Neidhart, Frank K., Jr. .... Chicago, IL
Neidich, George .... Great Falls, VA
Neidig, George B., Jr. .... Avalon, NJ
Neidig, John W. .... Portland, OR
Neidig, Richard D., The Law Offices of .... Columbia, MD
Neidinger, Richard P. .... Pittsburgh, PA
Neiditch, Alan M. .... New York, NY
Neiditz, Jonathan A. .... Atlanta, GA
Neiditz-Snow, Joyce H. .... Cleveland, OH
Neidl, Thomas .... Albany, NY
Neidle, Alan F. .... Washington, DC
Neidle, Gregory R. .... Livonia, MI
Neidle, Jeffrey R. .... Hartford, CT
Neidlinger, Olin E. .... Westbrook, CT
Neidorf, Richard P. .... Santa Monica, CA
Neier, Bryce Denman .... Fayetteville, NC
Neier, David .... New York, NY
Neier, Glen .... Kalispell, MT
Neier, Hal .... New York, NY
Neier, Melissa Zelen .... New York, NY
Neiers, David F. .... St. Louis, MO
Neiers, Nicholas J. .... Decatur, IL
Neifach, Jerome D. .... Cleveland, OH
Neifach, Michael .... Department of Justice, Immigration and Naturalization Service, GV
Neifeld, Cathy .... Wayne, PA
Neifeld, Marjorie .... Upper Montclair, NJ
Neifeld, Richard A. .... Arlington, VA
Neifeld, Shari .... Tampa, FL
Neifield, Marsha H. .... Philadelphia, PA
Neifield, Ronald M. .... Philadelphia, PA
Neigel, Jeff L. .... Canton, IL
Neiger, David S. .... Norcross, GA
Neighbor, David H. .... Overland Park, KS
Neighbor, R. Bradford .... Garland, TX
Neighborgall, Linda S. .... National Labor Relations Board, Office of Board Members, GV
Neighbors, Brent L. .... Oklahoma City, OK
Neighbors, Harry R., Jr. .... Marion, NC
Neighbors, Jenny L. .... Lexington, KY
Neighbors, John S. .... Overland Park, KS
Neighbors, Kenneth M. .... Atlanta, GA
Neighbors, Patrick Edward .... Fairfax Station, VA
Neighbors, Robert L. .... Little Rock, AR
Neighbors, Slade J. .... Encino, CA
Neighbors, Tracy C. .... Omaha, NE
Neighbors, Walter D., Jr. .... Rockville, MD
Neighbour, Hubbard B. .... Moline, IL
Neighbours, Doyle W. .... Lake Jackson, TX
Neighbours, John T. .... Indianapolis, IN
Neigher, Alan .... Westport, CT
Neiheisel, Michael E. .... Cincinnati, OH
Neihouse, John P. .... Springdale, AR
Neijna, Adam Mitchell .... Miami, FL
Neikirk, E. Bruce .... Louisville, KY
Neikirk, Frederick G. .... Somerset, KY
Neikrie, Mark H. .... Hartford, CT
Neil, A. B., Jr. .... Nashville, TN
Neil, Banks .... San Jose, CA
Neil, Benjamin A. .... Baltimore, MD
Neil, Burton .... West Chester, PA
Neil, Carl R. .... Portland, OR
Neil, David M. .... North East, PA
Neil, Dymott, Perkins, Brown & Frank, A Professional Corporation .... Palm Desert, CA
San Diego, CA
Neil, Fritz .... Southfield, MI
Neil, G. Eugene .... Phoenix, AZ
Neil, Gerald W. .... Tacoma, WA
Neil, Gerald W., P.S. .... Tacoma, WA
Neil, Gerard D. .... East Grand Forks, MN
Neil, James C. .... Los Angeles, CA
Neil, James S. .... San Jose, CA
Neil, M. Banks, IV .... Covington, GA
Neil, Mark L. .... Cambridge, MA
Neil, Mark Morse .... Beckley, WV
Neil, Mark T. .... Chicago, IL
Neil, Martha E. .... Chicago, IL
Neil, Michael I. .... San Diego, CA
Neil, Nicki Sue .... Okmulgee, OK
Neil, Peter M. .... Birmingham, AL
Neil, Philip A. .... San Antonio, TX
Neil, Rhonda L. .... Washington, DC
Neil, Steven A. .... New York, NY
Neil, W. R. (Bill) .... Dallas, TX
Neilan, Monte L. .... Kimball, NE
Neilan, Paul G. .... Chicago, IL
Neilander, Dennis K. .... Carson City, NV
Neild, William J. .... Rochester, NY
Neild, William J., P.C. .... Rochester, NY
Neiles, Joseph .... Sioux Falls, SD

Neiley & Alder .... Aspen, CO
Neiley, John F. .... Frisco, CO
Neiley, Richard Y., Jr. .... Aspen, CO
Neill, Andrew G. .... St. Louis, MO
Neill, Ann Mason .... Charlotte, NC
Neill, Benjamin J. .... Lenexa, KS
Neill, Brian P. .... Orange, CA
Neill, Catherine E. .... Dearborn, MI
Neill, Charles E., III .... Greensboro, NC
Neill, D. Samuel .... Hendersonville, NC
Neill, David J. .... Sacramento, CA
Neill, David S. .... New York, NY
Neill, Dennis R. .... Tulsa, OK
Neill, Duane .... Amarillo, TX
Neill, Edwin B. .... General Services Administration, Board of Contract Appeals, GV
Neill, Frederick W. .... Aurora, IL
Neill Griffin Jeffries Fowler Tierney & Neill, Chartered .... Fort Pierce, FL
Port St. Lucie, FL
Vero Beach, FL
Neill, Howard M. .... Pullman, WA
Neill, James K., Jr. .... Portland, OR
Neill, James P., Jr. .... Dallas, TX
Neill, John E. .... Burleson, TX
Neill, Jonathan H. .... Spokane, WA
Neill, Joseph V. .... St. Louis, MO
Neill, Julianne .... St. Paul, MN
Neill, K. Patrick .... Eugene, OR
Neill, Kenneth R. .... Great Falls, MT
Neill, Kyle E. .... San Antonio, TX
Neill, Margaret M. .... St. Louis, MO
Neill, Mark David .... Myrtle Beach, SC
Surfside Beach, SC
Neill, Mark H. .... St. Louis, MO
Neill, Nathan S. .... Alden, NY
Neill, Peter T. .... Uniondale, NY
Neill, Richard J. .... Clark, SD
Neill, Richard V. .... Fort Pierce, FL
Neill, Richard V., Jr. .... Fort Pierce, FL
Neill, Robert .... Larchmont, NY
Neill, Robert B. .... Fort Campbell, KY
Neill, Robert G., Jr. .... El Paso, TX
Neill, Robert H. .... Birmingham, AL
Neill, Robert H., Jr. .... Denver, CO
Neill, Ronald H. .... Cleveland, OH
Neill, Ronald L. .... McKinney, TX
Neill, Roy D. .... Hendersonville, NC
Neill, Sharla J. .... Wills Point, TX
Neill, William James .... Philadelphia, PA
Neill, William R. .... Weaverville, CA
Neill-Beckmann, Lisa .... Macon, GA
Neilly, Thomas D. .... Rye Brook, NY
Neilon, Robert P. .... Rochester, NY
Neilon, William J. .... Dallas, TX
Neils, Christopher B. .... San Diego, CA
Neils, Franz & Chirhart, P.A. .... St. Cloud, MN
Neils, Lynn A. .... New York, NY
Neils, Paul F. .... Washington, DC
Neils, Peggy A. .... Department of Commerce, Patent and Trademark Office, GV
Neils, Roger D. .... St. Cloud, MN
Neils, Theodore F. .... Minneapolis, MN
Neilsen, Craig H. .... Jackpot, NV
Neilsen, Daniel P. .... Traverse City, MI
Neilsen, Michael B. .... Pocatello, ID
Neilsen, Walter H. .... Nashville, TN
Neilson, Barbara L. .... Minneapolis, MN
Neilson, Benjamin R. .... Philadelphia, PA
Neilson, Bruce A. .... Fresno, CA
Neilson, Christopher Mark .... Hollywood, FL
Neilson, Claud D. .... Demopolis, AL
Neilson, George W. .... Madras, OR
Neilson, Gordon W. .... St. Louis, MO
Neilson, James D. .... Harrisburg, PA
Neilson, James M. .... Anoka, MN
Neilson, Jeffrey T. .... Troy, MI
Neilson, John F. .... Fairfield, CA
Neilson, Larry W. .... St. Paul, MN
Neilson, Leonard E. .... Salt Lake City, UT
Neilson, Leonard E., P.C. .... Salt Lake City, UT
Neilson, Lewis L., Jr. .... Philadelphia, PA
Neilson, Mary Beth .... Camden, NJ
Neilson, Michael R. .... Washington, DC
Neilson, Mikol S. B. .... Washington, DC
Neilson, Renn G. .... Dallas, TX
Neilson, Richard R. .... Los Angeles, CA
Neilson, Robert Davis .... Fort Lauderdale, FL
Neilson, Scott A. .... Minneapolis, MN
Neilson, Susan Bieke .... Detroit, MI
Neilson, Susan M. .... Stamford, CT
Neilson, Thomas L. .... Panama City Beach, FL
Neilson, Vernon L. .... Odenton, MD
Neilson, W. Lane .... Orlando, FL
Neilson, William A. .... Rochester, NY
Neilson, William L. .... New York, NY
Neilsson, Douglas Clark .... Palo Alto, CA
Neily, Warren S., Jr. .... Blacksburg, VA
Neiman, Adrian Dee .... Miami, FL
Neiman, Allen I. .... Los Angeles, CA
Neiman, Amy L. .... Los Angeles, CA
Neiman & Barnes, L.L.P. .... Lewisville, TX
Neiman, Dennis R. .... Detroit, MI
Neiman, Donald F. .... Des Moines, IA
Neiman, Eric J. .... Portland, OR
Neiman, Erwin B. .... Highland Park, IL
Neiman, Gerald D. .... Keene, NH
Neiman Ginsburg & Mairanz P.C. .... New York, NY
Neiman, Glenn C. .... Bensalem, PA
Neiman, Ira S. .... Chicago, IL
Neiman, Jan S., (Mr.) .... Boca Raton, FL
Miami, FL
Neiman, Jill .... San Francisco, CA
Neiman, John Braxton .... Milwaukee, WI

Neiman, John H. .... West Des Moines, IA
Neiman, Joseph .... Hackensack, NJ
Neiman, Kenneth P. .... Springfield, MA
Neiman, Kevin S. .... Miami, FL
Neiman, Lawrence M. .... Farmingdale, NY
Neiman, Marvin .... New York, NY
Neiman, Maurice P. .... Akron, OH
Neiman, Meryl J. .... Pittsburgh, PA
Neiman, Michelle L. .... Akron, OH
Neiman, Mitchell M. .... Brooklyn, NY
Neiman, Peter G. .... New York, NY
Neiman, Phillip L. .... Los Angeles, CA
Neiman, Robert E. .... Chicago, IL
Neiman, Robert K. .... Chicago, IL
Neiman, Ronald J. .... Lewisville, TX
Neiman, Sanford .... Pittsburgh, PA
Neiman, Shirah, (Ms.) .... New York, NY
Neiman, Stone, McCormick & Wendl, P.C. .... West Des Moines, IA
Neiman, Stuart M. .... Atlanta, GA
Neiman, Tanya .... San Francisco, CA
Neiman, William J. .... Chicago, IL
Neimann, Paul G. .... Minneapolis, MN
Neimark, Cort A. .... Fort Lauderdale, FL
Neimark & Nadel, P.A. .... Fort Lauderdale, FL
Neimark, Richard P. .... New City, NY
Neimark, Sheridan .... Washington, DC
Neimeier, Mary-Karen .... Detroit, MI
Neimeth, Albert C. .... Ithaca, NY
Neimeth, Clifford E. .... New York, NY
Neimeyer, Harry T. .... St. Paul, MN
Neimeyer, Paul C. .... Washington, DC
Nein, James R. .... Columbus, OH
Neinast, Steven H. .... Austin, TX
Neinast, Vera Callahan .... Austin, TX
Neinast, William H. .... Somerville, TX
Neinstein, Paul B. .... Universal City, CA
Neipris, Jonathan P. .... Wilmington, DE
Neira, Christian .... New York, NY
Neira, Mercedes .... Brooklyn, NY
Neira, Thelma .... Huntington Station, NY
Neirynck, Reginald P. .... Boston, MA
Neirynck, Robert W. .... Bloomington, IL
Neis & Callaway, P.C. .... Tucson, AZ
Neis, Diane E. .... Overland Park, KS
Neis, James M. .... Chicago, IL
Neis, John M. .... Tucson, AZ
Neis, Mark W. .... Topeka, KS
Neis & Michaux, P.A. .... Topeka, KS
Neis, Robert J. .... Atlanta, GA
Neis, Robert W. .... Schaumburg, IL
Neisen, Christopher A. .... New Prague, MN
Neisen, Jay S. .... Wilmington, NC
Neisent, Tracy Speck .... Oklahoma City, OK
Neiser, David D. .... St. Petersburg, FL
Neiser & Neiser, P.A. .... St. Petersburg, FL
Neiser, Richard W. .... St. Petersburg, FL
Neish, Laurence A. .... Pittsburgh, PA
Neishloss, Meyer .... Pittsburgh, PA
Neisig, Russell W. .... Midland, TX
Neisler, Alexandra D. .... Toledo, OH
Neisler, C. Andrew, Jr. .... Kings Mountain, NC
Neisler, Kirsten N. .... New York, NY
Neisler, Melvin B., Jr. .... Killington, VT
Neiss, Arthur M. .... White Plains, NY
Neiss, Dahlia I. .... Agency for International Development, Office of the General Counsel, GV
Neiss, Moshe S. .... New York, NY
Neisser, Eric .... Newark, NJ
Neisser, Joan L. .... Newark, NJ
Neisser, Peter A. .... Scottsdale, AZ
Neisser, Peter A., Attorney at Law, P.C. .... Scottsdale, AZ
Neistadt, Kim A. .... Beverly Hills, CA
Neistadt, Tracy C. .... Palo Alto, CA
Neistat, Douglas M. .... Santa Monica, CA
Neistein, Bernard S. .... Chicago, IL
Neiswender, Howard W. .... Tuscaloosa, AL
Neiswender, Jane Ann Roe .... Washington, DC
Neiswender, Kate M. .... Ventura, CA
Neiter, Gerald I. .... Los Angeles, CA
Neiter, Gerald I., A Professional Corporation .... Los Angeles, CA
Neiter, Richard M. .... Los Angeles, CA
Neithercut, Edward J. .... Flint, MI
Neithercut, Edward J., P.C. .... Flint, MI
Neithercut, Geoffrey L. .... Flint, MI
Neitlich, David E. .... Boston, MA
Neitz, Carol S. .... Philadelphia, PA
Neitzel, Charlotte Louise .... Denver, CO
Neitzel, Donald C. .... Spring Lake, MI
Neitzel, Stephanie J. .... Denver, CO
Neitzel, Warren J. .... Woodside, NY
Neitzke, Eric K. .... Daytona Beach, FL
Neives-Blas, Myrta Estrella .... Mayaguez, PR
Neiwirth, Arthur C. .... Fort Lauderdale, FL
Neiwirth, Arthur C., P.A. .... Fort Lauderdale, FL
Neiwirth, Leo .... Newark, NJ
Neiwirth & Neiwirth, P.A. .... Newark, NJ
Neiwirth, Ronald G. .... Miami, FL
Neizer, Joseph J. .... Phoenixville, PA
Nejaime, Nadia B. .... Washington, DC
NeJame, Karin A. .... Danbury, CT
NeJame, Mark A. .... Springfield, MA
NeJame, Mark E., P.A., Law Offices of .... Orlando, FL
NeJame, Mark Elias .... Orlando, FL
NeJame, Scott .... Albany, NY
Nejedlo, Todd W. .... Milwaukee, WI
Nejedly, John A. .... Walnut Creek, CA
Nekhom, Deborah L. .... Fort Worth, TX
Nekich, Michael A. .... Minneapolis, MN
Nekritz, Barry B. .... Chicago, IL

Nekritz, Felicia B .... Columbus, OH
Nekvasil, Kalju .... Clearwater, FL
Nelabovige, Joseph M. A. .... Hamburg, PA
Nelabovige, Joseph M. A., Inc., Law Offices of .... Hamburg, PA
Nelch, H. Gregory .... Redwood City, CA
Nelder, Maralee .... Grass Valley, CA
Nelder, Robert L. .... San Francisco, CA
Neligan & Averch, L.L.P. .... Dallas, TX
Neligan, Maura Victor .... Dallas, TX
Neligan, Patrick J., Jr. .... Dallas, TX
Nelinson, Mark Charles .... Sunset Hills, MO
Nelis, Mark C. .... Purcellville, VA
Nelivigi, Nandan S. .... New York, NY
Nelken, Melissa L. .... San Francisco, CA
Nelken, Sam .... Natchitoches, LA
Nelkin, Amy L. .... New York, NY
Nelkin, Carol .... Houston, TX
Nelkin, Henry D. .... Baldwin, NY
Nelkin, Leslie Andrew .... New York, NY
Nelkin & Nelkin, A Professional Corporation .... Houston, TX
Nelkin, Stuart M. .... Houston, TX
Nelkin-Rose, Barbara J. .... Sharon, MA
Nell, Gary L. .... Oceanside, CA
Nell, John D. .... Indianapolis, IN
Nell, Richard E .... De Pere, WI
Nell, Roger Eric .... Clarksville, TN
Nelle, Richard A. .... Blaine, WA
Nellen, A. Suzanne .... Bozeman, MT
Nellen, Annette M. Bomyea .... San Jose, CA
Nellen, David S. .... Department of Transportation, Surface Transportation Board, GV
Nellen, James W., II .... Green Bay, WI
Nellen, Richard C. .... Bozeman, MT
Neller, Kristen .... Washington, DC
Neller, Robert R. .... Walnut Creek, CA
Nellermoe, Barbara Hanson .... San Antonio, TX
Nellermoe, Leslie C. .... Seattle, WA
Nelles, Matthew S. .... Fort Lauderdale, FL
Nelles, Sharon L. .... New York, NY
Nelley, John W., Jr. .... Nashville, TN
Nelligan, John J. .... Glen Ellyn, IL
Nelligan, Kevin F. .... Canaan, CT
Nelligan, Maurice J., Jr. .... Liberty Corner, NJ
Nellinger, Michael A. .... Indianapolis, IN
Nellis, Anthony J. .... Detroit, MI
Nellis, Gregory D., P.C. .... Tulsa, OK
Nellis & Jahr .... Westland, MI
Nellis, James F., Jr. .... Atlanta, GA
Nellis, James R. .... Westland, MI
Nellis, Jeffrey C. .... Bancroft, MI
Nellis, Joseph L. .... Washington, DC
Nellis, Kenneth G. .... San Francisco, CA
Nellis, Noel W. .... San Francisco, CA
Nellis, William J. .... Rosemont, IL
Nellor, J. D. .... Vancouver, WA
Nellor, Nancy A. .... Vancouver, WA
Nellor, Susan A. .... Washington, DC
Nelmes, William G. .... Tucson, AZ
Nelms, Beverly Dean .... Knoxville, TN
Nelms, David O. .... Blackstone, VA
Nelms, E. Joan .... Redlands, CA
Nelms, F. Donald, Jr. .... New Bern, NC
Wilmington, NC
Nelms, Fielder F. .... Dallas, TX
Nelms, Frank D. .... Atlanta, GA
Nelms, Gary T. .... Springfield, MO
Nelms, John R. .... Dallas, TX
Nelms, Johnny L. .... Gulfport, MS
Nelms, K. Anderson .... Montgomery, AL
Nelms, K. Anderson, P.C. .... Montgomery, AL
Nelms, Kenneth Lee .... Saint Marys, GA
Nelms, Laura Diane .... Baltimore, MD
Nelms, Mark L. .... Tulsa, OK
Nelms, Robert L. .... Los Alamitos, CA
Nelms, Robert W. .... Irvine, CA
Nelms, Russell F. .... Dallas, TX
Nelms, William P., (P.C.) .... Murfreesboro, TN
Nelo, C. Mark .... Kyle, TX
Nelon, Robert D. .... Oklahoma City, OK
Nelowet, Richard T. .... New York, NY
Nelsch & Vrooman, LLC .... Denver, CO
Nelsch, William Dale .... Denver, CO
Nelsen & Brock .... Roseville, CA
Nelsen, Bruce J. .... Cozad, NE
Nelsen, David M. .... Mason City, IA
Nelsen, Edward P. .... San Francisco, CA
Nelsen, Eric W. .... New York, NY
Nelsen, Georgiana S. .... Waukee, IA
Nelsen Greenberg & Gohen .... San Francisco, CA
Nelsen, James D. .... Jacksonville, FL
Nelsen, James M. .... Denver, CO
Nelsen, James W. .... San Jose, CA
Nelsen, Justin B. .... Milwaukee, WI
Nelsen, Karin M. .... Minneapolis, MN
Nelsen, Leo W. .... St. Louis, MO
Nelsen, Michael A. .... Omaha, NE
Nelsen, Michelle Lynn .... Washington, DC
Nelsen, Ned R. .... Los Angeles, CA
Nelsen, Nels Raymond .... Palo Alto, CA
Nelsen & Nelsen .... Cozad, NE
Nelsen, Richard F. .... Cozad, NE
Nelsen, Robert .... Roseville, CA
Nelsen, Romain Oliver .... Santa Monica, CA
Nelsen, Stephen H. .... Lincoln, NE
Nelsen, Thompson, Pegue & Thornton, A Professional Corporation .... Los Angeles, CA
Santa Monica, CA
Nelsen, Timothy A. .... Chicago, IL
Nelsen, Timothy W. .... Humboldt, NE
Nelson, Aaron Alma .... Salt Lake City, UT
Nelson, Abbott L. .... Chicago, IL

Nelson, A. C. ....Brownsville, TX
Nelson, Adam ....Chicago, IL
Nelson, Adam R. ....Richmond, VA
Nelson, Adrian Van, II ....Washington, DC
Nelson, Alan S. ....Saco, ME
Nelson, Albert L. ....Du Bois, PA
Nelson, Albert Taylor, Jr. ....Troy, MI
Nelson, Albin James ....Minneapolis, MN
Nelson, Alice K. ....Gainesville, FL
Nelson, Alison R. ....Dearborn, MI
Nelson, Allan G. ....Bel Air, MD
Nelson, Allen G. ....Rapid City, SD
Nelson, Allen J. ....Flint, MI
Nelson, Allen W. ....Atlanta, GA
Nelson, Andrea L.
Department Of The Interior, Bureau of Land Management, GV
Nelson, Andréa Laurena ....New York, NY
Nelson, Andrea V. ....Tallahassee, FL
Nelson, Andrew ....San Francisco, CA
Nelson, Andrew ....Atlanta, GA
Nelson, Andrew F. ....Chicago, IL
Nelson, Andrew L. ....Madison, WI
Nelson, Andrew P. ....Calmar, IA
Decorah, IA
Nelson, Andrew W. ....New York, NY
Nelson, Angie ....Salt Lake City, UT
Nelson, Anthony J. ....Austin, TX
Nelson, April ....Delaware, OH
Nelson, Arne J. ....San Francisco, CA
Nelson, Arthur H. ....Weston, MA
Nelson, Arthur L. ....Wauwatosa, WI
Nelson, Arthur Sund ....Minneapolis, MN
Nelson, Arthur W. ....Minneapolis, MN
Nelson & Associates, P.A. ....Aventura, FL
Miami, FL
North Miami Beach, FL
Nelson & Associates, P.S. ....Seattle, WA
Nelson, B. Eric ....Pasadena, CA
Nelson, Barbara ....Claxton, GA
Nelson, Barbara A. ....New York, NY
Nelson, Barbara G. ....Boston, MA
Nelson, Barbara J. ....San Francisco, CA
Nelson, Barbara Strapp ....Princeton, NJ
Nelson, Barry A. ....Aventura, FL
West Palm Beach, FL
Nelson, Barry C. ....Boston, MA
Nelson, Barry E. ....Cincinnati, OH
Nelson, Barry G. ....Tucson, AZ
Nelson, Beckett & Nelson
St. Petersburg, FL
Nelson, Benjamin D. ....Dallas, TX
Nelson, Bernard ....Houston, TX
Nelson, Bernis Shapiro ....Peekskill, NY
Nelson, Bert A. ....Dallas, TX
Nelson, Beverly C. ....Boulder, CO
Nelson & Bice, P.C. ....Lynchburg, VA
Nelson, Bill ....Melbourne, FL
Nelson, Blake R. ....Eden Prairie, MN
Nelson, Bobby J. ....Austin, TX
Nelson, Bonnie G. ....Houston, TX
Nelson & Boswell ....Pascagoula, MS
Nelson, Boyd, III ....St. Petersburg, FL
Nelson, Boyd, MacDonald, Mitchell, Mason & Hedin ....San Rafael, CA
Nelson, Boyles, Niblock and Green
Winston-Salem, NC
Nelson, Bradley J. ....Denison, IA
Nelson, Bradley P. ....Chicago, IL
Nelson, Brandon B. ....Fairfield, IA
Nelson, Brandon, P.C. ....Fairfield, IA
Nelson, Brenda B. ....Los Angeles, CA
Nelson, Bret A. ....Houston, TX
Nelson, Brett Andrew ....Rock Island, IL
Nelson, Brian C. ....San Diego, CA
Nelson, Brian H. ....Miami, FL
Nelson, Brian L. ....West Lafayette, IN
Nelson, Brian S. ....Los Angeles, CA
Nelson, Brian S. ....Rock Island, IL
Nelson, Brian Stanton ....Houston, TX
Nelson, Brian W. ....Fargo, ND
Nelson, Bruce A. ....Winona, MN
Nelson, Bruce C. ....Chicago, IL
Nelson, Bruce E. ....Sacramento, CA
Nelson, Bruce J. ....Salt Lake City, UT
Nelson, Bruce L. ....Mission Hills, CA
Nelson, Bruce M. ....Spokane, WA
Nelson, Bruce W. ....Las Vegas, NV
Nelson, Bryan M. ....Carson City, NV
Nelson, Byron ....Laguna Hills, CA
Nelson, Byron G., Law Offices of
Redondo Beach, CA
Nelson, Byron, Prof. Corp.
Laguna Hills, CA
Nelson, C. David ....Glenwood, MN
Nelson, C. Krather, III ....Macon, GA
Nelson, C. Raymond ....Douglaston, NY
Nelson, C. Roger ....Bethesda, MD
Nelson, C. Stanley ....Salina, KS
Nelson, C. William ....Tallahassee, FL
Nelson, Carl B., Jr. ....Dallas, TX
Nelson, Carl K., Jr. ....Dublin, GA
Nelson, Carl P. A. ....Walnut Creek, CA
Nelson, Carl R. ....Tampa, FL
Nelson, Carl W. ....Franklin, NJ
Nelson, Carla S. ....Houston, TX
Nelson, Carlton G. ....Grand Forks, ND
Nelson, Carol S. ....Valley City, ND
Nelson, Carol Sue ....Birmingham, AL
Nelson, Caroline B. ....San Francisco, CA
Nelson, Carolyn B. ....Birmingham, AL
Nelson, Carolyn D. ....Newark, NJ
New York, NY
Nelson, Catherine ....Philadelphia, PA
Nelson, Catherine A. ....Chesapeake, VA
Nelson, Catherine A. T. ....Chicago, IL
Nelson, Catherine B. ....Chicago, IL
Nelson, Cathleen A. ....Denver, CO

Nelson, Cecil H., Jr. ....Greenville, SC
Nelson, Cecil H., Jr., LLC ....Greenville, SC
Nelson, Chandler A. ....South Boston, VA
Nelson, Charles A. ....Jackson, MI
Nelson, Charles D. ....Washington, DC
Nelson, Charles E. ....Washington, DC
Nelson, Charles I. ....Malibu, CA
Nelson, Charles L.
Indian Harbour Beach, FL
Nelson, Charles W., Jr. ....New Orleans, LA
Nelson, Charles Walter
South Lake Tahoe, CA
Nelson, Chas. D. ....Roseville, MN
Nelson, Chas. R. ....Seattle, WA
Nelson, Cheryl ....Beverly Hills, CA
Nelson, Cheryl ....New York, NY
Nelson, Chipman, Quigley & Hansen
Salt Lake City, UT
Nelson, Chris A. ....Woodbridge, NJ
Nelson, Christa M. ....Englewood, CO
Nelson, Christian W. ....Salt Lake City, UT
Nelson, Christina Gallagher
San Francisco, CA
Nelson, Christine K. ....Brookfield, WI
Nelson, Christopher A. ....St. Louis Park, MN
Nelson, Christopher D.
San Francisco, CA
Nelson, Christopher J. ....Detroit, MI
Nelson, Christopher J. ....Billings, MT
Nelson, Christopher M. ....Miami, FL
Nelson, Christopher P. ....New York, NY
Nelson, Christopher W. ....Boston, MA
Nelson, Cindy E. ....New York, NY
Nelson, Clark R. ....Wichita, KS
Nelson, Clifford E. ....Washougal, WA
Nelson, Clifford H., Jr. ....Atlanta, GA
Nelson, Clifford J. ....Kilmarnock, VA
Nelson, Clifford S. ....New York, NY
Nelson, Clyde A., Jr., (P.C.) ....Petaluma, CA
Nelson, Clyde E., III ....New York, NY
Nelson, Clyde G. ....Soda Springs, ID
Nelson, Colin T. ....Minneapolis, MN
Nelson, Constance S. ....Walnut Creek, CA
Nelson, Craig A. ....Centralia, WA
Nelson, Craig D. ....Los Angeles, CA
Nelson, Craig E. ....Chicago, IL
Nelson, Craig H. ....Augusta, ME
Nelson, Craig R. ....New Orleans, LA
Nelson, Craig S. ....Albert Lea, MN
Nelson, Craig W. ....Brookfield, WI
Nelson, Cynthia A. ....Charleston, WV
Nelson, Cynthia Brotman ....Dallas, TX
Nelson, Cynthia S. ....Richmond, VA
Nelson, D. Brit ....Red Bank, NJ
Houston, TX
Nelson, D. Marshall ....Alpharetta, GA
Nelson, Dale Ellen ....Burbank, CA
Nelson, Dan F. ....Decatur, AL
Nelson, Dan K. ....St. Paul, MN
Nelson, Dan R. ....Springfield, MO
Nelson, Dan S. ....Greenwood, AR
Nelson, Dana M. ....Seattle, WA
Nelson, Dane C. ....Adrian, MI
Nelson, Daniel A. ....Boston, MA
Nelson, Daniel C. ....St. Louis, MO
Nelson, Daniel E. ....Columbia City, IN
Nelson, Daniel L. ....Los Angeles, CA
Nelson, Daniel R. ....Houlton, ME
Nelson, Daniel R. ....Minneapolis, MN
Nelson, Daniel T. ....Oroville, CA
Nelson, Daniel W. ....Washington, DC
Nelson, Daniel W. ....Austin, TX
Nelson, Darren K. ....Salt Lake City, UT
Nelson, Darwin J. ....Tucson, AZ
Nelson, Daryl Andrew ....Culpeper, VA
Nelson, David ....Ukiah, CA
Nelson, David ....Wagoner, OK
Nelson, David ....Longview, WA
Nelson, David A. ....Chicago, IL
Nelson, David A. ....Cincinnati, OH
Nelson, David A. ....Dallas, TX
Nelson, David A. ....Bellingham, WA
Nelson, David B. ....Orlando, FL
Nelson, David C. ....Los Angeles, CA
Nelson, David C. ....Belleville, IL
Nelson, David C. ....Mattoon, IL
Nelson, David C. ....Bloomfield Hills, MI
Nelson, David C. ....Omaha, NE
Nelson, David C. ....Las Vegas, NV
Nelson, David Charles ....St. Louis, MO
Nelson, David D. ....Washington, DC
Nelson, David D. ....Des Moines, IA
Nelson, David E. ....Oakland, CA
Nelson, David E. ....San Francisco, CA
Nelson, David E. ....Cincinnati, OH
Nelson, David E., Jr. ....Chattanooga, TN
Nelson, David F. ....Charleston, WV
Nelson, David H. ....Newport Beach, CA
Nelson, David H. ....Monroe, LA
Nelson, David H. ....Brady, MT
Nelson, David H. ....Attica, NY
Nelson, David H. ....Charlottesville, VA
Nelson, David J. ....Geneva, IL
Nelson, David K. ....Santa Monica, CA
Nelson, David K. ....Baton Rouge, LA
Nelson, David K. ....Milwaukee, WI
Nelson, David L. ....Sausalito, CA
Nelson, David L. ....Golden, CO
Nelson, David L. ....Wichita, KS
Nelson, David L. ....Southfield, MI
Nelson, David L. ....Dallas, TX
Nelson, David L. ....Lubbock, TX
Nelson, David M. ....Waukegan, IL
Nelson, David MacKennett
San Francisco, CA
Nelson, David N. ....Macon, GA
Nelson, David P. ....Washington, DC
Nelson, David R. ....Phoenix, AZ

Nelson, David R. ....Colusa, CA
Nelson, David R. ....Sioux Falls, SD
Nelson, David R. ....San Antonio, TX
Nelson, David S. ....Santa Rosa, CA
Nelson, David S. ....Tampa, FL
Nelson, David S. ....Boston, MA
Nelson, David S. ....Canton, NY
Nelson, David V. ....Minneapolis, MN
Nelson, David W. ....Williston, ND
Nelson, David W. ....Austin, TX
Nelson, Dean M. ....Minneapolis, MN
Nelson, Dean R. ....Earlham, IA
Nelson, Deane D. ....Rancho Mirage, CA
Nelson, Deanna R. ....Watertown, NY
Nelson, DeAnne J. ....Morrisville, NC
Nelson, Deborah E. ....Boise, ID
Nelson, Deborah E. ....Short Hills, NJ
Nelson, Deborah L. ....Framingham, MA
Nelson, Debra A. ....Huntington, WV
Nelson, Debra Steinberg ....Orlando, FL
Nelson, Della S. ....Denver, CO
Nelson, Delos T. ....Cleveland, OH
Nelson, Dennis R. ....Tucson, AZ
Nelson, Denyse M. ....Miami, FL
Nelson, Dewey M. ....Eden Prairie, MN
Nelson, Dirk W. ....Bayfield, CO
Nelson, Don C. ....Houston, TX
Nelson, Don D. ....Los Angeles, CA
Nelson, Don I. ....Sapulpa, OK
Nelson, Don L. ....Loveland, CO
Nelson, Donald A. ....Shreveport, LA
Nelson, Donald E. ....Edina, MN
Nelson, Donald E., (P.C.) ....Leesburg, VA
Nelson, Donald G. ....Sacramento, CA
Nelson, Donald L. ....San Francisco, CA
Nelson, Donna L. ....Austin, TX
Nelson, Dorothy W. ....Pasadena, CA
Nelson, Douglas A. ....Eugene, OR
Nelson, Douglas C. ....Phoenix, AZ
Nelson, Douglas C., P.C. ....Phoenix, AZ
Nelson, Douglas G. ....Henderson, MN
Nelson, Douglas J. ....Palo Alto, CA
Nelson, Douglas M., II ....Cleveland, OH
Nelson, Douglas N. ....Port Huron, MI
Nelson, Douglas R. ....Idaho Falls, ID
Nelson, Douglas T. ....Washington, DC
Nelson, Dries, Connell & Kramer, S.C.
Brookfield, WI
Milwaukee, WI
Nelson, Duane L. ....Modesto, CA
Nelson, Duane R. ....Hartford, CT
Nelson, Dustin D. ....Mayville, NY
Nelson, E. Benjamin ....Omaha, NE
Nelson, E. Bradley ....Fairfield, CA
Nelson, E. Bradley ....Vacaville, CA
Nelson, E. Miles ....Phoenix, AZ
Nelson, Edward ....Palo Alto, CA
Nelson, Edward D. ....New York, NY
Nelson, Edward H.
Department of Commerce, Patent and Trademark Office, GV
Nelson, Edward J. ....Rapid City, SD
Nelson, Edward R., III ....Fort Worth, TX
Nelson, Edward S. ....Norwich, NY
Nelson, Edwin L. ....Birmingham, AL
Nelson, Elaine Edwards ....Dallas, TX
Nelson, Elaine T. ....Los Altos, CA
Nelson, Elizabeth A. ....Santa Barbara, CA
Nelson, Elizabeth A. ....West Des Moines, IA
Nelson, Elizabeth E. ....Minneapolis, MN
Nelson, Elizabeth F. ....Fort Lauderdale, FL
Nelson, Elizabeth S. ....Lubbock, TX
Nelson, Elizabeth Thayer
Department Of Health And Human Services, Office of the General Counsel, GV
Nelson, Ellen L. ....Attleboro, MA
Nelson, Ellis M. ....Macon, GA
Nelson, Emily H. ....Birmingham, AL
Nelson, Eric A. ....Glendale, CA
Nelson, Eric C. ....Topanga, CA
Nelson, Eric C. ....Minneapolis, MN
Nelson, Eric C. ....Milwaukee, WI
Nelson, Eric E.
Environmental Protection Agency, Office of Enforcement and Compliance Assurance, GV
Nelson, Eric H. ....Missoula, MT
Nelson, Eric H. ....Houston, TX
Nelson, Eric Jon ....Janesville, WI
Nelson, Eric K. ....Indianapolis, IN
Nelson, Eric L. ....Atlanta, GA
Nelson, Eric L. ....Minneapolis, MN
Nelson, Eric M. ....San Diego, CA
Nelson, Eric M. ....New York, NY
Nelson, Eric M. ....New York, NY
Nelson, Eric P. ....Tulsa, OK
Nelson, Eric S. ....Aberdeen, WA
Nelson, Eric S. ....Seattle, WA
Nelson, Erling W. ....Alexandria, VA
Nelson, Ernest J., Jr. ....Stone Mountain, GA
Nelson, Erven T. ....Las Vegas, NV
Reno, NV
Nelson, Eugene A. ....Lakeland, FL
Nelson, Evan C. ....Los Angeles, CA
San Francisco, CA
Nelson, F. David ....Wagoner, OK
Nelson, F. Dennis ....Chicago, IL
Nelson, F. Kirk ....Jackson, MS
Nelson, Farrell L. ....Irvine, CA
Nelson & Feldman, P.A.
Bay Harbor Islands, FL
Nelson, Ford R., Jr. ....Kansas City, MO
Nelson, Frank B. ....Spencer, IA
Nelson, Frank Lawrence ....Birmingham, AL
Nelson, Frank R. ....Laramie, WY
Nelson, Frank V. ....Salt Lake City, UT
Nelson, Franklin W. ....Sierra Madre, CA
Nelson, Fred G. ....Salt Lake City, UT

Nelson, Frederick D. ....Lexington, KY
Nelson, Frederick D. ....Cincinnati, OH
Nelson, Frederick H. ....Orlando, FL
Nelson, Frederick L. ....Oakland, CA
Nelson, Fredric C. ....San Francisco, CA
Nelson & Fromer ....Asbury Park, NJ
Nelson, G. Carey, P.C. ....Cartersville, GA
Nelson, G. Macy ....Baltimore, MD
Nelson, G. Macy ....Towson, MD
Nelson & Gai, P.C. ....Billings, MT
Nelson, Garry ....Miami, FL
Nelson, Gary A. ....Leavenworth, KS
Nelson, Gary B. ....Carbondale, IL
Nelson, Gary C. ....Modesto, CA
Nelson, Gary D. ....Peoria, IL
Nelson, Gary J. ....Pasadena, CA
Nelson, Gary K. ....Phoenix, AZ
Nelson, Gary M. ....Minneapolis, MN
Nelson, Gary M., (Ltd.) ....Reno, NV
Nelson, Gary Philip ....Pittsburgh, PA
Nelson, Gary Wayne ....Albuquerque, NM
Nelson, Geo. D. ....Shreveport, LA
Nelson, Geoffrey W. ....Bridgeport, CT
Nelson, George A. ....Cleveland, OH
Nelson, George D., Jr. ....Shreveport, LA
Nelson, George E. ....Hopkins, MN
Nelson, George E. ....Oklahoma City, OK
Nelson, George E., P.C. ....Oklahoma City, OK
Nelson, George H. ....Lubbock, TX
Nelson, George L. ....Ukiah, CA
Nelson, George Law Firm, A Professional Corporation ....Lubbock, TX
Nelson, George R. ....Houston, TX
Nelson, Gerald Michael ....Altoona, PA
Nelson, Gilbert F. ....Laguna Hills, CA
Nelson, Gillis & Smith, P.C. ....Dublin, GA
Nelson, Ginger Pearson ....Amarillo, TX
Nelson, Gini ....Santa Fe, NM
Nelson, Glen G. ....Westminster, CA
Nelson, Glenn D. ....Los Angeles, CA
Nelson, Glenn R. ....Seattle, WA
Nelson, Gordon D. ....Honolulu, HI
Nelson, Gordon E. ....Rowley, MA
Nelson, Grant J. ....Kent, CT
Nelson, Grant James ....Fairfax, VA
Nelson, Grant S. ....Los Angeles, CA
Nelson, Greg S. ....Yakima, WA
Nelson, Gregg B. ....North Oaks, MN
Nelson, Gregory ....Montesano, WA
Nelson, Gregory A. ....West Palm Beach, FL
Nelson, Gregory J. ....Phoenix, AZ
Nelson, Gregory L. ....Portland, OR
Nelson, Gregory P. ....Fort Pierce, FL
Nelson, Gregory V. ....Houston, TX
Nelson, Gregory W. ....Reno, NV
Nelson & Greif ....Baldwin, NY
Nelson, Gretchen M. ....Los Angeles, CA
Nelson • Griffin ....Los Angeles, CA
Nelson, Guggenheim, Felker & Levine, LLP
Los Angeles, CA
Nelson Gullen Bronson & Katz, LLP
Los Angeles, CA
Nelson, Gunnard A., Jr. ....Lenexa, KS
Nelson, Guy C. ....Pullman, WA
Nelson, H. Donald ....San Jose, CA
Nelson, Hal L. ....Austin, TX
Nelson, Hammons & Self, A Professional Law Corporation ....Shreveport, LA
Nelson, Harlan L. ....Fergus Falls, MN
Nelson, Harley ....Homosassa, FL
Nelson, Harold E. ....Grand Rapids, MI
Nelson, Harold M. ....Omaha, NE
Nelson, Harold S. ....Irvine, CA
Nelson, Harold S. ....Dawson, MN
Madison, MN
Nelson, Harry J. ....Chicago, IL
Nelson, Harry L., Jr.
Rolling Hills Estates, CA
Nelson, Harry L., Jr. ....Nashville, TN
Nelson, Harry M. ....Santa Ana, CA
Nelson, Harry R. ....Shreveport, LA
Nelson, Harry R., Ltd. ....Shreveport, LA
Nelson, Heather E. ....Houston, TX
Nelson, Hedy L. ....Washington, DC
Nelson, Helaine Q. ....Columbus, OH
Nelson, Helene W. ....New York, NY
Nelson, Helmer J. ....Chicago, IL
Nelson, Henry C., Jr. ....Columbia, SC
Nelson, Henry K. ....Ukiah, CA
Nelson, Henry P. ....Los Angeles, CA
Nelson, Herbert O. ....Chicago, IL
Nelson, Herbert R. ....Phoenix, AZ
Nelson, Herbert R., Ltd. ....Phoenix, AZ
Nelson & Herlin ....Walnut Creek, CA
Nelson • Hesse ....Sarasota, FL
Nelson, Hilary Fisher ....Hartford, CT
Nelson, Hill, Lord & Beasley, LLP
Athens, GA
Decatur, GA
Nelson, Howard E., (P.A.) ....Miami, FL
Nelson, Howard L. ....Washington, DC
Nelson, Howard T. ....St. Louis, MO
Nelson, Hugh F. ....Menasha, WI
Nelson, Hugh W. ....Columbus, OH
Nelson, Ilene Berenter ....Raleigh, NC
Nelson, Irving T. ....Flint, MI
Nelson, J. Alan ....Jackson, MS
Waco, TX
Nelson, J. Barlow ....Tulsa, OK
Nelson, J. Barlow, Inc. ....Tulsa, OK
Nelson, J. David ....Lubbock, TX
Nelson, J. David ....Sandy, UT
Nelson, J. Paul ....Louisville, KY
Nelson, J. Paul ....Henderson, TX
Nelson, J. Robert ....Los Angeles, CA
Nelson, J. Robt. ....Portland, OR
Nelson, Jack D. ....Chicago, IL
Nelson, Jack O., Jr. ....Lubbock, TX

Nelson, Jack R. ... Oakland, CA
Nelson, James ... Los Angeles, CA
Nelson & James ... Grants Pass, OR
Nelson, James A. ... Los Angeles, CA
Nelson, James A. ... Shelby, MT
Nelson, James A. ... Portland, OR
Nelson, James A. ... Darlington, SC
Nelson, James A. ... Toledo, WA
Nelson, James A., Jr. ... Greenville, NC
Nelson, James A., P.A. ... Darlington, SC
Nelson, James B. ... Atlanta, GA
Nelson, James B. ... Ypsilanti, MI
Nelson, James C. ... Oakland, CA
Nelson, James C.
Environmental Protection Agency, Office of the General Counsel, GV
Nelson, James C. ... Helena, MT
Nelson, James C. ... Portland, OR
Nelson, James D. ... Seattle, WA
Nelson, James E. ... Pasadena, CA
Nelson, James E. ... Denver, CO
Nelson, James E. ... Chicago, IL
Nelson, James E. ... Minneapolis, MN
Nelson, James E. ... Poughkeepsie, NY
Nelson, James E. ... Seattle, WA
Nelson, James F. ... Ventura, CA
Nelson, James F. ... Glenwood, MN
Nelson, James F., Jr. ... Dublin, GA
Nelson, James G. ... Albany, OR
Nelson, James H. ... Longmont, CO
Nelson, James I. ... Irvine, CA
Nelson, James J. ... Houston, TX
Nelson, James K. ... San Francisco, CA
Nelson, James L. ... Beatrice, NE
Nelson, James L. ... Austin, TX
Nelson, James M. ... Sacramento, CA
Nelson, James M. ... Walnut Creek, CA
Nelson, James O., II ... Jackson, MS
Nelson, James P. ... St. Paul, MN
Nelson, James R. ... Chicago, IL
Nelson, James R. ... Grand Rapids, MI
Nelson, James R. ... Kenilworth, NJ
Nelson, James R. ... Dallas, TX
Nelson, James R., II ... Chicago, IL
Nelson, James S. ... Rapid City, SD
Nelson, James T. ... Daytona Beach, FL
Nelson, James W. ... Brainerd, MN
Nelson, Jan Craig ... Redwood Falls, MN
Nelson, Janai S. ... New York, NY
Nelson, Jane Rakay ... Seattle, WA
Nelson, Janet Allie ... Milwaukee, WI
Nelson, Janice A. ... Columbus, OH
Nelson, Janice M. ... Clarkfield, MN
Montevideo, MN
Nelson, Janis C. ... Los Angeles, CA
Nelson, Jas. A. ... Columbus, OH
Nelson, Jason ... Spokane, WA
Nelson, Jay Scott ... Chicago, IL
Nelson, Jean Marie ... Miami, FL
Nelson, Jeanette M. ... Orange, CA
Nelson, Jeff V. ... New York, NY
Nelson, Jeffery S. ... Visalia, CA
Nelson, Jeffrey A. ... Merced, CA
Nelson, Jeffrey A. ... Bowling Green, OH
Nelson, Jeffrey B. ... Minneapolis, MN
Nelson, Jeffrey C. ... Santa Barbara, CA
Nelson, Jeffrey C. ... Washington, DC
Nelson, Jeffrey M. ... Treasury Department, Internal Revenue Service, GV
Nelson, Jeffrey M. ... St. Paul, MN
Nelson, Jeffrey M. ... Columbia, SC
Nelson, Jeffrey S. ... Kansas City, MO
Nelson, Jeffrey V., P.A.
Fort Lauderdale, FL
Nelson, Jeffrey W. ... Des Moines, IA
Nelson, Jeffry H. ... Arlington, VA
Nelson, Jennifer Charno
Kansas City, MO
Nelson, Jennifer E. ... Burlington, VT
Nelson, Jennifer N. ... Boston, MA
Nelson, Jeremy D. ... Palo Alto, CA
Nelson, Jerold O. ... Minneapolis, MN
Nelson, Jerold T. ... Chicago, IL
Nelson, Jerry C. ... Colorado Springs, CO
Nelson, Jerry M. ... Tampa, FL
Nelson, Jill B. ... Denver, CO
Nelson, Jill L.
Merit Systems Protection Board, Office of Appeals Counsel, GV
Nelson, Jo ... Houston, TX
Nelson, Joan L. ... Hyannis, MA
Nelson, Jodi L. ... Lincoln, NE
Nelson, Joel D. ... Lincoln, NE
Nelson, Joel Edward ... St. Paul, MN
Nelson, Joellyn ... Chicago, IL
Nelson, John A. ... Homosassa, FL
Inverness, FL
Nelson, John A. ... St. Cloud, MN
Nelson, John A. ... Willmar, MN
Nelson, John A. ... New York, NY
Nelson, John A. ... Milwaukee, WI
Nelson, John B. ... Dallas, TX
Nelson, John C. ... Fullerton, CA
Nelson, John C. ... Newport Beach, CA
Nelson, John C. ... Sioux City, IA
Nelson, John C. ... New York, NY
Nelson, John D. ... St. Paul, MN
Nelson, John E. ... Omaha, NE
Nelson, John E. ... Kent, WA
Nelson, John E., Jr. ... Johnstown, PA
Nelson, John F. ... Chambersburg, PA
Nelson, John G. ... Whittier, CA
Nelson, John G. ... Atlanta, GA
Nelson, John G. ... Shreveport, LA
Nelson, John H. ... Pasadena, CA
Nelson, John H. ... Williston Park, NY
Nelson, John K. ... Findlay, OH
Toledo, OH
Nelson, John Keith ... Wichita Falls, TX
Nelson, John L. ... Minneapolis, MN
Nelson, John M. ... Rockford, IL
Nelson, John M. ... Chickasha, OK
Nelson, John N. ... Yuma, AZ
Nelson, John P., II ... Louisville, KY
Nelson, John P., Jr. ... New Orleans, LA
Nelson, John R. ... Santa Barbara, CA
Nelson, John R. ... Westfield, NJ
Nelson, John R. ... Westbury, NY
Nelson, John R. ... Austin, TX
Nelson, John R. ... Milwaukee, WI
Nelson, John Randolph ... Lynchburg, VA
Nelson, John Ray ... Spokane, WA
Nelson, John S. ... Tucson, AZ
Nelson, John S. ... Orange, CA
Nelson, John S. ... Roswell, NM
Nelson, John S. ... Painesville, OH
Nelson, John W. ... Phoenix, AZ
Nelson, John W. ... Orange, CA
Nelson, John W., A Professional Corporation
Phoenix, AZ
Nelson, Johnson & Malloy, P.C. ... Ogden, IA
Nelson, Jon E. ... Memphis, TN
Nelson, Jon Mark ... Boston, MA
Nelson, Jon O. ... Chicago, IL
Nelson, Jonathan B. ... New York, NY
Nelson, Jonathan D. F. ... Fort Worth, TX
Nelson, Jonathan P. ... Greenwich, CT
Nelson, Jonathan Robert ... New York, NY
Nelson & Jones, Ltd. ... Henderson, MN
Nelson, Joni Lysett ... New York, NY
Nelson, Joseph B. ... Washington, DC
Nelson, Joyce ... San Diego, CA
Nelson, Judith S. ... Miami, FL
Nelson, Julia C. ... San Diego, CA
Nelson, Julie A. ... Washington, DC
Nelson, Julie A. ... Austin, TX
Nelson, Julie Collins ... Oakland, CA
Nelson, Julie Mathis ... Phoenix, AZ
Nelson & Kalbfleisch ... Shelby, MT
Nelson, Kara E. ... Milwaukee, WI
Nelson, Karen Cherese ... Jefferson City, MO
Nelson, Karen E. ... Boston, MA
Nelson, Karen S. ... Portland, OR
Nelson, Karen S. ... Dallas, TX
Nelson, Karl A. ... Shell Rock, IA
Nelson, Karl G. ... Dallas, TX
Nelson, Karl J. ... Baltimore, MD
Nelson, Karmen M. ... Minneapolis, MN
Nelson, Karolyn King ... Houston, TX
Nelson, Katharine F. ... Harrisburg, PA
Nelson, Katharine M. ... Kansas City, MO
Nelson, Katherine A. ... Enola, PA
Nelson, Katherine B. ... Austin, TX
Nelson, Katherine Parks ... Mobile, AL
Nelson, Kathleen A. ... Los Angeles, CA
Nelson, Kathleen A. ... Seattle, WA
Nelson, Kathleen E. ... Boston, MA
Nelson, Kathryn B. ... Tucson, AZ
Nelson, Kathryn J. ... Tacoma, WA
Nelson, Kathryn M. ... San Jose, CA
Nelson, Kathy Lynne ... Oklahoma City, OK
Nelson, Katy A. ... Los Angeles, CA
Nelson, Kay Neill ... Los Angeles, CA
Nelson, Keisha T. ... Chicago, IL
Nelson, Keith A. ... Long Beach, CA
Nelson, Keith M. ... Dallas, TX
Nelson, Keith R. ... Faribault, MN
Nelson, Keith R. ... Moultonborough, NH
Nelson, Kelly C. ... Warrenton, MO
Nelson & Kennard ... Sacramento, CA
Nelson, Kennard F. ... Laramie, WY
Nelson, Kenneth B. ... Chicago, IL
Nelson, Kenneth D. ... Minneapolis, MN
Nelson, Kenneth E. ... Kansas City, MO
Nelson, Kenneth L. ... Santa Barbara, CA
Nelson, Kenneth M. ... Portland, ME
Nelson, Kenneth W. ... Brockport, NY
Nelson, Kent E. ... Boise, ID
Nelson, Kerry P. ... Philadelphia, PA
Nelson, Kevin ... Oklahoma City, OK
Nelson, Kevin A. ... Charleston, WV
Nelson, Keys, Keys & Schultz, P.C.
Rock Island, IL
Nelson, Kilgus & Richey ... Morrison, IL
Nelson, Kimberly A. ... Winter Park, FL
Nelson, Kinder, Mosseau & Saturley, P.C.
Manchester, NH
Nelson, Kirby D. ... Boise, ID
Nelson, Kit L. ... Malibu, CA
Nelson, Kory A. ... Denver, CO
Nelson and Kreuger, Professional Corporation ... Grand Rapids, MI
Nelson, Kristen A. ... St. Paul, MN
Nelson, Kristen C. ... Minneapolis, MN
Nelson, Kristen Kay ... Orange, CA
Nelson, Kristi ... Chicago, IL
Nelson, Kristi A. ... Anchorage, AK
Nelson, Kristi P. ... Hebron, KY
Nelson, Krysia Carmel ... Charlottesville, VA
Nelson and Kuhn, Ltd. ... Glenwood, MN
Starbuck, MN
Nelson, Kurt A. ... Silver Spring, MD
Nelson, Kurt T., (P.C.) ... Houston, TX
Nelson, L. Bruce ... Denver, CO
Nelson, L. Michele ... Tulsa, OK
Nelson, L. Willard ... Morrison, IL
Nelson, Lance B. ... Anchorage, AK
Nelson, Lance J. ... West Chester, PA
Nelson, Larry A. ... Canton, SD
Lennox, SD
Nelson, Larry E. ... Dodgeville, WI
Nelson, Larry J. ... Leland, MI
Nelson, Larry N. ... Dublin, OH
Nelson, Larry R. ... Los Angeles, CA
Nelson, Laura S. ... Washington, DC
Nelson, Laurel M. ... Denver, CO
Nelson, Lauren Bethany ... Boston, MA
Nelson, Laurie C. ... New York, NY
Nelson Law Firm, P.C. ... Kansas City, MO
Nelson Law Firm, P.C. ... Billings, MT
Nelson Law Offices, P.A. ... Hopkins, MN
Nelson, Lawrence A. ... Rockford, IL
Nelson, Lawrence E. ... Puyallup, WA
Nelson, Lawrence J. ... San Francisco, CA
Nelson, Lawrence J. ... Bloomington, IL
Nelson, Lawrence W.
Englewood Cliffs, NJ
Nelson, Lawrence W. ... Seattle, WA
Nelson, Lee B. ... St. Paul, MN
Nelson, Lee Edward ... Tampa, FL
Nelson, Leif ... Grand Rapids, MN
Nelson, Leigh ... Houston, TX
Nelson, Leonard A. ... Chicago, IL
Nelson, Leonard J., III ... Birmingham, AL
Nelson, Leonard M. ... Portland, ME
Nelson, Leonard S. ... Ogden, IA
Nelson, LeRoy W. ... Kissimmee, FL
Nelson, Lester ... New York, NY
Nelson, Lewin G., Jr. ... Marshfield, MA
Nelson, Lewis N. ... Oakland, CA
Nelson, Liesl E. ... Hudson, WI
Nelson, Linda Ferroli ... Fort Lauderdale, FL
Nelson, Linda I. ... Greensburg, PA
Nelson, Linda J. ... New Orleans, LA
Nelson, Linda K. ... Tacoma, WA
Nelson, Linda M. ... Framingham, MA
Nelson, Linda Phyllis ... Tallahassee, FL
Nelson, Lisa A. ... Des Moines, IA
Nelson, Lisa B. ... Anchorage, AK
Nelson, Lisa E. ... Chicago, IL
Nelson, Lisa J. ... Minneapolis, MN
Nelson, Lisa "Li" Shearer ... Tallahassee, FL
Nelson, Lori Ellen ... Daytona Beach, FL
Nelson, Lori W. ... Salt Lake City, UT
Nelson, Louis V. ... Beaumont, TX
Nelson, Louise C. ... Los Angeles, CA
Nelson, Lowell H. ... Morris, MN
Wheaton, MN
Nelson, Lowell Y. ... Medford, OR
Nelson, Luella E. ... Oakland, CA
Nelson, Luther A., Jr. ... Denton, TX
Nelson, Lyle R. ... Oklahoma City, OK
Nelson, Lyle R., P.C. ... Oklahoma City, OK
Tulsa, OK
Nelson, Lyndon P. ... West St. Paul, MN
Nelson, Lynn Alan ... Keyser, WV
Nelson, Lynn B. ... Kansas City, MO
Nelson, Lynn F. ... Orlando, FL
Nelson, Lynn R. ... Gooding, ID
Nelson, M. Dean ... Daytona Beach, FL
Nelson, M. Forest ... Dallas, TX
Nelson, M. John ... Redwood City, CA
Nelson, M. Judith ... Sacramento, CA
Nelson & MacNeil, P.C. ... Albany, OR
Nelson, Malcolm D. ... Department of Labor, Office of Secretary, GV
Nelson, Manson ... Richmond Hill, GA
Nelson, Manuel C. ... New York, NY
Nelson, Marcia M. ... Seattle, WA
Nelson, Maren E. ... Los Angeles, CA
Nelson, Margaret A. ... Omaha, NE
Nelson, Margaret A. ... Lynchburg, VA
Nelson, Margaret H. ... San Bernardino, CA
Nelson, Margaret H. ... Concord, NH
Nelson, Margaret M. ... Gloucester, MA
Nelson, Maria K. ... Los Angeles, CA
Nelson, Marilyn E., Law Offices of
Washington, DC
Nelson, Marilyn E., Law Offices of
Bethesda, MD
Nelson, Marilyn H. ... Beverly Hills, CA
Nelson, Mark A. ... Oxnard, CA
Nelson, Mark A. ... Bradenton, FL
Nelson, Mark A. ... Atlanta, GA
Nelson, Mark A ... Hattiesburg, MS
Nelson, Mark C. ... Tuscaloosa, AL
Nelson, Mark C. ... Dallas, TX
Nelson, Mark D. ... Chicago, IL
Nelson, Mark E. ... Boston, MA
Nelson, Mark J. ... Union City, NJ
Nelson, Mark J. ... Charlottesville, VA
Nelson, Mark L. ... Los Angeles, CA
Nelson, Mark L. ... Schaumburg, IL
Nelson, Mark R. ... Indianapolis, IN
Nelson, Mark S. ... Modesto, CA
Nelson, Mark S. ... Brookfield, WI
Nelson, Mark T. ... Detroit, MI
Nelson, Mark W. ... Washington, DC
Nelson, Mark W. ... Department of Labor, Office of the Solicitor, GV
Nelson, Mark W. ... Bel Air, MD
Nelson, Marlene Mathes ... Chicago, IL
Nelson, Marshall J. ... Seattle, WA
Nelson, Martin R. ... Denver, CO
Nelson, Martin R. ... Littleton, CO
Nelson, Martin S. ... Kirkland, WA
Nelson, Mary Alleruzzo ... Woodbridge, NJ
Nelson, Mary Ann ... Boston, MA
Nelson, Mary E. ... Oklahoma City, OK
Nelson, Mary E. ... Milwaukee, WI
Nelson, Mary Elizabeth ... St. Louis, MO
Nelson, Mary P. ... Detroit, MI
Nelson, Matthew ... Denver, CO
Nelson, Matthew D. ... Lexington, KY
Nelson, Matthew L. ... Costa Mesa, CA
Nelson, Matthew W. ... San Diego, CA
Nelson, Maureen ... Washington, DC
Nelson, Maurice A. ... Niles, MI
Nelson, Maurice O. ... Fort Collins, CO
Nelson, Maurice S. ... Cambridge, MD
Nelson & McClellan ... Omaha, NE
Nelson, McCormick, Hancock & Newton
Houston, TX
Nelson, McMahan & Noblett
Chattanooga, TN
Nelson, McPherson, Summers & Santos, L.C.
Staunton, VA
Nelson, Melissa L. ... Hartford, CT
Nelson, Melissa Morgan ... Seattle, WA
Nelson, Mellie H. ... Department of Justice, Civil Rights Division, GV
Nelson, Merrill F. ... Salt Lake City, UT
Nelson, Michael ... New York, NY
Nelson, Michael A. ... Portland, ME
Nelson, Michael A. ... Spokane, WA
Nelson, Michael D. ... Danville, CA
Nelson, Michael D. ... Omaha, NE
Nelson, Michael D. ... New York, NY
Nelson, Michael D. ... West Fargo, ND
Nelson, Michael E. ... Seattle, WA
Nelson, Michael G. ... Newport Beach, CA
Nelson, Michael G. ... Erie, PA
Nelson, Michael H. ... Dallas, TX
Nelson, Michael J. ... Irvine, CA
Nelson, Michael J. ... Sacramento, CA
Nelson, Michael J. ... Newark, NJ
Nelson, Michael L., Sr. ... Cleveland, OH
Nelson, Michael O. ... Lafayette, CA
Nelson, Michael R. ... Sacramento, CA
Nelson, Michael R. ... Morristown, NJ
Nelson, Michael R. ... Philadelphia, PA
Nelson, Michael S. ... New York, NY
Nelson, Michael S. ... Pittsburgh, PA
Nelson, Michel W. ... Carroll, IA
Nelson, Michele ... Redondo Beach, CA
Nelson, Michele I. ... West Palm Beach, FL
Nelson, Michele J. ... Atlanta, GA
Nelson, Michele S. ... Daytona Beach, FL
Nelson, Michelle Clarice ... Tulsa, OK
Nelson, Miles R. ... Midland, TX
Odessa, TX
Nelson, Milton E., Jr. ... Park Ridge, IL
Nelson, Mitchell J. ... New York, NY
Nelson, Molly Anne ... Boston, MA
Nelson, Morrow & Waldron ... Omaha, NE
Nelson, Moses ... Bay Shore, NY
Nelson Mullins Riley & Scarborough, L.L.P.
Atlanta, GA
Charlotte, NC
Charleston, SC
Columbia, SC
Greenville, SC
Lexington, SC
Myrtle Beach, SC
Nelson, N. Royce ... Salina, KS
Nelson, Nancy ... New York, NY
Nelson, Nancy C. ... Stillwater, MN
Nelson, Nancy J. ... Chatsworth, CA
Nelson, Nancy Jo ... Washington, DC
Nelson, Nancy K. ... Lake Elsinore, CA
Nelson, Nancy Lee ... Minneapolis, MN
Nelson, Nancy Stockslager ... Jackson, TN
Nelson, Narissa G. ... Foley, AL
Nelson & Natale, LLP ... Los Angeles, CA
Nelson, Natalie Elaine ... Dobbs Ferry, NY
Nelson, Nathan J. ... Minneapolis, MN
Nelson, Neal H., Jr. ... Roseville, MN
Nelson, Neal P. ... Lincoln, NE
Nelson, Nehru R. ... Philadelphia, PA
Nelson, Neil G. ... Shakopee, MN
Nelson, Nels B., Jr. ... Tacoma, WA
Nelson & Nelson ... Orange, CA
Nelson & Nelson ... New York, NY
Nelson & Nelson ... Portland, OR
Nelson & Nelson ... Ebensburg, PA
Nelson & Nelson ... Lubbock, TX
Nelson & Nelson LLP ... Washington, DC
Bethesda, MD
Nelson & Nelson, P.C. ... Belleville, IL
Nelson, Nelson Story, (P.C.) ... Phoenix, AZ
Nelson, Nelson Story, (P.C.) ... Phoenix, AZ
Nelson, Nicole H. ... Portland, OR
Nelson, Nikole ... Albany, OR
Nelson, Noel J. ... Mobile, AL
Nelson, Norman B. ... Mount Vernon, WA
Nelson, Norman C. ... Chicago, IL
Nelson, Norman E. ... Washington, DC
Nelson, Norman J. ... Houston, TX
Nelson, Norman L. "Happy", Jr.
Dallas, TX
Nelson, Norman L. "Happy", Jr.
Richardson, TX
Nelson, Norman R. ... New York, NY
Nelson, O. Wade ... Nashville, TN
Nelson, Obenland and Doebbert
Glenwood, MN
Nelson, Oliver W. ... Rockford, IL
Nelson, Oliver W., P.C. ... Rockford, IL
Nelson, Otha C., Sr. ... Lake Charles, LA
Nelson Oyen Torvik ... Appleton, MN
Clarkfield, MN
Montevideo, MN
Nelson, P. Keith ... Salt Lake City, UT
Nelson, Pamela C.
Federal Deposit Insurance Corporation, Corporate Affairs Section, GV
Nelson, Pamela J. ... Jacksonville, FL
Nelson, Pamela Miller ... Orange, CA
Nelson, Parker ... Dallas, TX
Nelson, Patience Robinson ... Pittsburgh, PA
Nelson, Patricia S. ... Lexington, MA
Nelson, Patrick G. ... Huntsville, AL
Nelson, Patrick J. ... Kansas City, MO
Nelson, Patrick J. ... Kearney, NE
Nelson, Paul A. ... St. Petersburg, FL
Nelson, Paul A. ... Montevideo, MN
Nelson, Paul C. ... Chicago, IL
Nelson, Paul D. ... San Francisco, CA
Nelson, Paul D. ... St. Paul, MN
Nelson, Paul D. ... Media, PA
Nelson, Paul L. ... Grand Rapids, MI

Nelson, Paul M. ..... Lake Oswego, OR
Nelson, Paul S. ..... Chicago, IL
Nelson, Paul S. ..... Seattle, WA
Nelson, Peggy A., Law Offices of
Chicago, IL
Nelson, Peggy J. ..... Taos, NM
Nelson, Peggy L. ..... Moorhead, MN
Nelson, Perlov & Lee, A Professional Corporation ..... Los Altos, CA
Nelson, Peter A. ..... Department of Commerce, Patent and Trademark Office, GV
Nelson, Peter C. ..... Rochester, NY
Nelson, Peter H. ..... West Berlin, NJ
Nelson, Peter Martin ..... Los Angeles, CA
Nelson, Peter R. ..... Westlake Village, CA
Nelson, Peter S. ..... Appleton, WI
Nelson, Philip A., Jr. ..... Austin, TX
Nelson, Philip I. ..... Minneapolis, MN
Nelson, Philip L. ..... Astoria, OR
Nelson, Philip L. ..... Grants Pass, OR
Nelson, Philip P., (P.C.) ..... Jasper, AL
Nelson, Phillip J. ..... Grand Rapids, MI
Nelson, Phillip L. ..... Altus, OK
Nelson, Phillip M. ..... Madison, MS
Nelson, Polly J. ..... Washington, DC
Nelson, R. Scott ..... Denver, CO
Nelson, R. Stephen, Jr. ..... New York, NY
Nelson, Ralph S. ..... Kennesaw, GA
Nelson, Randall C. ..... Phoenix, AZ
Nelson, Randall C. ..... Redding, CA
Nelson, Randall G. ..... Billings, MT
Nelson, Randall L. ..... Chattanooga, TN
Nelson, Randy A. ..... Dallas, TX
Nelson, Randy S. ..... Milwaukee, WI
Nelson Rasmussen & Christensen, A Professional Corporation
Salt Lake City, UT
Nelson, Ray E. ..... Burnsville, MN
Nelson, Raymond H. ..... Des Plaines, IL
Nelson, Rebecca ..... Millburn, NJ
New York, NY
Nelson, Rebecca A. ..... Sioux City, IA
Nelson, Rebecca A.D. ..... St. Louis, MO
Nelson, Regina A. ..... Washington, DC
Nelson, Reid ..... Indianapolis, IN
Nelson, Reid A. ..... San Antonio, TX
Nelson, Rhonda L. ..... San Francisco, CA
Nelson, Richard A. ..... Arlington Heights, IL
Nelson, Richard A. ..... Minneapolis, MN
Nelson, Richard A., & Associates
Arlington Heights, IL
Nelson, Richard C. ..... Mankato, MN
Nelson, Richard C. ..... Minneapolis, MN
Nelson, Richard C. ..... Manchester, NH
Nelson, Richard C. ..... Seattle, WA
Nelson, Richard D. ..... San Francisco, CA
Nelson, Richard D. ..... Chicago, IL
Nelson, Richard D. ..... Cincinnati, OH
Nelson, Richard D. ..... Portland, OR
Nelson, Richard E. ..... Sarasota, FL
Nelson, Richard E. ..... Milwaukee, WI
Nelson, Richard F. ..... Mountain Home, AR
Nelson, Richard J. ..... San Jose, CA
Nelson, Richard J. L. ..... Walnut Creek, CA
Nelson, Richard L. ..... Charlotte, NC
Nelson, Richard L. ..... Dallas, TX
Nelson, Richard N. ..... Toledo, OH
Nelson, Richard R. ..... Los Angeles, CA
Nelson, Richard R. ..... Grosse Pointe Park, MI
Nelson, Richard R., II ..... Pittsburgh, PA
Nelson, Richard S. ..... Des Moines, IA
Nelson, Richard T. ..... San Diego, CA
Nelson, Richard W. ..... Roseville, MN
Nelson, Rick ..... Olivette, MO
Nelson & Riemenschneider ..... Ukiah, CA
Nelson, Robb A. ..... Englewood, CO
Nelson, Robert A. ..... Helena, MT
Nelson, Robert A. ..... Seaford, NY
Nelson, Robert A., Jr. ..... Washington, DC
Nelson, Robert Allan ..... Ponchatoula, LA
Nelson, Robert B. ..... Cleveland, OH
Nelson, Robert C. ..... Belleville, IL
Nelson, Robert C. ..... Wenatchee, WA
Nelson, Robert D. ..... Stockton, CA
Nelson, Robert D. ..... Chicago, IL
Nelson, Robert D. ..... Exira, IA
Nelson, Robert Don ..... Tucson, AZ
Nelson, Robert E. ..... Englewood, CO
Nelson, Robert E. ..... Aurora, IL
Nelson, Robert E. ..... Gresham, OR
Nelson, Robert E. ..... Green Bay, WI
Nelson, Robert F. ..... Brookfield, WI
Nelson, Robert J. ..... San Francisco, CA
Nelson, Robert L. ..... San Rafael, CA
Nelson, Robert L. ..... Washington, DC
Nelson, Robert L. ..... Grand Rapids, MI
Nelson, Robert L. ..... Cheyenne, WY
Nelson, Robert L., Jr. ..... Menlo Park, CA
Nelson, Robert M. ..... Cleveland, OH
Nelson, Robert N. ..... Baldwin, NY
Nelson, Robert P. ..... Madison, WI
Nelson, Robert R. ..... Elmhurst, IL
Nelson, Robert R. ..... Sioux Falls, SD
Nelson, Robert W. ..... Denver, CO
Nelson, Robert W. ..... El Reno, OK
Oklahoma City, OK
Nelson, Robert W. ..... San Antonio, TX
Nelson, Robt. T. ..... Orinda, CA
Nelson, Roderick K. ..... Birmingham, AL
Nelson, Rodney A. ..... Newark, OH
Nelson, Rodney K. ..... Yakima, WA
Nelson & Roediger ..... Phoenix, AZ
Nelson, Roger A.
Environmental Protection Agency, Program Office Attorneys, GV
Nelson, Roger A. ..... Portland, OR
Nelson, Roger A., P.C. ..... Portland, OR
Nelson, Roger C., Jr. ..... Wheaton, IL
Nelson, Rolf T. ..... Brooklyn Center, MN
Nelson, Ron ..... Great Falls, MT
Nelson, Ronald E. ..... Statesboro, GA
Nelson, Ronald Emery, P.C. ..... Statesboro, GA
Nelson, Ronald J. ..... Barrington, IL
Nelson, Ronald J. ..... Scotch Plains, NJ
Nelson, Ronald J. ..... Carrollton, TX
Nelson, Ronald L. ..... Pensacola, FL
Nelson, Ronald P. ..... Valparaiso, IN
Nelson, Ronald W. ..... San Francisco, CA
Nelson, Ronald W. ..... Overland Park, KS
Nelson, Roscoe C., Jr. ..... Portland, OR
Nelson, Rosemary ..... New York, NY
Nelson, Roy E. ..... Laurel, MD
Nelson, Roy H. ..... Milwaukee, WI
Nelson, Roy L., II ..... Las Vegas, NV
Nelson, Roy P. ..... Dearborn, MI
Nelson, Ruth L. ..... Woodstock, IL
Nelson Ryan & Kochems ..... Mercer, PA
Nelson, Ryan L. ..... Cincinnati, OH
Nelson, S. Anderson ..... Clarksville, VA
Nelson, Samuel M. ..... Winter Park, FL
Nelson, Sandra A. ..... Lebanon, NH
Nelson, Sandra M. ..... Fergus Falls, MN
Nelson & Schmeling ..... Green Bay, WI
Nelson, Schubert & McKechnie
Grand Forks, ND
Nelson, Scott ..... Chicago, IL
Nelson, Scott ..... Houston, TX
Nelson, Scott David ..... Houston, TX
Nelson, Scott J. ..... Dubuque, IA
Nelson, Scott L. ..... Washington, DC
Nelson, Scott M. ..... Scottsdale, AZ
Nelson, Scott M. ..... Chicago, IL
Nelson, Scott M. ..... Minneapolis, MN
Nelson, Scott Michael ..... Houston, TX
Nelson, Scott O. ..... Pascagoula, MS
Nelson, Shari Dennis ..... Los Angeles, CA
Nelson, Sharon D. ..... Baltimore, MD
Nelson, Sharon L. ..... Las Vegas, NV
Nelson, Sharon L. ..... Olympia, WA
Nelson, Sharon T. ..... Washington, DC
Nelson, Shawn J. ..... Los Angeles, CA
Nelson, Sheffield ..... Little Rock, AR
Nelson, Sheila Gropper ..... San Francisco, CA
Nelson, Shelton R. ..... Mabelvale, AR
Nelson, Sherlee Stanford ..... Bethesda, MD
Nelson, Sherwin M. ..... Hartford, CT
Nelson, Sheryl C. ..... Kansas City, MO
Nelson, Shirley A. ..... Sacramento, CA
Nelson, Siri C., (Ms.) ..... Seattle, WA
Nelson & Smith, L.L.P. ..... Macon, GA
Nelson, Snuffer & Dahle ..... Sandy, UT
Nelson, Stan F. ..... Houston, TX
Nelson, Stephanie ..... Houston, TX
Nelson, Stephanie, P.C. ..... Houston, TX
Nelson, Stephen ..... Arlington, VA
Nelson, Stephen A. ..... Olympia, WA
Nelson, Stephen C. ..... Cedar Rapids, IA
Nelson, Stephen G. ..... San Diego, CA
Nelson, Stephen H. ..... Miami, FL
Nelson, Stephen J. ..... St. Petersburg, FL
Nelson, Stephen L. ..... Mather, CA
Santa Monica, CA
Nelson, Stephen L. ..... St. Paul, MN
Nelson, Stephen P. ..... Jacksonville, FL
Nelson, Stephen R. ..... Albuquerque, NM
Nelson, Steven A. ..... Gold River, CA
Nelson, Steven A. ..... Lilburn, GA
Nelson, Steven A. ..... International Falls, MN
Nelson, Steven C. ..... San Diego, CA
Nelson, Steven C. ..... Minneapolis, MN
Nelson, Steven D. ..... Union, NJ
Nelson, Steven D. ..... Austin, TX
Nelson, Steven D. ..... Bellevue, WA
Nelson, Steven E. ..... Asbury Park, NJ
Nelson, Steven J. ..... Covina, CA
Nelson, Steven J. ..... Escondido, CA
Nelson, Steven L. ..... Rock Island, IL
Nelson, Steven L. ..... Des Moines, IA
Nelson, Steven L. ..... Milwaukee, WI
Nelson, Steven S. ..... Portsmouth, VA
Nelson, Steven V. ..... San Ramon, CA
Nelson & Stipp, Professional Corporation
Hoopeston, IL
Nelson, Stuart A. ..... Fort Lauderdale, FL
Nelson, Stuart K. ..... New York, NY
Nelson, Sue Ann ..... Minneapolis, MN
Nelson, Susan A. ..... San Diego, CA
Nelson, Susan B. ..... Toledo, OH
Nelson, Susan C. ..... St. Cloud, MN
Nelson, Susan H. ..... Bloomington, IN
Nelson, Susan I. ..... Dallas, TX
Nelson, Susan Jane ..... Madison, WI
Nelson, Susan M. ..... San Marino, CA
Nelson, Susan Rantala ..... Ada, MN
Nelson, Susan Richard ..... Minneapolis, MN
Nelson, Sven K. ..... Tacoma, WA
Nelson, Sweet & Hurley ..... Painesville, OH
Nelson, Sydney B. ..... Shreveport, LA
Nelson, T. Delbert, (P.C.) ..... Mesa, AZ
Nelson, T. Leverett ..... Chicago, IL
Nelson, Tad A., & Associates
Galveston, TX
Nelson, Tamara K. ..... Tallahassee, FL
Nelson, Tamara K. ..... Seattle, WA
Nelson, Ted J. ..... Tulsa, OK
Nelson, Teresa A. ..... Johnson City, TN
Nelson, Teresa L. ..... Oakland, CA
Nelson, Terry A. ..... Huntington Beach, CA
Nelson, Terry D. ..... Madison, WI
Nelson, Terry S. ..... Fort Myers, FL
Nelson, Thelma G. ..... Los Angeles, CA
Nelson, Theodore R.
Bay Harbor Islands, FL
Nelson, Theresa L. ..... Los Angeles, CA
Nelson, Thomas A. ..... New Roads, LA
Nelson, Thomas A. ..... Rhinelander, WI
Nelson, Thomas A., III ..... Elkins Park, PA
Nelson, Thomas A., Jr. ..... Denver, CO
Nelson, Thomas B. ..... Waukegan, IL
Nelson, Thomas C. ..... San Diego, CA
Nelson, Thomas C. ..... Lansing, MI
Nelson, Thomas C. ..... Dallas, TX
Nelson, Thomas E. ..... Washington, DC
Nelson, Thomas E. ..... St. Joseph, MI
Nelson, Thomas E., A Prof. Corp., Law Offices of ..... Salt Lake City, UT
Nelson, Thomas Edward ..... Nashville, TN
Nelson, Thomas F. ..... Los Altos, CA
Nelson, Thomas F. ..... Minneapolis, MN
Nelson, Thomas F. ..... Pittsburgh, PA
Nelson, Thomas G. ..... Boise, ID
Nelson, Thomas G. ..... Marshalltown, IA
Nelson, Thomas H. ..... Seattle, WA
Nelson, Thomas H., & Associates, Law Offices ..... Portland, OR
Nelson, Thomas J., III ..... Laguna Hills, CA
Nelson, Thomas Kevin ..... Amarillo, TX
Nelson, Thomas Patrick
Dearborn Heights, MI
Nelson, Thomas R. ..... Chicago, IL
Nelson, Thomas R. ..... Austin, TX
Nelson, Thomas S. ..... Carrollton, TX
Nelson, Thomas W. ..... Buffalo, NY
Nelson, Thomas W. ..... Ebensburg, PA
Nelson, Timothy A. ..... Phoenix, AZ
Nelson, Timothy C. ..... Sacramento, CA
Nelson, Timothy D. ..... San Francisco, CA
Nelson, Timothy F. ..... New York, NY
Nelson, Timothy W. ..... St. Cloud, MN
Nelson, Todd A. ..... Palo Alto, CA
Nelson, Todd A. ..... Tampa, FL
Nelson, Todd A. ..... Oklahoma City, OK
Nelson, Todd M. ..... Seattle, WA
Nelson, Todd N. ..... Las Vegas, NV
Nelson, Toni M. ..... Honolulu, HI
Nelson, Tracy Michelle ..... Atlanta, GA
Nelson, Troy D. ..... Friendswood, TX
Nelson, Troy Y. ..... Spokane, WA
Nelson and Tyler ..... Seattle, WA
Nelson & VanHon ..... Redwood Falls, MN
Nelson, Varuni ..... Brooklyn, NY
Nelson & Vencill ..... San Ramon, CA
Nelson, Vicki L. ..... Billings, MT
Nelson, Victor S. ..... Wichita, KS
Nelson, Victoria L. ..... Las Vegas, NV
Nelson, Vincent E. ..... Napa, CA
Nelson, Virginia C. ..... San Diego, CA
Nelson, W. Blair ..... Conroe, TX
Nelson, W. Dan ..... Edmond, OK
Nelson, W. Don ..... Lincoln, NE
Nelson, Wallace J. ..... Hampton, VA
Nelson & Walrod ..... Union City, NJ
Nelson, Walter E., Jr. ..... Moorestown, NJ
Nelson, Walter R. ..... Pacifica, CA
Nelson, Ward W. ..... Chattanooga, TN
Nelson, Warren H., Jr. ..... San Diego, CA
Nelson, Warren Lee ..... Newport Beach, CA
Nelson, Wayne C. ..... Zephyrhills, FL
Nelson, Wayne G. ..... Minneapolis, MN
Nelson, Wayne W. ..... Vancouver, WA
Nelson, Wesley D. ..... San Antonio, TX
Nelson & Widom LLP ..... Bronx, NY
Brooklyn, NY
New York, NY
Nelson, Wilbur T. ..... Boise, ID
Nelson, Wilfrid D. ..... Atlanta, GA
Houston, TX
Nelson, Will L. ..... Columbia, MO
Nelson, William A. ..... Alexandria, VA
Nelson, William B. ..... Houston, TX
Nelson, William C. ..... River Ridge, LA
Nelson, William C. ..... Lincoln, NE
Nelson, William D. ..... Tucson, AZ
Nelson, William D. ..... Denver, CO
Nelson, William E. ..... La Jolla, CA
Nelson, William E. ..... Hoopeston, IL
Nelson, William E. ..... Bethesda, MD
Nelson, William E. ..... Cincinnati, OH
Nelson, William F. ..... Atlanta, GA
Nelson, William F. ..... Vancouver, WA
Nelson, William J. ..... Fort Myers, FL
Nelson, William J. ..... Indianapolis, IN
Nelson, William J., Jr. ..... Michigan City, IN
Nelson, William K. ..... New City, NY
Nelson, William L. ..... Phoenix, AZ
Nelson, William L. ..... Los Angeles, CA
Nelson, William L. ..... Winston-Salem, NC
Nelson, William L., III ..... Irvine, CA
Long Beach, CA
Nelson, William M. ..... Columbus, OH
Nelson, William R. ..... Gallipolis, OH
Nelson, William W. ..... Raleigh, NC
Nelson, Wilson & Wilson, P.C.
Detroit, MI
Nelson, Wincel C., Jr. ..... Omaha, NE
Nelson, Wyman A. ..... Buffalo, MN
Nelson, Wyman E. ..... Blair, NE
Nelson, Wyman E., P.C. ..... Blair, NE
Nelson-Archer, Joshua C. ..... Texarkana, TX
Nelson-Holmdahl, Susan L. ..... San Jose, CA
Nelson-Laduca, Laurel M. ..... Escondido, CA
Nelson-Reade, Patricia A. ..... Portland, ME
Nelthropp, Albert V. F. ..... Allentown, PA
Neltner, Michael ..... Cincinnati, OH
Nelton, Peter S. ..... Balsam Lake, WI
Nelton & Swanson ..... Balsam Lake, WI
Neman, Albert H. ..... Cincinnati, OH
Neman, Patrick J. ..... Akron, OH
Nemanich, Scott E. ..... Chicago, IL
Nemanick, Colleen H. ..... Creve Coeur, MO
St. Louis, MO
Nemarow, Jeryl L. ..... Rye, NY
Nemazi, John E. ..... Southfield, MI
Nembach, Paul A. ..... Hauppauge, NY
Nemchek, Edward F. ..... Stamford, CT
Nemcik-Cruz, Rick ..... San Juan, PR
Nemec, Aaron H. ..... Boise, ID
Nemec, Alicia M. ..... Jarrell, TX
Nemec, Anna L. ..... Black River Falls, WI
Nemec, Douglas R. ..... New York, NY
Nemec, Gary A.
Department of Housing and Urban Development, Office of General Counsel, GV
Nemec, Gerald R. ..... Houston, TX
Nemec, Kenneth J., Jr. ..... Summit, IL
Nemec, Michael A. ..... Pittsburgh, PA
Nemec, Michael L. ..... Tulsa, OK
Nemec, Nicole V. ..... Peoria, IL
Nemecek & Cole, A Professional Corporation
Los Angeles, CA
Sherman Oaks, CA
Nemecek, David P., Jr ..... Los Angeles, CA
Nemecek, Frank W. ..... Sherman Oaks, CA
Nemecek, Jeffrey A. ..... New York, NY
Nemecek, Philip A. ..... New York, NY
Nemecek, Steven D. ..... Phoenix, AZ
Nemecek, Vennie E. ..... Anchorage, AK
Nemechek, Kathleen M. ..... Kansas City, MO
Nemechek, Timothy L. ..... Denver, CO
Nemeh, Katherine H. ..... Harper Woods, MI
Nemelka, Carl J. ..... Houston, TX
Nemelka, Joseph ..... Little Rock, AR
Nemelka, Richard S. ..... Salt Lake City, UT
Nemenoff, Brian M. ..... Peoria, IL
Nemer, Bruce A. ..... Minneapolis, MN
Nemer, David B., Jr. ..... San Francisco, CA
Nemer, Elaine F. ..... Foster City, CA
Nemer, Gary ..... San Francisco, CA
Nemer, R. Guy Eric ..... Birmingham, MI
Nemer, Raule Gail ..... Evergreen, CO
Nemer, Stanley ..... Minneapolis, MN
Nemer, William P. ..... Whitehall, WI
Nemergut & Duff ..... Woodbridge, NJ
Nemergut, Paul J., III ..... Woodbridge, NJ
Nemeroff, Michael A. ..... Washington, DC
Nemeroff, Michael A. ..... Chicago, IL
Nemeroff, Milton A. ..... Jenkintown, PA
Nemeroff, Richard I. ..... Dallas, TX
Nemeroff, Robert H. ..... Elkins Park, PA
Nemeroff, Scott M. ..... Washington, DC
Nemeroff, Steven M. ..... College Park, MD
Nemerov, Jeffrey A. ..... New York, NY
Nemerovski, Howard N.
San Francisco, CA
Nemerovski, Leonard J. ..... Wilmette, IL
Nemerovski, Steven H. ..... Chicago, IL
Nemerovsky, Edward M. ..... Jamaica, NY
Nemery, Harold ..... Boca Raton, FL
Nemes, Alan S. ..... St. Louis, MO
Nemes & Anderson ..... Farmington Hills, MI
Nemes, Thomas C. ..... Farmington Hills, MI
Nemeth, Andrew S. ..... Bensalem, PA
Nemeth Burwell, P.C. ..... Detroit, MI
Nemeth, Caborn & Butauski
Columbus, OH
Nemeth, Carol A. ..... Indianapolis, IN
Nemeth, Charles P. ..... Rosslyn Farms, PA
Nemeth, David E., Jr. ..... Costa Mesa, CA
Nemeth, Deborah L. ..... Cheshire, CT
Nemeth, Edward J. ..... Lafayette, IN
Nemeth, Elizabeth Anne ..... Chicago, IL
Nemeth, Eric J. ..... Short Hills, NJ
Nemeth, Eric M. ..... Southfield, MI
Nemeth, Feeney & Masters, P.C.
South Bend, IN
Nemeth, Fred H. ..... Philadelphia, PA
Nemeth, George G. ..... Mineola, NY
Nemeth, J. David ..... Cherry Hill, NJ
Nemeth, John C. ..... Columbus, OH
Nemeth, Joseph G., Jr. ..... Hauppauge, NY
Nemeth, Julius J. ..... Columbus, OH
Nemeth, Karen D. ..... New York, NY
Nemeth, Kathleen Lucas ..... Spokane, WA
Nemeth, Laura D. ..... Cleveland, OH
Nemeth, Lori J. ..... Upper Marlboro, MD
Nemeth, Lynda L. ..... Norwalk, CT
Nemeth, Mark S. ..... Buffalo, NY
Nemeth, Mary T. ..... Detroit, MI
Nemeth, Nick ..... Dallas, TX
Nemeth, Patricia ..... Detroit, MI
Nemeth, Peter G., P.C. ..... Houston, TX
Nemeth, Peter J. ..... South Bend, IN
Nemeth, Philip ..... Gatlinburg, TN
Nemeth, Sandra E. ..... Aztec, NM
Nemeth, Scott J. ..... Eugene, OR
Nemeth, Steven F. ..... Toms River, NJ
Nemeth, Tania M. ..... Butler, NJ
Nemeth, Valerie A. ..... Encinitas, CA
Nemeti, Frank R., Jr. ..... Oneida, NY
Nemeti, Frank R., Sr. ..... Oneida, NY
Nemeti, McDermott, Eppolito & Hedglon
Oneida, NY
Nemetz, Beverly A. ..... Sherman Oaks, CA
Nemetz, Edward ..... Oakland, CA
Nemetz, Gary L., (A P.C.) ..... Menlo Park, CA
Nemetz, J.C. ..... Sherman Oaks, CA
Nemetz, Jerold E. ..... Amityville, NY
Nemetz, Margaret Nottingham ..... Bowie, MD
Nemetz, Mary N. ..... Chesterfield, MO
Nemetz, Miriam R. ..... Washington, DC
Nemeyer, Lori T. ..... Jacksonville, FL
Nemhauser, Nancy ..... Tampa, FL
Nemia, Frank A. ..... Binghamton, NY
Nemiah, James C. ..... Canton, MA
Nemier, Craig L. ..... Farmington Hills, MI
Nemier, Tolari, Landry, Mazzeo & Johnson, P.C. ..... Detroit, MI
Farmington Hills, MI
Nemir, Cygne L. ..... El Paso, TX
Nemir, David W. ..... San Francisco, CA
Nemir, Donald ..... Mill Valley, CA

Nemire, Marleta L. ...Coral Gables, FL
Nemiroff, Alexander ...Rockville, MD
Nemiroff, Andrew P. ...Greenwich, CT
Nemiroff & Auslander, P.A. ...Miami, FL
Nemiroff, Craig ...New York, NY
Nemiroff, Lauren H. ...Van Nuys, CA
Nemiroff, Lori Ann ...Ventura, CA
Nemiroff, Paul G ...Miami, FL
Nemirow, Arnold M. ...Cedar Springs, GA
Nemirow & Hu, PC ...Washington, DC
Nemirow, Laurence E. ...Denver, CO
Nemirow, Lawrence H. ...Los Alamitos, CA
Nemirow, Ronald H. ...Denver, CO
Nemirow, Samuel B. ...Washington, DC
Nemirow, Steven J. ...Portland, OR
Nemish, Kathleen M. ...Dothan, AL
Nemitz, Eugene H., Jr.
New Philadelphia, OH
Nemko, Amy H. ...Washington, DC
Nemkov, Peter M. ...Denver, CO
Nemkov, Peter M., Esq., P.C. ...Denver, CO
Nemlaha, Beatrice H. ...Los Angeles, CA
Nemlaha, Beatrice H., P.C.
Los Angeles, CA
Nemmers, Barry H. ...New York, NY
Nemmers, James C. ...Cedar Rapids, IA
Nemmers, John T. ...Dubuque, IA
Nemo, Anthony J. ...Maplewood, MN
Minneapolis, MN
Nemo, Daniel A. ...New York, NY
Nemo, Fragale & Hypes Co., L.P.A.
Marion, OH
Nemo, Joseph M., Jr. ...Minneapolis, MN
Nemo, Robert C. ...Marion, OH
Nemo, Thomas E. ...Chicago, IL
Nemon, Nancy S. ...Boston, MA
Nemore, L. Richard ...Norwalk, CT
Nemore & Nemore ...Norwalk, CT
Nemoy, Paul I., (Ltd.) ...Chicago, IL
NeMoyer, Edgar C. ...Buffalo, NY
NeMoyer, Patrick H. ...Buffalo, NY
Nemphos, George J. ...Baltimore, MD
Nemrow, Anabel I. ...Miami, FL
Nemrow, Robert Jay ...Coconut Grove, FL
Nemschoff, Louise ...Beverly Hills, CA
Nemschoff, Louise ...Los Angeles, CA
Nemser, Alan ...Garden City, NY
Nemser, Benjamin L. ...North Miami, FL
Nemser, Earl H. ...New York, NY
Nemser, Kathy S. ...Garden City, NY
Nemser & Nemser ...Garden City, NY
Nemser, Paul E. ...Boston, MA
Nemser, Stanley ...New York, NY
Nemsick, Judith R. ...New York, NY
Nemtsev, Irina ...North Miami Beach, FL
Nemtzow, Bernard ...Key Biscayne, FL
Nemvalts, Janet K. ...Chicago, IL
Nemzer, Adam M.
National Labor Relations Board,
Office of Board Members, GV
Nemzer, Kenneth P. ...Belvedere-Tiburon, CA
Nemzin, Robert F. ...Chicago, IL
Nemzura, Marjorie ...Chicago, IL
Nendick, Michael ...Boston, MA
Nene, Frederick R. ...Pittsburgh, PA
Nenney, Milton J. ...Los Angeles, CA
Nenni, Linda J. ...Buffalo, NY
Nenni, Vanessa M. ...Bethlehem, PA
Nenni, Vanessa M. ...Easton, PA
Nennig, Robert E., Jr. ...Chicago, IL
Nenninger, Christopher S. ...Glens Falls, NY
Nenninger, Kyle E. ...Chicago, IL
Nenno, Michael L. ...Olean, NY
Nenno, Richard W. ...Wilmington, DE
Nenos, Byron J., Jr. ...Tampa, FL
Nepal, Rohit ...New York, NY
Neperud, George H. ...Litchfield, MN
Nepf, Ruthe A. ...New York, NY
Nephew, Robert A. ...Atlanta, GA
Nephew, Robert A., P.C. ...Atlanta, GA
Nepola, S. Richard ...Stamford, CT
Nepom, David R. ...Portland, OR
Nepom, Doreen L. ...Milwaukie, OR
Nepom, Marvin S. ...Portland, OR
Nepomuceno, Emmerico T. ...Houston, TX
Nepomuceno, Erwin A. ...Los Angeles, CA
Nepomuceno, Michelle E. ...San Diego, CA
Nepp, Douglas E. ...Minneapolis, MN
Nepper, Allen K. ...Denison, IA
Dunlap, IA
Ute, IA
Neppl, Daniel J. ...Chicago, IL
Neppl, Gregory E. ...Arlington, VA
Neppl, William J. ...Cedar Rapids, IA
Nepple & Associates, PLC
Rock Island, IL
Davenport, IA
Nepple, Frederick C. ...Madison, WI
Nepple, James A. ...Rock Island, IL
Muscatine, IA
Nepple Law Offices, PLC ...Muscatine, IA
Neptune, Frayne D. ...Golden, CO
Neptune, Robert H. ...Harlingen, TX
Neptune, Tyler G., Jr. ...Batavia, IL
Neptune-Rivera, Vivian I. ...San Juan, PR
Nepute, Patrick A. ...Erlanger, KY
Nepveu, Julie ...Washington, DC
Neraas, Nancy M. ...Seattle, WA
Nerat, Frank J., Jr. ...Lansing, MI
Nerath, Gustan ...Royal Oak, MI
Nere, John A., Jr. ...Fredericksburg, VA
Nereim, Mardell, (Ms) ...Chicago, IL
Neren, Sandra L. ...Minneapolis, MN
Nerenberg, Aaron ...Elkins Park, PA
Nerenberg, Eliot J. ...West Hartford, CT
Nerenberg, Jeffrey A. ...Philadelphia, PA
Nerenberg, Jonathon O. ...Hamilton, OH
Nerenberg, Kimberly B. ...Camden, NJ
Nerenberg, Mark E. ...New York, NY
Nerenberg, Mark J. ...Flushing, NY
Nerenberg, Roy ...Washington, DC
Nerenstone, Marc A. ...Fort Myers, FL
Neret, Eduardo E. ...Miami, FL
Nergaard, Diane M. ...New York, NY
Nergaard, Maryann L. ...Somerville, NJ
Nergenah, Regina M. ...Redondo Beach, CA
Nerheim, Lawrence E. ...San Francisco, CA
Neri, Joan M. ...Florham Park, NJ
Neri, Louis R. ...Albany, NY
Ravena, NY
Neri, Mannie ...Syracuse, NY
Neri, Michael G. ...Philadelphia, PA
Neri, Michael S. ...Boston, MA
Neri, Miguel A. ...San Francisco, CA
Neri, Veneard D. ...Boston, NY
Nering, Theodore D., III ...Indianapolis, IN
Nerio, Jesus A. ...Marietta, GA
Nerison, Jane P. ...Houston, TX
Nerison, R. G. ...Jamestown, ND
Nerko, Katherine Perrera ...Garden City, NY
Nerland, Bruce J. ...Minneapolis, MN
Nerland, Gregory S. ...Walnut Creek, CA
Nerland, Lynn Tracy ...Emeryville, CA
Nerlino, Gambale & Klapper LLP
New York, NY
Staten Island, NY
Nern, Christopher C. ...Detroit, MI
Nern, William F. ...Birmingham, MI
Nernberg, A. Richard ...Pittsburgh, PA
Nernberg, Maurice A. ...Pittsburgh, PA
Nernberg, Maurice A., & Associates
Pittsburgh, PA
Nerness, Barbara C. ...Minneapolis, MN
Nerness, Eric A. ...Minneapolis, MN
Nerney, Dennis M. ...San Francisco, CA
Nerney, Philip S. ...Honolulu, HI
Nerney, Susan C. ...Chicago, IL
Nero, Gregory P. ...New York, NY
Nero, James John ...Pebble Beach, CA
Nero, Kerry Gilligan ...Boston, MA
Nero, Margaret A. ...Cincinnati, OH
Nero, Mark J. ...Chicago, IL
Nero, Paul M. ...Naperville, IL
Nero, Roberta Moseley ...Troy, NY
Nero, Worrell D. ...Philadelphia, PA
Nerone, F. Regan ...Pittsburgh, PA
Nerone, J. Roger ...Pittsburgh, PA
Nerone, Michael F. ...Pittsburgh, PA
Neroni, Frederick J. ...Delhi, NY
Nerren, Michael J. ...Bossier City, LA
Nersesian, Richard A. ...New York, NY
Nersesian, Robert A., Law Offices of
Las Vegas, NV
Nersessian, David L. ...Boston, MA
Nersessian, Sonya ...Dedham, MA
Nershi, Michael T. ...Johnstown, NY
Nerud, Anthony F. ...Arlington, MN
Neruda, Francis D. ...Houston, TX
Nervell, Anders G. O. ...Honolulu, HI
Nervig, James E. ...Clive, IA
Nervig, Luther P. ...Wadena, MN
Nervig, Richard A., Law Offices of
Denver, CO
Nervo, Frank P. ...New York, NY
Nervo, Frederick A. ...San Francisco, CA
Nerz, C. Warren ...Indianapolis, IN
Nesbet, Barbara ...San Jose, CA
Nesbett, Raymond A. ...Anchorage, AK
Nesbit, Chad C. ...Troy, MI
Nesbit, Christine ...Eugene, OR
Nesbit, Christopher S. M. ...Charlotte, NC
Nesbit, Douglas C. ...Oklahoma City, OK
Nesbit, Ellyn E. ...San Jose, CA
Nesbit, Gordon ...Tulsa, OK
Nesbit, Justin M. ...Boston, MA
Nesbit, Mark M. ...Columbus, OH
Nesbit, Phyllis S. ...Fairhope, AL
Nesbit, Renee E. ...East Tawas, MI
Nesbit, Robert P. ...Buffalo Grove, IL
Nesbit, Thomas L. ...Winston-Salem, NC
Nesbit, Thomas L., P.C. ...Winston-Salem, NC
Nesbitt, Abigail R. ...Minneapolis, MN
Nesbitt, Alfred F. ...Miami, FL
Nesbitt, Arron ...San Jose, CA
Nesbitt & Associates ...Los Angeles, CA
Nesbitt, B. Woodrow, Jr. ...Shreveport, LA
Nesbitt, B. Woodrow, Jr., Ltd.
Shreveport, LA
Nesbitt, Charles ...Oklahoma City, OK
Nesbitt, Daniel F. ...Cincinnati, OH
Nesbitt, Deborah Ann ...Albuquerque, NM
Nesbitt, Dominic S. O. ...San Diego, CA
Nesbitt, Edward C. ...Tucson, AZ
Nesbitt, Gary Ian ...Miami, FL
Nesbitt, Henry B. ...Newark, NY
Palmyra, NY
Nesbitt, James T. ...Houston, TX
Nesbitt, Janet Staton ...Danville, KY
Nesbitt, John B. ...Newark, NY
Palmyra, NY
Nesbitt, John D. ...Kansas City, MO
Nesbitt, John R. (Jack) ...Rensselaer, IN
Nesbitt, John W. ...Cordele, GA
Nesbitt, Joseph ...Miami, FL
Nesbitt, Kevin L. ...Danville, KY
Nesbitt, La Fonte ...Washington, DC
Nesbitt Law Firm ...Rensselaer, IN
Nesbitt, Lenore C. ...Miami, FL
Nesbitt, Leroy ...Washington, DC
Nesbitt, Leroy, Jr. ...Washington, DC
Nesbitt, M. Bree ...Hartford, CT
Nesbitt, Mark T. ...Denver, CO
Nesbitt, Martin L., Jr. ...Asheville, NC
Nesbitt & Nesbitt ...Miami, OK
Nesbitt, Patrick M. ...Los Angeles, CA
Nesbitt, Patrick T. ...Cincinnati, OH
West Chester, OH
Nesbitt, Paul B. ...Los Angeles, CA
Nesbitt, Paul K. ...Houston, TX
Nesbitt, Randall J. ...Algoma, WI
Sturgeon Bay, WI
Nesbitt, Robert E. ...Miami, OK
Nesbitt, Robin A. ...Baton Rouge, LA
Nesbitt & Slawter ...Asheville, NC
Nesbitt, Stephanie A. ...Cary, NC
Nesbitt, Stephen L. ...Bridgewater, NJ
Nesbitt, Thomas Andrew ...Austin, TX
Nesbitt, Thomas P. ...Oshkosh, WI
Nesbitt, Thomas R., Jr. ...New York, NY
Nesbitt, Weldon E. ...Norman, OK
Nesbitt, William T. ...Washington, DC
Nesbitt & Williams, LLP ...Newark, NY
Palmyra, NY
Nesburg, Alan D. ...Chicago, IL
Nesburg, Kathryn S. ...Oak Park, IL
Nesburn, Judith ...Los Angeles, CA
Neschis, Janet C. ...New York, NY
Nesci, James ...Tucson, AZ
Nesci, James, P.C. ...Tucson, AZ
Nesci, Vincent P. ...White Plains, NY
Nescio, Joseph S. ...West Chester, PA
Nesdore, Bruce G. ...Columbus, OH
Nese, Joseph A. ...Pittsburgh, PA
Nesemann, Robert E. ...Appleton, WI
Nesenholtz, Lynda H. ...Austin, TX
Nesenoff, Ira S. ...New York, NY
Nesenoff & Miltenberg, LLP ...New York, NY
Neser, Arlin P. ...Irvine, CA
Neset, Catherine M ...Alexandria, MN
Nesfeder, Michael R. ...Allentown, PA
Nesgos, Nicholas J. ...Boston, MA
Nesgos, Peter D. ...New York, NY
Nesh, William ...Woodland Hills, CA
Neshat-Hersh, Kay M. ...Victorville, CA
Nesheim, Douglas ...Fargo, ND
Nesheim, John M. ...Houston, TX
Nesheim, Paul R. ...Houston, TX
Neshek, Laura S. ...Danville, IL
Neshek, Milton E. ...Elkhorn, WI
Neshek, Thomas R. ...Elkhorn, WI
Nesi, Anthony R. ...Boston, MA
Nesi, Kathleen Moro ...Detroit, MI
Nesis, Beth N. ...Boulder, CO
Nesis, Joseph J. ...Boulder, CO
Nesis & Nesis, LLP ...Boulder, CO
Nesius, John J. ...Charleston, WV
Neski, Gerald J. ...Bridgeton, NJ
Neskis, George A. ...Norfolk, VA
Neskora, Teanna West ...Baton Rouge, LA
Neslage, John Edward ...Houston, TX
Nesland, James E. ...Boulder, CO
Denver, CO
Neslen, Richard R. ...Salt Lake City, UT
Nesler, Joseph H. ...Chicago, IL
Nesler, Robert D. ...Portland, OR
Neslin, David S. ...Denver, CO
Neslund, Jeffrey ...Chicago, IL
Neslund, Verla S. ...Atlanta, GA
NeSmith, A. Newell ...Cochran, GA
NeSmith, Carl Dalton ...Oneonta, AL
NeSmith, Carl Dalton, Jr. ...Oneonta, AL
Nesmith, George C. ...Menasha, WI
NeSmith, Joseph Q. ...Herndon, VA
Nesmith, Joy ...Dallas, TX
NeSmith, Robert J. ...Decatur, GA
Nesmith, Roosevelt N. ...New York, NY
NeSmith, Stephen M. ...Montgomery, AL
Nesmith, Steven B. ...Philadelphia, PA
NeSmith, William D. ...Henderson, KY
NeSmith, William D., III ...Tifton, GA
NeSmith-Rosner, Joanna ...Saint Marys, GA
Nesnow, Dolores O. ...Raleigh, NC
Nesoff, Mark ...New York, NY
Nesom, H. Todd ...Oakdale, LA
Nesper, Ferber & DiGiacomo, LLP
Buffalo, NY
Nesper, James M. ...Buffalo, NY
Nesper, Paul T. ...Buffalo, NY
Nespica, Rose Anne, (P.C.)
Blue Springs, MO
Nespole, Gregory M. ...New York, NY
Nespole, James ...New York, NY
Nespor, Julieann Kimball ...Denver, CO
Nespor, Wesley D. ...Albion, NE
Fullerton, NE
Ness, Amanda A. ...Sacramento, CA
Ness, Andrew D. ...Washington, DC
Ness, Anton P. ...Wilmington, DE
Ness, Bari Stolmack ...San Francisco, CA
Ness, Dale S. ...Lexington, SC
Ness, David ...Safety Harbor, FL
Ness, David F. ...Chattanooga, TN
Ness, David M. ...Minneapolis, MN
Ness, Edwin N. ...Emeryville, CA
Ness, Howard L. ...Toledo, OH
Ness, Irvin C. ...Kansas City, MO
Ness, Jerome M. ...Hicksville, NY
Ness, Kenneth B. ...Milwaukee, WI
Ness, Lowell D. ...Menlo Park, CA
Ness Motley Loadholt Richardson & Poole, Professional Association
New Orleans, LA
Providence, RI
Barnwell, SC
Charleston, SC
Ness, Paul L. ...El Monte, CA
Ness, Peter G. ...Bedford, NH
Ness, Peter S. ...Greenwich, CT
Ness, Richard B. ...Bamberg, SC
Ness, Robert C. ...Owings Mills, MD
Ness, Ronald D. ...Port Orchard, WA
Ness, Shari A. ...New York, NY
Ness, Stanley M. ...Santa Ana, CA
Ness, Stephen C. ...Sioux Falls, SD
Ness, Steven E. ...Minnetonka, MN
Ness, Susan P.
Federal Communications Commission,
Office of the Commissioners, GV
Ness, Theodore ...New York, NY
Nessan, Douglas E. ...Minneapolis, MN
Nessary, Richard ...Los Angeles, CA
Nesse, Janet M. ...Washington, DC
Nesse, Madeline
Department Of Health And Human Services,
Office of the General Counsel, GV
Nesse, Paul S. ...San Jose, CA
Nesse, Paul S., A Professional Corporation
San Jose, CA
Nessel, Frank W. ...Warminster, PA
Nessel, Kerry A. ...Huntington, WV
Nessel, Mary Ann B. ...New York, NY
Nessel, MaryAnn ...St. Louis, MO
Nessel, Patricia E. ...Birmingham, MI
Nessel, Thomas ...Bethel, CT
Nesselquist, Edward J. ...Roseland, NJ
Nesselroth, Robert M. ...Hollywood, FL
Nesselrotte, Toni M ...Fairmont, WV
Nesselson, Debra Helene ...Glencoe, IL
Nessen, Maurice N. ...New York, NY
Nessen, R. Peter ...Chicago, IL
Nessenson, Ilene ...Portland, OR
Nessenson, Lawrence M. ...New York, NY
Nesser, Anita L. ...Dallas, TX
Nesser, Catherine L. ...Boston, MA
Nesser, J. Michael ...Columbus, OH
Nesser, John T., III ...New Orleans, LA
Nesser, Joseph G. ...Rochester, NY
Nesset, Curtis C. ...Salt Lake City, UT
Nesseth, Laurie H. ...Minneapolis, MN
Nesset-Sale, Jo Carol ...Athens, GA
Nessim, Daniel ...New York, NY
Nessim, Ronald J. ...Los Angeles, CA
Nesslage, Larry D. ...St. Peters, MO
Nessler, Cynthia L.
Department of Commerce,
Patent and Trademark Office, GV
Nessler, Frederic W. ...Springfield, IL
Nessler, L. Robert ...Rochester, NY
Nessler, Patricia Hart ...Mineola, NY
Nessler, Paul H., Jr. ...Spring Hill, FL
Nessler, Richard A. ...New York, NY
Nessler, Thomas G., Jr. ...Greenville, SC
Nessman, Alan C. ...Washington, DC
Nesson, Alexander M. ...Taunton, MA
Nesson, Barry E. ...Spring Valley, NY
Nesson, Benjamin ...Boston, MA
Nesson, Carol E. ...Boston, MA
Nesson, Charles R. ...Cambridge, MA
Nesson Law Office, P.C. ...Sioux Falls, SD
Nesson, Paul R., Jr. ...Madison, WI
Nesson, Richard B. ...New York, NY
Nesson, Steven R. ...Sioux Falls, SD
Nessralla, Philip C., Jr. ...Brockton, MA
Nessralla, Richelle A. ...Boston, MA
Nesta, JoAnn M. ...Fort Lauderdale, FL
Nestel, Denise L. ...Houston, TX
Nestel, Randy K. ...Hialeah, FL
Nester, Alexander J. ...Belleville, IL
Nester, Brian R. ...Washington, DC
Nester, Charles M. J. ...Pottstown, PA
Nester, Cheryl J. ...Columbus, OH
Nester, Daniel C. ...St. Louis, MO
Nester, David A. ...Belleville, IL
Nester, Elbert R. ...Columbus, OH
Nester, Elbert R., Associates & Co., L.P.A.
Columbus, OH
Nester, Gary W. ...New York, NY
Nester, Gerard A. ...St. Louis, MO
Nester, Gregory L. ...Philadelphia, PA
Nester, Joseph S. ...Jersey City, NJ
Nester, Kathryn N. ...Jackson, MS
Nester, Mary A. ...Portland, OR
Nester, Michael J. ...Belleville, IL
Nester, Nester & Whiteman ...Pottstown, PA
Nester, Norbert Dean ...Belleville, IL
Nester, Patrick A. ...Austin, TX
Nester, Raymond D. ...Pottstown, PA
Nester, Tracy Pierce ...Oklahoma City, OK
Nesterczuk, Christopher P. ...New York, NY
Nesteroff, Michael A. ...Seattle, WA
Nesthus, Kristine P. ...Irvine, CA
San Diego, CA
Nestico, John J. ...Somerset, NJ
Nesting, Richard O. ...Portland, OR
Nestingen, Carolyn S. ...Minneapolis, MN
Nestingen, David I. ...Milwaukee, WI
Nestingen, William E. ...San Diego, CA
Nestle, Jennifer J. ...Philadelphia, PA
Nestle, Lewis S. ...Albany, NY
Nestle, Manuel E. ...Forestville, CA
Nestler, Gary J. ...Garden City, NY
Nestler, Lawrence ...Sylva, NC
Nestler, Andrew, III ...Tulsa, OK
Nestor, Bruce D. ...Iowa City, IA
Nestor, Bruce D. ...Washington, IA
Nestor, Christopher R. ...Harrisburg, PA
Nestor, Daniel C. ...Chicago, IL
Nestor, Douglas R. ...Baltimore, MD
Nestor, Joann S. ...Boston, MA
Nestor, John A. ...Huntington, NY
Nestor, John N. ...Lynn, MA
Nestor, Joseph L. ...Endicott, NY
Nestor, Lorraine M. ...Columbus, OH
Nestor, Mark L. ...Fitchburg, MA
Nestor, Matthew J. ...Boston, MA
Nestor & Mercure ...Tecumseh, NE
Nestor, Michael F. ...Newark, NJ
Nestor, Michael R. ...Wilmington, DE
Nestor, Mirce M. ...Jackson, MI
Nestor, Paul J. ...Mission Viejo, CA
Nestor, Stacey ...Macon, GA

Nestor, Therese A. ....Trenton, NJ
Nestrick, Catherine A. ....Evansville, IN
Nestrud, Charles R. ....Little Rock, AR
Nesvig, Douglas M. ....Gaylord, MN
Nesvig, Mark A. ....Phoenix, AZ
Nesvig, Paul M. ....St. Paul, MN
Neswiacheny, Bohdan ....Fort Lauderdale, FL
Neswiacheny, Bohdan, Law Office of
Fort Lauderdale, FL
Sarasota, FL
Netanel, Neil W. ....Austin, TX
Netardus, Kenneth R. ....Wichita Falls, TX
Netburn, David ....Hartford, CT
Netburn, Peter C. ....Boston, MA
Netchert, Dineen & Hillmann, Esqs.
Closter, NJ
Netchert, William J. ....Closter, NJ
Netchin, Maurine ....New York, NY
Netemeyer, Margaret ....San Antonio, TX
Netemeyer, Ron ....Columbia, MO
Netterval, Jeffrey P. ....Boston, MA
Neterville, Adele Hebert
Baton Rouge, LA
Neth, Joann M. ....Washington, DC
Neth, Spencer ....Cleveland, OH
Nethercut, John H. ....Baltimore, MD
Nethercut, Richard A. ....Harmony, MN
Mabel, MN
Netherlin, Alton ....Ajo, AZ
Nethers, Mark R. ....Phoenix, AZ
Netherton, Darrell L.
Merit Systems Protection Board, Office of Regional Operations, GV
Netherton, J. Nick ....Houston, TX
Netherton, Lee ....Louisville, KY
Netherton, William E. ....Tucson, AZ
Nethery, D. Martin, (P.C.)
Indian Wells, CA
Nethery, John F. ....Chicago, IL
Nething, David E. ....Jamestown, ND
Netolicky, Sara R. ....Des Moines, IA
Netsch, Dawn Clark ....Chicago, IL
Netsch, Maitte R. ....Miami, FL
Netski, Christine M. ....Boston, MA
Nett, George J. ....Macomb, IL
Netta, Kim S. ....Irvine, CA
Netta, Kimberly ....Riverside, CA
Netteberg, Eric B. ....St. Paul, MN
Nettelblad, Karen Seymour
Overland Park, KS
Nettels, Charles F. ....Pasadena, CA
Nettels, J. Curtis ....St. Louis, MO
Nettels, John C., Jr. ....Wichita, KS
Netter, Arthur B. ....Old Greenwich, CT
Netter, Charles H., (P.A.) ....Miami, FL
Netter, Edith M. ....Boston, MA
Netter, Edith M., P.C. ....Boston, MA
Netter, George J. ....Pasadena, CA
Netter, Helene K., The Law Offices of
New York, NY
Netter, Miriam M. ....Troy, NY
Netter, Richard ....New York, NY
Netter, Robert E. ....Kingston, NY
Netterblad, John W. ....San Diego, CA
Netterfield, Kyle D. J. ....Seattle, WA
Nettesheim, Christoph T. ....Ventura, CA
Nettesheim, Gregory H.
Wisconsin Rapids, WI
Nettesheim, Neal ....Waukesha, WI
Nettesheim, Timothy A. ....Milwaukee, WI
Netti, John E., Jr. ....Lexington, KY
Nettiksimmons, Dennis ....Billings, MT
Nettis, John J. ....Rye, NY
Nettle, Amy ....Dallas, TX
Nettle, Donald B. ....San Antonio, TX
Nettleford, Leslie A. ....Washington, DC
Nettleford, Paul A. ....Baltimore, MD
Nettleingham, Brian A. ....Grand Rapids, MI
Nettler, Richard B. ....Washington, DC
Nettles, A. Bentley ....Houston, TX
Nettles, Alan R. ....Minneapolis, MN
Nettles, Bert S. ....Birmingham, AL
Nettles, Bryar C. ....Richmond, VA
Nettles, Charles R., Jr. ....Austin, TX
Nettles, Cory L. ....Milwaukee, WI
Nettles, Dexter C., Jr. ....Carthage, MS
Nettles, E. Carter, Jr. ....Wakefield, VA
Nettles, E. LeRoy ....Lake City, SC
Nettles, E. LeRoy, Jr. ....Lake City, SC
Nettles, Eugene M. ....Houston, TX
Nettles, F. Truett, II ....Charleston, SC
Nettles, Gaylon ....Indianapolis, IN
Nettles, Gaylon James, P.C.
Indianapolis, IN
Nettles, George C. ....Department of State, Foreign Service Officers (Overseas), GV
Nettles, John L. (Jack) ....Florence, SC
Nettles, John R. ....Gainesville, FL
Nettles, Joseph L. ....Columbia, SC
Nettles, Larry W. ....Houston, TX
Nettles, Laura C. ....Birmingham, AL
Nettles, Louis D. ....Florence, SC
Nettles, Malcolm S. ....Austin, TX
Nettles, Marian D. ....Lake City, SC
Nettles, Marsha Kay ....Detroit, MI
Nettles, McBride, Hoffmeyer, P.A.
Darlington, SC
Dillon, SC
Florence, SC
Nettles, Michael Gary ....Lake City, SC
Nettles, Michael J. ....Jacksonville, FL
Nettles, Nelson A. ....Indianapolis, IN
Nettles, Reginald C. ....Portland, OR
Nettles & Rhea ....Carthage, MS
Nettles, Robert M., Jr. ....Columbia, SC
Nettles, Thomas A., IV ....Tuscaloosa, AL

Nettles, Turbeville and Reddeck
Florence, SC
Kingstree, SC
Lake City, SC
Manning, SC
Sumter, SC
Nettles, Walter Jeff ....Brookhaven, MS
Nettles, William F., IV ....Camden, SC
Nettles, Zoe Sanders ....Columbia, SC
Nettleton, Alan T. ....Portland, OR
Nettleton, Carol J. ....Midland, MI
Nettleton, Gail A. ....Washington, DC
Annapolis, MD
Owings Mills, MD
Nettleton, James A., Jr. ....Lancaster, PA
Nettleton, Mark E. ....Grand Rapids, MI
Nettleton, Paul L. ....Miami, FL
Nettleton, Robert C. ....Haines City, FL
Nettleton, Ronald E. ....Glastonbury, CT
Nettlow, Donald R. ....St. Petersburg, FL
Nettum, Richard E. ....Americus, GA
Netty, Nicholas A. ....Orange, CA
Netusil, William L. ....Rocky Point, NY
Netz, Cheryn Leigh ....Jackson, MS
Netzel, Dawn M. ....Buffalo, NY
Netzel, Quin W. ....Fairview Heights, IL
Netzell, Timothy A. ....Eagan, MN
Netzer, Donald L. ....Sidney, MT
Netzer, Evin L. ....Tampa, FL
Netzer, Gary R. ....Los Angeles, CA
Netzer, Jonathan G. ....Modesto, CA
Netzer, Roger D. ....New York, NY
Netzky, Terrence F. ....Chicago, IL
Netzley, David C. ....Orlando, FL
Netzley, Willard P. ....La Puente, CA
Netzloff, Terry L. ....Birmingham, MI
Netzly, Dwight H. ....Massillon, OH
Netzorg & Caschette, P.C. ....Las Vegas, NV
Netzorg, Gordon W. ....Denver, CO
Netzorg, John M. ....Las Vegas, NV
Netzorg & McKeever, Professional Corporation ....Denver, CO
Neu, Arthur A. ....Carroll, IA
Glidden, IA
Neu, Arthur Eric ....Carroll, IA
Neu, Douglas B. ....Providence, RI
Neu, Douglas R. ....Boca Raton, FL
Neu, Harold A. ....New York, NY
Neu, Howard M. ....Pembroke Pines, FL
Neu, Howard M., Law Offices of, P.A.
Pembroke Pines, FL
Neu, John A. ....San Francisco, CA
Neu, John H. ....Manhattan Beach, CA
Neu, Mary E. ....New York, NY
Neu, Michael C. ....Las Vegas, NV
Neu, Minnich, Comito & Hall, P.C.
Carroll, IA
Glidden, IA
Neu, Nancy ....San Francisco, CA
Neu, Richard B. ....Quincy, IL
Neu, Roger L. ....Irvine, CA
Neu, Roger L., Inc. ....Irvine, CA
Neu, Rubin ....Sherman Oaks, CA
Neubardt, Andrew M. ....White Plains, NY
Neubauer, David M. ....Columbus, OH
Neubauer, Deborah Ann ....Akron, OH
Neubauer, Diane R. ....Los Angeles, CA
Neubauer, Ellen M. ....Treasury Department, Financial Management Service, GV
Neubauer, Hildegard ....Alden, NY
Neubauer & Hunsinger, P.S. ....Seattle, WA
Neubauer, John J., Jr. ....Baltimore, MD
Neubauer, John R. ....Tucson, AZ
Neubauer, Laura J. ....Brooklyn, NY
Neubauer, Lisa Stephens ....Milwaukee, WI
Neubauer, Mark A. ....Santa Monica, CA
Neubauer, Richard J. ....Nashville, TN
Neubauer, Robert J. ....Ellicott City, MD
Neubauer, Robert M. ....Los Angeles, CA
Neubauer, Ronald G.
Department of Defense, Office of the General Counsel, GV
Neubauer, Sara R. ....New York, NY
Neubauer, Terry J. ....Fairview Heights, IL
Neubauer, Timothy R. ....Mount Vernon, IL
Neubauer, William P. ....Iowa City, IA
Neubauer-Zoller, Brenda ....Bismarck, ND
Neubaum, Victor A. ....York, PA
Neubeck, Beman G. ....Plymouth, MI
Neubeck, Pamela L. ....Buffalo, NY
Neubeck, Stephen J. ....Cincinnati, OH
Neubecker, Mark Forrest ....Cleveland, OH
Neubeiser, Evan A. ....Denver, CO
Neuber, Frank William ....Bowling Green, KY
Neuberg, Susan E. ....Hartford, CT
Neuberger, Ari S. ....Brooklyn, NY
Neuberger, Carmen G. ....Washington, DC
Neuberger, Emily Koenig ....Chicago, IL
Neuberger, George L., Jr. ....Watertown, WI
Neuberger, Hallie ....Staten Island, NY
Neuberger, Isaac M. ....Baltimore, MD
Neuberger, James A. ....New York, NY
Neuberger, Jerome M. ....Staten Island, NY
Neuberger, Lorenz, Griggs & Sweet
Watertown, WI
Neuberger, Mark J. ....Aventura, FL
Neuberger, Ned Craig ....Staten Island, NY
Neuberger and Neuberger, LLP
Staten Island, NY
Neuberger, Quinn, Gielen, Rubin & Gibber, P.A. ....Baltimore, MD
Neuberger, Robert J. ....Portland, OR
Neuberger, Thomas S., P.A.
Wilmington, DE
Neuberger, Thomas Stephen
Wilmington, DE
Neuberger, Tracey ....New York, NY
Neuberger, Yaakov S. ....Baltimore, MD

Neubert, Deborah Monteith
New Haven, CT
Neubert, Eleanore S. ....Northfield, OH
Neubert, Hunter S. ....Nashville, TN
Neubert, Matthew Jon ....Phoenix, AZ
Neubert, Michael D. ....New Haven, CT
Neubert, Pepe & Monteith, P.C.
New Haven, CT
Southport, CT
Neubert, William T. ....Cleveland, OH
Neuborne, Helen R. ....New York, NY
Neuburger, Jeffrey D. ....New York, NY
Neuchterlein, Jeffrey D. ....Washington, DC
Neuckranz, Thomas H. ....Chicago, IL
Neudeck, Alexander J. ....Fort Collins, CO
Neudek, Dennis A. ....Fresno, CA
Neudorfer, Wolfgang E.
Department Of The Interior, Office of Hearings & Appeals, GV
Neue, Karyn S. ....Newport Beach, CA
Neue, Michael D. ....Irvine, CA
Neuen, Gary L. ....Fort Wayne, IN
Neuendorf, Louis E. ....Sandwich, IL
Yorkville, IL
Neuenschwander, Gordon E. ....Pittsburgh, PA
Neuenschwander, Jack L. ....Piqua, OH
Neuenschwander, Janet D.
Indianapolis, IN
Neuenschwander, Jeffrey J. ....Chicago, IL
Neuenschwander, John A. ....Kenosha, WI
Neuenschwander, Roy P. ....Knoxville, TN
Neuer, Paul A. ....Santa Rosa, CA
Neuer, Philip D. ....Newark, NJ
Parsippany, NJ
Neuer, Raymond A. ....Houston, TX
Neuerburg, James E. ....Ventura, CA
Neufeld, Alan S. ....Aventura, FL
Neufeld, Alison C. ....San Francisco, CA
Neufeld, Bradley E. ....Riverside, CA
Neufeld, David S. ....Princeton, NJ
Neufeld, David S. J. ....Melville, NY
New York, NY
Neufeld, Don O. ....Roseville, CA
Neufeld, Ellen G. ....Hutchinson, KS
Neufeld, Eva N. ....Omaha, NE
Neufeld, Fred ....Los Angeles, CA
Neufeld, Gerald J. ....New York, NY
Neufeld, Marjorie Nieset ....Burbank, CA
Neufeld, Michael A. ....Fairfield, CT
Neufeld & O'Leary ....Melville, NY
New York, NY
Neufeld, Raymond ....New York, NY
Neufeld, Russell T. ....Brooklyn, NY
Neufeld, Shawn M. ....Princeton, NJ
Neufeld, Stacie ....Minneapolis, MN
Neufeld, Thomas A. ....New York, NY
Neufeld, Timothy L. ....Los Angeles, CA
Neufeld, Warren R. ....Denver, CO
Neuffer, Brian E. ....Chicago, IL
Neuffer, Helen M. ....Barrington, IL
Neugarten, Jerrold L. ....Hannacroix, NY
Neugebauer, Brian D. ....West Fargo, ND
Neugebauer, Gerald P., Jr. ....Ebensburg, PA
Neugebauer, John (Ed.) ....Blue Bell, PA
Neugebauer, Lynn ....Jackson Heights, NY
Neugebauer, Paul L. ....White Plains, NY
Neugebauer, Robert D. ....Seattle, WA
Neugebauer, Walter M. F. ....Harrisburg, PA
Neugeboren, Craig A. ....San Jose, CA
Neugeboren, Steven M.
Environmental Protection Agency, Office of the General Counsel, GV
Neugent, Dean ....Texas City, TX
Neugent, Gerard D. ....West Des Moines, IA
Neugent, Vickers ....Lakeland, GA
Neuger, Charles J. ....Cleveland, OH
Neuger, Howard M. ....Cleveland, OH
Neuhard, James R. ....Detroit, MI
Neuhard, Thomas F. ....Lapeer, MI
Neuhardt, Amy L. ....New York, NY
Neuhardt, David A. ....Dayton, OH
Neuhardt, Sharen Swartz ....Dayton, OH
Neuhart, David M. ....Pittsburgh, PA
Neuharth, Gail Kosier ....Seattle, WA
Neuharth, Paul H., Jr., Law Offices of
San Diego, CA
Neuhaus, Gregory M. ....Grand Island, NE
Neuhaus, Howard L. ....Omaha, NE
Neuhaus, Joseph E. ....New York, NY
Neuhaus, Mary Lynn ....Dubuque, IA
Neuhaus, Thomas E. ....Oxnard, CA
Neuhaus, Wanda D. ....York, PA
Neuhauser, Frank L. ....Potomac, MD
Neuhauser, George Robert ....Atlanta, GA
Neuhauser, Maxine H. ....Newark, NJ
Neuhauser, Mitchell A. ....Louisville, KY
Neuhauser, Paul M. ....Iowa City, IA
Neuhauser, Stanley J. ....Towson, MD
Neuhauser, Stuart ....New York, NY
Neuheisel, Kathryn A. ....Tempe, AZ
Neuheisel & Neuheisel, P.C. ....Tempe, AZ
Neuheisel, Richard G. ....Tempe, AZ
Neuhof, Siegbert H. ....Pikesville, MD
Neuhoff, Christine S. ....San Francisco, CA
Neuhoff, Edward D. ....Reno, NV
Neuhoff, John D., Jr. ....Dallas, TX
Neuhoff, Richard C. ....San Francisco, CA
Neuhoff, Ronald E. ....Los Angeles, CA
Neuhoff, Thomas H., Jr. ....Dallas, TX
Neukamm, John B. ....Tampa, FL
Neukamm, Michael E. ....Orlando, FL
Neukom, Albert J. ....Hillsdale, MI
Neukom, William H. ....Redmond, WA
Neuland, Nordberg & Andrews, A Professional Law Corporation
Rancho Santa Margarita, CA
Neuland, Richard P.
Rancho Santa Margarita, CA

Neulight, Seth L. ....San Francisco, CA
Neuling, R. Bruce
Department of State, GV
Neumaier, Fredrick J. ....Milwaukee, WI
Neumaier, Mark ....Tampa, FL
Neumaier, Robert J. ....Crown Point, IN
Neuman, A. Bruce ....Media, PA
Neuman, Andrea B. ....New York, NY
Neuman, Andrea E. ....Irvine, CA
Neuman, Arthur E. ....Washington, DC
Neuman, Barry S. ....Washington, DC
Neuman, Bette ....Brookville, NY
Neuman, Bruce H. ....New York, NY
Neuman, Clifford L., (P.C.) ....Boulder, CO
Neuman & Comnas ....Bridgehampton, NY
Neuman, Craig H. ....Warren, OH
Neuman, Cyrus A. ....Miami Beach, FL
Neuman, David J. ....San Francisco, CA
Neuman, Douglas J. ....Niles, OH
Neuman, Edward B. ....Dayton, OH
Neuman, Eric P. ....Rockville, MD
Neuman, Eve F. ....New York, NY
Neuman, Farley J. ....San Francisco, CA
Neuman, Gail O'Sullivan ....Smyrna, TN
Neuman, Gerald L. ....New York, NY
Neuman, Glen ....Northbrook, IL
Neuman, Henry G. ....Davenport, IA
Neuman, Howard A. ....Summit, NJ
New York, NY
Neuman, Howard N. ....St. Louis, MO
Neuman, J. Fred ....Irvine, CA
Neuman, James E. ....New York, NY
Neuman, James M. ....Chicago, IL
Neuman, Jay S. ....Pittsburgh, PA
Neuman, Jeffrey J. ....Washington, DC
Neuman, Jeffrey N. ....New York, NY
Neuman, Jerold B., (P.C.)
Los Angeles, CA
Neuman, Jerome ....Brooklyn, NY
Neuman, Joel M. ....Atlanta, GA
Neuman, June Marie ....Dearborn, MI
Neuman, K. Sidney ....Pittsburgh, PA
Neuman, K. William ....San Francisco, CA
Neuman, Kenneth F. ....Birmingham, MI
Neuman, Kristin K.H. ....Stamford, CT
Neuman, Larry A. ....Cincinnati, OH
Neuman, Leonard ....St. Louis, MO
Neuman, Linda K. ....Davenport, IA
Neuman, Neva J. ....Los Angeles, CA
Neuman, Peter H ....Newburgh, NY
Neuman, Peter H., P.C. ....Goshen, NY
Newburgh, NY
Neuman, Phillip J. ....Southfield, MI
Neuman, Reed W. ....Washington, DC
Neuman, Reid S. ....Des Plaines, IL
Neuman, Rhonda Cook
Department of Commerce, Office of the General Counsel, GV
Neuman, Robert H. ....Washington, DC
Neuman, Rod B. ....Tampa, FL
Neuman, Sandra S. ....Butler, PA
Neuman, Sanford S. ....St. Louis, MO
Neuman, Scott M. ....East Lansing, MI
Neuman, Stephen ....Bergenfield, NJ
Neuman, Susan ....New York, NY
Neuman, Todd H. ....Columbus, OH
Neumann, Amy E. ....Syracuse, NY
Neumann, Amy Elliott ....Modesto, CA
Neumann, Andrea K. ....Los Angeles, CA
Neumann, Arthur W. ....Lakewood, OH
Neumann, Bruce A. ....Chicago, IL
Neumann, Calvin R. ....Clovis, NM
Neumann & Canjar ....Lansing, MI
Neumann, Carl A. ....Oakbrook Terrace, IL
Neumann, Cecilia M. ....Westport, CT
Neumann, Christine Yvonne Edwards
Hempstead, NY
Neumann, Christopher ....New York, NY
Neumann, Christopher J. ....Denver, CO
Neumann, Christopher J. ....New York, NY
Neumann, David C. ....Brevard, NC
Neumann, David F. ....Scotia, NY
Neumann, David M. ....Cleveland, OH
Neumann, De Wayne G. ....Milwaukee, WI
Neumann, Donald S., Jr.
Garden City, NY
Neumann, Elaine H. ....New York, NY
Neumann, Franklin W., III ....Birmingham, AL
Neumann, Gerard A. ....Hempstead, NY
Neumann, G. R. ....Des Moines, IA
Neumann, Howard P. ....Greensboro, NC
Neumann, Humke, Moir, Mueller & Bohrofen, S.C. ....Sheboygan, WI
Neumann, James R. ....Lansing, MI
Neumann, Janet H. ....Bethesda, MD
Neumann, Jon T. ....Phoenix, AZ
Neumann, Kathleen M. ....Encino, CA
Neumann, Liz ....Corpus Christi, TX
Neumann, Lynn W. ....Charlotte, NC
Neumann, Marilyn J. ....Columbia, KY
Neumann, Martin A. ....Los Angeles, CA
Neumann, Martin H. ....Lansing, MI
Neumann, Mary S. ....Englewood, CO
Neumann, Melanie J. ....Austin, MN
Neumann, Michael ....Phoenix, AZ
Neumann, Michael J. ....San Francisco, CA
Neumann, Michelle A. ....Houston, TX
Neumann, Michelle Dye ....Gainesville, FL
Neumann, Monica R. ....Houston, TX
Neumann, Otto C. ....Chicago, IL
Neumann, Patricia F. ....Southampton, NY
Neumann, Paul Gustav ....San Francisco, CA
Neumann, Peter Chase ....Reno, NV
Neumann, R. Randall ....Greenville, IL
Neumann, Richard E. ....Lake Elsinore, CA
Neumann, Richard K., Jr. ....Hempstead, NY
Neumann, Rita ....Las Cruces, NM
Neumann, Roland M., Jr. ....Sheboygan, WI

Neumann, Ronald M. ... New York, NY
Neumann, Sara R. ... San Diego, CA
Neumann, Sylvia J. ... Chicago, IL
Neumann, Theodore H. ... Trenton, TN
Neumann, Timothy J. ... Houston, TX
Neumann, Timothy P. ... Manasquan, NJ
Neumann, William G., Jr. ... Alvin, TX
Neumark, Avery E. ... New York, NY
Neumark, Dustin E. ... Chicago, IL
Neumark, Frederick A. ... Clarkston, MI
Neumark, Jason ... Chicago, IL
Neumark Law Offices, P.C. ... Clarkston, MI
Neumark, Michael H. ... Cincinnati, OH
Neumark, Neil T. ... Chicago, IL
Neumark, Philip ... San Francisco, CA
Neumark, Zoltan ... New York, NY
Neumayr, Carl A. ... Louisville, KY
Neumayr, Joe H. ... Gettysburg, SD
Neumayr, Mary B. ... San Francisco, CA
Neumayr & Smith ... Gettysburg, SD
Onida, SD
Neumeg, Richard W. ... St. Paul, MN
Neumeier, Edward J. ... Kentfield, CA
Neumeier, Joseph O'C. ... Excelsior, MN
Neumeier, Matthew M. ... Chicago, IL
Neumeier, Richard L. ... Boston, MA
Neumeister, David E. ... Chicago, IL
Neumeister, James R. ... Cleveland, OH
Neumeister, Kent J. ... Omaha, NE
Neumeister, William David ... Bakersfield, CA
Neumer, Stephen M. ... Chicago, IL
Neumeyer & Boyd, LLP ... Los Angeles, CA
Neumeyer, David B. ... Lynchburg, VA
Neumeyer, Debora Hewitt ... Cedar Rapids, IA
Neumeyer, Glenn B. ... Albuquerque, NM
Neumeyer, Gregory W. ... Cedar Rapids, IA
Neumeyer, Jeffrey D. ... Boise, ID
Neumeyer, Jerome J. ... St. Paul, MN
Neumeyer, Richard A. ... Los Angeles, CA
Neumeyer, Susan L. ... Minneapolis, MN
Neumiller & Beardslee, A Professional Corporation ... Galt, CA
Lodi, CA
Manteca, CA
Modesto, CA
Stockton, CA
Tracy, CA
Turlock, CA
Neumiller, Paul A. ... St. Helena, CA
Neun, Kristin M. ... Washington, DC
Neundorf, Ken ... Albuquerque, NM
Neundorf, Tanda L. ... Palo Alto, CA
Neuner, Francis X., Jr. ... St. Louis, MO
Neuner, Frank X., Jr. (P.C.)
Lafayette, LA
Neuner, George W., (P.C.) ... Boston, MA
Neuner, Jennifer L. ... New York, NY
Neuner, John, III ... Charleston, WV
Neuner, Lynn K. ... New York, NY
Neuner, Robert ... New York, NY
Neuner, Steven R. ... Marlton, NJ
Neuner, Thomas J. ... St. Louis, MO
Neuner, Thomas James ... Algonac, MI
Neuner, Tillman H. ... Washington, DC
Neuner and Ventura ... Marlton, NJ
Neunzig, Bradley E. ... Seattle, WA
Neupert, Charles J., Jr. ... Shreveport, LA
Neupert, David H. ... Port Angeles, WA
Neupert, John A. ... Lake Mills, WI
Neupert, John F., P.C. ... Portland, OR
Neupert, Marcus ... New York, NY
Neupert & Wakeman, S.C. ... Lake Mills, WI
Neureiter, N. Reid ... Denver, CO
Neuren, Herbert M. ... Purchase, NY
Neuren, Michael S. ... Atlanta, GA
Neurock, Mitchel ... Washington, DC
Neusch, Raymond D. ... Cincinnati, OH
Neuschaefer, William W. ... Burbank, CA
Neuschatz, Kevin Alan ... New York, NY
Neuschwander, Richard E. ... Lansdale, PA
Neuse, Karl W. ... Middlebury, VT
Neuse, Smith, Roper & Venman, P.C.
Middlebury, VT
Neuser, Daryll J. ... Madison, WI
Neuser, Mark ... Madison, WI
Neusner, David N. ... Groton, CT
Neusner, Frederick D. ... Department of Labor, Office of Secretary, GV
Neuson, Bridget A. ... Chicago, IL
Neussendorfer, Stacie A. ... Omaha, NE
Neustadt, Arthur I. ... Arlington, VA
Neustadt, Carol J.
Federal Maritime Commission, Office of the General Counsel, GV
Neustadt, David J. ... Pittsburgh, PA
Neustadt, Frederic L. ... New York, NY
Neustadt, Jeffrey B., Law Offices of
San Francisco, CA
Neustadt, John R. ... Woodland Hills, CA
Neustadt, Mark W. ... Dobbs Ferry, NY
Neustadt, Paul ... New York, NY
Neustadt, Stanley S. ... Washington, DC
Neustadter, Gary G. ... Santa Clara, CA
Neustadter, Jonathan P. ... Los Angeles, CA
Neustadter, Judith L. ... Wailuku, HI
Neustadter, Robert ... Mays Landing, NJ
Neustadter, Stanley ... New York, NY
Neustadter, Steven C. ... Sebastopol, CA
Neustaetter, Janet ... New York, NY
Neustein, Barry F. ... Clifton, NJ
Neustein, Charles L. ... Miami Beach, FL
Neustein, Miles B. ... Hackensack, NJ
Neustein, Stephen ... Pittsburgh, PA
Neustel, Michael S. ... Fargo, ND
Neustifter, Robert M. ... Jackson, MI
Neustrom, Patrik W. ... Salina, KS
Neuthaler, Howard ... New York, NY
Neuvens, Cecile ... Washington, DC
Neuville, Lisa A. ... Phoenix, AZ
Neuville, Thomas M. ... Northfield, MN
Neuwahl, Malcolm H. ... Miami, FL
Neuwald, Edward R. ... Mountain View, CA
Neuwelt, Klari, Law Office of
New York, NY
Neuwirt, Brenda Barton ... Dallas, TX
Neuwirth, Alan J. ... New York, NY
Neuwirth, Dean S. ... Denver, CO
Neuwirth, Elizabeth M. ... Great Neck, NY
Neuwirth, Francis ... New York, NY
Neuwirth, Gloria S. ... New York, NY
Neuwirth, Jessica ... New York, NY
Neuwirth, John A. ... New York, NY
Neuwirth, Laura H. ... Washington, DC
Neuwirth, Richard H. ... Atlanta, GA
Neuwirth, Stephen R. ... Armonk, NY
Neuwirth, Steven J. ... Huntington, NY
Neuwoehner, Russell A. ... Dubuque, IA
Neuworth, Richard P. ... Baltimore, MD
Neuzil, Ralph L. ... Iowa City, IA
Neuzil & Sanderson ... Iowa City, IA
Nevada, Eugene P. ... Columbus, OH
Nevadomski, Linda ... Boonton, NJ
Nevard, Donald B. ... Oklahoma City, OK
Nevares, Andrés R. ... San Juan, PR
Nevares, Dora ... San Juan, PR
Nevares, John F. ... San Juan, PR
Nevares, Mercedes M. ... New Port Richey, FL
Nevares, Sánchez-Alvarez & Mendez
San Juan, PR
Nevarez, David ... El Paso, TX
Nevarez, Kathrine N. ... Scottsdale, AZ
Nevarez, Kristin ... Santa Clara, CA
Nevas, Alan H. ... Bridgeport, CT
Nevas, Andrew B. ... Westport, CT
Nevas, Leo ... Westport, CT
Nevas, Nevas & Capasse ... Westport, CT
Nevas, Stephen E. ... Westport, CT
Neve, John R. ... Minneapolis, MN
Neve, Leslie E. ... Santa Cruz, CA
Neveaux, John L.(Jack), Jr. ... Wayzata, MN
Nevel, Ann Ariel ... New Milford, CT
Nevel, David H. ... Miami, FL
Nevel, Ira T. ... Chicago, IL
Nevel, Terry L. ... Atlanta, GA
Nevell, Todd F. ... Pasadena, CA
Neveloff, Jay A. ... New York, NY
Nevelow, Craig A. ... Austin, TX
Nevels, James E. ... New York, NY
Nevels, Michael ... Phoenix, AZ
Nevels, Randy N. ... Memphis, TN
Nevens, Robert Arthur ... Englewood, CO
Neverett, Meredith A. ... Tupper Lake, NY
Nevergold, Patricia Ann ... Bronx, NY
Neveril, Edward J. ... Chicago, IL
Nevers, Darryl K. ... Milwaukee, WI
Nevers, Gary W. ... Westlake Village, CA
Nevers, Laurie ... St. Paul, MN
Nevers, Palazzo, Maddux & Packard, A Professional Law Corporation
Los Angeles, CA
Ventura, CA
Westlake Village, CA
Neves, Arnold, Jr. ... La Jolla, CA
Neves & Crowther ... Galveston, TX
Neves, Jorge L. ... Holyoke, MA
Neves, Kerry Lane ... Galveston, TX
Neves, Michele J. ... Casper, WY
Nevett, Jonathon L. ... Washington, DC
Neveu, Debra Simmons ... New Orleans, LA
Neveu, Wayne J. ... New Orleans, LA
Neveux, David P. ... Bloomfield Hills, MI
Grosse Pointe Woods, MI
Nevias, Lori ... Kew Gardens, NY
Nevill, Guy L. ... Houston, TX
Nevill, Paul W. ... Bluffton, SC
Neville, Angela ... Bryan, TX
Neville, Arthur J. ... Chicago, IL
Neville, Brenda K. ... Chesapeake, OH
Neville, Brennan S. ... Lincoln, NE
Neville, Cara Lee ... Minneapolis, MN
Neville, Carole ... New York, NY
Neville, Constance M. ... Cambridge, MA
Neville, Dave ... San Francisco, CA
Neville, Deborah A. ... Palo Alto, CA
Neville, Douglas S. ... Kansas City, MO
Neville, Edward ... Belleville, IL
Neville, Edward J., III ... Boston, MA
Neville, Edward R. ... Pasadena, CA
Neville, Frank D. ... Casper, WY
Neville, Gary M. ... Dwight, IL
Neville, George W. ... Jackson, MS
Neville, Gregory J. ... Westport, CT
Neville, Jack L. (Drew), Jr.
Oklahoma City, OK
Neville, James ... Los Angeles, CA
Neville, James E. ... Belleville, IL
Neville, James M. ... St. Louis, MO
Neville, John A. ... Cleveland, OH
Neville, John B. ... Kenton, OH
Neville, John B. ... Salt Lake City, UT
Neville, John G. ... Denver, CO
Neville, John Richard ... Cumming, GA
Neville, Joseph B. ... Cincinnati, OH
Neville, Katherine ... New York, NY
Neville, Katherine Scurria ... Austin, TX
Neville, Kathryn A. ... Okemos, MI
Neville & Kelley ... Cambridge, MA
Springfield, MA
Neville, Lawrence H. ... Atlanta, GA
Neville, Leo D. ... Southfield, MI
Neville, Louise Holden ... New York, NY
Neville, Marcella M. ... Albuquerque, NM
Neville, Martin J. ... New York, NY
Neville, Michael W. ... San Francisco, CA
Neville & Neville ... Statesboro, GA
Neville, Paul M. ... Jackson, MS
Neville, Peterson & Williams
Washington, DC
New York, NY
Neville, Reba J., (Mrs.) ... Statesboro, GA
Neville, Richard E. ... Chicago, IL
Neville, Richard F., III ... San Antonio, TX
Neville, Richard M. ... Stamford, CT
New York, NY
Neville, Richards, DeFranco & Wuller
Belleville, IL
St. Louis, MO
Neville, Robert E. ... Cambridge, MA
Neville, Robert E. ... Milwaukee, WI
Neville, Robert T. ... Tempe, AZ
Neville, Robert T., P.C. ... Tempe, AZ
Neville, Ronald F. ... Chicago, IL
Neville Shaver Hubbard & McLean
Greenwich, CT
Norwalk, CT
Stamford, CT
New York, NY
White Plains, NY
Neville, Shepherd S. ... Waco, TX
Neville, T. Michael ... Houston, TX
Neville, Teri ... Los Angeles, CA
Neville, Terri-Lynne ... Boston, MA
Neville, Thomas F. ... Boise, ID
Neville, Thomas M. ... Waltham, MA
Neville, Warwick Fay ... Pinehurst, NC
Neville, William D. ... Meridian, MS
Neville, William D., Jr. ... Meridian, MS
Neville, William J. ... Statesboro, GA
Neville, William J. ... New York, NY
Neville, William J., Jr. ... Claxton, GA
Metter, GA
Statesboro, GA
Neville, William V., Jr. ... Eufaula, AL
Neville & Wilson ... Jackson, MS
Louisville, MS
Neville-Ewell, Florise ... Detroit, MI
Nevils, Mark J. ... Stoneham, MA
Nevils, Nancy Norfolk ... Boston, MA
Nevils, Richard C. ... Baton Rouge, LA
Nevils, Timothy F. ... Stoneham, MA
Nevils, Timothy F., Jr. ... Stoneham, MA
Nevin, Barbara Nilva ... Minneapolis, MN
Nevin, C. Brent ... Vancouver, WA
Nevin, Cathleen L. ... Indianapolis, IN
Nevin, Colleen M. ... Chicago, IL
Nevin, Craig S. ... Walnut Creek, CA
Nevin, David Z. ... Boise, ID
Nevin, Edward J. ... San Francisco, CA
Nevin Gruen, LLP ... Oakland, CA
Sacramento, CA
San Francisco, CA
Nevin, Herzfeld & Benjamin, LLP
Boise, ID
Nevin, Hugh W., Jr. ... Pittsburgh, PA
Nevin, Jack F. ... Tacoma, WA
Nevin, James F. ... Portland, OR
Nevin, Jeffrey G. ... Oakland, CA
Sacramento, CA
San Francisco, CA
Nevin, John S. ... Norfolk, VA
Nevin, Patricia M. ... Minneapolis, MN
Nevin, Ronald K. ... Nashville, TN
Nevin, Scott E. ... Baltimore, MD
Nevin, Thomas W. ... Denver, CO
Nevin, William J. ... Pierre, SD
Nevinny, Philip H. R. ... Los Angeles, CA
Nevins, Albert E., Jr. ... Hartford, CT
Nevins, Arnold ... Miami, FL
Nevins, Arthur G., Jr. ... Jersey City, NJ
New York, NY
Nevins, Francis M. ... St. Louis, MO
Nevins, Gavin R. ... Anthon, IA
Mapleton, IA
Nevins, Gregory R. ... San Francisco, CA
Nevins, Howard S. ... Sacramento, CA
Nevins, J. Patrick ... Washington, DC
Nevins, John E. ... Surf City, NJ
Nevins, John Mitchell ... Dallas, TX
Nevins, Joseph A., Jr. ... Olean, NY
Nevins, Joseph W. ... Maynard, MA
Nevins, Judith Babcock ... Seattle, WA
Nevins, Julie E. ... Miami, FL
Nevins, Kathleen M. ... Hartford, CT
Nevins, Kent S. ... Stamford, CT
New York, NY
Nevins, Louis H. ... Washington, DC
Nevins, Mary Jane ... Olean, NY
Nevins, Matthew J. ... Boston, MA
Nevins, Michael P. ... Olean, NY
Nevins & Nevins ... Hartford, CT
Nevins, Norman L. ... San Antonio, TX
Nevins, Patrick A. ... Cleveland, OH
Nevins, Paul L. ... Wellesley, MA
Nevins, Richard F. ... Los Angeles, CA
Nevins, Richard L. ... New York, NY
Nevins, Richard P. ... Hartford, CT
Nevins, Robert W., Jr. ... Marietta, GA
Nevins, Robert W., Jr., P.C. ... Marietta, GA
Nevins, Rosemary J. ... Springfield, MA
Worcester, MA
Nevins, Sheila S. ... Corte Madera, CA
Nevins, Thomas D. ... San Francisco, CA
Nevis, Christopher J. ... San Francisco, CA
Nevis, David L. ... San Jose, CA
Nevis, Heather S. ... San Francisco, CA
Nevis, Ralph R. ... Sacramento, CA
Nevitt, David R. ... Saipan, TT
Nevitt, G. Cornelius ... Atlanta, GA
Nevitt, W. Kenneth ... Louisville, KY
Nevitt, William R., Jr. ... San Diego, CA
Nevitte, David C. ... Columbia, MD
Nevius, Eugene S. ... Springfield, OH
Nevius, Garrett W. ... Farmington, CT
Nevius, John G. ... New York, NY
Nevius, Mary C. ... Burtonsville, MD
Nevius, Nancy ... Fort Lauderdale, FL
Nevler, Janis M. ... Kirkland, WA
Nevling, J. Kelley, Jr. ... New York, NY
Nevola, Roger P. ... Austin, TX
Nevola, Tracy C. ... Clinton, NJ
Nevolo, Gary J., Law Offices of
San Francisco, CA
Nevonen, Larry E. ... Los Angeles, CA
Nevonen, Patricia A. ... Los Angeles, CA
Nevoral, Bernard R. ... Chicago, IL
Nevoral, Bernard R., and Associates Ltd.
Chicago, IL
Nevrla, Martin J. ... Little Rock, AR
Nevue, Elizabeth J. ... Salem, OR
New, Arnold L. ... West Chester, PA
New, Cheryl M. ... Vienna, VA
New, Christina J. ... Los Angeles, CA
New, David W. ... Washington, DC
New, David W. ... Clifton, NJ
New, H. Steven ... San Diego, CA
New, Herbert, (P.A.) ... Clifton, NJ
New, Ilson W. ... San Francisco, CA
New, J. Craig ... Corpus Christi, TX
New, Jacob ... Dublin, GA
New, Jason G. ... Chicago, IL
New, Jennifer McCracken ... Chicago, IL
New, Jonathan B. ... New York, NY
New, Kimberly S. ... Mineola, NY
New, Laura L. ... Louisville, KY
New, Lee ... Los Angeles, CA
New, Leroy K. ... Carmel, IN
New, Lorraine F. ... Detroit, MI
New, Michael E. ... Germantown, TN
New & New ... Clifton, NJ
New, Paul ... Denver City, TX
New, Pauline A. ... Los Angeles, CA
New, Randy L. ... Atlanta, GA
New, Shelley Robins ... Philadelphia, PA
New, Stephen P. ... Beckley, WV
New, Timothy D. ... El Dorado, AR
New, Walter H. ... Quitman, GA
New, Warren ... Denver City, TX
Newa, Kenneth C. ... Detroit, MI
Newacheck, David J. ... Oakland, CA
Newacheck, David J., Law Offices of
San Leandro, CA
Neward, James E. ... Sarasota, FL
Newark, Nancy A. ... Wellesley, MA
Neway, Douglas W. ... Orlando, FL
Newbanks, Ronal R. ... Cincinnati, OH
Newbarr, David ... Los Angeles, CA
Newberg, Amy E. ... Warren, MI
Newberg, B. Alan ... Buffalo Grove, IL
Newberg, David A. ... New York, NY
White Plains, NY
Newberg, David M. ... Stillwater, MN
Newberg, Fred E. ... Bryn Mawr, PA
Newberg, Jamison D. ... Dallas, TX
Newberg, Janet A. ... Minneapolis, MN
Newberg, Joseph H. ... Boston, MA
Newberg, Joshua A.
Federal Trade Commission, Bureau of Competition, GV
Newberg, Marvin N. ... Monticello, NY
Newberg, Richard A. ... Monticello, NY
Newberger, Barry S. ... Austin, TX
Newberger, Mark D. ... Elkins Park, PA
Newberger, Martin ... Pompano Beach, FL
Newberger, Nancy A. ... Glencoe, IL
Newberger, Stuart H. ... Washington, DC
Newbern, C. George ... Valdosta, GA
Newbern, David ... Little Rock, AR
Newbern, St. Clair, III, A Professional Corporation ... Fort Worth, TX
Newbern, St. Clair, III ... Fort Worth, TX
Newberry, Brian C. ... Providence, RI
Newberry, Charles D. ... Gray, GA
Newberry, Deborah D. ... Daytona Beach, FL
Newberry, Edward J. ... Washington, DC
Newberry, Edward L., Jr. ... Savannah, GA
Newberry, FéLesia M. ... Chicago, IL
Newberry, Forde J. ... Kettering, OH
Newberry, Haden, Cowherd, Bullock, Keck & McGinnis, L.L.C. ... Springfield, MO
Newberry, J. Stuart ... Cincinnati, OH
Newberry, J. Stuart, Co., L.P.A.
Cincinnati, OH
Newberry, James H., Jr. ... Lexington, KY
Newberry, James S. ... Naperville, IL
Newberry, James W. ... Springfield, MO
Newberry, Jennifer Ann ... Washington, DC
Newberry, Jodi M. ... Palo Alto, CA
Newberry, Lawrence S. ... Pasadena, CA
Newberry, Mark D. ... Dalton, GA
Newberry, Molly Sullivan
Washington, DC
Newberry, Paul ... La Jolla, CA
Newberry, Peter C. ... Cincinnati, OH
Newberry, Robert D. ... Muscatine, IA
Newberry, William W. ... Fort Worth, TX
Newbery, C. David, (P.A.) ... Topeka, KS
Newbery, John A. ... Brooklyn, NY
Newbery & Ungerer ... Topeka, KS
Newblatt, Flora I. ... Glen Arbor, MI
Newblatt, Stewart A. ... Flint, MI
Newbold, Arthur ... Philadelphia, PA
Newbold, Arthur E., III ... Philadelphia, PA
Newbold, Edmund W. ... Miami, FL
Newbold, Gail L. ... Cochranville, PA
Newbold, J. William ... St. Louis, MO
Newbold, Keith ... Durango, CO
Newbold, Lynda S. ... Denver, CO
Newbold, Michael G. ... Kansas City, MO
Newbold, Robert C. ... Providence, RI
Newbold, Stephen A. ... Bloomington, IL
Newbold, Wiley W. ... Morgantown, WV
Newboles, Matthew A. ... Laguna Hills, CA

Newborn, Andrea R. ....Pleasantville, NY
Newborn, Ernest J., Jr. ....San Francisco, CA
Newborn, Herbert Alan ....Boston, MA
Newborn, Karen B. ....Cleveland, OH
Newborn, Norton N. ....Cleveland, OH
Newborn, Samuel R. ....New York, NY
Newborn, Steven A. ....Washington, DC
Newborough, Bruce A. ....Staten Island, NY
Newbould, A. L. ....Henderson, NV
Newbould, E. J. ....Alexandria, VA
Newbould, Kenneth H. ....Albany, NY
Newbould, Mary Z. ....Norwalk, CT
Newbre, Richard N. ....La Habra Heights, CA
Newbrough, Christy G. ....Houston, TX
Newbrough, D. R. ....Ames, IA
Newbrough, Gerald J. ....Des Moines, IA
Newbrough, Johnston, Brewer, Maddux and Sotak, L.L.P. ....Ames, IA
Newbrough, Kim H. ....San Diego, CA
Newbrough, Thomas C., Jr. ....Baltimore, MD
Newburg, Herman ....Lynn, MA
Newburg, Jeffrey D. ....Scottsdale, AZ
Newburg, Ronald F. ....Lynn, MA
Newburger, Cary L. ....New York, NY
Newburger, David J. ....St. Louis, MO
Newburger, Frank L., III
Philadelphia, PA
Newburger, Henry I. ....Pikesville, MD
Newburger, Manuel H. ....Austin, TX
Newburger & Vossmeyer ....St. Louis, MO
Newburgh, Morton ....New York, NY
Newburn, John L. ....La Jolla, CA
Newburry, Keith A. ....Los Angeles, CA
Newbury, Abigail Dunning ....Anchorage, AK
Newbury, Francene M. ....Southfield, MI
Newbury, Jeremiah D. ....Portland, ME
Newbury, Mary Jane Simmons ....Denver, CO
Newbury, Nathan, III ....Boston, MA
Newbury, Philip T., Jr. ....Hartford, CT
Newbury, Robert M. ....Chicago, IL
Newbury, Samuel P. ....Boston, MA
Newbury, Sandra L. ....Corpus Christi, TX
Newbury, Sarah R. ....Boston, MA
Newby, Brian C. ....Austin, TX
Fort Worth, TX
Newby, David A. ....Chicago, IL
Newby, Fred B. ....Myrtle Beach, SC
Newby, Harry L., Jr. ....Cloquet, MN
Newby, James G. ....San Diego, CA
Newby, Jane M. ....Boise, ID
Newby, Jeffrey D. ....Philadelphia, PA
Newby, John W. ....La Porte, IN
Newby, Jon W. ....Los Angeles, CA
Newby, Lewis, Kaminski & Jones
La Porte, IN
Michigan City, IN
South Bend, IN
Newby, Lingren & Skare, Ltd.
Cloquet, MN
Newby, Melanie A. ....Charlotte, NC
Newby, Melany Stinson ....Madison, WI
Newby, Narda M. ....Washington, DC
Newby, Paul M. ....Raleigh, NC
Newby, Pridgen & Sartip
Myrtle Beach, SC
Newby, Terrance C. ....St. Paul, MN
Newby, Thomas R. ....Indianapolis, IN
Newby, Tom L. ....Alva, OK
Enid, OK
Newcamp, Christine I. ....Pittsburgh, PA
Newcom, Charles W. ....Denver, CO
Newcom, Jennings J. ....Denver, CO
Newcomb, Allen J. ....Nashville, TN
Newcomb, Barbara A. ....Boston, MA
Newcomb, Brian W. ....Menlo Park, CA
Newcomb, Brian W. ....Santa Clara, CA
Newcomb, Christine J. ....Washington, DC
Newcomb, Christopher W. ....Chicago, IL
Newcomb, Danforth ....New York, NY
Newcomb, David R., Jr. ....St. Paul, MN
Newcomb, Elizabeth ....Portland, OR
Newcomb, Elliott S. ....Annapolis, MD
Newcomb, Frederick M., Attorney at Law, P.A.
Rockland, ME
Newcomb, Frederick M., III ....Rockland, ME
Newcomb, Harold E., Jr. ....White Plains, NY
Newcomb, Helen Frances Parker
St. Louis, MO
Newcomb, Jacqueline G. ....Spokane, WA
Newcomb, Jennifer ....New York, NY
Newcomb, Jon E. ....Bremen, IN
Newcomb, Jonathan B. ....Deerfield, IL
Newcomb, K. Kristen ....Lincoln, NE
Newcomb, Karen A. ....Bakersfield, CA
Newcomb, Mark D. ....Irvine, CA
Newcomb, Martha F. ....Providence, RI
Newcomb, Michael B. ....Simi Valley, CA
Newcomb, Michael W. ....Solana Beach, CA
Newcomb, Nancy Jo ....Department of Justice, Criminal Division, GV
Newcomb, Paula M. Eade ....Buffalo, NY
Newcomb, R. Hugo, Jr. ....Jackson, MS
Newcomb, R. Hugo, Sr. ....Jackson, MS
Newcomb, R. Richard ....Treasury Department, Departmental Offices, GV
Newcomb, Robert ....Little Rock, AR
Newcomb, Roberta B. ....Boston, MA
Newcomb, Sabin, Schwartz & Landsverk, LLP ....Portland, OR
Newcomb, Sterling E. ....Greenville, TX
Newcomb, Suzanne S. ....Indianapolis, IN
Newcomb, Teri L. ....Jackson, MS
Newcomb, Thomas E. ....Indianapolis, IN
Newcomb, Thomas W. ....St. Paul, MN
Newcomb, Tim ....Laramie, WY
Newcomb, Verne W. ....Portland, OR
Newcomb, Virginia L. ....Madison, WI
Newcomb, Wellington A. ....New York, NY
Newcomb, William A. ....Harriman, TN
Newcomb, William L., Jr. ....St. Louis, MO
Newcomb, William S., Jr. ....Columbus, OH
Newcombe, Bryan R. ....Rockville, MD
Newcombe, Edward J. ....Worcester, MA
Newcombe, George M. ....Palo Alto, CA
Newcombe, Jack ....Livonia, MI
Newcombe, Jason S ....Eugene, OR
Seattle, WA
Newcombe, Judith P. ....Concord, NH
Newcombe, Mary ....Los Angeles, CA
Newcombe, Ralph W. ....Lawton, OK
Newcombe and Redman, Inc. A Professional Corporation ....Lawton, OK
Newcombe, Scott J. ....Bay City, MI
Newcombe, Stephen K. ....Lawton, OK
Newcombe, Victoria M. ....Miami, FL
Newcome, Douglas S. ....Woodbridge, VA
Newcome, Richard N. ....St. Paul, MN
Newcome, Ron E. ....Columbus, OH
Newcome, Thomas W. ....St. Paul, MN
Newcome, Thomas W., III ....St. Paul, MN
Newcome, Victoria Ann ....Minneapolis, MN
Newcomer, Anne K. ....Detroit, MI
Newcomer, Arthur S. ....Bryan, OH
Newcomer, Bradley D. ....Perkasie, PA
Newcomer, Clarence C. ....Philadelphia, PA
Newcomer, David C. ....Bryan, OH
Newcomer, Ewing Durigon ....Uniontown, PA
Newcomer, James D. ....Columbus, OH
Newcomer, John H., Jr. ....Wilmington, DE
Newcomer, John R., Jr.
St. Petersburg, FL
Tampa, FL
Newcomer, Kerry N., (Mr.) ....Missoula, MT
Newcomer & McCarter ....Toledo, OH
Newcomer, Melvin E. ....Lancaster, PA
Newcomer, Michael S. ....Sacramento, CA
Newcomer, N. Stevens ....Toledo, OH
Newcomer, Paul M. ....Birmingham, MI
Newcomer, Philip W. ....Philadelphia, PA
Newcomer, Robert C. ....Atlanta, GA
Newcomer, Shaffer & Spangler
Bryan, OH
Montpelier, OH
Newcomm, Gregory J.
West Palm Beach, FL
Newcomm, Phillip G., (P.A.) ....Miami, FL
NewDelman, Allan D. ....Phoenix, AZ
NewDelman, Allan D., P.C. ....Phoenix, AZ
Newdorf, David B. ....San Francisco, CA
Newell & Adubato ....Freehold, NJ
Newell, Alfred T., IV ....Birmingham, AL
Newell, Ann Bounds ....Vienna, VA
Newell, Arlette Bolduc ....Long Beach, CA
Newell, Bernard A., Jr. ....San Diego, CA
Newell, Bernard A., Jr. A Prof. Corp., Law Offices of ....San Diego, CA
Newell, Betsy ....Barnstable, MA
Newell, C. Burt
Hot Springs National Park, AR
Newell & Canterbury, LLC
Tuscaloosa, AL
Newell, Carla S. ....Menlo Park, CA
Newell, Catherine L. ....Santa Monica, CA
Newell, Daniel W. ....Homer, LA
Newell, David M. ....Homer, LA
Newell, David W. ....Muscatine, IA
Newell, Deborah K. ....Richmond, VA
Newell, Dix A. ....San Francisco, CA
Newell, Donald P. ....San Diego, CA
Newell, Douglas K. ....Portland, OR
Newell, Edward L., II ....Lander, WY
Newell, Elaine S. ....Atlanta, GA
Newell, Elizabeth A. ....New York, NY
Newell, Emery J. ....North Palm Beach, FL
Newell, Eric P. ....Los Angeles, CA
Newell, Felton T., Jr. ....San Francisco, CA
Newell, Francis Patrick ....Philadelphia, PA
Newell, Frank B. ....Little Rock, AR
Newell, Frank R. ....Long Beach, CA
Newell, Gary J. ....Washington, DC
Newell, Hal H. ....Washington, DC
Newell, Herbert M., III ....Tuscaloosa, AL
Newell, Howard L. ....Framingham, MA
Newell, J. Ross, III ....Staunton, VA
Newell, James A. ....McLean, VA
Newell, James D. ....Pittsburgh, PA
Newell, James P. ....East Quogue, NY
Newell, Janice D. ....Boise, ID
Newell, Jeffrey J. ....Lafayette, IN
Newell, John C. ....Dallas, TX
Newell, John C., Jr. ....Peoria, IL
Newell, John D. ....Annapolis, MD
Newell, John F. ....Chicago, IL
Newell, John M. ....Los Angeles, CA
Newell, John O. ....Boston, MA
Newell, John P. ....Los Angeles, CA
Newell, Katherine A. ....Trenton, NJ
Newell, Kaylee A. ....Sacramento, CA
Newell, Larry M. ....Fort Worth, TX
Newell, Larry W.
Equal Employment Opportunity Commission, Office of Federal Operations, GV
Newell, Lisa ....Department of Justice, Criminal Division, GV
Newell, Lisa C. ....Boston, MA
Newell, Margaret M. ....Washington, DC
Newell, Mark A. ....Mobile, AL
Pensacola, FL
Newell, Mark E. ....Washington, DC
Newell & Martens ....Denver, CO
Newell, Mary Lynne ....Silver City, NM
Newell, Meg G. ....Minneapolis, MN
Newell, Michael E. ....Haleyville, AL
Newell, Michael J. ....San Francisco, CA
Newell, Michael K. ....Dover, DE
Wilmington, DE
Newell, Michael T. ....Lovington, NM
Newell, Neal C. ....Birmingham, AL
Newell, Paul A. ....Homer, LA
Newell, Paul D. ....Keystone Heights, FL
Newell, Paul E. ....Freehold, NJ
Newell, Paul F. ....Tucson, AZ
Newell, Phillip R. ....San Luis Obispo, CA
Newell, Richard F. ....Louisville, KY
Newell, Robert A. ....New York, NY
Newell, Robert D. ....Portland, OR
Newell, Robert D., Jr. ....Tallahassee, FL
Newell, Robert M. ....Los Angeles, CA
Newell, Robert M., Jr. ....Los Angeles, CA
Newell, Roger P. ....New York, NY
Newell, Ronald L. ....Glens Falls, NY
Newell, Russell R. ....Columbus Junction, IA
Newell & Sents ....Columbus Junction, IA
Newell, Sterling, Jr. ....Cleveland, OH
Newell, Steven R., (P.C.) ....Denver, CO
Newell, Susan Smith ....Alexandria, VA
Newell, T. Jamie ....Washington, DC
Newell & Terry, P.A. ....Tallahassee, FL
Newell, Thomas B. ....Fairfax, VA
Newell, Thomas J. ....Blooming Glen, PA
Newell, Thomas P. ....New York, NY
Newell, W. Thomas ....Canton, OH
Salem, OH
Newell, Warren L., Jr. ....Calumet City, IL
Newendorp, Paul W. ....Warren, OH
Newett, Frank R. ....Department of Justice, Criminal Division, GV
Newey, Paul D. ....Chicago, IL
Newey, Robert E. ....Houston, TX
Newey, Robt. L. ....Ogden, UT
Newfeld, Mark L. ....New York, NY
Newfield, Craig M. R. ....Newton, MA
Newfield, James S. ....Stamford, CT
New York, NY
White Plains, NY
Newfield, Jill E. ....New York, NY
Newfield, Lisa M. ....White Plains, NY
Newfield, Mayer U. ....Birmingham, AL
Newfield, Meyer ....New York, NY
Newgren, Richard A. ....Bloomington, MN
Newhall, David G. ....Minneapolis, MN
Newhall, David G. ....Portland, OR
Newhall, John B. ....Boston, MA
Newhall, Norman L. ....Minneapolis, MN
Newhall, Norman L. ....Great Falls, MT
Newhall, Sarra A. ....Marblehead, MA
Newhall, Timothy L. ....Bradenton, FL
Newhard, Eloise W. ....Decatur, GA
Newhard, James A. ....Troy, MI
Newhard, John F., Jr. ....Virginia Beach, VA
Newhard, Tracy L. ....Farmington Hills, MI
Newhart, Anita L. ....Marietta, OH
Newhart, Chester D., Jr. ....Wilkes-Barre, PA
Newhoff, Eleanor J. ....Cambridge, MA
Newholm, Timothy E. ....Milwaukee, WI
Newhook, Amber Marie ....Syracuse, NY
Newhouse, Andrew J. ....Coos Bay, OR
Newhouse, Brian E. ....Los Angeles, CA
Newhouse, Byers & Swaney, P.C.
Independence, MO
Newhouse, Cay A., Jr. ....Sterling Heights, MI
Newhouse, D. Wesley ....Columbus, OH
Newhouse, Daryl L. ....Gaithersburg, MD
Newhouse, David J. ....Tigard, OR
Newhouse, Dixie ....Hagerstown, MD
Newhouse, Eileen ....Minneapolis, MN
Newhouse, Elmer M. ....Baltimore, MD
Newhouse, George B., Jr.
Los Angeles, CA
Newhouse, Gerald W. ....Walnut, CA
Newhouse, J. Samuel ....Independence, MO
Newhouse, James H. ....Monterey, CA
Newhouse, John ....New York, NY
Newhouse, John S. ....Independence, MO
Newhouse, Julie A. ....Rushville, IN
Newhouse, M. Neal ....Boise, ID
Newhouse, Marilyn C. ....Columbia, MD
Newhouse, Martin J. ....Boston, MA
Newhouse, Mary Jo ....Seattle, WA
Newhouse, Michael J ....Wilmington, MA
Newhouse & Newhouse ....Rushville, IN
Newhouse, Norman C. ....San Mateo, CA
Newhouse, Paul F. ....Baltimore, MD
Newhouse, Richard H., Jr. ....Chicago, IL
Newhouse, Robert G. ....Boise, ID
Newhouse, Russell S. ....Dallas, TX
Newhouse, Thomas C. ....Houston, TX
Newhouse, Timothy R. ....Grandville, MI
Newhouse, Tracy J. ....Rushville, IN
Newhouse, W. Wesley ....Salem, NJ
Newhouse, William G., III
Oklahoma City, OK
Newill, Maria Paris ....Wilmington, DE
Newirth, Jerold ....New York, NY
Newitt & Bruny ....Charlotte, NC
Newitt, George B. ....Chicago, IL
Newitt, John G., Jr. ....Charlotte, NC
Newitt, Timothy B. ....Carol Stream, IL
Newitz, Noah B. ....New York, NY
Newkirk, Brett W. ....Miami, FL
Newkirk, Christie A. ....Dallas, TX
Newkirk, Colleen M. (Benedict)
Los Angeles, CA
Newkirk, David G. ....Overland Park, KS
Newkirk, Douglas R. ....Chicago, IL
Newkirk, Eileen McNeil ....Richmond, VA
Newkirk, Eric ....Little Rock, AR
West Memphis, AR
Newkirk, Frank E., Jr. ....Salem, IN
Newkirk, Henry M. ....Atlanta, GA
Newkirk, Jettie D. ....Philadelphia, PA
Newkirk, Krista L. ....Wilmington, NC
Newkirk, Krista Lyn ....Charlotte, NC
Newkirk, Lance Eric ....West Memphis, AR
Newkirk, Maria Ann ....Irvine, CA
Newkirk, Nancy W. ....Washington, DC
Newkirk, Newkirk & Rolin
Los Angeles, CA
Newkirk, Pamela J. ....Bedford, NH
Newkirk, Raymond ....Albany, NY
Newkirk, Robert B., III ....Charlotte, NC
Newkirk, Robert G. ....Minneapolis, MN
Newkirk, Robert St. Claire
Fort Worth, TX
Newkirk & Salada ....Albany, NY
Newkirk, Stephanie D. ....Dallas, TX
Newkirk, Stephanie K. ....Kansas City, MO
Newkirk, Thomas A.
West Des Moines, IA
Newkirk, Thomas C.
Securities and Exchange Commission, Division of Enforcement, GV
Newkirk, William H. ....Los Angeles, CA
Newkirk III, Robert B ....Charlotte, NC
Newkold, Richard H. ....San Mateo, CA
Newlan, Douglas H. ....Redding, CA
Newlan, Eric ....Lewisville, TX
Newlan, Geoff ....Santa Barbara, CA
Newlan, L. A., Jr. ....Lewisville, TX
Newlan & Newlan ....Lewisville, TX
Newland, Bart G. ....Washington, DC
Newland, Benjamin R. ....Washington, DC
Newland, D. Alden ....Charlottesville, VA
Newland, Floyd L. ....Seattle, WA
Newland, G. Daniel ....San Francisco, CA
Newland, Gary A. ....Arlington Heights, IL
Newland, Harold M. ....Detroit, MI
Newland, Howard T., Jr.
Office of Personnel Management, GV
Newland, James R., Jr. ....Falls Church, VA
Leesburg, VA
Newland, Leontyne P. ....Grand Rapids, MI
Newland, Michael A. ....Hamilton, OH
Newland, Stephen S. ....Libertyville, IL
Newlander, Deena S. ....Chicago, IL
Newlander, Roger A. ....Los Altos, CA
Newlands, Bruce W. ....Worcester, MA
Newlands, C. John ....Tacoma, WA
Newlands, Marcia ....Seattle, WA
Newlin, Charles F. ....Chicago, IL
Newlin, Clifton W. ....New Orleans, LA
Newlin, Deborah Lamont ....San Antonio, TX
Newlin, Donald F. ....Bruce, MS
Newlin, Eileen Sloan ....Chicago, IL
Newlin, Floyd W. ....Gretna, LA
Newlin, Henry H. ....Tecumseh, MI
Newlin, Jackson P. ....Pekin, IL
Newlin, Jennifer Stewart ....Lawrence, KS
Newlin, John R. ....Kettering, OH
Newlin, John W. ....Chicago, IL
Newlin, Joseph E. ....Middletown, OH
Newlin, Joseph H. ....Arlington, VA
Newlin, Lawrence E. ....Atlanta, GA
Newlin, Ronald Scott ....Silver Spring, MD
Newlin, Stephen T. ....Houston, TX
Newlin, Thomas C. ....Terre Haute, IN
Newlin, William R. ....Pittsburgh, PA
Newlon, Jeanne Louise ....Washington, DC
Newlon, Jon Eric ....Greenwood, SC
Newlon, Jonathan W. ....Tampa, FL
Newlon, Sharon R. ....Detroit, MI
Newlon, Thomas A. ....Seattle, WA
Newlon, Thornton L. ....Powhatan, VA
Newlove, John F. ....Bowling Green, OH
Newlove, Megan E. ....Bowling Green, OH
Newman, A. Marcy ....Chicago, IL
Newman Aaronson Vanaman, An Assn. of Attys., Not A Prtnrshp ....Sherman Oaks, CA
Newman, Abbie R. ....Philadelphia, PA
Newman, Adam J. ....Cerritos, CA
Newman, Adam T. ....New York, NY
Newman, Alan ....Oklahoma City, OK
Newman, Alan B. ....Marina Del Rey, CA
Newman, Alan H. ....Oceanside, NY
Newman, Alan L. ....Atlanta, GA
Newman, Alan N. ....Rochester, NY
Newman, Albert J., Jr. ....Knoxville, TN
Newman, Alfred W. ....Vallejo, CA
Newman, Alice B. ....Hackensack, NJ
Newman, Alison ....New York, NY
Newman, Alison L. ....Brick, NJ
Newman, Alizabeth S. ....Hempstead, NY
Newman, Alvin L. ....New York, NY
Newman, Amy B. ....Eden Prairie, MN
Newman, Amy E. ....Chicago, IL
Newman, Amy S. ....Jenkintown, PA
Newman, Amy S., P.C., The Law Offices of
Jenkintown, PA
Newman, Andrew ....West Palm Beach, FL
Newman, Andrew J. ....Boston, MA
Newman, Andrew R. ....Fort Lauderdale, FL
Newman, Andrew S. ....Washington, DC
Newman & Andriuzzi ....Clifton, NJ
Newman, Anne Davies ....Rochester, NY
Newman, Anthony G. ....Washington, DC
Newman, Anthony G. ....Bethesda, MD
Newman, Arnold S. ....Chicago, IL
Homewood, IL
Newman, Arthur G., Jr. ....Phoenix, AZ
Newman & Associates ....Los Angeles, CA
Newman & Associates ....Atlanta, GA
Newman, B. A. ....Houston, TX
Newman, Barbara Kaplan ....Morristown, NJ
Newman, Barbara L ....Clifton, NJ
Newman, Barry I., Law Offices of
San Diego, CA
Newman, Barry J. ....Minneapolis, MN
Newman, Barry K. ....Fairfield, CA
Newman, Benjamin W. ....Orlando, FL
Newman & Berger ....New York, NY

Newman, Paul A. ... Chardon, OH
Middlefield, OH
Newman, Paul Andrew ... Los Angeles, CA
Newman, Paul D. ... Salt Lake City, UT
Newman, Paul I. ... Syracuse, NY
Newman, Paula H. ... Stowe, VT
Newman, Pauline ...
United States Court Of Appeals For The Federal Circuit, GV
Newman, Penny G. ... Kansas City, MO
Newman, Perry Wayne ... Owasso, OK
Newman, Peter K. ... Cincinnati, OH
Newman, Peter M. ... Philadelphia, PA
Newman, Philip ... Asbury Park, NJ
Newman, Philip ... Bronx, NY
Newman, Philip H. ... Boston, MA
Newman, Philip H. ... Malden, MA
Newman, Phillip Robert ... Franklin, TN
Newman, R. Anthony ... Atlanta, GA
Newman, R. Ferrell ... Richmond, VA
Newman, Raleigh ... Lake Charles, LA
Newman, Randall S. ... Cleveland, OH
Newman, Randolph A. ... Clifton, NJ
Newman, Randy V. ... Camas, WA
Newman, Ray, Law Offices of
Pasadena, CA
Newman, Raymond F., Jr.
Fort Walton Beach, FL
Newman, Rebekah G. ... Farmington, NM
Newman, Renee C. ... Charleston, SC
Newman, Richard ... Newark, NJ
Newman, Richard ... New York, NY
Newman, Richard A. ... Washington, DC
Newman, Richard B. ... Hudson, MA
Newman, Richard D. ... Santa Ana, CA
Newman, Richard K. ... Chesterfield, VA
Newman, Richard L. ... Oakland, CA
Newman, Richard L. ... Bridgeport, CT
Newman, Richard L. ... New York, NY
Newman, Richard M. ... Chicago, IL
Newman, Richard P. ... Leesburg, FL
Newman, Robbin ... Fort Lauderdale, FL
Newman, Robert ... New York, NY
Newman, Robert A. ... Philadelphia, PA
Newman, Robert B. ... Cincinnati, OH
Newman, Robert C. ... Chicago, IL
Newman, Robert C. ... Pontiac, MI
Newman, Robert C. ... Arcade, NY
Newman, Robert C. ... Brooklyn, NY
Newman, Robert D., Jr. ... Los Angeles, CA
Newman, Robert E. ... Buffalo, NY
Newman, Robert E. ... Kenosha, WI
Newman, Robert G. ... San Antonio, TX
Newman, Robert H. ... Miami, FL
Newman, Robert Jon ... Los Angeles, CA
Newman, Robert L. ... Cherry Hill, NJ
Newman, Robert L., P.A. ... Cherry Hill, NJ
Newman, Robert P. ... Rogers, AR
Newman, Robert S. ... Washington, DC
Newman, Robert S. ... New York, NY
Newman, Robert Scott ... Miami, FL
Newman, Robert T., Sr. ... Asheboro, NC
Newman, Robert Thomas ... Chicago, IL
Newman, Robert W. ... Chicago, IL
Newman, Robert W. ... McMinnville, TN
Newman & Roberts ... Knoxville, TN
Newman, Roger H., Jr. ... Omaha, NE
Newman, Ronald C. ... Topeka, KS
Newman, Ronald D. ... Paramus, NJ
Newman, Ronald J. ... Tucson, AZ
Newman, Roxanne Stephanie ... Marrero, LA
Newman, Roy R. ... Cerritos, CA
Newman, Russell A. ... Modesto, CA
Newman, Russell A., A Professional Law Corporation ... Modesto, CA
Newman, Russell W. ... Redmond, WA
Newman, Samuel ... Boston, MA
Newman, Samuel ... South Padre Island, TX
Newman, Samuel L. ... New City, NY
Newman, Samuel W. ... Stroudsburg, PA
Newman, Sandra K. ... Chicago, IL
Newman, Sandra Schultz
West Conshohocken, PA
Newman, Sapp & Davis, L.L.P.
Atlanta, GA
Newman Schwartz & Greenberg
New York, NY
Newman, Scott ... Hutchinson, MN
Newman, Scott B. ... West Palm Beach, FL
Newman, Scott C. ... Indianapolis, IN
Newman, Scott D. ... New York, NY
Newman, Scott L. ... New York, NY
Newman, Sean ... Los Angeles, CA
Newman, Sharon D. ... San Diego, CA
Newman, Sharon G. ... Portland, ME
Newman, Sheree L. ... Birmingham, MI
Newman, Sheryl L. ... Newark, NJ
Newman & Simpson, LLP ... Hackensack, NJ
Newman, Stanley L. ... Washington, DC
Newman, Stefanie Malin
Fort Lauderdale, FL
Newman, Stephanie Graff ... New York, NY
Newman, Stephanie K. ... Las Vegas, NV
Newman, Stephen A. ... New York, NY
Newman, Stephen C. ... Chicago, IL
Newman, Stephen Elliot ... St. Louis, MO
Newman, Stephen G. ... Jefferson City, MO
Newman, Stephen H. ... Springfield, MA
Newman, Stephen J. ... Los Angeles, CA
Newman, Stephen M. ... Beverly Hills, CA
Newman, Stephen M. ... Boca Raton, FL
Buffalo, NY
New York, NY
Newman, Stephen T. ... Irvine, CA
Newman, Steve ... New York, NY
Newman, Steven F. ... New York, NY
Newman, Steven H. ... New York, NY
Newman, Stewart E. ... New Haven, CT
Newman, Stuart ... Atlanta, GA
Newman, Stuart B. ... New York, NY
Newman, Stuart J. ... Reno, NV
Newman, Stuart Mason ... Blue Bell, PA
Newman, Susan D. ... Chicago, IL
Newman, Tamsin J. ... Philadelphia, PA
Newman Tannenbaum Helpern Syracuse & Hirschtritt LLP ... New York, NY
Newman and Tempkins, P.A.
Miami Beach, FL
Newman, Terri D. ... Sacramento, CA
Newman, Terry E., (P.C.) ... Chicago, IL
Newman, Theodore R., Jr.
Charlotte Amalie, St. Thomas, VI
Newman, Thomas C. ... Portland, ME
Newman, Thomas F., Jr.
South Yarmouth, MA
Newman, Thomas J. ... Suffern, NY
Newman, Thomas J., Jr. ... Suffern, NY
Newman, Thomas, Jr. ... Anderson, IN
Newman, Thomas L. ... Pompano Beach, FL
Newman, Thomas L., Chartered
Pompano Beach, FL
Newman, Thomas M. ... Wheaton, IL
Newman, Thomas P. ... Washington, DC
Newman, Thomas R. ... New York, NY
Newman, Timothy G. ... Southfield, MI
Newman, Todd A. ... Washington, DC
Newman, Todd G. ... Monroe, LA
Newman, Todd H.
Christiansted, St. Croix, VI
Newman, Tracy L. ... New York, NY
Newman, Trockman, Lloyd, Flynn & Rheinlander ... Evansville, IN
Newman, Vicki A. ... Boston, MA
Newman, W. Leonard ... West New York, NJ
Newman, W. Martin ... Fair Oaks, CA
Newman, Walter G. ... Sumter, SC
Newman, Wayne L. ... Chicago, IL
Newman, William A. ... New York, NY
Newman, William A. ... Columbus, OH
Newman, William A. ... Dallas, TX
Houston, TX
Newman, William A. ... McLean, VA
Newman, William A., III ... Merced, CA
Newman, William C. ... Northampton, MA
Newman, William C. ... El Paso, TX
Newman, William David, Jr.
Hollywood, FL
Newman, William F. ... Columbus, OH
Newman, William J., Jr. ... Richmond, VA
Newman, William M. ... Muskegon, MI
Newman, William R. ... Hattiesburg, MS
Newman, William S., Sr. ... Chicago, IL
Newman, William T., Jr. ... Arlington, VA
Newman, Williams, Mishkin, Corveleyn, Wolfe & Fareri, A Professional Corporation ... Marshalls Creek, PA
Stroudsburg, PA
Newman, Winn I. ... Washington, DC
Newman, Zachary G. ... New York, NY
Newman, Zalman D. ... Newport, RI
Newman Aaronson, Edith S.
Sherman Oaks, CA
Newman Eckstein, Lisa ... Portland, OR
Newman Knowling, Marla Y.
Kansas City, MO
Newmann, David ... Washington, DC
Newman-Worrell, Terri ... Indianapolis, IN
Newmark, Allan J. ... Chappaqua, NY
Newmark, Andrea ... Department of Justice, Civil Division, GV
Newmark, Donald M. ... Sparta, NJ
Newmark, Edwin ... New York, NY
Newmark, Eileen Evans ... East Northport, NY
Newmark, Eric L. ... Minneapolis, MN
Newmark, Herbert L. ... Center Moriches, NY
Newmark Irvine, P.A. ... Phoenix, AZ
Newmark, Jodi Ann ... Chicago, IL
Newmark, Kara Turner ... Fenton, MO
Newmark, Lamb, Monohan & Marchisio
New York, NY
Syosset, NY
Newmark, Laurie L. ... Montclair, NJ
Newmark, Lawrence ... Riverhead, NY
Newmark, Linda A. ... Los Angeles, CA
Newmark, Lynn E. ... St. Louis, MO
Newmark, Martin A. ... Morristown, NJ
Newmark, Michael N. ... St. Louis, MO
Newmark, Milton Maxwell
Walnut Creek, CA
Newmark, Mitchell A. ... Trenton, NJ
Newmark, Richard D. ... New York, NY
Newmark, Robert L. ... St. Louis, MO
Newmark, Scott ... New York, NY
Newmark, Scott M. ... Fort Lauderdale, FL
Newmark, Stanley M. ... Miami, FL
Newmark, Stanley M., P.A. ... Miami, FL
Newmark, Stephen C. ... Phoenix, AZ
Newmark, Steven D. ... Charlotte, NC
Newmark, Thomas M. ... St. Louis, MO
Newmark, Tracy B. ... Hollywood, FL
Newmaster, T. Walter ... Ada, OK
Newmeyer, Barbara A. ... Edison, NJ
Newmeyer & Dillion LLP
Newport Beach, CA
Newmeyer, Robert J. ... Terre Haute, IN
Newmeyer, Thomas F.
Newport Beach, CA
Newmyer, Edward A. ... Muskegon, MI
Newnam, Benjamin T. ... Wilmington, DE
Newnam, George A. ... Trinidad, CO
Newnam, Stephen H. ... Shalimar, FL
Newnan, Lisa S. ... Los Angeles, CA
Newnham, Gary C. ... Toledo, OH
Newnham, M. Kathryn ... La Jolla, CA
San Diego, CA
Newnham, Stephen L. ... La Jolla, CA
San Diego, CA
Newnum, Paul D. ... Winter Park, FL
Newnum, Paul D., P.A. ... Winter Park, FL
Newport, Jeffrey Richard ... Houston, TX
Newport, Joel D. ... Towson, MD
Newport, John G. ... Los Alamitos, CA
Newport Law Associates, P.C. ... Newport, RI
Newport, Michael W. ... St. Louis, MO
Newport & Newport ... Davenport, IA
Newport, Stephany J. ... Kansas City, MO
Newport, Stephen W. ... Davenport, IA
Newport, Walter ... Davenport, IA
Newport, Wayne M. ... Davenport, IA
Newport, William Lamar ... Brentwood, TN
Newpower, William J., Jr. ... Eagan, MN
Newquist, Carl J. ... Fridley, MN
Newquist & Ekstrum, P.A. ... Fridley, MN
Newquist, Elaine T. ... Chicago, IL
Newquist, Lane W. ... East Greenwich, RI
Newquist, Michael L. ... Chicago, IL
Newsam, Raleigh William, II ... Dallas, TX
Newsham, George M. ... Anchorage, AK
Newsham, John F. ... St. Louis, MO
Newsham, Katie ... Chicago, IL
Newsom, Bernard D. (Skip), Jr.
Austin, TX
Newsom, Christian G. ... Dallas, TX
Newsom, Dan L. ... Memphis, TN
Newsom, Daniel O. ... Houston, TX
Newsom, Edward M. ... Atlanta, GA
Newsom, Elizabeth W.
Department of Justice, Civil Division, GV
Newsom, Eric A. ... Walnut Creek, CA
Newsom, Fred L., Jr. ... Columbus, OH
Newsom, Garmon, II ... Brooklyn, NY
Newsom, Graham, Hedrick & Kennon, P.A.
Durham, NC
Newsom, Gwyn P. ... Columbus, GA
Newsom, Hamlet T., Jr. ... San Antonio, TX
Newsom, Heather Elizabeth
Birmingham, AL
Newsom, J. Kent ... Dallas, TX
Newsom, James A. ... Houston, TX
Newsom, James L. ... Durham, NC
Newsom, James M., Jr. ... Madison, GA
Newsom, James R., III ... Memphis, TN
Newsom, James T. ... Kansas City, MO
Newsom, Jan R. ... Dallas, TX
Newsom, Jennifer R. ... Tampa, FL
Newsom, Kevin C. ... Washington, DC
Newsom, Larry J. ... Palatine, IL
Newsom, N. Kendall ... Richmond, VA
Newsom, Neil E. ... Dallas, TX
Newsom, Phillip F. ... Columbia, SC
Newsom, R. Kirk ... Dallas, TX
Newsom, Robert Edward
Sulphur Springs, TX
Newsom, Ruey A., II ... Erlanger, KY
Newsom, Scott D. ... Toledo, OH
Newsom, Sondra H. ... Topeka, KS
Newsom, Terry & Newsom ... Dallas, TX
Newsom, Tim D. ... Amarillo, TX
Newsom, Walter F. ... Valdosta, GA
Newsom, Walter F., P.C. ... Valdosta, GA
Newsom, William A. ... San Francisco, CA
Newsome, Amy Marie ... Dothan, AL
Newsome, C. Richard ... Orlando, FL
Newsome, Dan ... Del Rio, TX
Newsome, David, Jr.
Department of the Army, U.S. Army Legal Services Agency, GV
Newsome, George M. ... Washington, DC
Vienna, VA
Newsome, Heber H., III
Nuclear Regulatory Commission, Office of the General Counsel, GV
Newsome, Helene R. ... Treasury Department, Internal Revenue Service, GV
Newsome, Jack S. ... Tampa, FL
Newsome, James B. ... Atlanta, GA
Newsome, Jerry C. ... Atlanta, GA
Newsome, Jonathan K. ... Houston, TX
Newsome, Kelvin L. ... Norfolk, VA
Richmond, VA
Newsome, Larry D. ... Washington, DC
Newsome, Lynn Fontaine ... Short Hills, NJ
Newsome, P. David, Jr. ... Tulsa, OK
Newsome, Raina Spielman ... Houston, TX
Newsome, Randall J. ... Oakland, CA
Newsome, William Bruce ... Dallas, TX
Newsome, William G., III ... Columbia, SC
Newsome, William R., III ... San Diego, CA
Newson, Neil C. ... Beverly Hills, CA
Newson, Neil C., & Associates, P.C.
Beverly Hills, CA
Newson, Perry Y. ... Raleigh, NC
Newstadt, Jacqueline ... Laurel, MD
Newstadt, Stephen A. ... Beverly Hills, CA
Newstead, Jennifer G. ... New York, NY
Newsum, Clint Thomas
Overland Park, KS
Newsum, J. Hartly ... Bellevue, WA
NewTechLaw ... Palo Alto, CA
Newth, James F. ... Carrollton, TX
Newton, Albert H., Jr. ... Yreka, CA
Newton, Alex W. ... Birmingham, AL
Newton, Alexander D.
Agency for International Development, Legal Advisers-Overseas, GV
Newton, Alexander R. ... Tuscaloosa, AL
Newton, Angela M. ... Houston, TX
Newton, Anna ... Texarkana, AR
Newton, Arnaud ... Fort Collins, CO
Newton, Blake T., III ... Darien, CT
Newton, Bob H. ... Anthony, KS
Newton, Bonnie S. ... Seminole, FL
Newton, Brent E. ... Houston, TX
Newton, Bruce W. ... Eugene, OR
Newton, Brynn Gail ... Daytona Beach, FL
Newton, Carl K. ... Los Angeles, CA
Newton, Carla W. ... Springfield, MA
Newton, Carrie L. ... Chicago, IL
Newton, Carrie L. ... Parkersburg, WV
Newton, Carrie L. ... Ripley, WV
Newton, Catherine M. ... Brooklyn, NY
Newton, Charles Anthony ... Texarkana, TX
Newton, Charles D. ... Scottsdale, AZ
Newton, Charles L., II ... Atlanta, GA
Newton, Charles T., Jr. ... Houston, TX
Newton, Christian A. ... Chattanooga, TN
Newton, Christine M. ... Attica, NY
Newton, Christopher A. ... Terre Haute, IN
Newton, Clifford B. ... Jacksonville, FL
Newton, Clinton G. ... Kansas City, MO
Newton, Courtney B. ... San Antonio, TX
Newton, Cynthia F. ... San Francisco, CA
Newton, Dean A. ... Kansas City, MO
Newton, Debra M. ... Chicago, IL
Newton, Dinah ... Boulder, CO
Newton, Donald L. ... Glynco, GA
Newton, Elizabeth ... Jamaica, NY
Newton, Everett E. ... Hartford, CT
Newton, Everett W. ... Dallas, TX
Newton, F. Page ... Department of Justice, Executive Office for United States Attorneys, GV
Newton, Floyd C., III ... Atlanta, GA
Newton, Francis C., Jr. ... Boston, MA
Newton, Francis C., Jr., Law Firm
Boston, MA
Newton, Francis J., Jr. ... Detroit, MI
Newton, Frank C., Jr. ... Charlotte, NC
Newton, Frank W. ... Oakland, CA
Newton, Franklin Hobbs ... Houston, TX
Newton, Gary C. ... Kalamazoo, MI
Newton, Geo. A. ... St. Louis, MO
Newton, Geoffrey L. ... Dallas, TX
Newton, George D., Jr. ... Winston-Salem, NC
Newton, George F. ... Clifton Springs, NY
Newton, Germain D. ... West Hartford, CT
Newton, Gilbert E. ... El Cajon, CA
Newton, Grace A. ... Chicago, IL
Newton, Gregory ... Raleigh, NC
Newton, G. W. (Bill) ... Tulsa, OK
Newton, H. Dwayne ... Houston, TX
Newton, Harold W. ... Hawesville, KY
Newton, Heather ... Asheville, NC
Newton, Henry R. ... Easton, PA
Newton, Henry T. ... Everett, WA
Newton and Hoff, L.L.P.
Bay St. Louis, MS
Biloxi, MS
Diamondhead, MS
Gulfport, MS
Hattiesburg, MS
Jackson, MS
Long Beach, MS
Lucedale, MS
Mc Comb, MS
Natchez, MS
Pascagoula, MS
Pass Christian, MS
Newton, Howard P. ... San Antonio, TX
Newton & Howell, P.C. ... Griffin, GA
Newton, Hurst & Almand ... Jacksonville, FL
Newton, Iris S. ... Sacramento, CA
Newton & Ivins ... Sandy, UT
Newton, J. Alvin, Jr. ... Albany, GA
Newton, J. Gregory ... Raleigh, NC
Newton, J. Jefferson ... Beaufort, NC
Newton, J. Michael ... Mobile, AL
Newton, J. Michael ... Naperville, IL
Newton, J. Rita ... Cleveland, OH
Newton, J. Steven ... Sandy, UT
Newton, Jacqueline A. ... Wilmington, NC
Newton, James A. ... East Lansing, MI
Newton, James P. ... Butler, AL
Newton, James R. ... Bridgeport, CT
Southport, CT
Newton, Jane W. ... Texarkana, TX
Newton, Jeffrey J. ... Orlando, FL
Newton, Jennifer E. ... Boston, MA
Newton, Jerry L. ... Hermosa Beach, CA
Newton, Joel D. ... Houston, TX
Newton, Joel T. ... Las Cruces, NM
Newton, John D. C., II ... Tallahassee, FL
Newton, John F. ... Cos Cob, CT
Newton, John F. ... Weymouth, MA
Newton, John J. ... Beloit, WI
Newton, John P., Jr. ... Knoxville, TN
Newton, John R. ... Hillsborough, NJ
Newton, John Richard ... Wilmington, NC
Newton, John T., Jr. ... Griffin, GA
Newton, John W., III ... Beaumont, TX
Newton, Johnnie Lee ... Fallbrook, CA
Newton, Jon P. ... Hartford, CT
Newton, Jonathan B. ... Dallas, TX
Newton, Jonathan V.
Environmental Protection Agency, Office of the General Counsel, GV
Newton, Joseph ... Houston, TX
Newton, Joseph B. ... Waycross, GA
Newton, Joseph B. ... San Antonio, TX
Newton, Judith Sperling ... Madison, WI
Newton, Kastner & Remmel, A Professional Corporation ... Mountain View, CA
Newton, Kellie L. ... Washington, DC
Newton, Kenneth B. ... Boston, MA
Newton - Kight L.L.P. ... Everett, WA
Newton, L. Trammell, Jr. ... Atlanta, GA
Newton, Lauri A. ... Portland, OR
Newton Law Firm ... Beaufort, NC
Newton Law Office ... Anthony, KS
Newton, Lawrence L. ... Huntingdon, PA
Newton, Leslie Ann ... Hermosa Beach, CA

Nicholas, John E., Jr. ....Akron, NY
Nicholas, John J.
Securities and Exchange Commission, Office of the General Counsel, GV
Nicholas, Joseph F., Jr. ....Cleveland, OH
Nicholas, Kevin C. ....Phoenix, AZ
Nicholas, Kevin Dale ....Westminster, CO
Nicholas, Leslee Ann Clark ......Chesapeake, VA
Nicholas, Lisa V. ....Costa Mesa, CA
Nicholas, Louis K., II ....Miami, FL
Nicholas, Lynn ....Salt Lake City, UT
Nicholas, Mark H. ....Mountain View, CA
Nicholas, Mary Lynn ....New York, NY
Nicholas, Michele Monaghan
Camp Hill, PA
Nicholas, Nestor M., (P.C.) ....Boston, MA
Nicholas, Nick D. ....Houston, TX
Nicholas, Patricia E. ....Washington, DC
Nicholas, Perot & Strauss ....Akron, NY
Nicholas, Philip ....Laramie, WY
Nicholas, Robert A. ....Philadelphia, PA
Nicholas, Robert B. ....Washington, DC
Nicholas, Robert C. ....San Francisco, CA
Nicholas, Robert H., Jr. ....Houston, TX
Nicholas, Robert M. ....Santa Monica, CA
Nicholas & Robertson, L.L.P. ....Dallas, TX
Nicholas, Romel L. ....Pittsburgh, PA
Nicholas, Samuel J., Jr. ....Jackson, MS
Nicholas, Scott A. ....San Bernardino, CA
Nicholas, Scott A. ....Minneapolis, MN
Nicholas, Socrates Scott L. ....New York, NY
Nicholas, Stefan C. ....Washington, DC
Nicholas, Stephen A. ....Bellmore, NY
Nicholas, Stephen A. ....San Antonio, TX
Nicholas, Stephen W. ......Avondale Estates, GA
Nicholas, Steve C. ....Harrisburg, PA
Nicholas, Steven L. ....Mobile, AL
Nicholas, Susan Young ....Manheim, PA
Nicholas, Talbot J., II
Department of Transportation, U. S. Coast Guard, GV
Nicholas, T.B. "Nick", Jr. ....Dallas, TX
Houston, TX
Nicholas, Theodore L. ....Indianapolis, IN
Nicholas, Thomas A., III ....Cheyenne, WY
Nicholas, Vernon L. ....Mesa, AZ
Nicholas, Vernon L. ....Phoenix, AZ
Nicholas, William R. ....Los Angeles, CA
Nicholas, William T. ....Norristown, PA
Nicholas, W. J. ....Lander, WY
Nicholas, Steven A. ....Portland, OR
Nicholl, Peter T. ....Baltimore, MD
Nicholls, Albert E., Jr. ....Dunmore, PA
Nicholls & Associates, P.C. ....Denver, CO
Nicholls, Brent W. ....Denver, CO
Nicholls, Bruce G. ....Boston, MA
Nicholls & Crampton, P.A. ....Raleigh, NC
Nicholls, David H. ....Crown Point, IN
Nicholls, Dennis A. ....Sunnyvale, CA
Nicholls, Donald G. ....Mill Valley, CA
Nicholls, F. Timothy ....Raleigh, NC
Nicholls, Garth J. ....Colorado Springs, CO
Nicholls, Henry P. ....Newport Beach, CA
Nicholls, Jeffrey M. ....Anderson, IN
Nicholls, John C. ....Raleigh, NC
Nicholls, John F. ....Barre, VT
Nicholls, Jon S. ....Denver, CO
Nicholls, Lawrence P. ....Phoenix, AZ
Nicholls, Lawrence P., P.C. ....Phoenix, AZ
Nicholls, Lewis D. ....Greenup, KY
Nicholls, Lewis H. ....Greenup, KY
Nicholls, Malcolm B., III ....Boston, MA
Nicholls, Mary ....New York, NY
Nicholls & Maul ....Boston, MA
Nicholls, Richard H. ....New York, NY
Nicholls, Stephen C. ....Denver, CO
Nicholls-Car, Lori J. ....Durham, NC
Nichols, A. Shane ....Atlanta, GA
Nichols, Alan H. ....San Francisco, CA
Nichols, Alan H. ....Atlanta, GA
Nichols, Alan Shane ....Atlanta, GA
Nichols, Alexandra J. ....Towson, MD
Nichols, Alison M. ....Palo Alto, CA
Nichols, Andrea H ....Las Vegas, NV
Nichols, Andrew G. ....Baltimore, MD
Nichols, Andrew L., (P.C.) ....Boston, MA
Nichols, Andrew T. ....New York, NY
Nichols, Ann Kell ....Lakeville, MN
Nichols, Antoinette L. ....San Francisco, CA
Nichols & Arceneaux, A P.L.C.
Jennings, LA
Nichols, Arthur W., Jr. ....Kennebunkport, ME
Nichols, Ashley P. ....Atlanta, GA
Nichols & Associates ....Portland, OR
Nichols, Aubrey E. ....Columbus, MS
Nichols, A. W., III ....Palatka, FL
Nichols, B. Clarke ....Naples, FL
Nichols, Basil P. ....Houston, TX
Nichols, Bergere, Zauzig & Sandler, P.C.
Fairfax, VA
Lake Ridge, VA
Manassas, VA
Woodbridge, VA
Nichols, Bruce R. ....Grosse Pointe Farms, MI
Nichols, C. Philip, Jr. ....Upper Marlboro, MD
Nichols & Campbell, P.A. ....Little Rock, AR
Nichols, Candace A. ....Edgartown, MA
Nichols, Carl John ....Washington, DC
Nichols, Carol S. ....Tulsa, OK
Nichols, Carolyn ....Salt Lake City, UT
Nichols, Carolyn M. ....Albuquerque, NM
Nichols, Catherine A. ....Tucson, AZ
Nichols, Catterton, Downing & Reed, Inc.
Orinda, CA
Nichols, Chanda R. ....Columbus, OH
Nichols, Charles E., Jr. ....Raleigh, NC
Nichols, Charles L. ....San Diego, CA
Nichols, Charles L. ....Dearborn, MI
Nichols, Charles L., P.C. ....Dearborn, MI
Nichols, Charles S. ....Dallas, TX
Nichols, Cheryl C. ....Atlanta, GA
Nichols, Chris D. ....Reno, NV
Nichols, Christine Kelly ....New York, NY
Nichols, Christopher A. ....South Bend, IN
Nichols, Christopher C. ....Norwell, MA
Nichols, Christopher R. ....Asheville, NC
Charlotte, NC
Gastonia, NC
Hendersonville, NC
Hickory, NC
Nichols, Cisselon S. ....Beaumont, TX
Nichols, Clark G. ....Scottsbluff, NE
Nichols, Clark Reed ....Seattle, WA
Nichols, Clifford C. ....Lancaster, CA
Nichols, Colleen M. ....Auburn, CA
Nichols, Craig Allen ....Portland, OR
Nichols, Craig B. ....St. Paul, MN
Nichols, Craig K. ....Fayetteville, NY
Nichols, Curt M. ....Vienna, VA
Nichols, Curtis B. ....Marietta, OH
Nichols, Cynthia A. ....Santa Ana, CA
Nichols, Cynthia Leigh ....Jacksonville, FL
Nichols, Dale K. ....Chicago, IL
Nichols, Daniel J. ....Sioux Falls, SD
Nichols, Daniel K. ....Boynton Beach, FL
Nichols, Darrell S. ....Wiscasset, ME
Nichols, Darrin L. ....Saginaw, MI
Nichols, David A. ....Bellingham, WA
Nichols, David E.
Charlotte Amalie, St. Thomas, VI
Nichols, David E., P.C.
Charlotte Amalie, St. Thomas, VI
Nichols, David G., Jr. ....New York, NY
Nichols, David L. ....Chilton, WI
Nichols, David M. ....Tulsa, OK
Nichols, Dean M. ....Harrisonburg, VA
Nichols, Deborah L. ....Hayesville, NC
Nichols, Diane Christy ....Kansas City, MO
Nichols, Donald G. ....Jacksonville, FL
Nichols, Donald H. ....Minneapolis, MN
Nichols, Donald L. ....St. Louis, MO
Nichols, Donna S. ....Indianapolis, IN
Nichols, Douglas D. ....Ludlow, MA
Nichols, Douglas E. ....Hillsboro, OR
Nichols, Douglas, Kelly and Meade, A Professional Corporation ...Scottsbluff, NE
Nichols, Douglas R. ....Portland, OR
Nichols, Edward A. ....Devon, PA
Nichols, Edward C., Jr. ....Nashville, TN
Nichols, Edward M. ....Lake Charles, LA
Nichols, Edward P. ....Atlanta, GA
Nichols, Edward (Ted), Jr.
Lake Charles, LA
Nichols, E. L. ....Los Altos, CA
Nichols, Elaine K. ....Stowe, VT
Nichols, Elizabeth S. ....Albany, NY
Nichols, Elvin C.
Federal Labor Relations Authority, Authority Member Staff, GV
Nichols, Eric James Roy ....Houston, TX
Nichols, Errol B. ....Conyers, GA
Nichols, Eugene Bullard ....Jacksonville, FL
Nichols, F. Glenn, Law Offices of
Pasadena, CA
Nichols, F. Harris ....Buffalo, NY
Nichols, Frank K. ....St. Joseph, MO
Nichols, Frank Wilson ....Fairfield, ID
Nichols, Frederick E. ....Madisonville, KY
Nichols, G. Peter ....Chicago, IL
Nichols, Gary H. ....Dyersburg, TN
Nichols, Gary Richard ....San Diego, CA
Nichols, Gary V. ....Plymouth, MA
Nichols, Gary W. ....Hayesville, NC
Nichols, Geo. O. ....Terre Haute, IN
Nichols, Geoffrey Kemble
St. Petersburg, FL
Nichols, George D. ....Lamar, MO
Nichols, George F., Jr. ....Chicago, IL
Nichols, George N. ....Bridgeport, CT
Nichols, Georgia L. ....North Haven, CT
Nichols, Gordon Earle ....Nashville, TN
Nichols, Grace M. ....St. Charles, MO
Nichols, Gregory Martin ....Sunrise, FL
Nichols, Gregory T. ....Greensburg, PA
Nichols, H. Louis ....Dallas, TX
Nichols, H. Michael ....Wichita, KS
Nichols, Harrison W. ....Union Grove, WI
Nichols, H. E. ....Atlanta, GA
Nichols, Henry W. ....Oklahoma City, OK
Nichols, Hugh L., II ....Batavia, OH
Nichols, J. Erik ....Austin, TX
Nichols, J. Harold ....Memphis, TN
Nichols, J. Pat ....Parsons, WV
Nichols, Jack Britt ....Orlando, FL
Nichols, Jack Q. ....Austin, TX
Nichols, Jackson, Dillard, Hager & Smith, L.L.P. ....Dallas, TX
Nichols, Jacques B. ....Lake Oswego, OR
Nichols, James ....Markham, IL
Nichols, James A. ....Birmingham, MI
Nichols, James D. ....Los Angeles, CA
Nichols, James D. ....New Brunswick, NJ
Nichols, James D., Jr. ....Lawrenceville, GA
Nichols, James G. ....Batavia, OH
Nichols, James Henry ....Charlotte, NC
Nichols, James K. ....Ionia, MI
Nichols, James Larry ....Fort Myers, FL
Tupelo, MS
Nichols, James P. ....San Mateo, CA
Nichols, James R. ....Boston, MA
Nichols, James R., Jr. ....Santa Barbara, CA
Nichols, James V. ....Lamar, MO
Nichols, Jarret P. ....Columbus, MS
Nichols, Jas. E. ....Vicksburg, MS
Nichols, Jeff W. ....Madison, WI
Nichols, Jeffrey C. ....Deerfield, IL
Nichols, Jeffrey J. ....Houston, TX
Nichols, Jeffrey L. ....Glendale, CA
Nichols, Jeffrey R. ....Lake Success, NY
Nichols, Jeffrey T. ....Milwaukee, WI
Nichols, Jerry R. ....Tulsa, OK
Nichols, Jessica Armstrong ....Malvern, PA
Nichols, Joe Y. ....Woodbury, TN
Nichols, John A. ....Luverne, AL
Nichols, John C. ....Baltimore, MD
Nichols, John D. ....North Little Rock, AR
Nichols, John D. ....Portland, OR
Nichols, John F. ....Houston, TX
Nichols, John L. ....Tacoma, WA
Nichols, John M. ....Minneapolis, MN
Nichols, John M. ....Oklahoma City, OK
Nichols, John P. ....Terre Haute, IN
Nichols, John R. ....Grand Rapids, MI
Nichols, John S. ....Columbia, SC
Nichols, John W. ....Cartersville, GA
Nichols, John W. ....Kennett, MO
Nichols, Johnny L. ....Harrison, AR
Nichols, Jon A. ....Hamburg, NY
Nichols, Jonathan D. ....Hudson, NY
Nichols, Jones & McCown ....Tuscola, IL
Nichols, Jose A. ....Sanford, FL
Nichols, Joseph E. ....Glens Falls, NY
Nichols, Joseph P. ....Malone, NY
Nichols, Joyce Birkel ....Upper Marlboro, MD
Nichols, Judith A. ....Missouri City, TX
Nichols, Julie M. ....Chicago, IL
Nichols, Karen A. ....Denver, CO
Nichols, Karen M. ....Norwood, MA
Nichols Kaster & Anderson
Minneapolis, MN
Nichols, Kathleen MacMahon ....Miami, FL
Nichols, Kathleen P. ....Bedford, MA
Nichols, Kenneth A. ....Stockton, CA
Nichols, Kenneth L. ....New Kensington, PA
Nichols, Kevin F. ....Malone, NY
Nichols, Kimaka ....Greenville, SC
Nichols, Kristin A. ....Chicago, IL
Nichols, L. Wesley, (P.A.)
Palm Beach Gardens, FL
Nichols, Lara Simmons ....Charlotte, NC
Nichols, Laurel A. ....New York, NY
Nichols Law Office, P.C. ....Birmingham, AL
Nichols, Le Mans ....Salinas, CA
Nichols, Leon G. ....Miami, FL
Nichols, Leonard J. ....Roslyn, NY
Nichols, Leslie A. ....Denver, CO
Nichols, Leslie C. ....San Jose, CA
Nichols, Leslie H.
Hastings-On-Hudson, NY
Nichols, Lisa J. ....Houston, TX
Nichols, Lizabeth R. ....Birmingham, AL
Nichols, Logan L. ....Jennings, LA
Nichols, Lucille Pratt ....New York, NY
Nichols, Lyle D. ....Marietta, GA
Nichols, M. Jackson ....Raleigh, NC
Nichols, M. Jay ....Columbus, MS
Nichols, Madeleine M. ....New York, NY
Nichols, Malcolm G. ....Arlington, TX
Nichols, Margaret J. ....Ann Arbor, MI
Nichols, Maria P. ....Boston, MA
Nichols, Marilyn ....Salem, OR
Nichols, Mark ....Oklahoma City, OK
Nichols, Mark E. ....Lexington, KY
Nichols, Mark W. ....Little Rock, AR
Nichols, Marsha M. ....Houston, TX
Nichols, Martin Clark ....San Diego, CA
Nichols, Martin R. ....Soquel, CA
Nichols, Mary Alexander ....Biloxi, MS
Nichols, Mary Barrow ....Austin, TX
Nichols, Matthew B. ....Saco, ME
Nichols, Matthew W. ....Atlanta, GA
Nichols, Michael A. ....Sunnyvale, CA
Nichols, Michael C. ....Houston, TX
Nichols, Michael G. ....San Francisco, CA
Nichols, Michael S. ....Springfield, MO
Nichols, Michael W. ....Munfordville, KY
Nichols, Muriel Irwin ....Boston, MA
Nichols & Myers ....Erie, PA
Nichols, Myra W. ....Dixon, IL
Nichols, Nancy O. ....Las Vegas, NV
Nichols, Nathaniel C. ....Wilmington, DE
Nichols, Neal A. ....Austin, TX
Nichols Newman Logan & D'Eramo, P.C.
Christiansted, St. Croix, VI
Nichols, Nia J. ....Rochester, NY
Nichols & Nichols ....Madisonville, KY
Nichols and Nichols ....Lamar, MO
Nichols & Nichols ....Hayesville, NC
Nichols & Nichols ....Parsons, WV
Nichols, Nichols & Kennedy ....Tulsa, OK
Nichols & Nichols, P.C. ....Longview, TX
Nichols, Nick C., (P.C.) ....Houston, TX
Nichols, Nils N.
Federal Energy Regulatory Commission, Office of the General Counsel, GV
Nichols, Nina A. ....Washington, DC
Nichols, Norman C., IV
Sagamore Hills, OH
Nichols & Oliver ....Albuquerque, NM
Nichols, Orville W., Jr. ....Knox, IN
Nichols, O. T. ....Jesup, GA
Nichols, Pamela A. ....Albany, NY
Nichols, Patricia ....Berkeley, CA
Nichols, Patricia ....Jersey City, NJ
Nichols, Patricia A. ....Mountain View, CA
Nichols, Patricia E. ....Miami, FL
Nichols, Patrick ....Topeka, KS
Nichols, Patrick A. ....Parsons, WV
Nichols, Patrick R., Chartered ....Topeka, KS
Nichols, Patsy W. ....Austin, TX
Nichols, Paul F. ....Woodbridge, VA
Nichols, Paul M. ....Redwood City, CA
Nichols, Paul W. ....Los Angeles, CA
Nichols, Peter ....Los Angeles, CA
Nichols, Peter ....Wethersfield, CT
Nichols, Peter A. ....Pasadena, CA
Nichols, Philip M. ....Philadelphia, PA
Nichols, Philip R. ....Columbus, OH
Nichols, Phillip A. ....Stephenville, TX
Nichols, Phillip Anthony ....Birmingham, AL
Nichols, Phillip G. ....Los Angeles, CA
Nichols Professional Law Corporation, The
San Francisco, CA
Nichols, R. Thomas, Jr. ....Rockingham, NC
Nichols and Rabuck, P.C. ....Sioux Falls, SD
Nichols, Ralph A. ....Stamford, CT
Nichols, Randall E. ....Knoxville, TN
Nichols, Randall W. ....Birmingham, AL
Nichols, Raymond E. ....Manchester, NH
Nichols, R. E., Jr. ....Chesapeake, VA
Nichols, Rex A. ....Longview, TX
Nichols, Rex A., Jr. ....Longview, TX
Nichols, Richard D. ....Jacksonville, FL
Nichols, Richard L. ....Jacksonville, FL
Nichols, Richard M. ....Douglas, GA
Nichols, Richard M. ....Charleston, SC
Nichols, Richard S. ....Parsippany, NJ
Nichols, Richard W. ....Sacramento, CA
Nichols, Roann ....Baltimore, MD
Nichols, Robert ....Dedham, MA
Nichols, Robert B. ....Buffalo, NY
Hamburg, NY
Nichols, Robert C. ....Pasadena, CA
Nichols, Robert C. ....Newport News, VA
Nichols, Robert D. ....London, OH
Nichols, Robert F., Jr. ....Dana Point, CA
Nichols, Robert Gary ....Fort Lauderdale, FL
Nichols, Robert H. ....Rosemont, IL
Nichols, Robert H. ....Columbus, OH
Nichols, Robert J. ....New Orleans, LA
Nichols, Robert J. ....Tulsa, OK
Nichols, Robert S. ......Department of the Army, Office, Chief of Engineers/Headquarters, U.S. Army Corps of Engineers, GV
Nichols, Robert S. ....Corpus Christi, TX
Nichols, Robert W. ....Boulder, CO
Nichols, Robert W. ....Mosinee, WI
Nichols, Robt. E. ....Birmingham, MI
Nichols, Rodney H. ....Springfield, MO
Nichols, Roger J. ....North Hollywood, CA
Nichols, Roger J., A Prof. Corp., Law Offices of ....North Hollywood, CA
Nichols, Roger M. ....Abilene, TX
Nichols, Ron K. ....Ogden, UT
Nichols, Rosemary ....Watervliet, NY
Nichols, Rudy J. ....Pontiac, MI
Nichols, Sacks, Slank & Sweet, A Professional Corporation ...Ann Arbor, MI
Nichols, Sandi L. ....San Francisco, CA
Nichols, Sara S. ....Washington, DC
Nichols, Scott B. ....Portland, OR
Nichols, Scott E. ....Long Beach, CA
Nichols, Scott G. ....St. Paul, MN
Nichols, Shannon M. ....Detroit, MI
Nichols, Shawn E. ....Laconia, NH
Nichols, Sherry Raduenz ....Decorah, IA
Nichols & Skinner, L.C.
Charles Town, WV
Martinsburg, WV
Nichols, Speidel & Nichols ....Batavia, OH
Georgetown, OH
Nichols Stead Boileau & Kostoff, A Professional Corporation ....Claremont, CA
Nichols, Stephen C. ....Washington, DC
Nichols, Stephen M. ....Orange, CA
Nichols, Stephen W. ....Bethesda, MD
Nichols, Stephen W. ....Kansas City, MO
Springfield, MO
Nichols, Steve W. ....Bakersfield, CA
Nichols, Steven A. ....Costa Mesa, CA
Nichols, Steven D. ....St. Louis, MO
Nichols, Steven L. ....Washington, DC
Nichols, Steven P. ....Austin, TX
Nichols, Stonecipher & Flax ....London, OH
Nichols, Stuart J. ....San Jose, CA
Nichols, Sue K.A. (Totsy) ....Atlanta, GA
Nichols, Sumner E., II ....Erie, PA
Nichols, Susan M. ....Santa Monica, CA
Nichols, Taylor ....DeSoto, TX
Nichols, Ted ....Gainesville, FL
Nichols, Theodore J. ....Anthony, KS
Nichols, Thomas Britt ....Wamego, KS
Nichols, Thomas E., Jr. ....Farwell, TX
Nichols, Thomas J. ....Milwaukee, WI
Nichols, Thomas S. ....Denver, CO
Nichols, Thomson, Peek & Phelan
Westfield, NJ
Nichols, Timothy H. ....Chattanooga, TN
Nichols, Todd C. ....Everett, WA
Nichols, Tracy ....Miami, FL
Nichols, Valerie Nicole ....Charlotte, NC
Nichols, W. Edward ....Topeka, KS
Nichols, W. McDonald ....Jackson, MS
Nichols, Wade H., III ....New York, NY
Nichols, Wade R. ....Noblesville, IN
Nichols, Wallace V. ....London, OH
Nichols, Wallsmith & Weaver ....Knox, IN
Nichols, Walter F. ....Manchester, TN
Nichols, William Alan ....Chattanooga, TN
Nichols, William B., Jr. ....Jackson, MI
Nichols, William D. ....Birmingham, AL
Nichols, William D. ....Boston, MA
Nichols, William E. ....Williamsport, PA
Nichols, William F. ....Nyssa, OR
Ontario, OR
Nichols, William H. ....Chicago, IL
Nichols, William M. ....San Antonio, TX
Nichols, William Paul ....Monroe, MI
Nichols, William T. ....Topeka, KS
Nichols, William W. ....Dothan, AL
Nichols and Wolfe, Chartered ....Topeka, KS

Nicolai, Francis A. ... White Plains, NY
Nicolai, James ... Moorhead, MN
Nicolai, Joanne McCrossen ... Seattle, WA
Nicolai Law Group, P.C. ... Springfield, MA
Nicolai, Michael C. ... New York, NY
Nicolai, Paul P. ... Springfield, MA
Nicolai, Thomas R. ... Portland, OR
Nicolaides, Mark ... Plainfield, NJ
Nicolaides, Mary ... Chicago, IL
Nicolaides, Richard H., Jr. ... Chicago, IL
Nicolaidis, Natalia ... New York, NY
Nicolaievsky, Deborah L. ... Dallas, TX
Nicolais, John L. ... Mahopac, NY
Nicolais, Robert Fred ... White Plains, NY
Nicolaisen, Jay R. ... San Francisco, CA
Nicolaisen, Lee K. ... Lafayette, CA
Nicolaou, Carl C. ... Beverly Hills, CA
Nicolaou, Steve ... Tracy, CA
Nicolas, Corrinne ... Stockton, CA
Nicolas, Denise M. ... Bronx, NY
Nicolas, Julie L. ... Osceola, NE
Nicolas, Keller ... Rosedale, NY
Nicolas, Michael A. ... Chicago, IL
Nicolas, Morris & Gilbreath
Corpus Christi, TX
Nicolas, Samuel A., III ... Carlsbad, CA
Nicolas, Sandra R. ... Austin, TX
Nicolas, Toufic ... Corpus Christi, TX
Nicolas, Welsh & Hayward ... Louisville, KY
Nicolato, Elizabeth Thompson
White Plains, NY
Nicolau, George A. ... New York, NY
Nicolau, George A., P.C. ... New York, NY
Nicolau, Mary T. ... Chicago, IL
Nicolaus, Martin M. ... Oakland, CA
Nicolaus, Sheryl L. ... Fort Myers, FL
Davenport, IA
Nicolay, Christi L. ... Houston, TX
Nicolay, Harry J., Jr. ... New York, NY
White Plains, NY
Nicolay, John D. ... Chicago, IL
Nicolaysen, Gregory ... Beverly Hills, CA
Nicolaysen, Gregory, A Professional Corporation ... Beverly Hills, CA
Los Angeles, CA
San Francisco, CA
Nicolaysen, Pamela ... Haverford, PA
Nicolaysen, Peter C. ... Casper, WY
Nicolazzo, Frank J. ... Newton, MA
Nicole, Betina Font ... San Juan, PR
Nicoleau, Michael D. ... Washington, DC
Nicolella, Matthew J. ... Mansfield, MA
Nicolello, Richard J. ... Garden City, NY
Nicolet, Jeffrey S. ... Minneapolis, MN
Nicoletta, Vincent A. ... New York, NY
Nicolette, Alan K. ... Los Angeles, CA
Nicolette, Carol L. ... Baltimore, MD
Nicolette, David A., Jr. ... Hackensack, NJ
Nicolette & Perkins, P.A. ... Hackensack, NJ
Oradell, NJ
Nicoletti & Associates, P.C.
Bloomfield Hills, MI
Nicoletti Duffy & Edwards, Professional Association ... West Palm Beach, FL
Nicoletti, Frank M. ... New York, NY
Nicoletti, Frank P. ... Santa Clara, CA
Nicoletti, George N. ... Woodland Hills, CA
Nicoletti, Gonson & Bielat LLP
New York, NY
Nicoletti Hornig Campise & Sweeney
Hackensack, NJ
New York, NY
Nicoletti, John A. V. ... New York, NY
Nicoletti, Joseph D. ... Fraser, MI
Nicoletti, Paul J. ... West Palm Beach, FL
Nicoletti, Paul J. ... Bloomfield Hills, MI
Nicoletti, Richard A. ... Newton, MA
Nicoletti, Rick L. ... Denver, CO
Nicoletti-Jones, Jane E. ... Phoenix, AZ
Nicoli, David Paul ... Washington, DC
Nicoli, Olufemi F. ... Chicago, IL
Nicolia, John Paul ... Akron, NY
Nicolich, John G. ... New York, NY
Nicolini, Anthony J. ... Mineola, NY
Nicolini, Daniel A. ... Tucson, AZ
Nicolini, Maria ... Washington, DC
Nicolini & Paradise ... Mineola, NY
Nicolino, Lynda ... Lake Success, NY
Nicoll, Alison F. ... New York, NY
Nicoll, Christopher W. ... Seattle, WA
Nicoll, David L. ... Washington, DC
Nicoll, Frederick A. ... Paramus, NJ
Nicoll, Heather Leigh ... Bakersfield, CA
Nicoll, Jacquelyn Avin ... Baltimore, MD
Nicoll, James L. ... Seattle, WA
Nicoll, Richard F. ... Greenfield, MA
Nicoll, W. James ... Baltimore, MD
Nicolle, Lori A. ... Baltimore, MD
Nicolli, Zan M. ... Bloomfield Hills, MI
Nicolls, Donald J. ... New Castle, PA
Nicolls, Keith K. ... Oakbrook Terrace, IL
Nicolo, Anthony J. ... Portsmouth, VA
Nicolo, James J. ... Philadelphia, PA
Nicoloff, Nicolas G. ... Livonia, MI
Nicoloff Collett, Marsha ... Lorain, OH
Nicolosi & Associates ... Rockford, IL
Nicolosi, Benjamin A., Jr. ... Scranton, PA
Nicolosi, Christina ... Boston, MA
Nicolosi, Diane M. ... Manchester, NH
Nicolosi, Paul S. ... Rockford, IL
Nicolosi, Philip A. ... Rockford, IL
Nicolosi, Philip J. ... Rockford, IL
Nicolosi, Sherrill Boley, (P.A.)
Hot Springs National Park, AR
Hot Springs Village, AR
Nicolosi, Wendy A. ... Easton, PA
Nicols, Howard J.C. ... Cleveland, OH
Nicolson, Anne Carson Irvine ... Mobile, AL

Nicolson, Cheryl ... Media, PA
Nicolson, David F., III ... San Antonio, TX
Nicolson, W. Perrin ... Columbus, GA
Nicolucci, John P. ... Lansing, MI
Nicopoulos, John V. ... Charlotte, NC
Nicora, Albert J. ... Carmel, CA
Nicosia, Benedict R. ... Red Bank, NJ
Nicosia, Deborah E. ... East Aurora, NY
Nicosia, Frank R. ... Buffalo, NY
Nicosia, Giovanni ... Coral Springs, FL
Nicosia, Gregory ... Boca Raton, FL
Nicosia, Lisa R. ... New York, NY
Nicosia, Lydia M. ... Tampa, FL
Nicosia, Perry Michael ... New Orleans, LA
Nicosia, Peter J. ... Tyngsborough, MA
Nicosia, Ralph A. ... Buffalo, NY
Nicosia, Salvatore J. ... Farmingdale, NY
Nicoson, Kevin D. ... Lafayette, IN
Nicoson, William J. ... Washington, DC
Nicotera, Thomas Charles ... Albany, NY
Nicotra, Frances ... Jersey City, NJ
Nicotra, Joseph S. ... White Plains, NY
Nicotra, Nancy ... New York, NY
Nicou, George J. ... San Jose, CA
Nicoud, George A. ("Trey"), III
Dallas, TX
Nicoud, Robert M., Jr. ... Dallas, TX
Nicoulin, Louis M. ... Louisville, KY
Nicrosi, Michel ... Department of Justice, Tax Division, GV
Nicyper, Dean R. ... New York, NY
Nida, Charles ... Detroit, MI
Nida, Joseph E. ... Santa Barbara, CA
Nida & Maloney, LLP ... Los Angeles, CA
Santa Barbara, CA
Nida, Paul A. ... Troy, MI
Nida, Robert G. ... Alexandria, LA
Nida, Robert H. ... San Marino, CA
Niddrie, David A. ... San Diego, CA
Nidel, Richard O. ... Bronx, NY
Niderberg, Ben ... Mineola, NY
Nidey, Frank J. ... Cedar Rapids, IA
Nidich, Paul A. ... Cincinnati, OH
Nidiffer, Lisa D. ... Elizabethton, TN
Nidiry, Rosemary ... Department of Justice, Office of Legal Counsel, GV
Niditch, Stacey ... New York, NY
Nido, Loretta Crews ... Ponte Vedra Beach, FL
Nido, Luis M. ... Washington, DC
Nido, Michael P., Jr. ... Miami, FL
Nie, William L. ... Columbus, IN
Niebank, C. George ... Hilton Head Island, SC
Niebauer, David M. ... San Francisco, CA
Niebauer, Edward J. ... Erie, PA
Niebauer, Jean Kelleher ... Falls Church, VA
Niebauer, Peter W.
Department Of The Interior, Bureau of Land Management, GV
Niebaum, Joel T. ... Missouri Valley, IA
Nieberding, J. R. ... Cincinnati, OH
Nieberding, Michael J. ... Dayton, OH
Nieberg, Benjamin D. ... Los Angeles, CA
Niebergall, A. Thomas ... Beaverton, OR
Niebergall, Shane M. ... Omaha, NE
Niebes, Roger S. ... Mentor, OH
Niebisch, Stefanie ... New York, NY
Niebla, Vivian M. ... Miami, FL
Niebler, Andrew J. ... Milwaukee, WI
Niebler, Andrew K. ... Washington, DC
Niebler, John H. ... Menomonee Falls, WI
Niebler, Joseph C. ... Milwaukee, WI
Niebler, Joseph C., Jr. ... Milwaukee, WI
Niebler & Muren, S.C. ... Milwaukee, WI
Niebler Pyzyk Klaver & Wagner LLP
Menomonee Falls, WI
Niebling, F. Bradford ... Dallas, TX
Niebling, Jeffrey R. ... Honolulu, HI
Niebling, John F., Jr.
Department of Commerce, Patent and Trademark Office, GV
Niebow, Steven N. ... Sherman Oaks, CA
Niebruegge, Michael E. ... Houston, TX
Niebrugge, Thomas W. ... Denver, CO
Niebuhr, Frederick W. ... Minneapolis, MN
Niece, W. Samuel ... San Jose, CA
Nied, David ... San Francisco, CA
Nied, Joel R. ... Philadelphia, PA
Nied, Thomas H. ... New York, NY
Niedecken, Ben W., Jr. ... Dallas, TX
Niedelman, Louis ... Atlantic City, NJ
Niedenthal, Craig P. ... Birmingham, AL
Nieder, Douglas M. ... St. Louis, MO
Niederberg, Richard D. ... Studio City, CA
Niederberger, Jean K. ... New Orleans, LA
Niederdeppe, David L. ... Phoenix, AZ
Niederer, Donald ... Addison, IL
Niedergall, Alice Ann ... Grand Haven, MI
Niederhauser, J. Brian ... Indianapolis, IN
Niederhoffer, Jeffrey M. ... New York, NY
Niederlander, Ann Quill ... St. Louis, MO
Niederluecke, Earle J. ... Wayzata, MN
Niederluecke, Kurt J. ... St. Paul, MN
Niederman, Allan N. ... Chicago, IL
Niederman, Gerald A. ... Denver, CO
Niederman, Jay M. ... Manchester, NH
Niederman, Jerold ... Chicago, IL
Niederman & Stanzel ... Manchester, NH
Niedermann, John ... Encino, CA
Niedermann, Timothy P. ... Guilford, CT
Niedermayer, Alan B. ... Baltimore, MD
Niedermayer, Leonard H. ... Mount Holly, NJ
Niedermayer, Roy I. ... Washington, DC
Niedermayer, Roy I. ... Bethesda, MD
Niedermayer, V. ... New York, NY
Niedermeier, Christine M.
Securities and Exchange Commission, Office of Investor Education and Assistance, GV

Niedermeier, Jerome J. ... Burlington, VT
Niedermeyer, Deborah ... Seattle, WA
Niedermeyer, James C. ... Portland, OR
Niedermeyer, James P. ... Tulsa, OK
Niederpruem, Craig P. ... Utica, NY
Niederreuther, Thomas E.
Corte Madera, CA
Niederriter, Edward R. ... Memphis, TN
Niederwimmer, Theresa M. ... St. Louis, MO
Nieding, Dean C. ... Cleveland, OH
Niednagel, Timothy E. ... Indianapolis, IN
Niedner, Bodeux, Carmichael, Huff & Lenox
St. Charles, MO
Niedner, Charles W. ... St. Charles, MO
Niedner, Paul F. ... St. Charles, MO
Niedrach, John E. ... Rome, GA
Niedringhaus, Marcia Smith
St. Louis, MO
Niedritis, Aiga N. ... Bronx, NY
Nieds, Mark A. ... Chicago, IL
Niedt, Nancy Z. ... New York, NY
Niedweske, Linda J. ... West Orange, NJ
Niedwiewcki, Anthony S. ... Dallas, TX
Niedz, Alan R. ... Verona, NJ
Niedzielski, Marc P. ... Wilmington, DE
Niedzielski, Michael J. ... Toledo, OH
Niedzwiecki, Paul James ... Boston, MA
Niedzwiecki, Rachelle M. ... Chicago, IL
Niefeld, Evan M. ... Minneapolis, MN
Niefer, David L. ... Binghamton, NY
Niegowski, James A. ... Portland, OR
Nieh, Joe ... City of Industry, CA
Niehans, Daniel ... Menlo Park, CA
Niehans, Patricia Lazowska
Menlo Park, CA
Niehaus, Barron M. ... Cincinnati, OH
Niehaus, Bernard H. ... Cleveland, OH
Niehaus, Bernard H., Co., L.P.A.
Cleveland, OH
Niehaus, Charles D. ... Sylvania, OH
Niehaus, David J. ... Hamilton, OH
Niehaus, Frank ... Ypsilanti, MI
Niehaus, J. David ... Louisville, KY
Niehaus, James B. ... Cleveland, OH
Niehaus, Kimberly Ziev ... New York, NY
Niehaus, Mary C. ... Chicago, IL
Niehaus, Maurice A. ... Cincinnati, OH
Niehaus, Paul R. ... New York, NY
Niehaus, R. F. ... Omaha, NE
Niehaus, Richard A. ... Cincinnati, OH
Niehaus, Robert W. ... Ponte Vedra Beach, FL
Dawsonville, GA
Niehaus, Robt. L. ... Cincinnati, OH
Niehaus, Roccina S. ... Cincinnati, OH
Niehaus, Ronald R. ... Houston, TX
Niehaus, Russell R. ... Portland, OR
Niehaus, Susan Patricia ... San Antonio, TX
Niehoff, David O. ... Columbus, OH
Niehoff, H. C. Buck ... Cincinnati, OH
Niehoff, James F. ... Jamaica, NY
Niehoff, Leonard M. ... Ann Arbor, MI
Niehoff, Philip J. ... Chicago, IL
Niehoff & Santellani ... Columbus, OH
Niehoff, William J. ... St. Louis, MO
Niehoff, William P. ... Waterville, ME
Niehus, Grant R. ... Deerfield, IL
Niehus, Grant R., Ltd., P.C. ... Deerfield, IL
Niehuss, John M. ... Washington, DC
Niekamp, Christopher J. ... Akron, OH
Niekamp, Thomas J. ... Cincinnati, OH
Nielan, Kellie ... Daytona Beach, FL
Nieland, Maurice B. ... Sioux City, IA
Nieland, Robert G. ... Chicago, IL
Nielander, Timothy E. ... Seattle, WA
Nielander, William J. ... Lake Placid, FL
Nielander, William J., P.A. ... Lake Placid, FL
Nield, Edgar R. ... San Diego, CA
Nield, Laura V. ... Glens Falls, NY
Nields, Henry C. ... Concord, MA
Westborough, MA
Nields, John W., Jr. ... Washington, DC
Nields Lemack & Dingman ... Concord, MA
Westborough, MA
Nielsen, Andrew T. ... Everett, WA
Nielsen, Ann M. ... Corning, IA
Nielsen, Anne Marie L. ... Culver City, CA
Nielsen, Arlene Merino
Belvedere-Tiburon, CA
Nielsen, Arthur ... Minneapolis, MN
Nielsen & Birch ... North Platte, NE
Nielsen, Brad H. ... Irvine, CA
Nielsen, Bradley C. ... Kansas City, MO
Nielsen, Bradley J. ... Omaha, NE
Nielsen, Brenda T. ... Mesa, AZ
Nielsen, Brian R. ... Keizer, OR
Nielsen, Brooke A. ... Carson City, NV
Nielsen, Bruce S. ... Lewistown, PA
Nielsen, Bruce V. ... Hallock, MN
Nielsen, Caren R. ... Encino, CA
Nielsen, Carl D. ... Pasadena, CA
Nielsen, Carol M. ... Houston, TX
Nielsen, Catherine Roemer
Washington, DC
Nielsen, Christian ... Dallas, TX
Nielsen, Christian B. ... San Jose, CA
Nielsen, Christina Jeanette
Independence, MO
Nielsen, Clark R. ... Salt Lake City, UT
Nielsen, D. James ... Minneapolis, MN
Nielsen, D. Michael ... Bountiful, UT
Nielsen, David A. ... Torrance, CA
Nielsen, David J. ... Omaha, NE
Nielsen, David L. ... Helena, MT
Nielsen, David V. ... Boise, ID
Nielsen, Dean E. ... Warren, OH
Nielsen, Deryl K. ... Salem, OR
Nielsen & Dixon, P.C. ... Salt Lake City, UT
Nielsen, Donald A. ... San Marino, CA

Nielsen, Donald M. ... Winston-Salem, NC
Nielsen, Donald W. ... Fresno, CA
Nielsen, Drew ... Everett, WA
Nielsen, Edward H. ... Chicago, IL
Nielsen, Erik W. ... Chicago, IL
Nielsen, Erwin C. ... Bend, OR
Nielsen, Frank C. ... Tracy, MN
Nielsen, Gary W. ... Los Angeles, CA
Park City, UT
Nielsen, George B., Jr. ... Phoenix, AZ
Nielsen, George O. ... San Francisco, CA
Nielsen, Gerald J. ... Metairie, LA
Nielsen, Gerald T. ... Richardson, TX
Nielsen, Gerhardt M. ... Great Neck, NY
Nielsen, Gilbert L. ... Edison, NJ
Nielsen, Greg R. ... Salt Lake City, UT
Nielsen, Howard R. ... Eugene, OR
Nielsen, J. Bushnell ... Waukesha, WI
Nielsen, J. Susanne ... Greenwich, CT
Nielsen, Jack C. ... Fort Collins, CO
Nielsen, Jack H. ... Olympia, WA
Nielsen, James C. ... San Francisco, CA
Nielsen, Jan K. ... Van Buren, AR
Nielsen, Jeffry F. ... Caldwell, NJ
Nielsen, Jess C. ... North Platte, NE
Nielsen, John D. ... Winnsboro, SC
Nielsen, John Eric ... San Francisco, CA
Nielsen, John T. ... Salt Lake City, UT
Nielsen, Jorgen L. ... Los Angeles, CA
Nielsen, Joseph M. ... Metairie, LA
Nielsen, Karen L. ... New York, NY
Nielsen, Kathleen A. ... Winston-Salem, NC
Nielsen, Ken ... Hacienda Heights, CA
Nielsen, Ken R. ... Orange, CA
Nielsen, Ken W. ... Santa Ana, CA
Nielsen, Kenneth Edward, Jr.
Alexandria, VA
Nielsen, Kenneth P. ... Hacienda Heights, CA
Nielsen Law Firm ... Metairie, LA
New Orleans, LA
Nielsen Law Office, Inc., P.S. ... Seattle, WA
Nielsen, Leland C. ... San Diego, CA
Nielsen, Leslie R. ... Denver, CO
Nielsen, Lisa Ann ... St. Louis, MO
Nielsen, Lori A. ... Beverly Hills, CA
Nielsen, Louis B. ... Honesdale, PA
Nielsen, Lynn C. ... Flemington, NJ
Nielsen, Lynn M. ... Springfield, MA
Nielsen, Mark C. ... Washington, DC
Nielsen, Mark F. ... Racine, WI
Nielsen, Martin C. ... Silver Spring, MD
Nielsen, Matthew J. ... Chicago, IL
Nielsen, Merksamer, Parrinello, Mueller & Naylor, LLP ... Mill Valley, CA
Sacramento, CA
San Francisco, CA
Nielsen, Michael William
Winter Springs, FL
Nielsen, Morris L. ... Richland, MI
Nielsen, N. Andre ... Baltimore, MD
Nielsen, Neal A., III ... Eagle River, WI
Nielsen, Neal D., (P.C.) ... Brighton, MI
Nielsen & Nielsen ... Eagle River, WI
Nielsen and Nielsen, Inc., P.S. ... Everett, WA
Nielsen & Nielsen, P.C. ... Corning, IA
Nielsen & O'Donnell ... Lewistown, PA
Nielsen, Olaf ... Akron, OH
Nielsen, Patricia ... Salem, OR
Nielsen, Paul C. ... Chicago, IL
Nielsen, Paul J. ... Dayton, OH
Nielsen, Peter A. ... Tucson, AZ
Nielsen, Peter A., P.C., Law Offices of
Tucson, AZ
Nielsen, Phillip J. ... San Jose, CA
Nielsen, Randall E. ... Mason City, IA
Nielsen, Randy L. ... Kimball, NE
Nielsen, Richard A. ... Tampa, FL
Nielsen, Richard A. ... Seattle, WA
Nielsen, Richard D., II ... Corpus Christi, TX
Nielsen, Richard E. ... San Francisco, CA
Nielsen, Richard E. ... Bethesda, MD
Nielsen, Robert C. ... Brooklyn, NY
Nielsen, Robert E.
Department of Commerce, Office of the General Counsel, GV
Nielsen, Robert M. ... Rupert, ID
Nielsen, Robert N., Jr. ... Binghamton, NY
Nielsen, Robert R. ... San Francisco, CA
Nielsen, Robin L. ... Seattle, WA
Nielsen, Rod Pace ... Parma, ID
Nielsen, Roger H. ... San Diego, CA
Nielsen, Ruth ... Seattle, WA
Nielsen, Sally C. ... Atlanta, GA
Nielsen & Senior, A Prof. Corp.
Ogden, UT
Salt Lake City, UT
Nielsen, Sharon M. ... Eagle River, WI
Nielsen, Sherrill A. ... Hemet, CA
Nielsen, Steen C. ... Morgan Hill, CA
Nielsen, Stephen V. ... Des Moines, IA
Nielsen, Stuart D. ... Corning, IA
Nielsen, Tennessee ... Dallas, TX
Nielsen, Thérèse P. ... Hempstead, NY
Nielsen, Thomas D. ... Sacramento, CA
Nielsen, Todd A. ... Kansas City, MO
Nielsen, Todd G. ... Creston, IA
Nielsen, Todd W. ... Boise, ID
Nielsen, Vigo G., Jr., (P.C.)
Mill Valley, CA
Sacramento, CA
San Francisco, CA
Nielsen, W. Durrell, II ... Salt Lake City, UT
Nielsen, W. Joseph ... Stamford, CT
Nielsen, Walter W. ... Lake Forest, IL
Nielsen, Walter W. ... Minneapolis, MN
Nielsen, William H. ... Olympia, WA
Nielsen, William J. ... Great Neck, NY
Nielsen, Will[illegible] R. ... Battle Creek, MI

Niles, John B. ... Bethesda, MD
Niles, John F. ... Plattsburgh, NY
Niles, John Franklin ... Austin, TX
Niles, John G. ... Los Angeles, CA
Niles, Lawson R. ... Winston-Salem, NC
Niles, Margaret A. ... Seattle, WA
Niles, Mark C. ... Department of Justice, Civil Division, GV
Niles, Martha A. ... Chicago, IL
Niles, Mary Ellen ... Glen Burnie, MD
Niles, Michael J. ... Pittstown, NJ
Niles, N. Lawrence ... Woodstock, VT
Niles, Palmer A. ... South Miami, FL
Niles, Randall C. ... Laguna Beach, CA
Niles, Richard G. ... Wood Ridge, NJ
Niles, Robert A. ... Remington, VA
Niles, Stephen D. ... Washington, DC
Niles, Stewart E., Jr. ... New Orleans, LA
Niles, William E. ... Santa Monica, CA
Niles, William I. ... Boynton Beach, FL
Niles, William J. ... Santa Monica, CA
Niles-Spencer, Sharon L. ... Washington, DC
Nill, Douglas J. ... Minneapolis, MN
Nill, Rockwell & Keene, A Professional Corporation ... Flint, MI
Nill, Stephen C. ... Rancho Santa Margarita, CA
Nill, William C. ... Eastpointe, MI
Nilles, Andrew J. ... Milwaukee, WI
Nilles, Bruce E. ... Department of Justice, Environment and Natural Resources Division, GV
Nilles, David A. ... Chicago, IL
Nilles, Hansen & Davies, Ltd. ... Moorhead, MN; Fargo, ND; Williston, ND
Nilles, James E. ... Milwaukee, WI
Nilles, Kathleen M. ... Washington, DC
Nilles, Michael J. ... Milwaukee, WI
Nilles & Nilles, S.C. ... Milwaukee, WI; Racine, WI
Nilles, Terry E. ... Milwaukee, WI
Nilmeier, Lisa Jorgensen ... Fresno, CA
Nilon, James F., Jr. ... Wallingford, PA
Nilon, James P. ... Gainesville, FL
Nilon, John W., Jr. ... Media, PA
Nilon, Judith D. ... Upper Darby, PA
Nilsen, Arthur C. ... Roswell, GA
Nilsen, Cohn & Palmer ... Englewood, CO
Nilsen, D. Sean ... Louisville, KY
Nilsen, Eva S. ... Boston, MA
Nilsen, John A. ... Minneapolis, MN
Nilsen, Martin J. ... New York, NY
Nilsen, Peter H. ... Roseburg, OR
Nilsen, Susan Mealka ... Santa Ana, CA
Nilsen, Walter G. ... Murray Hill, NJ
Nilson, Christian C. ... Detroit, MI
Nilson, Clifford E. ... Tallahassee, FL
Nilson, Clifford E., Jr. ... Tallahassee, FL
Nilson, Deborah Ann ... New York, NY
Nilson, Edwin Erick ... Lincoln, NE
Nilson, Elizabeth L. ... Baltimore, MD
Nilson, George A. ... Baltimore, MD
Nilson, Norman F. ... Chicago, IL
Nilson, Richard P. ... Chicago, IL
Nilson, Stookal, Gleason & Caputo, Ltd. ... Chicago, IL
Nilson, Thomas W. ... Columbus, GA
Nilsson, Bradford A. ... San Francisco, CA
Nilsson, Byard G. ... Los Angeles, CA
Nilsson, Michael D. ... Washington, DC
Nilsson, Nils E. ... Akron, OH
Nilsson, Peter E. J. ... Livonia, NY
Nilsson, Rand W. ... Elkhart, IN
Nilsson, Richard L. ... Timonium, MD
Nilsson, Steven G. ... Clearwater, FL
Nilsson, Torgny R. ... Los Angeles, CA
Nilva and Frisch, P.A. ... St. Paul, MN
Nilva, Stephanie Mara ... New York, NY
Nimako, Joseph ... Livonia, MI
Niman, Kenneth P. ... Baltimore, MD
Niman, Shari Clark ... Portland, OR
Nimaroff, Carole W. ... New York, NY
Nimaroff, Ellen ... New York, NY
Nimaroff, Selwyn ... New York, NY
Nimatallah, Leila ... Arlington, VA
Nimblett, Donna Malgeri ... Salisbury, MA
Nimensky, Allen H. ... Livingston, NJ
Nimensky, Bruce D. ... Morristown, NJ
Nimer, Jonathan B. ... Palo Alto, CA
Nimeroff, Jami B. ... Philadelphia, PA
Nimetz, Everett N. ... Kew Gardens, NY
Nimetz, Marshall A. ... Floral Park, NY
Nimetz, Matthew ... New York, NY
Nimetz, Warren J. ... New York, NY
Nimick, C. Lockhart ... Department of Justice, Executive Office for Immigration Review, GV
Nimkin, Bernard William ... New York, NY
Nimkoff, Ronald A. ... New York, NY
Nimlo, John E. ... Willimantic, CT
Nimmer, David ... Los Angeles, CA
Nimmer, George R. ... Omaha, NE
Nimmer, Gerhardt E. ... Gatlinburg, TN
Nimmer, John C. ... Omaha, NE
Nimmer, Raymond T. ... Houston, TX
Nimmich, David L. ... Virginia Beach, VA
Nimmo, Anthony ... Chicago, IL
Nimmo, Dale Edward ... Research Triangle Park, NC
Nimmo, David L. ... Ada, OK
Nimmo, Elizabeth M. ... Minneapolis, MN
Nimmo, Hoehn, Kirt and Nimmo ... Nashville, TN; White Bluff, TN
Nimmo, M. R. ... Winfield, WV
Nimmo, Nick ... Denver, CO
Nimmo, Niles S. ... Nashville, TN
Nimmo, Penny Elaine ... Pounding Mill, VA
Nimmo, R. Price ... Nashville, TN
Nimmo, Rabin P. ... Nashville, TN
Nimmo, Ridley S., II ... Flint, MI
Nimmo, Scot G. ... Orlando, FL
Nimmo, Stephen H. ... Pittsburgh, PA
Nimmons, Deborah K. ... Dalton, GA
Nimmons, Ken M. ... Augusta, GA
Nimmons & Malchow ... Augusta, GA; Aiken, SC
Nimmons, Paul W., Jr. ... Houston, TX
Nimmons, Ralph W., Jr. ... Jacksonville, FL
Nimoy, Adam B. ... Los Angeles, CA
Nimri, Rami G. ... Salinas, CA
Nimrick, Sandra L. ... Cleveland, OH
Nimrod, Alfred F. ... Cleveland, OH
Nimrod, Raymond N. ... Chicago, IL
Nimrod, Timothy D. ... Chicago, IL
Nims, Arthur L., III ... United States Tax Court, GV
Nims, Barbara ... New York, NY
Nims, David E., III ... Detroit, MI
Nims, David E., Jr. ... Grand Rapids, MI
Nims, Eric J. ... Stockton, CA
Nims, Geoffrey R. ... Gunnison, CO
Nims, Howes, Collison, Hansen & Lackert ... New York, NY
Nims, J. Clarke ... Grand Rapids, MI
Nims, Mark Richard ... Del Mar, CA
Nims, Michael A. ... Cleveland, OH
Nims, Ronald K. ... Powell, OH
Nims, Sarah Morgan ... Versailles, KY
Nimsger, Kristin M. ... Minneapolis, MN
Nimtz, Robert O. ... Madison, NJ
Nimz, Jack D. ... Chicago, IL
Nimz, Jeffrey E. ... Chicago, IL
Nimz, Nancy M. ... Northfield, IL
Ninan, Emilie R. ... Wilmington, DE
Ninas, Nina F. ... St. Louis, MO
Nine, Paul L. ... Bloomfield Hills, MI
Nine, Paul L., P.C. ... Bloomfield Hills, MI
Ninfo, John C., II ... Rochester, NY
Ning, Ke-Ching ... Honolulu, HI
Ning, Lilly & Jones, Attorneys At Law, A Law Corporation ... Honolulu, HI
Ninivaggi, Daniel A. ... New York, NY
Ninneman, Mary Pat ... Milwaukee, WI
Ninneman, Maureen A. ... Evanston, IL
Ninneman, Richard C. ... Milwaukee, WI
Ninneman, Sheila M. ... Cleveland, OH
Ninnis, William R. ... Clovis, CA
Niño, Deanna H. ... Boston, MA
Nino, Dennis M. ... Campbell, CA
Nino, Edward Charles ... San Jose, CA
Nino, Edward D. ... San Jose, CA
Nino, Filice & Arata ... San Jose, CA
Niño, George ... Houston, TX
Nino, Katherine Ann ... Chicago, IL
Nino, Noël M. ... San Francisco, CA
Nino, Philip E. ... Spokane, WA
Ninos, Helen Marie ... Columbus, OH
Ninosky, John R. ... Harrisburg, PA
Nin-Torregrosa, Ana Matilde ... San Juan, PR
Niose, David A. ... Fitchburg, MA
Niosi, Corinne A. ... Washington, DC
Niosi, Peter T. ... Kansas City, MO
Niosi, Ruthann G. ... New York, NY
Niosi, Ruthann G., P.C., Law Offices of ... New York, NY
Niosi, Valerie ... Brooklyn, NY
Nip, Renton L. K. ... Honolulu, HI
Nip, Robert L. S. ... Honolulu, HI
Nip, Roland ... Honolulu, HI
Niparko, Steven J. ... Denver, CO
Nipe, Chris ... Mitchell, SD
Nipert, Richard F. ... Denver, CO
Nipp, John C. ... Charlotte, NC
Nipp, Tracy B. ... Charlotte, NC
Nippard, E. Josephine ... Ellicott City, MD
Nippard, Lewis Straughn ... Ellicott City, MD
Nippard, Lewis Straughn, P.A. ... Ellicott City, MD
Nippe, Wayne R. ... Las Vegas, NV
Nipper, Cheryl Lynn ... Jacksonville, FL
Nipper, J. Russell ... Raleigh, NC
Nipper, James L. ... Jacksonville, FL
Nipper, John M. ... Grenada, MS
Nipper, Oscar ... Houston, TX
Nipper, Oscar, A Prof. Corp., Law Offices of ... Houston, TX
Nipper, Paul T. ... Dallas, TX
Nipper, Stephen Michael ... Boise, ID
Nippert, Alfred K., Jr. ... Cincinnati, OH
Nippert, Glenn E. ... Newport, RI
Nippert, Grady Kendall ... Dallas, TX
Nippert & Nippert ... Cincinnati, OH
Nippert, William D., Jr. ... Childress, TX
Nippes, James Stanford ... Jackson, MS; Jackson, MS
Niquet, James A. ... Milwaukee, WI
Niquette & Niquette ... Winooski, VT
Niquette, Russell F., Jr. ... Winooski, VT
Nir, Esther ... Kew Gardens, NY
Nir, Randi Koch ... Kew Gardens, NY
Nir, Robyn G. ... New York, NY
Nir, Ronald Steven ... Kew Gardens, NY
Nirenberg, Alex J. ... Ellenville, NY
Nirenberg, Darryl D. ... Washington, DC
Nirenberg, David ... New York, NY
Nirenberg, Henry M. ... Southfield, MI
Nirenberg, Howard M. ... Hackensack, NJ; Trenton, NJ
Nirenberg, Jonathan I. ... Hackensack, NJ
Nirenberg, Lori Hecht ... United States Senate, Senatorial Assistants, GV
Nirenberg, Richard B. ... Tallahassee, FL
Nirenberg, Stanley S. ... Staten Island, NY
Nirenberg & Varano ... Hackensack, NJ; Trenton, NJ; Islandia, NY
Nirenstein, Alexander D. ... New York, NY
Nirenstein, David O. ... Minneapolis, MN
Nirenstein, Faith B. ... Boston, MA
Nirenstein, Horowitz & Associates ... Hartford, CT
Nirenstein, Jeffrey A. ... Hartford, CT
Nirenstein, Julius J. ... Los Angeles, CA
Nirenstein, Marcia R. ... Washington, DC
Nirken, Howard ... Austin, TX
Nirmel, Chittaranjan N. ... Washington, DC
Niro, Cheryl I. ... Chicago, IL
Niro, Dean D. ... Chicago, IL
Niro, Francis Anthony ... Milford, MA
Niro, Raymond P. ... Chicago, IL
Niro, Raymond P., Jr. ... Chicago, IL
Niro, Robert E. ... Tallahassee, FL
Niro, Scavone, Haller & Niro ... Chicago, IL
Niro, William L. ... Chicago, IL
Nisa, Joseph P. ... New York, NY
Nisall, David R. ... Van Nuys, CA
Nisberg, Alan J. ... Tampa, FL
Nisbet, A. Wyckliff, Jr. (P.A.) ... Little Rock, AR
Nisbet, Diane M. ... Cookeville, TN
Nisbet, Hugh Kenneth, Jr. ... Oklahoma City, OK
Nisbet, John Byers, III ... Cookeville, TN
Nisbet, Miriam M. ... National Archives And Records Administration, General Counsel Staff, GV
Nisbet, Steven A. ... Clearwater, FL
Nisbet, William A., III ... Madisonville, KY
Nisbet-Lance, Thomas ... Salem, OR
Nisbett, Robert S. ... Longview, TX
Nisby, Jacquelyn L. ... Houston, TX
Nischwitz, Jeffrey L. ... Cleveland, OH
Nischwitz, Pembridge & Chriszt Co., L.P.A. ... Cleveland, OH
Nisely, Robert L. ... New York, NY
Nisen, Charles M. ... Chicago, IL
Nisen & Elliott ... Chicago, IL
Nisen, Fern S. ... Los Angeles, CA
Nisenbaum, Nathan ... Indianapolis, IN
Nisenbaum, Steven ... Topsfield, MA
Nisenbaum, Sylvia T. ... Philadelphia, PA
Nisenson, Robert C. ... North Brunswick, NJ
Nisenson, Shari D. ... Red Bank, NJ; New York, NY
Nisenson, Stuart C. ... Newark, NJ
Nish, Robert J. ... Morristown, NJ
Nishanian, V. Rick ... Manassas, VA
Nishawala, Vipul N. ... New York, NY
Nisher, Michael Seth ... Philadelphia, PA
Nishi, Jin ... Oakland, CA
Nishi, John C. ... Palo Alto, CA
Nishi, Kazunobu ... New York, NY
Nishi, Sharon H. ... Honolulu, HI
Nishi, Susan M. ... Palo Alto, CA
Nishida, Rodney S. ... Honolulu, HI
Nishigaya, Daisy M. ... Palo Alto, CA
Nishigaya, Daniel T. ... San Jose, CA
Nishii, Harunobu E. ... Costa Mesa, CA
Nishikawa, Wendy K. K. ... Orange, CA
Nishimi, Lyle R. ... San Francisco, CA
Nishimitsu, Lorna A. ... Lihue, HI
Nishimoto, Cary H. ... Los Angeles, CA
Nishimoto, John S. ... Honolulu, HI
Nishimoto, Paul K. ... Department of Transportation, Surface Transportation Board, GV
Nishimura, Alan B. ... Los Angeles, CA
Nishimura, Ann M. ... Torrance, CA
Nishimura, Dennis D. ... Hilo, HI
Nishimura, Gilbert M. ... Los Angeles, CA
Nishimura, Keiichi ... San Francisco, CA
Nishimura, Nanci E. ... Los Angeles, CA
Nishimura, Rhonda A. ... Honolulu, HI
Nishimura & Saunders ... Los Angeles, CA
Nishinaka, Robert S. ... Los Angeles, CA
Nishino, Gilbert Y. ... Hemet, CA
Nishioka & Fujioka, Attorneys At Law, A Law Corporation ... Honolulu, HI
Nishioka, Greg I. ... Honolulu, HI
Nishioka, Krisida Jones ... Oakland, CA
Nishioka, Linnel T. ... Honolulu, HI
Nishioka, Wayne S. ... Richmond, CA
Nishiura, Diana H. ... Los Angeles, CA
Nishiyama, Daniel ... Long Beach, CA
Nishiyama, Kristine M. ... Los Angeles, CA
Nishiyama, Michael B. ... San Francisco, CA
Nishizawa, Eric Y. ... Los Angeles, CA
Nishizu, Mikio ... Indianapolis, IN
Nishkian, Michael A. ... Long Beach, CA
Nishnick, Larry W. ... San Diego, CA
Nisi, Frank P., Jr. ... Winter Park, FL
Nisi, Marina G. ... New York, NY
Nisi, Robert A. ... New York, NY
Nisidis, Jamie C. Hecht ... Saginaw, MI
Nisim, Joseph ... Los Angeles, CA
Nisimblat, Stephen ... West Hartford, CT
Nisivoccia, Anthony J. ... Bloomfield, NJ
Niskar, Joey S. ... Farmington Hills, MI
Niskar, Joseph Adam ... Birmingham, MI
Niskey, Eve-Marie ... Vineland, NJ
Nisley, James R. ... North Platte, NE
Nisnewitz, Craig M. ... New York, NY
Nisnewitz, David Z. ... Flushing, NY
Nisoff, Karl E. ... Albany, NY
Nison, Edward J. ... Los Angeles, CA
Nisonoff, Bert H. ... Forest Hills, NY
Nisonoff, Donald M. ... New York, NY
Nisonson, Ronald Seth ... Miami, FL
Nispel, David H. ... Madison, WI
Nisperos, Eleanor O. ... San Francisco, CA
Nissan, Ilan S. ... New York, NY
Nissan, Limor ... New York, NY
Nissan, Michael ... New York, NY
Nissan, Randy S. ... Bay Shore, NY
Nissel, J. Thomas ... Ellicott City, MD
Nissel, Stanley N. ... Hartford, CT
Nisselson, Alan ... New York, NY
Nissen, Alison Margaret ... Mount Laurel, NJ
Nissen, Arthur E. ... Damariscotta, ME
Nissen, Christopher D. ... Los Angeles, CA
Nissen, David R. ... Fullerton, CA
Nissen, David R., A Professional Law Corporation ... Fullerton, CA
Nissen & Douglas ... Gold River, CA; Sacramento, CA
Nissen, Elaine H. ... Fort Lee, NJ; New York, NY
Nissen, Irwin K. ... New York, NY
Nissen, J. Frederic ... Minneapolis, MN
Nissen, J. Harold ... New York, NY
Nissen, Jack H. ... Gold River, CA
Nissen, Jill L. ... Palo Alto, CA
Nissen, Karen M. ... West Palm Beach, FL
Nissen, Leif M. ... Haddonfield, NJ
Nissen, Louis A. ... Palm Springs, CA
Nissen, Pamela Hodges ... Minneapolis, MN
Nissen, Robert C. ... Washington, DC
Nissen, Spencer T. ... Environmental Protection Agency, Office of Administrative Law Judges, GV
Nissen, Steven A. ... San Francisco, CA
Nissen, Thomas D. ... Chicago, IL
Nissen, Todd L. ... Minneapolis, MN
Nissen, Walter I., Sr. ... Cleveland, OH
Nissen, Wesley G. ... Chicago, IL
Nissen, William F. ... Quincy, IL
Nissen, William J. ... Chicago, IL
Nissenbaum, Dale G. ... New York, NY
Nissenbaum, David ... New York, NY
Nissenbaum, Gary D. ... Newark, NJ
Nissenbaum, Gerald L. ... Boston, MA
Nissenbaum Law Offices ... Boston, MA
Nissenbaum, Mark L. ... San Francisco, CA
Nissenbaum, Morris ... Somerville, MA
Nissenbaum & Nissenbaum ... Somerville, MA
Nissenbaum, Paul D. ... Somerville, MA
Nissenbaum, Robert J. ... Cleveland, OH
Nissenbaum, Robert M. ... Merion Station, PA
Nissenbaum, Susan B. ... Grafton, MA
Nissenberg, David N. ... San Diego, CA
Nissenberg, Merel Grey ... La Jolla, CA
Nissenholtz, David M. ... St. Louis, MO
Nissensohn, Nancy Neis ... Barrington, RI
Nissim, Michael C. ... New York, NY
Nissim, Norris ... New York, NY
Nissim, Stuart H. ... Princeton, NJ
Nissim-Sabat, Charles ... Chicago, IL
Nissl, Colleen K. ... Columbus, OH
Nissle, Tod R. ... Scottsdale, AZ
Nissle, Tod R., P.C. ... Scottsdale, AZ
Nissler, Perry S. ... Denver, CO
Nissley, Kirk K. ... Ann Arbor, MI
Nissly, Barry L. ... Lancaster, PA
Nissly, Kenneth L. ... San Jose, CA
Nissly, Nedric L. ... Harrisburg, PA
Nissman, David M. ... Christiansted, St. Croix, VI
Nissman, Edward S. ... Los Angeles, CA
Nissman, Peter M. ... White Plains, NY
Nisson, C. Arthur, Jr. ... Tustin, CA
Nisson, David M. ... Tustin, CA
Nisson & Nisson ... Tustin, CA
Nisson, Peter L. ... Tustin, CA
Nisson & Pincin ... Redding, CA
Nisson, Scott H. ... Bakersfield, CA
Nisson, Timothy J. ... Redding, CA
Nist, Donald E. ... Prescott, AZ
Nistad, P. Gunnar ... Charleston, SC
Nistico, Charles G. ... Media, PA
Nistico, Joseph F., Jr. ... Houston, TX
Nistler, Heather L. ... Houston, TX
Nistler, Lawrence J. ... Polson, MT
Niswander, Rex Lee ... New York, NY
Niswanger, Stephen B. ... Little Rock, AR
Niswonger, J., Law Office of ... Corona, CA
Nita, Michael J. ... Florham Park, NJ
Nitao, John S. ... Honolulu, HI
Nitchals, Glenn P. ... Phoenix, AZ
Nitchals, Louis W. ... Algona, IA
Nitcher, Eric L. ... Houston, TX
Nitcher, John W. ... Lawrence, KS
Nitcher, Walter E. ... Columbus, GA
Nitchkey, Robert A., Jr. ... Easton, PA
Nitido, Vincent, Jr. ... Tucson, AZ
Nitikman, Franklin W. ... Chicago, IL
Nitikman, Mark A. ... Irvine, CA
Nitikman, Nancy J. ... Cambridge, MA
Nitka & Glover ... Ludlow, VT
Nitka, Joseph J. ... St. Louis, MO
Nitka, Martin ... Ludlow, VT
Nitkewicz, Andrew P. ... Woodbury, NY
Nitkewicz, Edward J. ... Commack, NY
Nitkin, Rebecca A. ... Rockville, MD
Nitkin, William ... Chestnut Hill, MA
Nitsch, Charles E. ... Houston, TX
Nitsch, Mary Lovett ... White Plains, NY
Nitsch, Patrick Andrew, Jr. ... McAllen, TX
Nitsche, Bradley W. ... Bellevue, WA
Nitsche, Caroline M. ... Miami, FL
Nitsche, Gary S. ... Wilmington, DE
Nitsche, James A. ... Louisville, KY
Nitsche, John C. B. ... Phoenix, AZ
Nitsche, Joseph E. ... Albany, NY
Nitschke, David F. ... Woodbridge, NJ
Nitschke, Peter D. ... Orange, CA

Noble, John W., Jr. .... Chicago, IL
Noble, Jonathan J. .... Menlo Park, CA
Noble, Julie A. .... Sacramento, CA
Noble, Katharine Carter .... Boston, MA
Providence, RI
Noble, Kelly S. .... Englewood, CO
Noble, Kenneth E. .... Chicago, IL
Noble, Kent A. .... Peoria, IL
Noble, Kraig E. .... Mendon, OH
St. Marys, OH
Noble, L. Oliver, Jr. .... Hickory, NC
Noble, Laura E. Washburn
Consumer Product Safety Commission, Office of Compliance, GV
Noble, Laurie A. .... Rangely, CO
Noble, Lawrence .... Ventura, CA
Noble, Lawrence C., P.C., & Associates
Ventura, CA
Noble, Lawrence M.
Federal Election Commission, Office of the General Counsel, GV
Noble, Leary, Leary & Lynch .... Auburn, NY
Noble & Lipstein, A Professional Association
Clinton, MD
Noble, Lorinda S. .... Colville, WA
Noble, M. Karen .... Hartford, CT
Noble, M. Scott .... Jacksonville, FL
Noble, Mary C. .... Lexington, KY
Noble, Melody L. .... Little Rock, AR
Noble, Michael .... Royal Oak, MI
Noble, Michael J. .... Dallas, TX
Noble, Michael R. .... Tacoma, WA
Noble, Michael R., P.S. .... Tacoma, WA
Noble, Michael Scott .... Jacksonville, FL
Noble, Michael T. .... Windsor, CT
Noble, Milton .... Valley Stream, NY
Noble, Montague & Moul .... Mendon, OH
St. Marys, OH
Noble & Noble .... Brookhaven, MS
Noble, Noble & Noble .... Hazard, KY
Noble, Painter & Bakshi .... Rockville, MD
Noble, Patricia E. .... Chicago, IL
Noble, Patrick H. .... Henderson, KY
Noble, Phillip D. .... Seattle, WA
Noble & Quinn .... Fayetteville, NC
Noble, Randolph, Jr. .... Greenville, MS
Noble, Raymond A. .... New Brunswick, NJ
Noble, Reed N. .... Fayetteville, NC
Noble, Richard G. .... Indianola, MS
Noble, Richard L. .... Pasadena, CA
Noble, Richard P. .... West Linn, OR
Noble, Richard W. .... Kansas City, MO
Noble, Ricky Duane .... Circleville, OH
Noble, Ritchard S. .... Boise, ID
Noble, Robert Dean .... Columbus, OH
Noble, Roger F., Jr. .... Library of Congress, Congressional Research Service, GV
Noble, Roger W. .... New York, NY
Noble, Ronald H. .... Tampa, FL
Noble, Roy A. .... Boston, MA
Noble, Rubye E. .... Metairie, LA
Noble, Russell E. .... Jackson, MI
Noble & Ryan, S.C. .... La Crosse, WI
Noble, Saundra Lea .... Pasadena, CA
Noble, Scott A. .... Cleveland, OH
Noble, Shannon .... Austin, TX
Noble, Sharon Marie .... Morris Plains, NJ
Noble, Susan D. .... New York, NY
Noble, Sybille Scott .... Memphis, TN
Noble, Theron G. .... Clearfield, PA
Noble, Travis L., Jr. .... St. Louis, MO
Noble, William J. .... Chicago, IL
Noble, Wm. M., Jr. .... Newton, MA
Noble, Young & O'Connor, P.C.
West Hartford, CT
Noble-Allgire, Alice M. .... Carbondale, IL
Noble-Choder, Joann .... Pittsburgh, PA
Nobleman, Eli E. .... United States Senate, Committee Legal Personnel, GV
Nobler, Alan L. .... San Jose, CA
Nobler, Alan L., Inc. .... San Jose, CA
Nobles, Andre T. .... New York, NY
Nobles, Anne .... Indianapolis, IN
Nobles & Associates .... Atlanta, GA
Nobles, David O. .... Longview, TX
Nobles, Dina D. .... San Francisco, CA
Nobles, Edw. B. .... Amarillo, TX
Nobles, Eric A. .... Escondido, CA
Nobles, Henry E. .... Tampa, FL
Nobles, James C., Jr. .... Atlanta, GA
Nobles, James H., Jr. .... El Dorado, AR
Nobles, James W., Jr. .... Jackson, MS
Nobles, Jeffery T. .... Houston, TX
Nobles, John E., Jr. .... Beaufort, NC
Nobles, Kimberley G. .... Costa Mesa, CA
La Jolla, CA
Nobles, Patricia J. .... St. Louis, MO
Nobles, T. Neal .... Houston, TX
Noblett, Lisa C. .... Chicago, IL
Noblett, Phillip A. .... Chattanooga, TN
Noblin, James E. .... Los Angeles, CA
Noblin, James Robert .... Los Angeles, CA
Noblin, J. T. .... Jackson, MS
Noblin, Kelly .... Dallas, TX
Noblin, William C., Jr. .... Jackson, MS
Noblit, David W. .... Chattanooga, TN
Noblitt, Daniel J. .... Phoenix, AZ
Noblitt, Jane Ann .... Fountaintown, IN
Noblitt, Larry .... Port Clinton, OH
Noblitt, V. Lesa .... Edgewater, MD
Nobori, Dean .... Pasadena, CA
Noborikawa, Bruce S. .... Honolulu, HI
Nobregas-Sancio, Millin A.
Miami Beach, FL
Nobumoto, Karen S. .... Los Angeles, CA
Nobunaga, Howard M. .... Honolulu, HI
Nocca, Jos. F. .... Yonkers, NY
Nocchi, Marguerite M. .... North Wales, PA
Nocco, Frank P. .... New York, NY
Noce, Anthony M., Jr. .... Danboro, PA
Noce & Buckley, L.L.C. .... Clayton, MO
St. Louis, MO
Noce, Charles T. .... Rochester, NY
Noce, David D. .... St. Louis, MO
Noce, Gerard T. .... St. Louis, MO
Noce, Philip S. .... Hackensack, NJ
Nocella, Joseph .... Los Angeles, CA
Nocella, Richard J. .... Marlton, NJ
Nocella, Thomas M. .... Philadelphia, PA
Nocenti, David M. .... Kew Gardens, NY
Nocera, David M. .... Westminster, CO
Nocera, John .... New York, NY
Nocera, Nicole .... Chicago, IL
Nocera, Robert R. .... Pawtucket, RI
Nocero, Patricia A. .... Painesville, OH
Nochimson, David .... Los Angeles, CA
Nochlin, Elizabeth R. .... New York, NY
Nochowitz, Matthew M. .... Chicago, IL
Nocito, Frank W. .... Wilkes-Barre, PA
Nocito, Joseph .... Wilkes-Barre, PA
Nocito, Judith L. .... Pittsburgh, PA
Nocjar, David E. .... Lorain, OH
Nock, George R. .... Tacoma, WA
Nock, James R. .... Minneapolis, MN
Nock, Louis L. .... New York, NY
Nock, Steven C. .... Costa Mesa, CA
Nock, Susan J. .... Boston, MA
Nocket, M. Keith .... El Segundo, CA
Nockett, Richard P. .... Department of Justice, Civil Division, GV
Nockleby, Brian E. .... Chevy Chase, MD
Nocon, James J. .... Indianapolis, IN
Noda, John A. .... San Francisco, CA
Nodd, Jeffrey D. .... Los Angeles, CA
Noddings, Sarah E. .... Burbank, CA
Nodel, Marvin B. .... Davie, FL
Nodell, Glass & Haskell, L.L.P.
Raleigh, NC
Nodell & Jones .... Morrisville, NY
Nodell, Kenneth E. .... Morrisville, NY
Nodell, Theodore A. .... Raleigh, NC
Noden, J. Wilson .... Trenton, NJ
Noderer, Eric W. .... Seville, OH
Nodes, Allan J. .... Trenton, NJ
Nodes, Dwight D. .... Columbus, OH
Nodgaard, John C. .... Wichita, KS
Nodier, Matthew C. .... Metairie, LA
Nodiff & Ellis .... St. Louis, MO
Nodiff, Eric W. .... New York, NY
Nodiff, Marvin J. .... St. Louis, MO
Nodine, Lawrence K. .... Atlanta, GA
Nodine, William E. .... Clearwater, FL
Nodland, Chad C. .... Bismarck, ND
Nodland, Irvin B. .... Bismarck, ND
Nodland, Jeffrey T. .... Minneapolis, MN
Nodland Law Offices .... Bismarck, ND
Nodtvedt, Craig L. .... Seattle, WA
Nodvin Firm, The .... Atlanta, GA
Nodvin, Marvin P. .... Atlanta, GA
Nodzenski, Thaddeus J. .... Naperville, IL
Noe, Alphonse R. .... Cambridge, MA
Noe, Anastasia .... Las Vegas, NV
Noe, Diane .... Denver, CO
Noe, Elizabeth Hardy .... Atlanta, GA
Noe & Foody .... Atlantic Beach, FL
Noe, G. Harold .... Meridian, MS
Noe, George T. .... Everett, WA
Noe, Glenn Carlyle .... Sulligent, AL
Noe, Gregory R. .... Moline, IL
Noe, Jack T. .... Hoover, AL
Noe, James A. .... Seattle, WA
Noe, James William .... New Orleans, LA
Noe, Jeffrey W. .... Los Angeles, CA
Noe, Jennifer F. .... Ashland City, TN
Noe, Keith F. .... West Greenwich, RI
Noe, Larry D. .... Campbellsville, KY
Noe, Larry D., P.S.C. .... Campbellsville, KY
Noe, Lawrence M. .... New York, NY
Noe, Michael E., Jr. .... Austin, TX
Noe, P. Renee .... Cincinnati, OH
Noe, Paul R. .... United States Senate, Committee Legal Personnel, GV
Noe, Paula H. .... Brookline, MA
Noe, Randal S. .... Norfolk, VA
Noe, Randolph .... Louisville, KY
Noe, Robert G. .... Oxnard, CA
Noe, Robert J. .... Moline, IL
Noe, Spencer D. .... Lexington, KY
Noe, Stephen L. .... Peoria, IL
Noe, Susan D. .... Houston, TX
Noe, Susan Y. .... Cary, NC
Noe, Thomas Augustine, III
Russellville, KY
Noe Valley Law Offices .... San Francisco, CA
Noe, William G., Jr. .... Atlantic Beach, FL
Noecker, A. Scott .... Orlando, FL
Noecker, Jeffrey Evan .... Charlottesville, VA
Noecker, John W. .... Greensboro, NC
Noecker, Kathlyn E. .... Minneapolis, MN
Noecker, Linda L. .... San Antonio, TX
Noecker, Lisa Carter .... Whiteville, NC
Noecker, Rebecca H.
Colorado Springs, CO
Noecker, Steve D. .... Colorado Springs, CO
Noeding & Moody, P.C.
Albuquerque, NM
Noeding, Nicholas J. .... Albuquerque, NM
Noehring, Arthur .... St. Paul, MN
Noel, Ann Marie .... San Francisco, CA
Noel, Anthony M. .... Nashville, TN
Noel, Art .... Detroit, MI
Noel & Associates .... Chicago, IL
Lombard, IL
Noel, Charles J. .... St. Paul, MN
Noel, Charolette F. .... Dallas, TX
Noel, D. Bobbitt, Jr. .... Houston, TX
Noel, David D. .... Knoxville, TN
Noel, Edmond F., Jr. .... Denver, CO
Noel, Edwin L., (P.C.) .... St. Louis, MO
Noel, Elijah, Jr. .... Memphis, TN
Noel, Frank G. .... Salt Lake City, UT
Noel, Franklin L. .... Minneapolis, MN
Noel, George P. .... Media, PA
Noel, George W. .... Huntsville, AL
Noel, Gerald T., Jr. .... Columbus, OH
Noel, Gregg A. .... Los Angeles, CA
Noel and Hackett .... Media, PA
Noel, Ian .... Los Angeles, CA
Noel, James B. .... Bristol, CT
Noel, James D., III .... San Juan, PR
Noel, James K., IV .... Lancaster, PA
Noel, James L. .... Englewood, CO
Noel, Jena M. .... Chicago, IL
Noel, John E. .... Lombard, IL
Noel, John O. .... New York, NY
Noel, Joseph M. .... Columbus, OH
Noel, Joseph P. .... Kokomo, IN
Noel, Kristin .... Chicago, IL
Noel, Kristin Graham .... Madison, WI
Noel, Leila J. .... Santa Barbara, CA
Noel, Mary K. .... El Dorado Hills, CA
Noel, Maxine A. .... Stuart, FL
Noel, Melbourne A., Jr. .... Hines, IL
Noel, Melody E. .... Indianapolis, IN
Noel, Nancy .... Palm Desert, CA
Noel, Nels P. .... Sublette, KS
Noel, Nicholas, III .... Easton, PA
Noel, Philip W. .... Providence, RI
Noel, Randall D. .... Jackson, MS
Memphis, TN
Noel, Rick L. .... Omaha, NE
Noel, Robert C. .... Houston, TX
Noel, Rochelle M. .... New York, NY
Noel, Ronald E. .... San Antonio, TX
Noel, Sheryl D. .... Fresno, CA
Noel, Stephen F. .... Ogden, UT
Noel, Stephen L. .... Monroe, GA
Noel, Thomas E. .... Baltimore, MD
Noel, Thomas R. .... Attleboro, MA
Providence, RI
Noel, Thomas R., P.C., Counselor at Law
Attleboro, MA
Providence, RI
Noel, W. Keith .... Cincinnati, OH
Noel, William C. .... Charleston, WV
Noel, William D. .... Houston, TX
Noel, William W., III .... Henderson, NC
Noelke, Carl B. .... San Francisco, CA
Noelke & English, L.L.P. .... Austin, TX
Noelke, Hal T. .... San Angelo, TX
Noelke, Lea C. .... Austin, TX
Noelke, Paul .... Milwaukee, WI
Noelker, Timothy F. .... St. Louis, MO
Noell, H. Theodore .... Mishawaka, IN
Noell, John S., Jr. .... Athens, GA
Noell, John W. .... Chicago, IL
Noell, Milburn K., Jr. .... Memphis, TN
Noell, William A., Jr. .... Norfolk, VA
Noelle, William J., III .... Chicago, IL
Noelte, Heather M. .... Los Angeles, CA
Noeltner, Barry S. .... Atlanta, GA
Noennig, Mark E. .... Billings, MT
Noerenberg, Charles .... Golden Valley, MN
Noeske, Abbo & Associates, P.C.
Grand Rapids, MI
Troy, MI
Noeske, Linda J. .... San Carlos, CA
Noeske, Walter F. .... Troy, MI
Noet, Nancy A. .... Milwaukee, WI
Noeth, Lawrence A. .... Northbrook, IL
Noeth, Thomas D., Jr. .... Vero Beach, FL
Noethe, Edward F. .... Omaha, NE
Noethiger, Robert A. .... Stamford, CT
Noethlich, Keith A. .... Pickerington, OH
Noetzel, Henry D. .... Peoria, IL
Noetzel, Henry D., & Associates Ltd.
Peoria, IL
Noey, R. Daniel .... Jacksonville, FL
Nofal, Carolyn Ossi .... Jacksonville, FL
Nofal, Philip A., Jr. .... Concord, NC
Nofer, Frank S. .... Collingswood, NJ
Philadelphia, PA
Nofer, George H. .... Philadelphia, PA
Nofer, Michelle Smith .... Malvern, PA
Nofer, Paul G. .... Philadelphia, PA
Noferi, Louis J., Jr. .... Milford, MA
Noferi, Michael J. .... Milford, MA
Noffke, Mai Lin P. .... Chicago, IL
Noffke, Rachel L. .... Austin, TX
Noffsinger, Henry O. .... Pleasant Hill, CA
Noffsinger, Terry .... Evansville, IN
Nofi, James A. .... New York, NY
Nofi, Susan Polla .... Kennesaw, GA
Flushing, NY
Nofi, Vincent J. .... Melville, NY
Nofri, Donald W. .... Stuart, FL
Nofsinger, Jodi L. .... Lewiston, ME
Noftz, Brenda A. .... Athens, OH
Nofziger, Phyllis Kay .... Elkhart, IN
Noga, Andrew L. .... Hartford, CT
Noga, Darrell Gerard-Marc .... Dallas, TX
Noga, Dorothy M. .... Pittsburgh, PA
Noga, John T. .... Orland Park, IL
Noga, Joseph L. .... New York, NY
Noga, Ronald B. .... Columbus, OH
Nogal, Richard J. .... Oak Brook, IL
Nogan, Thomas J. .... Mineola, NY
Nogaro, Thomas S. .... New York, NY
Nogay, Arlie R. .... Pittsburgh, PA
Nogay, Joseph G. .... Weirton, WV
Nogay, Michael Edward .... Weirton, WV
Nogee, Jeffrey L. .... Westbury, NY
Nogee & Wartel .... Westbury, NY
Nogg, Russell A. .... Anchorage, AK
Noggle, Michael C. .... Findlay, OH
Noggle, Robert B. .... Portland, OR
Noggler, Clifford J. .... Cincinnati, OH
Noggy, Joseph A. .... Buckhannon, WV
Nogi, Appleton, Weinberger & Wren, P.C.
Honesdale, PA
Scranton, PA
Nogi, Jacob .... Scranton, PA
Nogid, Amy F. .... New York, NY
Nogle, Marlene J. .... Minneapolis, MN
Noguchi, George K. .... Honolulu, HI
Nogueira, Jonathan Teixeira
New Bedford, MA
Nogueira, Mark W. .... Cincinnati, OH
Nogueira, Robert D. .... Beeville, TX
Noguera, Steven C. .... Sacramento, CA
Nogueras-Castro, Annette .... San Juan, PR
Nogues, Jean Pierre, (A Professional Corporation) .... Los Angeles, CA
Noh, Jerry H. .... Culver City, CA
Nohara, Sherry A. .... Honolulu, HI
Nohe, Cathy W. .... Ambler, PA
Nohe, David L. .... Brookfield, CT
Nohe, Kenneth M. .... Andover, KS
Nohinek, Sandra A. .... Arlington, TX
Nohl, James Dieter .... Boston, MA
Nohr, Jane E. .... Topeka, KS
Nohr, Jason L. .... Atlanta, GA
Nohr, Katharine M. .... Honolulu, HI
Nohr, Melissa McMath .... Marietta, GA
Nohr, Timothy William .... Topeka, KS
Nohra, Jennifer Welfley .... Cleveland, OH
Nohra, Jude J. .... Cleveland, OH
Nohrden, Patrick T. .... Las Vegas, NV
Nohrr, Donald A. .... Melbourne, FL
Nohrr, Philip F. .... Melbourne, FL
Nohsey, Henry A. .... Union City, TN
Noia, Ernest G. .... Palm Springs, CA
Noiray, Megan A. .... Westlake Village, CA
Noirot, Annette R. .... Mansfield, OH
Noiroux, Mary Ann .... Orange, CA
Nojay, William R. .... Rochester, NY
Nojeim, Gregory T. .... Washington, DC
Noji, Greg K. .... Honolulu, HI
Nojima, Cynthia M. .... Honolulu, HI
Nojima, John A. .... Los Angeles, CA
Nojima, Yoshiyuki .... New York, NY
Nojunas, Thomas M. .... Philadelphia, PA
Noker, David C. .... Lansdale, PA
Nokes, Beau James .... Newport Beach, CA
Nokes, Davis & Quinn, A Professional Corporation .... Laguna Beach, CA
Nokes, D.C., Jr. .... Johnstown, PA
Nokes, George .... Austin, TX
Nokes, Gregory B. .... Hartford, CT
Stamford, CT
Nokes, James C. .... Arlington, TX
Nokes, Laurence P. .... Laguna Beach, CA
Nokes, Shari E. .... Newport Beach, CA
Nolan, A. Michael .... Lutherville, MD
Nolan, Agnes F. .... New York, NY
Nolan, Al G. .... Vienna, VA
Nolan, Alan T. .... Indianapolis, IN
Nolan and Alderson .... El Dorado, AR
Nolan, Andrew J. .... Wichita, KS
Nolan, Angela .... Houston, TX
Nolan, Angela M. .... Sunnyvale, CA
Nolan, Anne C. .... Walthill, NE
Nolan, Anoma T. .... Phoenix, AZ
Nolan, Anthony J. .... Baltimore, MD
Nolan, Anthony R.G. .... New York, NY
Nolan, Armstrong & Barton, LLP
Palo Alto, CA
Redwood City, CA
San Jose, CA
Nolan, Arthur J. .... Federal Trade Commission, Bureau of Competition, GV
Nolan, Bennett S. .... Fort Smith, AR
Nolan, Beth .... Department of Justice, Office of Legal Counsel, GV
Nolan, Billie Schrecker .... Pittsburgh, PA
Nolan, Bobbe S. .... Dayton, OH
Nolan, Brendan W. .... New York, NY
Nolan, Brett .... Chicago, IL
Nolan, Brian D. .... Omaha, NE
Nolan, C. Duff, Jr. .... Stuttgart, AR
Nolan, Caddell & Reynolds, P.A.
Fort Smith, AR
Nolan, Carol Lucchesi .... Staten Island, NY
Nolan, Catherine R. .... Washington, DC
Nolan, Charles A., Jr. .... Manahawkin, NJ
Nolan, Charles J. .... West Boylston, MA
Nolan, Chas. T. .... West Bloomfield, MI
Nolan, Chris T. .... Akron, OH
Nolan, Christopher .... West Springfield, MA
Nolan, Christopher C. .... McLean, VA
Nolan, Christopher D. .... Salt Lake City, UT
Nolan, Christopher J. .... New York, NY
Nolan, Christopher M. .... New York, NY
Nolan, Craig S. .... Burlington, VT
Nolan, Cristina Clare .... St. Louis, MO
Nolan, Dailey, Gallo, Rothemich & Brunero, Ltd. .... Coventry, RI
Nolan, Dan L., Jr. .... Clarksville, TN
Nolan, Daniel J. .... Chicago, IL
Nolan, Daniel J. .... Marblehead, MA
Nolan, Daniel Mark .... Clarksville, TN
Nolan, Daniel P. .... Albany, NY
Nolan, David B. .... Department of Energy, Office of the General Counsel, GV
Nolan, David C. .... Walnut Creek, CA
Nolan, David D. .... Oakland, CA
Nolan, David L. .... Wrentham, MA
Nolan, Dayle .... Minneapolis, MN
Nolan, Deborah A. .... Los Angeles, CA
Nolan, Debra L. .... Walnut Creek, CA
Nolan, Denise M. .... Martinez, CA
Nolan, Dennis M. .... Chicago, IL

Nomura, Nelson T. .... New York, NY
Nonaka, Scott T. .... New York, NY
Nonberg, Randy E. .... Pacific Palisades, CA
Nondorf, Kurt D. .... Houston, TX
Nonemaker, Keith R. .... Hanover, PA
Noneman, Charles E. .... Los Angeles, CA
Noneman, Gary R. .... Keokuk, IA
Noneman, Kathleen F. .... Reno, NV
Nong, Yuvora .... Orlando, FL
Noniewicz, Thomas M. .... North Haven, CT
Nonna, John M. .... New York, NY
Nonnemaker, Philip E. .... Kansas City, MO
Nonnenmacher, John J. .... New York, NY
Nonnenmann, Gregory J. .... Mount Sinai, NY
Nooe, Charles J. .... Eden, NC
Nooe, John W. .... Eden, NC
Noojin, Frank K., Jr. .... Huntsville, AL
Noon, David D. .... Sunbury, PA
Noon, Hillis W. .... Des Moines, IA
Noon, Jody Ann .... Portland, OR
Noon, Meredith C. .... Greenville, SC
Noon, Philip M. .... Grandview, WA
Noon, Richd. E. .... Concord, MA
Noon, Susan M. .... Washington, DC
Noon, Timothy S. .... San Diego, CA
Noona, Stephen E. .... Norfolk, VA
Noonan, A. Shawn .... Houston, TX
Noonan, Andrew S. .... Albany, OR
Noonan, C. Brendan .... Waltham, MA
Noonan, Charles T. .... Allentown, PA
Noonan, D. Michael .... St. Cloud, MN
Noonan, D. Michael .... Concord, NH
Noonan, D. Sean .... Brockton, MA
Noonan, Daniel A. .... Milwaukee, WI
Noonan, Daniel J. .... Round Rock, TX
Noonan, David J. .... San Diego, CA
Noonan, Douglas T. .... Roswell, GA
Noonan, Edward R. .... Washington, DC
Noonan, E. J. .... Omaha, NE
Noonan, Elizabeth A. .... Washington, DC
Noonan, Elizabeth McDonough
Providence, RI
Noonan, Erin K. .... Norwalk, CA
Noonan, Gerald J. .... Brockton, MA
Noonan, Gerald M. .... Naugatuck, CT
Noonan, Gerald P. .... Chicago, IL
Noonan, Geralyn Farrell .... Fort Myers, FL
Noonan, Gregory R. .... Cherry Hill, NJ
King Of Prussia, PA
Royersford, PA
Noonan, Honorah .... Marshalltown, IA
Noonan, James C. .... St. Paul, MN
Noonan, James C. .... Stevens Point, WI
Noonan, James V. .... Chicago, IL
Noonan, James V., Ltd. .... Chicago, IL
Noonan, James W. .... Weston, MA
Noonan, Jean .... Farm Credit Administration,
Office of the General Counsel, GV
Noonan, Jennifer Horn .... Nashville, TN
Noonan, Jill .... Vallejo, CA
Noonan, Joann S. .... Jacksonville, FL
Noonan, John C. .... Kansas City, MO
Noonan, John D. .... Traverse City, MI
Noonan, John F. .... Detroit, MI
Noonan, John J. .... South San Francisco, CA
Noonan, John T., Jr. .... San Francisco, CA
Noonan, John W. .... New York, NY
Noonan, John W., Prof. Corp.
Pleasanton, CA
Noonan, Julie J. .... Denver, CO
Noonan, Kathleen G. .... Boston, MA
Noonan, Kathryn M. .... Newton, MA
Noonan, Kay G. .... Kansas City, MO
Noonan, Kelly Twiss .... Seattle, WA
Noonan, Kevin E. .... Chicago, IL
Noonan, Kevin M. .... Chicago, IL
Noonan, Linda .... Washington, DC
Noonan, Linda S. .... Allentown, PA
Noonan, Lionel W. .... Mobile, AL
Noonan, Lori A. .... Los Angeles, CA
Noonan, Mark E. .... Worcester, MA
Noonan, Mark J. .... Boston, MA
Noonan, Martin F. .... New York, NY
Noonan, Mary T. .... Salt Lake City, UT
Noonan, Michael A. .... Cumberland, MD
Noonan, Michael D.
Department of Housing and Urban Development,
Office of General Counsel, GV
Noonan, Michael J. .... Verona, NJ
Noonan, Michael K. .... Waukegan, IL
Noonan, Michael M. .... New Orleans, LA
Noonan, Michael P. .... Austin, TX
Noonan, Nancy A. .... Washington, DC
Noonan, Patricia M. .... Chicago, IL
Noonan, Patrick K. .... Milwaukee, WI
Noonan, Patrick M. .... Guilford, CT
Noonan & Prokup .... Allentown, PA
Bethlehem, PA
Noonan, Raymond J. .... Sea Girt, NJ
Noonan, Rebecca Lee .... New York, NY
Noonan, Robert C. .... Batavia, NY
Noonan, Robert E. .... Boston, MA
Noonan, Robert T.
Consumer Product Safety Commission,
Office of the General Counsel, GV
Noonan, Robert T. .... Boston, MA
Noonan, Robert W. .... Santa Cruz, CA
Noonan, Roger W. .... Denver, CO
Noonan, Susan J. .... Seattle, WA
Noonan, Susan M. .... Allentown, PA
Noonan, T. Scott .... Nashville, TN
Noonan, Thomas E. .... Des Moines, IA
Noonan, Thomas E. .... Boston, MA
Noonan, Thomas F. .... Meriden, CT
Noonan, Thomas J. .... St. Louis, MO
Noonan, Thomas J., P.C., The Law Offices of .... St. Louis, MO

Noonan, Thomas K. .... Allentown, PA
Noonan, Thomas K. .... Mahanoy City, PA
Noonan, Timothy R. .... Royal Oak, MI
Noonan, Todd M. .... Sacramento, CA
Noonan, Tracy M. .... Los Angeles, CA
Noonan, Virginia C. .... Bradford, MA
Noonan, W. Patrick .... Woodland Hills, CA
Noonan, W. Patrick, A Professional Corporation .... Los Angeles, CA
Woodland Hills, CA
Noonan, William D. .... Portland, OR
Noonan, William E. .... Fort Myers, FL
Noonan, William T. .... Pawtucket, RI
Noonan, Yunker & Friedman .... Batavia, NY
Noonan-Day, Heidi L. .... Cedar Falls, IA
Noonberg, Lewis A. .... Washington, DC
Noone, Anita M. .... San Diego, CA
Noone, Christopher S. .... Rochester, NY
Noone, George W. .... Boston, MA
Noone, James A. .... Washington, DC
Noone, James J. .... Wichita, KS
Noone, John J., Jr. .... Malden, MA
Noone, John T. .... South Barrington, IL
Noone, Joseph M. .... Boston, MA
Noone, Laura Palmer .... Phoenix, AZ
Noone, M. Caragh .... New York, NY
Noone, Margaret E. .... Malvern, PA
Noone, Mary Alice .... Chicago, IL
Noone, Mary-Ellen .... Washington, DC
Noone, Matthew F. .... Philadelphia, PA
Noone, Michael .... Denver, CO
Noone, Michael M. .... Fort Myers, FL
Naples, FL
Noone and Noone .... Malden, MA
Noone, Paul B. .... Malden, MA
Noone, Peter H. .... Boston, MA
Noone, Robert M. .... Glenwood Springs, CO
Noone, Robert M., P.C.
Glenwood Springs, CO
Noone, Robert T. .... Logan, WV
Noone, Thomas F., (P.C.) .... New York, NY
Noone, Thomas P. .... Malden, MA
Noonen, Martin M. .... Los Angeles, CA
Nooney, Christina Lynn .... Palo Alto, CA
Nooney, J. Scott .... Jacksonville, FL
Nooney, James F. .... Toledo, OH
Nooney, John K. .... Rapid City, SD
Nooney, Kathleen L. .... Chicago, IL
Nooney, Michael J. .... Palo Alto, CA
Nooney, Patrick J. .... Cumberland, MD
Hagerstown, MD
Nooney, Patrick J., P.A. .... Cumberland, MD
Hagerstown, MD
Noonoo, Robert E. .... Los Angeles, CA
Noonoo, Susan V. .... Los Angeles, CA
Noordsy, J. Mark .... Glens Falls, NY
Noorigian, Antonetta .... New York, NY
Noorigian, Antonetta L. .... New York, NY
Noorigian & Associates, P.C.
San Diego, CA
Noorigian, Kenneth C. .... San Diego, CA
Noorigian, Michael H. .... New York, NY
Noorlander, Willem J. .... Rice Lake, WI
Noorman, Jeffrey J. .... Traverse City, MI
Nooter, Thomas H. .... New York, NY
Nooter, William Ward .... Washington, DC
Rockville, MD
Nopar, Alan S. .... Palo Alto, CA
Nopper, Jas. J. .... Grandville, MI
Noppinger, John G. .... Baltimore, MD
Nora, John J. .... Plymouth, MI
Nora, Karen E. .... Huntington, NY
Nora, Mark J. .... Chicago, IL
Nora, Robert L. .... Chicago, IL
Nora, Suzanne M. .... Los Angeles, CA
Noranbrock, Randy Allan .... Alexandria, VA
Norat, Cecilia Elena .... New York, NY
Norat, David E. .... Lexington, KY
Norat, Richard N.V. .... Miami, FL
Norback, Ernest H. .... Menlo Park, CA
Norbeck, Suzanna Anstine .... Mesa, AZ
Norber, Samuel .... Los Angeles, CA
Norberg, Carl E. .... St. Paul, MN
Norberg, Charles Robert .... Washington, DC
Norberg, Deena Sherman .... Tempe, AZ
Norberg, Erin E. .... Washington, DC
Norberg, Jaron B. .... Phoenix, AZ
Norberg, John D. .... Boston, MA
Norberg, Scott F. .... Jackson, MS
Norberg, Willard P. .... San Francisco, CA
Norbert, William S. .... Portland, ME
Norbin, Carrie L. .... Milwaukee, WI
Norbitz, Todd C. .... New York, NY
Norblad, Albin W. .... Salem, OR
Norburg, David W. .... Kansas City, MO
Norbury, Terry .... New York, NY
Norbut, Alex S. .... Riverside, IL
Norbut & Associates .... Riverside, IL
Norbut, Gregory P. .... Poulsbo, WA
Norbut Law Firm .... Poulsbo, WA
Norbut, Nancy Ann .... Riverside, IL
Norby, Charlotta .... Atlanta, GA
Norby, Claudia M. .... Santa Rosa, CA
Norby, Dennis W. .... Spokane, WA
Norby, Eric S. .... Irvine, CA
Norby, Gary K. .... Dubuque, IA
Norby, Joseph M. .... Marshfield, WI
Norby, Mark A. .... Portland, OR
Norby, Scott J. .... Lincoln, NE
Norby, Steven G. .... Cedar Falls, IA
Norby, Thomas J. .... St. Paul, MN
Norchi, Kevin M. .... Cleveland, OH
Norcia, Joseph G. .... Sea Girt, NJ
Norcini, Joyce M. .... Palo Alto, CA
Norcom, Janet V.
Federal Deposit Insurance Corporation,
Resolutions Section, GV
Norcross, Angelea C. .... Manteo, NC

Norcross, David A. .... Washington, DC
Trenton, NJ
Norcross, Joe L. .... Hanford, CA
Norcross, John D. .... Chicago, IL
Norcross, Kathryn R.
Federal Deposit Insurance Corporation,
Appellate Litigation Section, GV
Norcross, Kenneth J. .... Morristown, NJ
New York, NY
Norcross, Mark D. .... Redding, CA
Norcross, Michelle Anne .... Denver, CO
Norcross, Philip A. .... Marlton, NJ
Norcross, William Ernest .... Cordova, TN
Nord, Amelia .... West Hartford, CT
Nord, Arvid D., III .... Orange, CA
Nord & Associates .... East Brunswick, NJ
Nord, Beryl A. .... Minneapolis, MN
Nord, David W. .... Caledonia, MN
Nord, Donald A. .... Glendale, AZ
Nord, Donald C. .... Chicago, IL
Nord, Eric Edward .... Manchester, NH
Nord, Henry J. .... Chicago, IL
Nord, Jill Cantor .... Baltimore, MD
Nord, Julie L. .... Pittsburgh, PA
Nord, Kent D. .... Tiffin, OH
Nord, Larry B. .... Eureka, CA
Nord, Larry M. .... Duluth, MN
Nord, Lori Ann .... San Francisco, CA
Nord, Macklin & Meinerts, P.A.
Lakeville, MN
Nord, Marcy Lee .... Pittsburgh, PA
Nord, Mary M. .... New Albany, IN
Nord, Melvin .... Glendale, AZ
Nord, Michael .... East Brunswick, NJ
Nord, Michael D. .... Baltimore, MD
Nord, Nancy A. .... Rochester, NY
Nord, R. Glenn .... Lakeville, MN
Nord, Robert E. .... Chicago, IL
Nord, Roger G. .... Fairfax, VA
Nord, Scott J. .... Beverly Hills, CA
Nord, Steven F. .... Merced, CA
Nord, Steven K. .... Huntington, WV
Nord, Thomas C. .... San Francisco, CA
Nord, Tim D.
Department of Justice, GV
Nordahl, Andrew C. .... Chicago, IL
Nordahl, Erik R. .... Quincy, MA
Nordahl, Natasha Leigh .... New York, NY
Nordahl, Stephen D. .... New York, NY
Nordale, Mary A. .... Fairbanks, AK
Nordan, Josh L. .... San Diego, CA
Nordan, Richard P. .... Raleigh, NC
Nordaune, Andrea J. .... Minneapolis, MN
Nordaune & Friesen .... Minneapolis, MN
Nordaune, Roselyn J. .... Minneapolis, MN
Nordberg, Carl A., Jr. .... Washington, DC
Nordberg, Daniel A.
Rancho Santa Margarita, CA
Nordberg, Edward P., Jr. .... Chevy Chase, MD
Nordberg, John A. .... Chicago, IL
Nordberg, Peter B. .... Philadelphia, PA
Nordboe-Tinker, Connie J. .... Wichita, KS
Nordbrock, Mark A. .... Santa Monica, CA
Nordby, Diane D. .... Anaheim, CA
Nordby, Eric C. .... Syracuse, NY
Nordby, Jack .... Minneapolis, MN
Nordbye, Rodger L. .... Minneapolis, MN
Nordeen, David .... Vancouver, WA
Nordeen, Roger A. .... Olathe, KS
Nordell, Keith C. .... Colorado Springs, CO
Nordell, Michael .... White Plains, NY
Norden, Dennis A. .... Kankakee, IL
Norden, Donald J. .... United States Senate,
Senatorial Assistants, GV
Norden, Irving .... New York, NY
Norden, Laura K. .... New Haven, CT
Norden, Lawrence D. .... New York, NY
Norden, Mark .... Fort Myers, FL
Norden, Mark, P.A. .... Fort Myers, FL
Norden, William B. .... New York, NY
Nordenberg, Arthur D. .... Chicago, IL
Nordenberg, Donna R. .... New York, NY
Nordenberg, Jon C. .... Madison, WI
Nordenberg, Mark A. .... Pittsburgh, PA
Nordenbrook, Ruth A. .... Brooklyn, NY
Nordeng, Mervin D. .... Fargo, ND
Nordeng, Richard K. .... Madison, WI
Sun Prairie, WI
Nordgren, Gerald P. .... Chicago, IL
Nordgren, Marcia L.
Overseas Private Investment Corporation,
GV
Nordgren, Timothy A. .... Raleigh, NC
Nordham, George W. .... Waldwick, NJ
Nordhaus, Haltom, Taylor, Taradash & Frye, LLP .... Washington, DC
Albuquerque, NM
Santa Fe, NM
Nordhaus, Robert J. .... Albuquerque, NM
Nordhaus, Robert R. .... Washington, DC
Nordheden, John A. .... Champaign, IL
Nordheim, Susan V. .... Chicago, IL
Nordhoff, Arthur C., Jr. .... Jasper, IN
Nordhoff, Crouse & Smith .... Jasper, IN
Nordhoff, Dennis Leo, II .... Franklin, TN
Nordhoff, John Michael .... Bloomington, IN
Nordhoff, Katherine DeSales .... Phoenix, MD
Nordholm, Jeffery D. .... Milwaukee, WI
Nordholt, James S., Jr. .... Tiffin, OH
Nordhougen, Curtis A. .... Moorhead, MN
Nordick, Larry F. .... Moorhead, MN
Nordigian, Peter J. .... Waukegan, IL
Nordin, H. Bertil .... New York, NY
Nordin, Hartley .... Minneapolis, MN
Nordin, John Eric, II .... Los Angeles, CA
Nordin, John Michael
Oklahoma City, OK
Nordin, Kathleen A. .... Santa Ana, CA

Nordin, Kenneth H. .... Palo Alto, CA
Nordin, Randy A. .... Atlanta, GA
Nording, Stephen J. .... Madison, WI
Nordlander, Nancy A. .... Tillamook, OR
Nordlicht & Hand .... New York, NY
Nordlicht, Harold .... Long Beach, NY
Nordlicht, Ira S. .... New York, NY
Nordling, Bernard E. .... Hugoton, KS
Nordling, Erick E. .... Hugoton, KS
Nordling, H. G. .... Washburn, WI
Nordlinger, Alan .... Mattituck, NY
Nordlinger, Bernard I. .... Washington, DC
Nordlinger, Edwin H. .... New York, NY
Nordlinger, Marjorie S.
Nuclear Regulatory Commission,
Office of the General Counsel, GV
Nordlinger, Stephanie .... Los Angeles, CA
Nordlof, Eric T. .... Pacific, WA
Nordloh, Christopher Scott
Crestview Hills, KY
Nordlund, D. Craig .... Palo Alto, CA
Nordlund, John V. .... Larkspur, CA
Nordlund, Randall .... Fort Lauderdale, FL
Miami, FL
Nordlund & Ryan .... Larkspur, CA
Nordlund, Sally .... Nashville, TN
Nordlund, William C. .... Dallas, TX
Nordman, Cormany, Hair & Compton
Los Angeles, CA
Oxnard, CA
Ventura, CA
Nordman, Eric R. .... Westerville, OH
Nordmann, Vicki Knight .... Louisville, KY
Nordmarken, Oliver G. .... Odessa, TX
Nordmeyer, Nancy A. .... Edina, MN
Nordone, August J. .... Syracuse, NY
Nordquist, Dale M. .... Centralia, WA
Nordquist, Joel P. .... Phoenix, AZ
Nordquist, Joyce D. .... Scotts Valley, CA
Nordquist, Karl R. .... Houston, TX
Nordquist, Kenneth L. .... Austin, TX
Nordquist Law Offices, Ltd. .... Rockford, IL
Nordquist, Marnie .... San Francisco, CA
San Jose, CA
Nordquist, Pamela S. .... Seattle, WA
Nordquist, Richard A., III .... Minneapolis, MN
Nordquist, Stephen G. .... New York, NY
Nordquist & Stern PLLC .... New York, NY
Nordquist, Steven L. .... Rockford, IL
Nordquist, Stuart B. .... Rockford, IL
Nordseth & Evans .... Sioux Falls, SD
Nordseth, Mary .... Sioux Falls, SD
Nordsletten, Paul M. .... Seattle, WA
Nordstrand, Scott J. .... Anchorage, AK
Nordstrandt, Renée J. .... Santa Barbara, CA
Nordstrom, Adrienne E. .... Pleasanton, CA
Nordstrom, Bruce A. .... Monroe, MI
Nordstrom, Christa Lee .... Sacramento, CA
Nordstrom, Donald H. .... Minneapolis, MN
Nordstrom, Erik R. .... Austin, TX
Nordstrom, James C. .... Wabasha, MN
Nordstrom, James P. .... Topeka, KS
Nordstrom, Kenneth J. .... Ashland, OH
Nordstrom & Locke .... Ashland, OH
Nordstrom, Lucia .... Los Angeles, CA
Nordstrom, Mark A. .... Fairfield, CT
Nordstrom, Michael N. .... Hanford, CA
Nordstrom, Nees & Janecek, P.S.
Spokane, WA
Nordstrom, Orrin B. .... Cincinnati, OH
Nordstrom, P. Christian .... Dayton, OH
Nordstrom, Paul E. .... Washington, DC
Nordstrom, Robert J. .... Columbus, OH
Nordstrom, Robert P. M. .... Atlanta, MI
Nordstrom, Russell E., (A Professional Corporation) .... Los Angeles, CA
Nordstrom, Steele, Nicolette, Blythe and Jefferson .... Kenai, AK
Los Angeles, CA
Orange, CA
Palm Desert, CA
Nordstrom, Stephen L. .... Spokane, WA
Nordstrom, Tamika R. .... Minneapolis, MN
Nordstrom, Ted R. .... Morgantown, WV
Nordstrom, Thomas A. .... Monroe, MI
Nordstrom, Vincent Alexander .... Salinas, CA
Nordstrom, William R., Law Office
Minneapolis, MN
Nordsven, Mary E. .... Dickinson, ND
Nordt, Glen A. .... Houston, TX
Nordt, Gregory M. .... Fort Lauderdale, FL
Nordtvedt, Anna K. .... Newport, WA
Nordwall, Blaine L. .... Bismarck, ND
Nordwall, Brian L. .... Seattle, WA
Nordwall, David R. .... Chicago, IL
Nordwall, Michael A. .... Peoria, IL
Nordwind, Betty L. .... Los Angeles, CA
Nordwind, William R. .... Washington, DC
Nordwind, Willy, Jr. .... Kalamazoo, MI
Nordyke and Denlinger .... Baton Rouge, LA
Nordyke, Keith B. .... Baton Rouge, LA
Nordyke, Robert E. .... Salem, OR
Nordyke, Stephen K. .... Butler, MO
Kansas City, MO
Nore, Jennifer P. .... Phoenix, AZ
Scottsdale, AZ
Nore, Jennifer P., P.C. .... Scottsdale, AZ
Nored, Alvin .... Burnet, TX
Nored, Anne M. .... Richardson, TX
Nored, Michael .... Corpus Christi, TX
Noreen, Robert .... Fairbanks, AK
Noreika, Keith A. .... Washington, DC
Noreika, Maryellen .... Wilmington, DE
Norek, Alfred M. .... Albany, NY
Norek, Charles J. .... Glendale, CA
Ontario, CA
Norek, Joan I., Law Office of .... Chicago, IL
Noreke, Anissa B. .... Boston, MA

Norelius & Nelson ... Denison, IA
Norelius, Wm. Q. ... Denison, IA
Norell, Andrew Oldland ... Tucson, AZ
Norell, Beverly E. ... Memphis, TN
Norell & Hatcher, P.L.C. ... Tucson, AZ
Norell, Lars R. ... New York, NY
Norell, Mark O. ... New York, NY
Norell, Peter H. ... Rancho Cucamonga, CA
Norelli, George H. ... Lake Success, NY
Norelli, Nancy Black ... Charlotte, NC
Norelli, Nancy Black, PLLC
Charlotte, NC
Noren, David C. ... Hillsboro, OR
Noren, David G. ... Chicago, IL
Noren, Douglas L. ... New York, NY
Noren, Marc B. ... Baltimore, MD
Noren, Ronald B. ... Southport, CT
Noretsky, Harry B. ... Newark, NJ
Norfleet, Brooks, Jr. ... Dallas, TX
Norfleet, Deatria M. ... Fort Worth, TX
Norfleet, Doren P. ... Oswego, NY
Norfleet, Eben C. ... Oswego, NY
Norfleet, Edward K., Jr. ... Amarillo, TX
Norfleet & Fletcher ... Memphis, TN
Norfleet, Kathleen D., (P.C.) ... Memphis, TN
Norfolk, Matthew D. ... Uniondale, NY
Norfolk, William A. ... Baton Rouge, LA
Norfolk, William R. ... New York, NY
Norford, Lawrence C. ... Philadelphia, PA
Norgaard, Anders J. ... Belle Plaine, IA
Norgaard, Anders J., P.C. ... Belle Plaine, IA
Norgaard, Christopher ... Los Angeles, CA
Norgaard, Gary K., P.C. ... Englewood, NJ
Norgaard, Philip J. ... Point Richmond, CA
Norgaard, Steven K. ... Glen Ellyn, IL
Norgard, David W. ... Highland Heights, OH
Norgard, John A. ... Sacramento, CA
Norgard, Robert A. ... Bartow, FL
Norgard, Tami L. ... Fargo, ND
Norgle, Charles R. ... Chicago, IL
Norgle, Gregory M. ... Chicago, IL
Norgle-Loewer, Christine R. ... Chicago, IL
Norgren, Paul W. ... Superior, WI
Norgress, Ben C. ... Denham Springs, LA
Norheim, Jon W. ... Las Vegas, NV
Norian, A. Catherine ... Los Angeles, CA
Noriega, Andrea L. Schneider ... Tucson, AZ
Noriega & Bradshaw, LLP
Bakersfield, CA
Noriega, James E. ... Bakersfield, CA
Noriega, Joseph ... Bakersfield, CA
Noriega, Luis A. ... Ponce, PR
Noriega, Raul ... San Antonio, TX
Noriega, Robert J. ... Bakersfield, CA
Norigian, Gerald G. ... Warwick, RI
Norin, Howard ... Pikesville, MD
Norin, Mitchell Alan ... Baltimore, MD
Norine, William L. ... Grantsburg, WI
Noris, Anna R. ... Union City, NJ
Noris, Anne ... Seattle, WA
Nork, Jeremy J. ... Reno, NV
Nork, Michael A. ... Glendale, CA
Nork, Thomas R. ... Houston, TX
Norken, David ... York, PA
Norkett, Brian W. ... Chicago, IL
Norko, Raymond R. ... Hartford, CT
Norkunas, Stanley W. ... Lowell, MA
Norkus, Nancy J. ... Pittsburgh, PA
Norland, Cynthia J. ... Bismarck, ND
Norland, Eric P. ... San Jose, CA
Norland & Kays ... San Jose, CA
Norland, Phillip N. ... Northwood, IA
Norlander, Gerald A. ... Albany, NY
Norlander, James D. ... Battle Creek, MI
Norlander, Karen S. ... Albany, NY
Norlander, Lisa D. ... Los Angeles, CA
Norley, Dolores ... DeLand, FL
Norlin, Janice ... Concordia, KS
Norlin, John W. ... Palm Beach Gardens, FL
Norling, Dennis ... Joliet, IL
Norling, John C. ... Phoenix, AZ
Norling, Jonathan M ... Portland, OR
Norling, Kolsrud, Sifferman & Davis, P.L.C.
Phoenix, AZ
Norling, Richard E. ... Phoenix, AZ
Norman, A. Scott ... Columbus, OH
Norman, A. Scott, LLC, Law Offices of
Columbus, OH
Norman, Alan H. ... St. Louis, MO
Norman, Albert G., Jr. ... Atlanta, GA
Norman, Andrew G. W. ... Baltimore, MD
Norman, Andy ... Chicago, IL
Norman, Angela Benzo ... Oakland, CA
Norman, Barbara Cohn ... Birmingham, MI
Norman, Barbara Mailly ... Chicago, IL
Norman, Brian K. ... Dallas, TX
Norman, Carol Nash ... Rock Hill, SC
Norman, Charles E. ... Tulsa, OK
Norman, Christopher ... Medford, NJ
Norman, Christopher H.
Sun City Center, FL
Tampa, FL
Norman, Christopher J. ... New York, NY
Norman, Collie E.
Greenwood Village, CO
Norman, Collie, P.C.
Greenwood Village, CO
Norman, Craig A. ... Columbus, OH
Norman, Craig H. ... Albany, NY
Norman, David C. ... Portland, ME
Norman, David J. ... Crofton, MD
Norman, David J., III ... Houma, LA
Norman, David L. ... Washington, DC
Norman, David Louis ... San Francisco, CA
Norman, David R. ... Dallas, TX
Norman, David S. ... Milwaukee, WI
Norman, Deborah L. ... St. Louis, MO
Norman, Dennis O. ... Cleveland, OH
Norman, Diane E. ... McFarland, WI
Norman, Donald H. ... Fort Lauderdale, FL
Norman, Donald H., P.A.
Fort Lauderdale, FL
Norman, Donald L., Jr. ... Chicago, IL
Norman, Donna Katherine ... Palo Alto, CA
Norman, Douglas K. ... Indianapolis, IN
Norman, Dowler, Sawyer, Israel, Walker & Barton ... Ventura, CA
Norman & Eames ... Auburn, CA
Norman, Edem, McNaughton & Wallace
Enid, OK
Norman, Edem, McNaughton & Wallace, P.L.L.C., A Professional Association
Enid, OK
Norman, Edem, McNaughton & Wallace, P.L.L.C. ... Oklahoma City, OK
Norman, Elena C. ... New York, NY
Norman, Eliot ... Richmond, VA
Norman, Elizabeth Marie ... Ukiah, CA
Norman, Ellington M. ... Bethesda, MD
Norman, Elton F. ... Washington, DC
Norman, Ernest J. ... Buffalo, NY
Norman, Fitzpatrick, Wood & Kendrick
Birmingham, AL
Norman, Forrest A. ... Cleveland, OH
Norman, Forrest A., III ... Cleveland, OH
Norman & Gardner ... Louisburg, NC
Norman, Gary E. ... Albany, OR
Norman, Geoffrey E. ... Newton, MA
Norman, George ... Olney, MD
Norman, George B. ... Davenport, IA
Norman, George L. ... Keokuk, IA
Norman, Gerald E. ... Worcester, MA
Norman, Gerald R. ... San Francisco, CA
Norman, Gilloon & Wright ... Dubuque, IA
Norman, H. Wayne, Jr. ... Bel Air, MD
Norman, H. Wayne, Jr., P.A. ... Bel Air, MD
Cambridge, MD
Norman, Hanson & DeTroy, LLC
Portland, ME
Norman, Horace H. ... Houston, TX
Norman, Jack, Jr. ... Nashville, TN
Norman, Jack O., P.C. ... Dallas, TX
Norman, James A. ... Des Moines, IA
Norman, James A. ... Coquille, OR
Norman, James B. ... Department of the Navy, Office of the Judge Advocate General, GV
Norman, James C. ... San Antonio, TX
Norman, James K. ... Auburn, CA
Norman, James M. ... Fort Lauderdale, FL
Norman, Jan B. ... Los Angeles, CA
Norman, Jane Carol ... Washington, DC
Norman, Jane Morrissey ... San Francisco, CA
Norman, Jas. S., Jr. ... Houston, TX
Norman, Jeffery S. ... Chicago, IL
Norman, Jeffrey A. ... Miami, FL
Norman, Jeffrey B.
Federal Energy Regulatory Commission, Office of the General Counsel, GV
Norman, Jeffrey P. ... Houston, TX
Norman, Jeffrey P., P.C. ... Houston, TX
Norman, Jim T., III ... Prattville, AL
Norman, Joan M. ... Boulder, CO
Norman, Joe B. ... New Orleans, LA
Norman, John Anderson, II ... Charlotte, NC
Norman, John B. ... Oklahoma City, OK
Norman, John K. ... Anchorage, AK
Norman, John L. ... Santa Ana, CA
Norman, John W. ... Belleville, IL
Norman, John W. ... Enid, OK
Oklahoma City, OK
Norman, Jonathan M. ... Columbus, OH
Norman, Judith A. ... New York, NY
Norman, Judith M. ... Rochester, NY
Norman, Kathie Z. ... Sheboygan, WI
Norman, Keith B. ... Montgomery, AL
Norman, Keith J. ... Detroit, MI
Norman, Kenneth A. ... Stuart, FL
Norman, Kenneth Eugene ... Oakland, CA
Norman, Kenneth J. ... Moorhead, MN
Norman & Kingsbury ... Medford, NJ
Norman, L. Bruce ... Los Angeles, CA
Norman, Larry E. ... Louisburg, NC
Norman, Laura Ouverson
Department of the Army, Office, Chief of Engineers/Headquarters, U.S. Army Corps of Engineers, GV
Norman, Laura S. ... New York, NY
Norman, Lawrence ... Beaumont, CA
Norman, Lawrence, Inc. ... Beaumont, CA
Norman, Lynn E. ... Chicago, IL
Norman, Marcus D. ... Dallas, TX
Norman & Marion ... Keokuk, IA
Norman, Mark A. ... Cincinnati, OH
Norman, Mark W. ... Los Angeles, CA
Norman, Martha, The Law Offices of
Oak Brook, IL
Norman, Mary Jane ... Indianapolis, IN
Norman, Matthew D. ... Marblehead, MA
Norman, Medrith Lee ... Lexington, KY
Norman, Melissa S. ... Louisville, KY
Norman, Merrick J., Jr. ... Lake Charles, LA
Norman, Michael H. ... Houston, TX
Norman, Michael T. ... Muskogee, OK
Norman, Milton ... New York, NY
Norman, Nancy A. ... San Antonio, TX
Norman, Nancy B. ... Boston, MA
Norman, Nancy L. Jones ... Anoka, MN
Norman & Norman ... Houston, TX
Norman & Paloucek ... Curtis, NE
North Platte, NE
Norman, Pamela Brady ... Worthington, OH
Norman, Patrick J. ... Vienna, VA
Norman, Paul M. ... Scottsdale, AZ
Norman, Paul R. ... Madison, WI
Norman, Paula R. ... Los Angeles, CA
Norman, Peter J. ... Philadelphia, PA
Norman, Phillip A. ... Valparaiso, IN
Norman, Pia ... Chicago, IL
Norman, Ralph R., III ... Montgomery, AL
Norman, Richard E. ... Houston, TX
Norman, Richard M. ... Ventura, CA
Norman, Richard William ... Spencer, IN
Norman, Rick J. ... Lake Charles, LA
Norman, Risë B. ... New York, NY
Norman, Robert C. ... Augusta, GA
Aiken, SC
Norman, Robert C., Jr. ... Macon, GA
Norman, Robert D. ... Birmingham, AL
Norman, Robert D., Jr. ... Birmingham, AL
Norman, Robert E. ... Oklahoma City, OK
Norman, Robert Eugene ... Atlanta, GA
Norman, Robert Paul ... Chicago, IL
Norman, Robin C. ... Shreveport, LA
Norman, Roger A. ... Benton, AR
Norman, Roger H. ... Lancaster, OH
Norman, Roger M. ... Fort Worth, TX
Norman, Ronald A. ... San Jose, CA
Norman, Ronald C. ... Albuquerque, NM
Norman, Ronald E. ... Newport Beach, CA
Norman, Roy A. ... San Luis Obispo, CA
Norman, Royce E. ... North Platte, NE
Norman, Sandra B. ... Long Beach, CA
Norman, Sanford B., (P.C.) ... Richmond, VA
Norman, Sarah Goss ... Cleveland, OH
Norman, Scott M. ... Ventura, CA
Norman, Seth W. ... Nashville, TN
Norman, Sheila D. ... Clearwater, FL
Tampa, FL
Norman, Sheila D., P.A. ... Clearwater, FL
Tampa, FL
Norman, Stephen ... Salem, OR
Norman, Stephen ... Burlington, VT
Norman, Stephen C. ... Wilmington, DE
Norman, Stephen P. ... Leonardtown, MD
Norman, Steve ... Portland, OR
Norman, Steven R. ... Westford, MA
Norman, Stuart R., Jr. ... Jewett City, CT
Norman, Susan ... Plano, TX
Norman, Telfer W. ... Lakewood, CO
Norman, Terry R. ... Brady, TX
Norman, Thomas ... Medford, NJ
Norman, Thomas E. ... Tallahassee, FL
Norman, Thomas F. ... San Francisco, CA
Norman, Thomas G. ... Spring, TX
Norman, Thomas "Jay" ... Nashville, TN
Norman, Thrall, Angle, Guy & Day, L.L.P.
Jacksonville, TX
Rusk, TX
Norman, Tiffany Taylor ... Atlanta, GA
Norman, Todd K. ... Orlando, FL
Norman, Vickie L. ... Chicago, IL
Norman, W. Caffey, III ... Washington, DC
Norman, Wayne A., Jr. ... Dubuque, IA
Norman, Wilfred H. ... Westfield, NJ
Norman, William A. ... Oakland, CA
Norman, William D. ... Salem, MA
Norman, William D., Jr.
New Orleans, LA
Norman, William H. G.
San Francisco, CA
Norman, William K. ... Los Angeles, CA
Norman, William R., Jr. ... Washington, DC
Norman, OK
Norman Wohlgemuth Chandler & Dowdell
Tulsa, OK
Normand, Charles W. ... Boston, MA
Providence, RI
Normand, Edmund A. ... Orlando, FL
Normand, Edward J. ... Armonk, NY
Normand, Elizabeth A. ... Portland, OR
Normand, James A. ... Manchester, NH
Normand, James T. ... Oak Ridge, TN
Normand, Jocelyn R. ... New York, NY
Normand, Marjorie Weiner ... New York, NY
Normand, Rick C. ... New Orleans, LA
Normand & Shaughnessy, P.A.
Manchester, NH
Normand, Tom ... Temple, TX
Normandeau, Andrew A. ... Fairfax, VA
Normandin, Charles P. ... Boston, MA
Normandin, Cheney & O'Neil
Laconia, NH
Normandin, Edward C. ... Middletown, NJ
Normandin, Paul L. ... Laconia, NH
Normandin, Tom Roddy ... Santa Ana, CA
Norman-Johnson, Sonia Y. ... Cambridge, MA
Normanly, John J. ... Santa Maria, CA
Normann, Caroline Potter ... Gainesville, FL
Normann, David R. ... New Orleans, LA
Normann, Robert P. ... Pittsburgh, PA
Normansell, Nicole A. ... Pittsburgh, PA
Normark, Per B. ... Jonesboro, GA
Norment, Russell J. ... Fort Worth, TX
Norment, Thomas K., Jr.
Williamsburg, VA
Norment, William B., Jr. ... Henderson, KY
Normile, Bruce ... Edina, MO
Normile, Hubert C., Jr. ... Melbourne, FL
Normile, James S. ... New York, NY
Normile, John J., Jr. ... New York, NY
Normile, John R. ... Binghamton, NY
Normile, John R., Jr. ... Binghamton, NY
Normile, Robert J. ... El Segundo, CA
Normille, Eileen Walsh ... Elizabeth, NJ
Normington, Dale A. ... Cleveland, OH
Normington, Richard V., III ... Oakland, CA
Norminton, Thomas M., (P.C.)
Beverly Hills, CA
Norminton & Wiita ... Beverly Hills, CA
Normoyle, Brent M. ... Olympia, WA
Nornes, Pamela J. ... Hauppauge, NY
Nornes, Timothy C. ... St. Paul, MN
Noroian, Edith M. ... Blythe, CA
Noronha, Peter A. ... Santa Ana, CA
Noronha, Sirikit M. ... New York, NY
Noronha-Advogados ... Los Angeles, CA
Miami, FL
Norooz, Al F. ... Los Angeles, CA
Norpell, Thomas E. ... Newark, OH
Norquest & Brisack, L.L.P. ... McAllen, TX
Norquest, Neil E. ... McAllen, TX
Norquist, Elliot ... Kansas City, MO
Norquist, James P. ... Vadnais Heights, MN
Norquist, John D.
Department Of Veterans Affairs, Office of Employment Discrimination Complaints Adjudication, GV
Norquist, Myron H. ... Colorado Springs, CO
Norquist, S. David ... Cleveland, MS
Norquist, S. Griffin ... Yazoo City, MS
Norr, Amy ... Philadelphia, PA
Norr, Daniel D. ... Las Vegas, NV
Norr, Paul ... Portland, OR
Norred, R. A. ... Birmingham, AL
Norred, Robert G., Jr. ... Chattanooga, TN
Norregard, G. Peter ... Santa Ana, CA
Norrell, David G. ... Washington, DC
Norrell, Mitchell Abbott ... Lancaster, SC
Norrett, Lisa Michele ... Washington, DC
Norrick, Floyd T. ... Hillsboro, MO
Norrie, Christopher ... Captain Cook, HI
Norrie, David T., Law Offices of
Mount Olive, NJ
Norrie, G. Kenneth ... Jacksonville, FL
Norris, Alan E. ... Columbus, OH
Norris, Alan James ... Monroe, LA
Norris, Alan R. ... Portland, OR
Norris, Albert B., Jr. ... San Francisco, CA
Norris, Allen L. ... Richmond, CA
Norris, Allen R. ... Dayton, OH
Norris, Amy ... San Francisco, CA
Norris, Andrea L. ... Akron, OH
Norris, Anne E. ... Indianapolis, IN
Norris, Anthony J. ... New York, NY
Norris, Arthur B. ... Bakersfield, CA
Norris & Assocs., P.C. ... Birmingham, AL
Norris, Benjamin R. ... Phoenix, AZ
Norris, Bruce Alan ... Winter Park, FL
Norris, Burnadette D. ... Hollywood, FL
Norris, Bush & Byrd ... Elizabethton, TN
Norris, C. Todd ... San Francisco, CA
Norris & Campbell, Professional Association
Hingham, MA
Norris, Candace ... Canyon, TX
Norris, Casey William ... Sacramento, CA
Norris, Cathy J. ... Denver, CO
Norris, Charlene D. ... Boone, NC
Norris, Charlene M. ... Kalispell, MT
Norris, Charles B. ... New York, NY
Norris, Charles K. ... Norwich, CT
Norris, Charles R. ... Charleston, SC
Norris, Charles S., Jr. ... Monroe, LA
Norris, Charles W. ... Culver City, CA
Norris, Choplin & Schroeder, LLP
Indianapolis, IN
Norris, Christina ... Nashville, TN
Norris, Christina R. L. ... Louisville, KY
Norris, Christopher T. ... Boston, MA
Norris, Clarence S. ... Sumter, SC
Norris, Clarissa Jatho ... Fort Wayne, IN
Norris, Craig D. ... Palo Alto, CA
Norris, Craig W. ... Chicago, IL
Norris, Dale Allen ... Kansas City, MO
Norris, Daniel O. ... Vale, OR
Norris, Daniel W. ... Cincinnati, OH
Norris, David B. ... Birmingham, AL
Norris, David B. ... San Diego, CA
Norris, David B. ... North Palm Beach, FL
Norris, David E. ... Orlando, FL
Norris, David M. ... Reno, NV
Norris, David S. ... Rutherfordton, NC
Norris, David Walter ... Chicago, IL
Norris, Dean E. ... Denver, CO
Norris, Diane M. ... Rocklin, CA
Norris, Donald G. ... Los Angeles, CA
New York, NY
Norris, Donald P. ... Phoenix, AZ
Norris, Donald T. ... Liberty, MO
Norris, D.W., Co., LPA ... Cincinnati, OH
Norris, Earl R. ... Albuquerque, NM
Norris, Edwin L. ... Los Angeles, CA
Norris, Eric B. ... San Jose, CA
Norris, Erika Kristine ... Evansville, IN
Norris, Floyd H. ... Los Angeles, CA
Norris, Franklyn K. ... Omaha, NE
Norris, G. William, Jr. ... Richmond, VA
Norris, Gail M. ... Rochester, NY
Norris, Gary G. ... McMinnville, OR
Norris, Gary W. ... Ventura, CA
Norris, Geoffrey A. ... Monterey, CA
Norris, George L. ...
Department of Housing and Urban Development, GV
Norris, Gilbert C. ... Weiser, ID
Norris, Glenn L. ... Des Moines, IA
Norris, Gloria J. ... Dallas, TX
Norris, Grady J. ... New Bern, NC
Norris, Gregory S. ... Arlington, TX
Norris, Guy W. ... Lake City, FL
Norris, Harold ... East Lansing, MI
Norris, Howard Lee ... Tyler, TX
Norris, J. Earle ... Rosemead, CA
Norris, J. Kenny ... Perryton, TX
Norris, James A., Jr. ... West Monroe, LA
Norris, James D. ... Orange, CA
Norris, James H. ... Department of Labor, Employment & Training Administration, GV
Norris, James H. ... Pittsburgh, PA
Norris, James L. ... Bismarck, ND
Norris, James L., P.C. ... Bismarck, ND
Norris, James M. ... London, KY
Norris, James M. ... Danvers, MA

Norris, James M. .... Parchman, MS
Norris, James R. .... Centerburg, OH
Norris, James W. .... Cheyenne, WY
Norris, Janet C. .... San Francisco, CA
Norris, Jeffrey A. .... Washington, DC
Reston, VA
Norris, Jeffrey B. .... Oxnard, CA
Norris, Jeffrey C. .... Dublin, OH
Norris, Jeffrey R. .... Washington, IN
Norris, Jeffrey R. .... Montrose, PA
Norris, Jeffrey W. .... Philadelphia, PA
Norris, Jerome J. .... Washington, DC
Norris, Jerry L. .... Omaha, NE
Norris, Jessica Schwedner .... Cupertino, CA
Norris, Joanne F. .... Denver, CO
Norris, John A.
Department Of Health And Human Services, Food & Drug Administration, GV
Norris, John Alan .... Miami, FL
Norris, John B., III .... Annapolis, MD
Norris, John D. .... Houston, TX
Norris, John E. .... Birmingham, AL
Norris, John E. .... Lake City, FL
Norris, John F. .... Brea, CA
Norris, John H. .... Bloomfield Hills, MI
Norris, John K., Jr. .... Sanibel, FL
Chicago, IL
Wood Dale, IL
Norris, John L. .... Nashville, TN
Norris, John R., III .... Dallas, TX
Norris, John S., Jr. .... Virginia Beach, VA
Norris, Johnson & Placke .... West Monroe, LA
Norris, Jon W. .... Washington, DC
Norris, Jonathan P. .... Newton, MA
Norris, Jonathan P., P.C. .... Newton, MA
Norris, Jonathan R. .... Lexington, KY
Norris, Joseph A.
Office of Personnel Management, Personnel in Non-Legal Positions, GV
Norris, Judy C. .... Dallas, TX
Norris, Karen S. .... Philadelphia, PA
Norris, Kathleen A. .... Carlsbad, CA
Norris, Kenneth M. .... Richland, WA
Norris & Keplinger, L.L.C.
Overland Park, KS
Kansas City, MO
Norris, Kevin A. .... Bala Cynwyd, PA
Norris, Kevin L. .... San Bernardino, CA
Norris, Kimberlee Dawn .... Fort Worth, TX
Norris & Koberlein, P.A. .... Lake City, FL
Norris, Lana L. .... San Mateo, CA
Norris, Lanny R. .... Elizabethton, TN
Norris, Larry O. .... Hattiesburg, MS
Norris, Larry O., P.A. .... Hattiesburg, MS
Norris, Lawrence G. .... Bonsall, CA
Norris, Linda B. .... Lincoln, NE
Norris, Lisa A. .... Sunnyvale, CA
Norris, Lisa D. .... Pensacola, FL
Norris, Lischer, Batts & Somerville, P.C.
Phoenix, AZ
Scottsdale, AZ
Sun City, AZ
Norris, Lloyd .... Philadelphia, PA
Norris, Lon D. .... Baton Rouge, LA
Norris, Lyonel F. .... Minnetonka, MN
Norris, M. Hatcher .... Hartford, CT
Hartford, CT
Norris, Mark S. .... Memphis, TN
Norris, Mary R. .... New Haven, CT
Norris, Matthew C. .... Bloomfield Hills, MI
Norris, Matthew J. .... Rochester, NY
Norris, McLaughlin & Marcus, P.A.
Bridgewater, NJ
Somerville, NJ
New York, NY
Norris, Megan P. .... Detroit, MI
Norris, Melanie Reynolds .... Lafayette, CA
Norris, Melvin .... Boston, MA
Norris, Michael .... Redondo Beach, CA
Norris, Michael D. .... Rochester, NY
Norris, Michael D. .... Fort Worth, TX
Norris, Michael G. .... Overland Park, KS
Kansas City, MO
Norris, Michael J. .... Indianapolis, IN
Norris, Michael J. .... Marlborough, MA
Norris, Michael J. .... Concord, NH
Norris, Michael P. .... Omaha, NE
Norris, Michael T. .... Schaumburg, IL
Norris, Nancy Morrow .... Los Angeles, CA
Norris, Nancy W. .... Charlotte, NC
Norris, Nathan Robert .... Birmingham, AL
Norris, Norman L. .... Philadelphia, PA
Norris & Norris .... Richmond, CA
Walnut Creek, CA
Norris & Norris .... Akron, OH
Norris, Oscar John, III .... Memphis, TN
Norris, Palmer W. .... Gardendale, AL
Norris, Patricia C. .... Dayton, OH
Norris, Patricia K. .... Phoenix, AZ
Norris, Patrick R. .... Birmingham, AL
Norris, Paul F. .... Seattle, WA
Norris, Paul W. .... New Brunswick, NJ
Norris & Peterson .... Burnsville, NC
Norris, Pleas M. .... Canton, MS
Norris, R. Wade .... Washington, DC
Norris, Randolph D. .... Trenton, NJ
Norris, Raymond M., Law Offices of
Phoenix, AZ
Norris, R. C. .... Akron, OH
Norris, Renee' C. .... Chicago, IL
Norris, Richard A. .... Somerville, NJ
Norris, Richard E. .... Richmond, CA
Walnut Creek, CA
Norris, Richard F. .... Omaha, NE
Norris, Richard L. .... Indianapolis, IN
Norris, Richard N. .... Clovis, NM
Norris, Rick D., Jr. .... Birmingham, AL
Norris, Robert B. .... Charlotte, NC
Norris, Robert D., Jr. .... Tulsa, OK
Norris, Robert E. .... Shenandoah, IA
Norris, Robert H. .... Sun City, AZ
Norris, Robert H. .... Hingham, MA
Norris, Robert N. .... Granada Hills, CA
Norris, Robert W. .... Birmingham, AL
Norris, Robert W. .... Montgomery, AL
Norris, Roderick G. .... Pittsburgh, PA
Norris & Rossi LLP .... San Mateo, CA
Norris & St. Clair, P.C. .... Norfolk, VA
Virginia Beach, VA
Norris, Scott V. .... Lansing, MI
Norris, Shane W. .... Salt Lake City, UT
Norris, Shannon D. .... Dallas, TX
Norris, Staunton .... Burnsville, NC
Norris, Stephen B. .... Fort Worth, TX
Norris, Stephen E. .... Los Angeles, CA
Norris, Stephen E. .... Mount Vernon, IL
Norris, Steve C. .... Nashville, TN
Norris, Steven P. .... New York, NY
Norris, Susan J. .... Richmond, VA
Norris, Teresa L. .... Columbia, SC
Norris, Thomas L., Jr. .... Raleigh, NC
Norris, Timothy J. .... Miami, FL
Norris, Todd A. .... Kansas City, KS
Norris, Trenton H. .... San Francisco, CA
Norris, Verle W. .... Corydon, IA
Norris, Veronica N. .... Tustin, CA
Norris, Vickie K. .... Everett, WA
Norris, Victor M. .... Bloomfield Hills, MI
Norris, Walker .... Birmingham, AL
Norris, Walter A. .... Woodbury, NJ
Norris, Walter F. .... Washington, DC
Norris, Wayne F. .... Berwyn, IL
Norris, Wendy I. .... New York, NY
Norris, Whitton E., III .... Boston, MA
Norris & Wicker .... Danvers, MA
Norris, William A. .... Los Angeles, CA
Norris, William A. .... Northampton, MA
Norris, William A., Jr. .... Bartow, FL
Norris, William B. .... Cleveland, OH
Norris, William C. .... Le Center, MN
Norris, William E. .... Hinsdale, IL
Norris, William F. .... Brookings, OR
Norris, William, III .... West Monroe, LA
Norris, William M., (P.A.) .... Miami, FL
Norris-York, Dover A. .... Portland, OR
Norrix, Pamela J. .... Albany, NY
Norrod, Gregory S. .... Chicago, IL
Norry, Lewis A. .... Rochester, NY
Norry, Lewis A., P.C. .... Rochester, NY
Norse, Kristin A. .... Ruskin, FL
Norseng, Charles G. .... Chippewa Falls, WI
Norsetter, John I. .... Madison, WI
Norsigian, Gregory C. .... Wethersfield, CT
Norsigian, Hrant, Jr. .... O'Fallon, IL
Norsworthy, Clinch G., III .... Atlanta, GA
Norsworthy, Elizabeth K. .... Concord, VT
Norsworthy, Jase O. .... Billings, MT
Norsworthy, Kenneth A. .... Anchorage, AK
Norsworthy, Levator, Jr.
Department of the Army, Office of the General Counsel, GV
Norsworthy, Thomas G. .... Naples, FL
Nortell, Bruce .... Lisle, IL
Norten, Stephen G. .... Burlington, VT
North, Alison Kathryn .... Tucson, AZ
North, Barbara A. .... Columbus, OH
North, Barbara C. .... New York, NY
North, Basil L., Jr. .... Kansas City, MO
North, Brent J. .... Newport Beach, CA
North, Brett A. .... New Orleans, LA
North, Brian S. .... Philadelphia, PA
North, Bruce A. .... Gretna, LA
North, Carol M. .... Valley Stream, NY
North, Cecil J., III .... Stamford, CT
North, Charles M. .... Waco, TX
North, Chris J. .... Columbus, OH
North, Christine M. .... San Francisco, CA
North, Christopher Colt
Newport News, VA
North & Cobb, P.A. .... Towson, MD
North, David A. .... Rockford, IL
North, Don Mark .... Nashville, TN
North, Douglas A. .... Seattle, WA
North, Edwin M. .... Salt Lake City, UT
North, Evans W. .... Rosslyn, VA
North, Florence M. .... Westlake Village, CA
North, Gloria O. .... Boca Raton, FL
North, Gloria O., P.A. .... Boca Raton, FL
North, H. Davis, III .... Greensboro, NC
North, Harold L., Jr. .... Chattanooga, TN
North, Harris J. .... Falls Church, VA
North, James L. .... Birmingham, AL
North, Jane A. .... Philadelphia, PA
North, Jane P. .... Winston-Salem, NC
North, Jeremy W. .... Towson, MD
North, Joe R. .... Columbia, SC
North, John C. .... Downers Grove, IL
North, John C., III .... Denver, CO
North, John D. .... Woodbridge, NJ
North, John E. .... Omaha, NE
North, John E., Jr. .... Omaha, NE
North, John F. .... Helena, MT
North, John L. .... Atlanta, GA
North, John-Clarence .... Easton, MD
North, Joseph R. .... Fort Myers, FL
North, Julia Palasek .... Clarksville, TN
North, Julie A. .... New York, NY
North, Karis Lynn .... Boston, MA
North, Kathleen M. .... Denver, CO
North, Kelly M. .... Denver, CO
North, Kenneth E. .... Virginia Beach, VA
North Law Firm, The, P.A. .... Fort Myers, FL
North Law Office, The .... Nashville, TN
North, Michael B. .... New Orleans, LA
North, Michael L. .... Wichita, KS
North, Michael P. .... St. Paul, MN
North, Omer C. .... Hondo, TX
North, Paul D., Jr. .... Lehigh Valley, PA
North, Paul R., Jr. .... New Haven, CT
North, Penelope .... Idaho Falls, ID
North, Philip E. .... Beaverton, OR
North, Phillip L. .... Nashville, TN
North, Phillip O. .... Hilton Head Island, SC
North, Pia J. .... Richmond, VA
North, Pursell & Ramos, PLC
Nashville, TN
North, Raymond E. .... Dallas, TX
North, Richard B., Jr. .... Atlanta, GA
North, Richard L. .... Baltimore, MD
North, Robert E. .... Topeka, KS
North, Robert H. .... Bethesda, MD
North, Robert J. .... Berkeley Heights, NJ
North, Sally .... Woodland Hills, CA
North, Scott E. .... Columbus, OH
North, Stanley U., III .... Newark, NJ
New York, NY
North, Stephen Adam .... Monroe, LA
North, Steve .... Nashville, TN
North, Steven E. .... New York, NY
North, Steven E., P.C. .... New York, NY
North, Susan C. .... Richmond, VA
North, Susan L. .... Oak Brook, IL
North Texas Family Law .... Carrollton, TX
Dallas, TX
Denton, TX
McKinney, TX
North, Thomas B. .... St. Ignace, MI
North, Thomas M. .... Woodbury, NJ
North, Vaughn W. .... Sandy, UT
North, W. A. Jerry .... Portland, OR
North, Wendy L. .... New York, NY
North, William C. .... Downers Grove, IL
North, William D. .... Arlington Heights, IL
North, William M. .... Lansdale, PA
North, William M., Jr. .... Auburn, CA
North, William T. .... Cottonwood Falls, KS
North, William V. .... Kansas City, MO
Northam, David E. .... Rushville, IN
Northam, Frank M. .... Washington, DC
Northam, Patrick R. .... Louisville, KY
Northam, Thomas L. .... Accomac, VA
Northam, Wescott B. .... Accomac, VA
Northcraft, H. Fred .... Kansas City, MO
Northcraft, Julian O. .... Pfafftown, NC
Northcraft, Mark S. .... Seattle, WA
Northcraft & Woods, P.C. .... Seattle, WA
Northcross, Wilson H., Jr. .... Ann Arbor, MI
Northcutt, C. Wayne .... Denton, TX
Northcutt, Clarence D. .... Ponca City, OK
Northcutt, Clark, Gardner, Hron & Tate
Ponca City, OK
Northcutt, David V. .... Madison, WI
Northcutt, Edwards, Gordon, Perrotta & Feingold .... Atlanta, GA
Northcutt, Gregory K. .... Calvert City, KY
Northcutt, Herrn .... Little Rock, AR
Northcutt, John E. .... Ponca City, OK
Northcutt, Michael L. .... Missoula, MT
Northcutt, Paul E. .... Ponca City, OK
Northcutt, Raymond E. .... Salem, OR
Northcutt, Robert F. .... Montgomery, AL
Northcutt & Seccombe .... Denver, CO
Northcutt, Stevan T. .... Lakeland, FL
Northcutt, William M. .... Tulsa, OK
Northcutt, William R.
Indian Harbour Beach, FL
Northcutt, William R., P.A.
Indian Harbour Beach, FL
Northen Blue, L.L.P. .... Chapel Hill, NC
Northen, John A. .... Chapel Hill, NC
Northen, Lora V. .... Mount Laurel, NJ
Northen, Patrick M. .... Cherry Hill, NJ
Philadelphia, PA
Northern, Ann C. .... New York, NY
Northern, Christina .... Washington, DC
Northern, Kathy Seward .... Columbus, OH
Northern, Richard .... Louisville, KY
Northern, Van W. .... Amarillo, TX
Northern Wyoming Law Associates
Sheridan, WY
Northey, John H., III .... Charlotte, NC
Northgrave, William W. .... Jersey City, NJ
Northington, D. Henry .... Princeton, NJ
Northington, Harold M., Jr.
San Antonio, TX
Northington, Hiawatha, II .... Jackson, MS
Northman, Tod A. .... Portland, OR
Northness, Robert C. .... Pickerington, OH
Northridge, Keith C. .... New Brunswick, NJ
Northridge, Michael Allen
Environmental Protection Agency, Office of Enforcement and Compliance Assurance, GV
Northrip, Robert E. .... Kansas City, MO
Northrop, Albert W. .... Bowie, MD
Northrop, Carl W. .... Washington, DC
Northrop, Charles P. .... Denver, CO
Northrop, David E. .... Columbus, OH
Northrop, Edward S. .... Baltimore, MD
Northrop, Frederick J. .... Pacifica, CA
Northrop, Geoffrey M. .... San Diego, CA
Northrop, James B. .... Salem, OR
Northrop, John K. .... Elkton, MD
Northrop, John L. .... Bensenville, IL
Northrop, Joseph S. .... Huntington, IN
Northrop, Margaret D. .... Stamford, CT
Northrop, Monroe .... Houston, TX
Northrop, Patricia T. .... New York, NY
Northrop, Stradar & Glenn, P.C.
Newburgh, NY
Northrop, Walsh, Becker & Colaresi
Bowie, MD
Northrup, Anne L. .... Seattle, WA
Northrup, Arthur H. .... Indianapolis, IN
Northrup, Charles H. .... Springfield, IL
Northrup, Charles J. .... Springfield, IL
Northrup, Donald W. .... Boston, MA
Northrup, George A. W. .... Madison, WI
Northrup, Judith A. .... Columbus, OH
Northrup, Kenneth A. .... Milford, MA
Northrup, Linda L. .... Los Angeles, CA
Northrup, Linda L., A Prof. Corp., Law Offices of .... Los Angeles, CA
Northrup, M. Kate .... West Palm Beach, FL
Northrup, Mark D. .... Seattle, WA
Northrup, Michael A. .... Zanesville, OH
Northrup, R. Michael .... Dallas, TX
Northrup, Richard D., Jr. .... Walton, NY
Northrup, Ryan T. .... Mobile, AL
Northrup, Thomas E. .... La Jolla, CA
Northrup, Vel .... San Antonio, TX
Northrup, B. V. (Bill) .... Cedar Rapids, IA
Northup, Douglas C. .... Phoenix, AZ
Northup, Julie S. .... Atlanta, GA
Northup, Kenneth P. .... Leonia, NJ
Northup, Nancy Jean .... New York, NY
Northup, Nathan C. .... San Diego, CA
Northup, Robert E. .... Richmond, VA
Northup, Robert W., Jr. .... Pasadena, CA
Northup, Ron A. .... Stockton, CA
Northup, Stephen A. .... Richmond, VA
Northway, Robert J., Jr. .... Houston, TX
Northwood, Edward C. .... Buffalo, NY
Northwood, Inez .... Covina, CA
Nortman, William .... Fort Lauderdale, FL
Norton, A. Dennis .... Salt Lake City, UT
Norton, A. Jay .... Lakewood, CA
Norton, Albert L., Jr. .... Norcross, GA
Norton, Alfred V., Jr. .... New York, NY
Norton, Andrew H. P. .... Brockton, MA
Norton, Ann Birgitta .... Los Angeles, CA
Norton, Anthony W. .... Ramona, CA
Norton, Arpert, Sheehy & Higgins, P.C.
Hackensack, NJ
Paterson, NJ
West Paterson, NJ
Norton, Arthur F. .... Department of Justice, Criminal Division, GV
Norton, Babette .... Golden, CO
Norton, Bradley Alan .... Seneca, SC
Norton, Bradley L. .... Lowden, IA
Norton, Brian P. .... Chicago, IL
Norton, Bruce .... Tarrytown, NY
Norton • Burgess .... Texarkana, TX
Norton, Burke F. .... Palo Alto, CA
Norton, C. Mac .... Pine Bluff, AR
Norton, C. Michael .... Nashville, TN
Norton, Carl L. .... Houston, TX
Norton, Carolyn Butler .... Far Hills, NJ
Norton, Charles E.
Greenwood Village, CO
Norton, Charles F., Jr. .... Birmingham, AL
Norton, Charles L., Jr. .... Atlanta, GA
Norton & Christensen .... Rochelle Park, NJ
Goshen, NY
Norton, Christopher .... Houston, TX
Norton, Christopher H. .... Los Angeles, CA
Norton, Constance E. .... Los Angeles, CA
Norton, Daniel A. .... Boca Raton, FL
Norton, Daniel F. .... Scottsdale, AZ
Norton, Daniel F. .... Sikeston, MO
Norton, Daniel J. .... Belvidere, IL
Norton, Daniel J. .... Columbus, IN
Norton, Daniel S. .... Sikeston, MO
Norton, David B., Law Offices of
Selma, AL
Norton, David C. .... Charleston, SC
Norton, David R. .... Dallas, TX
Houston, TX
Norton, David T. .... Dallas, TX
Norton, David W. .... Chicago, IL
Norton, David W. .... Chattanooga, TN
Norton, Debra A. .... Buffalo, NY
Norton, Dennis H. .... Chicago, IL
Norton & DeRose .... Westfield, NJ
Norton, Dianna M. .... Irving, TX
Norton, Donald A. .... Chicago, IL
Norton, Donald T. .... Hollywood, FL
Norton, Drew S. .... Troy, MI
Norton, Dwight W. .... Metairie, LA
Norton, Edward M., Jr. .... Columbia, MD
Norton, Edward V. .... Ann Arbor, MI
Norton, Edwin N. .... Kelso, WA
Norton, Eileen M. .... Seattle, WA
Norton, Elaine V. .... Malibu, CA
Norton, Eleanor Holmes .... Washington, DC
Norton, Elizabeth W. .... Minneapolis, MN
Norton & Fairman .... Los Angeles, CA
Norton, Floyd L., IV .... Washington, DC
Norton, Francis X., Jr. .... Athens, GA
Norton, Frank .... Dallas, TX
Norton, Frank C. .... Salina, KS
Norton, Fred C. .... St. Paul, MN
Norton, Fred R. .... Texarkana, TX
Norton, Frederic P. .... Kenmore, NY
North Tonawanda, NY
Norton, Frederick C. .... Stanhope, NJ
Norton, Gail Y., Law Offices of
Burlingame, CA
Norton, Gale A. .... Denver, CO
Norton, Gary .... Corpus Christi, TX
Norton, Gary A. .... Des Moines, IA
Norton, Gary A. .... El Paso, TX
Norton, Gary C. .... Roseville, MN
Norton, Gary C. .... Omaha, NE
Norton, Gary E. .... Bloomsburg, PA
Norton, Gary J. .... Bangor, ME
Norton, Geoffrey P. .... Encino, CA
San Francisco, CA
Norton, George H. .... Palo Alto, CA
Norton, Gerald P. .... Washington, DC
Norton, Gerard F., Jr. .... Pittsford, NY

Norton, Gerard P. ... New York, NY
Norton, Glen A. ... Chaska, MN
Norton, Glenn A. ... New London, MO
Norton, Gregory N. ... Anniston, AL
Norton, Gurley, Hammersley & Lopez, P.A.
Sarasota, FL
Norton, Harold Douglas ... Bel Air, MD
Norton, Harry D., Jr. ... West Paterson, NJ
Norton, Heather J. ... Camas, WA
Norton, Helen L. ... Washington, DC
Norton, Henry ... Miami, FL
Norton, Hubbard, Ruzicka & Kreamer, L.C.
Olathe, KS
Norton, Hugh A. ... Englewood, CO
Norton, Hunter ... Stamford, CT
Norton, Hunter N. ... New Haven, CT
Norton, Irena Leigh ... Los Angeles, CA
Norton, Jack ... Fort Lauderdale, FL
Norton, Jack F. ... Montgomery, AL
Norton, Jacobs, Kuhn & McTopy, L.L.P.
Houston, TX
Norton, James F. ... Freehold, NJ
Norton, James N. ... Ericson, NE
Norton, James T. ... Jacksonville, FL
Norton, Jane M. ... Falmouth, ME
Norton, Janet Barbre ... Indianapolis, IN
Norton, Janet M. ... Louisville, KY
Norton, Jay ... Olathe, KS
Norton, Jean L. ... Metairie, LA
Norton, Jefferson D. ... Bethesda, MD
Norton, Jeffery L. ... New York, NY
Norton, Jeffrey A. ... Encino, CA
Norton, Jeffrey J. ... Philadelphia, PA
Norton, Jennifer M. ... Boston, MA
Norton, Jerry E. ... Chicago, IL
Norton, Jo Betsy ... Austin, TX
Norton, Joe L. ... Olathe, KS
Norton, Joe L. ... Wichita, KS
Norton, John B.
Federal Communications Commission,
Cable Services Bureau, GV
Norton, John C. ... Selma, AL
Norton, John C. ... Atlanta, GA
Norton, John C. ... Keene, NH
Norton, John E. ... Chicago, IL
Wheaton, IL
Norton, John F. ... Cleveland, OH
Norton, John H. ... Berkley, MI
Norton, John H. ... Wayne, NJ
Norton, John H., III ... Shelbyville, TN
Norton, John H. (Jack) ... Kansas City, MO
Norton, John Howard ... Moscow, ID
Norton, John J. ... Boston, MA
Norton, John J., Jr. ... Brooklyn, NY
Norton, John L., III ... Cambridge, MD
Norton, John M. ... Long Beach, CA
Norton, John S., Jr. ... Daytona Beach, FL
Norton, John S., Jr., P.A.
Daytona Beach, FL
Norton, John W. ... Anniston, AL
Norton, John William ... St. Paul, MN
Woodbury, MN
Norton, Joseph A. ... Chicago, IL
Norton, Judith Trainor ... Boston, MA
Norton, Karin J. ... New York, NY
Norton, Kate M. Johnson ... Norristown, PA
Norton, Kevin ... Fort Worth, TX
Norton, Kimberly ... Galesburg, IL
Norton, Larry ... Peoria, IL
Norton, Lauren I. ... Boston, MA
Norton, Lawrence H.
Commodity Futures Trading Commission,
Division of Enforcement, GV
Norton, Lewis F. ... Huntington, WV
Norton • Lidstone, LLC ... Denver, CO
Englewood, CO
Norton, Lisa Kay ... Washington, DC
Norton, Lorna McGilvray ... Atlanta, GA
Norton & Luhn, P.C. ... Knoxville, TN
Norton, Lynette ... Pittsburgh, PA
Norton, Lynne L. ... Marriottsville, MD
Norton, Mallie M. ... Tulsa, OK
Norton, Mancini, Argentati, Weiler & DeAno
Chicago, IL
Wheaton, IL
Norton, Marcy L. ... Los Angeles, CA
Norton, Margaret Lee ... Baltimore, MD
Norton, Margaret M. ... Cleveland, OH
Norton, Marice Beth ... Rockville, MD
Norton, Marla Hirshman ... Wilmington, DE
Norton & Marryott, P.A. ... Punta Gorda, FL
Norton, Mary Katherine ... Detroit, MI
Norton, Mary Reed ... Springfield, MA
Norton, Matthew E. ... Chicago, IL
Norton, Matthew J. ... Charleston, SC
Norton, Maura ... Cleveland, OH
Norton, McCarty, Lanane, Broderick, Rock &
Pancol ... Anderson, IN
Norton, Melinda S. ... Fairfax, VA
Norton, Melissa L. ... Sunbury, PA
Norton, Melissa W. ... Portland, ME
Norton & Melnik ... Encino, CA
San Francisco, CA
Norton, Merrill L. ... Lovington, NM
Norton, Michael C. ... San Ramon, CA
Norton, Michael E. ... New York, NY
Norton, Michael E. ... Dallas, TX
Norton, Michael F. ... Omaha, NE
Norton, Michael J. ... Englewood, CO
Norton, Michael J. ... Wichita, KS
Norton, Michael P. ... Irvine, CA
Norton, Michael R. ... Stockton, CA
Norton, Michael T. ... Minneapolis, MN
Norton, Mitchell L. ... Los Angeles, CA
Norton, Nancy A. ... Liberty, MO
Norton, Nancy A. ... Seattle, WA
Norton, Nancy Ellen ... Boston, MA
Norton, Nancy J. ... Tacoma, WA

Norton, Nanette M. ... Chicago, IL
Norton, N. M. ... Little Rock, AR
Norton and Norton ... Sikeston, MO
Norton & Norton, LLP ... Encino, CA
Norton, Norton & Noland, P.C.
Kansas City, MO
Norton & Norton, P.C. ... Lowden, IA
Norton, P. Kay ... Greeley, CO
Norton, Parent & Cleary, P.C. ... Keene, NH
Norton, Patricia A. ... Boston, MA
Norton, Patrick J. ... Cleveland, OH
Norton, Peter ... Santa Ana, CA
Norton, Peter J. ... New York, NY
Norton, Philip J., Jr. ... Edgartown, MA
Norton, R. Franklin ... Knoxville, TN
Norton, R. Lynn ... Los Angeles, CA
Norton Radin Hoover Freedman
Kenmore, NY
North Tonawanda, NY
Norton, Ralph W. ... New York, NY
Norton, Randell Hunt ... Washington, DC
Rockville, MD
Arlington, VA
Norton, Raymond D. ... Tulsa, OK
Norton, Rebecca A. ... Moline, IL
Norton, Richard C. ... San Diego, CA
Norton, Richard D. ... Santa Monica, CA
Norton, Richard L. ... Cincinnati, OH
Norton, Richard P. ... San Francisco, CA
Norton, Richard Walsh ... Rutland, VT
Norton, Rick D. ... Hattiesburg, MS
Norton, Rita Faye ... Miami, FL
Norton, Robert C. ... Los Angeles, CA
Norton, Robert D. ... Evansville, IN
Norton, Robert E., II ... Livonia, MI
Norton, Robert E., Jr. ... Purchase, NY
Norton, Robert J. ... Punta Gorda, FL
Norton, Robert L. ... Miami, FL
Norton, Robert T. ... Boston, MA
Norton, Robert T. ... Westfield, NJ
Norton, Rodney K. ... Portland, OR
Norton, Ronald R. ... Conway, SC
Norton, Ronald R. ... Myrtle Beach, SC
Norton, Sally P. ... South Bend, IN
Norton, Sam D. ... Sarasota, FL
Norton, Sarah H. ... Beverly Hills, CA
Memphis, TN
Norton, Schwentker and Norton
Evansville, IN
Norton, Scott D. ... San Francisco, CA
Norton, Sharon Lynch ... Somerville, NJ
Norton and Smith ... Shelbyville, TN
Norton, Stanley R. ... Palo Alto, CA
Norton, Steven A. ... Jacksonville, FL
Norton & Sullivan ... Omaha, NE
Norton, Susan Potter ... Miami, FL
Norton, Suzanne Belot, Law Office of
Maumee, OH
Norton, Tait O. ... Jacksonville, FL
Norton, Teresa J. ... Santa Rosa, CA
Norton, Theo. M. ... Saratoga, CA
Norton, Thomas A. ... Detroit, MI
Norton, Thomas C. ... Aptos, CA
Norton, Thomas E., Jr. ... Birmingham, AL
Norton, Thomas F. ... Warren, OH
Norton, Thomas P. ... Evansville, IN
Norton, Thomas W., Jr. ... Pittsburgh, PA
Norton, Tiffaney A. ... Denver, CO
Norton, Timothy H. ... Portland, ME
Norton, Timothy O. ... Boston, MA
Norton, Todd A. ... Encino, CA
Norton, Tom, Jr. ... Bay Minette, AL
Gulf Shores, AL
Norton, Tom, Jr., P.C. ... Bay Minette, AL
Gulf Shores, AL
Norton, Vicki Gee ... La Jolla, CA
Norton, Warner D. ... New York, NY
Norton, Wasserman, Jones & Kelly
Salina, KS
Norton, W. B., Jr. ... Marion, SC
Norton & Weeks ... Bangor, ME
Norton, William A. ... West Palm Beach, FL
Norton, William B. ... Lowden, IA
Norton, William C. ... Marissa, IL
Sparta, IL
Norton, William F., Jr. ... Mineola, NY
Norton, William G.
House of Representatives,
Congressional Assistants, GV
Norton, William H. ... Osceola, NE
Norton, William J. ... Anderson, IN
Norton, William L., III ... Nashville, TN
Norton, William N. ... New Orleans, LA
Norton, William R. ... Cleveland, OH
Norton, William T. ... St. Paul, MN
Norton, Wm. Harrison ... Kansas City, MO
Norton-Larson, Mary J. ... Cambridge, MN
Norton-Moore, Ann Yukie ... Chula Vista, CA
Nortz, James A. ... Greenwich, CT
Norum, David P. ... Chicago, IL
Norum and Pearson, P.A. ... Wayzata, MN
Norum, Russell A. ... Wayzata, MN
Norval Bros. ... Seward, NE
Norval, Byron J. ... Seward, NE
Norval, J. Andy ... Austin, TX
Norvell & Associates, A Professional
Corporation ... Abilene, TX
Norvell, David L. ... Albuquerque, NM
Norvell, Edward P. ... Salisbury, NC
Norvell, Felicia A. ... Dallas, TX
Norvell, G. Todd, P.C. ... Portland, OR
Norvell, Joseph V. ... Chicago, IL
Norvell Law Firm, P.A. ... Albuquerque, NM
Norvell, Lipscomb, Jr. ... Beaumont, TX
Norvell, Louis C. ... Mobile, AL
Norvell, Mary K. ... San Diego, CA
Norvell, Michael C. ... Leesburg, FL
Norvell, Phillip E. ... Fayetteville, AR

Norvell, Ralph ... Columbia, SC
Norvell, Ray C., Sr. ... Decatur, GA
Norvell, Robert J. ... Boerne, TX
Norvell, Sam S. ... Dallas, TX
Norvell, William C., Jr. ... Houston, TX
Norvid, Walter ... Brooklyn, NY
Norviel, Vernon A. ... Santa Clara, CA
Norville, Craig H. ... Memphis, TN
Norville, Darcy M. ... Portland, OR
Norville, Forest M. ... Nashville, TN
Norville, Gerald J. ... Lake Oswego, OR
Norville, Oliver I. ... Portland, OR
Norville, Rod, Law Offices of, A Professional
Corporation ... Houston, TX
Norville, Rodney L. ... Houston, TX
Norwalk, L. Jeffrey ... New York, NY
Norwalk, Leslie V. ... Washington, DC
Norwell, Bruce H. ... Walpole, MA
Norwell, Gregory E. ... Chicago, IL
Norwich, Donald P. ... Minneapolis, MN
Norwich, William G. ... Cocoa Beach, FL
Norwick, Kenneth P. ... New York, NY
Norwick, Michael A. ... Roseland, NJ
Norwick, Robert J. ... Chagrin Falls, OH
Norwick & Schad ... New York, NY
Norwind, Edward L. ... Washington, DC
Bethesda, MD
Norwine, John C. ... Cincinnati, OH
Norwinski, Evelina J. ... Washington, DC
Norwitt, Glori J. ... Los Angeles, CA
Norwitz, Barry D. ... Deerfield Beach, FL
Norwitz, Jennifer S. ... Baltimore, MD
Norwitz, Trevor S. ... New York, NY
Norwood, Abraham R. ... Sarasota, FL
Norwood, Anthony W.
Department of Justice, Civil Division, GV
Norwood, Barry W. ... Richmond, VA
Norwood, C. Willard ... Mechanicsville, VA
Norwood, Colvin G., Jr., (P.C.)
New Orleans, LA
Norwood, Cynthia H. ... Richmond, VA
Norwood, Dan M. ... Memphis, TN
Norwood, David J. ... Dearborn, MI
Norwood, Deborah ... Midland, TX
Norwood, Deborah ... Olympia, WA
Norwood, Dorothy F. ... Montgomery, AL
Norwood, Doug ... Rogers, AR
Norwood, Edgar R. ... Liberty, TX
Norwood, Edward Andrew ... Nashville, TN
Norwood, Edward C. ... Houston, TX
Norwood, Felicia F. ... Blue Bell, PA
Norwood, Gary W. ... Midland, TX
Norwood, Jack G. ... Tyler, TX
Norwood, James E. ... West Monroe, LA
Norwood, Jeffrey S. ... Chattanooga, TN
Norwood, Jerry W. ... Bolivar, TN
Norwood, John A. ... Sacramento, CA
Norwood, John M. ... Fayetteville, AR
Norwood, John W., III ... Greenville, SC
Norwood, Kevin D. ... Nashville, TN
Norwood, Kimberly Jade ... St. Louis, MO
Norwood Law Firm, The ... Liberty, TX
Norwood, Leslie M. ... New York, NY
Norwood, Linda Bradley ... West Monroe, LA
Norwood, Linda H. ... San Diego, CA
Norwood, Linda Jo ... Atlanta, GA
Norwood, Mary Elizabeth ... Dallas, TX
Norwood, Matthew E. ... Denver, CO
Norwood, Naomi ... Santa Monica, CA
Norwood & Norwood, P.C. ... Midland, TX
Norwood, Paige C. ... Atlanta, GA
Norwood, Phillip L. ... Jackson, MS
Norwood, R. Bredt ... Irving, TX
Norwood, Ron O. ... Liberty, TX
Norwood, Ronald A. ... St. Louis, MO
Norwood, Ronald L. ... Huntsville, AL
Norwood, Timothy D. ... Portland, OR
Norwood, Wade E. ... Los Angeles, CA
Norwood, Walter V. ... Las Vegas, NV
Norwood, William U., III ... Atlanta, GA
Norwood, William Usher, III ... Atlanta, GA
Norwood, Wilson & Atchley ... Memphis, TN
Norwood-Lynch, Marcy B. ... Orlando, FL
Norych, Mark D. ... Coral Springs, FL
Norych and Tallis ... Coral Springs, FL
Brooklyn, NY
Nosal, Chester W. ... Washington, DC
Nosan, Bernard J. ... Cleveland, OH
Nosan & Jakubaitis ... Cleveland, OH
Nosan, Terry J. ... West Bloomfield, MI
Nosanchuk, Mathew S.
Department of Justice,
Office of Policy Development, GV
Nosce, Vidor A. ... New York, NY
Noschese, Gregory C. ... Dallas, TX
Nose, Kevin R. ... Columbus, OH
Nosef, Joe D., III ... Jackson, MS
Nosek, Anthony M. ... Buffalo, NY
Nosek, Francis J., (P.C.) ... Anchorage, AK
Nosek Law Group, LLC ... Anchorage, AK
Nosek, Peter C. ... Anchorage, AK
Nosek, Robert D. ... New York, NY
Nosek, Ronald R. ... Lombard, IL
Nosek, Steven B., (P.A.) ... Minneapolis, MN
Nosek, William G. ... Chicago, IL
Nosel, Mary Ellen M. ... Temecula, CA
Nosenchuck, Sharon Lynn ... Buffalo, NY
Noser, Richard C. ... Elkhart, IN
Noser, Stephen F. ... Houston, TX
Nosewicz, Thomas M. ... New Orleans, LA
Nosich, James J. ... Miami, FL
Noskin, Scott H. ... Encino, CA
Nosky, Richard E., Jr. ... Salinas, CA
Nosler, Michael D. ... Denver, CO
Nosonowitz, Stevan A. ... Poughkeepsie, NY
Nosowitz, Harvey ... Boston, MA
Nosowsky, Rachel ... Blue Bell, PA
Noss, David L. ... Tulsa, OK

Nossaman, Guthner, Knox & Elliott, LLP
Irvine, CA
Los Angeles, CA
Sacramento, CA
San Francisco, CA
Washington, DC
Nossel, Deon J. ... New York, NY
Nossen, Jeffrey F. ... Walnut Creek, CA
Nossiff, Alexander G. ... Salisbury, MA
Nossiff & Giampa, P.C. ... Salisbury, MA
Nossiff, John G., Jr. ... Boston, MA
Nossokoff, Ivan N. ... Charleston, SC
Nossokoff, Ivan N., LLC ... Charleston, SC
Nostdahl, James E. ... Minot, ND
Nostrame, Catherine A. ... Silver Spring, MD
Nostrame, Frank J. ... Jersey City, NJ
Nostramo, Philip T. ... Albany, NY
Nostramo, Robert F. ... New York, NY
Nostrand, G. Lott ... Tenafly, NJ
Nostrand, George W. ... Bellows Falls, VT
Nostrand, Ltd. ... San Diego, CA
Nostrand, Robert M. ... San Diego, CA
Nostro, Louis ... Miami, FL
Nota, Kenneth J. ... West Warwick, RI
Notar, Barbara A. ... Leesburg, VA
Notar, Susan A. ...
Department Of Health And Human Services,
GV
Notarbartolo, Jeffrey R. ... Brooklyn, NY
Notareus, Bruce M. ... Sacramento, CA
Notargiacomo, Edward ... Boston, MA
Notargiacomo, Moira
Federal Energy Regulatory Commission,
Office of Electric Power Regulation, GV
Notari, John C. ... Orlando, FL
Notarianni, Aldo G. ... Denver, CO
Notarianni, Gregory J. ... Denver, CO
Notarianni, Joseph J. ... Scranton, PA
Notarianni, Joseph J., Jr. ... Camp Hill, PA
Notarianni & Notarianni ... Denver, CO
Notarianni & Sernak ... Scranton, PA
Notarius, Joyce M. ... Washington, DC
Notarius, Milton ... New York, NY
Notarius, Susan J. ... Chicago, IL
Notaro, Angelo ... New York, NY
Orangeburg, NY
Notaro, Felicia G., Law Offices of
New York, NY
Notaro, Frank J. ... Buffalo, NY
Notaro, Karen Anne ... Riverwoods, IL
Notaro, Leslie ... Chicago, IL
Notaro, Mary G. ... New York, NY
Notaro & Michalos P.C. ... New York, NY
Orangeburg, NY
Notaro, Paul ... West Seneca, NY
Noteboom, Charles M. ... Hurst, TX
Noteboom and Gray ... Fort Worth, TX
Hurst, TX
Noteboom, James D. ... Bend, OR
Noteboom, Lowell J. ... Minneapolis, MN
Noteboom, Philip L. ... Wausau, WI
Noteboom, Todd A. ... Minneapolis, MN
Noterman, Peter A. ... Takoma Park, MD
Notestine, Jack R. ... Fort Wayne, IN
Notestine, Kerry E ... Houston, TX
Notestine, Robert John, III ... Nashville, TN
Notestine, W. E. ... Dallas, TX
Noteware, David F. ... Washington, DC
Noteware, David R. ... Houston, TX
Noteware, Ellen T. ... Philadelphia, PA
Noth, James G. ... Davenport, IA
Noth, William J. ... Des Moines, IA
Nothern, R. Austin ... Topeka, KS
Nothern, W. Thomas ... Sherman Oaks, CA
Nothnagle, Matthew J. ... Goshen, NY
Nothstein, Robert H. ... Stroudsburg, PA
Nothum, Lisa Ann ... Chicago, IL
Notias, Nicholas K. ... Brooklyn, NY
Notice, Melissa A. ... Fort Lauderdale, FL
Notigan, Robert, Jr. ... Washington, DC
Notine, Brett M. ... Rochester, NY
Notinger, Alan S. ... Dallas, TX
Notinger, Deborah A. ... Nashua, NH
Notinger, Ramona Stephens
Department of Justice, Tax Division, GV
Notinger, Steven M. ... Nashua, NH
Notini, Albert A. ... Billerica, MA
Notini, Jessica M. ... Orinda, CA
Notis, James S. ... New York, NY
Notis, Mitchell J. ... Boston, MA
Notis-McConarty, Edward ... Boston, MA
Notkin, Corrinne L. ... Burbank, CA
Notkin, Deborah J. ... New York, NY
Notkin, Nathan T. ... Chicago, IL
Notley, Nancy Luise ... Ann Arbor, MI
Noto, Aldo ... Washington, DC
Noto, Anne Doris ... Washington, DC
Noto, Anthony C. ... Rochester, NY
Noto, Dino G. ... Great Neck, NY
Noto, Gregory J. ... Chalmette, LA
Noto, Gwendolyn Field ... Stamford, CT
Noto, Ingolf ... Portland, OR
Noto, Janis M. ... Old Brookville, NY
Noto, Joseph C. ... Waldwick, NJ
Noto, Joseph M. ... Neenah, WI
Noto, Louis C. ... Rochester, NY
Noto, Margaret Hill ... Portland, OR
Noto, Mario T. ... Washington, DC
Noto, Michael A. ... West Palm Beach, FL
Noto, Michael A. ... Old Bridge, NJ
Noto & Oswald, P.C. ... Washington, DC
Noto, Paul J. ... Mamaroneck, NY
Noto, Robert A. ... East Lansing, MI
Noto, Thomas A. ... Fairfax, VA
Noto, Thomas J. ... Washington, DC
Notopoulos, Alexander A., Jr. ... Boston, MA
Notopoulos, Anastasios V. ... Miami, FL
Notopoulos, Philip J. ... Boston, MA

Notre, Kevin ... Los Angeles, CA
Notrica, Lewis E. ... Encino, CA
Nott, Lori B. Anker ... New York, NY
Nott, Michael G. ... Los Angeles, CA
Nott, Ross R. ... Sacramento, CA
Nott, Sheri E. ... Miami, FL
Nott, Suzanne D. ... Rochester, NY
Nottage, Rosaire M. ... Chicago, IL
Nottage and Ward ... Chicago, IL
Notte, Craig M. ... New York, NY
Notte, Gregg S. ... Atlanta, GA
Notte, John A., III ... Greenville, RI
Nottebaum, Walter E. ... Miami, FL
Nottebohm, Barbara H. ... New York, NY
Nottenburg, Carol ... Seattle, WA
Notti, John C. ... Glendale, CA
Nottie, Joseph T., III ... Cranston, RI
Nottingham, Catherine Casey
Department of Commerce, Office of the General Counsel, GV
Nottingham, Edward W. ... Denver, CO
Nottingham, Engel, Gordon & Kerr, LLP
Syracuse, NY
Nottingham, J. S. ... Chicago, IL
Nottingham, Prescott L. ... Atlanta, GA
Nottingham, Robin E. ... Lansing, MI
Nottingham, Wm. P. ... Indianapolis, IN
Nottoli, Eileen M. ... San Francisco, CA
Nottoli, Lynne ... Los Angeles, CA
Nottolini, Gene L. ... Geneva, IL
Nottonson, Ira N. ... Boulder, CO
Notturno and Karamanos ... Lancaster, PA
Notturno, Kenneth C. ... Lancaster, PA
Notvik, Donald E. ... St. Paul, MN
Notz, Edward U. ... Chicago, IL
Notz, Edward U., P.C., Law Offices of
Chicago, IL
Notz, John K., Jr. ... Chicago, IL
Notzen, Randall A. ... Pittsburgh, PA
Notzon, Denise A. ... Palo Alto, CA
Notzon, Marc A. ... San Antonio, TX
Notzon, Marcel C., II ... Laredo, TX
Notzon, Marcel C., III ... Laredo, TX
San Antonio, TX
Notzon, Monica Z. ... Laredo, TX
Notzon, Vincent A. ... San Antonio, TX
Noucas, James G., Jr. ... Portsmouth, NH
Noucas & Keenan, P.A. ... Portsmouth, NH
Noud, John L. ... Mason, MI
Noud & Noud ... Mason, MI
Noud, William H., Jr. ... Mason, MI
Noufer & Brown ... Wailuku, HI
Noufer, Steve ... Wailuku, HI
Nougué-Sans, Marguerite ... New York, NY
Nouhan, J. Jeffrey ... Chicago, IL
Nouhan, Joseph E. ... Paterson, NJ
Noulles, Richard B. ... Tulsa, OK
Noumair, George J. ... New York, NY
Noumair, George J., P.C. ... New York, NY
Nour, Firouzeh ... Dallas, TX
Nour, Ronald A. ... Ormond Beach, FL
Nourafchan, Poopak ... Los Angeles, CA
Nourani, Leila ... Los Angeles, CA
Nourani, Marc D. ... San Antonio, TX
Nouri, Lisa G. ... Kansas City, MO
Nourian, Morrie Pour ... Dallas, TX
Nourian, Robert B. ... Bryn Mawr, PA
Nourizadeh, Karen ... New York, NY
Nourmand, H. Joseph ... Los Angeles, CA
Nourse, Anthony H. ... Chantilly, VA
Nourse & Bowles, LLP ... Millburn, NJ
New York, NY
Nourse, David A. ... New York, NY
Nourse, Hazel W. ... Mount Kisco, NY
Nourse, Jodi L. ... Manchester, NH
Nourse, Philip G. ... Fort Pierce, FL
Nourse, Stephen L. ... Seattle, WA
Nourse, Steven T. ... Columbus, OH
Nouskajian, John, Jr.
South Pasadena, CA
Nouskajian, John, Jr., Prof. Corp. Law Office of ... Los Angeles, CA
South Pasadena, CA
Nouskajian, Norman ... San Diego, CA
Nouss, James L. ... St. Louis, MO
Nouss, James L., Jr. ... St. Louis, MO
Nova, Janet Lapidus ... New York, NY
Nova, Peter J. ... Sonoma, CA
Nova, Peter J., Law Offices of ... Sonoma, CA
Novacek, Stephen V. ... Reno, NV
Novacheck, Ann ... Minneapolis, MN
Novack, Barry ... Beverly Hills, CA
Novack, Barry ... Los Angeles, CA
Novack Burnbaum & Crystal, P.C.
New York, NY
Novack, Catherine G. ... Tampa, FL
Novack, Charles D. ... Oakland, CA
Novack, David ... Cherry Hill, NJ
Novack, David J. ... Short Hills, NJ
Novack, Debra Falduto ... Wheaton, IL
Novack, Edith M. ... Montclair, NJ
Novack, Edward J. ... Everett, WA
Novack, Gerald A. ... New York, NY
Novack, Janet L. ... Providence, RI
Novack, Jeffrey N. ... Cardiff-By-The-Sea, CA
Novack, John R. ... Bloomington, IL
Novack, Kenneth J. ... Boston, MA
Novack, Laura A. ... Washington, DC
Novack, Lawrence W. ... San Bernardino, CA
Novack, Lewis G. ... Cambridge, MA
Novack and Macey ... Chicago, IL
Novack, Martin ... New York, NY
Novack, Michael J. ... Albany, NY
Novack, Michael R. ... Fairfield, CT
Novack, Nancy A. ... Columbus, OH
Novack, Paul D. ... Miami, FL
Novack, Paul D., P.A. ... Miami, FL
Novack, Paul J. ... Chicago, IL

Novack, Robert ... Short Hills, NJ
Novack, Roslynne ... Trenton, NJ
Novack, Sheri M. ... Menlo Park, CA
Novack, Stephen ... Chicago, IL
Novack, Thomas J. ... Columbus, OH
Novajosky, Christina T. ... Scranton, PA
Novak, Alan Paul ... Coatesville, PA
Novak, Alan Paul ... Philadelphia, PA
West Chester, PA
Novak, Alan Paul ... West Chester, PA
Novak, Alan R. ... Washington, DC
Novak, Alessandra R. ... Elmsford, NY
Novak, Andrew ... Chicago, IL
Novak, Andrew G., II ... New Orleans, LA
Novak, Anthony E. ... Urbana, IL
Novak, Anthony S. ... Wethersfield, CT
Novak, Barbara ... Eugene, OR
Novak, Ben ... Bellefonte, PA
Novak, Carla T. ... Des Plaines, IL
Novak, Christina L. ... Washington, DC
Novak, Christopher C. ... New York, NY
Novak, Daniel F. ... Buffalo, NY
Novak, David
National Labor Relations Board, Office of Board Members, GV
Novak, David J. ... Johnstown, PA
Novak, David M. ... Chicago, IL
Novak, Douglas Lloyd ... Columbia, SC
Novak, Edward F. ... Phoenix, AZ
Novak, Edwin A. ... New York, NY
Novak, Ellen Avery ... Kenmore, NY
Novak, Eva M. ... Department of the Army, U.S. Army Court of Criminal Appeals, GV
Novak, Francis J., Jr. ... Buffalo, NY
Novak, Frank A., III ... Rochester, NY
Novak, G. Alexander ... Woodmere, NY
Novak, George D., II ... Washington, DC
Novak, George J. ... Rochester, NY
Novak, Gregory M. ... Lima, OH
Novak, Gregory P. ... Phoenix, AZ
Novak, Gregory V. ... San Antonio, TX
Novak, Harold Z. ... Lincolnwood, IL
Novak, Ira S. ... Somerville, NJ
Novak, James M. ... Pittsburgh, PA
Novak, Jane Cotton ... New York, NY
Novak, Jeffrey L. ... McLean, VA
Novak, Jennifer F. ... Los Angeles, CA
Novak, Jennifer L. ... Nashville, TN
Novak, Jerald ... Long Grove, IL
Novak, Jeremy E. ... New York, NY
Novak, Joanne M. ... Canton, NY
Novak, Joel A. ... Department of the Army, U.S. Army Court of Criminal Appeals, GV
Novak, Joel D. ... Des Moines, IA
Novak, John ... Houston, TX
Novak, John J. ... Lakewood, NJ
Novak, John J., Jr. ... Southport, CT
Novak, John M. ... Grand Rapids, MI
Novak, John P. ... Sag Harbor, NY
Novak, Joseph ... Salt Lake City, UT
Novak, Joseph S. ... Clinton, NJ
Novak & Juhase ... New York, NY
Novak, Karen A. ... Toledo, OH
Novak, Karen J. ... Strongsville, OH
Novak, Karen T. ... Redondo Beach, CA
Novak, Karl E. ... Charleston, SC
Novak, Lawrence John ... Lancaster, OH
Novak, Lawrence P. ... Brockton, MA
Novak, Lawrence P., P.C., Law Office of
Brockton, MA
Novak, Lawrence S. ... Uniondale, NY
Novak, Lee M. ... Kingman, AZ
Novak, Leslie H. ... Minneapolis, MN
Novak, Linda ... New York, NY
Novak, Louis C. ... Rancho Cucamonga, CA
Novak, Margo H. ... Rochester, NY
Novak, Mark ... Chicago, IL
Novak, Mark S. ... Encino, CA
Novak, Mary J. ... Santa Clara, CA
Novak, Matthew G. ... Cedar Rapids, IA
Novak, Michael Alan ... Detroit, MI
Novak, Michael E. ... St. Cloud, MN
Novak, Michael G. ... Baltimore, MD
Novak, Michael T. ... Washington, DC
Glenwood, IL
Novak, Michael T. ... Chicago, IL
Novak, Nathan E. ... Eau Claire, WI
Novak, Neal R. ... Chicago, IL
Novak & Novak ... Rochester, NY
Novak, Patrick E. ... Miami, FL
Novak, Paul F. ... Lansing, MI
Novak, Paul J. ... Lynbrook, NY
Novak, Paul M. ... Worcester, MA
Novak, Paul Stanley ... Baltimore, MD
Novak, Peter J. ... Phoenix, AZ
Novak, Ralph Martin, Jr. ... Austin, TX
Novak, Raymond A. ... Pittsburgh, PA
Novak, Rebecca A. ... New York, NY
Novak, Richard A. ... Omaha, NE
Novak, Richard A., Jr. ... Troy, MI
Novak, Richard E. ... West New York, NJ
Novak, Richard G. ... Los Angeles, CA
Novak, Richard J. ... Westport, CT
Novak, Richard S. ... Boston, MA
Novak, Rita M. ... Chicago, IL
Novak, Robert A. ... New York, NY
Novak, Robert J. ... Phoenix, AZ
Novak, Robert S. ... Pelham, NY
Novak, Scott J. ... Cleveland, OH
Novak, Scott L. ... Washington, DC
Novak, Sean M. ... Los Angeles, CA
Novak, Shirley ... Pittsburgh, PA
Novak, Stover & Furst ... Bellefonte, PA
Novak, Suzanne A. ... Daytona Beach, FL
Novak, Tabor R., Jr. ... Montgomery, AL
Novak, Theodore J., (P.C.) ... Chicago, IL
Novak, Thomas J. ... Phoenix, AZ
Novak, Thomas J., P.C. ... Phoenix, AZ

Novak, Thomas P. ... Philadelphia, PA
Novak, Thomas S. ... Newark, NJ
Novak, Thomas W. ... Pittsburgh, PA
Novak, Walter F. ... Dade City, FL
Novak, William J. ... Cleveland, OH
Novak-Krajewski, Alexa ... Tacoma, WA
Novakoski, Leo V. ... Santa Clara, CA
Novakov, Daniel P. ... Dallas, TX
Novakov Davidson & Flynn ... Dallas, TX
Novakov Davis, A Professional Corporation
Dallas, TX
Novakovic, Michael B. ... Philadelphia, PA
Novakowski, Janet M. ... Buffalo, NY
Noval, William F. ... Rochester, NY
Novander, Kenneth L. ... Chicago, IL
Novara, Gary W. ... Southfield, MI
Novara, James M. ... Mount Clemens, MI
Novara, Michael J. ... Pittsburgh, PA
Novara, Tesija, Michela & Priehs, P.C.
Southfield, MI
Novasitis, Anthony W., Jr. ... Philadelphia, PA
Novasky, Robert W. ... Tacoma, WA
Novatney, John F., Jr. ... Cleveland, OH
Novatney, Steven J. ... Chicago, IL
Novatt, Janine Rickman ... Scottsdale, AZ
Novatt, Jeff M. ... Naples, FL
Novatt, Maria S. ... Santa Barbara, CA
Novatt, Susan Westeen ... Oxnard, CA
Nove, Michael J. ... Milwaukie, OR
Noveck, Beth Simone ... New York, NY
Noveck, Daniel ... Birmingham, MI
Noveck, Harold ... Bingham Farms, MI
Noveck, Morton ... Bingham Farms, MI
Novela, Daniel ... Los Angeles, CA
Novell and Associates ... Claremont, CA
Los Angeles, CA
Pomona, CA
Riverside, CA
San Bernardino, CA
Ventura, CA
Novell, Jennifer A. ... Claremont, CA
Novell, Raymond A. ... Claremont, CA
Novell, Therese M. ... Detroit, MI
Novelle, Robert A. ... Chicago, IL
Novelli, Catherine A.
Executive Office Of The President, Office of the U.S. Trade Representative, GV
Novelli, Geoffrey M. ... Chicago, IL
Novelli, Harvie & Huzinec, P.C.
Houston, TX
Novelli, Susan R. ... Boulder, CO
Novello, Arthur S. ... Haddonfield, NJ
Philadelphia, PA
Novello, Christopher ... Boston, MA
Novello, David P. ... Washington, DC
Novello, John A. ... Media, PA
Novello, Leonard P. ... Newark, NJ
Novello, William J. ... Chicago, IL
November, Bernard L. ... Santa Ana, CA
November, Celine Y. ... Hackensack, NJ
November, Ellen J. ... New York, NY
November, Peter C. ... Atlanta, GA
November, Raymond R. ... Cleveland, OH
Novenstern, Kenneth J. ... Mount Kisco, NY
Novetsky, Terry D. ... New York, NY
Novey, Carol Victoria ... Staten Island, NY
Novey, Jerome M. ... Tallahassee, FL
Novey, Mendelson & Adamson
Panama City, FL
Tallahassee, FL
Novey, Michael S. ... Treasury Department, Internal Revenue Service, GV
Novey, Steven B. ... Emporia, VA
Novian, Farhad ... Los Angeles, CA
Novic, Lisa S. ... San Francisco, CA
Novich, Lee J. ... San Francisco, CA
Novick, Alan J. ... Bloomington, IL
Novick, Alan S. ... Naples, FL
New Bedford, MA
Novick, Alphonsus C. ... Santa Ana, CA
Novick, Amy R. ... Washington, DC
Novick, Andrea T. ... New York, NY
Novick, Andrew C. ... New Bedford, MA
Novick, Andrew Dean ... Millburn, NJ
Novick, Beth E. ... Princeton, NJ
Novick, David S. ... Sarasota, FL
Novick, Donald ... Huntington, NY
Novick, Edelstein, Lubell, Reisman, Wasserman and Leventhal, P.C. ... Yonkers, NY
Novick, Harold L. ... Washington, DC
Novick, Howard ... Boston, MA
Novick, Irving ... New Orleans, LA
Novick, Irving ... Bronx, NY
Novick, Jeffrey M. ... Garden City, NY
Novick, Jerold J. ... King Of Prussia, PA
Novick, Judith L. ... Stoughton, MA
Novick, Julie A. ... East Amherst, NY
Novick, Keith V. ... Dallas, TX
Novick Law Office ... Marion, IL
Novick, Lawrence G. ... New Rochelle, NY
Novick, Leonard ... Lowell, MA
Novick, Marsha E. ... Princeton, NJ
Novick, Michael T. ... Bridgeton, NJ
Novick, Michelle G. ... Chicago, IL
Novick, Mindy ... New York, NY
Novick, Mitchell P. ... Montclair, NJ
Novick, Robert M. ... New York, NY
Novick, Robert T.
Executive Office Of The President, Office of the U.S. Trade Representative, GV
Novick, Sheldon M. ... South Strafford, VT
Novick, Steven A. ... Tulsa, OK
Novick, Stuart J. ... Boston, MA
Novick, Sylvan R. ... New York, NY
Novick, Ted A. ... New York, NY
Novick, Ted Alan ... White Plains, NY
Novick, Walter E. ... La Jolla, CA
Novick, William J. ... Marion, IL

Novick, William P. ... Marion, IL
Novicki, Gertrude M. ... Miami, FL
Novicoff, Amy S. ... Los Angeles, CA
Novicoff, Benj. ... Lincoln, NE
Novicoff, Michael L. ... Beverly Hills, CA
Noviello, Matthew A. ... Sebring, FL
Noviello, Nicholas, Jr. ... Sebring, FL
Noviello & Noviello, P.C. ... Sebring, FL
Novik, Jos. ... Cincinnati, OH
Novikoff, Allen ... Brooklyn, NY
Novikoff, Harold S. ... New York, NY
Novikoff, Kenneth A. ... Uniondale, NY
Novikoff, Neil ... New York, NY
Novilla, Michael F. ... St. Petersburg, FL
Novin, Ferena ... Los Angeles, CA
Novins, Alan S. ... Washington, DC
Novins, Beth ... Toms River, NJ
Novins, Jeffrey A. ... Boston, MA
Novins, Michael S. ... New York, NY
Novins, Robert F. ... Toms River, NJ
Novins, Susan Donaldson ... Boston, MA
Novins, York & Pentony, A Professional Corporation ... Toms River, NJ
Novinsky, Norman ... Brockton, MA
Novinson, Carol B. ... Princeton, NJ
Novinson, Steven L. ... Detroit, MI
Novion, Laurie A. ... Kansas City, MO
Novis, James H. ... Detroit, MI
Novit, Herbert L. ... Hilton Head Island, SC
Novit, Kent E., (Ltd.) ... Chicago, IL
Novit, Nancy Ann ... Chicago, IL
Novit, Nancy Petrick ... Chicago, IL
Novit, Scarminach & Williams, P.A.
Beaufort, SC
Bluffton, SC
Hilton Head Island, SC
Novit, Sidney ... Chicago, IL
Novitch, Richard L. ... Marlborough, MA
Novitke, Robert E. ... Roseville, MI
Novitke, Robert E., P.C. ... Roseville, MI
Novitski, David E. ... Los Angeles, CA
Novitsky, David C. ... Philadelphia, PA
Novitt, Donald S. ... Kew Gardens, NY
Novitzke, Don Paul ... Amery, WI
Novitzke, Gust & Sempf ... Amery, WI
Novo, Guy P. ... Hartsdale, NY
Novo, Jesus, III ... Miami, FL
Novo, Maria Cristina ... Coral Gables, FL
Novo, Michael A. ... Miami, FL
Novoa, Ana M. ... San Antonio, TX
Novobilski, Jerome R. ... Clay, WV
Novodor, Alan G. ... Los Angeles, CA
Novogrod, John C. ... New York, NY
Novogroski, Arthur ... Providence, RI
Novogroski, Herbert A. ... Framingham, MA
Novok, Danl. A. ... Palm Beach, FL
Novom, Barri Lyn ... Los Angeles, CA
Novorr, Karen ... Tustin, CA
Novosad, Steven N. ... Chicago, IL
Novosad, Susan L. ... Chicago, IL
Novosat-Gradert, Lisa Marie ... Akron, OH
Novosedlik, Stephen J. ... Sewaren, NJ
Novosel, Brian S. ... Pittsburgh, PA
Novosel, Joseph Robert ... Marysville, MI
Novosel, Linda M. ... Blackwood, NJ
Novoseletsky, Ellen ... Miami, FL
Novoselsky, Benj. E. ... Chicago, IL
Novoselsky, David A. ... Chicago, IL
Novoselsky, David A., & Associates
Chicago, IL
Novoselsky, Henry N. ... Chicago, IL
Novotnak, Lynn M. ... Milwaukee, WI
Novotne, Alfred H. ... Department of the Army, Office of the Judge Advocate General, GV
Novotney, George C. ... Cleveland, OH
Novotney, Ralph J., Jr. ... West Hills, CA
Novotny, Arthur J. ... Forest Hill, MD
Novotny, David J. ... Chicago, IL
Novotny, Edmund J., Jr. ... Atlanta, GA
Novotny, Elizabeth F. ... South Burlington, VT
Novotny, F. Douglas ... Albany, NY
Novotny, F. Douglas, Law Offices of
Albany, NY
Novotny, Janae H. ... Palo Alto, CA
Novotny, Linda Coyle ... Buffalo, NY
Novotny, Lois M. ... Boston, MA
Novotny, Mark E. ... Omaha, NE
Novotny, Michael J. ... Oklahoma City, OK
Novotny, Michael J. ... Martinsburg, WV
Novotny, Norman E. ... Hartford, CT
Novotny, Patricia S. ... Seattle, WA
Novotny, Ronald W., (P.C.)
Los Angeles, CA
Novotny, Susan M. ... Pensacola, FL
Novotny, Thomas F. ... Oak Lawn, IL
Novotny, William ... Phoenix, AZ
Novotny-Price, Lisa ... Dallas, TX
Novy, Eugene ... Atlanta, GA
Novy, Fredric G. ... Chicago, IL
Novy, J. Scott ... Longview, TX
Novy, Michael D. ... Chicago, IL
Novy, Michael Ted ... Chicago, IL
Novy, Ralph M. ... Milwaukee, WI
Novy, Robert C. ... Lakehurst, NJ
Toms River, NJ
Novy, Steven B. ... Chicago, IL
Waukegan, IL
Nowachek, Anthony G. ... Mineola, NY
Nowachek, Deborah L. ... Goldsboro, NC
Nowachek, Deborah L., P.A.
Goldsboro, NC
Nowack, Andrew P. ... New York, NY
Nowack, George E., Jr. ... Atlanta, GA
Nowack, Robert W. ... Eugene, OR
Nowacki, Erik A. ... Irvine, CA
Nowacki, James N. ... Chicago, IL
Nowacki, Theodore J. ... Indianapolis, IN
Nowaczewski, Jeanne L. ... Chicago, IL

Null, Michael G. ... Spicewood, TX
Null, Miriam P. ... Jamaica, NY
Null, Richard D. ... Mayfield, KY
Null, Robert D. ... South Bend, IN
Null, Thomas & Samson, Law Offices of Mayfield, KY
Null, W. Gregory ... Atlanta, GA
Null, William C. ... Morris, IL
Null, William S. ... White Plains, NY
Nulle, Douglas E. Rancho Santa Margarita, CA
Nulman, James L. ... Fort Myers, FL
Nulman, Kalman I. ... New York, NY
Nulman, Mark A. ... Elmwood Park, NJ
Nulman, Michael B. ... Woonsocket, RI
Nulsen, William J. ... New Haven, CT
Nulton, Edmund W. ... Naples, FL
Nulton, Kevin L. ... Boston, MA
Providence, RI
Nulton, William C. ... Kansas City, MO
Nulty, Frank J. ... Wilton, CT
Nulty, John P., Jr. ... Jersey City, NJ
Nulty, Neil J. ... White River Junction, VT
Numbers, Audrey ... Boise, ID
Numbers, Charles H. ... Larkspur, CA
Nummi, Richard M. ... Tampa, FL
Numrich, Robert P. ... Leawood, KS
Kansas City, MO
Numrych, David C. ... Washington, DC
Nunalee, Mark I. ... Burgaw, NC
Hampstead, NC
Nunalee, Mary Margaret McEachern Wilmington, NC
Nunalee & Nunalee, L.L.P. Wilmington, NC
Nunalee, Thomas Hervey, IV Wilmington, NC
Nunan, Gerald A. ... Red Bank, NJ
Nunan, Nancy E. ... Washington, DC
Nunan, Terence S. ... Los Angeles, CA
Nunberg, Noah ... New York, NY
Nunberg, Rebecca Citron ... Uniondale, NY
Nunemaker, James P., Jr. Garden City, NY
Nunery, David A. ... Campbellsville, KY
Lexington, KY
Nunery, David A., P.S.C. Campbellsville, KY
Nunes, Gary H. ... McLean, VA
Nunes, Geoffrey ... Cambridge, MA
Nunes, Jeffrey W. ... Phoenix, AZ
Nunes, Jose M. ... Chicago, IL
Nunes, Louis S., III ... New Orleans, LA
Nunes, Manuel ... Santa Ana, CA
Nunes, Margaret M. ... Winchester, MA
Nunes, Melbourne ... New York, NY
Nunes, Michael A. (IBA) ... Houston, TX
Nunes, Morris A. ... Falls Church, VA
Nunes, Morris A., P.C. ... Falls Church, VA
Nunes, Paul V. ... Rochester, NY
Nunes, Peter F. ... Tampa, FL
Nunes, Rachel K. ... Santa Rosa, CA
Nunes, Rebecca ... Escondido, CA
Nunes, Richard A. ... Taunton, MA
Nunes, Robert F., Jr. ... Los Angeles, CA
Nuneviller, Christopher ... Lancaster, PA
Nunez, Adam G. ... Sulphur, LA
Nunez, Alexander G. ... Annapolis, MD
Nunez, Charles J. ... New Orleans, LA
Nunez, Dolores ... Dearborn, MI
Nunez, Felipe M. ... Atlanta, GA
Nunez, Gustalo ... Lorain, OH
Nuñez, Irene G. ... Los Angeles, CA
Nunez, Jose L. ... Miami, FL
Nuñez, Joseph L. ... Minneapolis, MN
Nuñez, Kelly Barcia ... Tampa, FL
Nuñez, Leticia ... El Paso, TX
Nunez, Linda S. ... Tustin, CA
Nuñez, Manuel, Law Offices of San Juan, PR
Nuñez, Maria D. ... Victoria, TX
Nuñez, Maria E. ... San Diego, CA
Nuñez, Mary Chris ... Miami, FL
Nuñez, Michael J. ... Los Angeles, CA
Nunez & Nunez ... New Orleans, LA
Nuñez, Paulino A., Jr. ... Miami, FL
Nunez, Ramon E. ... Miami, FL
Nunez, Randy S. ... Chalmette, LA
Nuñez, Ricardo J. ... Miami, FL
Nuñez, Richard J. W., L.L.P.C. Brownsville, TX
Nuñez, Richard J. W. ... Brownsville, TX
Nuñez, Rodolfo ... Tallahassee, FL
Nunez, Russell J., Jr. ... New Orleans, LA
Nunez, Sandra J. ... Teaneck, NJ
New York, NY
Nuñez, Vivian ... San Juan, PR
Nunez, Wilo B. ... Huntington Park, CA
Nunez-Arco, Victor R. ... San Juan, PR
Nunez-Hoyo, Esteban J. ... San Juan, PR
Nuñez-Salgado, Luis A. ... San Juan, PR
Nunez-Vivas, Carlos A. ... Miami, FL
Nungesser & Hill ... Meredith, NH
Nungesser, Kendall E. ... San Gabriel, CA
Nungesser, Nancy A. ... New Orleans, LA
Nungesser, William L., Jr. ... Meredith, NH
Nungester, William L. ... Twin Falls, ID
Nunheimer, David C. ... Boston, MA
Nunis, Robert P. ... Austin, TX
Nunley, A. M., III ... Midland, TX
Nunley, C. Patrick ... Waco, TX
Nunley, Caroline B. ... Charlottesville, VA
Nunley, D. Alan ... Sterling, VA
Nunley, Daniel Clarence ... Tulsa, OK
Nunley, E. Scott ... West Palm Beach, FL
Nunley, J. Ken ... Hondo, TX
Nunley & Jolley, L.L.P. ... Hondo, TX
Nunley, Lonnie D., III ... Richmond, VA
Nunley, Marvin P. ... Owensboro, KY
Nunley, P.A.L. ... Richmond, VA
Nunley, Pamela L. ... San Jose, CA
Nunley, Patricia Hart ... Waco, TX
Nunley, Richard L. ... Charlottesville, VA
Nunley, Spencer J. ... Pittsburgh, PA
Nunley, Troy L. ... Sacramento, CA
Nunley, Walter D., Jr. ... Medford, OR
Nunley-Farris, Sheila ... Henderson, KY
Nunlist, Cathryn C. ... Hanover, NH
Norwich, VT
Nunmaker, Charles A. ... New Orleans, LA
Nunn, Ann D. ... Mobile, AL
Nunn, Bill J. ... Stigler, OK
Nunn, Daniel B., Jr. ... Jacksonville, FL
Nunn, Darren L. ... Palo Alto, CA
Nunn, David L. ... Edmond, OK
Nunn, David L., P.C. ... Edmond, OK
Oklahoma City, OK
Nunn, David W. ... Columbus, OH
Toledo, OH
Nunn, Donald A. ... Poway, CA
Nunn, Frances L. ... Alexandria, VA
Nunn, Gary D. ... Jonesboro, LA
Nunn, George F., Jr. ... Perry, GA
Nunn & Greene Law Office, Professional Corporation ... Bloomington, IN
Nashville, IN
Nunn, J. Douglas, Jr. ... Camden, SC
Nunn, J. Roy ... Toledo, OH
Nunn, James T. ... Holly Hill, FL
Nunn, John E., III ... Chestertown, MD
Nunn, Kenneth L. ... Bloomington, IN
Nunn, Kent G. ... Kansas City, MO
Nunn, Leah E. ... New Orleans, LA
Nunn, Leslie E. ... Cynthiana, IN
Nunn, Louie B. ... Horse Cave, KY
Nunn, Marcia J. ... Dearborn, MI
Nunn, Mark S. ... Rochester, NY
Nunn, Michael M. ... Florence, SC
Nunn, Michael W. ... Santa Ana, CA
Nunn, Morris J. ... Kansas City, MO
Nunn Motschenbacher & Blattner LLP Portland, OR
Nunn, Rachel K. ... Orlando, FL
Nunn, Randall H. ... Richardson, TX
Nunn, Randall M. ... San Diego, CA
Nunn, Robert W. ... Portland, OR
Nunn, Robinson S. Small Business Administration, Office of the General Counsel, GV
Nunn, Sam A., Jr. ... Atlanta, GA
Nunn, Sandra L. ... Cincinnati, OH
Nunn & Share ... Holly Hill, FL
Nunn, Susan Andrea ... Grover Beach, CA
Nunn, Todd L. ... Seattle, WA
Nunn, William A., III ... White Stone, VA
Nunnallee, Hue E. ... Avon Park, FL
Nunnallee, Thomas L. ... Sebring, FL
Nunnallee, Walter H. ... Durham, NC
Nunnally, C. Talbot, III ... Atlanta, GA
Nunnally, Charles F., III ... Alexandria, LA
Nunnally, E. Russell ... Dallas, TX
Nunnally, John M. ... Gastonia, NC
Nunnally, Kevin C. ... Richmond, VA
Nunnally, Knox D. ... Houston, TX
Nunnally, Phillip L. ... Columbus, OH
Nunnally, R. Wayne ... Norfolk, VA
Nunnally & Robbins ... Norfolk, VA
Nunnally, Robert H., Jr. ... Los Angeles, CA
Nunnally, Timothy H. ... Tuscaloosa, AL
Nunnally, William S. ... Greeneville, TN
Nunnari, Jeffrey P. ... Perrysburg, OH
Nunneley, Barbara D. ... Hurst, TX
Nunnelley, Kenneth S. ... Daytona Beach, FL
Nunnelley, Richard A. ... Lexington, KY
Nunnelly, K. Colleen ... Liberty, MO
Nunnenkamp, Kenneth J. ... McLean, VA
Nunner, Michael K. ... Cadiz, OH
Nunnery, B. D., III ... Hazard, KY
Prestonsburg, KY
Nunnery, Dale E. ... Doniphan, MO
Nunnery, Edwin W., Jr. ... Atlanta, GA
Nunnery, J. Robert ... Hollandale, MS
Nunnery, Margaret A. ... Tulsa, OK
Nunnery, Willie J. ... Madison, WI
Nunn-Gibbs, Barbara L. Department of Defense, GV
Nunno, William R. ... Hackensack, NJ
Nunu, Paul E. ... Houston, TX
Nunziant, Francis ... Belleville, NJ
Nunziato, Carl A. ... Youngstown, OH
Nunziato, Dawn C. ... Washington, DC
Nunziato, Tom A. ... Los Angeles, CA
Nunziella, Amy B. ... West Palm Beach, FL
Nunzio, Colleen A. ... Sanford, FL
Nunzio, Kathryn Kraus Grand Rapids, MI
Nunzio, Nicholas S. ... Washington, DC
Nunzio, Rocco C. ... Rockville, MD
Nuovo, Betty A. ... Middlebury, VT
Nuovo, Marybeth C. ... Burlington, VT
Nuovo, Thomas C. ... Burlington, VT
Nurenberg, Marshall I. ... Cleveland, OH
Nurenberg, Plevin, Heller & McCarthy Co., L.P.A. ... Cleveland, OH
Nurenberg, Steven E. ... Detroit, MI
Nurge, Paul R. ... Ukiah, CA
Nurick, Herbert R. ... Harrisburg, PA
Nurick, Lester ... Washington, DC
Nuridin, Khadija ... Berkeley, CA
Nurieli, Eddie ... Hallandale Beach, FL
Nurik, Cary E. ... Pompton Lakes, NJ
Nurik, Jeffrey H. ... Fairfield, CA
Nurik & Lefkowitz ... Pompton Lakes, NJ
Nurik, Marc S. ... Fort Lauderdale, FL
Nuris, Thomas A. ... Daly City, CA
Nurkiewicz, Dennis J., Jr. ... Lansing, MI
Nurkin, Gary Howard ... Mineola, NY
Nurkin, John W. ... Charlotte, NC
Nurkin, Sidney J. ... Atlanta, GA
Nurmi, Thomas D. ... Washington, DC
Nurnberg, D. Tyler ... Chicago, IL
Nurnberg, Joseph ... New York, NY
Nurnberg, Ronald L. ... New York, NY
Nurre, Charlotte Camille ... Houston, TX
Nurre, Gabrielle S. ... Albuquerque, NM
Nurre, Richard L. ... Cincinnati, OH
Nurre, Thomas Charles ... Cincinnati, OH
Nursall, John G. ... Torrance, CA
Nurse, Brian M. ... New York, NY
Nursey, Joseph M. ... Atlanta, GA
Nusbacher, Gloria W. ... New York, NY
Nusbaum, Alan H. ... Cleveland, OH
Nusbaum, Ater and Wissler ... Chillicothe, OH
Nusbaum, Beryl ... Rochester, NY
Nusbaum, Carl ... Chicago, IL
Nusbaum, Edward ... Westport, CT
Nusbaum, Harriett Weiss ... Baltimore, MD
Nusbaum, Herbert S. ... Santa Monica, CA
Nusbaum, Jack H. ... New York, NY
Nusbaum, John (Jay) P. ... Portland, OR
Nusbaum, Joseph N. ... Boca Raton, FL
Nusbaum, Lawrence G., III New York, NY
Nusbaum, Lawrence G., Jr. ... New York, NY
Nusbaum, Marci Alboher ... Jersey City, NJ
Nusbaum, Mark E. ... Arlington, VA
Nusbaum, Maury D. ... Pittsburgh, PA
Nusbaum, Melvin G. ... Toledo, OH
Nusbaum, Mitchell S. ... Rochester, NY
Nusbaum & Parrino, P.C. ... Westport, CT
Nusbaum, Paul R. ... Succasunna, NJ
Nusbaum, Robert C. ... Norfolk, VA
Nusbaum, Scott W. ... Chillicothe, OH
Nusbaum, Simon J. ... New York, NY
Nusbaum, Stein, Goldstein & Bronstein, A Professional Corporation ... Succasunna, NJ
Nusbaum, Tacey J. ... Baltimore, MD
Nusbaum, William L. ... Norfolk, VA
Nuschler, Robin M. ... Washington, DC
Nusel, Rami ... Washington, DC
Nusgart, Cathy J. Nunziati ... Wheaton, IL
Nusgart, Jonathan D. ... Darien, IL
Nusich, Lee C. ... Portland, OR
Nusinow, Alan ... Northbrook, IL
Nusken, Ralph E. ... Columbus, OH
Nuspl, Nicholas J. ... Sherman, TX
Nuss, Brigitte T. ... Chicago, IL
Nuss, C. Lynne ... Solon, OH
Nuss, Craig S. ... Englewood, CO
Nuss, Eric J. ... Washington, DC
Nuss & Farmer ... Fort Scott, KS
Nuss, Henry ... Corpus Christi, TX
Nuss, James T. C. ... Stockton, CA
Nuss, Kenneth R. ... Colorado Springs, CO
Nuss, Larry D. ... Fort Scott, KS
Nuss Law Office, S.C. ... Fond du Lac, WI
Nuss, Lawton M. ... Salina, KS
Nuss, Richard J. ... Fond du Lac, WI
Nuss, Thomas F. ... Rancho Cucamonga, CA
Nuss, Thomas L. ... Minneapolis, MN
Nussbacher, Kenneth J. ... Santa Clara, CA
Nussbaum, Alan J. ... Little Rock, AR
Nussbaum, Amanda H. ... New York, NY
Nussbaum, Andrew J. ... New York, NY
Nussbaum, Andrew W. Upper Marlboro, MD
Nussbaum, Bernard J. ... Chicago, IL
Nussbaum, Bernard W. ... New York, NY
Nussbaum, Beth M. ... Somerville, MA
Nussbaum, Brett D. ... Great Neck, NY
Nussbaum, Brian E. ... San Francisco, CA
Nussbaum, Carolyn G. ... Rochester, NY
Nussbaum, David M. ... New York, NY
Nussbaum, Donald M. ... New York, NY
Nussbaum, Frank ... Miami, FL
Nussbaum, Gary ... Roseland, NJ
Nussbaum, Gerald S. ... Chicago, IL
Nussbaum, Harold J. ... Silver Spring, MD
Nussbaum, Harvey A. ... Boca Raton, FL
Nussbaum, Hendrix & Trussell, P.A., A Professional Association ... Little Rock, AR
Nussbaum, Howard J. ... Northlake, IL
Nussbaum, J. Michael ... Houston, TX
Nussbaum, Jan L. ... Oakland, CA
Nussbaum, Janet Adelle ... Houston, TX
Nussbaum, Jeffrey ... San Francisco, CA
Nussbaum, Jeremy ... New York, NY
Nussbaum, Jerold K. ... Annapolis, MD
Nussbaum, Joseph S. ... New York, NY
Nussbaum, Keith ... Beverly Hills, CA
Nussbaum, L. Martin Colorado Springs, CO
Nussbaum, Leana B. ... New York, NY
Nussbaum, Lenell ... Seattle, WA
Nussbaum, Linda P. ... New York, NY
Nussbaum, Mark S. ... West Palm Beach, FL
Nussbaum, Martin ... New York, NY
Nussbaum, Mary Stephenson Jacksonville, FL
Nussbaum, Michael ... Washington, DC
Nussbaum, Mitchell S. ... New York, NY
Nussbaum, Morton R. ... New York, NY
Nussbaum, Neil E. ... Moretown, VT
Nussbaum & Nussbaum ... Jacksonville, FL
Nussbaum, Paul A. ... Dallas, TX
Nussbaum, Paul M. ... Baltimore, MD
Columbia, MD
Nussbaum, Peter A. ... New York, NY
Nussbaum, Peter D. ... San Francisco, CA
Nussbaum, Peter E. ... Roseland, NJ
Nussbaum, Randy ... Phoenix, AZ
Nussbaum, Richard A., II ... South Bend, IN
Nussbaum, Richard D. ... Los Angeles, CA
Nussbaum, Robert B. ... Newark, NJ
Nussbaum, Robert E. ... Longmont, CO
Nussbaum, Robert S. ... Hackensack, NJ
Nussbaum, Robin Lynn ... New York, NY
Nussbaum, Ronald J. ... New York, NY
Nussbaum, Sheldon G. ... New York, NY
Nussbaum, Sue C. ... Lincoln Park, NJ
Nussbaum, Theodore ... New York, NY
Nussbaum & Wald ... Washington, DC
Nussbaum, William ... Jacksonville, FL
Nussbaum, William C. ... Alexandria, VA
Nussbaum, William D. ... Washington, DC
Nussbaum, William L. ... St. Louis, MO
Nussbaum-Bell, Mindy ... Des Moines, IA
Nussbaumer, John R. ... Lansing, MI
Nussbaumer, Kenneth M. ... Belleville, IL
Nussbaumer, Robert L. ... St. Louis, MO
Nussbaumer, Robert L., & Associates, A Prof. Corp. ... St. Louis, MO
Nussberger, Terry L., (Mr.) ... Ladysmith, WI
Nussdorf, Harry ... Kew Gardens, NY
Nussdorf, Lawrence C. ... Bethesda, MD
Nussdorf, Melanie F. ... Washington, DC
Nussel, Arthur H., Sr. ... Williston, FL
Nussenbaum, Adam J. ... Newton, MA
Nussenblatt, Michael P. ... Houston, TX
Nussinow, Bernard L. ... Mount Sinai, NY
Nussle, Herbert L. ... Cleveland, OH
Nusslock, Kathy L. ... Milwaukee, WI
Nussman, Aaron W. ... Hackensack, NJ
Nussman, Bruce L. ... Hackensack, NJ
Nusz, David B. ... Irvine, CA
Nuszbaum, Joyce M. ... Atlanta, GA
Nuta, Alan J. ... Frederick, MD
Gaithersburg, MD
Hagerstown, MD
Nutall, Dexter U. ... Washington, DC
Nute, Eugene F. ... Farmington, NH
Nute, Leslie F. ... Pittsburgh, PA
Nute, Stephanie T. ... Dover, NH
Nuterangelo, Brian ... Washington, DC
Nutgrass, David P. ... Lawrenceburg, KY
Nuth, Timothy E. ... Lake Forest, CA
Nuti, Gregory C. ... San Francisco, CA
Nutile, John F., Jr. ... North Haven, CT
Nutile, Maria ... Phoenix, AZ
Nutini, Dona A. ... Phoenix, AZ
Nutley, Ashley Steele ... Greenville, SC
Nutley, Deborah ... Chicago, IL
Nutman, Midge J. ... New York, NY
Nutovic, Isaac ... New York, NY
Nutt, Ann S. ... San Francisco, CA
Nutt, Brian C. ... Pasadena, CA
Nutt, C. David ... Houston, TX
Nutt, Claude L. ... Louisville, KY
Nutt, David, & Associates, P.C. Jackson, MS
Nutt, David H. ... Jackson, MS
Nutt, Douglas ... Englewood, CO
Nutt, Gilbert Hale ... Louisville, KY
Nutt, Harold L. ... Hollister, CA
Nutt, James E. ... West Palm Beach, FL
Nutt, Kathleen L. ... West Des Moines, IA
Nutt, Kimberly ... Treasury Department, Federal Law Enforcement Training Center, GV
Nutt, Laural Axsom ... Murfreesboro, TN
Nutt, Mary B. ... New York, NY
Nutt & Mayer ... Louisville, KY
Nutt, Milburn E. ... Wichita Falls, TX
Nutt, Robert L. ... Boston, MA
Nutt, Stephen D. ... San Francisco, CA
Nutt, Stephen Martin ... San Antonio, TX
Nutt, Wendy L. ... Chicago, IL
Nuttall Berman Attorneys ... Fresno, CA
Nuttall, Edward John ... Fairfax, VA
Nuttall, Glen L. ... Newport Beach, CA
Nuttall, James R. ... Chicago, IL
Nuttall, Roger T., (Inc.) ... Fresno, CA
Nuttall, Steven R. ... Olean, NY
Nuttall, Thomas J. ... Braintree, MA
Nutter, Coleman A. ... New York, NY
Nutter, David C. ... Atlanta, GA
Nutter, Donna Maria ... Dallas, TX
Nutter, Gina L. ... Covington, KY
Nutter, Guy B. ... Santa Monica, CA
Nutter, Harry T. ... Midland, TX
Nutter, Jack O., II ... Washington, DC
Nutter, Jennifer ... Los Angeles, CA
Nutter, Kim ... Boca Raton, FL
Nutter, McClennen & Fish, LLP Boston, MA
Hyannis, MA
Nutter, Melvin L. ... Long Beach, CA
Nutter, Michael K. ... Chicago, IL
Nutter, R. Gary ... Texarkana, AR
Nutter, Ralph H. ... Los Angeles, CA
Nutter, R. J., II ... Virginia Beach, VA
Nutter, Robert H. ... Tampa, FL
Nutter, Steven T. ... Los Angeles, CA
Nutter, Thomas E. ... St. Louis, MO
Nutter, Timothy J. ... Boston, MA
Nutting, Mary P. ... Momence, IL
Nutting, N. Joseph ... Waterloo, IA
Nutting, Norwood V. C., Jr. ... Winter Park, FL
Nutting, Stephen J. ... Saipan, TT
Nuttleman, David C. ... Port Charlotte, FL
Nuttman, Robert F. ... Santa Ana, CA
Nutto, Francis X. ... Anaheim, CA
Nutto, William J. ... Corpus Christi, TX
Nutty, John E. ... Ames, IA
Nutzman-Buller, Teresa J. ... Omaha, NE
Nuutinen, Arto Juhani ... Orange, CA
Nuxoll, Dennis R. ... Washington, DC
Nuxoll, Jay ... Bellevue, WA
Nuxoll, Libey, Ensley & Esser Colfax, WA
Pullman, WA
Nuxoll, Wanda J.R. ... Seattle, WA

Oatman, Jack L., Jr. ....San Diego, CA
Oatman, Jane H. ....Seal Beach, CA
Oatman Law Offices, P.C. ....Llano, TX
Oatman, Sam ....Llano, TX
Oatman, Wilburn, Jr. ....Llano, TX
Oats, Fred L. ....Reno, NV
Oats & Hudson ....Lafayette, LA
Oats, Stephen J. ....Lafayette, LA
Oatway, Andrew C. ....Quincy, MA
Oaxaca, Bernal & Associates ....El Paso, TX
Oaxaca, J. Roberto ....El Paso, TX
Oba, Gary G. ....St. Mary's, AK
Obadal, Anthony J. ....Alexandria, VA
Obadal & MacLeod, P.C. ....Alexandria, VA
Obade, Claire C. ....Philadelphia, PA
Obade, Claire C., & Associates, P.C.
Philadelphia, PA
Obadiah, Richard ....Boston, MA
Obama, Barack H. ....Chicago, IL
O'Ban, Steven T. ....Seattle, WA
O'Banion, Dana K. ....Chicago, IL
O'Banion, John P. ....Sacramento, CA
O'Banion & Ritchey LLP
Sacramento, CA
O'Bannon, A. Stewart, III ....Florence, AL
O'Bannon, A. Stewart, Jr. ....Florence, AL
O'Bannon, Earl, Jr. ....Louisville, KY
O'Bannon, Ernest L. ....New Orleans, LA
O'Bannon, Frank L. ....Corydon, IN
O'Bannon, James E. ....Dallas, TX
O'Bannon, Janet Kalt ....Kansas City, MO
O'Bannon, Linda ....Anchorage, AK
O'Bannon & O'Bannon, LLC
Florence, AL
O'Bannon, Robert O.
Oklahoma City, OK
O'Bannon, Thomas C. ....Jacksonville, FL
O'Bannon, Thomas C. ....Charlotte, NC
O'Bar, Rachael M. ....Boise, ID
O'Bara, Marianne ....Seattle, WA
Obara, Patricia E. ....Wilmington, DE
O'Barr, Bobby G. ....Biloxi, MS
O'Barr, Bobby G., P.A. ....Biloxi, MS
O'Barr, Walter M. ....Everett, WA
Obayashi, Lisa J. ....Department of Commerce, Office of the General Counsel, GV
Obbard, Philip ....Oakland, CA
Obdyke, Louis K., IV ....Austin, TX
Obear, George W. ....Delphi, IN
Obear, Henry N. ....Winnsboro, SC
Obear, Kirk B. ....Elkhart Lake, WI
Obear, Overholser, Huffer, Rider & Fouts
Delphi, IN
Obebe, Oluwasegun G. ....Washington, DC
Obecny, Carlton T. ....Bethesda, MD
Obedin, Glenn A. ....Central Islip, NY
Obee, John A. ....Southfield, MI
Obee, Mary Jo ....Oklahoma City, OK
Obegi & Brewer, P.C.
Newport Beach, CA
Obegi, Joseph C. ....Newport Beach, CA
Obegi, Melissa
Overseas Private Investment Corporation, GV
Obeid, Fran ....New York, NY
Obeidallah, Dean J. ....Montvale, NJ
O'Beirne, Anne ....New York, NY
O'Beirne, Daniel J. ....Natchez, MS
O'Beirne, Emmet C. ....Tulsa, OK
O'Beirne, Patricia L. ......Department of Justice, Civil Rights Division, GV
O'Beirne, Stephen F. ....New York, NY
O'Beirne, Thomas J. ....Natchez, MS
Obel, David I. ....New York, NY
Obel, Kenneth M. ....Chicago, IL
O'Bell, Frank G. ....Cleveland, OH
Obenauer, John P. ....Sacramento, CA
Obenauf, Lori Chapman ....Macon, GA
Obenberger, Thomas E. ....Milwaukee, WI
Obenchain, John R. ....South Bend, IN
Obenhaus, Stacy R. ....Dallas, TX
Obenland, Bruce D. ....Glenwood, MN
Obenour, John S., Jr. ....Tacoma, WA
Obenour, Malcolm D. ....Akron, OH
Obenschain & Chandler, L.L.C.
Atlanta, GA
Obenschain, Samuel L., Jr. ....Atlanta, GA
Obenshain, Elizabeth A. ....Atlanta, GA
Obenshain, Hinnant & Runkle, LLP
Richmond, VA
Obenshain, Mark D. ....Harrisonburg, VA
Obenshain, Wiley S., III ....Augusta, GA
Obenshain, Wiley S., III, P.C.
Augusta, GA
Ober, Angela D. ....Hartford, CT
Ober, David ....Washington, DC
Ober, David J. ....Union, NJ
Ober, Edward S. ....Sunrise, FL
Ober, Frank Fritz ....Southport, CT
Ober, Fred R. ....Miami, FL
Ober, Frederick H., III ....Cherry Hill, NJ
Ober, Joelle Ann ....Tampa, FL
Ober, John ....Indianapolis, IN
Ober, Kaler, Grimes & Shriver, A Professional Corporation
Washington, DC
Baltimore, MD
Ober, Louise C. ....Palo Alto, CA
Ober, Mark A. ....Tampa, FL
Ober, Matt D. ....Los Angeles, CA
Ober, Nancy L. ....San Francisco, CA
Ober, Norman R. ....Honolulu, HI
Ober, Paul R. ....Reading, PA
Ober, Paul R., & Associates ....Reading, PA
Ober, Peter C. ....Fredericksburg, VA
Ober, Richard F., Jr. ....Princeton, NJ
Ober, Richd. F. ....Baltimore, MD
Ober, Robin A. ....Burlington, VT

Ober, Russell J., Jr. ....Pittsburgh, PA
Ober, Scott T. ....Worcester, MA
Ober, William ....Baltimore, MD
Ober, William J. ....Greensburg, PA
Oberbauer, Earl J., Jr. ....Manassas, VA
Oberbeck, Arthur W. ....Westminster, CO
Oberbeck, D. Michael ....Santa Monica, CA
Oberbillig, Robert C. ....Des Moines, IA
Oberbillig, Robert H. ....Mesa, AZ
Oberbroeckling, Laura J.
Washington, DC
Oberc, Thaddeus A. ....West Caldwell, NJ
Oberdank, Lawrence M. ....Independence, OH
Oberdank, Lawrence M., Co., L.P.A.
Independence, OH
Oberdas, Jill ....Dallas, TX
Oberdick, David G. ....Pittsburgh, PA
Oberdick, Todd M. ....Stamford, CT
Oberdick, William J. ....Cleveland, OH
Oberdier, Carl W. ....New York, NY
Oberdier, Karal B. ....Jacksonville, FL
Oberdier, Ronald R. ....Jacksonville, FL
Oberding, Juliet M. ....Coronado, CA
Oberdorf, Cheryl J. ....Woodbridge, NJ
Oberdorf, John J. ....Newark, NJ
Oberdorf, Peter Scott ....New York, NY
Oberdorf, William P. ....Newark, NJ
Oberdorfer & Barry, P.A.
Jacksonville, FL
Oberdorfer, Carol B. ....Washington, DC
Oberdorfer, Daniel ....Minneapolis, MN
Oberdorfer, E. Charles ....Jacksonville, FL
Oberdorfer, John L. ....Washington, DC
Oberdorfer, Louis F. ....
United States District Court For The District Of Columbia, GV
Oberdorfer, Wilson ....Spring House, PA
Oberdorff, Marc L. ....Cleveland, OH
Oberembt, Laurie A. ....Department of Justice, Civil Division, GV
Oberer, Walter E. ....Salt Lake City, UT
Oberfeld, Neil B. ....Denver, CO
Oberfell, James W. ....South Bend, IN
Oberfest, Bruce D., (P.C.) ....Chappaqua, NY
Oberg, Amy Page ....Boston, MA
Providence, RI
Oberg, Cynthia J. H. ....Detroit, MI
Oberg, David D. ....Roseland, NJ
Oberg, David L., (A P.C.)
Beverly Hills, CA
Oberg, Frank D. ....Clay Center, KS
Oberg, Gregg O. ....Mesquite, TX
Oberg, Howard C. ....Rancho Cucamonga, CA
Oberg, H. W. ....Denver, CO
Oberg, John W. ....Phoenix, AZ
Oberg Law Office ....Mesquite, TX
Oberg, Lisa L. ....San Francisco, CA
Oberg and Malcolm ....Clay Center, KS
Oberg, Mary C. ....Vernon, CT
Oberg, Paul W. ....Wayzata, MN
Oberg, Philip A. ....Carmel, CA
Oberg, Scott K. ....Phoenix, AZ
Oberg, Steve G. ....St. Augustine, FL
Oberg, Steven J. ....Rapid City, SD
Obergfell, Brian D. ....New York, NY
Obergh & Berlin ....Washington, DC
Oberhand, Sandra J. ....Stamford, CT
Oberhansley, Philip D. ....Temecula, CA
Oberhardt, William P. ....Chicago, IL
Oberhaus, Geoffrey L. ....Cincinnati, OH
Oberhausen, Frank C., Jr. ....Sebring, FL
Oberhausen, Lawrence W. ....Pensacola, FL
Oberhausen, Thomas J. ....Indianapolis, IN
Oberhauser, Louis B. ....Wayzata, MN
Oberhauser & Neveaux ....Wayzata, MN
Oberheide, Frederick Brett .....St. Louis, MO
Oberhelman, Harry A., III ....Santa Cruz, CA
Oberhelman, William J., Jr., (P.C.)
New Orleans, LA
Oberholtzer & Centers ....Whittier, CA
Oberholtzer, David B. ....San Diego, CA
Oberholtzer, Filous & Lesiak, A Legal Professional Association ....Medina, OH
Oberholtzer, James ....Chicago, IL
Oberholtzer, Jay ....Whittier, CA
Oberholtzer, John C. ....Medina, OH
Oberholtzer, Kim R. ....Minerva, OH
Oberholtzer, Matthew W. ....Canton, OH
Oberholtzer, Scott K. ....Lancaster, PA
Oberholtzer, Steven L. ....Ann Arbor, MI
Oberholzer, Richard J. ....Bakersfield, CA
Oberkfell, Keith F. ....Chicago, IL
Oberkfell, Sandra L. ....Chicago, IL
Oberkircher, Peter J. ....Philadelphia, PA
Oberkoetter, Robert F. ....Providence, RI
Oberland, Gregory C. ....Milwaukee, WI
Oberlander, Benita ....Mineola, NY
Oberlander, David R. ....Cherry Hill, NJ
Oberlander, Jill K. ....New York, NY
Oberlander, Lynn B. ....New York, NY
Oberlander, Michael I. ....St. Louis, MO
Oberlander, Robert G. ....Kansas City, MO
Oberle, Cheryl B. ....Dayton, OH
Oberle, Christopher P. ....San Diego, CA
Oberle, Joseph F. ....Oceanside, CA
Oberle, Michael T. ....St. Paul, MN
Oberle, Patrick E. ....Pekin, IL
Oberle, Paul Douglas, Jr. ....Shreveport, LA
Oberlies, Hilary ....Indianapolis, IN
Oberlies, Jeffrey R. ....Indianapolis, IN
Oberlies, Joseph M. ....Cherry Hill, NJ
Paoli, PA
Philadelphia, PA
Oberlies, Katherine M. ....New York, NY
Oberlin, John C. ....Los Altos Hills, CA
Oberlin, Phillip S. ....Toledo, OH
Oberlin, Robert J. ....Massillon, OH
Oberlink, James R. ....Berkeley, CA

Oberly, Charles M., III ....Wilmington, DE
Oberly & Jennings, P.A. ....Wilmington, DE
Oberly, Kathryn A. ....New York, NY
Oberly, Robert P. ....Philadelphia, PA
Oberly, William B. ....Anchorage, AK
Obermaier, Otto G. ....New York, NY
Oberman, Caryl Andrea, The Law Offices of
Doylestown, PA
Philadelphia, PA
Oberman, Caryl Andrea, The Law Offices of
Willow Grove, PA
Oberman, Harold A. ....Charleston, SC
Oberman, J. Douglas ....Waterloo, IA
Oberman, James L. ....Oakland, CA
Oberman, Jeffrey B. ....Minneapolis, MN
Oberman, Joy D. ....New York, NY
Oberman, Martin J. ....Chicago, IL
Oberman, Marvin I. ....Charleston, SC
Oberman, Michael M. ....Munster, IN
Oberman, Michael S. ....New York, NY
Oberman & Oberman ....Charleston, SC
Oberman, Richard S. ....New York, NY
Oberman, Robert M. ....Omaha, NE
Oberman, Stacy I. ....New York, NY
Oberman, Steven ....Knoxville, TN
Oberman, Stewart J. ....Mill Valley, CA
Obermanns, James D.
Bloomfield Hills, MI
Obermayer, Rebmann, Maxwell & Hippel LLP ....Haddonfield, NJ
Harrisburg, PA
Philadelphia, PA
Pittsburgh, PA
Obermeier, Bradley C. ....Des Moines, IA
Obermeier, David J. ....Pittsburgh, PA
Wheeling, WV
Obermeier, Steven J. ....Olathe, KS
Obermeyer, Michael A. ....Brighton, CO
Obermeyer, Sarai K. ....San Francisco, CA
Obermiller, Wm. J. ....Whiting, IN
Oberndorfer Law Firm ....Milwaukee, WI
Oberndorfer, Michael H. ....Milwaukee, WI
Oberndorfer, Ron H. ....La Mesa, CA
Oberndorfer, William P. ....Norfolk, VA
Obernesser, Peter J. ....Colorado Springs, CO
Oberrecht, Phillip S. ....Boise, ID
O'Berry, Billie Jo ....Lansing, MI
O'Berry, Donna L.
Department of Transportation, Research and Special Programs Administration, GV
Oberscheven, Toni M. ....Los Angeles, CA
Oberschmidt, David W. ....Saginaw, MI
Oberschmidt, E. Richard ....Cincinnati, OH
Oberski, Edward M. ....Sterling Heights, MI
Oberst, Brett H. ....Los Angeles, CA
Oberst, E. Ernest ....Cheshire, CT
Oberst, Edward J. ....Pittsburgh, PA
Oberst, Gary ....Norwalk, CT
Oberst, Gary, P.C., Law Offices of
Norwalk, CT
Oberst, George W. ....Alstead, NH
Oberst, Mary J. ....Lake Oswego, OR
Oberst, Paul ....Lexington, KY
Oberst, Sharon T. ....Norwalk, CT
Oberstaedt, Mark J. ....Haddonfield, NJ
Oberstar, David R. ....Iron Mountain, MI
Duluth, MN
Oberstein, Alan C. ....Palm Desert, CA
Oberstein, Gary J. ....Boston, MA
Oberstein, Kibre & Horwitz LLP
Los Angeles, CA
Oberstein, Norman S., (A Professional Law Corporation) ....Los Angeles, CA
Obert, Keith D. ....Brandon, MS
Obert, Lisa M. ....Cleveland, OH
Obert, Mark Gene ....Salem, OR
Obert, Paul R. ....Long Grove, IL
Oberti, Mark J. ....Houston, TX
Oberting, Victor A., III ....Troy, NY
Oberto, Sheila K. ....Fresno, CA
Oberts, Stacie E. ....Minneapolis, MN
Oberts, William Bradley ....Chicago, IL
Oberts, William J. ....Chicago, IL
Obertubbesing, Edward ....White Plains, NY
Oberwetter, Thomas R. ....Madison, WI
Obetz, Peter S. ....Kansas City, MO
Obetz, Robin R. ....Columbus, OH
Obeysekere, Indrajit ....Oakland, CA
Obeysekere, Susan ....San Francisco, CA
Obi, Francis ....Irvington, NJ
Obiajulu, Heidi L. ....Rochester, NY
Obiala, John R. ....Chicago, IL
Obico, Paul Velasco ....Palo Alto, CA
Obidinski, Anne M. ....Shelton, CT
Obie, Damon D. ....Billings, MT
Obie, Stephen J.
Commodity Futures Trading Commission, Division of Enforcement, GV
Obie, Stephen Jay ....St. Louis, MO
O'Biecunas, Leo G., Jr. ....Los Angeles, CA
Obinata, Naomi ....Santa Clara, CA
Obiol, Richard C. ....Mineola, NY
Obiora, Leslye ....Indianapolis, IN
Obiorah, Edwin S.C. ....Rochester, NY
Obitts, Timothy R. ....McLean, VA
Oblachinski, Robert M. ....Riverside, CA
Oblath, Geoffry W. ....Los Angeles, CA
Obledo, Mario G. ....Sacramento, CA
O'Blenes, Ann Scowcroft ....Dallas, TX
O'Blenes, Carole ....New York, NY
O'Bleness, Brian K. ....Washington, DC
O'Blennis, M. Kathleen ....Pleasanton, CA
Obler, Elizabeth A. ....San Francisco, CA
Obler, Robert A. ....Trenton, NJ
Obletz, Bernard I. ....Buffalo, NY
Oblich, David ....Washington, DC
Obligato, Carlo A. ....Boston, MA

O'Block, Victor J. ....Chicago, IL
Oblon, David A. ....Arlington, VA
Oblon, Michael A. ....Washington, DC
Oblon, Norman F. ....Arlington, VA
Oblon, Spivak, McClelland, Maier & Neustadt, P.C. ....Washington, DC
Arlington, VA
Obloy, Edward J. ....Department of Defense, Defense Legal Services Agency, GV
Obloy, Gregory T. ....Bloomfield Hills, MI
Obninsky, Victor Peter ....Novato, CA
Obod, Barry G. ....Philadelphia, PA
Obod, Marjorie McMahon
Philadelphia, PA
Obod, Ramon R. ....Philadelphia, PA
Obold, Joseph K. ....Philadelphia, PA
Obold, Taylor H. ....Syracuse, NY
Obolensky, Michael N. ....New York, NY
Oborne, Scott W. ....Oakland, CA
Walnut Creek, CA
O'Boy, Francis M. ....Taunton, MA
O'Boy and Moniz ....Taunton, MA
O'Boyle, Bryan R.
Department of the Air Force, Office of the Judge Advocate General, GV
O'Boyle, David J. ....Naugatuck, CT
O'Boyle, David M. ....Pittsburgh, PA
O'Boyle, Dennis B. ....Chicago, IL
O'Boyle, Emmett ....Salinas, CA
O'Boyle, Francis J. ....New York, NY
O'Boyle, Gregory M.
Colorado Springs, CO
O'Boyle, Hugh ....New York, NY
O'Boyle, James D. ....New York, NY
O'Boyle, James G. ....Chevy Chase, MD
O'Boyle, John ....Englewood, NJ
O'Boyle, John J., Jr. ....Dallas, TX
O'Boyle, John M. ....Ellsworth, WI
O'Boyle, Kathleen Theresa ....Export, PA
O'Boyle, Kevin F. ....Seaford, NY
O'Boyle, Kevin J. ....Hamilton, NJ
O'Boyle, Kristina E. ....New Richmond, WI
O'Boyle, Mark E. ....St. Paul, MN
O'Boyle, Mary, II ....Stonewall, TX
O'Boyle, R. Michael ....Detroit, MI
O'Boyle, Robert M. ....Austin, TX
O'Boyle, Sheila Mary ....Simi Valley, CA
Oboz, Kim M. ....Washington, DC
Oboz, M. Kenneth ....Washington, DC
Obradovich, David J. ....Frankfort, KY
O'Bradovich, Greg J. ....New York, NY
O'Bradovich, Michael J. ....Omaha, NE
Obrand, Michael ....Irvine, CA
Newport Beach, CA
O'Brasky, Nancy Kase ....Hartford, CT
Obrecht, Charles F., Jr.
Severna Park, MD
Obrecht, George F., III
Severna Park, MD
Obrecht, John L. ....Northampton, PA
Obrecht and Obrecht ....Annapolis, MD
Severna Park, MD
O'Brecht, Richard P. ....Denver, CO
Obregon, Conrad J. ....Bronx, NY
Obregon, Rene Luis ....Dallas, TX
Obreholzer, Regina M. ....Harrisburg, PA
Obremskey, Peter L. ....Indianapolis, IN
Lebanon, IN
Obremski, Charles P. ....Cornwall, NY
Obrenski, Timothy V. ....Marina Del Rey, CA
O'Bresly, Michael P. ....San Francisco, CA
O'Brian, David M. ....Houston, TX
O'Brian, Harold S. ....Saddle Brook, NJ
O'Brian, Paul M. ....Mayville, NY
O'Brian, Perry H. ....Bangor, ME
O'Brian, Robert D. ....Fairfield, NJ
O'Brian, Susan E. Millican ....Redmond, WA
O'Brian, Valerie R. ....Department of Justice, Civil Rights Division, GV
O'Brian, William E., Jr. ....Washington, DC
O'Briant, Bunch, Robins & Stubblefield
Asheboro, NC
O'Briant, Eric H. ....Logan, WV
O'Briant, J. Michael ....Corpus Christi, TX
O'Briant, Lillian B. ....Asheboro, NC
O'Briant, Mark K. ....Dallas, TX
O'Briant, Patrick W. ....Houston, TX
O'Briant, Robert P. ....Amarillo, TX
O'Briant, Sheryl W. ....Houston, TX
O'Brien, Aaron J. ....Fort Myers, FL
O'Brien & Adamski ....Easthampton, MA
O'Brien, Albert J. ....East St. Louis, IL
O'Brien, Alice ....Washington, DC
O'Brien, Amy L. ....Atlanta, GA
O'Brien, Anderson, Burgy, Garbowicz & Brown, LLP ....Boulder Junction, WI
Eagle River, WI
O'Brien, Andrea I. ....Washington, DC
O'Brien, Andrea White ....Eatontown, NJ
O'Brien, Andrew A. ....St. Louis, MO
O'Brien, Andrew G.S. ....Buffalo, NY
O'Brien, Ann K. ....Los Angeles, CA
O'Brien, Ann Marie
West Palm Beach, FL
O'Brien, Ann Marie ....Akron, OH
Cleveland, OH
O'Brien, Anne Bedinghaus ....Idaho Falls, ID
O'Brien, Anne J. ....Washington, DC
O'Brien, Anne M. ....Chicago, IL
O'Brien, Anthony A. ....Washington, DC
O'Brien, Anthony N. ....Washington, DC
O'Brien, April A. ....Las Vegas, NV
O'Brien, Arthur R. ....Glenview, IL
O'Brien & Associates, P.C.
Oakbrook Terrace, IL
O'Brien & Associates, P.C. ......Philadelphia, PA
O'Brien, B. Wells ....Reno, NV
O'Brien, Barbara A. ....Milwaukee, WI

O'Brien, Mary ... Department of Commerce, National Oceanic and Atmospheric Administration, GV
O'Brien, Mary Ann C. ... Haddonfield, NJ
O'Brien, Mary Beth ... Chicago, IL
O'Brien, Mary Crowe ... Avon, CT
O'Brien, Mary E. ... Issaquah, WA
O'Brien, Mary Grace ... Manassas, VA
O'Brien, Mary K. ... Coal City, IL
O'Brien, Mary M. L. ... Minneapolis, MN
O'Brien, Mary Win ... Pittsburgh, PA
O'Brien, Maura McCauley ... Wellesley, MA
O'Brien, Maureen ... Miami, FL
O'Brien, Maureen ... Maywood, IL
O'Brien, Maureen A. Department of Agriculture, Office of the General Counsel, GV
O'Brien, Maureen Ann ... Newark, NJ
O'Brien, Maureen E. ... Brooklyn, NY
O'Brien, Maureen J. ... Denver, CO
O'Brien, Maureen J. ... Lakewood, CO
O'Brien, Maureen P. ... Wilmington, DE
O'Brien, Maureen T. ... Boston, MA
O'Brien, Maurice J. ... Haverhill, MA
O'Brien, Maurice W. ... Minneapolis, MN
O'Brien, Melanie P. ... Ridgefield, CT
O'Brien, Melvin F. ... Wheeling, WV
O'Brien, Merrill M. ... Paramus, NJ
O'Brien, Michael ... Clayton, MO
O'Brien, Michael ... Garden City, NY
O'Brien, Michael A. ... Talladega, AL
O'Brien, Michael C. ... Oxnard, CA
O'Brien, Michael D. ... Trenton, NJ
O'Brien, Michael D. ... Brooklyn, NY
O'Brien, Michael D. ... Eau Claire, WI
O'Brien, Michael E. ... Salem, MA
O'Brien, Michael E. ... New York, NY
O'Brien, Michael F. ... Geneva, IL
O'Brien, Michael F. ... Rockford, IL
O'Brien, Michael F. ... Columbus, OH
O'Brien, Michael F. ... Eau Claire, WI
O'Brien, Michael H. ... Dallas, TX
O'Brien, Michael J. ... Juneau, AK
O'Brien, Michael J. ... Chicago, IL
O'Brien, Michael J. ... Danville, IL
O'Brien, Michael J. ... Sioux City, IA
O'Brien, Michael J. ... Grand Rapids, MI
O'Brien, Michael J. ... Huntington Station, NY
O'Brien, Michael J. ... Syracuse, NY
O'Brien, Michael J. ... Cleveland, OH
O'Brien, Michael J. ... Oklahoma City, OK
O'Brien, Michael J. ... Forest Grove, OR
O'Brien, Michael J. ... Spokane, WA
O'Brien, Michael Joseph ... New York, NY
O'Brien, Michael J.T. ... Covina, CA
O'Brien, Michael L. ... Mattapoisett, MA
O'Brien, Michael M. ... Omaha, NE
O'Brien, Michael "Mick" ... Orlando, FL
O'Brien, Michael P. ... Marietta, GA
O'Brien, Michael P. ... Chicago, IL
O'Brien, Michael P. ... Boston, MA
O'Brien, Michael P. ... Corpus Christi, TX
O'Brien, Michael Patrick
Salt Lake City, UT
O'Brien, Michael R. ... St. Paul, MN
O'Brien, Michaela ... Mount Olive, NJ
O'Brien, Michele N. ... Houston, TX
O'Brien, Michelle Nadeau ... Boston, MA
O'Brien, Mike F. ... Claremont, CA
O'Brien, Mollie K. ... Roseland, NJ
O'Brien, Monica C. ... Chicago, IL
O'Brien, Monica M. ... Portland, OR
O'Brien & Morrissey ... Lafayette, IN
O'Brien, Murrough H. ... Portland, ME
Obrien, Neal J. ... Chicago, IL
O'Brien, Neil J. ... Dallas, TX
O'Brien & O'Brien ... Holyoke, MA
O'Brien and O'Brien ... Ann Arbor, MI
O'Brien & O'Brien ... Pomeroy, OH
O'Brien, O'Rourke & Hogan ... Chicago, IL
O'Brien, Pamela R. ... Boston, MA
O'Brien, Partlow & White ... Boston, MA
O'Brien, Pat ... Jacksonville, AR
O'Brien, Patrice S. ... Philadelphia, PA
O'Brien, Patricia ... Chicago, IL
O'Brien, Patricia A. ... New York, NY
O'Brien, Patricia Cadagin ... Wheaton, IL
O'Brien, Patricia Hickey ... Olympia, WA
O'Brien, Patricia L. ... St. Paul, MN
O'Brien, Patrick ... Boston, MA
O'Brien, Patrick A. ... New York, NY
O'Brien, Patrick B. ... United States Court Of Veterans Appeals, GV
O'Brien, Patrick C. ... Washington, DC
O'Brien, Patrick D. ... Washington, DC
O'Brien, Patrick H. ... Pomeroy, OH
O'Brien, Patrick J. ... Redwood City, CA
O'Brien, Patrick J ... Chevy Chase, MD
O'Brien, Patrick J. ... Lansing, MI
O'Brien, Patrick J. ... Armonk, NY
O'Brien, Patrick J. ... Mineola, NY
O'Brien, Patrick J. ... New York, NY
O'Brien, Patrick J. ... Staten Island, NY
O'Brien, Patrick M. ... Indianapolis, IN
O'Brien, Patrick S. ... St. Louis, MO
O'Brien, Patrick T. ... Fort Lauderdale, FL
O'Brien, Patrick T. ... Lincoln, NE
O'Brien, Patrick W. ... Chicago, IL
O'Brien, Paul D. ... Hauppauge, NY
O'Brien, Paul David ... Los Angeles, CA
O'Brien, Paul E. ... Greenwich, CT
O'Brien, Paul Edward
Department of Justice, Antitrust Division, GV
O'Brien, Paul F. ... Lexington, MA
O'Brien, Paul J. ... Auburn, MA
O'Brien, Paul L. ... Washington, DC
O'Brien, Paul T. ... Somerset, NJ
O'Brien, Paul V. ... New York, NY
O'Brien, Paul V. ... Rockville Centre, NY
O'Brien, Paul W. ... Rochester, NY
O'Brien, Peter ... Beverly, MA
O'Brien, Peter B. ... Los Angeles, CA
O'Brien, Peter J. ... Stroudsburg, PA
O'Brien, Peter K. ... New York, NY
O'Brien, Philip J., Jr. ... Newark, NJ
O'Brien, Philip, Jr. ... Holyoke, MA
O'Brien, Philip R. ... Milwaukee, WI
O'Brien, Phillip J. ... Deerfield Beach, FL
O'Brien, Phyllis Klein ... Short Hills, NJ
O'Brien, R. Frances ... Arlington, VA
O'Brien, Rae Ann ... Brookline, MA
O'Brien, Raymond A. ... Boston, MA
O'Brien, Raymond C. ... Washington, DC
O'Brien, Raymond D. ... Union, NJ
O'Brien, Rhonda A. ... St. Louis, MO
O'Brien, Richard D. M. ... Honolulu, HI
O'Brien, Richard E. ... Lambertville, MI
O'Brien, Richard E. ... New York, NY
O'Brien, Richard F., III ... South Miami, FL
O'Brien, Richard F., III ... Salem, NJ
O'Brien, Richard J. ... Auburn, ME
O'Brien, Richard J. ... Pittsfield, MA
O'Brien, Richard J., Jr. ... Chicago, IL
O'Brien, Richard J., Jr. ... Omaha, NE
O'Brien, Richard M. ... Chicago, IL
O'Brien, Richard W. ... New York, NY
O'Brien, Riemenschneider & Kancilia, P.A.
Melbourne, FL
O'Brien, Robert A. ... American Canyon, CA
O'Brien, Robert C. ... Greenwich, CT
O'Brien, Robert C., Jr. ... Los Angeles, CA
O'Brien, Robert D. ... Lemoyne, PA
O'Brien, Robert E.
Department Of Veterans Affairs, Board of Veterans Appeals, GV
O'Brien, Robert F. ... Cherry Hill, NJ
Northfield, NJ
Media, PA
O'Brien, Robert G. ... Dublin, OH
O'Brien, Robert H. ... Los Angeles, CA
O'Brien, Robert J. ... Hartford, CT
O'Brien, Robert J. ... New Haven, CT
O'Brien, Robert L. ... St. Paul, MN
O'Brien, Robert L. ... Carlisle, PA
O'Brien, Robert L., Jr. ... Atlanta, GA
O'Brien, Robert M. ... New York, NY
O'Brien, Robert P. ... Baltimore, MD
O'Brien, Robert P. ... Jericho, NY
O'Brien, Robert P., & Associates, P.C.
Jericho, NY
O'Brien, Robert P. O'Flynn
Wilmington, DE
O'Brien, Robert Terence ... Columbus, OH
O'Brien, Robert V., Jr. ... Portland, OR
O'Brien, Robert W. ... Valley Stream, NY
O'Brien, Roberta A. ... Hartford, CT
O'Brien, Robin Lynn ... Cedar Rapids, IA
O'Brien, Ronald J. ... Columbus, OH
O'Brien, Ronan Peter ... Newton, MA
O'Brien, Rondolyn R. ... Albuquerque, NM
O'Brien, Rosalie Wacker ... St. Louis, MO
O'Brien, Rulis and Bochicchio, LLC
Pittsburgh, PA
O'Brien, Russell L. ... Louisville, KY
O Brien, Ruth D. ... Harrisburg, PA
O'Brien, Ruth R. ... Boston, MA
O'Brien & Ryan, LLP ... Philadelphia, PA
Plymouth Meeting, PA
O'Brien, Saml. D. ... San Jose, CA
O'Brien, Saml. L. ... Alliance, NE
O'Brien, Samuel G. ... Des Moines, IA
O'Brien, Sandra MacGregor
Burlington, MA
O'Brien, Sandra Tremper ... Louisville, KY
O'Brien, Sarah B. ... Madison, WI
O'Brien, Scot Patrick ... Miami, FL
O'Brien, Scot W. ... Dallas, TX
O'Brien, Scott C. ... Petaluma, CA
O'Brien, Sean A. ... Costa Mesa, CA
O'Brien, Sean D. ... Kansas City, MO
O'Brien, Sean J. ... Reading, PA
O'Brien, Sean M. ... Des Moines, IA
O'Brien, Sean M. ... Brookings, SD
O'Brien, Sean P. ... Phoenix, AZ
O'Brien, Sean R. ... New York, NY
O'Brien, Sean W. ... Washington, DC
O'Brien, Shafner, Stuart, Kelly & Morris, P.C. ... Groton, CT
New London, CT
Norwich, CT
O'Brien, Sharon K. ... Sacramento, CA
O'Brien, Sharon Kelly ... Piscataway, NJ
O'Brien, Sharon M. ... Boston, MA
O'Brien, Shaun Healy ... Indianapolis, IN
O'Brien, Shawn R. ... Houston, TX
O'Brien, Signe B. ... Pittsburgh, PA
O'Brien, Stephanie Monaghan ... Newton, MA
O'Brien, Stephen C. ... Cherry Hill, NJ
Spring Lake Heights, NJ
O'Brien, Stephen J. ... Fairfield, CT
O'Brien, Stephen J. ... St. Louis, MO
O'Brien, Stephen J. ... Fairfax, VA
O'Brien, Stephen M. ... Clayton, MO
O'Brien, Stephen M., III ... Lexington, KY
O'Brien, Stephen R. ... Minneapolis, MN
O'Brien, Steven D. ... Lincoln, NE
O'Brien, Steven M. ... Cambridge, MA
O'Brien, Sullivan & Jensen
Walnut Creek, CA
O'Brien, Susan ... Rockford, IL
O'Brien, Susan R. ... Ventura, CA
O'Brien, Suzanne M. ... King Of Prussia, PA
O'Brien, Syndi S. ... Denver, CO
O'Brien, T. Michael, Jr. ... Oak Brook, IL
O'Brien, Tamara A. ... Akron, OH
O'Brien, Tamara Hayes ... Milwaukee, WI
O'Brien, Tanski & Young ... Hartford, CT
O'Brien and Taylor ... West Caldwell, NJ
O'Brien, Terence ... New York, NY
O'Brien, Terence K. ... Sacramento, CA
O'Brien, Terence K. ... Cleveland, OH
O'Brien, Teresa A. ... Sioux City, IA
O'Brien, Teri S. ... La Grange, IL
O'Brien, Terrence G. ... New Orleans, LA
O'Brien, Terrence L. ... Gillette, WY
O'Brien, Terrence M. ... Pittsburgh, PA
O'Brien, Terrence P. ... St. Paul, MN
O'Brien, Theodore H., Jr. ... Milton, MA
O'Brien, Theodore M. ... Miramar, FL
O'Brien, Theresa A. ... Huntsville, TX
O'Brien, Theresa B. ... Pittsburgh, PA
O'Brien, Thomas B., Jr. ... Philadelphia, PA
O'Brien, Thomas C. ... Chicago, IL
O'Brien, Thomas C. ... Ann Arbor, MI
O'Brien, Thomas C. ... Corning, NY
O'Brien, Thomas E. ... Toms River, NJ
O'Brien, Thomas E. ... Williamsville, NY
O'Brien, Thomas G. ... New Orleans, LA
Houston, TX
O'Brien, Thomas G., III
West Palm Beach, FL
O'Brien, Thomas I. ... New York, NY
O'Brien, Thomas J. ... South Bethany, DE
O'Brien, Thomas J. ... Washington, DC
O'Brien, Thomas J. ... Chicago, IL
O'Brien, Thomas J. ... Danville, IN
O'Brien, Thomas J. ... Lafayette, IN
O'Brien, Thomas J. ... Raytown, MO
O'Brien, Thomas J. ... Philadelphia, PA
O'Brien, Thomas J. ... Hudson, WI
O'Brien, Thomas J. ... Milwaukee, WI
O'Brien, Thomas M. ... Waterbury, CT
O'Brien, Thomas M. ... Coral Springs, FL
O'Brien, Thomas M. ... Chicago, IL
O'Brien, Thomas M. ... Lawrenceville, NJ
O'Brien, Thomas M. ... New York, NY
O'Brien, Thomas P., III ... Louisville, KY
O'Brien, Thomas P., Jr. ... Cincinnati, OH
O'Brien, Thomas R. ... Clinton, NJ
O'Brien, Thomas S. ... Hackensack, NJ
O'Brien, Thomas W. ... Milwaukee, WI
O'Brien, Timothy A., III ... Washington, DC
O'Brien, Timothy C. ... Chicago, IL
O'Brien, Timothy F. ... Cleveland, OH
O'Brien, Timothy F., Jr.
Newport Beach, CA
O'Brien, Timothy J. ... Chicago, IL
O'Brien, Timothy J. ... Portland, ME
O'Brien, Timothy J. ... Omaha, NE
O'Brien, Timothy J. ... Baldwin, WI
O'Brien, Timothy M. ... Overland Park, KS
O'Brien, Timothy M. ... Minneapolis, MN
O'Brien, Timothy Michael ... Savannah, GA
O'Brien, Timothy P. ... Greenbelt, MD
O'Brien, Timothy P. ... Haddonfield, NJ
O'Brien, Timothy W. ... Ukiah, CA
O'Brien, Todd W. ... Portland, OR
O'Brien, Victoria Klekamp
Department of Justice, Office of Justice Programs, GV
O'Brien, Vincent ... Miami, FL
O'Brien, Vincent A. ... Tampa, FL
O'Brien, Vincent J. ... Dover, MA
O'Brien, Vincent M. ... San Carlos, CA
O'Brien, W. Mark ... Saddle Brook, NJ
O'Brien, Walter F. ... Roseville, CA
O'Brien, Walter J., II
Oakbrook Terrace, IL
O'Brien, Walter P.
Department Of Health And Human Services, Social Security Administration, GV
O'Brien, Warren J. ... Longboat Key, FL
O'Brien Watters & Davis, LLP
Santa Rosa, CA
O'Brien, William A. "Rob"
Martinsburg, WV
O'Brien, William C., Jr. ... Haddonfield, NJ
O'Brien, William D. ... Boston, MA
O'Brien, William D. ... Irving, TX
O'Brien, William E. ... New York, NY
O'Brien, William F. ... Cincinnati, OH
O'Brien, William F., III ... Wampsville, NY
O'Brien, William F., Jr. ... New York, NY
O'Brien, William H. ... Detroit, MI
O'Brien, William H. ... New York, NY
O'Brien, William J. ... Los Angeles, CA
O'Brien, William J.
Department Of Health And Human Services, Social Security Administration, GV
O'Brien, William J. ... Minneapolis, MN
O'Brien, William J. ... Mineola, NY
O'Brien, William J. ... New York, NY
O'Brien, William J. ... New York, NY
O'Brien, William J. ... Sag Harbor, NY
O'Brien, William J. ... Cleveland, OH
O'Brien, William J. ... Philadelphia, PA
O'Brien, William J. Co., L.P.A.
Cleveland, OH
O'Brien, William J., II ... Washington, DC
O'Brien, William J., II ... Philadelphia, PA
O'Brien, William J., III ... Highland Park, MI
O'Brien, William J., III ... New York, NY
O'Brien, William J., Jr. ... Stow, MA
O'Brien, William J., Jr. ... Warwick, RI
O'Brien, William K. ... San Francisco, CA
O'Brien, William M. ... Boston, MA
O'Brien, William M. ... Cambridge, MA
O'Brien, William M. ... Winooski, VT
O'Brien, William P. ... Louisville, KY
O'Brien, William R. ... Washington, DC
O'Brien, William R. "Buster"
Virginia Beach, VA
O'Brien, William Scott ... Oklahoma City, OK
O'Brien, William T. ... Washington, DC
O'Brien, William T. ... Chicago, IL
O'Brien, Wm. J. ... White Plains, NY
O'Brien-Crum, Catherine ... Glendale, CO
O'Brien-Firack, Sheila E. ... Columbus, OH
O'Brien-Heinzen, M. Tess ... Madison, WI
O'Brien-Holcomb, Diane J.
United States Court Of Appeals District Of Columbia Circuit, GV
O'Brien-Reyes, Sharon A. ... Mesa, AZ
O'Brien-Reyes, Sharon A., P.C. ... Mesa, AZ
O'Brien Shepherd, Brigid
Indianapolis, IN
Obrig, Elwood M. ... Fort Lauderdale, FL
O'Brine, George T. ... Salem, MA
Obringer, Dave ... Chapel Hill, NC
Obringer, Michael J. ... Jacksonville, FL
Obringer, Robert A. ... Detroit, MI
Obringer, Timothy R. ... Cleveland, OH
OBrion, John H., Jr. ... Richmond, VA
Obritsch, Diane ... Las Vegas, NV
Obrokta, Thomas J., Jr. ... Huntington, WV
Obront, Curt D. ... Miami, FL
O'Bryan, Ann Whitford ... Menlo Park, CA
O'Bryan, Berton W. ... Indianapolis, IN
O'Bryan, Brazill & Drics, LLP
Indianapolis, IN
O'Bryan, Brown & Toner ... Fort Knox, KY
Lexington, KY
Louisville, KY
Pikeville, KY
O'Bryan, Christopher P. ... Louisville, KY
O'Bryan, D. Michael ... Birmingham, MI
O'Bryan, D. Wayne ... Norfolk, VA
O'Bryan, Daniel W. ... Columbus, OH
O'Bryan and Denbow ... Shively, KY
O'Bryan, George R. ... Shively, KY
O'Bryan, Henry R. ... Troy, NY
O'Bryan, J. D., Jr. ... Kingstree, SC
O'Bryan, John M. ... Chicago, IL
O'Bryan, John R. (Jack) ... Lafayette, IN
O'Bryan, Joseph C. ... Louisville, KY
O'Bryan, Joseph H. ... Cabot, AR
O'Bryan Law Center, P.C. ... Birmingham, MI
O'Bryan, Michael G. ... San Francisco, CA
O'Bryan, Michelle M. ... Shively, KY
O'Bryan & O'Bryan ... Kingstree, SC
O'Bryan, Patrick W. ... Des Moines, IA
O'Bryan, Rachel C. ... Denver, CO
O'Bryan, Rory ... Carmel, IN
Indianapolis, IN
O'Bryan, Sean Paul ... Lapeer, MI
O'Bryan, Sean Paul ... Metamora, MI
O'Bryan, Sean T. ... San Diego, CA
O'Bryan, Sheila M. ... Indianapolis, IN
O'Bryan, Stephen M. ... Cleveland, OH
O'Bryan, W. Howard, Jr.
Oklahoma City, OK
O'Bryan, William M. ... Fort Lauderdale, FL
O'Bryan, William M., Jr. ... Kingstree, SC
O'Bryan, William R., Jr. ... Nashville, TN
O'Bryant, Ann Graham ... Washington, DC
O'Bryant, David W. ... Salt Lake City, UT
O'Bryant, Jeffrey A. ... Fairbanks, AK
O'Bryant, Michael T. ... Washington, DC
Silver Spring, MD
O'Bryant, Ramona Cunningham
Greensboro, NC
O'Bryant, Theresa M. ... Roxbury, MA
O'Bryon, Kevin Cramer
New Orleans, LA
O'Bryon, Laurie E. ... Washington, DC
O'Bryon, Maureen ... Washington, DC
Obrzut, Ted ... Los Angeles, CA
Obsitnik, Cristin M. ... Chicago, IL
Obssuth, Raymond K. ... Wayne, NJ
Obst, Anthony K. ... New York, NY
Obstarczyk, Patricia A. ... Rochester, NY
Obstbaum, Merilee ... New York, NY
Obstfeld, Harold B. ... New York, NY
Obstler, Edward E. ... Baltimore, MD
Obstler, Harold ... Old Lyme, CT
Obstler, Mimi ... Old Lyme, CT
Obstler, Peter ... San Francisco, CA
Obten, J. Martin ... New York, NY
Obten, J. Martin, P.C. ... New York, NY
Obuch, Richard ... Elizabeth, NJ
Obuchowski Law Office ... Bethel, VT
Obuchowski, Raymond J. ... Bethel, VT
Obuhanych, Daniel Ko ... Honolulu, HI
Obus, Leslie J. ... New York, NY
Obus, Michael J. ... New York, NY
Obus, Steven E. ... New York, NY
Obut, Barry ... Teaneck, NJ
Oby, Matthew W. ... Akron, OH
O'Byrne, Christopher L.
Port Washington, WI
O'Byrne, Deirdre G. ... New York, NY
O'Byrne, Edward G. ... Totowa, NJ
O'Byrne, Francis J., Jr. ... Chicago, IL
O'Byrne, Francis J., Sr. ... Chicago, IL
O'Byrne, J. Michael ... Champaign, IL
O'Byrne, Joan de R. ... Rochester, NY
O'Byrne, John D. ... New York, NY
O'Byrne, Mary E. ... Sunnyvale, CA
O'Byrne, Stephen F. ... Chicago, IL
O'Byrne, Stephen M. ... Champaign, IL
O'Byrne, Sylvester G. ... New York, NY
O'Byrne, T. Leonard ... Portland, OR
O'Byrne, William F. ... San Anselmo, CA
Obzud, John M. ... Baltimore, MD
O'Cadiz, Sergio A. ... Department of Justice, Executive Office for Immigration Review, GV
O'Cain, Patrick J. ... New Orleans, LA
O'Callaghan & Associates
Los Angeles, CA

O'Connell & O'Connell ... Falls Church, VA
O'Connell, Patricia L. ... Springfield, MA
O'Connell, Patricia Mary ... Seattle, WA
O'Connell, Patrick J. ... South Bend, IN
O'Connell, Patrick J. ... Minneapolis, MN
O'Connell, Patrick J. ... Austin, TX
O'Connell, Patrick T. ... Wilkes-Barre, PA
O'Connell, Paul D. ... Fort Lauderdale, FL
O'Connell, Paul F. ... Gaylord, MI
O'Connell, Paul R., Jr. ... Millbury, MA
O'Connell, Paul V. ... Largo, FL
St. Petersburg, FL
O'Connell, Peter B. ... Bridgeport, CT
Westport, CT
O'Connell, Peter D. ... Washington, DC
O'Connell, Phil D., Jr., (P.A.)
West Palm Beach, FL
O'Connell, Philip A. ... Boston, MA
O'Connell, Philip A., Jr.
San Francisco, CA
O'Connell, Philip D., Jr. ... Auburn, MA
O'Connell, Philip J. ... St. Petersburg, FL
O'Connell, Philip J. ... Missoula, MT
O'Connell, Philip L. ... Bethesda, MD
O'Connell, Philip R. ... Southport, CT
O'Connell, Phyllis R. ... Waynesville, NC
O'Connell, Quinn ... Bethesda, MD
O'Connell, R. Sean ... Pittsburgh, PA
O'Connell, Richard E. ... Flushing, NY
O'Connell, Richard P. ... Quincy, IL
O'Connell, Richard P., Ltd. ... Quincy, IL
O'Connell, Richard T. ... Old Saybrook, CT
O'Connell, Richard T. ... Port Chester, NY
O'Connell, Richard T. ... Rye Brook, NY
O'Connell & Riley ... Montvale, NJ
Pearl River, NY
O'Connell, Robert A. ... Brighton, MA
O'Connell, Robert E. ... Boca Raton, FL
O'Connell, Robert E. ... Sioux City, IA
O'Connell, Robert E., Jr. ... Augusta, ME
O'Connell, Robert F. ... Boston, MA
O'Connell, Robert F. ... Rochester, NY
O'Connell, Robert J. ... Sacramento, CA
O'Connell, Robert John ... Atlanta, GA
O'Connell, Robert John ... New City, NY
O'Connell, Robert Joseph
New Providence, NJ
O'Connell, Robert L. ... Pontiac, MI
O'Connell, Robert L. ... Clarence, NY
O'Connell, Robert M., Jr. ... Boston, MA
O'Connell, Robert M., P.C. ... Chicago, IL
O'Connell, Robert S. ... Boston, MA
O'Connell & Robinson, LLP ... Austin, TX
O'Connell & Ryan ... Chicago, IL
O'Connell, Sean ... Pleasanton, CA
O'Connell, Sean T. ... Concord, NH
O'Connell, Sean V. ... Oklahoma City, OK
O'Connell, Sharon ... Quincy, IL
O'Connell, Shaun P. ... Taunton, MA
O'Connell & Silvis ... Greensburg, PA
O'Connell, Stephen ... White Plains, NY
O'Connell, Stephen B. ... Austin, TX
O'Connell, Stephen C. ... Tallahassee, FL
O'Connell, Stephen W. ... New York, NY
O'Connell, Susan L. ... Alexandria, VA
O'Connell, Susan Lee
Federal Communications Commission, International Bureau, GV
O'Connell, T. Joseph ... Worcester, MA
O'Connell, Terence J. ... Rockville, MD
O'Connell, Terrance ... New City, NY
O'Connell, Theresa Aurora ... Montclair, NJ
O'Connell, Thomas F. ... Montvale, NJ
Pearl River, NY
O'Connell, Thomas F. ... Wenatchee, WA
O'Connell, Thomas F., III ... Houston, TX
O'Connell, Thomas J. ... Washington, DC
O'Connell, Thomas J. ... Wilmington, NC
O'Connell, Thomas J. ... Columbus, OH
O'Connell, Thomas Michael ... Chicago, IL
O'Connell, Thomas R. ... St. Paul, MN
O'Connell, Thomas W. ... Rochester, NY
O'Connell, Thomas W. ... Philadelphia, PA
O'Connell, Thos. G. ... Palm City, FL
O'Connell, Timothy C. ... Linthicum, MD
O'Connell, Timothy G. ... Buffalo, NY
O'Connell, Timothy J. ... Indianapolis, IN
O'Connell, Timothy J. ... Harrisburg, PA
O'Connell, Timothy J. ... Seattle, WA
O'Connell, Timothy L. ... San Diego, CA
O'Connell, Timothy N. ... Dayton, OH
O'Connell, Timothy P. ... Charlestown, MA
O'Connell, Tom ... Plano, TX
O'Connell, Tracy Cullen ... Savannah, GA
O'Connell, Van Shellenbeck & Land
Austin, TX
O'Connell, Virginia M. ... New York, NY
O'Connell, William A. ... Walnut Creek, CA
O'Connell, William B., Jr. ... Arlington, VA
O'Connell, William C. ... Newport, RI
O'Connell, William Henry, Jr. ... Boston, MA
O'Connell, William J. ... Oak Brook, IL
O'Connell, William J., Jr. ... Boston, MA
O'Connell, William M., III ... Rockledge, PA
O'Connell, William P., Jr.
San Francisco, CA
O'Connell, William T. ... New York, NY
O'Connell-Burton, Kathleen ... Aurora, OH
O'Connell Clinton, Elizabeth
New Orleans, LA
O'Conner, Adele E. ... Columbus, OH
O'Conner, James V. ... Seattle, WA
O'Conner, Loretta R ... Pueblo, CO
O'Connor, A. Ashley ... Boulder, CO
O'Connor & Acciani ... Cincinnati, OH
O'Connor, Adina C. ... Brook Park, OH
O'Connor, Aidan P. ... Newark, NJ
O'Connor, Ailish C. ... Jacksonville, FL
O'Connor, Alan E. ... Merrillville, IN
O'Connor, Alan M. ... Los Angeles, CA
O'Connor, Amy S. ... Albany, NY
O'Connor, Ana M. ... Oakland, CA
O'Connor, Andrea B. ... Simsbury, CT
O'Connor, Andrew S. ... New York, NY
O'Connor, Ann ... Lawrence, MA
O'Connor, Ann Balmelli ... Boston, MA
O'Connor, Anna R. ... Basking Ridge, NJ
O'Connor, Anne L. ... Worcester, MA
O'Connor, Anthony D. ... St. Louis, MO
O'Connor, Anthony M., Jr. ... Dallas, TX
O'Connor, Arthur C. ... Medford, MA
O'Connor, Arthur E. ... Houston, TX
O'Connor & Associates ... Boston, MA
O'Connor & Associates, P.C.
Englewood, CO
O'Connor, B. Dennis ... Trenton, NJ
O'Connor, Barbara E. ... Washington, DC
O'Connor, Barbara Jean ... New York, NY
O'Connor, Barry E. ... Springfield, MA
O'Connor, Barry L. ... Riverside, CA
O'Connor, Basil F. ... Morristown, NJ
O'Connor and Bergmann ... New York, NY
O'Connor, Berman, Dotts & Banes, Law Offices of ... Saipan, TT
O'Connor, Bernard E., Jr. ... Torrance, CA
O'Connor, Bernard E., Jr., A Law Corporation ... Los Angeles, CA
Torrance, CA
O'Connor, Bernard G. ... Philadelphia, PA
O'Connor, Bernard T. ... Springfield, MA
O'Connor, Beth A. ... Chicago, IL
O'Connor, Beth Anne Dorsey ... Hudson, NY
O'Connor, Blair T. ... Department of the Army, U.S. Army Legal Services Agency, GV
O'Connor, Bonnie T. ... Buffalo, NY
O'Connor, Brian E. ... New York, NY
O'Connor, Brian F. ... Battle Creek, MI
O'Connor, Brian J. ... Sacramento, CA
O'Connor, Brian J. ... Baltimore, MD
O'Connor, Brian M. ... Washington, DC
Alexandria, VA
Arlington, VA
Fairfax, VA
Falls Church, VA
O'Connor, Brian M. ... Reston, VA
O'Connor, Brian P. ... Rochester, NY
O'Connor, Brian T. ... Stamford, CT
O'Connor, Brian T. ... Chicago, IL
O'Connor, Bridget ... Washington, DC
O'Connor, Brien T. ... Boston, MA
O'Connor, Bruce E. ... Seattle, WA
O'Connor & Brungard ... Koror, TT
O'Connor, Bryan J., III ... Chicago, IL
O'Connor, Bryan P. ... Cleveland, OH
O'Connor, Carey Anne ... Dallas, TX
O'Connor, Carolyn Flanagan ... Newark, NJ
O'Connor, Carrie ... Fullerton, CA
O'Connor, Carrie ... Le Mars, IA
O'Connor, Carroll A. ... Springfield, MA
O'Connor, Catherine ... Kennebunk, ME
O'Connor, Catherine Dugan
Stamford, CT
O'Connor, Cavanagh, Anderson, Killingsworth & Beshears, A Professional Association ... Phoenix, AZ
Sun City, AZ
O'Connor, Cecile
Department of Transportation, Federal Aviation Administration, GV
O'Connor, Cecilia M. ... Philadelphia, PA
O'Connor, Charles A., III
Washington, DC
O'Connor, Charles D. ... Shelbyville, IN
O'Connor, Charles E. ... Philadelphia, PA
O'Connor, Charles Edward, Jr.
Philadelphia, PA
O'Connor, Charles J. ... Brandon, FL
O'Connor, Charles J. ... Chicago, IL
O'Connor, Charles M. ... San Francisco, CA
O'Connor, Charles P. ... Washington, DC
O'Connor, Cheryl ... Santa Fe, NM
O'Connor, Christian ... McLean, VA
O'Connor, Christine A. ... Sandwich, MA
O'Connor, Christine Barrett
Washington, DC
O'Connor, Christopher J. ... Providence, RI
O'Connor, Cindy A. ... Andover, MA
O'Connor, Clarence J. ... Brightwaters, NY
O'Connor, Clarence P. ... Kaukauna, WI
O'Connor, Cohn, Dillon & Barr, A Law Corporation ... San Francisco, CA
O'Connor, Colin ... Redondo Beach, CA
O'Connor, Colleen A. ... Dallas, TX
O'Connor, Colleen E. ... Seattle, WA
O'Connor, Colleen P. ... Detroit, MI
O'Connor, Cornelius J. ... Bensenville, IL
O'Connor, Cornelius J., Jr. ... Albany, NY
O'Connor, Craig R.
Department of Commerce, National Oceanic and Atmospheric Administration, GV
O'Connor, Craig S. ... Pittsburgh, PA
O'Connor, Craig V. ... Morristown, NJ
O'Connor, D. Fredk. ... Manchester, NH
O'Connor, Damian J. ... Bethesda, MD
O'Connor, Daniel A. ... Larchmont, NY
O'Connor, Daniel Alan ... Pittsburgh, PA
O'Connor, Daniel E. ... Menlo Park, CA
O'Connor, Daniel J. ... Phoenix, AZ
O'Connor, Daniel J. ... Danville, CA
O'Connor, Daniel J. ... Chicago, IL
O'Connor, Daniel J. ... Brockton, MA
O'Connor, Daniel J. ... Chester, NJ
O'Connor, Daniel M. ... Detroit, MI
O'Connor, Daniel P. ... San Antonio, TX
O'Connor, Daniel P. J.
Fort Lauderdale, FL
O'Connor, Daniel S. ... Grayslake, IL
O'Connor, Daniel V. ... Chicago, IL
O'Connor, Danny B. ... Frederick, MD
O'Connor, Darrin Michael ... Metairie, LA
O'Connor, David A. ... Washington, DC
O'Connor, David C. ... Naples, FL
O'Connor, David E. ... Hartford, CT
O'Connor, David F. P. ... Seattle, WA
O'Connor, David J. ... Weedsport, NY
O'Connor, David M. ... Boston, MA
O'Connor, David M. ... Mequon, WI
O'Connor, David P. ... Philadelphia, PA
O'Connor, David W. ... Wilmington, DE
O'Connor, Davis O. ... Denver, CO
O'Connor, Dean W. ... Phoenix, AZ
O'Connor, Deborah F. ... Kansas City, MO
O'Connor, Deborah L. ... Irvine, CA
O'Connor, Debra L. ... Denver, CO
O'Connor, DeGrazia & Tamm, P.C.
Ann Arbor, MI
Bloomfield Hills, MI
Detroit, MI
O'Connor & Demas, P.C. ... Brick, NJ
Chatham, NJ
Morristown, NJ
O'Connor, Denise ... Hackensack, NJ
White Plains, NY
O'Connor, Denise L. ... New York, NY
O'Connor, Dennis E. W. ... Honolulu, HI
O'Connor, Dennis E. W., Jr. ... Honolulu, HI
O'Connor, Dennis L., Jr.
White Plains, NY
O'Connor, Dennis M. ... Louisville, KY
O'Connor, Dennis P., II
West Hartford, CT
O'Connor, Dennis Patrick
Steamboat Springs, CO
O'Connor, Dennis R. ... Orlando, FL
O'Connor, Diane K. ... Mequon, WI
O'Connor, Donald J. ... Denver, CO
O'Connor, Donald J. ... Cleveland, OH
O'Connor, Donald Joseph, Jr.
Binghamton, NY
O'Connor, Donald L. ... Hoboken, NJ
O'Connor, Donald T. ... New York, NY
O'Connor, Donald T. ... Pittsburgh, PA
O'Connor, Donna A. ... Bloomfield Hills, MI
O'Connor, Douglas M. ... Central Islip, NY
O'Connor, Douglas R. ... San Francisco, CA
O'Connor, Doyle ... Detroit, MI
O'Connor, Duane J. ... Herscher, IL
O'Connor, Duane L. ... Hastings, MI
O'Connor, Earl E. ... Kansas City, KS
O'Connor, Edna M. ... Lakewood, CO
O'Connor, Edward F.
Newport Beach, CA
O'Connor, Edward F. ... Rock Island, IL
O'Connor, Edward G. ... Pittsburgh, PA
O'Connor, Edward J. ... Buffalo, NY
O'Connor, Edward J., Jr.
Camp Springs, MD
O'Connor, Edward T., Jr. ... Jersey City, NJ
O'Connor, Edward V., Jr. ... Fairfax, VA
O'Connor, Edwin M., III ... Lubbock, TX
O'Connor, Eileen C. ... Washington, DC
O'Connor, Eileen M. ... Fort Lauderdale, FL
O'Connor, Elizabeth ... Gloucester, MA
O'Connor, Elizabeth A. ... New York, NY
O'Connor, Elizabeth R. ... Buffalo, NY
O'Connor, Ellen M. ... Indianapolis, IN
O'Connor, Ellen M. ... Worcester, MA
O'Connor, Emily ... Department of State, Office of the Legal Adviser, GV
O'Connor, Emily N. ... Pittsburgh, PA
O'Connor, Erin ... Redondo Beach, CA
O'Connor, Erin Marie ... Vernon Hills, IL
O'Connor, Eugene F. ... New York, NY
O'Connor, Eugene F., II ... Phoenix, AZ
O'Connor, Eugene J., Jr. ... New York, NY
O'Connor, Eugene M. ... Rochester, NY
O'Connor, Eugene P. ... Buffalo, NY
O'Connor, F. William ... Avon, CT
O'Connor, F. William ... Hartford, CT
O'Connor, Frances Magovern ... Roseland, NJ
O'Connor, Francis D.
Fort Lauderdale, FL
O'Connor, Francis J. ... Boston, MA
O'Connor, Francis P. ... Boston, MA
O'Connor, Francis X. ... Great Bend, PA
O'Connor, Frank C., III ... Albany, NY
O'Connor, G. Patrick ... Camp Hill, PA
O'Connor, Gacioch, Pope & Tait, L.L.P.
Binghamton, NY
O'Connor, Gaile ... San Rafael, CA
O'Connor, Gary B. ... Waterbury, CT
O'Connor, Gary E.
Department Of Veterans Affairs, Office of the General Counsel, GV
O'Connor, Gavin M. ... Pittsburgh, PA
O'Connor, Geoffrey J. ... Garden City, NY
O'Connor, George C., Jr.
Federal Energy Regulatory Commission, Office of the General Counsel, GV
O'Connor, George M. ... Topsfield, MA
O'Connor, Gerald B. ... Brick, NJ
Chatham, NJ
O'Connor, Gerald J. ... San Francisco, CA
O'Connor, Gerard E. ... Buffalo, NY
O'Connor, Gerard P. ... Boston, MA
O'Connor, Gregory W. ... Denver, CO
O'Connor & Hannan, L.L.P.
Washington, DC
Vienna, VA
O'Connor, Harry J., Jr. ... Greensboro, NC
O'Connor, Heather Shanan
Baltimore, MD
O'Connor, Heidi Roberts ... Boulder, CO
O'Connor, Henry F., III ... New Orleans, LA
O'Connor, Henry F., Jr. ... New Orleans, LA
New Orleans, LA
O'Connor, Henry, Jr. ... Greenfield, MA
O'Connor, Hilary J. ... Baltimore, MD
O'Connor, J. Fitzgerald, Jr.
Columbia, SC
O'Connor, J. Ford ... Bourne, MA
O'Connor, J. Gregory ... Knoxville, TN
O'Connor, J. Norman ... Adams, MA
O'Connor, J. Norman, Jr. ... Adams, MA
O'Connor, J. Robert, III ... San Diego, CA
O'Connor, J. Robt. ... Coronado, CA
O'Connor, James ... Little Rock, AR
O'Connor, James ... Stamford, CT
O'Connor, James C.
West Conshohocken, PA
O'Connor, James Duffy ... Minneapolis, MN
O'Connor, James E. ... Omaha, NE
O'Connor, James E. ... Annandale, VA
O'Connor, James E. (Jim) ... Washington, DC
O'Connor, James Francis, II
Englewood, CO
O'Connor, James Gavan
Grand Rapids, MI
O'Connor, James H. ... Syracuse, NY
O'Connor, James J. ... Chicago, IL
O'Connor, James J. ... New Orleans, LA
O'Connor, James J. ... Hastings, MN
O'Connor, James J. ... Bloomfield, NJ
O'Connor, James J. ... Philadelphia, PA
O'Connor, James J. ... Scranton, PA
O'Connor, James M. ... Cambridge, MA
O'Connor, James N. ... Seattle, WA
O'Connor, James P. ... Scarsdale, NY
O'Connor, James P. ... Valley Stream, NY
O'Connor, James R. ... Orleans, MA
O'Connor, James S.
Palos Verdes Estates, CA
O'Connor, James W. ... Chicago, IL
O'Connor, Jan ... Columbia, MD
O'Connor, Janet Bohon ... Athens, GA
O'Connor, Jeffrey S. ... Chicago, IL
O'Connor, Jeffrey T. ... Kansas City, MO
O'Connor, Jeffrey W. ... Rock Island, IL
O'Connor, Jennifer J. ... Lakeland, FL
O'Connor, Jennifer L. ... Seattle, WA
O'Connor, Jennifer M. ... Washington, DC
O'Connor, Jill M. ... Danbury, CT
O'Connor, Jo Ellen M. ... Saginaw, MI
O'Connor, Joan E. ... Boston, MA
O'Connor, John A. ... Boston, MA
O'Connor, John A. ... White Plains, NY
O'Connor, John A., Jr. ... Baltimore, MD
O'Connor, John C. ... Naples, FL
O'Connor, John C. ... Dubuque, IA
O'Connor, John Campbell ... Chicago, IL
O'Connor, John Christopher ... Seattle, WA
O'Connor, John D. ... San Francisco, CA
Santa Rosa, CA
O'Connor, John D. ... Pittsburgh, PA
O'Connor, John E. ... Forty Fort, PA
O'Connor, John E., III
Oakbrook Terrace, IL
O'Connor, John F. ... Buffalo, NY
O'Connor, John F., Jr ... Washington, DC
O'Connor, John G. ... Kansas City, KS
O'Connor, John I. ... Pittsburg, KS
O'Connor, John J. ... Thousand Oaks, CA
O'Connor, John J. ... Evanston, IL
O'Connor, John J. ... Geneva, IL
O'Connor, John J. ... Oak Lawn, IL
O'Connor, John J. ... Boston, MA
O'Connor, John J. ... Garden City, NY
O'Connor, John J. ... Manhasset Hills, NY
O'Connor, John J., III ... Phoenix, AZ
Washington, DC
O'Connor, John J., III ... Atlanta, GA
O'Connor, John J., Jr. ... Baltimore, MD
O'Connor, John J., Jr. ... Boston, MA
O'Connor, John J., Jr. ... Bronx, NY
O'Connor, John L. ... Clarkston, GA
O'Connor, John L. ... Spokane, WA
O'Connor, John M. ... Washington, DC
O'Connor, John M. ... Chicago, IL
O'Connor, John M. ... Fitchburg, MA
O'Connor, John M. ... Hackensack, NJ
New York, NY
O'Connor, John M. ... Newark, NJ
O'Connor, John M. ... Tulsa, OK
O'Connor, John Michael
San Francisco, CA
San Jose, CA
O'Connor, John P. ... Blue Jay, CA
O'Connor, John P. ... Cincinnati, OH
O'Connor, John P. ... Cincinnati, OH
O'Connor, John P. ... Providence, RI
O'Connor, John Patrick ... Kansas City, MO
O'Connor, John R. ... Garden City, NY
O'Connor, John R. ... Rochester, NY
O'Connor, John R. ... San Juan, PR
O'Connor, John Robert ... Union, MO
O'Connor, John S. ... Kitty Hawk, NC
O'Connor, John Sladek ... Brooklyn, NY
O'Connor, John T. ... New York, NY
O'Connor, John T., II ... Knoxville, TN
O'Connor, John V. ... Kenosha, WI
O'Connor, Joseph ... Hammond, IN
O'Connor, Joseph A. ... Philadelphia, PA
O'Connor, Joseph A., Jr. ... Philadelphia, PA
O'Connor, Joseph, & Associates
Hammond, IN
O'Connor, Joseph D. ... Bloomington, IN
O'Connor, Joseph E. ... San Diego, CA
O'Connor, Joseph E. ... Kingston, NY
O'Connor, Joseph F. ... Chicago, IL
O'Connor, Joseph J. ... Miller Place, NY

O'Dea, Arthur J. ....Arlington, VT
O'Dea & Associates ....Washington, DC
Lowell, MA
O'Dea, Brian M. ....Oakland, CA
O'Dea, Bruce B. ....Bradenton, FL
O'Dea, Candice Bogie ....Louisville, KY
O'Dea, Dennis M., (P.C.) ....New York, NY
O'Dea, Gregory P. ....Sacramento, CA
O'Dea, James L. ....Oakland, CA
O'Dea, James L., III ....Washington, DC
Lowell, MA
O'Dea, Jeffry ....Houston, TX
O'Dea, Joseph F., Jr. ....Philadelphia, PA
O'Dea, Joseph J. ....Manchester, VT
O'Dea, Joseph J., P.C. ....Manchester, VT
O'Dea, Kathleen K. ....Santa Fe, NM
O'Dea, Kathleen Maureen
Los Angeles, CA
O'Dea, Kevin L. ....New Orleans, LA
O'Dea, Mark P. ....Sacramento, CA
O'Dea, Mary C. ....New York, NY
O'Dea, Mary Jo ....Edina, MN
O'Dea, Patrick F. ....Myrtle Beach, SC
O'Dea, Patrick K. ....Bloomfield Hills, MI
O'Dea, Raymond J. ....Ironwood, MI
O'Dea, Sean W. ....Bothell, WA
O'Dea, Thomas E. ....Annandale, VA
O'Dea, Thomas P., Jr. ....Westport, CT
O'Dea, Timothy J., Jr. ....Louisville, KY
Odean, William C. ....St. Paul, MN
O'Dear, Craig S. ....Kansas City, MO
Odedra, Dhiren R. ....Washington, DC
Odedra, Kaushal R. ....Washington, DC
O'Deen, Kenneth L. ....Charlotte, MI
Odegaard, Douglas N. ....Phoenix, AZ
Odegard, Gregory J. ....El Paso, TX
Odegard, Mark ....Minneapolis, MN
Odegard, Sally A. ....Phoenix, AZ
Odeh, Elaine ....Lisle, IL
Odeku, Lenora F. ....New York, NY
Odell, Andrew L. ....New York, NY
O'Dell, Angela J. ....Oklahoma City, OK
Odell, Barry K. ....Brick, NJ
O'Dell, Christopher C. ....Denver, CO
O'Dell, Christopher L. ....New York, NY
O'Dell, Cynthia Ann ....Charleston, SC
Odell, Daniel Parker ....New York, NY
O'Dell, David B. ....Birmingham, AL
Odell, David M. ....Dallas, TX
O'Dell, Dennis C. ....San Diego, CA
O'Dell, Dennis E. ....Huntsville, AL
O'Dell, Diane Marie ....Virginia Beach, VA
Odell, Donald A. ....Pleasanton, CA
Odell, Donald A. ....Arkville, NY
O'Dell, Donald B. ....Huntington, WV
O'Dell, Donald E. ....Tulsa, OK
O'Dell, Donald L. ....Orlando, FL
O'Dell, Donald R. ....Lowell, IN
Odell, Donald W. ....Lone Pine, CA
O'Dell, Edward T., (P.C.) ....Boston, MA
Odell, Elizabeth D. ....St. Louis, MO
Odell, Frederick W. ....Wethersfield, CT
Odell, Gabriela Beatrice ....Livermore, CA
O'Dell, Harold G., Jr. ....Indianapolis, IN
Odell, Harris, Jr ....Savannah, GA
Odell, Herbert ....Bala Cynwyd, PA
O'Dell, H. J., Jr. ....Lexington, KY
Odell, James ....New York, NY
Odell, James Nellis ....Oakland, CA
Odell, James R. ....Lexington, KY
Odell, James R., P.S.C. ....Lexington, KY
Odell, Joan E. ....Lantana, FL
Odell, Jody H. ....South Bend, IN
O'Dell, John ....Lookout Mountain, GA
Odell, Jonathan C. ....Washington, DC
Odell, Kenneth A. ....Piedmont, CA
Odell, Kevin D. ....White Plains, NY
Odell, Kevin J. ....Hayward, CA
O'Dell, LaVerne F. ....Syracuse, NY
Odell, Lawrence ....San Juan, PR
O'Dell, L. W. ....Charleston, WV
Odell, Marilyn K. ....Eugene, OR
O'Dell, Michael E. ....Fort Payne, AL
O'Dell, Michael L. ....Bakersfield, CA
O'Dell, P. Leigh ....Colorado Springs, CO
Odell & Partners LLP ....Bala Cynwyd, PA
Philadelphia, PA
Odell, Paul M. ....Chicago, IL
O'Dell, Richard A. ....Chicago, IL
O'Dell, Robert B. ....Bloomington, IL
Odell, Robert B., Jr. ....Costa Mesa, CA
O'Dell, Robert E. ....Pascagoula, MS
Odell, Robert J. ....New York, NY
O'Dell, Robert S. ....Indianapolis, IN
Odell, Robert S., Jr. ....Palo Alto, CA
O'Dell, Robert W. ....Camas, WA
O'Dell, Sean M. ....Encino, CA
O'Dell, Sherilyn L. ....Irvine, CA
O'Dell, Stanley R. ....Flagstaff, AZ
Odell, Stephen J. ....Irvine, CA
O'Dell, Stephen P. ....Santa Ana, CA
Odell, Steven R. ....Riverside, CA
Santa Ana, CA
Odell, Timothy B. ....Everett, WA
O'Dell, Tony L. ....Charleston, WV
O'Dell, Veronica Carrozza
Glens Falls, NY
O'Dell, William A. ....Rome, GA
Odell, William D. ....Denver, CO
Odell, William G. ....Denver, CO
Odell-Gonzalez, Jennifer ....San Juan, PR
Odelson, Ann ....New York, NY
Odelson, Burton S. ....Evergreen Park, IL
Odem, Dennis N. ....Florence, AL
Odems, Sheryl A. ....New Orleans, LA
Oden, David H. ....Dallas, TX
Oden, Debra Hall ....Springfield, MO
Oden, Dennis ....Klamath Falls, OR

Oden, Edward K. ....Charlotte, NC
Oden, James C. ....Dallas, TX
Oden, Jon Marshall ....Orlando, FL
Oden, Jon T. ....Amarillo, TX
Odén, Joshua P., III ....Dallas, TX
Oden, Kenneth, Jr. ....Alice, TX
Oden, Kiyo D. ....Washington, DC
Oden, Lane D. ....Tucson, AZ
Oden, Layne R. ....Hughesville, PA
Oden, Natasha B. ....San Francisco, CA
Oden, Paul W., P.C. ....Seattle, WA
Oden, Sherry L. ....Oklahoma City, OK
Oden, Stephen ....Texarkana, TX
Oden, Walter M. ....Norfolk, VA
Oden, Wm. K., Jr. ....Greensboro, NC
Oden, W. T. (Tal), Jr. ....Altus, OK
Odenbrett, Harvey G. ....Milwaukee, WI
Odenbrett, Stacia A. ....Seaside, CA
Odence-Ford, Marion K. ....Boston, MA
Odendahl, John H. ....Los Angeles, CA
Newport Beach, CA
Odeneal, Logan ....Dallas, TX
Odeneal & Odeneal ....Dallas, TX
Odeneal, William C., Jr. ....Dallas, TX
Odenheimer, Shari J.
West Conshohocken, PA
Oden-Orr, Melvin D. ....Portland, OR
O'Dens, David M. ....Dallas, TX
Odensky, Lawrence I. ....Houston, TX
Odenthal, Grover T. ....Watkins Glen, NY
Odenwald, Kathrine ....Southfield, MI
Odenwald, Kurt S. ....St. Louis, MO
Odenwald, Paul W. ....New Orleans, LA
Odenweller, Fabrega & Hood, L.L.P.
Houston, TX
Odenweller, Keith H. ....Houston, TX
Oder, John Wayne ....Upland, CA
Oderberg, Simon W. ....Fort Worth, TX
Oderkirk, David P. ....Waterloo, IA
Oderman, Jeffrey M., (P.C.)
Costa Mesa, CA
Odermatt, Albert C. ....Pittsburgh, PA
O'Dess, M. Abigail ....Milwaukee, WI
Odesser, Edward H. ....White Plains, NY
Odessey, Edward B. ....Boise, ID
Odessky, Neil ....North Miami Beach, FL
Odette, Christopher R. ....Grand Blanc, MI
Odette, Kylee D. ....Costa Mesa, CA
Odette Law Firm, The, P.C.
Birmingham, MI
Odette, Michael James ....Birmingham, MI
Odette, Michael L. ....Clarkston, MI
Odgers, Richard W. ....San Francisco, CA
Odgers, Stephen L. ....Claremont, CA
Odgers, Stephen L., P.C. ....Claremont, CA
Odgers, Vincent E. ....Tucson, AZ
Odiaga, Neni ....Cambridge, MA
Odiaga, Ursula M.
Department of Commerce,
Office of the General Counsel, GV
O'Diam, Thomas M. ....Beavercreek, OH
Dayton, OH
O'Diam, Turner, McNamee, Hill & Stone, A
Legal Professional Assn. ....Dayton, OH
Beavercreek, OH
Odian, Bedros ....Buffalo, NY
Odierna & Beaumier ....Springfield, MA
Odierna, John A. ....Springfield, MA
Odierna, Lori K. ....Springfield, MA
Odierno, Joseph J. ....Melville, NY
Odierno, Lori Wentworth ....New York, NY
Odin, Dexter S. ....Fairfax, VA
Odin, Feldman & Pittleman, P.C.
Fairfax, VA
Odin, Rita M. ....Washington, DC
Odinga, John H. ....Mount Clemens, MI
Odinkemere, E. Nkem ....Irvington, NJ
Odintz, Joshua D. ....Novato, CA
Odio, Guillermo A. ....Bethesda, MD
Odiorne, Alice Quinn ....Austin, TX
Odiorne, Anthony C. ....Wichita Falls, TX
Odiorne, James T. ....Olympia, WA
Odioso, Michael M. ....Cincinnati, OH
Odita, Florence C. Uwandu ....Columbus, OH
Odjakjian, Karnick ....North Plainfield, NJ
Odland, Edwin M. ....Crookston, MN
Odland, Fitzgerald, Reynolds & Remick
Crookston, MN
Odland, James M. ....Minneapolis, MN
Odland, O. Harold ....Minneapolis, MN
Odland, Omar S. ....Chicago, IL
Odlaug, Bruce G. ....Minneapolis, MN
Odlaug, David J. ....St. Paul, MN
Odle, Bob Glen ....Washington, DC
Odle, Cynthia M. ....Nashville, TN
Odle, Kathleen A. ....Denver, CO
Odle, Lloyd D. ....Lewisville, TX
Odle, Robert C., Jr. ....Washington, DC
Odle, Robert P. ....Durango, CO
Odle, William C. ....Kansas City, MO
Odlum, James A. ....San Bernardino, CA
Odlum, Peter F. ....Hartford, CT
Odneal, Roger D. ....Kansas City, MO
Odo, Lyle Louis ....Platte City, MO
O'Doherty, David J. ....Lincoln, NE
O'Doherty, Dennis D., Jr. ....Sayville, NY
O'Doherty, F. X. Sean
Rancho Cucamonga, CA
O'Doherty, Kieran ....House of Representatives,
Committee on Post Office & Civil Service,
GV
O'Doherty, Marianne ....Simsbury, CT
O'Doherty, Patrick A. ....Baltimore, MD
Odom, Benjamin H. ....Norman, OK
Odom, Bob D. ....Belton, TX
Odom, Bobby Lee ....Fayetteville, AR
Odom, Bradley S. ....Pensacola, FL

Odom & Carp, A Professional Corporation
Houston, TX
Sealy, TX
Odom, Christine Carlisle ....Raleigh, NC
Odom, Clint E.
Federal Communications Commission,
Cable Services Bureau, GV
Odom, Conrad T. ....Fayetteville, AR
Odom, David E. ....Atlanta, GA
Odom, David T. ....Chicago, IL
Odom, David T., & Associates, P.C.
Chicago, IL
Odom & Des Roches, LLP ....Hahira, GA
Savannah, GA
Valdosta, GA
New Orleans, LA
Odom, Donald R. ....Tampa, FL
Odom, Edward E., Jr. ....Bethesda, MD
Odom, Elizabeth Ann ....Amory, MS
Odom & Elliott ....Fayetteville, AR
Odom, F. Perry ....Tallahassee, FL
Odom, Frank K. ....Greenwood, MS
Odom, G. Scott ....Dallas, TX
Odom, Gary R. ....Los Angeles, CA
Odom & Groves, P.C. ....Charlotte, NC
Odom, H. Edward ....
Department of State, GV
Odom, H. Parnell ....Newnan, GA
Odom, Harold A., III ....Houston, TX
Odom, Harold L. ....Chatom, AL
Odom, Hubert Turner, Jr. ....Sealy, TX
Odom, Hugh D. ....Salt Lake City, UT
Odom & Hurley ....Belton, TX
Odom, J. Huntington ....Baton Rouge, LA
Odom, J. Larry ....Kansas City, MO
Odom, James J., Jr. ....Birmingham, AL
Pelham, AL
Odom, Jan Waltman ....Houston, TX
Odom, Jennifer D. ....Atlanta, GA
Odom, John ....Houston, TX
Odom, John Gregory, PLC ....Hahira, GA
New Orleans, LA
Odom, John M. ....Tampa, FL
Odom, John S., Jr. ....Shreveport, LA
Odom, Lane ....Fort Worth, TX
Odom, Larry C. ....Mobile, AL
Odom, Lewis G., Jr. ....Mobile, AL
Montgomery, AL
Washington, DC
Odom, Linda C. ....Atlanta, GA
Odom, Lisa S. ....Jacksonville, FL
Odom, M. Glenn ....Florence, SC
Odom, Mark W. ....Shreveport, LA
Odom & McCain ....Greenwood, MS
Odom, M. Glenn ....Darlington, SC
Odom, Michael B. ....Birmingham, AL
Odom, Patricia Falletta ....Birmingham, AL
Odom, Preston O., III ....Tallahassee, FL
Odom, Ray H. ....San Antonio, TX
Odom, Raymond C. ....Chicago, IL
Odom, Reginald D. ....New York, NY
Odom, Richard C. ....Baton Rouge, LA
Odom, Richard S. ....Los Angeles, CA
Odom, Robert I. ....Seattle, WA
Odom, Robert R. ....Spartanburg, SC
Odom, Robert W. ....Albemarle, NC
Odom, Ronald R. ....Los Angeles, CA
Odom, Roy H., Jr. ....Shreveport, LA
Odom, Schmerin & Thomason ....Houston, TX
Odom, Stephen R. ....Seattle, WA
Odom, Suzanne C. ....Denver, CO
Santa Fe, NM
Odom, Suzanne Rolfsen
Department of Energy,
Office of the General Counsel, GV
Odom, T. LaFontine ....Charlotte, NC
Odom, Terry, Abernathy and Cantrell
Spartanburg, SC
Odom, Thomas H. ....Washington, DC
Odom, Thomas LaFontaine, Jr.
Charlotte, NC
Odom, Thomas M. ....Millen, GA
Odom, Wendell A. ....Lufkin, TX
Odom, William W., Jr. ....Corinth, MS
O'Donald, Lisa Erin ....Washington, DC
Odoner, Ellen J. ....New York, NY
O'Donel, Thomas F. ....Lynnfield, MA
O'Donnell, A. Jane ....Norwood, MA
O'Donnell, Aaron V. ....Cerritos, CA
O'Donnell, Alethea ....Boston, MA
O'Donnell, Andrew B. ....Worcester, MA
O'Donnell, Ann E. ....Braintree, MA
Waltham, MA
O'Donnell, Anne Wathen ....St. Louis, MO
O'Donnell, Anthony J., Jr. ....Miami, FL
O'Donnell, Arianne ....Stamford, CT
O'Donnell, Arthur J. ....Chicago, IL
O'Donnell, B. Patrick, Jr. ....Vernon, CT
O'Donnell, Barbara A. ....Boston, MA
O'Donnell, Barbara Bourdonnay
Metairie, LA
O'Donnell, Beatrice ....Philadelphia, PA
O'Donnell, Bernard J. ....Wilmington, DE
O'Donnell, Brendan ....Interlaken, NY
O'Donnell, Brian ....Hartford, CT
O'Donnell, Brian C. ....Bedford, MA
O'Donnell, Brian E. ....Morristown, NJ
O'Donnell, Brian J. ....Albany, NY
O'Donnell, Brian T. ....Alexandria, VA
O'Donnell, Bruce V. ....Atlanta, GA
O'Donnell, Carol Befanis ....Fairfield, CT
O'Donnell, Catherine R. ....Scranton, PA
O'Donnell, Charles M. ....Blue Bell, PA
Harrisburg, PA
O'Donnell, Charles W. ....McLean, VA
O'Donnell, Charles W., P.C.
Falls Church, VA
McLean, VA

O'Donnell, Christopher J. ....Brunswick, GA
O'Donnell, Christopher J. ....Enola, PA
Plymouth, PA
O'Donnell, Christopher M. ....Payson, AZ
O'Donnell & Clark LLP ....Portland, OR
Salem, OR
O'Donnell, Colin F. ....Mineola, NY
O'Donnell, Cory ....Los Angeles, CA
San Francisco, CA
O'Donnell, Cynthia L. ....Pittsburgh, PA
O'Donnell, Daniel A., Jr. ....Trenton, NJ
O'Donnell, Daniel E. ....Armonk, NY
O'Donnell, Daniel G. ....St. Charles, MO
O'Donnell, Daniel J. ....Trenton, NJ
O'Donnell, Daniel J. ....New York, NY
O'Donnell, Daniel J. ....New York, NY
O'Donnell, Daniel M. ....Santa Rosa, CA
O'Donnell, Daniel Patrick ....Sacramento, CA
O'Donnell, David D. ....Oxford, MS
O'Donnell, Deborah Toth ....Trenton, NJ
O'Donnell, Declan J. ....Denver, CO
O'Donnell, Declan Joseph, P.C. ....Denver, CO
O'Donnell, Deirdre Leigh
Camdenton, MO
O'Donnell, Denis A. ....Flushing, NY
O'Donnell, Denise E. ....Buffalo, NY
O'Donnell, Dennis C. ....New York, NY
O'Donnell, Dennis R. ....Wheeling, WV
O'Donnell, Dianne E. ....New York, NY
O'Donnell, Dianne M. ....Atlanta, GA
O'Donnell, Douglas Leroy ....San Diego, CA
O'Donnell, Earle H. ....Washington, DC
O'Donnell, Edward F., Jr. ....Hartford, CT
O'Donnell, Edward J. ....Livingston, NJ
O'Donnell, Edward M. ....Chicago, IL
O'Donnell, Edward T., Law Offices of
Miami, FL
O'Donnell, Eileen ....Neptune, NJ
O'Donnell, Eleanor M. ....Hershey, PA
O'Donnell, Elizabeth (Beth) ....Decatur, IL
O'Donnell, Elizabeth G. ....Los Angeles, CA
O'Donnell, Ellen A. ....Santa Clara, CA
O'Donnell, Erin L. ....Boston, MA
O'Donnell, Eugene P., Jr. ....Fitchburg, MA
O'Donnell, Ferebee, McGonigal & Stone, A
Professional Corporation ....Houston, TX
O'Donnell, Fox & Gartner, P.C.
New York, NY
O'Donnell, Frank ....Wilmington, DE
O'Donnell, G. Daniel ....Philadelphia, PA
O'Donnell, Garry W.
Fort Lauderdale, FL
O'Donnell, Gary J. ....Rochester, NY
O'Donnell, George F. ....Somerset, NJ
O'Donnell, George J. ....Garden City, NY
O'Donnell, Ger P. ....Chicago, IL
O'Donnell, Geraldine ....New York, NY
O'Donnell & Grosse ....Jacksonville, FL
O'Donnell, Guy T. ....Mount Holly, NJ
O'Donnell, H. David ....Harrisonburg, VA
O'Donnell, Harry B., IV ....Louisville, KY
O'Donnell, Heather ....Chicago, IL
O'Donnell, Hugh ....Dixon, CA
O'Donnell, Hugh C. ....Chicago, IL
O'Donnell, Hugh C. ....Cincinnati, OH
O'Donnell, Hugh F. ....Kansas City, MO
O'Donnell, J. Brian ....La Jolla, CA
O'Donnell, J. Michael ....Houston, TX
O'Donnell, Jack ....New Haven, CT
O'Donnell, Jack C. ....Austin, TX
O'Donnell, James D. ....Jacksonville, FL
O'Donnell, James E. ....Fairfield, CT
O'Donnell, James E. ....Seattle, WA
O'Donnell, James J. ....San Francisco, CA
Walnut Creek, CA
O'Donnell, James J. ....Baltimore, MD
O'Donnell, James J. ....Royal Oak, MI
O'Donnell, James J. ....Kansas City, MO
O'Donnell, James J. ....Mansfield, OH
O'Donnell, James J. ....Greendale, WI
O'Donnell, James J. ....New Berlin, WI
O'Donnell, James L. ....Sarasota, FL
O'Donnell, James M. ....Staten Island, NY
O'Donnell, James P. ....Herkimer, NY
O'Donnell, James R. ....Dearborn, MI
O'Donnell, Jane ....Irvine, CA
O'Donnell, Jane G. ....Philadelphia, PA
O'Donnell, Jeffrey M. ....Washington, DC
O'Donnell, Jeffrey T. ....Blue Bell, PA
O'Donnell, Jennie Lee A. ....Morristown, NJ
O'Donnell, Jill E. ....Baltimore, MD
O'Donnell, Joan M. ....Chesterfield, VA
O'Donnell, Joe, P.C. ....Philadelphia, PA
O'Donnell, John A. ....Chicago, IL
O'Donnell, John B., Jr. ....Raleigh, NC
O'Donnell, John Baldwin
San Francisco, CA
O'Donnell, John C., III ....Mansfield, OH
O'Donnell, John D. ....Fort Lauderdale, FL
O'Donnell, John F. ....Fort Lauderdale, FL
O'Donnell, John F. ....Paterson, NJ
O'Donnell, John F. ....West Orange, NJ
O'Donnell, John F. ....Buffalo, NY
O'Donnell, John F. ....Dallas, TX
O'Donnell, John H. ....Sacramento, CA
O'Donnell, John J. ....Orland Park, IL
O'Donnell, John J. ....Mendota Heights, MN
O'Donnell, John J. ....Morristown, NJ
O'Donnell, John J. ....New York, NY
O'Donnell, John J. ....Philadelphia, PA
O'Donnell, John J. ....Seattle, WA
O'Donnell, John J., Jr. ....St. Louis, MO
O'Donnell, John J., Jr. ....Alexandria, VA
O'Donnell, John Jude ....Washington, DC
Rockville, MD
O'Donnell, John L., Jr. ....Los Angeles, CA
O'Donnell, John Logan ....New York, NY
O'Donnell, John M. ....Sacramento, CA

Oestreich, Paul C. .... **Salt Lake City, UT**
Oestreich, Stephen D. .... **New York, NY**
Oestreicher, Charles R. .... **Portland, ME**
Oestreicher, David .... **Baltimore, MD**
Oestreicher & Ennis .... White Plains, NY
Oestreicher, Eugene L. .... Akron, OH
Oestreicher, John B. .... North Branford, CT
Oestreicher, John C. .... **Madison, WI**
Oestreicher, Julius Y. .... White Plains, NY
Oestreicher, Karen .... East Hartford, CT
Oestreicher, Kenneth .... **Baltimore, MD**
Oestreicher, Michael R. (IBA)
Cincinnati, OH
Oetgen, Stephen D. .... **Chicago, IL**
Oeth, Steven J. .... Ames, IA
Oetheimer, Richard A. .... **Boston, MA**
Oetjen, Bernard H. .... McLean, VA
Oetken, Amy K. .... Le Mars, IA
Oetken, J. Paul .... Department of Justice, Office of Legal Counsel, GV
Oetken, Randy P. .... Milwaukie, OR
Oettel, Melanie A. .... Okanogan, WA
Oetter, Bruce C. .... **St. Louis, MO**
Oetter, George C., Jr. .... Macon, GA
Oetter, Jennifer K. .... Portland, OR
Oetting, Barbara Taylor .... San Diego, CA
Oetting, David P. .... **St. Louis, MO**
Oetting, Martin C. .... **Detroit, MI**
Oetting, Richard F. .... **Los Angeles, CA**
Oetting, Roger H. .... **Grand Rapids, MI**
Oetting, Steven T. .... San Diego, CA
Oettinger, David, Jr. .... Rocky Mount, NC
Oettinger, Elmer R., Jr. .... Chapel Hill, NC
Oettinger, Gail Kane .... Cleveland, OH
Oettinger, Julian A. .... Deerfield, IL
Oettinger, Kenneth B. .... **Raleigh, NC**
Oettinger, Kenneth B., Jr. .... **Charlotte, NC**
Oettinger, Mark D. .... **Burlington, VT**
Oettinger, Michael D. .... Chicago, IL
Oettinger, Philip H.
Securities and Exchange Commission, Office of Compliance Inspections and Examinations, GV
Oettinger, Richard S. .... Seattle, WA
Oettle, Kenneth F. .... **Atlantic City, NJ**
Newark, NJ
Oettle, Randall T. .... **St. Louis, MO**
Oetzell, Walter K. .... **Los Angeles, CA**
Oexeman, Robert J. .... Clarendon Hills, IL
Oexmann, Richard .... Lexington, KY
Oey, S. Joseph .... Maywood, NJ
Of Counsel Law Center .... Fallbrook, CA
O'Fallon, Daniel A. .... **Minneapolis, MN**
O'Fallon, Shannon K. .... Juneau, AK
O'Farrell, Arthur S. .... Delta, CO
O'Farrell, Edward E. .... New Philadelphia, OH
O'Farrell, Heather L. .... **Chicago, IL**
O'Farrell, James T. .... Annapolis, MD
O'Farrell, John W. .... Morristown, NJ
O'Farrell, Robert A. .... Monterey, CA
O'Farrell, Rodney J. .... Saginaw, MI
O'Farrell, William E. .... Stamford, CT
O'farrill, Anthony J. .... Montebello, CA
Ofeldt, Richard F. .... Spring Lake Heights, NJ
Ofelt, Charles N. .... Albuquerque, NM
Ofelt, Jack Cortland, Jr. .... Wilsonville, OR
O'Ferrall, Alfred J., III .... Snow Hill, MD
O'Ferrall, Kirk H. .... **New York, NY**
Offen, Alan L. .... Rochester, NY
Offen, Frank .... Oakland, CA
Offen, Herman N. .... New York, NY
Offen, M. Louis .... Kensington, MD
Offen, Stephen M. .... **Somerville, NJ**
Offenbach, Daniel J. .... Chicago, IL
Offenbach, Kate M. .... Dallas, TX
Offenbach, Sigi M. .... Chicago, IL
Offenbacher, Kimberly .... Studio City, CA
Offenbacker, Phillip .... Seattle, WA
Offenbecher, Peter .... Seattle, WA
Offenberg, Amy .... Phoenix, AZ
Offen-Brown, David F. .... Oakland, CA
Offenhartz, Adam H. .... **New York, NY**
Offenhartz, Gilbert L. .... New York, NY
Offenhartz, Marc .... Tucson, AZ
Offenhauser, Tyler D. .... **Orange, CA**
Offenkrantz, Jonathan G. .... **New York, NY**
Offenkrantz, Ronald J. .... **New York, NY**
Offer, Mary Ellen B. .... **Montvale, NJ**
Offer, Robert .... **Beverly Hills, CA**
Offer, Stuart J. .... **San Francisco, CA**
Offerdahl, Charlotte L. .... Winston-Salem, NC
Offerdahl, John E. .... Mount Horeb, WI
Offergeld, Leslie .... **Belleville, IL**
Offerman & Associates .... Beaumont, TX
Offerman, Garry A. .... Beaumont, TX
Offerman, Phylis West .... Seguin, TX
Offermann, Cassano, Greco & Slisz
Buffalo, NY
Offermann, Francis J., Jr. .... Buffalo, NY
Office, Gerald, Jr. .... Plano, TX
Office, Gerald S., Sr. .... Clayton, OH
Office, James R. .... Springboro, OH
Officer, David J. .... **Worcester, MA**
Officer, John R. .... **Livingston, TN**
Officer, Julie E. .... **Livingston, TN**
Officer, Philip N. .... Santa Ana, CA
Officer, Robert L. .... **St. Louis, MO**
Officer, Susan L. .... Lutherville, MD
Offidani, Daniel R. .... Scottsdale, AZ
Offidani & Kresin, P.C. .... Scottsdale, AZ
Offill, Phillip W., Jr. .... Fort Worth, TX
Offit & Kurman .... Owings Mills, MD
Offit, Maurice .... Owings Mills, MD
Offit, Theodore A. .... Owings Mills, MD
Offley, Jon Eric .... Riverdale, MD
Offner, Alan L. .... **New Orleans, LA**
Offner, Daniel O'Connell .... Los Angeles, CA
Northampton, MA
New York, NY
Offner, Daniel O'Connell, P.C.
Los Angeles, CA
Northampton, MA
New York, NY
Offner, Donna L. .... St. Louis, MO
Offner, Eric D. .... Manhasset Hills, NY
Offner, Lawrence Steven .... Orange, CA
Offner, Michael L. .... **Red Cloud, NE**
Offner, Robin W. .... San Diego, CA
Offner, Stuart A. .... **Boston, MA**
Offredi, Cynthia M. .... Hartford, CT
Offret, Ronald A. .... Anchorage, AK
Offutt, David A. .... Yuba City, CA
Offutt, D. C., Jr. .... **Huntington, WV**
Offutt, Fisher & Nord .... **Ashland, KY**
Ironton, OH
Charleston, WV
Huntington, WV
Offutt, Gary S. .... Baltimore, MD
Offutt, Gerald M. .... **Chicago, IL**
Offutt, Horman, Burdette & Frey, P.A.
Frederick, MD
Offutt, James R.
Overseas Private Investment Corporation, GV
Offutt, M. Willson, IV .... Annapolis, MD
Offutt, Richard H., Jr. .... **Westminster, MD**
Offutt, Robt. B. .... Oklahoma City, OK
Offutt, W. Jerome .... **Frederick, MD**
O'Fiel, Hugh E. .... Port Arthur, TX
Ofiesh, Becky Ann .... Charleston, WV
O'Flaherty, Anna Wirt .... Swisher, IA
O'Flaherty, Brendan R. .... Fremont, CA
O'Flaherty, Cross, Martinez & Ovando LLP
Anaheim, CA
Los Angeles, CA
Woodland Hills, CA
O'Flaherty, Daniel F. .... Alexandria, VA
O'Flaherty, Eugene L. .... Boston, MA
O'Flaherty, Gerard J. .... **La Crosse, WI**
O'Flaherty, Ian M. .... Fairfax, VA
O'Flaherty, John F. .... Pleasanton, CA
O'Flaherty, John J. .... Tampa, FL
O'Flaherty, Kevin P. .... **Boston, MA**
O'Flaherty Law Firm .... Swisher, IA
O'Flaherty Law Offices
Newburyport, MA
O'Flaherty, Michael A.
Woodland Hills, CA
O'Flaherty, Michael G. .... **Kansas City, MO**
O'Flaherty, Michael J. .... **Washington, DC**
O'Flaherty, Neil F. .... **Washington, DC**
O'Flaherty, Paul B., Jr. .... Chicago, IL
O'Flaherty, Paul B., (P.C.) .... **Chicago, IL**
O'Flaherty, Sharon L. .... Cleveland, OH
O'Flaherty, Teresa W. .... Milton, MA
O'Flaherty, Thomas H. .... Cincinnati, OH
O'Flaherty, Thomas J. .... Swisher, IA
O'Flaherty, Vincent F.
Overland Park, KS
Kansas City, MO
O'Flaherty, William J. .... **Newburyport, MA**
O'Flanagan, Ann .... **Flanders, NJ**
O'Flanagan, Ann .... **Morristown, NJ**
O'Flanagan, John P. .... Annapolis, MD
O'Flanagan, John P. .... Plymouth, MA
O'Flanagan, William .... New York, NY
O'Flinn, Kathleen Tracy .... Mamaroneck, NY
O'Flinn, Peter R. .... **New York, NY**
O'Flynn, Augustine M.
San Francisco, CA
O'Flynn, Mark .... San Francisco, CA
Ofman, Lee .... **Franklin, TN**
Ofner, William B. .... Chino Hills, CA
Ofodu, Uzoma A. .... **Kansas City, MO**
O'Foghludha, Michael J. .... **Durham, NC**
Ofori-Acquaah, Anne-Marie .... Boston, MA
O'Friel, Daniel J. .... Santa Fe, NM
O'Friel, Joseph A. .... Tampa, FL
O'Friel, Michael F. .... Hampton, NH
O'Friel, Paul G. .... Newton, MA
Ofsa, Joyce Fleming .... **Charleston, WV**
Ofsevit, Samuel M. .... **New York, NY**
Ofseyer, Jeremy J. .... Chapel Hill, NC
Ofsink, Darren L. .... **New York, NY**
Ofsthun, D. Glenn .... **Chicago, IL**
Oftedal, Richard H. .... Los Alamitos, CA
Oftedal, Richard L. .... West Palm Beach, FL
Oftring, Susan M. .... Wellesley Hills, MA
O'Gallagher, Brian A. .... Wheaton, IL
O'Gallagher, James E. .... **Crown Point, IN**
O'Gallagher, James K. .... San Francisco, CA
Ogami, Carolyn E. .... **Honolulu, HI**
Ogan, Norman .... **Holyoke, MA**
Ogan, Sam .... Albuquerque, NM
Ogan, Uzoma Onyekwere .... Los Angeles, CA
Ogando, Janine C. .... **Walnut Creek, CA**
Ogar, Helen E. .... Bloomington, IL
O'Gara, Carol Lynn .... St. Paul, MN
O'Gara, Carolyn S. .... Glenview, IL
O'Gara, James V. .... **New York, NY**
O'Gara, John J., Jr. .... **Belleville, IL**
O'Gara, Lawrence D. .... Chicago, IL
O'Gara, Marie S. .... San Francisco, CA
O'Gara, Michael J. .... Los Angeles, CA
O'Gara, Paul M. .... **Trenton, NJ**
O'Gara, Robert M. .... **Lincoln, NE**
O'Gara, Scott Howard .... Kew Gardens, NY
O'Gara, Thomas F. .... Markham, IL
O'Gara, Thomas F. .... **Indianapolis, IN**
O'Gara, Vincent .... San Francisco, CA
O'Gara, William E. .... **Providence, RI**
O'Gary, Jennifer L. .... St. Paul, MN
Ogata, Clyde T. .... San Francisco, CA
Ogata, Jeffery M. .... Sacramento, CA
Ogata-Deal, Ann Masako .... Honolulu, HI
Ogawa, Albert H., (A Law Corporation)
Honolulu, HI
Ogawa, Audrey R. .... San Bruno, CA
Ogawa, Dean T. .... Colorado Springs, CO
Ogawa, Diane Harrison
Albuquerque, NM
Ogawa, Lisa A. .... Los Angeles, CA
Ogawa, Mitsuo Ken .... Aurora, CO
Ogawa, Richard Takashi .... **Palo Alto, CA**
Ogawa, Roy T. .... **Honolulu, HI**
Ogaz, Michael J. .... San Jose, CA
Ogborn, Michael J. .... **Denver, CO**
Ogborn, Murray .... **Denver, CO**
Lincoln, NE
Ogborn, Summerlin & Ogborn, L.L.C.
Denver, CO
Lincoln, NE
Ogburn, David W., Jr. .... **Richmond, VA**
Ogburn, J. Denis .... **Louisville, KY**
Ogburn, John N., Jr. .... **Asheboro, NC**
Greensboro, NC
Ogburn, Lee H. .... **Baltimore, MD**
Ogburn, Mary Margaret
Winston-Salem, NC
Ogburn, Matthew M. .... San Francisco, CA
Ogburn, Robert W. .... Monte Vista, CO
Ogburn, Rudy L. .... **Raleigh, NC**
Ogburn, Thomas L., III .... **Charlotte, NC**
Ogburn, W. Gary .... San Francisco, CA
Ogburn, Willard P. .... Boston, MA
Ogburn, William G. .... San Francisco, CA
Ogdahl, W. Wallace .... **Salem, OR**
Ogden, Alfred .... New York, NY
Ogden, Ann Penny .... Burlington, CO
Ogden, Bruce P. .... **Westfield, NJ**
Ogden, Bryan C. .... Tacoma, WA
Ogden, C. Robert .... Spokane, WA
Ogden, Carlos K. .... Deming, NM
Ogden, Carroll J. .... Mobile, AL
Ogden, Charlton B., II .... New Orleans, LA
Ogden, Charlton B., III .... **New Orleans, LA**
Ogden, David A. .... Los Angeles, CA
Ogden, David W. .... Department of Justice, Civil Division, GV
Ogden, Dennis P. .... **Des Moines, IA**
Ogden, Donald G. .... **Natchez, MS**
Ogden, Donald G., P.A. .... **Natchez, MS**
Ogden, E. Charles, III .... **Guntersville, AL**
Ogden, E. Jeannette .... Buffalo, NY
Ogden, Gary L. .... **Los Angeles, CA**
Ogden, Gary L., A Prof. Corp., Law Offices of .... **Los Angeles, CA**
Ogden, Gayle M. .... Liberty Lake, WA
Ogden, George E., Jr. .... Beaumont, TX
Ogden, Gibson, White & Broocks, L.L.P.
Houston, TX
Ogden, Gregory L. .... Malibu, CA
Ogden, Harry P. .... **Knoxville, TN**
Ogden, Henry M. .... Warren, NJ
Ogden, Herbert G., Jr. .... Rutland, VT
Ogden, J. Anthony .... Denver, CO
Ogden, James Ashley .... Jackson, MS
Ogden, James F. .... Covington, KY
Ogden, James P. .... St. Petersburg, FL
Ogden, James Russell .... Cuyahoga Falls, OH
Ogden, J. N. .... Mobile, AL
Ogden, John M. .... York, PA
Ogden, John V. .... **Stamford, CT**
Ogden, Larry F. .... **Torrance, CA**
Ogden, Laurie G. .... Syracuse, NY
Ogden, Len W., Jr. .... **Paducah, KY**
Ogden, Lesley L. .... Stratham, NH
Ogden, Louise R. .... San Francisco, CA
Ogden, M. Blair .... San Francisco, CA
Ogden, Mark .... **Phoenix, AZ**
Ogden, Mark H. .... **Cedar Rapids, IA**
Ogden, Marlin V. .... Sacramento, CA
Ogden, Marti M. .... **Baton Rouge, LA**
Ogden, Mary Kay .... **Washington, DC**
Ogden, Mindy King .... **Clearwater, FL**
Ogden Murphy Wallace, P.L.L.C.
Seattle, WA
Wenatchee, WA
Ogden Newell & Welch .... **Louisville, KY**
Ogden, Patricia L. .... **Indianapolis, IN**
Ogden, Philip W. .... **Colorado Springs, CO**
Ogden, Philip W. .... Bay City, MI
Ogden, Ralph .... Denver, CO
Ogden, Ralph C., III .... Modesto, CA
Ogden, Randy J. .... **Tampa, FL**
Ogden, Richard C. .... **Oklahoma City, OK**
Ogden, R. M. .... **Austin, TX**
Ogden, Robert S., Jr. .... **New York, NY**
Ogden, Roy E. .... San Luis Obispo, CA
Ogden, Sandra P. .... San Francisco, CA
Ogden, Seymour .... Chicago, IL
Ogden, Stasia L. .... **St. Louis, MO**
Ogden, Susan E. .... New Orleans, LA
Ogden, Thomas J. .... Stone Mountain, GA
Ogden, Thomas P. .... **New York, NY**
Ogden, Todd D. .... **Dallas, TX**
Ogden, W. Edwin .... **Reading, PA**
Ogden, Wendy Everett .... Des Moines, IA
Ogden, William Allen .... Annapolis, MD
Ogden, William Baldwin .... Grand Rapids, MI
Ogden, William (Bill) W. .... **Houston, TX**
Ogden, William F., Jr. .... Plymouth, MN
Ogden, William N. .... Somerville, NJ
Ogdie, Susan A. .... Oakland, CA
Ogene, Chidi J. .... **Washington, DC**
Ogens, Ronald L. .... **Bethesda, MD**
Ogenyi, Gloria C. .... Houston, TX
Ogg, E. Jerald, Jr. .... Martin, TN
Ogg, Gary J. .... **Pittsburgh, PA**
Ogg, Jack C. .... Houston, TX
Ogg, Jack C., & Associates .... Houston, TX
Ogg, Jack L. .... Prescott, AZ
Ogg, Joelle Kay .... **Washington, DC**
Ogg, Jones, Cordes & Ignelzi, L.L.P.
Johnstown, PA
Pittsburgh, PA
Ogg, Leslie L. .... Minneapolis, MN
Ogg, Nancy Neubauer .... Cincinnati, OH
Ogg, R. Danforth .... Kodiak, AK
Ogg, Ramsey L. .... **Monroe, LA**
Ogg, Randell C. .... **Washington, DC**
Ogg, Robert K. .... Missoula, MT
Ogg, W. Stuart .... **Dallas, TX**
Ogg, Wilson Reid .... Berkeley, CA
Oggel, Stephen P. .... **San Diego, CA**
Oggel, Stephen P., A P.C., The Law Offices of
San Diego, CA
Oggiani, Louis J. .... Great Barrington, MA
Ogi, Irene A. .... San Jose, CA
Ogibovic, Richard S., II .... Momence, IL
Ogier, Alton L. .... Charleston, SC
Ogier, Dwight E. .... Lakeland, FL
Ogier, Herbert L., Jr. .... Houston, TX
Ogier, Tamara Miles .... Atlanta, GA
Ogihara, Shigetaka .... New York, NY
Ogilby, Anne Phillips .... **Boston, MA**
Ogilby, Barry R. .... **San Francisco, CA**
Ogilby, John J., Jr. .... Miami, FL
Ogilby, Remsen B. .... Washington, DC
Ogilvie, Alan S. .... Wausau, WI
Ogilvie, Alison .... Ann Arbor, MI
Ogilvie, Andrew J. .... **San Francisco, CA**
Ogilvie, Curtis R. .... San Francisco, CA
Ogilvie, David A. .... **Denver, CO**
Ogilvie, David A., P.C. .... **Denver, CO**
Ogilvie, Denise M. .... West Greenwich, RI
Ogilvie, Dian D. .... **Torrance, CA**
Ogilvie, Gail .... Richmond, ME
Ogilvie, George F. .... Las Vegas, NV
Ogilvie, George F., III .... **Las Vegas, NV**
Reno, NV
Ogilvie, Ian M. .... **New York, NY**
Ogilvie, Jeffrey S. .... Redding, CA
Ogilvie, Jeffrey S. .... Boston, MA
Ogilvie, John W.L. .... **Salt Lake City, UT**
Ogilvie, Kathleen Murray .... Liberty, MO
Albuquerque, NM
Ogilvie, Lynley A. .... **Washington, DC**
Ogilvie, Moyahoena N. .... **Hartford, CT**
Ogilvie, Norman J., Jr. .... **Lancaster, OH**
Ogilvy, J. P. .... Washington, DC
Oginski, Gerald M. .... Great Neck, NY
Oginsky, James S. .... Flint, MI
Ogisaka, James H. .... Northlake, IL
Ogland, Kristina .... Hudson, WI
Oglander, Joseph M. .... **Washington, DC**
Oglanian, Ann F. .... **Chicago, IL**
Ogle, Alexander .... Somerset, PA
Ogle, Carl R., Jr. .... Jefferson City, TN
Ogle, Charles E., (A Professional Corporation) .... **Morro Bay, CA**
San Luis Obispo, CA
Ogle, Charles Patrick .... **Morro Bay, CA**
San Luis Obispo, CA
Ogle, Douglas .... Pasadena, TX
Ogle, Flint B. .... **Grand Junction, CO**
Ogle, Frederick C. .... **Houston, TX**
Ogle, Gail S. .... Charlottesville, VA
Ogle, Gary M. .... Oroville, CA
Ogle, Gass & Richardson, P.C.
Sevierville, TN
Ogle, H. Kelly .... Redwood City, CA
Ogle, Henry T. .... Knoxville, TN
Ogle, J. David .... **Oklahoma City, OK**
Ogle, Jerry M. .... Bannockburn, IL
Ogle, John D. .... Hannibal, MO
Ogle, Kurt A. .... **Billerica, MA**
Ogle, Le Roy M. .... Mount Clemens, MI
Ogle, Mark A. .... **Fort Wright, KY**
Ogle, Merzon & Kirschner
Morro Bay, CA
San Luis Obispo, CA
Ogle & Peterson, P.C. .... Charlottesville, VA
Ogle, Policicchio, Frantz & Scurfield
Somerset, PA
Ogle, Randall S. .... Kalispell, MT
Ogle, Rex Henry .... Sevierville, TN
Ogle, Richard F. .... **Birmingham, AL**
Ogle, Richard N. .... **Cleveland, OH**
Ogle, Robert D. .... Arcadia, CA
Ogle, Robert J. .... Boerne, TX
Ogle, Robert L., Jr. .... **Sevierville, TN**
Ogle, Ronald Eugene .... San Marcos, CA
Ogle, Stephen S. .... **Maryville, TN**
Ogle, William F. .... Wailuku, HI
Ogle, William H. .... Ormond Beach, FL
Ogle & Worm .... Kalispell, MT
Ogles, John .... Jacksonville, AR
Ogles Law Firm, P.A. .... Jacksonville, AR
Oglesbee, Miriam R. .... Chapel Hill, NC
Oglesby, Brian R. .... **Rutherfordton, NC**
Oglesby, Charles M. .... Salt Lake City, UT
Oglesby, Christopher B. .... Madisonville, KY
Oglesby, David E. .... **Birmingham, AL**
Oglesby, Edward T. .... **Little Rock, AR**
Oglesby, Edwin R. .... Farmington, MI
Oglesby, Gene T. .... Lincoln, NE
Oglesby, H. Patrick .... Chapel Hill, NC
Oglesby, James T. .... **Franklin, TN**
Oglesby, Jerry B. .... **Anniston, AL**
Oglesby, Jimmie D. .... **Midland, TX**
Oglesby Law Offices, P.C. .... Lincoln, NE
Oglesby, Michael J. .... Richmond, VA
Oglesby, Myrna L. .... **Ukiah, CA**
Oglesby, Nancy van Luyn .... Chesterfield, VA
Oglesby, Nicholas E., Jr. .... Wilmington, DE
Oglesby, Patricia L. .... Tulsa, OK
Oglesby, Robert E. .... West Palm Beach, FL
Oglesby, Robert E., P.A.
West Palm Beach, FL

Oglesby, Roger D. .... Costa Mesa, CA
Oglesby, Ronald G. .... Farmington, MI
Oglesby, Ursula D. .... Kernersville, NC
Ogletree, Anne C. .... Denton, MD
Ogletree, Benjamin R. .... Washington, DC
Ogletree, Charles .... Cambridge, MA
Ogletree, Charles J., Jr. .... Washington, DC
Ogletree, Charles W. .... Columbia, NC
Ogletree, Deakins, Nash, Smoak & Stewart, P.C. .... Birmingham, AL
Washington, DC
Atlanta, GA
Chicago, IL
Raleigh, NC
Winston-Salem, NC
Charleston, SC
Columbia, SC
Greenville, SC
Nashville, TN
Dallas, TX
Houston, TX
Ogletree, John L. .... Beverly Hills, CA
Ogletree and Livingston .... Sylacauga, AL
Ogletree, Powell G., Jr. .... Jackson, MS
Ogletree, Robert B. .... Jackson, MS
Ogletree, Robert S. .... Rome, GA
Ogletree, Sheila K. .... Decatur, GA
Ogletree, Tom R. .... Sylacauga, AL
Ogletree, William B. .... Gadsden, AL
Oglevie, Thomas R. .... Ulysses, KS
Ogline, Michael A. .... Alliance, OH
Oglukian, Tanya M. .... Greensboro, NC
Ogman, Abraham .... Wilmington, MA
Ognall, Andrew H. .... Portland, OR
Ogne, Alberts & Stuart, P.C. .... Detroit, MI
Troy, MI
Cleveland, OH
Columbus, OH
Toledo, OH
Ogne, Wayne L. .... Troy, MI
Toledo, OH
Ognelodh, Harold G. .... New York, NY
Ognibene, Charles A. .... Boston, MA
Ognibene, Michael A. .... Warren, OH
Ognisanti, E. Louis .... Saginaw, MI
Ognjanovic, Ivana .... Los Angeles, CA
Ogolin, William J., Jr. .... Pekin, IL
Ogolo, Chidi A .... Washington, DC
Ogomori, Ronald T. .... Honolulu, HI
Ogonowski, Matthew S., Jr. .... Utica, NY
Ogonowsky, Brian D. .... San Jose, CA
Ogorchock, James F. .... Manchester, NH
Ogorchock, Mary S. .... Milwaukee, WI
Ogorchock, Thomas A. .... Milwaukee, WI
Ogorek, Elky .... Brooklyn, NY
O'Gorman, Barrett Patrick .... Goleta, CA
O'Gorman, C. Brian .... Goleta, CA
O'Gorman, Carmella A. .... Somerville, NJ
O'Gorman, Daniel P. .... Orlando, FL
O'Gorman, Debra DuBritz
New York, NY
O'Gorman, Diane T. .... Anchorage, AK
O'Gorman, Edward J. .... New York, NY
O'Gorman, Hugh J. .... South Orange, NJ
O'Gorman, James E. .... Detroit Lakes, MN
O'Gorman, Jill Michele
Santa Barbara, CA
O'Gorman, Kevin Michael .... Houston, TX
O'Gorman & O'Gorman .... Goleta, CA
O'Gorman, P. Keith .... San Antonio, TX
O'Gorman, Patricia A. .... Cottage Grove, MN
O'Gorman, Rhea .... New York, NY
O'Gorman and Sandroni, A Professional Corporation .... St. Louis, MO
O'Gorman, Sean P. .... St. Louis, MO
O'Gorman, Thomas E. .... Scotch Plains, NJ
Ogorzalek, John F. .... Los Alamitos, CA
Ogorzalek, Lisa Lattal .... Glenwood, MD
Ogozalek, J. Francis, Jr. .... Chicopee, MA
Ogozalek & Pasterczyk .... Chicopee, MA
O'Grady, Brian J. .... Mountain View, CA
O'Grady, Catherine .... Tempe, AZ
O'Grady, Clive R. G. .... McLean, VA
O'Grady, Daniel W. .... Darien, CT
O'Grady & Darville, P.A. .... Belle Glade, FL
Boca Raton, FL
Kissimmee, FL
O'Grady, Dennis J. .... Morristown, NJ
O'Grady, Dermot P. .... Trenton, NJ
O'Grady, George W. .... Miami, FL
O'Grady, Gerald B., III .... Boston, MA
O'Grady, James B. .... Sunnyvale, CA
O'Grady, James F., Jr. .... Edison, NJ
O'Grady, James J. .... Columbus, OH
O'Grady, Janice K. .... San Jose, CA
O'Grady, Janice Kay .... Parker, CO
O'Grady, John Brad .... Richmond, VA
O'Grady, John E. .... San Francisco, CA
O'Grady, John F. .... Saginaw, MI
O'Grady, John J. .... Sparkill, NY
O'Grady, John J., III .... New York, NY
O'Grady, John J., Jr. .... Philadelphia, PA
O'Grady, John P. .... Chicago, IL
O'Grady, Keven M.P. .... Overland Park, KS
O'Grady, Kevin J. .... Fort Lauderdale, FL
O'Grady, Kevin M. .... Westport, CT
O'Grady, Kristin Moody .... Washington, DC
O'Grady, Liam .... Washington, DC
O'Grady, Lowell A. .... Sun City West, AZ
O'Grady, Matthew P. .... St. Louis, MO
O'Grady, Michael J. .... Scottsdale, AZ
O'Grady, Michael J. .... Washington, DC
O'Grady, Michael J. .... Cincinnati, OH
O'Grady, Noreen C. .... Philadelphia, PA
O'Grady & O'Neil, P.C. .... Saginaw, MI
O'Grady, Paul T. .... Falls Church, VA
O'Grady, Robert K. .... Philadelphia, PA
O'Grady, Sharon L. .... San Francisco, CA
Washington, DC
O'Grady, Terrance P. .... Rochester, NY
O'Grady, Thomas J. .... Maplewood, NJ
O'Grady, Thomas James .... Boca Raton, FL
Kissimmee, FL
O'Grady, Thomas S. .... Somers, CT
O'Grady, Timothy .... Council Bluffs, IA
O'Grady, Timothy P. .... Westwood, KS
O'Grady, Timothy S. .... St. Louis, MO
O'Grady, William J. .... Springfield, MA
O'Grady-Diamond, Colleen
San Francisco, CA
O'Grady-Parent, Erin M. .... Albany, NY
Ogram, Mark E. .... Tucson, AZ
Ogram & Teplitz, P.C. .... Tucson, AZ
O'Green, John R., II .... Auburn Hills, MI
Ogren, Arnold E. .... Los Angeles, CA
Ogren, David Isaac .... Santa Maria, CA
Ogren, J. Daniel .... Indianapolis, IN
Ogren, Jeffrey W. .... Philadelphia, PA
Ogren, Jennifer M. .... St. Louis Park, MN
Ogren, Kenneth R. .... Oakland, CA
Ogren, Quentin O. .... San Luis Obispo, CA
Ogren, Robert V. .... Springfield, IL
Ogren, Robert W. .... Washington, DC
Ogrey, Eric S. .... Jonesboro, GA
Ogrin, Kenneth Dean .... Sherman Oaks, CA
Ogrod, Gregory D. .... San Diego, CA
O'Grody, Jeffrey R. .... Bowling Green, KY
Ogron, Bruce D. .... Chicago, IL
Ogrosky, John Kirk .... Frankfort, KY
O'Grosky, Joy L. .... Madison, WI
Ogrosky, Kori Lyttle .... Miami, FL
Louisville, KY
Ogsbury, James D.
House of Representatives, Committee Legal Personnel, GV
Oguagha, Ifeyinwa .... New York, NY
Ogul, Michael Samuel .... Oakland, CA
Ogulnik, Rose B. .... Thousand Oaks, CA
Ogunlesi, Adebayo O. .... New York, NY
Oguntomilade, Bandele O. .... Frederick, MD
Ogura, Meiko .... Chicago, IL
Ogurak Law Offices, P.A.
Minneapolis, MN
Ogurak, Melvin .... Minneapolis, MN
Ogurek, Ruth Charolette .... San Antonio, TX
Ogus, Lonny B. .... Chicago, IL
Oh, Alex Young K. .... New York, NY
Oh, Allen J. .... Minneapolis, MN
Oh, Angela E. .... Redondo Beach, CA
Oh, Anne .... Boston, MA
Oh, April Unhui .... Baltimore, MD
Oh, Cindy S. .... Boston, MA
Oh, David .... Philadelphia, PA
Oh, David, P.C., The Law Firm
Philadelphia, PA
Oh, Edward H. .... Largo, MD
Oh, Edwin .... Washington, DC
Oh, Emma L. .... Philadelphia, PA
Oh & Harjani .... St. Paul, MN
Oh, Hyunjoo Susan .... New York, NY
Oh, James .... Palo Alto, CA
Oh, James J. .... Chicago, IL
OH, James W. .... Cleveland, OH
Oh, Juli .... San Diego, CA
Oh, Kenneth C. .... New York, NY
Oh, Matthew I. .... St. Paul, MN
Oh, Mona Y. .... Los Angeles, CA
Oh, Paul I. .... Englewood, CO
Oh, Peter B. .... New York, NY
Oh, Rachel Mihwan .... Silver Spring, MD
Oh, Ruth K. .... Honolulu, HI
Oh, Sam S. .... Los Angeles, CA
Oh, Seong-Kun .... San Francisco, CA
Oh, Seong-Mi .... New York, NY
Oh, Shinyung .... San Francisco, CA
Oh, Sung I. .... Los Angeles, CA
Oh, Susie H. .... Burbank, CA
Oh, Taeri Im .... Dallas, TX
O'Hagan, Cindy J. .... New York, NY
O'Hagan, Gary G. .... Wayzata, MN
O'Hagan, James J. .... Chicago, IL
O'Hagan, Jean K. .... Lansing, MI
O'Hagan, Kevin M. .... Chicago, IL
O'Hagan, Michael J. .... Cadillac, MI
O'Hagan, Michael M. .... Chattanooga, TN
O'Hagan & Reilly .... Islip, NY
O'Hagan, Robert W. .... Freehold, NJ
O'Hagan, Sean J. .... St. Louis, MO
O'Hagan, Smith & Amundsen
Chicago, IL
Geneva, IL
Rockford, IL
Waukegan, IL
Wheaton, IL
Woodstock, IL
Milwaukee, WI
Racine, WI
O'Hagan, Terrence J. .... Grand Ledge, MI
O'Hair, John D. .... Detroit, MI
O'Hair, Robert J. .... Sacramento, CA
O'Haire, Betty N. .... Jesup, GA
O'Haire, George V. .... Hicksville, NY
O'Haire, Karen A. .... Sacramento, CA
O'Haire, Kelly M. .... San Rafael, CA
O'Haire, Kevin G. .... Troy, NY
O'Haire, Michael .... Vero Beach, FL
O'Haire, Michael B. .... Clearwater, FL
O'Haire, Quinn & Candler, Chartered
Sebastian, FL
Vero Beach, FL
O'Haire, Sean M. .... Vero Beach, FL
O'Haire, Walter W. .... Menlo Park, CA
O'Hale, John P. .... Smithfield, NC
O'Hale, Robert .... Greensboro, NC
Ohall, Carl J. .... Tampa, FL
O'Hallaron, Janet P. .... St. Louis, MO
O'Halloran, Amanda .... Tacoma, WA
O'Halloran, Ann C. .... Staten Island, NY
O'Halloran, Brian .... Staten Island, NY
O'Halloran, C. Michael .... Hartford, CT
O'Halloran, Charles M. .... Hartford, CT
O'Halloran, Edw. J. .... Philadelphia, PA
O'Halloran, Elizabeth M. .... Greensburg, PA
O'Halloran, F. Thomas .... Providence, RI
O'Halloran, Hugh J. .... Milwaukee, WI
O'Halloran, James E., III .... Chicago, IL
O'Halloran, James E., Jr. .... Northbrook, IL
O'Halloran, James T. .... Jersey City, NJ
O'Halloran, Janice T. .... Youngstown, OH
O'Halloran, John .... Los Angeles, CA
O'Halloran, John .... Buffalo, NY
O'Halloran, John F. .... Bayonne, NJ
O'Halloran, John M. .... Chicago, IL
O'Halloran, John T. .... Ewing, NJ
O'Halloran, Joseph P. .... Chicago, IL
O'Halloran, Julie A. .... Milwaukee, WI
O'Halloran, Kevin M. .... Westwood, NJ
O'Halloran, Kosoff, Geitner & Cook, P.C.
Chicago, IL
Northbrook, IL
O'Halloran, M. Sheilah .... Morristown, NJ
O'Halloran, Michael J. .... Chicago, IL
O'Halloran, Michael T., The Law Office of
San Diego, CA
O'Halloran, Neil J. .... New York, NY
O'Halloran, Richard A.
Plymouth Meeting, PA
O'Halloran, Robert L. .... Portland, OR
O'Halloran, Roger E. .... Fort Myers, FL
O'Halloran & Schofield .... Philadelphia, PA
O'Halloran, Sean .... Portland, OR
O'Halloran, Sean R. .... San Jose, CA
O'Halloran, Terence .... Greensburg, PA
O'Halloran, Teresa E. .... Minneapolis, MN
O'Halloran, Vincent J. .... Kansas City, MO
Ohana, Gilad Y. .... Palo Alto, CA
Ohanesian, Ara .... Fresno, CA
Ohanesian, Barbara A. .... Bennettsville, SC
Ohanesian, Consuelo M. .... Phoenix, AZ
Ohanesian, Gail D. .... Sacramento, CA
Ohanesian, Glenn V. .... Myrtle Beach, SC
Ohanesian, Gordon K. .... Sacramento, CA
Ohanesian, Gregory H. .... Bennettsville, SC
Ohanesian, Karolan F. .... Myrtle Beach, SC
Ohanesian & Ohanesian .... Bennettsville, SC
Ohanesian and Ohanesian .... Myrtle Beach, SC
Ohanessian, Norayr .... Los Angeles, CA
Ohanian, Diron M. .... Glendale, CA
Ohanian, Eric J. .... Cleveland, OH
Youngstown, OH
Ohanian, H. Artoush .... Houston, TX
O'Hanian, Hunter .... Boston, MA
Ohanlan, Aram M. .... Canton, OH
O'Hanlan, Edward V. .... Stamford, CT
O'Hanlon, Daniel J. .... San Francisco, CA
O'Hanlon, Edward P. .... New York, NY
O'Hanlon, Erin M. .... New York, NY
O'Hanlon, G. John .... Washington, DC
O'Hanlon, George A. .... Port Chester, NY
O'Hanlon, George B.
Research Triangle Park, NC
O'Hanlon, Janet L. .... St. James, NY
O'Hanlon, Jerry M. .... Fairfield, CA
O'Hanlon, John P. .... Putnam Valley, NY
O'Hanlon, John R. .... New York, NY
O'Hanlon, John V. .... Boston, MA
O'Hanlon Law Offices .... Blair, NE
O'Hanlon, Mary T. .... McMinnville, OR
O'Hanlon, Neil R. .... Los Angeles, CA
O'Hanlon, Paul M. .... Kansas City, MO
O'Hanlon, Robert J. .... Florissant, MO
O'Hanlon, Susan G. .... Omaha, NE
O'Hanlon, Timothy J. .... Pendleton, OR
O'Hanlon, Trischa J. .... Pasadena, CA
O'Hanrahan, Ellenore .... Stamford, CT
O'Hara, Alfred P. .... New York, NY
O'Hara, Alison E. .... Chicago, IL
O'Hara, Alton C. .... Syracuse, NY
O'Hara, Andrew S. .... Charlotte, NC
O'Hara, Ann M. .... Indianapolis, IN
O'Hara, Anne M. .... St. Petersburg, FL
O'Hara, Barbara J. .... Dunmore, PA
O'Hara, Brendan Paul .... Treasury Department, Internal Revenue Service, GV
O'Hara, Brian C. .... Glendale, CA
O'Hara, Brian J. .... Chicago, IL
O'Hara, Brian J. .... Bloomfield Hills, MI
O'Hara, Callie C. .... Los Angeles, CA
O'Hara, Carolyn M. .... Englewood, CO
O'Hara, Chad T. .... Philadelphia, PA
O'Hara, Charles D., Jr. .... Bridgeport, CT
O'Hara, Charles G. .... Pittsburgh, PA
O'Hara, Charles J. .... Fairfax, VA
O'Hara, Christopher A. .... Phoenix, AZ
O'Hara, Christopher C. .... Charlotte, NC
O'Hara, Christopher P. .... Garden City, NY
O'Hara, Christopher R. .... Boston, MA
O'Hara, Daniel J., Jr. .... Summit, NJ
O'Hara, David .... Fremont, CA
O'Hara, David Patrick .... Cazenovia, NY
O'Hara, Dennis G. .... Syracuse, NY
O'Hara, Dennis J. .... Chicago, IL
O'Hara, Dennis M. .... Fort Lauderdale, FL
Miami, FL
O'Hara, Diane Kathleen .... New Orleans, LA
O'Hara, Edward A., III .... Syracuse, NY
O'Hara, Edward B. .... Lakewood, CO
O'Hara, Elaine Rose .... Kansas City, MO
O'Hara, Elizabeth A. .... Modesto, CA
O'Hara, Elizabeth M. .... Los Angeles, CA
O'Hara, Ellen M .... Visalia, CA
O'Hara, Ellen M. .... Salt Lake City, UT
O'Hara, Erin .... Arlington, VA
O'Hara, F. Peter .... Brooklyn, NY
Garden City, NY
O'Hara, Frances Suarez .... Atlanta, GA
O'Hara, Francis P. .... Norristown, PA
Ohara, Frank H. .... Woodside, CA
O'Hara, Frank J. .... Philadelphia, PA
O'Hara, Frank R. .... Pittsburgh, PA
O'Hara, G. Stuart, Jr. .... Sandusky, OH
O'Hara, Georgina L. .... Philadelphia, PA
O'Hara, Gerard J. .... White Plains, NY
O'Hara, Gregory L. .... Des Moines, IA
O'Hara, Gregory Paul .... San Jose, CA
O'Hara & Hanlon, LLP .... Cazenovia, NY
Syracuse, NY
O'Hara, Harold N. .... East Peoria, IL
O'Hara, Hedwig .... New York, NY
O'Hara, Henry J. .... Kulpsville, PA
O'Hara, J. Brian .... San Ramon, CA
O'Hara, J. Michael .... Fort Wayne, IN
O'Hara, J. Patrick .... Santa Barbara, CA
O'Hara, J. Stephen, Jr. .... Jacksonville, FL
O'Hara, James F. .... Los Angeles, CA
O'Hara, James J. .... Morristown, NJ
O'Hara, James P. .... Overland Park, KS
Kansas City, MO
O'Hara, James T. .... Washington, DC
O'Hara, Jane R. .... New York, NY
O'Hara, Jeffrey J. .... Grand Rapids, MI
O'Hara, Jeffrey L. .... Roseland, NJ
O'Hara, Jennifer .... Port Jervis, NY
O'Hara, Jerilynn M. .... Jacksonville, FL
O'Hara, John A. .... Newport Beach, CA
O'Hara, John C., Sr. .... Canton, MA
O'Hara, John D. .... Vallejo, CA
O'Hara, John D. .... Vallejo, CA
O'Hara, John F. .... Los Angeles, CA
O'Hara, John J. .... Portland, OR
O'Hara, John M. .... Detroit, MI
O'Hara, John P., Jr. .... Bloomfield Hills, MI
O'Hara, John V. .... Philadelphia, PA
O'Hara, Joseph F. .... Liberty, MO
O'Hara, Joseph J., Jr. .... Chicago, IL
O'Hara, Joseph Paul .... Burlington, VT
O'Hara, Katherine A. .... New York, NY
O'Hara, Kathleen E. .... Buffalo, NY
O'Hara, Keith A. .... Binghamton, NY
O'Hara, Kerry Anne
Department Of The Interior, Office of the Solicitor, GV
O'Hara, Kevin .... Irvine, CA
O'Hara, Kevin J. .... Scranton, PA
O'Hara, Kevin P. .... Nashville, TN
O'Hara, Kevin T. .... Sanford, FL
O'Hara, Kimerlee Petrik .... Des Moines, IA
O'Hara, Laura Proske .... Edison, NJ
O'Hara, Laura Reilly .... Dallas, TX
O'Hara Law Firm, P.A. .... Sanford, FL
O'Hara, Lawrence F. .... Trenton, NJ
O'Hara, Leslie E. .... Phoenix, AZ
O'Hara, Lisa Tinsley .... Mobile, AL
O'Hara, Lloyd H. .... Dayton, OH
O'Hara, Lorraine H. .... Los Angeles, CA
O'Hara, Malcolm B. .... Glens Falls, NY
O'Hara, Malcolm V. .... New Orleans, LA
O'Hara, Margaret .... Glendale, CA
O'Hara, Margaret L. .... Chicago, IL
O'Hara, Mark A. .... Herndon, VA
O'Hara, Mark S. .... Brownsburg, IN
O'Hara, Martin J. .... Chicago, IL
O'Hara, Mary Ann .... San Jose, CA
O'Hara, Mary Payton .... New York, NY
O'Hara, Matthew J. .... Chicago, IL
O'Hara, Maureen C. .... Los Angeles, CA
O'Hara, Michael .... Covington, KY
O'Hara, Michael A. .... Nashua, NH
O'Hara, Michael A. .... Livingston, NJ
O'Hara, Michael A. .... Cincinnati, OH
O'Hara, Michael A., III, P.C.
Steamboat Springs, CO
O'Hara, Michael J. .... Los Angeles, CA
O'Hara, Michael J. .... Omaha, NE
O'Hara, Michael P. .... Fort Wayne, IN
O'Hara, Michael W. .... Springfield, IL
O'Hara, Michael W. .... Cherry Hill, NJ
O'Hara, Milena D. .... Beverly Hills, CA
O'Hara, Nancy .... Los Angeles, CA
O'Hara, Nancy P. .... Philadelphia, PA
O'Hara, Nicholas V. .... St. Paul, MN
O'Hara & O'Connell, P.C. .... Syracuse, NY
O'Hara & O'Hara .... Bloomfield Hills, MI
O'Hara, Pat .... Elk City, OK
Oklahoma City, OK
Ohara, Patricia .... Honolulu, HI
O'Hara, Patricia A. .... Notre Dame, IN
O'Hara, Patrick .... Baton Rouge, LA
O'Hara, Patrick C., Jr. .... Somerville, NJ
O'Hara, Patrick J. .... Petersburg, IL
O'Hara, Patrick, Jr. .... Oklahoma City, OK
O'Hara, Patrick M.
West Palm Beach, FL
O'Hara, Patrick M., P.A.
West Palm Beach, FL
O'Hara, Raymond A., III .... Westport, CT
O'Hara, Richard L. .... Garden City, NY
O'Hara, Robert C. .... Wilmington, DE
O'Hara, Robert J. .... Hartford, CT
O'Hara, Robert J., III .... Pittsburgh, PA
O'Hara, Robert L. .... Detroit, MI
O'Hara, Robert S., Jr. .... New York, NY
O'Hara, Ruberg, Taylor, Sloan and Sergent
Covington, KY
Cincinnati, OH
O'Hara, Sara Towery .... Vienna, VA
O'Hara, Shellie Harvey .... Sanford, FL
O'Hara, Spradley, Jenson, Waters & McCall, P.A. .... Jacksonville, FL
O'Hara, Steven T. .... Anchorage, AK
O'Hara, Susan B. .... Newburyport, MA

O'Hara, Susan J. ....Palm Beach, FL
O'Hara, Susan M. ....Boston, MA
O'Hara, Terence J. ....San Jose, CA
Ohara, Thomas ....Tampa, FL
O'Hara, Thomas M. ....Mobile, AL
O'Hara, Thomas N. ....New Paltz, NY
O'Hara, Timothy D. ....Chicago, IL
O'Hara, Timothy D.A. ....Chicago, IL
O'Hara, Timothy J. ....Indianapolis, IN
O'Hara, Timothy W. ....Fresno, CA
O'Hara, Veronica B. ....Troy, MI
O'Hara, Vincent F. ....New York, NY
O'Hara, Vincent F., Sr. ....New York, NY
O'Hara, William D., Jr. ....Brainerd, MN
O'Hara, William J. ....New York, NY
O'Hare, Anne Liles ....Ashland, KY
O'Hare, Bernard F. ....New York, NY
O'Hare, Edward H. ....Newark, NJ
O'Hare, Eileen M. ....Fresno, CA
O'Hare, Fay A. ....Detroit, MI
O'Hare & Heitczman ....Bethlehem, PA
Easton, PA
O'Hare, James P. ....Baltimore, MD
O'Hare, James T. ....Nashville, TN
O'Hare, Jean A. ....New York, NY
O'Hare, Jennifer A. ....Miami, FL
O'Hare, John E. ....Tucson, AZ
O'Hare, John M. ....Chicago, IL
O'Hare, John P., Sr. ....Houston, TX
O'Hare, Kathleen McInerney ....Harrison, NY
O'Hare, Kathryn A. Sackett
Los Angeles, CA
O'Hare, Kevin F. ....Department of Justice, United States Marshals Service, GV
O'Hare, Kevin M. ....Marshalltown, IA
O'Hare, Mary V. ....Culver City, CA
O'Hare, Michael P. ....Philadelphia, PA
O'Hare Parnagian LLP ....New York, NY
O'Hare, Patrick A. ....Richmond, VA
O'Hare, Patrick K. ....Washington, DC
O'Hare, Richard C. ....Santa Rosa, CA
O'Hare, Richard J. ....Coral Gables, FL
O'Hare, Robert A., Jr. ....Wilmington, DE
O'Hare, Robert A., Jr. ....New York, NY
O'Hare, Robert J. ....New York, NY
O'Hare, Robert J. M., Jr. ....Johnston, RI
O'Hare, Rolland R. ....Detroit, MI
O'Hare, Sheila ....Dallas, TX
O'Hare, Stephen P. ....Hopewell Junction, NY
O'Hare, Terrence D. ....Omaha, NE
O'Hare, Thomas ....Silverdale, WA
O'Hare, Thomas F. ....Hopkinton, MA
O'Hare, Timothy J. ....Lewistown, MT
O'Hare, William J., P.C.
Hopewell Junction, NY
O'Hare, William S., Jr. ....Irvine, CA
O'Harra, Catherine ....Houston, TX
O'Harra, Colleen C. ....Oceanside, CA
O'Harra, Michael B. ....Sacramento, CA
Ohashi, John E. ....El Segundo, CA
Pasadena, CA
Ohashi & Priver ....El Segundo, CA
Pasadena, CA
O'Haver, James G. ....Kingman, AZ
Ohaver, Jane E. ....Peoria, IL
O'Hayer, Michael ....Wayne, PA
O'Hayre, Robert M. ....Gunnison, CO
O'Hea, June A. ....New York, NY
O'Heaghra, MacCrae ....Visalia, CA
O'Hear, Michael M. ....Chicago, IL
O'Hearn, Barbara ....Sacramento, CA
O'Hearn, Beverly G. ....Savannah, GA
O'Hearn, Christine ....Camden, NJ
Westmont, NJ
O'Hearn, L. Stephen, Jr. ....Savannah, GA
O'Hearn, Leo A. ....Oxnard, CA
O'Hearn, Marybeth Holland ....Barnstable, MA
O'Hearn, Michael J. ....Oxnard, CA
O'Hearn, Timothy J. ....Cleveland, OH
O'Hearn, William J., Jr. ....Nantucket, MA
O'Hearn, William W. ....Memphis, TN
O'Hearne, David B. ....Stamford, CT
Ohebsion, Amir ....Los Angeles, CA
O'Heir, Diane S. ....Bandera, TX
O'Hern, Billie Ann ....St. Petersburg, FL
O'Hern, Charles T. ....Delmar, NY
O'Hern, Daniel J. ....Red Bank, NJ
O'Hern, Daniel J., Jr. ....Newark, NJ
O'Hern, James E. ....Gig Harbor, WA
O'Hern, James Edward, III ....Fort Smith, AR
O'Hern, James I. ....Newark, NJ
O'Hern, J. L. ....Houston, TX
O'Hern, Patrick J. ....Livermore, CA
O'Hern, Steven K. ....Kansas City, MO
O'Hern, Thomas J. ....Albany, NY
O'Hern, Thomas M., Jr. ....St. Paul, MN
O'Hern, Tonya L. ....Kansas City, MO
O'Hern, William F. ....New York, NY
O'Heron, Joseph M. ....Los Angeles, CA
O'Herren, John ....Waco, TX
O'Herron, Felicity A. ....Englewood, CO
O'Herron, Margaret M.R.
Department of Justice, Executive Office for Immigration Review, GV
O'Herron, Matthew J. ....Falls Church, VA
O'Herron, Suzanne ....Mount Laurel, NJ
O'Herron, Thomas F.
Department of State, GV
Ohi, Eddie M., Jr. ....North Miami, FL
Ohigashi, Lee A. ....Wailuku, HI
Ohinata, Lori M. ....Honolulu, HI
Ohira, Michael T. ....Pasadena, CA
Ohl, Abigail Harriet Gummer
Ann Arbor, MI
Ohl, Charles N. ....Valencia, CA
Ohl, Dennis L. ....Lubbock, TX
Ohl, Donald J. ....Edwardsville, IL

Ohl, Mary Joan ....Los Angeles, CA
Ohlander, Jan H. ....Rockford, IL
Ohlandt, Greeley, Ruggiero & Perle
Stamford, CT
Ohlandt, John F. ....Stamford, CT
Ohlandt, Katherine ....Napa, CA
Ohlbaum, Edward D. ....Philadelphia, PA
Ohle, B. Robert ....St. Petersburg, FL
Ohlemeyer, William S. ....New York, NY
Ohlemiller, Marcia L. ....United States Senate, Senatorial Assistants, GV
Ohlenberg, Richard P. ....Shakopee, MN
Ohlenforst, Cynthia Morgan ....Dallas, TX
Ohler, Michael J. ....New York, NY
Ohler, Terrence B. ....Lakeport, CA
Ohleyer, Edward J. ....Indianapolis, IN
Ohleyer, Michael L. ....San Francisco, CA
Ohlgren, Joel R. ....Los Angeles, CA
Ohlhausen, Lisa T. ....Chicago, IL
Ohlhausen, Maureen K.
Federal Trade Commission, Offices of Commissioners, GV
Ohlhausen, Robert A. ....Oak Brook, IL
Ohlhausen, William G.
United States Information Agency, Office of the General Counsel, GV
Ohlig, Gretchan R. ....New York, NY
Ohlig, James J. ....New York, NY
Ohliger, Lee A. ....New York, NY
Ohliger, Paula C. ....San Francisco, CA
Ohlin, Charles E. ....Warren, OH
Ohlinger, Fred A. ....Tampa, FL
Ohlinger, Fred A., P.A. ....Tampa, FL
Ohlman, Jonathan D. ....Gainesville, FL
Ohlmann, Brent E. ....Wheaton, IL
Ohlmeyer, Alison F. ....Pittsburgh, PA
Ohlmeyer, Raleigh L., Jr. ....New Orleans, LA
Ohlms, Jacquelynn K. ....St. Louis, MO
Ohlms, Philip J. ....St. Charles, MO
Ohlms, Todd J. ....Chicago, IL
Ohlmuller, Raymond P. ....Franklin Lakes, NJ
Ohlrich, Roger C. ....Washington, DC
Ohlrogge, Kendel J. ....Minneapolis, MN
Ohlsen, Carolyn M. ....St. Louis, MO
Ohlsen, Mark A. ....Pueblo, CO
Ohlsen, Richard A. ....Brainerd, MN
Ohlsen, Robert W. ....Decatur, IL
Ohlsen-Johnson, Jonathan ....Eugene, OR
Ohlson, Barry J. ....Washington, DC
Ohlson, Carrol J. ....Louisville, KY
Ohlson, Elaine M. ....Boston, MA
Ohlson, Glenn W. ....Chicago, IL
Ohlson, John, Jr. ....Reno, NV
Ohlson, Kate E. ....San Francisco, CA
Ohlson, Kevin A. ....Department of Justice, Office of the Deputy Attorney General, GV
Ohlson, Kristin A. ....San Francisco, CA
Ohlson, Larry E. ....Rockford, IL
Ohlson, Richard W. ....Wellsville, NY
Ohlson, Robert D. ....Reading, MA
Ohlson & Springgate ....Reno, NV
Ohlstein, Myron ....San Antonio, TX
Ohlweiler, John W. ....New York, NY
Ohlwein, David ....Aurora, IL
Ohly, D. Christopher ....Baltimore, MD
Ohly, Frederick C. ....Washington, DC
Ohly, James C. ....Rochester, MN
Ohly, Louis M. ....Rochester, MN
Ohly, Robert S. ....Cleveland, OH
Ohm, Allan O. ....Ettrick, WI
Galesville, WI
Ohm, Alvin A. ....Dallas, TX
Ohm, Judith Mills ....Madison, WI
Ohm, Michael K. ....Chicago, IL
Ohm, Ralph, (P.A.)
Hot Springs National Park, AR
Ohm, Randall B. ....St. Paul, MN
Ohman, David John ....Fort Morgan, CO
Ohman, Earl R., Jr.
Occupational Safety and Health Review Commission, Office of the General Counsel, GV
Ohman, John C. ....New York, NY
Ohman, John M. ....Idaho Falls, ID
Ohme, Brennan Collins ....Birmingham, AL
Ohmer, Charles F. ....St. Louis, MO
Ohmer, Charles F., III ....St. Louis, MO
Ohmer & Ohmer, P.C. ....St. Louis, MO
Ohmer, Steven R. ....St. Louis, MO
Ohms, Mary Ann ....St. Louis, MO
Ohms, Timothy J. ....Spokane, WA
Ohmstedt, Marguerite R.
White Plains, NY
Ohnegian, Donald C. ....Mahwah, NJ
Ohnegian, Donald C. ....Ramsey, NJ
Ohnegian, Donald C. ....Ridgewood, NJ
Ohnegian, Scott A. ....Morristown, NJ
Ohneiser, Robert J. ....Ashburn, VA
Ohnesorge, Robert W. ....Houston, TX
Ohnick, Barbara ....Seattle, WA
Ohnstad, Dorinda J. M. ....Milbank, SD
Ohnstad, John V., Jr. ....Hanford, CA
Ohnstad, Mark G. ....Minneapolis, MN
Ohnstad Twichell, P.C. ....Moorhead, MN
Fargo, ND
Hillsboro, ND
Mayville, ND
West Fargo, ND
O'Hollaren, Paul J. ....West Linn, OR
O'Hop, Paul A., Jr. ....Washington, DC
O'Horo, Cathleen E. ....Canton, NY
O'Horo, Kristen L. ....Youngstown, OH
O'Horo, Robert A. ....Atlanta, GA
Ohr, Clara Juwon ....Omaha, NE
Ohr, Leslie A. ....Houston, TX
Ohrbach, Caryl E. ....San Rafael, CA
Ohre, Mark D. ....Phoenix, AZ
Ohren, Ronald L. ....Chicago, IL

Ohrenberger, Henry W. ....Boston, MA
Ohrenberger, William H., III ....Scituate, MA
Ohrenschall, John C. ....Denver, CO
Ohrenstein, Benjamin S. ....Haverford, PA
Ohrenstein & Brown, L.L.P.
Garden City, NY
New York, NY
Ohrenstein, David J. ....Washington, DC
Ohrenstein, John ....Santa Rosa, CA
Ohrenstein, Manfred ....New York, NY
Ohri, Shaila Lakhani ....Washington, DC
Ohrin, Lisa M. ....Baltimore, MD
Ohriner, Kenneth H. ....Los Angeles, CA
Ohringer, Arthur N. ....New York, NY
Ohringer, Mark J. ....Chicago, IL
Ohrn, Jon C. ....New York, NY
Ohrn, Luke ....Chicago, IL
McAllen, TX
Ohrnberger, John M. ....New York, NY
Ohrt, John C. ....Houston, TX
Ohrwashel, Norman A. ....New York, NY
Ohs, Larry D. ....Lincoln, NE
Ohsfeldt, Ronald A. ....Houston, TX
Ohsfeldt, Susan A. ....Houston, TX
Ohye, George H. ....Cranbury, NJ
Ohye, Yoshimi ....Uniondale, NY
Oie, Susan R. ....Sacramento, CA
Oien, Harold A., Jr. ....St. Paul, MN
Oien, Jessica Warner ....Los Angeles, CA
Oif, Barbara L. ....Hoboken, NJ
Oif, Leslie A.
Environmental Protection Agency, Office of Enforcement and Compliance Assurance, GV
Oifer, Edward G. ....Fairfax, VA
Oiffer, Michael C. ....Cleveland, OH
Oiknine, Joel S. ....Torrance, CA
Oill, Carolyn ....Beverly Hills, CA
Oines, Ronald P. ....Irvine, CA
Oisher, Jack ....New York, NY
Oistad, Jeffrey P. ....St. Cloud, MN
Oitzinger, John J. ....Helena, MT
Oium, Mark ....San Francisco, CA
Oja, Michael L. ....Santa Fe, NM
Oja, Richard W.
Rancho Santa Margarita, CA
Oja, Susan D. ....Denver, CO
Ojala, Carin L. ....Grand Rapids, MI
Ojala, Elizabeth M.
Environmental Protection Agency, Office of Enforcement and Compliance Assurance, GV
Ojala, Linda ....Minneapolis, MN
Ojalvo, Nisa Lynn ....New York, NY
Ojamaa, Elo-Kai ....Somerset, NJ
Ojan, Ourmazd S. ....Arlington, VA
Ojanen, Karuna ....Rochester, MN
Ojeda, Bernal P. ....Northridge, CA
Ojeda, Daniel A. ....San Francisco, CA
Ojeda, Elsa M. ....Miami, FL
Ojeda, Manuel R. ....New York, NY
Ojeda, Richard F. ....San Antonio, TX
Ojeda, Stephanie L. ....Charleston, WV
Ojeda-Castro, Diana L. ....San Juan, PR
Ojile, Frank M. ....Wichita, KS
Ojile, Fred ....Minneapolis, MN
Ojile, Michael E. ....Minneapolis, MN
Ojile, William M., Jr. ....Denver, CO
Ojiri, Rene E. ....Honolulu, HI
Ojserkis, Daniel S. ....Atlantic City, NJ
Ojserkis, Jill T. ....Atlantic City, NJ
Oka, Lynnette T. ....Honolulu, HI
Oka, Marcella C. ....Los Angeles, CA
Okabayashi, Neal K. ....Honolulu, HI
Okada, Dick M. ....San Francisco, CA
Okada, Michael ....Palo Alto, CA
Okada, Paul A. ....Palo Alto, CA
Okada, Raymond K. ....Honolulu, HI
Okada, Ronald S. ....Cleveland, OH
Okada, Shannon S., (Mr.) ....Wailuku, HI
Okafor, Ugo N. ....Atlanta, GA
Okai, Thomas K. ....Ontario, OR
Okal, Timothy H. ....Chicago, IL
Okali, Agwu U. ....New York, NY
Okami, Mika ....Atlanta, GA
Okamoto, Alan M. ....Hilo, HI
Okamoto, Duane E. ....Torrance, CA
Okamoto, James K. ....Palo Alto, CA
Okamoto, Jaye E. ....San Diego, CA
Okamoto, Jeri Christine ....Los Angeles, CA
Okamoto, Kenneth T. ....Honolulu, HI
Okamoto, Noriko Ellen ....Morristown, NJ
Okamoto, Quinn ....Playa Del Rey, CA
Okamoto, Yasuko ....New York, NY
Okamoto, Yasuo ....New York, NY
Okamura, George T. ....Honolulu, HI
O'Kane, Bernard P. ....Lakewood, CO
O'Kane, Brian P. ....Hempstead, NY
O'Kane, Brian Patrick ....Chicago, IL
O'Kane, Eileen Hanson ....Los Angeles, CA
O'Kane, Frank J., Jr. ....Santa Monica, CA
O'Kane, James G., Jr. ....Knoxville, TN
O'Kane, John, Jr. ....Honolulu, HI
O'Kane, Julie Hions ....Orlando, FL
Okane, Laura J. ....Sacramento, CA
O'Kane, Matthew R. ....Orlando, FL
O'Kane, Michael G. ....Dublin, OH
O'Kane, Michael J. ....Miami, FL
O'Kane, William J. ....Fort Washington, PA
O'Kane, William J., Jr. ....Haddonfield, NJ
Okano, Pamela A. ....Seattle, WA
Okano, Stephen M. ....Honolulu, HI
Okarma, Jerome D. ....Milwaukee, WI
Okaro, Ngozi ....New York, NY
O'Kasey, Karen ....Portland, OR
Okasinski, Damian Edward ....Dearborn, MI
Okawa, Gordon J. ....Sacramento, CA
Okawa, Iris R. ....Honolulu, HI

Okawachi, Stanley Kikuo ....Palo Alto, CA
Okay, Christopher M. ....Washington, DC
Okay Law Firm, The, L.L.C. ....Batavia, NY
Okay, Mehmet K. ....Batavia, NY
Okazaki, Brian K. ....Pasadena, CA
Pasadena, CA
Okazaki, James S. ....Laguna Hills, CA
Okazaki, Kenneth A. ....Salt Lake City, UT
Okazaki Law Offices ....Laguna Hills, CA
Pasadena, CA
Pasadena, CA
San Juan Capistrano, CA
Okazaki, Michel Andre ....Honolulu, HI
Okazaki, Theodore S. ....Glendale, CA
Okazaki, Zale T. ....Honolulu, HI
Okediji, Nike P. ....Nashville, TN
Okediji, Ruth Gana ....Oklahoma City, OK
O'Keefe, Andrew J. ....Bethlehem, CT
Hartford, CT
West Hartford, CT
O'Keefe, Arthur J. ....New Orleans, LA
O'Keefe, Ashenden, Lyons & Ward
Chicago, IL
O'Keefe, Bernard W. ....Pittsburgh, PA
O'Keefe, Brian D. ....Birmingham, MI
O'Keefe, Brian E. ....New York, NY
Okeefe, Brian L. ....Hauppauge, NY
O'Keefe, Brian T. ....Salem, MA
O'Keefe, Brian T. ....St. Clair Shores, MI
O'Keefe, Bridget M. ....Chicago, IL
O'Keefe, Carol L. ....Rochester, NY
O'Keefe, Christopher J. ....San Diego, CA
O'Keefe, Constance ....Washington, DC
O'Keefe, Daniel F., Jr. ....Washington, DC
O'Keefe, Daniel M. ....St. Louis, MO
O'Keefe, Daniel M. ....Springfield, OH
O'Keefe, Daniel P. ....Dallas, TX
O'Keefe, Daniel T. ....Orlando, FL
O'Keefe, David J. ....Los Angeles, CA
O'Keefe, David J. ....Chicago, IL
O'Keefe, Dennis M.
Commodity Futures Trading Commission, Division of Enforcement, GV
O'Keefe, Dennis P. ....Edison, NJ
O'Keefe, Diane J. ....New York, NY
O'Keefe, Donald E. ....Charlotte, NC
O'Keefe, Donald L. ....St. Louis, MO
O'Keefe, Douglas L. ....Miami, FL
O'Keefe, Dwight H., III ....Springfield, IL
O'Keefe, Edward F. ....Chappaqua, NY
O'Keefe, Edward F., (P.C.) ....Denver, CO
O'Keefe, Edward P. ....New York, NY
O'Keefe, Edward S., Jr. ....Clearwater, FL
O'Keefe, Egan & Peterman, L.L.P.
Austin, TX
O'Keefe, Eleanor M. ....New York, NY
O'Keefe, F. Ronald ....Cleveland, OH
O'Keefe, Garet D. ....San Francisco, CA
O'Keefe, Gerard P. ....Fairfax, VA
O'Keefe, J. Scott ....Philadelphia, PA
O'Keefe, Jack ....Dallas, TX
O'Keefe Jacobson Trial Lawyers, S.C.
La Crosse, WI
O'Keefe, James H. ....Grafton, ND
O'Keefe, James J. ....Portland, ME
O'Keefe, Jeffrey A. ....Fort Lauderdale, FL
O'Keefe, Jennifer Auer ....St. Louis, MO
O'Keefe, John A. ....Rockville Centre, NY
O'Keefe, John A., Jr. ....McLean, VA
O'Keefe, John E. ....Boston, MA
O'Keefe, John J. ....Salem, MA
O'Keefe, John J. ....New York, NY
O'Keefe, John J., III ....Chesapeake, VA
O'Keefe, John J., Jr. ....Florham Park, NJ
O'Keefe, John R. ....Minneapolis, MN
O'Keefe, John R., Jr. ....Pittsburgh, PA
O'Keefe, John W. ....Hartford, CT
O'Keefe, Joseph A. ....Fresno, CA
O'Keefe, Joseph C. ....Newark, NJ
O'Keefe, Joseph D. ....Philadelphia, PA
O'Keefe, Joseph J., Jr. ....Bethlehem, PA
O'Keefe, Joseph P. ....St. Louis, MO
O'Keefe, Julie Emmerich ....St. Louis, MO
O'Keefe, Katharine Susan ....Kansas City, KS
O'Keefe, Kathleen L. ....West Chester, PA
O'Keefe, Kathleen M. ....New York, NY
O'Keefe, Kelly A. ....Tallahassee, FL
O'Keefe, Kevin C. ....La Crosse, WI
O'Keefe, Kevin M. ....Chicago, IL
O'Keefe, Kevin M. ....St. Louis, MO
O'Keefe, Kevin P. ....New York, NY
O'Keefe, Kurt A. ....Detroit, MI
O'Keefe, Lawrence J. ....Peabody, MA
O'Keefe, Lisa ....Chicago, IL
O'Keefe, Lynne R. ....West Hartford, CT
O'Keefe, M. Rush, Jr. ....Memphis, TN
O'Keefe, Margaret M. ....New York, NY
O'Keefe, Matthew J. ....Bethlehem, CT
Hartford, CT
West Hartford, CT
O'Keefe, Maurice P., Jr. ....Atchison, KS
O'Keefe, Michael D. ....San Diego, CA
O'Keefe, Michael D. ....St. Louis, MO
O'Keefe, Michael E. ....Pacific Palisades, CA
O'Keefe, Michael H., Jr. ....New Orleans, LA
O'Keefe, Michael H., Sr. ....New Orleans, LA
O'Keefe, Michael J. ....Des Moines, IA
O'Keefe, Michael K. ....Washington, DC
O'Keefe, Michael R., III
New Orleans, LA
O'Keefe, Nicholas J. ....Chicago, IL
O'Keefe, Nicholas S. ....New York, NY
O'Keefe, O'Keefe & Bernstein, A Professional Law Corporation ....New Orleans, LA
O'Keefe, Patrick E. ....New Orleans, LA
O'Keefe, Patrick F. ....San Antonio, TX
O'Keefe, Patrick K. ....Washington, DC
O'Keefe, Peter K. ....Hartford, CT

Oldham, Sarah S. ....Greenwich, CT **Westport, CT**
Oldham, Scott M. ....**Akron, OH**
Oldham, Steve A. ....**Indianapolis, IN**
Oldham, Steven A. ....Sacramento, CA
Oldham, Susan S. ....**Rockville, MD**
Oldham, Theodore H. ....**Detroit, MI**
Oldham, William K. ....**Louisville, KY**
Oldham, William M. ....**Akron, OH**
Oldhouser, Wilson H., III ....**Baltimore, MD**
Olding, John H. ....Glen Cove, NY
Oldknow-Marshall, Sharon L. Cleveland, OH
Oldman, Cooley & Leighton, L.L.P. Encino, CA **Los Angeles, CA**
Oldman, Marshal A. ....**Los Angeles, CA**
Oldman, Oliver ....Cambridge, MA
Oldmen, Frank A. ....Costa Mesa, CA
Oldmixon, Colette A. ....**Poplarville, MS**
Oldroyd, J. Raymond ....Piscataway, NJ
Oldroyd, Jerold G. ....**Salt Lake City, UT**
Olds, Candace A. Department of Justice, GV
Olds, Charles B. ....Rogers, AR
Olds, Christopher Michael ....Frankfort, KY
Olds, David McN. ....Pittsburgh, PA
Olds, Edward A. ....Pittsburgh, PA
Olds, Eileen A. ....Chesapeake, VA
Olds, George R. ....Phoenix, AZ
Olds, Harry B., Jr. ....Novelty, OH
Olds, James, Jr. ....**Akron, OH**
Olds, Janeen-Ann A., (Atty. At Law, A Law Corp.) ....**Honolulu, HI**
Olds, Jeffrey S. ....**Vallejo, CA**
Olds, John R. ....Baton Rouge, LA
Olds, Julie Horn ....Syracuse, NY
Olds, Kenneth M. ....Wayne, NE
Olds Law Offices, P.A. ....Grangeville, ID
Olds & Mackinder ....Hartford, MI
Olds, Marjorie Z. ....Ithaca, NY
Olds, Michael J. ....**Platteville, WI**
Olds, Pieper and Connolly ....Wayne, NE
Olds, Russell S. ....Phoenix, AZ
Olds, Scott ....Grangeville, ID
Olds, Stuart K. ....**Richmond, KY**
Olds, Theodore W., III **Bloomfield Hills, MI**
Olds, Victoria A. ....Grangeville, ID
Olds, Warner S. ....Pompano Beach, FL
Oldshue, Jerry C., Jr. ....**Tuscaloosa, AL**
Oldstrom, Stephen C. ....Detroit, MI
Oldt, Charles L. ....**Easton, PA**
Oldweiler, Thomas P. ....**Mobile, AL**
Oldwin, Leonard E., Jr. ....Fairfield, CA
Olea, John ....**West Palm Beach, FL**
Olear, Conrad M. ....**Paramus, NJ**
Olear, Janice ....Department of Commerce, Patent and Trademark Office, GV
Olear, Kathleen Jane ....**Parsippany, NJ**
Olear, Leslie Inrig ....**Hartford, CT**
Olear, Stephen E. ....Orange, CA
Olearcek, Patrick Francis ....Springfield, MA
Olearcek, Steven F. ....Middletown, CT
O'Leary, Aileen P. ....Flushing, NY
O'Leary, Anne ....Hartford, CT
O'Leary & Associates ....**Los Angeles, CA**
O'Leary, Barbara-Cherrix Rehoboth Beach, DE
O'Leary, Brian C. ....Pittsburgh, PA
O'Leary, Brian M. ....Department of Justice, Executive Office for Immigration Review, GV
O'Leary, Caroline W. ....**Boston, MA**
O'Leary, Catherine Ann ....Tulsa, OK
O'Leary, Charles F. ....Manchester, NH
O'Leary, Clive A. ....Parker, CO
O'Leary, Colleen A. ....Treasury Department, Internal Revenue Service, GV
O'Leary, Colleen Elizabeth **San Diego, CA**
O'Leary, Cyril E. ....Fairhaven, MA
O'Leary, D. Michael ....**Tampa, FL**
O'Leary, Dan ....Olympia, WA
O'Leary, Daniel B. ....St. Paul, MN
O'Leary, Daniel E. ....**Portland, OR**
O'Leary, Daniel J. ....**Livonia, MI**
O'Leary, Daniel J. ....Bronx, NY
O'Leary, Daniel J. ....Kew Gardens, NY
O'Leary, Daniel J. ....**New York, NY**
O'Leary, Daniel P. ....San Diego, CA
O'Leary, Daniel V., Jr. ....**Chicago, IL**
O'Leary, David F. ....**Harrisburg, PA**
O'Leary, David G. ....**Chicago, IL**
O'Leary, David J. ....Janesville, WI
O'Leary, David Sean ....Denver, CO
O'Leary, Denis P. ....**New York, NY**
O'Leary, Dennis J. ....**Philadelphia, PA**
O'Leary, Dennis M. ....Albany, NY
O'Leary, Diane M. ....**Poughkeepsie, NY**
O'Leary, Dolores N. ....**New York, NY**
O'Leary, Donald M. ....St. Petersburg, FL
O'Leary, Donna Rowley ....**Jersey City, NJ** **New York, NY**
O'Leary, Edward P. ....**Boston, MA**
O'Leary, Elizabeth ....**New York, NY**
O'Leary, Elizabeth S. ....Anchorage, AK
O'Leary, Erin A. ....**New York, NY**
O'Leary, Eugene C. ....Guilford, CT
O'Leary, F. Douglas ....**St. Louis, MO**
O'Leary, Frank J. ....Chicago, IL
O'Leary, G. David ....Coral Gables, FL
O'Leary, G. Michael ....**Houston, TX**
O'Leary, Gerard E. ....Boston, MA
O'Leary, Gregory M. ....Seattle, WA
O'Leary, Harry Charles ....Janesville, WI
O'Leary, Harry J. ....Janesville, WI
O'Leary, Howard E., Jr. ....**Washington, DC**
O'Leary, J. Brian ....Comfrey, MN Sanborn, MN Springfield, MN
O'Leary, J. Cavanaugh ....**Houston, TX**
O'Leary, J. Dennis ....St. Louis, MO
O'Leary, James A. ....Providence, RI
O'Leary, James A., Jr. ....Worcester, MA
O'Leary, James C. ....Portland, OR
O'Leary, James D. ....**St. Louis, MO**
O'Leary, James F. ....Boston, MA
O'Leary, James L., II ....Bonita Springs, FL
O'Leary, James M. ....**Odessa, TX**
O'Leary, James S. ....**Lansing, MI**
O'Leary, James W. ....Oregon City, OR
O'Leary, Jane M. ....**Baltimore, MD**
O'Leary, Jeremiah L. ....**Short Hills, NJ**
O'Leary, JoErin ....**Pittsburgh, PA**
O'Leary, John A. ....Columbia, SC
O'Leary, John Andrew ....**Salina, KS**
O'Leary, John G. ....Staten Island, NY
O'Leary, John J. ....Chicago, IL
O'Leary, John J. ....Elmhurst, IL
O'Leary, John J. ....Middle Village, NY
O'Leary, John Patrick ....**Southfield, MI**
O'Leary, Joseph P. ....Baraga, MI
O'Leary, Joseph P. ....**Cincinnati, OH**
O'Leary, Joseph T. ....Brooklyn, NY
O'Leary, Joseph V. ....Chula Vista, CA
O'Leary, Kathleen E. ....Santa Ana, CA
O'Leary, Kathryn A. ....**Worcester, MA**
O'Leary, Kevin Boyd ....Boston, MA
O'Leary, Kevin D. ....**Los Angeles, CA**
O'Leary, Kevin D. ....**Hartford, CT**
O'Leary, Kevin J. ....**Norfolk, VA**
O'Leary Law Office ....**Sioux Falls, SD**
O'Leary, Lawrence F. ....Portland, OR
O'Leary, Leslie W. ....**Portland, OR**
O'Leary, Lynn A. ....**Los Angeles, CA**
O'Leary, Lynn A. ....**Hastings, MN**
O'Leary, Margaret M. ....Kansas City, MO
O'Leary, Marilyn C. ....**Albuquerque, NM**
O'Leary, Mark D. ....**Sioux Falls, SD**
O'Leary, Mark R. ....**Princeton, NJ**
O'Leary, Martin J. ....**San Francisco, CA**
O'Leary, Mary Ellen ....Shelton, CT
O'Leary, Matthew T. ....**Denver, CO**
O'Leary & McMahon ....Staten Island, NY
O'Leary, Meg ....**Albany, NY** **Saratoga Springs, NY**
O'Leary, Melissa (Dalla) ....**Denver, CO**
O'Leary, Michael ....Middletown, NY
O'Leary, Michael A. ....Millbury, MA
O'Leary, Michael B. ....Dearborn, MI
O'Leary, Michael F. ....**San Francisco, CA**
O'Leary, Michael J. ....Fall River, MA
O'Leary, Michael T. ....New York, NY
O'Leary, Molly ....**Boise, ID**
O'Leary & Moritz, Chartered ....Comfrey, MN Sanborn, MN Springfield, MN
O'Leary, Nancy ....Cambridge, MA
O'Leary, O'Leary, Jacobs, Mattson, Perry & Mason, P.C. ....**Detroit, MI** **Southfield, MI**
O'Leary, Patrick F. ....**Washington, DC**
O'Leary, Patrick F. ....Goshen, IN
O'Leary, Patrick, Jr. ....Pittsburgh, PA
O'Leary, Paul V. ....West Barnstable, MA
O'Leary, Prentice L. ....**Los Angeles, CA**
O'Leary, Richard A. ....Wheaton, IL
O'Leary, Richard P. ....**Newark, NJ**
O'Leary, Richard Raymond ....Lowell, MA
O'Leary, Robert M. ....Binghamton, NY
O'Leary, Robert P. ....Elizabeth, NJ
O'Leary, Robert P. ....Manlius, NY
O'Leary, Robert P., P.C. ....Manlius, NY
O'Leary, Robert T. ....Butte, MT
O'Leary, Robt. D. ....Quincy, MA
O'Leary, Robt. T. ....Baltimore, MD
O'Leary, Rosemary ....Syracuse, NY
O'Leary, Sara B. ....New Bedford, MA
O'Leary, Sarah E. ....Boston, MA
O'Leary, Sean ....Garden City, NY
O'Leary, Sean E. ....Easthampton, MA
O'Leary, Sean P. ....Haverhill, MA
O'Leary, Sean T. ....**New York, NY** West Warwick, RI
O'Leary, Shannon L. ....**Austin, TX**
O'Leary, Sharon A. ....**Englewood, CO**
O'Leary, Shawn T. ....**Walnut Creek, CA**
O'Leary, Sheila E. ....**Boston, MA**
O'Leary, Susan Wood ....Chicago, IL
O'Leary, Terence P. ....Walton, NY
O'Leary, Terrence V. ....**Granite City, IL**
O'Leary, Theodore H. ....**Los Angeles, CA**
O'Leary, Thomas J. ....**Summit, NJ**
O'Leary, Thomas M. ....**Pasadena, CA**
O'Leary, Thomas M. ....Barrington, IL
O'Leary, Thomas M. ....**Southfield, MI**
O'Leary, Thomas M. ....**Atlantic City, NJ** **Pleasantville, NJ**
O'Leary, Thomas N. ....Phoenix, AZ
O'Leary, Timothy D. ....**Kansas City, MO**
O'Leary, Timothy E. ....**Palo Alto, CA**
O'Leary, Timothy F. ....**San Francisco, CA**
O'Leary, Timothy J. ....**Belleville, IL**
O'Leary, Timothy J., Jr. ....Washington, DC
O'Leary, Timothy M. ....Winter Park, FL
O'Leary, Virginia M. ....Oakland City, IN
O'Leary, William A. ....**Jacksonville, FL**
O'Leary, William E. ....Helena, MT
O'Leary, William M. ....**Butte, MT**
O'Leary, William V. ....Albany, NY
O'Leary, Wm. J. ....Sacramento, CA
Olech, Carol Currie ....**Syracuse, NY**
Olechny, Steven J. ....Reno, NV
Oleck, Adrienne ....Washington, DC
Oleck, Howard L. ....St. Petersburg, FL
Oleck, Mary Kay ....Orlando, FL
Olecki, Joseph T. ....**Columbus, OH**
Olecki, Michael J. ....**Beverly Hills, CA**
Oleckna, Kenneth S. ....Rahway, NJ
Oleen, Jan Matthew ....Council Grove, KS
Oleen, Kent E. ....Manhattan, KS
Olefson, Shari B. ....Fort Lauderdale, FL
Oleinick, Arthur ....Ann Arbor, MI
Oleinik, Joel H. ....**Baltimore, MD**
Oleinik, Michael G. ....**Los Angeles, CA**
Oleisky, Allen ....Minneapolis, MN
Oleisky, Jill Ann ....Minneapolis, MN
Oleisky & Oleisky, P.A. ....Minneapolis, MN
Oleisky, Robert ....Minneapolis, MN
Olejar, Linda M. K. ....Morristown, NJ
Olejar & Olejar, P.C. ....Morristown, NJ
Olejar, Robert J. ....Morristown, NJ
Olejarczyk, Pamela A. ....Milford, CT
Olejarz, Karen ....Bensalem, PA
Olejko, Mitchell J. ....**San Francisco, CA**
Olejniczak, Julian M. ....Nashville, TN
Olejniczak, Thomas M. ....**Green Bay, WI**
Olejnik, Thomas J. ....Pontiac, MI
Olek, Donald H. ....Naperville, IL
Oleks, John T. ....Peabody, MA
Oleksa, Michelle ....**Fresno, CA**
Oleksak, Paul J. ....Grayslake, IL
Oleksiewicz, Lawrence M. ....Los Angeles, CA
Oleksy, Kathryn A. ....Miami, FL
Oleksyk, Kenneth J. ....Riverview, FL
Olem, Oscar J. ....East Meadow, NY
Olen, Elliot Mark ....Fairless Hills, PA
Olen & Nicholas P.C. ....**Mobile, AL**
Olen, Stephen C. ....**Mobile, AL**
Olena, Arnold T. ....**Buffalo, NY**
Olena, Kenneth A. ....Buffalo, NY
Olenczuk, Alexandra ....**Los Angeles, CA**
Olenczuk, David M. ....**Los Angeles, CA**
Olender, Jack H. ....**Washington, DC**
Olender, Jack H., and Associates, P.C. **Washington, DC**
Olender, Kurt D. ....**Newark, NJ**
Olender, Robert A. ....Royal Oak, MI
Olender, Robert J. ....Cleveland, OH
Olender, Robert L. ....Bethesda, MD
Olender, Terrys T. ....Los Angeles, CA
Olendorff, Catherine A. ....**Las Vegas, NV**
Oleniacz, Bernard S. ....Bethesda, MD
Olenich and Richardson ....Ridgewood, NJ
Olenich, Walter ....Ridgewood, NJ
Olenick, Alice ....Waitsfield, VT
Olenick, Dave ....Waitsfield, VT
Olenick, Donald J. ....Rego Park, NY
Olenick, Michael H. ....Tallahassee, FL
Olenick & Olenick, P.C. ....Waitsfield, VT
Olenick, Philip R. ....Boston, MA
Oleniczak, Paul M. ....**Grand Rapids, MI**
Oleniczak, Victoria A. ....East Troy, WI
Oleniewski, Walter A. ....Silver Spring, MD
Olenko, Mariana ....**New York, NY**
Olenn, J. Renn ....**Warwick, RI**
Olenn & Penza ....**Providence, RI** **Warwick, RI**
O'Leno, Philip L. ....Los Angeles, CA
Olens, Samuel S. ....Atlanta, GA
Olenski, Maribeth ....**Chicago, IL**
Oleon, Glenn P. ....Oakland, CA
Oler, Carren S. ....**Bethesda, MD**
Oler, Creighton G. ....San Francisco, CA
Oler, Curtis G. ....San Francisco, CA
Oler, Douglas B. ....**Richmond, IN**
Oler, Gayle E. ....**Dallas, TX**
Oler, Harriet L. B. ....Library of Congress, Copyright Office, GV
Oler, J. Wesley, Jr. ....Carlisle, PA
Oler & Oler ....San Francisco, CA
Oles, David E. ....**Atlanta, GA**
Oles, Douglas S. ....**Seattle, WA**
Oles, Frank J. ....Chicago, IL
Oles, Karl F. ....**Seattle, WA**
Oles, Morrison, Rinker & Baker, LLP **Anchorage, AK**
Oles, Morrison, Rinker & Baker L.L.P. **Seattle, WA**
Oles, Stuart G. ....**Seattle, WA**
Olesen, Anne K. ....Department of Justice, Civil Rights Division, GV
Olesen, Cheryl ....**Beaumont, TX**
Olesen, Elvi J. ....San Diego, CA
Olesen, Willard W. ....**Greenfield, IA**
Olesh, Martin H. ....**Flushing, NY**
Olesh, Stanley D. Department Of Health And Human Services, Office of the General Counsel, GV
Olesiuk, John M. ....Asheville, NC
Olesiuk, Walter W. J. ....Beverly Hills, CA
Oleske, Mary E. Laspakis ....Manhasset, NY
Oleske, Michael M. ....New York, NY
Olesker, Landis ....**New York, NY**
Oleskey, Stephen H. ....**Boston, MA**
Oleski, Nancy ....**Thousand Oaks, CA**
Oleskiewicz, Francis S. ....Framingham, MA
Olesky, David E. ....**Dallas, TX**
Olesnycky, Nestor L. ....East Hanover, NJ
Olesnyckyj, Myron F. ....New York, NY
Oleson, Debra Ann ....Mount Prospect, IL
Oleson, George D. ....Fayetteville, AR
Oleson, George T. ....Clive, IA
Oleson, Gregory R. ....Palm Desert, CA
Oleson, H. James ....Kalispell, MT
Oleson, Joseph M. ....Laguna Niguel, CA
Oleson, Kenneth D. ....San Francisco, CA
Oleson, Kimberly G. ....Rancho Mirage, CA
Oleson Law Corporation **Nevada City, CA**
Oleson Law Firm ....Kalispell, MT
Oleson, Raymond C. ....**Nevada City, CA**
Oleson, Richard C. ....**White Plains, NY**
Oleson, Stan D. ....Minneapolis, MN
Oleson, William S. ....**White Plains, NY**
Olesten, Christina ....**Santa Monica, CA**
Oleszczuk, Timothy K. ....Milwaukee, WI
Oleszewski, Richard Joint Committees And Commissions, GV
Oleszkiewicz, Robert T. ....**Chicago, IL**
Oleszkiewicz, Stephen M. ....Chicago, IL
Oleszkiewicz, Vincent S. ....**Chicago, IL**
Oleszkowicz, Michael J. ....Detroit, MI
Oleszycki, Charles R. Department of State, GV
Oletsky, Jason S. ....**Fort Lauderdale, FL**
Olevson, Ken ....Wallingford, CT
Olevson, Samuel Arthur ....Providence, RI
Olewiler, Norman R. ....York, PA
Olewinski, Mark A. ....Orlando, FL
Olewinski, Michael ....Morris, IL
Olewnik, Richard L. ....Pittsfield, MA
Olexa, Donald S. ....Roswell, GA
Olexa, Georgine A. ....**Allentown, PA**
Olexo, George R. ....Wilton, CT
Olexy, Peter D., (P.C.) ....**Washington, DC**
Oley, Jarlath ....Los Angeles, CA
Oleyer, George R. ....Bridgeport, CT
Oleyer, John M. ....**Hartford, CT**
Oleynik, Jeffrey E. ....**Greensboro, NC** **Raleigh, NC**
Oleynik, Ronald A. ....**Washington, DC**
Olf, Jerald R. ....Los Angeles, CA
Olfano, Robert R. ....New York, NY
Olfson, Herbert B. ....Glenview, IL
Olfson, James O. ....Baltimore, MD
Olgiati, Susan L. ....**Princeton, NJ**
Olgin, Deborah Cooley ....Louisville, KY
Olgin, Elise Anne ....New York, NY
Olgin, Jeffrey ....Branford, CT
Olgin, Steven B. ....New York, NY
Olgin, Tracy ....**Los Angeles, CA**
Olguin, Janet ....**Las Vegas, NV**
Oliak, Beth A. ....**New York, NY**
Olian, Irwin A., Jr. ....Los Angeles, CA
Olian, J. Robert ....Miami, FL
Olian, Jeffrey H. ....San Diego, CA
Olian, Robert M. ....**Chicago, IL**
Olian, Terri R. ....Highland Park, IL
Oliason, Tarl R. ....Seattle, WA
Olick, Alice D. ....New York, NY
Olick, Arthur S. ....**New York, NY**
Olick, Eric David ....Boston, MA
Olick, Jonathan A. ....**New York, NY**
Olick, Philip S. ....**New York, NY**
Olick, Robert S. ....Roseland, NJ
Olick, Susan Emma ....New York, NY
Olicker, Maury R. ....**Miami, FL**
Olidge, Darilyn T. ....**New York, NY**
Olien, Carl J. ....Owego, NY
Oliensis, Sheldon ....**New York, NY**
Olifant, Scott B. ....North Hollywood, CA
Olifer, Edward G. ....Washington, DC
Oliff, Alice Cole ....Boston, MA
Oliff & Berridge, PLC ....**Washington, DC** **Alexandria, VA** **Arlington, VA**
Oliff, James A. ....**Alexandria, VA**
Oliff, Jay R., (P.C.) ....**San Jose, CA**
Olijnyk, Roman ....Las Vegas, NM
Oliker, Jacob ....Venice, CA
Oliker, Robert P. ....Petaluma, CA
Olim, Max ....Atlanta, GA
Olimpi, Joseph M. ....Aliquippa, PA
Olimpia, Gary L. ....**San Jose, CA**
Olimpia, Whelan & Lively, A Professional Corporation ....**San Jose, CA**
Olin, Allen O. ....West Chester, PA
Olin, Caroline L. ....Albuquerque, NM
Olin, David M. ....Thief River Falls, MN
Olin, Dorothy E. ....Springfield, VA
Olin, Douglas H. ....**Greenwich, CT**
Olin, Elliott C. ....New York, NY
Olin, Jean K. ....Miami Beach, FL
Olin, John P. ....Chaska, MN
Olin, Joseph R. ....**Kentfield, CA**
Olin, Joyce A. Environmental Protection Agency, Office of Enforcement and Compliance Assurance, GV
Olin, Keith ....**Miami, FL**
Olin, Michael S. ....**Miami, FL**
Olin, Milton E., Jr. ....Los Angeles, CA
Olin, Mitchell J. ....Miami, FL
Olin, Nathan A. ....Hartford, CT
Olin, Neil & Haltrecht ....West Chester, PA
Olin, R. Brendan ....**Chattanooga, TN**
Olin, Robert ....**New York, NY**
Olin, Suzanne M. ....Lake Success, NY
Olincy, J. Dan ....**Los Angeles, CA**
Olincy & Karpel ....**Los Angeles, CA**
Olinde, Henry D. H., Jr. **Baton Rouge, LA**
Olinde, John F. ....**New Orleans, LA**
Oliner, Aron Mark ....**San Francisco, CA**
Oliner, Harris ....**New York, NY**
Oliner, Jacob ....Brooklyn, NY
Oliner, Jerome S. ....**New York, NY**
Oliner, Joyce L. ....**Washington, DC**
Oliner, Martin ....**New York, NY**
Oliner, Martin, P.C. ....**New York, NY**
Oliner, S. David ....Brooklyn, NY
Olinger, Benjamin R. ....**Asheville, NC**
Olinger, David Y., Jr. ....Lexington, KY
Olinger, Heather K. ....**Indianapolis, IN**
Olinger, Lovald, Robbennolt, McCahren and Reimers, P.C. ....**Pierre, SD**
Olinger, Nancy E. ....Austin, TX
Olinger, Philip S. ....Cincinnati, OH
Olinger, Robin M. ....Cincinnati, OH
Olinger, Ronald D. ....**Pierre, SD**

Olinger, William F. ... Cedar Rapids, IA
Olinick, Martin ... Beverly Hills, CA
O'Linn, Mildred K. ... Los Angeles, CA
Olins, Douglas F. ... San Diego, CA
Olins, Foerster & Hayes ... San Diego, CA
Santa Ana, CA
Olins, Jay S. ... Los Angeles, CA
Olins, Torrey A. ... Irvine, CA
Olinsky & DiMartino ... Oswego, NY
Olinsky, Howard D. ... Oswego, NY
Olinsky, Mark S. ... Newark, NJ
New York, NY
Olinsky, Wendy R. ... Methuen, MA
Olio, Louis ... Fontana, CA
Oliphant, C. Frederick, III
Washington, DC
Oliphant, Dara Beth ... Gainesville, FL
Oliphant, David J. ... Granada Hills, CA
Oliphant, Hammond, O'Hara & Atwell, L.L.C. ... Steamboat Springs, CO
Oliphant, James B. F., P.C.
Steamboat Springs, CO
Oliphant, James S. ... Columbus, OH
Oliphant, Jeff D. ... Indianapolis, IN
Oliphant, Jeffrey ... Westlake Village, CA
Oliphant, John H. ... North Hollywood, CA
Oliphant, L. Dee ... Purcell, OK
Oliphant, Lincoln C. ... United States Senate, Senatorial Assistants, GV
Oliphant, Neal D. ... Paducah, KY
Oliphant, R. Shawn ... Reno, NV
Oliphant, Robert E. ... St. Paul, MN
Oliphant, Scott E. ... New Orleans, LA
Oliphant, Susan E. ... Minneapolis, MN
Oliphant, Theotis F. ... San Francisco, CA
Oliss, Philip M. ... Cleveland, OH
Oliszewicz, Sandra D. ... Deerfield, IL
Olit, Lisa ... Madison Heights, MI
Olitsky, Andrea H. ... Buffalo, NY
Olitsky, Norman ... Portsmouth, VA
Olitt, Lance N. ... New York, NY
Oliva, Anthony J. ... Los Angeles, CA
Oliva, Bridgette Sopper ... San Antonio, TX
Oliva, Donna R. ... New York, NY
Oliva, Javier F. ... San Antonio, TX
Oliva, John E. ... White Plains, NY
Oliva, John G. ... Nashville, TN
Oliva, Joseph A. ... New York, NY
Oliva, Joseph E. ... Great Neck, NY
Oliva, Joseph L. ... San Marcos, CA
Oliva, Judith M. ... Albuquerque, NM
Oliva, Karin M. ... Los Angeles, CA
Oliva, Linda M. ... Great Neck, NY
Oliva, Louis Paul ... Long Island City, NY
Oliva, Michael G. ... Lansing, MI
Oliva, Pamela A. ... Windsor, CT
Oliva, Ruben ... Miami, FL
Oliva, Stephen E. ... Sacramento, CA
Oliva, Suzanne Dapra ... San Antonio, TX
Oliva, Thomas Medardo ... New York, NY
Olivadoti & Olivadoti ... Dallas, TX
Olivadoti, Paul S. ... Dallas, TX
Olivadoti, Peter J. ... Dallas, TX
Oliva-Dowdell, Catherine ... Fort Lee, NJ
Olivar, Harry A. ... Los Angeles, CA
Olivar, Harry A. ... Los Angeles, CA
Olivar, Harry A., Jr. ... Los Angeles, CA
Olivares, Alicia ... Los Angeles, CA
Olivares, Ernest Jay ... Norway, MI
Olivarez, Carla J. ... El Paso, TX
Olivarez, Leticia ... San Diego, CA
Olivas, Adolf ... Hamilton, OH
Olivas, Daniel A. ... Los Angeles, CA
Olivas, David A. ... Denver, CO
Olivas, David J. ... Los Angeles, CA
Olivas, Jane ... Los Angeles, CA
Olivas, Sean ... Albuquerque, NM
Oliva Sainz de Aja, Margarita
New York, NY
Olive, B. B. ... Durham, NC
Olive, Ben E. ... Dayton, OH
Olive, Carolyn D. ... Tallahassee, FL
Olive, Frank W. ... Summit, NJ
Olive, Graydon V., III ... Columbia, SC
Olive, Jack H. ... San Francisco, CA
Olive, Laurence H. ... Montclair, NJ
Olive, Laurence Leon ... Charlotte, NC
Olive, Leon ... Charlotte, NC
Olive, Mark G. ... Minneapolis, MN
Olive, Martha Corry ... Tallahassee, FL
Olive, Michael A., Jr. ... Houston, TX
Olive and Olive, P.A. ... Durham, NC
Raleigh, NC
Olive & Olive, P.C. ... Knoxville, TN
Olive, Patricia A. ... Los Angeles, CA
Olive, Patricia M. ... Eagan, MN
Olive, Richard L. ... Summit, NJ
Olive, Robert S. ... Knoxville, TN
Olive, Sabrena A. ... Charleston, WV
Olive, Sandra G. ... Knoxville, TN
Olive, Stewart W. ... Fort Collins, CO
Olive, Susan Freya ... Durham, NC
Olive, Taber & Owens, P.A.
Minneapolis, MN
Olive, Thomas H. ... Minneapolis, MN
Olive, W. Robert ... Tallahassee, FL
Oliveau, Maidie E. ... Los Angeles, CA
Oliveira, Ana ... Somerset, NJ
Oliveira, Belisa Marie ... St. Petersburg, FL
Oliveira, Carla ... New York, NY
Oliveira, David G. ... Brownsville, TX
Oliveira, David J. ... Providence, RI
Oliveira, Duane S. ... Sacramento, CA
Oliveira, F. Jeffrey ... Merrillville, IN
Oliveira, Jeffrey, & Associates
Merrillville, IN
Oliveira, Jeffrey J. ... Farmington, CT
Oliveira, Karen Auclair ... Lincoln, RI
Oliveira, Kevin Thomas ... Fairfax, VA
Oliveira, Kris E. ... Fall River, MA
Oliveira, Linda D. ... Boston, MA
Oliveira, Mario ... Blue Bell, PA
Oliveira, Michael J. ... Newark, NJ
Oliveira, Nelson R. ...
Overseas Private Investment Corporation, GV
Oliveira, Rene O. ... Brownsville, TX
Oliveira, Ronald E. ... Pittsfield, MA
Olivella, Miguel ... Titusville, FL
Olivella, Miguel A., Jr. ... Tallahassee, FL
Olive-Monnett, Laura, P.A. ... Charlotte, NC
Olive-Monnett, P.A. ... Charlotte, NC
Oliver, Aaron T. ... Des Moines, IA
Oliver, Alicia Brown ... Chattanooga, TN
Oliver, Anthony T., Jr. ... Los Angeles, CA
Oliver, Arlene Gordon ... Harrison, NY
Oliver, Arthur P. ... Pocatello, ID
Oliver, Arvid D. ... Des Moines, IA
Oliver, Augustus K., II ... New York, NY
Oliver, Bert Richard ... Weston, FL
Oliver, Bonnie Chessher ... Gainesville, GA
Oliver, Brooke, & Associates
San Francisco, CA
Oliver, Bruce D. ... Pleasanton, CA
Oliver, Bruce S. ... McLean, VA
Oliver, Carl R. ... San Antonio, TX
Oliver, Carl R., P.C., Law Offices of
San Antonio, TX
Oliver and Carney, P.C. ... Arvada, CO
Oliver, Carolyn K. ... Doylestown, PA
Oliver, Carolyn L. ... San Diego, CA
Oliver, Carrie N. ... Belleville, IL
St. Louis, MO
Oliver, Casey A. ... Merced, CA
Oliver, Catherine ... Taos, NM
Oliver, Charles A. ... Dallas, TX
Oliver, Charles A., A Professional Corporation ... Dallas, TX
Oliver, Charles C. ... Kansas City, MO
Oliver, Charles Douglas ... Pasadena, CA
Oliver, Charles M. ... Washington, DC
Oliver, Cheryl L. ... Atlanta, GA
Oliver, Choya G. ... Lexington, KY
Oliver, Christine P. ... Philadelphia, PA
Oliver, Christopher J. ... Chicago, IL
Oliver, Cindy Coles ... Denver, CO
Oliver, Cindy G. ... Raleigh, NC
Oliver, Close, Worden, Winkler & Greenwald ... Rockford, IL
Lake Geneva, WI
Oliver, Craig R. ... Springfield, MO
Oliver, Dale H. ... Los Angeles, CA
Oliver, Daniel A. ... Morgantown, WV
Oliver, DanielLee ... Evansville, IN
Oliver, Darlene M.
Commodity Futures Trading Commission, Division of Enforcement, GV
Oliver, David ... Bay St. Louis, MS
Biloxi, MS
Oliver, David ... Gulfport, MS
Oliver, David ... Hattiesburg, MS
Jackson, MS
Pascagoula, MS
Wiggins, MS
Oliver, David A. ... Columbia, MO
Oliver, David A. ... Houston, TX
Oliver, David B. ... Salt Lake City, UT
Oliver, David F. ... Kansas City, MO
Oliver, David P. ... Olympia, WA
Oliver, David S. ... Orlando, FL
Oliver, David W.
United States International Trade Commission, Office of the Commissioners, GV
Oliver, Deborah B. ... New York, NY
Oliver, Donald D. ... Syracuse, NY
Oliver, Donna F. ... Newtown Square, PA
Oliver, Douglas K. ... Redford, MI
Oliver, Duckworth, Sparger & Winkle, P.C.
Jonesboro, GA
Oliver, E. Joan ... Trenton, NJ
Oliver, Edward ... Oklahoma City, OK
Oliver, Edward Page
Clear Lake Shores, TX
Oliver, Edward Page ... Houston, TX
Oliver, Elaine B. ... Salem, OR
Oliver, Eric ... Washington, DC
Oliver, Eric J. ... Chattanooga, TN
Oliver, Eric Vincent ... Fort Worth, TX
Oliver, Erica J. ... San Francisco, CA
Oliver, Erik ... Palo Alto, CA
Oliver, Eugene R. ... Seattle, WA
Oliver, Fernando ... Hackensack, NJ
Oliver, Frank ... Austin, TX
Oliver, Frank W. ... Miami, FL
Oliver, Fred B. ... Sacramento, CA
Oliver, Fred B., Inc. ... Sacramento, CA
Oliver, G. Robert ... Jonesboro, GA
Oliver, Garvin L.
Federal Labor Relations Authority, Office of the Administrative Law Judges, GV
Oliver, Geoffrey D.
Federal Trade Commission, Bureau of Competition, GV
Oliver, George E. ... Savannah, GA
Oliver, George J. ... Raleigh, NC
Oliver, Georgiann ... Belleville, IL
Oliver, Glenn H. ... Southfield, MI
Oliver, Gregory S. ... Dallas, TX
Oliver, Harry Gordon, II
San Francisco, CA
Oliver, Harvey A., Jr. ... Aberdeen, SD
Oliver, Helen M. ... Raleigh, NC
Oliver, Henry E. ... Philadelphia, PA
Oliver, Howard C. ... Montgomery, AL
Oliver, Hugh G. ... Westwego, LA
Oliver, J. Van ... Dallas, TX
Oliver, James ... Raleigh, NC
Oliver, James A. ... Seattle, WA
Oliver, James C. ... Baltimore, MD
Oliver, James Craig ... Nashville, TN
Oliver, James D. ... Topeka, KS
Wichita, KS
Oliver, James E., Jr. ... Portland, OR
Oliver, James J. ... Mount Laurel, NJ
Norristown, PA
Pottstown, PA
Spring City, PA
West Chester, PA
Oliver, James N., Jr. ... Hampton, CT
Oliver, James P. ... Cleveland, OH
Oliver, James S. ... Pueblo, CO
Oliver, James S. ... Chester, NJ
Oliver, James W. ... Hartford, CT
Oliver, Jami S. ... Columbus, OH
Oliver, Jan P., (Mr.) ... Hollywood, FL
Oliver, Janet E. ... Kansas City, MO
Oliver, Jason F. ... Honolulu, HI
Oliver, Jason L. ... Sherman Oaks, CA
Oliver, Jeffrey C. ... Moline, IL
Oliver, Jerrold B. ... Winterset, IA
Oliver, Jerrold S. ... Orange, CA
Oliver, Jesse D. ... Austin, TX
Oliver, Jim U., Jr. ... Department of Justice, Civil Rights Division, GV
Oliver, Jody H. ... North Palm Beach, FL
Oliver, John C. ... San Antonio, TX
Oliver, John L., Jr. ... Cape Girardeau, MO
Oliver, John M. ... Albany, NY
Oliver, John M. ... Raleigh, NC
Oliver, John P. ... Dadeville, AL
Oliver, John P. ... Port Jefferson, NY
Oliver, John P., II ... Dadeville, AL
Oliver & Johnson, P.A. ... Minneapolis, MN
Oliver, Joseph E. ... Fairlawn, OH
Oliver, Joseph M., Jr. ... Washington, DC
Oliver, Julia Barnes
Research Triangle Park, NC
Oliver, Justin J. ... Washington, DC
Oliver, Katherine V. ... State College, PA
Oliver, Kathleen D. ... Houston, TX
Oliver, Kathryn ... San Francisco, CA
Oliver, Kelley Taylor ... Nashville, TN
Oliver, Kenneth J. ... Albany, NY
Oliver, Kenneth L. ... Newburgh, NY
Oliver, Kenneth L., Jr. ... Philadelphia, PA
Oliver, Kenneth M. ... Fort Lauderdale, FL
Oliver, Kenneth S. ... New York, NY
Oliver, Kenny L. ... Lafayette, LA
Oliver, Kent N. ... Hagerstown, MD
Oliver, Kevin ... Los Angeles, CA
Oliver, Kevin E. ... Dallas, TX
Oliver, Kevin Scott ... Southfield, MI
Oliver, Kevin T. ... Bay Shore, NY
Oliver, Kirk C. ... Sacramento, CA
Oliver, Kristen C. ... Houston, TX
Oliver, Kristin L. ... Tulsa, OK
Oliver, L. Scott ... Palo Alto, CA
Oliver, Larry L. ... Tulsa, OK
Oliver, Larry L., & Associates, P.C.
Tulsa, OK
Oliver, Lau, Lawhn, Ogawa & Nakamura, Attorneys At Law, A Law Corporation
Honolulu, HI
Kailua-Kona, HI
Lihue, HI
Wailuku, HI
Oliver, Laurie C. ... Syracuse, NY
Oliver Law Firm, P.C. ... Billings, MT
Oliver, Lawrence R. ... Department of Energy, Office of the General Counsel, GV
Oliver, Leland Chance ... Carrollton, TX
Oliver, Leonard L. ... San Antonio, TX
Oliver, Leslie Bakken ... Bismarck, ND
Oliver, Lewis B., Jr. ... Albany, NY
Oliver, Lewis M., III ... Orlando, FL
Oliver, Linda B. ... Walnut Creek, CA
Oliver, Linda L. ... Washington, DC
Oliver, Lloyd W. ... Houston, TX
Oliver, Lois A. ... Lebanon, OH
Oliver, Louis W., III ... Hendersonville, TN
Oliver, Luis A. ... San Juan, PR
Oliver, M. Leon ... Plano, TX
Oliver, M. Patricia Donnelly
Cleveland, OH
Oliver Maner & Gray LLP ... Atlanta, GA
Brunswick, GA
Savannah, GA
Statesboro, GA
Oliver, Manuel E. ... Orlando, FL
Oliver, Marcia B. ... Houston, TX
Oliver, Margaret L. ... Boston, MA
Oliver, Marianne ... Pittsburgh, PA
Oliver, Mark B. ... Lafayette, LA
Oliver, Marlo S. ... Palos Verdes Estates, CA
Oliver, Mary Ann ... Washington, DC
Oliver, Mary Margaret ... Decatur, GA
Oliver, Mary W. ... Chapel Hill, NC
Oliver, Matthew M. ... New York, NY
Oliver, Melinda ... Bronx, NY
Oliver, Melody W. ... Memphis, TN
Oliver, Michael D. ... Towson, MD
Oliver, Michael J. ... Pleasant Hill, CA
Oliver, Michael P. ... Overland Park, KS
Oliver, Michele Marie
Equal Employment Opportunity Commission, Office of Federal Operations, GV
Oliver, Milton M. ... Monroe, CT
Oliver, Morgan Dene ... San Diego, CA
Oliver, Nancy J. ... Wickford, RI
Oliver, Nancy K. ... Department of Justice, Criminal Division, GV
Oliver, Norman G., Jr. ... Los Angeles, CA
Oliver & Oliver ... Winchester, IN
Oliver & Oliver ... Berea, KY
Oliver & Oliver ... San Antonio, TX
Oliver & Oliver, P.C. ... Washington, DC
Reston, VA
Oliver, Oliver & Waltz, P.C. ... Anna, IL
Cairo, IL
Carbondale, IL
Marion, IL
Cape Girardeau, MO
Oliver, Orson ... Louisville, KY
Oliver, Owen L. ... Arvada, CO
Oliver, Patricia K. ... Los Angeles, CA
Oliver, Phillip R. ... Billings, MT
Oliver, Price and Rhodes ... Scranton, PA
Wilkes-Barre, PA
Oliver, R. Timothy ... Colorado Springs, CO
Oliver, Ralph S. ... Larimore, ND
Oliver, Randall C. ... Cleveland, OH
Oliver, Ranko Shiraki ... Little Rock, AR
Oliver, Raymond A. ... West Paterson, NJ
Oliver, Richard ... Tampa, FL
Oliver, Richard A. ... Washington, DC
Oliver, Richard B. ... Los Angeles, CA
Oliver, Richard B. ... Santa Clara, CA
Oliver, Ricky E. ... Nashville, TN
Oliver, Robert ... Los Angeles, CA
Oliver, Robert C. ... Houston, TX
Oliver, Robert C., Jr. ... Winchester, IN
Oliver, Robert C., Jr. ... Accomac, VA
Oliver, Robert C., Jr. ... Eastville, VA
Oliver, Robert G. ... New Haven, CT
Oliver, Robert H. ... Fresno, CA
Oliver, Robert J. ... Rockford, IL
Oliver, Robert L. ... San Marino, CA
Oliver, Robert L. ... Austin, TX
Oliver, Robert L. ... San Antonio, TX
Oliver, Robert W. ... Salem, OR
Oliver, Robert Webster ... Bay Shore, NY
Oliver, Rogelio R. ... Coral Gables, FL
Oliver, Roger M. ... Berea, KY
Oliver, Rosalind R. ... Los Angeles, CA
Oliver, Rose ... Walnut Creek, CA
Oliver, Roseann ... Chicago, IL
Oliver, Rufus W., III ... Houston, TX
Oliver, Sally J. ... Houston, TX
Oliver, Samuel ... Tavares, FL
Oliver, Samuel G. ... Darien, GA
Oliver, Samuel L. ... Gainesville, GA
Oliver, Samuel T., Jr. ... Raleigh, NC
Oliver, Samuel W., Jr. ... Birmingham, AL
Oliver, Scott ... Albuquerque, NM
Oliver, Shannon L. ... Albuquerque, NM
Oliver & Sims ... Dadeville, AL
Oliver, Solomon, Jr. ... Cleveland, OH
Oliver, Stephen A. ... Martinsville, IN
Oliver, Stephen E. ... Port Angeles, WA
Oliver, Stephen L. ... Portsmouth, OH
Oliver, Stephen R. ... San Jose, CA
Oliver, Steven D.
Hot Springs National Park, AR
Oliver, Steven Dow ... Gretna, LA
Oliver, Susan B. ... Greenwood, SC
Oliver, Susan G. ... Lynchburg, VA
Oliver, Susan L. ... San Diego, CA
Oliver, T. Walter, Jr. ... Tuscaloosa, AL
Oliver, Teel ... Washington, DC
Oliver, Terese S. ... Fullerton, CA
Oliver, Terri Kay ... Austin, TX
Oliver, Terry E. ... Tulsa, OK
Oliver, Thomas L., II ... Birmingham, AL
Oliver, Thomas M. ... Tyler, TX
Oliver, Thomas W. ... Dallas, TX
Oliver, Timothy A. ... Lebanon, OH
Oliver, Timothy J. ... Minneapolis, MN
Oliver, Tonya Y. ... Greenville, NC
Oliver, Vernon D. ... Glastonbury, CT
Oliver, Vincent J. ... Los Angeles, CA
Oliver, Vose, Sandifer, Murphy & Lee, A Professional Corporation
Los Angeles, CA
Oliver, Walker, Wilson & Ehrhardt, LLC
Columbia, MO
Jefferson City, MO
Oliver, Wallace L., Jr. ... Chicago, IL
Oliver, Wendell E. ... Normal, IL
Oliver, Wendy Beth ... Lake Oswego, OR
Oliver, Wesley A. ... Austin, TX
Oliver, Wesley MacNeil ... Nashville, TN
Oliver, Wiley E., Jr. ... Mineral Wells, TX
Oliver, William E. ... Roswell, GA
Oliver, William E. ... Lancaster, KY
Oliver, William H. ... San Antonio, TX
Oliver, William H., Jr. ... Asbury Park, NJ
Oliver, William Joseph ... Novi, MI
Oliver, William L., Jr. ... Wichita, KS
Oliver, William R. ... Cornelia, GA
Oliver, William W. ... Sugar Hill, NH
Olivera, Beatriz M. ... Chicago, IL
Olivera, Elizabeth Ufkes ... Chico, CA
Olivera, Gerard-Dominic T. ... Bakersfield, CA
Olivera, Keith R. ... Denver, CO
Oliveras, Héctor F. ... San Juan, PR
Oliveras, Hector G. ... San Juan, PR
Oliveras, R. Martin ... Chatham, NJ
Oliveras-Sifre, Oronte ... San Juan, PR
Oliverez, Peter E., Jr. ... Los Angeles, CA
Oliveri, Francis X. ... Somerville, MA
Oliveri, John M. ... Baltimore, MD
Oliveri, Leslie D. ... Lanham, MD
Oliveri, Paul F. ... New York, NY
Oliveri & Schwartz, P.C. ... New York, NY
Oliveri, Susan L. ... Easton, MD
Oliveri, Victor Alan ... Buffalo, NY
Oliveri, Warren S., Jr. ... Washington, DC
Gaithersburg, MD
Arlington, VA
Oliverio, B. P. ... Buffalo, NY

Oliverio, Daniel C. ... **Buffalo, NY**
Oliverio, M. Lawrence ... **Boston, MA**
Oliverio, Melissa K. ... **Morgantown, WV**
Olivero, David W. ... Peru, IL
Olivero, Douglas B. ... Peru, IL
Olivero, John ... Peru, IL
Tonica, IL
Olivero, Judy ... **Wayne, NJ**
Olivero, Kathy A. ... Bloomington, IL
Macomb, IL
Peoria, IL
Quincy, IL
Rushville, IL
Springfield, IL
Olivero, Lisa M. ... Peru, IL
Olivero, Louis E. ... Peru, IL
Olivero, Louis E., & Associates ... Peru, IL
Olivero, Manuel Jacobo Mendez
New York, NY
Olivero, Mark S. ... Fort Wayne, IN
Olivero, Noel M. ... Huntington, WV
Oliveros, Armando, Jr. ... **Miami, FL**
Oliveros, Edna Carmen ... Kansas City, KS
Oliver-Parrott, Alice ... **Houston, TX**
Oliver-Simon, Gloria C.
Department Of Veterans Affairs, Office of Human Resources Management, GV
Oliver-Vázquez, Gilberto ... San Juan, PR
Olives, F. Glen ... **Marysville, CA**
Olives Chavez, Marcia L.
Philadelphia, PA
Olivet, Jacqueline A. ... Catskill, NY
Olivetti, Armand E., Jr. ... **Scranton, PA**
Olivetti, Michael G.
Hilton Head Island, SC
Olivetti & Scacchitti ... **Honesdale, PA**
Milford, PA
Scranton, PA
Stroudsburg, PA
Wilkes-Barre, PA
Olivi, Ralph L., Jr. ... Chicago, IL
Olivia, Keith M. ... **Broomfield, CO**
Olivier and Brinkhaus ... Sunset, LA
Olivier, D. Craig ... Houston, TX
Olivier, Dan A. ... Houston, TX
Olivier, Daniel E. ... **Rancho Mirage, CA**
Olivier, Dena L. ... **New Orleans, LA**
Olivier, Elizabeth ... **Palm Desert, CA**
Olivier, Elizabeth A. ... **Portland, ME**
Olivier, Elizabeth M. ... Metairie, LA
Olivier, Frances M. ... New Orleans, LA
Olivier, Francis A., III ... Sunset, LA
Olivier, James D. ... Putney, VT
Olivier, James L. ... **Tampa, FL**
Olivier, Jason T. ... Metairie, LA
Olivier, Jeanne C. ... **New York, NY**
Olivier, John D. ... **Fort Lauderdale, FL**
Olivier, John D. ... Bartlesville, OK
Olivier, John L. ... Sunset, LA
Olivier, John T. ... New Orleans, LA
Olivier, Karla A. ... **New York, NY**
Olivier, Lynn M. ... **Farmington Hills, MI**
Olivier, Monique ... **San Francisco, CA**
Olivier and Olivier, P.C. ... **Ann Arbor, MI**
Detroit, MI
Farmington Hills, MI
Flint, MI
Lansing, MI
Mount Clemens, MI
Pontiac, MI
Olivier, Paul T., Jr. ... **Farmington Hills, MI**
Olivier, Rebecca M. ... Jefferson, LA
Olivier, Robert S. ... Frankenmuth, MI
Olivier, Roland E. ... **Manchester, NH**
Nashua, NH
Olivier, Sarah A. ... **Waltham, MA**
Olivier, Thomas P. ... **Boston, MA**
Olivier, Thomas T. ... Boston, MA
Olivier, William K. ... Department of Justice, Civil Division, GV
Olivieri, Alessandro G. ... New York, NY
Olivieri, Daniel R. ... Garden City, NY
Olivieri, Henry J., Jr. ... Mokena, IL
Olivieri, John M. ... **New York, NY**
Olivieri, José A. ... **Milwaukee, WI**
Olivieri, Richard J. ... **New York, NY**
Olivieri, Robert J. ... **Buffalo, NY**
Olivieri, Vincent R. ... Virginia Beach, VA
Olivieri-Barreto, Veronica ... **San Juan, PR**
Olivio, Michael A. ... **Charleston, WV**
Olivito, Dominick E. ... Steubenville, OH
Olivito, Dominick E., Jr. ... Carrollton, OH
Olivito, Peter S. ... Steubenville, OH
Olivito, William P. ... Oakland, CA
Olivo, Andrew C. ... **Carrollton, TX**
Olivo, Anthony ... Brooklyn, NY
Olivo, Anthony ... **New York, NY**
Olivo, Anthony M. ... Haddonfield, NJ
Olivo, Craig L. ... **Mineola, NY**
New York, NY
Olivo, Eduardo ... Los Angeles, CA
Olivo, Frank G. ... Hammonton, NJ
Olivo, John William, Jr. ... **Summit, NJ**
New York, NY
Olivo, Kenneth ... Rockville, MD
Olivo, Paul J. ... New York, NY
Olivo, Peter-Christian ... **Broomfield, CO**
Olivo, Steven M. ... **Danbury, CT**
Olix, Thomas J. ... **Columbus, OH**
Olizi, Albert J., Jr. ... Camden, NJ
Olk, Barbara E. ... New York, NY
Olk, Judith Kavanagh ... Wilmette, IL
Olk, Judith Kavanagh, Ltd. ... Wilmette, IL
Olk, Richard M. ... Antigo, WI
Olken, Robert Max ... Berkeley, CA
Olken, Scott M. ... **Los Angeles, CA**
Olkon, Ellis ... Minneapolis, MN
Olkon, Nancy K. ... Minneapolis, MN
Olkon & Olkon, P.A. ... Minneapolis, MN
Olkowitz, Robert A. ... Shrewsbury, NJ
Ollada, Anne M. ... Denver, CO
Ollanik, Stuart A. ... Arvada, CO
Ollar, Scott A. ... Martinsburg, WV
Ollari, Lambert R. ... Springfield, MA
Ollason, Lawrence ... Tucson, AZ
Ollason, Thomas ... **Lemoyne, PA**
Pittsburgh, PA
Olle, Dennis J. ... **Miami, FL**
Ollen, Daniel J. ... **New York, NY**
Ollen, Michael E. ... Fairfax, VA
Ollen, Walter T., Jr. ... Gardiner, ME
Ollenburg, Kristen N. ... **Mason City, IA**
Ollendorff, Scott Howard ... New York, NY
Ollendorff, Stephen A. ... **Tenafly, NJ**
New York, NY
Ollenschleger, Craig A. ... **Roseland, NJ**
Oller & Harding, L.L.C. ... **Rockaway, NJ**
Oller, Janet Petrey ... **Calabasas, CA**
Oller, John R. ... **New York, NY**
Oller, Mart B., IV ... **Fresno, CA**
Oller, Paul R. ... Wa Keeney, KS
Oller, R. Shawn ... **El Paso, TX**
Oller, Richard L. ... **Rockaway, NJ**
Oller, Richard S. ... Lafayette Hill, PA
Olley, Dennis W. ... Pocatello, ID
Olley, Michael J. ... **Bala Cynwyd, PA**
Ollie, Leandra ... **Washington, DC**
Olliff, Danny C. ... Metter, GA
Olliff, E. Ambrose, Jr. ... Jacksonville, FL
Olliff, E. A. (Stacey), III
Beverly Hills, CA
Olliff, R. Hudson ... Jacksonville, FL
Ollikainen, Curt ... Flint, MI
Ollila, Terry L. ... Concord, NH
Ollinger, Charles G., III ... Paradise Valley, AZ
Ollinger, George E., III ... Melbourne, FL
Ollinger, Thomas P., Jr. ... **Mobile, AL**
Ollinger, W. James ... **Cleveland, OH**
Olliphant, Stacy, P.C. ... Tempe, AZ
Ollis, Andrew M. ... **Arlington, VA**
Ollis, David C. ... New Albany, IN
Ollis, Robert W., Jr. ... **Chicago, IL**
Ollison, C. E. ... Austin, TX
Ollivier, Charles L. ... Waukegan, IL
Ollivierre, Dawn D. ... **Uniondale, NY**
Ollman, Robert C. ... New Rochelle, NY
Ollmann, Mark S. ... Waterbury, VT
Olm & Associates ... Whitewater, WI
Olm, Mark T. ... Whitewater, WI
Olman, Donald D. ... New York, NY
Olmedo, Armando A. ... **Dallas, TX**
Olmer, Jody R. ... Washington, DC
Olmer, Morris I. ... New Haven, CT
Olmert, Keith M. ... Upper Marlboro, MD
Olmert, Lynn B. ... **Atlanta, GA**
Olmo, Mark E. ... Pomona, CA
Olmon, John E. ... **Minneapolis, MN**
Olmos, Marcus ... Fresno, CA
Olmstead, Arthur E. ... Northport, NY
Olmstead, Brett N. ... **Urbana, IL**
Olmstead, Brian M. ... Nahant, MA
Olmstead, Cecil J. ... **Washington, DC**
Olmstead, Cecil Jay, III ... **Houston, TX**
Olmstead, Christopher D. ... **Atlanta, GA**
Olmstead, Clarence W., Jr. ... **New York, NY**
Olmstead, Clay F., III ... Ludington, MI
Olmstead, Craig D. ... **Foley, AL**
Olmstead, David ... **Lansing, MI**
Olmstead, Dina M. ... **Cincinnati, OH**
Olmstead, Donald L. ... Northfield, CT
Olmstead, Frank H. ... **Norwich, VT**
Olmstead, Frederick R., Law Office of
Reno, NV
Olmstead, G. Wayne ... Buffalo, OK
Olmstead, George E. ... **San Diego, CA**
Olmstead, Gregory J. ... Northbrook, IL
Olmstead, J. Steele ... Tampa, FL
Olmstead, Joan Wart
Environmental Protection Agency, Office of Enforcement and Compliance Assurance, GV
Olmstead, John C. ... **New York, NY**
Olmstead, John F. ... Deerfield Beach, FL
Olmstead, Judith ... **Pittsburgh, PA**
Olmstead, Michael Eric ... **St. George, UT**
Olmstead, Michael F. ... **Ogden, UT**
Olmstead, Neil R. ... Ogden, UT
Olmstead, Nils R. ... Phoenix, AZ
Olmstead & Olmstead, LLC
Bay Minette, AL
Foley, AL
Pensacola, FL
Olmstead, Patrick J. ... La Jolla, CA
Olmstead & Pizzuto ... **San Diego, CA**
Olmstead, Ray Howard, III ... Santa Rosa, CA
Olmstead, Rosanne L. ... **Foley, AL**
Olmstead, Steven D. ... **Jackson, WY**
Olmstead, Thea ... Boston, MA
Olmstead, Thomas J. ... **Fayetteville, AR**
Olmstead, William E. ... Juneau, AK
Olmsted, Betty A. ... Overland Park, KS
Olmsted, Christopher W.
Los Angeles, CA
Olmsted, Daniel H. ... New York, NY
Olmsted, David E. ... **Port Charlotte, FL**
Olmsted, Edward W. ... La Plata, MD
Olmsted, Elizabeth McLain ... New York, NY
Olmsted, Frances L. ... New York, NY
Olmsted, Franklin B. ... La Plata, MD
Olmsted, John E. ... Santa Rosa, CA
Olmsted, Kenneth A. ... Martinez, CA
Olmsted, Mark E. ... **Portland, OR**
Olmsted, Matthew L. ... **Washington, DC**
Olmsted & Olmsted ... La Plata, MD
Olmsted, R. Wayne ... **Costa Mesa, CA**
Olmsted, William F. ... La Plata, MD
Olmsted & Wilson, P.A.
Port Charlotte, FL
Punta Gorda, FL
Olness, Andrea ... Crystal Lake, IL
Olney, Austin P. ... **Washington, DC**
Olney, Claude W. ... Scottsdale, AZ
Olney, Daniel C. ... Santa Monica, CA
Olney, Garrett W. ... Quincy, CA
Olney, Gregory L. (Skip), II
St. Petersburg, FL
Olney, Kathryn ... Portland, OR
Olney, Lynn L. ... Colorado Springs, CO
Olney, Margaret S. ... Portland, OR
Olney, Michael E. ... New York, NY
Olney, Norman M. ... San Diego, CA
Olney, Norris G., Jr. ... Marathon, IA
Olney, P. David ... Lake Charles, LA
Olney, Patricia J. ... Ventura, CA
Olney, Patricia K., (P.A.) ... **Cocoa, FL**
Olney, Susan E. ... San Francisco, CA
Olney, William G. ... Naples, FL
Olney, William H. ... **Orlando, FL**
Olnick, Richard M. ... Columbus, GA
Olobri, Charles L. ... Santa Ana, CA
O'Lochlayne, D. Sean ... Milwaukee, WI
Oloffson, Richard W. ... **Chicago, IL**
Wheaton, IL
Olofson, Jill Elizabeth ... Long Beach, CA
Olofson, Peter J. ... Houston, TX
Olofsson, Thomas J. ... Chicago, IL
Olohan, Daniel P. ... **Boston, MA**
Olohan, Mary Kate ... **Boston, MA**
Oloko, Abimbola Olatokunbo
New York, NY
Oloko, Shamsey ... **New York, NY**
Olona, Arthur G. ... Albuquerque, NM
Olona & Associates, P.C. ... Denver, CO
Olona, Richard G. ... Denver, CO
O'Lone, Mary M.
Environmental Protection Agency, Office of the General Counsel, GV
Olonoff Asen & Olonoff ... **New York, NY**
Olonoff, Robert H. ... **New York, NY**
Olore, Hugo A., Jr. ... **Presque Isle, ME**
Olorunnisomo, Leora S. ... Dallas, TX
Olosunde, Kikelomo O. ... **New York, NY**
O'Loughlin, Daniel J. ... **Cleveland, OH**
O'Loughlin, Darcy L. ... **Chicago, IL**
O'Loughlin, Edward J. ... Boston, MA
O'Loughlin, Franklin D. ... **Denver, CO**
O'Loughlin, J. Patrick
Cape Girardeau, MO
O'Loughlin, James J. ... White Plains, NY
O'Loughlin, James Leo ... **Moberly, MO**
O'Loughlin, Johanna G. ... Pittsburgh, PA
O'Loughlin, John Brendan, Jr.
Washington, DC
O'Loughlin, John C. ... **Grand Rapids, MI**
O'Loughlin, John D. ... Los Angeles, CA
O'Loughlin, Joseph M. ... New York, NY
O'Loughlin, Michael C. ... Boston, MA
O'Loughlin, Michael F. ... Dayton, OH
O'Loughlin, Michael J. ... Minneapolis, MN
O'Loughlin, Michael T. ... **Farmington, NM**
O'Loughlin, Miles W. ... Pampa, TX
O'Loughlin, O'Loughlin and McManaman, L.C. ... **Cape Girardeau, MO**
O'Loughlin, Peter J. ... Houston, TX
O'Loughlin, Ruth A. ... Lincoln, NE
O'Loughlin, Sandra S. ... **Buffalo, NY**
O'Loughlin, Terence J. ... **St. Paul, MN**
O'Loughlin, Theresa C. ... San Francisco, CA
O'Loughlin, Thomas K., II
Cape Girardeau, MO
O'Loughlin, Thomas M. ... Pluckemin, NJ
O'Loughlin, William P. ... Chicago, IL
O'Loughlin-Salvest, Felicia F. ... Lakehurst, NJ
Olowinski, Don A. ... Boise, ID
Olpin, Owen ... **Los Angeles, CA**
Olpin, Tyler G. ... **Oakland, CA**
Olrich, Denise L. ... **Petaluma, CA**
Olsan, Jeremy L. ... **Santa Rosa, CA**
Olsan, Matthew D. ... **Oakland, CA**
Olsan, Michael S. ... **Philadelphia, PA**
Olsavick, Gregory S. ... **Altoona, PA**
Olsavsky, Charles R., Jr. ... **Cleveland, OH**
Olsavsky, Diane S. ... San Diego, CA
Olschansky, Craig A. ... **St. Louis, MO**
Olschner, Barbara F. ... **Birmingham, AL**
Olschner & Hart, P.C. ... **Birmingham, AL**
Olschwang, Alan P. ... **Cypress, CA**
Olsen, Alfred ... White Plains, NY
Olsen, Alfred J. ... **Phoenix, AZ**
Olsen, Alison ... **Chicago, IL**
Olsen, Allan E. ... **Cedar Falls, IA**
Dike, IA
Olsen, Allison J. ... Malibu, CA
Olsen, Angela L. ... Port Orchard, WA
Olsen, Anne Frassetto ... **Salinas, CA**
Olsen, Arlen L. ... **Latham, NY**
Olsen, Arnold J. ... Roswell, NM
Olsen & Associates ... Irvine, CA
Olsen, B. Joan ... Oklahoma City, OK
Olsen, Barry L. ... Yuma, AZ
Olsen, Brett J. ... **Santa Fe, NM**
Olsen, Brian M. ... Cokato, MN
Olsen, Byron D. ... **Minneapolis, MN**
Olsen, Carl R. ... Memphis, TN
Olsen, Charlene A. ... Waukesha, WI
Olsen & Christensen ... Billings, MT
Olsen, Christine M. ... **Los Angeles, CA**
Olsen, Christine R. H. ... Wausau, WI
Olsen, Christine V. ... Portland, OR
Olsen, Christopher J. ... Woodland Hills, CA
Olsen, Christopher N. ... **Washington, DC**
Olsen, Christopher T. ... **Long Beach, CA**
Olsen, Clifford B. ... Portland, OR
Olsen, Clifford E. ... Metairie, LA
Olsen, Craig R. ... Cold Spring Harbor, NY
Olsen, Cynthia S. ... **Houston, TX**
Olsen, Dan G. ... Newport Beach, CA
Olsen, Dan R. ... Hillsboro, OR
Olsen, Daniel E. ... Boulder, CO
Olsen, Daniel W. ... Raymore, MO
Olsen, David A. ... Fresno, CA
Olsen, David Bradley ... **Minneapolis, MN**
Olsen, David R. ... **Salt Lake City, UT**
Olsen, David W. ... Commack, NY
Olsen, David Worthington ... Cutchogue, NY
Olsen, Debra M. ... Orange, CA
Olsen, Dennis M. ... Pasadena, CA
Olsen, Don E. ... Salt Lake City, UT
Olsen, Douglas R. ... Pendleton, OR
Olsen, Douglas W. ... Baton Rouge, LA
Olsen, Edward L. ... Downers Grove, IL
Olsen, Elizabeth C. ... **Fort Lauderdale, FL**
Olsen, Elizabeth Y. ... **Dover, DE**
Olsen, Elliot L. ... **Minneapolis, MN**
Olsen, Eric G. ... **Moorhead, MN**
Olsen, Eric G., Law Offices of
Jensen Beach, FL
Olsen, Eric G., Law Offices of ... **Stuart, FL**
West Palm Beach, FL
Olsen, Eric J. ... **Minneapolis, MN**
Olsen, Eric L. ... **Pocatello, ID**
Olsen, Eric R. ... **Las Vegas, NV**
Olsen, Eric T. ... **Tallahassee, FL**
Olsen, Eric W. ... Salem, OR
Olsen, Filoramo, Jarvi & McNamara, P.C.
Escanaba, MI
Olsen, Francis J. ... Arlington, VA
Olsen, Frederick F., Jr. ... New Orleans, LA
Olsen, Fredrick H. ... **Salt Lake City, UT**
Olsen, Gail M. ... **Milwaukee, WI**
Olsen, Gary Flanner ... Cutchogue, NY
Olsen, Gary J. ... **Fort Lauderdale, FL**
Olsen, Gary K. ... **Los Angeles, CA**
Olsen, Gary L. ... Escanaba, MI
Olsen, Geoffrey G. ... Irwindale, CA
Olsen, George G. ... **Washington, DC**
Olsen, George H. ... Flossmoor, IL
Olsen, George H., P.C. ... Flossmoor, IL
Olsen, George, Jr. ... Islandia, NY
Olsen, George L. ... New York, NY
Olsen, Gloria Blaine
Mendota Heights, MN
Olsen, Gloria J. ... Denver, CO
Olsen, Gordon ... Phoenix, AZ
Olsen, Gregory G. ... **Fort Lauderdale, FL**
Olsen, Gretchen L. ... **Petoskey, MI**
Olsen, H. Peter ... **Boston, MA**
Providence, RI
Olsen, Harold A. ... **New York, NY**
Olsen, Harold F. ... **Seattle, WA**
Olsen, Harold C. ... Oceanside, CA
Olsen, Harold L. ... St. Helens, OR
Olsen, Harry F., Jr. ... Westbury, NY
Olsen, Heidi L. ... Clatskanie, OR
Olsen, Howard P., Jr. ... **Bridgeport, NE**
Scottsbluff, NE
Olsen, Huffman & Horn ... St. Helens, OR
Olsen, J. Bradley ... Denver, CO
Olsen, Jack F. ... Pendleton, OR
Olsen, James ... Maitland, FL
Olsen, James G. ... Muskegon, MI
Olsen, James Karge ... Scottsdale, AZ
Olsen, James M. ... **Wilmington, DE**
Olsen, James S. ... Piketon, OH
Olsen, Janet ... Vance, AL
Olsen, Janet D. ... **Chicago, IL**
Olsen, Jeffrey A. ... Manchester, NH
Olsen, Jeffrey G. ... Sacramento, CA
Olsen, Jeffrey J. ... Brooklyn, NY
Olsen, John E. ... Ashtabula, OH
Olsen, John K. M. ... Midway, UT
Olsen, John L. ... **Wilmington, DE**
Olsen, John M. ... Asheville, NC
Olsen, John R. ... Lake Forest, IL
Olsen & Johnson ... Albuquerque, NM
Olsen, Joleen Payeur ... Marion, MA
Olsen, Joseph C. ... San Jose, CA
Maxton, NC
Olsen, Joseph D. ... **Rockford, IL**
Olsen, Judith D. ... St. Paul, MN
Olsen, Juliana ... Albuquerque, NM
Olsen, Justin ... Orem, UT
Olsen, Karl Y. ... Las Vegas, NV
Olsen, Katherine E. ... **New York, NY**
Olsen, Katherine Koenig ... **Philadelphia, PA**
Olsen, Kenneth A. ... Lebanon, NJ
Olsen, Kenneth A. ... New Brunswick, NJ
Olsen, Kenneth L. ... **Tampa, FL**
Olsen, Kenneth L., The Law Firm of
Tampa, FL
Olsen, Kenneth P. ... Bronx, NY
Olsen, Kent E. ... **Menlo Park, CA**
San Jose, CA
Olsen, Kevin V. ... Pleasant Grove, UT
Olsen, Kloet, Gunderson & Conway
Sheboygan, WI
Olsen, Kristin E. ... Salem, OR
Olsen, Kristine L. ... **Beverly Hills, CA**
Olsen & Kuhn ... Memphis, TN
Olsen, Kurt C. ... Livermore, CA
Olsen, Kurt E. ... Chicago, IL
Olsen, Labhart, White & Hambidge
Evansville, IN
Olsen, Lance E. ... **Bellevue, WA**
Olsen, Leonard R., Jr. ... Exton, PA
Olsen, Lisa A. ... San Rafael, CA
Olsen, Lisa A. ... **Chicago, IL**
Olsen, Lisa K. ... Salt Lake City, UT
Olsen, M. Kent ... **Denver, CO**
Olsen, Mack W. (Herm) ... Logan, UT
Olsen, Margaret A. ... Brewster, MA

Olsen, Mark C. ....Fort Lauderdale, FL
Olsen, Mark D. ....Richland, WA
Olsen, Mark R. ....Portland, OR
Olsen, Mary Ann ....Bayonne, NJ
Olsen, Mary Elizabeth ....Mobile, AL
Olsen, Matthew G. ....Washington, DC
Olsen, Michael A. ....Chicago, IL
Olsen, Michael A. ....Las Vegas, NV
Olsen, Michael David ....Houston, TX
Olsen, Michael Don ....Washington, DC
Olsen, Michael E. ....San Francisco, CA
Olsen, Michael G. ....Redding, CA
Olsen, Michael T. ....Spokane, WA
Olsen, Michelle ....Springfield, VA
Olsen, Mitchell J. ....Midvale, UT
Olsen, Nancy E. ....Carlsbad, CA
Olsen, Neil A. ....Torrance, CA
Olsen, Nolan J. ....Midvale, UT
Olsen, Norman C. ....Van Nuys, CA
Olsen, Ole J., Jr. ....Evansville, IN
Olsen & Olsen ....Fort Lauderdale, FL
Olsen & Olsen ....Bainbridge Island, WA
Olsen & Pahl ....Pendleton, OR
Olsen and Parsons, LLP ....Cedar Falls, IA
Dike, IA
Grundy Center, IA
Waterloo, IA
Olsen, Paul A. ....Washington, DC
Olsen, Paul G. ....Billings, MT
Olsen, Pauline B. ....Baltimore, MD
Olsen, Perry E. ....Watsonville, CA
Olsen, Perry E., Inc. ....Watsonville, CA
Olsen, Peter A. ....Morristown, NJ
Olsen, Peter B. ....Wickford, RI
Olsen, Peter Conrad ....New York, NY
Olsen, Philip A. ....Reno, NV
Olsen, Philip S. ....Boston, MA
Olsen, Priscilla Almquist ....Warwick, NY
Olsen, R. Stephen ....Ann Arbor, MI
Olsen, R. Stephen, P.C. ....Ann Arbor, MI
Olsen, Randy M. ....Fairbanks, AK
Olsen, Richard H. ....Palm Beach, FL
Olsen, Richard W. ....Beaverton, OR
Olsen, Robert A. ....Kansas City, KS
Olsen, Robert C. ....Salt Lake City, UT
Olsen, Robert E. ....McLean, VA
Olsen, Robert E. ....Madison, WI
Olsen, Robert K. ....Irvine, CA
Olsen, Robert L. ....Tampa, FL
Olsen, Robt. W. ....Orlando, FL
Olsen, Rodney C. ....Manhattan, KS
Olsen, Roger M., A Professional Corporation
Los Angeles, CA
Olsen, Roger Milton ....Los Angeles, CA
Olsen, Ronald E., Jr. ....Aurora, CO
Olsen, Rory R. ....Houston, TX
Olsen, Rosalia (Sally) Van Dyke
St. Paul, MN
Olsen, Sally F. ....Bainbridge Island, WA
Olsen, Sam'l H. ....West Bloomfield, MI
Olsen, Scott D. ....Camarillo, CA
Olsen, Shirley H. ....Frazier Park, CA
Olsen, Siri A. ....Frisco, CO
Olsen, Stanley H. ....Salt Lake City, UT
Olsen, Stephanie Shaw ....Leadville, CO
Olsen, Stephen R. ....Santa Rosa, CA
Olsen, Steven J. ....Atlanta, GA
Olsen, Steven L. ....Bainbridge Island, WA
Olsen, Steven LaMar ....Boise, ID
Olsen, Steven W. ....Scottsbluff, NE
Olsen, Sturla ....St. Louis, MO
Olsen, Susan ....Anchorage, AK
Olsen, Susan Baker ....Galveston, TX
Olsen, Sverre M., Jr. ....Bloomington, IL
Olsen & Talpers, P.C. ....Kansas City, MO
Olsen, Tamara Hjelle ....Minneapolis, MN
Olsen, Terri L. ....Redondo Beach, CA
Olsen, Tex R. ....Richfield, UT
Olsen, Theodore A. ....Denver, CO
Olsen, Thomas J. ....Irvine, CA
Oakland, CA
Olsen, Thomas J., IV ....Parsippany, NJ
Olsen, Thomas Richard ....Orlando, FL
Olsen, Timothy L. ....Wewoka, OK
Olsen, Tonya A. ....Minneapolis, MN
Olsen, Troy L. ....Washington, DC
Olsen, Troy R. ....Colorado Springs, CO
Olsen, Walter H., Jr. ....Seattle, WA
Olsen, Warren E. ....Washington, DC
Olsen, Warren J. ....New York, NY
Olsen, William E. ....Irving, TX
Olsen-Smith, Ltd. ....Phoenix, AZ
Olsen-Tjensvold, Ingrid ....Cortland, NY
Olshaker, Clifford ....New York, NY
Olshan, Adam J. ....East Hartford, CT
Olshan, Alan ....Milwaukee, WI
Olshan Grundman Frome Rosenzweig & Wolosky LLP ....New York, NY
Olshan, Joseph R. ....Walpole, MA
Olshan, Marvin L. ....New York, NY
Olshan, Regina ....New York, NY
Olshan, Stefanie P. ....New York, NY
Olshan, William A. ....New York, NY
Olshansky, Barbara J. ....New York, NY
Olshansky, Emily ....New York, NY
Olshein, Cookie Lea ....Las Vegas, NV
Olsher, Robert A. ....Black River Falls, WI
Sparta, WI
Olshever, Robert M. ....Manhasset, NY
Olshever, Robert M., P.C. ....Manhasset, NY
Olshin, Joshua M. ....New York, NY
Olshin, Lewis R. ....Wayne, PA
Olshonsky, Michael A. ....Washington, DC
Olsman, Jules B. ....Farmington Hills, MI
Olsoff, Jonathan A. ....New York, NY
Olson, A. Andrew, III ....Chicago, IL
Olson, A. Charles ....Duluth, MN
Olson, A. Conrad ....Louisville, KY
Olson, A. Dean ....Groton, CT
Olson, A. William ....Pasadena, CA
Olson, Alan J. ....Chicago, IL
Olson, Alan R. ....Milwaukee, WI
Olson, Allan J. ....Bend, OR
Olson, Allen E. ....Wichita, KS
Olson, Allen I. ....St. Paul, MN
Olson, Althauser & Lawler ....Centralia, WA
Olson, Amy E. ....Glencoe, MN
Olson, Andrea I. ....Port Orchard, WA
Olson, Arden J. ....Eugene, OR
Olson, Arne M. ....Chicago, IL
Olson, Arthur R., Jr. ....Fargo, ND
Olson & Associates, P.C. ....Chicago, IL
Olson, B. Tucker ....Chicago, IL
Olson & Baker ....Louisville, KY
Olson, Barbara K. ....Washington, DC
Olson, Barbara K. ....Boca Raton, FL
Olson, Barney, II, (Ltd., A Prof. Service Corp.)
Galesburg, IL
Olson, Barry T. ....Great Falls, MT
Olson, Bennett A. ....Faribault, MN
Olson, Beth J. ....Washington, DC
Olson, Betsy J. ....Palo Alto, CA
Olson, Blaine W. ....Germantown, TN
Olson, Bob L. ....Las Vegas, NV
Olson, Bonita L. ....Bothell, WA
Olson, Bradley C. ....Minneapolis, MN
Olson, Bradley J. ....Washington, DC
Olson, Bradley P. ....Carterville, IL
Olson & Breddan ....Thousand Oaks, CA
Olson, Brent A. ....Minneapolis, MN
Olson, Brent M. ....Minot, ND
Olson, Brian L., P.C. ....St. George, UT
Olson, Brian R. ....Washington, DC
Olson, Bruce A. ....Appleton, WI
Olson, Bruce L. ....Salt Lake City, UT
Olson, Bryan Scott ....Dallas, TX
Olson Burns Lee & Larson, P.C. ....Minot, ND
Olson, Camille A. ....Chicago, IL
Olson, Carl E. J. ....New York, NY
Olson, Carl R. ....Peekskill, NY
Olson, Carol Duane ....Cincinnati, OH
Olson, Carole D. ....Dallas, TX
Olson, Carolyn J. ....Ames, IA
Olson, Carolyn M. ....Lake Oswego, OR
Olson, Charles D. ....Waco, TX
Olson, Charles E. ....Roseville, MN
Olson, Charles R. ....San Francisco, CA
Olson, Cheri ....Thousand Oaks, CA
Olson, Christian J. ....Fort Lauderdale, FL
Olson, Christine A. ....Hartford, CT
Olson, Christine L. ....Chicago, IL
Olson, Christopher G. ....Clemson, SC
Olson, Christopher J. ....Los Gatos, CA
Olson, Christopher S. ....Detroit, MI
Olson Cichy Attorneys ....Bismarck, ND
Olson, Claire M., (Mr.) ....Bismarck, ND
Olson, Clifford B. ....Augusta, ME
Olson, Clifford R. ....Linthicum Heights, MD
Olson, Cynthia J. ....Denver, CO
Olson, D. Wayne, Jr. ....Winter Garden, FL
Olson, Daisy ....Jacksonville, AR
Olson, Daniel E. ....Riverside, CA
Olson, Daniel P. ....Hopkins, MN
Olson, Darrell L., (P.C.)
Newport Beach, CA
Olson, David A. ....New Orleans, LA
Olson, David B. ....Orange, CA
Olson, David B. ....Newport News, VA
Olson, David C. ....Santa Ana, CA
Olson, David C. ....Plymouth, MN
Olson, David C. ....Albuquerque, NM
Olson, David C. ....Cincinnati, OH
Olson, David C. ....Portland, OR
Olson, David E. ....Minneapolis, MN
Olson, David L. ....Minneapolis, MN
Olson, David M. ....Dallas, TX
Olson, David P. ....Las Vegas, NV
Olson, David P. ....Milwaukee, WI
Olson, David R. ....Milwaukee, WI
Olson, David Russell ....Miami, FL
Olson, David S. ....Los Angeles, CA
Olson, David W. ....Minneapolis, MN
Olson, David W. ....Buffalo, NY
Olson, Dean A. ....Los Angeles, CA
Olson, Dean A. ....Gun Barrel City, TX
Olson, Dean S., Jr. ....Waterloo, IA
Olson, Dennis D. ....San Jose, CA
Olson, Dennis E. ....Seattle, WA
Olson, Dennis L. ....Las Vegas, NV
Olson, Dennis O. ....Dallas, TX
Olson, Diana C. ....Chicago, IL
Olson, Donald H. ....Easton, MD
Olson, Donald J. ....Grand Forks, ND
Olson, Donald N. ....Spokane, WA
Olson, Doreen Marie ....Los Angeles, CA
Olson, Douglas E., (A Professional Corporation) ....La Jolla, CA
Olson, Douglas G. ....Silvis, IL
Olson, Douglas H.R. ....Minneapolis, MN
Olson, Douglas K. ....Washington, DC
Olson, Douglas V. ....Coralville, IA
Olson, D. P. ....Springfield, IL
Olson, Duane A. ....Phoenix, AZ
Olson, E. Van ....Indianapolis, IN
Olson, Ebert D. ....Naples, FL
Olson, Edmund Eugene ....Macon, GA
Olson, Edward C. ....Portland, OR
Olson, Edward G. ....Minneapolis, MN
Olson, Edward, Jr. ....Berlin, CT
Olson, Edward M. ....Troy, MI
Olson, Edwin J. ....St. Louis, MO
Olson, Elaine J. ....Albany, CA
Olson, Elena B. ....Boston, MA
Providence, RI
Olson, Elizabeth Graham ....Los Angeles, CA
Olson, Elliott D. ....Los Angeles, CA
Olson, Elton R. ....Roseville, CA
Olson, Emily ....South Windsor, CT
Olson, Eric ....Glendale, CA
Olson, Eric ....Kenosha, WI
Olson, Eric A. ....Seattle, WA
Olson, Eric C. ....Department of Agriculture, Office of the General Counsel, GV
Olson, Eric C. ....Salt Lake City, UT
Olson, Eric D. ....Los Angeles, CA
Olson, Eric D. ....Miami Shores, FL
Olson, Eric J. ....Winona, MN
Olson, Eric L. ....Minneapolis, MN
Olson, Eric T. ....Minneapolis, MN
Olson, Eric W. ....West Orange, NJ
Olson, Erik D. ....Washington, DC
Olson, Erik J. ....Palo Alto, CA
Olson, Erin K. ....Boston, MA
Olson, Eugene E. ....Des Moines, IA
Olson, Evan J. ....Midland, TX
Olson, Everett N. ....Minot, ND
Olson, F. Thomas ....Milwaukee, WI
Olson, G. Christopher ....Raleigh, NC
Olson, Gary ....Los Angeles, CA
Olson, Gary O. ....Meriden, CT
Olson, Gary O. ....Renton, WA
Olson, Gary W. ....Ganado, TX
Olson, Gene C. ....Minneapolis, MN
Olson, George A. ....San Antonio, TX
Olson, George A., A Prof. Corp., Law Offices of ....San Antonio, TX
Olson, George E. ....Boston, MA
Olson, Gerald E. ....San Diego, CA
Olson, Gerald W. ....Pocatello, ID
Olson Gibbons Nicoud Birne Sussman & Gueck, L.L.P. ....Plano, TX
Olson Gibbons Wilbur Nicoud Birne & Gueck, L.L.P. ....Dallas, TX
Olson, Gordon H., (P.C.)
Newport Beach, CA
Olson, Gordon R. ....Sabetha, KS
Olson, Grabill & Hoffman
Northbrook, IL
Olson, Grabill, Hoffman & Louis
Chicago, IL
Olson, Greggory M. ....Barrow, AK
Olson, Gregory A. ....Indiana, PA
Olson, Gregory C. ....Owatonna, MN
Olson, Gregory P. ....San Diego, CA
Olson, Hagel, Leidigh, Waters & Fishburn, LLP ....Sacramento, CA
Olson, Harriett Jane ....Nashville, TN
Olson, Harry O. ....Green Bay, WI
Olson & Hierl, Ltd. ....Chicago, IL
Olson & Hoggan ....Tremonton, UT
Logan, UT
Olson, Hope K. ....Milwaukee, WI
Olson, Ingrid M.
Federal Energy Regulatory Commission, Office of the General Counsel, GV
Olson, J. Peter ....San Diego, CA
Olson, J. Phillip ....Altus, OK
Olson, Jack D. ....St. Louis, MO
Olson, Jack F. ....Portland, OR
Olson, Jacqueline Casey
Minneapolis, MN
Olson, James A. ....Madison, WI
Olson, James C. ....San Francisco, CA
Olson, James C. ....Baltimore, MD
Olson, James D. ....Minneapolis, MN
Olson, James F. ....Spokane, WA
Olson, James J. ....Mishawaka, IN
Olson, James M. ....Traverse City, MI
Olson, James R. ....New Ulm, MN
Olson, James R. ....Las Vegas, NV
Olson, James W. ....Washington, DC
Olson, James W. ....Rapid City, SD
Olson, James W. ....Salt Lake City, UT
Olson, Jan P. ....Seattle, WA
Olson, Jane Sharpe ....Nashville, TN
Olson, Janice Radler ....Salt Lake City, UT
Olson, Jantsch, Bakker & Blakey, P.A.
Phoenix, AZ
Olson, Jared P. ....Omaha, NE
Olson, Jason A. ....Marion, IL
Olson, Jeff Scott ....Madison, WI
Olson, Jeffrey H. ....Washington, DC
Olson, Jeffrey H. ....Eden Prairie, MN
Olson, Jeffrey M. ....Los Angeles, CA
Olson, Jeffry G. ....Stillwater, MN
Olson, Jennifer L. ....Albuquerque, NM
Olson, Jerald E. ....Seattle, WA
Olson, Jeryl ....Chicago, IL
Olson, Jill A. ....Seattle, WA
Olson, Jocelyn Furtwangler ....St. Paul, MN
Olson, Joe D. ....Branson, MO
Olson, John A. ....Twin Falls, ID
Olson, John D. ....Freeport, TX
Olson, John Eric ....Jersey City, NJ
New York, NY
Olson, John F. ....Washington, DC
Olson, John F. ....Houston, TX
Olson, John K. ....Tampa, FL
Olson, John L. ....Captain Cook, HI
Olson, John L. ....Rockford, IL
Olson, John M. ....Bismarck, ND
Olson, John M. ....Milwaukee, WI
Olson, John O. ....Lake Geneva, WI
Olson, John P. ....Los Angeles, CA
Olson, John R., Law Office of
Placerville, CA
Olson, John S. ....Newport Beach, CA
Olson, John S. ....Chicago, IL
Olson, Jon A. ....St. Paul, MN
Olson, Jon S. ....Minneapolis, MN
Olson, Jonathan W. ....New York, NY
Olson, Joseph Edward ....St. Paul, MN
Olson, Joseph R. ....Kenosha, WI
Olson, Judith F. ....Pittsburgh, PA
Olson, Julie M. ....Dayton, OH
Olson, Karen ....White Plains, NY
Olson, Karen D. ....St. Paul, MN
Olson, Kari L. ....Hartford, CT
Olson, Karin A. ....Chicago, IL
Olson, Karl ....San Francisco, CA
Olson, Karl Tage ....Des Moines, IA
Olson, Karli L. ....Portland, OR
Olson, Katharyn E. ....Murray Hill, NJ
Olson, Kathryn E. ....Los Angeles, CA
Olson, Kathy A. ....Columbus, OH
Olson, Kelin R., Sr ....Waukesha, WI
Olson, Ken R. ....Salt Lake City, UT
Olson, Kenneth R. ....Great Falls, MT
Olson, Kent C. ....Charlottesville, VA
Olson, Kerry B. ....Glencoe, MN
Olson, Kevin L. ....Phoenix, AZ
Olson, Kim M. ....Austin, TX
Olson, Kirk Alan ....Oklahoma City, OK
Olson, Kirk M. ....Fullerton, CA
Olson, Kirk Michael ....Santa Ana, CA
Olson, Kirk R. ....Long Prairie, MN
Olson, Kristen K. ....Littleton, CO
Olson, Kristin G. ....Bellevue, WA
Olson, Kristine A. ....Winnetka, IL
Olson, Kristopher R. ....Swampscott, MA
Olson, Kulkoski, Galloway & Vesely, S.C.
Green Bay, WI
Olson, Kurt H. ....Seattle, WA
Olson, Kurt J. ....Raleigh, NC
Research Triangle Park, NC
Olson, Kurt S. ....Andover, MA
Olson, Lamont R. ....San Francisco, CA
Olson, Lance H. ....Sacramento, CA
Olson, Larry J. ....Department of Defense, Defense Legal Services Agency, GV
Olson, Laura A. ....Tampa, FL
Olson, Laurel A. ....San Diego, CA
Olson Law Group, LLC ....Appleton, WI
Olson, Lawrence D. ....St. Paul, MN
Olson, Layton E. ....Chicago, IL
Olson, Len ....Amarillo, TX
Olson, Leonard A. ....Youngstown, OH
Olson, Leslie R. ....Irvine, CA
Olson, Lester E. ....Pasadena, CA
Olson, Linda J. ....Denver, CO
Olson, Linda R. ....Milwaukee, WI
Olson, Lisa Ann ....Department of Justice, Civil Division, GV
Olson, Lisa Michelle ....Minneapolis, MN
Olson, Loeffler & Landis ....Spokane, WA
Olson, Lonnie ....Devils Lake, ND
Olson, Lonnie J. ....Helena, MT
Olson, Lowell W., Esq. ....Atlanta, GA
Olson, Lynda D. ....Salem, OR
Olson, Lyndon ....Waco, TX
Olson, Lynn C. ....Anoka, MN
Olson, Marcella L. ....Arlington, TX
Olson, Margaret H. ....Salt Lake City, UT
Olson, Margaret H. ....Salt Lake City, UT
Olson, Marion A., Jr. ....San Antonio, TX
Olson, Mark A. ....San Francisco, CA
Olson, Mark A. ....Burnsville, MN
Olson, Mark D. ....Covina, CA
Olson, Mark D. ....Georgetown, DE
Wilmington, DE
Olson, Mark D. ....Chicago, IL
Olson, Mark D. ....Seattle, WA
Olson, Mark D., & Company, L.L.C.
Georgetown, DE
Wilmington, DE
Olson, Mark L. ....Milwaukee, WI
Olson, Mark S. ....Minneapolis, MN
Olson, Martha J. ....San Jose, CA
Olson, Mary Ellen ....Irvine, CA
Olson, Michael C. ....Newport Beach, CA
Olson, Milo V. ....Los Angeles, CA
Olson, Mitchel J. ....Rancho Santa Fe, CA
Olson, Mitchell ....Fargo, ND
Olson, Mitchell R. ....Rhinelander, WI
Olson, Monica E. ....Irvine, CA
Olson, Nancy L. ....Cleveland, OH
Olson, Nancy M. ....Chicago, IL
Olson, Neil ....Irvine, CA
Olson, Neil E. ....San Francisco, CA
Olson, Nelson, Wood & Berry
Litchfield, MN
Olson, Nijole C. ....Harrisburg, PA
Olson, Noonan & Bzdok, P.C.
Traverse City, MI
Olson, Norman L., Jr. ....Northbrook, IL
Olson, O. Russell ....Rochester, MN
Olson & Olson ....Houston, TX
Olson & Olson ....Kenosha, WI
Olson & O'Neill ....Lafayette, LA
Olson, Pamela F. ....Washington, DC
Olson, Pamela L. ....Ponte Vedra Beach, FL
Olson, Paul A. ....Kenedy, TX
Olson, Paul E. ....Anchorage, AK
Olson, Paul E. ....Sarasota, FL
Olson, Paul N. ....Brattleboro, VT
Olson, Paula M. ....Burbank, CA
Olson, Per C. ....Portland, OR
Olson, Perry V. ....Menlo Park, CA
Olson, Peter G. ....Liberal, KS
Olson, Peter L. ....St. Paul, MN
Olson, Peter M. ....Department of State, Office of the Legal Adviser, GV
Olson, Peter M. ....Chicago, IL
Olson, Peter M. ....Clarksville, TN
Olson, Peter R. ....Cartersville, GA
Olson, Peter S. ....Bridgeport, CT
Olson, Peter W. ....San Mateo, CA
Olson, Peter W. ....Honolulu, HI
Olson, Philip J., II ....Flint, MI
Olson, Phillip A. ....Wheaton, IL
Olson & Pierce ....San Jose, CA
Olson, R. Brent ....West Point, PA

Olson, R. Thomas ... Seattle, WA
Olson, Ralph E. ... Centralia, WA
Olson, Randall E. ... Lafayette, LA
Olson, Raymond E. ... Minneapolis, MN
Olson, Raymond, Jr. ... Chicago, IL
Olson, Rebecca G. ... Stowe, VT
Olson, Rebecca G., & Associates ... Stowe, VT
Olson, Rebecca J. McGee ... Norman, OK
Olson, Richard E. ... Minneapolis, MN
Olson, Richard E. ... Roswell, NM
Olson, Richard E., Jr. ... Bishop, CA
Olson, Richard J. ... Clinton, IL
Olson, Richard J. ... Poughkeepsie, NY
Olson, Richard J. ... Merrill, WI
Olson, Richard James ... Edina, MN
Olson, Richard L. ... Fresno, CA
Olson, Richard L. ... Madison, WI
Olson, Richard P. ... Portland, ME
Olson, Richard P. ... Minot, ND
Olson, Richard W. ... Grand Forks, ND; Larimore, ND
Olson, Rick E. ... Flagstaff, AZ
Olson, Rick L. ... Des Moines, IA
Olson, Ricky W. ... Vancouver, WA
Olson, Robert A. ... Beverly Hills, CA
Olson, Robert A. ... Los Angeles, CA
Olson, Robert A. ... Minneapolis, MN
Olson, Robert A. ... Concord, NH
Olson, Robert C. ... Chicago, IL
Olson, Robert Carter ... Florence, AZ
Olson, Robert D. ... Cody, WY
Olson, Robert G. ... St. Louis, MO
Olson, Robert G. ... Cut Bank, MT
Olson, Robert H. ... Phoenix, AZ
Olson, Robert J. ... Minneapolis, MN
Olson, Robert L. ... Seattle, WA
Olson, Robert M., Jr. ... Pasadena, CA
Olson, Robert S. ... Lebanon, OH
Olson, Robert T. ... Aurora, IL
Olson, Robert W. ... Cincinnati, OH
Olson, Robert W., Jr. ... Santa Barbara, CA
Olson, Robin J. ... Boston, MA
Olson, Roger A. ... Buffalo, NY
Olson, Roger D. ... New York, NY
Olson, Roger J. ... Portland, OR
Olson, Ronald D. ... St. Paul, MN
Olson, Ronald H. ... Lindon, UT
Olson, Ronald L., (A Professional Corporation) ... Los Angeles, CA
Olson, Ronald W. ... Chicago, IL
Olson, Rosalise ... Spirit Lake, IA
Olson, Ross E. ... Bottineau, ND
Olson, Roy A. ... Lake Forest, IL
Olson, Roy G., Jr. (P.C.) ... Golden, CO
Olson, Russell A. ... Cleveland, OH
Olson, Ruth E. ... New York, NY
Olson, Sarah L. ... Chicago, IL
Olson, Scott L. ... Houston, TX
Olson, Scott P. ... Albany, NY
Olson, Scott W. ... Boston, MA
Olson, Sheri L. ... Baltimore, MD
Olson, Sherry D. ... Norcross, GA
Olson, Sherry D., P.C. ... Atlanta, GA; Norcross, GA
Olson, Sletten C. ... Bemidji, MN
Olson, Smith, Jordan & Cox, P.A. ... Clemson, SC; Easley, SC
Olson, Sonali ... Encino, CA
Olson, Stephanie A. ... Uniontown, PA
Olson, Stephen G. ... Omaha, NE
Olson, Stephen G., II ... Omaha, NE
Olson, Stephen J. ... Boise, ID
Olson, Stephen L. ... Oklahoma City, OK
Olson, Stephen L. ... Montesano, WA
Olson, Stephen M. ... Pittsburgh, PA
Olson, Stephen R. ... Naperville, IL
Olson, Stephen T. ... Troy, MI
Olson, Stephen W. ... Pasadena, CA
Olson, Steven F. ... Minneapolis, MN
Olson, Steven J. ... Los Angeles, CA
Olson, Steven J. ... Chicago, IL
Olson, Steven J. ... Minneapolis, MN
Olson, Steven J. ... Omaha, NE
Olson, Steven M. ... Santa Rosa, CA
Olson, Steven R. ... Chicago, IL
Olson, Steven R. ... Manitowoc, WI
Olson, Stewart O. ... St. Petersburg, FL
Olson, Susan A. ... Sacramento, CA
Olson, Susan Danner ... Stillwater, MN
Olson, Susan E. ... Houston, TX
Olson, Susan J. ... San Francisco, CA
Olson, Susan T. ... Los Angeles, CA
Olson, Suzann M. ... Madelia, MN; St. James, MN
Olson, Teresa J. ... New York, NY
Olson, Theodore B. ... Los Angeles, CA; Washington, DC
Olson, Theodore H. ... Seattle, WA
Olson, Theresa Ann ... Seattle, WA
Olson, Thomas A. ... Bozeman, MT
Olson, Thomas A. ... Spokane, WA
Olson, Thomas B. ... Minneapolis, MN
Olson, Thomas E. ... Ventura, CA
Olson, Thomas F. ... Berkeley, CA
Olson, Thomas L. ... Tyler, TX
Olson, Thomas L. ... De Pere, WI
Olson, Thomas M. ... Omaha, NE
Olson, Thomas M. ... Morristown, NJ
Olson, Thomas M. ... La Crosse, WI
Olson, Thomas O. ... Albuquerque, NM
Olson, Thomas O. ... Madison, WI
Olson, Thomas P. ... Washington, DC
Olson, Thomas R. ... Moorhead, MN; Fargo, ND
Olson, Thomas R., & Associates ... Minneapolis, MN
Olson, Thomas R., & Associates ... St. Paul, MN
Olson, Thomas W. ... Santa Fe, NM
Olson, Thomas W., Jr. ... Sacramento, CA
Olson, Tiffany A. ... Phoenix, AZ
Olson, Tim Phillip ... Jacksonville, IL
Olson, Timothy K. ... Omaha, NE
Olson, Timothy P. ... Chicago, IL
Olson, Tobin E. ... San Antonio, TX
Olson, Usset & Weingarden ... Minneapolis, MN
Olson, Valerie ... Diamond Springs, CA
Olson, Victoria V. ... Metairie, LA
Olson, Wade D. ... Alhambra, CA
Olson, Waldine H. "Dean" ... Omaha, NE
Olson, Walter G. ... San Francisco, CA
Olson, Walter L. ... Troy, MI
Olson, Wanda J. ... New York, NY
Olson, Warren S. ... Issaquah, WA
Olson, Wayne E. ... Rochester, NY
Olson, Wayne K. ... Fort Worth, TX
Olson, Wendy J. ... Pocatello, ID
Olson, William A. ... Houston, TX
Olson, William A. ... Seattle, WA
Olson, William A., Jr. ... Houston, TX
Olson, William D. ... Pocatello, ID
Olson, William D. ... Grinnell, IA
Olson, William E. ... Lancaster, OH
Olson, William E., Jr. ... Lincoln, NE
Olson, William J. ... Washington, DC; McLean, VA
Olson, William J., P.C. ... Washington, DC; McLean, VA
Olson, William R. ... Bakersfield, CA
Olson, Winter & Fox ... Two Rivers, WI
Olson, Wm. Kelly ... Portland, OR
Olson, Zabriskie & Campbell, Inc., Inc. ... Montesano, WA
Olson-Elm, Norine ... St. Paul, MN
Olsrud, John D. ... Bismarck, ND
Olsson, Andrew W. ... San Jose, CA
Olsson, Brent K. ... Fort Collins, CO
Olsson, Brently C. ... Chickasha, OK; Oklahoma City, OK
Olsson, Carl Eric ... Boise, ID
Olsson, Donald E. ... Ronan, MT
Olsson, Eric J. ... Tucson, AZ
Olsson, Frank and Weeda, P.C. ... Washington, DC
Olsson, Harry R., Jr. ... Douglaston, NY
Olsson, Hope W. ... Rochester, NY
Olsson, John E. ... Newark, NJ
Olsson, Loren G. ... Scottsbluff, NE
Olsson, Patricia M. ... Boise, ID
Olsson, Philip C. ... Washington, DC
Olsson, Stephen C. ... Natick, MA
Olsson, Thomas S. ... Grand Rapids, MI
Olstein, Charles ... New York, NY
Olstein, David Carey ... New York, NY
Olstein, Elliot M. ... Roseland, NJ
Olsten, Jann L. ... Edina, MN
Olster, Jeffrey D. ... Los Angeles, CA
Olster, Kathleen M. ... Pasadena, CA
Olster, Stuart L. ... Encino, CA
Olswang, Daniel H. ... Chicago, IL
Olswang, Steven G. ... Seattle, WA
Olswanger, Jill A. ... Chicago, IL
Olswing, Gordon Bennett ... Memphis, TN
Olszak, Daniel D., Jr. ... Oradell, NJ
Olszewski, Carol B. ... Albany, NY
Olszewski, Deborah D. ... Pittsburgh, PA
Olszewski, Edmund L., Jr. ... Pittsburgh, PA; Wheeling, WV
Olszewski, Edward Bryan ... Glenwood Springs, CO
Olszewski, Jeffrey M. ... Pittsburgh, PA
Olszewski, John L. ... Montgomery, AL
Olszewski, Kevin T. ... Bel Air, MD
Olszewski, Kevin T., P.A., Law Office of ... Bel Air, MD
Olszewski, Michael E. ... Fairfax, VA
Olszewski, Monica L. ... Cincinnati, OH
Olszewski, Nancy ... Department of Labor, GV
Olszewski, Paul J. ... Downers Grove, IL
Olszewski, Peter Paul ... Wilkes-Barre, PA
Olszewski, Peter Paul, Jr. ... Wilkes-Barre, PA
Olszewski, Veronica Noonan ... Philadelphia, PA
Olszewski-Szczur, Margaret ... Buffalo, NY
Olszowa, Izabel ... Brooklyn, NY
Olszowka, Deborah A. ... Niagara Falls, NY
Olszowy, Colleen Rachel ... Washington, DC
Olt, Joseph W., Jr. ... Cortez, CO
Olt, Joseph W., Jr., P.C. ... Cortez, CO
Olt, Schuyler J. ... Louisville, KY
Olt, Theodore F., III ... Davenport, IA
Oltarsh, David E. ... New York, NY
Oltarsh, Jennifer M. ... New York, NY
Oltarsh, Kenneth S. ... New York, NY
Oltarsh & Oltarsh, P.C. ... New York, NY
Oltarsh, William H. ... New York, NY
Oltarz-Schwartz, Sara ... West Bloomfield, MI
Olters, Sandra C. ... Fairfax, VA
Oltersdorf, James C. ... San Antonio, TX
Olthoff, Linda M. ... Chicago, IL
Olthoff, Mark A. ... Kansas City, MO
Oltman, Bernard L. ... Pekin, IL
Oltman, C. Megan ... Hartsdale, NY
Oltman, Flynn and Kubler ... Boca Raton, FL; Fort Lauderdale, FL; Miami, FL
Oltman, Glenn W. ... Tulsa, OK
Oltman, Gregory ... Chicago, IL
Oltman, John ... Ellsworth, WI
Oltman, John H. ... Boca Raton, FL; Fort Lauderdale, FL; Miami, FL
Oltman, William C. ... Tacoma, WA
Oltmans, Curtis G. ... Indianapolis, IN
Olton, C. Matthew ... Hopkinton, MA
Olton, Laura Schotsky ... Boston, MA
Olton, Tina M. ... Momence, IL
Oltrogge Law Office, P.C. ... Clear Lake, IA
Oltrogge, M. Wayne ... Clear Lake, IA
Olup & Associates ... Minneapolis, MN
Olup, Jeffrey T. ... Charleroi, PA; Washington, PA
Olup, Linda A. ... Minneapolis, MN
Olvany, Eisner & Donnelly ... Garden City, NY
Olver, Korts, Korona & Russell LLP ... Pittsford, NY
Olver, Melvin L. ... Pittsford, NY
Olver, Michael L. ... Seattle, WA
Olvera, A. John ... Montebello, CA
Olvera, Antonio, Jr. ... Dallas, TX
Olvera, J. Rolando, Jr. ... Brownsville, TX
Olvera, Michael H. ... Dallas, TX
Olverson, Frederick A. ... Callao, VA
Olvey, Thomas N. ... Indianapolis, IN
Olwell, David H. ... Bellevue, WA
Olwell, Lee ... Westminster, CO
Olyarchuk, Janice ... New York, NY
Olynick, Mary R. ... Mountain View, CA
Olzark, Roland L. ... Detroit, MI
Omachi, Joseph I. ... Stockton, CA
Omahana, Gail Allyn ... Chicago, IL
Omahana, Robin J. ... Chicago, IL
O'Mahoney, Denis A. ... Costa Mesa, CA
O'Mahoney, P.J. Benedict ... San Mateo, CA
O'Mahoney, William P. ... Kokomo, IN
O'Mahony, Christian D. ... Miami, FL
O'Mahony, Gregory G. ... Quincy, MA
O'Mahony, Kevin P. ... Atlanta, GA
O'Mahony & Vancil, LLP ... Atlanta, GA
O'Mahony, William J. ... Uniondale, NY
O'Maley, Jeffrey L. ... Houston, TX
O'Maley & O'Maley, P.C. ... Richmond, IN
O'Maley, Robert L. ... Richmond, IN
O'Maley, Terry ... Richmond, IN
O'Malia, Patrick J. ... Pittsburgh, PA
O'Malie, Sean D. ... Arlington, VA
O'Malley, Andrew M. ... Tampa, FL
O'Malley, Ann ... Boston, MA
O'Malley, Anthony J. ... Cleveland, OH
O'Malley, Anthony L. ... Fond du Lac, WI
O'Malley, Barbara Ann ... Centereach, NY
O'Malley, Barbara B. ... Department of Justice, Civil Division, GV
O'Malley, Barbara J. ... New York, NY
O'Malley, Bernard J. ... Des Moines, IA
O'Malley, Brian S. ... Walnut Creek, CA
O'Malley, Brian S. ... Woodbury, NJ
O'Malley, Bryan P. ... North Olmsted, OH
O'Malley, C. Timothy ... Los Angeles, CA
O'Malley, Carlon M. ... Scranton, PA
O'Malley, Carrie H. ... Richmond, VA
O'Malley, Cheryl Ng ... Pittsburgh, PA
O'Malley, Christopher B. ... New York, NY
O'Malley, Daniel J. ... Orlando, FL
O'Malley, Daniel W. ... Quincy, MA
O'Malley, David T. ... Kerman, CA
O'Malley, Deborah Anne ... Boston, MA
O'Malley, Deneen, Leary, Messina & Oswecki ... Windsor, CT; Windsor Locks, CT
O'Malley, Denise ... Chicago, IL
O'Malley, Dennis ... Portland, OR
O'Malley, Dennis M. ... Minneapolis, MN
O'Malley, Diane Marie ... San Francisco, CA
O'Malley, Dianne Chabot ... Boston, MA
O'Malley, E. Raymond ... Grand Rapids, MI
O'Malley, Edward F. ... New York, NY
O'Malley, Edward Francis ... Belleville, IL
O'Malley, Edward J. ... Paoli, PA
O'Malley, Edward J., III ... Fort Washington, PA
O'Malley, Edwin J., Jr. ... Brick, NJ; Manchester, NJ
O'Malley, F. Jerome ... New London, CT
Omalley, Faith ... Lake Peekskill, NY
O'Malley, Francis T. ... Clinton, MA
O'Malley, Francis W. ... Chicago, IL
O'Malley, G. Thomas, III ... Denver, CO
O'Malley, Grace D. ... Washington, DC
O'Malley & Harris, P.C. ... Easton, PA; Scranton, PA; Stroudsburg, PA; Wilkes-Barre, PA; Williamsport, PA
O'Malley and Harvey ... Boston, MA
O'Malley, Henry J. ... Clinton, MA
O'Malley, J. Patrick ... Three Rivers, MI
O'Malley, J. Peter ... Lansing, MI
O'Malley, J. Terence ... San Diego, CA
O'Malley, James D. ... Chicago, IL
O'Malley, James F. ... Johnstown, PA
O'Malley, James J. ... Topeka, KS
O'Malley, James, Jr. ... New York, NY
O'Malley, James K. ... Pittsburgh, PA
O'Malley, James T. ... Madison, WI
O'Malley, Jean D., P.C. ... Annandale, VA
O'Malley, Jeffrey S. ... Dayton, OH
O'Malley, Jennifer A. ... Chicago, IL
O'Malley, John ... Sacramento, CA
O'Malley, John A. ... Los Angeles, CA
O'Malley, John C. ... Los Angeles, CA
O'Malley, John F. ... Geneva, NY
O'Malley, John G. ... Chicago, IL
O'Malley, John J. ... Chicago, IL
O'Malley, John J. ... Chicago, IL
O'Malley, John Joseph ... Philadelphia, PA
O'Malley, John M. ... Chicago, IL
O'Malley, John P. ... Chicago, IL
O'Malley, John R. ... Kansas City, MO
O'Malley, John T. ... Scranton, PA
O'Malley, Josefa E. ... Department Of The Interior, Office of the Solicitor, GV
O'Malley, Joseph B. ... Federal Energy Regulatory Commission, Office of the General Counsel, GV
O'Malley, Joseph M. ... Bethlehem, PA
O'Malley, Joseph M., Jr. ... New York, NY
O'Malley, Joseph P. ... Redwood City, CA
O'Malley, Joseph P. ... Cleveland, OH
O'Malley, Joseph S. ... Fairfield, CT
O'Malley, Julian L. ... Jefferson City, MO
O'Malley, Karen ... Boston, MA
O'Malley, Katherine S. ... Evanston, IL
O'Malley, Kathleen A. ... Jacksonville, FL
O'Malley, Kathleen A. ... Cherry Hill, NJ
O'Malley, Kathleen McDonald ... Cleveland, OH
O'Malley, Kevin C. ... East Lansing, MI
O'Malley, Kevin E. ... Phoenix, AZ
O'Malley, Kevin F. ... St. Louis, MO
O'Malley, Kevin J. ... Raynham, MA
O'Malley, Kevin Matthew, Law Office of ... Houston, TX
O'Malley, Kevin P. ... Medford, MA
O'Malley, Kevin P. ... Tappan, NY
O'Malley, Kevin R. ... Pittsburgh, PA
O'Malley, Kevin T. ... St. Paul, MN
O'Malley & Langan, A Professional Corporation ... Pittston, PA; Scranton, PA
O'Malley Law Firm, The, P.C. ... St. Louis, MO
O'Malley, Lisa ... Chicago, IL
O'Malley, M. Donald ... Montrose, PA
O'Malley, M. Megan ... Chicago, IL
O'Malley, Margaret Ann ... Johnstown, PA
O'Malley, Marion ... Montrose, PA
O'Malley, Martha Oberle ... San Francisco, CA
O'Malley, Martin D. ... Houston, TX
O'Malley, Martin J. ... San Francisco, CA
O'Malley, Martin J. ... Baltimore, MD
O'Malley, Martin J., Jr. ... Hyannis, MA
O'Malley, Mary P. ... Newton, MA
O'Malley, Matthew P. ... Newark, NJ
O' Malley, Michael A. ... Chicago, IL
O'Malley, Michael C. ... Little Rock, AR
O'Malley, Michael C. ... Santa Ana, CA
O'Malley, Michael E. ... Ottawa, OH
O'Malley, Michael J. ... Honolulu, HI
O'Malley, Michael J. ... Belleville, IL
O'Malley, Michael J. ... Lawrenceville, NJ
O'Malley, Michael J. ... Pittsburgh, PA
O'Malley, Michael P. ... Cleveland, OH
O'Malley, Michael R. ... Boston, MA
O'Malley, Michael R. ... Omaha, NE
O'Malley, Michael V. ... Central Falls, RI
O'Malley, Michael W. ... Des Moines, IA
O'Malley, Miles, Nylen & Gilmore, P.A. ... Annapolis, MD; Greenbelt, MD; Waldorf, MD
O'Malley, Nancy E. ... Oakland, CA
O'Malley, Nick ... Santa Ana, CA
O'Malley & O'Malley ... Clinton, MA
O'Malley, Owen L. ... Cohasset, MA
O'Malley, Patrick J. ... Cleveland, OH
O'Malley, Patrick J., Ltd. ... Alsip, IL
O'Malley, Patrick T. ... New York, NY
O'Malley, Patrick T. ... New York, NY
O'Malley, Paul W., Jr. ... Fort Wayne, IN
O'Malley, Peter F. ... Greenbelt, MD
O'Malley, Peter G. ... New York, NY
O'Malley, Peter J. X. ... New York, NY
O'Malley, Peter Michael ... Oakbrook Terrace, IL
O'Malley, Rena L. ... Los Angeles, CA
O'Malley, Richard F., Jr. ... Chicago, IL
O'Malley, Richard L. ... Louisville, KY
O'Malley, Robert C. ... Madison, WI
O'Malley, Robert E. ... Chicago, IL
O'Malley, Robert E. ... Chicago, IL
O'Malley, Robert F., Jr. ... Miami, FL
O'Malley, Rosanne Pinzok ... Philadelphia, PA
O'Malley, Salie B. ... Sarasota, FL
O'Malley, Stephanie Y. ... Denver, CO
O'Malley, Stephen P., Jr ... Boston, MA
O'Malley Surman & Michelini ... Brick, NJ; Manchester, NJ; Whiting, NJ
O'Malley, Suzanne Higgins ... Department of Transportation, Federal Highway Administration, GV
O'Malley, Terence M. ... Kansas City, MO
O'Malley, Terence P. ... Boston, MA
O'Malley, Terrance ... Irvine, CA
O'Malley, Terrance ... New York, NY
O'Malley, Terry ... Denver, CO
O'Malley, Theodore J. ... Cleveland, OH
O'Malley, Thomas ... Olympia, WA
O'Malley, Thomas A. ... West Palm Beach, FL
O'Malley, Thomas F. ... Cleveland, OH
O'Malley, Thomas F., III ... Phoenix, AZ
O'Malley, Thomas F., Jr. ... Cleveland, OH
O'Malley, Thomas J. ... San Diego, CA
O'Malley, Thomas J. ... Windsor, CT
O'Malley, Thomas J. ... Philadelphia, PA
O'Malley, Thomas J., Jr. ... Media, PA
O'Malley, Thomas M. ... Rockville, MD
O'Malley, Thomas N. ... Fort Wayne, IN
O'Malley, Thomas P. ... New York, NY
O'Malley, Thomas R. ... Clearwater, FL

O'Malley, Todd J. ... Scranton, PA
O'Malley, Vincent J. ... San Mateo, CA
O'Malley, Virginia ... Paradise Valley, AZ
O'Malley, William A. ... Walnut Creek, CA
O'Malley, William C. ... Brockton, MA
O'Malley, William D. ... Cleveland, OH
O'Malley, William J. ... Columbus, OH
O'Malley, William P. ... Scranton, PA
O'Malley-Harpel, Nancy ... San Antonio, TX
Oman, Charles E., III ... Waterbury, CT
Oman, Gentry & Yntema, P.A.
Albuquerque, NM
Oman, John D. ... Findlay, OH
Oman, Kester L. ... Albuquerque, NM
Oman, Lisa James ... Seattle, WA
Oman, Patrick A. ... Austin, MN
Oman, Ralph ... Washington, DC
Oman, Richard Heer ... Columbus, OH
Oman, Sherrill R. ... Minneapolis, MN
Omansky, Joseph H. ... Towson, MD
Omansky, Paula J. ... New York, NY
Omar, Riyad ... New York, NY
Omar, Sharif L. ... Kew Gardens, NY
O'Mara, Aloysius B. ... Blissfield, MI
O'Mara, Bernard G. ... Easton, ME
O'Mara, Edwin J., Jr. ... Greenwich, CT
O'Mara, Esther L. ... West Covina, CA
O'Mara, Frank Anthony ... Little Rock, AR
O'Mara, Gary J. ... Sacramento, CA
O'Mara, J. Kent ... Sacramento, CA
O'Mara, James D. ... Washington, DC
O'Mara, James W. ... Jackson, MS
O'Mara, John F. ... Elmira, NY
O'Mara, John P., Jr. ... Brooklyn, NY
O'Mara, John T. ... Buffalo, NY
O'Mara, John W. ... West Long Branch, NJ
O'Mara, L. Kevin, Jr. ... New York, NY
O'Mara, Laine Alee ... Pittsburgh, PA
O'Mara, Mark M. ... Orlando, FL
O'Mara, Mark M. ... Winter Park, FL
O'Mara, Mary Ellen ... Boston, MA
O'Mara, Michael D. ... Malvern, PA
O'Mara, Michael J. ... Cherry Hill, NJ
O'Mara, Patrick J. ... Ossining, NY
O'Mara, Peter M. ... Red Bank, NJ
O'Mara, Scott Alan ... San Diego, CA
O'Mara, T. Michael ... Cookeville, TN
O'Mara, Thomas F. ... Elmira, NY
O'Mara, Timothy M. ... Amherst, NY
Buffalo, NY
Eden, NY
O'Mara, Timothy P. ... Louisville, KY
O'Mara, Timothy P. ... St. Louis, MO
O'Mara, William M. ... Reno, NV
O'Marra, John L. ... Morristown, NJ
O'Marra, Thomas R. ... Manchester, CT
O'Marro, Meg Colleen ... Milwaukee, WI
Omata, Richard J. ... Seattle, WA
Omberg, Robert A. ... Richmond, VA
Omberg, Robert E.
National Labor Relations Board,
Office of the General Counsel, GV
Ombres, Alexander J. ... Orlando, FL
Ombres, Douglas E. ... Tequesta, FL
Ombres, Marian Elinor ... Tequesta, FL
Ombres, Richard S. ... Pittsburgh, PA
Ombres, Teresa ... Whitestone, NY
Omdahl, James C. ... Bethlehem, PA
Omdahl, Thomas ... Grand Forks, ND
Omdahl, Thomas D. ... Appleton, WI
Omdahl, Torger G. ... Iron River, MI
O'Mealia, Harry A., III ... Oldwick, NJ
O'Meally, Edmund J. ... Baltimore, MD
O'Meara, Andrew P., III ... Boston, MA
O'Meara, Anna M. ... Chicago, IL
O'Meara, Arthur C. ... Palos Heights, IL
O'Meara, Benedict J. ... Elkader, IA
O'Meara, Corbett Edge ... Detroit, MI
O'Meara, Daniel C. ... Chicago, IL
O'Meara, Daniel J. ... Larkspur, CO
O'Meara, Daniel P. ... Paoli, PA
O'Meara, Dennis E. ... Pasadena, CA
O'Meara, Donald J., Jr. ... Chicago, IL
O'Meara, Donald J., (P.C.) ... Chicago, IL
O'Meara, Donald P. ... Milwaukee, WI
O'Meara, Douglas J. ... New Philadelphia, OH
O'Meara, Eckert, Pouros & Gonring, LLP
West Bend, WI
O'Meara, Edward J. ... Irving, TX
O'Meara, Eric M. ... New York, NY
O'Meara, Frances Mary
Santa Monica, CA
O'Meara, Francis A., III ... Boston, MA
O'Meara, Gerard R. ... Tucson, AZ
O'Meara, Gregory R. ... Hingham, MA
O'Meara, Herbert J. ... Woodland Hills, CA
O'Meara & Hight, P.C. ... Bloomfield, NJ
O'Meara, James P. ... Baltimore, MD
O'Meara, James P. ... St. Paul, MN
O'Meara, John Corbett ... Detroit, MI
O'Meara, John J. ... Washington, DC
O'Meara, John K. ... Milwaukee, WI
O'Meara, John V. ... Westlake Village, CA
O'Meara, John W. ... Alexandria, VA
O'Meara & Kinnealey ... Hingham, MA
O'Meara Law Offices
New Philadelphia, OH
O'Meara, Mark R. ... Chicago, IL
O'Meara, Mary Joy ... Milwaukee, WI
O'Meara, Matt ... Seattle, WA
O'Meara, Matthew D. ... Chicago, IL
O'Meara, Michael B. ... Des Moines, IA
O'Meara, Michael S. ... Chicago, IL
O'Meara, Nicolas P. ... Honolulu, HI
O'Meara, Patrick J. ... Half Moon Bay, CA
O'Meara, Richard L. ... Portland, ME
O'Meara, Richard M. ... Bloomfield, NJ
O'Meara, Robert A. ... Boston, MA
O'Meara, Robert S. ... Chicago, IL
O'Meara, S. Charles ... West Bend, WI
O'Meara, Scott M. ... Riverside, CA
O'Meara, Sean T. ... Haddonfield, NJ
O'Meara, Shamus P. ... Minneapolis, MN
O'Meara & Smith ... Woodland Hills, CA
O'Meara, Stephen Patrick ... Des Moines, IA
O'Meara, Terence T. ... Chicago, IL
O'Meara, Thomas J. ... St. Paul, MN
O'Meara, Thomas J., Jr. ... Austin, TX
O'Meara, Thomas P. ... St. Louis Park, MN
O'Meara, Vicki A. ... Miami, FL
O'Meara, William P. ... Denver, CO
O'Meara, Wm. F., Jr. ... Joliet, IL
O'Melia, Brendan A. ... Long Beach, CA
O'Melia, John F., II ... Rhinelander, WI
O'Melia, Michael J. ... Phoenix, AZ
O'Melia, Patrick F. ... Rhinelander, WI
O'Melia, Richard J. ... Bethesda, MD
O'Melia, Schiek & McEldowney, S.C.
Crandon, WI
Rhinelander, WI
O'Melia, Scott L. ... Atlanta, GA
O'Melia, Tammy Sue ... Albany, NY
Omelko, Nancy L.
Department of Commerce,
Patent and Trademark Office, GV
O'Melveny, John P. ... Tacoma, WA
O'Melveny & Myers LLP
Los Angeles, CA
Newport Beach, CA
San Francisco, CA
Washington, DC
New York, NY
Omer, Douglas B. ... Nashville, TN
Omer, Edie Carol ... Upper Marlboro, MD
Omer, Gregory Davis ... St. Louis, MO
Omer, James R. ... Nashville, TN
Omer, James R., & Associates
Nashville, TN
Omer, James R., Jr. ... Nashville, TN
Omer, Michael L. ... Houston, TX
Omer, Orhan Kelley ... Baltimore, MD
Omer, Robert L. ... Wichita, KS
Omer, Robin L. ... Lansing, MI
Omerberg, Maynard J. ... Los Angeles, CA
Omerberg, Mitchell Kevin
San Francisco, CA
Omerza, Raphael J. ... Cleveland, OH
Ometer, Jo Marie ... Monterey, CA
Omichinski, Nancy M. ... Detroit, MI
Omid, Lilly M. ... Oakland, CA
Omilian, Susan M. ... West Hartford, CT
Ominsky, Alan J. ... Philadelphia, PA
Ominsky, Albert ... Philadelphia, PA
Ominsky, Andrew M. ... Philadelphia, PA
Ominsky, Emma G. ... Philadelphia, PA
Ominsky, Harris ... Philadelphia, PA
Ominsky, Marc A. ... Baltimore, MD
Ominsky & Messa, P.C. ... Marlton, NJ
Philadelphia, PA
Omlie, Lynne J. ... Washington, DC
Ommaya, Shana E. ... Washington, DC
Omni Law Chartered ... Naples, FL
Omodt, Donald J. ... Minneapolis, MN
Omohundro, Herschel C. ... Scottsdale, AZ
Omohundro, Scott R. ... San Diego, CA
Omohundro, William D. ... Buffalo, WY
Gillette, WY
Omohundro, William D., P.C., Law Offices of
Buffalo, WY
Gillette, WY
Omoigui, Eghosa D. ... Portland, OR
Omolecki, Leonard R., Jr. ... Nanticoke, PA
Omolecki, Stephen H. ... Ottawa, IL
Omonaka, Joy S. ... Honolulu, HI
Omoniyi, A. Olusanjo ... Springfield, IL
Omoniyi Law Firm ... Springfield, IL
O'Moore, Anne ... Torrance, CA
Omori, Morio ... Honolulu, HI
Omorogbe, Benjamin I. ... Minneapolis, MN
Omoto, Dennis T. ... Payson, AZ
Omrod, Robert M. ... Baltimore, MD
Oms, Michelle ... Fort Lauderdale, FL
Omsberg, Keith S. ... Oakland, CA
Omsberg, Philip H. ... Tarrytown, NY
Oms de Picó, Ingrid ... San Juan, PR
Omslaer, Rhonda Lee ... Orlando, FL
Omstead, Eric A. ... Redding, CA
O'Mullan & Brady ... Whippany, NJ
O'Mullan, Daniel W. ... Whippany, NJ
O'Mullan, Michael P. ... New York, NY
Omura, Anne T. ... Berkeley, CA
Omura, Kenneth I. ... Northbrook, IL
Omuro, Lennes N. ... Honolulu, HI
Omvedt, Jack N. ... Minneapolis, MN
Omvig, Kristin L. ... Billings, MT
Omwenga, Samuel N. ... Washington, DC
On Call Legal Resources ... Kalamazoo, MI
Onacewicz, Walter J. ... West Hartford, CT
Onaga, Elena J. ... Honolulu, HI
Onaga, Grace S. ... New York, NY
O'Naghten, Juan Tomas ... Miami, FL
O'Naghten, Luis M. ... Miami, FL
Onaitis, Matthew W. ... Atlanta, GA
Onak, Mark H. ... Houston, TX
O'Nan, Gerald D. ... Lakewood, CO
Onan, Robert C., Jr. ... Minneapolis, MN
Onbargi, Fouad S. ... Chicago, IL
Oncale, Charlene D. ... Birmingham, AL
Oncale, Shane M. ... Birmingham, AL
Onchuck, Dale E. ... Phillips, WI
Onchuck Law Office, S.C. ... Phillips, WI
Oncidi, Anthony J. ... Los Angeles, CA
Oncken, Denise ... Houston, TX
Oncken, J. Kevin ... San Antonio, TX
Oncken, Kevin ... San Antonio, TX
Oncken, Kirk J. ... Houston, TX
Onco, Eldridge ... Arlington, TX
Oncu, Melike S. ... Washington, DC
Onda, Robert J. ... Columbus, OH
Onda, Thomas Mandel
San Francisco, CA
Ondak, Robert C., Jr. ... Cleveland, OH
Ondeck, Christopher E. ... Washington, DC
Onder, James G. ... St. Louis, MO
Onderdonk, A. Michael ... Chatom, AL
Mobile, AL
Onderdonk, Laurie J. ... San Jose, CA
Onderdonk, Philip B., Jr. ... Indianapolis, IN
Onders, Edward A. ... Greenlawn, NY
Onders, Kathleen Donovan
Fairview Park, OH
Ondich, Lisa ... Pittsburgh, PA
Ondov, Raymond B. ... Austin, MN
Ondrasek, Douglas J. ... Fond du Lac, WI
Ondrasek, Keith G. ... Chilton, WI
Ondrasek, Keith G., Law Offices of, S.C.
Chilton, WI
Ondrasek Law Office ... Fond du Lac, WI
Ondrasik, Paul J., Jr. ... Washington, DC
Ondrey, Albert C. ... Dushore, PA
Ondrey, David M. ... Chardon, OH
Ondrey-Gruber, Lynn F. ... Cleveland, OH
Ondrovic, Robert S. ... White Plains, NY
Ondrush, Laura ... Hartford, CT
One, Joan ... Macedonia, OH
O'Neal, Anna K. ... Newnan, GA
O'Neal, Ardra M. ... Washington, DC
O'Neal & Booth, P.A. ... Fort Lauderdale, FL
O'Neal, Brown & Sizemore, A Professional Corporation ... Atlanta, GA
Macon, GA
O'Neal, C. Duane ... Indianapolis, IN
O'Neal, Carl S., Jr. ... Leeds, AL
O'Neal, Charles D. ... Acton, MA
O'Neal, Dale, Jr. ... Fort Worth, TX
Oneal, Dan ... San Jose, CA
O'Neal, David P. ... Houston, TX
O'Neal, Denis G. ... San Jose, CA
O'Neal & Driggers ... North Charleston, SC
O'Neal, Dudley L., Jr. ... United States Senate,
Committee Legal Personnel, GV
O'Neal, Edward A. ... Elizabeth City, NC
O'Neal, Elizabeth M. ... King, NC
O'Neal, Faith E. ... Kew Gardens, NY
O'Neal, Forbeck, Elliott & Monahan, S.C.
Beloit, WI
Orfordville, WI
O'Neal, Frances Gossen ... Lafayette, LA
O'Neal, Frederic B. ... Orlando, FL
O'Neal, G. Michael ... Kansas City, MO
O'Neal, Gregory W. ... Memphis, TN
O'Neal, H. Sanders ... Houma, LA
O'Neal, Hodge, III ... Monroe, LA
O'Neal, Horace L. ... Angel Fire, NM
O'Neal, Horace V., Jr. ... Birmingham, AL
O'Neal, J. Loyd ... Grants Pass, OR
O'Neal, James A. ... Minneapolis, MN
O'Neal, James B. ... Costa Mesa, CA
O'Neal, James E. ... Leucadia, CA
O'Neal, James P. ... Birmingham, AL
O'Neal, Jan ... Fremont, CA
O'Neal, Jerry D. ... Fort Worth, TX
O'Neal, Jim A. ... Indianapolis, IN
O'Neal, Joanne P. ... United States Senate,
Senatorial Assistants, GV
O'Neal, John F. ... Washington, DC
O'Neal, John Maston ... Phoenix, AZ
O'Neal, John T. ... Greensboro, NC
O'Neal, Katherine ... San Francisco, CA
O'Neal, Kenneth E. ... Sikeston, MO
O'Neal, Kevin L. ... Houston, TX
O'Neal, Kristin L. ... Dallas, TX
O'Neal, Larry R. ... Kansas City, MO
O'Neal, Laura R. ... Blythewood, SC
O'Neal, Laurie Lynne ... Denver, CO
O'Neal & Leavoy ... De Ridder, LA
O'Neal, Lee C. ... Greensboro, NC
O'Neal, Leslie K. ... Diboll, TX
O'Neal, Leslie King ... Orlando, FL
O'Neal, Lisa D. ... San Diego, CA
Oneal, Louis, Law Offices of ... San Jose, CA
O'Neal, L. W. ... Greenfield, IN
O'Neal, Lynne Stephens ... Birmingham, AL
O'Neal, Mariclare Foster ... Waltham, MA
O'Neal, Martha Ann ... De Ridder, LA
O'Neal, Mary E. ... Boston, MA
O'Neal, Maston A., Jr. ... Apopka, FL
O'Neal, Michael K. ... Dallas, TX
O'Neal, Michael L. ... Dallas, TX
O'Neal, Michael R. ... Hutchinson, KS
Wichita, KS
O'Neal, Michael R. ... Houston, TX
O'Neal, Michael S. ... Jacksonville, FL
O'Neal, Michael S. ... North Charleston, SC
O'Neal, Mike E. ... Malibu, CA
O'Neal & Norris, L.L.P. ... Monroe, LA
Vidalia, LA
O'Neal, Patrick ... Fort Lauderdale, FL
O'Neal, Patrick J. ... Dallas, TX
O'Neal, R. Michael ... Cleveland, OH
O'Neal, Raymond G. ... Fulton, MS
O'Neal, Raymond G., III ... Fulton, MS
O'Neal, Rex R. ... Boulder, CO
Denver, CO
O'Neal, Richard E. ... Birmingham, AL
O'Neal, Robert C. ... St. Louis, MO
O'Neal, Robert F. ... Sacramento, CA
O'Neal, Robert M. ... Dayton, OH
O'Neal, Rock ... Madeira Beach, FL
O'Neal, Roger D. ... Beloit, WI
O'Neal, Roosevelt, Jr. ... Sacramento, CA
O'Neal, Silas, Jr. ... Marksville, LA
O'Neal, Solon F., Jr. ... Tampa, FL
O'Neal, Stephen V. ... San Francisco, CA
O'Neal, Sterling, Jr. ... Bloomington, IN
O'Neal, Steven M. ... San Diego, CA
O'Neal, Susan A. ... Los Angeles, CA
Oneal, Terry L. ... Fort Worth, TX
O'Neal, Thomas H., (P.C.)
Chattanooga, TN
O'Neal, Thomas J. ... Kansas City, MO
Springfield, MO
O'Neal, Thomas W. ... Peoria, IL
O'Neal, Velma P. ... Hammond, LA
O'Neal, Vivian D. Mack ... Oakland, CA
O'Neal, Walker & Boehm
Chattanooga, TN
O'Neal, William C. ... Gainesville, FL
O'Neale, L. J. ... San Diego, CA
O'Neale, Robert S. ... Chester, SC
Oneale, Tracy R. ... Boise, ID
O'Neale, Trey ... York, SC
O'Neal-Jones, Rikki ... Dallas, TX
O'Neall, Cris K. ... Los Angeles, CA
O'Neall, Kathryn B. ... Rensselaer, IN
O'Neall, Michael D. ... Remington, IN
Onebane, Bernard, Torian, Diaz, McNamara & Abell ... Lafayette, LA
Monroe, LA
Onebane, Helen ... Lafayette, LA
Oneglia, Catherine S. ... Waterbury, CT
Oneglia, Gregory S. ... Torrington, CT
Oneglia, Roderic M. ... Torrington, CT
Oneglia, Stewart B. ... Highland, MD
O'Neil, A. Gerard ... Laconia, NH
O'Neil, A.G., Jr. ... Laconia, NH
O'Neil & Allen ... Lebanon, MO
O'Neil, Angela ... Crystal River, FL
Melbourne, FL
Orlando, FL
O'Neil, Augustin F. ... Akron, OH
O'Neil, Barry A. ... Minneapolis, MN
O'Neil, Bennie ... North Little Rock, AR
O'Neil, Bonnie Irvin ... Columbus, OH
O'Neil, Brian J. ... Chicago, IL
O'Neil, C. Richard ... Columbus, OH
O'Neil, Cannon & Hollman, S.C.
Milwaukee, WI
O'Neil, Carol Q. ... Washington, DC
O'Neil, Christina A. ... Dallas, TX
O'Neil, Colleen Ann ... New York, NY
O'Neil, Colleen Moran ... Cleveland, OH
O'Neil, Constance P. ... Bath, ME
O'Neil, D. Michael, Jr. ... Oklahoma City, OK
O'Neil, Daniel E., III ... Chicago, IL
O'Neil, Daniel F. ... Denver, CO
O'Neil, Daniel J., III ... Wappingers Falls, NY
O'Neil, Daniel P. ... Traverse City, MI
O'Neil, Daniel R. ... Mount Pleasant, MI
O'Neil, Daniel T. ... New York, NY
O'Neil, David G. ... Washington, DC
O'Neil, David S. ... The Woodlands, TX
O'Neil, Deborah L. ... Troy, MI
O'Neil, Dennis D. ... Irvine, CA
O'Neil, Diane J. ... Newark, NJ
O'Neil, Donald J. ... Worcester, MA
O'Neil, Donald S. ... San Antonio, TX
O'Neil, E. Joseph ... Boston, MA
O'Neil, Elaine M. ... San Francisco, CA
O'Neil, Frank D. ... Dana Point, CA
O'Neil, Fred ... Thayer, MO
O'Neil, Gary A. ... Bakersfield, CA
O'Neil, Holland Neff ... Dallas, TX
O'Neil, J. Brian ... Marietta, GA
O'Neil, Jalen ... Topeka, KS
O'Neil, James D. ... Phoenix, AZ
Oneil, James E., III ... Saginaw, MI
O'Neil, James J. ... Chatham, NJ
O'Neil, James P. ... San Diego, CA
O'Neil, James P. ... Green Bay, WI
O'Neil, James W. ... Los Angeles, CA
O'Neil, James W., Jr. ... Dorset, VT
O'Neil, Jeannine ... Walnut Creek, CA
O'Neil, Jennifer R. Tocci ... Albany, NY
O'Neil, John ... St. Paul, MN
O'Neil, John A. ... Springfield, MA
O'Neil, John C. ... Fall River, MA
O'Neil, John H. ... Fall River, MA
O'Neil, John H., Jr. ... Saco, ME
O'Neil, John J. ... Lynn, MA
O'Neil, John J. ... New York, NY
O'Neil, John J. ... Woodbury, NY
O'Neil, John J., Jr. ... Hartford, CT
O'Neil, John P. ... Cleveland, OH
O'Neil, John R. ... Chicago, IL
O'Neil, John W., Jr. ... St. Louis, MO
O'Neil, Joseph C. ... Bellevue, WA
O'Neil, Joseph E. ... Mount Laurel, NJ
Philadelphia, PA
O'Neil, Joseph F. ... Boston, MA
O'Neil, Joseph F., P.C. ... Boston, MA
O'Neil, Joseph W. ... Defiance, OH
O'Neil, Katherine H. ... Portland, OR
O'Neil, Kelley ... Memphis, TN
O'Neil, Kenton R. ... Clarion, PA
O'Neil, Kevin C. ... Akron, OH
O'Neil, Kristin Michelle ... Los Angeles, CA
O'Neil, Lawrence J. ... Tampa, FL
O'Neil, Lorain Jo ... Bartow, FL
O'Neil, Lynch & Bloem, P.C.
Mount Pleasant, MI
O'Neil, Margaret E. ... New York, NY
O'Neil, Mark W. ... Bridgewater, NJ
O'Neil, Mary Ann J. ... Royal Oak, MI
O'Neil, Mary E. ... Fall River, MA
O'Neil, Maura E. ... Dedham, MA
O'Neil, Michael ... Chicago, IL
O'Neil, Michael A. ... Dallas, TX
O'Neil, Michael A., P.C. ... Dallas, TX
O'Neil, Michael D. ... King City, OR
O'Neil, Michael J. ... Washington, DC

O'Neil, Michael J. ... Newark, NJ
O'Neil, Michael P. ... Indianapolis, IN
O'Neil, Michael R. ... Sacramento, CA
O'Neil, Michael R. ... Santa Ana, CA
O'Neil, Michael W. ... Orinda, CA
O'Neil, Michael W. ... Cleveland, OH
O'Neil, Michael W., A L.C. ... Orinda, CA
O'Neil, Monica C. ... Chico, CA
O'Neil, Nancy Doerr ... Washington, DC
Baltimore, MD
O'Neil, Nancy M. ... Norwich, CT
O'Neil and O'Neil ... Dedham, MA
O'Neil, Parker and Williamson
Knoxville, TN
O'Neil, Patience Jane ... New York, NY
O'Neil, Patricia A. ... Hartford, CT
O'Neil, Patrick A. ... Milwaukee, WI
O'Neil, Patrick J. ... Livonia, MI
O'Neil, Patrick J. ... Milwaukee, WI
O'Neil, Patrick T. ... Cambridge, MN
O'Neil, Paul ... Seattle, WA
O'Neil, Paul Matthew ... Houston, TX
O'Neil, Peter ... Seattle, WA
O'Neil & Pierson ... Akron, OH
O'Neil, Richard D. ... San Antonio, TX
O'Neil, Richard P. ... Manchester, NH
O'Neil, Rickard T. ... Milwaukee, WI
O'Neil, Robert A. ... Washington, DC
O'Neil, Robert E. ... Fort Lauderdale, FL
O'Neil, Robert J. ... Charleston, WV
O'Neil, Robert J., Jr. ... St. Louis, MO
O'Neil, Robert M. ... Charlottesville, VA
O'Neil, Roger W., Jr. ... Plymouth, MA
O'Neil, Sean T. ... Missoula, MT
O'Neil, Sharon Brennan ... Geneva, IL
O'Neil, Shauna H. ... Salt Lake City, UT
O'Neil, Shawn M. ... Portland, OR
O'Neil, Stephen E. ... Los Angeles, CA
O'Neil, Stephen E. ... New York, NY
O'Neil, Stephen J. ... Los Angeles, CA
O'Neil, Stephen J. ... Chicago, IL
O'Neil, Stuart B. ... Dallas, TX
O'Neil, Terence M. ... Mineola, NY
New York, NY
O'Neil, Thomas A. ... Chevy Chase, MD
O'Neil, Thomas F., III ... Washington, DC
O'Neil, Thomas G. ... Sidney, NY
O'Neil, Thomas J. ... Lebanon, MO
O'Neil, Thomas M. ... Los Angeles, CA
O'Neil, Timothy D. ... Aurora, IL
O'Neil, Timothy P. ... Manchester, CT
O'Neil, Timothy P., P.C. ... Manchester, CT
O'Neil, Vincent A. ... Syracuse, NY
O'Neil, W. Sean ... New Orleans, LA
O'Neil, Wallace & Fegen, P.C. ... Denver, CO
O'Neil & Widelock ... Bakersfield, CA
O'Neil, William A. ... Woodland Hills, CA
O'Neil, William E. ... New Orleans, LA
O'Neil, William E. ... Dedham, MA
O'Neil, William F., III, P.C. ... Conway, SC
Myrtle Beach, SC
North Myrtle Beach, SC
O'Neil, William F. (Rick), III
Myrtle Beach, SC
O'Neil, William G. ... Boca Raton, FL
O'Neil, William J. ... Florence, AZ
O'Neil, William J. ... Northampton, MA
O'Neil, William J. ... Springfield, MA
O'Neil, William J. ... Manchester, NH
O'Neil, William J., Jr. ... Carmichael, CA
O'Neil, William Patrick ... Oakland, CA
O'Neil, William T. ... Washington, DC
O'Neil-Jenkins, Merilou P.
Lake Elsinore, CA
O'Neil Jr., Joseph ... New York, NY
O'Neill, Albert C., Jr. ... Tampa, FL
O'Neill, Alexander R. ... East Hanover, NJ
O'Neill, Alison Ayers ... Ventura, CA
O'Neill, Andrew J. ... New Haven, CT
O'Neill, Andrew T. ... Wilmington, DE
O'Neill, Ann M. ... Quincy, MA
O'Neill, Arthur J. ... Southbury, CT
O'Neill, Arthur S., Jr. ... Norristown, PA
O'Neill, Athy & Casey, P.C.
Washington, DC
O'Neill & Balega, P.C. ... San Antonio, TX
O'Neill, Barbara A.
National Labor Relations Board, Office of the General Counsel, GV
O'Neill, Barry E. ... Westborough, MA
O'Neill, Bernard C., Jr. (P.A.)
Orlando, FL
O'Neill, Bernard V., Jr. ... Kansas City, MO
O'Neill, Beth Ann C. ... Miami, FL
O'Neill, Bethany ... San Francisco, CA
O'Neill, Blake R. ... San Francisco, CA
O'Neill & Bockelman, P.C. ... Lake Forest, IL
O'Neill & Borges ... San Juan, PR
O'Neill, Bracken C. ... Greens Farms, CT
O'Neill, Bragg & Staffin, P.C.
Philadelphia, PA
Plymouth Meeting, PA
O'Neill, Brian ... Santa Monica, CA
O'Neill, Brian B. ... Minneapolis, MN
O'Neill, Brian D. ... Washington, DC
O'Neill, Brian D. ... Lyndhurst, NJ
O'Neill, Brian E. ... Philadelphia, PA
O'Neill, Brian J. ... Philadelphia, PA
O'Neill, Brian M. ... New York, NY
O'Neill, Brian M. ... Cleveland, OH
O'Neill, Brian P. ... Chicago, IL
O'Neill, Brian T. ... Boston, MA
O'Neill, Brian T., P.C., Law Offices of
Boston, MA
O'Neill, Bridget R. ... Chicago, IL
O'Neill, Bruce A. ... Westmont, NJ
Philadelphia, PA
O'Neill, Bruce C. ... Milwaukee, WI
O'Neill, C. William ... Columbus, OH
O'Neill, Carol B. ... Oakland, CA
Walnut Creek, CA
O'Neill, Caroline Page ... Charlottesville, VA
O'Neill, Cathryn A. ... South Dartmouth, MA
O'Neill, Chapin, Liebman & Cooper
Orlando, FL
Sanford, FL
Winter Park, FL
O'Neill, Charles K. ... New York, NY
O'Neill, Charles S., Jr. ... Honolulu, HI
O'Neill, Charles T. ... Boston, MA
Waltham, MA
O'Neill, Charles V. ... New York, NY
O'Neill, Charron ... San Luis Obispo, CA
O'Neill, Chris P. ... Portland, OR
O'Neill, Christopher ... Somers, NY
O'Neill, Christopher R. ... Washington, DC
O'Neill, Clare ... New York, NY
O'Neill, Colin H. ... Waco, TX
O'Neill, Colin X. ... New York, NY
O'Neill, Colleen P. ... Atlanta, GA
O'Neill, Constance R. ... Chicago, IL
O'Neill Crawford & Green, P.C.
Burlington, VT
O'Neill, Cynthia ... Mountain View, CA
O'Neill, Cynthia L. ... Manchester, NH
O'Neill, Dana Jones ... West Hartford, CT
O'Neill, Daniel I. ... Sacramento, CA
O'Neill, Daniel J. ... San Luis Obispo, CA
O'Neill, Daniel J. ... Indianapolis, IN
O'Neill, Daniel J. ... New York, NY
O'Neill, Daniel J. ... New York, NY
O'Neill, Daniel P. ... Summit, NJ
O'Neill, Daniel R. ... St. Louis, MO
O'Neill, Dawn Weiger ... Clearwater, FL
O'Neill, Debora A. ... Philadelphia, PA
O'Neill, Deborah Piperni ... Columbus, OH
O'Neill, Dennis E. ... Mount Pleasant, SC
O'Neill, Dennis E., L.L.C.
Mount Pleasant, SC
Seabrook Island, SC
O'Neill, Dennis Patrick ... Romulus, MI
O'Neill, Dennis S. ... San Diego, CA
O'Neill, Dennis W. ... Wilmington, DE
O'Neill, Derrick J. ... Boise, ID
O'Neill, Desmond ... Santa Barbara, CA
O'Neill, DiManno & Kelly ... New York, NY
O'Neill, Douglas A. ... St. Louis, MO
O'Neill, Douglas W. ... St. Louis, MO
O'Neill & Dyer, A Professional Corporation
Dallas, TX
O'Neill, E. Jack ... Houston, TX
O'Neill, Edgar L., Jr. ... Gulfport, MS
O'Neill, Edward F. ... Massapequa Park, NY
O'Neill, Edward J., Jr. ... Houston, TX
O'Neill, Edward S. ... Washington, DC
O'Neill, Edward W. ... San Francisco, CA
O'Neill, Eileen F. ... Houston, TX
O'Neill, Eileen M. ... New York, NY
O'Neill, Elizabeth M. ... Sacramento, CA
O'Neill, Elizabeth M. ... Atlanta, GA
O'Neill, Elizabeth M. ... New York, NY
O'Neill, Ellen C. ... Sacramento, CA
O'Neill, Ellen M. ... Rochester, NY
O'Neill, Emmett ... Pipestone, MN
O'Neill, Eugene J. ... Vero Beach, FL
O'Neill, Evans, Swogger & Cowan
Salem, OR
O'Neill, Finbarr J. ... Fountain Valley, CA
O'Neill, Francis M. ... Scranton, PA
O'Neill, Francis P. ... Chicago, IL
O'Neill, Geoffrey A. ... Berkeley, CA
O'Neill, George B. ... San Luis Obispo, CA
O'Neill, Gerald F., Jr. ... Boston, MA
O'Neill, Greg ... Bend, OR
O'Neill, Gregory W. ... New York, NY
O'Neill, Grills & O'Neill, P.L.L.P.
Minneapolis, MN
St. Paul, MN
O'Neill, Hampton K. ... Casper, WY
O'Neill, Harriet ... Houston, TX
O'Neill, Harry J. ... Fairfax, VA
O'Neill, Harry J. J. ... Philadelphia, PA
O'Neill, Harry St. A. ... Fallston, MD
O'Neill, Henry E. ... Honolulu, HI
O'Neill, Holly M. ... Boca Raton, FL
O'Neill, Hugh P., III ... Philadelphia, PA
O'Neill, Huxtable & Abelson
Los Angeles, CA
O'Neill, J. Brendan ... Santa Monica, CA
O'Neill, J. Dan ... Tucson, AZ
O'Neill, J. Norman, Jr. ... San Marino, CA
O'Neill, J. Patrick ... Birmingham, MI
O'Neill, J. Patrick, Jr. ... Superior, WI
O'Neill, J. Timothy ... Washington, DC
O'Neill, James A.
Cape May Court House, NJ
O'Neill, James C. ... St. Paul, MN
O'Neill, James D., III ... Laconia, NH
O'Neill, James E. ... Pipestone, MN
O'Neill, James E., III ... Flint, MI
Saginaw, MI
O'Neill, James E., III ... Philadelphia, PA
O'Neill, James G. ... Costa Mesa, CA
O'Neill, James J. ... New York, NY
O'Neill, James K. ... New York, NY
O'Neill, James L. ... Providence, RI
O'Neill, James P. ... Santa Maria, CA
O'Neill, James P. ... New York, NY
O'Neill, James P. ... Cleveland, OH
O'Neill, James P. ... Milwaukee, WI
O'Neill, James Richard ... Washington, DC
O'Neill, James T. ... Wheeling, IL
O'Neill, James W., Jr. ... Gulfport, FL
O'Neill, Janet M. ... San Luis Obispo, CA
O'Neill, Jas. D. ... Laconia, NH
O'Neill, Jean C. ... Colchester, VT
O'Neill, Jeanne E. ... Long Island City, NY
O'Neill, Jeanne E. ... Plano, TX
O'Neill, Jennifer G. ... Middletown, RI
O'Neill, Jerome F. ... Burlington, VT
O'Neill, Joan ... Portland, OR
O'Neill, John ... St. Paul, MN
O'Neill, John D. ... Palm Beach, FL
O'Neill, John D., Jr. ... Richmond, VA
O'Neill, John E. ... Houston, TX
O'Neill, John E., Jr. ... Burbank, CA
O'Neill, John F.
Treasury Department, GV
O'Neill, John F. ... Burlington, IA
O'Neill, John F., Jr. ... Atlanta, GA
O'Neill, John G. ... Boston, MA
O'Neill, John H., Jr. (P.C.)
Washington, DC
O'Neill, John I. ... White Plains, NY
O'Neill, John J. ... San Francisco, CA
O'Neill, John J. ... Garden City, NY
O'Neill, John J. ... Milwaukee, WI
O'Neill, John J., Jr. ... Rockville, MD
O'Neill, John J., Jr. ... Boston, MA
O'Neill, John M. ... Wailuku, HI
O'Neill, John P. ... Chicago, IL
O'Neill, John P. ... Birmingham, MI
O'Neill, John P. ... Ravenna, OH
O'Neill, Jos. E. ... Youngstown, OH
O'Neill, Joseph A. ... Yardley, PA
O'Neill, Joseph D. ... Vineland, NJ
O'Neill, Joseph D., A Professional Corporation ... Vineland, NJ
O'Neill, Joseph M. ... Norristown, PA
Philadelphia, PA
O'Neill, Joseph M. ... Rutland, VT
O'Neill, Joseph T. ... St. Paul, MN
O'Neill, Joyce A. ... Rockford, IL
O'Neill, Judith C. R. ... Phoenix, AZ
O'Neill, Judith D. ... New York, NY
O'Neill, Judy A. ... Detroit, MI
O'Neill, Julia K. ... Boston, MA
O'Neill, Julie Gearty ... Boston, MA
O'Neill, Justin J. ... New York, NY
O'Neill, Karen P. ... Chicago, IL
O'Neill, Kathleen ... Chicago, IL
O'Neill, Kathleen Buckley ... Grand Blanc, MI
O'Neill, Kathleen M. ... Brooklyn, NY
O'Neill, Kathleen Marie ... New York, NY
O'Neill, Kathleen Suzanne ... Philadelphia, PA
O'Neill, Kathy A. ... Philadelphia, PA
O'Neill, Keelin G. ... Cleveland, OH
O'Neill, Kevin ... Sunnyvale, CA
O'Neill, Kevin E. ... Baltimore, MD
O'Neill, Kevin F. ... Timonium, MD
O'Neill, Kevin F. ... Richmond Hill, NY
O'Neill, Kevin F. ... Cleveland, OH
O'Neill, Kevin H. ... Naples, FL
Manchester, NH
O'Neill, Kevin J. ... New York, NY
O'Neill, Kevin M. ... Buffalo, NY
O'Neill, Kevin P. ... Wilmington, DE
O'Neill, Kirt S. ... San Antonio, TX
O'Neill, Lambert J. ... Staten Island, NY
O'Neill, Laura A. ... Chicago, IL
O'Neill, Lauren Koffler ... Roseland, NJ
O'Neill, Lawrence J. ... Fresno, CA
O'Neill, Lawrence J., III ... Livermore, CA
O'Neill, Leigh C. ... Carson City, NV
O'Neill, Lisa O. ... Miami, FL
O'Neill, Lynne Turel ... Massillon, OH
O'Neill, Lysaght & Sun LLP
Los Angeles, CA
Santa Monica, CA
O'Neill, M. Beth ... Birmingham, AL
O'Neill, M. Elizabeth ... Milwaukee, WI
O'Neill, M. Sean ... Department of Justice, Federal Bureau of Investigation, GV
O'Neill, Margaret E. ... Deerfield, IL
O'Neill, Mark ... Cleveland, OH
O'Neill, Mark Edward ... Madison, WI
O'Neill, Mark L. ... Staten Island, NY
O'Neill, Mark M. ... Racine, WI
O'Neill, Martha E. ... Nashua, NH
O'Neill, Martin J. ... Stratford, CT
O'Neill, Mary Catherine ... Albany, NY
O'Neill, Mary Keating
Virginia Beach, VA
O'Neill, Mary L. ... Los Angeles, CA
O'Neill, Mary O'Keefe
Marina Del Rey, CA
O'Neill, MaryEllen ... Washington, DC
O'Neill, Matthew H. ... Polson, MT
Ronan, MT
O'Neill, Matthew W. ... Milwaukee, WI
O'Neill, Maura A. ... Framingham, MA
O'Neill, Maureen A. ... Chicago, IL
O'Neill, Maureen B. ... Morristown, NJ
O'Neill, Maureen E. ... Atlanta, GA
O'Neill, Maureen E. ... Pennington, NJ
O'Neill, Megan ... Hartford, CT
O'Neill, Melissa A. ... Worcester, MA
O'Neill, Michael D. ... St. Paul, MN
O'Neill, Michael D. ... Tacoma, WA
O'Neill, Michael E. ... Hammond, IN
O'Neill, Michael E. ... Rochester, NY
O'Neill, Michael F. ... San Francisco, CA
O'Neill, Michael F. ... Atlanta, GA
O'Neill, Michael F. ... Bedminster, NJ
O'Neill, Michael G. ... New York, NY
O'Neill, Michael G. ... Dallas, TX
O'Neill, Michael J. ... Los Angeles, CA
O'Neill, Michael J. ... Boston, MA
O'Neill, Michael J. ... New York, NY
O'Neill, Michael J. ... Columbus, OH
O'Neill, Michael J. ... Philadelphia, PA
O'Neill, Michael J. ... Dallas, TX
O'Neill, Michael J., Jr. ... Warren, NJ
O'Neill, Michael K. ... Costa Mesa, CA
O'Neill, Michael P. ... Bloomfield Hills, MI
O'Neill, Michael R. ... Irvine, CA
O'Neill, Molly ... Sandusky, OH
O'Neill, Monica E. ... Philadelphia, PA
O'Neill, Nancy J. ... Tucson, AZ
O'Neill, Nancy L. ... San Francisco, CA
O'Neill, Neill J., II ... Mendota Heights, MN
O'Neill, Netterville & Burton ... Gretna, LA
O'Neill & Neylon ... Boston, MA
Waltham, MA
O'Neill, Noreen E. ... Baltimore, MD
O'Neill, Norris L. ... Hartford, CT
O'Neill, Olivia A. ... Boston, MA
O'Neill, O'Neill & Barduson
Pipestone, MN
O'Neill, Oren ... Bakersfield, CA
O'Neill, Owen Roe ... Boston, MA
O'Neill, P. Bradley ... New York, NY
O'Neill, Patricia A. ... Wilmington, DE
O'Neill, Patricia B. ... Fresno, CA
O'Neill, Patricia M. ... Wilmington, DE
O'Neill, Patrick C. ... Menomonee Falls, WI
O'Neill, Patrick D. ... San Juan, PR
O'Neill, Patrick H. ... Fort Worth, TX
O'Neill, Patrick H., Jr. ... St. Paul, MN
O'Neill, Patrick H., Jr., Ltd. ... St. Paul, MN
O'Neill, Patrick H., Law Offices of
Fort Worth, TX
O'Neill, Patrick K. ... Philadelphia, PA
O'Neill, Patrick M. ... Columbus, OH
O'Neill, Paul J. ... Edwardsville, IL
O'Neill, Paul J., Jr. ... New York, NY
O'Neill, Paul T. ... Melrose, MA
O'Neill, Paul T. ... Detroit, MI
O'Neill, Pauline E. ... Newark, OH
O'Neill, Peter M. ... Princeton, NJ
O'Neill, Peter Sean ... Glen Burnie, MD
O'Neill, Philip D., Jr. ... Boston, MA
O'Neill, Philip E. ... Gretna, LA
O'Neill, Philip L. ... Washington, DC
O'Neill and Proctor ... Carbondale, IL
O'Neill, Ralph J. ... Honolulu, HI
O'Neill, Raymond B., Jr. ... Rochester, NY
O'Neill, Raymond C. ... San Juan, PR
O'Neill, Rebecca J. ... Carbondale, IL
O'Neill, Richard E. ... Eagleville, PA
O'Neill, Richard J. ... Springfield, OH
O'Neill, Richard, Jr. ... Wakefield, MA
O'Neill, Richard T. ... Lansing, MI
O'Neill, Richard W. ... Boston, MA
O'Neill, Robert B. ... Hollywood, CA
O'Neill, Robert E. ... Lake Forest, IL
O'Neill, Robert E. ... Franklin, VA
O'Neill, Robert F. ... La Jolla, CA
O'Neill, Robert F. ... Burlington, VT
O'Neill, Robert J. ... San Diego, CA
O'Neill, Robert J. ... Front Royal, VA
O'Neill, Robert Joseph, Jr. ... Dover, DE
O'Neill, Robert O. ... New Prague, MN
O'Neill, Robert P. ... New York, NY
O'Neill, Robert W. ... Birmingham, AL
O'Neill, Schimmel, Quirk & Carroll, S.C.
Milwaukee, WI
O'Neill, Scott William ... Irvine, CA
O'Neill, Sean A. ... Kennett Square, PA
Malvern, PA
O'Neill, Sean F. ... San Antonio, TX
O'Neill, Sean K. ... New York, NY
O'Neill, Sean W. ... La Crosse, WI
O'Neill, Shane ... New York, NY
O'Neill, Shannon & Mills
Bloomfield Hills, MI
O'Neill, Shari Winget ... Columbus, OH
O'Neill, Shawn P. ... Lafayette, LA
O'Neill, Stacey A. ... Liverpool, NY
O'Neill, Stephanie M. ... Chicago, IL
O'Neill, Stephen F. ... Santa Rosa, CA
O'Neill, Stephen M. ... Rochester, NY
O'Neill, Stephen T. ... Palo Alto, CA
O'Neill, Stephen T. ... Providence, RI
O'Neill, Steven J. ... Seattle, WA
O'Neill, Steven P. ... Westlake Village, CA
O'Neill, Steven T. ... Norristown, PA
O'Neill, Susan G. ... San Francisco, CA
O'Neill, Susan M. ... Philadelphia, PA
O'Neill, Susan R. ... Boulder, CO
O'Neill, Sylvia Park ... San Francisco, CA
O'Neill, Tamara Maria ... Minneapolis, MN
O'Neill, Tanya C. ... Madison, WI
O'Neill, Terence ... Attleboro, MA
O'Neill, Terence J. ... Flint, MI
Saginaw, MI
O'Neill & Thatcher, LLP ... Poughkeepsie, NY
O'Neill, Theresa S. ... Tampa, FL
O'Neill, Thomas E. ... Columbia, SC
O'Neill, Thomas Emmet ... Elmhurst, IL
O'Neill, Thomas J. ... Stamford, CT
O'Neill, Thomas J. ... Poughkeepsie, NY
O'Neill, Thomas J. ... Syracuse, NY
O'Neill, Thomas J. ... West Chester, PA
O'Neill, Thomas J., III ... Hartford, CT
O'Neill, Thomas L. ... Arlington, VA
O'Neill, Thomas N., Jr. ... Philadelphia, PA
O'Neill, Thomas P. ... Andover, MA
O'Neill, Thomas S. ... Chicago, IL
O'Neill, Thomas T. ... Kansas City, KS
O'Neill, Tim ... Lincoln, NE
O'Neill, Timothy B. ... Salem, OR
O'Neill, Timothy E. ... Detroit, MI
O'Neill, Timothy G. ... Phoenix, AZ
O'Neill, Timothy G. ... McLean, VA
O'Neill, Timothy J. ... Princeton, NJ
O'Neill, Timothy J. ... New York, NY
O'Neill, Timothy P. ... Chicago, IL
O'Neill, Timothy P. ... Boston, MA
O'Neill, Traxler, Zard, Neisen & Morris, Ltd.
New Prague, MN
O'Neill, Treva H. ... Carbondale, IL

O'Neill, Trevor Quaid ... **New York, NY**
O'Neill, Virginia E. ... Arlington, VA
O'Neill, W. James, Jr. ... Barnstable, MA
O'Neill, Wallace & Doyle, P.C. ... **Flint, MI**
Saginaw, MI
O'Neill, William ... **Washington, DC**
O'Neill, William ... Vashon, WA
O'Neill, William D. ... **Washington, DC**
O'Neill, William E. ... Richmond, VA
O'Neill, William G. ... Williston, FL
O'Neill, William G. ... New York, NY
O'Neill, William G.
Plymouth Meeting, PA
O'Neill, William G., P.A. ... Williston, FL
O'Neill, William H. ... Allen Park, MI
O'Neill, William, III ... Sacramento, CA
O'Neill, William J. ... Poughkeepsie, NY
O'Neill, William J. ... Staten Island, NY
O'Neill, William J. ... **Cleveland, OH**
O'Neill, William J. ... Westlake, OH
O'Neill, William J., Jr. ... Cambridge, MA
O'Neill, William J., Jr. ... Cleveland, OH
O'Neill, William M. ... Cleveland, OH
O'Neill, William P. ... **Washington, DC**
O'Neill, William P. ... Springfield, MA
O'Neill, William P. ... Bryn Mawr, PA
O'Neill, William R. ... **Naples, FL**
O'Neill, Woolpert, Terhune & Hindmarsh
San Luis Obispo, CA
O'Neill & Young ... Santa Monica, CA
O'Neill and Young, P.C. ... Cambridge, MA
O'Neill Font, Jose E. ... **San Juan, PR**
O'Neill III, James J. ... **Baltimore, MD**
O'Neill-Killy, Ann Cecile
Christiansted, St. Croix, VI
O'Neill- Stephens, Ellen ... Seattle, WA
O'Neill-Taylor, Kathleen
Department of Justice,
Federal Bureau of Investigation, GV
O'Neil-White, Alphonso ... Silver Spring, MD
Onek, Brian N. ... Titusville, FL
Onel, Suzan ... **Washington, DC**
O'Nell, William E. ... **San Diego, CA**
Onello, Anthony P., Jr. ... **Boston, MA**
Onello, Harriet Holzman ... Lexington, MA
Onerheim, Neil E. ... Lawrence, MA
Onesian, John ... Santa Monica, CA
Onesto, Anthony J. ... Chicago, IL
Onesto, John L. ... Columbus, OH
Oneto, James S. ... Ellicott City, MD
Oney, Claudia, & Associates, P.C.
Chicago, IL
Oney, Claudia, P.C., & Associates
Chicago, IL
Oney, Joan M. ... Chicago, IL
Oney Law Firm ... Phoenix, AZ
Oney, Patricia A. ... Palmer, MA
Oney, Richard E. ... Phoenix, AZ
Oney, Thomas E. ... **Dallas, TX**
Ong, Cynthia C. ... San Francisco, CA
Ong, Donna ... **Phoenix, AZ**
Ong, Fiona W. ... **Baltimore, MD**
Ong, George E. ... Oakland, CA
Ong, Helen ... New York, NY
Ong, James J. ... **New Philadelphia, OH**
Ong, Johanna Yao ... **Los Angeles, CA**
Ong, John Whitelaw ... **Charlotte, NC**
Ong, Julian K. ... San Jose, CA
Ong, Justin ... Houston, TX
Ong, Kara W. ... **Atlanta, GA**
Ong, Kathleen T. ... Boston, MA
Ong, Luke H. ... Bountiful, UT
Ong, Luke H., P.C. ... Bountiful, UT
Ong, Michael R. ... Leawood, KS
Ong, Richard ... Washington, DC
Ong, Richard S. ... Boston, MA
Ong, Roxanne K. Song ... Phoenix, AZ
Ong, Tomson T. ... San Pedro, CA
Ong, Winfield D. ... Indianapolis, IN
Ongaro, David R. ... **San Francisco, CA**
Ongert, Kathy Dean ... **Houston, TX**
Ongert, Steven W. ... **Houston, TX**
Ongerth, Richard H. ... Fair Oaks, CA
Ongie, Kelly Christie ... Maitland, FL
Ongioni & Borrelli ... Greenport, NY
Ongioni, Marie ... Greenport, NY
Ongkeko, Doyle & Nicholas, A Professional Corporation ... **Pasadena, CA**
Ongkeko, Rafael A. ... **Pasadena, CA**
Ongley, Craig G. ... **Dallas, TX**
Onglingswan, Alastair ... **New York, NY**
Ongman, John Will ... **Washington, DC**
Onichimowski, Dianne M. ... Chicago, IL
O'Niell, Herbert E. ... **Houston, TX**
O'Niell, Juliana ... **New York, NY**
Onifer, Michael J., III ... **Elkton, MD**
Onimus, Noreen Hibbard
Philadelphia, PA
Onion, James C. ... San Antonio, TX
Onion, John F., Jr. ... Austin, TX
Onion, John Frank, III ... **San Antonio, TX**
Onixt, David T. ... Schaumburg, IL
Onixt, Micah R. ... **Chicago, IL**
Onka, Thomas J. ... **Princeton, NJ**
Onken, Judith Slayman ... Oklahoma City, OK
Onken, Nancy C. ... Hartford, CT
Onley, Douglas S. ... **Washington, DC**
Onneflod, Christer P. ... Fresno, CA
Onnen, Dennis R. ... Kansas City, MO
Onnen, Ivan L. ... Omaha, NE
Ono, Allan S. ... **Los Angeles, CA**
Ono, James N. ... San Jose, CA
Ono, Jeffrey T. ... Honolulu, HI
Ono, Jon R. ... Hilo, HI
Ono, Naomi ... **Costa Mesa, CA**
Onoda, Ayako ... **San Francisco, CA**
Onoda, H. Sam ... **Chicago, IL**
Onofri, Angelo J. ... Princeton, NJ
Onofrio, Adrienne ... Hempstead, NY
Onofrio, Charles J. ... Denver, CO
Onofrio, Dara L. ... **New York, NY**
Onofry, Charles D. ... Port Jervis, NY
Onofry, Robert A. ... Port Jervis, NY
Onoprienko, George ... Coral Gables, FL
Onorata, Anastasia ... Albany, NY
Onorata, Gerard J. ... **River Edge, NJ**
New York, NY
Onorati, Annette C. ... Coral Gables, FL
Onorato, Alfred J. ... **New Haven, CT**
Onorato, Brian E. ... **Denver, CO**
Onorato, David C. ... Lansdale, PA
Onorato, David J. ... **Atlanta, GA**
Onorato, Donald M. ... Hackensack, NJ
Onorato, Frederick J. ... New York, NY
Onorato, Joanna R. ... **Washington, DC**
Onorato, Joseph R. ... Mineola, NY
Onorato, Linda Herko ... Warminster, PA
Onorato, Maria A. ... **Stamford, CT**
Onorato, Martin A. ... **Hartford, CT**
Onorato, Philip J. ... **New York, NY**
Onorato, Stephanie ... Haddonfield, NJ
Onorato, Susan J. ... **Mineola, NY**
New York, NY
White Plains, NY
Onore, Eric ... Manchester, CT
Onore, Harvey M. ... Lakewood, NJ
Onorevole, Richard M. ... Lake Hiawatha, NJ
Onouye, Galen K. ... Honolulu, HI
Onsager, Christian Carl ... Denver, CO
Onsager, David J. ... **Seattle, WA**
Onsager, Kristen Pugsley ... Seattle, WA
Onsager, Richard C. ... **Phoenix, AZ**
Onsager, Richard C., P.C. ... **Phoenix, AZ**
Onsdorff, Keith A. ... **Philadelphia, PA**
Onsdorff, Kim R. ... **Secaucus, NJ**
Onsi, Douglas E. ... Boston, MA
Onstad Law Firm, The ... **Austin, TX**
Onstad, Rockne W. ... **Austin, TX**
Onstot, Stephen R. ... **Los Angeles, CA**
Onstot, W. Stephen ... **Santa Paula, CA**
Ontell, David J. ... Washington, DC
Ontell, Jeffrey L. ... Boston, MA
Ontell, Milton J. ... Cranbury, NJ
Ontiveras, Jose Marcelino ... Oxnard, CA
Ontiveros, Aide C. ... **Los Angeles, CA**
Ontiveros, Bertha A. ... Oakland, CA
Ontiveros, Cheryl, Law Offices of
Monterey, CA
Ontiveros, Cheryl, Law Offices of
Salinas, CA
Santa Cruz, CA
Ontiveros, Janel Tritch ... Fresno, CA
Ontiveros, Kevin J. ... Salt Lake City, UT
Ontiveros, Maria L. ... San Francisco, CA
Ontiveros, Patrick Anton Carlon
Palo Alto, CA
Ontko, David A. ... **Lake Buena Vista, FL**
Ontko, Elizabeth A. ... Harrisburg, PA
Ontra, Joseph A. ... Houston, TX
Onufrak, Joseph J. ... **New York, NY**
Onufrak, Michael N. ... **Philadelphia, PA**
Onufrak, Rachel A. ... Florham Park, NJ
Onuma, Susan J. ... **New York, NY**
Onur, Gamze ... **Los Angeles, CA**
Onuscheck, David ... **Raleigh, NC**
Onuska, Paul R. ... Farmington, NM
Onusko, Thomas J. ... **Cleveland, OH**
Onwaeze & Nwabuzor ... Los Angeles, CA
Onwaeze, Ogochukwu Victor
Los Angeles, CA
Onwuachi-Willig, Angela ... **Cleveland, OH**
Onwualu, Emeka Godfrey ... Lawndale, CA
Onwuanibe, Anthony C. ... Baltimore, MD
Onwudinjo, Andrew C. ... Pottsville, PA
Onwukwe, Helen Ekenma ... Pikesville, MD
Onychuk, Nick G. ... Detroit, MI
Onyeije, Uzoma C. ... **Washington, DC**
Onyejekwe, Moses O. ... Los Angeles, CA
Onyemaechi, Pauline C. ... Baltimore, MD
Onyia, Cosmas M. ... Phoenix, AZ
Onyia, Cosmas M., P.C. ... Phoenix, AZ
Onyirimba & Associates, P.C. ... Atlanta, GA
Onyirimba, Charles ... Atlanta, GA
Onysko, Peter ... Cleveland, OH
Oogjen, Martin H., III ... Buffalo, NY
Oole, Richard B. ... Grand Rapids, MI
Ooley, Michael D. ... Los Angeles, CA
Oommen, Kuruvilla ... **Fort Worth, TX**
Oonk, Lisa A. ... **Tampa, FL**
Oonk, Toby Andrew ... Punta Gorda, FL
Oostdyk, Robert H., Jr. ... Riverdale, NJ
Oostdyk, Scott C. ... **Richmond, VA**
Oostema, John R. ... **Grand Rapids, MI**
Oosterbaan, Jennifer S. ... **Chicago, IL**
Oosterbaan, John ... Kalamazoo, MI
Oosterhouse, Carl, P.C.
Grand Rapids, MI
Oosterhouse, Donald F.
Grand Rapids, MI
Oosterhouse, Kenneth R.
Grand Rapids, MI
Oosterhouse, Kurt T. ... Charlotte, NC
Oosterhout, Barbara Ann ... Laurel, MD
Oosterhuis, Paul W. ... **Washington, DC**
Oosting, Susan S. ... **Jacksonville, FL**
Oostingh, Reina Winifred
Charlottesville, VA
Oostmeyer, Melissa M. ... **Toledo, OH**
Oostra, Bierma & Schouten
Sioux Center, IA
Oostra, Ronald J. ... Sioux Center, IA
Oot & Associates ... Syracuse, NY
Oot, Earl L. ... East Syracuse, NY
Oot Law Offices ... East Syracuse, NY
Oot, Michael P. ... De Witt, NY
Oot & Stratton ... De Witt, NY
Oot, Suzanne E. ... East Syracuse, NY
Oot, Thaddeus B. ... Syracuse, NY
Oothout, Raymond B. ... Rochester, MA
Ooyama, Clara Michiko ... Rochester, NY
Opacki, Dennis G. ... Bellevue, WA
O'Pake, Malsnee & Parisi, P.C. ... Reading, PA
O'Pake, Michael A. ... Reading, PA
Opal, Jacques E. ... Baltimore, MD
Opal, Walter A. ... Shoreview, MN
Opala, Marian P. ... Oklahoma City, OK
Opalenik, Stanley J. ... Stamford, CT
Opalinski, Christopher R. ... **Pittsburgh, PA**
Opalisky, Mark E. ... **Philadelphia, PA**
Opalka, Robert J. ... Philadelphia, PA
Opalko, Bryan H. ... **Chicago, IL**
Opanashuk, Leonard ... Warsaw, NY
Opar, John A. ... Wayne, NJ
Opar, John L., Jr. ... **New York, NY**
Opara, Clay C. ... Baltimore, MD
Opara, Opara & Huffine ... Baltimore, MD
Opara, Patrick A. U. ... Baltimore, MD
Oparaku, Bertram C. ... Houston, TX
Oparil, Richard J. ... **Washington, DC**
Opat, Matthew J. ... Chatfield, MN
Opat, Steven L. ... **Junction City, KS**
Opatrny, Donald C. ... Cleveland, OH
Opatrny, Robert B. ... New York, NY
Opdahl, Clark D. ... **Minneapolis, MN**
Opderbeck, David W. ... **Newark, NJ**
Opdycke, Stuart W. ... Chicago, IL
Opdyke, Mona E. ... Auburn, CA
Opdyke, Robert F. ... Washington, NJ
Opdyke, T. William ... **Los Angeles, CA**
Opel, Gordon A. ... Pasadena, CA
Opel, James C. ... **Los Angeles, CA**
Opel, John E. ... Los Angeles, CA
Opel, Paul F. ... Santa Monica, CA
Opel, Robert H. ... Montpelier, VT
Opel, Robert N., II ... Kingston, PA
Opel, W. Glenn ... **Dallas, TX**
Opelt, Lyn C. ... Madison, WI
Opelt, Vivian L. ... **Dublin, OH**
Openchowski, Charles A.
Environmental Protection Agency,
Office of the General Counsel, GV
Openshaw, Blaine L. ... Salt Lake City, UT
Openshaw, Glen R. ... **Boston, MA**
Opera, Robert E. ... **Irvine, CA**
Operhall, Harrie Marie Pollok
Houston, TX
Operini, Edward G. ... **Victorville, CA**
Opert, Jon I. ... **Washington, DC**
Opert, Lawrence R. ... Boston, MA
Opert & Sandler ... Boston, MA
Opett, Edward J. ... Cleveland, OH
Opfel, Gregory L. ... Chicago, IL
Opfell, Christopher K. ... Woodland Hills, CA
Opfer, James D., Jr. ... Vernon, NJ
Opferman, Thomas G. ... **Chicago, IL**
Opgenorth, Joanne ... Kensington, MD
Ophaug, John M. ... **Northfield, MN**
Opheim & Rantala ... Ada, MN
Opheim, Steven C. ... **St. Paul, MN**
Opheim, Thomas A. ... Ada, MN
Ophelia, Dianne R. ... Fresno, CA
Opher, Ron Z. ... Valley Forge, PA
Ophir, Gal C. ... **New York, NY**
Ophoff, Daniel A. ... Grand Rapids, MI
Ophoven, Jerry ... **Grand Rapids, MN**
Opich, Joseph P. ... **New York, NY**
Opich, Martha Evensen ... Sacramento, CA
Opie, Glenn E. ... **Great Bend, KS**
Opie, Marvin W. ... Tipton, MO
Opilo, Theodore J. ... San Bernardino, CA
Opinante, Nicholas J. ... Brooklyn, NY
Opincar, Scott N. ... **Cleveland, OH**
Opinsky, Heidi E. ... New York, NY
Opitz, John P.
Department of Housing and Urban Development,
Office of General Counsel, GV
Opitz, Mary Painter ... **Norfolk, VA**
Opland, Robert N. ... Anchorage, AK
O'Planick, Richard B. ... **Milwaukee, WI**
Oplatka, William ... Berwyn, IL
Opler, Stephen A. ... **Atlanta, GA**
Oplinger, Jon C. ... Frazer, PA
Opoku, Lisa F. ... Palo Alto, CA
Opolski, Leon A. ... San Diego, CA
Opotowsky, Randy ... **New Orleans, LA**
Opotowsky, Stuart B. ... New York, NY
Opotzner, Robert M. ... **Danbury, CT**
Ridgefield, CT
Opp, Christine A. ... Chicago, IL
Opp, Clifford R., Jr. ... Tampa, FL
Opp, Craig Allen ... **New York, NY**
Opp, Richard A. ... Billings, MT
Oppat, Robert J. ... Mount Clemens, MI
Oppedahl, Carl ... **Frisco, CO**
Oppedahl & Larson LLP ... **Frisco, CO**
Oppedahl, Mary C. ... **Oakland, CA**
Oppedisano, David J. ... San Diego, CA
Oppegard, Paul R. ... **Moorhead, MN**
Oppel, Curt A. ... **Davenport, IA**
Oppel, Jeffrey W. ... **Houston, TX**
Oppel, Jerald J. ... **Baltimore, MD**
Oppel, Margaret S. ... Santa Barbara, CA
Oppel, Matthew Robert ... Kingfisher, OK
Oppel, R. Craig ... **Muscatine, IA**
West Liberty, IA
Oppenberg, Gale L.
National Mediation Board, GV
Oppeneer, Brian K. ... **Eau Claire, WI**
Oppenheim & Associates ... **Miami, FL**
Oppenheim, Avivith ... Springfield, NJ
Oppenheim, Bernard K. ... Metairie, LA
Oppenheim, Charles B. ... **Los Angeles, CA**
Oppenheim, Daniel P. ... Washington, DC
Oppenheim, David L.
Commodity Futures Trading Commission,
Division of Enforcement, GV
Oppenheim, David S.
Greenwood Village, CO
Oppenheim, David W. ... **Philadelphia, PA**
Oppenheim, Elliot Arnold ... Beverly Hills, CA
Oppenheim, Eric C. ... Detroit, MI
Oppenheim, Gordon A. ... Dedham, MA
Oppenheim, Ian S. ... Halifax, MA
Oppenheim, James N. ... Monticello, NY
Oppenheim, Jay B. ... Philadelphia, PA
Oppenheim, Jeffrey A. ... **New York, NY**
Oppenheim, Jeffrey W. ... Falmouth, MA
Oppenheim, Jerrold N. ... Boston, MA
Oppenheim, Jerry ... **New York, NY**
Oppenheim, Jerry, P.C. ... **New York, NY**
Oppenheim, Jessica S. ... Trenton, NJ
Oppenheim, John P. ... **Englewood, CO**
Oppenheim, Joyce M. ... Detroit, MI
Oppenheim, Judy B. ... Chicago, IL
Oppenheim, Lanny A. ... **New York, NY**
Oppenheim, Leonard J. ... Rumson, NJ
Oppenheim, Louis J. ... New York, NY
Oppenheim, Lucille Cass ... White Plains, NY
Oppenheim & Maire, P.C. ... Halifax, MA
Oppenheim, Martha H.
Federal Trade Commission,
Bureau of Competition, GV
Oppenheim, Mary E. ... Portland, CT
Oppenheim, Mary G. ... Chicago, IL
Oppenheim, Matthew J. ... **Washington, DC**
Oppenheim, Maurice H. ... Roseville, CA
Oppenheim, Mona Hirsch ... Kings Point, NY
Oppenheim, Morris J. ... Rumson, NJ
Oppenheim, Moshe R.
West Palm Beach, FL
Oppenheim, Nancy Ann
Steamboat Springs, CO
Oppenheim & Oppenheim ... Rumson, NJ
Oppenheim, Patrice W. ... **Metairie, LA**
Oppenheim, Patricia G. ... Roseville, CA
Oppenheim & Pilelsky, P.A.
Fort Lauderdale, FL
Weston, FL
Oppenheim, Rhonda J. ... Edison, NJ
Oppenheim, Richard D., Jr.
Los Angeles, CA
Oppenheim, Robert L. ... Los Angeles, CA
Oppenheim, Robert P. ... **New York, NY**
Oppenheim, Roger D. ... Houston, TX
Oppenheim, Roy D. ... **Fort Lauderdale, FL**
Oppenheim, Scott D. ... Encino, CA
Oppenheim, Stephanie E. ... New York, NY
Oppenheim, Stephen D. ... **Hartford, CT**
Oppenheim, Stephen J. ... Rumson, NJ
Oppenheim, Steven D. ... **New York, NY**
Oppenheim, Steven P. (IBA) ... **Miami, FL**
Oppenheim, Trudy H. ... New Orleans, LA
Oppenheimer, Amy J. ... Berkeley, CA
Oppenheimer, Arthur M. ... Boca Raton, FL
Oppenheimer, Bennett ... Fort Lauderdale, FL
Oppenheimer, Blend, Harrison & Tate, Inc.
Edinburg, TX
San Antonio, TX
Oppenheimer, Brett ... **Louisville, KY**
Oppenheimer, Carla ... **Kansas City, MO**
Oppenheimer, Carol ... Santa Fe, NM
Oppenheimer, Charles D. ... **Ashland, KY**
Oppenheimer, Charles H. ... **Kenilworth, NJ**
Oppenheimer, David B. ... San Francisco, CA
Oppenheimer, Douglas L. ... Miami, FL
Oppenheimer, Eleanor F. ... Jamaica, NY
Oppenheimer, Franz M. ... **Washington, DC**
Oppenheimer, Gail C. ... **Louisville, KY**
Oppenheimer, Gordon S. ... New York, NY
Oppenheimer, Gregg ... Los Angeles, CA
Oppenheimer, Houston ... **Louisville, KY**
Oppenheimer, J. David ... **San Antonio, TX**
Oppenheimer, Jack C.
Department Of Health And Human Services,
Public Health Service, GV
Oppenheimer, James Chadwick
Washington, DC
Oppenheimer, James R. ... **St. Paul, MN**
Oppenheimer, Jerry L. ... **Washington, DC**
Oppenheimer, Jesse A. ... San Antonio, TX
Oppenheimer, Jesse H. ... **San Antonio, TX**
Oppenheimer, Joan I.
Department of Justice, Tax Division, GV
Oppenheimer, Joe L. ... **Bethesda, MD**
Oppenheimer, Kay ... Strafford, NH
Oppenheimer, Laurence B. ... **Buffalo, NY**
Oppenheimer, Lori Segal ... New York, NY
Oppenheimer, M. Randall
Los Angeles, CA
Oppenheimer, Mark H. ... **Louisville, KY**
Oppenheimer, Mark V. ... Monroe, CT
Oppenheimer, Martin J. ... **New York, NY**
Oppenheimer, Martin J. ... **New York, NY**
Oppenheimer, Mary E. ... Treasury Department,
Internal Revenue Service, GV
Oppenheimer, Max Stul, (P.C.)
Baltimore, MD
Oppenheimer, Michelle Reed
Lummi Island, WA
Oppenheimer, Nanette L. ... Washington, DC
Oppenheimer, Peter H. ... Washington, DC
Oppenheimer, Peter J. ... **Miami, FL**
Oppenheimer, Randolph C. ... **Buffalo, NY**
Oppenheimer, Robert ... **Rochester, NY**
Oppenheimer, Robert J. ... **New York, NY**
Oppenheimer, Ronald S. ... New York, NY
Oppenheimer, Steven J. ... **Los Angeles, CA**
Oppenheimer, Susan L. ... **Columbus, OH**
Oppenheimer, Theodore N. ... Oceanside, NY
Oppenheimer, Thomas J. ... Springfield, MA
Oppenheimer, William J. ... San Jose, CA

Oppenheimer Wolff & Donnelly (Illinois)
Chicago, IL
Oppenheimer Wolff Donnelly & Bayh LLP
Washington, DC
Oppenheimer Wolff & Donnelly LLP
Los Angeles, CA
Newport Beach, CA
Palo Alto, CA
Minneapolis, MN
St. Paul, MN
New York, NY
Oppenhoff & Rädler Linklaters & Alliance
New York, NY
New York, NY
Oppenneer, G. E. ... Denver, CO
Opper, Edward A. ... Valley Stream, NY
Opper, Joseph ... New York, NY
Opper, Loren M. ... Dearborn, MI
Opper, Michael B. ... Sacramento, CA
Opper, Richard G. ... San Diego, CA
Opper, Ronald Allen ... Houston, TX
Opperer, Joshua F. ... Detroit, MI
Opperman & Associates, P.C. ... Denver, CO
Opperman, Craig P. ... Palo Alto, CA
Opperman, Daniel S. ... Bay City, MI
Mount Pleasant, MI
Opperman, David R. ... Baton Rouge, LA
Opperman, Dwight D. ... Eagan, MN
Opperman, Harriet Elizabeth
Shreveport, LA
Opperman, Joanna D. ... San Francisco, CA
Opperman, John R. ... Portland, ME
Opperman, Kathleen M. ... Landing, NJ
Opperman, Leonard ... Indianapolis, IN
Opperman, Marlin D. ... Denver, CO
Opperman, Vance K. ... Eagan, MN
Oppermann, Gus David, V ... Houston, TX
Opperthauser, Glen A.
Huntington Woods, MI
Opperthauser, Glen A. ... Royal Oak, MI
Opperwall, Kathleen R. ... East Lansing, MI
Opperwall, Stephen G., Law Offices of
Pleasanton, CA
Opperwall, Stephen G., Law Offices of
San Jose, CA
Opperwall, Theodore R. ... Birmingham, MI
Detroit, MI
Oppewal, Jacob ... Whitinsville, MA
Oppinger, Anouchka M. ... Houston, TX
Oppito, Wayne J. ... Trenton, NJ
Oppleman, Jeffrey A. ... Richmond, VA
Oppler, Edward P.
Department of Transportation,
Office of the Secretary, GV
Oppliger, David E. ... Lansing, MI
Oppliger, James Robert ... Fresno, CA
Oppliger, Trevor Z ... Fresno, CA
Oppman, Suzanne M. ... Pittsburgh, PA
Oppold, Thomas J. ... Des Moines, IA
Oprendek, Matthew J. ... Houston, TX
Opri, Debra A. ... Beverly Hills, CA
Opri, Debra A., A Professional Corporation
Beverly Hills, CA
Opria, Ryan M. ... Chicago, IL
Oprian, Linda M. ... Santa Ana, CA
Oprisko, Brian S. ... Bala Cynwyd, PA
Opryszek, Sharon D. ... Chicago, IL
Opsahl, Erick R. ... Fond du Lac, WI
Opsahl, Kurt B. ... Menlo Park, CA
Opsahl, Richard B. ... Rantoul, IL
Opshal, Lisa S. ... Bethesda, MD
Opsitnick, Allan J. ... Pittsburgh, PA
Opsitnick, Timothy M. ... Cleveland, OH
Opstelten, Joseph W. ... Golden, CO
Opstelten, Joseph W., P.C. ... Golden, CO
Opton, Edward M., Jr. ... Oakland, CA
Opton Handler & Feiler, LLP ... Edison, NJ
New York, NY
Opton, Michael P. ... Portland, OR
Opton & Underwood, P.C. ... Portland, OR
Oquendo, Lilia E. ... San Juan, PR
Oquendo, Ricardo E. ... New York, NY
Oquin, Erin L. ... Inola, OK
O'Quin, Gregory B. ... Alexandria, LA
O'Quinn, David S. ... Fort Pierce, FL
O'Quinn, John M. ... Houston, TX
O'Quinn, Kathy McCoy ... Mesa, AZ
St. Martinville, LA
O'Quinn & Laminack ... Houston, TX
O'Quinn, M. Darren ... Little Rock, AR
O'Quinn, Michael ... San Antonio, TX
O'Quinn, Michael A. ... McDonough, GA
O'Quinn, Michael A., P.C.
McDonough, GA
O'Quinn, Michael A. U. ... Orlando, FL
O'Quinn, Osborne Walker ... Fort Pierce, FL
O'Quinn, Pam Gates ... Dallas, TX
O'Quinn, Robert A. ... Wilmington, NC
O'Quinn, Robert E., Jr. ... Jacksonville, FL
O'Quinn, Tim J. ... Tucumcari, NM
O'Quinn, William L. ... Denver, CO
O'Quinn, William L., Jr. ... Wilson, NC
Or, Olivia ... New York, NY
Oradell Law Offices ... Oradell, NJ
O'Rafferty, Garry S. ... Scottsdale, AZ
Orahood, Harper M. ... Wheat Ridge, CO
Orahood, Jane R. ... Atlanta, GA
Oraker, Jeffrey E. ... Denver, CO
Oram, Cole H. ... New York, NY
Oram, George E., Jr. ... Washington, DC
Oram, John C., Jr. ... New York, NY
Oram, Judi L. ... Biloxi, MS
Oram, Kathleen
Equal Employment Opportunity
Commission,
Office of Legal Counsel, GV
Oram, Nell Anne (IBA) ... Portland, OR
Oram, Peter D. ... New York, NY

Oram, Stephen W., (P.C.) ... Adrian, MI
Oram, Steven H. ... Chevy Chase, MD
Oram, Steven H., Chartered
Chevy Chase, MD
Oram, Susan E. ... Lewiston, ME
Oramas, John E. ... Miami, FL
Oram-Smith, Jennifer Dobbs
Virginia Beach, VA
Oran, Alan K. ... Austin, TX
Oran, Michael L., (A Professional Corporation)
Las Vegas, NV
Orand, Rebecca R. ... Miami, FL
Orander, A. D., Jr. ... Easley, SC
Orander, William D., III ... Goldsboro, NC
Orange, Charles R. ... Russellville, KY
Orange, Jan H. ... New York, NY
Orange, Laurie J. ... San Diego, CA
Orange, Vincent B. ... Washington, DC
Orans, Elsen & Lupert LLP
New York, NY
Oransky, Charles ... Newark, NJ
Oransky, Emanuel ... Roseland, NJ
Oransky, Scaraggi, Borg & Abbamonte
Roseland, NJ
Oratio, Gerald J. ... Westwood, NJ
Oratz, Lisa T. ... Bellevue, WA
Orava, Stephen J. ... Washington, DC
Oravec, Alan M. ... Sarasota, FL
Oravetz, Kalman A. ... New York, NY
Oray, Lauren Cabot ... Denver, CO
Orbach, David M. ... Los Angeles, CA
Orbach, Frank ... Princeton, NJ
Orbach & Huff LLP ... Los Angeles, CA
Orbach, Louis ... Syracuse, NY
Orbach, Morton ... Miami, FL
Orban, Alex J. ... Wilbraham, MA
Orban, Frank A., III ... Lancaster, PA
Orban, Frank A., Jr. ... Somerset, PA
Orban, Joseph S. ... New Brunswick, NJ
Orban, Mary J. ... Rancho Cucamonga, CA
Orban, Russell ... Falls Church, VA
Orband, James W. ... Binghamton, NY
Orbas, Sallie-Carol ... Sacramento, CA
Orbe, Lawrence F., III ... Aspen, CO
Orbe, Octavius A. ... Ridgewood, NJ
Orbe, Roland ... West New York, NJ
Orbe, William Q. ... New York, NY
Orbeck, Dale C. ... Austin, TX
Orbeck, Kim S. ... Irvine, CA
Orberson, William B. ... Louisville, KY
Orbeton, Jane ... Hallowell, ME
Orbison, Beth L. F. ... Greensburg, PA
Orbison, Charles E. ... Denton, TX
Orbison, James C. ... Tulsa, OK
Orbison, Michael H. ... New York, NY
Orbison, Robert H. ... Indianapolis, IN
Orbock Bowden Ruark & Dillard, P.L.L.C.
Winston-Salem, NC
Orbock, Jessica Kahn ... Atlanta, GA
Orbock, Maureen Tierney
Winston-Salem, NC
Orbon, John A. ... New York, NY
Orbon, Margaret J. ... Chicago, IL
Orbovich & Gartner, Chartered
St. Paul, MN
Orbovich, Samuel D. ... St. Paul, MN
Orbuch, Paul Marshall ... Denver, CO
Orce, Kenneth W. ... New York, NY
Orchard, Arlen R. ... Sacramento, CA
Orchard, Jack L., Jr. ... Portland, OR
Orchard, John T. ... Whitefish Bay, WI
Orchard, Merle P. ... Ukiah, CA
Orchard, Nancy Nolan ... Solvang, CA
Orchard, Scott E. ... Providence, RI
Orchard, Susan L. ... Tulsa, OK
Orchid, Harold L. ... Los Angeles, CA
Orchid, Lance R. ... Richmond, VA
Orchinik, Jeffrey S. ... Bensalem, PA
Orcino, Rose Marie ... San Diego, CA
Orcutt, Charles E. ... Hutchinson, KS
Orcutt, David S. ... Wilson, NC
Orcutt, Gregory J. ... Tampa, FL
Orcutt, Kenneth D. ... Hagåtña, GU
Orcutt, Shelly H. ... Costa Mesa, CA
Orcutt, Steven Y. ... Portland, OR
Orcutt, Steven Y., P.C. ... Portland, OR
Orcutt, William S. ... Manchester, NH
Ord, Edward O. C. ... San Francisco, CA
Ord, George P., (P.A.) ... Palm Beach, FL
Vero Beach, FL
Ord, Isabelle L. ... Costa Mesa, CA
Ord & Norman ... Los Angeles, CA
San Francisco, CA
Ordal, Kaseburg & Mitchell, PLLC
Seattle, WA
Ordal, Robert E. ... Seattle, WA
Ordas, Dale E. ... Sacramento, CA
Ordas Timmons Owen & Owen, Inc.
Sacramento, CA
Ordas, William J. ... Sacramento, CA
Ordaz, Steven P. ... Bannockburn, IL
Ordelheide, Kris ... Englewood, CO
Ordell, David J. ... Seattle, WA
Ordemann, Floyd J. ... Minneapolis, MN
Ordemann, Marshall F., Jr. ... Harvey, LA
Orden, Bonnie L. ... New York, NY
Orden, Jeremy F. ... New York, NY
Orden, Stewart L. ... New York, NY
Scarsdale, NY
Order, Richard S. ... Hartford, CT
Orderica, Lionel E. ... San Diego, CA
Ordet, Larry ... Miami, FL
Ordin, Andrea Sheridan ... Los Angeles, CA
Ordin, Robert L. ... Los Angeles, CA
Ordine, Charles J. ... Seattle, WA
Ording, Kenneth G. ... Hauppauge, NY
Ording, Michael K. ... Columbus, OH
Ordman, Morgan J. ... Chicago, IL

Ordman, Theodore ... Stanfordville, NY
Ordnung, Michael J. ... Savannah, MO
Ordon, Kimberly ... Marysville, WA
Ordonez, Alberto J. ... Miami, FL
Ordonez, Edward M. ... Chicago, IL
Ordonez, George E. ... Encino, CA
Ordóñez, Gustavo Adolfo ... New York, NY
Ordonez, Juan C. ... New York, NY
Ordoñez, Luis E. ... Miami, FL
Ordonez, Maria G. ... Chicago, IL
Ordonez, Raul G., Jr. ... Miami, FL
Ordoñez, Rene ... El Paso, TX
Ordos, Wayne L. ... Sacramento, CA
Ordoubadian, Margaret H ... Murfreesboro, TN
Ordover, Abraham P. ... Atlanta, GA
Ordover, Jerald ... New York, NY
Ordover, Marilyn G. ... Brooklyn, NY
Ordover, Morris H. ... New York, NY
Ordoveza, Domingo L. ... Arlington, VA
Ordower, Benj. ... Chicago, IL
Ordower, Lawrence B. ... Chicago, IL
Ordower & Ordower, P.C. ... Chicago, IL
Ordower, Peter ... Chicago, IL
Ordowski, James E. ... Las Vegas, NV
Ordubegian, Aram ... Santa Ana, CA
Orduno, Ramon R. ... Oceanside, CA
Ordway, David J. ... Stamford, CT
Ordway, David R. ... Biddeford, ME
Ordway, Dustin P. ... Grand Rapids, MI
Ordway, Eric ... New York, NY
Ordway, Gary D. ... Des Moines, IA
Ordway, John A., Jr. ... Washington, DC
Ordway, John M. ... Department of State,
Foreign Service Institute, GV
Ordway, Randy J. ... Troy, MI
Ordway, Sidney G. ... San Antonio, TX
Ore, Joseph Y. ... City of Industry, CA
O'Rear, Caine, III ... Mobile, AL
O'Rear, Caine, Jr. ... Jasper, AL
O'Rear, Griff ... Jasper, AL
O'Rear, Kevin D. ... South Bend, IN
O'Rear & O'Rear ... Jasper, AL
O'Rear, Stephen B. ... Fort Worth, TX
Orebic, Matthew J. ... Berkeley, CA
Orecchia, Paul V. ... Freehold, NJ
Orecchio, Maria ... New York, NY
Oreck, Bradley, Crighton, Adams & Chase,
LLC ... Boulder, CO
New Orleans, LA
Oreck, Bruce J. ... Boulder, CO
Oreck, Eugene R. ... Oakland, CA
Orefice, James A.
United States Tax Court, GV
Orefice, Stephanie M. ... White Plains, NY
O'Regan, Ann M. ... Fremont, CA
O'Regan, Deborah J. ... Anchorage, AK
O'Regan, Deirdre C. ... East Falmouth, MA
O'Regan, Dustin ... Evanston, IL
O'Regan, Francis M. ... New York, NY
O'Regan, James J. ... Northbrook, IL
O'Regan, Kevin ... Springfield, MA
O'Regan, Laura M. ... Ship Bottom, NJ
O'Regan, Patrick T., Jr. ... Falmouth, MA
O'Regan, Robert J. ... Boston, MA
O'Regan, William D., III ... La Place, LA
Oreh, John Paul ... Cleveland, OH
Oreh, Kim Moses ... Cleveland, OH
Oreh, Kimberly M. ... Solon, OH
Oreh and Sweeney, P.L.L. ... Cleveland, OH
Orehek, Frederick A. ... North Riverside, IL
O'Reilley, D. Patrick ... Washington, DC
O'Reilly, Alessandra L. ... Philadelphia, PA
O'Reilly, Ann C. ... South St. Paul, MN
O'Reilly, Brendan Peter ... Forest Hills, NY
O'Reilly, Brian ... Hackensack, NJ
O'Reilly, Brian T. ... Springfield, VA
O'Reilly, Charles A. ... Department of Justice,
Tax Division, GV
O'Reilly, Charles B. ... Marina Del Rey, CA
O'Reilly, Christine K. ... Philadelphia, PA
O'Reilly, Colleen Marie ... New York, NY
O'Reilly, Collins & Danko, A Professional
Corporation ... Menlo Park, CA
O'Reilly, D. Kevin, (Co., L.P.A.)
Chardon, OH
O'Reilly, Daniel J. ... Brooklyn, NY
O'Reilly, David ... Westlake Village, CA
O'Reilly, Deirdre A. ... San Mateo, CA
O'Reilly, Dennis E. ... Newport Beach, CA
O'Reilly, Dennis M. ... Sacramento, CA
O'Reilly, Edward J. ... Kansas City, MO
O'Reilly, Edward V. ... Eugene, OR
O'Reilly, Gerald J. ... Chicago, IL
O'Reilly, Gerald J. ... Buffalo, NY
O'Reilly, Gregory W. ... Chicago, IL
O'Reilly, Herbert M. ... Hardinsburg, KY
O'Reilly, Hugh A. ... Boston, MA
O'Reilly, Hugh T. ... Key Biscayne, FL
O'Reilly, James Francis ... Washington, DC
Baltimore, MD
O'Reilly, James M. ... Farmington Hills, MI
O'Reilly, James M. ... Gardnerville, NV
O'Reilly, James T. ... Cincinnati, OH
O'Reilly, Janice Griffin ... Pittsburgh, PA
O'Reilly, John A., Jr. ... Farmington, CT
O'Reilly, John D., III ... Southborough, MA
O'Reilly, John F. ... Wheaton, IL
O'Reilly, John F., (A Professional
Corporation) ... Las Vegas, NV
O'Reilly, John H. ... San Francisco, CA
O'Reilly, John J. ... Morristown, NJ
O'Reilly, John M. ... Florham Park, NJ
O'Reilly, Joseph W. ... Frankfort, KY
O'Reilly, Joyce Glason
Christiansted, St. Croix, VI
O'Reilly, Juliana Schulte ... Washington, DC
O'Reilly, Kathleen G. ... Keene, NH
O'Reilly & Kelly ... Corpus Christi, TX

O'Reilly, Kelly C. ... Columbus, OH
O'Reilly, Kelly P. ... Burlington, WI
O'Reilly, Kelly Shane ... Pasadena, CA
O'Reilly, Kenneth D. ... New York, NY
O'Reilly, Kevin E. ... Chicago, IL
O'Reilly, Kevin R. ... Glenwood Springs, CO
O'Reilly, Kevin R. ... Lafayette, IN
O'Reilly, Kevin T. ... Basking Ridge, NJ
O'Reilly, Kevin W. ... Woodbury, NY
O'Reilly, Laurie Pyne ... Alexandria, VA
O'Reilly Law Offices ... Wheaton, IL
O'Reilly, Lawrence ... Trenton, NJ
O'Reilly, Lawrence X. ... Chicago, IL
O'Reilly, M. Dylan ... Albuquerque, NM
O'Reilly, Margaret A. ... Belmont, MA
O'Reilly, Mark & Peelman, L.L.C.
Washington, DC
Bethesda, MD
O'Reilly, Marsh & Corteselli, P.C.
Garden City, NY
Mineola, NY
O'Reilly, Mary Ann ... Chicago, IL
O'Reilly, Mary E. ... Akron, OH
O'Reilly, Mary Sean ... Houston, TX
O'Reilly, Matthew C. ... Atlanta, GA
O'Reilly, Maureen A. ... Dedham, MA
O'Reilly, Mel B., Law Offices of
Albuquerque, NM
O'Reilly, Michael J. ... Lafayette, IN
O'Reilly, Michael J. ... Dearborn, MI
O'Reilly, Michael J. ... Pittsburgh, PA
O'Reilly, Michael J., Law Offices of
Columbus, OH
O'Reilly, Michael L. ... Vienna, VA
O'Reilly, Michael P. ... Corpus Christi, TX
O'Reilly, Michael T. ... Los Angeles, CA
O'Reilly, Molly M. ... Wheaton, IL
O'Reilly, Nancy J. ... Vienna, VA
O'Reilly, Patrick C. ... Buffalo, NY
O'Reilly, Patrick C. ... New York, NY
O'Reilly, Patrick W. ... Phoenix, AZ
O'Reilly, Paul ... Torrance, CA
O'Reilly, Paul E. ... Perrysburg, OH
O'Reilly, Paul J. ... Washington, DC
Bethesda, MD
O'Reilly, Paul J. ... Sterling Heights, MI
O'Reilly, Peter L. ... Chicago, IL
O'Reilly, Philip F. ... New York, NY
O'Reilly, Philip J. ... Garden City, NY
O'Reilly, Philip N. ... Norristown, PA
O'Reilly, Rancilio, Nitz, Andrews, Turnbull
& Scott, P.C. ... Mount Clemens, MI
Sterling Heights, MI
O'reilly, Richard C. ... Watertown, MA
O'Reilly, Robert J., Jr. ... Sacramento, CA
O'Reilly, Roger Kevin ... Wheaton, IL
O'Reilly, Terrence ... Detroit, MI
O'Reilly, Terrence J. ... Los Angeles, CA
O'Reilly, Terrence M. ... Milwaukee, WI
O'Reilly, Terrence P. ... New York, NY
O'Reilly, Terry ... Menlo Park, CA
O'Reilly, Thomas P. ... Lanham, MD
O'Reilly, Thomas P. ... Boston, MA
O'Reilly, Timothy B., Law Offices of
Springfield, MO
O'Reilly, Timothy L. ... Long Beach, CA
O'Reilly, Timothy P. ... Rochester, NY
O'Reilly, Timothy P. ... Philadelphia, PA
O'Reilly, Timothy P. ... Pittsburgh, PA
O'Reilly, Tricia Bevelock ... Roseland, NJ
O'Reilly, Vincent F. ... Miami, FL
O'Reilly, William J. ... Olean, NY
O'Reilly, William L. ... Whippany, NJ
O'Reilly, William M. ... Stevens Point, WI
O'Reilly, William R., Jr. ... Boston, MA
O'Reilly, William V. ... Washington, DC
O'Reilly, Wm. M. ... Albany, NY
Orejuela, Kathleen W. ... Boston, MA
Orel, James D. ... Oak Brook, IL
Orel, Stephen H. ... New York, NY
Orellana, Robert R. ... Ventura, CA
Orelup, Elizabeth A. ... Milwaukee, WI
Orem, Belinda K. ... Los Angeles, CA
Orem, Clyde ... Memphis, TN
Orem, Robert E. ... Knoxville, TN
Oremland, Annalisa ... Washington, DC
Oremland, Lawrence R. ... Tucson, AZ
Oremland, Nancy K.
Securities and Exchange Commission,
Division of Corporation Finance, GV
Oremus, Dorothy A. ... Chicago, IL
Oremus, Frederick L. ... Athens, OH
Oren, Brandon A. ... Macon, GA
Oren, Charles D. ... Fresno, CA
Oren, Craig N. ... Camden, NJ
Oren, David C. ... Alexandria, VA
Oren, Donald E. ... Fresno, CA
Oren, Eric P. ... Fresno, CA
Oren, Kipling ... New York, NY
Oren, Laura ... Houston, TX
Oren & Oren, Inc. ... Fresno, CA
Oren, Thomas C. ... Lansing, MI
Orenbach, Kenneth Barry ... New York, NY
Orenberg, Allen H. ... Washington, DC
Orendain, Abel A. ... McAllen, TX
Orendain, Amada R. ... San Diego, CA
Orendain, Helen H. ... Missoula, MT
Orendain, Nina M. ... Dallas, TX
Orendorf, Jo T. ... Bowling Green, KY
Orendorff, James M. ... Pasadena, CA
Orendorff, Melinda Badgley ... Pueblo, CO
Orendorff, William K. ... Sallisaw, OK
Orenic, Paul M. ... Oakbrook Terrace, IL
Orens, Morris ... New York, NY
Orens, Robert M. ... Lido Beach, NY
Orens, Stephen J. ... Gaithersburg, MD
Orensky, Andrew J. ... Coram, NY
Orenstein, Andrew J. ... New York, NY

Ormsby, Michael C. ....**Coeur d'Alene, ID**
Spokane, WA
Ormseth, Kris ....**Boise, ID**
Ormseth, Leif M. ....**Seattle, WA**
Ormseth, Milo E. ....**Portland, OR**
Ormsten & Evangelist ....Jericho, NY
Ormsten, Franklin D. ....Jericho, NY
Orna, Susan V. ....Philadelphia, PA
Ornburn, Lannie C., Jr. ....Olathe, KS
Orndahl, Michael L. ....Rolling Meadows, IL
Orndorff, Brian Patrick ....New York, NY
Orndorff, David L. ....Buckhannon, WV
Orndorff, Jeffrey T. ....**Chardon, OH**
Orndorff, Jon B. ....**Huntington, WV**
Orndorff Law Offices ....**Boise, ID**
Nampa, ID
Orndorff, Owen H. ....**Boise, ID**
Orndorff, Terry O. ....Oklahoma City, OK
Orndorff, Terry S. ....Zebulon, NC
Ornduff, Jason S. ....**Chicago, IL**
Orne, Jonathan B. ....Richmond, VA
Ornelas, Virginia S. ....Paradise Valley, AZ
Laguna Niguel, CA
Ornelas, Xavier ....Edinburg, TX
Ornell, Craig T ....Worcester, MA
Ornellas, Mark F. ....**Sonora, CA**
Stockton, CA
Orner, Dan R. ....Cincinnati, OH
Orner, Robert T. ....Irving, TX
Orner, Ronald A. ....Chicago, IL
Orner, Seymour B. ....Highland Park, IL
Ornish, Marty Chapman ....La Mesa, CA
Ornitz, Barbara E. ....**Aspen, CO**
Ornitz, Richard M. ....**New York, NY**
Ornoff & Arnold, P.C. ....Virginia Beach, VA
Ornoff, Michael E. ....Virginia Beach, VA
Ornsteen, Pamela ....San Antonio, TX
Ornstein, Alexander T. ....Southfield, MI
Ornstein, Chantel Renee ....**Annapolis, MD**
Fort Washington, MD
Waldorf, MD
Ornstein, Debra ....Washington, DC
Ornstein, Elizabeth B. ....**Boston, MA**
Ornstein, Fred ....Palm Beach Gardens, FL
Ornstein and Harris ....Santa Barbara, CA
Ornstein, Jules ....**Denver, CO**
Ornstein, Mark L. ....**Orlando, FL**
Ornstein, Maurice J. ....Brooklyn, NY
Ornstein & Ornstein, P.C. ....Brooklyn, NY
Ornstein, Paul N. ....**Central Valley, NY**
Ornstein, Peter M. ....Denver, CO
Ornstein, Robert M. ....Santa Barbara, CA
Ornstein, Sheldon S. ....Brooklyn, NY
Ornstein, Stanley E. ....Cleveland, OH
Ornstein, Stephen F. J. ....**Washington, DC**
Ornstein, Warren K. ....Cleveland, OH
Ornstein & Woll, PLLC ....Southfield, MI
Ornstil, Michael G. ....San Francisco, CA
Oro, Barbara ....Boston, MA
O'Roark, Dulaney L., Jr. ....St. Petersburg, FL
O'Roark, Walter N., III ....**Baton Rouge, LA**
Orodenker, Daniel E. ....Kailua, HI
Orodenker, Norman G. ....**Providence, RI**
Oroho, John Patrick ....Riverdale, NJ
O'Roke, Sharon ....Oklahoma City, OK
Orol, Elliot S. ....**New York, NY**
Orol, Harriet ....**New York, NY**
Orona, M. Maurice ....Bellevue, WA
Oronoz, Mario R. ....**San Juan, PR**
Oronoz-Rodriguez, Lilly A. ....**San Juan, PR**
Oropallo, Michael A. ....**Syracuse, NY**
Oropeza, M. Anthony ....Sacramento, CA
Oropollo, Michael B. ....**Hackensack, NJ**
O'Rorke, James F., Jr. ....**New York, NY**
O'Rorke, Karen A. ....Atlantic City, NJ
O'Rorke, Patricia A. ....**Salt Lake City, UT**
Oros, Delbert W. ....Sacramento, CA
Oros, George ....Mound City, IL
Oros, James F., Jr. ....Birmingham, AL
Orosco, Rene ....Omaha, NE
Orosz, David L. ....Fort Myers, FL
Orosz, Donald G. ....Glendale, CA
Orosz, Florence Upjohn ....Kalamazoo, MI
Orosz, Gina R. ....**Parsippany, NJ**
Orosz, Kimiko ....**Chicago, IL**
Orosz, Richard T. ....Painesville, OH
Orosz, Stephen C. ....New Brunswick, NJ
O'Rourk, Ieva Karklins
Treasury Department,
Office of Regulations and Rulings, GV
O'Rourke, Allan & Fong, LLP
Burbank, CA
Glendale, CA
Los Angeles, CA
Pasadena, CA
San Bernardino, CA
O'Rourke, Andrew P. ....White Plains, NY
O'Rourke, Ann M. ....Braintree, MA
O'Rourke, Ann M. ....**Cleveland, OH**
O'Rourke & Associates Co., L.P.A.
Akron, OH
Cleveland, OH
O'Rourke & Associates, LLC
Greenwich, CT
New Canaan, CT
Stamford, CT
White Plains, NY
O'Rourke, Bartholomew J. ....Stuart, FL
O'Rourke, Brendan J. ....**New Canaan, CT**
Stamford, CT
O'Rourke, Brendan J. ....**New York, NY**
O'Rourke, Brendan Michael ....**Boston, MA**
O'Rourke, Bridget K.
Steamboat Springs, CO
O'Rourke, C. Larry ....**Palo Alto, CA**
O'Rourke, Carol L. ....**Garden City, NY**
O'Rourke, Charles F. ....Marysville, CA
O'Rourke, Christopher J. ....**New York, NY**

O'Rourke, Clifford F. ....Camden, ME
O'Rourke & Cundra ....**Washington, DC**
O'Rourke, Daniel ....**Chicago, IL**
O'Rourke, Daniel ....**Spokane, WA**
O'Rourke, Daniel Charles ....**Destin, FL**
O'Rourke, Daniel J. ....**Cherry Hill, NJ**
Philadelphia, PA
O'Rourke, Daniel P. ....**Essex Junction, VT**
O'Rourke, Denis M. ....**Glendale, CA**
O'Rourke, Denise Michelle ....**Glendale, CA**
O'Rourke, Dennis ....Colorado Springs, CO
O'Rourke, Dennis C. ....**Mineola, NY**
O'Rourke, Edward M. ....Olympia Fields, IL
O'Rourke, Francis J. ....Santa Ana, CA
O'Rourke, Frederick H. ....Syracuse, NY
O'Rourke & Friedman ....Brooklyn, NY
O'Rourke, Gerard M. ....**Wilmington, DE**
O'Rourke, Helen E. McL. ....Boston, MA
O'Rourke, Howard G. ....Valley Stream, NY
O'Rourke, James F., Jr. ....Portland, OR
O'Rourke, James G. ....Stratford, CT
O'Rourke, James J. ....Hauppauge, NY
O'Rourke, James J., Jr. ....**Raynham, MA**
O'Rourke, James L. ....Stratford, CT
O'Rourke, James M. ....Chicago, IL
O'Rourke, James P. ....Boonville, NY
O'Rourke, James P. ....New York, NY
O'Rourke, Jason J. ....**Rock Island, IL**
O'Rourke, Jerome F. ....**Flint, MI**
O'Rourke, John C. ....Bayside, NY
O'Rourke, John C., Jr. ....**Chicago, IL**
O'Rourke, John G. ....Hanford, CA
O'Rourke, John M. ....**Anderson, SC**
O'Rourke, John P. ....Danville, IL
O'Rourke, John P. ....East Meadow, NY
O'Rourke, John R. ....Los Angeles, CA
O'Rourke, John R., Jr. ....**Norristown, PA**
O'Rourke, John T., Law Offices of
Washington, DC
O'Rourke & Joseph, P.C. ....**Flint, MI**
O'Rourke, Kathleen ....Chicago, IL
O'Rourke, Kenneth J. ....Department of State,
Office of the Legal Adviser, GV
O'Rourke, Kenneth R. ....**Los Angeles, CA**
O'Rourke, Kevin D. ....**Spokane, WA**
O'Rourke, Kevin G. ....New York, NY
O'Rourke, Kevin P.
Securities and Exchange Commission,
Division of Enforcement, GV
O'Rourke, Lawrence J. ....Jersey City, NJ
O'Rourke, Lawrence M. ....Washington, DC
O'Rourke, Margaret Mary ....Mendocino, CA
O'Rourke, Marie A. ....Department of Justice,
Criminal Division, GV
O'Rourke, Marilyn ....San Francisco, CA
O'Rourke, Mary E. ....Cranston, RI
O'Rourke, Maureen T. ....**New York, NY**
O'Rourke McCloskey & Moody
Chicago, IL
O'Rourke, Melissa R. ....**Huron, SD**
Mitchell, SD
O'Rourke, Michael E. ....Fond du Lac, WI
ORourke, Michael Francis ....Randolph, MA
O'Rourke, Michael J. ....Jacksonville, FL
O'Rourke, Michael J. ....Bloomington, IL
O'Rourke, Michael J. ....**Chicago, IL**
O'Rourke, Michael J. ....Minneapolis, MN
O'Rourke, Michael J. ....Brooklyn, NY
O'Rourke, Michael J. ....Pottsville, PA
O'Rourke, Michael J., Jr.
Board of Governors Of The Federal Reserve
System,
Office of the General Counsel, GV
O'Rourke, Michael P. ....Troy, MI
O'Rourke, Michael P. ....**Las Vegas, NV**
O'Rourke, Michael S. ....**Washington, DC**
New York, NY
O'Rourke, Neil G. ....**Winston-Salem, NC**
O'Rourke, Norman F. ....Fort Lauderdale, FL
O'Rourke, Pamela Sellnow ....Brainerd, MN
O'Rourke, Patrick A. ....San Leandro, CA
O'Rourke, Patrick J. ....Bloomington, IL
O'Rourke, Patrick T. ....**Denver, CO**
O'Rourke, Paul ....Passaic, NJ
O'Rourke, Paul J., Jr. ....**Fresno, CA**
O'Rourke, Paul R. ....**Memphis, TN**
O'Rourke, Peter E. ....Detroit, MI
O'Rourke, Peter E., P.C. ....Detroit, MI
O'Rourke, Peter J. ....**New York, NY**
O'Rourke, Philip J. ....**White Plains, NY**
O'Rourke, R. Joseph ....**Rutland, VT**
O'Rourke, R. Russell ....**Cleveland, OH**
O'Rourke, Ralphine Newlin ....Colchester, VT
O'Rourke, Renée W. ....**Denver, CO**
O'Rourke, Richard L. ....**Rye, NY**
White Plains, NY
O'Rourke, Robert B. ....**Sunnyvale, CA**
O'Rourke, Robert E. ....**Pendleton, OR**
O'Rourke, Robert E., Jr. ....Stockton, CA
O'Rourke, Robert K. ....Berkley, MI
O'Rourke, Samuel ....**Menlo Park, CA**
O'Rourke, Sean D. ....Madison, WI
O'Rourke, Sean T. ....**Fresno, CA**
O'Rourke, Shawn P. ....**Boston, MA**
O'Rourke, Sheila ....Berkeley, CA
O'Rourke, Stephanie ....**San Antonio, TX**
O'Rourke, Terrence J. ....**Pittsburgh, PA**
O'Rourke, Theresa A. ....**New York, NY**
O'Rourke, Thomas A. ....**New York, NY**
O'Rourke, Thomas H. ....New York, NY
O'Rourke, Thomas J. ....**Washington, DC**
Rockville, MD
O'Rourke, Thomas M. ....Denver, CO
O'Rourke, Thomas W. ....Boulder, CO
O'Rourke, Timothy A. ....Lansing, MI
O'Rourke, Timothy C. ....East Meadow, NY
O'Rourke, Timothy J. ....**Washington, DC**
O'Rourke, Timothy J. ....**Columbia, SC**

O'Rourke, Timothy P. ....**Pendleton, OR**
O'Rourke, Vincent F., Jr. ....**Worcester, MA**
O'Rourke, William A. ....**Munster, IN**
O'Rourke, William A., III ....**Rutland, VT**
O'Rourke, William F. ....**Houston, TX**
O'Rourke, William J., Jr. ....Pittsburgh, PA
Orovitz, Robert J. ....Miami, FL
Oroza, Stephen ....San Francisco, CA
Orozco, Constance E. ....Pasadena, CA
Orozco, Cynthia E. ....St. Petersburg, FL
Orozco, Deborah L. ....Bethesda, MD
Orozco, Francisco L. ....Los Angeles, CA
Orozco, Margarita Lopez ....San Jose, CA
Orozco, Patricia A. ....Yuma, AZ
Orozco, Richard E. ....El Monte, CA
Orozco, Robert L. ....Bryan, TX
Orozco, Sergio O. ....Beverly Hills, CA
Orozco & Willoughby ....San Jose, CA
Orozco, Yolanda ....**Santa Monica, CA**
Orozo-martinez, Maria E. ....Santa Ana, CA
Orpett, Mitchell A. ....**Chicago, IL**
Orphan, Jas. G. ....Glenview, IL
Orphanides, Gust G. ....New Port Richey, FL
Orque-Lee, Jean Malia ....Honolulu, HI
Orr, A. Summey, III ....**Atlanta, GA**
Orr, Albert S. ....**Milwaukee, WI**
Orr, Alexander, Jr. ....New York, NY
Orr, Allen L. ....**Salt Lake City, UT**
Orr, Anne Holladay ....Atlanta, GA
Orr, Arthur W. ....Decatur, AL
Orr, Barbara Jean ....**San Diego, CA**
Orr, Bette M. ....**Washington, DC**
Orr, Bruce H. ....**Portland, OR**
Orr, Bryan R. ....**Chicago, IL**
Orr, C. Meghan ....Baltimore, MD
Orr, Charles W. ....Iowa City, IA
Orr, Cheryl A. ....**Los Angeles, CA**
Orr, Cheryl D. ....**San Francisco, CA**
Orr, Claudia D. ....**Detroit, MI**
Orr, Craig N. ....**Laurel, MS**
Orr, Cynthia Hujar ....**San Antonio, TX**
Orr, Dan M. ....Ash Flat, AR
Orr, David A. C. ....Los Angeles, CA
Orr, David L. ....**Austin, TX**
Orr, David S. ....Olympia, WA
Orr, Debra A ....Caldwell, ID
Orr, Dennis P. ....**New York, NY**
Orr, Diane L. ....Los Angeles, CA
Orr, Donald E. ....Stamford, CT
Orr, Donna J. ....**Sevierville, TN**
Orr, Dudley W. ....**Concord, NH**
Orr, Dvorak and Associates, Ltd.
East Peoria, IL
Orr, E. Wycliffe ....**Gainesville, GA**
Orr and Edwards, Attorneys at Law, P.C.
Atlanta, GA
Decatur, GA
Orr, Edwin W., Jr. ....**Florham Park, NJ**
Orr, Edwin W., Law Offices of
Columbia, MO
Orr, Francis A. ....Philadelphia, PA
Orr, Gail L. ....**Los Angeles, CA**
Orr, Gary E. ....East Peoria, IL
Orr, Geoffrey J. ....**Metairie, LA**
Orr, George A., Jr. ....Niagara Falls, NY
Orr, Heidi L. G. ....**Bellevue, WA**
Orr, J. Douglas ....Clinton, NJ
Orr, Jack G. ....Seattle, WA
Orr, Jacquelyn J. ....**Washington, DC**
Orr, James A. ....**Atlanta, GA**
Orr, James C., Jr. ....**Hurst, TX**
Orr, James Crawford ....**Newark, NJ**
Orr, James J. ....Broken Bow, NE
Orr, James M. ....**Dallas, TX**
Orr, James M., Jr. ....Mobile, AL
Orr, James P. ....Rome, GA
Orr, James R. ....Prairie Village, KS
Orr, James W. ....**Columbia, SC**
Orr, Janice C. ....Orlando, FL
Tallahassee, FL
Orr, Jay E. ....Riverside, CA
Orr, Jefferson C. ....**Nashville, TN**
Orr, Jeffrey A., P.C. ....Salt Lake City, UT
Orr, Jeffrey C. ....Bloomington, IL
Orr, Jeffrey K. ....Indianapolis, IN
Orr, Jeffrey L. ....**Kearney, NE**
Orr, Jimmie G., Jr. ....Georgetown, KY
Orr, Jimmie G., Jr., P.S.C. ....Georgetown, KY
Orr, Joanne ....Indianapolis, IN
Orr, Joe L. ....Fort Worth, TX
Orr, John C. ....**Ventura, CA**
Orr, John F. ....Seaside, OR
Orr, John M. ....**San Francisco, CA**
Orr, John M. ....**Austin, TX**
Orr, John R. ....Charlotte, NC
Orr, John T., Jr. ....Atlanta, GA
Orr, Joseph B. ....Los Angeles, CA
Orr, Julie L. ....Wichita, KS
Orr, Kathleen Field ....**Chicago, IL**
Crystal Lake, IL
Orr, Kathleen L. ....Northwood, NH
Orr, Kevin J. ....**Jonesboro, AR**
Orr, Kevyn D. ....Department of Justice,
Executive Office for United States Trustees,
GV
Orr, Kristine E. ....**Gainesville, GA**
Orr Law Firm, The ....**Jonesboro, AR**
Orr, Lawrence B. ....**Florence, SC**
Orr, Lawrence G. ....Alamosa, CO
Orr, Lee Rand ....Menlo Park, CA
Orr, Leslie E. ....Walnut Creek, CA
Orr, Lynda Wilson ....Atlanta, GA
Orr, Marcia B. ....Skokie, IL
Orr, Margarita Brose ....New York, NY
Orr, Mark E. ....Ozark, MO
Orr, Mary L. B. ....Irvine, CA
Orr, Michael D. ....**Gulfport, MS**
Orr, Michael F. ....New York, NY

Orr, Michael S. ....**Newport Beach, CA**
Orr, Michael W. ....Lansing, MI
Orr, Michelle F. ....Cleveland, OH
Orr, Norman D. ....**Troy, MI**
Orr, Norman McLeod ....**Jackson, MS**
Orr & Orr ....**Gainesville, GA**
Orr, Parker M. ....**Cleveland, OH**
Orr, Patricia J. ....Guilderland, NY
Orr, Patricia S. ....**Burlington, VT**
Orr, Peter D. ....Lake Mary, FL
Orr, Randall L. ....Columbus, OH
Orr & Reno, Professional Association
Concord, NH
Orr, Richard D. ....Appleton, WI
Orr, Richard F. ....Hartford, CT
Orr, Richard J. ....**Princeton, NJ**
Orr, Richard M. ....Indianapolis, IN
Orr, Richard M. ....Cherry Hill, NJ
Orr, Rick W. ....**Sioux Falls, SD**
Orr, Robert F. ....Raleigh, NC
Orr, Robert, Jr. ....**Nashville, TN**
Orr, Robert M. ....Long Beach, CA
Orr, Robert W. ....**Chicago, IL**
Orr, Robin Hugh ....**Tampa, FL**
Orr, Roger G. ....Port St. Lucie, FL
Orr, Ron, & Professionals, Inc.
Marina Del Rey, CA
Orr, Ronald S. ....**Marina Del Rey, CA**
Orr, Roselie M. ....Lawrence, KS
Orr, Samuel J. ....Naples, FL
Orr, Samuel J., III ....Beaver, PA
Orr, San W., Jr. ....Wausau, WI
Orr, San Watterson, III ....New York, NY
Orr, Sarah Berryhill ....Davis, CA
Orr, Scott ....**Columbia, MO**
Orr, Scott J. ....**The Woodlands, TX**
Orr, Stanton R. ....Coral Gables, FL
Orr, Stefanie S. ....**Houston, TX**
Orr, Stephen T. ....Wyandotte, MI
Orr, Steven R. ....**Los Angeles, CA**
Orr, Susan D. ....Covington, IN
Orr, Susan M. ....**Hartford, CT**
Orr, Theresa A. ....Detroit, MI
Orr, Thomas ....Missoula, MT
Orr, Thomas B. ....Newport, RI
Orr, Thomas J. ....Burlington, NJ
Orr, Thomas Michael ....**Eugene, OR**
Orr, Timothy L. ....Palmdale, CA
San Fernando, CA
Orr, Tina McCree ....**Detroit, MI**
Orr, Tonja M. ....Minneapolis, MN
Orr, Trent W. ....San Francisco, CA
Orr, Twila Russell ....**Effingham, IL**
Orr, W. Fred, II ....**Decatur, GA**
Orr, Walter ....Dallas, TX
Orr, Wilbur A. ....**Washington, GA**
Orr, William J. ....**Atlanta, GA**
Orr, William L. ....Minneapolis, MN
Orr, William M. ....**New York, NY**
Orr, William R. ....**Astoria, OR**
Orr, William W. ....Asheville, NC
Orr, Wm. A., Jr. ....Bay City, TX
Orrantia, Lisa M. ....**Hudson, NY**
Poughkeepsie, NY
Orrell, John E., Jr. ....**Des Moines, IA**
Orrell, Nancy I. ....Orinda, CA
Orrell-Jones, Richard D. ....**Atlanta, GA**
Orren, David E. ....St. Paul, MN
Orren, Gary A. ....Abilene, TX
Orren, Harding A. ....Rancho Mirage, CA
Orren, Klemp & Stanton ....St. Paul, MN
Orren, Marna Wolf ....St. Paul, MN
Orren, Royal C. ....St. Paul, MN
Orrick, Andrew D. ....San Francisco, CA
Orrick, Herrington & Sutcliffe LLP
Los Angeles, CA
Menlo Park, CA
Sacramento, CA
San Francisco, CA
Washington, DC
New York, NY
Orrick, John R., Jr. ....**Silver Spring, MD**
Orrick, Sandra L. ....Chico, CA
Orrick, Timothy P. ....**Lenexa, KS**
Orrick, William H., III
San Francisco, CA
Orrick, William H., Jr. ....San Francisco, CA
Orrico, Vicki E. ....**Seattle, WA**
Orrill & Cordell, L.L.C. ....**Lafayette, LA**
New Orleans, LA
Orrill, R. Ray, Jr. ....**New Orleans, LA**
Orrio, Bryan J. ....Salem, OR
Orris, Gary D. ....Minneapolis, MN
Orris, Harry A. ....Lakewood, OH
Orris, Thomas L. ....**St. Louis, MO**
Orrison, Brenda Krebs ....**Atlanta, GA**
Orriss, Christopher J. ....Union City, NJ
Orrock, Higson & Kurta ....**Ventura, CA**
Orrock, R. Dennis ....**Ventura, CA**
Orrock, Stanley O. ....**Riverside, CA**
Orron, David E. ....**Cranbury, NJ**
Ors, Rose D. ....Culver City, CA
Orsag, Gregg ....**Pittsburgh, PA**
Orsak, Michael E. ....Richmond, TX
Orsatti, Chad T. ....**Bradenton, FL**
Orsatti, Ernest B. ....Pittsburgh, PA
Orsatti, Victor Anthony ....La Jolla, CA
Orsbon, R. Anthony ....**Charlotte, NC**
Orsborn, Allan C. ....**Ottumwa, IA**
Orsborn, Bauerle & Milani
Centerville, IA
Ottumwa, IA
Orsburn, Charles C. ....**Houston, TX**
Orsburn, D. Keith ....Denton, TX
Orschel, Alan Rauh ....**Chicago, IL**
Orscheln, Phillip A. ....**Leawood, KS**
Kansas City, MO
Orseck, Eric I. ....Waldwick, NJ

Orseck, Gary A. .... **Washington, DC**
Orseck, Gerald ....Liberty, NY
Orseck, Jeffrey I. ....Fort Lauderdale, FL
Orseck, Jeffrey, P.A. ....Fort Lauderdale, FL
Orser, H. Stanton ....San Francisco, CA
Orseth, Robert W. ....Fargo, ND
Orsey, Dennis J. ....Granite City, IL
Orsey, Dennis J., P.C. ....Granite City, IL
Orshan, Janice V. ....Centereach, NY
Orshan, Paul L. ....**Miami, FL**
Orshan, Robert Dale ....Miami, FL
Orshefsky, David M. ....Fort Lauderdale, FL
Orshefsky, Debbie M.
Fort Lauderdale, FL
Orsi, Anne K. ....Spokane, WA
Orsi, Peter John ....Wichita, KS
Orsi, Philip A. ....**Fort Lauderdale, FL**
Orsi, Robert ....**Boston, MA**
Orsic, Eric ....**Chicago, IL**
Orsic, Karin ....**Chicago, IL**
Orsinger & Nardone ....**Westerly, RI**
Orsinger, Richard R. ....**San Antonio, TX**
Orsinger, Victor J. ....**Westerly, RI**
Orsini, David ....Little Rock, AR
Orsini, Diane L. ....Burbank, CA
Orsini & Rose, P.A. ....St. Petersburg, FL
Orsini, Rosemary ....**Englewood, CO**
Orsini, Scott T. ....St. Petersburg, FL
Orsini, Victor R. ....Elizabeth, NJ
Orsini-Capo, Francisco ....**San Juan, PR**
Orsini-Ford, Joan ....**Doylestown, PA**
Orsini-Herencia, Eugenia I. .....**San Juan, PR**
Orsino, Richard Brent ....**Fairfax, VA**
Orsley & Cripps, P.A.
West Palm Beach, FL
Orsley, Jack E. ....**West Palm Beach, FL**
Orsmond, Gareth Iain ....**Boston, MA**
Orso, Gregory J. ....**York, ME**
Orso, Joseph F., III ....Williamsport, PA
Orso, Joseph F., Jr. ....Williamsport, PA
Orso, Stephen K. ....Mobile, AL
Orsoff, Beth H. ....**Burbank, CA**
Orson, Marshall D. ....Atlanta, GA
Orson, Mary Beth Miller ....**Phoenix, AZ**
Orson, Theodore ....**Providence, RI**
Orszag, Paul, III ....Glendale, CA
Orszula, Stanley Franz ....Bremerton, WA
Orszulak, Francis A. ....Putnam, CT
Orszulak, Joseph L., II ....**Pittsburgh, PA**
Ort, Beate A. ....Department of Justice,
Immigration and Naturalization Service, GV
Ort, John T. ....**Chalfont, PA**
Ort, Mark Philip ....Pickerington, OH
Ort, Steven E. ....New London, IA
Ort, Victor M. ....Oyster Bay, NY
Orta, David M. ....**Washington, DC**
Orta, Genevieve S. ....**Oakland, CA**
Orta, Leslie ....San Jose, CA
Orta, Rodolfo Ortegon, Jr. ......San Antonio, TX
Orta, Vanessa A. ....**Oklahoma City, OK**
Ortal, Avraham ....New York, NY
Ortale, Kelley, Herbert & Crawford
Nashville, TN
Ortale, Robert M. ....Kingston, NY
Ortale, William P. ....**Nashville, TN**
Ortbal, Thomas J. ....Quincy, IL
Ortbals, Gerald R. ....**St. Louis, MO**
Ortbals, Mary Beth ....St. Louis, MO
Ortega, Angelique ....Miami, FL
Ortega, Anthony ....Walnut Creek, CA
Ortega, Beverly Ann ....Department of Justice,
Tax Division, GV
Ortega, Carla Jean ....Los Angeles, CA
Ortega, Carlos Alejandro ....**Miami, FL**
Ortega, Cynthia P. ....**Kalamazoo, MI**
Ortega, Daniel ....Albuquerque, NM
Ortega, Daniela ....**New York, NY**
Ortega, David L. ....**San Antonio, TX**
Ortega, David Richard ....Merced, CA
Ortega, Edward R. ....Los Angeles, CA
Ortega, Emalie Monarrez ....Santa Clara, CA
Ortega, Evelina ....**El Paso, TX**
Ortega, Gary A. ....**Brownsville, TX**
Ortega, Gary A., P.C., Law Offices of
Brownsville, TX
Ortega, Hugo G. ....Lake Success, NY
Ortega, Jennifer Rae ....**Los Angeles, CA**
Ortega, Joe C. ....Los Angeles, CA
Ortega, John R. ....Compton, CA
Ortega, Juan Carlos ....Mobile, AL
Ortega, Lotario D. ....Santa Fe, NM
Ortega, M. Elizabeth ....**Atlanta, GA**
Ortega, Marlene ....Miami, FL
Ortega, Michael A., Jr. ....Danbury, CT
Ortega, Michael B. ....**Kalamazoo, MI**
Ortega, Nina A. ....Littleton, CO
Ortega, Orlando N. ....San Francisco, CA
Ortega, Reuben A. ....Los Angeles, CA
Ortega, Ricardo E. ....Las Cruces, NM
Ortega, Ricardo E., P.C. ....Las Cruces, NM
Ortega, Richard ....Oakland, CA
Ortega, Roberto D. ....**Albuquerque, NM**
Ortega, Stacy L., P.A., Law Office of
Wichita, KS
Ortega, Stacy Lynne ....Wichita, KS
Ortega, Teresa L. ....**Los Angeles, CA**
Ortega, Victor R. ....**Santa Fe, NM**
Ortega-Piron, D. Jean ....Chicago, IL
Ortego, Adam L. ....Lake Charles, LA
Ortego & Dupre ....Ville Platte, LA
Ortego, Ellis J. ....Santa Fe, TX
Ortego, Gary J. ....Ville Platte, LA
Ortego, Joseph Bradley ....Eunice, LA
Ortego, Joseph Bradley, A Professional Law
Corporation ....Eunice, LA
Ortego, Joseph J. ....**Garden City, NY**
Ortego, Kenneth O. ....**Alexandria, LA**
Ortego, Shirley Bedor ....Long Beach, NY

Ortelere, Brian T. ....**Philadelphia, PA**
Ortell, Michael N. ....Pasadena, CA
Orten, Hindman & Jordan, P.C.
Wheat Ridge, CO
Orten, Jerry C. M. ....Wheat Ridge, CO
Ortenberg, Michael A ....Edison, NJ
Ortenberg, Reuben ....**Suffern, NY**
Ortengren, Janel D. ....**Atlanta, GA**
Ortenstone, Lori L. ....San Diego, CA
Ortenzio, Albert J. ....Canfield, OH
Ortez, David G. ....San Francisco, CA
Orth, Andrea D. ....**Seattle, WA**
Orth, Beverly J. ....Portland, OR
Orth, Carole ....Fort Worth, TX
Orth, Charles A., Jr. ....**Milwaukee, WI**
Orth, Charles E., Jr. ....Baltimore, MD
Orth, D. Gerry ....Fort Worth, TX
Orth, Daniel A., III ....Rockford, IL
Orth, Felicia L. ....Los Alamos, NM
Orth, Frances Piccoli ....Bryn Mawr, PA
Orth, Frederick J. ....Seattle, WA
Orth, H. Louise ....Moorestown, NJ
Orth, Hrabal & Orth, L.L.P. ......Fort Worth, TX
Orth, John D. ....**Hackensack, NJ**
Orth, John V. ....Chapel Hill, NC
Orth & Laskowski, S.C. ....**Milwaukee, WI**
Orth, Paul W. ....**Hartford, CT**
Orth, Robert F. ....**Akron, OH**
Orth, Scott Alan, Law Offices of
Miami, FL
Orth, Susan L. ....New Albany, IN
Orth, William M. ....**Minneapolis, MN**
Orth, William M., P.A. ....**Minneapolis, MN**
Orthmann, George J. ....Ridgewood, NJ
Orthuber, Gerhard W. ....Ventura, CA
Orthwein, Adolphus B., Jr. ....Atlanta, GA
Orthwein, Stephen A. ....St. Louis, MO
Orticelli, David J. ....Stamford, CT
Orticelli, Samuel A. ....Oak Brook, IL
Ortins, J. Bradley ....Washington, DC
Ortique, Revius O., Jr. ....New Orleans, LA
Ortis, Amy R. ....**Baton Rouge, LA**
Ortisi, Dominic R. ....Eastpointe, MI
Ortisi, Frank R. ....Southfield, MI
Ortisi, John R. ....Detroit, MI
Ortiz, A. Luis ....Indianapolis, IN
Ortiz, Alejandro ....**Dallas, TX**
Ortiz, Ana Violeta ....**San Juan, PR**
Ortiz, Angela ....**Chicago, IL**
Ortiz, Anna C. ....Globe, AZ
Ortiz, Antonio F., Jr ....Santa Fe, NM
Ortiz & Associates ....Indianapolis, IN
Ortiz, Barbara Macri ....Oxnard, CA
Ortiz, Carlos G. ....Secaucus, NJ
Ortiz, Celso D. ....**Oakland, CA**
Ortiz, Chandra M. ....Garden City, NY
Ortiz, Criselda ....Department of Justice,
Environment and Natural Resources
Division, GV
Ortiz, Daniel S. ....New York, NY
Ortiz, Donnasue Smith
Rancho Cucamonga, CA
Ortiz, Elizabeth Burton ....Mesa, AZ
Ortiz, Filemon, Jr. ....Del Rio, TX
Ortiz, Francis R. ....**Detroit, MI**
Ortiz, Frank A. ....Brooklyn, NY
Ortiz, Frank A. ....Brooklyn, NY
Ortiz, Frank M. ....**New York, NY**
Ortiz, Frederic A. ....Dallas, TX
Ortiz, Ginger T. ....Morro Bay, CA
Ortiz, Hector A. ....Flushing, NY
Ortiz, Hector N. ....San Francisco, CA
Ortiz, Herman E. ....**Las Cruces, NM**
Ortiz, J. Damian ....Chicago, IL
Ortiz, Jennifer A. ....Milwaukee, WI
Ortiz, Jesse S., III ....Sacramento, CA
Ortiz, John A. ....**New York, NY**
Ortiz, Jonathan L. ....**Honolulu, HI**
Ortiz, Jorge L. ....Fox Lake, IL
Ortiz, Juan Antonio ....San Juan, PR
Ortiz, Juan U. ....Jackson Heights, NY
Ortiz & Katano, Attorneys at Law, A Law
Corporation ....**Honolulu, HI**
Ortiz, Leslie A. Richards ....Troy, NY
Ortiz, Lissette Benitez ....**Miami, FL**
Ortiz, Luis M. ....**Dallas, TX**
Ortiz, Luz Aurora ....Los Angeles, CA
Ortiz, Maria D. ....Miami, FL
Ortiz, Marian Kent ....Bonita, CA
Ortiz, Martha Harden ....Topeka, KS
Ortiz, Martine M. ....Boston, MA
Ortiz, Mary R. ....Lubbock, TX
Ortiz, Matthew Edward ....Santa Fe, NM
Ortiz, Michael ....Miami, FL
Ortiz, Michael A. ....**Sarasota, FL**
Ortiz, Michael R. ....**Durham, NC**
Ortiz, Miguel R. ....**San Juan, PR**
Ortiz, Nelda J. ....San Antonio, TX
Ortiz, Nelda J., P.C. ....San Antonio, TX
Ortiz, Nicholas L. ....**Philadelphia, PA**
Ortiz, Norma E. ....Brooklyn, NY
Ortiz & Ortiz ....Brooklyn, NY
Ortiz & Ortiz ....San Juan, PR
Ortiz & Paster ....West New York, NJ
Ortiz, Patrick T. ....Albuquerque, NM
Ortiz, Paul J. ....Department of the Air Force,
Office of the Judge Advocate General, GV
Ortiz, Raho N. ....**Washington, DC**
Ortiz, Ramona L. ....**Houston, TX**
Ortiz, Raquel M. ....Cambridge, MA
Ortiz, Ray R. ....**San Antonio, TX**
Ortiz, Raymond Z. ....**Santa Fe, NM**
Ortiz, Reynaldo ....McAllen, TX
Ortiz, Robert ....**Cherry Hill, NJ**
Ortiz, Robert M. ....Albuquerque, NM
Ortiz, Robert M. ....**Woodbury, NY**
Ortiz, Rudy A. ....Alexandria, VA
Ortiz, Sandra M. ....**Los Angeles, CA**

Ortiz, Scott E. ....**Casper, WY**
Ortiz, Tony F. ....**Santa Fe, NM**
Ortiz, Victor M. ....New Orleans, LA
Ortiz, Victoria ....San Francisco, CA
Ortiz, Wilfredo Jose, II ....West New York, NJ
Ortiz-Abreu, Luis D. ....**San Juan, PR**
Ortiz-Alvarez, Pedro E. ....**Ponce, PR**
Ortiz-Castro, Dyana L. ....Guayama, PR
Ortíz-Colón, Ricardo L. ....**San Juan, PR**
Ortiz-de-Montellano, Victor M.
San Francisco, CA
Ortiz Gordils, Humberto ....Humacao, PR
Ortiz-Le, Juan ....Andover, MA
Ortiz-Marcano, Myrlena ....**San Juan, PR**
Ortiz Morales, Carlos A. ....**San Juan, PR**
Ortiz Morales, Igor José ....San Juan, PR
Ortiz Morales, Kermit ....San Juan, PR
Ortiz-Murias, Jacobo ....San Juan, PR
Ortiz-Murias & Saldaña ....San Juan, PR
Ortiz-Olinger, Haydee ....**Oak Brook, IL**
Ortiz-Ortiz, Ana M. ....Newark, NJ
Ortiz-Palmieri, Ramon I. ....**Ponce, PR**
Ortiz-Ponce, Vivian ....San Juan, PR
Ortiz-Rivera, Edwin ....Juana Diaz, PR
Ortiz-Rodríguez, Claribel ....**San Juan, PR**
Ortiz-Segura, Luis Ramón ....**San Juan, PR**
Ortiz-Soto, Neville ....**San Juan, PR**
Ortiz Vélez, JoséR. ....San Juan, PR
Ortiz-White, Aleene J. ....Denver, CO
Ortler, Lisabeth ....Los Altos, CA
Ortley, David M. ....Kalispell, MT
Ortlieb, Frederick M. ....San Diego, CA
Ortlieb, Mark R. ....Chicago, IL
Ortlieb, Randolph W. ....**Escondido, CA**
Ortlip, Diane W. ....**St. Louis, MO**
Ortloff, Thomas W. ....**Midland, TX**
Ortman & Associates, PLC
Minneapolis, MN
Ortman, David B. ....Washington, DC
Ortman, Glen L. ....**Washington, DC**
Ortman, Jerome J. ....Omaha, NE
Ortman, Julianne E. ....Minneapolis, MN
Ortman, Love & Huckabay
Washington, DC
Bethesda, MD
Rockville, MD
Ortman, Mahlon H. ....Summit, NJ
Ortman, Raymond C., Jr. ....Minneapolis, MN
Ortman, Ronald A. ....Ventura, CA
Ortman, Sue Culpepper, Law Offices of
Gonzales, TX
Ortman, Sue Culpepper, Law Offices of
San Antonio, TX
Ortmann, Dale A. ....**Pasadena, CA**
Ortmann, Laura A. ....**St. Louis, MO**
Ortmann, Sheryl Cudd Blenis
Columbia, SC
Ortman-Scott, Deborah S.
San Ramon, CA
Ortmayer, Russell A. ....Boone, NC
Ortmeier, Julie A. ....**Richmond, VA**
Ortmeyer, Charles P. ....**San Francisco, CA**
Ortmeyer, Edmund F. ....Evansville, IN
Ortmeyer, Susan ....Pasadena, CA
Ortner, Anthony J. ....Maitland, FL
Ortner, Ava K. ....**Detroit, MI**
Ortner, Charles B. ....**New York, NY**
Ortner, Eric R. ....Chico, CA
Ortner, Francis C., Jr. ....Malvern, PA
Ortner, Kenneth N. ....Cleveland, OH
Ortner Law Firm, L.L.C. ....Charleston, SC
North Charleston, SC
Ortner, Leon Martin ....Charleston, SC
North Charleston, SC
Ortner, Melvin L. ....**Stamford, CT**
Ortner, Michael P. ....Hot Springs, SD
Ortner, Sally K. ....Denver, CO
Ortolani, Frank R. ....Rehoboth Beach, DE
Ortolani, Frank R., Jr. ....**Fairfax, VA**
Ortolani, Mark E. ....Newark, NJ
Ortolano, Joan S. ....Los Angeles, CA
Ortolano-Chambers, Lisa ....Bronx, NY
Ortoleva, John E., Jr. ....**Birmingham, MI**
Ortoli, Richard J. F. ....**New York, NY**
Orton, Byron K. ....Des Moines, IA
Orton, Catherine Curran ....Mauston, WI
Orton, Christopher M. ....**Warwick, RI**
Orton, Christopher N. ....**Albuquerque, NM**
Orton, Edward ....North East, PA
Orton, Gary A. ....**San Mateo, CA**
Orton & Jeffery, P.C. ....North East, PA
Orton, John E., III ....**Providence, RI**
Orton, John R. ....Mauston, WI
Orton, John S. ....**Houston, TX**
Orton, Leroy W. ....Lincoln, NE
Orton, Luther Kent ....**Palo Alto, CA**
Orton, Michelle D. ....Chicago, IL
Orton, R. Willis ....**Salt Lake City, UT**
Orton, Robert F. ....**Salt Lake City, UT**
Orton, Susan J. ....Sacramento, CA
Orton, Thomas & Peterson ....Lincoln, NE
Orton, Thorpe P. ....Boise, ID
Orton, Tooman, Hale, McKown and Kiel,
P.C. ....**Allegan, MI**
Saugatuck, MI
Orton, William H. ....**Washington, DC**
Salt Lake City, UT
Orts, Eric W. ....Philadelphia, PA
Ortsman-Dauer, Nicole A. ....**New York, NY**
Orttel, Rebecca L. ....**Minneapolis, MN**
Ortwein & Associates, P.C.
Chattanooga, TN
Ortwein & Bellafatto, Professional
Corporation ....**Bethlehem, PA**
Easton, PA
Reading, PA
Ortwein, Bernard M., II ....Boston, MA
Ortwein, Dennis P. ....**Easton, PA**

Ortwein, F. Lee ....Chattanooga, TN
Ortwein, J. Otto ....Grosse Pointe, MI
Ortwein, William H. ....Chattanooga, TN
Ortwein, William S. ....**Atlanta, GA**
Ortwerth, Craig M. ....**St. Louis, MO**
Ortwine, Bruce A. ....**New York, NY**
Oruaga, Dorothy ....Houston, TX
Orum, Keith H. ....Chicago, IL
Orum, Wilbur C., Jr. ....Inglewood, CA
Orvell, Betty J. ....**Oakland, CA**
Orvick, Rebecca M. ....**Madison, WI**
Orvik, Charles D. ....Rugby, ND
Orvik, Larry Dean ....Crookston, MN
Orvis, Douglas D., II ....**Washington, DC**
Orvis, John J. ....Dallas, TX
Orvis, Kenneth Gordon ....Troy, NY
Orvis, Mary E. ....Irving, TX
Orwasher, Abram H. ....New York, NY
Orwick, Karen S. ....Alexandria, VA
Orwig, George E., II ....Williamsport, PA
Orwig, Matthew D. ....Dallas, TX
Orwin, D. Bruce ....**Somerset, KY**
Orwitz, Carol Lunine ....Cherry Hill, NJ
Orwoll, Gregg S. ....Rochester, MN
Ory, Christine M. ....Wheaton, IL
Ory, Nancy A. ....**Washington, DC**
Ory, Paul J. ....New Orleans, LA
Ory, Samuel S. ....**Kansas City, MO**
Oryol, Yuliya A. ....San Francisco, CA
Oryshkewych, George R. ....Parma, OH
Oryshkewych, George V. ....Parma, OH
Orza, Eugene D. ....New York, NY
Orzame, Arthur F. ....Detroit, MI
Orzame, Gabriel, Jr. ....**Detroit, MI**
Orze, Walter J. ....Missoula, MT
Orzechowski, Barbara F. ....**Sioux City, IA**
Orzechowski, Karen Lee ......**Washington, DC**
Orzechowski, Victor J. ....Lockport, NY
Orzel, John A. ....**New York, NY**
Orzel, William A. ....**San Diego, CA**
Orzeske, Donald G. ....Indianapolis, IN
Orzeske, Julia Lauderdale ....Indianapolis, IN
Orzick, Eric S. ....New York, NY
Orzoff, Stewart C. ....Northbrook, IL
Orzynski, Stephen J. ....**Denver, CO**
Osach, Ronald C. ....**New Haven, CT**
Osadchey, Earl ....Northridge, CA
Osadjan, Marie Frances ....**Chicago, IL**
Osagie, Emmanuel O. ....Los Angeles, CA
Osagiede, Osamwonyi Ehi ....Boston, MA
Osajda, Michael C. ....Rolling Meadows, IL
Osajima, Glenn K. ....Santa Ana, CA
Osaki, Carl H. ....**Honolulu, HI**
Osaki, Isaac ....**New York, NY**
Osaki, Keli N. ....**Los Angeles, CA**
Osaki, Kerry G. ....Fullerton, CA
Long Beach, CA
Osako, David P. ....**Emeryville, CA**
San Francisco, CA
Osanloo, O. Michael ....Chicago, IL
Osantowski, William E.
Bloomfield Hills, MI
Osar, Robert L. ....**White Plains, NY**
Osband, Marvin B. ....Arcadia, CA
Osbeck, Mark K. ....**Denver, CO**
Osber, Keith F. ....**Binghamton, NY**
Osber, Steven H. ....**Fort Lauderdale, FL**
Osberg, Randi L. ....**Eau Claire, WI**
Osborn, Amy L. ....**Tulsa, OK**
Osborn, Baugher, Roule & Raelson
La Porte, IN
Michigan City, IN
Osborn, Bert L. ....Payette, ID
Osborn, Bert L., Chartered ....Payette, ID
Osborn, Cathleen M. ....Denver, CO
Osborn, Chris L. ....Belleville, IL
St. Louis, MO
Osborn, Christopher J. ....Los Angeles, CA
Osborn, Christopher R. ....**Seattle, WA**
Osborn, Cloyce R. ....Moore, OK
Osborn, Cynthia L. ....Houston, TX
Osborn, D. Christopher ....Charlotte, NC
Osborn, Daniel A. ....**New York, NY**
Osborn, David C. ....Mentor, OH
Osborn, David D. ....**La Porte, IN**
Osborn, David H. ....Falls Church, VA
Osborn, David L. ....Fort Collins, CO
Osborn, Debra L. ....Chicago, IL
Osborn, Donald R. ....Glendale, CA
Osborn, Donald R. ....**New York, NY**
Osborn, Donna M. ....**Las Vegas, NV**
Osborn, Duncan F. ....Del Mar, CA
Osborn, Emily ....Stoughton, WI
Osborn & Fox, L.P.A. ....Sycamore, OH
Osborn, Fred G. ....Kokomo, IN
Osborn, Fred G., P.C. ....Kokomo, IN
Osborn, Geoffrey D. ....**Dallas, TX**
Osborn, George P. ....**Marion, IN**
Osborn, Gerald T. ....Anacortes, WA
Osborn, Harold W. ....Prescott, AZ
Osborn, Harvey J. ....Portland, OR
Osborn, Heidi S. ....Portland, ME
Osborn Hiner & Lisher, P.C.
Indianapolis, IN
Osborn, J. Kirk ....**Chapel Hill, NC**
Osborn, J. Kirk
Research Triangle Park, NC
Osborn, Jeffrey T. ....Huntington Beach, CA
Osborn, Jim T. ....Odessa, TX
Osborn, Jo E. ....**Elmhurst, IL**
Osborn, Joe ....**Austin, TX**
Osborn, Joel W. ....Tulsa, OK
Osborn, John C. ....Pittsford, NY
Rochester, NY
Osborn, John D. ....**Saipan, TT**
Osborn, John E. ....Chappaqua, NY
New York, NY
Osborn, John E. ....West Chester, PA

Osborn, John E., P.C. ....Chappaqua, NY
New York, NY
Osborn, John G. ....**Portland, ME**
Osborn, John J., Jr. ....Scottsdale, AZ
Osborn, John S., Jr. ....**Louisville, KY**
Osborn, John W. ....**New York, NY**
Osborn, Jone S. ....Manhattan Beach, CA
Osborn, Jones, II ....**Phoenix, AZ**
Osborn, Judith L. ....Department of State, Office of the Legal Adviser, GV
Osborn, Julia A. ....Los Angeles, CA
Osborn, Kathy A. ....Colorado Springs, CO
Osborn, Kevin C. ....**Seattle, WA**
Osborn, L. John ....**Washington, DC**
Osborn, Laurence C. ....**Los Angeles, CA**
Osborn, Leslie M. ....Kenbridge, VA
Osborn, Lynn R. ....**Stillwater, OK**
Osborn, Malcolm E. ....**Winston-Salem, NC**
Osborn, Malcolm E., P.A.
Winston-Salem, NC
Osborn Maledon, P.A. ....**Phoenix, AZ**
Tucson, AZ
Osborn, Margaret Ann ....Rock Island, IL
Osborn, Mark M. ....**Denver, CO**
Osborn, Mark N. ....**El Paso, TX**
Osborn, Marla Raucher
San Francisco, CA
Osborn, Mary K. ....Rockford, IL
Osborn, Max N. ....El Paso, TX
Osborn, Maxwell E. ....Cheyenne, WY
Osborn, Melinda R. ....Chicago, IL
Osborn, Mitchell E. ....Cheyenne, WY
Osborn, Patrick J. ....**Bakersfield, CA**
Osborn, Paul A. ....**Sterling, IL**
Osborn, Paula D. ....**Minneapolis, MN**
Osborn, Peter N. ....Los Angeles, CA
Osborn, Preston ....**Marion, IN**
Osborn, R. Michael ....**Lexington, KY**
Osborn, Raymond A., III ....Gretna, LA
Osborn, Reed & Burke, LLP
Pittsford, NY
Rochester, NY
Osborn, Richard L. ....Broomfield, CO
Osborn, Rick C. ....Columbia, TN
Osborn, Rittman & Osborn ....**Marion, IN**
Osborn, Robert G. ....Lufkin, TX
Osborn, Rodney A. ....Holdrege, NE
Osborn, Roy A. ....Phoenix, AZ
Osborn, Russell B. ....Kenmore, NY
Osborn, Sarah C. ....**New York, NY**
Osborn, Scott D. ....**Dallas, TX**
Osborn, Sean T. ....**Costa Mesa, CA**
Osborn, Simeon J. ....**Seattle, WA**
Osborn Smith, P.L.L.C. ....**Seattle, WA**
Osborn, Thomas A. ....Commack, NY
Osborn, Thomas E. ....**Kansas City, KS**
Osborn, Thomas E. ....Sycamore, OH
Osborn, Timothy R. ....**Seattle, WA**
Osborn, Virgil L. ....Salem, OR
Osborn, William M. ....**Indianapolis, IN**
Osborn, William S. ....Houston, TX
Osborn, William Sheffield ....**Austin, TX**
Osborne, Alfred H. ....**Reno, NV**
Osborne, Andrew M. ....Dedham, MA
Osborne, Anna Stowe ....Asheville, NC
Osborne & Baker ....**Fayetteville, AR**
Osborne, Brian A. ....Ventura, CA
Osborne, Bruce D. ....**New York, NY**
Osborne, C. Barry ....Dallas, TX
Osborne, Carl K. ....Beverly Hills, CA
Osborne, Carol S. ....Dallas, GA
Osborne, Caroline L. ....**Charlotte, NC**
Osborne, Christopher E. ....**Nashville, TN**
Osborne, Christopher J. ....**Scranton, PA**
Osborne, Christopher R.L.
San Francisco, CA
Osborne, Christy Lynn Campbell
Birmingham, AL
Osborne, Clyde W. ....Youngstown, OH
Osborne, Craig C. ....**Truckee, CA**
Osborne, Crystal Lynn ....**Lexington, KY**
Osborne, Curtis C. ....Monroe, NC
Osborne, Curtis C., P.A. ....Monroe, NC
Osborne, David M. ....**Boston, MA**
Osborne, David R. ....**Des Moines, IA**
Osborne, David S. ....**Chicago, IL**
Osborne, David W. ....Orange, CA
Osborne, David W. ....**Sandy, UT**
Osborne, Dee S. ....Houston, TX
Osborne and Deutsch ....**Washington, DC**
Osborne, Diana T. ....Del Mar, CA
Osborne, Douglas V. ....Klamath Falls, OR
Osborne, Duncan Elliott ....**Austin, TX**
Osborne, Edward B. ....Batavia, OH
Osborne, Edwin M. ....Ojai, CA
Osborne, Frank E. ....Cincinnati, OH
Osborne, Frank R. ....**Cleveland, OH**
Osborne, Gary W. ....**San Diego, CA**
Osborne, Gary W. ....Chicago, IL
Osborne, Gary W. ....Holland, OH
Osborne, George M. ....St. Petersburg, FL
Osborne, George R. ....New York, NY
Osborne, Glenn R. ....Youngstown, OH
Osborne, Grant B. ....**Asheville, NC**
Osborne, H. Harrison, III ....Burke, VA
Osborne, Hamilton, Jr. ....**Columbia, SC**
Osborne, Harry A. ....Jonesboro, GA
Osborne, Harry A., P.C. ....Jonesboro, GA
Osborne, Harry V., II
Ocean Township, NJ
New York, NY
Osborne, J. Gregory ....Tempe, AZ
Osborne, J. Lee E. ....Roanoke, VA
Osborne, Jack B., P.C. ....Beaumont, TX
Osborne, James C., Jr. ....**Washington, DC**
Osborne, James D. ....Craig, CO
Osborne, James G. ....Edgewood, KY
Osborne, James J. ....**Phoenix, AZ**
Osborne, James R. ....Dallas, GA
Osborne, James William ....Bristol, VA
Osborne, Jane ....Mayfield, KY
Osborne, Janne Berry ....Orangeburg, SC
Osborne, Jay L. ....Raleigh, NC
Osborne, Jerry R. ....**New Orleans, LA**
Osborne, Jill K. ....Lexington, KY
Osborne, Jim R. ....Vincennes, IN
Osborne, John E. ....Sierra Vista, AZ
Tucson, AZ
Osborne, John S., Jr. ....**New York, NY**
Osborne, John W. ....**New York, NY**
Osborne, John W. ....Ravensdale, WA
Osborne, Jonathan L. ....**Washington, DC**
Osborne, Joseph A. ......**West Palm Beach, FL**
Osborne, Julia L. ....Las Vegas, NV
Osborne, Kenneth L. ....**Fayetteville, AR**
Osborne, Kevin B. ....**Richmond, VA**
Osborne, Kevin E. ....Harrisburg, PA
Osborne, Kimberly L. ....Galax, VA
Osborne, LaRaye M. ....Minneapolis, MN
Osborne Law Office, Chartered, A Prof. Corp. ....**Reno, NV**
Osborne Law Offices, P.C.
Washington, DC
Osborne, Lee S. ....Jacksonville, FL
Osborne, Leslie Scott ....**Boca Raton, FL**
Osborne, Leutrell M. C., II ....Washington, DC
Osborne, Lorraine W. ....Hartford, CT
Osborne, Lowe, Helman & Smith, L.L.P.
Austin, TX
Osborne, Margot Willson ....Babson Park, FL
Osborne, Maribel D. ....**San Francisco, CA**
Osborne, Martin L. ....Treasury Department, Internal Revenue Service, GV
Osborne, Martin Lee ....**Prestonsburg, KY**
Osborne, Matthew O. ....**San Diego, CA**
Osborne, Maura B. Murphy
Hartford, CT
Osborne, McComiskey, Gobert & Reasonover, L.L.P. ....Metairie, LA
Osborne & McGowan, P.C.
East Hampton, NY
Osborne, Michael ....Metairie, LA
Osborne, Michael C. ....**San Francisco, CA**
Osborne, Michael F. ....**New York, NY**
Osborne, Michelle M. ....Mountain View, CA
Osborne, Nancy Rose ....Frankfort, KY
Osborne & Nesbitt ....**San Diego, CA**
Osborne, Norman ....Las Cruces, NM
Osborne, O. Leland ....San Mateo, CA
Osborne & Osborne ....Edgewood, KY
Osborne & Osborne, Co., L.P.A.
Youngstown, OH
Osborne & Osborne, P.A.
Boca Raton, FL
Osborne, Paul M. ....**Wakefield, MA**
Osborne, Paul R. ....Mission Viejo, CA
Osborne, Peter L. ....**Portland, OR**
Osborne, Philip H. ....Princeton, NJ
Osborne, R. Brady, Jr. ....**Boca Raton, FL**
Osborne, Ralph E. ....Sparta, WI
Osborne, Randall S. ....Dallas, TX
Osborne, Ray C. ....**Boca Raton, FL**
Osborne, Rebecca J. ....Salem, OR
Osborne, Richard L. ....Eutaw, AL
Osborne, Richard L. ....Treasury Department, Internal Revenue Service, GV
Osborne, Richard N. ....St. Louis Park, MN
Osborne, Richard P. ....Fayetteville, AR
Osborne, Richard W. ....**Tampa, FL**
Osborne, Richard W. ....Schaumburg, IL
Osborne, Robert A., Jr. ....Kernersville, NC
Osborne, Robert C. ....**East Hampton, NY**
Osborne, Robert J. ....**Philadelphia, PA**
Osborne, Robert S., (P.C.) ....**Chicago, IL**
Osborne, Rodney W. ....Hinsdale, IL
Osborne, Roxanne Burgett
Klamath Falls, OR
Osborne, Ruth C. ....**Orlando, FL**
Osborne, Samuel L. ....Wilkesboro, NC
Osborne, Samuel S. ....**Seattle, WA**
Osborne, Scott B. ....**Seattle, WA**
Osborne, Solomon C. ....Greenwood, MS
Osborne, Stanley I.
Department of Commerce, Patent and Trademark Office, GV
Osborne, Stephen H. ....**Reno, NV**
Osborne, Stephen M. ....**Springfield, IL**
Osborne, Stephen T. ....**Kennewick, WA**
Osborne, Thomas B. ....Ventura, CA
Osborne, Thomas I. ....Mexico, MO
Osborne, Thomas J. ....**East Hampton, NY**
Osborne, Thomas L. ....**Paducah, KY**
Osborne, Thomas L., P.S.C. ....**Paducah, KY**
Osborne, Tina L. ....Farmington, CT
Osborne & Visconti ....Dedham, MA
Osborne, W. Glenn, (Co., L.P.A.)
Youngstown, OH
Osborne, Wallace S. ....Charlotte, NC
Osborne, William David ....San Diego, CA
Osborne, William G. ....**Orlando, FL**
Osborne, William G., P.A. ....**Orlando, FL**
Osborne, William T. ....Chatham, NJ
Osborne, William W., Jr. ....**Washington, DC**
Osborne, Woodley B. ....**Washington, DC**
Osborne, Zachary ....**Hartford, CT**
Osborne, Zebulon L. ....Mount Dora, FL
Osborne-Anderson, Marla D. ....Salinas, CA
Osborne-Pikelny, Julia L. ....Columbus, OH
Osbourn, Mark A. ....**Louisville, KY**
Osbron, Todd A. ....Rockford, IL
Osburn, Alice M. ....**Detroit, MI**
Osburn, C. Dixon ....Washington, DC
Osburn, Gerald T. ....Harrisburg, PA
Osburn, Hine, Kuntze & Yates, L.L.C.
Cape Girardeau, MO
Osburn, Jeffrey B. ....**Manchester, NH**
Osburn, John R. ....**Portland, OR**
Osburn, John W., (P.C.) ....**Portland, OR**
Osburn, Judith E. ....Johnson City, NY
Osburn, Kimberly A. ....**Houston, TX**
Osburn, Lana K. ....Oklahoma City, OK
Osburn, Michael E. ....**Binghamton, NY**
Osburn, Robert H. ....**Dallas, TX**
Osburn, Robert H., & Associates, P.C.
Dallas, TX
Osburn, Robert J., Jr. ....**Orlando, FL**
Osburn, Sarah ....**Ann Arbor, MI**
Osburn, Ted R. ....**Cape Girardeau, MO**
Osby, Mark W. ....Yukon, OK
Oscadal, John M. ....Buffalo, NY
O'Scannlain, Brendan N. ....**Portland, OR**
O'Scannlain, Diarmuid F. ....Portland, OR
O'Scannlain, Kevin S. ....**Portland, OR**
Oscar, Gerald M. ....New York, NY
Oscar, Lawrence E. ....**Cleveland, OH**
Oscar, Leonard ....Aurora, OR
Oscar, Sharon J. ....Phoenix, AZ
Oschal, James C. ....**Wilkes-Barre, PA**
Osder, Jonathan N. ....**Mill Valley, CA**
Oakland, CA
Ose, Paul A. ....**Cincinnati, OH**
Oseasohn, Nancy M. ....San Antonio, TX
Oseekey, Cheryl Lynn ......Treasury Department, Internal Revenue Service, GV
Oseff, Harold R. ....**Southfield, MI**
O'Sell, Mark E. ....Oakdale, MN
Osemene, Justin C. ....**Seattle, WA**
Osen, Andrew C. ....Madison, WI
Osen, Frank S. ....Beverly Hills, CA
Osen, Max N. ....Oradell, NJ
Osen, Richard W. ....**Sacramento, CA**
Osenbaugh, Kimberly W. ....**Seattle, WA**
Osenbaugh, Kurt V. ....**Los Angeles, CA**
Osensky, Tanya S. ....Atlanta, GA
Osenton, O. Reginald ....Logan, WV
Oser, Aaron M. ....**Washington, DC**
Oser, Andrea ....Albany, NY
Oser, Diane Brock ....**Winston-Salem, NC**
Oser, Janice A. ....**New York, NY**
Oser, Judi ....Piedmont, CA
Oser, Rebecca S. ....Covington, LA
Oser, Roy B. ....**New York, NY**
Oseran, Deborah ....**Tucson, AZ**
Oseran, Hahn, Spring & Watts, P.S.
Bellevue, WA
Seattle, WA
Oseran, Melville ....**Bellevue, WA**
Oseran, Richard ....**Tucson, AZ**
Oserow, Beverly W. ....Denver, CO
Oset, Nancy J. ....Clearwater, FL
Osetek, Peter J. ....**Ann Arbor, MI**
Osga, Kristi A. ....Oak Park, IL
Osgard, James L. ....Tacoma, WA
Osgathorpe, John D. ....**Jacksonville, FL**
Osgood, Alfred M. ....Chevy Chase, MD
Osgood & Harris, L.L.C. ....Boulder, CO
Osgood, Helen ....**Buffalo, NY**
Osgood, Jeffrey S., (P.C.) ....**Dallas, TX**
Osgood, Jerry W. ....Galt, CA
Osgood, John R. ....Lee's Summit, MO
Osgood, Judy P. ....**Reno, NV**
Osgood, Marla F. ....Toledo, OH
Osgood, Marsha L. ....Ellsworth, ME
Osgood, Patricia M. ....Malden, MA
Osgood, Russell K. ....Boulder, CO
Osgood, Russell K. ....Ithaca, NY
Osgood, Scott R. ....Boulder, CO
Osgood, Steven P. ....Woburn, MA
Osgood, Susanne Mykel ....Newark, NJ
Osgood, Vicki L. ....**Everett, WA**
Osgood, Warren C. ....**Stockton, CA**
Osha, J. Frank ....**Washington, DC**
Osha, Jonathan P. ....**Houston, TX**
O'Shaughnessy, Brian C. ....Stamford, CT
O'Shaughnessy, Brian P. ....**Alexandria, VA**
O'Shaughnessy, Christopher T.
Columbus, OH
O'Shaughnessy, Francis A. ....Evanston, IL
O'Shaughnessy, Gerald E. ....Wichita, KS
O'Shaughnessy, James P. ....Seal Beach, CA
O'Shaughnessy, James S. ....Middleboro, MA
O'Shaughnessy, Jennifer Downs
Kansas City, MO
O'Shaughnessy, John C.
New Brunswick, NJ
O'Shaughnessy, John F. ....Seaford, NY
O'Shaughnessy, Kevin M. ....Denver, CO
O'Shaughnessy, Kevin T. ....Spokane, WA
O'Shaughnessy, Lindsay K. ....**Millburn, NJ**
O'Shaughnessy, Lizbeth S.
Grand Rapids, MI
O'Shaughnessy, Maureen F. ....Weston, CT
O'Shaughnessy, Michael B.
Manchester, NH
O'Shaughnessy, Michael J.
Bloomfield Hills, MI
O'Shaughnessy, Michael L. ....**Chicago, IL**
O'Shaughnessy, Patrick M. ....Campbell, CA
O'Shaughnessy, Phillips P.
Fort Lauderdale, FL
Baltimore, MD
O'Shaughnessy, Phillips P., P.A.
Fort Lauderdale, FL
Baltimore, MD
O'Shaughnessy, Susan E.
Staten Island, NY
O'Shaughnessy, Thomas E. ....Versailles, KY
O'Shaughnessy, Thomas M. ....Danville, IL
O'Shaughnessy, Timothy J. ....New York, NY
O'Shaughnessy, Timothy J. ....Cleveland, OH
O'Shaughnessy, Timothy J. ....**Dallas, TX**
Weatherford, TX
O'Shaughnessy, William J. ....**Newark, NJ**
O'Shaughnessy, William J., Jr.
New York, NY
O'Shaugnessy, Timothy ....**New York, NY**
O'Shea, Ann E. ....**New York, NY**
O'Shea, Annemarie C. ....San Francisco, CA
O'Shea Barnard Martin P.S.
Bellevue, WA
Seattle, WA
O'Shea, Brendan C. ....**Albany, NY**
O'Shea, Brian ....Los Angeles, CA
O'Shea, Brian J. ....**Atlanta, GA**
O'Shea, Daniel F. ....Miami, FL
O'Shea, Daniel J. ....Oldsmar, FL
O'Shea, Deborah Bergeron ....Buffalo, NY
O'Shea, Dennis F. ....Fort Lauderdale, FL
O'Shea & Downes, LLP
Southampton, NY
O'Shea, Edward B., Jr. ....Forest Park, IL
O'Shea, Elizabeth Melzer ....Bethesda, MD
O'Shea, Ethan ....**Lansdale, PA**
O'Shea, Eugene K. ....Bedford Hills, NY
O'Shea & Forcum, P.C. ....Lubbock, TX
O'Shea, Frank M., III ....Englewood Cliffs, NJ
O'Shea, Gregory D. ....LeMay, MO
O'Shea, Heather M. ....**Washington, DC**
O'Shea, J. Kevin ....**Rome, NY**
O'Shea, James A. ....**Syracuse, NY**
O'Shea, James C. ....**Rome, NY**
O'Shea, James M. ....**Southampton, NY**
O'Shea, James P. ....Boston, MA
O'Shea, Jeremiah J. ....Mineola, NY
O'Shea, Jill T. ....**Cincinnati, OH**
O'Shea, John D., Jr. ....**Laconia, NH**
O'Shea, John F. ....**Houston, TX**
O'Shea, John J. ....**Detroit, MI**
O'Shea, John J. ....Manhasset, NY
O'Shea, John J. C. ....Lubbock, TX
O'Shea, John Joseph ....Margate City, NJ
O'Shea, John L. ....**Cincinnati, OH**
O'Shea, John N. ....Morris Plains, NJ
O'Shea, John T. ....**St. Louis, MO**
O'Shea, John T. ....**Bellevue, WA**
Oshea, Joseph A. ....Staten Island, NY
O'Shea, Joseph G. ....New York, NY
O'Shea, Julie S. ....**New York, NY**
O'Shea, Karen P. ....**Seattle, WA**
O'Shea, Kerry A. ....**Newark, NJ**
O'Shea, Kevin F. ....**Bloomfield Hills, MI**
O'Shea, Kevin J. ....Chicago, IL
O'Shea, Kevin J. ....**New York, NY**
O'Shea, Laurent G., III ....Pasadena, CA
O'Shea, Martin T. ....Elmhurst, NY
O'Shea, Maurice F. ....Paramount, CA
O'Shea, McDonald & Stevens, LLP
Rome, NY
O'Shea, Michael A. ....**Washington, DC**
O'Shea, Michael D. ....**Pasadena, CA**
O'Shea, Michael F. ....**East Meadow, NY**
O'Shea, Michael J. ....Paterson, NJ
O'Shea, Michael J. ....Cleveland, OH
O'Shea, Michael P., Jr. ....Cairo, IL
O'Shea, Patrick J. ....Lombard, IL
O'Shea, Patrick J. ....**Boston, MA**
O'Shea, Patrick J. ....**New York, NY**
O'Shea, Peter J., Jr. ....**New York, NY**
O'Shea, Philip J., Jr. ....**Buffalo, NY**
O'Shea and Quan ....Forest Park, IL
O'Shea, Regina ....**New York, NY**
O'Shea, Reynolds & Cummings
Buffalo, NY
O'Shea, Robert J. ....**Cedar Rapids, IA**
O'Shea, Robert J., Jr. ....**Philadelphia, PA**
O'Shea, Robert S. ....Springfield, IL
O'Shea, Rosemary ....**Orlando, FL**
O'Shea, Sean F. ....**New York, NY**
O'Shea, Sean P. ....St. Louis, MO
O'Shea, Shannon F. ....**Chicago, IL**
O'Shea, Sharon A. ....Forest Park, IL
O'Shea, Sheila ....**Hackensack, NJ**
O'Shea, Sheila ....**New York, NY**
O'Shea, Stefanie A. ....**Madison, WI**
O'Shea, Stephen M. ....**Boston, MA**
O'Shea, Suzanne Matt
Department Of Health And Human Services, Food & Drug Administration, GV
O'Shea, Terence M.
San Juan Capistrano, CA
O'Shea, Thomas D. ....**Red Lion, PA**
York, PA
O'Shea, Thomas J. ....**Hartford, CT**
O'Shea, Thos. M. ....St. Louis, MO
O'Shea, Timothy Brian ....**Rome, NY**
O'Shea, Timothy M. ....Madison, WI
O'Shea, Timothy P. ....**Washington, DC**
O'Shea, William F., III ....**Philadelphia, PA**
O'Shea, William J. ....**New York, NY**
O'Shea, William P. ....Treasury Department, Internal Revenue Service, GV
O'Shea-Carter, Kathleen ....Severna Park, MD
O'Shee, Michael J. ....**Alexandria, LA**
O'Sheehan, Edward J.
Fort Lauderdale, FL
Osheff, Alan ....Chicago, IL
O'Sheill, Rockwell ....Warren, PA
Osheim, Donald E., (P.C.) ....Watertown, SD
Oshel, David B. ....Oklahoma City, OK
Oshel, Michael V. ....**Harrisburg, IL**
Oshel, Michael V., P.C. ....**Harrisburg, IL**
O'Shell, Kevin ....**Glens Falls, NY**
Osher, Daniel A. ....**Monterey, CA**
Osher, Irwin Spiegel ....Los Angeles, CA
Osher, James W. ....Department of Labor, Office of Secretary, GV
Osher, Jeremy J. ....**Los Angeles, CA**
Osher, Kenneth A. ....Corvallis, OR
Osher Law Firm, The, PC ....Los Angeles, CA
Osher, Loren Mark ....**New York, NY**
Osher, Nathaniel Albert ....Venice, CA

Osher, Robert M. .... Los Angeles, CA
Osherenko, Gail .... Hanover, NH
Osheroff, Carolyn S. .... Reno, NV
Osheroff, Mauri L.
Securities and Exchange Commission, Division of Corporation Finance, GV
Osheroff, Samantha .... Los Angeles, CA
Osherow, Mark R. .... Boca Raton, FL
Fort Lauderdale, FL
New York, NY
Osherow, Mark R., P.A. .... Boca Raton, FL
Fort Lauderdale, FL
Osherow, Randolph N. .... San Antonio, TX
Osherow, Randolph N., P.C.
San Antonio, TX
Oshie, Patrick J. .... Zillah, WA
O'Shields, H. Joseph .... Jacksonville, FL
O'Shields, Reginald T. .... Atlanta, GA
O'Shieles, Kelly .... Austin, TX
Oshikawa, Tomohiko .... New York, NY
Oshiki, Alice M. .... Los Angeles, CA
Oshima, Alan Makoto .... Honolulu, HI
Oshima, Chun, Fong & Chung
Honolulu, HI
Oshima, June M. .... Columbus, OH
Oshima, Leighton K. .... Honolulu, HI
Oshima, Michael W. .... New York, NY
Oshima, Robert M. .... Boulder, CO
Oshin, Heidi Bogin .... White Plains, NY
Oshin, Jeffrey A. .... Springfield, NJ
Oshin, Jill B. .... New York, NY
Oshins & Associates, P.C. .... Las Vegas, NV
Oshins, Jason A. .... Hoboken, NJ
Brooklyn, NY
Oshins, Michael .... Utica, NY
Oshins, Richard A. .... Las Vegas, NV
Oshins, Steven J. .... Las Vegas, NV
Oshinski, Allen W. .... Arlington Heights, IL
Oshinski, Richard A. .... Carson City, NV
Oshinskie, Mark D. .... Trenton, NJ
Oshinsky, Carol .... Chevy Chase, MD
Oshinsky, Daniel V. .... New York, NY
Oshinsky, David B. .... Los Angeles, CA
Oshinsky, Jeffrey M. .... Miami, FL
Oshinsky, Jerold .... Washington, DC
Oshinsky, John S. .... Department of Justice, Executive Office for Immigration Review, GV
Oshinsky, Leonard .... Hallandale Beach, FL
Oshinsky, Matthew .... Menlo Park, CA
Oshinsky, Samuel J. .... Department of Labor, Office of the Solicitor, GV
Oshinsky, William S. .... Washington, DC
Oshinsky, William S. .... Bethesda, MD
Oshiro, Anna H. .... Honolulu, HI
Oshiro, Arthur A. .... Los Angeles, CA
Oshiro, Blake K. .... Honolulu, HI
Oshiro, Carl .... San Francisco, CA
Oshiro, Carolyn M. .... Honolulu, HI
Oshiro, Cynthia N. .... Menlo Park, CA
Oshiro, Donna A. .... Honolulu, HI
Oshiro, Hiroshi .... Honolulu, HI
Oshiro, James K. .... Honolulu, HI
Oshiro, Lester D. .... Hilo, HI
Oshiro, Lisa Mei Tomita .... Seattle, WA
Oshiro, Robert C. .... Wahiawa, HI
Oshlag, Jeffrey D. .... Batavia, NY
Oshlag & Saleh .... Batavia, NY
Oshman, Gene J. .... Houston, TX
Oshman & Helfenstein, LLP .... New York, NY
Oshman, Karen A. .... Houston, TX
Oshman, Matthew .... New York, NY
Oshman, Michele T. .... Baltimore, MD
Oshman, Rick .... Houston, TX
Oshman, Theodore .... New York, NY
Osho, Lucky Theophilus .... Charlotte, NC
Oshoway, F. John .... Grantsville, WV
Oshoway, Rebecca .... Rockville, MD
Oshrin, Alan D. .... Riverhead, NY
Oshrin, Milton .... Ridge, NY
Oshrine, Theodore B. .... Baltimore, MD
Oshtry, Daniel I. .... Washington, DC
Oshtry, Joel E. .... Philadelphia, PA
Osias, David L. .... Los Angeles, CA
San Diego, CA
Osiason, Lee J. .... Miami, FL
Osiason & Singer, P.A. .... Miami, FL
Osick, James P. .... Chicago, IL
Osier, Catherine M. .... Santa Ana, CA
Osier, Robert M. .... San Francisco, CA
Osimetha, Clement H. .... Dallas, TX
Osimitz, Dennis V. .... Chicago, IL
Osinoff, Joanne Schwartz .... Santa Monica, CA
Osinoff, Peter R. .... Los Angeles, CA
Osinski, Charles R. .... Allentown, PA
Osinski, Patrick J. .... Dobbs Ferry, NY
Osinski, Val L. .... Coral Springs, FL
Osinski, Val L., P.A. .... Coral Springs, FL
Osipowicz, Edward W., Jr. .... Salem, CT
Osis, Daiga G. .... Bridgeport, CT
Osis, Imants .... Tualatin, OR
Ositis, Andrew P. .... Salem, OR
Osius, Victoria M. .... Chicago, IL
Osk, Victoria .... Islandia, NY
Oskam, Gerard L. .... Reno, NV
Oskandy, David L. .... Chicago, IL
Oskie, David .... St. Paul, MN
Osko, Eugene .... Covina, CA
Oskorep, John J. .... San Diego, CA
Oslakovic, Charles S. .... Rockford, IL
Oslan, Reed S. .... Chicago, IL
Osler, Hoskin & Harcourt LLP
New York, NY
Osler, Lois Bonsal .... Department of Justice, Civil Division, GV
Oslick, Harold .... Lyndhurst, NJ
Oslick, Marci L. .... Belle Mead, NJ
Oslinker, Cheryl L. .... Orange, CA
Oslund, David E. .... Minneapolis, MN
Osman, Alyson R. .... Miami Beach, FL
Osman, David S. .... Laconia, NH
Osman, Dina S. .... Alexandria, VA
Osman, Edith G. .... Miami, FL
Osman, Harold S. .... North Caldwell, NJ
Osman, James P. .... Roseville, CA
Osman, Joel A. .... Los Angeles, CA
Osman, Kathleen W. .... Houston, TX
Osman, Lee R. .... Denver, CO
Osman & Levine, LLP .... San Diego, CA
Osman, Linda A. .... New Brunswick, NJ
Somerset, NJ
Osman, Lisa A. .... Denver, CO
Osman, Mark A. .... San Diego, CA
Osman, Michael J. .... Miami, FL
Osman, Michael J., P.A. .... Miami, FL
Osman, Randa A. F. .... Los Angeles, CA
Osman, Richard M. .... New York, NY
Osman, Rita .... San Jose, CA
Osman, Ronald E. .... Dongola, IL
Osman, Scott E. .... Stephenville, TX
Osman, Steven H. .... Grandview, MO
Osman, Thomas J. .... Denver, CO
Osmars, K. Jill .... San Diego, CA
Osment, Gregory Thomas .... Monroe, MI
Osment, Jeffrey S. .... Monroe, MI
Osment, Pamela S. .... Conway, AR
Osmer, Gerald Michael .... San Andreas, CA
Osmer, James D. .... Troy, MI
Osmon, David L. .... Mountain Home, AR
Osmon, Ethredge & Drake, P.A.
Mountain Home, AR
Osmond, Darin V. .... Chicago, IL
Osmond, Debra A. .... Chicago, IL
Osmond, Gordon C. .... New York, NY
Osmond, William K. .... Tulsa, OK
Osmun, Jeffrey T. .... New York, NY
Osmundsen, Lori A. .... Honolulu, HI
Osmundsen, Robert C.
Elk Grove Village, IL
Osmundson, Anthony D. .... Sacramento, CA
Osmundson, Brad J. .... Minnetonka, MN
Osnato, John E. .... New York, NY
Osnato, John, Jr. .... Brooklyn, NY
Osnato, Michael J., Jr. .... New York, NY
Osner, Donna K. .... Media, PA
Philadelphia, PA
Osnos, David M. .... Washington, DC
Osnos, Jean .... New York, NY
Osnos, Matthew D. .... Greenbelt, MD
Osnowitz, Samuel .... Toledo, OH
Osnowitz, Steven J.
Federal Trade Commission, Bureau of Competition, GV
Osoba, Wayne F. .... Chicago, IL
Osofsky, Debra .... Washington, DC
Osofsky, Gene L. .... Hayward, CA
Osofsky, Herman .... Clifton, NJ
Osofsky, Hilary M. .... Orinda, CA
Osofsky, Howard R. .... Avondale Estates, GA
Osofsky, Irving B. .... Torrance, CA
Osofsky, Joseph A. .... West Hempstead, NY
Osofsky, Larry C. .... Middletown, NY
Osofsky, Lisa Kate .... Department of Justice, Federal Bureau of Investigation, GV
Osofsky, Marshall J. .... West Palm Beach, FL
Osofsky & Replansky .... Pine Plains, NY
Osofsky, Richard A. .... Pine Plains, NY
Osojnak, Daniel J. .... Garden City, NY
Osol, Robert .... Worcester, MA
Osolinik, Carolyn P. .... Washington, DC
Osorio, John .... Richardson, TX
Osorio, John H. .... Cherry Hill, NJ
Osorio, Sandra M. .... Millbrae, CA
Osowiecki, Jennifer A. .... Hartford, CT
Osowik, Thomas John .... Toledo, OH
Osowski, Beth Driscoll .... Oshkosh, WI
Osowski, Edward L. .... Chicago, IL
Osowski, Paul Joseph .... Charlotte, NC
Osowski, Samuel D. .... San Diego, CA
Osowski, Shane J. .... Anchorage, AK
Ospenson, James A. .... Newark, NJ
Osper, George P. .... San Diego, CA
Osradker, Dorothy .... Memphis, TN
Osran, Joan .... Barrington, IL
Oss, Frederick M. .... Minneapolis, MN
Ossé, Reginald J. .... New York, NY
Osséé Woods .... New York, NY
Ossen, Jeffrey P. .... Mansfield Center, CT
Ossen & Murphy .... Hartford, CT
Ossen, Neal .... Hartford, CT
Ossenfort, Elizabeth J. .... Austin, TX
Ossenfort, Kristine M. .... Augusta, ME
Ossentjuk, David A. .... Irvine, CA
Westlake Village, CA
Osser, A. Irving .... Beverly Hills, CA
Osser, Jeffrey S. .... Beverly Hills, CA
Osserman, Richard A. .... New York, NY
Ossi, Butler, Najem & Rosario, P.A.
Jacksonville, FL
Ossi, Christina S. .... Bronx, NY
Ossi, John T. .... Tampa, FL
Ossi, Judy C. .... Jacksonville, FL
Ossi, Michael A. .... Jacksonville, FL
Ossian, Kathryn L. .... Detroit, MI
Ossian, Mark A. .... Clearwater, FL
Ossias, Richard B.
Environmental Protection Agency, Office of the General Counsel, GV
Ossick, John J., Jr. .... Kingsland, GA
Ossick, John J., Jr., P.C. .... Kingsland, GA
Ossin, Stacy Lynn .... Miami, FL
Ossinsky, Arthur M. .... Daytona Beach, FL
Ossinsky & George .... Daytona Beach, FL
Ossinsky and Krol .... Daytona Beach, FL
Ossinsky, Louis, Jr. .... Daytona Beach, FL
Ossinsky, Marc P. .... Winter Park, FL
Ossinsky, Marc P., P.A. .... Winter Park, FL
Ossip, Michael J. .... Philadelphia, PA
Ossman, Julian J. .... Jefferson City, MO
Ossmann, Carl W. .... Topeka, KS
Ossoff, Daniel J. .... Boston, MA
Ossola, Charles D. .... Washington, DC
Ossola, Thomas W. .... Glenwood Springs, CO
Osson, Ronald Edmond .... Brooklyn, NY
Ossorio, Peter M. .... Las Cruces, NM
Osstyn, Bays, Ferns & Quinnell
Marquette, MI
Osstyn, Randolph B. .... Marquette, MI
Osswald, David E. .... Milwaukee, WI
Osswald, Jack .... Chicago, IL
Osswald Law Offices, P.C. .... Chicago, IL
Ossyra, James D. .... Chicago, IL
Ost, Barton B. .... Indianapolis, IN
Ost, Herbert E. .... Sunrise, FL
Ost, Roger D., Jr. .... Seattle, WA
Osta, William Gerard .... Schenectady, NY
Ostad, Joseph H. .... Baltimore, MD
Ostad, Joseph H., P.A. .... Baltimore, MD
Ostad, Karen .... New York, NY
New York, NY
O'Stafy, Stacey A. .... Toledo, OH
Ostapenko, Nicholas .... Duluth, MN
Ostapiuk, Sharon M. .... Riverwoods, IL
Ostapoff, Tatjana .... West Palm Beach, FL
Ostapuk, Benjamin R. .... Palo Alto, CA
Ostapuk, David R. .... Tucson, AZ
Ostar, William L. .... New York, NY
Ostarch, Gerald W. .... Corpus Christi, TX
Ostas, Daniel T. .... College Park, MD
Ostaseski, Jeanette M. .... Lake Success, NY
Ostaszewski, Dolores J. .... New York, NY
Ostby, Byron C. .... Madison, WI
Ostby, Carolyn S. .... Billings, MT
Ostby, Elena L. .... St. Paul, MN
Ostdiek, Jerald L. .... Scottsbluff, NE
Ostdiek, Thomas R. .... Omaha, NE
Ostebee, M. Alan .... Des Moines, IA
Osteen, C. Joel .... Hinesville, GA
Osteen, Carolyn M. .... Boston, MA
Osteen, Donald E. .... Los Angeles, CA
Osteen, J. Noel .... Hinesville, GA
Osteen, James N., Jr. .... Hinesville, GA
O'Steen, J. C. .... Tallahassee, FL
Osteen, Jeffery N. .... Hinesville, GA
Osteen, Kathleen J. .... Riverside, CA
San Diego, CA
Osteen, Michael D. .... Richmond, VA
O'Steen, Molly K. .... Athens, GA
Osteen and Osteen .... Hinesville, GA
O'Steen, Regan Gayle .... Dallas, TX
Osteen, Stephanie .... Dallas, TX
O'Steen, Van .... Phoenix, AZ
O'Steen, Van, and Partners .... Phoenix, AZ
Tucson, AZ
Osteen, William L. .... Knoxville, TN
Osteen, William L., Jr. .... Greensboro, NC
Osteen, William L., Sr. .... Greensboro, NC
Ostema, Lawrence L. .... Denver, CO
Osten, Judd F. .... Atlanta, GA
Ostendarp, Gary D. .... Batavia, OH
Ostendorf, Gregory A. .... Chicago, IL
Ostendorf, James A., Jr. .... St. Paul, MN
Ostendorf, Lance S. .... Metairie, LA
Ostendorf, Marika McVey .... Baltimore, MD
Ostendorff, William C. .... Shreveport, LA
Ostendorp, Louis A. .... Berwyn, IL
Ostenso, Ned E. .... Hopkins, MN
Ostenson, James Edwin .... Atlanta, GA
Ostenson, Thomas L. .... Jackson, MS
Oster, Barry A. .... Garden City, NY
Oster, Bernard .... Los Angeles, CA
Oster, Craigen J. .... St. Clair Shores, MI
Oster, Daniel H. .... Bismarck, ND
Oster, David J. .... San Francisco, CA
Oster, Edwin A. .... Newport Beach, CA
Oster, Ellen .... New York, NY
Oster, J. Berle .... Pompano Beach, FL
Oster, James C. .... Utica, NY
Oster, Jeffrey B. .... Seattle, WA
Oster, Jody Michelle .... Columbus, OH
Oster, Joel L. .... Kansas City, MO
Oster, Jonathan C. .... Denver, CO
Oster, Jonathan F. .... Lincoln, RI
Oster, Karen Dana .... Portland, OR
Oster & Kaufman .... Dallas, TX
Oster, Kenneth L. .... Glasgow, MT
Oster Law Offices .... Lincoln, RI
Oster, Matthew X. .... Los Angeles, CA
Oster, Robert D. .... Lincoln, RI
Oster, Robert M. .... Newport Beach, CA
Oster, Roma K. .... Rockaway, NJ
Oster, Ronald M., (P.C.) .... Los Angeles, CA
Oster, Shari Grant .... Smithtown, NY
Oster, Stephen G. .... Tampa, FL
Oster, Stephen G., P.A. .... Tampa, FL
Oster, Steven M. .... Washington, DC
Oster, Timothy C. .... Rolla, MO
Oster, Warren .... Oregon City, OR
Oster & Wegener, A P.L.C.
New Orleans, LA
Slidell, LA
Osterbauer, Joseph J. .... Minneapolis, MN
Osterbauer, Mary A. .... Southbridge, MA
Osterbauer, Michelle Barone
Minneapolis, MN
Osterberg, Edward C., Jr. .... Houston, TX
Osterberg, Eric .... New York, NY
Osterberg, Kevin M. .... Riverside, CA
Osterberg, Richard B. .... Boston, MA
Osterberg, Robert C. .... New York, NY
Osterberger, Domenica .... Joliet, IL
Osterberger, Thomas R. .... Joliet, IL
Osterbrock, Andrew C. .... Miamisburg, OH
Osterdale, Ann P. .... Basking Ridge, NJ
Ostergaard, Joni H. .... Seattle, WA
Ostergaard & Roach, LLP .... Seattle, WA
Ostergar, Allen C., III .... Costa Mesa, CA
Ostergard, Kyle A. .... Irvine, CA
Ostergard, Paul M. .... Fairfield, CT
Ostergren, Alan R. .... Muscatine, IA
Ostergren, Jennifer Lerner .... Clinton, IA
Osterhage, John J. .... Warsaw, KY
Osterhage, Lawrence E. .... Louisville, KY
Osterhaus, Timothy D. .... Washington, DC
Osterhoff, Michael R. .... Chicago, IL
Osterholm, Orrin C. .... Omaha, NE
Osterholt, Christopher A. .... Oakland, CA
Osterholt, M. Lynne .... Louisville, KY
Osterholt, Thomas E., Jr. .... St. Louis, MO
Osterhoudt, Charles H. .... Roanoke, VA
Osterhoudt, Ferguson, Natt, Aheron & Agee, A Professional Corporation .... Roanoke, VA
Osterhoudt, William L.
San Francisco, CA
Osterhout, Anna B. .... New Bern, NC
Osterhout, Bruce N. .... Orange, CA
Osterhout, David E. .... Washington, DC
Osterhout, Julie .... Fort Myers, FL
Osterhout, Julie, P.A. .... Fort Myers, FL
Osterhout, Karl E. .... Pittsburgh, PA
Osterhout, Mark C. .... Rocky Mount, NC
Osterhout, Richard C. .... Feasterville, PA
Osterhout, Suzanne .... Irvine, CA
Astericher, Scott R. .... Chicago, IL
Osterkamp, Jeffrey M. .... Chicago, IL
Osterkamp, Kevin J. .... Columbus, OH
Osterland, Charles E. .... North Royalton, OH
Osterland, Gerry D. .... Los Angeles, CA
Osterloh, Curtis J. .... Austin, TX
Osterloh, David Erwin .... San Rafael, CA
Osterloh, Douglas D. .... Seattle, WA
Osterloh, Henry J. .... Little Rock, AR
Osterloh, Karen .... Treasury Department, Office of Thrift Supervision, GV
Osterloth, Gregory W. .... Denver, CO
Osterlund, Paul B. .... Toledo, OR
Osterlund, Paul B., Attorney, P.C.
Toledo, OR
Osterman, Bruce S. .... San Francisco, CA
Osterman, David S. .... Newark, NJ
Osterman, David W. .... Denver, CO
Osterman, Edward J. .... Pittsburgh, PA
Osterman, Elizabeth G.
Securities and Exchange Commission, Division of Investment Management, GV
Osterman, Garth A. .... Oakland, CA
Osterman, Howard C. .... Boynton Beach, FL
Osterman, Jeffrey D. .... New York, NY
Osterman, Melvin H. .... Albany, NY
Osterman, Michael .... Warren, NJ
Osterman, R. Dennis .... Bethesda, MD
Fairfax, VA
Osterman, Richard J., Jr.
Federal Deposit Insurance Corporation, Appellate Litigation Section, GV
Ostermayer, Eric M. .... Dallas, TX
Ostermeyer, Michael J. .... Milwaukee, WI
Ostermiller, Peter L. .... Louisville, KY
Osterndorf & Associates, P.A.
Daytona Beach, FL
Osterndorf, Daniel P. .... Orlando, FL
Osterndorf, MaryEllen P.
Daytona Beach, FL
Osterndorf, Richard J.
Daytona Beach, FL
Palm Coast, FL
Osterrieder, Erik J. .... Houston, TX
Ostertag, Dale .... Sandusky, MI
Ostertag, James J. .... San Francisco, CA
Ostertag, Jüergen R. .... New York, NY
Ostertag & O'Leary .... Poughkeepsie, NY
Ostertag, Robert L. .... Poughkeepsie, NY
Ostertag, Thomas J. .... New York, NY
Osterud, S. Dwight .... Perrysburg, OH
Osterweil, Alan M. .... Columbia, SC
Osterweil, Alfred G., (A Prof. Corp.)
Edgewater, NJ
Osterweis, Harry L. .... New York, NY
Ostfeld, David M., (P.C.) .... Houston, TX
Ostfeld, Lynne R. .... Chicago, IL
Ostfeld, Lynne R., P.C. .... Chicago, IL
Ostfeld, Naomi S. .... Houston, TX
Ostfield, Alan J. .... Washington, DC
Ostgard, Dennis A. .... Seattle, WA
Ostgard, James E., II .... Minneapolis, MN
Ostheimer, David R. .... New York, NY
Ostheimer, Michael
Federal Trade Commission, Bureau of Consumer Protection, GV
Osthimer, Charles E., III
San Francisco, CA
Osthus, Marlin O. .... Minneapolis, MN
Ostiller, Cathy J. .... Los Angeles, CA
Ostiller, David B. .... San Rafael, CA
Ostiller, Patricia V. .... Los Angeles, CA
Ostin, Mila A. .... Atlanta, GA
Osting, Clayton P. .... Delphos, OH
Ostis, Algird R. .... Oak Brook, IL
Ostler, Blake T. .... Salt Lake City, UT
Ostler, Brian Clark .... Los Angeles, CA
Ostler, Duane Lowell .... St. George, UT
Ostler, George H. .... Norwich, VT
Ostler, James P., Jr. .... Chicago, IL
Ostler, Mark R. .... Palo Alto, CA
Ostler, Raymond J. .... Chicago, IL
Ostlie, Cynthia E. .... Crookston, MN
Ostlie, Steven D. .... St. Paul, MN
Ostling Ensign & Barry .... Bloomington, IL
Decatur, IL
Eureka, IL
Pontiac, IL

Ostling, Eric E. ... Redding, CA
West Sacramento, CA
Ostling, Gregory E. ... New York, NY
Ostling, Herbert F. ... Woodland Hills, CA
Ostling, Lars Eric ... Bloomington, IL
Pontiac, IL
Ostling, Paul J. ... New York, NY
Ostlund, Dow Glenn ... Phoenix, AZ
Ostlund, Jon E. ... Bellingham, WA
Ostlund, Lloyd J. ... Sun City West, AZ
Ostlund, Richard T. ... Minneapolis, MN
Ostlund, William C. ... Jefferson, IA
Ostman, Ellen D. ... Tampa, FL
Ostman, Robert A. ... Hempstead, TX
Ostmann, James Buckley ... Washington, DC
Ostmann, Robert A. ... Arlington, VA
Ostner, Steven M. ... New York, NY
Ostoich, Mark A. ... Riverside, CA
San Bernardino, CA
Ostoja-starzewski, Nga C. ... Little Rock, AR
Ostojic, John R. ... Chicago, IL
Ostojic, Radusa ... Chicago, IL
Ostolaza, Yvette ... Dallas, TX
Ostomel, Jeffrey A. ... Reno, NV
Ostovich, Carolyn Conklin
Wichita Falls, TX
Ostovitz, Linda Sorg ... Ellicott City, MD
Ostow, M. Jeremy ... Roseland, NJ
Ostow, S. Michael ... St. Petersburg, FL
Ostoyich, Joseph A. ... Washington, DC
Ostrach, Michael S. ... Hayward, CA
Ostrager, Allen M.
Department of Commerce,
Patent and Trademark Office, GV
Ostrager, Barry R. ... Palo Alto, CA
New York, NY
Ostrager Chong Flaherty & Onofrio, P.C.
Honolulu, HI
New York, NY
Ostrager, Fieldman, Kachmar & Nirenberg
Hackensack, NJ
Ostrager, Glenn F. ... New York, NY
Ostrager, Jeffrey N. ... New York, NY
Ostrander, Angela J. ... Fort Dodge, IA
Ostrander, David M. ... Walnut Creek, CA
Ostrander, David W. ... Northampton, MA
Ostrander, Donald M. ... Denver, CO
Ostrander, Frank W., Jr. ... Boston, MA
Ostrander, George W. ... Northport, NY
Ostrander, Joel W. ... Oak Park, IL
Ostrander, John D. ... Portland, OR
Ostrander, Judy L. ... Grand Rapids, MI
Ostrander & Kelly ... Grand Rapids, MI
Ostrander, Leslie L. ... Cincinnati, OH
Ostrander, Michelle M. ... Westminster, MD
Ostrander, Remsen B. ... Southampton, NY
Ostrander, Richard A. ... New York, NY
Ostrander, Thomas H. ... Bradenton, FL
Ostrander, Thomas H. ... Tampa, FL
Ostrander, Thomas W. ... Philadelphia, PA
Ostrander-Krug, Karen ... Denver, CO
Ostrau, Mark S. ... Palo Alto, CA
Ostrau, Norman M. ... Fort Lauderdale, FL
Ostreich, Peter D. ... Tallahassee, FL
Ostreicher, Jeffrey I. ... Phoenix, AZ
Ostreicher, Randy Kaston ... Boston, MA
Ostreicher & Vatz, P.C. ... Phoenix, AZ
Ostrelich, Michelle ... Wildwood, NJ
Media, PA
Ostrem, Donald L. ... Great Falls, MT
Ostrem, Mark A. ... Rochester, MN
Ostrer, Benjamin ... Chester, NY
Ostrer, Benjamin, & Associates, P.C.
Chester, NY
Goshen, NY
Ostrer, Mitchel E. ... Newark, NJ
New York, NY
Ostrin, Baker B. ... Los Angeles, CA
Ostrin, Benjamin B. ... North Hollywood, CA
Ostrin, Robert A. ... Santa Maria, CA
Ostrin, Ronald E., Law Offices of
Los Angeles, CA
Ostrochovsky, Rene ... Albuquerque, NM
Ostroff, Brad S. ... Phoenix, AZ
Ostroff, Donna ... Philadelphia, PA
Ostroff, Gary E. ... Garden City, NY
Ostroff, Janet J. ... Miami, FL
Ostroff, Jonathan ... Lansdale, PA
Philadelphia, PA
Ostroff, Joseph S. ... Washington, DC
Ostroff, Michael ... Universal City, CA
Ostroff, Nathan ... Buffalo, NY
Ostroff, Paul M. ... Portland, OR
Ostroff, Peter I. ... Los Angeles, CA
Ostroff, Ron ... Iselin, NJ
Ostroff, Sheldon A. ... San Diego, CA
Ostrofsky, Bonnie G. ... Erdenheim, PA
Ostrolenk, Faber, Gerb & Soffen, LLP
Washington, DC
New York, NY
Ostrom, Carolyn Collins ... Austin, TX
Ostrom, Gregory J. ... Lansing, MI
Ostrom, Jennifer Ann ... Denver, CO
Ostrom, Jesse R. ... Neenah, WI
Ostrom, Michael B. ... Overland Park, KS
Ostrom, Robert B. ... Greenbelt, MD
Rockville, MD
Ostrom, Ruth Y. ... Minneapolis, MN
Ostronic, Patrick ... Baltimore, MD
Ostroskey, Michael J. ... Boston, MA
Ostroski, Janell Schoenbeck
Wilmington, DE
Ostroski, Kara Krystina ... Dallas, TX
Ostroski, Raymond B. ... Princeton, NJ
Ostrov, Eric ... Chicago, IL
Ostrov, Frank E. ... Los Angeles, CA
Ostrov, George E. ... Lauderdale Lakes, FL
Ostrov, Jerome ... Washington, DC
Ostrov, Lester G. ... Santa Monica, CA
Ostrov, Richard E. ... Schenectady, NY
Ostrov, Robert ... Wheeling, IL
Ostrove, David ... Los Angeles, CA
Ostrove, Elliot D. ... Morristown, NJ
Ostrove, Fredric David ... Carle Place, NY
Ostrove, Kenneth E. ... Los Angeles, CA
Ostrove, Krantz & Ostrove, A Professional Corporation ... Los Angeles, CA
Ostrove, Nona L. ... Atlantic City, NJ
Voorhees, NJ
Voorhees, NJ
Ostrove, Steven M. ... Los Angeles, CA
Ostrover, Marla Miller ... New York, NY
Ostrovsky, Cyd C. ... Southborough, MA
Ostrovsky, Eric ... United States Senate,
Senatorial Assistants, GV
Ostrovsky, Jan Samuel ... Seattle, WA
Ostrovsky, Lawrence Z. ... Anchorage, AK
Ostrovsky, Mark L. ... Fort Myers, FL
Ostrow, Alan C. ... Philadelphia, PA
Ostrow, Alan D. ... Brooklyn, NY
Ostrow, Alec P. ... New York, NY
Ostrow, Andrew A. ... West Palm Beach, FL
Ostrow, David S. ... Owings Mills, MD
Ostrow, David S., P.A. ... Owings Mills, MD
Ostrow, Edwin ... New York, NY
Ostrow, Eleanor J. ... New York, NY
Ostrow, Gary S. ... Fort Lauderdale, FL
Ostrow, George ... Plantation, FL
Ostrow, Jack M. ... Beverly Hills, CA
Ostrow, Jeffrey E. ... New York, NY
Ostrow, Jeffrey M. ... Boca Raton, FL
Ostrow, Joel S. ... Chicago, IL
Chicago, IL
Ostrow, John B. ... Miami, FL
Ostrow, John B., P.A. ... Miami, FL
Ostrow, Joseph ... Beverly Hills, CA
Ostrow, Kenneth A. ... Los Angeles, CA
Ostrow, Loren S. ... Los Angeles, CA
Ostrow, Marc D. ... New York, NY
Ostrow, Max L. ... Memphis, TN
Ostrow, Michael J. ... Garden City, NY
Ostrow, Paul T. ... St. Paul, MN
Ostrow, Richard D. ... Chicago, IL
Ostrow, Ronald I. ... Laguna Niguel, CA
Ostrow, Seth H. ... New York, NY
Ostrow, Shirley ... Los Alamitos, CA
Ostrow, Stacia ... New York, NY
Ostrow, Stanley V. ... Pittsburgh, PA
Ostrow, Stephen I. ... Cardiff-By-The-Sea, CA
Ostrow, Stephen R. ... Marco Island, FL
Ostrow, Steven E. ... Philadelphia, PA
Ostrow and Taub, LLP ... Garden City, NY
Mineola, NY
Ostrow, Winston A. ... Green Bay, WI
Ostrower, Donald A. ... Roslyn Heights, NY
Ostrowitz, Alan R. ... Manalapan, NJ
Ostrowitz, Martha D. F. ... Manalapan, NJ
Ostrowitz & Ostrowitz ... Manalapan, NJ
Ostrowski, Andrew J. ... Harrisburg, PA
Ostrowski, Dennis M. ... Louisville, KY
Ostrowski, Edward L., Jr. ... Columbus, OH
Ostrowski, James ... Buffalo, NY
Ostrowski, John M. ... Topeka, KS
Ostrowski, Joseph Thomas ... Lakewood, OH
Ostrowski, Kenneth W. ... New York, NY
Ostrowski, Leo A. ... Griffith, IN
Ostrowski, Mark ... Markham, IL
Ostrowski, Mark K. ... Hartford, CT
Ostrowski, Peter J., Jr. ... Eureka, SD
Ostrowski, Robert J. ... Tarzana, CA
Ostrowski, Sharon L. ... Chicago, IL
Ostrowski, Stacy H. ... Washington, DC
Ostrowski, Thomas W. ... Cleveland, OH
Ostrowski, William J. ... Buffalo, NY
Ostrowsky, Barry H. ... Livingston, NJ
Ostrowsky, Howard ... New York, NY
Ostrowsky, Lenore S. ... Washington, DC
Ostrowsky, Michael L. ... Livingston, NJ
Ostroy, Joan Patsy ... Los Angeles, CA
Ostrum, Dean G. ... New York, NY
Ostrye, Michelle K. ... Amarillo, TX
Ostwald, David H. ... New York, NY
Ostwald, Mitchell S. ... Sacramento, CA
Ostwald, Peter B. ... Albany, NY
Osty, Michael J. ... Chicago, IL
Osuch, Lawrence T. ... San Diego, CA
O'Sullivan, Allan T. ... Long Beach, NY
O'Sullivan & Associates, P.C. ... Norwell, MA
O'Sullivan, Barry J. ... White Plains, NY
O'Sullivan, Benjamin C. ... Fishkill, NY
O'Sullivan & Blotch, PLLC ... Seattle, WA
O'Sullivan & Bray ... Greenfield, MA
O'Sullivan, Brendan P. ... Tampa, FL
O'Sullivan, Brian J. ... New York, NY
O'Sullivan, Brian P. ... Deerfield Beach, FL
O'Sullivan, Brian P., P.A.
Deerfield Beach, FL
O'Sullivan, Catherine G.
Department of Justice,
Antitrust Division, GV
O'Sullivan, Christine B. ... Westport, CT
O'Sullivan, Ciarán ... Oakland, CA
O'Sullivan, Cornelius J., Jr.
Cleveland, OH
O'Sullivan, Daniel F. ... Cincinnati, OH
O'Sullivan, Daniel S. ... Santa Ana, CA
O'Sullivan, Dennis J. ... Long Beach, CA
O'Sullivan, Dennis J. ... Flushing, NY
O'Sullivan, Dennis P. ... Belvidere, IL
O'Sullivan, Desmond J. ... Port Jefferson, NY
O'Sullivan, Desmond J., P.C.
Port Jefferson, NY
O'Sullivan, Donald ... New York, NY
O'Sullivan, Eileen M. ... Bloomington, IL
Chicago, IL
O'Sullivan, F. Patrick ... Bristol, CT
O'Sullivan, Frederick T. ... Peabody, MA
O'Sullivan, Freek & O'Sullivan
Belvidere, IL
O'Sullivan, George P. ... New York, NY
O'Sullivan Graev & Karabell, LLP
New York, NY
O'Sullivan, James C. ... Greenfield, MA
O'Sullivan, James G. ... Mission, KS
O'Sullivan, James K. ... Jericho, NY
O'Sullivan, James M. ... Norwell, MA
O'Sullivan, James P. ... Phoenix, AZ
O'Sullivan, James P.
Office of Government Ethics,
Office of General Counsel and Legal Policy,
GV
O'Sullivan, James P. ... Mount Clemens, MI
O'Sullivan, James P., Sr. ... Fairfax, VA
O'Sullivan, Jane M. ... Haverhill, MA
O'Sullivan, Jay D. ... Seattle, WA
O'Sullivan, Jean M. ... Sacramento, CA
O'Sullivan, Jennifer Walker ... Oakland, CA
O'Sullivan, Jeremiah J. ... Boston, MA
O'Sullivan, Jeremiah T., (P.C.)
Boston, MA
Osullivan, Jill Elizabeth ... Pearl River, NY
O'Sullivan, Joan L. ... Baltimore, MD
O'Sullivan, Joanne M. ... Falmouth, MA
Raynham, MA
O'Sullivan, John A. ... Sacramento, CA
O'Sullivan, John B. ... Washington, DC
O'Sullivan, John F. ... Miami, FL
O'Sullivan, John J. ... Miami, FL
O'Sullivan, John P. ... Mineola, NY
New York, NY
White Plains, NY
O'Sullivan, Joseph D. ... San Francisco, CA
O'Sullivan, Joseph P., III ... Hutchinson, KS
O'Sullivan, Judith R. ... Department of Justice,
Criminal Division, GV
O'Sullivan, Kathleen M. ... Seattle, WA
O'Sullivan, Kieran H. D. ... Bronxville, NY
O'Sullivan, Laura H G ... Annapolis, MD
O'Sullivan, Lauren M. ... Roseland, NJ
O'Sullivan, Lynda Troutman
Washington, DC
O'Sullivan, Maria P. ... Bethesda, MD
O'Sullivan, Maura E. ... New York, NY
O'Sullivan, Maureen ... Boston, MA
O'Sullivan, Maureen Naomi ... Halifax, PA
O'Sullivan, Maurice J., Jr.
Kansas City, MO
O'Sullivan, Michael C. ... New York, NY
O'Sullivan, Michael J. ... Los Angeles, CA
O'Sullivan, Michael W. ... New York, NY
O'Sullivan, Patrick J. ... Syracuse, NY
O'Sullivan, Patrick J. ... White Plains, NY
O'Sullivan, Robert C.
Overseas Private Investment Corporation,
GV
O'Sullivan, Robert J. ... Andover, MA
O'Sullivan, Roger C. ... Scottsdale, AZ
O'Sullivan, Sean J. ... Albertson, NY
O'Sullivan, Sean M. ... Greenfield, MA
O'Sullivan, Shawn L. ... New Haven, CT
O'Sullivan, Sheila D. ... Albany, NY
O'Sullivan, Stephen D. ... Skokie, IL
O'Sullivan, Susan M. ... Washington, DC
O'Sullivan, Terrence B. ... Bend, OR
O'Sullivan, Thomas E. ... Los Angeles, CA
O'Sullivan, Thomas J. ... Milford, CT
O'Sullivan, Thomas J. ... New York, NY
O'Sullivan, Timothy J. ... Albany, NY
O'Sullivan, Timothy J. ... Raleigh, NC
O'Sullivan, Timothy O. ... St. Louis, MO
O'Sullivan, Timothy P. ... Wichita, KS
Kansas City, MO
O'Sullivan, William F. ... Kansas City, MO
O'Sullivan, William J. ... Wethersfield, CT
O'Sullivan, William P. ... Herndon, VA
Osuna, Jesse ... Chula Vista, CA
Osuna, Juan P. ... Washington, DC
Osur, Ian G. ... Miami, FL
Osur, Ian G., P.A. ... Miami, FL
Osvald-Mruz, Christine ... Roseland, NJ
Oswald, Andrew L. ... Hutchinson, KS
Oswald, Billy R., & Associates
West Columbia, SC
Oswald, Bruce A. ... Palm Springs, CA
Oswald, Carol ... Lawrenceville, NJ
Oswald, Carolyn Boyd ... Kansas City, MO
Oswald, Charles E., Jr. ... Evansville, IN
Indianapolis, IN
Oswald, Christina Metcalf ... Burbank, CA
Oswald, Cottey & Templeton, A Professional Corporation ... Kirksville, MO
Oswald, David H. ... Seattle, WA
Oswald, Donald E. ... Fort Lauderdale, FL
Oswald, Douglas H. ... Ocala, FL
Oswald, Edwin G. ... Washington, DC
Oswald & Feil, A P.C. ... Salt Lake City, UT
Oswald, Frank A. ... New York, NY
Oswald, Gary P. ... San Rafael, CA
Oswald, Henry P. ... Salem, NY
Oswald, Hugo E., Jr. ... Seattle, WA
Oswald, James A. ... New Orleans, LA
Oswald, James A. ... Brooklyn, NY
Oswald, James D. ... Seattle, WA
Oswald, James R. ... Providence, RI
Oswald, Janelle M. ... Littleton, CO
Oswald, Jennifer Inglis ... Atlanta, GA
Oswald, John E. ... Seattle, WA
Oswald, John K. ... Fort Edward, NY
Oswald, John Michael ... Portland, OR
Oswald, John P. ... New York, NY
Oswald, John T. ... Duluth, MN
Oswald, Joseph H. ... Fort Edward, NY
Oswald, Joseph M. ... Cedar Park, TX
Oswald, Julius M. ... Blue Springs, MO
Oswald, Kelly J. ... Moorestown, NJ
Philadelphia, PA
Oswald, Kenneth F. ... Orlando, FL
Oswald, Kenneth L. ... Eldon, MO
Oswald, Lynda K. ... Montgomery, AL
Oswald, Lynne ... Orlando, FL
Oswald, Mark G. ... Eugene, OR
Oswald, Michael A. ... Irvine, CA
Oswald, R. Scott ... Washington, DC
Oswald and Reed ... Gulfport, MS
Pascagoula, MS
Oswald, Robert H. ... Pascagoula, MS
Oswald, Robert L. ... Washington, DC
Oswald, Robert L. ... Norfolk, VA
Oswald, Rod ... Deadwood, SD
Oswald, Stanton S. ... Philadelphia, PA
Oswald, Suellen ... Cleveland, OH
Oswald, Thomas R. ... Kirksville, MO
Oswald, Timothy J. ... Los Angeles, CA
Oswald, Victoria Kathleen ... Berkeley, CA
Oswald, William D. ... Salt Lake City, UT
Oswald & Yap, A Professional Corporation
Irvine, CA
Oswalt, D. Stewart, (P.A.) ... Hutchinson, KS
Oswalt, Deborah D. ... Richmond, VA
Oswalt, Frank A., III ... El Centro, CA
Oswalt, J. David ... Los Angeles, CA
Oswalt, James S. ... Hutchinson, KS
Oswalt, Kenneth W. ... Newark, OH
Oswalt, Oswalt & Arnhold ... Hutchinson, KS
Oswalt, Robert D. ... Oklahoma City, OK
Oswalt, Susan H. ... Little Rock, AR
Oswalt, W. Lee, III ... Altoona, PA
Oswecki, Jane C. ... Department of Commerce,
Patent and Trademark Office, GV
Oswecki, Vincent W., Jr. ... Windsor, CT
Oswell, Allis Milkovich ... Pittsburgh, PA
Oswell, Judith Ann ... Allen Park, MI
Oswell, Lisa A. ... Jacksonville, FL
Oswood, Deborah Rodgers ... Great Falls, MT
Oszewski, Patrick R. ... Milwaukee, WI
Oszustowicz, John C. ... Carlisle, PA
Ota, Cathy Miyo ... Irvine, CA
Ota, Ed K., Jr. ... Philadelphia, PA
Ota, Henry Y. ... Costa Mesa, CA
Ota, John ... San Francisco, CA
Ota, Russell A. ... Honolulu, HI
Ota, William N. ... Honolulu, HI
Ota & Yuen ... Honolulu, HI
Otaguro, Lynn M. ... Honolulu, HI
Otaguro, Steven Y. ... Honolulu, HI
Otaka, Sandra Reiko ... Chicago, IL
Otamura-Kester, Judith K. ... Los Angeles, CA
Otani, Ann H. ... Honolulu, HI
Otani, Caroline S. ... Honolulu, HI
Otano-Guilbe, Jorge Miguel
Los Angeles, CA
Otchet, Michael I. ... Lancaster, PA
Otchy, Arthur A. ... Mantoloking, NJ
Otepka, Thomas A. ... Omaha, NE
Otera, Richard H. ... Los Angeles, CA
Otera, Steven Y. ... Long Beach, CA
Oteri, Joseph S. ... Boston, MA
Oteri, Weinberg & Lawson, P.A.
Boston, MA
Otero, Brian V. ... Richmond, VA
Otero, David E. ... Jacksonville, FL
Otero, Dolores C. ... New York, NY
Otero, Eduardo ... Philadelphia, PA
Otero, Jack A. ... Santa Barbara, CA
Otero, John B., Jr. ... Lorain, OH
Otero, Jorge E. ... Miami, FL
Otero, Jose ... Washington, DC
Otero, Jose G. ... San Diego, CA
Otero, Juan B. ... Santa Clara, CA
Otero, Judith ... Slidell, LA
Otero, Lisa M. ... Boston, MA
Otero & Otero Co., L.P.A. ... Lorain, OH
Otero, Philip V. ... Princeton, NJ
Otero, Ramon, Jr. ... Pomona, CA
Otero, S. James ... Los Angeles, CA
Otero, Samantha S. ... Richmond, VA
Otero, Sandra B. ... New York, NY
Otero, Stephen D. ... Richmond, VA
Otero Suro & Otero Suro ... San Juan, PR
Otero Tomlin & Tomlin, P.A. ... Miami, FL
Otero-Fernandez, Pedro A. ... San Juan, PR
Otero-Phillips, Camille V. ... Roseland, NJ
Otero-Silva, Eugenio ... San Juan, PR
Otero Suro, Jose ... San Juan, PR
Otero Suro, Rodrigo ... San Juan, PR
Otey, Brian Alan ... Philadelphia, PA
Otey, Charles F. ... Brooklyn, NY
Otey, David W. ... Williamsburg, VA
Otey, David W., Jr. ... Williamsburg, VA
Otey, George N., III ... Tulsa, OK
Otey, John Dubiel ... Ardmore, OK
Otey, Millie E. ... Tulsa, OK
Othman, Linda Berg ... Fresno, CA
Othman, Nehad S. ... Chicago, IL
Othmer, Craig ... Santa Fe, NM
Othrow, Randi L. ... McFarland, WI
Oths, Heiser, Regan and Miller
Jackson, OH
Wellston, OH
Oths, Joseph A. ... Wellston, OH
Oths, Michael J. ... Boise, ID
Otieno, Rosalyn W. ... Minneapolis, MN
O'Tierney, Daniel Patrick ... Anchorage, AK
Otillar, Steven P. ... Houston, TX
Otipoby, Lisa Beth ... Lawrence, KS
Otis, Andrew D. ... New Paltz, NY
Otis, Anthony ... Montpelier, VT
Otis, Clyde L., III ... Englewood, NJ
Otis, Coan and Stewart, LLC ... Greeley, CO
Otis, David J. ... Media, PA
Otis, David K. ... Lansing, MI
Otis, Fred L. ... Greeley, CO

Ottosen Trevarthen Britz Dooley & Kelly, Ltd. .... Elburn, IL
McHenry, IL
Schaumburg, IL
Wheaton, IL
Ottoson, Gary C., (A Professional Corporation) .... Santa Monica, CA
Ottoson, Mary R. .... St. Louis, MO
Otts, Lee M. .... Brewton, AL
Otts, Mark G. .... New Orleans, LA
Otts, Moore & Jordan .... Brewton, AL
Ottsen, Heidi M. .... St. Louis, MO
Ottsen, Lamar E. .... St. Louis, MO
Ottsen, Mauzé, Leggat & Belz, L.C.
St. Louis, MO
Otubusin & Associates, P.C. .... Chicago, IL
Otubusin, Paul O. .... Chicago, IL
O'Tuel, John W., III .... Raleigh, NC
Otuteye, Maxy Rush .... Irvine, CA
Otway, James L. .... Salisbury, MD
Otwell, Brian T. .... Springfield, IL
O'Tyson, Nicolle A. .... Atlanta, GA
Otzel, Paul Lewis .... Milford, CT
Oualline, Charles E. .... San Antonio, TX
Oualline, David M. .... Houston, TX
Ouborg, Peter .... San Francisco, CA
Oubre, David A. .... Houston, TX
Oubre, Edward P. .... Boulder, CO
Oubre, Jerry A. .... Lafayette, LA
New Iberia, LA
Oubre, Louis O. .... Metairie, LA
Oubre, Trenton J. .... Baton Rouge, LA
Ouchterloney, Megan J. .... Stamford, CT
Ouchterloney, Robert D. .... New York, NY
Ouda, Peter A. .... Morris Plains, NJ
Oudemool, Dirk J. .... Syracuse, NY
Oudenhoven, Julie A. .... Green Bay, WI
Ouderkirk, James F. .... Newport, OR
Ouderkirk, John W. .... Los Angeles, CA
Ouderkirk Law Firm .... Indianola, IA
Ouderkirk, Mason G. .... Indianola, IA
Ouderkirk, Mason J. .... Indianola, IA
Oudsema, William R. .... Kalamazoo, MI
Ouellet, Jeffrey P. .... Harrisburg, PA
Ouellette, Alfred P. .... Boston, MA
Ouellette, Daniele M. .... Boston, MA
Ouellette, Eileen M. .... Boston, MA
Ouellette, Gerard L. .... Springfield, MA
Ouellette, Hallisey, Dibble & Tanguay, Professional Association .... Dover, NH
Ouellette, Lawrence A., Jr. .... New Haven, CT
Ouellette, Linda A. .... Boston, MA
Ouellette, Margaret A. .... Albany, NY
Ouellette, Michelle .... Riverside, CA
Ouellette, Patricia M. .... Lansing, MI
Ouellette, Raymond R. .... Dover, NH
Ouellette, Robert R. .... Columbus, OH
Ouellette, Roberta A. .... Raleigh, NC
Ouellette, Scott A. .... Providence, RI
Ouellette, Stephen M. .... Beverly, MA
Ouellette, Steven J. .... Fort Wayne, IN
Ouellette, Suzanne E. .... Rochester, NY
Ouer, Richard .... Carrollton, TX
Oufnac, Kevin L. .... Charleston, SC
Oughourli, Diana .... Ashland, VA
Oughterson, Sundheim & Woods, P.A.
Stuart, FL
Oughterson, William A. .... Stuart, FL
Oughton, Kimberly Ann .... Los Angeles, CA
Ouida, Herbert .... New York, NY
Ouimet, John A. .... Rensselaer, NY
Ouimet, Lilianne Voigt .... Coral Gables, FL
Ouimet, Patrick M. .... Chicago, IL
Ouimet, Robert D. .... Leominster, MA
Ouimette, David J. .... Phoenix, AZ
Ouimette, Goldstein & Andrews, P.C.
Kingston, NY
Middletown, NY
New Windsor, NY
Poughkeepsie, NY
Ouimette, James H. .... Vergennes, VT
Ouimette, Mary L. .... Frederick, MD
Ouimette, Robert A. .... New York, NY
Ouimette & Runcie .... Vergennes, VT
Ouimette, Wilfred T. .... Poughkeepsie, NY
Oujesky, J. Ray .... Hurst, TX
Oulahan, Courts .... Washington, DC
Ould, James P., Jr. .... Richmond, VA
Ould, Susan E. .... New York, NY
Oulds, Valarie K. .... Baltimore, MD
Oulsnam, Donald R. .... Milledgeville, GA
Oulton, Donald P. .... Natick, MA
Oulton, Richard J. .... Richmond, VA
Oulundsen, Donald C. .... East Hartford, CT
Ounan, Francis X. .... Totowa, NJ
Ounanian, Harding M. .... Needham, MA
Ounsworth, James A. .... Wayne, PA
Our Pal Asija .... Shelton, CT
Ourada, Eric James .... Charlotte, NC
Ourada, Michael J. .... Fremont, NE
Ourada, Norman L. .... Washington, DC
Ouradnik, Eugene R. .... Bagley, MN
Ourfalian, Sarkis A. .... Glendale, CA
Ours, G. Fred .... New Orleans, LA
Ours, John Winthrop .... Cleveland, OH
Ours, Josh Shannon .... Virginia Beach, VA
Ours, Stuart C. .... Washington, NJ
Oursler, Timothy J. .... Towson, MD
Ourso, A. Justin, III .... Baton Rouge, LA
Ourso, Candace A. .... Houston, TX
Ourso, Corbett L., Jr. .... Hammond, LA
Ourso, Jason G. .... Baton Rouge, LA
Ourth, Joe .... Chicago, IL
Oury, Dennis J. .... Hackensack, NJ
Oury, Loren H. .... Downers Grove, IL
Oury & Mizdol, P.C. .... Hackensack, NJ
Oury, Shannon C. .... Denver, CO
Ousey, Roger William .... Medford, OR
Oushalem, Robert .... San Jose, CA
Ouska, John A. .... Chicago, IL
Ousky, Ronald D. .... Bloomington, MN
Ouslander, Andrew .... Treasury Department, Internal Revenue Service, GV
Ouslander, Charles .... Trenton, NJ
Ouslander, Morris .... New York, NY
Ousley, Bernard V. .... Claremont, CA
Ousley, Bobette Smiley .... Cleveland, OH
Ousley, Daniel .... Toledo, OR
Ousley, Mary B. .... Walnut Creek, CA
Oussani, Rita C. .... Brooklyn, NY
Oustad, Ann .... Reno, NV
Ousterhout, Donald G.
San Francisco, CA
Ousterhout, Glenn A. .... New York, NY
Ousterling, Lisa R. .... San Francisco, CA
Outcalt, Peter Louis .... Cincinnati, OH
Outen, Boyce C. .... Richmond, VA
Outerbridge, Cheryl .... Golden, CO
Outhier, Philip J. .... Enid, OK
Outhwaite, Richard A. .... Springfield, NJ
Outis, Robert R. .... Albany, CA
Outis, Robert R., A Professional Corp.
Albany, CA
Outka, Ann E. .... Des Moines, IA
Outland, Denise Y. .... Cambridge, MA
Outland, Gray, O'Keefe & Hubbard
Chesapeake, VA
Norfolk, VA
Outland, Grover C., III .... Millersville, MD
Outland, Grover C., Jr. .... Chesapeake, VA
Outland, Robert J. .... Grosse Pointe Woods, MI
Outlaw Firm, The .... Atlanta, GA
Decatur, GA
Outlaw, Larry A. .... Raleigh, NC
Outlaw, M. DeAnn .... St. Louis, MO
Outlaw, Rondrew A. .... Los Angeles, CA
Outlaw, Shelby A. .... Decatur, GA
Outler, Thomas A. .... Albuquerque, NM
Outman, James B. .... Atlanta, GA
Outman, William D., II .... New York, NY
Outten, Angela E. .... Palm Harbor, FL
Outten, Barrett, Burr & Sharrett, P.C.
Emporia, VA
Lawrenceville, VA
Outten & Golden LLP .... New York, NY
Outten, Robert L. .... Kitty Hawk, NC
Outten, Samuel Wright .... Greenville, SC
Outten, W. Curtis, Jr. .... Lawrenceville, VA
Outten, Wayne N. .... New York, NY
Outterson, M. Kevin .... Nashville, TN
Outtrim, Elissa R. .... Bryn Mawr, PA
Outwater, David E. .... Newport Beach, CA
Outwater, Lynn C. .... Pittsburgh, PA
Ouweleen, Mark S. .... Denver, CO
Chicago, IL
Ouyang, Michael K. .... Minnetonka, MN
Ouzts, Cynthia Hall .... Columbia, SC
Ouzts, Steven W. .... Columbia, SC
Ouzts, Wm. C. .... Columbia, SC
Ovadia, Vera M. .... New York, NY
Ovando, Lynn E. .... Anaheim, CA
Woodland Hills, CA
Ovanezian, Daniel E. .... Sunnyvale, CA
Ovard, David L. .... Dallas, TX
Ovard, John .... Dallas, TX
Ovca, Jodi E. ....
Department of Commerce, GV
Oveisi, Paul .... Austin, TX
Ovella, Dominic J. .... Metairie, LA
Ovelmen, Richard J. .... Miami, FL
Oven, Gwynn & Miller, P.A.
Tallahassee, FL
Over, Edward R. .... Redmond, WA
Over, Eugene A., Jr. .... Englewood, CO
Over, Oliver O., Jr. .... Council Bluffs, IA
Over, Oscar O. .... Council Bluffs, IA
Over, Over & Over, P.C. .... Council Bluffs, IA
Over, Susan Carol .... Wilmington, DE
Overall, Don B. .... Tucson, AZ
Overall, Gene .... Clayton, MO
Overall, Martha R. .... New York, NY
Overall, Scott C. .... Washington, DC
Overall, Thomas W. .... Greeneville, TN
Overbay, Allison K. .... Greensboro, NC
Overbeck, Daniel H. .... Rochester, NY
Overbeck, John H., Jr. .... Chicago, IL
Overbeck, Karl .... Monticello, IN
Overbeck, Michael J.
West Palm Beach, FL
Overbeek, Donald E. .... Portage, MI
Overberg, Kathryn Atkinson
Des Moines, IA
Overberg, Nathan J. .... Des Moines, IA
Overbey, Amy F. .... Houston, TX
Overbey, Daniel L. .... Chicago, IL
Overbey, Geo. Edward, Jr. .... Frankfort, KY
Overbey Graham & Strigel, PLC
Little Rock, AR
Overbey, Hawkins & Selz .... Lynchburg, VA
Rustburg, VA
Overbey, J. Douglas .... Knoxville, TN
Overbey, Jesse W. .... Chatham, VA
Overbey Law Firm .... Murray, KY
Overbey, Terry L. .... Cincinnati, OH
Overbey, Thomas L. .... Little Rock, AR
Overbey, W. Hutchings, Jr. .... Rustburg, VA
Overbey, Wm. Donald .... Murray, KY
Overboe, David A. .... West Fargo, ND
Overby, A. Brooke .... New Orleans, LA
Overby, C. Frederick .... Atlanta, GA
Columbus, GA
Overby, David S. .... Hannibal, MO
Overby, Donald W. .... Raleigh, NC
Overby, Earl F. .... Pensacola, FL
Overby, Enoch .... Calhoun, GA
Overby, Eric A. .... Salt Lake City, UT
Overby, J. Allen .... Nashville, TN
Overby, J. Jefferson .... Key West, FL
Overby, James O. .... Murray, KY
Overby, John C. .... New Orleans, LA
Overby, Michelle Lynn .... Harrisonburg, VA
Overby, Richard J. .... Plentywood, MT
Overby, Robert G. .... Santa Ana, CA
Overby, Russell J. .... Murfreesboro, TN
Overcash, Allen L. .... Lincoln, NE
Overcash, Bert L. .... Lincoln, NE
Overcash, Edward H., Jr. .... Spartanburg, SC
Overcash, Kathleen M. .... Englewood, CO
Overcash, Kathleen M., P.C.
Englewood, CO
Overcash, Marcy M. .... Lincoln, NE
Overcash, W. Hugh .... Atlanta, GA
Overcash, Wendell H. .... Frankfort, KY
Overcast, Thomas D. .... Edmonds, WA
Overchuck, John R. .... Orlando, FL
Tallahassee, FL
Overchuck, Newsome & Schwerer, LLP
Orlando, FL
Overchuk, Karen E. .... Hartford, CT
Overdier, Frederick C. .... Saginaw, MI
Overdorff, John S. .... Phoenix, AZ
Overdyke & Clawson .... Shreveport, LA
Overdyke, Donald F., III .... Shreveport, LA
Overend, Charles A. .... Hartford, CT
Overend, George D., Jr. .... Chattanooga, TN
Overend, William R. .... San Francisco, CA
Overfelt, Aaron F. .... Bowling Green, KY
Overfelt, Gary .... Aloha, OR
Overfelt, Leslie .... Los Angeles, CA
Overfelt, Samuel E. .... Jefferson City, MO
Overfield, J. Landon .... Henderson, KY
Overfield, John Covington
Greensboro, NC
Overfield, Kelly Ayers .... Tampa, FL
Overgaard, Cordell J., (P.C.) .... Chicago, IL
Overgaard & Davis .... Barrington, IL
Chicago, IL
Homewood, IL
Overgaard, Mitchell J. .... Chicago, IL
Homewood, IL
Overhardt, Kurt F. .... Denver, CO
Overhauser, Paul B. .... Greenfield, IN
Overholser, Carl Dean .... Delphi, IN
Overholser, Gloria J. .... Rockville, MD
Overholser, Heather Lynn
New Haven, CT
Overholser, James N. .... Dayton, OH
Overholser, John W. .... Montrose, CO
Overholser & Slee, P.C. .... Montrose, CO
Overholser, Sonia D. .... Phoenix, AZ
Overholt, David G. .... Los Angeles, CA
Overholt, David W. .... Salt Lake City, UT
Overholt, Don R. .... Waterloo, NE
Overholt, E. Llewellyn, Jr. .... Anaheim, CA
Overholt, Elizabeth M. .... Phoenix, AZ
Overholt, H. Scott .... Greenville, NC
Overholt, Hugh R. .... New Bern, NC
Overholt, James A. .... Phoenix, AZ
Overholt, Judy M. .... Rochester, NY
Overholt, Keith F. .... Phoenix, AZ
Overholt, Mary Ann .... Cincinnati, OH
Overholt, Ralph J. .... Hopkins, MN
Overholt, Weston C., Jr. .... Media, PA
Philadelphia, PA
Overing, Michael S. .... San Fernando, CA
Overland, Allan L. .... Tacoma, WA
Overland, Barbara C. .... Pacific Palisades, CA
Overland, Carol A. .... Northfield, MN
Overland & Gits .... Santa Monica, CA
Overland, Jody D. .... Ames, IA
Overland, Mark E. .... Santa Monica, CA
Overlander, Clare V. .... Northampton, MA
Overlander, Lewis & Russell .... Pasadena, CA
Overlander, Thomas F. .... Pasadena, CA
Overley, Thomas G. .... Holland, OH
Overlock, Marc E. .... Nashville, TN
Overlock, Willard J. .... Stamford, CT
Overly, Michael R. .... Los Angeles, CA
Overly, Niles C. .... Dublin, OH
Overly, Sannie .... Lexington, KY
Overly & Spiker, A Legal Professional Association .... Dublin, OH
Overly, Steven D. .... Princeton, NJ
Overman, Carl D. .... Indianapolis, IN
Overman, Charles H., III .... Pensacola, FL
Overman, Cowardin & Martin, P.L.C.
Newport News, VA
Overman, Dean L. .... Washington, DC
Overman, Eric M. .... New York, NY
Overman, G. Curtis, Jr. .... Newport News, VA
Overman, James B. .... Kansas City, MO
Overman, John Wm. .... Sun City, AZ
Overman, Larry Jack, II .... Fayetteville, GA
Overman, Michael C. .... Houston, TX
Overman, Robert D. .... Wichita, KS
Overman, William H. .... Atlanta, GA
Overman, William H., P.C. .... Atlanta, GA
Overmann, Michael L. .... Chicago, IL
Overmyer, Jenifer K. .... Hammond, IN
Overmyer, Linda D. .... Southfield, MI
Overn, Michael P. .... New York, NY
Overom, Steven C. .... Duluth, MN
Overpeck, Destie Lee .... San Francisco, CA
Overs, Peter W., Jr. .... New York, NY
Overshiner, George W. .... Fort Worth, TX
Overson, Lyle B., (Ltd.) .... Mankato, MN
Overson, Paul E. .... Minneapolis, MN
Overson, Wesley E., Jr.
San Francisco, CA
Overstreet, Adrian M., Jr. .... Austin, TX
Overstreet, Ann Hurst .... Enid, OK
Overstreet & Associates, P.C.
Alamogordo, NM
Overstreet, Cornele A. .... Phoenix, AZ
Overstreet, David J. .... Minneapolis, MN
Overstreet, David K. .... Mount Vernon, IL
Overstreet, David M., IV .... Fresno, CA
Overstreet, David Matthew
Las Cruces, NM
Overstreet, David R. .... Harrisburg, PA
Overstreet, Dwayne V. .... Kountze, TX
Overstreet, Gary F. .... Los Angeles, CA
Overstreet, J. Carlisle .... Augusta, GA
Overstreet, James S., Jr. .... Jackson, MS
Overstreet, Jesse R., Jr. .... Clarksville, VA
Overstreet, Julie V. .... Owensboro, KY
Overstreet, Karen A. .... Seattle, WA
Overstreet, Kent .... Owensboro, KY
Overstreet, Lana Beth .... Dallas, TX
Overstreet, Marian B. .... Eldorado, TX
Overstreet, Mark R. .... Frankfort, KY
Overstreet, Martin V. .... Vancouver, WA
Overstreet, Mary Marshall .... Clarksville, VA
Overstreet, Miles, Ritch & Cumbie, P.A.
Kissimmee, FL
St. Cloud, FL
Overstreet, Murray .... Kissimmee, FL
Overstreet, Raymond .... Liberty, KY
Overstreet, Rebecca M. .... Lexington, KY
Overstreet, Rhonda L. .... Roanoke, VA
Overstreet, Robert B. .... Versailles, KY
Overstreet, Roy .... Atlanta, GA
Overstreet, S. Thomas .... Alamogordo, NM
Overstreet & Taylor .... Owensboro, KY
Overstreet, Wm. Dean .... Little Rock, AR
Overton, A. L. (Sid) .... Englewood, CO
Overton, Alan D. .... Essex Junction, VT
Overton, Allan G. .... Atlanta, GA
Overton, Amy E. .... Washington, DC
Overton, Babiarz & Sykes, P.C.
Englewood, CO
Overton, Barbara E. .... Miami, FL
Overton, Benjamin F. .... Daytona Beach, FL
Maitland, FL
Overton, Bruce L.
Executive Office Of The President, Office of the U.S. Trade Representative, GV
Overton, Christopher W. P.
Los Angeles, CA
Overton, Dabney, Jr. .... Harrisonburg, VA
Overton, Daniel L. .... Essex Junction, VT
Overton, Elizabeth R. .... Lexington, KY
Overton, Elvin E. .... Knoxville, TN
Overton & Feeley, A Professional Corporation .... Denver, CO
Overton, G. Byron .... Washington, IN
Overton, George R. .... San Jose, CA
Overton, George W. .... Chicago, IL
Overton, George W. .... Philadelphia, PA
Overton, J. Bradley .... Baton Rouge, LA
Overton, Jack A., Jr. .... Clifton Park, NY
Overton, JeanPaul P. .... New Orleans, LA
Overton, Joel M., Jr. .... Dallas, TX
Overton, John B. .... Sausalito, CA
Overton, John W. .... Houston, TX
Overton, John W., Jr. .... Savannah, TN
Overton, John W., The Law Office of, P.C.
Houston, TX
Overton, Julie Burroughs .... Houston, TX
Overton, Kathryn Reichel
Library of Congress, Congressional Research Service, GV
Overton, Larry S. .... Ahoskie, NC
Overton, Leslie .... Washington, DC
Overton, Lyman & Prince, LLP
Los Angeles, CA
Overton, Nelson T. .... Hampton, VA
Overton, Pamela M. .... Phoenix, AZ
Overton, Paul Eugene .... San Diego, CA
Overton, Richard L. .... Baton Rouge, LA
Overton, Russell & Doerr .... Clifton Park, NY
Overton, Sarah L. .... San Bernardino, CA
Overton, Saundra P. .... Baton Rouge, LA
Overton, Shana L. .... Fairfax, VA
Overton, Suellen .... Council Bluffs, IA
Overton, Suellen .... Omaha, NE
Overton, Thomas J. .... Denver, CO
Overton, Thomas K. .... St. Paul, MN
Overton, Thomas Travis .... Nashville, TN
Overton, Todd H. .... Amarillo, TX
Overton, Troy B. .... Redwood City, CA
Overton, W. Jeffrey .... Suffolk, VA
Overton, W. Lee .... Baton Rouge, LA
Overtoom, Douglas L. .... Cherry Hill, NJ
Philadelphia, PA
Overtree, Edward L. .... Houston, TX
Overturf, Judith E. .... Indianapolis, IN
Overturf, Mark C. .... Denver, CO
Overturf, Tad L. .... La Junta, CO
Overzat, Peter K. .... New York, NY
Overzyl, Robert John .... Ventura, CA
Ovesey, Michele M. .... New York, NY
Ovestrud, Richard .... Columbus, OH
Ovey, Glycon L., Jr. .... Eddyville, KY
Ovey & Johnson .... Eddyville, KY
Ovian, Douglas A. .... Enfield, CT
Oviatt, Clark & Gross, L.L.P.
Denver, CO
Wheat Ridge, CO
Oviatt, Clifford R., Jr. .... Washington, DC
Oviatt, Janice P. .... Houston, TX
Oviatt, Jonathan J. .... Rochester, MN
Oviatt, Lincoln P. .... Wooster, OH
Oviatt, Melinda Brooks .... Westlake, OH
Oviatt, Nancy L. .... Watertown, SD
Oviatt, Percival D., Jr. .... Rochester, NY
Oviatt, Richard A. .... Cleveland, OH
Oviatt, Richard B. .... Cleveland, OH
Oviatt, Thad M. .... Wheat Ridge, CO
Ovieda, James G. .... Hacienda Heights, CA
Oviedo, Richard .... Santa Ana, CA
Oviedo, Theresa .... Washington, DC

Oviedo-Reyes, Alfonso ... Miami, FL
Ovington, Gordon G. ... Rockville, MD
Ovington, J. Patrick ... Greenville, SC
Ovington, Mark D. ... Kansas City, MO
Ovington, Sharon L. ... Dayton, OH
Ovink, B. John ... Tampa, FL
Ovits, Eric U. ... Fort Lauderdale, FL
Ovletrea, Shirley W. ... St. Louis, MO
Ovrom, Arthur P. ... Keosauqua, IA
Ovrom, Eliza J. ... Des Moines, IA
Ovrut, Barnett D. ... Boston, MA
Ovsak, Catherine M. ... Minneapolis, MN
Ovsenik, Edward C. ... Midland, MI
Ovson, David F. ... Birmingham, AL
Ovson, Richard G. ... Golden, CO
Owano, Keith R. ... Rockford, IL
Owczarek, Denise Stellmach ... Detroit, MI
Owczarski, John W. ... Washington, DC
Owczarski, Lester A. ... West Bloomfield, MI
Owdom, Bruce A. ... Fresno, CA
Oweis, Merette ... Lakeland, FL
Owel, Daniel L. ... Rockville, MD
Owen, Allan J. ... Sacramento, CA
Owen, Allison MacLeod ... Columbus, OH
Owen, Amanda A. ... Seattle, WA
Owen, Amy Sanborn ... McLean, VA
Owen, Andrew W. ... Columbus, OH
Owen, Anessa Jean ... Washington, DC
Owen, Ann Pearl, (P.S.) ... Seattle, WA
Owen, Anna Hall ... Canon City, CO
Owen, Arlene G.
Research Triangle Park, NC
Owen, Aubrey J. ... Winchester, VA
Owen, B. Erin ... Palos Verdes Estates, CA
Owen, Ben ... Columbus, MS
Owen, Bogart and Rogers ... Bastrop, TX
Elgin, TX
Owen, Borron J., Jr. ... Orlando, FL
Owen & Bradley ... Rialto, CA
Owen, Brent H. ... Des Moines, IA
Owen, Brent M. ... Wethersfield, CT
Owen, Bret C. ... Topeka, KS
Owen, Brian ... Chicago, IL
Owen, Bruce G. ... Decatur, IL
Owen, C. Medferd, Jr. ... Midland, TX
Owen, Carla Rendina ... Chicago, IL
Owen, Caroline M. ... Amherst, NH
Owen, Catherine D. ... Minneapolis, MN
Owen, Charles C., (P.A.) ... Little Rock, AR
Owen, Charles E., II ... Garden City, KS
Owen, Charles E., II, P.A. ... Garden City, KS
Owen, Charles R. ... Richardson, TX
Owen, Christina L. ... Long Beach, CA
Owen, Christopher T. ... New York, NY
Owen, Clyde C., Jr. ... Montgomery, AL
Owen, Constance C. ... Overland Park, KS
Owen, Crawford & Owen
St. Petersburg, FL
Owen, Curtis L. ... Omaha, NE
Owen, D. Adele ... Baton Rouge, LA
Owen, D. Glynne ... Memphis, TN
Owen, D. June ... Gainesville, FL
Owen, D. Ray, Jr. ... Salt Lake City, UT
Owen, Daniel D. ... Overland Park, KS
Kansas City, MO
Owen, Daryl H. ... United States Senate,
Senatorial Assistants, GV
Owen, David ... Columbus, MS
Owen, David ... Montclair, NJ
Owen, David A. ... Lexington, KY
Owen, David B. ... Sherman Oaks, CA
Owen, David B. ... Fort Worth, TX
Owen, David C. ... Palo Alto, CA
Owen, David C. ... Richmond, VA
Owen, David E. ... Covington, TN
Owen, David M. ... Fort Myers, FL
Owen, David M., Jr. ... Orlando, FL
Owen, David R. ... Baltimore, MD
Owen, David R. ... New York, NY
Owen & Davis PC ... New York, NY
Owen, Deborah K. ... Lancaster, PA
Owen, Donald T. ... Concord, MA
Owen, Douglas B. ... Dallas, TX
Owen & Eddy ... White Plains, NY
Owen & Edwards ... Knoxville, TN
Owen, Ellen Gray ... Richmond, VA
Owen, Erin A. ... Los Angeles, CA
Owen, Errol ... Texarkana, TX
Owen Farnell & Garner
Hot Springs National Park, AR
Owen, Frank, Associate, P.C. ... El Paso, TX
Owen, Frank C. ... San Diego, CA
Owen, Frank, III ... El Paso, TX
Owen & Galloway ... Biloxi, MS
Gulfport, MS
Jackson, MS
Owen, Gene V. ... Plainview, TX
Owen, George E. ... Tallahassee, FL
Owen, George E., Jr. ... St. Petersburg, FL
Owen, Gregory N. ... San Francisco, CA
Owen, G. T., III ... Prairieville, LA
Owen, H. Andrew ... Atlanta, GA
Owen, H. Dean, Jr. ... Fort Worth, TX
Owen, H. Martyn ... Brunswick, ME
Owen, H. Rex ... St. Petersburg, FL
Owen, Hank ... Lake Wylie, SC
Owen, Harry Dale ... Jackson, MS
Owen, Harvey & Carter ... Benton, KY
Owen, Heather A. ... Jacksonville, FL
Owen, Irvin ... Shawnee, OK
Owen, J. Worth ... Tallahassee, FL
Owen, Jack B., Jr. ... Palm Beach Gardens, FL
Owen, Jack E., Jr. ... Austin, TX
Owen, Jack F. ... Rhinelander, WI
Owen, Jackie L. ... Medina, OH
Owen, James A. ... Santa Monica, CA
Owen, James C. ... St. Louis, MO
Owen, James C., Jr. ... Griffin, GA
Owen, James H. ... Athens, TX
Owen, James M., Jr. ... Baton Rouge, LA
Owen, James R. ... Bay Minette, AL
Owen, James R. ... Knoxville, TN
Owen, James W. ... Wilmington, DE
Owen, James W., P.A. ... Wilmington, DE
Owen, Janee Shaw ... Waterville, ME
Owen, Jean C. ... Mission, KS
Owen, Jeffrey N. ... Chicago, IL
Owen, Jeffrey R. ... Pittsburgh, PA
Owen, Jeffrey W. ... Redwood City, CA
Owen, Jennifer L. ... Rhinelander, WI
Owen, Jill Casson ... Tucson, AZ
Owen, Jim D. ... Knoxville, TN
Owen, Joe A. ... Benton, KY
Owen, Joe Sam ... Gulfport, MS
Owen, John A. ... Oakland, CA
Owen, John H. ... Albany, NY
Owen, John R. ... Kansas City, MO
Owen, John R. ... Cary, NC
Owen, John R. ... Dallas, TX
Owen, John R., III ... Pittsburgh, PA
Owen, John Ryan ... Richmond, VA
Owen, Jon C. ... Kendallville, IN
Owen, Joseph A. ... Goshen, NY
Owen, Joseph G. ... Goshen, NY
Owen, Joseph Lee ... Birmingham, AL
Owen, Joyce G. ... Wichita, KS
Owen, J. R. ... Taylor, TX
Owen, Judson L., III ... Key Biscayne, FL
Owen, Julie A. ... Miami, FL
Owen, Kathy J. ... Dallas, TX
Owen, Kelley G. ... Pittsburgh, PA
Owen, Kenneth E. ... Los Angeles, CA
Owen, Kimberly B. ... Lexington, KY
Owen, Kip R. ... Chicago, IL
Owen, Lail & McClure ... Memphis, TN
Owen, Langdon T., Jr. ... Salt Lake City, UT
Owen, Laura M. ... San Mateo, CA
Owen, Laura Z. ... Columbia, SC
Owen, Laurie Ann ... Groton, MA
Owen, L. D., III ... Bay Minette, AL
Owen, L. D., III, P.C. ... Bay Minette, AL
Owen, Lea Carol ... Nashville, TN
Owen, Lester W. ... Sylva, NC
Owen, Loretta Cantu ... Victoria, TX
Owen, Louis H., III ... Austin, TX
Owen, Loyd E., Jr. ... Kansas City, MO
Owen, Lyle, Voss & Owen, P.C.
Plainview, TX
Owen, Marc C.
Department of Transportation,
St. Lawrence Seaway Development
Administration, GV
Owen, Marguerite S.
Federal Deposit Insurance Corporation,
Trial Litigation Section, GV
Owen, Marianne Mitten ... Lafayette, IN
Owen, Mark M. ... Worcester, MA
Owen, Mark W., (P.C.) ... Bastrop, TX
Elgin, TX
Owen, Mary E. ... Spokane, WA
Owen, Marye Helen ... Memphis, TN
Owen, Maureen T. ... Indianapolis, IN
Owen & Melbye, A Professional Corporation
Redwood City, CA
Owen, Melinda Belew ... Ventura, CA
Owen, Melville ... San Francisco, CA
Owen, Michael E. ... Tucson, AZ
Owen, Michael G. ... West Chester, PA
Owen, Michael L. ... Los Angeles, CA
Owen, Michael L. ... Chicago, IL
Owen, Michael S. ... Manchester, NH
Owen, Michael W. ... Indianapolis, IN
Owen, Nancy W. ... Mattoon, IL
Owen, Nathan P. ... Chicago, IL
Owen, Norman M. ... Santa Rosa, CA
Owen, P. John ... Kansas City, MO
Owen, Pat ... Louisville, KY
Owen, Patrick H. ... Boise, ID
Owen, Paul R. ... Santa Fe, NM
Owen, Paul W., Jr. ... Columbia, SC
Owen, Peter ...
Department of Justice, GV
Owen & Post, P.C. ... Los Angeles, CA
Rolling Hills, CA
Owen, R. Christopher ... White Plains, NY
Owen, R. Prewitt ... Lexington, KY
Owen, Ray, Jr.
Hot Springs National Park, AR
Owen, Richard ... New York, NY
Owen, Richard B. ... Casselberry, FL
Owen, Richard D. ... Bakersfield, CA
Owen, Richard D. ... Charleston, WV
Owen, Richard W.
Federal Deposit Insurance Corporation,
Resolutions Section, GV
Owen, Rick L. ... Anchorage, AK
Owen, Robert A. ... Rialto, CA
Owen, Robert D. ... New York, NY
Owen, Robert H. ... Atlanta, GA
Owen, Robert H., Jr. ... Middleton, WI
Owen, Robert I. ... Oklahoma City, OK
Owen, Robert J. ... Pembroke Pines, FL
Owen, Robert J., Jr. ... Arlington, VA
Owen, Robert M. ... Decatur, IL
Owen, Robert O. ... Costa Mesa, CA
Owen, Roberts B. ... Washington, DC
Owen, Ronald E. ... Santa Ana, CA
Owen, Ronald M. ... Jacksonville, FL
Owen, Rosaria Vivo ... Chicago, IL
Owen, Rudd F. ... Plainview, TX
Owen, Sally T. ... Quincy, MA
Owen, Samuel J. ... Golden, CO
Owen, Samuel J., P.C. ... Golden, CO
Owen, Sandra D. ... Seattle, WA
Owen, Scott M. ... Houston, TX
Owen, Stanford B. ... Salt Lake City, UT
Owen, Stephen F., Jr. ... Washington, DC
Falls Church, VA
Owen, Stephen L. ... Washington, DC
Baltimore, MD
Owen, Stephen R. ... Portland, OR
Owen, Stephen T. ... Arlington, VA
Owen, Steve C. ... New York, NY
Owen, Steven A. ... Fort Worth, TX
Owen, Steven L. ... Paoli, IN
Owen, Steven L. ... Lansing, MI
Owen, Steven P. ... Los Angeles, CA
Owen, Steven S. ... San Diego, CA
Owen, Sylvia S. ... Tupelo, MS
Owen, T. Alan ... Arlington, TX
Owen, Tammy J. ... Charleston, WV
Owen, Thomas E. ... Bloomfield Hills, MI
Owen, Thomas H., Jr. ... Houston, TX
Owen, Thomas J. ... San Francisco, CA
Owen, Thomas R. ... Neenah, WI
Owen, Timothy R. ... Rolling Hills, CA
Owen, Trevor B. ... New York, NY
Owen & Truban ... Winchester, VA
Owen, Vance J. ... Corpus Christi, TX
Owen, Victoria Combs ... Midway, KY
Owen, W. James ... Dayton, OH
Owen, W. Joseph, III ... Richmond, VA
Owen, Wickersham & Erickson, A Professional Corporation
Menlo Park, CA
San Francisco, CA
Owen, William B. ... Brentwood, TN
Owen, William C. ... Tallahassee, FL
Owen, William C., Jr. ... West Palm Beach, FL
Owen, William E., Jr. ... Corpus Christi, TX
Owen, William H. ... Redwood City, CA
Owen, William J. ... Sacramento, CA
Owen, William J. ... Columbus, OH
Owen, William L. ... Little Rock, AR
Owen, William L. ... Lonoke, AR
Owen, William L. ... Sacramento, CA
Owen, William L. ... Altamonte Springs, FL
Owenby, Ruth L. ... West Covina, CA
Owendoff, Michael S. ... Cleveland, OH
Owendoff, Stephen P. ... Cleveland, OH
Owens, A. Anne ... Bartow, FL
Owens, A. Dean ... Eugene, OR
Owens, A. Douglas ... Baltimore, MD
Owens, A. Dow ... Pulaski, VA
Owens, Alan P. ... Norfolk, VA
Owens & Almond, LLP ... Birmingham, AL
Tuscaloosa, AL
Owens, Alvarene N. ... Dayton, OH
Owens, Alvarene N., Co., L.P.A.
Dayton, OH
Owens, André E. ... Washington, DC
Owens, Andrew D., Jr. ... Sarasota, FL
Owens, Andrew G., Jr. ... Los Angeles, CA
Owens, Andrew H. ... Memphis, TN
Owens, Angela Pergrem ... Richmond, KY
Owens, Angela R. ... Houston, TX
Owens, Ann H. ... Hartford, CT
Owens, Arthur F. ... Des Moines, IA
Owens & Associates of Illinois, P.C.
Chicago, IL
Owens, Audrey G. ... Upland, CA
Owens, B. Shea ... New York, NY
Owens & Beck ... Pensacola, FL
Owens, Bernard C. ... Scottsdale, AZ
Owens, Betty R. ... Houston, TX
Owens, Beverly Ray ... Memphis, TN
Owens, Bevin C. ... Albuquerque, NM
Owens, Bill A. ... South Pasadena, CA
Owens, B. J. ... Melbourne, FL
Owens, Bob ... Jackson, MS
Owens, Bobby D. ... Bentonville, AR
Owens, Bradley D. ... Anchorage, AK
Owens, Bradley T. ... Phoenix, AZ
Owens, Brent A. ... Gainesville, FL
Owens, Brenton C. ... Cherry Hill, NJ
Owens, Bruce R. ... Globe, AZ
Owens, Bryce D. ... Pendleton, IN
Owens, C. Camille ... Dallas, TX
Owens, C. Philip ... Newport, TN
Owens, Carol Elizabeth ... Rochester, NY
Owens, Carolyn Richardson
Los Angeles, CA
Owens, Carroll L. ... Benton, IL
Owens, C. D., Jr. ... Scottsdale, AZ
Owens, Charles L. ... Oklahoma City, OK
Owens, Charles W. ... Durango, CO
Owens, Cherry ... Lexington, KY
Owens, Chris A. ... Towson, MD
Owens, Christine L. ... Takoma Park, MD
Owens, Clark V., II ... Wichita, KS
Owens, Clary & Aiken, L.L.P. ... Dallas, TX
Owens, Claude M. ... Santa Ana, CA
Owens, Clifton G. ... Milwaukee, WI
Owens, Collins L., Jr. ... Newport News, VA
Owens, D'Ambrosio & Nescio
West Chester, PA
Owens, Dan L. ... Louisville, KY
Owens, Daniel L. ... Oklahoma City, OK
Owens, Darrow A. ... Indianapolis, IN
Owens, Darryl T. ... Louisville, KY
Owens, David ... New York, NY
Owens, David F. ... Brooklyn, NY
Owens, David J. ... Houston, TX
Owens, David L. ... Rochester, NY
Owens, David Lynn ... Columbus, OH
Owens, David R. ... Palo Alto, CA
Owens, David R. ... Walnut Creek, CA
Owens, David W. ... Chapel Hill, NC
Owens Davies Mackie, P.S., A Professional Services Corporation ... Olympia, WA
Owens, Deborah Ann ... Atlanta, GA
Owens, Deborah Karazin ... New York, NY
Owens, Deborah W. ... Hinsdale, IL
Owens, Deke Slayton ... Jacksonville, NC
Owens, Delia R. ... Jackson, MS
Owens, Denis J. ... Park Ridge, IL
Owens, Dennis G. ... Longview, WA
Owens, Dennis J. C. ... Kansas City, MO
Owens, Dennis N. ... Indianapolis, IN
Owens, Don G., III ... Memphis, TN
Owens, Don G., Jr. ... Memphis, TN
Owens, Donald G. ... Richmond, VA
Owens, Donald Patrick ... Dallas, TX
Owens, Donald S. ... Lansing, MI
Owens, Dorothy S. ... Austin, TX
Owens, Douglas P. ... Anacortes, WA
Owens, Edward J. ... Lowell, MA
Owens, Edward L. ... Flowery Branch, GA
Owens, Edward M. ... Pine Bluff, AR
Owens, Elisabeth P. ... San Francisco, CA
Owens, Ella U. ... Boerne, TX
Owens, Ellen M. ... Little Rock, AR
Owens, Evan L. ... Benton, IL
Owens, F. Herbert, III ... Cherry Hill, NJ
Owens, F. Joseph, Jr. ... New York, NY
Owens, Floyd Wesley ... Tulsa, OK
Owens, Frank J. ... Olympia, WA
Owens, Frederick J. ... Wilmington, NC
Owens, G. Douglass ... Pendleton, IN
Owens & Gach Ray ... Los Angeles, CA
Owens, Garry D. ... Currituck, NC
Owens, Gary E. ... Blue Springs, MO
Owens, Gary R. ... Philadelphia, PA
Owens, George W. ... Tulsa, OK
Owens, Gerald D. ... Benton, IL
Owens, Gerald T. ... Carmel Valley, CA
Owens, Gregg L. ... Spirit Lake, IA
Owens, Gregory M. ... New York, NY
Owens, H. Douglas ... Salt Lake City, UT
Owens, Henry F., III ... Boston, MA
Owens, Hewson L. ... Charlotte, NC
Owens, Hewson L., P.A. ... Charlotte, NC
Owens, Hollis M., Jr. ... Rutherfordton, NC
Owens, Howell C. ... Houston, TX
Owens, Hubert F. ... Big Canoe, GA
Owens, Irmina Rivero ... Atlanta, GA
Owens, J. Andrew ... Rome, GA
Owens, J. Bentley, III ... Birmingham, AL
Owens, J. David ... Ann Arbor, MI
Owens, J. Kevin ... Spartanburg, SC
Owens, J. Robert ... Atlanta, GA
Owens, J. Sam, Jr. ... Daytona Beach, FL
Owens, Jack ... El Paso, TX
Owens, Jack B. ... Modesto, CA
Owens, Jack F., Jr. ... Harrisonburg, LA
Owens, Jacqueline A. ... Albany, NY
Owens, James D. ... Benkelman, NE
Owens, James Franklin ... Los Angeles, CA
Owens, James J. ... Agoura Hills, CA
Owens, James J. ... Grand Rapids, MI
Owens, James J., Law Offices of
Albuquerque, NM
Taos, NM
Taos, NM
Owens, James M. ... Chico, CA
Owens, James M. ... Los Angeles, CA
Owens, James S., Jr. ... Atlanta, GA
Owens, James T. ... West Chester, PA
Owens, James W. ... Paducah, KY
Owens, James W. ... Chattanooga, TN
Owens, James W. ... Casper, WY
Owens, James W., Chartered
Mayfield, KY
Paducah, KY
Owens, James W., Jr. ... Cheyenne, WY
Owens, Jane E. ... Scottsdale, AZ
Owens, Jane S. ... Olney, MD
Owens, Jeffrey R. ... Cherry Hill, NJ
Owens, Jene William, Jr. ... Mobile, AL
Owens, Jennifer ... Austin, TX
Owens, Jerome P., Jr. ... Woodville, TX
Owens, Jerrolyn M. ... Jackson, MS
Owens, Jerry H. ... Pittsburgh, PA
Owens, Jill C. ... New York, NY
Owens, Joel P. ... Azle, TX
Owens, John A. ... Tuscaloosa, AL
Owens, John E. ... Santa Fe, NM
Owens, John E., Jr. ... Park Ridge, IL
Owens, John Jay ... Cleveland, OH
Owens, John Linwood ... Erdenheim, PA
Owens, John R. ... Indianapolis, IN
Owens, John R., Jr. ... Clearwater, FL
Owens, John V. ... Park Ridge, IL
Owens, John W. ... Houston, TX
Owens, Jon Nathan ... Irvine, CA
Owens, Jonathan M. ... Washington, DC
Owens, Jonathan O. ... Palo Alto, CA
Owens, Joseph C. ... Los Angeles, CA
Owens, Joseph C. ... Chicago, IL
Owens, Joseph C., P.C. ... Chicago, IL
Owens, Joseph E. ... Rockville, MD
Owens, Joseph F. ... New Berlin, WI
Owens, Joseph H. ... Washington, DC
Owens, Joseph H., Jr. ... Washington, DC
Owens, Judith L. ... Benkelman, NE
Owens, Karen Carter ... Phoenix, AZ
Owens, Katherine Leigh ... Tuscaloosa, AL
Owens, Kathy Gear ... Hampton, VA
Owens, Kathy Gear ... Newport News, VA
Owens, Kenneth D. ... Austin, TX
Owens, Kermit P. ... Spokane, WA
Owens, Kerry H. ... Washington, DC
Towson, MD
Owens, Kerry L. ... Austin, TX
Fort Worth, TX
Houston, TX
Owens, Kerry L. ... Salt Lake City, UT
Owens, Kevin G. ... Chicago, IL
Owens, Kevin Mitchel ... Washington, DC
Owens, Kimberly A. ... Juneau, AK
Owens, Kimberly Anne ... Chicago, IL
New York, NY

Owens, Kimberly Sipes ... Charlotte, NC
Owens, L. Dale ... Atlanta, GA
Owens, Laura Lewis ... Atlanta, GA
Owens, Laurel D. ... Huntsville, TX
Owens Law Firm ... Jackson, MS
Owens Law Firm, The, P.C. ... Tulsa, OK
Owens, Lee Ryan ... Austin, TX
Fort Worth, TX
Houston, TX
Owens, Leroy Scott ... Minneapolis, MN
Owens, Lori A. ... Chicago, IL
Owens, Luke C. ... Buffalo, NY
Owens, Lynn L. ... Philadelphia, PA
Owens, M. Diane ... Atlanta, GA
Owens, M. Edward, Jr. ... Knoxville, TN
Owens & Manning ... Coshocton, OH
Owens, Margaret A. ... Treasury Department, Internal Revenue Service, GV
Owens, Margaret Ann ... Needham, MA
Owens, Margaret W. ... Oklahoma City, OK
Owens, Mark D. ... Bakersfield, CA
Owens, Mark D. ... Odessa, TX
Owens, Mark E. ... Canton, OH
Owens, Mark E. ... Dayton, OH
Owens, Mark, Jr. ... San Francisco, CA
Owens, Mark W. ... Sacramento, CA
Owens, Mark W., III ... Greenville, NC
Owens, Mark W., Jr. ... Farmville, NC
Greenville, NC
Owens, Martha D. ... Chicago, IL
Owens, Mary ... Grand Rapids, MI
Owens, Mary Burkey ... Richmond, VA
Owens, Matthew L. ... Harrisburg, PA
Owens, Melvin J. ... Phoenix, AZ
Owens, Michael J. ... Boston, MA
Owens, Michael J. ... Aurora, NE
Owens, Michael R. ... Charleston, SC
Owens, Mitchell N. ... Jacksonville, FL
Owens and Moore ... Wilmington, NC
Owens, Myles A. ... Houston, TX
Owens, N. Todd ... Charlotte, NC
Owens, Nancy J. ... Rockland, MA
Owens, Nathaniel D. ... Anniston, AL
Owens & Owens ... Oxnard, CA
Owens and Owens ... Benton, IL
Owens & Owens ... Brenkelman, NE
Owens and Owens ... Memphis, TN
Owens, Owens & Rinn, Ltd. ... Chicago, IL
Park Ridge, IL
Owens, Pamela Claire ... Redding, CA
Owens, Patrick D. ... Park Ridge, IL
Owens, Paul D., Jr. ... Brewton, AL
Owens & Perkins, P.C. ... Scottsdale, AZ
Owens, Philip G. ... Louisville, KY
Owens, Philip M. ... Irvine, KY
Owens, Philip W. ... Washington, DC
Owens, Phillip P., II ... Oklahoma City, OK
Owens & Pyper, P.L.C. ... Phoenix, AZ
Owens, R. Bruce ... Coeur d'Alene, ID
Owens, R. Kevin ... San Luis Obispo, CA
Owens, R. Michael ... Wayne, PA
Owens, R. Vann ... Signal Mountain, TN
Owens, Randall C. ... Houston, TX
Owens, Randall W. ... Omaha, NE
Owens, Raymond E., Jr. ... Charlotte, NC
Owens, Raymond L. ... Rochester, NY
Owens, Richard C. ... Department of Justice, Criminal Division, GV
Owens, Richard J. ... Chicago, IL
Owens, Richard P. ... Boston, MA
Owens, Richard S., III ... Wilmington, NC
Owens, Robert A. ... Oxnard, CA
Owens, Robert B. ... Los Angeles, CA
Owens, Robert C. ... Coral Gables, FL
Owens, Robert E., Jr. ... Cincinnati, OH
Owens, Robert F. ... St. George, UT
Owens, Robert J. ... Boston, MA
Owens, Robert John ... Garden City, NY
Owens, Robert L. ... Dallas, TX
Owens, Robert M. ... Columbus, OH
Owens, Robert P. ... Anchorage, AK
Owens, Robert P. ... Department of Justice, Executive Office for Immigration Review, GV
Owens, Robert T. ... Santa Clara, CA
Owens, Robert W., Jr. ... Minneapolis, MN
Owens & Robertson, P.A. ... Baltimore, MD
Owens, Robyn ... Tulsa, OK
Owens, Rock W. A. ... Houston, TX
Owens, Rodney J. ... Dallas, TX
Owens, Rodney Parker ... Bentonville, AR
Owens, Roger P. ... Des Moines, IA
Owens, Ross Collins, III ... Cincinnati, OH
Owens, Rouse & Nelson, PLLC
Farmville, NC
Greenville, NC
Owens, Schine & Nicola, P.C.
Bridgeport, CT
Fairfield, CT
Trumbull, CT
Owens, Sheila A. ... Chicago, IL
Owens, Stephen H. ... Evansville, IN
Owens, Stephen J. ... Kansas City, MO
Owens, Stephen T. ... Los Angeles, CA
Owens, Stephen W. ... Calistoga, CA
Salt Lake City, UT
Owens, Steve ... Phoenix, AZ
Owens, Steven R. ... Sedona, AZ
Owens, Steven S. ... Las Vegas, NV
Owens, Susan Brown ... St. Louis, MO
Owens, Susan J. ... Forks, WA
Owens, Tench P. ... Clinton, SC
Owens, Terry J. ... Department of Commerce, Patent and Trademark Office, GV
Owens, Terry R. ... Dallas, TX
Owens, Terryn D. ... Raleigh, NC
Owens, Thaddeus E. ... Brooklyn, NY
Owens, Theodore E ... Newport Beach, CA
Owens, Theresa R. ... San Francisco, CA
Owens, Thomas C. ... Overland Park, KS
Owens, Thomas F. ... Port Jefferson, NY
Owens, Thomas J. ... Seattle, WA
Owens, Thomas L. ... Minneapolis, MN
Owens, Thomas M. ... Albany, NY
Owens, Thomas P., III ... Anchorage, AK
Owens, Thomas P., Jr. ... Anchorage, AK
Owens, Thomas R. ... San Francisco, CA
Owens, Thomas R. ... Lubbock, TX
Owens, Thomas W. ... Philadelphia, PA
Owens, Timothy J. ... Columbus, OH
Owens, Tony ... Arlington, TX
Owens & Turner, A Professional Corporation
Anchorage, AK
Owens, V. Jean ... Ruskin, FL
St. Petersburg, FL
Tampa, FL
Owens, W. Dean ... Salina, KS
Owens, W. Lance ... Jonesboro, AR
Owens, Walter R., Jr. ... Dallas, TX
Owens, Wendy S. ... Casper, WY
Owens, Wilbur D., III ... Savannah, GA
Owens, Willard P. ... Bethesda, MD
Owens, William B. ... Alexandria, LA
Owens, William B., Jr. ... Austin, TX
Owens, William C., Jr. ... San Antonio, TX
Owens, William H. ... Baltimore, MD
Owens, William H., Jr. ... Washington, DC
Owens, William L. ... Naples, FL
Owens, William L. ... Plattsburgh, NY
Owens, William Leon ... Sacramento, CA
Owens, William Leon, Law Office of
Sacramento, CA
Owens, William M. ... Coshocton, OH
Owens, William Robert, Jr. ... Walhalla, SC
Owens, William S. ... Ottumwa, IA
Owens, William W. ... Norwalk, OH
Owens, Windell C. ... Monroeville, AL
Owens, Wroe ... Austin, TX
Owens, Xanath ... Los Angeles, CA
Owens, Yvonne ... Chicago, IL
Owensby, J. Richard ... Springfield, MO
Owensby, Jeffery ... Sacramento, CA
Owensby, Lois ... Pasadena, CA
Owensby, Tracy ... Sacramento, CA
Owen-Sherr, Maria Christina, M.D.
Hurst, TX
Owens-Ruff, Tina ... Marysville, OH
Owers, James E. ... Concord, NH
Owings, Alfred J. ... Richmond, VA
Owings, Alice G. ... Chicago, IL
Owings, Benjamin T. ... Louisville, KY
Owings, Karen J. ... Little Rock, AR
Owings, Randal J. ... Columbia, MO
Owings, Steven A. ... Little Rock, AR
Owings, William A. ... Little Rock, AR
Owings, William D. ... Centreville, AL
Owlett, Edward H. ... Elkland, PA
Knoxville, PA
Wellsboro, PA
Owlett, Edward H., III ... Wellsboro, PA
Owlett & Lewis, P.C. ... Elkland, PA
Knoxville, PA
Wellsboro, PA
Owlett, Thomas M. ... Wellsboro, PA
Ownbey, Amos B. ... Denver, CO
Ownbey, Lloyd C., Jr. ... Los Angeles, CA
Ownbey, Lloyd C., Jr. ... Pasadena, CA
Ownbey, Nancy E. ... Albuquerque, NM
Ownby, Ashley L. ... Cleveland, TN
Ownby, Edward C. ... Marietta, GA
Ownby, Gordon Lee, Jr. ... Knoxville, TN
Ownby, Gordon T. ... Los Angeles, CA
Ownby, Jere Franklin ... Knoxville, TN
Owoc, Vincent J. ... Davie, FL
Owoc, Vincent J., P.A. ... Davie, FL
Owren, Gilbert E. ... Summit, NJ
Owren, Turid L. ... Portland, OR
Owsen, John D. ... Irving, TX
Owsen, John D., P.C. ... Irving, TX
Owsiany, Michael J. ... Grosse Pointe, MI
Owsiany, Robert M. ... Pittsburgh, PA
Owsley, Alvin ... Houston, TX
Owsley, Arvid ... Kansas City, MO
Owsley & Associates ... Houston, TX
Owsley, Jason W. ... West Palm Beach, FL
Owsley, Jonathan H. ... Boston, MA
Owsley, Lisa Suzanne ... Newton, NC
Owsley, Mark D. ... Talladega, AL
Owsley, Michael A. ... Bowling Green, KY
Owsley, Robert ... New Orleans, LA
Owsley, Sheila ... Houston, TX
Owsley, Steven A. ... Houston, TX
Owsley, Thomas L. ... Baltimore, MD
Owsley, William B. ... Lexington, KY
Owusu, Frederick K. ... St. Paul, MN
Owyang, Albert D. ... Alameda, CA
Owyang, Emmeline Kim ... Boston, MA
Owyang, Raymond ... San Francisco, CA
Owyang, Steven C. ... San Francisco, CA
Oxamendi, Miguel ... Tallahassee, FL
Oxandale, Richard E. ... Topeka, KS
Oxberger, Leo E. ... Des Moines, IA
Oxborough, Sharon K. ... Los Angeles, CA
Oxenberg, Arthur D. ... New York, NY
Oxenberg, Jonathan J. ... Forest Hills, NY
Oxenburg, Barry H. ... Philadelphia, PA
Oxenburg & Franzel ... Philadelphia, PA
Oxendine & Associates, P.C. ... Snellville, GA
Oxendine, Henry W. ... Pembroke, NC
Oxendine, James W. ... Lawrenceville, GA
Oxendine, John W. ... Snellville, GA
Oxendine, Lee W. ... Snellville, GA
Oxendine, Robert H. ... Tampa, FL
Oxendine, Selene R. ... Tampa, FL
Oxenford, David D. ... Washington, DC
Oxenham, J. Preston ... Denver, CO
Oxenham, Thomas H., III ... Staunton, VA
Oxenham, Thomas H., Jr. ... Richmond, VA
Oxenhandler, Gary ... Columbia, MO
Oxfeld, Eric J. ... Washington, DC
Oxfeld, Nancy Iris ... Newark, NJ
Oxfeld, Sanford R. ... Newark, NJ
Oxford, Alan James, II ... Tahlequah, OK
Oxford, Brinkley L. ... Edinburg, TX
Oxford, Clifford ... Atlanta, GA
Oxford, David A. ... East Hampton, NY
Oxford, Gregory R. ... Los Angeles, CA
Oxford, Hubert, III ... Beaumont, TX
Oxford, Judy A. ... Franklin, TN
Oxford, Lamar D. ... Orlando, FL
Oxford, Larry B. ... San Antonio, TX
Oxford, Oxford & González ... Edinburg, TX
Oxford, Patrick C. ... Houston, TX
Oxford, R. Bradley ... San Antonio, TX
Oxford, Roderick L. ... Houston, TX
Oxford, Terrell W., (P.C.) ... Dallas, TX
Oxford, William H. ... Stephenville, TX
Oxholm, Carl (Tobey), III
Philadelphia, PA
Oxholm-Uribe, José M. ... New York, NY
Oxhorn, Melanie L. ... New York, NY
Oxley, A. Winston ... Dallas, TX
Oxley, Anthony W., III ... Atlanta, GA
Oxley, Dana L. ... Cedar Rapids, IA
Oxley, Elizabeth Lerch ... Raleigh, NC
Oxley, Joel M. ... San Antonio, TX
Oxley, John L. ... Madisonville, TX
Oxley, Laura L. ... Rumson, NJ
Oxley, Leon K. ... Huntington, WV
Oxley, Lisa B. ... Los Angeles, CA
Oxley, Malone, Fitzgerald & Hollister
Findlay, OH
Oxley, Maureen ... Detroit, MI
Oxley, Perry W. ... Huntington, WV
Oxley, Scott G. ... Dayton, OH
Oxley, Suzanne McGinnis
Huntington, WV
Oxley, Timothy J. ... Chicago, IL
Oxley, Warren G. ... Davenport, IA
Oxley, William T. ... Ashland, OH
Oxley, William W. ... Los Angeles, CA
Oxman, Bernard
Treasury Department, GV
Oxman, David C. ... New York, NY
Oxman Geiger Natale & Tulis, P.C.
Hawthorne, NY
New York, NY
White Plains, NY
Oxman, Harry J. ... Bensalem, PA
Philadelphia, PA
Oxman, Irving I. ... Denver, CO
Oxman and Jaroscak ... Santa Fe Springs, CA
Oxman, Jason D.
Federal Communications Commission, Office of Plans and Policy, GV
Oxman, Jon S. ... Auburn, ME
Oxman, Levitan, Goodstadt & Krevitz, A Prof. Corp. ... Voorhees, NJ
Bensalem, PA
Philadelphia, PA
Oxman, Marc S. ... Hawthorne, NY
Oxman, Michael ... New York, NY
Oxman, Michelle L. ... Tallahassee, FL
Oxman & Oxman, P.C. ... Denver, CO
Oxman, Peter M. ... Houston, TX
Oxman, Stephen A. ... Short Hills, NJ
Oxman, Stephen E. ... Denver, CO
Oxman, Thomas K. ... San Francisco, CA
Oxner, G. Dewey, Jr. ... Greenville, SC
Oxner, J. Carlisle, Jr. ... Columbia, SC
Oxner, Todd P. ... Greensboro, NC
Oxner, Vallerie ... Metairie, LA
Oxtoby, Robert B. ... Springfield, IL
Oxton, Charles M. ... Santa Barbara, CA
Oxton, Glen T. ... New York, NY
Oyakawa, Denis H. ... Los Angeles, CA
Oyama, James T. ... Aiea, HI
Oyarzo, Edwin M., III ... San Francisco, CA
Oyaski, Paul F. ... Euclid, OH
Oye, Ronald A. ... Santa Clara, CA
Oyebolu, Olusola ... New York, NY
Oyen, Kendra M. ... Grand Junction, CO
Oyen, Nancy G. ... Phoenix, AZ
Oyen, Sigvald B. ... Montevideo, MN
Oyer, Barbara J. ... Lansing, MI
Oyer, Clinton C. ... Arcadia, CA
Oyer, Eve H. ... Concord, NH
Oyer, Harvey E., III
West Palm Beach, FL
Oyer, Jay H. ... Madison, NJ
Oyer, Roselee M. ... Golden, CO
Oyer, Sarah E. ... Seattle, WA
Oyer, Timothy J. ... Boston, MA
Oyewole, G. Godwin ... Washington, DC
Oygard, Susan C. ... Springfield, MA
Oyler, Caroline Miller ... Louisville, KY
Oyler, Connolly ... Santa Monica, CA
Oyler, Daniel M. ... Louisville, KY
Oyler, Donald G. ... Gettysburg, PA
Oyler, Gregory K. ... Washington, DC
Oyler, John S. ... Harrisburg, PA
Oyler, Karen Clark ... Gettysburg, PA
Oyler, Mac ... Oklahoma City, OK
Oyler, Michael W. ... Louisville, KY
Oyler & Pauzauskie ... Topeka, KS
Kansas City, MO
Oyler, Ralph D. ... Gettysburg, PA
Oyler, Randall L. ... Chicago, IL
Oyler, Stanley E. ... Topeka, KS
Oyler, Theodore T., III
Colorado Springs, CO
Oyler, W. Tedd ... Whitmore Lake, MI
Oyos, Martin ... Sioux Falls, SD
Oyster, Elizabeth J. ... Becker, MN
Oyster, James L. ... Castleton, VA
Oz, Ernest C. ... Dearborn, MI
Ozaki, DeAnne H. ... Los Angeles, CA
Ozalas & McKinley ... Jim Thorpe, PA
Ozalas, Michael L. ... Jim Thorpe, PA
Ozan, Gerald M. ... Euclid, OH
Ozan, Gerald M., Co., L.P.A. ... Euclid, OH
Ozanne, Brendan K. ... San Diego, CA
Ozanne, Dominic L. ... Cleveland, OH
Ozanne, Ismael R. ... Madison, WI
Ozanne, Peter A. ... Portland, OR
Ozar, I. I. ... Kansas City, MO
Ozark, Damian M. ... Bradenton, FL
Ozark & Pierce, P.A. ... Bradenton, FL
Ozarow, Alan ... Livingston, NJ
Ozaruk, Bohdan S. ... New York, NY
Ozawa, Steve H. ... Lakewood, CO
Ozbirn, David W. ... Dallas, TX
Ozbolt, Anthony C. ... San Bernardino, CA
Ozburn, Christopher J. ... Austin, TX
Ozburn, Julie L. ... Daytona Beach, FL
Ozburn, Renee A. ... Lansing, MI
Ozburn, Samuel D. ... Covington, GA
Ozcomert, Stephen M. ... Decatur, GA
Ozcomert, Stephen M., P.C. ... Decatur, GA
Özdögan, M. Catherine ... Houston, TX
Ozell, Robert M. ... Los Angeles, CA
Ozello, Frank J., Jr. ... Los Angeles, CA
Ozenberger, Laura L. ... Westwood, KS
Ozenberger, Lawrence ... New Orleans, LA
Ozer, Cem ... New York, NY
Ozer, Erika Leigh ... Boston, MA
New York, NY
Ozer, Irwin S. ... Germantown, MD
Ozer, Marilyn G. ... Chapel Hill, NC
Ozer, Renee C ... Denver, CO
Ozer, Robert C. ... Denver, CO
Ozer, Ron ... Mesa, AZ
Ozeran, David J. ... Los Angeles, CA
Ozerden, Halil S. ... Gulfport, MS
Ozeroff, Antonia ... Denver, CO
Ozeroff, Christopher D. ... Broomfield, CO
Ozeroff, Myfanwy J. ... Palo Alto, CA
Ozete, Andrew C. ... Evansville, IN
Ozga, Martin J. ... Des Moines, IA
Ozga, Patricia Ann ... Marlton, NJ
Ozgu, Murat ... Washington, DC
Ozhekim, Greg ... Sherman Oaks, CA
Ozias, Charles, Jr. ... Denver, CO
Ozias, Teresa ... Dallas, OR
Oziel, Robert I. ... New York, NY
Ozier, Charles T. ... Jackson, MS
Ozier, William N. ... Nashville, TN
Ozimkowski, Lester E. ... Great Neck, NY
Ozinga, Lepore, Campbell & Lord
Evergreen Park, IL
Ozinga, Martin G. ... Oklahoma City, OK
Ozkan, Lisa Marie Sotir ... Dayton, OH
Ozlu, John A. ... Washington, DC
Ozman, Brandon ... Walden, NY
Ozment, J. Franklin ... Birmingham, AL
Ozment, Kenneth Drake
Fort Lauderdale, FL
Ozment, Sarah Arnott ... Emigrant, MT
Ozmint, Jonathan Edward ... Columbia, SC
Ozmint, Lee T. ... Gadsden, AL
Ozmon, Laird M. ... Joliet, IL
Ozmon, Laird M., Ltd. ... Joliet, IL
Ozmon, Nat P. ... Chicago, IL
Ozmun, Elizabeth Collum ... Austin, TX
Ozmun, Kent F. ... Grove City, OH
Ozmun, Richard R. ... Department of the Navy, Office of the Judge Advocate General, GV
Ozmun, Scott A. ... Austin, TX
Ozoa, Teresa F. ... Irvine, CA
Ozog, Ann M. ... Caro, MI
Ozog, Edward J. ... Chicago, IL
Ozog, James W. ... Downers Grove, IL
Ozol, James R. ... Toms River, NJ
Ozols, Andra C. ... Denver, CO
Ozone, Reem Elias ... Dedham, MA
Ozorowski, Edward J. ... Harleysville, PA
Ozowski, Richard M. ... Dallas, TX
Oztan, Omer ... New York, NY
Ozuna, Alan Troy ... Weslaco, TX
Ozur, Miriam D. ... Department of Labor, Office of the Solicitor, GV
Ozzard, William E. ... Bridgewater, NJ
Ozzello, Mark A. ... Los Angeles, CA
Ozzi, Wayne M. ... Staten Island, NY

Paajanen, Reynold A. ... Warren, OH
Paalborg, Andrew M. ... Memphis, TN
Paape, Jeffrey Dean ... La Mesa, CA
Paar, Christopher R. ... Dubuque, IA
Paar, James S. ... Commack, NY
Paar, Louis H. ... Canton, OH
Paarlberg, Russell T. ... South Holland, IL
Paarz, Master & Koernig ... Haddonfield, NJ
Pleasantville, NJ
Paarz, Robert E. ... Haddonfield, NJ
Pleasantville, NJ
Paasch, Michael A. ... Orlando, FL
Paasch, Rod J. ... Nederland, TX
Paasch, William E., Jr. ... St. Louis, MO
Paasche, Franz W. ... Rye Brook, NY
Paavola, Samuel H. ... Annapolis, MD
Pabarcus, William N. ... La Jolla, CA
Pabarue, James A. A., Jr.
Philadelphia, PA
Paben, Mark Charles ... Seattle, WA
Pabian, Brian ... West Palm Beach, FL
Pabian, Ilene Linda ... Miami, FL
Pabian, Jay M. ... Boston, MA
Pabian, Michael S. ... Hoffman Estates, IL
Pabis, Ronald J. ... Washington, DC
Pablo, Christopher G. ... Honolulu, HI

Pacula, E. Scott .... **Orlando, FL**
Pacun, Norman .... Chatham, MA
Pac-urar, Mary Lynn .... Canton, OH
Pacyga, Joseph S. .... Brighton, CO
Pacynski, Rick .... Taylor, MI
Paczak, Susan .... **Pittsburgh, PA**
Paczelt, Anna Elizabeth .... Austintown, OH
Paczesny, Elizabeth A. .... Ontonagon, MI
Pazier, Aladar E., (P.A.) .... Key Largo, FL
Paczkowski, John F. .... Dracut, MA
Paczosa, Dorothy J. .... Fairfax, VA
Padamadan, Michelle T. .... Akron, OH
Padams, Allison K. .... Department of Labor, Pension and Welfare Benefits, GV
Padawer, Joseph .... Lake Mary, FL
Padberg, Godfrey P. .... **St. Louis, MO**
Padberg, Jean E. .... Atlanta, GA
Padberg Law Firm, The .... **St. Louis, MO**
Padberg, Matthew J. .... **St. Louis, MO**
Padda, Darshpaul S. .... Department of Justice, Civil Division, GV
Padden, Amy L. .... **Denver, CO**
Padden & Associates .... St. Paul, MN
Padden, Daniel G. .... **Cambridge, OH**
Padden, Edward M. .... Franklin, MA
Padden, Jeff C. .... **Phoenix, AZ**
Padden, Mary Louise .... **Louisville, KY**
Padden, Michael B. .... St. Paul, MN
Padden, Michael P. .... **Chicago, IL**
Padden, Richard J. .... **Seattle, WA**
Padden, Ted J. .... Erie, PA
Padden, Timothy J. .... **Morgantown, WV**
Paddison, David R. .... Covington, LA
Paddison, Fletcher W. .... **San Diego, CA**
Paddison, Jane I. .... **Denver, CO**
Paddleford, James H. .... Oklahoma City, OK
Paddock, Anthony C. .... New York, NY
Paddock, Barbara L. Department of the Navy, GV
Paddock, Brian .... Oak Ridge, TN
Paddock, David S. .... Rockford, IL
Paddock, Edward M. .... Northville, MI
Paddock, Harold D., III .... Columbus, OH
Paddock, James W. .... Lawrence, KS
Paddock, John A. G. .... Louisville, KY
Paddock, John R., Jr. .... **Denver, CO**
Paddock, Laurie Scott .... Denver, CO
Paddock, Lisa .... Cape May Court House, NJ
Paddock, Michael B. .... Fort Worth, TX
Paddock, Mona A. .... Bloomfield, IN
Paddock, Robert .... **Houston, TX**
Paddock, Robert B. .... Tulsa, OK
Paddock, William A. .... **Denver, CO**
Paddock, William S. .... **Atlanta, GA**
Paddor, Garrett B. .... **Los Angeles, CA**
Paddor, Richard S. .... Beverly Hills, CA
Pade, Jeffrey A. .... Alexandria, VA
Padegimas, Julius V. .... Chicago, IL
Padegs, Juris .... **New York, NY**
Padelford, William B. .... **Bradenton, FL**
Padell, Bert .... New York, NY
Padella, Arthur M. .... McLean, VA
Padellaro, Joseph J., Jr. .... Princeton, MA
Padellaro, Marc D. .... Cambridge, MA
Paden, Gary L. .... Visalia, CA
Paden Group, The, L.L.C. Independence, MO
Paden, Jan P. .... **Harrisburg, PA**
Paden, Kristine M. .... **Los Angeles, CA**
Paden, Lee W. .... United States Senate, Senatorial Assistants, GV
Paden, Lyman R., (P.C.) .... **Houston, TX**
Paden & Paden .... **Bessemer, AL** Hoover, AL
Paden, Peter R. .... **New York, NY**
Paden, R. Shan .... **Bessemer, AL** Hoover, AL
Paden, Richard S. .... Mountain Home, AR
Paden, Robert B. .... Maysville, MO
Paden, Robert C., Jr. .... Independence, MO
Paden, Robert C., Sr. .... Independence, MO
Paden, Robert E. .... **Bessemer, AL** Hoover, AL
Paden, Robin Christy .... Independence, MO
Paden, Shawn Patrick .... **Costa Mesa, CA**
Paderewski, Alexander G. .... Sarasota, FL
Paderewski & Sweeting, P.A. .... Sarasota, FL
Paderick, Clifton W. .... Clinton, NC
Padernacht, Sheri S. .... Scarsdale, NY
Padesky, Ellen C. .... **Detroit, MI**
Padfield, Adrienne F. .... Houston, TX
Padfield, Alan B. .... Fort Worth, TX
Padfield, Law Firm, P.C. .... Houston, TX
Padfield, M. Kathleen .... **St. Louis, MO**
Padgen, Kimberly A. .... **Chicago, IL**
Padget, Cynthia D. .... **Fort Worth, TX**
Padget, Thomas M. .... Costa Mesa, CA
Padgett, A. Gary, Jr. .... **Jacksonville, FL**
Padgett, Alison L. .... Montgomery, AL
Padgett, Anne .... **Las Vegas, NV**
Padgett, Barbara K. .... Louisville, KY
Padgett, Carroll D., Jr. .... Loris, SC
Padgett, Carroll D., Jr., P.A. .... Loris, SC
Padgett, Carson Epes .... **San Antonio, TX**
Padgett, Christian D. .... Gaffney, SC
Padgett, Donald F. .... Dallas, TX
Padgett, Frank D. .... Kula, HI
Padgett, Gail B. .... Department of Justice, Executive Office for Immigration Review, GV
Padgett, George A. .... Edison, NJ
Padgett, Glenn R. .... Daytona Beach, FL
Padgett, Gregory L. .... **Indianapolis, IN**
Padgett, Herman D. .... **Mobile, AL**
Padgett, J. Rogers .... Tampa, FL
Padgett, James L. .... Lincolnshire, IL
Padgett, James L., Jr. .... Crescent City, FL
Padgett, Jill F. .... **Oklahoma City, OK**
Padgett, John D. .... **Norfolk, VA**
Padgett, John F. .... Orleans, MA
Padgett, Kenneth M. .... New York, NY
Padgett, Kenneth Patrick .... Lakeside Park, KY
Padgett, L. Richard, Jr. .... **Salem, VA**
Padgett, L. Richard, Jr., P.C. .... **Salem, VA**
Padgett, Lucas C., Jr. .... **Charleston, SC**
Padgett, Mahlon E., IV .... **Bennettsville, SC**
Padgett, Mark .... **Minneapolis, MN**
Padgett, Matthew N. .... **Athens, GA**
Padgett, Michael W. .... **Indianapolis, IN**
Padgett, Miles C. .... **Washington, DC**
Padgett & Morris .... Crescent City, FL
Padgett, Nancy .... United States Court Of Appeals District Of Columbia Circuit, GV
Padgett, Pat A. .... Tulsa, OK
Padgett, Randall A. .... Sacramento, CA
Padgett, Richard G. .... Spring Hill, FL
Padgett, Richard G., P.A. .... Spring Hill, FL
Padgett, Sandra A. .... St. Louis, MO
Padgett, Shaw & Associates, P.A. Coral Gables, FL
Padgett, Shelton E. .... **San Antonio, TX**
Padgett, Stanley T. .... **Tampa, FL**
Padgett, Tammy .... **Phoenix, AZ**
Padgett, Thomas H., Jr. .... **Houston, TX**
Padgett, Timothy Daniel .... Tallahassee, FL
Padgett, Troy Allen .... Victorville, CA
Padgett, Virgil W. .... Memphis, TN
Padgett, Wares & Day, A Professional Corporation .... Belleville, MI Farmington Hills, MI
Padgett, Whitworth, Donohue & Ward Memphis, TN
Padgett, William E. .... **Indianapolis, IN**
Padgham, Charles R. Hot Springs National Park, AR
Padgham, Kenneth A., Jr. .... Chicago, IL
Padgitt, D. Lee .... **Winnetka, IL**
Padgitt, D. L., & Associates Ltd. **Winnetka, IL**
Padgitt, Donald L. .... **Winnetka, IL**
Padgitt, Sarah M. .... **Chicago, IL**
Padian, Gerald .... Allendale, NJ **New York, NY**
Padien, Mary Anne J. .... West Medway, MA
Padien, Paul P. .... **Media, PA**
Padierne & Associates, P.A. .... Miami, FL
Padierne, Rafael E. .... Miami, FL
Padilla, Adoralida (Dora) .... **San Jose, CA**
Padilla, Agnes Fuentevilla **Albuquerque, NM**
Padilla, Alfredo .... Brownsville, TX
Padilla, Angela L. .... **San Francisco, CA**
Padilla, Anthony Alan .... Portland, OR
Padilla, Arnold .... Corrales, NM
Padilla, D. Laurence .... Liberty Corner, NJ
Padilla, Ernest L. .... Santa Fe, NM
Padilla, Fernando, II .... Little Rock, AR
Padilla, Frank .... Frederiksted, St. Croix, VI
Padilla, Frank S. .... Taos, NM
Padilla, Gerald V. .... **Southfield, MI**
Padilla, Janelle S. .... **Dallas, TX**
Padilla, Javier .... San Antonio, TX
Padilla, Jeffrey W. .... New York, NY
Padilla, Joaquin A. .... **Denver, CO**
Padilla, John J. .... Greenville, NC
Padilla, John M. .... **San Jose, CA**
Padilla, John M. .... **Houston, TX**
Padilla, John R. .... Corpus Christi, TX
Padilla, Jose A., Jr. .... New York, NY
Padilla, José D. .... Chicago, IL
Padilla, Jose L., Jr. .... **Los Angeles, CA**
Padilla, Jose S. .... Phoenix, AZ
Padilla, Julio A. .... Miami Beach, FL
Padilla, Karla K. .... **Palo Alto, CA**
Padilla, Kenneth A. .... Denver, CO
Padilla Law Firm .... **San Jose, CA**
Padilla Law Firm, P.A. .... Santa Fe, NM
Padilla, Luis F. .... San Juan, PR
Padilla, Margarita .... Oakland, CA
Padilla, Mark F. .... Alpharetta, GA
Padilla, Michael .... **Seattle, WA**
Padilla, Michael D., (P.C.) .... San Diego, CA
Padilla & O'Leary LLP .... Los Angeles, CA
Padilla, Richard M. .... **Albuquerque, NM**
Padilla, Robin L. .... **Las Vegas, NV**
Padilla, Steff .... San Gabriel, CA
Padilla, Stephanie S. .... **Denver, CO**
Padilla, Stephen M. .... Los Angeles, CA
Padilla, Timothy M. .... Albuquerque, NM
Padilla, Timothy M., and Associates, P.C. Albuquerque, NM
Padilla-Diaz, Linda .... **New York, NY**
Padilla-Taylor, Laura M. .... San Diego, CA
Padilla-Velez, Carlos A. .... **San Juan, PR**
Padin, Mark A. .... Redondo Beach, CA
Padin, Mercedes .... **Aventura, FL**
Padish, James .... Phoenix, AZ
Padjen, Ann E. .... **Allentown, PA**
Padjen, Robert .... **Denver, CO**
Padleschat, Joyce A. .... **San Diego, CA**
Padley, Albert F., III .... Altadena, CA
Padley & Dudden, P.C. .... Ogallala, NE
Padley, Pamela K. .... Oklahoma City, OK
Padley, Susan E. .... **Bloomfield Hills, MI**
Padley, William A. .... Lodi, WI
Padlo, Victor A. .... Rahway, NJ
Padmanabhan, Devan V. **Minneapolis, MN**
Padmanabhan, Ram .... **Chicago, IL**
Padmore, Gerald .... **Denver, CO** **New York, NY**
Padmore, Shirley A. .... **St. Louis, MO**
Padnes, David R. .... Liberty Corner, NJ
Padnick, Glenn A. .... Beverly Hills, CA
Padnick, Jennifer C. .... **New York, NY**
Padnos, Norman B. .... Oak Brook, IL
Padnos, Todd L. .... **Chicago, IL**
Padon, Mark A. .... **Houston, TX**
Padova, Daniel J. .... **Los Angeles, CA**
Padova, Donald Michael .... Philadelphia, PA
Padova, John R. .... Philadelphia, PA
Padovani, Anthony .... Hammonton, NJ
Padovano, Gregg A. .... **Montvale, NJ**
Padovano, Margaret E. .... West Orange, NJ
Padovano, Philip J. .... Tallahassee, FL
Padovano, Ralph J. .... **Montvale, NJ**
Padovano, Robert K. .... Raleigh, NC
Padove, Burton A. .... Hammond, IN
Padove, Susan B. Commodity Futures Trading Commission, Division of Enforcement, GV
Padover, Mitchell S. .... **Phoenix, AZ**
Padow, Judith I. .... Nutley, NJ
Padowitz, Kenneth D. .... Fort Lauderdale, FL
Padrick, H. Thomas, Jr. .... Virginia Beach, VA
Padrick, Jack O. .... San Rafael, CA
Padrick, Kevin D. .... Sunriver, OR
Padrick, Robert G. .... Encino, CA
Padrino, James Lee .... Encino, CA
Padrnos, Dennis R. .... Mitchell, SD
Padrnos, John P. .... New York, NY
Padro, Eduardo .... Bronx, NY
Padro, Efrain M. .... Denver, CO
Padro, Lizzie M. .... **San Juan, PR**
Padro Diaz, Gilberto R. .... Arecibo, PR
Padrón, Carol A. .... Spring Valley, NY
Padron, Eric C. .... Miami, FL
Padron, James P. .... **Merced, CA**
Padrón, Luis E. .... **San Juan, PR**
Padron, Luis M. .... Miami, FL
Padron, Luis M., & Associates, P.A. Miami, FL
Padron-Fragetta, Ameli .... Miami Lakes, FL
Padrow, Kim S. .... Des Moines, WA
Padua, Charmagne A. .... **New Orleans, LA**
Padua, Vincent .... West Covina, CA
Padua Flores, Noelia .... Ponce, PR
Paduano, Anthony .... **New York, NY**
Paduano, James A. .... New York, NY
Paduano, Michael S. .... Toms River, NJ
Paduck, Paul .... Grass Valley, CA
Paduda, Marcie E. .... **Birmingham, AL**
Paduda, Michael J., Jr. .... Bogalusa, LA
Paduhovich, Janet L. .... **Columbia, SC**
Padula, Geo. T. .... Quincy, MA
Padula, Peter E. .... Franklin, MA
Padula, Stephen J. .... **Boca Raton, FL**
Padula, Vincent P. .... New York, NY
Padwa, Jeffrey M. .... Providence, RI
Padwa, Sabrina I. .... New York, NY
Padway, Laurence F. .... Alameda, CA
Padway, M. Nicol .... Milwaukee, WI
Padway & Padway, Ltd. .... Milwaukee, WI
Padway, Robert A. .... **San Francisco, CA**
Padway, William A. .... Milwaukee, WI
Padys, Danny J. .... **Minneapolis, MN**
Padzieski, Richard J. .... Detroit, MI
Pae, Jessica .... **Los Angeles, CA**
Paek, J. Hyung .... **New York, NY**
Paek, Sang Y. .... Washington, DC
Paek, Steve S. .... Los Angeles, CA
Paelet, Lawrence D. .... **New Haven, CT**
Paepke, C. Owen .... **Phoenix, AZ**
Paepke, Gail C. .... Hawthorne, CA
Paer, Gary S. .... Santa Ana, CA
Paer, Tracey B. .... **New York, NY**
Paes, Fern H. .... **Norwalk, CT**
Paes, Michael T. .... Newburgh, NY
Paese, James P. .... Rolling Meadows, IL
Paese, Michael M. .... **New York, NY**
Paessler, Robert N. .... New York, NY
Paetkau, Tyler M. .... **San Francisco, CA**
Paetro, Anthony S. .... Miami, FL
Paetsch, Christopher E. .... **Chicago, IL**
Paetzold, Raymond M. .... Oakland, CA
Paetzold, White & Brodsky, A Professional Corporation .... Oakland, CA
Paez, Eileen .... Albuquerque, NM
Paez, Jacqueline M. .... **Chicago, IL**
Paez, Mauricio F. .... **Roseland, NJ**
Páez-Rodríguez, Rebecca .... **San Juan, PR**
Paff, Lester .... Des Moines, IA
Paffenbarger, Thomas L. .... **Norwalk, OH**
Pafford, John W. .... Jacksonville, FL
Pafford, John W., P.A., The Law Offices of Jacksonville, FL
Pafford, Keith .... Kansas City, MO
Pafford, Leon Keith .... **Overland Park, KS**
Paffrath, Stephen E. .... **San Francisco, CA**
Pafundi, Richard T. .... Honolulu, HI
Pafundi, Robert N., Law Offices of Thousand Oaks, CA
Pagac, Christine A. .... **Los Angeles, CA**
Pagac, Shelly R. .... **Pittsburgh, PA**
Pagalilauan, Tisha F. .... **Seattle, WA**
Pagan, Carmen M. .... San Juan, PR
Pagan, Deborah Lee .... Memphis, TN
Pagán, Ed, Jr. .... Flemington, NJ
Pagan, Greer Humphreys .... **Houston, TX**
Pagan, Gregory .... San Francisco, CA
Pagan, John R. .... Little Rock, AR Richmond, VA
Pagan, Juan S. .... San Juan, PR
Pagan, Kevin D. .... McAllen, TX
Pagán, Lisa Riveland .... **Seattle, WA**
Pagán, Lourdes Teresa .... **San Juan, PR**
Pagan, Luis M. .... San Juan, PR
Pagan, Maria L. .... Department of Commerce, Office of the General Counsel, GV
Pagan, Ramon W. .... **Bronx, NY**
Pagan, William .... New York, NY
Paganelli, F. Anthony .... **Indianapolis, IN**
Paganetti, Steven E. .... **Fresno, CA**
Pagán Gutierrez, Diego .... San Juan, PR
Pagan Hernandez, Ivan Luis .... Carolina, PR
Paganini, Kenneth J. .... New York, NY
Paganini & Malmud .... New York, NY
Paganis, Karen T. .... **Houston, TX**
Pagan-Marin, Nora H. .... Ponce, PR
Pagano, Anthony .... San Francisco, CA
Pagano, Anthony F. .... Manchester, CT
Pagano, Anthony James .... Rockville, MD
Pagano, Anthony M. .... **Toms River, NJ**
Pagano, Carmen V. .... Charlotte, NC
Pagano, Catherine V. United States Postal Service, Law Department, GV
Pagano, Christine C. .... Oakland, CA
Pagano, Daniel A. .... Poughkeepsie, NY
Pagano, Eva A. .... Atlantic City, NJ
Pagano, George A. .... Media, PA
Pagano, James L., Law Offices of San Jose, CA
Pagano, James P. .... New York, NY
Pagano, Jeanette Wallag .... Vero Beach, FL
Pagano, Jeffrey W. .... **New York, NY**
Pagano, Joseph C. .... **Birmingham, MI**
Pagano, Joseph R. .... **Springfield, NJ**
Pagano, Laura A. .... **Minneapolis, MN**
Pagano, Matthew J. .... **Chicago, IL**
Pagano, Melanie M. .... Salem, NH
Pagano, Nicholas .... Mableton, GA
Pagano, Philip G. .... Wall Township, NJ
Pagano, Ralph V. .... **New York, NY**
Pagano, Richard C. .... **Rosemont, IL**
Pagano, Vincent, Jr. .... **New York, NY**
Pagano, William .... **Hackensack, NJ**
Pagano, William F. .... Burlingame, CA
Pagano, Yolanda F. .... Philadelphia, PA
Pagano & Zuboff .... Manchester, CT
Pagán Rosado, Diana Lynn .... **San Juan, PR**
Paganucci, Michael J. .... **Chicago, IL**
Paganucci, Paul D. .... Hanover, NH
Paganuzzi, O. Stephen, Jr. .... New York, NY
Pagar, Charulata B. .... **New York, NY**
Pagay, Malhar S. .... **San Francisco, CA**
Page, Adam D. .... **Worcester, MA**
Page, Adele Hedley .... **Fargo, ND**
Page, Akulian & Baker, Inc. Walnut Creek, CA
Page, Alan C. .... St. Paul, MN
Page, Alan G. .... New York, NY
Page, Alfred E., Jr. .... **White Plains, NY**
Page, Alice K. .... Portsmouth, NH
Page, Alice Nystel .... **Albuquerque, NM**
Page, Allison A. .... Richmond, VA
Page, Anderson .... Philadelphia, PA
Page, Arden E. .... **Anchorage, AK**
Page, Arthur B. .... **Boston, MA**
Page, Arthur L. .... Fort Wayne, IN
Page & Associates, A Professional Corporation Dallas, TX
Page & Bacek LLP .... **Atlanta, GA**
Page, Bambi Couch .... Mansfield, OH
Page, Bart J. .... **Phoenix, AZ**
Page, Beatty B. .... **New York, NY**
Page, Benjamin J. .... Seattle, WA
Page, Bradley D. .... **Milwaukee, WI**
Page, Brenda B. .... **Atlanta, GA**
Page, Brenda J. .... Hartford, CT
Page, Brian J. .... **Grand Rapids, MI**
Page, Bruce Dean .... Jacksonville, FL
Page, Carl R. .... Louisville, KY
Page, Carter R. .... **Columbus, GA**
Page, Catherine M. .... **Irvine, CA**
Page, Charles H. .... Monterey, CA
Page, Christina M. .... **Winter Park, FL**
Page, Christine A. .... **Los Angeles, CA**
Page, Christopher A. .... **Raleigh, NC**
Page, Clemson North, Jr. .... Reading, PA
Page, Craig A. .... Atlanta, GA
Page, Cyd Sheree .... **Lafayette, LA**
Page, David K. .... **Detroit, MI**
Page, David M. .... Boston, MA
Page, David P. .... **Tulsa, OK**
Page, Deborah G. .... Northbrook, IL
Page, Debra K. .... **Minneapolis, MN**
Page, Denise .... **Indianapolis, IN**
Page, Denise L. .... **Boston, MA**
Page, Dennis A. .... **Los Angeles, CA**
Page, Donald A. .... Thomaston, GA
Page, Donald W., Jr. .... Cambridge, MA
Page, Dorothy L. .... Department of Labor, Office of the Solicitor, GV
Page, Douglas R. .... Walnut Creek, CA
Page, Edward John .... Washington, DC
Page & Eichenblatt, P.A. **Winter Park, FL**
Page, Elizabeth D. .... Denver, CO
Page, Eric Michael .... **Glen Allen, VA** **Richmond, VA**
Page, Ernest M., III .... Live Oak, FL
Page, Ernest M., Jr. .... **Madison, FL**
Page, Eston W. .... Laurens, SC
Page, F. Scott .... **Los Angeles, CA**
Page Firm, The, A P.C. .... **San Diego, CA**
Page, Frederick D. .... **Jacksonville, FL**
Page, G. Keyes, III .... **Houston, TX**
Page, Garilou .... Columbus, GA
Page, Garrett D. .... Norristown, PA
Page, George A., Jr. .... **Boston, MA**
Page, George O. .... Gilmanton, NH
Page, Geraldine H. Carnes New Orleans, LA
Page, Gimi D. .... **Vancouver, WA**
Page, Glenn J. .... Detroit, MI
Page, Gregg A. .... **Winter Park, FL**
Page, Gregory D. .... Department of Justice, Environment and Natural Resources Division, GV
Page, Gregory P. .... **Des Moines, IA**

Painter, Andrew D. ... Atlanta, GA
Painter, Ann Marie ... Dallas, TX
Painter, Barrett T. ... Cleveland, TN
Painter, Brett C. ... Denver, CO
Painter, Charles S. ... Sacramento, CA
Painter, Christopher Martin Edward
Los Angeles, CA
Painter, David ... Lake Charles, LA
Painter, Delanie D.
Federal Election Commission,
Office of the General Counsel, GV
Painter, Donald L. ... Casper, WY
Painter, Donald L., P.C. ... Casper, WY
Painter, Douglas R. ... Glendale, CA
Painter, Elizabeth C. ... Phoenix, AZ
Painter, Enver W., Jr. (A Law Corporation)
Honolulu, HI
Painter, George H.
Commodity Futures Trading Commission,
Office of Proceedings, GV
Painter, George M., III ... King Of Prussia, PA
Painter, J. Marcus ... Boulder, CO
Painter, Jack W. ... Cincinnati, OH
Painter, James D. ... Pittsburgh, PA
Painter, James M. ... Boca Raton, FL
Painter, James M., P.A. ... Boca Raton, FL
Painter, James V. ... Savannah, GA
Painter, Jane Foy ... Gastonia, NC
Painter, Jennifer H. ... Los Angeles, CA
Painter, Jerry L. ... Federal Way, WA
Painter, J. H., III ... Houston, TX
Painter, John H. ... Monroe, NC
Painter, Jonathan W. ... Waltham, MA
Painter, Joseph Graham, Jr. ... Blacksburg, VA
Painter, L. Harlen ... Cleveland, TN
Painter & Long ... Monroe, NC
Painter, Lori Burns ... Columbus, OH
Painter, Marjorie Seber ... Beaumont, TX
Painter, Mark P. ... Cincinnati, OH
Painter, Mark S., Sr. ... Royersford, PA
Painter, Mattison C. ... Nashville, TN
Painter, Michael A. ... Beverly Hills, CA
Painter, Michael J. ... San Francisco, CA
Painter, Michael L. ... Beaumont, TX
Painter, Michael M. ... Muncie, IN
Painter, Michael W. ... Seattle, WA
Painter, Patricia A., Law Offices of
Redondo Beach, CA
Painter, Paul ... Longview, TX
Painter, Paul W. ... Rossville, GA
Painter, Paul W., Jr. ... Savannah, GA
Painter, Richard E. ... Rockville, MD
Painter, Robert K. ... Silver Spring, MD
Painter, Robert W. ... Houston, TX
Painter, Robin A. ... Boston, MA
Painter, Sam S. ... Billings, MT
Painter, Samuel F. ... Columbia, SC
Painter & Schafer ... Muncie, IN
Painter, Scott C. ... Reading, PA
Painter, Sidney ... San Anselmo, CA
Painter, Simon M., Jr. ... Staunton, VA
Painter, Susan A. ... Chula Vista, CA
Painter, Thomas M. ... Waynesboro, PA
Painter, William H. ... Kansas City, MO
Painter, William S. ... Jackson, MS
Nashville, TN
Painter Bohn, Thayla ... Tulsa, OK
Paintin, Francis A. ... Philadelphia, PA
Painton, Larry R., Jr. ... Trabuco Canyon, CA
Painton, Russell E. ... Austin, TX
Pair, Arnold D. ... Arlington, TX
Pair, James R. ... Seattle, WA
Pair, Quentin C. ... Department of Justice,
Environment and Natural Resources
Division, GV
Pairo, Preston A., Jr. ... Ellicott City, MD
Pais, Louise C. ... Thousand Oaks, CA
Pais, Mara Devine ... Aberdeen, MD
Bel Air, MD
Pais, Ralph M. ... Palo Alto, CA
Pais, Randall M. ... Houston, TX
Paisley, Andrew A. ... Cleveland, OH
Paisley, Barbara Davis ... Philadelphia, PA
Paisley, Bonnie J. ... Albuquerque, NM
Paisley, Bradley T. ... Taylorville, IL
Paisley, Carol ... Lexington, KY
Paisley, Douglas A., II ... Houston, TX
Paisley, J. Scott ... San Diego, CA
Paisley, James A. ... New Orleans, LA
Paisley, John P., Jr. ... Graham, NC
Paisley, Lewis G. ... Lexington, KY
Paisley, Louis ... Cleveland, OH
Paisley, Marian ... Galena, OH
Paisley, Mark R. ... Alice, TX
Paisley, Megan ... Monticello, IL
Paisley, Russell Kevin ... Bronx, NY
Paisley, Vicki A. ... McLean, VA
Paisner, Bruce L. ... New York, NY
Paisner, Joel R. ... Seattle, WA
Paisner, Michael S. ... Old Tappan, NJ
Paisner, Richard D. ... Washington, DC
Paisner, S. Barry ... Santa Fe, NM
Paisner, Steven R. ... Cherry Hill, NJ
Philadelphia, PA
Paist, Debra ... Harrisburg, PA
Paitsel, James D., Jr. ... Hickman, KY
Paiva, Chad S. ... Stuart, FL
Paiva, Frank, Jr. ... Philadelphia, PA
Paiva, Suzan DeBusk ... Philadelphia, PA
Paixao, Robert ... Springfield, MA
Paja, Marilyn G. ... Port Orchard, WA
Paja, Ronald P. ... Stockton, IL
Paja, Salvador I. ... Los Angeles, CA
Pajak, David J. ... Buffalo, NY
Pajak, Gregory V. ... Buffalo, NY
Pajak, John J. ... United States Tax Court,
Special Trial Judges, GV
Pajak, John J. ... Springfield, MA
Pajak, Kenneth W. ... Beaumont, TX
Pajala, Ulla M. ... Oakland, CA
Pajares, Raymond J. ... Covington, LA
Pajcic, Curry Gary ... Jacksonville, FL
Pajcic, Curtis Stephen ... Jacksonville, FL
Pajcic, Gary ... Jacksonville, FL
Pajcic & Pajcic, P.A. ... Jacksonville, FL
Pajcic, Stephen J., III ... Jacksonville, FL
Pajda, Thomas A. ... St. Louis, MO
Pajonas, Todd R. ... New York, NY
Pajonk, Arthur D. ... Ridgefield, NJ
Pajonk, Morris ... Ridgefield, NJ
Pajonk & Pajonk ... Ridgefield, NJ
Pajoohi, Nilie ... New York, NY
Pajtas, Richard M. ... Charlevoix, MI
Pak, Alvin S. ... Palo Alto, CA
Pak, Bliss Burdett ... Dallas, TX
Pak, Byongchae ... New York, NY
Pak, Byung Jin ... Springfield, IL
Pak, Charles C. ... Los Angeles, CA
Pak, Chul ... Federal Trade Commission,
Bureau of Competition, GV
Pak, Chung K. ... Department of Commerce,
Patent and Trademark Office, GV
Pak, Dongkwan James ... Washington, DC
Pak, Dorothy D. ... Birmingham, AL
Pak, Eugene M. ... San Francisco, CA
Pak, James L. ... Phoenix, AZ
Pak, Jong Pil ... Los Angeles, CA
Pak, Katherine S. ... San Jose, CA
Pak, Kevin Y. ... Chicago, IL
Pak, Mitchell E. ... New York, NY
Pak, Richard U. ... Flushing, NY
Pak, Ronald J. ... Doraville, GA
Pak, Song A. ... Washington, DC
Pak, Song H. ... Dallas, TX
Pak, Thomas ... New York, NY
Pakalka, William R. ... Houston, TX
Pakchar, Jay W. ... Atlanta, GA
Pake, Lisa A. ... St. Louis, MO
Pakel, Edward Dennis ... Port Washington, NY
Pakele, Gary M. ... Reno, NV
Pakenham, Kathleen M. ... New York, NY
Pakenham, Linda C. ... Milwaukee, WI
Pakenham, Timothy J. ... Atlanta, GA
Pakes, Kathleen A. ... Louisville, KY
Pakis, Giotes, Beard & Page ... Temple, TX
Waco, TX
Pakis, William R. ... Waco, TX
Pakiz, J. Derek ... Santa Ana, CA
Pakkala, Mark D. ... Grand Rapids, MI
Paknik-Nagem, Brenda A.J.
Department of the Air Force,
Office of the Judge Advocate General, GV
Pakradouni, Nairi ... Whittier, CA
Pakradouni, Viken K. ... Pasadena, CA
Pakrashi, Sara S. ... Mentor, OH
Paksarian, Paul ... Albany, NY
Paksoy, Ali, Jr. ... Shelby, NC
Pakula, David B. ... Fort Lauderdale, FL
Pakula, Kenneth R.
Environmental Protection Agency,
Office of the General Counsel, GV
Pakula, Philip D. ... New York, NY
Pakula, Rina J. ... Los Angeles, CA
Pakuris, Christopher J. ... Philadelphia, PA
Pal, Andrew J. ... New York, NY
Pal, Eugene R., Jr. ... Kansas City, MO
Pal, Indra ... Brooklyn, NY
Pal, Koushik Shiek ... Department of Justice,
Antitrust Division, GV
Pala, Nina A. ... Wilmington, DE
Pala, Theodore S. ... Newport Beach, CA
Palace, Eric S. ... Boston, MA
Palace, Herbert M. ... Spring Valley, NY
Palace, Kristin M. ... Boston, MA
Palace, Thomas W. ... Hackensack, NJ
Palace, William ... Boston, MA
Palachuk, O. Marie ... Spokane, WA
Palacino, Richard A ... Miami, FL
Palacio, Cristina ... Gainesville, FL
Palacio, José A., Law Offices of
Santa Ana, CA
Palacio, Ricardo ... Wilmington, DE
Palacios, Alejandro J. ... Washington, DC
Palacios, Ernest ... Fort Worth, TX
Palacios, Fernando M. ... Miami, FL
Palacios, Jaime J. ... Edinburg, TX
Palacios, Oscar ... Pharr, TX
Palacios, Patrick K. ... San Jose, CA
Palacios, Pedro P. ... Las Cruces, NM
Palacios, Ricardo D. ... Laredo, TX
Palacios, Rosa Liliana ... Boston, MA
Palacios, Victor S. ... Fontana, CA
Palacios de Vizzio, Sergio ... New York, NY
Paladin, John ... Sherman Oaks, CA
Paladin, Joseph C. ... Trinidad, CA
Paladin, Lawrence G., Jr. ... Pittsburgh, PA
Paladina, Jeffrey M. ... Monaca, PA
Paladini, Jon M. ... Sedona, AZ
Paladini, Vincent M.
Federal Communications Commission,
Common Carrier Bureau, GV
Paladino, Alfred Paul ... San Francisco, CA
Paladino, Carl P. ... Buffalo, NY
Paladino, Cavan & Quinlivan ... Buffalo, NY
Paladino, Christopher J. ... Trenton, NJ
Paladino, Daniel R. ... New York, NY
Paladino, James ... New York, NY
Paladino, Jeanette M. ... Philadelphia, PA
Paladino, Peter T., Jr. ... Pittsburgh, PA
Paladino, Ralph ... Hauppauge, NY
Paladino, Richard ... Old Saybrook, CT
Paladino, Richard ... West Palm Beach, FL
Paladino, Theodore R. ... Pittsburgh, PA
Paladino, Victor G. ... Albany, NY
Palaferri, Julie A. ... Carlsbad, CA
Palaferri, Julie A. ... San Diego, CA
Palafox, Gina M. ... El Paso, TX
Palafox, Julie A. ... Santa Ana, CA
Palagano, Michael ... Youngstown, OH
Palagi, Ronald J. ... Omaha, NE
Palagi, Ronald J., The Law Offices of, P.C.
Omaha, NE
Palahach, Michael, III, (P.A.)
Melbourne, FL
Miami, FL
Palaigos, Anthony P. ... Baltimore, MD
Palais, Douglas M. ... Richmond, VA
Palakow, Gregory J. ... Philadelphia, PA
Palamar, Randal C. ... Fredericksburg, VA
Palamara, A. Thos. ... Jersey City, NJ
Palamara, Sarah R. ... Woodsville, NH
Palamountain, Kathryn C.
San Francisco, CA
Palan, Barbara Lerner ... Overland Park, KS
Palan, Perry ... Washington, DC
Palan, Stephen W. ... Alexandria, VA
Palanca, Christopher L. ... Chicago, IL
Palanca, Georgiana V. ... Los Angeles, CA
Palandech, Douglas J. ... Chicago, IL
Palange, Dawn M. ... Reading, PA
Palank, Mary A. ... St. Louis, MO
Palans, Lloyd A. ... St. Louis, MO
Palansky, IJay ... Washington, DC
Palardy, Shirley L. ... Detroit, MI
Palarz, Herman S. ... Los Angeles, CA
Palash, Andrea Leigh ... San Francisco, CA
Palast, Geri D.
Department of Labor, GV
Palat, Milton ... Yardley, PA
Palatnik, Eric ... New York, NY
Palatucci, Armond L. ... Glendale, NY
Palatucci, William J. ... Cranford, NJ
Palau, Henry S. ... Alexandria, VA
Palau, Manuel A.
Federal Deposit Insurance Corporation,
Appellate Litigation Section, GV
Palavoy, Kim M. ... Philadelphia, PA
Palay, Alfred ... Beachwood, OH
Palay, Daniel J. ... Ventura, CA
Palay, Linda Coren ... Deerfield, IL
Palay, Susan Bartell ... Carlsbad, CA
Palazzese, Jeffrey P. ... Philadelphia, PA
Palazzi, Daniel F. ... Hackensack, NJ
Palazzo, Donald J. ... Westlake Village, CA
Palazzo, Eugene O. ... Rochester, NY
Palazzo, John T. ... Fullerton, CA
Palazzo, Lisa M. ... Akron, OH
Palazzo, Michele A. ... Newark, NJ
Palazzo, Richard J. ... Lancaster, PA
Palazzo, Robert P. ... Darwin, CA
Los Angeles, CA
Palazzo, T. Louis ... Las Vegas, NV
Palazzo, Tina L. ... New York, NY
Palazzolo, Andrea ... Mineola, NY
Palazzolo, Anna C. ... Atlanta, GA
Palazzolo, Frank J. ... Clinton, MI
Palazzolo, Linda A. ... Roseland, NJ
Palazzolo, Steven A. ... Ada, MI
Palazzolo, Thomas J. ... St. Louis, MO
Palchick, Mark J. ... Washington, DC
Palchikoff, Jay F. ... Irvine, CA
Palda, George W. ... Cleveland, OH
Paldino, F. Joseph ... New York, NY
Paldino, Patrice ... Fort Lauderdale, FL
Paldy, David L. ... New York, NY
Palecek, James F. ... Escondido, CA
Palecek, James J. ... Wadsworth, OH
Palecek, McIlvaine, Paul & Hoffmann Co.,
L.P.A. ... Wadsworth, OH
Palecki, Scott C. ... Topeka, KS
Kansas City, MO
Palefsky, Cliff ... San Francisco, CA
Palek, Michael G. ... Washington, DC
Palek, Roger William ... Appleton, WI
Palella, Charles ... New York, NY
Palella, Charles, P.C. ... New York, NY
Palen, Benedict T., Jr. ... Denver, CO
Palen, Frank S. ... West Palm Beach, FL
Palen, John B. G. ... Newton, MA
Palen, Marion A. ... Bronx, NY
Palenchar, James L. ... Denver, CO
Chicago, IL
Palenchar, Richard J. ... San Francisco, CA
Palenica, Matthew ... Phoenix, AZ
Palenko, John M. ... Meadow Vista, CA
Palenscar, Alexander J., Jr. ... Annapolis, MD
Palenscar, Lynn S. ... Villanova, PA
Palenske, Robin R. ... Greensboro, NC
Palenski, Ronald J. ... Arlington, VA
Palenz, John A. ... Wichita, KS
Palenzuela, Alexander L. ... Miami, FL
Palenzuela, Roberto L. ... Deerfield Beach, FL
Paleologos, Arthur A. ... Woburn, MA
Paleos & Krieger, P.C. ... Washington, DC
Annapolis, MD
Alexandria, VA
Paleos, W. Steven ... Washington, DC
Alexandria, VA
Palerm, Silda ... New York, NY
Palerm-Cruz, Ivonne ... San Juan, PR
Palermino, Anthony J., Law Office of
Hartford, CT
Palermino, Donna L. ... Boston, MA
Palermino, Paul A. ... Boston, MA
Palermo, Anthony R. ... Rochester, NY
Palermo, Barbaro, Chinen & Pitzer
Pasadena, CA
Palermo, Christopher C. ... New York, NY
Palermo, Christopher J. ... San Jose, CA
Palermo, Don P. ... Philadelphia, PA
Palermo, Frank A. ... Cliffside Park, NJ
Palermo, J. Rock ... Lake Charles, LA
Palermo, James D. ... Tampa, FL
Palermo, John C. ... Rochester, NY
Palermo, John R. ... Denver, CO
Palermo, Joseph M. ... Elmhurst, IL
Palermo, Joseph P., III ... Atlanta, GA
Palermo, Lark Jurev ... Boston, MA
Palermo, Mario C. ... Chicago, IL
Palermo, Maryann ... White Plains, NY
Palermo, Michael ... Boston, MA
Palermo, Nancy M. ... Bethesda, MD
Palermo, Norman A.
Colorado Springs, CO
Palermo, Norman A., P.C.
Colorado Springs, CO
Palermo, Paul D. ... Metairie, LA
Palermo, Peter R. ... Miami, FL
Palermo, Peter R., (Professional
Corporation) ... Pasadena, CA
Palermo, Renee J. ... San Diego, CA
Palermo, Robert F. ... Phillipsburg, NJ
Palermo, Rose ... Nashville, TN
Palermo, Samuel Roy ... Houston, TX
Palermo, Stephanie ... New York, NY
Palermo, Virgen Milagros ... Boston, MA
Palese, Luke Allan ... Chicago, IL
Palestine, Steven M. ... New York, NY
Palestini, Karen L. ... Princeton, NJ
Paletou, Wallace H. ... Metairie, LA
Paletou, Wallace H. ... New Orleans, LA
Paletta, Beth A. ... New Kensington, PA
Paletta, David R. ... Boone, NC
Paletta, Joseph A. ... Pittsburgh, PA
Paletta-Davis, Lori ... Morgantown, WV
Paletti, Paul R., Jr. ... Louisville, KY
Paletz, Susan E. ... Farmington Hills, MI
Paletz, Susan E., & Associates, PC
Farmington Hills, MI
Paleudis, John George ... St. Clairsville, OH
Paleveda & Rome, LLC ... Marietta, GA
Palevitz, Stephen F. ... Tucson, AZ
Palewicz, Jonathan L. ... San Francisco, CA
Palewski and Palewski ... New York Mills, NY
Palewski, Peter S. ... New York Mills, NY
Paley, Alan H. ... New York, NY
Paley, Alvin ... North Hollywood, CA
Paley, Andrew Marc ... Los Angeles, CA
Paley, David R. ... New York, NY
Paley, Donald W. ... New York, NY
Paley, Eileen Y. ... Columbus, OH
Paley, Eric R. ... Rochester, NY
Paley, Gerald E. ... New York, NY
Paley, Gerald L. ... Rochester, NY
Paley, Gregg Michael ... Deerfield Beach, FL
Paley, Gregory S. ... Seattle, WA
Paley, Joan Lawton ... New York, NY
Paley, Kenneth R. ... New York, NY
Paley Law Offices, P.S. ... Seattle, WA
Paley, Lloyd S. ... Royal Oak, MI
Paley, Marc ... New York, NY
Paley, Mark A. ... Morristown, NJ
Paley, Marsha I. ... Cleveland, OH
Paley, Michael D. ... Chicago, IL
Paley, Michael D. ... New York, NY
Paley, Paul M. ... New York, NY
Paley, Paula J. ... San Francisco, CA
Paley, Phillip Lewis ... New Brunswick, NJ
Paley, Richard J. ... New York, NY
Paley, Robert J. ... Chicago, IL
Paley, Roberta L. ... Monsey, NY
Paley, Robin E. ... Encino, CA
Paley, Rothman, Goldstein, Rosenberg &
Cooper, Chartered ... Bethesda, MD
Paley, Stephen H. ... Bethesda, MD
Paley, Stewart ... Philadelphia, PA
Paley, Stuart M. ... New York, NY
Palffy, Thomas ... Pasadena, CA
Palfi, Alfred M. ... Michiana Shores, IN
Palfi, Csaba ... Beverly Hills, CA
Palfreyman, Ross H. ... Glendale, CA
Palgon, Ira M. ... New York, NY
Palgut, Paul J. ... Southfield, MI
Palguta & Hesselgrave ... Indianapolis, IN
Palguta, J. Paul ... Indianapolis, IN
Palguta, Larry J. ... South Bend, IN
Palia, Colleen G. ... Castro Valley, CA
Paliani, Alfred R. ... Short Hills, NJ
New York, NY
Paliath, Dilip B. ... Baltimore, MD
Palica, Peter M. ... Marshfield, MA
Palid, Michael J. ... Marinette, WI
Paliga, John R.
Pension Benefit Guaranty Corporation,
Office of the General Counsel, GV
Palik, Anthony J. ... Sacramento, CA
Palik, Douglas D. ... Chappell, NE
Palik, Evan J. ... Seven Hills, OH
Palik, James N. ... New York, NY
Palikan, J. Michael ... Huntington Beach, CA
Palillo, Frank W. ... New York, NY
Palillo, Michael B. ... New York, NY
Palilonis, Robert W. ... Gibbstown, NJ
Palilonis, Stewart P. ... Lambertville, NJ
Palin, Cynthia Caruso ... Irvine, CA
Palin, Mark T. ... Irvine, CA
Palincsar, John E. ... Dearborn, MI
Palinkas, Laura T. ... Cleveland, OH
Palinski, Kathleen ... Columbia, SC
Paliobeis, Bill J. ... Cincinnati, OH
Paliotta, Armand ... Oklahoma City, OK
Paliotti, David J. ... Boston, MA
Palisano, Samuel J. ... Buffalo, NY
Palisi, Thomas M. ... Westfield, NJ
Palisin, John W. ... Houston, TX
Palisin, John W., P.C. ... Houston, TX
Palisoul, Alan A.
Department Of The Interior,
Office of the Solicitor, GV
Palistrant, Robert H. ... Dallas, TX
Palitto, Debra Shore ... Philadelphia, PA

Palmer, Lansing R., P.C., The Law Firm of ... New York, NY
Palmer, Larry I. ... Ithaca, NY
Palmer, Laura Ann ... Lawrence, KS
Palmer Law Firm ... Dyersburg, TN
Palmer Law Firm, Inc. ... Marshall, TX
Palmer Law Firm, The ... Beaufort, SC
Hilton Head Island, SC
Palmer Legal Services ... Middlebury, VT
Palmer, Leslie Allen, Jr. ... Waco, TX
Palmer, Linda Corwin ... Brookline, MA
Palmer, Lisa Marable ... Columbus, OH
Palmer, Liza E. ... New York, NY
Palmer, Lizzette M. ... Houston, TX
Palmer, Louis A. ... Ocean City, MD
Palmer, Louise M. ... Portland, OR
Palmer, Lowry, Leatherman & White, LLP ... Topeka, KS
Palmer, M. Dale ... Plainfield, IN
Palmer, M. Janet ... Richmond, VA
Palmer, Margaret A. ... Ocala, FL
Palmer, Margaret A., P.A. ... Ocala, FL
Palmer, Margaret M.H. ... Chicago, IL
Palmer, Mark A. ... Atlanta, GA
Palmer, Mark A. ... Indianapolis, IN
Palmer, Mark B. ... Santa Monica, CA
Palmer, Mark D. ... Lanham, MD
Palmer, Mark D. ... Syracuse, UT
Palmer, Mark J. ... Columbus, OH
Palmer, Mark L., & Associates ... Rockville, MD
Palmer, Mark Shriver ... Pittsburgh, PA
Palmer, Martin ... Hagerstown, MD
Palmer, Martin W. ... Tampa, FL
Palmer, Mary Ann ... Austin, TX
Palmer, Mary Helen ... Grand Rapids, MI
Palmer, Mary Jane ... Memphis, TN
Palmer, Mary M. ... Spokane, WA
Palmer, Melissa E. ... Galveston, TX
Palmer, Meredith L. ... Gainesville, GA
Palmer, Meredith Susan ... Lexington, VA
Palmer, Michael ... Middlebury, VT
Palmer, Michael D. ... Houston, TX
Palmer, Michael G. ... Coeur d'Alene, ID
Palmer, Michael J. ... Bakersfield, CA
Palmer, Michael P. ... Chicago, IL
Palmer, Michael T. ... Washington, DC
Palmer, Michele D. ... Treasury Department, Internal Revenue Service, GV
Palmer, Michelle L. ... Orange, CA
Palmer, Michelle T. ... Washington, DC
Palmer, Mickey R. ... Houston, TX
Palmer, Mitchell O. ... Bradenton, FL
Palmer, Molly E. ... Michigan City, IN
Palmer, N. Sue Van Sant ... Nashville, TN
Palmer, Nana ... Irvine, CA
Palmer, Nancy S. ... Orlando, FL
Palmer, Nikki Jo ... Dayton, OH
Palmer, Noel ... Utica, NY
Palmer, Oliver S. ... Treasury Department, GV
Palmer, P. Bruce ... Pocatello, ID
Palmer & Palmer ... Newton Falls, OH
Palmer & Palmer, L.C. ... Ogden, UT
Syracuse, UT
Palmer & Palmer, P.A. ... Orlando, FL
Palmer & Palmer, P.C. ... Dallas, TX
Palmer, Pamela J. ... Kansas City, MO
Palmer, Pamela S. ... Los Angeles, CA
Palmer, Patrick J. ... Stevensville, MD
Palmer, Patti ... Pawhuska, OK
Palmer, Paul ... Miami, FL
Palmer, Paul C. ... Washington, DC
Palmer, Paul E. ... Lake Charles, LA
Palmer, Paul T. ... Austin, TX
Palmer, Peter A. ... Worcester, MA
Palmer, Peter C. ... Tolland, CT
Palmer, Peter D. ... Louisville, KY
Palmer, Peter E. ... Los Angeles, CA
Palmer, Peter J. ... Troy, MI
Palmer, Philip I., Jr. ... Dallas, TX
Palmer, R. Chase ... Marshall, TX
Palmer, R. Evan ... Anderson, SC
Palmer, R. Nicholas ... Denver, CO
Palmer, R. Scott ... West Palm Beach, FL
Palmer, R. Scott ... Eugene, OR
Palmer, Randall B. ... Des Moines, IA
Palmer, Randall D. ... Stockton, MO
Palmer, Randall P., III ... Beaumont, TX
Palmer, Raymond Buckley ... Gulf Breeze, FL
Palmer, Rebecca L. ... Orlando, FL
Palmer, Rex A. ... Chicago, IL
Palmer, Rexford L. ... Missoula, MT
Palmer, Richard A. ... Sterling, IL
Palmer, Richard A. ... New York, NY
Palmer, Richard A., Jr. ... Macon, GA
Palmer, Richard B., Jr. ... New York, NY
Palmer, Richard C. ... Chicago, IL
Palmer, Richard C., Jr. ... Stonington, CT
Palmer, Richard D. ... Greenville, MI
Palmer, Richard D. ... Columbus, OH
Palmer, Richard J. ... Modesto, CA
Palmer, Richard M. ... Brooklyn, NY
Palmer, Richard N. ... Hartford, CT
Palmer, Richard W. ... Philadelphia, PA
Palmer, Robert ... Garden City, NY
Palmer, Robert A. ... Pomona, CA
Palmer, Robert A. ... San Francisco, CA
Palmer, Robert A. ... Oberlin, OH
Palmer, Robert B. ... Department of Energy, Office of Hearings and Appeals, GV
Palmer, Robert C. ... Toledo, OH
Palmer, Robert C., III ... Pensacola, FL
Palmer, Robert D. ... Lima, OH
Palmer, Robert E. ... Irvine, CA
Palmer, Robert E. ... Ponchatoula, LA
Palmer, Robert Gray ... Columbus, OH
Palmer, Robert J. ... South Bend, IN
Palmer, Robert L. ... Birmingham, AL
Palmer, Robert L. ... Phoenix, AZ
Los Angeles, CA
Palmer, Robert M. ... Boca Raton, FL
Palmer, Robert M., P.A. ... Boca Raton, FL
Palmer, Robert M. N. ... Springfield, MO
Palmer, Robert M. N., P.C., Law Offices of ... Springfield, MO
Palmer, Robert N. ... Poughkeepsie, NY
Palmer, Robert P. ... Dallas, TX
Palmer, Robert S. ... Middletown, CT
Palmer, Robert T. ... Chicago, IL
Palmer, Robert T., P.C. ... Chicago, IL
Palmer, Robert W. ... Ann Arbor, MI
Palmer, Robert W. ... Portland, OR
Palmer, Robin L. ... Houston, TX
Palmer, Robt. L. ... Peoria, AZ
Palmer, Rodney J. ... Ainsworth, NE
Palmer, Ronald J. ... Troy, MI
Palmer, Ronald Joseph ... Washington, DC
Palmer, Ronald L. ... Jacksonville, FL
Palmer, Ronald L. ... Dallas, TX
Palmer, Ronald L., Law Offices of ... Jacksonville, FL
Palmer, Russell ... Middletown, CT
Palmer, Russell R., Jr. ... Pasadena, CA
Palmer, Samuel C., III ... Fresno, CA
Palmer, Scott H. ... Dallas, TX
Palmer, Scott H., P.C. ... Dallas, TX
Denton, TX
Palmer, Sheldon ... New York, NY
West Nyack, NY
Palmer, Shelly L. ... Syracuse, NY
Palmer, Stacey C. ... Pittsburgh, PA
Palmer, Stephanie A. ... Utica, NY
Palmer, Stephen ... Lexington, KY
Palmer, Stephen ... Loretto, MN
Palmer, Stephen A. ... West Point, VA
Palmer, Stephen A. K. ... Chicago, IL
Palmer, Stephen C. ... Washington, DC
Palmer, Stephen C. ... Lincoln City, OR
Palmer, Stephen D. ... Atlanta, GA
Palmer, Stephen E. ... Columbus, OH
Palmer, Stephen H. ... Media, PA
Palmer, Stephen K. ... Rock Springs, WY
Palmer, Stephen L. ... Boston, MA
Palmer, Stephen L. ... Hickory, NC
Palmer, Stephen M. ... Sioux Falls, SD
Palmer, Stephen M., P.C. ... Sioux Falls, SD
Palmer, Stephen R. ... Sacramento, CA
Palmer, Stephen R. ... Oklahoma City, OK
Palmer, Steven C. ... Omaha, NE
Palmer, Steven David ... Troy, MI
Palmer, Steven G., (P.C.) ... Dallas, TX
Palmer, Steven J. ... Kennewick, WA
Palmer, Sue Ann ... St. Joseph, MO
Palmer, Susan A. ... Raleigh, NC
Palmer, Susan T. ... San Antonio, TX
Palmer, Suzanne Elizabeth ... Reading, PA
Palmer, T. Lawrence ... Pittsburgh, PA
Palmer, Tamra A. ... Englewood, CO
Palmer, Tekla Ann ... Concord, CA
Palmer, Thomas A. ... Oakland, CA
Palmer, Thomas A. ... West Des Moines, IA
Palmer, Thomas A. ... Buffalo, NY
Palmer, Thomas Allan ... Buffalo, NY
Palmer, Thomas C., Jr. ... Manassas, VA
Palmer, Thomas E. ... Dayton, OH
Palmer, Thomas H. ... Newton Falls, OH
Palmer, Thomas L. ... Flagstaff, AZ
Palmer, Thomas N. ... Galion, OH
Palmer, Thomas P. ... Portland, OR
Palmer, Thomas R. ... Schaumburg, IL
Palmer, Thomas S. ... San Diego, CA
Palmer, Thomas T. ... Roanoke, VA
Palmer, Thomas W. ... Toledo, OH
Palmer, Tiffany L. ... Philadelphia, PA
Palmer, Timothy A. ... Birmingham, AL
Palmer, Timothy D. ... Washington, DC
Palmer, Todd E. ... Madison, WI
Palmer, Todd F. ... Cleveland, OH
Palmer, Toni M. ... Racine, WI
Palmer, Tracie D. ... Detroit, MI
Palmer, Venrice R. ... San Francisco, CA
Palmer, Vernon V. ... New Orleans, LA
Palmer, Victor D. ... Michigan City, IN
Palmer, Victor W. ... Chevy Chase, MD
Palmer, Victoria Smith ... Eastpointe, MI
Palmer, Virginia ... Oakland, CA
Palmer, W. Rockne ... Westfield, MA
Palmer, W. Scott ... Santee, SC
Palmer, Wallace ... Independence, MO
Palmer, Walter ... Denver, CO
Palmer, Walter B., III ... Denton, MD
Palmer, Walter H. ... Princeton, IN
Palmer, Walter W. ... West Palm Beach, FL
Palmer, Wayne D. ... Portland, OR
Palmer, Wayne M. ... Dallas, TX
Palmer, Weston H. ... Penn Yan, NY
Palmer, W. F. ... Marshall, TX
Palmer, William A. ... Colorado Springs, CO
Palmer, William B., II ... Las Vegas, NV
Palmer, William C. ... Lenoir, NC
Palmer, William D. ... Bakersfield, CA
Palmer, William D. ... Orlando, FL
Palmer, William E. ... Rockford, IL
Palmer, William Jay ... Miami, FL
Palmer, William M. ... Washington, DC
Palmer, William N. ... Bangor, ME
Palmer, William R. ... Orange Park, FL
Palmer, William R. ... Elmira, NY
Palmer, William R. ... South Boston, VA
Palmer, William R., Jr. ... Greenup, KY
Palmer, William W. ... Sacramento, CA
Palmer, Wilma L. ... Tulsa, OK
Palmer, Wright & Williamson ... Jackson, MS
Meridian, MS
Palmer-House, Gail E. ... Grayslake, IL
Palmeri, Charles J. ... Cleveland, OH
Palmeri, Charles J., Co., L.P.A. ... Cleveland, OH
Palmeri, Denise A. ... New York, NY
Palmeri & Gaven ... New York, NY
Palmeri, John J. ... Cheshire, CT
Palmeri, John J. ... New York, NY
Palmeri, John M. ... Denver, CO
Cheyenne, WY
Palmeri, Michael F. ... Baldwin, NY
Palmeri, Patricia E. ... Mineola, NY
Palmeri, Rock & Talbot, P.C. ... Cheshire, CT
Palmerino, Anthony J. ... Waltham, MA
Palmerino, Kim A. ... Treasury Department, Internal Revenue Service, GV
Palmerlee, David F. ... Buffalo, WY
Gillette, WY
Palmerlee and Durrant ... Buffalo, WY
Gillette, WY
Palmer-Royston, Sharon E. ... Department of State, Bureau of Consular Affairs, GV
Palmersheim, Karen R. ... Los Angeles, CA
Palmersheim, Kevin J. ... Madison, WI
Palmersheim, Richard J. ... Brookfield, WI
Palmersheim, Robert J. ... Chicago, IL
Palmer-Stanford, Tina Marie ... Buffalo, NY
Palmerton, Charles I. ... Seattle, WA
Palmese, Maria L. ... New York, NY
Palmesi Kaufman Goldstein & Petrucelli, PC ... Trumbull, CT
Palmesi, Ralph L. ... Trumbull, CT
Palmeter, N. David ... Washington, DC
Palmgren, Nadine R. ... Geneseo, IL
Palmie, Ross ... Houston, TX
Palmier, Jane B. ... Orlando, FL
Palmier, Joseph P. ... Anchorage, AK
Palmiere, Mark J. ... Rochester, NY
Palmiere, Norman A. ... Rochester, NY
Palmiere, Norman Andrew ... Rochester, NY
Palmieri, Andrew F. ... Washington, DC
Palmieri, Angela ... Garden City, MI
Palmieri, Ann L. ... Boston, MA
Palmieri, Anthony G., Jr. ... Cleveland, OH
Palmieri, Catherine T. ... New Britain, CT
Palmieri, Christine A. ... New York, NY
Palmieri, Dana K. ... Garden City, NY
Palmieri, Daniel ... Mineola, NY
Palmieri, Denise L. ... McLean, VA
Palmieri, Dennis A. ... Garden City, MI
Palmieri, Francis W. ... Princeton, NJ
Palmieri, Francis W. ... McLean, VA
Palmieri, Joseph ... Providence, RI
Palmieri, Joseph Anthony ... Providence, RI
Palmieri, Joseph R. ... San Jose, CA
Palmieri, Laura ... Mineola, NY
Palmieri, Michael J. ... Stamford, CT
Palmieri, Nicola W. ... Mount Olive, NJ
Palmieri & Palmieri ... Providence, RI
Palmieri, Phyllis ... Morganton, NC
Palmieri, Ralph V. ... Los Angeles, CA
Palmieri, Ronald J. ... Los Angeles, CA
Palmieri, Thomas J., (P.A.) ... Miami, FL
Palmieri, Tyler, Wiener, Wilhelm & Waldron, LLP ... Irvine, CA
Palmieri, Victor H. ... New York, NY
Palmieri, Vincent L. ... Libertyville, IL
Palmieri, Vito A. ... Mineola, NY
Palmieri, William S. ... New Haven, CT
Palmintere, Nanci Goldman ... Santa Clara, CA
Palmintier, Daniel C. ... Lafayette, LA
Palmintier, Michael C. ... Baton Rouge, LA
Palmiotto, Michael J. ... Schenectady, NY
Palmiotto, Vincent J. ... Wheeling, WV
Palmisano, Ann Tomeny ... Metairie, LA
Palmisano, Anthony, Jr ... Newark, NJ
Palmisano, Carl J. ... Woodbridge, NJ
Palmisano, Charles S. ... Allston, MA
Palmisano, Deana D. ... New Orleans, LA
Palmisano & Goodman ... Woodbridge, NJ
Palmisano, James A. ... Palos Heights, IL
Palmisano, James Anthony, Ltd. ... Chicago, IL
Palos Heights, IL
Palmisano, John P. ... Elmwood Park, NJ
Palmisano, Joseph D., (P.C.) ... Chicago, IL
Palmisano, Nancy A. ... Tinley Park, IL
Palmisano, Nick ... Modesto, CA
Palmisano, Ralph J. ... Akron, OH
Palmisano, Robin Spencer ... New Orleans, LA
Palmisano, Samuel C. ... Williston, VT
Palmisciano, Nancy A. ... Providence, RI
Palmiter, Alan R. ... Winston-Salem, NC
Palmore, Fred W., III ... Richmond, VA
Palmore, John S. ... Frankfort, KY
Lexington, KY
Palmore, Roderick A. ... Chicago, IL
Palmore, Russell V., Jr. ... Richmond, VA
Palmos, Bill ... Hearne, TX
Palmos, Russ, McCullough & Russ, L.L.P. ... Hearne, TX
Palmour, Albert C. ... Summerville, GA
Palmour, Frank M. ... Apopka, FL
Palmour, Frank M., & Associates, P.A. ... Apopka, FL
Palmour, James E., III ... Gainesville, GA
Palmour, John R. ... Dahlonega, GA
Palmquist, Daniel L. ... Minneapolis, MN
Palmquist, Elizabeth Mooers ... Denver, CO
Palmquist, James B., III ... Medina, OH
Palmquist, James B., III, Co., L.P.A. ... Medina, OH
Palmquist, James P. ... St. Paul, MN
Palmquist, Jennifer L. ... Portland, OR
Palmquist, Jill M. ... St. Louis, MO
Palmquist, John L. ... Denver, CO
Palmquist, Jonathon B. ... San Antonio, TX
Palmquist, Robert F. ... Tucson, AZ
Palmquist, Steven K. ... Clarksville, IN
Palms, H. Norman, Jr. ... Dallas, TX
Palms, Margaret A. ... Boone, NC
Palms, Stephen G. ... Troy, MI
Palmunen, Arthur A. ... Blue Bell, PA
Palnick, Lazar M. ... Pittsburgh, PA
Palo, Bryce ... Grand Junction, CO
Palo, David B. ... Grand Junction, CO
Palo, Margaret Reid-Alvarez ... Los Angeles, CA
Palo, Ralph R. ... New Brunswick, NJ
Palochak, John B. ... Sunnyvale, CA
Paloci, Henry D., III, P.A. ... Fort Myers, FL
LaBelle, FL
Paloci, Henry Davis, III ... Fort Myers, FL
LaBelle, FL
Paloian, Gus A. ... Chicago, IL
Palomar, Joyce Dickey ... Norman, OK
Palomar, Linda L. ... Chicago, IL
Palomares, Henry ... El Paso, TX
Palomba, Tarz F. ... New York, NY
Palombaro, Albert A. ... Youngstown, OH
Palombo, Anthony N. ... Cleveland, OH
Palombo, Armand Anthony ... Scottsdale, AZ
Palombo, Kenneth M. ... Franklin, TN
Palombo, Lisa A. ... Los Angeles, CA
Palombo, Lisa L. ... Sacramento, CA
Palombo, Michael A. ... Pittsburgh, PA
Palombo, Salvatore D. ... Center Line, MI
Palomino, Carmelo "Carl" D. ... Marathon, FL
Palomino, Fabian G. ... Brooklyn, NY
Palomino, Jacinto ... Las Cruces, NM
Palomino, Maria ... Los Angeles, CA
Palomino, Raul C., Jr. ... Tampa, FL
Palomino, Raul C., Jr., P.A. ... Tampa, FL
Palomino, Rene, Jr. ... Coral Gables, FL
Palomo, Carmen M. ... Chico, CA
Palomo, M. Francis ... Northampton, MA
Palomo, William A. ... New York, NY
Palopoli, Stephen J., III ... Allentown, PA
Reading, PA
Palos, Nicholas J. ... Bronx, NY
Palotas, Thomas L. ... Seattle, WA
Palotay, Marc R. ... Universal City, CA
Paloucek, James J. ... North Platte, NE
Palou-Sabater, Miguel ... San Juan, PR
Paloutzian, Dirk B. ... Fresno, CA
Palozola, Janice Lauer ... St. Louis, MO
Pals, Mark A. ... Chicago, IL
Pals, Steven C. ... Orange City, IA
Palsa, Susan C. ... San Francisco, CA
Palsho, Edward R. ... West Trenton, NJ
Palso, Dennis A. ... St. Petersburg, FL
Paltell, Eric ... Baltimore, MD
Palten, Paul M. ... Hartford, CT
Paltenghi, Bruce C. ... Martinez, CA
Palter, Alan D. ... Palo Alto, CA
Palter, Daniel S. ... Honesdale, PA
Palter, John T. ... Dallas, TX
Palter, Kathleen Bagwell ... Irving, TX
Palter, Lisa ... San Francisco, CA
Paltiel, Ellen ... New York, NY
Paltiel, Rae G. ... Morris Plains, NJ
Paltron, Mary-Elizabeth ... New Orleans, LA
Paltrow, Barbara L. ... Massapequa, NY
Paltrow & Paltrow ... Massapequa, NY
Paltrowitz, J. Lawrence ... Glens Falls, NY
Paltrowitz, Ronald I. ... New York, NY
Palty, Joseph L. ... Encino, CA
Palty, Robert L. ... Encino, CA
Paltz, Robert C. ... Syracuse, NY
Paltzik, David M. ... Bellevue, WA
Palu, Jayne M. ... Denver, CO
Palubinsky, Kathleen A ... Shenandoah, PA
Paluch, Ann Marie ... New York, NY
Paluch, Doreen T. ... Woodstock, IL
Paluch, Edw. J. ... Chicago, IL
Paluch, Martha Ann ... Denver, CO
Paluda, Andrew J. ... Troy, MI
Paluf, Timothy G. ... Cleveland, OH
Paluga, Pamela J. ... Long Beach, CA
Palughi, Delano J. ... Mobile, AL
Palughi, Peter J. ... Mobile, AL
Palumbo, Anthony J. ... Phoenix, AZ
Palumbo, Anthony N. ... Cranford, NJ
Palumbo, Blase P. ... Buffalo, NY
Palumbo, Brian Michael ... New York, NY
Palumbo, Bruce ... Pasadena, CA
Palumbo, Carla M. ... Rochester, NY
Palumbo, Corey ... Charleston, WV
Palumbo, Daniel R. ... Olean, NY
Palumbo, Diane O. ... Irvine, CA
San Diego, CA
San Francisco, CA
Palumbo, Francis X.B. ... Hunt Valley, MD
Palumbo, Gary L. ... Denver, CO
Palumbo, Guy L. ... Louisville, KY
Palumbo, James P. ... New York, NY
Palumbo, Jeffery D. ... Buffalo, NY
Palumbo, Joann T. ... New York, NY
Palumbo, Joanne M. ... Newton, MA
Palumbo, John ... Altamonte Springs, FL
Palumbo, John A. ... Lexington, KY
Palumbo, John P. ... Covington, KY
Palumbo, John Patrick ... Scottsdale, AZ
Chicago, IL
Palumbo, John R. ... Waterbury, CT
Palumbo, Joseph J. ... Pittsburgh, PA
Palumbo, Joseph R., Jr. ... Middletown, RI
Palumbo, Judith A. ... Corning, NY
Palumbo, Julianne ... Boston, MA
Providence, RI
Palumbo, Katherine ... Bethesda, MD
Palumbo, Leonard, Wilson, Powell & Vukelic ... Steubenville, OH
Palumbo, Lisa M. ... Stamford, CT

Pannozzo, John R., Jr. ....San Francisco, CA
Pannucci, Ronald H. ....Muskegon, MI
Pannullo, Deborah ....Cranston, RI
Panny, Christopher J. ....Brooklyn, NY
Panoff, Arthur J. ....New York, NY
Panoff, Robert E. ....Miami, FL
Panoff, Robert E., P.A. ....Miami, FL
Panopoulos, Frank ....Washington, DC
Panopoulos, Gus V. ....New York, NY
Panora, Lauren C. ....New York, NY
Panos, Athena A. ....Chevy Chase, MD
Panos, Christine ....Cincinnati, OH
Panos, Christopher J. ....Boston, MA
Panos, Christopher Louis ....Baltimore, MD
Panos, Dean G. ....Denver, CO
Panos, Dean N. ....Chicago, IL
Panos, George E. ....Palos Park, IL
Panos, Harry S. ....Milwaukee, WI
Panos, James ....Lake Success, NY
Panos, Johnny N. ....Decatur, GA
Panos, Laura A. ....Braintree, MA
Panos, Nicholas C. ....Chicago, IL
Panos, Perry G. ....Lowell, MA
Panos, Samuel W. ....Chesterfield, MO
Panos, Tas ....Del Mar, CA
Panos, William S. ....Sterling Heights, MI
Panosian, Chas. G. ....West Allis, WI
Panourgias, John T. ....Troy, MI
Panourgias, Jonathan T. ....Detroit, MI
Panouses, Kurt D. ....Cocoa Beach, FL
Indialantic, FL
Panouses, Kurt D., P.A. ....Cocoa Beach, FL
Indialantic, FL
Panousis, Christ T. ....Rock Island, IL
Panovka, Robin ....New York, NY
Panowicz, Thomas E. ....Jackson, MS
Panse, Robert G. ....West Palm Beach, FL
Pansegrau, Phaedra R. ....Charlotte, NC
Pansegrau, Robert J. ....Los Angeles, CA
Panser, Maynard O. ....Brooklyn Center, MN
Pansing, Arthur F. ....Denver, CO
Pansing, James E. ....Denver, CO
Pansing, Thomas R., Jr. ....Omaha, NE
Pansini & Lessin ....Philadelphia, PA
Pansini, Michael O. ....Philadelphia, PA
Pansius, David K. ....San Jose, CA
Pansius, Jonathan E. ....Tulsa, OK
Pansky, Ellen A. ....South Pasadena, CA
Pansky & Markle ....South Pasadena, CA
Pansler, Karl F. ....Bartow, FL
Pansler & Moody, P.A. ....Bartow, FL
Pansulla, Robert J. ....Short Hills, NJ
Pansya-Shah, Sonal ....Plainsboro, NJ
Pansza, J. Terrence ....Oklahoma City, OK
Pansza, J. Terrence, Inc., A Professional
Corporation ....Oklahoma City, OK
Panszi, Mary Foley ....Indianapolis, IN
Pant, Christina M. ....Dallas, TX
Pantages, James L. A. ....Livingston, NJ
Pantages, Louis J. ....Livingston, NJ
Pantages, Pamela E. ....Shaker Heights, OH
Pantalena, David M. ....Seattle, WA
Pantalena, Lynne L. ....Hartford, CT
Pantaleo, Carl V. ....Branford, CT
Pantaleo, Frances M. ....Rye, NY
White Plains, NY
Pantaleo, Lorraine H. ....Chappaqua, NY
Pantaleo, Peter S. ....Washington, DC
Pantaleo, Peter V. ....New York, NY
Pantaleon, I. Ed ....Orlando, FL
Pantaleoni, Anthony ....New York, NY
Pantaleoni, Michael ....New York, NY
Pantaleoni, Patricia ....Oneonta, NY
Pantaleoni & Weiss, LLP ....New York, NY
Pantalion, Thomas A. ....Minneapolis, MN
Pantani, Edmund L. ....New Haven, CT
Pantano, Anthony ....West Orange, NJ
Pantano, B. Thomas ....Franklin Square, NY
Pantano, Paul J., Jr. ....Washington, DC
Pantaze, Diamond J. ....Dallas, TX
Pantazis, Dennis George ....Birmingham, AL
Pantazis, Eleni S. ....Chicago, IL
Pantazis, Thomasine Lowry ....Houston, TX
Pantea, Thomas M. ....Milwaukee, WI
Pantel, Glenn S. ....Florham Park, NJ
Pantel, Lisa K. ....Morristown, NJ
Pantel, Nicholas J. ....Cincinnati, OH
Pantelakis, Katherine J. ....Rockville, MD
Pantelakis, Marianne Emanuel ....Salem, MA
Pantelas, Nicholas ....Nashua, NH
Pantele, William J. ....Richmond, VA
Pantelis, Irene N. ....Washington, DC
Pantelis, Thomas V. ....Garden City, NY
Pantell, Laurie Judith ....San Francisco, CA
Pantell, Lloyd S., A Professional Law
Corporation ....Calabasas, CA
Pantell, Lloyd S., (P.C.) ....Calabasas, CA
Pantello, Mark S. ....Fort Wayne, IN
Pantelopoulos, Nicholas E. ....New York, NY
Panter, Angela Stewart ....Blue Ridge, GA
Panter, Brett Alan ....Miami, FL
Panter, Danielle R. ....Albuquerque, NM
Panter, Deborah L. ....San Francisco, CA
Panter, Gerald M. ....Beverly Hills, CA
Panter, H. Dennis ....Atlanta, GA
Panter, H. Dennis, & Associates, LLC
Atlanta, GA
Panter, Irwin ....Chicago, IL
Panter, James F. ....Atlanta, GA
Panter, Michael J. ....New York, NY
Panter, Michael R., & Associates
Chicago, IL
Oak Brook, IL
Waukegan, IL
Panter, Mitchell J. ....Miami, FL
Panter & Panter, P.A. ....Miami, FL
Panter, Ronald L. ....Chicago, IL
Panter, S. Craig ....Jackson, MS
Panteris, George ....Great Neck, NY
Panther, James B., Law Offices of
Oceanside, CA
Panther, John P. ....Houston, TX
Panther, Todd E. ....Nashville, TN
Pantiliat, Eddie A. ....Scottsdale, AZ
Pantina, Maria J. ....New York, NY
Pantino, Thomas R. ....New York, NY
Pantirer, Larry ....Union, NJ
Pantis, Yianni Dennis ....Carmichael, CA
Pantoga, Ann Addis ....Chicago, IL
Pantoja, Joseph A. ....New York, NY
Panton, Jo-Jean M. ....Boca Raton, FL
Pantone, B. James ....San Diego, CA
Pantone & Spangler ....San Diego, CA
Pantoni, Anthony F. ....La Jolla, CA
Pantoni, Anthony F. ....San Diego, CA
Pantony, Angela ....New York, NY
Pantos, Andrew J. ....Houston, TX
Pantsios, Joan L. ....Waukegan, IL
Pantuliano, Michael J. ....New York, NY
Pantuso, Anthony J., III ....Stratford, CT
Pantzer, Kurt F., Jr. ....Indianapolis, IN
Pantzer, Robert T. ....Missoula, MT
Panunzio, Mindy Sheps ....Los Angeles, CA
Panus & Associates, L.C.
Kansas City, MO
Panus, Stephen B. ....New Orleans, LA
Panus, Victor C., Jr. ....Kansas City, MO
Panush, Don B. ....New York, NY
Panuthos, Peter J. ....United States Tax Court,
Special Trial Judges, GV
Panza, Christopher ....Pittsburgh, PA
Panza, Mariah A. ....San Francisco, CA
Panza, Maurer, Maynard & Neel, P.A.
Fort Lauderdale, FL
Tallahassee, FL
Panza, Richard D. ....Lorain, OH
Panza, Thomas F. ....Fort Lauderdale, FL
Panzarella, Charles J. ....Tucson, AZ
Panzarella, Christina M. ....Metairie, LA
Panzarella, David T. ....Phoenix, AZ
Panzarella, Frank G. ....Horseheads, NY
Panzarella, Jay L. ....Pittsburgh, PA
Panzarella, John F. ....Tampa, FL
Panzarella, Michael G. ....San Antonio, TX
Panzarella, Raymond V. ....Tucson, AZ
Panzarino, Jeanne L. ....Boston, MA
Panzeca & D'Angelo ....Metairie, LA
Panzeca, Salvatore ....Metairie, LA
Panzella, Bernadette ....Staten Island, NY
Panzella, Bernadette, P.C. ....Staten Island, NY
Panzer, Alvin M. ....Elizabeth, NJ
Panzer, Bryce D. ....Salt Lake City, UT
Panzer, Charles N. ....Parsippany, NJ
Panzer, Curtis C. ....Rahway, NJ
Panzer, David S. ....La Plata, MD
Panzer, Irving J. ....Bronx, NY
Panzer, Irving R. M. ....Washington, DC
Panzer, Jason M. ....Austin, TX
Panzer, Jonathan J. ....Los Angeles, CA
Panzer, Mitchell E. ....Philadelphia, PA
Panzer, Thomas E. ....Blue Bell, PA
Panzer, William C. ....Southfield, MI
Panzer, William G. ....Oakland, CA
Panzera, Guido ....New York, NY
Panzera, Philip M. ....San Diego, CA
Panzer-Howell, Nancy L. ....Kansas City, MO
Panzeri, Mark A. ....St. Louis, MO
Panzeri, Richard W. ....Houston, TX
Panzica, Anthony N. ....Chicago, IL
Panzica, Edward Martin ....Clearwater, FL
Panzica, Frank V., (P.C.) ....Houston, TX
Panzik, Susan J. ....Washington, DC
Panzini-Romeo, Frances J. ....West Orange, NJ
Panzitta, Leonard J. ....Savannah, GA
Panzl, Joseph R. ....Orlando, FL
Panzone, Anthony T. ....Utica, NY
Panzone, John A. ....Rome, NY
Pao, Ellen K. ....Boston, MA
Paola, Francis D., Jr. ....Wallingford, CT
Paola, Frederick Adolf ....Oldsmar, FL
Paolano, Mary J. ....Cleveland, OH
Paolella, John B. ....Hackensack, NJ
Paolella, Raymond L. ....Yakima, WA
Paoletti, C. Jeffry ....Salt Lake City, UT
Paoletti, Douglas P. ....New York, NY
Paoletti, Frederick D., Jr. ....Bridgeport, CT
Paoletti, Jodie A. ....Philadelphia, PA
Paoli, A. C. ....Hollywood, FL
Paoli, Anita ....Hollywood, FL
Paoli, August C., P.A., The Law Offices of
Hollywood, FL
Paoli & Bratter ....Oakland, CA
Paoli & Brown, P.C. ....Livingston, MT
Paoli, Charles E., Jr. ....Hollywood, FL
Paoli, Charles E., Jr., Professional Association
Hollywood, FL
Paoli, David R. ....Missoula, MT
Paoli, Elena I. ....Federal Trade Commission,
Bureau of Consumer Protection, GV
Paoli, Fred, Jr. ....Livingston, MT
Paoli & Geerhart, LLP ....San Francisco, CA
Paoli, James P. ....Atlantic City, NJ
Paoli, Maria Dolores ....New York, NY
Paoli & Paoli, Inc. ....La Mirada, CA
Paoli, Peter J. ....La Mirada, CA
Paoli, Sylvia L. ....La Mirada, CA
Paoli, Thomas Alan ....San Francisco, CA
Paoli, William D. ....Oakland, CA
Paoli, William Delli ....Newport Beach, CA
Paolicelli, Diane ....New York, NY
Paolillo, Charles D.
Agency for International Development,
Other Offices of A.I.D., GV
Paolillo, Christopher P. ....Newton, MA
Paolillo, Lisa A. ....Boston, MA
Paolillo, Michael P. ....Stamford, CT
Paolin, Gerald J. ....Greenville, DE
Paolini, Ezio M. ....San Francisco, CA
Paolini, Mario G. ....San Francisco, CA
Paolini, Mario G., Jr. ....San Francisco, CA
Paolini, Michael R. ....West Roxbury, MA
Paolini & Paolini ....San Francisco, CA
Paolini, Robert M. ....Barre, VT
Paolini-Mori, Anne Marie
San Francisco, CA
Paolino, Eugene T. ....Jersey City, NJ
Paolino, Guy N. ....Media, PA
Paolino, John M. ....Philadelphia, PA
Paolo, Richard A. ....Cincinnati, OH
Paolone, Ralph A. ....Pleasantville, NJ
Williamstown, NJ
Paoloni, Robert J. ....Kent, OH
Paolucci, Joseph M., Jr. ....Chicago, IL
Paolucci, Lawrence J. ....Detroit, MI
Paolucci, Marylou A. ....Smithtown, NY
Paolucci, Michael A. ....Cincinnati, OH
Paolucci, Michael J. ....Detroit, MI
Paolucci, Peter J. ....Lacon, IL
Paone, Anthony J. ....Bronx, NY
Paone, Arthur J. ....Dallas, TX
Paone Callahan McHolm & Winton, LLP
Irvine, CA
Newport Beach, CA
Paone, Frank ....Brooklyn, NY
Paone, James A. ....Avon-By-The-Sea, NJ
Paone, John P., Jr. ....Billerica, MA
Paone, John P., Jr. ....Woodbridge, NJ
Paone, John P., Jr., A Prof. Corp., Law
Offices of ....Woodbridge, NJ
Paone, Kathleen Carothers ....Irvine, CA
Paone, Nicholas L. ....New York, NY
Paone, Tim ....Irvine, CA
Pap, Patricia A. ....Hyannis, MA
Papa, Frank R. ....Amherst, NY
Papa, Gino C. ....Mineola, NY
Papa, Herman D. ....San Francisco, CA
Papa, James Anthony ....Brentwood, NY
Papa, John S., Jr. ....Bristol, CT
Papa, John Stephen ....Hartford, CT
Manchester, CT
Papa, John T. ....Granite City, IL
Papa, Jolene M. ....Lincoln, NE
Papa, Joseph A., Jr. ....Albany, NY
Papa, Joseph F. ....Boca Raton, FL
Papa, Julie Nolan ....Washington, DC
Papa, Kenneth J. ....New Haven, CT
Papa, Laura Miller ....Lake Success, NY
Papa, Louis S. ....Vienna, VA
Papa, Mario J. ....Gloversville, NY
Papa, Nicholas Anthony ....Pepper Pike, OH
Papa, Nicole J. ....Baltimore, MD
Papa & Papa ....New Castle, PA
Papa, Philip R. ....New York, NY
Papa, Robert L. ....Charleston, SC
Papa, Ronald R. ....New York, NY
Papa, Rose M. ....Baltimore, MD
Papa, Salvatore F. ....Albany, NY
Papa, Susan M. ....New Castle, PA
Papa, Thomas W. ....Richmond, VA
Papa, Vincent J. ....New York, NY
Papa-Cacace, Claudia Marie ....Yonkers, NY
Papachristos, John ....New York, NY
Papada, James M., III ....Philadelphia, PA
Papadakis, Alec ....Atlanta, GA
Papadakis, Dean J. ....Chicago, IL
Papadakis, Ellen M. ....San Francisco, CA
Papadakis, Felix N. ....New York, NY
Papadakis, Victor N. ....Fresno, CA
Papadatos, Caroline ....New York, NY
Papademas Law Firm ....Lebanon, NH
Papademas, N. George ....Lebanon, NH
Papademas, Nancy A. ....Lebanon, NH
Papademetriou, Barbara ....Miami, FL
Papademetriou, Constantine Dean
Boston, MA
Papademetriou, Ourania ....Philadelphia, PA
Papadia, John ....Chicago, IL
Papadimitriou, Jon ....Alpharetta, GA
Papadimos, Peter J. ....Columbus, OH
Papadopoulos, Helena C. ....Houston, TX
Papadopoulos, Imogen S. ....Houston, TX
Papadopoulos, Mark E. ....Washington, DC
Papadopoulos, Panagiotis (Peter)
Department of Housing and Urban
Development, GV
Papadopoulos, Paul G. ....Charleston, WV
Papadopoulos-Papandreou, Christina
Houston, TX
Papageorge, Chris ....Gardena, CA
Papageorge, George ....Milwaukee, WI
Papageorge, Janet E. ....Chesterfield, MO
Papageorge, John D. ....Indianapolis, IN
Papageorge, Lee J. ....Los Angeles, CA
Papageorge, Thomas A. ....Los Angeles, CA
Papagianakis, Peter ....Tampa, FL
Papagjika, Mary A. ....Gaithersburg, MD
Papagoda, Suzann E. ....Los Angeles, CA
Papahronis, John A. ....Oklahoma City, OK
Papain, Nicholas ....Mineola, NY
New York, NY
Papaj, William E. ....Chicago, IL
Papajcik, Dale E. ....Cleveland, OH
Papajohn, John N. ....Alexandria, VA
Papak, Paul J. ....Cedar Rapids, IA
Papakhian, Victor ....Detroit, MI
Papalas, Menelaos K. ....Tampa, FL
Papalas, Michael A. ....Dallas, TX
Papale, Antonio E., Jr., (P.L.C.)
Metairie, LA
Papale, George M. ....New Orleans, LA
Papale, Lawrence G. ....St. Helena, CA
San Francisco, CA
Papale, Thomas E. ....Marksville, LA
Papalia, Bridget H. ....Louisville, KY
Papalia, Frank D. ....New York, NY
Papalia, Kathryn T. ....Sacramento, CA
Papalia, Patrick ....Hackensack, NJ
Papalia, Roy C. ....Watertown, MA
Papalia, Vincent F. ....Newark, NJ
Papalini, Joseph I. ....Philadelphia, PA
Papan, Diane D. ....San Francisco, CA
Papan, Virginia I. ....Los Angeles, CA
Papandon, John C. ....Bethesda, MD
Papandon, Stephen N. ....Sayville, NY
Papandrea, John F. ....Meriden, CT
Papandrea, John F. ....Washington, DC
Papandrea, Joseph J. ....Port Charlotte, FL
Papandrea, Mary-Rose ....Washington, DC
Papandrea, Ronald J. ....Warren, MI
Papandreas, Fahrer & Corso ....Cleveland, OH
Papandreas, John G. ....Cleveland, OH
Papandreou, Alexander C. ....Houston, TX
Papanek, Andrea ....Boston, MA
Papanek, Samuel, III ....Northbrook, IL
Papanickolas, Emmanuel N. ....Peabody, MA
Papanikolas, Demetrios ....Pasadena, CA
Papano, Susan G. ....New York, NY
Papantones, Melissa J. ....New Haven, CT
Papantonio, J. Michael ....Pensacola, FL
Papantonio, Kathy W. ....Cumming, GA
Papantonis, Perry C. ....Bedminster, NJ
Papapanagiotou, Jennifer L. ....Houston, TX
Paparazzo, Louis F. ....Greenfield, MA
Paparella, Christopher M. ....New York, NY
Paparella, Joseph F. ....Holden, MA
Paparella, Kathleen A.
West Palm Beach, FL
Paparelli, Angelo A. ....Irvine, CA
Paparelli & Partners LLP ....Irvine, CA
Paparian, Glenn T. ....New York, NY
Paparian, William M. ....Pasadena, CA
Paparo, Edward ....New York, NY
Paparo, Vincenzo ....Hackensack, NJ
Paparodis, Chris O. ....Hilliard, OH
Paparone & Associates, P.C. ....Trevose, PA
Paparone, Salvatore A., Jr. ....Trevose, PA
Papas & Atkinson ....Stockton, CA
Papas, Caroline E. ....San Francisco, CA
Papas, Chris Wm. ....Stockton, CA
Papas, Constantine W. ....Tampa, FL
Papas, Katerina C. ....Akron, OH
Papas, Leo S. ....San Diego, CA
Papasian, Vahak A. ....Tarzana, CA
Papasodora, Karen S. ....Virginia Beach, VA
Papastavros, Angelica N. ....New Haven, CT
Papastavros, Nicholas G. ....Boston, MA
Papastratakos, Nick ....Northbrook, IL
Papathemetrios, Constantine ....Concord, CA
Papavasiliou, Elaine ....Alexandria, VA
Papavizas, Constantine G.
Washington, DC
Papay, Debbie J. ....Toledo, OH
Papay, Debbie J., Co., L.P.A. ....Toledo, OH
Papay, Jacob A., Jr. ....Clinton, NJ
Papazekos, Joanna P. ....Pittsburgh, PA
Papazekos, Pantelis T. ....Pittsburgh, PA
Papazian, Edmund R. ....Larchmont, NY
Papazian, Gerald S.
Palos Verdes Estates, CA
Papazian, Mark S. ....Bloomfield Hills, MI
Papazian, Simona S. ....New York, NY
Papazian-Ross, Jessica L. ....Providence, RI
Papazicos, George ....New York, NY
Papazoglou, George S. ....Danbury, CT
Pape, Alwin E., Jr. ....Seguin, TX
Pape, Arthur E., (P.C.) ....Wheaton, IL
Pape, Christopher D. ....Racine, WI
Pape, Daniel C. ....Omaha, NE
Pape, Donald A. ....Norman, OK
Oklahoma City, OK
Pape, Donald A., P.C. ....Norman, OK
Pape, James M. ....San Marcos, TX
Pape, Jeffrey B. ....Clovis, CA
Pape, John A. ....Atlanta, GA
Pape, Julie ....New York, NY
Pape, Kara A. ....Los Angeles, CA
Pape, Kathy Lee ....Voorhees, NJ
Pape, Kenneth L. ....Old Bridge, NJ
Pape, Lella Amiss E. ....Silver Spring, MD
Pape, Leonard ....Los Angeles, CA
Pape, Mary ....Round Rock, TX
Pape, Matthew S. ....El Paso, TX
Pape, Michael J. ....Minneapolis, MN
Pape, Patrick J. ....San Antonio, TX
Pape, Ralph C. ....Ravena, NY
Pape, Rebecca H. ....Great Falls, MT
Pape, Robert J., Jr. ....Manhasset, NY
New York, NY
Pape, Robert J., Jr. ....Mineola, NY
Pape, Scott C. ....Sherman Oaks, CA
Pape, Stephen G. ....Fairview, NJ
Pape, Stuart M. ....Washington, DC
Pape, Susan F. ....Omaha, NE
Pape, Timothy M. ....Fort Wayne, IN
Papel, Laurence M. ....Nashville, TN
Papelian, Jeanmarie ....Manchester, NH
Papelian, Joseph E. ....Troy, MI
Papell, Ronald M. ....Los Angeles, CA
Papell, Ronald M., A Prof. Corp., Law
Offices of ....Los Angeles, CA
Papenbrock, William A. ....Cleveland, OH
Papendick, Rolland L. ....Red Bluff, CA
Papendorf, Jarrod J. ....Appleton, WI
Papenfuss, Francis D. ....La Crosse, WI
Papenfuss, Herbert ....Reseda, CA
Papenheim, Gary R. ....Parkersburg, IA
Papenthien, Janet L. ....Cedar Rapids, IA
Paper, Lawrence N. ....Pittsburgh, PA
Paper, Lewis J. ....Washington, DC
Papera, John L., Jr ....Highland Beach, FL
West Palm Beach, FL
Parsippany, NJ

Papera, John L., Jr., P.A. Highland Beach, FL; West Palm Beach, FL; Parsippany, NJ
Papermaster, Daniel I. **Hartford, CT**
Papermaster, Gail E. Austin, TX
Papermaster, Meyer B., (S.C.) Milwaukee, WI
Papermaster, Stephen J. **Rockville, MD**
Papermaster & Weltmann, A Professional Corporation **Washington, DC; Greenbelt, MD; Landover, MD; Rockville, MD**
Paperner, Howard, (P.C.) **St. Louis, MO**
Paperner, Leslie J. **Reston, VA**
Papernick, Alan **Pittsburgh, PA**
Papernick & Gefsky, A Professional Corporation **Pittsburgh, PA**
Papernick, Stephen M. **Pittsburgh, PA**
Papernik, Brian G. **Los Angeles, CA**
Papernik, Joel I. **New York, NY**
Paperno, Jill L. Rochester, NY
Paperno, Pearl R. Milford, CT
Paperny, Alan K. Enfield, CT
Papetti, Randy **Phoenix, AZ**
Papez, Danny L. Ely, NV
Papiano, Neil **Los Angeles, CA**
Papica, Francis P. Orange, CA
Papier, David J. **Newark, NJ**
Papier, Philip B., Jr. Princeton, NJ
Papier, Philip B., Jr., A Professional Corporation Princeton, NJ
Papiernick, Jacqueline I. New York, NY
Papiernik, Gregory A. **Chicago, IL**
Papiewski, Suzanne M. **Washington, DC**
Papik, James E. **Osceola, NE**
Papik, James E. Shelby, NE; **Stromsburg, NE**
Papile, Christopher R. **Norfolk, VA**
Papillion, Darrel J. **Baton Rouge, LA**
Papillo, Anthony F. Boston, MA
Papillo, Jeanette P. Rockville, MD
Papillon, Mona **Washington, DC**
Papirio, Mark A. Springfield, MA
Papirmeister, James N. Upper Marlboro, MD
Papish, Pamela J. New York, NY
Papke, Alicia A. Manchester, NH
Papke, Jerome J. Richardson, TX
Papke, Letecia J. Eau Claire, WI
Papke, Melissa **New York, NY**
Papke, William L. Glen Ellyn, IL
Papkin, Carol Sandy Fort Lauderdale, FL
Papkin, Rachel F. Chevy Chase, MD
Papkin, Robert D. **Washington, DC**
Papkin, Steven C. **Los Angeles, CA**
Papleacos, Nicholas S. **Atlanta, GA**
Paplos, Elaine Ann Saipan, TT
Papner, Donald F. Cincinnati, OH
Papol, Sheela Marian Deer Park, NY
Papoutsis, John N. Lancaster, PA
Papp, Allen N. Woodbridge, NJ
Papp, Bernard K. Harvard, IL
Papp, Bernard K., P.C. Harvard, IL
Papp, Dennis M. Columbus, OH
Papp, Edward D. **Cleveland, OH**
Papp, Eric M. **Las Vegas, NV**
Papp, Joseph R. **Troy, MI**
Papp, Leo Detroit, MI
Papp, Lisa M. **Newark, NJ**
Papp, Robert J. New London, CT
Pappa, Donald J. Allenhurst, NJ
Pappa, Kristina K. Woodbridge, NJ; **New York, NY**
Pappa, Michael J. Hazlet, NJ
Pappachen, George V., Jr. **New York, NY**
Pappacoda, Joseph J. Fort Lauderdale, FL
Pappadia, Priscilla A. Hartford, CT
Pappafotis, Michael S. Glen Burnie, MD
Pappafotis, Michael S., P.A. Glen Burnie, MD
Pappafotis, Rachel E. Baltimore, MD
Pappagianis, George S. Nashua, NH
Pappajohn, Shriver, Eide & Nicholas, P.C. **Mason City, IA**
Pappajohn, Socrates G. **Mason City, IA**
Pappal, Nancy A. **Rochester, NY**
Pappalardo, A. John **Boston, MA**
Pappalardo, Angelo C. Lawrence, MA
Pappalardo, Bradford D. Sacramento, CA
Pappalardo, Carla F. Elk Grove Village, IL
Pappalardo, Denise M. Franklin, MA
Pappalardo, Fauna M. Rochester, NY
Pappalardo, Frank D. Rochester, NY
Pappalardo, Frederick C. Basking Ridge, NJ
Pappalardo, Gregory J. Scarsdale, NY
Pappalardo, Jack D. **Atlanta, GA**
Pappalardo, John A. Roseland, NJ; **White Plains, NY**
Pappalardo, John J. Eastchester, NY
Pappalardo, Joseph S. New Orleans, LA
Pappalardo, Joseph W. **Cleveland, OH**
Pappalardo, Marc F. **Phoenix, AZ**
Pappalardo, Victor A. Auburn, CA
Pappanastos, John N. **Montgomery, AL**
Pappanastos, Wilson & Associates, P.C. **Montgomery, AL**
Pappano & Breslin Brookhaven, PA
Pappano, Daniel G. **Chicago, IL**
Pappano, John A. **Buffalo, NY**
Pappano, Robert F. Brookhaven, PA
Pappas, Albert G. **Atlanta, GA**
Pappas, Alexa B. **Boston, MA**
Pappas, Alexia **Washington, DC**
Pappas, Andrew Staten Island, NY
Pappas, Ann Hogue Raleigh, NC
Pappas, Barbara M. New York, NY
Pappas, Brian J. Tallahassee, FL
Pappas, C. Andrew **Syracuse, NY**
Pappas, Callie Georgeann Pittsburgh, PA
Pappas, Carol L. Akron, OH
Pappas, Catherine A Boston, MA
Pappas, Catherine E. Philadelphia, PA
Pappas, Chris **New York, NY**
Pappas, Chris I. Boston, MA
Pappas, Christie Eufaula, AL
Pappas, Christina Jessica **Baltimore, MD**
Pappas, Christina S. Astoria, NY
Pappas, Christopher C. **Houston, TX**
Pappas, Christopher P. **Irvine, CA**
Pappas, Cleopatra **Baltimore, MD**
Pappas, Daniel C. Houston, TX
Pappas, Daniel C., P.C. Houston, TX
Pappas, Daniel G. Fort Wayne, IN
Pappas, David C. Deerfield, WI
Pappas, Dean **Los Angeles, CA**
Pappas, Dean A. **Redwood City, CA**
Pappas, Dean G. Austin, TX; **Houston, TX**
Pappas, Dean T. Baltimore, MD
Pappas, Dennis J. Syosset, NY
Pappas, Diane Thousand Oaks, CA
Pappas, Diane E. **Chicago, IL**
Pappas, Diane H. **Beverly Hills, CA**
Pappas, Douglas R. **New York, NY**
Pappas, Edward H. **Bloomfield Hills, MI**
Pappas, Eric W. Indialantic, FL
Pappas, F. Richard Austin, TX
Pappas & Garcia Orlando, FL
Pappas, Gary A. Boston, MA
Pappas, Gary M. **Miami, FL**
Pappas, Geo. Akron, OH
Pappas, George Chicago, IL
Pappas, George Fort Wayne, IN
Pappas, George C. **La Jolla, CA**; Schaumburg, IL
Pappas, George C. Spring Lake, NJ
Pappas, George C. Akron, OH
Pappas, George, Co., L.P.A. Akron, OH
Pappas, George F. **Washington, DC; Baltimore, MD**
Pappas, George N. Hoboken, NJ
Pappas, George P. **East Lansing, MI**
Pappas, George P. **Houston, TX**
Pappas, George R. New City, NY
Pappas, George S. **Daytona Beach, FL; Maitland, FL**
Pappas, Gregory J. Leawood, KS; **Kansas City, MO**
Pappas, Gus Chula Vista, CA
Pappas, Gus E., (P.C.) Houston, TX
Pappas, Harold N. **New York, NY**
Pappas, Harry J. Cincinnati, OH
Pappas, Hercules Gibbsboro, NJ; Marlton, NJ; Philadelphia, PA
Pappas, James A. Springfield, IL
Pappas, James G. Fort Lee, NJ
Pappas, James L. Traverse City, MI
Pappas, James, (Ltd.) Flossmoor, IL
Pappas, James P. New York, NY
Pappas, Jeanette Spring Lake, NJ
Pappas, Jeannette D. New York, NY
Pappas, Jim D. Boise, ID
Pappas, Joanne N. Maynard, MA
Pappas, John D. Corpus Christi, TX
Pappas, John E. Portsmouth, VA
Pappas, John J. **Miami, FL; Tampa, FL**
Pappas, John J., Sr. **Chicago, IL**
Pappas, John T. Concord, NH
Pappas, Jordan E. Rochester, NY
Pappas, Laurence E. Rochester, NY
Pappas, Leah P. Astoria, NY
Pappas and Lenzo Boston, MA
Pappas, Leonard J. Canton, OH; **Cleveland, OH**; Youngstown, OH
Pappas, Louis C. Tulsa, OK
Pappas, Louis W. **Los Angeles, CA**
Pappas, M. Lynn **Jacksonville, FL**
Pappas, Maria Chicago, IL
Pappas, Mary Atlanta, GA
Pappas, Matthew J. United States Senate, Committee Legal Personnel, GV
Pappas, Matthew P. **Rock Island, IL**
Pappas Metcalf Jenks Miller & Reinsch, P.A. **Jacksonville, FL**
Pappas, Michael D. Securities and Exchange Commission, Office of Administrative Law Judges, GV
Pappas, Michael L. Waltham, MA
Pappas, Michael P. **New York, NY**
Pappas, Milton J. New York, NY
Pappas, Nicholas C. **Indianapolis, IN**
Pappas, Nicholas J. West Bethesda, MD
Pappas, Nicholas J. **New York, NY**
Pappas, Nicholas S. **Fort Worth, TX**
Pappas, Nicole M. **Chicago, IL**
Pappas, Pamela Nichols **Houston, TX**
Pappas & Pappas Spring Lake, NJ; Astoria, NY
Pappas and Pappas Rochester, NY
Pappas, Perry A. **Princeton, NJ; New York, NY**
Pappas, Pete F. Springfield, OH
Pappas, Peter C. Antioch, CA
Pappas, Peter C. Orlando, FL
Pappas, Peter G. **Atlanta, GA**
Pappas, Peter G. **Greensboro, NC**
Pappas, Peter G. La Crosse, WI
Pappas, Power & Marcus **Chicago, IL**
Pappas & Richardson, L.L.C. Marlton, NJ; Philadelphia, PA
Pappas, Robert T. **Columbus, OH**
Pappas, Samuel L. **Chicago, IL**
Pappas & Schnell, P.C. **Moline, IL; Rock Island, IL; Davenport, IA**
Pappas, Sherri Lynn Department of Transportation, Research and Special Programs Administration, GV
Pappas, Sophia G. Metairie, LA
Pappas, Sophia H. Wayland, MA
Pappas, Stacey P. **Chicago, IL**
Pappas, Stanley R. Wauwatosa, WI
Pappas, Stephanie E. Akron, OH
Pappas, Stephanie L. **Detroit, MI**
Pappas, Stephen R., Esq. **Palo Alto, CA**
Pappas, Steven J. **Uniondale, NY**
Pappas, T. G. **Nashville, TN**
Pappas, Theodore Sherman Oaks, CA
Pappas, Thomas G. **Dallas, TX**
Pappas, Thomas John **Manchester, NH**
Pappas, Thomas P. **Columbus, OH**
Pappas, Thomas R. **New York, NY**
Pappas, Tinsley & Russell, P.A. **Daytona Beach, FL; Orange City, FL; Palm Coast, FL**
Pappas, Valeri **Denver, CO**
Pappas, Virginia C. **Blue Bell, PA**
Pappas, William G. New York, NY
Pappas, William G. **Raleigh, NC**
Pappaterra, Martin S. Mount Holly, NJ; Princeton, NJ
Pappayliou, George S. **Dayton, OH**
Papp-Campbell, Carolyn Ann Bronx, NY
Pappenfus, Thomas J. Alexandria, MN
Papper, Richard N. New York, NY
Papperman, Raymond S. **Livingston, NJ**
Papperman, Solomon Silver Spring, MD
Pappert, Edward B. Evanston, IL
Pappert, Michael J. **Houston, TX**
Pappin, James R. Seattle, WA
Pappo, Donna Neudecker Glenview, IL
Pappone, Michael J., (P.C.) **Boston, MA**
Papps, Thos. G. Toledo, OH
Pappy, Elizabeth M. **San Jose, CA**
Papy, George A. Burbank, CA
Paprocki, Paul E. Chicago, IL
Paprocki, Thomas J. Chicago, IL
Paprota, Frank J., Jr. South River, NJ
Papsdorf, Cynthia S. **Los Angeles, CA**
Papson, Costa L. New York, NY
Papson, Cristina S. Harrisburg, PA
Papson, John A. Jeannette, PA
Papson, Thomas C. **Washington, DC**
Papst, Edward Pittsburgh, PA
Papst, Richard J. Bakersfield, CA
Papuc, Michael A. San Francisco, CA
Papuga, John P. **Pittsburgh, PA**
Papuga, Stanley W. Chicago, IL
Papushak, Deborah J. **Cleveland, OH**
Papushkewych, Darka Chicago, IL
Papushkewych, Gerri Springfield, IL
Papy, Charles C., III **Miami, FL**
Papy, Charles C., Jr. **Miami, FL**; Tampa, FL
Papy, Donald M. Miami, FL
Papy & Weissenborn, P.A. **Miami, FL**
Papy Weissenborn Poole & Vraspir, P.A. Tampa, FL
Paque, Anita M. Santa Clara, CA
Paquet, Susan I. **Fort Worth, TX**; Weatherford, TX
Paquette, Danielle A. Lincoln, RI
Paquette, Deborah A. New York, NY
Paquette, Dennis A. Department of Labor, Office of the Solicitor, GV
Paquette, Jerold G. Gardner, MA
Paquette, Nicole G. Washington, DC
Paquette, Paul N. Los Angeles, CA
Paquette, Roxanne J. Mineola, NY
Paquette, Steven A. Syracuse, NY
Paquette, Susan Pfeifer Houston, TX
Paquin, Jeffrey D. Atlanta, GA
Paquin, Jerome F. Minneapolis, MN
Paquin, Joseph H., Jr. **Chicago, IL**
Paquin, Judith E. South Windsor, CT
Paquin, Paul J. Charlotte Amalie, St. Thomas, VI
Paquin, Thomas C. **Barnstable, MA; Yarmouth Port, MA**
Paquin, William F. Warwick, RI
Par, Matthew T. Elk Grove Village, IL
Para, Bruno G. Glen Ellyn, IL
Para, Gerard A. Long Grove, IL
Para, Noel J. **New York, NY**
Parachini, Donald G. **San Francisco, CA**
Parachini, Maria N. Manhattan Beach, CA
Parachini, Thomas G. **Detroit, MI**
Paracuellos, Amanda J. **Washington, DC**
Parad, Boris Skokie, IL
Parada, Oswald Los Angeles, CA
Paradee, John W. **Dover, DE**
Paradeis, Todd A. **New York, NY**
Paradela, Robert E. **Fort Lauderdale, FL**
Paradice, William L., III San Francisco, CA
Paradies, Beth H. Marietta, GA
Paradine, Danielle Helen **Washington, DC**
Paradis, David B. Springfield, MA
Paradis, David B. **Medford, OR**
Paradis, Gary L. Manchester, NH
Paradis, Jacquelyn C. Allentown, PA
Paradis, Jon Pierre **Santa Ana, CA**
Paradis, Jon Pierre, Inc., A Law Corporation **Santa Ana, CA**
Paradis, Joseph A., III Louisville, KY
Paradis, Kenneth J. Natick, MA
Paradis, Maurice L. Napa, CA
Paradis, Paul O. **New York, NY**
Paradis, Raoul E. Old Orchard Beach, ME
Paradis, Suzanne Lisinski Batavia, IL
Paradis, Vincent A. **Essex Junction, VT**
Paradis, Wendy J. **Portland, ME**
Paradise, Alberts & Fisher LLP Boca Raton, FL; **New York, NY**
Paradise, April **Los Angeles, CA**
Paradise, David T. **Chicago, IL**
Paradise, Francine Caren Elgin, IL
Paradise, Gregg A. **New York, NY**
Paradise, Gregory J. Madison, WI
Paradise, James C. Cincinnati, OH
Paradise, Leone P. Pittsburgh, PA
Paradise, Melvin **New York, NY**
Paradise, Michael S. **New York, NY**
Paradise, Robert D. Fort Worth, TX
Paradise, Robt. E. Arcadia, CA
Paradise, Stacey E. **New York, NY**
Paradise, Stephen J. United States Senate, Committee Legal Personnel, GV
Paradise, Steven R. **New York, NY**
Paradise, Thomas D. **Voorhees, NJ**
Paradise, Thomas W. **Fort Lauderdale, FL**
Paradise, Vincent J. **Mineola, NY**
Paradiso, Anthony J. **Detroit, MI**
Paradiso, Christina L. Worcester, MA
Paradiso, Dack, Taub & Oler, P.C. **Washington, DC; Bethesda, MD; Vienna, VA**
Paradiso, Don A. West Palm Beach, FL
Paradiso, F. Joseph **Stafford Springs, CT**
Paradiso, Joseph C. **Washington, DC; Bethesda, MD**
Paradiso, Marisa Y., The Law Offices of Riverdale, NJ
Paradiso, Michela G. Staten Island, NY
Paradiso & Muska **Stafford Springs, CT; Willimantic, CT**
Paradiso, Robert J. **New York, NY**
Paradoski, Adam J. Houston, TX
Paradoski, Ronald C., Jr. **Detroit, MI**
Parady, Christopher A. **Boston, MA**
Parady, Robert W. Monument Beach, MA
Parady, William A. Fort Lauderdale, FL
Parady & Zikakis, P.A. Fort Lauderdale, FL
Paragano & Benvenuto, P.C. Bernardsville, NJ; Springfield, NJ
Paragano, John Union, NJ
Paragano, Vincent D. Bernardsville, NJ
Paragas, C. David **Columbus, OH**
Paragas, William Randall Omaha, NE
Parajeckas, Kristen C. Solana Beach, CA
Parakilas, Charles M. Enfield, CT
Parakilas, Kathryn M. Westfield, MA
Paralusz, Kathleen M. **Washington, DC**; Washington, DC
Parambath, Reena E. **Philadelphia, PA**
Parameswaran, Prabha **Chicago, IL**
Paramore, Kenneth D. Greenville, NC
Paramore, Phyllis Naomi Turnham Birmingham, AL
Paramore, W.H., III **Jacksonville, NC**
Paran, Mark L. Euless, TX
Paranac, Joseph P., Jr. **Newark, NJ**; Philadelphia, PA
Paranczak, Gene **Philadelphia, PA**
Parandeh, Nayssan L. **Los Angeles, CA**
Parang, Touraj **Palo Alto, CA**
Parangi, Mahsa **New York, NY**
Paranica, Kristine J. Bismarck, ND
Paranicas, Dean J. Franklin Lakes, NJ
Paranzino, Gary A. Sunnyvale, CA
Paras, Apy & Reiss, P.C. **North Brunswick, NJ; Red Bank, NJ**
Paras, Danae A. Sacramento, CA
Paras, George C. Merrillville, IN
Paras, George E. **Sacramento, CA**
Paras, Harry M. **Pittsburgh, PA**
Paras, Helen Sacramento, CA
Paras, James C. **San Francisco, CA**
Paras, Peter C. **Red Bank, NJ**
Parascandola, Anthony J. Venice, CA
Parascandola, Frank C. Phoenix, AZ
Parascandola, Pamela S. **Harrisburg, PA**
Parascandola, Stephen T. **Raleigh, NC**
Parascandolo, Gerald **Providence, RI**
Paraschos, Arik C. Huntington, WV
Paraschos, John P. **New York, NY**
Parash, William H. **New York, NY**
Parashes, Peter T. **Philadelphia, PA**
Parashos, Tom San Diego, CA
Paraskevas, Theodore H. **New York, NY**
Paraskevas-Thadani, Elena **New York, NY**
Paraskou, Gregory C. San Jose, CA
Parauda, John E. **New York, NY**
Paravano, Jeffrey H. **Cleveland, OH**
Paravati, Peter P. Utica, NY
Paravati, Peter P., Jr. Utica, NY
Paravati, Peter P., P.C. Utica, NY
Paravecchio, James Russell Littleton, CO
Paravola, Thomas J. **Chicago, IL**
Paray, Paul E. Berkeley Heights, NJ
Parcel, Howard E. Portland, OR
Parcel, Randy L. **Denver, CO**
Parcell, John H. Treasury Department, Departmental Offices, GV
Parcell, Webb, Honey & Wallerstein, P.C. Richmond, VA
Parcell, William H., III Richmond, VA
Parcella, Mark F. **San Francisco, CA**
Parcellin, John W. Malden, MA
Parcells, Dayton B., III Los Angeles, CA

Parchem, David F. ...Westlake, OH
Parchem, Robert P. ...Tinley Park, IL
Parcher, Frederic C. ...Columbus, OH
Parcher, Hayes & Snyder, P.C.
New York, NY
Parcher, L. Peter ...New York, NY
Parcher, Laura Tuell ...Washington, DC
Parchert, Brett M. ...Department of Justice, Immigration and Naturalization Service, GV
Parcheta, Mark E. ...Denver, CO
Parchman, Daniel K. ...Mount Vernon, TX
Parchman, Wynette G. ...Azle, TX
Parchment, Monica Charisse
Washington, DC
Parchment, Nathalie R. ...Davie, FL
Parde, Glynna Christian
Tysons Corner, VA
Parde, Kristianna M. ...San Bernardino, CA
Pardee, Candyce B. ...Globe, AZ
Pardee, David R. ...Globe, AZ
Pardee, David R. ...Payson, AZ
Safford, AZ
Pardee, Edward L. ...White Bear Lake, MN
Pardee, Katherine ...Silver Spring, MD
Pardee, Vera P. ...San Diego, CA
Pardee, William Lyon ...Boston, MA
Pardee, William R. ...Los Angeles, CA
Parden, Shannon A. ...Albuquerque, NM
Pardes and Pardes ...Tarrytown, NY
Pardes, Richard S. ...Tarrytown, NY
Pardes, Robert M. ...Tarrytown, NY
Pardes, Sondra K. ...Huntington, NY
Pardes, Steven A. ...Point Pleasant Beach, NJ
Pardew, Wendy Mia ...Albany, NY
Pardi, James J., II ...Columbus, OH
Pardi, Jessica F. ...Atlanta, GA
Pardi, Michael E. ...Alexandria, VA
Pardieck, Gill, Vargo & MacTavish, A Professional Corporation
Indianapolis, IN
Seymour, IN
Pardieck, Margarett S. ...Seymour, IN
Pardieck, Roger L. ...Indianapolis, IN
Seymour, IN
Pardillo, Armando A. ...Coral Gables, FL
Pardington, Robert ...Portland, OR
Pardini, Anton U. ...Portland, OR
Pardini, Julian ...San Francisco, CA
Pardini, Julian J. ...San Francisco, CA
Santa Rosa, CA
Pardini, Thomas J. ...Alexandria, VA
Pardo, Adrienne Friesner ...Miami, FL
Pardo, Angelo ...Riviera Beach, FL
Pardo, Beth A. ...Portland, OR
Pardo, Christie ...Tampa, FL
Pardo, James A. ...New York, NY
Pardo, James A., Jr. ...Atlanta, GA
Pardo, Jason A. ...Washington, DC
Baltimore, MD
Rockville, MD
Pardo, Jeffrey J. ...Miami, FL
Pardo, Jose E., 2nd ...New York, NY
Pardo, Joseph ...Miami, FL
Pardo, Joseph A. ...New York, NY
Pardo, Kate ...Porterville, CA
Pardo, Mark E. ...New York, NY
Pardo, Michelle C. ...Washington, DC
Pardo & Pardo, P.A. ...Miami, FL
Pardo, Robert ...Los Angeles, CA
Pardo, Stevan J. ...Miami, FL
Pardo, Thomas Stanley ...New York, NY
Pardo de Zela, Gonzalo ...New York, NY
Pardo-Kronemann, Jose
Department of Housing and Urban Development, Office of General Counsel, GV
Pardo-Marquez, Joanne ...San Juan, PR
Pardubsky, Kristin A. ...Rock Island, IL
Parducci, Pilar S. ...Los Angeles, CA
Pardue & Associates ...Austin, TX
Pardue, Benjamin Wesley ...Tampa, FL
Pardue, Chuck R. ...Augusta, GA
Pardue, David L. ...Atlanta, GA
Pardue, Hobart O. ...Springfield, LA
Pardue, James L. ...Midland, TX
Pardue, Janice E. ...Houston, TX
Pardue, Keith A. ...Austin, TX
Pardue, Tobias L. ...Clearwater, FL
Pardue, W. Davidson ...Oklahoma City, OK
Pardue, William R. ...Marietta, GA
Pardy, Thomas J. ...Billings, MT
Pardy, Thomas R. ...Howard, SD
Madison, SD
Pardyjak, Patrick W. ...Fairport, NY
Pardys, David F. ...Waukegan, IL
Pardys, David N. ...Haddonfield, NJ
Pardys, Michael ...Chicago, IL
Pardys and Vargas ...Chicago, IL
Pare, Anne M. ...Augusta, ME
Paré , Armand M., Jr. ...New York, NY
Paré, Claire M. ...New York, NY
Pare, David F. ...San Diego, CA
Pare, Edward D., Jr. ...Providence, RI
Paré, John G. ...Tampa, FL
Paré, John Zachary ...Orlando, FL
Paré, Laura Fisher ...Berkeley, CA
Paredes, Laurence D. ...New York, NY
Paredes, Leo R. ...Garden Grove, CA
Paredes, Rachel ...Phoenix, AZ
Paredes, Roger F. ...Los Angeles, CA
Paredes, Troy A. ...Los Angeles, CA
Paregol, Ian M. ...Franklin, MA
Pareigat, Thomas G. ...St. Cloud, MN
Pareigis, Maria P. ...Olympia, WA
Pareira, Judith A. ...Malone, NY
Pareja, Mary Leto ...Indianapolis, IN
Paré-Johnson, Alice ...Germantown, MD
Paré-Johnson, Alice ...North Potomac, MD

Parekh, Behram V. ...Los Angeles, CA
Parekh, Keaton S. ...New York, NY
Parekh, Milind ...Detroit, MI
Parel, S. Scott ...Dallas, TX
Parelius, M. Ronald ...Portland, OR
Parella, Sharon ...New York, NY
Parello, Laura J. ...Iselin, NJ
Parelman, A. Robert ...Kansas City, MO
Parelskin, Howard A. ...Washington, DC
Parent, Alfred J. ...Grand Rapids, MI
Parent, Annette S. ...San Francisco, CA
Parent, Daniel J. ...North Highlands, CA
Parent, Daniel J. ...Pittsburgh, PA
Parent, Denise M. ...Providence, RI
Parent, Edmund ...Santa Barbara, CA
Parent, Gerald B. ...Santa Barbara, CA
Parent & Godoff ...Wellesley, MA
Parent, Gregory J. ...Atlanta, GA
Parent, James E. ...Wellesley, MA
Parent, Jane Guenther ...Cleveland, OH
Parent, Jennifer L. ...Manchester, NH
Parent, Joni McNamara ...New Orleans, LA
Parent, Lea M. ...Chicago, IL
Parent, Louise Marie ...New York, NY
Parent, Mary Hannan ...Fresno, CA
Parent, Nancy L. ...Pittsburg, CA
Parent, Neil P., (P.C.) ...New York, NY
Parent, Philip P. ...Van Buren, ME
Parent, Philip R ...Madison, SD
Parent, Randall O. ...San Francisco, CA
Parent, Rebecca Matthews ...Hartford, CT
Parent, Richard J. ...Culver City, CA
Parent, Robert ...De Pere, WI
Parent, Roland R. ...Boynton Beach, FL
Parent, Theodore H. ...Keene, NH
Parent, Thomas B. ...Lafayette, IN
Parente, Alan M. ...Garden City, NY
Parente, Bonnie L.S. ...Woodbury, NY
Parente, C. Albert ...Westbury, NY
Parente, Clemente J. ...Albany, NY
Parente, James J. ...Chicago, IL
Parente, John J. ...San Francisco, CA
Parente, John W. ...Miami, FL
Parente, Libien & Christopher
San Francisco, CA
Parente, Oscar M. ...New Haven, CT
Parente, Scott T. ...Somerville, NJ
Parente, William J., Jr. ...Philadelphia, PA
Parente, William M. ...New York, NY
Parenteau, Jacques J. ...New London, CT
Parenteau, Jacques N. ...Quincy, MA
Parenteau, Joseph (IBA) ...New York, NY
Parenti, Andrea C. ...Butler, PA
Parenti, Carmen R. ...Lyons, NY
Parenti, Christopher M. ...Lexington, KY
Parenti, Deloris Jean ...Nitro, WV
Parenti, Falk, Waas, Hernandez & Cortina, P.A. ...Coral Gables, FL
Miami, FL
Parenti, Gail Leverett ...Coral Gables, FL
Parenti, James Aladino ...San Ramon, CA
Parenti, Janis M. ...Oakland, CA
Parenti, Meredith B. ...Houston, TX
Parenti, Michael J., III ...Coral Gables, FL
Parenti, Peter J. ...San Antonio, TX
Parenti, Peter J., A Prof. Corp.
San Antonio, TX
Parenti, Philip C. ...Chicago, IL
Parenti, Philip C., Ltd. ...Chicago, IL
Parenti, Robert V. ...Stuart, FL
Parenti-Ancone, Vera M. ...Pocopson, PA
Parenton, O'Neil J., Jr. ...Donaldsonville, LA
Parenzan, Annie R. Dozier
Huntington Beach, CA
Pareres, Joseph T. ...New York, NY
Parés, James W. ...Bayville, NY
Pares, Thomas C. ...Buffalo, NY
Parese, John A. ...New Haven, CT
North Haven, CT
Parese, Stanley E. ...Williamstown, MA
Paresky, David S. ...Miami, FL
Pareti, Harold J. ...Bernardsville, NJ
Paretsky, Jonathan ...Topeka, KS
Paretti, James A., Jr. ...Boston, MA
Paretti, Kenneth L. ...Miami, FL
Paretzky, Raymond ...Washington, DC
Parfitt, Anne Marie ...Langhorne, PA
Parfitt, Chris ...Troy, MI
Parfitt, Michelle A. ...Washington, DC
Parfomak, Andrew N. ...New York, NY
Parga, Denise M. ...Los Angeles, CA
Parga, Miguel ...San Juan, PR
Parga, Rhonda N. ...Phoenix, AZ
Parga, Rodolfo, Jr. ...Phoenix, AZ
Pargaman, William D. ...Austin, TX
Pargament, Jeffrey J. ...Washington, DC
New York, NY
Pargament, Michael ...Los Angeles, CA
Pargman, Benjamin C. ...Atlanta, GA
Parham, A. Bradley ...Greenville, SC
Parham, Austin ...Hannibal, MO
Parham, Candace Jeanne ...Tulsa, OK
Parham, Cheryl A. ...Mineola, NY
Parham, Clayton E. ...Pinehurst, NC
Parham, Dale ...Yorba Linda, CA
Parham, David L. ...Cleveland, OH
Parham, David R. ...Williamstown, NJ
Parham, David W. ...Dallas, TX
Parham, Eric J. ...Charlotte, NC
Parham, Feltus, Brawner & Bartholomew
Memphis, TN
Parham, George ...Boise, ID
Parham, Gregory C. ...Denver, CO
Parham, Harry C. ...Bradenton, FL
Parham, Helms, Harris, Blythe & Morton
Charlotte, NC
Monroe, NC
Parham, J. Randolph ...St. Louis, MO

Parham, Jackson E. ...Irvine, CA
Parham, James C., Jr. ...Greenville, SC
Parham, James R. ...Belleville, IL
Parham, James S. ...Tampa, FL
Parham, Jeffrey W. ...Martin, TN
Parham, Jennifer R. ...Richmond, VA
Parham, Jones & Shiver ...Dallas, TX
Parham, Lewis H., Jr. ...Charlotte, NC
Parham, Michael ...Greenville, SC
Parham, Michael A. ...Phoenix, AZ
Parham, Michael A., P.L.C., Law Offices of
Phoenix, AZ
Parham, Michael G. ...Ellijay, GA
Parham, Michael L. ...Dallas, TX
Parham, Michael M. ...Chicago, IL
Parham, Monica G. ...Washington, DC
Parham, Nancy McRoberts ...Tampa, FL
Parham, Nathaniel W. ...Memphis, TN
Parham, Patrick Greg ...Los Angeles, CA
Parham & Rajcic ...Irvine, CA
Parham & Smith, L.L.C. ...Anderson, SC
Greenville, SC
Spartanburg, SC
Parham, W. Travis ...Nashville, TN
Parhiala, Peter J. ...Windham, NH
Parhms, Carlton Lashayne ...Port Allen, LA
Pari, Joseph M. ...Washington, DC
Pari, Phyllis M. ...New Haven, CT
Parichan, Harold A. ...Fresno, CA
Parichan, Renberg, Crossman & Harvey, Law Corporation ...Fresno, CA
Paridy, Nancy E. ...Chicago, IL
Pariente, Barbara J. ...West Palm Beach, FL
Parietti, George E. ...Harrington Park, NJ
Parigi, Frank A. ...Dallas, TX
Parikh, Abhijat R. ...Austin, TX
Parikh, Kevin S. ...Los Angeles, CA
Parikh, Lopa B. ...Akron, OH
Parikh, Nirav Raj D. ...Toledo, OH
Parikh, Ramdas M. ...Sugar Land, TX
Parikh, Rita D. ...New York, NY
Parikh, Sudarshana (Mona) ...Sugar Land, TX
Parikh, Sujay ...New York, NY
Parilla & Gellman, P.C. ...New York, NY
Parilla, John G. ...New York, NY
Parilla, Militzok & Shedden, LLP
Irvine, CA
Parilla, Paul H. ...Irvine, CA
Parillo, Michael Patrick ...Flint, MI
Parilo, Lisa M. ...Dayton, OH
Parinello, David A. ...Old Bridge, NJ
Parini, Matthew J. ...Falls Church, VA
Parins, Jeffrey C. ...Greeley, CO
Parins Law Firm, S.C. ...Green Bay, WI
Parins, Robert J. ...Green Bay, WI
Parins, Thomas J. ...Green Bay, WI
Parins, Thomas J., Jr. ...Green Bay, WI
Paris, Andrew E. ...Los Angeles, CA
Paris, Anthony J ...Syracuse, NY
Paris & Associates, P.A. ...Tampa, FL
Paris, Bette S. ...Santa Monica, CA
Paris, Blank & Brown ...Chesterfield, VA
Richmond, VA
Paris, Candida O. ...New York, NY
Paris, Carolyn E. C. ...New York, NY
Paris, Catherine M.
West Palm Beach, FL
Paris, D. Todd ...Salisbury, NC
Paris, Daniel T. ...San Jose, CA
Paris, David ...Bath, ME
Paris, David M. ...Nutley, NJ
Paris, David M. ...Cleveland, OH
Paris, Deborah M. ...Tampa, FL
Paris, Dominic A. ...Treasury Department, Internal Revenue Service, GV
Paris, Don C. ...Georgetown, KY
Paris, Douglas S. ...San Mateo, CA
Paris, Elizabeth Crewson ...Denver, CO
Paris, Eric D. ...Pomona, CA
Paris, F. Donald ...Florham Park, NJ
Paris, Gerald C. ...Pittsburgh, PA
Paris, Grant A. ...Anniston, AL
Paris, Jack ...Miami, FL
Paris, Jack L., Jr. ...Greenville, TX
Paris, Jack L., Jr., P.C. ...Greenville, TX
Paris, James R. ...Chattanooga, TN
Paris, Jeffrey A. ...Santa Monica, CA
Paris, John M., Jr. ...Virginia Beach, VA
Paris, Jonathan S. ...Rye Brook, NY
Paris, Karen M. ...Santa Monica, CA
Paris, Leonard ...Lexington, MA
Paris, Leonard A. ...Richmond, VA
Paris, LeRoy H., II ...Jackson, MS
Paris, Lissa J. ...Hartford, CT
Paris, Margaret L. ...Eugene, OR
Paris, Michael G. ...Boston, MA
Paris, Michael J. ...Hollywood, FL
Paris, Michelle Louise ...Cleveland, OH
Paris, Pamela ...Sacramento, CA
Paris and Paris ...San Rafael, CA
Los Angeles, CA
Santa Monica, CA
Paris, Philip T. ...Phoenix, AZ
Paris, Reynold F. ...San Rafael, CA
Santa Monica, CA
Paris, Richard E. ...Santa Monica, CA
Paris, Richard J., Jr. ...Atlanta, GA
Paris, Sanford P. ...Encino, CA
Paris, Simon B. ...Cherry Hill, NJ
Paris, Stephen J. ...Boston, MA
Paris, Theodore William ...Houston, TX
Paris, Thomas ...Cleveland, OH
Paris, Wendy J. ...Salem, OR
Paris, William C., III ...Chico, CA
Paris, Zachary T. ...Cleveland, OH
Parise, Angelo S. ...San Diego, CA
Parise, Anthony F. ...Ithaca, NY
Parise, Carl A. ...Pittsburgh, PA

Parise, Frank J. ...Kenosha, WI
Parise, John Peter ...Nutley, NJ
Parise, John S. ...El Dorado Hills, CA
Parise, Joseph M. ...Moorhead, MN
Parise, Joseph R. ...New York, NY
Parise, Michael J. ...Anchorage, AK
Parise, Phyllis H. ...Phoenix, AZ
Parise, Rachelle A. ...Portland, ME
Parise, Robert J. ...Dover, NJ
Parise, Sandra R. ...Columbia, SC
Pariseau, Shane R. ...Newport Beach, CA
Parisella, Jerald A. ...Beverly, MA
Pariser, Brian W. ...Miami, FL
Pariser, Brian W., P.A. ...Miami, FL
Pariser, Burton C. ...Mendham, NJ
Pariser, Daniel S. ...Washington, DC
Pariser, David B. ...Columbus, OH
Pariser, Jeffrey D. ...Washington, DC
Pariser, Jennifer L. ...New York, NY
Pariser, Michael ...Brooklyn, NY
Pariser, Wayne D. ...Los Angeles, CA
Parish, Andrew M. ...Fort Lauderdale, FL
Parish, Andrew M., P.A.
Fort Lauderdale, FL
Parish, Barbara S. ...Orange, CA
Parish, Brad ...New York, NY
Parish, Bruce D. ...Medina, OH
Parish, Cooke, Russ & Bullard
Fayetteville, NC
Parish, Darrel F. ...Decatur, IL
Parish, David ...New York, NY
Parish, David F. ...Miami, FL
Parish, Donald E. ...Huntingdon, TN
Parish, Elinor T. ...Sandusky, OH
Parish, Frank R. ...Houston, TX
Parish, Gary D. ...Corpus Christi, TX
Parish, Gary E. ...Denver, CO
New York, NY
Parish, George J. ...Clinton Township, MI
Parish, George J., & Associates, P.C.
Clinton Township, MI
Parish, Gerald J. ...Springfield, MA
Parish, G. R., Jr. ...Indianapolis, IN
Parish, Gregg Allen ...Lakewood, CO
Parish, J. Michael ...New York, NY
Parish, James D. ...Houston, TX
Parish, James R. ...Fayetteville, NC
Parish, Jeffrey J. ...San Francisco, CA
San Jose, CA
Parish, Joan V. ...Edmonds, WA
Parish, Lawrence W. ...Okemah, OK
Parish, Lori D. ...Memphis, TN
Parish, Mary A. ...Brea, CA
Parish, Michael S. ...Springfield, MA
Parish, Neal A. ...Oakland, CA
Parish & Nelson, A Professional Corporation
Stockton, CA
Parish & Nutting ...Momence, IL
Parish, O. L., Jr. ...Ballinger, TX
Parish, Rhonda J. ...Spartanburg, SC
Parish, Richard L. ...Helena, MT
Parish, Robert S., Jr. ...Redwood City, CA
Parish, Ronda G. ...Springfield, MA
Parish, Stephen P. ...Chattanooga, TN
Parish, Tat ...Watervliet, MI
Parish, Terry L. ...Reading, PA
Parish, Tiffany L. ...El Cajon, CA
Parish, William H. ...Stockton, CA
Parish, William W. ...Memphis, TN
Parish, William W., Law Offices of
Dallas, TX
Parish-Ramón, Rose M. ...Miami, FL
Parisi, Adam G. ...Schenectady, NY
Parisi, Albert L. ...Rochester, NY
Parisi, Alfred J. ...Flushing, NY
Parisi, Andrew A. ...Norwood, MA
Parisi, Anthony, III ...New York, NY
Parisi, Anthony Philip ...Poughkeepsie, NY
Parisi, Barbara E. ...Washington, DC
Parisi, Donna M. ...New York, NY
Parisi, Englert, Stillman, Coffey & McHugh
Schenectady, NY
Parisi, Francis D. ...Cranston, RI
Parisi, Frank M. ...Portland, OR
Parisi, Frank N. ...Schenectady, NY
Parisi, Georgianna I. ...Dayton, OH
Parisi and Gerlanc, P.A. ...Hackensack, NJ
Parisi, Gregory, Law Offices of
Mineola, NY
New York, NY
Parisi, Guy T. ...White Plains, NY
Parisi, Janet Praver ...Houston, TX
Parisi, John C. ...Clayton, MO
Parisi, John J. ...Federal Trade Commission, Bureau of Competition, GV
Parisi, John M. ...Kansas City, KS
Overland Park, KS
Kansas City, MO
Parisi, Joseph S. ...Chicago, IL
Parisi, Joyce A. ...Hackensack, NJ
Parisi, Mark L. ...Philadelphia, PA
Parisi, Matthew B. ...New York, NY
Parisi, Matthew G. ...White Plains, NY
Parisi, Michael ...Chicago, IL
Parisi, Nicolette ...Harrisburg, PA
Parisi, Paige ...Boston, MA
Parisi & Parisi, P.C. ...Portland, OR
Parisi, Patricia Michelena
Los Angeles, CA
Parisi, Patrick A. ...Flossmoor, IL
Parisi, Patrick A., & Associates, Ltd.
Flossmoor, IL
Parisi, Phillip E. ...Cleveland, OH
Parisi, Robin B. ...Portland, OR
Parisi, Stephen J. ...Philadelphia, PA
Parisi, Stephen T. ...Cleveland, OH
Parisi, Theodore A., Jr., Law Offices of
Castleton, VT

Parker, Douglas A. ....New York, NY
Parker, Douglas G. ....Phoenix, AZ
Parker, Douglas H. ....Provo, UT
Parker, Douglas L. ....Washington, DC
Parker, Douglas L. ....Washington, DC
Parker, Douglas M. ....Orleans, MA
Parker, Douglas S. ....Anchorage, AK
Parker, Douglas S. ....Bloomfield Hills, MI
Parker, Drew ....Peoria, IL
Parker, Drew J. ....Marlton, NJ
Parker, Druella A. ....East St. Louis, IL
Parker and DuFresene ....Jacksonville, FL
Parker Duryee Rosoff & Haft, A Professional Corporation ....New York, NY
Parker, Dvora ....Belvedere-Tiburon, CA
Parker, E. Allen ....Mariemont, OH
Parker, E. Clay ....Orlando, FL
Parker, E. Peter ....Boston, MA
Parker, Earl Warren (Chip), Jr.
Jacksonville, FL
Parker, E. B. Borden ....Goldsboro, NC
Parker, Edward A. ....Brightwaters, NY
Parker, Edward B., II, Law Offices of
Montgomery, AL
Parker, Edward C. ....Providence, RI
Parker, Edward C. ....Dallas, TX
Parker, Edward G. ....West Des Moines, IA
Parker, Edward J. ....St. Paul, MN
Parker, Edward L. ....Tyler, TX
Parker, Edward R. ....Richmond, VA
Parker, Edward W. ....Phoenix, AZ
Parker, Edwin L. ....Indianola, MS
Parker, Edwin W., II ....Houston, TX
Parker, E. L., III ....Etowah, TN
Parker, Eleanor A. ....Helena, MT
Parker, Elissa A. ....Washington, DC
Parker, Elizabeth V. ....Rockville, MD
Parker, Ella S. ....Grand Rapids, MI
Parker, Ellen F. ....Orlando, FL
Parker, Ellen Wahl ....New York, NY
Parker, Ellis J., III ....Rockville, MD
Parker, Elton L. ....Cleveland, OH
Parker, Emily A. ....Dallas, TX
Parker, Emily D. ....Eden, NC
Parker, Emily Moore ....Purvis, MS
Parker, Eric G. ....Barre, VT
Parker, Eric J. ....Waukegan, IL
Parker, Eric J. ....Boston, MA
Parker, Erick S. ....Chicago, IL
Parker, Ericka S. ....Toledo, OH
Parker, Eugene ....New York, NY
Parker, Eugene E. ....Fort Wayne, IN
Parker, Eugene F. ....Sugar Grove, IL
Parker, Eugene L. ....Beaverton, OR
Parker, Everett H. ....Boston, MA
Parker, F. Byron, Jr. ....Richmond, VA
Parker, F. Thomas ....Rapid City, SD
Parker, Florence Knight ....San Antonio, TX
Parker, F. M. (Jack) ....Kearney, NE
Parker, Fran Mulnick ....New York, NY
Parker, Francis I. ....Charlotte, NC
Parker, Frank ....Fort Worth, TX
Parker, Frank G. ....Massapequa, NY
Parker, Frank J. ....Chestnut Hill, MA
Parker, Frank L., Jr. ....Mobile, AL
Parker, Frank M. ....Granby, CO
Parker, Frank M., Jr. ....Hillsborough, NC
Parker, Frank R. ....Atlanta, GA
Parker, Frank R. ....Madison, WI
Parker, Franklin E. ....Cumming, GA
Norcross, GA
Parker, Fred I. ....Burlington, VT
Parker, Fred P., III ....Raleigh, NC
Parker, Frederick B. ....Bryan, OH
Parker, Frederick R., Jr. ....Shreveport, LA
Parker, Freestone & Angerhofer
Salt Lake City, UT
Parker, G. Edgar ....Winston-Salem, NC
Parker, G. Stephen ....Atlanta, GA
Parker, G. Waring ....Summerville, SC
Parker, Gary ....Decatur, GA
Parker, Gary A. ....Birmingham, AL
Parker, Gary, Law Group, P.C., The
Decatur, GA
Parker, Gary W. ....Southfield, MI
Parker, Gene E. ....The Dalles, OR
Parker, Geo. A. ....Fort Worth, TX
Parker, George E., III ....Detroit, MI
Parker, George F., III ....Boston, MA
Parker, George H., Jr. ....Franklin, VA
Parker, George, Jr. ....San Antonio, TX
Parker, George L. ....Rochester, NY
Parker, George M., & Associates
McKinney, TX
Plano, TX
Parker, George P. ....Louisville, KY
Parker, George P., Jr. ....San Antonio, TX
Parker, George R. ....Montgomery, AL
Parker, George W. ....Millbrae, CA
Parker, George W. ....Ann Arbor, MI
Parker, Georgenne ....Kearney, NE
Parker, Gerald C. ....Greensboro, NC
Parker, Gerald M. ....Canton, OH
Parker, Gilbert E. ....Portland, OR
Parker, Gina ....Waco, TX
Parker, Glenn C. ....Baltimore, MD
Parker, Grant D. ....Missoula, MT
Parker, Gregg A. ....Media, PA
Parker, Gregory J. ....Santa Barbara, CA
Parker, Gregory J. ....Seattle, WA
Parker, Gregory K. ....El Reno, OK
Parker, Gregory S. ....Perry, FL
Parker, Grossart, Bahensky & Beucke
Kearney, NE
Parker, Guila P. ....Menomonee Falls, WI
Parker, Guy ....Peachtree City, GA
Parker, H. Brad ....Houston, TX
Parker, H. Bryce ....South Padre Island, TX

Parker, H. Earl, Jr. ....Marysville, CA
Parker, H. Grady, Jr. .....Oklahoma City, OK
Parker, H. James ....New Port Richey, FL
Parker, H. James ....New Orleans, LA
Parker & Hafner, P.A. ....Clearwater, FL
Largo, FL
Parker & Haggas ....New York Mills, NY
Parker & Halliday ....Peoria, IL
Parker, Harold A. ....San Francisco, CA
Parker, Harold C. ....Perry, NY
Parker, Harold E. ....Fort Belvoir, VA
Parker, Harold F. ....Hagåtña, GU
Parker, Harold G. ....Akron, OH
Parker, Harry J. ....Sacramento, CA
Parker, Harvey M. ....Pasadena, CA
Parker, Hayes & Lovinger, P.C.
Adrian, MI
Coldwater, MI
Hillsdale, MI
Parker, Heidi ....Charlottesville, VA
Parker, Helen B. ....Point Pleasant, NJ
Parker, Helene G. ....Dallas, TX
Parker, Henrik D. ....Philadelphia, PA
Parker, Henry Clay, IV ....Orlando, FL
Parker, Herbert ....Brooklyn, NY
Parker, Herbert J. ....Jonesboro, AR
Parker, Hillery A. K. L. ....Honolulu, HI
Parker, Howard J. ....San Francisco, CA
Parker & Howes, L.L.P. ....Statesville, NC
Parker, Hudson, Rainer & Dobbs LLP
Tallahassee, FL
Atlanta, GA
Parker, Hugh F., III ....Knoxville, TN
Parker, Hugh S. ....Dallas, TX
Parker, Ira H. ....Burlington, MA
Parker, Irvin D. ....Columbia, SC
Parker & Irwin, A Professional Corporation
Pomona, CA
San Bernardino, CA
San Diego, CA
Santa Ana, CA
Parker, J. Branson ....Athens, GA
Parker, J. Chad ....Tyler, TX
Parker, J. Gwynn ....Tallahassee, FL
Parker, J. Peyton, Jr. ....Baton Rouge, LA
Parker, J. Randolph ....Charlottesville, VA
Parker, J. Wilson ....Winston-Salem, NC
Parker, Jack G. ....Portland, OR
Parker, Jacqueline M. ....Spokane, WA
Parker, Jacqueline Y. ....Boston, MA
Parker, James A. ....McDonough, GA
Parker, James A. ....Chicago, IL
Parker, James A. ....Albuquerque, NM
Parker, James B. ....Hillsdale, MI
Parker, James C. ....San Francisco, CA
Parker, James D. ....Virginia Beach, VA
Parker, James F. ....Dallas, TX
Parker, James J. ....Houston, TX
Parker, James K. ....Pembroke Pines, FL
Parker, James K., P.A. ....Pembroke Pines, FL
Parker, James L. ....Pittsburgh, PA
Parker, James M. ....Enterprise, AL
Parker, James M. ....Newport Beach, CA
Parker, James M. ....Albuquerque, NM
Parker, James M. ....San Antonio, TX
Parker, James O. ....Memphis, TN
Parker, James P. ....Washington, DC
Parker, James R. ....Troy, MI
Parker, James R., Jr. ....Bakersfield, CA
Parker, James S. ....Arcadia, FL
Parker, James S. ....Buffalo, NY
Parker, James Scott ....Gainesville, FL
Orlando, FL
Parker, James T. ....Gastonia, NC
Parker, James W. ....Orange, CA
Parker, James W. ....Cincinnati, OH
Parker, Jamie D. ....Lafayette, LA
Parker, Jane E. ....New Orleans, LA
Parker, Janice H. ....Birmingham, AL
Parker, Janice M. ....Chicago, IL
Parker, Janice S. ....Dallas, TX
Parker, Jann M. ....Marlborough, CT
Parker, Jared G. ....Phoenix, AZ
Parker, Jay A. ....Baton Rouge, LA
Parker, J. B. Riggs ....Chilmark, MA
Parker, J.E., Jr. ....Denver, CO
Parker, Jean K. ....Crawfordville, FL
Parker, Jeff E. ....Carson City, NV
Parker, Jeffrey D.
Department Of Veterans Affairs, Board of Veterans Appeals, GV
Parker, Jeffrey D. ....Killeen, TX
Parker, Jeffrey J. ....Los Angeles, CA
Parker, Jeffrey L. ....Torrance, CA
Parker, Jeffrey L. ....Tulsa, OK
Parker, Jeffrey M. ....New York, NY
Parker, Jeffrey M. ....Pittsburgh, PA
Parker, Jeffrey R. ....Phoenix, AZ
Parker, Jeffrey S. ....Arlington, VA
Parker, Jeffrey Scott ....Waycross, GA
Parker, Jeffrey T. ....Dallas, TX
Parker, Jeffrey W. ....Warrenton, VA
Parker, Jennifer A. ....St. Petersburg, FL
Parker, Jennifer A. ....Columbus, OH
Parker, Jennifer E. ....Worcester, MA
Parker, Jennifer J. ....Santa Monica, CA
Parker, Jerome H., Jr. ....Fort Worth, TX
Parker, Jerome R. ....Toledo, OH
Parker, Jerrold S. ....Great Neck, NY
New York, NY
Parker, Jerry C. ....Tyler, TX
Parker, Jerry D., Jr. ....Dunn, NC
Parker, Jerry P. ....Detroit, MI
Parker, Jerry R. ....Tampa, FL
Parker, Jessica Ferrell ....Boston, MA
Parker, Jim ....Austin, TX

Parker, Joakim E.
Agency for International Development, Office of the General Counsel, GV
Parker, Joe ....Clovis, NM
Parker, Joe, P.C. ....Clovis, NM
Parker, Joel L. ....Jersey City, NJ
Parker, Joel S. ....Encino, CA
Parker, John A. ....Houston, TX
Parker, John C. ....Westport, CT
Parker, John C. ....Atlanta, GA
Parker, John C. ....Birmingham, MI
Parker, John D. ....Cleveland, OH
Parker, John D. ....Houston, TX
Parker, John D., II, P.C. ....Phoenix, AZ
Parker, John D., Jr. ....Kingsport, TN
Parker, John E. ....New Orleans, LA
Parker, John E. ....Philadelphia, PA
Parker, John E. ....Hampton, SC
Parker, John F. ....San Bernardino, CA
Parker, John F. ....New York, NY
Parker, John F., Jr. ....Louisville, KY
Parker, John G. ....Atlanta, GA
Parker, John H. ....Eden Prairie, MN
Parker, John H. ....Raleigh, NC
Parker, John H. ....Bay Village, OH
Parker, John H. ....Memphis, TN
Parker, John H., III ....Live Oak, FL
Parker, John H., Jr. ....Atlanta, GA
Parker, John J. ....White Plains, NY
Parker, John J., III ....Charlotte, NC
Parker, John (Jay) A. ....New Orleans, LA
Parker, John L. ....Joliet, IL
Parker, John L., Jr. ....Tallahassee, FL
Parker, John M. ....Manchester, NH
Parker, John Michael ....Baton Rouge, LA
Parker, John Patrick
Federal Deposit Insurance Corporation, Appellate Litigation Section, GV
Parker, John R. ....Orange, CA
Parker, John R. ....Melbourne, FL
Parker, John R. ....Minneapolis, MN
Parker, John R. ....Manteo, NC
Parker, John R., Jr. ....Atlanta, GA
Parker, John R., Jr. ....Clinton, NC
Parker, John Robert ....Mobile, AL
Parker, John S. ....Santee, CA
Parker, John S. ....Lowville, NY
Parker, John Shay ....Greenbelt, MD
Parker, John V. ....Baton Rouge, LA
Parker, John W. ....Ventura, CA
Parker, John W., III ....Syracuse, NY
Parker, John W., Law Offices of
Mobile, AL
Parker, Johnson & Parker, P.S.
Hoquiam, WA
Parker, Jolene L. ....San Diego, CA
Parker, Jon C. ....Hoquiam, WA
Parker, Jonathan H. ....Coral Gables, FL
Summit, NJ
Parker, Jordan M. ....Fort Worth, TX
Parker, Joseph C. ....Marietta, GA
Parker, Joseph C., Jr. ....Austin, TX
Parker, Joseph M. ....Costa Mesa, CA
Parker, Joseph M. ....Raleigh, NC
Parker, Joseph P. ....Fort Worth, TX
Parker, Joyce ....Bloomfield Hills, MI
Parker, Joyce R. ....Rochester, NY
Parker, Juanita T. ....New Orleans, LA
Parker, Judy C. ....Lubbock, TX
Parker, Julian A., II ....New Orleans, LA
Parker, Julianne M. ....Dallas, TX
Parker, Julie A. ....Morristown, NJ
Parker, Julie K. ....San Diego, CA
Parker, Julius F., III ....Tallahassee, FL
Parker, Julius F., Jr. ....Tallahassee, FL
Parker, Kara A. ....Rockville, MD
Parker, Karen A. ....Hackensack, NJ
Parker, Karen E. M. ....San Francisco, CA
Parker, Karen Z. ....Grand Rapids, MI
Parker, Katharine H. ....New York, NY
Parker, Katharine Blackwell
Clarksdale, MS
Parker, Kathleen A. ....San Luis Obispo, CA
Parker, Kathleen King ....Boston, MA
Parker, Kathryne Lee ....Redondo Beach, CA
Parker, Kathy Blackwell ....Pascagoula, MS
Parker, Keenan A. ....Encinitas, CA
Parker, Keith Edward ....Portland, OR
Parker, Keith M. ....Irvine, CA
Parker, Kelley D. ....New York, NY
Parker, Kellis E ....New York, NY
Parker, Kelly ....Salem, MO
Parker, Kelly W. ....Salem, MO
Parker, Kenneth A. ....Los Angeles, CA
Parker, Kenneth G. ....Newport Beach, CA
Parker, Kenneth L. ....Cincinnati, OH
Parker, Kenneth T. ....Brooklyn, NY
Parker, Kerri Page ....Birmingham, AL
Parker, Kerry M. ....Newark, NJ
Parker, Kevin ....Indianola, IA
Parker, Kevin ....Philadelphia, PA
Parker, Kevin J. ....Phoenix, AZ
Parker, Kevin P. ....Houston, TX
Parker, Kim Marie ....Scarsdale, NY
Parker, Kim Terese ....Wichita, KS
Parker, Kimberlee S. ....Albany, NY
Parker, Kimberly ....Washington, DC
Parker, Kimberly A.
Federal Communications Commission, Common Carrier Bureau, GV
Parker, Kimberly E. ....Palo Alto, CA
Parker, Kimberly M. ....Boston, MA
Parker & Knabeschuh, P.C. ....Houston, TX
Parker, Kurt J. ....Jackson, MI
Parker, L. Craig ....Atlanta, GA
Parker, L. Lyle ....Alexandria, LA
Parker, L. Stevenson ....Washington, DC
Parker, L. Thomas ....Aberdeen, WA

Parker, Lainie Elyse ....Dobbs Ferry, NY
Parker, Landerman & Parker, P.A.
Clermont, FL
DeLand, FL
Eustis, FL
Orlando, FL
Parker, Lane ....Oakland, CA
Parker, Larri A. ....Worcester, MA
Parker, Larry B. ....San Diego, CA
Parker, Larry H. ....Long Beach, CA
Parker, Larry J. ....Cincinnati, OH
Parker, Larry S. ....Tyler, TX
Parker, Laura Savage ....New York, NY
Parker, Laurie Stone ....South Burlington, VT
Parker Law Firm ....Nevada, IA
Parker Law Firm ....Billings, MT
Parker Law Firm, The ....Tallahassee, FL
Parker, Lawrence B. ....Valley Village, CA
Parker, Lawrence, Cantrell & Dean
Nashville, TN
Parker & Layne ....Brooklyn, NY
Parker, Leann P. ....Tampa, FL
Parker, Lee S. ....New York, NY
Parker, Lee W. ....Houston, TX
Parker, Leon S. ....Danville, IL
Parker, Leonard C. ....Bend, OR
Parker, Leroy F., Jr. ....Stockton, CA
Parker, Linda L. ....Kansas City, MO
Parker, Linda S. ....San Diego, CA
Parker, Lisa Janice ....Chicago, IL
Parker, Lisa P. ....Englewood, NJ
Newark, NJ
Parker, Lloyd A., III ....Spartanburg, SC
Parker, Lloyd J., Jr. ....Spartanburg, SC
Parker, Lorie C. ....Seattle, WA
Parker, Lorne H. ....San Francisco, CA
Parker, Lorraine C. ....Newton, NJ
Parker, Lorraine E. ....Denver, CO
Parker, Louis C., III ....Atlanta, GA
Parker, Louis M. ....Phoenix, AZ
Parker and Lundy ....Cedartown, GA
Rome, GA
Parker, Lynette M. ....Oakland, CA
Parker, Lynn McKnight ....Jonesboro, AR
Parker, Lynn Perry ....Arlington, VA
Parker, Lynne M. ....Wilmington, DE
Voorhees, NJ
Parker, M. Kathleen ....Rockville, MD
Parker, M. Michelle ....Alexandria, LA
Parker, M. Steven ....Menlo Park, CA
Parker, Maclyn T. ....Fort Wayne, IN
Parker & Maloney ....Coral Gables, FL
Summit, NJ
Parker, Marc W. ....Wood River, IL
Parker, Marea ....New York, NY
Parker, Margaret Lund
San Francisco, CA
Parker, Margaret M. ....Santa Ana, CA
Parker, Maria Salinas ....Houston, TX
Parker, Marilyn Loch ....Maumee, OH
Parker, Mark B. ....Baltimore, MD
Parker, Mark D. ....Billings, MT
Parker, Martin L. ....White Plains, NY
Parker, Mary A. ....Nashville, TN
Parker, Mary C. ....Redwood City, CA
Parker, Mary Carol ....St. Louis, MO
Parker, Mary Caroline ....Orange, TX
Parker, Mary Lou ....Morristown, NJ
Parker, Mary Louise ....Stroudsburg, PA
Parker, Mary Margaret ....Beaumont, TX
Parker, Mary S. ....Los Angeles, CA
Parker, Max ....San Angelo, TX
Parker, Max W. ....Murray, KY
Parker, M.B. ....Las Vegas, NV
Parker, McCay & Criscuolo, P.A.
Cherry Hill, NJ
Lawrenceville, NJ
Marlton, NJ
Parker, McElwain & Jacobs, P.C.
Charlottesville, VA
Parker, Michael ....Chicago, IL
Parker, Michael C. ....Chicago, IL
Parker, Michael D. ....Springfield, MA
Parker, Michael Dean ....Monroe, NC
Parker, Michael E. ....Lafayette, LA
Parker, Michael H. ....New York, NY
Parker, Michael J. ....Mocksville, NC
Parker, Michael L. ....Berkeley, CA
Parker, Michael L. ....Portland, ME
Parker, Michael L. ....Pierre, SD
Parker, Michael M. ....San Antonio, TX
Parker, Michael M. ....Spokane, WA
Parker, Michael O. ....Little Rock, AR
Parker, Michael R. ....Los Angeles, CA
Parker, Michael R. ....New York, NY
Parker, Michael T. ....Jackson, MS
Parker, Michael W. ....Boston, MA
Parker, Midgett S., Jr. ....Greenbelt, MD
Parker, Mike ....Carthage, TX
Parker, Mike, A Prof. Corp., Law Offices of
Carthage, TX
Parker, Miller & Kehoe ....Howell, MI
Parker, Milliken, Clark, O'Hara & Samuelian, A Professional Corporation
Los Angeles, CA
Parker Mills & Patel LLP
Los Angeles, CA
Parker, Myles A. ....Jackson, MS
Tupelo, MS
Parker, Nadine H. ....New York, NY
Parker, Nancy L. ....Roseville, CA
Parker, Naomi E. ....Campbell, CA
Parker, Nathan K., Jr. ....Pittsburgh, PA
Parker, Neal B. ....Rockville, MD
Parker & Nelson ....Ventura, CA
Parker, Nelson & Arin, Chtd.
Las Vegas, NV
Parker, Nelson R. ....Manning, SC

Parker, Nina M. .... Winchester, MA
Parker, Norman E., Jr. .... Baltimore, MD
Parker & O'Connell, PLLC
Louisville, KY
Parker, Olan, Jr. .... Jonesboro, AR
Parker, Olive B. .... Miami, FL
Parker, Oliver A. .... Fort Lauderdale, FL
Parker, Ollen & Carmody, LLP
New York, NY
Parker, Omar S. .... Hoquiam, WA
Parker, Omar S., Jr. .... Seattle, WA
Parker, Paige Alan .... Boise, ID
Parker, Pamela Ann .... Bradenton, FL
Parker, Pamela K. .... Seattle, WA
Parker, Pamela M. .... San Diego, CA
Parker, Pamela McGinty .... Scottsboro, AL
Parker & Parker .... El Toro, CA
New Orleans, LA
Parker and Parker .... Howell, MI
Parker & Parker .... Minneapolis, MN
Brooklyn, NY
Parker & Parks, L.L.P. .... Port Arthur, TX
Parker, Patric A. .... Flint, MI
Parker, Patricia L. .... Jacksonville, FL
Parker, Patrick N., IV .... Jackson, TN
Parker, Paul .... Los Angeles, CA
Parker, Paul A. .... Rochester, NY
Parker, Paul E. .... Knoxville, TN
Parker, Paul E. .... Fairmont, WV
Parker, Paul E., III .... Fairmont, WV
Parker, Paul J. .... Bartlesville, OK
Parker, Paul L. .... Minneapolis, MN
Parker, Paul S. .... Nashville, TN
Parker, Paul S. .... San Angelo, TX
Parker, Paul T. .... Seattle, WA
Parker, Paulette P. .... Portland, ME
Parker, Penelope .... Twin Falls, ID
Parker, Pennee .... Sacramento, CA
Parker, Penny Ann .... Novi, MI
Parker, Penny L. .... Irving, TX
Parker, Perry .... Yuba City, CA
Parker, Philip W. .... Roanoke, VA
Parker, Phillip D. .... Washington, DC
Parker, Phyllis F. .... Auburn, AL
Parker, Phyllis Maza .... Philadelphia, PA
Parker, Poe, Adams & Bernstein L.L.P.
Charlotte, NC
Gastonia, NC
Raleigh, NC
Columbia, SC
Greenville, SC
Rock Hill, SC
Rock Hill, SC
Spartanburg, SC
Parker, Pollard & Brown, P.C.
Richmond, VA
Virginia Beach, VA
Parker, Quanah .... Abilene, TX
Parker, Quay F. .... Anson, TX
Parker, Quentin G. .... Baltimore, MD
Parker, R. Clyde, Jr. .... Houston, TX
Parker, R. Craig .... Gladewater, TX
Parker, R. Eugene, Jr. .... Vicksburg, MS
Parker, R. Frank .... Chicago, IL
Parker, R. Joseph .... Cincinnati, OH
Parker, R. Michael .... Elkhart, IN
Parker, Ralph S., II .... Minneapolis, MN
Parker, Ralph W. .... Westminster, MD
Parker, Randall A. .... San Antonio, TX
Parker, Randall S. .... St. Louis, MO
Parker, Randolph E. .... Schroon Lake, NY
Parker, Raymond A., II .... Jonesville, NC
Parker, Raymond P. .... Pittsburgh, PA
Parker, Raymond S., III .... Collegeville, PA
Parker, Rebecca .... Brighton, CO
Parker, Rebecca A. .... Windsor, CT
Parker, Rebekah L. .... Los Angeles, CA
Parker, Richard .... Alexandria, VA
Parker, Richard D. .... Houston, TX
Parker, Richard D., P.C. .... Houston, TX
Parker, Richard Davies .... Cambridge, MA
Parker, Richard E. .... Indianapolis, IN
Parker, Richard G. .... New York Mills, NY
Parker, Richard H. .... Miami, FL
Parker, Richard J. .... Chicago, IL
Parker, Richard J. .... Portland, OR
Parker, Richard K. .... Arlington, TX
Parker, Richard L. .... San Diego, CA
Parker, Richard L. .... Bethany, MO
Parker, Richard L. .... Middletown, NY
Parker, Richard L. .... New York, NY
Parker, Richard Lee, Jr. .... Gainesville, FL
Parker, Richard N. .... Warren, MI
Parker, Richard O. .... Nevada, IA
Parker, Richard R. .... Harrison, AR
Parker, Richard R. .... Nashville, TN
Parker, Richard W. .... Jackson, MS
Parker, Richard W. .... Norfolk, VA
Parker, Robert A., Jr. .... Atlanta, GA
Parker, Robert B. .... Long Beach, CA
Parker, Robert B. .... Houston, TX
Parker, Robert C. .... El Toro, CA
Parker, Robert C., Jr. .... Crawfordville, FL
Parker, Robert E. .... Howell, MI
Parker, Robert E. .... Nashville, TN
Parker, Robert E., and Associates .... Tulsa, OK
Parker, Robert F. .... Hammond, IN
Parker, Robert J., Jr. .... Hastings, NE
Parker, Robert K. .... Westminster, MD
Parker, Robert M. .... South Bend, IN
Parker, Robert M. .... Trevose, PA
Parker, Robert M. .... Tyler, TX
Parker, Robert P. .... Washington, DC
Parker, Robert R. .... Scottsdale, AZ
Parker, Robert R. .... Roswell, GA
Parker, Robert S. .... Providence, RI
Parker, Robert S., Jr. .... Richmond, VA
Parker, Robert Ted .... San Francisco, CA
Parker, Robert V. .... West Palm Beach, FL
Parker, Robert W.
General Services Administration, Board of Contract Appeals, GV
Parker, Robert W. .... Traverse City, MI
Parker, Robin L. .... Oxford, OH
Parker, Robin, (Mr.) .... Trenton, NJ
Parker, Robt. W. .... Missoula, MT
Parker, Rodney R. .... Salt Lake City, UT
Parker, Rodney S. .... Anniston, AL
Parker, Roger N. .... New York, NY
Parker, Rom B., Jr. .... Enfield, NC
Parker, Ronald G. .... Fullerton, CA
Parker, Ronald I. .... Livingston, NJ
Parker, Ronald J. .... Jackson, MI
Parker, Ronald S. .... Los Angeles, CA
Parker, Ronald W. .... White Marsh, MD
Parker, Ross .... Detroit, MI
Parker, Ross H. .... Dallas, TX
Parker, Roy O. .... Tupelo, MS
Parker, Roy O., Jr. .... Tupelo, MS
Parker, Russell J. .... Marietta, GA
Parker, Russell John, Jr. .... Douglasville, GA
Parker, S. Jill .... Morrison, CO
Parker, Sandra Dooley .... Lexington, SC
Parker, Sandra G. .... Irving, TX
Parker, Sandra L. .... Augusta, ME
Parker, Sandra M. .... Los Angeles, CA
Parker, Sara L. .... Santa Ana, CA
Parker, Saraann .... St. Louis, MO
Parker, Sarah Elizabeth .... Raleigh, NC
Parker, Satrom, O'Neil & Benjamin, P.A.
Cambridge, MN
Parker, Scott Edward .... Carrollton, TX
Parker, Scott G. .... Berkeley, CA
Parker, Scott H. .... Oregon City, OR
Parker, Sean Riley .... Bartow, FL
Parker, Sharon L. .... Marion, NC
Parker, Sheldon H. .... Charlottesville, VA
Parker, Sheryl L. .... Brooklyn, NY
Parker, Siemer, Austin, Resch & Fuhr
Casey, IL
Effingham, IL
Parker, Southwick & Parker, L.L.P., Attorneys at Law, P.A. .... Raleigh, NC
Parker, Stacy M. .... New York, NY
Parker, Staggs & Associates .... Tulsa, OK
Parker • Stanbury LLP .... Los Angeles, CA
Sacramento, CA
San Bernardino, CA
San Diego, CA
Santa Ana, CA
Parker, Stanley Joel .... Pittsburgh, PA
Parker, Stanley R. .... Topeka, KS
Parker, Steffanie D. .... Alexandria, VA
Parker, Stephanie E. .... Atlanta, GA
Parker, Stephen C. .... Newark, NJ
Parker, Stephen Conrid .... Memphis, TN
Parker, Stephen D. .... Dallas, TX
Parker, Stephen E. .... Atlanta, GA
Parker, Stephen E. .... Westlake, OH
Parker, Stephen L. .... Washington, DC
Parker, Stephen L. .... Kansas City, MO
Parker, Stephen Landis, Sr. .... Fayetteville, AR
Parker, Stephen O. .... Jacksonville, FL
Parker, Stephen S. .... Oklahoma City, OK
Parker, Stephen W. .... Albany, NY
Parker, Stephen Wade .... Little Rock, AR
Parker, Stev Y. .... Portland, ME
Parker, Steve D. .... Tampa, FL
Parker, Steven C. .... Washington, DC
Parker, Steven J. .... Brea, CA
Parker, Steven J.
Department of the Navy, GV
Parker, Steven L. .... Phoenix, AZ
Parker, Steven L. .... Tecumseh, OK
Parker, Stuart E. .... Dallas, TX
Parker, Stuart I. .... New York, NY
Parker, Stuart M. .... Newport Beach, CA
Parker, Suellen J. .... Flint, MI
Parker, Suellen J., P.C. .... Flint, MI
Parker, Sumner L. .... Pittsburgh, PA
Parker, Susan G. .... White Plains, NY
Parker, Susan Milner .... Raleigh, NC
Parker, Suzanne G. .... Garden City, NY
Parker, Suzanne M. .... Washington, DC
Parker, T. Gilbert .... Howell, MI
Parker, Talley F., Jr. .... Irving, TX
Parker, Tamara R. .... Washington, DC
Parker, Tammi D. .... Atlanta, GA
Parker, Tammy Griner .... Marietta, GA
Parker, Tammy L. .... Lafayette, LA
Parker, Ted C., Jr. .... Dallas, TX
Parker, Terrence L. .... Providence, RI
Parker, Terrence M. .... Belfast, NY
Parker, Terri Kay .... United States Senate, Committee Legal Personnel, GV
Parker, Terri L. .... Jefferson City, MO
Parker, Terrill A. .... Atlanta, GA
Parker, Terry M. .... Phoenix, AZ
Parker, Theodore .... Sarasota, FL
Parker, Theodore A. .... Lancaster, PA
Parker, Theodore, III .... Las Vegas, NV
Parker, Theresa A. .... Hillsdale, MI
Parker, Thomas C. .... Grand Rapids, MI
Parker, Thomas D. .... Charlotte, NC
Parker, Thomas E., Jr. .... Huntsville, AL
Parker, Thomas F., IV .... Montgomery, AL
Parker, Thomas J. .... New York, NY
Parker, Thomas M. .... Miami, FL
Parker, Thomas M. .... Belleville, IL
Parker, Thomas M. .... Akron, OH
Parker, Thomas M. .... Knoxville, TN
Parker, Thomas N., Jr. .... Clarksville, VA
Parker, Thomas O. .... Salt Lake City, UT
Parker, Thomas R. .... Irving, TX
Parker, Thomas Reed .... Placerville, CA
Parker, Thomas W. .... Salt Lake City, UT
Parker, Thornley & Critchlow .... Ogden, UT
Parker, Timothy J. .... Linden, NJ
Parker, Timothy J. .... Seattle, WA
Parker, Timothy S. .... Eureka Springs, AR
Parker, Toni Campbell .... Memphis, TN
Parker, Tyler F. .... Federal Way, WA
Parker, V. Duane .... Easton, MD
Parker, Vance R. .... Winston-Salem, NC
Parker, Vaughan & Werlein .... Houston, TX
Parker, Vawter "Buck" .... San Francisco, CA
Parker, Vernon G. .... Fort Pierce, FL
Parker, Viveca D. .... Philadelphia, PA
Parker, W. Bradley .... Fort Worth, TX
Parker, W. Carey .... United States Senate, Senatorial Assistants, GV
Parker, W. Gale .... Raleigh, NC
Parker, W. Todd .... Tyler, TX
Parker & Waichman .... Newark, NJ
Great Neck, NY
New York, NY
Parker, Walter E., Jr. .... Dallas, TX
Parker, Walter J., Jr. .... Rochester, NY
Parker, Walton C. .... Rockport, TX
Parker, Wanda I. L. .... Los Angeles, CA
Parker, Warr & Brown, L.L.P.
Twin Falls, ID
Parker, Warrington S. .... Los Angeles, CA
Parker, Wayne R., Jr. .... Kent, WA
Parker, Wendy P. .... Norfolk, VA
Parker, Whilden S. .... West Palm Beach, FL
Parker, Wiley P. .... Lebanon, PA
Parker, Will .... Meridian, MS
Parker, Willard C., II .... Easton, MD
Parker, William A. .... Asheville, NC
Parker, William A., III .... Birmingham, AL
Parker, William B. .... Ventura, CA
Parker, William B. .... Chattanooga, TN
Parker, William E. .... San Jose, CA
Parker, William E., III .... Raleigh, NC
Parker, William H., III .... Lafayette, LA
Parker, William H., Jr. .... Danville, VA
Parker, William J. .... Honesdale, PA
Parker, William Jerry
Bowling Green, KY
Parker, William L. .... Boston, MA
Parker, William L. .... Seattle, WA
Parker, William L., Jr. .... Nashville, TN
Parker, William Leslie .... Bloomfield Hills, MI
Parker, William M. .... Western Springs, IL
Parker, William O. .... Covina, CA
Parker, William P. .... Oklahoma City, OK
Parker, William P., P.C. .... Oklahoma City, OK
Parker, William R. .... Walnut Creek, CA
Parker, William R. .... Atlanta, GA
Parker, William Shelley, Jr.
Chattanooga, TN
Parker, Wilmer, III .... Atlanta, GA
Parker, W. L. (Dean), Jr. .... Ocala, FL
Parker, Wm. E. .... Dallas, TX
Parker, Wylie F. .... Goldsboro, NC
Parker, Yvonne M. .... San Francisco, CA
Parker/Scheer .... Boston, MA
Parker-Bass, Harriet .... Ketchum, ID
Parker-Burns, Sandra .... Sacramento, CA
Parkerhaase, Melanie E. .... Santa Ana, CA
Parker-Jackson, Loren .... Dallas, TX
Waxahachie, TX
Parker-Perry, Rebecca .... Bend, OR
Parkerson, Frank J. .... Chicago, IL
Parkerson, G. Bruce .... New Orleans, LA
Parkerson, Hal B. .... Secaucus, NJ
Parkerson, Hardy M. .... Lake Charles, LA
Parkerson, I. J. .... Decatur, GA
Parkerson, J. Gary .... West Monroe, LA
Parkerson, John E., Jr. .... Atlanta, GA
Parkerson, John W.
Hot Springs National Park, AR
Parkerson Law Firm, The .... Lake Charles, LA
Parkerson, Maquiling B. .... Norfolk, VA
Parkerson, Robert B. .... Richmond, VA
Parkerson, Shelfer & Groff .... Decatur, GA
Parkerson, William F., Jr. .... Richmond, VA
Parkerton, Prosper K. .... Brooklyn, NY
Parkes, John H. .... Philadelphia, PA
Parkes, John Russell .... Columbia, TN
Parkes, Melissa J. .... Las Cruces, NM
Parkes, Nancy Morse .... Jackson, MS
Parkes, Robert J. .... Fayetteville, TN
Parkes, Susan A. .... Anchorage, AK
Parkes, Thomas J. .... Tacoma, WA
Parkes, Wright C. .... Cleveland, OH
Parkhill, Don R. .... Coshocton, OH
Parkhill, Gayle E. .... Columbus, OH
Parkhill, Henry B. .... Grand Prairie, TX
Parkhill, Parkhill, Cowden & Runge
Grand Prairie, TX
Parkhill, Weldon .... Grand Prairie, TX
Parkhurst, Arthur B. .... Fort Lauderdale, FL
Parkhurst, Arthur B., P.A.
Fort Lauderdale, FL
Parkhurst, Beverly Susler .... Chicago, IL
Parkhurst, Cameron M. .... Minneapolis, MN
Parkhurst, Clement W. .... Richland, WA
Parkhurst, David G. .... Los Angeles, CA
Parkhurst, Eliot F. .... Boston, MA
Parkhurst, Gail S. .... Mount Pleasant, MI
Parkhurst, J. Kory .... Wichita, KS
Parkhurst, John M. .... Portland, OR
Parkhurst, Jonathan T. .... Brighton, MA
Parkhurst, Joshua S. C. .... New York, NY
Parkhurst, Kelly Marie .... Union City, TN
Parkhurst, Lindsay A. .... Chicago, IL
Parkhurst, Roger W. .... Alexandria, VA
Parkhurst, Steven L. .... Orange, TX
Parkhurst, Todd S. .... Chicago, IL
Parkhurst, Vance C. .... Peoria, IL
Parkhurst & Wendel, L.L.P.
Alexandria, VA
Arlington, VA
Parkhurst, William J. .... Geneva, IL
Parkhurst-Stein, Dawn .... Germantown, TN
Parkin & Cameron .... Fairfield, IA
Parkin, David S. .... Glendale, CA
Parkin, Eric G. .... Fullerton, CA
Parkin, Gregory L. .... Fullerton, CA
Parkin, Lafe S. .... Santa Ana, CA
Parkin, Matthew S. .... San Antonio, TX
Parkin, Robert W. .... Los Angeles, CA
Parkin, Robt. D. .... Fairfield, IA
Parkin & Woodland, Inc. .... Santa Ana, CA
Parkins, James M. .... Spokane, WA
Parkins, John A., Jr. .... Wilmington, DE
Parkins, Lenard M. .... Houston, TX
Parkins, Walter C. .... Minneapolis, MN
Parkinson, Barry D. .... Petaluma, CA
Parkinson, Benjamin Henry, Jr.
San Francisco, CA
Parkinson, C. Jay .... Salt Lake City, UT
Parkinson, David O. .... Salt Lake City, UT
Parkinson, David R. .... Salt Lake City, UT
Parkinson, Dawn M. .... Yardley, PA
Parkinson, Don .... Hagåtña, GU
Parkinson, Donald R. .... Urbana, IL
Parkinson, Donna Taylor .... Sacramento, CA
Parkinson, Durward W. .... Kennebunk, ME
Parkinson, Earl Vernon .... Pittsburgh, PA
Parkinson, Edwin Brown, Jr.
Greenville, SC
Parkinson, Edwin R. .... Springfield, IL
Parkinson, Eric J. .... San Luis Obispo, CA
Parkinson, Erin Fury .... New Orleans, LA
Parkinson, Foth & Orrick, L.L.P.
Lenexa, KS
Kansas City, MO
Parkinson, J. Louis .... Englewood, CO
Parkinson, James F., III .... Richmond, VA
Parkinson, James W., The Law Offices of
Palm Desert, CA
Parkinson, Jared G. .... Salt Lake City, UT
Parkinson, Jerry R. .... Norman, OK
Parkinson, John T. .... Syracuse, NY
Parkinson, Kenneth .... Provo, UT
Parkinson, L. Marie .... Pinckneyville, IL
Parkinson, Larry R. .... Department of Justice, Federal Bureau of Investigation, GV
Parkinson, Leslie .... Idaho Falls, ID
Parkinson, Lisa M. .... Baltimore, MD
Parkinson, Mark V. .... Lenexa, KS
Parkinson, Michael G. .... Pinckneyville, IL
Parkinson, Nancy B.
Environmental Protection Agency, Office of Enforcement and Compliance Assurance, GV
Parkinson & Parkinson .... Pinckneyville, IL
Parkinson, Paul .... Macon, MO
Parkinson, Philip I. .... Rhinelander, WI
Parkinson, Richard J. R. .... Orlando, FL
Parkinson, Robynne Thaxton .... Seattle, WA
Parkinson, Roger A. .... Woodland Hills, CA
Parkinson, S. Lynn .... Oregon City, OR
Parkinson, Stacy A. .... Lenexa, KS
Parkinson, Stephen T. .... Seattle, WA
Parkinson, Susan .... San Rafael, CA
Parkinson, Terry Arnold .... St. Louis, MO
Parkinson, Thomas I., Jr. .... New York, NY
Parkinson, Ward .... Boise, ID
Parkinson, William C., Jr. .... Richmond, VA
Parkinson, William C., Jr., P.C.
Richmond, VA
Parkison, Willis E. .... Glenwood Springs, CO
Parkman, Allen M. .... Albuquerque, NM
Parkman, Harold D. .... Mobile, AL
Parkman, James W., III .... Dothan, AL
Parkman, Samuel L. .... Cambridge, MA
Parkman, Steven T. .... South Bend, IN
Parkman, W. Henry .... Atlanta, GA
Parkman, Winston W., (Inc.) .... Inglewood, CA
Parkoff, I. David .... Park Ridge, NJ
Parkowski, F. Michael .... Dover, DE
Parkowski, Noble & Guerke, Professional Association .... Dover, DE
Parks, A. Colby .... Tacoma, WA
Parks, A. Lauriston .... Providence, RI
Parks, A. Lee, Jr. .... Atlanta, GA
Parks, Amy L. .... Reno, NV
Parks, Andrew .... Miami, FL
Parks, Angela .... Lancaster, PA
Parks, Anna Lee .... Upper Marlboro, MD
Parks, Anthony .... Rochester, NY
Parks, Armond O. .... Athens, GA
Parks & Associates .... Houston, TX
Parks, Barbara Hanson
Eden Prairie, MN
Parks, Bauer, Sime & Winkler .... Salem, OR
Parks & Beard .... Tulsa, OK
Parks, Benjamin F. .... San Diego, CA
Parks, Benjamin G. .... Naples, FL
Parks, Bill .... Vista, CA
Parks, Bob .... Monahans, TX
Parks, Brenda Jean .... Wichita, KS
Parks, Brett T. .... Memphis, TN
Parks, C. Michael .... Metairie, LA
Parks, C. Tracey .... Gallatin, TN
Parks, Carolyn Anita .... Newark, NJ
Parks, Catherine B. .... Miami, FL
Parks, Charles G., Jr. .... Shelton, CT
Parks, Charles L. .... Anniston, AL
Parks, Charles T., Jr. .... Minneapolis, MN
Parks, Chesin & Miller, P.C. .... Atlanta, GA
Parks, Christopher M. .... Port Arthur, TX
Parks, Clyde R. .... Dallas, TX
Parks, Connie S. .... Arlington, VA
Parks, Corey J. .... Portland, OR
Parks, Curtis A. .... Tulsa, OK

Parks, Cynthia E. ... Novato, CA
Parks, D. Anthony ... Newport, RI
Parks, Dana L. ... Kansas City, MO
Parks, Daniel J. ... Sonoma, CA
Parks, Daniel L. ... Corona, CA
Parks, Daniel L. ... Fond du Lac, WI
Parks, Daniel S. ... The Woodlands, TX
Parks, David B., Sr.
Department Of The Interior, Office of the Solicitor, GV
Parks, David G. ... Omaha, NE
Parks, David M. ... Arlington, TX
Parks, Diana M.
General Services Administration, Office of Regional Counsel, GV
Parks, D'Juana Bellue ... Beaumont, TX
Parks, Donald W. ... Sarasota, FL
Parks, Douglas H. ... Dallas, TX
Parks, Edgar K. ... Fairfax, VA
Parks, Edward B., II ... Washington, DC
Parks, Edward Y. A. ... Columbus, OH
Parks, Edwin K., III ... Kingman, AZ
Parks, Elwyn E. ... Houston, TX
Parks, Erin R. ... Santa Barbara, CA
Parks, Eve ... Phoenix, AZ
Parks, Floyd L., Jr. ... Chestertown, MD
Parks, Frank A. ... Phoenix, AZ
Parks, Fred ... Houston, TX
Parks, Gary Abbott ... Lake Oswego, OR
Parks, Gary E. ... Houston, TX
Parks, George ... Detroit, MI
Parks, Gerald T., Jr. ... Seattle, WA
Parks, Graham M. ... Galax, VA
Parks, Gregory T. ... Columbus, OH
Parks, Gregory T. ... Philadelphia, PA
Parks, Gwendolyne S. ... Phoenix, AZ
Parks, H. Emslie ... Towson, MD
Parks, Harry L., Jr. ... Decatur, GA
Parks, Howard E., Jr. ... Denver, CO
Parks, Hubbard S. ... San Antonio, TX
Parks Huffman McVay & Shepard, A Professional Corporation ... Arlington, TX
Parks, J. Douglas ... Dahlonega, GA
Parks, J. Duncan ... Oklahoma City, OK
Parks, J. Gregory
Department of Transportation, Research and Special Programs Administration, GV
Parks, J. Manly ... Philadelphia, PA
Parks, J. Philip ... Salem, OR
Parks, James Edward ... Fresno, CA
Parks, James G.
Department of Transportation, U. S. Coast Guard, GV
Parks, James J. ... Bloomfield Hills, MI
Parks, James R. ... North Miami, FL
Parks, Jared ... Boca Raton, FL
Parks, Jeanus B., Jr. ... Washington, DC
Parks, Jeffrey A. ... Allentown, PA
Parks, Jennifer A. ... Boston, MA
Parks, Jessica L. ... Washington, DC
Parks, Jimmy B. ... San Antonio, TX
Parks, John A. ... Hermitage, MO
Humansville, MO
Parks, John Cardinal ... Denver, CO
Parks, John Emory ... Honolulu, HI
Parks, John H. ... Somers, CT
Parks, John M. ... Augusta, ME
Parks, John Paul ... Lakeland, FL
Parks, John R. ... Americus, GA
Parks, John R. ... Atlanta, GA
Parks, John Randolph ... Warrenton, VA
Parks, Jonathan C. ... Pittsburgh, PA
Parks, Joseph ... Bennington, VT
Parks, Julie Kincaid ... New Orleans, LA
Parks, Katherine L. ... Boston, MA
Parks, Ken ... Burbank, CA
Parks, Kenneth F. ... Leesburg, VA
Parks, Kenneth R. ... New York, NY
Parks, Kevin J. ... Houston, TX
Parks, Kim M. ... St. Louis, MO
Parks, Larry ... Austin, TX
Parks, Larry Deaton ... Miami, FL
Parks, Larry G. ... Pensacola, FL
Parks, Lawrence D. ... Colorado Springs, CO
Parks, Lee S. ... New York, NY
Parks, Leonard C., Jr. ... Gainesville, GA
Parks, Leonard R. ... Philadelphia, PA
Parks, Leta S. ... Houston, TX
Parks, Lewis H. ... Chatham, MA
Parks, Linda S. ... Wichita, KS
Parks, Lois Bruckner
Pension Benefit Guaranty Corporation, Office of the General Counsel, GV
Parks, Malcolm ... Richmond, VA
Parks, Margaret Caroline ... Boston, MA
Parks, Martin O. ... Painesville, OH
Parks, Mary A. ... Oakland, CA
Parks, Mary Ann ... Jackson, MS
Parks, Matthew W. ... Trenton, NJ
Parks, Merle E. ... Lenexa, KS
Shawnee, KS
Parks, Michael A. ... Chicago, IL
Parks, Michael C. ... Albuquerque, NM
Parks, Michael D. ... McAlester, OK
Parks, Michael E. ... New Roads, LA
Parks, Michael L. ... Houston, TX
Parks, Michael W. ... Los Angeles, CA
Parks, Mitchell ... New York, NY
Parks, N. Houston ... Columbia, TN
Parks, Neil Ann ... Baton Rouge, LA
Parks, Norman S. ... Lexington, KY
Parks, Owen Tracy, III ... Pinehurst, NC
Parks & Parks ... New Roads, LA
Parks, Pate & Scarborough, L.L.P.
Pinehurst, NC
Parks, Patricia J. ... Seattle, WA
Parks, Patricia J., P.S. ... Seattle, WA

Parks, Patrick C. ... Fort Worth, TX
Parks, Philip M. ... New Haven, CT
Parks, Preston ... Somerville, TN
Parks, Prudence M. H. ... Fairfax, VA
Parks, Rachelle ... Monterey, CA
Parks, Randall S. ... Richmond, VA
Parks, Rebecca D. ... Mobile, AL
Parks, Richard J. ... Erie, PA
Parks, Richard K. ... Denver, CO
Parks, Robert B. ... New York, NY
Parks, Robert E., II ... Union, MO
Parks, Robert G. ... Wellesley Hills, MA
Parks, Robert G. ... New York, NY
Parks, Robert J. ... San Diego, CA
Parks, Robert L. ... Miami, FL
Parks, Robert Scott ... Searcy, AR
Parks, Rosaline Chustz ... New Roads, LA
Parks, Roxanne Story ... San Diego, CA
Parks, Russell W., Jr. ... Washington, DC
Parks, Sandra K. ... Columbus, OH
Parks, Scott B. ... Jacksonville, FL
Parks, Sharon R. ... Jacksonville, FL
Parks, Sherman A. ... Topeka, KS
Parks, Sherman A., Jr. ... Topeka, KS
Parks, Sidney ... Atlanta, GA
Parks, Stephen T. ... Dallas, TX
Parks, Steven C. ... Escanaba, MI
Parks & Stewart, Law Firm of
Naples, FL
Parks, Suzanne Montague ... Chicago, IL
Parks, Tammy Koester ... Madison, WI
Parks, Thomas S. ... Medford, OR
Parks, Timothy M. ... Portland, OR
Parks, William A., Jr. ... Hot Springs, VA
Parks, William C.
Hot Springs National Park, AR
Parks, William Hays
Department of the Army, Office of the Judge Advocate General, GV
Parks, William L. ... Evanston, IL
Parks, William Land ... Durham, NC
Parks, William O., III ... Phoenix, AZ
Parks, William R., III ... Newport Beach, CA
Parks, William Raymond, II
Kernersville, NC
Parks, William S. ... Waycross, GA
Parks, William Stuart ... Spartanburg, SC
Parks, Yvonne M. ... Frisco, TX
Parkulo, John F. ... Beckley, WV
Parlade, Alberto J. ... Miami, FL
Parlamis, Franklin M. ... New York, NY
Parlapiano, Alan R. ... Gainesville, FL
Parlapiano, Carl ... Pueblo, CO
Parlapiano, David C. ... Pueblo, CO
Parlapiano, Joseph J. ... Newark, NJ
Parlato, Carmelo A. ... Buffalo, NY
Parlato, Carolyn S. ... New York, NY
Parlato, Charles A. ... Larchmont, NY
Parlato, Frank J. ... Buffalo, NY
Parlato, Frank R. ... Buffalo, NY
Parlato, Lucian C. ... Buffalo, NY
Parlato, Raymond F. ... Danielson, CT
Parlato LeDonne, Lisa ... Morristown, NJ
Parlatore, Anthony M. ... Coram, NY
Parlee, Gayle E. ... Boston, MA
Parlee, Randy S. ... Milwaukee, WI
Parler, Rembert D. ... White Stone, VA
Parler, William C. ... Rockville, MD
Parler, William C., Jr. ... Towson, MD
Parler & Wobber, L.L.P. ... Towson, MD
Parles, Craig E. ... Hackensack, NJ
Parles, Lisa M. ... Hackensack, NJ
Parlett, W. Timothy ... Upper Marlboro, MD
Parlette, Robert L. ... Wenatchee, WA
Parley, Louis I. ... New Haven, CT
Parliman, Edwin C. ... Sioux Falls, SD
Parliman, Gregory C. ... Morristown, NJ
Parliman & Parliman ... Sioux Falls, SD
Parliman, Thomas W., P.C. ... Sioux Falls, SD
Parlin, Allison L. ... Philadelphia, PA
Parlin, C. Christopher ... Washington, DC
Parlin, Charles C., Jr. ... Silver Bay, NY
Parlin, Eugene ... Fishkill, NY
Parlin, George S., Jr. ... Bethlehem, PA
Parlipiano, Marty D. ... Metairie, LA
Parlo, Christopher A. ... New York, NY
Parlongue & Riegel ... New Orleans, LA
Parlongue, Sydney J. ... New Orleans, LA
Parlow, Dianne N.
Department Of Veterans Affairs, Office of the General Counsel, GV
Parlow, Michael ... Bensalem, PA
Parlow, Robert A. ... Cambridge, MA
Parma, Andrew Patrick ... Houston, TX
Parma, Floyd D. ... San Bruno, CA
Parma, Rowena T. ... Chicago, IL
Parman & Associates ... Kansas City, MO
Oklahoma City, OK
Parman, Claudette M. ... Fairfield, CA
Parman, David B. ... Albany, MO
Parman, Donald F. ... Philadelphia, PA
Parman, John P. ... Winter Haven, FL
Parman, Larry V. ... Oklahoma City, OK
Parman, Mark W. ... Wausau, WI
Parman, Steven D. ... Nashville, TN
Parmar, Pankaj R. ... Houston, TX
Parmele, Daniel A. ... Springfield, MO
Parmele, Laura M. ... Tulsa, OK
Parmele, Paul W. ... Cincinnati, OH
Parmele, Thomas H. ... Brockport, NY
Parmelee, Berkley ... Boca Raton, FL
Parmelee, Christopher L. ... Medina, OH
Parmelee, G. Kendall ... Stamford, CT
Parmelee, Joan B. ... Diamondhead, MS
Parmelee, Kara Ann ... Washington, DC
Parmelee, Mark L. ... New York, NY
Parmelee, Michael K. ... Newark, NJ
New York, NY

Parmelee, Robert A. ... Fort Worth, TX
Parmelee, Robert D. ... Sonoma, CA
Parmelee, Steven W. ... Seattle, WA
Parmely, Laurine Symula ... Detroit, MI
Parmenter, Andy Brian ... Gainesville, FL
Parmenter, Carolyn S. ... Baton Rouge, LA
Parmenter, Dennis W. ... Huxley, IA
Parmenter, Frederick H.
Department of Justice, Antitrust Division, GV
Parmenter and Humke ... Huxley, IA
Parmenter, Lester L. ... Covington, LA
Parmenter, Matthew ... Vincennes, IN
Parmenter O'Toole ... Muskegon, MI
Parmenter, Roselyn R. ... Ann Arbor, MI
Parmer, Carolyn A. ... Leavenworth, KS
Parmer, Carolyn J.N. ... Winnetka, IL
Parmer, David L. ... Hinton, WV
Parmer, Diana ... Newark, NJ
Parmer, Elizabeth ... Fort Worth, TX
Parmer, Geoffrey E. ... St. Petersburg, FL
Tampa, FL
Parmer, Jeffrey W. ... Birmingham, AL
Parmer, Jo Lindsey ... Douglasville, GA
Parmer, Thomas E. ... Carrollton, GA
Parmes, Penelope ... Costa Mesa, CA
Parmet, Donald J. ... Melville, NY
Parmet, Jeff C. ... Washington, DC
Parmet, Philip M. ... New York, NY
Parmet, Suzanne ... Washington, DC
Parmet, Wendy Ellen ... Boston, MA
Parmet, Wendy J. ... New York, NY
Parmeter, Daniel J., Jr.
Grand Rapids, MI
Parmeter, John, Jr. ... Watertown, NY
Parmeter, John M. ... Des Moines, IA
Parminter, Steven R. ... Los Angeles, CA
Parmley, Bruce E. ... Washington, DC
Parmley, Richard A. ... Ogden, UT
Parmley, Richard J., Jr. ... Farmington, NM
Parmley, Robert D. ... Overland Park, KS
Parmley, Robert J. ... Kerrville, TX
Parmly, Jeffrey A. ... Northbrook, IL
Parms, Edwin L. ... Akron, OH
Parms, Rebecca ... Akron, OH
Parnacott, Robert W. ... Wichita, KS
Parnagian, Christopher P. ... New York, NY
Parnagian, Steven K. ... Boston, MA
Parnall, Bertrand R. ... Albuquerque, NM
Parnall, Theodore ... Albuquerque, NM
Parnall, William E. ... Albuquerque, NM
Parnas, Michael J. ... St. Louis, MO
Parnas, Susan M. ... Herndon, VA
Parnass, Geoffrey W.
Upper Saddle River, NJ
Parnass, John H. ... Seattle, WA
Parnass, Larry S. ... Dallas, TX
Parnell, Albert H. ... Atlanta, GA
Parnell, Amy Kathleen ... Arnold, MO
Parnell, April Denise ... Tulsa, OK
Parnell & Associates, A Professional Corporation ... Las Vegas, NV
Parnell & Associates, P.C. ... Lakewood, CO
Parnell, B. Todd ... Little Rock, AR
Parnell, Barbara A. ... Cheyenne, WY
Parnell, Bruce F. ... Lake Ronkonkoma, NY
Parnell, Charles N., III ... Montgomery, AL
Parnell, Charles S. ... San Francisco, CA
Parnell, Charles S. ... Lakewood, CO
Parnell, Covert E., III ... Irwindale, CA
Parnell & Crum, P.A. ... Montgomery, AL
Wetumpka, AL
Parnell, E. Fitzgerald, III ... Charlotte, NC
Parnell, Eve A. ... Flagstaff, AZ
Parnell, George F. A. ... Somerset, NJ
Parnell, Jeffrey C. ... Rochester, NY
Parnell, Joe Michael ... Mesquite, TX
Parnell, John G. ... Cincinnati, OH
Parnell, K. Mark ... Birmingham, AL
Parnell, Ledford A., Jr. ... Lauderhill, FL
Parnell, Lisa J. ... Los Angeles, CA
Parnell, Lorna Kay ... Santa Monica, CA
Parnell, Mary Carol Mertz ... Haverhill, MA
Parnell & McKay ... Derry, NH
Parnell, Meredith ... San Rafael, CA
Parnell, Richard B. ... Las Vegas, NV
Parnell, Ron ... Conyers, GA
Parnell, Schoen R. ... Virginia Beach, VA
Parnell, Séan R. ... Anchorage, AK
Parnell, Terri S. ... Little Rock, AR
Parnell, Thomas E. ... Tampa, FL
Parnell, W. Chris ... Charlotte, NC
Parnell, W. Chris, P.A. ... Charlotte, NC
Parnell, Wendy T. ... Los Angeles, CA
Parnell, William B. ... Derry, NH
Parnes, Alan P. ... New York, NY
Parnes, Andrew ... Ketchum, ID
Parnes, H. Elliot ... Southfield, MI
Parnes, Helene ... Tampa, FL
Parnes, Lydia Bloom
Federal Trade Commission, Bureau of Consumer Protection, GV
Parnes, Mark ... Palo Alto, CA
Parnes, Sanford J.
Department of Energy, GV
Parness, Alan M. ... New York, NY
Parness, Hillel Ira ... New York, NY
Parness, Jeffrey A. ... De Kalb, IL
Parness, Steven K. ... Morristown, NJ
Parnham, George J. ... Houston, TX
Parnham, John T. ... Pensacola, FL
Parnie, A. David ... Monterey, CA
Parnisari, Eugene ... Laguna Hills, CA
Parnoff, Laurence V. ... Bridgeport, CT
Parnoff, Laurence V., P.C. ... Bridgeport, CT
Parnon, Frederic W. ... New York, NY
Parnon & Pratt, L.L.P. ... New York, NY
Parobek, Drew T. ... Cleveland, OH

Parobek, James S. ... Lorain, OH
Parode, Ann ... La Jolla, CA
Parodi & Bush ... Hudson, NH
Parodi, Michael R. ... Marietta, GA
Parodi, Robert ... Hudson, NH
Parodneck, Lloyd ... New York, NY
Paroff, Jason M. ... New City, NY
Paroff, Melvin D. ... New York, NY
Paroff, Philip S. ... Kew Gardens, NY
Parola, Frederick E., Jr. ... Wantagh, NY
Parola, Gross & Marino ... Wantagh, NY
Parola, Tracy L. ... San Francisco, CA
Parolisi, Cheryl Anne ... Boston, MA
Parolisi, Nicholas J., Jr. ... Chicago, IL
Parolski, Richard A. ... Ocean City, MD
Paroly, Matthew K. ... Troy, MI
Parone, Anthony D. ... Niagara Falls, NY
Paronish, Joseph ... Belleville, MI
Paronish, Terry Lee ... Girard, OH
Paroutaud, Richard A. ... Chehalis, WA
Paroz, Roger C. ... Brookfield, OH
Parquette, Jack R. ... Citrus Heights, CA
Parquette, William P. ... Auburn, CA
Parr, Adair Draughn Freeman
New Orleans, LA
Parr, Ann L. ... Lincoln, NE
Parr, Atlee M. ... Corpus Christi, TX
Parr, Audrey C. ... Boston, MA
Parr, Bernard ... Baltimore, MD
Parr, Carolyn M.
United States Tax Court, GV
Parr, Clayton J. ... Salt Lake City, UT
Parr, Cynthia O. ... Boston, MA
Parr, Daniel Loyd, Sr. ... Gainesville, GA
Parr, Darren K. ... Pittsburgh, PA
Parr, David D., (A Professional Corporation)
Irvine, CA
Parr, David W. ... Boston, MA
Parr, Dolores Ann ... Baltimore, MD
Parr, Douglas L. ... Oklahoma City, OK
Parr, E. Glenn ... Vero Beach, FL
Parr, Edward J., Jr. ... New Orleans, LA
Parr, Henry L., Jr. ... Columbia, SC
Greenville, SC
Parr, Jack R. ... Oklahoma City, OK
Parr, James F. ... Charlotte, NC
Parr, James N., Jr. ... Columbia, SC
Parr, Jerry D. ... Lewisville, TX
Parr, Jo Karen ... Montgomery, AL
Parr, John C. ... St. Albans, WV
Parr, John D. ... Denver, CO
Parr, John McCutcheon ... Olympia, WA
Parr, Josh H. ... Odessa, TX
Parr, Keely D. ... Newport Beach, CA
Parr, Keith D. ... Chicago, IL
Parr, Kent C. ... Concord, CA
Parr, Lillian Webb ... Greenville, SC
Parr, Michael F. ... Santa Ana, CA
Parr, Michael F., A Law Corporation
Santa Ana, CA
Parr, Michael T. ... Austin, TX
Parr, Nancy G. ... Chesapeake, VA
Parr, Patricia Singleton ... Florence, SC
Parr, Rebecca S. ... Salt Lake City, UT
Parr, Richard A., II ... Addison, TX
Parr, Richard M. ... Houston, TX
Parr, Richard S. ... Rahway, NJ
Parr Richey Obremskey & Morton
Indianapolis, IN
Lebanon, IN
Parr, Robert ... Indianapolis, IN
Parr, Robert Alan ... Troy, MI
Parr, Rudolph V. ... Syracuse, NY
Parr, S. Gail ... Huntsville, TX
Parr, Stephanie ... Menlo Park, CA
Parr Waddoups Brown Gee & Loveless, A Professional Corporation
Salt Lake City, UT
Parr & Younglove, P.S. ... Olympia, WA
Parra, Cynthia D. ... Garden City, NY
Parra, Del Valle, Frau & Limeres
Ponce, PR
Parra, Gabriel M. ... Albuquerque, NM
Parra, J. Wensles, Jr. ... Metairie, LA
Parra, Olga E. ... Hollywood, FL
Parra, Oscar C. ... Los Angeles, CA
Parra, Oscar C. ... Pasadena, CA
Parra, Phillip A. ... Pasadena, CA
Parra, Victoria R. ... Montpelier, VT
Parrack, David H. ... Elkton, MD
Parraguirre, Julie A. ... Houston, TX
Parraguirre, Paul C. ... Las Vegas, NV
Parramore, John L. ... Cedar Hill, TX
Parranto & Davis ... St. Paul, MN
Parranto, Julia J. ... Santa Rosa, CA
Parranto, Val Marie ... St. Paul, MN
Parras, Arthur H. ... South Houston, TX
Parras, John ... Houston, TX
Parratt, Norman D. ... Albany, NY
Parravani, James V. ... New York, NY
Parravano, Ronald A. ... Monterey, CA
Parrell, Mark J. ... Chicago, IL
Parrella, Keith A. ... Gilbert, AZ
Parrella, Keith M.
Hilton Head Island, SC
Parrella, Lisa J. ... Las Vegas, NV
Parrent, Ann ... Hartford, CT
Parrent, Homer B., Jr. ... Louisville, KY
Parrent, Homer, III ... Louisville, KY
Parrent, Mark P. ... San Francisco, CA
Parrent & Vish ... Louisville, KY
Parres, John R. ... St. Louis, MO
Parres, Lawrence E. ... St. Louis, MO
Parret, Charles W. ... Costa Mesa, CA
Parrett, James R. ... Santa Ana, CA
Parrett, Noreen J. ... Madison, WI

Parsons, David W. ....Los Angeles, CA
Parsons, Davies, Kinghorn & Peters, P.C.
Salt Lake City, UT
Parsons, Deborah J. ....Ketchikan, AK
Parsons and Destian ....Los Angeles, CA
Parsons, Donald F., Jr. ....Wilmington, DE
Parsons, Donald H. ....Bloomfield Hills, MI
Charlevoix, MI
Parsons, Donald S. ....Dagsboro, DE
Parsons, Dwight ....Akron, OH
Parsons, Earl B., III ....Atlanta, GA
Parsons and Eberhardt ....Huntsville, AL
Parsons, Edward E. ....Eureka, CA
Parsons, Edward F. ....Richmond, VA
Parsons, Eileen L. ....Miami, FL
Parsons, Elbert H., Jr. ....Huntsville, AL
Parsons, Elizabeth A. ....Pensacola, FL
Parsons, Elizabeth F. ....Smithfield, NC
Parsons, Elizabeth S. ....Pell City, AL
Parsons, Eugene A. ....Scottsdale, AZ
Parsons, Frank R. ....Birmingham, AL
Parsons, Frederick C., II, P.A.
Surfside Beach, SC
Parsons, Fredrick C., III ....Surfside Beach, SC
Parsons & Funnell, L.L.P. ....Denver, CO
Dallas, TX
Parsons, Gary D. ....Livonia, MI
Parsons, Gary S. ....Raleigh, NC
Parsons, George H. ....Richmond, VA
Parsons, George W., Jr. ....Hackensack, NJ
Parsons, Gerald P. ....San Francisco, CA
Santa Clara, CA
Parsons, Glenn C. ....North Baltimore, OH
Parsons & Goltry ....Phoenix, AZ
Parsons, Grant W. ....Traverse City, MI
Parsons, Grant W., P.C. ....Traverse City, MI
Parsons, Gregory P. ....Lexington, KY
Parsons & Guyton ....Fairfield, AL
Parsons, H. Thomas ....Manchester, TN
Parsons, Henry ....Orcas, WA
Parsons, Henry W. ....Moline, IL
Parsons, Huber R., Jr. ....Miami, FL
Parsons, Inga L. ....New York, NY
Parsons, J. Kenton ....Baton Rouge, LA
Parsons, J. Lester, III ....Bernardsville, NJ
Parsons, J. Michael ....Atlanta, GA
Parsons, James A. ....Roanoke, VA
Parsons, James B. ....Bellevue, WA
Parsons, James B., P.S. ....Bellevue, WA
Parsons, James D. ....Chicago, IL
Parsons, James E. ....San Jose, CA
Parsons, James E. ....Elsmere, KY
Parsons, James E. ....Irving, TX
Parsons, James L., Jr. ....Bethesda, MD
Parsons, James N., III ....Palestine, TX
Parsons, Jeffrey B. ....Raleigh, NC
Parsons, Jeffrey R. ....Houston, TX
Parsons, Joan F. ....Boston, MA
Parsons, John D. ....Portland, OR
Parsons, John E. ....Alpharetta, GA
Parsons, John M. ....Houston, TX
Parsons, John M. ....Salt Lake City, UT
Parsons, John P. ....Cookeville, TN
Parsons, John R. ....Denver, CO
Parsons, John R. W. ....Miami, FL
Parsons, John W. ....Independence, VA
Parsons, John W. ....Richmond, VA
Parsons, Jon R. ....Palo Alto, CA
Parsons, Jonathan D. ....Newton, MA
Parsons, Judson A., Jr. ....Summit, NJ
Parsons, Julia L. ....Seattle, WA
Parsons, Katherine Dunn ....Houston, TX
Parsons, Kevin D. ....Wallingford, CT
Parsons, Kevin V. ....Charlotte, NC
Parsons, Kimberly A. ....Boston, MA
Parsons, L. Keith ....Jackson, MS
Parsons, Larry M. ....Austin, TX
Parsons, Lee & Juliano, P.C.
Birmingham, AL
Parsons, Lester S. ....Norfolk, VA
Parsons, Lisa B. ....Chicago, IL
Parsons, Lynne Wyatt ....Houston, TX
Parsons, M. Anthony, II ....Dallas, TX
Parsons, Marc L. ....Boston, MA
Parsons, Marcia B. ....Augusta, GA
Parsons, Mari ....Sebastian, FL
Parsons, Mark C. ....Glenside, PA
Parsons, Mark E. ....St. Augustine, FL
Parsons, Martha M. ....Tracy, CA
Parsons, Mary Porter ....Nashville, TN
Parsons, Mary T. ....Cheyenne, WY
Parsons, Michael D. ....Dallas, TX
Parsons, Michael F. ....Franklin, MI
Parsons, Michael Lee ....Nashville, TN
Parsons, Michael T. ....Cupertino, CA
Parsons & Nardelli ....Red Bank, NJ
Parsons, Neal E. ....Falls City, NE
Parsons & Nichols ....Manchester, TN
Parsons, Pamela G. ....Richmond, VA
Parsons & Parsons ....Shawnee, OK
Parsons, Paul ....Austin, TX
Parsons, Paul, P.C. ....Austin, TX
Parsons, P.C. ....Roseburg, OR
Parsons, Philip G. ....Johnston, RI
Parsons, Philip S. ....Tallahassee, FL
Parsons & Powell ....Old Bridge, NJ
Parsons, Rachel ....Kansas City, MO
Parsons, Randy A. ....Norman, OK
Parsons, Randy C. ....Shawnee, OK
Parsons, Randy D. ....Riverside, CA
Parsons, Richard A. ....Carrizozo, NM
Parsons, Richard D. ....New York, NY
Parsons, Richard E. ....Roseburg, OR
Parsons, Richard H. ....Peoria, IL
Parsons, Robert A. ....Phoenix, AZ
Parsons, Robert B. ....Torrance, CA
Parsons, Robert E. ....Birmingham, AL
Parsons, Robert G. ....Tallahassee, FL
Parsons, Robert J., II ....Baltimore, MD
Parsons, Robert J., (P.A.)
San Bernardino, CA
Parsons, Robert K. ....Charleston, WV
Parsons, Robert M. ....Columbus, OH
Parsons, Robin T. ....Baltimore, MD
Parsons, Rodney H. ....Fullerton, CA
Parsons, Rodney H., A Professional Corporation
Fullerton, CA
Parsons, Ronald A., Jr. ....Sioux Falls, SD
Parsons, Ronald C. ....West Jefferson, OH
Parsons, Ronald S. ....Woodland Hills, CA
Parsons, Scott A. ....Old Bridge, NJ
Parsons, Smith & Stone, LLP ....Burley, ID
Parsons, Stanley S. ....Oklahoma City, OK
Parsons, Stephen H. ....Minneapolis, MN
Parsons, Stephen P. ....Greeneville, TN
Parsons, Steven J. ....Las Vegas, NV
Parsons, Stewart E. ....Chattahoochee, FL
Parsons, Terry Diane ....Cedar Falls, IA
Dike, IA
Parsons, Theodore C. ....Cleveland, OH
Parsons, Theodore D., Jr. ....Red Bank, NJ
Parsons, Thomas, III ....Darien, CT
Parsons, Thomas M. ....Tucson, AZ
Parsons Thompson & Hill
Martinsburg, WV
Wheeling, WV
Parsons, Timothy J. ....Denver, CO
Parsons, Tomie K. ....Joplin, MO
Parsons, W. Cameron ....Tuscaloosa, AL
Parsons, W. Douglas ....Clinton, NC
Parsons, W. Stuart ....Milwaukee, WI
Parsons, Wade H. ....Fort Myers, FL
Parsons, Walter B., Sr. ....St. Paul, MN
Parsons, Wayne D. ....Honolulu, HI
Parsons, Wesley R. ....Miami, FL
Parsons, Willard E. ....Fernandina Beach, FL
Parsons, William ....New York, NY
Parsons, William A. ....Laguna Hills, CA
Parsons, William A. ....Burley, ID
Parsons, William A., (P.A.)
Daytona Beach, FL
Parsons, William E., II ....Wheeling, WV
Parsons, William H., Jr. ....Denver, CO
Parsons, William, Jr. ....New York, NY
Parsons, William X. ....Roanoke, VA
Parsons and Wilson, P.C.
Cape Girardeau, MO
Dexter, MO
Parsons-Salem, Diane L. ....Greenville, NC
Parssinen, Trevor A. ....Atlanta, GA
Part, Marvin L. ....Los Angeles, CA
Partaker, Robert C. ....Anoka, MN
Partacz, James A. ....West Seneca, NY
Partain, Bruce M. ....Beaumont, TX
Partain, David O. ....Van Buren, AR
Partain, Eugene G. ....Atlanta, GA
Partain and Forester ....Logan, WV
Partain, George L. ....Logan, WV
Partain, Jack M., Jr. ....San Antonio, TX
Partain, Lisa N. ....Los Angeles, CA
Partain, Michael M. ....Fairfield, AL
Partain, William A. ....Pittsburgh, PA
Partaka, Chad Richard ....Lexington, MI
Partan, Daniel G. ....Boston, MA
Partch, Richard C. ....Houston, TX
Partee, Albert L., III ....Nashville, TN
Partee, Andrew C., Jr. ....New Orleans, LA
Partee, Goodloe M. ....Little Rock, AR
Partee, Hoyt F. ....Greenville, SC
Partee, Monte ....Woodbury, NJ
Partee, Peter Stone ....Richmond, VA
Partee, Ronald E. ....Kansas City, MO
Partee, Tracey P. ....Providence, RI
Partelow, John E. ....Chicago, IL
Parten, Anne ....Alexandria, VA
Parten, Ben L., Jr. ....Austin, TX
Parten, John R. ....Crockett, TX
Partenheimer, R. Scott ....Princeton, IN
Partenheimer, Verner P. ....Princeton, IN
Partenheimer, Wayne ....Philadelphia, PA
Parter, Alan S. ....New York, NY
Parthasarathy, Jayshree ....New York, NY
Parthemer, Linda L. ....Cherry Hill, NJ
Philadelphia, PA
Parthemer, Mark R. ....Harrisburg, PA
Parthemos & Bryant, P.C.
Winchester, VA
Parthemos, George P. ....New York, NY
Parthemos, Nikolas E. ....Winchester, VA
Parthemos, Stylian P. ....Chesterfield, VA
Parthum, Donald J. ....Detroit, MI
Parthum, Donald J., Jr.
Bloomfield Hills, MI
Parthum, Irene E. ....Milwaukee, WI
Particelli, Robert A. ....Philadelphia, PA
Partida, Cristina M. ....Dallas, TX
Partida, Gilbert A. ....San Diego, CA
Partida, Juan R. ....Edinburg, TX
Partida-Kipness, Robbie S. ....Dallas, TX
Houston, TX
Partigan, John C. ....Rochester, NY
Partilla, Shelly A. ....Chicago, IL
Partin, Anne Marie ....Columbia, SC
Partin, C. Fred ....Louisville, KY
Partin, Charles C. ....Bay Minette, AL
Partin, Dan F. ....Harlan, KY
Partin, James W. (Jack) ....Elkin, NC
Partin, Joanne K. ....New Bern, NC
Partin, John P. ....Columbus, GA
Partin, Mark S. ....Austin, TX
Partin, Matthew K. ....Kansas City, MO
Partin & Partin ....Kansas City, MO
Partin, Patrick D. ....Camden, SC
Partin, Robert W. ....Richmond, VA
Partin, Robin R. ....Columbus, OH
Partin, William C. ....Kansas City, MO
Partin, William H., Jr. ....Brentwood, TN
Partin, Wilson B., Jr. ....Raleigh, NC
Partington, Bruce D. ....Pensacola, FL
Partington, Donald E. ....Irvine, CA
Partington, Donald H. ....Pensacola, FL
Partington, Doretta Hahn
Winter Springs, FL
Partington, Earle A. ....Honolulu, HI
Partington, Elizabeth J. ....Pensacola, FL
Partington and Foley ....Honolulu, HI
Partipilo, Anthony J. ....Simi Valley, CA
Partipilo, Francesco L. ....Port Huron, MI
Partland, Donald P. ....New York, NY
Partlow, David L. ....Tampa, FL
Partlow, Elizabeth B. ....Columbia, SC
Greenville, SC
Partlow, Graham ....Blytheville, AR
Partlow, James J. ....Sanford, FL
Partlow, Jeanette Glose ....Baltimore, MD
Partlow, Michael A. ....Cleveland, OH
Partlow, R. Keith ....Boston, MA
Partlow, Ralph V., III ....Baltimore, MD
Partlow, Robert J. ....Marlton, NJ
Partnow, Mark I. ....Brooklyn, NY
Partnow, Peter C. ....Anchorage, AK
Partnoy, Robert W. ....New York, NY
Partnoy, Ronald A. ....Wilmington, DE
Partoll, Alfred C. ....Basking Ridge, NJ
Parton, Craig A. ....Santa Barbara, CA
Parton, David H. ....Gatlinburg, TN
Parton, James, III ....San Francisco, CA
Parton, Maureen Brown ....Mill Valley, CA
Partos, Michael J. ....Los Angeles, CA
Partoyan, Garo A. ....McLean, VA
Partrich, Spencer M. ....Farmington Hills, MI
Partrick, Cornelius T., Jr. ....Washington, NC
Partrick, Cornelius T., Jr., P.A.
Washington, NC
Partrick, Kathryn L. ....San Diego, CA
Partrick, Sean T. ....Greenville, NC
Partridge, Anthony ....Washington, DC
Partridge, B. Waring, III ....Washington, DC
Partridge, Benjamin W., Jr. ....Montpelier, VT
Partridge, Charles E., Jr. ....Baltimore, MD
Partridge, Dennis P. ....Detroit, MI
Partridge, Donald C. ....Mobile, AL
Partridge, Elizabeth W. ....Berkeley, CA
Partridge, Ellen L. ....Chicago, IL
Partridge, Gerald N. ....Washington, IA
Partridge Group, The, Chartered
Washington, DC
Partridge, Jack C. ....Corpus Christi, TX
Partridge, James Syme ....Castro Valley, CA
Partridge, Jean Marie ....White Plains, NY
Partridge, John Henry ....Herndon, VA
Partridge, John J. ....Providence, RI
Partridge, Kathryn ....Middlebury, CT
Partridge, Kay B. ....Ellicott City, MD
Partridge, Mark V. B. ....Chicago, IL
Partridge, Michelle C. ....Jackson, MS
Partridge, Olivia Lowe ....Alameda, CA
Partridge & Perkins ....Falls Church, VA
Partridge, Philip H. ....Mobile, AL
Partridge, Philip L. ....Orlando, FL
Partridge, Robert G. ....Lafayette, CA
Partridge, Sanborn ....Shelburne, VT
Partridge, Sandra Tucker ....Benton, AR
Partridge, Scott F. ....Washington, DC
Houston, TX
Partridge, Scott S. ....New Orleans, LA
Partridge, Shelley Graves
New London, CT
Partridge Snow & Hahn, LLP ....Boston, MA
Partridge Snow & Hahn LLP
Providence, RI
Partridge, Terri L. Burden ....Boston, MA
Partridge, W. Frank, Jr. ....Newberry, SC
Partridge, William E. ....Sarasota, FL
Partridge, William S. ....Mankato, MN
Partritz, Joan E. ....Pomona, CA
Partyka, Edward Joseph ....Springfield, MA
Partyka, Karen A. ....Amsterdam, NY
Partyka, Mary D. ....Chicopee, MA
Paruch, Lawrence S. ....Detroit, MI
Paruch, Patricia ....Troy, MI
Paruk, Ann Hagman ....Lansing, MI
Paruk, Paul J. ....Hamtramck, MI
Parulkar, G. D. ....Topeka, KS
Parulski, Susan Linder ....Rochester, NY
Parum, Burns ....Grand Prairie, TX
Parum, Michael L. ....Grand Prairie, TX
Parven, Scott D. ....Hartford, CT
Parver, Alan K. ....Washington, DC
Parver, Corrine Propas ....Washington, DC
Parver, James F. ....New York, NY
Parver, Jane W. ....New York, NY
Parver, Ronald
Federal Communications Commission,
Cable Services Bureau, GV
Parvex, Guy C., Jr. ....Oxnard, CA
Parvey, Allan M. ....Fort Myers, FL
Parvey and Frankel, Attorneys, P.A.
Fort Myers, FL
Parvin, Cordell M. ....Dallas, TX
Parvin, Curtis D. ....Irvine, CA
Parvin, Gary R. ....Coffeeville, MS
Parvin, Gregory S. ....Kotzebue, AK
Parvin, John M. ....Woodbridge, NJ
Parvin, Ruth Ann ....De Kalb, IL
Parvin, Vanessa L. ....Minneapolis, MN
Parvis, Barbara Anne ....New York, NY
Parvis, Peter P. ....Baltimore, MD
Parwani Manson, Rinky
Beverly Hills, CA
Parys, Joseph H. ....Foster, RI
Parz, Daniel J. ....Tampa, FL
Parzen, Stanley J. ....Chicago, IL
Parzen, Tad Seth ....San Diego, CA
Parziale, James V. ....San Diego, CA
Parziale, John R. ....Alexandria, VA
Parzianello, Eric A. ....Detroit, MI
Parzych, Gregory T. ....Mesa, AZ
Parzygnat, Peter R. ....Orlando, FL
Pasahow, Lynn H. ....Palo Alto, CA
San Francisco, CA
Pasak, Roger A. ....Orlando, FL
Pasalis, Dean J. ....Cleveland, OH
Pasano, Armand J. ....Montebello, CA
Pasano, Michael S. ....Fort Lauderdale, FL
Miami, FL
Pasarela, Richard J. ....Muskegon, MI
Pasarow, Averill C. ....Van Nuys, CA
Pasarow, Stephen C. ....Glendale, CA
Pasca, Anthony C ....Riverhead, NY
Pascal, Albert ....Fort Lauderdale, FL
Pascal, Christopher B. ....Rockville, MD
Pascal, Erica ....Chicago, IL
Pascal, Jason L. ....New York, NY
Pascal, Larry B. ....Dallas, TX
Pascal, Larry D. ....San Jose, CA
Pascal, Lawrence J. ....Alexandria, VA
Pascal, Muriel-Theresa M. ....Richmond, VA
Pascal, Paul L. ....Washington, DC
Pascal, Richard J. ....Groton, CT
Norwich, CT
Pascal, Robert A. ....Fort Lauderdale, FL
Pascal, Robert F. ....Bellevue, WA
Pascal, Robert Frederick ....Washington, DC
Pascal, Robt. A. ....Baton Rouge, LA
Pascal, Roger ....Chicago, IL
Pascal, Ross A. ....Boston, MA
Pascal, Stephen C. ....New York, NY
Pascal & Weiss, P.C. ....Washington, DC
Pascale, Anthony P. ....Rahway, NJ
Pascale, Connie M., (Mr.) ....Edison, NJ
Pascale, Gregory J. ....Scranton, PA
Pascale, Jon S. ....Burke, VA
Pascale, Joseph K.
Securities and Exchange Commission,
Division of Corporation Finance, GV
Pascale, Karen L. ....Wilmington, DE
Pascale, Kevin J. ....Baltimore, MD
Pascale, Lia N. ....New York, NY
Pascale, Matthew S. ....Los Angeles, CA
Pascale, Sebastian G. ....White Plains, NY
Pascale, Susan Marie ....Garden City, NY
Pascalli, Lewis G. ....Fairfield, CA
Pascarell, William A. ....Newark, NJ
Pascarella & Associates ....Red Bank, NJ
Pascarella, Cassandra S. ....New Haven, CT
Pascarella, David A. ....Albany, NY
Pascarella, Henry W. ....Greenwich, CT
Pascarella, Kim A. ....Seaside Heights, NJ
Pascarella, Lisa M. ....New York, NY
Pascarella, Stephen M. ....Red Bank, NJ
Pasch, Robert A. ....Madison, WI
Pasch, Susan M. ....Minneapolis, MN
Pasch, Thomas K. ....Philadelphia, PA
Pasch, William H. ....Waynesville, NC
Paschal, Baxter Worth, III
Fayetteville, NC
Paschal, Catherine ....Wake Forest, NC
Paschal, Chas. M., Jr. ....New Orleans, LA
Paschal, Edward ....Wake Forest, NC
Paschal, Evangeline C. ....Washington, DC
Paschal, Guy ....New York, NY
Paschal, Howard W. Pat, Jr.
Greenville, SC
Paschal, Janet Altman ....Florence, SC
Paschal, Kay F. ....West Columbia, SC
Paschal, Marti Yvonne ....San Francisco, CA
Paschal, Richard A. ....Tulsa, OK
Paschal, Robert C. ....Raleigh, NC
Paschal, Robert C., Jr. ....Austin, TX
Paschal, Wade H., Jr. ....Siler City, NC
Paschall, Belker D., III ....Fort Worth, TX
Paschall, Dale ....Deer Park, TX
Paschall, David L. ....Dallas, TX
Paschall, Evita A. ....Augusta, GA
Paschall, Evita A., P.C. ....Augusta, GA
Paschall, James C. ....Lisle, IL
Paschall, James R. ....Norfolk, VA
Paschall, John C. ....Hearne, TX
Paschall, Michael Alexander ....Charlotte, NC
Paschall, Nancy Borders ....Gastonia, NC
Paschall, Samuel S. ....Washington, DC
Paschall, Stephen P. ....Pittsburgh, PA
Paschburg, Donald B. ....Iselin, NJ
Pasche, Paul W. ....Chicago, IL
Paschetto, John J. ....Wilmington, DE
Paschke, John F. ....Chicago, IL
Paschke, Lehlia K. ....Minneapolis, MN
Paschke, Raymond J. ....Pittsburgh, PA
Paschon & Feurey ....Toms River, NJ
Paschon, Michael G. ....Roseville, CA
Paschon, Robert V. ....Toms River, NJ
Paschos, Thomas ....Westmont, NJ
Philadelphia, PA
Pasciullo, Nicholas A. ....Pittsburgh, PA
Pasciuto, Karen K. ....Rockville, MD
Pasciuto, Robert C. ....Cambridge, MA
Pasco, Charles ....Bellevue, WA
Pasco, Charles M. ....Fort Lauderdale, FL
Pasco, Charles M., P.A. ....Fort Lauderdale, FL
Pasco, Dabney L. ....Covington, VA
Pasco, Dabney Lancaster, Jr ....Covington, VA
Pasco and Dascher, P.C. ....Covington, VA
Pasco, H. Merrill ....Richmond, VA
Pasco, John S. ....San Jose, CA
Pasco, John S., Jr. ....Walnut Creek, CA
Pasco, Karen Elisabeth ....White Plains, NY
Pasco, Richard E. ....Washington, DC
Pascocello, Susan Keller
Securities and Exchange Commission,
Office of International Affairs, GV
Pascoe, Bruce E. ....Tucson, AZ

Pascoe, D. Monte ... Denver, CO
Pascoe, John R. ... San Francisco, CA
Pascoe, P. Larry ... Dallas, TX
Pascoe & Rafton ... San Rafael, CA
Pascoe, William J. ... Winter Park, FL
Pascoe, William R. ... San Rafael, CA
Pascoe, William T. ... Temecula, CA
Pascotto, Alvaro ... Los Angeles, CA
Pascotto & Gallavotti ... Los Angeles, CA
Pascover, Kathryn W. ... Memphis, TN
Pascrell, David J. ... Trenton, NJ
Pascrell, William J., III ... Roseland, NJ
Pascual, Glen Ramos ... Wailuku, HI
Pascual, Jorge A. ... Miami, FL
Pascual, Mitchell L. ... Hackensack, NJ
Roseland, NJ
Pascual, Reinaldo ... Atlanta, GA
Pascual-Amadeo, Francisco X.
San Juan, PR
Pascual-Villaronga, Ricardo
San Juan, PR
Pascucci, Daniel T. ... San Diego, CA
Pascucci, Erminia ... West Hartford, CT
Pascucci, Janice M. ... Boston, MA
Pascucci, John A. ... Jacksonville, FL
Pascucci, Nancy C. ... Chicago, IL
Pascucci, Raymond J. ... Syracuse, NY
Pascucci, Robert M. ... Great Neck, NY
Pascucci, Victor, III ... Chicago, IL
Pascucci, Vincent J. ... Chicago, IL
Pascucci, Vincent S. ... New York, NY
Pascucci, William R. ... Norwalk, CT
Pasculli, Janice D. ... Newton, NJ
Pasculli, Leonard P. ... New York, NY
Pasculli, Mark A. ... Fresno, CA
Pascus, Keith D. ... Chicago, IL
Pascutoi, Diane G. ... Rochester, NY
Pascutoi, Victor M. ... Rochester, NY
Pascuzzi, David J. ... Boca Raton, FL
Pascuzzi, Harry ... Fresno, CA
Pascuzzi, Harry, A Professional Corporation
Fresno, CA
Pascuzzi, Paul J. ... Sacramento, CA
Pasek, Charles J. ... Miami, FL
Pasek, Gary B. ... Midland, MI
Pasek, Jeffrey Ivan ... Philadelphia, PA
Pasek, Melissa A. ... Irvine, CA
San Jose, CA
Pasek, Myra J. ... San Francisco, CA
Pasek, Rita A. ... Butler, NJ
Pasekoff, Andrea Weisstuch
Gaithersburg, MD
Pasekoff, Marc Eric ... Washington, DC
Greenbelt, MD
Pasekoff, Robert L. ... Miami, FL
Paseltiner, David E. ... New York, NY
Woodbury, NY
Paseltiner, Ellen Kettler ... Glencoe, IL
Paseltiner, Philip J. ... Stamford, CT
Paseornek, Steven M. ... Paramus, NJ
Paserba, Diana M. ... Chicago, IL
Paset, Gustave ... Chicago, IL
Pasetsky, Alan E. ... Norwalk, CT
Paseur, Deborah Bell ... Florence, AL
Paseur, Geraldine M. ... Houston, TX
Paseur, Henry L., Jr. ... Atlanta, GA
Pasewark, Mark D. ... St. Louis, MO
Pasewark, Virginia Gaddy ... St. Louis, MO
Pasfield, W. Bruce ... Department of Justice, Environment and Natural Resources Division, GV
Pash, Clifford G., Jr.
Federal Communications Commission, Office of the General Counsel, GV
Pash, David Andrew ... Los Angeles, CA
Pash, Jeffrey ... New York, NY
Pash, Joseph J., Jr. ... New York, NY
Pashby, Gary J. ... Sioux Falls, SD
Pashkin, Mitchell L. ... Huntington, NY
Pashkoff, Dana Barrie ... Washington, DC
Pashkoff, Lionel E. ... Washington, DC
Pashkoff, Lisa ... New York, NY
Pashkoff, Paul H. ... Washington, DC
Pashler, Peter L. J. ... Des Moines, IA
Pashman, David J. ... New York, NY
Pashman, Louis ... Hackensack, NJ
Pashman, Morris ... Hackensack, NJ
Pashman Stein, A Professional Corporation
Hackensack, NJ
Pashos, Kay E. ... Plainfield, IN
Pashos, Michael L. ... Atlanta, GA
Pashos, Theodore G. ... St. Louis, MO
Pasiadis, Christopher F. ... Lyndhurst, OH
Pasiak, Richard W. ... Detroit, MI
Pasic, Djenita ... Louisville, KY
Pasich, Kirk A. ... Los Angeles, CA
Pasichnyk, David P. ... Lansing, MI
Pasierb, John C. ... Alexandria, VA
Arlington, VA
Pasierb, Theodore J., Jr. ... Danville, IL
Pasik, Elliot B. ... Long Beach, NY
Pasik, Laura F. ... Seattle, WA
Pasin, Audry Roth ... Coral Springs, FL
Pasin, Mario A. ... Chicago, IL
Pasin, Mitchell C. ... Highland Beach, FL
Pasin, Robert ... Margate, FL
Pasini, Lawrence A. ... New York, NY
Pasinkoff, Eric M. ... New York, NY
Pasion, Rod ... San Francisco, CA
Pasionek, Robert A. ... West Bloomfield, MI
Paskach, David M. ... Marshall, MN
Paskal and Benson ... Clayton, MO
Paskal, Robert M. ... Clayton, MO
Paskal, Steven S. ... Riva, MD
Paskalakis, Elaina Kara ... Jacksonville, FL
Paskay, Alexander L. ... Tampa, FL
Paske, Donna L. ... Madison, WI
Paskel, Clifford ... Southfield, MI
Paskell, Gregory E. ... Kalispell, MT
Paskerian, Matthew W. ... Irvine, CA
Paskert, Jeffrey M. ... Tampa, FL
Paskett, Herbert A. ... Lodi, CA
Paskevicius, Ruta ... Concord, CA
Paskewitz, Donald P. ... La Mirada, CA
Paskey, Paul J. ... Bayonne, NJ
Paskey, Stephen ... Department of Justice, Washington, D.C. District Office, GV
Paskiewicz, Lorraine S. ... Saginaw, MI
Paskin and Oberwetter, Law Offices, Ltd.
Madison, WI
Paskin, Ronald B. ... Madison, WI
Paskin, Wendy Edyth ... San Francisco, CA
Paskind, Martin B. ... Albuquerque, NM
Paskind, Martin B., Attorney at Law, P.C.
Albuquerque, NM
Pasko, Arlene E. ... Basking Ridge, NJ
Pasko, Cristina ... Chicago, IL
Pasko, Margaret Ann ... Chattanooga, TN
Paskoff, Adam ... Fort Lee, NJ
Paskoff, Elliot ... Southold, NY
Paskoff, Martin ... Teterboro, NJ
Paskoff, Stephen M. ... Atlanta, GA
Paskow, Anne C. ... Trenton, NJ
Paskowitz, Laurence D. ... New York, NY
Paskowitz, Michael ... Buffalo, NY
Paskowitz, Michael A. ... La Mesa, CA
Paskus, Robert Vidas ... Santa Monica, CA
Paskvan, Bonnie J. ... Anchorage, AK
Paskvan, Joseph L. ... Fairbanks, AK
Paslay, James B. ... Spartanburg, SC
Paslay, Michael R. ... Nashville, TN
Paslay, Paul W. ... Anchorage, AK
Pasley, Clarke A. ... Ames, IA
Pasley & Farabough ... Ardmore, OK
Pasley, R. Scott ... Boise, ID
Pasley, Robert S. ... Treasury Department, Office of the Comptroller of the Currency, GV
Pasley, Robert S., Jr. ... Sarasota, FL
Pasley, Suzanne ... Wildwood, NJ
Pasley, Ted J. ... Ardmore, OK
Pasley, Vickie L. ... Chicago, IL
Pasley, William B. ... Dallas, TX
Paslin, Deborah B. ... Burlingame, CA
Pasman, Nora J. ... Lansing, MI
Pasman, Robert F. ... Southfield, MI
Pasmantier, Jeanne F. ... West Orange, NJ
Pasnik, Margaret M. ... Buffalo, NY
Pasnik, Michael J. ... Basking Ridge, NJ
Pasqua & Pasqua ... De Witt, NY
Pasqua, Thomas F., Jr. ... De Witt, NY
Pasqual & Chumbley, A Professional Corporation ... San Antonio, TX
Pasqual, Jack ... San Antonio, TX
Pasqual, Jack D., Jr. ... San Antonio, TX
Pasqual, Morris ... Chicago, IL
Pasquale, Gennaro L. ... Oyster Bay, NY
Pasquale, Gregory B. ... Florham Park, NJ
Pasquale, H. Donald ... Melbourne Beach, FL
Pasquale, Jack M. ... Manchester, CT
Pasquale, John J. ... Jamaica, NY
Pasquale, Kenneth ... New York, NY
Pasquale, Margaret Marie ... New York, NY
Pasquale, Maria E. ... New York, NY
Pasquale, Michael P. ... Newark, NJ
Pasquale, Robert ... Wilmington, DE
Pasqualetto, Joseph P. ... Hazlet, NJ
Pasqualini, David A. ... Redondo Beach, CA
Pasqualini, Martin J. ... Boston, MA
Pasqualone, Gary L. ... Geneva, OH
Pasqualone, Terry G. ... El Paso, TX
Pasquantonio, Anthony ... Pelham, NY
Pasquantonio, Jennifer A.
Mount Vernon, NY
Pasquarella, Augustus L. ... Philadelphia, PA
Pasquarelli, Anthony P. ... Rahway, NJ
Pasquarelli, Robert J. ... Pittsburgh, PA
Pasquarelli, Samuel J. ... Pittsburgh, PA
Pasquarette, Lizanne T. ... New Hope, PA
Pasquariello, Ann Agnes ... Philadelphia, PA
Pasquariello, Anthony J. ... Clifton, NJ
Pasquariello, Anthony J. & Associates, P.C.
Clifton, NJ
Pasquariello, Arthur A. ... Schenectady, NY
Pasquariello, Julie A. ... Buffalo, NY
Pasquariello, Mark J. ... Adams, MA
Pasquerella, Anna A. ... White Plains, NY
Pasquesi Associates, P.C.
Highland Park, IL
Pasquesi, David J. ... Chicago, IL
Pasquesi, Frank E. ... Chicago, IL
Pasquesi, Mark A. ... Chicago, IL
Pasquesi, Theodore A. ... Highland Park, IL
Pasquesi, Thomas A. ... Highland Park, IL
Pasquesi, Victoria L. ... Chicago, IL
Pasquier, Evelyn W. ... Baltimore, MD
Pasquier, Richard P. ... Chicago, IL
Philadelphia, PA
Pasquina, Edward F., Jr. ... Gloucester, MA
Pasquina, William J., P.C.
West Newbury, MA
Pasquinelli, James R. ... Palos Heights, IL
Pasquinelli, Joseph ... Cypress, CA
Pasquinelli & Pasquinelli ... San Jose, CA
Pasquinelli, Robert L. ... San Jose, CA
Pasquini, Francis J. ... Philadelphia, PA
Pasquini, Gina A. ... Westport, CT
Pasquini, Peggy Clements ... Dallas, TX
Pass, Brian J. ... Los Angeles, CA
Pass & Carlson, A Law Corporation
Torrance, CA
Pass, Caryn G. ... Washington, DC
Pass, Charles R. ... Pittsburgh, PA
Pass, Henry Ian ... Bala Cynwyd, PA
Pass, Henry Ian ... Philadelphia, PA
Pass, Herbert L. ... Revere, MA
Pass, Jeffrey H. ... St. Louis, MO
Pass, Joseph J., Jr. ... Pittsburgh, PA
Pass Law Offs., P.C. ... Revere, MA
Pass, Leonard E. ... Revere, MA
Pass, Richard D. ... Riverside, RI
Pass, Robert N. ... Potomac, MD
Pass, Robert W. ... Tallahassee, FL
Pass, Robin Kaplan ... Chicago, IL
Pass, Ronald C. ... Torrance, CA
Pass, Stephen C. ... Sacramento, CA
Passafaro, Jeffrey G. ... Dunkirk, NY
Passafiume, Clara M. ... Louisville, KY
Passafuime, Phillip A. ... Scotts Valley, CA
Passage, Daniel F. ... Los Angeles, CA
Passaglia, Charles T. ... Denver, CO
Passaic, Joseph G., Jr. ... Washington, DC
Passalacqua, Frank J. ... Santa Rosa, CA
Passalacqua, Jill A. ... Menlo Park, CA
Passalacqua, John P. ... Sacramento, CA
Passalacqua, Joseph Richard
Healdsburg, CA
Passalacqua, Karen M. ... Geyserville, CA
Passalacqua, Lisa Silva ... Walnut Creek, CA
Passalacqua, Mazzoni & Gladden
Healdsburg, CA
Passalacqua & Passalacqua ... Healdsburg, CA
Passalacqua, Richard Joseph
Healdsburg, CA
Passalacqua, Thomas R. ... Healdsburg, CA
Passalaqua, Anthony ... Franklin Lakes, NJ
Passalaqua, Martha L. ... Walnut Creek, CA
Passalaris, Tina ... New York, NY
Passales, Richard K. ... Treasury Department, Internal Revenue Service, GV
Passalino, James J. ... Lake Forest, IL
Passamaneck, Daniel ... San Mateo, CA
Passamano & Hunt, A Professional Corporation
Morristown, NJ
Passamano, James A. ... Houston, TX
Passamano, Russell J. ... Morristown, NJ
Passanante, Paul J. ... North Little Rock, AR
St. Louis, MO
Passanante, Philip J. ... Princeton, NJ
Passananti, Mari J. ... Washington, DC
Passanise, Joseph S. ... Springfield, MO
Passanisi, Michael ... Boston, MA
Passannante, Mark G. ... Portland, OR
Passannante, William G. ... New York, NY
Passante, Brian J. ... Macon, GA
Passante, Rebekah Myers ... Macon, GA
Passantino, Alexander J. ... Nashville, TN
Passantino, Stefan C. ... Atlanta, GA
Passar, Arthur L. ... Department of the Army, Office of the Judge Advocate General, GV
Passarella, Frank J. ... Totowa, NJ
Passarella, Steven T. ... Runnemede, NJ
Passarelli, Derek G. ... Denver, CO
Passarelli, Edward J. ... Department of Justice, Environment and Natural Resources Division, GV
Passarelli, John P. ... Omaha, NE
Passarelli, Robert J. ... Babylon, NY
Passarelli, Ronald J. ... St. Charles, IL
Passarelli, Thomas R. ... McLean, VA
Passarello, Darya M. ... Washington, DC
Passarello, John A., Jr. ... Staten Island, NY
Passarello, Kevin Louis ... Washington, DC
Passarello & LaRosa ... Staten Island, NY
Passarello, Lisa M. ... Pittsburgh, PA
Passarello, Steven P. ... Altoona, PA
Passaretti, Anthony Peter ... San Jose, CA
Passaretti, Jos. S. ... Hingham, MA
Passaretti, Joseph J., Jr. ... Glastonbury, CT
Passarino, Gary J. ... Santa Rosa, CA
Passaro, Geralyn M. ... Fort Lauderdale, FL
Passaro, Karen A. ... Hackensack, NJ
Passaro, T. J. (Tim) ... St. Joseph, MI
Passe, Kevin E. ... Redwood Falls, MN
Passe, Michael D. ... Yonkers, NY
Passe, Michele Arens ... Towson, MD
Passek, Stephen P. ... Berkeley, CA
Passen, Richard B. ... Norwood, NJ
Passen, Stephen C. ... Nashville, TN
Passen, Stephen M. ... Chicago, IL
Passen, Stephen M., Ltd. ... Chicago, IL
Passenger, Donald H. ... Grand Rapids, MI
Passer, Jay D. ... Tampa, FL
Passer, Jay D., P.A. ... Tampa, FL
Passer, Sanford H. ... Bloomfield Hills, MI
Passer, Steven L. ... Overland Park, KS
Passer-Muslin, Juliette M. ... New York, NY
Passero, Donna L. ... Murray Hill, NJ
Passero, Karen E. ... River Edge, NJ
Passero, Michael E. ... Milford, CT
Passero, Robert J. ... Paterson, NJ
Passero, Ronald J. ... Rochester, NY
Passey, Alan K.
Department of the Air Force, Office of the Judge Advocate General, GV
Passey, W. Lee ... Salt Lake City, UT
Passiatore, Joseph L. ... Orlando, FL
Passick, Irving ... Brooklyn, NY
Passidomo, John A. ... White Plains, NY
Passidomo, John M. ... Naples, FL
Passidomo, Kathleen C. ... Naples, FL
Passidomo, Peter J. ... New York, NY
Passin, Allan ... New York, NY
Passin, Courtney E. ... Philadelphia, PA
Passin, Mark D. ... Los Angeles, CA
Passin, Robert F. ... Northridge, CA
Passineau, Theodore L. ... Okemos, MI
Passino, David R. ... Atlanta, GA
Passino, Michael J. ... Nashville, TN
Passis, Dennis P. ... Northfield, IL
Passler, Mark D. ... West Palm Beach, FL
Passler, Richard G. ... New Orleans, LA
Passley, Shanann Pinkham ... Tulsa, OK
Passman, Aaron ... Boulder, CO
Passman, Donald S. ... Beverly Hills, CA
Passman, Edward H. ... Washington, DC
Passman, Eugene ... Suffern, NY
Passman, James Morgan ... Alexandria, LA
Passman & Jones, A Professional Corporation ... Dallas, TX
Passman, Julie P. ... Mount Kisco, NY
Passman & Kaplan, P.C. ... Washington, DC
Passman, Lex A. ... White Plains, NY
Passman, Sam ... Dallas, TX
Passman, Sanford M. ... Los Angeles, CA
Passman, Scott Eric ... Chestnut Hill, MA
Passman, Steven M. ... East Hanover, NJ
Passmore, J. Lincoln ... Dover, MA
Passmore, Lauren E. ... Denver, CO
Passmore, Leonard ... Austin, TX
Passmore, Lynda G. ... Chico, CA
Passmore, Walker & Twenhafel, L.L.P.
Brownsville, TX
McAllen, TX
Rio Grande City, TX
Passmore, Walter J. ... McAllen, TX
Passo, William O. ... Santa Ana, CA
Passodelis, Christopher, Jr. ... Pittsburgh, PA
Passodelis, Constantine J. (Dean)
Pittsburgh, PA
Passodelis, William C. ... Pittsburgh, PA
Passolt, James C., Jr. ... Downers Grove, IL
Passon, Kenneth D. ... Irvine, CA
Santa Ana, CA
Passonneau, Polly N., P.C. ... New York, NY
Passonneau, Polly Nicole ... New York, NY
Passovoy, Susan J. ... San Francisco, CA
Passy, Victor ... New York, NY
Pasta, Diane ... Seattle, WA
Pastel, Christopher R. ... Ithaca, NY
Pastel, Clifford A. ... Pittsburgh, PA
Pastel, Marvin Paul, II
Fort Lauderdale, FL
Pastel, Robert S. ... Albany, NY
Pastel, Wayne R. ... Chelmsford, MA
Pastena, Joseph A. ... West Orange, NJ
Paster, Barry N. ... West Barnstable, MA
Paster, Benjamin G. ... Providence, RI
Paster, Darrell L. ... New York, NY
Paster & Greenberg ... West Orange, NJ
Paster, Gregg F. ... West New York, NJ
Paster & Harpootian, Ltd. ... Providence, RI
Paster, Janice D. ... Albuquerque, NM
Paster, Jay E. ... West Palm Beach, FL
Paster, Jeffrey G. ... West Orange, NJ
Paster, Kimberly Kozemchak ... Boston, MA
Paster, Neal H. ... Houston, TX
Paster, Neal H., & Associates ... Houston, TX
Paster, Paula ... New York, NY
Paster, Phillip J. ... St. Louis, MO
Paster, Richard D. ... Quincy, MA
Paster, Robert W. ... St. Louis, MO
Paster, West & Kraner, P.C.
St. Louis, MO
Pasterak, Helene Kamenar ... Cleveland, OH
Pasterczyk, Catherine Ellen
Albuquerque, NM
Pasterczyk, Michael J. ... Chicopee, MA
Pasternack, Alan L. ... Portland, OR
Pasternack, Barry A. ... San Diego, CA
Pasternack, Bruce E. ... Albuquerque, NM
Pasternack, Gregg S. ... Los Angeles, CA
Pasternack, Harvey ... State College, PA
Pasternack, Jay S. ... Clifton, NJ
Pasternack, Jay S., P.A. ... Clifton, NJ
Pasternack, Jessica ... Walnut Creek, CA
Pasternack, Kenneth C. ... Goleta, CA
Pasternack, Marshall R. ... Miami, FL
Pasternack, Melvin ... Mineola, NY
Pasternack, Michael P. ... Brooklyn, NY
Pasternack, Sam, (P.C.) ... Boston, MA
Pasternack, Scott ... San Francisco, CA
Pasternack, Tina Dianne ... Santa Monica, CA
Pasternack, Victor ... Brooklyn, NY
New York, NY
Pasternack, Winifred ... Garden City, NY
Pasternak, Alvin ... New York, NY
Pasternak, Arthur David ... Washington, DC
Pasternak, Barton A. ... Philadelphia, PA
Pasternak, Bernice A. ... Boston, MA
Pasternak, Cynthia F. ... Los Angeles, CA
Pasternak, Dahna S. ... Menlo Park, CA
Pasternak, Daniel B. ... Chicago, IL
Pasternak, David J. ... Los Angeles, CA
Pasternak, Feldman & Plutnick, A Professional Association ... Livingston, NJ
Pasternak & Fidis, P.C. ... Bethesda, MD
Pasternak, Frank T. ... Mequon, WI
Milwaukee, WI
Racine, WI
Pasternak, I. Joel ... Des Moines, IA
Pasternak, Joel H. ... Winston-Salem, NC
Pasternak, Jonathan S. ... Harrison, NY
Pasternak, Kathryn L. ... New Canaan, CT
Pasternak, Michael B. ... Cleveland, OH
Pasternak, N. Alfred ... Bethesda, MD
Pasternak, Phyllis F. ... Roseland, NJ
Pasternak, Steven ... Livingston, NJ
Pasternak, Thomas G. ... Chicago, IL
Pasteur, Julie G. ... Racine, WI
Pasteur, Michelyn E. ... Lansing, MI
Pasti, Pamela ... San Francisco, CA
Pastin, Max ... Chicago, IL
Pastirik, Daniel R. ... St. Paul, MN
Pastis, Alix G. ... Medina, OH
Pastis, Stephan T. ... San Francisco, CA
Pasto, James H. ... San Diego, CA
Pasto, John R. ... Lafayette, CA
Paston, Michael J. ... Mount Laurel, NJ
Pastoor Law Office, LTD ... St. Paul, MN
Pastoor, Maria K. ... St. Paul, MN
Pastor, Adele V. ... Rutland, VT

Pastor, Bernard .... Miami, FL
Pastor, Bonnie .... Beverly Hills, CA
Pastor, Brian B. .... **Atlanta, GA**
Pastor, Carlos .... Miami, FL
Pastor, David .... **Boston, MA**
Pastor, David B. .... Walnut Creek, CA
Pastor, Dennis A. .... **Los Angeles, CA**
Pastor, E. William .... Blue Bell, PA
Pastor, Frederick A., P.C. .... Lewisville, TX
Pastor, Frederick A., The Law Offices of, P.C.
Lewisville, TX
Pastor, L. Stephen .... **Princeton, NJ**
Pastor Law Group, A, P.C. .... **Atlanta, GA**
Pastor & Leonard .... **Los Angeles, CA**
Encino, CA
Pastor, M. Veronica .... Washington, DC
Pastor, Mark D. .... **Los Angeles, CA**
Pastor, Michael E. .... Los Angeles, CA
Pastor, Nina L. .... Great Neck, NY
Pastor, Rafael .... New York, NY
Pastor, Roy W. .... Harvard, MA
Pastor, Sergio R. .... **Parsippany, NJ**
Pastor, Sherilyn .... **Newark, NJ**
Pastor, Stuart H. .... Dallas, TX
Pastor de Rovira, Carmen G. .... San Juan, PR
Pastore, Albert Gustav .... **New York, NY**
Pastore, Clare .... Los Angeles, CA
Pastore, Daniel J. .... **Erie, PA**
Pastore, Dominic .... Department of Justice,
Office of Intelligence Policy and Review, GV
Pastore, James J. .... **Greenwich, CT**
Pastore, James J. .... **New York, NY**
Pastore, John P. .... Clifton Park, NY
Pastore, Joseph A. .... San Diego, CA
Pastore, Joseph M., III .... **Stamford, CT**
Pastore, Michael M. .... **Stamford, CT**
Pastore, Nicholas .... **San Jose, CA**
Pastore, Paul C. .... **Albany, NY**
Pastore, Peter A. .... **Albany, NY**
Pastore, Pietra .... Albany, NY
Pastore, Richard S. .... **Greenwich, CT**
Pastore, Richard S., P.C. .... **Greenwich, CT**
Pastore, Robert .... Monte Vista, CO
Pastore, Thomas A. .... **Indianapolis, IN**
Pastore, Thomas M. .... **Auburn Hills, MI**
Pastore & Trujillo, P.C. .... Monte Vista, CO
Pastorek, Paul G. .... **New Orleans, LA**
Pastori, Terri L. .... **Manchester, NH**
Pastorick, William Dirk .... **Philadelphia, PA**
Pastoriza, Gilberto .... **Miami, FL**
Pastoriza, Julio .... Coral Gables, FL
Pastor-Klucens, Caridad .... Detroit, MI
Pastorkovich, Anne-Marie C.
Environmental Protection Agency,
Program Office Attorneys, GV
Pastor-Perez, David .... San Juan, PR
Pastors, Calvin R. .... Nashville, TN
Pastors, Charles R., II .... Chicago, IL
Pastrana, Armando, Jr. .... **Austin, TX**
Pastrana, David E., (A Prof. Corp.)
Huntington Beach, CA
Pastrana, Joseph C. .... Brooklyn, NY
Pastrana Law Firm .... Austin, TX
El Paso, TX
Pastrana, Marcia Denise .... Austin, TX
Pastrana, Raul Steven .... Austin, TX
El Paso, TX
Pastreich, Philip Edward .... Greenwich, CT
Pastrnak, Candy K. .... **Rock Island, IL**
Pastrnak Law Firm, P.C. .... Moline, IL
Davenport, IA
Pastrnak, Thomas J. .... Moline, IL
Davenport, IA
Pastroff, Sanford M. .... **Chicago, IL**
Pastryk, John R. .... **Charlotte, NC**
Pastucha, Edward J. .... Irvington, NY
Pastula, Perry G. .... **Wyoming, MI**
Pastuszek & Associates .... Mandeville, LA
Pastuszek, Harry P., Jr. .... Mandeville, LA
Pastuszenski, Brian E. .... **Boston, MA**
Pastuszenski, Erin S. .... Boston, MA
Pasula, Angela M. .... St. Joseph, MI
Pasulka, David P. .... **Chicago, IL**
Pasulka, David P., & Associates, P.C.
Chicago, IL
Pasulka, Donald C. .... **Chicago, IL**
Pasulka, Kathleen A. .... **San Diego, CA**
Pasulka, Margaret M. .... **Chicago, IL**
Pasulka, Matthew P. .... **Chicago, IL**
Pasulka, Michael D. .... San Diego, CA
Pasulka, Robert T. .... San Diego, CA
Pasulka, W. Raymond .... Chicago, IL
Pasulka-Brown, Kathleen R. .... **Chicago, IL**
Pasvogel, Glenn E., Jr. .... Little Rock, AR
Pasz, David J. .... **Strongsville, OH**
Paszamant, Brian S. .... **Philadelphia, PA**
Paszamant, Melissa B. .... **Philadelphia, PA**
Pasztory, Blaise G. A. .... **New York, NY**
Patacca, Angelo M., Jr. .... **Jacksonville, FL**
Patacca, Paul J. .... **Garden City, NY**
Patack, Melissa B. .... United States Senate,
Senatorial Assistants, GV
Patafio, John T. .... Amityville, NY
Patail, Michelle L. .... **Chicago, IL**
Patak, Terri Imbarlina .... **Pittsburgh, PA**
Pataki, George E. .... Peekskill, NY
Pataki, Leonard I. .... **Tulsa, OK**
Patalan, Timothy A. .... Durango, CO
Patalano, Anthony .... Los Angeles, CA
Patalano, Sylvia S. .... Cambridge, MA
Patamia, Steven E. .... Miami, FL
Patane, Arthur .... Albany, NY
Patane, John A. .... Oneida, NY
Patane, Joseph M. .... San Francisco, CA
Patané , Michael A. .... **Philadelphia, PA**
Patane, Nina M. .... **Salinas, CA**
Patanella, James S. .... Sykesville, MD

Patanelli, John M. .... Colorado Springs, CO
Patangan, Patrick P. .... **Metairie, LA**
Patarini, Val R. .... Wauchula, FL
Patashnick, Scott L. .... Pittsfield, MA
Patashnik, Moss .... Seattle, WA
Patay, Christopher H. .... **Los Angeles, CA**
Patberg, Rolf L. .... Pittsburgh, PA
Patberg, William L. .... **Toledo, OH**
Patch, Andrew John .... **Arlington, VA**
Patch, Daniel .... Upper St. Clair, PA
Patch, Douglas J. .... **Milwaukee, WI**
Patch, Edward F. .... Manchester, NH
Patch & Fitzgerald, Professional Association
Manchester, NH
Patch, Howard W. .... **Jackson, MI**
Patch, Howard W., P.C. .... **Jackson, MI**
Patch, Kathryn V. Woodward .... Old Lyme, CT
Patch, Kelly Ann .... Beloit, WI
Patch, Lee .... Mountain View, CA
Patch, Mary K.W. .... **Moline, IL**
Patch, Ralph J. .... Wolf Point, MT
Patch, Renn M. .... United States Senate,
Committee Legal Personnel, GV
Patch, Richard R. .... **San Francisco, CA**
Patch, Robert John .... **Arlington, VA**
Patch, Robert L., II .... **Fresno, CA**
Patch, Ryan Mark .... **Irvine, CA**
Patch, Sabrina M. .... Homewood, IL
Patch, T. W. .... Anchorage, AK
Patchan, Joseph .... **Cleveland, OH**
Patchel, Kathleen .... Indianapolis, IN
Patchell, Robert D. .... Treasury Department,
Internal Revenue Service, GV
Patchell, Stanley L. .... Phoenix, AZ
Patchen, Brian P. .... **Miami, FL**
Patchen, Gregory G. .... **New York, NY**
Patchen, Jerry D. .... Houston, TX
Patchen, Joseph M. .... **Columbus, OH**
Patchen, Michael N., Law Office of
Gillette, WY
Patchen, Richard V. .... **Columbus, OH**
Patchen, Robert J. .... **New York, NY**
Patchen, Robert W. .... Columbus, OH
Patchen, Stanley D. .... New Rochelle, NY
Patchen, Stuart .... Philadelphia, PA
Patchett, David B. .... **St. Paul, MN**
Patchett, John E. .... Chicago, IL
Patchett, John R. (Randy) .... **Marion, IL**
Patchin, Daniel F. .... **Houston, TX**
Patchin, Daniel M. .... Boring, OR
Patchin, Michael J. .... **Virginia, MN**
Patchke, Carl W. .... New York, NY
Pate, A. John (Jack) .... **Salt Lake City, UT**
Pate, Allen C. .... **Florence, SC**
Pate, Allen C., P.A. .... **Florence, SC**
Pate, Anne H. .... Dallas, TX
Pate, Bailey & Rigney .... Elizabethtown, KY
Pate, Barbara A. Linch
House of Representatives,
Congressional Assistants, GV
Pate, Christine V. .... San Diego, CA
Pate, Collier H. .... **Oklahoma City, OK**
Pate, C. W. (Bill) .... Tulsa, OK
Pate, Dennis W. .... La Mesa, CA
Pate, Diana C. .... Austin, TX
Pate & Dodson .... **Beaumont, TX**
Pate, Donna S. .... **Huntsville, AL**
Pate, Dorothy H. .... Jacksonville, FL
Pate, Frank .... Wellesley, MA
Pate, Gordon R. .... **Beaumont, TX**
Pate, H. D. .... Bridge City, TX
Pate, Imelda J. .... Kinston, NC
Pate, J. Gary .... Birmingham, AL
Pate, Jack C. .... **Dallas, TX**
Pate, James L., Jr. .... Elizabethtown, KY
Pate, James L., (P.C.) .... **Lafayette, LA**
Pate, James R., (P.A.) .... **Russellville, AR**
Pate, James S. .... **Erwin, TN**
Johnson City, TN
Pate, Kandi K. Jepsen .... Oklahoma City, OK
Pate, Kara K. .... Minneapolis, MN
Pate, Kempf & Knarr, A Professional
Corporation .... **Oklahoma City, OK**
Pate, Kimberly W. .... Los Angeles, CA
Pate, Lenora W. .... **Birmingham, AL**
Pate, Linda Wallace .... Los Angeles, CA
Pate, Lisa L. .... San Francisco, CA
Pate, Lisa M. .... **Chattanooga, TN**
Pate, Lloyd, Fuston & Cochrun, L.L.P.
Birmingham, AL
Pate, Mark A. .... Searcy, AR
Pate, Mary Ann .... Columbus, OH
Pate, Mary L. .... Anchorage, AK
Pate, Michael L. .... **Washington, DC**
Pate, Michael L. .... **Tulsa, OK**
Pate, Michael T. .... Louisville, KY
Pate, Michael T. .... **Towson, MD**
Pate, Page A. .... **Atlanta, GA**
Pate, Pat .... Poteau, OK
Pate, Paul A. .... **Huntsville, AL**
Pate, R. Gordon .... **Birmingham, AL**
Pate, R. Hewitt .... **Richmond, VA**
Pate, Richard F. .... Mobile, AL
Pate, Richard F., & Associates, P.C.
Mobile, AL
Pate, Rickey Ray .... Indianapolis, IN
Pate, Ridge .... Waco, TX
Pate, Robert C. .... Corpus Christi, TX
Pate, Samuel A. .... Steubenville, OH
Pate, Sherri D. .... Richmond, KY
Pate, Stephen P. .... **Houston, TX**
Pate, Stephen W. .... **Murfreesboro, TN**
Pate & Swain .... **Clarksville, AR**
Russellville, AR
Pate, Teri D. .... Brawley, CA
Pate, Tracey N. .... **Baltimore, MD**
Pate, Victoria J. .... Platte City, MO
Pate, W. Daniel .... **Pinehurst, NC**

Pate, Wanda L. .... Winston-Salem, NC
Pate, Whit .... Poteau, OK
Pate, William A. (Bill) .... Gulfport, MS
Pate, William C. .... San Diego, CA
Pate, William F., III
Department of Commerce,
Patent and Trademark Office, GV
Pate, William H. .... Gilmer, TX
Pate, William M. .... Orange, CA
Patea, Elvis R. Pila .... Wailuku, HI
Patek, Barbara A. .... **Detroit, MI**
Patek, James M. .... Chicago, IL
Patek, Jewell .... **Chillicothe, MO**
Patel, Aarti J. .... **Pittsburgh, PA**
Patel, Ahmed A. .... Chicago, IL
Patel, Ajay A. .... **Los Angeles, CA**
Patel, Amal S. .... Boston, MA
Patel, Andrew G. .... New York, NY
Patel, Anil .... **Palo Alto, CA**
Patel, Anjana D. .... **Saddle Brook, NJ**
New York, NY
Patel, Apexa .... Indianapolis, IN
Patel, Apur R. .... Minneapolis, MN
Patel, Arun S. .... Garden Grove, CA
Patel, Bijal M. .... **San Francisco, CA**
Patel, Binal J. .... **Chicago, IL**
Patel, C. Aaron .... Hackensack, NJ
Patel, Chirag V. .... **Baltimore, MD**
Patel, Chirag V., & Associates, P.A.
Baltimore, MD
Patel, Dahesh D. .... **Roseland, NJ**
Patel, Darshan V. .... **New York, NY**
Patel, Deborah J. .... Milwaukee, WI
Patel, Dharma .... Chicago, IL
Patel, Dilip .... Clearwater, FL
Patel, Dilip B. .... **Woodbridge, NJ**
Patel, Dilipkumar .... Tampa, FL
Patel, Farhad K. .... **Chicago, IL**
Minneapolis, MN
Patel, Hersh P. .... **New York, NY**
Patel, Himanshu M. .... **Miami, FL**
Patel, Jamshed J. .... **Milwaukee, WI**
Patel, Jasmin N. .... San Francisco, CA
Patel, Jayesh .... **Los Angeles, CA**
Patel, Jighnasa .... **Atlanta, GA**
Patel, Jigna P. .... **Los Angeles, CA**
Patel, Ken K. .... Cincinnati, OH
Patel, Ketan K. .... **Cleveland, OH**
Patel, Kiran M. .... San Francisco, CA
Patel, Kirtan, (L.L.C.) .... **Atlanta, GA**
Patel, Krishna .... **New York, NY**
Patel, Mahesh I. .... Lubbock, TX
Patel, Marilyn H. .... San Francisco, CA
Patel, Mehul T. .... San Francisco, CA
Patel, Mona J. .... **New York, NY**
Patel, Mona Mahendra .... Hanover, MA
Patel, Mona R. .... **Boston, MA**
Patel, Mukesh M. .... Edison, NJ
Patel, Narendra B. .... **Palo Alto, CA**
Patel, Nikesh R. .... **Washington, DC**
Patel, Nilesh S. .... **Kansas City, MO**
Patel, Nimesh B. .... **Atlanta, GA**
Patel, Nimesh M. .... Department of Justice,
Bureau of Prisons, GV
Patel, Nimesh R. .... **Atlanta, GA**
Patel, Nimish P. .... **La Jolla, CA**
Patel, Niranjan D. .... Artesia, CA
Patel, Nitin (Nick) M. .... Phoenix, AZ
Patel, Panna P. .... **Chicago, IL**
Patel, Parag .... **Los Angeles, CA**
Patel, Parag P. .... South Orange, NJ
Patel, Pravinchandra J. .... New York, NY
Patel, Purvi J. .... **Dallas, TX**
Patel, Rahul .... **Atlanta, GA**
Patel, Rajan .... **Parsippany, NJ**
Patel, Rajiv P. .... **Palo Alto, CA**
Patel, Rakhee .... **Dallas, TX**
Patel, Rena .... **Philadelphia, PA**
Patel, Rita M. .... Department of Justice,
Executive Office for Immigration Review,
GV
Patel, Ritu .... Fremont, CA
Patel, Salil P. .... **Philadelphia, PA**
Patel, Samir R. .... **Syosset, NY**
Patel, Sandip H. .... **Chicago, IL**
Patel, Sanjay S. .... Chicago, IL
Patel, Shashi .... **Houston, TX**
Patel, Shennie .... **Midland, TX**
Patel, Shilpa .... Philadelphia, PA
Patel, Sonia .... **Irvine, CA**
Patel, Stephanie Collings .... **Atlanta, GA**
Patel, Sujyot S. .... **Cincinnati, OH**
Patel, Tejas B. .... **Torrance, CA**
Patel, Tina S. .... **Palo Alto, CA**
Patel, Trupti S. .... **New York, NY**
Patel, Vipal J. .... **Los Angeles, CA**
Patel, Vipanj B. .... **Atlanta, GA**
Patel, Yoginee B. .... Riverside, CA
Patella, Christopher L. .... Union, NJ
Patella, Joseph Anthony .... New York, NY
Patella & Plaia .... Union, NJ
Patella, Raymond M. .... **Philadelphia, PA**
Patellaro, Geralynn .... Santa Clara, CA
Pateman, Mark L. .... **West Palm Beach, FL**
Patenaude, Craig W. .... **Washington, DC**
Patenaude & Felix .... San Diego, CA
Patenaude, Norman J. .... Concord, NH
Patenaude, Raymond A. .... San Diego, CA
Patenaude, Richard H. .... Taunton, MA
Patenode, Timothy J. .... **Chicago, IL**
Patent, Lawrence B.
Commodity Futures Trading Commission,
Division of Trading and Markets, GV
Patents & TMS, P.C. .... **Chicago, IL**
Pater, Clem, III .... Hamilton, OH
Pater, Dorothy M. .... Hampton, VA
Pater, Gerald L. .... Hamilton, OH
Pater, Mary Ann .... St. Joseph, MI

Pater, Pater & Pater Co., L.P.A.
Hamilton, OH
Pater, Raymond J. .... **Holland, MI**
Patera, Lisa M. .... **Arlington, VA**
Pateracki, John A., Jr. .... **New York, NY**
Paterick, Barbara Block
Ponte Vedra Beach, FL
Paterniti, Stephen T. .... **Boston, MA**
Paterniti, Thos. W. .... Erie, PA
Paterno, Louie A., Jr. .... Charleston, WV
Paterno, Peter T. .... **Los Angeles, CA**
Paterno, Ralph M. .... Oakland, CA
Paterno, Robert J. .... Miami, FL
Paternó, Sandro S. .... East Hanover, NJ
Paternó , Sandro S., & Assoc., P.C.
East Hanover, NJ
New York, NY
Paternoster, Charles J. .... **Elmira, NY**
Paternoster, Francis R. .... Walton, NY
Paternoster, John M. .... Taos, NM
Paternoster, Paul F. .... **Detroit, MI**
Paternoster, Rocco R. .... **Sacramento, CA**
Paternostro, Andrew L. .... **Charleston, WV**
Paternostro, Charles J. .... Dallas, TX
Paternostro, Peter J. .... **Armonk, NY**
Paterra, Carmine G. .... **Detroit, MI**
Paterson, Allan G., Jr. .... **San Antonio, TX**
Paterson, Andrea S. .... Washington, DC
Paterson, Andrew A., Jr. .... Southfield, MI
Paterson, Basil A. .... **Mineola, NY**
Paterson, Charles B. .... **Montgomery, AL**
Paterson, Charlotte A. .... Englewood, CO
Paterson, Clayton H. .... New Brunswick, NJ
Paterson, David G. .... Somerset, NJ
Paterson, David Grant .... Toledo, OH
Paterson, Dennis M., III .... **Portland, OR**
Paterson, Eva .... San Francisco, CA
Paterson, Gordon .... Marshall, MN
Paterson, Gordon R. .... **Stamford, CT**
Paterson, James .... Hazel Park, MI
Paterson, John M. R. .... **Portland, ME**
Paterson, John S. .... Sandusky, MI
Paterson, Joy Fellenzer .... Chatham, NJ
Paterson, Keith E. .... Mount Tabor, NJ
Paterson, Laurie L. .... **Valdosta, GA**
Paterson Law Office, P.C. .... Southfield, MI
Paterson, Lee T. .... **Los Angeles, CA**
Paterson, Leonard J. .... Sandusky, MI
Paterson, Mary T. Gardier .... **Scranton, PA**
Paterson, Nancy L. .... New York, NY
Paterson, Neil J. .... **Boston, MA**
Paterson & Paterson .... Sandusky, MI
Paterson, Paul K. .... Seattle, WA
Paterson, Richard W. .... Champaign, IL
Paterson, Robert E. .... **San Francisco, CA**
Paterson & Roberts .... **Stamford, CT**
Paterson, Thomas W. .... **Houston, TX**
Paterson & Walke, P.C. .... **Montpelier, VT**
Paterson, William E. .... **Ventura, CA**
Pates, James M. .... Fredericksburg, VA
Patestides, Michael .... **New York, NY**
Patete, A. Richard, Jr. .... Bala Cynwyd, PA
Patetta, Carl .... Westfield, NJ
Patey, Jon Mark .... **Jackson, TN**
Patey, Teel & McCormack, P.L.C.
Jackson, TN
Path, Dennis E. .... Charlotte, MI
Okemos, MI
Pathak, Ajay S. .... **Washington, DC**
Pathak, Anand S. .... **Cleveland, OH**
Pathak, Hemant .... **Redwood City, CA**
Pathare, Vijay W. .... New York, NY
Patheja, Jay S. .... **Merrillville, IN**
Pathman, Ronald C. .... Miami, FL
Paticchio, Michael A. .... Warren, NJ
Paticoff, Harvey .... **New York, NY**
Patience, Steve .... **Mesa, AZ**
Patient, Robert J. .... St. Paul, MN
Patierno, Christina Lynn Huiatt
Denver, CO
Patin, Anne M. .... **New York, NY**
Patin, C. Snyder .... **Anaheim, CA**
Patin, Charles L., Jr. .... **Baton Rouge, LA**
Patin, Claire B. .... Indianola, IA
Patin, Douglas L. .... **Washington, DC**
Patin, James R. .... **Houston, TX**
Patin, John A. .... **Lake Charles, LA**
Patinelli, Jamie A. .... **New York, NY**
Patinkin, Debra L. .... Deerfield, IL
Patinkin, Howard P. .... Chicago, IL
Patinkin, Hugh M. .... Chicago, IL
Patinkin & Patinkin .... Deerfield, IL
Patinkin, Richard E. .... Deerfield, IL
Patino & Associates, P.A.
Coral Gables, FL
Miami, FL
Patino, Elizabeth J. .... Dearborn, MI
Patiño, Jose L. .... **Dearborn, MI**
Patino, Leticia G. .... Tiffin, OH
Patino, Nadia A. .... **Dearborn, MI**
Patino, Ralph G. .... **Coral Gables, FL**
Patino, Susan Grombacher .... Evanston, IL
Patino, Vivian S. .... El Paso, TX
Patino-Treat, Marita .... Cherry Hill, NJ
Patino-Treat and Rosen .... Cherry Hill, NJ
Patish, Lawrence A. .... **Norfolk, VA**
Patish, Lawrence A., P.C. .... **Norfolk, VA**
Virginia Beach, VA
Patison, James L. .... Ventura, CA
Patitucci, Serena F. .... **Palo Alto, CA**
Patitucci, Wendy E. .... New York, NY
Patka, Carl F. .... Albany, NY
Patka, Thomas J. .... Tampa, FL
Patke, Marshall P. .... Lake Forest, IL
Patkin, Bertram S. .... Lexington, MA
Patkin, Roger A. .... Sharon, MA
Patko, Yvette A. G. .... Laguna Niguel, CA
Patkus, John P. .... Philadelphia, PA

Patla, Straus, Robinson & Moore, P.A.
Asheville, NC
Patler, Steven Y. ... Bloomfield Hills, MI
Patlin, Scott ... Colorado Springs, CO
Patman, Carrin F. ... Houston, TX
Patman, Connor ... Texarkana, TX
Patman & Osborn ... Austin, TX
Patman, Philip F. ... Austin, TX
Patman, Wm. N. ... Ganado, TX
Patmon, William W., III ... Columbus, OH
Patmont, Robert E. ... San Francisco, CA
Patnaik, Goutam ... New York, NY
Patnaude, Edmond T. ... Oakbrook Terrace, IL
Patnaude, Raymond ... New Bedford, MA
Patnaude, Suzanne N. ... Newark, NJ
Patnaude, Videbeck & Marsh
Oakbrook Terrace, IL
Patneaude-Krahulik, Christine M.
Middletown, NY
Patner, Bruce D. ... Chevy Chase, MD
Patner, Marshall ... Chicago, IL
Patner, Marshall, & Associates, P.C.
Chicago, IL
Patno, Christian R. ... Cleveland, OH
Patno, Judy M. ... Fullerton, CA
Patnode, Patrick K. ... Schenectady, NY
Patnoi, Stanley G. ... Encino, CA
Patoile, Marc C. ... Castle Rock, CO
Patoir, Steven ... Randolph, NJ
Paton, Adam Blaine ... Boston, MA
Paton, Brian A. ... Cleveland, OH
Paton, Cathryn R. ... Irving, TX
Paton, Geo. R. ... Leesburg, IN
Paton, Kimberly A. ... Paramus, NJ
Paton, Michael G. ... Indianapolis, IN
Paton, Scott C. ... Albany, NY
Paton, Vance D. ... Corpus Christi, TX
Patouris, Nicholas ... New York, NY
Patout, Edwin S. ... New Iberia, LA
Patout, Leslie M. ... Metairie, LA
Patramanis, Mike G. ... Moline, IL
Patrao, Raj C. ... Los Angeles, CA
Patras, Patrick L. ... Chicago, IL
Patras, Socrates H. ... Perth Amboy, NJ
Patrenos, Cathy L. ... Glendale, CA
Patrenos, James H., Jr. ... Livingston, AL
Patria, Kristen Jay ... Fitchburg, MA
Patriaco, Andrew A. ... River Edge, NJ
Patriarca, Francis J. ... Providence, RI
Patricco, Raymond E. ... Washington, DC
Patrich, Barry A. ... Woodbridge, NJ
Patrich, Kenneth D. ... Washington, DC
Patricia, Kenneth A. ... Buffalo, NY
Patricio, Jewell A. ... Houston, TX
Patricios, Leon N. ... Miami, FL
Patrick, A. Elizabeth ... Atlanta, GA
Patrick, Albert Jack ... Auburn, CA
Patrick, Albert W., III ... Hampton, VA
Patrick, Allison Snead ... Charleston, SC
Patrick, Angela, & Associates
Mount Sterling, KY
Patrick, Angie D. ... San Antonio, TX
Patrick, Bailey, Jr. ... Charlotte, NC
Patrick, Beard, Schulman & Jacoway, P.C.
Chattanooga, TN
Patrick, Bentley H. ... Birmingham, AL
Patrick, Bradford A. ... Redmond, WA
Patrick, Bruce D. ... Florham Park, NJ
Patrick, Carl E. ... Sarasota, FL
Patrick, Carl E., P.A. ... Sarasota, FL
Patrick, Casimir C., II ... New York, NY
Port Washington, NY
Patrick, Chandler & Campbell, LLC
Georgetown, SC
Litchfield Beach, SC
Myrtle Beach, SC
Surfside Beach, SC
Patrick, Charles B. ... Miami, FL
Patrick, Charles L. ... San Diego, CA
Patrick, Charles W., Jr. ... Charleston, SC
Patrick, Cheri C. ... Durham, NC
Patrick, Clayton B. ... Frankfort, KY
Patrick, Clayton C. ... Salem, OR
Patrick, Craig M. ... Dallas, TX
Patrick, Dane ... San Antonio, TX
Patrick, Daniel L. ... Surfside Beach, SC
Patrick, David ... Harrodsburg, KY
Patrick, David, P.S.C. ... Harrodsburg, KY
Patrick, Dean R. ... Groveland, CA
Patrick, Denise ... Lindale, TX
Patrick, Dennis M. ... Minneapolis, MN
Patrick, Diane ... Miami, FL
Patrick, Diane B. ... Boston, MA
Patrick, Donald Wood ... Austin, TX
Patrick, Douglas F. ... Greenville, SC
Patrick, Edward R. ... Knoxville, TN
Patrick, Frank G. ... Portland, OR
Patrick, Gary Ray ... Chattanooga, TN
Patrick, George W. ... Philadelphia, PA
Patrick, Glen E. ... Tyler, TX
Patrick, Granville R. ... Richmond, VA
Patrick, H. Brent ... Nashville, TN
Patrick, Harold Scott ... Opelika, AL
Patrick, Harper & Dixon L.L.P.
Hickory, NC
Newton, NC
Patrick, Herbert E., Law Offices of
Clarksville, TN
Patrick, Hunter ... Cody, WY
Patrick, J. Steven ... Gunnison, CO
Patrick, J. Vernon, Jr. ... Birmingham, AL
Patrick, J. Vernon, Jr., & Associates, P.C.
Birmingham, AL
Patrick, Jack W. ... Menomonee Falls, WI
Patrick, Jackie B. ... Department of Justice,
Criminal Division, GV
Patrick, James A., III ... Murrells Inlet, SC
Patrick, James D. ... Columbus, GA
Patrick, James J. ... San Francisco, CA
Patrick, James P. ... Lima, OH
Patrick, James S. ... New Philadelphia, OH
Patrick, James S., Co., L.P.A.
New Philadelphia, OH
Patrick, Jane F. ... Santa Cruz, CA
Patrick, John ... Department of the Army,
Office of the Judge Advocate General, GV
Patrick, John ... Cleveland, OH
Patrick, John B. ... Richmond, TX
Patrick, John B. ... Torrington, WY
Patrick, John C., III ... Greenwood, SC
Patrick, John C., Jr. ... Southfield, MI
Patrick, John R. ... Kansas City, MO
Patrick, Johnson & King, P.C.
Detroit, MI
Southfield, MI
Patrick, Kathy D. ... Houston, TX
Patrick, Kelley D. ... Bakersfield, CA
Patrick, Kennett L. ... Vista, CA
Patrick, Kennett M. ... Burbank, CA
Patrick, Kerry L. ... Leawood, KS
Patrick, Kevin L. ... Aspen, CO
Patrick, Kim J. ... Sioux Falls, SD
Patrick, Kirk A. ... Los Angeles, CA
Patrick, Kirk A., III ... Baton Rouge, LA
Patrick, L. Elizabeth ... Greenville, SC
Patrick, Lawrence C., Jr. ... Detroit, MI
Patrick, Leslie S. ... San Francisco, CA
Patrick, Leslie S., A Law Corporation
San Francisco, CA
Patrick, Linda ... Sacramento, CA
Patrick, Lisa Mitts ... Fullerton, CA
Patrick, Mark E. ... Dallas, TX
Patrick, Martha C. ... Phoenix, AZ
Patrick, Marty ... Miami, FL
Patrick, Marty, P.A. ... Miami, FL
Patrick and Meadowbrook ... Salem, OR
Patrick, Melanie Peirron
Baton Rouge, LA
Patrick, Michael A. ... Louisville, CO
Patrick, Michael D. ... New York, NY
Patrick, Michael J. ... Palo Alto, CA
Patrick, Michael W. ... Durham, NC
Patrick, Michelle Dwyer ... Riverwoods, IL
Patrick, Miller, Burnside & Belleau, LLC
New Orleans, LA
Patrick, N. Edward ... Takoma Park, MD
Patrick, P. Howard ... Derwood, MD
Patrick & Patrick ... Indianapolis, IN
Patrick, Patrick H. ... New Orleans, LA
Patrick, Paula A. ... Philadelphia, PA
Patrick, Paula A., P.C., Law Office of
Philadelphia, PA
Patrick, Peter ... Cheboygan, MI
Patrick, Phillip J. ... The Woodlands, TX
Patrick, Phillip J., P.C. ... The Woodlands, TX
Patrick, R. Alfred ... Greenville, NC
Patrick, R. Rex ... Tallahassee, FL
Patrick, Ralph C. ... Upper Darby, PA
Patrick, Richard E. ... Alexandria, VA
Patrick, Richard G. ... Phoenix, AZ
Patrick, Robert F. ... Colfax, WA
Pullman, WA
Patrick, Roger W. ... Washington, DC
Patrick, Roy M. ... Houston, TX
Patrick, Sara E. ... Eagan, MN
Patrick, Scott S. ... Washington, DC
Patrick, Shari L. ... New York, NY
Patrick, Shawn J. ... Clifton Park, NY
Patrick, Steven C. ... Thousand Oaks, CA
Patrick, Steven Dennis ... Los Angeles, CA
Patrick & Stowell, P.C. ... Aspen, CO
Patrick, Susan ... Olympia, WA
Patrick, Susan N ... Chantilly, VA
Patrick, Tandy C. ... Louisville, KY
Patrick, Teresa L. ... Department of Justice,
Environment and Natural Resources
Division, GV
Patrick, Thomas M. ... Chicago, IL
Patrick, Thomas M., Jr. ... Greenville, SC
Patrick, Todd G. ... Chesapeake, VA
Patrick, Victor P. ... Morristown, NJ
Patrick, W. Lawrence ... Ellicott City, MD
Patrick, W. Terry ... Youngstown, OH
Patrick, Walter ... Lawrenceburg, KY
Patrick, William ... Neshanic Station, NJ
Patrick, William B. ... Los Angeles, CA
Patrick, William B., Jr. ... Greenwood, SC
Patrick, William H., III, A Professional Law
Corporation ... Baton Rouge, LA
Patrick, William Hardy, III
Baton Rouge, LA
Patrick, William J. ... Berwick, PA
Patrick, William Lewis ... Lawrenceburg, KY
Patrick, William R. ... Oroville, CA
Patrick, Wm. B. ... Indianapolis, IN
Patricof, Allan J. ... Hewlett, NY
Patricoff, George B. ... Dayton, OH
Patricoff, Harold E., Jr. ... Miami, FL
Patricoski, Matthew T. ... Chicago, IL
Patricoski, Paul T. ... Aurora, IL
Patridge, Billy W. ... Brandon, MS
Patridge, James C. ... Oklahoma City, OK
Patridge, John J. ... Stockton, CA
Patrikis, Ernest T. ... New York, NY
Patrin, Derek A. ... Minneapolis, MN
Patrino, Anthony V. ... Akron, OH
Patrinostro, Stephen C. ... Lakeland, FL
Patriquin, Herbert F. ... West Harwich, MA
Patriquin, Robert S. ... Baton Rouge, LA
Patrissi, Patrick ... Fort Lauderdale, FL
Patrizi, Vanessa Pappas ... Cherry Hill, NJ
Patrizia, Charles A. ... Washington, DC
Patrizio, Eugene A. ... San Diego, CA
Patrizio, Frank J. ... Piqua, OH
Patrizio, Mark D. ... San Francisco, CA
Patrizio, Michael G. ... Chicago, IL
Des Plaines, IL
Patrizio, Stephen P. ... Philadelphia, PA
Patrón, David L. ... New Orleans, LA
Patrón, Mindy Brickman
New Orleans, LA
Patron, Robert Lawrence ... Plantation, FL
Patronas, Patrick ... Birmingham, AL
Patrone, Andre J. ... Fort Myers, FL
Patrone, Andre J., P.A. ... Fort Myers, FL
Patrone, John D. ... El Segundo, CA
Patrone, Vincent R. ... Providence, RI
Patronella, David M. ... Houston, TX
Patronella, Michael Blase ... Houston, TX
Patronik, Susan T. ... Sacramento, CA
Patronite, Gerald J. ... Cleveland, OH
Patronite, James M., Jr. ... Covina, CA
Patronite, Janice M. ... Irvine, CA
Patronite, Sal J. ... Rocky River, OH
Patross, Lloyd W. ... Pittsburgh, PA
Patrucco, Jon ... Meriden, CT
Patrusky, Bernard ... Los Angeles, CA
Patrusky, Bernard ... Jericho, NY
New York, NY
Patryk, Robb W. ... New York, NY
Patryn, Bruce J. ... Springfield, MA
Patsalos, Pano Z. ... Goshen, NY
Patsalos, Peter C. ... Goshen, NY
Patsavos, Estelle C. ... River Forest, IL
Patsavos, Evelyn C. ... Chicago, IL
Patsch, Glenn F. ... South Euclid, OH
Patsey, Richard L. ... Martinez, CA
Patsfall, Stephen J. ... Cincinnati, OH
Patsis, George ... Lindenhurst, NY
Patsko, Joseph T. ... Tampa, FL
Patsos, Christopher James, The Law Offices of ... New York, NY
Patsos, William S., Jr. ... Quincy, MA
Patsourakos, Vasilios P. ... Lowell, MA
Patsouras, Peter L. ... Lakewood, OH
Patt, Aldon W. ... Chicago, IL
Patt, Anthony G. ... Boston, MA
Patt, Christopher ... St. Louis, MO
Patt, Emily C. ... San Francisco, CA
Patt, Eric G. ... Chicago, IL
Patt, Herbert Jacob ... Santa Ana, CA
Patt, Jeffrey R. ... Chicago, IL
Patt, John E. ... Lafayette, LA
Patt, Kathryn Robertson ... Houston, TX
Patt, Mark S. ... Los Angeles, CA
Patt, P. Jules ... Hollidaysburg, PA
Patt, Raymond M. ... New York, NY
Patt, Stephen P. ... Chicago, IL
Glenview, IL
Patta, John David ... Lakewood, OH
Youngstown, OH
Patte, George D., Jr. ... Ithaca, NY
Spencer, NY
Pattee, Jeffrey C. ... Chicago, IL
Pattee, Michelene B. ... Grand Rapids, MI
Pattee, Phillip J. ... San Diego, CA
Pattee, Randall J. ... Minneapolis, MN
Pattee, Steven D. ... Minneapolis, MN
Patten, Alisan M. B. ... Phoenix, AZ
Patten, Andrew Lee ... Tampa, FL
Patten, Anthony W. ... White Plains, NY
Patten, Bernard M. ... Westwood, MA
Patten, Bonnie Lynne ... New Haven, CT
Patten, Bradley J. ... Gainesville, GA
Patten, Brenda L ... Sarasota, FL
Patten, C. Brent ... Martinez, CA
Patten, Charles D., III ... Baton Rouge, LA
Patten, Charles M. ... Indianapolis, IN
Patten, Clark W. ... Walnut Creek, CA
Patten, David C. ... West Chester, PA
Patten, Donald N. ... Waynesville, NC
Patten, Donald N. ... Newport News, VA
Richmond, VA
Patten, Edward E., Jr. ... Hazlehurst, MS
Patten, Edward T. ... Boston, MA
Patten, Faith & Sandford
Los Angeles, CA
Monrovia, CA
Patten, Gary ... Tempe, AZ
Patten, Gerland P. ... Little Rock, AR
Patten, Gordon L. ... Tulsa, OK
Patten, James A. ... Billings, MT
Patten, James R. ... Wolfeboro, NH
Patten, Jeffrey L. ... Tucson, AZ
Patten, Jocelyne H. ... Baton Rouge, LA
Patten, John D. ... New York, NY
Patten, John G., Jr. ... Fort Thomas, KY
Patten, John P. ... Fayetteville, NC
Patten, Keith D. ... University City, MO
Patten Law Offices, P.C. ... Tempe, AZ
Patten, Lisa Daugherty ... Miami, FL
Patten, Michael E. ... Poplarville, MS
Patten, Michael W. ... Phoenix, AZ
Patten, Nancy P. ... St. Louis, MO
Patten, Neal J. ... Newport News, VA
Patten, Patricia A. ... Tulsa, OK
Patten & Patten ... Norman, OK
Patten, Rebecca J. ... Norman, OK
Oklahoma City, OK
Patten, Robert ... Boston, MA
Patten, Scott A. ... Boulder, CO
Patten, Stacy J. ... Richmond, VA
Patten, Teresa M. ... Boston, MA
Patten, Thomas L. ... Washington, DC
Patten, Valerie L. ... Palo Alto, CA
Patten, Warren ... Salt Lake City, UT
Patten, Wendy L. ... Department of Justice,
Office of Policy Development, GV
Patten, William E. ... Tulsa, OK
Patten, William F. ... Fall River, MA
Patten, William R. ... Norman, OK
Patten, William W., II ... New York, NY
Patten, Woolvin ... Seattle, WA
Patten, Wornom, Hatten & Diamonstein, L.C. ... Newport News, VA
Pattenaude, Susan Seligson
West Sand Lake, NY
Patten-Greene, Melissa A.
Salt Lake City, UT
Patter, Jeffrey J. ... Dublin, OH
Patterman, Patricia ... Boulder, CO
Pattermann, Laura Laubenthal
Council Bluffs, IA
Pattermann, T. J. ... Council Bluffs, IA
Patterson, A. Gerard ... Appleton, WI
Patterson, Adele V. ... Bridgeport, CT
Patterson, Albert D. ... Anchorage, AK
Patterson, Albert John ... Montgomery, AL
Patterson, Alexander W. ... Atlanta, GA
Patterson, Alice S. ... Louisville, KY
Patterson, Alisa L. ... Chicago, IL
Patterson, Amy S. ... Columbia, SC
Patterson, Andrea L. ... Eagan, MN
Patterson, Andrea P. ... Boise, ID
Patterson, Andrew S. ... Palm Desert, CA
Patterson, Ann Crowley ... Chicago, IL
Patterson, Annabelle Lee ... Texarkana, TX
Patterson, Anne M. ... Morristown, NJ
Patterson, Anthony W. ... Indianapolis, IN
Patterson, Archibald A. ... New York, NY
Patterson, Arthur E., II ... Boulder, CO
Patterson & Associates
Corpus Christi, TX
Patterson, A. W., Jr. ... Dallas, TX
Patterson, B. Todd ... Red Bank, NJ
Houston, TX
Patterson, Barbara J. ... Akron, OH
Patterson, Barking & Thompson ... Ogden, UT
Patterson, Bart J. ... Scottsdale, AZ
Patterson, Belknap, Webb & Tyler LLP
New York, NY
Patterson, Ben L., Jr. ... Marietta, GA
Patterson, Benjamin E. ... Chicago, IL
Patterson, Benjamin R., III ... Tallahassee, FL
Patterson, Beth Ann ... Miami, FL
Patterson, Beth S. ... New York, NY
Patterson & Bleiweiss ... Willoughby, OH
Patterson, Bond & Latshaw, P.A.
Jacksonville, FL
Jacksonville Beach, FL
Patterson, Bonnie Claire ... New Orleans, LA
Patterson, Boyd & Lowery, P.C.
Houston, TX
Patterson, Bradley A. ... Irvine, CA
Patterson, Bradley D. ... Salt Lake City, UT
Patterson and Brencher ... Branford, CT
Patterson, Brent A. ... Gastonia, NC
Patterson, Brian D. ... Washington, DC
Patterson, Brian Vance ... Atlanta, GA
Patterson, Bruce M. ... Santa Ana, CA
Patterson, Burton H. ... El Paso, TX
Patterson, Byron L. ... Los Angeles, CA
Patterson, C. Cary ... Daingerfield, TX
Patterson, C. Duane ... Wausau, WI
Patterson, Carl N., Jr. ... Raleigh, NC
Patterson, Carol J. ... New York, NY
Patterson, Caroline J. ... Berwyn, PA
Patterson, Carolyn H. ... Hutchinson, KS
Patterson, Cecil B., Jr. ... Phoenix, AZ
Patterson, Chaka M. ... Denver, CO
Chicago, IL
Patterson, Charles ... San Francisco, CA
Patterson, Charles ... Jackson, TN
Patterson, Charles B. ... Greenville, SC
Patterson, Charles E. ... Los Angeles, CA
Patterson, Charles F., Jr. ... East Northport, NY
Patterson, Charles T. ... Sioux City, IA
Patterson, Cheryl W. ... Memphis, TN
Patterson, Chris L. ... Orem, UT
Patterson, Christie A. ... Southfield, MI
Patterson, Christine C. ... San Gabriel, CA
Patterson, Christine Danave
Providence, RI
Patterson, Christine J. ... Pineland, FL
Patterson, Christine Steffen
Virginia Beach, VA
Patterson, Christopher C. ... Rochester, NY
Patterson, Christopher M. ... Lancaster, PA
Patterson, Christopher N.
Panama City, FL
Patterson, Christopher N., P.A.
Panama City, FL
Patterson, Christopher T.
North Kansas City, MO
Patterson, Christopher W.
Westlake Village, CA
Patterson, Colleen Sue ... Hemet, CA
Patterson, Craig R. ... Fort Wayne, IN
Patterson, Cynthia J. ... Albuquerque, NM
Patterson, Dan ... Dallas, TX
Patterson, Dan A. ... Columbus, IN
Patterson, Daniel C. ... Greenville, SC
Patterson, Daniel W. ... Denver, CO
Patterson, Daniel W., & Associates, P.C.
Denver, CO
Patterson, David, & Associates, Inc., P.S.
Everett, WA
Patterson, David C. ... Berlin, NJ
Patterson, David C. ... Columbus, OH
Patterson, David D. ... Newton, MA
Patterson, David F. ... Tampa, FL
Patterson, David H. ... Philadelphia, PA
Pittsburgh, PA
Patterson, David J. ... New York, NY
Patterson, David L. ... Dallas, TX
Patterson, David L. ... Salt Lake City, UT
Patterson, David N. ... Willoughby, OH
Patterson, David R. ... Shrewsbury, MA
Patterson, David R. ... Trenton, NJ
Patterson, David S. ... New York, NY
Patterson, David T. ... Columbus, OH

Patterson, David T. ... Everett, WA
Patterson, Dawn M. ... Hayward, CA
Patterson, Dawn M. ... Troy, MI
Patterson, Deborah H. ... Louisville, KY
Patterson, Deborah K. ... Sacramento, CA
Patterson, Debra J. ... Wauwatosa, WI
Patterson, Dennis L. ... Dayton, OH
Patterson, Dennis M. ... Camden, NJ
Patterson, Dexter, A Professional Corporation
The Woodlands, TX
Patterson, Dickie W. ... Hammond, LA
Patterson, Dilthey, Clay & Bryson, L.L.P.
Raleigh, NC
Wilmington, NC
Patterson, Don L. ... Amarillo, TX
Patterson, Donald ... Topeka, KS
Patterson, Donald B. ... Brookhaven, MS
Patterson, Donald E. ... Richmond, CA
Patterson, Donald H. ... Florence, AL
Patterson, Donald J., Jr. ... Washington, DC
Patterson, Donald R. ... Tyler, TX
Patterson, Donna E. ... Washington, DC
Patterson, Douglas J. ... Leawood, KS
Patterson, Dwight F., Jr. ... Spartanburg, SC
Patterson, Earle J. ... Kennebunk, ME
Patterson & Edquist ... Angleton, TX
Lake Jackson, TX
Patterson, Edward J., III ... Houston, TX
Patterson, Edward J., Jr. ... Galveston, TX
Patterson, Edward M. ... Montgomery, AL
Patterson, Edward M. ... Pasadena, CA
Patterson, Edwin W., III ... Cincinnati, OH
Patterson, Elizabeth Biddison ... Houston, TX
Patterson, Elizabeth H. ... Washington, DC
Patterson, Elizabeth J. ... Dallas, TX
Patterson, Elizabeth Kay Harris ... Fairfax, VA
Patterson, Elizabeth L. ... Greeneville, TN
Patterson, Elizabeth Marie ... New York, NY
Patterson, Ellen R. ... New York, NY
Patterson, Erin Hunter ... Houston, TX
Patterson, Errol R. ... Washington, DC
Patterson, Eskin & Ball ... Cape Coral, FL
Patterson, Eudox
Hot Springs National Park, AR
Patterson, Floyd N. ... New York, NY
Patterson, Forbes ... Columbia, SC
Patterson, Forest R. ... Waco, TX
Patterson, Forrest T. ... Cranbury, NJ
Patterson, Frank B. ... Roswell, NM
Patterson, Franklin D. ... Englewood, CO
Patterson, Fred R. ... Union, NJ
Patterson, Frederick A ... Walnut Creek, CA
Patterson, G. Clifton, III ... Rockville, MD
Patterson, G. Douglas ... Lincolnshire, IL
Patterson, Gale ... Fort Worth, TX
Patterson, Gary ... Englewood, CO
Patterson, Gary B. ... Richmond, VA
Patterson, Gary D. ... Saginaw, MI
Patterson, Gary E. ... Wichita, KS
Patterson, Gaylene Gordon ... Princeton, NJ
Patterson, Geo. F., Jr. ... Cincinnati, OH
Patterson, Geoffrey D. ... Seattle, WA
Patterson, George A. ... Deerfield Beach, FL
Patterson, George A., III ... Charleston, WV
Patterson, George C. ... Boise, ID
Patterson, George E., Jr. ... Miami, FL
Patterson, George M. ... Midland, TX
Patterson, George M., Jr. ... Beaver Falls, PA
Patterson, George P.
Upper Marlboro, MD
Patterson, Gerald G. ... Nashville, TN
Patterson, Gerald S. ... San Francisco, CA
Patterson, Gerlad G., P.C. ... Nashville, TN
Patterson, Gina D. ... Houston, TX
Patterson, G. L. "Pat", II ... Springerville, AZ
Patterson, Glenn R. ... Merrillville, IN
Patterson, Glenn W., Jr. ... Houston, TX
Patterson, Grady L., III ... Columbia, SC
Patterson, Grady L., Jr. ... Columbia, SC
Patterson, Grady S., Jr. ... Raleigh, NC
Patterson, Gregory J. ... Los Angeles, CA
Patterson, Gregory L. ... Columbus, OH
Patterson, Gregory S. ... Cleveland, OH
Patterson, Gruber, Kennedy, Gill & Milster
Bay City, MI
Patterson, Hal B. ... Nanuet, NY
Patterson, Harkavy & Lawrence, L.L.P.
Greensboro, NC
Raleigh, NC
Patterson & Harmon, P.A.
Deerfield Beach, FL
Patterson, Henry N., Jr. ... Raleigh, NC
Patterson, Henry Newton, V ... Durham, NC
Patterson, Herbert W. ... Washington, DC
Patterson, Howard L., Jr. ... Hattiesburg, MS
Patterson, Hugh L. ... Norfolk, VA
Patterson, J. Michael ... San Jose, CA
Patterson, J. Phillip ... Oklahoma City, OK
Patterson, J. Randall ... Jackson, MS
Patterson, J. Randall ... San Antonio, TX
Patterson, J. Steven ... Washington, DC
Patterson, J. Timothy ... Pontiac, MI
Patterson, J. A. (Tony), Jr. ... Dallas, TX
Patterson, Jacqueline ... Greenville, SC
Patterson, Jacqueline A. ... Los Angeles, CA
Patterson, Jamee Jordan ... San Diego, CA
Patterson, James Allan
Newport News, VA
Patterson, James E. ... Whittier, CA
Patterson, James E. ... Ellsworth, ME
Patterson, James E. ... Parsippany, NJ
Patterson, James H. ... Phoenix, AZ
Patterson, James H. ... Minneapolis, MN
Patterson, James M., III ... Dallas, TX
Patterson, James McMahan, Jr.
Nashville, TN
Patterson, James O., Jr. ... Memphis, TN
Patterson, James R. ... Chicago, IL
Patterson, James R. ... Columbus, OH
Patterson, James S. ... Colorado Springs, CO
Patterson, James S. ... Addison, TX
Patterson, James W. ... Oklahoma City, OK
Patterson, James W. ... Philadelphia, PA
Patterson, James W. ... Kerrville, TX
Patterson, James W. ... Fairfax, VA
Patterson, Jan P. ... Aberdeen, MS
Patterson, Jan Powell ... Austin, TX
Patterson, Janet Lynne ... Phoenix, AZ
Patterson, Janice E. ... Cedar Rapids, IA
Patterson, Jay ... Dallas, TX
Patterson, Jay, A Prof. Corp., Law Offices of
Dallas, TX
Patterson, J. D. ... Lawrenceville, GA
Patterson, Jeanene F. ... Salt Lake City, UT
Patterson, Jeffery S. R. ... Rancho Mirage, CA
Patterson, Jeffrey D. ... Las Vegas, NV
Patterson, Jeffrey P. ... Mukwonago, WI
Patterson, Jeffrey R. ... San Diego, CA
Patterson, Jeffrey S. ... Columbia, SC
Patterson, Jeffrey S. ... Dallas, TX
Patterson, Jeffry D. ... Lincoln, NE
Patterson, Jennifer ... Minneapolis, MN
Patterson, Jennifer B. ... New York, NY
Patterson, Jennifer J. ... Concord, NH
Patterson, Jennifer K. ... Austin, TX
Patterson, Jerome A.
Agency for International Development,
Office of the General Counsel, GV
Patterson, Jerry D. ... Marshall, AR
Patterson, Jerry M. ... Costa Mesa, CA
Patterson, Jill S. ... Dayton, OH
Patterson, J. M., Jr. ... Austin, TX
Patterson, Joe M., Jr. ... Florence, AL
Patterson, John ... Searcy, AR
Patterson, John ... Sarasota, FL
Patterson, John C. ... Elk Grove, CA
Patterson, John C. ... Seattle, WA
Patterson, John C., Jr. ... Sarasota, FL
Patterson, John D., Jr. ... Boston, MA
Patterson, John E. ... Vista, CA
Patterson, John E., Jr. ... Oklahoma City, OK
Patterson, John E., Jr., P.C.
Oklahoma City, OK
Patterson, John F., Jr. ... Missoula, MT
Patterson, John G. ... Minneapolis, MN
Patterson, John G. ... Houston, TX
Patterson, John H., Jr. (P.A.) ... Miami, FL
Patterson, John H., (P.A.) ... Miami, FL
Patterson, John J. ... New York, NY
Patterson, John K. ... Burlington, NC
Patterson, John N. ... Santa Fe, NM
Patterson, John, P.A. ... Searcy, AR
Patterson, John R. "Bob" ... Roanoke, VA
Patterson, John R., Jr. ... Albany, NY
Patterson, John S. ... Clarksville, AR
Patterson, John S. ... Sarasota, FL
Patterson, John T. ... Findlay, OH
Patterson, John T. ... Waco, TX
Patterson, Jon-Mark C. ... Loveland, CO
Patterson, Joseph ... Angleton, TX
Patterson, Joseph C. ... Harrisburg, PA
Patterson, Joseph Redwine ... Dallas, TX
Patterson, Joseph William, Jr. ... McAllen, TX
Patterson, Joyce L. ... Dresher, PA
Patterson, J. R., Jr. ... Henderson, TX
Patterson, Judith ... Dallas, TX
Patterson, Judy S. ... Baton Rouge, LA
Patterson, Julie E. ... Irvine, CA
Patterson, Julie Yates ... Washington, DC
Patterson, Justin P.
Department Of The Interior,
Office of the Solicitor, GV
Patterson, Kathleen D. ... San Francisco, CA
Patterson, Kathleen F. ... Washington, DC
Patterson, Kelly T. ... Winston-Salem, NC
Patterson, Kendrick ... Washington, DC
Patterson, Kenneth O., Jr. ... Englewood, CO
Patterson, Kenneth W.
Environmental Protection Agency,
Office of Enforcement and Compliance
Assurance, GV
Patterson, Kent H. ... Camp Hill, PA
Patterson, Kent H. ... Harrisburg, PA
Patterson & Keough, P.A.
Minneapolis, MN
Patterson, Kevin ... New York, NY
Patterson, Kevin Glenn ... Memphis, TN
Patterson & Kiersz, P.C. ... Greencastle, PA
Waynesboro, PA
Patterson, Kim E. ... Milwaukee, WI
Patterson, Kinney & Ruga
Grand Rapids, MI
Patterson, Kirk ... San Antonio, TX
Patterson, L. Brooks ... Pontiac, MI
Patterson, Laird D. ... Washington, DC
Patterson, Lamberty & Robinson, A
Professional Corporation ... Dallas, TX
Patterson, Larry R. ... Greenville, SC
Patterson, Laurie A. ... Tulsa, OK
Patterson, Laverne D. ... San Francisco, CA
Patterson Law Firm, P.A. ... Greenville, SC
Patterson Law Offices ... Boise, ID
Patterson, Lawrence F. ... Oak Brook, IL
Patterson, Lawrence N., Jr. ... Centreville, MD
Patterson, Lawrence R.
Jacksonville Beach, FL
Patterson, Lee A., II ... Durham, NC
Patterson, Leeanne Y. ... Vallejo, CA
Patterson, Leigh-Ann M. ... Boston, MA
Patterson, Lennox C. ... Brooklyn, NY
Patterson, Lennox C., P.C. ... Brooklyn, NY
Patterson, Leonard M. ... San Francisco, CA
Patterson, Leslie J. ... Southfield, MI
Patterson, Linda J. ... Seattle, WA
Patterson, Linda S. ... Tigard, OR
Patterson, Lindsay ... Jackson, MS
Patterson, Lorentzen, Duffield, Timmons,
Irish, Becker & Ordway, L.L.P.
Des Moines, IA
Patterson, Lori Hackleman ... Memphis, TN
Patterson, Lori S. ... Jacksonville, FL
Patterson, Lorin E. ... Salt Lake City, UT
Patterson, Lowell H., III ... Washington, DC
Patterson, Lyman Ray ... Athens, GA
Patterson, M. Kenneth ... San Antonio, TX
Patterson, M. Susan ... Plymouth, MI
Patterson, Maloney & Maisel
Fort Lauderdale, FL
Patterson, Margaret J. ... Bartlesville, OK
Patterson, Margaret K.
Department of the Army,
Office of the Judge Advocate General, GV
Patterson, Maria M. ... New York, NY
Patterson, Marie A. ... Norristown, PA
Patterson, Mark A. ... United States Senate,
Senatorial Assistants, GV
Patterson, Mark C. ... Cincinnati, OH
Patterson, Mark J. ... Nashville, TN
Patterson, Mark L. ... Dallas, TX
Patterson, Mark R. ... New York, NY
Patterson, Mark R. ... Tacoma, WA
Patterson, Mark W. ... Las Vegas, NV
Patterson, Mark William ... Corpus Christi, TX
Patterson, Martha Geisler ... Buena Park, CA
Patterson, Mary Kathleen ... Everett, WA
Patterson, Matthew T. ... Dublin, OH
Patterson, Melinda L. ... Houston, TX
Patterson, Melvin K. ... Daly City, CA
Patterson, Michael A. ... Baton Rouge, LA
Patterson, Michael A. ... Seattle, WA
Patterson, Michael D. ... Detroit, MI
Patterson, Michael E. ... New York, NY
Patterson, Michael H. ... Arlington, TX
Patterson, Michael J. ... Anchorage, AK
Patterson, Michael L. ... Birmingham, AL
Patterson, Michael P. ... Port Clinton, OH
Patterson, Michael S. ... Burbank, CA
Patterson, Mike ... Dallas, TX
Patterson, Mildred L., (Miss) ... Guthrie, OK
Patterson & Miller ... Palm Desert, CA
Patterson, N. Paul ... Washington, DC
Patterson, Nancy A. ... New Bloomfield, PA
Patterson, Nancy L. ... Houston, TX
Patterson, Nancy Phelps ... Addison, TX
Patterson, Neal C., Jr., (P.A.)
Cape Coral, FL
Patterson, Neal J. ... Cleveland, OH
Patterson, Nicki Elizabeth ... Mobile, AL
Patterson & Nuss, P.C., Law Offices of
Englewood, CO
Patterson, P. Andrew ... Atlanta, GA
Patterson, Pamela ... Santa Ana, CA
Patterson, Parker & White ... Burlington, NC
Patterson, Patricia L.
Grosse Pointe Woods, MI
Patterson, Patricia L. ... Hixson, TN
Patterson, Patrick A. ... St. Louis, MO
Patterson, Patrick C. ... Dallas, TX
Patterson, Patrick Hyder ... San Diego, CA
Ann Arbor, MI
Patterson, Patrick O. ... Fox Point, WI
Patterson & Patterson ... Whittier, CA
Patterson & Patterson ... Aberdeen, MS
Columbus, MS
Starkville, MS
Tupelo, MS
Patterson, Paul ... Tuscaloosa, AL
Patterson, Paul A. ... Philadelphia, PA
Patterson, Paul S. ... Downey, CA
Patterson, Peggy E. ... Ashland, KY
Patterson, Perry S. ... Coudersport, PA
Patterson, Perry S., Jr. ... Ridgecrest, CA
Patterson, Peter A. ... Grand Rapids, MI
Patterson, Peter R. ... Pittsburgh, PA
Patterson, Peter T. ... Houston, TX
Patterson, Phifer & Phillips, P.C.
Detroit, MI
Mount Clemens, MI
Pontiac, MI
Patterson, Philip C. ... Ogden, UT
Patterson, R. Scott ... North Haven, CT
Patterson, R. Wayne ... Los Angeles, CA
Patterson, R.A., III ... Tampa, FL
Patterson, Ralph M., Jr.
North Little Rock, AR
Patterson, Randal M. ... Odessa, TX
Patterson, Randall L. ... Houston, TX
Patterson & Reese ... Fairfax, VA
Patterson, Reid E. ... Centerville, OH
Patterson, René R. ... Dallas, TX
Patterson, Richard A. ... East Lansing, MI
Patterson, Richard A., P.C. ... East Lansing, MI
Patterson, Richard B., Jr. ... Lynn, MA
Patterson, Richard C. ... Tazewell, VA
Patterson, Richard D. ... Branford, CT
Patterson, Richard H. ... San Diego, CA
Patterson, Richard H., Jr.
Los Angeles, CA
Patterson, Richard J. ... Rocky Hill, CT
Patterson, Richard M. ... Indianapolis, IN
Patterson, Richard North ... San Francisco, CA
Patterson, Richard O. ... Houston, TX
Patterson, Richard S. ... Baltimore, MD
Patterson, Richard S. ... Houston, TX
Patterson, Richard W. ... Omaha, NE
Patterson, Rick J. ... Auburn Hills, MI
Patterson, Ritner, Lockwood, Gartner &
Jurich ... Bakersfield, CA
Los Angeles, CA
San Bernardino, CA
Ventura, CA
Patterson, Robert A. ... Charleston, SC
Patterson, Robert B. ... Chicago, IL
Patterson, Robert B. ... Middleburg, VA
Patterson, Robert B., Jr. ... Portland, ME
Patterson, Robert B., Jr.
Minneapolis, MN
Patterson, Robert B., Ltd., Law Offices of
Chicago, IL
Patterson, Robert Charles ... Easton, PA
Patterson, Robert D. ... Bakersfield, CA
Patterson, Robert D. ... Aberdeen, MS
Patterson, Robert E. ... Palo Alto, CA
Patterson, Robert E. ... Boston, MA
Patterson, Robert E. ... Jacksonville, NC
Patterson, Robert E. ... Olympia, WA
Patterson, Robert E., P.A. ... Jacksonville, NC
Patterson, Robert Earl ... Huntsville, AL
Patterson, Robert H. ... Detroit, MI
Patterson, Robert H., Jr. ... Richmond, VA
Patterson, Robert J. ... Corpus Christi, TX
Patterson, Robert L. ... Rancho Mirage, CA
Patterson, Robert M. ... Santa Cruz, CA
Patterson, Robert P., Jr. ... New York, NY
Patterson, Robert S. ... Santa Barbara, CA
Patterson, Robert S. ... Nashville, TN
Patterson, Robert W. ... Rochester, MN
Patterson, Robert W. ... Buffalo, NY
Patterson, Robert W., (P.C.) ... Chicago, IL
Patterson, Rod ... Fort Worth, TX
Patterson, Roger J. ... Washington, DC
Baltimore, MD
Patterson, Roger K. ... San Diego, CA
Patterson, Ron ... Austin, TX
San Antonio, TX
Patterson, Ronald B. ... Alexandria, VA
Patterson, Ronald J. ... Philadelphia, PA
Patterson, Ronald S. ... Hayesville, NC
Patterson, Rosemarie F. ... Whittier, CA
Patterson, Rudolph N. ... Albany, GA
Macon, GA
Patterson, Russell P.
Hilton Head Island, SC
Patterson, R. Y., Jr. ... Winter Park, FL
Patterson, S. James ... Omaha, NE
Patterson, S. Jane ... Gresham, OR
Patterson, Samuel T., Jr. ... Petersburg, VA
Patterson, Sandy G. ... Southern Pines, NC
Patterson, Sarah F. ... Rocky Mount, NC
Patterson, Scott ... Houston, TX
Patterson, Scott D. ... Berwyn, PA
Patterson, Scott E. ... Solana Beach, CA
Patterson, Scott G. ... Easton, MD
Patterson, Scott T. ... Troy, MI
Patterson, Sean P. ... Reno, NV
Patterson, Shari Cassin ... Las Vegas, NV
Patterson, Sharon Byrd ... Huntsville, AL
Patterson, Sharon F. ... Knoxville, TN
Patterson, Shaunda A. ... Washington, DC
Patterson, Sheila I. ... Laguna Beach, CA
Patterson, Sherrod G. ... Atlanta, GA
Patterson, Sheryl Noel ... Sacramento, CA
Patterson & Siceloff ... Houston, TX
Patterson, South Trimble
Newport News, VA
Patterson, Spencer C. ... Dallas, TX
Patterson, Stacie L. ... San Diego, CA
Patterson, Stacie Wagner
State College, PA
Patterson, Stacy S. ... Clinton, MS
Patterson, Stephanie Kinsley ... Madison, CT
Patterson, Stephen E. ... Greencastle, PA
Waynesboro, PA
Patterson, Stephen J. ... Boston, MA
Patterson, Stephen J. ... Concord, NH
Patterson, Stephen R., (P.C.)
Longview, TX
Patterson, Stephen T. ... Englewood, CO
Patterson, Stephen W. ... Houston, TX
Patterson, Steven K. ... Carmel, NY
Patterson, Steven L. ... Sacramento, CA
Patterson, Steven R. ... Fullerton, CA
Patterson, Susan C. ... Sanford, NC
Patterson, Susan L. ... Kerrville, TX
Patterson, Susan R. ... Dallas, TX
Patterson, Susan S. ... San Antonio, TX
Patterson & Sweeny ... Miami, FL
Patterson, T. B., Jr., P.A.
Hot Springs National Park, AR
Patterson, Terri S. ... Atlanta, GA
Patterson, Thomas E. ... Los Angeles, CA
Patterson, Thomas E. ... Chicago, IL
Patterson, Thomas E. ... La Crosse, KS
Patterson, Thomas G. ... Long Beach, CA
Patterson, Thomas K. ... Beckley, WV
Patterson, Thomas L. ... Washington, DC
Patterson, Thomas R. ... Rochester, MN
Patterson, Thos. G. ... Madison, WI
Patterson, Thurman B., Jr.
Hot Springs National Park, AR
Patterson, Timothy G. ... Palo Alto, CA
Patterson, Timothy J. ... Hillsboro, MO
Patterson, Timothy R. ... San Diego, CA
Patterson, Tracy V. ... Memphis, TN
Patterson & Traynham ... Tallahassee, FL
Patterson, Trent M. ... Bluffton, IN
Ossian, IN
Patterson, Uhl P. F., (Mrs.) ... Gautier, MS
Patterson, Urban J.W., P.A. ... Islamorada, FL
Patterson, Urban J.W. ... Islamorada, FL
Patterson, Van Abel & Lindeman
Anchorage, AK
Patterson, Vicki J. ... Bloomfield Hills, MI
Patterson, Virginia Calvert
Birmingham, AL
Patterson, Virginia E. ... Savannah, GA
Patterson, Virginia E., P.C., A Professional
Corporation ... Savannah, GA
Patterson, W. Bruce ... Houston, TX
Patterson, W. Drake ... Dallas, TX
Patterson, W. Ralph ... Tulsa, OK
Patterson, W. Scott ... Tampa, FL

Patterson, W. Wayne ..... Houston, TX
Patterson and Wagner ..... San Antonio, TX
Patterson, Walter B. ..... Statesville, NC
Patterson, Wayne ..... Port Arthur, TX
Patterson, Weldon E. ..... Knoxville, TN
Patterson, William ..... Lapeer, MI
Patterson, William A. ..... St. Petersburg, FL
Patterson, William A. ..... Jackson, MS
Patterson, William Bruce ..... Red Bank, NJ
Houston, TX
Patterson, William D., (P.C.) ..... Midland, TX
Patterson, William F., Jr. ..... Greensboro, NC
Patterson, William J. ..... Charlotte, NC
Patterson, William John ..... Tulsa, OK
Patterson, William Lin ..... Tulsa, OK
Patterson, William R. ..... Atlanta, GA
Patterson, William Russell, Jr.
Atlanta, GA
Patterson, William S. ..... Raleigh, NC
Patterson, Wm. F. ..... Johnstown, PA
Patterson, Woodrow W. ..... Austin, TX
Patterson, W. R. (Pat), Jr. ..... Louisville, KY
Patterson & Wright ..... Florence, AL
Patterson, Yasma Michelle McGowan
Atlanta, GA
Patterson-Hollenberg, Rorie E. ..... Concord, NH
Patterson-Lavery, Mary P.
Harrisburg, PA
Patterson Wimes, Michelle
Kansas City, MO
Patteson, Ann L. ..... Green Bay, WI
Patteson, John H., Jr. ..... Atlanta, GA
Patteson, Richard Busch ..... Tyler, TX
Patteson, Sara S. ..... Tyler, TX
Patti, Anthony J. ..... Los Angeles, CA
Patti, Anthony P. ..... Ann Arbor, MI
Patti, Carmen B. ..... Chicago, IL
Patti, Clement S. ..... Yonkers, NY
Patti, Clement S., Jr. ..... White Plains, NY
Patti, Debra D. ..... Pittsburgh, PA
Patti, Frank L. ..... Sparta, NJ
Patti, Frederick S. ..... Philadelphia, PA
Patti, Gregory P., Jr. ..... New York, NY
Patti, James P. ..... Chicago, IL
Patti, John C. ..... Chicago, IL
Patti, Mary Ann ..... Fort Walton Beach, FL
Panama City, FL
Pensacola, FL
Patti, Mary P. ..... Brookfield, WI
Patti, Rose A. ..... Twinsburg, OH
Patti & Sgro ..... Las Vegas, NV
Patti, Stephen J. ..... New York, NY
Patti, Steven J. ..... Sausalito, CA
Patti, Timothy Lee ..... Gastonia, NC
Pattie, Bernard C.
Christiansted, St. Croix, VI
Pattie & Daley
Christiansted, St. Croix, VI
Charlotte Amalie, St. Thomas, VI
Pattie, Hinshaw, Danielson & Kloberdanz, P.C.
Marshalltown, IA
Pattie, Hugh L. ..... Woodburn, OR
Pattie, J. Warren ..... Marshalltown, IA
Pattie, John H. ..... Simi Valley, CA
Patti-Jelsvik, Alaine ..... Las Vegas, NV
Pattillo, Albert D., III ..... Kerrville, TX
Pattillo, Andrew G., Jr. ..... Ocala, FL
Pattillo, Darryl L. ..... Austin, TX
Pattillo, James G. ..... Sacramento, CA
Pattillo, James L. ..... Santa Barbara, CA
Pattillo, John T. ..... Winter Park, FL
Pattillo, McKeever & Bice, P.A. ..... Ocala, FL
Pattillo, R. D. (Spike), III ..... Waco, TX
Pattillo, Vicki Howard ..... Seguin, TX
Pattinson, Catherine E. ..... Los Angeles, CA
Pattinson, Christie L. ..... Covington, KY
Pattinson, Jeffrey I. ..... Crystal River, FL
Pattinson, Michael J. ..... Moscow, ID
Pattinson, William J. ..... Ames, IA
Pattis, Norman A. ..... New Haven, CT
Pattisall, Richard C. ..... Roanoke, VA
Pattishall, Beverly W. ..... Chicago, IL
Pattishall, McAuliffe, Newbury, Hilliard &
Geraldson ..... Washington, DC
Chicago, IL
Pattison, Daphne L. ..... Ocean Springs, MS
Pattison & Flannery ..... New York, NY
Pattison, George E. ..... Batavia, OH
Pattison, James B. ..... Manassas, VA
Pattison, Jason J. ..... Madison, IN
Pattison, John T. ..... Rochester, NY
Pattison, Joseph E. ..... Philadelphia, PA
Pattison, Kelly J. ..... Los Angeles, CA
Pattison, Richard A. ..... Battle Creek, MI
Pattison, Richard G. ..... Monona, IA
Pattison, Richard M. ..... Framingham, MA
Pattison, Robert K. ..... Sturgis, MI
Pattison, Robert M. ..... San Francisco, CA
Pattison, Sampson, Ginsberg & Griffin, P.C.
Albany, NY
Troy, NY
Pattison, Sarah Foxman ..... El Macero, CA
Pattison, Thomas R. ..... New York, NY
Pattison, William H., Jr. ..... Cambridge, MD
Easton, MD
Pattiz, Davidson M. ..... Los Angeles, CA
Pattiz, Henry A. ..... Beverly Hills, CA
Pattiz, Keith M. ..... New York, NY
Pattno, John W. ..... Cheyenne, WY
Patton, Amy E. ..... Overland Park, KS
Kansas City, MO
Patton, Anna Gaston ..... Atlanta, GA
Patton, Arthur G., Sr. ..... Melbourne, FL
Patton Boggs LLP ..... Denver, CO
Washington, DC
Dallas, TX
Seattle, WA
Patton, Brainard L., Jr. ..... New York, NY
Patton, Bruce V. ..... San Francisco, CA
Patton, C. Benton ..... Nashville, TN
Patton, C. Bradley ..... Carlsbad, CA
Patton, C. Bradley, A Professional
Corporation ..... Carlsbad, CA
San Diego, CA
Vista, CA
Patton, C. Raymond, Jr. ..... Tulsa, OK
Patton, Catherine Patiño ..... Costa Mesa, CA
Patton & Chamberlain, Attorneys At Law,
P.C. ..... Liberty, MO
Patton, Charles C. ..... Los Angeles, CA
Patton, Charles E. ..... Syracuse, NY
Patton, Cindy M. ..... Charlotte, NC
Patton, Claire L. ..... Boston, MA
Patton, Claude E. ..... Mobile, AL
Patton, Craig A. ..... El Paso, TX
Patton, Cynthia J. ..... San Jose, CA
Patton, Cynthia J. ..... Topeka, KS
Patton, Cynthia M. ..... Long Beach, CA
Patton, D. Wayne ..... Leadville, CO
Patton, Dale K., Jr. ..... Holbrook, AZ
St. Johns, AZ
Patton, Dale K., Jr. ..... Winslow, AZ
Patton, David A. ..... San Jose, CA
Patton, David D. ..... Baltimore, MD
Patton, David D. ..... Bloomfield Hills, MI
Patton, David D., & Associates, P.C.
Bloomfield Hills, MI
Detroit, MI
Patton, David L. ..... Dodge City, KS
Patton, David M. ..... Houston, TX
Patton, David U. ..... Athens, AL
Patton, David Wm. ..... Storm Lake, IA
Patton & Davison ..... Cheyenne, WY
Patton, Dennis P. ..... Westlake, OH
Patton, Diana R. ..... Cleveland, OH
Patton, Dorothy E.
Environmental Protection Agency,
Program Office Attorneys, GV
Patton, Dorothy P.
Federal Trade Commission,
Office of the General Counsel, GV
Patton, Douglas H. ..... Salt Lake City, UT
Patton, Douglas J. ..... Washington, DC
Patton, Douglas K. ..... Oakland, CA
Patton, Edward L. ..... Treasury Department,
Internal Revenue Service, GV
Patton, Edward O. ..... Cleveland, OH
Patton, Eileen Evers ..... Long Beach, NY
Patton, Frances A. ..... Washington, DC
Patton, Frances E. ..... Oklahoma City, OK
Patton, Frank C., III ..... Marion, NC
Patton, Frank, Jr. ..... New York, NY
Patton, Frank R., Jr. ..... Tulsa, OK
Patton, Frederick J., II ..... Topeka, KS
Patton, Frederick P. ..... Rock Island, IL
Patton, Gary A. ..... Sacramento, CA
Patton, Gary K. ..... Liberty, MO
Patton, Gary N. ..... Murfreesboro, TN
Patton, Gary P. ..... Dallas, TX
Patton, Gary W. ..... Huntington Beach, CA
Patton, Geo. T. ..... South Bend, IN
Patton, Geoffrey L.
Department of Housing and Urban
Development,
Office of General Counsel, GV
Patton, George Thomas, Jr.
Indianapolis, IN
Patton, Glenn G. ..... Atlanta, GA
Patton, Gordon S. ..... New Orleans, LA
Patton, Gregory F. ..... Hillsville, VA
Patton, Gregory P. ..... Clarksville, TN
Patton, Haltom, Roberts, McWilliams &
Greer, L.L.P. ..... Texarkana, AR
Texarkana, TX
Patton, Harold R. ..... Minneapolis, MN
Patton & Hofstetter ..... Plainfield, IN
Patton, Hoversten & Berg, P.A.
Waseca, MN
Patton, J. Jeffrey ..... Chicago, IL
Patton, J. Matthew ..... Eugene, OR
Patton, J. Maurice ..... Gary, IN
Patton, Jack A. ..... Atlanta, GA
Patton, James A. ..... Tuscumbia, AL
Patton, James A. ..... Hiawatha, KS
Patton, James A., Jr. ..... Birmingham, AL
Patton, James H. ..... Tulsa, OK
Patton, James L., Jr. ..... Wilmington, DE
Patton, James M. ..... Birmingham, AL
Patton, James Monroe ..... Richmond, KY
Patton, James R. ..... Moline, IL
Patton, James R., Jr. ..... Washington, DC
Patton, James W. ..... Cincinnati, OH
Patton, Jay D. ..... Cincinnati, OH
Patton, Jeffery R. ..... Winchester, VA
Patton, Jeffrey D. ..... Winston-Salem, NC
Patton, Jerry A. ..... Prestonsburg, KY
Patton, Jerry L. ..... Decatur, IL
Patton, Jerry L. ..... University, MS
Patton, John C. ..... Atlanta, GA
Patton, John C. ..... Cheyenne, WY
Patton, John E. ..... Newark, NJ
Patton, John H. ..... Walnut Creek, CA
Patton, John J. ..... Anahuac, TX
Patton, John J. ..... Houston, TX
Patton, John M.
Treasury Department, GV
Patton, John R. ..... Austin, TX
Patton, John S. ..... Atlanta, GA
Patton, John T. ..... Cleveland, OH
Patton, John W. ..... Dallas, TX
Patton, John W., IV ..... Lewisville, AR
Patton, John W., Jr. ..... Woodland Hills, CA
Patton, John W., Jr. ..... Chicago, IL
Patton, Judith Chapman ..... Cheyenne, WY
Patton, Kathleen A. ..... Joliet, IL
Patton, Kathryn L. ..... Houston, TX
Patton, Katrina L. ..... Charleston, SC
Patton, Kenneth E. ..... Baltimore, MD
Patton and Kerbs ..... Dodge City, KS
Patton, Kevin W. ..... Birmingham, AL
Patton, Kirk, (P.C.) ..... Texarkana, TX
Patton, L. Diane ..... Plainfield, IN
Patton, L. Scott ..... Monroe, LA
Patton, Larry D. ..... Oklahoma City, OK
Patton, Larry R. ..... San Antonio, TX
Patton, Latham, Legge & Cole
Athens, AL
Decatur, AL
Huntsville, AL
Patton Law Offices ..... Omaha, NE
Patton, Lawrence A. ..... El Cajon, CA
Patton, Lawrence M., Jr. ..... Franklin, NC
Patton, Lee C. ..... Southfield, MI
Patton, Leroy J. ..... Oklahoma City, OK
Patton, Lynn Hawkins ..... Jackson, MS
Patton, Lynn S. ..... Longview, TX
Patton, M. Leigh-Anne ..... Cincinnati, OH
Patton, Martha Jane ..... Birmingham, AL
Patton, Mary B. ..... Chicago, IL
Patton, Matthew H. ..... Atlanta, GA
Patton, Matthew R., III ..... Gilmer, TX
Patton, McKelvey & Kennemer
Tuscumbia, AL
Patton, Michael ..... Warrington, PA
Patton, Michael C. ..... Memphis, TN
Patton, Michael F. ..... Washington, DC
Patton, Michael G. ..... Emporia, KS
Patton, Michael J. ..... Springfield, MO
Patton and Miller ..... St. Louis, MO
Patton, Nan J. ..... Oklahoma City, OK
Patton, Nat, Jr. ..... Crockett, TX
Patton, Neal G. ..... Atlanta, GA
Patton, Nicholas H. ..... Texarkana, TX
Patton, Nix & Young, L.L.P.
Longview, TX
Patton, Norman T. ..... Cleveland, OH
Patton, Paige C. ..... Houston, TX
Patton, Patricia Ann ..... Boonsboro, MD
Patton & Patton ..... Topeka, KS
Patton, Paul David ..... Jersey City, NJ
Patton, Peter M. ..... Philadelphia, PA
Patton, Phillip R. ..... Glasgow, KY
Patton, Phillip R. ..... Secaucus, NJ
Patton, Putnam & Hollembeak, P.A.
Emporia, KS
Patton, R. David ..... Atlanta, GA
Patton, Ray V., (P.C.) ..... Houston, TX
Patton, Rebecca ..... Dallas, TX
Patton, Richard E. ..... Colusa, CA
Patton, Richard E. ..... New Hope, PA
Patton, Richard F. ..... North Olmsted, OH
Patton, Richard L. ..... Greenville, SC
Patton, Rita S. ..... Bloomfield Hills, MI
Patton, Robert C. ..... Newport, KY
Patton, Robert F. ..... Pittsburgh, PA
Patton, Robert J. ..... Chicago, IL
Patton, Robert J. ..... Prestonsburg, KY
Patton, Robert J. ..... Cleveland, OH
Patton, Robert J., Jr.
Department of Transportation,
Maritime Administration, GV
Patton, Robert James ..... Rochester, NY
Patton, Robert L. ..... Fort Worth, TX
Patton, Robert M. ..... Abilene, TX
Patton, Robert W. ..... Tampa, FL
Patton, Roger L., Jr. ..... Beverly Hills, CA
Patton, Roger W. ..... Oakland, CA
Patton, Roy H., Jr. ..... Waynesville, NC
Patton, S. Kendall ..... San Francisco, CA
Patton, S. Lee ..... St. Louis, MO
Patton, Samuel C. ..... Springfield, IL
Patton, Sara ..... Seattle, WA
Patton, Scott D. ..... Oakland, CA
Patton, Shannon K. ..... Cleveland, OH
Patton, Sharon H. ..... Boston, MA
Patton, Shelley A. ..... Carlsbad, CA
Patton, Starnes, Thompson, Aycock, Teele &
Ballew, P.A. ..... Morganton, NC
Patton, Stephen Michael ..... Milwaukee, WI
Patton, Stephen R. ..... Chicago, IL
Patton, Sylvia K. ..... Pasadena, CA
Patton, Tad ..... Wichita, KS
Patton, Terence M. ..... Belleville, IL
Patton, Teresa K. ..... Minneapolis, MN
Patton, Terry E. ..... Akron, OH
Patton, Terry J. ..... Omaha, NE
Patton, Thomas Earl ..... Washington, DC
Patton, Thomas H. ..... Gainesville, FL
Patton, Thomas M. ..... Carson City, NV
Patton, Thomas R. ..... Provo, UT
Patton, Thomas W. ..... Springfield, IL
Patton, Thomas W. ..... Knoxville, TN
Patton, Tidwell & Sandefur, L.L.P.
Texarkana, AR
Texarkana, TX
Patton, Timothy ..... San Antonio, TX
Patton & Veigas, P.C. ..... Birmingham, AL
Sheffield, AL
Patton, W. Andrew ..... Cincinnati, OH
Patton, W. Randolph ..... Las Vegas, NV
Patton, Wayne G. ..... St. Louis, MO
Patton, Wilbur P. ..... Piedmont, OK
Patton, William B. ..... Waseca, MN
Patton, William H. ..... Seattle, WA
Patton, William J. ..... Baltimore, MD
Patton, William L. ..... Boston, MA
Patton, William L., Jr. ..... Little Rock, AR
Patton, William T. ..... Portland, OR
Patton, William W. ..... Costa Mesa, CA
Patton, Wolan & Boxer ..... Oakland, CA
Patton-Hulce, Vicki R. ..... Richardson, TX
Patton-Schmitt, Ginger K. ..... Atlanta, GA
Pattridge, Frederick J. ..... Golden, CO
Pattullo, John G. ..... Phoenix, AZ
Pattullo, Robert L., Jr. ..... Chicago, IL
Pattwell, Jane R. ..... Rumson, NJ
Patty, Claibourne W., Jr.
North Little Rock, AR
Patty, Clarence R., Jr. ..... Hendersonville, NC
Patty, Clifton M., Jr. ..... Ringgold, GA
Patty, Clinton E. ..... Topeka, KS
Patty, Hubert D. ..... Maryville, TN
Patty, R. Andrew, II ..... Baton Rouge, LA
Patty, Rebecca E. ..... Montgomery, AL
Patty, Seldon E. ..... Greensboro, NC
Patty, Willard J., Jr. ..... Minneapolis, MN
Patty, William F. ..... Montgomery, AL
Patula & Associates ..... Chicago, IL
Patula, Rodney R. ..... San Francisco, CA
Patula, Timothy T. ..... Chicago, IL
Patunas, Michael E. ..... Rutherford, NJ
Paturick, Charles ..... Washington, DC
Paturis, E. Michael ..... Alexandria, VA
Patusky, Christopher ..... Washington, DC
Patuto, James P. ..... Hackensack, NJ
Paty, B. F., Jr. ..... West Palm Beach, FL
Paty, Charles D. ..... Chattanooga, TN
Paty, Rymer & Ulin, P.C. ..... Chattanooga, TN
Paty, Selma Cash ..... Chattanooga, TN
Paty, Sherry Bailey ..... Chattanooga, TN
Patyi, Frank J. ..... Syracuse, NY
Patyrn, Mary Higby ..... Ludlow, MA
Patz, Christopher A. ..... San Francisco, CA
Patz, Darren E. ..... Miami, FL
Patz, Edward F. ..... Baltimore, MD
Patz, Janice M. ..... Syracuse, NY
Patz, Linda M. ..... Canaan, CT
Patz, Nathan ..... Baltimore, MD
Patz, Richard L. ..... Providence, RI
Patzakis, John M. ..... Los Angeles, CA
Patzakis, Theresa A. ..... San Marino, CA
Patzer, Colleen O'Connor ..... Milwaukee, WI
Patzer, David H. ..... Milwaukee, WI
Patzik, Alan B. ..... Chicago, IL
Patzik, Frank & Samotny Ltd.
Chicago, IL
Patzke, Jeffry J. ..... Milwaukee, WI
Patzke, John C. ..... Milwaukee, WI
Patzke, Michelle ..... Chicago, IL
Patzke, Pamela McKenna ..... Dodgeville, WI
Patzman, Andrew D. ..... Washington, DC
Patzman, David F. ..... Kansas City, MO
Patzner, Faye A. ..... Madison, WI
Pau, Andrew Y. ..... New York, NY
Pauca, Janet F. ..... Winston-Salem, NC
Pauchnik, Elizabeth A. ..... Oklahoma City, OK
Pauciulo, John W. ..... Philadelphia, PA
Pauciulo, Paul A. ..... Philadelphia, PA
Pauck, Thaddeus G. ..... Medford, OR
Paudler, Pamela Ann ..... Olympia, WA
Pauel, Linda J. ..... Chicago, IL
Pauerstein, Jonathan David
San Antonio, TX
Paugh, David W. ..... Seymour, IN
Paugh, Jon
Department of Commerce, GV
Paugh, Leslie J. ..... Tallahassee, FL
Paugh, Richard D. ..... Rockville, MD
Pauk, Edgar ..... New York, NY
Pauka, Andre M. ..... Denver, CO
Chicago, IL
Pauka, Mary Beth S. ..... Chicago, IL
Pauken, Margaret M. ..... Cleveland, OH
Pauken, Patrick J. ..... Cleveland, OH
Pauken, Thomas W. ..... Dallas, TX
Pauker, David H. ..... Chicago, IL
Pauker, Lawrence ..... Norristown, PA
Pauker, Molly ..... Washington, DC
Pauker & Rubin, Ltd. ..... Chicago, IL
Paukert, George J. ..... Los Angeles, CA
Paukert, Kathleen H. ..... Spokane, WA
Paukert, Michael J. ..... Spokane, WA
Paukstelis, Peter J. ..... Los Angeles, CA
Paul, Aaron ..... Oakland, CA
Paul, Abe R. ..... Neosho, MO
Paul, Adam C. ..... Alexandria, VA
Paul, A. J. Drexel, Jr. ..... Philadelphia, PA
Paul, Alexander P. ..... St. Louis, MO
Paul, Alfred J. ..... Chicago, IL
Paul, Alison L. ..... Helena, MT
Paul, Amy M. ..... Petaluma, CA
Paul, Amy N. ..... San Francisco, CA
Paul, Andrea B. ..... Philadelphia, PA
Paul, Andrew J. ..... New York, NY
Paul, Andrew J. ..... New York, NY
Paul, Angela ..... Columbus, OH
Paul, Angelique M. ..... Columbus, OH
Paul, Anne M. ..... Mount Laurel, NJ
Paul, Ashley C. ..... New Brunswick, NJ
Paul, Barbara ..... Haddon Heights, NJ
Paul, Barbara H. ..... Roswell, GA
Paul, Bernadette K. ..... Harrisburg, PA
Paul, Bernard A. ..... Marion, IL
Paul, Bernard Z. ..... De Kalb, IL
Paul, Bette Lynn ..... Waterbury, CT
Paul, Blair Frederick ..... Seattle, WA
Paul, Bonnie L. ..... Harrisonburg, VA
Paul, Brian G. ..... Lawrenceville, NJ
Paul, Bruce B. ..... Denver, CO
Paul, Carl E., Jr. ..... Wheeling, WV
Paul, Cathy R. ..... Beverly Hills, CA
Paul, Charles H. ..... Rancho Cucamonga, CA
Paul, Charles S. ..... Universal City, CA
Paul, Charles W. ..... Philadelphia, PA
Paul, Chris A. ..... Tulsa, OK
Paul, Christina Chen ..... Stamford, CT
Paul, Christopher Allan ..... El Paso, TX
Paul, Christopher H. ..... New York, NY
Paul, Christopher J. ..... Hazard, KY
Paul, Daniel ..... Jamestown, NC
Paul, Daniel J. ..... Indianapolis, IN
Paul, Darryl J. ..... Dana Point, CA

Paul, David ... **Portland, OR**
Paul, David J. ... Omaha, NE
Paul, David Joseph ... **San Francisco, CA**
Paul, David L. ... Torrance, CA
Paul, Dean F. ... Springfield, MA
Paul, Debora N. ... Cameron Park, CA
Paul, Deborah L. ... **New York, NY**
Paul, Denise M. ... Springfield, IL
Paul, Dennis E. ... Wadsworth, OH
Paul, Dennis L. ... Milwaukee, WI
Paul, Diane B. ... **Los Angeles, CA**
Paul, Diane Fox ... Winston-Salem, NC
Paul, Donald P. ... **Nashville, TN**
Paul, Donald S. ... Lincoln Park, MI
Paul, Doris B., (Mrs.) ... Atlanta, GA
Paul, Douglas A. ... Mountain View, CA
Kansas City, MO
Paul, Douglas J. ... **Cleveland, OH**
Paul, Douglas K. ... Aurora, OH
Paul, D. P. S. ... **Miami, FL**
Paul, Drummond, Jr. ... Miami, FL
Paul, E. Blake ... **Lakeland, FL**
Lake Wales, FL
Winter Haven, FL
Paul, Edward L. ... **Haddonfield, NJ**
Paul, Edward R. ... **Media, PA**
Paul, Edwin H. ... **Boston, MA**
Paul, Edwin, Law Offices of, The
Tustin, CA
Paul, Eric ... Department of Agriculture, Office of the General Counsel, GV
Paul, Eric G. ... West Seneca, NY
Paul, Eve W. ... New York, NY
Paul, Francis A. ... McAfee, NJ
Paul, Frank & Collins, Inc.
Burlington, VT
Paul, Gary M. ... **Santa Monica, CA**
Paul, Gary P. ... **St. Louis, MO**
Paul, George L. ... **Phoenix, AZ**
Paul, George L. ... **Washington, DC**
Paul, Gerad C. ... **Grand Forks, ND**
Paul, Gerald G. ... **New York, NY**
Paul, Glenn J. ... **DeLand, FL**
Paul, Gregory G. ... **Pittsburgh, PA**
Paul, Gregory M. ... **Los Angeles, CA**
Paul, H. Edward ... **Grand Rapids, MI**
Paul, Harlan L. ... **DeLand, FL**
Paul, Harold W ... Westport, CT
New York, NY
Paul, Hartley ... **Seattle, WA**
Paul, Hastings, Janofsky & Walker LLP
Costa Mesa, CA
Los Angeles, CA
Newport Beach, CA
San Francisco, CA
Stamford, CT
Washington, DC
Atlanta, GA
New York, NY
Paul, Henry J. ... Milwaukee, WI
Paul, Henry Lee ... **Tampa, FL**
Paul, Herman S. ... **Jacksonville, FL**
Paul, Holly R. ... **Los Angeles, CA**
Paul, Howard R. ... Memphis, TN
Paul, Irving "Buddy" ... **Coeur d'Alene, ID**
Spokane, WA
Paul, J. Scott ... **Omaha, NE**
Paul, Jack ... **Los Angeles, CA**
Paul, Jack D. ... Mandan, ND
Paul, James C. ... **Gold River, CA**
Paul, James C. N. ... Newark, NJ
Paul, James E. ... Atlanta, GA
Paul, James L. ... **Atlanta, GA**
Paul, James M. ... **Neosho, MO**
Paul, James M. ... **St. Louis, MO**
Paul, James P. ... **Fort Lauderdale, FL**
Miami, FL
Paul, James R. ... Great Falls, MT
Paul, James T. ... **Honolulu, HI**
Paul, James W. ... **Los Angeles, CA**
Paul, James W. ... **New York, NY**
Paul, Janice Perrin ... Durham, NC
Paul & Janofsky ... **Los Angeles, CA**
Santa Monica, CA
Paul, Jeffrey Philip ... Pottsville, PA
Paul, Jeffrey W. ... **Davenport, IA**
Paul, Jennifer J. ... **Dallas, TX**
Paul, Jeremy R. ... Hartford, CT
Paul, Jerry ... **Port Charlotte, FL**
Paul, Jerry Neil ... Encino, CA
Paul, J. J., III ... Indianapolis, IN
Paul, Joan ... **Burlingame, CA**
San Jose, CA
Paul, JoAnn P. ... Tolland, CT
Paul, John A. ... Ponte Vedra Beach, FL
Paul, John A. ... Harrisonburg, VA
Paul, John C. ... **Washington, DC**
Paul, John D. ... Wilton, CT
Paul, John D., & Associates, P.C.
Wilton, CT
Paul, John P. ... **Great Falls, MT**
Paul, John R. ... **Tulsa, OK**
Paul, John W. ... **Englewood, CO**
Paul, Johnson, Park & Niles, Attorneys At Law, A Law Corporation ... **Honolulu, HI**
Wailuku, HI
Paul, Jonathan A. ... Austin, TX
Paul, Jonathan W. ... **Pittsburgh, PA**
Paul, Joshua ... **New York, NY**
Paul, Joyce E. ... **Los Angeles, CA**
Paul, Julia M. ... LaBelle, FL
Paul, Julia Morris ... Manchester, CT
Paul, Kāren C. ... Phoenix, AZ
Paul, Katherine L. ... **Philadelphia, PA**
Paul, Kendall W. ... Virginia Beach, VA
Paul, Kenneth A. ... New York, NY
Paul, Kenneth A. ... Houston, TX
Paul, Kevin Carter ... Denver, CO

Paul Law Firm, The ... **Pineville, MO**
Paul Law Firm, The, A Professional Corporation ... **Tulsa, OK**
Paul Law Firm, The, P.C. ... **Neosho, MO**
Paul, Lee G. ... **Costa Mesa, CA**
Paul, Lisa C. ... **Milwaukee, WI**
Paul, Lisa D. ... Everett, WA
Paul, Louis C. ... **New York, NY**
Paul, Lowell C. ... Topeka, KS
Paul, Lyssa Kaye ... **Rosemont, IL**
Paul, Mack A., IV ... Raleigh, NC
Paul, Marc A. ... **Washington, DC**
Paul, Marc R. ... **Washington, DC**
Paul, Marcia B. ... **New York, NY**
Paul, Mardinly, Durham, James, Flandreau & Rodger, A Professional Corporation
Media, PA
Paul, Mark P. ... **Hampton, NH**
Paul, Marshall B. ... **Baltimore, MD**
Paul, Matthew E. ... **Washington, DC**
Paul, Maurice M. ... Gainesville, FL
Paul, Michael ... Woodmere, NY
Paul, Michael A. ... Washington, NC
Paul, Michael A. ... Media, PA
Paul, Michael G. ... Philadelphia, PA
Paul, Michael S. ... Lansdale, PA
Paul, Michael T. ... Department of Defense, Armed Services Board of Contract Appeals, GV
Paul, Nathan A. ... **New York, NY**
Paul, Niall A. ... **Charleston, WV**
Paul, Norman A. ... Treasury Department, Internal Revenue Service, GV
Paul, Norman L., Jr. ... San Antonio, TX
Paul, Pamela Sisk ... Newport Beach, CA
Paul, Patricia G. ... **New York, NY**
Paul, Patricia N. ... Dunbar, WV
Paul, Patricia Tanzer ... **Savannah, GA**
Paul, Patrick A. ... Ventura, CA
Paul, Patrick J. ... **Phoenix, AZ**
Paul, Patrick L. ... Great Falls, MT
Paul & Paul ... **Harrisburg, PA**
Media, PA
Philadelphia, PA
Valley Forge, PA
Paul, Perry and Bloom ... Baltimore, MD
Paul, Peter A. ... **Cashiers, NC**
Paul, Peter C. ... Cambridge, MD
Paul, Philip S. ... Los Gatos, CA
Paul Plevin & Sullivan, L.L.P.
San Diego, CA
Paul, R. Allan ... **Burlington, VT**
Paul, R. Kathleene ... Santa Ana, CA
Paul, R. Rushton, Jr. ... Charlottesville, VA
Paul, Randolph M. ... **Alamo, CA**
Paul, Randolph M. ... **Los Angeles, CA**
Paul, Reymont ... Bloomfield Hills, MI
Paul, Richard A. ... El Cerrito, CA
Paul, Richard A. ... San Diego, CA
Paul, Richard J. ... **Syracuse, NY**
Paul, Richard J., Law Offices of
Charleston, SC
Paul, Richard M., III ... **Kansas City, MO**
Paul, Richard S. ... Newport Beach, CA
Paul, Richard S. ... **Stamford, CT**
Paul, Richard W. ... **Bloomfield Hills, MI**
Paul, Robert ... **Miami, FL**
Paul, Robert A. ... Pittsburgh, PA
Paul, Robert C. ... **New York, NY**
Paul, Robert D. ... **Washington, DC**
Paul, Robert E. ... Washington, DC
Paul, Robert E. ... **Boston, MA**
Paul, Robert E. ... New York, NY
Paul, Robert J. ... Chicago, IL
Paul, Roger D. ... Bellevue, OH
Paul, Roland A. ... **Greenwich, CT**
Paul, Ronald C. ... **Bloomfield Hills, MI**
Paul, Ronald S. ... Ventura, CA
Paul, Ronda Fields ... Lexington, KY
Paul & Rosen, LLP ... **New York, NY**
Paul, Ross R. ... Cleveland, OH
Paul, Roy E. ... **Savannah, GA**
Paul, Roy L. ... Downey, CA
Paul, Russell D. ... **Philadelphia, PA**
Paul, Russell E. ... Woodbury, NJ
Paul, Santi J. ... Warwick, RI
Paul, Sarah E. ... **New York, NY**
Paul, Scott B. ... **San Francisco, CA**
Paul, Scott D. ... **West Palm Beach, FL**
Paul, Selma ... Tucson, AZ
Paul, Sheila J. B. ... Hudson, WI
Paul & Singer, P.A. ... **Tampa, FL**
Paul, Sophia P. ... Pittsburgh, PA
Paul, Stephen H. ... **Indianapolis, IN**
Paul, Stephen R. ... Burlington, NC
Paul, Steven Jon ... **Colorado Springs, CO**
Paul, Steven L. ... **Boston, MA**
Paul, Steven R. ... Salt Lake City, UT
Paul, Steven W. ... **Burbank, CA**
Paul & Sugerman, P.C. ... **Portland, OR**
Paul, Susan B. ... **Savannah, GA**
Paul, Susan L. ... St. Cloud, MN
Paul, Sven R. ... Schenectady, NY
Paul, Sydney W. ... New Castle, PA
Paul, Teri L. ... **Torrance, CA**
Paul, Thaddeus I. ... **Seattle, WA**
Paul, Thomas D. ... **Houston, TX**
Paul, Thomas F. ... Seattle, WA
Paul, Timothy M. ... New Brunswick, NJ
Paul, Tracie DeMatteis ... **Everett, WA**
Paul, Tracy ... **Park City, UT**
Paul, Trisha J. ... **Fort Wayne, IN**
Paul, Urvashi R. ... Boston, MA
Paul, Varnum ... **San Francisco, CA**
Paul, Vivian ... Cathedral City, CA
Paul, Walter ... Downingtown, PA

Paul, Weiss, Rifkind, Wharton & Garrison
Washington, DC
New York, NY
Paul, Wesley J. ... **New York, NY**
Paul, William B. ... **Atlanta, GA**
Paul, William D. ... Duluth, MN
Paul, William G. ... **Oklahoma City, OK**
Paul, William J. ... Geneva, AL
Paul, William M. ... **Washington, DC**
Paul, William R. ... **Tampa, FL**
Paula, Carlos R. ... **San Juan, PR**
Paula, Richard L. ... Matawan, NJ
Paulan, Alverna M. ... Fairfax, VA
Paulantis, James T. ... Albuquerque, NM
Paulauskis, Vincent P. ... Kankakee, IL
Paulazzo, Anthony J. ... Trenton, NJ
Paulding, Judith ... Hempstead, NY
Paulding, Mark ... **Washington, DC**
Paulding, Theodore R. ... **Hartford, CT**
Paulding, T. R., Jr. ... Glastonbury, CT
Paule, Camazine & Blumenthal, A Professional Corporation ... **St. Louis, MO**
Paule, Donald W. ... **St. Louis, MO**
Paule, Edward P., Jr. ... Pomona, CA
Paule, Jeffrey ... **Burbank, CA**
Paule, Leon S. ... Santa Monica, CA
Paule, Robert Matthew ... Minneapolis, MN
Paulekas, Walter E. ... **Hartford, CT**
Paulen, Richard W. ... **Elkhart, IN**
Paulet, Harry E. ... St. Paul, MN
Paulett, H. Kenneth ... Strongsville, OH
Paulette, Janet S. ... Hickory, NC
Pauletto, Anthony J. ... Skokie, IL
Pauletto, James M. ... Northlake, IL
Pauletto, Michael A. ... **Chicago, IL**
Pauletto, Nannini & Catrambone
Maywood, IL
Paulett-Toumert, Mary Jo ... Cleveland, OH
Pauley, Barbara Maggio ... Frankfort, KY
Pauley & Barney, P.C. ... Rochester, NY
Pauley, Bradley S. ... **Los Angeles, CA**
Pauley, Bruce A. ... Dallas, TX
Pauley, Curry, Sturgeon & Vanderford
Charleston, WV
Huntington, WV
Winfield, WV
Pauley, David C. ... Lincoln, NE
Pauley, Douglas G. ... Hastings, NE
Pauley, Douglas H. ... **Hoffman Estates, IL**
Pauley, J. Renard ... Chesterfield, MO
Pauley, James L., Jr. ... **Jefferson, IA**
Scranton, IA
Pauley, Karen L. ... **Colorado Springs, CO**
Pauley, K. D. ... **Charleston, WV**
Pauley, Lawrence L. ... Huntington, WV
Pauley, Michael S. ... Columbia, SC
Pauley, Nicholas J. ... **Los Angeles, CA**
Pauley Petersen Kinne & Fejer
Chicago, IL
Hoffman Estates, IL
Pauley, Robert U., Jr. ... Forest, VA
Pauley, Robert U., Jr., P.C. ... Forest, VA
Pauley, Roger A. ... Department of Justice, Criminal Division, GV
Pauley, Timothy J. ... **Seattle, WA**
Pauley, Travis M. ... New York, NY
Pauley, William H., III ... New York, NY
Pauli, Christel H. ... **Los Angeles, CA**
Pauli, Dan J. ... Cheyenne, WY
Pauli, Diana L. ... Los Angeles, CA
Pauli, James G. ... Silver Spring, MD
Pauli, Joseph A. ... Yuma, AZ
Pauli, Mary ... Boston, MA
Pauli, Norman W., Jr. ... **Hattiesburg, MS**
Pauli, Rebecca Cohen ... **Anchorage, AK**
Paulich, John, III ... Naples, FL
Paulich, Kevin M. ... **Seattle, WA**
Paulich, Patrick M. ... **Seattle, WA**
Paulich, Slack & Wolff, P.A. ... Naples, FL
Paulick, Louis R. ... Pittsburgh, PA
Paulig, Gretchen ... Austin, TX
Paulig, Karl E. ... **Urbana, OH**
Paulig and Singer ... **Bellefontaine, OH**
Urbana, OH
Paulin, David J. ... **Kenilworth, NJ**
Paulin, Joseph H. ... Englewood, CO
Pauline, G. David ... Glenrock, WY
Pauling, Carlos L. ... **Charlotte, NC**
Pauling, Corie Diane ... **Charlotte, NC**
Pauling, David L. ... Tulsa, OK
Pauling, G. Thomas ... **Boston, MA**
Pauling, Gerald L., II ... **Chicago, IL**
Pauling, Theresa A. ... Washington, DC
Pauling, Wendy ... Columbia, SC
Paulino, Cesar Porfirio ... Flushing, NY
Paulino, Harry R. ... Columbus, OH
Paulis, Edward T., III ... **New York, NY**
Paulisick, Gerri V. ... Butler, PA
Paulissen, Barbara Hunt ... **San Antonio, TX**
Paulius, Thomas David ... **Chicago, IL**
Paulk, Alton O. ... Panama City, FL
Paulk, Carol A. ... Atlanta, GA
Paulk, George T., II
Indian Harbour Beach, FL
Paulk, Gerald R. ... **Scottsboro, AL**
Paulk, Gerald R., P.C., Law Offices of
Scottsboro, AL
Paulk, James R., Jr. ... **Atlanta, GA**
Paulk, Jeff Council ... Tampa, FL
Paulk, Joseph H. ... **Tulsa, OK**
Paulk, L. Auburn ... Marietta, GA
Paulk, L.A., P.C. ... Marietta, GA
Paulk, Laura Faye ... **Gulfport, MS**
Paulk, Terrence J. ... Fitzgerald, GA
Paulk, Terrence J., P.C. ... Fitzgerald, GA
Paulk, Thomas B., Jr. ... Union Springs, AL
Paull, Christopher J. ... **Wellsburg, WV**
Paull, Debra Woods ... Oklahoma City, OK

Paull, Diane L. ... **Tampa, FL**
Paull, Dolora ... Mount Clemens, MI
Paull, Edward L. ... St. Louis, MO
Paull, Ira ... United States Senate, Committee Legal Personnel, GV
Paull, James, IV ... Gainesville, FL
Paull, Jeffrey S. ... St. Louis, MO
Paull, Joel Henry ... Buffalo, NY
Paull, John H., Jr. ... Canton, MI
Paull, Joseph ... Washington, DC
Paull, Lindy L. ... United States Senate, Committee Legal Personnel, GV
Paull, Michael ... **Chicago, IL**
Highland Park, IL
Paull, Peter L., Jr. ... New Bedford, MA
Paull, Richard ... Chicago, IL
Paull & Seguin ... New Bedford, MA
Paull, Sidney W. ... Warwick, RI
Paull, Stephen M. ... Southfield, MI
Paull, Walter J. ... Canton, OH
Paullin, Mark S. ... **Richmond, VA**
Paulling & James ... **Darlington, SC**
Paullin-Hebden, Linda ... **Southfield, MI**
Paully, Denise G. ... **Los Angeles, CA**
Paulmann, Frederick H., IV
New York, NY
Paulos, Clay H. ... **Roswell, NM**
Paulos, Nicholas ... **Santa Ana, CA**
Paulos, Stephanie E. ... **New York, NY**
Paulose, Rachel K. ... Department of Justice, Executive Office for United States Attorneys, GV
Pauloski, Thomas J. ... **Chicago, IL**
Paulousky, Peter J. ... **Franklin, MA**
Paulowsky, Michael G. ... Las Cruces, NM
Pauls, Brian C. ... Fort Wayne, IN
Pauls, Janice Long ... Hutchinson, KS
Pauls, Jason E. ... **Milwaukee, WI**
Pauls, John C. ... Kansas City, MO
Pauls, Robert J. ... Addison, IL
Paulsen, Angela McSpadden ... **Tulsa, OK**
Paulsen, Anita C. ... Seattle, WA
Paulsen, Arthur R. ... Tacoma, WA
Paulsen, Brett F. ... **Salt Lake City, UT**
Paulsen, Bruce G. ... **New York, NY**
Paulsen, Buechel, Swenson, Uri & Brewer, Chartered ... Concordia, KS
Paulsen, Carrie ... **San Francisco, CA**
Paulsen, Clarence ... Concordia, KS
Paulsen, Curtis A. ... **Milwaukee, WI**
Paulsen, Cynthia B. ... **Irvine, CA**
Paulsen, Dale J. ... St. John, KS
Paulsen, David E. ... Sacramento, CA
Paulsen, David J. ... Watertown, NY
Paulsen & Davis, A Professional Corporation
Auburn, CA
Paulsen, Diane Margosian
Hawthorn Woods, IL
Paulsen, Donald L. ... West Des Moines, IA
Paulsen, Donna L. ... Des Moines, IA
Paulsen, Dwight C., III ... **New Orleans, LA**
Paulsen, Edward (Ted) B. ... Draper, UT
Paulsen, Frederick S. ... **Boston, MA**
Paulsen, Gary D. ... Onaga, KS
Paulsen, Glenn R. ... **Trenton, NJ**
Paulsen, Gordon W. ... **New York, NY**
Paulsen, Harvey A. ... Chicago, IL
Paulsen, James G. ... New York, NY
Paulsen, James H. ... Sandpoint, ID
Paulsen, James P. ... Challis, ID
Paulsen, Jeffrey F. ... Lake Forest, IL
Paulsen, Jeffrey S. ... Minneapolis, MN
Paulsen, John H. ... Auburn, CA
Paulsen & Malec, Ltd. ... Chicago, IL
Paulsen, Maria E. ... Mineola, NY
Paulsen, Marilyn E. ... San Jose, CA
Paulsen, Peter W. ... **Washington, DC**
Paulsen, Randall John ... Westminster, CO
Paulsen, Roger P. ... **Milwaukee, WI**
Paulsen, Sandy J. ... **Staten Island, NY**
Paulsen, Scott R. ... **Peoria, IL**
Paulsgrove, Steven G. ... Goliad, TX
Paulsin, Joanna L. ... Long Beach, CA
Paulson, Alvin C. ... Belleville, IL
Paulson & Associates, A Professional Law Corporation ... **Santa Ana, CA**
Paulson & Associates, P.C.
Virginia Beach, VA
Paulson, Bradley S. ... Tucson, AZ
Paulson, Bruce L. ... Plymouth, MN
Paulson, C. Gordon ... **Rhinelander, WI**
Paulson, Chad E. ... **Portland, OR**
Paulson, Charles ... **Portland, OR**
Paulson, Christopher R. ... **Denver, CO**
Paulson, David ... **San Francisco, CA**
Paulson, David E. ... Bend, OR
Paulson, David F., Jr. ... **Charlotte, NC**
Paulson, David W. ... Fairfield, CA
Paulson, David W. ... **Racine, WI**
Paulson, Diane F. ... Worcester, MA
Paulson, Duane L. ... **Minneapolis, MN**
Paulson, Elias William ... Virginia Beach, VA
Paulson, Gary L. ... **Houston, TX**
Paulson, Gerald S. ... Monticello, MN
Paulson, Gordon P. ... **Chicago, IL**
Paulson, Greg S. ... **Minneapolis, MN**
Paulson, Gregory ... **Lancaster, PA**
Paulson, Gregory L. ... Minneapolis, MN
Paulson, Harold J. ... Seattle, WA
Paulson, Heidi C. ... Boston, MA
Paulson, Hilary S. ... Redwood City, CA
Paulson, Howard W. ... **Sioux Falls, SD**
Paulson, J. Larry ... Bremerton, WA
Paulson, J. Robert, Jr. ... Minneapolis, MN
Paulson, James M. ... **Boston, MA**
Paulson, Jane ... **Portland, OR**
Paulson, Jean E. ... Cokato, MN
Paulson, Jeffrey C. ... **Minneapolis, MN**

Payette, Peter C., P.C. .... **Flint, MI**
Payette, Steven E. .... San Francisco, CA
Payeur-Olsen, Joleen .... Marion, MA
Paykel, Joseph S. .... Washington, DC
Paykel, Neela A. .... **Washington, DC**
Paykin, Joseph N. .... New York, NY
Paylo, John L. .... Whiting, IN
Paylor, Alice F. .... **Charleston, SC**
Paylor, John J. .... Philadelphia, PA
Payment, Kenneth A. .... **Rochester, NY**
Payment, M. Shawn .... **San Diego, CA**
Payne, Alanson E. .... Philadelphia, PA
Payne, Alton W., Jr., (P.C.) .... **Houston, TX**
Payne, Andrew L. .... **Dallas, TX**
Payne, Anne M. .... **San Ramon, CA**
Payne, Anne M. .... Cottekill, NY
Payne, Anthony Cardozo
Department of Justice, Executive Office for Immigration Review, GV
Payne, Arthur L. .... Pompano Beach, FL
Payne & Associates .... **Washington, DC**
Payne, Barbara C. .... Denver, CO
Payne, Barbara Lee .... Pittsburgh, PA
Payne, Beverly C. .... Colorado Springs, CO
Payne, Bill F. .... **Paris, TX**
Payne, Billy M. .... **Bryan, TX**
Payne, Blake Alan .... Jasper, AL
Payne & Blanchard, L.L.P. .... **Dallas, TX**
Payne, Bobby S. .... **Danbury, CT**
Payne, Brett .... **Dallas, TX**
Payne, Brian K. .... Brooklyn, NY
Payne, Brian Lavoy .... Dumas, AR
Payne, Bridget Ann .... Tacoma, WA
Payne, Candace Torgerson .... **Helena, MT**
Payne, Carol A. .... Englewood, CO
Payne, Carol Collins .... **Dallas, TX**
Payne, Carroll L. .... Miami Lakes, FL
Payne, Cary Colt .... Las Vegas, NV
Payne, Cathleen C. .... Columbus, OH
Payne, Charles E. .... **Norfolk, VA**
Payne, Charles L. .... East Liverpool, OH
Payne, Charles Tom .... Montgomery, AL
Payne, Cheryl R. .... Naples, FL
Payne, Christopher A. .... **Dallas, TX**
Payne, Christopher D. .... **Phoenix, AZ**
Payne, Christopher W. .... **Denver, CO**
Payne, Clare Hudson .... **Bangor, ME**
Payne, Clifford J. .... **Salt Lake City, UT**
Payne, Clifford L. .... Lovington, NM
Payne, Clinton S. .... **Miami, FL**
Payne, Connie J., Law Offices of
Houston, TX
Payne, Crillon C., II .... Denton, TX
Payne, Cymier .... **Boston, MA**
Payne, Cynthia Howard .... Bridgeport, CT
Payne, Cynthia M. .... Albuquerque, NM
Payne, Cynthia S. .... Williamsburg, VA
Payne, D. Mark .... Plantation, FL
Payne, Daniel C., Jr. .... San Francisco, CA
Payne, Daniel G. .... Albany, NY
Payne, Daniel H. .... San Francisco, CA
Payne, Daniel J. .... Newport Beach, CA
Payne, Darrell W. .... **Miami, FL**
Payne & Dart, P.C. .... Palmyra, VA
Payne, David .... Ironton, OH
Payne, David A. .... **Atlanta, GA**
Payne, David C. .... Owensboro, KY
Payne, David H. .... Salt Lake City, UT
Payne, David M. .... Stamford, CT
Payne, David M. .... Marion, IN
Payne, David N. .... **Newport News, VA**
Payne, David R. .... **Wayne, PA**
Payne, David T. .... **Birmingham, AL**
Payne, David W. .... **Sarasota, FL**
Payne, David W. .... **Morristown, NJ**
Payne, David Y. .... Ogden, UT
Payne, Deborah Ann .... **Birmingham, AL**
Payne, Della Capozzi .... **Philadelphia, PA**
Payne, Diana J. .... **Aurora, CO**
Payne, Dinah .... New Orleans, LA
Payne, Donald N., II .... Detroit, MI
Payne, Donna Gooden .... **Elizabethtown, NC**
Payne, Douglas B. .... New York, NY
Payne, Douglas J. .... **Brunswick, ME**
Payne, Douglas J. .... **Salt Lake City, UT**
Payne, Douglas L. .... **Greeneville, TN**
Payne, Douglas Paul .... St. Maries, ID
Payne, Dwight .... **Rome, GA**
Payne, Edward M., III .... **Beckley, WV**
Payne, Elizabeth Mee .... Oklahoma City, OK
Payne, Emarie S. .... **Baltimore, MD**
Payne, Eugene C., III .... **San Francisco, CA**
Payne & Fears LLP .... **Irvine, CA**
Payne, Francis M. .... Cleveland Heights, OH
Payne, Frank W. .... Federal Way, WA
Payne, Frederick J. .... Cleveland, OH
Payne, Frederick W. .... **Charlottesville, VA**
Payne, Gale, & Associates
Fort Lauderdale, FL
Payne, Gary E. .... Oklahoma City, OK
Payne, Gates, Farthing & Radd, P.C.
Chesapeake, VA
Norfolk, VA
Portsmouth, VA
Virginia Beach, VA
Payne, Gaylen B. .... Federal Way, WA
Payne, Geoffrey S. .... Irvine, CA
Payne, George .... **Houston, TX**
Payne, Gordon D. .... Villa Park, IL
Payne, H. Dudley .... Arlington, VA
Payne, H. Dudley, Jr. .... Warrenton, VA
Payne, H. Thomas .... **Overland Park, KS**
Payne, H. Vern .... Albuquerque, NM
Payne & Hall, P.C. .... Albuquerque, NM
Payne, Harry E., Jr. .... Raleigh, NC
Payne, Harvey .... **Pawhuska, OK**
Payne, Harvey, III .... San Diego, CA
Payne, Harvey M. .... **San Diego, CA**
Payne, Harvey M. .... West Covina, CA
Payne, Hershel R. .... **Fort Worth, TX**
Payne & Hodous .... **Charlottesville, VA**
Payne, Hope V. .... **Charlottesville, VA**
Payne, Horace P., Jr. .... Pittsburgh, PA
Payne, Hunter Andrew .... Charlotte, NC
Payne, J. Michael .... **Cape Girardeau, MO**
Payne, J. Stanley, Jr. .... High Point, NC
Payne, J. Timothy .... Rochester, NY
Payne, Jackson M. .... **Birmingham, AL**
Payne, Jacqueline Kathleen .... **Chicago, IL**
Payne, James A. .... **Minneapolis, MN**
Payne, James A. .... Hemphill, TX
Payne, James A., Jr. .... **Houston, TX**
Nacogdoches, TX
Payne, James B. .... St. Cloud, FL
Payne, James D. .... **Beaumont, TX**
Payne, James E. .... Akron, OH
Payne, James E. .... **Beaumont, TX**
Payne, James H. .... Muskogee, OK
Payne, James L. .... **Irvine, CA**
Payne, James P. .... Austin, TX
Payne, James S. .... South Point, OH
Payne, James Tillman, Jr. .... **Acworth, GA**
Payne, James W. .... Indianapolis, IN
Payne, Janette O. .... **New York, NY**
Payne, Janice .... **New York, NY**
Payne, Janice C. .... Lubbock, TX
Payne, Jason H. .... **Chicago, IL**
Payne, Jeff Paul .... Grangeville, ID
Payne, Jeffrey L. .... **Florence, SC**
Payne, Jennifer J. .... Chicago, IL
Payne, Jerome A. (Jay), Jr. .... **Akron, OH**
Payne, Jerry O. .... Louisville, KY
Payne, Jerry O., P.S.C. .... Louisville, KY
Payne, Jestyn G. .... **Reading, PA**
Payne, Joe L. .... **Huntsville, AL**
Payne, John .... **Benton, AR**
Payne, John Abb .... **Cary, NC**
Payne, John B. .... **Dearborn, MI**
Payne, John C. .... Tuscaloosa, AL
Payne, John D. .... **Houston, TX**
Payne, John E. .... Dixon, IL
Payne, John F. .... Kansas City, MO
Payne, John F. .... North Platte, NE
Payne, John G. .... **Tyler, TX**
Payne, John H. .... Plantation, FL
Payne, John M. .... Department of the Navy, Office of the Judge Advocate General, GV
Payne, John M. .... Newark, NJ
Payne, John M. .... **Seattle, WA**
Payne, John M., Jr. .... **Springfield, MA**
Payne, John R. .... Los Angeles, CA
Payne, John R., Jr. .... Westerly, RI
Payne, John T. .... San Francisco, CA
Payne, John William .... **Dallas, TX**
Payne, Jon A. .... **Seattle, WA**
Payne, Jon M. .... **Dallas, TX**
Payne & Jones, Chartered
Kansas City, KS
Olathe, KS
Overland Park, KS
Kansas City, MO
Payne, Joseph H., III .... Department of Justice, Criminal Division, GV
Payne, Joseph Leon .... Austin, IN
Payne, Joshua A. .... **Palm Beach, FL**
Payne, Judith .... **New York, NY**
Payne, Judith E. .... **Minneapolis, MN**
Payne, Julie Thomas .... **Atlanta, GA**
Payne, Karen S. .... **Salisbury, MD**
Payne, Katherine S. .... **Atlanta, GA**
Payne, Kathlein K. .... Kissimmee, FL
Payne, Kellie Renee .... **Birmingham, AL**
Payne, Kelly L. .... Austin, TX
Payne, Kenneth E. .... **Washington, DC**
Payne, Kenneth E. .... **Davenport, IA**
Payne, Kenneth W. .... Lincoln, NE
Payne, Kent B. .... Baton Rouge, LA
Payne, Kevin F. .... Cleveland, OH
Payne, Konrad F. .... **New York, NY**
Payne, Kristina L. .... Columbus, OH
Payne, L. Howard .... **Sarasota, FL**
Venice, FL
Payne, Larissa U. .... Harker Heights, TX
Payne, Laurel L. .... **Augusta, GA**
Payne, Lee .... Covington, GA
Payne, Leslie C. .... **Stephenville, TX**
Payne, Leslie J. .... **Cambridge, MA**
Payne, Leslie V. .... **Houston, TX**
Payne, Linda Helene .... Costa Mesa, CA
Payne, Lindsey A. .... **Fort Lauderdale, FL**
Payne, Lisa .... Pasadena, CA
Payne, Lisa A. .... Owensboro, KY
Payne, Lisa Oppedisano
East Greenbush, NY
Payne, Loeb & Ray .... **Charleston, WV**
Payne, Lucy Salsbury .... Notre Dame, IN
Payne, Lundeen, D'Ambrosio & Arismendi, L.L.P. .... **Houston, TX**
Payne, M. Blair .... **Lake City, FL**
Payne, M. Travis .... Raleigh, NC
Payne, Margaret Anne .... **San Diego, CA**
Payne, Mark A. .... Indianapolis, IN
Payne, Mark C. .... Tampa, FL
Payne, Mark C., P.A. .... Tampa, FL
Payne, Mark J. .... **Irvine, CA**
Payne, Mark K. .... **Denver, CO**
Payne, Martha J. .... Portland, OR
Payne, Mary H. .... Milwaukee, WI
Payne, Mary Libby .... Jackson, MS
Payne, Mary Lou .... Jackson, MS
Payne, Mary Penelope .... United States Senate, Committee Legal Personnel, GV
Payne, Mary-Susan Parnell .... Palmyra, VA
Payne, Matthew T. .... **Omaha, NE**
Payne, Melvin M. .... Washington, DC
Payne, Michael D. .... **Los Angeles, CA**
Payne, Michael D. .... **Atlanta, GA**
Payne, Michael F. .... Wichita Falls, TX
Payne, Michael H. .... **Fort Washington, PA**
Payne, Mitchell C. .... Rock Hill, SC
Payne, Mitchell C., P.A. .... Rock Hill, SC
Payne, Nell .... **Washington, DC**
Payne, Nolan Lee .... Kalamazoo, MI
Payne, Pamela McOwen .... **Pensacola, FL**
Payne, Patricia A. .... Monmouth Junction, NJ
Payne, Patricia L. .... **Washington, DC**
Payne, Patti .... Lockhart, TX
Payne, Paula G. .... Houston, TX
Payne Payne & Cook .... Cleveland, OH
Payne, Penn .... **Atlanta, GA**
Payne, Peter J. .... White Oak, PA
Payne, Philip S. .... Charlotte, NC
Payne, Phillip D., IV .... Lovingston, VA
Payne, Phillis .... **Washington, DC**
Payne, Phoebe Joyce .... Boston, MA
Payne, R. Morrison M. .... Edisto Island, SC
Walterboro, SC
Payne, R. Thomas .... **Stamford, CT**
Payne, Ralph Lucian .... Alexandria, VA
Payne, Randal .... **Houston, TX**
Payne, Raymond J. .... **Hartford, CT**
Payne, Raymond L., Jr. .... Denver, CO
Payne, Rebecca Graves .... Denver, CO
Charleston, WV
Payne, Richard .... **San Francisco, CA**
Payne, Richard B. .... Kansas City, KS
Payne, Richard D. .... Towson, MD
Payne, Richard E. .... Virginia Beach, VA
Payne, Richard G. .... Key West, FL
Payne, Richard S. .... Larchmont, NY
Payne, Richard T. .... Greenfield, IN
Payne, Richard W., Jr. .... Norfolk, MA
Payne, Richmond A. .... Cape Girardeau, MO
Payne, Richmond A., & Associates, L.C.
Cape Girardeau, MO
Payne, R. J. .... Atlanta, GA
Payne, Robert A. .... McMinnville, OR
Payne, Robert A. .... **Fairfax, VA**
Payne, Robert A. K. .... Richmond, VA
Payne, Robert B. .... **Dallas, TX**
Payne, Robert B., Jr. .... **Dallas, TX**
Payne, Robert E. .... Richmond, VA
Payne, Robert J. .... Blue Springs, MO
Payne, Robert L. .... Springfield, MO
Payne, Robert L. .... Salt Lake City, UT
Payne, Robert S. .... Oklahoma City, OK
Payne, Robert Thomas .... Fort Wayne, IN
Payne, Robert W. .... **Monterey, CA**
San Jose, CA
Payne, Robert W. .... **Salt Lake City, UT**
Payne, Rod D. .... **Louisville, KY**
Payne, Ronald .... **Fort Lauderdale, FL**
Payne, Ronald D. .... San Jose, CA
Payne, Ronald K. .... Asheville, NC
Payne, Ronald R. .... Dallas, TX
Payne, Ross E. .... Orlando, FL
Payne, Roy S. .... Shreveport, LA
Payne, R. W., Jr. .... **Miami, FL**
Payne, S. Giles .... **Southport, CT**
Payne, S. Mark .... **Raleigh, NC**
Payne, Samuel D. .... **Nashville, TN**
Payne, Samuel H. .... Chattanooga, TN
Payne, Samuel L. .... Jacksonville, FL
Payne, Sharon .... **Peoria, IL**
Payne, Sharon A. .... Southfield, MI
Payne, Shirley .... **Madison, MS**
Payne, Stephanie Karen .... **Houston, TX**
Payne, Stephen R. .... **Washington, DC**
Payne, Steven S. .... **Washington, DC**
Payne, Sue .... **Chicago, IL**
Payne, T. Michael .... San Ramon, CA
Payne, Terri Lynn .... Grangeville, ID
Payne, Thomas .... Zanesville, OH
Payne, Thomas E. .... Biloxi, MS
Payne, Thomas F. .... Montgomery, OH
Payne, Thomas W. .... **Bingham Farms, MI**
Payne, Timothy G. .... **Chicago, IL**
Payne, Timothy J. .... **Fort Lauderdale, FL**
Payne, Timothy J., P.A.
Fort Lauderdale, FL
Payne, Timothy P. .... **Bingham Farms, MI**
Payne, Timothy R. .... Rockville, MD
Payne, Todd S. .... Hollywood, FL
Payne, Tom & Associates, P.L.L.C.
Biloxi, MS
Payne, Tommy D. .... Nashville, TN
Payne, Tracy Helen .... **Bridgewater, NJ**
Payne, Ulice, Jr. .... **Milwaukee, WI**
Payne & Verzani .... Federal Way, WA
Payne, W. James .... Shallotte, NC
Payne, Walter A., III .... **Detroit, MI**
Payne, Walter R. J., Jr. .... Heath, OH
Payne, Watson, Kling, Miller & Malechek, P.C. .... **Bryan, TX**
Payne, Wesley R., IV .... Philadelphia, PA
Payne, William A. .... Cleveland, OH
Payne, William B. .... **Minneapolis, MN**
Payne, William C. .... **Charleston, WV**
Payne, William H. .... Dallas, TX
Payne, William J. .... **West Palm Beach, FL**
Payne, William J. .... **Wayne, PA**
Payne, William T. .... **Los Angeles, CA**
Pittsburgh, PA
Payne, William T. .... Decatur, GA
Payne, Wood & Littlejohn
Bridgehampton, NY
Hauppauge, NY
Locust Valley, NY
Melville, NY
Mineola, NY
Riverhead, NY
Paynter, Bruce D. .... **Chicago, IL**
Paynter, C. Frederick, Jr. .... **Atlanta, GA**
Paynter, Craig B. .... **Columbus, OH**
Paynter, David B. .... **San Francisco, CA**
Paynter, Donald G. .... **Columbus, OH**
Paynter, Ed, (P.C.) .... Abilene, TX
Paynter, Frank R. .... **Tulsa, OK**
Paynter, Harry S. .... Jeffersonville, IN
Paynter, L. Scott .... **Indianapolis, IN**
Paynter, Richard B. .... Denver, CO
Paynter, Richard T. .... Santa Barbara, CA
Paynter, T. Noel .... **Phoenix, AZ**
Paynter, W. B., P.C. .... **Akron, CO**
Paynter, Walter R. .... **Dallas, TX**
Paynter, Walter R. .... **Plano, TX**
Paynter, William B., Jr. .... **Akron, CO**
Paynter, William H. .... Sonoma, CA
Payntor, Carl S. .... Akron, OH
Payonk, James A., Jr. .... Chicago, IL
Payseno, John P. .... Seattle, WA
Payseur, Cynthia L. .... Kansas City, MO
Paysinger, Robert B. .... Golden, CO
Payson, Anthony, II .... Tucson, AZ
Payson, Curtis M. .... **Rockland, ME**
Payson, Earl A. .... Davenport, IA
Payson, Earl A., P.C. .... Davenport, IA
Payson, Frank M. .... Dayton, OH
Payson, Frank M., P.C. .... Dayton, OH
Payson, Kenneth E. .... **Seattle, WA**
Payson, Marcus A. .... **Milwaukee, WI**
Payson, Marian W. .... New York, NY
Payson, Martin D. .... New York, NY
Payson, Martin F. .... **White Plains, NY**
Payson, Robert K. .... **Wilmington, DE**
Payson, Steven B. .... Lamesa, TX
Payson, Suzanne H. .... West Palm Beach, FL
Paysour, Conrad E., III .... Belhaven, NC
Paysse, Julie Lee .... New Orleans, LA
Paysse, René S. .... **New Orleans, LA**
Paysse, Rene S., Jr. .... **New Orleans, LA**
Paytas, Antoinette D. .... **Washington, DC**
Baltimore, MD
Paytas, Henry R. .... **Phoenix, AZ**
Payte, John M. .... St. Paul, MN
Payton & Carlson, P.A.
Fort Lauderdale, FL
Miami, FL
Payton, Dan Lloyd .... Lawton, OK
Payton, Donald L. .... **Farmington Hills, MI**
Payton, G. Michael .... Columbus, OH
Payton, Harry A. .... **Miami, FL**
Payton, Henry N. .... Newnan, GA
Payton, Janet G. .... Chesterland, OH
Payton, Jeffrey L. .... Hartford, CT
Payton, Joan M. .... Houston, TX
Payton, John .... **Washington, DC**
Payton, John A. .... Indianapolis, IN
Payton, Kinney & Tardio .... Greenville, KY
Payton, Koreen A. .... **Chicago, IL**
Payton, Leslie A. .... New York, NY
Payton, Leslie L. .... Philadelphia, PA
Payton, Lloyd .... Muskogee, OK
Payton, Mark F., III, (P.C.) .... Tulsa, OK
Payton, Mildred B. .... Greensboro, NC
Payton, Nolan H. .... Los Angeles, CA
Payton, Patrick H. .... Des Moines, IA
Payton, Patrick H., & Associates, P.C.
Des Moines, IA
Payton, Ray G. .... Springfield, MO
Payton, Robert M. .... Boston, MA
Payton, Rusty A. .... Chicago, IL
Payton, Sallyanne .... Ann Arbor, MI
Payton, Willis C. .... Washington, DC
Payumo, Kenneth C. .... New York, NY
Payzant, Scott S. .... **Minneapolis, MN**
Paz, Debra Collins .... **Nashville, TN**
Paz, F. Bryan .... **Walden, NY**
Paz, Frank P. .... Tarentum, PA
Paz, James Lawrence .... Tarentum, PA
Paz, John N. .... Tarentum, PA
Paz, JoséR. .... Pasadena, CA
Paz, Paz & Paz .... Tarentum, PA
Paz, Rafael A. .... **Miami, FL**
Pazak, Cheryl A. .... Pittsburgh, PA
Pazan, Stephen P. .... Haddonfield, NJ
Pazar, Charles E. .... Department of Justice, Civil Division, GV
Pazar, Christopher E. .... Limington, ME
Pazar, Christopher E., P.A. .... Limington, ME
Pazdernik, Michael K. .... Sacramento, CA
Pazdon, Walter A., Jr. .... Concord, NH
Pazen, Thea M. .... **Chicago, IL**
Pazer and Epstein .... New York, NY
Pazienza, Marc V. .... Washington, DC
Pazin, Richard J., Jr. .... Pontiac, MI
Pazner, Bruce K. .... Bloomfield Hills, MI
Pazner, Eric Laurence .... **Southfield, MI**
Pazniokas, Paul M. .... Norwood, MA
Pazniokas, Rita .... **Baltimore, MD**
Pazol, James L. .... **Warren, OH**
Youngstown, OH
Pazol, Judith Armstrong .... **Rosemont, IL**
Pazol, Lawrence Z. .... Bloomfield Hills, MI
Pazornick, Marvin I. .... Baltimore, MD
Pazornik, Arnold .... Silver Spring, MD
Pazos, Alphonse L. .... Upland, CA
Pazos, Carlos A. .... Tampa, FL
Pazos, James M. .... **Los Angeles, CA**
Paz-Soldan, Carlos M. .... **Washington, DC**
Pazuhanich, Mark P. .... Stroudsburg, PA
Pazuniak, George .... **Wilmington, DE**
Pazzanita, Anthony G. .... Wellesley Hills, MA
Pazzol, Ross .... **Chicago, IL**
Pcolinski, John J., Jr. .... **Wheaton, IL**
Pea, Barry G. .... Seattle, WA
Pea, Janice Farrell .... Danville, IL
Peabody, A. Douglas .... New York, NY
Peabody & Arnold LLP .... **Portland, ME**
Boston, MA
Providence, RI

Peabody, Arthur A. ... Portland, ME
Peabody, Arthur E., Jr.
Department of Justice, Civil Rights Division, GV
Peabody, Barbara W. ... New York, NY
Peabody, Bradford C. ... Baltimore, MD
Peabody, Brian W. ... Berkley, MI
Peabody & Brown ... Washington, DC
Boston, MA
Manchester, NH
Providence, RI
Peabody, Bruce A. ... Bartlesville, OK
Peabody, Bruce R. ... New Haven, CT
Peabody, Daniel L. ... Naples, ME
Peabody, Endicott ... Nashua, NH
Peabody, Eric S. ... Austin, TX
Peabody, George E. ... Oklahoma City, OK
Peabody, George F. ... Bangor, ME
Peabody, J. Ross ... San Diego, CA
Peabody, J. Royden, Jr. ... Louisville, KY
Peabody, James A. ... Oklahoma City, OK
Peabody, John C. ... Louisville, KY
Peabody, Karen K. ... Santa Barbara, CA
Peabody, Laura S. ... Boston, MA
Peabody, Lionel H. ... Duluth, MN
Peabody, Mark B. ... Philadelphia, PA
Peabody, Martin H. ... Atlanta, GA
Peabody, Max N. ... Seattle, WA
Peabody, Robert L. ... Boston, MA
Peabody, Thomas M. ... Long Beach, CA
Peabody, Timothy P.
Rancho Cucamonga, CA
Peabody, W. Tyler, Jr. ... Moylan, PA
Peace, Breon S. ... New York, NY
Peace, Daniel S. ... Farmington Hills, MI
Peace, David L. ... Irving, TX
Peace, Edward D. ... Buffalo, NY
Peace, Ernest J. ... Mineola, NY
Peace, Gerard L. ... Plainview, NY
Peace, Jack ... Princeton, MO
Trenton, MO
Peace, Jerome L. ... Thomasville, NC
Peace, Jerry A. ... Oklahoma City, OK
Peace, John B. ... Little Rock, AR
Peace, John C. ... Roanoke, VA
Peace, Kenneth J. ... Phoenix, AZ
Peace, M. Alan ... Columbia, SC
Peace, Miriam S. ... Lawrenceville, GA
Peace, Nora Curley ... Glenshaw, PA
Peace, Rosanna L. ... Lexington, KY
Peace, Sharon M.
Department Of Veterans Affairs, Board of Veterans Appeals, GV
Peace-Jackson, Marva M.
Department of Labor, Office of the Solicitor, GV
Peaceman, Karen L. ... Chicago, IL
Peach, Charles ... Suquamish, WA
Peach, John W. ... Jasper, FL
Peach, Matthew W. ... Bellingham, WA
Peach, Randall ... Morristown, NJ
Peach, Roxanne O. ... Phoenix, AZ
Peach, Sam ... Bellingham, WA
Peach, Timothy W. ... Ontario, CA
Riverside, CA
San Bernardino, CA
Peach & Weathers, A Law Corporation
Ontario, CA
Riverside, CA
San Bernardino, CA
Peachee, Russell L. ... Los Alamitos, CA
Peacher, Kenneth L., II ... Oklahoma City, OK
Peacher-Ryan, Carla ... Memphis, TN
Peachey, Carol M. ... Boston, MA
Peachey, Douglas M. ... Groton, CT
Peachey, Thomas C. ... The Dalles, OR
Peachey, William C. ... Department of Justice, Civil Division, GV
Peaco, James W., Jr.
Department of Commerce, National Oceanic and Atmospheric Administration, GV
Peacock, Aaron Michael ... Lincoln, IL
Peacock, Albert ... Tallahassee, FL
Peacock, Albert E., III ... Long Beach, CA
Peacock, Aleta D. ... Austin, TX
Peacock, Andrew S. ... Indianapolis, IN
Peacock, Bradley R. ... Jackson, MS
Tupelo, MS
Peacock, Bruce E. ... Dayton, OH
Peacock, Carol Davis ... Tallahassee, FL
Peacock, Carolyn Taylor ... New Bern, NC
Peacock, D. Denise ... Colorado Springs, CO
Peacock, D. Grant ... Pittsburgh, PA
Peacock, D. Lee ... Warner Robins, GA
Peacock, Deborah A. ... Albuquerque, NM
Peacock, Doli ... Fort Worth, TX
Peacock, Dorinda L. ... Raleigh, NC
Peacock, Douglas L. ... Phoenix, AZ
Peacock, Edward P., III ... Clarksdale, MS
Peacock, Emily A. ... St. Petersburg, FL
Tampa, FL
Peacock, Erle E., Jr. ... Raleigh, NC
Peacock & Gaffney, P.A. ... Clearwater, FL
Peacock, Gregg A. ... Minneapolis, MN
Peacock, Gregory T. ... New Bern, NC
Peacock, Heidi R. ... Federal Way, WA
Peacock & Ingleson, Professional Corporation
Sault Ste. Marie, MI
Peacock, J. Hoke, II ... Beaumont, TX
Peacock, J. Hoke, III ... Houston, TX
Peacock, James D. ... Baltimore, MD
Peacock, James F. ... Laguna Niguel, CA
Peacock, James L. ... Morris, IL
Peacock, James R., III ... Dallas, TX
Peacock, Jim L., The Law Offices of
Houston, TX
Peacock, Jimmy W. ... Odessa, TX
Peacock, Joe N. ... Augusta, AR
Peacock, Joe N. ... McCrory, AR
Peacock, Joe V. ... Fulton, TX
Peacock, John D. ... Morris, IL
Peacock, John D. ... Sault Ste. Marie, MI
Peacock Keller Ecker & Crothers, LLP
Washington, PA
Waynesburg, PA
Peacock, Lauren Hudgins ... Dallas, TX
Peacock & Le Beau ... Long Beach, CA
Peacock, Linda J. ... Birmingham, AL
Peacock, McFarland & Belt, P.C. ... Morris, IL
Peacock, Michael F. ... Kellogg, ID
Peacock, Mike ... St. Petersburg, FL
Tampa, FL
Peacock, Milton Dale ... Monroe, LA
Peacock, Myers & Adams, P.C.
Albuquerque, NM
Peacock, P. Dexter ... Houston, TX
Peacock, Peter W. ... Mount Clemens, MI
Peacock, Raymond J. ... Clearwater, FL
Peacock, Robert J. ... San Leandro, CA
Peacock, Robert T. ... Department of the Army, Office, Chief of Engineers/Headquarters, U.S. Army Corps of Engineers, GV
Peacock, Robert W., Jr. ... Orlando, FL
Peacock, Rosalyn R. ... Dallas, TX
Peacock, Sally B. ... Indianapolis, IN
Peacock, Sandra J. ... New Orleans, LA
Peacock, Sandra L. ... Tampa, FL
Peacock, Sara Beth ... Houston, TX
Peacock, Shea W. ... Boston, MA
Peacock, Stephen Prosser ... Long Beach, CA
Peacock, Stuart L. ... Washington, DC
Peacock, Thomas P. ... Amagansett, NY
Peacocke, Lee Morgan ... Metairie, LA
Peaden, Paula L. ... Richmond, VA
Peaden, Porter L., Jr. ... Orlando, FL
Peaden, Timothy J. ... Atlanta, GA
Peagler, Desiree Sutton ... Decatur, GA
Peagler, George M., Jr. ... Americus, GA
Peahl, Kathleen C. ... Manchester, NH
Peahl, Robert H. ... New York, NY
Peairs, Jeffrey D. ... Sarasota, FL
Peak, Carla J. ... Shepherdsville, KY
Peak, Christopher B. ... Kansas City, KS
Peak, Daniel Clifton ... San Jose, CA
Peak, Daniel S. ... Riverside, MO
Peak, Deborah L. ... Danville, CA
Peak, Gary D. ... Eastland, TX
Peak, Helen Holmes ... Escondido, CA
Peak, Jack E ... Cleveland, OH
Peak, James H. ... Delaware, OH
Peak, Jane E. ... Morgantown, WV
Peak, John A. ... San Jose, CA
Peak, John T. ... Department of Transportation, Office of the Secretary, GV
Peak, John T. ... Kansas City, MO
Peak, Peter Alan ... Bradenton, FL
Peak, Robert M. ... New York, NY
Peak, Terrence F. ... Indianapolis, IN
Peak, Theodore Blakey ... Denver, CO
Peak, Thomas R. ... Baton Rouge, LA
Peak, W. Judd ... Memphis, TN
Peake, Alan J. ... Bakersfield, CA
Peake, Charnell C. ... Columbia, SC
Peake, Darryl L. ... Buffalo Grove, IL
Peake, Ernest F. ... Minneapolis, MN
Peake, Joseph C., III ... Norcross, GA
Peake, Larry F. ... Bakersfield, CA
Peake Law Firm, P.A. ... Columbia, SC
Peake, Lloyd E. ... San Bernardino, CA
Peake, Mark J. ... Lynchburg, VA
Peake, Merwin W. ... McLean, VA
Peake, Robert F. ... New York, NY
Peake, Sandra J. ... Houston, TX
Peake, Sarah K. ... Provincetown, MA
Peake, Thomas R., II ... Burlington, NC
Peake, Walter H., III ... Roanoke, VA
Peake, Walter S. ... Valley Forge, PA
Peakes, James L. ... Dexter, ME
Peal, Gary W. ... Sarasota, FL
Peal, S. Audiway ... Skillman, NJ
Peale, David Earl ... Pasadena, CA
Peale, Frances A. ... Bethesda, MD
Peale, Michael O'Hara, Jr.
Fort Washington, PA
Peale, Richard N. ... Concord, NH
Peale, Willie E., Jr. ... Frankfort, KY
Pealer, Charles E. ... Warren, OH
Pealer & Pealer Co., L.P.A. ... Warren, OH
Pear, Brian Richard ... Taunton, MA
Pear, Charles E., Jr. ... Honolulu, HI
Pear, Edwin L. ... Ann Arbor, MI
Pear, Michael J. ... Santa Ana, CA
Pear Sperling Eggan & Muskovitz, P.C.
Ann Arbor, MI
Ypsilanti, MI
Pearce, Alan S. ... New York, NY
Pearce, Alden G., (A P.C.)
Los Angeles, CA
Pearce, Barbara L. ... North Haven, CT
Pearce, Beth J. ... Rosemead, CA
Pearce, Betty J. ... Greensboro, NC
Pearce, Braddock S. ... Dundee, NY
Pearce, Bradley E. ... Charlotte, NC
Pearce, Bruce E. ... Detroit, MI
Pearce, C. Jack ... Washington, DC
Pearce, Charles A. ... Southfield, MI
Pearce, Clyde C. ... Salinas, CA
Pearce, Colin L. ... San Francisco, CA
Pearce, David B. ... Lexington, KY
Pearce, David E. ... Madison, AL
Pearce, David F. ... New York, NY
Pearce, Derrick A. ... Overland Park, KS
Pearce, Dixon F., II ... Charleston, SC
Pearce, Douglas C. ... Dubuque, IA
Pearce, Douglas C, II ... Louisville, CO
Pearce and Durick, PLLP ... Bismarck, ND
Pearce, Edith A. ... Philadelphia, PA
Pearce, Edwin B. ... San Jose, CA
Pearce, Elizabeth A. ... Philadelphia, PA
Pearce, Elizabeth Quinn ... New York, NY
Pearce, Frank G. ... Richardson, TX
Pearce, George M. ... Chicago, IL
Pearce, Harry J. ... Detroit, MI
Pearce, Herbert H. ... Lenoir, NC
Pearce & Howard ... Noblesville, IN
Pearce, Hugo A., III ... Charlotte, NC
Pearce, J. David ... Las Vegas, NV
Salt Lake City, UT
Pearce, Janine A. ... New York, NY
Pearce, Jennifer K. ... Oakland, CA
Pearce, John A. ... Salt Lake City, UT
Pearce, John G. ... Covington, LA
Pearce, John M. ... Phoenix, AZ
Pearce, John R., III ... Dallas, TX
Pearce, John S. ... Noblesville, IN
Pearce, John Y. ... New Orleans, LA
Pearce, Jon R. ... Des Moines, IA
Pearce, Julia M. ... Mandeville, LA
Pearce, Julie Davis ... Birmingham, AL
Pearce, Karola K. ... San Francisco, CA
Pearce, Kathleen Solner ... Naples, FL
Pearce, Kenneth H. ... Houston, TX
Pearce, Krisann A. ... United States Senate, Senatorial Assistants, GV
Pearce, Laura Boyd ... Tallahassee, FL
Pearce & Lett ... Tipton, IN
Pearce, Lewis R. ... Merritt Island, FL
Pearce, M. Jane ... Sacramento, CA
Pearce, Mark D. ... Alexandria, LA
Pearce, Mark G. ... Buffalo, NY
Pearce, Marshall R. ... Shreveport, LA
Pearce, Mary Sinclair ... Chicago, IL
Pearce & Massler ... Hackensack, NJ
Pearce, Michael A. ... New York, NY
Pearce, Michael J. ... Phoenix, AZ
Pearce, Michael J. ... Long Beach, CA
Pearce, Michael J. ... Portland, ME
Pearce, Michael R. ... Sacramento, CA
Pearce, Nancy A. ... Lynn, MA
Pearce, Nancy Harris
Farmington Hills, MI
Pearce, Owen B. ... Spring Lake, NJ
Pearce, Owen B., P.C. ... Spring Lake, NJ
Pearce, Patrick H.W.F. ... Riverside, CA
Pearce, Patrick S. ... Seattle, WA
Pearce, Paul K., Jr. ... Dallas, TX
Pearce, R. Edwin ... Dallas, TX
Pearce, Randy T. ... Hackensack, NJ
Pearce, Richard C. ... Portland, OR
Pearce, Richard L. ... Aiken, SC
Pearce, Richard W. ... Fayetteville, NC
Pearce, Robert K. ... Wilmington, DE
Pearce, Robert W., Jr. ... Charleston, SC
Pearce, Robert Wayne ... Boca Raton, FL
Pearce, Robert Wayne
Fort Lauderdale, FL
Pearce, Robert Wayne
West Palm Beach, FL
Pearce, Roger A. ... Seattle, WA
Pearce, Rosemary ... Valhalla, NY
Pearce, Russell C. ... New York, NY
Pearce, Saul ... New York, NY
Pearce, Stephanie Jo ... Louisville, KY
Pearce, Stephen L. ... Utica, NY
Pearce, Theodore P. ... Charlotte, NC
Pearce, W. Gregory ... Charleston, SC
Pearce, W. Ruffin, Jr. ... Charlotte, NC
Pearce, William D. ... Clyde, OH
Pearce, William F., Jr. ... Conyers, GA
Pearce, William M., III ... Houston, TX
Pearce, William P. ... Bismarck, ND
Pearce, William R. ... Des Moines, IA
Pearce Reggio, Deborah ... Dallas, TX
Pearce-Smith, David W. ... Alcoa Center, PA
Pearcey, Roderick K. ... Temple Terrace, FL
Pearcy, Brian C. ... Riverside, CA
Pearcy, C. W., III ... Hico, TX
Pearcy, Donald W. ... San Diego, CA
Pearcy, Loyd Gerald ... Denver, CO
Pearcy, Loyd Gerald, P.C. ... Denver, CO
Pearcy, Marian M. ... Corydon, IN
Pearcy, Paul R. ... Miami, FL
Pearcy, Virginia ... Palo Alto, CA
Pearcy, William R. ... Nashville, IL
Peard, Patricia A. ... Portland, ME
Peare, Dan C. ... Wichita, KS
Pearigen, Michael D. ... Nashville, TN
Pearis, Resseguie, Kline & Barber, LLP
Binghamton, NY
Pearis, Stuart M. ... Binghamton, NY
Pearl, Alan B. ... Syosset, NY
Pearl, Allen B. ... Livingston, NJ
Pearl, Andrew ... Reno, NV
Pearl, Andrew J. ... Los Angeles, CA
Pearl, Anthony J. ... Los Angeles, CA
Pearl, Bernard D. ... West Caldwell, NJ
Pearl, Blaine H. ... Canton, OH
Pearl, Brian S. ... Fort Lauderdale, FL
Pearl, Clifford R. ... Denver, CO
New York, NY
Pearl, Daniel ... La Jolla, CA
Pearl, David A. ... Miami, FL
Pearl, David H. ... Melville, NY
Pearl, David R. ... San Francisco, CA
Pearl, David S. ... Owings Mills, MD
Pearl, Edward M. ... Chicago, IL
Pearl, Elizabeth L. ... Greenbelt, MD
Pearl, Elliot D. ... Sacramento, CA
Pearl, Erwin M. ... Chevy Chase, MD
Pearl, F. L. ... Louisville, KY
Pearl, Frank H. ... Washington, DC
Pearl and Gohman ... Radcliff, KY
Pearl, Helen Z. ... New Britain, CT
Pearl, Howard M. ... Chicago, IL
Pearl, James ... Los Angeles, CA
Pearl, James H. ... San Antonio, TX
Pearl, James R., Jr. ... Northfield, OH
Pearl, Jane ... New York, NY
Pearl, Jason E. ... New Britain, CT
Pearl, Jeremy K. ... San Diego, CA
Pearl, Jonathan A. ... Chicago, IL
Pearl, Judson W., (P.C.) ... New York, NY
Pearl, Julie ... San Francisco, CA
Pearl, Kenneth B. ... Chicago, IL
Pearl, Laurence D.
Department of Housing and Urban Development, GV
Pearl Law Office, A Professional Corporation
Sacramento, CA
Pearl Levy and Cohen ... West Caldwell, NJ
Pearl, Lisa B. ... New York, NY
Pearl & MacKenzie, P.C. ... Syosset, NY
Pearl, Marc A. ... Arlington, VA
Pearl, Mark J. ... Los Angeles, CA
Pearl, Mary Catherine ... Redding, CA
Pearl, McNiff, Crean, Cook & Sheehan
Peabody, MA
Pearl, Melvin E., (P.C.) ... Chicago, IL
Pearl, Michael A. ... New York, NY
Pearl, Michael R. ... White Plains, NY
Pearl, Michael S. ... Owings Mills, MD
Pearl, Mitchell L. ... Middlebury, VT
Pearl, Nancy L. ... Denver, CO
Pearl, Nicholas L. ... Radcliff, KY
Pearl, Nicole M. ... Los Angeles, CA
Pearl, Norman L. ... Tarzana, CA
Pearl, Peter M. ... Atlanta, GA
Pearl Professional Corporation
Bridgeport, CT
Stamford, CT
Westport, CT
Pearl, Quinn F., Sr. ... Elizabethtown, KY
Pearl, Richard B. ... Philadelphia, PA
Pearl, Richard M., Law Offices of
San Francisco, CA
Pearl, Robert F. ... Detroit, MI
Pearl, Robert J. ... Rochester, NY
Pearl, Robin A. ... Department of Labor, Pension and Welfare Benefits, GV
Pearl, Robin L. ... Sacramento, CA
Pearl, Robin Leslie ... Sacramento, CA
Pearl, Rudolph ... San Pedro, CA
Pearl, Russell P. ... Winchester, MA
Pearl, Sara L. ... Washington, DC
Pearl, Scott W. ... New York, NY
Pearl & Smith, Law Offices of
Rochester, NY
Pearl, Steven G. ... Encino, CA
Pearl, Stewart W. ... Westport, CT
Pearlberg, Alex J. ... Boca Raton, FL
Pearlberg, Felicia S. ... Washington, DC
Pearlberg, Van ... Marietta, GA
Pearle, Howard ... Mahopac, NY
Pearle, Lynn K. ... Washington, DC
Pearlin, Marc Alan ... Fairfield, CT
Purchase, NY
Pearlman, A. Clifford ... Philadelphia, PA
Pearlman, Alan ... Northbrook, IL
Pearlman, Alan D. ... Chicago, IL
Pearlman, Alan H. ... Providence, RI
Pearlman, Alan J. ... Jersey City, NJ
Pearlman, Alan, Ltd. ... Northbrook, IL
Pearlman, Allan R. ... New York, NY
Pearlman, Arvin J. ... Southfield, MI
Pearlman, Barry S. ... Encino, CA
Pearlman, Benjamin H. ... Boulder, CO
Pearlman, Borska & Wax ... Encino, CA
Pearlman, Brian Andrew
Fort Lauderdale, FL
Pearlman, Charles B.
Fort Lauderdale, FL
Pearlman, Chosnek, Morrissey & Hopson, P.C. ... Lafayette, IN
Pearlman, Cindi L. ... Albuquerque, NM
Pearlman, Craig S. ... Orlando, FL
Pearlman & Dalton, P.C. ... Denver, CO
Pearlman, Daniel D. ... Berkeley, CA
Pearlman, David J. ... Boston, MA
Pearlman, David T. ... Charleston, SC
Pearlman, Donald H. ... Washington, DC
Pearlman, Donald J. ... Lowell, MA
Pearlman, Elihu ... Malden, MA
Pearlman, Ellen S.
United States Court Of Appeals District Of Columbia Circuit, GV
Pearlman, Elyse G. ... Homewood, IL
Pearlman, Eva Brindisi ... Utica, NY
Pearlman, Fred D. ... Great Neck, NY
Pearlman, Gus H. ... Charleston, SC
Pearlman, Harvey R. ... Rutherford, NJ
Pearlman, Heidi C. ... Washington, DC
Pearlman, Henry S. ... White Plains, NY
Pearlman, Howard L. ... San Francisco, CA
Pearlman, Jay S. ... Houston, TX
Pearlman, Jay W. ... Cleveland, OH
Pearlman, Jeffrey D. ... Los Angeles, CA
Pearlman, Jenny ... New York, NY
Pearlman, Joel ... Bethesda, MD
Pearlman, Joseph D. ... Charlotte, NC
Pearlman, Joshua P., Law Offices of
Pawtucket, RI
Pearlman, Julie M. ... Philadelphia, PA
Pearlman, Kenneth D. ... New York, NY
Pearlman, Kenneth T. ... Columbus, OH
Pearlman, Kerry E. ... Austin, TX
Pearlman, Lee R. ... Lloyd Harbor, NY
Pearlman, Leonard W. ... Portland, OR
Pearlman, Lise A. ... Oakland, CA
Pearlman, Marc J. ... Chicago, IL
Pearlman, Marina ... New York, NY

man, Marshall M. ... **Newport Beach, CA**
arlman, Marshall M., A Prof. Corp., Law Offices of ... **Newport Beach, CA**
Pearlman, Mel, P.A. ... Fern Park, FL
Pearlman, Melvin ... Fern Park, FL
Pearlman, Michael ... Rochester, NY
Pearlman, Mike ... Rochester, MN
Pearlman, Mitchell W. ... Hartford, CT
Pearlman, Morton I. ... New York, NY
Pearlman, Patrick W. ... Charleston, WV
Pearlman, Paul S. ... **New York, NY**
Pearlman, Peter S. ... **Saddle Brook, NJ**
Pearlman, Philip A. ... Denver, CO
Pearlman and Pianin ... **Southfield, MI**
Pearlman, Reid A. ... **Akron, OH**
Pearlman, Richard L. ... **Tallahassee, FL**
Pearlman, Richard Mark ... **Pittsburgh, PA**
Pearlman, Robert Alan ... Southfield, MI
Pearlman, Robert B. ... **Charleston, SC**
Pearlman, Robert I. ... **New York, NY**
Pearlman, Ronald A. ... **Washington, DC**
Pearlman, Ruth W. ... Jersey City, NJ
Pearlman, Samuel B. ... Miami Beach, FL
Pearlman, Samuel S. ... **Cleveland, OH**
Pearlman, Sandra L. ... **Washington, DC**
Pearlman, Sherri L. ... **New York, NY**
Pearlman, Stephen B. ... **Newark, NJ**
Pearlman, Steven J. ... Los Angeles, CA
Pearlman, Steven W. ... Washington, DC
Pearlman, Susan T. ... Wethersfield, CT
Pearlman, Thomas A. ... Ferndale, MI
Pearlman, Thomas A., P.C. ... Ferndale, MI
Pearlman, Thomas W. ... **Providence, RI**
Pearlman, Trevor L. ... **Dallas, TX**
Pearlman & Wick ... Providence, RI
Pearlman, William H. ... Boulder, CO
Pearlmutter, Fredi L. ... **Summit, NJ**
Pearlroth, Jonathan S. ... New York, NY
Pearlson, A. Ross ... **Newark, NJ**
New York, NY
Pearlson, Albert ... Culver City, CA
Pearlson, Herbert D. ... Culver City, CA
Pearlson, Jonathan Z. ... **Boston, MA**
Pearlson, Paul R. ... **Long Beach, CA**
Pearlstein, Andrew
Environmental Protection Agency, Office of Administrative Law Judges, GV
Pearlstein, Andrew M. ... **Boston, MA**
Pearlstein, Arthur B. ... Beltsville, MD
Pearlstein, Brian K. ... **Gaithersburg, MD**
Pearlstein, Debra J. ... **New York, NY**
Pearlstein, Gerald ... Boston, MA
Pearlstein, Jonathan J. ... Los Angeles, CA
Pearlstein, Jonathan M. ... **Seattle, WA**
Pearlstein, Judith L. ... New York, NY
Pearlstein, Lisa C. ... Brooklyn, NY
Pearlstein, Lynn M. ... **Phoenix, AZ**
Pearlstein, Mark D. ... **Chicago, IL**
Pearlstein, Mark S. ... Camden, NJ
Wayne, PA
Pearlstein, Marvin B. ... **San Francisco, CA**
Pearlstein, Mitchell D. ... **Garden City, NY**
Pearlstein, Paul D., & Associates
Washington, DC
Pearlstein, Seth L. ... **New York, NY**
Pearlstein, Susan ... Philadelphia, PA
Pearlstein, Susan J. ... Mc Keesport, PA
Pearlstein, Suzan V. ... **Phoenix, AZ**
Pearlstein, William G. ... **New York, NY**
Pearlstine & Associates, P.C. ... Lansdale, PA
Pearlstine, Jules, (P.A.) ... Miami, FL
Pearlstine, Neal R. ... Lansdale, PA
Pearlstine, Raymond ... **Blue Bell, PA**
Pearlston, Carl B. ... Torrance, CA
Pearlston, Melvin B. ... Eureka, CA
Pearlstone, Burt ... New York, NY
Pearlstone, Scott L. ... Independence, MO
Pearman, Charles N. ... **Columbia, SC**
Pearman, E. Shaun ... **Denver, CO**
Pearman & Galamba, L.C.
Overland Park, KS
Kansas City, MO
Pearman, Greg W. ... **Springfield, MO**
Pearman, Jayne A. ... Overland Park, KS
Kansas City, MO
Pearman, Joel E. ... Kingston, TN
Pearman, John ... **Paris, IL**
Pearman, Joseph ... **Merrillville, IN**
Pearman, J.R. ... Pawhuska, OK
Pearman, Kim H. ... Los Angeles, CA
Pearman, Larry W. ... Greensboro, NC
Pearman, Peter E. ... Tucson, AZ
Pearman, Ralph S. ... **Paris, IL**
Pearman, Richard M., Jr. ... Greensboro, NC
Pearman, Robert C., Jr. ... Los Angeles, CA
Pearman, Robert L. ... Van Nuys, CA
Pearn, James F., Jr. ... Philadelphia, PA
Pearne, Gordon, McCoy & Granger
Cleveland, OH
Pearre, Courtney N. ... **Nashville, TN**
Pears, Gary C. ... Birmingham, AL
Pearsall, Doreen M. ... **Minneapolis, MN**
Pearsall, Elizabeth ... **Washington, DC**
Pearsall, Henry B. ... Oak Park, IL
Pearsall, Joel K. ... Salem, OR
Pearsall, John W. ... Richmond, VA
Pearsall, John W., III ... Richmond, VA
Pearsall, Mack B. ... Rocky Mount, NC
Pearsall, Melissa M. ... **New York, NY**
Pearsall, Michael J. ... **New York, NY**
Pearsall, Otis Pratt ... **New York, NY**
Pearsall & Pearsall ... Richmond, VA
Pearsall, Stephen John ... Decatur, GA
Pearsall, Steven W. ... Stamford, CT
Wilton, CT
White Plains, NY
Pearsall, Susan Carter ... Madison, WI
Pearsall, Todd ... **San Diego, CA**
Pearsall, Wayne G. ... Tampa, FL
Pearse, Charleston S. ... Sacramento, CA
Pearse, Richard L., Jr. ... **Clearwater, FL**
Pearse, Richard L., Jr., P.A.
Clearwater, FL
Pearse, Richard W. ... **Chicago, IL**
Pearson, A. Hugo ... Cayucos, CA
Pearson, Alan L. ... Dubuque, IA
Pearson, Albert M., III ... **Atlanta, GA**
Pearson, Alfred E. ... Somerville, MA
Pearson, Amanda Kay ... Alamosa, CO
Pearson, Anthony Allan
Grand Rapids, MI
Pearson, April V. ... Brea, CA
Pearson, Arthur V. ... **Sacramento, CA**
San Francisco, CA
Pearson, B. Howard ... **Stanford, CA**
Pearson, Barbara M. ... San Rafael, CA
Pearson, Barbara Savitt ... Lowell, MA
Pearson, Barclay Howard ... Palo Alto, CA
Pearson, Ben C. ... Phoenix, AZ
Pearson, Benita ... **Cleveland, OH**
Pearson, Beth S. ... **Seattle, WA**
Pearson, Beverly S. ... San Diego, CA
Pearson, Beverly S. ... **Oklahoma City, OK**
Pearson, Bob ... Spearman, TX
Pearson, Brad L. ... **Kansas City, MO**
Pearson, Brian V. ... Phoenix, AZ
Pearson, Brooke ... Montpelier, VT
Pearson, Bruce A. ... **Glendale, CA**
Pearson, Bruce Edward ... Tampa, FL
Pearson, C. Alden ... **Brooklyn Park, MN**
Pearson, C. Judson ... Charleston, WV
Pearson, C. Thomas, Jr. ... Fayetteville, AR
Pearson, Cannon ... **Tustin, CA**
Pearson, Caroline ... **New York, NY**
Pearson & Chadwick ... Fayetteville, AR
Pearson, Charles A.
Department of Commerce, Patent and Trademark Office, GV
Pearson, Charles E. ... **Tuscaloosa, AL**
Pearson, Chris A. ... **Austin, TX**
Pearson, Christensen, Larivee, Clapp, Fiedler, Fischer & Jensen ... Grand Forks, ND
Pearson, Claude M. ... **Tacoma, WA**
Pearson, Claudia H. ... **Birmingham, AL**
Pearson, Clifford H. ... **Tarzana, CA**
Pearson, Clinton O. ... Brunswick, GA
Pearson, Clinton R. ... Memphis, TN
Pearson, Colone L., (Mr.) ... Detroit, MI
Pearson, Craig T. ... Toledo, OH
Pearson & Crass, P.A. ... Woodbury, NJ
Pearson, Curtis A., (P.A.) ... Minneapolis, MN
Pearson, Cynthia Beattie ... Atlanta, GA
Pearson, D. Blake ... **Sikeston, MO**
Pearson, D. Bruce ... Department of Justice, Antitrust Division, GV
Pearson, Daniel L. ... Los Angeles, CA
Pearson, Daniel S. ... **Miami, FL**
Pearson, Darrell D. ... Pasadena, CA
Pearson, David A. ... **Orlando, FL**
Pearson, David A. ... McFarland, WI
Pearson, David B. ... **Washington, DC**
Pearson, David C. ... Seattle, WA
Pearson, David P. ... **Minneapolis, MN**
St. Paul, MN
Pearson, David S. ... Fresno, CA
Pearson, Debra Bryant ... **McLean, VA**
Pearson, Dennis R. ... **Burlington, VT**
Pearson, Denton J. ... Sitka, AK
Pearson, Don ... Muskogee, OK
Pearson, Don C. ... Tacoma, WA
Pearson, Don M., (A Professional Corporation) ... **Los Angeles, CA**
Pearson, Donald V. ... Heber Springs, AR
Pearson, Douglas A. ... **Pittsburgh, PA**
Pearson, Edward F. ... **Los Angeles, CA**
Pearson, Edward O. ... Jackson, MS
Pearson, Edward O. ... Glenshaw, PA
Pearson, Edward R. ... Albuquerque, NM
Pearson, Eric B. ... **Media, PA**
Pearson, Eric D. ... **Dallas, TX**
Pearson, Eric Welch ... **Los Angeles, CA**
Salt Lake City, UT
Pearson, Ernest C. ... **Raleigh, NC**
Pearson, Floyd S. ... **Decorah, IA**
Pearson, Frederic C. ... Chicago, IL
Pearson, Frederick H., Jr. ... Saratoga, CA
Pearson, Frederick J. V. ... St. Petersburg, FL
Pearson, Fredric H. ... Union, NJ
Pearson, Gail R. ... Point Pleasant Beach, NJ
Pearson, Gale D. ... Wayzata, MN
Pearson, Garry A. ... Grand Forks, ND
Pearson, Gary M. ... **Warrenton, VA**
Pearson, Gary R. ... Lincoln, NE
Pearson, Gayle M. ... Houston, TX
Pearson, George H., III ... Wichita, KS
Pearson, George O. ... Lexington, KY
Pearson, Gerald E. ... Jonesboro, AR
Pearson, Gillian E. ... Boston, MA
Pearson, Glenn A. ... Escanaba, MI
Pearson, Gordon ... **Washington, DC**
Pearson, Grant ... Phoenix, AZ
Pearson, Gregory A. ... **Pittsburgh, PA**
Pearson, Gregory C. ... Santa Monica, CA
Pearson, H. Clyde ... Roanoke, VA
Pearson, H. Gregory ... Tuscaloosa, AL
Pearson, Hank E. ... **Phoenix, AZ**
Pearson & Hanson ... Sitka, AK
Pearson, Hazel Bob ... Conway, AR
Pearson, Henry W. ... Massapequa, NY
Pearson, Holly ... Sacramento, CA
Pearson, J. Keith ... **Oxford, MS**
Pearson, J. Kent, Jr. ... **Portland, OR**
Pearson, J. Richmond ... Birmingham, AL
Pearson, J. Robert ... Theodore, AL
Pearson, James ... Sweetwater, TX
Pearson, James A. ... Hollywood, FL
Pearson, James A. ... Eugene, OR
Pearson, James D. ... Fairfield, IA
Pearson, James H. ... **Houston, TX**
McAllen, TX
Pearson, James O., Jr. ... San Francisco, CA
Pearson, James V. ... **Denver, CO**
Pearson, James W., Jr. ... **Philadelphia, PA**
Pearson, Jane ... **Seattle, WA**
Pearson, Jane A. ... **Houston, TX**
Pearson, Janet L. ... Westlake Village, CA
Pearson, Janice L. ... Clovis, CA
Pearson, Jas. A. ... Columbus, OH
Pearson, Jeane W. ... Fort Dodge, IA
Pearson, Jeanne A. ... **Rock Hill, SC**
Pearson, Jeffrey G. ... **Denver, CO**
Pearson, Jeffrey T. ... Plymouth, MN
Pearson, Jennifer ... **Round Rock, TX**
Pearson, Jennifer J. ... **Brooklyn, NY**
Pearson, Jerry W. ... San Francisco, CA
Pearson, Jim ... **Oklahoma City, OK**
Pearson, Joan E. ... **Florham Park, NJ**
Pearson, Joel H. ... **Montgomery, AL**
Pearson, John D. ... Denver, CO
Pearson, John D. ... Tipp City, OH
Pearson, John E. ... **Miami, FL**
Pearson, John E. ... Springfield, MA
Pearson, John H. ... Notre Dame, IN
Pearson, John H., Jr. ... **Lowell, MA**
Pearson, John J. ... San Francisco, CA
Pearson, John K. ... Wichita, KS
Pearson, John L. ... Rosedale, MS
Pearson, John R. ... **Houston, TX**
Pearson, John Y., Jr. ... **Norfolk, VA**
Pearson, Joi Gardner ... **Salt Lake City, UT**
Pearson, Jonathan P. ... **Charlotte, NC**
Columbia, SC
Pearson, Joyce J. ... Woodland Hills, CA
Pearson, Julia A.B. ... **Salem, MA**
Pearson, Julia C.C. ... Honolulu, HI
Pearson, Juliet S. ... **Los Angeles, CA**
Pearson, Karen E. ... **Santa Ana, CA**
Pearson, Karen Louise ... Englewood, CO
Pearson, Karl E. ... **Maitland, FL**
Pearson, Karl Stephen ... Phoenix, AZ
Pearson, Keith ... **Glendale, CA**
Pearson, Kenneth ... New York, NY
Pearson, Kenneth W. ... Minneapolis, MN
Pearson, Kenneth W. ... **Dallas, TX**
Pearson, Kerry W. ... Arlington Heights, IL
Pearson, Kevin L. ... **Vinton, VA**
Pearson, Kevin T. ... **Portland, OR**
Pearson, Krista M. ... Tacoma, WA
Pearson, Laura J. ... Key Biscayne, FL
Pearson, Laurence H. ... New York, NY
Pearson, Laurice ... **New York, NY**
Pearson, Lawrence D. ... Armonk, NY
Pearson, Lennart Jon ... Los Angeles, CA
Pearson, Leslie M. ... Minneapolis, MN
Pearson, Linley E. ... Frankfort, IN
Pearson, Lisa B. ... Minneapolis, MN
Pearson, Lisa Madsen ... Palo Alto, CA
Pearson, Lisa R. ... Orlando, FL
Pearson, Lisa Schilit ... **New York, NY**
Pearson, Lois G. ... **Warrenton, VA**
Pearson, Lowell D. ... **Jefferson City, MO**
Pearson, Lynne A. ... San Diego, CA
Pearson, Mark ... **Los Angeles, CA**
Pearson, Mark L. ... Jackson, MS
Pearson, Mark W. ... Santa Fe, NM
Pearson, Martha McMasters
Gainesville, GA
Pearson, Mary Bain ... **Houston, TX**
Pearson, Mary Black ... Temple, TX
Pearson, Mary E. ... New York, NY
Pearson, Mary F. ... United States Senate, Committee Legal Personnel, GV
Pearson, Matthew G. ... **Bellevue, WA**
Pearson, Matthew M. ... Harrison, NY
Pearson, Matthew R. ... **Houston, TX**
Pearson, Maureen Dolan ... Chicago, IL
Pearson, McKay M. ... **Salt Lake City, UT**
Pearson, Melynda ... Texarkana, TX
Pearson • Merriam, P.C. ... **Seattle, WA**
Pearson, Michael P. (IBA) ... **Houston, TX**
Pearson, Michael T. ... **Cleveland, OH**
Pearson, Michael V. ... Bowling Green, KY
Pearson, Michael W. ... Mesa, AZ
Pearson, Milligan & Horowitz, P.C.
Denver, CO
Pearson, Neil R. ... **New York, NY**
Pearson, Nels R. ... Fort Lauderdale, FL
Pearson, Nicole Grattan ... **Los Angeles, CA**
Pearson, Niels L. ... **Las Vegas, NV**
Pearson, Nigel G. ... **Los Angeles, CA**
Pearson, Pamela M. ... **Rock Hill, SC**
Pearson, Patton, Shea, Foley & Kurtz, P.C.
Las Vegas, NV
Reno, NV
Pearson, Paul C., III ... **Corpus Christi, TX**
Pearson, Paul D. ... **Buffalo, NY**
Pearson, Paul R. ... **Falls Church, VA**
Pearson, Paul W. ... Dallas, TX
Pearson & Pearson ... **El Paso, TX**
Pearson & Pearson ... Temple, TX
Pearson & Pearson, A Professional Corporation ... **Houston, TX**
McAllen, TX
Pearson & Pearson, LLP ... **Boston, MA**
Lowell, MA
Pearson and Pearson, P.C.
Warrenton, VA
Pearson, Peter J. ... **Atlanta, GA**
Pearson, Phil C. ... **Aurora, CO**
Pearson, Phil C. ... **Denver, CO**
Pearson, Philip E. ... Berkeley, CA
Pearson, Phillip R. ... Agoura Hills, CA
Pearson, Phyllis E. ... **Des Moines, IA**
Pearson & Price, PLLC
Corpus Christi, TX
Pearson, R. Dugald ... Cleveland, OH
Pearson, R. Lynn, Jr. ... Huntsville, AL
Pearson, Ralph J. ... Austin, TX
Pearson, Ralph J., Jr. ... Houston, TX
Pearson, Ralph W. ... Salt Lake City, UT
Pearson, Ray ... **El Paso, TX**
Pearson, Ray H. ... **Miami, FL**
Pearson, Rebecca E. ... **Washington, DC**
Pearson, Richard ... Edmonds, WA
Pearson, Richard A. ... Rutland, VT
Pearson, Richard C. ... **Los Angeles, CA**
Pearson, Richard J. ... New Brighton, MN
Pearson, Richard L. ... **Birmingham, AL**
Pearson, Richard P. ... **St. Cloud, MN**
Pearson, Rita P. ... Phoenix, AZ
Pearson, Robert A. ... Kansas City, MO
Pearson, Robert C. ... **Duluth, MN**
Pearson, Robert E. ... Tustin, CA
Pearson, Robert F. ... Santa Rosa, CA
Pearson, Robert T. ... **El Paso, TX**
Pearson, Robin M. ... **San Ramon, CA**
Pearson, Robin Messier ... **Farmington, CT**
Pearson, Roderic A. ... West Des Moines, IA
Pearson, Roger C. ... Salem, OR
Pearson, Roger D. ... New York, NY
Pearson, Roger J. ... **Stamford, CT**
New York, NY
Pearson, Ronald C. ... **Los Angeles, CA**
Pearson, Ronald E. ... Temple, TX
Pearson, Ronald G. ... Charleston, WV
Pearson, Russell R. ... Seattle, WA
Pearson, S. Tammy ... **Atlanta, GA**
Pearson, Scott M. ... **Los Angeles, CA**
Pearson & Shapiro ... Union, NJ
Pearson, Shawn G. ... **Las Vegas, NV**
Reno, NV
Pearson, Shirley McGregor ... Houston, TX
Pearson & Silver ... Hollywood, FL
Pearson, Skipper J. ... St. Cloud, MN
Pearson & Smithart, P.C. ... **Tuscaloosa, AL**
Pearson, Stanley G. ... Burbank, CA
Pearson, Stephen J. ... Juneau, AK
Pearson, Stephen L. ... Boston, MA
Pearson, Stephen W. ... **Monterey, CA**
Salinas, CA
Pearson, Steven C. ... **Birmingham, AL**
Pearson, Steven D. ... **Chicago, IL**
Pearson, Steven W. ... **Richmond, VA**
Pearson, Suzanne Marsh ... **Clarksville, TN**
Pearson, Teresa H. ... **Portland, OR**
Pearson, Theodore B., Jr. ... Birmingham, AL
Pearson, Thomas A. ... Minneapolis, MN
Pearson, Thomas C. ... **Brainerd, MN**
Pearson, Thomas C. ... Madison, WI
Pearson, Thomas Calvin ... Honolulu, HI
Pearson, Thomas L. ... Tulsa, OK
Pearson, Thomas Y. ... Illiopolis, IL
Springfield, IL
Pearson, Tillman ... Tallahassee, FL
Pearson, Timothy G. ... Des Moines, IA
Pearson, Todd C. ... Minneapolis, MN
Pearson, Tommy H. ... Victoria, TX
Pearson, Travis A. ... **Wichita, KS**
Pearson, Vernon R. ... Olympia, WA
Pearson, Victor D. ... Boise, ID
Pearson, Victoria N. ... Washington, DC
Pearson, W. Beatty ... Daphne, AL
Pearson, W. Brent ... **Alexandria, LA**
Pearson, W. Robert
Department of State, GV
Pearson, Wayne ... **Dallas, TX**
Pearson, Wayne C. ... Portland, OR
Pearson, Wendy S. ... **Seattle, WA**
Pearson, William G. ... Lyons, IL
Pearson, William J. ... Virginia Beach, VA
Pearson, William M. ... Clarksville, AR
Pearson, William M. ... **Key West, FL**
Naples, FL
Pearson, William M. ... Miami, FL
Pearson, William R. ... Woodbury, NJ
Pearson, William S. ... Detroit, MI
Pearson, William S. ... Saginaw, MI
Pearson, William W. ... **Phoenix, AZ**
Pearson, Z. L., Jr. ... Denver, CO
Pearson-Browne, Kristine
San Francisco, CA
Pearson-Wise, Lori ... Maitland, FL
Pearston, Karen A. ... Des Moines, IA
Peart, Charles K. ... Davenport, IA
Peart, Jonathan F. ... Cody, WY
Peart, Sharon M. ... Chicago, IL
Peartree, Audrey P. ... Rochester, NY
Peartree, David S. ... Rochester, NY
Peartree, Frank T. ... Arlington, VA
Peartree, Kevin F. ... **Rochester, NY**
Peartree & Peartree, LLP ... Rochester, NY
Peasback, David R. ... New York, NY
Peasco, Albert J., Jr. ... North Brunswick, NJ
Pease, Alan C. ... Tenants Harbor, ME
Pease, Alison Maude ... Sacramento, CA
Pease, Allen B. ... Vinita, OK
Pease, Allen F. ... Detroit, MI
Pease, Allen H. ... **Kensington, CT**
Oak Bluffs, MA
Pease, Ann M. Caviani ... **Palo Alto, CA**
Pease, Cameron C. ... **Boston, MA**
Pease, Clark ... Merchantville, NJ
Philadelphia, PA
Pease, Daniel S. ... Massena, NY
Pease, David W. ... **Anchorage, AK**
Pease, Donald E. ... Wilmington, DE
Pease, Douglas C. ... **Los Angeles, CA**
Pease, Edgar B., III ... Los Angeles, CA
Pease, Edwin C. ... **Boston, MA**
Pease, Eleanor Thompson ... Wilmington, DE
Pease, Elizabeth D. ... Cincinnati, OH

Pecoraro, Margaret Louise
Middle Village, NY
Pecoraro, Nunzio G. ....Flushing, NY
Pecoraro, Peter J. ....Buffalo, NY
Pecoraro, Raymond G. ....Brooklyn, NY
Pecoraro & Schiesel ....New York, NY
Pecoraro, Steven ....New York, NY
Pecore, Jama H. ....Norman, OK
Pecore, Jeffrey M. ....Baltimore, MD
Pecore, Jeffrey M. ....Columbia, MD
Pecore, John W. ....New York, NY
Pecorelli, Frank J., Jr. ....Albertson, NY
Pecori, E. Robert, III ....Oakdale, PA
Pecori, Emil R. ....Oakdale, PA
Pecori, Emil R., Jr. ....Oakdale, PA
Pecori, John V. ....Oakdale, PA
Pecori & Pecori ....Oakdale, PA
Pecorino, J. Victor ....Huffman, TX
Pecoulas, George A. ....Chicago, IL
Pecquet, Janet E. ....Cincinnati, OH
Pecquet, Janet Eileen ....Cincinnati, OH
Pecquet, Philip N. ....Port Allen, LA
Pecquet, William J. ....Chicago, IL
Pecsenye, Timothy D. ....Philadelphia, PA
Pecsok, Marilyn S. ....Pacific Palisades, CA
Pectol, Cynthia Bibb ....Lexington, KY
Pectol, Richard W. ....Johnson City, TN
Pectol, Richard W., & Associates P.C.
Johnson City, TN
Pecunies, Russell P. ....Corona, NY
Pecyna, Daniel W. ....Chicago, IL
Ped, Thomas A. ....Eugene, OR
Pedas, George Theodore ....Washington, DC
Pedas, Joanna M. ....Washington, DC
Pedata, Martin A., Law Office of
DeLand, FL
Pedati, Brian D. ....Washington, DC
Pedder, Robert J. ....Lafayette, CA
Pedder, Stanley ....Lafayette, CA
Pedder, Stover, Hesseltine & Walker, LLP
Lafayette, CA
Pedder, William Robert ....Alameda, CA
Pedder, William Robert, A Professional Corporation ....Alameda, CA
Peddicord, Jarvis R. ....Hobart, IN
Peddicord, Randall H. ....Coshocton, OH
Peddicord, Roland D. ....Des Moines, IA
Peddicord, Thomas J., Jr. ....Towson, MD
Peddicord, Wharton, Thune and Spencer, A Professional Corporation
Des Moines, IA
Peddie, Collyn A. ....Houston, TX
Peddie, Richard Byron ....Boulder, CO
Peddrick, Martha Taylor ....Greensboro, NC
Peddy, A. Joe ....Birmingham, AL
Peddy, Robert B., Jr. ....Lakeland, FL
Peddy, Steven J. ....Garden City, NY
Peddy, Tracie P. ....Garden City, NY
Peddycord, John H. ....South Bend, IN
Peddycord, Robert K. ....San Diego, CA
Pedelty, Jay D. ....Denver, CO
Peden, David D., Jr. ....Houston, TX
Peden, Derrel W. ....Ridgeland, MS
Peden, Donald E. ....Arlington, VA
Peden, F. Gary ....Bellville, TX
Houston, TX
Peden, F. Gary, P.C. ....Houston, TX
Peden, Harry E., III ....Greenwich, CT
Peden, Harry E., Jr. ....Greenwich, CT
Peden, J. Brooks ....Austin, TX
Peden, James A., Jr. ....Jackson, MS
Peden, James K., III, (P.C.) ....Dallas, TX
Peden, James M. ....Lansing, MI
Peden, Jeanne W. ....Bakersfield, CA
Peden, John ....Columbus, OH
Peden, Keith S. ....Houston, TX
Peden, L. Bruce ....Columbia, TN
Peden, Mark ....Martinsville, IN
Peden, Michael P. ....San Antonio, TX
Peden, Michelle ....Tampa, FL
Peden, Paley & Associates Co., L.P.A.
Columbus, OH
Peden, Phil ....Houston, TX
Peden, Robert F., Jr. ....Bay City, TX
Peden, Steven E. ....Los Angeles, CA
Peden, William B. ....Louisville, KY
Pedersdotter, Deb C. ....San Diego, CA
Pedersen, Alan E. ....Omaha, NE
Pedersen, Alden W. ....Billings, MT
Pedersen, Amy Joseph ....Portland, OR
Pedersen, Anne D. ....Beverly Hills, CA
Pedersen, Anne E. ....Philadelphia, PA
Pedersen, A. W. ....Portland, OR
Pedersen, Barbara Lynn ....New York, NY
Pedersen, Bill, Jr. ....Nacogdoches, TX
Pedersen, Birgit ....Athens, OH
Pedersen, Brett ....San Francisco, CA
Pedersen, Brian C. ....San Francisco, CA
Pedersen, C. Richard ....Ridgefield, CT
Pedersen, C. Whitney ....Boston, MA
Pedersen, Carla J. ....Minneapolis, MN
Pedersen, Carrie A. ....Houston, TX
Pedersen, Chris A.F.
Department of Commerce, Patent and Trademark Office, GV
Pedersen & Company, PLLC ....Boise, ID
Pedersen, Craig S. ....Pasadena, CA
Pedersen, Dale W. ....Colorado Springs, CO
Pedersen, Dana R. ....Seattle, WA
Pedersen, David M. ....Omaha, NE
Pedersen, Dennis R. ....Walnut Creek, CA
Pedersen, Donald B. ....Fayetteville, AR
Pedersen, Douglas M. ....St. Louis, MO
Pedersen, Edward C.
Bloomfield Hills, MI
Pedersen, Edward K., Jr.
Bloomfield Hills, MI
Pedersen, Erika E. ....Chicago, IL

Pedersen, Frances A. ....Herndon, VA
Pedersen, Fred C. ....Dallas, TX
Pedersen, Gilbert J. ....St. Paul, MN
Pedersen & Hardy ....Billings, MT
Pedersen, Harvey L., Law Offices of
El Cajon, CA
Pedersen, Henry F., Jr. ....Estes Park, CO
Pedersen & Houpt, A Professional Corporation ....Chicago, IL
Lake Forest, IL
Pedersen, James F. ....Minneapolis, MN
Pedersen, James L. ....Mt. Ayr, IA
Pedersen, James L., P.C. ....Mt. Ayr, IA
Pedersen, Jamie D. ....Seattle, WA
Pedersen, Ji-Zhou Z. ....Washington, DC
Pedersen, Joan H. ....Philadelphia, PA
Pedersen, Jorden N. ....Hoboken, NJ
Pedersen, Keenan, King, Wachsberg & Andrzejak, P.C. ....Detroit, MI
Farmington Hills, MI
Traverse City, MI
Pedersen, Kenneth F. ....Milwaukee, WI
Pedersen, Kenneth J. ....Boise, ID
Pedersen, Kenneth J. ....Seattle, WA
Pedersen, Kenneth L. ....Twin Falls, ID
Pedersen, Kenneth L., (Chartered)
Twin Falls, ID
Pedersen, Kjell ....Fort Myers Beach, FL
Pedersen, Kristin ....San Francisco, CA
Pedersen, Kurt M. ....Sacramento, CA
Pedersen, L. Jay ....San Francisco, CA
Pedersen, Lance A. ....Hardin, MT
Pedersen, Lars ....Tucson, AZ
Pedersen, Lloyd D. ....Hartford, CT
Pedersen, Luke K. ....Dallas, TX
Pedersen, Mark William ....Rochester, NY
Pedersen, Mary J. ....Cherry Hill, NJ
Harrisburg, PA
King Of Prussia, PA
Pedersen, Maryanne Foronjy
New York, NY
Pedersen & McCaughey ....San Jose, CA
Pedersen, Michael M. ....Waterloo, IA
Pedersen, Nancy Bedford ....Houston, TX
Pedersen, Neils K. ....Kirkwood, NY
Pedersen, Nils E. ....Washington, DC
Pedersen, Norman A. ....Los Angeles, CA
Pedersen, Norman A., III ....Concord, MA
Pedersen, Paul E. ....Farmington Hills, MI
Traverse City, MI
Pedersen & Pedersen ....Harrisburg, PA
Pedersen, Peer ....Chicago, IL
Pedersen, Peer T. ....Greenwich, CT
Pedersen, Richard J. ....Omaha, NE
Pedersen, Richard R. ....San Jose, CA
Pedersen, Rita Harmening ....Jefferson, IA
Pedersen, Robert E. ....New York, NY
Pedersen, Robert H. ....Jackson, MS
Pedersen, Roberta O. ....Rego Park, NY
Pedersen, Scott P. ....Chicago, IL
Pedersen & Scott, P.C. ....Charleston, SC
Pedersen, Sigrid H., (Miss) ....New York, NY
Pedersen, Stephen R. ....Harrisburg, PA
Pedersen, T. E. ....Charleston, SC
Pedersen, Thomas S. ....Lancaster, PA
Pedersen, Willard S. ....Seattle, WA
Pedersen, William F. ....Washington, DC
Pedersen-Reed, Shawn ....Covington, LA
Pederson, Anastasia (Stacy)
Oklahoma City, OK
Pederson, Arthur W. ....Phoenix, AZ
Pederson & Baber, PC ....Gallup, NM
Pederson, Charles B., Law Offices of
La Jolla, CA
Pederson, Charles B., Law Offices of
San Diego, CA
Pederson, David W. ....North Platte, NE
Pederson, Donald W. ....North Platte, NE
Pederson, Durward L. ....Ivanhoe, MN
Pederson & Freedman, L.L.P.
Washington, DC
Rockville, MD
Pederson, Gerald R. ....Portland, OR
Pederson, James A.
Federal Energy Regulatory Commission, Office of the General Counsel, GV
Pederson, Jan M., (P.C.) ....Washington, DC
Pederson, Janet C. ....McKinney, TX
Pederson, Jeffrey D. ....Wadena, MN
Pederson, Jeffrey W. ....Cleveland, OH
Pederson, Jerome B. ....Minneapolis, MN
Pederson, John E. ....Milwaukee, WI
Pederson, John J. ....Tucson, AZ
Pederson, Justina L. ....Philadelphia, PA
Pederson, Karen Rae ....Seattle, WA
Pederson, Lawrence A. ....Anchorage, AK
Pederson, L. D. ....Eastsound, WA
Pederson, Lee M. ....San Jose, CA
Pederson, Leonard C., Jr. ....Washington, DC
Pederson, Lynda M. ....Phoenix, AZ
Pederson, Marvin ....Santa Rosa, CA
Pederson, Merle T. ....Des Moines, IA
Pederson, Michael D., Law Office of
Chaska, MN
Pederson, Michael E. ....New York, NY
Pederson, Michael L. ....Englewood, CO
Pederson, R. David ....Gallup, NM
Pederson, Roger Otto ....Washington, DC
Pederson, Sally Mayne ....Madison, WI
Pederson, Scott E. ....Grand Rapids, MI
Pederson, Steven C. ....Minneapolis, MN
Pederson, Steven K. ....Thousand Oaks, CA
Pederson, Steven M. ....Winona, MN
Pederson, Timothy J. ....Wadena, MN
Pederson, William R. ....Edina, MN
Pederzani, Paul P., III ....Warwick, RI
Pederzani, Paul P., Jr. ....North Kingstown, RI
Pederzani, Robert W. ....Orange, CA

Pedgrift & Orozco ....St. Petersburg, FL
Pedgrift, Robert J. ....St. Petersburg, FL
Pedicin, Gregory M. ....Philadelphia, PA
Pedicini, Michael N. ....Morristown, NJ
Pedicone, Alfred J. ....Loveland, OH
Pedicone, Henry, Jr. ....Albany, NY
Pedicone, Michael A. ....Wilmington, DE
Pedigo, Carl S., Jr. ....Savannah, GA
Pedigo, Clay L. ....Jackson, MS
Pedigo, Dewey, Jr. ....Brentwood, TN
Pedigo, Douglas F. ....Houston, TX
Pedigo, Haley Austin ....Chattanooga, TN
Pedigo, Helen J. ....Topeka, KS
Pedigo, James D. ....Hope, AR
Pedigo, James L., Jr. ....Norfolk, VA
Pedigo, Joseph H. ....Houston, TX
Pedigo, Katie B. ....Garland, TX
Pedigo, Kerry Lawson ....Dallas, TX
Pedigo, N. Annette ....Atlanta, GA
Pedigo, Paul F. ....Charlotte, NC
Pedigo, Scott W. ....Jackson, MS
Pedigo, Stephany Skaggs
Chattanooga, TN
Pedisich, Anton J. ....New York, NY
Pedlar, Alan ....Los Angeles, CA
Pedley, David M. ....Atlanta, GA
Pedley, James K. ....Fort Lauderdale, FL
Pedley, Lawrence L. ....Louisville, KY
Pedley, Michael G. ....Cincinnati, OH
Pedley Zielke Gordinier Olt & Pence, PLLC
Louisville, KY
Pedlow, Bernard B. ....Santa Rosa, CA
Pedlow, Edward B., IV ....Lima, OH
Pedlow, Edward B., Jr. ....Lima, OH
Pedone, John ....Worcester, MA
Pedone, Melissa ....New York, NY
Pedone, Richard C. ....Boston, MA
Pedone, Rose M. ....Buffalo, NY
Pedorella, Marni Beck ....New York, NY
Pedowitz, Arnold H. ....New York, NY
Pedowitz, James M. ....Garden City, NY
Pedowitz, Lawrence B. ....New York, NY
Pedowitz, Loraine L. ....San Diego, CA
Pedranghelu, John P., Jr. ....Hicksville, NY
Pedraza, Francisco ....Palo Alto, CA
Pedraza, George I. ....Miami, FL
Pedraza, Miguel A., Jr. ....Springfield, OH
Pedraza-Reyes, Angela ....Rochester, NY
Pedregal, Natalie ....Tampa, FL
Pedreira, Carollynn ....New York, NY
Pedreira, Jorge ....New York, NY
Pedreira, Thomas A. ....Fresno, CA
Pedreira, Virginia Miller ....Fresno, CA
Pedre-Mestre, Lisette ....Fairfax, VA
Pedretti, Mark G. ....New York, NY
Pedri, Charles R. ....Hazleton, PA
Pedrick, Daniel E. ....Albuquerque, NM
Pedrick, Gregory J. ....Los Angeles, CA
Pedrick, J. Edmund ....Waycross, GA
Pedrick, Michael J. ....Philadelphia, PA
Pedrick, W. Grady ....Alma, GA
Douglas, GA
Folkston, GA
Pedrick, W. Grady ....Waycross, GA
Pedrick, Willard H. ....Tempe, AZ
Pedrini, Bruna E. ....Tempe, AZ
Pedro, Diane C. ....Louisville, KY
Pedro, Kristina M. ....Glendale, CA
Pedro, Patrick J. ....Syracuse, NY
Pedroli & Gauthier ....St. Louis, MO
Pedroli, Robert H., Jr. ....St. Louis, MO
Pedroni, A. Thomas, Jr. ....Baltimore, MD
Pedrosa, Eliot ....Miami, FL
Pedrosa, Juan A. ....Ponce, PR
Pedrosa Lewis, Marco A. ....Plano, TX
Pedroso, Filipe ....Newark, NJ
Pedroso, Viviana Irene ....Bartow, FL
Pedrotty, Frank W. ....Richmond, VA
Pedrow, Brian D. ....Philadelphia, PA
Pedroza, Christine L. ....Los Angeles, CA
Pedroza, Kenneth R. ....Los Angeles, CA
Pedroza, Octavio A. ....Los Angeles, CA
Pedroza, Rina ....San Francisco, CA
Pedrozo, Raul A. ....Kidron, OH
Pedulla, Diane M. ....Department of Labor, Office of the Solicitor, GV
Pedulla Lake, Mary ....Michigan City, IN
Peduto, Gustave A. ....Jersey City, NJ
Peduto, James R. ....Binghamton, NY
Peduto, John M. ....Jersey City, NJ
Peduto, Leonard A., Jr. ....Roseland, NJ
Peduto, Mark B. ....Pittsburgh, PA
Peduzzi, Edward F. ....Ebensburg, PA
Peduzzi, Edward F., Jr. ....Pittsburgh, PA
Peduzzi, Robert E. ....New York, NY
Pedzimaz, Barbara A. ....Scottsdale, AZ
Peebles, Alex D. ....Hermitage, MO
Peebles, Betty & Brantley, L.L.P.
Fort Worth, TX
Peebles, Brent M. ....Baytown, TX
Peebles, C. David ....Fort Wayne, IN
Peebles, C.D. ....Fort Worth, TX
Peebles, Charles F. ....Norcross, GA
Peebles, Clay B. ....Fort Worth, TX
Peebles, David C. ....Cleveland, OH
Peebles, David E. ....Syracuse, NY
Peebles, David S. ....Crawfordsville, IN
Peebles, Dianne D. ....Oakland, CA
Peebles, Douglas A. ....Bradenton, FL
Peebles, E. B., III ....Mobile, AL
Peebles, Edith T. ....Omaha, NE
Peebles & Gracy, P.A. ....Dunedin, FL
Peebles, Jack C. ....New Orleans, LA
Peebles, James M., Jr. ....Pulaski, TN
Peebles, James M., Jr. ....Arlington, TX
Peebles, Jane ....Irvine, CA
Los Angeles, CA

Peebles, John M. ....Washington, DC
Omaha, NE
Peebles, Lisa A. ....Central Square, NY
Peebles, Monique M. ....Durham, NC
Raleigh, NC
Peebles, Paul L. ....Fort Worth, TX
Peebles, Rand L. ....Ketchum, ID
Peebles, Richard A. ....Baytown, TX
Peebles, Richard A., P.C. ....Baytown, TX
Peebles, Robert J.
Chesterfield Township, MI
Peebles, Robert R., Jr. ....New Orleans, LA
Peebles, Sam R. ....Fort Walton Beach, FL
Panama City, FL
Pensacola, FL
Peebles, Sandra R. ....Houston, TX
Peebles & Schramm ....Winston-Salem, NC
Peebles, Stafford R., Jr. ....Winston-Salem, NC
Peebles, Terry L. ....Cahokia, IL
Peebles, Thomas D., Jr. ....Springfield, MO
Peebles, Thomas G. ....Salina, KS
Peebles, Thomas H., III ....Nashville, TN
Peebles, Thomas H., IV ....Columbia, TN
Peebles, Todd M. ....Winston-Salem, NC
Peebles, William L. ....Hattiesburg, MS
Peed, Charles O., Jr. ....Winston-Salem, NC
Peed, F. Gates ....Statesboro, GA
Peed, F. Gates, P.C. ....Statesboro, GA
Peed, Fred M. ....Orlando, FL
Peed, Mary Jo ....Atlanta, GA
Peed, Roger ....North Fort Myers, FL
Peeira Eseves, Pedro J. ....Juncos, PR
Peek, Alan J. ....Sheboygan, WI
Peek, Barry J. ....Mineola, NY
Peek, Cobb, Edwards & Ashton, Professional Association ....Jacksonville, FL
Ocala, FL
Peek, David H. ....Jacksonville, FL
Peek, Edward M. ....St. Louis, MO
Peek, Eugene G., III ....Jacksonville, FL
Peek, Eve K. ....Sacramento, CA
Peek, G. Houston, Jr. ....Fort Worth, TX
Peek, Gail L. ....Tempe, TX
Peek, George S. ....New Baltimore, MI
Peek, Harold B. ....Washington, DC
Peek, Harold F., Jr. ....Valparaiso, FL
Peek, J. Corbett, Jr. ....Atlanta, GA
Peek, J. Jacob R. ....Jacksonville, FL
Peek, J. Stephen ....Las Vegas, NV
Reno, NV
Peek, James Garland ....Atlanta, GA
Peek, Jeffrey ....Indianapolis, IN
Peek, Jerry B. ....Monterey Park, CA
Peek, John M. ....Andalusia, AL
Peek, Jule W., Jr. ....Rome, GA
Peek, Kathleen E. ....Munster, IN
Peek, Kathryn Collins ....Jacksonville, FL
Peek, Kristy R. ....Vancouver, WA
Peek, Lawrence F. ....Colorado Springs, CO
Peek, Leigh Ann ....Hillsborough, NC
Peek, Lon E. ....Fountain Valley, CA
Peek, Michael C. ....Indianapolis, IN
Peek, Michael D. ....Texarkana, TX
Peek, Michael S. ....Nashville, TN
Peek, Perry L. ....Amarillo, TX
Peek, Richard H. ....Smithland, KY
Peek, Richard H. ....Casper, WY
Peek, Richard H., Jr. ....Smithland, KY
Peek, R. K. ....Du Quoin, IL
Peek, Samuel M. ....Niceville, FL
Peek, Stanley C. ....Greeley, CO
Peek, Thomas L. ....Oklahoma City, OK
Peek and Whaley ....Atlanta, GA
Peek, William D. ....Westfield, NJ
Peek, William D. ....Portland, OR
Peek, William L., Jr. ....Texarkana, TX
Peek, William M. ....Denver, CO
Peel, Beatty, Motil & Walters
Edwardsville, IL
Peel, Colby, P.A. ....Chipley, FL
Peel, Daniel F. B. ....Memphis, TN
Peel, Donna Alberts ....Department of Justice, Antitrust Division, GV
Peel, Drew G.A. ....Chicago, IL
Peel, Edward B. ....Ridgefield, CT
Peel, Frederick Colby ....Chipley, FL
Peel, Gary E. ....Edwardsville, IL
Peel, Gregory, Spangler & Brown
Henderson, NV
Peel, Hal T. ....Claxton, GA
Peel, Hal T., P.C. ....Claxton, GA
Statesboro, GA
Peel, J. Edward ....Memphis, TN
Peel and James ....Williamston, NC
Peel, James R. ....Los Angeles, CA
Peel, James W. ....Fresno, CA
Peel, John R. ....Russellville, AR
Peel, Joseph C. ....Nashville, TN
Peel, Kelly C. ....Naples, FL
Peel, Lucia C. ....Raleigh, NC
Peel, Michael ....Bronx, NY
Peel, Paul C. ....Memphis, TN
Peel, Paul E. ....Plymouth Meeting, PA
Peel, Richard L. ....Russellville, AR
Peel, Richard L. ....Henderson, NV
Peel, Richard V. ....Rancho Cucamonga, CA
Peel, Robert C. ....Williamston, NC
Peel, Robert D. ....Chattanooga, TN
Peel, Sherry L. ....Austin, TX
Peel and Simmons, P.A. ....Russellville, AR
Peel, Virginia A. ....Boston, MA
Peel, Wesley D. ....Columbia, SC
Peel, Wm. E. ....Cherry Hill, NJ
Peele, B. Thomas, III ....Washington, DC
Peele, Jo Anne ....Washington, DC
Peele, M. Bruce ....Plano, TX
Peele, S. Austin, (P.A.) ....Lake City, FL
Peele, Stanley ....Chapel Hill, NC

Peele, Vernell Yp ....Burtonsville, MD
Peelen, Jeffrey D. ....Milwaukee, WI
Peeler, Cartwright & Mann
Corpus Christi, TX
Peeler, Clarence, Jr. ....Decatur, GA
Peeler, Clarence L., III
Federal Trade Commission,
Bureau of Consumer Protection, GV
Peeler, David R. ....Mobile, AL
Peeler, Donald D. ....Omaha, NE
Peeler & Hollis ....Camden, TN
Peeler, John W. ....Austin, TX
Peeler, K. Kyle ....Pleasanton, TX
Peeler, Karen Britt ....Raleigh, NC
Peeler, Philip L. ....Memphis, TN
Peeler, Ray, Jr. ....Bonham, TX
Peeler, Robert W. ....Mason, OH
Peeler, Ronald L. ....Des Moines, IA
Peeler, Stuart T. ....Dallas, TX
Peeler, Thomas L. ....Trucksville, PA
Peeler, Travis A. ....Corpus Christi, TX
Peeler, Wm. J. ....Waverly, TN
Peeling, Mary Alice ....Wilmington, DE
Peelle, Carol S. ....Wilmington, OH
Peelle Law Offices Co., L.P.A.
Wilmington, OH
Peelle, Robert E. ....Wilmington, OH
Peelle, William E. ....Wilmington, OH
Peelman, Danny L. ....Rancho Cucamonga, CA
Peelman, James ....Bethesda, MD
Peelman, James S. ....Germantown, MD
Peelor, Pamela K. ....Pittsburgh, PA
Peelor, Sharon G. ....Irvine, CA
Peeples, Aimee Melton ....Naples, FL
Peeples, Andrea Cheryl ....Columbus, OH
Peeples, Arthur N. ....Bronx, NY
Peeples, C. Perry ....Naples, FL
Peeples, Clayburn L. ....Trenton, TN
Peeples, Darrel L. ....Olympia, WA
Peeples, David ....San Antonio, TX
Peeples, David C. ....West Memphis, AR
Peeples, H. E. Christian ....Oakland, CA
Peeples, James E. ....Arlington, VA
Peeples, John C. ....Savannah, GA
Peeples, John N. ....Valdosta, GA
Peeples, L. Grant ("Jack") ....Miami, FL
Peeples, Lloyd Chandler, III
Washington, DC
Peeples, Mary Kay ....Long Beach, CA
Peeples, Maurice L., Jr. ....San Antonio, TX
Peeples, Michael E. ....New York, NY
Peeples, O. Benjamin ....Charleston, SC
Peeples, Ralph A. ....Winston-Salem, NC
Peeples, Ralph L. ....Brookhaven, MS
Peeples, Richard H., (P.C.) ....Dallas, TX
Peeples, Robert I. ....Houston, TX
Peeples, Rodney A. ....Barnwell, SC
Peeples & Stringer ....Charleston, SC
Peeples, Veleka R. ....Columbia, SC
Peeples, William H. ....Miami, FL
Peer, Arnold C. ....Troy, NY
Peer, Arnold C., P.C. ....Troy, NY
Peer, Carl Louis ....Westfield, NJ
Peer, John E. ....Los Angeles, CA
Peer Mallinckrodt & Mallinckrodt
Kansas City, MO
Peer, Nelson & Braland ....Earlham, IA
Peer, Norman J. ....Woodbridge, NJ
Peer, Peter M., II ....Kansas City, MO
Salt Lake City, UT
Peer, Rodney R. ....Wichita, KS
Peer, Rodney R., P.A. ....Wichita, KS
Peer, William B. ....Washington, DC
Peerce, Marjorie J. ....New York, NY
Peerman, Lisa Ezell ....Brentwood, TN
Peers, Olga S. ....Louisville, KY
Peers, Richard A. ....Palo Alto, CA
Peery, Charles E. ....Seattle, WA
Peery, Dennis C. ....San Antonio, TX
Peery, Donald P. ....Roanoke, VA
Peery, Donna R. S. ....Fort Worth, TX
Peery, Gordon F. ....Los Angeles, CA
Peery, Hiscock, Pierson, Kingman & Peabody, Inc., P.S. ....Seattle, WA
Peery, Lisa N. Gale ....Burlington, VT
Peery, Liza A. ....New York, NY
Peery, Mark C. ....Greenbrae, CA
Peery, Mark W. ....Minneapolis, MN
Minnetonka, MN
Peery, Pamela J. ....San Rafael, CA
Peery, R. Briggs ....Atlanta, GA
Peery, Reta J. ....Atlanta, GA
Peery, Stephen C. ....Austin, TX
Beaumont, TX
Peery, W. W. ....Milton-Freewater, OR
Pees, Randall W. ....Columbus, OH
Pees, Robert H. ....New York, NY
Peesapati, V. Leelakumar ....Washington, DC
Peet, Charles D, Jr. ....New York, NY
Peet, Fred F. ....Hampton, VA
Peet, J. Carlisle, III ....Wilmington, DE
Peet, Richard C. ....Washington, DC
Peete, Duncan Albert ....Billings, MT
Peete, Raymond K. ....Billings, MT
Peeters, Jayne Ann ....San Francisco, CA
Peeters, John L. ....Kaukauna, WI
Peeters, Robert S. ....Stamford, CT
Peetluk, Ellis W. ....Marietta, GA
Peetris, Harry V. ....Los Angeles, CA
Peets, Alphonso O. ....Fort Lauderdale, FL
Peets, Randolph D., III ....Jackson, MS
Peetz, Forrest F. ....O'Neill, NE
Peetz, Jeffery T. ....Columbus, NE
Peetz, John P., III ....Lincoln, NE
Peetz, Nancy Z. ....O'Neill, NE
Peetz and Peetz ....O'Neill, NE
Peetz, Sonntag & Goodwin, P.C.
Sidney, NE

Peevers, Nancy L. ....Reno, NV
Peevy, Alan S.
Department Of Veterans Affairs,
Board of Veterans Appeals, GV
Peffer, H. Ray ....San Ramon, CA
Peffer, J. Michael ....Covington, KY
Peffer, Michael J. ....Santa Ana, CA
Peffer, Nicole ....Houston, TX
Peffer, Thomas P. ....Cedar Rapids, IA
Pefka, David D. ....West Palm Beach, FL
Pegalis, Andrew M. ....Silver Spring, MD
Pegalis, Steven E. ....Great Neck, NY
Philadelphia, PA
Pegalis, Wachsman & Erickson, P.C.
Great Neck, NY
Philadelphia, PA
Pegan, John R. ....Las Vegas, NV
Pegan, John R. ....Pittsburgh, PA
Pege, Deborah A ....Boston, MA
Pegg, Brendan ....Ventura, CA
Pegg, Grant D. ....Sacramento, CA
Pegg, Leon E. ....Houston, TX
Pegg, Lori E. ....San Jose, CA
Pegg, Richard E. ....Madison, WI
Pegg, Robert L. ....Vero Beach, FL
Pegg, William D. ....Washington, DC
Pegg, William L., Jr. ....Morristown, NJ
Peggins, Nichole D. ....Greensboro, NC
Peggs, Jack ....Wichita, KS
Pegher, Charles F. ....Pittsburgh, PA
Pegler, Fred S. ....Scottsdale, AZ
Pegler, Laurie A. ....Schaumburg, IL
Peglow, Paul C. ....Marshalltown, IA
Pegnato, Carol ....Chicago, IL
Pegnia, Anthony F., Jr. ....Buffalo, NY
Pegnim, Thomas M. ....Antioch, CA
Pegno, David S. ....New York, NY
Pegram, Joe D. ....Oxford, MS
Pegram, John B. ....New York, NY
Pegram, Marshall L. ....Winston-Salem, NC
Pegram, Melissa J. ....Dallas, TX
Pegram, Patricia Ann Greene ....Charlotte, NC
Pegue, Jaymeson ....Santa Monica, CA
Peguero, Antonio, Jr. ....New York, NY
Pegues, Billy J. ....Texas City, TX
Pegues, Donna Spragg ....Juneau, AK
Pegues, Michael D. ....Dallas, TX
Pegues, Rodger W. ....Juneau, AK
Pegues, William C., III ....De Ridder, LA
Pegues, Wm. T. ....Mansfield, LA
Peharda, Kresimir ....Los Angeles, CA
Pehler, Terrence P. ....Indianapolis, IN
Pehlivanian, Charles H. ....Racine, WI
Pehlivanian, John S. ....Toms River, NJ
Pehlke, Robert E. ....Northbrook, IL
Pehowski, Carla Mary ....New York, NY
Pehrson, Douglas K. ....Salt Lake City, UT
Pehrson, Elizabeth S. ....San Francisco, CA
Pehrson, Gordon O., Jr. ....Washington, DC
Pehrson, Mark A. ....Scottville, MI
Pehrsson, Kirsten Margot ....Bethesda, MD
Pei, Liane ....New York, NY
Pei-Cheng Huang, Paul ....Atlanta, GA
Peick, John C. ....Bellevue, WA
Peick, John C., P.S. ....Bellevue, WA
Peifer, Jeffrey D. ....Wichita, KS
Peifer, Charles R. ....Albuquerque, NM
Peifer, James F. ....Springfield, OH
Peifer, Jo E. ....Mount Laurel, NJ
Philadelphia, PA
Peifer, K. Lee, Law Offices of
Albuquerque, NM
Peifer, Stephen F. ....Portland, OR
Peiffer, Gary D. ....Hawthorne, NJ
Peiffer, Joseph A. ....Cedar Rapids, IA
Peiffer Law Office, P.L.C.
Cedar Rapids, IA
Peiffer, Sharyn J. ....Hackensack, NJ
Peiffer, William A. ....New Bern, NC
Peiffle, Steven J. ....Arlington, WA
Peikes, Lawrence ....New York, NY
Peikes, Ronald D. ....Hartford, CT
Peikin, Jodi Misher ....New York, NY
Peikin, Vivian Benz ....Radnor, PA
Peikoff, Jodi D. ....Los Angeles, CA
Peil, Michael A. ....Chicago, IL
Peiler, Alice M. ....San Ramon, CA
Peim, David ....Los Angeles, CA
Peim, Joyce ....Pasadena, CA
Peinado, Arnold B., III ....New York, NY
Peinado, Arthur G. ....San Diego, CA
Peinado, Daniel ....Irvine, CA
Peine, Douglas ....St. Paul, MN
Peiper, Jeffrey A. ....Dallas, TX
Peirano, Christine M. ....Miami, FL
Peirano, John J. ....Newark, NJ
Peirats, Jorge I. ....San Juan, PR
Peirce, Calista L. ....Aspen, CO
Peirce, Charles A. ....Palermo, ME
Peirce, Dorothy S. ....Lakeville, MA
Peirce, Dudley B. ....Silver Spring, MD
Peirce, Frederick F. ....Aspen, CO
Peirce, G. Michael ....Newton, MA
Peirce, George A. B. ....Department of Justice,
Environment and Natural Resources
Division, GV
Peirce, Hester Maria ....Washington, DC
Peirce & Hughes ....Ludlow, KY
Peirce, John C. ....Washington, DC
Peirce, Kenneth B., Jr. ....Holland, MI
Peirce, Kenneth E. ....Hutchinson, KS
Peirce, Lara M. ....Dallas, TX
Peirce, Raimond, Osterhout, Wade, Carlson and Coulter, P.C. ....Pittsburgh, PA
Peirce, Raimond, Osterhout, Wade, Carlson, and Coulter, P.C. ....Huntington, WV
Peirce, Richard M. ....Providence, RI
Peirce, Robert A. ....White Plains, NY

Peirce, Robert N., III ....Pittsburgh, PA
Peirce, Robert N., Jr. ....Pittsburgh, PA
Peirce, Steve A. ....San Antonio, TX
Peirez, Ackerman & Levine, L.L.P.
Great Neck, NY
Peirez, David H. ....Garden City, NY
Peirez, Joshua L. ....New York, NY
Peirez, William K. ....Elmhurst, NY
Peirsol & Associates ....Maitland, FL
Peirsol, Frederick W. ....Maitland, FL
Peirson, Chris A. ....Dallas, TX
Peirson & Patterson ....Arlington, TX
Dallas, TX
Peirson, Robert M., Jr.
Colorado Springs, CO
Peirson, William H. ....Dallas, TX
Peisak, Steven A. ....Forest Hills, NY
Peisch, Alice Hanlon ....Wellesley, MA
Peisch, Thomas E. ....Boston, MA
Peischl, Charles J. ....Nazareth, PA
Peischl, Kara L. ....Philadelphia, PA
Peisen, John G. ....Dallas, TX
Peisen, William D. ....Edinburg, TX
Peisen, William D., Law Office of
Edinburg, TX
Peiser, J. Virginia, Law Offices of
Walnut Creek, CA
Peisner, Bruce D. ....Winter Park, FL
Peisner, Kathi ....New York, NY
Peisner, Michael B. ....Portland, ME
Peiss, John H. ....Western Springs, IL
Peissel, Charles R. ....Austin, TX
Peissel & Garwood, L.L.P. ....Houston, TX
Peist, Kenneth W. ....Florham Park, NJ
Peister, Joel K. ....New York, NY
Peithman, Robert C. ....Springfield, IL
Peithmann Law Office ....Farmer City, IL
Peithmann, Ortheldo A. ....Farmer City, IL
Peithmann, William A. ....Farmer City, IL
Peitler, Arthur J. ....New Milford, CT
Peitsch, David T. ....Odenton, MD
Peitz, Ruth A. ....Chico, CA
Peitzman, Glassman & Weg
Los Angeles, CA
Peitzman, Lawrence ....Los Angeles, CA
Peixoto, Marvin A. ....Sacramento, CA
Peizer, Alan J. ....Seattle, WA
Peizer, Donna M. ....Moraga, CA
Peizer, Richards & Ziontz, P.S.
Everett, WA
Seattle, WA
Pejic, Nenad ....Cleveland, OH
Pejic, P. Branko ....Reston, VA
Pejovic-Mandich, Natasha
Los Angeles, CA
Pekala, Beverly A. ....Chicago, IL
Oakbrook Terrace, IL
Pekala, Robyn H. ....Walnut Creek, CA
Pekale, Saara J. ....West Palm Beach, FL
Pekar, John C. ....Memphis, TN
Pekar, Patricia R. ....Portsmouth, OH
Pekarsky, Michael J. ....Syracuse, NY
Pekas, John R. ....Sioux Falls, SD
Pekay, Marc M. ....Chicago, IL
Pekay, Michael, (P.C.) ....Chicago, IL
Pekelder, Ruth E. ....Gresham, OR
Pekelis, Rosselle ....Olympia, WA
Pekelner, Alan D. ....New York, NY
Pekerman, Victoria R. ....Philadelphia, PA
Pekich, Donald M. ....Long Beach, CA
Pekin, D. James ....Clark, NJ
Pekin, Elizabeth Bialow ....Chicago, IL
Pekin & Levin ....Chicago, IL
Pekin, Marshall J. ....Chicago, IL
Pekin, Michael S. ....Chicago, IL
Pekin, Richard J., Jr. ....San Diego, CA
Peklo, Gary S. ....Ellicott City, MD
Pekow, Eugene ....Chicago, IL
Pekowsky, Holly ....New York, NY
Pekowsky, Michael G. ....New York, NY
Pekowsky, Robert R. ....Madison, WI
Pelaez, Anthony D. ....Tampa, FL
Pelaez, Alfred S. ....Pittsburgh, PA
Pelaez, Perry J. ....Dayton, OH
Pelafas, Peter G. ....River Forest, IL
Pelagalli, Paul ....Clifton Park, NY
Pelagatti, Gustine J., (P.C.) ....Philadelphia, PA
Pelagatti, Thomas Michael
Prince Frederick, MD
Upper Marlboro, MD
Pelaia, Maria Theresa ....Wilmington, DE
Pelaia, Ralph F., Jr. ....Gilmer, TX
Pelak, Mark ....Wilkes-Barre, PA
Pelanda, Dorothy Liggett ....Marysville, OH
Pelanda, Kevin ....Marysville, OH
Pelander, A. John ....Tucson, AZ
Pelandini, William A. ....Seattle, WA
Pelavin, Alvin H. ....San Francisco, CA
Pelavin, Mark J. ....Washington, DC
Pelavin, Michael A. ....Flint, MI
Pelavin, Peter N. ....San Francisco, CA
Pelavin, Powers and Behm, P.C.
Corunna, MI
Flint, MI
Saginaw, MI
Southfield, MI
Pelay, Anthony, Jr. ....Portland, OR
Pelc, Brad G. ....Belleville, IL
St. Louis, MO
Pelc, David S. ....Los Angeles, CA
Pelc, Julia M. ....Spokane, WA
Pelc, Larissa A. ....Hackensack, NJ
Pelch, Dale R. ....Pasadena, CA
Pelchat, Zachary P. ....Riverside, CA
Pelcher, Stephen R. ....Moncks Corner, SC
Pelcin, Martin K. ....Los Angeles, CA

Pelcovits, Pamela M.
Department of Transportation,
U. S. Coast Guard, GV
Pelcyger, Robert S. ....Louisville, CO
Pelczarski, Karen A. ....Providence, RI
Pelczynski, Melissa Jones
Washington, DC
Peldyak, Paul E. ....Chicago, IL
Pelech, Bernard W. ....Portsmouth, NH
Peled, Avraham R. ....Department of the Navy,
Office of the Judge Advocate General, GV
Peled, Daphna ....Greenbelt, MD
Pelegrin, Jon Slaughter ....Lakewood, CO
Pelegrin, Jon Slaughter, P.C. ....Lakewood, CO
Pelegrin, Julie A. ....Denver, CO
Pelehach, John A. ....Greensboro, NC
Pelekoudas, Daniel L. ....Irvine, CA
Pelella, Noel A. ....Daytona Beach, FL
Pelella, William C. ....Binghamton, NY
Pelerose, Debbie C. ....Marietta, GA
Pelerose, Debbie Crosby, P.C., Law Offices of
Canton, GA
Marietta, GA
Pelersi, Mark S. ....Albany, NY
Peles, Ronald P. ....Stewartsville, NJ
Peles, Tal T. ....Los Angeles, CA
Pelesh, Mark L. ....Washington, DC
Peletz, Peter, Jr. ....Fair Lawn, NJ
Pelfrey, D. Patton ....Louisville, KY
Pelfrey, Melissa D. ....Norlina, NC
Pelfrey, Patricia A. ....Phoenix, AZ
Pelfrey & Pelfrey ....Norlina, NC
Pelfrey, Stephen Walter ....Norlina, NC
Pelfrey, Vincent E. ....Gary, IN
Pelger, William R. ....Munhall, PA
Pelgrift, Robert Y. ....Wethersfield, CT
Pelgrift, Robert Y., Jr. ....New York, NY
Pelgro, Michael J. ....Cambridge, MA
Pelham, Douglas S. ....Hartford, CT
Pelham, John C., Jr. ....Tallahassee, FL
Pelham, Pierre ....Mobile, AL
Pelham, Thomas G. ....Tallahassee, FL
Pelhan, William J. ....Lancaster, PA
Pelias, Harry ....New Orleans, LA
Pelias, Mary Zengel ....New Orleans, LA
Pelican, Edward J. ....Chicago, IL
Pelican, Joseph P. ....Washington, DC
Pelican, Patricia A. Palma ....Paramus, NJ
Pelican, Steven T. ....Colorado Springs, CO
Pelikan, Ann Lawlor ....Riverside, CA
Pelikan, Daniel G. ....St. Charles, MO
Pelikan, Ehlmann & Guinness, P.C.
St. Charles, MO
Pelikan, Lisa W. ....Clayton, MO
Pelikow, Alan S. ....New York, NY
Pelikow, Arthur ....New York, NY
Pelini, Craig G. ....Canton, OH
Pelini & Fischer, Ltd. ....Canton, OH
Pelini, Gregory E. ....Champaign, IL
Pelino, Andrew M.
North Palm Beach, FL
Pelino, John W. ....Philadelphia, PA
Pelino & Lentz ....Haddonfield, NJ
Philadelphia, PA
Pelinsky, Michael ....Island Park, NY
Pelio, Robert E. ....Totowa, NJ
Pelios, Elia A., The Law Office of
Bridgewater, NJ
Pelisek, Frank J. ....Milwaukee, WI
Pelish, James A. ....Rice Lake, WI
Pelka, Joann C. ....Chicago, IL
Pelka, Karen M. ....North Olmsted, OH
Pelker, Kenneth A. ....South Plainfield, NJ
Pelkey, Bruce A. ....Washington, DC
Pelkey, Bryan R. ....Rochester, NY
Pelkey, James A. ....St. Albans, VT
Pelkey, John F. ....Calumet City, IL
Pelkey, John M. ....Arlington, VA
Pelkey & Pelkey ....Rochester, NY
Pelkey, Walter M. ....Rochester, NY
Pelkofer, Peter ....Sacramento, CA
Pelkofer, Ronald F. ....Pittsburgh, PA
Pelkowsky, Jennifer T. ....Bay Shore, NY
Pelky, Paul Lloyd ....Oswego, NY
Pell, Carol C. ....Wilmette, IL
Pell, Daniel M. ....York, PA
Pell, David A. ....Jackson, MI
Pell, Deborah Owen ....Baltimore, MD
Pell, Edward G. ....Santa Monica, CA
Pell, Elliott Louis ....Bridgewater, NJ
New York, NY
Pell, Elliott Louis, P.A. ....Bridgewater, NJ
New York, NY
Pell, Frank M. ....Albany, NY
Pell, Gerald A. ....Greensboro, NC
Pell, H. Alan ....Raleigh, NC
Pell, James E. ....Greensboro, NC
Pell, Kimberly F. ....Panama City, FL
Pell & LeViness, P.C. ....New York, NY
Pell, Nancy L. ....Washington, DC
Pell, Owen C. ....New York, NY
Pell and Pell, L.L.P. ....Greensboro, NC
Pell, Reed C. ....Yakima, WA
Pell, Richard W. ....Wilmington, DE
Pell, Robert A. ....Panama City, FL
Pell, Robert A. ....Brazil, IN
Pell, Steve ....Ventura, CA
Pell, Suzanne P. ....Wentworth, NC
Pell, Terence J. ....Washington, DC
Pell, Thomas B. ....Boston, MA
Pell, Wilbur F., III ....Northfield, IL
Pell, Wilbur F., Jr. ....Chicago, IL
Pelland, Francis J. ....Washington, DC
Pelland, James M. ....Detroit, MI
Pellar, Daniel E. ....Houston, TX
Pellar, Richard ....Gainesville, FL
Pellarchy, Shirley D. ....Clearwater, FL
Pellard, Alfred S. ....Elmhurst, NY

Pellathy, Gabriel S. .... Latrobe, PA
Pelle, Anthony H. .... Miami, FL
Pelle, David D. .... Massapequa, NY
Pelle, John R. .... Santa Ana, CA
Pelle, Lisa Della .... East Hanover, NJ
Pellecchia, Donald E. .... Fort Myers, FL
Pellecchia, John M. .... Trenton, NJ
Pellecchia, Robert F. .... Newark, NJ
Pellecchio, Ralph L. .... New York, NY
Pellegrin, Anthony J. .... Chicago, IL
Pellegrin, Daniel S. .... White Plains, NY
Pellegrin, Ernest B. .... Gallatin, TN
Pellegrin, Glynn P. .... Baton Rouge, LA
Pellegrin, Jennie P. .... Lafayette, LA
Pellegrin, Joan K. .... Cleveland, OH
Pellegrin, John .... Gallatin, TN
Pellegrin, John D. .... Burke, VA
Pellegrin, John D., Chartered
Washington, DC
Burke, VA
Pellegrin, Michael P. .... Houma, LA
Pellegrin & Zone .... Cleveland, OH
Pellegrini, Anne V. .... Chicago, IL
Pellegrini, Anthony A. .... Los Angeles, CA
Pellegrini, Anthony D. .... Worcester, MA
Pellegrini, Ben E. .... Atlanta, GA
Pellegrini, Carl J. .... Washington, DC
Pellegrini, Charles Joseph .... Tallahassee, FL
Pellegrini, Dan .... Pittsburgh, PA
Pellegrini, Frank .... Oak Park, IL
Pellegrini, Frank L. .... St. Louis, MO
Pellegrini, Frank L. .... White Plains, NY
Pellegrini, Frederick N. .... Dedham, MA
Pellegrini, Geary A. .... Newton, MA
Pellegrini, Gerard L. .... Springfield, MA
Pellegrini, Greg A. .... New Orleans, LA
Pellegrini, Gregory .... Framingham, MA
Pellegrini, James A. .... Milwaukee, WI
Pellegrini, John B. .... New York, NY
Pellegrini, Joseph .... Leominster, MA
Pellegrini & Kostas .... Dedham, MA
Pellegrini, Lora M. .... Boston, MA
Pellegrini, Nadine .... Boston, MA
Pellegrini, Nicholas A. .... New York, NY
Pellegrini & O'Keefe, A Professional Corporation .... St. Louis, MO
Pellegrini, Robert J. .... Worcester, MA
Pellegrini, Robert R. .... Newburyport, MA
Pellegrini, Rosemarie .... La Grange, IL
Pellegrini & Seeley, P.C.
North Adams, MA
Pittsfield, MA
Springfield, MA
Worcester, MA
Pellegrini, Sheri .... Yorkville, IL
Pellegrini, Terry C. .... New Milford, CT
Pellegrini, Walter J. .... Yonkers, NY
Pellegrini, Wayne P. .... Seattle, WA
Pellegrino, Ann M. .... Dallas, TX
Pellegrino, Anthony W. .... Fort Lauderdale, FL
Pellegrino & Associates, P.A.
Fort Lauderdale, FL
Pellegrino, Bernard .... New Haven, CT
Pellegrino, Bernard A. .... New Haven, CT
Pellegrino, David A. .... New York, NY
Pellegrino, Dominic .... Rochester, NY
Pellegrino, Dominick F. .... Compton, CA
Pellegrino, Jeffrey J. .... New York, NY
Pellegrino, Joanne Maria .... New York, NY
Pellegrino, Joseph H. .... Waterbury, CT
Pellegrino, June L. .... Flemington, NJ
Pellegrino, Kathleen .... Louisville, KY
Pellegrino, Kimberly A. .... Brooklyn, NY
Pellegrino Law Firm, The, A Professional Corporation .... New Haven, CT
Pellegrino, Lawrence B. .... Milford, CT
Pellegrino, Mark A. .... Chicago, IL
Pellegrino, Michael G. .... Parsippany, NJ
Pellegrino, Michael T. .... Philadelphia, PA
Pellegrino & O'Connell, P.C.
Springfield, MA
Pellegrino, Raipher .... Springfield, MA
Pellegrino, Robert J. .... Fort Myers, FL
Pellegrino, Robert L. .... New Haven, CT
Pellegrino, Robert M. .... New York, NY
Pellegrino, Sandra M. .... Peoria, IL
Pellegrino & Steier, P.A. .... Fort Myers, FL
Pellegrino, Thomas C. .... New Haven, CT
Pellegrino, Victor J. .... Tampa, FL
Peller, Charlotte A. .... Gary, IN
Peller, Joel P. .... Buffalo, NY
Clifton Park, NY
Peller, Laurie .... New Orleans, LA
Peller, Michael S. .... New York, NY
Peller & Williams .... New Orleans, LA
Pellerin, Bryan L. .... Concord, NH
Pellervo, Duane H. .... Washington, DC
Pelleteri, Maura Zivalich
New Orleans, LA
Pelleteri, Raymond A., Jr.
New Orleans, LA
Pelleteri, Raymond, & Associates, L.L.C.
New Orleans, LA
Pelletier, Andrew T. .... Albany, NY
Pelletier, Angela M. .... Washington, DC
Pelletier, Claudette A. .... Vero Beach, FL
Pelletier, Colleen M. .... Providence, RI
Pelletier, Dan C. .... Cherry Hill, NJ
Pelletier, Dawn M. .... Bangor, ME
Pelletier, Dean A. .... Chicago, IL
Pelletier, Denise Ann .... Boston, MA
Pelletier, Douglas S. .... Bristol, CT
Pelletier, Elisabeth A. .... Boston, MA
Pelletier, Eric J. .... Rockville, MD
Pelletier, Franklin D., Law Offices of
Woodland Hills, CA
Pelletier, George A., Jr. .... Dallas, TX
Pelletier, J. Dan .... Atlanta, GA

Pelletier, James L. .... Lafayette, LA
Pelletier, John E. .... Boston, MA
Pelletier, John M. .... Fall River, MA
Pelletier, Kristin .... Los Angeles, CA
Pelletier, Michael C. .... Chester, NJ
Pelletier, Michael J. .... Chicago, IL
Pelletier, Nancy Frankel .... Springfield, MA
Pelletier, Nelson E. .... Kalamazoo, MI
Pelletier, Nelson E., P.C. .... Kalamazoo, MI
Pelletier, Nina J. .... Boston, MA
Pelletier, Nina S. .... Department of Justice, Civil Division, GV
Pelletier, Paul E. .... Miami, FL
Pelletier, Raymond A., Jr. .... Portland, ME
Pelletier, Richard A. .... Woodbridge, VA
Pelletier, Richard J. .... Palmer, MA
Pelletier, Robert G. .... Sanford, ME
Pelletier, Rudolph T. .... Madawaska, ME
Pelletier, Sean A. .... Des Moines, IA
Pelletier, Thomas J. .... Caribou, ME
Pelletreau, Alderson & Cabral
Richmond, CA
Pelletreau & Pelletreau, L.L.P.
Central Islip, NY
Hauppauge, NY
Patchogue, NY
Pelletreau, Robert H. .... Patchogue, NY
Pelletreau, Robert H., Jr.
Washington, DC
Pelletreau, Robert W. .... Richmond, CA
Pelletreau, William A. .... Norwalk, CT
Pelletreau, William A., L.L.C.
Norwalk, CT
Pellett, Clark D. .... Chicago, IL
Pellett, Jon M. .... Tampa, FL
Pellett, Lawrence R. .... Waterbury, CT
Pellett, Marilyn Clark .... Southington, CT
Pellett, Susan J. Olson .... Atlantic, IA
Pellette, Jacques .... Birmingham, MI
Pelletter, James J. .... Silver Creek, NY
Pelletter, McKelvey & Pelletter
Silver Creek, NY
Pelletteri, Gerolama M.
Manhasset Hills, NY
Pellettieri, Carl A., Jr. .... Chicago, IL
Pellettieri, Rabstein and Altman
Mount Holly, NJ
Princeton, NJ
Pelley, Douglas S. .... Washington, DC
Pelley, Richard A. .... Sherman, TX
Pelley, Russell A. (Chip) .... Sherman, TX
Pelley, Scott .... Sherman, TX
Pelli, Stanley A. .... Philadelphia, PA
Pellicane, Richard .... Southampton, NY
Pelliccio, Richard J. .... White Plains, NY
Pelliccioni, Daniel M., (P.C.)
Los Angeles, CA
Pelliccioni, Lori S R .... Los Angeles, CA
Pellicciotti, Joseph M. .... Munster, IN
Pellicer, Charles E. .... St. Augustine, FL
Pellicer, Ramon B., Jr. .... Santa Ana, CA
Pelligra, Ronald J. .... Syracuse, NY
Pellinen, Herbert W. .... Boise, ID
Pellinen, Robert D. .... Beverly Hills, CA
Pelling, Carolyn H. .... New York, NY
Pellinger, Scott D. .... Towanda, PA
Pellington, Joseph O. ....
Department of State, GV
Pellini, Michael A. .... Ridgefield Park, NJ
Pellino, Charles E., Jr. .... Madison, WI
Pellino, Rose M. .... Redondo Beach, CA
Pellino, Rosen, Mowris & Kirkhuff, S.C.
Madison, WI
Pellis, Joseph L., II .... Washington, DC
Pellis, Mark .... New York, NY
Pellis, Thomas P. .... Greensburg, PA
Pellish, Joseph M. .... St. Paul, MN
Pellish, Linda Susan .... Pottsville, PA
Pellish & Pellish .... Pottsville, PA
Pellish, Ronald R. .... Pottsville, PA
Pellish, Stuart .... Chicago, IL
Pellish, Thomas J. .... Pottsville, PA
Pellissier, Charles M. .... Atlanta, GA
Pellissier, Kimberly S. .... San Jose, CA
Pellitta, Nicholas F. .... Somerville, NJ
Pellittiere, Timothy .... Rochester, NY
Pellizzari, Christine A. .... Morristown, NJ
Pellizzari, Dana A. .... Durham, NC
Pellizzari, William F. .... Hines, IL
Pellman, Amy M. .... Los Angeles, CA
Pellman, Irving R. .... Alexandria, VA
Pellman, Lloyd W. .... Los Angeles, CA
Pellmann, John Harold .... Milwaukee, WI
Pellot-Gonzalez .... San Juan, PR
Pellot-Gonzalez, Luis M. .... San Juan, PR
Pellow, David M. .... Syracuse, NY
Pellow, James A., III .... Pittsburgh, PA
Pellow, Wendy Marie .... Washington, DC
Pellow, William P. .... Highland, CA
Pellowski, Kathleen .... New York, NY
Pells, Richard R. .... Maple Heights, OH
Pelofsky, Eric J. .... New York, NY
Pelofsky, Joel .... Kansas City, MO
Pelofsky, Lawrence H. .... Overland Park, KS
Peloian, James H. .... Fresno, CA
Peloquin, James B. .... Boston, MA
Péloquin, Louis O. .... Denver, CO
Peloquin, Norman A., II .... Boston, MA
Providence, RI
Peloquin, Robt. D. .... Rockville, MD
Peloquin, Suzanne Kari Tillitt
Colorado Springs, CO
Pelosi, John A. .... New York, NY
Pelosi, Nancy D. .... Fort Lauderdale, FL
Pelosi, Samantha J. .... Washington, DC
Pelosi, William K. .... Philadelphia, PA
Pelosi & Wolf, LLP .... New York, NY
Peloso, John F. X. .... New York, NY

Peloso, John F. X., Jr. .... Stamford, CT
Peloso, Matthew T. .... New York, NY
Peloso, Wendy Imatani .... Costa Mesa, CA
Pelosof, Serena L. .... Houston, TX
Pelot, Reuben Nisbet, IV .... Knoxville, TN
Pelphrey, Gary .... Marietta, GA
Pelphrey, Joyce .... Marietta, GA
Pelphrey & Pelphrey .... Marietta, GA
Pelrine, Mildred E. .... Utica, NY
Pelrine, Raymond L. .... Eau Claire, WI
Pels, Anderson & Lee, L.L.C.
Rockville, MD
Alexandria, VA
Pels, David J. .... Fort Worth, TX
Pels, Gerald J. .... Houston, TX
Pels, Jon D. .... Rockville, MD
Pels, Paula C. .... Rockville, MD
Pels, Valerie A. .... New York, NY
Pelshaw, Capri L. .... Auburn Hills, MI
Pelsinger, Kenneth S. .... Margate, FL
Pelsozy, Dale F. .... Cleveland, OH
Pelster, Martin P. .... Omaha, NE
Pelster, William C. .... New York, NY
Pelstring, R. James .... Cincinnati, OH
Pelt, Kent D. .... Irvine, CA
Pelt, Roland B. .... Dallas, TX
Pelta, Edward J. .... Rochester, NY
Pelta, Eleanor .... Washington, DC
Pelta, Lisa G. .... Rochester, NY
Peltan, David G. .... Clewiston, FL
Pelteson, Edward F. .... Columbus, OH
Pelteson, Edward F., Co., L.P.A.
Columbus, OH
Peltier, Annette N. .... Lake Charles, LA
Peltier, David C. .... Thibodaux, LA
Peltier, Donald L. .... Thibodaux, LA
Peltier, F. Johanna .... Detroit, MI
Peltier, Gary M. .... Hammond, LA
Peltier, Robert B. .... Houston, TX
Peltier, Stephen G. .... Thibodaux, LA
Peltin, Michael J. .... Woodland Hills, CA
Peltin, Sherwin C. .... Milwaukee, WI
Peltin, Steven R. .... Seattle, WA
Pelto, Don J. .... Washington, DC
Pelton, Annette A. .... Glendale, CA
Pelton & Associates, P.A. .... Albuquerque, NM
Pelton, August W. .... Los Angeles, CA
Pelton, Balland, Young, Demsky, Baskin & O'Malie, P.C. .... Arlington, VA
Pelton, Benjamin D. .... Arlington, VA
Pelton, Bruce D. .... Kirkland, WA
Pelton, Charles H. .... Clinton, IA
Pelton, David C. .... Rochester, NY
Pelton, Delbert L. .... Bellevue, NE
Pelton, Eric J. .... Birmingham, MI
Detroit, MI
Pelton, Gregory V. .... Albuquerque, NM
Pelton & Gunther, Professional Corporation
San Francisco, CA
Pelton, Joe .... Abilene, TX
Pelton, Robert .... Houston, TX
Pelton, Robert D. .... Hicksville, OH
Pelton, Russell G. .... Larchmont, NY
Pelton, Russell M. .... Chicago, IL
Pelton, Valerie J. .... Chantilly, VA
Pelton, William E. .... New York, NY
Peltonen, John E. .... Concord, NH
Manchester, NH
Peltoniemi, Carl W. S. .... Wadena, MN
Pelton-Roby, Ruth .... Keenesburg, CO
Peltosalo, Eric .... Annapolis, MD
Peltosalo, Eric, P.A. .... Annapolis, MD
Pelts, Mark J. .... Kennett, MO
Pelts, McMullan & Edgington .... Kennett, MO
Peltyn, Ilona Z. .... Los Angeles, CA
Peltz, Alexander .... New York, NY
Peltz, Arvin .... Miami, FL
Peltz, Audrey Lynn .... Syosset, NY
Peltz, Brynn D. .... New York, NY
Peltz, Fillmore K. .... Massapequa, NY
Peltz, Gordon L. .... Towson, MD
Peltz, Harry, Jr. .... Jericho, NY
Peltz, Howard M. .... Northfield, IL
Peltz, Jacqueline Rosenberg .... Chicago, IL
Peltz, Jan Michelle .... Miami, FL
Peltz, Jan Rose .... Miami, FL
Peltz, Jason L. .... Denver, CO
Chicago, IL
Peltz, Jay M. .... Scarsdale, NY
Peltz, Jeffrey B. .... Brooklyn, NY
Peltz, Jeffrey B., P.C. .... Brooklyn, NY
Staten Island, NY
Peltz, Jeffrey S. .... New York, NY
Peltz, Jennifer M. .... San Francisco, CA
Peltz, Maxwell S. .... San Francisco, CA
Peltz, Paulette B. .... Vienna, VA
Peltz, Richard B. .... Cleveland, OH
Peltz, Richard J. .... Baltimore, MD
Peltz, Robert D. .... Miami, FL
Peltz, Thomas M. .... Denver, CO
Peltz & Walker .... Bronx, NY
Brooklyn, NY
New York, NY
White Plains, NY
Peltz, William R. .... Wilmington, DE
Peltzer, Vernon A. .... San Marcos, CA
Peltzer, Wesley Watson .... San Marcos, CA
Peltzman, Lee J. .... Washington, DC
Pelusi, Anthony R., Jr. .... Cambridge, MA
Pelusi, Joseph L. .... Revere, MA
Peluso, Carl T. .... New York, NY
Peluso, Charles J. .... Modesto, CA
Peluso, Charles J., Law Office of, A Professional Corporation .... Modesto, CA
Peluso, Dana C. M. .... Richmond, VA
Peluso, Frank A. .... Milwaukee, WI
Peluso, Frank N. .... Stamford, CT
Pelham, NY

Peluso, Frank N., P.C., Law Offices of
Stamford, CT
Pelham, NY
Peluso, Gino F. .... Lower Burrell, PA
Peluso, Giovanni .... New York, NY
Peluso, James R. .... Boston, MA
Peluso, John .... New York, NY
Peluso, Joseph Roy .... Richmond, VA
Peluso, Marie K. .... San Diego, CA
Peluso, Matthew A. .... Haddonfield, NJ
Peluso, Peter J. .... New York, NY
Peluso, Rachelle A. .... New York, NY
Peluso, Stephen F. .... Nashville, TN
Peluso, Tina A. .... Garden City, NY
Peluso & Touger .... New York, NY
Peluso, Valentino & Iacobelli
New York, NY
Peluzzo-Perotin, Antonio M.
San Juan, PR
Pelych, Joseph G. .... Hornell, NY
Pelypenko, Elizabeth .... Atlanta, GA
Pelypenko Law Firm, The, P.C.
Atlanta, GA
Pelz & Associates, P.C. .... Denver, CO
Pelz, Harlan P. .... Denver, CO
Pelz, Joel T. .... Chicago, IL
Pelz, Richard K. .... Washington, DC
Pelz, Robert L. .... New York, NY
Pelzel, Janet L. .... Hunt Valley, MD
Pelzel, Leigh H. .... Seattle, WA
Pelzer, J. Randolph .... Charleston, SC
Pelzer, James E. .... Brooklyn, NY
Pelzer, John H. .... Fort Lauderdale, FL
Naples, FL
Pelzer, Max O. .... Estherville, IA
Ringsted, IA
Pelzer and Salisbury, Professional Association
Charleston, SC
Pelzl, Carol J. .... Denver, CO
Pelzman, Henry .... Newark, NJ
Pelzman, Joseph .... Bethesda, MD
Pelzner, Howard N. .... Miami, FL
Pelzner, Howard N., P.A. .... Miami, FL
Pember, George E. .... Northborough, MA
Pemberton, Alan A. .... Washington, DC
Pemberton, Bradley P. .... Kansas City, MO
Pemberton, Christian A. .... Sicklerville, NJ
Pemberton, Christian A., P.C.
Sicklerville, NJ
Pemberton, David L. .... Lewis Center, OH
Pemberton, Dennis R. .... Clearwater, FL
Pemberton, Douglas E. .... Houston, TX
Pemberton, Elizabeth Nelson
Washington, DC
Pemberton, Gary A. .... Newport Beach, CA
Pemberton, Green, Newcomb and Weis
Greenville, TX
Pemberton, Gregory L. .... Indianapolis, IN
Pemberton, Heidi .... Chicago, IL
Pemberton & Hoogestraat, P.S.
Bellingham, WA
Pemberton, James A. .... Washington, DC
Pemberton, James L. .... Schenectady, NY
Pemberton, James S. .... Kansas City, KS
Pemberton, John de J., Jr. .... Monte Rio, CA
Pemberton, John W. .... Montgomery, AL
Pemberton, Joseph T., Jr. .... Bellingham, WA
Pemberton, Margaret Lindeberg
Kansas City, MO
Pemberton, Margaret Uhlig .... Austin, TX
Pemberton, Michael S. .... Knoxville, TN
Pemberton, Ogden H. .... Houston, TX
Pemberton, Paul J. .... Bay City, MI
Pemberton, Richard L. .... Fergus Falls, MN
Pemberton, Richard L., Jr.
Minneapolis, MN
Pemberton, Rosalie V. .... Staunton, VA
Pemberton, Sam .... Tacoma, WA
Pemberton, Sorlie, Rufer & Kershner, P.L.L.P. .... Fergus Falls, MN
Pemberton, Stanton B. .... Temple, TX
Pemberton, Stephen C. .... Oregon, IL
Pemberton, Timothy J. .... Treasury Department, Office of the Comptroller of the Currency, GV
Pemberton, William B., II .... Jackson, MS
Pemberton, William R. .... Crockett, TX
Pemberton, William R., P.C. .... Crockett, TX
Pemberton, Wm. L., Jr. .... St. Louis, MO
Pemberton-Heard, Denielle
Alexandria, VA
Pemble, Geoffrey C. .... Washington, DC
Pembleton, Robert E. .... Richmond, VA
Pembridge, D. Timothy .... Cleveland, OH
Pembroke & Brown, A Prof. Corp. of Attys.
Park Ridge, IL
Pembroke, Christine R. .... Washington, DC
Pembroke, James D. .... Washington, DC
Pembroke, John .... Zanesville, OH
Pembroke, John J. .... Park Ridge, IL
Pembroke, Joseph P. .... Northfield, IL
Pembroke, R. David .... Hagerstown, MD
Pempus, Eric O. .... Cleveland, OH
Pemrick, Keith M. .... Franklin, PA
Pemsler, Barry A. .... Coral Gables, FL
Pemstein, Bernard D. .... Boston, MA
Pemstein, Bernard D. .... Boston, MA
Pemstein, E. David .... Boston, MA
Pemstein, Jason M. .... Los Angeles, CA
Pemstein, Rachel Krongrad .... Boston, MA
Pena, Alberto J. .... San Antonio, TX
Pena, Amalia Gisela .... New York, NY
Pena, Angel R. .... Fort Lee, NJ
Peña, Anneris M. .... Syosset, NY
Pena, Antonio .... Banning, CA
Peña, Bert R. .... Washington, DC
Peña, Carlos E. .... Danbury, CT
Peña, Carlos F. .... El Paso, TX

Peña, Carlos R. ....Austin, TX
Pena, Cervini & Wittstruck
Jackson Heights, NY
Pena, David L. ....Department of Labor, Office of the Solicitor, GV
Pena, Diego J. ....San Antonio, TX
Pena, Dulce L. ....Riverside, CA
Peña, Eduardo, Jr. ....Silver Spring, MD
Pena, Enrique H. ....El Paso, TX
Pena, Gilbert J. ....Austin, TX
Pena, Guillermo, Law Offices of
Miami, FL
Peña, Gustavo ....San Francisco, CA
Peña, Holly Sherman ....Dallas, TX
Peña, Horacio, Jr., Law Office of
Mission, TX
Pena, Humberto R. ....Joint Committees And Commissions, GV
Peña, Ivette ....Palos Verdes Estates, CA
Pena, Jaime ....San Jose, CA
Pena, Jeanne Siebert ....Miami Shores, FL
Peña, Jesus A. ....New Brunswick, NJ
Pena, Jesus J. ....Jackson Heights, NY
Peña, Jorge A. ....Fort Lauderdale, FL
Peña, Juan M. ....Edinburg, TX
Peña, L. Aron ....Edinburg, TX
Peña, Leonard ....Los Angeles, CA
Peña, Leslie Lavin ....Aventura, FL
Pena, Manuel M., Jr. ....San Antonio, TX
Pena, Maritza ....Miami, FL
Peña, Marvin G. ....Palo Alto, CA
Pena, Miguel D. ....West Chester, PA
Pena, Oscar J. ....Laredo, TX
Pena, Peter ....Paterson, NJ
Pena, Raymundo G. ....Rupert, ID
Pena, Richard ....Austin, TX
Brownsville, TX
Harlingen, TX
McAllen, TX
Pena, Richard C. ....West Palm Beach, FL
Pena, Richard C., P.A.
West Palm Beach, FL
Pena, Richard, P.C. ....Austin, TX
Brownsville, TX
Harlingen, TX
McAllen, TX
Pena, Rogelio ....Berwyn, IL
Pena, Ronald ....Miami, FL
Peña, Rosendo, Jr. ....Fresno, CA
Peña, Ruben R. ....Harlingen, TX
Peña, Steven J. ....Los Angeles, CA
Peña, Steven M. ....Miami, FL
Penache, Perry P. ....Flushing, NY
Penachio, Anne J. ....Eastchester, NY
Penachio, Joseph D. ....New York, NY
Pena Fonseca, Emilio ....Guaynabo, PR
Peña-García, Teodoro ....San Juan, PR
Peñagarícano, Gabriel A. ....San Juan, PR
Penagaricano, Juan T., Jr. ....San Juan, PR
Peñagarícano-Suárez, Dora M.
San Juan, PR
Penaloza, Caroline Achatz ....Lakewood, CO
Penalta, C. Richard ....West Palm Beach, FL
Penaluna, Barbara Davis ....San Mateo, CA
Peñalver, Aurora ....Miami, FL
Penalver, Charisse ....New York, NY
Penalver, Luis R. ....New York, NY
Penalver, Moises ....Brooklyn, NY
Peñalver & Peñalver, Professional Association
Miami, FL
Peñalver, Rafael A., Jr. ....Miami, FL
Pena-Perez, Enrique ....New York, NY
Penar, Gary R. ....Spokane, WA
Penarczyk, Matthew J. ....Boston, MA
Penas, Dwight J. ....Minneapolis, MN
Penate, Rafael A. ....Brentwood, NY
Penati, Francesco ....Chicago, IL
Penava, Silvana ....New York, NY
Penberthy, Edward A. ....Moorestown, NJ
Penberthy, Francisco ....Utica, NY
Penberthy, James G., Ltd. ....Minnetonka, MN
Penca, Gerald F. ....Cleveland, OH
Pencak, Christopher
Chesterfield Township, MI
Pencak, Paul C. ....Oak Brook, IL
Pence, Angela G. ....Houston, TX
Pence, B. Jeffery ....Little Rock, AR
Pence, Barbara L. ....Chicago, IL
Pence, Brenda J. ....Sacramento, CA
Pence, Christopher C. ....Seattle, WA
Pence, David T. ....Chicago, IL
Pence, David W. ....Hillsboro, OH
Pence & Dawson LLP ....Seattle, WA
Pence & Friedel ....McLean, VA
Pence & Housley ....Norman, OK
Pence, James E. ....Norman, OK
Pence, James M. ....Chamblee, GA
Pence, Jeffrey N. ....Livingston, MT
Pence, John E. ....Covington, KY
Cincinnati, OH
Pence, Kyle D. ....Fort Lauderdale, FL
Pence, Linda L. ....Indianapolis, IN
Pence, Lisa ....Stephenville, TX
Pence, Lynn ....Little Rock, AR
Pence and MacMillan ....Laramie, WY
Pence, Mark E. ....Tulsa, OK
Pence, Mary S. ....Washington, DC
Rockville, MD
Pence, O. Gordon ....Peoria, IL
Pence, Randall G. ....United States Senate, Senatorial Assistants, GV
Pence, Richard Franklin ....Roanoke, VA
Pence, Robert F. ....McLean, VA
Pence, Stephen B. ....Louisville, KY
Pence, Steven L. ....Marquette, MI
Pence, Thomas C. ....Milwaukee, WI
Pence, Thomas R. ....Cedar Rapids, IA
Pence, William L. ....Orlando, FL
Pence-Lavy, M. Melissa ....Columbus, OH
Penchef, Esther ....Glendale, CA
Pencheff, Peter M., (Co., L.P.A.)
Columbus, OH
Penchina, Robert ....New York, NY
Pencoske, Edward L. ....Pittsburgh, PA
Pendarvis, Clay C.
Federal Communications Commission, Mass Media Bureau, GV
Pendarvis, David B. ....San Diego, CA
Pendarvis, Robert L. ....Norman, OK
Pendarvis, Thomas A. ....Columbia, SC
Pendas, Luzardo ....Orlando, FL
Pendell, Charles R. ....Los Angeles, CA
Pendell, Terry A. ....Oklahoma City, OK
Pender & Coward, A Professional Corporation ....Chesapeake, VA
Newport News, VA
Norfolk, VA
Virginia Beach, VA
Pender, David R.
Federal Trade Commission, Bureau of Competition, GV
Pender, George H. ....Raleigh, NC
Pender, James M. ....Boston, MA
Pender, James R. ....Little Rock, AR
Pender, John H. ....Annandale, VA
Pender, John M. ....Boston, MA
Pender, John T. ....New Orleans, LA
Pender, Joseph W. ....Rahway, NJ
Pender, Kathleen Henry ....Chicago, IL
Pender, Mary Beth ....Annandale, VA
Pender, McCastlain & Ptak, A Professional Association ....Little Rock, AR
Pender, Michael J. ....Atlantic City, NJ
Pender, Michael J. ....Mineola, NY
Pender, Robert B., Jr. ....Washington, DC
Pender, Thomas R. ....Chicago, IL
Pender, Thomas R. ....St. Paul, MN
Pender, William L. ....Charlotte, NC
Pender, Wm. E. ....Atlanta, GA
Pendergast & Blum, P.C. ....Atlanta, GA
Pendergast, David T. ....Houston, TX
Pendergast, Donna Claire ....Houston, TX
Pendergast, Dorothy D. ....Rockville, MD
Pendergast, Francis J., III ....Chicago, IL
Pendergast, Gary M. ....New Orleans, LA
Pendergast, Gene E., Jr. ....Sacramento, CA
Pendergast, John C. ....Chicago, IL
Pendergast, John F., Jr. ....Atlanta, GA
Pendergast, John J., III ....Boston, MA
Providence, RI
Pendergast, John W. ....Whitinsville, MA
Pendergast, Joseph E., III ....Renton, WA
Pendergast, Kathleen M. ....Framingham, MA
Pendergast, Margaret A. ....San Francisco, CA
Pendergast, Michael C. ....St. Louis, MO
Pendergast, Michael J. ....Novato, CA
Pendergast, Paul E. ....Irving, TX
Pendergast, Rick L. ....Eau Claire, WI
Pendergast, Robert E. ....Pittsburgh, PA
Pendergast, William F. ....Washington, DC
Pendergast, William J., III ....Vallejo, CA
Pendergast, William R. ....Washington, DC
Pendergraft, Clayton E. ....Wichita, KS
Pendergraft, Jeffrey R. ....Houston, TX
Pendergraft, Michael R. ....Greensboro, NC
Pendergraft, Neal R. ....Fayetteville, AR
Pendergrass, Alphonso W. ....Washington, DC
Pendergrass, C. Walter, III
Stockbridge, GA
Pendergrass, Carl ....Del Rio, TX
Pendergrass, G. Lee ....Puyallup, WA
Pendergrass, James K., Jr. ....Raleigh, NC
Pendergrass, Jere E. ....Taylor, MI
Pendergrass, John A. ....Washington, DC
Pendergrass, John M. ....Dowagiac, MI
Pendergrass, Joseph C., Jr. ....Gainesville, GA
Pendergrass & Kaukl ....Puyallup, WA
Pendergrass, Rita K. ....Colleyville, TX
Pendergrass, Robert A. ....Tulsa, OK
Pendergrass, Robert W. ....San Rafael, CA
Pendergrass, Samantha D. ....Charlotte, NC
Pendergrass, Walter H. ....Portland, OR
Pendergrass, Wesley L. ....Hampton, VA
Pendergrast, Craig K. ....Atlanta, GA
Pendergrast, Teresa W. ....Atlanta, GA
Penders, John P. ....Philadelphia, PA
Penders, Kevin Francis ....Boston, MA
Penders, Michael
Environmental Protection Agency, Office of Enforcement and Compliance Assurance, GV
Pendery, Julia F. ....Dallas, TX
Pendery, Mark S. ....Grand Rapids, MI
Pendery, Susan E. ....Cherry Hill, NJ
Philadelphia, PA
Pendino, Sam D. ....Tampa, FL
Pendland, James L., Jr. ....High Springs, FL
Pendland, Karen D. ....Kansas City, MO
Pendleton, Abby ....Royal Oak, MI
Pendleton, Alan F. ....Anoka, MN
Pendleton, Alan R. ....Medford, OR
Pendleton, Alexander T. ....Milwaukee, WI
Pendleton, B. John, Jr. ....Newark, NJ
Pendleton, Brian ....Denver, CO
Pendleton, C. Jean ....Des Moines, IA
Pendleton, Charles F. ....Corona, CA
Pendleton, Christopher ....Okemos, MI
Pendleton, Clay ....Lincolnton, NC
Pendleton, Constance Morrow
Washington, DC
Pendleton, Dianna Lynn ....Houston, TX
Pendleton, Don M. ....Lincolnton, NC
Pendleton, Donald M. ....Sioux City, IA
Pendleton, Douglas H. ....San Jose, CA
Pendleton, Edmond V. ....New York, NY
Pendleton, Edmund ....Washington, DC
Pendleton, Elisabeth M. ....Washington, DC
Pendleton, Friedberg, Wilson & Hennessey, P.C. ....Boulder, CO
Denver, CO
Pendleton, G. Franklin, II ....Clover, SC
Pendleton, Garrett & Henderson, P.C.
Amherst, VA
Lovingston, VA
Lynchburg, VA
Pendleton, Gary W. ....St. George, UT
Pendleton, James K. ....St. Louis, MO
Pendleton, Jane E. ....Weatherford, TX
Pendleton, John T. ....Henniker, NH
Pendleton, Jonathan D.
San Francisco, CA
Pendleton, Laurence ....Denver, CO
Pendleton, Lea B. ....Waltham, MA
Pendleton, LeRoy ....Clover, SC
Pendleton, Lewis S., Jr. ....Reidsville, NC
Pendleton, Mary B. ....San Diego, CA
Pendleton, Melissa B. ....Charlotte, NC
Pendleton, Michael J., Jr. ....Dallas, TX
Pendleton, Paul B. ....Pine Bluff, AR
Pendleton & Pendleton, P.A.
Lincolnton, NC
Pendleton, Philip E. ....Shamrock, TX
Pendleton, Robert Edward, III ....Pasadena, TX
Pendleton, Robert L. ....Ridgecrest, CA
Pendleton, Roxanne J. ....Kansas City, MO
Pendleton, Stephen R. ....Angel Fire, NM
Pendleton, Thomas A. ....Erie, PA
Pendleton, Wendell ....Homosassa, FL
Inverness, FL
Pendleton, William B. ....Lawrence, KS
Pendley, Elisabeth Young ....Evergreen, CO
Pendley, F. Scott ....Orlando, FL
Pendley, John L. ....Frankfort, KY
Pendley, Kevin W. ....Atlanta, GA
Pendley, Michael C. ....Jacksonville, FL
Pendley, Pamela Marian ....Plaquemine, LA
Pendley, Patrick W. ....Plaquemine, LA
Pendley, Patrick W., A Professional Law Corporation ....Plaquemine, LA
Pendolphi, Michael A. ....Wilkes-Barre, PA
Pendorf, Stephan A. ....Miami, FL
Pendracki, Michael J. ....Southfield, MI
Pendrey, Jeremy E. ....Los Angeles, CA
Pendry, Christine B. ....New York, NY
Pendry, David L. ....Xenia, OH
Pendry, Reita P. ....Washington, DC
Pendygraft, George W. ....Indianapolis, IN
Pendygraft, George W., P.C.
Indianapolis, IN
Pendzick, Elizabeth M. ....Mineola, NY
Pene, Katherine B. ....Sherman Oaks, CA
Penebad, Coralee G. ....Miami, FL
Penegar, Kenneth L. ....Dallas, TX
Penegor, Robert J. ....Brookfield, WI
Pener, Ben E. ....Kansas City, MO
Pener, Michael A. ....Overland Park, KS
Penetar, Daniel L., Jr. ....Scranton, PA
Penetar, Danl. L. ....Scranton, PA
Penett, Thomas K. ....Staten Island, NY
Penfield, Carole ....Phoenix, AZ
Penfield, D. Kent ....Manchester, NH
Penfield, George R. ....Fairview Park, OH
Penfield, James R. ....San Diego, CA
Penfield, Jason ....Washington, DC
Penfield, John W. ....Sacramento, CA
Penfield, Liong Lie Gan ....San Diego, CA
Penfield, Thomas D. ....San Diego, CA
Penfil, Elizabeth K. ....Newport Beach, CA
Penfold, Craig ....Dallas, TX
Peng, Chuan R. ....New York, NY
Peng, Elizabeth Chun-Yun ....Seattle, WA
Peng, Linda Y.
Commodity Futures Trading Commission, Division of Enforcement, GV
Peng, Phillip ....Los Angeles, CA
Peng, Tammy C. ....San Bernardino, CA
Peng & Weber ....Seattle, WA
Pengelly, David L. ....Missoula, MT
Pengelly, Vaughn A. ....Milwaukee, WI
Pengilly, Charles R. ....Fairbanks, AK
Pengilly, J Ronald ....Piedmont, CA
Pengilly, James W. ....Las Vegas, NV
Pengilly, Mark E. ....Portland, OR
Pengra, Brian L. ....Chicago, IL
Penhaligen, Jane K. ....Oakland, CA
Penhallegon, John R. ....Baltimore, MD
Penhallurick, Kent W. ....Chardon, OH
Penich, Harry A. ....San Diego, CA
Peniche, Carlos A. ....Houston, TX
Peniche, Laurel A. ....Anaheim, CA
Peniche & Singleton ....Houston, TX
Penichet, Luis Andrew ....White Plains, NY
Penichet, Paul F. ....Coral Gables, FL
Penichet, Paul F., P.A. ....Coral Gables, FL
Miami, FL
Penick, Bridget R. ....Chicago, IL
Penick, Charles D. ....Bastrop, TX
Penick, Edward M. ....Little Rock, AR
Penick, Giles A., Jr. ....Tulsa, OK
Penick & Greening, P.C. ....Dallas, TX
Penick, Henry Lee ....Birmingham, AL
Penick, J. Edward, Jr. ....Skillman, NJ
Penick, James H., III ....Little Rock, AR
Penick, Janet L. C. ....Palo Alto, CA
Penick, Julia S. ....Morris Plains, NJ
Penick, Michael P. ....Dallas, TX
Penick, Paul M. ....Lexington, VA
Penick, Thomas E., Jr. ....St. Petersburg, FL
Penick, William S. ....New Orleans, LA
Penico, Stephen J. ....Rolla, MO
Penico, Victor L. ....Treasury Department, Internal Revenue Service, GV
Penicook, Mary Ellen ....Oak Brook, IL
Penilla, David R. ....Phoenix, AZ
Yuma, AZ
Penino, Stephen J. ....White Plains, NY
Peninsula I.P. Group ....Morgan Hill, CA
Penirian, Frank K., Jr. ....Detroit, MI
Peniston, Richard A. ....Charlotte, NC
Penix, Bill ....Jonesboro, AR
Penke, Thomas H. ....Omaha, NE
Penkethman, William C., Jr. ....Plymouth, MA
Penkethman, William C., Jr., P.C., The Law Offices of ....Plymouth, MA
Penkoff, Stephen D. ....Fallbrook, CA
Penkovsky, Nicholas A., P.C., Law Offices of
New York, NY
Penkovsky, Nicholas Alexander
New York, NY
Penkowsky, Gregory D. ....Denver, CO
Penkwitz, Martin Wm. ....Houston, TX
Penland & Block, P.A. ....Jacksonville, FL
Penland, Gene B. ....Salina, KS
Penland, James W. ....Atlanta, GA
Penland, Kathleen A. ....Chicago, IL
Penland, Lisa ....Eldora, IA
Penland Munther Boardman, Chartered
Boise, ID
Penland, Paul S. ....Boise, ID
Penland, Robert Tideman, Jr ....Ruston, LA
Penland, S. Perry ....Jacksonville, FL
Penland, S. Perry, Jr. ....Jacksonville, FL
Penland, S. Perry, Jr., P.A. ....Jacksonville, FL
Penland, Talmage N. ....Asheville, NC
Penland, Thomas L., Jr. ....Atlanta, GA
Penley, Alexander C. ....Sacramento, CA
Penley, J. Mark ....Dallas, TX
Penley, James L., Jr. ....Vicksburg, MS
Penley, James W. ....Huntsville, AL
Penman, Gordon R. ....Boston, MA
Providence, RI
Penman, Robert A., III ....Atlanta, GA
Penman, Sharon K. ....Pleasantville, NJ
Penn, Alan ....Allentown, PA
Penn, Amir N. ....Chicago, IL
Penn, Andrew S. ....Largo, MD
Penn, Arthur ....Mount Holly, NJ
Princeton, NJ
Penn, Arthur S. ....New York, NY
Penn, Barbara F. L. ....St. Paul, MN
Penn, Barry F. ....Cherry Hill, NJ
Philadelphia, PA
Philadelphia, PA
Wynnewood, PA
Penn, Carleton, III ....Fairfax, VA
Penn, Carmella Johnson ....Aurora, IL
Penn, Carol Horne ....Philadelphia, PA
Penn, Charles E. ....Philadelphia, PA
Penn, Cheryl G. ....Texarkana, TX
Penn, Craig Eric ....New York, NY
White Plains, NY
Penn, Cyril C. ....Jamaica, NY
Penn, D. Gaines ....Bowling Green, KY
Penn, Dale W. ....Salem, OR
Penn, Dara A. ....Jenkintown, PA
Penn, Darren W. ....Atlanta, GA
Penn, David G. ....Springfield, IL
Penn, Douglas R. ....Denver, CO
Penn, Edward D. ....Princeton, NJ
Penn, Ethan N. ....New Orleans, LA
Penn, George E., II ....Columbia, MD
Penn, Harlan W. ....Dublin, CA
Penn, Homer J. ....New Orleans, LA
Penn, James W. ....Decatur, IL
Penn, John C. ....Washington, DC
Penn, John D. ....Fort Worth, TX
Penn, John Garrett ....
United States District Court For The District Of Columbia, GV
Penn, Jonathan B. ....Santa Clara, CA
Penn, Karen R. ....Department of Justice, Office of Justice Programs, GV
Penn, Laura Hardy ....Miami, FL
Penn, Laureen R. ....Falls Church, VA
Penn, Marian R. ....Monterey, CA
Penn, Marsha A. ....Houston, TX
Penn, Melinda Carter ....Martinsville, VA
Penn, Michael A. ....Atlanta, GA
Penn, Michael C. ....Chicago, IL
Penn, Michéal Leslie ....Lake Charles, LA
Penn, Myron Cordell ....Birmingham, AL
Penn, Nicholas S. ....Washington, DC
Penn & Pate, LLP ....Atlanta, GA
Penn, Philip J. ....Charlotte, NC
Penn, Phyllis A. ....Houston, TX
Penn, Ralph W. ....Huber Heights, OH
Penn, Richard W. ....Circleville, OH
Penn, Robert F. ....Stevens Point, WI
Penn & Robinson ....Cherry Hill, NJ
Philadelphia, PA
Washington Crossing, PA
Wynnewood, PA
Penn, Robt. W. ....Toledo, OH
Penn, Shelton C. ....Battle Creek, MI
Penn, Stephen H. ....New York, NY
Penn, Stephen W. ....Saratoga, CA
Penn, Steven R. ....Chicago, IL
Penn, Thomas A. ....Harleysville, PA
Penn, Timothy Harold ....Hartford, CT
Penn, Tyrrel J. ....Chicago, IL
Penn, Walter L., III ....Martinsville, VA
Penn, Wayne P. ....Alhambra, CA
Penn, William ....Kingman, AZ
Penn, William C. ....Phoenix, AZ
Penn, William E. ....East Lansing, MI
Penn, William L. ....Dearborn, MI
Penn, William R. ....Joliet, IL
Penn, William R., P.C. ....Kingman, AZ
Penna, Christopher E. ....Atlanta, GA
Penna, Dominic A. ....Ambler, PA
Penna, Grabois & Associates ....Ambler, PA

Penna, Joseph E. ....Monmouth, OR
Penna, Richard A. ....Washington, DC
Penna, Thomas F. ....Simsbury, CT
Pennacchini, Steven W. ....Warwick, RI
Pennachio, Robert A. ....Englewood, NJ
Pennak, Arthur F. ....Cincinnati, OH
Pennak, Mark W. ....Department of Justice, Civil Division, GV
Pennamped, Bruce M. ....Indianapolis, IN
Pennant, Stephanie P. ....Philadelphia, PA
Pennarola, Francis G. ....Danbury, CT
Pennartz, David A. ....Glendale, AZ
Pennas, Perry Pandelis ....Bayside, NY
Penne, Jeffrey S. ....Omaha, NE
Pennebaker, Douglas E. ....San Antonio, TX
Pennebaker, George ....Dallas, GA
Pennebaker, John D. ....New Albany, MS
Pennebaker, John T. ....Sacramento, CA
Pennebaker, Ray W. ....DeLand, FL
Pennebaker, Susan ....Houston, TX
Pennebaker, W. F. ....Midland, TX
Pennefather, Marcia C.
Winston-Salem, NC
Pennekamp, J. Michael ....Miami, FL
Pennekamp, Lisa A. ....Cincinnati, OH
Pennekamp, Tom, Jr ....Miami, FL
Sarasota, FL
Pennell, Barbara A. ....Philadelphia, PA
Pennell, Carlene A. ....Boston, MA
Pennell, Frances E. ....Seattle, WA
Pennell, John S. ....Chicago, IL
Pennell, Marcia F. ....Dallas, TX
Pennell, Michael N., (A Professional Corporation) ....San Bernardino, CA
Pennell, Nancy H. ....Oklahoma City, OK
Pennell, Robert G. ....St. Louis, MO
Pennell, Robin Lynn ....San Francisco, CA
Pennell, Stephen R. ....Lafayette, IN
Pennell, William B. ....Canaan, NY
Pennella & Claps ....Dover, NJ
Pennella, David C. ....Dover, NJ
Pennella, Neil V. ....New York, NY
Pennella, Rosanne ....New York, NY
Penner, C. Scott ....Seattle, WA
Penner, Daniel L. ....Fort Worth, TX
Penner, David J. ....Los Angeles, CA
Penner, Deborah J. ....Lubbock, TX
Penner, Deborah J., P.C. ....Lubbock, TX
Penner, Douglas Eugene ....Norfolk, VA
Penner, Eileen ....Washington, DC
Penner, Gerald M., (P.C.) ....Chicago, IL
Penner, Herman L., Jr. ....Arlington, VA
Penner, Ingeborg E. ....San Francisco, CA
Penner, Kimberly S. ....New York, NY
Penner, Michael J. ....San Francisco, CA
Penner, Nancy J. ....Cedar Rapids, IA
Penner, Randall M. ....Fresno, CA
Penner, Ronald L. ....Akron, OH
Penner, Stephen E. ....Santa Barbara, CA
Penner, Tami Johnson ....San Diego, CA
Penner, Vernon D. ....Phoenix, AZ
Penner, William
Commodity Futures Trading Commission, Division of Enforcement, GV
Penner, William A., Jr. ....Birmingham, MI
Detroit, MI
Penners, Ann K. ....Los Angeles, CA
Pennes, Carol G. ....Camden, NJ
Pennet, David S. ....Van Nuys, CA
Pennewill, Elizabeth C. ....Tampa, FL
Penney, Charles A. ....Palm Beach, FL
Penney, Charles R. ....Lockport, NY
Penney, Douglass F. ....Sacramento, CA
Penney, Forrest E. ....Gonzales, TX
Penney, James A. ....Seattle, WA
Penney, James F. ....Laguna Beach, CA
Penney, Jamie ....North Reading, MA
Penney, Jeffrey S. ....Auburn, CA
Penney, John C. ....Newport Beach, CA
Penney, Larry B. ....Las Vegas, NV
Penney, Maier, Wallach & Crowe
Buffalo, NY
Penney, Miriam F. ....Las Vegas, NV
Penney & Penney ....Las Vegas, NV
Penney, Robert A. ....Oak Bluffs, MA
Penney, Susan L. ....San Francisco, CA
Penney, Todd D. ....Dayton, OH
Penney, William H. ....Arvada, CO
Penney-Martin, T. F. N. F. G. Chris
New York, NY
Penneys, Jeffrey ....Philadelphia, PA
Penneys, Sylvia Sohn ....Miami, FL
Pennfield, Edward B. ....New York, NY
Pennica, Kenneth ....Fairport, NY
Pennick, Edward C. ....Cincinnati, OH
Pennick, Neil V.
Hot Springs National Park, AR
Pennick, Paul P.
Hot Springs National Park, AR
Pennie, Daniel R. ....Bloomington, MN
Pennie & Edmonds LLP ....Palo Alto, CA
Washington, DC
New York, NY
Pennie, Nancy L. ....New York, NY
Penniman, Alford R. ....Belvidere, IL
Penniman, Rebecca Fariss
Baton Rouge, LA
Penniman, William H. ....Washington, DC
Penning, Ann Cooper, Mrs. ....Washington, DC
Penning, Dan A. ....Farmington Hills, MI
Penninger, Margaret A. ....St. Joseph, MI
Penninger, Robert ....Springfield, MO
Penninger, Una Lee ....Springfield, MO
Penninger, William Holt, Jr.
Springfield, MO
Pennings, Richard W. ....Lansing, MI
Pennington, Alyce L. ....Tucson, AZ
Pennington, Andrea P. ....Mobile, AL
Pennington, Anthony B. ....Springfield, OH
Pennington, Beth ....San Francisco, CA
Pennington, Brenda K. ....Washington, DC
Pennington, C. Richard ....Denver, CO
Pennington, C. Rufus, III
Jacksonville, FL
Pennington, Caren N. ....New York, NY
Pennington, Carl R., Jr. ....Tallahassee, FL
Pennington, Catharina ....San Francisco, CA
Pennington, Christopher L.
New York, NY
Pennington, D. Ashley ....Charleston, SC
Pennington, David A. ....Philadelphia, PA
Pennington, David L. ....Cherry Hill, NJ
New York, NY
Philadelphia, PA
Pennington, David S. ....Carson City, NV
Pennington, Deanna L. ....Elkins, WV
Pennington, Deborah K. ....Indianapolis, IN
Pennington, Dennis A. ....Baton Rouge, LA
Pennington, Dennis A., A Prof. Law Corp.
Baton Rouge, LA
Pennington, Diana ....Washington, DC
Pennington, E. Justin ....Albuquerque, NM
Pennington, Edward A. ....Washington, DC
Pennington, Eric S. ....Newark, NJ
Pennington, Francis E., III ....St. Louis, MO
Pennington, Gail ....Boston, MA
Pennington, Gary C. ....Columbia, SC
Pennington, Gregory S. ....Brick, NJ
Pennington, H. Allen, Jr. ....Fort Worth, TX
Pennington, H. Joan ....Trenton, NJ
Pennington, Hal H. ....Duncan, OK
Pennington, Harvey T. ....Morehead, KY
Pennington, Henry Vincent, III
Danville, KY
Pennington, J. Gordon ....Washington, DC
Pennington, James C. ....Birmingham, AL
Pennington, James E. ....Dallas, TX
Pennington, James P. ....Houston, TX
Pennington, Jane L. ....Norman, OK
Pennington, Janice Robinson ....Dallas, TX
Pennington, Jean Z. ....New York, NY
Pennington, Jerry V. ....Orange, TX
Pennington, Jill C. ....Midland, TX
Pennington, Jill J. ....Landover, MD
Pennington, Joan ....Chicago, IL
Pennington, John C. ....Atlanta, GA
Pennington, John C., P.C. ....Atlanta, GA
Pennington, John M. ....Birmingham, AL
Pennington, John M. ....Houston, TX
Pennington, John R. ....Los Angeles, CA
Pennington, John W., III ....Miami, FL
Pennington, Karen H. ....Dallas, TX
Pennington, Kathleen M.
Department of Justice, Civil Rights Division, GV
Pennington, Kathryn Hunt ....Nashville, TN
Pennington, Kenneth W.
Wilkes-Barre, PA
Pennington, Kim Allen ....St. Cloud, MN
Pennington, L. Robert ....Chanute, KS
Pennington, Lara B. ....Morristown, NJ
Pennington, Laurence M.
Hacienda Heights, CA
Pennington, Laurie Atkins ....Orlando, FL
Pennington Law Firm, P.A. ....Columbia, SC
Pennington & Lies, P.A. ....St. Cloud, MN
Pennington, Lisa H. ....Houston, TX
Pennington, Lucinda W.
Thousand Oaks, CA
Pennington, Mark C. ....New York, NY
Pennington, Mark S. ....Des Moines, IA
Pennington, Michael R. ....Birmingham, AL
Pennington, Michael T. ....Denver, CO
Pennington, Mickey R. ....Uvalde, TX
Pennington, Moore, Wilkinson, Bell & Dunbar, P.A. ....Tallahassee, FL
Tampa, FL
Pennington, Nicholas I. ....Marietta, GA
Pennington, Oliver ....Houston, TX
Pennington, Philip C. ....Kansas City, MO
Pennington, Phyllis S. ....San Luis Obispo, CA
Pennington, Ralph, Jr ....New York, NY
Pennington, Ralph S. ....Wilmington, NC
Pennington, René Webb ....New Orleans, LA
Pennington, Richard D. ....Anchorage, AK
Pennington, Richard L.
Peterborough, NH
Pennington, Robert ....Chanute, KS
Pennington, Robert G. ....Atlanta, GA
Pennington, Robert J. ....Madisonville, TN
Pennington, Robert L. ....Atlanta, GA
Pennington, Rollie M. ....Stockton, CA
Pennington, Ronald R.
Charlotte Amalie, St. Thomas, VI
Pennington, Stephen S. ....Harrisburg, PA
Philadelphia, PA
Pennington, Stephen T. ....Toledo, OH
Pennington, Thomas T. ....Nashville, TN
Pennington, Thomas W. ....Fort Smith, AR
Pennington, Thomas W. ....Bethesda, MD
Pennington & Thompson ....Cherry Hill, NJ
Pennington, Walter Allen ....Dallas, TX
Pennington, Warren Y. ....Houston, TX
Pennington, Warren Y., P.C. ....Houston, TX
Pennington, William L. ....Morgantown, WV
Pennington-Cross, Carla G.
Philadelphia, PA
Pennini, Karen Faber ....New Bedford, MA
Pennisi, Albert F. ....Lake Success, NY
Pennisi, Daniels and Norelli
Lake Success, NY
Pennisi, Janet L. ....Millburn, NJ
Pennisi, Monica V. ....Moorestown, NJ
Pennison, Christopher R. ....Tucson, AZ
Pennix, Brian G. ....Truckee, CA
Penn-Jenkins, Monique
Federal Energy Regulatory Commission, Office of the General Counsel, GV
Pennock & Breedlove, LLP
Clifton Park, NY
Pennock & Cooper ....Houston, TX
Pennock, David S. ....New York, NY
Pennock, Harold H., III ....Centralia, IL
Pennock, Harold H., Jr. ....Centralia, IL
Pennock, John H., Jr. ....Clifton Park, NY
Pennock, Lewis F. ....Houston, TX
Pennock, Lisa M. ....Belleville, IL
Pennock, Paul J. ....New York, NY
Pennock, Scott R. ....Midland, MI
Pennoni, Lawrence D. ....Houston, TX
Pennow, Mark A. ....Green Bay, WI
Pennoyer, James E. ....Farmington, MO
Pennoyer, Paul G., Jr. ....New York, NY
Pennoyer, Robert M. ....New York, NY
PennStuart ....Bristol, TN
Johnson City, TN
Kingsport, TN
Abingdon, VA
Bristol, VA
Richmond, VA
Pennsylvania Land Titles ....Wexford, PA
Penny, Ann ....Pittsburgh, PA
Penny, Barbara Jean ....Granada Hills, CA
Penny, Botticello, O'Brien & Higgins, P.C.
Manchester, CT
Penny, David M. ....Boise, ID
Penny, Diana L. ....Sacramento, CA
Penny, Douglas R. ....Riverhead, NY
Penny, Gordon M. ....Lawrence, KS
Penny, Ian M. ....New York, NY
Penny, J. Curt ....Burlington, CO
Penny, James B. ....Tempe, AZ
Tucson, AZ
Penny, James D. ....Houston, TX
Penny, James M., Jr. ....Philadelphia, PA
Penny, Jane Gowen ....Harrisburg, PA
Penny, John C. ....Burlington, CO
Penny, John J., Jr. ....Washington, DC
Penny and Penny ....Burlington, CO
Penny, Robert J. ....Fort Collins, CO
Penny, Robert M. ....Los Angeles, CA
Penny, Ronald T. ....Sanford, NC
Penny, Roy W., Jr. ....Denver, CO
Penny, Stephen T. ....Manchester, CT
Penny, Theodore A. ....Los Angeles, CA
Penny, William E. ....Scarsdale, NY
Penny, William L. ....Nashville, TN
Penny, William M., Jr. ....Fort Worth, TX
Pennycooke, Colin ....New York, NY
Pennypacker, B. F. "Biff", III
San Antonio, TX
Pennypacker, Paula K. ....Point Pleasant, NJ
Pennypacker, Philip H. ....San Jose, CA
Pennywell, Kenneth B. ....Denver, CO
Penot, Charles R., Jr. ....New Orleans, LA
Penovich, Gerald George ....Chicago, IL
Penoyar, Elizabeth B. ....South Bend, WA
Penoyar, Joel M. ....South Bend, WA
Penoyer, Eve Grace ....Boston, MA
Penrod, Craig W. ....Tempe, AZ
Las Vegas, NV
Penrod, David A. ....Harrisonburg, VA
Penrod, Deborah L. ....Philadelphia, PA
Penrod, Earl G. ....Princeton, IN
Penrod, Jack R. ....Naperville, IL
Penrod, James N. ....San Francisco, CA
Penrod, Paul R. ....San Antonio, TX
Penrod, Samuel W. ....Phoenix, AZ
Penrod, William A. ....Pittsburgh, PA
Penrose, James F. ....New York, NY
Penrose, James W. ....Carson City, NV
Penrose, John F. ....San Francisco, CA
Penrose, Steven D. ....Salinas, CA
Penrose, William L. ....St. Petersburg, FL
Penry, George A. ....Omaha, NE
Penry, J. Anthony ....Raleigh, NC
Penry, J. Rodwell, Jr. ....Lexington, NC
Penry, Phyllis S. ....Lexington, NC
Penry-Williams, Susan J. ....New York, NY
Pensa, Marianne S. ....New Orleans, LA
Pensabene, Judith K. ....Fairfax, VA
Pensabene, Marc J. ....New York, NY
Pensabene, Michele F. ....Orangeburg, NY
Penserini, Daniel ....Sacramento, CA
Penshorn, Edward W. ....San Antonio, TX
Pensig, Paul A. ....Beverly Hills, CA
Pensinger, John ....Department of Justice, Office of Justice Programs, GV
Pensinger, Kathryn A. ....Tucson, AZ
Pensinger, Richard L. ....Nashville, TN
Penskar, Alan D. ....Flint, MI
Penskar, Mark H. ....San Francisco, CA
Penski, Anthony E. ....Boston, MA
Penski, Frank H. ....New York, NY
Penslar, Robin Levin ....Bloomington, IN
Penso, Marc Gentry, Law Office of
Los Angeles, CA
Penso, Sally Jo ....Vista, CA
Penson, Albert Craig ....Panama City, FL
Tallahassee, FL
Penson, Andrew S. ....New York, NY
Penson, Dominique A. ....New York, NY
Penson, Edward I. ....New York, NY
Penson, John L. ....Miami, FL
Penson, Lauren C. ....Forest Hills, NY
Penstein, Marvin H. ....Coram, NY
Pensyl, Claire E. ....Chicago, IL
Pensyl, Jon P. ....Fort Valley, GA
Pent, Michael R. ....San Diego, CA
Pentak, William J. ....Altamont, NY
Pentecost, Alexander J. ....Pittsburgh, PA
Pentecost, B. H. ....Knoxville, TN
Pentecost, Cayce L. ....Dresden, TN
Pentecost, James I. ....Jackson, TN
Pentecost, John P. ....Santa Ana, CA
Pentecost, Michael R. ....Dayton, OH
Pentecost, Ronald R. ....Lansing, MI
Pentecost, William B., Jr. ....Pittsburgh, PA
Pentelovitch, William Z.
Minneapolis, MN
Penterman, Lester L. ....Scottsdale, AZ
Penterman, Lester L., P.C. ....Scottsdale, AZ
Pentico, Julie M. ....Williamsport, PA
Penticuff, Mark T. ....Irvine, CA
Penticuff, Paul S. ....Kansas City, MO
Pentima, Vincent J. ....Philadelphia, PA
Pentis, Carl J. ....Los Angeles, CA
Pentis, Charles J., Jr. ....Chelsea, MA
Pentiuk, Couvreur & Kobiljak, P.C.
Detroit, MI
Monroe, MI
Taylor, MI
Pentiuk, Randall A. ....Taylor, MI
Pentkowski, David H. ....Clifton Park, NY
Pentkowski, Pastore & Freestone
Clifton Park, NY
Pentland, David L. ....St. Louis, MO
Pentland, Richard J. ....Worcester, MA
Pentlarge, James B. ....Anchorage, AK
Pentlarge, Joel ....Ware, MA
Pentolino, Angelo A. ....Pigeon, MI
Penton, Janis S. ....Los Angeles, CA
Penton, John S., Jr. ....Pensacola, FL
Penton, Patricia Cowen ....Metairie, LA
Penton, Simeon F. ....Montgomery, AL
Penton, Wheeler & Spring, L.C.
Pensacola, FL
Covington, LA
Pentoney, Howard A. ....Eureka, CA
Pentoney, Stephen L. ....Los Angeles, CA
Pentony, Kenneth R. ....Toms River, NJ
Pentony, Peter Ashby ....Charles Town, WV
Pentore, Richard H. ....Kensington, CT
Penttila, Jane Eileen ....Cleveland, OH
Pentuic, Carol M. ....Rock Island, IL
Pentz, Ada R. ....Los Angeles, CA
Pentz, Chris A. ....Clearfield, PA
Pentz, John J., Jr. ....Stroudsburg, PA
Pentz, Martin C. ....Boston, MA
Pentz, Matthew A. ....Niles, OH
Pentz, Peter A. ....Erie, PA
Pentz, Ronald A. ....Bloomfield Hills, MI
Pentz, Stephen I. ....Seattle, WA
Pentz, William H. ....Horsham, PA
Penuel, Stephen G. ....La Habra, CA
Penuela, Marlene Rose ....Walnut Creek, CA
Penuela, Roy ....Sylmar, CA
Penwell, C. Bennett ....Whitewater, WI
Penwell, J. David ....Bozeman, MT
Penwell, Scott C. ....Harrisburg, PA
Penwell, Tonya L. ....Vancouver, WA
Penwell, Wm. Christopher
Minneapolis, MN
Penz, Janet A. ....Washington, DC
Penza, Jill ....West Simsbury, CT
Penza, Joseph F., Jr. ....Warwick, RI
Penza, Robert A. ....Wilmington, DE
Penza, Robert L. ....Livingston, NJ
Penzato, Allison Hopkins ....Metairie, LA
Penzato, Frank J. ....Taylor, MI
Penzel, Arthur L. ....New Rochelle, NY
Penzel, Markus L. ....Boston, MA
Penzell, Kris E. ....Miami Beach, FL
Penzer, Abraham M. ....Lakewood, NJ
Penzer, Eric W. ....Uniondale, NY
Penzer, Mark ....Hialeah, FL
Penzer, Michèle O. ....New York, NY
Penzien, Bernard P. ....Imlay City, MI
Penzien, Eugene C. ....Auburn, MI
Peo, Ernest R. (Rick), III ....Lincoln, NE
Peoples, Aunna L. ....Kansas City, MO
Peoples, A. V., III ....Oklahoma City, OK
Peoples, Brian ....Cedar Knolls, NJ
Peoples, Charles W., Jr. ....Huntington, WV
Peoples, Donald A. ....Helena, MT
Peoples, Elizabeth Lancaster ....Portland, ME
Peoples, Howell N. ....Chattanooga, TN
Peoples, Hugh H. ....Mount Airy, NC
Peoples, John F. ....Broomall, PA
Peoples, John T. ....Red Bank, NJ
Peoples, Linda Auger ....Florham Park, NJ
Peoples, Mark Alan ....Little Rock, AR
Peoples, Richard R. ....San Jose, CA
Peoples, Sean M. ....Hartford, CT
Peoples, Thomas G., Jr. ....Hollidaysburg, PA
Peoples, Veo, Jr. ....St. Louis, MO
Peoples, William R. ....Carrollton, TX
Peoples, Zenobia J. ....Richmond, VA
Pepe, Christopher J. ....New York, NY
Pepe, David P. ....Woodbridge, NJ
Pepe, Dean G. ....Daytona Beach, FL
Pepe, Gregory J. ....New Haven, CT
Pepe & Hazard LLP ....Bridgeport, CT
Hartford, CT
New Haven, CT
Southport, CT
Boston, MA
Pepe, Joan S. ....Norcross, GA
Pepe, Liisa Beth L'Huillier ....Roseland, NJ
Pepe, Louis R. ....Hartford, CT
Pepe & Nemire, P.A. ....Coral Gables, FL
Pepe, Pasquale ....Ansonia, CT
Pepe, Raymond P. ....Harrisburg, PA
Pepe, Russell A. ....Hackensack, NJ
Pepe, Stephen A. ....Tuckerton, NJ
Pepe, Stephen P. ....Los Angeles, CA
Newport Beach, CA
Pepe, Steven ....New York, NY
Pepe, Steven D. ....Ann Arbor, MI
Pepe, Steven J. ....New York, NY
Pepe, Thomas F. ....Coral Gables, FL

Pepe, Valerie ... Moorestown, NJ
Pepek, John E. ... West Springfield, MA
Pepek, Michael J. ... Los Angeles, CA
Pepelnjak, Anna M. ... Milwaukee, WI
Peper, Christian B. ... St. Louis, MO
Peper, Christian B., Jr. ... St. Louis, MO
Peper, Edmund G. ... Napoleon, OH
Peper, Graham B. ... Denver, CO
Peper, John H. ... Houston, TX
Peper Law Firm ... Napoleon, OH
Peper, Margaret E. ... Denver, CO
Peper, Martin, Jensen, Maichel and Hetlage
Belleville, IL
St. Louis, MO
Peper, Richard C., Jr. ... Jacksonville, FL
Pepe-Robbins, Suzanne Marie
Stamford, CT
Peperone, E. Joseph ... Williamsville, NY
Pepi, Jennifer ... Winthrop, MA
Pepi, Lora C. ... Boston, MA
Pepicelli, Alan L. ... Meadville, PA
Pepicelli, Youngs and Youngs P.C.
Meadville, PA
Pepich, Steven W. ... San Diego, CA
Pepin, Alfred L., Jr. ... San Francisco, CA
Pepin, Andrew G. ... Newport, VT
Pepin, Arthur W. ... Haddonfield, NJ
Pepin, Gerald N. ... New Bedford, MA
Pepin, Joan M. ... Department of Justice, Environment and Natural Resources Division, GV
Pepin, Michael K. ... Wallace, MI
Pepin, Rebecca M. ... Longmont, CO
Pepin, Richard G., Jr. ... Minneapolis, MN
Pepin, Robert W. ... Denver, CO
Pepin, Suzanne J. ... Minneapolis, MN
Pepino, Ralph W. ... Flagstaff, AZ
Pepinsky, Eugene E., Jr. ... Harrisburg, PA
Pepinsky, Harold E. ... Bloomington, IN
Pepitone, Paul C. ... Baton Rouge, LA
Pepitone, Quinn Jo Ann
Yorktown Heights, NY
Pepitone, Susan R. ... New York, NY
Pepitone & Trosclair ... Baton Rouge, LA
Pepka & Balzer ... St. Louis, MO
Pepka, Gene R. ... St. Louis, MO
Pepka, William A., Jr. ... Oxford, MA
Pepke, Michael T. ... Milwaukee, WI
Pepkin, Cari E. ... New York, NY
Peplau, Karl F. ... Eau Claire, WI
Pepler, Frank T. ... San Francisco, CA
Peplinski, John J. ... New York, NY
Peplow, Gary M. ... Peoria, IL
Peplowski, Gerard ... Detroit, MI
Peplowski, Joseph C. ... Beverly, MA
Pepmeyer, John T. ... Galesburg, IL
Pepmeyer & Pepmeyer, P.C. ... Galesburg, IL
Pepmeyer, Thomas L. ... Galesburg, IL
Peppard, Andrew B. ... Fall River, MA
Peppard and Littman ... Fall River, MA
Peppard, Joan S. ... Miami, FL
Peppard, Patricia ... Littleton, CO
Peppard, Ralph E. ... Omaha, NE
Peppard, Terry F. ... Madison, WI
Peppe, Richard R. ... Pembroke, NH
Peppe, Ronald W., II ... Point of Rocks, MD
Peppe, Vincent H. ... Nashville, TN
Peppel, Gomes & MacIntosh, P.C.
Memphis, TN
Peppel, Howard R. ... Memphis, TN
Peppelman, Raymond J., Jr. ... Media, PA
Philadelphia, PA
Pepper, Alan L., (A Professional Corporation) ... Los Angeles, CA
Pepper, Allan M. ... New York, NY
Pepper, Amelia S. ... Washington, DC
Pepper, Andrew L. ... Honolulu, HI
Pepper, Anthony M. ... Hartford, CT
Pepper, Beth ... Baltimore, MD
Pepper & Corazzini, L.L.P.
Washington, DC
Pepper, Daniel A. ... Iselin, NJ
Pepper, David C. ... Brooklyn, NY
Pepper, David E. ... Oklahoma City, OK
Pepper, Dixie L. ... Nashville, TN
Pepper, Duke ... Harrisburg, PA
Pepper, Elyse ... New York, NY
Pepper, Eugene ... Denver, CO
Pepper, Frederick W. ... Uniondale, NY
Pepper, Gordon, Breen & Weinberg, P.C.
Voorhees, NJ
Norristown, PA
Philadelphia, PA
Pepper, H. Harris, Jr. ... Bowling Green, KY
Pepper Hamilton LLP ... Wilmington, DE
Washington, DC
Detroit, MI
Cherry Hill, NJ
New York, NY
Berwyn, PA
Harrisburg, PA
Philadelphia, PA
Pittsburgh, PA
Pepper, J. Ross ... Nashville, TN
Pepper, Jack M. ... Plano, TX
Pepper, Jack M., P.C. ... Plano, TX
Pepper, Jack R., Jr. ... Brooksville, FL
Pepper, James A.
Federal Energy Regulatory Commission, Office of the General Counsel, GV
Pepper, Jeanne E. ... Newport Beach, CA
Pepper, Jeffrey D. ... Dearborn, MI
Pepper, Jeffrey W. ... Tallahassee, FL
Pepper, Joyce M. ... Chicago, IL
Pepper, L. Kimberly ... Beverly Hills, CA
Pepper, Lawrence, Jr. ... Hammonton, NJ
Vineland, NJ
Pepper, Lawrence S. ... Bingham Farms, MI
Pepper, Leonard ... Tallahassee, FL
Pepper, Leslie Wilson ... Oklahoma City, OK
Pepper, Letitia E. ... Los Angeles, CA
Pepper, Lisa R. ... Garden City, NY
Pepper, Louis A. H. ... Great Neck, NY
Pepper, Margaret A. ... New York, NY
Pepper, Marilyn G. ... Chalmette, LA
Pepper, Matthew Louis ... New Orleans, LA
Pepper, Michael A. ... New Haven, CT
Pepper, Murray S. ... Beverly Hills, CA
Pepper, Nason & Hayes ... Charleston, WV
Pepper, Nathan H. ... Galveston, TX
Pepper, Pamela ... Milwaukee, WI
Pepper & Pepper ... Tallahassee, FL
Pepper, Raymond ... San Diego, CA
Pepper, Richard H. ... Lehigh Valley, PA
Pepper, Robert M., Jr. ... Riverside, CA
Pepper & Rubin, P.C. ... Denver, CO
Pepper, Sheila F. ... New York, NY
Pepper, Steven A. ... Atlanta, GA
Pepper, T. Sergeant ... Philadelphia, PA
Pepper, Tasha K. ... Miami, FL
Pepper, Vincent A. ... Washington, DC
Pepper, W. Allen, Jr. ... Cleveland, MS
Pepper, W. Allen, Jr., P.A. ... Cleveland, MS
Pepper, William ... Ottumwa, IA
Pepper, William W. ... Charleston, WV
Pepperbloom, Richard J. ... Margate, FL
Pepperdine, Larry G. ... Topeka, KS
Pepperl, Donald J. ... Lincoln, NE
Pepperl & McMahon-Boies, Law Offices, P.C.
Lincoln, NE
Pepperman, Ann S. ... Williamsport, PA
Pepperman, Carla R. ... Leesburg, FL
Pepperman, Donald R. ... Los Angeles, CA
Pepperman, Lewis J. ... Princeton, NJ
Pepperman, Michael S. ... Philadelphia, PA
Pepperman, Richard C., II ... New York, NY
Pepperman, Steven C. ... New York, NY
Pepperman, Walter L., II ... Oquossoc, ME
Pepperney, Kenneth R. ... Pittsburgh, PA
Peppers, Jeffrey D. ... San Antonio, TX
Peppers, Jerry P. ... New York, NY
Peppers, Nicholas S. ... Rosemont, IL
Peppers, Samuel Asa, III ... Columbus, OH
Peppers, Sanford B. ... Riverview, MI
Pepper Sr., William W. ... Dover, DE
Peppet, Jennifer T. ... Boston, MA
Peppey, Brooke L. B. ... Winnetka, IL
Pepping, Jerry J. ... Silvis, IL
Pepple, Daniel P. ... Seattle, WA
Pepple, Donald J. ... Colorado Springs, CO
Pepple, Frederick D. ... Wapakoneta, OH
Pepple Johnson Cantu & Schmidt, PLLC
Seattle, WA
Pepple & Waggoner ... Cleveland, OH
Pepple, William C. ... Cleveland, OH
Peppler, Charles V. ... Pensacola, FL
Peppler, Dennis A. ... Harper Woods, MI
Peppler, Donald W., Jr. ... Freehold, NJ
Peppler, Laurence H. ... Mount Clemens, MI
Peppler, Laurence H., & Associates, P.C., A Prof. Corp ... Detroit, MI
Mount Clemens, MI
Peppler, Lori A. ... Sault Ste. Marie, MI
Peppler, Thomas A., P.C. ... Phoenix, AZ
Peppler, Thomas R. ... Oviedo, FL
Pepples, Ernest C., Jr. ... Louisville, KY
Pepples, Ronald J. ... Parkersburg, IA
Peppy, Renee V. ... Heathrow, FL
Pepyne, Edward W. ... Ashfield, MA
Pepyne, Edward W., Jr. ... Greenfield, MA
Pepyne, Edward W., P.C. ... Ashfield, MA
Pepys, Mark B. ... Long Beach, CA
Pequignot, Margot ... Largo, FL
Pequignot, Margot, P.A., Law Office
Clearwater, FL
Largo, FL
Pequignot, Stanley E. ... Warsaw, IN
Pera, David W. ... Merrillville, IN
Pera, John R. ... Merrillville, IN
Pera, Lonnie Anne ... Washington, DC
Pera, Lucian T. ... Memphis, TN
Pera, Marc G. ... Dayton, OH
Pera, Thomas P. ... Memphis, TN
Perabo, Fred H. ... St. Louis, MO
Peracca, Roland M., Jr. ... San Juan, PR
Peracchio, John R. ... Harper Woods, MI
Perachi, Paul E. ... Pittsfield, MA
Peradotto, Erin M. ... Buffalo, NY
Peraertz, Louis E. ... Department of Justice, Civil Rights Division, GV
Peragine, Frank J. ... New Orleans, LA
Peragine, Paul F. ... New York, NY
Peraic, Tomislav (Tom) ... San Francisco, CA
Peraica, Anthony J., (P.C.) ... Chicago, IL
Peraino, Vito C. ... Los Angeles, CA
Perakis, Christine V. ... Santa Monica, CA
Perakis, Harold A. ... Sterling Heights, MI
Perakis, Monica M. ... Daytona Beach, FL
Perakis, Stefanie Margaret ... Detroit, MI
Perakos, Peter G., II ... Hartford, CT
Perakos & Zitser, P.C. ... Hartford, CT
Peral, Enrique ... San Juan, PR
Peraldo, Jeffrey K. ... Greensboro, NC
Perales, Gabriel, Jr. ... Richardson, TX
Perales, Michael A. ... Denver, CO
Perales, Nina ... San Antonio, TX
Perales, Paul S. ... Denver, CO
Perales, Ralph ... Atlanta, GA
Peralez, Gil P. ... McAllen, TX
Peralez, Ilene ... Edinburg, TX
Peralez, Ilene S. ... McAllen, TX
Peralta, Armando ... El Paso, TX
Peralta, Gilligan & Vitali ... Lynn, MA
Peralta, John A. ... Austin, TX
Peralta, Katja Dunbar ... Greenville, SC
Peralta, Montgomery Suzuki
San Francisco, CA
Peralta, Nelson L. ... Minneapolis, MN
Peralta, Paul J. ... South Bend, IN
Peralta, Salvador J. ... Denver, CO
Peraner-Sweet, Andrea ... Boston, MA
Peranteau, Mary Elizabeth
Milwaukee, WI
Peranteau, Patrick T. ... San Antonio, TX
Perantie, Carol A. ... New Port Richey, FL
Perantinides & Nolan Co., L.P.A.
Akron, OH
Cleveland, OH
Perantinides, Paul G. ... Akron, OH
Perasso, Claude D. ... San Francisco, CA
Peratis, Kathleen ... New York, NY
Peratis, Kathleen, P.C. ... New York, NY
Peraza, Angie M. ... Metairie, LA
Peraza, Frank J. ... New York, NY
Peraza, Lisa M. ... Albany, NY
Perazich, John ... Washington, DC
Perazich, John ... Rockville, MD
Perbix, James L. ... Havana, IL
Perbix, Michael ... Anaheim, CA
Perbix and Morgan ... Havana, IL
Perbix, Steven W. ... Decatur, IL
Perbohner, Julene M. ... Crystal Lake, IL
Percario, Michael A. ... New Brunswick, NJ
Perce, Bruce F. ... Chicago, IL
Perce, Legrand W., III ... Bedford, PA
Perceful, Bill R. ... Pocola, OK
Percell, Dennis W. ... Eugene, OR
Percell, Marion, (Ms.) ... Newark, NJ
Percello, Louis J. ... Yorktown Heights, NY
Percely, Alan S. ... Houston, TX
Perch, Barry J. ... Lehigh Acres, FL
Perch and Hill, P.A. ... Fort Myers, FL
Lehigh Acres, FL
Perchem, Costa ... Chester, NJ
Perchick, Mark I. ... Cleveland, OH
Perchik, Jerrold R. ... Louisville, KY
Perciaccante, Marianne
Federal Labor Relations Authority, Authority Member Staff, GV
Perciballi, Henry P. ... Williamsport, PA
Percifull, Mary B. ... Boston, MA
Percilla, Del, Jr. ... Albany, GA
Percio, David R. ... Westlake, OH
Percio, Joseph M. ... Rocky River, OH
Percival, Albert E., III ... Austin, TX
Percival, Ana C. ... West Palm Beach, FL
Percival, Cindy J. ... Oklahoma City, OK
Percival, Donald E. ... Seattle, WA
Percival, James L. ... Norman, OK
Percival, James R. ... Irvine, CA
Percival, John F. ... Oklahoma City, OK
Percival, Mark R. ... Massillon, OH
Percival, Peter C. ... Des Moines, IA
Percival, Richard E. ... North Bend, WA
Percival, Robert V. ... Baltimore, MD
Perconti, John J. ... Chicago, IL
Percy, Billups P. ... New Orleans, LA
Percy, E. Farish ... Oxford, MS
Percy, J. Michael ... Alexandria, LA
Percy, James D. ... South Windsor, CT
Percy, Jerry G. ... Denver, CO
Percy, John H. ... St. Louis, MO
Percy, John R. ... Sykesville, MD
Percy, Linda Eve ... Timonium, MD
Percy, Michael D. ... Oxnard, CA
Simi Valley, CA
Percy, Michelle Palmer ... Lead, SD
Percy, Pujol & Wall ... Baton Rouge, LA
Donaldsonville, LA
Gonzales, LA
Percy, Robert J. ... Hartford, CT
Percy, Robert Ryland, III
Baton Rouge, LA
Gonzales, LA
Percy, Smith, Foote & Gadel
Alexandria, LA
Percy, Terry V. ... Miami, FL
Percy, Thomas J. ... Taunton, MA
Percy, Thomas J., P.C. ... Taunton, MA
Percy, Valencia E. ... Tampa, FL
Perczak, Greg L. ... Denver, CO
Perczak, Mari K. ... Denver, CO
Perczek, Jacqueline ... Miami, FL
Perdian, Richard A. ... New York, NY
Perdigao, James G. ... New Orleans, LA
Perdion, Jason P. ... Cleveland, OH
Perdomo, Luis J. ... Coral Gables, FL
Perdomo, Michelle L.
North Miami Beach, FL
Perdomo, Saul Anthony ... Kenilworth, IL
Perdue, Allen Eugene, Jr. ... Birmingham, AL
Perdue, Beth A. ... Acton, MA
Perdue, Christine H. ... McLean, VA
Perdue, Clyde H., Jr. ... Rocky Mount, VA
Perdue, D. Wayne ... Prattville, AL
Perdue, Dale C. ... Pittsburgh, PA
Perdue, Dale K. ... Columbus, OH
Perdue, David G. ... Winchester, KY
Perdue, David K. ... Washington, DC
Perdue, Edward P. ... Grand Rapids, MI
Perdue, Elizabeth S. ... Chicago, IL
Perdue, Herman E. ... Salisbury, MD
Perdue, Howard W. ... Arlington, TX
Perdue, Jacob C., Jr. ... Phenix City, AL
Perdue, Jane Adams ... Pearl, MS
Perdue, Jim M. ... Houston, TX
Perdue, Jim M., Jr. ... Houston, TX
Perdue, K. Alan ... Charleston, WV
Perdue, Lance D. ... Portland, OR
Perdue Law Firm, The, L.L.P.
Houston, TX
Perdue, Mark D. ... Dallas, TX
Perdue, Michael G. ... Carlsbad, CA
Perdue, Nicole ... Houston, TX
Perdue, Pamela D. ... St. Louis, MO
Perdue, Paul R. ... San Francisco, CA
Perdue, Randall T. ... Staunton, VA
Perdue, Rayne, White & Heidt, P.A.
Ocean City, MD
Salisbury, MD
Perdue, Rhodes ... Atlanta, GA
Perdue, Roderick Burke ... Wetumpka, AL
Perdue, Sandra Rider ... Houston, TX
Perdue, Stanley E. ... Spokane, WA
Perdue, Wendy Collins ... Washington, DC
Perdue, William Garrett Roberts
Department of the Navy, Office of the Judge Advocate General, GV
Pere, John G. ... Akron, OH
Perea, Juan F. ... Boston, MA
Perea, Kenneth A. ... Los Angeles, CA
Perea, Paul F. ... Houston, TX
Perea, Valerie J. ... Alexandria, VA
Perednia, Julia Hall ... Staten Island, NY
Perednia, Richard W. ... Spokane, WA
Perednia, Richard W., P.S., Inc.
Spokane, WA
Perego, Charles F. ... Pittsburgh, PA
Peregord, Jennifer J. Stan ... Detroit, MI
Peregoy, Kathleen M. ... Newark, NJ
Peregoy, Robert M. ... Washington, DC
Peregrin, Mark J. ... Oklahoma City, OK
Peregrin, Robert M. ... Oklahoma City, OK
Peregrine, Michael W. ... Chicago, IL
Peregrine, Moore W. ... Oak Park, IL
Peregrine, Robert B. ... Milwaukee, WI
Peregrine & Roth, S.C. ... Milwaukee, WI
Peregrine, Roy I. ... Wheaton, IL
Peregrine, Stime, Newman, Ritzman & Bruckner, Ltd. ... Wheaton, IL
Pereira, Andres C. ... Houston, TX
Pereira, Christoph A. ... New York, NY
Pereira, Elizabeth A. ... Tampa, FL
Pereira, Ivy M. ... Tampa, FL
Pereira, John ... Lawton, OK
Pereira, John David ... Cameron Park, CA
Pereira, John M. ... Malden, MA
Pereira, John S. ... New York, NY
Pereira, Julio C. ... Westbury, NY
Pereira, Leslie A. ... Los Angeles, CA
Pereira, Maytee ... New York, NY
Pereira, Neal ... Visalia, CA
Pereira, Paul A. ... Sacramento, CA
Pereira, Philip A. ... Redwood City, CA
Pereira, Rita Gordon ... Boston, MA
Pereira, Sheryl Lynn ... San Francisco, CA
Pereira, Stephen F. ... West Bloomfield, MI
Pereira, Steven M. ... New York, NY
Pereira, Steven R. ... Fall River, MA
Pereira, Susan ... Portland, ME
Pereira, Thomas J. ... Farmington Hills, MI
Pereira, Thomas J., P.C. ... Detroit, MI
Farmington Hills, MI
Southfield, MI
Pereira-Santiago, Amado A. ... Ponce, PR
Pereiro, Francisco J. ... Chicago, IL
Perel, Andrew J. ... Newark, NJ
New York, NY
Perel, Erica G. ... Brooklyn, NY
Perel, Liza Gail ... Los Angeles, CA
Perel, Marshall ... Olympia Fields, IL
Perel, Nelson ... Buffalo, NY
Perel, Robert ... El Paso, TX
Perel, Rochelle G. ... New York, NY
Perel, Sabrina Hodges ... New York, NY
Perel, Stephen ... Houston, TX
Perel, Stephen, & Associates, P.C.
Houston, TX
Pereles, Edward A. ... Philadelphia, PA
Pereles, Joseph B. ... St. Louis, MO
Pereles, Susan M. ... Washington, DC
Perell, Edward A. ... New York, NY
Perella, Hanni C. ... San Francisco, CA
Perella, Marie L. ... Cleveland, OH
Perelli-Minetti, C. Robton ... Greenwich, CT
Perellis, Andrew H. ... Chicago, IL
Perellis, Florie Shertzer ... Northbrook, IL
Perello, Patricia M. ... Colorado Springs, CO
Perelman, Bruce ... Santa Monica, CA
Perelman, Charles R. ... Los Angeles, CA
Perelman, David S. ... Cleveland, OH
Perelman, Dell E. ... Philadelphia, PA
Perelman, Donald L. ... Philadelphia, PA
Perelman, Jane E. ... Houston, TX
Perelman, Jeffrey S. ... Glencoe, IL
Perelman, Mark S. ... San Francisco, CA
Perelman, Richard B. ... Los Angeles, CA
Perelman, Richard S. ... Philadelphia, PA
Perelmutter, Potash & Ginzberg, P.C.
Seymour, CT
Waterbury, CT
Perelson, Stephen J. ... Mill Valley, CA
Perelstein, Michael A. ... Minneapolis, MN
Perenchio, John Gardner ... Los Angeles, CA
Perenich, Carroll, Perenich, Avril & Caulfield, P.A. ... Clearwater, FL
Perenich, Gregory J. ... Clearwater, FL
Perenich, Guy N. ... Clearwater, FL
Perenich Law, Professional Association
Palm Harbor, FL
Perenich, Mark H. ... Clearwater, FL
Perenich, Terence A. ... Palm Harbor, FL
Perenich, Timothy B. ... Palm Harbor, FL
Perenich, Timothy B. ... Palm Harbor, FL
Pereno, August J. ... Hialeah, FL
Perentesis, John L. ... Detroit, MI
Pereos, C. Nicholas ... Reno, NV
Pereos, C. Nicholas, Ltd. ... Reno, NV
Pereplyotchik, Sergei Y. ... Brooklyn, NY
Perer, Alan H. ... Pittsburgh, PA
Perer, Diane W. ... Pittsburgh, PA

Perera, Lawrence T. ... Boston, MA
Perera, Piyasena C. ... San Francisco, CA
Perera-Riveroll, Mario ... McAllen, TX
Peres, Isaac H. ... Boston, MA
Peres, Javier S. ... San Francisco, CA
Peres, Leonard ... Scottsdale, AZ
Peresich, Ronald G. ... Biloxi, MS
Peresich, Stephen G. ... Biloxi, MS
Peress, Sasson David ... Wilmington, DE
Peret, Andrew R. ... Milwaukee, WI
Peretore, Frank ... Sparta, NJ
Peretore, Janis Migliorise ... Sparta, NJ
Peretore & Peretore ... Sparta, NJ
Perets-Kaner, Yael ... Sherman Oaks, CA
Peretti, Brian ... Washington, DC
Peretti, Gene G. ... Alameda, CA
Peretti, Robert A. ... Providence, RI
Peretz, Andrew B., P.A.
Fort Lauderdale, FL
New York, NY
Peretz, Avi S. ... Los Angeles, CA
Peretz, Ralph L. ... Encino, CA
Peretz, Steven I. ... Miami, FL
Perey, Ron, Law Office of ... Seattle, WA
Pereyda, Lorenzo A., Jr. ... Los Angeles, CA
Perez, A. Alex ... Austin, TX
Perez, Albert ... Fort Worth, TX
Perez, Albert, Jr. ... Covina, CA
Perez, Alex T. ... Irwindale, CA
Perez, Alfonso J. ... Miami, FL
Perez, Alfred A. ... Campbell, CA
Perez, Alfredo R. ... Houston, TX
Perez, Alina M. ... Miami Beach, FL
Perez, Angel Modesto ... Tarrytown, NY
Perez, Anthony M. ... Sacramento, CA
Perez, Antonio F. ... Washington, DC
Perez, Armando A. ... Miami, FL
Perez, Arnaldo ... Miami, FL
Perez, Assunta DiBiase ... Hull, MA
Perez, Barbara ... Miami, FL
Perez, Benjamin ... Washington, DC
Pérez, Bertin Henry ... Washington, DC
Perez, Brenda Eileen ... El Paso, TX
Pérez, Carlos E. Aguilar ... San Juan, PR
Perez, Carlos R. ... Los Angeles, CA
Perez, Carmen I. ... El Paso, TX
Perez, Carmenelisa ... Malden, MA
Perez, Carol Lonergan ... Whitehouse, NJ
Perez, Carole C. ... Rockville, MD
Rockville, MD
Swanton, MD
Perez, Cesar Alexander ... New York, NY
Perez, Cesar R. ... Edinburg, TX
Perez, Chalin O. ... Braithwaite, LA
Perez, Christa D. ... Los Angeles, CA
Perez, Christina R.
Federal Trade Commission,
Bureau of Competition, GV
Perez, Christopher G. ... Bernalillo, NM
Perez, Cora ... Phoenix, AZ
Perez, Daniel F. ... Dallas, TX
Perez, Daniel, Jr. ... Houston, TX
Perez, Dario ... New York, NY
Perez, Dario A. ... Miami, FL
Perez, David A., II ... Troy, MI
Perez, David D. ... Santa Monica, CA
Perez, David H. ... Sterling Heights, MI
Perez, David W. ... Milwaukee, WI
Perez & Davis ... Chicago, IL
Perez, Dennis ... Beverly Hills, CA
Perez, Dinah ... Los Angeles, CA
Perez, Edith R. ... Los Angeles, CA
Perez, Enrique ... Chicago, IL
Perez, Ernesto J. ... West Sacramento, CA
Perez, Ernesto R. ... Miami, FL
Perez, Eustorgio ... Laredo, TX
Perez, Fernando, III ... Tampa, FL
Perez, Flora R. ... Fort Lauderdale, FL
Perez, Francisco H. ... Baton Rouge, LA
Pérez, Frank E. ... Brownsville, TX
Perez, Franklyn ... New York, NY
Perez, George H. ... Bernalillo, NM
Perez, Gerald Anthony ... Tampa, FL
Perez, Gilbert R. ... Rochester, NY
Perez Gonzalez, Freddie, & Assoc.
San Juan, PR
Perez, Gonzalo, Jr. ... Miami, FL
Perez, Gonzalo, Jr., P.A. ... Miami, FL
Perez, Goran & Rodriguez, P.A. ... Miami, FL
Perez, Gustavo J. ... Newark, NJ
Perez, H. Hugo ... Arlington, VA
Perez, H. A. Tico ... Orlando, FL
Perez, Hector ... San Juan, PR
Perez, Hector A. ... Orlando, FL
Perez, Hector C. ... Los Angeles, CA
Perez, Ignacio ... Jersey City, NJ
Perez, Ismael D. ... San Jose, CA
Perez, Israel, Jr. ... Miami, FL
Perez, James O. ... Fullerton, CA
Perez, James T. ... Beverly Hills, CA
Perez, Jay G ... Columbus, OH
Perez, Jeanie Branham ... Orlando, FL
Perez, Jesus D. ... Van Nuys, CA
Perez, Jesus R. ... Van Nuys, CA
Perez, Jonathan David ... Little Rock, AR
Perez, Jose I. ... Miami, FL
Perez, Jose Luis ... Brooklyn, NY
Perez, Jose Rafael, Jr. ... Houston, TX
Perez, Joseph J. ... Portsmouth, VA
Perez, Joseph L. ... Lafayette, LA
Perez, Joseph M. ... Washington, DC
Perez, Juan C. ... Miami Beach, FL
Perez, Juan C. ... Cherry Hill, NJ
Pérez, Juan José G. ... Columbus, OH
Perez, Juan Ramon ... Los Angeles, CA
Perez, Julie Cobb ... San Antonio, TX
Perez, Karen A. ... Troy, MI
Perez, Kenneth A. ... Irving, TX
Perez, Kent J. ... Tallahassee, FL
Perez, Kevin P. ... Denver, CO
Perez, Lane B. ... Covington, LA
Metairie, LA
Perez Law Firm, The, Co., L.P.A.
Cincinnati, OH
Perez, Lennie F. ... Baton Rouge, LA
Perez, Lionel ... McAllen, TX
Perez, Lisa A. ... West Orange, NJ
Perez, Lori Peterson
Rio Grande City, TX
Perez, Louis A., Jr. ... Philadelphia, PA
Perez, Louis A., Jr. ... San Angelo, TX
Perez, Louis J. ... Niagara Falls, NY
Perez, Louis J. ... Pawtucket, RI
Perez, Lucia Thompson ... Harlingen, TX
Perez, Luis A. ... Coral Gables, FL
Perez, Luis A. ... Miami, FL
Perez, Luis A. ... New Orleans, LA
Houston, TX
Perez, Luis A., P.A., Law Offices of
Miami, FL
Perez, Luis J. ... Miami, FL
Perez, Luis N. ... Miami, FL
Perez, Lydia ... New York, NY
Perez, Manuel ... Ontario, OR
Perez, Maria del Carmen
United States Postal Service,
Postal Inspection Service, GV
Perez, Maria Estella ... Brownsville, TX
Perez, Mario E. ... Greenville, NC
Perez, Mario J. ... Woodstock, IL
Perez & McNabb, A Professional Corporation ... Orinda, CA
Walnut Creek, CA
Perez, Melvyn J. ... Chalmette, LA
Perez, Michael A.
Department of Justice, GV
Perez, Michael A., Law Office of
Chicago, IL
Perez, Michael J. ... San Diego, CA
Perez, Michael J. ... Hagåtña, GU
Perez, Michael S. ... Houston, TX
Perez, Michelle ... Brooklyn, NY
Perez, Milagros ... New York, NY
Perez, Monique V. ... Miami, FL
Perez, Nancy ... West Palm Beach, FL
Perez, Nidia ... Miami, FL
Perez, Omar, Jr. ... Miami, FL
Perez, Orestes ... Miami, FL
Miami, FL
Perez, Orestes, P.A. ... Miami, FL
Perez, Orlando ... Tampa, FL
Perez, Patricia M. ... New York, NY
Perez, Paul G. ... Houston, TX
Perez, Paul I. ... Jacksonville, FL
Perez, Plinio ... Wallingford, CT
Perez, Rafael ... Morristown, NJ
Perez, Rafael A. ... Miami, FL
Perez, Ralph ... Torrance, CA
Perez, Ramona Godoy ... Los Angeles, CA
Perez, Raquel G. ... San Antonio, TX
Pérez, Raul ... Los Angeles, CA
Perez, Raymond W. ... Marysville, OH
Perez, Renato ... Miami, FL
Perez, Rey ... San Antonio, TX
Perez, Ricardo A. ... Ontario, CA
Perez, Richard A. ... Miami, FL
Perez, Richard J. ... Willoughby, OH
Perez, Richard L. ... Orinda, CA
Perez, Robert ... New York, NY
Perez, Robert A. ... Kirkland, WA
Perez, Robert Armand, Sr.
Cincinnati, OH
Perez, Robert C. ... San Francisco, CA
Perez, Robert H. ... San Francisco, CA
Perez, Robert J. ... San Antonio, TX
Perez, Roger A. ... San Antonio, TX
Perez, Romeo R. ... Edinburg, TX
Perez, Ronald E. ... Los Angeles, CA
Perez, Rose Helen ... Fremont, CA
Perez, Ruben ... Corpus Christi, TX
Perez, Salinas & Canas ... Fort Worth, TX
Pérez, Sigifredo, III ... Laredo, TX
Perez, Silvia T. ... Fort Lauderdale, FL
Perez, Sonia ... Bronx, NY
Perez, T. Christine ... Fort Lauderdale, FL
Tampa, FL
West Palm Beach, FL
Perez, Terilynn ... Menlo Park, CA
Perez, Terri A. ... San Diego, CA
Perez, Una M. ... Towson, MD
Pérez & Urbis, A Professional Corporation
Brownsville, TX
Perez, Vicente S. ... Glendale, CA
Perez, Victor J. ... Woodcliff Lake, NJ
Perez, Victor Manuel ... Visalia, CA
Perez, Vincent T. ... Hagåtña, GU
Perez, William C. ... Dallas, TX
Perez-Abreu, Javier ... Coral Gables, FL
Perez-Albuerne, Carlos ... Boston, MA
Perez Andreu, Adaljisa ... San Juan, PR
Pérez-Bachs, Rafael ... San Juan, PR
Perez-Benitoa, Antonio J. ... Naples, FL
Perez-Benitoa, Antonio J., P.A.
Naples, FL
Perez-Cervera, Agustin A. ... Coral Gables, FL
Perez Colon, Fernando ... San Juan, PR
Pérez-Colon, Fernando A. ... San Juan, PR
Perez-Cruz, Marcos ... San Juan, PR
Perez Diaz, Jorge ... San Juan, PR
Perez-Dominguez, Nelson ... San Juan, PR
Pérez-Fowler, Carmina ... Baltimore, MD
Perez-Gimenez, Juan M. ... San Juan, PR
Perez-Giusti, Luis R. ... San Juan, PR
Perez Gonzalez, Cristina ... Los Angeles, CA
Perez-Gonzalez, Freddie ... San Juan, PR
Perez-Guerrero, Arturo ... San Juan, PR
Perez-Hernandez, Alberto J. ... San Juan, PR
Pérez-Hernández, José ... San Juan, PR
Perez-Jaqvez, Eridania ... New York, NY
Perez-Jimenez, Efrain ... Guaynabo, PR
Perez-Llorca, Carmen ... New York, NY
Perez Marrero, Plinio ... San Juan, PR
Peréz-Medrano, Juan ... Tucson, AZ
Perez-Mesa, Carlos D., Jr. ... Honolulu, HI
Perez-Orama, Arturo ... San Juan, PR
Pérez-Otero, Juan Carlos ... San Juan, PR
Perezous, Michael J. ... Lancaster, PA
Perez-Platt, Rebecca E. ... Palo Alto, CA
Perez-Posner, Sylvie ... Fort Lauderdale, FL
Perez-Quiñones, Maria Victoria
San Juan, PR
Perez-Roman, Edna E. ... San Juan, PR
Perez-Selsky, Gregorio A. ... Salem, OR
Perez-Serrano, Rebeca ... San Diego, CA
Perez Sosa, Ivan ... Arecibo, PR
Perez-Sotolongo, Michelle M.
Orlando, FL
Perez-Webel, Lizette ... Coral Gables, FL
Perfater, Paul S. ... Charleston, WV
Perfetti, David W. ... Cortland, NY
Perfetti, Heather Fae ... Caruthersville, MO
Perfetti, John P. ... New York, NY
Perfetti, Louise C. ... Miami, FL
Perfetto, Carlo M. ... Buffalo, NY
Perfetto, Louis A. ... New York, NY
Perfido, Ruth S. ... New York, NY
Pittsburgh, PA
Perfili, Michelle A. ... San Diego, CA
Perfilio, Joseph P. ... Hoboken, NJ
Perfilio & Marquet ... Hoboken, NJ
Perfit, Rosemary E. ... Tampa, FL
Perfrement, Lisa F. ... Denver, CO
Perfrement, Steven J. ... Denver, CO
Perga, Mary Ann S. ... Turtle Lake, WI
Pergament, Arthur Jay ... Melville, NY
Pergament, Heidi E. ... Minneapolis, MN
Pergament, Ira A. ... Poughkeepsie, NY
Wappingers Falls, NY
Pergament, Marc A. ... Garden City, NY
Pergament, Stuart P. ... Washington, DC
Pergande, Gerald W. ... Bay City, MI
Pergande, Joseph E. ... Bay City, MI
Pergande, K. William ... Irvine, CA
Pergande & Pergande ... Bay City, MI
Pergericht, Frances L. ... Chicago, IL
Pergerson, Donald D. ... Henderson, NC
Pergine, Gail Dimarco ... Philadelphia, PA
Pergola, Anthony O. ... Roseland, NJ
Pergola, Michael P. ... Washington, DC
Pergola, Philip ... Stoughton, MA
Pergolizzi, Frank J. ... Washington, DC
Pergolizzi, James J., Jr. ... Brooklyn, NY
Pergolizzi, Joseph V. ... Brooklyn, NY
Pergolizzi & Pergolizzi ... Brooklyn, NY
Pergolizzi, Stephen R. ... Brooklyn, NY
Pergram, Dennis L. ... Columbus, OH
Delaware, OH
Pergue, Charles ... New York, NY
Perhacs, Pablo ... New York, NY
Perhacs, Richard W. ... Erie, PA
Perhacs, Sheldon ... Birmingham, AL
Perhalla, Rudolph F. ... Ironwood, MI
Perham, Nancy E. ... San Francisco, CA
Peri, John, Jr. ... Long Beach, NY
Peri, Steven B. ... Maplewood, NJ
New York, NY
Peri & Stewart, L.L.C. ... Maplewood, NJ
New York, NY
Periard, Mark B. ... Grand Rapids, MI
Periard, Ronald W. ... Mattoon, IL
Perica, Bob L. ... Alton, IL
Perica, Jacob ... Warren, MI
Perica, Nicholas M. ... Scottsdale, AZ
Pericak, John G. ... Rochester, NY
Pericak, William C. ... Albany, NY
Perich, James N. ... Pittsburgh, PA
Perich, S. Ana ... Chicago, IL
Perich, Shelly A. ... Mount Vernon, IL
Perich, Thomas J. ... Houston, TX
Periconi, James J. ... New York, NY
Perides-Gross, Maria H. ... Albuquerque, NM
Peries, Rohan ... Palo Alto, CA
Perigard, Gregory P. ... Fairfax, VA
Perigo, Jerry E. ... Tulsa, OK
Perigo, Timothy Wayne ... Neosho, MO
Periharos Spiliopoulos, Maria L.
Fort Lauderdale, FL
Perikles, John N. ... Miami, FL
Perillat, Alexis J. ... Hillsborough, CA
Perillat, Alexis J., Jr. ... San Francisco, CA
Perille, Christine Ciabotti ... Chicago, IL
Perilli, Marc A. ... Rolling Meadows, IL
Perillo, Anna Mae ... Red Bank, NJ
Perillo, Anne M. ... Wilmington, DE
Perillo, Danl. R. ... Cleveland, OH
Perillo, Frank R. ... Palo Alto, CA
Andover, MA
Perillo, Frederick ... Milwaukee, WI
Perillo, Joseph A. ... Houston, TX
Perillo, Joseph M., Jr. ... New York, NY
Perillo, Kathleen M. ... Philadelphia, PA
Perillo, Mary Scalise ... Albany, NY
Perillo, Michael J., Jr. ... Waukegan, IL
Perillo, Michele T. ... Boston, MA
Perillo, Robert J. ... Bronx, NY
Perillo, Robert R. ... Orangeburg, NY
Perillo, Salvatore ... Atlantic City, NJ
Perillo, Salvatore J. ... Calhoun, GA
Perilloux, Aimee ... Dallas, TX
Perilloux, Roy J. ... Jackson, MS
Perilman, J. Bryan ... Greenbelt, MD
Perilstein, Joel P. ... Cherry Hill, NJ
Blue Bell, PA
Perilstein, Joel P. ... Philadelphia, PA
Periman, Carl ... Amarillo, TX
Periman, Deborah K. ... Anchorage, AK
Perin, Charles H., Jr. ... Columbus, OH
Perin, James P. ... Bloomington, IN
Perin, Martha H. ... Cincinnati, OH
Perin, Susan Goldfaden ... Houston, TX
Perington, Lamont Lee ... Geneva, IL
Perini, Cindy J. ... Houston, TX
Perini, Daniel T. ... Denver, CO
Perini, David B. ... Framingham, MA
Perini & Hoerger ... Hauppauge, NY
Perini, Kimberly S. ... Washington, DC
Perini, Raymond G. ... Hauppauge, NY
Perini, Victor J., Jr. ... Washington, DC
Perini, Vincent Walker ... Dallas, TX
Perini, Vincent Walker, P.C. ... Dallas, TX
Perini-Hegarty, Stephanie Ann ... Boston, MA
Perino, Michael A. ... Jamaica, NY
Perino, Michael E. ... Madison, WI
Periolat, John R. ... Minneapolis, MN
Periolat, Mary K. ... Chicago, IL
Perisho, Joel T. ... Stockton, CA
Perisho, Russell L. ... Seattle, WA
Perisich, John M. ... Lake Forest, CA
Perisin, Mary C. ... Chicago, IL
Perison, E. A. ... Rancho Palos Verdes, CA
Perison, Eben Paul ... Los Angeles, CA
Perisutti, Stephen J. ... Cleveland, OH
Perito, James J. ... New Haven, CT
Perito, Mahlia L. ... Miami, FL
Perito, Paul L. ... Washington, DC
Peritore, Michael A. ... Sacramento, CA
Peritz, Loreen ... New York, NY
Peritz, Marc A. ... Charlottesville, VA
Peritz, Revelle G. ... Chicago, IL
Peritz, Rudolph J. ... New York, NY
Perivolidis, Arthur C. ... Chicago, IL
Perk, Daniel P. ... Kalamazoo, MI
Perk, Ralph J., Jr. ... Cleveland, OH
Perk, Robert H. ... Buffalo, NY
Perka, Daniel J. ... Washington, DC
Perka, Suzanne Mackall ... Berryville, VA
Perkal, Donald W. ... Department of Defense,
Defense Legal Services Agency, GV
Perkal, Lee ... Beverly Hills, CA
Perkal, M. Jay ... Skokie, IL
Perkal, Richard L. ... Washington, DC
Perkal, Ross B. ... Albuquerque, NM
Perkaus, Robt. P. ... Wilmette, IL
Perkel, Bertram ... New York, NY
Perkel, Felix ... Ridgewood, NY
Perkel, Jonathan E. ... New York, NY
Perkel, Morris A. ... Teaneck, NJ
Perkerson, Barbara J. ... Dallas, TX
Perkerson, Edgar J., III ... Lithonia, GA
Perkerson, T. Robert ... Atlanta, GA
Perkes, Gregory T. ... Corpus Christi, TX
Perkes, Kenneth L.
Charlotte Amalie, St. Thomas, VI
Perkes, Lawrence A. ... Visalia, CA
Perkett, Christopher E.
South Burlington, VT
Perkiel, Mitchel H. ... New York, NY
Perkin & Associates ... Allentown, PA
Bethlehem, PA
Easton, PA
Perkin, Frank S., Jr.
Grosse Pointe Woods, MI
Perkin, Henry S. ... Allentown, PA
Perkin & Hosoda ... Honolulu, HI
Perkin, John Francis ... Honolulu, HI
Perkins, A. Michelle ... Shreveport, LA
Perkins, Alan C. ... San Francisco, CA
Perkins, Alan G. ... Sacramento, CA
Perkins, Alan J. ... Dallas, TX
Perkins, Albert Dashiell, IV
Montgomery, AL
Perkins, Albert G. ... White Plains, NY
Perkins, Alexander ... Seattle, WA
Perkins, Alfred H., Jr. ... Birmingham, AL
Perkins, Allyson L. ... Dallas, TX
Perkins, Alphonse B. ... Jacksonville, FL
Perkins, Andrew H. ... Washington, DC
Perkins, Ann R. ... Chicago, IL
Perkins, Ann-Margaret ... Carrollton, GA
Perkins, Anthony E. ... Portland, ME
Perkins, Arthur Val, P.C. ... Houston, TX
Perkins, Arthur W. ... Concord, NH
Perkins, Bascom T. ... Mount Pleasant, TX
Perkins, Benjamin G. ... Richmond, VA
Perkins, Blake ... New York, NY
Perkins, Bruce ... Austin, TX
Perkins, Bryan D. ... Dallas, TX
Perkins, Byron R. ... Birmingham, AL
Perkins, C. Jackson ... Birmingham, AL
Perkins, Carlisle E.
Securities and Exchange Commission,
Division of Enforcement, GV
Perkins, Carlton L., Jr. ... Houston, TX
Perkins, Carson D. ... Nashville, GA
Perkins, C. C. ... Carrollton, GA
Perkins, Cecilia A. ... Irvine, CA
Perkins, Charles B. ... Los Gatos, CA
Perkins, Charles E. ... San Francisco, CA
Perkins, Charles G. ... Macon, MS
Perkins, Charles H. ... St. Louis, MO
Perkins, Charles M. ... Georgetown, KY
Perkins, Charles R., Law Offices of
Memphis, TN
Perkins, Cherrie R. ... Wakefield, RI
Perkins, Cheryl F. ... Columbia, SC
Perkins, Christine L. ... Norwood, MA
Perkins, Christopher L. ... Richmond, VA
Perkins, Cindy Leadley
Saratoga Springs, NY
Perkins, Clayton M., Jr.
St. Francisville, LA
Perkins, Cliff ... Carrollton, GA

Perkins Coie LLP ... **Anchorage, AK**
Los Angeles, CA
Menlo Park, CA
San Francisco, CA
Santa Monica, CA
Denver, CO
Washington, DC
Boise, ID
Portland, OR
Bellevue, WA
Olympia, WA
Seattle, WA
Spokane, WA
Perkins, Courtney W. ... Kansas City, MO
Perkins, D. Kendall ... Sandy, UT
Perkins, Daniel C. ... Dallas, TX
Perkins, Daniel J. ... **Greenville, TX**
Perkins, Daniel W. ... Ames, IA
Perkins, Daren W. ... **Phoenix, AZ**
Perkins, David A. ... **San Diego, CA**
Perkins, David A. ... **Peoria, IL**
Perkins, David A. ... Detroit, MI
Perkins, David B. ... Louisville, KY
Perkins, David J. ... **Portland, ME**
Perkins, David L. ... **Fort Lauderdale, FL**
Perkins, David P. ... Shippensburg, PA
Perkins, David S. ... **Boise, ID**
Perkins, David W. ... Downey, CA
Perkins & Day, L.L.C. ... **Shreveport, LA**
Perkins, Dean Standish, Jr. ... Seattle, WA
Perkins, Dennis J. ... **Bellevue, WA**
Perkins, Dennis L. ... **Howell, MI**
Perkins, Dennis L., P.C. ... **Howell, MI**
Lansing, MI
Perkins, Djuna E. ... Boston, MA
Perkins, Donald D. ... Seattle, WA
Perkins, Donald H. ... Framingham, MA
Perkins, Donald J. ... Middle Village, NY
Perkins, Donald W. ... **Portland, ME**
Perkins, Donna Becker ... Dallas, TX
Perkins, Dosite H., Jr. ... Shreveport, LA
Perkins, Douglas A. ... **Irvine, CA**
Perkins, Douglas C. ... **Anchorage, AK**
Perkins, Drew A. ... **Casper, WY**
Perkins & Dunnegan ... **New York, NY**
Perkins, Dwight C. ... Lincoln, NE
Perkins, Edgar, Jr. ... De Quincy, LA
Perkins, Edward C. ... Bethlehem, PA
Perkins, Edward L. ... Bend, OR
Perkins, Edward L. ... **Media, PA**
Perkins, Elizabeth C. ... **Providence, RI**
Perkins, Elizabeth Eve ... **Lexington, KY**
Perkins, Ellen M. M.
Rolling Hills Estates, CA
Perkins, Elvin D. ... Emporia, KS
Perkins, Eric C. ... **Richmond, VA**
Perkins, Eric M. ... Trenton, NJ
Perkins, Eric R. ... **Hackensack, NJ**
Perkins, F. Lee ... **Cartersville, GA**
Perkins, Francis E., Jr. ... **Boston, MA**
Perkins, Francis R. ... **Newark, NJ**
Perkins, Fred Blake ... **Emmetsburg, IA**
Perkins, Fred H. ... **New York, NY**
Perkins, Fred M., III ... **Little Rock, AR**
Perkins, G. Alan ... **Little Rock, AR**
Perkins, Gary B. ... Rochester Hills, MI
Perkins, Gary H. ... Fort Lauderdale, FL
Perkins, George C. ... South Dartmouth, MA
Perkins, George W. ... **Skowhegan, ME**
Perkins, Giles Gilpin ... **Birmingham, AL**
Perkins, Gregory W. ... **Vail, CO**
Perkins, G.S. Brant ... **Jonesboro, AR**
Perkins, Guy W. ... **Bluefield, WV**
Perkins, Hannah ... Washington, DC
Perkins, Happy R. ... **Louisville, KY**
Perkins, Harold W. ... Concord, NH
Perkins, Harriet E. ... **Philadelphia, PA**
Perkins, Harry, III ... **Des Moines, IA**
Perkins, Harry, Jr. ... Des Moines, IA
Perkins, Howard D., Jr. ... Tulsa, OK
Perkins, Howard R., Jr. ... **Andover, MA**
Perkins, J. Carter ... **Tavares, FL**
Perkins, Jack E. ... Department of Justice, Executive Office for Immigration Review, GV
Perkins, Jacob N. ... **Lanham, MD**
Perkins, James A. ... San Antonio, TX
Perkins, James A. ... **Yakima, WA**
Perkins, James A., P.C. ... San Antonio, TX
Perkins, James D. ... Liberty Lake, WA
Perkins, James H. ... **Fresno, CA**
Perkins, James I. ... Rusk, TX
Perkins, James J. ... **Los Angeles, CA**
Perkins, James K. ... **Los Angeles, CA**
Perkins, James L. ... Chicago, IL
Perkins, James W. ... **Boston, MA**
Perkins, James W. ... **New York, NY**
Perkins, Jan T. ... **Fresno, CA**
Perkins, Jane ... Baltimore, MD
Perkins, Jefferson ... **Chicago, IL**
Perkins, Jeffrey J. ... **Toledo, OH**
Perkins, Jennifer L. ... **Kansas City, MO**
Perkins, Jennifer S. ... **Washington, DC**
Perkins, Jerry F., Jr ... **Birmingham, AL**
Perkins, Joan ... Chicago, IL
Perkins, Joan Unger ... Atlanta, GA
Perkins, John A. ... **Boston, MA**
Perkins, John D. ... **Falls Church, VA**
Perkins, John H. ... Pittsburgh, PA
Perkins, John H., Jr. ... Bedford, NY
Perkins, John M. ... Fort Dodge, IA
Perkins, John R. ... **Des Moines, IA**
Perkins, John R. ... **Jefferson City, MO**
Perkins, John R. ... Youngstown, OH
Perkins, John R., Jr. ... **Columbus, OH**
Perkins, John S. ... San Jose, CA
Perkins, Jonathan N. ... Milford, CT
Perkins, Joseph J., Jr. ... **Anchorage, AK**
Perkins, Joseph L. ... Marshall, TX
Perkins, Joseph M., Jr. ... Columbus, IN
Perkins, Joseph T. ... **Albany, NY**
Perkins, Judith L. ... **Milwaukee, WI**
Perkins, Julia A. ... Hanover, MD
Perkins, Julia A. ... **Detroit, MI**
Perkins, Julia H. ... **Chicago, IL**
Perkins, Julie R. ... Boston, MA
Perkins, Karon E. ... Columbus, IN
Perkins, Kathleen L.Y. ... Chicago, IL
Perkins, Kathryn Bennett
Little Rock, AR
Perkins, Kelly ... Eagan, MN
Perkins, Kenneth D. ... Sewickley, PA
Perkins, Kenneth L., Jr. ... **Irvine, CA**
Perkins, Kevin M. ... Nashua, NH
Perkins, Kirk B. ... Bakersfield, CA
Perkins, Lanny E. ... Dallas, TX
Perkins Law Group ... **Lexington, KY**
Perkins Law Office ... Fort Dodge, IA
Perkins Law Office ... **Jefferson City, MO**
Perkins Law Office, L.L.C. ... Thayer, MO
Perkins, Lee B. ... **Atlanta, GA**
Perkins, Lee-Anne ... **Miami, FL**
Perkins, Leigh P. ... Boston, MA
Perkins, Leonard F. ... Arlington Heights, IL
Perkins, Linwood, Jr. ... Phoenix, AZ
Perkins, Lloyd W. ... Sherman, TX
Perkins, LouAnna C. ... Bucksport, ME
Perkins, Louis J. ... West Sacramento, CA
Perkins, Lynn L. ... **Howard, KS**
Perkins, Mahlon R. ... Dryden, NY
Perkins, Mahlon R., P.C. ... Dryden, NY
Perkins, Malcolm D. ... Boston, MA
Perkins, Mann & Everett ... **Fresno, CA**
Perkins, Mariette J. ... Laguna Niguel, CA
Perkins & Mario, P.C. ... Milford, CT
Perkins, Mark A. ... **Shreveport, LA**
Perkins, Mark D. ... Downers Grove, IL
Perkins, Martha L. ... **Washington, DC**
Perkins, Mary Ellen ... Panora, IA
Perkins, Matthew R. ... **Denver, CO**
Perkins, Matthew W. ... **Quincy, MA**
Perkins, Michael A. ... Pensacola, FL
Perkins, Michael K. ... **Redwood City, CA**
Perkins, Michael K. ... Des Moines, IA
Perkins, Michael R. ... **Austin, TX**
Perkins, Michelle J. ... Scottsdale, AZ
Perkins & Miltner, LLP ... **San Diego, CA**
Perkins, Nancy L. ... **Washington, DC**
Perkins, Nancy L. ... Youngstown, OH
Perkins, Nancy Paula ... Athens, TX
Perkins, Oliver C. ... Austin, TX
Perkins, Olson & Pratt, P.A.
Camden, ME
Portland, ME
Perkins, Orinthia Elouise ... New York, NY
Perkins, Patricia A. ... San Francisco, CA
Perkins, Patricia B. ... Hartford, CT
Perkins, Patricia D. ... **Jefferson City, MO**
Perkins, Patrick T. ... **New York, NY**
Perkins, Patty L. ... Sparta, IL
Perkins, Paul C., Jr. ... **Orlando, FL**
Perkins, Paul F. ... **Boston, MA**
Perkins & Perkins ... Carrollton, GA
Perkins & Perkins ... Saratoga Springs, NY
Mount Pleasant, TX
Perkins, Philip R. ... Tucson, AZ
Perkins, Phillips & Puckhaber, Professional Association ... **Concord, NH**
Perkins, R. Ben., Jr. ... Lombard, IL
Perkins, R. Edward ... **Houston, TX**
Perkins, R. Kevin ... San Diego, CA
Perkins, R. Paul, Jr. ... **Dayton, OH**
Perkins, Ralph B. ... San Diego, CA
Perkins, Ralph L. ... Newport, WA
Perkins, Randal K. ... **Louisville, KY**
Perkins, Randolph M. ... **Lake Forest, IL**
Perkins, Ray H. ... El Segundo, CA
Perkins, Raymond ... **Chicago, IL**
Perkins, Raymond A. ... Newburyport, MA
Perkins, Richard A. ... Madison, WI
Perkins, Richard C. ... Le Center, MN
Perkins, Richard K. ... Honolulu, HI
Perkins, Richard P. ... St. Louis, MO
Perkins, Richard W. ... Bowie, MD
Perkins, Richard W. ... Salt Lake City, UT
Perkins, Richie E. ... Moss Point, MS
Perkins, Robert ... Carmel, CA
Perkins, Robert A. ... Austin, TX
Perkins, Robert A., & Associates
Chicago, IL
Perkins, Robert C. ... Augusta, ME
Perkins, Robert H. ... Silver Spring, MD
Perkins, Robert J. ... **Wichita, KS**
Perkins, Robert S.
Agency for International Development, Other Offices of A.I.D., GV
Perkins, Robert S. ... **Portland, OR**
Perkins, Robert W. ... **Tallahassee, FL**
Perkins, Robert W. ... Portland, ME
Perkins, Roberta D. ... Oakland, CA
Perkins, Robin K. ... **Sacramento, CA**
Perkins, Rodney L. ... Kingsport, TN
Perkins, Roger A. ... **Annapolis, MD**
Perkins, Roger A. ... **Glen Burnie, MD**
Perkins, Roger G. ... **San Diego, CA**
Perkins, Ronald L. ... **Morristown, TN**
Perkins, Ronald W. ... Ogden, UT
Perkins, Roy F., Jr. ... Herndon, VA
Perkins, Russell N. ... Murfreesboro, TN
Perkins, Russell T. ... Nashville, TN
Perkins, Ryan F. ... Fort Bragg, CA
Perkins, S. Linn ... **Peoria, IL**
Perkins, S. Scott ... Saratoga Springs, NY
Perkins, Salvador T. ... North Potomac, MD
Perkins, Sam G. ... Olathe, KS
Perkins, Samuel ... **Boston, MA**
Perkins, Samuel L. ... **Lexington, KY**
Perkins, Samuel Lee ... Memphis, TN
Perkins, Samuel T. ... **Washington, DC**
Perkins, Sandra Lynn ... **Seattle, WA**
Perkins, Sara ... Dallas, TX
Perkins Schildnecht ... Pittsburgh, PA
Perkins & Schroeder ... Gonzales, TX
Perkins, Smith, Cohen & Crowe, LLP
Washington, DC
Perkins, Smith & Cohen, LLP
Boston, MA
Perkins, Stacey Jackson ... Woodbridge, CT
Perkins, Stephanie Sessions ... Roseville, CA
Perkins, Stephen B. ... Dallas, TX
Perkins, Stephen L. ... Portland, ME
Perkins, Stephen T. ... Richmond, VA
Perkins, Susan N. ... Delray Beach, FL
Perkins, Suzanne K. ... Tyler, TX
Perkins, Terence R. ... **Daytona Beach, FL**
Perkins, Thomas C. ... **Palo Alto, CA**
Fort Collins, CO
Perkins, Thomas C. ... Sacramento, CA
Perkins, Thomas D. ... Indianapolis, IN
Perkins, Thomas E. ... Minden, NV
Perkins, Thomas E. ... **Albuquerque, NM**
Perkins, Thomas G. ... **San Jose, CA**
Perkins, Thomas L. ... **Peoria, IL**
Perkins, Thomas P., III (P.C.)
Baltimore, MD
Perkins, Thomas W. ... **Arlington, VA**
Perkins, Thompson, Hinckley & Keddy, P.A.
Portland, ME
Perkins, Timothy S. ... **Dallas, TX**
Perkins, Todd Russell ... Detroit, MI
Perkins, Townsend & Shay, P.A.
Skowhegan, ME
Perkins, Tracy Suzanne ... **St. Louis, MO**
Perkins, Vicki ... Tulsa, OK
Perkins, Victoria J., (P.C.)
Washington, DC
Perkins, W. Swain ... Thayer, MO
Perkins, Walter T. ... Greensburg, PA
Perkins, Wendy S. ... Worcester, MA
Perkins, William B. ... Scottsdale, AZ
Perkins, William B., P.C. ... Scottsdale, AZ
Perkins, William Drew ... Lufkin, TX
Perkins, William H. ... **Portland, OR**
Perkins, William J. ... Columbia, LA
Perkins, William L., III
Virginia Beach, VA
Perkins, William O., Jr. ... Jersey City, NJ
Perkins, William P. ... **New York, NY**
Perkins, William S. ... **Boston, MA**
Perkins, Willie J., Sr. ... Greenwood, MS
Perkins & Zayed, P.C. ... Downers Grove, IL
Perkins-Brown, Lynne ... Madison, GA
Perkins-Hooker, Patrise M. ... Atlanta, GA
Perkins-Meyers, Holly Knotts ... Lufkin, TX
Perkinson, Charles A., Jr. ... Lawrenceville, VA
Perkinson, Cynthia R. ... **Reston, VA**
Perkinson, Diana M. ... Roanoke, VA
Perkinson, Doyle E. ... Houston, TX
Perkinson, Frank N., Jr. ... Roanoke, VA
Perkinson, Jacob B. ... South Burlington, VT
Perkinson, John R., Jr.
Winston-Salem, NC
Perkinson, Linda Barreca ... Portsmouth, VA
Perkinson, M. L. ... La Grange, KY
Perkinson and Perkinson ... Roanoke, VA
Perkinson, Ronald L. ... **Sanford, NC**
Perkins-Reed, Marcia A. ... Beaverton, OR
Perkiss, Gary M. ... Philadelphia, PA
Perkiss, Lewis ... New York, NY
Perkiss, Robert J. ... **San Francisco, CA**
Perkit, Joyce ... Jamaica Plain, MA
Perko, Brian M. ... Portland, OR
Perko, Douglas J. ... Arvada, CO
Perko, Gary V. ... **Tallahassee, FL**
Perko, Kenneth A., Jr. ... Scarsdale, NY
Perko, Phyllis J. ... West Dundee, IL
Perkoski, James P. ... Attleboro, MA
Perkoski, Joseph J. ... **Milwaukee, WI**
Perkosky, John D. ... **Pittsburgh, PA**
Perkovich, D. M. ... Sacramento, CA
Perkovich, George R., Jr. ... Los Angeles, CA
Perkovich, Joseph I. ... Naples, FL
Perkovich, Nancy ... Sacramento, CA
Perkovich & Perkovich ... Sacramento, CA
Perkovich, Robert ... Chicago, IL
Perkowitz, Vicki W. ... Pasadena, CA
Perkowitz, William T. ... Burr Ridge, IL
Perkowski, Peter E. ... **Los Angeles, CA**
Perkowski, Thomas J. ... **Stamford, CT**
Perkowski, Thomas J., Esq., P.C.
Stamford, CT
Perks, Benjamin W. ... Costa Mesa, CA
Perkun, Olga ... Pittsburgh, PA
Perl, Andrew ... New York, NY
Perl, Arnold E. ... **Memphis, TN**
Perl, David A. ... **New York, NY**
Perl, Deirdre June ... Philadelphia, PA
Perl, Else S. ... Harrison, NY
Perl, Erica Sarah ... New York, NY
Perl, Gary B. ... **San Diego, CA**
Perl, Iris Kate ... Los Angeles, CA
Perl, Jeffrey Samuel ... New York, NY
Perl, Justin H. ... **Minneapolis, MN**
Perl, Mark Meyer ... Los Angeles, CA
Perl, Norman ... **Minneapolis, MN**
Perl, Norman, & Associates, P.A.
Minneapolis, MN
Perl, Raphael ... Library of Congress, Congressional Research Service, GV
Perl, Ronald L. ... **Princeton, NJ**
Perl, Sander ... Passaic, NJ
Perl, Sanford E. ... **Chicago, IL**
Perl, Steven M. ... Santa Rosa, CA
Perl, Warren R. ... Cleveland, OH
Perla & Associates ... **Orlando, FL**
Perla, Henry L. ... **Orlando, FL**
Perla, Herbert H. ... Cleveland, OH
Perla, Jeffray A. ... Buffalo, NY
Perla, John P. ... Brookfield, WI
Perla, Mary E. ... Buffalo, NY
Perla, Peter J. ... **Denver, CO**
Perla, Peter Paul, Jr ... **Roseland, NJ**
New York, NY
Perla, Randall M. ... **Cleveland, OH**
Perla, Russell T. ... Buffalo, NY
Perla, Saul N. ... Chicago, IL
Perla, Vivian Lee ... **Denver, CO**
Perlah, Philip M. ... New York, NY
Perlberg, Dennis M. ... **Melville, NY**
New York, NY
Perlberg, Jules M. ... **Chicago, IL**
Perlberg, Larry J. ... Toms River, NJ
Perlberg, Michael T. ... **Chicago, IL**
Perlberger, Jillian ... **New York, NY**
Perlberger Law Associates, P.C.
Norristown, PA
Perlberger, Martin ... Los Angeles, CA
New York, NY
Perlberger, Norman ... Norristown, PA
Perlberger, Ralph ... New York, NY
Perle, E. Gabriel ... **Stamford, CT**
Perle, Ellen ... **New York, NY**
Perle, Lawrence P. ... Woodland Hills, CA
Perle, Linda E. ... Washington, DC
Perle, Michael R., (P.C.) ... Weehawken, NJ
Perle, Scott Ian ... Charlotte, NC
Perlee, J. Reynolds ... Jamestown, NY
Perlee, Jeffrey S. ... Schenectady, NY
Perlee, Kiersta D. ... Sacramento, CA
Perlee & Perlee ... Jamestown, NY
Perlee, Willard E. ... Jamestown, NY
Perles, Henry A. ... **Southport, CT**
Perles, Jerome A. ... New York, NY
Perles, Richard M. ... **New Orleans, LA**
Perles, Richard S. ... Atlanta, GA
Perlet, Terry L. ... Colorado Springs, CO
Perley, Barbara ... Metamora, IL
Perley, James F. ... Fremont, CA
Perley, Michael F. ... Buffalo, NY
Perley-Robertson, Panet, Hill & McDougall
Washington, DC
Perlich, Diane E. ... Cincinnati, OH
Perlich, John J. ... La Crosse, WI
Perlik, Stuart ... Northbrook, IL
Perlik, William R. ... Washington, DC
Perlin, Alan S. ... Worcester, MA
Perlin, Alex H. ... Brooklyn, NY
Perlin, Alice S. ... Chicago, IL
Perlin, Brian C. "Chuck" ... Coral Gables, FL
Perlin, Bruce ... **Alexandria, VA**
Perlin, Daniel ... Deerfield, IL
Perlin, Darryl G. ... Santa Barbara, CA
Perlin, Ellen H. ... Norwood, MA
Perlin, Jan ... Brooklyn, NY
Perlin, Marc G. ... Boston, MA
Perlin, Marshall ... New York, NY
Perlin, Michael L. ... New York, NY
Perlin, Morton J. ... Miami, FL
Perling, Lester J. ... **Fort Lauderdale, FL**
Perling, Lewis P. ... **Atlanta, GA**
Perlinger, Kathryn M. ... Eagan, MN
Perlini, Richard ... Fort Lauderdale, FL
Perlioni, Ellen L. ... **Dallas, TX**
Perlis, David G. ... Metairie, LA
Perlis, Deborah M. ... Waycross, GA
Perlis & Hogg ... Metairie, LA
Perlis, Mark L. ... **Washington, DC**
Perlis, Marvin E. ... Rockville, MD
Perlis, Michael F. ... **Los Angeles, CA**
Perlis, Robert
Environmental Protection Agency, Office of the General Counsel, GV
Perlis, Samuel ... Silver Spring, MD
Perlis, Saul ... Missouri City, TX
Perlis, Sharon A., (P.L.C.) ... Metairie, LA
Perliss, Steven C. ... Mount Prospect, IL
Perliss, Sanford H. ... Los Angeles, CA
Perlite, Diane M. ... Pleasant Hill, CA
Perlitsh, Stephen M. ... New York, NY
Perlitsh, Stephen M., P.C. ... New York, NY
Perlman, Adam L. ... **Washington, DC**
Perlman, Alan J. ... **Miami, FL**
Perlman, Alan M. ... Silver Spring, MD
Perlman, Alex G. ... Des Moines, WA
Perlman, Alice L. ... Santa Rosa, CA
Perlman, Amy R. ... **Chicago, IL**
Perlman, Andrew M. ... Chicago, IL
Perlman & Associates ... New York, NY
Perlman & Associates, ALC
Beverly Hills, CA
Perlman, B. Arthur ... Littleton, CO
Perlman, Bernard ... New York, NY
Perlman, Bruce M. ... **Danbury, CT**
Perlman, Burton ... Cincinnati, OH
Perlman, C. Max ... **Boston, MA**
Perlman, Cary R. ... **Chicago, IL**
Perlman, Catherine ... Santa Barbara, CA
Perlman, Charles H. ... **Chicago, IL**
Perlman, Clifford ... New York, NY
Perlman, Dana M. ... Beverly Hills, CA
Perlman, Daniel J. ... **Chicago, IL**
Perlman, Daniel T. ... **Princeton, NJ**
Perlman, David B. ... Lyndhurst, NJ
Perlman, David H. ... Brooklyn, NY
Perlman, David H. ... Madison, WI
Perlman, David J. ... Philadelphia, PA
Perlman, David M. ... Baltimore, MD
Perlman, David O. ... Southfield, MI
Perlman, Deborah K. ... **Beverly Hills, CA**
Perlman, Diane B. ... Detroit, MI
Perlman, Douglas L. ... New York, NY
Perlman & Duncan ... **Bakersfield, CA**

Perlman, Edward F. .... **Boston, MA**
Perlman, Edward P. .... Niagara Falls, NY
Perlman, Elliott R. .... Southfield, MI
Perlman, Felicia L. Gerber .... **Chicago, IL**
Perlman, Gail L. .... Northampton, MA
Perlman, Gary M. .... New York, NY
Perlman, George D. .... **Miami, FL**
Perlman, Glen K. .... Lexington, MA
Perlman, Ira M. .... New York, NY
Perlman, Irving .... Baldwin, NY
Perlman, Irwin Frank .... Memphis, TN
Perlman, James M. .... **Toledo, OH**
Perlman, Jay H.
Securities and Exchange Commission, Division of Enforcement, GV
Perlman, Jeffrey C. .... **Miami, FL**
Perlman, Jerald L. .... Shreveport, LA
Perlman, Jonathan E. .... **Miami, FL**
Perlman, Jonathan S. .... Dallas, TX
Perlman, Joseph N. .... Largo, FL
Perlman, Judy Platt .... **Chicago, IL**
Perlman, Julian S. .... New York, NY
Perlman, Kenneth S. .... **Chicago, IL**
Perlman Law Office .... **Minneapolis, MN**
Perlman, Lawrence .... Bloomington, MN
Perlman, Lee M. .... Cherry Hill, NJ
Perlman, Leonard S. .... **Los Angeles, CA**
Perlman, Leslie Canfield
Department of Labor, Office of the Solicitor, GV
Perlman, Linda S. .... Takoma Park, MD
Perlman, Lissa .... Woodbridge, CT
Perlman, Lori J. .... **New York, NY**
Perlman, Louise .... Seattle, WA
Perlman, Marjorie R. .... Canton, OH
Perlman, Mark .... **Hallandale Beach, FL**
Perlman, Mark, P.A.
Hallandale Beach, FL
Perlman, Matthew S. .... **Washington, DC**
Perlman, Michael B. .... **Southfield, MI**
Perlman, Michael L. .... **Minneapolis, MN**
Perlman, Michael M. .... Mineola, NY
Perlman, Nancy B. .... Jacksonville, FL
Perlman, Norman .... New York, NY
Perlman, Pamela D. .... Lexington, KY
Perlman, Paul I. .... **Buffalo, NY**
Perlman & Perlman .... New York, NY
Perlman, Peter .... **Lexington, KY**
Perlman, Peter A. .... **New York, NY**
Perlman, Peter, Law Offices, P.S.C.
Lexington, KY
Perlman, Rachel C. .... **Chicago, IL**
Perlman, Randy S. .... **Eureka, CA**
Perlman, Raymond L. .... Rancho Santa Fe, CA
Perlman, Richard B. .... Longboat Key, FL
Norristown, PA
West Chester, PA
Perlman, Richard R. .... **Chicago, IL**
Perlman, Robert S. .... Boston, MA
Perlman, Robin .... Phoenix, AZ
Perlman & Robison .... **Dallas, TX**
Plano, TX
Perlman, Rodney M., (P.C.)
Los Angeles, CA
Perlman, Ronald S. .... **Washington, DC**
Perlman, Rubin & Stein, P.C. .... Braintree, MA
Perlman, Samuel S. .... Braintree, MA
Perlman, Scott D. .... **Bakersfield, CA**
Perlman, Scott P. .... **Washington, DC**
Perlman, Seth I. .... New York, NY
Perlman, Sheri L. .... Salinas, CA
Perlman, Stephen B. .... **Boston, MA**
Perlman, Steven E. .... New York, NY
Perlman, Stuart D. .... **Chicago, IL**
Perlman, Susan D. .... Valhalla, NY
Perlman, T. S. L. .... Washington, DC
Perlman, Wendy J. .... Boston, MA
Perlman, William L. .... **Dallas, TX**
Perlmeter, Rosemary C. .... Irving, TX
Perlmuter, Gary E. .... **Torrance, CA**
Westland, MI
Perlmuth, William A. .... **New York, NY**
Perlmutter, Adam D. .... Kew Gardens, NY
Perlmutter, Benjamin .... Maplewood, NJ
Perlmutter, Beth .... New York, NY
Perlmutter, David M., & Associates
New York, NY
Perlmutter, Donald S. .... **Denver, CO**
Perlmutter, Edwin G. .... **Denver, CO**
Perlmutter, Gary Alan .... **San Diego, CA**
Perlmutter, Gerald .... Merrick, NY
Perlmutter, Irving H. .... New Haven, CT
Perlmutter, Jack .... Melbourne, FL
Perlmutter, Jack, P.A. .... Melbourne, FL
Perlmutter, Jerome A. .... **Greensboro, NC**
Perlmutter, Joel A. .... Cleveland, OH
Perlmutter, Joyce M. .... Briarcliff Manor, NY
Perlmutter, Lawrence Mark .... Boston, MA
Perlmutter, Leslie Ann
Commodity Futures Trading Commission, Division of Enforcement, GV
Perlmutter, Lisa Ann .... Indialantic, FL
Perlmutter, Mark L. .... Austin, TX
Perlmutter, Michael A. .... Encino, CA
Perlmutter, Mitchell D. .... Jersey City, NJ
Perlmutter, Patricia P. .... Newark, NJ
Perlmutter & Reagan, L.L.P. .... Austin, TX
Perlmutter, Richard M. .... Boston, MA
Perlmutter, Robert S. .... San Francisco, CA
Perlmutter, Sam .... Los Angeles, CA
Perlmutter, Sandra Zavodnick
Totowa, NJ
Perlmutter, Sharon R. .... New Canaan, CT
Perlmutter, Shira .... Library of Congress, Copyright Office, GV
Perlmutter, Stephen D. .... New York, NY
Perlmutter, Steven J. .... Toledo, OH
Perlmutter, Steven P. .... **Boston, MA**

Perlmutter, Stuart .... **New York, NY**
Perlmutter, Willa B. .... **Washington, DC**
Perlo, Ezekiel P. .... Encino, CA
Perlo, Lionel H. .... Boston, MA
Perlo, Stanley .... Los Angeles, CA
Perlof, Abraham .... Bronx, NY
Perloff, Hal J. .... **Vienna, VA**
Perloff, James W. .... Dresher, PA
Perloff, Jean M. .... Ventura, CA
Perloff, John W., (P.C.)
Fort Lauderdale, FL
Perloff, Michael J. .... New York, NY
Perloff, Neil S. .... Philadelphia, PA
Perloff, R. Jeffrey .... Mobile, AL
Perloff, Saul H. .... **San Antonio, TX**
Perlos, Alexander C. .... Jackson, MI
Perlos, Charles A. .... Jackson, MI
Perlotto, Joel D. .... Torrington, CT
Perlov, Florence T. .... **Los Altos, CA**
Perlove, Warren J. .... **Flint, MI**
Perlow, Barry A., Law Offices
Bridgeton, NJ
Perlow, Glenn A. .... **Concord, NH**
Perlow, Jeffrey M. .... **Aventura, FL**
Perlow, Jeffry S. .... Cranston, RI
Perlow, Mark D.
Securities and Exchange Commission, Division of Enforcement, GV
Perlow, Matthew G. .... **St. Louis, MO**
Perlow, S. James .... Broadview, IL
Perlow, Sidney H. .... Salem, MA
Perlowitz, Alan J. .... New York, NY
Perlowski, Henry M. .... **Atlanta, GA**
Perlowski, Stanley T. .... Millburn, NJ
Perlroth, Wm. S. .... New Haven, CT
Perls, N. Lynn .... **Albuquerque, NM**
Perls, N. Lynn .... **Rio Rancho, NM**
Perlson, David A. .... **Chicago, IL**
Perlson, J. Lewis .... **Milwaukee, WI**
Perlstadt, Sidney M. .... **Chicago, IL**
Perlstein, Allen .... **Jericho, NY**
Perlstein, Arnold L. .... Fort Lauderdale, FL
Perlstein, Barry D. .... New York, NY
Perlstein, Edwin .... Encino, CA
Perlstein, Hildegarde Conte
Department of the Air Force, Office of the Judge Advocate General, GV
Perlstein, Howard E.
National Labor Relations Board, Office of the General Counsel, GV
Perlstein, Jan I. .... Los Angeles, CA
Perlstein, Janet .... **Denver, CO**
Perlstein, Jerold I. .... **Milwaukee, WI**
Perlstein, Joel T. .... San Francisco, CA
Perlstein, John Julius .... Los Angeles, CA
Perlstein, John R. .... Bloomfield, CT
Perlstein, Loren S.
Department of the Air Force, Office of the Judge Advocate General, GV
Perlstein, Mary A. .... **Champaign, IL**
Perlstein, Matthew N., Law Office of
Farmington, CT
Perlstein, Matthew N., Law Office of
Hartford, CT
Perlstein, Michael A. .... Chicago, IL
Perlstein, Michael J. .... Los Angeles, CA
Perlstein, Michele S. .... Princeton, NJ
Perlstein, Mitchell L. .... Boca Raton, FL
Perlstein, Paul Mark .... **Exton, PA**
Philadelphia, PA
Perlstein & Robbins .... Los Angeles, CA
Perlstein, Robert S. .... **New York, NY**
Perlstein, Steven W. .... **New York, NY**
Perlstein, William J. .... **Washington, DC**
Perlsweig, Leon .... Los Angeles, CA
Perluss, Dennis M. .... **Los Angeles, CA**
Perluss, Irving H. .... **Sacramento, CA**
Permakoff, Patricia E. .... New York, NY
Perman, Corey M. .... Department of Labor, Office of the Solicitor, GV
Perman, Gerald A. .... Malibu, CA
Perman & Green, LLP .... **Fairfield, CT**
Permar, David B. .... Columbus, OH
Permar, David H. .... **Raleigh, NC**
Permar, James B. .... Clearwater, FL
Permaul, Lawrence G. .... Monterey Park, CA
Perme, Michael R. .... Euclid, OH
Permenter, Fred C., Jr. .... Ripley, MS
Permenter, J. Ray, Jr. .... Miami, FL
Permenter, James R. .... El Paso, TX
Permenter, R. Douglas .... Pensacola, FL
Permenter, Tommy D., Jr. .... **Greenville, SC**
Permigiani, Rodney .... Pittsburgh, PA
Permut, Barry M. .... **Denver, CO**
Permut, David A. .... Treasury Department, Office of Thrift Supervision, GV
Permut, David L. .... **Washington, DC**
Permut, Jacob .... Washington, DC
Permut, Michael .... **Garden City, NY**
Permut, Philip V. .... **Washington, DC**
Permut, Stephen R. .... Wilmington, DE
Permut, Steven L. .... **Troy, MI**
Permut, Susan I. .... **Hopkinton, MA**
Permuter, Lawrence J. .... **St. Louis, MO**
Permutt, James L. .... **Birmingham, AL**
Permutt, Neal A. .... Scarsdale, NY
Permutt & Permutt .... Scarsdale, NY
Permutt, William M. .... Scarsdale, NY
Perna, Anthony J., Jr. .... **Goshen, NY**
Perna, Barbara Britzke .... Philadelphia, PA
Perna, D. Georgette
Charlotte Amalie, St. Thomas, VI
Perna, Elizabeth Plaskon .... Hackensack, NJ
Perna, Frank M. .... Kennett Square, PA
Perna, James F. .... **Washington, DC**
Perna, Jo-Anne E. .... Philadelphia, PA
Perna, Lance E. .... Dallas, TX
Perna, Michael R. .... Kennett Square, PA

Perna, Michael W. .... Oakland, CA
Perna, Philip A. .... Buffalo, NY
Perna, Richard C. .... **Chicago, IL**
Perna, Robert J. .... **Chicago, IL**
Perna, Rocco R. P. .... Riverside, CT
Perna, Terrance .... Hackensack, NJ
Pernas, Frank N. .... Lutz, FL
Pernas, Guillermo A., Jr. .... **Tampa, FL**
Pernell, Janel M. .... Burgettstown, PA
Pernell, Kevin Derek .... **Denver, CO**
Pernell, LeRoy .... Columbus, OH
Perner, Michael W. .... **Philadelphia, PA**
Pernerewski, Colleen B. .... Simsbury, CT
Pernerewski, Paul K., Jr. .... Hartford, CT
Perney, David A. .... **St. Louis, MO**
Pernicano, Frank J. .... San Diego, CA
Pernice, Charles A., III .... Irvine, CA
Pernice, Thomas J. .... Gainesville, FL
Pernice-Knefel, Deborah Lynne
Anaheim, CA
Perniciaro & Lambert .... Staten Island, NY
Perniciaro, William P. .... Staten Island, NY
Pernick, David A. .... Detroit, MI
Pernick, Irwin .... Department of State, Director General—Foreign Service, GV
Pernick, John D. .... **San Francisco, CA**
Pernick, Lisa K. .... **Southfield, MI**
Pernick, Marc J. .... **Palo Alto, CA**
Pernick, Matthew H.
Department of State, GV
Pernick, Nat .... Royal Oak, MI
Pernick, Norman L. .... **Wilmington, DE**
Pernick, Ralph .... **Rockville Centre, NY**
Pernick, Steven L. .... Wilmette, IL
Pernick, Susan Goldenkranz .... Glen Head, NY
Pernicone, Carl J. .... **New York, NY**
Pernicone, Isabella M. .... Yonkers, NY
Pernini, David M. .... Atlanta, GA
Pernini, Teresa Brazzel .... **Atlanta, GA**
Pernitz, Mark W. .... **Madison, WI**
Pernitz, Scott G. .... **Madison, WI**
Pernoud, A. Stephen .... **St. Louis, MO**
Pero, Brian V. .... Englewood, CO
Pero, Jeffrey T. .... **San Francisco, CA**
Pero & Kaplan .... **Los Angeles, CA**
Pero, Matthew J. .... **Los Angeles, CA**
Perocchi & Fernandez, LLP
North Andover, MA
Perocchi, Joyce G. .... **North Andover, MA**
Perocchi, Paul P. .... **Boston, MA**
Peroff, Mark I. .... **Livingston, NJ**
New York, NY
Peron, Gayle L. .... **San Luis Obispo, CA**
Peron & Pratt .... **San Luis Obispo, CA**
Peron, Rochelle L. .... Laguna Niguel, CA
Perona, Alison Ryan .... Chicago, IL
Perona, James T. .... **Long Beach, CA**
Perona, Langer, Beck & Lallande, A Professional Corporation
Long Beach, CA
Los Angeles, CA
Perona Law Offices .... Peru, IL
Perona, Louis J. .... Ottawa, IL
Perona, Paul D. .... Peru, IL
Perona, Paul R. .... Manalapan, NJ
Perone, A. Ralph .... Margate City, NJ
Perone, Anne M. .... North Plainfield, NJ
Perone, F. Frederick .... Margate City, NJ
Perone, Fred N. .... North Plainfield, NJ
Perone, John M. .... White Plains, NY
Perone & Perone .... North Plainfield, NJ
Perone, Susan R. .... **White Plains, NY**
Perone, Thomas M. .... **New York, NY**
Peroni, Robert J. .... New Orleans, LA
Peronti, Gino M. .... Skokie, IL
Peronti, Maryann .... **New York, NY**
Peros, Michael V. .... Los Angeles, CA
Orange, CA
Peros, Nicholas J. .... Burlingame, CA
Perot, James F., Jr. .... Metairie, LA
Perot, Lawrence A. .... Akron, NY
Perot, Remy R. .... Binghamton, NY
Perot, Sczerina A. .... Washington, DC
Perotin, Gary A. .... Placentia, CA
Perotti, Candida F. .... United States Senate, Senatorial Assistants, GV
Perotti, Dawn C. .... **Dallas, TX**
Perotti, Patrick J. .... **Painesville, OH**
Perotti, Rose N. .... **St. Louis, MO**
Peroutka, Dale J. .... Anaheim, CA
Peroutka, Michael A. .... Pasadena, MD
Peroutka & Peroutka .... Pasadena, MD
Peroutka, Raymond J., Jr. .... Baltimore, MD
Perovich, William S. .... Sutter Creek, CA
Peroz, Michael L. .... St. Paul, MN
Perozzi, Joseph R. .... Chicago Heights, IL
Perpall, Peter R. .... Falmouth, MA
Perpenia, Victor R. .... Hartford, CT
Perper, Phoebe M. .... Philadelphia, PA
Perpich, Joseph G. .... Bethesda, MD
Perpiglia, Paul J. .... Philadelphia, PA
Perplies, Edward V. .... Arleta, CA
Perque, Chris P. .... **Austin, TX**
Perr, Cindy M. .... **Westmont, NJ**
Perr, Irwin N. .... Piscataway, NJ
Perr, Joel S. .... Pittsburgh, PA
Perr, Karolina F. .... Cincinnati, OH
Perr, Mortimer H. .... Yonkers, NY
Perr, Richard J. .... **Philadelphia, PA**
Perra, Craig Lyle .... **Hartford, CT**
Perra, Kevin J. .... **New York, NY**
Perra, Raymond P. .... **Brattleboro, VT**
Perra, Richard D. .... **Brattleboro, VT**
Perra, Salvatore J. .... Lynnfield, MA
Perrapato, Jamie M. .... **Philadelphia, PA**
Perras, Henry A. .... **Phoenix, AZ**
Perras, Louis A., Jr. .... East Freetown, MA
Perras, Richard A. .... **Boston, MA**

Perrault, David L. .... **Sacramento, CA**
Perrault, Donald J. .... **Manchester, NH**
Perrault, Jean-Paul .... **Baton Rouge, LA**
Perrault, John .... Portsmouth, NH
Perrault, John D. .... West Palm Beach, FL
Perrault, Joseph A., Jr. .... Baton Rouge, LA
Perrault, Laura Estelle .... Denver, CO
Perrault, Margaret M. .... Tulsa, OK
Perrault, Margaret M., P.C. .... Tulsa, OK
Perreault, Cynthia A. .... Exeter, NH
Perreault, Dennis N. .... Bedford, NH
Perreault, Donald J. .... Boston, MA
Perreault, Laurie S. .... **Amherst, NH**
Perreault, Mark D. .... **Norfolk, VA**
Perreault, Reneé .... San Diego, CA
Perreault, Thomas Darwin .... Albany, NY
Perrecone, Frank A. .... **Rockford, IL**
Perrell, Charlotte B. .... **Atlanta, GA**
Perrell, Glenn M. .... Los Angeles, CA
Perrell, Joel L., Jr. .... **Baltimore, MD**
Perrella, Domenico C. .... **San Francisco, CA**
Perrella, Donald J. .... **New York, NY**
Perrella, Nicholas R. .... Kingston, PA
Perrella, Patrick A. .... Hauppauge, NY
Perrella, Stephen .... San Diego, CA
Perrella, Stephen G. .... **New Brunswick, NJ**
Perrelli, Katherine E. .... **Boston, MA**
Perrelli, Sante J. .... Lansing, MI
Perrelli, Thomas J. .... Department of Justice, Office of the Attorney General, GV
Perrello, Stephen J., Jr. .... San Diego, CA
Perren, Steven Z. .... Ventura, CA
Perrenot, Richard B. .... **El Paso, TX**
Perrenoud, Scott .... **Sioux Falls, SD**
Perrero, Bryan M. .... **Dayton, OH**
Perrero, Robin G. .... **Shreveport, LA**
Perres, Lee Scott .... Chicago, IL
Perret, David W., Jr. .... Marrero, LA
Perret Doise, A Professional Law Corporation .... **Lafayette, LA**
New Orleans, LA
Perret, Henry C., Jr. .... **Lafayette, LA**
Perret, Karen .... Seattle, WA
Perret, Paul F. .... Menlo Park, CA
Perret, Robert, Jr. .... Brooklyn, NY
Perreten, Paul F. .... Hastings-On-Hudson, NY
Perreten, Paul F., Attorney and Counsellor at Law P.C. .... Hastings-On-Hudson, NY
Perrett, George T. .... **Battle Creek, MI**
Perrett, Michael F. .... Ventura, CA
Perrett, Michael Kevin .... Mobile, AL
Perrett, Patrick J. .... Goleta, CA
Perretta, Charlotte Anne .... Boston, MA
Perretta, Frank J. .... **Pleasanton, CA**
Perretta, Michael A. .... Canastota, NY
Perretta, Susan R. .... Branchville, NJ
Perrette, John E. .... Cleveland, OH
Perretti, Mel E. C. .... Schaumburg, IL
Perretti, Patrick J. .... Glen Ellyn, IL
Perretti, Peter N., Jr. .... **Morristown, NJ**
Perrey, Philip E .... **Bradenton, FL**
Perrey, Philip E., P.A. .... Bradenton, FL
Perrey, Richard A. .... Spokane, WA
Perri, Adam B. .... **New York, NY**
Perri, Audrey A. .... **Ontario, CA**
Perri, C. Kenneth .... Geneva, NY
Perri, Daniel C. .... **Destin, FL**
Perri, Daniel C. .... **Fort Walton Beach, FL**
Perri, David P. .... **Turnersville, NJ**
Philadelphia, PA
Perri, Dennis D. .... Chicago, IL
Perri, Frank Saverio .... **Wheaton, IL**
Perri, Ingrida D. .... **Oak Brook, IL**
Perri, Kenneth S. .... **San Diego, CA**
Perri, Mary Ellen .... New York, NY
Perri, Michael R. .... **Oklahoma City, OK**
Perri, Saverio .... Bronx, NY
Perri, Victor M. .... Las Vegas, NV
Perricelli, William J. .... Kissimmee, FL
Perricone, Anthony L. .... **New York, NY**
Perrien, Stephen T. .... **New Orleans, LA**
Perrier, Allen O. .... Palm Springs, CA
Perrier, E. M. .... St. James, MN
Perrier, Eugene A. .... Vicksburg, MS
Perrier, Guy D. .... **New Orleans, LA**
Perrige, Michelle E. .... **Minneapolis, MN**
Perrigo, James M. .... Dillon, CO
Perrill, J. W. .... Glenville, WV
Perrill, Peter M. .... Rock Hill, SC
Perrilloux, Scott M. .... **Hammond, LA**
Perriman, Janet C. .... Denver, CO
Perrin, Andrew F. .... **Minneapolis, MN**
Perrin, Arvid B. .... Lansing, MI
Perrin, Carol .... **Los Angeles, CA**
Perrin, Chas. J. .... Venice, FL
Perrin, Christopher G. .... **Springfield, IL**
Perrin, Clifford W., Jr. .... Arlington, VA
Perrin & DeMore .... Lafayette, NY
Fabius, NY
Perrin, Diane V. .... **Houston, TX**
Perrin, Donald F. .... **Inverness, FL**
Perrin, Doug .... **Arlington, TX**
Perrin, Doug .... **Dallas, TX**
El Paso, TX
Perrin, Edward P. .... **Spartanburg, SC**
Perrin, Edward P., Jr. .... **Dallas, TX**
Perrin, Ellen A. .... **Charlotte, NC**
Perrin, Gregory J. .... Brooklyn, NY
Perrin, Harry A. .... **Houston, TX**
Perrin, James A. .... Collingswood, NJ
Perrin, James Kirk .... **Chicago, IL**
Perrin, John M. .... **Detroit, MI**
Perrin, John P. .... Kansas City, MO
Perrin, John R. .... Colorado Springs, CO
Perrin, Jonathan M. .... Athens, OH
Perrin, Karen B. .... Atlantic Beach, FL
Perrin, L. Timothy .... Malibu, CA

Perrin, Landry, deLaunay & Durand
Erath, LA
Perrin, Landry, de Launay & Durand
Lafayette, LA
Perrin, Lawrence J. .... San Jose, CA
Perrin, Lois K. .... San Francisco, CA
Perrin, Marc D. .... Eugene, OR
Perrin, Mark W. .... Eugene, OR
Perrin, Martha C. .... Atlanta, GA
Perrin, Maureen A. .... Fabius, NY
Lafayette, NY
Perrin, Michael W. .... Houston, TX
Perrin, Patrick K. .... Broomfield, CO
Perrin, Perrin, Mann & Patterson, L.L.P.
Spartanburg, SC
Perrin, Richard P. .... Washington, DC
Perrin, Robert W. .... Los Angeles, CA
Perrin, Ronald J. .... Cleveland, OH
Perrin, Roy A., III .... New Orleans, LA
Perrin, Scotty Lee .... Mesa, AZ
Perrin, Steven K. .... Thousand Oaks, CA
Perrin & Thayer, LLP .... Eugene, OR
Perrin, Warren A. .... Erath, LA
Lafayette, LA
Perrin, Wm. Gardner .... Boston, MA
Perrine, Amos W. .... Charleston, WV
Perrine, David E. .... San Diego, CA
Perrine, David S. .... Redding, CA
Perrine, Harlin .... Salem, VA
Perrine, Mark .... Ashland, WI
Perrine, Robert E., Jr. .... Albany, GA
Perrine, Robert G. .... Norman, OK
Perrine, Rosanne P.
Jacksonville Beach, FL
Perrine, Thomas E. .... Kansas City, MO
Perrine, William D. .... Tulsa, OK
Perrini, John J., (Co., L.P.A.)
Columbus, OH
Perrini, Tessie M. .... Garden City, NY
Perrino, Anastasia Welsh .... Barnstable, MA
Yarmouth Port, MA
Perrino, Dominic F. .... Cincinnati, OH
Perrino, John M., Jr. .... Valley Stream, NY
Perrino, Nicholas A. .... Cincinnati, OH
Perrino, P. J., Jr. .... Augusta, ME
Perrino, Rudy R. .... Los Angeles, CA
San Diego, CA
San Francisco, CA
Perrino, Thomas J. .... Barnstable, MA
Yarmouth Port, MA
Perrino, Tina .... San Francisco, CA
Perrion, Jeanne A. .... Burnsville, MN
Perris, Alex C. .... Akron, OH
Perris, Elizabeth L. .... Portland, OR
Perris, Terrence G. .... Cleveland, OH
Perris-Fitch, Ellen .... Santa Clara, CA
Perritano, Judith A. .... Boston, MA
Perritt, H. Franklin, Jr. .... Jacksonville, FL
Perritt, Harvey H., Jr. .... Fairfax, VA
Perritt, Ricky B. .... Denton, TX
Perrizo, Mark J. .... Downey, CA
Perrochet, George M. .... San Francisco, CA
Perrochet, Lisa .... Los Angeles, CA
Perron, Andre R. .... Bradenton, FL
Perron, Carla Marie .... Lafayette, LA
Perron, Edward A. .... Los Angeles, CA
Perron, Jean M. .... Washington, DC
Perron, Jerry D. .... St. Paul, MN
Perron, Maria V. .... St. Louis, MO
Perron, Martin L. .... East St. Louis, IL
St. Louis, MO
Perron, Peter P. .... Bellevue, WA
Perron, William P. .... Burnsville, MN
Perrone, Frank A. .... Houston, TX
Perrone, Gregory .... Lexington, KY
Perrone, John H. .... Haverhill, MA
Perrone, John Jay .... New Brunswick, NJ
Perrone, Joseph J. .... New York, NY
Perrone, Mary-Ann .... Morristown, NJ
Perrone, Mathew R. P., Jr. .... Algonquin, IL
Perrone, Michael J. .... Norwich, CT
Perrone, Pamela G. .... Chicago, IL
Perrone, Patrick J. .... Newark, NJ
Perrone, Paul J., Jr. .... Department of the Army,
U.S. Army Legal Services Agency, GV
Perrone, Paula .... Metairie, LA
Perrone, Perry Paul .... White Plains, NY
Perrone, Robert A. .... Worcester, MA
Perrone, Stephen L., (P.A.) .... Miami, FL
Perrone, Vincent L. .... Santa Monica, CA
Perrone, William A. .... Stamford, CT
Perrone, William J. .... Lansing, MI
Perroni and James .... Little Rock, AR
Perroni, Samuel A. .... Little Rock, AR
Perrot, Linda Jean .... Little Rock, AR
Perrott, Frank R. .... Stockton, CA
Perrott, Lisa A. .... Los Angeles, CA
Perrotta, Austin D. .... Bloomfield Hills, MI
Perrotta, Carmine J. .... St. Clair Shores, MI
Perrotta, Charles F. .... San Jose, CA
Perrotta, Chas. F. X. .... Brooklyn, NY
Perrotta, Fioravante G. .... New York, NY
Perrotta, Frank G. .... Smithtown, NY
Perrotta, Joseph D. .... Atlanta, GA
Perrotta, Joseph E., Jr. .... Tampa, FL
Perrotta, Justin M. .... Boston, MA
Perrotta, Kathryn E. .... Andover, MA
Perrotta, Louis M. .... New Castle, PA
Perrotta, Michael F. .... Huntington, NY
Perrotta, Paul G. .... Boston, MA
Perrotta, Susan T. .... North Woodmere, NY
Perrotta, Teresa L. .... Atlanta, GA
Perrotti, Janet A. .... Hartford, CT
Perrotti, Paula A. .... New York, NY
Perrotto, Joseph L. .... Norwood, MA
Perrotto, Joseph L., P.C. .... Norwood, MA
Perrow, Edgar J. T. .... Lynchburg, VA
Perrow, G. Turner .... Georgetown, SC
Perrow, G. Turner, P.A., Law Office of
Georgetown, SC
Perrow, Mosby G., III .... Lynchburg, VA
Perrow, Robert D. .... Richmond, VA
Perrucci, Angelo M., Jr. .... Washington, NJ
Perrucci, Michael J. .... Phillipsburg, NJ
Perruso, Roxane J. .... Denver, CO
Perruzza, John N. .... Hermosa Beach, CA
Perruzzi, Christopher A. .... Easton, MA
Perruzzi, John E. .... Alexandria, VA
Perruzzi, Sean O. .... Secaucus, NJ
Perry, Achilles M. .... New York, NY
Perry, Adam W. .... Buffalo, NY
Perry, Alan J. .... Hingham, MA
Perry, Alan R. .... San Diego, CA
Perry, Alan R., Jr. .... Atlanta, GA
Perry, Alan W. .... Jackson, MS
Perry, Albert J., III .... Baltimore, MD
Perry, Alexa D. .... Wayne, NJ
Perry, Alexander B. .... Hoosick Falls, NY
Perry, Alice L. .... Stamford, CT
Perry, Alison Lawton .... Aptos, CA
Salinas, CA
Perry, Allan R. .... Phoenix, AZ
Perry, Allen L. .... Cleveland, OH
Perry, Allison M. .... Tampa, FL
Perry, Alvin P., Jr. .... Chalmette, LA
Perry, Alvin R. .... Woodland Hills, CA
Perry, A. N. .... Surfside, FL
Perry, Ann Marie .... California, MO
Perry, Ann R. .... Washington, DC
Perry, Anna M. .... Northport, NY
Perry, Anne B. .... Washington, DC
Perry, Anne Kristina .... San Diego, CA
Perry, Archie .... Bogalusa, LA
Perry, Arthur J. .... South Bend, IN
Perry, Arthur Thaddeus .... Indianapolis, IN
Perry, Audy M., Jr. .... Huntington, WV
Perry, B. Dwight .... Washington, DC
Perry, Barbara L. .... Houston, TX
Perry, Barbara S. .... Beverly Hills, CA
Perry, Barbara S. .... Kinston, NC
Perry, Belvin, Jr. .... Orlando, FL
Perry, Bennett H., Jr. .... Henderson, NC
Perry, Blair L. .... Boston, MA
Perry, Brad .... Alamogordo, NM
Perry & Bray .... Colonial Heights, VA
Perry, Brendan J., & Associates
Holliston, MA
Perry, Brent C. .... Houston, TX
Perry, Brett A. .... Columbia, SC
Perry, Brett Alan .... Minneapolis, MN
Perry, Brett M. .... Denver, CO
Perry, Brian D., Sr. .... New Orleans, LA
Perry, Brian P. .... Cincinnati, OH
Perry, Brian W. .... Harrisburg, PA
Perry, Brock E. .... Lawrenceville, GA
Perry, Brown and Levin .... Rocky Mount, NC
Perry, Bruce R. .... Modesto, CA
Perry, Buddy D. .... Winchester, TN
Perry, Bundy, Plyler & Long, L.L.P.
Monroe, NC
Perry, C. Jones, Jr. .... New York, NY
Perry, C. Kenneth, Jr. .... Southfield, MI
Perry, C. Robert .... Stanton, MI
Perry, Carl E. .... Weber City, VA
Perry, Carl G. .... Kansas City, MO
Perry, Carlyle V. .... Columbus, OH
Perry, Carol A. .... Salem, MA
Perry, Carol A. .... Fairfax, VA
Perry, Carolyn J. .... Department of Defense,
Defense Legal Services Agency, GV
Perry, Carolyn Madden
Harrisonburg, VA
Perry, Carolyn Pratt .... Baton Rouge, LA
Fort Belvoir, VA
Perry, Catherine D. .... St. Louis, MO
Perry, Cathleen D.
National Labor Relations Board,
Office of Board Members, GV
Perry, Cathleen J. .... Indianapolis, IN
Perry, Charles .... Clearwater, FL
Perry, Charles A. .... Atlanta, GA
Perry, Charles E. .... Wichita Falls, TX
Perry, Charles F. .... Paoli, IN
Perry, Charles L. .... Dallas, TX
Perry, Charles R. .... Palm Springs, CA
Perry, Charles R. .... San Francisco, CA
Perry, Charles R. .... Cumming, GA
Perry, Charles Stanton .... Beaumont, TX
Houston, TX
Perry, Chase .... Dallas, TX
Perry, Cheryl A. .... Raleigh, NC
Perry, Christopher D. .... Washington, DC
Perry, Christopher D. .... Boston, MA
Perry, Christopher J. .... Boston, MA
Perry, Christopher James
Oklahoma City, OK
Perry, Christopher L. .... New York, NY
Perry, Christopher R. .... Phoenix, AZ
Perry, Christopher Thomas .... Chelmsford, MA
Perry, Cindy Gayle .... Los Angeles, CA
Perry, Clifford R., III .... Chicago, IL
Perry, Clifton B. .... Auburn, AL
Perry, Connie M. .... San Francisco, CA
Perry, Courtland D., II .... Augusta, ME
Perry, Craig K. .... Las Vegas, NV
Perry, Curtis L. .... Kansas City, MO
Perry, D. Max .... Los Angeles, CA
Perry, Dan C. .... San Antonio, TX
Perry, Dan E. .... Kinston, NC
Perry, Dana B. .... Chattanooga, TN
Perry, Daniel A. .... Scranton, PA
Perry, Daniel C. .... New Bedford, MA
Perry, Daniel J. .... Bangor, ME
Perry, Daniel J. .... Pittsburgh, PA
Perry, Daniel L. .... Tampa, FL
Perry, Daniel M. .... Tulsa, OK
Perry, Daniel Thaddeus, III
Fayetteville, NC
Perry, Daniel W. .... Orlando, FL
Perry, Darlene G. .... Upper Marlboro, MD
Perry, Danya E. .... New York, NY
Perry, David .... Philadelphia, PA
Perry, David A. .... Livonia, MI
Perry, David A. .... Cincinnati, OH
Perry, David C. .... Hamilton, MT
Perry, David E. .... Albany, GA
Perry, David E. .... Roanoke, VA
Perry, David Francis .... San Francisco, CA
Perry, David J. .... Newport Beach, CA
Perry, David L. .... San Carlos, CA
Perry, David L. .... Washington, DC
Perry, David L. .... Corpus Christi, TX
Perry, David L., Jr. .... West Palm Beach, FL
Perry, David M. .... Logan, UT
Perry, David W. .... Lynnfield, MA
Perry, Davida S. .... New York, NY
Perry, Dawn S. .... Seattle, WA
Perry, Deborah M. .... Dallas, TX
Perry, Debra M. .... Newark, NJ
Perry, Denise A. .... Chicago, IL
Perry, Denise M. .... Bethesda, MD
Perry, Dominic V. .... Cleveland, OH
Perry, Don R. .... Santa Ana, CA
Perry, Donald C. .... Monroe, NC
Perry, Donald G. .... Bay Shore, NY
Perry, Donald R. .... New Bedford, MA
Perry, Donna King .... Louisville, KY
Perry, Douglas E. .... Washington, DC
Perry, Douglas J. .... Boston, MA
Perry, Douglas P. .... Mineola, NY
New York, NY
Smithtown, NY
Perry, Dow M., Jr. .... Decatur, AL
Perry, E. Jay .... Eugene, OR
Perry, E. Lynn .... San Francisco, CA
Perry, Edward M. .... Reading, MA
Perry, Edward N. .... Boston, MA
Perry, Edward T. .... San Francisco, CA
Perry, Edward T. .... San Rafael, CA
Perry, Edwin C. .... Lincoln, NE
Perry, Edwin C. .... Portland, OR
Perry, Edwin H. .... Louisville, KY
Perry, Edwin J., III .... Bainbridge, GA
Perry, Eileen P. .... Manlius, NY
Perry, Elizabeth A. .... Wise, VA
Perry, Elizabeth A. .... Vancouver, WA
Perry, Emil B. .... Orangevale, CA
Perry, Ezra B., Jr. .... Birmingham, AL
Perry, F. Edwin .... Oxford, MS
Perry, F. Martin .... West Palm Beach, FL
Perry, F. Martin & Assocs., P.A.
West Palm Beach, FL
Perry, Fialkowski & Perry
Clementon, NJ
Philadelphia, PA
Perry Firm, The .... Lawrenceville, GA
Perry, Francine Jackson .... Gulfport, MS
Perry, Frank B. .... Ringgold, GA
Perry, Frank B., III .... Fairfax, VA
Perry, Franklin H. .... Dallas, TX
Perry, Fred N. .... Westbury, NY
Perry, Frederick V. .... Miami, FL
Perry and Freeman .... Carmel, CA
Salinas, CA
Perry, G. Chad, III .... Paintsville, KY
Perry, G. Michael .... Northbrook, IL
Perry, Gail A. .... Department of Labor,
Office of the Solicitor, GV
Perry, Gail S. .... Lincoln, NE
Perry, Gail V. .... Madison, WI
Perry, Garry A. .... Lexington, KY
Perry, Gary G. .... Sacramento, CA
Perry, Gentry, Perry & Marsh
Hobart, OK
Perry, George A. .... Newton, MA
Perry, George H. .... Shenandoah, IA
Perry, George M. .... San Francisco, CA
Perry, George W. .... Cleveland, OH
Perry, George W. .... Arlington, TX
Perry, Gina K. .... Montclair, NJ
Perry, Giovanni Isabel .... Oklahoma City, OK
Perry, Glen R. .... Virginia Beach, VA
Perry, Glenn A. .... Longview, TX
Perry, Glenn J. .... Washington, DC
Perry, Greg A. .... Jefferson City, MO
Perry, Gregory E. .... Austin, TX
Perry, Gregory H. .... Lincoln, NE
Perry, Gregory J. .... Chicago, IL
Perry, Gregory L. .... Memphis, TN
Perry, Gregory M. .... Wilton, CT
Perry, Gregory M. .... Commerce, GA
Perry, Guthery, Haase & Gessford, P.C.
Lincoln, NE
Perry, Guy .... Newport Beach, CA
Perry Haas, L.L.P. .... Corpus Christi, TX
Perry, Harvey P. .... Monroe, LA
Perry, Henry Larry .... Panama City, FL
Perry, H. H., Jr. .... Albany, GA
Perry, Hicks, Crotty and Deshaies
New Bedford, MA
Perry, Hugh J. .... Storm Lake, IA
Perry, Hugh W. .... West Palm Beach, FL
Perry, J. Lee .... Cumming, GA
Perry, J. Scott .... Dallas, TX
Perry, Jack G. .... Las Vegas, NV
Perry, Jack W. .... Houston, TX
Perry, Jack Y. .... Minneapolis, MN
Perry, James A. .... Midland, MI
Perry, James A. .... Salem, OR
Perry, James B. .... Detroit, MI
Perry, James D. .... Long Beach, CA
Perry, James D., Jr. .... Huntington, WV
Perry, James Douglas .... Stone Mountain, GA
Perry, James E. C. .... Orlando, FL
Perry, James F. .... Pittsboro, NC
Perry, James K. R. Jisho .... Santa Barbara, CA
Perry, James L. .... Santa Ana, CA
Perry, James Lynn .... Mobile, AL
Perry, James M. .... Brewton, AL
Perry, James M. .... North Tonawanda, NY
Perry, James N. .... Cincinnati, OH
Perry, James O., IV .... Pittsburgh, PA
Perry, James Stockton .... Kinston, NC
Perry, James T. .... Wilmington, DE
Perry, James W. .... Sault Ste. Marie, MI
Perry, Jane P. .... Columbus, OH
Perry, Janet G. .... Philadelphia, PA
Perry, Jean Louise .... Danville, CA
Perry, Jeffrey Kevin .... Atlanta, GA
Perry, Jennifer F. .... Indianapolis, IN
Perry, Jennifer L. .... Orlando, FL
Perry, Jerold L. .... Pomona, CA
Perry, Jerome W., Law Offices
Rochester, MN
Perry, Jill D. .... San Diego, CA
Perry, Joan E. .... Lansing, IL
Perry, Joe R. .... Marianna, AR
Perry, John A. .... Hoffman Estates, IL
Perry, John B. .... New Orleans, LA
Perry, John C. .... Spokane, WA
Perry, John E. .... Pittsburgh, PA
Perry, John F. .... Pittsburgh, PA
Perry, John F. .... Sulphur Springs, TX
Perry, John F., III .... Jackson, MS
Perry, John H., III .... Riviera Beach, FL
Perry, John J. .... Houston, TX
Perry, John M., III .... Oklahoma City, OK
Perry, John M., Jr. .... Lynchburg, VA
Perry, John R. .... Detroit, MI
Perry, John R. .... Friendswood, TX
Perry, John R. .... Buffalo, WY
Perry, John W. .... Washington, DC
Perry, John W., Jr. .... Baton Rouge, LA
Perry, Johnson, Murray, Anderson & Miller
LLP .... Santa Rosa, CA
Perry, Jon C. .... Palo Alto, CA
Perry, Jon R. .... Pittsburgh, PA
Perry, Jonathan M. .... Atlanta, GA
Perry, Jonathan R. .... Morristown, TN
Perry, Joseph E. .... New Bedford, MA
Perry, Joseph P. .... Bonner Springs, KS
Perry, Joy Ann (Jan) .... Northbrook, IL
Perry, Julian S. .... Downers Grove, IL
Perry, Juliana Fahrbach .... Roanoke, VA
Perry, Justin S. .... Macon, GA
Perry, Kara McCarthy .... Morristown, NJ
Perry, Karen MacMillan .... Phoenix, AZ
Perry, Karl G. .... Ogden, UT
Perry, Kate M.
Environmental Protection Agency,
Program Office Attorneys, GV
Perry, Katharine S. .... Boston, MA
Perry, Kathy R. .... New York, NY
Perry, Kearon & Campanelli, LLP
New York, NY
Westbury, NY
Perry, Kellogg & Fitzsimons, L.L.P.
San Antonio, TX
Perry, Kenneth D. .... Indiahoma, OK
Perry, Kenneth G. .... Jackson, MS
Perry, Kenneth M. .... Birmingham, AL
Perry, Kenneth M. .... Washington, DC
Perry, Kenneth M. .... New York, NY
Perry, Kenneth R. .... Portland, OR
Perry, Kent T. .... Overland Park, KS
Perry, Kim E. .... Boston, MA
Perry, Kimberly V. .... Westfield, NJ
Perry, Kittrell, Blackburn & Blackburn
Henderson, NC
Perry, Kristin M. .... Bowling Green, MO
Perry, Larry D. .... Knoxville, TN
Perry, Larry Stephen .... Houston, TX
Perry, Larry W. .... Louisville, KY
Perry, Lars A. .... Reno, NV
Perry, Laura A. .... Morgan Hill, CA
Perry, Laura D. .... Morristown, TN
Perry Law Firm, The .... Scranton, PA
Perry Law Firm, The .... Dallas, TX
Perry Law Office .... Little Falls, MN
Perry, Lawrence S. .... New York, NY
Perry, Leah B. .... Philadelphia, PA
Perry, Lee N. .... Gulfport, MS
Perry, Leonard C. .... Brook Park, OH
Perry, Lerner & Quindel, S.C.
Milwaukee, WI
Perry, Leroy F. .... Bridgeport, WV
Perry, Leslie Ecotlyn .... Aliquippa, PA
Perry, Leslie R. .... Santa Rosa, CA
Perry, Lester A. .... Salt Lake City, UT
Perry, Levis H., Jr. .... Cleveland, OH
Perry, Linda L. .... Boca Raton, FL
Perry, Lisa R. .... Denver, CO
Perry & Logan .... North Tonawanda, NY
Perry, Lona Triplett .... Washington, DC
Perry, Lori Lewis .... Santa Barbara, CA
Perry, Lorraine D.H. .... Alameda, CA
Perry, Lynn .... Cleveland, TN
Perry, Lynn M. .... Grand Rapids, MI
Perry, M. Kirk .... Guntersville, AL
Perry, M. Toni .... Huntington Beach, CA
Perry, M. Virginia .... Phoenix, AZ
Perry, Malmberg & Perry .... Logan, UT
Perry, Mansco, III .... St. Paul, MN
Perry, Marc H. .... Philadelphia, PA
Perry, Marcus S. .... Sanford, NC
Perry, Margaret H. .... Baton Rouge, LA
Perry, Margaret J. .... Department of Justice,
Civil Division, GV
Perry, Marjorie R. .... Tucson, AZ
Perry, Mark A. .... Washington, DC
Perry, Mark A. .... Eddington, ME
Perry, Mark B. .... Boise, ID

Perry, Mark B. ... Salisbury, NC
Perry, Mark C. ... Fort Lauderdale, FL
Perry, Mark L. ... Foster City, CA
Perry, Mark T. ... Scranton, PA
Perry, Martin K. ... New Brunswick, NJ
Perry, Marvin Glenn, Jr.
Birmingham, AL
Perry, Mary G. Florendo ... Salinas, CA
Perry, Mary J. ... Tampa, FL
Perry, Mary Lou ... Omaha, NE
Perry, Mary Lynne ... San Diego, CA
Perry, Mary Moran ... Boston, MA
Perry, Mary-Helen ... Washington, DC
Perry, Matthew Hart ... Tampa, FL
Perry, Matthew J. ... Columbia, SC
Perry, Matthew W., Jr. ... Palmyra, VA
Perry and McKendry ... Wilton, CT
Perry, Megan F. ... Walnut Creek, CA
Perry, Michael ... Scranton, PA
Perry, Michael B. ... Saint Marys, GA
Perry, Michael G. ... Coleman, WI
Perry, Michael H. ... Lansing, MI
Perry, Michael J. ... Marina Del Rey, CA
Perry, Michael J. ... Chicago, IL
Perry, Michael Kiah ... Wake Forest, NC
Perry, Michael N. ... El Paso, TX
Perry, Michael P. ... Little Falls, MN
Perry, Michael R. ... Phoenix, AZ
Perry, Michael R. ... Irvine, CA
Perry, Michael R. ... Boston, MA
Perry, Michael S. ... Sarasota, FL
Perry, Michael T. ... Baton Rouge, LA
Perry, Michael V. ... Phoenix, AZ
Perry, Michelle ... Daphne, AL
Perry, Michelle Diane ... Oakland, CA
Perry, Michelle Gibeaut ... Wellesley, MA
Perry, Mike ... Naperville, IL
Perry, Morton G. ... Staten Island, NY
Perry, Morton L. ... Stuart, FL
Perry & Murr ... Bay St. Louis, MS
Biloxi, MS
Gulfport, MS
Hattiesburg, MS
Jackson, MS
Pascagoula, MS
Perry, Nancy ... Savannah, GA
Perry, Natalie M. ... Chicago, IL
Perry, Nathaniel Charles, III ... Flint, MI
Perry, Nellie ... Hobart, OK
Perry, Nichelle Jones ... Durham, NC
Perry, Norman R. ... Berrien Springs, MI
Perry & O'Brien LLP ... Cleveland, OH
Perry, Pamela I. ... Miami, FL
Perry, Patricia H. ... San Francisco, CA
Perry, Patricia M. ... Attleboro, MA
Perry, Patrick Austin ... Los Angeles, CA
Perry, Patrick, Farmer & Michaux, P.A.
Charlotte, NC
Raleigh, NC
Perry, Patrick H. ... Gainesville, FL
Perry, Patrick J. ... San Luis Obispo, CA
Perry, Paul D. ... Ridgeland, MS
Perry, Paul E. ... Markham, IL
Perry, Paul E. ... Bloomfield Hills, MI
Perry & Perry ... Montgomery, AL
Perry & Perry ... Washington, DC
Storm Lake, IA
Perry & Perry ... Morristown, TN
Perry, Perry & Perry ... Minneapolis, MN
Perry, Perry & Perry ... Kinston, NC
Perry, Peter A. ... Sparks, NV
Perry, Peter E., Jr. ... Bristol, PA
Perry, Peter P. ... Allentown, PA
Perry, Philip E. ... Bradenton, FL
Perry, Philip J. ... Washington, DC
Perry, Phillip B. ... New York, NY
Philadelphia, PA
Perry, Preston & Miller ... Paintsville, KY
Perry, Priscilla Ellen ... Dallas, TX
Perry, Putnam H. ... Hartford, CT
Perry, R. Scott, Jr. ... Fort Wayne, IN
Perry, R.W., Law Offices of ... Portland, OR
Perry, Ralph B., III ... Los Angeles, CA
Perry, Ralph W. ... Santa Rosa, CA
Perry, Randall B. ... Huntsville, AL
Perry, Randall J. ... Rutherford, NJ
Perry, Randolph H. ... Fairfax, VA
Perry, Randolph S. ... Detroit, MI
Perry, Raymond S., Jr. ... Manchester, NH
Perry, Reid D. ... Farmington Hills, MI
Perry & Reuter, L.C. ... Overland Park, KS
Kansas City, MO
Perry, Richard ... Easton, MD
Perry, Richard ... Milwaukee, WI
Perry, Richard A. ... Ocala, FL
Perry, Richard J. ... Norwich, CT
Perry, Richard J., Jr. ... Washington, DC
Perry, Richard, LLC ... Easton, MD
Perry, Richard M. ... Enid, OK
Perry, Richard O. ... Brewster, MA
Perry, Richard P., (J.D., P.C.)
Roswell, GA
Perry, Richard T. ... Mattawa, WA
Perry, Richard W. ... Amarillo, TX
Perry, Richd. A. ... Republic, WA
Perry, Rife, Walters, Sullivan & Cain
Oklahoma City, OK
Perry, Robert ... Reno, NV
Perry, Robert A. ... Sacramento, CA
Perry, Robert A. ... Maynard, MA
Perry, Robert B. ... Dallas, TX
Perry, Robert E. ... Jackson, MS
Perry, Robert E., Jr. ... Charlotte, NC
Perry, Robert F. ... New York, NY
Perry, Robert H., Ltd. ... Carson City, NV
Reno, NV
Perry, Robert J. ... Clearwater, FL
Perry, Robert J. ... Auburn, KS
Perry, Robert J. ... South Burlington, VT
Perry, Robert J. ... Dillwyn, VA
Perry, Robert J., & Associates
Columbus, OH
Perry, Robert L., Jr. ... Ashland City, TN
Perry, Robert M. ... Gainesville, FL
Perry, Robert P. ... Boca Raton, FL
Naples, FL
Palm Beach Gardens, FL
Birmingham, MI
Perry, Robert R. ... New York, NY
Perry, Robert X., Jr. ... Washington, DC
Perry, Robin ... Chula Vista, CA
Perry, Robin L. ... Woodstock, IL
Perry, Robt. S. ... Americus, GA
Perry, Roger ... Benton, KY
Perry, Roger F. ... Philadelphia, PA
Perry, Roger J. ... Charles Town, WV
Perry, Roger, Law Offices, P.S.C.
Benton, KY
Perry, Ronald ... York, PA
Perry, Ronald D. ... Spring, TX
Perry, Ronald K. ... San Pedro, CA
Perry, Ronald K. ... Santa Barbara, CA
Perry, Rory L., II ... Charleston, WV
Perry, Rosario ... Santa Monica, CA
Perry, Rotraud M., (Mrs.) ... Washington, DC
Perry, Roya R. ... Los Angeles, CA
Perry, R. R. ... Lincoln, NE
Perry, Russell G. ... Saratoga, CA
Perry, R.W., Law Offices of ... Tualatin, OR
Perry, Ryan L. ... Detroit, MI
Perry, S. Brian ... Lafayette, LA
Perry, Sam R. ... Austin, TX
Perry, Samuel M. ... New York, NY
Perry, Samuel S. ... Cleveland, OH
Perry, Samuel S., and Associates
Cleveland, OH
Perry, Sandra J. ... Peoria, IL
Perry & Schmucker ... South Burlington, VT
Perry & Schwarz ... New York, NY
Perry, Scott ... Hartford, CT
Perry, Scott D. ... Long Beach, CA
Perry, Scott M. ... Washington, DC
Perry, Sequoyah, Jr. ... Lubbock, TX
Perry, Shan B. ... Idaho Falls, ID
Perry, Shane C. ... Minneapolis, MN
Perry, Shaun Watchie ... Seattle, WA
Perry, Shawn ... Minneapolis, MN
Perry, Sheldon ... Los Angeles, CA
Perry, Sherryl R. ... Philadelphia, PA
Perry & Spann, A Professional Corporation
Las Vegas, NV
Reno, NV
Perry, Spence W.
Federal Emergency Management Agency, Office of the General Counsel, GV
Perry, Stanley A. ... Arlington Heights, IL
Perry, Stanley L. ... Galliano, LA
Perry, Stephen F. ... Cleveland, OH
Perry, Stephen H. ... Providence, RI
Perry, Stephen M. ... Boston, MA
Perry, Steve M. ... Sandy, UT
Perry, Steven L. ... Stuart, FL
Perry, Steven M. ... Los Angeles, CA
Perry, Stewart R. ... Minneapolis, MN
Perry, Stuart ... New York, NY
Perry & Stuursma, LLP ... Grand Rapids, MI
Perry, Susan E. ... Santa Clarita, CA
Perry, Susan E. ... Atlanta, GA
Perry, Susan M. ... Racine, WI
Perry, Suzanne M. ... Washington, DC
Perry, T. Dudley ... Montgomery, AL
Perry, T. Dudley, Jr. ... Montgomery, AL
Perry, Tallien ... Los Angeles, CA
Perry, Taylor T., Jr. ... Demopolis, AL
Perry, Terance P. ... Holliston, MA
Perry, Terese Marie ... San Francisco, CA
Perry, Theodore S. ... Logan, UT
Perry, Thomas A. ... Kew Gardens, NY
Perry, Thomas J. ... Morristown, NJ
Perry, Thomas, Jr. ... Atlanta, GA
Perry, Thomas O. ... Stockton, CA
Perry, Thomas W. ... Boston, MA
Perry, Timothy F. ... San Francisco, CA
Perry, Timothy J. ... Boston, MA
Providence, RI
Perry, Timothy J. ... Syracuse, NY
Perry, Timothy S. ... Atlanta, GA
Perry, Twila L. ... Newark, NJ
Perry, Valerie H. ... Houston, TX
Perry, Vanessa L. ... Vallejo, CA
Perry, Veronica A. ... White Plains, NY
Perry, Victor A. ... Las Vegas, NV
Reno, NV
Perry, Virginia Dante ... Colonial Heights, VA
Perry & Vloedman ... Gainesville, FL
Perry, W. Wayne ... Durham, NC
Perry, Wade B., Jr. ... Mobile, AL
Perry, Walter ... Salem, OR
Perry & Walters, LLP ... Albany, GA
Perry, Warren R. ... San Anselmo, CA
Perry, Warren S. ... Kinston, NC
Perry, Wayne M. ... Redmond, WA
Perry, Weldon W. 'Chip', Jr. ... Lexington, MO
Perry & Wildman ... Modesto, CA
Perry, William A., Jr. ... Evergreen, CO
Perry, William A., Jr. ... Nyack, NY
Perry, William B. ... Storm Lake, IA
Perry, William E. ... Washington, DC
Perry, William E., III ... Ajo, AZ
Perry, William F. ... Livingston, NJ
Perry, William H., III ... Joplin, MO
Perry, William J. ... Chicago, IL
Perry, William J. ... Covington, LA
Perry, William J. ... Pawnee, OK
Perry, William K. ... Washington, DC
Perry, William M. ... Commack, NY
Perry, William R. ... Washington, DC
Perry, William T. ... Agua Dulce, CA
Perry, Willie R., Jr. ... Durham, NC
Perry, Wilson D. ... Milwaukee, WI
Perry & Windels ... New York, NY
Dillwyn, VA
Perry, Wm. D. ... Washington, DC
Perry & Womack ... Longview, TX
Perry, W. S. ... Nashville, GA
Perry-Harris, Deborah ... Riverdale, MD
Perry-Isaacson, Misty A. ... Orange, CA
Perry Jr., Robert J. ... Jacksonville, FL
Perry-Lehnert, Dawn E. ... Fort Myers, FL
Perryman, Bruce A. ... Waco, TX
Perryman, David G. ... Atlanta, GA
Perryman, David L. ... Chickasha, OK
Oklahoma City, OK
Perryman, Eric ... Denver, CO
Perryman, Joan M. ... New York, NY
Perryman, K. C. ... Sayre, OK
Perryman, Nancy Adams ... Athens, TX
Perryman, Neal F. ... St. Louis, MO
Perryman, Steven ... La Mirada, CA
Perryman, Ted L. ... Belleville, IL
St. Louis, MO
Perryman, Zachary
United States Tax Court, GV
Perry-Miller & Blount, L.L.P. ... Dallas, TX
Perry-Miller, Ralph C. ... Dallas, TX
Pers, Elaine M. ... Albany, NY
Pers, Herman ... Pound Ridge, NY
Pers, Jessica S. ... San Francisco, CA
Persa, John G. ... Milwaukee, WI
Persad, Teeluck ... Orlando, FL
Persampieri, Nicholas F.
Department of Justice, Environment and Natural Resources Division, GV
Persandi, George C. ... Miami, FL
Persante, Patricia McNair
Palm Beach Gardens, FL
Persante, Robert ... Clearwater, FL
Persaud & Decker ... Coral Gables, FL
Persaud, Horace H. ... Jamaica, NY
Persaud, Horace H., P.C. ... Jamaica, NY
Persaud, Samuel A. ... Coral Gables, FL
Persaud, Sharmine ... Woodbury, NY
Persaud, Veena D. ... Los Angeles, CA
Perschall, Clement F., Jr. (P.L.C.)
Metairie, LA
Perschbach, James E. ... Corpus Christi, TX
Perschbacher, Rex R. ... Davis, CA
Perscheid, Kenneth M. ... Walnut Creek, CA
Perschetz, Arthur D. ... Washington, DC
Baltimore, MD
Perschetz, Martin L. ... New York, NY
Perse, Karen G. ... Denver, CO
Perse, Michael S. ... Miami, FL
Persechino, Nancy M. ... Washington, DC
Perselay, Lee A. ... Concord, NH
Persell, Charles B. ... New York, NY
Persels, Jimmy Burdette ... Makanda, IL
Perseo, Mariann G. ... New York, NY
Perser, Peggy Roberts ... Houston, TX
Pershall, Keith E. ... Sacramento, CA
Pershall, Sallye N. ... Boise, ID
Pershan, Lee ... New York, NY
Pershan, Richard H., Jr. ... Hartford, CT
Pershe, Ratimir M. ... San Juan, PR
Pershes, Robert E. ... Coral Springs, FL
Pershes & Schwartz, P.A.
Coral Springs, FL
Fort Lauderdale, FL
Pershing, Jennifer A. ... Phoenix, AZ
Pershing, Laura M. ... Boise, ID
Pershing, Lenore M. ... Cleveland, OH
Pershing, Melissa Anne ... Cary, NC
Pershing, Richard W. S. ... Corona, CA
Pershing, Stephen B. ... Department of Justice, Civil Rights Division, GV
Pershkow, Barry I. ... Washington, DC
Persian, Eric M. ... Washington, DC
Fairfax, VA
Persian, Gary E. ... Minneapolis, MN
Persian, MacGregor & Thompson
Minneapolis, MN
Persiani, John B. ... West Palm Beach, FL
Persichilli, J. Roger ... Trenton, NJ
Persichilli, Susan P. ... New York, NY
Persichilli, Thomas ... Deer Park, NY
Persick, Lawrence J. ... West Chester, PA
Persico, Anthony ... Boca Raton, FL
Persico, Joseph L. ... Wilkes-Barre, PA
Persico, Richard A. ... Saratoga Springs, NY
Persily, Marc A. ... New York, NY
Persin, Dennis N. ... Greensburg, PA
Persin, Milton F. ... Lisle, IL
Persin, Nicholas E. ... Grundy, VA
Persin, Raymond C. ... Chicago, IL
Persin, Raymond C., Law Offices of
Chicago, IL
Persina, William E.
Federal Labor Relations Authority, Office of the Solicitor, GV
Persinger, Craig R. ... Marion, IN
Persinger, Howard M., Jr. ... Williamson, WV
Persinger, Howard M., Jr., L.C.
Williamson, WV
Persinger, Howard Moses, III
Charleston, WV
Persinger, James P. ... Santa Ana, CA
Persinger, Joseph M. ... New York, NY
Persinger, Richard B. ... New York, NY
Persinger, Richard D. ... Holland, MI
Persinger, Roger E. ... Bismarck, ND
Persinger, Thomas ... Charleston, WV
Persio, Dino S. ... Ebensburg, PA
Persio, Kevin D. ... Ebensburg, PA
Persion, Kenneth I. ... Los Angeles, CA
Perske, Anne Marie ... Englewood, NJ
Perskie, Lawrence M. ... Atlantic City, NJ
Perskie Nehmad & Perillo, A Professional Corporation ... Atlantic City, NJ
Perskie, Philip J. ... Atlantic City, NJ
Perskie, Steven P. ... Atlantic City, NJ
Perskin, Brian D. ... Brooklyn, NY
Perskin, Randy S. ... New York, NY
Perskin, Robert S. ... Bayside, NY
Perskin, Robert S., P.C. ... Bayside, NY
Persky, Arnold ... Newtown, CT
Persky, Bernard ... New York, NY
Persky, David ... New York, NY
Persky, David W. ... Tampa, FL
Persky, J., & Associates, P.C.
New York, NY
Persky, Jerry ... Los Angeles, CA
Persky, Joel ... Saginaw, MI
Pittsburgh, PA
Persky, Marla S. ... Deerfield, IL
Persky, Raphael ... New York, NY
Persky, Robert S. ... Jersey City, NJ
Persky, Robert S. ... New York, NY
Persky, Seymour H. ... Chicago, IL
Persky, Shapiro, Salim, Esper, Arnoff & Nolfi Co., L.P.A. ... Cleveland, OH
Persky, Tom Ernest ... Irvine, CA
Persley, Kathryn Renee ... Kansas City, MO
Persley, Sidney ... Fort Lee, NJ
Persoff, Dan ... Woodland Hills, CA
Persoff, Stephan ... Carle Place, NY
Persohn, Leroy L., IV ... Alice, TX
Person, Allen S. ... Perrysburg, OH
Person, Barbara Ebers ... Omaha, NE
Person, Blair A. ... Detroit, MI
Person, Carl E. ... New York, NY
Person & Craver LLP ... Washington, DC
Person, Curtis, Jr. ... Memphis, TN
Person, Cynthia Ranck ... Williamsport, PA
Person, David B. ... San Antonio, TX
Person, David Wayne ... Houston, TX
Person, Dier, Person, Osborn & Cox
Alma, NE
Holdrege, NE
Person, Douglas P. ... Omaha, NE
Person, Eric Oliver ... New Orleans, LA
Person, Gary D. ... Fort Smith, AR
Person, George J. ... Laredo, TX
Person, J. Brad ... West Liberty, IA
Person, James C., Jr. ... Newport Beach, CA
Person, Jean F. ... Camden, NC
Person, John C. ... Washington, DC
Person, John C. ... New Orleans, LA
Person, John C. ... Alma, NE
Person, John D. ... New Orleans, LA
Person, John E., III ... Wilmore, KY
Person, John R. ... Edina, MN
Person, John W. ... East Lansing, MI
Person, John W. ... Brainerd, MN
Person, Kent E. ... Holdrege, NE
Person, Michele E. ... Macon, GA
Person & Miester, L.L.P. ... New Orleans, LA
Person, Rebecca F. ... Fayetteville, NC
Person, Richard E. ... Holdrege, NE
Person, Roland E. ... Chicago, IL
Person, Terry McKenney ... East Lansing, MI
Person, Victor H. ... Pasadena, CA
Person, Whitworth, Ramos, Borchers & Morales, L.L.P. ... Laredo, TX
Person, W. L., Jr. ... Williamsburg, VA
Personette, Carol Ann ... Hackensack, NJ
Personette, Donald B. ... Treasury Department, United States Secret Service, GV
Personette, Robert E. ... Hackensack, NJ
Personius, James E. ... Elmira, NY
Personius, Prechtl, Mattison & Palmer
Bath, NY
Corning, NY
Elmira, NY
Watkins Glen, NY
Personius, Rodney O. ... Buffalo, NY
Persons, Alan R. ... Rochester, NY
Persons, Benton H. ... Andalusia, AL
Persons, Bonnie B. ... San Jose, CA
Persons, David K. ... Metairie, LA
Persons, Edgar N., III ... Philadelphia, PA
Persons, Fred K. ... Detroit, MI
Persons, Henry Z. ... Chicago, IL
Persons, J. Robert ... Atlanta, GA
Persons, James B. ... Gulfport, MS
Persons, John D., III ... Richmond, VA
Persons, John P. ... New York, NY
Persons, John W. ... Farmingdale, NY
Persons, Jonathan Michael ... New York, NY
Persons, Kaye J. ... Biloxi, MS
Persons & Miller ... Chico, CA
Persons, Oscar N. ... Washington, DC
Atlanta, GA
Persons, Paul T. ... Chico, CA
Persons, Robert B., Jr.
Jacksonville Beach, FL
Persons, Robert K. ... Chico, CA
Persons, Sondra J. ... Santa Rosa, CA
Persons, W. Ray ... Atlanta, GA
Persons, Wilton B., Jr. ... Savannah, GA
Personte, Michael J. ... Rochester, NY
Persse, Robert Lawrence ... Springfield, GA
Persson, Darrold E. ... Hibbing, MN
Persson, David P. ... Sarasota, FL
Persson, Dion D. ... Denver, CO
Persson, E. Hjalmar ... Hamilton, OH
Persson, Larry ... Hamilton, MT
Persson, Randolph ... Scottsdale, AZ
Persson, Tommy ... Los Angeles, CA
Persun, Lloyd R. ... Harrisburg, PA
Persun, Mark D. ... Somerset, PA
Persyn, Mary G. ... Valparaiso, IN

Perta, Alan E. ... Utica, NY
Pertcheck, Darcy M. ... San Francisco, CA
Pertchek, Kerri M. ... Denver, CO
Pertchik, Jonathan M. ... Washington, DC
Pertel, Joseph A. ... Santa Monica, CA
Perten, John H. ... Framingham, MA
Perticari, Amy Lynne ... Annapolis, MD
Perticone, John L. ... Binghamton, NY
Perticone, Maria ... Rochester, NY
Perticone, Michael J. ... Baltimore, MD
Pertierra, José ... Washington, DC
Pertierra, Roberto E. ... Miami, FL
Pertierra, Roberto E., P.A. ... Miami, FL
Pertile, Arthur L., III ... Waco, TX
Pertile, Cynthia L. ... Los Angeles, CA
Pertner, O. Fredrich ... Northville, MI
Pertnoy, Leonard D. ... Miami, FL
Pertnoy, Sidney M. ... Miami, FL
Pertnoy, Solowsky, Allen & Haber, P.A.
Miami, FL
Perttula, Heather L. ... Dallas, TX
Perttula, Joshua M. ... Los Angeles, CA
Perttunen, Maryann Pierce
Bloomfield Hills, MI
Pertz, Richard ... Utica, NY
Pertzik, Marvin J. ... St. Paul, MN
Perugini, John T. ... Chicago, IL
Perugini, Maria A. ... Washington, DC
Perugino, Robert ... Tulsa, OK
Perullo, John F. ... Boston, MA
Perun, Angela L. ... New Providence, NJ
Perun, Robert K. ... San Francisco, CA
Perun, William D., Jr. ... Richmond, VA
Perunovich, James ... Hibbing, MN
Perusek, Ginger Lynch ... Bradenton, FL
Lakeland, FL
Perusse, Catherine Vance ... Stamford, CT
Perusse, Michele C. ... Farmington, CT
Perutelli, Barbara Jones ... Nashville, TN
Peruto, A. Charles, Jr. ... Philadelphia, PA
Peruto, A. Charles, Sr. ... Philadelphia, PA
Peruto, James A. ... Philadelphia, PA
Peruto, John M. ... Philadelphia, PA
Peruto, Lori N. ... Philadelphia, PA
Peruto & Peruto ... Philadelphia, PA
Peruzzi, Linda M. ... Manchester, NH
Pervere, Maude H. ... Stanford, CA
Pervis, Donald E. ... Sarasota, FL
Perwich, Daniel J. ... San Diego, CA
Perwich, Goff & Karavatos
Newport Beach, CA
San Diego, CA
Perwin, David S. ... Houston, TX
Perwin, Jean S. ... Miami, FL
Perwin, Joel S. ... Miami, FL
Perwin, Scott E. ... Miami, FL
Peryam, Alan W. ... Denver, CO
Peryam, Alan W., LLC ... Denver, CO
Peryer, Kevin L. ... Plattsburgh, NY
Perz, Frederick C. ... Tomball, TX
Perzan, Christopher P. ... Springfield, IL
Perzan, Howard L. ... Philadelphia, PA
Perzan, Jeffrey ... Brookfield, WI
Perzan, Joseph C. ... Oviedo, FL
Perzan, Karen DaCosta ... Whitefish Bay, WI
Perzell, Philip J. ... Chicago, IL
Perz-Fresard, Patricia ... Mount Clemens, MI
Perzik, James L. ... Inglewood, CA
Perzin, Michael ... New Haven, CT
Perzley, Alan H. ... Newark, NJ
Perzley, Laurie B. ... Portland, ME
Pesant, Guillermo ... Coral Gables, FL
Pesant, Guillermo, P.A. ... Coral Gables, FL
Pesante, Wilfredo, Jr. ... Charlottesville, VA
Pesarchick, Stephen G. ... Syracuse, NY
Pesaresi, Gina A. ... Breinigsville, PA
Pesavento, Raymond R. ... Chicago, IL
Pescatello, Michael C. ... San Francisco, CA
Pescatello, Paul R. ... Hartford, CT
Pescatore, Alfred C., Jr. ... Hackensack, NJ
Pescatore, Richard M. ... Vineland, NJ
Pesce, Carl J. ... St. Louis, MO
Pesce, Christopher A. ... Seattle, WA
Pesce, Edward J. ... Ellicott City, MD
Pesce, Edward J., P.A. ... Ellicott City, MD
Pesce, Frank V. ... Mineola, NY
Pesce, Michael ... Clifton, NJ
Pesce, Michael L. ... Brooklyn, NY
Pesce, Nick ... Memphis, TN
Pesce, Paula M. ... Houston, TX
Pesce, Randal J. ... New York, NY
Pesce, Teresa ... New York, NY
Pesce, William J., II ... Sacramento, CA
Pesce-Fusto, Eleanor ... Bronx, NY
Pesch, Ellen P. ... Chicago, IL
Pesch, Susan Marie ... Wheaton, IL
Pesch, William D. ... Hagåtña, GU
Peschcke-Koedt, Lisa D. V. ... Palo Alto, CA
Peschel, Brian J. ... Seattle, WA
Peschel, Dwight E. ... Seguin, TX
Peschel, John L. ... New Orleans, LA
Peschel, Mark J. ... Minneapolis, MN
Pesciotta, Gregg ... Freehold, NJ
Pescosolido, Dana N. ... Baltimore, MD
Pescosolido, Pamela J. ... Visalia, CA
Pesek, Charles J. ... Geneva, IL
Pesek, Fred A. ... Brecksville, OH
Pesek, Leon F. ... Texarkana, TX
Pesek, Leon F., Jr. ... New Boston, TX
Pesek, Paul E., (P.C.) ... Dallas, TX
Pesek, Phillip A. ... Little Rock, AR
Pesek, Rebecca B. ... Dallas, TX
Pesel, David A. ... Houston, TX
Peseski, Michael J. ... Grosse Pointe, MI
Pesesky, Amy G. ... Norfolk, VA
Pesetsky, Ian Alexander
Upper Marlboro, MD
Pesetsky, Walter S. ... North Miami Beach, FL
Pesetsky, Warren B. ... New York, NY
Pesetsky & Zack, P.A.
North Miami Beach, FL
Peshek, Linda M. ... Canton, OH
Peshek, Peter A. ... Madison, WI
Peshel, Elsbeth T. ... Vero Beach, FL
Peshel, Mary J. ... San Diego, CA
Peshell, Rinehart L. ... Midvale, UT
Peshkin, Joy Kony ... Westport, CT
Peshkin Kotalik & Burghart, A Professional Corporation ... Phoenix, AZ
Peshkin, Lawrence A. ... Phoenix, AZ
Peshkin, S. David ... Scottsdale, AZ
Pesick, Jerome P. ... Southfield, MI
Pesik, Eric Roring ... Santa Cruz, CA
Pesikoff, Bette ... Houston, TX
Pesin, Byron I. ... Palm Springs, CA
Pesin, Edward ... North Bergen, NJ
Pesin, Edward, A Professional Corporation
North Bergen, NJ
Pesin, Morris ... Jersey City, NJ
Pesiri, Emil G. ... San Francisco, CA
Peska, David J. ... West Haven, CT
Peska, Kevin R. ... Department of Commerce, Patent and Trademark Office, GV
Peskar, Stanley G. ... St. Paul, MN
Peskin, Bernard M. ... Chicago, IL
Peskin, Bonnie Gust ... Cleveland, OH
Peskin, Judd L. ... Springfield, MA
Peskin, Lawrence F. ... Cleveland, OH
Peskin, Lester ... New York, NY
Peskin, M. Scott ... Atlanta, GA
Peskin, Neal C. ... Los Angeles, CA
Peskin, Richard S. ... New York, NY
Peskin, Sandra R. ... Tempe, AZ
Peskin, Stacy P. ... New York, NY
Peskin, Stephen H. ... New York, NY
Peskind, E. J. ... Scottsdale, AZ
Peskind Hymson & Goldstein, P.C.
Phoenix, AZ
Scottsdale, AZ
Peskind, Neal S. ... Denver, CO
Peskind & Peskind, Ltd. ... Geneva, IL
Peskind, Steven N. ... Geneva, IL
Peskin-Shepherd, Alisa A.
Farmington Hills, MI
Peskoe, Andrew C. ... New York, NY
Peskoe, Florence R. ... Freehold, NJ
Peskoe, Howard E. ... New York, NY
Peskoe, Michael P. ... Madison, NJ
Peskoff, Joanne B. ... Plymouth Meeting, PA
Peskowitz, Michael ... New York, NY
Peslak, Arthur M. ... Freehold, NJ
New York, NY
Peslar, Norman G. ... Warren, MI
Pesnell, A. Matt ... Jackson, MS
Pesnell, Billy R. ... Shreveport, LA
Pesnell, J. Whitney ... Shreveport, LA
Pesnell, John Whitney ... Baton Rouge, LA
Pesnell, W. Alan ... Alexandria, LA
Pesner Law Group, The, PLC
McLean, VA
Pesner, Steven M., (P.C.) ... New York, NY
Pesner, Susan M. ... McLean, VA
Pesola, Taisto A. ... Keizer, OR
Pesota, John P. ... Scranton, PA
Pesquera, Ricardo R. ... Orlando, FL
Pessa, Ingrid E. ... New York, NY
Pessala, Elizabeth Dalal ... Westbury, NY
Pessala, John B. ... Mineola, NY
Pessel, William O., Jr. ... Princeton, NJ
Pessen, Abigail ... New York, NY
Pesses, Ian D. ... Southfield, MI
Pessia, Michael W. ... Canton, MA
Pessillo, Dorothy M. ... Clearwater, FL
Pessin, Andrew S.
Department of Transportation, U. S. Coast Guard, GV
Pessin, Baird, Wells & Ward ... Belleville, IL
Pessin, David N. ... Towson, MD
Pessin, Gregg ... Miami, FL
Pessin, Karol M. ... Thousand Oaks, CA
Pessin, Myron Stuart ... Boston, MA
Pessin, Norman E. ... Laurel, MD
Pessin, Sam S. ... Belleville, IL
Pessina, Cyril C. ... Harper Woods, MI
Pessis, Surekha A. ... Los Angeles, CA
Pesso, Mark S. ... Washington, DC
Pesso, Steven M. ... Boca Raton, FL
Pessoa, Ignacio B. ... Alexandria, VA
Pessolano, Mark P. ... Bloomfield, NJ
Pessolano, Robert W. ... Louisville, KY
Pesta, Ben Walter ... Los Angeles, CA
Pestaina, Kaye L. ... Silver Spring, MD
Pestana, Frank S. ... Los Angeles, CA
Pestana, Georgia Mary ... New York, NY
Pestano, Lisa A. ... Los Angeles, CA
Pestarino, Angelo T. ... Saratoga, CA
Pestcoe, Bernard C. ... Hollywood, FL
Pestello-Sharf, Stephanie ... Columbus, OH
Pester, Goldberg & Schiff ... Carle Place, NY
Pester, Miriam K. ... New York, NY
Pester, Monroe ... Carle Place, NY
Pester, Pamela J. ... San Francisco, CA
Pester, Tamara ... Atlanta, GA
Pesterfield, Leslie R. ... Seattle, WA
Pesticci, Christine E. ... Scottsdale, AZ
Pestine & Neuman ... Northbrook, IL
Pestine, Ronald G. ... Northbrook, IL
Pestinger, R. Samuel ... Irving, TX
Pestka, Steven M. ... Grand Rapids, MI
Pestle, John W. ... Grand Rapids, MI
Pesto, Marilyn M. ... Kansas City, MO
Pesto, Richard M. ... Westfield, MA
Pestone, Wayne
Securities and Exchange Commission, Office of Compliance Inspections and Examinations, GV
Pestotnik, Timothy R. ... San Diego, CA
Pestronk, Mark ... Fairfax, VA
Peszko, Mark J. ... Buffalo, NY
Petacchi, Erica L.
Department Of The Interior, Bureau of Land Management, GV
Petacque, Gerald M. ... Chicago, IL
Petajan, Albert H. ... Milwaukee, WI
Petak, Devera L. ... Los Angeles, CA
Petak, Ronald L. ... Fond du Lac, WI
Petak, Steven M. ... Houston, TX
Petal, Malcolm R. ... New Orleans, LA
Petalas, Daniel A. ... Washington, DC
Petas, Marc E. ... Los Angeles, CA
Petaway, Dana Rene ... Hartford, CT
Petche, Mark A. ... Tampa, FL
Petchenik, Larry A. ... Chicago, IL
Petchesky, Harry J. ... New York, NY
Petchul, Dirk E. ... Santa Ana, CA
Pete, Colette A. ... Philadelphia, PA
Pete, Robert A. ... Crown Point, IN
Peteet, Jerry Lee ... Gary, IN
Peteet, Porter W. ... Greenwood, MS
Petefish, Immel & Heeb, L.L.P.
Lawrence, KS
Petefish, Olin K. ... Lawrence, KS
Petelle, James F. ... Orland Park, IL
Petelos, Teresa Bearden ... Pleasant Grove, AL
Petentler, John A. ... Billings, MT
Peter, Alois, Jr. ... Los Angeles, CA
Peter, Arnold P. ... Los Angeles, CA
Peter, Bernard G., Jr. ... Chicago, IL
Peter, Bonnie Jean ... Basking Ridge, NJ
Peter, Bradley S. ... Napa, CA
Peter, David L. ... Washington, DC
Peter, Donna J. ... Roseville, CA
Peter E.J. Nilsson ... Livonia, NY
Peter, Frank T. ... Fort Lauderdale, FL
Peter, Gary E. ... St. Paul, MN
Peter, Jacalyn W. ... Tulsa, OK
Peter, James P. ... Richmond, VA
Peter, Karl A. ... Providence Forge, VA
Peter, Kevin N. ... Houston, TX
Peter, Laura A. ... San Francisco, CA
Peter, Linda L. ... San Diego, CA
Peter, Paul J. ... Lincoln, NE
Peter, Phillips S. ... Washington, DC
Peter, Robert L. ... Ellinwood, KS
Peter, Robert L., P.A. ... Ellinwood, KS
Peter, Thomas G. ... Baltimore, MD
Peter, Werner B. ... Mantoloking, NJ
Peterffy, Jan L.A. von ... Huntersville, NC
Peterfreund, Joshua ... Greenwich, CT
Peterfy, Agota ... St. Louis, MO
Petering, Robert R. ... San Diego, CA
Petering, Roland ... Kansas City, MO
Peterka, Edward R. ... Aurora, IL
Chicago, IL
Peterka, Karin E. ... Los Angeles, CA
Peterka, Kristine M. ... Los Angeles, CA
Peterkin, Michael W. ... Bend, OR
Peterkin, Rachel S. ... Tampa, FL
Peterkort, Carol F. ... Salt Lake City, UT
Peterlin, Gary L. ... Peru, IL
Peterlin, Tracy K. ... Rancho Cucamonga, CA
Peterman, Alan R. ... Syracuse, NY
Peterman, Amy E. ... Southfield, MI
Peterman, Amy E., P.C. ... Southfield, MI
Peterman, Anthony E. ... Round Rock, TX
Peterman & Bohn ... Chicago, IL
Peterman, Brian W. ... Austin, TX
Peterman, Carleton H. ... Cockeysville, MD
Peterman, David S., (P.C.) ... Houston, TX
Peterman, Eric J. ... New York, NY
Peterman, George F., III ... Macon, GA
Peterman, Jody D. ... Valdosta, GA
Peterman, Jody D., P.C. ... Valdosta, GA
Peterman, Kevin J. ... Albuquerque, NM
Peterman, Laura M. ... Columbus, OH
Peterman, Mark H. ... Portland, OR
Peterman, Michael B. ... Detroit, MI
Peterman, Michael J. ... Mayfield Heights, OH
Peterman, Nancy A. ... Chicago, IL
Peterman, Nathan S. ... West Bloomfield, MI
Peterman, Patricia D. ... Billings, MT
Peterman, Randall A. ... Boise, ID
Peterman, Roger C. ... Haworth, NJ
Peterman, Roger L. ... Covington, KY
Louisville, KY
Peterman, Scott D. ... Washington, DC
Peterman & Stotts, L.L.P.
Albuquerque, NM
Peterman, T. Russell, Jr. ... New Bern, NC
Peterman, Thomas A. ... Las Vegas, NV
Peterman, William C. ... Chicago, IL
Petermann, Conrad D. ... Beverly Hills, CA
Petermann, Douglas G. ... Milwaukee, WI
Petermann, Richard P., (P.A.)
Fort Walton Beach, FL
Petermann, Thomas J. ... Chicago, IL
Petermann, Tonya C. ... Shalimar, FL
Peternell, Mark ... Wenatchee, WA
Peteros, Karen H. ... Palo Alto, CA
Peterpaul, Anthony J. ... Springfield, NJ
Peterpaul, Clark, Corcoran & Costello, P.C.
Springfield, NJ
Peterpaul, Frank J. ... Springfield, NJ
Peterpaul, Luanne M. ... Springfield, NJ
Peters, A. Allen ... Arlington Heights, IL
Peters, Albert C., II ... Harrisburg, PA
Peters, Alec, Jr. ... Los Angeles, CA
Peters, Alexander McC. ... Raleigh, NC
Peters, Alexandra M. ... Minneapolis, MN
Peters, Allen C. ... Los Angeles, CA
Peters, Allison Lynn ... Wilmington, DE
Peters, Alvin L. ... Panama City, FL
Peters, Amanda D. ... Waycross, GA
Peters, Amos, Jr. ... Taylor, TX
Peters, Angela ... Buffalo Grove, IL
Peters, Ann Davis ... Inglewood, CA
Peters, Ann Marie H. ... Washington, DC
Peters, Anne Marie ... Palo Alto, CA
Peters, Arthur M., Jr. ... Danville, PA
Peters, Aulana L. ... Los Angeles, CA
Washington, DC
Peters, Barbara J. ... Santa Monica, CA
Peters, Barry ... Eagle, ID
Peters, Barry, P.A. ... Eagle, ID
Peters, Barry W. ... Philadelphia, PA
Peters, Bart F. ... Stamford, CT
Peters, Benjamin M. ... Monroe, LA
Peters, Berger & Koshel, P.C. ... Brooklyn, NY
Peters, Beth A. ... Dallas, TX
Peters, Beverlee Richter ... Norfolk, VA
Virginia Beach, VA
Peters, Beverly S., The Law Office of
Elkhart, IN
Peters, Bill Thomas ... Salt Lake City, UT
Peters, Bobby G. ... Columbus, GA
Peters, Bonnie S. ... Smithtown, NY
Peters, Brandon S. ... Orlando, FL
Peters, Brian D. ... Los Angeles, CA
Peters, Brian Earl ... Department of Labor, Office of the Solicitor, GV
Peters, Brian M. ... Philadelphia, PA
Peters, Brian W. ... Dubuque, IA
Peters, Bruce W. ... Pittsford, NY
Peters, Cameron ... Albuquerque, NM
Santa Fe, NM
Peters, Carl F. ... Elizabethton, TN
Peters, Carl L. ... Indianapolis, IN
Peters, Carol A. ... Los Angeles, CA
Peters, Carol A. ... Pasadena, CA
Peters, Carol Sparkman ... Irving, TX
Peters, Carolyn V. ... St. Paul, MN
Peters & Carter ... Indianapolis, IN
Peters, Caryl Shortridge ... Janesville, WI
Peters, Chad B. ... Cleveland, OH
Peters, Charles ... Falmouth, MA
Peters, Charles H.R. ... Chicago, IL
Peters, Charles J. ... Baltimore, MD
Peters, Charles M. ... Amana, IA
Peters, Charles R. ... Canandaigua, NY
Peters, Christopher E. ... Mobile, AL
Peters, Christopher Jon ... New York, NY
Peters & Chunka, P.C. ... Lincoln, NE
Peters, Cindy V. ... Akron, OH
Peters, Clayburn H. ... Los Angeles, CA
Peters, Colin ... Palo Alto, CA
Peters, Colin M. ... San Diego, CA
Peters, Conrad A. ... Willimantic, CT
Peters, Craig M. ... Harrison, OH
Peters, Dan M. ... Oklahoma City, OK
Peters, Daniel A. ... Brighton, MA
Peters, Daniel H. ... Los Angeles, CA
Peters, Daniel S. ... St. Louis, MO
Peters, Daniel W. ... Kansas City, KS
Peters, Danny G. ... Department of the Navy, Office of the Judge Advocate General, GV
Peters, Darleene Darensbourg
New Orleans, LA
Peters, Darrell, P.C. ... Detroit, MI
Peters, David ... Portland, OR
Peters, David ... Bountiful, UT
Peters, David E. ... Chicago, IL
Peters, David F. ... Richmond, VA
Peters, David L. ... Fort Wayne, IN
Peters, David M. ... Encinitas, CA
Peters, David W. ... Los Angeles, CA
San Diego, CA
Peters, Dawn M. ... Norfolk, VA
Peters, Deborah F. ... Brooklyn, NY
Peters, Deborah L. ... Cleveland, OH
Peters, Dennis S. ... Jackson, MS
Peters, Diana L.S. ... Washington, DC
Peters, Donald ... Santa Rosa, CA
Peters, Donald C. ... Gainesville, FL
Peters, Donald F. ... Chicago, IL
Peters, Donald H. ... Southfield, MI
Peters, Donald J. ... Worcester, MA
Peters, Donald L. ... Kerrville, TX
Peters, Donald M. ... Phoenix, AZ
Peters, Donald M., P.C. ... Phoenix, AZ
Peters, Dorathea J. ... Alexandria, VA
Peters, Douglas D. ... Selah, WA
Peters, Douglas N. ... Decatur, GA
Peters, Duke L. ... Los Angeles, CA
Peters, E. Richard ... San Diego, CA
Peters, Edmund A. ... Chicago, IL
Peters, Edward J. ... Jackson, MS
Peters, Edward J., Jr. ... Portland, CT
Peters, Eliza Leventis ... Charlottesville, VA
Peters, Elizabeth ... New York, NY
Peters, Elizabeth L. ... Troy, MI
Peters, Ellen A. ... Hartford, CT
Peters, Elliot R. ... San Francisco, CA
Peters, Emily ... Los Angeles, CA
Peters, Eric G. ... Lynchburg, VA
Peters, Eric L. ... Edgartown, MA
Peters, Erik A. ... Mason, OH
Peters, Eugene F. ... Washington, DC
Peters, Ferdinand M. ... Warren, MI
Peters, Fortelka & Buckwalter ... Chicago, IL
Peters & Fowler, Inc., P.S. ... Selah, WA
Peters, Frances C. ... New York, NY
Peters, Franklin ... Oakland, MD
Peters, Fred E. ... Lexington, KY
Peters, Frederick W. ... Washington, DC
Peters & Freedman ... Encinitas, CA
Peters, Gary A. ... Bloomfield Hills, MI
Peters, Gary Arthur ... Chicago, IL
Peters, Gary J. ... New York, NY
Peters, Gary W. ... Santa Rosa, CA
Peters, Geoffrey J. ... Cleveland, OH
Peters, Geoffrey W. ... Vienna, VA
Peters, Geoffrey W., P.C. ... Vienna, VA

Peters, George A. ....Santa Monica, CA
Peters, George A., Jr. ....Santa Ana, CA
Peters, George B., Jr. ....Athens, GA
Peters, George T. ....Burbank, CA
Peters, Georgeann G. ....Columbus, OH
Peters, Gerald E. ....El Cajon, CA
Peters, Gerald P. ....Thousand Oaks, CA
Peters, Glenn E. ....Arroyo Grande, CA
Peters, Grant H. ....Chicago, IL
Peters, Gregory A. ....Long Prairie, MN
Peters, Gregory G. ....Manchester, NH
Peters, Gregory Hoerr ....Champaign, IL
Peters, Gregory L. ....Minneapolis, MN
Peters, Harry ....New York, NY
Peters, Harvey R. ....Boston, MA
Peters, Heather ....Los Angeles, CA
Peters, Heather E. ....Cincinnati, OH
Peters, Helen L., Law Offices of
Pleasanton, CA
Peters, Helen L., Law Offices of
San Ramon, CA
Peters, Henry T. ....Salinas, CA
Peters, Herbert G. ....Bristol, VA
Peters, Holly S. ....Roanoke, VA
Peters, Howard M. ....Palo Alto, CA
Peters, J. Christopher ....Alexandria, LA
Peters, J. Douglas ....Detroit, MI
Peters, J. Michael ....Wichita, KS
Peters, J. Robt., Jr. ....Hampton, SC
Peters, J. Roumain, III ....New Orleans, LA
Peters, J. Tyler ....Overland Park, KS
Peters, Jackson L. ....Miami, FL
Peters, Jackson Levick, Jr.
Cripple Creek, CO
Peters, Jacob J. ....Council Bluffs, IA
Peters, James A. ....Tallahassee, FL
Peters, James H. ....Glenview, IL
Peters, James J. ....Denver, CO
Peters, James M.
Agency for International Development, Office of the General Counsel, GV
Peters, James M. ....Cedar Rapids, IA
Peters, James M. ....Cincinnati, OH
Columbus, OH
Peters, James M. ....Oklahoma City, OK
Peters, James P. ....Atlanta, GA
Peters, James P. ....Doylestown, PA
Peters, James T. ....Independence, IA
Peters, James W. ....Woodsfield, OH
Peters, Janice Roark ....Kalamazoo, MI
Peters, Jason M. ....Houston, TX
Peters, Jeffery D. ....Pittsburgh, PA
Peters, Jeffrey ....Brooklyn, NY
Peters, Jeffrey A. ....Arlington Heights, IL
Peters, Jeffrey S. ....Tustin, CA
Peters, Jeffrey W. ....Bath, ME
Peters, Jennifer C. ....Santa Monica, CA
Peters, Jerome D., Jr. ....Chico, CA
Peters, Jerry R. ....San Francisco, CA
Peters, Jimmie C. ....Jena, LA
Peters, Joan S. ....San Juan, PR
Peters, Joann F. ....San Diego, CA
Peters, Joanne S. ....Columbus, OH
Peters, John C. ....West Hartford, CT
Peters, John C., P.C. ....Hartford, CT
West Hartford, CT
Peters, John E. ....Jersey City, NJ
Peters, John E. ....Columbia, SC
Peters, John H. ....Studio City, CA
Peters, John I. ....Pataskala, OH
Peters, John I., Co., L.P.A. ....Pataskala, OH
Peters, John J. ....Richland, MI
Peters, John M. ....Council Bluffs, IA
Peters, John M. ....Fort Dodge, IA
Peters, John O. ....Richmond, VA
Peters, John R. ....Iselin, NJ
Peters, John R., Jr. ....New Orleans, LA
Peters, John T., Jr. ....Detroit, MI
Farmington Hills, MI
Peters, John T., Jr. ....Kalamazoo, MI
Peters, John W. ....Portage, IN
Peters, Jonathan C. ....Atlanta, GA
Peters, Jordan H. ....Chicago, IL
Peters, Joseph J. ....Edison, NJ
Peters, Joseph J., A Professional Corporation
Edison, NJ
Peters, Joseph L., Jr. ....Heathsville, VA
Peters, Joyce E. ....Department of Justice, Office of Legislative Affairs, GV
Peters, Juliet ....Phoenix, AZ
Peters, Kai ....San Francisco, CA
Peters, Karen Breeding ....Roanoke, VA
Peters, Karen L. ....Phoenix, AZ
Peters, Karna M. ....Glenwood, MN
Peters, Kathryn D. ....Evansville, IN
Peters, Kathryn Pruessner
Overland Park, KS
Kansas City, MO
Peters, Keith ....Blue Bell, PA
Peters, Kelly A. ....Simsbury, CT
Peters, Kenneth D. ....Chicago, IL
Peters, Kenneth D. ....Chicago, IL
Peters, Kenneth G. ....McLean, VA
Peters, Kevin ....Chicago, IL
Peters, Kevin D. ....Denver, CO
Peters, Kevin J. ....Wilmington, NC
Peters, Kevin T. ....Boston, MA
Peters, Kristen Thall ....Walnut Creek, CA
Peters, Laurence ....Boston, MA
Peters Law Firm ....Fort Wayne, IN
Peters Law Firm, P.C. ....Council Bluffs, IA
Omaha, NE
Peters, Lawrence F. ....Canton, MA
Peters, Lee E. ....Las Cruces, NM
Peters, Lee I., Jr. ....Live Oak, FL
Peters, Leonard E. ....Houston, TX
Peters, Leslie G. ....Avoca, IA
Peters, Linda Law ....Sacramento, CA
Peters, Lindsay ....Shawnee, OK
Peters, Lisa A. ....Bend, OR
Peters, Lloyd S. ....Milwaukee, WI
Peters, Loren W. ....San Antonio, TX
Peters, Loretta M. ....Scottsdale, AZ
Peters, Lori Ashmore ....Dallas, TX
Peters, Lori-Ann S. ....Washington, DC
Peters, Lynda A. ....Chicago, IL
Peters & Lyons, Ltd. ....Chicago, IL
Peters, M. Anne ....Waterbury, CT
Peters, M. Elizabeth ....Washington, DC
Peters, M. Powell ....Virginia Beach, VA
Peters, M. Stephen ....Wheat Ridge, CO
Peters, Margaret H. ....Pittsburgh, PA
Peters, Marie E. ....Dade City, FL
Peters, Marilyn
Department Of Veterans Affairs, Office of Employment Discrimination Complaints Adjudication, GV
Peters, Marilyn A. ....Bloomfield Hills, MI
Peters, Mark ....Boston, MA
Peters, Mark B. ....Pomona, CA
Peters, Mark C. ....San Francisco, CA
Peters, Mark D. ....Santa Rosa, CA
Peters, Mark S. ....Cocoa, FL
Peters, Mark T. ....Peoria, IL
Peters, Mark T., Sr. ....Sterling Heights, MI
Peters, Mark W. ....Detroit, MI
Peters, Mark W. ....Nashville, TN
Peters, Marshall F. ....Oak Park, IL
Peters, Mary Donne ....Atlanta, GA
Peters, Mary Lou ....New York, NY
Peters, Marybeth ....Library of Congress, Copyright Office, GV
Peters, Massad & Rodolakis ....Worcester, MA
Peters, Maxey, Short & Maxey, P.A.
Coral Gables, FL
Peters, Megan Jones ....Columbus, OH
Peters, Melvin D. ....Los Angeles, CA
Peters, Michael A. ....Costa Mesa, CA
Peters, Michael A. ....Orlando, FL
Peters, Michael A. ....Albuquerque, NM
Peters, Michael A. ....Oklahoma City, OK
Peters, Michael E. ....Baltimore, MD
Peters, Michael L. ....Las Vegas, NV
Peters, Michael M. ....Long Beach, CA
Peters, Michael S. ....Oklahoma City, OK
Peters, Michael T. ....Houston, TX
Peters, Michael W. ....Springfield, IL
Peters, Michael W. ....Albany, NY
Peters, Mildred G. ....Northfield, IL
Peters, Mitchell A. ....Merrillville, IN
Peters, Moore & Delfine ....Portage, IN
Peters, Moritz, Peischl, Zulick & Landes
Nazareth, PA
Peters & Mullins ....Alexandria, VA
Peters, Murdaugh, Parker, Eltzroth & Detrick, P.A. ....Hampton, SC
Ridgeland, SC
Peters, Nancy Furey ....Omaha, NE
Peters, Neal H. ....Golden, CO
Peters, Neill T. ....Metamora, MI
Peters, Nichole M. ....Oklahoma City, OK
Peters, Norman W., Jr. ....Houston, TX
Peters, Oliver D., Jr. ....Decatur, GA
Peters, Oliver D., Jr. ....Decatur, GA
Peters, Pamela A. ....Winter Park, FL
Peters, Pamela Lee ....Chicago, IL
Peters, Pamela R. ....Oakland, CA
Peters, Patricia M. ....Atlanta, GA
Peters, Patrick C. ....Iowa City, IA
Lone Tree, IA
North Liberty, IA
Peters, Patrick W. ....Kansas City, MO
Peters, Paul A. ....San Francisco, CA
Peters, Paul A. ....Buffalo, NY
Peters, Paul F. ....Omaha, NE
Peters, Paula J. ....Los Angeles, CA
Peters, Paula J. ....Annapolis, MD
Peters, Paulette Lemay ....New York, NY
Peters, Peter J., (P.C.) ....Council Bluffs, IA
Peters & Peters ....Santa Monica, CA
Peters & Peters ....Santa Rosa, CA
Peters & Peters ....Taylor, TX
Peters, Peters & Ellingson, A Professional Corporation ....Palo Alto, CA
Peters, Philip D.
Federal Energy Regulatory Commission, Office of the Commissioners, GV
Peters, Philip G. ....Manchester, NH
Peters, Philip G., Jr. ....Columbia, MO
Peters, Philip W. ....San Francisco, CA
Peters & Ploetz ....Salamanca, NY
Peters, Priscilla D. ....Scotts Valley, CA
Peters, R. Delacy, Jr. ....Chicago, IL
Peters, R. Norman ....Worcester, MA
Peters, R. Timothy ....Clearwater, FL
Peters, R. Wayne ....Chattanooga, TN
Peters, Ralph W. ....San Diego, CA
Peters, Randall F. ....Chicago, IL
Peters, Randall J. ....Los Angeles, CA
Peters, Register & McEachern
Wilmington, NC
Peters, Rich J. ....Phoenix, AZ
Peters, Richard H. ....Toledo, OH
Peters, Richard L. ....Washington, DC
Peters, Richard L. ....New York, NY
Peters, Richard T. ....Los Angeles, CA
Peters, Rise J. ....Washington, DC
Peters, Robert F. ....Somers, CT
Peters, Robert F. ....Merrillville, IN
Peters, Robert J. ....Sacramento, CA
Peters, Robert J. ....Chicago, IL
Peters, Robert N. ....Eugene, OR
Peters, Robert R., II ....Tulsa, OK
Peters, Robert S. ....Winchester, TN
Peters, Robert W. ....Carroll, IA
Peters, Robert W. ....New York, NY
Peters, Robert W., P.C. ....Carroll, IA
Peters, Robert Y. ....Greensboro, NC
Peters, Roberts, Borsuk & Taylor
Decatur, GA
Peters Robertson DeMahy Parsons Mowers Passaro & Drake P.A.
Fort Lauderdale, FL
Fort Myers, FL
Miami, FL
Sarasota, FL
West Palm Beach, FL
Peters, Robt. L. ....Cincinnati, OH
Peters, Roger A. ....Ventura, CA
Peters, Roger Allen, II ....Charlotte, NC
Peters, Roger C. ....San Francisco, CA
Peters, Roger J. ....San Francisco, CA
Peters, Roger J. ....Clairton, PA
Peters, Roger P. ....Laguna Niguel, CA
Peters, Ronald A. ....San Francisco, CA
Peters, Ronald J. ....Sacramento, CA
Peters, Ronald L. ....Honolulu, HI
Peters, Rose Collantes ....San Pedro, CA
Peters & Rose, LLP ....Los Angeles, CA
San Diego, CA
Peters, Ross A. ....Ellicottville, NY
Salamanca, NY
Peters, Ross J. ....Waukegan, IL
Peters, Roy F. ....Redding, CA
Peters, Rush, Habib & McKenna
Chico, CA
Oroville, CA
Quincy, CA
Red Bluff, CA
Redding, CA
Sacramento, CA
Willows, CA
Peters, Sally M. ....Houston, TX
Peters, Samuel A. ....Los Alamitos, CA
Peters, Scott C. ....Cleveland, OH
Peters, Scott H. ....San Diego, CA
Peters, Scott H. ....Council Bluffs, IA
Peters, Scott L. ....Philadelphia, PA
Peters, Scott N. ....Oak Brook, IL
Peters, Scott N. ....Sioux Falls, SD
Peters, Scott V. ....Evanston, IL
Peters, Scott W. ....Atlanta, GA
Peters, Sharon Jane ....Fort Wayne, IN
Peters, Sherri Moreland ....Des Moines, IA
Peters, Shirley L. ....Oakland, CA
Peters, Stephanie J. ....Washington, DC
Peters, Stephen ....New York, NY
Peters, Stephen C. ....Denver, CO
Peters, Stephen F. ....Pasadena, CA
Peters, Stephen H. ....Clinton, IL
Peters, Stephen J. ....Indianapolis, IN
Peters, Stephen K. ....Baton Rouge, LA
Peters, Stephen M. ....Palo Alto, CA
Peters, Stephen Q. ....Claremore, OK
Tulsa, OK
Peters, Steven D. ....Mountain View, CA
Peters, Steven J. ....Eaton Rapids, MI
Peters, Susan Perry ....Okemos, MI
Peters, Suzanne ....Cleveland, OH
Peters, Ted L. ....Wichita, KS
Peters, Theodore C. ....Boise, ID
Peters, Thomas A. ....Kingsport, TN
Peters, Thomas H. ....Santa Monica, CA
Peters, Thomas J., IV ....Atlanta, GA
Peters, Thomas M. ....Chicago, IL
Peters, Thomas M. ....Detroit, MI
Peters, Thomas P. ....New York, NY
Peters, Thomas P., II ....Lewiston, ME
Peters, Thomas R. ....Belleville, IL
St. Louis, MO
Peters, Troy A. ....Jacksonville, NC
Peters & Varco, LLP ....San Diego, CA
Peters, Verny, Jones & Biksa, L.L.P.
Palo Alto, CA
Peters, Victor B. ....Kansas City, MO
Peters, Victor C. ....Chicago, IL
Peters, Victor S., Jr. ....Winnetka, IL
Peters, Victoria J. ....Chicago, IL
Peters, Victoria L. ....Denver, CO
Peters, Ward, Bright & Hennessy
Shreveport, LA
Peters, Warren ....Lincoln, IL
Peters & Wasilefski ....Harrisburg, PA
Peters, Wes W. ....Jackson, MS
Peters, William C. ....Moultrie, GA
Peters, William C., Jr. ....Gering, NE
Peters, William D., Jr. ....Kansas City, KS
Peters, William E. ....Bay City, MI
Peters, William E. ....Lincoln, NE
Peters, William F. ....Meadville, PA
Peters, William F., Jr. ....Fort Worth, TX
Peters, William J. ....Los Angeles, CA
Peters, William J. ....San Francisco, CA
Peters, William J. ....Frankfort, IL
Peters, William J. ....Blue Springs, MO
Peters, William J. ....Toledo, OH
Peters, William J. ....Harrisburg, PA
Peters, William R. ....New York, NY
Peters, William V., Law Offices of
Scranton, PA
Peters & Wilmering ....Farmington, MI
Peters, Yvonne M. ....Canby, OR
Petersberger, Ralph I. ....Washington, DC
Petersburg, Paula J. Larson ....Decorah, IA
Peterschmidt, James J. ....Parker, CO
Petersdorf, Rudolph ....Ojai, CA
Petersen, A. Lee, Law Offices of, P.C.
Houston, AK
Petersen, A. Lee, Law Offices of, (P.C.)
Houston, AK
Petersen, Aaron R. ....Solvang, CA
Petersen, Agnes M. ....St. Helens, OR
Petersen, Amanda Anna ....Dallas, TX
Petersen, Andrew J. ....Tucson, AZ
Petersen, Ann Bach ....Chapel Hill, NC
Petersen, Ann C. ....Chicago, IL
Petersen, Ann C. ....Southern Pines, NC
Petersen, Antje C. ....Indianapolis, IN
Petersen, Arthur L. ....Saginaw, MI
Petersen, Arthur L., P.C. ....Saginaw, MI
Petersen, Arthur R. ....Fort Worth, TX
Petersen Associates, Inc. ....Norman, OK
Petersen, Barbara B. H. ....Port Clinton, OH
Petersen, Barker & Dunfield ....Corvallis, OR
Petersen, Bartlett C. ....Milwaukee, WI
Petersen, Bert D. ....Clear Lake, WI
Petersen, Brian J. ....Sherman Oaks, CA
Petersen, Bronwyn Whittaker ....Irvine, CA
Petersen, Byron G. ....Fort Lauderdale, FL
Petersen, Carl J. ....Atlantic, IA
Petersen, Catherine Holland ....Norman, OK
Petersen, Charlene J. ....Jacksonville, FL
Petersen, Charles E. ....Aurora, IL
Petersen, Christian A. ....Tampa, FL
Petersen, Christian C.D. ....Washington, DC
Petersen, Christopher J. ....Oklahoma City, OK
Petersen, Craig A. ....Woodland Hills, CA
Petersen, Dale R. ....Chicago, IL
Petersen, Dana C. ....Baltimore, MD
Petersen, Dana J. ....Denver, CO
Petersen, Daniel R. ....San Antonio, TX
Petersen, Daniel S. ....Augusta, ME
Petersen, David A. ....Duluth, MN
Petersen, David A. ....McMurray, PA
Petersen, David Bruce ....Los Angeles, CA
Petersen, David C. ....Austin, TX
Petersen, David E. ....Bend, OR
Petersen, David J. ....San Francisco, CA
Petersen, David L. ....Naples, FL
Petersen, David L. ....Grafton, ND
Petersen, David L. ....Pasco, WA
Petersen, David P. ....Portland, OR
Petersen, Dean L. ....Sacramento, CA
Petersen, Deborah L. ....Council Bluffs, IA
Petersen, Dennis R. ....Idaho Falls, ID
Petersen, Don E. ....Huron, SD
Mitchell, SD
Petersen, Don R. ....Provo, UT
Petersen, Donald C. ....Glendale, CA
Petersen, Donald E. ....Orlando, FL
Petersen, Donald K. S. ....Bloomfield Hills, MI
Petersen, Donald S. ....Chicago, IL
Petersen, Dori K. ....Salt Lake City, UT
Petersen, Eddy & Judge ....Clinton, IA
Petersen, Edith M. ....Hartland, WI
Petersen, Edward H. ....La Habra, CA
Petersen, Eileen R.
Christiansted, St. Croix, VI
Petersen, Einar C. ....Long Beach, CA
Petersen, Elisabeth S. ....Durham, NC
Petersen, Ellen A. ....Marblehead, MA
Petersen, Eric S. ....New York, NY
Petersen, Erik Anders ....Washington, DC
Petersen, F. Gregory ....Fort Bragg, CA
Petersen, Fonda, Farley, Mattoon, Crockenberg, Garcia & Mattoon, P.C.
Colorado Springs, CO
Pueblo, CO
Petersen, Frank R. ....Reno, NV
Petersen, Frederick J. ....Thousand Oaks, CA
Petersen, G. Chapman ....Barrington, IL
Petersen, G. Russell ....Vero Beach, FL
Petersen, G. Russell, P.A. ....Vero Beach, FL
Petersen, Gary H. ....Westford, MA
Petersen, Gene A. ....Peoria, IL
Petersen, George C., Jr. ....Idaho Falls, ID
Petersen, George O. ....St. Paul, MN
Petersen, Gerald K. ....Corvallis, OR
Petersen, Glen R. ....Baton Rouge, LA
Petersen, Grant D. ....Tampa, FL
Petersen, Gregory G. ....Costa Mesa, CA
Petersen, Harry Tom ....El Paso, TX
Petersen, Howard E. ....LaGrange, IN
Petersen & Ibold ....Chardon, OH
Petersen, J. Chapman ....McLean, VA
Petersen, J. David ....Portland, OR
Petersen, Jack M. ....Des Moines, IA
Petersen, James
Department Of Veterans Affairs, Office of the General Counsel, GV
Petersen, James D. ....Franklin, TN
Petersen, James E. ....Bend, OR
Petersen, James H. ....Milwaukee, WI
Petersen, James L. ....Indianapolis, IN
Petersen, James M. ....New Orleans, LA
Petersen, Jan, (Mr.) ....St. Cloud, MN
Petersen, Jerry A. ....Chardon, OH
Petersen, John D. ....Overland Park, KS
Petersen, John L. ....Geneva, IL
Petersen, John M. ....Portland, OR
Petersen, Jon G. ....Dallas, TX
Petersen, Joseph E. ....New York, NY
Petersen, Karen A. ....Irvine, CA
Petersen, Kathryn W. ....Mobile, AL
Petersen, Keith Blaine ....San Diego, CA
Petersen, Keith J. ....St. Paul, MN
Petersen, Kenneth E., Jr.
Corona Del Mar, CA
Petersen, Kenneth L., Jr. ....Austin, TX
Petersen, Kimberly A. ....Boston, MA
Petersen, Kirk H. ....Springfield, IL
Petersen, Kirk L. ....Des Moines, IA
Petersen, Kurt M. ....Denver, CO
Petersen, L. Chris ....Washington, DC
Atlanta, GA
Petersen, L. Dena ....Seattle, WA
Petersen, Laurence W. ....Billings, MT
Petersen, Laurette ....Chicago, IL
Petersen, Laurie A. ....Milwaukee, WI
Petersen, Lauris G. ....Lakeland, FL
Petersen Law Offices, P.C. ....Omaha, NE
Petersen, Lee ....Akron, OH

Peterson, James P. ... San Antonio, TX
Peterson, James P. ... Milwaukee, WI
Peterson, James R. ... Chicago, IL
Peterson, James R. ... Dundee, IL
Peterson, James R. ... Grand Rapids, MI
Peterson, James R. ... St. Paul, MN
Peterson, James R. ... Buffalo, NY
Peterson, James W. ... La Jolla, CA
Peterson, James W. ... Redwood City, CA
Peterson, James W. ... Twain Harte, CA
Peterson, James W., Jr. ... Florence, SC
Peterson, Jamie Scott ... San Francisco, CA
Peterson, Jan Eric ... Seattle, WA
Peterson, Jan Marc ... Chicago, IL
Peterson, Janeanne ... Portland, OR
Peterson, Janice C.
Administrative Office Of The United States Courts, GV
Peterson, Janice S. ... Keene, NH
Peterson, Jaqualin Friend
Washington, DC
Peterson, Jason W. ... Pensacola, FL
Peterson, Jay A. ... San Luis Obispo, CA
Peterson, Jay K. ... Vail, CO
Peterson, Jean R., (Mrs.) ... Buffalo, NY
Peterson, Jeanne Tiller ... Lansing, MI
Peterson, Jeffery M. ... Birmingham, MI
Detroit, MI
Peterson, Jeffrey C. ... Atlantic Beach, FL
Peterson, Jeffrey J. ... Bowbells, ND
Peterson, Jeffrey Joseph ... Denver, CO
Peterson, Jeffrey L. ... Nashville, TN
Peterson, Jeffrey N. ... Palm Coast, FL
Peterson, Jennifer ... Sioux City, IA
Peterson, Jennifer E. ... Minneapolis, MN
Peterson, Jennifer K. ... Philadelphia, PA
Peterson, Jerod H. ... Minneapolis, MN
Peterson, Jerrold B. ... Gretna, LA
Peterson, Jerry B. ... Houston, TX
Peterson, Jerry G. ... Atlanta, GA
Peterson, Jill Carla ... San Francisco, CA
Peterson, Jill M.
Securities and Exchange Commission, Division of Enforcement, GV
Peterson, Jim Neil, Jr. ... Atlanta, GA
Peterson, Jo Ann ... Phoenix, AZ
Peterson, Joan C. ... Minneapolis, MN
Peterson, Joan Carol ... Minneapolis, MN
Peterson, Joel D. ... Redlands, CA
Peterson, Joel H. ... Wellesley, MA
Peterson, John ... Austin, TX
Peterson, John ... Beeville, TX
Peterson, John A. ... Los Angeles, CA
Peterson, John A., Jr. ... Seaside Park, NJ
Peterson, John C. ... Topeka, KS
Peterson, John C. ... Bethesda, MD
Peterson, John C. ... Mankato, MN
Peterson, John C. ... Harrisburg, PA
Peterson, John C. ... Appleton, WI
Peterson, John D. ... Hillsboro, OR
Peterson, John E. ... Fresno, CA
Peterson, John E. ... La Jolla, CA
Peterson, John E. ... Plainfield, IL
Peterson, John E. ... Rock Hill, SC
Peterson, John E., Jr. ... Long Beach, CA
Peterson, John F. ... Sherman Oaks, CA
Peterson, John H. ... Pasadena, CA
Peterson, John L. ... Milford, CT
Peterson, John L. ... Kansas City, KS
Peterson, John L. ... Houston, TX
Peterson, John L. (Jack) ... Butte, MT
Peterson, John M. ... Chicago, IL
Peterson, John M. ... New York, NY
Peterson, John M. ... Norfolk, VA
Peterson, John M., Jr. ... Palo Alto, CA
Peterson, John P. ... Sioux Falls, SD
Peterson, John R. ... Albert Lea, MN
Peterson, John R. ... McMinnville, OR
Peterson, John S. ... Glendale, CA
Peterson, John S. ... San Pedro, CA
Peterson, John S. ... Kingston, WA
Peterson, John T. ... Buffalo, NY
Peterson, John W. ... Ketchikan, AK
Peterson, John W. ... Mount Ida, AR
Peterson, John W. ... Los Angeles, CA
Peterson, John W. ... Lynn Center, IL
Peterson, Johnson & Murray, S.C.
Madison, WI
Milwaukee, WI
Peterson, Jon L. ... Minneapolis, MN
Peterson, Jonathan M. ... New York, NY
Peterson, Jonathan M. ... Philadelphia, PA
Peterson, Jonathan R. ... Honolulu, HI
Peterson, Joseph L., Jr. ... San Antonio, TX
Peterson, Joyce Courtney ... Melbourne, FL
Peterson, Judith Bakes ... Lisle, IL
Peterson, Julie A. ... Northbrook, IL
Peterson, K. Charles, Law Office of
Houston, TX
Peterson, K. Craig ... Rockford, IL
Peterson, K. Greg, Law Office of
Sacramento, CA
Peterson, Kami L. ... Salt Lake City, UT
Peterson, Karen A. ... Carson City, NV
Peterson, Karen L. ... Portola Valley, CA
Peterson, Karen L. ... Boston, MA
Peterson, Karen L. ... Kenmore, NY
Peterson, Karen Lynn ... San Francisco, CA
Peterson, Karen M. ... St. Paul, MN
Peterson, Karen S. ... Richmond, VA
Peterson, Karrin ... Seattle, WA
Peterson & Kasper ... Ellsworth, KS
Peterson, Kathleen Flynn
Minneapolis, MN
Peterson, Kathleen O. ... Irvine, CA
Peterson, Kathryn A. ... Washington, DC
Boston, MA
Peterson, Kathryn E. ... Dallas, TX

Peterson, Kay M. ... Houston, TX
Peterson, Keith A. ... Kalamazoo, MI
Peterson, Keith H. ... New York, NY
Peterson, Keith R. ... Panama City, FL
Peterson & Kell ... Sacramento, CA
Peterson, Ken M. ... Wichita, KS
Peterson, Kendall S. ... Salt Lake City, UT
Peterson, Kenneth A. ... Chicago, IL
Peterson, Kenneth A., Jr. ... Chicago, IL
Peterson, Kenneth B. ... Oakland, CA
Peterson, Kenneth B. ... Memphis, TN
Peterson, Kenneth D. ... Billings, MT
Peterson, Kenneth G. ... Sacramento, CA
Peterson, Kenneth W. ... Carson, ND
Peterson, Kent M. ... Des Moines, IA
Peterson, Kevin C. ... East Islip, NY
Peterson, Kevin D. ... Plano, TX
Peterson, Kevin R. ... Grand Rapids, MI
Peterson, Kevin R. ... Billings, MT
Peterson, Kimberley J. ... San Jose, CA
Peterson, Kimberly ... San Francisco, CA
Peterson, Kimberly A. ... West Hartford, CT
Peterson, Kirk A. ... Kansas City, MO
Peterson, Kirk L. ... Chicago, IL
Peterson, Kirk S. ... Portland, OR
Peterson, Kirstin R. ... New York, NY
Peterson, Kurt A. ... Phoenix, AZ
Peterson, Kurt B. ... Seattle, WA
Peterson, Kurt C. ... Los Angeles, CA
Peterson, Kurt N. ... Atlanta, GA
Peterson, Kurt S. ... Des Moines, IA
Peterson, Kurt W. ... Lakewood, CO
Peterson, L. Charles ... St. Paul, MN
Peterson, Larry A. ... Los Angeles, CA
Peterson, Larry J. ... St. Paul, MN
Peterson, Laura A. ... Dallas, TX
Peterson, Laura L. ... Anaheim, CA
Peterson, Laura L. ... San Diego, CA
Peterson, Laurel J. ... Anchorage, AK
Peterson, Laurel J., P.C. ... Anchorage, AK
Peterson, Laurence E. ... La Jolla, CA
Peterson, Laurie ... Kew Gardens, NY
Peterson Law Firm ... Kenyon, MN
Peterson Law Firm, P.C. ... Philadelphia, PA
Peterson Law Office ... Bowbells, ND
Peterson, Lawrence K. ... Lake Oswego, OR
Peterson, Lawrence R., Jr.
Salt Lake City, UT
Peterson, Leary E. ... Prairie du Chien, WI
Peterson, Lee H. ... Salem, OR
Peterson, Lee T. ... St. Paul, MN
Peterson, Leon Lewis ... Santa Ana, CA
Peterson, LeRoy D. ... Omaha, NE
Peterson, Lesli Bailey
Oklahoma City, OK
Peterson, Leslie A. ... Waukegan, IL
Peterson, Linda S. ... Los Angeles, CA
Peterson, Linda S. ... Los Angeles, CA
Peterson & Lipps ... Algona, IA
Peterson, Lisa ... Seattle, WA
Peterson, Lisa A. ... Fort Worth, TX
Peterson, Lisa L. ... Sweetwater, TX
Peterson, Lisa N. ... Larchmont, NY
Peterson, Lloyd E., Jr. ... Lake City, FL
Peterson, Louis D. ... Seattle, WA
Peterson, Lowell G. ... Mineola, NY
Peterson, Lowell L. ... Hartford, CT
Peterson, Lynn ... New York, NY
Peterson, Lynn C. ... Knoxville, TN
Peterson, Lynn P. ... Glendale, CA
Peterson, M. Christopher ... Phoenix, AZ
Peterson, M. Dale ... San Diego, CA
Peterson, M. Shannon ... Minneapolis, MN
Peterson, Mac ... Albuquerque, NM
Peterson, Marc ... Gainesville, FL
Peterson, Marcia Leslie ... Cody, WY
Peterson, Margaret M. ... Utica, NY
Peterson, Maria P. ... Barrington, IL
Peterson, Marilyn Wolf ... Gainesville, FL
Peterson, Mark ... Omaha, NE
Peterson, Mark A. ... Concord, CA
Peterson, Mark A. ... Columbus, OH
Peterson, Mark A. ... Milwaukee, WI
Peterson, Mark Allen ... Concord, CA
Peterson, Mark Arthur ... Prairie du Chien, WI
Peterson, Mark B. ... Minneapolis, MN
Peterson, Mark B. ... Charlottesville, VA
Peterson, Mark C. ... Birmingham, AL
Peterson, Mark D. ... Irvine, CA
Peterson, Mark D., Law Offices of
Irvine, CA
Peterson, Mark F. ... Dundee, IL
Peterson, Mark R. ... San Francisco, CA
Peterson, Mark W. ... Minneapolis, MN
Peterson, Marsha Carpenter
Oakland, CA
Peterson, Marshall E. ... Xenia, OH
Peterson, Marshall H. ... Knoxville, TN
Peterson, Martha A. ... Topeka, KS
Peterson, Martin L. ... Meridian, TX
Peterson, Martin W. ... Algona, IA
Peterson, Mary ... Memphis, TN
Peterson, Mary S. ... Atlanta, GA
Peterson, Matthew A. ... San Diego, CA
Peterson, Matthew D. ... Washington, DC
Peterson, Matthew K. ... Anchorage, AK
Peterson, Matthew R. ... Waterbury, CT
Peterson, Max G. ... Aurora, IL
Peterson, Maximilian R.
Department of Commerce, Patent and Trademark Office, GV
Peterson, Melissa H. ... Houston, TX
Peterson, Melissa M. ... Houston, TX
Peterson, Melvin J., Sr. ... Robbinsdale, MN
Peterson, Meredith Oakes ... Hastings, NE
Peterson, Michael A. ... Arlington, TX
Peterson, Michael B. ... Richmond, CA
Peterson, Michael H. ... Cleveland, OH

Peterson, Michael J. ... Kansas City, KS
Peterson, Michael J. ... Portland, OR
Peterson, Michael L. ... Apollo Beach, FL
Peterson, Michael L. ... Orlando, FL
Peterson, Michael N. ... Philadelphia, PA
Peterson, Michael P. ... South Miami, FL
Peterson, Michael R. ... Davis, CA
Peterson, Michael R. ... Cleveland, OH
Peterson, Milton M. ... Corning, NY
Peterson, Mrk D.S.
Federal Trade Commission, Bureau of Competition, GV
Peterson, Murphy H. ... Cedar Hill, TX
Peterson & Myers, P.A. ... Bartow, FL
Lakeland, FL
Lake Wales, FL
Sebring, FL
Winter Haven, FL
Peterson, Mylene A. ... Minneapolis, MN
Peterson, Myra T. ... Oradell, NJ
Peterson, Nancy Anne ... Mankato, MN
Peterson, Nancy K. ... Milwaukee, WI
Peterson, Nancy L. ... San Jose, CA
Peterson, Nancy L. ... Portland, OR
Peterson, Nancy R. ... Philadelphia, PA
Peterson, Natalie L. ... Cleveland, OH
Peterson, Natalie Y. ... Lee's Summit, MO
Peterson, Neal N. ... Minneapolis, MN
Peterson & Nelson ... St. Paul, MN
Peterson, Nils George ... Arlington, VA
Peterson, Norman C. ... Helena, MT
Peterson, Norman M. ... Bettendorf, IA
Peterson, O. P. (Pete), Jr. ... Kansas City, KS
Peterson, Oscar P. (Pete) ... Shawnee, KS
Peterson, Osler L. ... Medfield, MA
Newton, MA
Peterson, P. Kurt ... San Francisco, CA
Peterson, Paige ... Walker, MN
Peterson, Pamela A. ... Newburyport, MA
Peterson, Patricia ... Denver, CO
Peterson, Patricia L.
Colorado Springs, CO
Peterson, Patricia L. ... Minneapolis, MN
Peterson, Patricia Pierce
Walnut Creek, CA
Peterson, Patricia S. ... Oakland, CA
Peterson, Patricia Schuett ... Omaha, NE
Peterson, Paul A. ... San Diego, CA
Peterson, Paul A. ... Marquette, MI
Peterson, Paul C. ... Minneapolis, MN
Peterson, Paul D. ... St. Paul, MN
Stillwater, MN
Peterson, Paul D., Ltd. ... Minneapolis, MN
St. Paul, MN
Peterson, Paul L. ... Chicago, IL
Peterson, Paul M. ... Phoenix, AZ
Peterson, Paul R. ... Chicago, IL
Peterson, Paulette ... Seattle, WA
Peterson, Peter C. ... New Bedford, MA
Peterson, Peter E. ... Bellevue, WA
Peterson, Peter H. ... Grand Rapids, MI
Peterson, Peter L. ... Salina, KS
Peterson, Peter P. ... Garden City, NY
Peterson, Peter W. ... New Haven, CT
Peterson & Peterson ... Faribault, MN
Peterson & Peterson ... Xenia, OH
Peterson & Peterson, P.C. ... Mineola, NY
Peterson, Peterson & Shors, P.C.
Cut Bank, MT
Peterson, Petit & Peterson, L.L.P.
Beaumont, TX
Peterson, Philip A. ... Nampa, ID
Peterson, Philip B. ... New Smyrna Beach, FL
Peterson, Philip C. ... Chicago, IL
Peterson, Philip E. ... Lewiston, ID
Peterson, Philip H., Jr. ... Wayne, PA
Peterson, Phillip D. ... Houston, TX
Peterson, P. L. ... Woodburn, OR
Peterson & Prause, L.L.P. ... McMinnville, OR
Peterson & Price, A Professional Corporation ... San Diego, CA
Peterson, Priscilla T. ... Seattle, WA
Peterson, R. Alan ... Sioux Falls, SD
Peterson, R. Bertil ... Mineola, NY
Peterson, R. Eric ... Denver, CO
Peterson, R. Glen ... Morehead City, NC
Peterson, R. Gwen ... San Francisco, CA
Peterson, R. Michael ... Houston, TX
Peterson, R. Russ ... Redding, CA
Peterson, R. Thomas ... Costa Mesa, CA
Peterson, Ralph A. ... Pensacola, FL
Peterson, Ralph B. K. ... Escanaba, MI
Peterson, Ralph H. ... Albert Lea, MN
Peterson, Ralph W. ... St. Paul, MN
Peterson & Ramirez, P.A. ... Tulsa, OK
Peterson, Raymond A. ... Newport, VT
Peterson, Raymond R. ... Minneapolis, MN
Peterson Reed L.L.C. ... Salt Lake City, UT
Peterson, Regina Kwan ... Oak Park, IL
Peterson & Rekshan ... Marquette, MI
Peterson, Renno L., (P.A.) ... Sarasota, FL
Peterson, Reuben W., Jr. ... Milwaukee, WI
Peterson, Richard A.
Department of the Air Force, Office of the Judge Advocate General, GV
Peterson, Richard A. ... Hutchinson, MN
Peterson, Richard A. ... Minneapolis, MN
Peterson, Richard A. ... Lincoln, NE
Peterson, Richard A. ... Greenville, PA
Peterson, Richard B. ... Minneapolis, MN
Peterson, Richard E. ... Chicago, IL
Peterson, Richard F. ... Northbrook, IL
Peterson, Richard F., Jr. ... Burlington, VT
Peterson, Richard G. ... Englewood, CO
Peterson, Richard H. ... San Francisco, CA
Peterson, Richard J. ... Eagan, MN
Peterson, Richard L. ... Issaquah, WA
Peterson, Richard L. ... Port Orchard, WA

Peterson, Richard M. ... El Cajon, CA
Peterson, Richard M.
Rancho Santa Margarita, CA
Peterson, Richard M. ... Seattle, WA
Peterson, Richard N. ... Rosemont, IL
Peterson, Richard N. ... Rosemont, IL
Peterson, Richard P., II ... Ann Arbor, MI
Peterson, Richard T. ... Washington, DC
Peterson, Richard W. ... Council Bluffs, IA
Peterson, R. L. ... St. Paul, MN
Peterson, Robert A. ... Irvine, CA
Peterson, Robert A. ... Washington, DC
Peterson, Robert A. ... Salt Lake City, UT
Peterson, Robert C. ... Odessa, TX
Peterson, Robert D. ... Ventura, CA
Peterson, Robert E. ... Rochester, IN
Peterson, Robert F. ... Omaha, NE
Peterson, Robert F., Jr. ... Ventura, CA
Peterson, Robert G. ... Chicago, IL
Peterson, Robert H. ... Tacoma, WA
Peterson, Robert J. ... Washington, DC
Peterson, Robert J. ... Cleveland, OH
Peterson, Robert L. ... Sacramento, CA
Peterson, Robert L. ... Roseville, MN
Peterson, Robert M. ... Los Angeles, CA
San Francisco, CA
Peterson, Robert M. ... Pasadena, CA
Peterson, Robert T. ... Banning, CA
Peterson, Robert V. ... Bloomfield Hills, MI
Peterson, Robert W. ... Santa Clara, CA
Peterson, Robin J. ... Cleveland, OH
Peterson, Rocky L. ... Trenton, NJ
Peterson, Rodney M. ... Cut Bank, MT
Peterson, Rodney R. ... Kasson, MN
Peterson, Roger ... Ellsworth, KS
Peterson, Roger A. ... South Lake Tahoe, CA
Peterson, Roger A. ... Minneapolis, MN
Peterson, Roger F. ... Waterloo, IA
Peterson, Rollie A. ... Sacramento, CA
Peterson, Ronald A. ... Colorado Springs, CO
Peterson, Ronald B. ... Minneapolis, MN
Peterson, Ronald C. ... Los Angeles, CA
Peterson, Ronald C. ... San Francisco, CA
Peterson, Ronald D. ... Jacksonville, FL
Peterson, Ronald R. ... Chicago, IL
Peterson, Ronald S. ... San Francisco, CA
Peterson, Rosanna M. ... Spokane, WA
Peterson & Ross ... Los Angeles, CA
Chicago, IL
New York, NY
San Juan, PR
Austin, TX
Peterson, Ross D. ... Homewood, IL
Peterson, Ross W. ... Las Vegas, NV
Peterson, Roy E. ... Monrovia, CA
Peterson, Royce G. ... Fresno, CA
Peterson Russell Cofano PLLC
Bellevue, WA
Seattle, WA
Peterson, Russell D. ... Broken Arrow, OK
Peterson, Samuel R., Jr. ... Anchorage, AK
Peterson, Sandra D. ... Menlo Park, CA
Peterson, Sandra Heims ... Lake City, FL
Peterson, Sara Ann ... Roseville, MN
Peterson, Sara Louise ... San Francisco, CA
Peterson, Savelkoul, Schlichting & Davies, Ltd. ... Albert Lea, MN
Peterson & Scannell, P.C.
New Bedford, MA
Peterson and Schofield ... Billings, MT
Peterson, Scot M. ... Denver, CO
Peterson, Scott A. ... Seattle, WA
Peterson, Scott C. ... Des Moines, IA
Peterson, Scott D. ... Wellesley Hills, MA
Peterson, Scott D. ... Omaha, NE
Peterson, Scott K. ... Andover, MA
Peterson, Scott R. ... Houston, TX
Peterson, Shane Douglas ... Williston, ND
Peterson, Sharon Shields ... San Diego, CA
Peterson, Shaun D. ... Wilmington, OH
Peterson, Sheila J. ... Morgan Hill, CA
Peterson, Sheral K. ... El Paso, TX
Peterson, Sheral K., P.C. ... El Paso, TX
Peterson, Sherilyn ... Bellevue, WA
Peterson, Sherry ... Dublin, CA
Peterson, Sherry Clark ... Tacoma, WA
Peterson, Shirley D. ... Frederick, MD
Peterson, Sid C., II ... New Smyrna Beach, FL
Peterson, Sieglinde T. ... Greenbelt, MD
Peterson & Simpson ... Salt Lake City, UT
Peterson, Sonja Dunnwald ... Minneapolis, MN
Peterson, Sonja J. ... Faribault, MN
Peterson, Sonja L. ... Spokane, WA
Peterson, Stephen ... Oklahoma City, OK
Peterson, Stephen D. ... Atlanta, GA
Peterson, Stephen J. ... Los Angeles, CA
Peterson, Stephen L. ... Washington, DC
Peterson, Stephen L. ... St. Paul, MN
Peterson, Stephen W. ... San Diego, CA
Peterson, Steven ... Minneapolis, MN
Peterson, Steven A. ... Chanhassen, MN
Peterson, Steven D. ... Twin Falls, ID
Peterson, Steven D. ... Slidell, LA
Houston, TX
Peterson, Steven D. ... Salt Lake City, UT
Peterson, Sue-Ann A. ... Burbank, CA
Peterson, Susan B. ... Salt Lake City, UT
Peterson, Susan L. ... Seattle, WA
Peterson, Susan M. ... New Orleans, LA
Peterson, Susan M., A Professional Law Corporation ... New Orleans, LA
Peterson, Susan P. ... Sacramento, CA
Peterson, Tamara Beatty ... Las Vegas, NV
Peterson, Tari L., P.A. ... Tampa, FL
Peterson, Tari Logsdon ... Tampa, FL
Peterson, Terrence R. ... St. Paul, MN
Peterson, Thayne L. ... Cleveland, OH
Peterson, Theodie L., III ... Harrisburg, PA

Peterson, Theresa K. ....Salem, OR
Peterson, Theresa M. ....Hollywood, FL
Peterson, Thomas A. ....Moraga, CA
Peterson, Thomas A. ....Pomona, CA
Peterson, Thomas A. ....Beaumont, TX
Peterson, Thomas E. ....Minneapolis, MN
Peterson, Thomas F. ....Chicago, IL
Peterson, Thomas F. ....Seattle, WA
Peterson, Thomas F. ....Prairie du Chien, WI
Peterson, Thomas H. ....San Antonio, TX
Peterson, Thomas J. ....North Windham, ME
Peterson, Thomas J. ....Minneapolis, MN
Peterson, Thomas K., (Ltd.) ....Glenview, IL
Peterson, Thomas L. ....Santa Ana, CA
Peterson, Thomas L. ....Washington, DC
Peterson, Thomas M. ....San Francisco, CA
Peterson, Thomas M. ....St. Paul, MN
Peterson, Thomas P. ....Pittsburgh, PA
Peterson, Thomas R. ....Indianapolis, IN
Peterson, Thomas W. ....Indianapolis, IN
Peterson, Thomas W. ....Ballston Spa, NY
Peterson, Tim D. ....Flagstaff, AZ
Peterson, Timothy A.
Federal Communications Commission, Common Carrier Bureau, GV
Peterson, Timothy E. ....Indianapolis, IN
Peterson, Timothy J. ....Lindstrom, MN
Peterson, Timothy P. ....Washington, DC
Peterson, Todd A. ....Portland, OR
Peterson, Todd D. ....Washington, DC
Peterson, Todd Lind ....San Francisco, CA
Peterson, Todd M. ....Chico, CA
Peterson, Tom Loomis ....Lexington, MA
Peterson, Torsten E., Jr. ....Hopewell, VA
Peterson, Torsten E., Jr. ....Hopewell, VA
Peterson, Tracy A. ....Chicago, IL
Peterson, Travis S. ....New Rockford, ND
Peterson, Trev E. ....Lincoln, NE
Peterson, Trevor H. ....New York, NY
Peterson, V. Scott ....Brevard, NC
Peterson, Valerie L. ....Manhattan, KS
Peterson, Vance W. ....Spokane, WA
Peterson, Virginia B. ....Dunwoody, GA
Peterson, W. Thatcher ....Oshkosh, WI
Peterson & Waggoner ....Rochester, IN
Peterson, Walter W. ....Toledo, OH
Peterson, Warren E. ....St. Paul, MN
Peterson, Warren H. ....Delta, UT
Peterson, Warren R. ....Indianapolis, IN
Peterson, Wayne E., (A Professional Corporation) ....Santa Monica, CA
Peterson, Wayne R. ....Green Bay, WI
Peterson, Wendy W. ....Brighton, MI
Peterson, Wicks, Nemer & Kamrath, P.A.
Minneapolis, MN
Peterson, Wieting, Calewarts, Duffy & Maxwell
Green Bay, WI
Peterson • Wilka • Weyand • Martin, LLP
San Francisco, CA
Peterson, William A. ....Baltimore, MD
Peterson, William A. ....Marshall, MO
Peterson, William, and Associates, Ltd.
Bloomington, MN
Peterson, William B. ....New York, NY
Peterson, William B. ....Fort Worth, TX
Peterson, William D. ....Denver, CO
Peterson, William D., P.C. ....Denver, CO
Peterson, William E. ....Reno, NV
Peterson, William G. ....San Diego, CA
Peterson, William G. ....Bloomington, MN
Peterson, William L. ....Oklahoma City, OK
Peterson, William M. ....Warner Robins, GA
Peterson, William N. ....Ada, OK
Peterson, Woody N. ....Washington, DC
Peterson, Young, Putra, Fletcher & Zeder
Seattle, WA
Peterson Bekx, Nancy ....Appleton, WI
Peterson-Buie, Becky Jo ....Greensboro, NC
Peterson-Colasacco, Laureen J.
White Plains, NY
Peterson-Gleason, June ....Waukegan, IL
Peterson-Hutto, Anne Louise
North Charleston, SC
Peterson-Lee, Deborah ....San Diego, CA
Peterson-Muth, Bettie Jane ....Meadville, PA
Peterson-Ross, Cheri R. ....New York, NY
Petersons, Arvids V. ....Kansas City, MO
Peterson-Schon, Lisa Kay ....San Jose, CA
Peterson-Smith, Berta ....Santa Ana, CA
Peterson-Stromgren, Christine L.
Minneapolis, MN
Peterson-Theuriet, Dana
San Francisco, CA
Peters-Weaver, Claudia Ann ....Lancaster, CA
Peterzalek, Jeffrey C. ....Waterloo, IA
Peterzeil, Shrimattie ....Denver, CO
Peterzell, Betsy Vance ....Atlanta, GA
Peterzell, Marc L., (P.C.) ....Atlanta, GA
Petesch, Bruce A. ....Raleigh, NC
Petesch, Gregory J. ....Helena, MT
Petesch, Peter J. ....Washington, DC
Petesch, Richard T. ....Aurora, IL
Petesch, Sabrina M. (Doll) ....Peoria, IL
Petgrave, Randolph O. ....Seattle, WA
Peth, Fred J. ....Prairie View, IL
Pethel, Branson A. ....Salisbury, NC
Petherbridge, Richard W. ....Santa Ana, CA
Pethers, Sheryl A. ....Chicago, IL
Pethick, David A. ....Lynchburg, VA
Pethick, Jeffrey D. ....New Bedford, MA
Petho, Douglas A. ....Charlotte, NC
Forest City, NC
Pethybridge, Matthew D. ....Norfolk, VA
Petica, Ron, P.C. ....Bullhead City, AZ
Petica, Ronald H. ....Bullhead City, AZ
Peticolas, E. K. ....El Paso, TX
Peticolas, J. Michael ....El Paso, TX
Peticolas, Shapleigh, Brandys & Kern, PLLC
El Paso, TX
Peticolas, Susanne ....Newark, NJ
Peticolas, W. C. ....El Paso, TX
Petigrow, Daniel ....Fishkill, NY
Petigrow, Paul M. ....West Orange, NJ
Petilla, Rodolfo Enriquez ....Fresno, CA
Petilla, Rudy ....Fresno, CA
Petillo, Angela ....Beverly Hills, CA
Petillo, Diane C. ....Rockville Centre, NY
Petillo, Irene Darmochwal
Liberty Corner, NJ
Petillo, Joseph C. ....New York, NY
Petillo, Lynne ....Fair Haven, NJ
Petillon & Hansen ....Los Angeles, CA
Torrance, CA
Petillon, Lee R. ....Torrance, CA
Petit, Bruce E. ....Carmel, IN
Petit, Dale J. ....Hester, LA
Petit, Elizabeth C. ....Beaumont, TX
Petit Hess Atherly & Petit, P.A. ....Carmel, IN
Petit, Jeffrey A. ....Newark, NJ
Petit, John M. ....Medina, OH
Petit, Maurice R. ....Carmel, IN
Petit, Michael S. ....Beaumont, TX
Petit, Miriam L. ....Carmel, IN
Petit, Paul J. ....Missoula, MT
Petit, Russell W. ....Department of the Army, Office, Chief of Engineers/Headquarters, U.S. Army Corps of Engineers, GV
Petit-Clair, Alfred J., Jr. ....Metuchen, NJ
Petite, John E. ....St. Louis, MO
Petitjean, Barbara A. ....Windsor, CT
Petitjean, David L. ....Columbus, OH
Petitjean, John R. ....Green Bay, WI
Petitjean, Martin, II ....Rayne, LA
Petito, Bruce A. ....Poughkeepsie, NY
Petito, Christopher S. ....Washington, DC
Petito, Deborah Hanna ....Los Angeles, CA
Petito, Eileen ....St. Louis, MO
Petito, Maria Angelina ....Detroit, MI
Petito, Robert A. ....Woodbridge, NJ
Petito, Susan R. ....New York, NY
Petito & Tomlins ....Poughkeepsie, NY
Petitt, Carol Schureck ....Louisville, KY
Petitt, Michele C. ....Croton-On-Hudson, NY
Petitt, Richard Thomas ....Tampa, FL
Petitt, Teri L. ....Denver, CO
Petitt, Tylor J. ....Scottsbluff, NE
Petitte, Mark H. ....Syracuse, NY
Petitti, Michael J., Jr. ....Phoenix, AZ
Petitto, Charles A. ....New York, NY
Petix, Robert G., Jr. ....Atlanta, GA
Petix, Stephen V. ....San Diego, CA
Petizon, Alice T. ....Basking Ridge, NJ
Petkanics, Bryan G. ....New York, NY
Petkanics, Donna M. ....Palo Alto, CA
Petkevis, Edward R. ....Roebling, NJ
Petkin, Lauren S. ....Beverly Hills, CA
Petko, Thomas E. ....Dearborn, MI
Petkoff, George S. ....Memphis, TN
Petkoff, Gregory H.
Department of the Air Force, Office of the General Counsel, GV
Petkoff and Lancaster ....Memphis, TN
Petkofsky, Jane E. ....
Supreme Court Of The United States, GV
Petkovich, Michael N. ....Chicago, IL
Petkovsek, Debra A. ....Sun Prairie, WI
Petkun, David S. ....Philadelphia, PA
Petkun, Lisa B. ....Philadelphia, PA
Petkun, Richard M. ....Englewood, CO
Petkus, Tomas ....Chicago, IL
Petlak, Alan S. ....Los Angeles, CA
Petlak, Elliott E. ....Berwyn, IL
Petler, Gary S. ....Shaker Heights, OH
Petlow, James J. ....Toledo, OH
Petmecky, Kalla C. ....Los Angeles, CA
Petmecky, Robert J. B. ....Atlanta, GA
Petmecky, William M. ....Williamsville, NY
Houston, TX
Peto, Guy B. ....El Dorado, CA
Peto, John G. ....Cleveland, OH
Peto, Terri M. ....Cleveland, OH
Petock, Michael F. ....Philadelphia, PA
Petock, Michael F. ....Valley Forge, PA
Petok, Gary S. ....King Of Prussia, PA
Petok, Seth D. ....New York, NY
Petosa, Frank M. ....Boca Raton, FL
Petosa, John J. ....Syracuse, NY
Petosa, Joseph J. ....Des Moines, IA
Petosa, Petosa, Boecker & Nervig
Clive, IA
Petosa, Ronald ....Bristol, CT
Petosa, Stephen J. ....Clive, IA
Petosa, Susan Sherman ....Boca Raton, FL
Petoskey, Elizabeth M. ....Ann Arbor, MI
Petoskey, Michael D. ....Traverse City, MI
Petow, Patricia A. ....Belmont, MA
Petoyan, Marcus A. ....Beverly Hills, CA
Petr, John J. ....Indianapolis, IN
Petr, John L. ....Omaha, NE
Petr, Joseph R. ....Towson, MD
Petracca, Ronald B., Jr.
Department of Education, Office of the General Counsel, GV
Petracek, Kevin L. ....Kansas City, MO
Petraglia, Catherine T. ....Youngstown, OH
Petraglia, Edward G. ....New York, NY
Petragnani, Amy M. ....Albany, NY
Petraitis, Karel C. ....College Park, MD
Petraitis, Martin F. ....New York, NY
Petrak, Jonathan ....Los Angeles, CA
Petrak, Keith D. ....Seattle, WA
Petrak, Russell H. ....Chicago, IL
Petrakes, Andrew N. ....San Diego, CA
Petrakis, Jonathan M. ....Cherry Hill, NJ
Norristown, PA
Philadelphia, PA
Petrakis, Peter ....Chicago, IL
Petrakis, Peter T. ....Chicago, IL
Petrakos, Theodore J. ....Boston, MA
Petralia, Arnold R. ....Rochester, NY
Petralia, Joseph ....Washington, DC
Petralia, Louis M. ....White Plains, NY
Petralia, Webb & O'Connell, P.C.
Rochester, NY
Petralito, Frank, II ....New York, NY
Petrallia, Robert A. ....Maplewood, NJ
Petramale, Frank R. ....Poughkeepsie, NY
Petramalo, Frank, Jr. ....Washington, DC
Petrangelo & Bondy ....Monroe, MI
Petrangelo, James G. ....Monroe, MI
Petranovich, Milo ....Portland, OR
Petranto, Nancy A. ....San Francisco, CA
Petrantoni, Rosemary M. ....Pittsburgh, PA
Petrara, Madeleine C. ....Brooklyn, NY
Petrarca, Christopher L. ....Chicago, IL
Chicago Heights, IL
Petrarca, Justino D. ....Chicago, IL
Chicago Heights, IL
Petrarca, Louis A., Jr. ....West Warwick, RI
Petraro, Vincent L. ....New York, NY
Petrarulo, Edward W., Jr. ....Albany, NY
Petras & Associates Co., L.P.A.
Cleveland, OH
Petras, David J. ....Hilliard, OH
Petras, Frank B. ....Cleveland, OH
Petras, George J., IV ....Austin, TX
Petras, Mary M. ....Washington, DC
Petras, Nicholas G. ....Manhasset, NY
Petras, Paul J. ....Atlanta, GA
Petras, Stephen J., Jr. ....Cleveland, OH
Petras, Wieser, Merriam & Lee, P.C.
Washington, DC
Petras, William J., Jr. ....Pittsburgh, PA
Petrash, Jeffrey M. ....Washington, DC
Petrasic, Kevin L. ....Treasury Department, Office of Thrift Supervision, GV
Petrasich, John ....Irvine, CA
Petraske, Eric W. ....Hartford, CT
Petrauskas, Jeanne D. ....Bronx, NY
Petrauskas, Mark S. ....Greenbelt, MD
La Plata, MD
Petravicius, Adam V. ....Chicago, IL
Petravicius, Beverly G. ....Chicago, IL
Petre, Courtney G. ....Glenwood Springs, CO
Petre, Daniel B. ....Glenwood Springs, CO
Petre, David C. ....Stamford, CT
Petre, George J. ....Glenwood Springs, CO
Petre & Petre, A Professional Corporation
Glenwood Springs, CO
Petre, Richard J., Jr. ....Lafayette, LA
Petrecca, Catherine ....San Diego, CA
Petrecca, Michael A. ....Columbus, OH
Petredis, Nicholas P. ....San Jose, CA
Petree, Charles R. ....Columbus, OH
Petree, Jeffrey H. ....Lawrenceville, GA
Petree, John A. ....Bethany, OK
Petree, Reyno B. ....Atlanta, GA
Petree, Robert G. ....Orlando, FL
Petree Stockton, L.L.P. ....Charlotte, NC
Raleigh, NC
Winston-Salem, NC
Petree, William H. ....Winston-Salem, NC
Petree-McCoy, Leah T. ....Greenville, SC
Petrek, Francis R., Jr. ....Chicago, IL
Petrel, David B. ....Columbus, OH
Petrell, Jeffrey ....Pittsburgh, PA
Petrella & Associates, P.C. ....Southfield, MI
Petrella, Barbara Jo ....Columbus, OH
Petrella, Daniel J. ....Westland, MI
Petrella, James J. ....Hackensack, NJ
Petrella, John C. ....Livingston, NJ
Petrella, Marisa C. ....Southfield, MI
Petrella, Michael E. ....Roseland, NJ
Petrella, Patricia J. ....Warwick, RI
Petrella, Siobhan M. J. ....Worcester, MA
Petrelli, Frederick E., Jr. ....Wethersfield, CT
Petrelli, Susan C. ....Harrison, NY
Petrellis, Luann M. ....Hockessin, DE
Petrello, Anthony G. ....New York, NY
Petrello, Colleen H. ....Cleveland, OH
Petren, Carol Ann ....Washington, DC
Petren, Suzanne M. ....Kansas City, MO
Petrenchak, Joyce K. ....Allentown, PA
Petrenko, George P. ....Parma, OH
Petrequin, Brian L. ....Newark, NJ
Petretti, Cheryl A. ....Litchfield Park, AZ
Petretti, Richard S. ....New York, NY
Petrey, Ann Marie C. ....New York, NY
Petrey, Curtis N. ....Shreveport, LA
Petrey, Karl R. ....Beverly Hills, CA
Petrey, Katherine G. ....Cleveland, OH
Petrey, Kenneth D. ....Cleveland, OH
Petrey, R. Claybourne, Jr. ....Brentwood, TN
Petrey, Roderick N. ....Miami, FL
Petri, Henry A., Jr. ....Houston, TX
Petri, Hilda N., (Mrs.) ....Bancroft, NE
Petri, Keller & Zeisler ....Galion, OH
Petri, Kenneth M. ....Galion, OH
Petri, Leslie A. ....Denver, CO
Petri, Marinus (Rick) J.W. ....Madison, WI
Petri, Mark G. ....Milwaukee, WI
Petri, Scott A. ....Richboro, PA
Petri, Steven R. ....Miami, FL
Petri, Thomas E. ....Fond du Lac, WI
Petri, Vernon J., & Associates
Indianapolis, IN
Petric, Christian ....West Palm Beach, FL
Petricca, Arcangelo J. ....Lackawanna, NY
Petricca, Perri C. ....Pittsfield, MA
Petricca Reszel, Catherine A.
Lackawanna, NY
Petrich, Alexandra ....San Francisco, CA
Petrich, Annmarie ....Seattle, WA
Petrich, David B. ....Tacoma, WA
Petrich, David S. ....Chicago, IL
Petrich, Elizabeth ....Olympia, WA
Petrich, Frank A. ....St. Louis, MO
Petrich, Gail Sears ....Oak Park, IL
Petrich, George M. ....Burnham, IL
Petrich, Jeffrey P. ....House of Representatives, Committee Legal Personnel, GV
Petrich, John A. ....Tacoma, WA
Petrich, Kathleen Thomas ....Seattle, WA
Petrich, Louis P. ....Los Angeles, CA
Petrich, Peter T. ....Tacoma, WA
Petrich, R. Mark ....Tulsa, OK
Petrick, Edward J. ....Baltimore, MD
Petrick, Frederick G., Jr.
Treasury Department, Office of the Comptroller of the Currency, GV
Petrick, Gregory M. ....New York, NY
Petrick, Holly ....Chicago, IL
Petrick, James B. ....Chevy Chase, MD
Petrick & Kapur ....Endicott, NY
Petrick, Lisa W. ....Pittsburgh, PA
Petrick, Nancy Elizabeth ....Chicago, IL
Petrick, Paul L. ....Endicott, NY
Petrick, Robert J. ....Tulsa, OK
Petrick, W. W. ....Oakland, CA
Petricka, LuAnn M. ....Minneapolis, MN
Petricoff, M. Howard ....Columbus, OH
Petricone, Michael D. ....Washington, DC
Petrics, C. William ....Chester, NJ
Petrides, Randall J. ....Flint, MI
Petrides, Thomas H. ....Los Angeles, CA
Petrie, Amanda Hammond ....Lexington, KY
Petrie, Andrew J. ....Denver, CO
Petrie, Arthur R., II ....Anaheim, CA
Petrie & Associates, The Law Offices of
Laguna Niguel, CA
Petrie, Bauer, Vriesman & Hecht, LLP
Denver, CO
Petrie, Bernard ....San Francisco, CA
Petrie, Bruce I. ....Cincinnati, OH
Petrie, Bruce I., Jr. ....Cincinnati, OH
Petrie, C. Daniel, Jr. ....Fort Lauderdale, FL
Petrie, C. Daniel, Jr., P.A.
Fort Lauderdale, FL
Petrie, Charles E. ....Harrisburg, PA
Petrie, D. Bruce ....Danville, KY
Petrie, Donald A. ....New York, NY
Petrie, Donald B. ....Phoenix, AZ
Petrie, Gair B. ....Spokane, WA
Petrie, Gayle ....Jacksonville, FL
Petrie, Gordon W. ....Emmett, ID
Petrie, Granville E. ....Tallahassee, FL
Petrie, Granville E., Jr., P.A. ....Tallahassee, FL
Petrie, Gregory S. ....Seattle, WA
Petrie, Harold J. ....Tacoma, WA
Petrie, J. David ....Fresno, CA
Petrie, James G. ....Stamford, CT
Petrie, James G. ....Columbus, OH
Petrie, James L. ....Waverly, TN
Petrie, James R. ....Milwaukee, WI
Petrie, James S. ....Chicago, IL
Petrie, Jason Kelly ....Elkton, KY
Russellville, KY
Petrie, Jim R. ....Raytown, MO
Petrie, Joanne ....Department of Transportation, Office of the General Counsel, GV
Petrie, John T. ....Seattle, WA
Petrie, Kenneth P. ....Riverdale, NJ
Petrie, Laura J. ....Newport Beach, CA
Petrie, Laura J. ....Milwaukee, WI
Petrie, Laura S. ....Cincinnati, OH
Petrie, Leroy H. ....Denver, CO
Petrie, Linda C. ....Spokane, WA
Petrie, Michael E. ....Laguna Niguel, CA
Petrie, Paul E. ....Chicago, IL
Petrie, Richard A. ....Milwaukee, WI
Petrie, Richard E. ....Kansas City, MO
Petrie, Robert A. ....Mesa, AZ
Petrie, Robert A., P.C. ....Mesa, AZ
Petrie, Sean J. ....Palo Alto, CA
Petrie, Sherman V., Jr. ....Bronxville, NY
Petrie & Stocking S.C. ....Milwaukee, WI
Petrie, William W. ....Laguna Hills, CA
Petriello, John J. ....Newark, NJ
Petriello, Joseph C. ....Wayne, NJ
Petriello, Louis J. ....Blue Bell, PA
Petriello & Royal, LLP ....Blue Bell, PA
Philadelphia, PA
Petrig, A. M. Christina ....Gainesville, GA
Petrik & Frieze ....Broken Arrow, OK
Petrik, Joe ....Cleveland, OH
Petrik, John J. ....Minot, ND
Petrik, Michael T. ....Atlanta, GA
Petrikin, J. Ronald ....Tulsa, OK
Petrikin, Wellman, Damico, Brown & Petrosa, A Professional Corporation
Media, PA
Petrikis, Steven M. ....Pittsburgh, PA
Petrila, John P. ....Albany, NY
Petrilla, Antony R. ....Washington, DC
Petrilla, Shannan Stamper
Washington, DC
Petrille, Donald, Jr. ....Cherry Hill, NJ
Harrisburg, PA
King Of Prussia, PA
Petrilli, Jennifer A. ....New York, NY
Petrilli, John A. ....Long Beach, NY
Petrilli, Kathleen L. ....Philadelphia, PA
Petrilli, Susan M. ....New York, NY
Petrillo, Ann L. ....Englewood Cliffs, NJ
Petrillo, Anthony J. ....Tampa, FL
Petrillo, Concetta ....Bronx, NY
Petrillo, F. Charles ....Wilkes-Barre, PA
Petrillo, Guy ....New York, NY

Petrillo, Jessie V. .... Syracuse, NY
Petrillo, John S. .... Arlington, VA
Petrillo, Joseph E. .... San Francisco, CA
Petrillo, Joseph J. .... Washington, DC
Petrillo, Kathleen M. .... St. Louis, MO
Petrillo, Maria L. .... Philadelphia, PA
Petrillo, Mary Ann .... Monroeville, PA
Petrillo & Powell, P.L.L.C.
Washington, DC
Petrillo, Richard T. .... White Plains, NY
Petrillo, Robert M. .... Clearwater, FL
Petrillo, Stephen L. .... Roseland, NJ
Petrillo, Thomas W. .... Rochester, NY
Petrillo, William Scott .... Mineola, NY
Petrin, Helen Fite .... Salem, NJ
Petrina, Gilbert E. .... Hershey, PA
Petrina, William T. .... Clifton, NJ
Petrine, Alan K. .... Miami, FL
Petrine, Kenneth J. .... Cave Creek, AZ
Petring, Walter A. .... Florissant, MO
Petrini, Christopher J. .... Boston, MA
Petrini, Edward L. .... Richmond, VA
Petrini, John F. .... Bakersfield, CA
Petrini, Julie O'Brien .... Cambridge, MA
Petrini, Kenneth R. .... Allentown, PA
Petrini, Marla S. .... Denver, CO
Jacksonville, FL
Petrinjak, Gregory A. .... Jackson, TN
Petrino, Frank J. .... Trenton, NJ
Petrinovic, Peter .... Cleveland Heights, OH
Petris, Nicholas C. .... Campbell, CA
Petrizzi, Maribeth .... Department of Justice, Antitrust Division, GV
Petrizzo, Joseph P. .... Newburgh, NY
Petrizzo, Louis J. .... Babylon, NY
Petrizzo, Michael A., Jr. .... New York, NY
Petro, Caroline E. .... Washington, DC
Petro Cohen .... Northfield, NJ
Petro, Douglas J. .... Orlando, FL
Petro, Dyana L. .... Clermont, FL
Petro, Frank A. .... Northfield, NJ
Petro, Frank W. .... Chicago, IL
Petro, James M. .... Columbus, OH
Petro, John D. .... Albany, NY
Petro, John J. .... Columbus, OH
Petro, John P. .... Columbus, OH
Petro, Joseph A. .... Los Angeles, CA
Petro, Laura .... Birmingham, AL
Petro, Lee G. .... Washington, DC
Petro, Michael J. .... Chicago, IL
Petro, Michael J. .... Springville, UT
Petro, Nancyjean P. .... Philadelphia, PA
Petro, Nerino J., Jr. .... Loves Park, IL
Petro, P. Mark .... Birmingham, AL
Petro, P. Mark, P.C. .... Birmingham, AL
Petro, Patricia Ann M. .... Denville, NJ
Petro, Paul M. .... Donora, PA
Petro, Susan .... Northfield, NJ
Petro, Thomas K. .... Kingston, NY
Petrocca, Anthony T. .... Millis, MA
Petrocchi, Anthony A. .... Dallas, TX
Petrocchi, Mark J. .... Fort Worth, TX
Petroccia, Malcolm W. .... Coraopolis, PA
Petroccio, William M. .... Southport, CT
Petroccione, Emilio A. F. .... Albany, NY
Cedarhurst, NY
Petroccione, Patricia M. .... Arlington, VA
Petrocelli & Christy .... New York, NY
Petrocelli, Daniel M., (A Professional Corporation) .... Los Angeles, CA
Petrocelli, Laura R. .... Flushing, NY
Petrocelli Law Offices, P.C. .... Providence, RI
Petrocelli, Mandy M. .... Arlington, VA
Petrocelli, Richard N. .... New York, NY
Petrocelli, Richard W. .... Providence, RI
Petrocine, Alfonse R. .... Bronx, NY
Petrock & Fendel, P.C. .... Denver, CO
Petrock, James J. .... Denver, CO
Petroff, David .... New York, NY
Petroff, Donald Z. .... Oregon, OH
Petroff, Dragan D. .... Oklahoma City, OK
Petroff, Ernest A., III .... Huntsville, TN
Petroff, Gregory A. .... Trenton, NJ
Petroff, Kip A. .... Dallas, TX
Petroff, Kip, P.C. .... Dallas, TX
Petroff, Laura R. .... Los Angeles, CA
Petroff, Martin B. .... New York, NY
Petroff, Rose Caroline .... Charlotte, NC
Petroff, Samuel J. .... Springfield, OH
Petroff, Svetlana V. .... New York, NY
Petrofsky, Richard C. .... St. Louis, MO
Petrokaitis, Gina M. .... Waterbury, CT
Petrokofsky, Robert .... Laguna Niguel, CA
Petrolle, Michael A. .... Newark, NJ
Petronack, Paul S. .... St. Paul, MN
Petrone, Angela M. .... Chicago, IL
Petrone, Anthony J. .... Philadelphia, PA
Petrone, Anthony M. .... Chicago, IL
Petrone, Charles D. .... Cherry Hill, NJ
Petrone, Donna J. .... Houston, TX
Petrone, Evelyn .... White Plains, NY
Petrone, John R., II .... Syracuse, NY
Utica, NY
Petrone, Joseph E. .... Scarsdale, NY
Petrone, Lori E. .... Syracuse, NY
Utica, NY
Petrone, Louis S. .... Syracuse, NY
Utica, NY
Petrone, Michael G. .... Princeton, NJ
Petrone, Peter J. .... East Hartford, CT
Petrone & Petrone, P.C. .... Buffalo, NY
Rochester, NY
Syracuse, NY
Utica, NY
Petrone, Rafael L. .... New York, NY
Petrone, Ricky L. .... Las Vegas, NV
Petrone, Robert Felix .... Philadelphia, PA
Petrone, Victor P. .... Plymouth Meeting, PA

Petronella, P. Neill .... Chicago, IL
Petronella, Richard L. .... Houston, TX
Petronella & Yarborough, P.C. .... Houston, TX
Petronelli, Jack L. .... Cleveland, OH
Petronelli, Montez L. .... San Jose, CA
Petroni, Gloria M. .... Reno, NV
Petroni, Louis A. .... Cherry Hill, NJ
Philadelphia, PA
Petroni, Robert L. .... Las Vegas, NV
Petroni, Romeo G. .... New Haven, CT
Petroni, Thomas Richard .... Lansing, MI
Petronio, Andrea Hogarth .... Mendon, MA
Petronio, Arthur .... Waterloo, NY
Petronio, Everett A. .... Johnston, RI
Petronio, Michael C. .... New York, NY
Petronio, Richard E. .... Cranston, RI
Petronio, Thomas M. .... Johnston, RI
Petronis, Joe .... Killeen, TX
Petronis, Karen L.
Department of Transportation, Federal Aviation Administration, GV
Petronko, John, Jr. .... Rahway, NJ
Petrony, John F. .... Youngstown, OH
Petronzio, Anna M. .... Cleveland, OH
Petronzio, Schneier & Willis .... Cleveland, OH
Petropoulos, Anthony N.
Elk Grove Village, IL
Petropoulos, Gary .... Garden City, NY
Petropoulos, Michael .... Garden City, NY
Petroro, Jill .... Morristown, NJ
Petros, Christina G. .... Manitowoc, WI
Petros, George Z. .... Annapolis, MD
Camp Springs, MD
Petros, Gerald J. .... Boston, MA
Providence, RI
Petros, Peter P. .... Chicago, IL
Petros, Raymond L. .... Denver, CO
Petros & White, LLC .... Denver, CO
Petros, William L. .... Miami, FL
Petros, William L., P.A. .... Miami, FL
Petrosa, Donald T. .... Media, PA
Petrosinelli, Joseph G. .... Washington, DC
Petrosino, Frank V. .... Burlington, VT
Petrosino, Joan S. .... New York, NY
Petrosino, Joseph A. .... Brooklyn, NY
Petrosino, Karen M. .... New York, NY
Petrosino, Sharon L. Campot
Hackensack, NJ
Petroske, Clifford J. .... East Islip, NY
Petroski, Daniel J. "Pete", Jr.
Houston, TX
Petroski, Mary Chinnock .... Laramie, WY
Petroski, Walter W. .... St. Paul, MN
Petrosky, Brent A. .... Lock Haven, PA
Petrosky, Edward F., Jr. .... New York, NY
Petrosky, Robert .... Kittanning, PA
Petrosky, Sylvia A. .... Akron, OH
Petrossian, Alen .... Los Angeles, CA
Petrossian, Elaine T. .... Philadelphia, PA
Petrou, Anastasia M. .... McLean, VA
Petrou, Ioana .... San Francisco, CA
Petrou, Peter .... Parsippany, NJ
Petrouski, Carolyn Sue
San Francisco, CA
Petrov, Alan M. .... Cleveland, OH
Petrov, Alan P. .... Houston, TX
Petrov, Geoffrey S. .... Austin, TX
Petrovic, Jablanka .... Chicago, IL
Petrovich, Emilie Koers .... Marietta, GA
Petrovich, George J., Jr. .... Fort Worth, TX
Petrovich & Giraud, Law Office of
Fort Worth, TX
Petrovich, John G. .... Los Angeles, CA
Petrovich, Luke A. .... Buras, LA
Petrovich, Mark J. .... Springfield, VA
Petrovich, Michael P. .... Tallahassee, FL
Petrovich, Robert G. .... Pasadena, CA
Petrovich, Stephen C. .... Alpharetta, GA
Petrovich, Susan F. .... Santa Barbara, CA
Petrovits, Eugene A. .... Phoenix, AZ
Petrovits, James J. .... Montrose, CA
Petrow, George J. .... New York, NY
Petrow, Joel R. .... Memphis, TN
Petrow, John E. .... Department of Justice, Office of Intelligence Policy and Review, GV
Petrow-Cohen, Julie .... New York, NY
Petrowitz, Harold C.
Department of the Army, Office, Chief of Engineers/Headquarters, U.S. Army Corps of Engineers, GV
Petrowski, Lawrence C. .... Phoenix, AZ
Petrozella, Philip .... Coral Springs, FL
Petroziello, Jo Ann C. .... Washington, DC
Petrozzi, Paul J. .... Fair Oaks, CA
Petrozzi, Ursula A. .... Detroit, MI
Petrozzo, Michael A. .... Brooklyn, NY
Petrozzo, Vincent J. .... Syosset, NY
Petruccelli, Christopher L.
St. Petersburg, FL
Tampa, FL
Petruccelli, Don A. .... Davenport, IA
Petruccelli, Gerald F. .... Portland, ME
Petruccelli & Martin, LLP .... Portland, ME
Petruccelli, Mary B. .... Chalmette, LA
Petruccelli, Michael A.
Fort Lauderdale, FL
Petruccelli, Paul J. .... Northfield, IL
Petrucci, Gretchen L. .... Columbus, OH
Petrucci, James E. .... Boston, MA
Petrucci, Mark C. .... Columbus, OH
Petrucci, Michael J. .... Columbus, OH
Petrucci, Michael L. .... Cincinnati, OH
Petrucci, Richard J. .... Providence, RI
Petrucci, Richard J., Jr. .... Providence, RI
Petrucci, Robert M. .... New York, NY
Petrucelli, Donna M. .... New York, NY
Petrucelli, James Michael .... Kerman, CA

Petrucelli, Jodi M. .... Boston, MA
Petrucelli, Leonard J. .... Mount Prospect, IL
Petrucelli, Nora Angeli .... Iron Mountain, MI
Iron River, MI
Petrucelli & Petrucelli, P.C.
Iron Mountain, MI
Iron River, MI
Petrucelli, Robert R. .... Trumbull, CT
Petrucelli, Vincent R. .... Iron Mountain, MI
Iron River, MI
Petrucelly, Jeffrey .... Boston, MA
Petrucelly & Nadler, P.C. .... Boston, MA
Petruchius, Mary F. .... St. Charles, IL
Petruff, Patricia A. .... Bradenton, FL
Petrulakis, Dean P. .... Modesto, CA
Petrulakis, George A. .... Modesto, CA
Petrulakis Jensen & Friedrich, LLP
Modesto, CA
Petrulakis, Karen Jensen
Los Angeles, CA
San Francisco, CA
Petrulis, Donald L. .... Troy, MI
Petrulis, John B. .... Frankfort, IL
Petrulis, Kenneth G. .... Los Angeles, CA
Petrulis, Richard D. .... Cleveland, OH
Petrulis, Robert C. .... Cleveland, OH
Petrulis, Vytas A. .... Houston, TX
Petrullo, John P. .... Los Angeles, CA
Petrungaro, Barbara N. .... Joliet, IL
Petrunoff, Andre B. .... New York, NY
Petrus, Barbara A. .... Honolulu, HI
Petrus, Brad S. .... Honolulu, HI
Petrus, Desiree A. .... Harrisburg, PA
Petrus, Edmond A., Jr. .... San Diego, CA
San Francisco, CA
Petrus, William G., Jr. .... Springfield, MO
Petrusek, Robert A. .... Muscle Shoals, AL
Petrush, John J. .... Beaver, PA
Petruska, David C. .... Dallas, TX
Petruska, Julius G. .... Orlando, FL
Petruska, Lynette M. .... Erie, PA
Petruska, Paul E. .... St. Louis, MO
Petruso, John D. .... Meadville, PA
Petrutsas, George .... Washington, DC
Arlington, VA
Petruzzell, Christine D. .... Woodbridge, NJ
Petruzzelli, Jerrold F. .... Palo Alto, CA
Petruzzelli, Julie A. .... Washington, DC
Petruzzelli, Lori A. .... New Haven, CT
Petruzzelli, Michele A. .... Albany, NY
Petruzzelli, Nanette .... Library of Congress, Copyright Office, GV
Petruzzelli, Robert A. .... Cherry Hill, NJ
Petruzzi, Anthony R. .... Cleveland, OH
Petruzzi, Frank M. .... Youngstown, OH
Petruzzi, James D. .... Dallas, TX
Petruzzi, Paul D. .... Miami, FL
Petruzzi, Paul D., P.A. .... Miami, FL
Petruzziello, Elaine J. .... Cherry Hill, NJ
Petruzziello, Luigi R. .... Boston, MA
Petruzzo, Jennifer K. .... Jericho, NY
Petry & Gonzalez .... Carrizo Springs, TX
Petry, John J. .... San Francisco, CA
Petry, John L. .... Eaton, OH
Petry, John W. .... Carrizo Springs, TX
Petry, Marvin .... Alexandria, VA
Petry, Paul Andrew .... Seattle, WA
Petry, Samuel Richard, II .... Cleveland, OH
Petrycki, Alison R. .... Philadelphia, PA
Petrycki, John V., Jr. .... New Providence, NJ
Petryha, Jerry G. .... Santa Monica, CA
Petryk, Richard Charles .... Fort Lauderdale, FL
Petrylak, Joseph F. .... Sterling Heights, MI
Petrzelka, Matthew J. .... Cedar Rapids, IA
Petsas, Kosta J. .... Moss Beach, CA
Petsch, Joe S. .... Del Rio, TX
Petsch, Roy R. .... Scottsdale, AZ
Petsche, Frank J. .... South Bend, IN
Petsche, James L. .... Woodbridge, NJ
Petsche, Randy .... Iowa City, IA
Petshaft, David Bryan .... New Haven, CT
Petshow, John M. .... Portland, OR
Petska, Denice Marie .... Cedar Rapids, IA
Petsko, John .... Moneta, VA
Petso, Lora L. .... Edmonds, WA
Petsonk, Carol A. .... Washington, DC
Pett, Craig R. .... Atlanta, GA
Pett, Curtis C. .... Department of Justice, Tax Division, GV
Pett, Harry .... Totowa, NJ
Pett, Kristina B. .... Boca Raton, FL
Pett, Richard S. .... Totowa, NJ
Pett, Russo & Pett .... Totowa, NJ
Pettaway, Collins, Jr. .... Selma, AL
Pettay, Lee .... Bloomington, IN
Pettay, Mosser & Tabacchi .... Cadiz, OH
Pette, Monica L. .... Kirkwood, CA
Pettee, Susan .... Federal Trade Commission, Bureau of Competition, GV
Pettegrew, Hillary L. .... Washington, DC
Pettengill, Darnell Wayne
Jefferson City, MO
Pettengill, Lori L. .... Los Angeles, CA
Pettepit, Marguerite M. .... Wakefield, MA
Petter, Leslie Zinkand .... Atlanta, GA
Pettersen, Andrew M. .... New York, NY
Pettersen, Katherine A. .... Denver, CO
Pettersen, Kristen D. .... Anchorage, AK
Pettersen, Robert G. .... Longmeadow, MA
Pettersen, Scott P. .... Long Grove, IL
Petterson, Bruce N. .... Alpharetta, GA
Petterson, James D. .... Carlsbad, CA
Petterson, Jay R. .... Sylmar, CA
Petterson, Kenneth M. .... Traverse City, MI
Petterson, Paul S. .... Washington, DC
Pettey, Christopher A. .... Decatur, AL
Pettey, Louis S. .... Gaithersburg, MD
Pettey, Robert H., Jr. .... Opelika, AL

Pettey, Rodney E. .... Raleigh, NC
Pettey, Susan M. .... Alexandria, VA
Pettey, Virginia L. .... Dallas, TX
Pettey, Walter G., III .... Dallas, TX
Pettey, William H., Jr. .... Gulfport, MS
Petti, Angel .... Fort Lauderdale, FL
Petti, Christopher J. .... Englewood, CO
Petti, Dana J. .... Atlanta, GA
Petti, David A. .... New York, NY
Petti, Edgar P. .... Geneva, IL
Petti, Edgar P., & Associates, P.C.
Geneva, IL
Petti, Frederick R. .... Phoenix, AZ
Petti, Gary M. .... Akron, OH
Petti, Jerome D. .... Union, NJ
Petti, Luanna Bennett .... Atlanta, GA
Petti, Maria J. .... New York, NY
Petti, Philip T. .... Chicago, IL
Petti, Russell G. .... Los Angeles, CA
Pettibone, Craig B.
Office of Personnel Management, Personnel in Non-Legal Positions, GV
Pettibone, Douglas J. .... Tustin, CA
Pettibone, James P. .... Sacramento, CA
Pettibone, John S., III .... Philadelphia, PA
Pettibone, Jon E. .... Phoenix, AZ
Pettibone, Peter J. .... New York, NY
Pettibone, Russell O. .... Ocean City, NJ
Petticord, Damon J. .... Tigard, OR
Petticord, Daniel F. .... Cleveland, OH
Petticrew, Paul S. .... Indianapolis, IN
Pettiet, Bradley M. .... Lubbock, TX
Pettiette, Alison .... Houston, TX
Pettiette, Armand, Dunkelman, Woodley & Byrd, L.L.P. .... Shreveport, LA
Pettiette, John K. .... Dallas, TX
Pettiette, John K. .... Dallas, TX
Pettiette, Lawrence W., Jr.
Shreveport, LA
Pettiette, Tom L. .... Houston, TX
Pettiford, Nadine S. .... Toledo, OH
Pettig, David C. .... Pittsford, NY
Pettig, David C., P.C. .... Pittsford, NY
Rochester, NY
Pettigrass, David J. .... San Diego, CA
Pettigrew, Albert H. .... Biloxi, MS
Pettigrew, Anne S. .... Walnut Creek, CA
Pettigrew & Associates, P.C. .... Atlanta, GA
Pettigrew, A. W., Jr. .... Houma, LA
Pettigrew, C. Keith .... Indianapolis, IN
Pettigrew, Charles R. .... Jackson, TN
Pettigrew, Edward W. .... Seattle, WA
Pettigrew, Frank W. .... Grand Prairie, TX
Pettigrew, Grady L., Jr. .... Columbus, OH
Pettigrew, Gregory M. .... Los Angeles, CA
Pettigrew, Harry W. .... Atlanta, GA
Pettigrew, Jamie L., (Miss)
Montgomery, AL
Pettigrew, John D. .... Bradenton, FL
Pettigrew, Judith Reif .... Los Angeles, CA
Pettigrew, Karen Bailey .... Austin, TX
Pettigrew, Karen Beth .... New York, NY
Pettigrew, Kathleen T. .... Charleston, WV
Pettigrew, Lewis F. .... New Philadelphia, OH
Pettigrew, M. Jane .... Anchorage, AK
Pettigrew, Mark H. .... York, PA
Pettigrew, R. Matthew, Jr. .... Philadelphia, PA
Pettigrew, Richard A. .... Miami, FL
Pettigrew, Sam W., Jr. .... Grand Prairie, TX
Pettigrew, Stephen H. .... San Jose, CA
Pettigrew & Wagner .... Grand Prairie, TX
Pettigrew, William D. .... Oklahoma City, OK
Pettigrew, William S. .... Sun City, AZ
Pettijohn, Bruce A. .... Phoenix, AZ
Pettinari, Mark Lee .... San Francisco, CA
Pettinato, David J. .... Tampa, FL
Pettinato, Joseph J., Jr. .... Rego Park, NY
Pettinato, Mark D. .... Aiea, HI
Pettine, Andrea B. .... West Chester, PA
Pettine, Mark V. .... San Diego, CA
Pettine, Paul A., III .... Santa Barbara, CA
Pettine, Raymond J. .... Providence, RI
Pettinella, John P. .... Scarsdale, NY
Pettinelli, Joan E. .... Cleveland, OH
Pettinelli, Virginia M. .... Park Ridge, NJ
Pettinga, Gayle Gerling .... Evansville, IN
Pettingell, Richard H. .... Boston, MA
Pettinger, Pierre E. .... Lincoln, NE
Pettingill, Kathleen A. .... Cleveland, OH
Pettingill, Michael .... San Francisco, CA
Pettingill, Norman A. .... New Orleans, LA
Pettingill, William L. .... San Diego, CA
Pettini, L. Robert .... Wheeling, WV
Pettinicchi, Thomas P. .... Waterbury, CT
Pettis, Alan W. .... Costa Mesa, CA
Pettis, Clay B. .... Holdenville, OK
Pettis, David W., Jr. .... Tampa, FL
Pettis, Eugene K. .... Fort Lauderdale, FL
Pettis, Faith L. .... Seattle, WA
Pettis, Glenn A., Jr. .... Omaha, NE
Pettis, James L., III .... Jackson, MS
Pettis, Jim Cole .... Shawnee, OK
Pettis, John A. .... Martinez, CA
Pettis Law Firm .... Omaha, NE
Pettis, Philip L. .... Exeter, NH
Pettis, R. Leon .... Beaumont, TX
Pettis & Van Royen, P.A. .... Tampa, FL
Pettit, Aaron R. .... Chicago, IL
Pettit, Allison G. .... Seattle, WA
Pettit, Alvin D. .... Baltimore, MD
Pettit, Anne E. .... New York, NY
Pettit, Aubrey L., Jr. .... Stamford, CT
Pettit, Bernard F. .... Philadelphia, PA
Pettit, Bill W. .... Schulenburg, TX
Pettit, Calvin F. .... Linthicum Heights, MD
Pettit, Charles K. .... Bloomfield, IA
Pettit, Christopher R. .... Columbus, OH
Pettit, D. Bradley .... Charlottesville, VA

Pettit, Daniel J. ... **Racine, WI**
Pettit, David ... **Los Angeles, CA**
Pettit, David H. ... **Charlottesville, VA**
Pettit, Debra Rectenbaugh ... **Des Moines, IA**
Pettit, Douglas A. ... Los Angeles, CA
San Diego, CA
Santa Ana, CA
Pettit, George R. ... **Washington, DC**
Pettit, George W. ... Woodridge, IL
Pettit, H. Boyd, III ... **Cartersville, GA**
Pettit, H. Foster ... **Lexington, KY**
Pettit, James J. ... Philadelphia, PA
Pettit, Jeffrey L. ... **Philadelphia, PA**
Pettit, Jerry L. ... Omaha, NE
Pettit, John C. ... Washington, PA
Pettit, John E. ... Department of the Air Force, Office of the General Counsel, GV
Pettit, John J., Jr. ... Philadelphia, PA
Pettit, John W. ... **Washington, DC**
Pettit, Jonathan L. ... **Los Angeles, CA**
Pettit, Joseph A. ... Fort Pierce, FL
Pettit, Julia R. ... Salt Lake City, UT
Pettit, Kenton K. ... **Cincinnati, OH**
Pettit, Kim M., Law Office of ... **San Antonio, TX**
Pettit, Kristi S. ... Grand Forks, ND
Pettit, Laurence ... **New York, NY**
Pettit Law Office, P.C. ... Bloomfield, IA
Pettit, Lori L. ... Machias, NY
Pettit, Mark, Jr. ... Boston, MA
Pettit, Mary Frances Koch ... **Dallas, TX**
Pettit, Michael ... Pullman, WA
Pettit, Michael W. ... Naples, FL
Pettit, Mitchell S. ... Washington, DC
Pettit, Otho E., Jr. ... Kosciusko, MS
Pettit, Peter R. ... Memphis, TN
Pettit & Pettit, P.C. ... Aurora, MO
Pettit, Philip J. ... New York, NY
Pettit, Richard R. ... Portland, OR
Pettit, Richard R. ... **Chattanooga, TN**
Pettit, Robert E. ... Little Rock, AR
Pettit, Robert L. ... **Washington, DC**
Pettit, Roger L. ... **Milwaukee, WI**
Pettit, Ronald M. ... Columbus, OH
Pettit, Rosser J. ... Baltimore, MD
Pettit, Scott R. ... Aurora, MO
Pettit, Sharon E. ... Lansing, MI
Pettit, Stacy L. ... Albany, NY
Pettit, Stephen J. ... Houston, TX
Pettit, Susan ... Columbus, OH
Pettit & Taragin ... Baltimore, MD
Pettit, Ted N. ... **Honolulu, HI**
Pettit, Thomas W. ... **Huntington, WV**
Pettit, Tristan R. ... **Milwaukee, WI**
Pettit, Walter S., Jr. ... Aurora, MO
Pettit, William F. ... Mason, MI
Pettit, William R. ... Terrace Park, OH
Pettit, William Walt ... **Charlotte, NC**
Pettit, William Walt, P.A. ... **Charlotte, NC**
Pettitt, Anthony N. ... **Dallas, TX**
Fort Worth, TX
Pettitt, B. Buck ... **McAllen, TX**
Pettitt, Blaine ... **Fresno, CA**
Pettitt, Krishna L. ... Oakland, CA
Pettitt, Marcy A. ... Sherman Oaks, CA
Pettitt, Patrick R. ... **Newport News, VA**
Pettitt, Roger C. ... Los Angeles, CA
Pettker, John D. ... **Los Angeles, CA**
Pettler, Peter D. ... Torrance, CA
Pettler, Richard J. ... **San Francisco, CA**
Pettler, Robert J. ... Los Angeles, CA
Pettlon, N. Trey ... **Olathe, KS**
Pettorini, Timothy B. ... **Wooster, OH**
Pettoruto, Albert P., Jr. ... North Andover, MA
Pettrone, Claire R. ... **Alexandria, VA**
Pettrone, George J. ... Pittsburgh, PA
Pettus, A. C. G., Sr. ... Montgomery, AL
Pettus, Don K. ... Little Rock, AR
Pettus, Donna C. ... Fayetteville, AR
Pettus, Erle, Jr. ... Birmingham, AL
Pettus, J. Donald ... San Francisco, CA
Pettus, Lamar ... Fayetteville, AR
Pettus Law Firm, P.A. ... Fayetteville, AR
Pettus, Marvin K. ... New York, NY
Pettus, Nancy M. ... **Santa Ana, CA**
Pettus, Reginald H. ... Keysville, VA
Pettus, Reginald H. Law Office of, P.C. ... Keysville, VA
Pettus, Richard C. ... **New York, NY**
Pettus & Smith, L.L.C. ... Montgomery, AL
Pettus, William B. ... Frankfort, KY
Pettus-Dotson, Lita ... **Hayward, CA**
Pettway, James R. ... **Monroe, LA**
Pettway, Jo Celeste ... Camden, AL
Petty, Amy Campbell ... **Raleigh, NC**
Petty, Bruce ... Fort Worth, TX
Petty, Carl F. ... Cleveland, TN
Petty, Charles W., Jr. ... **Washington, DC**
Petty, D. Paul ... Searcy, AR
Petty, David K. ... **Guymon, OK**
Petty, David K., A Professional Corporation ... **Guymon, OK**
Petty, David T., Jr. ... **Lynchburg, VA**
Petty, Denis K. ... Los Angeles, CA
Petty, Gary C. ... Administrative Office Of The United States Courts, GV
Petty, J. Gordon ... Chattanooga, TN
Petty, Jack H. ... Bethany, OK
Petty, James Guy ... Searcy, AR
Petty, Jim K. ... **Chattanooga, TN**
Petty, John Reese ... Reno, NV
Petty, Jonathan M. ... **Atlanta, GA**
Petty, Keith ... Palo Alto, CA
Petty, Keith, A Professional Corporation ... Palo Alto, CA
Petty, Kenneth E. ... **Seattle, WA**

Petty, Lewis F. ... Great Meadows, NJ
Petty, Linda J. ... **New York, NY**
Petty, Livingston, Dawson & Richards, A Professional Corporation ... **Lynchburg, VA**
Petty, Lynette F. ... Topeka, KS
Petty, Mark T. ... Arcola, IL
Petty, Mark T., P.C., Law Office of ... Arcola, IL
Petty, Mark W. ... Rocky Hill, CT
Petty, Melvin E. ... **Pine Bluff, AR**
Petty, Michael D. ... **Washington, DC**
Petty, Michael D. ... **Dallas, TX**
Petty, Michael S. ... Raleigh, NC
Petty, Michele ... San Antonio, TX
Petty, Myrle Rountree ... **San Bernardino, CA**
Petty, Neil E. ... **Chicago, IL**
Petty, Norman H., Jr. ... **Princeton, NJ**
Petty, P. Alex ... Searcy, AR
Petty, Patricia L. ... Department of Justice, Criminal Division, GV
Petty, Philip A. ... **Towson, MD**
Petty, Philip C. ... **Fairmont, WV**
Petty, Phillip A. ... Orange, CA
Petty, R. Larry ... Reno, NV
Petty, Ralph C. ... **Salt Lake City, UT**
Petty, Regina A. ... **San Diego, CA**
Petty, Richard S. ... Harrison, NY
Petty, Ross David ... Wellesley, MA
Petty, Ross M. ... **San Francisco, CA**
Petty, Sarah ... **Irvine, CA**
Petty, Sharon Lee ... **Memphis, TN**
Petty, Shaw and Densmore ... Bethany, OK
Petty, Stephan R. ... Midland, TX
Petty, Thomas R. ... **Washington, DC**
Petty, W. Scott ... **Atlanta, GA**
Petty, Wayne G. ... **Salt Lake City, UT**
Petty, Weldon R., Jr. ... Midland, TX
Petty, William E. ... Antioch, IL
Petty, William G. ... Lynchburg, VA
Petty, William W. ... **Knoxville, TN**
Petty-Hankins, Juanita ... Houston, TX
Pettyjohn, David E. ... Kansas City, MO
Pettyjohn, Frederick P. ... Anchorage, AK
Pettyjohn, Shirley E. ... Louisville, KY
Pettyjohn, Thomas W., Jr. ... Lynchburg, VA
Pettys, N. William, Jr. ... Acworth, GA
Pettys, Todd Edward ... Seattle, WA
Petuchowski, Jonathan M. ... Columbus, OH
Petuchowski, Samuel J. ... **Boston, MA**
Petula, Brian J. ... Factoryville, PA
Petulla, Amy Abernathy ... **Rossville, GA**
Petumenos, Timothy J. ... **Anchorage, AK**
Petway, Blackshear & Cain, L.L.P. ... Nashville, TN
Petway, D. Bruce ... **Birmingham, AL**
Petway, Patricia D. ... Irmo, SC
Petyak, Robert P. ... Ebensburg, PA
Petyk, Roman ... Philadelphia, PA
Petz & Associates, P.C. ... Grosse Pointe Woods, MI
Petz, Edwin V. ... New York, NY
Petz, Frederick A. ... Grosse Pointe Woods, MI
Petzall, Gerhard J. ... **St. Louis, MO**
Petze & Hodgdon ... Norwell, MA
Petze, John ... Norwell, MA
Petze, John E. ... **El Cajon, CA**
Petze, John E. ... **San Diego, CA**
Petzel, William J. ... Oakland, CA
Petzinger, Walter F. ... New York, NY
Petzke, James J. ... San Francisco, CA
Petzke, Roger A. ... **St. Joseph, MI**
Petznick, Eliza L. ... **Birmingham, AL**
Petznick, Heather ... **Kansas City, MO**
Petzold, Guy D. ... Stockton, CA
Petzold, Herman G., III ... Detroit, MI
Petzold, John P. ... Dayton, OH
Petzold, Lewis M. ... Atlantis, FL
Peugeot, Brad Jon ... Los Angeles, CA
Peugh, James E. ... Milledgeville, GA
Peuler, John B. ... **New Orleans, LA**
Peurach, Robert A. ... **Detroit, MI**
Peurifoy, J. Colbert ... Farmersville, TX
Pevar, Stephen L. ... Denver, CO
Pevec, Davor Z. ... **Honolulu, HI**
Pevehouse, Cynthia L. ... **Houston, TX**
Peven, Jerrold M. ... **Chicago, IL**
Peverada, Anthony J., Jr. ... Topsham, ME
Peverada, Robert ... **Whitehouse Station, NJ**
Peverini, Nancy ... Sacramento, CA
Pevers, Marc W. ... Palm Desert, CA
Peveto, Eric T. ... Orange, TX
Peveto, Wayne ... Orange, TX
Pevey, Marcia ... Houston, TX
Pevey and Segura, PLLC ... Houston, TX
Pevney, David B. ... **Melville, NY**
Pevos, Daniel N. ... Farmington Hills, MI
Pevos, Debra Beth ... **Southfield, MI**
Pevos, Raphael I. ... Farmington Hills, MI
Pevsner, Donald L. ... Merritt Island, FL
Pevsner, Joseph S. ... **Dallas, TX**
Pew, Curtis E. ... **New York, NY**
Pew, Douglas J. ... Farmington, CT
Pew, J. Edgar ... Novato, CA
Pew, Jack, Jr. ... **Dallas, TX**
Pew, James S. ... Washington, DC
Pew, Michael T. ... **Warwick, RI**
Pew, Nancy ... St. Louis, MO
Pew, W. Ralph ... **Mesa, AZ**
Pew, W. Ralph, P.C. ... **Mesa, AZ**
Pew, Wendy L. ... Philadelphia, PA
Pewarski, Glen T. ... **New York, NY**
Pewe, Jeffrey L. ... **Seattle, WA**
Pewett, Edwin H. ... Chevy Chase, MD
Pewitt, Douglas S. ... Miami, OK
Pewitt, James P. ... **Birmingham, AL**
Pewsey, Wilmar A. ... Lincoln City, OR
Pexa, E. Joseph, Jr. ... Simsbury, CT

Pey, Christopher E. ... **New York, NY**
Peycke, Mark A. ... Dallas, TX
Peyer, Sibyl C. ... New York, NY
Peyerwold, David L. ... Berkeley, CA
Peyla, Gregory L. ... **Joliet, IL**
Peyrat, Paul ... Sonoma, CA
Peyron, Marie R. ... **Purchase, NY**
Peyronnet, Douglas R. ... Richmond, VA
Peyronnin, Edgar U. ... Ojai, CA
Peyronnin, Paul L. ... **New Orleans, LA**
Peyser, Andrea ... **New York, NY**
Peyser, Daniel B. ... Springfield, VA
Peyser, Josephine L. ... Montpelier, VT
Peyser, Lilyanna L. ... **Washington, DC**
Peyser, Mark W. ... **Detroit, MI**
Peyser, Mary Driscoll ... Portsmouth, NH
Peyser, Robert J. ... New York, NY
Peyser, Robert M. ... Malden, MA
Peyser, Roxane D. ... Birmingham, AL
Peyser, Theodore D. ... **Washington, DC**
Peyster, Richard I. ... Federal Deposit Insurance Corporation, Liquidation Branch, GV
Peytavin, John L. ... Lutcher, LA
Peytavin, Malcolm J. ... Lutcher, LA
Peytavin, Michael D. ... **Gretna, LA**
Peyton, Angus E. ... **Charleston, WV**
Peyton, Barbara ... Sacramento, CA
Peyton, Bradley J. ... Warren, MN
Peyton, Bradley R. ... West Des Moines, IA
Peyton, Charles E. ... Louisville, KY
Peyton, Deborah M. ... **Baltimore, MD**
Hunt Valley, MD
Peyton, Donald R. ... New Port Richey, FL
Peyton and Dunsmore ... Knightstown, IN
Peyton, Erin ... **New York, NY**
Peyton, Evelyn A. ... **San Jose, CA**
Peyton, George S., Jr. ... **Oakland, CA**
Peyton, Gordon P. ... **Alexandria, VA**
Peyton, Gordon P., P.C. ... **Alexandria, VA**
Peyton, Gregory J. ... Racine, WI
Peyton, Harold M. ... Tempe, AZ
Peyton, Harvey D. ... **Nitro, WV**
Peyton, James J. ... Greeley, CO
Peyton, James P. ... Naperville, IL
Peyton, Janet P. ... **Richmond, VA**
Peyton, Janie O. ... Charleston, WV
Peyton, Jerri A. ... Towson, MD
Peyton, John ... Racine, WI
Peyton, John B., Jr. ... **Dallas, TX**
Peyton, John F., Jr. ... Honolulu, HI
Peyton, Mary K. ... **Metairie, LA**
New Orleans, LA
Peyton, Michael D. ... Knightstown, IN
Peyton, Norman C. ... Houston, TX
Peyton, Parenti & Whittington
Charleston, WV
Nitro, WV
Peyton, Patrick T. ... Beaumont, TX
Peyton, Richard E. ... **Madisonville, KY**
Peyton, Robert D. ... **New Orleans, LA**
Peyton, Robert E. ... **New Orleans, LA**
Peyton, Robert W. ... Los Angeles, CA
Peyton, Stan ... Las Vegas, NV
Peyton, Suzette B. ... Nashville, TN
Peyton, Theresa M. ... **Chicago, IL**
Peyton, Timothy J. ... Madison, WI
Peyton, Troy E. ... **Las Vegas, NV**
Peyton, Walter B. ... Binghamton, NY
Peyton, Wesley E. ... Hewitt, TX
Pezalla, Stephan A., Jr. ... Golden Valley, MN
Pezanoski, Diane M. ... Chicago, IL
Pezanosky, Stephen M. ... **Dallas, TX**
Pezda, Ralph W. ... Southfield, MI
Pezdek, John Victor ... Lexington, KY
Pezely, Martin J. ... Midvale, UT
Pezenik, Alfred J. ... Rockville Centre, NY
Pezhman, Payman ... **Los Angeles, CA**
Pezman, Alfred L. ... Quincy, IL
Pezold, Caruso, Barker & Woltz
Tulsa, OK
Pezold, Daniel G. ... **Santa Ana, CA**
Pezold, George Carl ... **Huntington, NY**
Pezold, R. K. ... **Tulsa, OK**
Pezoldt, Kenneth W. ... Fort Lauderdale, FL
Pezza, Guglielmo A. ... Beverly Hills, MI
Pezza, Michael A., Jr. ... **Boston, MA**
Pezza, Raymond R. ... Providence, RI
Pezzaglia, James A. ... **Martinez, CA**
Pezzani, Angelo M. ... Palo Alto, CA
Pezzano, Lisa J. ... **Bridgewater, NJ**
Pezzano, Tony V. ... **New York, NY**
Pezzaro, Edward R. ... New York, NY
Pezze, Debra A. ... Greensburg, PA
Pezze, Ronald G., Jr. ... **Milwaukee, WI**
Pezzetti, Elizabeth M.
Bloomfield Hills, MI
Pezzetti, Michael John ... Troy, MI
Pezzetti, Thomas A. ... **Traverse City, MI**
Pezzillo, Brian J. ... **Albuquerque, NM**
Pezzini, Danielle Modeste ... Alamo, CA
Pezzino, Margaret L. ... **Mineola, NY**
Pezzlo, Benjamin A. ... Stafford, VA
Pezzner, Ashley I. ... **Wilmington, DE**
Pezzner, Harold ... **Wilmington, DE**
Pezzo, Raymond M. ... Poughkeepsie, NY
Pezzola, Stephen P. ... **Oakland, CA**
Pezzoli, Raymond J. ... Staten Island, NY
Pezzolo, Peter E. ... Metuchen, NJ
Pezzoni, William M. ... **Framingham, MA**
Pezzulich, Matthew C. ... **Bennington, VT**
Pezzulla, James Stephen ... Towson, MD
Pezzulla, Kenneth D. ... Towson, MD
Pezzulla & Pezzulla ... Towson, MD
Pezzulli, Giuseppe ... **New York, NY**
Pezzulli & Loewinsohn, L.L.P. ... **Dallas, TX**
Pezzulli, Michael F. ... **Dallas, TX**
Pezzullo, Michael S. ... Providence, RI

Pezzulo, Christina M. ... Syracuse, NY
Pezzulo, Glenn E. ... **Rochester, NY**
Pezzuolo, Garland P. ... Hatboro, PA
Pezzuti, Vincent G. ... Jersey City, NJ
Pezzutti, William ... Jacksonville, FL
Pezzy, Roxanna ... San Francisco, CA
Pfabe, Howard C. ... **New York, NY**
Pfadenhauer, Diane M.
Long Island City, NY
Pfadenhauer, Glenn J. ... **Washington, DC**
Pfadt, Sue Anthony ... Erie, PA
Pfadt, William E. ... Erie, PA
Pfaehler, Kenneth J. ... **Washington, DC**
Pfaelzer, Mariana R. ... Los Angeles, CA
Pfaender, John A. ... St. Paul, MN
Pfaff, Alan R. ... **Wichita, KS**
Pfaff, Brotherson & Killoren, LLP
Elkhart, IN
Goshen, IN
South Bend, IN
Pfaff, Bruce Robert ... Chicago, IL
Pfaff, Derek J. ... **Las Vegas, NV**
Houston, TX
Pfaff, E. Peter ... East Aurora, NY
Pfaff, E. Peter, P.A. ... East Aurora, NY
Pfaff, Ellen O. ... Seattle, WA
Pfaff, Garner & Terlizzi ... Salem, IL
Pfaff, J. Lawrence ... Banner Elk, NC
Pfaff, Jeffrey M. ... Kansas City, MO
Pfaff, J.S. ... Greensboro, NC
Pfaff, L. Benjamin ... Elkhart, IN
Pfaff, McIntyre, Dugas & Hartye
Hollidaysburg, PA
Pfaff, Robert A. ... **Elkhart, IN**
Pfaff, Robert E. ... Cleveland, OH
Pfaff, Robert J. ... Hollidaysburg, PA
Pfaff, Samuel H. ... Palm Desert, CA
Pfaff, Stephen C. ... Boston, MA
Pfaffenberger, William J.
North Palm Beach, FL
Pfaffenroth, Peter A. ... Chester, NJ
Pfaffly, Philip A. ... **Minneapolis, MN**
Pfaffmann, Carol A. ... **Los Angeles, CA**
Pfaffmann, Lori Lea ... Oakland, CA
Pfaff-Pierce, Mary F. ... Port Angeles, WA
Pfahl, Charlotte W. ... New York, NY
Pfahl, Scott B. ... **Cleveland, OH**
Pfahler, Stephen P. ... **Los Angeles, CA**
Pfaller, Eberhard W., Jr. ... **Washington, DC**
Pfaltz, Hugo M., Jr. ... **Summit, NJ**
Pfaltz & Woller, P.A. A Professional Corporation ... **Summit, NJ**
Pfaltzgraff, Albert J. ... Kailua, HI
Pfalzer, Thomas E. ... **Walnut Creek, CA**
Pfalzer, William R. ... Buffalo, NY
Pfalzgraf, Amy ... Treasury Department, Departmental Offices, GV
Pfalzgraf, David R. ... Buffalo, NY
Pfalzgraf, David R., Jr. ... **Buffalo, NY**
Pfalzgraf, H. Douglas ... **Wellington, KS**
Pfalzgraf, Harold A. ... **Wellington, KS**
Pfalzgraf Law Offices ... **Wellington, KS**
Pfander, James E. ... Champaign, IL
Pfann, George R., Jr. ... Ithaca, NY
Pfann, Susan D. ... Los Angeles, CA
Pfannebecker, Robert L. ... **Columbia, PA**
Lancaster, PA
Lititz, PA
Quarryville, PA
Pfannerstill & Camp ... Wauwatosa, WI
Pfannerstill, John A. ... Wauwatosa, WI
Pfannkuche, Christopher E. K. ... Chicago, IL
Pfanstiel, Carl Eric ... Tulsa, OK
Pfarr, John S. ... **Providence, RI**
Pfarrer, David A. ... Dayton, OH
Pfarrer & Squires ... Dayton, OH
Pfarrer, Stephen M. ... **Dayton, OH**
Pfatteicher, Carl ... Pittsburgh, PA
Pfatteicher, Linda E. S. ... Los Angeles, CA
Pfau, Ann T. ... New York, NY
Pfau, Edward L. ... Columbus, OH
Pfau, James M. ... **Minneapolis, MN**
Pfau, John C. ... **Youngstown, OH**
Pfau, John E. ... **Rockford, IL**
Pfau, Michael E. ... **Santa Barbara, CA**
Pfau, Michael J. ... **Milwaukee, WI**
Pfau, Michael T. ... **Tacoma, WA**
Pfau, Peggy Taylor ... Gillette, WY
Pfau, Peggy Taylor, P.C. ... Gillette, WY
Pfau, Pfau & Marando ... **Warren, OH**
Youngstown, OH
Pfau, Sandra K. ... Washington, DC
Pfau, William E., III ... **Youngstown, OH**
Pfau, William E., Jr. ... **Youngstown, OH**
Pfeffer, A. Antony ... **New York, NY**
Pfeffer, A. Robert ... Department of Labor, Office of the Solicitor, GV
Pfeffer, Alan ... New York, NY
Pfeffer, Alan A. ... Albany, NY
Pfeffer, Anne T. ... Los Angeles, CA
Pfeffer, Charles A. ... Bloomfield Hills, MI
Pfeffer, David H. ... **New York, NY**
Pfeffer, David J. ... **New York, NY**
Pfeffer, Eric R. ... New York, NY
Pfeffer, Howard J. ... **Fairfield, NJ**
Pfeffer, Irving ... **San Francisco, CA**
Pfeffer, James M. ... **Omaha, NE**
Pfeffer, Joel ... **Pittsburgh, PA**
Pfeffer, Kathleen Purtill ... Glastonbury, CT
Pfeffer, Lisa D. ... **Los Angeles, CA**
Pfeffer, Louis P. ... **West Palm Beach, FL**
Pfeffer, Mark ... Atlantic City, NJ
Pfeffer, Martin ... **New York, NY**
Pfeffer, Matthew B. ... Chicago, IL
Pfeffer, Maxine S. ... New York, NY
Pfeffer, Michael S. ... Oakland, CA
Pfeffer, Michael S. ... Ripley, OH
Pfeffer, Nancy S. ... New York, NY

Pfeffer, Paul E. .... **Houston, TX**
Pfeffer, Paul E., Law Office .... Clinton, IA
Pfeffer, Philip E. .... Covington, LA
Pfeffer, Richard M. .... Department of Labor, Office of the Solicitor, GV
Pfeffer, Robert .... **New York, NY**
Pfeffer, Sam E. .... Chicago, IL
Pfeffer, Sanford L. .... Philadelphia, PA
Pfeffer, Sheldon E. .... Houston, TX
Pfeffer, Stephen D. .... Santa Fe, NM
Pfeffer, Steven I. .... **Jackson, NJ**
Pfeffer & Williams, A Professional Corporation .... **San Francisco, CA**
Pfefferkorn, David M. .... Bethesda, MD
Pfefferkorn, Michael G. .... Ballwin, MO
Pfefferkorn, William G., P.A. Winston-Salem, NC
Pfefferkorn, William Gottholdt Winston-Salem, NC
Pfefferle, Ben L., III .... **Columbus, OH**
Pfefferle & Galloway .... Sandusky, OH
Pfefferle, Jas. O. .... Madison, WI
Pfefferle, John A. .... Sandusky, OH
Pfefferle, René J. .... **Baton Rouge, LA**
Pfefferle, Steven J. .... **Minneapolis, MN**
Pfeifer, Agnes A. .... Upper Sandusky, OH
Pfeifer, Barry A. .... New York, NY
Pfeifer, Chad H. .... **San Francisco, CA**
Pfeifer, Charles H. .... Los Angeles, CA
Pfeifer, Clarence J. .... Minneapolis, MN
Pfeifer, Daniel H. .... **South Bend, IN**
Pfeifer, David A. .... San Francisco, CA
Pfeifer & Davidson .... **Santa Ana, CA**
Pfeifer, Dennis E. .... Upper Sandusky, OH
Pfeifer, E. Michael .... Upper Sandusky, OH
Pfeifer, Eugene M. .... **Washington, DC**
Pfeifer & Fabian, P.A. .... Baltimore, MD
Pfeifer, Frank M. .... Springfield, IL
Pfeifer, George S. .... Evanston, IL
Pfeifer, Gregory J. .... **Pittsburgh, PA**
Pfeifer, Harry .... **San Francisco, CA**
Pfeifer, James W. .... San Diego, CA
Pfeifer, Jerome M. .... Longmeadow, MA
Pfeifer, J. J. .... Zanesville, OH
Pfeifer, Joan M. .... San Jose, CA
Pfeifer, John F. .... **Syracuse, NY**
Pfeifer, K. Amy .... Helena, MT
Pfeifer, Kathleen M. .... Byfield, MA
Pfeifer, Mark E. .... **Owensboro, KY**
Pfeifer, Maxwell S. .... Hallandale Beach, FL
Bronx, NY
New York, NY
Pfeifer, Maxwell S. .... **Mount Vernon, NY**
Yonkers, NY
Pfeifer, Michael George .... Washington, DC
Pfeifer, Michael L. .... Garden City, NY
Pfeifer, Michael R. .... **Santa Ana, CA**
Pfeifer & Pfeifer .... Upper Sandusky, OH
Pfeifer, Philip J. .... Oak Ridge, TN
Pfeifer, Phillip A., and Associates Houston, TX
Pfeifer, Robert M. .... Newport News, VA
Pfeifer, Ronald T. .... **Green Bay, WI**
Pfeifer, Susan E. .... **Cabin John, MD**
Pfeifer, Susan E. .... **Chevy Chase, MD**
Pfeifer, William Arthur .... Alpena, MI
Pfeifer, William C. .... Topeka, KS
Pfeifer, William L., Jr. .... Foley, AL
Pfeiffenberger, Michelle M.
New York, NY
Pfeiffer, Alfred C., Jr. .... **San Francisco, CA**
Pfeiffer, Andrea J. .... Brooklyn, NY
Pfeiffer, Arnold .... Parker, SD
Pfeiffer, Astrid .... Miami, FL
Pfeiffer, Barbara J. .... Columbus, OH
Pfeiffer, Bernard A. .... Columbus, GA
Pfeiffer, Beverly Y. .... Columbus, OH
Pfeiffer, Brown, Brennan & Di Nicola Pottsville, PA
Pfeiffer, Carl H. .... San Antonio, TX
Pfeiffer, Christine M. .... Glendale, CA
Pfeiffer, Cynthia J. .... Largo, FL
Pfeiffer, Douglas B. .... **Baltimore, MD**
Pfeiffer, Eileen M. .... Albany, NY
Pfeiffer, Eugene L. .... Portland, OR
Pfeiffer, Fred N. .... San Antonio, TX
Pfeiffer, Frederick T. .... Orlando, FL
Pfeiffer, Fredrick S. .... **Greenville, SC**
Pfeiffer, G. Steven .... Tallahassee, FL
Pfeiffer and Gantt, PA .... **Anderson, SC**
Greenville, SC
Spartanburg, SC
Pfeiffer, Geoffrey E. .... Phoenix, AZ
Pfeiffer, George J. .... Sarasota, FL
Pfeiffer, George W. .... **Walnut Creek, CA**
Pfeiffer, Gordon W. .... Pasadena, CA
Pfeiffer, Guy D. .... **Cordele, GA**
Pfeiffer, Hudnall A. .... **Indianapolis, IN**
Pfeiffer, James J. .... Sylvania, OH
Pfeiffer, James L. .... **Phillipsburg, NJ**
Pfeiffer, James W. .... **Rolling Meadows, IL**
Pfeiffer, Jason W. .... **Kansas City, MO**
Pfeiffer, Jessica M. .... **Chicago, IL**
Pfeiffer, John G. .... Chicago, IL
Pfeiffer, John T., III .... Pottsville, PA
Pfeiffer, Jon A. .... **Santa Monica, CA**
Pfeiffer, Laura A. .... **Minneapolis, MN**
St. Paul, MN
Pfeiffer, Loc .... **Richmond, VA**
Pfeiffer, Marcia G. .... Jennings, LA
Pfeiffer, Margaret K. .... **Washington, DC**
Pfeiffer, Mark .... **Philadelphia, PA**
Pfeiffer, Mark D. .... **Columbia, MO**
Pfeiffer, Mark William .... **Indianapolis, IN**
Pfeiffer, Michael R. .... Escondido, CA
Pfeiffer, Neal P. .... Sacramento, CA
Pfeiffer, Paul N. .... Washington, DC
Pfeiffer & Pfeiffer, P.C. .... Buffalo, NY
Pfeiffer, Philip J. .... **San Antonio, TX**
Pfeiffer, Raymond M. .... Buffalo, NY
Pfeiffer, Richard C., Jr. .... Columbus, OH
Pfeiffer, Robert M. .... **Lexington, KY**
Pfeiffer, Ron E. .... Houston, TX
Pfeiffer, Ronald C. .... Findlay, OH
Pfeiffer, Rosemary Phipps Redwood City, CA
Pfeiffer, Sophia D. .... Brunswick, ME
Pfeiffer, Stan L. .... Houston, TX
Pfeiffer, Steven B. .... **Washington, DC**
Pfeiffer, Steven L. .... **Portland, OR**
Pfeiffer, Theresa L. .... Los Gatos, CA
Pfeiffer, W. Dean .... Department of the Navy, Office of the Judge Advocate General, GV
Pfeiffer, William E. .... **Omaha, NE**
Pfeiffer, William J. .... Aberdeen, SD
Pfeiffer, William M. .... Los Angeles, CA
Pfeiffer & Winegar, A Professional Corporation .... **Phillipsburg, NJ**
Pfeifle, Craig A. .... **Rapid City, SD**
Pfeifle, David A. .... **Sioux Falls, SD**
Pfeifle, Elmer L. .... Troy, MI
Pfeifle, Jane Wipf .... **Rapid City, SD**
Pfeifle, Thomas Nash .... Franklin, MA
Pfeil, C. Eric .... **Pittsburgh, PA**
Pfeil, Richard H. .... Fontana, WI
Pfeil, Todd M. .... Plain, WI
Pfeiler, Louis P. .... **Dubuque, IA**
Pfeiler, Thomas A. .... Chicago, IL
Pfeilsticker, Jack L. .... Newark, NJ
Pfeilsticker, Robert C., Jr. .... Philadelphia, PA
Pfendler, Christopher C. .... Canton, OH
Pfennig, Jon C., (P.C.) .... **Baytown, TX**
Pfennigs, Robert B. .... **Great Falls, MT**
Pfenning, Suzanne Sara .... Melville, NY
Pfenninger, Lisa M. .... Washington, DC
Pfenninger, P. Frederick .... Indianapolis, IN
Pferdehirt, Ronald H. .... Pittsburgh, PA
Pferdesteller, Vondy, Professional Corporation Denver, CO
Pfeuffer, David G. .... **New Braunfels, TX**
Pfeuffer, Richard H. .... Pittsburgh, PA
Pfeuffer, Robert T. .... **New Braunfels, TX**
Pfeuffer, William A. .... **Naples, FL**
Pfiester, R. Edward, Jr. .... Los Angeles, CA
Pfiester, R. Edward, Jr., A Law Corporation Los Angeles, CA
Pfiffner, Anthony L. .... Venice, FL
Pfiffner, Frank A. .... **Anchorage, AK**
Pfiffner, Hans P. .... Sterling Heights, MI
Pfiffner, Robert F. .... Chippewa Falls, WI
Pfingst, Joseph P. .... Mission Viejo, CA
Pfingstl, Stefanie .... Gastonia, NC
Pfirrman, Barbara W. .... **Boston, MA**
Pfirrman, Christina R. .... **Reno, NV**
Pfirrman, Christopher K. .... **Hartford, CT**
Pfirrman, Drew J. .... Boston, MA
Pfirrmann, Frederick A. .... Valley Forge, PA
Pfister, Alfred J. .... Tempe, AZ
Pfister, Betty D. .... Cincinnati, OH
Pfister, C. Michael, Jr. .... **Metairie, LA**
Pfister, Charles B. .... Bakersfield, CA
Pfister, Edward J. .... **Miami, FL**
Pfister, Elizabeth A. Westhampton Beach, NY
Pfister, Ellen L. .... Shepherd, MT
Pfister, Harold Francis .... **Chicago, IL**
Pfister, James W. .... Manitou Beach, MI
Pfister, Jeanne N. .... Powell, OH
Pfister, Jeffery M. .... **Tavares, FL**
Pfister, Jeffery M., P.A. .... **Tavares, FL**
Pfister, Karen D. .... Columbus, OH
Pfister, Kevin T. .... Midland, TX
Pfister, Lewis Mark, Jr. .... Vienna, VA
Pfister, Mark L. .... **Minneapolis, MN**
Pfister, Peter J. .... **San Francisco, CA**
Pfister, R. Jerome .... **Rockford, IL**
Pfister, Robert E. .... Lusk, WY
Pfister, Ronald P. .... Staten Island, NY
Pfister, Thomas L. .... **Los Angeles, CA**
Pfister, Timothy J. .... **Princeton, NJ**
Pfister, Todd B. .... **Tampa, FL**
Pfister, William R., Sr. .... Lawrenceburg, IN
Pfisterer, David L. .... Melville, NY
Pfitzinger, Brian A. .... Juneau, WI
Pfitzner, G. Richard .... Woodbridge, VA
Pfitzner, Morley, Brickley & Borsley Woodbridge, VA
Pfizenmayer, Francis J. .... Los Angeles, CA
Pfizenmayer, Frank J. .... Burbank, CA
Pfizenmayer, Rickard F. .... White Plains, NY
Pflaging, Lea Morgan .... Raleigh, NC
Pflanz, Fred C. .... **Spokane, WA**
Pflanz, Karl E. .... **New York, NY**
Pflaster, Herbert .... Roslyn, NY
Pflaster, James .... Los Angeles, CA
Pflaum, David J. .... **Nashville, TN**
Pflaum, Freda Wagner .... Sarasota, FL
Pflaum, Frederick S. .... Sarasota, FL
Pflaum, Jeffrey D. .... Minneapolis, MN
Pflaum, Keith J. .... **Birmingham, AL**
Pflaum, Michael L. .... **New York, NY**
Pflaum, Stephen R. .... **Minneapolis, MN**
Pflaum, Steven F. .... **Chicago, IL**
Pflaum, Thomas M. .... Micanopy, FL
Pflaumer, Harry .... Cambria, CA
Pflaumer, John S. .... Chicago, IL
Pflaumer, Katrina C. .... Seattle, WA
Pflederer, Gail .... **Danbury, CT**
Pflederer, Kent A. .... **Chicago, IL**
Pfleeger, Gary S. .... Carrollton, TX
Pfleegor, Clyde K. .... Miami, FL
Pfleger, Edmund P. .... **Tucson, AZ**
Pfleging, Daniel J. .... Noblesville, IN
Pflepsen, Keith A. .... Albany, GA
Pflepsen, Waldemar J., Jr.
Washington, DC
Pfluam, Jeffrey D. .... Minnetonka, MN
Pflueger, Kim C. .... **Seattle, WA**
Pflueger, Robert Hunter Altamonte Springs, FL
Pflueger, Robert R. .... Ortonville, MN
Pflug, Andrea J. .... **Los Angeles, CA**
Pflug, Christopher R. .... **Los Angeles, CA**
Pflug, John .... Westfield, NJ
Pflug, Mark D. .... **Charlotte, NC**
Pflug, Ronald M. .... Glen Rock, NJ
Morristown, NJ
Pflug, Victoria H. .... Venice, FL
Pflugarth, William J. .... Albuquerque, NM
Pfluger, George .... Huntington, NY
Pfluger, Walter W. .... San Angelo, TX
Pflugheber, Ellen Fern .... Watertown, NY
Pflughoeft, Pederson & Johnsrud Winona, MN
Pflughoeft, Wayne E. .... Winona, MN
Pflugner, J. Geoffrey .... **Sarasota, FL**
Pflum, Daniel L. .... Connersville, IN
Pflum, Joseph F. .... Cincinnati, OH
Pfohl, Edward J. .... Syracuse, NY
Pfohl, Mary Beth .... **Pittsburgh, PA**
Pfohl, Peter A. .... **Washington, DC**
Pfordte, Richard Securities and Exchange Commission, Division of Investment Management, GV
Pforr, Geoffrey H. .... **Mineola, NY**
New York, NY
Smithtown, NY
Pforzheimer, Margaret Y. .... Cambridge, MA
Pfotenhauer, Carolyn V. .... South Bend, IN
Pfotenhauer, Jay .... Walnut Creek, CA
Pfotenhauer, Jeanette .... Washington, DC
Pfotenhauer, Mark .... Incline Village, NV
Pfountz, Harold J. .... Denver, CO
Pfrang, Pamela .... Chicago, IL
Pfrommer, Fredk. G. .... San Mateo, CA
Pfrommer, Michael P. .... **Memphis, TN**
Pfuhler, Robert J. .... **Staten Island, NY**
Pfuhlmann, Gustav A. .... Bayside, NY
Pfullmann, Robert C., Jr. .... San Antonio, TX
Pfund, David T. .... **Hackensack, NJ**
Pfund, Peter H. .... Department of State, Office of the Legal Adviser, GV
Pfund, Peter J. .... Laguna Beach, CA
Pfund, William J. .... Richmond, VA
Pfunder, Curtis C. .... **Boston, MA**
Pfunder, Malcolm R. .... **Washington, DC**
Pfunder, Margaret S. General Services Administration, Board of Contract Appeals, GV
Pfundstein, Donald J. .... **Concord, NH**
Pfundstein, Joseph A. .... **Solon, OH**
Pfundstein, Michael A. .... Miami, FL
Phadden, Kathleen M. .... Highland Park, NJ
Phadke, Ajit Arun .... Lake Oswego, OR
Phagan, Jimmie R. .... **Dallas, TX**
Phair, George A. .... Houston, TX
Phair, Joseph B. .... Palo Alto, CA
Phair, Patricia A. .... Reno, NV
Phalan, Kenneth L. .... West Roxbury, MA
Phalan and Lowery, P.C. .... West Roxbury, MA
Phalen, David C. .... **Boston, MA**
Phalen, James R. .... House of Representatives, Committee Legal Personnel, GV
Phalen, James T. .... **Washington, DC**
Phalen, John M., Jr. .... Dallas, TX
Phalen, Karin S. .... **Sacramento, CA**
Phalen, Michael J. .... **Phoenix, AZ**
Phalen, Paul R. .... Torrington, CT
Phalen, Ralph .... **Independence, MO**
Phalen, Thomas F., Jr. .... Cincinnati, OH
Phalen, Thomas J. .... Phoenix, AZ
Phalen, Tonda Micshel Federal Election Commission, Office of the General Counsel, GV
Phaler, Karl J. .... San Diego, CA
Phalin, Lawrence J. .... **Orlando, FL**
Phalin, Michael K. .... Phoenix, AZ
Pham, Anh-Bang Bill .... **Los Angeles, CA**
Pham & Associates, P.C. .... Houston, TX
Pham, Brandon L. .... **Newport Beach, CA**
Pham, Chinh H. .... **Boston, MA**
Pham, Christine Thu .... **New York, NY**
Pham, Chuong H. .... **Baltimore, MD**
Pham, Curt H. .... Salem, OR
Pham, Dung Hong .... Santa Clara, CA
Pham, Hanh T. .... **San Francisco, CA**
Pham, Hanh T. .... **Jersey City, NJ**
Pham, Kay-Linh H. .... **Houston, TX**
Pham, Le-Huyen T. .... Boston, MA
Pham, Lu .... **Fort Worth, TX**
Pham, Mai-Lan .... **New York, NY**
Pham, Pho Van .... Westminster, CA
Pham, Phuong N. .... San Francisco, CA
Pham, Robert Bad .... Houston, TX
Pham, T. Christine .... Baltimore, MD
Pham, Teri T. .... **Beverly Hills, CA**
Pham, Thao Phuong .... McLean, VA
Pham, Tien D. .... Arlington, VA
Pham, Tracie M.T. .... **Los Angeles, CA**
Pham, Trang T. .... Houston, TX
Pham, Tu Minh .... **Chicago, IL**
Pham, Tuan A. .... **Los Angeles, CA**
Pham, William L. .... **New York, NY**
Pham, Yen T. .... Houston, TX
Phan, H. Le .... **St. Paul, MN**
Phan, Luan K. .... **Santa Monica, CA**
Phan, Nguyen D. .... Monterey Park, CA
Phan, Nhat D. .... **Alexandria, VA**
Phan, Peter G. .... **Los Angeles, CA**
Phan, Trong Tu .... Houston, TX
Phaneuf, Carrie Johnson .... **Dallas, TX**
Phaneuf, Chris H. .... Commerce Township, MI
Phaneuf, Frederic John .... Santa Cruz, CA
Phaneuf, Paula C. .... Ann Arbor, MI
Phansalkar, Kiran A. .... **Oklahoma City, OK**
Phansalkar, Mohan V. .... Los Angeles, CA
Phanumas, Joy .... **New York, NY**
Phares, Ana L. Ventura .... Santa Cruz, CA
Phares, Banker .... **Port Arthur, TX**
Phares & Chickris .... East Moline, IL
Phares, Gil K. .... Kerrville, TX
Phares, Gloria C. .... **New York, NY**
Phares, Mark .... **Missoula, MT**
Phares, Rhett B. .... **Houston, TX**
Phares, Robert M. .... Denver, CO
Phares, William T., (P.C.) .... East Moline, IL
Pharies, S. Andrew .... **San Diego, CA**
Pharis, Allison R. .... Sebastopol, CA
Pharis, Charlie C. .... Monticello, KY
Pharis, F. Jean .... Alexandria, LA
Pharis, Fred A. .... Alexandria, LA
Pharis, G. Michael .... **Baton Rouge, LA**
Pharis, James A., Jr. .... Alexandria, LA
Pharis Law Offices .... Alexandria, LA
Pharis, Stewart Shaw .... Cleveland, OH
Phariss, Mark A. .... San Antonio, TX
Pharo, James W. .... New York, NY
Pharo, Milam Randolph .... Denver, CO
Pharo, Sandra K. .... Sells, AZ
Pharo, William G. .... Denver, CO
Pharr, Ann L. .... **Newport News, VA**
Pharr, David K. .... **Jackson, MS**
Pharr, Douglas A. .... Ukiah, CA
Pharr, Henry N., II .... **Charlotte, NC**
Pharr, Henry N., III .... Charlotte, NC
Pharr, John C. .... Anchorage, AK
Pharr, John D. .... Memphis, TN
Pharr, Mark R., III .... **Houston, TX**
Pharr, Newton T. .... New Iberia, LA
Pharr, Samuel S. .... Austin, TX
Pharr, Steve M. .... **Winston-Salem, NC**
Pharris, Charles A. .... **Albuquerque, NM**
Pharris, Danial D. .... **Seattle, WA**
Pharris, James K. .... Olympia, WA
Pharris, John W. .... Fort Collins, CO
Phaup, F. Allen, II .... **Alexandria, VA**
Phaup, Lee Timmerman .... Middleburg, VA
Phay, Robert E. .... Chapel Hill, NC
Phay, Robert E., Jr. .... **New York, NY**
Phayer, Dennis J. .... **Metairie, LA**
Pheanis, Mark A. .... **Geneva, IL**
Phears, H. Wayne, (P.C.) .... **Norcross, GA**
Phears & Moldovan .... **Atlanta, GA**
Norcross, GA
Pheasant, Merle E., Jr. .... Sylvania, OH
Phebus, Annette Talley .... **Birmingham, AL**
Phebus, Darius E. .... **Urbana, IL**
Phebus, Earla J. .... Fresno, CA
Phebus, John .... Surprise, AZ
Phebus, Joseph W. .... **Urbana, IL**
Phebus, R. Michael .... **Cincinnati, OH**
Phebus & Winkelmann .... **Champaign, IL**
Urbana, IL
West Chester, PA
Pheffer, Jeffrey Ian .... Los Angeles, CA
Phegley, Luvern W. .... Hurst, TX
Pheil, David B. .... Long Beach, CA
Pheil & Kelepecz .... Long Beach, CA
Pheils, David R. .... Perrysburg, OH
Pheils, Jon D. .... **San Francisco, CA**
Phelan, A. Grant .... **King Of Prussia, PA**
Phelan, Albert F. .... Villanova, PA
Phelan, Andrew C. .... **Boston, MA**
Phelan, Bernard Q. .... Cheyenne, WY
Phelan, Brian P. .... **Washington, DC**
Phelan, Burke & Scolamiero, LLP
Albany, NY
Rensselaer, NY
Saratoga Springs, NY
Schenectady, NY
Phelan, Charles S. .... Millington, NJ
Phelan, Cori E. .... Brooksville, FL
Phelan, Daniel D. .... **Atlanta, GA**
Phelan, Daniel J. .... Philadelphia, PA
Phelan, David C. .... **Boston, MA**
Phelan, Denise Martino .... **Hartford, CT**
Phelan, Donald M. .... Bolingbrook, IL
Naperville, IL
Phelan, Edward J. .... Hobe Sound, FL
Phelan, Elizabeth Ann .... **Denver, CO**
Phelan, Francis J. .... Schaumburg, IL
Phelan, Gary E. .... **New Haven, CT**
Phelan, Harold Anthony .... Cleveland, OH
Phelan, J. Daniel .... **Denver, CO**
Phelan, James E. .... **Chicago, IL**
Phelan, James E. .... Kansas City, KS
Phelan, James J., Jr. .... Narberth, PA
Philadelphia, PA
Phelan, James L. .... Memphis, TN
Phelan, Jeanne M. .... **Baltimore, MD**
Phelan, Jeremiah L., Jr. .... St. Louis, MO
Phelan, Jerry J. .... Oakland, CA
Phelan, John C. .... **New York, NY**
Phelan, John E. .... **Miami, FL**
Phelan, John E., P.A. .... **Miami, FL**
Phelan, John F. .... Waterbury, CT
Phelan, John F. .... Newport, RI
Phelan, John J. .... Buffalo, NY
Phelan, John J. .... **White Plains, NY**
Phelan, John J., III .... **Albany, NY**
Phelan, John J., III .... **New York, NY**
Phelan, John J., III, P.C. .... **New York, NY**
Phelan, John M. .... **Chicago, IL**
Phelan, John M. .... **Detroit, MI**
Phelan, John M. .... **Philadelphia, PA**
Phelan, John T. .... Schenectady, NY
Phelan, John W. .... Collingswood, NJ
Philadelphia, PA
Phelan, Joseph Edward .... Quincy, MA
Phelan, Joseph F. .... Chicago, IL
Phelan, Kevin J. .... Fall River, MA
Phelan, Kimberly Ann .... Buffalo, NY

Phelan, Kim-Marie .... Revere, MA
Phelan, Laurie E. .... Detroit, MI
Phelan, Lawrence J. .... Grand Rapids, MI
Phelan, Lawrence T. .... Philadelphia, PA
Phelan, Lisa C. .... Los Angeles, CA
Phelan, Lisa Marie .... Department of Justice, Antitrust Division, GV
Phelan, M. Thomas .... Joliet, IL
Phelan, Margaret Madison .... Vancouver, WA
Phelan, Marie V. .... Hartford, CT
Phelan, Maureen .... Department of State, Foreign Service Officers (Overseas), GV
Phelan, Maurice E., (Ltd.) .... Oak Lawn, IL
Phelan and McDonald .... Memphis, TN
Phelan, Melinda R. .... Dallas, TX
Phelan, Michael G. .... Mount Pleasant, MI
Phelan, Michael G. .... Richmond, VA
Phelan, Michael J. .... Newhall, CA
Phelan, Michael J. .... San Francisco, CA
Phelan, Michael L., Jr. .... Springfield, MA
Phelan & Mitri .... Greenwich, CT
Norwalk, CT
Stamford, CT
White Plains, NY
Phelan, Mollie .... Dallas, TX
Phelan & Nolan .... Joliet, IL
Phelan, Pamela E. .... Concord, NH
Phelan, Patrick J., Jr. .... Tallahassee, FL
Phelan, Pettit & Biedrzycki
Collingswood, NJ
Philadelphia, PA
Phelan & Phelan .... Lynn, MA
Phelan, Richard J. .... Chicago, IL
Phelan, Richard W. .... San Luis Obispo, CA
Phelan, Robert E. .... San Francisco, CA
Phelan, Robert G. .... Lynn, MA
Phelan, Robin Bartlett .... Albany, NY
Phelan, Robin E. .... Dallas, TX
Phelan, Rod .... Dallas, TX
Phelan, Sarah .... Hawthorne, NY
Phelan, Sean M. .... Charlotte, NC
Phelan, Sean T. .... Georgetown, SC
Phelan, Shawn W. .... Dallas, TX
Phelan, Shirley A. .... Lynn, MA
Phelan, Tara L. .... Hackensack, NJ
Phelan, Thomas C. .... Westfield, NJ
Phelan, Thomas C. .... Vancouver, WA
Phelan, Thomas M. .... Cape May, NJ
Phelan, Thomas P. .... Mineola, NY
Phelan, Tucker, Mullen, Walker, Tucker & Gelman, L.L.P. .... Iowa City, IA
Phelan, Vincent R. .... Shelby, OH
Phelan — Watson Law Offices
Cheyenne, WY
Phelan, William G. .... Mosinee, WI
Phelan, William H., Jr. .... Ocala, FL
Phelan, William J. .... Stamford, CT
Phelan, William J. .... Joliet, IL
Phelan, William J. .... Quincy, MA
Phelan, William R., Jr. .... Baltimore, MD
Phelan, William V. .... Iowa City, IA
Pheley, James R. .... Eastpointe, MI
Phelon, FitzGerald & Wood, P.C.
Hartford, CT
Manchester, CT
Phelon, Herbert A., Jr. .... Manchester, CT
Phelon, Jeffrey V. .... West Hartford, CT
Phelosof, Benjamin .... Rochester, NY
Phelps, Alfred S. .... South Holland, IL
Phelps, Andrea, P.C. .... Chesapeake, VA
Phelps, Andrea W. .... Chesapeake, VA
Phelps & Andreatta, P.C. .... St. Louis, MO
Phelps, Arthur E., Jr. .... Cincinnati, OH
Phelps, Ashton, Jr. .... New Orleans, LA
Phelps, Beauford H. .... Los Angeles, CA
Phelps, Betty J. .... Topeka, KS
Phelps, Betty Lee .... Encinitas, CA
Phelps, Bob G. .... Manassas, VA
Phelps, Bob G., P.C. .... Manassas, VA
Phelps, C. Vincent, Jr. .... Brighton, CO
Phelps Campbell and Webb .... Elberton, GA
Phelps, Carl B. .... Glendale, CA
Phelps, Carol B. .... Marlborough, CT
Phelps, Charlie P. .... Richmond, VA
Phelps, Christian J. .... Spokane, WA
Phelps, David A. .... Perry, FL
Phelps, David S. .... Costa Mesa, CA
Phelps, Dee .... North Palm Beach, FL
Phelps, Dennis L. .... Wichita, KS
Phelps, Donald T. W. .... Baton Rouge, LA
Phelps, Douglas D. .... Spokane, WA
Phelps Dunbar, L.L.P. .... Baton Rouge, LA
New Orleans, LA
Jackson, MS
Tupelo, MS
Houston, TX
Phelps, E. Ray .... Roswell, NM
Phelps, Edward M. .... Pasadena, CA
Phelps, Edward W. .... Greensboro, NC
Phelps, Elizabeth M. .... Topeka, KS
Phelps, Eric W. .... Traverse City, MI
Phelps, Erik J. .... Madison, WI
Phelps, Esmond, II .... New Orleans, LA
Phelps, F. Jerry .... Dallas, TX
Phelps & Fara .... Indianapolis, IN
Phelps, Frank K. .... Oak Lawn, IL
Phelps, G. William .... Encinitas, CA
Phelps, Gail Bransford .... Harrisburg, PA
Phelps, Gale M. .... Indianapolis, IN
Phelps, George A. .... Department of Justice, Executive Office for Immigration Review, GV
Phelps, Gerald A. .... Quincy, MA
Phelps, Gray & Hewitt .... Niagara Falls, NY
Phelps, Harry B., Jr. .... Oakley, KS
Phelps, J. Andrew .... Hattiesburg, MS
Phelps, J. Barton .... Palo Alto, CA
Phelps, J. Mark .... Seminole, OK
Phelps, J. Michael .... San Francisco, CA
Phelps, James E. .... St. Louis, MO
Phelps, James R. .... Washington, DC
Phelps, James R. .... Sylvester, GA
Phelps, James T. .... San Antonio, TX
Phelps, James V. .... Pueblo, CO
Phelps, Jenkins, Gibson & Fowler, L.L.P.
Eutaw, AL
Tuscaloosa, AL
Phelps, John M., II .... Raleigh, NC
Phelps, John Michael .... Whitefish, MT
Phelps, John O. .... Carthage, MO
Phelps, John R. .... Niagara Falls, NY
Phelps, John V. .... Jonesboro, AR
Phelps, Jon H. .... Wenatchee, WA
Phelps, Jonathan B. .... Topeka, KS
Phelps, Joseph D. .... Montgomery, AL
Phelps, Joseph G. .... Chicago, IL
Phelps, Joseph P., Jr. .... Blue Bell, PA
Phelps, Judson H., Jr. .... San Antonio, TX
Phelps, Kasten, Ruyle, Burns, Carmody & Sims .... Carlinville, IL
Phelps, Kathleen M. .... Boston, MA
Phelps, Kathy Bazoian .... Los Angeles, CA
Phelps, Kelley Ray .... Marion, IL
Phelps & King .... Warren, OH
Phelps, Lauren M. .... Davenport, IA
Phelps Law Office .... Monticello, IA
Phelps, Lawrence W. .... Scottsdale, AZ
Phelps, Lisa E. .... Houston, TX
Phelps, Lisa M. .... Santa Barbara, CA
Phelps, Lou Ann .... Durham, NC
Phelps, Margaret A. .... Irvine, CA
Phelps, Mark .... Houston, TX
Phelps, Mark E. .... Chicago, IL
Phelps, Mark J. .... Seattle, WA
Phelps, Mark M. .... Eugene, OR
Phelps, Martha F. .... Boston, MA
Phelps, Mary Jane Wilhoit .... Versailles, KY
Phelps, Melinda M. .... Springfield, MA
Phelps, Michael R. .... Minneapolis, MN
Phelps, Michael W. .... Bloomington, IN
Phelps, Michele J. .... Simsbury, CT
Phelps, N. Nelson .... Washington, DC
Phelps, Nancy .... Milwaukee, WI
Phelps, Nancy, Attorney at Law, S.C.
Milwaukee, WI
Phelps, P.L. Pat, P.C. .... Durant, OK
Phelps, P. Michael .... Chicago, IL
Phelps, Paul J. .... Woodbury, MN
Phelps & Phelps .... Davenport, IA
Phelps, P.L. Pat .... Durant, OK
Phelps, R. Chris .... Elberton, GA
Phelps, Richard E. H., II .... Monticello, IA
Phelps, Richard W. .... Prince Frederick, MD
Phelps, Robert C. .... San Francisco, CA
Phelps, Robert F. .... Larchmont, NY
Phelps, Robert F., Jr. .... New York, NY
Phelps, Robert J. .... Davenport, IA
Phelps, Robert L., II .... Topeka, KS
Phelps, Rodney M. .... Durant, OK
Phelps, Ronald C. .... Austin, TX
Phelps, Ronald W., Law Office of
Kingfisher, OK
Phelps, Ross A. .... La Crescent, MN
Phelps, R. S. .... Laredo, TX
Phelps, Ruth A. .... Pasadena, CA
Phelps, S. Don .... Olympia, WA
Phelps, S. Don, P.S. .... Olympia, WA
Phelps, Sam M. .... Tuscaloosa, AL
Phelps, Sarah Catherine .... Atlanta, GA
Phelps, Schwarz & Phelps, A Professional Law Corporation .... Pasadena, CA
Phelps, Scott M. .... Birmingham, AL
Phelps, Seth M. .... Durham, NC
Phelps, Singer & Dunn, LLC .... Denver, CO
Phelps, Stephany .... Boston, MA
Phelps, Stephen E. .... Gilbert, AZ
Phelps, Terri Elms .... Louisville, KY
Phelps, Thomas A. .... Grand Rapids, MI
Phelps, Thomas D., (P.C.)
Los Angeles, CA
Phelps, Timothy Bryan .... Topeka, KS
Phelps, W. Robert, Jr. .... Newport News, VA
Phelps, William C. .... Houston, TX
Phelps, William G. .... Encinitas, CA
Phelps, William H. .... Los Angeles, CA
Phelps, William H. .... Redding, CA
Phelps, William R., Jr. .... Costa Mesa, CA
Phelps, William Sabin .... San Francisco, CA
Phelps, Winthrop H. .... Buffalo, NY
Phemister, Bonnie B. .... Skokie, IL
Phemister, James M. .... Lexington, VA
Phemister, Thomas A.
Department of Transportation, Federal Railroad Administration, GV
Pheney, Dennis J. .... Farmington Hills, MI
Phenicie, Kelly Brown, Ms. .... Harrisburg, PA
Phenicie, Mark E. .... Harrisburg, PA
Phenicie, R. William .... Burlington, WI
Salem, WI
Phenix, Dudley R. .... San Francisco, CA
Phenix, Jas. N., Sr. .... Henderson, TX
Phenix, Lisa M. .... Sacramento, CA
Phenner, Michael E., (P.C.) .... Chicago, IL
Pherson, Bruce E., Jr. .... Woodland Hills, CA
Pherson, Sheryl M. .... Monticello, IN
Pherson, Steven P. .... Chicago, IL
Pheterson, I. Jeffrey .... Boca Raton, FL
Pheterson, Irving .... Rochester, NY
Pheterson & Pheterson .... Rochester, NY
Pheterson, Steven J. .... Rochester, NY
Phethean, Carol .... New York, NY
Phetteplace, Katrina L.
San Francisco, CA
Phi, Tram Thi .... Palo Alto, CA
Phiambolis, Margaret S. .... Spring House, PA
Phibbs, Henry C., II .... Jackson, WY
Phibbs & Resor, P.C. .... Jackson, WY
Phifer, Dennis B. .... Newark, DE
Phifer, Dwight L. .... Jacksonville, TX
Phifer, Elizabeth L. .... Dallas, TX
Phifer, Forrest K. .... Rusk, TX
Phifer, Franklin C. .... Toms River, NJ
Phifer, George H. .... Washington, DC
Phifer, Gregory L. .... Amarillo, TX
Phifer, H. Craig, III .... Pinehurst, NC
Phifer, Howard Middleton, Jr.
Department of Defense, Defense Legal Services Agency, GV
Phifer, Kimberly Ann Davis
Ocean Springs, MS
Phifer, Michael L. .... Austin, TX
Houston, TX
Phifer, Noel L. .... New Ulm, MN
Phifer, Randolph D. .... Detroit, MI
Phifer, Rebecca R. .... Morganton, NC
Phifer & Richards .... Jacksonville, TX
Phifer, Robert S. .... Charlotte, NC
Phifer, Scott C. .... Irvine, CA
Phifer, Sky D .... Lander, WY
Phifer, Valerie Hafner .... Lander, WY
Phiffer, Misty Borland .... Midland, TX
Philabaum, Laura Blanchard .... Coshocton, OH
Philabaun, Michael A. .... Columbus, OH
Philadelphia, Michael A. .... Reston, VA
Philbeck, J. Heydt .... Raleigh, NC
Philbeck, John H. .... Raleigh, NC
Philbin, David A. .... Clinton, MA
Philbin, Dax W. .... Houston, TX
Philbin, Donald R. .... Oklahoma City, OK
Philbin, Donald R., A Professional Corporation
Oklahoma City, OK
Philbin, Donald R., Jr. .... San Antonio, TX
Philbin, James P., III .... New York, NY
Philbin, John A. .... Oklahoma City, OK
Philbin, John J. .... New York, NY
Philbin, Joseph M. .... Evergreen Park, IL
Philbin, Kenneth A. .... New York, NY
Philbin, Kevin J. .... New York, NY
Philbin, Kimberley Ann .... North Andover, MA
Philbin, Margaret M. .... Falls Church, VA
Philbin, Michael J. .... Nashville, TN
Philbin, Michael J., P.C. .... Nashville, TN
Philbin, Neil P. .... Peace Dale, RI
Philbin, Patrick F. .... Washington, DC
Philbin, Paul A. .... Houston, TX
Philbin, Paul A. & Assoc., P.C.
Houston, TX
Philbin, Peter S. .... Vienna, VA
Philbin, Phillip B. .... Dallas, TX
Philbin, Scott M. .... Hamburg, NY
Philbin, Stephanie .... Washington, DC
Philbin, Stephen J. .... Clinton, MA
Philbin, Vivian A. .... Lakewood, CO
Philbrick, Allen J. .... Ann Arbor, MI
Philbrick, Charles L. .... Chicago, IL
Philbrick, Donald L. .... Portland, ME
Philbrick, Jon R. .... Columbus, OH
Philbrick, Melissa D. .... Nantucket, MA
Philbrick, Melissa D., P.C.
Nantucket, MA
Philbrick, Michael J. .... Muskegon, MI
Philbrick, Suzanne N. .... Chesterton, IN
Philbrick, Tammie J. .... St. Louis, MO
Philbrick, William L. .... Eugene, OR
Philbrook, Burnham J. .... St. Paul, MN
Philbrook, Julia A. .... Portland, OR
Philbrook, Malcolm W., Jr. .... Auburn, ME
Philbrook, Paula L. .... Brookline, NH
Philhours, Randy F. .... Paragould, AR
Philibin, Gary J. .... Youngstown, OH
Philibosian, Alan G. .... Englewood, NJ
Philibosian, Emil H.
North Brunswick, NJ
Philibosian, J. Timothy .... Denver, CO
Philibosian, Robert H. .... Los Angeles, CA
Philion, Norman J., III .... Washington, DC
Philip, Carrington F. .... Atlanta, GA
Philip, Elizabeth J. .... Charleston, SC
Philip, George M. .... Albany, NY
Philip, John B. .... Memphis, TN
Philip, John Van Ness, III .... New York, NY
Philip, Karen M. .... Los Angeles, CA
Philip, Michael, Jr. .... Albany, NY
Philip, Sherly A. .... Houston, TX
Philip & Wimmer .... Palmerton, PA
Philipchuck, John F. .... Aurora, IL
Naperville, IL
Philiph, Douglas P. .... Des Moines, IA
Philiph, E. H. .... Sibley, IA
Philipp, Adam L.K. .... San Diego, CA
Philipp, Albert E., Jr. .... Ridgewood, NJ
Philipp, Brian C. .... Towson, MD
Philipp, Christopher R. .... Lafayette, LA
Philipp, Douglas H. .... Oldsmar, FL
Philipp, Elizabeth R. .... New York, NY
Charlotte, NC
Philipp, Guenther M., (P.C.) .... Chicago, IL
Philipp, Joel G. .... Sacramento, CA
Philipp, Jonathan W. .... Woodbridge, NJ
Philipp, Michael G. .... Naperville, IL
Philipp, Michael M. .... Chicago, IL
Philipp, Norine M. .... Cambridge, MA
Philipp, Robert D.
Department Of Veterans Affairs, Board of Veterans Appeals, GV
Philipp, Shirin .... Boston, MA
Philipp, Timothy P. .... St. Louis, MO
Philippakis, Katherine .... Phoenix, AZ
Philippart, Howard L., Jr. .... Redford, MI
Philippe, Marcel J. .... New York, NY
Philippi, Michael J. .... Chicago, IL
Philippi, Michael R. .... Walnut Creek, CA
Philippi, Reed S. .... Troy, NY
Philippides, Christopher .... Sacramento, CA
Philippone, Alex F. .... Rochester, NY
Philippone, David J. .... Syracuse, NY
Philippone, James V. .... Rochester, NY
Philippone, John E. .... Rochester, NY
Philippone Law Offices .... Rochester, NY
Philippone, Martin A. .... Rochester, NY
Philipps, Charles J. .... Corte Madera, CA
Philipps, David J. .... Chicago, IL
Philipps, David S. .... Toledo, OH
Philipps, John N., Jr. .... Buffalo, NY
Philipps, Kurt A. .... Covington, KY
Philipps, Laura M. .... Burlington, VT
Philipps, Linda J. .... Corte Madera, CA
Philipps, Lyn K. .... Calabasas, CA
Philipps, Mary E. .... Chicago, IL
Philipps, Randall J. .... Menominee, MI
Philipps, Randall J., P.C. .... Menominee, MI
Philips, A. Lewis, III .... Mobile, AL
Philips, A. Merrill .... Washington, DC
Philips, Abe L., Jr. .... Mobile, AL
Philips, Ann Patricia-Woodrick
Traverse City, MI
Philips, Ben B. .... Columbus, GA
Philips, Ben B., P.C. .... Columbus, GA
Philips, Brian P. .... Brevard, NC
Philips, Bruce G. .... Cherry Tree, PA
Philips, Charles C. .... McKinney, TX
Philips, Charles, P.C. .... McKinney, TX
Philips, Charles S. .... New Port Richey, FL
Philips, Claudia Lee .... New York, NY
Philips, Curtin & Di Giacomo
Cherry Hill, NJ
Philadelphia, PA
Philips, David M. .... Riverside, CA
Philips, David P. .... Dallas, TX
Philips, Eva C. .... New York, NY
Philips, George O. .... Philadelphia, PA
Philips, Grace .... Santa Fe, NM
Philips, H. Shelton .... St. Petersburg, FL
Philips, Harry J. ("Skip"), Jr.
Baton Rouge, LA
Philips, H. H., Jr. .... Tarboro, NC
Philips, Hopkins, Eames & Cobb, P.C.
Denton, TX
Philips, Howard R. .... Fairfax, VA
Philips, J. Michael .... Seattle, WA
Philips, James A. .... Mobile, AL
Philips, Janet M. .... Huntington, NY
Philips, J.J. .... Houston, TX
Philips, John E. .... San Diego, CA
Philips, Jonathan .... New York, NY
Philips, Kathleen G. .... San Francisco, CA
Philips, Louis C. .... New Orleans, LA
Philips, Malcolm H., Jr. .... Washington, DC
Philips, Margaret A. .... Jacksonville, FL
Tampa, FL
Philips, Marian B. .... New York, NY
Philips, Mary Anne .... Fort Lauderdale, FL
Philips, Mary Anne, P.A.
Fort Lauderdale, FL
Philips, Merrill .... Washington, DC
Philips, Michael R. .... Durham, NC
Philips, Paul N. .... Los Angeles, CA
Philips, Rebecca .... Houston, TX
Philips, Richard T. .... East Hanover, NJ
Philips, Robert M. .... Los Angeles, CA
Philips, Ruth B. .... New York, NY
Philips, Sidney T. .... Birmingham, AL
Philips, Susan Scarle .... Berkeley, CA
Philips & Vesy .... New Orleans, LA
Philips, William P., Jr. .... Denton, TX
Philipsborn, John T. .... San Francisco, CA
Philipse, Patti J. .... Fairfax, VA
Philipson, Alice .... Berkeley, CA
Philipson, Bruce G. .... Silver Spring, MD
Philipson, David J. .... Big Bear Lake, CA
Philipson, Lisa Gayle .... New York, NY
Philipson, Lori .... New York, NY
Philipson, Robert A. .... Santa Monica, CA
Philipson, Stephen L. .... Anaheim, CA
Philis, Duane G. .... Neenah, WI
Philis, Elaine C. .... New York, NY
Philla, Dustin D. .... Miami, FL
Phillabaum, Ledlin, Matthews & Gaffney-Brown .... Spokane, WA
Phillabaum, Sheryl S. .... Spokane, WA
Phillabaum, Stephen D. .... Spokane, WA
Philleo, Jessica .... Appleton, WI
Philley, Steven M. .... Houston, TX
Phillion, D. William .... Richardson, TX
Philliou, Peter J. .... Winchester, MA
Phillip, Francis .... New York, NY
Phillip, Harvey G. .... Cincinnati, OH
Phillip, Kelli Station .... New York, NY
Phillipe, Frank V. .... Taunton, MA
Phillipes, Peter M. .... Quincy, MA
Phillipi, P. Bane .... Austin, TX
Phillipi, Steven V. .... Pasadena, CA
Phillipoff, Mark J. .... South Bend, IN
Phillipp, James G. .... Los Angeles, CA
Phillippay, Wendy J. .... Sonoma, CA
Phillippe, Belton, Sullivan & Cabler
Brownsville, TX
McAllen, TX
Phillippe, Christopher Lee
Brownsville, TX
Phillippe, Donald R. .... Anderson, IN
Phillippi, James M. .... Glendale, CA
Phillippi, Kenneth Troy .... Oakland, CA
Phillippi, Polly N. .... Chicago, IL
Phillippi, William C., (P.A.)
Fort Lauderdale, FL
Phillippo, Matthew K. .... Providence, RI
Phillipps & Carson .... Cincinnati, OH
Phillipps, James E. .... Cincinnati, OH
Phillipps, Kenneth E. .... Everett, WA
Phillipps, Stephanie M. .... Washington, DC
Phillips, Adam D. .... Fort Lauderdale, FL

Phillips, Adrian B. ....San Francisco, CA
Phillips & Akers, A Professional Corporation
Austin, TX
Houston, TX
Phillips, Alan M. ....Half Moon Bay, CA
Phillips, Alan S. ....Monsey, NY
Phillips, Alane A. ....Birmingham, AL
Phillips, Albert E. ....Atlanta, GA
Phillips, Alberta M. ....Ogden, UT
Phillips, Alexander D. ....Palo Alto, CA
Phillips, Alfred C. ....Lexington, MA
Phillips, Alice M. ....New York, NY
Phillips, Alma F. ....Oakland, CA
Phillips, Althea M., (Ms) ....Utica, NY
Phillips, Amy K. ....Washington, DC
Phillips, Amy L. ....Cleveland, OH
Phillips, Andrea L. ....Chicago, IL
Phillips, Andrea L. ....Nashville, TN
Phillips, Andrew J. ....Virginia, MN
Phillips, Andrew J. ....Oshkosh, WI
Phillips, Angela Marie ....Frederick, MD
Phillips & Angley, P.C. ....Boston, MA
Phillips, Ann E. ....Watertown, NY
Phillips, Ann Holsonback ....Asheville, NC
Phillips, Ann K. ....Minneapolis, MN
Phillips, Ann M. ....Daytona Beach, FL
Phillips, Anna R. ....Worcester, MA
Phillips, Anne Haase ....Scottsdale, AZ
Phillips, Anthony F. ....New York, NY
Phillips, Anthony L. ....Muncie, IN
Phillips, Arden T. ....Washington, DC
Phillips, Arnold F. ....McHenry, MD
Phillips, Arsine B. ....Los Angeles, CA
Phillips, Arthur A., (Ltd.) ....Chicago, IL
Phillips, Arthur L. ....Macon, GA
Phillips, Arthur L. ....Jamesburg, NJ
Phillips, Asa E., III ....Wellesley, MA
Phillips, Asa E., Jr. ....Washington, DC
Ogunquit, ME
Seal Harbor, ME
Boston, MA
Phillips, Ashley D. ....Atlanta, GA
Phillips & Associates
San Luis Obispo, CA
Phillips, B. Wayne ....Marietta, GA
Phillips, B. Wayne, P.C. ....Marietta, GA
Phillips, Barbara J. ....Andover, MA
Phillips, Barbara W. ....Evanston, IL
Phillips, Barbara Y. ....University, MS
Phillips, Barnet, IV ....New York, NY
Phillips, Barry ....Atlanta, GA
Phillips & Bartlett, P.C.
Williamsburg, VA
Phillips, Beckwith & Hall ....Fairfax, VA
Phillips, Benjamin J. ....Santa Fe, NM
Phillips, Bernard ....New York, NY
Phillips, Bernard R., III ....Herndon, VA
Phillips, Betsy ....Mays Landing, NJ
Phillips, Betsy H. ....Rustburg, VA
Phillips, Blaine T. ....Wilmington, DE
Phillips, Blaine T. ....Charlottesville, VA
Phillips, Bobby J. ....Carthage, TX
Phillips, Bohn E. ....Houston, TX
Phillips & Bohyer, P.C. ....Missoula, MT
Phillips & Bordallo, P.C. ....Hagåtña, GU
Phillips, Brad A. ....South Hamilton, MA
Phillips, Bradley S. ....Los Angeles, CA
Phillips, Brian ....Everett, WA
Phillips, Brian Lee ....Lubbock, TX
Phillips, Brian W. ....Piqua, OH
Phillips, Brinel Joy ....Lauderdale Lakes, FL
Phillips, Brock D. ....San Francisco, CA
Phillips, Bruce H. ....Monticello, KY
Phillips, Bruce H. ....Nashville, TN
Phillips, Bruce J. ....Pittsburgh, PA
Phillips, Bruce J. ....Wilkes-Barre, PA
Phillips, Bruce L. ....Philadelphia, PA
Phillips, Bruce M. ....Phoenix, AZ
Phillips, Bruce W. ....Palo Alto, CA
Phillips, Bryan R. ....Washington, DC
Phillips, C. Allen ....Jackson, MS
Phillips, C. Alton ....Jackson, MS
Phillips, C. Deborah ....Fitchburg, MA
Phillips, C. Gorham ....New York, NY
Phillips, C. Gregory ....Salem, VA
Phillips, C. William ....New York, NY
Phillips, Cameron ....Coeur d'Alene, ID
Phillips, Camille S. ....Austin, TX
Phillips & Caputo ....Chattanooga, TN
Phillips, Carol A. ....Stockton, MO
Phillips, Carol W. ....Belmont, MA
Phillips, Carol-Lisa ....Fort Lauderdale, FL
Phillips, Carolyn D. ....Martinez, CA
Phillips, Carolyn Del ....Fresno, CA
Phillips, Carolyn Nivia Bell ....Placerville, CA
Phillips, Carolyn P. ....Hillsville, VA
Phillips, Carter G. ....Washington, DC
Phillips, Catherine L. ....Tacoma, WA
Phillips, Catherine R. ....St. Louis, MO
Phillips, Celeste ....Washington, DC
Phillips, Charles A. ....Huntsville, AL
Phillips, Charles A. ....San Diego, CA
Phillips, Charles B. ....Salem, VA
Phillips, Charles B. ....Walla Walla, WA
Phillips, Charles D. ....Evanston, WY
Phillips, Charles E. ....College Park, GA
Phillips, Charles I. ....Waukesha, WI
Phillips, Charles J. ....Wyomissing, PA
Phillips, Charles K. ....Des Moines, IA
Phillips, Charles M. ....Tarpon Springs, FL
Phillips, Charles M., Jr. ....Dunedin, FL
Phillips, Charles R. ....New York, NY
Phillips, Charles R. ....Houston, TX
Phillips, Cheryl S. ....Houston, TX
Phillips, Chester J., Jr. ....Salinas, CA
Phillips, Christine M. ....Denver, CO
Phillips, Christopher D. ....Omaha, NE
Phillips, Christopher Weis ....Savannah, GA
Phillips, Christy L. ....Birmingham, AL
Phillips, Clarence E. "Bud" ....Castlewood, VA
Phillips, Clarence W. ....Shelbyville, TN
Phillips, Claude C., III ....Humble, TX
Phillips, Claudia London ....Los Angeles, CA
Phillips, Clay H. ....Chicago, IL
Phillips, Clifford J. ....Los Angeles, CA
Phillips, Clifford L. ....Warren, OH
Phillips, Clinton E. ....Houston, TX
Phillips & Cohen ....San Diego, CA
San Francisco, CA
Washington, DC
Phillips, Connie Sullivan
Campbellsville, KY
Phillips, Constance Baker
Indianapolis, IN
Phillips, Cook & Lowe, L.L.P. ....Atlanta, GA
Phillips, Cornelius W., III ....Springfield, MA
Phillips, Craig W. ....Phoenix, AZ
Phillips, Curt ....Atlanta, GA
Phillips, Cynthia A. ....Sand Springs, OK
Phillips, Cynthia L. ....Cleveland, OH
Phillips, Cyrus E., IV ....Washington, DC
Phillips, D. Andrew ....Oxford, MS
Phillips, D. Gene ....Pasadena, CA
Phillips, Dale ....Paintsville, KY
Phillips, Dalton F.
Department Of Health And Human Services, GV
Phillips, Dan C. ....Sacramento, CA
Phillips, Dana ....Fort Lauderdale, FL
Phillips, Dana W. ....Sacramento, CA
Phillips, Daniel E. ....Novato, CA
Phillips, Daniel E. ....Fargo, ND
Phillips, Daniel H. ....Wichita, KS
Phillips, Daniel M. ....Ann Arbor, MI
Phillips, Daniel P. ....Washington, DC
Phillips, Darlene Fischer, (P.C.)
Los Angeles, CA
Phillips, Darrin M. ....Naples, FL
Phillips, Darrin M., P.A. ....Naples, FL
Phillips, Darryl M. ....New Orleans, LA
Phillips, David ....Atlanta, GA
Phillips, David A. ....Gastonia, NC
Phillips, David B. ....West Hempstead, NY
Phillips, David C. ....San Francisco, CA
Phillips, David C., III ....Tulsa, OK
Phillips, David Earl ....Nashville, TN
Phillips, David J. ....Kansas City, KS
Phillips, David J. ....Eugene, OR
Phillips, David K. ....Wichita Falls, TX
Phillips, David L. ....West Des Moines, IA
Phillips, David L. ....Las Vegas, NV
Phillips, David L. ....Austin, TX
Phillips, David L. ....Houston, TX
Phillips, David L. ....Houston, TX
Phillips, David M. ....Pasadena, CA
Phillips, David M. ....Chillicothe, OH
Phillips, David O. ....Alexandria, VA
Phillips, David P. ....Denver, CO
Phillips, David P. ....Chattanooga, TN
Phillips, David Peter ....Lauderdale Lakes, FL
Phillips, David R. ....Merrillville, IN
Phillips, David S. ....Manchester, NH
Phillips, David T. ....Kenansville, NC
Phillips, David W. ....Newark, NJ
Phillips, David W. ....Sand Springs, OK
Phillips, David W. ....Vienna, VA
Phillips, David W., III ....Marysville, OH
Phillips, Dawn G. ....Norfolk, VA
Phillips, Dawn L. ....Ann Arbor, MI
Phillips, Dawn M. ....Chicago, IL
Phillips, D.C., & Associates, P.C. ....Tulsa, OK
Phillips, Dean E. ....Portland, CT
Phillips, Dean K. ....Jupiter, FL
Phillips, Dean M. ....Portland, OR
Phillips, Dean R. ....Philadelphia, PA
Phillips, Deborah A. ....McLean, VA
Phillips, Deborah A. L. ......Fort Lauderdale, FL
Phillips, Deborah J. ....Seattle, WA
Phillips, Deborah L. ....San Ramon, CA
Phillips, Deborah M. ....Hood River, OR
Phillips, Dee Anne ....Birmingham, AL
Phillips, Delbert R. ....Springville, UT
Phillips, Denise V. ....Kansas City, MO
Phillips, Dennis J. ....Glens Falls, NY
Phillips, Dennis L. ....Department of Justice, Civil Division, GV
Phillips, Diane ....New York, NY
Phillips, Diane E. ....Encino, CA
Phillips, Dianne R. ....Boston, MA
Phillips, Don ....Corsicana, TX
Phillips, Donald D. ....Colby, KS
Phillips, Donald D. ....Smithville, NJ
Phillips, Donald L. ....Pittsburgh, PA
Phillips, Donald M. ....Lanett, AL
Phillips, Donald T. ....Smyrna, GA
Phillips, Donald T. ....Garden City, NY
Phillips, Donohue & Cymerman, S.C.
Milwaukee, WI
Phillips, Dorothy A. ....Brooklyn, NY
Phillips, Dorothy K. ....Cherry Hill, NJ
Philadelphia, PA
Wynnewood, PA
Phillips, Douglas C. ....Los Angeles, CA
Phillips, Douglas E. ....Washington, DC
Phillips, Douglas L. ....Sioux City, IA
Phillips, Douglas L. ....Bellevue, WA
Phillips, Douglas R. ....Denver, CO
Phillips, Douglas R., P.C. ....Denver, CO
Phillips, Douglas S. ....Dulles, VA
Phillips, Douglas S., (P.C.)
Rancho Mirage, CA
Phillips, Douglas W. ....Boston, MA
Phillips, Drew C. ....New York, NY
Phillips, Duane T. ....Pleasantville, NJ
Phillips, Dudley C. ....New Canaan, CT
Phillips, Dwight W. ....Detroit, MI
Phillips, E. Louise R. ....Washington, DC
Phillips, E. Lynn ....Philippi, WV
Phillips, E. Stuart ....Austin, TX
Phillips, Earl Ernest ....New York, NY
Phillips, Earl W., Jr. ....Hartford, CT
Phillips, Edmund J., Jr. ....Newton, MS
Phillips, Edmund P., Jr. ....San Antonio, TX
Phillips, Edward B. ....Knoxville, TN
Phillips, Edward G. ....Knoxville, TN
Phillips, Edward H. ....Chicago, IL
Phillips, Edward J. ....New York, NY
Phillips, Edward P. ....Boca Raton, FL
Phillips, Edward P. ....Coral Springs, FL
Phillips, Edward R. ....Lindenhurst, NY
Phillips, Eisinger, Koss, Rothstein & Rosenfeldt, P.A. ....Hollywood, FL
Phillips, Elizabeth A. ....Anchorage, AK
Phillips, Elizabeth A ....Kansas City, MO
Phillips, Elizabeth Barnes ....Houston, TX
Phillips, Elizabeth Shoman ....Lexington, KY
Phillips, Elizabeth T. ....Pittsburgh, PA
Phillips, Elizabeth Vaughn ....Houston, TX
Phillips, Ellen D. ....New Smyrna Beach, FL
Phillips, Elliot ....Mineola, NY
Phillips, Elvin W. ....Sarasota, FL
Phillips, Elwood ....Orlando, FL
Phillips, Eric ....Washington, DC
Phillips, Eric ....Chicago, IL
Phillips, Eric J. ....Oakland, CA
Phillips, Eric J. ....Doylestown, PA
Phillips & Erlewine LLP
San Francisco, CA
Phillips, Ernest A. ....Lansing, MI
Phillips, Erwin D. ....Sand Springs, OK
Phillips, Ettinger & Prikryl, L.L.P.
Austin, TX
Phillips, Eugene H. ....Winston-Salem, NC
Phillips & Ezell ....Phenix City, AL
Phillips, F. Peter ....New York, NY
Phillips & Faldowski, P.C.
Washington, PA
Phillips Farrell ....Baiting Hollow, NY
New York, NY
Riverhead, NY
Phillips, Felix M. ....Minneapolis, MN
Phillips, Felix P. ....Houston, TX
Phillips, Florence J. ....Arvada, CO
Phillips, Floyd M. ....Grants Pass, OR
Phillips, Frances E. ....Dallas, TX
Phillips, Francine H. ....Martinsburg, WV
Phillips, Frank J. ....Stony Point, NY
Phillips, Frank Smithson, Jr. ....Easton, MD
Phillips, Frank W. ....Marion, OH
Phillips, Frederick C. ....San Diego, CA
Phillips, Frederick S. ....Washington, DC
Phillips, G. Kent ....Robinson, IL
Phillips, G. Mark ....Charleston, SC
Phillips, G. William ....Niles, IL
Phillips, Gail V. ....Sherman Oaks, CA
Phillips and Galanter, Professional Corporation
Pittsburgh, PA
Phillips & Gale, P.A. ....Fort Pierce, FL
Phillips, Gardill, Kaiser & Altmeyer
Wheeling, WV
Phillips, Garrison L. ....Chicago, IL
Phillips, Gary A. ....Decatur, AL
Phillips, Gary A. ....Hackensack, NJ
Phillips, Gary D. ....Louisville, KY
Phillips, Gary L. ....Washington, DC
Phillips, Gary R. ....Phoenix, AZ
Phillips, Gary R. ....Los Angeles, CA
Phillips, Gary R. ....Honolulu, HI
Phillips, Gary S. ....Beverly Hills, CA
Phillips, Gary S. ....Hollywood, FL
Phillips, Gavin L. ....Rochester, NY
Phillips & Gemignani ....Waukesha, WI
Phillips, Gene M., (Ltd.) ....Highland Park, IL
Phillips, George A. ....New York, NY
Phillips, George B. ....Lansing, MI
Phillips, George E. ....Carmichael, CA
Phillips, George F. ....Winston-Salem, NC
Phillips, George L. ....United States Senate, Senatorial Assistants, GV
Phillips, George P. ....Broken Arrow, OK
Phillips, George R. ....Los Angeles, CA
Phillips, George R. ....Bay City, MI
Phillips, George R., Jr. ....Los Angeles, CA
Phillips, George W. ....Tampa, FL
Phillips, George W. ....Chicago, IL
Phillips, George W., P.A. ....Tampa, FL
Phillips, Gerald A. ....Reno, NV
Phillips, Gerald A., A Prof. Corp., Law Offices of ....Reno, NV
Phillips, Gerald F. ....Los Angeles, CA
Phillips, Gerald J. ....Newport Beach, CA
Phillips, Gerstein, Holber & Channen
Haverhill, MA
Exeter, NH
Phillips, Gladys ....Aberdeen, WA
Phillips, Glenn D. ....Kilgore, TX
Phillips, Glenn M. ....Lynden, WA
Phillips, Glenn S. ....Tyler, TX
Phillips, Goldman & Spence, P.A.
Wilmington, DE
Phillips, Gordon G., Jr. ....Irvine, CA
Phillips, Gordon G., Jr., Inc., Law Office of
Irvine, CA
Phillips, Graham A., Jr. ....Wallace, NC
Phillips, Greenberg, Strain & Hauser
San Francisco, CA
Phillips, Greer L. ....New York, NY
Phillips, Gregory D. ....Los Angeles, CA
Phillips, Gregory D. ....Salt Lake City, UT
Phillips, Gregory G. ....Ventura, CA
Phillips, Gregory James ....Washington, DC
Phillips, Gregory L. ....Boston, MA
Phillips, Gregory L. ....Houston, TX
Phillips, Gregory R. ....Austin, TX
Phillips, Gregory T. ....Rochester, NY
Phillips, Grisham A. ....Benton, AR
Phillips & Hale ....Rogersville, TN
Phillips, Hans J. ....Baltimore, MD
Phillips, Harold ....Wichita, KS
Phillips, Harold C. ....Austin, TX
Phillips, Harris A., III
Oklahoma City, OK
Phillips, Harry A., Jr. ....Houston, TX
Phillips, Harry L. "Don", Jr.
Greenville, SC
Phillips, Harry Shannon, Jr. ....Austin, TX
Phillips, Haskett & Ingwalson, A Professional Corporation ....San Diego, CA
Phillips, Healy & Allen, P.C. ....Chicago, IL
Phillips, Heaney & Schofield ....Beacon, NY
Phillips, Hector ....El Paso, TX
Phillips, Helen E. ....Linwood, NJ
Phillips, Helen E. ....Charlottesville, VA
Phillips, Herbert C. ....Denver, CO
Phillips, Herbert P., (P.C.) ....Haverhill, MA
Phillips, Howard E. ....Pittsburgh, PA
Phillips, Howard E. ....Dallas, TX
Phillips, Howard & Grubb ....Memphis, TN
Phillips, Howard K. ....Denver, CO
Phillips & Ingrum ....Gallatin, TN
Phillips, J. Brantley, Jr. ....Greenville, SC
Phillips, J. Dickson, III ....Chapel Hill, NC
Phillips, J. Dickson, Jr. ....Chapel Hill, NC
Phillips, J. Harrison, III ....Ocean City, MD
Phillips, J. Henry, III ....Dexter, NY
Phillips, J. Hunter, III ....Birmingham, AL
Phillips, J. Olcott ....Fort Worth, TX
Phillips, J. Russell ....Atlanta, GA
Phillips, J. Russell ....Macon, GA
Phillips, J. Taylor ....Macon, GA
Phillips, J. William ....Murray, KY
Phillips, Jack E. ....New York, NY
Phillips, Jack M. ....Templeton, CA
Phillips, Jacqueline ....Baton Rouge, LA
Phillips, Jacqueline ....New York, NY
Phillips, Jacqueline M. ....Burlingame, CA
Sarasota, FL
Phillips, Jacqueline W. ....Pittsburgh, PA
Phillips, James A. ....Springdale, AR
Phillips, James A. ....Memphis, TN
Phillips, James A., Jr. ....Albemarle, NC
Phillips, James C. ....Sacramento, CA
Phillips, James Chrisman ....Austin, TX
Phillips, James D. ....Lake Oswego, OR
Phillips, James D. ....Richmond, VA
Phillips, James E. ....Cleveland, OH
Phillips, James E. ....Columbus, OH
Phillips, James E. ....Evanston, WY
Phillips, James E., Jr. ....Florham Park, NJ
Phillips, James G. ....Melrose, MA
Phillips, James H. ....Dalton, GA
Phillips, James H., III ....Little Rock, AR
Phillips, James J. ....Hayward, CA
Pleasanton, CA
Phillips, James J. ....Worcester, MA
Phillips, James J. ....Bay City, MI
Phillips, James J., A Professional Corporation ....Hayward, CA
Pleasanton, CA
Phillips, James K. ....Winston-Salem, NC
Phillips, James L. ....Seattle, WA
Phillips, James M. ....Fresno, CA
Phillips, James M. ....New York, NY
Phillips, James N. ....Milwaukee, WI
Phillips, James O., III ....Rogersville, TN
Phillips, James P., Jr. ....Lake Ariel, PA
Scranton, PA
Phillips, James R. ....Tempe, AZ
Phillips, James S. ....Vienna, VA
Phillips, James S., Jr. ....Wichita, KS
Phillips, James S., Sr. ....Wichita, KS
Phillips, James T. ....Dallas, TX
Phillips, James W. ....Hailey, ID
Phillips, James W. ....Rego Park, NY
Phillips, Jamey Laney ....Lubbock, TX
Phillips, Jana Ault ....Springfield, MO
Phillips, Jane ....Bridgeport, CT
Phillips, Jane E.
Federal Communications Commission, Wireless Telecommunications Bureau, GV
Phillips, Janet L. ....Mansfield, OH
Sandusky, OH
Phillips, Janine ....New York, NY
Phillips, Jas. N. ....Baltimore, MD
Phillips, Jason Wade ....Austin, TX
Phillips, Javonne M. ....Modesto, CA
Phillips, Jeanne M. ....Chicago, IL
Phillips, Jeffrey Evan ....New York, NY
Phillips, Jeffrey J. ....Boston, MA
Phillips, Jeffrey K. ....Charleston, WV
Phillips, Jeffrey L. ....Phoenix, AZ
Phillips, Jerome ....Toledo, OH
Phillips, Jerrel E. ....Tallahassee, FL
Phillips, Jerrold K. ....Tampa, FL
Phillips, Jerry J. ....Knoxville, TN
Phillips, Jerry L. ....Kansas City, MO
Phillips, Jerry M. ....Fairfax, VA
Phillips, Jerry S. ....Beverly Hills, CA
Phillips, Jill A. ....Dearborn, MI
Phillips, Jill Patterson ....Enid, OK
Phillips, Jim W., Jr. ....Greensboro, NC
Raleigh, NC
Phillips, Jimmy, Jr. ....Angleton, TX
Phillips, Joanne ....Philadelphia, PA
Phillips, Jodie Anne ....Portland, OR
Phillips, Joe ....Kansas City, MO
Phillips, Joe ....Houston, TX
Phillips, Joe B. ....Houston, TX
Phillips, Joelle James ....Nashville, TN
Phillips, John Allen, II ....Durant, OK
Phillips, John B. ....Denver, CO
Phillips, John B. ....Nashville, TN

Phillips, John B., Jr. ... Chattanooga, TN
Phillips, John C. ... Washington, DC
Phillips, John C. ... Westfield, NJ
Phillips, John C. ... Austin, TX
Phillips, John C. ... Sandy, UT
Phillips, John C., Jr. ... Wilmington, DE
Phillips, John D. ... Stockton, CA
Phillips, John D. ... Albuquerque, NM
Phillips, John D. ... Columbus, OH
Phillips, John D. ... Wheeling, WV
Phillips, John D., Jr. ... Denver, CO
Kansas City, MO
Phillips, John E. ... Prescott, AZ
Phillips, John E. ... Tampa, FL
Phillips, John E. ... Canton, OH
Phillips, John E. ... Seattle, WA
Phillips, John E., (P.C.) ... Dallas, TX
Phillips, John F. ... Houston, TX
Phillips, John G. ... San Diego, CA
Phillips, John G. ... Chicago, IL
Phillips, John G., & Associates ... Chicago, IL
Phillips, John Gordon
North Little Rock, AR
Phillips, John H. ... Berkeley, CA
Phillips, John H. ... Morehead City, NC
Phillips, John H. ... Dallas, TX
Phillips, John H., P.A. ... Morehead City, NC
Phillips, John J. ... Overland Park, KS
Phillips, John J. ... Towson, MD
Phillips, John J. ... Boston, MA
Phillips, John J. ... Independence, MO
Phillips, John J., Jr. ... Miami, FL
Phillips, John, Jr. ... Austin, TX
Phillips, John L. ... West Palm Beach, FL
Phillips, John L., Jr. ... Brooklyn, NY
Phillips, John M. ... Salinas, CA
Phillips, John M. ... Milwaukee, WI
Phillips, John P. ... San Francisco, CA
Phillips, John R. ... Anniston, AL
Phillips, John R. ... Englewood, CO
Phillips, John R. ... Washington, DC
Phillips, John R. ... Clearwater, FL
Phillips, John R. ... Cochran, GA
Phillips, John R. ... Kansas City, MO
Phillips, John R., Jr. ... Gallatin, TN
Phillips, John S. ... Denver, CO
Chicago, IL
Phillips, John T. ... Prescott, AZ
Phillips, John T. ... Waukegan, IL
Phillips, John W. ... Fresno, CA
Phillips, John W. ... Louisville, KY
Phillips, John W. ... Gettysburg, PA
Phillips, John W. ... Greer, SC
Phillips, John W. ... Seattle, WA
Phillips, Jonathan L. ... Houston, TX
Phillips, Jonathan Peter ... Stamford, CT
Phillips, Joseph B. ... Stockton, MO
Phillips, Joseph C. ... Harrisburg, PA
Phillips, Joseph F., Jr. ... Williamsburg, VA
Phillips, Joseph K. ... Lebanon, OR
Phillips, Joseph W. ... Ann Arbor, MI
Phillips, Joy H. ... Dallas, TX
Phillips, Joy Lambert ... Gulfport, MS
Phillips, Joy LaNelle ... Baltimore, MD
Phillips, Judith J. ... Springfield, MA
Phillips, Julie K. ... Kalamazoo, MI
Phillips, K. Todd ... Charlotte, NC
Phillips, K. Todd ... Dallas, TX
Phillips, Karen Jean ... Boston, MA
Phillips, Karen K. ... Chicago, IL
Phillips, Karen T. ... Springfield, VA
Phillips, Kate ... New York, NY
Phillips, Kathleen A. ... Houston, TX
Phillips, Kathleen J. ... North Andover, MA
Phillips, Kathleen M. ... Coral Gables, FL
Phillips, Kathryn H. ... Laguna Beach, CA
Phillips, Kathryn Sevier ... Nashville, TN
Phillips, Keith C. ... McLean, VA
Phillips, Keith L. ... Richmond, VA
Phillips, Kelly L. ... Bloomington, MN
Phillips, Kendall J. ... Fort Pierce, FL
Phillips, Kenneth Barrett ... Natick, MA
Phillips, Kenneth F. ... San Francisco, CA
Phillips, Kenneth Morgan ... Los Angeles, CA
Phillips, Kerry O. ... Pontiac, MI
Phillips, Kevin E. ... Cape Girardeau, MO
Phillips, Kevin L. ... Mankato, KS
Phillips, Kevin Michael ... Chicago, IL
Phillips, Kevin P. ... Bethesda, MD
Phillips, Kevin P. ... Marshfield, MA
Phillips, Kimberley A. ... Towson, MD
Phillips, Kimberly D. ... Los Angeles, CA
Phillips, Kimberly M. ... San Francisco, CA
Phillips, Kirsa ... New York, NY
Phillips, Krause & Brown ... Aberdeen, WA
Phillips, Kristine A. ... Cherry Hill, NJ
Phillips, L. Lee, (P.C.) ... Los Angeles, CA
Phillips & Lancaster, P.C. ... Evanston, WY
Phillips, Lance Boyd ... Oklahoma City, OK
Phillips, Larry E. ... Pittsburgh, PA
Phillips, Larry S. ... Edina, MO
Phillips, Laura A. ... Southfield, MI
Phillips, Laura Brodbeck
Washington, DC
Phillips, Laura Hathaway
Washington, DC
Phillips, Laurel Gilbert ... New York, NY
Phillips, Lauren B. ... Mechanicsburg, PA
Phillips, Lauren D. ... San Antonio, TX
Phillips, Laurie Paravati ... Rochester, NY
Phillips Law Firm, P.A. ... Columbia, MS
Phillips, Lawrence ... Bonita, CA
Phillips, Lawrence A. ... Sherman, TX
Phillips, Lawrence J. ... Louisville, KY
Phillips, Layn R. ... Newport Beach, CA
Phillips, Lee ... New Orleans, LA
Phillips, Lee Anne ... San Antonio, TX
Phillips, Lee Brooke ... Flagstaff, AZ

Phillips, Leigh Keyser ... South Burlington, VT
Phillips, Leo H., Jr. ... Gaithersburg, MD
Phillips, Leo J. ... Franklin, NC
Phillips, Leo L., Jr. ... Cochran, GA
Phillips, Leroy, Jr. ... Chattanooga, TN
Phillips, Leslie G. ... Lexington, KY
Phillips, Linda A. ... Plymouth, MI
Ypsilanti, MI
Phillips, Linda A., P.C., Law Offices of
Plymouth, MI
Ypsilanti, MI
Phillips, Linda Conway
Treasury Department,
Internal Revenue Service, GV
Phillips, Linda Wohlbruck ... Charlotte, NC
Phillips, Lisa Lopin ... Costa Mesa, CA
Phillips, Lloyd A., Jr. ... Sacramento, CA
Phillips, Lois F. ... Baiting Hollow, NY
New York, NY
Phillips, Lois R. ... Albany, NY
Phillips, Loren C. ... Diamond Bar, CA
Phillips, Lori Lynn ... Seattle, WA
Phillips, Lorraine K. ... Georgetown, DE
Phillips, Louis Middleton ... Baton Rouge, LA
Phillips, Lunsford D. ... Honolulu, HI
Phillips, Lyndelle Tolliver ... New York, NY
Phillips, Lynette ... Austin, TX
Phillips, Lynn A. ... Bethesda, MD
Phillips & Lyon, P.A. ... Phoenix, AZ
Phillips, Lytle, Hitchcock, Blaine & Huber LLP ... Buffalo, NY
Fredonia, NY
Jamestown, NY
New York, NY
Niagara Falls, NY
Rochester, NY
Phillips, M. Alan ... Beverly Hills, CA
Phillips, Malcolm C. ... Bronx, NY
Phillips, Mallory E., III ... Atlanta, GA
Phillips, Marc A. ... Spokane, WA
Phillips, Margaret C. ... San Francisco, CA
Phillips, Margaret Coullard ... Houston, TX
Phillips, Margaret L. ... Buffalo, NY
Phillips, Margo ... Los Angeles, CA
Phillips, Marilyn C. ... Edwardsville, IL
St. Louis, MO
Phillips, Marina Liacouras ... Norfolk, VA
Phillips, Mark A. ... Cleveland, OH
Phillips, Mark A. ... Brookfield, WI
Phillips, Mark A., Law Offices of, S.C.
Brookfield, WI
Phillips, Mark C. ... Encino, CA
Phillips, Mark C. ... Walnut Creek, CA
Phillips, Mark D. ... West Chester, PA
Phillips, Mark E. ... Columbus, OH
Phillips, Mark J. ... Los Angeles, CA
Phillips, Mark J. ... Santa Monica, CA
Phillips, Mark K. ... Boonville, IN
Phillips, Mark L. ... La Porte, IN
Phillips, Mark T. ... Albany, GA
Phillips, Mark W. ... Atlanta, GA
Phillips, Marsha V. ... Skokie, IL
Phillips, Martha J. ... Tulsa, OK
Phillips, Marty R. ... Jackson, TN
Phillips, Mary A. ... Boston, MA
Phillips, Mary Ann ... Northbrook, IL
Phillips, Mary Beth ... Phoenix, AZ
Phillips, Mary Fields ... Paintsville, KY
Phillips, Mary Kleyla ... Jacksonville, FL
Phillips, Mary M. ... Denver, CO
Phillips, Mary Susan ... Wallace, NC
Phillips, Mary V. ... Washington, DC
Phillips, Mary Wisehart ... Middletown, IN
Phillips, Matthew A. ... Chicago, IL
Phillips, Matthew T. ... Pittsburgh, PA
Phillips, Maureen A. ... St. Paul, MN
Phillips, Maureen K. ... Harvard, MA
Phillips, McCollom, Kozlowski & Vald, PLC
West Des Moines, IA
Phillips McCullough Wilson Hill & Fikso, P.S. ... Seattle, WA
Phillips, McElligott, Ewan & Hall, P.C.
Independence, MO
Phillips, McElyea, Walker & Carpenter, P.C.
Camdenton, MO
Osage Beach, MO
Phillips McFall McCaffrey McVay & Murrah, P.C. ... Norman, OK
Oklahoma City, OK
Phillips & McMichen, P.A. ... Orlando, FL
Phillips, Megan ... St. Louis, MO
Phillips, Melinda B. ... Tifton, GA
Phillips, Melissa W. ... Akron, OH
Phillips & Merica, P.C. ... Austin, TX
Phillips, M. H. ... New Orleans, LA
Phillips, Michael ... Hackensack, NJ
Phillips, Michael ... Eugene, OR
Phillips, Michael ... Houston, TX
Phillips, Michael B.
Federal Deposit Insurance Corporation,
Resolutions Section, GV
Phillips, Michael C. ... Palo Alto, CA
Raleigh, NC
Phillips, Michael C. ... Kansas City, MO
Phillips, Michael C., (P.C.)
Los Angeles, CA
Phillips, Michael D. ... Boston, MA
Phillips, Michael D. ... Cleveland, OH
Phillips, Michael F. ... Hagåtña, GU
Phillips, Michael G. ... Wilmington, DE
Phillips, Michael J. ... Freeport, IL
Phillips, Michael J. ... Schenectady, NY
Phillips, Michael K. ... San Francisco, CA
Phillips, Michael K. ... Boonville, IN
Phillips, Michael Kregg ... Austin, TX
Phillips, Michael M. ... Angleton, TX
Phillips, Michael P. ... Santa Barbara, CA
Phillips, Michael R. ... Chicago, IL

Phillips, Michael R. ... New Orleans, LA
Phillips, Michael Scott ... Columbus, GA
Phillips, Michael W. ... Oklahoma City, OK
Phillips, Michelle E. ... New York, NY
Phillips, Mildred N. ... Brookline, MA
Phillips and Mille Co., L.P.A.
Middleburg Heights, OH
Phillips, Mimi ... Memphis, TN
Phillips, Mireille Leruth ... Troy, MI
Phillips, Monte C. ... Kansas City, MO
Phillips & Moore, P.S.C. ... Harrodsburg, KY
Phillips, Morris B. ... New Orleans, LA
Phillips, Morris C., Jr. ... Carthage, MS
Phillips, Morris S. ... Swampscott, MA
Phillips, Morrison & Alexander
Rustburg, VA
Phillips and Mueller ... Crystal Lake, IL
Phillips, N. Scott ... Baltimore, MD
Phillips, N. William ... Milan, MO
Phillips, Nancy A. ... Media, PA
Phillips, Nancy Crocker ... Elizabethtown, NC
Phillips, Nancy I.
Department Of Veterans Affairs,
Board of Veterans Appeals, GV
Phillips, Nancy Pat ... Atlanta, GA
Phillips, Nancy Williams ... Nashville, TN
Phillips, Nathaniel P., Jr. ... New Orleans, LA
Phillips, Natonya C. ... Cherry Hill, NJ
Phillips, Neal A. ... Newark, DE
Phillips, Neil Franklin ... New York, NY
Phillips, Neil P. ... Norwalk, CT
Phillips, Nicholas B. ... Iuka, MS
Phillips, Nicholas E.
Middleburg Heights, OH
Phillips, Nina W. ... Los Angeles, CA
Phillips Nizer Benjamin Krim & Ballon LLP
Garden City, NY
New York, NY
Phillips, Norman A. ... Beaverton, OR
Phillips, Norman W. ... Seymour, IN
Phillips, Norwood ... El Dorado, AR
Phillips, Olivia Harrison ... Ocean City, MD
Phillips, Olore, Dunlavey & York, P.A.
Caribou, ME
Houlton, ME
Presque Isle, ME
Phillips, P. Scott ... Meridian, MS
Phillips, Packard E. ... New Orleans, LA
Phillips, Paige Michaux ... Greensboro, NC
Phillips, Pamela ... San Francisco, CA
Phillips, Pamela ... Dallas, TX
Phillips, Pamela A. ... New York, NY
Phillips, Pamela K. ... Jacksonville, FL
Phillips, Pat W. ... Dickinson, TX
Phillips, Patricia Dominis
Los Angeles, CA
Phillips, Patricia Lea ... Richmond, VA
Phillips, Patrick J. ... St. Louis, MO
Phillips, Patrick M. ... Oklahoma City, OK
Phillips, Patrick P. ... Reynoldsburg, OH
Phillips, Paul A. ... Birmingham, AL
Phillips, Paul Allen ... Jackson, TN
Phillips, Paul D. ... Denver, CO
Phillips, Paul E. ... Providence, RI
Phillips, Paul J. ... Montpelier, VT
St. Johnsbury, VT
Phillips, Paul M. ... Pismo Beach, CA
Phillips, Paul P. ... Fox Lake, IL
Phillips, Paul W. ... Department of Energy,
Office of the General Counsel, GV
Phillips, Paula G. ... Effingham, IL
Phillips, Paula J. ... Miami, FL
Phillips, Peggy A. ...
Federal Emergency Management Agency,
GV
Phillips, Penelope A. ... San Diego, CA
Phillips, Penelope J. ... Minneapolis, MN
Phillips, Perry A. ... Atlanta, GA
Phillips, Perry W. ... Columbia, MS
Phillips, Peter J. ... New York, NY
Phillips, Peyton Paul ... Frederick, MD
Phillips, Phil E. ... Malibu, CA
Phillips, Philip B. ... Detroit, MI
Phillips, Philip B., Jr. ... Jacksonville, FL
Phillips, Philip D. ... Arlington, TX
Phillips, Philip S. ... Zanesville, OH
Phillips & Phillips ... Anniston, AL
Phillips & Phillips ... Lauderdale Lakes, FL
Phillips & Phillips ... Cochran, GA
Phillips & Phillips ... Macon, GA
Phillips & Phillips ... St. Louis, MO
Phillips & Phillips, Chartered ... Wichita, KS
Phillips, Phillips & Hull ... Monticello, KY
Phillips & Phillips, P.A. ... Miami, FL
Phillips, Phillips & Phillips ... Angleton, TX
Phillips, P. N. ... Marshalltown, IA
Phillips & Potach, P.A. ... Minneapolis, MN
Phillips, Quentin ... Chicago, IL
Phillips, R. Bruce ... Little Rock, AR
Springfield, MO
Phillips, R. Bruce ... Denver, CO
Phillips, R. Bruce ... Warsaw, IN
Phillips, R. Gerald (Jerry) ... Buford, GA
Phillips, R. Glenn ... Redmond, WA
Phillips, R. Patrick ... Orlando, FL
Phillips, Ralph E. ... Ripley, WV
Phillips, Ralph, Jr. ... Union, SC
Phillips, Ralph M. ... Encino, CA
Phillips, Ralph W. ... Greenfield, OH
Phillips, Randall E. ... Bloomfield Hills, MI
Phillips, Randall J. ... Jackson, TN
Phillips, Randall M. ... Booker, TX
Perryton, TX
Phillips, Randel E. ... Charlotte, NC
Phillips, Randolph H. ... Albany, GA
Phillips, Ray Chappell ... Durham, NC
Phillips, Reid L. ... Greensboro, NC
Raleigh, NC

Phillips, Reneé J. ... Detroit, MI
Phillips, Rex C. ... Daly City, CA
Phillips, Reynier & Sumerfield
Hood River, OR
Phillips, Richard A. ... Encino, CA
Phillips, Richard A. ... Chicago, IL
Phillips, Richard A. ... Statesville, NC
Phillips, Richard D. ... Ludowici, GA
Phillips, Richard F. ... Houston, TX
Phillips, Richard G. ... Sidney, MT
Phillips, Richard G. ... Philadelphia, PA
Phillips, Richard G., Associates, P.C.
Philadelphia, PA
Phillips, Richard G., Jr.
Department of Justice, Civil Division, GV
Phillips, Richard G., Jr. ... Olympia, WA
Phillips, Richard H. ... Miami, FL
Phillips, Richard I. ... San Luis Obispo, CA
Phillips, Richard J. ... Clinton, OK
Phillips, Richard L. ... Burlingame, CA
Phillips, Richard L. ... Cleveland, OH
Phillips, Richard L. ... Seattle, WA
Phillips, Richard M. ... Washington, DC
Phillips, Richard R. ... Muscatine, IA
Phillips, Richard S. ... Chicago, IL
Phillips, Richard S. (Dick) ... Easton, MD
Phillips, Richard T. ... Batesville, MS
Phillips, Richard W. ... Cleveland, OH
Phillips, Richard W. ... Dallas, TX
Phillips, Richards, Mayew & Corrigall, S.C.
Kenosha, WI
Phillips, Robert A. ... Burnsville, NC
Phillips, Robert B. ... Accomac, VA
Phillips, Robert Buchanan, II
Birmingham, AL
Phillips, Robert C. ... San Diego, CA
Phillips, Robert D. ... Hudson, OH
Phillips, Robert D., Jr. ... Walnut Creek, CA
Phillips, Robert E. ... Wilmington, DE
Phillips, Robert G. ... Ruskin, FL
Phillips, Robert J. ... Missoula, MT
Phillips, Robert J., Jr. ... New York, NY
Phillips, Robert J., Jr. ... Fort Worth, TX
Phillips, Robert K. ... Fresno, CA
San Francisco, CA
San Luis Obispo, CA
Phillips, Robert L. ... Boise, ID
Phillips, Robert M. ... Cleveland, OH
Phillips, Robert M., III ... Austin, TX
Phillips, Robert M., III ... Georgetown, TX
Phillips, Robert N. ... Menlo Park, CA
Phillips, Robert O. ... White Plains, NY
Phillips, Robert Paul, III ... Savannah, GA
Phillips, Robert S. ... Crystal Lake, IL
Phillips, Robert S. ... Hopedale, MA
Phillips, Robert W. ... St. Louis, MO
Phillips, Robert W. ... Columbus, OH
Phillips, Robin A. ... Scarsdale, NY
Phillips, Robin E. ... Dallas, TX
Phillips, Robin S. ... Ann Arbor, MI
Phillips, Robin W. ... Seattle, WA
Phillips, Robyn L. ... Salt Lake City, UT
Phillips, Roger B. ... Concord, NH
Phillips, Roger C. ... Simsbury, CT
Phillips, Roger M. ... Leawood, KS
Phillips, Ronald A. ... Nyack, NY
Phillips, Ronald Allan ... Fordyce, AR
Phillips, Ronald F. ... Malibu, CA
Phillips, Ronald L. ... Charleston, SC
Phillips, Ronnie ... Denton, TX
Phillips, Rosalind Ann ... Washington, DC
Phillips, Rosemary E. ... Goodlettsville, TN
Phillips, Rosemary Leeds
Pension Benefit Guaranty Corporation,
Office of the General Counsel, GV
Phillips, Roy H. ... Phenix City, AL
Phillips, Russell A., Jr. ... New York, NY
Phillips, Russell D., Jr. ... Santa Ana, CA
Phillips, S. Albert ... Louisville, KY
Phillips, S. Kay ... Tonawanda, NY
Phillips, S. Larry ... Brunswick, GA
Phillips, S. Larry, P.C. ... Brunswick, GA
Saint Simons Island, GA
Phillips, Salman & Stein ... Los Angeles, CA
New York, NY
Phillips, Sam R. ... Franklin, KY
Phillips, Sam S. ... Springfield, MO
Phillips, Samantha M. ... Los Angeles, CA
Phillips, Samuel L. ... Modesto, CA
Phillips, Samuel W. ... Richmond, VA
Phillips, Sandra L. ... Houston, TX
Phillips, Sandra Trotter ... Pine Bluff, AR
Phillips, Sarah Fiona ... New York, NY
Phillips, Sarah J. ... Kenwood, CA
Phillips & Schisler ... Bay City, MI
Phillips, Scott D. ... Cincinnati, OH
Phillips, Scott Hamilton ... Baltimore, MD
Phillips, Scott M. ... San Rafael, CA
Phillips, Scott P. ... Milwaukee, WI
Phillips, Scott R. ... Atlanta, GA
Phillips, S.E. ... East Lansing, MI
Phillips, Seth R. ... St. Paul, MN
Phillips, Shannon E. ... Seattle, WA
Phillips, Shannon M. ... Round Rock, TX
Phillips, Sharon K. ... Tulsa, OK
Phillips, Shawn P. ... Lehigh Valley, PA
Phillips & Sheehan Co., L.P.A. ... Canton, OH
Phillips, Sheri Sensing ... Clarksville, TN
Phillips, Sherrie Lynn ... Birmingham, AL
Phillips, Sherrie R. ... Andalusia, AL
Phillips, Sherry M. ... Columbus, OH
Phillips, Silver, Talman & Aframe, P.C.
Worcester, MA
Phillips, Sloan & Silverman, P.A.
Baltimore, MD
Phillips, Sonya C. (Sunny) ... Corinth, MS

Phillips & Spallas, LLP ... Fresno, CA
San Francisco, CA
San Luis Obispo, CA
Phillips & Spencer, P.C. ... Milan, MO
Phillips, Stacy D. ... Los Angeles, CA
Phillips, Stanley A. ... Virginia Beach, VA
Phillips, Stanley S. ... Dayton, OH
Phillips, Stanton ... Arlington, VA
Phillips, Stanton Lee ... Los Angeles, CA
Phillips, Stephanie L. ... Buffalo, NY
Phillips, Stephen D. ... Chicago, IL
Phillips, Stephen G. ... Greenwich, CT
Phillips, Stephen J. ... Huntsville, AL
Phillips, Stephen L. ... Austin, TX
Phillips, Stephen M. ... Atlanta, GA
Phillips, Stephen R. ... West Palm Beach, FL
Phillips, Stephen R. ... Brattleboro, VT
Phillips, Stephen R., P.A.
West Palm Beach, FL
Phillips, Stephen S. ... Philadelphia, PA
Phillips, Stevan D. ... Seattle, WA
Phillips, Steve ... Newport Beach, CA
Phillips, Steven B. ... West Palm Beach, FL
Phillips, Steven B. ... Durham, NC
Phillips, Steven C. ... Ventura, CA
Phillips, Steven D. ... Lexington, KY
Phillips, Steven D. ... Philadelphia, PA
Phillips, Steven E. ... Atlanta, GA
Phillips, Steven J. ... New York, NY
Phillips, Steven M. ... Minneapolis, MN
Phillips, Steven R. ... Washington, DC
Phillips, Steven W. ... Tucson, AZ
Phillips, Steven W. ... Boston, MA
Phillips, Stirling S.R. ... Dallas, TX
Phillips & Street ... Chillicothe, OH
Phillips, Stuart J. ... Doylestown, PA
Phillips, Sue ... Kansas City, MO
Phillips, Sue A. ... St. Louis, MO
Phillips, Sue Ellen ... Cleveland, OH
Phillips, Susan ... Washington, DC
Phillips, Susan B. ... San Diego, CA
Phillips, Susan Conlon ... Chicopee, MA
Phillips, Susan D. ... Denver, CO
Phillips, Susan D. ... Louisville, KY
Phillips, Susan G. ... Walnut Creek, CA
Phillips, Susan J. ... Tiffin, OH
Phillips, Susan L.
San Juan Capistrano, CA
Phillips, Susan Mara ... New London, CT
Phillips, Susan O. ... Charleston, WV
Phillips, Susan P. ... Boston, MA
Phillips, Susan Z. ... West Des Moines, IA
Phillips, Suzanne D. ... St. Louis, MO
Phillips and Swanson ... Salem, VA
Phillips, T. Ray, III ... Oklahoma City, OK
Phillips, T. Stephen ... Cincinnati, OH
Phillips, Terry D. ... San Diego, CA
Phillips, Terry G. ... Decatur, GA
Phillips, Thelma D. ... Pembroke, NC
Phillips, Theodore N., II ... Norwich, CT
Phillips, Theodore W. ... San Francisco, CA
Phillips, Thomas A. ... Spartanburg, SC
Phillips, Thomas B. ... Houston, TX
Phillips, Thomas C. ... Lansing, MI
Phillips, Thomas C., Jr. ... Johnson City, TN
Abingdon, VA
Phillips, Thomas D. ... Cameron Park, CA
Sacramento, CA
Phillips, Thomas J. ... Boston, MA
Phillips, Thomas J. ... Traverse City, MI
Phillips, Thomas J. ... Milwaukee, WI
Phillips, Thomas J., Jr. ... Milledgeville, GA
Phillips, Thomas L. ... Traverse City, MI
Phillips, Thomas L. ... Rustburg, VA
Phillips, Thomas L., Jr. ... Rustburg, VA
Phillips, Thomas M. ... Los Angeles, CA
Phillips, Thomas M. ... Dayton, OH
Phillips, Thomas M. ... Dublin, OH
Phillips, Thomas P. ... Pacific Palisades, CA
Phillips, Thomas R. ... Chicago, IL
Phillips, Thomas R. ... Austin, TX
Phillips, Thomas W. ... Knoxville, TN
Phillips, Timothy C. ... Lincoln, NE
Phillips, Timothy J. ... St. Louis, MO
Phillips, Tod A. ... Galveston, TX
Phillips, Todd R. ... New York, NY
Phillips, Tom F. ... Baton Rouge, LA
Phillips, Tondra J. ... Joplin, MO
Phillips, Tracy A. ... Houston, TX
Phillips, Travis R. ... Austin, TX
Phillips, Troy D. ... Dallas, TX
Phillips, Trudie Anne ... Anniston, AL
Phillips, Van Fossen ... Monticello, KY
Phillips, Vel R. ... Milwaukee, WI
Phillips, Victoria F.
Federal Communications Commission,
Mass Media Bureau, GV
Phillips, Virginia A. ... Los Angeles, CA
Phillips, Virginia M. ... Greenville, SC
Phillips, W. Alan ... Nashville, TN
Phillips, W. Brantley, Jr ... Nashville, TN
Phillips, W. Bruce ... Grand Junction, CO
Phillips, W. Daniel ... Port Orchard, WA
Phillips, W. Newton ... Richmond, VA
Phillips, Walter J. ... Grand Junction, CO
Phillips, Walter J. ... Pittsburgh, PA
Phillips, Walter M. ... San Mateo, CA
Phillips, Walter M., Jr. ... Philadelphia, PA
Phillips, Walter R. ... Athens, GA
Phillips, Walton M. ... Orinda, CA
Phillips, Ward D. ... Elkhorn, WI
Phillips, Wayne W., II ... Zanesville, OH
Phillips, W. B. ... Killeen, TX
Phillips, Webb & Wallerstein, P.C.
Richmond, VA
Phillips & Weir ... Virginia, MN
Phillips, Wendy G. ... Irvine, CA

Phillips & Whisnant, LLP
Newport Beach, CA
Phillips, Wilbur L. ... Omaha, NE
Phillips, Will E. ... Irving, TX
Phillips, William A. ... Greenwich, CT
Phillips, William A. ... Detroit, MI
Phillips, William B. ... Chicago, IL
Phillips, William B., III ... Healdsburg, CA
Phillips, William C. ... Fort Worth, TX
Phillips, William D. ... Washington, DC
Phillips, William D. ... Washington, PA
Phillips, William E. ... Chicago, IL
Phillips, William E. ... Laurel, MS
Phillips, William E. ... Anderson, SC
Phillips, William E. ... Rogersville, TN
Phillips, William E. ... Lynchburg, VA
Phillips, William G. ... St. Louis, MO
Phillips, William J. ... Peterborough, NH
Phillips, William J. ... New York, NY
Phillips, William L. ... Chicago, IL
Phillips, William L. ... St. Paul, MN
Phillips, William L., III ... Birmingham, AL
Phillips, William L., III ... Johnson City, TN
Phillips, William M. ... Ringgold, GA
Phillips, William M. ... Cleveland, OH
Phillips, William M. ... Lynchburg, VA
Phillips, William M., Jr. ... Birmingham, AL
Phillips, William P. ... Huntsville, TN
Phillips, William R. ... Las Vegas, NV
Phillips, William R. ... Fairlawn, OH
Phillips, William Rinaudo ... Tacoma, WA
Phillips, William S ... Columbia, MS
Phillips, William T. ... Glenwood Springs, CO
Phillips, Wilson Cary, Jr. ... Overland Park, KS
Phillips, Wilson Cary, Jr.
Overland Park, KS
Phillips, Wm. ... Miami, FL
Phillips, Wm. E., Jr. ... Naples, FL
Phillips, Wm. L. ... St. Paul, MN
Phillips-Harris, Tammy L. ... Little Rock, AR
Phillipson, Donald E. ... Golden, CO
Phillipson, Herbert E., Jr. ... Dowagiac, MI
Phillipson, John ... Culver City, CA
Phillips Sherry, Sherry M. ... Dublin, OH
Phillips-Williams, Bonnie ... Miami, FL
Phillis, Jana L. ... Pittsburgh, PA
Washington, PA
Phillis, Mark T. ... Pittsburgh, PA
Phillpott, Robert W., Jr. ... Houston, TX
Philman, J. Edward ... Trenton, FL
Philo, DuWayne A. ... La Mesa, CA
Philo, Gregory J. ... Tallahassee, FL
Philo, Harry M. ... Detroit, MI
Philo, John C. ... Detroit, MI
Philo, Robert E., Jr. ... Dallas, TX
Philo, Sharron J. ... Battle Creek, MI
Philo, Spivey & Henning, P.A.
Franklin, NC
Highlands, NC
Philo, Steven E. ... Franklin, NC
Philomena, James A. ... Canfield, OH
Philos, Conrad ... Vienna, VA
Philp, Elizabeth J. ... New York, NY
Philp, Graeme ... New York, NY
Charleston, SC
Philp, Jay P. W. ... Fort Lauderdale, FL
Philp, Lisa ... Atlanta, GA
Philp, Mary Susan ... Washington, DC
Philp, P. Robert, Law Office of
La Jolla, CA
Philp, P. Robert, Law Office of
San Diego, CA
Philpitt, Frederick C. ... Bethesda, MD
Philpitt, Stephen R. ... Jamesburg, NJ
Philpot, Brian G. ... Lakeland, FL
Philpot, Edward D., Jr. ... Laconia, NH
Philpot, Elizabeth H. ... Greenville, SC
Philpot, Eric Holcombe ... Greenville, SC
Philpot, I. Henry, Jr. ... Greenville, SC
Philpot, Irvin H., III ... Greenville, SC
Philpot, Jeffrey T. ... Laconia, NH
Philpot, Jeffrey T., P.C. ... Laconia, NH
Philpot, Kenneth J. ... San Francisco, CA
Philpot Law Firm, P A ... Greenville, SC
Philpot, Ransdell, Roach & Wier, PLLC
Lexington, KY
Philpot, Sidney G., P.A. ... Lakeland, FL
Philpot, Susan Cooper ... San Francisco, CA
Philpot, Timothy N. ... Lexington, KY
Philpot, W. Martyn, Jr. ... New Haven, CT
Philpot, W. Martyn, Jr., L.L.C., Law Office of ... New Haven, CT
Philpott, William H., Jr. ... Mobile, AL
Philpott, William H., Jr., P.C. ... Mobile, AL
Philpott, William, Jr. ... Laconia, NH
Philpott, A. Richard ... Honolulu, HI
Philpott, Benjamin G. ... Lexington, NC
Philpott, Claire J. ... Portland, OR
Philpott, Douglas M. ... Flint, MI
Philpott, H. Julian, Jr. ... Raleigh, NC
Philpott, J. Michell ... Atlanta, GA
Philpott, James A., Jr. ... Lexington, KY
Philpott, Jami E. ... Atlanta, GA
Philpott, Jay G., Jr. ... Fairfax, VA
Philpott, Jerry A. ... Duncannon, PA
Philpott, John J. ... San Diego, CA
Philpott, Kathleen R. ... Washington, DC
Philpott, Peter J. ... Flint, MI
Philpott, Steven L. ... Eugene, OR
Philpott, Susan A. ... Milwaukee, WI
Philpott-Bryant, Marcelle ... Decatur, GA
Philson, Robert M. ... Somerset, PA
Philson-Skalski, Rita Anne ... Washington, DC
Phin, Donald A. ... San Diego, CA
Phinizy, Coles H., Jr. ... New York, NY
Phinney, A. W., III ... Boston, MA
Phinney, Kara D. ... Miami, FL
Phinney, Kathleen S. ... Provo, UT

Phinney, Paul B., III ... Pearl River, NY
Phinney, Richard Allison ... Charleston, SC
Greenville, SC
Phinney, Thomas R. ... Sacramento, CA
Phippard, James R.
Agency for International Development,
Other Offices of A.I.D., GV
Phippard, William J. ... San Diego, CA
Phippen, David P. ... Washington, DC
Phipps, Adam A. ... Norwalk, CA
Phipps, Allan Rogers ... Denver, CO
Phipps, Ann M. ... Champaign, IL
Phipps, Anson D. ... Houston, TX
Phipps, Arral A. ... Modesto, CA
Phipps, Benjamin K. ... Tallahassee, FL
Phipps, Blaine R. ... El Cajon, CA
Phipps, Chad F. ... Harrisburg, PA
Phipps, Charles E. ... New York, NY
Phipps, Christopher D. ... Las Vegas, NV
Phipps, Christopher D., Chartered
Las Vegas, NV
Phipps, David L. ... Des Moines, IA
Phipps, David L. ... Xenia, OH
Phipps, Errol S. ... Dallas, TX
Phipps, Evanthea P. ... New Orleans, LA
Phipps Firm, The ... Tallahassee, FL
Phipps, Greg A. ... San Jose, CA
Phipps, Harve H., Jr. ... Spokane, WA
Phipps, Herbert E. ... Albany, GA
Phipps, J. Blaine ... Des Moines, IA
Phipps, Jacqueline A. ... Rochester, NY
Phipps, James D. ... Washington, DC
Phipps, James E. ... Portland, ME
Phipps, James M. ... Chicago, IL
Phipps, James Wm. ... Greencastle, IN
Phipps, Jill L. ... Fort Collins, CO
Phipps, John G. ... Estes Park, CO
Phipps, John T. ... Champaign, IL
Phipps, John T., Law Offices, P.C.
Champaign, IL
Urbana, IL
Phipps, Joyce ... Newark, NJ
Phipps, K. Clark ... Tulsa, OK
Phipps, Kathryn B. ... Dublin, OH
Phipps, Kent C. ... Ponca City, OK
Phipps, Kim T. ... Dallas, TX
Phipps, Love ... Daytona Beach, FL
Phipps, Martin J. ... San Antonio, TX
Phipps, Meg Scott ... Mebane, NC
Phipps, Melissa Perrell ... Winston-Salem, NC
Phipps, Patrick J. ... Kingsley, IA
Phipps, Paul L. ... Wise, VA
Phipps, Peter J. ... Columbus, OH
Phipps, Rand ... Oklahoma City, OK
Phipps, Rebecca Coleman ... Corinth, MS
Phipps, Robert M. ... Mayfield, KY
Phipps & Rolfe ... Lamoni, IA
Phipps, Sherman W. ... Lamoni, IA
Phipps, Stephanie Dinsmore ... Tulsa, OK
Phipps, Victoria Martin ... Houston, TX
Phipps, W. Michael ... Manassas, VA
Phipps, William R.
Hilton Head Island, SC
Phipps, William R., P.A. ... Beaufort, SC
Hilton Head Island, SC
Phipps, William Winslow ... Tabor City, NC
Phlegar, Jacquelyn K. ... Burbank, CA
Santa Barbara, CA
Phleger, Gary L. ... Wayzata, MN
Phleger, Peter M. ... San Francisco, CA
Phocas, George A. ... Philadelphia, PA
Phocas, Robert J. ... Washington, DC
Phoebe, Timm Owen ... West Chester, PA
Phoebus, David G. ... Fort Pierce, FL
Phoebus, Edgar W. ... Evanston, IL
Phoebus, John K. ... Salisbury, MD
Phoenix, David D. ... Bloomington, IL
Phoenix, David G. ... Crystal Lake, IL
Phoenix, E. Chilton ... Pocatello, ID
Phoenix, G. Keith ... Belleville, IL
St. Louis, MO
Phoenix, Joy L. ... Tucson, AZ
Phoenix, R. Timothy ... Portsmouth, NH
Pholeric, Karen J. ... Media, PA
Photiadis, Gregory P. ... Buffalo, NY
Photiadis, Lynn ... Charleston, WV
Photis, Dore Valavanes ... Lancaster, PA
Photopoulos, Harry P. ... Boston, MA
Photopulos, Todd P. ... Memphis, TN
Phufas, John M. ... New York, NY
Phufas, John Michael, P.C. ... New York, NY
Phufas, Katherine C. ... North Tonawanda, NY
Phulwani, Michael ... Edison, NJ
Phung, Thu-Cuc T. ... Westminster, CA
Phy, Paul W., (P.C.) ... Dallas, TX
Phythyon, Daniel B. ... Washington, DC
Pia, Joseph ... Birmingham, MI
Pia, Robert J. ... Salinas, CA
Pia, Robert Joseph ... San Francisco, CA
Pia, Robert, Law Offices of
San Francisco, CA
Piacente, Robert V. ... Fresno, CA
Piacentini, Anthony J. ... Port Washington, NY
Piacentini, Charles P., Jr. ... Portland, ME
Piacentini, Donald W. ... Richmond, VA
Piacentini, Gary T. ... Glen Allen, VA
Piacentino, C. Michael ... Marion, OH
Piacentino & Piacentino Co., L.P.A.
Marion, OH
Piacenza, Dominic S. ... New London, CT
Piacquad, Joseph A. ... Boston, MA
Piacun, Joseph S. ... New Orleans, LA
Piaggione, Rocky ... Albany, NY
Piaia, David M. ... Rock Springs, WY
Piaker, Matthew H. ... Wellesley, MA
Pialis, Stefania ... Chicago, IL
Piampiano, James J. ... Rochester, NY
Piampiano, Robert J. ... Portland, ME

Piana, Ann Marie ... Belleville, IL
St. Louis, MO
Piane, Lucian Vincent ... Kansas City, MO
Pianelli, James V. ... Houston, TX
Pianin, Michael ... Southfield, MI
Pianka, Andrew J. ... Norwalk, CT
Pianko, Howard ... New York, NY
Pianko, Theodore A. ... Irvine, CA
Piano, John G. ... Beverly Hills, CA
Pianowski, Michael A. ... Elkhart, IN
Piantadosi, Richard N.
Manhattan Beach, CA
Piantanida, Donald A. ... Pittsburg, CA
Piantini, Albert J. ... Miami, FL
Piantino, Paul, III ... Newark, NJ
Piar, Daniel F. ... Atlanta, GA
Piar, Kimberly Sue ... Atlanta, GA
Piarulli, Frank A. ... Cherry Hill, NJ
Piarulli, Jayne A. ... Philadelphia, PA
Piarulli, Michael J. ... Cherry Hill, NJ
Pias, Scott J. ... Lake Charles, LA
Piasecki, Alison Smith ... Boston, MA
Piasecki, Brandon William
Niagara Falls, NY
Piasecki, Carmen M. ... South Bend, IN
Piasecki, Chris E. ... Middlesex, NJ
Piasecki, Christopher J. ... Lafayette, LA
Piasecki, John A. ... Malone, NY
Piasecki, Mark J. ... South Bend, IN
Piasecki, Ronald L. ... Grand Rapids, MI
Piaskoski & Associates, S.C. ... Franklin, WI
Milwaukee, WI
Piaskoski, Paul A. ... Franklin, WI
Milwaukee, WI
Piaskowy, Walter A., Jr. ... Westmont, IL
Piassick, Joel B. ... Atlanta, GA
Piasta, Eric S. ... New York, NY
Piasta, Joseph A., II ... Santa Rosa, CA
Piatak, Thomas J. ... Cleveland, OH
Piatchek, Thomas J. ... St. Louis, MO
Piatek, Anthony S. ... New Castle, PA
Piatek, Frank J. ... New Castle, PA
Piatek, Michael J. ... Sterling Heights, MI
Piatek, Stephen Patrick ... Wilmington, CA
Piatkowski, Jerzy L. ... Scottsdale, AZ
Piatnicia, Andrew Y. ... Menlo Park, CA
Piatoff, Mindy S. ... New York, NY
Piatt, James H. ... Pomona, CA
Piatt, Justin M. ... New York, NY
Piatt, Lee S. ... Wilkes-Barre, PA
Piatt, Noreen Maley ... Philadelphia, PA
Piatt, Norma ... Berkeley, CA
Piatt, Paul ... Mount Clemens, MI
Piatt, Robert L. ... Portage, MI
Piatt, Robert W. ... Lubbock, TX
Piatt, Rosanne ... Lubbock, TX
Piatt, Theodore D. ... Pomona, CA
Piatt, Timothy R. ... Youngstown, OH
Piatt, William M. ... Phoenix, AZ
Piatt, William M., Professional Corporation
Phoenix, AZ
Piazza, A.E. ... Medford, OR
Piazza, Angelo J., III ... Marksville, LA
Piazza, Anthony A. ... Stamford, CT
Piazza, Anthony E. (Gene) ... Medford, OR
Piazza, Anthony F., II ... St. Louis, MO
Piazza, Anthony J. ... Rochester, NY
Piazza, Anthony J., Jr. ... Scranton, PA
Piazza, Anthony M. ... Cleveland, OH
Piazza, Barbara A. ... Buffalo, NY
Piazza, Basil R. ... Buffalo, NY
Piazza, Ben J., Jr. ... Jackson, MS
Piazza, Carl F. ... Las Vegas, NV
Piazza, Carl F., & Associates, Ltd.
Las Vegas, NV
Piazza, D'Addario & Frumin ... Brooklyn, NY
Piazza, Deborah J. ... New York, NY
Piazza, Debra ... Denver, CO
Piazza, Donna J. ... Minneapolis, MN
Piazza, Edward F. ... New Haven, CT
Piazza, Ethna M.S. ... San Diego, CA
Piazza, Eugene J. ... Medford, OR
Piazza, Eugene, Jr. ... Hingham, MA
Piazza, Frank ... Naples, FL
Piazza, George C. ... Houston, TX
Piazza, Harold D., Jr. ... New York, NY
Piazza, James P. ... Des Moines, IA
Piazza, Jeffrey A. ... Jamestown, NY
Piazza, Leonard J. ... Las Cruces, NM
Piazza, Mark S. ... Staten Island, NY
Piazza, Mark T. ... Warsaw, IN
Piazza, Michael A. ... Dallas, TX
Piazza, Michael D. ... Naples, FL
Piazza, Michael G. ... Gulfport, MS
Piazza, Nickolas ... Berwick, PA
Piazza, Pascal Paul ... Houston, TX
Piazza, Paul ... Sudbury, MA
Piazza, Peter R. ... New York, NY
Piazza & Pickel ... Greenwich, CT
Hartford, CT
Norwalk, CT
Stamford, CT
Piazza, Robert A. ... Elyria, OH
Piazza, S. Joseph ... Orlando, FL
Piazza, Salvatore ... Brooklyn, NY
Piazza, Samuel P. ... Baltimore, MD
Piazza, Vincent J. ... Boca Raton, FL
Piazza, Vincent J. ... Baltimore, MD
Piazza-Ryan, Rita ... Garden City, NY
Piazzolla, Mario ... Brooklyn, NY
Pibel, E. Douglas, Jr. ... Monroe, WA
Pibel & Marston ... Monroe, WA
Pibl, Roman C. ... Salisbury, NC
Pic, Zane M. ... Greeley, CO
Pica, Derek A. ... Boise, ID
Pica, Diane M. ... Madison, WI
Pica, John A., Jr. ... Baltimore, MD
Pica, Mary Rose ... Troy, OH

Pica, Nicholas R. ... Albuquerque, NM
Pica & Olson LLP ... Albuquerque, NM
Picadio, Anthony P. ... Pittsburgh, PA
Picadio McCall Miller & Norton
Butler, PA
Greensburg, PA
Pittsburgh, PA
Washington, PA
Waynesburg, PA
Picard, B. Donovan ... Washington, DC
Picard, Barbara Smith ... Richmond, VA
Picard, Clifford J. ... Beverly Hills, CA
Picard, Daniel C. ... Lapwai, ID
Picard, Daniel J. ... Middletown, OH
Picard, Donald S. ... Herndon, VA
Picard, Irving H. ... New York, NY
Picard, James D. ... Madison, WI
Picard, John A. ... Saginaw, MI
Picard, Matthew ... Mineola, NY
Picard, Nancy ... Metairie, LA
Picard, Raymond V. ... Fall River, MA
Picard, Roberta A. ... Seattle, WA
Picard, Tyron D. ... Lafayette, LA
Picard, Valerie C. ... New York, NY
Picardi, Ferdinand L. ... Syracuse, NY
Picardi, Kenneth E. ... Pottstown, PA
Picardi, Mariano H. ... Little Falls, NJ
Picardi, Matthew J. ... Syracuse, NY
Picardi, Ralph G. ... Boston, MA
Picardi, Steven J. ... Denver, CO
Picardo, Beth Mattler ... Seattle, WA
Picardo, Raul S. ... San Francisco, CA
Picarello, Anthony R., Jr.
Washington, DC
Picarello, Robert A. ... Fort Wayne, IN
Picariello, John ... New York, NY
Picariello, Pasquale ... Philadelphia, PA
Picariello, Salvatore ... Irvine, CA
Picariello, Suzanne Sierra ... Morristown, NJ
Picascia, Stacy T. ... Garden Grove, CA
Picazio, Carl A. ... Somerville, NJ
Picazio, Kim L. ... Miami, FL
Picazio, Mark J. ... Florham Park, NJ
Picca, Dominic J. ... New York, NY
Picca, Victoria R. ... New York, NY
Piccard, Mary M. ... Tallahassee, FL
Piccarreta, Carl A. ... Tucson, AZ
Piccarreta & Davis, P.C. ... Tucson, AZ
Piccarreta, Michael L. ... Tucson, AZ
Piccarreto, Louis J. ... Rochester, NY
Piccerilli, Albert L. ... Philadelphia, PA
Picchi, Blaise ... Fort Lauderdale, FL
Picchi, Blaise, P.A. ... Fort Lauderdale, FL
Picchi, David J. ... San Rafael, CA
Picchi, Joseph S. ... Walnut Creek, CA
Picciano, Constance Lee ... Sacramento, CA
Picciano, Dante J. ... Washington, DC
Picciano, James R. ... Deepwater, NJ
Picciano, John F. ... Garden City, NY
Picciano, Rosemary ... Mineola, NY
New York, NY
Picciano, William P. ... Hauppauge, NY
Piccin & Glynn ... Gainesville, FL
Inverness, FL
Leesburg, FL
Ocala, FL
Piccin, John H. ... Ocala, FL
Piccini, Alfredo ... Coral Gables, FL
Piccini, Juliette ... Department of Justice, Antitrust Division, GV
Piccininni, Dominick A., Jr. ... Merrick, NY
Piccininni, Nicholas R. ... New York, NY
Piccininni, Patrick J. ... Columbus, OH
Piccioli, Thomas C. ... St. Louis, MO
Picciolo, Warren A. ... Harrisonburg, VA
Piccione, Anthony M. ... New York, NY
Piccione, Brenda Sibille ... Lafayette, LA
Piccione, James Kirk ... Lafayette, LA
Piccione, John A. ... Waltham, MA
Piccione, John J. ... Wheaton, IL
Piccione, Joseph J.
Department Of Health And Human Services, GV
Piccione, Joseph James ... Lafayette, LA
Piccione, Keeley & Associates, Ltd.
Wheaton, IL
Piccione, Michael C. ... Lafayette, LA
Piccione, Peter C., Jr. ... Lafayette, LA
Piccione, Peter C., Jr., P.C. ... Lafayette, LA
Piccione & Piccione, L.L.P. ... Lafayette, LA
Piccione, Thomas M. ... New Castle, PA
Piccionelli, Gregory A. ... Los Angeles, CA
Piccioni, Lou ... Cheyenne, WY
Picciotti, Anthony L. V. ... Berwyn, PA
Picciotti, Dean ... Downingtown, PA
Picciotti, Joseph D. ... Rochester, NY
Picciotti, Romulus A. ... Pittsburgh, PA
Picciotto, John A. ... Owings Mills, MD
Piccirilli, Dawn M. ... Boston, MA
Piccirilli, Dominic ... Tucson, AZ
Piccirilli, Gerald L. ... Tucson, AZ
Piccirilli, Gregory P. ... Cranston, RI
Piccirilli, Vincent J. ... Cranston, RI
Piccirillo, Antonio N. ... New York, NY
Piccirillo, Charles S. ... Madison, WV
Piccirillo, Danielle ... New York, NY
Piccirillo, Francis C. ... Hudson, OH
Piccirillo, Joan L. ... Valley Stream, NY
Piccirillo, Mark J. ... Valley Stream, NY
Piccirillo, Michael R. ... Youngstown, OH
Picco, Gregory L. ... Santa Monica, CA
Picco Herbert Kennedy, A Professional Corporation ... Trenton, NJ
Picco & Presley ... Santa Monica, CA
Picco, Steven A. ... Sacramento, CA
Picco, Steven J. ... Princeton, NJ
Piccola, Jeffrey E. ... Harrisburg, PA
Piccola, Stephen ... Glendale, CA
Piccoli, Marie A. ... Simsbury, CT
Piccoli, Russell ... Phoenix, AZ
Piccoli, Russell, Ltd. ... Phoenix, AZ
Piccolo, David M. ... West Palm Beach, FL
Piccolo, David M., P.A., Law Offices
West Palm Beach, FL
Piccolo, Frank A. ... Woodland Hills, CA
Piccolo, Frank A. ... New Orleans, LA
Piccolo, Gerard A. ... Grand Island, NE
Piccolo, Joseph G.
Department of Commerce, Patent and Trademark Office, GV
Piccolo, Lisa J. ... Jersey City, NJ
Piccolo, Michael J. ... Spokane, WA
Piccolo, Rick A. ... Miami, FL
Piccolo, V. Brian ... Honolulu, HI
Piccone, Arthur L. ... Wilkes-Barre, PA
Piccone, Irene ... Northville, MI
Piccone, James M. ... Denver, CO
Piccone, Marsha M. ... Denver, CO
Picconi, John S. ... Hershey, PA
Piccony, Gary G. ... Aurora, IL
Piccotti, Carolyn M. ... Department of Justice, Executive Office for Immigration Review, GV
Piccus, Todd Olen ... El Segundo, CA
Picetti, Gary M. ... Hayward, CA
Picetti, Lawrence P. ... Oakland, CA
Picha, George J. ... Rockford, IL
Picha & Salisbury ... Rockford, IL
Pichan, Barbara T. ... Detroit, MI
Pichardo, Mario A. ... Los Angeles, CA
Piché, Dianne Marie ... Washington, DC
Piché, Gregory Russell ... Denver, CO
Piche, Peter E. ... New York, NY
Picheca, Anthony F., Jr. ... Far Hills, NJ
Pichel, Michael J. ... Ithaca, NY
Picheny, Richard L. ... Palo Alto, CA
Picher, Robt. L. ... Winooski, VT
Picher, Thomas C. ... Boston, MA
Pichette, George J. ... Owosso, MI
Pichette, Richard ... Danvers, MA
Pichichero, Mark Lawrence ... Pacifica, CA
Pichini, Roberta D. ... Philadelphia, PA
Pichon, Emily E. ... Fort Wayne, IN
Pichon, John N., Jr. ... Fort Wayne, IN
Pichon, Larry E. ... Lake Charles, LA
Pichot, Cindee ... Noble, OK
Pichowicz, Michael R. ... Harrison, NJ
Picillo Caruso, A Professional Corporation
West Orange, NJ
Picillo, Joseph Ives ... West Orange, NJ
Picillo, Martin G. ... West Orange, NJ
Picillo, Natalee A. ... Iselin, NJ
Picillo, S. John ... New Brunswick, NJ
Picini, Richard D. ... Newark, NJ
Picinich & McClure ... Hackensack, NJ
Picinich, Ronald J. ... Hackensack, NJ
Picione, Anthony A. ... Trenton, NJ
Piciucco, Marirose ... San Francisco, CA
Pick, Alan B. ... Los Angeles, CA
Pick, Bernard J. ... Malibu, CA
Pick & Boydston, LLP ... Los Angeles, CA
Pick, Daniel E. ... Albuquerque, NM
Pick, David ... Beverly Hills, CA
Pick, David, Law Corporation
Beverly Hills, CA
Pick, Dennis A. ... Houston, TX
Pick, Douglas J. ... New York, NY
Pick, Kay L. ... Chicago, IL
Pick, Lenard I. ... Santa Monica, CA
Pick, Lisa D. ... Troy, MI
Pick, Mark Laurence ... Los Angeles, CA
Pick, Randall J. ... Taylor, TX
Pick, Steven D. ... Chicago, IL
Pick, T. Daniel ... New Orleans, LA
Pickard, Andrew D., II ... San Antonio, TX
Pickard, Berniece R. ... Memphis, TN
Pickard, Carol Hill ... San Jose, CA
Pickard, Carolyn Anne ... Miami, FL
Pickard, Carolyn Anne, P.A. ... Miami, FL
Pickard, Dana T. ... Palm Beach, FL
Pickard, Daniel B.
Department Of Veterans Affairs, Board of Veterans Appeals, GV
Pickard and Djinis LLP ... Washington, DC
Pickard, Florence T. ... Los Angeles, CA
Pickard, Fred ... Birmingham, AL
Pickard, Gregory L. ... Boston, MA
Pickard, Hardy O. ... Bartow, FL
Pickard, Howard B. ... Germantown, TN
Pickard, Jeffrey W. ... Chicago, IL
Pickard & Jenkins ... Torrington, CT
Pickard, Joe ... Denver, CO
Pickard, John W. ... Torrington, CT
Pickard, Joseph C. ... New York, NY
Pickard, Kenneth C. ... Coupeville, WA
Pickard, Lamar L. ... Hazlehurst, MS
Pickard, Lee A. ... Washington, DC
Pickard, Lynn ... Santa Fe, NM
Pickard, Marcie J. ... Chicago, IL
Pickard, Mary A. ... Mineola, NY
Pickard, Mary K. ... Atlanta, GA
Pickard, Orren Taylor, Jr. ... Kingsport, TN
Pickard, Randall S., (P.C.) ... Tulsa, OK
Pickard, Richard R. ... Campbell, CA
Pickard, Robert F. ... Providence, RI
Pickard, Stephen R. ... Alexandria, VA
Pickard, Stephen R., P.C. ... Alexandria, VA
Pickard, Terry R. ... Syracuse, NY
Pickard, Timothy P. ... Adrian, MI
Pickard, Todd S. ... New York, NY
Pickard & Waters, P.C. ... Denver, CO
Pickarski, Karen Anne ... St. Paul, MN
Pickart, Gail P. ... Corona Del Mar, CA
Pickart, Joseph A. ... Milwaukee, WI
Pickel, Alan Scott ... Stamford, CT
Pickel, Mary Lynn ... Houston, TX
Pickel, Robert G. ... New York, NY
Pickell, Brian S. ... Troy, MI
Pickell, Ervin B.
Environmental Protection Agency, Office of Enforcement and Compliance Assurance, GV
Pickell, J. Slocum ... Pine Bluff, AR
Pickell, James B. ... Los Angeles, CA
Pickell, Robert J. ... Newport Beach, CA
Riverside, CA
Pickell, Robert J., A Law Corporation
Newport Beach, CA
Riverside, CA
Pickell, R. W. ... Salem, OR
Pickell, Timothy V. ... Westwood, KS
Pickelman, Matthew R. ... Dallas, TX
Pickelner, Daniel B. ... Bellaire, TX
Pickelner, Joel M. ... Moab, UT
Pickels, John C. ... Alexandria, LA
Pickels, Robert L. ... Monticello, FL
Pickels, Stephanie A. ... Dallas, TX
Picken, Cyrus S., Jr. ... Lanham, MD
Picken, Gregory C.
North Palm Beach, FL
Picken, Mary E. ... Dublin, OH
Picken, R. David ... London, OH
Pickens, Ace ... Austin, TX
Pickens, Andrew L. ... Houston, TX
Pickens, Andrew T. ... St. Louis, MO
Pickens, Barnes & Abernathy
Cedar Rapids, IA
Pickens, Barry L. ... Kansas City, MO
Pickens, Bruce Andrew, Jr. ... Charlotte, NC
Pickens, David W. ... Cochranton, PA
Pickens, Deborah A. ... Birmingham, AL
Pickens, Dwain D. ... Scottsdale, AZ
Pickens, Henry B. ... Denver, CO
Pickens, James F. ... Cedar Rapids, IA
Pickens, Jeffery A. ... Lincoln, NE
Pickens, Joe H. ... Palatka, FL
Pickens, Kenneth W. ... Omaha, NE
Pickens, Kenneth W., P.C. ... Omaha, NE
Pickens, Kirby K. ... Little Rock, AR
Pickens, Larry Duane ... Chicago, IL
Pickens, Linda McKnight ... Enid, OK
Pickens, Lynn E. ... Baltimore, MD
Pickens, Mark A. ... Birmingham, AL
Pickens, Mary Jane Valentine
Charleston, WV
Pickens, Richard W. ... Enid, OK
Pickens, Robert J. ... Houston, TX
Pickens, S. Kevin ... Seattle, WA
Pickens, Sandra-Mae ... Carson City, NV
Pickens, Scott E. ... Washington, DC
Pickens, Scott E. ... Chicago, IL
Pickens, Steven A. ... Lawrenceville, GA
Pickens, Thomas H., Jr. ... Houston, TX
Picker, Bennett G. ... Philadelphia, PA
Picker, Christine A. ... Chicago, IL
Picker, Colin Benjamin ... Washington, DC
Picker, David B. ... Philadelphia, PA
Picker, David J. ... Norristown, PA
Picker, David P. ... Albany, NY
Picker, Harold F. ... Tucson, AZ
Picker, Jane M. ... Cleveland, OH
Picker, Jeffrey T. ... Tallahassee, FL
Picker & Leibowitz ... Norristown, PA
Picker, Leonard I. ... New York, NY
Picker, Marc ... Reno, NV
Picker, Randal C. ... Chicago, IL
Picker, Robert K., Jr. ... Atlanta, GA
Picker, Sidney I., Jr. ... Cleveland, OH
Picker, Todd Andrew ... Irvine, CA
Pickeral, David E. ... McLean, VA
Pickerell, Loretta ... Wilsonville, OR
Pickering, Benjamin E. ... Dallas, TX
Pickering, C. Russell ... Atlanta, GA
Pickering, Charles W., Sr. ... Hattiesburg, MS
Pickering, Christopher F.
Kansas City, MO
Pickering, Cotogno & Dunn
New Orleans, LA
Pickering, David F. ... Fort Worth, TX
Pickering, Gretchen Anderson
Philadelphia, PA
Pickering, Hardy E., Jr. ... Atlanta, GA
Pickering, Harold K. ... Los Altos, CA
Pickering, Harry E. ... Huron, OH
Pickering, James H., Jr. ... Noblesville, IN
Pickering, James H., Jr.
Cape May Court House, NJ
Pickering, Jason W. H. ... Philadelphia, PA
Pickering, Jerrald K. ... Fresno, CA
Pickering, Jerrald K. ... Redding, CA
Pickering, John D. ... Birmingham, AL
Pickering, John H. ... Washington, DC
Pickering, Joseph M. ... Bangor, ME
Pickering, Judith M. ... Southfield, MI
Pickering, Kathleen Ann ... Fort Collins, CO
Pickering, Kathryn J. ... Houston, TX
Pickering, Kenneth C. ... Boston, MA
Pickering, Kenneth E. ... New Orleans, LA
Pickering Law Corporation ... Redding, CA
Pickering Law Firm, The, P.C.
Fort Collins, CO
Cheyenne, WY
Pickering, Leonard L. ... Lubbock, TX
Pickering, Linda ... Roseland, NJ
Pickering, Margaret S. ... Department of State, Office of the Legal Adviser, GV
Pickering, Mark C. ... San Francisco, CA
Pickering, Mark L. ... Carlsbad, NM
Pickering, Mark R. ... Beaumont, TX
Houston, TX
Pickering, Mary Kristina ... Las Vegas, NV
Reno, NV
Pickering, Michael L. ... Redding, CA
Pickering, Michael R. ... Houston, TX
Pickering, Michael T. ... Springfield, TN
Pickering, Millard C. ... Oklahoma City, OK
Pickering, Robert G. ... Fort Collins, CO
Cheyenne, WY
Pickering, Steven Lee ... San Francisco, CA
Pickering, Timothy Scott ... Little Rock, AR
Pickering, Wayne ... McAllen, TX
Pickering, Wayne, P.C. ... McAllen, TX
Pickering, William C. ... Milwaukee, WI
Pickering, William H. ... Chattanooga, TN
Pickersgill, Dianne S. ... Washington, DC
Pickerstein, Harold James ... Hartford, CT
Southport, CT
Pickert, Alan M. ... Jacksonville, FL
Pickert, Lisa Lloyd ... Panama City, FL
Pickert, Paul C. ... Palo Alto, CA
Pickert, Stephen W. ... Orlando, FL
Picket, David L. ... New York, NY
Picket, Geoffrey P. ... New York, NY
Pickett, A. Dean ... Flagstaff, AZ
Pickett, Albert M. ... Augusta, GA
Pickett, Andrew C. ... Boston, MA
Pickett, Angela R. ... Los Angeles, CA
Pickett, Arthur C. ... Boston, MA
Pickett, Barbara B. ... Mount Kisco, NY
Pickett, Bradford ... Liberty, TX
Pickett, C. Robert ... Auburndale, FL
Pickett, Carl N. ... Liberty, TX
Pickett, Charles J. ... Waterloo, IA
Pickett, Charles L., Jr.
West Palm Beach, FL
Pickett, Charles L., Jr.
West Palm Beach, FL
Pickett, Cynthia C. ... Mobile, AL
Pickett, D. Lyndell ... Treasury Department, Internal Revenue Service, GV
Pickett, David E. ... Dallas, TX
Pickett, David S. ... Simsbury, CT
Pickett, Donald A. ... West Palm Beach, FL
Pickett, Donn P. ... San Francisco, CA
Pickett, Douglas G. ... Portland, OR
Pickett & Dow, LLP ... Kennewick, WA
Pickett, Edward B. ... Liberty, TX
Pickett, Elizabeth A. ... Many, LA
Pickett, Francine S. ... Staten Island, NY
Pickett, Francis J., Jr. ... Riverside, RI
Pickett, Fremont O. ... Shoals, IN
Pickett, Garth E. ... San Jose, CA
Pickett, George A. ... Plattsburg, MO
Pickett, George, Jr. ... Jackson, MS
Pickett, Hal F. ... San Antonio, TX
Pickett, J. Michael ... Washington, DC
Pickett, J. Randolph ... Portland, OR
Pickett, J. Randolph, P.C. ... Portland, OR
Pickett, Jack C. ... Pascagoula, MS
Pickett, James D. ... Chicago, IL
Pickett, James R. ... Laguna Beach, CA
Pickett, Jeffrey S. ... Houston, TX
Pickett, John D. ... San Diego, CA
Pickett, John J. ... Albany, NY
Pickett, John M. ... Washington, DC
Pickett, John M. ... Texarkana, TX
Pickett, John W. ... Many, LA
Pickett, John W. ... Boston, MA
Pickett, Judith ... Boston, MA
Pickett, Karen A. ... Boston, MA
Pickett and Kober ... Waterloo, IA
Pickett, Lawrence M. ... Las Cruces, NM
Pickett, Leslie Dean ... Houston, TX
Pickett, Leslie S. ... Savannah, GA
Pickett, Mark ... Las Cruces, NM
Pickett, Mark L. ... Albany, GA
Pickett, Martha C. "Marty" ... Aspen, CO
Pickett, Michael R. ... Kennewick, WA
Pickett, Michelle E. ... Portland, OR
Pickett, Michelle L. ... Santa Barbara, CA
Pickett & Miyares ... Boston, MA
Pickett & Murphy ... Las Cruces, NM
Pickett, Norman N. ... Houston, TX
Pickett, Patrick M. ... Columbus, OH
Pickett & Pickett ... Liberty, TX
Pickett, Pickett & Pickett ... Jasper, GA
Pickett, R. Wayne ... Concord, NC
Pickett & Raynes ... Trenton, MO
Pickett, Richard C. ... Columbus, OH
Pickett, Richard F. ... Cheyenne, WY
Pickett, Russell N. ... Trenton, MO
Pickett, Sean William ... Kansas City, MO
Pickett, Sharon Baker ... Athens, GA
Pickett, Stanley S. ... Chevy Chase, MD
Greenbelt, MD
Hyattsville, MD
Potomac, MD
Pickett, Stanley Sinclair ... Greenbelt, MD
Pickett, Stephanie Wright ... Seattle, WA
Pickett, Stephen E. ... Rosemead, CA
Pickett, Therence O. ... Greensboro, NC
Pickett, Thomas O. ... Trenton, MO
Pickett, W. Hays ... Jasper, GA
Pickett, Walter M., Jr. ... Litchfield, CT
Pickett, Will H., Jr. ... Jasper, GA
Pickett, William D. ... Fairfax, VA
Pickett, William D. ... Yakima, WA
Pickett, William H. ... Kansas City, MO
Pickford & Barkley ... Charlottesville, VA
Pickford, Carey C. ... Temecula, CA
Pickford, Thomas M. ... Houston, TX
Pickford, William G. ... Charlottesville, VA
Pickhardt, Walter A. ... Minneapolis, MN
Pickholtz, Andrew ... San Francisco, CA
Pickholz, Jason ... New York, NY
Pickholz, Joyce Merrick
Securities and Exchange Commission, Division of Investment Management, GV
Pickholz, Marvin G. ... New York, NY
Pickhover & Gehman ... Attleboro, MA
Pickhover, Lyn A. ... Mansfield, MA
Picking, Jay H. ... Long Beach, CA

Pickle, Anne .... Jasper, TX
Pickle, Cecyl L. .... Miami, FL
Pickle, David .... Washington, DC
Pickle, G. Edward .... Houston, TX
Pickle, Jerry R. .... Temple, TX
Pickle, L. Scott .... Kosciusko, MS
Pickle, Robert Douglas .... St. Louis, MO
Pickler, Harold T. .... Wichita, KS
Pickler, Richard M. .... Ulysses, KS
Pickles, Timothy F. .... Cocoa, FL
Picklesimer, Max D. .... Lexington, KY
Louisville, KY
Pickman-Thoon, Rennika Hom
San Rafael, CA
Picknally, Carmen W., Jr. .... Springfield, MA
Picknally, Ernest F. .... Westmont, NJ
Pickner, James H. .... Hawarden, IA
Pickner, Theresa A. .... Boulder, CO
Pickney, Donald J. .... Metairie, LA
Pickover, Glen Howard .... Troy, MI
Pickrel, John S. .... Dayton, OH
Pickrel, Patricia A. .... Princeton, NJ
Pickrel, Schaeffer & Ebeling
Beavercreek, OH
Dayton, OH
Lebanon, OH
Middletown, OH
Springboro, OH
Troy, OH
Xenia, OH
Pickrel, Timothy R. .... Cincinnati, OH
Pickrell, Charles Mark .... Nashville, TN
Pickrell, Christopher L. .... Seattle, WA
Pickrell, Greg L. .... Palo Alto, CA
Pickrell, James M. .... Norfolk, VA
Pickrell, James M., Jr. .... Norfolk, VA
Pickrell, Jane Cetlin .... Boston, MA
Pickrell, Juliana Holway .... Bellevue, WA
Pickrell, Maryellen Sullivan .... Nashville, TN
Pickrell, Thomas W. .... Phoenix, AZ
Pickren, Gary A. .... Columbia, SC
Pickren, Jack L. .... Houston, TX
Pickren, William Terry .... Atlanta, GA
Pickron, M. Celeste .... Atlanta, GA
Pickslay, Peter H. .... La Mesa, CA
Pickup, James A. .... Washington, DC
Pickus, Albert P. .... Cleveland, OH
Pickus, Bob .... Berkeley, CA
Pickus, Evan N. .... New Brunswick, NJ
Pickus and Landsberg .... New Brunswick, NJ
Pickus, Miriam I. .... Chicago, IL
Pickus, Philip B. .... New York, NY
Pickwell, Timothy A. (IBA) .... San Diego, CA
Pickwick, George S. .... Bronxville, NY
Pickworth, Donald A. .... Naples, FL
Pickworth, Donald A., P.A. .... Naples, FL
Pic'l, Dean R. .... Covina, CA
Picl, Frank M. .... Peoria, IL
Picó, Alberto .... San Juan, PR
Picó, Alberto J., Jr. .... San Juan, PR
Pico, Deborah L. .... Fair Lawn, NJ
Pico, Francis Leland .... Cheyenne, WY
Picó, Guillermo R. .... San Juan, PR
Pico, James F. .... Las Vegas, NV
Pico, Javier F. .... Boston, MA
Pico, John J. .... Youngstown, OH
Pico, Juliette Galicia .... Boston, MA
Pico, Kristen A. .... San Francisco, CA
Picó, Maria Emilia .... San Juan, PR
Pico, Martin .... Miami, FL
Pico & Mitchell .... Las Vegas, NV
Reno, NV
Pico, Steven A. .... Chicago, IL
Pico, Timothy A. .... Los Angeles, CA
Pico, Tristan R. .... Glendora, CA
Picon, David A. .... New York, NY
Picone & Defilippis, A Prof. Law Corp.
San Jose, CA
Picone, Jill S. .... Sacramento, CA
Picone, John V., III .... San Jose, CA
Picone, Joseph C. .... Peekskill, NY
Picone, Joseph C., P.C. .... Peekskill, NY
Picone, Lawrence E. .... Los Angeles, CA
Picone, Samuel B. .... Los Angeles, CA
Picone, Stephen S. .... San Jose, CA
Picot, Christopher T. .... Alexandria, VA
Picot, Grissel C. .... Miami, FL
Picot, Pierre .... Forest Hills, NY
Picott, Allison E. .... Boston, MA
Picotte, Gene A. .... Helena, MT
Picotte, Peter J., II .... Philadelphia, PA
Picotte, Susan Carroll .... Albany, NY
Picou, Curtis R. .... Belleville, IL
St. Louis, MO
Picou, Cynthia B. .... St. Francisville, LA
Picou, J. Daniel .... Metairie, LA
Picou, Leon A. .... St. Francisville, LA
Picou, Robert L., Jr. .... Houma, LA
Picou, Vicki .... Baton Rouge, LA
Picozzi, James M. .... Irvine, CA
Picquet, Roger .... San Luis Obispo, CA
Picton, Kenneth Clark .... Rutland, VT
Pictor, Henry A. .... Batesville, IN
Picucci, John J. .... New York, NY
Piculell, Gene .... Bellevue, WA
Pidala, Joseph P. .... Bedford, OH
Pidala & Pidala .... Bedford, OH
Pidala, Sherry A. .... Bedford, OH
Pidcock, Andrew L. .... Denver, CO
Pidcock, Robert L. .... Albuquerque, NM
Pidcock, William S. .... Canton, OH
Piddoubny, Peter .... Astoria, NY
Pidduck, Carol Newell .... Seattle, WA
Pidgeon, James M. .... Bloomfield Hills, MI
Pidgeon, John C. .... Newark, NJ
Pidgeon, John R. .... Princeton, NJ
Pidgeon, Julia Caroff .... Detroit, MI
Pidgeon, Kathryn A. .... Phoenix, AZ
Pidgeon, Lawrence M. .... Salem, MA
Pidgeon, Mary Ann Kenny .... Princeton, NJ
Pidgeon & Pidgeon, P.C. .... Princeton, NJ
Pidgeon, Steven D. .... Phoenix, AZ
Pidgeon, Tina M. .... Washington, DC
Pidgeon, William Joseph, Jr .... Waltham, MA
Pidgeon, William S. .... Reading, MA
Pidgirsky, Andrew .... Dallas, TX
Pidlak, Rebecca L. .... Hartford, CT
Pidot, Jeffrey R. .... Augusta, ME
Pidot, Whitney D. .... New York, NY
Pidoux, Rae Fallon .... Los Angeles, CA
Pié, Maureen F. .... Philadelphia, PA
Pié, Pierre B., II .... Philadelphia, PA
Pie, Susan Schmidt .... Philadelphia, PA
Piecewicz, Walter M. .... Chicago, IL
Piech, David A. .... Chicago, IL
Piech, Hanna T. .... Chicago, IL
Piech, Kenneth S. .... New York, NY
Piech, Melanie M. .... San Francisco, CA
Piechota, David M. .... Milford, CT
Piechta, Leon B. .... West Orange, NJ
Piechura, Lori L. .... Miami, FL
Pieck, Manfred .... Omaha, NE
Piecuch, Michael F. J. .... Philadelphia, PA
Piecuch, Stacey J. .... Philadelphia, PA
Piecuch, Stanley W. .... Augusta, ME
Piecuch, Stephen A. .... Los Angeles, CA
Pieczonka, James P. .... Chicago, IL
Pieczynski, Linda S. .... Hinsdale, IL
Piedade, Anne M. .... Greenwich, CT
Piedalue, Daniel A. .... Missoula, MT
Piedalue Law Offices, P.C. .... Missoula, MT
Piedfort, Pascual L. .... Austin, TX
Piedfort, Pascual L., P.C. .... Austin, TX
Piedimonte & Associates, A Professional Corporation .... Independence, MO
Piedimonte, James R. .... Independence, MO
Piedimonte, William A. .... Independence, MO
Piedimonte, William A., P.C.
Independence, MO
Piedimonte, William D.
Independence, MO
Piediscalzi, Nicholas J. .... San Francisco, CA
Piediscalzz, Terry A. .... Madison, WI
Piedmont Associated Consultants
Greenville, SC
Piedmont Legal Associates, P.A.
Mocksville, NC
Piedmont, Richard S. .... Albany, NY
Piedra, David A. .... New York, NY
Piedra, Emil .... Bronx, NY
Piedra, Jorge L. .... Hollywood, FL
Piedra & Miller .... Hollywood, FL
Piedra, Ricardo H. .... Hollywood, FL
Piedrahita, Athena B. .... Baton Rouge, LA
Piedrahita, Randolph A.
Baton Rouge, LA
Piedrahita, Sandro F. .... Los Angeles, CA
Piedrahita-Sicard, Patricia .... Sanford, FL
Piefer, Sally A. .... Waukesha, WI
Piegore, John J. .... Chicago, IL
Piehler, Arthur E. .... Seattle, WA
Piehler, David A. .... Wausau, WI
Piehler & Strande, S.C. .... Wausau, WI
Piekara, Thomas P. .... White Plains, NY
Piekarski, Thaddeus F. .... Yonkers, NY
Piekarski, Victor J. .... Chicago, IL
Piekarski, Vincent A. .... Honolulu, HI
Piekarski, Virginia A. .... Winston-Salem, NC
Piekarsky, Scott B. .... Wayne, NJ
Piekarz, Michael A. .... Citrus Heights, CA
Pieksen, John O., Jr. .... New Orleans, LA
Pieku, Kenneth E. .... Chicago, IL
Piel, Andrew B. .... Fort Worth, TX
Piel, Anna Evans .... Arlington, TX
Piel, Eleanor Jackson .... New York, NY
Piel, Gregory A. .... Denver, CO
Piel, Karen L. .... Wausau, WI
Piel, Loren A. .... Las Vegas, NV
Piel, Peter .... North Andover, MA
Piel, Walter A., Jr. .... Milwaukee, WI
Piela, Andrew .... Manchester, NH
Pielemeier, James R. .... St. Paul, MN
Pielke, Emil B. .... Baltimore, MD
Piell, Hilda Harris .... Chicago, IL
Piell, Jeffrey S. .... Chicago, IL
Piell, Joel L. .... Detroit, MI
Piels, Barry Y. .... Fairfield, CT
Piels, William B. .... San Francisco, CA
Pielsticker, J. W. .... Tulsa, OK
Piemont, Jeffrey L. .... New York, NY
Piemonte, George C. .... Charlotte, NC
Piemonte Law Office .... Syracuse, NY
Piemonte, Salvatore J. .... Syracuse, NY
Pieniek, Tobias .... New York, NY
Pieniek, Tobias, P.C. .... New York, NY
Pienknagura, Jose M. .... Indianapolis, IN
Pienkny, Seymour .... Babylon, NY
Pienkos, John T. .... Milwaukee, WI
Pienkos, Thomas J. .... Milwaukee, WI
Pieno, Larry C. .... Marrero, LA
Piepenbrink, Gary L. .... San Diego, CA
Piepenburg, Marianne B. .... Dallas, TX
Piepenburg, Matthew R. .... Miami, FL
Pieper & Anderson .... Stoughton, WI
Pieper, Bryan E. .... Nashville, TN
Pieper, Carl G. .... Stoughton, WI
Pieper, Daniel F. .... North Charleston, SC
Pieper, Darold D. .... Los Angeles, CA
Pieper, David B. .... Nashville, TN
Pieper, Gabrielle P. .... Chicago, IL
Pieper, Gregg A. .... Fairfield, IA
Pieper Hoban & Royce, P.C. .... Mineola, NY
Pieper, J. Gardiner .... Mineola, NY
Pieper, James J. .... Raritan, NJ
Pieper, James S. .... Omaha, NE
Pieper, Joel G. .... Atlanta, GA
Pieper, John N. .... Oakbrook Terrace, IL
Pieper, Mark A. .... Omaha, NE
Pieper, Michael E. .... Wayne, NE
Pieper, Nathaniel G. W.
Cape Canaveral, FL
Tampa, FL
Pieper, Paul B. .... Arlington, VA
Pieper, Roland L. .... Milwaukee, WI
Pieper, Thomas C. .... Matawan, NJ
Pieper, Timothy R. .... Wellington, OH
Pieper, Troy G. .... Uniondale, NY
Piepes, Eric J. .... Rego Park, NY
Piepho, John R. .... St. Louis, MO
Piepho, Scott R. .... Canton, OH
Piepkorn, Timothy L. .... Minneapolis, MN
Pieples, Gary J. .... Cincinnati, OH
Pieplow, Kathryn W. .... Sioux Falls, SD
Pieplow, Kathryn W., P.C. .... Sioux Falls, SD
Pieplow, Richard A. .... Lancaster, OH
Piepmeier, Mark E. .... Cincinnati, OH
Pieprz, William .... Reston, VA
Piepszak, Richard J. .... Trenton, NJ
Piepul, Joseph M. .... New York, NY
Pier, John T. .... Bloomfield, CT
Pier, Kinchen C., III .... Fort Worth, TX
Pier, Richard F. .... St. Louis, MO
Pier, Steven L. .... Yankton, SD
Pier, Tamara M. .... Rapid City, SD
Pier, William S. .... Palo Alto, CA
Pieragostini, Anthony J.
Mount Kisco, NY
Pierangeli, David M. .... Grand Rapids, MI
Pierantoni, Fred A., III .... Pittston, PA
Pieras, Jaime, Jr. .... San Juan, PR
Pieratt, Anita R. .... Huntington Beach, CA
Pieratt, Robert S. .... Houston, TX
Pierce, A. Robert, Jr. .... Detroit, MI
Pierce, Aaron M. .... Syracuse, NY
Pierce, A. C. .... Orange, CA
Pierce, Alan J. .... Syracuse, NY
Pierce, Alan K. .... New York, NY
Pierce, Alan S. .... Salem, MA
Pierce, Alfred R. .... Camden, NJ
Pierce, Alfred S. .... Nazareth, PA
Pierce, Allen S. .... Chicago, IL
Pierce, Allin H. .... Martinez, CA
Pierce, Andrew F. .... Palo Alto, CA
Pierce, Andrew R. .... Atlanta, GA
Pierce, Anne .... Ventura, CA
Pierce, Anne Cole .... Franklin, MI
Pierce, Anthony T. .... Washington, DC
Pierce, Archie Carl .... Austin, TX
Pierce, Arthur R. .... Chicago, IL
Pierce & Associates .... Chicago, IL
Pierce Atwood .... Augusta, ME
Portland, ME
Newburyport, MA
Pierce, B. Dean .... Columbia, SC
Pierce, Barry W. C. .... Dover, DE
Pierce, Ben. .... Augusta, GA
Pierce, Bradley D. .... Los Angeles, CA
Pierce, Bradley D. .... St. Louis, MO
Pierce, Brenda J. .... Mobile, AL
Pierce, Brian D. .... Marietta, GA
Pierce, Brian M. .... Akron, OH
Pierce, Bryan C. .... Louisville, KY
Pierce, C. Fenning .... Coshocton, OH
Pierce, Cameron S. .... Atlanta, GA
Pierce, Carl .... Beverly, MA
Pierce, Carl Arthur .... Knoxville, TN
Pierce, Carl Everette, II .... Charleston, SC
Pierce, Carl H. .... Philadelphia, PA
Pierce, Catherine L. .... Irvine, CA
Pierce, Charles A. .... Belleville, IL
Pierce, Charles R. .... Huntington Station, NY
Pierce, Charles R., Jr. .... New York, NY
Pierce, Chris W. .... Albuquerque, NM
Pierce, Christina J. .... Costa Mesa, CA
Pierce, Christopher P. .... Baton Rouge, LA
Pierce, Clay J. .... New York, NY
Pierce, Clifford D., Jr. .... Memphis, TN
Pierce, Clifford M. .... Boston, MA
Pierce, Constance E. .... Youngstown, OH
Pierce, Corey L. .... Dallas, TX
Pierce Couch Hendrickson Baysinger & Green, L.L.P. .... Oklahoma City, OK
Tulsa, OK
Pierce, Craig F. .... Bushnell, IL
Pierce, Daley, Baffes, O'Sullivan & Mussar
Chicago, IL
Pierce, Daniel J. .... Chicago, IL
Pierce, Daniel J. .... Bingham Farms, MI
Pierce, Daniel K. .... Brownsville, TX
Pierce, Daniel M. .... Chicago, IL
Pierce, Daniel R. .... Boston, MA
Pierce, Darell R. .... Bowling Green, KY
Pierce, Darrel E. .... Placerville, CA
Pierce, Darrell W. .... Chicago, IL
Pierce, David A. .... Beverly Hills, CA
Pierce, David A. .... Neosho, MO
Pierce, David Benjamin .... Baltimore, MD
Pierce, David C. .... Los Angeles, CA
Pierce, David E. .... Topeka, KS
Pierce, David H. .... Ventura, CA
Pierce, David J. .... Norfolk, VA
Pierce, David K. .... Muskogee, OK
Pierce, David L. .... San Marino, CA
Pierce, David M. .... Los Angeles, CA
Pierce, David M. .... Perry, GA
Pierce, David N. .... Salt Lake City, UT
Pierce, David P. .... Dayton, OH
Pierce, David R. .... Westfield, NJ
Pierce, David R. .... El Paso, TX
Pierce, Davis, Fahey & Perritano, LLP
Boston, MA
Pierce, Deborah A. .... Vauxhall, NJ
Pierce, Debra H. .... Fort Pierce, FL
Pierce, Debra Stachowski .... St. Louis, MO
Pierce, Delana S. .... Covington, KY
Pierce, Delila F. .... Minneapolis, MN
Pierce, Denis B. .... Chicago, IL
Pierce, Denise Nance .... Austin, TX
Pierce, Don, P.C. .... St. Joseph, MO
Pierce, Donald A., Jr. .... Troy, MI
Pierce, Donald F. .... Mobile, AL
Pierce, Donald J. .... Huntington Beach, CA
Pierce, Donald M., A Professional Law Corporation .... New Orleans, LA
Pierce, Donna L. .... Sewanee, TN
Pierce, Douglas F. .... Austin, TX
Pierce, Douglas R. .... San Diego, CA
Nashville, TN
Pierce, Douglas W. .... Eugene, OR
Pierce, Dudley W. .... Wisconsin Rapids, WI
Pierce Duke Mengel .... Bloomfield Hills, MI
Pierce, Edward J. .... Los Angeles, CA
Pierce, Edwin A. .... St. Marys, OH
Pierce, Edwin C. .... Akron, OH
Pierce, Edwin R., Jr. .... Alexandria, VA
Pierce, Eliot N. .... San Diego, CA
Pierce, Elizabeth M. .... Minneapolis, MN
Pierce, Ellen Gean .... Fort Smith, AR
Pierce, Ellen Lewis .... Anaheim, CA
Pierce, Elmer B. .... Wheaton, IL
Pierce, Emily G. .... Jacksonville, FL
Pierce, Eugene H., Jr. .... Columbus, OH
Pierce, Francis D. .... Sun City, AZ
Pierce, Francis E., III .... Orlando, FL
Pierce, Francis E., Jr. .... Orlando, FL
Pierce, Frank P. .... San Antonio, TX
Pierce, Franklin A. .... Auburn, MA
Pierce, Franklin H. .... Augusta, GA
Pierce, G. Carter .... Warrington, PA
Pierce, Gary D.E. .... Salt Lake City, UT
Pierce, George A. .... New York, NY
Pierce, George H. .... Alachua, FL
Pierce, Gerald W. .... Fort Myers, FL
Pierce, Ginger L. .... Mobile, AL
Pierce, Glenda J. .... Lincoln, NE
Pierce • Gorman .... Beverly Hills, CA
Los Angeles, CA
Pierce, Greg .... Austin, TX
Pierce, Gregory P. L. .... Chicago, IL
Pierce, H. Cynthia .... Tulsa, OK
Pierce and Hahn .... Ann Arbor, MI
Pierce, Hal .... Overland Park, KS
Kansas City, MO
Pierce, Harold W. .... Portland, OR
Pierce, Harry A. .... Boston, MA
Pierce, Hart B., Jr. .... Palmyra, NY
Pierce & Havas .... Harrisburg, PA
Hershey, PA
Pierce, Herbert I., III .... Billings, MT
Pierce, Hinton R. .... Augusta, GA
Pierce & Howard .... Richmond, VA
Pierce, Howard L. .... Hartford, CT
Pierce & Hughes .... Broomall, PA
Pierce, Hyrum O., Jr. .... Conyers, GA
Pierce, Irwin A. .... Denver, CO
Pierce, J. Brian .... Chicago, IL
Pierce, J. Michael .... Boston, MA
Pierce, J. Scott .... Montgomery, AL
Pierce, J. Wayne .... Atlanta, GA
Pierce, J. William, Jr. .... Memphis, TN
Pierce, Jack .... Nacogdoches, TX
Pierce, Jack E. .... Minneapolis, MN
Pierce, Jack W. .... Tallahassee, FL
Pierce, Jacqueline M., Law Offices of
Monterey, CA
Pierce, James A. .... Proctorville, OH
Pierce, James B. .... Fort Smith, AR
Pierce, James B. .... Long Beach, CA
Pierce, James D. .... Houston, TX
Pierce, James J. .... Lanoka Harbor, NJ
Pierce, James L. .... Mount Shasta, CA
Pierce, James Michael .... Wayne, PA
Pierce, James R. .... Gainesville, FL
Pierce, James R. .... Cincinnati, OH
Pierce, James V. .... St. Petersburg, FL
Pierce, James W., Jr. .... Baton Rouge, LA
Pierce, Jan R. .... Portland, OR
Pierce, Janice .... Austin, TX
Pierce, Jason Rupert .... Scottsboro, AL
Pierce, Jean William .... Washington, GA
Pierce, Jean William, P.C. .... Washington, GA
Pierce, Jesse R. .... Houston, TX
Pierce, JoAnne Aylward .... Boston, MA
Pierce, Jody L. .... Orange, CA
Pierce, Joel F. .... Boston, MA
Pierce, John A. .... Oakland, CA
Pierce, John A. .... Savannah, GA
Pierce, John A. .... Hamilton, OH
Pierce, John A., P.C. .... Savannah, GA
Pierce, John C. .... New York, NY
Pierce, John Charles S. .... Mobile, AL
Pierce, John D. .... Boston, MA
Pierce, John E. .... San Jose, CA
Pierce, John E. .... Danville, IN
Pierce, John G. .... Orlando, FL
Pierce, John H. .... Seattle, WA
Pierce, John L., II .... Navasota, TX
Pierce, John M. .... Annville, PA
Pierce, John P. .... San Diego, CA
Pierce, John P. .... Philadelphia, PA
Pierce, John R. .... Richmond, CA
Pierce, John R. .... Cambridge, MA
Pierce, John R. .... Salem, OR
Pierce, John S. .... San Francisco, CA
Pierce, Jonathan .... Houston, TX
Pierce, Jonathan M. .... New Orleans, LA
Pierce, Jonyson Allen .... Irvine, CA
Pierce, Joseph Aaron .... Palo Alto, CA
Pierce, Joseph B. .... Phoenix, AZ
Pierce, Joseph G. .... Tuscaloosa, AL
Pierce, Joseph K. .... Harrisburg, PA
Pierce, Jotham D., Jr. .... Portland, ME

Pietrandrea, Peter J., II
Cranberry Township, PA
Pietrangelo, Anthony Charles ... Memphis, TN
Pietrangelo, Michael A. ... Memphis, TN
Pietrangelo, Wendy D. ... Rocky River, OH
Pietrangelo, William A. ... Media, PA
Pietrantone, Mark J. ... Austin, TX
Pietrantoni, Julio ... San Juan, PR
Pietrantoni, Manuel R. ... San Juan, PR
Pietrantoni Méndez & Alvarez, LLP
San Juan, PR
Pietrantonio, Frank ... Washington, DC
Pietrantonio, Jacqueline
Port Washington, NY
Pietras, J. Scott ... Garfield Heights, OH
Pietras, James G. ... Mount Laurel, NJ
Pietras, Judith Ellen ... Wilbraham, MA
Pietrasz, Margaret A. ... San Mateo, CA
Pietraszkiewicz, Robert A. ... Warren, MI
Pietrek, Wendy L. ... Los Angeles, CA
Pietrick, Steven G. ... Chicago, IL
Pietrini, Jill M. ... Los Angeles, CA
Pietrkowski, Henry ... Chicago, IL
Pietro, Frank W., II ... Dover, OH
Pietro, Gino P. ... Costa Mesa, CA
Pietrobono, Rex M. ... Coral Gables, FL
Mount Kisco, NY
Pietrofeso, Richard J.
Department of Justice, Tax Division, GV
Pietroforte, Gerald D. ... New York, NY
Pietropaoli, Patrick J. ... Rochester, NY
Pietropaoli, Paul D. ... Portland, ME
Pietropaolo, Vincent P. ... Washington, DC
Pietrosimone, Frank W., Jr. ... Hamden, CT
Pietroski, David A. ... Warren, MI
Pietrovito, Guy R.
General Accounting Office,
Office of the General Counsel, GV
Pietrowicz, Richard R.
Department Of Health And Human Services,
Social Security Administration, GV
Pietrowski, Edward F. V. ... Scranton, PA
Pietrowski, Moira H. ... Akron, OH
Pietrowski, R. Scott ... Jackson, TN
Pietrowski, Robert F., Jr.
Washington, DC
Pietrusiak, Stanley, Jr. ... San Antonio, TX
Pietrusinski, Mark A. ... Kittanning, PA
Pietruska, Stanley R. ... Jersey City, NJ
Pietruszka, Michael F. ... Buffalo, NY
Pietruszkiewicz, Christopher M.
Department of Justice,
Tax Division, GV
Pietryga, Terry E. ... Farmington Hills, MI
Pietrykowski, Mark L. ... Toledo, OH
Pietrykowski, Michael J.
San Francisco, CA
Pietrykowski, Robert J. ... Mentor, OH
Pietrykowski, William F.
Port Clinton, OH
Pietrzak, A. Robert ... New York, NY
Pietrzyk, George ... Park Ridge, IL
Pietrzyk, Joseph W. ... Chicago, IL
Pietsch & Cuchna ... Wheaton, IL
Pietsch, Jay A. ... Fort Worth, TX
Pietsch, Leigh R. ... Wheaton, IL
Pietsch, Matthew V. ... Kahului, HI
Pietschmann, Candace ... Cary, IL
Piette Law Firm, S.C. ... Brookfield, WI
Milwaukee, WI
Piette, Mary R. (Molly) ... Savannah, GA
Piette, Michael A. ... Buffalo, NY
Piette, Robert M. ... Brookfield, WI
Piette, Ronald L. ... Brookfield, WI
Piette, Susan E. ... Urbana, IL
Piette, Thomas A. ... Brookfield, WI
Piety, Christopher G. ... Westlake Village, CA
Piety, Margaret E. ... Indianapolis, IN
Piety, Philip A. ... Des Arc, AR
Pietz, Colin D. ... Wausau, WI
Pietz, James M. ... Pittsburgh, PA
Pietz, James T. ... Independence, MO
Pietz, Lynne P. ... Dayton, OH
Pietz, Nancy L. ... Clive, IA
Pietz, William R. ... Indianapolis, IN
Pietzsch, Michael E. ... Phoenix, AZ
Pifer, Dean David ... Germantown, TN
Pifer, George L. ... Truckee, CA
Pifer, Karen R. ... Bloomfield Hills, MI
Pifer, Matthew E.C. ... Burlington, VT
Piff, Linda L. ... Wall, NJ
Piffat, Kathryn A. ... Danvers, MA
Pifher, Mark T. ... Denver, CO
Pifher, Wendy J. ... Colorado Springs, CO
Pifko, Michael J. ... Jackson, NJ
Piga, Stephen M. ... New York, NY
Pigato, Joseph R. ... Chicago Heights, IL
Pigeaud, Martine ... Irvine, CA
Pigeon, G. Steven ... Buffalo, NY
Pigeon, Joann R. ... Dallas, TX
Pigeon, Sharon M. B. ... Kansas City, MO
Pigford, Howard R. ... Meridian, MS
Pigford, Thomas H. ... Memphis, TN
Pigford, Walter S. ... Beaumont, TX
Pigg, Alan W. ... Tyler, TX
Pigg, Gail P. ... Nashville, TN
Pigg, Harold H. ... Lubbock, TX
Pigg, J. Steven ... Topeka, KS
Pigg, James F. ... Glen Allen, VA
Pigg, Sammie E., Jr. ... Lexington, KY
Pigg, Sharon Sutton ... Silverton, TX
Piggins, John T. ... Grand Rapids, MI
Piggitts, Cameron H. ... Detroit, MI
Piggott, Gary J. ... Flint, MI
Piggott, Gary J., P.C. ... Flint, MI
Piggott, George B. ... Irvine, CA
Piggott, George B., A Prof. Corp., Law Offices of ... Irvine, CA

Piggott, John W. ... Bay City, MI
Piggott, L. Patrick ... Stockton, CA
Piggott, Philip G. ... Birmingham, AL
Piggush, James R. ... Lansing, MI
Piggush, Nancy Arends ... Lansing, MI
Piglia, Marynell L. ... New Orleans, LA
Pigman, Edwin P. ... Euclid, OH
Pigman, Gary H. ... Hayden Lake, ID
Pigman, George W., Jr. ... New Orleans, LA
Pigman, Heather A. ... Tampa, FL
Pigman, Jack R. ... Columbus, OH
Pigman, Paul O. H., (P.C.)
New Orleans, LA
Pignataro, Fiore J. ... Seattle, WA
Pignatelia, Michael A. ... Shelton, CT
Pignatella and Kern ... New Britain, CT
Pignatella, Michael A. ... Hartford, CT
Pignatella, Ralph C. ... New Britain, CT
Pignatelli, Francis M. ... Akron, OH
Pignatelli, Louis F. ... Rock Falls, IL
Pignatelli, Michael A. ... Concord, NH
Nashua, NH
Pignatello, Elizabeth F. ... Washington, DC
Pignatiello, Richard A. ... Seven Hills, OH
Pignato, A. Alexander ... Westbury, NY
Pignato, Gerard F. ... Oklahoma City, OK
Pignato, Michael K. ... San Francisco, CA
Pignone, Mike ... Manassas, VA
Pignotti, Jill A. ... Chicago, IL
Pignuolo, Charles J. ... Houston, TX
Pigorsh, Mary Rachel ... Grand Rapids, MI
Pigott, Charles F. ... Chicago, IL
Pigott, Charles M. ... Lake Park, FL
Pigott, David R. ... Newport Beach, CA
Pigott, Eugene F., Jr. ... Buffalo, NY
Pigott, James E. ... Syracuse, NY
Pigott, James R. ... Foley, AL
Pigott, Jane DiRenzo ... Chicago, IL
Pigott, Joe N. ... Mc Comb, MS
Pigott, John T. ... Los Angeles, CA
Pigott, Kevin T. ... New York, NY
Pigott, Richard J. ... Chicago, IL
Pigott, Stephen E. ... Cleveland, OH
Pigsley, Jerry L. ... Lincoln, NE
Pigsley, Mary Jude ... Boston, MA
Pigue, William C. ... Hermitage, TN
Pigue, Wm. Ritchie ... Nashville, TN
Pih, Jerri Hoi ... La Canada Flintridge, CA
Pihart, Mark A. ... Davenport, IA
Pihl, Holger M., Jr. ... Hillsboro, OR
Pihlstrom, Gary D. ... Woodbury, MN
Pihlstrom, Kimberly K. ... St. Paul, MN
Pihlstrom, Mark D. ... Washington, DC
Piibe, Alary Endel ... Santa Monica, CA
Piibe, Anne-Marie P. ... Los Angeles, CA
Piibe, Mark A. ... New York, NY
Piilola, Mariel E. ... Minneapolis, MN
Piirimae, Karl F. ... Philadelphia, PA
Pijls, Hans H. J. ... Detroit, MI
Pijoan, G. Nicholas ... Denver, CO
Pijor, David W. ... Fairfax, VA
Pijut, Terry L. ... St. Louis, MO
Pikala, James S. ... Minneapolis, MN
Pikarski, Maureen C. ... Chicago, IL
Pikarski, Thomas Michael ... Chicago, IL
Pikcunas, Charles R. ... Kalamazoo, MI
Pike, Andrew D. ... Washington, DC
Pike, Anne M. ... Houston, TX
Pike & Bliss ... North Little Rock, AR
Pike, Burlyn ... Shepherdsville, KY
Pike, C. Ashley ... Lisbon, OH
Pike, Carl W. ... New York, NY
Pike, Cathy S. ... Louisville, KY
Pike, Chan Poyner ... La Jolla, CA
Pike, Charles R. ... Great Bend, KS
Pike, Charles W. ... Denver, CO
Pike, Dale E. ... Great Bend, KS
Pike, David A. ... Frankfort, KY
Frankfort, KY
Shepherdsville, KY
Pike, David F. ... Waukesha, WI
Pike, David M. ... Palo Alto, CA
Pike, Dixon P. ... Portland, ME
Pike, Donald W. ... Los Angeles, CA
Pike, Donna Meek ... Gainesville, FL
Pike, Donna Meek, P.A. ... Gainesville, FL
Pike, Douglas R. ... Las Vegas, NV
Pike & Draskovich ... Las Vegas, NV
Pike, Ed ... North Weymouth, MA
Pike, Edward W. ... Idaho Falls, ID
Pike, Emil F., Jr. ... Twin Falls, ID
Pike, Emil F., Jr., P.A. ... Twin Falls, ID
Pike, Evelyn ... Irvine, CA
Pike, Fred D. ... Lenoir, NC
Pike, Frederic ... Framingham, MA
Pike, Gary E. ... San Diego, CA
Pike, Geoffrey R. ... Houston, TX
Pike, George E., Jr.
North Little Rock, AR
Pike, George H., III ... Pittsburgh, PA
Pike, Gerald L. ... Lacey, WA
Pike, Gregg A. ... Frederick, MD
Pike, Gregory D. ... Oakland, CA
Pike, Helene C. ... Dedham, MA
Pike, J. William ... Crownsville, MD
Pike, James C., Jr.
North Myrtle Beach, SC
Pike, James H. ... Dothan, AL
Pike, James M. ... Waterford, MI
Pike, Jay N. ... Tampa, FL
Pike, John A. ... Boston, MA
Pike, John B. ... Erie, PA
Pike, John G. ... Wichita, KS
Pike, John H. ... Oxford, NC
Pike, Joseph P. ... Louisville, KY
Pike, Julia M. ... Louisville, KY
Pike, Kenneth L. ... Banning, CA
Pike, Kenneth R. ... Medford, NJ

Pike, Kim Purcell ... Atlanta, GA
Pike, Larry S. ... Atlanta, GA
Pike, Laurence B. ... Brattleboro, VT
Pike Legal Group ... Frankfort, KY
Shepherdsville, KY
Pike, Linda ... Moscow, ID
Pike, Losson G. ... Ashland, KS
Pike, Malane S. ... Columbia, SC
Pike, Mark W. ... Glendale, CA
Pike, Mary Boresz ... Brooklyn, NY
Pike, Mary Carolyn ... Washington, DC
Pike, N. Neal ... Salisbury, MA
Pike, Nelson E. ... Gates Mills, OH
Pike, Patrick M. ... Baltimore, MD
Pike, Paul H. ... Dover, NH
Laconia, NH
Wolfeboro, NH
Pike, Peter J. ... Bellmore, NY
Pike & Pike ... Bellmore, NY
Pike, Randall H. ... Las Vegas, NV
Pike, Robert B. ... Moscow, ID
Pike, Robert D. ... Riverhead, NY
Pike, Robert K. ... Grand Rapids, MI
Pike, Robert L. ... Irvine, CA
Pike, Robert S., Jr. ... Santa Ana, CA
Pike, Robert W. ... Santa Barbara, CA
Pike, Robert W. ... Northbrook, IL
Pike, Roberta Cohen ... Bellmore, NY
Pike, Roy W. ... Pascagoula, MS
Pike, Russell R. ... El Cajon, CA
Pike, Russell W. ... Portland, OR
Pike & Schmidt Law Office, P.S.C.
Shepherdsville, KY
Pike & Shurtliff, A Professional Association
Boise, ID
Idaho Falls, ID
Pike, Stacy K. ... Chicago, IL
Pike, Stephen E. ... Wailuku, HI
Pike, Stephen L. ... Boston, MA
Pike, Stephen M. ... Oklahoma City, OK
Pike, Therese A. ... Delray Beach, FL
Pike, Therese A., P.A. ... Boca Raton, FL
Delray Beach, FL
Pike, Timothy J. ... Milwaukee, WI
Pike, William B. ... Cuyahoga Falls, OH
Pike, William G., Jr. ... Atlanta, GA
Pike, William R. ... Atlanta, GA
Pike-Bokhari, Paulita A. ... Chicago, IL
Pikel, Howard J. ... Chicago, IL
Pikel, Patricia J. ... Fort Wayne, IN
Pike-Masteralexis, Lisa L. ... Amherst, MA
Piken, Gerald ... North Miami Beach, FL
Piken, Gerald, Law Offices, P.A.
North Miami Beach, FL
Piken, Marilyn D. ... New York, NY
Piken, Robert W. ... New York, NY
Piker, Edward P., Jr. ... San Antonio, TX
Piker, James L. ... Baton Rouge, LA
Pikkarainen, A. John ... Howell, MI
Pikl, James A. ... McKinney, TX
Pikl, James A., P.C. ... McKinney, TX
Piklor, Nicholas S. ... Ann Arbor, MI
Pikna, Raymond J., Jr. ... Dayton, OH
Pikoff, Andrew S. ... Houston, TX
Pikoff, Nelson & Riff, L.L.P. ... Houston, TX
Pikofsky, Seymour ... Milwaukee, WI
Pikor, Richard E. ... Rocky Hill, CT
Pikowsky, Harry ... Chicago, IL
Pikrallidas, Charles E. ... Alexandria, VA
Pikrallidas, Demetrios C. ... Fairfax, VA
Pikrallidas, Susan Gustafson
Washington, DC
Pikser, Meredith P. ... New York, NY
Pikul, David Joseph ... Fayetteville, NC
Pikula, Edward M. ... Springfield, MA
Pikulski, Diana ... Barre, VT
Waitsfield, VT
Pikus, David H. ... Florham Park, NJ
New York, NY
Pikus, Irwin M.
Department of Commerce, GV
Pikus, James X. ... Cleveland, OH
Pikus, Kelly ... New York, NY
Pil, Kristin A. ... Dearborn, MI
Pilacek, Thomas J. ... Maitland, FL
Pilachowski, Patrick M. ... Baltimore, MD
Pilafian, James ... Key Biscayne, FL
Pilafian, Nerisa Gay ... Tampa, FL
Pilalis, Labros E. ... Harrisburg, PA
Piland, Bruce A. ... Sacramento, CA
Piland, Deborah Dech ... Reston, VA
Piland, E. Mark ... Colorado City, TX
Piland, John C. ... Urbana, IL
Piland, Steven G. ... Kansas City, MO
Pilant, David L. ... Houston, TX
Pilant, Jeannie L. ... Richmond, VA
Pilant, Tanya K. ... Houston, TX
Pilarska, Halina ... Philadelphia, PA
Pilarski, John H. ... Milwaukee, WI
Pilarski, John L. ... Fort Myers, FL
Pilarz, Michael ... Buffalo, NY
Pilat, George V. ... Cleveland, OH
Pilat, William R. ... Houston, TX
Pilate, Cheryl A. ... Kansas City, MO
Pilati, August A. ... Chicago, IL
Pilato, Joseph C. ... Rochester, NY
Pilato, Louis P. ... Rochester, NY
Pilato & Pilato ... Rochester, NY
Pilato, Samuel C. ... Rochester, NY
Pilatsky, Judith ... Syosset, NY
Pilawa, Dennis M. ... Cleveland, OH
Pilawski, Eugene W. ... Long Grove, IL
Pilch, Caroline A. ... Phoenix, AZ
Pilch, Frederic H., III ... Atlanta, GA
Pilch, Gennady ... Washington, DC
Pilch, Howard D. ... Los Angeles, CA
Pilch, Richard J. ... Stockton, NJ
Pilchak, Lynn B. ... Monrovia, CA

Pilchak, William E. ... Detroit, MI
Farmington Hills, MI
Pilchard, Jeffrey A. ... Ocean City, MD
Pilchen, Saul M. ... Washington, DC
Pilcher, Alan F. ... Gainesville, GA
Pilcher, Gary L. ... Naples, FL
Pilcher, Gregory F. ... Oklahoma City, OK
Pilcher, James B. ... Atlanta, GA
Pilcher, James B., P.C. ... Atlanta, GA
Pilcher, John C. ... Mount Dora, FL
Pilcher, John E. ... Selma, AL
Pilcher, John H. ... Washington, DC
Pilcher, John J., II ... Wrens, GA
Pilcher, Lawrence C. ... Rocky Hill, CT
Pilcher, Mary E. ... Pensacola, FL
Pilcher, Matthew B., IV ... Sewanee, TN
Pilcher, Paul S. ... Hanover, NH
Pilcher & Pilcher, P.C. ... Selma, AL
Pilcher, Roger D. ... St. Louis, MO
Pilcher, Stephen R. ... San Antonio, TX
Pilcher, Susan L. ... South Pasadena, CA
Pilcher, Toby C. ... Chicago, IL
Pilcher, Walter Todd ... Washington, DC
Pilchowski, Thomas S., (P.C.)
Los Angeles, CA
Pilcowitz, Robert ... Southfield, MI
Pildes, Michael E. ... Chicago, IL
Pildes, Richard H. ... Ann Arbor, MI
Pile, Robert J. ... Atlanta, GA
Pile, Roscoe ... Lakewood, CO
Pile, Ruel B. ... Washington, DC
Pileckas, Joseph J. ... Rome, NY
Pileckas, Paul L. ... Rome, NY
Pileckas, Paul L. ... Utica, NY
Pilecki, Elizabeth M. ... New York, NY
Pilecki, Paul S., (P.C.) ... Washington, DC
Pilegard, Cris A. ... Fresno, CA
Pileggi, Daniel A. ... Bangor, ME
Pileggi, Dominic F. ... Woodlyn, PA
Pileggi, Francis G., Sr. ... Woodlyn, PA
Pileggi, Francis G. X. ... Wilmington, DE
Pileggi, James J. ... Mc Keesport, PA
Pileggi, Patricia A. ... Brooklyn, NY
Pileggi, Pileggi & Pileggi ... Woodlyn, PA
Pileggi, William G. ... Chicago, IL
Pilelsky, Ellen B. ... Fort Lauderdale, FL
Piles, Juan J. ... Miami, FL
Piles, Juan J., P.A. ... Miami, FL
Piletich, Urosh ... Stillwater, MN
Pilewski, Steven A. ... Brooklyn, NY
Pilger, Carlton C. ... Atlanta, GA
Pilger, Donald M. ... San Diego, CA
Pilger, Karl W. ... Vienna, VA
Pilger, Richard C. ... Department of Justice,
Criminal Division, GV
Pilgram, William M. ... Golden Valley, MN
Pilgreen, Terry C. ... Wichita, KS
Pilgrim, Caleb M., Law Offices of
New Haven, CT
Pilgrim, Carl O. ... Montgomery, AL
Pilgrim, Gail L. ... Philadelphia, PA
Pilgrim, Gary Wayne ... Tulsa, OK
Pilgrim, J. Jerry ... Mobile, AL
Pilgrim, Larry ... Sacramento, CA
Pilgrim, Lily T. ... Washington, DC
Pilgrim, Lois E. ... New York, NY
Pilgrim, Lynda K. ... Little Rock, AR
Pilgrim, Michelle A. ... Washington, DC
Pilgrim, Shirleen M. ... Washington, DC
Pilibosian, Paul ... El Paso, TX
Pilic, Dominka M. ... Ventura, CA
Pilicy, Franklin G. ... Watertown, CT
Pilicy, Robert F. ... Waltham, MA
Pilié, Denise M. ... New Orleans, LA
Pilie, Glen M. ... New Orleans, LA
Pilié, M. Arnaud ... New Orleans, LA
Pilié, Pilié & Landry ... New Orleans, LA
Piliero, Alfred S. ... Forest Hills, NY
Piliero Goldstein Jenkins & Sullivan, LLP
San Francisco, CA
Washington, DC
Carlstadt, NJ
New York, NY
Piliero, Mazza & Pargament, PLLC
Washington, DC
New York, NY
Piliero, Robert D. ... Washington, DC
Carlstadt, NJ
New York, NY
Piliponis, John A. ... Chicago, IL
Pilipshen, Kenneth S. ... Armonk, NY
Pilja, George Daniel ... Chicago, IL
Pilka & Associates, P.A. ... Brandon, FL
Lakeland, FL
Tampa, FL
Pilka, Daniel F. ... Brandon, FL
Pilkenton, Jill I. ... St. Louis, MO
Pilkington, Jeffrey R. ... Denver, CO
Pilkington, John H. ... Las Vegas, NV
Pilkington, Joseph H. ... Toledo, OH
Pilkington, Joseph H., & Co., L.P.A.
Toledo, OH
Pilkington, Kathy L. ... Charlotte, NC
Pilkington, Laura M. ... Seattle, WA
Pilkington-Casey, Mary T. ... Concord, NH
Pilkinton, James H., Jr. ... Hope, AR
Pilkinton, Pilkinton & Yocom ... Hope, AR
Pill, David D. ... Martinsburg, WV
Pill, David M. ... Los Angeles, CA
Pill, Michael ... Shutesbury, MA
Pill & Pill ... Berkeley Springs, WV
Charles Town, WV
Martinsburg, WV
Pill, Richard A. ... Martinsburg, WV
Pilla, Alan C. ... Tuckahoe, NY
Pilla, Kenneth J. ... Baltimore, MD
Pilla, Kenneth J., P.A. ... Baltimore, MD
Pilla, Mary Lee ... Solon, OH

Pillai, James S. .... Carle Place, NY
Pillai, K. G. Jan .... Philadelphia, PA
Pillai, Xavier .... Washington, DC
Pillans, C. Palmer, IV .... Nashville, TN
Pillans, Charles P., III .... Jacksonville, FL
Pillar, John A. .... Pittsburgh, PA
Pillar • Mulroy & Ferber, Professional Corporation .... Pittsburgh, PA
Pillard, Cornelia T. L. .... Washington, DC
Pillari, Thomas .... Mineola, NY
Pillari, Thomas .... Lorain, OH
Pille, Glenn E. .... Des Moines, IA
Pille, Richard H. .... Binghamton, NY
Pillemer, David B. .... Van Nuys, CA
Piller, Donald .... Houston, TX
Piller, Geoffrey .... San Francisco, CA
Piller, Michael C. .... Carol Stream, IL
Piller, Neil E. .... Longmont, CO
Piller, Ruth E. .... Houston, TX
Piller, Susan J. .... Houston, TX
Piller, Susanna S. .... Plattsburgh, NY
Pillers, G. Wylie, III .... Clinton, IA
Pillers, James L. .... Clinton, IA
Pillers, Pillers & Pillers, P.C. .... Clinton, IA
Pillersdorf, Gary B. .... New York, NY
Pillersdorf, Gary B., & Associates, P.C. New York, NY
Pillersdorf, Ned B. .... Prestonsburg, KY
Pillets, Daniel P. .... Wilkes-Barre, PA
Pillette, John .... Washington, DC
Pilley, Mark B. .... Warsaw, MO
Pilli, Dominick A. .... Fairfax, VA
Pilli, Dominick A., P.C. .... Fairfax, VA
Pillick, Aleta M. .... Florence, SC
Pilling, Laurie H. .... Lawrenceville, NJ
Pilling, William S., III .... Philadelphia, PA
Pillinger, James J. .... Bayside, NY
Pillinger, Marc H. .... New York, NY
Pillinger, Terry H. .... Phoenix, AZ
Pillinger, Terry H., P.C. .... Phoenix, AZ
Pilliod, Jane E. .... Baltimore, MD
Pilliod, Mark E. .... Beaverton, OR
Pillion, Kevin P. .... Washington, DC
Pillion, Kieran E., Jr. .... Princeton, NJ
Pillion, Michael L. .... Philadelphia, PA
Pillischer, Eric S. .... Commack, NY
Pillittieri, Peter A. .... Jamestown, NY
Pilloff, Benson Dale .... Cleveland, OH
Pillon, Charles G. .... Rowayton, CT
Pillon, Fred L. .... San Francisco, CA
Pillot, Jonathan .... New York, NY
Pillote, Cynthia .... Phoenix, AZ
Pillote, Robert L. .... Bethesda, MD
Pillote, Robert L., Jr. .... Bethesda, MD
Pillote, Robert L., P.C. .... Bethesda, MD
Pillote, Vernon J. .... Rockford, IL
Pillow, Julie K. .... Covington, TN
Pillow, Michael F. .... Orlando, FL
Pillow, Roger F. .... Washington, DC
Pillow, Rosemary T. .... Baton Rouge, LA
Pillsbury, Andrew P. .... Chicago, IL
Pillsbury, Charles A. .... New Haven, CT
Pillsbury, D. Taylor, Jr. .... San Francisco, CA
Pillsbury, David L. .... Richmond, VA
Pillsbury, Donaldson C. .... New York, NY
Pillsbury, Dorothy A. .... Quincy, MA
Pillsbury, John S., Jr. .... Minneapolis, MN
Pillsbury, L. Harrison .... Washington, DC
Pillsbury, Laurence L. .... La Jolla, CA
Pillsbury & Levinson, LLP San Francisco, CA
Pillsbury, Luci S. .... Nashua, NH
Pillsbury Madison & Sutro LLP Costa Mesa, CA; Los Angeles, CA; Palo Alto, CA; Sacramento, CA; San Diego, CA; San Francisco, CA; Washington, DC; New York, NY; Vienna, VA
Pillsbury, Mark H. .... Dallas, TX
Pillsbury, Philip L., Jr. San Francisco, CA
Pillsbury & Pillsbury .... Nashua, NH
Pillsbury, Rodney F. .... Greenville, SC
Pillsbury, Rodney F., P.A. .... Greenville, SC
Pillsbury, Samuel H. .... Los Angeles, CA
Pillsbury, Wm. T. .... Long Beach, CA
Pilmer & Barnhart .... Yorkville, IL
Pilmer, R. Alexander .... Los Angeles, CA
Pilmer, Robert P. .... Yorkville, IL
Pilney, Mark A. .... St. Paul, MN
Pilnick, Gary H. .... Chicago, IL
Pilo, Barbara .... Dallas, TX
Pilo, Marvin .... Hartford, CT
Pilon, James A. .... Naples, FL
Pilon, Lawrence Joseph, Jr. .... Springfield, MA
Pilon, Lawrence R. .... Chicago, IL
Pilon, Margaret M. .... Falmouth, MA
Pilon, Mark D. .... Duluth, MN
Piloseno, Daniel A. .... Rye, NY
Pilosof, Maurice B. .... Los Angeles, CA
Pilot, Debora E. .... Newark, OH
Pilot, Edward W. .... Beverly Hills, CA
Pilot, Larry R. .... Washington, DC
Pilot, Sidney I. .... Los Angeles, CA
Pilot, Todd A. .... Department of Commerce, Patent and Trademark Office, GV
Piloto, Hilda .... Miami, FL
Pilotte, Frank T., (P.A.) .... Palm Beach, FL; Vero Beach, FL
Pilotte, Michele .... Boston, MA
Pilotti, Eric .... Forest Hills, NY
Pilpel, Heidi E. Securities and Exchange Commission, Division of Market Regulation, GV

Pilsecker, C. Ellen .... San Diego, CA
Pilshaw, Rebecca L. .... Wichita, KS
Pilsk, W. Eric .... Washington, DC
Pilskaln, Harold, Jr. .... Minneapolis, MN
Pilsner, Toby J. .... Bronx, NY
Pilson, Allan S. .... New York, NY
Pilson, Howard C. .... Stuart, VA
Pilson, Jack M. .... Temecula, CA
Pilson, Judith L. .... San Bernardino, CA
Pilson, Neal H. .... New York, NY
Pilson, Robert Michael .... Morton Grove, IL
Piltch, Deborah Reina .... Boston, MA
Piltch, Sanford J. .... Allentown, PA
Piltzer, David S. .... Clark, NJ
Piltzer & Piltzer .... Clark, NJ
Piluso, Charles J. .... Setauket, NY
Pilver, Joan E. .... Hartford, CT
Pilzer, Donald L. .... Greenville, SC
Pilzer, Leonard .... Hauppauge, NY
Pilzner, Antoinette M. .... Detroit, MI
Pimenta, David A. .... Boston, MA
Pimentel, Carlos J., Jr. .... North Bellmore, NY
Pimentel, David T. .... New Orleans, LA
Pimentel, Eligio C. .... Chicago, IL
Pimentel, Frank T. .... Washington, DC
Pimentel, James William Green Cove Springs, FL
Pimentel, Jay D. .... San Leandro, CA
Pimentel, Julio G. .... Chicago, IL
Pimentel, Leonard A. .... Miami, FL
Pimentel, Mario A. .... New Bedford, MA
Pimentel, Paul J. .... Fresno, CA
Pimentel, Philip A. .... Modesto, CA
Pimlott, Mark F. .... Redford, MI
Pimm, Shirley E. .... Cherry Hill, NJ
Pimpinelli, Michael J. .... Woodbury, NJ
Pimstone, Gregory N. .... Los Angeles, CA
Pin, Robert A. .... Park Ridge, NJ
Piña, David Aaron .... Austin, TX
Piña, Edward L. .... San Antonio, TX
Piña, Edward L., P.C. .... San Antonio, TX
Piña, Kenneth R. .... Collegeville, PA
Pina, Mary Ellen Fitzgerald .... Paoli, PA
Piña, Mercy Blasa .... Miami, FL
Pina, Michael A. .... Santa Barbara, CA
Pina, Olga M. .... Tampa, FL
Pina, Ronald A., & Associates New Bedford, MA
Piña, Rosalba .... Franklin Park, IL
Pina, Theodore Samuel, Jr. Jacksonville, FL
Pinaire, Joan T. .... Newark, NJ
Pinaire, Richard A. .... Junction City, KS
Pinal, Randall A. .... Fresno, CA
Pinales, Martin S. .... Cincinnati, OH
Pinamont, Bernadette J .... Mount Laurel, NJ
Pinamont, William J. .... Philadelphia, PA
Pinansky, David M. Federal Deposit Insurance Corporation, GV
Pinansky, William D. .... South Portland, ME
Pinao, Noralynne K. .... Hilo, HI
Pinarchick, Cheryl B. .... Boston, MA
Pinarchick, Scott J. .... Boston, MA
Pinard, Jeanette L. .... Stamford, CT
Pinard, Robert J. .... Trenton, NJ
Pinasco, Debra A. .... Redding, CA
Pinasco, Luana A. .... Elk Grove, CA
Pinaud, Donald E., Jr. .... Jacksonville, FL
Pinault, Rene J. .... South Yarmouth, MA
Pincelli, Frank .... Rochester, NY
Pincelli, John A. .... Columbia, SC
Pincelli & Lang, P.A. .... Columbia, SC
Pinch, David E. .... Woodland Hills, CA
Pinch, Thomas A. .... Bloomfield Hills, MI; Detroit, MI
Pinchak, Ann .... Houston, TX
Pinchak, Frank P. .... Chattanooga, TN
Pinchak, George L., Jr. .... Cleveland, OH
Pinchak, Michael H. .... Tarzana, CA
Pincham, R. Eugene .... Chicago, IL
Pinchas, David E. .... Los Angeles, CA
Pinchbeck, Kimberly A. .... Richmond, VA
Pincher, Mike .... Palmdale, CA
Pinchiaroli, Christopher .... White Plains, NY
Pinchiff, Edward C. .... Long Beach, CA
Pinchoff, Allan M. .... Buffalo, NY
Pinchot, Dov J. .... Chicago, IL
Pinchuk, Leslie .... Los Angeles, CA
Pinchuk, Sheldon .... Woodland Hills, CA
Pinci, Marcantonio .... New York, NY
Pinciaro, David .... New Haven, CT
Pincin, James W. .... Redding, CA
Pinciotti, Cynthia J. .... Detroit, MI
Pinciss, Ann J. .... New York, NY
Pinck, Lawrence R. .... Clifton, NJ
Pinckard, Elizabeth E. .... Denver, CO
Pinckard, Kenneth R. .... Scottsdale, AZ
Pinckard, Richard L. .... San Diego, CA
Pinckert, Eric G. .... Los Angeles, CA
Pinckes, Randi Ellen .... Irvine, CA
Pincket, Brian G. .... Jacksonville, FL
Pincket, Michelle O. .... Lakeland, FL
Pinckney, C. Cotesworth .... Richmond, VA
Pinckney, Charles C. .... Birmingham, AL
Pinckney, Francis M. .... Charlotte, NC
Pinckney, Francis Morris, III Charlotte, NC
Pinckney, Fred J. .... Atlanta, GA
Pinckney, Joanne P. .... Wilmington, DE
Pinckney, John McPherson, III San Antonio, TX
Pinckney, Lynn D. .... Salem, OR
Pinckney, Marc L. .... San Jose, CA
Pinckney, Michael J. .... New York, NY
Pinckney, Obie, Jr. .... Upper Marlboro, MD
Pinckney, Obie, Jr., P.C. Upper Marlboro, MD
Pinckney, Robert P. .... Houston, TX

Pinckney, Ronald R. .... Bremerton, WA
Pinckney, Thomas M., Jr. .... Nashville, TN
Pinckney, Vicki A. .... Lansing, MI
Pinco, Robert G. .... Washington, DC
Pincock, Garth S. .... Pocatello, ID
Pincourt, A. Kenneth, Jr. West Palm Beach, FL
Pincu, Robert L. .... Springfield, NJ
Pincura, John D., III .... Avon Lake, OH
Pincus, Alisa A. .... New York, NY
Pincus, Andrea J. .... New York, NY
Pincus, Andrew .... Roseland, NJ
Pincus, Arthur .... Bethesda, MD
Pincus, & Associates, P.C. .... Tucson, AZ
Pincus, Beth .... Department of Justice, Civil Rights Division, GV
Pincus, Brian P. .... Philadelphia, PA
Pincus, David I. .... Department of Justice, Tax Division, GV
Pincus, Diane .... New Brunswick, NJ
Pincus, Edward K. .... Brooklyn, NY
Pincus, Elkin .... Chicago, IL
Pincus, Elliott N. .... Norristown, PA
Pincus, Erwin L. .... Philadelphia, PA
Pincus, George A. .... Boca Raton, FL
Pincus, Glenn .... Buffalo, NY
Pincus & Gordon .... North Brunswick, NJ
Pincus, Harry, Jr. .... Norfolk, VA
Pincus, I. Meyer .... New York, NY
Pincus, I. Meyer, & Associates, P.C. New York, NY
Pincus, Iris S. .... Philadelphia, PA
Pincus, Jacqueline A. .... Scottsdale, AZ
Pincus, Jane E. .... Phoenix, AZ
Pincus, Jeffrey M. .... Melville, NY
Pincus, Kathryn Ann .... Wilmington, DE
Pincus, Laura B. .... Chicago, IL
Pincus, Mark H. .... Burbank, CA
Pincus, Martin B. .... Middlesex, VT
Pincus, Marvin .... Livingston, NJ
Pincus, Mary C. P. .... Iowa City, IA
Pincus, Michele A. .... Melville, NY
Pincus, Paul H. .... New York, NY
Pincus, Robert .... Cross River, NY
Pincus, Robert B. .... Wilmington, DE
Pincus, Roger W. .... Department of Justice, Office of Intelligence Policy and Review, GV
Pincus, S. Bruce .... San Ramon, CA
Pincus, S. Richard .... Chicago, IL
Pincus, Sheldon H. .... Clifton, NJ
Pincus, Sheryl G. .... Philadelphia, PA
Pincus, Stephen M. .... New Haven, CT
Pincus, Steven H. .... Tucson, AZ
Pincus, Steven M. .... Minneapolis, MN
Pincus, Steven R. .... Syracuse, NY
Pincus, William Hoffman West Palm Beach, FL
Pincus, Wm. .... New York, NY
Pinczewski, Benjamin M. .... Garden City, NY
Pinczewski, Benjamin M., Law Offices of Garden City, NY
Pinczower, Kenneth E. .... New York, NY
Pindar, Patricia J. .... Roseland, NJ
Pindar, Therese Forrester .... Savannah, GA
Pindel, Donna D. .... Winfield, IL
Pindell, Ngai .... Baltimore, MD
Pinder, Edward T. .... Baltimore, MD
Pinder, Jessalyn R. .... Los Angeles, CA
Pinder, Keven K. .... Baltimore, MD
Pinder, Michele D. .... New York, NY
Pinder, Peggy .... Grinnell, IA
Pinder, Susan D. .... Washington, DC
Pinder, Wilma W. .... Los Angeles, CA
Pinderhughes, Alice G. .... Baltimore, MD
Pinderhughes, Alice G., P.A. Baltimore, MD
Pinderski, James A. .... Chicago, IL
Pinderski, Jerome W., Jr. .... Palatine, IL
Pinderski, Paul C. .... Palatine, IL
Pinderski & Pinderski, Ltd. .... Chicago, IL; Palatine, IL
Pinderski, Polly J. .... Palatine, IL
Pindle, Robert A. .... Philadelphia, PA
Pindulic, Robert T. .... Paramus, NJ
Pindyck, Bruce Eben .... Milwaukee, WI
Pindyck, Suzanne .... Huntington, NY
Pine, Alfred M. .... Jersey City, NJ
Pine, Barry Evan .... Manhattan Beach, CA
Pine, Bennett .... New York, NY
Pine, Beverly Tillett .... Los Angeles, CA
Pine, Cathryn R. .... Thousand Oaks, CA
Pine, Charlotte W., (Mrs.) .... Towson, MD
Pine, Clyde A., Jr. .... El Paso, TX
Pine, Daniel H. .... New York, NY
Pine, Dianne F.G. .... Great Neck, NY
Pine, Elizabeth Woodruff .... Rochester, NY
Pine, Francine Jaffe .... Chicago, IL
Pine, Gregory B. .... El Paso, TX
Pine, Jacob .... Brooklyn, NY
Pine, James A. .... Towson, MD
Pine, Jane .... Sunnyvale, CA
Pine, Jeffrey A. .... Evanston, IL
Pine, Jeffrey B. .... Providence, RI
Pine, Jordan R. .... Rock Hill, NY
Pine, Kathleen L. .... Belleville, IL; St. Louis, MO
Pine, Laura Gay .... St. Louis, MO
Pine, Leila C. .... Madison, WI
Pine, Marcia B. .... Los Angeles, CA
Pine, Nancy Worth .... Paoli, PA
Pine, Norman .... Los Angeles, CA
Pine, Norman J. .... Parkesburg, PA
Pine, Norman J., II .... Parkesburg, PA
Pine & Pine .... Los Angeles, CA
Pine and Pine .... Parkesburg, PA
Pine, R. Dean .... Kintnersville, PA
Pine, Robert A. .... Hawthorne, NJ

Pine, Robert M. .... Beverly Hills, CA
Pine, Rosel R. .... Jacksonville, FL
Pine, Selma K. .... Phoenix, AZ
Pine, Shari L. .... New York, NY
Pine, Sheldon L. .... McLean, VA
Pine, V. Ronald .... San Jose, CA
Pine, William L. Department Of Veterans Affairs, Board of Veterans Appeals, GV
Pineau, John Kenneth .... Boulder, CO
Pineau, Maureen A. .... Rochester, NY
Pineau, Robert J. .... Detroit, MI
Pineault, Michael J. .... Boston, MA
Pineda, Andre G. Federal Election Commission, Office of the General Counsel, GV
Pineda, Ernesto .... El Paso, TX
Pineda, Jose .... Dallas, TX
Pineda, Michael S. .... Chattanooga, TN
Pineda, Patricia Salas .... Fremont, CA
Pineda, Robert O. .... Philadelphia, PA
Pineda, Susanna Carballo .... Phoenix, AZ
Pineda, Victor H. .... Oakland, CA
Pineda-Kirwan, Diccia Trinidad Jamaica, NY
Pinedo, Anna T. .... New York, NY
Pinedo, Craig A. .... Walnut Creek, CA
Pinedo, Frank, & Associates .... Houston, TX
Pinedo, James Austin .... Houston, TX
Pinegar, Kevin R. .... Salt Lake City, UT
Pineiro, A. J., Jr. & Associates, P.A. Miami, FL
Pineiro, Andrew A. Palm Beach Gardens, FL
Piñeiro, Héctor E. .... Boston, MA
Pineiro, Michael A. .... New York, NY
Pineiro, Roberto M. .... Miami, FL
Pinel, Robert A. .... Bernardsville, NJ
Pinelli, Anthony .... Chicago, IL
Pinelli, Anthony F. .... San Jose, CA
Pinelli, Michael V. .... Stoneham, MA
Pinelli, Vincent D. .... Chicago, IL
Pinelo, Armando J. .... Springfield, IL
Pineo, Gordon C. .... Virginia, MN
Pineo, Paul, Jr. .... Rochester, NY
Piner, Amy M. .... Bloomfield Hills, MI
Pines, Adam .... Los Angeles, CA
Pines, Allan A. .... New York, NY
Pines, Andrea .... New York, NY
Pines, Burt, (P.C.) .... Los Angeles, CA
Pines, David A., Law Offices of Woodland Hills, CA
Pines, Dennis S. .... Lisle, IL
Pines, Emily .... Medford, NY
Pines, Geoffrey W. .... Miami, FL
Pines, James M. .... Bethesda, MD
Pines, Joseph I. .... Baltimore, MD
Pines, Judi Smith Solon .... Elgin, IL
Pines & Kessler .... Hackensack, NJ; New York, NY
Pines, Lawrence M. .... San Francisco, CA
Pines, Lester A. .... Madison, WI
Pines, Lois G. .... Newton, MA
Pines, Lori L. .... New York, NY
Pines, M. Harvey .... St. Louis, MO
Pines, Michael A. .... La Jolla, CA
Pines, Mitchell .... Hackensack, NJ; New York, NY
Pines, Newcomb B. .... Farmingdale, NY
Pines, Noah Howard .... Decatur, GA
Pines, Ricardo E. .... Coral Gables, FL
Pines, Ricardo E., P.A. .... Coral Gables, FL
Pines, Richard Thomas .... Hoffman Estates, IL
Pines, Spero .... Binghamton, NY
Pines, Zygmont A. .... Philadelphia, PA
Pinet, Robert L. .... Ottawa, KS
Ping, Christine M. .... Sebastopol, CA
Pingatore, Joseph J. .... St. Paul, MN
Pingel, G. Brian .... Des Moines, IA
Pingel, Heidi L. .... Dallas, TX
Pingel, Kimberly Ann .... Jamaica, NY
Pingel, Steven R. .... Seal Beach, CA
Pingel & Templer, P.C. .... Des Moines, IA; West Des Moines, IA
Pingelton, Daniel J. .... Columbia, MO
Pingelton, Daniel J., P.C. .... Columbia, MO
Pingelton, Jerod .... Dumas, TX
Pingenot, David J. .... Toledo, IA
Pingenot, Hilmer C. .... San Antonio, TX
Pingeon, James R. .... Boston, MA
Pingitore, Linda .... Pittsburgh, PA
Pingitore, Peter J. .... Boston, MA
Pingitore, Peter J., P.C., Law Office of Boston, MA
Pingon, Francois E. .... Princeton, NJ
Pingpank, Jeffrey C. .... Hartford, CT
Pingree, Bruce D. .... Dallas, TX
Pingree, Hedley G. .... Goffstown, NH
Pingree, Stephen P. .... Honolulu, HI
Pings, Anne .... Washington, DC
Pinguelo, Fernando M. .... Somerville, NJ
Pinhasik, Annette E. .... Chicago, IL
Pinheiro, Brian Michael .... Philadelphia, PA
Pinheiro, John A. .... Bridgeport, CT
Pinheiro, John F. .... Santa Clara, CA
Pinheiro, Melissa G. .... Philadelphia, PA
Pinheiro-Palmer, Cristina Fort Lauderdale, FL; Miami, FL; West Palm Beach, FL
Pinhey, Edward L. .... Three Rivers, CA
Pinho, John M. .... Harrison, NJ
Pinilis, Russell J. .... New York, NY
Pinilis, William J. .... Livingston, NJ
Pinion, G. Bryan .... Fresno, CA
Pinion, Karla J. .... New York, NY
Pinizzotto, Anthony .... Spring, TX
Pinizzotto, Joseph .... Toms River, NJ

Pinizzotto, Robert J. ... Hammonton, NJ
Pinjuh, Joseph M. ... O'Fallon, IL
Pink, Andrea Sloan ... Irvine, CA
Pink, Bevon Barrington ... New York, NY
Pink, Brian R. ... Orlando, FL
Pink, Clement Bernard ... Houston, TX
Pink, John R. ... Kansas City, MO
Pink, Jonathan S. ... Costa Mesa, CA
Pink, Karen M. ... Evanston, IL
Pink, Michael Howard ... Minneapolis, MN
Pink, Scott W. ... Rocklin, CA
Pinkala, Catherine C. ... Boston, MA
Pinkard, Charles E., Jr. ... Rockmart, GA
Pinkas, Debora L. ... El Cerrito, CA
Pinkasewicz, Michael E. ... Syracuse, NY
Pinkel, Mary B. ... Anchorage, AK
Pinker, Eric W., P.C. ... Dallas, TX
Pinkerman, Connie Redbird
Los Angeles, CA
Pinkernell, Denis R. ... New York, NY
Pinkert, Daniel B. ... Chicago, IL
Pinkert, Dean A. ... Washington, DC
Pinkert, James H. ... Chicago, IL
Pinkert, Jill A. ... St. Cloud, MN
Pinkert, Jon Robert ... Sturgeon Bay, WI
Pinkert, Roger ... Sturgeon Bay, WI
Pinkert, Smith, Weir, Jinkins, Nesbitt, Hauser & Weber ... Algoma, WI
Sister Bay, WI
Sturgeon Bay, WI
Pinkert-Lieb, Karen ... Chicago, IL
Pinkerton, A. Duane ... Portland, OR
Pinkerton, A. Duane, II
Walnut Creek, CA
Pinkerton, Bobby L. ... Healdton, OK
Pinkerton, Brooke A. ... Washington, DC
Rockville, MD
Pinkerton, Bruce D. ... Moses Lake, WA
Pinkerton, C. Frederick ... Reno, NV
Pinkerton, Catherine L. ... McLean, VA
Pinkerton, Cheryl Lee ... Little Rock, AR
Pinkerton, David L. ... Irving, TX
Pinkerton Doppelt & Associates, LLP
Rancho Bernardo, CA
Pinkerton, Drew S., (P.A.)
Fort Walton Beach, FL
Pinkerton, Ernest E. ... Novato, CA
Pinkerton & Finn, P.C. ... Tulsa, OK
Pinkerton and Friedman ... Crown Point, IN
Hammond, IN
Highland, IN
Merrillville, IN
Munster, IN
Pinkerton, Glenn L. ... Houston, TX
Pinkerton, Harlan S. ... Tulsa, OK
Pinkerton, Hulbert B. ... Madison, WI
Pinkerton, James C. ... Tulsa, OK
Pinkerton, Jess A. ... Atlanta, GA
Pinkerton, John C. ... Sarasota, FL
Pinkerton, John P. ... Dallas, TX
Pinkerton, Kirk A. ... Munster, IN
Pinkerton, Kyle A. ... Dickinson, TX
Pinkerton, Laurence L. ... Tulsa, OK
Pinkerton, Linda ... Asheville, NC
Pinkerton, Linda F. ... Asheville, NC
Pinkerton, Margery B. ... Richmond, VA
Pinkerton, Michael H. ... New Orleans, LA
Pinkerton, Michael L. ... Sacramento, CA
Pinkerton and Pinkerton, A Professional Corporation ... Tulsa, OK
Pinkerton, Russell D. ... Indianapolis, IN
Pinkerton, Susan B. ... Oklahoma City, OK
Pinkerton, Thomas M., Jr. ... San Diego, CA
Pinkerton, W. Stewart, Jr. ... New York, NY
Pinkerton, Walter E., Jr.
Rancho Bernardo, CA
Pinkes, Andrew J. ... Hartford, CT
Pinkham, Francis H. ... New York, NY
Pinkham, Margaret M. ... Boston, MA
Pinkham, Nancy Barclay ... Kansas City, MO
Pinkiert, Robert S. ... Hollywood, FL
Pinkley, Patricia Markus ... Raleigh, NC
Pinkley, T. Harold ... Nashville, TN
Pinkner, Jeffrey S. ... Pikesville, MD
Pinkney, A. Drew ... Ann Arbor, MI
Pinkney, Betty K. ... Cleveland, OH
Pinkney, Crystal E. ... Suitland, MD
Pinkney, J. Dominique ... Oakland, CA
Pinkney, John O. ... Rancho Mirage, CA
Pinkney, Padrick A. ... Port St. Lucie, FL
Pinkos, Cynthia ... Los Angeles, CA
Pinkos, Stephen M.
House of Representatives, Committee Legal Personnel, GV
Pinkowitz, David A. ... Montclair, NJ
Pinkowski, Andrew H. ... Hartford, CT
Pinkowski, Brian Jude ... Wheat Ridge, CO
Pinkowski & Flanders ... Washington, DC
Fairfax, VA
Manassas, VA
Tysons Corner, VA
Pinkowski, James E. ... Fairfax, VA
Pinkowski, Michelle A. ... Denver, CO
Pinks, Arbeit, Lewis & Nemeth
Hauppauge, NY
Pinks, Lester R. ... Trenton, MI
Pinks, Steven G. ... Hauppauge, NY
Pinks, Tracy L. ... Chester, IL
Pinkstaff, John C. ... McMinnville, OR
Pinkstaff, K. Ray, Jr. ... Knoxville, TN
Pinkstaff, K. Ray, P.C. ... Knoxville, TN
Pinkstaff, R. Steven ... Chicago, IL
Pinkston, Arnold A. ... Scottsdale, AZ
Pinkston, Calder F. ... Macon, GA
Pinkston and Cohen, P.A. ... Jacksonville, FL
Pinkston, David J. ... Jacksonville, FL
Pinkston, David L. ... Salt Lake City, UT
Pinkston, Donald O. ... New Orleans, LA
Pinkston, Frank C. ... Macon, GA
Pinkston, J. Murray, III ... Chicago, IL
Pinkston, Jean L. ... Oklahoma City, OK
Pinkston, Julian S. ... Jacksonville, FL
Pinkston, Loretta L. ... Atlanta, GA
Pinkston, Mark A. ... Asheville, NC
Pinkston, Nat A. ... Dallas, TX
Pinkston, Patrick D. ... Wetumpka, AL
Pinkston, Reuben C., Jr. ... Bryant, AR
Pinkston, Shannon Evans ... Nashville, TN
Pinkston, Susan G. ... Ridgeland, MS
Pinkston, William E. ... Paducah, KY
Pinkstone, Wayne E. ... Newark, NJ
Pinkus, Barry C. ... Hamden, CT
Pinkus, Craig ... Indianapolis, IN
Pinkus, D. C. ... Chicago, IL
Pinkus, Edward C. ... Boston, MA
Pinkus, Fredric ... Toledo, OH
Pinkus, Gene A. ... Crown Point, IN
Pinkus, I. Marshall ... Indianapolis, IN
Pinkus, Morton ... Congers, NY
Pinkus, Myron A. ... Scranton, PA
Pinkus, Ralph S. ... Philadelphia, PA
Pinkus, Roslyn ... Los Angeles, CA
Pinkusiewicz, Tomer ... New York, NY
Pinkwasser, Alan H. ... Boynton Beach, FL
Pinn, Godfrey T. ... Richmond, VA
Pinn, Jerome D. ... Knoxville, TN
Pinna Johnston & Burwell, P.A.
Raleigh, NC
Research Triangle Park, NC
Pinna, William P. ... Raleigh, NC
Pinnegar, Terry A. ... San Diego, CA
Pinnel, Alison C. ... New York, NY
Pinnell, Joan A. ... Columbia, MO
Pinnell, Julia M. ... Maitland, FL
Pinnell, Kathleen M. ... Wichita, KS
Pinnell, Philip E. ... Tulsa, OK
Pinnell, Robert E. ... Wichita, KS
Pinnell, W. H. ... Monett, MO
Pinneo, John M. ... Santa Clara, CA
Pinner, Alan J. ... San Jose, CA
Pinner, Edward K. ... New Orleans, LA
Pinner, James F. ... New Orleans, LA
Pinnero, Robert J. ... Albany, GA
Pinney, A. Searle ... Danbury, CT
Pinney & Caldwell, A P.C. ... El Centro, CA
Pinney, Charles A., Jr. ... El Centro, CA
Pinney, John B. ... Florence, KY
Cincinnati, OH
Pinney, John S. ... Bloomfield, CT
Pinney, Paul B. ... Oakland, CA
Pinney, Payne, Van Lenten, Burrell, Wolfe & Dillman, P.C. ... Danbury, CT
Pinney, Sidney D., Jr. ... Hartford, CT
Pinney, Thomas M. ... Philadelphia, PA
Pinney, Willard F., Jr. ... Hartford, CT
Pinney, William M., Jr. ... San Francisco, CA
Pinney-Hawkins, Alesia L. ... Seattle, WA
Pinnick, Brooks C. ... Warsaw, IN
Pinnick, Jon M. ... Indianapolis, IN
Pinnie, Anthony F. ... Media, PA
Pinnie, Anthony S. ... Philadelphia, PA
Pinnie, Mark S. ... Media, PA
Pinnisi, Michael D. ... Ithaca, NY
Pinnix, John L. ... Raleigh, NC
Pinnix, Lorita K. ... Raleigh, NC
Pinno, Lawrence P., Jr. ... Bel Air, MD
Pinnock, Blondel A. ... New York, NY
Pinnock, Donald M. ... Albuquerque, NM
Pinnola & Bomstein ... Philadelphia, PA
Pinnola, Peter J. ... Philadelphia, PA
Pinnola, Robert ... Islip, NY
Pinnolis, Barry R. ... Santa Barbara, CA
Pinnolis, Brona E. ... Danvers, MA
Piñon, Michelle ... El Paso, TX
Pinnow, John A. ... Greenwood, IN
Pino & Associates, LLP ... New York, NY
White Plains, NY
Pino, Carmen J. ... Buffalo, NY
Pino, Deborah E. ... Fort Lauderdale, FL
Pino, Haydee C. ... Miami, FL
Pino, Jim ... Pelham, AL
Pino, Jim, & Associates, P.C.
Columbiana, AL
Pelham, AL
Pino, John A. ... Brockton, MA
Pino, Kenneth A. ... Grand Prairie, TX
Pino, L. Kimball ... Attleboro, MA
Pino, Linda ... San Francisco, CA
Pino, Mark Jerome ... Alexandria, VA
Pino, Mary Cornelia ... St. Johns, MI
Pino, Paul G. ... Brockton, MA
Providence, RI
Pino, Ralph C. ... Gloucester, MA
Pino, Raul F. ... Miami, FL
Pino, Richard A. ... Commack, NY
Pino, Rudolph V., Jr. ... White Plains, NY
Pino & Shea ... Gloucester, MA
Pinon, Dwayne A. ... Deerfield, IL
Piñon, Gema M. ... Miami, FL
Pinover, Diana Elzey ... New York, NY
Pinover, Eugene A. ... New York, NY
Pins, Richard W. ... Minneapolis, MN
Pinsel, David L., Law Offices of
Northbrook, IL
Pinsel, David L., Law Offices of
Park Ridge, IL
Pinsel, David L., Law Offices of
Skokie, IL
Pinsel, Elliot A. ... Waukegan, IL
Pinsel, Michael J. ... Arlington Heights, IL
Pinsker, Jerrold B. ... Greensboro, NC
Pinsker, Robert H. ... Palo Alto, CA
Pinsker, Steven ... Santa Barbara, CA
Pinskey, Ralph B. ... Harrisburg, PA
Pinski, Avivah R.Z. ... Philadelphia, PA
Pinski, Ronald L. ... Chicago, IL
Pinsky, Albert H. ... Rochester, NY
Pinsky, Bradley M. ... Syracuse, NY
Pinsky, H. Rhett ... Grand Rapids, MI
Pinsky, Irving J. ... New Haven, CT
Pinsky, Lawrence S. ... Houston, TX
Pinsky, Marlene ... Miami, FL
Pinsky, Michael D. ... Middletown, NY
Pinsky, Michael D., P.C. ... Middletown, NY
Pinsky, Michael S. ... Chicago, IL
Pinsky, Michele Dougherty ... New York, NY
Pinsky, Morris W. ... Westmont, NJ
Pinsky, Philip C. ... Syracuse, NY
Pinsky, Ronald D. ... Treasury Department, Internal Revenue Service, GV
Pinsky, Roy D. ... Syracuse, NY
Pinsky, Seth ... New York, NY
Pinsky & Skandalis ... Albany, NY
Syracuse, NY
Pinsky, Smith, Fayette & Hulswit
Grand Rapids, MI
Pinsley, George ... New York, NY
Pinsley, George, P.C. ... New York, NY
Pinsly, Mitchell S. ... Philadelphia, PA
Pinsof, Michael W. ... Des Plaines, IL
Pinson & Associates, P.C., Law Offices of
Houston, TX
Pinson, Brandon W. ... Midland, TX
Pinson, Chad M. ... Dallas, TX
Pinson, Harley F. ... Los Angeles, CA
Pinson, James B. ... Austin, TX
Pinson, Jerry D. ... Harrison, AR
Pinson, Paul E. ... Williamson, WV
Pinson, Sandra ... Longview, TX
Pinson, Theo W. ... Houston, TX
Pinson, William H., Jr. ... Savannah, GA
Pinsoneault, Harold J. ... Missoula, MT
Pinson-Harvey, Jennifer C. ... Lilburn, GA
Pinsonneault, David K. ... Nashua, NH
Pinstein, Robert J. ... Memphis, TN
Pinta, Howard A. ... Woburn, MA
Pinta, Howard A., P.C. ... Woburn, MA
Pinta, Michael R. ... Boston, MA
Pintado, John Paul ... New Orleans, LA
Pintar, Michael A. ... Carson City, NV
Pintar, Susan K. ... Los Angeles, CA
Pintar, Theodore J. ... San Diego, CA
Pintard, Claude, Jr. ... Natchez, MS
Pintard & Pintard ... Natchez, MS
Pintard, Scott Janvier ... Natchez, MS
Pintarelli, John C., Jr. ... Arcadia, CA
Pintas, William G. ... Chicago, IL
Pintauro, Douglas L. ... Garden City, NY
Pintek, John ... Bisbee, AZ
Pintek, Michael D. ... Los Alamitos, CA
Pintel, Ira Seth ... New York, NY
Pinter, Alexander V. ... Columbus, GA
Pinter, Douglas M. ... Appleton, WI
Pinter, Edward M. ... New York, NY
Pinter, Gregory S. ... New York, NY
Pinter, Julianne ... San Francisco, CA
Pinter, Keith M. ... New York, NY
Pinter, Kristen M. ... Inverness, IL
Pinter, Laszlo L. ... Danbury, CT
Pinter, Michael R. ... Naples, FL
Pinter, Steven I. ... Treasury Department, Departmental Offices, GV
Pinter, Zoltan ... Coral Gables, FL
Pintner, James Charles ... Palo Alto, CA
Pinto, Anthony M. ... Chicago, IL
Pinto, Arthur R. ... Brooklyn, NY
Pinto, Barry ... Kew Gardens, NY
Pinto and Butler ... Princeton, NJ
Pinto, Celeste ... Los Angeles, CA
Pinto Coates Kyre & Brown, PLLC
Greensboro, NC
Pinto, Conssuela A. ... Department of Labor, Office of the Solicitor, GV
Pinto, Consuela A. ... Washington, DC
Pinto, Craig A. ... El Cerrito, CA
Pinto, Daniel ... Los Angeles, CA
Pinto, Darin D. ... Westfield, NJ
Pinto, Donald R., Jr. ... Boston, MA
Pinto & Dubia, LLP ... Irvine, CA
Pinto, E. Nicholas ... New York, NY
Pinto, Edward J. ... Washington, DC
Pinto, Francine B. ... Department of Energy, Office of the General Counsel, GV
Pinto, Harry J., Jr. ... Morristown, NJ
Pinto, James A. ... Denver, CO
Pinto, James T ... Houston, TX
Pinto, Joseph M. ... Roebling, NJ
Pinto, Joseph V. ... Philadelphia, PA
Pinto, Joseph W., Jr. ... Troy, NY
Pinto, Kathleen M. ... Philadelphia, PA
Pinto, Libert ... Cleveland, OH
Pinto, Lillian H. ... Greensboro, NC
Pinto, Michael ... Teaneck, NJ
Pinto, Nicholas V. ... Philadelphia, PA
Pinto, Patricia A. ... Irvine, CA
Pinto & Prestifilippo ... Westfield, NJ
Pinto, Radovan Z. ... Mill Valley, CA
Pinto, Ralph D. ... Charlottesville, VA
Pinto, Richard J. ... Laguna Niguel, CA
Pinto, Richard J. ... Princeton, NJ
Pinto, Richard L. ... Greensboro, NC
Pinto, Robert H. ... Lakeport, CA
Pinto, Robert J. ... Princeton, NJ
Pinto, Robert L. ... Media, PA
Pinto Rodgers & Kopf ... Morristown, NJ
Pinto, Rosalyn Suna ... Atlanta, GA
Pinto, Rosemary ... Philadelphia, PA
Pinto, Sara K. ... New York, NY
Pinto, Saul B. ... Irvine, CA
Pinto, Stephen G. ... Chicago, IL
Pinto, Theodore F. ... Ocala, FL
Pinto, Timothy M. ... Chicago, IL
Pinto, Tricia L. ... Norwalk, CT
Pinto, Vito A. ... Newark, NJ
Pintoff, Craig A. ... New York, NY
Pintoff, Scott E. ... New York, NY
Pinto-Leite, Francisco ... Houston, TX
Pinto-Lugo, René ... San Juan, PR
Pinto-Lugo & Rivera ... San Juan, PR
Pintozzi, Barbara ... Elgin, IL
Pintro Armstrong, Linda M.
Washington, DC
Pintzuk, Marcia D. ... Philadelphia, PA
Pinyan, Clinton R. ... Greensboro, NC
Pinza, Ernest C. ... Los Gatos, CA
Pinza, Gloria A. ... Portland, ME
Pinzel, Frank B. ... Buffalo, NY
Lockport, NY
Niagara Falls, NY
Williamsville, NY
Pinzer, Norton ... Bronx, NY
Pinzino, Gerald J. ... Oak Brook, IL
Pinzler, William M. ... New York, NY
Pinzolo, Rosemarie ... New York, NY
Pinzon, Albert J. ... New York, NY
Pinzone, Charles R., Jr. ... Cleveland, OH
Pinzone, Scott R. ... Findlay, OH
Pinzon-Mantovani, Yesica ... Miami, FL
Pinzow-Naidoff, Jane E. ... New York, NY
Pinzur & Hartstein, Ltd.
Buffalo Grove, IL
Chicago, IL
Long Grove, IL
Waukegan, IL
Pinzur, Robert S. ... Long Grove, IL
Pioch, Susan M. ... Toledo, OH
Pioli, Janet A. ... Chicago, IL
Pioli, Robert J. ... Columbus, OH
Pioli, Victor J. ... Chicago, IL
Piombino, Ronald J. ... Madison, CT
Piombo, Frank ... Redwood City, CA
Piomelli, Ascanio A. ... San Francisco, CA
Pion, John T. ... Pittsburgh, PA
Pionk, Nancy L. ... Portland, OR
Pionke, Lorette M. ... Chicago, IL
Pionkowski, Michelle A. ... Philadelphia, PA
Piontek, Luke F. ... Baton Rouge, LA
Piontek, Mark C. ... Washington, MO
Piontek, Michael ... Chicago, IL
Piontek, Michael J. ... Racine, WI
Piontkowski, Bruce ... San Jose, CA
Piontnica, Abraham D. ... New York, NY
Pionzio, Christen Gilmore ... Lansdale, PA
Piorkowski, Joseph D., Jr.
Washington, DC
Piosa, Hixson, Giordano, & Reilly, P.C.
Coplay, PA
Piosa, Hixson & Reilly, P.C. ... Allentown, PA
Piosa, Michael J. ... Allentown, PA
Pioske, Brian R. ... Minneapolis, MN
Piotrkowski, Irv ... Petaluma, CA
Piotrkowski, Joel S. ... Miami Beach, FL
Piotroski, Anton ... Mineola, NY
Piotrowicz, Michael S. ... Philadelphia, PA
Piotrowski, Bruce K. ... Rochester, MN
Piotrowski, Elizabeth A.
Federal Trade Commission, Bureau of Competition, GV
Piotrowski, James E. ... Hartford, CT
Piotrowski, James Marshall
Albuquerque, NM
Piotrowski, Lemke and Zdanio, P.C.
Warren, MI
Piotrowski, Leonard R. ... Gallup, NM
Piotrowski, Paul S. ... Buffalo, NY
Piotrowski, Thomas Stanley ... Detroit, MI
Piotrowski, Wallace Christopher
West Seneca, NY
Piovarcy, Lee L. ... Memphis, TN
Pipa, Michael D. ... Harrisburg, PA
Pipak, Francis E., Jr. ... Pittsburgh, PA
Pipal, David E. ... Hollister, CA
Pipal, Faustin A., Jr. ... Chicago, IL
Pipal, Frank F. ... Chicago, IL
Pipal, John R. ... Dodgeville, WI
Pipal, Susan A. ... Chicago, IL
Piper, Alika Leilani ... Honolulu, HI
Piper, Angela F. ... Xenia, OH
Piper, Annette J. ... Troy, MI
Piper, Arlene J. ... Honolulu, HI
Piper & Associates ... Shreveport, LA
Piper, Brian S. ... Columbus, OH
Piper, Curtis W. ... Nashville, TN
Piper, David A. ... Eugene, OR
Piper, David A., P.C. ... Eugene, OR
Piper, David D. ... Aurora, CO
Piper, David R. ... Knoxville, TN
Piper, David S. ... Houston, TX
Piper, Diane Buchbinder ... Dover, MA
Piper, Donald A. W. ... Klamath Falls, OR
Piper, Donald H. ... Milwaukee, WI
Piper, Donald R., Jr. ... Philadelphia, PA
Piper, Edwin E., Jr. ... Albuquerque, NM
Piper, Ernest W. ... San Diego, CA
Piper, Esteva, Green, Karvonen & Lewis
St. Petersburg, FL
Piper, Gary A. ... Mansfield, OH
Piper, George C. ... Lexington, KY
Piper, Gordon H. ... Boston, MA
Piper, Harry C. ... Skokie, IL
Piper, Harry C., III ... Bozeman, MT
Piper, Henry B. ... State College, PA
Piper, Jack W., Jr. ... Knoxville, TN
Piper, James G. ... Chicago, IL
Piper, James P. ... Grand Haven, MI
Piper, Jan J. ... St. Petersburg, FL
Piper, Jeffrey Scott ... Honolulu, HI
Piper, John A. ... Paris, IL
Piper, John T., (P.S.) ... Seattle, WA
Piper, Jonathan ... Chicago, IL
Piper, Jonathan S. ... Portland, ME
Piper, Joseph K. ... Seattle, WA

Piper, Julian M. ... St. Petersburg, FL
Piper, Karen L. ... Detroit, MI
Piper, Kathryn A. ... Lower Waterford, VT
Piper, Kenneth L. ... Geneva, OH
Piper, Kerry F. ... Lubbock, TX
Piper, LaMar T. ... St. James, MN
Piper Law Firm ... St. James, MN
Piper Law Offices ... Paris, IL
Piper Law Offices ... Hamilton, OH
Piper, Ludin, Howie & Werner, P.A.
St. Petersburg, FL
Piper, M. Harry ... Flint, MI
Piper, Madeline ... Milton, MA
Piper & Marbury L.L.P. ... Baltimore, MD
Easton, MD
Philadelphia, PA
Piper Marbury Rudnick & Wolfe LLP
Washington, DC
Tampa, FL
Princeton, NJ
New York, NY
Dallas, TX
Reston, VA
Piper, Martin N. ... Fair Lawn, NJ
Piper, Michael B. ... St. Petersburg, FL
Piper, Michael H. ... Metairie, LA
Piper, Michael R. ... Fort Lauderdale, FL
Piper, Perry Howard ... Chattanooga, TN
Piper, Randolph ... Flint, MI
Piper, Robert E., Jr. ... Shreveport, LA
Piper, Robert N. ... Hamilton, OH
Piper, Robert N., III ... Hamilton, OH
Piper, Robert N.E. ... Honolulu, HI
Piper, Scott D. ... Rochester, NY
Piper, Sharon ... Collingswood, NJ
Piper, Stephen M. ... Bethesda, MD
Piper, Stephen R. ... Camden, NJ
Piper, Thomas H. ... White Hall, IL
Piper, Virginia L. ... Bastrop, TX
Piper, Wellman & Bowers ... Lexington, KY
Piper, William B. ... Montpelier, VT
St. Johnsbury, VT
Piper, William F. ... Kalamazoo, MI
Piper, William R. ... St. Louis, MO
Piper, William S. ... Chicago, IL
Piper & Witt ... Knoxville, TN
Piperi, Ronald A. ... Houston, TX
Piper-Maurer, Joanne ... Duluth, MN
Piperni-O'Neill, Deborah A. ... Columbus, OH
Pipes, Glenn W. ... Fort Worth, TX
Pipes, H. Minor, III ... New Orleans, LA
Pipes, Jeffrey W. ... Paso Robles, CA
Pipes, John Casey ... Mobile, AL
Pipes, L. Douglas ... Martinez, CA
Pipes, Matthew D. ... Dallas, TX
Pipes, Richard A., (A Law Corporation)
Tamuning, GU
Pipes, Richard H. ... Monroe, LA
Pipes, Robert Trent ... Oklahoma City, OK
Pipes, Roger J. ... Dallas, TX
Pipes, S. Wesley, V ... Mobile, AL
Pipes, W. Ransom ... Baton Rouge, LA
Pipes, Wesley ... Mobile, AL
Pipes, W. F., Jr. ... Monroe, LA
Pipestem, F. Browning ... Norman, OK
Pipestem, Wilson K ... Washington, DC
Pipher, Bernard T. ... Tekamah, NE
Piphus, Carolyn F. ... Nashville, TN
Pipino, James D. ... Youngstown, OH
Pipino, Samuel M. ... Columbus, OH
Pipito, Frank T. ... Albany, NY
Pipitone, Daniel D. ... Corpus Christi, TX
Pipitone, Marie ... Riverside, CT
Pipitone, Patricia Chanson
Corpus Christi, TX
Pipitone, Paul J. ... Houston, TX
Pipitone & Seger, P.C.
Corpus Christi, TX
Pipkin, Anna Catherine ... Tupelo, MS
Pipkin, Ashmead P. ... Raleigh, NC
Pipkin, John E. ... Houston, TX
Pipkin, Knott, Clark & Berger, L.L.P.
Cary, NC
Raleigh, NC
Research Triangle Park, NC
Pipkin, Leigh Lichty ... Mobile, AL
Pipkin, Marvin G. ... San Antonio, TX
Pipkin, Marvin L. ... Darien, GA
Pipkin, Mike F. ... Dallas, TX
Pipkin & Oliver ... San Antonio, TX
Pipkin, R. Michael ... Chapel Hill, NC
Pipkin, R. Michael, P.A. ... Chapel Hill, NC
Pipkin, Richard S. ... Sebring, FL
Pipkin, Robin E. ... Raleigh, NC
Pipkin, Stephen C. ... Dallas, TX
Pipkin, William A. ... Moore, OK
Pipkin, William E., Jr. ... Mobile, AL
Pippen, Albert C. ... West Point, MS
Pippen, David L. ... Indianapolis, IN
Pippen, Joseph F., Jr. ... Largo, FL
Pippen, Joseph F., Jr., & Associates, Law Office of ... Largo, FL
Pippenger, David L. ... Towson, MD
Pippenger, Mark Andrew
Chattanooga, TN
Pippenger, Philip M. ... Baton Rouge, LA
Pippenger, Phillip M. ... Chicago, IL
Pippert, Thomas W. ... New York, NY
Pippett, Christopher J. ... Wayne, PA
Pippin & Bocci ... Lake Oswego, OR
Pippin, Don R. ... Norton, VA
Pippin, Harry M. ... Fargo, ND
Williston, ND
Pippin, James D. ... San Diego, CA
Pippin, James M. ... Lake Oswego, OR
Pippin, Joe D. ... Norton, VA
Pippin, Mark S. ... Montgomery, AL
Pippin & Pippin, P.C. ... Norton, VA
Pippin, Robert L. ... Palm Desert, CA
Pippin, Tra C., (Mr.) ... Oklahoma City, OK
Pippinger, Richard G. ... Tampa, FL
Pippinger, Richard G., P.A. ... Tampa, FL
Piquette, Edward L., Jr. ... Bridgeport, CT
Piquette, William J. ... Miami Springs, FL
Pirages, James R. ... Rockford, IL
Piraino, Andrew N. ... Syracuse, NY
Piraino, Edwin ... Champaign, IL
Piraino, Katherine D. Wood ... Cleveland, OH
Piraino, Michael C. ... Seattle, WA
Piraino, Robert A. ... Bloomfield Hills, MI
Piraino, Russell W. ... St. Louis, MO
Piraino, Thomas A. ... Oberlin, OH
Piraino, Thomas A., Jr. ... Cleveland, OH
Piras, Alessandra ... Miami, FL
Pircher, Leo J. ... Los Angeles, CA
Pircher, Nichols & Meeks
Los Angeles, CA
Chicago, IL
Pire, David J. ... Dallas, TX
Piré, Shari Lisa ... New York, NY
Pirelli, Arthur ... San Francisco, CA
Pires, Alexander J., Jr. ... Washington, DC
Pires, Anthony P., Jr. ... Naples, FL
Pirfo, Oreste Russ ... Treasury Department, Internal Revenue Service, GV
Pirich, John D. ... Lansing, MI
Pirie, Ellen ... Santa Cruz, CA
Pirie, Sophie H. ... Palo Alto, CA
Pirik, Christine M. T. ... Columbus, OH
Pirilla, Brian G. ... Belle Vernon, PA
Pirina, John, Jr. ... Hartford, CT
Pirio, Maurice J. ... Seattle, WA
Pirk, William R. ... New York, NY
Pirkey, Jonathan L. ... Hudson, MA
Pirkey, Louis T. ... Austin, TX
Pirkey, Nancy L. ... Milwaukee, WI
Pirkey, Will Jay ... Los Angeles, CA
Pirkle, Gregory D. ... Tupelo, MS
Pirkle, James J. ... Greensboro, GA
Pirkle, John E. ... Hinesville, GA
Pirkle, John P. ... Department of Justice, Tax Division, GV
Pirkle, Lawrence ... Mount Vernon, WA
Pirkle, Neal E. ... Waco, TX
Pirkle, Robert F. ... Hinesville, GA
Pirko, John A. ... Glen Allen, VA
Richmond, VA
Pirkola, Gerald N. ... Iron Mountain, MI
Pirnar, Staci C. ... Dallas, TX
Pirner, Deborah ... Portland, OR
Pirner, Rachael K. ... Wichita, KS
Pirnie, Patricia Curtis ... Midland, MI
Pirnie, Thomas H. ... Cedar Rapids, IA
Pirnot, John D. ... Wilmington, DE
Piro, Clare A. ... Hartsdale, NY
Piro, James M. ... Nutley, NJ
Piro, Joseph N. ... Los Angeles, CA
Piro & Lilly, L.L.P. ... Houston, TX
Piro, Peter A. ... Florham Park, NJ
Piro, Robert J. ... Houston, TX
Piro, Zinna, Cifelli & Paris ... Nutley, NJ
Pirog, John B. ... New York, NY
Pirog, John F. ... Sioux City, IA
Pirog, Matthew ... New York, NY
Pirogovsky, Alex ... Chicago, IL
Pirolli, Linda T. ... Millville, NJ
Pirolli, Michael A. ... Bridgeton, NJ
Pirolli & Pirolli ... Bridgeton, NJ
Millville, NJ
Pirone, Vincent A. ... Bloomfield, NJ
Piroozfar, Ahtossa K. ... San Francisco, CA
Pirozzi & Levine, LLP ... New York, NY
Pirozzi, Mark C. ... Twinsburg, OH
Pirozzi, Thomas J. ... New York, NY
Pirozzolo, Jack R. ... Boston, MA
Pirozzolo, Jack W. ... Boston, MA
Pirozzolo, Lisa J. ... Boston, MA
Pirpiris, Irene V. ... Chicago, IL
Pirraglia, P. Edward ... White Plains, NY
Pirraglia, Peter L. ... New York, NY
Pirraglia, Raymond T. ... Staten Island, NY
Pirraglia, Robert K. ... Cranston, RI
Pirraglia, Rosenblatt & McGarrity
White Plains, NY
Pirrello, Mario J. ... Rochester, NY
Pirrello, Ronald L. ... Rockford, IL
Pirretti, James J. ... New York, NY
Pirri, Kathleen S. ... Washington, DC
Pirro, Albert J., Jr. ... New York, NY
White Plains, NY
Pirro, Charles A., III ... Norwalk, CT
Pirro, Church & Cook, L.L.C. ... Norwalk, CT
Pirro, Collier, Cohen, Halpern & Bock, LLP
Stamford, CT
New York, NY
Pirro, Collier, Cohen & Halpern, LLP
White Plains, NY
Pirro, Jeanine Ferris ... White Plains, NY
Pirro, Kendall R. ... Schenectady, NY
Pirrone, Christopher J. ... San Francisco, CA
Pirrone, Vincent A. ... Long Beach, NY
Pirrotti, Anthony J. ... Ardsley, NY
Pirrotti, Nina T. ... New York, NY
Pirruccello, Frank W., Jr. ... Chicago, IL
Pirruccello, Jeffrey J. ... Omaha, NE
Pirruccello, Salvatore ... Augusta, ME
Pirsch, P. Elizabeth ... Alexandria, VA
Pirsch, Perry A. ... Lincoln, NE
Pirslin, Nancy A. ... Huntington Woods, MI
Pirt, Nancy E.
Department Of Health And Human Services, Food & Drug Administration, GV
Pirtle, Alan G. ... East St. Louis, IL
Pirtle, B. Timothy ... McMinnville, TN
Pirtle, Charles R. ... Houston, TX
Pirtle, Elmer B., Jr. ... La Jolla, CA
Pirtle, Harry C. ... Jacksonville, IL
Pirtle, Jane D. ... Fort Worth, TX
Pirtle, Joe M. ... Houston, TX
Pirtle, Lawrence J. ... Houston, TX
Pirtle, Michael W. ... Omaha, NE
Pirtle, Patrick A. ... Amarillo, TX
Pirtle, Robert L. ... Seattle, WA
Pirtle, Steven E. ... Fort Worth, TX
Pirtle, Sue M. ... Rockwall, TX
Pirtle, Thomas E. ... La Jolla, CA
Pirtle, Thomas W. ... Houston, TX
Pirtle, Timothy A. ... Columbus, OH
Pirtle, William F. ... Los Angeles, CA
Pisa, Albert A. ... New York, NY
Pisa, Regina M., (P.C.) ... Boston, MA
Pisacano, Dean Alan ... Covington, KY
Pisacano, Don A. ... Lexington, KY
Pisacano, Margaret M. ... Lexington, KY
Pisacreta, Edward A. ... New York, NY
Pisanelli, Andrew F. ... Mount Kisco, NY
Pisanelli, David A. ... Poughkeepsie, NY
Pisanelli, Ernest C. ... Cleveland, OH
Pisanelli, Gerard J. ... Poughkeepsie, NY
Pisanelli, James J. ... Las Vegas, NV
Reno, NV
Pisanelli, Mary Ellen ... Toledo, OH
Pisani, Arthur A. ... Plymouth, MI
Pisani, Arthur A., P.C. ... Plymouth, MI
Pisani, Dominic M. ... Uniondale, NY
Pisani, Eduardo ... Deerfield, IL
Pisani, Fred J. ... Tenafly, NJ
Pisani, Michael J. ... Highland Park, IL
Pisani, Michael J. ... New York, NY
Pisani, Otto C. ... Fairfield, CA
Pisani, Robert J. ... Treasury Department, Office of Regulations and Rulings, GV
Pisani, Robert P. ... Chicago, IL
Pisani, Stanley ... Flossmoor, IL
Pisano, Alfonso L. ... Cranford, NJ
Pisano, Carmen M. ... Department of Defense, Defense Legal Services Agency, GV
Pisano, Carol A. ... New York, NY
Pisano, Charles J. ... Kenner, LA
Pisano, Charles M. ... New Orleans, LA
Pisano, Christopher M. ... Los Angeles, CA
Pisano, Denise M. ... Fort Lauderdale, FL
Pisano, Frank, III ... Montville, NJ
Pisano, Frank M. ... Houston, TX
Pisano, George A. ... Los Angeles, CA
Pisano, Joanne ... Yonkers, NY
Pisano, Joel A. ... Newark, NJ
Pisano, John J. ... Cranford, NJ
Pisano, Joseph Francis Stephen
San Francisco, CA
Pisano, Mills & Isgard, L.L.P.
New York, NY
Pisano, Nicola A. ... Palo Alto, CA
Pisano & Pisano ... Huron, OH
Pisano, Ralph C. ... Huron, OH
Pisano, Ralph C., Jr. ... Huron, OH
Pisano, Steven ... Redwood City, CA
Pisano, Triarsi & Betancourt ... Cranford, NJ
Pisano, Vincent J. ... New York, NY
Pisansky, Janet L. ... Morristown, NJ
Pisansky, John ... Elizabeth, NJ
Pisansky, Michael J. ... New Brighton, MN
Pisapia, Michael Forster ... Kew Gardens, NY
Pisapia, Peter E. ... New York, NY
Pisarcik, Edward J. ... Philadelphia, PA
Pisarcik, Gerard J. ... Lemoyne, PA
Pisa-Relli, John C. ... Treasury Department, Departmental Offices, GV
Pisarello, William J. ... Farmingdale, NY
Pisarich, Keith ... Biloxi, MS
Pisaris, John B. ... Columbus, OH
Pisarra, David T. ... Santa Monica, CA
Pisarri, Joseph A. ... Boston, MA
Pisarri, Mari-Anne ... Washington, DC
Pisarri, McEnroe & Careri ... Hackensack, NJ
Pisarri, Thomas J. ... Hackensack, NJ
Pisaturo, Catherine C. ... Department of Justice, Environment and Natural Resources Division, GV
Pisaturo, Charles A. ... Providence, RI
Pisaturo, Charles A., Jr. ... Providence, RI
Pisaturo, John J. ... Spencerport, NY
Pisaturo, Laura A. ... Providence, RI
Pisaturo, Michael J. ... Boston, MA
Providence, RI
Pisauro, Michael L., Jr. ... Hackensack, NJ
Piscal, Francis P. ... Toms River, NJ
Piscatelli, Louis R. ... New Haven, CT
Piscatelli, Patrick A. ... Hartford, CT
Piscevich & Fenner ... Reno, NV
Piscevich, Margo ... Reno, NV
Pischel, Dawn H. ... Troy, MI
Pischke, Vail W. ... Falls Church, VA
Pischnotte, William W. "Zeb"
Department of the Air Force, Office of the Judge Advocate General, GV
Piscionere, Anthony G. ... Rye, NY
Piscionere & Nemarow ... Rye, NY
Pisciotta, Aileen A. ... Washington, DC
Pisciotta, Cathyanne A. ... Lawrenceville, NJ
Pisciotta, Donna M. ... Beverly, MA
Minneapolis, MN
Pisciotti, Anthony M. ... Hackensack, NJ
New York, NY
Piscitelli, Alyson M. ... New York, NY
Piscitelli, Domenico & Murphy
Brockton, MA
Piscitelli, Frank E., Jr. ... Cleveland, OH
Piscitelli, Kathryn S. ... Orlando, FL
Piscitelli, Lisa K. ... Lincoln, NE
Piscitelli, Mike ... Fort Lauderdale, FL
Piscitelli, Peter A. ... Albany, NY
Piscitello, Jacqueline L. ... Palo Alto, CA
Piscitello, Joseph T ... Philadelphia, PA
Piscopo, Joseph C. ... Elmsford, NY
Piscopo, Joseph P. ... Clifton, NJ
Piscopo, Joseph P., P.A. ... Clifton, NJ
Piscopo, Philip J. ... Geneva, IL
Piscopo, Richard S., Jr. ... San Diego, CA
Pise, Michael J. ... Boston, MA
Pisegna, Vincent J. ... Boston, MA
Pisella, Bart ... New York, NY
Pisem, Elliot ... New York, NY
Pisem, Rosanne R. ... New York, NY
Piser, Steven B. ... Oakland, CA
Piserchia, Gary F. ... Marlton, NJ
Piserchia, John Joseph ... Roseland, NJ
Pishevar, Afshin ... Rockville, MD
Pishko, Bernard A. ... Norfolk, VA
Pishko, David C. ... Winston-Salem, NC
Pishny, Lyle D. ... Overland Park, KS
Pisias, J. Michael, Jr. ... San Francisco, CA
Pisieczko, Charles J. ... St. Petersburg, FL
Pisini, Stephen C. ... Milford, MA
Piskadlo, Suzanne B. ... Westminster, CO
Piskadlo, Suzanne B., LLC ... Westminster, CO
Piskiel, Susan G. ... Short Hills, NJ
Piskorowski, Chester A. ... New York, NY
Piskorski, David A. ... New Britain, CT
Piskorski, John J. ... Arlington, VA
Piskorski, Thomas J. ... Chicago, IL
Piskun, Jennifer ... Austin, TX
Pismeny, Miriam ... Great Neck, NY
Pisoni, Jeanine M. ... Chicago, IL
Pistell, Joseph K. ... Stony Brook, NY
Pistella, Frank J. ... Pittsburgh, PA
Pisterzi, Albert J. ... Kansas City, MO
Pistey, Nora E. ... Hartford, CT
Pistilli, Augusta J. ... Woodbury, NJ
Pistilli, Louis V. ... Joliet, IL
Pistillo, Donald J. ... Omaha, NE
Pistillo, Michael F. ... Omaha, NE
Pistillo & Pistillo, P.C. ... Omaha, NE
Pisto, Laird A. ... Tacoma, WA
Pisto, Lawrence W.
Securities and Exchange Commission, Division of Investment Management, GV
Pistocchi, John A. ... New York, NY
Pistol, Jeffrey T. ... Trenton, NJ
Pistolas, Nicholas J. ... Towson, MD
Pistole, Valerie ... Sonoma, CA
Piston, Michael E. ... Troy, MI
Piston, Michael E., P.C. ... Troy, MI
Pistone, Anthony D. ... Flushing, NY
Pistone, Baruch & Wolder, LLP
Irvine, CA
Pistone, Dominick ... Kew Gardens, NY
Pistone, Joseph ... Forest Hills, NY
Pistone, Julianne ... Beachwood, OH
Pistone, Thomas A. ... Irvine, CA
Pistorino, Charles L. ... McLean, VA
Pistorino, James C. ... Houston, TX
Pistorio, Francis T. ... Roselle, IL
Pistorio, Francis T., P.C. ... Roselle, IL
Pistorius, B. Luke ... San Diego, CA
Pistorius, Eric S. ... Jerseyville, IL
Pistorius, K. Mark ... Dallas, TX
Pistorius, Myles C. ... New York, NY
Pistorius, William P. ... Chicago, IL
Pistotnik, Brian D. ... Wichita, KS
Pistotnik Law Offices ... Wichita, KS
Piszczatowski, Walter J.
Bloomfield Hills, MI
Piszczek, Gerald D. ... Medina, OH
Piszczek, Walter J. ... Osceola, WI
Pita, Frank J. ... Raleigh, NC
Pita, Henry M. ... New York, NY
Pita, Howard Kraft ... Miami, FL
Pita, Howard (Skip) K. ... Washington, DC
Pita, Marina K. ... Houston, TX
Pitakskul, K. Kristann ... Chicago, IL
Pitalo, J. Michael ... Fresno, CA
Pitard, Andree F. ... New Orleans, LA
Pitard, Robert F. ... New Orleans, LA
Pitaro, Eugene D. ... Flushing, NY
Pitaro, Lara K. ... New York, NY
Pitaro, Nicholas L. ... Kew Gardens, NY
Pitaro, Nicholas R. ... Cohasset, MA
Pitaro & Pitaro ... Flushing, NY
Pitaro, Thomas F. ... Las Vegas, NV
Pitaro, Vincent D. ... Flushing, NY
Pitarresi, Charles F. ... Buffalo, NY
Pitassi, Mary E. ... Madison, WI
Pitassi, Robert A. ... Pawtucket, RI
Pitassy, Caesar L. ... New York, NY
Pitassy, Richard N. ... White Plains, NY
Pitcairn, John E. ... Rochester, NY
Pitcairn, Robert A., Jr. ... Cincinnati, OH
Pitcairn, Rodger ... Department of Labor, Office of the Solicitor, GV
Pitcaithley, Alan L. ... La Mesa, CA
Pitcaithley, Bruce E. ... Cupertino, CA
Pitcaithley & Hobbs ... La Mesa, CA
Pitch, Myron E. ... Helena, MT
Pitchal, Laura S. ... New York, NY
Pitchayan, Bathmanaban
Jackson Heights, NY
Pitchel, Sheldon H. ... Sudbury, MA
Pitchenik, David E. ... Stamford, CT
Pitcher, Charles A. ... Gautier, MS
Pitcher, Clark A. ... Syracuse, NY
Pitcher, David E., Jr. ... New York, NY
Pitcher, David M. ... Washington, DC
Pitcher, Edmund R. ... Boston, MA
Pitcher, Freddie, Jr. ... Baton Rouge, LA
Pitcher, George P. ... Vinita, OK
Pitcher, George S. ... Portland, OR
Pitcher, Griffith F. ... Atlanta, GA
Pitcher, J. William ... Annapolis, MD
Pitcher, Jeffrey S. ... Phoenix, AZ
Pitcher, John F. ... Sarasota, FL
Pitcher, Joseph R. ... Greenwood, IN

Pitcher, Kelly Bauman ....Indianapolis, IN
Pitcher, Neal R. ....Elgin, IL
Pitcher & O'Neal, P.A. ....Madeira Beach, FL
Pitcher, Shannon H. ....Flint, MI
Pitcher, Stephen R. ....San Francisco, CA
Pitcher, Thomas B. ....Irvine, CA
Pitcher, William C. ....Wichita, KS
Pitcher-Hartley, Pamela R. ....Vinita, OK
Pitchess, Peter J., II ....Santa Monica, CA
Pitchford, Aliya ....Washington, DC
Pitchford, David L. ....New York, NY
Pitchford, Jan Walters ....Sarasota, FL
Pitchford, Malcolm J. ....Sarasota, FL
Pitchford, Mark B. ....Palo Alto, CA
Pitchford, Raymond B. ....Houston, TX
Pitchford, Susan D. ....Vancouver, WA
Pitchie, R. Brooks ....Kingsport, TN
Pitchkolan, Margaret Anderson
San Diego, CA
Pitchlynn, Gary S., (P.C.) ....Norman, OK
Pitchlynn, Morse, Ritter & Morse, A
Professional Association ....Norman, OK
Pitcock, Charles L. ....Cleveland, OH
Pitcock, Donald L. ....Oakland, CA
Pitcock, Stephen R. ....Oklahoma City, OK
Pitcoff, Beth C. ....Woodbury, NY
Pitcoff, Roy David ....New York, NY
Pite, David C. ....New Haven, CT
Pite, Steven W. ....El Cajon, CA
Pitegoff, Jeffrey I. ....Las Vegas, NV
Pitegoff Law Office ....White Plains, NY
Pitegoff, Peter ....Buffalo, NY
Pitegoff, Thomas M. ....White Plains, NY
Pitet, Patrick G. ....Cody, WY
Pitfield, John R. ....Boston, MA
Pitisci, D. Lee ....Tampa, FL
Pitisci, Silvia P. ....Tampa, FL
Pitkiel, Joseph A. ....Arlington, VA
Pitkin, David R. ....Gold Bar, WA
Pitkin, Jerald R. ....Naples, FL
Pitkin, John M. ....Irvine, CA
Pitkin, Martha ....Houston, TX
Pitkin, Peter J. ....Toledo, OH
Pitkin & Ponds ....Naples, FL
Pitkin, Robert M. ....Kansas City, MO
Pitkin, Roger F. ....Department of Defense,
Office of the General Counsel, GV
Pitkin & Young ....Houston, TX
Pitkofsky, Nancy S. ....New York, NY
Pitkow, Hal C. ....Washington Crossing, PA
Pitkow, Martin B. ....Philadelphia, PA
Pitkowsky, Herbert G. ....Oceanside, NY
Pitler, Barry A. ....Chicago, IL
Pitler & Mandell ....Chicago, IL
Pitler, Randall B. ....Detroit, MI
Pitler, Robert L. ....Englewood, CO
Pitler, Robert M. ....Brooklyn, NY
Pitler, Sanford E. ....Seattle, WA
Pitler, Stephen H. ....Hampton, VA
Pitler, Steven P. ....Washington, DC
Pitlick, Harris A. ....Arlington, VA
Pitluck, Haskell M. ....Woodstock, IL
Pitluck Kido Sato & Stone ....Honolulu, HI
Pitluck, Wayne Marshall ....Honolulu, HI
Pitman, Bruce M. ....Springfield, NJ
Pitman, David J. ....Los Angeles, CA
Pitman, Debora A. ....New York, NY
Pitman, Donald Lloyd ....Boston, MA
Pitman, Eugene J. ....Houston, TX
Pitman, Henry B. ....New York, NY
Pitman, Jeffrey A. ....Milwaukee, WI
Pitman, Joel L. ....Springfield, NJ
Pitman, Lewis H., Jr. ....Jeanerette, LA
Pitman, Michael M. ....Murray, KY
Pitman, Pitman and Mindas, P.C.
Springfield, NJ
Pitman, Robert J. ....Salinas, CA
Pitman, Robert Lee ....Austin, TX
Pitman, Ronald F. ....Denville, NJ
Pitman, Sheila O'Connor ....Metairie, LA
Pitman & Stilwell ....Palestine, TX
Pitman, Thomas A. ....Indianapolis, IN
Pitman, Thomas J. ....Jacksonville, NC
Pitman, William K. ....Wendover, NV
Pitman, William L. ....Richmond, VA
Pitner, Albert W. ....Chattanooga, TN
Pitner, Jay J. ....Milwaukee, WI
Pitner, Joseph A., III ....Austin, TX
Pitner, Thomas J. ....Gilbert, AZ
Pitner, Timothy R. ....Denver, CO
Pitney, Brian R. ....Richmond, VA
Pitney, Ernest W. ....Gold Beach, OR
Pitney, Hardin, Kipp & Szuch LLP
Morristown, NJ
New York, NY
Pitney, James C. ....Morristown, NJ
Pitney, James C., Jr. ....Augusta, ME
Pitney, Maria Menard ....Worcester, MA
Pitnof, Nathaniel D. ....Worcester, MA
Pitnof-Mahoney, Nancy ....Brockton, MA
Pitocchelli, Mary Claire ....Palm Beach, FL
Pitocco, Joseph A. ....Cincinnati, OH
Pitock, Jordon R. ....Philadelphia, PA
Pitofsky, Alexander H. ....Washington, DC
Pitofsky, Donald A. ....New York, NY
Pitofsky, Robert ......Federal Trade Commission,
Office of the Chairman, GV
Pitofsky, Sally Forman
Federal Trade Commission,
Bureau of Consumer Protection, GV
Pitonyak, Jack F., (P.C.) ....Rochester, MI
Pitre, Bobby K. ....Lake Charles, LA
Pitre, Carole M. ....San Dimas, CA
Woodland, CA
Pitre, David P. ....New Orleans, LA
Pitre, Earl G. ....Lake Charles, LA
Pitre, Earl G., Jr. ....Lake Charles, LA
Pitre, Elizabeth Randall ....Phoenix, AZ
Pitre, Frank M. ....Burlingame, CA
Los Angeles, CA
Pitre, Halley & Sikich L.L.P.
Lake Charles, LA
Pitre, Joshua J. ....Opelousas, LA
Pitre, Kenneth ....Eunice, LA
Pitre, Loulan J., Jr. ....Cut Off, LA
Thibodaux, LA
Pitre, Marcus A. ....Port Neches, TX
Pitre, Norman J. ....Luling, LA
Pitre, Randall J. ....San Dimas, CA
Pitre, Robert A., Jr. ....Gretna, LA
Pitre & Teunisse ....Los Angeles, CA
Pomona, CA
Rancho Cucamonga, CA
San Dimas, CA
Woodland, CA
Pitrof, Elizabeth A. ....Chicago, IL
Pitrof, Eugene Edward
Upper Marlboro, MD
Pitrof & Starkey ....Prince Frederick, MD
Upper Marlboro, MD
Pitrolo, Jo Marie ....Fairmont, WV
Pitrowski, Ellen S. ....Santa Maria, CA
Pitruzzella, Vincenzo D. ....Sunnyvale, CA
Pitruzzello, Philip R. ....New York, NY
Pitschmann, David W. ....Houston, TX
Pitsenbarger, Jeffrey J. ....Moorhead, MN
Pitsenbarger, Roger ....Moorhead, MN
Pitsenberger, William H., Jr. ....Topeka, KS
Pitsiokos, Judith W. ....Wading River, NY
Pitsiokos, Peter ....St. James, NY
Pitstick, Joseph V. ....Cincinnati, OH
Pitstick, Mark J. ....London, OH
Pitstick, Terri L. ....Springfield, OH
Pitt, Alan S. ....Beverly Hills, CA
Pitt, Andrew S. ....Los Angeles, CA
Pitt, Brent W. ....Oklahoma City, OK
Pitt, Christopher S. ....Boston, MA
Pitt, Donald ....Tucson, AZ
Pitt, Dorothy M. ....Louisville, KY
Pitt, Ernest M., Jr. ....Ashland, KY
Pitt, Fenton & Smith ....Louisville, KY
Pitt & Frank ....Louisville, KY
Pitt, George ....Chicago, IL
Pitt, Harold T. ....Hartford, CT
Pitt, Harry W. ....Floral Park, NY
Pitt, Harvey L. ....Washington, DC
New York, NY
Pitt, Hubbard & Marshall, LLP
Boston, MA
Pitt, Jane Hanify ....Boston, MA
Pitt, Jerome O. ....Indianapolis, IN
Pitt, Joseph B., Jr. ....Nashville, TN
Pitt, Kenneth P. ....Golden, CO
Pitt, Larry ....Glenside, PA
Lansdowne, PA
Philadelphia, PA
Pitt, Larry, & Associates, P.C.
Doylestown, PA
Glenside, PA
Lansdowne, PA
Media, PA
Norristown, PA
Philadelphia, PA
Pitt, Lawrence B. ....Lake Buena Vista, FL
Pitt, Loretta Reid
Federal Deposit Insurance Corporation,
Trial Litigation Section, GV
Pitt, M. Stephen ....Louisville, KY
Pitt, Michael H. ....Portsmouth, VA
Pitt, Pamela O. ....San Francisco, CA
Pitt, Patricia Meigs ....Ashland, KY
Pitt, Paulette L. ....Weehawken, NJ
Pitt & Pitt ....West Chester, PA
Pitt, R. Michael ....Louisville, KY
Pitt, Richard L. ....Coupeville, WA
Pitt, Robbie S. ....Washington, DC
Pitt, Robert D. ....Pinetops, NC
Pitt, Robert Francis, Jr. ....Wethersfield, CT
Pitt, Thomas A., III ....West Chester, PA
Pitt, Thomas A., Jr. ....West Chester, PA
Pitt, Valerie E. ....Hollywood, FL
Pitt, Walter W., Jr. ....Winston-Salem, NC
Pitta, Herbert, Jr. ....Chelmsford, MA
Pitta, Vincent F. ....New York, NY
Pittacora, James R. ....Chicago, IL
Pittaluga, Christiane M.
Fort Lauderdale, FL
Pittaluga, Cindy Hide ....Dublin, OH
Pittaluga, Elisabeth A. ....New York, NY
Pittaluga, Rodolfo, Jr. ....Miami, FL
Pittaluga, Stephanie A. ....Irvine, CA
Pittam, Richard O. ....Denver, CO
Pittard, Cynthia M. ....Smithfield, NC
Pittard, David B. ....Austin, TX
Pittard, Elizabeth Frost ....Philadelphia, PA
Pittard, Jesse F. ....Raeford, NC
Southern Pines, NC
Pittard, John B. ....Murfreesboro, TN
Pittarelli, Anthony R. ....Syracuse, NY
Pittari, Stephen J. ....White Plains, NY
Pittaro, Frederick J. ....Boston, MA
Pittas, John E. ....Astoria, NY
Pittas, John F. ....Arlington Heights, IL
Pittas • Koenig ....Boston, MA
Winchester, MA
Pittas, Sydelle ....Winchester, MA
Pittas-Giroux, Alexia ....Charleston, SC
Pittaway, David B. ....New York, NY
Pittel, Wayne A. ....Grosse Pointe, MI
Pittelkow, Miles, Jr. ....Houston, TX
Pittell, Jeffrey G. ....New York, NY
Pittella, Anna-Maria ....Toms River, NJ
Pittenger & Associates, P.C. ....Frisco, TX
Pittenger, Bradford L. ....Mission, KS
Pittenger, Dwight W. ....Neptune, NJ
Pittenger, Gordon L. ....Indianapolis, IN
Pittenger, Gregory C. ....McCall, ID
Pittenger, James E. ....Denver, CO
Pittenger, Michael A. ....Wilmington, DE
Pittenger, Perry A. ....Springfield, NJ
Pittenger & Smith, P.C. ....Denver, CO
Pittenger, T. Todd ....Orlando, FL
Pittenger, William A. ....Frisco, TX
Pittenger, William B. C. ....Frisco, TX
Pitter, Anne E. ....New York, NY
Pitterich, Joseph W. ....Bethesda, MD
Pitterich & Snedegar, P.C. ....Bethesda, MD
Pitterle, Peter T. ....Torrance, CA
Pitterman, Bernard ....New Milford, CT
Pitters, Amardo Wesley ....Montgomery, AL
Pitters, Amardo Wesley, P.C.
Montgomery, AL
Pittillo, Nila R. ....South Charleston, WV
Pittinger, Christopher J. ....New York, NY
Pittinsky, David H. ....Philadelphia, PA
Pittle, Herbert ....Washington, DC
Pittleman, James B. ....Fairfax, VA
Pittleman, Linda J. ....New York, NY
Pittleman, Steven H. ....New York, NY
Pittler, Alan M. ....Pittsburgh, PA
Pittler, Leslie M. ....Towson, MD
Pittler, William J. ....Baltimore, MD
Pittluck, Norman ....San Diego, CA
Pittman, Adam A. ....Batesville, MS
Pittman, Alan ....Fayetteville, NC
Pittman, Alisa L. ....Atlanta, GA
Pittman, Alton R. ....Indian Rocks Beach, FL
Pittman, Ashley ....Jackson, MS
Pittman, Ashley G. ....Boston, MA
Pittman, Aubrey Nick ....Dallas, TX
Pittman, Barbara J. ....Tampa, FL
Pittman, Barry V. ....Kings Park, NY
Pittman, Bob W. ....Jackson, MS
Pittman, Bryan W. ....Charlotte, NC
Pittman, C. Wes ....Panama City, FL
Pittman, Charles D., Jr. ....Virginia Beach, VA
Pittman, Charles W. ....Tampa, FL
Pittman, Christopher J. ....Clarksville, TN
Pittman, Cindy S. ....San Diego, CA
Pittman, Craig S. ....Mobile, AL
Pittman, Crymes G. ....Jackson, MS
Pittman, Crymes M. ....Jackson, MS
Pittman, Darryl E. ....Cleveland, OH
Pittman, Darryl E., & Assoc Co. L.P.A. The
Law Off. of ....Cleveland, OH
Pittman, David B. ....Rock Hill, SC
Pittman, David S. ....Slidell, LA
Pittman & Davis ....Rockingham, NC
Pittman, Dawn S. ....Los Angeles, CA
San Francisco, CA
Pittman, Donald S. ....Enterprise, AL
Pittman, Dorn C., Jr. ....Burlington, NC
Pittman, Edmund S. ....Richmond, VA
Pittman, Edward L. ....Washington, DC
Pittman, Edwin L. ....Jackson, MS
Pittman, Elizabeth D. ....Norfolk, NE
Pittman, Elizabeth L. ....Chicago, IL
Pittman, Eric L., & Associates
Denham Springs, LA
Pittman & Fink, P.C. ....Austin, TX
Pittman, Frank P. ....Carrollton, TX
Pittman, Galen W. ....La Crosse, WI
Pittman, Germany, Roberts & Welsh, L.L.P.
Jackson, MS
Pittman, Glenda L. ....Austin, TX
Pittman, Guy Bradley ....Riverside, CA
Pittman, Guy O. ....Jefferson, GA
Pittman, H. C. ....Austin, TX
Pittman, Hooks, Dutton & Hollis, P.C.
Birmingham, AL
Pittman, Iddo, Jr. ....Hammond, LA
Pittman, Ira B. ....Rockingham, NC
Pittman, Jack H. ....Hattiesburg, MS
Pittman, James Bradford, Jr. ....Mobile, AL
Pittman, James C., Jr. ....Hattiesburg, MS
Pittman, James Clinton ....Birmingham, AL
Pittman, James David ....Houston, TX
Pittman, James G. ....Bedford, IN
Pittman, James L. ....Chicago, IL
Pittman, Jan N. ....Raleigh, NC
Pittman, Jeffrey R. ....Jonesboro, AR
Pittman, Jerry F. ....Douglasville, GA
Pittman, Jerry M. ....Dallas, TX
Pittman, Jerry M., P.C. ....Dallas, TX
Pittman, Joe S. ....Enterprise, AL
Pittman, John B. ....Rockingham, NC
Pittman, John Mauzy ....Little Rock, AR
Pittman, Jonathan Hale ....Washington, DC
Pittman, Juan A. ....Culver City, CA
Pittman, Judy A. ....Roswell, NM
Pittman, Judy Markham ....Panama City, FL
Pittman, Julie W. ....Birmingham, AL
Pittman, Karen M. ....Clayton, MO
Pittman, Karen M. ....St. Louis, MO
Pittman, Keith A. ....Atlanta, GA
Columbus, GA
Pittman, Keith E. ....New Orleans, LA
Pittman Law Office ....Hattiesburg, MS
Pittman, Leta V. ....Pittsburgh, PA
Pittman, Lisa Etta .....House of Representatives,
Committee on Resources, GV
Pittman, Malcolm G., III ....Boston, MA
Pittman, Marcus P., Jr. ....Pascagoula, MS
Pittman, Margaret L. ....Department of Defense,
Defense Legal Services Agency, GV
Pittman, Mark ....Fort Worth, TX
Pittman, Mark L. ....Memphis, TN
Pittman, Nancy Sue Short ....Springfield, IL
Pittman, Nicole ....New Orleans, LA
Pittman, Pat Leigh ....New Bern, NC
Pittman, Paul M. ....Indianapolis, IN
Pittman & Perry, P.A. ....Panama City, FL
Pittman, Pittman, Carwie & Fuquay
Enterprise, AL
Mobile, AL
Pittman, R. Clinton ....Tarpon Springs, FL
Pittman, Raymond H., III ....Toledo, OH
Pittman, Robert C. ....Tacoma, WA
Pittman, Robert H. ....Rialto, CA
Pittman, Robert J. ....Sun City Center, FL
Pittman, Robert L. ....Montgomery, AL
Pittman, Robert W. ....Miami, FL
Pittman, Ross H. ....Tifton, GA
Pittman, Samuel Ira, Jr. ....Greenville, MS
Pittman, Sheri Soderberg ....Mound, MN
Pittman, Stephanie Robin ....Randolph, MA
Pittman, Steuart L., (P.C.)
Washington, DC
Pittman, Steven W. ....Memphis, TN
Pittman, Susan V. ....Miami, FL
Pittman, Thomas H. ....Tifton, GA
Pittman, Virgil ....Mobile, AL
Pittman, W. Lee ....Birmingham, AL
Pittman, William B. ....Raleigh, NC
Pittmann, Ross Henry, III ....Hinesville, GA
Pittman-Waller, M. V. Victoria ....Austin, TX
Pittner, Kurt T. ....Fort Dodge, IA
Pittner, Nicholas A. ....Columbus, OH
Pittocco, Louis P. ....Greenwich, CT
Pitton Law Offices, P.A. ....Iowa City, IA
Minneapolis, MN
Pitton, Michael J. ....Iowa City, IA
Minneapolis, MN
Pittoni, Bonchonsky & Zaino, LLP
Garden City, NY
Pittoni, Luke M. ....Stamford, CT
New York, NY
Pittoni, M. John ....Garden City, NY
Pittore, Ronald ....Lambertville, NJ
Pittroff, Kelley M. ....San Jose, CA
Pitts, Adrienne Banks ....Chicago, IL
Pitts, Albert L. ....Roswell, NM
Pitts, Alton G. ....Orlando, FL
Pitts, Alton G., P.A. ....Orlando, FL
Pitts, Annette ....Homestead, FL
Pitts, Arthur G. ....Lindenhurst, NY
Pitts, B. Wesley ....Gretna, LA
Pitts, Benjamin Younger ....Chattanooga, TN
Pitts, Bernard R. ....Cheyenne, WY
Pitts, Brian C. ....Hilton Head Island, SC
Pitts and Brittian, P.C. ....Knoxville, TN
Pitts, Carroll M., Jr. ....Rock Hill, SC
Pitts, Christina Terrell ....Nashville, TN
Pitts, Christopher J. ....Fairfield, NJ
Pitts, Clover S. ....Jackson, MS
Pitts & Collard, L.L.P. ....Houston, TX
Pitts, Conrad C. ....Florence, AL
Orlando, FL
Pitts, Cornelius ....Detroit, MI
Pitts, David A. ....Ellensburg, WA
Pitts, David L. ....Denver, CO
Pitts, Deborah ....Los Angeles, CA
Pitts, Donald F. ....Torrance, CA
Pitts, Donald W.
Yosemite National Park, CA
Pitts, Dugan & Diaz, P.C. ....Wood River, IL
Pitts, Edmund M. ....Wells, ME
Brookline, MA
Pitts, Edmund R. ....Wells, ME
Brookline, MA
Taos, NM
Pitts, Edward I. ....Syracuse, NY
Pitts, Frances ....Detroit, MI
Pitts, Gary B. ....Houston, TX
Pitts, George R. ....Washington, DC
Pitts, Gregory ....Fort Worth, TX
Pitts, H. Craig ....Oklahoma City, OK
Pitts, H. Keith ....Gadsden, AL
Pitts, Hay, Hugenschmidt & Devereux, P.A.
Asheville, NC
Pitts, Henry L. ....Chicago, IL
Pitts, Howard J. ....Wausau, WI
Pitts & Irons, P.C. ....Florence, AL
Pitts, J. Terry ....Cordova, TN
Pitts, Jack D. ....Greenville, RI
Pitts, James A. ....Racine, WI
Pitts, James T. ....Washington, DC
Pitts, Jamie ....Tulsa, OK
Pitts, Jeffrey W. ....Phoenix, AZ
Pitts, Jeffrey W. ....New York, NY
Pitts, Jennifer Bailey ....Elizabethtown, KY
Pitts, Jerry Owen ....Lima, OH
Pitts, Joe W. (Chip), III ....Irving, TX
Pitts, John R. ....Austin, TX
Pitts, Larry W. ....Newton, NC
Pitts, Lawrence J. ....Springfield, MO
Pitts, Lewis, Jr. ....Durham, NC
Pitts, Lydia M. ....New York, NY
Pitts, M. Bruce ....Huntsville, AL
Pitts, Marina B. ....Walnut Creek, CA
Pitts, Mark G. ....Albany, GA
Pitts, Marshall B., Jr. ....Fayetteville, NC
Pitts, Michael E. ....Redwood City, CA
Pitts, Michael L. ....Lansing, MI
Pitts, Michael S. ....Greenville, SC
Pitts, Morris W. ....Bay Village, OH
Pitts, Neal P. ....Orlando, FL
Pitts, Neal P., Professional Association
Orlando, FL
Pitts, Orville E. ....Milwaukee, WI
Pitts, Pamela D. ....Memphis, TN
Pitts, Patrice M. ....Washington, DC
Pitts, Paul E. ....Ardmore, OK
Pitts, Philip Henry ....Selma, AL
Pitts, Phillip ....Jefferson City, MO
Pitts and Pitts, A Professional Association
Wells, ME
Brookline, MA
Taos, NM
Pitts & Pitts, Inc., P.C. ....Phoenix, AZ

Platek, Todd L. ... **Hoboken, NJ**
New York, NY
Plater, D. Frank, Jr. ... Oklahoma City, OK
Plater, David D. ... Thibodaux, LA
Plater, Joseph R., III ... Reno, NV
Plater, Lori A. ... Reno, NV
Plater, Zygmunt J.B. ... Newton, MA
Plath, James P. ... Grosse Pointe Woods, MI
Plath, R. Russell ... Billings, MT
Plath, Robert W. ... Mill Valley, CA
Plati, Michael ... **Phoenix, AZ**
Platiau, Paul E. ... Johnston, RI
Platine, Ralph W. ... Margate City, NJ
Platis, Harry B. ... Lynnwood, WA
Platis, Tom G. ... Topeka, KS
Platke & Berkowitz, L.L.P. ... **St. Louis, MO**
Platke, Lee ... **St. Louis, MO**
Platkin, Charles S. ... New York, NY
Platkin, Lawrence P. ... **Madison, NJ**
Platkin, Richard ... Albany, NY
Platko, Jeffrey J. ... Cleveland, OH
Platner, Andrea J. ... **New York, NY**
Platner, Bronson ... Ellsworth, ME
Platner, Michael G. ... **Fort Lauderdale, FL**
Platner, Michael L. ... Washington, DC
Platner, Ronold P. ... **Phoenix, AZ**
Platnick, Barry H. ... **New York, NY**
Platnick, Penny Tibke ... **Rapid City, SD**
Platnik, Harry ... Silver Spring, MD
Plato, Edward D. ... **Farmington Hills, MI**
Platock, Neil W. ... **West Palm Beach, FL**
Platon, Benjamin V., II ... Fair Oaks, CA
Platón, Jaime S. ... San Juan, PR
Platow, William E. ... **Fort Lauderdale, FL**
Platsis, George J. ... Okemos, MI
Platsis, Maria E. ... Chicago, IL
Platt, Abe A. ... New York, NY
Platt, Alexander Hartley ... Washington, DC
Platt, Alison R. ... Los Angeles, CA
Platt, Allen C., II ... Louisville, KY
Platt, Allen C., III ... **New Albany, IN**
Platt, Amy L. ... Minneapolis, MN
Platt, Andrea Nicole ... Portland, OR
Platt, Anthony D. ... **Orange, CA**
Platt, Arlene A. ... Eugene, OR
Platt & Associates ... Los Angeles, CA
Platt, Barbara Juliet ... Denver, CO
Platt, Bob S. ... Granada Hills, CA
Platt & Brown ... Oakland, CA
Platt, Bruce D. ... **Tallahassee, FL**
Platt, Carol A. ... St. Louis, MO
Platt, Carrie A. ... **Houston, TX**
Platt, Charles C. ... **New York, NY**
Platt, Charles C.J. ... Boston, MA
Platt, Charles F. ... Houston, TX
Platt, Charles I. ... Junction City, KS
Platt, Christopher J. ... **New York, NY**
Platt, Clayton A. ... Austin, TX
Platt, Clyde A., Jr. ... **Seattle, WA**
Platt, Constance Adams ... Florence, MA
Platt, Cynthia Ann ... **Albany, NY**
Platt, Dana Lynn ... **New York, NY**
Platt, Daniel A. ... Los Angeles, CA
Platt, David ... **Hartford, CT**
Platt, David M. ... **East Lansing, MI**
Platt, David R. ... Junction City, KS
Platt, Dennis L. ... **Philadelphia, PA**
Platt, DiGiorgio & DiFabio ... Marlton, NJ
Paoli, PA
Platt, Elaine ... New York, NY
Platt, Elliot B. ... Philadelphia, PA
Platt, Falise J. ... Lisle, IL
Platt, Frank B. ... **Port Angeles, WA**
Platt, Frank D. ... New York, NY
Platt, Gary R. ... **Morristown, NJ**
Platt, Gene L. ... **McMinnville, OR**
Platt, George I., III ... **Fort Lauderdale, FL**
Platt, George L. ... New York, NY
Platt, George M. ... Eugene, OR
Platt, Gordon T. ... New York, NY
Platt, H. Jay ... St. Johns, AZ
Platt, Harold K. ... **Southampton, NY**
Platt, Harvey B. ... Phoenix, AZ
Platt, Harvey J. ... New York, NY
Platt, Henry A. ... **Washington, DC**
Platt, Henry N., Jr. ... Narberth, PA
Platt, Herman ... Ormond Beach, FL
Platt, Ian J. ... **Boston, MA**
Platt, Irwin, Taylor, Colley, Oliver & Moriarty ... **Bremerton, WA**
Port Angeles, WA
Port Townsend, WA
Sequim, WA
Platt, Jack M. ... New York, NY
Platt, James B. ... **Minneapolis, MN**
Platt, James R. ... Elmwood Park, IL
Platt, Janet D. ... Anchorage, AK
Platt, Jason ... Pleasantville, NY
Platt, Jeffrey R. ... Chicago, IL
Platt, Jeffrey S. ... San Diego, CA
Platt, Jennifer C. ... **Boston, MA**
Platt & Jenson, P.C. ... Coolidge, AZ
Platt, Joel R. ... Niles, IL
Platt, John C. ... Garden Grove, CA
Platt, John H., Jr. ... Northfield, IL
Platt, Jonathan A ... **Cleveland, OH**
Platt, Jonathan J. ... **Southampton, NY**
Platt, Jos. C. ... Forest Park, IL
Platt, Joseph L. ... Kaysville, UT
Platt, Karen Kay ... South El Monte, CA
Platt, Karen M. ... **Menlo Park, CA**
Platt, Katherine B. L. ... West Chester, PA
Platt, Kenneth M. ... Denver, CO
Platt, L. Steven ... Chicago, IL
Platt, L. Stuart ... Tyler, TX
Platt, Laurence E. ... **Washington, DC**
Platt, Lawrence B. ... South El Monte, CA
Platt & Lee, P.C. ... Holbrook, AZ
St. Johns, AZ
Platt, Leslie A. ... **Washington, DC**
Platt, Leslie K. ... Pittsburgh, PA
Platt, Lewis M. ... New Britain, CT
Platt, Loretta S. ... Concord, NH
Platt, Lyle C. ... **West Palm Beach, FL**
Platt, Lynnette N. M. ... Treasury Department,
Internal Revenue Service, GV
Platt, Mark ... **New York, NY**
Platt, Mark A. ... **Dallas, TX**
Platt, Marshall Douglas ... **Hollywood, FL**
Platt, Marshall Douglas, P.A.
Fort Lauderdale, FL
Hollywood, FL
Pembroke Pines, FL
Platt, Marvin S. ... Akron, OH
Platt, Mary F. ... **Cherry Hill, NJ**
Philadelphia, PA
Platt, Melanie McGee ... Atlanta, GA
Platt, Michael ... Chicago, IL
Platt, Michael D. ... Los Angeles, CA
Platt, Michael L. ... **Boulder, CO**
Denver, CO
Platt, Michael T. ... **Washington, DC**
Platt, Milton L. ... Brooklyn, NY
Platt, Mitchel D. ... **St. Johns, AZ**
Platt, Myra ... New York, NY
Platt, Nancy E. Kessler
National Labor Relations Board,
Office of the General Counsel, GV
Platt, Neal R. ... New York, NY
Platt, Nora M. ... **Milwaukee, WI**
Platt, Pamela J ... Concord, CA
Platt & Platt ... Junction City, KS
Platt & Platt, P.C. ... New York, NY
Platt, Platt & Platt ... **Southampton, NY**
Platt, R. James, Attorney at Law, P.A.
Lakeland, FL
Platt, R. James, Jr. ... **Lakeland, FL**
Platt, R. Sherman ... San Diego, CA
Platt, Richard ... Detroit, MI
Platt, Richard L. ... Newport Beach, CA
Platt, Richard Stephen ... Newport Beach, CA
Platt, Richard T. ... Florence, AZ
Platt, Robert A. ... Windsor, CT
Platt, Robert C. ... Oakland, CA
Platt, Robert C. ... **Washington, DC**
Platt, Robert D. ... Fairfax, CA
Platt, Robert H. ... **Los Angeles, CA**
Platt, Robert J. ... Elmhurst, IL
Platt, Robert M. ... Williamston, MI
Platt, Robert M., Jr. ... Cortland, OH
Warren, OH
Platt, Robert M., Sr. ... Cortland, OH
Warren, OH
Platt, Rona L. ... **Garden City, NY**
Platt, Ronald L. ... Boca Raton, FL
Platt, Ronald S., P.C. ... New York, NY
Platt, Rutherford H., Jr. ... Amherst, MA
Platt, Sean ... **Palo Alto, CA**
Platt, Shearn H. ... **San Diego, CA**
Platt, Sheldon ... New York, NY
Platt, Sheldon, P.C., The Law Offices of
New York, NY
Platt, Shelley Ann ... Richmond, VA
Platt, Stephen E. ... Elkhart, IN
Platt, Steven I. ... Upper Marlboro, MD
Platt, Steven Keith ... Chicago, IL
Platt, Stuart A. ... Pennsauken, NJ
Platt, Stuart I. ... St. Louis, MO
Platt, Susan J. ... Baltimore, MD
Platt, Thomas C. ... Uniondale, NY
Platt, Thomas C., III ... Merrimack, NH
Platt, Thomas E. ... **Seattle, WA**
Platt, Todd E. ... **Newport Beach, CA**
Platt, Vincent E. ... St. Paul, MN
Platt, W. Edward ... Houston, TX
Platt, Warren E. ... **Phoenix, AZ**
Platt and Westby, P.C. ... Phoenix, AZ
Platt, William B., III ... **Southampton, NY**
Platt, William E. ... Coolidge, AZ
Platt, William H. ... Allentown, PA
Platt, William I. ... New York, NY
Platt, William L. ... Manitowish Waters, WI
Platt, William R. ... **Tampa, FL**
Platte, David E. ... Belleair, FL
Platte, Jeffrey M. ... New York, NY
Platte, Paul M. ... **Columbia, SC**
Platte, Richard C. ... Bellingham, WA
Platte, Walter R. ... Columbus, OH
Platten, Christopher E. ... **San Jose, CA**
Platten, Jack R. ... Portland, OR
Platten, Peter ... **Limerick, PA**
Platten, Peter ... **Philadelphia, PA**
Platter, H. Lingo ... Houston, TX
Platter, Holly B. ... **Salt Lake City, UT**
Platter, Lawrence ... Charlotte, NC
Platter, Patrick J. ... **Springfield, MO**
Plattner, Daniel D. ... Denver, CO
Plattner, Dean R. ... Fort Myers, FL
Plattner, Francis B. ... Malabar, FL
Plattner, Frank T. ... Belleville, IL
Plattner, Glenn J. ... **Los Angeles, CA**
Plattner, Leslie A. ... **Phoenix, AZ**
Plattner, Richard S. ... **Phoenix, AZ**
Plattner, Robert D. ... **Albany, NY**
Plattner, Schneidman & Schneider, P.C.
Phoenix, AZ
Plattner Verderame, P.C. ... **Phoenix, AZ**
Platto, Charles (IBA) ... **Norwich, VT**
Platto, Charles, PLC, Law Offices of
Norwich, VT
Platton, Brian J. ... **New York, NY**
Platts, Henry S., Jr. ... Houston, TX
Platts, Michael J. ... Wenatchee, WA
Platts, William R. ... Kennewick, WA
Plattsmier, Charles B. ... Morgan City, LA
Plattsmier, Charles B., Ltd.
Morgan City, LA
Plattsmier, Don C. ... **Fort Worth, TX**
Plattus, Seth P. ... New York, NY
Platz, David Benjamin ... Bentonville, AR
Platz, Deborah Susan
Fort Lauderdale, FL
Platz, George A. ... **Chicago, IL**
Platz, Harlan ... New York, NY
Platz, John F. ... **Palo Alto, CA**
Platz, Lisa Michelle ... Oakland Township, MI
Platz, Richard S. ... Blue Lake, CA
Platz, Sarah L. ... Toledo, OH
Platz & Thompson, P.A. ... **Lewiston, ME**
Platzer, Ann R. ... **Prospect Heights, IL**
Platzer, Kathleen S. ... Columbus, OH
Platzer, Kenneth J. ... **New York, NY**
Platzer, Philip ... Massapequa, NY
Platzer Swergold Karlin Levine Goldberg & Jaslow, LLP ... Gibbsboro, NJ
New York, NY
Platzer, Sydney G. ... **New York, NY**
Platzer, Victoria ... Miami Beach, FL
Platzer, Victoria, P.A. ... Miami Beach, FL
Platzer, William J. ... Washington, DC
Platzkere, Jennifer J. ... **Philadelphia, PA**
Platzman, Jerome J. ... White Plains, NY
Plauché, A. Lane ... **Lake Charles, LA**
Plauché, Andrew L., Jr. ... **New Orleans, LA**
Plauché, Désireé M. ... Franklin, MA
Plauché, Gael ... Houston, TX
Plauché, George C. ... **Lafayette, LA**
Plauché & Hartley ... **Lafayette, LA**
Plauché Maselli Landry & Parkerson L.L.P.
Metairie, LA
New Orleans, LA
Plauché, Samuel W., IV ... **Seattle, WA**
Plauché Smith & Nieset, A Professional Law Corporation ... **Lake Charles, LA**
Plauché, S. W., III ... **Lafayette, LA**
Plauche, W. Evan ... **Metairie, LA**
Plauda, Daniel D. ... Naperville, IL
Plaum, Eric S. ... Philadelphia, PA
Plaum & Thompson, P.C. ... Philadelphia, PA
Plaushines, Peter J. ... **Waukesha, WI**
Plaut, Benjamin ... **Houston, TX**
Plaut, Bernard C. ... Cincinnati, OH
Plaut, Cathleen M. ... **Raleigh, NC**
Plaut, Christopher R. ... **New York, NY**
Plaut, David L. ... **Austin, TX**
Plaut, Diane Marcovici ... **New York, NY**
Plaut, Frank ... Lakewood, CO
Plaut, Marcel R. ... West New York, NJ
Plaut, Michael F. ... **New York, NY**
Plaut, N. Michael ... **Keene, NH**
Plaut, Peter K. ... Irving, TX
Plaut, Rebecca Mautner ... Allston, MA
Plaut, Tanya M. ... Orlando, FL
Plaut, Tanya M., P.A. ... Orlando, FL
Plautz, David R. ... White Plains, NY
Plautz, Robert ... New York, NY
Plavan, Frank P. ... Sacramento, CA
Plave, Erica Frohman ... Gaithersburg, MD
Plave, Lee J. ... **Washington, DC**
Plave, Mitchell E. F. ... Washington, DC
Plave, Ruth Z. ... **New York, NY**
Plavner, Jodi Trager ... **Philadelphia, PA**
Plavnick, Gary S. ... San Diego, CA
Plavnick, Lawrence R. ... Salem, MA
Plavnicky, David J. ... **Houston, TX**
Plavnicky Wheat & Marshall
Houston, TX
Plavoukos, Lee J. ... Syracuse, NY
Plawer, Henry J. ... Springfield, IL
Plawker, K. Roger ... **Roseland, NJ**
Plax, Karen A. ... Kansas City, MO
Plaxco, Dale ... Fort Smith, AR
Plaxco, R. Frank ... **Greenville, SC**
Plaxen & Adler, P.A. ... Columbia, MD
Plaxen, Bruce M. ... Columbia, MD
Plaxico, Charles M., Jr. ... Vienna, VA
Plaxico, Robert H. ... San Diego, CA
Plaxton, Kenneth D. ... **Alma, MI**
Playdon, Frances B. ... San Francisco, CA
Playdon, George W., Jr. ... **Honolulu, HI**
Playdon, Pamela J. ... Newport Beach, CA
Player, Charles P. ... Dallas, TX
Player, Jeanne M. L. ... Tallahassee, FL
Player, Judith Ann ... **Santa Clara, CA**
Player, Lea A. ... **Louisville, KY**
Player, Lonnie M., Jr. ... **Fayetteville, NC**
Player, Mack A. ... Santa Clara, CA
Player & McMillan, L.L.C. ... **Sumter, SC**
Player, Michael Scott ... Kilgore, TX
Player, Stephen W., Law Offices
Palo Alto, CA
Player, Suzanne Catherine ... Farmingdale, NY
Player, Theresa J. ... San Diego, CA
Player, Thomas A. ... **Washington, DC**
Atlanta, GA
Player, Thomas Andrew ... Winter Park, FL
Player, Thomas E., Jr. ... **Sumter, SC**
Player, William E. ... **Washington, DC**
Playfair, M. Brian ... Portland, OR
Playle, Darin E. ... **Nashville, TN**
Playter, Caroline ... Lynn, MA
Playton, Christina Laura ... Miami, FL
Playton, Dona ... Laramie, WY
Plaza, Ann M. ... **Washington, DC**
Plaza, Bernadette M. ... Wilmington, DE
Plaza, Christian E. ... **Washington, DC**
Plaza, Edward J. ... Chatham, NJ
Plaza, Edwin M. ... Chicago, IL
Plaza, Jeffrey William ... **Newark, NJ**
Plaza, Thomas M. ... **Sioux City, IA**
Plaza, Wayne F. ... **Chicago, IL**
Plaza de Jennings, Carmen
San Francisco, CA
Plazak, Douglas Allen ... **San Francisco, CA**
Plaza Mariota, Luis A. ... **San Juan, PR**
Plaze, Robert E.
Securities and Exchange Commission,
Division of Investment Management, GV
Plazibat, Stephen E. ... Chicago, IL
Pleas, Alexa ... **Tallahassee, FL**
Pleas, Coral D. ... **Milwaukee, WI**
Pleasant, James S. ... **Dallas, TX**
Pleasant, Laurie L. ... **Houston, TX**
Pleasant, Ray K. ... Angier, NC
Pleasant, Robert S. ... **Wadesboro, NC**
Pleasant, Robert W. ... New York, NY
Pleasant, Timothy Wayne
Colorado Springs, CO
Pleasanton, David F. ... West Palm Beach, FL
Pleasants, Donald A. ... Tampa, FL
Pleasants, Donald A., P.A. ... Tampa, FL
Pleasants, Edith E. ... Indianapolis, IN
Pleasants, James F. ... Bellevue, WA
Pleasants, James V. ... Brunswick, GA
Pleasants, Larry, (P.C.) ... Indianapolis, IN
Pleasants Law Firm ... **Memphis, TN**
Pleasants, Michael F. ... **Memphis, TN**
Pleasure, Robert J. ... Silver Spring, MD
Pleat & Associates, P.A. ... **Destin, FL**
Pleat, David Brand ... **Destin, FL**
Pleatman, Amy R. ... Los Angeles, CA
Pleatman, Debra S. ... **Covington, KY**
Pleau, Carol A. ... Worcester, MA
Pleban, C. John ... **St. Louis, MO**
Pleban, Sarah Shelledy ... **St. Louis, MO**
Plecas, Mary Ann ... Lakeland, FL
Plechner, Richard F. ... New Brunswick, NJ
Pleckan, Barbara J. ... Buffalo, NY
Pledger & Feord P.L.C. ... **Washington, DC**
Fairfax, VA
McLean, VA
Pledger, James L. ... Austin, TX
Pledger, Kevin D. ... **McLean, VA**
Pledger, Michael J. ... Houston, TX
Pledger, R. Harrison, Jr. ... **McLean, VA**
Pledger, Richard T. ... **Richmond, VA**
Pledger, Ruth ... Houston, TX
Pledger, T. Christopher ... **Austin, TX**
Pledger, Timothy C. ... **Houston, TX**
Pledl, Robert W. (Rock) ... Milwaukee, WI
Pleet, Eric L. ... Treasury Department,
Internal Revenue Service, GV
Pleet, Jesse L. ... **Reading, PA**
Pleet, Jesse L., P.C., Law Offices of
Lebanon, PA
Reading, PA
Pleeter, Elizabeth ...
Department of Labor, GV
Plefka, Walter C. ... St. Louis, MO
Pleger, Ernest W. ... **Marinette, WI**
Pleger, Gary L. ... Athens, GA
Pleger, Gary L., P.C. ... Athens, GA
Pleger, Katherine L. ... **Green Bay, WI**
Plegge, Brian R. ... **St. Louis, MO**
Plegge, Christopher Craig
Department of Labor,
Office of Secretary, GV
Plegge, Jerrie House ... **St. Louis, MO**
Plegge, John B. ... Little Rock, AR
Plegge, Lisa Doussard ... Washington, DC
Pleicones, Costa M. ... Columbia, SC
Pleier, Donna M. ... **Newtown Square, PA**
Plein, Thomas A. ... Oshkosh, WI
Pleines, Robert L. ... Sacramento, CA
Pleines, Thomas J. ... Chicago, IL
Pleiss, Larry T. ... **Tustin, CA**
Pleitz, Dan ... **Waco, TX**
Plemer, Kathleen S. ... **New Orleans, LA**
Plemmons, Gregory Scott ... Roswell, GA
Plemmons, James A. ... **Detroit, MI**
Plemmons, Loren E. ... Lenoir City, TN
Plemmons, Lynn F. ... Conway, AR
Plenge, Charles F. ... **Dallas, TX**
Pleninger, Stanley B. ... Anchorage, AK
Plenk, Bruce M. ... Topeka, KS
Plepelits, Marc O. ... New York, NY
Plepler, Andrew D. ... Department of Justice,
Tax Division, GV
Plepler & Barlow ... **Manchester, CT**
Plepler, Sanford J. ... **Manchester, CT**
Plescia, Joseph S. ... Hawthorne, NY
Plescia-Schultz, Michele ... Culver City, CA
Plese, David J. ... Rochester, MI
Plesec, William Thomas ... **Cleveland, OH**
Plesent, Nora Elizabeth ... New York, NY
Plesent, Stanley ... **New York, NY**
Plesha, Gregory G. ... Chicago, IL
Plesha, Robert A. ... Duluth, MN
Plesha & Vranicar ... Chicago, IL
Pleshaw, Robert J. ... Washington, DC
Pleshe, Dorothy C. ... **Salt Lake City, UT**
Plesich, Gregory T. ... Akron, OH
Pleska, Kenneth W. ... Mentor, OH
Pleska, P. Michael ... **Charleston, WV**
Pleska, Philip L. ... Atlanta, GA
Plesko, Andrew E. ... **St. Paul, MN**
Pleskow, Alan H. ... **New York, NY**
Pleskow, Susan I. ... **Buffalo, NY**
Pleskus, Susan ... Tarzana, CA
Plesnarski, Robert T.
Securities and Exchange Commission,
Division of Corporation Finance, GV
Pless, Erik J. ... **Green Bay, WI**
Pless, Habeeb & Slowinski ... Hackensack, NJ
Newark, NJ
New York, NY
Pless, Laurance D. ... **Atlanta, GA**
Pless, Robert J. ... Hackensack, NJ
Newark, NJ
Pless, Robert S. ... Tucker, GA
Plessala, Brian M. ... **Los Angeles, CA**

Plummer, Dana Hamilton ....Santa Monica, CA
Plummer & Farmer ....Houston, TX
Plummer, Franklin R. ....Concord, NC
Plummer, Herbert G. ....Hauppauge, NY
Plummer, Hubert George ....Hauppauge, NY
Plummer, Hugh J. ....Houston, TX
Plummer, J. Paul ....Houston, TX
Plummer, James C. ....Houston, TX
Plummer, James P. ....San Antonio, TX
Plummer, John M., III ....Bedford, IN
Plummer, John M., Jr. ....Bedford, IN
Plummer, Joyce M. ....Baton Rouge, LA
Plummer, Kathleen Mock ....St. Paul, MN
Plummer, Kerrie M. ....Des Moines, IA
Plummer Law Offices ....Bedford, IN
Plummer, Lee J. ....Jerseyville, IL
Plummer, Mark B. ....Orange, CA
Plummer, Mary Beth ....Indianapolis, IN
Plummer, Matthew W., Sr. ....Houston, TX
Plummer & Means, L.L.C. ....Mansfield, LA
Plummer, Mercedes Lara ....Bedford, IN
Plummer, Michael E. ....Covington, KY
Plummer, Michael R. ....Pittsburgh, PA
Plummer, Mott V. ....Newport, KY
Plummer, Noël S. ....Berkeley, CA
Plummer, Pamela J. Zepka ....Gettysburg, PA
Plummer, Patrick ....Phoenix, AZ
Plummer, Patrick Richard
Federal Labor Relations Authority, Authority Member Staff, GV
Plummer, Peter L. ....Marquette, MI
Plummer & Plummer, LLP ....Hauppauge, NY
Plummer, Raymond E. ....Anchorage, AK
Plummer, Risque W. ....Baltimore, MD
Plummer, Robert E. ....Mansfield, LA
Plummer, Robert H., Jr. ....Franklin, TN
Plummer, Robert P. ....Little Rock, AR
Plummer, Rosalind M. ....Philadelphia, PA
Plummer, Scott R. ....Minneapolis, MN
Plummer, Stacey J. ....St. Petersburg, FL
Plummer, Stacey J., P.A.
St. Petersburg, FL
Plummer, Steven ....Cold Spring, KY
Plummer, Terry L. ....San Diego, CA
Plummer, Vernon L., II ....Shelbyville, IL
Plummer, W. Hubert ....Hauppauge, NY
Plummer, William G. ....Annandale, NJ
Plummer, William J. ....Green Bay, WI
Plummer, William T. ....Oildale, CA
Plump, Andrew R. ....Washington, DC
Plump, Carolyn M. ....United States Senate, Office of Senate Chief Counsel for Employment, GV
Plump, Joan E. Danielson
Doylestown, PA
Philadelphia, PA
Plump, Leslie ....Jericho, NY
Plump, Leslie, P.C. ....Jericho, NY
Plumpe, Robert W. ....Detroit, MI
Plumridge, Richard R. ....Denver, CO
Plunk, Crolin E. ....Tullahoma, TN
Plunk, Dennis W. ....Savannah, TN
Plunk, Jay E., Jr. ....Moorestown, NJ
Plunk, John ....Athens, AL
Plunk, Robert M. ....West Des Moines, IA
Plunkert, Thomas J. ....St. Louis, MO
Plunket, Jas. C. ....Kingston, NY
Plunket, Thomas J. ....Kingston, NY
Plunkett, Andrew ....New York, NY
Plunkett, Barry C. ....Albany, NY
Plunkett, Barry W. ....Salem, MA
Plunkett, Brian F. ....Boston, MA
Plunkett, Charles E. ....Camden, AR
Plunkett, Christopher L. ....Salem, MA
Plunkett, Clifford W. ....Little Rock, AR
Plunkett & Cooney, P.C. ....Ann Arbor, MI
Bloomfield Hills, MI
Detroit, MI
Flint, MI
Gaylord, MI
Grand Rapids, MI
Kalamazoo, MI
Lansing, MI
Marquette, MI
Mount Clemens, MI
Petoskey, MI
Pittsburgh, PA
Plunkett, Daniel T. ....New Orleans, LA
Plunkett, David E. ....Chicago, IL
Plunkett, David J. ....Lowell, MA
Plunkett, Edward A., Jr. ....Stuarts Draft, VA
Plunkett, Eliska Marie ....New Orleans, LA
Plunkett, Gary D. ....Dayton, OH
Plunkett & Gibson, Inc. ....San Antonio, TX
Plunkett, Harry L. ....Glendale, CA
Plunkett, Hugh V., III ....Minneapolis, MN
Plunkett, J. Jerome ....St. Paul, MN
Plunkett, J. Matthew ....Tonawanda, NY
Plunkett, J. Patrick ....St. Paul, MN
Plunkett & Jaffe, P.C. ....Albany, NY
New York, NY
White Plains, NY
Plunkett, James T. ....Augusta, GA
Plunkett, Jimmy D. ....Thomson, GA
Plunkett, John Eugene ....Ridgewood, NJ
Plunkett, John L. ....San Diego, CA
Plunkett, Johnny J. ....Smyrna, GA
Plunkett, Joseph ....New York, NY
Plunkett, Joseph J. ....Allentown, PA
Plunkett, Joseph J., P.C. ....Allentown, PA
Plunkett, Kara E. ....Miami, FL
Plunkett, Kevin J. ....New York, NY
White Plains, NY
Plunkett, Kevin M. ....Chicago, IL
Plunkett, Lance R. ....New York, NY
Plunkett, Lawrence R., Jr. ....Metairie, LA
Plunkett, Lewin ....San Antonio, TX
Plunkett, Lorna Shaffer ....Albany, NY
Plunkett, Maureen A. ....Madison, WI
Plunkett, Michael A. ....Charleston, IL
Plunkett, Michael E. ....Philadelphia, PA
Plunkett, Michael O. ....Emeryville, CA
Plunkett & Oehlschlaeger PLC
Roanoke, VA
Plunkett, Patrick F. ....Lowell, MA
Plunkett, Paul B. ....Minneapolis, MN
Plunkett, Paul E. ....Chicago, IL
Plunkett, Peter D. ....Austin, MN
Plunkett & Plunkett ....Lowell, MA
Plunkett, Richard H. ....Rochester, MN
Plunkett, Richard P. ....Silver Spring, MD
Plunkett, Robert L. ....Lancaster, CA
Plunkett, Robert W., Jr. ....Bloomington, MN
Plunkett, Robt. W. ....St. Paul, MN
Plunkett, Roger S. ....Rochester, MN
Plunkett, Roma R. ....Williamsburg, VA
Plunkett, Sandra E. ....Ann Arbor, MI
Plunkett, Schwartz, Peterson, P.A.
Minneapolis, MN
Plunkett, Sean Murphy ....Scottsdale, AZ
Plunkett, Sharon G. ....Jackson, MS
Plunkett, Shepard, Plunkett & Hamilton, LLP ....Augusta, GA
Plunkett, Stephen O. ....Minneapolis, MN
Plunkett, Stuart C. ....San Francisco, CA
Plunkett, Theodore R. ....Minneapolis, MN
Plunkett, Thomas C. ....St. Paul, MN
Plunkett, Thomas C. ....Providence, RI
Plunkett, Thomas G. ....Birmingham, MI
Plunkett, T. L., Jr. ....Roanoke, VA
Plunkett, Tom ....Baton Rouge, LA
Plunkett, Wade M.
Office of Personnel Management, Compensation Division, GV
Plunkett, Warren F. ....Austin, MN
Plunkett, Warren F., & Associates
Austin, MN
Plunkett, William F., Jr. ....New York, NY
White Plains, NY
Plush, Mark D. ....New York, NY
Pluskey, Mark C. ....Fort Worth, TX
Pluss, Douglas A. ....Denver, CO
Pluss, Edward A. ....Denver, CO
Pluta, Carol A. ....Setauket, NY
Pluta, Joseph ....Bakersfield, CA
Pluta, Thomas A.
Department Of Veterans Affairs, Board of Veterans Appeals, GV
Pluth, Gerald E., Jr. ....Spokane, WA
Pluth, Robert R., Jr. ....Chicago, IL
Plutnick, Beverly A. ....Livingston, NJ
Pluto, John M. ....Caribou, ME
Plutte, James M. ....Fairfax, VA
Plutzik, Alan R. ....Walnut Creek, CA
Plutzker, Robert B. ....New York, NY
Pluymert, James H. ....Hoffman Estates, IL
Ply, Kenneth P. ....Newark, NJ
Plybon, Christopher J. ....Charleston, WV
Huntington, WV
Plybon, Suzanne Tucker ....Atlanta, GA
Plybon, William T. ....Atlanta, GA
Plyler, Cranford O., III ....Thomasville, NC
Plyler, Dale Ann Wilkinson ....Monroe, NC
Plyler & Elliott ....Thomasville, NC
Plyler, Joyce E. ....Charlotte, NC
Plyler, M. Matthew ....Charlotte, NC
Plyler, Matthew R. ....Fayetteville, NC
Plyler, W. Scott ....Santa Barbara, CA
Plyler, William Webb ....Raleigh, NC
Plymale & Associates ....Columbus, OH
Plymale, Richard E. ....Lexington, KY
Plymale, Ronald E. ....Columbus, OH
Plymale, Thomas M. ....Wayne, WV
Plymire, Cynthia D. ....Nashville, TN
Pnewski, Floyd A., III ....Minneapolis, MN
Png, Margaret L.H. ....Washington, DC
Po, Jennifer A. ....Lincolnshire, IL
Poach, William G., Jr. ....Phoenix, AZ
Sun City, AZ
Poag, Christopher C. ....Ketchikan, AK
Poag, D. Mark ....Houston, TX
Poag, James William, Jr.
West Columbia, SC
Poag, Judy L. ....Atlanta, GA
Poag, Mary Woodson (Molly)
Washington, DC
Poage, David R. ....Houston, TX
Poage, Rebecca L. ....New York, NY
Poage, Tammara K. ....Topeka, KS
Poague, Wall, Eshelman, Cox & Adams
Clinton, MO
Poarch, David A. ....Norman, OK
Poareo, Paul W. ....Los Angeles, CA
Poast, D. Michael ....Cincinnati, OH
Poats, Grayson M.
United States Postal Service, Law Department, GV
Pobedinsky, Alexander ....Syracuse, NY
Pober, Elizabeth Citrin ....New York, NY
Pober, Richard J. ....Westport, CT
Pober, Ross & Pasquini ....Westport, CT
Pobereyko, Paul P. ....Chicago, IL
Pobiner, Howard J. ....Dobbs Ferry, NY
Pobjecky, J. David ....Winter Haven, FL
Pobjecky, Thomas A. ....Tallahassee, FL
Poblete, Annette L. ....New York, NY
Poblete, Marizelle D. ....West Palm Beach, FL
Poblocki, Kathryn J. ....Fort Lauderdale, FL
Pocan, William S. ....Waukesha, WI
Pocaro, Jeffrey R. ....Bedminster, NJ
Pocaro, Ralph J. ....Summit, NJ
Pocaterra, Jan Long ....Los Angeles, CA
Pocchia, Anthony Joseph ....Staten Island, NY
Pocchia, James M. ....Chatham, NJ
Pocchiari, Daniel ....New York, NY
Pocchiari, Susan K. ....New York, NY
Poch, Joel M. ....Cheektowaga, NY
Poch, R. John ....Alpena, MI
Poch, Thomas B. ....St. Paul, MN
Pochal, Susan B. ....Mystic, CT
New London, CT
Poché, Camille Bienvenu ....Lafayette, LA
Poche, Charles A., Jr. ....Dallas, TX
Poche, Clifford E. ....Metairie, LA
Poche, Clifford E., A P.L.C. ....Metairie, LA
Poché, Laura C. ....Baton Rouge, LA
Poche, Marcel B. ....San Francisco, CA
Poche, Stephen S. ....Shalimar, FL
Poche, Stephen S., P.A.
Fort Walton Beach, FL
Shalimar, FL
Poche, Thomas F. ....Washington, DC
Poché, Timothy J. ....Baton Rouge, LA
Pochepan, Paul M. ....Buffalo, NY
Poches, Charles, Jr. ....Fort Pierce, SD
Poches and Lee Law Office ....Fort Pierre, SD
Pochick, Laura E. ....Charleston, WV
Pochiro, Patrick R. ....Youngstown, OH
Pochis, David S. ....Chicago, IL
Pochoday, Donna T. ....Chatham, NJ
Pochop, Stephanie E. ....Gregory, SD
Sioux Falls, SD
Pochopien, Donald J. ....Chicago, IL
Pochucha, Larry A. ....Richmond, VA
Pociask, Jack R. ....Atlanta, GA
Pocius, James E. ....Scranton, PA
Pocius, Kenneth J. ....Waterbury, CT
Pocius, Kenneth John ....Detroit, MI
Pocker, Beth Bird ....New Rochelle, NY
Pocker, Richard J. ....Las Vegas, NV
Pockrass, Steven F. ....Indianapolis, IN
Pockross, Keith M. ....Denver, CO
Pocock, Brian L. ....Eugene, OR
Pocock, Laura S. ....Rutherfordton, NC
Pocock, Sharon A. ....Washington, DC
Pocock, T. Keith ....Mission Viejo, CA
Pocras, Joyce M. ....Lincoln, NE
Pocrass, Gregory M. ....Pittsburgh, PA
Pocrass, James L. ....Los Angeles, CA
Pocsik, Darren B. ....New York, NY
Poczatek, Donna M. ....Deerfield, IL
Poda, Phyllis Kaye ....New York, NY
Podair, Leonard Lee ....New York, NY
Podawiltz, Jeffery L. ....Walnut Creek, CA
Podbelsek, Glenn ....Chicago, IL
Podberesky, Samuel
Department of Transportation, Office of the General Counsel, GV
Podberesky, Vicki I. ....Santa Monica, CA
Podbielski, Cheryl A. ....Beverly Hills, CA
Podbielski, John T.; Jr. ....Milwaukee, WI
Podboy, Alvin M., Jr. ....Cleveland, OH
Podboy, Ronald August ....Denver, CO
Podcasy, Bernard J. ....Wilkes-Barre, PA
Poddar, Ranjini ....New York, NY
Pode, Charles S. ....Ventura, CA
Podein, Michael W. ....Grand Rapids, MI
Podel, Louis ....Medford, NJ
Philadelphia, PA
Podell, Albert N. ....New York, NY
Podell, Barbara A. ....Philadelphia, PA
Podell, Bari S.
Securities and Exchange Commission, Division of Enforcement, GV
Podell, Gary ....New York, NY
Podell, George W. ....Fort Lee, NJ
Podell, Herbert S. ....New York, NY
Podell, James J. ....Milwaukee, WI
Podell, Kenneth E. ....Appleton, WI
Podell, Margaret Ansell ....New York, NY
Podell, Mortimer I. ....Miami Beach, FL
Podell, Owen Lee ....Sherman Oaks, CA
Podell, Peggy L. ....Milwaukee, WI
Podell & Podell ....Milwaukee, WI
Podell, Richard J. ....Milwaukee, WI
Podell, Richard J., & Associates, S.C.
Milwaukee, WI
Podell, Sidney B. ....Madison, WI
Podell, Todd M. ....Sunnyvale, CA
Podell, Ugent, Haney & Delery, S.C.
Milwaukee, WI
Podemski, Marilyn R. ....Portland, OR
Poder, Susan M. ....Chicago, IL
Podeschi, Kenneth R. ....Taylorville, IL
Podesta, Cari A. ....Palm Beach Gardens, FL
Podesta, Cari A., P.A.
Palm Beach Gardens, FL
Podesta, Eugene J., Jr. ....Memphis, TN
Podesta, Gerard B. ....Glen Ridge, NJ
Podesta, John D.
Executive Office Of The President, GV
Podesta, John H. ....Redwood City, CA
Podesta, Mary S. ....Washington, DC
Podesta, Myers & Crammond
Bloomingdale, NJ
Podesta, Roger E. ....New York, NY
Podewils, Lisa A. ....New York, NY
Podgers, James ....Chicago, IL
Podgor, Benjamin ....Massapequa Park, NY
Podgorny, Chester ....Sanibel, FL
Wayne, MI
Podgorny, George, Jr. ....Greensboro, NC
Podgorski, Norbert J. ....Dearborn Heights, MI
Podgorsky, Arnold B. ....Washington, DC
Podgurski, John A. ....Cleveland, OH
Podheiser, Ira L. ....Pittsburgh, PA
Podheiser, James F. ....Philadelphia, PA
Podheiser, Linda E. ....Boston, MA
Podhorzer, Elliot ....New York, NY
Podhradsky, Scott J. ....Wagner, SD
Podhurst, Aaron ....Miami, FL
Podhurst, Orseck, Josefsberg, Eaton, Meadow, Olin & Perwin, P.A.
Fort Lauderdale, FL
Miami, FL
Podis, Mark R. ....Nashville, TN
Podkopacz, Jerry S. ....Minneapolis, MN
Podkowa, Daniel ....Chicago, IL
Podkowirow, Waleri ....Rolling Meadows, IL
Podlas, James J. ....Blairstown, NJ
Podlas, Kimberlianne ....New York, NY
Podlasek, Robert M. ....Chicago, IL
Podlesak, John C. ....Chicago, IL
Podleski, John J. ....Carthage, MO
Podlesney, Francis A. ....Arlington, VA
Podlewski, Joseph R., Jr. ....Chicago, IL
Podlin, Mark J. ....Saint Simons Island, GA
Podliska, John F. ....Chicago, IL
Podlofsky, Ira C. ....New York, NY
Podlofsky & Orange ....New York, NY
Podnos, Marvin ....Brooklyn, NY
Podobinski, James R. ....Long Island City, NY
Podobnik, Raymond V. ....Lemont, IL
Podol, Michael ....Waltham, MA
Podolak, Edwin M. ....Hadley, MA
Podolefsky, Ronnie L. ....Waterloo, IA
Podoll and Podoll, P.C. ....Denver, CO
Podoll, Richard B. ....Denver, CO
Podoll, Robert C. ....Denver, CO
Podolnick, Andrew ....New Orleans, LA
Podolnick, Benjamin ....Atlantic City, NJ
Northfield, NJ
Podolnick, Matthew ....Pennsauken, NJ
Podolny, Janice B. ....Department of Justice, Immigration and Naturalization Service, GV
Podolski, Alfred L. ....Dedham, MA
Podolski, Michael A. ....Wellesley Hills, MA
Podolsky, Andrea G. ....New York, NY
Podolsky, Arnold M. ....Birmingham, MI
Podolsky & Associates, P.C.
Birmingham, MI
Podolsky, Bonnie D. ....New York, NY
Podolsky, David R. ....Rockville, MD
Podolsky, Melissa E. ....Tampa, FL
Podolsky, Meryl C. ....Southfield, MI
Podolsky, Ronald ....New York, NY
Podolsky, Seymour E. ....Lincoln Park, MI
Podolsky, Steven M. ....Pennsauken, NJ
Podolsky, Susan R. ....Washington, DC
Podorefsky, Arthur ....Newark, NJ
Podorowsky, Leon ....Hartford, CT
Podpeskar, Kenneth A. ....Minneapolis, MN
Podrasky, Mark ....Everett, WA
Podrasky, Sara E. ....New York, NY
Podrasky & Tweedie ....Everett, WA
Podraza, Joseph R., Jr. ....Philadelphia, PA
Podraza, Sharon M. ....Robbinsville, NJ
Podrebarac, Louis A. ....Meade, KS
Podrecca, Adolfo A. ....Fort Lauderdale, FL
Podren, Cynthia ....Berkeley, CA
Podrid, Albert ....Bayside, NY
Podrid, Paul A. ....Redwood City, CA
Podrug, Junius T. ....Beverly Hills, CA
Podryhula, Oleh ....Washington, DC
Podsaid, Patrick A. ....Miami, FL
Podsedly, Susan V. ....Centerville, OH
Podszus, Edward S. ....Boston, MA
Podurgiel, Bernard J. ....Boston, MA
Poduska, Joseph J. ....Chicago, IL
Poduslenko, Nicholas ....Philadelphia, PA
Poduval, Teri Diane Smith ....Marietta, GA
Podvey, Robert L. ....Newark, NJ
Podvey, Sachs, Meanor, Catenacci, Hildner & Cocoziello ....New York, NY
Newark, NJ
Podvia, Mark Wayne ....Carlisle, PA
Podvin, F. John, Jr. ....Dallas, TX
Podvin, Francis J. ....Wisconsin Rapids, WI
Podwika, Joseph A. ....Memphis, TN
Podwil, Robert C. ....Philadelphia, PA
Podwill, Loren D. ....Portland, OR
Pody, Dean H. ....Seattle, WA
Podzamsky, Susan B. ....Jacksonville, FL
Poe, Alexandra Porges ....New York, NY
Poe, Anita Harper ....Missoula, MT
Poe, Brian David ....Atlanta, GA
Poe, Charla ....Marietta, GA
Poe, David R. ....Washington, DC
Poe, Edgar A., Jr. ....Charleston, WV
Poe, Fielding ....St. Louis, MO
Poe Firm, The, P.C. ....Cordova, TN
Poe, Franklin A. ....Boothbay Harbor, ME
Poe & Freireich, P.A. ....Florham Park, NJ
Poe, G. Jona, Jr. ....Durham, NC
Poe, Grace Y. ....Chicago, IL
Poe, H. Sadler ....Atlanta, GA
Poe, Harvey C., Jr. ....Melbourne, FL
Poe, Harvey R. ....Florham Park, NJ
Poe, Hazel C. ....Clemson, SC
Poe, Heather K. ....Cincinnati, OH
Poe, Hoof & Reinhardt ....Durham, NC
Poe, Hoyt & Roediger, P.C. ....St. Louis, MO
Poe, Ivan O. ....Wichita, KS
Poe, James E. ....Tulsa, OK
Poe, James M. ....Atlanta, GA
Poe, Jeanne Early ....Cleveland, OH
Poe, Jennifer R. ....Dallas, TX
Poe, Josh L. ....Tampa, FL
Poe, Karla K. ....Albuquerque, NM
Poe, Kimberly D. ....Madisonville, KY
Poe, Kip ....Lubbock, TX
Poe & Klatt, P.A. ....Ocala, FL
Poe, Kristen J. ....New York, NY
Poe, L. Harvey, Jr. ....Washington, DC
Annapolis, MD
Owings Mills, MD
Poe, Leonard ....Burnsville, NC
Poe, Michael A. ....Columbus, OH
Poe, Michael K. ....Melbourne, FL

Poe, Myron F. ...... Royal Oak, MI
Poe & Poe, P.A. ...... Melbourne, FL
Poe, Richard S. ...... Charlotte, NC
Poe, Richard W. ...... San Mateo, CA
Poe, Richard W. ...... Maspeth, NY
Poe, Robert Alan ...... Greenwood Village, CO
Poe, Ronald E. ...... Cordova, TN
Poe, Sheena E. ...... Winston-Salem, NC
Poe, Stephen D. ...... Winston-Salem, NC
Poe, Stephen L. ...... Denton, TX
Poe, Steven F. ...... Chicago, IL
Poe, Ted ...... Houston, TX
Poe, Vera Leigh ...... Dallas, TX
Poe, W. Edward, Jr. ...... Charlotte, NC
Poe, Wellon B., Jr. ...... Oklahoma City, OK
Poe, William E. ...... Charlotte, NC
Poe, William H. ...... Elk Grove, CA
Poehler, Andrea McDowell ...... Eagan, MN
Poehler, Bryan W. ...... Vancouver, WA
Poehlmann, Eric A ...... Burlington, VT
Poehlmann, John J., S.C. ...... Milwaukee, WI
Poehlmann, Paul F. ...... Milwaukee, WI
Poehlmann, Theodore A.E., P.C., Law Office of ...... Woodstock, IL
Poehlmann, Theodore A. E.
Woodstock, IL
Poehls, Susan G. ...... Los Angeles, CA
Poehner, Maria J. ...... Wilmington, DE
Poekel, Charles A., Jr. ...... Verona, NJ
New York, NY
Poel & Foster ...... San Jose, CA
Poel, Lee E. ...... San Jose, CA
Poelke, Mark J. ...... Charlotte, NC
Poelking, Thomas F. ...... Chicago, IL
Poell, Joseph R. ...... Waukegan, IL
Poellnitz, Farley A. ...... Tuscaloosa, AL
Poellnitz, Richard H. ...... Greensboro, AL
Poelman, B. Lloyd ...... Salt Lake City, UT
Poelman & Langa ...... Wailuku, HI
Poelman, LLoyd ...... Wailuku, HI
Poelman, Roch P. ...... New Orleans, LA
Poelman, Ronald E. ...... Salt Lake City, UT
Poelman, Ronald S. ...... Salt Lake City, UT
Poelman, Stuart L. ...... Salt Lake City, UT
Poelstra, David A. ...... Lafayette, IN
Poenisch, Gary M. ...... San Antonio, TX
Poeppel, Sarah L. ...... Naperville, IL
Poepplein, Ronald F. ...... Mineola, NY
Poepsel, Michael J. ...... Omaha, NE
Poer, DL ...... Bloomington, IN
Poer, Jonathan L. ...... Adrian, MI
Poer, Stephen L. ...... Birmingham, AL
Poerio, James M. ...... Pittsburgh, PA
Poerio, Joseph Mark ...... Washington, DC
Poertner, Emil L. ...... St. Louis, MO
Poeschl, Kohn & Epstein LLP
Oakland, CA
Poeschl, Patrick L. ...... Stamford, CT
Poeschl, Thomas F., Jr. ...... Oakland, CA
Poese, Kimberly S. ...... Santa Ana, CA
Poeta, John R. ...... Cherry Hill, NJ
Philadelphia, PA
Poetting, Gary M. ...... Des Moines, IA
Poetzel, Megan B. ...... Chicago, IL
Poey, Dennis B. ...... Los Angeles, CA
Pofahl, Brady C. ...... Albuquerque, NM
Pofahl, C. F. ...... Dallas, TX
Pofahl, Nancy Gene ...... Houston, TX
Pofcher, DiSciullo & Petruzziello
Boston, MA
Poff, Craig Joseph ...... Beaufort, SC
Poff, Franklin A., Jr. ...... Texarkana, TX
Poff, James E. ...... Mount Olive, NJ
Poff, Joe S. ...... Houston, TX
Poff, Pamela S. ...... Weehawken, NJ
Poff, Phyllis G. ...... Auburn, IN
Poff, Randall E. ...... Portland, OR
Poff, Richard G., Jr. ...... Birmingham, AL
Poff, Richard H. ...... Richmond, VA
Poff, Robert L. ...... Roanoke, VA
Poff, William B. ...... Roanoke, VA
Poffenbarger, John E. ...... Seattle, WA
Poffenbarger, John T. ...... Charleston, WV
Poffenbarger, Richard M. ...... Eagle, CO
Poffenbarger, William H. ...... Frederick, MD
Poffenberger, Clara M. ...... Washington, DC
Poffenberger, J. Dwight, Jr.
Cincinnati, OH
Poffenberger, John D. ...... Cincinnati, OH
Poffenberger, Leanne King ...... Yardley, PA
Poffenberger, Max V. ...... Oklahoma City, OK
Poffenberger, Richard L. ...... Perry, IA
Poffenberger, Virginia Joy ...... Perry, IA
Poffinbarger, Judd N., Jr. ...... Pittsburgh, PA
Pofit, Jeffrey William ...... Bradford, MA
Pogach, Harry A. ...... Towson, MD
Pogal, Patricia B. ...... Atlanta, GA
Pogalies, Kristine ...... San Diego, CA
Pogany, Andras H. ...... South Orange, NJ
Pogany, Andrew T.
General Accounting Office, Office of the General Counsel, GV
Pogar, Joseph, Jr. ...... Treasury Department, Office of the Comptroller of the Currency, GV
Pogarsky, Alan J. ...... Toms River, NJ
Pogarsky, Louis & Santangelo
Toms River, NJ
Pogeler, Gary D. ...... New York, NY
Poger, Arthur L. ...... St. Louis, MO
Poger, Gerald M. ...... St. Louis, MO
Pogge, Mariann ...... Springfield, IL
Pogge, R. Ronald ...... Des Moines, IA
Poggi, Francis A., Jr. ...... Mobile, AL
Poggi, John J., Jr. ...... Santa Clara, CA
Poggi, Paul ...... New York, NY
Poggi, Thomas F. ...... Orinda, CA
Poggio, Maria Paula ...... Indianapolis, IN
Poglaze, Debra M. ...... Hackensack, NJ
Pogledich, Philip J. ...... San Francisco, CA
Poglinco, Patricia A. ...... New York, NY
Pogoda, Daniel E ...... Somerville, MA
Pogoda, I. Edward ...... New York, NY
Pogoda, Kevin T. ...... McLean, VA
Pogoloff, Donald D. ...... Fresno, CA
Pogorelec, John D. ...... Clifton, NJ
Pogoriler, Harvey W. ...... Milwaukee, WI
Pogorzelski, Henry M. ...... Houston, TX
Pogostin, Abraham J. ...... New Rochelle, NY
Pogostin, Marc ...... New Rochelle, NY
Pogostin, Richard D. ...... New York, NY
Pogrebin, Bertrand B. ...... Mineola, NY
New York, NY
Pogrow, Jeffrey O. ...... Bronx, NY
Pogrund, David B. ...... Chicago, IL
Pogrund, Sherwin I., (P.C.) ...... Chicago, IL
Pogson, Christopher A. ...... Binghamton, NY
Pogson, Mara J. ...... Coraopolis, PA
Pogson, Stephen W. ...... Phoenix, AZ
Pogue, Alan D. ...... Greenwood Village, CO
Pogue, Brian V. W. ...... Irwindale, CA
Pogue, Donald C. ...... New York, NY
Pogue, G. Michael ...... La Crescenta, CA
Pogue, John L. ...... Warren, OH
Pogue, Leonard F., III ...... Nashville, TN
Pogue, Mark A. ...... Providence, RI
Pogue, Mary Elizabeth ...... Indianapolis, IN
Pogue, Michael D. ...... Palo Alto, CA
Pogue, Peter A. ...... Long Beach, CA
Pogue, Peter H. ...... Indianapolis, IN
Pogue, Ralph E. ...... Aberdeen, MS
Pogue, Richard W. ...... Cleveland, OH
Pogue, Robert ...... New Hampton, NY
Pogue, Sharon Kay ...... Sacramento, CA
Pogue Stark Law Firm ...... Aberdeen, MS
Pogue, Thomas L. ...... Tuscaloosa, AL
Pogue, Timothy H. ...... Florence, SC
Pogue, Timothy H. ...... Marion, SC
Pogue, Timothy H. ...... Mullins, SC
Pogust, Glenn J. ...... New York, NY
Pogust, Harris L. ...... Pennsauken, NJ
Pogwizd, James L. ...... Chicago, IL
Pohan, Armand ...... North Bergen, NJ
Pohl, Amelia E. ...... Boca Raton, FL
Pohl, Amy Kirby ...... Pittsburgh, PA
Pohl, Arnold M. ...... New York, NY
Pohl, Beverly A. ...... Fort Lauderdale, FL
Pohl, Christopher ...... Boston, MA
Pohl, Dale L. ...... Eureka, KS
Pohl, Frank L. ...... Winter Park, FL
Pohl, Geoffrey V. ...... Omaha, NE
Pohl, Glenn K. ...... Irvine, CA
Pohl, Howard A. ...... Miami, FL
Pohl, Irwin P. ...... Cleveland, OH
Pohl, J. Scott ...... Wichita, KS
Pohl, James E. ...... Dallas, TX
Pohl, Janice Swimmer ...... San Diego, CA
Pohl, Jeffrey M. ...... Albany, NY
Pohl, Joanne Theobald ...... Red Wing, MN
Pohl, John B. ...... Glens Falls, NY
Pohl, Joseph P., III ...... Pittsburgh, PA
Pohl, Karen N. ...... Lexington, KY
Pohl, Kathleen H. ...... Canandaigua, NY
Pohl, Lisa M. ...... Toledo, OH
Pohl, LLoyd E. K. ...... Banning, CA
Pohl, Mark R. ...... Washington, DC
Pohl, Michael A. ...... Cleveland, OH
Pohl, Michael A. ...... Houston, TX
Pohl, Nelson A. ...... Woodland, CA
Pohl, Paul Michael ...... Pittsburgh, PA
Pohl, Robert W. ...... Prairie Village, KS
Kansas City, MO
Pohl, Ronald S. ...... New York, NY
Pohl & Short, P.A. ...... Kissimmee, FL
Orlando, FL
Winter Park, FL
Pohl, Stephen C. ...... Bozeman, MT
Pohl, Steven D. ...... Boston, MA
Pohl, Steven R. ...... Royal Oak, MI
Pohl, Stuart M. ...... Williamsville, NY
Pohl, Timothy R. ...... Chicago, IL
Pohl, W. Timothy ...... Voorhees, NJ
Pohland, David C. ...... Greensburg, PA
Pohle, Carl C. ...... St. Louis, MO
Pohle, Timothy A. ...... Washington, DC
Pohle, William H., Jr. ...... Monterey Park, CA
Pohlen, Patrick A. ...... Palo Alto, CA
Pohlen, Paul D., Jr. ...... Bellflower, CA
Pohlenz, Julius ...... Westmont, IL
Pohlers, Nicolette M. ...... Denver, CO
Pohli, Laura Anne ...... Dallas, TX
Pohlig, Francis Marion ...... Miami, FL
Pohlig, Helen M. ...... Phoenix, AZ
Pohlkamp, Francis W., Jr. ...... Madison, WI
Pohlman, Berentje C. M. ...... Enderlin, ND
Pohlman, Dolphy O. ...... Butte, MT
Pohlman, Herbert C. ...... Naples, FL
Pohlman, James D. ...... Spencerville, OH
Pohlman, James E. ...... Washington, DC
Columbus, OH
Pohlman, Jay A. ...... Blasdell, NY
Pohlman, Jill M. ...... Salt Lake City, UT
Pohlman, Katherine J. ...... Minneapolis, MN
Pohlman, Richard C. ...... Buffalo, NY
Pohlman, Robert J. ...... Phoenix, AZ
Pohlman, Scott W. ...... Lemoyne, PA
Pohlman, William J. ...... Columbus, OH
Pohlmann, Karen Pieslak
Philadelphia, PA
Pohlmann, William H. ...... Ardsley, NY
Pohlmeyer, Michael J. ...... Mexico, MO
Pohls, Robert R., & Associates
Walnut Creek, CA
Pohlson, Gary M. ...... Laguna Hills, CA
Pohlson, Moorhead & Goethals, RLLP
Huntington Beach, CA
Irvine, CA
Laguna Hills, CA
Mission Viejo, CA
Newport Beach, CA
Santa Ana, CA
Pohly, Lawrence M. ...... Melville, NY
Pohly, Linda A. ...... Flint, MI
Pohly, Linda A., P.C. ...... Flint, MI
Poholek, Constant S., Jr. ...... Pawtucket, RI
Pohorelsky, John R. ...... Lake Charles, LA
Pohorelsky, Viktor V. ...... New York, NY
Pohorille, Cecilia ...... Greenwich, CT
Pohoryles, Louis ...... Washington, DC
Pohren, Edward F. ...... Omaha, NE
Pohrer, Jack E. ...... St. Louis, MO
Pohrer, William J. ...... St. Louis, MO
Poidmore, Anthony J., Law Offices of
Sacramento, CA
Poile, Henry J. ...... Mount Prospect, IL
Poindexter, Alan ...... Lebanon, TN
Poindexter, Anne Hensley ...... Carmel, IN
Poindexter Associates ...... Lafayette Hill, PA
Poindexter, Carol A. ...... Overland Park, KS
Poindexter, Dale W. ...... Ruston, LA
Poindexter & Doutré, Inc.
Los Angeles, CA
San Francisco, CA
Poindexter, E. Timothy ...... Lafayette Hill, PA
Poindexter, Gammiel G. ...... Surry, VA
Poindexter, Georgette C. ...... Lafayette Hill, PA
Poindexter, Gerald G. ...... Surry, VA
Poindexter, Gordon W., Jr. ...... Waynesboro, VA
Poindexter, Gwendolyn Ryder
Los Angeles, CA
Poindexter, James W. ...... San Francisco, CA
Poindexter, Jamiel E. ...... Boston, MA
Poindexter, Jeffrey E. ...... Springfield, MA
Poindexter, John A. ...... New Orleans, LA
Poindexter, John O., III ...... Mount Laurel, NJ
Poindexter, John T. ...... Santa Cruz, CA
Poindexter, Mark D. ...... Washington, DC
Poindexter, Martha M. ...... Norfolk, VA
Poindexter, Michael L. ...... Denver, CO
Poindexter, Miles, II ...... Danville, VA
Poindexter, Obrea O. ...... Washington, DC
Poindexter, Paul O. ...... Los Angeles, CA
Poindexter and Poindexter ...... Surry, VA
Poindexter, Portia J. ...... New York, NY
Poindexter, Robert R. ...... San Francisco, CA
Poindexter & Schorsch, A Professional Corporation ...... Waynesboro, VA
Poindexter, Thomas C. ...... Washington, DC
Poindexter, Tiffany Gabeheart
Paducah, KY
Poindexter, Travis D. ...... Kansas City, MO
Poindexter, Virginia McNeill ...... Richmond, VA
Poindexter, William M. ...... Los Angeles, CA
Poinsett, Richard G. ...... Hampton, VA
Poinsett, Roy M. ...... Terrell, TX
Poinsett, Royce P. ...... Dallas, TX
Poinsette, Cheryl L. ...... San Francisco, CA
Point, James N. ...... Rogersville, TN
Point, Juli ...... Coos Bay, OR
Point, Lawrence W. ...... Woodstown, NJ
Pointer, Ann E. ...... St. Petersburg, FL
Pointer, Ann Margaret ...... Atlanta, GA
Pointer, D. Michael, II ...... St. Petersburg, FL
Pointer, David B. ...... Kansas City, MO
Pointer, Edward J. ...... New Orleans, LA
Pointer, Elizabeth Sue ...... Little Rock, AR
Pointer, Homer S. ...... Department of Justice, Federal Bureau of Investigation, GV
Pointer, J. Edgar, Jr. ...... Gloucester, VA
Pointer, Jack Dempsey ...... Oklahoma City, OK
Pointer, Karen E. ...... Los Angeles, CA
Pointer, Richard P. ...... San Jose, CA
Pointer, Sam C., Jr. ...... Birmingham, AL
Pointer, Susie ...... Little Rock, AR
Pointner, Thomas D. ...... Charlevoix, MI
Pointner, Thomas D., P.C. ...... Charlevoix, MI
Pointon, Louis R. ...... Elgin, IL
Points, Beverly J. ...... York, PA
Points, Chad D. ...... Houston, TX
Points, David C., Jr. ...... Huntsville, AL
Poir é, Alfonso L. ...... American Canyon, CA
Poiré, Karin A. ...... Oakland, CA
Poirier, Aldric C., Jr. ...... Metairie, LA
New Orleans, LA
Poirier, Brent ...... Las Cruces, NM
Poirier, Brian W. ...... Hamden, CT
Poirier, C.J., Law Office, P.A.
Fairway, KS
Poirier, Carla T. ...... Honolulu, HI
Poirier, C.J. ...... Fairway, KS
Poirier, David J. ...... Chicago, IL
Poirier, David W. ...... Stamford, CT
Poirier, Dean R. ...... Raleigh, NC
Poirier, Dominique T. ...... Fairfax, VA
Poirier, G. R. ...... Diamond Bar, CA
Poirier, James W. ...... Department of Justice, Civil Division, GV
Poirier, John R. ...... Carteret, NJ
Poirier, Joseph M. ...... Belleville, IL
St. Louis, MO
Poirier, Kenneth P. ...... Lansing, MI
Poirier, Marc R. ...... Newark, NJ
Poirier, Mary Ann ...... Washington, DC
Poirier, Omer G. ...... Chicago, IL
Poirier, Phillip L., Jr. ...... San Diego, CA
Poirier, Robin W. ...... Baton Rouge, LA
Poirier, Ronald J. ...... Franklin, MA
Poirier, Ronald R. ...... Roseville, CA
Poirier-Whitley, Kirstin D.
Los Angeles, CA
Poirot, Carl R. ...... San Diego, CA
Poirot, Marla Thompson ...... Houston, TX
Poirot, Paul E. ...... Washington, DC
Poirot, Rod L. ...... Dallas, TX
Poirrier, Dwight D. ...... Gonzales, LA
Poirrier, Michael J. ...... Pierre Part, LA
Poissant, Brian M. ...... New York, NY
Poissant, Joseph M. ...... Malone, NY
Poissant, Margaret A., P.C. ...... Houston, TX
Poissant, Margaret Anne ...... Houston, TX
Poissant & Nichols, P.C. ...... Malone, NY
Poissant, Robert J. ...... El Paso, TX
Poisson, David E. ...... Washington, DC
Poisson, Fred D., Sr. ...... Wadesboro, NC
Poisson, Frederick D., Jr. ...... Wadesboro, NC
Poisson & Hackett, P.C. ...... Garden City, NY
Poisson, Jack ...... Asheville, NC
Poisson, Pierre Charles
House of Representatives, Office of Legislative Counsel, GV
Poisson, Poisson, Bower & Clodfelter
Wadesboro, NC
Poisson, Robert R. ...... Hyattsville, MD
Poisson, William J. ...... Garden City, NY
Poissonnier, Gerard A. ...... Waterville, ME
Poitevent, Benjamin E. ...... Tallahassee, FL
Poitevent, Earl S., III ...... Jacksonville, FL
Poitevent, Edward B., II
New Orleans, LA
Poitevent, John ...... Mandeville, LA
Poitinger, Jack L., Jr. ...... Tallahassee, FL
Poitras, Alison Faltersack ...... Enfield, CT
Poitras, David M., (A Professional Corporation) ...... Los Angeles, CA
Poitras, Gregory B. ...... Portland, ME
Poitras, Norma S. ...... Portland, OR
Poitrast, Francis G. ...... Boston, MA
Pojani, Dennis ...... Worcester, MA
Pojanowski, Joseph A., III ...... Clifton, NJ
Pojednic, Leonard C. ...... New York, NY
Pojman, Paul J. ...... Parma Heights, OH
Poka, John A. ...... Monroe, NY
Pokalsky, Ann R. ...... Garden City, NY
Pokalsky, John S. ...... New York, NY
Pokart, Joseph ...... New York, NY
Pokart & Pokart ...... New York, NY
Pokart, Stephen P. ...... New York, NY
Pokela, A. Thomas ...... Sioux Falls, SD
Pokela, David S. ...... Greensboro, NC
Pokempner, Joseph K. ...... Baltimore, MD
Poker, Mark S. ...... Milwaukee, WI
Pokiniewski, Stephen J., Jr.
Philadelphia, PA
Pokladnik, Frank ...... Lamarque, TX
Poklar, Michael A. ...... Cleveland, OH
Poklar, Robert A. ...... Cleveland, OH
Poklar, Robert A., & Associates, L.L.P.
Cleveland, OH
Poklemba, Hobbs & Ulasewicz, L.L.C.
Albany, NY
Glens Falls, NY
Lake Placid, NY
Saratoga Springs, NY
Poklemba, John J. ...... Albany, NY
Saratoga Springs, NY
Pokoik, Gary M. ...... New York, NY
Pokoj, Stephen J. ...... Detroit, MI
Pokojny, Nancy P. ...... New York, NY
Pokora, Tammy Huskey ...... Columbia, SC
Pokornicky, Edward J.
Department of Veterans Affairs, Office of the General Counsel, GV
Pokorny and Associates, Ltd. ...... La Grange, IL
Pokorny, James F. ...... San Diego, CA
Pokorny, James F., A.P.C., Law Offices of
San Diego, CA
Pokorny, Joseph K. ...... Towson, MD
Pokorny, Julie L. ...... Lincoln, NE
Pokorny, Norman ...... San Diego, CA
Pokorny, Sally D. ...... Independence, KS
Pokorny, Stephen J. ...... Chicago, IL
Pokorny, William H. ...... La Grange, IL
Pokorny, William H., Jr. ...... La Grange, IL
Pokorski, Jody Kathleen ...... Phoenix, AZ
Pokorski, Patricia J. ...... Barrington, IL
Pokotilow, Manny D. ...... Philadelphia, PA
Pokotilow, Steven B., (P.C.)
New York, NY
Pokras, Bruce A. ...... Peapack, NJ
Pokras, Sheila, (Mrs.) ...... Long Beach, CA
Pokrass, Gregory S. ...... Brookfield, WI
Pokrass, Tyler Seth ...... Durham, NC
Pokross, David R. ...... Boston, MA
Pokross, David R., Jr. ...... Boston, MA
Pokusa, Robert E. ...... Washington, DC
Pola, Frank, Jr. ...... Metairie, LA
San Juan, PR
Polacco, Frank A. ...... Hempstead, NY
Polacek, Alan C. ...... Bridgehampton, NY
Locust Valley, NY
Melville, NY
Polacek, Fred T. ...... Providence, RI
Polacek, Michael ...... Salt Lake City, UT
Polacek, Pamela C. ...... Harrisburg, PA
Polacek, Peggy Jo ...... Lincoln, NE
Polacek, Timothy C. ...... San Diego, CA
Polach, Patricia ...... Washington, DC
Polach, Raymond F. ...... Schaumburg, IL
Polacheck, Allan ...... Glendale, WI
Polacheck, Joan F. ...... Chicago, IL
Polacheck, Judy ...... Boston, MA
Polacheck, Laura R. ...... Washington, DC
Polacheck, Mary K. Eads ...... Lemoyne, PA
Polacheck, R. Steven ...... Park Ridge, IL
Polachek, Michael J. ...... Addison, IL
Polachek, Pecile & Smith, P.C.
Scranton, PA
Wilkes-Barre, PA
Polachek, R. Steven ...... Barrington, IL
Polachek, Ralph R. ...... Chantilly, VA

Polachek, Richard A. ... **Wilkes-Barre, PA**
Polachek, Thomas A. ... **Chicago, IL**
Polack, Gail ... Santa Ana, CA
Polack, James ... **Omaha, NE**
Polack, Joseph ... **Omaha, NE**
Polack, Robert ... **Indianapolis, IN**
Polack, Rosenberg, Endom & Riess, L.L.P.
New Orleans, LA
Polack, Stanley J. ... Passaic, NJ
Polackwich, Alan S., Sr. (P.A.)
Vero Beach, FL
Polaczyk, Chris B. ... Plymouth, MI
Poladian, Tamar ... Glendale, CA
Polaha, Stephen J. ... **Media, PA**
Polak, Aaron J. ... **New York, NY**
Polak, Alan G. ... New York, NY
Polak, Bernard B. ... New York, NY
Polak, Frederick B. ... **Roseland, NJ**
New York, NY
Polak, Hans G. ... **Newark, NJ**
Polak, John J. ... **Charleston, WV**
Polak, John Joseph, Jr. ... Fall River, MA
Polak, Jonathan G. ... **Dallas, TX**
Polak, Karyn S. ... **New York, NY**
Polak, Rebecca ... **Dallas, TX**
Polak, Samuel J. ... **Dallas, TX**
Polak, Simone Charlotte ... Wailuku, HI
Polak, Stanley J. ... Chelmsford, MA
Polak, Vivian L. ... **New York, NY**
Polak, Werner L. ... **New York, NY**
Polakoff, Benjamin L. ... **Towson, MD**
Polakoff, Stephen K. ... **New York, NY**
Polakov, Anthony S. ... Los Angeles, CA
Polakovic, John M.
Rancho Cucamonga, CA
Polakovic, Michael J.
Highlands Ranch, CO
Polakovic, Ray ... Bellevue, WA
Polales, Dean J. ... Chicago, IL
Polales, John C., (P.C.) ... Chicago, IL
Polan, A. Ronald ... Milwaukee, WI
Polan, David J. ... Tucson, AZ
Polan, Diane ... **New Haven, CT**
Polan, Jack H. ... Palm Beach Gardens, FL
Polan, James R. ... **Tulsa, OK**
Polan, Laura B. ... Mamaroneck, NY
Polan, Lisa Gail ... Shelton, CT
Polan, Mark S. ... Van Nuys, CA
Polan, Michael S. ... Del Mar, CA
Polan, Steven M. ... **New York, NY**
Polance, Jack ... Portland, OR
Polance, Michael E. ... Chicago, IL
Polanco, Arnold G. ... **Houston, TX**
Polanco, Pedro J. ... **San Juan, PR**
Poland, Arlette S. ... Palm Desert, CA
Poland, Christian M. ... **Chicago, IL**
Poland, David D. ... Santa Rosa, CA
Poland, Depler and Shepherd Co., L.P.A.
Mansfield, OH
Shelby, OH
Poland, Douglas ... **Muskegon, MI**
Poland, Douglas M. ... **Chicago, IL**
Poland, F. Herbert ... **Shelby, OH**
Poland, G. James ... Brighton, CO
Poland, George W. ... St. Louis, MO
Poland, Hugh R., Jr. ... Clarksville, TN
Poland, Jacquelyn L. ... **New Brunswick, NJ**
Poland, James E. ... Ravenna, OH
Poland, James E. ... Portland, OR
Poland, James L. ... Dallas, TX
Poland, John P. ... **St. Louis, MO**
Poland, Kenneth R. ... Houston, TX
Poland, Kevin T. ... Ravenna, OH
Poland, Kim Brown ... **Charleston, WV**
Poland, Linda O. ... **Lufkin, TX**
Poland, Michelle R. ... Knoxville, TN
Poland, Paul A. ... Fort Myers, FL
Poland, Peter J. ... **Houston, TX**
Poland and Poland ... Ravenna, OH
Poland & Poland ... Clarksville, TN
Poland, R. Michael ... Cameron, MO
Poland, Richard C. ... St. Augustine, FL
Poland, Richard L. ... Long Beach, CA
Poland, Sandra S. ... Albany, NY
Poland, Scott ... Lakewood, CO
Poland, Sherman S. ... Bethesda, MD
Poland, Suellen S. ... **Baltimore, MD**
Poland, Susan L. ... **Stamford, CT**
Poland, Todd M. ... **Newark, NJ**
Poland, W. Charles ... Waynesboro, VA
Poland, William D., Jr. ... **Baltimore, MD**
Harrisburg, PA
Poland, William H. ... Clarksville, TN
Polaner, Melissa ... New York, NY
Polani, Leron ... **New York, NY**
Polaniecki, Elliott ... **Cincinnati, OH**
Polanin, John, Jr. ... New York, NY
Polanowski, Rosalind M. ... **Buffalo, NY**
Polans, Christine M. ... **Tampa, FL**
Polanski, Daniel A. ... Easton, PA
Polanski, Margaret A. ... Greensburg, IN
Polansky & Baraty, S.C. ... Milwaukee, WI
Polansky, Burton B. ... Milwaukee, WI
Polansky, Larry P. ... Lake Harmony, PA
Polansky, Marc A. ... **Chicago, IL**
Polansky, Michael D. ... Plainview, NY
Polansky, Mitchell S. ... **Miami, FL**
Polansky, Paul J. ... Austin, TX
Polansky, Paul Michael ... Baltimore, MD
Polansky, Paul Michael, P.A. ... Baltimore, MD
Polansky, Rica J. ... New Orleans, LA
Polansky, Ronald V. ... Corpus Christi, TX
Polansky, Steven J. ... **Moorestown, NJ**
Philadelphia, PA
Polansky, William G. ... **New York, NY**
Polanzi, Craig W. ... Aiea, HI
Polard, Steven G. ... **Santa Monica, CA**
Polaschek, Joseph A. ... **Rock Island, IL**

Polasek, John T. ... **Houston, TX**
Polasek, Ronald L. ... Barrington, IL
Polashuk, David J. ... Baltimore, MD
Polashuk, Robyn R. ... **Burbank, CA**
Polashuk, Stacie S. ... **Los Angeles, CA**
Polaski, Alan P. ... Portland, OR
Polaski, Anne Spencer ... **Chicago, IL**
Polaski, Paul J. ... Brookfield, WI
Polaski, Susan Joyce ... Reston, VA
Polaski, Thomas W. ... South Orange, NJ
Polasky, Frank M. ... **Saginaw, MI**
Polastri, Pablo E. ... New York, NY
Polaszek, Christopher S. ... Tampa, FL
Polatin, Jacob N. ... **Boston, MA**
Polatnick, Stephen Jay ... Miami, FL
Polatsek, David F.
Department of Housing and Urban Development,
Office of General Counsel, GV
Polatsek, Frederick A.
Fort Lauderdale, FL
Polatsek, Harry D. ... Coral Gables, FL
Fort Lauderdale, FL
Lake Worth, FL
Polatsek, Harry D., P.A.
Fort Lauderdale, FL
Lake Worth, FL
Coral Gables, FL
Polatsek, William ... Lakewood, OH
Polatty, George J., Jr. ... Roswell, GA
Polatty, George J., Sr. ... Roswell, GA
Polatty, Robert W. ... Dawsonville, GA
Roswell, GA
Polatty & Sullivan ... Dawsonville, GA
Roswell, GA
Polay, Neil A. ... Poughkeepsie, NY
Polayes, Faye M. ... New York, NY
Polcari, Jerome A. ... Belmont, MA
Polcari, Meryl M. ... Morganville, NJ
Polcari, Ralph E. ... **Red Bank, NJ**
Polce, Anthony Paul ... Dearborn, MI
Polchinski, Peter D. ... **Huntington, NY**
Polchinski, Peter D. ... **New York, NY**
Polchinski, Peter D. ... **White Plains, NY**
Polcyn, Frank R. ... St. Louis, MO
Polcyn, Laura R. ... **St. Louis, MO**
Polcyn, Thomas A. ... **St. Louis, MO**
Poldberg, Mindy Larsen ... **Des Moines, IA**
Polden, Donald J. ... Des Moines, IA
Polden, Lorelei J. Alterwein
Fort Lauderdale, FL
Poldy, Megan Rae ... Washington, DC
Pole, Christopher W.
Fort Lauderdale, FL
Pole, Debra E. ... **Los Angeles, CA**
Polebaum, Elliot E. ... **Washington, DC**
Polebaum, Mark N. ... **Boston, MA**
Polednak, Donald T. ... **Las Vegas, NV**
Polega, Gary R. ... **Chicago, IL**
Polek, Frank J. ... **San Diego, CA**
Polek O'Brien, Anastasia ... **Chicago, IL**
Polelle, Michael J. ... Chicago, IL
Polemeni, Mark A. ... **New York, NY**
Polen, Albert B. ... Willoughby, OH
Polen, Charles A. "Pete"
Virginia Beach, VA
Polen, Dennis J. ... Woodland Hills, CA
Polen, Esther ... Philadelphia, PA
Polen, Jean Speiser ... West Chester, PA
Polen, Jeri ... Los Angeles, CA
Polen, Larry ... Towson, MD
Polen, Mark E. ... West Palm Beach, FL
Polen, Raymond ... Rego Park, NY
Polentz, Michael C. ... **San Jose, CA**
Polentz, Rod S. ... San Mateo, CA
Polenzani, Joseph E. ... **Waukegan, IL**
Polera, John C. ... **Stamford, CT**
Tarrytown, NY
Tarrytown, NY
Poles, John G. ... **New York, NY**
Poles, Michael Philip ... New Rochelle, NY
Poles, Tublin, Patestides & Stratakis, LLP
New York, NY
Polese, James F. ... **Phoenix, AZ**
Polese, Pietzsch, Williams & Nolan, A Professional Association ... **Phoenix, AZ**
Poleselli, Nicole L. ... San Mateo, CA
Polesetsky, Matthew P. ... **Los Angeles, CA**
Poleski, Earl G., Jr. ... Jackson, MI
Poleski, Edward G. ... Henderson, NV
Polesky, Joelle E. ... **Wilmington, DE**
Polestino, Frank S. ... Jamaica, NY
Polette & Lynn ... Kansas City, MO
Poletti, Thomas J. ... **Beverly Hills, CA**
Poletto, Janet L. ... **Springfield, NJ**
Poletto, Kim David ... **Denver, CO**
Polevoy, Jason T. ... **New York, NY**
Polevoy, Martin D. ... **New York, NY**
Polevoy, Nancy T. ... New York, NY
Polevoy, Pamela L. ... **New York, NY**
Polewski, John P. ... **DeSoto, TX**
Polewski & Loomis ... **DeSoto, TX**
Poley, Brooks F. ... **Minneapolis, MN**
St. Paul, MN
Poley, D. Scott ... **Cincinnati, OH**
Poley, Jeffrey A. ... **Raleigh, NC**
Poley, John D. ... Denver, CO
Poley, John D. ... Dayton, OH
Poley, Lawrence I. ... Hackensack, NJ
Poley, M. Robert ... Hackensack, NJ
Poley & Poley ... Hackensack, NJ
Poley, Richard Edward ... Boulder, CO
Poleynard, Kelley B. ... **Los Angeles, CA**
Polgar, Gary B. ... **Merced, CA**
Polgar, Matthew J.
Grosse Pointe Woods, MI
Polgar, Richard ... Warren, MN

Polglase, Holly M. ... **Hartford, CT**
Portland, ME
Boston, MA
Concord, NH
Polglase, Janice E. ... Fresno, CA
Polglaze, Daniel J. ... **Minneapolis, MN**
Polgrean, John S. ... Sacramento, CA
Polhamus, Danny Thomas
Long Beach, CA
Polhamus, William R. ... Columbus, OH
Polhemus, Richard V. ... Dover Plains, NY
Polhemus, Steven J. ... **LaBelle, FL**
Polhill, Freddie ... Orange, NJ
Poli, Carl E. ... **Chicago, IL**
Poli, Francis C. ... New York, NY
Poli, Michael N. ... **Phoenix, AZ**
Poli, Michelle M. ... **Ann Arbor, MI**
Poliak, Daniel C. ... **Seattle, WA**
Poliak, Paul M. ... **Seattle, WA**
Poliakoff, Abba David ... **Baltimore, MD**
Poliakoff, Andrew N. ... Spartanburg, SC
Poliakoff, Edward E. ... **Columbia, SC**
Poliakoff, Gary A. ... **Clearwater, FL**
Fort Lauderdale, FL
Fort Myers, FL
Maitland, FL
Miami, FL
Naples, FL
St. Petersburg, FL
Sarasota, FL
West Palm Beach, FL
Poliakoff, Gary W., (P.A.)
Spartanburg, SC
Poliakoff, Poole & Associates
Spartanburg, SC
Poliakoff, Ryan D. ... **New York, NY**
Policar, Raymond ... **Fairfield, CA**
Policastro, Anthony V. ... **Clearwater, FL**
Policastro, Kristen A. ... White Plains, NY
Policastro & LeRoux, P.A.
Clearwater, FL
Policastro, Marc D. ... **Woodbridge, NJ**
Policastro, Michael John ... Newark, NJ
Policastro, William ... Hackensack, NJ
Policelli, Frank ... **Utica, NY**
Polich, Barbara K. ... **Salt Lake City, UT**
Polich, John E. ... Los Angeles, CA
Polich, Joseph J., Jr. ... **Winter Park, FL**
Polich, Judith ... Santa Fe, NM
Polich, Melissa K. ... **Chicago, IL**
Polich, Roy P. ... Iron River, MI
Polich, Steve J. ... Iron River, MI
Polich, Theodore P., Jr. ... **Los Angeles, CA**
Polich, Thomas A. ... Denver, CO
Polich, Thomas A., P.C. ... Denver, CO
Polichio, Susan M. ... Sacramento, CA
Policicchio, Joseph B. ... Somerset, PA
Policinski, Henry J. ... **Fairfield, CT**
Policinski, Thomas P. ... Cassopolis, MI
Polick, Joseph M. ... Wheaton, IL
Polick, Steven P. ... Des Plaines, IL
Policriti, Annamarie ... Jamaica, NY
Policy, Carmen A. ... Santa Clara, CA
Policy, Edward R. ... **Cleveland, OH**
Policy, Sindy J. ... **Cleveland, OH**
Policy, Vincent Mark J. ... **Washington, DC**
Policzer, Milton A. ... Los Angeles, CA
Polidor, Barry J. ... Springfield, VT
Polidora, Roxane A. ... **San Francisco, CA**
Polidore, Alfred C. ... **New York, NY**
Polidori & Bussler ... Milwaukee, WI
Polidori, Cecilia Fagan ... Herkimer, NY
Polidori, Charles F. ... Milwaukee, WI
Polidori, David ... Warren, MI
Polidori, Gary L. ... **Lakewood, CO**
Polidori, Gerome, Franklin and Jacobson, L.L.C. ... **Denver, CO**
Lakewood, CO
Polidori, Steven R. ... Denver, CO
Polidoro, Monique R. ... **Hartford, CT**
Polidoro, Paul D. ... Patterson, NY
Polier, Jonathon Wise ... **New York, NY**
Polier, Tulin & Cohn ... New York, NY
Poliferno, Richard J. ... **Boston, MA**
Polifka, John C. ... Sioux City, IA
Polifka, Pearl ... **New York, NY**
Polifka, Robert ... **New York, NY**
Polifron, Pamela Cohen ... Millburn, NJ
Polifroni, Robert L. ... **Springfield, NJ**
Polignani, William K. ... **Long Beach, NY**
Polikoff, Alan M. ... Deerfield, IL
Polikoff, Alexander ... Chicago, IL
Polikoff, Bernard A. ... Deerfield, IL
Polikoff & Clareman, P.C. ... New York, NY
Polikoff, Gary M. ... Gladwyne, PA
Polikoff, Harry ... New York, NY
Polikoff, Marvin M. ... Baltimore, MD
Polikov, E. Scott ... Austin, TX
Polikov, Leon K. ... Papillion, NE
Polimeni, Eleanor L. ... Newburgh, NY
Polimeni, John A. ... Canandaigua, NY
Polimeni, Thomas G. ... **Boston, MA**
Polin, Alan J. ... Coral Springs, FL
Polin, Andrew D. ... Glen Cove, NY
Polin, David L. ... Petaluma, CA
Polin, Eva ... Washington, DC
Polin, Kenneth D. ... **San Diego, CA**
Polin, Kenneth L. ... Scarsdale, NY
Polin, Lorraine Berlund ... Hauppauge, NY
Polin, Martin ... San Luis Obispo, CA
Polin, Michael R. ... Los Angeles, CA
Santa Ana, CA
Polin, Prisco & Villafane ... Glen Cove, NY
Polin, Richard L. ... Philadelphia, PA
Polin, Robert A. ... Philadelphia, PA
Polin, Sandra Jyll ... Durham, NC
Polin, Sandra Segal, Law Offices of
Santa Monica, CA

Polin, Theodore L. ... New York, NY
Poliner, Bernard ... **Middletown, CT**
Poliner, Elizabeth S. ... **Washington, DC**
Poliner, Gary A. ... Milwaukee, WI
Poliner, Jason M. ... **Albany, NY**
Poliner, L. Joseph ... Los Angeles, CA
Poliner, Michael C. ... **Washington, DC**
Poliner, Myron J. ... **Middletown, CT**
Poliner, Phillip R. ... Long Beach, CA
Poliner, Poliner & Antin, P.C.
Hartford, CT
Middletown, CT
Poliner, Robert S. ... **Middletown, CT**
Poling, Amy Sapper ... **San Diego, CA**
Poling, Beverly A. ... Sewickley, PA
Poling, Brant E. ... Columbus, OH
Poling & Casey ... **Charlotte, NC**
Poling, Christopher ... **Indianapolis, IN**
Poling, Dan W. ... Depoe Bay, OR
Poling, Darl W. ... Beckley, WV
Poling, David M. ... Rancho Cucamonga, CA
Poling, Douglas L. ... Westport, CT
Poling, Jan Wade ... Department of Agriculture,
Office of the General Counsel, GV
Poling, Jason A. ... **Huntington, WV**
Poling, Kathleen U. ... **Martinez, CA**
Poling, McGaw & Poling, P.C.
Detroit, MI
Troy, MI
Poling & Poling ... **Concord, CA**
Martinez, CA
Walnut Creek, CA
Poling, Raymond L. ... Sea Isle City, NJ
Poling, Richard B. ... **Troy, MI**
Poling, Richard B., Jr. ... **Troy, MI**
Poling, Richard D. ... **Charlotte, NC**
Poling, Scott E. ... **Martinez, CA**
Poling, Steven Clark ... **Southfield, MI**
Poling, Susan A. ... General Accounting Office,
Office of the General Counsel, GV
Poling, William Compton, Jr
Washington, DC
Polinger, Thomas M. ... Hermosa Beach, CA
Polino, Joseph F. ... Roebling, NJ
Polino, Joseph F., P.C. ... Roebling, NJ
Polino, Steven T. ... **Dallas, TX**
Polino, Teresa M. ... **Washington, DC**
Polinske, Brian L. ... Edwardsville, IL
Polinske, Lisa A. ... Elm Grove, WI
Polinske, Teresa Ann ... Lynchburg, VA
Polinski, Thomas J., & Associates
Chicago, IL
Polinski, Thomas John ... Chicago, IL
Polinsky, Andrew M. ... **Goleta, CA**
Polinsky, Audrey Lynn ... New York, NY
Polinsky, David ... **Tarzana, CA**
Polinsky, David B. ... Greensboro, NC
Polinsky, Eric A. ... **Hartford, CT**
Polinsky, H. Gilbert ... Brooklyn, NY
Polinsky, Harriet M. ... **New York, NY**
Polinsky, Irwin B. ... Woodbury, NY
Polinsky, Jeffrey ... **Hartford, CT**
Polinsky, Laurie H. ... **Philadelphia, PA**
Polinsky, Santos & Polinsky, LLC
Hartford, CT
Polinsky, Sara ... Los Angeles, CA
Polinsky, Steven S. ... East Brunswick, NJ
Polintan, Odette ... **Seattle, WA**
Poliquin, Gerard S.
National Credit Union Administration,
Office of General Counsel, GV
Poliquin, Goodspeed, Mulder & Skripko
Santa Ana, CA
Poliquin, James D. ... **Portland, ME**
Poliquin, Mark P. ... **Santa Ana, CA**
Poliquin, Shawn A. ... Portsmouth, NH
Polis, Bertram ... Tucson, AZ
Polis, George N. ... Ventnor City, NJ
Polis, Gerald D. ... Riverside, CA
Polis & Hartshorne, P.C. ... Tucson, AZ
Polis, Michael Gaspar ... **Sacramento, CA**
Polis, Nancy S. ... Houston, TX
Polis, Thomas J. ... **Irvine, CA**
Polisar, Leonard M. ... **New York, NY**
Polisar, Steven ... Miami Beach, FL
Polise, David W. ... Houston, TX
Polise, David W., PLLC ... Houston, TX
Polish, George A. ... San Juan, PR
Polish, Jack B. ... New York, NY
Polish, James ... **Los Angeles, CA**
Polish, Jonathan S. ... **Chicago, IL**
Polish, Sheldon S. ... **Fort Lauderdale, FL**
Polishan, Timothy P., Law Offices of
Wilkes-Barre, PA
Polisher, Edward N. ... **Philadelphia, PA**
Polishook, Lewis A. ... **New York, NY**
Polisini, John ... **Houston, TX**
Polisky, Joel S. ... **Chicago, IL**
Polisky, Philip Scott ... **Chicago, IL**
Chicago, IL
New York, NY
Polisner, Jeffrey D. ... **Walnut Creek, CA**
Polisoto, Catherine M. ... Los Angeles, CA
Polis-Pearson, Carol ... **New York, NY**
Polisson, James G. ... Boston, MA
Polit, Robert B. ... **Chicago, IL**
Politan, John R. ... **Scottsdale, AZ**
Politan, Mark J. ... **Roseland, NJ**
Politan, Nicholas H. ... Newark, NJ
Politan, Nicholas H. ... **New York, NY**
Politano, Frank L. ... Basking Ridge, NJ
Politano, Thomas P. ... Wilmington, VT
Polite, Audrey ... St. Louis, MO
Politeo, Deanne B. ... **Oakland, CA**
Santa Rosa, CA
Polites, Thomas G ... **Lexington, KY**
Prestonsburg, KY
Politi, Diane ... Youngstown, OH

Politi, Joan E. ....Boston, MA
Politi, Stephen M. ....Boston, MA
Politis, John N. ....Los Angeles, CA
Politis, Michael J. ....Daytona Beach, FL
Deltona, FL
Politis, Nicholas J. ....Los Angeles, CA
Politis, Nicholas S. ....Long Beach, CA
Politis & Politis ....Los Angeles, CA
Politis, Steven ....Long Island City, NY
Politiski, Gregory J. ....Orange, CA
Politiski, Richard-James ....Santa Ana, CA
Politiski, Robert C. ....Santa Ana, CA
Polito, Andrew S. ....Newark, NJ
Polito, Anthony J. ....Pittsburgh, PA
Polito, Bruno ....New York, NY
Polito, Denise L. ....San Diego, CA
Polito, Francis A.
Equal Employment Opportunity Commission, Office of Legal Counsel, GV
Polito, Frank D. ....Los Angeles, CA
Polito, Humbert J., Jr. ....New London, CT
Polito, John A. ....Cleveland, OH
Polito, John J. ....Bellevue, WA
Polito, John R. ....Summerville, SC
Polito, John S. ....Cleveland, OH
Polito, Joseph C. ....Joliet, IL
Polito, Joseph C., Ltd. ....Joliet, IL
Polito, Joseph L. ....Loves Park, IL
Polito, Joseph M. ....Detroit, MI
Polito, Joseph R., Jr. ....West Chester, PA
Polito, Karyn E. ....Worcester, MA
Polito, LuAnn A. ....Cleveland, OH
Polito, Margaret R. ....New York, NY
New York, NY
Polito, Melissa Suzanne ....Rockville, MD
Polito, Michael G. ....Fairview Park, OH
Polito, Nat N. ....Washington, DC
Polito & Russo ....Fairview Park, OH
Polito, Salvatore A. ....St. Petersburg, FL
Polito & Smock, P.C. ....Pittsburgh, PA
Polito, Stephen C. ....Lake Charles, LA
Polito, Steven M. ....San Diego, CA
Polito, William P. ....Webster, NY
Politte, Keith D. ....San Francisco, CA
Politte & Thayer ....Washington, MO
Politz, Bennett L. ....Shreveport, LA
Politz, Henry A. ....Shreveport, LA
Politz, Nyle A. ....Shreveport, LA
Politz, Paul J. ....New Orleans, LA
Politzer, Jerome F., Jr. ....Monterey, CA
Salinas, CA
Politzer, M. Arnold ....Baltimore, MD
Polivick, John P. ....Clearwater, FL
Polivick, Lew ....Sikeston, MO
Polivka, James J. ....Louisville, KY
Polivka, Maureen O. ....Fairfax, VA
Polivy, Calvin ....Cedarhurst, NY
Polivy, Denise R. ....Hartford, CT
Polivy, Gail L. ....Washington, DC
Polivy, Margaret (Margot) ....Washington, DC
Polivy, Richard B. ....Hartford, CT
Polivy, Steven P. ....New York, NY
Polivy & Taschner, LLC ....Hartford, CT
Polizano, Frank ....New York, NY
Polizio, Tiziana Ester Adelaide ....Boston, MA
Polizotto, Bruce A. ....Indianapolis, IN
Polizzi, Anthony ....Kingston, NY
Polizzi, Arturo ....Toledo, OH
Polizzi, Carol Anne ....New York, NY
Polizzi, Catherine M. ....Palo Alto, CA
Polizzi, Dennis G. ....Totowa, NJ
Polizzi, John M. ....Dearborn, MI
Polizzoto, Fran ....Kew Gardens, NY
Polizzotto, Alfred ....Brooklyn, NY
Polizzotto, Alfred J., III ....Brooklyn, NY
Polizzotto, Dominic F. ....Indianapolis, IN
Polizzotto, Fran S. ....Jamaica, NY
Polizzotto, Joseph ....New York, NY
Polizzotto, Julie E. ....Indianapolis, IN
Poljak, Rebecca Kearney ....Pittsburgh, PA
Poljak, Stephen J. ....Pittsburgh, PA
Polk, Angela Lauer ....Santa Clara, CA
Polk, Arnold S. ....Beaverton, OR
Polk & Associates ....Dallas, TX
Polk, Benjamin M. ....New York, NY
Polk, Beverly Benton ....Lexington, KY
Polk, C. Edward, Jr. ....Washington, DC
Polk, Charles E., Jr. ....St. Louis, MO
Polk, Christopher ....Los Angeles, CA
Polk, Christopher F. ....Louisville, KY
Polk, Corinna B. ....Los Angeles, CA
Polk, Deborah A. ....Kansas City, MO
Polk, Dennis B. ....Golden, CO
Polk, Donald L. ....Boston, MA
Polk, Douglas J. ....Chicago, IL
Polk, Ed ....San Francisco, CA
Polk, Edward S. ....Miami, FL
Polk, Elizabeth Rice ....Columbia, SC
Polk, Eugene K. ....Pensacola, FL
Polk, Frank L. ....Oklahoma City, OK
Polk, Franklin G. ....United States Senate, Committee Legal Personnel, GV
Polk, Herbert P. ....New York, NY
Polk, Ivan Roger ....Ashland, OR
Polk, James E. ....Midlothian, TX
Polk, Jay M. ....Phoenix, AZ
Polk, Joe A. ....Little Rock, AR
Polk, John C. ....Washington, DC
Polk, John J. ....Wilmington, DE
Polk, John L. ....Punta Gorda, FL
Polk, John R. ....Albuquerque, NM
Polk, John W. ....Washington, DC
Polk, Jonathan I. ....New York, NY
Polk, Kenneth J. ....Pittsburgh, PA
Polk, Larry R. ....Detroit, MI
Polk, Lee T. ....Chicago, IL
Polk, Lewie R. ....Memphis, TN
Polk, Loretta P. ....Washington, DC
Polk and Lynch ....Louisville, KY
Polk, Marc A. ....Boston, MA
Polk, Marlon A. ....Omaha, NE
Polk, Martha Quinn ....Henderson, KY
Polk, Melanie C. ....Las Vegas, NV
Polk, Michael A. ....Rapid City, SD
Polk, Michael F. ....Omaha, NE
Polk, Michael J. ....Columbia, SC
Polk, Michael R. ....Chicago, IL
Polk, Michael S. ....Woodland Hills, CA
Polk, Michael S. ....Hastings, MN
Polk and Polk ....Henderson, KY
Polk, Rhonda S. ....Miami, FL
Polk, Richard A. ....Southfield, MI
Polk, Richard L. ....Richmond, VA
Polk, Robert L. ....Washington, DC
Polk, Ross B. ....Hattiesburg, MS
Polk, Rustin S. ....Dallas, TX
Polk, S. Lawrence ....Atlanta, GA
Polk, Samuel C. ....Santa Monica, CA
Polk, Samuel S. ....New York, NY
Polk, Scheer & Prober, A Law Corporation
Woodland Hills, CA
Polk, Susan M. ....Chino Hills, CA
Polk, Teresa L. ....Irvine, CA
Polk, Victor H., Jr. ....Boston, MA
Polk & Waldman ....Omaha, NE
Polk, Wendy A. ....Fort Worth, TX
Polk, William F., Jr. ....Henderson, KY
Polk, William P. ....Alexandria, LA
Polk, William P., II ....Alexandria, LA
Polka, Matthew M. ....Pittsburgh, PA
Polke, Dennis J. ....Cleveland, OH
Polkes, Jonathan D. ....New York, NY
Polking Law Office ....Breda, IA
Carroll, IA
Polking, Paul J. ....Charlotte, NC
Polking, Thomas W. ....Carroll, IA
Jefferson, IA
Polking, William G. ....Breda, IA
Carroll, IA
Polkinghorn, Henry ....Venice, FL
Polkinghorn, James C., (P.A.)
Fort Lauderdale, FL
Polkinghorn, William A., Jr.
Los Angeles, CA
Polkowitz, Stuart Jeffrey ....Roseland, NJ
Poll, Albert ....West Orange, NJ
Poll, Brian N. ....San Francisco, CA
Poll, David N. ....San Jose, CA
Poll, Edward ....Venice, CA
Poll, Edward, A Professional Corporation
Venice, CA
Poll, Harvey S. ....Seattle, WA
Poll, Jeffrey C. ....Washington, DC
Poll, Michael Alan ....Birmingham, AL
Poll, N. Craig ....Englewood, CO
Poll, N. Craig, & Associates, P.C.
Denver, CO
Englewood, CO
Poll, Susan J. ....Danbury, CT
Pollack, Adam ....Los Angeles, CA
Pollack, Adam Paul ....New York, NY
Pollack, Alan A. ....New York, NY
Pollack, Alan M. ....New York, NY
Woodbury, NY
Pollack, A.M. "Fenway" ....Summersville, WV
Pollack, Andrea J. ....New York, NY
Pollack, Andrew R. ....Menlo Park, CA
Pollack, Ann K. ....St. Paul, MN
Pollack, Ari B. ....Concord, NH
Pollack, Barry A. ....Los Angeles, CA
Pollack, Barry J. ....Washington, DC
Pollack, Barry S. ....Boston, MA
Pollack, Bernard ....Palm Springs, CA
Pollack, Beth D. ....Toms River, NJ
Pollack, Billi K. ....Miami, FL
Pollack, Bonnie L. ....Garden City, NY
Pollack, Bradley G. ....Woodstock, VA
Pollack, Caleb ....New York, NY
Pollack, Caren L. ....Indianapolis, IN
Pollack, Carol Wendelin ....Los Angeles, CA
Pollack, Catherine Evans
Washington, DC
Pollack, Charles I. ....Atlanta, GA
Pollack, Conrad E. ....New York, NY
Pollack, Daniel ....Columbus, OH
Pollack, Daniel A. ....New York, NY
Pollack, Daniel M. ....Vero Beach, FL
Pollack, David ....Arlington, VA
Pollack, David A. ....Miami, FL
Pollack, David A. ....New York, NY
Pollack, David C. ....Miami, FL
Pollack, David J.
Department of Housing and Urban Development, GV
Pollack, David L. ....Philadelphia, PA
Pollack, David L. ....Pittsburgh, PA
Pollack, David M. ....New York, NY
Pollack, David M. ....White Plains, NY
Pollack, David S. ....Port Washington, NY
Pollack, Dean ....Oakland, CA
Pollack, Edward T. ....Boston, MA
Pollack, Edward Vail, (A Professional Corporation) ....San Francisco, CA
Pollack, Eli ....Great Neck, NY
Pollack, Elisa B. ....New York, NY
Pollack, Ellen G. ....Poughkeepsie, NY
Pollack, Ellen H. ....Nashville, TN
Pollack, Elliott B. ....Bridgeport, CT
Hartford, CT
Stamford, CT
Pollack, Elon A. ....Los Angeles, CA
Pollack, Elon A., A Prof. Corp., Law Offices of ....Los Angeles, CA
Pollack, Enid C. ....San Rafael, CA
Pollack, Erwin E. ....Jersey City, NJ
Pollack, Fanette ....New York, NY
Pollack, Frank S. ....Chicago, IL
Pollack, Fred L. ....Mineola, NY
Pollack, Gary ....Farmington Hills, MI
Pollack, Gary, P.C., Law Office of
Detroit, MI
Farmington Hills, MI
Pollack, Gary W. ....Coral Gables, FL
Pollack, Gary W., P.A. ....Coral Gables, FL
Pollack, Gayle E. ....New York, NY
Pollack, George ....Atlantic Beach, NY
Pollack, Gerald J. ....White Plains, NY
Pollack, Gerald L. ....Lake Bluff, IL
Pollack, Gloria E. ....New York, NY
Pollack, Grant E. ....New York, NY
Pollack & Greene, LLP ....Woodbridge, NJ
New York, NY
Pollack, Gregory W. ....San Diego, CA
Pollack, Henry A. ....New York, NY
Pollack, Howard A.
Department of Agriculture, Office of Administrative Law Judges, GV
Pollack, Howard A. ....Milwaukee, WI
Pollack, Howard G. ....Menlo Park, CA
Pollack, Howard J. ....Denver, CO
Pollack & Hyman, LLP ....White Plains, NY
Pollack, I. Miles ....White Plains, NY
Pollack, Ira B. ....Whitestone, NY
Pollack, Ira C. ....San Francisco, CA
Pollack, Irving ....Philadelphia, PA
Pollack, Irving M. ....Washington, DC
Pollack, Jacob N. ....Plano, TX
Pollack, James F. ....Coral Gables, FL
Pollack, James F., P.A. ....Coral Gables, FL
Pollack, Jan Bell ....Miami, FL
Pollack, Janine L. ....New York, NY
Pollack, Jason A., Law Offices of
San Francisco, CA
Pollack, Jeffrey D. ....New York, NY
Pollack, Jeffrey R. ....White Plains, NY
Pollack, Jessica Glass ....New York, NY
Pollack, Joel M. ....Denver, CO
Pollack, Jonathan K. ....New York, NY
Pollack, Jonathan S. ....Santa Monica, CA
Pollack, Jonathan V. ....Franklin Square, NY
Pollack, Joseph D. ....Cleveland, OH
Pollack, Joshua J. ....New York, NY
Pollack, Joyce A. ....Chicago, IL
Pollack & Kaminsky ....New York, NY
Pollack, Kenneth L. ....Washington, DC
Pollack, Kevin Andrew ....New York, NY
Pollack & Kotler ....Mineola, NY
Pollack, Larry M. ....Passaic, NJ
Pollack, Lawrence ....Nashville, TN
Pollack, Lawrence D. ....Cleveland, OH
Pollack, Lawrence W. ....New York, NY
Pollack, Lawrence W. ....New York, NY
Pollack, Lester ....New York, NY
Pollack, Lisa D. ....Newark, NJ
Pollack, Marc R. ....Coral Springs, FL
Pollack, Mark B. ....Milwaukee, WI
Pollack, Mark D. ....Chicago, IL
Pollack, Mark E. ....Miami, FL
Pollack, Martin D. ....New York, NY
Pollack, Matthew E. ....Topsham, ME
Pollack, Melvin ....Bethesda, MD
Pollack, Michael ....New York, NY
Pollack, Michael ....Philadelphia, PA
Pollack, Michael A. ....Milwaukee, WI
Pollack, Michael B. ....West Hartford, CT
Pollack, Michael B. ....Philadelphia, PA
Pollack, Michael J. ....Washington, DC
Pollack, Michael J. ....New York, NY
Pollack, Milton ....New York, NY
Pollack, Mindy ....Greenwich, CT
Pollack, Mitchell B. ....White Plains, NY
Pollack, Morris J. ....Van Nuys, CA
Pollack, Morton C. ....Baltimore, MD
Pollack, Noah C. ....Dallas, TX
Pollack, Pamela J. ....Brooklyn, NY
Pollack, Paul ....Miami, FL
Pollack, Paul B. ....Philadelphia, PA
Pollack Pollack Isaac & DeCicco
New York, NY
Pollack and Quirion, P.A. ....Topsham, ME
Pollack, Randy ....Sacramento, CA
Pollack, Richard A. ....New York, NY
Pollack, Richard Steven ....New York, NY
Pollack, Robert Lawrence ....Naples, FL
Pollack, Robert M. ....New York, NY
Pollack, Robyn F. ....Philadelphia, PA
Pollack, Ronald S., Law Offices of
Mount Laurel, NJ
Philadelphia, PA
Pollack & Rosen, P.A. ....Miami, FL
Pollack, Roslyn G. ....Philadelphia, PA
Pollack, Roy A. ....Austin, TX
Pollack, Russell H. ....New York, NY
Pollack, Ruth M. ....Mineola, NY
Pollack, S. Thomas ....Los Angeles, CA
Pollack, Samuel M. ....Boston, MA
Pollack, Scott M. ....Jenkintown, PA
Pollack, Sidney L. ....Granada Hills, CA
Pollack, Stanley M. ....Window Rock, AZ
Pollack, Stanley P. ....New York, NY
Pollack, Stephanie ....Boston, MA
Pollack, Steven I. ....New York, NY
Pollack, Stuart B. ....New City, NY
Pollack, Stuart E. ....New York, NY
Pollack, Susan F. ....New York, NY
Pollack, Todd D. ....New York, NY
Pollack & Weis ....Chicago, IL
Pollack, Wendy ....Chicago, IL
Pollack, William ....Clifton, NJ
Pollack & Zuckerman ....Kenilworth, NJ
Pollack-Matz, Fran M.
Securities and Exchange Commission, Division of Investment Management, GV
Pollaczek, Peter E. ....Roseburg, OR
Pollak, Andrew B. ....Sacramento, CA
Pollak, Bertram L. ....Northbrook, IL
Pollak, Cary D. ....Washington, DC
Pollak, Cathy J. ....Woodcliff Lake, NJ
Pollak, Cheryl Louise ....Brooklyn, NY
Pollak, Claudia R. ....New York, NY
Pollak, Craig ....New York, NY
Pollak, Daniel J. ....Secaucus, NJ
Pollak, David W. ....New York, NY
Pollak, Gwen ....Brooklyn, NY
Pollak, Harold R. ....Seattle, WA
Pollak, Harry R. ....New York, NY
Pollak & Hicks, P.C ....Omaha, NE
Pollak & Hoffman Ltd. ....Chicago, IL
Northbrook, IL
Pollak, Jay M. ....Northbrook, IL
Pollak, Jeffrey S. ....Los Angeles, CA
Pollak, Joanne E. ....Baltimore, MD
Pollak, John H. ....Mill Valley, CA
Pollak, Kevin B. ....New York, NY
Pollak, Larry S. ....Columbus, OH
Pollak, Lee ....New York, NY
Pollak, Lisa J. ....Morristown, NJ
Pollak, Louis H. ....Philadelphia, PA
Pollak, Mark ....Baltimore, MD
Pollak, Martin A. ....Bayside, NY
Pollak, Martin M. ....New York, NY
Pollak, Michael E. ....Northbrook, IL
Pollak, Michael M. ....Los Angeles, CA
Pollak, Michele C. ....Washington, DC
Pollak, Oliver B. ....Omaha, NE
Pollak, Richard ....Green Bay, WI
Pollak, Richard M. ....Tysons Corner, VA
Pollak, Rita S. ....Brookline, MA
Pollak, Robert K. ....Novato, CA
Pollak, Robert L. ....San Francisco, CA
Pollak, Roger ....Washington, DC
Pollak & Slepian ....Bayside, NY
Pollak, Stephen J. ....Washington, DC
Pollak, Stephen P. ....New York, NY
Pollak, Steven I. ....Millbrae, CA
Pollak, Stewart D. ....New York, NY
Pollak, Stuart R. ....San Francisco, CA
Pollak, Tom ....Washington, DC
Pollak, Vida & Fisher ....Los Angeles, CA
Pollak, William M. ....New York, NY
Pollak, William S. ....Miami, FL
Pollak, William T. ....Mill Valley, CA
Pollan, David Paul ....Decatur, GA
Pollan, Lynn E. ....Nashville, TN
Pollan, Phil J. ....Dallas, TX
Pollan, Robert J. ....Philadelphia, PA
Pollan, Stephen M. ....New York, NY
Pollan, Stephen M., P.C. ....New York, NY
Pollan, Thomas M. ....Austin, TX
Polland & Cook, L.L.P. ....Houston, TX
Polland, Elliot R. ....New York, NY
Polland, Gary M. ....Houston, TX
Polland, Jonathan ....San Francisco, CA
Polland, Wm. ....Milwaukee, WI
Pollara, Dominique A. ....Sacramento, CA
Pollard & Albertson, P.C.
Bloomfield Hills, MI
Detroit, MI
Mount Clemens, MI
Pontiac, MI
Pollard, Brian ....Waco, TX
Pollard, Bryan K. ....Hartford, CT
Pollard, C. William ....Downers Grove, IL
Pollard, Clare S. ....Totowa, NJ
Pollard, Clarence T. ....San Francisco, CA
Pollard, Daniel A. ....Bay City, MI
Pollard, David M. ....Philadelphia, PA
Pollard, David M., Jr. ....Goodlettsville, TN
Pollard, Dennis R. ....Bloomfield Hills, MI
Pollard, Douglas F. ....New Baden, TX
Pollard, E.A. "Bo" ....Incline Village, NV
Pollard, Edward D. ....Westfield, MA
Pollard, Edward N. ....Raleigh, NC
Pollard, Frank E. ....Westfield, MA
Pollard, Fred G. ....Richmond, VA
Pollard, Gary E. ....Bethesda, MD
Pollard, Henry ....Los Angeles, CA
Pollard, Henry R., V ....Richmond, VA
Pollard, H. R., IV ....Richmond, VA
Virginia Beach, VA
Pollard, James H. ....Marblehead, MA
Pollard, Jennifer Bloess ....Alexandria, VA
Pollard, Jerry L. ....Yankton, SD
Pollard, John J., III
House of Representatives, Congressional Assistants, GV
Pollard, John N. ....Spring, TX
Pollard, John O. ....Charlotte, NC
Pollard, JoLynn M. ....Los Angeles, CA
Pollard, Krista Leigh ....Sacramento, CA
Pollard, Laurie K. ....Lufkin, TX
Pollard, Leonard W., II ....San Diego, CA
Pollard, Lynn B. ....Oak Hill, WV
Pollard, Malcolm L. ....Erie, PA
Pollard, Marcia Swistock ....Tequesta, FL
Pollard, Margaret A. ....Houston, TX
Pollard, Marilyn A. ....Phoenix, AZ
Pollard, Mark D. ....Dallas, TX
Pollard, Mark R. ....Treasury Department, Internal Revenue Service, GV
Pollard, Mary Sheehan ....Raleigh, NC
Pollard, Michael ....Pasadena, CA
Pollard, Michael A. ....Chicago, IL
Pollard, Michael A. ....Tulsa, OK
Pollard, Michael R. ....Washington, DC
Pollard, Odell ....Searcy, AR
Pollard, Oliver A., Jr. ....Petersburg, VA
Pollard, Oliver Amos, III ....Charlottesville, VA
Pollard, Overton P. ....Richmond, VA
Pollard, Patricia S. ....Houston, TX
Pollard, Phyllis M. ....Austin, TX

Pollard, Ralph L. .... Concord, CA
Pollard, Randle B. .... Washington, DC
Pollard, Richard A. .... Pittsburgh, PA
Pollard, Robert W. .... Birmingham, AL
Pollard, Ronald L. .... Baltimore, MD
Pollard, Scott T. .... Charlotte, NC
Pollard, T. Lawrence .... Raleigh, NC
Pollard, Thomas B., Jr. .... Columbia, SC
Pollard, Thomas C. .... Wilmington, NC
Pollard, Thomas W. .... Kerrville, TX
Pollard, Tiffany A. .... New York, NY
Pollard, Tomas G., Jr. .... Tyler, TX
Pollard, Trisha S. .... Houston, TX
Pollard, Vicky L. .... New Orleans, LA
Pollard, W. Scott .... Florissant, MO
Pollard, Walter S., Jr. .... Boston, MA
Pollard, Wilbur L. (Will) .... Spickard, MO
Pollard, Willard L. G. .... St. Petersburg, FL
Pollard, William A. .... Columbia, SC
Pollard, William B., III .... New York, NY
Pollard, William C. .... Austin, TX
Pollard, William Nichols .... Richmond, VA
Pollaro, Anne C. .... Garden City, NY
Pollart, Christopher J. .... Boston, MA
Pollart, Eric J. .... Denver, CO
Pollastrini, Patricia (Tia)
San Francisco, CA
Pollastrino, Philip A. .... Mount Kisco, NY
Pollatschek, Julius R.
West Long Branch, NJ
Pollatsek, Jack A. .... San Francisco, CA
Polle, Ronald C. .... Des Moines, IA
Polleck, Laurie Schenker .... Wilmington, DE
Polledri, Sandro .... Livingston, NJ
Pollen, Raymond J. .... Milwaukee, WI
Pollenz, Kenneth A. .... Boston, MA
Poller, Jennifer L. .... Pittsburgh, PA
Poller, Jeri A. .... Miami, FL
West Palm Beach, FL
Poller, Judith L. .... New York, NY
Poller, Kenneth G. .... Hackensack, NJ
Poller, Kenneth G. .... Paramus, NJ
Poller, Neale J. .... Miami, FL
Poller, Stuart M. .... Williston, VT
Pollet, Andrew F. .... Los Angeles, CA
Pollet & Felleman, LLP .... New York, NY
Pollet, Gerald M. .... Seattle, WA
Pollet, Michael N. .... New York, NY
Pollet, Richard .... New York, NY
Pollet, Sybil H. .... New York, NY
Pollet & Woodbury, A Law Corporation
Los Angeles, CA
Pollets, John .... Braintree, MA
Polletta, Leonard D. .... New York, NY
Pollex, Charles A. .... Friendship, WI
Pollex, Dagmar .... Milton, MA
Pollex, Robert C. .... Bowling Green, OH
Pollex, Yvonne Tertel .... Toledo, OH
Polley, Alan J. .... Deerfield Beach, FL
Polley, Alan K. .... Bisbee, AZ
Polley, Alan S. .... Mount Vernon, NY
Polley, Daniel S. .... Fort Lauderdale, FL
Miami, FL
West Palm Beach, FL
Polley, David C. .... Las Vegas, NV
Polley, James L. .... Richmond, VA
Polley, John E. .... Cincinnati, OH
Polley, John W. .... Minneapolis, MN
Polley, Kent A. .... Oklahoma City, OK
Polley, Michael .... Aurora, IL
Polley, Oliver .... Center, TX
Polley, Richard C. .... Pittsburgh, PA
Wheeling, WV
Polley, Richard J. .... Portland, OR
Polley, Tamara M. .... Reno, NV
Polley, Terry L., (A Professional Corporation) .... Los Angeles, CA
Polley, Vincent I. .... Sugar Land, TX
Polley, Wesley E. .... Bisbee, AZ
Polley, William G. .... Sonora, CA
Polley-Abramson, Jennifer C.
Salt Lake City, UT
Polleys, E. Hardwick, Jr. .... Columbus, GA
Polli, Anita M. .... Boston, MA
Polli, Robert P. .... Tampa, FL
Polli, Robert P., P.A. .... Tampa, FL
Pollicino, Kristine .... New York, NY
Pollick, David M. .... York, PA
Pollick, Jody Lynn .... Tampa, FL
Pollick, John F. .... Chicago, IL
Pollick, Marissa W. .... Ann Arbor, MI
Pollick, Mark .... San Diego, CA
Pollick, Philip J., (Co., L.P.A.)
Reynoldsburg, OH
Pollick, Sidney E. .... Southfield, MI
Pollihan, Thomas H. .... St. Louis, MO
Pollin, Edra Jan .... Denver, CO
Pollin, Myles C. .... New York, NY
Pollina, Charles J. .... Smithtown, NY
Pollina, Daniel T. .... Cleveland, OH
Pollina, Denis R. .... Schaumburg, IL
Pollina & Phelan .... Schaumburg, IL
Pollina, Robert B. .... Smithtown, NY
Pollinger, Arnold N. .... Boston, MA
Pollinger, Cathryn P. .... Arlington, VA
Pollinger, Richard E. .... New York, NY
Pollinger, Steven J. .... Austin, TX
Pollinger, William J. .... Hackensack, NJ
Pollinger, William J., P.A. .... Hackensack, NJ
Pollingue, Eugene F., Jr.
New Orleans, LA
Pollino, Christopher J. .... Mount Vernon, WA
Pollino, John E. .... Salem, OR
Pollins, Eric S. .... San Mateo, CA
Pollins, John W., III .... Greensburg, PA
Pollins, Merle S. .... Kettering, OH
Pollio, Benedict J. .... Garden City, NY
Pollio, John W., Jr. .... Houston, TX
Pollio, Ronald A. .... Garden City, NY
Pollioni, Marcia A. .... San Francisco, CA
Pollis, Andrew S. .... Cleveland, OH
Pollis, Nicholas L., Jr. .... Turnersville, NJ
Pollish and Heisick .... Minneapolis, MN
Pollish, Janet G. .... Minneapolis, MN
Pollison, Joyce Wilkins .... Hackensack, NJ
Pollitt, Abby E. .... Santa Monica, CA
Pollitt, Basil R. .... Brooklyn, NY
Pollitt, Douglas B. .... New York, NY
Pollitt, Jeffrey G. .... Phoenix, AZ
Pollitt, John R. .... Santa Monica, CA
Pollitt & Pollitt .... Santa Monica, CA
Pollitt, Robert D. .... Charleston, WV
Pollitz, Edith Elizabeth .... Tallahassee, FL
Pollitzer, David J. .... Albany, NY
Pollitzer, Patricia M.
Consumer Product Safety Commission, Office of the General Counsel, GV
Pollman, Cheryl E. .... Dallas, TX
Pollman, Harold A. .... Dallas, TX
Pollmann, Daniel L. .... Chicago, IL
Pollmann, Linda .... Mendota Heights, MN
Pollner, Daniel E. .... Washington, DC
Pollner, Glenn R. .... New York, NY
Pollner, Martin R. .... New York, NY
Pollock, Adam N. .... Pittsburgh, PA
Pollock, Alan J. .... Deerfield Beach, FL
Pollock, Alison L. .... Chicago, IL
Pollock, Andrew S. .... Lincoln, NE
Pollock, Ann H. .... Chicago, IL
Pollock, Arthur J. .... Redwood City, CA
Pollock, Bernard I. .... Baltimore, MD
Pollock, Bradley P. .... Steamboat Springs, CO
Pollock, Brian H. .... Miami, FL
Pollock, Brian J. .... Phoenix, AZ
Pollock, Bruce G. .... West Warwick, RI
Pollock, C. Fred .... Madison, WI
Pollock, Candace M. .... Cleveland, OH
Pollock, Cynthia R. .... Lancaster, CA
Pollock, David .... Encino, CA
Pollock, David F. .... Waynesburg, PA
Pollock, David H. .... Sacramento, CA
Pollock, David J. .... Newburgh, NY
Pollock, David S. .... Pittsburgh, PA
Pollock, David S., & Associates
Pittsburgh, PA
Pollock, Donald I. .... Miami Beach, FL
Pollock, Donald W. .... Menlo Park, CA
Pollock, Douglas Ian .... Beverly Hills, CA
Pollock, E. Kears .... Pittsburgh, PA
Pollock, Earl E. .... Chicago, IL
Pollock, Edward M. .... Foster City, CA
Pollock, Elizabeth .... Denver, CO
Pollock, Elizabeth A. .... Los Angeles, CA
Pollock, Ennis & Heck .... Quincy, IL
Pollock, Eugenea C. .... Johnson City, TN
Pollock, Ewing B. .... Waynesburg, PA
Pollock, Gerald A. .... Phoenix, AZ
Pollock, Harold .... Cleveland, OH
Pollock, Harold, Co., L.P.A. .... Cleveland, OH
Pollock, Harold Lee .... Burgaw, NC
Pollock, James .... Boston, MA
Pollock, James E. .... Del Mar, CA
Pollock, Jeffrey L. .... Pittsburgh, PA
Pollock, Jeffrey M. .... Newark, NJ
New York, NY
Pollock, Jeffrey M. .... Philadelphia, PA
Pollock, Jeffrey R. .... Lakewood, WA
Pollock, Jerome F. .... Fort Lauderdale, FL
Pollock, John J. .... Binghamton, NY
Pollock, John M. .... Bloomfield Hills, MI
Pollock, John M., PLC
Bloomfield Hills, MI
Pollock, John P. .... Los Angeles, CA
Pollock, Joseph A. .... Anchorage, AK
Pollock, Joy E. .... Huntingdon Valley, PA
Pollock, Julie .... San Antonio, TX
Pollock, Julie Beth .... Los Angeles, CA
Pollock, Karen M. .... Boca Raton, FL
Pollock, Karol .... Los Angeles, CA
Pollock, Kenneth B. .... Atlanta, GA
Pollock, Kenneth C. .... Atlanta, GA
Pollock, Kenneth E. .... Orange, CA
Las Vegas, NV
Pollock, Kenneth S. .... Boca Raton, FL
Pollock, Kristen M. .... Atlanta, GA
Pollock, Lee A. .... White Plains, NY
Pollock, Linda J. .... Phoenix, AZ
Pollock, Linda Jacobsen .... Atlanta, GA
Pollock, Lorne M. .... Los Angeles, CA
Pollock & Maguire .... New York, NY
White Plains, NY
Pollock, Mark S. .... Napa, CA
Pollock, Martin M. .... Atlanta, GA
Pollock, Melissa Ann .... Wilmington, NC
Pollock, Melody Anne .... Pittsburgh, PA
Pollock, Meyers, Eicksteadt & Weech, Ltd.
Marengo, IL
Pollock, Michael J. .... San Francisco, CA
Pollock, Norman J. .... Marengo, IL
Pollock, Paul E. .... Bridgeport, CT
Pollock, Paul J. .... New York, NY
Pollock, Peter L., Jr. .... Orlando, FL
Pollock, Philip M. .... Peoria, IL
Pollock, Philip S. .... San Antonio, TX
Pollock, Phillip R. .... San Francisco, CA
Pollock, Pollock, Thomas & Morris, P.C.
Waynesburg, PA
Pollock, R. Jeffrey .... Cleveland, OH
Pollock, Rachel .... Brooklyn, NY
Pollock, Randy Sue .... Oakland, CA
Pollock, Ray L. .... Duncanville, TX
Pollock, R. F. Hoke .... Southern Pines, NC
Pollock, Richard C. .... Miami, FL
Pollock, Robert A. .... Washington, DC
Pollock, Robert E. .... Toledo, OH
Pollock, Robert M. .... Annapolis, MD
Pollock, Ronald H., Jr. .... Lancaster, PA
Pollock, Russell D. .... San Francisco, CA
Pollock, Russell X. .... Boston, MA
Pollock, Scott D., & Associates
Chicago, IL
Pollock, Stacy J. .... Washington, DC
Pollock, Stanley H. .... Atlanta, GA
Pollock, Stephen G. .... Philadelphia, PA
Pollock, Steven S. .... Madison, WI
Pollock, Stewart G. .... Morristown, NJ
Pollock, Sue Robin .... Santa Monica, CA
Pollock, Terri Ann .... Seattle, WA
Pollock, Theodore .... Chicago, IL
Pollock, Theodore .... Great Neck, NY
Pollock, Thomas E. .... Oakland, CA
Pollock, Thomas Philip .... Universal City, CA
Pollock, Thomas R. .... New York, NY
Pollock, Timothy S. .... Atlanta, GA
Pollock, Vande Sande & Amernick, R.L.L.P.
Washington, DC
Pollock, William W. .... Raleigh, NC
Pollock-Byrne, Joycelyn M. .... Houston, TX
Pollok, Benton H. .... Urbanna, VA
Pollok, Donald A. .... Santa Clarita, CA
Pollok, John L. .... New York, NY
Pollok, Julian A. .... Los Angeles, CA
Pollok, Julian A., A Professional Corporation
Los Angeles, CA
Pollok, Michael S. .... New York, NY
Pollok, Steven J. .... Lansing, MI
Pollow, Ronald A. .... Boca Raton, FL
Pollow, Ronald A., P.A. .... Boca Raton, FL
Pollowitz, David I. .... New Britain, CT
Pollowitz, Robert R. .... Hoboken, NJ
Polly, Dianne K. .... Memphis, TN
Polly, Felix W., III .... Fayetteville, WV
Polly, Ronald G. .... Whitesburg, KY
Polly, Ronald G., Jr. .... Atlanta, GA
Polly & Smallwood .... Whitesburg, KY
Pollyea, Susan L. .... Los Angeles, CA
Polly-Murphy, Michelle L. .... Kansas City, MO
Polma, Geoffrey R. .... Dallas, TX
Polmer, Henry M. .... Purchase, NY
Polner, Beth L. .... Islandia, NY
Polner, Eli .... Buffalo, NY
Polner, Frederick A. .... Washington, DC
Pittsburgh, PA
Polner, Richard B. .... New York, NY
Polo, Devanee P. .... Tampa, FL
Polo, Kevin A. .... Edwardsville, IL
Polo, Sylvia T. .... Coral Gables, FL
Polodna, Scott D. .... Orlando, FL
Polofka, John R. .... Toledo, OH
Pologeorgis, Elaine B. .... New York, NY
Pologeorgis, George C.
Department of Commerce, Patent and Trademark Office, GV
Polom, Michelle S. .... Boca Raton, FL
Polo-Martinez, Carlos E. .... San Juan, PR
Polomsky, John V., II .... Saginaw, MI
Polon, Burl S. .... San Jose, CA
Polon, Burl S. .... Santa Cruz, CA
Polon, Ira H. .... Washington, DC
Polon, James A. .... Freehold, NJ
Poloncarz, Kevin J. .... Dallas, TX
Poloncarz, Mark C. .... Buffalo, NY
Polonczyk, James T. .... Grand Rapids, MI
Poloner, Stuart S. .... New York, NY
Polonsky, Albert E. .... San Mateo, CA
Polonsky, Alex S. .... Washington, DC
Polonsky, Arlene E. .... Boston, MA
Polonsky, Jonathan E. .... New York, NY
Polonsky, Louis K., (P.C.) .... Atlanta, GA
Polonsky, Rita S. .... Audubon, NJ
Polony, Richard B. .... Chicago, IL
Polos, Peter John .... Newport Beach, CA
Polosky, Edward .... Las Vegas, NV
Polotko, Steven M. .... Houston, TX
Polott, Andrew R. .... Bethesda, MD
Polott, Arthur J. .... Houston, TX
Polott, Leon A. .... Cleveland, OH
Polovin, Robert K. .... Chicago, IL
Polovischak, Andrew, Jr. .... Youngstown, OH
Polovoy, Albert B. .... Hunt Valley, MD
Polovoy, Brian H. .... New York, NY
Polovoy, Kristen E. .... Cherry Hill, NJ
Philadelphia, PA
Polovoy, Norman .... Hunt Valley, MD
Polovoy, Turner & Broderick, LLC
Hunt Valley, MD
Polovy, Marian .... New York, NY
Polow, Bertram .... Livingston, NJ
Polow, David L. .... Hyde Park, VT
Polow, Ian L. .... New York, NY
Polowitz, Steven H. .... Buffalo, NY
Polowy, Carolyn I. .... Washington, DC
Polowy, Daniel R. .... Fredonia, NY
Poloyac, Denise S. .... Chicago, IL
Polozie, Michael A. .... Rochester, NY
Polozie, Stephen M. .... Washington, DC
Polozola, Frank J. .... Baton Rouge, LA
Polozola, Gordon D. .... Baton Rouge, LA
Polozola, Gregory D. .... Baton Rouge, LA
Polozola, Kyle P. .... Lafayette, LA
Pols, Donald J. .... New York, NY
Pols, E. Benet .... Brunswick, ME
Polsby, Allen I.
Department of Housing and Urban Development, Office of General Counsel, GV
Polsby, Daniel D. .... Chicago, IL
Polscer, Diane L. .... Portland, OR
Polsdofer, Edwin C. .... Dallas, TX
Polse, Richard G. .... Santa Cruz, CA
Polse, Roberta Rae .... Santa Cruz, CA
Polsenberg, Daniel F. .... Las Vegas, NV
Polsinelli, James A. .... Kansas City, MO
Polsinelli, Michael Louis .... Detroit, MI
Polsinelli, Vincent E. .... Miami, FL
Polsinelli, White, Vardeman & Shalton, A Professional Corporation
Overland Park, KS
Topeka, KS
Jefferson City, MO
Kansas City, MO
St. Louis, MO
Polski, Norman .... Baltimore, MD
Polski, Perry M. .... Inglewood, CA
Polski, Robert J., Jr. .... St. Paul, MN
Polski, Scott D. .... Milwaukee, WI
Polsky, Alan .... Bohemia, NY
Polsky, Alan R. .... Los Angeles, CA
Polsky, Alexander S. .... Long Beach, CA
Polsky & Associates, Ltd. .... Chicago, IL
Polsky, Barbara S. .... Los Angeles, CA
Polsky, Carl A. .... Philadelphia, PA
Polsky, Claudia .... San Francisco, CA
Polsky, Cope & Knapp .... Lincoln, NE
Polsky, Gregg D. .... Miami, FL
Polsky, Howard D. .... Bethesda, MD
Polsky, Hyman .... Lincoln, NE
Polsky, Jeffrey D. .... San Francisco, CA
Polsky, Kenneth P. .... New York, NY
Polsky, Larry Mark .... Daytona Beach, FL
Polsky, Leon B. .... New York, NY
Polsky, Michael S. .... Milwaukee, WI
Polsky, Robert L. F. .... Miami, FL
Polsky, Samuel J. .... Chicago, IL
Polsky, Scott .... Philadelphia, PA
Polsky, Tina Scott .... New York, NY
Polsley, David L. .... Onalaska, WI
Polsley, Kathryn S.S. .... Onalaska, WI
Polson, Edward W. .... Pleasanton, CA
Polson, Gary A. .... Westlake Village, CA
Polson, John M. .... Newport Beach, CA
Polson, Lee .... Austin, TX
Polson, Marilyn M. .... St. Petersburg, FL
Seminole, FL
Polson, Mark B. .... Birmingham, AL
Polson, Mary Koch .... Fort Walton Beach, FL
Polson, Mary Koch, P.A.
Fort Walton Beach, FL
Polson & Robbins, P.C. .... Birmingham, AL
Polson, Sherrie C. .... Hartsville, SC
Polstein, Ferrara, Dwyer & Speed, P.C.
Newark, NJ
New York, NY
Polstein, Neil .... Minneapolis, MN
Polstein, Robert .... New York, NY
Polster, Carl C. .... St. Louis, MO
Polster, Dan A. .... Cleveland, OH
Polster, David .... Chicago, IL
Polster, Dorothea M. .... Cleveland, OH
Polster, Harold .... Cleveland, OH
Polster, J. Philip .... St. Louis, MO
Polster, John C. .... Deerfield, IL
Polster, John R. .... Schenectady, NY
Polster, Lee M., (Professional Corporation)
Los Angeles, CA
Polster, Lieder, Woodruff & Lucchesi, L.C.
Belleville, IL
Louisville, KY
Clayton, MO
St. Louis, MO
Polster, Morton A. .... Rochester, NY
Polster, Neil E. .... Tampa, FL
Polster, Neil E., P.A. .... Tampa, FL
Polster, Philip B. .... St. Louis, MO
Polster, Philip B., II .... St. Louis, MO
Polster, Robert W. .... Jacksonville, FL
Polster, Scott H. .... Walton Hills, OH
Polster, Zvi .... Grayslake, IL
Polston, Bernard .... Tarzana, CA
Polston, Dean & Healy, P.A.
Tallahassee, FL
Polston, Kevin B. .... Atlanta, GA
Polston, Ricky L. .... Tallahassee, FL
Polston, Ronald W. .... Raymond, IL
Polston, Schwartz, Hamilton & Fenster
Beverly Hills, CA
Polstra, Ryan M. .... Sacramento, CA
Polt, Leslie J. .... Baltimore, MD
Polt, Max .... Baltimore, MD
Poltarak, William J. .... New York, NY
Poltenstein, Jerome .... Philadelphia, PA
Poltorack, Ronald D. .... Fort Lauderdale, FL
Poltorack, Ronald D., Law Office of
Fort Lauderdale, FL
Poltrack, Stephen E. .... New York, NY
Poltrock, Harold J. .... Millburn, NJ
Poltrock, Jennifer K. .... Chicago, IL
Poltrock, Lawrence A. .... Chicago, IL
Poltrock, Victor .... Los Angeles, CA
Poltronieri, Jeanine
Federal Communications Commission, Wireless Telecommunications Bureau, GV
Poltz, Judith T. .... Peoria, IL
Polubinski, Edmund, Jr. .... Boston, MA
Polucki, Robert D. .... West Caldwell, NJ
Polumbo, Carol (C.D.) .... Austin, TX
Polumbus, Gary M. .... Denver, CO
Polumbus, Richard T. .... Englewood, CO
Polunsky, Allan B. .... San Antonio, TX
Polunsky & Beitel, A Prof. Corp.
Dallas, TX
San Antonio, TX
Polur, Shari .... Washington, DC
Polus, Ann E. .... San Francisco, CA
Poluse, Janet J. .... St. Petersburg, FL
Polverari, Joseph R., Jr. .... Redwood City, CA
Polverari, Joseph R., Sr. .... Los Altos, CA
Polvere, Daniel M. .... Boston, MA
Polverino, Frank .... New York, NY
Polverino, Sam J. .... San Jose, CA
Polvino, Andrea R. .... Buffalo, NY
Polvino, Anthony Thomas .... Atlanta, GA

Polyakov, Karen B. .... Orange, CA
Polyakov, Leonard .... Santa Ana, CA
Polyakova, Kira .... New York, NY
Polycarpe, Yanick E. .... Chicago, IL
Polydoroff, Theodore .... Rockville, MD
Polydoros, George N., Jr. .... Houston, TX
Polyn, Denis A. .... Rochester, NY
Polywko, Walentyn .... Glendale, NY
Polzak, James A. .... Crosslake, MN
Polzin, Charles H. .... Birmingham, MI
Polzin, John T. .... Evanston, IL
Polzin, Lawrence G. .... Shorewood, WI
Polzin, Mark F. .... Hudson, OH
Poma, John M. .... Richmond, VA
Poma, Kelly M. .... Upper Marlboro, MD
Pomaco, Frank .... Belleville, NJ
Pomainville, Roger L.
Charlotte Amalie, St. Thomas, VI
Pomajevich, James J. .... Vancouver, WA
Pomann, John J. .... Westland, MI
Pomar, Francis P. .... New Milford, NJ
Pomar, Olga D. .... Haddonfield, NJ
Pomares, Carmen R. .... Department of Justice, Drug Enforcement Administration, GV
Pomaro, Nicholas T. .... Rolling Meadows, IL
Pomarole, Michael J. .... Boston, MA
Pomatto, Douglas J. .... Rockford, IL
Pombert, Jeffrey L. .... Atlanta, GA
Pombrio, Emy Lee .... Plattsburgh, NY
Pomento, Eileen A. .... Pottsville, PA
Pomerance, A. Jaye .... New York, NY
Pomerance, Anita L. .... New York, NY
Pomerance, Bradley E. .... Hollywood, CA
Pomerance, Brenda .... New York, NY
Pomerance & Collins .... New York, NY
Pomerance, Drew E. .... Los Angeles, CA
Pomerance, Edward Drew .... Los Angeles, CA
Pomerance, Jeffrey M. .... Los Angeles, CA
Pomerance, John R. .... Boston, MA
Pomerance, Leon .... Atlanta, GA
Pomerance, Philip L. .... Chicago, IL
Pomerance, Robert .... New York, NY
Pomerance, Robert S.
United States Tax Court, GV
Pomerance, Roger M. .... Boca Raton, FL
Pomerance, Roger M., P.A.
Boca Raton, FL
Pomerance, Ronald V. .... New York, NY
Pomerance & Snitow .... New York, NY
Pomerants, Alex J. .... Columbus, OH
Pomerantz, Adam Lee .... Armonk, NY
Pomerantz, Alan J. .... New York, NY
Pomerantz, Andrew S. .... Los Angeles, CA
Pomerantz, Anne P. .... Los Angeles, CA
Pomerantz, Burton D. .... Great Neck, NY
Pomerantz, Crane M. .... Washington, DC
Pomerantz and Crosby Co., L.P.A.
Cleveland, OH
Pomerantz, Dale L. .... Orange, CA
Pomerantz, Dana L. .... Hempstead, NY
Pomerantz, David .... Dix Hills, NY
Pomerantz, David I. .... Cleveland, OH
Pomerantz, Devorah I. .... New York, NY
Pomerantz, Frederick J. .... New York, NY
Pomerantz, Gerald Jay .... Elkins Park, PA
Philadelphia, PA
Pomerantz, Glenn D. .... Los Angeles, CA
Pomerantz, Gloria .... Fort Lauderdale, FL
Pomerantz, Gloria, P.A. .... Fort Lauderdale, FL
Pomerantz, Harold B. .... Chicago, IL
Pomerantz Haudek Block Grossman & Gross LLP .... New York, NY
Pomerantz, Hope M. .... Newark, NJ
Pomerantz, Howard L.
Fort Lauderdale, FL
Pomerantz, Jason S. .... Los Angeles, CA
Pomerantz, Jay L. .... New York, NY
Pomerantz, Jeffrey N. .... Los Angeles, CA
Pomerantz, Jerald M. .... McAllen, TX
Pomerantz, Jerald M. .... Weslaco, TX
Pomerantz, Julie M. .... Atlanta, GA
Pomerantz, Kami A. .... Denver, CO
Pomerantz, Kimberly A. .... Los Angeles, CA
Pomerantz, Lance .... Boston, MA
Pomerantz, Leonard H. .... Pasadena, CA
Pomerantz, Lisa Renee .... Melville, NY
Pomerantz, Madeline Beth .... Commack, NY
Pomerantz, Mark F. .... New York, NY
Pomerantz, Mark S. .... New York, NY
Pomerantz, Michael M. .... New York, NY
Pomerantz, Neil .... Denver, CO
Pomerantz, Nicole Blohm
Los Angeles, CA
Pomerantz, Nora E. .... Philadelphia, PA
Pomerantz, Norman S. .... Cleveland, OH
Pomerantz, Randi N. .... Morristown, NJ
Pomerantz, Reuben G. .... Woodland Hills, CA
Pomerantz, Rhonda S. .... New City, NY
Pomerantz, Richard M. .... New Milford, CT
Pomerantz, Robert .... Brooklyn, NY
Pomerantz, Sanford E. .... St. Louis, MO
Pomerantz, Scott F. .... Chicago, IL
Pomerantz, Steven Mark .... Landover, MD
Pomerantz, Stewart A. .... New York, NY
Pomerantz, William A. .... Chicago, IL
Pomeranz, Alfred J. .... Jacksonville, FL
Pomeranz, Anthony V. .... Philadelphia, PA
Pomeranz, David A. .... San Diego, CA
Pomeranz, Drayton & Stabnick
Glastonbury, CT
Pomeranz, Edward H. .... New York, NY
Pomeranz, Edwin S. .... Scottsdale, AZ
Pomeranz, Gottlieb & Mushkin, LLC
New York, NY
Pomeranz, Harold B. .... New York, NY
Pomeranz, Jacob .... Chicago, IL
Pomeranz, James L. .... Glastonbury, CT
Pomeranz, John Putnam .... Washington, DC
Pomeranz, Joseph .... New York, NY
Pomeranz, Mark L. .... North Miami, FL
Pomeranz, Morton .... Washington, DC
Pomeranz, Sharon Jane
General Services Administration, Office of the General Counsel, GV
Pomerene, Burns & Skelton
Coshocton, OH
Pomerene, Robert J. .... Boston, MA
Pomerenk, David D. .... San Mateo, CA
Pomerenk, Robert B. .... Washington, DC
Pomerico, Louis R. .... New Castle, PA
Pomerleau, Lilo D. .... Austin, TX
Pomeroy, Armstrong, Baranello & Casullo, LLP .... Cortland, NY
Pomeroy, Charles H., IV .... Los Angeles, CA
Pomeroy, Chas. A. .... Portland, ME
Pomeroy, Christopher D. .... Richmond, VA
Pomeroy, Daniel J. .... Springfield, NJ
Pomeroy, David W. .... Santa Ana, CA
Pomeroy, Denise J. .... Birmingham, AL
Pomeroy, Earl R., III .... Bismarck, ND
Pomeroy, Edward C. .... Redwood City, CA
Pomeroy, Edward C., Law Office of
Redwood City, CA
Pomeroy, Ellen R. C. .... New York, NY
Pomeroy, Elwaine F. .... Topeka, KS
Pomeroy, Emerson M. .... Topeka, KS
Pomeroy, Gary Louis .... Chanute, KS
Pomeroy, Gay M. .... Syracuse, NY
Pomeroy, George B. .... Fort Lauderdale, FL
Pomeroy, Gregg J. .... Fort Lauderdale, FL
Pomeroy, Harlan .... Washington, DC
Pomeroy, J. Paul, Jr. .... Brenham, TX
Pomeroy, James B. .... New York, NY
Pomeroy, Jeffrey G .... Cortland, NY
Pomeroy, Jeffrey Matthew
Birmingham, AL
Pomeroy, Jeremy .... New York, NY
Pomeroy, John H. .... Washington, DC
Pomeroy, John J. .... Johnston, RI
Pomeroy, John S. .... Brookline, MA
Pomeroy, Joseph H. .... Fond du Lac, WI
Pomeroy, Kent S. .... Los Angeles, CA
Pomeroy, L. David .... Oklahoma City, OK
Pomeroy, Laura O. .... Richmond, VA
Pomeroy, Mark C. .... Columbus, OH
Pomeroy, Martin C. .... Boston, MA
Pomeroy, Maureen F. .... Lexington, MA
Pomeroy and Pomeroy .... Topeka, KS
Pomeroy, Pomeroy & Beauchamp, P.A.
Fort Lauderdale, FL
Pomeroy, Randall L. .... Portage, MI
Pomeroy, Rebecca J. .... Lincolnton, NC
Pomeroy, Richard L. .... Anchorage, AK
Pomeroy, Robert B. .... Lynnfield, MA
Pomeroy, Robert C., (P.C.) .... Boston, MA
Pomeroy, Robert M., Jr.
Greenwood Village, CO
Pomeroy, Roger A. .... Fort Lauderdale, FL
Pomeroy, Ron .... Beaverton, OR
Pomeroy, Rosemary Ebner
Columbus, OH
Pomeroy, Scott K. .... Providence, RI
Pomeroy, Thomas W., Jr. .... Pittsburgh, PA
Pomeroy, Toni Lee .... Charlestown, MA
Pomeroy, W. Todd .... Lincolnton, NC
Pomeroy, Wayne W. .... Fort Lauderdale, FL
Pomeroy, Wesley A. .... Miami, FL
Pomeroy, William Jeffrey .... Cortland, NY
Pomes, David E. .... Dallas, TX
Pomfret, Ellen K. .... Cherry Hill, NJ
Philadelphia, PA
Pomfret, Mark D. .... Boston, MA
Pomfret, Scott D. .... Concord, NH
Pomianek, Theodore C. .... Clinton, NJ
Pomidor, John J. .... Vallejo, CA
Pomierski, William R. .... Chicago, IL
Pomije, Gregory M. .... Portsmouth, VA
Pomilio, Anthony K. .... Rome, NY
Pominville, Henry A. .... Bay City, MI
Pominville, Henry A., P.C. .... Bay City, MI
Pommer, Eric S. .... Ventura, CA
Pommer, Robert W., III .... Washington, DC
Pommer, Russell E. .... Washington, DC
Pommer, Virginia Rowan .... Washington, DC
Pommeranz, Melvin R. .... Toledo, OH
Pommerening, David G. .... Washington, DC
Pommerening, Edwin C. .... Milwaukee, WI
Pommerening, Glen E. .... Washington, DC
Pommerening Law Office SC
Milwaukee, WI
Pommerening, Louis A. .... Mount Clemens, MI
Pommersheim, Frank R. .... Rosebud, SD
Pommersheim, Peter .... Boston, MA
Pommert, G. Steven .... Washington, DC
Pommerville, Gerald A. .... Duluth, MN
Pommerville, Robert W. .... Fort Smith, AR
Pommier, Raneen .... Oceanside, OR
Pommier, Warren D. .... Wabasha, MN
Pomo, Matthew R., Jr. .... Kearny, NJ
Pomodore, Debra Lynn .... Kew Gardens, NY
Pomp, Richard D. .... Hartford, CT
Pompa, Renata C. .... New York, NY
Pompan, Gerard B. .... New York, NY
Pompan, Jacob B. .... Alexandria, VA
Pompeani, Fred J. .... Cleveland, OH
Pompei, Diane M. .... Newark, NJ
Pompei, Kenneth G. .... Albuquerque, NM
Pompelio, Richard D. .... Sparta, NJ
Pompeo, Joan E. .... Somerville, NJ
Pompeo, Michael P. .... Florham Park, NJ
Pompeo, Michael R. .... Washington, DC
Pompeo, Paul E. .... Washington, DC
Pomper & Barnett .... York, PA
Pomper, Brian .... Washington, DC
Pomper, Brooks K. .... York, PA
Pomper, David E. .... Washington, DC
Pomper, Diane Martin .... Raleigh, NC
Pomper, George Frank .... Pittsburgh, PA
Pomper, Howard .... Chicago, IL
Pomper, Neal M. .... Brookline, MA
Pomper, Robert F. .... Winston-Salem, NC
Pompey, Asahi .... New York, NY
Pompey, Brenda Montgomery
Birmingham, AL
Pompey, Dawn L. .... Tallahassee, FL
Pompey, Tina M. .... El Segundo, CA
Pompey, William M. .... Camden, AL
Pompliano, Robert J. .... Hackensack, NJ
Pompo, Vincent M. .... West Chester, PA
Pomponio, Bren J. .... Charleston, WV
Pomponio, Joseph R.
Department of Transportation, Federal Railroad Administration, GV
Pomputius, Mary-Alice .... Seattle, WA
Pomrantz, Barry Robert .... Encino, CA
Pomrenke, Kurt J. .... Bristol, VA
Pomrenze, Bonnie H. .... Highland Park, IL
Pomrenze, Nathaniel J. .... Chicago, IL
Pomroy, Anne C. .... Old Orchard Beach, ME
Poms, William .... Los Angeles, CA
Pomykala, Timothy .... Sacramento, CA
Pon, Henry L. .... New York, NY
Pon, Jane .... San Francisco, CA
Pon, Lillian .... Palo Alto, CA
Pon, Tyler B. .... San Francisco, CA
Pona, Charles Gerard .... Brooklyn Heights, OH
Ponader, David W. .... Indianapolis, IN
Ponader, Erick D. .... Indianapolis, IN
Ponader, Wayne C. .... Indianapolis, IN
Ponader, Wendy Wright .... Indianapolis, IN
Ponce, Carmen A. .... Monterey, CA
Ponce, Eric A. .... Indian Harbour Beach, FL
Ponce, Francisco .... Carrizo Springs, TX
Ponce, Mario .... New York, NY
Ponce, Michael J. .... Westminster, CA
Ponce & Ritter .... Victorville, CA
Ponce, Robert A. .... Victorville, CA
Ponce, Robert D. .... Monterey, CA
Ponce, S. Daniel .... Miami, FL
Ponce, Susan M. .... Houston, TX
Ponce de Leon, Agustin .... Painesville, OH
Ponce de Leon, Edmund .... Chicago, IL
Ponce Fantauzzi, Juan M. .... San Juan, PR
Ponce-Gomez, Diana S. .... Los Angeles, CA
Thousand Oaks, CA
Poncelet, Peter T. .... Goodhue, MN
Poncelow, Charles D. .... Colorado Springs, CO
Ponchak, Terrance .... San Pedro, CA
Poncin, Allan R. .... Minneapolis, MN
Poncin, William E. .... Macomb, IL
Pond, Deborah L. .... Atlanta, GA
Pond, Frank D. .... San Francisco, CA
Pond, George .... Warren, OH
Pond, George Mcn .... Buffalo, NY
Pond, George McNabb .... Albany, NY
Pond, Gregory R. .... Sanford, FL
Pond, Jeffrey C., (P.C.) .... Denver, CO
Pond, Joel T. .... Boston, MA
Pond, John Daniel, II .... Front Royal, VA
Pond, Jonathan R. .... Richmond, VA
Pond, Joseph H. .... Grahamsville, NY
Pond, Karl J. E. .... Atlanta, GA
Pond, Karl S .... Salem, OR
Pond, Lawrence J. .... Atlanta, GA
Pond, Michael G. .... Jackson, MS
Pond, Nigel .... Wilmington, DE
Pond, North & Hugo, P.C.
San Francisco, CA
Pond, Paul L. .... Mound, MN
Pond, Ralph C. .... Seattle, WA
Pond, Robert A. .... Chicago, IL
Pond, Robert K. .... Bolton, MA
Pond, Roesch, Rahn & Nelson, P.S.
Longview, WA
Pond, Roger A. .... Richmond, VA
Pond, Samuel H. .... Philadelphia, PA
Pond, Stanley E. .... San Mateo, CA
Pond, Steven H. .... Longview, WA
Ponda, Ameek Ashok .... Boston, MA
Pondelick, Frank L. .... Wayne, NJ
Ponder, Amos L., Jr. .... New Orleans, LA
Ponder, Andrew G. .... Hardy, AR
Ponder, Anita J. .... Chicago, IL
Ponder, B. Weldon, Jr. .... Austin, TX
Ponder, B. Weldon, Jr., P.C., Law Offices of
Austin, TX
Ponder, Bruce J. .... El Paso, TX
Ponder, Charles M., III .... New Orleans, LA
Ponder, David E. .... Norman, OK
Ponder, Deborah C. .... Atlanta, GA
Ponder, Harry L. .... Walnut Ridge, AR
Ponder, J. Lynn .... Amite, LA
Ponder, J. Michael .... Cape Girardeau, MO
Ponder, Jack G. .... Richardson, TX
Ponder, Jacqueline Bowman
Indianapolis, IN
Ponder & Jarboe .... Walnut Ridge, AR
Ponder, Jason M. .... Manchester, TN
Ponder, Jerry D. .... St. Louis, MO
Ponder, John E. .... San Diego, CA
Ponder, L. Barbee, IV .... New Orleans, LA
Ponder, Lester M. .... Indianapolis, IN
Ponder, Michael Elven .... Baton Rouge, LA
Ponder, Pamela R. .... Charlotte, NC
Ponder, Patricia E. .... Corpus Christi, TX
Ponder, Patricia J. .... Mobile, AL
Ponder, P.J. .... Tallahassee, FL
Ponder, Rhinold Lamar .... New Brunswick, NJ
Ponder, Stephen R. .... Daytona Beach, FL
Ponder, Teresa Ransom .... Irvine, CA
Ponder, Todd W. .... Indianapolis, IN
Ponder, William A. .... Dalton, GA
Ponder, William N. .... Livonia, MI
Pondo, Stanley L. .... Merrillville, IN
Pondolfi, Robert .... Miami, FL
Pondolfino, Joseph T., Jr. .... Oneonta, NY
Pondrom, Lisa .... San Diego, CA
Pondrom, Ruth D. .... Savannah, GA
Ponds, Billy L. .... Washington, DC
Ponds, Gary N. .... Naples, FL
Ponds Law Firm, The .... Washington, DC
Ponds, Navron .... Washington, DC
Pone, Edward A. .... Fayetteville, NC
Pone, Sal R. .... Warren, MI
Poneck, Douglas A. .... San Antonio, TX
Poneman, Daniel B. .... Washington, DC
Ponessa, Russell S. .... Minneapolis, MN
Ponfil, Theodore D. .... Chesterfield, MO
Pongetti, J. Victor .... Albuquerque, NM
Pongetti, Robert P. .... Los Angeles, CA
Pongrace, Donald R. .... Washington, DC
Pongracic, Elizabeth M. .... Universal City, CA
Pongracz, Louise F. .... Philadelphia, PA
Pongratz, Stephen G. .... Sacramento, CA
Poniatowski, Donald H. .... Lapeer, MI
Poniatowski, Mark D., Law Offices of
Castro Valley, CA
Oakland, CA
Ponichtera & DeNardis, P.C.
New Bedford, MA
Ponichtera, James R. .... New York, NY
Ponick, Duke W., Jr. .... Kansas City, MO
Ponick, Franklin J. .... Cleveland, OH
Ponikvar, Dale L. .... New York, NY
Ponitz, John A. .... Troy, MI
Ponkowski, Nancy Drolshagen
Grosse Pointe Woods, MI
Ponn, Enid Miller .... Coral Gables, FL
Ponomarchuk, Leonid (Les) .... Seattle, WA
Ponomarenko, Xenia M. .... Washington, DC
Ponoroff, Lawrence .... New Orleans, LA
Pons, Anthony J. .... San Antonio, TX
Pons, Elaine M. .... Salem, OR
Pons, Florence M. .... Greensboro, NC
Pons, J. Edwin .... Greensboro, NC
Pons, John M. .... Phoenix, AZ
Pons, Joseph P., Jr. .... Bel Air, MD
Pons, Martin E. .... Miami, FL
Pons, Mary E. .... Montgomery, AL
Pons, Victor M., Jr. .... San Juan, PR
Ponsa-Feliu, Francisco .... San Juan, PR
Ponsetto, James P. .... Boston, MA
Ponsetto, John R. .... Burlington, VT
Ponsetto, Joseph L. .... Chicago, IL
Ponsetto, K. Noelle .... Costa Mesa, CA
Ponsetto, Richard T., Jr. .... Flint, MI
Ponsford, Terrence V. .... San Francisco, CA
Ponsoldt, William Raymond, Jr.
Stuart, FL
Ponsor, Dennis J. .... Riverside, CA
Santa Ana, CA
Ponsor, Michael A. .... Springfield, MA
Pont, James K. .... Myrtle Beach, SC
Pont, Lloyd A. .... Southfield, MI
Pontacoloni, Edward J. .... Hartford, CT
Pontani, Thomas C. .... New York, NY
Pontaoe, Sheldon R. .... New York, NY
Pontarelli, Michael L. .... Park Ridge, IL
Pontarelli, Thomas .... Lincolnshire, IL
Pontarolo, Michael J. .... Spokane, WA
Ponte, Bruce .... San Francisco, CA
Pontell, Bonnie J. .... Honolulu, HI
Pontell, Steven .... Fort Lee, NJ
Pontello, Louis A., Jr. .... Houston, TX
Ponterio, Angelo F. .... Rio Vista, CA
Ponterio, Barbara A. .... Staten Island, NY
Ponterio, John J. .... Philadelphia, PA
Ponterio, Michael A. .... Buffalo, NY
Pontes, Audra L. .... Fall River, MA
Pontes, Thomas E. .... Raynham, MA
Ponti, Jennifer L. .... Dallas, TX
Ponti, R. Gary .... Walla Walla, WA
Ponticelli, Barry A. .... Washington, DC
Ponticelli, Michael I. .... Park Ridge, IL
Ponticello, Barry W. .... San Diego, CA
Ponticello, Christopher G. .... Pittsburgh, PA
Ponticello, Frank M. .... Las Vegas, NV
Ponticello, Teresita L. .... Las Vegas, NV
Ponticiello, Stephen .... Department of Justice, Tax Division, GV
Pontifex, Kenneth J. .... Santa Bbara, CA
Pontiff, Paul E. .... Glens Falls, NY
Pontigas, Susan J. .... Miami, FL
Pontikes & Garcia .... Chicago, IL
Pontikes, George C., & Associates
Chicago, IL
Pontikes, Rebecca .... Cambridge, MA
Pontikes, Steven M. .... Chicago, IL
Pontikis, Thomas J. .... Chicago, IL
Pontillo, Clement J., Jr. .... Glastonbury, CT
Pontillo, Salvatore B .... Farmingdale, NY
Pontious, Andrew Howard
San Francisco, CA
Pontious, Victor D., Jr.
Washington C. H., OH
Pontisakos, Demetra M. .... Gloucester, MA
Pontisakos, John D. .... Long Island City, NY
Mineola, NY
Pontius, Dale .... Department Of The Interior, Office of the Solicitor, GV
Pontius, David E. .... Ashtabula, OH
Pontius, Dean .... Vancouver, WA
Pontius, Donald H. .... Columbus, OH
Pontius, Gary D. .... St. Paul, MN
Pontius, Jarrod B. .... Cincinnati, OH
Pontius, Kevin L. .... Reston, VA
Pontius, Lisa M. .... Salinas, CA
Pontius, Nancy L. .... Syracuse, NY
Pontius, Robert A. .... Canton, OH
Ponto, Geraldine E. .... Newark, NJ
Ponto, Michael A. .... Minneapolis, MN
Ponto, Nancy L. .... Inver Grove Heights, MN

Ponton, Carol J. .... **Orlando, FL**
Ponton, Ellyn M. .... Grapevine, TX
Ponton, George G. .... Frankfort, IN
Ponton, Karen J. .... Sacramento, CA
Ponton & Mohler .... Frankfort, IN
Ponton, R. Darryl .... Pittsburgh, PA
Ponton, R. Darryl, & Associates
Pittsburgh, PA
Ponton, Robert A., Jr. .... **Raleigh, NC**
Pontone, Kathleen .... **Baltimore, MD**
Pontoppidan, Henrik A. .... New Orleans, LA
Pontrelli, Anne .... New York, NY
Pontrelli, Michael A. .... Camarillo, CA
Pontrelli, Michael R. .... Santa Barbara, CA
Pontrelli, Michael R. .... **Boston, MA**
Pontrelli, Paul Jay .... **Atlanta, GA**
Pontrello, Wm. G. .... **Clearwater, FL**
Pontz, Curtis M. .... Valley Forge, PA
Pontz, Evan H. .... **Atlanta, GA**
Pontz, Robert W. .... **Lancaster, PA**
Pontzer, David .... **Ridgway, PA**
Pontzer and Dickinson .... Ridgway, PA
Pontzer & Foradora .... **Brookville, PA**
Ridgway, PA
Pontzer, John F. .... Ridgway, PA
Pontzer, Kathryn M. .... Washington, DC
Pontzer, Norbert J. .... **Ridgway, PA**
Pontzer, Peter F. .... Department of Justice,
Bureau of Prisons, GV
Ponvert, Antonio, III .... **New Haven, CT**
Ponzi, Curtis R. .... San Francisco, CA
Ponzi, Matthew S. .... **Chicago, IL**
Ponziani, Peter J. .... **Hartford, CT**
Ponzini, John Lino .... **Stamford, CT**
Ponzini, Robert J. .... **Tarrytown, NY**
Ponzini, Spencer & Geis, L.L.P.
Tarrytown, NY
Ponzio, Anthony V. .... Chicago, IL
Ponzio, James T. .... **Santa Rosa, CA**
Ponzo & Ponzo .... Newport News, VA
Ponzo, Robt. P. .... Newport News, VA
Ponzoli, Ronald P. .... **Miami, FL**
Ponzoli, Ronald P., Jr.
West Palm Beach, FL
Ponzoli, Wassenberg & Sperkacz, P.A.
Fort Lauderdale, FL
Miami, FL
Poochigian, Charles S. .... Sacramento, CA
Poock, Arlen Long .... Muscatine, IA
Poock, Ronald B. .... Dallas, TX
Poock, Steven D. .... **Houston, TX**
Poohar, Stephen L. .... San Francisco, CA
Pool, Aaron .... **Houston, TX**
Pool, Benjamin E. .... **Montgomery, AL**
Pool, Blankenship, Vincent & Pool, A Professional Association .... **Del City, OK**
Oklahoma City, OK
Pool, C. Randy .... Marion, NC
Pool, Daniel .... New York, NY
Pool, Delby B., (Ms.) .... Clarksburg, WV
Pool, Donald J. .... **Fresno, CA**
Pool, Douglas W. .... **Indianapolis, IN**
Pool, Ernest H., Jr. .... **Ottawa, IL**
Pool, Eugene K. .... **Tampa, FL**
Pool, Franz L. .... Hartford, CT
Pool, Garrett N. .... **Del City, OK**
Oklahoma City, OK
Pool, Gregory R. .... Chicago, IL
Pool, Henry S. .... **Pittsburgh, PA**
Pool, Jack E. .... Natchez, MS
Pool, James M. .... **Birmingham, AL**
Pool, James M. .... Clarksburg, WV
Pool, Jimmy B. .... Montgomery, AL
Pool, Jo Anne .... Tulsa, OK
Pool, John L. .... Andrews, TX
Pool, Joseph H. .... Amarillo, TX
Pool, Kelly .... Jefferson City, MO
Pool, Lance A. .... Dallas, TX
Pool, Leigh & Fabricius .... **Ottawa, IL**
Rock Island, IL
Pool, Patsy A. .... Duncanville, TX
Pool, Paul E. .... Johnson City, NY
Pool, Rebecca J. .... Edinburg, TX
Pool, Robert A. .... Bellaire, TX
Pool, Roger B. .... San Francisco, CA
Pool, Rothwell B. .... Terrell, TX
Pool, Scot V. .... **Savannah, GA**
Pool, Ted N. .... **Del City, OK**
Oklahoma City, OK
Pool, Terry W. .... **Dallas, TX**
Pool, Tilman E., Jr. .... Tulsa, OK
Pool, Vanderver R. .... **Statesboro, GA**
Pool, Vanderver R., P.C. .... **Statesboro, GA**
Pool, Willard R. .... Garden Grove, CA
Poole, A. Gregory .... **Marietta, GA**
Poole, Albert H. .... **Chesterfield, VA**
Virginia Beach, VA
Poole, Anthony .... **Northbrook, IL**
Poole, Arnold W. .... Albany, OR
Poole & Associates, A Professional Service Corporation .... **Seattle, WA**
Poole, Benton J. .... **Rockwall, TX**
Poole, Beverly A.
Charlotte Amalie, St. Thomas, VI
Poole, Beverly D. .... Jackson, MS
Poole, Billie L. .... **Clinton, NC**
Poole, Bradley B., (Chartered) .... **Boise, ID**
Poole, Bradley B., Chtd. .... **Boise, ID**
Poole, Brooke D.
Nuclear Regulatory Commission,
Office of the General Counsel, GV
Poole, Bruce D. .... San Diego, CA
Poole, C. Thomas .... Bowling Green, KY
Poole, Calvin, III .... **Greenville, AL**
Poole, Carlyn G. .... **Raleigh, NC**
Poole, Carroll F. .... Hockessin, DE
Poole, Charles, & Associates, PLLC
Sevierville, TN
Poole, Charles I. .... **Sevierville, TN**
Poole, Charles Ruffin .... Raleigh, NC
Poole, Chris .... Chattanooga, TN
Poole, Christopher S. .... **Lynn, MA**
Poole, Cleveland .... Greenville, AL
Poole, Clinton L. .... Barrington, RI
Poole, D. Bruce .... Hagerstown, MD
Poole, Daniel L. .... **Denver, CO**
Poole, David K., Jr. .... Hagerstown, MD
Poole, David P. .... **Dallas, TX**
Poole, David S. .... **Los Angeles, CA**
Poole, Deborah L. .... **Sacramento, CA**
Poole, Debra Anne .... **Columbia, MD**
Poole, Dennis K. .... Salt Lake City, UT
Poole, Dennis K., & Associates, P.C.
Salt Lake City, UT
Poole, Don W. .... **Chattanooga, TN**
Poole, Donald C. .... **Sacramento, CA**
Poole, Donza M. .... Cleveland, OH
Poole, Doreen Smith .... Canton, OH
Poole, Dorothy Braun .... Pasadena, CA
Poole, Douglas W. .... **Galveston, TX**
Poole, Edward G. .... **San Francisco, CA**
Poole, Elisha C. .... **Greenville, AL**
Poole, Ellen K. .... Phoenix, AZ
Poole, Garth J. .... **San Jose, CA**
Poole, Gary R. .... Chapel Hill, NC
Poole, Gary R., P.A., Law Office of
Chapel Hill, NC
Poole, George A., Jr. .... Carmel, CA
Poole, Gerald B. .... Dearborn Heights, MI
Poole, Gordon L. .... **San Francisco, CA**
Poole, H. Price, Jr. .... Fernandina Beach, FL
Poole, H. Ronald .... Roseburg, OR
Poole, H. Scott .... **Ephrata, PA**
Lancaster, PA
Lititz, PA
Poole, Heather M. .... **Oklahoma City, OK**
Poole, J. Gregory .... **Greensboro, NC**
Poole, J. Michael, & Associates
Jeffersonville, IN
La Grange, KY
Poole, J. Michael, & Associates
Louisville, KY
Poole, J. Ray .... Tallahassee, FL
Poole, J. Roger .... **Spartanburg, SC**
Poole, J. Terry .... **Barnwell, SC**
Poole, James D. .... **Birmingham, AL**
Poole, James K. .... Dobbs Ferry, NY
Poole, Jay J. .... Chicago, IL
Poole, Jeanine L. .... **Concord, NH**
Poole, Jeffrey G. .... **Seattle, WA**
Poole, Jocelyn .... **Miami, FL**
Poole, Joel A. .... **St. Louis, MO**
Poole, John H. .... Pasadena, CA
Poole, John L. .... Belmont, CA
Poole, John S. .... Louisville, KY
Poole, John W., Jr. .... Department of Justice,
Antitrust Division, GV
Poole, Joseph N., III .... Pike Road, AL
Poole, Katherine S.
South San Francisco, CA
Poole, Kathleen M. .... Independence, OR
Poole, Keith .... Marietta, GA
Poole, Keith, P.C .... Marietta, GA
Poole, Kimbel and Deeb
Bowling Green, KY
Poole, Klask & Rivard, P.C.
Dearborn Heights, MI
Poole, Kristine L. .... **Chicago, IL**
Poole, L. Eric .... Redwood City, CA
Poole, Laurie S. .... Encinitas, CA
Poole, Leslie P. .... Chicago, IL
Poole, Lisa Lee .... **Washington, DC**
Poole, Lisa Shank .... Hagerstown, MD
Poole, Lynn D.
United States Postal Service,
Mid-Atlantic Office, GV
Poole, Marilynn .... Spring, TX
Poole, Mark Allan .... **New York, NY**
Poole, Medea D. .... **Orlando, FL**
Poole, Mitchell .... **Los Angeles, CA**
Poole, Nicole N. .... Garden City, NY
Poole, Pamela .... Houston, TX
Poole, Pamela J. .... Winter Springs, FL
Poole, Patricia A. .... **Cleveland, OH**
Poole, Patricia F. .... **Winston-Salem, NC**
Poole, Phillip L. .... Southfield, MI
Poole & Poole .... **Greenville, AL**
Poole and Poole .... **Richmond, VA**
Poole & Poole, P.A. .... Fernandina Beach, FL
Poole & Poole, P.A. .... Hagerstown, MD
Poole, Preston L., Jr. .... Post, TX
Poole, R. Edward .... **Washington, DC**
Poole, Ramon V. .... Pasadena, CA
Poole, Renee E. .... Shreveport, LA
Poole, Richard Alan .... Department of Justice,
Criminal Division, GV
Poole, Richard C. .... Greenville, NC
Poole, Richard E. .... **Wilmington, DE**
Poole, Ricky J. .... **San Antonio, TX**
Poole, Robert Lawrence .... Newport, KY
Poole, Rodney M. .... **Richmond, VA**
Poole, Ron .... Wichita Falls, TX
Poole, Ronny Ned .... Wichita Falls, TX
Poole, Russell C. .... **Fort Worth, TX**
Poole, Sam N., Jr. .... **Alexandria, LA**
Poole, Samuel E., III
Fort Lauderdale, FL
Poole, Samuel H. .... Washington, DC
Raleigh, NC
Poole, Samuel H., Jr. .... **Charlotte, NC**
Poole, Scott R. .... **Jefferson City, MO**
Poole & Shaffery, LLP .... **Los Angeles, CA**
Poole, Sharon .... St. Augustine, FL
Poole, Shelley V. .... Austin, TX
Poole, Susie Ross .... Little Rock, AR
Poole, Thornbury, Morgan & Richardson
Chattanooga, TN
Poole, Tracy A. .... **Oklahoma City, OK**
Poole, Tracy E. .... New York, NY
Poole, Victor P., Jr. .... **Tuscaloosa, AL**
Poole, Wesley R. .... Fernandina Beach, FL
Poole, William F., IV, Law Offices of
Orlando, FL
Poole, William H. .... Indian Wells, CA
Poole, William H., Jr. .... York, PA
Poole, William M. .... **Atlanta, GA**
Poole, William S., Jr. .... **Demopolis, AL**
Poole, William S., Jr. .... **Linden, AL**
Poole, Wm. H. .... Mullins, SC
Poole-Khatib, Patricia A. .... Oakland, CA
Pooler, Catherine M. .... Miami, FL
Pooler, Delia B. .... Portland, ME
Pooler, J. Richard .... **Syracuse, NY**
Pooler, Noel Louis .... Muncie, IN
Pooler, Randall B. .... Jacksonville, FL
Pooler, Rosemary S. .... Syracuse, NY
Pooler, Sanford M., Jr. .... Boston, MA
Pooley, Christopher J. .... **Toledo, OH**
Pooley, Douglas .... Denver, CO
Pooley, Edward C. .... Mount Clemens, MI
Pooley, Elizabeth A. .... Gainesville, FL
Pooley, James .... **Palo Alto, CA**
Pooley, Josephine .... Newburgh, NY
Pooley, Lisa M. .... **San Francisco, CA**
Pooley, Montgomery G. .... Buffalo, NY
Pooley, Phyllis K. .... Augusta, ME
Pooley, Thomas J. .... Greensboro, NC
Poon, Christine P. .... **New York, NY**
Poon, Chung S. .... **San Francisco, CA**
Poon, Enoch M. .... **Louisville, KY**
Poon, Gary P. .... Washington, DC
Poon, Helen M. .... Alexandria, VA
Poon, Linda .... **New York, NY**
Poon, Melinda .... **New York, NY**
Poon, Pamela G. .... Bozeman, MT
Poon, Peter N. .... Rockville, MD
Poon, Ricky W. .... Los Angeles, CA
Poon, Wena .... **New York, NY**
Poon, William .... Monterey Park, CA
Poon, Yee Ling .... New York, NY
Pooner, Jeffrey H. .... Marlton, NJ
Poonja, Zaitun .... **Palo Alto, CA**
Poor, Brian W. .... **Seattle, WA**
Poor, E. King .... **Chicago, IL**
Poor, J. Stephen .... **Chicago, IL**
Poor, Nona Smith .... Beaumont, TX
Poor, Ryan M. .... **Indianapolis, IN**
Poor, Sarah Thompson .... Littleton, CO
Poorak, Sharon C. .... Atlanta, GA
Poore, Curtis O. .... **Cape Girardeau, MO**
Poore, Gregory R. .... Cleveland, OH
Poore & Hopkins, PLLP .... **Butte, MT**
Helena, MT
Missoula, MT
Poore, J. Thomas .... Tucson, AZ
Poore, J. Timothy .... Williamson, WV
Poore, James A., III .... **Missoula, MT**
Poore, James A., Jr. .... **Butte, MT**
Poore, Jennie E. .... Fort Lauderdale, FL
Poore, Marvin A. .... Indianapolis, IN
Poore, Michaelle .... Spruce Pine, NC
Poore, Regina M. .... **Indianapolis, IN**
Poore & Riddle .... Tucson, AZ
Poore, Robert A. .... **Butte, MT**
Poore, Robert L. .... Orlando, FL
Poore, Roger S. .... San Rafael, CA
Poore & Rosenbaum .... **Providence, RI**
Poore, Roth & Robinson, P.C.
Anaconda, MT
Butte, MT
Deer Lodge, MT
Dillon, MT
Poore, Shannon L. .... **Fayetteville, AR**
Poore, Shelley L. .... **New Orleans, LA**
Poore, Steven G. .... Indianapolis, IN
Poore, Susan Minton .... **Dallas, TX**
Poore, William A. .... **Providence, RI**
Poorman, Anne Wilt .... Bronxville, NY
Poorman, Donald Harris .... Philadelphia, PA
Poorman, Gary L. .... Wauseon, OH
Poorman, J. D. .... Ogden, UT
Poorman, John Kevin .... Chicago, IL
Poorman, Scott L. .... Hayden, ID
Poormon, Richard P. .... **Tulsa, OK**
Poorten, William N., III .... **Tucson, AZ**
Poorvu, Sumner L. .... Boston, MA
Pooser, Christopher .... **Boise, ID**
Pooser, Wankard L. .... Auburn, NY
Poosikian, Glenn Z. .... Paterson, NJ
Poots, Jeffery L. .... Omaha, NE
Poovey, James D. .... Eureka, CA
Poovey, Kenneth M. .... San Francisco, CA
Poovey, Mark N. .... **Winston-Salem, NC**
Poovey, Nathaniel J. .... **Newton, NC**
Poovey, William P. .... **Menlo Park, CA**
Pop, Jeffrey S. .... Beverly Hills, CA
Popa, Ervin A. .... New York, NY
Popa, Mary-Theresa .... **Pittsburgh, PA**
Popa, Robert .... **Los Angeles, CA**
Popalisky, William M. .... **New York, NY**
Popa-Ravagnan, Alda M. .... **New York, NY**
Popcheff, George T. .... Speedway, IN
Popcke, Michael R. .... **San Diego, CA**
Pope, A. Harrell .... Greensboro, NC
Pope, A. Mark .... **San Diego, CA**
Pope, Adele J. .... **Columbia, SC**
Pope, Adele J., P.C. .... **Columbia, SC**
Pope, A. J., III .... Medina, TX
Pope, A. J. (Jack), Jr. .... Austin, TX
Pope, Alan J. .... Walnut Creek, CA
Pope, Alan J. .... **Binghamton, NY**
Pope, Alan W. .... **Charlotte, NC**
Pope, Amy Lee .... Fresno, CA
Pope, Andrea C. .... **Columbia, SC**
Pope, Andrea Sylvia Piccirilli
Birmingham, AL
Pope, Anna B. .... **San Francisco, CA**
Pope, Anne D. .... Hauppauge, NY
Pope, Anthony J. .... Elmhurst, IL
Pope, Anthony J .... **Newark, NJ**
Pope, Barrett E. .... **Richmond, VA**
Pope & Berger .... **San Diego, CA**
Pope, Beth Rodgers .... Purchase, NY
Pope, Blaise M. .... San Diego, CA
Pope, Bob G. .... Marietta, GA
Woodstock, GA
Pope, Brian Francis .... Burbank, CA
Pope, Bryan H. .... **Atlanta, GA**
Pope, Bryan T. .... **Dallas, TX**
Pope, C. Braxton .... Atlanta, GA
Pope, C. Elizabeth .... **Atlanta, GA**
Pope, C. Neal, (P.C.) .... **Atlanta, GA**
Columbus, GA
Pope, Calvin A. .... Tampa, FL
Pope, Carol Waller
Federal Labor Relations Authority,
Office of the General Counsel, GV
Pope, Cathy A. Hinton .... **Cary, NC**
Pope, Cecilia Ann .... Huntsville, AL
Pope, C. H., Jr. .... **New Bern, NC**
Pope, Charles E. .... Woodbridge, VA
Pope, Charles J. .... Ypsilanti, MI
Pope, Charles Parks .... Memphis, TN
Pope, Clara A. "Zazi" .... **Burbank, CA**
Pope, Cynthia A. .... Poughkeepsie, NY
Pope, Cynthia Lee .... Bellingham, WA
Pope, D. Bruce .... Denver, CO
Pope, D. Lucetta .... **South Bend, IN**
Pope, Dale E. .... Edgerton, WI
Pope, Daniel B. .... Seattle, WA
Pope, Daniel C. .... Fall River, MA
Seekonk, MA
Providence, RI
Pope, Daniel Carter, Jr. .... **Cary, NC**
Pope, Daniel J. .... **Chicago, IL**
Pope, Daniel M. .... Salt Lake City, UT
Pope, David A. .... **Macon, GA**
Pope, David F. .... **Tampa, FL**
Pope, David H. .... **Atlanta, GA**
Pope, Deborah L. .... Matthews, NC
Pope, Don G. .... **Norman, OK**
Pope, Don G., & Associates, P.C.
Norman, OK
Pope, Donnie R. .... Littleton, CO
Pope, Dougal C. .... Houston, TX
Pope, Douglas .... **Anchorage, AK**
Pope, Douglas N. .... Sacramento, CA
Pope, Douglas V. .... **Washington, DC**
Pope and Drayer .... **Clarion, PA**
Pope, Eddie M. .... **Austin, TX**
Pope, Edward C. .... United States Senate,
Committee Legal Personnel, GV
Pope, Elaine R. .... **Atlanta, GA**
Pope, F. Starr, Jr. .... **Corpus Christi, TX**
Pope, F. Wallace, Jr. .... **Clearwater, FL**
Tampa, FL
Pope Firm, The .... **Dallas, TX**
Pope, Gary R. .... Kingman, AZ
Pope, Gary T. .... **Newberry, SC**
Pope and Gentile .... Hesperia, CA
Pope, Geoffrey .... **Atlanta, GA**
Pope, Geoffrey S. .... **New York, NY**
Pope, George Cleveland .... Charlotte, NC
Pope, Glenn A., Jr. .... Sacramento, CA
Pope, Gregory A. .... **Buffalo, NY**
Lockport, NY
Niagara Falls, NY
Williamsville, NY
Pope, Gregory A., & Associates, Law Firm of
Buffalo, NY
Lockport, NY
Niagara Falls, NY
Williamsville, NY
Pope, Gregory S. .... **Columbus, OH**
Westerville, OH
Pope, Grossman, Bergrin, Verdesco & Bross, A Professional Corporation .... **Newark, NJ**
Pope, H. Cranston .... **Panama City, FL**
Pope, Hardwicke, Christie, Harrell, Schell & Kelly, L.L.P. .... **Fort Worth, TX**
Pope, Harold C. .... **Los Angeles, CA**
Pope, Harold D., III .... **Detroit, MI**
Pope, Harold G. .... Whiteville, NC
Pope, Harold N. .... Chicago, IL
Pope & Henninger, P.A. .... St. Petersburg, FL
Pope, Henry R., III .... **Clarion, PA**
Pope and Hudgens, P.A. .... **Newberry, SC**
Saluda, SC
Pope & Hughes, A Professional Association
Baltimore, MD
Towson, MD
Pope, James Arthur .... Raleigh, NC
Pope, James C. .... **Arlington, VA**
McLean, VA
Pope, James Mathews .... Courtland, VA
Pope, James R. .... **Plainfield, IN**
Pope, James R. .... Dodgeville, WI
Pope, James S. .... Columbia, SC
Pope, James W. .... **Charlotte, NC**
Pope, Janet Childers .... Oklahoma City, OK
Pope, Jaquelynn C. .... Hermosa Beach, CA
Pope, Jay Christopher .... Bel Air, MD
Pope, Jean Harvey, (Mrs.) .... Longview, WA
Pope, Jennifer Robinson .... **Jacksonville, NC**
Pope, Jerome W. .... **Chicago, IL**
Pope, Jim L. .... Greeley, CO
Pope, John A., III .... Rio Grande City, TX
Pope, John E. .... Newport Beach, CA
Pope, John F. .... Bradenton, FL
Pope, John Houston .... **New York, NY**
Pope, John M. .... Scottsdale, AZ

Porch, Brooks L. .... Atlanta, GA
Porch, C. Edward .... Stuart, FL
Porch, George A. .... Evansville, IN
Porch, Jerry C. .... Russellville, AL
Porch, Peeler, Williams & Thomason, A Professional Corporation .... Waverly, TN
Porch, Priscilla Elizabeth .... Philadelphia, PA
Porch, Ralph D. .... Anniston, AL
Porch, Rowland B. .... Pitman, NJ
Porch, William W. .... Oklahoma City, OK
Porche, Edward M., Jr. .... Metairie, LA
Porche, Edward M., Jr. .... New Orleans, LA
Porche, Marina .... Los Angeles, CA
Porcher, Corinne Tutuska .... Miami, FL
Porcher, Randall T. .... West Palm Beach, FL
Porcino, Peter R. .... New York, NY
Porco, Domenick J. .... New York, NY
Porco, John .... Weirton, WV
Wheeling, WV
Porco, John A. .... Carmel, NY
Cold Spring, NY
Westhampton Beach, NY
Porco, John A., P.C. .... Carmel, NY
Porco, John A., P.C. .... Cold Spring, NY
Porco, John A., P.C. .... New York, NY
Porco, Michael J. .... New York, NY
Porco, Peter R. .... Delmar, NY
Porco, Vittorio E. .... East Lansing, MI
Porcora, John E. .... Ramsey, NJ
Pordan, George W. .... Lorain, OH
Pordos, Mark J. .... Chandler, OK
Pordum, Karen J. .... Marina Del Rey, CA
Pordy, David A. .... Washington, DC
Rockville, MD
McLean, VA
Pordy, Ronald S. .... New York, NY
Poreda, Christopher .... Burlington, MA
Poreda, Heidi C. .... Brooklyn, NY
Poree, Victor J. .... Pleasanton, CA
Poree, Victor J., Law Offices of
Pleasanton, CA
Poremba, Carol A. .... Chicago, IL
Poremba, Daniel .... San Mateo, CA
Porembski, Chester P. .... Cincinnati, OH
Porembski-Perry, Elizabeth M. .... Liberty, MO
Pores, Joel Michael, The Law Office of
Laguna Hills, CA
Poresky, Donna .... Glastonbury, CT
Poret, Charles I. .... New York, NY
Poret, Hal L. .... Boston, MA
Poret, Hilary Ames .... Boston, MA
Poretsky, Beth L. .... White Plains, NY
Poretsky, Joel A. .... New York, NY
Poretta, Michael J. .... Hamburg, NY
Porette, Maureen Ann .... Uniondale, NY
Poretti, Daniel Q. .... Minneapolis, MN
Poretz, Alexi .... New York, NY
Poretz, Barry R. .... Alexandria, VA
Poretz, Jeffrey Scott .... McLean, VA
Poretz, Ted .... New York, NY
Porfido, Eugene J. .... Succasunna, NJ
Porfido, James M. .... Succasunna, NJ
Porfido, Margaret E. .... Boulder, CO
Porfilio, John Carbone .... Denver, CO
Porfiri, Raymond C. .... Boston, MA
Porges, Ellen R. .... New York, NY
Porges, Gregory J. .... Bradenton, FL
Porges, Janet Stodgell .... Bradenton, FL
Porges, Jennifer .... Penn Valley, PA
Porges, John .... New York, NY
Porges-Dodson, Ann .... Macon, GA
Pori, Tim A. .... Vallejo, CA
Porick, Dennis B. .... Joliet, IL
Porick, Dennis B., Ltd. .... Joliet, IL
Poris, Jil M. .... Granada Hills, CA
Poris, Kenneth E. .... Lisle, IL
Poris & Lawrence, Ltd. .... Lisle, IL
Poriss, Emily J. .... Hartford, CT
Poritz, Deborah Tobias .... Princeton, NJ
Poritz, Samuel N. .... Paterson, NJ
Pornprinya, Puemsuk T. .... Miami, FL
Porobil, Gregory M. .... New Orleans, LA
Porotsky, Richard D., Jr. .... Cincinnati, OH
Porper, Daniel S. .... Raleigh, NC
Porper, Julia .... New York, NY
Porr & Associates, P.C. .... Lancaster, PA
Porr, Norman W. .... Omaha, NE
Porr, Steven N. .... Omaha, NE
Porras, Antonio, Jr. .... Portland, OR
Porras, Carin Marie .... Fort Lauderdale, FL
Porras, D. Daniel .... Cleveland, OH
Porras, David J. .... Riverside, CA
Porras, Jorge A. .... Boston, MA
Porrata-Doria, Rafael A., Jr.
Philadelphia, PA
Porrazzo, Michael H. .... San Jose, CA
Porrazzo, Romy M. .... Brooklyn, NY
Porreca, Charles G. .... Rochester, NY
Porreca, Chas. G. .... Brighton, NY
Porreca, Christopher G. .... Livingston, NJ
Porreca, James M. .... Treasury Department, Office of Thrift Supervision, GV
Porreca, Martellus A. .... Los Angeles, CA
Porreca, Mary Anne I. Breslin .... Lansdale, PA
Porreca, Paul R. .... Northfield, NJ
Porreca & Porreca .... Lansdale, PA
Porreca, Raymond J., Jr. .... Lansdale, PA
Porreca, R. J. .... Ambler, PA
Porrello, Joseph A. .... Tampa, FL
Porretta, Charles .... Chicago, IL
Porretta, Francis H. .... Troy, MI
Porretta, Paul L. .... New York, NY
Porretto, James .... Melville, NY
Porricelli, Gerald J. .... Old Greenwich, CT
Porrini, Paul T. .... Berwyn, PA
Porrino, Christopher S. .... Woodbridge, NJ
Porritt, James R., Jr. .... Lake Orion, MI
Porritt, Nicholas .... Washington, DC
Porritt, Russell W., II .... Bloomfield Hills, MI
Toledo, OH
Porro, Hilda Montalvo
West Palm Beach, FL
Porro, Janet L. .... Pompton Plains, NJ
Porro, Kenneth A. .... Lyndhurst, NJ
Porroni, Albert .... Trenton, NJ
Porr Sweeney, Linda .... Lancaster, PA
Pors, Thomas M. .... Seattle, WA
Porsborg, Scott K. .... Bismarck, ND
Port, Alan D. .... Burlington, VT
Port, Andrew I. .... San Francisco, CA
Port, Barry S. .... Jamaica, NY
Port, Brian E. .... Aventura, FL
Port, Cameron A. .... Los Angeles, CA
Port, Charles S. .... New York, NY
Port, David F. .... Naples, FL
Port, Gail S. .... New York, NY
Port, Gary .... Woodmere, NY
Port, Gregory D. .... Columbus, OH
Port, Harold R. .... Lake Worth, FL
Port, Howard A. .... East Syracuse, NY
Port, Jason De Winter .... Philadelphia, PA
Port, Jennifer D. .... Greenwich, CT
Port, Joseph C., Jr. .... Washington, DC
Port, Kenneth L. .... Wauwatosa, WI
Port, Kenric E. .... Atlanta, GA
Port, Larry N. .... White Plains, NY
Port, Leon R. .... Brooklyn, NY
Port, Linda B. .... Boston, MA
Port, L. L., (Mrs.) .... Redwood City, CA
Port, M. L. .... Chicago, IL
Port, P. Allan .... Houston, TX
Port, Peter S. .... New York, NY
Port, Robert C. .... Atlanta, GA
Port, Sidney L. .... Des Plaines, IL
Port, Thomas R. .... Danville, CA
Port, Wayne H. .... Uniontown, PA
Port, William S. .... St. Louis, MO
Porta, David A. .... Clayton, MO
Porta, Earnest W., Jr. .... Washington, DC
Porta, Frank R. .... Ann Arbor, MI
Porta, Libretta A. .... Washington, DC
Porta, Lisa R. .... Durham, NC
Porta, Michelle G. .... Oklahoma City, OK
Portal, David M. .... New York, NY
Portales, Roberto Ernest .... Denver, CO
Portanova, Thomas A. .... Union City, NJ
Portanova, Victor E. .... Beverly Hills, CA
Portanova, Victor E., A Law Corporation
Beverly Hills, CA
Portanova, William J. .... Sacramento, CA
Portararo, Dennis P. .... Middletown, NY
Portasik, Linda Sue .... Atlanta, GA
Porte, Randall J. .... Stroudsburg, PA
Porte, Stephen A. .... Columbus, OH
Portee, Scheryl C.
Department of Transportation, Federal Transit Administration, GV
Portegello, Robert S. .... New York, NY
Portela, Gloria M. .... Houston, TX
Portela, Jose D. .... Miami, FL
Portela, Jose M. .... Dallas, TX
Portela, Joseph G. .... New York, NY
Portela, Lizzie M. .... San Juan, PR
Portell, C. William, Jr. .... Ballwin, MO
Portell, Stephen T. .... Tucson, AZ
Portella, Matthew V. .... Camden, NJ
Portelli, James M. .... Merrillville, IN
Portelli, Joseph A. .... Clifton, NJ
Portelli, Thomas F. .... Clifton, NJ
Portello, William L. .... Sacramento, CA
Walnut Creek, CA
Portenga, Roy J. .... Muskegon, MI
Porteous, David C. .... Memphis, TN
Porteous, David L. .... Grand Rapids, MI
Lansing, MI
Porteous, David W. .... Chicago, IL
Porteous, G. Thomas, Jr. .... New Orleans, LA
Porteous, Hainkel, Johnson & Sarpy, L.L.P.
Baton Rouge, LA
Covington, LA
New Orleans, LA
Thibodaux, LA
Porteous, William A., III
New Orleans, LA
Porter, A. Steven .... Madison, WI
Porter, Adam M. .... Beverly Hills, CA
Washington, DC
Porter, Adam Michael .... Birmingham, AL
Porter, Alan B. .... San Francisco, CA
Porter, Alan C. .... Washington, DC
Porter, Alexander W. .... Austin, TX
Porter, Allen D. .... Princeton, NJ
Porter, Allison Rae .... Monterey, CA
Porter, Amy D. .... Boston, MA
Porter, Amy R. .... Phoenix, AZ
Porter, Andrea Tofanelli
San Francisco, CA
Porter, Andrew C. .... Chicago, IL
Porter, Andrew Eliot .... Chicago, IL
Porter, Andrew L. .... Roseland, NJ
Porter, Andrew M. .... Boston, MA
Holliston, MA
Porter, Andy .... Longview, TX
Porter, Ann C. .... Stone Mountain, GA
Porter, Anne Hoffman .... Columbus, OH
Porter, Anne L. .... Cleveland, OH
Porter, Annette A. .... Alexandria, VA
Porter, Arthur L. .... Huntsville, AL
Porter, Austin, Jr. .... Little Rock, AR
Porter, Barbara Malloy .... Surprise, AZ
Porter & Barrett .... Atlanta, GA
Porter, Benjamin D. .... Winston-Salem, NC
Porter, Benjamin G. .... Seattle, WA
Porter, Bernald C. .... Mesa, AZ
Porter, Bernard A. .... Tampa, FL
Porter, Bernard W., Jr. .... Los Angeles, CA
Porter, Bonita R. .... Worcester, MA
Porter, Brian K. .... Dayton, OH
Porter, C. David .... Lufkin, TX
Porter, Calvin V., Jr. .... Los Angeles, CA
Porter, Carla Volpe .... New York, NY
Porter, Carolyn .... Bryson City, NC
Porter, Carson P. .... Washington, DC
Porter, Cary .... Los Angeles, CA
Porter, Catherine Anne .... Newtown, PA
Porter, Catherine Tift .... Washington, DC
Porter, Cecil Lee .... North Wilkesboro, NC
Porter, Charles .... Columbia, SC
Porter, Charles A., Jr. .... Minneapolis, MN
Porter, Charles D. .... New York, NY
Porter, Charles E., Jr. .... Osterville, MA
Porter, Charles J., P.C. .... Birmingham, MI
Porter, Charles L. .... New Iberia, LA
Porter, Charles R., Jr. .... Corpus Christi, TX
Porter, Charles W. .... Charlotte, NC
Porter, Charles W., P.C. .... Charlotte, NC
Porter, Chas. O. .... Eugene, OR
Porter, Cheairs Mayes .... Montgomery, AL
Porter, Chris A. .... Denver, CO
Porter, Christian P. .... Honolulu, HI
Porter, Christopher Allen .... Wheat Ridge, CO
Porter, Christopher James King .... Reston, VA
Porter, Cindy L. .... Nashville, TN
Porter, Claire M. .... Jackson, MS
Porter, Clark M. .... Phoenix, AZ
Porter, Claud .... Owensboro, KY
Porter & Coakley .... Gloucester, MA
Porter & Cohn, L.L.C.
Overland Park, KS
Kansas City, MO
Porter, Connie L. .... Clare, MI
Porter, Craig .... San Angelo, TX
Porter, Cynthia R. .... Washington, DC
Porter, D. Ross .... Des Moines, IA
Porter, Damon S. .... Jefferson City, MO
Porter, Dan C. .... Grand Rapids, MI
Porter, Daniel L. .... Washington, DC
Porter, David B. .... San Francisco, CA
Porter, David J. .... Pittsburgh, PA
Porter, David K. .... Minneapolis, MN
Porter, David Kevin .... Victorville, CA
Porter, David M. .... Baltimore, MD
Porter, David M., Law Offices of
San Francisco, CA
Porter, David P. .... Cleveland, OH
Porter, David S. .... Long Beach, CA
Porter, David W. .... Shirley, IN
Porter, David William .... Chicago, IL
Porter, Dawn M. .... Washington, DC
Porter, Dean D. .... Basking Ridge, NJ
Porter, Delmer W. .... Oklahoma City, OK
Porter, Dennis L. .... Redding, CA
Porter, Denton & Kobetz, A Professional Law Corporation .... Lafayette, LA
Porter, Diana L. .... Plano, TX
Porter, Diane Elizabeth Martin
Birmingham, AL
Porter, Diane Glee .... Lompoc, CA
Porter, Don L. .... Porterville, CA
Porter, Donald A. .... Rapid City, SD
Porter, Donald D. .... Syracuse, NY
Porter, Donald E. .... Elm Grove, WI
Porter, Donald J. .... Pierre, SD
Porter, Donald L. .... La Porte, IN
Porter, Donna Y. .... Boston, MA
Porter, Douglas G. .... Melbourne, FL
Porter, Douglas K. .... Rosemead, CA
Porter, Drew .... New York, NY
Porter, Dudley, Jr. .... Chattanooga, TN
Porter & Duran .... Lufkin, TX
Porter, Earl J., Jr. .... Nashville, TN
Porter, Edward A. .... Tampa, FL
Porter, Edward D. .... Houston, TX
Porter, Eileen M. .... New York, NY
Porter, Elise W. .... Columbus, OH
Porter, Elizabeth Catherine
Minneapolis, MN
Porter, Felicia G. .... Seattle, WA
Porter, Fia F. .... New York, NY
Porter, Frank B., Jr. (P.C.) .... Boston, MA
Porter, Frank W., Jr. .... Racine, OH
Porter, Frederick M. .... Holmes Beach, FL
Porter, G. David .... Kansas City, MO
Porter, G. Dennis .... Fairhope, AL
Porter, G. Terris .... Show Low, AZ
Porter, G. William .... Glen Ellyn, IL
Porter & Gair, P.C. .... Fairfax, VA
Porter, Garth R. .... Fairfax, VA
Porter, Gary A. .... Mesa, AZ
Porter, Gary D. .... Mobile, AL
Porter, Gary L. .... Oklahoma City, OK
Porter, Gene E., Jr. .... Jacksonville, FL
Porter, Gene T. .... Las Vegas, NV
Porter, George J. .... Huntsville, AL
Porter, George L., III .... Lawton, OK
Porter, George W. .... Ontario, CA
Porter, Gerald M. .... Cleveland, OH
Porter, Gigi Wynne .... Los Angeles, CA
Porter, Gilbert D. .... New York, NY
Porter, Glen L. .... Bangor, ME
Porter, Glenn M. .... Fort Lauderdale, FL
Porter, Grant A. .... Lakewood, CO
Porter, Gregg A. .... New Orleans, LA
Porter, Gregg M. .... Atlanta, GA
Porter, Gregory A. .... Manassas, VA
Porter, Gregory D.
Research Triangle Park, NC
Porter, Gregory E. .... Los Angeles, CA
Porter, Gregory Lawrence .... Austin, TX
Porter, Gregory S. .... Dallas, TX
Porter, Gregory Y. .... Washington, DC
Porter, Groff & Lodwick, A Law Corporation .... Long Beach, CA
Los Angeles, CA
Porter, H. Boone, III .... Kansas City, MO
Porter, H. Wayne .... Tampa, FL
Porter, Haigh .... Florence, SC
Porter & Hedges, L.L.P. .... Houston, TX
Porter, Helen Viney .... Northfield, IL
Porter, Henry B. .... Dumas, TX
Porter, Henry C. .... Beverly, MA
Porter, Henry M. .... Buffalo, NY
Porter, Henry Thomas .... Columbia, MS
Porter, Holly A. .... Washington, DC
Porter, Howard C. .... South Dennis, MA
Porter, Hugh .... Lakehurst, NJ
Porter, Irving C. J. .... Baltimore, MD
Porter, J. Alexander .... Atlanta, GA
Porter, J. Andrew .... Salisbury, NC
Porter, J. Chester .... Shepherdsville, KY
Porter, J. Chester, & Associates
Louisville, KY
Shepherdsville, KY
Taylorsville, KY
Porter, J. David .... Lexington, KY
Porter, J. Gregory .... Des Moines, IA
Porter, J. Kenneth .... Newport, TN
Porter, J. Richard, III .... Cairo, GA
Porter, J. Ridgely, III .... Portsmouth, VA
Porter, J. Terrence .... Fort Myers, FL
Porter, J. William .... Charlotte, NC
Porter, Jack A. .... West Palm Beach, FL
Porter, Jack A., Jr. .... Richardson, TX
Porter, James A. .... Houston, TX
Porter, James A., (P.A.) .... Boca Raton, FL
Porter, James B. .... Jacksonville, FL
Porter, James B. .... Tyler, TX
Porter, James D. .... Oklahoma City, OK
Porter, James D. .... Salt Lake City, UT
Porter, James D. .... Seattle, WA
Porter, James D., Jr. .... Morristown, NJ
Porter, James E., (Inc.) .... San Antonio, TX
Porter, James E. W. .... Arlington, TX
Porter, James F. .... Fort Myers, FL
Porter, James H. .... Nashville, TN
Porter, James H., Jr. .... Pocomoke City, MD
Porter, James H., Jr., P.A.
Pocomoke City, MD
Porter, James Herrin, III .... Montgomery, AL
Porter, James J. .... Tampa, FL
Porter, James L. .... Little Rock, AR
Porter, James L. .... Belleville, IL
Porter, James L. .... Albuquerque, NM
Porter, James L., Jr. .... Truckee, CA
Reno, NV
Porter, James M. .... Miami, FL
Porter, James M. .... Cleveland, OH
Porter, James O. .... Las Vegas, NV
Porter, James O. .... Huntington, WV
Porter, James S. .... Oklahoma City, OK
Porter, James T. .... Dallas, TX
Porter, James W. .... Topeka, KS
Porter, James W. .... Kalamazoo, MI
Porter, James W., II .... Birmingham, AL
Porter, Jamie Lynn .... Hartford, CT
Porter, Janet K. .... Appleton, WI
Porter, Janie C. .... Nashville, TN
Porter, Janis Sue .... Portland, OR
Porter, Jay P. .... Akron, OH
Porter, Jean B. J. .... Cape Canaveral, FL
Porter, Jeffrey J. .... Dallas, TX
Porter, Jeffrey R. .... Boston, MA
Porter, Jeffrey W. .... Wilmington, NC
Porter, Jennifer Elizabeth
Shepherdsville, KY
Porter, Jennifer M. .... Washington, DC
Porter, Jennifer R. .... Sacramento, CA
Porter, Jerome .... Garden City, NY
Porter, Jerome V. .... Denver, CO
Porter, Jerry D. .... Austin, TX
Porter, Jesse E., Jr. .... West Helena, AR
Porter & Jessell .... Fort Myers, FL
Porter, Jill Braunwald .... Lexington, MA
Porter, Jody E. .... Torrance, CA
Porter, Joel A. .... Oklahoma City, OK
Porter, Joel D. .... Hudson, WI
Porter, Joel H. .... Memphis, TN
Porter, John A. .... Belmont, MI
Porter, John C. .... Castro Valley, CA
Porter, John C. .... San Francisco, CA
Porter, John C. .... Bolivar, MO
Porter, John Clark, Jr. .... Atlanta, GA
Porter, John E. .... Los Angeles, CA
Porter, John Edward .... Deerfield, IL
Porter, John F., III, (P.C.) .... Scottsboro, AL
Porter, John H. .... Bethany, OK
Porter, John J. .... Pittsburgh, PA
Porter, John M. .... San Bernardino, CA
Porter, John M. .... Knoxville, TN
Porter, John McGavock .... Montgomery, AL
Porter, John N. .... Brunswick, OH
Porter, John P. .... Lyons, NY
Porter, John R. .... Moscow, ID
Porter, John R., Jr .... Bloomington, IL
Porter, John R., Jr. .... Portsmouth, VA
Porter, John T. .... Albuquerque, NM
Porter, John T. .... Columbus, OH
Porter, John T. .... Yankton, SD
Porter, John V., Jr. .... Paintsville, KY
Porter, John W. .... Fort Wayne, IN
Porter, John W. .... Houston, TX
Porter, Jon H. .... Geneseo, NY
Porter, Joseph B. .... Albany, NY
Porter, Joseph D. .... Houston, TX
Porter, Joseph E., III .... Seal Beach, CA
Porter, Joseph H. .... Sharon, MA
Porter, Joseph T., Jr. .... St. Louis, MO
Porter, Joseph W., Jr. .... Baton Rouge, LA
Porter, Josephine T. .... Albuquerque, NM
Porter, Julie M. .... Newport Beach, CA
Porter, Julie Sonenshine .... Atlanta, GA
Porter, Karen A. .... St. Louis, MO

Pose, Christopher R. .... Des Moines, IA
Pose, Walter E. .... Novato, CA
Posedly, Gloria J. .... Tucson, AZ
Posegate, Carol Hansen .... Springfield, IL
Posegate, David R. .... Tempe, AZ
Posel, Ramon L. .... Philadelphia, PA
Posel, Sherab .... Armonk, NY
Posell, Jerome V. .... Canoga Park, CA
Posell, Jerome V., A Law Corporation
Canoga Park, CA
Posell, Richard E. .... Los Angeles, CA
Posen, Kevin E. .... Chicago, IL
Posen, Richard L. .... New York, NY
Posen, Susan O. .... New York, NY
Posener, Daniel M. .... Burbank, CA
Poser, John F. .... McFarland, WI
Poser, Nicholas E. .... New York, NY
Poser, Norman S. .... Brooklyn, NY
Poserina, Robert J., Jr. .... Sea Isle City, NJ
Poses & Halpern .... Miami, FL
Poses, Mark .... Miami, FL
Posess, Charles F. .... Boca Raton, FL
Posess, Stanley .... Flushing, NY
Posewitz, Brian J. .... Portland, OR
Posey, Allen M., Jr. .... Baton Rouge, LA
Posey, David L. .... Payette, ID
Posey, Donald R. .... Hickory, NC
Posey, G. Harold .... Columbus, GA
Posey, Ivan M. .... Los Angeles, CA
Posey, James M. .... Anchorage, AK
Posey, James N. .... Bethany, OK
Posey, James P. .... Fort Wayne, IN
Posey, Janette R. .... Tustin, CA
Posey, Jennifer R. .... Tustin, CA
Posey, John D. .... San Rafael, CA
Posey, John T. .... Buffalo Grove, IL
Posey, Kimberly Ann .... Indianapolis, IN
Posey, Marona .... Madison, AL
Posey, Melissa A. .... Atlanta, GA
Posey, Moye & Cartledge .... Columbus, GA
Posey, Omiga C. .... Vienna, VA
Posey & Posey .... Tustin, CA
Posey, Richard B. .... Department of the Navy, Office of the Judge Advocate General, GV
Posey, Sonya Marie .... Boston, MA
Posey, Stanley W. .... White Springs, FL
Posey, Terry Wayne .... Dayton, OH
Posey, Thomas Lawson .... Houston, TX
Posey, Timothy S. .... Tulsa, OK
Posey, Tulane E., Jr. .... Plantersville, MS
Posey, Tyler S.
Agency for International Development, Office of the General Counsel, GV
Posey, Walter D. .... Orange, CA
Posey, Webster W. .... Cincinnati, OH
Posey, William A. .... Cincinnati, OH
Posey, William A., Jr. .... Pontiac, MI
Posey, Wyla M. .... Murfreesboro, TN
Posgay, Matthew N.
West Palm Beach, FL
Posgay, Raymond J. .... Fort Lauderdale, FL
Posilippo, Richard .... Mountain View, CA
Posillico, Joseph F. .... Philadelphia, PA
Posin, Debra E. .... Rockville, MD
Posin, Eric A. .... Las Vegas, NV
Posin, Jeffrey S. .... Las Vegas, NV
Posin, Mitchell .... Las Vegas, NV
Posin, Murray .... Las Vegas, NV
Posin & Posin .... Las Vegas, NV
Posinoff, Eli J. .... Carson, CA
Posinoff & Rowe .... Carson, CA
Positan, Wayne J. .... Roseland, NJ
Positano, John A. .... Brooklyn, NY
Poskanzer, Steven G. .... Chicago, IL
Poskozim, James G. .... Chicago, IL
Poskozim, Judy H. .... Schaumburg, IL
Poskus, Bernard A. .... Denver, CO
Posler, Donald M. .... Dearborn, MI
Posman, Eva H. .... New York, NY
Posmantier, Eric R. .... Greenwich, CT
Posmantur, Peter T. .... New York, NY
Posnak, Bruce A. .... Macon, GA
Posnak, Louis .... Delray Beach, FL
Posner, Alan B. .... Detroit, MI
Posner, Alan K. .... Boston, MA
Posner, Alan M. .... Chicago, IL
Posner, Amy K. .... New York, NY
Posner, Ashley D. .... Los Angeles, CA
Posner, Avram E. .... New York, NY
Posner, Barbara Manolakos .... Brooklyn, NY
Posner, Barry A. .... Clifton Park, NY
Posner, Barry A. .... Elmsford, NY
Posner, Bernard .... Eastchester, NY
Posner, Beth Sheba .... Raleigh, NC
Posner, Constance L. .... San Jose, CA
Posner, Curtis E. .... Toledo, OH
Posner, Cydney S. .... San Francisco, CA
Posner, Daniel B. .... Flushing, NY
Posner, David A. .... Cleveland, OH
Posner, David H. .... Millburn, NJ
Posner, David L. .... Poughkeepsie, NY
Posner, David M. .... New York, NY
Posner, David S. .... Washington, PA
Posner, Edward M. .... Philadelphia, PA
Posner, Ellen F. M. .... Jacksonville, FL
Posner, Ernest G. .... Valley Forge, PA
Posner, Ethan M. .... Washington, DC
Posner, Gary S. .... Baltimore, MD
Posner, Gayle R. .... Los Alamitos, CA
Posner, Gene .... Milwaukee, WI
Posner, Gerald F. .... Detroit, MI
Posner, Gordon P. R. .... New York, NY
Posner, Harriet S. .... Los Angeles, CA
Posner, Harvey H. .... Baton Rouge, LA
Posner, Herbert A. .... Jamaica, NY
Posner, Herbert N. .... Bronx, NY
Harrison, NY
Posner, Herbert T. .... East Windsor, NJ

Posner, Howard .... Chatsworth, CA
Posner, Jane Y. .... White Plains, NY
Posner, Jeffrey J. .... Sacramento, CA
Posner, Jeffrey P. .... Cleveland, OH
Posner, Joseph .... Encino, CA
Posner, Joseph, Inc. .... Encino, CA
Posner, Katherine B. .... New York, NY
Posner, Kenneth F. .... West Bloomfield, MI
Posner & Krasnow .... New York, NY
Posner, Lance A. .... Roseland, NJ
Posner, Lara M. .... New York, NY
Posner, Laurence P. .... Los Angeles, CA
Posner, Lawrence H. .... Jersey City, NJ
Posner, Linda Orlansky .... Baton Rouge, LA
Posner, Lorane L. .... Newark, NJ
Posner, Lori M. .... New York, NY
Posner, Louis .... New York, NY
Posner, M. Jon .... Detroit, MI
Posner, Margery S. .... Pacific Palisades, CA
Posner, Mark A. .... Department of Justice, Civil Rights Division, GV
Posner, Marlene A. .... Lauderhill, FL
Posner, Marlene A., P.A., Law Offices of
Lauderhill, FL
Posner, Marshall .... New York, NY
Posner, Martin Louis .... White Plains, NY
Posner, Marvin .... Memphis, TN
Posner, Michael H. .... New York, NY
Posner, Michael J. .... West Palm Beach, FL
Posner, Michael P. .... Los Angeles, CA
Posner, Morton J. .... Washington, DC
Posner, Neil B. .... Chicago, IL
Posner, Paul M. .... Paso Robles, CA
Posner, Philip B. .... Wakefield, MA
Posner, Posner & Associates, PC
Stamford, CT
Mahwah, NJ
Paramus, NJ
Carmel, NY
New City, NY
New York, NY
White Plains, NY
Posner, Posner & Posner .... Detroit, MI
Posner, Richard .... Chicago, IL
Posner, Robert A. .... New York, NY
Posner & Rosen, LLP .... Los Angeles, CA
Posner, S. Paul .... New York, NY
Posner, Samuel .... Detroit, MI
Posner, Samuel .... Long Beach, NY
Posner, Seymour .... Providence, RI
Posner, Seymour F. .... Southfield, MI
Posner, Stephanie G. .... Baltimore, MD
Posner, Steven B. .... Sands Point, NY
Posner, Suzanne L. .... Baltimore, MD
Posner, William .... New York, NY
Posner, William M. .... Burlington, NJ
Posner-Wedes, Sandra .... Detroit, MI
Posnick, Milton T. .... San Jose, CA
Posnik, Jay Allen .... Springfield, MA
Posnock, Leslie B. .... Asbury Park, NJ
Posnock, Michael A. .... Asbury Park, NJ
Posnock, Stuart .... Clark, NJ
Posorske, Laurence H. .... Washington, DC
Pospis, Joseph P. .... Paterson, NJ
Pospishil, Frank F. .... Omaha, NE
Pospishil, John I. .... Carmel Valley, CA
Pospisil, Gwen E. .... Philadelphia, PA
Poss, Anita M. .... Swampscott, MA
Poss, Charles W. .... Chattanooga, TN
Poss, Gerald, (P.A.) .... South Orange, NJ
Poss, J. Michael .... Dallas, TX
Poss, Jeffrey R. .... New York, NY
Poss, Michael Alan .... Oak Park, MI
Poss, Samuel .... Los Angeles, CA
Poss, Stephen C. .... Baton Rouge, LA
Poss, Stephen D., (P.C.) .... Boston, MA
Possa, Joseph C. .... Baton Rouge, LA
Possavino, Eva M. .... Uniondale, NY
Posselius, Edward J., III .... Denver, CO
Possenti, Cheryl A. .... Buffalo, NY
Possenti, Valerie .... Plantation, FL
Possessky, Edward F. .... Washington, DC
Possessky, Laura A. .... Washington, DC
Possi, John C. .... Milwaukee, WI
Possi, John C., Jr. .... Milwaukee, WI
Possick, Howard B. .... Washington, DC
Possin, James L. .... Madison, WI
Possinger, Paul V. .... Chicago, IL
Possler, Helga K. .... Chicago, IL
Posson, Craig A. .... Dakota City, NE
Post, Alan N. .... High Point, NC
Post, Alan R. .... Wichita, KS
Post, Barry J. .... San Pedro, CA
Post, Barton L. .... Philadelphia, PA
Post, Benjamin A. .... Philadelphia, PA
Post, Bernard G. .... New York, NY
Post, Blake .... Topeka, KS
Post, Bradley .... Wichita, KS
Post, Bradley A. .... Modesto, CA
Post, Charles C. .... Columbus, IN
Post, Charles D. .... Boston, MA
Post, Charles L. .... Sacramento, CA
Post, Charles W., Jr. .... Spring, TX
Post, Cheryl L. .... Englewood, CO
Post, Chris A. .... Nebraska City, NE
Syracuse, NE
Post, Clifford L., Jr. .... Rancho Cordova, CA
Post, Craig A. .... Spring Valley, NY
Post, Daniel A. .... Metairie, LA
Post, Daniel A. .... Albany, OR
Post, Daniel E. .... Santa Rosa, CA
Post, David F. .... Farmerville, LA
Post, David G. .... Portland, OR
Post, David M. .... Charlottesville, VA
Post, David N. .... Sacramento, CA
Post, David W. .... Sacramento, CA
Post, Deborah W. .... Marina Del Rey, CA
Post, Debra A. .... New York, NY

Post, Dianne L. .... Muscoda, WI
Post, Donna M. .... Celina, OH
Post, Douglas F. .... Los Angeles, CA
Post, Dynda .... Pryor, OK
Post, Edda Sara .... Cleveland, OH
Post, Edward N. .... High Point, NC
Post, Edward R. .... Grand Haven, MI
Post, Elizabeth Anne .... Phoenix, AZ
Post, Frederick R. .... Holland, OH
Post, Frederick W. .... Edmonds, WA
Post, G. Roger .... Columbus, OH
Post, Gary V. .... Fort Worth, TX
Post, Gregory A. .... San Diego, CA
Post, Harry C., III .... Dallas, TX
Post & Heymann, LLP .... Jericho, NY
Post, Hillary J. .... Los Angeles, CA
Post, Ira A. .... Arlington Heights, IL
Post, Iris J. .... Des Moines, IA
Post, J. Douglas .... Rolling Hills, CA
Post, James H. .... Jacksonville, FL
Post, Jamie L. .... Pierre, SD
Post, Jeffrey W. .... Minneapolis, MN
Post, Jennifer A. .... Boston, MA
Post, Jennifer K. .... San Francisco, CA
Post, Jerry .... Batesville, AR
Post, Joanne Lee .... Detroit, MI
Post, Joel G. .... New York, NY
Post, John .... Chevy Chase, MD
Post, John Osborn .... Boulder, CO
Post, John S. .... Hialeah, FL
Post, Joseph A. .... New York, NY
Post, Joseph C. .... Forest Grove, OR
Post, Karen A. .... Washington, DC
Post, Keenan M. .... Topeka, KS
Post, Keith D. .... Miami, FL
Post, Kenneth D. .... Grand Haven, MI
Post & Kervick .... Windsor Locks, CT
Post Kirby Noonan & Sweat LLP
San Diego, CA
Post, Kirk J. .... Atlanta, GA
Post, Kristi A. .... Metairie, LA
Post, Linda Farber .... Bronx, NY
Post, Lisa S. .... New York, NY
Post, M. Catharine .... Tampa, FL
Post, Marilyn R. .... Carrollton, TX
Post, Mary H. .... Roseland, NJ
Post, Norman C., Jr. .... Sanford, NC
Post, Pamela A. .... Philadelphia, PA
Post, Patricia K. .... Denver, CO
Post, Paul D. .... Topeka, KS
Post, Paul D., P.A. .... Topeka, KS
Post, Paul R. .... Barling, AR
Post, Peter D. .... Pittsburgh, PA
Post, Philip A. .... Windsor Locks, CT
Post, Philip O. .... Cherry Hill, NJ
Post, Philomena L. .... Wayne, PA
Post, Polak, Goodsell & MacNeill, P.A.
Elizabeth, NJ
Morristown, NJ
Newark, NJ
Paterson, NJ
Roseland, NJ
New York, NY
Post & Pond, LLP .... Atlanta, GA
Post & Post .... High Point, NC
Post, Robert .... Wakefield, MA
Post, Robert C. .... Berkeley, CA
Post, Robert E. .... Cleveland, OH
Post, Robert G. .... Miami, FL
Post, Robert M. .... Indiantown, FL
Post, Robert P. .... San Angelo, TX
Post, Robert S. .... Tulsa, OK
Post, Roger C. .... Columbus, OH
Post & Romero .... Miami, FL
Post, Russell L., Jr. .... Hartford, CT
Post, Russell S. .... Houston, TX
Post, Ruth Frances-Leve
White Plains, NY
Post, Ruth-Ellen .... Nashua, NH
Post & Schell, P.C. .... Voorhees, NJ
Allentown, PA
Harrisburg, PA
Lancaster, PA
Philadelphia, PA
Reading, PA
Post, Scott E. .... West Allis, WI
Post, Sharon L. .... Columbus, OH
Post, Stephanie H. .... Akron, OH
Post, Steven M. .... New York, NY
Post, Steven M. .... Dallas, TX
Post & Syrios .... Wichita, KS
Post, Tamara J. .... Oceanside, NY
Post, Terry R. .... Kansas City, MO
Post, Thomas R. .... Miami, FL
Post, Thomas R., P.A. .... Miami, FL
Post, Timothy P. .... Reno, NV
Post, Vanessa L. .... Houston, TX
Post, William A. .... Dunnellon, FL
Post, William A. .... Inverness, FL
Ocala, FL
Post, William F., Jr. .... Minneapolis, MN
Post, William G., Jr. .... Burlington, VT
Post, William J. .... Vail, CO
Post, William Noble, II .... San Francisco, CA
Post, William W. .... Jericho, NY
Posta, Jeffrey S. .... Trenton, NJ
Posta, John J., Jr. .... Woodland Hills, CA
Postal, David R. .... Phoenix, AZ
Postalakis, Stephen P. .... Dublin, OH
Postar, Adeen J. .... Washington, DC
Postar, Michael R. .... Washington, DC
Postawko, Robert E. .... Los Angeles, CA
Postel, Elizabeth K. .... Pacific Palisades, CA
Postel, Geo. .... New York, NY
Postel, John J. .... Rochester, NY
Postel, Joseph P. .... Chicago, IL
Postel, Lloyd F. .... San Francisco, CA

Postel, Theodore R. .... Chicago, IL
Postel, Waldo F., Jr. .... Novato, CA
Postell, Guy H. .... Dunwoody, GA
Postelle, Donald G. .... San Jose, CA
Postelli, Connie J. .... Munster, IN
Postelli, F. Ronald .... Coloma, MI
Postelli, John C. .... Benton Harbor, MI
Postelnek, Marc J. .... Miami Beach, FL
Postelnek, Stephen A. .... New York, NY
Postema, Howard H. .... Berkley, MI
Postema, Miles J. .... Grand Rapids, MI
Postema, Stephen K. .... Ann Arbor, MI
Posten, William S. .... Minneapolis, MN
Poster, Harold S. .... New York, NY
Poster, Jeffrey C. .... Dallas, TX
Poster, Marc J. .... Beverly Hills, CA
Poster, Michael S. .... New York, NY
Poster, Nancy D. .... Great Falls, VA
Poster, Robert L. .... New York, NY
Poster, Stephanie L. .... Boston, MA
Posteraro, David R. .... Cleveland, OH
Posternak, Blankstein & Lund, L.L.P.
Boston, MA
Posternak, Noel G., P.C. .... Boston, MA
Posternock, Daniel .... Philadelphia, PA
Poster-Zimmerman, Lynn D.
Huntington, NY
Posthauer, John S. .... Redwood City, CA
Posthuma, Matthew A. .... Chicago, IL
Posthuma, Richard A. .... West Lafayette, IN
Posthumus, John R. .... Denver, CO
Postian, Gregory G. .... Englewood Cliffs, NJ
Postic & Babb, L.L.C. .... Marietta, GA
Greensboro, NC
Postic & Bates, A Professional Corporation
Oklahoma City, OK
Postic, Lionel J. .... Marietta, GA
Postic, Martin, Jr. .... Oklahoma City, OK
Postiglione, Leonard .... New York, NY
Postilion, Laura G. .... Chicago, IL
Postilion Law Firm .... Chicago, IL
Postilion, Michael H. .... Chicago, IL
Postizzi, Joseph R. .... Clark, NJ
Postizzi and Sayer .... Clark, NJ
Postl, John O. .... Quincy, MA
Postler, Charles A. .... Tampa, FL
Postlethwait & Hudson .... Durham, NC
Postlethwait, Raymond W., Jr. .... Durham, NC
Postlewait, R. Samuel .... Decatur, IL
Postlewaite, Ann C. .... Portland, OR
Postlewaite, Charles C. .... Columbus, OH
Postlewaite, David M. .... Columbus, OH
Postlewaite, Jack A. .... Eau Claire, WI
Postlewaite & Jordan .... Columbus, OH
Postlewaite, Philip F. .... Chicago, IL
Postlewaite, Robert E. .... San Rafael, CA
Postlewaite, William N., Sr. .... Columbus, OH
Postley, Elaine M. .... New York, NY
Postma, Ann Lynn .... Abilene, TX
Postma, James L. .... Lawrence, KS
Postma, Larry .... Sheldon, IA
Postma, Richard .... Grand Rapids, MI
Postma, Richard William, Jr .... Denver, CO
Postman, Alan L. .... Miami, FL
Postman, Barry Adam .... Miami, FL
Postman, Harold .... Port Washington, NY
Postman & Postman .... Hasbrouck Heights, NJ
Postman, William R., Jr.
Hasbrouck Heights, NJ
Postner, Marya A. .... Palo Alto, CA
Postner & Rubin .... Holmdel, NJ
New York, NY
Postner, William J. .... New York, NY
Postnikoff, Joseph F. .... Fort Worth, TX
Postol, Lawrence P. .... Washington, DC
Poston, Anita O. .... Norfolk, VA
Poston, Beverly Paschal .... Cullman, AL
Poston, Brett M. .... Dallas, TX
Poston, Carl C. .... Houston, TX
Poston, Carl C., Jr. .... Saginaw, MI
Poston, Carolyn Jo Boeka .... Blue Jay, CA
Poston, Catherine Micklitsch
Department of Justice, Office of Policy Development, GV
Poston, Chalmers W., Jr. .... Charleston, SC
Poston, Charles E. .... Norfolk, VA
Poston, Christine L. .... Fort Belvoir, VA
Poston, Daniel D. .... Glendale, CA
Poston, David G. .... Dothan, AL
Poston, David S. .... Wilmington, DE
Poston, David W. .... Pickerington, OH
Poston, E. Delance .... Johnsonville, SC
Poston, E. Taylor .... Tulsa, OK
Poston, Fellrath & Ogden, P.C.
Oklahoma City, OK
Poston, J. Edwin .... Tulsa, OK
Poston, James R., Jr. .... Newport, KY
Poston, Janet N. .... Minneapolis, MN
Poston, Jeffrey L. .... Washington, DC
Poston, John M. .... Modesto, CA
Poston, John P. .... Helena, MT
Poston, Kenneth W. .... Greenwood, SC
Poston, Kevin D. .... Bloomfield Hills, MI
Poston, Marianne .... Tucson, AZ
Poston, Marvin B. .... Aiken, SC
Poston, McCracken .... Dalton, GA
La Fayette, GA
Poston, McCracken .... Ringgold, GA
Poston, Met R. .... Asheville, NC
Poston, Rebekah J. .... Miami, FL
Poston, Sam E. .... St. Louis, MO
Poston, Sarah W. .... Bridgeport, CT
Poston Seifried & Schloemer .... Newport, KY
Poston, Steven S. .... Denton, TX
Poston, Tammy Lynn .... McMinnville, TN
Poston, T. C. .... Corydon, IA
Poston, William G. .... Marietta, GA
Poston, William R. .... Tucson, AZ

Postow, Charles Jay ... Cincinnati, OH
Postula, James E. ... Elmhurst, IL
Postula, Walter J. ... West Palm Beach, FL
Postula, Walter J., P.A.
West Palm Beach, FL
Postweiler, John G. ... Orland Park, IL
Posvolsky, Harry L. ... New York, NY
Poswall, John M. ... Sacramento, CA
Poswall & White, A Law Corporation
Sacramento, CA
Poswistilo, Frank S. ... Easton, PA
Poswistilo, Margaret H. ... Easton, PA
Poswistilo, Susan M. ... Boston, MA
Poswolsky, Melvyn ... Plainview, NY
Posy, David H. ... New York, NY
Posz, David G. ... Troy, MI
Potach, Steven G. ... Minneapolis, MN
Potack, Frederick B. ... Bronx, NY
Potadle, Paul N. ... Lincoln, NE
Potako, Stephen T. ... Philadelphia, PA
Potamianos, Antigone
General Services Administration,
Office of Inspector General, GV
Potamianos, Constantine S.
New York, NY
Potanka, Edward P. ... Bloomfield, CT
Potanka, Paul E. ... Canton, CT
Potanovic, John F., Jr. ... Fort Myers, FL
Potarf, Michael C. ... Colorado Springs, CO
Potash, Arnold M. ... Seymour, CT
Potash, Charles ... Blue Bell, PA
Potash, Christopher M. ... Rochester, NY
Potash, Daniel V. ... Oakland, CA
Potash, Eileen J ... Mount Vernon, NY
Potash, Eileen M. ... Philadelphia, PA
Potash, Howard J. ... Dennis, MA
Potash, Howard J. ... Worcester, MA
Potash, Howard K. ... San Diego, CA
Potash, Kenneth ... Seymour, CT
Potash, Lester S. ... Cleveland, OH
Potash, Loree E. ... Cleveland, OH
Potash, M. Steven ... Cleveland, OH
Potash, Patti F. ... New York, NY
Potash, Randi ... Peabody, MA
Potash, Richard J., P.A. ... Boca Raton, FL
Potash, Robert B. ... Greenwich, CT
Potashnick, David A. ... Sikeston, MO
Potashnick, Fielding ... Sikeston, MO
Potashnick, Hillary A. ... New York, NY
Potashnick Law Offices ... Sikeston, MO
Potashnick, Mark ... Los Angeles, CA
Potashnick, Sam ... Sikeston, MO
Potasiak, Joseph T. ... Chicago, IL
Potasz, Frank J. ... Foster City, CA
Potchen, E. James ... Okemos, MI
Potchen, Joseph E. ... Lansing, MI
Pote, Daniel R. ... Phoenix, AZ
Pote, Doris R. ... Brookline, MA
Pote, Mitchell M. ... Indianapolis, IN
Poteat, Chad E. ... Columbia, SC
Poteat, Earmine L., Jr. ... Raleigh, NC
Poteat, Robert M. ... Oak Ridge, TN
Poteat, Robert M., P.C. ... Oak Ridge, TN
Poteat, Shannon Till ... Columbia, SC
Poteat, Thena G. ... Charleston, SC
Poteat, Thomas S. ... Owensboro, KY
Poteate, Linda R. ... Alexandria, VA
Potebnya, Walter N. ... Marysville, WA
Potee, Russell T., Jr. ... Glen Burnie, MD
Poteet, Cherry Lynne ... Columbus, OH
Poteet, Derek A. ... Dumfries, VA
Poteet, Dewey ... Austin, TX
Poteet, John G., Jr. ... Lafayette, LA
Poteet, Joseph M. ... Normangee, TX
Poteet, Lawrence Jay ... Los Angeles, CA
San Juan Capistrano, CA
Poteet, Sam H., Jr. ... Nashville, TN
Poteet, Timothy B. ... Austin, TX
San Antonio, TX
Potel, David ... Boston, MA
Potel, Mark J. ... New York, NY
Potemken, Bertram L. ... Baltimore, MD
Potenberg, Stephen ... Livingston, MT
Potenle, Alex ... Chicago, IL
Potenza, Austin D., II ... Phoenix, AZ
Potenza, Betty J. ... Poughkeepsie, NY
Potenza, John D. ... Jersey City, NJ
Potenza, Joseph M. ... Washington, DC
Potenza, Maryjeanne C. Guth ... Mahwah, NJ
Potenza, Paul L. ... Hackensack, NJ
Potenza, Robert J. V. ... Chicago, IL
Potenza, Rocco D., Jr. ... Akron, OH
Potenza, Valerie A. ... New York, NY
Potenza, Vito T. ... Department of Defense,
Defense Legal Services Agency, GV
Potenziani, Frank A. ... Albuquerque, NM
Potenzone, Mary Jean M. ... New York, NY
Potepan, James C. ... Pasadena, CA
Poteracke, Michele M. ... Fairfield, CA
Poteracki, Lee ... Rosemont, IL
Poterala, Michael R. ... East Lansing, MI
Potere, Robert F. ... Rochester, MI
Potero, Timothy J. ... New York, NY
Potesta, Woodrow A. ... Morgantown, WV
Potestio, Deanne ... Denver, CO
Potestivo, Brian A. ... Sterling Heights, MI
Potestivo, Brian A., P.C.
Sterling Heights, MI
Poth, Christine M. ... Columbus, OH
Poth, Gregory E. ... Roseville, CA
Poth, Harry A., Jr. ... New York, NY
Poth, James L. ... Irvine, CA
Poth, Jeffery M. ... Columbus, OH
Poth, Konrad ... La Grange, KY
Poth, Phillip J. ... Seattle, WA
Pothering, Christine A. ... Portland, OR
Pothier, Mary Jo ... Saugus, MA
Pothier, Robert ... Haverhill, MA
Pothier, Robert S. ... Wichita, KS
Pothier, Rose, & Associates
Santa Ana, CA
Pothin, Margaret A. ... New Haven, CT
Pothin, Timothy P. ... New Haven, CT
Pothitakis, Nicholas G. ... Burlington, IA
Pothoven, Dennis J ... Seattle, WA
Pothoven, Marion H. ... Sacramento, CA
Oskaloosa, IA
Pothoven & Stravers ... Oskaloosa, IA
Potiker, Brian R. ... Beverly Hills, CA
Potiris, Martha Ellis ... Sacramento, CA
Potis, Kenneth James ... Manalapan, NJ
Potisk, Steven F. ... Stroudsburg, PA
Potkai, John W. ... Philadelphia, PA
Potkay, Barbara K. ... Trenton, NJ
Potkin, Lane H. ... Washington, DC
Potkonjak, Theodore S., Law Office of
Waukegan, IL
Potkul, David J. ... Los Angeles, CA
Potler, B. Marvin ... Baltimore, MD
Potocki, Joseph P. ... San Diego, CA
Potoczak, Paula M. ... Washington, DC
Potoka, Judith A. ... Pittsburgh, PA
Potolsky, Marc L. ... Hackensack, NJ
Potolsky, Steven M. ... Miami, FL
Potolsky, Steven M., P.A. ... Miami, FL
Potomac, L. Lawrence ... La Jolla, CA
Potoroka, Walter ... Lake Orion, MI
Potosnak, Christine A. ... Philadelphia, PA
Potratz, Douglas D. ... Garden Grove, CA
Potratz & Hollander, P.C. ... Chicago, IL
Potratz, William G. ... Chicago, IL
Potruch, Alexander ... Mineola, NY
Potrykus, Clarence P. ... Kingston, MA
Potrykus, Robert J., Jr. ... Denver, CO
Potrzebowski, Robert E., Jr.
Milwaukee, WI
Potskowski, William J. ... Port Henry, NY
Pott, Carlton N., II ... Schenectady, NY
Pott, Claudia Anne ... Washington, DC
Pott, Jeffrey A. ... Wilmington, DE
Pott, Michael W. ... Sacramento, CA
Pott and Naviasky, LLP ... Schenectady, NY
Pott, Roger A. ... San Jose, CA
Pott, Roger A., Law Corporation
San Jose, CA
Pottash, Bruce ... New York, NY
Potteiger, David O. ... Harrisburg, PA
Pottenger, Jason M. ... Kansas City, MO
Pottenger, John L., Jr. ... New Haven, CT
Pottenger, Julie L. ... Tipton, IN
Pottenger, M. Tyler ... Honolulu, HI
Pottenger, Thomas A. ... Cincinnati, OH
Potter, Adam Lee ... Houston, TX
Potter, Alan L. ... Locust Grove, VA
Potter, Albert L., II ... Bowling Green, OH
Potter, Alice D. ... Columbia, SC
Potter, Allan L. ... Corpus Christi, TX
Potter, Alton W. ... Flossmoor, IL
Potter, Alvin E. ... San Mateo, CA
Potter Anderson & Corroon LLP
Wilmington, DE
Potter, Andrew G. ... Irvine, CA
Potter, Anthony S. ... Harrisburg, PA
Potter, B. Emory ... Atlanta, GA
Potter, Barbara Campbell
Department of Commerce,
Office of the General Counsel, GV
Potter, Barr B. ... Los Angeles, CA
Potter, Bertram L. ... Pasadena, CA
Potter, Brent J. ... Bowling Green, KY
Potter, C. Ann ... Charlotte, NC
Potter, Cal J., III ... Las Vegas, NV
Potter, Carniak, Anderson & DeAgostino
Auburn Hills, MI
Potter, Carol Ann ... Palo Alto, CA
Potter, Carolyn A. ... Covington, KY
Potter, Caryl A., III ... Washington, DC
Potter, Catherine L. ... Herndon, VA
Potter, Chad G. ... Eugene, OR
Potter, Charles A. ... Texarkana, AR
Potter, Charles A. ... Traverse City, MI
Potter, Charles A., Jr. ... Santa Ana, CA
Potter, Charles E., Jr. ... Los Angeles, CA
Potter, Charles J. ... Wayland, MA
Potter, Charles L., Jr. ... Pittsburgh, PA
Potter, Cheryl Lynn ... Coral Gables, FL
Potter, Clarissa C. ... Washington, DC
Potter, Clement Dale ... McMinnville, TN
Potter, Clement & Lowry
Mount Dora, FL
Potter, Cohen & Samulon ... Pasadena, CA
Potter, Daniel E. ... New Bern, NC
Potter, Daniel J. ... Milwaukee, WI
Potter, David B. ... Bakersfield, CA
Potter, David B. ... Minneapolis, MN
Potter, David D. ... Sacramento, CA
Potter, David E. ... New York, NY
Potter, David J. ... Texarkana, TX
Potter, Day & Associates, P.C.
San Diego, CA
Potter, Deborah ... Damariscotta, ME
Potter, Deborah L. ... Lewiston, ME
Potter, Deborah L. ... Annapolis, MD
Potter, Deborah L., P.A. ... Annapolis, MD
Potter, Debra B. ... Fort Lauderdale, FL
Potter, Del G. ... Mount Dora, FL
Potter, Dennis L. ... Seattle, WA
Potter, Diane Kay ... Omaha, NE
Potter, Diane S. ... Sacramento, CA
Potter & Dickson ... Princeton, NJ
Potter, Dirk ... Chico, CA
Potter, Donald C. ... Los Angeles, CA
Potter, Donald C. ... Chicago, IL
Potter, Donald F. ... Rochester, NY
Potter, Douglas G. ... Coeur d'Alene, ID
Potter, E. Bronson ... Vancouver, WA
Potter, Earl W. ... Santa Fe, NM
Potter, Edward B. ... Old Lyme, CT
Potter, Edward E. ... Washington, DC
Reston, VA
Potter, Elizabeth F. ... Boston, MA
Potter, Elizabeth Page ... Raleigh, NC
Potter, Elizabeth R. ... San Diego, CA
Potter, Ernest L. ... Huntsville, AL
Potter, Ervin W. ... Salem, OR
Potter, Ethan ... Leavenworth, KS
Potter, Foster D. ... Muskegon, MI
Potter, Frank B., Jr. ... Houston, TX
Potter, Fred L. ... Concord, NH
Potter, Frederick H. ... Rock Island, IL
Potter, Frenchette C. ... St. Louis, MO
Potter, G. Richard ... Indianapolis, IN
Potter, Gary T. ... Denver, CO
Potter, Geoffrey ... New York, NY
Potter, George E. ... Jackson, MI
Potter, George F., Jr. ... Tacoma, WA
Potter, George L., Jr. ... Dallas, TX
Potter & Girodat, LLP ... Jackson, MI
Potter, Gregory J. ... Boca Raton, FL
Potter, Gregory J. ... Wisconsin Rapids, WI
Potter, H. Clifford ... Colorado Springs, CO
Potter, H. David ... New York, NY
Potter, Harold W., Jr. ... Boston, MA
Potter, Harry ... Roseland, NJ
Potter, Henry J., Jr. ... Bowling Green, KY
Potter, Herbert S. ... Stateline, NV
Potter, Howard H. ... Denver, CO
Potter, Hugh J. ... Vancouver, WA
Potter, Ina L. ... Palo Alto, CA
Potter, Ira M. ... St. Louis, MO
Potter, Irving W. ... Portland, OR
Potter, J. Craig ... Washington, DC
Potter, James ... Barrington, IL
Potter, James M. ... Reading, PA
Potter, James R. ... Chicago, IL
Potter, James R. ... Springfield, IL
Potter, James R. ... Clarksville, TN
Potter, James T. ... Albany, NY
Potter, James W. ... O'Fallon, MO
Potter, James W. ... Columbia, SC
Potter, Jane E. R. ... Seattle, WA
Potter, Janet Smith ... Gainesville, FL
Potter, Janice Ann ... Bellevue, WA
Potter, Jeffrey E., (P.C.) ... Eugene, OR
Potter, Jeffrey H. ... Durham, NC
Potter, Joanie ... Jackson, MS
Potter, John ... Chicago, IL
Potter, John A. ... Grand Rapids, MI
Potter, John C. ... Farmington, IL
Potter, John F. ... Erie, PA
Potter, John M. ... Los Angeles, CA
Potter, John M. ... Clewiston, FL
Potter, John R. ... Vancouver, WA
Potter, John V., Jr.
White Sulphur Springs, MT
Potter, John W. ... Louisville, KY
Potter, John W. ... Toledo, OH
Potter, Jonathan ... Washington, DC
Potter, Joshua W. ... Pasadena, CA
Potter, Katherine Cranston
San Francisco, CA
Potter, Kathleen A. ... Lawrence, MA
Potter, Kathy ... Washington, DC
Potter, K. C. ... Nashville, TN
Potter, Kelley P. ... Los Angeles, CA
Potter, Kevin C. ... Madison, WI
Potter, Kim ... Atlanta, GA
Columbus, OH
Potter, Kimberly D. ... Louisa, KY
Potter, Larry E. ... Memphis, TN
Potter, Laura Van Harlingen
Portland, OR
Potter Law Offices, A Professional
Corporation ... Las Vegas, NV
Potter, Lawrence T. ... Waterville, ME
Potter, Lee J., Jr. ... New York, NY
Potter, Lee, (Miss) ... North Hollywood, CA
Potter, Leonard A. ... New York, NY
Potter, Leslie B. ... Glen Mills, PA
Potter, Lon G. ... Irving, TX
Potter, Lori ... Denver, CO
Potter, Marcus B., Jr. ... Kansas City, KS
Potter, Margaret A. ... Pittsburgh, PA
Potter, Mark A. ... La Jolla, CA
Potter, Mark Christopher
San Bernardino, CA
Potter, Mark H., II ... Santa Rosa, CA
Potter, Mark L. ... Pasadena, MD
Potter, Mark W. ... Portland, OR
Potter, Marshall O., Jr. ... Vienna, VA
Potter, Mary B. ... Shelbyville, KY
Potter, Mary J. ... Santa Barbara, CA
Potter, Mary L. ... United States Senate,
Senatorial Assistants, GV
Potter, Mary M. ... San Antonio, TX
Potter, Matthew R. ... Manchester, CT
Potter, Maureen ... Grand Haven, MI
Potter, McCarl & Whisnant, P.A.
Lenoir, NC
Potter, McClelland & Healy, P.A.
Melbourne, FL
Potter, Michael F. ... San Francisco, CA
Potter, Michael L. ... San Diego, CA
Potter, Michael R. ... Chapel Hill, NC
Potter, Michelle Lafond ... Maumee, OH
Potter & Mills, P.A. ... Santa Fe, NM
Potter, Minton, Roberts, Davis & Jones, A
Professional Corporation ... Tyler, TX
Potter, Nancy N. ... San Francisco, CA
Potter, Neil B. ... Fort Myers, FL
Potter, Nicholas F. ... New York, NY
Potter, P. Stephen ... Gothenburg, NE
Potter, P. Stephen, P.C. ... Gothenburg, NE
Potter, Pamela H. ... Ashland, KY
Potter, Patrick John ... Washington, DC
Potter, Paul E. ... Pasadena, CA
Potter, Paul F. ... San Diego, CA
Potter, Paul W., Jr. ... Riviera Beach, FL
Potter, Philip C., Jr. ... New York, NY
Potter, R. Clifford ... Chicago, IL
Potter, R. Michael ... Memphis, TN
Potter, R. William ... Princeton, NJ
Potter, Ralph M. ... Fayetteville, NC
Potter, Ralph R. ... Dubuque, IA
Potter, Randolph J. F., P.A. ... Plantation, FL
Potter, Randolph J. F. ... Plantation, FL
Potter, Richard A. ... Buffalo Center, IA
Potter, Richard E. ... Everett, WA
Potter, Richard T., Jr. ... New York, NY
Potter, Richard W. ... Eugene, OR
Potter, Robert A. ... Washington, DC
Potter, Robert D. ... Charlotte, NC
Potter, Robert D., Jr. ... Charlotte, NC
Potter, Robert H. ... Morrison, IL
Potter, Robert L. ... Pittsburgh, PA
Potter, Robert M., III
Fort Lauderdale, FL
Potter, Robert R. ... Atlanta, GA
Potter, Robert V., Jr. ... Clearwater, FL
Potter, Robin B. ... Chicago, IL
Potter, Roger A. ... Kansas City, MO
Potter, Ronald C. ... Tulsa, OK
Potter, Roy E. ... Government Printing Office,
Office of General Counsel, GV
Potter, Russell F., Jr. ... Willimantic, CT
Potter, Russell L. ... San Francisco, CA
Potter, Russell L. ... Alexandria, LA
Potter, S. Brent ... Indianapolis, IN
Potter, Sam C., Jr. ... Bowling Green, KY
Potter, Sandra L. ... Denver, CO
Potter, Sara E. ... Washington, DC
Potter & Schaffner ... Chicago, IL
Potter, Shanley & Shanley ... Montrose, CA
Potter, Sharon W. ... Pensacola, FL
Potter, Standlee G. ... Eugene, OR
Potter, Stephanie Elizabeth ... Little Rock, AR
Potter, Stephen B. ... Newark, DE
Wilmington, DE
Potter, Stephen B., and Associates, P.A.
Wilmington, DE
Newark, DE
Potter, Stephen J. ... St. Louis, MO
Potter, Steve B. ... Lenoir, NC
Potter, Steven B. ... Cleveland, OH
Potter, Steven J. ... Baltimore, MD
Potter, Steven M. ... Auburn Hills, MI
Potter, Stuart L. ... New York, NY
Potter, Susan B. ... Norfolk, VA
Potter, Suzanne N. ... Oakmont, PA
Potter, Teresa M. ... Houston, TX
Potter, Terry L. ... St. Louis, MO
Potter, Theodore Alan ... Toledo, OH
Potter, Theresann J. ... New York, NY
Potter, Thomas A. ... Texarkana, AR
Potter, Thomas A. ... New York, NY
Potter, Thomas A. ... Grand Forks, ND
Potter, Thomas A., P.A. ... Texarkana, AR
Potter, Thomas E. ... Charleston, WV
Potter, Thomas H. ... Nashville, TN
Potter, Thomas J. ... Morrison, IL
Potter, Thomas J. ... Syracuse, NY
Potter, Thomas K., III ... New Orleans, LA
Potter, Thomas L. ... Milwaukee, WI
Potter, Timothy V. ... Dickson, TN
Potter, Tony A. ... Hill City, KS
Potter, Tracy L. ... Chicago, IL
Potter, Trevor ... Washington, DC
Potter, Wilfred L. ... Springfield, OH
Potter, William C. ... Melbourne, FL
Potter, William C. ... Baton Rouge, LA
Potter, William C., Jr. ... Detroit, MI
Potter, William H., Jr. ... Raleigh, NC
Potter, William R. ... Eugene, OR
Potterfield, Amanda ... Cedar Rapids, IA
Iowa City, IA
Waterloo, IA
Potterfield, Ashlin Blanchard
Columbia, SC
Potterfield, John C. ... Columbia, SC
Potterfield, Phyllis M. ... Charleston, WV
Potter-Hall, Traevena ... Des Moines, IA
Potters, Bobby A. ... Indianapolis, IN
Potters, David E. ... Charleston, WV
Potters, Gary ... Newark, NJ
Potters, Robert S. ... Boston, MA
Potters, Robert S., P.C. ... Boston, MA
Potters, Sanford B. ... New York, NY
Pottharst-Wagner, Hyla ... New York, NY
Potthast, Catherine A. ... Towson, MD
Potthast, James W. ... Chicago, IL
Potthast, Theodore J., Jr. ... Towson, MD
Potthast, Theodore J. Jr., P.A. ... Towson, MD
Potthoff, Courtney R. ... Eufaula, AL
Potthoff, Dale R. ... Peru, IL
Pottinger, David C. ... Louisville, KY
Pottinger, O. Glen ... Woodbridge, NJ
Pottinger, Robert C. ... Rockford, IL
Pottinger, Stephen H. ... Lexington, KY
Pottinger, Susan M. ... Clearwater, FL
Pottish Freyberg Marcus & Velazquez, LLP
New York, NY
Pottish, Morris ... New York, NY
Pottish, Sol ... New York, NY
Pottle, Gregory L. ... Boston, MA
Pottle, Steven L. ... Atlanta, GA
Pottle, Willard M., Jr. ... Vero Beach, FL
Buffalo, NY
Pottle, Willard M., Jr., P.C.
Vero Beach, FL
Buffalo, NY
Pottmeyer, Jerome J., III ... Pittsburgh, PA
Pottorf, Fred A. ... Tulsa, OK

…Greg ... Overland Park, KS
Kansas City, MO
…orff, Julie F. ... Des Moines, IA
…ttorff, Mark G. ... Atlanta, GA
…ottow, Michael T. ... Santa Fe, NM
Pottratz, Dennis H. ... Veradale, WA
Pottratz, Robert E. ... Melrose, MN
Pottroff, Robert L. ... Manhattan, KS
Potts, A. Christopher ... Charleston, SC
Summerville, SC
Potts, Allen J. ... Marina Del Rey, CA
Potts, Allen J. ... Omaha, NE
Potts, Andrew J. ... Birmingham, AL
Potts, Andrew S. ... Washington, DC
Chicago, IL
Potts, Anne E. ... Ann Arbor, MI
Potts, Arthur G., Jr. ... Stamford, CT
Potts, Arthur N., Jr. ... Belton, TX
Potts, Barbara ... Philadelphia, PA
Potts, Bobby E. ... Austin, TX
Potts, Bryan H. ... Baltimore, MD
Potts, Byron Lee ... Columbus, OH
Potts, C. Richard ... Phoenix, AZ
Potts, Cecelia J. ... Mt. Orab, OH
Potts, Charles J. ... Mobile, AL
Potts, Christopher C. ... South Bend, IN
Potts, David William ... Birmingham, MI
Potts, Dennis W. ... Honolulu, HI
Potts, Dennis W., Attorney At Law, A Law Corporation ... Honolulu, HI
Potts, Ewell C., III ... Chalmette, LA
Potts, Frank B. ... Florence, AL
Potts, Frank S. ... Columbia, SC
Potts, Frank V. ... Florence, AL
Potts, Gary A. ... Gates Mills, OH
Potts, Gary W. ... Monticello, AR
Potts, Grover C., Jr. ... Louisville, KY
Potts, Harold G. ... Berryville, VA
Potts, Howard A. ... Huntington Beach, CA
Potts, Howard M. ... Kansas City, MO
Potts, Hugh S., Jr. ... Kosciusko, MS
Potts, Ivan J. ... Thousand Oaks, CA
Potts, J. Brian ... Boston, MA
Potts, Jack H. ... Brevard, NC
Potts, James G. ... Oklahoma City, OK
Potts, James G., P.C. ... Oklahoma City, OK
Potts, James H., II ... Atlanta, GA
Potts, James I. ... Houston, TX
Potts, James R. ... Philadelphia, PA
Potts, James Watson, III ... Fremont, CA
Potts, Janice E. ... Houston, TX
Potts, Jas. L. ... Inglewood, CA
Potts, Jeffrey A. ... Houston, TX
Potts, Jerry R. ... San Diego, CA
Potts, John D. ... Columbus, OH
Potts, John F. ... Toledo, OH
Potts, John H. ... Radnor, PA
Potts, John J. ... Valparaiso, IN
Potts, Joseph, III ... Lancaster, PA
Potts, Julie Anna ... Washington, DC
Potts, Karen A. ... Phoenix, AZ
Potts, Kathy L. ... Dallas, TX
Potts, Kenneth N. ... Wayzata, MN
Potts, Kyle L. ... New Orleans, LA
Potts, Lee E. ... Austin, TX
Potts, Lee W. ... Los Angeles, CA
Potts, Matthew C. ... Elmwood, IL
Potts, Millicent B.
Department of Housing and Urban Development,
Office of General Counsel, GV
Potts, Nancy E. ... Philadelphia, PA
Potts & Novotney ... Cleveland, OH
Potts, Oliver A. ... Arlington, VA
Potts, Phillip C. ... South Bend, IN
Potts & Potts ... Chalmette, LA
Potts, Ramsay D., (P.C.) ... Washington, DC
Potts, Ray H. ... Oklahoma City, OK
Potts & Reilly, L.L.P. ... Austin, TX
Potts, Richard G. ... Phoenix, AZ
Potts, Robert E. ... Lake Forest, IL
Potts, Robert H. ... Grand Rapids, MI
Potts, Robert L. ... Florence, AL
Potts, Robert L. ... Elmwood, IL
Potts, Roberta. J. ... Tulsa, OK
Potts, Stephen D.
Office of Government Ethics,
Office of the Director, GV
Potts, Stephen G. ... Greenville, SC
Potts, Stephen M. ... Dallas, TX
Potts, Stephen M., & Associates, Inc.
Dallas, TX
Potts, Steven S. ... Chicago, IL
Potts, Steven T. ... Malibu, CA
Potts, Steven T. ... Great Falls, MT
Potts, Susan E. ... Austin, TX
Potts, Thomas G. ... Tulsa, OK
Potts, Thomas J. ... Sidney, OH
Potts, Timothy C. ... Bellingham, WA
Potts, Timothy J. ... Cleveland, OH
Potts, Tracy M. ... Sacramento, CA
Potts, William E., Jr. ... Washington, DC
Potts, William F., Jr. ... Charlotte, NC
Potts & Young, Attorneys, LLP
Florence, AL
Pottschmidt, Faith L. ... Indianapolis, IN
Potts-Dupre, David H. ... Washington, DC
Potucek, John A., II ... Wellington, KS
Poturalski, Steven J. ... Toledo, OH
Poturica, Frank M. ... Torrance, CA
Poturica, Melanie M. ... Los Angeles, CA
Potuto, Josephine R. ... Lincoln, NE
Potuto, Tina
United States International Trade Commission,
Office of the General Counsel, GV
Potuznik, Carrozza, Wilson, Fisher & Catalino
Muskegon, MI

Potuznik, Charles L. ... Minneapolis, MN
Potuznik, Denis V. ... Muskegon, MI
Potvin, Carl W. ... Rochester, NH
Potvin, D. Joseph ... Houston, TX
Potvin, Gregg R. ... Alexandria, VA
Potvin, John F. ... Mount Clemens, MI
Potym, Igor ... Chicago, IL
Pou, Angelo R. ... Miami, FL
Pou, E. Lynne ... New York, NY
Pou, John W. ... Shreveport, LA
Pou, Juan Carlos ... San Juan, PR
Pou, Peggy J. ... San Antonio, TX
Pou, Robert L., III ... Dallas, TX
Pou, Robert L., IV ... Dallas, TX
Pouch, Natalie ... Toms River, NJ
Poucher, Allen L. ... Jacksonville, FL
Poucher, Allen L., Jr. ... Jacksonville, FL
Poucher, David G. ... Tallahassee, FL
Poucher, John S. ... Santa Barbara, CA
Poucher, Ralph L. ... Denver, CO
Pouder, R. Keith ... Nashville, TN
Pouget, Claire S. ... Ann Arbor, MI
Pough, W. Newton ... Orangeburg, SC
Pougiales, Ann M. ... San Francisco, CA
Pougiales, Mary E. ... Oakland, CA
Pouk, Robert J. ... Chicago, IL
Poul, Debra J. ... Philadelphia, PA
Poul, Franklin ... Philadelphia, PA
Poul, Herman B. ... Philadelphia, PA
Poul, Thomas J. ... Minneapolis, MN
Poula, David P. ... Iowa City, IA
Poulakidas, Alexander G. ... Chicago, IL
Poulakidas, Angelos G. ... Chicago, IL
Poulakidas, Dean M. ... San Francisco, CA
Poulakidas, Mark G. ... Chicago, IL
Poulakidas, Michael J. ... Aurora, IL
Poulin, Christopher J. ... Manchester, NH
Poulin, Douglas M. ... Seattle, WA
Poulin, Heather Ann ... Roanoke, VA
Poulin, Michael R. ... Auburn, ME
Poulin, Richard A. ... Anchorage, AK
Poulin, Talitha L. ... Newark, NJ
Poulin, Thomas J. ... Washington, DC
Poulin, Warren M. ... Winslow, ME
Poulios, Ann ... Wilmington, DE
Pouliot, Colleen M. ... San Jose, CA
Pouliot, David M. ... San Leandro, CA
Pouliot, Gerald J. ... Pawtucket, RI
Pouliot, John A. ... New York, NY
Pouliot, Roger R. ... Chicopee, MA
Pouliot, Thomas A. ... Helena, MT
Pouliquen, Corinne M. ... Washington, DC
Poulis, William Ernest ... Santa Barbara, CA
Poulliard, Marcus J. ... New Orleans, LA
Poulos, Audrey E. ... Texarkana, TX
Poulos, Beth A. ... Arlington, TX
Poulos, Beth A. ... Fort Worth, TX
Poulos, Bradley C. ... Fort Worth, TX
Poulos, Charles S. ... Yuba City, CA
Poulos, Christopher A. ... West Covina, CA
Poulos, Christopher Gary ... Flushing, NY
Poulos, David T. ... Chicago, IL
Poulos, Deborah ... Hauppauge, NY
Poulos, Denise A. ... Portsmouth, NH
Poulos & Dickey, L.L.P. ... Alamogordo, NM
Las Cruces, NM
El Paso, TX
Poulos, Eric G. ... Brooklyn, NY
Poulos, George K. ... Islip, NY
Poulos, Gregory C. ... Brooklyn, NY
Poulos, Gregory W. ... San Francisco, CA
Poulos, James A., III ... Washington, DC
Poulos, Jason N. ... Atlanta, GA
Poulos, Joan G. ... Bodega Bay, CA
Davis, CA
Poulos, John A. ... Canton, OH
Poulos, John H. ... West Allis, WI
Poulos, John S. ... Sacramento, CA
Poulos, John W. ... Davis, CA
Poulos, Karen Kazel ... Chicago, IL
Poulos, Kieran Sherlock
Virginia Beach, VA
Poulos, Larry G. ... Akron, OH
Poulos, Mary Ellen ... Milwaukee, WI
Poulos, Michael D. ... Evanston, IL
Poulos, Michael D., P.C. ... Evanston, IL
Poulos, Michael S. ... Chicago, IL
Poulos, Nicholas A. ... North Chicago, IL
Poulos, Nikki M. ... New York, NY
Poulos, Peter M. ... Cleveland, OH
Poulos, Peter P. ... Maplewood, NJ
Poulos, Peter W. ... Chicago, IL
Poulos, Richard E. ... Portland, ME
Poulos, Sara A. ... Minneapolis, MN
Poulos, Sengstock & Budny, S.C.
West Allis, WI
Poulos, Theodore ... Plainville, CT
Poulos, Theodore J. ... West Allis, WI
Poulos, Theodore T. ... Chicago, IL
Poulos, Victor F. ... El Paso, TX
Pouls, Charles G. ... Fort Worth, TX
Poulsen, Edward C. "Ted" ... Sioux City, IA
Poulsen and Jones, P.C. ... South Jordan, UT
Poulsen, Robert A. ... Poway, CA
Poulsen, Robert J. ... South Jordan, UT
Poulson, Jack Garyth ... Juneau, AK
Poulson, Jeffrey L. ... Sioux City, IA
Poulson, Jon C. ... Accomac, VA
Poulson, Lynn O., (Mr.) ... Los Angeles, CA
Poulson, Odell & Peterson, LLC
Denver, CO
Poulson, Paul D. ... Iron Mountain, MI
Poulson, Peter D. ... East Wenatchee, WA
Poulson, Richard E., Jr. ... Hales Corners, WI
Poulson, Richard J. M. ... Washington, DC
Poulson, Robert D. ... Denver, CO
Poulson, Robert E. ... Albuquerque, NM

Poulson, Robert J., Jr. ... Cooperstown, NY
New York, NY
Poulten, Stephen D. ... Saunderstown, RI
Poulter, Cristina M. ... Boston, MA
Poulter, Michael I. ... Charlottesville, VA
Poulter, Susan R. ... Salt Lake City, UT
Poulton, Jennifer A. ... Atlanta, GA
Poulton, John C. ... Baltimore, MD
Poulton, Richard J. ... Edina, MN
Poulton, Thomas W. ... Orlando, FL
Poulton, Timothy P. ... West Palm Beach, FL
Pouncey, Gerald L., Jr. ... Atlanta, GA
Pound, Frank R., Jr. ... Viera, FL
Pound, John B. ... Santa Fe, NM
Pound, Larry J. ... Salem, OR
Pound, Theodore E. G. ... Atlanta, GA
Pound, Theodore F., III ... Houston, TX
Pound, William C. ... Columbus, GA
Pounders & Associates ... Memphis, TN
Pounders, Dorothy Johnson ... Memphis, TN
Pounders, Tracy A. ... Dallas, TX
Pounds, Dallas M. ... Lumberton, NC
Pounds, Herbert E., Jr. ... San Antonio, TX
Pounds, Herbert E., P.C. ... San Antonio, TX
Pounds, Kenneth R. ... Austin, TX
Fort Worth, TX
Houston, TX
Pounds, Leeann Morgan ... Birmingham, AL
Pounds, Mary P. ... Portland, OR
Pounds, Minor E. ... Dallas, TX
Pounds, Todd K. ... Annapolis, MD
Fort Washington, MD
Waldorf, MD
Poundstone, Robert E., III ... Montgomery, AL
Pounian, Steven R. ... New York, NY
Poupard, Patricia M. ... Monroe, MI
Pouratian, Lara ... Greenvale, NY
Pouravelis, Maxine P. ... Portland, ME
Pourciau, Charles L., Jr. ... Tampa, FL
Pournaras, Stephen W. ... McLean, VA
Pournaras, Susan Springer
Washington, DC
Pouros, James G. ... West Bend, WI
Pourvali, Robert H. ... Los Angeles, CA
Pous, Robert T. ... Arlington, VA
Poushter, Bruce M. ... Syracuse, NY
Pousman, Mike ... Atlanta, GA
Pousoulides, Dimitrios S. ... Canton, OH
Pouss, William R. ... Harrisburg, PA
Pousson, Joseph R., Jr. ... Lake Charles, LA
Poust, Alex I. ... Portland, OR
Poust, Brian ... Chicago, IL
Poust, John G. ... Chicago, IL
Poust, Linda M. ... New York, NY
Poust, Teresa Elaine ... Atmore, AL
Poutasse, John D. ... Washington, DC
Poutasse, Judith Woo ... Portland, OR
Povalitis, Leslie A. ... Visalia, CA
Povall, Allie S., Jr. ... Charlotte, NC
Povall, J. Kirkham ... Cleveland, MS
Povall, J. Kirkham, P.A. ... Cleveland, MS
Povanda, Peter C. ... Scranton, PA
Povell, Elizabeth O. ... San Ramon, CA
Povell, Roy Albert ... New York, NY
Poverman, Christopher W. ... Towson, MD
Poverny, Marvin G. ... Woodland Hills, CA
Poveromo, Carl J. ... Scranton, PA
Povich, Albert S. ... Bethesda, MD
Povich, David ... Washington, DC
Povich, Douglas L. ... Washington, DC
Povich, Ilissa Kimball ... Lexington, MA
Povich, Lon F. ... Boston, MA
Povich, Michael E. ... Ellsworth, ME
Povich, Susan ... New York, NY
Povich/Kelly Associates P.C. ... New York, NY
Povilaitis, John F. ... Harrisburg, PA
Povinelli, Lawrence ... Washington, DC
Povlitz, John J., Jr. ... Algonac, MI
Povlitz, William G. ... Naples, FL
Povlitz, William G., P.C. ... Naples, FL
Povman, Bruce Stuart ... Forest Hills, NY
Povman, Linda S. ... Elmhurst, NY
Povman, Michael D. ... New York, NY
Povman, Morton ... Forest Hills, NY
Povodator, Kenneth B. ... Stamford, CT
Povondra, Robert M. ... San Diego, CA
Povtak, Dave W. ... Gaithersburg, MD
Pow, Tamara B. ... San Jose, CA
Powalowski, Joseph H. ... Barrington, IL
Powals, Matthew H. ... Atlantic City, NJ
Powalski, Lynn Marie
Federal Deposit Insurance Corporation,
Professional Liability Section, GV
Powanda, Allen ... Greensburg, PA
Powar, Lee D. ... Cleveland, OH
Powar, Madhurani S. ... New York, NY
Powars, Jefferson F. ... Ogden, UT
Powars-Bahr, Eve D. ... State College, PA
Powasnik, Jack ... Department of Labor,
Office of the Solicitor, GV
Powder, Gari ... New York, NY
Powderly, William H., III ... Pittsburgh, PA
Powders, Michael ... Oakbrook Terrace, IL
Powe, Douglas G. ... East Lansing, MI
Powe, E. K. ... Durham, NC
Powe, Kim Denise ... New York, NY
Powe, Larry E. ... Mount Clemens, MI
Powe, Lynn A. ... Horsham, PA
Powe, Thomas W., Jr. ... Tuscaloosa, AL
Powel, Benjamin R. ... Galveston, TX
Powel, William A., III ... Akron, OH
Powell, A. Gregory ... Salida, CO
Powell, Aaron ... Minneapolis, MN
Powell, Abner R., III ... Andalusia, AL
Powell, Abner Riley, IV ... Andalusia, AL
Powell, Agnes Cowan ... Greenbelt, MD
Powell, Alan B. ... High Point, NC
Powell, Alex ... Compton, CA

Powell, Alfred J., Jr. ... Camilla, GA
Powell, Alfred J., Jr., P.C. ... Camilla, GA
Powell, Alfred O. ... Mount Holly, NJ
Powell, Alice Rae ... Corpus Christi, TX
Powell, Allison D. ... New York, NY
Powell, Amy ... San Francisco, CA
Powell, Amy R. ... Independence, MO
Powell, Andrew K. ... Deerfield, IL
Powell, Ann Lavelle ... Scranton, PA
Powell, Annie ... Fort Smith, AR
Powell, Anthony J. ... Wichita, KS
Powell, Anthony O. L. ... Lawrenceville, GA
Powell, Archie C., III ... Hammond, LA
Powell, Arthur T., III ... Mobile, AL
Powell, Arthur T., III, PC ... Mobile, AL
Powell, Asa M., Jr. ... Newnan, GA
Powell, Austin T. ... Boston, MA
Powell, Ava Susan ... Crestview, FL
Powell, B. Jill ... Greenville, NC
New Bern, NC
Powell, Barbara B. ... Washington, DC
Powell, Barbara Bonn ... New York, NY
Powell, Barbara K.
Department of Commerce,
Office of the General Counsel, GV
Powell, Barry E. ... Los Angeles, CA
Powell, Barry H. ... Jackson, MS
Powell, Barry J. ... Kirkland, WA
Powell, Benjamin A. ... Washington, DC
Powell, Benjamin H., III ... Houston, TX
Powell, Bernard M. ... Tuckahoe, NJ
Powell, Beverly Constance ... Richmond, VA
Powell, Birchmeier & Powell
Atlantic City, NJ
Tuckahoe, NJ
Woodbury, NJ
Powell, B. J. ... Atlanta, GA
Powell, Blair A. ... Chatham, NJ
Powell, Blake G. ... Austin, TX
Powell, Bolling R., Jr. ... Alexandria, VA
Powell, Bradford J. ... New York, NY
Powell, Bradley A. ... Cincinnati, OH
Powell, Bradley L. ... Seattle, WA
Powell, Bret P. ... Burlington, VT
Powell & Brewer, L.L.P. ... Wichita, KS
Powell, Bruce Harrison ... Baltimore, MD
Powell, Bruce R. ... Portland, OR
Powell, Bruce W. ... Columbus, OH
Powell, Bryan E. ... Portland, OR
Powell Burke & Croke LLP, P.C.
Denver, CO
Powell, Burnele V. ... Kansas City, MO
Powell, Byron G. ... Spokane, WA
Powell, Byron M. ... Chicago, IL
Powell, C. Allison ... Birmingham, AL
Powell, C. Glenn ... Tuscaloosa, AL
Powell, C. Kenneth ... Columbia, SC
Powell, Cameron C. ... Washington, DC
Powell, Carleton D.
United States Tax Court,
Special Trial Judges, GV
Powell, Carney, Hayes & Silverstein, P.A.
St. Petersburg, FL
Powell, Carol B. ... Atlanta, GA
Powell, Carol B., P.C. ... Atlanta, GA
Marietta, GA
Powell, Carol D. ... Monroe, LA
Powell, Carol L. ... Oakland, CA
Powell, Caroline Lewis ... Birmingham, AL
Powell, Catherine Stevens ... Milwaukee, WI
Powell, Chance & Leon, L.L.P. ... Austin, TX
Powell, Charles A. ... Chicago, IL
Powell, Charles A., III ... Birmingham, AL
Powell, Charles A., IV ... Birmingham, AL
Powell, Charles D. ... Dallas, TX
Powell, Charles D. ... Houston, TX
Powell, Charles L. ... Carpinteria, CA
Powell, Charles L. ... San Francisco, CA
Powell, Charles L. ... Woodstock, VT
Powell, Charles M., Jr. ... New York, NY
Powell, Charles R. ... Bemidji, MN
Powell, Charles R., III ... Manchester, NH
Powell, Charmaine C. ... Miami, FL
Powell, Chas. A., Jr. ... Macon, MO
Powell, Cheryl A., Law Office of
Mount Vernon, IL
Powell, Christian F. ... Bonita Springs, FL
Powell, Christopher T., Jr. ... Scranton, PA
Powell, Cindy Willard ... Mobile, AL
Powell, Clabron Ann ... Dunwoody, GA
Powell, Cleo E. ... Richmond, VA
Powell, Cleve W. ... Ponca City, OK
Powell, Clifford K. ... Louisville, KY
Powell, Cole A. ... Oakland, CA
Powell, Cornelius P. ... Allentown, PA
Powell, Craig K. ... Sacramento, CA
Powell, Craig S. ... Osawatomie, KS
Powell, Cynthia M. ... Los Angeles, CA
Powell, D. Richard, Jr. ... Allentown, PA
Powell, D. Royce ... Raleigh, NC
Powell, D. Scott ... Columbus, OH
Powell, Daniel P. ... Los Angeles, CA
Powell, Daniel P. ... Boulder, CO
Powell, Daniel P., P.C. ... Boulder, CO
Powell, Darlene Wright ... Greenbelt, MD
Powell, Darlene Wright, P.A. ... Greenbelt, MD
Powell, David A. ... Gainesville, GA
Powell, David C. ... San Francisco, CA
Powell, David D. ... Vale, OR
Powell, David D., Jr. ... Denver, CO
Powell, David D., Law Offices of
Gulfport, MS
Powell, David E. ... Anadarko, OK
Powell, David F. ... Tallahassee, FL
Powell, David F. ... Buffalo, NY
Powell, David G. ... Lexington, KY
Powell, David J. ... Bellevue, WA
Powell, David L. ... Tallahassee, FL

Powell, David M. ... **Little Rock, AR**
Powell, David M. ... **Denver, CO**
Powell, David N. ... Worthington, IN
Powell, David T. M. ... **Kansas City, MO**
Powell, David W. ... **Washington, DC**
Powell, Dean M.
National Science Foundation, Office of the General Counsel, GV
Powell, Deborah P. ... **Pittsburgh, PA**
Powell, Dennis ... Orange, TX
Powell, Dennis E. ... **Monterey, CA**
Powell, Dennis K. ... Houston, TX
Powell, Dennis R. ... Salinas, CA
Powell, Dennis R., Inc. ... Salinas, CA
Powell & Denny, P.C. ... Birmingham, AL
Powell & Deutsch ... Asheville, NC
Powell, DeWayne A. ... New York, NY
Powell, Diana L. ... **Denver, CO**
Powell, Diane E. ... Pittsfield, MA
Powell, Dixie Dan ... **Crestview, FL**
Niceville, FL
Powell, Don E. ... Richland, WA
Powell, Donald A. ... **Tuckahoe, NJ**
Woodbury, NJ
Powell, Donald A. ... Akron, OH
Powell, Donald F. ... **Riverside, CA**
Powell, Donald N. ... Tacoma, WA
Powell, Donald S. ... Iron River, MI
Powell, Donald W. ... **Phoenix, AZ**
Powell, Dorothy A. ... **Birmingham, AL**
Powell, Douglas A. ... Eagan, MN
Powell, Douglas F. ... Morganton, NC
Powell, Douglas J. ... Austin, TX
Powell, Douglas J., P.C. ... Austin, TX
Powell, Douglas R. ... **Atlanta, GA**
Powell, E. Wayne ... Richmond, VA
Powell, E. D. ... Sullivan, IN
Powell, Edward E., Jr. ... **San Francisco, CA**
Powell, Edward O. ... Tupelo, MS
Powell, Edwin E., Jr. ... Gatesville, TX
Powell, Elias ... Los Angeles, CA
Powell, Elizabeth Benson
Minneapolis, MN
Powell, Elizabeth P. ... Alexandria, VA
Powell, Elwood P. ... Ogden, UT
Salt Lake City, UT
Powell, Emily Pate ... Lawrenceville, GA
Powell, Eric S. ... **Houston, TX**
Powell, Ernest M., III ... Houston, TX
Powell, Ernest N., Jr. ... Chicago, IL
Powell, Errol H. ... Tallahassee, FL
Powell & Fancher ... Canton, MS
Powell, Florence Annette ... **Marion, VA**
Powell, Francis R. ... **Boston, MA**
Powell, Frank Grey ... Winston-Salem, NC
Powell, Frank M. ... St. Augustine, FL
Powell, Fredric A. ... Syosset, NY
Powell, G. Deacon ... **New Orleans, LA**
Powell, Garrison & Swanson
Minneapolis, MN
Powell, Gary A. ... **Springfield, MO**
Powell, Gary E. ... **Cincinnati, OH**
Powell, Gary R. ... **Dallas, TX**
Powell, Gary W. ... San Diego, CA
Powell, Gene A. ... Sacramento, CA
Powell, George L. ... Bethesda, MD
Powell, George T., III ... Columbia, SC
Powell, George W. ... Bonita, CA
Powell, Georgene B. ... Akron, OH
Powell, Geraint D. ... **Minneapolis, MN**
Powell, Gerald A. ... West Hempstead, NY
Powell, Gerald R. ... **Dallas, TX**
Powell, Gillis E., Jr. ... **Crestview, FL**
Powell, Gillis E., Sr. ... **Crestview, FL**
Powell, Glenn ... **Wethersfield, CT**
Powell, Goldstein, Frazer & Murphy LLP
Washington, DC
Atlanta, GA
Powell, Greg, P.C. ... Salida, CO
Powell, Gregory C. ... Riverdale, MD
Powell, Gregory L. ... **Portland, OR**
Powell, Gregory T. ... Houston, TX
Powell, Gregory V. ... **Chevy Chase, MD**
Powell, Gregory W. ... Portland, ME
Powell & Gunter ... Richland, WA
Powell, Gwendolyn A. ... **Washington, DC**
Powell, H. David ... **Charlotte, NC**
Powell, H. Douglas ... **Plantation, FL**
Powell, H. Douglas, P.A. ... **Plantation, FL**
Powell, H. Robert ... **Austin, TX**
Powell & Hamilton ... Greenville, AL
Powell, Hanno T. ... Fresno, CA
Powell, Harlan C. ... **Chicago, IL**
Powell, Harold E., Jr. ... Mifflintown, PA
Powell, Harold F. ... Syosset, NY
Powell, Harold Jackson ... Charleston, WV
Powell, Hedy M. ... St. Davids, PA
Powell, Herbert W. ... Houston, TX
Powell, H. J. ... Durham, NC
Powell, Hoda N. ... Kokomo, IN
Powell, Hugh R. (Rick), Jr. ... **Atlanta, GA**
Powell, Hugh R. (Rick), Jr. ... **Doraville, GA**
Powell, Ida A. ... Washington, DC
Powell, J. Bradley ... **Birmingham, AL**
Powell, J. Coburn ... **Whiteville, NC**
Powell, J. Fred ... **Birmingham, AL**
Powell, J. Gregory ... **Joplin, MO**
Powell, J. Hughes, Jr. ... Dallas, TX
Powell, J. Michael ... **Madison, VA**
Stanardsville, VA
Powell, Jack N. ... Kenosha, WI
Powell & Jackson, P.C. ... Houston, TX
Powell & Jacobs ... New York, NY
Powell, Jacqueline Loughman ... Newark, DE
Powell, James C. ... **Foley, AL**
Powell, James C. ... Parkersburg, WV
Powell, James E. ... Cleveland, OH
Powell, James H. ... New York, NY
Powell, James J., III ... **Scranton, PA**
Powell, James L. ... **Jackson, MS**
Powell, James M. ... **Anchorage, AK**
Powell, James M. ... **Columbia, MO**
Powell, James M. ... **Greensboro, NC**
Powell, James M. ... Parkersburg, WV
Powell, James N. ... **St. Petersburg, FL**
Powell, James Spaulding ... Gloucester, VA
Powell, James W. ... Memphis, TN
Powell, Janet D. ... **Murfreesboro, TN**
Powell, Janice M. ... Savannah, GA
Powell, Janice M. ... **Peoria, IL**
Powell, Jason C. ... **Wilmington, DE**
Powell, Jay E. ... **San Francisco, CA**
Powell, Jay W. ... Visalia, CA
Powell, J. C. ... Charleston, WV
Powell, Jean E. ... Raeford, NC
Powell, Jeanne Varner ... Casa Grande, AZ
Powell, Jeffrey A. ... **Chattanooga, TN**
Powell, Jeffrey D. ... **Garden City, NY**
Powell, Jeffrey Kenneth ... **New York, NY**
Powell, Jeffrey S. ... **Chicago, IL**
Powell, Jennifer Archimbaud ... Austin, TX
Powell, Jennifer F. ... Morgantown, WV
Powell, Jennifer L. ... Syracuse, NY
Powell, Jerome ... Washington, DC
Powell, Jerry W. ... Birmingham, AL
Powell, Joan E. ... Chicago, IL
Powell, Joanne I. ... Wheaton, IL
Powell, Joe A. ... **Avon Lake, OH**
Powell, Joe B. ... Decatur, AL
Powell, John ... **Scottsdale, AZ**
Powell, John A. ... Asheville, NC
Powell, John A., Jr. ... Tampa, FL
Powell, John B. ... **Fort Wayne, IN**
Powell, John Brentnall, Jr.
Baltimore, MD
Powell, John C. ... Perry, IA
Powell, John Davis ... Houston, TX
Powell, John E. D. ... **Seattle, WA**
Powell, John Eris ... Chevy Chase, MD
Powell, John F. ... Carlsbad, CA
Powell, John G. ... Denver, CO
Powell, John M. ... Falls Church, VA
Powell, John P. ... Kailua-Kona, HI
Powell, John R. ... New Braunfels, TX
Powell, John R. ... **McLean, VA**
Powell, John S., III ... Pearland, TX
Powell, John W. ... **Pittsburgh, PA**
Powell, Jon Steven ... **Dunn, NC**
Powell, Jon T. ... **Houston, TX**
Powell, Joseph ... **San Juan Capistrano, CA**
Powell, Joseph A. ... Akron, OH
Powell, Joseph, A Law Corporation
San Juan Capistrano, CA
Powell, Joseph E. ... San Francisco, CA
Powell, Joseph Edward ... **Tuscaloosa, AL**
Powell, Joseph M. ... Old Bridge, NJ
Powell, Joseph W., II ... **Columbus, GA**
Powell, Josephine A. ... Detroit, MI
Powell, Josephine A., P.C. ... Detroit, MI
Powell, J. R. ... Pitman, NJ
Powell, Judith A. ... **Beverly Hills, CA**
Powell, Judith A. ... **Atlanta, GA**
Powell, Judith A. ... Steubenville, OH
Powell, Judith L. ... Great Neck, NY
Powell, Julius A., Jr. ... Macon, GA
Powell, Justin C. ... **Washington, DC**
Powell, K. Laliah H. ... Savannah, GA
Powell, Karen D. ... **Washington, DC**
Powell, Karen Pitts ... Frankfort, KY
Powell, Kathleen Lynch ... Avon, CT
Powell, Keenan ... Anchorage, AK
Powell, Keith L. ... Towson, MD
Powell, Keith Robert ... Columbia, MO
Powell, Kelly D. ... Scottsville, KY
Powell, Ken ... El Paso, TX
Powell, Kenneth D., Jr. ... Philadelphia, PA
Powell, Kenneth E. ... **Tarrytown, NY**
Powell, Kenneth J., Jr. ... Philadelphia, PA
Powell, Kenneth L. ... **Pasadena, CA**
Powell, Kirsten Murphy ... San Jose, CA
Powell, Klysta J. ... Palm Desert, CA
Powell, Kurtis A. ... **Atlanta, GA**
Powell, Larry S. ... Pomeroy, OH
Powell, Laura A. ... Rutherfordton, NC
Powell, Lavatus V. ... **New York, NY**
Powell Law Firm, The, P.C.
Des Moines, IA
Norwalk, IA
Powell Law Group, The ... West Hazleton, PA
Powell Law Offices ... Charleston, WV
Powell Law Offices ... Parkersburg, WV
Powell, Leland T., Jr. ... Charlotte, NC
Powell, Lesley G. ... **Charlotte, NC**
Powell, Leslie A. ... **Frederick, MD**
Powell, Leslie N. ... Miami, FL
Powell, Leta Karam ... El Paso, TX
Powell, Lewis F., III ... **Richmond, VA**
Powell, Lewis F., Jr.
Supreme Court Of The United States, GV
Powell, Lewis W., III ... Chicago, IL
Powell, Linda Ann ... Arlington, VA
Powell, Linda E. ... **Irvine, CA**
Powell, Linda Peterson ... Fort Wayne, IN
Powell, Linda Wanell ... **Liberal, KS**
Powell, Lisa ... **McAllen, TX**
Powell, Lisa A. ... **Houston, TX**
Powell, Lisa Holland ... **Durham, NC**
Powell, Lloyd E. ... Ann Arbor, MI
Powell, Lorene C. ... Tallahassee, FL
Powell, Louise C. ... Silver Spring, MD
Powell, Lucinda Beth ... Kansas City, MO
Powell, Lyman T., III ... **Fond du Lac, WI**
Powell, M. Catherine ... **Minneapolis, MN**
St. Paul, MN
Powell, M. Channing ... **Gulfport, MS**
Powell, M. Frank ... Houston, TX
Powell, M. Kevin ... **Lake Charles, LA**
Powell & Mack ... **Tallahassee, FL**
Powell, Marc ... Traer, IA
Powell, Marc A. ... **Wichita, KS**
Powell, Marc Baden ... **Fairfield, NJ**
Powell, Marcia R. ... Columbia, SC
Spartanburg, SC
Powell, Marjorie E. ... Washington, DC
Powell, Marjorie L. ... **Irving, TX**
Powell, Mark ... Laguna Beach, CA
Powell, Mark A. ... **Springfield, MO**
Powell, Mark E. ... Hendersonville, NC
Powell, Mark J. ... **Scranton, PA**
Powell, Marta Brown ... Olympia, WA
Powell, Martin F. ... Seattle, WA
Powell, Marvin J. ... **New York, NY**
Powell, Mary E. ... **Palo Alto, CA**
Powell, Mary H. ... Harrisburg, PA
Powell, Mary Lou ... **Columbia, SC**
Powell, Mary Lynn ... West Palm Beach, FL
Powell, Matthew D. ... **Tampa, FL**
Powell, Matthew D. ... Conroe, TX
Powell, Matthew W. ... **Sacramento, CA**
Powell, Maurice D. ... Kirkland, WA
Powell, Maurice W. ... Sacramento, CA
Powell, Max Courtney ... Toledo, OH
Powell, Maxwell M. ... Great Neck, NY
Powell, M. Channing ... **Biloxi, MS**
Powell, Meghan O'Ryan
San Francisco, CA
Powell, Melodie A. ... **Kansas City, MO**
Powell, Michael A. ... **Edwardsville, IL**
Powell, Michael A. ... Frederick, MD
Powell, Michael A. ... Tulsa, OK
Powell, Michael C. ... **Baltimore, MD**
Powell, Michael D. ... **Palo Alto, CA**
Powell, Michael D. ... Department of Justice, Tax Division, GV
Powell, Michael E. ... Lebanon, OH
Powell, Michael E., III ... Shreveport, LA
Powell, Michael H. ... Buffalo Grove, IL
Powell, Michael H. ... Aurora, NE
Powell, Michael J. ... **Atlanta, GA**
Powell, Michael J. ... Austin, TX
Powell, Michael J., Jr. ... Milton, MA
Powell, Michael K.
Federal Communications Commission, Office of the Commissioners, GV
Powell, Michael L. ... Knoxville, TN
Powell, Michael T. ... **Houston, TX**
Powell, Michael V. ... **Dallas, TX**
Powell, Michael W. ... **Peoria, IL**
Powell & Minehart, P.C. ... Philadelphia, PA
Powell, Morgan K. ... Collinsville, OK
Powell & Morris, P.S. ... **Spokane, WA**
Powell, Nancy E. ... San Francisco, CA
Powell, Nancy Noonan ... **Norristown, PA**
Powell, Nancy V. ... Palo Alto, CA
Powell, Nancy V., A Prof. Corp., Law Offices of ... Palo Alto, CA
Powell, Newton B. ... Decatur, AL
Powell, Norbert J. ... Johnsonburg, PA
Powell, Norman C. ... **Miami, FL**
Powell, Norman E. ... Plainview, NY
Powell, Norman M. ... **Wilmington, DE**
Powell, Norman R. ... Louisville, KY
Powell, O. Eugene, Jr. ... Columbia, SC
Powell, Owen N. ... Bonifay, FL
Powell, Patricia ... **Vineland, NJ**
Powell, Patricia A. ... Philadelphia, PA
Powell, Paul L., Jr. ... Oakland, CA
Powell & Payne ... Shallotte, NC
Powell, Peek & Weaver ... **Andalusia, AL**
Brewton, AL
Enterprise, AL
Evergreen, AL
Greenville, AL
Luverne, AL
Powell, Peter E. ... Raleigh, NC
Powell, Phillip L. ... Minneapolis, MN
Powell, Polly F. ... **Austin, TX**
Powell & Poston ... Aiken, SC
Powell & Powell ... Decatur, AL
Powell & Powell ... **Whiteville, NC**
Powell and Powell ... Akron, OH
Powell & Powell ... Kirkland, WA
Powell, Powell & Light ... **Bemidji, MN**
Powell, Powell & Powell
Fort Walton Beach, FL
Niceville, FL
Powell, Powell & Powell ... **Honesdale, PA**
Scranton, PA
Wilkes-Barre, PA
Powell, Powell & Powell, P.A.
Crestview, FL
Powell, R. Clay ... **Valdosta, GA**
Powell, R. Joseph ... Richardson, TX
Powell, R. Page, Jr. ... **Atlanta, GA**
Powell, Ralph B., Jr. ... **Harrisburg, PA**
King Of Prussia, PA
Powell, Ralph W. ... **Athens, GA**
Powell, Raymond H. J., Jr. ... **Arlington, VA**
Powell & Reggio ... **Dallas, TX**
Powell, Regina Licata ... San Antonio, TX
Powell & Reilly, P.C. ... **Chicago, IL**
Powell, Rhonda Edwards ... **New York, NY**
Powell, Richard ... Montgomery, TX
Powell, Richard G. ... **New York, NY**
Powell, Richard H.
Fort Walton Beach, FL
Powell, Richard L. ... **Marietta, GA**
Powell, Richard L. ... Steubenville, OH
Powell, Rick D. ... College Station, TX
Powell, Rick L. ... **Fort Worth, TX**
Powell, Ringer & Bischof ... Dexter, MO
Powell, Robert ... Traer, IA
Powell, Robert C. ... Lincolnton, NC
Powell, Robert E. ... Baltimore, MD
Powell, Robert H., III ... **Norfolk, VA**
Powell, Robert H., Jr. ... Canton, MS
Powell, Robert J. ... West Hazleton, PA
Powell, Robert L. ... Pearisburg, VA
Powell, Robert R. ... Palo Alto, CA
Powell, Robert Stanley ... Arlington, VA
Powell, Robert W. ... Detroit, MI
Powell, Robt. A. ... Denver, CO
Powell, Rod ... **Norwalk, IA**
Powell, Roger N. ... Pikesville, MD
Powell, Roger T. ... Taft, TX
Powell, Roger W. ... Fort Lauderdale, FL
Powell, Rom W. ... Winter Park, FL
Powell, Romaine R. ... **Bemidji, MN**
Powell, Ronald W. ... **Minneapolis, MN**
Powell, Ronnie Ann ... **Livingston, NJ**
Powell, Roy A. ... **Pittsburgh, PA**
Powell, Roy D. ... Madison, MS
Powell, Roy N. ... San Antonio, TX
Powell, Russell ... **Kansas City, MO**
Powell, Russell A. ... **Palo Alto, CA**
Powell, Russell C. ... **Alexandria, VA**
Powell, Samuel T. ... Williamsburg, VA
Powell, Sandra P. ... Ogden, UT
Powell, Sara J. ... Phoenix, AZ
Powell, Sarah Elizabeth ... Salisbury, NC
Powell, Scott A. ... **Birmingham, AL**
Powell and Senff ... Aurora, NE
Powell, Shannon L. ... **Birmingham, AL**
Powell, Shannon L. ... **Chicago, IL**
Powell, Sherman B. ... Decatur, AL
Powell, Sherman B., Jr. ... Decatur, AL
Powell, Sidney K. ... **Dallas, TX**
Powell, Sinclair ... Ann Arbor, MI
Powell & Slaten LLC ... Anchorage, AK
Powell, Sonya L. ... **Virginia Beach, VA**
Powell, Stanley Bruce ... **Niceville, FL**
Powell, Stanley Bruce, P.A. ... **Crestview, FL**
Destin, FL
Fort Walton Beach, FL
Niceville, FL
Powell, Stephanie C. ... **Durham, NC**
Powell, Stephen D. ... Dallas, TX
Powell, Stephen E. ... **New York, NY**
Powell, Stephen J. ... **Washington, DC**
Powell, Stephen J.
Department of Commerce, Office of the General Counsel, GV
Powell, Stephen J. ... **Waterloo, IA**
Powell, Stephen R. ... Mill Creek, WA
Powell, Steven B. ... New York, NY
Powell, Steven D. ... Ventura, CA
Powell, Steven L. ... **Houston, TX**
Powell, Steven Michael ... Findlay, OH
Powell & Strom, P.A. ... **Crestview, FL**
De Funiak Springs, FL
Destin, FL
Fort Walton Beach, FL
Niceville, FL
Powell, Susan ... **New York, NY**
Powell, Susie R. ... Hillsborough, NC
Powell, Sweet & Coleman, L.L.P.
Dallas, TX
Powell, Sylvester, Jr. ... Kansas City, MO
Powell & Tante ... **Columbus, GA**
Powell, Terrell D. ... Los Angeles, CA
Powell, Theron M ... **Springfield, IL**
Powell, Thomas A. ... Portland, ME
Powell, Thomas E., II ... **Louisville, KY**
Powell, Thomas J. ... **McLean, VA**
Powell, Thomas L. ... Newport Beach, CA
Powell, Thomas L. ... **Tallahassee, FL**
Powell, Thomas M. ... **Birmingham, AL**
Powell, Thomas O. ... **Atlanta, GA**
Powell & Thomas, P.C. ... Dallas, TX
Powell, Thomas R. ... **Wichita, KS**
Powell & Thompson, P.C. ... Alexandria, VA
Powell, Tim A. ... **Canton, OH**
Powell, Todd D. ... Topeka, KS
Powell, Tonia Jones ... **Washington, DC**
Baltimore, MD
Rockville, MD
Powell, Tonya Bunn ... Greensboro, NC
Powell, Trachtman, Logan, Carrle, Bowman & Lombardo, A Professional Corporation
Cherry Hill, NJ
Harrisburg, PA
King Of Prussia, PA
Philadelphia, PA
Powell, Tracy A. ... Rochester, NY
Powell, Tracy A. ... **Nashville, TN**
Powell, Tracy O., II ... Sacramento, CA
Powell, Trisha A. ... Flat Rock, MI
Powell, Tyler ... Tallahassee, FL
Powell, Tyson H. ... **San Francisco, CA**
Powell, Verne E. ... San Antonio, TX
Powell, Victoria A. ... Ada, MI
Powell, Victoria Jane ... Brainerd, MN
Powell, Virginia Ann ... Fredericksburg, VA
Powell, Virginia W. ... **Richmond, VA**
Powell, W. Brent ... Platte City, MO
Powell, W. Michael ... Sherwood, AR
Powell, W. Scott ... **Maitland, FL**
Powell, W. Thomas ... Wheaton, IL
Powell, W. Thomas ... Jefferson, OH
Powell, Walter V. ... Slippery Rock, PA
Powell, Warren C., Jr. ... **Columbia, SC**
Powell, Wesley C ... Orlando, FL
Powell, Wesley R. ... **New York, NY**
Powell, William A. ... Shallotte, NC
Powell, William B. ... **Rockford, IL**
Powell, William D. ... Columbia, MO
Powell, William D. ... **Springfield, MO**
Powell, William D. ... Dunn, NC
Powell, William D. ... **Dallas, TX**
Powell, William E., III ... **Washington, DC**
Powell, William G. ... **Parkersburg, WV**
Powell, William H. ... Lake San Marcos, CA

Powell, William H. ....Chicago, IL
Powell, William J. ....Spokane, WA
Powell, William J. ....Charleston, WV
Powell, William Jay ....Columbia, MO
Powell, William L., Jr. ....Goldsboro, NC
Powell, William M. ....Cape Coral, FL
Powell, William M., P.A. ....Cape Coral, FL
Powell, William P., Jr. ....Torrance, CA
Powell, William P., Jr. ....Raleigh, NC
Powell, William P., Jr., A Prof. Corp., Law Offices of ....Los Angeles, CA
Torrance, CA
Powell, William R. ....Sheboygan, WI
Powell, William V., Jr. ....Birmingham, AL
Powell, W. M. ....Little Rock, AR
Powell, Wm. J. ....Minneapolis, MN
Powell-Cosio, Sofia ....Miami, FL
Powell-Woodson, Dorthula H.
Washington, DC
Powelson, Donald L. ....Bakersfield, CA
Powelson, Robbie L. ....Ishpeming, MI
Powen, John T. ....Chicago, IL
Power, Amy M. ....Atlanta, GA
Power, Austin J., Jr. ....New York, NY
Power, Barbara B. ....Vero Beach, FL
Power, Beck & Matzureff ....Martinsburg, WV
Power, Berve M. ....Chicago, IL
Power, Bowen & Valimont, LLP
Doylestown, PA
Sellersville, PA
Power, Brick ....Salt Lake City, UT
Power, Christopher B. ....Charleston, WV
Power, Craig E. ....Beaumont, TX
Corpus Christi, TX
Houston, TX
Power & Cronin, Ltd. ....Oakbrook Terrace, IL
Power, Curtis G., III ....Martinsburg, WV
Power, Dale J. ....El Cerrito, CA
Power, Daniel L. ....Des Moines, IA
Power, David Edwin ....Fairfield, CA
Power, David J. ....San Jose, CA
Power, David S. ....Fort Collins, CO
Power & Deatherage ....Irving, TX
Power, Deirdre Waldron ....Bronx, NY
Power, Elizabeth S. ....Charleston, WV
Power, Frank G. ....Leland, MS
Power, Garrett ....Baltimore, MD
Power, Gerald J. ....Worcester, MA
Power, Gerald R. ....Jacksonville, FL
Power, Gregory J. ....Sodus, NY
Power, Gregory M. ....St. Louis, MO
Power, J. Edward ....Des Moines, IA
Power, James A., Jr. ....New York, NY
Power, James A., & Marguerite Del Valle
New York, NY
Power, James H. ....New York, NY
Power, James J. ....Plainview, NY
Power, James P. ....New York, NY
Power, James W. ....San Mateo, CA
Power, Jan Geiselman ....Findlay, OH
Power, Jeffrey B. ....Grand Rapids, MI
Power, John B. ....Los Angeles, CA
Power, John F. ....Chicago, IL
Power, John F., III ....Oakbrook Terrace, IL
Power, John H. ....Vero Beach, FL
Power, John K. ....Kansas City, MO
Power, John M. ....Boca Raton, FL
Livingston, NJ
New York, NY
Power, John M. ....Chicago, IL
Power, John R.
Agency for International Development, Office of the General Counsel, GV
Power, John S. ....Brielle, NJ
Power, Joseph A., Jr. ....Chicago, IL
Power, Justin J. ....Chicago, IL
Power, Karen P. ....Vienna, VA
Power, Katherine C.
Federal Communications Commission, Wireless Telecommunications Bureau, GV
Power, L. Patrick ....Kankakee, IL
Power Law Group, P.A.
Overland Park, KS
Power, Layton A. ....Kirkland, WA
Power, Leona A. ....Frankfort, KY
Power, Lisa M. ....El Paso, TX
Power, Little & Little ....Frankfort, IN
Power, Margaret M. ....Chicago, IL
Power, Marjorie J. ....Waterbury, VT
Power, Mark T. ....New York, NY
Power & Masi ....Vero Beach, FL
Power, Melinda L. ....Chicago, IL
Power, Michael D. ....Ambler, PA
Power, Michael J. ....Kenner, LA
Power, Michael S. ....Denver, CO
Power, Michele L. ....Bethel, AK
Power, Nancy E. ....Tustin, CA
Power, Patrick E. ....Winsted, CT
Power, Philip J. ....New York, NY
Power & Power ....Washington, DC
Arlington, VA
Power, Richard J. ....Washington, DC
Power, Richard J., Jr. ....McLean, VA
Power, Richard W. ....Santa Rosa, CA
Power, Robert C ....Harrisburg, PA
Power, Robert Christopher ....Orlando, FL
Power, Robert D. ....Boston, MA
Power, Robert G. ....Worcester, MA
Power, Robert H. ....Irving, TX
Power Rogers & Smith, P.C. ....Chicago, IL
Power, Russell B. ....Dallas, TX
Power, Samuel H. ....Frankfort, IN
Power, Sarah M. ....Helena, MT
Power, Susan H. ....Washington, DC
Power, Thomas C.
Federal Communications Commission, Office of the Commissioners, GV
Power, Thomas M. ....Chicago, IL
Power, Thomas W. ....Arlington, VA
Power, Tim ....Humble, TX
Power, Timothy A. ....Reston, VA
Power, Timothy E. ....Overland Park, KS
Power, Timothy H. ....Walnut Creek, CA
Power, Tracy J. ....Washington, DC
Arlington, VA
Power, Wallace M. ....Cincinnati, OH
Power, Warren R. ....Griffin, GA
McDonough, GA
Power, Weiss & Kurnit, LLP
Boca Raton, FL
Livingston, NJ
New York, NY
Power & Westbury, LLP ....Griffin, GA
McDonough, GA
Power, William A. ....San Juan, PR
Power, William C. ....Martinsburg, WV
Power, William H., Jr. ....Massena, NY
Power, William R. ....Chicago, IL
Power, William R. ....Arlington, TX
Power, William R., P.C. ....Arlington, TX
Power, William Scott ....Burlington, IA
Power, William V. ....Denver, CO
Power, Wm. J. ....Sacramento, CA
Powers, Alexander L.
Department of Commerce, Patent and Trademark Office, GV
Powers, Amy S. ....Golden, CO
Powers, Ann ....White Plains, NY
Powers, Ann R. ....Austin, TX
Powers, Anne P. ....Boston, MA
Powers, Arlene J. ....Boston, MA
Powers, Arthur J. ....New York, NY
Powers, Arthur, Jr. ....Sullivan, IL
Powers, Barry R. ....Southfield, MI
Powers, Benjamin R. ....Bristol, TN
Powers, Bernard J. ....Racine, WI
Powers, Beth L. ....Boston, MA
Powers, Betty Jo ....Houston, TX
Powers & Bigoness, P.C. ....Oak Brook, IL
Powers, Bradley E. ....Tampa, FL
Powers, Brendan O'Rourke ....Denver, CO
Powers, Brian A. ....Washington, DC
Powers, Brian C. ....Lake Worth, FL
Powers, Brian E. ....Bowie, TX
Powers, Brian J. ....New York, NY
Powers, Brian P. ....Chicago, IL
Powers, Bridget Brown ....Petoskey, MI
Powers, Bruce N. ....Tulsa, OK
Powers, Bruce S. ....Houston, TX
Powers, Cara W. ....Dayton, OH
Powers, Carol L. ....Rowley, MA
Powers, Catherine A. ....Herndon, VA
Powers, Chad M. ....Huntington, NY
Powers, Chapman, DeAgostino, Meyers & Milia, Professional Corporation
Pontiac, MI
Troy, MI
Powers, Charles C. ....South Fork, CO
Powers, Charles E. ....Chesterfield, VA
Powers, Charles E., Jr. ....Hackensack, NJ
Powers, Charles F., III ....Raleigh, NC
Powers, Christopher M. ....Northport, NY
Powers, Claudia Kay ....Portland, OR
Powers, Clifford W. ....Portland, OR
Powers, Constance P. ....Manchester, NH
Powers, Craig L. ....Tacoma, WA
Powers, Dale D. ....Cleveland, OH
Powers, David A., III ....Chesterfield, VA
Powers, David Earle ....Trenton, NJ
Powers, David J., (P.A.) ....Boca Raton, FL
Powers, David L. ....Bay City, MI
Powers, David N. ....Washington, DC
Powers, David P. ....Columbiana, OH
Powers, Deborah J. ....Milwaukee, WI
Powers, Delton W., Jr. ....Bennettsville, SC
Powers, Delton W., Jr., P.A.
Bennettsville, SC
Powers, Denise V. ....Coral Gables, FL
Powers, Denise V., P.A. ....Coral Gables, FL
Powers, Dennis J. ....Chicago, IL
Powers, Dennis M. ....Ashland, OR
Powers, Dennis N. ....Highland, MI
Powers, Dennis P. ....Springfield, MA
Powers, Dennis P. ....Newark, NJ
Powers, Dennis Wade ....Gallatin, TN
Powers, Diane M. ....Saginaw, MI
Powers, DiCicco & Sahagian ....Boston, MA
Powers, Donald B., Jr. ....Stamford, CT
Powers, Donald G. ....Verona, VA
Powers, Donald H. ....Cleveland, OH
Powers, Donald L. ....Richardson, TX
Powers, Donald R. (Tad) ....Middlebury, VT
Powers, Donna J. ....Cleveland, OH
Powers, Douglas Dormire ....Fort Wayne, IN
Powers, E.A. Ohnesorge ....Minneapolis, MN
Powers, Edward C. ....Painesville, OH
Powers, Edward H. ....Flint, MI
Powers, Edward J. ....Kitty Hawk, NC
Norfolk, VA
Powers, Edward L. ....New York, NY
Powers, Edward W. ....Boston, MA
Powers, Edwin T., Jr. ....Knoxville, TN
Powers, Eileen E. ....Annapolis, MD
Powers, Eleanor ....Houston, TX
Powers, Elizabeth Enayati
Menlo Park, CA
Powers, Elizabeth Oliver ....Baton Rouge, LA
Powers, Elizabeth W. ....New York, NY
Powers, English, Carroll & Ritter, Ltd.
Middlebury, VT
Powers, Erika K. ....Chicago, IL
Powers, Eugene D. ....St. Louis, MO
Powers, Eva ....Topeka, KS
Powers, F. William ....Charlotte, NC
Powers, Florence Schreiber ....Trenton, NJ
Powers, Francis J. ....Chicago, IL
Powers, Frank I. ....Phoenix, AZ
Powers, Frederick W., III ....Norcross, GA
Powers & French ....Freeport, ME
Powers & Frost, L.L.P. ....Houston, TX
Powers, G. Alan ....Bridgeport, TX
Decatur, TX
Powers, G. Brent ....St. Joseph, MO
Powers, Galen D. ....Washington, DC
Powers, Gary ....Providence, RI
Powers, George E., Jr. ....Cheyenne, WY
Powers, George R. ....Austin, TX
Powers, George R. ....South Charleston, WV
Powers, Gerald A. ....Boston, MA
Powers, Gerald F. ....Ottawa, KS
Powers, Gerard J. ....Boston, MA
Powers, Grace Pangilinan ....Portland, OR
Powers, Greg M. ....Harlingen, TX
Powers & Groh-Wargo ....Berea, OH
Cleveland, OH
Powers, H. Wayne ....Overland Park, KS
Powers, Hallowell & Nickolai ....Highland, MI
Powers, Harold J. ....Natick, MA
Powers, Heidi Schultz ....Somerset, KY
Powers, Helen V. ....Walnut Creek, CA
Powers, Howard J., II ....Phoenix, AZ
Powers, Hugh J. ....Wakefield, MA
Powers, Irving ....St. Louis, MO
Powers, J. Brian ....Sacramento, CA
Powers, J. Pat ....Palo Alto, CA
Powers, J. Patrick ....Atlanta, GA
Powers, Jack, Jr. ....Beeville, TX
Powers, James ....Phoenix, AZ
Powers, James A. ....Washington, DC
Powers, James B. ....Englewood, CO
Powers, James C. ....Los Angeles, CA
Powers, James E. ....Madison, WI
Powers, James F. ....Charlotte, NC
Powers, James F., Jr. ....Boston, MA
Powers, James F., Jr. ....Fairfax, VA
Powers, James G. ....Omaha, NE
Powers, James H. ....Houston, TX
Powers, James J. ....Chicago, IL
Powers, James K. ....Orlando, FL
Powers, James L. ....Denver, CO
Powers, James M. ....Cedar Rapids, IA
Powers, James N. ....Orlando, FL
Powers, James N., P.A. ....Orlando, FL
Powers, James P. ....Chicago, IL
Powers, James W. ....Prineville, OR
Powers, Jan, (A Professional Corporation)
Los Angeles, CA
Powers, Janet L. S. ....Irvine, CA
Powers, Janis S. ....Oklahoma City, OK
Powers, Jason M. ....Houston, TX
Powers, Jean C. ....Buffalo, NY
Powers, Jean Fleming ....Houston, TX
Powers, Jean M. ....Mobile, AL
Powers, Jeffrey B. ....Boston, MA
Powers, Jeffrey N. ....Macon, GA
Powers, Jeffry G. ....Southfield, MI
Powers, Jeniffer A. ....Los Angeles, CA
Powers, Jennifer A. ....Tampa, FL
Powers, Jennifer V. ....Madison, WI
Milwaukee, WI
Powers, Jessica L. ....Glenside, PA
Powers, Jill Fisher ....Clearwater, FL
Powers, Joan S. ....Washington, DC
Powers, John ....Portland, OR
Powers, John A. ....Cincinnati, OH
Powers, John C. ....Far Rockaway, NY
Powers, John D. ....Dania, FL
Powers, John D. ....Milford, MA
Powers, John D. ....New York, NY
Powers, John Dale ....Baton Rouge, LA
Powers, John E. ....Chicago, IL
Powers, John E. ....Austin, TX
Powers, John E., II ....St. Louis, MO
Powers, John G. ....Washington, DC
Powers, John G., (A Professional Corporation) ....Los Angeles, CA
Powers, John J. ....San Francisco, CA
Powers, John J. ....Bethel, CT
New Milford, CT
Powers, John J. ....Champaign, IL
Powers, John J. ....New York, NY
Powers, John J., III ....Department of Justice, Antitrust Division, GV
Powers, John K. ....Albany, NY
Powers, John L. ....Wayzata, MN
Powers, John M. ....Los Angeles, CA
Powers, John M. ....Vallejo, CA
Powers, John P. ....Syracuse, NY
Powers, John T., Jr. ....Spokane, WA
Powers, John W. ....Chicago, IL
Powers, John Weed ....Poland, OH
Powers, John Y. ....Chattanooga, TN
Powers, Jon M. ....Minneapolis, MN
Powers, Joseph K. ....New York, NY
Powers, Joseph M. ....Mobile, AL
Powers, Joseph P., Jr. ....San Francisco, CA
Powers, Joshua A. ....Chattanooga, TN
Powers, Jude Thaddeus A. ....Hemet, CA
Powers, Julie A. ....St. Louis, MO
Powers, K. Stephen ....Chattanooga, TN
Powers, Kathleen M. ....Providence, RI
Powers, Kathryn L. ....Denver, CO
Powers, Kenneth C. ....Anchorage, AK
Powers, Kenneth R.
Department of the Army, Office, Chief of Engineers/Headquarters, U.S. Army Corps of Engineers, GV
Powers, Kevin J. ....Center Moriches, NY
Powers, Kinder & Keeney, Incorporated
Providence, RI
Powers, Krista Lee ....Laguna Hills, CA
Powers, Larry A. ....Sulphur Springs, TX
Powers, Laurence J. ....Cleveland, OH
Powers Law ....San Francisco, CA
Powers Law Offices, P.C. ....Braintree, MA
Powers, Lawrence ....Baltimore, MD
Powers, Lawrence M. ....Englewood, NJ
Powers, Lawrence P. ....Princeton, NJ
Powers Legal Services ....East Palestine, OH
Lisbon, OH
Darlington, PA
Powers, Leonard J. ....Meriden, CT
Powers, Leonard R. ....Beaverton, OR
Powers, LeRoy A. ....Oklahoma City, OK
Powers, Leslie A. ....Yakima, WA
Powers, Leslie H. ....Lexington, MA
Powers & Lewis ....Washington, DC
Powers, Lisa M. ....Rochester, NY
Powers, Lonnie A. ....Boston, MA
Powers, Marc D. ....New York, NY
Powers, Marcus E. ....Malibu, CA
Powers, Margaret A. ....Santa Ana, CA
Powers, Margaret M. ....San Francisco, CA
Powers, Mark A. ....Chicago, IL
Powers, Mark G. ....Spokane, WA
Powers, Mark L. ....Schenectady, NY
Powers, Mark L. ....Toledo, OH
Powers, Mark L. ....Wauseon, OH
Powers, Mark W. ....Worcester, MA
Powers, Martin Thomas ....Bedford, OH
Powers, Mary A. ....Morristown, NJ
Powers, Mary Ellen ....Washington, DC
Powers, Mary Murphy ....St. Paul, MN
Powers, Matthew D. ....Menlo Park, CA
Powers, Matthew F. ....Gulfport, MS
Powers, Matthew T. ....San Jose, CA
Powers, Maureen ....Austin, TX
Powers, McCulloch & Bennett, LLP
Portland, OR
Powers, McNalis, Moody & Groelle
Lake Worth, FL
Powers, Melissa A. ....Cincinnati, OH
Powers, Melissa H. ....Orlando, FL
Powers, Michael A. ....Harvard, MA
Powers, Michael B. ....Buffalo, NY
Powers, Michael David ....Boston, MA
Powers, Michael E. ....Boise, ID
Powers, Michael E. ....Oak Brook, IL
Powers, Michael E. ....Shrewsbury, MA
Powers, Michael F. ....Indianapolis, IN
Powers, Michael H. ....Sacramento, CA
Powers, Michael J. ....Chicago, IL
Powers, Michael J. ....Joliet, IL
Powers, Michael J. ....Braintree, MA
Powers, Michael J. ....Springfield, MA
West Springfield, MA
Powers, Michael J. ....Hackensack, NJ
Powers, Michael M. ....Frankfort, KY
Powers, Michael P. ....Boulder, CO
Powers, Michael R. ....Atlanta, GA
Powers, Michael S. ....San Diego, CA
Powers, Michael S. ....Trenton, NJ
Powers, Michael T. ....Rochester, NY
Powers, Michele A. ....Los Angeles, CA
Powers, N. Richard ....Wilmington, DE
Powers, N. Thompson ....Washington, DC
Powers, Nancy A. ....Los Angeles, CA
Powers, Nancy D. ....Ely, MN
Powers, Nancy L. ....San Francisco, CA
Powers, Noah Edward, II ....Middletown, OH
Powers, P. Stacy ....Treasury Department, Office of Thrift Supervision, GV
Powers, Pamela E. ....Houston, TX
Powers, Patricia ....Philadelphia, PA
Powers, Patricia Ann ....Bedford, MA
Powers, Patricia Owen ....Nashville, TN
Powers, Paul ....Austin, TX
Fort Worth, TX
Houston, TX
Powers, Paul Bannon ....St. Louis, MO
Powers, Paul D. ....Ventura, CA
Powers, Paul F. X. ....Belmont, MA
Powers, Paul J., Jr. ....New York, NY
Powers, Peter G. ....Washington, DC
Powers, Peter J. ....New York, NY
Powers, Peter L. ....Buffalo, NY
Powers, Peter L. ....Newport, OR
Powers, Philip T. ....Chicago, IL
Powers Phillips, P.C. ....Denver, CO
Powers, Pike, Jr. ....Austin, TX
Powers and Powers ....Bethel, CT
New Milford, CT
Powers & Powers ....Rome, NY
Powers & Powers, P.A. ....Baltimore, MD
Powers, Pyles, Sutter & Verville, P.C.
Washington, DC
Powers, Quaschnick & Tischler
Tallahassee, FL
Powers, R. Eric, III ....Montgomery, AL
Powers, Ragan L. ....Seattle, WA
Powers, Ralph W., Jr.
Upper Marlboro, MD
Powers, Raymond D. ....Boise, ID
Powers, Richard A. ....Chicago, IL
Powers, Richard E. ....Boston, MA
Falmouth, MA
Wellesley, MA
Powers, Richard E., Jr. (P.C.)
Washington, DC
Powers, Richard J. ....Key West, FL
Powers, Richard J. ....Bellevue, WA
Powers, Richard M. ....Tallahassee, FL
Powers, Richard M., P.A. ....Tallahassee, FL
Powers, Richard S. ....Miami, FL
Powers, Richard W. ....White Plains, NY
Powers, Rick L. ....Knoxville, TN
Powers, Robert B. ....Springfield, IL
Powers, Robert C. ....Binghamton, NY
Powers, Robert C., (A Professional Corporation) ....Los Angeles, CA
Powers, Robert E. ....Boston, MA
Powers, Robert E. ....Bridgewater, NJ

Powers, Robert F. ... Montgomery, AL
Powers, Robert P. ... Boston, MA
Powers, Robert S. ... Providence, RI
Powers, Robert W. ... Des Moines, IA
Powers, Robin K. ... Chicago, IL
Powers, Rocky L. ... Durant, OK
Powers, Ron D. ... Chattanooga, TN
Powers, Ronald C. ... Rome, NY
Powers, Ronald D. ... Pittsburgh, PA
Powers, Ruth L. ... Stamford, CT
Powers & Santola ... Albany, NY
Powers, Sarah Ann ... Houston, TX
Powers, Sarah E. ... Medford, NJ
Powers, Scott M. ... Newport, KY
Powers, Scott Michael ... Sheridan, WY
Powers, Scott T. ... Johnson City, TN
Kingsport, TN
Powers, Sean J. ... Birmingham, MI
Powers, Sheila M. ... Tulsa, OK
Powers, Sheri ... Oakland, CA
Powers, Sheryl A. ... Westbury, NY
Powers, Sheryl J.
Equal Employment Opportunity Commission, Office of the General Counsel, GV
Powers, Stephen E. ... Marlboro, NJ
New York, NY
Powers, Susan A. ... Brooklyn, NY
Powers, Susan M. ... Los Angeles, CA
Powers, Suzanne LaTaif, (Mrs.) ... Bethel, CT
New Milford, CT
Powers, Tassma A. ... Casper, WY
Powers, Tassma Ann ... Casper, WY
Powers, Taya G ... Denver, CO
Powers, Teri L. ... Portland, OR
Powers, Theodore James ... Chicago, IL
Powers, Theresa ... Boston, MA
Powers & Therrien, P.S. ... Yakima, WA
Powers, Thomas B. ... Boston, MA
Powers, Thomas B. ... Portland, OR
Powers, Thomas D. ... Fort Worth, TX
Powers, Thomas E. ... Portland, ME
Powers, Thomas J. ... Minneapolis, MN
Powers, Thomas M. ... Portage, MI
Powers, Thomas P. ... Washington, DC
Powers, Timothy E. ... Dallas, TX
Powers, Timothy E. ... Denton, TX
Powers, Todd M. ... Cincinnati, OH
Powers, Tony G. ... Atlanta, GA
Powers, Tornatore & Amster
Upper Marlboro, MD
Powers, Troy ... Baltimore, MD
Powers, Valerie Ann ... Sellersville, PA
Powers, Van Stuart ... Hyattsville, MD
Powers, Victoria ... South Portland, ME
Powers, Victoria E. ... Columbus, OH
Powers, Vincent M. ... Lincoln, NE
Powers, W. Kevin ... Department of Defense, Defense Legal Services Agency, GV
Powers, Walter J. ... Rockport, MA
Powers, Walter W. ... Sacramento, CA
Powers, Ward D. ... Troy, MI
Powers, Ward M. ... Northville, MI
Powers, Ward M., P.C. ... Northville, MI
Powers, Werner A. ... Dallas, TX
Powers & Willard, L.L.P.
Baton Rouge, LA
Powers, William A. ... Littleton, CO
Powers, William B. ... Indianapolis, IN
Powers, William E., Jr., (P.A.)
Tallahassee, FL
Powers, William F. ... Burbank, CA
Powers, William F. ... Tulsa, OK
Powers, William F., Jr. ... Chatsworth, CA
Powers, William J. ... Seattle, WA
Powers, William J., Jr. ... Pascagoula, MS
Powers, William, Jr. ... Austin, TX
Houston, TX
Powers, William K. ... Tulsa, OK
Powers, William L. ... Houston, TX
San Antonio, TX
Powers, William M. E., III ... Medford, NJ
Powers, William M. E., Jr. ... Medford, NJ
Powers, William M. E., Jr., Chartered
Medford, NJ
Powers, William P., III ... Columbiana, AL
Powers, William R., Jr. ... Mount Laurel, NJ
Powers, William T. ... Portland, OR
Powers, William T., Jr. ... New York, NY
Powers, William V., Jr ... Portsmouth, VA
Powers-Denklau, Andrea R.
Benton Harbor, MI
Power-Wolfinger, Patricia ... Pittsburgh, PA
Powhatan, Becky A. ... Atlanta, GA
Powis, Patricia M. ... Richmond, VA
Powlan, Roy K. ... Moraga, CA
Powlan, Roy Y. ... Lafayette, CA
Powlen, David M. ... Indianapolis, IN
Powlen, Michael S. ... San Francisco, CA
Powles, Justine K. ... Chicago, IL
Powles, Peter B. ... Chicago, IL
Powless, Holly Beth ... Sault Ste. Marie, MI
Powless, Jeffrey D. ... San Antonio, TX
Powless, Kenneth B. ... Marion, IL
Powlette, Louis D. ... Stroudsburg, PA
Powley, Brian E. ... Oklahoma City, OK
Powley, Brian E., P.L.L.C.
Oklahoma City, OK
Powley, Douglas J. ... Akron, OH
Powley, Robert L. ... New York, NY
Powley, Susan E. ... Dallas, TX
Powlick, Jill Tabor ... Indianapolis, IN
Powlus, JoAnn Y. ... Columbus, OH
Pownall, Dixie L. ... Cumberland, MD
Pownall, Frederick M. ... San Francisco, CA
Pownall, Kimberly A. ... Atlanta, GA
Powrie, Diane E. ... Bend, OR
Powrie, Douglas B. ... Bend, OR
Powsner, David J. ... Boston, MA
Powsner, Ethan M. ... Grand Rapids, MI
Powsner, Robert H. ... Beverly Hills, CA
Powsner, Robert H.
Point Reyes Station, CA
Powsner, Robert H. ... San Francisco, CA
Poxon, John P., Jr. ... Pasadena, CA
Poxon, T. Michael ... Philadelphia, PA
Poxson, Elijah ... Detroit, MI
Poy, Henry A. ... Oakland, CA
Poy, John T. ... Indianapolis, IN
Poyatt, John J., Jr. ... Berkeley Heights, NJ
Poyatt, Michael ... Damascus, MD
Poydasheff, Robert S. ... Columbus, GA
Poydasheff, R. S., Jr. ... Columbus, GA
Poyfair, D.J. ... Denver, CO
Poyfair, Edwin L. ... Vancouver, WA
Poyner, B. Lynn ... Jacksonville, FL
Poyner, James M. ... Raleigh, NC
Poyner, John R. ... Colusa, CA
Poyner, Roger W. ... Los Gatos, CA
Monterey, CA
Poyner & Spruill, LLP ... Charlotte, NC
Raleigh, NC
Rocky Mount, NC
Poynor, James M. ... Sinton, TX
Poynor, Jeffery T. ... Montgomery, AL
Poynor, Lana P. ... Charlotte, NC
Poynor, Michael B. ... San Diego, CA
Poynor, Phillip J. ... Farmingdale, NY
Poynter & Gearhart, P.A.
Mountain Home, AR
Poynter, Jennifer A. ... Englewood, CO
Poynter, Mannear & Colomb, A Professional Law Corporation ... Baton Rouge, LA
Poynter, Pamela F. Sorensen ... Chicago, IL
Poynter, Richard L., (P.C.) ... Indianapolis, IN
Poynter, Robert E. ... Lafayette, IN
Poynter, Terry M. ... Mountain Home, AR
Poynter, Wandaleen ... Jacksonville, FL
Poyourow, Robert ... Los Angeles, CA
Poyourow, Robert L. ... Wayne, NJ
Poythress, David B. ... Atlanta, GA
Poyton, Andrew R. ... Wheaton, IL
Poyzer, Laura J. ... Macedon, NY
Poza, Carlos K. ... San Francisco, CA
Pozaric, Steven E. ... St. Louis, MO
Pozdol, Richard J. ... Chicago, IL
Pozefsky, Bramley & Murphy ... Albany, NY
Pozefsky, Martin W. ... Saratoga Springs, NY
Pozefsky, Steven A. ... Lake Success, NY
Pozefsky, William ... Albany, NY
Pozega, George Gregory ... Raleigh, NC
Pozehl, Rhonda Spencer ... Southfield, MI
Pozen, Denise ... Oak Brook, IL
Pozen, Ira, (P.A.) ... Miami, FL
Pozen, Joseph P. ... Chicago, IL
Pozen, Robert C. ... Boston, MA
Pozen, Robert C. ... Philadelphia, PA
Pozen, Sharis Arnold ... Washington, DC
Pozen, Thorn L. ... Washington, DC
Pozen, Walter ... Washington, DC
Pozenel, Jay W. ... New York, NY
Pozgay, Jon R. ... Phoenix, AZ
Pozgay, Jon R., Ltd. ... Phoenix, AZ
Pozin, Daniel ... White Plains, NY
Pozin, Robert M. ... Irvine, CA
San Diego, CA
Poznak, James L. ... Oak Brook, IL
Poznak Law Firm Ltd ... Oak Brook, IL
Poznak, Morton M. ... Chicago, IL
Poznak, Peter A. ... Midland, MI
Poznanski, Margot M. ... Kalamazoo, MI
Poznansky, Jonathan H. ... Staten Island, NY
Poznansky, Roslyn ... Boston, MA
Pozner, Daniel A. ... Ithaca, NY
Pozner, Larry, P.C. ... Denver, CO
Pozner, Larry S. ... Denver, CO
Pozner, Louis-Jack ... Albany, NY
Pozner, Louis-Jack, P.C. ... Albany, NY
Pozniak, Frank P. ... Boston, MA
Poznick, Jill L. ... Washington, DC
Pozo, Berti ... Key Biscayne, FL
Pozo, Miguel A. ... Roseland, NJ
Pozo, Rafael DeJesus ... Coral Gables, FL
Pozo, Zaedy R. ... Coral Gables, FL
Pozo-Diaz, Martha ... Miami, FL
Pozorski, Anthony J. ... Lancaster, WI
Pozorski, Edward G. ... Los Angeles, CA
Pozorski, Joseph M., Jr. ... Manitowoc, WI
Pozycki, Harry S., Jr. ... Metuchen, NJ
Pozza, Clarence L., Jr. ... Detroit, MI
Pozza, Daniel V. ... San Antonio, TX
Pozza, John S. ... Temecula, CA
Pozza, Karen H. ... San Antonio, TX
Pozza & Patton ... San Antonio, TX
Pozzerle, Sergio A. ... Houston, TX
Pozzi, Brian M. ... Philadelphia, PA
Pozzi, Donald R. ... Victoria, TX
Pozzi, Francis A., Jr. ... Sudbury, MA
Pozzi, Jeffrey R. ... San Diego, CA
Pozzi, Joseph D. ... Syracuse, NY
Pozzi, Kathleen A. ... Santa Rosa, CA
Pozzi, Michael F. ... Seattle, WA
Pozzi, Pamela M. ... Syracuse, NY
Pozzi Wilson Atchison, LLP ... Portland, OR
Pozzuoli, Edward J. ... Fort Lauderdale, FL
Pozzuoli, Frank A. ... New York, NY
Pozzuoli, Georgina R. ... Fort Lauderdale, FL
Pozzuoli, Joseph A. ... White Plains, NY
Pozzuoli-Buecker, Renee ... Westmont, NJ
Pozzuolo, Joseph R. ... Philadelphia, PA
Pozzuolo & Perkiss, P.C. ... Philadelphia, PA
Pozzuto, Andrew T. ... Ocala, FL
Pozzuto, Vincent P. ... New York, NY
P'Pool, William C. ... Nashville, TN
Prabhu, Jay V. ... Washington, DC
Prabhu, Jean M. ... Staten Island, NY
Prachar, William E. ... Los Angeles, CA
Pracher, Douglas J. ... Homestead, FL
Pracher, Maria C. ... San Francisco, CA
Pracht, Joseph M. ... Greenwood, SC
Pracht, Michael T. ... Davenport, IA
Prachthauser, Don C. ... Mequon, WI
Milwaukee, WI
Racine, WI
Prada, Cynthia Beier ... Oakland, CA
Prada, Vincent F. ... Washington, DC
Pradat, Diane V. ... Jackson, MS
Pradat, Edward H. ... Tuscaloosa, AL
Pradat, Edward H., P.C. ... Tuscaloosa, AL
Pradell and Associates ... Anchorage, AK
Pradell, Steven ... Anchorage, AK
Pradhan, Serra S. ... New York, NY
Pradhan, Varsha R. ... Philadelphia, PA
Prado, Edward C. ... San Antonio, TX
Prado, Maria T. ... New York, NY
Prado, Marta Maria ... Washington, DC
Prado, Mary Lou ... Miami, FL
Prado, Nanci I. ... New York, NY
Prado, Priscilla M. ... Fort Pierce, FL
Prados, David M. ... New Orleans, LA
Praed, Jon L. ... Washington, DC
Praefke, Jacqueline ... Flint, MI
Praeger, Andrea M. ... New York, NY
Praeger, Helene C. ... New York, NY
Praeger, John R. ... Seattle, WA
Praeger, Lawrence J. ... Dallas, TX
Prael, Charles F. ... San Francisco, CA
Praet, Bruce D. ... Santa Ana, CA
Praete, Arthur V. ... New Rochelle, NY
Praete, Frank C., Jr. ... New Rochelle, NY
Praetzel, Robert P. ... San Rafael, CA
Prag, Jeffrey E. ... Stockton, CA
Prag, Julie ... New York, NY
Prag, Kenneth S. ... Redding, CA
Praga, Lawrence ... Rye, NY
White Plains, NY
Prager, Adolph ... Brooklyn, NY
Prager, Adrienne C. ... San Diego, CA
Prager, Alan N. ... Dallas, TX
Prager, Albert U. ... Coronado, CA
Prager, Barbara J. ... Plantation, FL
Prager, Beth Greenberg
Highland Park, IL
Prager, Bruce J. ... New York, NY
Prager, David ... Topeka, KS
Prager, David A. ... New York, NY
Prager, David E. ... New York, NY
Prager, David, III ... Topeka, KS
Prager, David J. ... Santa Monica, CA
Prager, David M. ... Commack, NY
Prager, Donald L. ... Fort Worth, TX
Prager, Donald L., P.C. ... Fort Worth, TX
Prager, Eric A. ... New York, NY
Prager, Frank P. ... Denver, CO
Prager, Gerald David ... Cincinnati, OH
Prager, Ira Carl ... Patchogue, NY
Prager, Irving ... La Verne, CA
Prager, Isaac L. ... Boston, MA
Prager, Jerome L. ... Dallas, TX
Prager, John W., Jr. ... Santa Ana, CA
Prager, Judith L. ... New York, NY
Prager, Julian D. ... Staten Island, NY
Prager, Laura C. ... New York, NY
Prager, Laurel J. ... Oakland, CA
Prager, Linda C. ... New York, NY
Prager, Lisa A. ... Washington, DC
Prager, Lutz Alexander ... Washington, DC
Prager, Mark L. ... Chicago, IL
Prager, Marvin ... Los Angeles, CA
Prager, Metzger & Kroemer PLLC
Dallas, TX
Prager, Nancy C. ... Atlanta, GA
Prager, Pamela J. ... Des Moines, IA
Prager, Robin E. ... Baltimore, MD
Prager, Ruth ... Los Angeles, CA
Prager, Stanley B. ... Coral Gables, FL
Prager, Steven D. ... New York, NY
Prager, Stuart ... New York, NY
Prager, Susan Westerberg ... Hanover, NH
Prager, Vicki J. ... Buffalo, NY
Prager, Wendy L. ... New York, NY
Praggastis, Thomas C. ... Ketchum, ID
Praglin, Gary A. ... Los Angeles, CA
Prague, Owen H. ... Woodland Hills, CA
Prague, Ronald J. ... Parsippany, NJ
Prahinski, Leo F. X. ... Burtonsville, MD
Prahl, Cori Lynn ... Brookfield, WI
Prahl, Dennis S. ... New York, NY
Prahl, Eric L. ... Boston, MA
Prahl, Heino H. ... Buffalo, NY
Prahl, John T. ... Coral Gables, FL
Prahl, Margaret M. ... Sioux City, IA
Prahl & McBride, A Professional Corporation ... San Diego, CA
Prahl, Robert A. ... San Diego, CA
Prahler, James M. ... Philadelphia, PA
Prahofer, Nancy ... New York, NY
Prairie, J. Michael ... Eau Claire, WI
Prairie, Michael W. ... San Diego, CA
Praiss, Donna M. ... New York, NY
Praiss, Omri E. ... St. Louis, MO
Praitis, Judith M. ... Los Angeles, CA
Prajsner, Mark P. ... Toledo, OH
Prajzner, Norman G. ... Philadelphia, PA
Prak, Mark J. ... Greensboro, NC
Raleigh, NC
Prakash, Ambari ... Washington, DC
Prakel, Judith M. ... Phoenix, AZ
Prakel, Judith M., P.C. ... Phoenix, AZ
Prakke, Kevin A. ... Raleigh, NC
Prakken, William D. ... Grand Junction, CO
Praley, James C. ... Glen Burnie, MD
Pralgever, Alan S. ... Roseland, NJ
Prall, David S. ... Burbank, CA
Prall, Dwight E. ... Newton, IA
Prall, G. Michael ... Bloomington, IL
Prall, Jerry E. ... Columbus, IN
Prall, Stacy L. ... Indianapolis, IN
Prall, Thomas J. ... Weston, WV
Prall, Willow J. ... Washington, DC
Pramaggiore, Anne R. ... Chicago, IL
Pramas, Timothy J. ... Minneapolis, MN
Pramberg, John W. ... Newburyport, MA
Prame, Christine Liverzani
Washington, DC
Prame, Michael J. ... Washington, DC
Pramov, Henry P., Jr. ... Los Angeles, CA
Pramudji, Ari O. ... Houston, TX
Pramuk, Daniel A. ... Canton, OH
Salem, OH
Pranaitis, Alphonse J. ... Alton, IL
Edwardsville, IL
Prance, Norman R. ... Springfield, MA
Prando, Carla ... Santa Fe, NM
Prange, Claire G. ... Denver, CO
Prange, David E. ... Portland, OR
Prange, Eugene Hanly ... Annandale, VA
Prange, Karen Fischer ... Kansas City, MO
Prange, Patricia J. ... Chicago, IL
Prange, Roy L., Jr. ... Madison, WI
Prange, Stacey L. ... Chicago, IL
Pranger, Charlyn M. ... San Bernardino, CA
Pranger, James R. ... Chicago, IL
Pranger, Pamela S. ... Atlanta, GA
Prangle, Michael E. ... Chicago, IL
Pranin & Muldoon ... Wilmington, CA
Pranin, Rodney C. ... Wilmington, CA
Pranke, Lynn Marie ... Santa Ana, CA
Pranschke & Holderle, L.C.
St. Louis, MO
Pranschke, Leonard J. ... St. Louis, MO
Pransky, Alan J. ... Dedham, MA
Pransky, Irwin ... Laguna Beach, CA
Prante, Stafford W. ... El Cajon, CA
Prantil, Richard G. ... San Diego, CA
Pranzo, Gene M. ... New York, NY
Prappas, Elaine Faye ... Fort Worth, TX
Houston, TX
San Antonio, TX
Prappas, George J. ... Houston, TX
Prappas, James D. ... Houston, TX
Prasad, Ashish S. ... Chicago, IL
Prasad, Sanjay ... Redwood City, CA
Praschan, Edwards and Conormon
Fayetteville, NC
Praschan, Kenneth C. ... Fayetteville, NC
Prasco, Victor H. ... Merrillville, IN
Prasher, Gregory G. ... Grand Rapids, MI
Prashker, Audrey E. ... New York, NY
Prashker, David ... Gloucester, MA
Prashker, David, P.C. ... Gloucester, MA
Prashker, Lucy ... Alford, MA
Prashker, Lucy ... Great Barrington, MA
Prashner, Daniel F. ... Houston, TX
Prashner, E. S. ... San Antonio, TX
Prasifka, David W. ... Houston, TX
Prasifka, Karrén M. ... O'Fallon, MO
Prasil, Linda A. ... Glenview, IL
Prasinos, Alexander ... Harwich, MA
Prasinos, Anthony G. ... North Reading, MA
Pracko, Joseph J. ... Santa Monica, CA
Praskin, Susan D. ... Los Angeles, CA
Prass, Frank E. ... Bath, MI
Prass, Ronald E., Jr. ... Alexandria, VA
Prasse, David W. ... Atlanta, GA
Prasse, Frederick C. ... Chagrin Falls, OH
Prasse, Richard T. ... Cleveland, OH
Prassinos, Constant A. ... Canfield, OH
Prasso, Thomas M. ... Bellerose, NY
Praszkier, Herman ... St. Louis, MO
Prata, Robert J. ... Los Angeles, CA
Pratcher, Franklin R. ... Buffalo, NY
Prater, Alan Jay ... Shreveport, LA
Prater, Arlene ... San Diego, CA
Prater, Carol E. ... Temple, TX
Prater, Claude J. ... Stratford, OK
Prater, Dennis ... Lawrence, KS
Prater, Earl M., Jr. ... Treasury Department, Office of Director of Practice, GV
Prater, Erik S. ... Detroit, MI
Prater, Gabriele Margit ... San Diego, CA
Prater, Harlan I., IV ... Birmingham, AL
Prater, James Edward ... Paris, KY
Prater, James Edward, P.S.C. ... Paris, KY
Prater, Jill I. ... Washington, DC
Prater, John R. ... Littleton, CO
Prater, Kristin E. ... Ephrata, WA
Prater, Mark A. ... United States Senate, Committee Legal Personnel, GV
Prater, Nathan C. ... Montgomery, AL
Prater, Penny Lynn ... Fairfax, VA
Prater, R. Keith ... Newnan, GA
Prater, R. Keith, P.C. ... Newnan, GA
Peachtree City, GA
Prater & Ridley ... Temple, TX
Prater, Ronald E. ... Fort Wayne, IN
Prater, Wendy L. ... Houston, TX
Pratesi, Emil G. ... Clearwater, FL
Prather, Alicia A. ... Kansas City, MO
Prather, Alvin Eugene ... Adelphi, MD
Prather, Andrew, II ... Columbus, GA
Prather & Associates, P.C. ... Detroit, MI
Prather, Beth A. ... Fort Myers, FL
Prather, Charles I. ... McPherson, KS
Prather, Charles N. ... Orlando, FL
Prather, Claude R. ... Louisville, KY
Prather, Damien M. ... Louisville, KY
Nashville, TN
Prather, David C. ... West Palm Beach, FL
Prather, Donald T. ... Shelbyville, KY
Prather, Gene ... Marysville, CA

Prather, James A. .... **Abita Springs, LA**
New Orleans, LA
Prather, Janet Marin .... Indianapolis, IN
Prather, Jason D. .... **Fort Worth, TX**
Prather, J. D. .... **Raleigh, NC**
Prather, Jeffrey S. .... Modesto, CA
Prather, J.N., Jr. .... Abbeville, LA
Prather, John Christopher .... New York, NY
Prather, John G. .... **Somerset, KY**
Prather, John G., Jr. .... **Somerset, KY**
Prather, John G., The Firm of
Somerset, KY
Prather, John R. .... St. Clairsville, OH
Prather, Jon Lee .... Tulsa, OK
Prather, Karen R. .... Santa Ana, CA
Prather, Kenneth E. .... **Detroit, MI**
Prather, Laura E. .... **Tampa, FL**
Prather, Lee W. .... **Augusta, GA**
Prather, Lenore L. .... Jackson, MS
Prather, M. Joel .... Tallahassee, FL
Prather, Mark D. .... Meadville, PA
Prather, Pamela .... **Jackson, MS**
Prather, Paul E. .... **Memphis, TN**
Prather, Paul F. .... Tulsa, OK
Prather, R. Anthony .... **Carmel, IN**
Prather, Richard W. .... Indianapolis, IN
Prather, Robert C., Sr. .... **Dallas, TX**
Prather, Robert E. .... Louisville, KY
Prather, Ronald W. .... Crystal Lake, IL
Prather, Sharon L. .... Woodstock, IL
Prather, Stewart L. .... Louisville, KY
Prather, Susan Blake .... Phenix City, AL
Prather, William C. .... Macon, GA
Prather, William C. .... Toledo, IL
Prati Perugia, Beatrice .... **New York, NY**
Prato & Associates, P.C. .... **Bensenville, IL**
Berwyn, IL
La Grange Park, IL
Lombard, IL
Naperville, IL
Prato, Gioacchino (Jack) Vincent
La Grange Park, IL
Prato, Samuel F. .... Rochester, NY
Prato, Thomas M. .... Rochester, NY
Prats, Catherine C. .... St. Petersburg, FL
Prats, Luis .... **Tampa, FL**
Pratscher, Darryl D. .... Springfield, IL
Pratt, A. Kingman, Jr. .... Fryeburg, ME
Pratt, A. Michael .... **Philadelphia, PA**
Pratt, Albert .... Osterville, MA
Pratt, Alexander H., Jr. .... **Boston, MA**
Pratt, Andrew F. .... **Seattle, WA**
Pratt, Andrew R. .... Piqua, OH
Pratt & Bator, L.L.P. .... **Boston, MA**
Pratt, Benjamin R., Jr. .... **Glens Falls, NY**
Pratt, Bernadette M. .... **Seattle, WA**
Pratt, Brett & Luce, P.C. .... **Doylestown, PA**
Pratt, Carla D. .... **Philadelphia, PA**
Pratt, Carmen Cavazos .... **Houston, TX**
Pratt, Carol A. .... **Portland, OR**
Pratt, Carol Hempfling .... **Boston, MA**
Pratt, Carrie G. .... **San Francisco, CA**
Pratt, Catherine A. .... Bloomington, IL
Pratt, Catherine J. .... Los Angeles, CA
Pratt, Catherine Randall
Department of Commerce,
Office of the General Counsel, GV
Pratt, Chad T-W .... **Los Angeles, CA**
Pasadena, CA
Pratt, Channing L. .... **Monmouth, IL**
Pratt, Charles A. .... Kalamazoo, MI
Pratt, Charles A. .... Cincinnati, OH
Pratt, Charles E. .... Corpus Christi, TX
Pratt, Charles E., III .... Corpus Christi, TX
Pratt, Charles F. .... Fort Wayne, IN
Pratt, Charles J., Jr. .... **Bradenton, FL**
Pratt, Charles M. .... **Denver, CO**
Pratt, Charles M. .... **New York, NY**
Pratt, Charles W. .... Laguna Hills, CA
Pratt, Christa C. .... **Charlotte, NC**
Pratt, Christopher C. .... Fairport, NY
Pratt, Claire Bledsoe .... Cary, NC
Pratt, Clyde R. .... Newbury Park, CA
Pratt, Corlin J. .... **Wichita, KS**
Pratt, Cynthia Mather .... **Washington, DC**
Pratt, Dana S. .... New York, NY
Pratt, Daniel S. .... Norwalk, CA
Pratt, Darrell .... Wayne, WV
Pratt, Darren G. .... Washington, DC
Pratt, Darryl V. .... Dallas, TX
Pratt, David .... Aventura, FL
Boca Raton, FL
Fort Lauderdale, FL
West Palm Beach, FL
Pratt, David A. .... **Albany, NY**
Pratt, David F. .... Lexington, KY
Pratt, David H. .... Westminster, MD
Pratt, David L. .... **Dallas, TX**
Pratt, Dawn E. .... **Tulsa, OK**
Pratt, Denise V. .... Houston, TX
Pratt, Dennis C. .... Lilburn, GA
Pratt, Dennis L. .... Jacksonville, FL
Pratt, Diana V. .... Detroit, MI
Pratt, Donald O. .... **Arlington, TX**
Pratt, Donald R., Jr. .... Downers Grove, IL
Pratt, Donna F. .... **Bloomington, IN**
Pratt, Elma Hum .... **Washington, DC**
Pratt, Elizabeth Brandes .... **Beaumont, TX**
Pratt, Elliott L. .... **Salt Lake City, UT**
Pratt, Emron M., Jr. .... Dallas, TX
Pratt, Ernest J. .... Pawtucket, RI
Pratt, Eugene F., III .... Kennewick, WA
Pratt and Fossard .... Springfield, MO
Pratt, Frank G. .... Utica, NY
Pratt & Frank, P.C. .... Okemos, MI
Pratt, Frederic .... New York, NY
Pratt, George C. .... New York, NY
Pratt, George W. .... **Salt Lake City, UT**

Pratt, Gerald D. .... Denver, CO
Pratt, Gibson E. .... San Diego, CA
Pratt, Glendon B. .... **Columbus, OH**
Pratt, Gregory H. .... **Tacoma, WA**
Pratt, Gregory K. .... Middletown, OH
Pratt, Gregory T. .... **Dallas, TX**
Pratt, Grey Douglas .... Pittsburgh, PA
Pratt, Gwynne T. .... Auburn, CA
Pratt, H. Jonathan .... Olathe, KS
Pratt, Harold I. .... **Boston, MA**
Pratt, Harry Joe .... Hoxie, KS
Pratt, Irving A. .... Laughlintown, PA
Pratt, J. Burdette .... Vale, OR
Pratt, Jack S. .... Oklahoma City, OK
Pratt, James A. .... Council Bluffs, IA
Pratt, James E. .... New York, NY
Pratt, James J. .... Jacksonville, FL
Pratt, James M., Jr. .... Camden, AR
Camden, AR
Pratt, James R. .... **Winter Park, FL**
Pratt, James R. .... Eufaula, OK
Pratt, James R., III .... **Birmingham, AL**
Pratt, Jane Hartley .... **Monmouth, IL**
Pratt, Janet Hammett .... Bangor, ME
Pratt, Janet L. .... Sumas, WA
Pratt, Jas. R. .... Shorewood, MN
Pratt, Jeffrey E. .... Mill Creek, WA
Pratt, Jennifer L. .... Delaware, OH
Pratt, Joe N. .... **Austin, TX**
Pratt, Joe N. .... Victoria, TX
Pratt, John B., Sr. .... White Hall, IL
Pratt, John E. .... Lancaster, TX
Pratt, John L. .... Bloomington, IL
Pratt, John L. .... Kalispell, MT
Pratt, John L. .... Odessa, TX
Pratt, John M. .... **San Luis Obispo, CA**
Pratt, John Patrick .... Miami, FL
Pratt, John S. .... **Atlanta, GA**
Pratt, John S. .... Springfield, MO
Pratt, John T. .... Bloomington, IL
Pratt, Justin R. .... Stigler, OK
Pratt, Katherine M. .... **New York, NY**
Pratt, Kathleen M. .... **San Francisco, CA**
Pratt, Kathryn Mary .... **Portland, OR**
Pratt, Kenneth .... Yountville, CA
Pratt, Kent S. .... West Palm Beach, FL
Pratt, Kevin B. .... Bradenton, FL
Pratt, Kim Adams .... **Kent, WA**
Pratt, Larissa S. .... **Portland, ME**
Pratt, Laurie K. .... **Tuscaloosa, AL**
Pratt, Lawrence D. .... Columbus, OH
Pratt, Leslie C. .... Montpelier, VT
Pratt, Lewellyn H. .... **Bloomington, IN**
Pratt, Linda Raspolich .... Fort Lauderdale, FL
Pratt, Lisa .... Bradenton, FL
Pratt, Marcel A., Jr. .... Philadelphia, PA
Pratt, Marcia W. .... Birmingham, AL
Pratt, Mark David .... Birmingham, AL
Pratt, Mark F. .... Hillsboro, TX
Pratt, Mary E. .... **Morristown, NJ**
Pratt & Melville, LLP .... Lexington, KY
Pratt, Merle B. .... Liverpool, NY
Pratt, Michael C. .... Rutland, VT
Pratt, Michael K. .... **Brevard, NC**
Pratt, Michael M. .... **Washington, DC**
Pratt, Neal F. .... **Portland, ME**
Pratt, P. Edward .... **Huntsville, TN**
Knoxville, TN
Pratt, Paul C. .... Okemos, MI
Pratt, Paul E. .... Salt Lake City, UT
Pratt, Paula P. .... **Orlando, FL**
Pratt, Peter E., Jr. .... Houston, TX
Pratt, Peter R. .... Las Vegas, NV
Pratt & Pratt .... **Bloomington, IN**
Pratt & Pratt .... Corpus Christi, TX
Pratt & Pratt, A Legal Professional Association
Piqua, OH
Pratt and Pratt, P.C. .... Bloomington, IL
Pratt, Preston A. .... Oakley, KS
Oberlin, KS
Pratt, R. Wesley .... **San Francisco, CA**
Pratt, Ralph D. .... New Castle, PA
Pratt, Ralph E. .... Independence, MO
Pratt, Randal D. .... Yorktown Heights, NY
Pratt, Randall E. (IBA) .... **Kansas City, MO**
Pratt, Randall L. .... **Danvers, MA**
Pratt, Reagan D. .... **Houston, TX**
Pratt, Rex K. .... Ridgeway, SC
Pratt, Richard G. .... Charlotte, NC
Pratt, Richard Hale .... **Doylestown, PA**
Pratt, Richard J. .... **Washington, DC**
Pratt, Richard L. .... Eudora, AR
Pratt, Richard Wesley .... Santa Rosa, CA
Pratt, Robert A. .... **Santa Rosa, CA**
Pratt, Robert A. .... Piqua, OH
Pratt, Robert L. .... **Raleigh, NC**
Pratt, Robert M. .... Columbia, NJ
Pratt, Robert S. .... **Rutland, VT**
Pratt, Robert W. .... Wilmette, IL
Pratt, Robert W. .... Des Moines, IA
Pratt, Russell .... Denver, CO
Pratt, S. Mason, Jr. .... **Portland, ME**
Pratt, Samuel H. .... Canton, OH
Pratt & Sanderford, P.C. .... **Arlington, TX**
Dallas, TX
Fort Worth, TX
Pratt, Sara K.
Department of Housing and Urban
Development,
Office of General Counsel, GV
Pratt, Sarah L. .... Springfield, IL
Pratt, Scott O. .... Portland, OR
Pratt, Scott R. .... Houston, TX
Pratt, Scott R., P.C. .... Houston, TX
Pratt, Scott T. .... **Long Beach, CA**
Pratt, Sharon Glenn .... **San Jose, CA**
Pratt, Shawn Borrelli .... Rhinebeck, NY

Pratt, Sherease R.
Pension Benefit Guaranty Corporation,
Office of the General Counsel, GV
Pratt, Sherman W. .... Arlington, VA
Pratt and Singer .... Middletown, OH
Pratt, Stacey L. .... **San Francisco, CA**
Pratt, Staci J. .... **Kansas City, MO**
Pratt, Stacy J. .... **Wichita, KS**
Pratt, Stanley S. .... Yakima, WA
Pratt, Stanley S., Inc., P.S. .... Yakima, WA
Pratt, Stephen R. .... Kansas City, MO
Pratt, Steven H. .... **Indianapolis, IN**
Pratt, Steven H. .... **Medford, OR**
Pratt, Stewart D. .... Utica, NY
Pratt, Susan C. .... Tacoma, WA
Pratt, Teresa Garrison .... Eufaula, OK
Pratt, Thomas K. .... **Chicago, IL**
Pratt, Thomas V. .... Rancho Cucamonga, CA
Pratt, Timothy A. .... **Kansas City, MO**
Pratt & Tobin, P.C. .... East Alton, IL
Pratt, Victoria F. .... **Roseland, NJ**
Pratt Vreeland Kennelly Martin & White Ltd. .... **Rutland, VT**
Pratt, Walter G. .... New Hartford, NY
Pratt, Warren T. .... **Philadelphia, PA**
Pratt, Wayne F. .... Detroit, MI
Pratt, Willard R., III .... Vernon, NY
Pratt, William D. .... Mineral Wells, TX
Pratt, William H. .... **Washington, DC**
Pratt, William H. .... **New York, NY**
Pratt, William H. .... New York, NY
Pratt, William H. .... **Fairfax, VA**
Pratt, William J., Jr. .... Daingerfield, TX
Pratt, William K. .... Northridge, CA
Pratt, William L. .... **New Orleans, LA**
Pratt, William R. .... **Clinton, TN**
Pratt, William T. .... New York, NY
Pratt, Wyatt B. .... Princeton, NJ
Pratta, Matthew .... Spring House, PA
Pratte, Deborah .... **Tucson, AZ**
Pratte, Geoffrey L. .... Farmington, MO
Pratte, Kenneth W. .... Farmington, MO
Pratte, Robert J. .... **Minneapolis, MN**
Pratte, Robert P. .... Pasadena, CA
Pratter, Gene E. K. .... **Philadelphia, PA**
Pratter, Robert L. .... **Philadelphia, PA**
Pratter, S. Jerome .... **St. Louis, MO**
Pratt-Thomas, E. Douglas .... **Charleston, SC**
Pratt-Thomas, Pearce, Epting & Walker, P.A. .... **Charleston, SC**
Pratzel, Alan David .... **St. Louis, MO**
Praught, Allan .... Dedham, MA
Praul, Douglas R. .... Doylestown, PA
Prause, Carol J. .... McMinnville, OR
Prause, D. Marsh .... **Greensboro, NC**
Prause, Ty .... Columbus, TX
Prauser, Larry A. .... **Columbus, KS**
Pravda, David A. .... Scarsdale, NY
Pravda, Howard .... **San Juan, PR**
Pravda, Joel A. .... New City, NY
Pravda, Richard E. .... **New York, NY**
Pravda, Susan E. .... **Boston, MA**
Pravecek, Jody K. .... **Chicago, IL**
Pravel, Bernarr Roe .... **Houston, TX**
Pravel Intellectual Property Law, P.C.
Alexandria, VA
Pravel, James W. .... Alexandria, VA
Praver, David L. .... **Ventura, CA**
Praver, Roy A. .... Titusville, FL
Pravlik, Carolyn Smith .... Washington, DC
Praw, Albert Z. .... Los Angeles, CA
Prawer, Bonnie L. .... Minneapolis, MN
Prawer, Harry S. .... **New York, NY**
Prawer, Murray H. .... **New York, NY**
Pray, Amelia Greeson .... Austell, GA
Pray, Donald E. .... **Tulsa, OK**
Pray, Eileen W. .... Madison, WI
Pray, Francis C., Jr. .... **Charlotte, NC**
Pray, Francis (Frank) X. .... Irvine, CA
Pray, James L. .... **Des Moines, IA**
Pray, James P. .... Tucson, AZ
Pray, Price, Williams & Russell
Long Beach, CA
Los Angeles, CA
Pray, Ralph M., III .... **San Diego, CA**
Pray, Richard .... San Diego, CA
Pray, Stephen H. .... Eureka, MT
Pray, Susan G. .... **Denver, CO**
Pray, Thorsten John .... **San Francisco, CA**
Pray, Walker, Jackman, Williamson & Marlar, A Professional Corporation
Oklahoma City, OK
Tulsa, OK
Pray, William E. .... Leavenworth, KS
Prayor, Sharon E. .... Chicago, IL
Praywell, Diane Yuen .... **Honolulu, HI**
Prazak, Muriel .... Clinton, WI
Prazan, Susan E. .... Omaha, NE
Prazen, Raymond R. .... El Cajon, CA
Prchal, Honza Jan Ferdinand
Birmingham, AL
Preacher, Thomas H. .... Bettendorf, IA
Preate, Christopher J. .... **Princeton, NJ**
Preate, Elizabeth D. .... **Cherry Hill, NJ**
Philadelphia, PA
Preate, Robert A. .... **Scranton, PA**
Preaus, Eugene R. .... **New Orleans, LA**
Preaus, Frederick F. .... San Diego, CA
Preaus, Roddy & Krebs, L.L.P.
New Orleans, LA
Prebeg, Matthew J.M. .... **Houston, TX**
Prebenda, Donald J. .... Bloomfield Hills, MI
Prebensen, Eileen A. .... Winchester, MA
Prebich, Richard E. .... Hibbing, MN
Prebil, Kathleen A. .... Phoenix, AZ
Prebil, Richard L. .... Elk Grove Village, IL
Prebil, Thomas J. .... **St. Louis, MO**
Prebil, William J. .... **St. Paul, MN**

Prebish, Gregory A. .... Miami, FL
Prebish, Ronald F. .... Deerfield, IL
Prebish, Steven M. .... **Chicago, IL**
Preble, Gary A. .... Olympia, WA
Preble, Judith .... New York, NY
Preble, Laurence G. .... **Los Angeles, CA**
New York, NY
Preble, Louise H. .... Gaithersburg, MD
Preble, Robin L. .... **Minneapolis, MN**
Preblud, Arlan I. .... Denver, CO
Prebula, Mary A. .... **Duluth, GA**
Prebula, Mary A., P.C. .... **Atlanta, GA**
Duluth, GA
Lawrenceville, GA
Prebut, David S. .... **New York, NY**
Precario, Peter A. .... Columbus, OH
Precella, Karen S. .... **Fort Worth, TX**
Precht, Robert .... Mesa, AZ
Precht, Robert E. .... New York, NY
Prechtel, David R. .... **Indianapolis, IN**
Prechtel-Kluskens, Claire
National Archives And Records
Administration,
Office of Records Services-Washington,
D.C., GV
Prechtl, Jerome S. .... **Elmira, NY**
Prechtl, Roderick V., Jr. .... Ormond Beach, FL
Preciado, Arthur C. .... Pasadena, CA
Preciado, Gerry .... **Modesto, CA**
Preckel, Allan J. .... San Diego, CA
Preckwinkle, George W. .... Springfield, IL
Precobb, John T. .... Newton, MA
Precopio, Lizbeth A. .... **Fort Washington, PA**
Precour, Penny J. .... Tomah, WI
Precourt, Lyman A. .... **Milwaukee, WI**
Precup, Ronald G. .... **Alexandria, VA**
Pred, Deborah R. .... Omaha, NE
Pred, Ronald S. .... **Denver, CO**
Pred, Ronald S., P.C. .... **Denver, CO**
Pred, Stanley M. .... North Miami Beach, FL
Predan, Robert A. M. .... **Oak Brook, IL**
Preddie, LaVerne T.
Department of Commerce,
Patent and Trademark Office, GV
Preddy, Daniel .... **Fremont, CA**
Preddy, Laurie Bradsher .... Butner, NC
Preddy, Margery Sickles .... Broomall, PA
Preddy, Rose Marie Karadsheh
Jacksonville, FL
Prediletto, Halpin, Scharnikow, & Smart, P.S.
Yakima, WA
Prediletto, L. E. .... Yakima, WA
Predko, Christopher J.
Grand Rapids, MI
Predmore, Paul M. .... **Syracuse, NY**
Predovich, Walter J. .... Pueblo, CO
Pree, James Matthew .... St. Louis, MO
Pree, Mark W. .... Olympia, WA
Preece, James E. .... Bemidji, MN
Preece, Jane S. .... Los Angeles, CA
Preece, Joshua J. .... **Seattle, WA**
Preece, Katherine Jean .... New York, NY
Preece, Larry D. .... **Santa Ana, CA**
Preece, Lynn S. .... **Chicago, IL**
Preece, Robert S. .... Dallas, TX
Preefer, Jeffrey J., P.C. .... Cupertino, CA
Preefer, John J. .... New York, NY
Preeo, Robert L. .... **Denver, CO**
Preeo, Silverman & Green, P.C.
Denver, CO
Preg, Nancy Worgan .... **Seattle, WA**
Preg O'Donnell & Gillett PLLC
Seattle, WA
Preg O'Donnell Sargeant & Gillett PLLC
Anchorage, AK
Preg, Theodore L. .... **Seattle, WA**
Pregaldin, Anton J. .... Clayton, MO
Pregeant, Gene .... Hammond, LA
Pregel, Leslie E. .... Harrisburg, PA
Pregenzer, Ruth O. .... **Albuquerque, NM**
Pregerson, Dean D. .... Los Angeles, CA
Pregerson, Harry .... Woodland Hills, CA
Pregerson, James A. .... Santa Monica, CA
Pregerson, Scott B. .... Los Angeles, CA
Pregler, Bruce M. .... **Royal Oak, MI**
Pregliasco, Delores Hill .... **Louisville, KY**
Pregmon, Patricia L. .... **Philadelphia, PA**
Pregmon, Patricia L.
Plymouth Meeting, PA
Prego, Mayda .... **Miami, FL**
Pregulman, Betsy .... Phoenix, AZ
Preheim, Elissa J. .... **Washington, DC**
Preheim, Lynn D. .... **Wichita, KS**
Preheim, Randall F. .... Middletown, OH
Preheim, Randall L. .... Denver, CO
Prehn, David W. .... **Corpus Christi, TX**
Prehn, John C., Jr. .... Joliet, IL
Prehn, Roger B. .... Tucson, AZ
Prehoda, Donald P., Jr. .... **Laramie, WY**
Prehoda, Leonard and Janack, L.L.C.
Laramie, WY
Prehoditch, Thomas P. .... **Austin, TX**
Preier, Katalin S. .... West Hartford, CT
Preikszas, Otto J., Jr. .... **Boston, MA**
Prein, Edward J. .... **Indianapolis, IN**
Preiner, Barbara Ann .... Chicago, IL
Preira, Richard J. .... Miami Beach, FL
Preis, Aron .... **Pittsburgh, PA**
Preis, Bergeron & Atchison
Baton Rouge, LA
Preis, E. Fredrick, Jr. .... **New Orleans, LA**
Preis, Edwin G., Jr. .... **Lafayette, LA**
New Orleans, LA
Preis, James J. .... Los Angeles, CA
Preis, Julie C. .... **Los Angeles, CA**

Preis Kraft & Roy, A Professional Law Corporation ....Baton Rouge, LA
Lafayette, LA
New Orleans, LA
Houston, TX
Preis, Lehman K. ....Baton Rouge, LA
Preis, Michael Stuart ....Pasadena, CA
Preis, Nancy E. ....Arlington, MA
Preis, Phillip W. ....Baton Rouge, LA
Preisel, Clayton E. ....Lapeer, MI
Preiser, Godfrey K., Jr. ....Murray Hill, NJ
Preiser, Janice L. ....Getzville, NY
Preiser, Stanley E. ....West Palm Beach, FL
Charleston, WV
Preisig, Anne Curi ....Newton, MA
Preiskel, Barbara Scott ....New York, NY
Preiskel, Robert H., (P.C.) ....New York, NY
Preisler, Sarah ....Burbank, CA
Preisner, Peter J. ....Colchester, CT
Preiss, David L. ....Oakland, CA
Preiss, Jeremy O. ....Washington, DC
Preiss, Richard T. ....New York, NY
Preiss, Tamara L.
Federal Communications Commission, Common Carrier Bureau, GV
Preiss, William S. ....St. Louis, MO
Preisse, Dana ....Columbus, OH
Preisser, Stephen P. ....Pensacola, FL
Preissman, Bruce ....Southampton, PA
Preissman, Isidore Gordon ....Baltimore, MD
Preite, Daniel A. ....Walnut Creek, CA
Preite, Ralph E. ....New York, NY
Prejean, Steven L. ....New Orleans, LA
Prejeant, Robert J. ....Houma, LA
Prejeant, Robert J., A Prof. Law Corp.
Houma, LA
Prekel, Leonard J. ....Troy, MI
Preketes, Susan Philpott ....Flint, MI
Prekop, Joseph Emil ....Cleveland, OH
Prelac, John M. ....Canton, OH
Preleski, David J. ....Bristol, CT
Preleski, Stephen G. ....Bristol, CT
Prelipp, Sandra U. ....Raleigh, NC
Prell, Cheryl S. ....Los Angeles, CA
Prell, Frances E. ....Chicago, IL
Prell, Frog, III ....Stillwater, MN
Prell, Owen T. ....San Francisco, CA
Preller, David J., Jr. ....Towson, MD
Preller, David J., Sr. ....Towson, MD
Preller, Laura Virginia ....Albany, GA
Preller, Patrick Shane ....Bel Air, MD
Preller and Preller ....Towson, MD
Prelock, Edward P. ....North Hollywood, CA
Preloznik and Associates, S.C. ....Madison, WI
Preloznik, Joseph F. ....Madison, WI
Prelutsky, Steven D. ....Atlanta, GA
Prem, David Lawrence ....Cincinnati, OH
Prem, F. Herbert, Jr. ....New York, NY
Prem, Robert Curtis ....Baltimore, MD
Ellicott City, MD
Prem, Saltzman & Jablon, LLC
Baltimore, MD
Ellicott City, MD
Severna Park, MD
Prem, Wayne T. ....Baltimore, MD
Premack, Budd A. ....Minneapolis, MN
Premack, Paul ....San Antonio, TX
Preman, Vance C. ....Overland Park, KS
Kansas City, MO
Preman, Vance C., A Prof. Corp.
Overland Park, KS
Kansas City, MO
Premeau, Donald C. ....Globe, AZ
Premeau, Patricia A. ....Phoenix, AZ
Preminger, Clifford J. ....Washington, DC
Preminger, Daniel M. ....Cape May, NJ
Philadelphia, PA
Preminger, Daniel M., P.C. ....Camden, NJ
Cape May, NJ
Philadelphia, PA
Preminger, David S. ....New York, NY
Preminger, Eve M. ....New York, NY
Preminger, Katherine M. ....New York, NY
Preminger, Richard J. ....Westport, CT
Premisler, Andrew M. ....New York, NY
Premisler, Michael M. ....Carle Place, NY
Premo, Brian D. ....Albany, NY
Premo, Edward F., II ....Rochester, NY
Premo, Gilbert J. ....San Francisco, CA
Premo, John G. ....Western Springs, IL
Premo, Patrick E. ....Palo Alto, CA
Premo, Roger L. ....Farmington Hills, MI
Premo, Stephen W. ....Santa Cruz, CA
Prempas, Louis J. ....Westchester, IL
Prempeh, Henry Kwasi ....Washington, DC
Premysler, Debra ....Department of Justice, Executive Office for Immigration Review, GV
Prena, Karen L. ....Chicago, IL
Prena, Ronald A. ....Farmington Hills, MI
Prenda, Brian J. ....Fall River, MA
Prenda, Bruce J. ....Lincoln, NE
Prendergast, Barbara L. ....Syracuse, NY
Prendergast, Bradley E. ....Chicago, IL
Prendergast, Brian J. ....Baton Rouge, LA
Prendergast, D. Elizabeth ....New York, NY
Prendergast, David A. ....Eureka, CA
Prendergast & DelPrincipe
Evergreen Park, IL
Prendergast, George ....Marshall, TX
Prendergast, Gerald A. ....Evergreen Park, IL
Prendergast, Harold J. ....Laredo, TX
Prendergast, Heather A. ....Joplin, MO
Prendergast, James ....Chicago, IL
Prendergast, James D. ....Los Angeles, CA
Prendergast, James E. ....Wayne, PA
Prendergast, James J. ....Philadelphia, PA
Prendergast, James W. ....Boston, MA
Prendergast, Jean M. ....Chicago, IL
Prendergast, John A. ....Washington, DC
Prendergast, Kevin P. ....Cleveland, OH
Prendergast, M. Lisa ....Owensboro, KY
Prendergast, Marlene H. ....Palo Alto, CA
Prendergast, Maurice E. ....Cleveland, OH
Prendergast, Michael G. ....Jacksonville, FL
Prendergast, Michael J. ....Pittsburgh, PA
Prendergast, Norman W. ....New Orleans, LA
Prendergast, Patrick J. ....Murphysboro, IL
Prendergast, Paul A. ....Littleton, CO
Prendergast, Paul G. ....Murphysboro, IL
Prendergast, Richard F. ....Chicago, IL
Prendergast, Richard J. ....Chicago, IL
Prendergast, Richard J., Ltd. ....Chicago, IL
Prendergast, Richard M.
Department of Justice, GV
Prendergast, Robin M. ....Los Angeles, CA
Prendergast, Stephen D. ....Fort Wayne, IN
Prendergast, Terry N. ....Sioux Falls, SD
Prendergast, Virginia A. ......Western Springs, IL
Prendergast, William F. ....Montgomery, AL
Prendergast, William F. ....Chicago, IL
Prendergast, William P. ....Maywood, IL
Prendergast Lesnett, Angela ....McLean, VA
Prendeville, Mark T. ....Belleville, MI
Prendiville, John R. ....Chicago, IL
Prenetta, James P., Jr. ....Stamford, CT
Prenger, Ronald J. ....Jefferson City, MO
Prenger, Ronald J. ....Jefferson City, MO
Prenkert, Jamie D. ....Indianapolis, IN
Prenn, Kathryn J. ....Eau Claire, WI
Prenner, Lisa-Joy ....Walnut Creek, CA
Preno, Thomas W. ....Overland Park, KS
Prenovost, Normandin, Bergh & Dawe, A Professional Corporation ...Santa Ana, CA
Prenovost, Thomas J., Jr. ....Santa Ana, CA
Prensky, David N. ....Washington, DC
Prensky, Harriet P. ....Mill Valley, CA
Prensky & Tobin ....Mill Valley, CA
Prensky, William J. ....Hartford, CT
Prensner, Robert C. ....Boston, MA
Prentakis, Konstantinos E. ....Salem, MA
Prentice, Barbara Mayzik ....Montpelier, VT
Prentice, Chad M. ....Santa Barbara, CA
Prentice, Chris D. ....Plainview, TX
Prentice, Dara Derryberry ....Atlanta, GA
Prentice, David A. ....Sacramento, CA
Prentice, Dixon W. ....Indianapolis, IN
Prentice, E. Miles, III ....New York, NY
Prentice, F. Sheldon ....Burlington, VT
Prentice, John F. ....San Francisco, CA
Prentice Law Firm, The ....Plainview, TX
Prentice, Lois ....San Francisco, CA
Prentice, M. Scott ....Sacramento, CA
Prentice, Paul E. ....Portland, OR
Prentice, Rebecca L. ....Hollywood, CA
Prentice, Richard D. ....Florham Park, NJ
Prentice, R. J. ....Clarksville, IN
Prentice, Robert A. ....Philadelphia, PA
Prentice, Sally A. ....Richfield, OH
Prentice & Scott ....San Francisco, CA
Prentice, Stephen P. ....San Diego, CA
Prentice, Timothy H. ....Elkins, WV
Prentice, Walter C. ....Austin, TX
Prentice, William H. ....Portland, OR
Prentis, Richard F., Jr. ....Durham, NC
Prentiss, Charles J. ....New York, NY
Prentiss, David G. ....New Bedford, MA
Prentiss, David G., P.C. ....New Bedford, MA
Prentiss, David M. ....Boston, MA
Prentiss, Donald C. ....Elizabeth City, NC
Prentiss, John M., Jr. ....Littleton, CO
Prentiss, Linda H. ....Morristown, NJ
Prentiss, Paul E. ....Milwaukee, WI
Prentiss, Paul F. ....Omaha, NE
Prentiss, R. Daniel ....Providence, RI
Prentiss, Richard J., Jr. ....Palm Beach, FL
Prentiss, Robert A. ....Tallahassee, FL
Prentiss, Stephen M. ....Roseland, NJ
Prentke, Richard Ottesen ....Seattle, WA
Prentnicks, Mary ....St. Paul, MN
Prenton, James H. ....San Diego, CA
Prenty, Mark ....Department of Commerce, Patent and Trademark Office, GV
Preonas, George E. ....Los Angeles, CA
Preovolos, Michael J. ....Vallejo, CA
Preovolos, Penelope Athene
San Francisco, CA
Prephan, Michael ....Toledo, OH
Prephan, Michael, Jr. ....Perrysburg, OH
Prero, Elisha Michael ....Skokie, IL
Prero, Judah ....Corona, NY
Presant, Howard B. ....New York, NY
Presant, Sanford C. ....Los Angeles, CA
Presberg, Andrew D. ....Islandia, NY
Presberg, Andrew D., P.C., Law Offices of
Central Islip, NY
Islandia, NY
Mineola, NY
Riverhead, NY
Presberg, Leonard ....Fayetteville, GA
Presbrey & Amoni, P.C. ....Aurora, IL
Presbrey, Kim Edward ....Aurora, IL
Presburger, Paul ....Culver City, CA
Presby, Ellen A. ....Dallas, TX
Presby, Rosamond A. ....Lebanon, PA
Presby, Wayne W., II ....Littleton, NH
Prescott, Allie J., III ....Memphis, TN
Prescott, Andrew B. ....Providence, RI
Prescott, Arthur C.
Department of Commerce, Patent and Trademark Office, GV
Prescott, Barbara C. ....Hanover, NH
Prescott, Bryan K. ....Montgomery, AL
Prescott, Bullard & McLeod
New Bedford, MA
Prescott, Byron C. ....Dallas, TX
Prescott, Carol S. ....Denver, CO
Prescott, Charles A. ....New York, NY
Prescott, Charles J. ....Sarasota, FL
Prescott, Charles J., P.A. ....Sarasota, FL
Prescott, Christopher A. ....Portland, OR
Prescott & Company ....Point Roberts, WA
Prescott, Dana E. ....Saco, ME
Prescott, Darrell ....New York, NY
Prescott, David P. ....Princeton, NJ
Prescott, Elizabeth A. ....Denver, CO
Prescott, Emily ....San Francisco, CA
Prescott, Gary M. ....Columbus, OH
Prescott, George M. ....Lincoln, RI
Prescott, Harris Howard ....Tulsa, OK
Prescott, Howitt, Manchester & Andruschat
East Aurora, NY
Springville, NY
Prescott, J. Phillip ....Dallas, TX
Prescott, Jack L. ....New Brighton, MN
Prescott, Jack W. ....Belton, TX
Prescott, John C., Jr. ....Boston, MA
Prescott, John F., Jr. ....Indianapolis, IN
Prescott, John F., Jr. ....Tonawanda, NY
Prescott, Karen Comisar ....Cincinnati, OH
Prescott, Larry W. ....Houston, TX
Prescott Lemoine Jamieson & Nelson, P.A.
Old Orchard Beach, ME
Portland, ME
Saco, ME
Prescott, Loren D. ....Seattle, WA
Prescott, Loren D., Jr. ....Bellevue, WA
Prescott, Margaret ....Manchester, NH
Prescott, Michael K. ....Providence, RI
Prescott, Michael R. ....Oklahoma City, OK
Prescott and Pearson, P.A.
New Brighton, MN
Prescott & Prescott ....Orange, CA
Prescott & Prescott ....Dallas, TX
Prescott, R. David ....Tallahassee, FL
Prescott, Richard ....Minneapolis, MN
Prescott, Rita E. ....Media, PA
Prescott, Ronald Alan ....Castle Rock, CO
Prescott, Tom ....Point Roberts, WA
Prescott, Tonya E. ....Orange, CA
Prescott, Valerie E. ....Orange, CA
Prescott, Victoria ....Fort Worth, TX
Prescott, Walter H. ....Mystic, CT
Prescott, Warren P. ....Bloomingdale, IL
Prescott, Wayne H. ....Austin, TX
Prescott, William G. ....Boise, ID
Prescott, William P. ....Lorain, OH
Prescott, William S. ....Glenmont, NY
Prescott, Wm. Gordon ....Pittsfield, MA
Prescott, Wm. Roger ....Burlington, VT
Presel, Alan Marc ....Raleigh, NC
Present, Harris L. ....New York, NY
Present, Jeffrey A. ....Milwaukee, WI
Present, Jeffrey D. ....Garden City, NY
Present, Lewis A ....San Diego, CA
Present, Michael ....New York, NY
Present, Thomas R. ....Detroit, MI
Present, Thomas R., P.C. ....Detroit, MI
Present, Wendy D. ....Chicago, IL
Present-Podolak, Stephanie ....Brooklyn, NY
Presenza, Louis J. ....Philadelphia, PA
Preservati, Nicholas S. ....Chicago, IL
Presher, Daniel A. ....Oakland, CA
Presiado, Leo J. ....Irvine, CA
Presicci, Danny D. ....Boca Raton, FL
Preska, Loretta A. ....New York, NY
Presky, Joan E. ....San Francisco, CA
Preslan, Thom R. ....Denver, CO
Preslar, Holly A. ....Grants Pass, OR
Preslar, Janis W. ....Oklahoma City, OK
Preslar, Nancy R. ....Fort Oglethorpe, GA
Preslar, Stephen F. ....El Paso, TX
Presley, Buddy B., Jr. ....Chattanooga, TN
Presley, Gene F. ....Atlanta, GA
Presley, J. Hobson, Jr. ....Birmingham, AL
Presley, Joseph K. ....Nashville, TN
Presley, Kirk R. ....Kansas City, MO
Presley, M. Suzanne ....Boston, MA
Presley, Margaret G. ....Santa Monica, CA
Presley, Mari M. ....Tallahassee, FL
Presley, Nikki A. ....Newport Beach, CA
Presley, R. Carlton ....Austin, TX
Presley, Russell Vern, II ....Grundy, VA
Presley, Susan M. ....Fort Wayne, IN
Presley, Wilma E. ....Orange, CA
Presley, Wilma E., A Professional Corporation ....Orange, CA
Presnal & Associates, P.C. ....Austin, TX
Presnal, James K. ....Austin, TX
Presnell, E. Todd ....Nashville, TN
Presnell, Gary L. ....Raleigh, NC
Presnell, Gregory A. ....Orlando, FL
Presnell, Lacy M., III ....Raleigh, NC
Presnell, Misti D. ....Indianapolis, IN
Presnell, Paul T., Jr. ....Quincy, FL
Presney, Kelly and Presney ....Chatham, IL
Springfield, IL
Presney, Paul E. ....Springfield, IL
Presney, Paul E., II ....Springfield, IL
Presnick, David M. ....Cocoa, FL
Melbourne, FL
Presnick, John S. ....New York, NY
Preso, Timothy J. ....Washington, DC
Presperin, Thomas S. ....Wheaton, IL
Press, Adelita C. ....New York, NY
Press, Alan R. ....Arlington Heights, IL
Press, Allen P. ....St. Louis, MO
Press, Anthony L. ....Los Angeles, CA
Press, Barbara H. ....New York, NY
Press, Bryan D. ....Bloomfield, NJ
Press, Caren S. ....Englewood, CO
Press, Carol L. ....Philadelphia, PA
Press, Caroline S. ....New York, NY
Press, Carolyn B. ....Cumberland, MD
Press, Charles J. ....San Francisco, CA
Press, Cheryl E. ....Treasury Department, Internal Revenue Service, GV
Press, Daniel M. ....McLean, VA
Press, Daniel S. ....Washington, DC
Press, Danya Renee ....New York, NY
Press, David ....Twin Peaks, CA
Press, David ....New York, NY
Press, David L. ....New York, NY
Press, Dionne Susan ....Houston, TX
Press, Donald ....New York, NY
Press, Douglas M. ....Walnut Creek, CA
Press, Elliot ....New York, NY
Press, Elliot R. ....Brooklyn, NY
Press, Erich P. ....St. Louis, MO
Press, Estaire R. ....Victorville, CA
Press, Fredric A. ....Bethesda, MD
Press, Howard S. ....Fairfield, NJ
Press, Ira M. ....New York, NY
Press, J. Bertram ....Minneapolis, MN
Press, J. Jeffrey ....Montclair, NJ
Press, Jay A. ....Woodbury, NY
Press, Joel C. ....New York, NY
Press, Joseph R. ....Bayonne, NJ
Press, Katherine J. ....Columbus, OH
Press, Lawrence S. ....Gahanna, OH
Press & Long ....Northfield, NJ
Press, Lyle Bennett ....Treasury Department, Internal Revenue Service, GV
Press, Marc B. ....Providence, RI
Press, Marc P. ....Roseland, NJ
Press, Mark D. ....Miami Beach, FL
Press, Mark David, Law Offices of, P.A., Law Offices of ....Miami Beach, FL
Press, Mark L. ....Ardsley, NY
Press, Martin R., (P.A.)
Fort Lauderdale, FL
Press, Matthew ....New York, NY
Press, Michael R. ....West Orange, NJ
Press, Michael S. ....New York, NY
Press, Michelle Lynn ....Washington, DC
Press, Michelle R. ....Los Angeles, CA
Press, Morton H., Law Offices of
Washington, DC
Press, Richard L. ....Northfield, NJ
Press, Russell G., Jr. ....Glastonbury, CT
Press, Samuel H. ....Burlington, VT
Press, Sharon B. ....Tallahassee, FL
Press, Stephen M. ....Los Angeles, CA
Press, Steve ....West Palm Beach, FL
Press, Steven M. ....Minneapolis, MN
Press, Steven R. ....Atlanta, GA
Press, Theodore L. ....Washington, DC
Press, Thomas Jay ....Houston, TX
Press, Tony ....Sacaton, AZ
Pressberg, Harold M. ....Rochelle Park, NJ
Goshen, NY
Presse, Philip R. ....Austin, TX
Pressel, Wayne M. ....Washington, DC
Pressentin & Associates ....Seattle, WA
Pressentin, Patrick E. ....Seattle, WA
Presser, Edwin ....Jacksonville, FL
Presser, Jay E. ....Chicago, IL
Presser, Jay M. ....Springfield, MA
Worcester, MA
Presser, Lawrence M. ....Lauderhill, FL
Presser, Leopold ....Garden City, NY
Presser, Lisa B. ....New York, NY
Presser, Lisa S. ....Princeton, NJ
Presser, Mitchell S. ....New York, NY
Presser, Ronald L. ....Owensboro, KY
Presser, Sheldon W. ....Burbank, CA
Presser, Stefan ....Philadelphia, PA
Presser, Stephen B. ....Chicago, IL
Pressey, James C. ....Sag Harbor, NY
Pressgrove, A. L., Jr. ....Southaven, MS
Pressgrove, L. Wayne, Jr. ....Atlanta, GA
Pressinger, Wigg & Goodstein
New York, NY
Pressler, David A. ....Hackensack, NJ
Pressler, George W. ....East Brunswick, NJ
Pressler, H. Paul, III ....Houston, TX
Pressler, James W., Jr. ....Washington, DC
Pressler, Larry ....Washington, DC
Pressler, Paul R. ....Elkhart, IN
Pressler, Robert L. ....Merrillville, IN
Pressler, Sheldon H. ....East Hanover, NJ
Pressler, Sylvia B. ....Hackensack, NJ
Pressler, Timothy A. ....Columbus, OH
Pressley, Dianah L. ....Birmingham, AL
Pressley, Donald S. ....Sacramento, CA
Pressley, Fred G., Jr. ....Columbus, OH
Pressley, Janice Y. ....Fort Myers, FL
Pressley, John F., Jr. ....Washington, DC
Pressley, Robert S. ....Austin, TX
Pressley, Ronald J. ....Philadelphia, PA
Pressley, Ronald L. ....Durham, NC
Raleigh, NC
Pressley, Samuel Nixon ....Nashville, TN
Pressley, Theresa K. ....Yanceyville, NC
Pressley, William O., Jr. ......Spartanburg, SC
Pressly, David S. ....West Palm Beach, FL
Pressly, Edwin A. ....Statesville, NC
Pressly, J. Grier, III
West Palm Beach, FL
Pressly, James B., Jr. ....Greenville, SC
Pressly, James G., Jr.
West Palm Beach, FL
Pressly & Jiloty, P.C. ....Rutland, VT
Pressly, John L., Jr. ....Columbia, SC
Pressly & Pressly, P.A. ....Palm Beach, FL
West Palm Beach, FL
Pressly, Thomas J., II ....Rutland, VT
Pressly & Thomas, P.A. ....Statesville, NC
Pressman, Adam D. ....Albany, CA
Pressman, Adam M. ....Redding, CA
Pressman, Alan ....Islandia, NY
Pressman, Alan ....New York, NY

Pressman, Arthur L. ....**Philadelphia, PA**
Pressman, Barbara W. ....Philadelphia, PA
Pressman, Charles, (P.C.) ....Chicago, IL
Pressman, David ....San Francisco, CA
Pressman, Glenn S.
Colorado Springs, CO
Pressman, Gregory P. ....**New York, NY**
Pressman, Hayward Richard ......New York, NY
Pressman, Herbert ....Philadelphia, PA
Pressman, Howard C. ....Cherry Hill, NJ
Pressman, Jay H. ....West Chester, PA
Pressman, Jennifer S. ....Baltimore, MD
Pressman, Joel M. ....**San Diego, CA**
Pressman, Judy Kolodny ....**San Diego, CA**
Pressman & Kruskal ....Cambridge, MA
Pressman, Kurt M. ....Cambridge, MA
Pressman, Mara Lynn ....**Los Angeles, CA**
Pressman, Marianne ....Cincinnati, OH
Pressman, Michael E. ....New York, NY
Pressman, Mitchell S. ....Rockville, MD
Pressman, Norman W. ....**St. Louis, MO**
Pressman, Paul B. ....Laguna Beach, CA
Pressman, Paul R. ....Department of the Army, Office, Chief of Engineers/Headquarters, U.S. Army Corps of Engineers, GV
Pressman, Paula G. ....**Hartford, CT**
Pressman & Pressman ....Philadelphia, PA
Pressman, Richard B. ....Philadelphia, PA
Pressman, Robert A. ....Conshohocken, PA
Pressman, Robert G. ....Chicago, IL
Pressman, Robert G., Ltd. ....Chicago, IL
Pressman, Ronald A. ....Malden, MA
Pressman, Sandra D. ....Rockville, MD
Pressman, Sheldon B. ....New York, NY
Pressman, Stephen G.
Environmental Protection Agency, Office of the General Counsel, GV
Pressman, Steven D. ....New York, NY
Pressman, Stewart ....**Honolulu, HI**
Pressment, Jonathan D. ....**New York, NY**
Pressnall, Christopher R. ....Springfield, IL
Presson, Jerry M. ....Orange, CT
Presson, Michelle C.
United States Court Of Appeals For The Armed Forces, GV
Presson, Robert L. ....Jefferson City, MO
Presson, Sarah Ann ....**Little Rock, AR**
Presson, Thomas F. ....**New York, NY**
Presson, William R. ....Jackson, MS
Presswood, Kendra D. ....**Bradenton, FL**
Presswood, Kendra D., P.A., Law Office of
Bradenton, FL
Prest, Joseph G. ....**Steubenville, OH**
Presta, Frank P. ....**Arlington, VA**
Presta, Joseph S. ....**Arlington, VA**
Prestage, John A. ....Houston, TX
Prestash, Patricia L. ....Oconomowoc, WI
Prestegaard, Linda ....**Rochester, NY**
Presten, D.C., III ....**Atlanta, GA**
Prester, Jackie G. ....**Memphis, TN**
Prestholt, David A. ....**Los Angeles, CA**
San Francisco, CA
Prestholt, Kleeger, Fidone & Villasenor
Los Angeles, CA
San Francisco, CA
Presti, Diane C. ....**Austin, TX**
Presti, Geralyn M. ....Cleveland, OH
Presti, John B. ....Chicago, IL
Presti, Marta L. ....**Reno, NV**
Presti, Rosario, Jr. ....Carlstadt, NJ
Presti, Vincent J., III ....**Palo Alto, CA**
Prestia, Clayton J. ....Pittsburgh, PA
Prestia, Joanne M. Scanlon ......Wilmington, DE
Prestia, Joseph ....Edinburg, TX
Prestia, Michael G., & Associates
Biloxi, MS
Prestia, Michael G., & Associates
Gulfport, MS
Prestia & Ornelas ....Edinburg, TX
Prestia, Paul F. ....**Wilmington, DE**
Valley Forge, PA
Prestia, Paul Valentine ....Brooklyn, NY
Prestia, Rosa ....Lindenhurst, NY
Prestiano, James A. ....New York, NY
Prestidge, Myra J. ....**Los Angeles, CA**
Palo Alto, CA
Prestifilippo, Rosann C. ....Westfield, NJ
Prestigiacomo, Antonina ....**Madison, WI**
Prestigiacomo, MaryAnn ....New Albany, IN
Prestininzi, James M. ....Orange, CA
Prestley, Linda Pearce ....Hartford, CT
Prestley, Martha Watts ....**Hartford, CT**
Prestley, Peter B. ....**Hartford, CT**
Presto, Dominick ....Rutherford, NJ
Presto, Frank D., III ....Pleasanton, CA
Presto, Robert S. ....Brewton, AL
Presto, Vincent F. ....Philadelphia, PA
Preston, Albert W., Jr. ....**Philadelphia, PA**
Preston, Ann ....Indianapolis, IN
Preston, Ann M. ....Pittsburgh, PA
Preston, Anne F. ....**Seattle, WA**
Preston, Arthur G., Jr. ....St. Joseph, MI
Preston, Barry L. ....Los Angeles, CA
Preston, Benjamin R. ....**Washington, DC**
Boston, MA
Preston, Brett A. ....Schenectady, NY
Preston, Brett J. ....**Tampa, FL**
Preston, Brett J. ....**Charleston, WV**
Preston, Brian ....San Jose, CA
Preston, Bruce M. ....**Phoenix, AZ**
Preston, C. Kathryn ....Columbus, OH
Preston, Carlton L.
Equal Employment Opportunity Commission, Office of the General Counsel, GV
Preston, Charles A. ....Westerville, OH
Preston, Charles G. ....Great Falls, VA
Preston, Charles G., P.C. ....Great Falls, VA
Preston, Charles M. ....Salisbury, MD
Preston, Charles M. ....**Westminster, MD**
Preston, Cheryl Bailey ....Provo, UT
Preston & Cowan, L.L.P.
New Orleans, LA
Houston, TX
Preston, Craig ....Accomac, VA
Preston, Damon Loyd ....Richmond, KY
Preston, David E. ....**Grand Rapids, MI**
Preston, David M. ....**Bloomfield Hills, MI**
Preston, David R. ....San Diego, CA
Preston, David S. ....**Sarasota, FL**
Preston, David W. ....**Kansas City, MO**
Preston, Diana L. ....**Washington, DC**
Preston, Douglas G. ....New York, NY
Preston, Dwight ....**Elizabethtown, KY**
Preston, E. Page ....Virginia Beach, VA
Preston, Edward F. ....**Valdosta, GA**
Preston and Elliott ....Chevy Chase, MD
Preston, Eric Likins ....**Omaha, NE**
Preston & Flick ....**Flagstaff, AZ**
Sedona, AZ
Preston, Frank E. ....**Santa Rosa, CA**
Preston, Frank W. ....**San Francisco, CA**
Preston, Frederick M. ....Ashland, OH
Preston, G. Kline, IV ....**Nashville, TN**
Preston, Gabriel N. ....**West Chester, PA**
Preston, Gary R. ....**St. Louis, MO**
Preston Gates & Ellis LLP
Anchorage, AK
Irvine, CA
Los Angeles, CA
San Francisco, CA
Coeur d'Alene, ID
Portland, OR
Seattle, WA
Spokane, WA
Preston Gates Ellis & Rouvelas Meeds LLP
Washington, DC
Preston, George ....Scottsdale, AZ
Preston, George L. ....Paris, TX
Preston, George W. ....**Logan, UT**
Preston, Gregory R. ....Forest Hills, NY
Preston, Gregory W. ....**Irvine, CA**
Preston, H. LeBaron ....Columbia, MD
Preston, Harry S. ....Flint, MI
Preston, Henry A. ....Chicago, IL
Preston, Hilde D. ....Great Falls, VA
Preston, Hubert M. ....Muskegon, MI
Preston, Hugh L. ....Ukiah, CA
Preston, J. Scott ....Paintsville, KY
Preston, James B. ....Visalia, CA
Preston, James B., A Professional Corporation
Visalia, CA
Preston, James E. ....Phoenix, AZ
Preston, James E. ....**Burlington, VT**
Preston, James G. ....Oyster Bay, NY
Preston, James M. ....Cambridge, MA
Preston, James Y. ....**Charlotte, NC**
Preston, Janet D. ....**Parsons, WV**
Preston, Jeffrey ....Catlettsburg, KY
Preston, Jerome, Jr. ....Boston, MA
Preston, John A., (P.C.) ....Chino Valley, AZ
Preston, John B. ....Camillus, NY
Preston, John B. ....Virginia Beach, VA
Preston, John D. ....Paintsville, KY
Preston, John E. ....Woodland Hills, CA
Preston, John G. ....Brookfield, IL
Preston, John G. ....**Worcester, MA**
Preston, John M. ....San Diego, CA
Preston, John R. ....**Oklahoma City, OK**
Preston, John S. ....**Los Angeles, CA**
Preston, Joseph A. ....Manchester, MO
Preston, Joseph E. ....Petersburg, VA
Preston, Joseph R. ....McAllen, TX
Preston, Judith C. ....Department of Justice, Civil Rights Division, GV
Preston, Kenneth G. ....Berea, OH
Preston, Kevin F. ....**Middletown, NY**
Preston, Kevin M. ....Berea, OH
Preston, Kristen K. ....Sacramento, CA
Preston, Larry L. ....**Saginaw, MI**
Preston Law Offices, P.S.C. ....Paintsville, KY
Preston, Lee S. ....Chicago, IL
Preston, Leslie J. ....Los Angeles, CA
Preston, Mariannina Erra ....Phoenix, AZ
Preston, Mark A. ....Chillicothe, OH
Preston, Mark Woolman ....Atlanta, GA
Preston, Marlene Micheel ....Austin, TX
Preston, Mary M.
Securities and Exchange Commission, Office of the General Counsel, GV
Preston, Matthew L. ....**Cedar Rapids, IA**
Preston, Matthew M. ....Louisville, KY
Preston, Michael A. ....**Kansas City, MO**
Preston, Michael L. ....**Los Angeles, CA**
Preston & Michel ....Rochester, NY
Preston, Nathaniel S. ....Chevy Chase, MD
Preston, Paul G. ....**New Orleans, LA**
Houston, TX
Preston, Peter D. ....Seattle, WA
Preston, Peter W. ....Portland, OR
Preston & Preston, P.C. ....**Douglas, GA**
Preston, Ray C. ....Juneau, AK
Preston & Reed, P.L.C.
New Smyrna Beach, FL
Preston, Richard K., II
Department of Justice, U. S. Parole Commission, GV
Preston, Richard McKim
Washington, DC
Preston, R.J. Sims ....**Boston, MA**
Preston, Robert ....**Columbus, OH**
Preston, Robert A., Jr. ....New Orleans, LA
Preston, Robert B. ....Morris Plains, NJ
Preston, Robert B. ....**Cleveland, OH**
Preston, Robert F. ....**St. Davids, PA**
Preston, Robert H. ....**Douglas, GA**
Preston, Robert H. ....Minnetonka, MN
Preston, Robert J. ....**Portland, OR**
Preston, Robert M. ....Melville, NY
Preston, Robin J. ....Seattle, WA
Preston, Roger G., Jr. ....Rochester, NY
Preston, Ronald K. ....Sonoma, CA
Preston, Russell Power ....Monroe, GA
Preston, S. Mason ....Lewisburg, WV
Preston, Scott A. ....**Los Angeles, CA**
Preston, Shawn D. ....**Fort Lauderdale, FL**
Preston, Stacey R. ....**Santa Monica, CA**
Preston, Stanley J. ....**Salt Lake City, UT**
Preston, Stanley W., III ....Chicago, IL
Preston, Stephen T. ....Park City, UT
Preston, Steven H. ....**Orlando, FL**
Preston, Susan L. ....**Kirkland, WA**
Preston, Susan P. ....Morristown, NJ
Preston, Susan T. ....**Baltimore, MD**
Preston, T. Michael ....Baltimore, MD
Preston, Thomas ....Wharton, NJ
Preston, Thomas B. ....Ochelata, OK
Preston, Thomas B. ....Houston, TX
Preston, Thomas B., Law Office of
Houston, TX
Preston, Thomas Foster ....**Memphis, TN**
Preston, Thomas M., Jr.
Treasury Department, Internal Revenue Service, GV
Preston, Thomas P. ....**Wilmington, DE**
Preston, Tracy ....**San Francisco, CA**
Preston, Vernon L. ....Findlay, OH
Preston, Victor H. ....Laguna Hills, CA
Preston, Wilbur D., Jr. ....**Baltimore, MD**
Preston & Wilkins ....Hoboken, NJ
Forest Hills, NY
Preston, William C. ....Charlottesville, VA
Preston, William D. ....**Tallahassee, FL**
Preston, William R., Jr. ....**Flagstaff, AZ**
Preston, William T.
New Smyrna Beach, FL
Preston, William W. ....**Douglas, GA**
Preston, Wilson & Crandley
Virginia Beach, VA
Preston-Cooper, Dolores ....Detroit, MI
Preston-Cooper, Dolores, P.C. ....Detroit, MI
Preston-Holguin, Rebecca A. ....Temple, TX
Prestridge, Jerry C. ....Dale, TX
Prestridge, Rogers M. ....Shreveport, LA
Prestridge, Tom H. ....Paris, TX
Prestrud, Jack E. ....Cleveland, OH
Prestwich, Howard H. ....Freeport, IL
Prestwich, Thomas L. ....**San Francisco, CA**
Prestwood, Alvin T. ....**Montgomery, AL**
Prestwood, James M. ....Andalusia, AL
Presutti & Coniglio, P.C. ....Geneseo, NY
Presutti, Margaret A. ....West Palm Beach, FL
Presutti, Michael J. ....Winter Park, FL
Presutti, Richard A., Jr. ....**New York, NY**
Presutti, Robert A. ....Geneseo, NY
Preszler, Terry J. ....Kennewick, WA
Preta, John ....**Reston, VA**
Prete, Andrew W. ....**Boston, MA**
Providence, RI
Prete, Francis C. ....Cross River, NY
Prete, Gregory T. ....Media, PA
Prete, Lorraine M. B. ....**Frederick, MD**
Pretekin, Ronald S. ....**Dayton, OH**
Prether, Amy ....Lexington, KY
Preti, Flaherty, Beliveau, Pachios & Haley, LLC ....**Augusta, ME**
Bath, ME
Portland, ME
Preti, Robert F. ....**Portland, ME**
Preti, Todd J. ....**Norfolk, VA**
Pretl, Michael A. ....Baltimore, MD
Pretlow, Eason & Pretlow, A Professional Corporation ....**Suffolk, VA**
Pretlow, Joshua, Jr. ....**Suffolk, VA**
Pretlow, T. Kirk ....**Suffolk, VA**
Pretnar, Alan A. ....Taylor Springs, IL
Pretorius, Murvel, Jr. ....**Peoria, IL**
Pretre, Andrea G. ....Long Beach, CA
Pretsch, William D. ....Kingston, NY
Pretschner, Robert M. ....**Sarasota, FL**
Pretsfelder, Steven S. ....**New York, NY**
Pretsky, Helene E. ....**Los Angeles, CA**
Pretter, Alan S. ....**Pittsburgh, PA**
Pretti, Richard A. ....**New York, NY**
Pretto, Charles J. ....San Diego, CA
Pretto, Robert A. ....Beaver Dam, WI
Pretty, George H., II ....**Charlotte, NC**
Columbia, SC
Spartanburg, SC
Pretty, Laurence H. ....**Los Angeles, CA**
Pretty, Schroeder & Poplawski, A Professional Corporation
Los Angeles, CA
Pretty, William ....Washington, DC
Pretty, William A.
United States Tax Court, GV
Prettyman, E. Barrett, Jr.
Washington, DC
Prettyman, George B.
Department of Defense, Defense Legal Services Agency, GV
Prettyman, H. C., Jr. ....Johns Island, SC
Summerville, SC
Prettyman, Henry S. ....Boca Raton, FL
Prettyman, Keith A. ....Lincoln, NE
Prettyman, Loretta Kallay ....Boca Raton, FL
Prettyman, W. Marshall ....Newark, NJ
Pretz, L. Dale ....Reading, PA
Pretz, Linda ....Pittsburgh, PA
Pretzat, Mark F. ....**Washington, DC**
Pretzel, Barry L. ....Worcester, MA
Pretzel, Lorie C. ....Raleigh, NC
Pretzel & Stouffer, Chartered ....**Chicago, IL**
Pretzer, Arthur L. ....San Leandro, CA
Preuett-Armour, Bonita K.
Alexandria, LA
Preuhs, Sandra ....Pittsburgh, PA
Preuit, Terry D. ....Gillette, WY
Preus, Christian Andrew
Minneapolis, MN
Preus, David H. ....Osceola, WI
Preusen, Scott E. ....**Waukegan, IL**
Preuss, Charles F. ....**San Francisco, CA**
Preuss, Ronald S. ....St. Louis, MO
Preuss, Stephen C. ....Tampa, FL
Preuss & Vaughn, P.A. ....Tampa, FL
Preuss Walker & Shanagher LLP
San Francisco, CA
Preusser, Donald Harold ....Richfield, MN
Prevallet, Donald E. ....**Blytheville, AR**
Prevas, John N. ....Baltimore, MD
Prevas, Konstantine J. ....Baltimore, MD
Prevas, Peter A. ....Baltimore, MD
Prevas & Prevas ....Baltimore, MD
Prevas, Stephen L. ....Baltimore, MD
Prevatt, James W., Jr. ....**Live Oak, FL**
Prevatt, Karen J. ....**Tampa, FL**
Prevatt, Preston L. ....**Miami, FL**
Prevatt & Taylor ....**Tampa, FL**
Prevatte, Elias J. ....**Southport, NC**
Prevatte, Gilbert ....**Myrtle Beach, SC**
Prevatte, James R., Jr. ....**Southport, NC**
Prevatte, Prevatte & Campbell
Southport, NC
Prevaux, Steven D. ....Tallahassee, FL
Preves, Gregory P. ....Libertyville, IL
Prevete, Diana Centrella
Garden City, NY
Prevett, Robert J. ....Dedham, MA
Prevette, Robert C. ....Grand Rapids, MI
Previant, Goldberg, Uelmen, Gratz, Miller & Brueggeman, S.C. ....Green Bay, WI
Milwaukee, WI
Waukesha, WI
Previdi, Helen Joy ....Newtown, CT
Preville, Eileen ....**Alameda, CA**
Preville•Frey, L.L.P. ....**Alameda, CA**
Hayward, CA
Oakland, CA
Previn, Matthew P. ....**New York, NY**
Previs, John R. ....**Pittsburgh, PA**
Previte, Albert S., Jr. ....Lawrence, MA
Previte, Farber & Rosen, P.C.
Rego Park, NY
Previte, Joseph J. ....Rego Park, NY
Previte, Paul V. ....Fort Worth, TX
Previte, Peter A. ....Ada, OH
Previte, Sarah E. ....Lawrence, MA
Previtera, Christine E. ....**Boston, MA**
Previti, Charles R. ....Atlantic City, NJ
Previti, Daphne J. ....San Antonio, TX
Previti, Leo ....Reno, NV
Previti, Peter ....South Miami, FL
Previto, Joseph J. ....Roslyn, NY
Previto, Michael L. ....Mineola, NY
Prévost, Ann Marie ....**New York, NY**
Prevost, Earle G. ....**Greenville, SC**
Prevost, Jeffrey J. ....Upland, CA
Prevost, Mary Frances ....San Diego, CA
Prevost, Mary L. ....Seattle, WA
Prevost, Phyllis R. ....Waynesville, NC
Prevost, Robert ....Monroe, NC
Prevot, Rapheal M., Jr. ....New York, NY
Prevoznik, John C. ....**Stroudsburg, PA**
Prevoznik, Michael E. ....Collegeville, PA
Prew, Brian M. ....Binghamton, NY
Prew, John R. ....**Detroit, MI**
Prew, Jonathan ....Amherst, NH
Prew, Paul T. ....**Boston, MA**
Prewett, David E. ....Russellville, AR
Prewett, Hartford H. ....Houston, TX
Prewett, M. Todd ....**Atlanta, GA**
Prewett, Matthew M. ....**Houston, TX**
Prewett, Scott B. ....**Fort Worth, TX**
Prewett, William I. ....**El Dorado, AR**
Prewitt, Allen, Jr. ....Frankfort, KY
Prewitt, Brenda P. ....Dallas, TX
Prewitt, Brian Wayne ....**Charlotte, NC**
Prewitt, Cathy E. ....**Corbin, KY**
Prewitt, David E. ....**Philadelphia, PA**
Prewitt, H. Caywood, Jr. ....**Lexington, KY**
Prewitt, Henry C. ....Paris, KY
Prewitt, J. Coleman, Jr.
West Palm Beach, FL
Prewitt, J. Frank, Jr. ....Anchorage, AK
Prewitt, James K. ....Springfield, MO
Prewitt, James V. ....Conroe, TX
Prewitt, Janet R. White ....**Winchester, KY**
Prewitt, Jean M. ....Washington, DC
Prewitt, Jo Beth ....West Plains, MO
Prewitt, Leah J. ....Knoxville, TN
Prewitt, Mark W. ....Vicksburg, MS
Prewitt, Matthew F. ....**New York, NY**
Prewitt, Michael L. ....Leland, MS
Prewitt, Patricia Williams ....**Houston, TX**
Prewitt, Philip E. ....St. Louis, MO
Prewitt & Prewitt ....Frankfort, KY
Prewitt, Richard A. ....Frankfort, KY
Prewitt, Stephanie Hall ....Lexington, KY
Prewitt, Thomas A. ....**Florence, KY**
Cincinnati, OH
Prewitt, Thomas R. ....**Memphis, TN**
Prewitt, Thomas R., Jr. ....**Memphis, TN**
Prewitt, Thomas W. ....Ridgeland, MS
Prewitt, Tracy S. ....Louisville, KY
Prewitt, Tracy Sullivan ....**Louisville, KY**
Prey, Marc L. ....**Farmington Hills, MI**
Preyer, H. Mark ....Kennett, MO
Preyer, L. Richardson ....Greensboro, NC
Preyer, Virgel H. ....Little Rock, AR
Preysner, John P., Jr. ....**Hartford, CT**

Price, Patricia A.
Merit Systems Protection Board, Office of the General Counsel, GV
Price, Patrick E. .... Flemingsburg, KY
Price, Patty .... Merced, CA
Price, Paul H. .... Scranton, PA
Price, Paul L. .... Chicago, IL
Price, Paul M. .... Binghamton, NY
Price, Paul O. .... Corpus Christi, TX
Price, Paula A. .... Salisbury, MD
Price, Perkins & Larkin
Virginia Beach, VA
Price, Peter O. .... New York, NY
Price, Peter P. .... Grand Rapids, MI
Price, Peter R. .... Westhampton Beach, NY
Price, Philip B. .... Chico, CA
Price, Philip, Jr. .... Philadelphia, PA
Price, Phillip B., Sr. .... Huntsville, AL
Price, Phillip V. .... Indianapolis, IN
Price, Phyllis Y. .... Waukesha, WI
Price, Pine Scott .... Punta Gorda, FL
Price, Polly J. .... Atlanta, GA
Price, Postel & Parma LLP
San Luis Obispo, CA
Santa Barbara, CA
Santa Maria, CA
Price & Price .... Anchorage, AK
Price & Price .... Tucson, AZ
Price & Price .... Salem, OR
Price & Price, Chartered .... Bradenton, FL
Price & Price, L.L.C. .... Centreville, MD
Price, Priscilla Annette .... St. Louis, MO
Price & Pyles, P.C. .... Carrollton, GA
Price, Quentin D. .... Orange, TX
Price, R. A., & Associates, P.C.
Philadelphia, PA
Price, R. Daniel .... Rincon, GA
Price, R. Eben .... Dallas, TX
Price, R. Edward .... Washington, DC
Price, R. Scott .... Naples, FL
Price, R. Thomas .... Fort Dodge, IA
Price, R. Thomas .... Philadelphia, PA
Price, Ralph M. .... Chicago, IL
Price, Randall E. .... Indianapolis, IN
Price, Randall J. .... Wichita, KS
Price, Randall K. .... Dallas, TX
Price, Randall L. .... Seattle, WA
Price, Ray T. .... Hattiesburg, MS
Price, Ray T., P.A. .... Hattiesburg, MS
Price, Rebecca L. .... Dallas, TX
Price, Ricardo A. .... Houston, TX
Price, Richard A.B. .... Fairfax, VA
Price, Richard B. .... Omak, WA
Price, Richard B., P.S., Inc. .... Omak, WA
Price, Richard C. .... Fort Worth, TX
Price, Richard E. .... San Antonio, TX
Price, Richard F., Jr. .... New Orleans, LA
Price, Richard G.
Department Of Health And Human Services, Food & Drug Administration, GV
Price, Richard G. .... Morganville, NJ
Price, Richard G. .... Portland, OR
Price, Richard H., Jr. .... Wichita, KS
Price, Richard L. .... Bronx, NY
Price, Richard M. .... Washington, DC
Price, Richard M. .... Clayton, NC
Price, Richard M. .... Centerville, TX
Price, Richard S., II .... Fullerton, CA
Price, Robert A., IV .... San Antonio, TX
Price, Robert Allan .... Enterprise, AL
Price, Robert B. .... Claremont, CA
Price, Robert B. .... Tulsa, OK
Price, Robert C. .... Bloomington, IN
Price, Robert D. .... Holden, MA
Price, Robert D., PC .... Holden, MA
Price, Robert E. .... Anchorage, AK
Price, Robert E. .... Atlanta, GA
Price, Robert E. .... Greenville, MI
Price, Robert E. .... Rowland, NC
Price, Robert E. .... Claremore, OK
Price, Robert E. .... Philadelphia, PA
Price, Robert E. .... Dallas, TX
Price, Robert E. .... Houston, TX
Price, Robert E., Jr. .... Winston-Salem, NC
Price, Robert E., Jr. & Associates, P.A.
Winston-Salem, NC
Price, Robert F. .... Baltimore, MD
Price, Robert G. .... Columbia, SC
Price, Robert J., P.A. .... Little Rock, AR
Price, Robert L. .... Washington, DC
Price, Robert L. .... Hull, MA
Price, Robert L. .... Minneapolis, MN
Price, Robert M., Law Offices of
Washington, DC
Price, Robert N. .... Tulsa, OK
Price, Robert Q. .... Langdon, ND
Price, Robert R. .... Raleigh, NC
Price, Robert R., III .... Centreville, MD
Price, Robert R., Jr. .... Centreville, MD
Price, Robert S. .... Philadelphia, PA
Price, Roberta M. .... Albuquerque, NM
Price, Robin F. .... Palm Beach, FL
Price, Robt. .... New York, NY
Price, Roger L. .... Chicago, IL
Price, Ronald F. .... Salt Lake City, UT
Price, Ronald M. .... Winston-Salem, NC
Price, Roselee .... Watertown, MA
Price, Roy E., Jr. .... Longview, TX
Price & Runnells .... Bloomington, IN
Price, Russell E. .... Fremont, MI
Price, Russell E., P.C. .... Fremont, MI
Price, Ruth Ann .... Philadelphia, PA
Price, S. John, Jr. .... Ashland, PA
Pottsville, PA
Price, Sam David .... Carrollton, GA
Price, Samuel A. .... Fort Lauderdale, FL
Price, Samuel M. .... Newberry, SC
Price, Samuel P., Jr. .... Jamestown, NY
Price, Samuel P., Sr. .... Chautauqua, NY
Price, Samuel S. .... Luray, VA
Price, Sandra B. .... San Francisco, CA
Price, Sandra E. .... Phoenix, AZ
Price, Sandra L. .... San Jose, CA
Price, Sara .... Miami, FL
Price, Scott D. .... New York, NY
Price, Scott M. .... Longwood, FL
Price, Scott M. .... Salina, KS
Price, Scott Thomas .... Columbia, SC
Price, Scott Todd .... Nashville, TN
Price, Seth .... Atlanta, GA
Price, Seth J. .... Washington, DC
Price and Sherman .... San Antonio, TX
Price, Sherri Lynn .... Kansas City, MO
Price, Shirley M. .... Torrance, CA
Price, Siket & Solis, LLP .... Naples, FL
Price, Smith, Hargett, Petho & Anderson
Charlotte, NC
Forest City, NC
Price, Sol .... La Jolla, CA
Price, Somers S., Jr. .... Wilmington, DE
Price, Stacie L. .... Wheeling, WV
Price, Stanley B., (P.A.) .... Miami, FL
Price, Stanley E. .... Little Rock, AR
Price, Stephen C. .... Fairfax, VA
Leesburg, VA
Price, Stephen E. .... Houston, TX
Price, Stephen H. .... Reading, PA
Price, Stephen H. .... Nashville, TN
Price, Stephen J. .... Washington, DC
Price, Stephen M. .... Beverly Hills, CA
Price, Stephen M. .... Grand Rapids, MI
Price, Stephen R., Sr. .... Louisville, KY
Price, Stephen S. .... Los Angeles, CA
Price, Steven .... New York, NY
Price, Steven B. .... Boise, ID
Price, Steven E. .... El Segundo, CA
Price, Steven H. .... Los Angeles, CA
Price, Steven J. .... Minneapolis, MN
Price, Steven L. .... Hillsboro, OR
Price, Steven O'Brien .... Hermitage, TN
Price, Steven P. .... San Antonio, TX
Price, Stevenson H. .... El Paso, TX
Price, Stuart M. .... Encino, CA
Price, Stuart W. .... Irvine, CA
Price, Susan B. .... Littleton, CO
Price, Susan E. .... Anchorage, AK
Price, Susan E. .... Los Angeles, CA
Price, Susan R. .... Tucson, AZ
Price, Suzanne I. .... Alameda, CA
Price, T. Britt .... Department Of The Interior, Office of Hearings & Appeals, GV
Price, T. David .... Atlanta, GA
Price, T. David .... Newark, OH
Price, Teresa L. .... Clayton, MO
Price, Terry .... Birmingham, AL
Price, Thelma Thomas .... Columbus, OH
Price, Thomas A. .... Mayville, NY
Price, Thomas A. .... Charlotte, NC
Price, Thomas B. .... Goodwater, AL
Price, Thomas D. .... Tucson, AZ
Price, Thomas E. .... Kingman, AZ
Price, Thomas E. .... Mount Carmel, IL
Price, Thomas E. .... Salem, OR
Price, Thomas H., III .... Silver Spring, MD
Price, Thomas H., III, P.A.
Silver Spring, MD
Price, Thomas J. .... Northville, MI
Price, Thomas N. .... Elk River, MN
Price, Thornton W., III .... Durango, CO
Price, Tilghman Earle .... Baltimore, MD
Price, Timothy C. .... Atlanta, GA
Price, Timothy D. .... Jamestown, KY
Price, Timothy R. .... San Antonio, TX
Price, Todd Alan .... Boca Raton, FL
Price, Tom .... Dallas, TX
Price, Tom .... Charleston, WV
Price, Tracey Michelle .... Baltimore, MD
Price, Troy A. .... Little Rock, AR
Price Tunney Reiter & Bruton, A
Professional Corporation .... Chicago, IL
Price, V. Clark .... Greenville, SC
Price, Val P. .... Jonesboro, AR
Price, Valerie A. .... Pound Ridge, NY
Price, Velva L. .... Austin, TX
Price, Veronica Morgan .... Houston, TX
Price, Victoria S. .... Boston, MA
Price, Virginia S. .... Ridgewood, NJ
Price, W. Joseph .... Washington, DC
Price, Walter J., III .... Birmingham, AL
Price, Walter L. .... Johnson City, TN
Price, Wanda Kay Hannon
Department of Commerce, Patent and Trademark Office, GV
Price, Warren, III .... Honolulu, HI
Price, William A. .... Warrenville, IL
Price, William A. .... Des Moines, IA
Price, William A. .... Buffalo, NY
Price, William C. .... Long Beach, CA
Price, William C. .... Los Angeles, CA
Price, William C. .... Washington, DC
Price, William C. .... Cincinnati, OH
Price, William C., Jr. .... Pittsburgh, PA
Price, William Clinton III, P.A.
Bradenton, FL
Price, William Clinton, III (P.A.)
Bradenton, FL
Price, William Evan, II .... Columbus, OH
Price, William F. .... Newport Beach, CA
Price, William H. .... Granbury, TX
Price, William H., II .... Easton, MD
Price, William H., Jr. .... Greenport, NY
Price, William Ray, Jr. .... Jefferson City, MO
Price, William S. .... Chicago, IL
Price, William W. .... West Palm Beach, FL
Price, William W., P.A.
West Palm Beach, FL
Price, Wilson C., III .... Jamestown, NY
Price, Wm. E., Inc. .... White City, OR
Price, W. W., Jr. .... Olney, TX
Price & Zirulnik .... Jackson, MS
Price-Cates, Sharon .... Parsippany, NJ
Price-Crosby, Katrina Marie .... Seattle, WA
Price-Harper, Roshunda L.
Bloomfield Hills, MI
Price-Sladich, Shawn D. .... Spokane, WA
Price-Testerman, Connie .... Dayton, OH
Prichard, Chelye E. .... Jackson, MS
Prichard, David M. .... San Antonio, TX
Prichard, Donald L. .... Redondo Beach, CA
Prichard, E. Allen .... Charlotte, NC
Prichard, Edgar Allen .... McLean, VA
Prichard, Harold C. .... Falls City, NE
Prichard Hawkins & Young, LLP
San Antonio, TX
Prichard, J. Leslie .... Meridian, MS
Prichard, James M. .... Storm Lake, IA
Prichard, James Y. .... Northfield, MN
Prichard, Joseph W., Jr. .... Jacksonville, FL
Prichard, M. Patricia .... Houston, TX
Prichard, Mark R. .... Wausau, WI
Prichard, Michael .... Minneapolis, MN
Prichard, Michael S. .... Chattanooga, TN
Prichard, Philip A. .... Mannington, WV
Prichard, Robert I., III .... Purvis, MS
Prichard, Ronald A. .... Overland Park, KS
Kansas City, MO
Prichard, Thomas D. .... Austin, TX
Prichard, Thomas W. .... Minneapolis, MN
Prichard, Vincent M. .... Evergreen, CO
Prichason, Fred G. .... North Miami Beach, FL
Prichason, Fred G., P.A.
North Miami Beach, FL
Prickett, Anne R. .... Naples, FL
Prickett, C. Lane .... Austin, TX
Prickett, Carlton S., Jr. .... Wilmington, NC
Prickett, Dave R. .... Chattanooga, TN
Prickett, F. Lee, Jr. .... St. Matthews, SC
Prickett, Gregory L. .... Fullerton, CA
Prickett, James M. .... Albion, IN
Fort Wayne, IN
Prickett, Jones & Elliott, P.A. .... Dover, DE
Wilmington, DE
Kennett Square, PA
Prickett, Pamela K. .... Los Angeles, CA
Prickett, R. C. .... Des Moines, IA
Prickett, Russell O. .... Department of State, Director General—Foreign Service, GV
Prickett & Saunders, PLLC .... Austin, TX
Prickett, Thomas B., II .... Oneonta, AL
Prickett, Thomas B., II, P.C. .... Oneonta, AL
Prickett, William .... Wilmington, DE
Prickett, William L. .... Boston, MA
Pricopoulos, Rosemarie .... Malden, MA
Prida, Antonio M. .... New York, NY
Houston, TX
Pridavka, Gary M. .... Dallas, TX
Priddle, Michael A. .... Wichita, KS
Priddle, Steven J.
Securities and Exchange Commission, GV
Priddy, Alton D. .... New Albany, IN
Louisville, KY
Priddy, Britt R. .... Albany, GA
Priddy, John E. .... Tulsa, OK
Priddy, Joseph E. .... Basking Ridge, NJ
Priddy, Laurance L. .... Fort Worth, TX
Priddy, Laurance L., P.C., Law Office of
Fort Worth, TX
Priddy, Mary Moffett Hutcheson
Glen Allen, VA
Priddy, Robert R. .... Potomac, MD
Priddy, S. Vernon, III .... Richmond, VA
Pride, Allison .... Oklahoma City, OK
Pride, Andrew S. .... Detroit, MI
Pride, D. Jason .... Morganfield, KY
Pride, E. Eugene .... Richland, WA
Pride, Elisabeth K. .... Verona, PA
Pride, Hemphill P., II .... Columbia, SC
Pride, Nathan B. .... Jackson, TN
Pridemore, Katherine E. .... Cincinnati, OH
Pridgen, Bill M. .... Myrtle Beach, SC
Pridgen, Craig A. .... San Francisco, CA
Pridgen, Elton C. .... Smithfield, NC
Pridgen, Eugene C. .... Charlotte, NC
Pridgen, John C. .... Cordele, GA
Pridgen, Mack D., III .... Raleigh, NC
Pridgen, Otto K., II .... Wilmington, NC
Pridgen, Randall B. .... Rocky Mount, NC
Pridgen, S. Raymond .... Mullins, SC
Pridgen, William D. .... Kingstree, SC
Pridgeon, J. Stratis .... Orlando, FL
Pridgeon, Jeffrey C. .... Newport, OR
Pridgeon, Mark A. .... Minneapolis, MN
Pridham, Grenville Thomas .... Las Vegas, NV
Pridham, Herbert H. .... Youngstown, OH
Pridjian, John V. .... Los Angeles, CA
Pridmore, Howard J. .... Bloomfield Hills, MI
Pridmore, Mary Louise .... Detroit, MI
Pridmore, Timothy T. .... Lubbock, TX
Priebe, David .... Palo Alto, CA
Priebe, David C. .... Bloomington, MN
Priebe, Dennis L. .... St. Louis, MO
Priebe, James A. .... Atlanta, GA
Priebe, Jason K. .... Macon, GA
Priebe, John H. .... Rhinelander, WI
Priebe, Kathy Collum .... Maplewood, MO
Priebe Law Offices .... Rhinelander, WI
Priebe, Timothy A. .... Dickinson, ND
Priebus, Reince R. .... Milwaukee, WI
Priefer, Jean Mary .... Rancho Cucamonga, CA
Priegues, Lauren Jorgensen .... Miami, FL
Prieguez, Raquel M. .... San Diego, CA
Priehs, David A. .... Southfield, MI
Priehs, William J. .... Flushing, MI
Priem, Kenneth R. .... Austin, TX
Prier, Marci L. .... Glenwood, IA
Prier, Robert J. .... Nyack, NY
Prier, Robert W. .... Suffern, NY
Pries, Edward J., Jr. .... Valley Stream, NY
Pries, H. J. .... Davenport, IA
Pries, John Putnam .... Eugene, OR
Pries, Renee J. .... Troy, MI
Pries, Stephanie M. .... Washington, DC
Pries, William E. .... Mineola, NY
Priesing, Dana .... Washington, DC
Priesmeyer, Margaret M. .... San Antonio, TX
Priess, Howard K., II .... Chicago, IL
Priest, Alan G. .... Washington, DC
Priest, Alan I. .... Salem, OR
Priest, Benny C. .... Marietta, GA
Priest, C. Reid .... Greencastle, IN
Priest, Carol C. .... Department of Justice, Tax Division, GV
Priest, Charles R. .... Augusta, ME
Priest, Donald E. .... Everett, WA
Priest, Donald M., Jr. .... Woodbridge, CT
Priest, Ellen Carroll .... Syracuse, NY
Priest, Gordon Webb, Jr. .... Baltimore, MD
Priest, Gwenda .... Lexington, NC
Priest, Jade Marie .... New York, NY
Priest, James M., Jr. .... Jackson, MS
Priest, Jim T. .... Oklahoma City, OK
Priest, Kathy K. .... New Haven, CT
Priest Law Offices .... Syracuse, NY
Priest, Maurice A., Jr. .... Sacramento, CA
Priest, Melissa L. .... San Antonio, TX
Priest, Morey G. .... Seattle, WA
Priest, Pamela Disilvestri .... Niagara Falls, NY
Priest, Park L. .... Louisville, KY
Priest, Pat .... San Antonio, TX
Priest, Richard A., Jr. .... Lahaina, HI
Priest, Richard D. .... Syracuse, NY
Priest, Timothy A. .... Knoxville, TN
Priest, Timothy S. .... Winchester, TN
Priest, W. Cravens, III
Bowling Green, KY
Priest, Whayne C., Jr.
Bowling Green, KY
Priest, William G., Jr. .... San Jose, CA
Priest, William James .... Decatur, IL
Priest, William R. .... Amarillo, TX
Priestap, Gary T. .... Southfield, MI
Priestap, Stephen T. .... Toledo, OH
Priester, Amos U., IV .... Raleigh, NC
Priester, Brian D. .... Ballston Spa, NY
Priester, Jack M. .... Madison, WI
Priester, James L. .... Birmingham, AL
Priester, John .... Iowa City, IA
Priester, Melvin V. .... Jackson, MS
Priester, Theodore J. .... Davenport, IA
Priestley, Elizabeth M. .... Los Angeles, CA
Priestley, James E. .... Schaumburg, IL
Priestley, Joseph A., Jr. .... Westerly, RI
Priestley, Robert F. .... Newark, NJ
Priesz, Arthur W., Jr. .... Minneapolis, MN
Priesz Law Firm .... Minneapolis, MN
Prieto, Andres G. .... New York, NY
Prieto, Claudio R. .... Albany, NY
Prieto, Diana .... West Lafayette, IN
Prieto, Edward C. .... Miami, FL
Prieto, Ernest .... Mandeville, LA
Prieto, Ivonne .... San Jose, CA
Prieto, Joseph V., Jr. .... Chicago, IL
Prieto, Kathleen M. .... Atlanta, GA
Prieto, Louis .... Bronx, NY
Prieto, M. Lucia .... Houston, TX
Prieto, Malise .... Covington, LA
Prieto, Margarita M. .... Department of Justice, Civil Rights Division, GV
Prieto, Mercedes M. .... Miami, FL
Prieto, Michael A. .... Atlanta, GA
Prieto, Peter .... Miami, FL
Prieto, Richard A. .... Long Beach, CA
Prieto, Tulio R. .... New York, NY
Prieto, Vanessa L. .... Fort Lauderdale, FL
Prieto-Rivera, Zaida .... San Juan, PR
Prietto, Carlos A., III
Newport Beach, CA
San Diego, CA
Prietto, James Anthony .... Garden Grove, CA
Prietz, Eve E. .... Baltimore, MD
Prietz, George N., III .... Milwaukee, WI
Prifogle, Robert S. .... West Bend, WI
Prifti, William M. .... Amesbury, MA
Prifti, William M. .... Boston, MA
Prifty, Frederick S. .... Harvard, MA
Prigal, Alan .... Hackensack, NJ
Prigge, Richard L. .... Butte, MT
Prigge, William N. .... Keene, NH
Prigmore, Gene .... Oklahoma City, OK
Prigmore, Nancy L. .... Alva, OK
Prigmore, Terence D. .... Joplin, MO
Prignano, Pascal A. .... Columbia, CT
Manchester, CT
Prignano, Stephen M. .... Providence, RI
Prignoli, Robert .... Staten Island, NY
Prigoff, Bruce E. .... San Francisco, CA
Prigoff, Michael L. .... Englewood, NJ
Prigoff, Milton .... North Palm Beach, FL
Englewood, NJ
Prikryl, Latius R. .... Austin, TX
Prill, Danielle A. .... New York, NY
Prillaman, Alton B. .... Roanoke, VA
Prillaman, Fred C. .... Springfield, IL
Prillaman, G. Garner, Jr. .... Washington, DC
Prillaman & Prillaman, Ltd. .... Urbana, IL
Prillaman, Roger L. .... Urbana, IL
Prillaman, Terry Smith, Jr. .... Urbana, IL
Prillwitz, Bruce B. .... Rochester, MI
Prillwitz, Bruce B., P.C., Law Offices of
Rochester, MI
Rochester Hills, MI
Priluker, Louis B. .... Jenkintown, PA

Prim, Brian Alan ... Huntington, WV
Prim, Craig M. ... Palo Alto, CA
Prim, Joseph A., Jr. ... Philadelphia, PA
Prim, Mary Kannan ... Charleston, WV
Prim, Richard F. ... New Ulm, MN
Prim, Wayne L. ... Stateline, NV
Primack, Jordan ... Round Lake, IL
Primack, Marc A. ... Chicago, IL
Primack, Ronald N. ... Lansing, IL
Primak, L. Scott ... San Jose, CA
Primas, Emmett E., Jr. ... Woodbury, NJ
Primason, Webb F. ... Lynn, MA
Primavera, Carl S. ... Philadelphia, PA
Primavera, Catherine A. ... Somerset, PA
Primavera, Dennis R. ... Philadelphia, PA
Primavera, Donald A. ... Sacramento, CA
Primavera, Henry M. ... Mineola, NY
New York, NY
Smithtown, NY
Primavera, Patrick M. ... Houston, TX
Prime, Eric W. ... Indianapolis, IN
Prime, Jamison S.
Federal Communications Commission, Wireless Telecommunications Bureau, GV
Prime & Malcarney ... Medford, NJ
Prime, R. Case ... Glens Falls, NY
Prime, Timothy M. ... Medford, NJ
Prime, William ... Madison, IN
Primeau, Charles W. ... San Diego, CA
Primeau, John C. ... Hollywood, FL
Primeau, John D. ... Manassas, VA
Primeau, Michele S. ... Miami, FL
Primeau, Richard G. ... Fort Lauderdale, FL
Primeau, Robert J. ... Livonia, MI
Primeaux, Lawrence ... Meridian, MS
Primeaux, Russel O. ... Baton Rouge, LA
Primerano, Andrew J. ... Hazleton, PA
Primerano, William A. ... New York, NY
Primes, Brian D. ... Tarrytown, NY
Primes, Joel S. ... Sacramento, CA
Primes, Marlon A. ... Cleveland, OH
Primiani, Marc S. ... Los Angeles, CA
Primiano, Michael P. ... Phoenix, AZ
Primis, Craig S. ... Washington, DC
Primis, Tara Brennan ... Washington, DC
Primm, C. Wayne ... St. Louis, MO
Primm, D. Ruth ... Atlanta, GA
Primm, James D., Jr. ... Lisbon, OH
Primm, James L. ... Santa Monica, CA
Primm, William C. ... Santa Fe, NM
Primmer, John L. ... Montpelier, VT
St. Johnsbury, VT
Primmer, Patricia E. ... South Bend, IN
Primmer & Piper, Professional Corporation
Montpelier, VT
St. Johnsbury, VT
Primo, David M. ... Liverpool, NY
Primo, Robert N. ... Liverpool, NY
Primoff, L. Robert ... New York, NY
Primoff, Madlyn Gleich ... New York, NY
Primoff, Richard G. ... New York, NY
Primoli, Salvator J. ... St. Paul, MN
Primomo, Gene V. ... Muskogee, OK
Primomo, Marilyn Theurer ... San Antonio, TX
Primos, Noel E. ... Dover, DE
Primosch, Robert D. ... Washington, DC
Primost, Paula Lynn ... Washington, DC
Primozic, Eileen K. ... Naperville, IL
Primozic, William ... San Francisco, CA
Primps, Deborah A. ... Fairfield, CT
Primps, William G. ... New York, NY
Primrose, Lyons and Quigley
Mount Pocono, PA
Stroudsburg, PA
Primrose, Mark A. ... Mount Pocono, PA
Stroudsburg, PA
Primus, Brent Wm. ... Minneapolis, MN
Primus, Charles ... Waterford, CT
Primus, Edna Smith ... Columbia, SC
Primus Law Office, P.A. ... Minneapolis, MN
Primus, Loris P. ... New York, NY
Primus, Michael J. ... Walnut Creek, CA
Primuth, Richard A. ... Minneapolis, MN
Prince, A. Cheryl ... New York, NY
Prince, Alan J. ... Atlanta, GA
Prince, Allen L. ... Dallas, TX
Prince, Allison Carney ... Washington, DC
Fairfax, VA
Prince, Andrew S.
Department of the Navy, GV
Prince, Andrew S. ... Rahway, NJ
Prince, Annette Hooper ... Oklahoma City, OK
Prince, Anthony D. ... Oakland, CA
Prince, Arlene Elise Bailey ... Seattle, WA
Prince, Arnold E. ... Encino, CA
Prince, Barecki, Nicholas & Burrows, LLP
Hart, MI
Shelby, MI
Prince, Brice D. ... Washington, DC
Prince & Brien, P.S.C. ... Benton, KY
Prince, Charles M. ... Fort Lauderdale, FL
Prince, Charles O., III ... New York, NY
Prince, Cheryl M. ... Duluth, MN
Prince, Chesley H. ... West Des Moines, IA
Prince, Christopher E. ... Los Angeles, CA
Prince, Christopher S. ... Atlanta, GA
Prince, Clifford W. ... Shelby, MI
Prince, David C. ... Atlanta, GA
Prince, David L. ... Los Angeles, CA
Prince, David L. ... Miami, FL
Prince, David S. ... Houston, TX
Prince, David Scott
Colorado Springs, CO
Prince, Deborah S. ... Norfolk, VA
Prince, Dena Drury ... Tuscaloosa, AL
Prince, Dennis M. ... Las Vegas, NV
Prince & Diment, P.C. ... Carrollton, GA
Prince, Douglas C. ... Cincinnati, OH
Prince, Douglas R. ... Seattle, WA
Prince, Edd D. ... Houston, TX
Prince, Edward M. ... Washington, DC
Prince, Edward M., Jr. ... Washington, DC
Prince, Ellis T., III ... New York, NY
Prince, Franklin ... West Palm Beach, FL
Prince, Frederick S., Jr. ... Salt Lake City, UT
Prince, Gary A., Jr. ... Short Hills, NJ
Prince, Gary M. ... Knoxville, TN
Prince, George D. ... San Francisco, CA
Prince, Glick & McFarlane, P.A., Law Offices ... Fort Lauderdale, FL
Prince, Harold H. ... Pottstown, PA
Prince & Hellinger, P.C. ... Nashville, TN
Prince, J. Ritchie MacPherson
Mobile, AL
Prince, James C. ... Oklahoma City, OK
Prince, James G. ... Baltimore, MD
Prince, James L. ... New York, NY
Prince, James M. ... Houston, TX
Prince, James R. ... Hart, MI
Prince, James R. ... Dallas, TX
Prince, Jeannine L. ... Omaha, NE
Prince, Jeffrey C. ... San Antonio, TX
Prince, Jennifer J. ... Blue Bell, PA
Prince, John J. ... Cleveland, OH
Prince, John Matthew ... Raleigh, NC
Prince, John T. ... Boston, MA
Prince, Jonathan M. ... Baltimore, MD
Prince, Joseph B., IV ... Midlothian, VA
Prince, Judith Martin ... Houston, TX
Prince, Julaan Derrick ... Conway, SC
Prince, Karen L. ... Oaklyn, NJ
Prince, Kelley, Marshall & Coombs, P.S.
Seattle, WA
Prince, Kenneth C. ... Chicago, IL
Prince, Kenneth S. ... New York, NY
Prince, Keri C. ... Raleigh, NC
Prince, Larry E. ... Boise, ID
Prince Law Firm, The, P.S. ... Seattle, WA
Prince, Leland ... Detroit, MI
Prince, Leslie ... Fairfield, CA
Prince, Lionel A. ... Philadelphia, PA
Prince, Lobel & Tye LLP ... Boston, MA
Prince, Marvin C. ... Benton, KY
Prince, McKean, McKenna & Broughton, L.L.C. ... Mobile, AL
Prince, Michael ... Dallas, TX
Prince, Milton ... Brooklyn, NY
Prince, Pamela Yvonne ... Sumter, SC
Prince, Patricia ... San Francisco, CA
Prince, Patricia Gormely
Farmington Hills, MI
Prince, Patricia Gormely, P.C.
Detroit, MI
Farmington Hills, MI
Prince, Paul A. ... Pottstown, PA
Prince, Poole & Cross, P.C.
Tuscaloosa, AL
Prince, Prescott L. ... Richmond, VA
Prince & Prince, P.C. ... Pottstown, PA
Prince, Ralph H. ... Avila Beach, CA
Prince, Raymond G. ... Nashville, TN
Prince, Richard A. ... Chicago, IL
Prince, Richard G. ... Bartow, FL
Prince, Robert E. ... Lawton, OK
Prince, Robert E. ... Seattle, WA
Prince, Robert F. ... Tuscaloosa, AL
Prince, Robert H. ... Portsmouth, NH
Prince, Robert H. ... Philadelphia, PA
Prince, Robert L. ... Benton, KY
Prince, Robert S. ... Salt Lake City, UT
Prince, Robert W. ... La Jolla, CA
Prince, Robt. S. ... Boston, MA
Prince, Robyn ... Boston, MA
Prince, Roger P. ... Portland, ME
Prince, Rosalind S. ... Bangor, ME
Prince, Russell C. ... New York, NY
Prince, Samantha J. ... Harrisburg, PA
Prince, Schmidt & Lazar ... Santa Fe, NM
Prince, Sharon E. ... Escondido, CA
Prince, Sherry Dew ... Tabor City, NC
Prince, Sydney R., III ... Mobile, AL
Prince, Thomas A. ... Conway, AR
Little Rock, AR
Prince, Thomas E. ... Oklahoma City, OK
Prince, Timothy P. ... San Bernardino, CA
Prince, Vanedda ... Union City, TN
Prince, Wallace ... Brooklyn, NY
Prince, Walter B. ... Boston, MA
Prince, Warren H. ... Bechtelsville, PA
Prince, Wayman L. ... Houston, TX
Prince, Wendy L. ... New York, NY
Prince, William A. ... Columbia, SC
Prince, William B. ... Salt Lake City, UT
Prince, William C. ... Springfield, MO
Prince, William T. ... Norfolk, VA
Prince, Winston H., Jr. ... Cleveland, TN
Prince, Yeates & Geldzahler
Park City, UT
Salt Lake City, UT
Prince, Youngblood & Massagee
Hendersonville, NC
Princehorn, Rebecca Coleman
Columbus, OH
Princer, Jennifer ... New York, NY
Princi, Anthony ... New York, NY
Princi, Joseph M. ... Beverly, MA
Princi & King Co., L.P.A. ... Troy, OH
Princi, Michael J. ... Hyannis, MA
Princi, Paul R. F. ... Troy, OH
Princic, Richard A. ... Canton, OH
Princiotta, Jas. ... Bronx, NY
Principal, Quedel ... Purchase, NY
Principato, Salvatore, Jr. ... Blackwood, NJ
Principato-Phipps, Elizabeth A.
Oakland, CA
Principe, David L. ... Buffalo, NY
Principe, Frank A. ... Tampa, FL
Principe, Gerald L.
North Palm Beach, FL
Palm Beach, FL
Principe, Jane A. ... Treasury Department, Office of the Comptroller of the Currency, GV
Principe, John F., Law Office of
Garden City, NY
Principe, Joseph V. ... Carle Place, NY
Principe, Paul E. ... San Francisco, CA
Principe, Philip R. ... Arlington, VA
Principe, Shelly ... Troy, MI
Principe, Thomas J. ... New York, NY
Principe, Timothy D. ... San Diego, CA
Principe, William Keith ... Atlanta, GA
Principi, Anthony J. ... La Jolla, CA
Principi, Elizabeth A. ... La Jolla, CA
Principi & McClain, LLP ... La Jolla, CA
San Diego, CA
Prindable, Thomas K. ... Chicago, IL
Prindible, Michael C. ... Dallas, TX
Prindiville, Dale J. ... Barrington, IL
Prindiville, John C. ... Brick, NJ
Prindle, Brian E. ... Manchester, CT
Prindle, Decker & Amaro, L.L.P.
Long Beach, CA
Los Angeles, CA
Riverside, CA
San Francisco, CA
Santa Ana, CA
Prindle, Kenneth B. ... Long Beach, CA
San Francisco, CA
Prindle, Maland, Sellner, Stennes and Knutsen, Chartered ... Clara City, MN
Montevideo, MN
Prindle, Patrick L. ... San Diego, CA
Prindle, Rachel H. ... Boston, MA
Prindle, W. D. ... Montevideo, MN
Prine, Andrew W. ... Saginaw, MI
Prine, Arthur C., Jr. ... Indian Wells, CA
Northfield, IL
Prine, Barry C. ... Mobile, AL
Prine, Charley E., Jr. ... Houston, TX
Prine & Corsello ... Des Moines, IA
Prine, David E. ... Howell, MI
Prine, Kenneth A. ... Minneapolis, MN
Prine, Malcolm M. ... Pittsburgh, PA
Prine, Susan K. ... Saginaw, MI
Prine, Ted E. ... Des Moines, IA
Prineas, Zachary T. ... Long Beach, CA
Pring, Cynthia M. ... Colorado Springs, CO
Pring, George W. (Rock) ... Denver, CO
Pring, Raymond R., Jr. ... Alexandria, VA
Pring, Roy I. ... Colorado Springs, CO
Pringle, Andrew C., Jr.
Farmington Hills, MI
Pringle, Andrew L. ... Phoenix, AZ
Pringle and Associates ... Farmington Hills, MI
Pringle, B. Ross ... Austin, TX
Pringle, Brantley, Sr. ... Fort Worth, TX
Pringle, Bruce D. ... Denver, CO
Pringle, Charles K. ... Biloxi, MS
Pringle, Daniel M. ... Richmond, VA
Pringle, Douglas S. ... Wichita, KS
Pringle, Dwight L. ... Denver, CO
Pringle, Edward E. ... Denver, CO
Pringle, Eric J. ... Denver, CO
Pringle, Harry R. ... Portland, ME
Pringle & Herigstad, P.C. ... Minot, ND
Pringle & Herzog, A Prof. Law Corp.
Shreveport, LA
Pringle, Homer S. ... Northbrook, IL
Pringle, James J. ... New Philadelphia, OH
Pringle, James T., Jr. ... Winfield, KS
Pringle, John D., Law Offices of
Austin, TX
Pringle, John J., Jr. ... Columbia, SC
Pringle, John P. ... Los Angeles, CA
Pringle, Johnson & Kersey ... Fort Worth, TX
Pringle, Katherine L. ... New York, NY
Pringle, Kenneth ... Wichita, KS
Pringle, Kenneth E. ... Belmar, NJ
Pringle, Laura Nan Smith
Oklahoma City, OK
Pringle, Lawrence D. ... New York, NY
Pringle, Lynn A. ... Oklahoma City, OK
Pringle, Paul C. ... Los Angeles, CA
San Francisco, CA
Pringle & Pringle, A Professional Corporation ... Oklahoma City, OK
Pringle & Quinn ... Belmar, NJ
Pringle, R. Kent ... Chanute, KS
Pringle, R. Perry ... Shreveport, LA
Pringle, Richard E. ... Irving, TX
Pringle, Richard W. ... Fort Myers, FL
Pringle, Robert B. ... San Francisco, CA
Pringle, Robert C. ... Paterson, NJ
Pringle and Roemer, P.L.L.C. ... Biloxi, MS
Pringle, Shawn R. ... Washington, DC
Pringle, Stuart H., Jr. ... New York, NY
Pringle, Timothy J., Law Office of
Topeka, KS
Pringle, Victor B., Jr. ... Biloxi, MS
Pringle, William B., III ... Orlando, FL
Pringle, Woodrow W., III ... Biloxi, MS
Pringle, Woodrow W., III ... Gulfport, MS
Prinkey, Otis H. ... St. Paul, MN
Prinner, Martin C. ... Poughkeepsie, NY
Prins, Alexander D. ... Live Oak, FL
Prins, Jenelle C. ... San Francisco, CA
Prins, Richard H. ... Chicago, IL
Prins, Richard T. ... New York, NY
Prins, Russell E. ... Lansing, MI
Prins, William G. ... Miami, FL
Prinsell, Joel David ... Orlando, FL
Prinsell, William A. ... Brooklyn, NY
Prinsell, William A. ... New York, NY
Prinsen, A. Peter ... Philadelphia, PA
Prinster, Gordon D. ... St. Charles, MO
Prinster, Patrick K. ... Los Angeles, CA
Printemps, Edwin E. ... Santa Ana, CA
Printers, Vicky Lynn ... Houston, TX
Printup, Scott Charles ... Buffalo, NY
Printy, Gary L. ... Tallahassee, FL
Printy, Michael Patrick ... Henderson, NV
Printy, Suzanne G. ... Tallahassee, FL
Printz, Carrie ... New York, NY
Printz, Charles F., Jr. ... Martinsburg, WV
Printz, Jacqueline M. ... Roseland, NJ
Printz, Jana M. ... Del Mar, CA
Printz, Jane G. ... Albuquerque, NM
Printz, Matthew H. ... San Diego, CA
Printz, Nancy B. ... Denver, CO
Printz, Peter E. ... Birmingham, AL
Printz, Randall B. ... Vancouver, WA
Printz, Stanley V. ... Allentown, PA
Printz, Steven J. ... Alpharetta, GA
Printzlau, Jay E. ... Londonderry, NH
Prinz, Arno S. ... Los Angeles, CA
Prinz, Beth Teardo ... Stuart, FL
Prinz, Richard ... Houston, TX
Prinzivalli, Paul J. ... White Plains, NY
Prio, Maria Elena ... Miami, FL
Priola, Danielle ... Haddonfield, NJ
Priola, Victoria C. ... Chicago, IL
Prioleau, Florence Weatherly
Washington, DC
Prioleau, Oscar Eugene, Jr. ... Atlanta, GA
Priolo, Dennis J. ... Rancho Cordova, CA
Priolo, Frank L. ... White Plains, NY
Priolo, James S. ... Brooklyn, NY
Priolo, Nicole M. ... Boston, MA
Priolo, Toby A. ... Amarillo, TX
Prior, Christopher J. ... Great Neck, NY
Prior, Douglas ... Clearwater, FL
Prior, Francis B. ... Wilmington, NC
Prior, Francis J., Jr. ... Fairfax, VA
Prior, Gary L. ... Chicago, IL
Prior, George T. ... Braintree, MA
Prior, Glen ... Fife, WA
Prior, Glen, Inc., P.C., Law firm of
Fife, WA
Prior, H. David ... Philadelphia, PA
Prior, James H. ... Columbus, OH
Prior, Jennifer ... West Palm Beach, FL
Prior, John D., Jr. ... San Jose, CA
Prior, Karl L. ... Philadelphia, PA
Prior, Kimberly J. ... Atlanta, GA
Prior, Mark L. ... Paoli, PA
Prior, Michael J. ... New York, NY
Prior, Michelle Sheehan ... Great Neck, NY
Prior, Nancy ... Arkville, NY
Prior, Nancy D. ... Boston, MA
Prior, Norman V. ... Sacramento, CA
Prior, Patricia L. ... Dayton, OH
Prior & Prior ... Arkville, NY
Prior, Robert A. ... Hollister, CA
Prior, Robert D. ... Eureka, CA
Prior, Thomas E. ... Atlanta, GA
Prior, Vincent W. ... Arkville, NY
Prior, William A., Jr. ... Madison, GA
Priore, Donna J. ... Tulsa, OK
Priore, Matthew T. ... Paterson, NJ
Priore, Nicholas S. ... Utica, NY
Priore, Philip D. ... Marlton, NJ
Philadelphia, PA
Priory, Joseph D. ... Princeton, NJ
Prioste, Tanya E. ... San Mateo, CA
Pripas, Howard J. ... Bronx, NY
Pripeton, Arlene L. ... Fairfax, VA
Pripeton, Arlene Lyles, P.C. ... Fairfax, VA
Pripstein, Shirley M. ... Hartford, CT
Prisament, Gloria K.
Hastings-On-Hudson, NY
Prisamt, George ... Great Neck, NY
Prisbe, John T. ... Baltimore, MD
Prisbrey, Aaron ... St. George, UT
Prisbrey, Grant M. ... Salt Lake City, UT
Prisby, Paul A. ... Salem, MA
Prisco, Armand J. ... Glen Cove, NY
Prisco, Joseph J., Jr. ... New York, NY
Prisco, Matthew Luke ... New York, NY
Prisco, Peter G. ... Woodbury, NY
Prisco, Ralph C. ... Hauppauge, NY
Prisco, Richard S. ... Locust Valley, NY
Prisco, Ronald J. ... Milford, DE
Prisco, Thadd A. ... Washington, DC
Priselac, David M. ... Monroeville, PA
Priser, Michael J. ... Bel Air, MD
Prish, Gary S. ... Newark, NJ
Prisk, Simon H. ... New York, NY
Prislipsky, Thomas A. ... Cleveland, OH
Prislovsky, Mark Allen ... Kerrville, TX
Prisock, Edward C. ... Louisville, MS
Pristave, Robert J. ... Chicago, IL
Pristelski, James S. ... Schaumburg, IL
Pristo, Christine M. ... Chicago, IL
Pritchard, B. Holland ... Atlanta, GA
Pritchard, Cathleen Kent
Virginia Beach, VA
Pritchard, Charles C. ... Atlanta, GA
Pritchard, Charles C., P.C. ... Atlanta, GA
Pritchard, Charles E. ... Salem, OR
Pritchard, Christina E. ... Dallas, TX
Pritchard, Claudius H., V ... Atlanta, GA
Pritchard, Clyde B. ... Franklin, MI
Pritchard, Curtis E. ... Cleburne, TX
Pritchard, D. Barry, Jr. ... Norristown, PA
Pritchard, Daniel P. ... Jefferson City, MO
Pritchard, David E. ... Cincinnati, OH
Pritchard, David H. ... New York, NY
Pritchard, David J. ... Chicago, IL
Pritchard, David L. ... Fort Worth, TX
Pritchard, Diane E. ... San Francisco, CA
Pritchard, Edw. S., Jr. ... Fort Worth, TX

Pritchard, Edward B. ... Tampa, FL
Pritchard, Edward K., III ... Charleston, SC
Pritchard, Edward K., Jr. ... Charleston, SC
Pritchard, Elizabeth Akins ... Tampa, FL
Pritchard, Eric J. ... Haddonfield, NJ
Philadelphia, PA
Pritchard, Francis B. ... Grand Island, NY
Pritchard, Gary M. ... Riverside, CA
Pritchard, Glen R. ... Columbus, OH
Pritchard, Howard P. ... Memphis, TN
Pritchard, J. Brett ... Chicago, IL
Pritchard, James Wesley, III ... Annandale, VA
Pritchard, Jayne S. A.
Ridgefield Park, NJ
Pritchard, Joan Allison ... Columbus, MS
Pritchard, John F. ... New York, NY
Pritchard, John F. ... New York, NY
Pritchard, John L. ... Union, NJ
Pritchard, John R., III ... Williamsburg, VA
Pritchard, John R., III, P.L.L.C
Williamsburg, VA
Pritchard, Keith F. ... San Jose, CA
Pritchard & Kennedy ... Grand Island, NY
Pritchard, Kenneth G. ... Ridgecrest, CA
Pritchard, Laurence C. ... Jacksonville, FL
Pritchard, LaVern A., Law Office of
Minneapolis, MN
Pritchard, Llewelyn G. ... Seattle, WA
Pritchard, Marion C. ... Waycross, GA
Pritchard, McCall & Jones, L.L.C.
Birmingham, AL
Columbiana, AL
Pritchard, Michael Gregg ... Springdale, AR
Pritchard, Michelle C. ... Morganton, NC
Pritchard, Peter Keith ... Los Angeles, CA
Pritchard & Pritchard Law Firm, P.A.
Charleston, SC
Pritchard, R. Alan, Jr. ... Memphis, TN
Pritchard, R. Wayne ... El Paso, TX
Pritchard, Robert A. ... Gulfport, MS
Pritchard, Robert A. ... Harriston, MS
Pascagoula, MS
Pritchard, Robert A. ... Jackson, MS
Pritchard, Robert H. ... Jacksonville, FL
Pritchard, Robert H., Jr. ... New York, NY
Pritchard, Robert O., Jr. ... New York, NY
Pritchard, Robert W. ... Orange, CA
Pritchard, Robert W. ... Colmar, PA
Pritchard, Robert W. ... Pittsburgh, PA
Pritchard, Susan K. ... Akron, OH
Pritchard, Suzanne K. ... Palo Alto, CA
Pritchard, Suzanne N. ... Philadelphia, PA
Pritchard, Therese D. ... Washington, DC
Pritchard, Thomas A. ... Biloxi, MS
Pritchard, Thomas B. ... Charleston, SC
Pritchard, Thomas C. ... Lake Charles, LA
Houston, TX
Pritchard, W. John ... Columbus, OH
Pritchard, William E., III ... Mobile, AL
Pritchard, William H. ... Holbrook, MA
Pritchard, William L. ... San Francisco, CA
Pritchard, William R. ... Davis, CA
Pritchard, William S., III
Birmingham, AL
Pritchard, William S., Jr.
Birmingham, AL
Pritchard, William W. ... Tulsa, OK
Pritchard-Kelly, Ruth ... Washington, DC
Pritchard-Williams, Amy ... Charlotte, NC
Pritcher, Jacob R., Jr. ... Dallas, TX
Pritchett, Ashby R. ... Martinsville, VA
Pritchett, Bruce M. ... Salt Lake City, UT
Pritchett & Burch, PLLC ... Edenton, NC
Plymouth, NC
Windsor, NC
Pritchett, Charles M. ... Louisville, KY
Pritchett, Clark P., Jr. ... Columbus, OH
Pritchett, Daniel M., III ... Washington, DC
Pritchett, Daniel V. ... Dallas, TX
Pritchett, David C. ... Cloquet, MN
Pritchett, Deborah J ... Dallas, TX
Pritchett, Diane P. ... Washington, DC
Pritchett, E. Edd ... Oklahoma City, OK
Pritchett, James H., Jr. ... Atlanta, GA
Pritchett, Janet R. ... Midland, TX
Pritchett, Jonita ... Dallas, TX
Pritchett, L. Bow ... Wheaton, IL
Pritchett, M. Jed, Jr. ... Boise, ID
Pritchett, Mary Sue ... Kingfisher, OK
Pritchett, Michael E.C. ... Jefferson City, MO
Pritchett, Michael M. ... Poplar Bluff, MO
Pritchett, M. J. ... San Francisco, CA
Pritchett, Monty C. ... Tulsa, OK
Pritchett, Newton G., Jr. ... Raleigh, NC
Pritchett, Patricia J. ... Birmingham, AL
Pritchett, Rebecca Wright
Montgomery, AL
Pritchett, S. Douglas, Jr. ... Houston, TX
Pritchett, Scott M. ... Washington, DC
Pritchett, Snyder & Pendell
Oklahoma City, OK
Pritchett, Stephen N., Jr. ... Gulf Shores, AL
Pritchett, Susie ... Kingfisher, OK
Pritchett, Tod M. ... Salinas, CA
Pritchett, William W., Jr. ... Windsor, NC
Pritel, Randolph ... Sonoma, CA
Pritikin, Daniel W. ... Los Angeles, CA
Pritikin, David T. ... Chicago, IL
Pritikin, James B. ... Chicago, IL
Pritikin, James B., P.C. ... Chicago, IL
Pritikin, Kenneth W. ... Lafayette, CA
Pritikin, Nancy E. ... San Francisco, CA
Pritikin, Renee Zarbin ... Chicago, IL
Pritschet, Marybeth ... Kalamazoo, MI
Pritsker, Keith W. ... Los Angeles, CA
Pritt, Jeffry A. ... Union, WV
Pritt, Robert D. ... Sanibel, FL
Pritti, Joseph B. ... New York, NY
Pritts, George W., Jr. ... United States Senate,
Senatorial Assistants, GV
Pritts, Joy Lea ... Chevy Chase, MD
Pritts, Matthew P. ... Roanoke, VA
Pritz, Jennifer A. ... Chicago, IL
Pritz, Jerome L. ... Deerfield, IL
Pritz, Kristan J. ... Boulder, CO
Pritz, Kurt J. ... Glendale, CA
Pritz, Richard D. ... New York, NY
Pritzke & Davis ... Greenfield, IN
Pritzke, Ronald R. ... Greenfield, IN
Pritzker and Associates, P.A.
Minneapolis, MN
Pritzker, Bruce E. ... Larkspur, CA
Pritzker, Daniel F. ... Chicago, IL
Pritzker, David M.
General Services Administration,
Office of Governmentwide Policy, GV
Pritzker, Eli ... Philadelphia, PA
Pritzker, Elizabeth ... Oakland, CA
Pritzker, Fred H. ... Minneapolis, MN
Pritzker, Jay A. ... Chicago, IL
Pritzker, J. B. ... Chicago, IL
Pritzker, Jeffrey N. ... Baltimore, MD
Pritzker, M. Frederick ... Boston, MA
Pritzker, Malcolm L. ... Washington, DC
Pritzker, Nicholas J. ... Chicago, IL
Pritzker, Penny Sue ... Chicago, IL
Pritzker & Pritzker ... Chicago, IL
Pritzker, Randy J. ... Boston, MA
Pritzker, Thomas J. ... Chicago, IL
Pritzkur, Lewis Henry ... Wilmington, DE
Priu, Pablo Eduardo ... Reston, VA
Privat, George R. ... Lafayette, LA
Privat, Kenneth O. ... Crowley, LA
Privat & Regan ... Crowley, LA
Privateer, Christopher A. ... Lockport, NY
Priven, Carole Ann ... San Francisco, CA
Priver, Mark S. ... El Segundo, CA
Pasadena, CA
Prives, Loretta Kirsch ... Princeton, NJ
Prives, Melvin A. ... Boston, MA
Privetera, Lora ... Barnegat, NJ
Privett, Caryl Penney ... Birmingham, AL
Privett, Howard J. ... Los Angeles, CA
Privett, Kenneth B. ... Pawnee, OK
Privett, Pamela J. ... Oxnard, CA
Privett, Pamela J., A Professional Law
Corporation ... Oxnard, CA
Privette, Anthony S. ... Statesville, NC
Privette, Christopher H. ... Atlanta, GA
Privette, Howard M. ... Los Angeles, CA
Privette, Ivan T. ... Knoxville, TN
Privette, Melinda H. ... Chapel Hill, NC
Privette, Mitzi Lilly ... Johnson City, TN
Privette, Steven A. ... Willow Springs, MO
Privette, Thomas, Jr. ... Knoxville, TN
Privitera, Frances D. ... Somerville, MA
Privitera, Francis D., Jr. ... Somerville, MA
Privitera, John J. ... Albany, NY
Privitera, Nora ... San Francisco, CA
Privitera, Philip J. ... Boston, MA
Privitt, Bill R. ... Bartlesville, OK
Privratsky, Mark R. ... Minneapolis, MN
St. Paul, MN
Priwall, Heidi Marie ... Bridgeport, CT
Prizant, Bruce D. ... Louisville, KY
Prizant, James ... New York, NY
Prizant, Roger M. ... Louisville, KY
Prizer, Franklin S. ... Boston, MA
Prizy, Randall R. ... Quincy, IL
Prizzi, John J. ... Latrobe, PA
Pro, Lisa K. ... San Diego, CA
Pro, Michael L. ... Merced, CA
Pro, Philip M. ... Las Vegas, NV
Proakis, James N. ... Fairfax, VA
Proano, Galo M. ... Honeoye Falls, NY
Proaps, Robert E., Jr. ... Carmichael, CA
Probandt, Felix B. ... Temecula, CA
Probasco, E. Lou Bjorgaard ... Topeka, KS
Probasco, G. Wayne ... Topeka, KS
Probasco, Gene A. ... Sioux City, IA
Probasco, Kevin C. ... Syracuse, UT
Probasco, Peggy Lee ... Butte, MT
Probate Law Center, P.C. ... St. Louis, MO
Prober, Charles J. ... Palo Alto, CA
Prober, Dean R. ... Woodland Hills, CA
Prober, Joshua Lee ... Chicago, IL
Probert, Reina Janette ... Pittsburg, KS
Probert, Richard W. ... New Haven, CT
Probert, Walter ... Gainesville, FL
Probes, Harold B., Jr. ... Tampa, FL
Probinsky, Brent L. ... Homestead, FL
Probish, Antoinette ... Commack, NY
Probish, Margaret E. ... Manchester, NH
Probst, Alane C. ... Jersey City, NJ
Probst, Bernard I. ... Miami, FL
Probst, Christina M. ... Union, ME
Probst, David G. ... Oklahoma City, OK
Probst, Gregory L. ... Bountiful, UT
Probst, Janet H. ... Newport Beach, CA
Probst, Karl A. ... Merrick, NY
Probst, Leo R. ... Portland, OR
Probst, Mary E. ... St. Paul, MN
Probst, Patricia Anania ... Phoenix, AZ
Probst, Paul F., Jr. ... Clearwater, FL
Probst, Robert C. ... Albion, IN
Probst, Robert E. ... Winston-Salem, NC
Probst, Robert R. ... Los Angeles, CA
Probst, Valdemar B. ... Windsor, CT
Probst, Walter F., Jr. ... Fort Wayne, IN
Probstein, Jon M. ... Los Angeles, CA
Probstein & Weiner ... Los Angeles, CA
Probus, Bernadette E. ... San Diego, CA
Probus, Matthew B. ... Houston, TX
Probus, William D. ... Cynthiana, KY
Proby, Lucien C., Jr. ... Gainesville, FL
Proc, Karen S. ... Denver, CO
Procaccini & Associates ... Providence, RI
Procaccini, Daniel A. ... Providence, RI
Procaccino, Joseph A., Jr.
Department of the Air Force,
Office of the Judge Advocate General, GV
Procario, Gary J. ... Canton, OH
Procas, Simone ... New York, NY
Procelli, Robert S. ... McLean, VA
Proceviat, Jerry Ronald ... San Jose, CA
Prochaska, Bradley J. ... Wichita, KS
Prochaska, Gary G. ... Oklahoma City, OK
Prochaska, Jane Hendrick ... Omaha, NE
Prochaska, Joseph R. ... Nashville, TN
Prochaska, Patricia A. ... Berkeley, CA
Prochaska & Scott ... Wichita, KS
Prochaska, Wm. J. ... Staten Island, NY
Prochazka, Jerry E. ... Pasadena, CA
Prochazka, Richard D. ... San Diego, CA
Prochnow, C. Tyler ... Kansas City, MO
Prochnow, Dan K. ... Hutchinson, MN
Prochnow, Douglas L. ... Chicago, IL
Prochnow, Herbert V., Jr. ... Chicago, IL
Prochnow, James R. ... Denver, CO
Prochnow, Kenneth H. ... Palo Alto, CA
Prochnow, Thomas H. ... New York, NY
Prochot, W. William ... Washington, DC
Prochovnick, Ora S. ... San Francisco, CA
Prochowski, Mark Zdzislaw
Costa Mesa, CA
Procida, Brent W. ... Garden City, NY
Procida, Mary A. ... Haddonfield, NJ
Procida, Richard D. ... Media, PA
Procino, Michele L. ... Georgetown, DE
Prock, Charles M. ... Abilene, TX
Prock, Charles R. ... Des Plaines, IL
Prockiw, Orest M. ... Granada Hills, CA
Prockop, Jonathan (Jamie) ... Tampa, FL
Procopio, Cory ... Pittsburgh, PA
Procopio, Cory, Hargreaves & Savitch LLP
San Diego, CA
Procopio, Joan M. ... Long Beach, CA
Procopio, Joseph ... Wolcott, CT
Procopio, Mark J. ... Menlo Park, CA
Procopio, Michael J. ... Orange, CA
Procopio, Patricia C ... Wilmington, DE
Procopio, Phyllis T. ... Pittsburgh, PA
Procter, Arthur W., Jr. ... Stamford, CT
Procter, Ben R. ... Washington, DC
Procter, J. Elaine ... Fort Collins, CO
Procter, James N., II ... Ventura, CA
Procter, Kelly Ann ... Fort Smith, AR
Procter-Murphy, Janice ... Phoenix, AZ
Procton, Lloyd W., (P.A.)
Fort Lauderdale, FL
Proctor, Albert C. ... Fort Worth, TX
Proctor, Benjamin D. ... Eau Claire, WI
Proctor, Brian D. ... Chicago, IL
Proctor, Bruce N. ... Atlanta, GA
Proctor, Carol ... Chicago, IL
Proctor & Chambers ... Atlanta, GA
Proctor, Charles F. ... Oxford, MA
Proctor, Claude W. ... Denver, CO
Proctor, Constance L. ... Seattle, WA
Proctor, Craig E. ... Kansas City, MO
Proctor, Daniel Charles ... Concord, NH
Proctor, Darcy L. ... Chicago, IL
Proctor, David Dale ... Oklahoma City, OK
Proctor, David J. W. ... Des Moines, IA
Proctor, David R. ... Springfield, VA
Proctor, David W. ... Birmingham, AL
Proctor, E. Knox, V ... New Bern, NC
Proctor, Edward G. ... Chicago, IL
Proctor, Edward G., Jr. ... Chicago, IL
Proctor, Edward O. ... Wellesley, MA
Proctor, Elizabeth A. ... Laurel, MD
Proctor, Fletcher D. ... Springfield, VT
Proctor, Frank G. ... Waterford, MI
Proctor, G. Burns, Jr. ... Birmingham, AL
Proctor, G. Edwin, Jr. ... Cameron, MO
Kansas City, MO
Proctor, Gary L. ... Santa Ana, CA
Proctor, Gary R. ... Houston, TX
Proctor, George L. ... Jacksonville, FL
Proctor, H. Palmer ... Tallahassee, FL
Proctor, Harry J., (P.C.) ... San Diego, CA
Proctor, J. Bradley ... Sylacauga, AL
Proctor, James Crowell ... Fayetteville, NC
Proctor, James M., II ... Birmingham, AL
Proctor, James M., III ... Bethesda, MD
Proctor, James P. ... Canton, OH
Proctor, James T. ... San Rafael, CA
Proctor, James W. ... Toledo, OH
Proctor, Jamie K. ... Tampa, FL
Proctor, Jamie K., P.A. ... Tampa, FL
Proctor, Jan L. ... Chesapeake, VA
Proctor, Jane ... Phoenix, AZ
Proctor, Janet C. ... Carbondale, IL
Proctor, Jerry B. ... Miami, FL
Proctor, Jimmie C. ... Trenton, NC
Proctor, John Anderson ... Huntington, WV
Proctor, John F. ... Chattanooga, TN
Proctor, John H., III ... Jackson, MS
Proctor, John L. ... Enid, OK
Proctor, John P. ... Washington, DC
Proctor, John W. ... Fort Worth, TX
Proctor, Judy B.
Administrative Office Of The United States
Courts, GV
Proctor, K. Donald ... Towson, MD
Proctor, Kathleen ... Tacoma, WA
Proctor, K. Donald, P.A. ... Baltimore, MD
Towson, MD
Proctor, Kimberly A. ... San Francisco, CA
Proctor, Laura ... New York, NY
Proctor, Laura E. ... Birmingham, AL
Proctor, Lester T., Jr. ... Valparaiso, IN
Proctor, Lister H. ... Sylacauga, AL
Proctor, Llewellyn A., Sr. ... Baton Rouge, LA
Proctor, Lori ... Houston, TX
Proctor, M. Julian, Jr. ... Tallahassee, FL
Proctor, Mamie M. ... Houston, TX
Proctor, Marcia L. ... Detroit, MI
Proctor, Marcia Mace ... Carlsbad, CA
Proctor, Margaret S. ... Wilmington, DE
Proctor, Mark J. ... Pensacola, FL
Proctor, Marlan A., Jr. ... Burbank, CA
Proctor, Marsha Phillips ... Jacksonville, FL
Proctor, Martha A. ... Detroit, MI
Proctor, Martin W. ... Tallahassee, FL
Proctor, Max Houston ... Hobbs, NM
Proctor, Michael A. ... Tucson, AZ
Proctor, Michael G. ... Bridgeport, CT
Stamford, CT
Proctor, Michael J. ... San Francisco, CA
Proctor, Nathan H. ... Oxford, MA
Proctor, Patricia ... Philadelphia, PA
Proctor, Patricia ... Houston, TX
Proctor, Patrick L. ... Fort Wayne, IN
Proctor, Penelope A. ... Columbus, OH
Proctor and Proctor ... Burbank, CA
Proctor, R. Brent ... Abilene, TX
Proctor, R. David ... Birmingham, AL
Proctor, Richard L. ... Wynne, AR
Proctor, Robert C., Jr. ... Sierra Madre, CA
Proctor, Robert C., Jr., A Professional
Corporation ... Sierra Madre, CA
Proctor, Robert E. ... Lansing, MI
Proctor, Robert J. ... Atlanta, GA
Proctor, Sharon H. ... Gainesville, FL
Proctor, Shemin V. ... Washington, DC
Proctor, Sol H. ... Jacksonville, FL
Proctor, Stanley T. ... Houston, TX
Proctor, Stephen E. ... Logan, OH
Proctor, Stephen M. ... Chicago, IL
Cincinnati, OH
Proctor, Steven J. ... Pottstown, PA
Proctor, Susan C. ... Roanoke, VA
Proctor, Susan D. ... Denver, CO
Proctor, Susan Tully ... Tallahassee, FL
Proctor, Terrell W. ... Houston, TX
Proctor and Vaughn ... Sylacauga, AL
Proctor, Venable Bland, Jr. ... Victoria, TX
Proctor, Vernon R. ... Wilmington, DE
Proctor, W. Thomas ... Houston, TX
Proctor, W. Thomas, P.C. ... Houston, TX
Proctor, Wendy M. ... Kansas City, MO
Proctor, Willard, Jr. ... Little Rock, AR
Proctor-Donald, Beverly P.
North Canton, OH
Proctor-Williams, Stephanie ... Blue Bell, PA
Procyk, Frank G. ... Allentown, PA
Proczko, Taras R. ... Chicago, IL
Prodan, Angela J. ... Brattleboro, VT
Prodan, Pamela ... Wilton, ME
Prodanov, Elena ... New York, NY
Prodanov, Margaret ... San Diego, CA
Prodehl, Steven J. ... Joliet, IL
Prodgers, Toby B. ... Marietta, GA
Prodnuk, Stephen D. ... Salt Lake City, UT
Prodoehl, John A., Jr. ... Media, PA
Prodromo, Karen Lynn
Redwood City, CA
Chicago, IL
Prodromos, Debra ... Northfield, IL
Proenza & Roberts, P.A. ... Miami, FL
Proesel, Mark K. ... Winnetka, IL
Proett, Stephen G. ... Denver, CO
Profaci, Anthony J. ... Linden, NJ
Profaci, Dominic J. ... New York, NY
Profaci, Joseph R. ... Linden, NJ
Profaci, Vincent J. ... Winter Park, FL
Profaci, Vincent J., P.A. ... Orlando, FL
Winter Park, FL
Profant-Turner, Elaine ... Eureka, CA
Profera, Louis J. ... Merrick, NY
Profeta & Eisenstein ... New York, NY
Profeta, Fred R., Jr. ... New York, NY
Profeta, Jacqueline P. ... Garden City, NY
Profeta, Laura ... Washington, DC
Profeta, Lawrence J. ... New York, NY
Profeta, Sharon M. ... Pittsburgh, PA
Proffit, David S. ... Albuquerque, NM
Proffit, John B., Jr. ... Richmond, VA
Proffitt, David L. ... Louisville, KY
Proffitt, Geoffrey H. ... Sarasota, FL
Proffitt, J. Preston, Jr. ... Duluth, GA
Proffitt, James K. ... Louisville, KY
Proffitt, James L. ... Pana, IL
Proffitt, John D. ... Carmel, IN
Proffitt, Judith S. ... Noblesville, IN
Proffitt, Monica Tamar ... Philadelphia, PA
Proffitt, Nancy A. ... St. Paul, MN
Proffitt, Stephanie H. ... Irvine, CA
Proffitt, Susan R. ... Chicago, IL
Proffitt, Thomas D. ... Mesa, AZ
Proffitt, Thomas D. ... Phoenix, AZ
Profilet, David C. ... Miami, FL
Profilet Vazquez & Hess ... Miami, FL
Profili, Annmarie S. ... Bel Air, MD
Profio, Debra A. ... New York, NY
Profit, Kirk A. ... Lansing, MI
Profit, Michelle D.
Board of Governors Of The Federal Reserve
System,
Office of the General Counsel, GV
Profita, Michael ... Englewood, NJ
Profita & Philibosian ... Englewood, NJ
Profitt, Dale, Attorney, P.C. ... Floyd, VA
Profitt, Kenneth R. ... Stanton, KY
Profitt, S. Dale ... Floyd, VA
Profumo, Dante J. ... San Francisco, CA
Profumo, Laura S. ... Columbus, OH
Profusek, Robert A. ... New York, NY
Profy, Joseph M. ... Philadelphia, PA
Profy, Thomas J., III ... Bristol, PA
Langhorne, PA

Profy, Thomas J., IV .... **Bristol, PA**
Langhorne, PA
Progar, Michael J. .... **Chicago, IL**
Progen, Donald H. .... Worcester, MA
Proger, Phillip A. .... **Washington, DC**
Progoff, Susan .... **New York, NY**
Prohaska, Barbara M. .... **Lisle, IL**
Prohaska, Daniel W. .... Coeur d'Alene, ID
Prohaska, Glenn H. .... Portland, OR
Prohaska, J. Raymond .... **Columbus, OH**
Prohaska, Kevin R. .... **Minneapolis, MN**
Prohaska, Thomas C. .... Omaha, NE
Prohaska, Thomas F. .... **Coeur d'Alene, ID**
Prohias, Rafael G. .... **Miami, FL**
Prohl, Emil K. .... Kerrville, TX
Prohofsky, Dennis E. .... St. Paul, MN
Prohov, Fredric B. .... **Chicago, IL**
Proia, Andrea M. .... **New York, NY**
Proietti, Donald J. .... **Merced, CA**
Proietti, Ralph Anthony .... Chicago, IL
Proietti, Stephen A. .... Fairview, NJ
Proietto, William D. .... Woodbury, NY
Proios, George N. .... **Englewood Cliffs, NJ**
New York, NY
Proios, John J. .... Uniondale, NY
Projansky, David M. .... New York, NY
Projansky, Dawn A. .... Chicago, IL
Projansky, Robert M. .... **New York, NY**
Projansky, Sidney H. .... Chicago, IL
Prokes, Lori Ann .... **Chicago, IL**
Prokes, Roger M. .... Maryville, MO
Prokey, John W. .... **San Jose, CA**
Proko, Jeanne M. .... **Media, PA**
Prokoff, William W. .... Philadelphia, PA
Prokop, Edward C. .... Los Angeles, CA
Prokop, John A., Jr. .... Washington, DC
Prokop, Joseph A., Jr. .... **Baton Rouge, LA**
Prokop, Joseph A., Jr., PLC
Baton Rouge, LA
Prokop, Joseph M. .... Painesville, OH
Prokop, Michael A. .... **Morristown, NJ**
Prokop, Michele Butler .... **Metairie, LA**
Prokop, Paul J. .... River Ridge, LA
Prokop, R. Peter .... **Southfield, MI**
Prokop, Ruth Timberlake .... Chevy Chase, MD
Prokop, Stanley A. .... **Detroit, MI**
Prokopik, Linda C. .... Towson, MD
Prokopik, Michael W. .... Baltimore, MD
Prokopius, Donn W. .... Las Vegas, NV
Prokopowicz, Gerald J. .... Chicago, IL
Prokos, Frank .... Easton, MA
Proksch, Michael A. .... Portland, OR
Proksel, William W. .... Corona, CA
Prokup, Michael .... **Allentown, PA**
Prol, Jeffrey D. .... **Roseland, NJ**
Proller, Judith M. .... Bellingham, WA
Prolman, Andrew A. .... Nashua, NH
Prolman, Susan .... **Washington, DC**
Proly & Laporte, P.A. .... **Port Richey, FL**
Proly, Peter A. .... **Port Richey, FL**
Prom, Stephen G. .... **Jacksonville, FL**
Proman, James B. .... Minneapolis, MN
Promer, Alan C. .... **Philadelphia, PA**
Prominski, Henry J. .... Weirsdale, FL
Prominski, John E., Jr. .... **Washington, DC**
Fairfax, VA
Promis, Victoria G. .... Denver, CO
Promisel, Valorie Joy
Yorktown Heights, NY
Promislo, Daniel .... **Philadelphia, PA**
Promislo, Jacqueline .... **Philadelphia, PA**
Prommersberger, Lynne B. .... **Syosset, NY**
Promoff, Adrienne F. .... **Miami, FL**
Promoff, Adrienne F., P.A. .... **Miami, FL**
Promuto, Vincent L. .... Bronx, NY
Pronai, Stephen .... London, OH
Pronchick, David M. .... King Of Prussia, PA
Prone, Joseph G. .... Andover, MA
Proner, A. Stanley .... New York, NY
Proner, Arthur .... Fort Lauderdale, FL
Proner, Mitchell L. .... New York, NY
Pronesti, Suzanne M. .... **Teaneck, NJ**
New York, NY
Prongay & Borderud .... Los Angeles, CA
Prongay, Kevin M. .... Los Angeles, CA
Pronin, Irwin .... **San Francisco, CA**
Pronk, Mark R. .... **Atlanta, GA**
Pronk, Thomas F. .... Garner, IA
Pronley, Edward J. .... **Milwaukee, WI**
Pronske, Gerrit M. .... Santa Fe, NM
Dallas, TX
Pronske, Gerrit M., P.C. .... Santa Fe, NM
Dallas, TX
Pront, Peter E. .... **New York, NY**
Pronteau, Robert E. .... New Hartford, NY
Proost, Gerald .... Racine, WI
Proost, Robert L. .... St. Louis, MO
Proost, Thomas E. .... **St. Louis, MO**
Propas, Demetria A. .... East Sandwich, MA
Propeck, Debra E. .... Evergreen, CO
Proper, David M. .... New York, NY
Proper, Donald V. .... New York, NY
Proper, Jeffrey M. .... Phoenix, AZ
Proper, Roger D., Jr. .... **Wooster, OH**
Propert, Christopher B. .... **Washington, DC**
Propes, Larry W. .... Columbia, SC
Propes, Lorna E. .... **Chicago, IL**
Propester, Richard P. .... **Oklahoma City, OK**
Prophater, William H., Jr. .... **Columbus, OH**
Prophete, Donald S. .... Kansas City, MO
Propp, Deborah L. .... Salem, MA
Propp, Eugene .... Chicago, IL
Propp, Judith J. .... San Luis Obispo, CA
Propp, Kenneth R. .... Department of State,
Office of the Legal Adviser, GV
Propp, Leland J. .... Auburn, CA
Propp, Schultz & Kaye .... Chicago, IL
Propp, Sharman T. .... Briarcliff Manor, NY
Propp, Theodore .... **New York, NY**
Propp, William W. .... El Segundo, CA
Proppe, Edward J. .... Farmington Hills, MI
Proppe, Phyllis S. .... Portland, OR
Propper, Eugene M. .... **Washington, DC**
Propper, Grant E. .... **Los Angeles, CA**
Propper, Susan E.
Federal Election Commission,
Office of the General Counsel, GV
Propps, Floyd K. .... Oklahoma City, OK
Propp-Schmarak, Gina Alexis .... Chicago, IL
Propson, Thomas E. .... **Minneapolis, MN**
Propst, Andrea J. .... Grand Blanc, MI
Propst, Beverly Lucas .... **St. Louis, MO**
Propst, Floyd E., III .... Atlanta, GA
Propst, John L. .... Pittsburgh, PA
Propst, Joseph W., II .... Decatur, AL
Propst, Marty D. .... Hilton Head Island, SC
Propst, Robert B. .... Birmingham, AL
Propst, Stephen F. .... **Washington, DC**
Propst, Tristan E. .... **Houston, TX**
Propstra, John A. .... Phoenix, AZ
Prorok, Charles J. .... Rockford, IL
Prorok, John H. .... Pittsburgh, PA
Prorok, Robert F. .... **Pittsburgh, PA**
Prosch, Philip S. .... Sarasota, FL
Prosch, William F., Jr. .... Birmingham, AL
Proschek, Eric E. .... Bay City, MI
Proscia, Frank Paul .... **Roseland, NJ**
Proscia, James .... **Southfield, MI**
Prose, Thomas P. .... Phoenix, AZ
Prosek, Bryan K. .... **Columbus, OH**
Prosen, Lawrence M. .... **Washington, DC**
Proser, Eric S. .... **Atlanta, GA**
Proser, Sylvan D. .... Myrtle Beach, SC
Proses, Charles W., Jr. .... San Francisco, CA
Proshan, David A. .... **New York, NY**
Prosise, Mark A. .... Canton, OH
Prosise, Richard L. .... Madison, WI
Proskauer Rose LLP .... **Los Angeles, CA**
Washington, DC
Boca Raton, FL
Newark, NJ
New York, NY
Proske, Jeffrey E. .... Sun Valley, CA
Proske, Jeffrey M. .... **St. Louis, MO**
Proskin, Arnold W. .... Albany, NY
Proskin Law Firm, The .... Albany, NY
Prosmushkin, Greg .... Glassboro, NJ
Philadelphia, PA
Prosmushkin, Greg, P.C. .... Glassboro, NJ
Philadelphia, PA
Prosnitz, Mary Beth .... Wellesley, MA
Prosnitz, Susan M. .... Boston, MA
Prospect, Richard W. .... Daytona Beach, FL
Prosper, Michael A.
Environmental Protection Agency,
Office of the General Counsel, GV
Prospere, Peyton D. .... **Jackson, MS**
Prospere, Reed W. .... **Dallas, TX**
Prospere & Russell .... **Dallas, TX**
Prosperi, Louis A., Law Office of
Pittsburgh, PA
Prosperi, Mark S. .... Chicago, IL
Pross, Michael B. .... Salisbury, NC
Pross, Peter N. .... **Pittsburgh, PA**
Prosser, Andrew B. .... Burlington, IA
Prosser, Colleen Sinclair .... **Bowie, MD**
Prosser, David T., Jr. .... Appleton, WI
Prosser, Deborah C. .... **Riverside, CA**
Prosser, Don E. .... **Carbondale, IL**
Prosser, Eric J. .... **San Diego, CA**
Prosser, Everett .... **Carbondale, IL**
Prosser, James E. .... Ventura, CA
Prosser, James T. .... **Neenah, WI**
Prosser, John Murdock, Jr. .... Johnsonville, SC
Prosser, John R. .... Winchester, VA
Prosser, Jordan H. .... Marietta, GA
Prosser, Linda J. .... La Crescenta, CA
Prosser, Nathaniel L. .... Memphis, TN
Prosser, Raymond J. .... Chicago, IL
Prosser, Raymond L. .... **Fort Wayne, IN**
Prosser, Richard C. .... **Tampa, FL**
Prosser, Sarah S. .... **Memphis, TN**
Prosser, Sean T. .... **San Diego, CA**
Prosser, Ted C., III .... **Ocala, FL**
Prosser, Timothy J. .... **St. Louis, MO**
Prosser, Tracy L. .... **Chicago, IL**
Prosser, Tyrrell M. .... **San Francisco, CA**
Prost, Christine C. .... **Haddonfield, NJ**
Prost, David J. .... Downers Grove, IL
Prost, Frederick J. .... Troy, MI
Prost, Mark A. .... Quincy, IL
Prost, Michael G. .... Phoenix, AZ
Prosterman, Rosamond .... New York, NY
Prosterman, Roy L. .... Seattle, WA
Prostick, Arthur Isom .... **New York, NY**
Prostko, James A. .... Pittsburgh, PA
Prostok, Jeff P. .... **Fort Worth, TX**
Proszak, John P. .... **New York, NY**
Proszek, James J. .... Tulsa, OK
Protas, Henry R. .... Philadelphia, PA
Protas, Martin S. .... **Bethesda, MD**
Protas, Martin S., P.C. .... **Washington, DC**
Bethesda, MD
Protas & Spivok, Chartered .... Bethesda, MD
Arlington, VA
Protasiewicz, Janet Claire .... Milwaukee, WI
Protass, Harlan J. .... **New York, NY**
Protass, Joshua .... **New York, NY**
Proteau, Paul J. .... Oak Park, IL
Prothero, John T. .... Butte, MT
Prothero, Mark C. .... Spokane, WA
Prothro, Gwendolyn .... **Washington, DC**
Prothro, James F. .... Dallas, TX
Prothro, Jerry R. .... Dallas, TX
Midland, TX
Prothro, John E., Jr. .... **Wichita Falls, TX**
Prothro, Joseph A. .... Bakersfield, CA
Prothro, Patricia C. .... New York, NY
Prothro, R. King, Jr. .... Redwood City, CA
Protigal, Stanley N. .... San Jose, CA
Protil, Karl J., Jr. .... **Rockville, MD**
McLean, VA
Proto, Neil T. .... **Washington, DC**
Proto, Paul E. .... North Haven, CT
Proto, Rosemary .... New York, NY
Proto, Vincent J. .... **Short Hills, NJ**
Protogyrou, Andrew A. .... **Norfolk, VA**
Williamsburg, VA
Protogyrou & Rigney, P.L.C. .... **Norfolk, VA**
Williamsburg, VA
Protokowicz, Stanley E., Jr. .... **Bel Air, MD**
Protonentis, Kenneth G. .... **Tampa, FL**
Protopapas, Lydia T. .... **Dallas, TX**
Protsch, Gregory .... Howard, SD
Woonsocket, SD
Protsch, Vincent J. .... Howard, SD
Madison, SD
Protter, Howard .... **Walden, NY**
Protzel, Bernard .... Newark, NJ
Protzeller, Marilyn H. .... Augusta, GA
Protzmann, Bruce .... Madison, WI
Proud, Clifford J. .... East St. Louis, IL
Proud, James .... **New York, NY**
Proud, James F. .... Media, PA
Proud, James W. .... Louisville, KY
Proud, Jennifer Robinson .... **Louisville, KY**
Proud, Richard F. .... Omaha, NE
Proudfit, John G. .... New York, NY
Proudfit, Lori L. .... Phoenix, AZ
Proudfit, Nancy W. .... Newark, NJ
Proudfoot, David W. .... **Lihue, HI**
Proudfoot, Don A., Jr. .... **Los Angeles, CA**
Proudfoot, Dorothy Chou
San Francisco, CA
Proudfoot, Matthew M. .... Irvine, CA
Prough, Michael D. .... **Walnut Creek, CA**
Prough, Steven J. .... **Los Angeles, CA**
Proujansky, Adam .... **Washington, DC**
Proujansky, Albert N. .... **New York, NY**
Proul, Eric K. .... **Laguna Hills, CA**
Proulx, Albert P. .... New Britain, CT
Proulx, Alfred C. .... Falls Church, VA
Proulx, Dana K. .... Washington, DC
Proulx, David .... Victorville, CA
Proulx, Ernest E. .... Holyoke, MA
Proulx, Geoffrey E. .... New York, NY
Proulx, Laurence R. .... Amherst, NH
Proulx, Mary F. .... Boston, MA
Proulx, Nicholle R. .... Holyoke, MA
Proulx, Robert M. .... Brockton, MA
Prounis, Othon A. .... **New York, NY**
Prousis, Danae K. .... Chicago, IL
Prousis, Michael T. .... Northbrook, IL
Proust-Bonnin, Dominique .... **New York, NY**
Prout, D. Bruce .... **Pasadena, CA**
Prout, James E. .... **Troy, NY**
Prout, Kelly C. .... **Chicago, IL**
Prout, Linda D. .... San Francisco, CA
Prout, Maita Deal .... **Los Angeles, CA**
Prout, R. Mac .... **Sacramento, CA**
Prout, Richard L. .... **Seattle, WA**
Prout, Stephen C. .... **Chicago, IL**
Prout, Susan W. .... Chicago, IL
Prout, William F. .... **Minneapolis, MN**
Prout, William H., Jr. .... **New Haven, CT**
Proutt, Robert J. .... **Baltimore, MD**
Prouty, David M. .... New York, NY
Prouty, Douglas M. .... Truckee, CA
Prouty, Erin L. .... **Los Angeles, CA**
Prouty, Gehring C. .... Redding, CA
Prouty, Steven W. .... **Bradenton, FL**
Prouty, Vicki L. .... Argonne, IL
Provan & Associates, P.C. .... Austin, TX
Provan, J. Allan .... Wayne, NJ
Provan, J. Scot .... **New York, NY**
Provan, Michael J. .... San Diego, CA
Provan, Robert .... Austin, TX
Provanzano, Joseph S. .... Peabody, MA
Provatas, Rita .... **New London, CT**
Provda, Bruce .... Brooklyn, NY
Proven, Lisa A. .... Watertown, NY
Proven and Quencer .... Watertown, NY
Provence & Provence .... El Cajon, CA
Provence, Ross C. .... El Cajon, CA
Provencher, Dawn .... New York, NY
Provencher, Douglas B. .... Santa Rosa, CA
Provencher, James R. .... Orlando, FL
Provencher, Lauri .... Los Angeles, CA
Provencher, Scott D. .... **Little Rock, AR**
Provencher, Shelby L. .... **Washington, DC**
Provencio, Carlos E. .... **Washington, DC**
Provencio, Donald .... Albuquerque, NM
Provencio, Elizabeth M. .... **San Antonio, TX**
Provenghi, Ruggero (Reg) .... El Paso, TX
Provenmire, Ross M. .... **Concord, NH**
Manchester, NH
Provenza, James C. .... Glenview, IL
Provenza, James R. .... Sacramento, CA
Provenza, Kenneth J. .... Lorain, OH
Provenza, Michael K. .... Lorain, OH
Provenza & Provenza .... Lorain, OH
Provenza, Russell D. .... Lorain, OH
Provenza, S. Paul, Jr. .... **Baton Rouge, LA**
Provenza, Tony P. .... Greenville, MS
Provenzale, Leonard Thomas .... Sunrise, FL
Provenzale, Mary E. .... Wheaton, IL
Provenzano, Adrienne J. .... Glenside, PA
Provenzano, Anthony .... **Atlanta, GA**
Provenzano, Anthony F., Jr. .... Plymouth, MA
Provenzano, Susan Ehrmann .... **Chicago, IL**
Provenzano, Vincent P. .... **Jackson, MI**
Providenti, Anthony C. .... **New York, NY**
Province, J. Thomas .... Madison, WI
Province, James A. .... Silverdale, WA
Province, Sharon G. .... Fairfield, NJ
Provine, Jack C. .... **Walnut Creek, CA**
Provine, John C. .... **New York, NY**
Provini, Guerin J. .... **San Jose, CA**
Provinzino, John C. .... St. Cloud, MN
Provis, Timothy A. .... Madison, WI
Provitera, Joseph J. .... Cliffside Park, NJ
Provitola, Anthony I. .... DeLand, FL
Provitola, Anthony I., P.A. .... DeLand, FL
Provizer, Harold M. .... **Bloomfield Hills, MI**
Provizer & Phillips, P.C.
Bloomfield Hills, MI
Detroit, MI
Southfield, MI
Provo, John W. .... **Minneapolis, MN**
Provonsha-Lentz, Donna .... Tampa, FL
Provoost, Jonathan .... Florham Park, NJ
Provo-Petersen, Jeannie .... **Minneapolis, MN**
Provorny, Craig S. .... **Warren, NJ**
Provorny, Frederick A. .... Silver Spring, MD
Provost, Chris .... Bethel, AK
Provost, Christine A. .... Chicago, IL
Provost, Christopher A. .... **New York, NY**
Provost, Denise .... Somerville, MA
Provost, Eugene P. .... Newark, NJ
Provost, Ginger R. .... Roseland, NJ
Provost, Jim E. .... Brooklyn, NY
Provost, Melissa A. .... **Newark, NJ**
Provost, Norman J. .... Los Angeles, CA
Provost, Thomas J. .... Boston, MA
Provost & Umphrey Law Firm, L.L.P.
Washington, DC
Norristown, PA
Nashville, TN
Beaumont, TX
Port Arthur, TX
Provost, Wendy A. .... Commack, NY
Provosty, A. Allain .... **Austin, TX**
Provosty, Albin A., III .... **Alexandria, LA**
Provosty, Michel O. .... New Orleans, LA
Provosty, Sadler & deLaunay
Alexandria, LA
Marksville, LA
Natchitoches, LA
Provosty, Shelley Hammond
New Orleans, LA
Provvidera, Marco R. .... New York, NY
Prow, William C. .... Madisonville, KY
Prowant-Hircock, Barbara
Kansas City, MO
Seattle, WA
Prowda, Judith B. .... **New York, NY**
Prowell, William P. .... **Cedar Rapids, IA**
Prows, Bennett J. .... Kirkland, WA
Prows, Lee S. (Tex) .... **San Diego, CA**
Prowse, Patricia G. .... Seattle, WA
Prowse, Stanley D. .... Carlsbad, CA
Proxmire, Douglas C. .... **Washington, DC**
Proyect, Dana Kennedy .... **Ellicott City, MD**
Proyect, Joel M. .... Parksville, NY
Proyect, Louis R. .... Santa Fe, NM
Proyect, Martin H. .... Santa Fe, NM
Prozan, Michael W. .... **Menlo Park, CA**
Prozanski, Floyd F., Jr. .... Eugene, OR
Prozeller, Bradley .... Geneva, NY
Prozzi, James A. .... **Pittsburgh, PA**
Prucha, Deborah J. .... Sacramento, CA
Prucha, Gerald L. .... Lorain, OH
Prucha, James T. .... Miami, FL
Pruchnicki, John B. .... Flushing, MI
Pruchnik, Walter C., Jr. .... Windber, PA
Prucino, Diane L. .... **Atlanta, GA**
Prucker, Brian W. .... Stafford Springs, CT
Pruden, George E., II
Department of Justice,
Bureau of Prisons, GV
Pruden, J. Norfleet, III .... **Charlotte, NC**
Pruden, James L. .... Boca Raton, FL
Pruden, Jonathan E. .... **Norfolk, VA**
Pruden, Michael I. .... Sacramento, CA
Prudente, Stephen C. .... **Albany, NY**
Prudenti, Angela M. .... East Moriches, NY
Prudhomme, Angela M.
Department Of Veterans Affairs,
Office of the General Counsel, GV
Prud'homme, Gerard J. .... **Washington, DC**
Prud'homme, Gilbert .... Austin, TX
Prudhomme, Joan S. .... Thousand Oaks, CA
Prudhomme, Kathleen L.
Minneapolis, MN
Prud'homme, M. Edwin .... Houston, TX
Prudhomme, M. Keith .... **Lake Charles, LA**
Prud'Homme, Michelle Renée
Denver, CO
Prud'homme, Tommy .... Austin, TX
Prudich, Gregory S. .... **Princeton, WV**
Prudich, Joseph .... Charleston, WV
Prue, June P. .... North Reading, MA
Prue, Nancy J. Floyd .... Baltimore, MD
Prue, Patrick M. .... Willimantic, CT
Prue, Patrick M., & Associates, P.C., Law
Offices of .... Willimantic, CT
Prueitt, Janet P. .... Gatesville, TX
Pruell, Joseph J. .... Norwood, MA
Pruellage, John K. .... **St. Louis, MO**
Pruessner, David M. .... **Dallas, TX**
Pruessner & Shilling .... **Dallas, TX**
Pruet, Bennett E. .... Birmingham, AL
Pruet, Gene V. .... **Columbia, SC**
Prueter, Susan M. .... Lima, OH
Pruett, Alice B. .... Gadsden, AL
Pruett, Benjamin H. .... **Atlanta, GA**
Pruett, Carl R. .... Houston, TX
Pruett, Cecil M. .... Borger, TX
Pruett, David P. .... **Long Beach, CA**
Pruett, H. Douglas .... **Austin, TX**
Pruett, H. Lee .... **Atlanta, GA**
Pruett, J. Albert, Jr. .... Houston, TX

Pruett, James D. ... **Gadsden, AL**
Pruett, James E. ... Greensburg, IN
Pruett, Jennifer J. ... **Albuquerque, NM**
Pruett, Jody Jacobson ... Richmond, VA
Pruett, Leo M. ... Phoenix, AZ
Pruett, Mary Ann ... Missouri City, TX
Pruett, Michael C. ... **Athens, GA**
Pruett, Noble J. ... Sterling Heights, MI
Pruett, Rebecca Lynne ... **Alamogordo, NM**
Pruett, Ricky L. ... Little Rock, AR
Pruett, Ronnie A. ... **Charlotte, NC**
Pruett, Sandra S., (P.C.) ... Austin, TX
Pruett, Susan M. ... Atlanta, GA
Pruett, Theresa E. ... **Seattle, WA**
Pruett & Waldrup, L.L.C. ... **Gadsden, AL**
Pruett, William D. ... Arlington, TX
Pruett, William H. ... Oklahoma City, OK
Pruette, Eileen Clark
Research Triangle Park, NC
Pruette, Henry W. ... Durham, NC
Pruetz, Adrian M. ... **Los Angeles, CA**
Prugar, Todd P. ... **Harrisburg, PA**
Pruger, Raoul ... Pittsburgh, PA
Prugh & Associates ... Tampa, FL
Prugh, David C. ... Cleveland Heights, OH
Prugh, George S. ... Orinda, CA
Prugh, R. Mitchell ... Melrose, FL
Prugh, Sara Sopkin ... Tampa, FL
Prugh, Timothy F. ... Tampa, FL
Prugh, Virginia Patton ... Orinda, CA
Prugh, Wallace D. ... **Denver, CO**
Prugh, William B. ... **Kansas City, MO**
Pruhs, Martin J. ... **Milwaukee, WI**
Pruiti, Graziella ... New York, NY
Pruiti, Graziella, P.C., Law Offices of
New York, NY
Pruitt, Abby G. ... Sacramento, CA
Pruitt, Andrea D. ... **Washington, DC**
Pruitt, Bart N. ... **Amarillo, TX**
Pruitt, Bobby M. ... Spartanburg, SC
Pruitt, Bradley H. ... **Atlanta, GA**
Louisville, KY
Pruitt, C. Daniel ... **Greenville, SC**
Pruitt, Carl Eugene, Jr. ... Russell, KY
Pruitt, Charles J. ... **Portland, OR**
Pruitt, Charles W. ... Millington, TN
Pruitt, Christopher J. ... **Fort Worth, TX**
Pruitt, David ... **Washington, DC**
Pruitt, Dean W. ... Bronson, FL
Pruitt, Deana K. ... Atlanta, GA
Pruitt, Deborah N. ... Houston, TX
Pruitt and de Bourbon Law Firm
Pikeville, KY
Pruitt, E. Scott ... Tulsa, OK
Pruitt, Eric Lloyd ... **Montgomery, AL**
Pruitt, F. Smith ... Anderson, SC
Pruitt, Friberg & Heatly ... Vernon, TX
Pruitt, G. Dwayne ... Brownfield, TX
Pruitt, Garis L. ... Catlettsburg, KY
Pruitt, Gary B. ... Sacramento, CA
Pruitt, Gerald ... **Fort Worth, TX**
Pruitt, Glyndon C. ... Buford, GA
Pruitt, Gregory D. ... Clinton, KY
Pruitt, Gushee & Bachtell
Salt Lake City, UT
Pruitt, Helen Rives ... **Portland, OR**
Pruitt, Ira D., Jr. ... **Livingston, AL**
Memphis, TN
Pruitt, J. Calhoun ... Anderson, SC
Pruitt, J. Calhoun, Jr. ... Anderson, SC
Pruitt, J. Michael ... Houston, TX
Pruitt, Jacob E., Jr. ... Columbus, OH
Pruitt, James C. ... Washington, DC
Pruitt, James P., Jr. ... Pikeville, KY
Pruitt, Jana Lee ... **Los Angeles, CA**
Pruitt, Jerry D. ... Fort Smith, AR
Pruitt, John E., Jr. ... Fredericksburg, VA
Pruitt, John S. ... **Newark, NJ**
Pruitt, John T., Jr. ... **Somerset, KY**
Pruitt, John W. ... Austin, TX
Pruitt, Karen G. ... Central, SC
Pruitt, Kristin L. ... **Washington, DC**
Pruitt, Kyle D. ... Greenwood, SC
Pruitt, Laura S.
Securities and Exchange Commission,
Office of the General Counsel, GV
Pruitt, Lyn Peeples ... **Little Rock, AR**
Pruitt, Michael R. ... **Mesa, AZ**
Payson, AZ
Pruitt, Nancy C. ... **Tulsa, OK**
Pruitt, Paul D. ... Tyler, TX
Pruitt, Prentice P. ... Tallahassee, FL
Pruitt & Pruitt ... Anderson, SC
Pruitt & Pruitt, P.A.
West Palm Beach, FL
Pruitt, Pruitt and Watkins, P.A.
Demopolis, AL
Eutaw, AL
Linden, AL
Livingston, AL
Pruitt, R. Eugene, Jr. ... **Abbeville, SC**
Pruitt, Renee Colette ... New York, NY
Pruitt, Robert G., III ... **Salt Lake City, UT**
Pruitt, Robert G., Jr. ... **Salt Lake City, UT**
Pruitt, Robert R. ... Houston, TX
Pruitt, Robin R. ... San Diego, CA
Pruitt, Ronald B. ... Houston, TX
Pruitt, Shirley Maring ... **Raleigh, NC**
Pruitt, Steven M. ... **Greenwood, SC**
Pruitt, Thomas L. ... Grundy, VA
Pruitt, Timothy J. ... **Racine, WI**
Pruitt, Tom F. ... **Baytown, TX**
Pruitt, Virginia A. ... Brooklyn, NY
Pruitt, William E. ... **West Palm Beach, FL**
Pruitt, William H. ... **West Palm Beach, FL**
Pruitt, William Howard ... **Las Vegas, NV**
Pruitt-Hamm, Bruce K. ... Colville, WA
Prukop, Georgia A. ... San Jose, CA
Prukop, Harold K. ... Norwalk, CA
Prukop, Harold K.(Hal), Jr. ... Issaquah, WA
Prulhiere, Jeffrey N. ... Tallmadge, OH
Pruna, Laura M. ... Miami, FL
Pruneda, M. Ilda ... Grover Beach, CA
Pruner, Mark ... Rye, NY
Pruner, Mark A. ... Sacramento, CA
Pruneski, Stephen J. ... **Akron, OH**
Prunhuber, Lynn S. ... Seattle, WA
Prunhuber, Patti ... Northampton, MA
Prunier, Gerald R. ... Nashua, NH
Prunier & Leonard, P.A. ... Nashua, NH
Pruniski, John E., III ... **Little Rock, AR**
North Little Rock, AR
Pruniski, Mary J. ... Little Rock, AR
Prunskis, Maria ... Hallandale Beach, FL
Prunte, Thomas J. ... Columbus, OH
Prunty, Allen R. ... **Charleston, WV**
Prunty, James A. ... Portland, OR
Prunty, Katherine M. ... Mount Vernon, WA
Prunty Law Offices ... Huntington, WV
Prunty, Paul J. ... Huntington, WV
Prunty, Samuel V., Jr. ... Shreveport, LA
Prunty, Steven M. ... **Morgantown, WV**
Prunty, W. Merton ... Huntington, WV
Prupis, Ernest ... Seabrook Island, SC
Prupis, Neil L. ... **West Orange, NJ**
Prus, Eric I. ... Brooklyn, NY
Prus, Karen L.
Research Triangle Park, NC
Prusa, Sheila A. ... Seattle, WA
Prusak, Gregory J ... **Miami, FL**
Prusak, Maximilian M. ... **Peoria, IL**
Prusak & Winne, Ltd. ... **Galesburg, IL**
Peoria, IL
Prusaski, Christopher W.
Fort Lauderdale, FL
Prusek, Ronald E. ... **Toms River, NJ**
Pruser, Elizabeth R. ... New York, NY
Prusher, Craig S. ... **Miami, FL**
Prusiecki, Drew W. ... **Jacksonville, FL**
Prusiecki, John F. ... **Chicago, IL**
Prusik, David ... Rochester, NY
Prusik, John P. ... **Chicago, IL**
Prusik, Matthew J., Jr. ... Sayreville, NJ
Prusik, Selby & Daley ... **Chicago, IL**
Prusinowski, Cindy A. ... Garden City, NY
Pruski, Gina M. ... Madison, WI
Pruski, Jennifer L. ... **Tahoe City, CA**
Prusky, Andrew R. ... **Philadelphia, PA**
Prusky, Byron R. ... **Landover, MD**
Cherry Hill, NJ
Philadelphia, PA
Prusky Law Associates, P.C.
Landover, MD
Cherry Hill, NJ
Philadelphia, PA
Prusnofsky, Jeff S. ... **New York, NY**
Pruss, James D. ... Omaha, NE
Pruss, Marion F., Law Offices of
Omaha, NE
Pruss, Mary K. ... **Washington, PA**
Waynesburg, PA
Pruss, Stephen J. ... Dallas, TX
Pruss, Stephen L. ... **Nampa, ID**
Prussack, Andrew H. ... **Atlanta, GA**
Prusse, Joan Hilton ... Denver, CO
Prussin, H. Adam ... **New York, NY**
Prussin, Shari L. ... **New York, NY**
Prussing, Robert E. ... Santa Monica, CA
Prusynski, Mark S. ... **Boise, ID**
Pruter, Michael C. ... **San Diego, CA**
Prutting, George A., Jr. ... **Audubon, NJ**
Prutting & Lombardi, Law Offices of
Audubon, NJ
Camden, NJ
Prutton, Douglas A., Law Offices of
Berkeley, CA
Prutton, Douglas A., Law Offices of
Oakland, CA
Prutzman, Deborah S. ... New York, NY
Prutzman, L. Donald ... **New York, NY**
Pruyn, Bernadette ... Houston, TX
Pruyne, James A. ... Dushore, PA
Le Raysville, PA
Towanda, PA
Pruyne, Robert S. ... **New York, NY**
Pruzan, Carl ... **Seattle, WA**
Pruzan, Gloria E. ... Chicago, IL
Pruzan, Howard P. ... **Seattle, WA**
Pruzan, Jerry Z. ... Washington, DC
Pruzan, Mark S. ... **New York, NY**
Pruzan, Steven R. ... **Seattle, WA**
Pruzansky, Joshua M. ... **Smithtown, NY**
Pruzansky, Lawrence M. ... Bronx, NY
Pruzansky, Steven R. ... Bronx, NY
Pruzansky, Wallace ... Bronx, NY
Pruzinsky, Anthony J. ... **Jersey City, NJ**
New York, NY
Pruzynski, Kimberly A. ... Las Vegas, NV
Pry, C. Nicholas ... Findlay, OH
Pry, James W., II ... Bucyrus, OH
Pry, Lawrence W. ... St. Paul, MN
Pry, Russell M. ... Akron, OH
Pryatel, August ... Solon, OH
Pryatel, Keith L. ... **Cleveland, OH**
Pryatel, Mark R. ... Shaker Heights, OH
Pryatel, Robert L. ... Shaker Heights, OH
Pryatel, Steven E. ... **Cleveland, OH**
Prybylski, Mark C. ... **Winston-Salem, NC**
Pryce, Deborah D. ... Columbus, OH
Pryce, Douglas R. ... Golden, CO
Pryce, Jeffrey F
Department of Defense, GV
Pryce, Mary E. ... **Saratoga, CA**
Pryce, Robert D. ... Los Angeles, CA
Pryce, Susanne ... **Southfield, MI**
Pryde, James P. ... **Kansas City, MO**
Pryde, Marc Harry ... Bellevue, WA
Pryde, Robert E. ... Kittanning, PA
Prye, Steven M. ... Champaign, IL
Pryer, Mary J. ... Santa Ana, CA
Pryer, Rex A. ... Eureka, CA
Pryga & Petronko ... **Rahway, NJ**
Prygoski, Philip J. ... Lansing, MI
Prygrosky, Carol R. ... **Chicago, IL**
Prynkiewicz, Peter C. ... **Phoenix, AZ**
Pryor, Aline E. ... **Overland Park, KS**
Pryor, Andrew ... Mission Viejo, CA
Pryor, Anita ... **Jacksonville, FL**
Pryor, Anthony D. ... **Houston, TX**
Pryor, Barbara L. ... **Albuquerque, NM**
Pryor, Barry, Smith, Karber and Alford
P.L.C. ... **Fayetteville, AR**
Fort Smith, AR
Van Buren, AR
Pryor, C. Scott ... **Orlando, FL**
Pryor, Calvin C. ... Montgomery, AL
Pryor, Caroline T. ... **Mobile, AL**
Pryor, Carranza M. ... **Birmingham, AL**
Pryor Cashman Sherman & Flynn LLP
New York, NY
Pryor, David E. ... Columbus, OH
Pryor, David H. ... Little Rock, AR
Pryor, David M. ... **Dallas, TX**
Pryor, David T. ... **Dover, DE**
Pryor, David W. ... **Columbus, OH**
Pryor, Dianne M. Mullins ... Dallas, TX
Pryor, Doyle R. ... New York, NY
Pryor, Flynn, Priest & Harber
Knoxville, TN
Pryor, Francis W., Jr. ... Jasper, TN
Pryor, Gregory P. ... **New York, NY**
Pryor, Jackie Vencil ... **Minneapolis, MN**
Pryor, James K. ... Boonton, NJ
Pryor, Jill A. ... **Atlanta, GA**
Pryor Johnson Montoya Carney & Karr,
P.C. ... **Denver, CO**
Pryor, Juliette Williams
Annapolis Junction, MD
Pryor, Kathryn A. ... **Little Rock, AR**
Pryor, Kenneth A. ... New York, NY
Pryor, Kevin R. ... **Chicago, IL**
Pryor, Linda K. ... Indianapolis, IN
Pryor, Lindsey Stansfield ... New York, NY
Pryor, Louis S. ... **New Canaan, CT**
Pryor & Mandelup, L.L.P. ... **Mineola, NY**
Westbury, NY
Pryor, Mark G. ... **Minneapolis, MN**
Pryor, Mark L. ... Little Rock, AR
Pryor, Mary G. ... **Phoenix, AZ**
Pryor, Matthew W. ... Baton Rouge, LA
Gonzales, LA
Pryor, Melvin J. ... Baltimore, MD
Pryor, Michael H. ... **Washington, DC**
Pryor, Pamela ... Harahan, LA
Pryor, Patricia Anderson ... **Cincinnati, OH**
Pryor, Peter M. ... Albany, NY
Pryor, Peter W. ... **Denver, CO**
Pryor, Raymond E. ... Towson, MD
Pryor, Richard E. ... **Dayton, OH**
Pryor, Richard E., II ... Princeton, NJ
Pryor, Richard G. ... Norman, OK
Pryor, Robert E. ... **Knoxville, TN**
Pryor, Robert E., Jr. ... **Knoxville, TN**
Pryor, Robert H. ... **Charlotte, NC**
Pryor, Robert J. ... Bridgeton, NJ
Pryor, Robert L. ... **Westbury, NY**
Pryor, Roger J. ... Torrance, CA
Pryor, Samuel F. ... New York, NY
Pryor, Samuel F., III ... **New York, NY**
Pryor, Samuel R. ... **Los Angeles, CA**
Pryor, Saul P. ... Lakewood, CO
Pryor, Shepherd G., III ... Atlanta, GA
Pryor, Thomas B. ... **Fort Smith, AR**
Pryor, Thomas E., Jr. ... **Orlando, FL**
Pryor, Thomas J. ... **Princeton, NJ**
Pryor, Victor C. (Vic) ... Jacksboro, TN
Pryor, Vikki L. ... Park Forest, IL
Pryor, Virgil F. ... San Francisco, CA
Pryor, Walter O. ... Department of Justice,
Tax Division, GV
Pryor, Wilbert D. ... **Shreveport, LA**
Pryor, Wilbur M. ... **Denver, CO**
Pryor, Will ... Dallas, TX
Pryor, William A. ... Springfield, IL
Pryor, William B. ... New York, NY
Pryor, William C. ... Washington, DC
Pryor, William H., Jr. ... Montgomery, AL
Pryor, William T. ... Arlington, VA
Pryor, William Y. ... Essex Fells, NJ
Pryor-Baze, Holli V. ... **Houston, TX**
Pryor-Karangekis, Amy Lynne
Medway, MA
Prypchan, Andre Bohdan ... Chicago, IL
Prys, Kevin Charles ... Fresno, CA
Prysak, Suzanne J. ... **Chicago, IL**
Pryse, Gail Glassmeyer ... **Cincinnati, OH**
Prysock, Gregory D. ... **Orlando, FL**
Prystowsky, Steven B. ... **New York, NY**
Prywes, Daniel I. ... **Washington, DC**
Pryzanski, Corinne ... **New York, NY**
Pryzant, Joseph R. ... Houston, TX
Pryzbylski, David A. ... Fairless Hills, PA
Pryzwansky, David T. ... **Raleigh, NC**
Przekop, Charles R. ... **Princeton, NJ**
Przekop-Shaw, Susan ... Lansing, MI
Przelomiec, Debra J. ... **Woodland Hills, CA**
Przepis, Bruce E. ... New Port Richey, FL
Przetacznik, Frank ... New York, NY
Przetak, Laura ... **Oakland, CA**
Przybeck, Ruth A. ... St. Louis, MO
Przyborowski, Thaddeus A. ... Clark, NJ
Przyborski, Thomas G. ... Countryside, IL
Przybyla, Thomas J. ... Buffalo, NY
Przybylek, Charles S. ... Albuquerque, NM
Przybylinski, Donald
Department Of Health And Human Services,
Social Security Administration, GV
Przybylko, Eric J. ... **New York, NY**
Przybylo, Chester M. ... Chicago, IL
Przybylo, Kerry Ryan ... **Lansing, MI**
Przybylowicz, Arthur R. ... Okemos, MI
Przybyszewski, Sandra J. ... Lake Forest, IL
Przypyszny, John R. ... **Washington, DC**
Przystawski, Christine M. ... Louisville, KY
Przywara, Kathryn Knue ... **Cincinnati, OH**
Przywozny, Matthew E. ... **Iselin, NJ**
Short Hills, NJ
Psak, George L. ... Middlesex, NJ
Psak, Graziano, Piasecki & Whitelaw
Middlesex, NJ
Psalidas, Andrew ... Miami, FL
Psaltis, Edmond G.
Department of Agriculture,
Animal and Plant Health Inspection Service,
GV
Psarakis, Emanuel N. ... **Hartford, CT**
Psarellis & Carr, L.L.C.
New Orleans, LA
Psarellis, Erin E. ... **New Orleans, LA**
Psarellis, Steven E. ... **New Orleans, LA**
Psaris & Allen ... Red Hill, PA
Psaris, Ronald J. ... Red Hill, PA
Psaropoulos, Robert C. ... **Cleveland, OH**
Psaty, Martin M. ... Forest Hills, NY
Psencik, E. Dwain ... Eden, TX
San Angelo, TX
Psenda, Richard L. ... Houston, TX
Psetas, George C. ... Port Richey, FL
Psetas, George C., P.A. ... Port Richey, FL
Pshedesky, Edward ... Hauppauge, NY
Psihos, Christopher J. ... Edina, MN
Psimos, Harry A. ... Merrillville, IN
Psimos, Mark A. ... Merrillville, IN
Psimos & Psimos ... Merrillville, IN
Pskowski, Harold W. ... Rockville, MD
Psoinas, Laura A. ... Hempstead, NY
Psoinos, George D. ... West Palm Beach, FL
Psoinos, George D., P.A.
West Palm Beach, FL
Psomadelis, Paul ... Crown Point, IN
Psoras, Cynthia L. ... New York, NY
Psoras, Dennis J. ... Towson, MD
Psoras, Dennis J., P.A. ... Towson, MD
Psoras, Gregory J. ... Towson, MD
Psota, Paul ... **Cleveland, OH**
Psutka, Stephen J. ... **Pittsfield, MA**
Psyhogeos, Nicholas J. ... Washington, DC
Psyllos, Michael Peter ... Bayside, NY
Ptacek, Edward A. ... Chicago, IL
Ptacek, Gerald P. ... Racine, WI
Ptacek, Louise A. ... Milwaukee, WI
Ptacek, Susan J.
Department Of Veterans Affairs,
Office of the General Counsel, GV
Ptacek, Tammie S. ... St. Paul, MN
Ptak, David H. ... **Norfolk, NE**
Ptak, Edwin A. ... Chicago, IL
Ptak, LaValle D. ... **Scottsdale, AZ**
Ptak, Michael J. ... **Little Rock, AR**
Ptak & Rooney ... Cicero, IL
Ptak, Sylvester J. ... Cicero, IL
Ptashek, Jay M. ... **New York, NY**
Ptashnik, Neil B. ... **New York, NY**
Ptasiewicz, Seth ... **Newark, NJ**
Ptasinski, Lawrence J. ... Niles, IL
Ptasinski & Smith ... Niles, IL
Ptasnik, Edward R. ... Sterling Heights, MI
Ptaszek, Edward G. ... Jefferson, OH
Ptaszek, Edward G., Jr. ... **Cleveland, OH**
Ptasznik, Heather Gelfand ... Philadelphia, PA
Ptasznik, Victor F. ... **Detroit, MI**
Ptomey, William R., Jr. ... Tavernier, FL
Pu, Richard ... **New York, NY**
Pu, Robert M. ... Brattleboro, VT
Puathasnanon, Sam ... **Los Angeles, CA**
Publicover, Adrienne C.
San Francisco, CA
Publicover, Daniel H. ... Santa Ana, CA
Publow, Harry F. ... Las Vegas, NV
Puca, Michael J. ... Kalamazoo, MI
Pucci, Albert ... Putnam, IL
Pucci, George X. ... **Boston, MA**
Pucci, Gerard ... Miami, FL
Pucci, Jeanne F. ... **New York, NY**
Pucci, John P. ... **Northampton, MA**
Pucci, Louis J. ... Baltimore, MD
Pucci, Patrice A. ... St. Petersburg, FL
Pucci, Robert J. ... Mahwah, NJ
Pucci, Thomas D. ... **Providence, RI**
Puccia, Frank J. ... Albany, NY
Pucciarelli, Albert J. ... New York, NY
Pucciarelli, William J. C. ... Newton, MA
Puccinelli, Andrew J. ... **Elko, NV**
Puccinelli, Leo J. ... **Elko, NV**
Puccinelli & Puccinelli ... **Elko, NV**
Puccini, Arthur V. ... Fairfield, CT
Puccini, Lido L. ... **New York, NY**
Puccini, Louis, Jr. ... **Albuquerque, NM**
Puccini & Meagle, P.A. ... **Albuquerque, NM**
Puccio, Anthony J. ... Garden City, NY
Puccio, Carmen P. ... Corning, NY
Puccio, Cyrece ... **Walnut Creek, CA**
Puccio, Domenic, II ... Santa Ana, CA
Puccio, Frank S., Jr. ... Boston, MA
Worcester, MA
Puccio, James S. ... Cape Coral, FL
Puccio, Mark V. ... Des Plaines, IL
Puccio, Thomas P., Law Offices of
New York, NY
Pucel, Jody M. ... Seattle, WA
Puchades, Michael A. ... **Miami, FL**
Puchalla, Helge M. ... St. Louis, MO

Pullen, John S. ... **Ellsworth, ME**
Pullen, Lisa Anne ... Costa Mesa, CA
Pullen, Lisa Entress ... **Albuquerque, NM**
Pullen, Lucius W. ... **Raleigh, NC**
Pullen, Matthew A. ... **Albuquerque, NM**
Pullen, Michael L. ... **Easton, MD**
Pullen, Michael L., P.A. ... **Easton, MD**
Pullen, Myron D. ... Manhattan Beach, CA
Pullen, Peter J. ... **Sacramento, CA**
Pullen, Richard O. ... Arlington, VA
Pullen, Ronald J. ... Chula Vista, CA
Pullen, Susanna V. ... **Cameron Park, CA**
Pullen, Tera D. ... Atlanta, GA
Pullen, Thomas L. ... Department of Justice, Executive Office for Immigration Review, GV
Puller, A. Damien ... **Boston, MA**
Pulles, Gregory J. ... Minneapolis, MN
Pulley, Arthur L. ... New Rochelle, NY
Pulley, Brent H. ... **Dallas, TX**
Pulley, Daryl M. ... Portland, OR
Pulley, Diane G. ... **Atlanta, GA**
Pulley, F. Bert ... **Courtland, VA**
Pulley, Glenn W. ... **Danville, VA**
Pulley, J. Waverly, III ... **Richmond, VA**
Pulley, Jack I. ... **Midland, MI**
Pulley, Karl E. ... Nashville, TN
Pulley, Lewis C.
Federal Communications Commission, Mass Media Bureau, GV
Pulley, Lydia R. ... **Richmond, VA**
Pulley, Navarro
Equal Employment Opportunity Commission, GV
Pulley, Pamela Abney ... **Long Beach, CA**
Pulley, Ralph W. ... Dallas, TX
Pulley & Rowe ... **Courtland, VA**
Pulley, W. Paul, Jr. ... **Durham, NC**
Pulley, Warren A. ... **Oakland, CA**
Pulley, Watson, King & Lischer, P.A.
Durham, NC
Pulliam, Andrew J. ... **Nashville, TN**
Pulliam, Arthur Woodson ... Munfordville, KY
Pulliam, David C. ... **Des Moines, IA**
Pulliam, Edward H. ... Department of Energy, Office of the General Counsel, GV
Pulliam, G. Donald ... Gainesville, GA
Pulliam, Gary A. ... Las Vegas, NV
Pulliam, James H. ... **Charlotte, NC**
Pulliam, Janet L. ... **Little Rock, AR**
Pulliam, Karen A. ... Los Angeles, CA
Pulliam, Kathryn O'Neill ... **Atlanta, GA**
Pulliam, Leisa ... Little Rock, AR
Pulliam, Marie Haraka ... Norcross, GA
Pulliam, Mark S. ... **San Diego, CA**
Pulliam, Maxwell H., Jr. ... **Birmingham, AL**
Pulliam, Michael A. ... **Columbia, SC**
Pulliam, Paul A. ... Dallas, TX
Pulliam, Randall K. ... **Jacksonville, AR**
Pulliam, Royce C. ... Cynthiana, KY
Pulliam, Thomas E. ... **St. Louis, MO**
Pulliam, Thomas W., Jr.
San Francisco, CA
Pulliam, Tomi Anne Blevins
Lexington, KY
Louisville, KY
Pulliam, Virgil R. ... Dallas, TX
Pulliam, W. C. ... Cross Lanes, WV
Pulliam and Wright, P.A. ... **Little Rock, AR**
Pullin, Allan L. ... Woodbury, NY
Pullin, Betty Adkins ... Charleston, WV
Pullin, Diana C. ... Lexington, MA
Pullin, Gary E. ... **Charleston, WV**
Pullin, Gary W. ... Plano, TX
Pullin, Inna ... **Milwaukee, WI**
Pullin, Kirsten M. ... **Washington, DC**
Pullin, Knopf, Fowler & Flanagan
Beckley, WV
Charleston, WV
Huntington, WV
Pullins, John A. ... Silver Spring, MD
Pullis, Robert M. ... **Conroe, TX**
Pullman, Andrew B. ... **Pittsburgh, PA**
Pullman & Comley, L.L.C.
Bridgeport, CT
Hartford, CT
New Haven, CT
Southport, CT
Stamford, CT
Pullman, Craig ... Sarasota, FL
Pullman, Gust P. ... **Buffalo, NY**
Pullman, Mark Allan ... Syracuse, NY
Pullman, Richard D., (P.C.) ... **Dallas, TX**
Pullman, Saul A. ... Eastland, TX
Pullman, Terry L. ... Wichita, KS
Pullman & WarnerLaw Group, P.A.
Wichita, KS
Pullo, Andrew J. ... Boston, MA
Pullum, J. Stephen ... **Crystal River, FL**
Leesburg, FL
Pullum, Marybeth L. ... **Crystal River, FL**
Leesburg, FL
Pullum, Paul L. ... Omaha, NE
Pullum & Pullum, P.A. ... **Leesburg, FL**
Pullum, Roberta H. ... Detroit, MI
Pully, William A. ... Raleigh, NC
Pulman, Charles D. ... **Dallas, TX**
Pulman, Randall A. ... **San Antonio, TX**
Pulman, Shari Pullen ... **San Antonio, TX**
Pulner, Louis M. ... Providence, RI
Pulner, Warren M. ... El Paso, TX
Pulone, Robert J. ... Los Alamitos, CA
Pulos and Rosell, LLP ... Hornell, NY
Pulos, Theodore ... Stratford, CT
Pulos, Victoria ... Portsmouth, NH
Pulos, William W. ... Hornell, NY
Puls, Carl A., Jr. ... Decatur, GA
Puls & Chambers, L.L.P. ... **Fort Worth, TX**
Puls, Fritz L. ... Danvers, MA
Puls, W. Kelly ... **Fort Worth, TX**
Pulsfus, Dwight W. ... Sauk City, WI
Pulsifer, Howard A. ... **Wood Dale, IL**
Pulsifer, Kelly L. ... Falls Church, VA
Pulsifer, Marc D. ... Tempe, AZ
Pulsifer, Marion ... New York, NY
Pulsifer, Robert W. ... Saratoga Springs, NY
Pulsifer, Sharon L. ... Moline, IL
Pulsifer, Thomas R. ... **Wilmington, DE**
Pulsinelli, Gary ... Palo Alto, CA
Pulskamp, Arthur R. ... Lighthouse Point, FL
Pulskamp, Cassandra C. ... **Oakland, CA**
Pulskamp, John J. ... Sutter Creek, CA
Pulter, Daniel L. ... **Lansing, MI**
Pultman, Adeena Dresdner ... **Montclair, NJ**
Pultman, Jacob S. ... **New York, NY**
Pultz, Edward M. ... Farmington, MO
Pultz, George S. ... **Lynn, MA**
Pultz, William C. ... **Carlsbad, CA**
Pulver, Barry M. ... **Parsippany, NJ**
Pulver, George J., Jr. ... Catskill, NY
Pulver, Ira ... Flushing, NY
Pulver, Janice K. ... Chattanooga, TN
Pulver, Michael A. ... **Baltimore, MD**
Pulver, Robert A. ... Washington, DC
Pulver, Roberto ... Phoenix, AZ
Pulvermacher, Louis C. ... Millbrook, NY
Pulverman, Martin E. ... **Santa Barbara, CA**
Pulverman & Pulverman
Santa Barbara, CA
Pulverman, Raymond J.
Santa Barbara, CA
Pulvers, Marvin ... **New York, NY**
Pulvers, Patrice M. ... **New York, NY**
Pulvers, Pulvers, Thompson & Kutner, P.C.
New York, NY
Pulvers, Roy E. ... **Portland, OR**
Pulvirenti, Joseph L. ... New York, NY
Pum, Maria K. ... **San Diego, CA**
Puma, Anthony J. ... Bronx, NY
Puma, David J. ... Salem, NJ
Puma, Marie Elena R. ... **Westbury, NY**
Puma, Scott A. ... Chicago, IL
Puma, Vincent T. ... **New York, NY**
Pumarada, Pedro ... **San Juan, PR**
Pumilia, Adamec & Stephens, LLP
Costa Mesa, CA
Pasadena, CA
Pumilia, Richard B. ... **Pasadena, CA**
Pummell, Carly A. ... **Troy, MI**
Pummill, Brian S. ... Toledo, OH
Pummill, Robert A. ... Overland Park, KS
Pump, Ronald E. ... Washington, DC
Pumphrey, C. Michael ... **Jackson, MS**
Pumphrey, Gerald R.
Palm Beach Gardens, FL
Pumphrey, Gerald R., P.A.
Palm Beach Gardens, FL
Pumphrey, Janet Hetherwick ... Lenox, MA
Pumphrey, Joe D., II ... Dallas, TX
Pumphrey, John M. ... **Philadelphia, PA**
Pumphrey, Penny ... Dallas, TX
Pumphrey, Peter C. ... Stockton, CA
Pumphrey, William R. ... **Winchester, KY**
Pumphrey, Wm. H. ... Little Rock, AR
Pumpian, Mark A. ... Milwaukee, WI
Pumpian, Ryan T. ... West Palm Beach, FL
Pumroy, Jay F. ... **Anniston, AL**
Puñales, Rosalind S. ... **Union City, NJ**
Punancy, Karlene Ann ... Miami, FL
Punancy, Shelley M. ... West Palm Beach, FL
Puncer, William O. ... Miamisburg, OH
Punch, James P. ... Albion, NY
Punchatz, Ivan J. ... **Princeton, NJ**
Punches, Robert R. ... **Natchez, MS**
Pund, John L., Jr. ... Philadelphia, PA
Pundeff, Michael V. ... **San Diego, CA**
Punderson, Ebenezer ... Middlebury, VT
Pundt, Richard A., Law Offices
Cedar Rapids, IA
Pundt, Steven C. ... **Minneapolis, MN**
Puneky, Warren R., Jr. ... Metairie, LA
Punelli, Frank, Jr. ... **Newport Beach, CA**
Puner, Nicholas W. ... Chappaqua, NY
Puner, Polly M. ... Brookline, MA
Punger, Douglas ... Winston-Salem, NC
Punke, Timothy E. ... **Washington, DC**
Punnett, Spencer M., II ... Tampa, FL
Punshon, W. Wayne ... Media, PA
Puntch, James E., Jr. ... Wichita, KS
Puntenney, Keith deT. ... Des Moines, IA
Punter, Lawrence P. V. ... Los Angeles, CA
Puntigam, Clark A. ... **Seattle, WA**
Puntil, Ronald M., Jr. ... **Pittsburgh, PA**
Puntillo, Lisa K. ... **San Francisco, CA**
Puntureri, Larry J. ... New Castle, PA
Puntureri, Rocco L. ... Grove City, PA
Punturi, Michele R. ... **Philadelphia, PA**
Puntus, Marc D. ... **New York, NY**
Punzak, David R. ... **St. Petersburg, FL**
Puopolo, Edward V. ... Dedham, MA
Puopolo, Robert E. ... **Boston, MA**
Puopolo, Timothy M. ... Chandler, AZ
Pupatelli, Peter Paul ... Rochester, NY
Pupel, Daniel S., Jr. ... Battle Creek, MI
Pupillo, Teresa Dale ... **St. Louis, MO**
Pupke, Donald V., Jr. ... New York, NY
Pupke, Peter G. ... New York, NY
Pupkin, Barry A. ... **Washington, DC**
Pupkin, Randi Alper ... Baltimore, MD
Puplava, Jennifer A. ... **Grand Rapids, MI**
Pupo, Roberto R. ... **Miami, FL**
Pupo-Mayo, Gustavo A. ... Miami Beach, FL
Puppa, Thomas J. ... **New York, NY**
Puppio, Andrea Belefonte ... **Media, PA**
Puppio, Michael V., Jr. ... Media, PA
Puppo, Laura M. ... **New York, NY**
Purbaugh, John C. ... Tacoma, WA
Purbaugh, Kim ... Riverside, CA
Purce, Kenneth P. ... Port Jervis, NY
Purcel, Jerry P., L.P.A. ... Toledo, OH
Purcell, A. Craig ... **Central Islip, NY**
Purcell, A. Craig ... **Hauppauge, NY**
Purcell, A. Craig ... **Riverhead, NY**
Purcell, Anita Tedesco
Securities and Exchange Commission, Office of the General Counsel, GV
Purcell, Anne
National Labor Relations Board, Office of the General Counsel, GV
Purcell, Anne M. ... Department of Justice, Antitrust Division, GV
Purcell, Arthur K. ... **New York, NY**
Purcell & Associates, L.L.C.
St. Louis, MO
Purcell, Brian C. ... **Virginia Beach, VA**
Purcell, Byron Michael ... **Los Angeles, CA**
Purcell, C. William ... **Wickliffe, OH**
Purcell, Cary W. ... Columbus, OH
Purcell, Charles F. ... Louisa, VA
Purcell, Charles H. ... **Seattle, WA**
Purcell, Charles K. ... **Albuquerque, NM**
Purcell, Charles M. ... **Jackson, TN**
Purcell, Charles R. ... Chicago, IL
Purcell, Christopher H. ... Chicago, IL
Purcell, Coy W. ... **Flourtown, PA**
Purcell, D. Paul ... Newport Beach, CA
Purcell, Daniel E. ... **San Francisco, CA**
Purcell, Daniel P. ... **Rochester, NY**
Purcell, David M. ... Albany, NY
Purcell, David S. ... **St. Louis, MO**
Purcell, David V. ... Pewaukee, WI
Purcell, David W. ... Boulder City, NV
Purcell, Davis ... **Fort Worth, TX**
Purcell, Deborah Ann ... **Denver, CO**
Purcell, Donald H. ... Ashton, ID
Purcell, Douglas W. ... Lynnwood, WA
Purcell, Edgar G., Jr. ... Glens Falls, NY
Purcell, Edw. K. ... Sacramento, CA
Purcell, Edward A., Jr. ... New York, NY
Purcell, Edward B., Jr. ... Columbia, SC
Purcell, Edward C. ... Chicago, IL
Purcell, Edward R. ... Mountain Lakes, NJ
Purcell, Elizabeth A. ... Treasury Department, Internal Revenue Service, GV
Purcell, Elizabeth Higgins ... Atlanta, GA
Purcell, Eugene M. ... **Bedminster, NJ**
Philadelphia, PA
Purcell, Flanagan & Hay, P.A.
Jacksonville, FL
Tallahassee, FL
Purcell, Francis E., Jr. ... **Washington, DC**
Purcell, Gary M. ... Oklahoma City, OK
Purcell, Gilbert L. ... **Novato, CA**
Purcell, Graham B., Jr. ... Wichita Falls, TX
Purcell, Harold H. ... Louisa, VA
Purcell, Heather A. ... **Washington, DC**
Purcell & Ingrao, P.C. ... **Commack, NY**
Garden City, NY
Mineola, NY
New York, NY
Staten Island, NY
Purcell, Irving G. ... New York, NY
Purcell, Jack B. ... Mill Valley, CA
Purcell, James E. ... Butte, MT
Purcell, James E. ... **Providence, RI**
Purcell, James J. ... Seattle, WA
Purcell, James L. ... Williamstown, KY
Purcell, James L. ... **New York, NY**
Purcell, James L., Jr. ... **Jacksonville, FL**
Purcell, James W., (P.C.) ... **Augusta, GA**
Purcell, Jane A. ... New York, NY
Purcell, Jeffrey W. ... Boston, MA
Purcell, Joe R. ... Phoenix, AZ
Purcell, John B., Jr. ... Richmond, VA
Purcell, John C. ... Oakland, CA
Purcell, John F., P.C. ... **Portland, OR**
Purcell, John J. ... New York, NY
Purcell, John J., III ... **New York, NY**
Purcell, John M. ... Uniontown, PA
Purcell, John S. ... **Los Angeles, CA**
Purcell, John W. ... **Indianapolis, IN**
Purcell, John W. ... **Harrisburg, PA**
Purcell, John W., II ... Jefferson City, MO
Purcell, John W., Jr. ... **Harrisburg, PA**
Purcell, Joseph A., Jr. ... Bronx, NY
Purcell, Joseph J. ... Bronx, NY
Purcell, Joseph M. ... **New York, NY**
Purcell, Joseph R. ... **Bedminster, NJ**
Purcell, Kathleen J. ... **San Francisco, CA**
Purcell, Kenneth J. ... **El Segundo, CA**
Purcell, Kenneth P. ... **Chicago, IL**
Purcell, Kermit K. ... San Jose, CA
Purcell, Kevin ... Cleveland, OH
Purcell, Kristine Bogardus ... **Roseland, NJ**
Purcell, Krug & Haller ... **Harrisburg, PA**
Purcell, Laura M. ... Rochester, NY
Purcell, Madalyn ... **Honolulu, HI**
Purcell, Marda H. ... Tampa, FL
Purcell, Martin A. ... **Palm Beach, FL**
Purcell, Martin J. ... Kansas City, MO
Purcell, Mary Dey ... Kansas City, MO
Purcell, Mary Eileen ... Akron, OH
Purcell, Meabh ... **Boston, MA**
Purcell, Michael Sean ... **Washington, DC**
Purcell, Michael T. ... Portland, OR
Purcell, Michael T., P.C. ... Portland, OR
Purcell, Mikel L. ... Atlanta, GA
Purcell, Miles J. ... Saginaw, MI
Purcell, Morris D., Jr. ... **Tampa, FL**
Purcell, Nicholas J. ... **Livingston, NJ**
Purcell, Patrick J. ... **Mineola, NY**
Purcell, Paul M. ... **Saginaw, MI**
Purcell, Pierce T. ... Madison, WI
Purcell & Purcell ... Louisa, VA
Purcell, Regina B. ... Garden City, NY
Purcell, Richard Fick ... Westfield, NJ
Purcell, Richard J. ... Briarcliff Manor, NY
Purcell, Ricky D. ... Tucumcari, NM
Purcell, Ries, Shannon, Mulcahy & O'Neill
Bedminster, NJ
Belvidere, NJ
Bridgewater, NJ
Camden, NJ
Elizabeth, NJ
Flemington, NJ
Hackensack, NJ
Jersey City, NJ
Marlton, NJ
Morristown, NJ
Newark, NJ
New Brunswick, NJ
Newton, NJ
Paterson, NJ
Princeton, NJ
Somerville, NJ
Trenton, NJ
Philadelphia, PA
Purcell, Robert Dewey ... Sacramento, CA
Purcell, Robert E. ... **Denver, CO**
Purcell, Robert L. ... Kansas City, MO
Purcell, Robert M., Jr.
Whitehouse Station, NJ
Purcell, Robert R. ... **Houston, TX**
Purcell & Russell ... Lynnwood, WA
Purcell, Stephen G. ... **Chatham, NJ**
Toms River, NJ
Purcell, T. David ... **Mount Vernon, IL**
Purcell, Ted M. ... Newport Beach, CA
Purcell, Terri L. ... **Atlanta, GA**
Purcell, Thomas ... San Francisco, CA
Purcell, Thomas F. ... Carmel, NY
Purcell, Thomas K. ... **Jacksonville, FL**
Purcell, Thomas M. ... Orange, VA
Purcell, Thomas M., P.C. ... Orange, VA
Purcell, Thomas R. ... New York, NY
Purcell, Timothy M. ... **Houston, TX**
Purcell, Tunison & Boardman, P.C.
Bay City, MI
Saginaw, MI
Purcell, W. Riker ... **Richmond, VA**
Purcell, Wade H. ... **Atlanta, GA**
Purcell & Wardrope, Chartered ... Chicago, IL
Purcell, Wayne D. ... Longview, WA
Purcell, William C. ... Fort Lauderdale, FL
Purcell, William J. ... **Woodbridge, NJ**
Staten Island, NY
Purcell, William L. ... Chicago, IL
Purcell, William O. ... **New York, NY**
Purcell, William P., III ... Nashville, TN
Purcell, William R., II ... **Laurinburg, NC**
Purcell, Young & Sperber ... Cincinnati, OH
Purcella, James C. ... Portland, OR
Purchase, Eric J. ... **Erie, PA**
Purchase, Robert L. ... Slingerlands, NY
Purchis, Frederick Allen ... Homewood, AL
Purcigliotti, Robert A. ... New York, NY
Purcupile, J. Stephen ... Pittsburgh, PA
Purdie, Alan M. ... **Grenada, MS**
Jackson, MS
New Albany, MS
Oxford, MS
Purdie, Bridget O'Toole ... **Houston, TX**
Purdie, Denise W. ... Washington, DC
Purdom, Atchley and Pettiet, Law Offices of
Lubbock, TX
Purdom, Daniel M. ... **Lisle, IL**
Purdom, Eugene W. ... **Greensboro, NC**
Purdom, Kathryn V. ... **Greensboro, NC**
Purdom, Rebecca S. ... Pawlet, VT
Purdom, Seaton D. ... **Atlanta, GA**
Purdom, Thomas J. ... **Lubbock, TX**
Purdom, Wayne M. ... Decatur, GA
Purdon, Richard L. ... Kansas City, MO
Purdon, Roger A. ... Florence, MA
Purdon, Timothy Q ... Bismarck, ND
Purdue, Ann Roberts ... **Jacksonville, FL**
Purdue, Beverly ... Bethesda, MD
Purdue, David C. ... Toledo, OH
Purdue, Glenn E. ... Minneapolis, MN
Purdue, Glenn, P.A. ... Minneapolis, MN
Purdue, Jas. C. ... Cincinnati, OH
Purdue, John C. ... Toledo, OH
Purdue Law Offices ... Toledo, OH
Purdue, Marsha K. ... Cohoes, NY
Purdue, Robert A. ... **Seattle, WA**
Purdue, William T. ... **Providence, RI**
Purdum, David B. ... Baltimore, MD
Purdum, R. E. Lee ... Lutherville, MD
Purdy, Brad M. ... Boise, ID
Purdy, Carroll F. ... **Harrisburg, PA**
Purdy, Charles A. ... Santa Fe, NM
Purdy, Charles E., IV ... **San Diego, CA**
Purdy, Charles H. ... San Antonio, TX
Purdy, Court Bryant ... **Newport Beach, CA**
Purdy, Dan K. ... Osceola, MO
Purdy, Daniel C. ... Waldoboro, ME
Purdy, Don M. ... **Celina, OH**
Purdy, Donald A. ... Wallingford, PA
Purdy, Donald A., Jr. ... Washington, DC
Purdy, Donna Jeanne ... Denver, CO
Purdy, Dorrit W. ... Chesterland, OH
Purdy, Douglas C. ... **Los Angeles, CA**
Purdy, Douglas C. ... Quincy, MA
Purdy, Dwight G. ... Springfield, OR
Purdy, Eugene K. ... Cincinnati, OH
Purdy, Eugene K., Co., L.P.A.
Cincinnati, OH
Purdy and Flynn, P.A.
Fort Lauderdale, FL
Miami, FL
Palm Beach, FL
Purdy, Frank T. ... Cincinnati, OH

Purdy, Geoffrey P. M. ..... Los Angeles, CA
Purdy, George A. ..... Seattle, WA
Purdy, George E. ..... Indianapolis, IN
Purdy, H. Mark ..... Fort Lauderdale, FL
Purdy and Herron ..... San Diego, CA
Purdy, Howard E. ..... Salida, CO
Purdy, James A. ..... Miami, FL
New York, NY
Purdy, James K. ..... Tampa, FL
Purdy, James N. ..... Bismarck, ND
Purdy, James Rhoderick ..... Heathrow, FL
Purdy, Jennifer Randolph ..... Columbia, SC
Purdy, John D., Jr. ..... Oak Brook, IL
Purdy, John W. ..... Cape Canaveral, FL
Purdy, Lammers & Schiavone
Celina, OH
Purdy, Leslie A.W. ..... Washington, DC
Purdy, Linda A. ..... Waterbury, VT
Purdy, Lisa Ruoff ..... Albany, NY
Purdy, Mark F. ..... Minot, ND
Purdy, Meredyth Ashley ..... Dallas, TX
Purdy, Monica McCoy ..... Dallas, TX
Purdy, R. Lawrence ..... Minneapolis, MN
Purdy, Raymond A. ..... Lansing, MI
Purdy, Richard A. ..... Fort Lauderdale, FL
Purdy & Ring ..... Georgetown, OH
Purdy, Sherry M. ..... Superior, CO
Purdy, Stanley K. ..... Georgetown, OH
Purdy, William F., Jr. ..... Silver Spring, MD
Purdy, William G. ..... Medford, OR
Purdy, William J. ..... Paterson, NJ
Purdy, William J., III ..... Aptos, CA
Purdy, William M. ..... Bronx, NY
Purdy, William R. ..... Jackson, MS
Pure, Samuel W. ..... Mount Kisco, NY
Purello, Alfred C. ..... Albany, NY
Puretz, Jeffrey S. ..... Washington, DC
Purevich, Katherine A. ..... Chicago, IL
Purewal, Navroop Kaur
San Francisco, CA
Pureza, David R. ..... Greenville, NC
Purgatorio, Robert E. ..... Houston, TX
Purham, Albert L., Jr. ..... Peoria, IL
Puri, Bobby ..... Manassas, VA
Puri, Christopher Connell ..... Nashville, TN
Puri, K. Antonio ..... Roselle, IL
Puri, Rajnish ..... Los Angeles, CA
Puri, Vedica S. ..... Walnut Creek, CA
Puri, Vik ..... Chicago, IL
Puricelli, Firmin A. ..... St. Louis, MO
Puricelli, John R. ..... Princeton, MA
Puricelli, Michelle R. ..... Bloomfield Hills, MI
Detroit, MI
Puricelli, Paul J. ..... St. Louis, MO
Purificacion, Leslie J. ..... Hawthorne, NY
Purifoy, Cindy A. ..... Los Angeles, CA
Purifoy, Patrick T. ..... Los Angeles, CA
Purifoy, Philip B. ..... Texarkana, AR
Purington, Mary K. ..... Portland, ME
Purington, Thomas A. ..... Portland, ME
Purinton, Cindy D. ..... Arlington, TX
Purinton, Alan R. ..... De Smet, SD
Purintun, Ann-Elizabeth ..... New York, NY
Purintun, Orin ..... Milwaukee, WI
Purisch, Arthur C. ..... Weston, FL
Purisch, Marjorie H. ..... Basking Ridge, NJ
Purish, Arthur C., P.A. ..... Weston, FL
Puritz, Andrew M. ..... Oneonta, NY
Puritz, Lawrence A. ..... Chico, CA
Puritz, Steven Michael ..... Tallahassee, FL
Purkey, Harry R., Jr. ..... Virginia Beach, VA
Purkey, Harry R., Jr., P.C.
Virginia Beach, VA
Purkey, Lori L. ..... Kalamazoo, MI
Purkiss, Linda M. ..... Emeryville, CA
Purks, Darryl N. ..... Culver City, CA
Purks, David K.
Research Triangle Park, NC
Purmal, Barnes & Cohen ..... Chicago, IL
Purmal, Marthe C. ..... Chicago, IL
Purmort, Susan D. ..... Independence, MO
Purnell, Allen D., Jr. ..... Louisville, KY
Purnell, C. Adam ..... Okemos, MI
Purnell, Carolyn J. ..... Seattle, WA
Purnell, Charles G. ..... Dallas, TX
Purnell, Charles R. ..... San Francisco, CA
Purnell, Daniel D. ..... Richmond, CA
Purnell, David R. ..... Urbana, IL
Purnell, Edward ..... Cleveland, OH
Purnell, Harold F. X. ..... Tallahassee, FL
Purnell, Harold W. T., II ..... Georgetown, DE
Purnell, Jacqueline L. ..... Columbus, MS
Purnell, Maurice E., Jr. ..... Dallas, TX
Purnell, Norman ..... Akron, OH
Purnell, Oliver James, III ..... Vernon, CT
Purnell, Paul A. ..... West Point, MS
Purnell, Sarah M. (Sally) ..... Greenville, SC
Purnell, Simon B. ..... Corpus Christi, TX
Purnell, Timothy M. ..... Manassas, VA
Purnell, Tom ..... Dallas, TX
Purnhagen, Vincent John
South Windsor, CT
Puro, Nicholas J. ..... New York, NY
Puro, Samantha ..... Bronx, NY
Purohit, Tara ..... New York, NY
Purol, Matthew F. L. ..... Greenfield, IN
Indianapolis, IN
Purow, Malcolm A. ..... Hollywood, FL
Purow, Tammie A. Rosen ..... New York, NY
Purple, Donald G. ..... Bath, NY
Purple, James D. ..... Chattanooga, TN
Purpura, Mark V. ..... Wilmington, DE
Purpura, Michael M. ..... New York, NY
Purpura, William B., Law Office of
Baltimore, MD
Purrazzella, Joseph ..... Toms River, NJ
Purrazzella and Purrazzella, P.A.
Toms River, NJ
Purrazzella, Sally ..... Toms River, NJ
Purrington, A. Nicholas ..... Greensboro, NC
Purrington, Alfred L., III ..... Raleigh, NC
Purrington, Debra L. ..... Longmeadow, MA
Purrington & Edwards ..... Kilmarnock, VA
Purrington, John Ward ..... Raleigh, NC
Purrington & McConnell ..... New York, NY
Purrington, Philip P., Jr. ..... Kilmarnock, VA
Purrington, Roliff H., Jr. ..... Austin, TX
Houston, TX
Pursel, Charles B. ..... Bloomsburg, PA
Pursel, David F. ..... Hoffman Estates, IL
Pursel, David G. ..... Milpitas, CA
Pursel, Gail Singleton ..... Albany, GA
Pursel, John H. ..... Flemington, NJ
Pursel, Thomas L. ..... Las Vegas, NV
Pursel, Thomas L., Ltd. ..... Las Vegas, NV
Pursel, Timothy John ..... Towson, MD
Pursell, David B. ..... Kansas City, MO
Pursell, Jimmie W., Jr. ..... Phoenix, AZ
Pursell, Michael D. ..... Fountain Valley, CA
Pursell, R. H. ..... Nashville, TN
Pursell, Ronald J. ..... New Orleans, LA
Pursell, Thomas B. ..... Fairfield, CT
Pursell, Thomas F. ..... St. Paul, MN
Purser, Charles A. ..... Tulsa, OK
Purser, Donald J. ..... Salt Lake City, UT
Purser, Donald Joseph, & Associates, P.C., Law Offices ..... Salt Lake City, UT
Purser, Earle R. ..... Raleigh, NC
Purser, Edward R. ..... Cortland, NY
Purser, Fred H., Jr. ..... Jackson, MS
Purser, Kenneth W. ..... Carthage, MO
Purser, Robert B. ..... Lafayette, LA
Purser, Rodney L. ..... Charlotte, NC
Pursglove, Joseph, II ..... Columbus, OH
Pursiano, David T., (A Professional Corporation) ..... San Diego, CA
Pursley, C. Robert ..... Safford, AZ
Pursley, Charles N., Jr. ..... Atlanta, GA
Pursley, David A. ..... San Francisco, CA
Pursley, Denise Dicicco ..... Garden City, NY
Pursley, Evelyn M. ..... Durham, NC
Pursley, Howell, Lowery & Meeks, LLP
Atlanta, GA
Pursley, John L. ..... Butler, MO
Pursley, Kenneth L. ..... Boise, ID
Pursley, Thomas A. ..... Boston, MA
Pursley, Thomas A., III
Federal Energy Regulatory Commission,
Office of the General Counsel, GV
Purtan, Jill L. ..... Bingham Farms, MI
Purtan & Swoish, P.C. ..... Bingham Farms, MI
Purtell, Brian R. ..... Madison, WI
Purtell, Daniel T. ..... San Francisco, CA
Purtell, Dennis J. ..... Milwaukee, WI
Purtell, Gregory S. ..... Northville, MI
Purtell, J. Joseph ..... Bay City, MI
Purtell, Lawrence R. ..... Pittsburgh, PA
Purtell, Rosemary ..... Boston, MA
Purtell, Steven W. ..... Wellsboro, PA
Purtell, Thomas A. ..... Woodland, CA
Purtell, Vincent A. ..... Sioux Falls, SD
Purtha, Paul L. ..... Garland, TX
Purtich, Richard R. ..... Los Angeles, CA
Purtill, George Morrow ..... Glastonbury, CT
Purtill, John F. ..... Schaumburg, IL
Purtill, Joseph J. ..... New London, CT
Purtill, Purtill & Pfeffer ..... Glastonbury, CT
Purtill, Sharon Holland ..... Glastonbury, CT
Purtle, Glynn R. ..... Wichita Falls, TX
Purtle, John I. ..... Little Rock, AR
Purtle, John I., P.A. ..... Little Rock, AR
Purtz, Richard Lee ..... Cape Coral, FL
Fort Myers, FL
Port Charlotte, FL
Purtzer, Brett A. ..... Tacoma, WA
Purul, Joseph A., Jr. ..... Philadelphia, PA
Purut, Rita M.K. ..... Durham, NC
Purver, Jonathan M. ..... Novato, CA
Purves, Edmund S. ..... Larchmont, NY
Purves, John T. ..... Rochester, NY
Purves, Samuel A. ..... Chicago, IL
Purviance, E. Kenneth ..... San Diego, CA
Purviance, Farris C., III ..... El Cajon, CA
Purviance, Lorraine ..... El Cajon, CA
Purviance & Purviance ..... El Cajon, CA
Purvin, Benjamin ..... East Meadow, NY
Purvin, Saul ..... Brooklyn, NY
Purvines, Verne E., Jr. ..... St. Louis, MO
Purvis, Allen R. ..... Washington, DC
Purvis, Barbara A. ..... Riverside, CA
Purvis, Barbara K. ..... Denver, CO
Purvis, Claude M. ..... Hernando, MS
Purvis, Cynthia Pearson ..... Indianapolis, IN
Purvis, G. Frank, Jr. ..... New Orleans, LA
Purvis, Gray & Gordon, LLP
Boulder, CO
Denver, CO
Purvis, Gregory A. ..... Indianapolis, IN
Purvis, James M. ..... San Francisco, CA
Purvis, James Steven ..... Conyers, GA
Purvis, Jeannette B. ..... Fredericksburg, VA
Purvis, Jeffrey G. ..... Clovis, CA
Purvis, Jennifer A. ..... Washington, DC
Purvis, John A. ..... Boulder, CO
Denver, CO
Purvis, Joseph A. ..... Jackson, MS
Purvis, Joseph H. ..... Little Rock, AR
Purvis, Kristine Anne ..... Kansas City, MO
Purvis, Michael C. ..... Santa Barbara, CA
Purvis, Michael J. ..... New York, NY
Purvis, Mitchell M. ..... Atlanta, GA
Purvis, Nigel H. ..... Department of State,
Office of the Legal Adviser, GV
Purvis, Paige L. ..... Jackson, MS
Purvis, Randall W. B. ..... Colorado Springs, CO
Purvis, Robert D. ..... Towson, MD
Purvis, Russell C. ..... Kansas City, MO
Purvis, Stephanie B. ..... Fort Myers, FL
Sarasota, FL
Tampa, FL
Purvis, V. Russell, Jr. ..... Jonesville, LA
Purvis, Winston Wendt ..... New Orleans, LA
Purwin, Paul E. ..... Florham Park, NJ
Puryear, Daniel H. ..... Nashville, TN
Puryear, David B., Jr. ..... Greensboro, NC
Puryear, Edgar F., Jr. ..... Madison, VA
Puryear, Jeffrey W. ..... Jonesboro, AR
Puryear, Jennifer Herndon
Securities and Exchange Commission,
Office of the General Counsel, GV
Puryear, John M. ..... Tuscaloosa, AL
Puryear and Lingle, P.L.L.C.
Greensboro, NC
High Point, NC
Puryear, Mark L. ..... Dallas, TX
Puryear, Michael P. ..... Temple, TX
Puryear, Robert B., IV ..... Lafayette, CO
Puryear, Rob't. B., III ..... Nashville, TN
Puryear, S. B. ..... Madison, VA
Purzak, Robert ..... Garden City, NY
Pusatere, Ross E. ..... Albany, NY
Pusateri, David P. ..... Pittsburgh, PA
Pusateri, James A. ..... Topeka, KS
Pusateri, Julia E. ..... St. Louis, MO
Pusateri, Lawrence X. ..... Chicago, IL
Pusateri, Paul J. ..... Canton, OH
Pusateri, Philip J., Jr. ..... Metairie, LA
Pusateri, Robert M. ..... Lockport, NY
Pusateri, Salvador J. ..... New Orleans, LA
Pusateri, Sylvia Louise ..... Fitchburg, MA
Pusateri, Vincent P. ..... Fitchburg, MA
Pusatier, Sherman & Abbott ..... Kenmore, NY
Pusatier, Stephen F. ..... Kenmore, NY
Pusavat, Keith N. ..... La Habra, CA
Puscas, Victor E., Jr. ..... Joliet, IL
Pusch, Brian W., Law Offices of
New York, NY
Pusch, Gerard A., Jr. ..... Houston, TX
Pusch, Gregory D. ..... Minneapolis, MN
Pusch, Gregory T. ..... Boston, MA
Pusch, Jeffrey W. ..... Boise, ID
Pusch, William G. ..... Seattle, WA
Pusch, William L. ..... Little Rock, AR
Puscheck, Bret Allen ..... Rochester, NY
Puschnig, Luke ..... Las Vegas, NV
Pusey, J. Scott ..... Denver, CO
Pusey, John R. ..... Peoria, IL
Pusey, N. Woodrow ..... Charlotte, NC
Pusey, Noah Locke ..... New York, NY
Pusey, Robert Devin ..... Sandy, UT
Pusey, Robert T. ..... San Bernardino, CA
Pusey, William A. ..... Washington, DC
Pusey, William A., Jr. ..... Charleston, SC
Charlottesville, VA
Pushaw, Karen R. ..... Philadelphia, PA
Pushinsky, Jon ..... Pittsburgh, PA
Pushkar, Raymond S. E. ..... Washington, DC
Pushkin, Marc L. ..... Timonium, MD
Pushko, Michael Scott ..... Union, NJ
Pushor, John A. ..... Columbus, IN
Pusich, Maizie Whalen ..... Reno, NV
Puskar, M. Catharine ..... Arlington, VA
Puskar, Paul M. ..... Hollidaysburg, PA
Puskaric, Blane Michael ..... Pittsburgh, PA
Puskarich, Matthew P. ..... Steubenville, OH
Puskas & Orosz ..... New Brunswick, NJ
Puskas, William B., Jr. ..... New Brunswick, NJ
Puskuldjian, Robert P. ..... Brooklyn, NY
Staten Island, NY
Pusser, Charles R., Jr. ..... Chesterfield, SC
Pust, Tammy L. ..... St. Paul, MN
Pustay, Melanie ..... Department of Justice,
Office of Information and Privacy, GV
Pustilnik, Alix S. ..... New York, NY
Pustilnik, David D. ..... Hartford, CT
Pustilnik, Robert A. ..... Richmond, VA
Pustorino, Pederson, Tilton & Parrington
Edina, MN
Pustorino, Peter J. ..... Edina, MN
Putbrese, Cortland Christopher
Charleston, WV
Putbrese Hunsaker & Trent, P.C.
Washington, DC
Sterling, VA
Putbrese, Keith E. ..... Sterling, VA
Puterbaugh, David J. ..... Fortville, IN
Puterbaugh, Robert E. ..... Lakeland, FL
Lake Wales, FL
Winter Haven, FL
Puteska, David M. ..... Newark, NJ
Putetti, Michael A. ..... New York, NY
Putfark, Matthew M. ..... Metairie, LA
Puth, Jonathan C. ..... Washington, DC
Puthoff, Frank M. ..... Braintree, MA
Putinsky, Thomas F. ..... Pittsburgh, PA
Putka, Andrew C. ..... Rocky River, OH
Putka, Edward J. ..... Kelso, WA
Putkoski-Chodos, Gina Marie
Los Angeles, CA
Putlak, Kenneth J. ..... Chicago, IL
Putman, Berthold ..... New Bedford, MA
Putman, David J. ..... Birmingham, AL
Putman, Forest S., Jr. ..... Albuquerque, NM
Putman, Frank ..... Houston, TX
Putman, Harold D., Jr. ..... San Antonio, TX
Putman, J. Michael ..... San Antonio, TX
Putman, Lewis T., Jr. ..... Washington, DC
Putman, Marlene L. ..... Salem, OR
Putman, Patrice A. ..... Augusta, ME
Putman, Patricia K. ..... Honolulu, HI
Putman & Putman, Inc. ..... San Antonio, TX
Putman, Susette Camille Horton
Columbus, OH
Putman, Timothy J. ..... Canton, OH
Putnam, Vick ..... San Antonio, TX
Putman, William B. ..... Fayetteville, AR
Putnak, Robert J. ..... Monongahela, PA
Putnal, Bryan L. ..... Jacksonville, FL
Putnal, J. David, Jr. ..... Atlanta, GA
Putnal, Karen A. ..... Tallahassee, FL
Putnam, Abel A. ..... Lakeland, FL
Putnam, Alfred W., Jr. ..... Philadelphia, PA
Putnam, Amy L. ..... Harrisburg, PA
Putnam & Behrendt ..... Findlay, OH
Putnam, Charles D. ..... Benton Harbor, MI
Putnam, Charles T. ..... Concord, NH
Putnam, Christopher W. ..... Minneapolis, MN
Putnam, Dale Lee ..... Decorah, IA
Putnam, David H. ..... Columbus, OH
Putnam, David R. ..... Hanover, NH
Norwich, VT
Putnam, Debra Robinson ..... Chicago, IL
Putnam, Earle W. ..... Washington, DC
Putnam, Elizabeth A. ..... Findlay, OH
Putnam, Frederic L., Jr. ..... Lowell, MA
Putnam, Gary L. ..... Burlington, IA
Putnam, George, III ..... Boston, MA
Putnam, Glendora M. ..... Boston, MA
Putnam, Harold ..... Vero Beach, FL
Putnam, J. Bryan ..... Sarasota, FL
Putnam, Jack H., Jr. ..... Knoxville, TN
Putnam, Jay G., & Associates
Santa Rosa, CA
Putnam, Jeffrey F. ..... Omaha, NE
Putnam, Jeffrey J. ..... Houston, TX
Putnam, Jennifer M. ..... New York, NY
Putnam, Jerry W. ..... Edmond, OK
Putnam, Joe ..... Irving, TX
Putnam, John E. ..... Denver, CO
Washington, DC
Putnam, John G., Jr. ..... Buffalo, NY
Putnam, John L. ..... Hanover, NH
Norwich, VT
Putnam, John R. ..... Harrison, AR
Putnam, Jonathan F. ..... New York, NY
Putnam, Kent R. ..... Tallahassee, FL
Putnam, Kim R. ..... Olympia, WA
Putnam, Larry J. ..... Emporia, KS
Putnam & Lieb ..... Olympia, WA
Putnam, Lon J. ..... Lakewood, CO
Putnam, M. Maila ..... Culver City, CA
Putnam, M. Warren ..... Cardiff-By-The-Sea, CA
Putnam, Marilyn E. ..... San Francisco, CA
Putnam, Marilyn E., A Law Corporation
San Francisco, CA
Putnam, Martin S. ..... Oakland, CA
Putnam, Marvin S., Jr.
Santa Monica, CA
Putnam, Michael A. ..... Minneapolis, MN
Putnam, Michael R. ..... Glendale, CA
Putnam, Michael R. ..... Dallas, TX
Putnam, Nathaniel S. ..... Bangor, ME
Putnam, Neil W. ..... Hapeville, GA
Putnam, Philip C., (P.C.) ..... Los Angeles, CA
Putnam, Ralph C., Jr. ..... Aurora, IL
Putnam, Ralph L. ..... Fresno, CA
Putnam, Randal S. ..... Omaha, NE
Putnam, Richard E. ..... Omaha, NE
Putnam, Richard J. ..... Lafayette, LA
Putnam, Richard L., Jr. ..... Abbeville, LA
Putnam, Robert H., Jr. ..... Atlanta, GA
Putnam, Robert N., II
St. Petersburg Beach, FL
Putnam, Robert S. ..... Fair Oaks, CA
Putnam, Robin Christine ..... Fayetteville, AR
Putnam, Roger A. ..... Portland, ME
Putnam, Russell H., Jr. ..... Lexington, SC
Putnam, Stan M., Jr. ..... Austin, TX
Putnam & Strand ..... Decorah, IA
Putnam, Sylvia Audigier ..... Dallas, TX
Putnam, T. Michael ..... Birmingham, AL
Putnam, Thomas B., Jr. ..... Lakeland, FL
Lake Wales, FL
Winter Haven, FL
Putnam, Virginia Kozak ..... Bangor, ME
Putney, Bradley L. ..... Traverse City, MI
Putney, Catherine M. ..... Bedford, MA
Putney, David H. ..... Las Vegas, NV
Putney, F. Taylor, Jr. ..... Atlanta, GA
Putney, Herbert A. ..... Medford, OR
Putney, Joan E. ..... Richmond, VA
Putney, John C. ..... Mount Morris, NY
Putney, Kelly A. ..... Minneapolis, MN
Putney, Lacey E. ..... Bedford, VA
Putney, Laura L. ..... New York, NY
Putney, Louis D. ..... Tampa, FL
Putney, Louis W. ..... Tampa, FL
Putney, Louis W., P.A. ..... Tampa, FL
Putney, Macon C. ..... Bedford, VA
Putney, Mark E. ..... Grand Rapids, MI
Putney, Paul Wm. ..... Philadelphia, PA
Putney and Putney ..... Bedford, VA
Putney, Ray P. ..... Houston, TX
Putney, Scott W. ..... Department of Justice,
Tax Division, GV
Putney, Twombly, Hall & Hirson LLP
Iselin, NJ
Manhasset, NY
New York, NY
Putnick, Joseph J. ..... Chicago, IL
Putnick, Otto F. ..... Cincinnati, OH
Putnicki, William G. ..... San Antonio, TX
Puto, Christine E. ..... Marathon, FL
Putonti, Michelle M. ..... Pasadena, CA
Putonti, Stephen M. ..... Tustin, CA
Putorti, Frank M., Jr. ..... Schenectady, NY
Putorti, Frank M., Jr., P.C. ..... Schenectady, NY
Putra, Brian A. ..... Seattle, WA
Putrich-Lira, Celeste ..... San Antonio, TX
Putrino, Cary P. ..... Sarasota, FL
Putrino, Chas. ..... Endicott, NY
Putsavage, Telisport W. ..... Washington, DC

Putt, Christopher R. ..... South Bend, IN
Putta, Barbara J. ..... Chicago, IL
Putter, David ..... Plattsburgh, NY
Montpelier, VT
Putter, Michael G. ..... Rome, NY
Putter, Michael G. ..... Utica, NY
Putterman, Alan S. ..... San Francisco, CA
Putterman, Arnold L. ..... New York, NY
Putterman, Barry E. ..... Houston, TX
Putterman, Barry T. ..... Boston, MA
Putterman, Charles M. ..... Raleigh, NC
Putterman, Donald J. ..... San Francisco, CA
Putterman & Putterman ..... New York, NY
Putterman, Robert S. ..... Boca Raton, FL
Putters, Bianca E. ..... Los Angeles, CA
Putthoff, Laurie A. ..... Kansas City, MO
Puttock, John ..... Pasadena, CA
Puttre, Edward A. ..... San Francisco, CA
Puttré, Richard P. ..... Charlotte, NC
Puttroff, Paul A. ..... Oklahoma City, OK
Putz, A. Frank ..... Milwaukee, WI
Putzel, Constance K. ..... Baltimore, MD
Putzel, Constance K. ..... Towson, MD
Putzel, Henry, III ..... New York, NY
Putzel, Henry, Jr. ..... Munsonville, NH
Putzel, John M. ..... St. Louis, MO
Putzell, Edwin J., Jr. ..... St. Louis, MO
Putzer, Carl T. ..... North Syracuse, NY
Putzi, David Patrick ..... Annapolis, MD
Putzi, Patrick ..... Treasury Department,
Internal Revenue Service, GV
Putzier, Daphne L. ..... Houston, TX
Putzier, Frederick J. ..... St. Paul, MN
Putzier, Peter K. ..... Juneau, AK
Putziger, Michael T. ..... Boston, MA
Putziger, Myrna ..... Boston, MA
Puvogel, Linda S. ..... Oak Park, IL
Puya, Keith J. ..... West Palm Beach, FL
Puyanic, Max D. ..... Miami, FL
Puz, Rodger L. ..... Pittsburgh, PA
Puzder, Andrew F. ..... Irvine, CA
Newport Beach, CA
Puzella, Carolyn ..... Salem, MA
Puzey, James W. ..... Carson City, NV
Puzio, Ronald C. ..... Warren, MI
Puzo, Joseph M. ..... Merrick, NY
Puzo, Michael J. ..... Boston, MA
Puzone, Katherine I. ..... New York, NY
Puzzo, Edward L. ..... Glenview, IL
Puzzo, Edward L., Ltd. ..... Glenview, IL
Puzzo, Thomas E. ..... Seattle, WA
Puzzuole, Bernadette L. ..... Pittsburgh, PA
Puzzuoli, Gina Ursula ..... Southfield, MI
Puzzuoli, Hribar, Iafrate, Majerowicz, Gaber,
Seay & Jansen ..... Mount Clemens, MI
Puzzuoli, Joseph P. ..... Mount Clemens, MI
Puzzuoli, R. Dante ..... Stamford, CT
Py, Jamie ..... Brunswick, ME
Py, John D. ..... Sandusky, OH
Pyatenko, Eugene W. ..... Detroit, MI
Pyatt, Gayl Simonds ..... Pinckneyville, IL
Pyatt, Jonathan S. ..... San Diego, CA
Pyatt, Richard J. ..... Las Vegas, NV
Pyatt & Silvestri, Chtd., A Prof. Law Corp.
Las Vegas, NV
Pyatt, William L. ..... Columbia, SC
Pybas, Michael ..... Annapolis Junction, MD
Pybon, Theresa Tilton ..... Tacoma, WA
Pyburn, Jeffrey T. ..... Phoenix, AZ
Pyburn, Keith M., Jr., (P.C.)
New Orleans, LA
Pybus, David L. ..... Houston, TX
Pybus, Kenneth R. ..... Houston, TX
Pye, A. Kenneth ..... Dallas, TX
Pye, Anthony I. ..... Morristown, NJ
Pye, Chadwick D. ..... Spartanburg, SC
Pye, Dobbs & Berry, P.C. ..... Tyler, TX
Pye, James T. ..... Duxbury, MA
Pye, Loretta A. ..... Brooklyn, NY
Pye, Robert B. ..... Woodland, CA
Pye, Rosemary ..... Boston, MA
Pye, Thomas G. ..... Boca Raton, FL
Pye, Tom ..... Doraville, GA
Pyeatte, H. Charles ..... Phoenix, AZ
Pyeatte, Vicky S. ..... Pensacola, FL
Pyers, Edward C. ..... Fort Lauderdale, FL
Pyes & Cherin ..... Chicago, IL
Pyes, Harvey ..... Chicago, IL
Pyes, Hugo H. ..... Los Angeles, CA
Pyfer, John F., Jr. ..... Lancaster, PA
Willow Street, PA
Pyfer & Reese, A Professional Corporation
Lancaster, PA
Willow Street, PA
Pyfer, Richard J. ..... Helena, MT
Pyfer, Robert C. ..... Helena, MT
Pyfer, Scott C. ..... Princeton, NJ
Pyffer, Mary Kane ..... Vineland, NJ
Pyfrom, Gregory C., & Associates
Agoura Hills, CA
Pyka, Andrew J. ..... Santa Ana, CA
Pyke, Charles B., Jr. ..... Atlanta, GA
Pyke, David M. ..... Dallas, TX
Pyke, F. Gregory ..... San Diego, CA
Pyke, John S., Jr. ..... Cleveland, OH
Pyke, Kathryn S. ..... Cupertino, CA
Pyke, Thomas E. ..... Palo Alto, CA
Pykett, Daniel J. ..... White Plains, NY
Pykon, Francis H. ..... Newark, NJ
Pykosh, Michael J. ..... Camp Hill, PA
Pyland, Carie P. ..... Dallas, TX
Pyland, Christy M. ..... Los Angeles, CA
Pylant, Tracy L. S. ..... Dallas, TX
Pylate, Seale ..... Greenville, MS
Pyle, Alexander H. ..... Boston, MA
Pyle, Antonio D. ..... Pittsburgh, PA
Pyle, Antonio D., P.C. ..... Pittsburgh, PA
Pyle, B. C. ..... Winter Park, FL
Pyle, Beverly J. ..... Cleveland, OH
Pyle, C. Victor, Jr. ..... Greenville, SC
Pyle, David S. ..... Boston, MA
Pyle, Donald H. ..... Portland, OR
Pyle, Dreher, Mills & Dye, P.A.
Jackson, MS
Pyle, E. Thomas, III ..... Hutchinson, KS
Pyle, Edmund B., III ..... Valley Forge, PA
Pyle, Edwin S. ..... Nashville, TN
Pyle and Entwistle ..... Laurel, MD
Gettysburg, PA
Pyle, Eugene A. ..... Hillsboro, OH
Pyle, Frank J., Jr. ..... Orlando, FL
Pyle, Gail Luhn ..... Seattle, WA
Pyle, H. Thomas ..... Gettysburg, PA
Pyle, Howard, III ..... Washington, DC
Pyle, James W. ..... Newark, OH
Pyle, Jean M. ..... Gowanda, NY
Pyle, Jeffrey A. ..... Houston, TX
Pyle, Jennifer M. ..... Washington, DC
Pyle, John F., Law Office of ..... Amherst, VA
Pyle, John S. ..... Cleveland, OH
Pyle, John T. ..... Clarksburg, WV
Pyle, Jones, Hurley & Hand, P.A.
Winter Park, FL
Pyle, Kevin W. ..... Albuquerque, NM
Pyle, Kirk B. ..... Eufaula, OK
Pyle, Kurt H. ..... Santa Barbara, CA
Pyle, L. Arnold ..... Jackson, MS
Pyle, M. Scott ..... Dallas, TX
Pyle, Michael A. ..... Daytona Beach, FL
Ormond Beach, FL
Pyle, Michael A., P.A. ..... Daytona Beach, FL
Ormond Beach, FL
Pyle, Michael T. ..... Palo Alto, CA
Pyle, Michele M. ..... New York, NY
Pyle & Moccia ..... Valley Forge, PA
Pyle, Pamela J. ..... Buffalo, NY
Pyle, Ransford C. ..... Orlando, FL
Pyle, Ray S. ..... Tampa, FL
Pyle, Raymond D. ..... San Bernardino, CA
Pyle, Robert B. ..... Chattanooga, TN
Pyle, Robert E. ..... Bartow, FL
Pyle, Robert L. ..... Arvada, CO
Pyle, Robert M., Jr. ..... New York, NY
Pyle, Roger E. ..... Gowanda, NY
Pyle, Rome & Lichten, P.C. ..... Boston, MA
Pyle, Ronald G. ..... Richmond, IN
Pyle, Ronny D. ..... Oklahoma City, OK
Pyle, Ross M. ..... San Diego, CA
Pyle, Russell W. ..... Chicago, IL
Pyle Sims Duncan & Stevenson
San Diego, CA
Pyle, Steven P. ..... Winter Park, FL
Pyle, Terrence F. ..... Sun City Center, FL
Pyle, Thomas ..... Stockton, MO
Pyle, Thomas J., Jr. ..... Roseland, NJ
Pyle, Walter K. ..... Berkeley, CA
Pyle, Warren H. ..... Boston, MA
Pyle, William A. ..... Jackson, MS
Pyle, William R. ..... Fallston, MD
Pyles, Bradley G. ..... Macon, GA
Pyles, Bradley J. ..... Charleston, WV
Pyles, Bryan D. ..... Laguna Niguel, CA
Pyles, Christopher J. ..... Charleston, WV
Pyles, Clement W. ..... Columbus, OH
Pyles, Cynthia J. ..... Orlando, FL
Pyles, Dixon L. ..... Jackson, MS
Pyles, Dortha Larene ..... Beverly Hills, CA
Pyles, Gary Scott ..... Joliet, IL
Pyles, Gretchen E. ..... Charleston, WV
Pyles, James C. ..... Washington, DC
Pyles, John E. ..... Wichita, KS
Pyles, Phyllis ..... Department of Justice,
Civil Division, GV
Pyles, Pia ..... Philadelphia, PA
Pyles, Richard B. ..... Miami, FL
Pyles, T. Christopher ..... Carrollton, GA
Pylitt, Bernard L. ..... Indianapolis, IN
Pylman, Donna M. ..... Irvington, NY
Pylman, Norman H., II
Grand Rapids, MI
Pylypiw, Linda L. ..... Flint, MI
Pym, Bruce M. ..... Seattle, WA
Pym, Sheri ..... San Diego, CA
Pymm, Jennifer H. ..... New York, NY
Pynchon, Victoria ..... Los Angeles, CA
Pyne, Christopher M. ..... Princeton, NJ
Pyne, Daniel F., III ..... San Jose, CA
Pyne & Derry, P.C. ..... Washington, DC
Chevy Chase, MD
Pyne, Donna C. ..... Westfield, NJ
Pyne, Douglas R. ..... Memphis, TN
Pyne, James G. ..... Towson, MD
Pyne, Jane Surran ..... Waldoboro, ME
Pyne, John J. ..... Chevy Chase, MD
Pyne, Rebecca Kettelle
Department of Justice,
Criminal Division, GV
Pyne, Susan L. ..... Sunnyvale, CA
Pynes, William F. ..... Dallas, TX
Pynes, Benjamin E., Jr. ..... Carlsbad, CA
Pynes, Steven J. ..... San Diego, CA
Pynn, Verne H. ..... Concord, CA
Pynnonen, Brett D. ..... Detroit, MI
Pyon, Stevie ..... Los Angeles, CA
Pyott, F. Bradley ..... Tazewell, VA
Pyott, Mardi F. ..... Dover, DE
Odessa, DE
Pyper, David J. ..... Miami, FL
Pyper, Mark B. ..... Phoenix, AZ
Pyper, Richard L. ..... Montgomery, AL
Troy, AL
Pyper, Thomas H. ..... Dayton, OH
Pyper, Thomas M. ..... Madison, WI
Pyrah, James V., III ..... Kingston, PA
Pyrak, Theodore J. ..... Buffalo, NY
Pyrich, Alissa ..... Morristown, NJ
Pyron, Rob L. ..... Seminole, OK
Pyscher, Daniel H. ..... Mount Pleasant, MI
Pyser, Steven N. ..... Philadelphia, PA
Pysher, Paul A. ..... Boston, MA
Pyshos, Basil N. ..... Arlington Heights, IL
Pysno, Michael A. ..... Minneapolis, MN
Pysz, Michael ..... Hamburg, NY
Pyszka, Blackmon, Levy & Savola, P.A.
Miami Lakes, FL
Pyszka, Gerard E. ..... Miami Lakes, FL
Pytel, H. Jack, Jr. ..... San Antonio, TX
Pytel, H. Jack, Jr., P.C. ..... San Antonio, TX
Pytel, Melissa J. ..... Minneapolis, MN
Pytell, Robert H. ..... Detroit, MI
Pytell & Varchetti, P.C. ..... Detroit, MI
Grosse Pointe Farms, MI
Pytlik, Paul J. ..... Milwaukee, WI
Pytte, John Erling ..... Hinesville, GA
Pytynia, Thomas L. ..... Indianapolis, IN
Pyun, C. Sandra ..... Denver, CO
Pyun, Daniel J. Y. ..... Honolulu, HI
Pyun, James H. ..... Garden City, NY
Pyun, Matthew S.K., Jr., A Law Corporation
Honolulu, HI
Pyun, Matthew S. K., Jr. ..... Honolulu, HI
Pyune-McEldowney, Catherine
Philadelphia, PA
Pyzel, Cynthia A. ..... Carson City, NV
Pyzyk, Robert G. ..... Menomonee Falls, WI
Pyzyk, Roger C. ..... West Allis, WI

Q Auto Accident Attorneys ..... Bradenton, FL
Brandon, FL
Clearwater, FL
Holly Hill, FL
Lakeland, FL
Port Charlotte, FL
Port Richey, FL
St. Petersburg, FL
Sarasota, FL
Tampa, FL
Qadar, Sohaib ..... Bakersfield, CA
Qasim, Imad I. ..... Chicago, IL
Qayyum, Ayesha ..... New York, NY
Qian, Kevin Yi ..... San Francisco, CA
Qua, Hall, Harvey & Walsh
Chelmsford, MA
Qua, J. Corey ..... Battle Creek, MI
Saratoga Springs, NY
Quaadman, Thomas ..... Staten Island, NY
Quach, Kimberly A. ..... Aloha, OR
Quackenbos, Barbara ..... Newark, NJ
Quackenbos, Carol D. ..... San Francisco, CA
Quackenboss, Robert T. ..... Atlanta, GA
Quackenboss, Robert T.
North Brunswick, NJ
Quackenbush, Barbara P. ..... Houston, TX
Quackenbush, Cessario & Hamlin
Buffalo, NY
Quackenbush, Charles J. ..... New York, NY
Quackenbush, Edwin S. ..... Santa Barbara, CA
Quackenbush, Gary A. ..... San Diego, CA
Quackenbush, James E. ..... Madison, WI
Quackenbush, James H., Jr.
Columbia, SC
Quackenbush, John J., Jr. ..... Buffalo, NY
Quackenbush, Justin L. ..... Spokane, WA
Quackenbush, Karl J. ..... Seattle, WA
Quackenbush, Laura G. ..... San Mateo, CA
Quackenbush, Nancy
Maryland Heights, MO
Quackenbush & Quackenbush
San Mateo, CA
Quackenbush, William C. ..... San Mateo, CA
Quackenbush, William J. ..... San Diego, CA
Quade, Barbara C. ..... Denver, CO
Quade, Calvin E., Jr. ..... Department of Labor,
Office of Secretary, GV
Quade, David R. ..... Waukegan, IL
Quade, Dennis H. ..... Pasadena, CA
Quade, Fontana & Bonin, P.C.
Denver, CO
Quade, Joan Marie ..... Minneapolis, MN
Quade, Loretta C. ..... Cleveland, OH
Quade, Michael W. ..... San Diego, CA
Quade, Paul E. ..... Reno, NV
Quade, Stephanie Lee ..... Houston, TX
Quade, Stephen Gary ..... Fresno, CA
Quadlander, Cheryl A. ..... Austin, TX
Quadra, James A. ..... San Francisco, CA
Quadracci, Harry V. ..... Pewaukee, WI
Quadres, Harold L. ..... Costa Mesa, CA
Quadri, Sherri M. ..... San Bernardino, CA
Quadrino, George A. ..... Washington, DC
Quadrino, Richard J. ..... Garden City, NY
Quadrino & Schwartz, P.C.
Garden City, NY
Quadros & Associates ..... Newport News, VA
Quadros & Johnson, LLP ..... San Mateo, CA
Quadros, Katherine M. ..... San Mateo, CA
Quadros, Robert P. ..... Newport News, VA
Quaglia, Eugene A. ..... White Plains, NY
Quaglia, Jan ..... Burbank, CA
Quaglia, Paul L., Jr. ..... Department of State,
Foreign Service Institute, GV
Quaglia, Raymond Adam
Philadelphia, PA
Quaglia, Raymond J., P.C. ..... Philadelphia, PA
Quagliana, Angelo J. ..... Buffalo, NY
Quagliana, Rhonda ..... Charlottesville, VA
Quagliano & Seeger ..... Washington, DC
Quagliato, Fred C. ..... Peekskill, NY
Quagliato, John V. ..... Washington, DC
Quaglietta, James J. ..... Wayne, NJ
Quaglino, John Vito ..... Metairie, LA
Quaid, Charles J. ..... Dallas, TX
Quaid, Dennis E. ..... Chicago, IL
Quaid, Julie H. ..... Dallas, TX
Quaid, Mary F. ..... Baton Rouge, LA
Quaid & Quaid, LLC ..... Dallas, TX
Quaid, Rachel ..... Garden City, NY
Quaid, Rachel, PC ..... Garden City, NY
Quaid, Warren W. ..... Mineola, NY
Quaide, Chesley D. ..... Pleasanton, CA
Quaife, Nancy J. ..... New York, NY
Quail, Beverly J. ..... Denver, CO
Quail, Keith F. ..... Prescott, AZ
Quail, Robert J., III ..... Birmingham, MI
Quail, Robert L. ..... Santa Rosa, CA
Quain, Cheryl L. ..... Philadelphia, PA
Quaini, Duane C. ..... Chicago, IL
Quaintance, Charles, Jr.
Minneapolis, MN
Quaintance, Charles Lee
Highland Falls, NY
Quaintance, Donald C., II ..... Palo Alto, CA
Quaintance, Hauck & Mullen, P.C.
Sioux Falls, SD
Quaintance, Joe M. ..... Seattle, WA
Tacoma, WA
Quaintance, John C. ..... Sioux Falls, SD
Quaintance, Richard C. ..... Chicago, IL
Quaintance, Robert F., Jr. ..... New York, NY
Quaintance, Robert J. ..... Fruitland Park, FL
Quaintence, Alan Charles, Jr. ..... Houston, TX
Quaka, John Mark ..... Brandon, MS
Quakenbos, Ellen P. ..... New York, NY
Qual, Shirley J. ..... Minneapolis, MN
Quale, Andrew C., Jr. ..... New York, NY
Quale, Christopher D. ..... New Town, ND
Quale, Feldbruegge, Calvelli, Thom &
Croke, S.C. ..... Milwaukee, WI
Quale, Glenn R. ..... Baraboo, WI
Quale, Hartmann, Reynolds, Pulsfus &
Groeneweg, S.C. ..... Baraboo, WI
Sauk City, WI
Quale, Jane ..... Tucson, AZ
Quale, John C. ..... Washington, DC
Quale, L. J. ..... Hopkins, MN
Quale, Susan V. ..... Jefferson, WI
Qualey, Joseph K. ..... Charleston, SC
Qualey, M. Paul, Jr. ..... Atlanta, GA
Qualey, Robert S. ..... Las Vegas, NV
Qualey, Terryl K. ..... St. Paul, MN
Qualiana, Mary K. ..... Washington, DC
Qualkenbush, Roberta ..... Evanston, IL
Qualkinbush & Dazey ..... Indianapolis, IN
Qualkinbush, Jeffery J. ..... Indianapolis, IN
Qualkinbush, William E. ..... Haines City, FL
Quall, Matthew J. ..... Lake Forest, IL
Quall, Matthew W. ..... Fresno, CA
Qualley & Boulton ..... Canby, MN
Qualley, George T. ..... Sioux City, IA
Qualley, John E. ..... Canby, MN
Qualley, Steven R. ..... Pequot Lakes, MN
Qualls, Dan E. ..... Riverside, CA
Qualls, Daniel H. ..... San Francisco, CA
Qualls, Gary S.
Research Triangle Park, NC
Qualls, John R. ..... Cincinnati, OH
Qualls, Kimberly Webb ..... Memphis, TN
Qualls, Kriston D. ..... Los Angeles, CA
Qualls, Michael A. ..... Chula Vista, CA
Qualls, Steven D. ..... Cookeville, TN
Qualls & Workman, L.L.P.
San Francisco, CA
Qualmann, Christopher R., P.A.
Maitland, FL
Qualmann, Christopher Rumsey
Maitland, FL
Qualseth, Shon ..... Lawrence, KS
Qualtere, Graham & Redder ..... Kingston, NY
Qualtrough, Kerrie Jo ..... Austin, TX
Quam, Darrin J. ..... Tampa, FL
Quam, David C. ..... Washington, DC
Quam, Jay M. ..... Minneapolis, MN
Quam, John C. ..... Detroit Lakes, MN
Quam, Lester ..... Chicago, IL
Quam, Steven J. ..... Minneapolis, MN
Quamina, Lesia H. ..... Burtonsville, MD
Quamme, Steven J. ..... Washington, DC
Quammen, Thomas James ..... Greeley, CO
Quan, Carol ..... Los Angeles, CA
Quan, Cary K. ..... Santa Ana, CA
Quan, Cohen, Kurahashi, Yang, Scholtz &
Hirano, A Professional Corporation
Los Angeles, CA
Quan, David J. ..... Houston, TX
Quan, Donna L. ..... San Francisco, CA
Quan, Gordon J. ..... Houston, TX
Quan, Heidi C. ..... San Francisco, CA
Quan, John J. ..... Forest Park, IL
Quan, Jonathan R. ..... Hagåtña, GU
Quan, Judy A. ..... Newport Beach, CA
Quan, Kelvin P. ..... San Leandro, CA
Quan, Larry W. ..... San Francisco, CA
Quan, Lucinda Y. ..... San Diego, CA
Quan, Richard ..... New York, NY
Quan, Richard K. ..... Los Angeles, CA
Quan, Sheldon J. ..... Palo Alto, CA
Quan, Stacy ..... Beaverton, OR
Quan, Steven Y. ..... Washington, DC
Quanbeck, Kirsten K. ..... East Lansing, MI
Quanbeck, Maridee A. ..... Chicago, IL
Quance, Peter D. ..... Greenfield, OH
Quance, Rebecca J. ..... Greenfield, OH
Quandahl, Mark C. ..... Omaha, NE
Quander, Bethel McCoy ..... Baytown, TX
Quander, Donald W. ..... Billings, MT
Quander, Rohulamin ..... Washington, DC
Quandt, Eric F. ..... Chicago, IL
Quandt, Eric W. ..... Tulsa, OK
Quandt, Giffels & Buck Co., L.P.A.
Cleveland, OH
Quandt, Joseph E. ..... Traverse City, MI

Quigley, Laura A., P.A. ....Orlando, FL
Quigley, Laurie L. ....Fresno, CA
Quigley, Lawrence M. ....Fair Haven, NJ
Quigley, Lawrence W. ....Cassopolis, MI
Quigley, Leonard V. ....New York, NY
Quigley, Lewis B. ....Salt Lake City, UT
Quigley, Mallette C. ....Florence, AL
Quigley, Marc T. ....Indianapolis, IN
Quigley, Mark A. ....Everett, WA
Quigley, Mark Rian ....Boston, MA
Quigley, Mark T. ....Santa Monica, CA
Quigley, Michael ....Washington, DC
Quigley, Michael, Incorporated
Orange, CA
Quigley, Michael J. ....Orange, CA
Quigley, Michael J.
Environmental Protection Agency,
Program Office Attorneys, GV
Quigley, Neil ....Denver, CO
Quigley, Patrick J., Jr. ....New York, NY
Quigley, Patrick M. ....San Francisco, CA
Quigley, Patrick S. ....Galveston, TX
Quigley, Paul E. ....Oklahoma City, OK
Quigley, Peter C. ....Chicago, IL
Quigley, Peter J. ....Stroudsburg, PA
Quigley, Richard Q. ....Kennewick, WA
Quigley, Richard W., Jr. ....Fremont, OH
Quigley, Robert A. ....Harrisburg, PA
Quigley, Robert J., Jr. ....Providence, RI
Quigley, Robert M. ....Venice, FL
Quigley, Ron L. ....Atlanta, GA
Quigley, Sandra Ann ....San Francisco, CA
Quigley, Sean W. ....Milford, CT
Quigley, Stephen J. ....New York, NY
Quigley, Tang & Whitehill, P.L.C.
Tucson, AZ
Quigley, Theresa K. ....Melville, NY
Quigley, Thomas A. ....Orange, CT
Quigley, Thomas D. ....Indianapolis, IN
Quigley, Thomas E. ....Hartford, CT
Quigley, Thomas J. ....Washington, DC
Quigley, Thomas J. ....New York, NY
Quigley, Thomas M. ....Phoenix, AZ
Quigley, Thurl M. ....Minneapolis, MN
Quigley, Tricia R. ....Pontiac, MI
Quigley, William ....Pine Ridge, SD
Quigley, William Byron ....Valentine, NE
Quigley, William E., III ....Richardson, TX
Quigley, William E., Jr. ....Richardson, TX
Quigley, William P. (Pat) ....Merced, CA
Quigley, William Patrick ....New Orleans, LA
Quigley, William T. ....Buffalo, NY
Quigley, Wm. C. ....Salt Lake City, UT
Quigley, Zelica ....Boca Raton, FL
Quigley-Rick, Mary H. ....Iowa City, IA
Quigly, James W. ....Detroit, MI
Quihillalt, Michel E. ....San Francisco, CA
Quijada, Virginia R. ....Miami, FL
Quijano, Annette ....Roseland, NJ
Quijano, Dolph, Jr. ....El Paso, TX
Quijano, Eddy M. ....Baton Rouge, LA
Quijano, Peter E. ....New York, NY
Quildon, Jennifer P. ....Miami, FL
Quiles, Alan L. ....Miami, FL
Quiles, Edgardo Nieves ....San Juan, PR
Quiles-Mariani, Pedro D. ....San Juan, PR
Quiles Rosado, Domingo Arturo
San Juan, PR
Quiles Rosado, Mario A. ....San Juan, PR
Quilichini, Carlos J. ....San Juan, PR
Quilichini, Manuel A. ....San Juan, PR
Quilici, Belinda B. ....Lovelock, NV
Quilici, Peter A. ....Chicago, IL
Quilici, Victor D., Sr. ....Des Plaines, IL
Quill, Adrienne M. ....Indianapolis, IN
Quill, Donald J. ....Boston, MA
Quill, Edward S., Jr. ....Washington, DC
Quill, Eileen M. ....Boston, MA
Quill, Gary J. ....Birmingham, MI
Quill, Henry F. ....Winchester, MA
Quill, John F. ....Raleigh, NC
Quill, Joseph F. ....Indianapolis, IN
Quill, Kevin E. ....Newport, KY
Quill, Patrick B. ....New York, NY
Quill, Robert M. ....Atlanta, GA
Quill, Terry F. ....Washington, DC
Quill, Timothy M. ....Stafford, TX
Quillen, Amy B. ....Gainesville, FL
Quillen, Cecil D., Jr. ....Washington, DC
Quillen, Dale M., P.C. ....Nashville, TN
Quillen, Ford C. ....Gate City, VA
Quillen, Gwyn ....Los Angeles, CA
Quillen, Hamilton & Jorgensen, Law Firm of
Gate City, VA
Quillen, James, II ....Tampa, FL
Quillen, Jeffrey L. ....Boston, MA
Quillen, Lynda C. ....Tallahassee, FL
Quillen, Michael C. ....Birmingham, AL
Quillen, Myrl D. ....Kingsport, TN
Quillen, Patricia H. ....Salem, VA
Quillen, Roger K. ....Atlanta, GA
Quillen, Stephen M. ....Lebanon, VA
Quillen, Whitney S. ....New York, NY
Quillen, William T. ....Wilmington, DE
Quilliam, W. Reed, Jr. ....Lubbock, TX
Quillian, Abda Lee ....Savannah, GA
Quillian, Alfred A. ....Winder, GA
Quillian, Alfred A., Jr. ....Atlanta, GA
Quillian, Barbara H. ....Atlanta, GA
Quillian, Causy C., III ....Kenedy, TX
Quillian, Celia P. ....Atlanta, GA
Quillian, Harry W. ....Washington, DC
Quillian, Henry M., III ....Atlanta, GA
Quillian, H. T., Jr. ....La Grange, GA
Quillian, J. Kirk ....Atlanta, GA
Quillian, Robert M. ....Olympia, WA
Quillian, Roy D., III ....San Antonio, TX
Quillian, William F., III ....Lynchburg, VA

Quillin, Daniel B. ....Akron, OH
Quillin, Daniel W. ....Washington, DC
Quillin, Dennis J. ....Clayton, MO
Quillin, Edgar N. ....Arabi, LA
Quillin, Edward P. ....Dallas, TX
Quillin, George E. ....Washington, DC
Quillin, George W., Jr. ....Columbus, OH
Quillin, Mary L. ....Pasadena, CA
Quillin, Paula J. ....Tulsa, OK
Quillin, Ronald J. ....La Crosse, WI
Quillin, Ronald W. ....Fort Worth, TX
Quillinan, James V. ....Mountain View, CA
Quillinan, Kasia ....Salem, OR
Quillinan & Luce, LLP
Mountain View, CA
Quillinan, Michael J. ....White Plains, NY
Quilling, Michael J. ....Dallas, TX
Quilling, Selander, Cummiskey & Lownds, P.C. ....Dallas, TX
Quilling, Thomas F. ....Irvine, CA
Quilter, Caryn S. ....Jackson, MS
Quilter, Matthew P. ....Palo Alto, CA
Quilter, Thomas R., III ....Detroit, MI
Quilty, Dennis A. ....Boston, MA
Quilty, James R. ....Des Moines, IA
Quilty, Patrick J. ....Waukegan, IL
Quimby, B. Douglas
Colorado Springs, CO
Quimby, David W. ....Austin, TX
Quimby Higgins & McDonald LLP
Colorado Springs, CO
Quimby, Janice V. ....Cherry Hill, NJ
Philadelphia, PA
Quimby, Karen Michelle ....Spartanburg, SC
Quimby, Kathleen H. ....Washington, DC
Quimby, Robert F. ....Sarasota, FL
Quimby, Teri L. ....Lansing, MI
Quimby, Thomas L. ....Shoreview, MN
Quimby-Pennock, Lynne A. ....Tallahassee, FL
Quimper, James R. ....Chesapeake Beach, MD
Quin, Alison J. ....Memphis, TN
Quin, Ann Mandle ....Harahan, LA
Quin, George M. ....Gulfport, MS
Quin, Gordon D. ....Morristown, NJ
Quin, James N., Jr. ....San Antonio, TX
Quin, Jane J. ....Pearl River, NY
Quin, Kevin C. ....San Jose, CA
Quin, Paul M. ....Kansas City, MO
Quin, Whayne S. ....Washington, DC
Quin, William M. ....Kentwood, LA
Quin, William M., II ....New Orleans, LA
Quina, Marion A., Jr. ....Mobile, AL
Quinalty, Keats A.
Department of Commerce,
Patent and Trademark Office, GV
Quinan, Deborah Pechet ....Boston, MA
Quinan, Michael J. ....Richmond, VA
Quinan, Robert L. ....Boston, MA
Quinan, Robert L., Jr. ....Boston, MA
Quinby, Carter ....San Francisco, CA
Quinby, Joseph P. ....Irvine, CA
Quinby, Katherine A. ....Dallas, TX
Quinby, Richard E. ....Boston, MA
Quinby, William A. ....Oakland, CA
Quince, Peggy A. ....Lakeland, FL
Quince-Colbert, Thelma ....Fort Worth, TX
Quincey, Becker, Schuessler, Militello & Chase, S.C. ....Beaver Dam, WI
Mayville, WI
Quincey, Irene Kennedy
West Palm Beach, FL
Quincey, James S. ....Gainesville, FL
Quincey, Kenneth J. ....Beaver Dam, WI
Quincy Law Group ....Chicago, IL
Quincy, Stephanie ....Phoenix, AZ
Quindel, Barbara Zack ....Milwaukee, WI
Quindry, Charles L. ....Benton, IL
Quindry, Curtis G. ....Newton, IL
Quindry, Gerald T. ....Fairfield, IL
Quine, Stephen J. ....New York, NY
Quine, Susan C. ....Albany, NY
Quiner, Mark ....Cheyenne, WY
Quinlan, Amy Arnott ....Wilmington, DE
Quinlan, Amy S. ....Hingham, MA
Quinlan, Anne K.
Department of Transportation,
Surface Transportation Board, GV
Quinlan, Catherine M. ....New York, NY
Quinlan, Christopher G. ....Addison, NY
Quinlan & Crisham, Ltd. ....Chicago, IL
Quinlan, Dale K. ....San Juan Capistrano, CA
Quinlan, David J., Jr. ....Rye, NY
Quinlan, David M. ....Princeton, NJ
Quinlan, David M., P.C. ....Princeton, NJ
Quinlan, Denis J. ....Chicago, IL
Quinlan, Diane Murphy ....Manchester, NH
Quinlan, Dunne & Daily ....Merchantville, NJ
Quinlan, E. Michael ....Boston, MA
Quinlan, Edward J. ....Norwood, MA
Quinlan, Edward J., Jr. ....Brooklyn, NY
Quinlan, Elsie M. ....Hudson, NY
Quinlan, Emily Samuelsen
Mission Viejo, CA
Quinlan, Erin Marie ....Chicago, IL
Quinlan, Francis E. ....Corona Del Mar, CA
Quinlan, Francis X. ....Jaffrey, NH
Quinlan, Francis X., P.A. ....Jaffrey, NH
Quinlan, Fredk. J. ....Boston, MA
Quinlan, Gerald S. ....Metairie, LA
Quinlan, Gerard R. ....Clearwater, FL
Quinlan, Gregory Mark ....Alamogordo, NM
Quinlan, Guy C. ....New York, NY
Quinlan, Ian James Quincy ....Austin, TX
Quinlan, Jack A. ....Topeka, KS
Quinlan, James J. ....New York, NY
Quinlan, James L. ....Omaha, NE
Quinlan, James W., IV ....Atlanta, GA
Quinlan, Jeremiah ....Hastings-On-Hudson, NY

Quinlan, John ....Houston, TX
Quinlan, John L., III ....San Antonio, TX
Quinlan, John M. ....Corpus Christi, TX
Quinlan, John R. ....Spokane, WA
Quinlan, John V. ....Bradenton, FL
Quinlan, Joseph Mike ....Springfield, VA
Quinlan, Karen Ross ....Canton, OH
Quinlan, Kathleen J. ....Madison, WI
Quinlan, Kershaw & Fanucchi
Fresno, CA
Quinlan, Kevin S. ....Tuckerton, NJ
Quinlan, Lawlor F., III ....Buffalo, NY
Quinlan, Lesley Jane ....Summit, NJ
Quinlan, Louis H. ....Troy, NY
Quinlan, Margaret M. ....Chicago, IL
Quinlan, Mary E. ....Rancho Cucamonga, CA
Quinlan, Mary H. ....Tampa, FL
Quinlan, Maura K. ....Harrisburg, PA
Quinlan, Michael D. ....St. Louis, MO
Quinlan, Michael D.
Whitehouse Station, NJ
Quinlan, Michael J. ....Portland, ME
Quinlan, Nancy Vorpe ....Miami, FL
Quinlan, Pamela D. ....Salem, OR
Quinlan, Patrick ....Providence, RI
Quinlan, Patrick E. ....West Palm Beach, FL
Quinlan, Patrick P. ....Tonawanda, NY
Quinlan, Paul T. ....Palo Alto, CA
Quinlan, Regina L. ....Boston, MA
Quinlan and Reilly ....Troy, NY
Quinlan, Rene David ....Pittsburgh, PA
Quinlan, Richard M. ....Glastonbury, CT
Quinlan, Robert E. ....Gaithersburg, MD
Quinlan, Robert F. ....Bay Shore, NY
Quinlan, Robert F., Jr. ....Westport, CT
Quinlan, Robert J. ....Great Falls, VA
Quinlan, Russell T. ....Buffalo, NY
Hamburg, NY
Quinlan & Sadowski, P.C. ....Norwood, MA
Quinlan, Shannon M. ....Boston, MA
Quinlan, Shaun L., P.C. ....Anniston, AL
Quinlan, Shaun Leigh ....Anniston, AL
Quinlan, Terence M. ....Garden City, NY
Quinlan, Terrence E. ....Fort Wayne, IN
Quinlan, Thomas F. ....Wheaton, IL
Quinlan, Thomas J. ....Modesto, CA
Quinlan, Thomas J. ....Oakland, CA
Quinlan, Thomas P. ....Fircrest, WA
Quinlan, Timothy C. ....Jaffrey, NH
Quinlan, Timothy J. ....Dearborn, MI
Quinlan, Timothy J. P. ....Merchantville, NJ
Quinlan, V. Paul ....Omaha, NE
Quinlan, W. Scott ....Fresno, CA
Quinlan, William A. ....Fresno, CA
Quinlan, William A. ....Silver Spring, MD
Quinlan, William A. ....Buffalo, NY
Quinlan, William J. ....Berlin, CT
Quinlan, William J. ....Rockford, IL
Quinlan, William J., Jr. ....Chicago, IL
Quinlan, William John ....Chicago, IL
Quinlan, William R. ....Chicago, IL
QuinlanAdvocates Law Firm, LLC
Atlanta, GA
Quinland, Roger M. ....New York, NY
Quinlevan, John J., Jr. ....Mequon, WI
Quinley, Wilson ....Hagåtña, GU
Quinlisk, John J. ....Chicago, IL
Quinlisk, Wallace G. ....Fresno, CA
Quinlisk, Wallace G., Professional Corp.
Fresno, CA
Quinlivan & Hughes, P.A. ....Rochester, MN
St. Cloud, MN
Quinlivan, J. Mark ....South Miami, FL
Quinlivan, James S. ....Buffalo, NY
Quinlivan, John D. ....St. Cloud, MN
Quinlivan, Joseph D., Jr. ....Mobile, AL
Quinlivan & Kaniewski
Newport Beach, CA
Quinlivan, Marc A. ....Chicago, IL
Quinlivan, Margaret C.F. ....Miami, FL
Quinlivan, Mark T. ....Department of Justice,
Civil Division, GV
Quinlivan, Michael P. ....San Jose, CA
Quinlivan, Michael R. ....Minneapolis, MN
Quinlivan, Patrick C. ......Newport Beach, CA
Quinlivan, Patrick J. ....Buffalo, NY
Quinlivan, Robert D. ....Chicago, IL
Quinlivan, Robert D., P.C. ....Chicago, IL
Quinlivan, Stephen M. ....Minneapolis, MN
Quinlivan, Timothy J. ....Buffalo, NY
Quinn, A. James ....Lorain, OH
Quinn, A. Peter, Jr. ....Hartford, CT
Quinn, Adrienne E. ....Seattle, WA
Quinn, Allison R. ....Worcester, MA
Quinn, Andrew D. ....Lansing, MI
Quinn, Andrew H. ....Westmont, NJ
Philadelphia, PA
Quinn, Andrew W. ....San Diego, CA
Quinn, Anne M. ....Stamford, CT
Quinn, Anne V. ....Boston, MA
Quinn, Anthony B. ....Salt Lake City, UT
Quinn, Anthony Bernard
Philadelphia, PA
Quinn, Anthony J. ....Dubuque, IA
Quinn, Anthony P. ....Astoria, NY
Quinn, Arthur E. ....Memphis, TN
Quinn, Barbara A. ....Miami, FL
Quinn, Barbara J. ....Los Angeles, CA
Quinn, Barbara M. ....Middletown, CT
Quinn, Barry E. ....New York, NY
Quinn, Bernard ....Madison, NJ
Quinn, Bernard E. Jude ....Moorestown, NJ
Philadelphia, PA
Quinn, Beth Doherty ....Denver, CO
Quinn, Beverly Wilson
Rancho Cucamonga, CA
Quinn, Borella, Stockton & Amsbaugh, P.C.
Plymouth, MI

Quinn, Brendan G. ....Albany, NY
Quinn, Brian C. ....Washington, DC
Quinn, Brian E. ....Philadelphia, PA
Quinn, Brian F. ....Washington, DC
Quinn, Brian J. ....Great Barrington, MA
Pittsfield, MA
Quinn, Brian J. ....New City, NY
Quinn, Brian O. ....Washington, DC
Quinn, Brian P. ....Amarillo, TX
Quinn, Buseck, Leemhuis, Toohey & Kroto, Inc. ....Erie, PA
Quinn, C. Michael ....Birmingham, AL
Quinn, C. Rayford, Jr. ....Woburn, MA
Quinn, Cameron James ....Newport Beach, CA
Quinn, Cameron P. ....Providence, RI
Quinn, Cameron P., Miss ....Arlington, VA
Quinn, Camille M. ....Tulsa, OK
Quinn, Camille M., P.C. ....Tulsa, OK
Quinn, Carol A. ....Stamford, CT
Quinn, Carol A. ....Argonne, IL
Quinn, Carole A. ....Los Angeles, CA
Quinn, Caroline F. ....Wilson, NC
Quinn, Carolyn ....Chicago, IL
Quinn, Casey J. ....Omaha, NE
Quinn, Charles ....New York, NY
Quinn, Charles N. ....Philadelphia, PA
Quinn, Charles R. ....Stow, OH
Quinn, Charles V. ....Morristown, NJ
Quinn, Charles W. ....Pittsburgh, PA
Quinn, Christi D. ....Houston, TX
Quinn, Christopher ....Newton, MA
Quinn, Christopher D. ....Newton, NJ
Quinn, Christopher David ....Caldwell, ID
Quinn, Christopher E.V. ....Chicago, IL
Quinn, Christopher G. ....Mineola, NY
Quinn, Christopher W. ....Southfield, MI
Quinn, Clayton J. ....Hartford, CT
Quinn, Colin MaGuire ....Teaneck, NJ
Quinn, Colleen Marea ....Richmond, VA
Quinn, Cornelius P. ....Littleton, CO
Quinn & Correa, P.C. ....Plymouth, MA
Quinn, Cris ....Beaumont, TX
Quinn, Daniel E. ....Fort Collins, CO
Quinn, Daniel F. ....Modesto, CA
Oakland, CA
Sacramento, CA
Quinn, Daniel F. ....Stockton, CA
Quinn, Daniel T. ....Anchorage, AK
Quinn, Darren J. ....San Diego, CA
Quinn, David Brian ....Boston, MA
Quinn, David C. ....Buffalo, NY
Quinn, David C. ....North Salem, NY
Quinn, David M. ....Albany, NY
Quinn, David Michael ....Columbus, OH
Quinn, David P. ....Albany, NY
Quinn, Day & Barker, P.L.L.C.
Belle Fourche, SD
Rapid City, SD
Quinn, Dean ....Houston, TX
Quinn, Deanna M. ....Chicago, IL
Quinn, Deborah Ann ....Garnerville, NY
Quinn, Deborah Lee ....Aiken, SC
Quinn, Deborah McLean ....Rochester, NY
Quinn, Denis J. ....New York, NY
Quinn, Dennis C. ....San Francisco, CA
Quinn, Dennis J. ....Washington, DC
Quinn, Dennis J. ....Sea Isle City, NJ
Quinn, Dennis M. ....Chicago, IL
Quinn, Donald J. ....Kansas City, MO
Quinn, Donald J., II ....Kansas City, MO
Quinn, Donald P. ....Plymouth, MA
Quinn, Donald P., P.C. ....Plymouth, MA
Quinn, Donna M. ....Framingham, MA
Quinn, Donna M., P.C., Law Offices of
Framingham, MA
Quinn, Donna Underwood ....Clovis, NM
Quinn, Douglas E. ....Omaha, NE
Quinn, E. Paul ....Chicago, IL
Quinn, Edw. J. ....Philadelphia, PA
Quinn, Edward J., Jr. ....Sacramento, CA
Quinn, Elizabeth A. ....Washington, DC
Quinn Emanuel Urquhart Oliver & Hedges, LLP ....Indian Wells, CA
Los Angeles, CA
Palm Springs, CA
Palo Alto, CA
Quinn, Francine Corcoran ....Brooklyn, NY
Quinn, Francis F. ....Mount Laurel, NJ
New York, NY
Philadelphia, PA
Quinn, Francis J. ....New Brunswick, NJ
New York, NY
Quinn, Francis R. ....Norwich, CT
Quinn, Francis X. ....Rockville, MD
Quinn, Francis X., Jr. ....Portsmouth, NH
Quinn, Frank M. ....Bay City, MI
Quinn, Gerald T. ....Northbrook, IL
Quinn, Gerald T., Chartered ....Northbrook, IL
Quinn, Gerard J. ....New York, NY
Quinn, Gerard W. ....Atlantic City, NJ
Quinn, Gordon D. ....Springfield, MA
Quinn, Graceanne T. Snyder
New Hartford, NY
West Winfield, NY
Quinn, Gregory F. ....Manchester, MO
Quinn, Ground & Banton ....Manchester, MO
Quinn, H. Eugene ....Tacoma, WA
Quinn, Harold P., Jr. ....Washington, DC
Quinn, Harris P. ....Memphis, TN
Quinn, H. B. ....Cadiz, KY
Quinn, Heidi ....Woodside, CA
Quinn, Helen Emma ....Palo Alto, CA
Quinn, Helena M. ....Philadelphia, PA
Quinn, Hugh F., III ....Miami, FL
Quinn, Hugh P. ....Washington, DC
Quinn, J. Bartlett ....Chattanooga, TN
Quinn, J. Patrick ....Taylor, TX
Quinn, Jack ....Washington, DC

Quintrall, Albert F. .... San Diego, CA
Quintrell, Thomas A. .... Cleveland, OH
Quiogue, Manuel .... Palo Alto, CA
Quiram, Bryan W. .... Boulder, CO
Quirantes, Albert M. .... Miami, FL
Quirey, William O., Jr. .... Richmond, VA
Quirico, Francis J. .... Pittsfield, MA
Quirico, Thomas J. .... Hackensack, NJ
Quirion, Colleen M. .... Schenectady, NY
Quirion, Jane E. .... Topsham, ME
Quirk, Ashlin Carter .... Norwalk, CT
Quirk and Bakalor, P.C. .... New York, NY
Quirk, Barbara L. .... San Antonio, TX
Quirk, Brian P. .... New Orleans, LA
Quirk, Catherine Ann .... Chicago, IL
Quirk and Chamberlain, P.C.
Barnstable, MA
Yarmouth Port, MA
Quirk, Edward J. .... Las Vegas, NV
Quirk, Edward J., Jr. .... Bakersfield, CA
Quirk, Elizabeth .... Morristown, NJ
Quirk, Frank E. .... Akron, OH
Quirk, Ilana Marie .... Boston, MA
Quirk, J. Richard .... Seattle, WA
Quirk, Jack A. .... Muncie, IN
Quirk, James .... Citrus Heights, CA
Quirk, James H. .... San Francisco, CA
Quirk, James H. .... South Yarmouth, MA
Quirk, James H., Jr. .... Barnstable, MA
Yarmouth Port, MA
Quirk, Jeremy O. .... Fort Wayne, IN
Quirk, JoAnn C. .... Little Rock, AR
Quirk, JoAnn C., P.A. .... Little Rock, AR
Quirk, John .... Glendale, CA
Quirk, John F. .... Porterville, CA
Quirk, John T., Jr. .... Springfield, MA
Quirk, Joseph M. .... Rockville, MD
Quirk, Joseph P. .... Atlanta, GA
Quirk, Joseph P. .... Geneseo, NY
Quirk, Julie Espeseth .... Harrisburg, PA
Quirk, Karen Caraher .... Chicago, IL
Quirk, Katherine Karam
New Orleans, LA
Quirk, Kathryn L. .... New York, NY
Quirk, Kevin .... Atlanta, GA
Quirk, Lawrence T., III .... Asbury Park, NJ
Quirk, Madeline .... Providence, RI
Quirk, Marion M. .... Philadelphia, PA
Quirk, Martin G. .... Atlanta, GA
Quirk, Mary E. .... Springfield, MA
Quirk, Michael L. .... Milwaukee, WI
Quirk, Michael R. .... Walnut Creek, CA
Quirk, Neal J. .... Atlanta, GA
Quirk, Noreen .... Stamford, CT
Quirk, Patrick M. .... Baton Rouge, LA
Quirk and Quirk .... Geneseo, NY
Quirk & Quirk, P.C. .... Atlanta, GA
Quirk & Rivers .... Muncie, IN
Quirk, Robert C. .... San Antonio, TX
Quirk, Robert E. .... New York, NY
Quirk, Rory F. .... Washington, DC
Quirk, Sean R. .... Atlanta, GA
Quirk, Sherry A. .... Washington, DC
Quirk, Thomas E. .... San Antonio, TX
Quirk, Thomas J. .... Baltimore, MD
Quirk, Thomas M. .... Chicago, IL
Quirk, Thomas M. .... Charlotte, NC
Quirk, Thomas P. .... Lake Charles, LA
Quirk, Thos. E. .... Fort Wayne, IN
Quirk, Timothy W. .... Spokane, WA
Quirk & Tratos, Chartered
Las Vegas, NV
Quirk, William E. .... Kansas City, MO
Quirk, William H., III .... San Antonio, TX
Quirk, William J. .... Gainesville, FL
Quirke, Barry J. .... Chicago, IL
Quirke, John P. .... Philadelphia, PA
Quirós, Paul A. .... Atlanta, GA
Quiroz, Kathleen .... San Antonio, TX
Quisenberry & Barbanel, LLP
Los Angeles, CA
San Diego, CA
Quisenberry, C. Dale .... Houston, TX
Quisenberry, Carl G. .... Wichita Falls, TX
Quisenberry, Daniel J. .... Los Angeles, CA
Quisenberry, Jas. E. .... Roanoke, VA
Quisenberry, John A. .... New York, NY
Quisenberry, John N. .... Los Angeles, CA
San Diego, CA
Quisenberry, Quisenberry & Dant
Calhoun, KY
Quisenberry, Roy Graham, III
Weatherford, TX
Quisenberry, William E. .... Calhoun, KY
Quisenberry, William E., Jr. .... Calhoun, KY
Quisling, Kristine M. .... Elmhurst, IL
Quisling, Rolf W. .... Dearborn, MI
Quissell, Barbara C. .... Albuquerque, NM
Quist, Brian C. .... Knoxville, TN
Quist, Brooke W. .... Seattle, WA
Quist, Carl W. .... Pierre, SD
Quist, Darvid D. .... Blair, NE
Quist, David W. .... Albany, NY
Quist, Eric N. .... Tacoma, WA
Quist, Erik S. .... Knoxville, TN
Quist, Gordon J. .... Grand Rapids, MI
Quist, Karen L. .... Wasilla, AK
Quist, Marcelle Compton
Southern Pines, NC
Quist, Marinus .... New Orleans, LA
Quist, Richard J. .... Lowell, MI
Quist, Richard J., Jr. .... Westwood, MA
Quist, Scott .... Sandy, UT
Quitiquit, Sylvester V. .... Kailua-Kona, HI
Quitmeier, William M. .... Kansas City, MO
Quitmeier, William M., and Associates, P.C.
Kansas City, MO
Quitmeyer, John M. .... Danbury, CT

Quitt, Daniella .... New York, NY
Quittman, Peter F. .... Oakland, CA
Quittmeyer, David R. .... Mobile, AL
Quittmeyer, Peter C. .... Atlanta, GA
Quittmeyer, Robert T. .... Port Washington, NY
Quittner, Andrew L. .... Corpus Christi, TX
Quittner, Arnold M. .... Los Angeles, CA
Quittner, Marvin .... Plantation, FL
Quittschreiber, Bradley J. .... Belvidere, IL
Quivey, Douglas J. .... Charleston, IL
Quivey, Lara L. .... Urbana, IL
Qulia, Robert G. .... Cleveland, OH
Quock, Kevin J. .... Los Angeles, CA
Quon, Douglas T. .... Las Vegas, NV
Quon, Nancy .... Las Vegas, NV
Quon, Robin Marie Fagg .... Chicago, IL
Quon, Teresa J.A. .... Honolulu, HI
Quow, Franklin G.
Christiansted, St. Croix, VI
Quoyeser, Peter C. .... New Braunfels, TX
Qureshi, Abid .... New York, NY
Qureshi, Abid Riaz .... Washington, DC
Qureshi, Sarah Nafees
Small Business Administration,
Office of the General Counsel, GV
Qureshi, Sarah Q. .... Dallas, TX
Qusba, Sandeep .... New York, NY
Qushair, Ann H. .... Los Angeles, CA
Quynn, Russell H., Jr. .... Richmond, VA

R.E. Wheelan & Associates .... Houston, TX
Ra, Joseph J. .... Valley Stream, NY
Raab, Ariel .... Fort Lauderdale, FL
Raab, Daniel W. .... Miami, FL
Raab, Daniel W., P.A. .... Miami, FL
Raab, David S. .... New York, NY
Raab, Douglas J. .... Portland, OR
Raab, Edward Leon .... New York, NY
Raab, Frederick A. .... Baltimore, MD
Raab, Howard .... Fort Lauderdale, FL
Raab, Ira J. .... Woodmere, NY
Raab, Jonarde .... Sacramento, CA
Raab, Katie R. .... Brooklyn, NY
Raab, Mitchell .... New York, NY
Raab & Raab .... Fort Lauderdale, FL
Raab, Richard .... New York, NY
Raab, Ronald .... New York, NY
Raab, Sharon K. .... San Jose, CA
Raab, Sheldon, (P.C.) .... New York, NY
Raab, Stephen R. .... San Francisco, CA
Raab & Sturm LLP .... New York, NY
Raab, Susan Humes .... Jacksonville, FL
Raabe, Craig A. .... Hartford, CT
Raabe, Helen Eckardt .... Denver, CO
Raabe, Katherine Ann .... Denver, CO
Raabe, Michael E. .... Laguna Hills, CA
Raabe, Susan E. .... Cleveland, OH
Raabe, Wayne C. .... Department of Justice,
Criminal Division, GV
Raack, David W. .... Ada, OH
Raack, William J. .... Clayton, MO
Raad, Amal Ann .... New York, NY
Raad, Joseph L. .... Rock Hill, SC
Ra'anan, Michael .... Department of Defense,
Defense Legal Services Agency, GV
Raanan, Uzzi O. .... Los Angeles, CA
Raas, Daniel A. .... Bellingham, WA
Raas, Johnsen & Stuen, P.S.
Bellingham, WA
Raasch, E. John .... Waukesha, WI
Raasch, Jeffrey Paul .... Atlanta, GA
Raasch, Kevin W. .... Minneapolis, MN
Raasch, Ralph W. .... Milwaukee, WI
Raasch, Thomas F. .... Milwaukee, WI
Raaths, Bradley W. .... Madison, WI
Raattama, Henry H., Jr. .... Miami, FL
Raattama, M. Kristina .... Nashville, TN
Raatz, David Malcolm .... Wailuku, HI
Raatz, Gretchen E. .... Austin, TX
Raatz, Kenneth H. .... Trenton, NJ
Raatz, Les .... Phoenix, AZ
Raatz, Melvin E. .... Sacramento, CA
Raaum, Bruce .... Grand Junction, CO
Raaum, Care McInnis .... Grand Junction, CO
Rab, John P. .... Keene, NH
Rab and Neiman, P.A. .... Keene, NH
Rab, Sydney E. .... Woodbridge, VA
Raba, Angela S. .... San Antonio, TX
Raba, Elizabeth Alma .... Longmont, CO
Raba, Ernest A. .... San Antonio, TX
Raba, John T. .... San Antonio, TX
Rabadjija, Neven .... Boston, MA
Rabago, Anthony Adam .... San Antonio, TX
Rabago, Daniel L. .... Palo Alto, CA
Rabago, Roberto D. .... Jerome, AZ
Rabalais, David R. .... Lafayette, LA
New Orleans, LA
Rabalais Hanna & Hays .... Lafayette, LA
Rabalais Law Firm, The, A Professional Corporation .... Baton Rouge, LA
Rabalais, Paul A. .... Baton Rouge, LA
Rabalais, Ralph T. .... New Orleans, LA
Rabalais, Raphael J., Jr. .... New Orleans, LA
Rabalais, Robert René .... Houston, TX
Rabalais, Rodney M., Law Office of
Marksville, LA
Rabalais, Steven B. .... Lafayette, LA
Raban, Reginald J. .... Beach Haven, NJ
Raba-O'Connor, L.L.P. .... San Antonio, TX
Rabasco, Edward, Jr. .... Lewiston, ME
Rabassa, Maria M. .... Los Angeles, CA
Rabassa, Santiago C. .... Reston, VA
Rabaut, James C. .... Detroit, MI
Rabaut, James J. .... Grand Rapids, MI
Rabaut, John J. .... Detroit, MI
Rabaut, Louis C. .... Grand Rapids, MI
Rabaut, Vincent C., Jr. .... Detroit, MI

Rabaut, William F. .... Southfield, MI
Rabaya, Violet C. .... Los Angeles, CA
Rabb, Bridget .... La Crosse, WI
Rabb, Bruce .... New York, NY
Rabb & Davis .... Cleveland, OH
Rabb, Harriet S.
Department Of Health And Human Services,
Office of the General Counsel, GV
Rabb, Howard S. .... Painesville, OH
Rabb, John W., Jr. .... Camden, SC
Rabb, Joseph .... Indianapolis, IN
Rabb, Lawrence J. .... Brownsville, TX
Rabb, Lawrence W. .... Meridian, MS
Rabb, Lloyd L., III .... Tempe, AZ
Tucson, AZ
Amarillo, TX
Rabb, Maxwell M. .... New York, NY
Rabb, Richard A. .... Cleveland, OH
Rabb, Sheldon E. .... Cleveland, OH
Rabb, William E. .... Woodbridge, NJ
Rabbach, David J. .... New York, NY
Rabbani, Robert A. .... Los Angeles, CA
Rabbat and Rabbat .... Totowa, NJ
Rabbat, Victor K. .... Totowa, NJ
Rabbat, William F. .... Totowa, NJ
Rabben, Robert G. .... Department of Energy,
Office of the General Counsel, GV
Rabbideau, Richard E. .... Detroit, MI
Rabbin, Gille Ann .... New York, NY
Rabbin, Richard S. .... Ventura, CA
Rabbiner, Michele J. .... Plainview, NY
Rabbino, Anne Adams .... New York, NY
Rabbino, David A. .... San Francisco, CA
Rabbino, Mitchell W. .... Kingston, NY
Rabbino, Robert A., Jr. .... New York, NY
Rabbino, Stacey D. .... Washington, DC
Rabbito, Joseph J. .... Miami, FL
Rabbitt, Daniel T. .... St. Louis, MO
Rabbitt, Donna J. .... Fairfield, CT
Rabbitt, James S. .... Sandusky, OH
Rabbitt, Peter J. J. .... St. Louis, MO
Rabbitt, Pitzer & Snodgrass, P.C.
Belleville, IL
St. Louis, MO
Rabbitt, Richard J. .... San Francisco, CA
Rabby, Christopher L. .... Pensacola, FL
Rabchenuk, Paul Thomas .... Salem, MA
Rabdau, Matthew D. .... Portland, OR
Rabe, Brian C. .... Houston, TX
Rabe, Cynthia K. .... Anchorage, AK
Rabe, Edward R., Jr. .... Chicago, IL
Rabe, Genice A. G. .... Dallas, TX
Rabe, George F. .... Lexington, KY
Rabe, Herman E. .... Medina, OH
Rabe, Katherine S. .... Dallas, TX
Rabe, Mark D. .... St. Louis, MO
Rabe, Randall S. .... Columbus, OH
Rabe, Richd. F. .... Des Moines, IA
Rabecs, Robert N. .... Washington, DC
Rabekoff, Elise J. .... Washington, DC
Rabel, John V. .... Houston, TX
Rabel, Melissa Lynne .... Chicago, IL
Rabel, Timothy R. .... Chicago, IL
Rabell Méndez, Jesús R. .... San Juan, PR
Raben, David .... Miami, FL
Raben, Jesse .... Washington, DC
Raben, Margaret Sind .... Birmingham, MI
Raben, Seymore M. .... Davenport, IA
Rabena, John F. .... Washington, DC
Rabenau, Karen M. .... Raleigh, NC
Rabenberg, Keith A. .... St. Louis, MO
Rabenn, Glen L. .... Seal Beach, CA
Rabenn, Thomas O. .... Milwaukee, WI
Rabenold, Elizabeth L. .... Pittsburgh, PA
Rabenold, Keith M. .... Cincinnati, OH
Rabens, Formusa & Glassman, Ltd.
Chicago, IL
Rabens, Geo. C. .... Chicago, IL
Rabens, Ronald B.
Department of State, GV
Rabenseifner, Hanna C. .... Miami, FL
Raber, James S. .... Dallas, TX
Raber, Kimberly Allen .... Columbia, SC
Raber, Laurence B. .... Columbia, MD
Raber, Robert A. .... New York, NY
Raber, Scott R. .... San Francisco, CA
Raber, Stephen D. .... Washington, DC
Raber & Vandivier .... Danville, IN
Rabern, Tracy Lee .... Santa Fe, NM
Rabette, Thomas P. .... Clarkston, MI
Rabia, Vered .... New York, NY
Rabichow, Phillip H. .... Los Angeles, CA
Rabideau, Christopher J. .... Muskegon, MI
Rabideau, Guy .... Palm Beach, FL
Rabideau, Michael Thomas
West Palm Beach, FL
Rabidoux, Mark K. .... Detroit, MI
Rabie, Aseel M. .... Washington, DC
Rabieh, Maria N. .... New Orleans, LA
Rabiej, John
Administrative Office Of The United States
Courts, GV
Rabii, Susan M. .... Philadelphia, PA
Rabik, Bernard J. .... Pittsburgh, PA
Rabil, George J. .... Alexandria, VA
Rabil & Harris, L.L.C. .... Haddonfield, NJ
Moorestown, NJ
Rabil, Louis .... Washington, DC
Rabil, Michael J. .... Raleigh, NC
Rabil, Mitchell J. .... Haddonfield, NJ
Moorestown, NJ
Rabil, S. Mark .... Winston-Salem, NC
Rabil, Vincent F. .... Winston-Salem, NC
Rabil, William E., Jr. .... Winston-Salem, NC
Rabin, Alison J. .... Denver, CO
Rabin, Barry S. .... Downingtown, PA
Rabin, Benjamin Clair .... Syracuse, NY

Rabin, Bennett L. .... Clearwater, FL
Tampa, FL
Rabin, Bonnie .... New York, NY
Rabin, Byron M. .... Santa Ana, CA
Rabin & Champagne, P.C. .... Washington, DC
Rabin, Charles R. .... New York, NY
Rabin, Corey B. .... White Plains, NY
Rabin, Daniel S. .... Overland Park, KS
Kansas City, MO
Rabin, David A. .... Atlanta, GA
Rabin, David E. .... Stamford, CT
Rabin, Edward H. .... Davis, CA
Rabin, Edwin H. .... Flint, MI
Rabin, Frederick H. .... New York, NY
Rabin, Gary S. .... Lakeland, FL
Rabin, Gilbert .... White Plains, NY
Rabin, H. Mark .... Bethesda, MD
Rabin, Howard .... Westbury, NY
Rabin, Howard, P.C. .... Westbury, NY
Rabin, Howard R. .... New York, NY
Rabin, I. Stephen .... New York, NY
Rabin, Jack .... New York, NY
Rabin, Jay Harris .... New York, NY
Rabin, Jeffrey A. .... Los Angeles, CA
Rabin, Jeffrey A. .... Brooklyn, NY
Rabin, Jeffrey W. .... Bronx, NY
Rabin, Jonathon A. .... Detroit, MI
Rabin, Joseph .... Santa Barbara, CA
Rabin, Julie E. .... Cleveland, OH
Rabin, Kathy S. .... Cleveland, OH
Rabin, Mark .... Springfield, IL
Rabin, Mary Ann .... Cleveland, OH
Rabin, Matthew McLean
Washington, DC
Rabin, Myers & Hanken, P.C.
Springfield, IL
Rabin, Paul E. .... Redwood City, CA
Rabin & Peckel LLP .... New York, NY
Rabin & Rabin Co., L.P.A. .... Cleveland, OH
Rabin, Raymond .... Washington, DC
Rabin, Richard J. .... New York, NY
Rabin, Robert A. .... Miami, FL
Rabin, Robert B. .... North Palm Beach, FL
Rabin, Robert F. .... Chicago, IL
Rabin, Robert J. .... Syracuse, NY
Rabin, Robert L. .... Palo Alto, CA
Rabin, Rochelle S. .... West Chester, PA
Rabin, Samuel J., Jr. .... Miami, FL
Rabin, Samuel J., Jr., P.A. .... Miami, FL
Rabin, Steven M. .... Washington, DC
Rabin, Susan .... Mill Valley, CA
Rabin, Walter D. .... Jersey City, NJ
Rabin, Walter W. .... Miami, FL
Rabine, Joel H. .... Bronx, NY
Rabine, Laurie B. .... Bronx, NY
Rabine, Lawrence S. .... Dobbs Ferry, NY
Rabine, Merle C. .... Santa Ana, CA
Rabine & Nickelsberg .... Bronx, NY
Rabineau, Allan B. .... Baltimore, MD
Rabineau, Larry, (P.C.) .... Los Angeles, CA
Rabineau, Norman .... Silver Spring, MD
Rabiner, Bruce .... Jamaica, NY
Rabiner, Sheri Lynn .... New York, NY
Rabinkoff, Penny
Department of the Navy, GV
Rabino, Dvora Wolff .... New York, NY
Rabinoff, Regina .... New York, NY
Rabinor, Arnold James .... Lido Beach, NY
Rabinor, George B. .... Boca Raton, FL
Rabinove, Saml. .... White Plains, NY
Rabinovich, Anatoly .... New York, NY
Rabinovich, Barry .... New York, NY
Rabinovich, Irina .... Marina Del Rey, CA
Rabinovich, Laurence J. .... New York, NY
Rabinovich, Maria .... New York, NY
Rabinovich, Marina .... New York, NY
Rabinovich, Nathaniel .... New York, NY
Rabinovich, Pyotr S. .... New York, NY
Rabinovich, Pyotr S., P.C. .... New York, NY
Rabinovitz & Associates, P.C. .... Tucson, AZ
Rabinovitz, Bernard I. .... Tucson, AZ
Rabinovitz, Bruce H. .... Washington, DC
Rabinovitz, Daniel M. .... Boston, MA
Rabinovitz, Daniel S. .... Boston, MA
Rabinovitz, Edward .... Boston, MA
Rabinovitz, Joel, (P.C.) .... Los Angeles, CA
Rabinovitz, Lewis .... Hartford, CT
Rabinovitz, Mayer
Cumberland Foreside, ME
Rabinovitz, Peter .... Boston, MA
Rabinovitz, Steven, P.C.
Bloomfield Hills, MI
Rabinovitz, Zev Peter .... Boston, MA
Rabinow, Jean .... Trumbull, CT
Rabinowe, Fredric J. .... New Windsor, NY
Rabinowitch, Michael .... Indianapolis, IN
Rabinowitz, Adam .... Fort Lauderdale, FL
Rabinowitz, Adrienne .... Brooklyn, NY
Rabinowitz, Alan J. .... Westborough, MA
Rabinowitz, Alan Jay .... Dallas, TX
Rabinowitz, Alan S. .... San Diego, CA
Rabinowitz, Alan S. .... New York, NY
Rabinowitz, Amy Ginsburg
Westborough, MA
Rabinowitz, Asher .... Tampa, FL
Rabinowitz, Barbara W. .... Dallas, TX
Rabinowitz, Benjamin .... East Amherst, NY
Rabinowitz, Beth Ann
West Palm Beach, FL
Rabinowitz, Boudin, Standard, Krinsky & Lieberman, P.C. .... New York, NY
Rabinowitz, Brad D. .... Melville, NY
Rabinowitz, Bruce .... New York, NY
Rabinowitz, Clarice B. .... San Diego, CA
Rabinowitz, Daniel A. .... New York, NY
Rabinowitz, Daniel L. .... New York, NY
Rabinowitz, David .... New York, NY
Rabinowitz, David J. .... Newark, NJ

Rabinowitz, Denise Germain
New York, NY
Rabinowitz, Francine H. ... Cranbury, NJ
Rabinowitz, Fred ... Clifton, NJ
Rabinowitz, Gail ... Chicago, IL
Rabinowitz, Gregory L. ... Hicksville, NY
Rabinowitz, Hannah R. ... Jericho, NY
Rabinowitz, Howard A. ... New York, NY
Rabinowitz, Jacob ... White Plains, NY
Rabinowitz, Jason E. ... Sacramento, CA
Rabinowitz, Jay A. ... Fairbanks, AK
Rabinowitz, Jonathan I. ... West Orange, NJ
Rabinowitz, Jordy E. ... Great Neck, NY
Rabinowitz, Joshua P. ... San Diego, CA
Rabinowitz, Joshua T. ... New York, NY
Rabinowitz, Judith Ellen
Department of Justice, Civil Division, GV
Rabinowitz, Julie M. ... Washington, DC
Rabinowitz, Julius ... New York, NY
Rabinowitz, Karen B. ... Rochester, NY
Rabinowitz, Laurence P. ... New York, NY
Rabinowitz, Mark A. ... Chicago, IL
Rabinowitz, Mark I. ... Philadelphia, PA
Rabinowitz, Mark P. ... Orlando, FL
Rabinowitz, Martin J. ... New York, NY
Rabinowitz, Maynard ... Lantana, FL
Rabinowitz, Milton C. ... New York, NY
Rabinowitz, Mitchell L. ... Washington, DC
Rabinowitz & Rabinowitz, A Professional Corporation ... Dallas, TX
Rabinowitz, Rafal, Swartz, Taliaferro & Gilbert, P.C. ... Norfolk, VA
Virginia Beach, VA
Rabinowitz, Ralph ... Norfolk, VA
Rabinowitz, Randi L. ... New York, NY
Rabinowitz, Renee G.
Colorado Springs, CO
Rabinowitz, Robert Ira
Department of Commerce, Patent and Trademark Office, GV
Rabinowitz, Roberts & Silverberg
Glastonbury, CT
Rabinowitz, Samuel N. ... Philadelphia, PA
Rabinowitz, Scott H.
United States Tax Court, GV
Rabinowitz, Seymour ... Great Neck, NY
Rabinowitz, Stephen L. ... New York, NY
Rabinowitz, Stephen S. ... New York, NY
Rabinowitz, Steven J. ... New York, NY
Rabinowitz, Steven M. ... New York, NY
Rabinowitz, Stewart ... Dallas, TX
Rabinowitz, Susan C. ... Eatontown, NJ
Rabinowitz, Trenk, Lubetkin & Tully, P.C.
Newark, NJ
Roseland, NJ
West Orange, NJ
Rabinowitz, Victor ... New York, NY
Rabinowitz, Wayne I. ... White Plains, NY
Rabinowitz, Wilbur M. ... Boca Raton, FL
Rabis, Richard A. ... San Francisco, CA
Rabishaw, Fred S. ... Fayetteville, AR
Rabiteau, Marsha J. ... Midland, MI
Rabito, Frank J. ... New Orleans, LA
Rabits, Patricia H. ... Lexington, KY
Rabitz, Steven W. ... New York, NY
Rabizadeh, Ralph R. ... Philadelphia, PA
Rabke, Lisa A. ... Bridgewater, NJ
Rabkin, Alan B. ... Reno, NV
Rabkin, Beth ... Pittsburgh, PA
Rabkin, Gary M. ... Palo Alto, CA
Rabkin, Hannah ... San Francisco, CA
Rabkin, Ira ... Cherry Hill, NJ
Rabkin, Judy A. ... Westport, CT
Rabkin Law Offices, P.C. ... Cherry Hill, NJ
Rabkin, Lawrence B. ... San Francisco, CA
Rabkin, Lee W. ... Boston, MA
Rabkin, Maryann J. ... Cherry Hill, NJ
Rabkin, Michael W. ... Los Angeles, CA
Rabkin, Morton ... Cincinnati, OH
Rabkin, Peggy A. ... Florham Park, NJ
Rabkin, Richard H. ... Los Angeles, CA
Rabkin, Richard M. ... Secaucus, NJ
Rabkin, Ronald ... New York, NY
Rabkin, Sandor ... Lynn, MA
Rabkin, Sol ... Brooklyn, NY
Rablin, Dawn M. ... Milwaukee, WI
Rabner, Allcorn, Baumgart & Ben-Asher, P.C. ... Montclair, NJ
Newark, NJ
Rabner, Harold ... Montclair, NJ
Rabner, John B. ... Potomac, MD
Rabner, Monte J. ... Pittsburgh, PA
Rabney, Arthur E. ... New York, NY
Rabogliatti, Mark G. ... Minneapolis, MN
Raboin & Aakhus Law Offices, P.A.
Baxter, MN
Raboin, Christopher J. ... Phoenix, AZ
Raboin, John S. ... Baxter, MN
Rabold, C. Steven ... Avon Lake, OH
Rabold, Jennifer Fox ... Pittsburgh, PA
Rabolli, Charles, Jr. ... Paramus, NJ
Rabon, Barry S. ... Houston, TX
Rabon, Bob ... Hugo, OK
Rabon, Charles H., Jr. ... Charlotte, NC
Rabon, R. O'Neil, Jr. ... Greenville, SC
Rabon, Robert L. ... Hugo, OK
Rabon, Wolf & Rabon ... Hugo, OK
Raborn, Burta Rhoads ... Houston, TX
Raborn, J. Jeffery ... Baton Rouge, LA
Raborn, James A. ... Morristown, NJ
Raborn, James R. ... Houston, TX
Raborn, Robert L. ... Baton Rouge, LA
Raborn, Stanford L. ... Baton Rouge, LA
Rabourn, D. Arthur ... Cincinnati, OH
Rabovsky, Barry R. ... Naperville, IL
Rabowsky, Brent ... Los Angeles, CA
Rabren, Kimberly W. ... Atlanta, GA
Rabren, Wanda M. ... Andalusia, AL
Rabren, Wilton W. ... Columbiana, AL
Rabson, Saml. ... West Palm Beach, FL
Rabstein, Ruth ... Princeton, NJ
Rabuck, Robert J. ... Concord, NH
Rabuck, Steven K. ... Sioux Falls, SD
Rabun, Bruce H. ... Denver, CO
Rabun, Daniel W. ... Dallas, TX
Rabun, John P., Jr. ... Atlanta, GA
Rabun, Yolanda W.
Research Triangle Park, NC
Rabunski, Alan E. ... Larchmont, NY
New York, NY
Rabunski & Katz, L.L.P. ... Larchmont, NY
New York, NY
Raburn, Janice K.
Environmental Protection Agency, Program Office Attorneys, GV
Raburn, Patricia ... Jamaica, NY
Rabus, Michael J. ... New York, NY
Rabuse, Dwight G. ... Eagan, MN
Rabuse, Nathalie S. ... Minneapolis, MN
Rabushka, Gerald K. ... St. Louis, MO
Rabushka, Stanley D. ... St. Louis, MO
Rabuzzi, Douglas L. ... Pittsburgh, PA
Raby, Burgess J. W. ... Tempe, AZ
Raby, Craig A. ... Scottsdale, AZ
Raby, Gerald E., (P.C.) ... Scottsdale, AZ
Raby, Harold J. ... Old Greenwich, CT
Raby, Jennifer E. ... Rockwood, TN
Raby, John N. ... Denver, CO
Raby, Karen M. ... Atlanta, GA
Raby, Kenneth Alan ... Atlanta, GA
Raby Law Office ... Phoenix, AZ
Tempe, AZ
Tucson, AZ
Raby, Mark C. ... Department of Justice, Civil Division, GV
Raby, Paul E. ... Las Vegas, NV
Raby and Stafford ... Alexandria, VA
Raby, Vivian M. ... Cincinnati, OH
Rabyne, Milton ... Northfield, IL
Rac, Frank C. ... Torrance, CA
Racanelli, Janine ... New York, NY
Racanelli, John ... Melville, NY
Racanelli, Mark A. ... New York, NY
Racanelli, Martin J. ... New York, NY
Racanelli, Michael ... New York, NY
Racano, Frank A. ... Bronx, NY
Racca, Randall J. ... Breaux Bridge, LA
Raccagno, Susan Martin ... LeMay, MO
Raccah, Erin E. ... New York, NY
Racciatti, Lorraine ... Roseland, NJ
Raccio, Lynn M. ... Wallingford, CT
Raccio, William M. ... New Haven, CT
Raccuglia, Anthony C., & Associates
Ottawa, IL
Peru, IL
Raccuglia, Anthony C., & Associates
Princeton, IL
Raccuglia, Cynthia M. ... Ottawa, IL
Race, Annette S. ... Department of Agriculture, Farm Service Agency, GV
Race, Deborah ... Tyler, TX
Race, Dennis M. ... Washington, DC
Race, Geoffrey S. ... Denver, CO
Race, John P. ... Elkhorn, WI
Race, Joseph A. ... New Orleans, LA
Race, Kevin P. ... Atlanta, GA
Race, Peter S.
Department of Housing and Urban Development, Office of General Counsel, GV
Race, Richard K. ... Oklahoma City, OK
Race, Shannon L. ... Chicago, IL
Race, Terry P. ... Whitewater, WI
Racek, Frank L. ... Fargo, ND
Racer, Charles Bryan ... Monroe, LA
Racette, Gregory T. ... Des Moines, IA
Racette, Michael J. ... Boston, MA
Racette, Peter D. ... Plattsburgh, NY
Racette, Thomas C. ... Chicago, IL
Racey, Kermit L. ... Woodstock, VA
Racey, Kermit L., II ... Woodstock, VA
Racey & Racey ... Woodstock, VA
Racey, Susan L. ... Cleveland, OH
Rachadell, Claudia ... New York, NY
Rachal, Hal, Jr. ... Dallas, TX
Rachal, Robert ... New Orleans, LA
Rachal, Steven M. ... Alexandria, LA
Rachanow, Gerald M.
Department Of Health And Human Services, Food & Drug Administration, GV
Rachel, John A. ... Manchester, NH
Rachel, Kevin B.
United States Postal Service, Mid-Atlantic Office, GV
Rachels, Terry E. ... Knoxville, IA
Rachels, Warren A. ... Tampa, FL
Rachels, William E., Jr. ... Norfolk, VA
Rachelson, Aaron D. ... Chicago, IL
Rachelson, Gerald J. ... Atlanta, GA
Rachelson, Ira L. ... Atlanta, GA
Rachelson, Jani K. ... New York, NY
Rachelson & White, P.C. ... Atlanta, GA
Racher, Peter M. ... Indianapolis, IN
Rachetto, Jerry C. ... Deadwood, SD
Rachetto Law Office ... Deadwood, SD
Rachford, Laurie A. ... Houston, TX
Rachid Piñeiro, Michel ... San Juan, PR
Rachie, Cyrus ... Edina, MN
Rachie, John B. ... Forest Lake, MN
Rachie, Paul C. ... Minneapolis, MN
Rachles, Doris ... Lake Worth, FL
Rachles, Vivien ... New York, NY
Rachlin, Alan ... New York, NY
Rachlin, Alan R. ... Great Falls, VA
Rachlin, Carl ... New York, NY
Rachlin, Gary ... Houston, TX
Rachlin, Joan ... Boston, MA
Rachlin, Joseph S. ... Hartford, CT
Rachlin, Joy Barron ... Chestnut Hill, MA
Rachlin, Lauren D. ... Buffalo, NY
Rachlin, Leila ... New York, NY
Rachlin, Mark ... Danbury, CT
Rachlin, Marvin ... Westbury, NY
Rachlin, Mitchell ... Hempstead, NY
Rachlin, Paul I. ... New York, NY
Rachlin, Richard S.
North Palm Beach, FL
Rachlin, Richard S., P.A.
North Palm Beach, FL
West Palm Beach, FL
Rachlin, Robert D. ... Burlington, VT
Rachlin, Steven B. ... Cooper City, FL
Rachlin, Susan K. ... Houston, TX
Rachlinski, Irene L. ... Elsmere, KY
Rachlinski, Jeffrey J. ... Ithaca, NY
Rachlis, Michael ... Chicago, IL
Rachman, Marc J. ... New York, NY
Rachman, Peter H. ... Fort Lauderdale, FL
Rachmansky, Gene ... New York, NY
Rachmiel, Joel I. ... Springfield, NJ
Rachofsky, David J. ... Philadelphia, PA
Rachofsky, Marcia C. ... Austin, TX
Rachofsky, Robert S. ... New York, NY
Rachow, Edwin C. ... Elm Grove, WI
Rachow, Susan ... Webster, NY
Rachstein, Irving A. ... Boston, MA
Rachstein, Norman & Buchman, LLP
Newton, MA
Racht, Elizabeth M. ... Allentown, PA
Racht, Jody A. ... Burlington, VT
Racht, Theresa ... New York, NY
Rachwal, Barton C. ... Southfield, MI
Racich, Christopher J. ... Washington, DC
Racicot, Diane M. ... San Diego, CA
Racicot, John B. ... Boston, MA
Racicot, Marc F. ... Helena, MT
Racila, Raymond L. ... Cape Coral, FL
Fort Myers, FL
Lehigh Acres, FL
Naples, FL
Port Charlotte, FL
Racin, John P. ... Washington, DC
Easton, MD
Racin, Stephanie J. ... Newton, MA
Racine, Aaron J. ... Kansas City, MO
Racine, Barbara Eby ... Department of Labor, Office of the Solicitor, GV
Racine, Brian A. ... Boca Raton, FL
Racine, Charles E. ... Toledo, OH
Racine, John P., Jr. ... Traverse City, MI
Racine, Karl A.
Executive Office Of The President, GV
Racine, Louis F., Jr. ... Pocatello, ID
Racine, Marie T. ... Detroit, MI
Racine, Marie T., P.C. ... Detroit, MI
Racine, Norman H. ... Sycamore, IL
Racine, Olson, Nye, Budge & Bailey, Chartered ... Pocatello, ID
Racine, Richard B. ... Washington, DC
Racine, Scott H. ... Los Angeles, CA
Racines, Audrey Gardner ... Allentown, PA
Emmaus, PA
Racioppi, Joseph G. ... Newark, NJ
Racioppi, Nicholas, Jr. ... Morristown, NJ
Raciti, Eric P. ... Boston, MA
Rack, Kevin B. ... Virginia Beach, VA
Rack, Robert W. ... Cincinnati, OH
Rack, Robert W., Jr. ... Cincinnati, OH
Rack, Thomas P. ... Honolulu, HI
Rack, Vale, Burke, Fitzgerald, Burns & Balash
Cincinnati, OH
Rackauckas, Anthony J., Jr. ... Santa Ana, CA
Rackauckas, Vivian L. ... Ventura, CA
Rackay, Emil V., Jr. ... Tampa, FL
Rackear, Andrew D. ... Piscataway, NJ
Rackear, Bernard, (P.C.) ... Somers, NY
Rackear, Gary S. ... Miami, FL
Rackemann, Sawyer & Brewster, Professional Corporation ... Boston, MA
Rackers, Christopher P.
Jefferson City, MO
Rackers, Jane A. ... Jefferson City, MO
Rackett, Christina M. ... New York, NY
Rackis, Linda A. ... Staten Island, NY
Rackleff, Kathryn K. ... Denver, CO
Rackleff, Neal J. ... Houston, TX
Rackley, Chole Vilas ... Baton Rouge, LA
Rackley, Claude L., Jr. ... Fredericksburg, VA
Rackley, Elizabeth A. ... St. Paul, MN
Rackley, R. Robert ... Baton Rouge, LA
Rackley, Victoria L. ... Muskogee, OK
Rackley, W. John ... Beaver, PA
Rackliffe, Gail D. ... Los Angeles, CA
Racklin, Dimitri P. ... Boston, MA
Rackman, Joseph R. ... New York, NY
Rackman, Michael I. ... New York, NY
Rackner, Laura E. ... Portland, OR
Rackner, Lisa ... Portland, OR
Rackoff, Maryanne R. ... Akron, OH
Rackoff, Nancy L. ... Pittsburgh, PA
Rackow, Jeffrey A. ... Washington, DC
Rackow, Julian P. ... Wilmington, DE
Philadelphia, PA
Racobs, James B. ... Carson City, NV
Racobs, Peter E. ... Irvine, CA
Palm Desert, CA
Riverside, CA
Racoosin, Samuel Israel ... Vienna, VA
Racoosin, Stanley A. ... Bethesda, MD
Racoosin, Stanley A., P.A. ... Bethesda, MD
Racouillat, Richard N. ... San Luis Obispo, CA
Racouillat, Richard N., A Professional Law Corporation ... San Luis Obispo, CA
Racster, Lon R. ... Portland, IN
Racunas, Nancy E. ... Kansas City, MO
Racunas, Robert V. ... Falls Church, VA
Racusin, Barry L., P.C. ... Houston, TX
Racusin & Wagner, L.L.P. ... Houston, TX
Racusin, Warren K. ... Morristown, NJ
Racy, John A. ... New York, NY
Racy, Mike L. ... Kansas City, MO
Racz, Gregory N. ... New York, NY
Raczenbek, David F. ... Bridgeton, NJ
Raczka, Christine A. ... Cheektowaga, NY
Raczka, James K. ... Addison, IL
Raczka & Raczka ... Middletown, CT
Raczka, Theodore J. ... Middletown, CT
Raczka, Theodore V. ... Middletown, CT
Raczkowski, Annette T. ... Livonia, MI
Raczkowski, Dale J. ... Long Grove, IL
Raczkowski & Krenzel ... Sayreville, NJ
Raczkowski, Thaddeus C. ... Sayreville, NJ
Rad, Juliet M. ... New York, NY
Rad, Nader ... Tustin, CA
Rada, Lynn Layne ... San Antonio, TX
Rada, Milan ... Woodbury, NY
Rada, William J. ... New York, NY
Radabaugh, Ann Noden ... Lakeland, FL
Radabaugh, Carolyn J. ... Menlo Park, CA
Radabaugh, James M. ... Troy, MI
Radabaugh, John M. ... Lakeland, FL
Radabaugh, Tom B. ... Dayton, OH
Radack, Andrew T. ... Jamestown, NY
Radack, David V. ... Pittsburgh, PA
Radack, Stephen M. ... San Francisco, CA
Radak, Lawrence W. ... Detroit, MI
Radakovich, Daniel E. ... Chicago, IL
Radakovich, Danny J. ... Lewiston, ID
Radakovich, Dorthy A. ... Pueblo, CO
Radakovich & Eyler, P.C. ... Pueblo, CO
Westcliffe, CO
Radakovich, Karen J. ... Boulder, CO
Radano, Christiane D'Haese
New York, NY
Radano & Lide ... Vineland, NJ
Radano, Nicholas G. ... Vineland, NJ
Radano, Robert J. ... Drexel Hill, PA
Radanof, R. Gary ... Barberton, OH
Radanovic, Lawrence R. ... Washington, DC
Radasevich, Robert ... Chicago, IL
Radasky, David J. ... Prairie Village, KS
Radcliff, Barbara M. ... Upper Marlboro, MD
Radcliff, David H. ... Wormleysburg, PA
Radcliff, Diane G. ... Camp Hill, PA
Radcliff, Donald C. ... Mobile, AL
Radcliff, Frandsen & Dongell
Los Angeles, CA
San Francisco, CA
Radcliff, Jules G., Jr. ... Los Angeles, CA
San Francisco, CA
Radcliff, Patrick N. ... Parkersburg, WV
Radcliff, William F. ... Muncie, IN
Radcliffe, Albert E. ... Eugene, OR
Radcliffe, Barry ... Galveston, TX
Radcliffe, Conrad J.J. ... Philadelphia, PA
Radcliffe, DeHaas & Monaghan
Uniontown, PA
Radcliffe, Gene B. ... Black River Falls, WI
Radcliffe, George M. ... Cambridge, MD
Radcliffe, Gerald E. ... Chillicothe, OH
Radcliffe, James H. ... Wilmington, CA
Radcliffe, James M. ... Belleville, IL
Radcliffe, John A. ... West Covina, CA
Radcliffe, Kerry E. ... San Antonio, TX
Radcliffe, Kim ... Orlando, FL
Radcliffe, M. Sean ... Tulsa, OK
Radcliffe, M. Stanley ... Towson, MD
Radcliffe, Mark A. ... Winona, MN
Radcliffe, Mark F. ... Palo Alto, CA
Radcliffe, Martha Clark ... Moraga, CA
Radcliffe, Michael S. ... Towson, MD
Radcliffe, Michael T. ... Columbus, OH
Radcliffe, Michelle ... Costa Mesa, CA
Radcliffe, R. Thomas, Jr. ... Baltimore, MD
Radcliffe, Richard ... Irvine, CA
Radcliffe, Richard ... Tomah, WI
Radcliffe, Robert A. ... Seattle, WA
Radcliffe, Robert R. ... Chico, CA
Radcliffe, Robert W. ... Black River Falls, WI
Radcliffe, Ross J. ... Houston, TX
Radcliffe, Sania ... Portland, OR
Radcliffe, Susan ... Alpharetta, GA
Radcliffe, Thomas R. ... Palo Alto, CA
Radcliffe, Walter H. ... Lincoln, NE
Radcliffe, Wanda W. ... Pensacola, FL
Radcliffe, William L. ... Chino Hills, CA
Radcliffe, William M. ... Uniontown, PA
Radcliff-Morfe, Cherie ... Plantation, FL
Radd, Anthony F. ... Norfolk, VA
Radd, John D. ... Virginia Beach, VA
Radda, James L. ... Jackson, WY
Raddatz, Mark R. ... Milwaukee, WI
Raddatz, Peggy M. ... La Grange, IL
Radde, Susan M. ... Chicago, IL
Radden, Lawrence N. ... Detroit, MI
Raddie, Terese M. ... Burlingame, CA
Radding, Andrew ... Baltimore, MD
Radding, Eugene ... Ventura, CA
Radding, Jeffrey C. ... San Luis Obispo, CA
Radding, Ronald S. ... Jersey City, NJ
Radding, Rory J. ... New York, NY
Rade, Debra S. ... Northbrook, IL
Radebach, Robert G. ... Harrisburg, PA
Radecker, H. Philip, Jr. ... Metairie, LA
Radecki, Alison J. ... New York, NY
Radeff, Christina ... Lakewood, CO
Radek, Lee J. ... Department of Justice, Criminal Division, GV
Radeke, Sandra K. ... Minneapolis, MN
Radeker, Gwynn G. ... Shelby, NC
Radel, Dwayne C. ... St. Paul, MN
Radel, F. Robert, II ... Tampa, FL

Radel, Myra ... Pasadena, CA
Radel, Robert R. ... Buffalo, NY
Radelat, Paul B. ... Houston, TX
Radelet, David P. ... Chicago, IL
Radelet, Timothy J. ... Madison, WI
Radelfinger, Brook A. ... San Francisco, CA
Radelfinger, Brook A. ... San Mateo, CA
Radell, Lisa M. ... Wildwood, NJ
Radell, Marc M. ... Chicago, IL
Radell, Michael E. ... Miami, FL
Rademacher, Brian I. ... Tucson, AZ
Rademacher, James A. ... Escanaba, MI
Rademacher, John J. ... Park Ridge, IL
Rademacher, John P. ... Kearney, NE
Rademacher, Leigh A. ... Omaha, NE
Rademacher, Mark ... Hamden, CT
Rademacher, Mark A. ... Alexandria, VA
Rademacher, Mark H. ... Beverly Hills, CA
Rademacher, Patricia E. ... Chicago, IL
Rademacher, Robert B. ... Cameron Park, CA
Rademacher, Robin Ann ... Chicago, IL
Rademacher, Ronald Joseph ... Pittsburgh, PA
Rademacher, Wm. J. ... Chelsea, MI
Rademaekers, Iwana M. ... Dallas, TX
Rademaker, Amy M. ... Grand Rapids, MI
Rademaker, Bradley F. ... Chicago, IL
Rademaker, Dennis A. ... Cleveland, OH
Rademaker, Julie K. ... Chicago, IL
Rademaker, Matty, McClelland & Greve
Cleveland, OH
Rademaker, Randall J. ... Chicago, IL
Rademaker, William, Jr. ... Seattle, WA
Raden, James B. ... Chicago, IL
Radensky, Joseph H. ... Fullerton, CA
Radensky, Madeleine ... Orange, CA
Radensky, Paul W. ... Miami, FL
Rader, Adam James ... New York, NY
Rader, Alan ... Los Angeles, CA
Rader, Andrew J. ... New City, NY
Rader, Bruce J. ... New York, NY
Rader, C. David ... San Diego, CA
Rader, Campbell, Fisher & Pyke, A Professional Corporation ... Dallas, TX
Rader, Candace E. ... Carrollton, GA
Rader, Carol A. ... Sacramento, CA
Rader, Carolyn W. ... Indianapolis, IN
Rader, Dale A. ... Boise, ID
Rader, Daniel H., III ... Cookeville, TN
Rader, Daniel S.
Executive Office Of The President, Office of National Drug Control Policy, GV
Rader, Dennis W. ... Green Bay, WI
Rader & Eisenberg, P.C. ... Detroit, MI
Rader, Elizabeth H. ... Palo Alto, CA
Rader, Fishman, Grauer & McGarry PLLC
Grand Rapids, MI
Rader, Fishman & Grauer PLLC
Denver, CO
Washington, DC
Bloomfield Hills, MI
Detroit, MI
Rader, Harold ... Manchester, KY
Rader, James ... Springfield, IL
Rader, James A. ... Cincinnati, OH
Rader, James N. ... Austin, TX
Rader, Jean M. ... Houston, TX
Rader, John A. ... Williamsport, IN
Rader, Joseph ... Lorain, OH
Rader, Joseph P. ... Boulder, CO
Rader, Joseph P., P.C. ... Boulder, CO
Rader, Karen H. ... Southfield, MI
Rader, Kermit L. ... Bala Cynwyd, PA
Rader, Larry L. ... Sacramento, CA
Rader, Lindsey A. ... Baltimore, MD
Rader, Mark S. ... Riverside, CA
Rader, Mark S. ... Ontario, OR
Rader, Martin A., Jr. ... Danbury, CT
Rader, Marvin L. ... League City, TX
Rader, Marvin L., & Associates
League City, TX
Rader, Michael R. ... Terre Haute, IN
Rader, Philip S. ... North Conway, NH
Rader, Rader, Goulart & Gray
Sacramento, CA
Rader, Ralph Terrance
Bloomfield Hills, MI
Rader, Randall R. ...
United States Court Of Appeals For The Federal Circuit, GV
Rader, Richard E. ... Sacramento, CA
Rader, Richard E. ... Santa Barbara, CA
Rader, Rob ... Santa Monica, CA
Rader, Robert B. ... Raleigh, NC
Rader, Robert E., Jr. ... Dallas, TX
Rader, Robert M. ... Washington, DC
Rader, Robert N. ... Costa Mesa, CA
Rader, Roger L. ... Findlay, OH
Rader, Ronald ... Detroit, MI
Rader, Sanford ... Perth Amboy, NJ
Rader, Sharon Holt ... Winston-Salem, NC
Rader, Shawn G. ... Orlando, FL
Rader, Sheila C. ... Boston, MA
Rader, Stanley R. ... Pasadena, CA
Rader, Stephen P. ... Los Angeles, CA
Rader, Stuart A. ... Boca Raton, FL
Rader, Stuart A., P.A. ... Boca Raton, FL
Rader, Stuart C. ... Anchorage, AK
Rader, Wilma R. K. ... Berkeley, CA
Raderman, David E. ... Baltimore, MD
Raders, John M. ... Los Angeles, CA
Raders, M. Lou ... Denver, CO
Radeski, Robert M. ... Pasadena, CA
Radetic, Edward P. ... St. Louis, MO
Radetic, Kelly-Ann Benson ... St. Louis, MO
Radetic & Radetic, A Professional Corporation
St. Louis, MO
Radetich, Peter P. ... Buffalo, NY
Radetsky, Gregg E. ... Dallas, TX
Radetsky, James B. ... Denver, CO
Radetsky, Jay Stuart ... Denver, CO
Radetsky, Jay Stuart, P.C. ... Denver, CO
Radetsky, Lisa R. ... New York, NY
Radey, John ... Tallahassee, FL
Radey, Neil ... New York, NY
Radez, Patricia S. ... San Francisco, CA
Radford, Bruce W. ... Washington, DC
Radford, Cameron M. ... Arlington, VA
Radford, Emily Anne
Department of Justice, Civil Division, GV
Radford, Francine Terhune
San Francisco, CA
Radford, G. Robert ... Huntingdon, TN
Radford, Lee ... Idaho Falls, ID
Radford, Michael Eugene ... Asheville, NC
Radford, Michael J. ... Chula Vista, CA
Radford, Michael K. ... Brentwood, TN
Radford, Patricia Lee ... Louisville, KY
Radford, R. S. ... Sacramento, CA
Radford, Scott M. ... Great Falls, MT
Radford, Stephen F., Jr.
West Palm Beach, FL
Radford & Wandrei, P.C. ... Bedford, VA
Radford, Wendell C. ... Beaumont, TX
Radford, William N. ... Dallas, TX
Radford, William R. ... Miami, FL
Radford, Wynn L., III ... Hopkinsville, KY
Radice, Alex ... Baltimore, MD
Radice, Anthony M. ... New York, NY
Radice, Charles F. ... Fort Lauderdale, FL
Radice, Christine E. ... Boston, MA
Radice, Robert J. ... St. Louis, MO
Radich, Aleksander D. ... Cheyenne, WY
Radich, Miriam J. ... New York, NY
Radich, Patricia ... Media, PA
Radich, Rita M. ... Minneapolis, MN
Radick, Alicia J. ... Chicago, IL
Radick, Neil F. ... Los Angeles, CA
Radick, Rob M. ... Brooklyn, NY
Radick, Sallie Ann ... Pittsburgh, PA
Radick, Stuart A. ... Hamilton, NJ
Radig, Eugene L. ... Iowa City, IA
Radig, James W. ... Cedar Rapids, IA
Radigan, A. T. ... Gainesville, VA
Radigan, Brendan J. ... West Greenwich, RI
Radigan, C. Raymond ... Mineola, NY
Radigan, Charles McDonnell
Arlington, VA
Radigan & Garnett, A Professional Corporation ... Arlington, VA
Radigan, Kevin P. ... Albany, NY
Radigan, Michael G. ... New York, NY
Radigan, Raymond C. ... Garden City, NY
Radigan, William M. ... Louisville, KY
Radike, Pamela S. ... Bloomfield Hills, MI
Radil, Gary W. ... Omaha, NE
Radillo, Antonia D. ... Sacramento, CA
Radin, Anthony B. ... New York, NY
Radin, Bruce D. ... New York, NY
Radin, Carl ... New City, NY
Radin, Daniel J. ... Seattle, WA
Radin, David ... Brea, CA
Radin, Edward C., III ... Rochester, NY
Radin, Ellen ... Scotch Plains, NJ
Radin, Gerald L. ... Kenmore, NY
North Tonawanda, NY
Radin, John L. ... Idaho Falls, ID
Radin, Jonathan
Federal Communications Commission, Wireless Telecommunications Bureau, GV
Radin, Lee D. ... New York, NY
Radin, Louise Rembar ... New York, NY
Radin, Marc S. ... Hermosa Beach, CA
Radin, Margaret Jane ... Stanford, CA
Radin, Matthew E. ... Commack, NY
Radin, Melvin J. ... Norfolk, VA
Radin, Michael J. ... Boston, MA
Radin, Mitchell E. ... New York, NY
Radin, Neila B. ... New York, NY
Radin, Peter M., Jr. ... San Francisco, CA
Radin, Royal S. ... Staten Island, NY
Radin, Sam ... New York, NY
Radin, Sara K. ... Santa Monica, CA
Radin, Scott M. ... Los Angeles, CA
Radin, Stephen A. ... New York, NY
Radin, Steven S. ... Newark, NJ
New York, NY
Radin & Webb ... Idaho Falls, ID
Radinsky, Adam W. ... Santa Monica, CA
Radinsky, Gregory Scott ...
Department Of Health And Human Services, GV
Radinsky, Kathleen U. ... Denver, CO
Radinson-Perez, Francisco ... San Juan, PR
Radio, Thomas J. ... Minneapolis, MN
Radis, David J. ... Los Angeles, CA
Radis, Richard A. ... Fort Lauderdale, FL
Radis, Richard A., P.A. ... Fort Lauderdale, FL
Radisch, Jack B. ... Berkeley, CA
Radisch, Lois J. ... New York, NY
Radius, Karen M. ... Honolulu, HI
Radka, Elmer L. ... Rogers City, MI
Radke, Alan W. ... San Antonio, TX
Radke, Arthur F. ... Chicago, IL
Radke, Aryka Steele ... Merrillville, IN
Radke, Barbara K. ... Waseca, MN
Radke, Brian L. ... Sioux Falls, SD
Radke, Bruce A. ... Chicago, IL
Radke, Chris A. ... Houston, TX
Radke, Christopher J. ... Saginaw, MI
Radke, Dean F. ... Wethersfield, CT
Radke, Dwight D. ... Lyons, KS
Radke, Frederick Scott ... San Antonio, TX
Radke, Gregory J. ... New York, NY
Radke, Jack W. ... Pittsburgh, PA
Radke, Kirk A. ... New York, NY
Radke, Lynne E. ... Farmington Hills, MI
Radke, Mark S. ... Washington, DC
Radke, Mark S. ... Minneapolis, MN
Radke, R. Kent ... Lincoln, NE
Radke, Richard, Jr. ... Grand Rapids, MI
Radke, Richard W. ... Tampa, FL
Radke, Robert E. ... Van Nuys, CA
Radke, Terrance J. ... Stratford, CT
Radke, Victoria Ann ... Escanaba, MI
Radkey, William A. ... Springfield, IL
Radkiewicz, Theodore F., Jr.
Colorado Springs, CO
Radkins, Mary B. ... Tallahassee, FL
Radko, Joseph ... Beltsville, MD
Radlauer, Barbara J. ... New London, CT
Radlauer, David G. ... New Orleans, LA
Radlauer, Leonard A., Prof. Law Corp.
New Orleans, LA
Radler, Barbara W. ... Portland, OR
Radler, Charles M., Jr. ... Cranford, NJ
Radler, Daniel G. ... Milwaukee, WI
Radler, Jean M. ... Rochester, NY
Radler, Kirsten L. ... Chicago, IL
Radler, Monte P. ... Middletown, CT
Radler, Robert J. ... Lake Oswego, OR
Radler, Warren S. ... Chicago, IL
Radley, David B. ... Peoria, IL
Radley, David B., P.C. ... Peoria, IL
Radley, Gordon L. ... San Rafael, CA
Radley, Grover W., Jr. ... Ilion, NY
Radley, Philippe D. ... New York, NY
Radley, Ross ... Seattle, WA
Radley, Ross, Inc., P.S. ... Seattle, WA
Radlick, Janice M. ... Dearborn, MI
Radliff, Heather ... Dallas, TX
Radlin, Barry L. ... Amherst, NY
Radlin, Barry L. ... Buffalo, NY
Radlinski, Christopher A. ... Bonsall, CA
Radlinski, Gregory K. ... Jacksonville, FL
Radlo, Edward J. ... Palo Alto, CA
Radloff, Floyd E. ... Bellaire, TX
Radloff, Gwyneth J.
Department of Transportation, Office of the General Counsel, GV
Radloff, John E. ... Palo Alto, CA
Radloff, Michael K. ... Mattoon, IL
Radloff & Riske ... St. Louis, MO
Radloff, Stuart J. ... St. Louis, MO
Radmacher, B. Frank, III ... Louisville, KY
Radmacher, Brenda Kosma
Los Angeles, CA
Radmacher, Jonathan M. ... Portland, OR
Radman, Robert ... New York, NY
Radman, Scott S. ... Morgantown, WV
Radmer, Michael J. ... Minneapolis, MN
Radmilovich, Michael C. ... Reno, NV
Radmin, Andrew I. ... North Plainfield, NJ
Radmonovich, Barbara H. ... Houston, TX
Radmore, James R. ... Cherry Hill, NJ
Newtown, PA
Philadelphia, PA
Plymouth Meeting, PA
Radner, Cathi L. ... Glens Falls, NY
Radner, Cathy E. ... Clinton Township, MI
Radner, David M. ... Southfield, MI
Radner, Howard J. ... Southfield, MI
Radner, Howard L. ... Naples, FL
Radner, Jane S. ... Lansing, MI
Radner, Keith G. ... Chicago, IL
Radner, Marcia R. Peterson ... Springfield, MA
Radner and Radner, P.C.
West Bloomfield, MI
Radner, Richard E. ... West Bloomfield, MI
Radner, Robert M. ... West Bloomfield, MI
Radner, Samuel Marc ... Hartford, CT
Radney, Radney & Brown, P.A.
Alexander City, AL
Radney, Terry L. ... Houston, TX
Radney, Thomas Anderson
Alexander City, AL
Radney, Tom ... Alexander City, AL
Radney, W. Larkin, III ... Alexander City, AL
Radney, William Larkin, IV
Birmingham, AL
Radnick, Robert A.
Grosse Pointe Woods, MI
Radnofsky, Barbara A. ... Houston, TX
Radnor, Alan T. ... Columbus, OH
Rado, Danielle S. ... Waterbury, CT
Rado, Peter T. ... New York, NY
Radoccia, Evandro R., Jr.
North Kingstown, RI
Radocha, Dennis L. ... Boise, ID
Radoff, Franklin ... Encino, CA
Radoff, Henry V., (P.C.) ... Houston, TX
Radoff, Mark A. ... Bishop, CA
Radoff, Perry J., (P.C.) ... Houston, TX
Radoff, Phillip L. ... Chantilly, VA
Radogno, Joseph A. ... Northbrook, IL
Radogno, Nunzio C. ... Chicago, IL
Radol, Roger B. ... Teaneck, NJ
Radolinski, Anne M. ... Minneapolis, MN
Radolovich, F. R. ... Louisville, KY
Radom, Carl C. ... Kansas City, MO
Radom, Mark F. ... New York, NY
Radom, Susan J. ... Somerville, NJ
Radom, Thomas B. ... Birmingham, MI
Radon, Jenik ... New York, NY
Radon, Paul A. ... Toledo, OH
Radonich, John N. ... Anaconda, MT
Radonjich, Rajko ... Akron, OH
Rados, James L. ... Chicago, IL
Rados, Lilla J. ... San Mateo, CA
Rados, Richard P. ... San Francisco, CA
Radosevich, Andrea B. ... New York, NY
Radosevich, Donald J. ... Manitowoc, WI
Radosevich, John G. ... Waukegan, IL
Radosevich, Michele G. ... Seattle, WA
Radosevich, Mozinski & Cashman
Manitowoc, WI
Radosevich, Paul E. ... Denver, CO
Radosevich, Ted C. ... Oakland, CA
Radosevich, William J. ... Hudson, WI
Radosh, Richard M. ... Carlsbad, CA
Radostitz, Rita J. ... Eugene, OR
Radovich, Charles A. ... Geneva, IL
Radovich, David A. ... San Diego, CA
Radovich, George T. ... Billings, MT
Radovich, Joan ... Chicago, IL
Radovich, Joseph ... Geneva, IL
Radovich Law Offices
San Luis Obispo, CA
Radovich, M. Scott ... San Luis Obispo, CA
Radovich & Radovich ... Geneva, IL
Radovich, Scott Douglas ... Honolulu, HI
Radovsky, Joseph S. ... San Francisco, CA
Radow, Ellen L. ... Princeton, NJ
Radow, Sandy Khine ... Jackson Heights, NY
Radow, Tom A. ... Atlantic Beach, NY
Radowich, Jeffrey J. ... Baltimore, MD
Radowitz, Melvin ... Washington, DC
Radsch, Richard T. ... New York, NY
Radson, Marion J. ... Gainesville, FL
Radtke, Craig C. ... Boerne, TX
Radtke, Debra J. ... Fayetteville, NC
Radtke, Derek P. ... Edmonds, WA
Radtke, Kathryn R. ... Daytona Beach, FL
Radtke, Keith P. ... Minneapolis, MN
Radtke, Melva D. ... Lakeland, MN
Radtke, Michael J. ... Chicago, IL
Radtke & Nusbaum ... Chicago, IL
Radtke, Stephen D. ... Bloomington, MN
Radtke, Stephen D., P.A. ... Bloomington, MN
Radtke, Steven R. ... Chicago, IL
Raduano, Dawn ... Fort Lauderdale, FL
Raduazo, Anthony F. ... Jackson, MI
Radue, Jane S. ... Madison, WI
Raduege, Tammy J. ... Toledo, OH
Raduenz, Gary A. ... Lisle, IL
Raduenz, Nanette K. ... Hammond, IN
Radulescu, David C. ... New York, NY
Radulovic, Adrienne W. ... Atlanta, GA
Radulovich, Monna R. ... Alameda, CA
Radulski, Raymond M. ... Wilmington, DE
Radulski, Walter T., Law Office of
Lowell, MA
Radunz, Douglas P. ... Minneapolis, MN
Radus, Sidney L. ... Anaheim, CA
Radwan, Ralph J. ... Orchard Park, NY
Radwan, Tarik M. ... McLean, VA
Radwan, Theresa J. Pulley ... Cleveland, OH
Radwaner, Valerie E. ... New York, NY
Radway, Robert J. ... New York, NY
Radway, Robert R. ... Farmingdale, ME
Radway, Tedford B. ... Cranston, RI
Radwin, Jill O. ... Birmingham, AL
Rady, Arnold I. ... New York, NY
Rady, John M. ... Birmingham, MI
Rady, Marie M. ... Berea, OH
Rady, Nancy L. ... San Diego, CA
Rady, Thomas F., III ... Vernon, CT
Radzely, Edward S. ... Middletown, NY
Radzely, Howard M. ... Washington, DC
Radzik, Donna L. ... Prospect Heights, IL
Radzik, Edward C. ... New York, NY
Radzinski, Pamela Fae ... Ferndale, MI
Radzinski, Patricia L. ... Tampa, FL
Radziunas, John A. ... New Haven, CT
Radzyner, Mark H. ... New York, NY
Rae, Anne-Marie P. ... New York, NY
Rae, Bergstrom & Forbes, P.C.
Virginia Beach, VA
Rae, David B. ... Houston, TX
Rae, David L. ... Murray Hill, NJ
Rae, Donna L. ... Danville, PA
Rae, Donneve Starr ... Denver, CO
Rae, Glen Alexander ... New York, NY
Rae, J. Paterson ... Springfield, MA
Rae, James M. ... New York, NY
Rae, John J. ... Midland, MI
Rae, Mark N. ... New York, NY
Rae, Matthew S., Jr. ... Los Angeles, CA
Rae, Max ... Salem, OR
Rae, Michael J. ... Battle Creek, MI
Rae & Nelson LLP ... New York, NY
Rae, Priscilla M. ... Virginia Beach, VA
Rae, Renelle P.
Environmental Protection Agency, Program Office Attorneys, GV
Rae, Robert B. ... Virginia Beach, VA
Rae, Stephen M. ... Blue Bell, PA
Rae, Thomas W. ... New York, NY
Raeber, Michael M. ... Atlanta, GA
Raeburn, Charles F. ... New York, NY
Raeder & DeRespino, P.C. ... Philadelphia, PA
Raeder, James A. ... Cleveland, OH
Raeder, Lowell F. ... Philadelphia, PA
Raeder, Myrna ... Los Angeles, CA
Raehsler, Robert R. ... Hudson, WI
Raekes, John P. ... Kennewick, WA
Rael, Anita ... Denver, CO
Rael, Gregory L. ... Eureka, CA
Rael, Pedro G. ... Los Lunas, NM
Rael & Sanchez ... Los Lunas, NM
Raelson, Arthur I. ... La Porte, IN
Raelson, Douglas A. ... New York, NY
Raemisch, Richard F. ... Madison, WI
Raeon, Richard J. ... Rockville, MD
Raepple, Carolyn S. ... Tallahassee, FL
Raessler, Claudia D. ... Portland, ME
Raesz, Chris ... Denton, TX
Raether, Charles ... Charlotte, NC
Raether, H. C. ... Brookfield, WI
Raether, Ronald I., Jr. ... Dayton, OH
Rae-Venter, Barbara ... Palo Alto, CA

Rae-Venter Law Group, A Professional Law Corporation ... Palo Alto, CA
Raevis, Robert ... Department of Commerce, Patent and Trademark Office, GV
Raezer, Mark N. ... Reading, PA
Raezer, Timothy A. ... Department of Defense, Defense Legal Services Agency, GV
Rafa, Mike ... Palo Alto, CA
Rafaelle, John B. ... Collinsville, IL
Rafailides, Ernest S. ... Baltimore, MD
Rafal, Adam S. ... Norfolk, VA
Rafal, Edwin J. ... Norfolk, VA
Rafal, John W. ... Essex, CT
Rafala, Nella R. ... Middletown, CT
Rafalco, Roy D. ... Indianapolis, IN
Rafalko, Walter A. ... Timonium, MD
Rafalli, Leslie A. ... Miami, FL
Rafaloff, Jill C. ... New York, NY
Rafalovich, Rachel Beth ... San Francisco, CA
Rafalowicz, Joseph ... White Plains, NY
Rafalsky, Thomas R. ... New York, NY
Rafalson, Bruce ... New York, NY
Rafanelli, Cara Moore ... Chicago, IL
Rafanelli, Kerry I. ... Warwick, RI
Rafanelli, Toni-Lynne ... Chelmsford, MA
Rafanello, Richard A. ... Bernardsville, NJ
Rafano, Christopher ... South River, NJ
Rafano, Robert C. ... South River, NJ
Rafano and Wood, P.C. ... South River, NJ
Rafatjah, Sophia L. ... Austin, TX
Rafatjoo, Hamid R. ... Irvine, CA
Rafaty, Laura Jean ... Palo Alto, CA
Rafeedie, Edward ... Los Angeles, CA
Rafeedie, Fredrick A. ... Los Angeles, CA
Rafel, Anthony L. ... Seattle, WA
Rafel, Bonny G. ... Florham Park, NJ
Rafert, Cheryl A. ... St. Louis, MO
Rafey, Judd A. ... Washington, DC
Raff & Becker ... New York, NY
Raff, Christopher C. ... Searcy, AR
Raff, David A. ... New York, NY
Raff, Donald L. ... Paterson, NJ
Raff, Douglass A. ... Seattle, WA
Raff, Elliot D. ... Philadelphia, PA
Raff & Galloway ... Helena, AR
West Helena, AR
Raff, Gene ... Helena, AR
Raff, Jeffrey G. ... Fort Wayne, IN
Raff, Joshua E. ... New York, NY
Raff, Lawrence B. ... Newark, NJ
Raff, Lois M. ... Kew Gardens, NY
Raff, Martin Jay ... Louisville, KY
Raff, Spencer J. ... Palo Alto, CA
Raff, William F. ... Encino, CA
Raffa, Connie A. ... New York, NY
Raffa, Frank S. ... Naples, FL
Raffa, James J. ... Tacoma, WA
Raffa, Mark S. ... Bedford, MA
Raffa, Marshall V. ... Elizabeth, NJ
Raffa, Sam J. ... Syosset, NY
Raffa-Dietz, Camille A. ... Detroit, MI
Raffaele, Donna Marie ... Baltimore, MD
Raffaele, Michael A. ... Media, PA
Raffaelli, Elizabeth L. ... Redwood City, CA
Raffaelli, Giovanna M. ... Morrisville, PA
Raffaelli, John ... Orlando, FL
Raffaelli, Paolo ... Santa Clara, CA
Raffaelo, Sabatini ... Newark, NJ
Raffaldini, Barbara C. ... Deerfield, IL
Raffalli, Henri C ... New York, NY
Raffalow, Richard E. ... Sherman Oaks, CA
Raffanello, Michael J. ... Elmont, NY
Raffaniello, Patrick J. ... Washington, DC
Raffanti, Susan M. ... Oakland, CA
Raffath, Bernard A., Jr. ... Stow, OH
Raffe, Charles E. ... Riverhead, NY
Raffe, Daniel D. ... New York, NY
Raffee, Jill ... Del Mar, CA
Raffel, Blair A. ... Homestead, FL
Raffel, Doris R. ... Rockville, MD
Raffel, Erica ... Tampa, FL
Raffel, Keith ... United States Senate, Committee Legal Personnel, GV
Rafferty, Alex T., III ... Waukegan, IL
Rafferty, Carolyn A. ... Waterloo, IA
Rafferty, Catherine ... Fort Lauderdale, FL
Rafferty, Catherine Mary
Washington, DC
Rafferty, Dan ... Yankton, SD
Rafferty, Dennis B. ... Greensburg, PA
Latrobe, PA
Rafferty, Donal ... Palos Park, IL
Rafferty, Donald J. ... Gulfport, MS
Rafferty, Donald J. ... Cincinnati, OH
Rafferty, Donald J., P.A., Law Offices of
Gulfport, MS
Rafferty, Edson Howard ... Boston, MA
Rafferty, F. Thomas, III ... Baltimore, MD
Rafferty, Gary L. ... El Segundo, CA
Rafferty, Gerald J. ... Denver, CO
Rafferty, Gutiérrez & Sánchez-Aballí, P.A.
Miami, FL
Rafferty, James G. ... Washington, DC
Rafferty, John C., Jr. ... Lansdale, PA
Rafferty, John F. ... Raleigh, NC
Rafferty, John L. ... Great Falls, VA
Rafferty, John M. ... Washington, DC
Rafferty, John R. ... Chicago, IL
Rafferty, John T. ... Los Angeles, CA
Rafferty, John T. ... Montvale, NJ
Rafferty, Joseph A., Jr. ... Bethesda, MD
Rafferty, Leo P. ... Munhall, PA
Rafferty, Mary D. ... Duluth, GA
Rafferty, Michael F. ... Memphis, TN
Rafferty, Michael G. ... Washington, DC
Rafferty, Michaelle D. ... Reno, NV
Rafferty, Neil R. ... Champaign, IL
Rafferty, Owen P. ... Los Angeles, CA
Rafferty, Patrick H. ... Houston, TX
Rafferty, Patrick K. ... Santa Rosa, CA
Rafferty, Paul F. ... Costa Mesa, CA
Rafferty & Rafferty, PLLC
Washington, DC
Rafferty, Richard D. ... Dallas, TX
Rafferty, Richard J., Jr. ... Worcester, MA
Rafferty, Robert C. ... Columbus, OH
Rafferty, Robert L. ... Davenport, IA
Rafferty, Scott J. ... Washington, DC
Rafferty, Sharon R. ... Malvern, PA
Rafferty, Shaun B. ... New Orleans, LA
Rafferty, Shawn D. ... Atlanta, GA
Rafferty, Stephen J. ... Honolulu, HI
Rafferty, Susan B. ... Minneapolis, MN
Rafferty, Thomas G. ... New York, NY
Rafferty, Timothy M., (P.A.) ... Hockessin, DE
Rafferty, Troy Alan ... Pensacola, FL
Rafferty, William L., Jr. ... Miami, FL
Rafferty Thompson, Deirdre
Saddle Brook, NJ
Raffesberger, Wayne Alan ... San Diego, CA
Raffetto, Frederick C. ... Neptune, NJ
Raffetto, Shackley F. ... Wailuku, HI
Raffety, Mark D. ... Norfolk, NE
Raffety, Norman K. ... Hennepin, IL
Raffiani, Jeanne M. ... Woodbridge, NJ
Raffkind, Eliot D. ... Dallas, TX
Raffle, Beth A. ... Morgantown, WV
Raffle, Bradley I. ... Houston, TX
Raffle, John Thomas ... Palo Alto, CA
Raffman, Mark S. ... Washington, DC
Raffo, Anthony A. ... Springfield, PA
Raffo, Edward R. ... Edison, NJ
Raffol, Thos. J. ... Natick, MA
Raffony, Ronald J. ... Coral Springs, FL
Rafford, Michael S. ... Phoenix, AZ
Rafftery, James A. ... Edgerton, WI
Raffucci, Vanessa I. ... San Juan, PR
Rafi, Michael M. ... Baltimore, MD
Rafidi, Mark A. ... Youngstown, OH
Rafie, Darius F. ... Las Vegas, NV
Rafiei, Stella ... Beverly Hills, CA
Rafique, Tariq ... New York, NY
Rafiullah, Raana C. ... Chicago, IL
Rafkin, Andrew D. ... West Palm Beach, FL
Rafkin, Glen ... Fort Lauderdale, FL
Rafkin, Jodi B., (Ms.) ... Washington, DC
Rafkin, John M. ... Chicago, IL
Rafkin, Seth A. ... San Diego, CA
Rafkin, Steven A. ... Columbia, MD
Rafky, L. Michael
Nuclear Regulatory Commission, Office of the General Counsel, GV
Rafla-Hatzimemos, Mara ... New York, NY
Rafner, Douglas S. ... San Diego, CA
Rafner, Herbert M. ... Allentown, PA
Rafool & Bourne ... Peoria, IL
Rafool, Brandon J. ... Winter Haven, FL
Rafool, Gary T. ... Peoria, IL
Rafool & Rafool, P.A. ... Lakeland, FL
Winter Haven, FL
Rafool, Raymond J., II ... Winter Haven, FL
Raforth, John H. ... Rapid City, SD
Rafoth, Carl D. ... Youngstown, OH
Rafoth, James ... Youngstown, OH
Rafshoon, G. Scott ... Atlanta, GA
Rafsky, Gary D. ... Stamford, CT
Rafsky, Murray ... New York, NY
Raft, David B. ... Newport Beach, CA
Rafte, G. Alan ... Houston, TX
Rafter, Carmen Rojas ... Killeen, TX
Rafter, C. T., Jr. ... Kansas City, MO
Rafter, Heather Dembert ... Palo Alto, CA
Rafter, John A. ... Washington, DC
Rafter, John A., Jr. ... Los Angeles, CA
Rafter, John R. ... Houston, TX
Rafter, John T. ... New York, NY
Rafter, Joseph B. ... Troy, NY
Rafter, Katherine Abagail ... Charleston, WV
Rafter, Kenneth G. ... Baltimore, MD
Rafter, Michael K. ... Atlanta, GA
Rafter, Patricia S. ... Larchmont, NY
Rafter, Robert J. ... Port Chester, NY
Rafter, Thomas D. ... Chicago, IL
Rafterman, Alan S. ... New York, NY
Raftery and Associates, P.C. ... Southfield, MI
Raftery, Brian E. ... Roseland, NJ
Raftery, George A. ... New York, NY
Raftery Grainger Rosenbloom & Drew
New York, NY
Raftery, James J. ... Southfield, MI
Raftery, John B. ... Bethesda, MD
Raftery, John E. ... Sheboygan, WI
Raftery, Kelly ... San Jose, CA
Raftery, Loretta Gherna ... Santa Monica, CA
Raftery, Mark R. ... San Diego, CA
Raftery, Mary K. ... Redwood City, CA
Raftery, Michael R. ... Riverside, CA
Raftery, Michelle ... Boston, MA
Raftery, Rebecca L. ... Chicago, IL
Raftery, Robert W. ... Oklahoma City, OK
Raftery, Ruth Flynn ... New York, NY
Raftery, Sheila Marie ... Mount Laurel, NJ
Philadelphia, PA
Raftery, Susan L. ... Lynn, MA
Raftery, T. David ... Boston, MA
Raftery, Thomas J. ... Carlisle, MA
Raftery, W. Brian ... New York, NY
Raftice, Robert M., Jr. ... South Portland, ME
Raftis, Edmund B. ... Tacoma, WA
Rafton, Karen A. ... San Rafael, CA
Rafton, Michael G. ... Piedmont, CA
Raftopol, Anthony V. ... New York, NY
Raful, Lawrence ... Omaha, NE
Rafuse, Calvin E., Jr. ... Hauppauge, NY
Rafuse, H. Avery ... Mountain City, TN
Rafuse, Nancy E. ... Atlanta, GA
Rafuse, Robert O. ... Wichita Falls, TX
Ragab Hacking, Amany ... St. Louis, MO
Ragade, Anjani ... Palo Alto, CA
Ragaglia, Joseph C. ... Cherry Hill, NJ
Philadelphia, PA
Ragain, James M. ... Billings, MT
Ragains, Meredith H. ... Atlanta, GA
Ragalevsky, Stanley V. ... Boston, MA
Ragalie, Gregg Stephen ... River Forest, IL
Ragals, William C., Jr. ... New York, NY
Ragan, Alan K. ... Jacksonville, FL
Ragan, Billy H. ... Houston, TX
Ragan, Charles A. ... Chevy Chase, MD
Ragan, Charles O., Jr. ... Chattanooga, TN
Ragan, Charles R. ... Palo Alto, CA
Ragan, Darlene ... Lancaster, CA
Ragan, Dianna R. ... Louisville, KY
Ragan, Elizabeth A. ... Chicago, IL
Ragan, Gerald E. ... San Francisco, CA
Ragan, Hudson B. ... Orinda, CA
Ragan, Hughie ... Jackson, TN
Ragan, James Arthur ... Austin, TX
Ragan, James B. ... Corpus Christi, TX
Ragan, James B., P.C.
Corpus Christi, TX
Ragan, James E., III ... Bayboro, NC
Ragan, James W. ... Charlotte, NC
Ragan, Jennifer L. ... Santa Rosa, CA
Ragan, Jerry Neil ... Gastonia, NC
Ragan, Keith W. ... Phoenix, AZ
Ragan, Maureen ... Burlington, VT
White River Junction, VT
Ragan, Patrick Brian ... Dickson, TN
Ragan, Richard Scott
Department Of Veterans Affairs, Office of the General Counsel, GV
Ragan & Russell ... Houston, TX
Ragan, Sherry E. ... Provo, UT
Ragan, Thomas C. ... New York, NY
Ragan, Timothy D. ... Fair Oaks, CA
Ragan, W. Peter, Esq. ... Neptune, NJ
Ragan, William A., Jr. ... Howard, OH
Ragan, William James ... Buffalo, NY
Raganelli, Genevieve E. Shields ... Trenton, NJ
Ragano, Arnold H. ... Richmond Hill, NY
Ragano, Chris E. ... Tampa, FL
Ragano, Frank ... Tampa, FL
Ragano, James M. ... Tampa, FL
Ragano, John F. ... Richmond Hill, NY
Ragano & Ragano ... Richmond Hill, NY
Ragar, Thurman, Jr. ... Van Buren, AR
Ragatz, Eric C. ... Jacksonville, FL
Ragatz, Ronald R. ... Madison, WI
Ragatz, Teresa ... Miami, FL
Ragatz, Thomas G. ... Madison, WI
Ragazzo, Corina-Maria ... Houston, TX
Ragazzo, Denis J. ... Yonkers, NY
Ragazzo, Joseph A., Jr. ... Sacramento, CA
Ragen, Brian R. ... Spokane, WA
Ragen, Dennis A. ... San Diego, CA
Ragen, Douglas M. ... Portland, OR
Ragen, Frank J. ... San Diego, CA
Ragen, James J. ... Seattle, WA
Ragen, James J., P.S., Law Office of
Seattle, WA
Ragen, Laurie N. Cromwell ... Seattle, WA
Ragen, Lisa Reid
Securities and Exchange Commission, Office of the General Counsel, GV
Ragen, Ronald K. ... Portland, OR
Ragen, Sheryl A. ... Los Angeles, CA
Ragent, David S. ... Pacific Grove, CA
Rager, H. Raymond ... San Bernardino, CA
Rager, Jeffrey A. ... Los Angeles, CA
Rager, John M. ... Fontana, CA
Rager, John M., Law Offices of
Fontana, CA
Rager, Kathleen N. ... Orange, CA
Rager, Kurt T. ... South Sioux City, NE
Rager Law Office, P.C.
South Sioux City, NE
Rager, R. Russell ... Albuquerque, NM
Rager, R. Russell, P.C. ... Albuquerque, NM
Rager, R. Scott ... South Sioux City, NE
Rager, Susan Godman ... Coles Point, VA
Rager, Susan Godman, P.C. ... Coles Point, VA
Rager-White, Terri Spencer ... Freeman, MO
Ragghianti • Freitas • Montobbio • Wallace LLP ... San Rafael, CA
Ragghianti, Gary T. ... San Rafael, CA
Raggi, Reena ... Brooklyn, NY
Raggio, A. Matthew ... Oakland, CA
Raggio, Cappel, Chozen & Berniard
Lake Charles, LA
Sulphur, LA
Raggio, Caroline Craddock
Santa Monica, CA
Raggio, Grier H., Jr. ... New York, NY
Dallas, TX
Raggio, James J. ... Ellicott City, MD
Raggio, Kenneth G. ... Dallas, TX
Raggio, Louise B. ... Dallas, TX
Raggio, Michael T. ... Troy, MI
Raggio and Raggio, P.L.L.C. ... Dallas, TX
Raggio, Thomas L. ... Lake Charles, LA
Raggio, Thomas L. ... Dallas, TX
Raggio, William J. ... Las Vegas, NV
Reno, NV
Raghavan, Diane Verlangier ... Anaheim, CA
Raghavan, Latha ... Albany, NY
Raghavan, Vikram ... New York, NY
Ragheb, Mona ... Baltimore, MD
Ragheb, Nadia ... Dearborn, MI
Ragheb, Nadia ... Farmington Hills, MI
Ragione, Frank J. ... Annapolis, MD
Ragir, S. Eric ... Dallas, TX
Ragland, Andrew J. ... Portland, OR
Ragland, Carroll A. (Ms.) ... Chico, CA
Ragland, Daniel A. ... Atlanta, GA
Ragland, Denton E., Jr. ... Houston, TX
Ragland, Douglas W. ... Phoenix, AZ
Ragland, Edwin F. ... Cape Girardeau, MO
Ragland, G. Russell ... Dallas, TX
Ragland, Gary W. ... Clayton, NC
Ragland, George A. ... Winston-Salem, NC
Ragland, George H., Jr. ... Falls Church, VA
Ragland, Gerald F., Jr. ... Reston, VA
Ragland, James D. ... Quincy, MA
Ragland, Joe M. ... Jackson, MS
Ragland, Joel D. ... Clarksville, TN
Ragland, John W. ... Austin, TX
Ragland, Karen A. ... Pasadena, CA
Ragland and Kawamoto, P.C.
Falls Church, VA
Ragland, Kenneth N. ... Pompton Plains, NJ
Ragland, Lance A. ... Tampa, FL
Ragland Law Firm ... Austin, TX
Ragland, Mangrum & Young, L.L.P.
Waco, TX
Ragland, Michael J., Sr. ... Annapolis, MD
Ragland, Ned H., Jr. ... Beckley, WV
Ragland, Pattie J. ... Denver, CO
Ragland, Rebecca K. ... Louisville, KY
Ragland, Stephen William ... Memphis, TN
Ragland, Thomas K. ... Department of Justice, Executive Office for Immigration Review, GV
Ragland, Tim T. ... Idabel, OK
Ragland, Tom L. ... Waco, TX
Ragland, W. Frank ... Dallas, TX
Ragland, William E., III ... Chattanooga, TN
Ragland, William M., Jr. ... Atlanta, GA
Ragle, C. Allen ... Knoxville, TN
Ragle, Virginia B. ... Juneau, AK
Ragley, Michele G. ... Cleveland, OH
Ragley, Phyllis A. ... Lawrence, KS
Raglin, Dennis E. ... San Francisco, CA
Ragno, Deirdra M. ... Flemington, NJ
Ragno, Joseph G. ... Secaucus, NJ
Ragno, Joseph J., Jr. ... Riverdale, NJ
Rago, Albert R. ... Moorestown, NJ
Rago, Cynthia Marie ... Valley Stream, NY
Rago, Daniel A. ... Plano, TX
Rago, Frank N. ... Chicago, IL
Rago, Frank R. ... Markham, IL
Rago, Louis P. ... Parsippany, NJ
Rago, Matthew, (Ltd.) ... Chicago, IL
Rago, Michelle ... White Plains, NY
Rago, Richard F. ... Rehoboth Beach, DE
Wilmington, DE
Ragold, Laura Cadarette ... Detroit, MI
Ragon, Heartsill, III, (P.A.)
Little Rock, AR
Ragon, Stacy A. ... Akron, OH
Ragona, Lawrence T. ... Alexandria, LA
Ragona, Philip J. ... New York, NY
Ragona, Steven M. ... Los Angeles, CA
Ragone, Brennen C. ... Lexington, KY
Ragone, Mark A. ... New York, NY
Ragone, Peter A. ... New York, NY
Ragonese, Samuel J. ... Runnemede, NJ
Ragonetti, Anthony P. ... Staatsburg, NY
Ragonetti, Thomas J. ... Denver, CO
Ragosa, Emilio ... Princeton, NJ
New York, NY
Ragosta, John A. ... Washington, DC
Ragosta, Paul D. ... Providence, RI
Ragosta, Vincent A. F. ... Providence, RI
Ragosta, Vincent F., Jr. ... Providence, RI
Ragovin, Marc ... New York, NY
Ragovis, George ... Washington, DC
Ragozino, Anthony ... New York, NY
Ragozzine, Joseph B. ... Shelton, CT
Ragozzino, Toni A. ... Oakland, CA
Ragsdale, Barry A. ... Jasper, AL
Ragsdale, Beals, Hooper & Seigler
Atlanta, GA
Ragsdale, C. Gregory ... Lawrenceville, GA
Ragsdale, Calvin E. ... Green River, WY
Ragsdale, Cheryl Grissom ... Richmond, VA
Ragsdale, Dana M. ... Rochester, NY
Ragsdale, David Robert ... Dallas, TX
Ragsdale, Dennis B. ... Knoxville, TN
Ragsdale, Duncan E., Jr. ... Memphis, TN
Ragsdale, Forrest W., III ... Lexington, KY
Ragsdale, Fred L., Jr. ... Albuquerque, NM
Ragsdale, Fred T. ... Los Angeles, CA
Ragsdale, George R. ... Raleigh, NC
Ragsdale, Howell W., Jr. ... Atlanta, GA
Ragsdale, Jeffrey R. ... Washington, DC
Ragsdale, John D. ... Lincoln, NE
Ragsdale, John W., Jr. ... Atlanta, GA
Columbia, SC
Ragsdale, Julie E. ... Indianapolis, IN
Ragsdale, Kent M. ... Dubuque, IA
Ragsdale, Leslie M. ... San Francisco, CA
Ragsdale Liggett, PLLC ... Cary, NC
Raleigh, NC
Research Triangle Park, NC
Ragsdale, Lois V. ... Jacksonville, FL
Ragsdale, M. Clay ... Birmingham, AL
Ragsdale, Mary C. ... Washington, DC
Ragsdale, Michael E. ... Bridgewater, NJ
Ragsdale, Noel M. ... Los Angeles, CA
Ragsdale, Philip W. ... Little Rock, AR
Ragsdale, Richard A. ... Florham Park, NJ
Princeton, NJ
Ragsdale, Robert W. ... Santa Ana, CA
Ragsdale, Stanley D. ... Columbia, SC
Ragsdale, Susan E. H. ... San Diego, CA
Ragsdale, Terry D. ... Tulsa, OK
Ragsdale, Tracy G. ... Tucson, AZ
Ragsdale, Ursula V.
Department Of Veterans Affairs, Board of Veterans Appeals, GV
Ragsdale, William L. ... Raleigh, NC

Ragucci, Frederic L. ... New York, NY
Ragucci, Maria Sarath ... New York, NY
Rague, James T. ... Wellsboro, PA
Ragus, Dale Smolen ... Weston, MA
Ragusa, Anne M. ... Newtown, CT
Ragusa, Anthony D., Jr. ... Belle Chasse, LA
Buras, LA
Ragusa, Joseph M. ... San Diego, CA
Ragusa, Joseph W. ... New York, NY
Ragusa, Katherine P. ... Daly City, CA
Ragusa, Marc S. ... Hicksville, NY
Ragusa, Mark James ... Tampa, FL
Ragusa, Paul A. ... New York, NY
Ragusa, Robert F. ... New York, NY
Ragusa, Sebastian ... Hicksville, NY
Ragusan, Francis J. ... Garden City, NY
Raguse, Rick A. ... Chicago, IL
Ragusin, T. Andrew ... Highlands Ranch, CO
Raguso, Thomas ... Clarkston, MI
Raguso, Thomas, P.C. ... Clarkston, MI
Rah, John S. ... Washington, DC
Rah, Young ... New York, NY
Rahaim, Andrew D. ... Wilmington, DE
Rahaim, John J., II ... Jacksonville, FL
Rahaim, Richard D., Jr. ... Boca Raton, FL
Rahaim & Saints ... Wilmington, DE
Rahaim, Stephen ... Wilmington, DE
Rahal, Andrea F. ... Atlanta, GA
Rahal, Fred, Jr. ... Tulsa, OK
Rahal, Linda A. ... Washington, DC
Rahal, N. David ... Harrisburg, PA
Rahal, Ronald L. ... Maumee, OH
Rahal, Yasmina ... Chicago, IL
Rahall, David A. ... Atlanta, GA
Rahauser, David W. ... Chambersburg, PA
Rahavy, Stephen Paul ... Boston, MA
Rahbari, Robert C. ... New York, NY
Rahbeck, Jeffrey K. ... Zephyr Cove, NV
Rahbeck, Jeffrey K., A Professional Law Corporation ... Zephyr Cove, NV
Rahders, Richard R. ... Santa Cruz, CA
Rahdert, Anderson, McGowan & Steele, P.A.
St. Petersburg, FL
Tampa, FL
Rahdert, George K. ... St. Petersburg, FL
Rahdert, Mark C. ... Philadelphia, PA
Rahdert, Sara Warren ... St. Petersburg, FL
Rahe, Frank W. ... Indianapolis, IN
Rahe, Paul A. ... Chicago, IL
Rahe, S. Syd ... Beverly Hills, CA
Raheb, Joseph ... Lincoln, RI
Raheb, Michael M. ... Miami, FL
Raheb, Michael M., P.A. ... Miami, FL
Raheem, Antoinette R. ... Detroit, MI
Raher, Patrick M. ... Washington, DC
Rahhal, Anthony L. ... Oklahoma City, OK
Rahhal, Franklin D. ... Okemah, OK
Rahhal, Susan J. ... Oklahoma City, OK
Rahie, John G. ... Detroit, MI
Rahija, Michelle A. ... Cleveland, OH
Rahill, Daniel F., III ... Chicago, IL
Rahill, Michael F. ... Department of Justice, Executive Office for Immigration Review, GV
Rahilly, Lisa Richards ... Boston, MA
Rahilly, Lyn Michele ... Washington, DC
Rahim, Subhana ... New York, NY
Rahimi, Joseph Y., II ... Savannah, GA
Rahimi, Pouneh V. ... Lexington, MA
Rahimian, Paul ... Los Angeles, CA
Rahimzadeh, Haleh ... Long Beach, CA
Rahinsky, Sherri L. ... Fort Myers, FL
Rahjoo, Haleh ... Palo Alto, CA
Rahl, Christopher R. ... Baltimore, MD
Rahl, J. Andrew, Jr. ... New York, NY
Rahl, Richard H. ... Oakland, CA
Rahlfs, Roger E. ... Seattle, WA
Rahm, Antoinette L. ... Victoria, TX
Rahm, Brenda D. ... Sedalia, MO
Rahm, David A. ... New York, NY
Rahm, Elinor G. ... Warrensburg, MO
Rahm, Emmett J. ... San Antonio, TX
Rahm, J. Kirk ... Sedalia, MO
Warrensburg, MO
Rahm & Johnsen ... Des Moines, IA
Rahm, Rahm & Koenig, P.C.
Warrensburg, MO
Rahm, Rahm & McVay, P.C. ... Sedalia, MO
Rahm, Richard ... San Francisco, CA
Rahm, Susan Berkman ... New York, NY
Rahm, Timothy J. ... Des Moines, IA
Rahman, Aleya ... Minneapolis, MN
Rahman, Anika ... New York, NY
Rahman, Habib ... Weston, MA
Rahman, Joshua Hartley ... Richmond, VA
Rahman, M. Shakil ... Los Angeles, CA
Rahman, Michael A. ... Washington, DC
Rahman, Musa ... Baton Rouge, LA
Rahman, Nashra ... Seattle, WA
Rahman, S. Whitney ... Reading, PA
Rahman, Shaana ... San Francisco, CA
Rahman, Sofia S. ... New York, NY
Rahmanan, Anthony ... New York, NY
Rahmanan, Jacob ... Kings Point, NY
Rahmas, D. Steve ... Charlotteville, NY
Rahmati, Behrouz K. ... Huntsville, AL
Rahmati & Gray, P.C. ... Huntsville, AL
Rahmaty, Alireza ... Santa Ana, CA
Rahmeier, Larry E. ... Claremore, OK
Rahmes, Gordon R., Jr. ... Niceville, FL
Rahmes, Todd W. ... Fremont, CA
Rahmeyer, Dwight E. ... Springfield, MO
Rahmeyer, Nancy Steffen ... Springfield, MO
Rahmlow, John H. ... Bryn Mawr, PA
Rahn, A., III ... Reidsville, GA
Rahn, Abby ... Paw Paw, MI
Rahn, Betsy Fitzgerald ... Walnut Creek, CA
Rahn, Darryl B. ... Utica, NY
Rahn, Drivon & McCarthy ... Sacramento, CA
Rahn, George E., Jr. ... Philadelphia, PA
Rahn, J. Gail ... Charleston, SC
Rahn, Jeffrey A. ... Springfield, MA
Rahn, Kevin D. ... Longview, WA
Rahn, LeRoy T. ... Pasadena, CA
Rahn, Michael T. ... Sacramento, CA
Rahn, Paul R. ... Charleston, SC
Rahn, Richard F. ... Sioux Falls, SD
Rahn, Robert W. ... Avon, CT
Rahn, Stephen E. ... Fort Wayne, IN
Rahn, Steven C. ... Springfield, IL
Rahn, William F. ... Little Rock, AR
Rahnama, Roshanak ... Beverly Hills, CA
Rahnema, Shireen Bitha ... Los Angeles, CA
Rahner, James J. ... Havertown, PA
Rahner, William L. ... Memphis, TN
Rahoy, John D. ... St. Louis, MO
Rahoy, John P. ... St. Louis, MO
Rahrick, Mark J. ... Owatonna, MN
Rahter, J. Richard ... St. Petersburg, FL
Rahtz, Cristopher ... Pasadena, CA
Rai, Grace S. ... Los Angeles, CA
Rai, Rina K. ... Phoenix, AZ
Rai, Ritin ... Cleveland, OH
Rai, Shambhu K. ... Santa Ana, CA
Rai, Susan S. ... New York, NY
Raia, Camille A. ... Brooklyn, NY
Mineola, NY
New York, NY
Raia, Dominique ... New York, NY
Raia, Frank J. ... Uniondale, NY
Raia, Joseph A. ... Hackensack, NJ
Raia, Joseph L. ... Miami, FL
Raia, Marilyn ... San Francisco, CA
Raia, Matthew D. ... West Orange, NJ
Raia & Rondos ... Brooklyn, NY
Mineola, NY
New York, NY
Raiano, Holly L. ... Providence, RI
Raible, James R. ... Beacon, NY
Raible, Mark Justin ... Little Rock, AR
Raible, Mark Justin, P.A. ... Little Rock, AR
Raible, Philip S. ... New York, NY
Raibman, Michael D. ... Washington, DC
Raibourn, D. Dee, III ... Dallas, TX
Raice, Pinchus D. ... South Orange, NJ
Raich, Robert A. ... Oakland, CA
Raich, Robert A., P.C. ... Oakland, CA
Raiche, Bernard Marcel ... Bethesda, MD
Raiche, Herbert L. ... Vienna, VA
Raiche, Robert E., Sr. ... Manchester, NH
Raichelson, Michael H. ... Ventura, CA
Raichle, Banning, Weiss & Stephens
Buffalo, NY
Raicht, Geoffrey T. ... New York, NY
Raicht, Robert D. ... New York, NY
Raichur, Arvind A. ... Albuquerque, NM
Raicus, Marcia K. ... Forest Hills, NY
Raider, Daniel F. ... Palo Alto, CA
Raider, Jeffrey M. ... Olyphant, PA
Raider, Mark H. ... Natick, MA
Raider, Ronald L. ... Washington, DC
Raidle, Joyce M. ... Tampa, FL
Raidt, Kathryn T. ... Edina, MN
Raidy, Cherie Spence ... Los Angeles, CA
Raies, Elizabeth A. ... Canton, OH
Raiff, Michael L. ... Dallas, TX
Raifman & Edwards LLP
San Francisco, CA
Raifman, Gregory R. ... San Francisco, CA
Raifman, Lawrence J. ... Reisterstown, MD
Raiford, Dixon & Thackston, LLP
Atlanta, GA
Raiford, Jane C. ... New Orleans, LA
Houston, TX
Raiford, John D. ... Malibu, CA
Raiford, R. Chase ... Burlington, NC
Raiford, Wanda Sybil ... Denver, CO
Raiford, William B., III ... Clarksdale, MS
Raifsnider, Michael J. ... San Francisco, CA
Raig, Don A. ... San Diego, CA
Raihala, John W. ... Madison, WI
Raihle, David H. ... Chippewa Falls, WI
Raihofer, Karen ... Morristown, NJ
Raijman, Arlene ... Miami Beach, FL
Raiken, Larry S. ... Montville, NJ
Raiken, Michael Allan ... Clearwater, FL
Raikes, Charles F. G. ... New York, NY
Raikes, Larry D. ... Bardstown, KY
Raikes, William E., III ... Fort Pierce, FL
Raikin, Steven G. ... Washington, DC
Raikos, Gustin J. ... Indianapolis, IN
Raileanu, Ina ... San Jose, CA
Railey, Corinne A. ... Smithfield, NC
Railey, Lilburn R., III ... Orlando, FL
Railey, Richard E. ... Courtland, VA
Railing, James B. ... Scottsburg, IN
Railley, Amber ... New York, NY
Railo, Matt J. ... Los Angeles, CA
Railsback, D. Scott ... Keota, IA
Railsback, David E. ... Mt. Vernon, OH
Railsback, David Phillips ... Concord, MA
Railsback, Marcy ... Beverly Hills, CA
Railsback, Thomas C. ... Dallas, TX
Railsback, Thomas F. ... Washington, DC
Railton, W. Scott ... McLean, VA
Raim, David M. ... Washington, DC
Raimer, Steven L. ... New York, NY
Raimi, Burton L. ... Naples, FL
Sarasota, FL
Raimi, Charles N. ... Detroit, MI
Raimi, Diana ... Ann Arbor, MI
Raimi, Shepherd ... New York, NY
Raimi, Stephen A. ... Bingham Farms, MI
Raimo, Angela M. ... South Orange, NJ
Raimo & Murphy, P.C. ... Manchester, NH
Raimo, Ray ... Manchester, NH
Raimo, Thomas M. ... Dallas, TX
Raimo, Victor E. ... Barnegat, NJ
Raimon, Arthur J. ... Livingston, NJ
Raimon, Martha L. ... Brooklyn, NY
Raimond, Louis A. ... Pittsburgh, PA
Raimond, Roger A. ... New York, NY
Raimondi, Anthony J. ... New York, NY
Raimondi, Barbara L. ... Auburn, ME
Raimondi, Carole ... Berkeley, CA
Raimondi, Guy C., Jr. ... Brooklyn, NY
Raimondi, Hillary J. ... White Plains, NY
Raimondi, John F. ... Philadelphia, PA
Raimondi, Josephine A. ... Greenwich, CT
Raimondi, Lawrence N., Jr. ... Atlanta, GA
Raimondi, Lisa M. ... Chicago, IL
Raimondi, Lorenzo A. ... Danvers, MA
Raimondi, Marco A. ... Chicago, IL
Raimondi, Michael G. ... Baltimore, MD
Raimondi & Orton, Ltd. ... Chicago, IL
Raimondi, Thomas P. ... Baltimore, MD
Raimondi, Thomas R. ... Wayne, NJ
Raimondo, Antonio ... Dunkirk, NY
Raimondo, David J. ... Lake Grove, NY
Raimondo, Jacey A. ... Fort Lee, NJ
Raimondo, Janet L. ... Hopewell Junction, NY
Raimondo, Lynne M. ... Chicago, IL
Rain, James T. ... Dallas, TX
Rain, John W. ... Dallas, TX
Rain, Mary E. ... Oswego, NY
Rain, Robert E., Jr. ... Dallas, TX
Rain, Talbot ... Dallas, TX
Rainach, Rex D. ... Baton Rouge, LA
Rainbird, Jan ... Irvine, CA
Rainboldt, James A. ... Cypress, CA
Rainbolt, Charles P. ... Cordell, OK
Rainbolt, Geffrey D. ... Indianapolis, IN
Rainbolt, Harold E. ... San Antonio, TX
Rainbolt, John V., II ... Washington, DC
Rainbolt, Kenneth D. ... Durant, OK
Rainbolt Law Office ... Washington, DC
Rainboth, Michael P. ... Portsmouth, NH
Rainbow, Cindy ... Bronx, NY
Rainbow, Douglas R. ... Minneapolis, MN
Raine, C. Macon ... Corpus Christi, TX
Raine, C. Randall ... Lexington, KY
Raine, David L. ... Kilmarnock, VA
Raine, J. D., Jr. ... Louisville, KY
Raine, Michaux, III ... Rocky Mount, VA
Raine, Paul James ... Southfield, MI
Raine & Perdue ... Rocky Mount, VA
Raine, Stanley M. ... Denver, CO
Raine, William D. ... Springfield, MO
Rainear, Dennis H. ... Richmond, VA
Rainen, Edward A., (P.C.) ... Andover, MA
Rainer, Anding & McLindon
Baton Rouge, LA
Rainer, Andrew A. ... Boston, MA
Rainer, G. Bradley ... Media, PA
Rainer, Gisele C. ... San Francisco, CA
Rainer & Hyche ... Brandon, MS
Rainer, I. Warren ... North Hollywood, CA
Rainer, J. Edward ... Brandon, MS
Rainer, J. Kenyon, Sr., M.D., J.D.
Mobile, AL
Rainer, J. Marbury ... Atlanta, GA
Rainer, Nancy Jo ... Montgomery, AL
Rainer, Randall R. ... New York, NY
Rainer, Robert R. ... Baton Rouge, LA
Rainer, Ronald H. ... Boston, MA
Raineri, Eugene, Jr. ... Treasury Department, Internal Revenue Service, GV
Raineri, Joseph ... Los Gatos, CA
Raineri, Joseph C. ... Los Gatos, CA
Raineri, Joseph C., Sr. ... Scottsdale, AZ
Raineri, Mark B ... Los Angeles, CA
Raineri, Walter T. ... Palo Alto, CA
Rainerman, Jamie B. ... New York, NY
Rainero, David ... Oakmont, PA
Rainero, Julian ... New York, NY
Raines, Alan P. ... New York, NY
Raines, Albert M. ... Seattle, WA
Raines, Andrew H. ... Los Angeles, CA
Raines, Andrew H. ... Memphis, TN
Raines, C. Christopher, Jr.
Mount Carmel, TN
Raines, C. Ted, Jr. ... Dallas, TX
Raines, Carolyn K. ... Lake Forest, CA
Raines, Carolyn Konicek ... Dallas, TX
Raines, Christopher A. ... Lexington, NC
Raines, David S. ... Biloxi, MS
Raines, David S. ... Gulfport, MS
Raines, David S. ... Hattiesburg, MS
Jackson, MS
Raines, Deborah J. ... Albuquerque, NM
Raines, Edward P. ... Lincoln, NE
Raines, Jack ... Fort Worth, TX
Raines, Jack W. ... Fort Worth, TX
Raines, James G. ... Dawson, GA
Raines, James M. ... Chatham, NJ
Raines, Jeffrey A. ... New Orleans, LA
Raines, Jeffrey H. ... Covington, KY
Raines, J. N. ... Memphis, TN
Raines, John D., III ... Macon, GA
Raines, John Mark ... Amarillo, TX
Raines, Jonathan E. ... Laurelton, NY
Raines, Julie P. ... Raleigh, NC
Raines, June Camille Bush
Oklahoma City, OK
Raines, Karen I. ... Issaquah, WA
Raines, Keith R. ... Portland, OR
Raines, Kenneth R. ... Bay Minette, AL
Raines, Mark Wayne ... Memphis, TN
Raines, Marshall A. ... Jasper, TN
Raines, Mary E. ... Atlanta, GA
Raines, Murry A. ... Bowling Green, KY
Raines, Paula M. ... Big Sur, CA
Raines, Radford R., III ... St. Louis, MO
Raines, Randolph A., Jr. ... Suffolk, VA
Raines, Richard C. ... Danville, CA
Raines, Richard C. ... Memphis, TN
Raines, Thomas E. ... Norcross, GA
Raines, Thomas E., P.C. ... Atlanta, GA
Norcross, GA
Rainey, Arthur H. ... Philadelphia, PA
Rainey, Becky Ragland ... San Antonio, TX
Rainey, Carol Horan ... Bremerton, WA
Rainey, Charles E., Jr. ... Harrisburg, PA
Rainey, Charles J. ... Milwaukee, WI
Rainey, Charles R., ... Naples, FL
Rainey, Charles R., Jr. ... Vienna, VA
Rainey, Charles R., Jr., P.C. ... Vienna, VA
Rainey, Clifford W., Sr. ... Orlando, FL
Rainey, Craig L. ... Tulsa, OK
Rainey, Elisa Dillard ... Waco, TX
Rainey, F. Dean, Jr. ... Greenville, SC
Rainey, Gordon F., Jr. ... Richmond, VA
Rainey, J. Lynn ... Marietta, GA
Rainey, J. Scott ... Washington, DC
Rainey, James E. ... Franklin, VA
Rainey, James F. ... East Lansing, MI
Rainey, James H. ... West Palm Beach, FL
Rainey, James H., P.A.
West Palm Beach, FL
Rainey, James W. ... Irving, TX
Rainey, John D. ... Houston, TX
Rainey, John G., Jr. ... New York, NY
Rainey, John S. ... Geneva, IL
Rainey, John S. "Chip" ... Houston, TX
Rainey, John S., Jr. ... Raleigh, NC
Rainey, Kizer, Butler, Reviere & Bell
Jackson, TN
Rainey, L. Bratton, III ... Mobile, AL
Rainey, Lola Clayton ... Tucson, AZ
Rainey, Lola Clayton, P.C. ... Tucson, AZ
Rainey, M. Ellis, II ... Overland Park, KS
Rainey, Marion W. ... Macon, GA
Rainey, Marvin E. ... Overland Park, KS
Rainey, Michael B. ... Woodland Hills, CA
Rainey, P. James ... Waco, TX
Rainey, R. Marshall ... Tampa, FL
Rainey, Rainey & Sutton, L.C.
Overland Park, KS
Rainey, Richard L. ... Atlanta, GA
Rainey, Richard L. ... Charlotte, NC
Rainey, Robert Lee ... Oklahoma City, OK
Rainey, Ron S. ... Houston, TX
Rainey, Ronald I. ... San Jose, CA
Rainey, Ronald P. ... Caldwell, ID
Rainey, Ross, Rice & Binns
Oklahoma City, OK
Rainey, Roy A. H. ... Silverdale, WA
Rainey, Sally D. ... Washington, DC
Rainey, Stacey L. ... Kansas City, MO
Rainey, Sylvia L. ... Sunnyvale, CA
Rainey, Thomas H. ... Jackson, TN
Rainey, T. O., III ... Dinwiddie, VA
Petersburg, VA
Rainey, Valencia ... Upper Marlboro, MD
Rainey, William J. ... Topeka, KS
Rainey, William M. ... Gulfport, MS
Rainey, William Palma ... Marion, AR
Rainey, William V. ... San Antonio, TX
Rainey, William V., P.C., Law Offices of
San Antonio, TX
Rainford, Martin L. ... Boston, MA
Rainie, James C. ... Fort Bragg, CA
Rainis, Lynn Bromley ... Baltimore, MD
Rainis, Matthew ... Melville, NY
Rainis, Richard David
Belvedere-Tiburon, CA
Rainold, Robert R. ... New Orleans, LA
Rainone, Dominic E. ... Irvine, CA
Rainone, John D. ... Wheaton, IL
Rainone, Louis N. ... Sayreville, NJ
Rainone, Michael C. ... Philadelphia, PA
Rainone and Rainone ... Philadelphia, PA
Rainone, Salvatore ... Livingston, NJ
Rainone, Sebastian M. ... Philadelphia, PA
Rainone & Theisen, P.C. ... Wheaton, IL
Rains, Block and Ettlinger ... Walled Lake, MI
Ypsilanti, MI
Rains, Cameron Jay ... San Diego, CA
Rains, Charles E. ... Phoenix, AZ
Rains, D. Rainell ... Chicago, IL
Rains, Darryl P. ... San Francisco, CA
Rains, David A. ... Fort Payne, AL
Rains, David E. ... Tuscaloosa, AL
Rains, Elizabeth J. ... Kansas City, MO
Rains, Jack M. ... Houston, TX
Rains, John Harrison, III ... Tampa, FL
Rains, Lowry A., Jr. ... Adrian, MI
Rains, M. Greg ... Paducah, KY
Rains, M. Neal ... Cleveland, OH
Rains, Mark C. ... Victoria, TX
Rains, Mark C., & Associates, P.C.
Victoria, TX
Rains, Mark E. ... Blue Springs, MO
Rains, Mark S. ... Tulsa, OK
Rains, Meryl A. ... Saratoga, CA
Rains, Omer L. ... Carmichael, CA
Rains & Pogrebin, P.C. ... Mineola, NY
New York, NY
Rains, Robert E. ... Carlisle, PA
Rains, Russell E. ... Austin, TX
Rains, Senator Omer L. ... Carmichael, CA
Rains, Stephen A. ... Santa Ana, CA
Rains, Stephen L. ... Jamestown, TN
Rains, Stuart A. ... Tulsa, OK
Rains, William J. ... Conyers, GA
Rainsberger, Ben Allen ... Chillicothe, OH
Rainsberger, Kirby C. ... Tampa, FL
Rainsford, Edmund J. ... Weymouth, MA
Rainville, A. Gregory ... St. Albans, VT
Rainville & Associates, P.C.
St. Albans, VT
Rainville, Christina ... Philadelphia, PA

Rainville, Gay Parks ... Philadelphia, PA
Rainville, Gerard A. ... Annapolis, MD
Rainville, Michael J. ... Sacramento, CA
Rainville, Paul S. ... Worcester, MA
Rainville, Peter J. ... Hartford, CT
Rainville & Riese ... Sacramento, CA
Rainville, Robert E. ... Providence, RI
Rainwater, B. W. ... Augusta, GA
Rainwater, David N. ... Cordele, GA
Rainwater, Forgety & Jones ... Dandridge, TN
Rainwater & Humble ... Knoxville, TN
Rainwater, J. Earl ... Knoxville, TN
Rainwater, Lesa B. ... Humboldt, TN
Rainwater, Manford W. ... Tucumcari, NM
Rainwater, Michael R. ... Little Rock, AR
Rainwater, Paul S. ... Crossett, AR
Rainwater, Randy ... Mena, AR
Rainwater, Sloan, Jr. ... Jonesboro, AR
Rainwater, Tonya Baccus ... Viera, FL
Rainwater, Vickie ... Fort Worth, TX
Raio, Frank J. ... North Haven, CT
Raio, John F., Jr. ... New York, NY
Rair, David K. ... Honolulu, HI
Rair, Michael L. ... Bangor, ME
Rairigh, Ivona ... Lansing, MI
Raisanen, Gordon P. ... Cokato, MN
Raisanen, Kenneth P. ... Detroit, MI
Raisbeck, Michael N. ... Forge Village, MA
Raisbeck, Robert H., Jr. ... Mocksville, NC
Raisbeck, Thomas E. ... Cincinnati, OH
Raisch, Jerry W. ... Boulder, CO
Raisch, Kenneth L. ... Staten Island, NY
Raisch, William F. ... Grimes, IA
Raisfeld, Lawrence S. ... Atlantic Beach, NY
Raisfeld, Ruth D. ... New York, NY
Raish, David L. ... Boston, MA
Raish, Leonard R. ... Washington, DC
Arlington, VA
Raish, Todd A. ... Cleveland, OH
Raisher, Scott A. ... Kansas City, MO
Raisig, Paul J., Jr. ... Sanford, NC
Raisin, Bradley A. ... Los Angeles, CA
Raiskin, Daniel L. ... Los Angeles, CA
Raiskin, Morey ... Orlando, FL
Raiskin & Revitz ... Los Angeles, CA
Raiskin, Samuel M. ... New York, NY
Raiskin, Sol A. ... New York, NY
Raisler, Kenneth M. ... New York, NY
Raisman, Helene B. ... Fort Lauderdale, FL
Raisman, Myron S. ... Smithtown, NY
Raisman, Nancy B. ... Smithtown, NY
Raisner, Christian L. ... Oakland, CA
Raisner, Jack A. ... New York, NY
Raison, Margo A. ... Bakersfield, CA
Raison, Pamella Arnold ... Camp Hill, PA
Raisor, Thomas L. ... Muncie, IN
Raiss, Lawrence D. ... West Orange, NJ
Raissi, Jahan P. ... San Francisco, CA
Raissi, Laudan S. ... San Francisco, CA
Raissinia, Abdolreza ("Abdy")
Menlo Park, CA
Raisty, Laura M. ... New York, NY
Rait, Mitchell ... Woodbridge, NJ
Raitanen, Kauko K. ... Boston, MA
Raiter, Shawn M. ... St. Paul, MN
Raith, Gina R. ... Chicago, IL
Raith, John C. ... Chicago, IL
Raith, Mark Alan ... Reading, PA
Raith, Peter A. ... Kansas City, MO
Raithel, George S. ... Milwaukee, WI
Raithel, Renée M. ... Irvine, CA
Raithel, Thomas R. ... Kansas City, MO
Raitt & Associates, A Professional Law Corporation ... Irvine, CA
Raitt, Cecil G. ... Detroit, MI
Raitt, David H. ... Detroit, MI
Raitt, G. Emmett, Jr. ... Irvine, CA
Raitt, Robert M. ... Southfield, MI
Raitt, Ronald D. ... Toledo, OH
Raitt, Ruby L. ... Santa Monica, CA
Raitzin, Morris ... Mamaroneck, NY
Raives, Robert M. ... New York, NY
Raivio, H. Scott ... Portland, OR
Raiz, Michael J. ... Chicago, IL
Raizes, Maurice P. ... Chicago, IL
Raizes, Sheldon F. ... El Segundo, CA
Raizin, Jamie Wayne ... Bellmore, NY
Raizman, David H. ... Santa Monica, CA
Raizman, Dorothy L. ... Pittsburgh, PA
Raizman & Frischman, P.C.
Pittsburgh, PA
Raizner, Jeffrey L. ... Houston, TX
Raj, Sapna V. ... Memphis, TN
Raja, Aleem ... San Francisco, CA
Rajala, Alex ... Pe Ell, WA
Rajala, Eric C. ... Kansas City, KS
Rajala, Eric C. ... Overland Park, KS
Rajala, Eric C. ... Kansas City, MO
Rajalingam, Shyami U. ... New York, NY
Rajamani, Prakash ... Washington, DC
Rajan, Anandhi S. ... Atlanta, GA
Rajan, Paul ... New City, NY
Rajan, Raja G. ... Harrisburg, PA
Rajan, Raji ... Sunnyvale, CA
Rajapakse, Sayuri ... Library of Congress, Copyright Office, GV
Rajaram, V. ... Rolling Meadows, IL
Rajaratnam, Arjun
Research Triangle Park, NC
Rajchel, Mary Lou ... Tallahassee, FL
Rajcic, John ... Irvine, CA
Rajek, Michael M. ... Eau Claire, WI
Rajfer, Sol ... Chicago, IL
Rajguru, Suvarna Umakant
Washington, DC
Rajki, Walter A. ... Fort Myers, FL
Rajkovich, Marco M., Jr. ... Lexington, KY
Rajkowski, Frank J. ... St. Cloud, MN
Rajkowski Hansmeier Ltd. ... St. Cloud, MN
Rajkowski, Michael C. ... St. Cloud, MN
Rajkowski, Paul A. ... St. Cloud, MN
Rajkowski, Shauna T. ... San Francisco, CA
Rajkumar, Roshini A. ... Fargo, ND
Rajnoha, Sally Swyers ... Ballwin, MO
Rajt, Mark T. ... Detroit, MI
Rajt, Michael A. ... Detroit, MI
Rajtar, Michael Adrian
Hallandale Beach, FL
Rajtar, Steven A., (P.A.) ... Longwood, FL
Raju, Ajay ... Philadelphia, PA
Raju, Radhika P. ... Plantation, FL
Raju, Srinivas M. ... Wilmington, DE
Raju, Vijay K. ... Cherry Hill, NJ
Philadelphia, PA
Rak, Andrew G. ... Old Greenwich, CT
Rak, Jonathan P. ... Fairfax, VA
Rak, Ronald C. ... Newark, NJ
Rak, Samuel ... Leonia, NJ
Rak, Walter N. ... Raleigh, NC
Rakacky, Joseph W. ... Fort Myers, FL
Rakas, Rosemary T.
Agency for International Development, Legal Advisers-Overseas, GV
Rakatansky, Carol R. ... Reston, VA
Rakatansky, Ira ... Framingham, MA
Rakauski, Jill A. ... Chicago, IL
Rakay, Peter J. ... Dayton, OH
Rake & Catanese, A Professional Corporation
Phoenix, AZ
Rake, Doug ... Dallas, TX
Rake, M. E. "Buddy", Jr. ... Phoenix, AZ
Rake, Paul A. ... Hammond, IN
Raker, Arthur F. ... Toledo, OH
Raker, Colleen M. ... Houston, TX
Raker, David C. ... Williamsport, PA
Raker, Irma S. ... Rockville, MD
Raker, Keith H. ... Cleveland, OH
Rakers, Connie S. ... Belleville, IL
Rakers, Kevin C. ... Chicago, IL
Rakes, Elizabeth Ellen ... Hillsville, VA
Rakes, Gerald S. ... Oklahoma City, OK
Rakes, Lorie Brown ... Shepherdsville, KY
Rakes, Richard C. ... Roanoke, VA
Rakes, William R. ... Roanoke, VA
Rakestraw, Ann H. ... Washington, DC
Rakestraw, Frederick E. ... Rochester, IN
Rakestraw, Gregory A. ... Findlay, OH
Rakestraw & Rakestraw ... Findlay, OH
Rakestraw, Russell E. ... Findlay, OH
Rakestraw, W. Vincent ... Columbus, OH
Rakich Law Office ... Joliet, IL
Mokena, IL
Olympia Fields, IL
Rakich, Steven D. ... Mokena, IL
Rakinic & Associates ... Jenkintown, PA
Rakinic, Dana ... Jenkintown, PA
Rakita, Richard J. ... Milwaukee, WI
Rakley, Barbara J. ... Chicago, IL
Rakley, Martin L. ... San Diego, CA
Rako, Jennifer S. ... Boston, MA
Rakoczy, Mark E. ... Chicago, IL
Rakoczy, Richard E. ... Racine, WI
Rakoczy, William A. ... Chicago, IL
Rakoff, Jed S. ... New York, NY
Rakoff, Rosalie L. ... Santa Monica, CA
Rakoff, Todd D. ... Cambridge, MA
Rakonitz, David ... San Francisco, CA
Rakos, Maria E. ... Edison, NJ
Rakoski, Michael ... Marlton, NJ
Rakosky, Michael A. ... New London, CT
Rakosky, Ronald J. ... New Orleans, LA
Rakov, David A. ... Chicago, IL
Rakove, Helen S. ... San Jose, CA
Rakow, Eugene ... Rutland, VT
Rakow, J. Jay ... Los Angeles, CA
Rakow, John W., III ... San Francisco, CA
Rakow, Laura E. ... Nashville, TN
Rakow, Ross R. ... Goldendale, WA
Rakow and Smith ... Neligh, NE
Rakow, Terry L. ... Phoenix, AZ
Rakower, Eileen A. ... New York, NY
Rakowitz, Leonard ... Stamford, CT
Rakowski, Henry E. ... New York, NY
Rakowski, Kevin C. ... Westmont, NJ
Philadelphia, PA
Rakowski, L. Steven ... Northbrook, IL
Rakowski, L. Steven, Ltd. ... Chicago, IL
Northbrook, IL
Rakowski, Thomas R. ... Chicago, IL
Rakowsky, Connie L. ... Concord, NH
Rakowsky, Donna J. ... Louisville, KY
Rakowsky, Ihor G. ... New York, NY
Rakowsky, John R. ... West Columbia, SC
Rakowsky, Katherine E. ... Chicago, IL
Raksphal, Anirma ... Washington, DC
Rakusin, Stephen ... Fort Lauderdale, FL
Rakusin, Stephen, P.A.
Fort Lauderdale, FL
Ralabate, Frank T. ... Williamsville, NY
Ralabate & Galbo ... Williamsville, NY
Ralabate, James J. ... Williamsville, NY
Ralabate, Joseph M. ... Williamsville, NY
Ralbovsky, Stephen F. ... Scottsdale, AZ
Raldiris, Hiram Anthony ... Glendale, CA
Raldiris-Aguayo, Miguel A. ... San Juan, PR
Raleigh, Bruce W. ... Grosse Ile, MI
Raleigh & Cahill, P.C. ... Chicago, IL
Raleigh, Christopher ... New York, NY
Raleigh, Christopher J. ... Las Vegas, NV
Raleigh, Donald T. ... Lake Elmo, MN
Raleigh, Elizabeth A. ... Lake Elmo, MN
Raleigh, George Warfield ... West Chester, PA
Raleigh, Harry S., Jr.
Fort Lauderdale, FL
Raleigh, Helms & Finke ... Chicago, IL
Raleigh, Hunt & McGarry, P.C.
Las Vegas, NV
Raleigh, John K. ... Whittier, CA
Raleigh, John P. ... Berkley, MI
Raleigh, Karen O. ... San Antonio, TX
Raleigh, Kerry A. ... Miami, FL
Raleigh, Kirsten McAuliffe ... Wayne, PA
Raleigh, Lisa M. ... Tallahassee, FL
Raleigh, Mary J. ... Oak Park, IL
Raleigh, Michael F. ... Manchester, NH
Raleigh, Paul J. ... Corpus Christi, TX
Raleigh, Philip M. ... Chicago, IL
Raleigh, Rebecca A. ... Minneapolis, MN
Raleigh, Richard J. R., Jr. ... Birmingham, AL
Raleigh, Robert G. ... Alton, IL
Raleigh, Stuart W. ... Syracuse, NY
Raleigh, Thomas E. ... Chicago, IL
Raleigh, Thomas L., III ... Orlando, FL
Raleigh, W. Ray ... St. Louis, MO
Raleigh, William J. ... Chicago, IL
Raley, Bennett W. ... Denver, CO
Raley, Bill R. ... Fort Worth, TX
Raley & Bluestein, P.A. ... Charleston, SC
Raley, C. Clarke ... Leonardtown, MD
Raley, Charles E. ... McLean, VA
Raley, Charles H., Jr. ... Charleston, SC
Raley, F. Robert ... Macon, GA
Raley, G. Brian ... Atlanta, GA
Raley, Jacquelyn V. ... Lexington Park, MD
Raley, James W. ... Mandeville, LA
Raley, Jeff F. ... Norman, OK
Raley, Jeffrey E. ... Houston, TX
Raley, John W., Jr. ... Ponca City, OK
Raley, John Wesley ... Houston, TX
Raley, Landy ... Athens, AL
Raley, Michele ... Sacramento, CA
Raley, Patrick A. ... Winter Park, FL
Raley, Phillip A. ... Pine Bluff, AR
Raley, Robert Thames ... Wagoner, OK
Raley, Robert W. ... Bossier City, LA
Raley, Shane P. ... Dallas, TX
Ralidis, Kenneth W. ... Los Angeles, CA
Ralidis & Lee ... Los Angeles, CA
Ralis, Maryann ... Washington, DC
Ralis, Robert John ... Chicago, IL
Michigan City, IN
Rall, Caroline E. ... Columbus, OH
Rall, John P. ... Murray, KY
Rall, Lauris G. L. ... New York, NY
Rall, Martin M. ... Portland, OR
Rall, Thomas A. ... Rochester, NY
Ralles, Mark T. ... Tucson, AZ
Ralli, Constantine P. ... New York, NY
Ralli, Donna K. ... Houston, TX
Rallings, Thomas B., Jr. ... Charlotte, NC
Rallis & Chinen ... La Habra, CA
Rallis, Chris A. ... Durham, NC
Rallis, Dean C. ... Sioux Falls, SD
Rallis, Dean G., Jr. ... Los Angeles, CA
Rallis, Gus ... El Paso, TX
Rallis, Irene R. ... Manhasset, NY
Rallis, John G. ... Providence, RI
Rallis, Kirk Dean ... Fullerton, CA
Rallis, Ronald D., Sr. ... La Habra, CA
Rallo, Christina A. ... Newark, NJ
Rallo, David T. ... Chicago, IL
Rallo, Douglas ... Libertyville, IL
Rallo, Victor, Jr. ... Red Bank, NJ
Ralls, Chris ... Maryville, TN
Ralls, David L. ... Charlotte, NC
Ralls, David L. ... Charlotte, NC
Ralls, John W. ... San Francisco, CA
Ralls, Mary Ann ... Washington, DC
Ralls, Morgan S., Jr. ... Manhattan Beach, CA
Ralls, Nancy E. ... Cleveland, OH
Ralls, Nathan Mark ... San Antonio, TX
Ralls, Richard D. ... Kansas City, MO
Ralls, Stephen G. ... Tucson, AZ
Ralls, Valenzuela & Marshall, P.C.
Tucson, AZ
Ralls-Morrison, Desiree A. ... West Point, PA
Ralph, A. Laurence ... Augusta, ME
Ralph, Alice M. ... Arlington Heights, IL
Ralph, Amauda S. ... Columbus, OH
Ralph, Amy E. ... Washington, DC
Ralph, Arthur A. ... Rye, NY
Ralph, Arthur B. ... Salt Lake City, UT
Ralph, Bethany A. ... New York, NY
Ralph, Bradley C. ... Dodge City, KS
Ralph, David E. ... Baltimore, MD
Ralph, David E. ... Elmira, NY
Ralph, Francis P. ... Troy, AL
Ralph, Frank W. ... Ottawa, IL
Ralph, Gary A. ... Naples, FL
Ralph, Gordon P. ... Milwaukee, WI
Ralph, Gwendolyn Mary ... Erie, PA
Ralph, H. Lowell ... Columbus, OH
Ralph, James R. ... Memphis, TN
Ralph, Jesse Clyde ... Sacramento, CA
Ralph, Kenneth ... Hackensack, NJ
Ralph, Kenneth E. ... Au Gres, MI
Ralph, Michael L. ... Vernon Hills, IL
Ralph, Paul W. ... Laguna Hills, CA
Ralph, Regan Elisabeth ... Washington, DC
Ralph, Richard A. ... Newton, NJ
Ralph, Roberta ... Los Angeles, CA
Ralph, S. Lester ... Reading, MA
Ralph, Sheldon D.C. ... Encino, CA
Ralph, Theodore J. ... San Antonio, TX
Ralph, Thomas A. ... Philadelphia, PA
Ralph, Thomas D. ... Cambridge, MA
Ralph, Thomas V. ... Webster, MA
Ralph, Walter S. ... Toledo, OH
Ralph, William J. ... Chicago, IL
Ralphs, George L. ... Las Vegas, NV
Ralstin, G. Todd, Inc. ... Oklahoma City, OK
Ralstin, Martha Z. ... Dallas, TX
Ralston, A. Henry ... Middlesboro, KY
Ralston & Alvarez ... Seattle, WA
Ralston, Andrew ... Houston, TX
Ralston, Brian C. ... Wilmington, DE
Ralston, Bruce A. ... Memphis, TN
Ralston, Camille Taylor ... Seattle, WA
Ralston, Cary A. ... Richmond, VA
Ralston, Charles S. ... New York, NY
Ralston, David ... Houston, TX
Ralston, David E. ... Blue Ridge, GA
Ralston, David T., Jr. ... Washington, DC
Ralston, David W. ... Dallas, TX
Ralston, David W. ... Reston, VA
Ralston, Douglas R. ... Dallas, TX
Ralston, E. Randall ... Charlottesville, VA
Ralston, Eugene B. ... Topeka, KS
Ralston, Henry H. ... Charlotte, NC
Ralston, J. Christopher ... Columbus, OH
Ralston, J. Scott ... Las Vegas, NV
Ralston, James A. ... Memphis, TN
Ralston, Jeffrey C. ... Stanford, KY
Ralston, John J. ...
Department of Defense, GV
Ralston, Joseph R. ... Lancaster, OH
Ralston, Katherine McKusick
South Portland, ME
Ralston, Leonard J., Jr. ... Rockville, MD
Ralston, Mark H. ... Dallas, TX
Ralston, Michael A. ... Redding, CA
Ralston & Panter ... Blue Ridge, GA
Ralston, Peter N. ... Anchorage, AK
Seattle, WA
Ralston & Pope, LLC ... Topeka, KS
Ralston, R. Bruce ... Butler, PA
Ralston, Richard H. ... Kansas City, MO
Ralston, Richard S. ... Seattle, WA
Ralston, Robert L. ... Bloomington, IN
Ralston, Robert S. ... San Francisco, CA
Ralston, Robert W. ... Wilmington, DE
Ralston, Scott Andrew ... Houston, TX
Ralston, William H. ... Albany, NY
Ralston, William H., Jr.
Harrisonburg, VA
McLean, VA
Ralton, Deborah H. ... New York, NY
Raluy, Anthony George ... Louisville, KY
Ram, Candice Singer ... New York, NY
Ram, Eric D. ... New York, NY
Ram, James F. ... Chesterfield, MO
Ram, James J. ... New York, NY
Ram, Michael ... Petaluma, CA
Ram, Michael F. ... San Francisco, CA
Ram, Michael J. ... Los Angeles, CA
Ramach, Jennifer B. ... Fort Lauderdale, FL
Ramadan, Mahmoud ... Newark, NJ
Ramadan, Virginia Sher ... New York, NY
Ramaeker, Gary W. ... Sierra Vista, AZ
Ramaeker, Gary W., P.C., Law Offices of
Sierra Vista, AZ
Ramage, Andrew M. ... Springfield, IL
Ramage, Barbara K. ... Elyria, OH
Ramage, Bruce E. ... Houston, TX
Ramage, Colleen E. ... Pittsburgh, PA
Ramage, Gary R. ... Indianapolis, IN
Ramage, Jeffrey M. ... Philadelphia, PA
Ramage, Michael R. ... Tallahassee, FL
Ramage, Michael S. ... Bala Cynwyd, PA
Ramage, Sharon F. ... Austin, TX
Irving, TX
Ramage, Susan M. ... Grand Rapids, MI
Ramage & Valles ... Pittsburgh, PA
Ramage, W. Edward ... Nashville, TN
Ramah, Peter G. ... Saginaw, MI
Ramaker, Sara E. ... Green Bay, WI
Ramakrishna, Ranjani ... San Francisco, CA
Ramaley, Jeffrey A. ... Pittsburgh, PA
Ramalho, Louis F. ... Philadelphia, PA
Ramalingam, Sunil ... McCall, ID
Ramamurthy, Sunitha ... New York, NY
Raman, Albert J. ... Philadelphia, PA
Raman, Anand S. ... Washington, DC
Raman, James J. ... Spartanburg, SC
Raman, Kartik Kalyan
Department of Justice, Criminal Division, GV
Raman, Mythili ... Greenbelt, MD
Raman, Sachida R. ... Hammond, LA
Raman, William D. ... Austin, TX
Ramana, Marjorie J. ... Oklahoma City, OK
Ramanathan, Erik D. ... New York, NY
Ramanathan, Radha ... Edison, NJ
Ramanathan, Subhasri ... Washington, DC
Ramani, George T. ... Miami, FL
Ramanow, Joseph S. ... Newton, MA
Ramar, John J. ... Detroit, MI
Ramaswamy, Anand P. ... Burlington, NC
Ramatowski, Christine M. ... St. Louis, MO
Ramatowski, Deborah A. ... Port Jefferson, NY
Ramatowski, Jean M. ... New Brunswick, NJ
Ramazzini, Stephen L. ... Sacramento, CA
Ramba, David E. ... Tallahassee, FL
Ramba, David Eugene ... Tallahassee, FL
Rambach, Jeffrey C. ... Tulsa, OK
Rambacher, John J. ... Canton, OH
Rambalakos, Elena ... Atlanta, GA
Rambarran, Moses V. ... White Plains, NY
Rambaum, William ... Clearwater, FL
Rambaum, William, P.A. ... Clearwater, FL
Rambeau, James E., Jr. ... Atlanta, GA
Ramberg, Catherine L.
San Francisco, CA
Ramberger, Timothy R. ... St. Louis, MO
Rambert, Michael A. ... Trenton, NJ
Rambicure, Miller & Kuebler, PSC
Lexington, KY
Rambicure, William C. ... Lexington, KY
Rambin, W. Neil ... Dallas, TX
Rambler, William A. ... Tewksbury, MA
Rambo, Andrew C. ... Shelbyville, TN

Rambo, Andrew C., P.C. ....Fayetteville, TN
Lewisburg, TN
Shelbyville, TN
Rambo, Daphne A. ....Houston, TX
Rambo, Deborah Price ....Cincinnati, OH
Rambo, G. Dan ....Norman, OK
Rambo, Glenn L. ....Toledo, OH
Rambo, Harold E., Jr. ....Washington, DC
Rambo, J. David ....Norman, OK
Rambo, J. David, P.C. ....Norman, OK
Rambo, J. Wilson ....Monroe, LA
Rambo, James E., Jr. ....Glen Burnie, MD
Rambo, Jay Allen ....Spokane, WA
Rambo, John E. ....Joliet, IL
Rambo, Kelly Clifford ....Allentown, PA
Rambo, Lynne H. ....Fort Worth, TX
Rambo, Madeline ....Athens, OH
Rambo, Richard B. ....Klamath Falls, OR
Rambo, Rick L. ....Houston, TX
Rambo, Sylvia H. ....Harrisburg, PA
Rambo, William S. ....Anderson, SC
Rambo, Wm. Cates ....Cincinnati, OH
Rambosek, Theresa J. ....Bellevue, WA
Rambow, John C. ....Tucson, AZ
Rambow & Miller, P.A. ....Minneapolis, MN
Rambow, Paul R. ....Minneapolis, MN
Rambus, Johnnie B. ....Birmingham, MI
Rambusch, Lennard K. ....New York, NY
Rambuski, Edwin J. ....San Luis Obispo, CA
Ramchandani, Debra M.
Santa Monica, CA
Ramcharan, R. E. ....Topeka, KS
Ramczyk, Daniel E. ....Albuquerque, NM
Ramdas, Stacy S. ....Minneapolis, MN
Ramde, Rakesh ....Palo Alto, CA
Rameaka, Gregory P. ....Warwick, RI
Rameden, David A. ....Overland Park, KS
Ramee, Thomas M. ....Savannah, GA
Rameker, William J. ....Madison, WI
Ramel, Gregory J., Sr. ....Chicago, IL
Ramella, Raymond K. ....Phoenix, AZ
Ramelli, Rudolph R. ....New Orleans, LA
Ramello, Richard J. ....Rosemont, IL
Ramelmeier, Rolf ....Columbia, MD
Ramelow, Geo. E. ....Chicago, IL
Ramenda, Joseph T. ....Odessa, FL
Ramenian, Donald R. ....Los Angeles, CA
Ramer, Amelia L. ....Reston, VA
Ramer, Bruce M. ....Beverly Hills, CA
Ramer, Claude O., II ....Nashville, TN
Ramer, Daniel E. ....Piqua, OH
Ramer, Elaine G. ....Nashville, TN
Ramer, Glenna M. ....Chattanooga, TN
Ramer, Henry ....Hawthorne, NJ
Ramer, Henry, P.A. ....Hawthorne, NJ
Ramer, James T. ....Harbor Springs, MI
Ramer, Jeffrey S. ....Greenwich, CT
Ramer, Laurence ....Jamaica, NY
Ramer, Moore & Glass ....Detroit, MI
Harbor Springs, MI
Petoskey, MI
Ramer, Nancy N. ....Greenwich, CT
Ramer, Norman A. ....Vernon, NJ
Ramer & Ramer ....Greenwich, CT
Ramer, Samuel ....New York, NY
Ramer, Thomas F. ....Asheville, NC
Ramerman, Dale B. ....Seattle, WA
Ramers, M. Katherine ....Dunedin, FL
Ramers & Stephens, P.A. ....Dunedin, FL
Rames, Peter B. ....Albuquerque, NM
Ramesh, Elaine M. ....Chicago, IL
Rameson, Jack A., III
Woodland Hills, CA
Rametra, Munish Kukli ....New York, NY
Ramette, James E. ....Burnsville, MN
Ramey, Alfred E., Jr. ....Trenton, NJ
Ramey, Ancil G. ....Charleston, WV
Ramey, Bryan D. ....Easley, SC
Ramey, Bryan D., P.A. ....Easley, SC
Ramey, Carl R. ....Washington, DC
Ramey, Cecil E., Jr. ....Shreveport, LA
Ramey, Christopher B. ....Houston, TX
Ramey, Cole B. ....Dallas, TX
Ramey, Curtis E. ....Fort Worth, TX
Ramey, Douglas ....Madisonville, KY
Ramey, Drucilla S. ....San Francisco, CA
Ramey, E. Allan ....De Funiak Springs, FL
Ramey, Edward T. ....Denver, CO
Ramey, Fenton R. ....Yukon, OK
Ramey, Fenton R., Inc. ....Yukon, OK
Ramey & Flock, A Professional Corporation
Tyler, TX
Ramey, Fred L., P.A. ....Boise, ID
Ramey, Frederick L. ....Boise, ID
Ramey, George H. ....Yukon, OK
Ramey & Hailey ....Aspen, CO
Indianapolis, IN
Ramey, Hardin R. ....Dallas, TX
Ramey, James W. ....Des Moines, IA
Ramey, Jerome ....Greenville, NC
Ramey, Jerry D. ....Russellville, AR
Ramey, John F. ....Los Angeles, CA
Ramey, J. R. ....Sulphur Springs, TX
Ramey, Judith A. ....Chicago, IL
Ramey, Karen W. ....Richmond, VA
Ramey, Kathryn A. ....Richmond, VA
Ramey, Kimberly Dobbs ....Decatur, AL
Ramey, Leonard L., Jr. ....San Bernardino, CA
Ramey, Lynn Van Hyning ....Tampa, FL
Ramey, M. Scott ....Sylvania, OH
Ramey, Mark S. ....Tampa, FL
Ramey, Mary Beth ....Indianapolis, IN
Ramey, Mary Ellen Dubec ....Seattle, WA
Ramey, Owen D. ....Kalamazoo, MI
Ramey, Ramey & Kampf, P.A.
Tampa, FL
Ramey, Robert L. ....Corpus Christi, TX
Ramey, Robert L. ....Houston, TX
Ramey, Robert L., P.C. ....Houston, TX
Ramey, Ron ....Houston, TX
Ramey, Ron, Inc., A Texas Professional Corporation ....Houston, TX
Ramey & Sheffield ....Sulphur Springs, TX
Ramey, Sherry W. ....Houston, TX
Ramey, Shon C. ....Houston, TX
Ramey, Stephen E. ....Shreveport, LA
Ramey, Steven Arthur ....Lansing, MI
Ramey & Tharp ....El Reno, OK
Yukon, OK
Ramey, Todd K. ....Houston, TX
Ramey, Tom B., Jr. ....Tyler, TX
Ramey, William J. ....Marina Del Rey, CA
Ramfjord, Per A. ....Portland, OR
Ramgopal, Mahendra M. ....New York, NY
Ramgren, Peter ....Boston, MA
Ramich, Thomas E. ....Elmira, NY
Ramier, George R. ....Minneapolis, MN
Ramier & Murray, P.A. ....Minneapolis, MN
Ramig, Christopher J. ....Fayetteville, GA
Ramik, Vincent L. ....Annandale, VA
Ramil, Antonio V. ....Wailuku, HI
Ramil, Mario R. ....Honolulu, HI
Ramin, Bruce P. ....Framingham, MA
Raming, Renee J. ....Edina, MN
Raming, Richard J. ....Edina, MN
Ramirez, Alann Martin ....Sewell, NJ
Ramirez, Andrew R. ....Lawrence, KS
Ramirez, Anthony B. ....St. Louis, MO
Ramirez, Anthony B., P.C. ....St. Louis, MO
Ramirez, Antonio ....San Francisco, CA
Ramirez, Arturo V. ....Houston, TX
Ramirez & Associates, P.C. ....Dallas, TX
Ramirez, Bethzaida Jordan ....Mayaguez, PR
Ramirez, Bob J. ....San Antonio, TX
Ramirez, Carlos A. ....Tampa, FL
Ramirez, Carlos J. ....San Antonio, TX
Ramirez, Carlos S. ....Cincinnati, OH
Ramirez, Carrie M. ....Dallas, TX
Ramirez, Christina Kizirian ....Tampa, FL
Ramirez, Daniel ....McAllen, TX
Ramirez, Daniel R. ....Edinburg, TX
Ramirez, David E. ....Denver, CO
Ramirez, David M. ....El Dorado Hills, CA
Ramirez, David P. ....San Diego, CA
Ramirez, Deborah A. ....Boston, MA
Ramirez, Dorian Evans ....Houston, TX
Ramirez, Eddie D. ....Tulsa, OK
Ramirez, Eddie R. ....San Juan, PR
Ramirez, Edith ....Los Angeles, CA
Ramirez, Edmundo O. ....McAllen, TX
Ramirez, Edward ....Beverly Hills, CA
Ramirez, Edward Robert ....Clovis, CA
Ramirez, Elisabeth Wolfe ....Covington, LA
Ramirez, Enrique ....El Paso, TX
Ramirez, Eugene P. ....Los Angeles, CA
Ramirez, Florencio (Larry) ....Las Cruces, NM
Ramirez, Florentino, Jr. ....Dallas, TX
Ramirez, Florentino A. ....Dallas, TX
Ramirez, Francis Lee ....Turlock, CA
Ramirez, Francisco J. ....New York, NY
Ramirez, Frank T. ....Fresno, CA
Ramirez, Frederick, (P.A.)
Pembroke Pines, FL
Ramirez, G. Allen ....Roma, TX
Ramirez, Gary E. ....Corpus Christi, TX
Ramirez, Genaro C. ....San Diego, CA
Ramirez, Gregory J. ....Oxnard, CA
Ramirez, Hector C. ....Laredo, TX
Ramirez, Hector R. ....Tucson, AZ
Ramirez, Henry ....Jamaica, NY
Ramirez, Ignacio, Sr. ....Baytown, TX
Ramirez, Israel G. ....San Jose, CA
Ramirez, Jack ....Des Plaines, IL
Ramirez, James A. ....New Orleans, LA
Ramirez, Javier B. ....Norwalk, CA
Ramirez, John A. ....Costa Mesa, CA
Ramirez, John A. ....Houston, TX
Ramirez, John M. ....Baltimore, MD
Ramirez, Jorge Alberto ....Houston, TX
Ramirez, Jose R. ....Bolton, CT
Ramirez, Joseph ....Morristown, NJ
Ramirez, Joseph A. ....Pasco, WA
Ramirez, Joseph M. ....Pittsburgh, PA
Ramirez, Josephine L. ....McAllen, TX
Ramirez, Juan, Jr. ....Miami, FL
Ramirez, Juan M. ....Edinburg, TX
Ramirez, Julian ....Houston, TX
Ramirez, Kenneth ....Austin, TX
Ramirez, Larry, P.A., Law Offices of
Las Cruces, NM
Ramirez, Les W. ....Albuquerque, NM
Ramirez, Linda Friedman ....Portland, OR
Ramirez, Linda Friedman, P.C. ....Portland, OR
Ramirez, Lori A. ....Pasadena, CA
Ramirez, Luis R. ....McAllen, TX
Ramirez, M. Carmen ....Oxnard, CA
Ramirez, M. Christina ....Encino, CA
Ramirez, Manuel ....New Orleans, LA
Ramirez, Manuel A. ....Riverside, CA
Ramirez, Manuel J. ....Miami, FL
Ramirez, Manuel L., (Inc.) ....Irvine, CA
San Diego, CA
Ramirez, Maria ....Compton, CA
Ramirez, Maria Eugenia ....San Juan, PR
Ramirez, Mario E. ....Edinburg, TX
Ramirez, Mary K. ....Topeka, KS
Ramirez, Matthew Damon ....Denver, CO
Ramirez, Maureen S. ....Providence, RI
Ramirez, Michael I. ....San Antonio, TX
Ramirez, Michelle L. ....New York, NY
Ramirez, Mina ....Modesto, CA
Ramirez, Nancy ....Los Angeles, CA
Ramirez, Nancy A. ....Los Angeles, CA
Ramirez, Patricia A. ....Juneau, WI
Ramirez, Paul ....Westborough, MA
Ramirez, Pete L. ....Denver, CO
Ramirez, Peter J. ....Dodge City, KS
Ramirez, Peter L. ....Milwaukee, WI
Ramirez, Philip A. ....Dallas, TX
Ramirez, Porfirio F., Jr. ....New York, NY
Ramirez, Ralph M. ....Waukesha, WI
Ramirez, Raul A. ....Sacramento, CA
Ramirez, Raymond R. ....Plano, TX
Ramirez, Rene ....Pharr, TX
Ramirez, Rene, (Mr.) ....Franklin, TN
Ramirez, Richard ....Richardson, TX
Ramirez, Richard B. ....New Orleans, LA
Ramirez, Richard E. ....El Paso, TX
Ramirez, Rion Joaquin ....Seattle, WA
Ramirez, Robert ....San Antonio, TX
Ramirez, Robert B. ....Glenview, IL
Ramirez, Robert B., P.C. ....Glenview, IL
Ramirez, Robert P. ....Phoenix, AZ
Ramirez, Roberto L. ....McAllen, TX
Ramirez, Rolando Rene ....Alice, TX
Ramirez, Ronald W. ....Forest Hills, NY
Ramirez, Russell ....Austin, TX
Ramirez, Sergio J. ....Department of Justice, Executive Office for Immigration Review, GV
Ramirez, Shirley D. ....Los Angeles, CA
Ramirez, Silverio A. ....Elizabeth, NJ
Ramirez, Steven A. ....Topeka, KS
Ramirez, Suzanne Marie ....Chula Vista, CA
Ramirez, Ted L. ....Columbus, OH
Dayton, OH
Ramirez, Teresita Villa ....Tomball, TX
Ramirez, Vic ....Austin, TX
Ramirez, Victor A. ....Boise, ID
Ramírez-Ball, Rafael ....San Juan, PR
Ramirez-Becerra, Maria Soledad
San Juan, PR
Ramirez-Browning, Yvonne
Newport Beach, CA
Ramirez-Cardenas, Julie W. ....San Diego, CA
Ramirez-Cuebas, Nestor D.
Federal Deposit Insurance Corporation, Corporate Affairs Section, GV
Ramírez de Arellano, Carlos F.
San Juan, PR
Ramirez de Arellano, Max ....Jersey City, NJ
Ramirez de Arellano, Sergio A.
San Juan, PR
Ramirez de Arellano-Oliver, Liza M.
San Juan, PR
Ramirez-Eaves, Linda L. ....Denver, CO
Ramírez-MacDonald, Alfredo F.
San Juan, PR
Ramirez-Meadows, Gabriela
San Juan Capistrano, CA
Ramirez-Rivera, Francisco M.
San Juan, PR
Ramirez-Uy, Lillian ....Honolulu, HI
Ramirez-Vincenty, Elmer ....Mayaguez, PR
Ramis, Crew, Corrigan & Bachrach
Portland, OR
Salem, OR
Vancouver, WA
Ramis, Timothy V. ....Portland, OR
Ramish, Timothy E. ....Department of State, Office of the Legal Adviser, GV
Ramist, Roselyn B. ....Stamford, CT
Ramiu, Maria F. ....San Francisco, CA
Ramji, Mohammad A. ....Houston, TX
Ramler, Douglas M. ....Minneapolis, MN
Ramler, Richard A. ....Belgrade, MT
Ramlo, Kurt E. ....Los Angeles, CA
Ramlow, James M. ....Kalispell, MT
Ramlow, Todd A. ....Rockford, IL
Ramm, Brian N. ....Cleveland, OH
Ramm, Carolyn E. ....Burlington, MA
Ramm, Peter H. ....Winston-Salem, NC
Ramm, Walter C. ....Wilmette, IL
Rammelkamp, Bradney, Kuster, Keaton, Fritsche & Lindsay, P.C.
Jacksonville, IL
Rammelkamp, David A.
Albuquerque, NM
Rammelkamp, Theodore C.
Jacksonville, IL
Rammelkamp, Theodore C., Jr.
Jacksonville, IL
Rammell, Bron M. ....Pocatello, ID
Rammell, Phelon S. (Scott)
Brigham City, UT
Rammelt, David A. ....Chicago, IL
Rammer, Gerald H. ....Neenah, WI
Rammes, Lisa M. ....Cincinnati, OH
Ramming, Brad ....Denver, CO
Ramming, Brian J. ....Pasco, WA
Ramming, John B. ....Granger, IN
Ramniceanu, Nicolas ....Los Angeles, CA
Ramo, Bruce S. ....Scottsdale, AZ
Ramo, Nashak & Brown ....Glendale, NY
Ramo, Roberta Cooper ....Albuquerque, NM
Ramón, Alberto M. ....Eagle Pass, TX
Ramón, Alberto M., L.L.P.C.
Eagle Pass, TX
Ramon, Hector E. ....San Jose, CA
Ramón, Jaime ....Dallas, TX
Ramón, Jaime (Jim) ....McAllen, TX
Ramon, Lois Cannell ....Belvidere, IL
Ramon, Sofia A. ....McAllen, TX
Ramon, Sonia ....Miami, FL
Ramonas, George A. ....Washington, DC
Ramos, A. Gregory ....Nashville, TN
Ramos, Alfonso F. ....Springfield, NJ
Ramos, Alonzo ....Laredo, TX
Ramos, Andrea V. ....Los Angeles, CA
Ramos, Andres Aaron ....Laredo, TX
Ramos, Anita M. ....Brook Park, OH
Ramos, Anthony M. ....Oxnard, CA
Ramos, Barron Edward ....San Diego, CA
Ramos, Carey R. ....New York, NY
Ramos, Carlos J. ....Tallahassee, FL
Ramos, Carlos R. ....Fort Wayne, IN
Ramos, Charles E. ....New York, NY
Ramos, Constance F. ....San Francisco, CA
Ramos, Cynthia ....Miami, FL
Ramos, Daniel J. ....Washington, DC
Ramos, David G. ....Napa, CA
Ramos, Debi A. ....Altadena, CA
Ramos, Dianna Lynn ....Buffalo, NY
Ramos, Diego A. ....San Juan, PR
Ramos, Dion ....Houston, TX
Ramos, Donato D. ....Laredo, TX
Ramos, Edgar A. ....Cleveland, OH
Ramos, Edgardo ....Garden City, NY
Ramos, Ena Acevedo ....San Juan, PR
Ramos, Eva C. ....Austin, TX
Ramos, Francisco, Jr. ....Miami, FL
Ramos, Fred P. ....Cleveland, OH
Ramos, Fred P., Co., L.P.A.
Cleveland, OH
Independence, OH
Ramos, Frederick ....St. Paul, MN
Ramos, G. Ernie, Jr. ....Batavia, OH
Ramos, G. Ernie, Jr. ....Cincinnati, OH
Ramos, Gene M. ....Los Angeles, CA
Ramos, George L. ....Akron, OH
Ramos, Gregory J. ....Denver, CO
Ramos, James R. ....Sacramento, CA
Ramos, John P. ....Syracuse, NY
Ramos, Jose M. ....Bayamon, PR
Ramos, Jose S. ....Riverside, CA
Ramos, Joseph ....Charleston, AR
Ramos, Joseph V. ....Beverly Hills, CA
Ramos, Karen A. ....New York, NY
Ramos, Kiki ....Culver City, CA
Ramos & Latoni ....Bayamon, PR
Ramos, Laura J. ....Albuquerque, NM
Ramos & Lewis, L.L.P. ....Shallotte, NC
Ramos, Louis ....New York, NY
Ramos, Luis Miguel ....Santa Cruz, CA
Ramos, Manuel ....Norwalk, CA
Ramos, Marco A. ....McAllen, TX
Ramos, Marcos A. ....Los Angeles, CA
Ramos, Maria D. ....San Francisco, CA
Ramos, Marilyn J. ....Stamford, CT
Ramos, Mario ....Nashville, TN
Ramos, Melvin H. ....New Orleans, LA
Ramos, Merle A. ....Tucker, GA
Ramos, Michael A. ....Los Angeles, CA
Ramos, Michael L. ....Daytona Beach, FL
Ramos, Michael L., P.A.
Daytona Beach, FL
Ramos, Michael R. ....Shallotte, NC
Ramos, Patrick B. ....Boulder, CO
Ramos, Pearlette J. ....Detroit, MI
Ramos, Pedro A. ....Philadelphia, PA
Ramos, Pilar S. ....New York, NY
Ramos, Rene A. ....South Pasadena, CA
Ramos, Ricardo A. ....McAllen, TX
Ramos, Richard T. ....St. Louis, MO
Ramos, Robert ....El Paso, TX
Ramos, Robert Troy ....San Diego, CA
Ramos, Rodrigo V. ....El Paso, TX
Ramos, Sandra G. ....Chicago, IL
Ramos, Stephen D. ....Philadelphia, PA
Ramos, Steven T. ....Dallas, TX
Ramos, Suzanne G. ....San Diego, CA
Ramos, Vanessa ....New York, NY
Ramos, Ventura V. ....Granada Hills, CA
Ramos, William G. ....Bristol, RI
Ramos, Zunilda ....San Francisco, CA
Ramos-Collazo, Reinaldo ....San Juan, PR
Ramos-Cruz, Lydia M. ....San Juan, PR
Ramos-Diaz, Hector R. ....San Juan, PR
Ramos-Diaz, Juan A., Law Offices of
San Juan, PR
Ramos Lugo, Santos ....San Juan, PR
Ramos Luiña, Guillermo J. ....San Juan, PR
Ramos Martinez, Gail ....San Juan, PR
Ramos-Rivera, Migdali ....San Juan, PR
Ramos-Smith, Vanessa M.
Salt Lake City, UT
Ramos-Soler, Sonsire ....San Juan, PR
Ramos-Tomasini, Mario A. ....San Juan, PR
Ramp, David L. ....Minneapolis, MN
Ramp, Edward J. ....East Brunswick, NJ
Ramp, Fredrick L. ....Kolonia, TT
Ramp, John J. ....Huntington Beach, CA
Ramp, Kenneth A. ....Tenafly, NJ
Ramp & Pisani, LLP ....Tenafly, NJ
Ramp and Renaud ....East Brunswick, NJ
Ramp, Stephen W. ....Princeton, NJ
Rampacek, Anne S. ....Atlanta, GA
Rampe, James M. ....Fort Lauderdale, FL
Rampell, Paul ....Palm Beach, FL
Rampenthal, Charles E. ....Los Angeles, CA
Rampey, Denver L., Jr. ....Elberton, GA
Rampilla, Narayana R. ....Washington, DC
Rampino, Kenneth J. ....Warwick, RI
Rampson, Edward J. ....Wheaton, IL
Rampton, Anthony L. ....Salt Lake City, UT
Rampton, Calvin L. ....St. George, UT
Salt Lake City, UT
Rampton, Vincent C. ....Salt Lake City, UT
Rampulla, John F., III ....Lexington, KY
Rampulla, Robert B. ....New York, NY
Ramputi, William ....Ocala, FL
Rampy, Matthew C. ....Washington, DC
Ramras, Ari ....Phoenix, AZ
Ramras, Christopher Andrew
San Diego, CA
Ramras, David N. ....Phoenix, AZ
Ramras Law Offices, P.C. ....Phoenix, AZ
Ramras, Steven R. ....San Diego, CA
Ramrath, Joseph R. ....Boston, MA
Ramsammy, Dasree V. ....Clearwater, FL
Ramsauer, Kirk L. ....Westborough, MA
Ramsaur, David J. ....Lumberton, NC

Ramsaur, James W. ..... Oakland, CA
Ramsaur, Jimmie Lynn ..... Nashville, TN
Ramsay, Allan R. ..... Toccoa, GA
Ramsay, Bridgforth, Harrelson & Starling
Pine Bluff, AR
Ramsay, Charles R., Jr. ..... San Marcos, TX
Ramsay, Christopher Dominic ..... Denver, CO
Ramsay, Christopher L. ..... New York, NY
Ramsay, Dana L. ..... West Bloomfield, MI
Ramsay, David E. ..... Columbus, OH
Ramsay, Don Douglas ..... St. Petersburg, FL
Ramsay, Donald C. ..... Leawood, KS
Ramsay, Ernest C. ..... Norcross, GA
Ramsay, George B., Jr. ..... Toccoa, GA
Ramsay, J. Bradford ..... Washington, DC
Ramsay, J. Robert ..... Hattiesburg, MS
Ramsay, Jan M. ..... Dallas, TX
Ramsay, Janice A. ..... Irvine, CA
Ramsay, John M. ..... Washington, DC
New York, NY
Ramsay & Johnson, A Law Corporation
Irvine, CA
Ramsay, Kathleen Parker
Department of the Navy, GV
Ramsay, Louis L., Jr. ..... Pine Bluff, AR
Ramsay, Martha L. ..... Charlotte, NC
Ramsay, O'Malley & O'Connor
Tappan, NY
Ramsay, Philip D. ..... Walnut, CA
Ramsay, Raymond M. ..... Salem, OR
Ramsay, Reed ..... Des Moines, IA
Ramsay, Rhona H. ..... New York, NY
Ramsay, Richard E. ..... Washington, DC
Ramsay, Richard E. ..... Des Moines, IA
Ramsay, Richard G. ..... Tappan, NY
Ramsay, Richard L. ..... Little Rock, AR
Ramsay, Robert G. ..... Pascagoula, MS
Ramsay, Robin A. ..... Denton, TX
Ramsay, Rosemary E. ..... Roseland, NJ
Ramsay, Samuel H., Jr. ..... Providence, RI
Ramsay, Sharon ..... Glastonbury, CT
Ramsay, Sheldon C. ..... San Francisco, CA
Ramsay & Stein, P.C. ..... Salem, OR
Ramsay, Thomas Glendon ..... Rochester, NY
Ramsay Title Group, L.L.C. ..... Norcross, GA
Ramsayer, George B. ..... Cleveland, OH
Ramsbacher, John F. ..... San Jose, CA
Ramsberger, Peter R. ..... Clearwater, FL
Ramsberger, Thomas Mark ..... Orlando, FL
Ramsberger, Timothy T. ..... Orlando, FL
Ramsburg, Cheryl L. ..... North Canton, OH
Ramsdale, Marie-Louise A. ..... Columbia, SC
Ramsdell & Associates, P.C.
Springfield, MO
Ramsdell, Barry D. ..... Boston, MA
Ramsdell, Daniel T., P.C. ..... Springfield, MO
Ramsdell, Edward Louis ..... Newburyport, MA
Ramsdell, Jeffrey M. ..... Seattle, WA
Ramsdell, Kelly R. ..... Moorestown, NJ
Philadelphia, PA
Ramsdell, Michael D. ..... Concord, NH
Ramsdell, Patricia P. ..... Cazenovia, NY
Ramsdell, Robert A. ..... Madison, WI
Ramsdell, Steven B. ..... Alexandria, VA
Ramsdell, Thomas J. ..... Chicago, IL
Ramsden, Linda G. ..... Medfield, MA
Ramsden, Lisa M. ..... Chicago, IL
Ramsden & Lyons ..... Coeur d'Alene, ID
Lewiston, ID
Spokane, WA
Ramsden, Mary K. ..... Los Angeles, CA
Ramsden, Mary Suzanne ..... Pittsburgh, PA
Ramsden, Michael E. ..... Coeur d'Alene, ID
Ramseier, William Frederic
Alexandria Bay, NY
Clayton, NY
Ramsell & Associates ..... Wheaton, IL
Ramsell, Donald J. ..... Wheaton, IL
Ramsen, John ..... New York, NY
Ramser, John F. ..... Allison Park, PA
Ramseur, Donald E., Sr. ..... Gastonia, NC
Ramseur, Joseph M., Jr. ..... Greenville, SC
Ramseur, Thomas M., Jr. ..... New York, NY
Ramsey, A. Allen ..... Homewood, AL
Ramsey, A. Allen, P.C. ..... Homewood, AL
Ramsey, A. Benjamin ..... Houston, TX
Ramsey, Albert C. S. ..... Long Beach, CA
Ramsey, Alice L. ..... Sacramento, CA
Ramsey, Ann Lockridge ..... Baltimore, MD
Ramsey, Austin Lee, III ..... Atlanta, GA
Ramsey, B. Harold ..... Poughkeepsie, NY
Ramsey & Bauer ..... Plainwell, MI
Ramsey, Baxley & McDougle ..... Dothan, AL
Ramsey, Ben ..... Houston, TX
Ramsey, Beverley A. ..... Falls Church, VA
Ramsey, Beverly J., Jr. ..... Jefferson City, TN
Ramsey & Black ..... Vincennes, IN
Ramsey, Bobby C. ..... Jay, OK
Ramsey, Bronstein & Dayton
Los Angeles, CA
Ramsey, Bruce A. ..... San Francisco, CA
Ramsey, Bruce E. ..... Modesto, CA
Ramsey, Bruce Mitchel
West Palm Beach, FL
Ramsey, Charles B. ..... Treasury Department,
Internal Revenue Service, GV
Ramsey, Charles S. (Buck), Jr.
Manchester, TN
Ramsey, Charles T. ..... Oakland, CA
Ramsey, Cheryl A. ..... Stillwater, OK
Ramsey, Christopher A. ..... Vincennes, IN
Ramsey, Christopher K. ..... Pittsburgh, PA
Ramsey, Christopher P. ..... Los Angeles, CA
Ramsey, Clayton G. ..... Seattle, WA
Ramsey, Coe W. ..... Greensboro, NC
Raleigh, NC
Ramsey, Cynthia L. ..... Detroit, MI
Ramsey, D. Wade ..... Birmingham, AL
Ramsey, Daena G. ..... Dallas, TX
Ramsey, Dale K. ..... Overland Park, KS
Ramsey, Daniel W. ..... Richmond, VA
Ramsey, Dean C. ..... Clarksburg, WV
Ramsey, Dennis F., Jr. ..... Leesburg, FL
Ramsey, Diane M.O. ..... Phoenix, AZ
Ramsey & Dismuke, P.C. ..... Arlington, TX
Dallas, TX
Fort Worth, TX
Ramsey, Donald L. ..... Sandusky, OH
Ramsey, Donald T. ..... San Francisco, CA
Ramsey, Donald W., Jr. ..... Savannah, GA
Ramsey, Drew B. ..... Rochester, NY
Ramsey, E. Jerrell ..... Brunswick, GA
Ramsey, Edward L. ..... Birmingham, AL
Ramsey, Edwin P. ..... Los Angeles, CA
Ramsey, Elizabeth A. ..... Washington, DC
Ramsey, Erich M. ..... Arlington, TX
Dallas, TX
Ramsey, Francis W., 3rd ..... Cambridge, MA
Ramsey, Gary D. ..... Dickinson, ND
Ramsey, Gayle E. ..... Brevard, NC
Ramsey, George E., III ..... Austin, TX
Ramsey, Gordon P. ..... Boston, MA
Ramsey, H. Vaughn ..... Greensboro, NC
Ramsey, Heather S. ..... Salem, MA
Ramsey, Hill, Smart, Ramsey & Pratt, P.A.
Brevard, NC
Ramsey, Holly Elizabeth ..... Jackson, MS
Ramsey, Homer B. ..... New York, NY
Ramsey, Ian T. ..... Louisville, KY
Ramsey, J. David ..... Morristown, NJ
Ramsey, J. Kevin ..... Canton, OH
Ramsey, J. Timothy ..... Chicago, IL
Ramsey, James E. ..... Boston, MA
Ramsey, James E. ..... Kansas City, MO
Ramsey, James E. ..... Roxboro, NC
Ramsey, James F. ..... Houston, TX
Ramsey, James G. ..... Nashville, TN
Ramsey, James M. ..... Kansas City, MO
Ramsey, James N. ..... Clinton, TN
Ramsey & Janssen, P.A. ..... Leesburg, FL
Ramsey, Jeffrey E. ..... Indianapolis, IN
Ramsey, Jeffrey F. ..... Chicago, IL
Ramsey, Jeffrey T. ..... Dallas, TX
Ramsey, Jennifer ..... Austin, TX
Ramsey, Jerry A. ..... Los Angeles, CA
Ramsey, Joe ..... Sacramento, CA
Ramsey, Joe F., Jr. ..... Lanham, MD
Ramsey, Joel W. ..... Dothan, AL
Ramsey, John Arthur ..... Denver, CO
Greenwood Village, CO
Ramsey, John C. ..... Pittsburgh, PA
Ramsey, John E. ..... Atlanta, GA
Ramsey, J. R. ..... Houston, TX
Ramsey, Julie A. ..... Roxboro, NC
Ramsey, Karlyn L. ..... Connellsville, PA
Ramsey, Katherine E. ..... Richmond, VA
Ramsey, Kelly ..... Detroit, MI
Ramsey, Kelly Erin McMurdo
Louisville, KY
Ramsey, Kenneth E. ..... Strongsville, OH
Ramsey, Kim E., (P.C.) ..... San Antonio, TX
Ramsey, Kimberlee Harris ..... Richmond, VA
Ramsey, Lance J. ..... Austin, TX
San Antonio, TX
Ramsey, Larry A. ..... San Jose, CA
Ramsey, Laura C. ..... Chicago, IL
Ramsey, Lawrence E. ..... Dickson, TN
Ramsey, Lawrence R. ..... Torrance, CA
Ramsey, Leith C. ..... Albany, NY
Ramsey, Lewis B., Jr. ..... Philadelphia, PA
Ramsey, Linda F. ..... Chatham, VA
Ramsey, Linda L. ..... Fresno, CA
Ramsey, Lisa K. ..... Lexington, KY
Ramsey, Lloyd J. ..... Middleburg Heights, OH
Ramsey, Maja K. ..... San Francisco, CA
Ramsey, Mari Strong ..... Tulsa, OK
Ramsey, Mark ..... Houston, TX
Ramsey, Mark Allen ..... Chattanooga, TN
Ramsey, Mark P. ..... Chicago, IL
Ramsey, Mark R. ..... Tell City, IN
Ramsey, Martha T. ..... Hyannis, MA
Ramsey, Martin S. ..... Earlham, IA
Ramsey, Mary Gayle, A Prof. Corp.
Terrell, TX
Ramsey, Matthew S. ..... Houston, TX
Ramsey, Max C., III ..... Minneapolis, MN
Ramsey, Max E. ..... Odessa, TX
Ramsey, Michael ..... Houston, TX
Ramsey, Michael D. ..... San Diego, CA
Ramsey, Michael D. ..... Indianapolis, IN
Ramsey, Michael G. ..... San Diego, CA
Ramsey, Michael K. ..... Garden City, KS
Ramsey, Michael L. ..... Oroville, CA
Ramsey, Michael O. ..... Baltimore, MD
Ramsey, Michael R. ..... Beaumont, TX
Ramsey & Murray ..... Boston, MA
Ramsey & Murray, A Professional
Corporation ..... Houston, TX
Ramsey, Nancy A. ..... Los Angeles, CA
Ramsey, Natalie D. ..... Philadelphia, PA
Ramsey, Norris C. ..... Baltimore, MD
Ramsey, Norris C., P.A. ..... Baltimore, MD
Ramsey, Patricia K. ..... Santa Barbara, CA
Ramsey, Patricia Smith ..... Carmel, CA
Ramsey, Patrick A. ..... Los Angeles, CA
Ramsey, Patty S. ..... Nashville, TN
Ramsey, Paul R. ..... Sacramento, CA
Ramsey & Price ..... Los Angeles, CA
Ramsey, R. Scott, Jr. ..... Morgan City, LA
Ramsey, R. Scott, Jr., Ltd., A Professional Law
Corporation ..... Morgan City, LA
Ramsey, Ramsey & Long ..... Roxboro, NC
Ramsey, Randall ..... Phoenix, AZ
Ramsey, Raymond J. ..... Hayward, CA
Ramsey, Regina J. Eliot ..... Providence, RI
Ramsey, Reynard ..... Salem, OR
Ramsey, Richard D. ..... Winston-Salem, NC
Ramsey, Richard E. ..... Orlando, FL
Ramsey, Richard H., III ..... Dothan, AL
Ramsey, Richard H., IV ..... Dothan, AL
Ramsey, Robert ..... Trenton, NJ
Ramsey, Robert B., III ..... Pittsburgh, PA
Ramsey, Robert, Jr. ..... Los Angeles, CA
Ramsey, Robert K., Jr. ..... Terrell, TX
Ramsey, Robert L. ..... Houston, TX
Ramsey, Robert R. ..... Crossville, TN
Ramsey, Robinson C. ..... San Antonio, TX
Ramsey, Rodney A. ..... Shreveport, LA
Ramsey, Rodney C. ..... Oklahoma City, OK
Ramsey, Roger L. ..... Zephyr Cove, NV
Ramsey, Russell B. ..... New Orleans, LA
Ramsey, Russell J. ..... Houston, TX
Ramsey, Ruth Lauren ..... Peace Corps,
Office of the General Counsel, GV
Ramsey, Sam W., Jr. ..... Fayetteville, GA
Ramsey, Sarah H. ..... Syracuse, NY
Ramsey, Scott ..... Houston, TX
Ramsey & Sorey, P.A. ..... Vicksburg, MS
Ramsey, Stephen D. ..... Fairfield, CT
Ramsey, Stephen D. ..... Owego, NY
Ramsey, T. Lee, Jr. ..... Bellaire, TX
Ramsey, Ted ..... Towson, MD
Ramsey, Thomas A. ..... Long Beach, CA
Ramsey, Thomas A., A Professional
Corporation ..... Long Beach, CA
Ramsey, Thomas D. ..... Boston, MA
Ramsey, Thomas R., III ..... Knoxville, TN
Ramsey, Timothy J. ..... Atlanta, GA
Ramsey, Todd H. ..... Dallas, TX
Ramsey, Tonya Moffat ..... Dallas, TX
Ramsey, Virginia L. ..... East Hartford, CT
Ramsey, W. Forbes ..... McLean, VA
Ramsey, Walter T. ..... West Hempstead, NY
Ramsey, Wendy G. ..... Denver, CO
Ramsey, William B. ..... Wyncote, PA
Ramsey, William G. ..... Memphis, TN
Ramsey, William J. ..... Lawton, OK
Ramsey, William S. ..... Washington, DC
Ramsey, William T. ..... Nashville, TN
Ramsey, William W. ..... Vicksburg, MS
Ramsey, Zachary S. ..... Lexington, KY
Ramseyer, Craig A. ..... San Diego, CA
Ramseyer, James W. ..... Waukesha, WI
Ramseyer, John Allen ..... Los Angeles, CA
Ramseyer, Judith H. ..... Seattle, WA
Ramseyer & Kuhlman, A P.L.C.
San Diego, CA
Ramseyer, S. Randall ..... Abingdon, VA
Ramseyer, William L. ..... Los Angeles, CA
Ramseyer, William M. ..... Pasadena, CA
Ramsey-Kacena, Ellen R.
Cedar Rapids, IA
Ramsfelder, Jonathan
Whitehouse Station, NJ
Ramshaw, Paul D.
Equal Employment Opportunity
Commission,
Office of the General Counsel, GV
Ramshur Law Office, P.C. ..... Piedmont, MO
Ramshur, Robert M. ..... Piedmont, MO
Ramshur, Wilson R. ..... St. Francisville, LA
Ramsier, Floyd A. ..... Fort Wayne, IN
Ramsingh, Omyra M. ..... Washington, DC
Ramskill, George E. ..... Burlingame, KS
Ramson & Associates, LLC
Baltimore, MD
Burtonsville, MD
Laurel, MD
Silver Spring, MD
Ramson, Julie A. ..... Chicago, IL
Ramson, Romeo A. ..... Jamaica, NY
Ramson, Shanta ..... Burtonsville, MD
Ramspeck, George D., P.C. ..... Osprey, FL
Ramstack, Douglas A. ..... Wauwatosa, WI
Ramstad, Charles J. ..... Detroit Lakes, MN
Ramstad, Daylen D. ..... Fargo, ND
Ramstad, Dean D. ..... Santa Barbara, CA
Ramstad, James M. ..... Bloomington, MN
Ramstad, James O. ..... Detroit Lakes, MN
Ramstad, Rick L. ..... Sioux Falls, SD
Ramstad, Roger J. ..... Eagan, MN
Ramstead, John H. ..... Minneapolis, MN
Ramthun, Daniel P. ..... San Francisco, CA
Ramthun, Diane M. ..... Madison, WI
Ramthun, Phillip J. ..... Milwaukee, WI
Ramundo, Clifford J. ..... Paramus, NJ
Ramundo, Frank A. ..... Cincinnati, OH
Ramundo, Katherine E. Hargrove
New York, NY
Ramundo, Paolo A. ..... New York, NY
Ramunni, Steven A. ..... LaBelle, FL
Ramunno, Charles A. ..... Denver, CO
Ramunno, Christy A. ..... Parsippany, NJ
Ramunno, L. Vincent ..... Wilmington, DE
Ramunno, Lawrence A. ..... Wilmington, DE
Ramunno, Leo John ..... Wilmington, DE
Ramunno, Lorenzo ..... Ocala, FL
Ramunno, Lorenzo, P.A. ..... Ocala, FL
Ramunno, Lorraine Mary ..... Wilmington, DE
Ramunno, Louis A. ..... Short Hills, NJ
Ramunno & Ramunno, P.A.
Wilmington, DE
Ramynke, Mildred D. ..... Peever, SD
Ramzel, Andrew ..... Houston, TX
Ran, Ronald S. ..... Cincinnati, OH
Rana, H. Singh ..... Warren, NJ
Rana, Kulpreet S. ..... Palo Alto, CA
Rana, Lisa R. ..... Brooklyn, NY
Rana, Najma Q. ..... New York, NY
Ranadive, Rahul P. ..... Miami, FL
Ranaghan, William L. ..... Pompano Beach, FL
Ranaghan, William L., Jr. ..... Cincinnati, OH
Ranahan, Michael D. ..... Walnut Creek, CA
Ranahan, Terrence D. ..... Walnut Creek, CA
Ranalli, Daniel J. ..... Troy, NY
Ranalli, George M. ..... Las Vegas, NV
Ranalli, Kathleen M. ..... Philadelphia, PA
Ranalli, Laura C. ..... Dallas, TX
Ranalli, Michael D. ..... Scarsdale, NY
Ranalli, Regina ..... Springdale, AR
Ranallo, Edmund G. ..... Princeton, NJ
Ranallo, Michael J. ..... Chicago, IL
Ranallo, Robert A. ..... Mayfield Village, OH
Ranando, Paul S. ..... Cheshire, CT
Ranard, William W. ..... Rockford, IL
Ranatza, Colette C. ..... Metairie, LA
Ranby, John W. ..... Phoenix, AZ
Rancan, Robert ..... Cresskill, NJ
Rancano, Juan C. ..... Modesto, CA
Rance, Brian D. ..... New York, NY
Rance, Pritchett, Brantner, Robison & Keller
Co., L.P.A. ..... Columbus, OH
Rance, William E. ..... Columbus, OH
Ranche, Valerie J. ..... Martinez, CA
Ranchod, Kaushik ..... San Francisco, CA
Rancilio, Susan A. ..... Sterling Heights, MI
Ranck, Christopher J. ..... Orlando, FL
Ranck, Jeffrey L. ..... Redmond, WA
Ranck, Matthew Allan ..... Baltimore, MD
Ranck, Michael H. ..... Lancaster, PA
Ranck and Ranck ..... Lancaster, PA
Ranck, Robert B. ..... Jackson, WY
Ranck, Samuel C. ..... Sunbury, PA
Ranck, Schwartz & Day, LLC
Jackson, WY
Rancke, Robert K. ..... Springfield, MA
Rancourt, Charles G. ..... Salem, MA
Rancourt, Craig J. ..... Biddeford, ME
Rancourt, Robert G. ..... Lindstrom, MN
Rand, Algeier, Tosti & Woodruff, A
Professional Corporation
Morristown, NJ
Newark, NJ
Rand, Anthony E. ..... Fayetteville, NC
Rand, Barbara J. ..... Little Rock, AR
Rand, Charles M. ..... Altamonte Springs, FL
Rand, Charles M. ..... Cherry Hill, NJ
Rand, Charles S. ..... Rockville, MD
Rand, Connie J. ..... San Diego, CA
Rand, David B. ..... Morristown, NJ
Rand, David B. ..... McLean, VA
Rand, David E. ..... Los Angeles, CA
Rand, David S. ..... San Francisco, CA
Rand, Deborah E. ..... New York, NY
Rand, Debra Sue ..... Harrisburg, PA
Rand, Douglas H., II ..... Pasadena, CA
Rand, E. Cooke ..... New York, NY
Rand, Ezor & Olens, P.C. ..... Atlanta, GA
Rand, Frederick H. ..... San Diego, CA
Rand, Gary ..... Van Nuys, CA
Rand, Gary, & Suzanne E. Rand-Lewis,
Professional Law Corporations
Van Nuys, CA
Rand, George A. ..... Andover, MA
Rand, Gregory Jonathan ..... Hollywood, FL
Rand, Gurley, Hanahan & Koerner
Painesville, OH
Rand, Harry ..... Atlanta, GA
Rand, Harry I. ..... New York, NY
Rand, Heidi ..... Oakland, CA
Rand, Howard ..... Bellmore, NY
Rand, Jacob ..... Long Branch, NJ
Rand, Jay S. ..... New York, NY
Rand, John C. ..... Alexandria, VA
Rand, John S. ..... White Plains, NY
Rand, Jon S. ..... New York, NY
Rand, Joseph L. ..... Lake Forest, IL
Rand, Karl A. ..... San Diego, CA
Rand, Kathryn R. L. ..... Milwaukee, WI
Rand, Kenan S., Jr. ..... New Orleans, LA
Rand, Lee W., Mr. ..... New Orleans, LA
Rand, Lindsay Preston ..... Braintree, MA
Rand, Louis V., II ..... Metairie, LA
Rand, Marjorie ..... Philadelphia, PA
Rand, Martin G. ..... Dover, NJ
Rand, Michael J. ..... Encino, CA
Rand, Pamela J. ..... San Diego, CA
Rand, Patrick M. ..... Canton, MS
Jackson, MS
Rand, Richard M. ..... Honolulu, HI
Rand, Robert C. ..... Palo Alto, CA
Rand Rosenzweig Smith Radley Gordon &
Burstein LLP ..... New York, NY
Rand, S. Richard ..... Department of State,
Foreign Service Officers (Overseas), GV
Rand, Samuel G. ..... Jacksonville, FL
Rand, Scott C. ..... Omaha, NE
Rand, Scott M. ..... San Diego, CA
Rand, Sheldon M ..... New York, NY
Rand, Steven R. ..... New York, NY
Rand, Steven S. ..... New York, NY
Rand, Steven W. ..... Westbrook, ME
Rand, Susan S. ..... Roslyn, NY
Rand, Theodora M. ..... Chicago, IL
Rand, Thomas S., Jr. ..... Rockville, MD
Rand, Tom Slade, Jr. ..... Wilson, NC
Rand, Victoria S. ..... Woodbury, NJ
Rand, Walter ..... Greensboro, NC
Rand, William ..... New York, NY
Rand, William C. ..... New York, NY
Rand, William R. ..... Wilson, NC
Randa, Rudolph T. ..... Milwaukee, WI
Randaccio, Brad F. ..... Buffalo, NY
Williamsville, NY
Randall, Albert B. ..... Washington, DC
Randall, Albert B., Jr. ..... Baltimore, MD
Randall, Alexander A. ..... Boston, MA
Randall, Ann Coolidge ..... Schenectady, NY
Randall, Anne Loridas
Bloomfield Hills, MI
Randall, Anthony H. ..... Spartanburg, SC
Randall, Anthony T. ..... Haslett, MI

Randall, B. Wayne ... Tuscaloosa, AL
Randall, Benjamin C. ... Minneapolis, MN
Randall, Benjamin J. ... Chicago, IL
Randall, Blake & Cox, P.A. ... Lewiston, ID
Moscow, ID
Clarkston, WA
Randall, Boxx & Associates, P.C.
Monett, MO
Randall, Boyd ... Provo, UT
Randall, Bradley N. ... Beaumont, TX
Randall, Brendan W. ... Minneapolis, MN
Randall, Bret F. ... Salt Lake City, UT
Randall, Brian C. ... Milwaukee, WI
Randall, Bruce ... Phoenix, AZ
Randall, Carey A. ... Madison, MS
Randall, Charles B. ... Wauwatosa, WI
Randall, Charles P. ... Boca Raton, FL
Randall, Charles T. ... Albany, NY
Randall, Chas. H., Jr. ... Columbia, SC
Randall, Christopher ... Wichita, KS
Randall, Clarke L. ... Oklahoma City, OK
Randall, Clay R. ... Spokane, WA
Randall, Corey D. ... Las Vegas, NV
Randall, Craig Z. ... Lafayette, CA
Randall, Cynthia L. ... Philadelphia, PA
Randall & Danskin, P.S. ... Spokane, WA
Randall, David ... Boston, MA
Randall, David A. ... Los Angeles, CA
Randall, David V. ... Philadelphia, PA
Randall, Deborah A. ... Washington, DC
Randall, Deborah H. ... Anchorage, AK
Randall, Dehn & Goodrich ... Anoka, MN
Randall, Denise McCarthy ... Albany, NY
Randall, Donald A. ... Washington, DC
Randall, Donald A., Law Offices of
Washington, DC
Randall, Donn A. ... Boston, MA
Randall, Douglas A. ... Quincy, MA
Randall, Elizabeth E. ... East Rutherford, NJ
Randall, Ellis R. ... Vallejo, CA
Randall, Evan L. ... Kansas City, MO
Randall, Fred ... Livingston, NJ
Randall, Fred, P.A. ... Livingston, NJ
Randall, Gail A. ... Department of Justice, Drug Enforcement Administration, GV
Randall & Galbraith, P.C. ... Indianapolis, IN
Randall, Gary B. ... Department of Justice, Environment and Natural Resources Division, GV
Randall, Gary C. ... Spokane, WA
Randall, Gary E. ... Woodinville, WA
Randall, Geoffrey ... Miami, FL
Randall, George E. ... Frederick, MD
Randall, Gerald J. ... Glastonbury, CT
Randall, Gerald M. ... Anoka, MN
Randall, Geraldine M. ... San Anselmo, CA
Randall, Glen Paul ... Lowell, MA
Randall, Glenn ... Ambler, PA
Randall, Glenn ... Philadelphia, PA
Randall, Harry, Jr. ... Westwood, NJ
Randall, Harvey ... Schenectady, NY
Randall, Jack ... St. Louis, MO
Randall, James D. ... Houston, TX
Randall, James D., Jr. ... Washington, DC
Randall, James E. ... Albuquerque, NM
Randall, James H. ... Las Vegas, NV
Randall, James J. ... Monett, MO
Randall, Jane M. ... Rock Hill, SC
Randall, Jane M., P.A., The Law Offices of
Rock Hill, SC
Randall, Jane S. ... Toledo, OH
Randall, Jeffrey G. ... Palo Alto, CA
Randall, Jeffrey M. ... Chicago, IL
Glenview, IL
Randall, Jerome E. ... Milwaukee, WI
Randall, Jervis & Hill ... Durham, NC
Randall, Jesse T. ... Mound City, KS
Randall, John C. ... Durham, NC
Randall, John J., III ... Locust Valley, NY
Randall, John J., IV ... Locust Valley, NY
Randall, John S. ... Mandeville, LA
Randall, Jon H. ... Dallas, TX
Randall, Josephine H. ... Dallas, TX
Randall, Karen ... Universal City, CA
Randall, Karen B. ... Hartford, CT
Randall, Karen Painter ... Roseland, NJ
Randall, Karl W. ... Waterford, MI
Randall, Katherine ... Lexington, KY
Randall, Kenneth D. ... Dixon, CA
Randall, Kenneth Dale ... Midland, MI
Randall, Kerry L. ... Lakewood, OH
Randall, Kevin C. ... Cincinnati, OH
Randall, Kim Alison ... Boston, MA
Randall, Larry E. ... Fort Smith, AR
Randall, Laura M. ... San Francisco, CA
Randall, Leigh J. ... New York, NY
Randall, Leslie C. ... Houston, TX
Randall, Lisa Harriman ... St. Paul, MN
Randall, Lucinda D. ... Dayton, OH
Randall, Lynn B. ... Birmingham, AL
Randall, Mark E. ... Blue River, WI
Randall, Mark H. ... Longwood, FL
Randall, Mark L. ... Portland, ME
Randall, Mark S. ... Washington, DC
Randall, Martin E. ... Garden City, NY
New York, NY
Randall, Mary E. ... Canton, OH
Randall, Meredith ... Koror, TT
Randall, Michael ... Princeton, NJ
Randall, Michael R. ... Concord, NH
Randall, Mitchell S. ... Walnut Creek, CA
Randall, Neal S. ... Idaho Falls, ID
Randall, Pat ... San Diego, CA
Randall, Patricia ... Salem, NH
Randall, Paula Vincich ... Waukegan, IL
Randall, Preston ... Austin, TX
Randall, R. Nathan ... Chicago, IL
Randall, R. A. (Jim) ... St. Paul, MN
Randall, Ralph E. ... Scottsburg, IN
Randall, Randall & Stevens, LLP
Westwood, NJ
Randall, Raymond L. ... Colorado Springs, CO
Randall, Richard ... Phoenix, AZ
Randall, Richard A. ... Ludington, MI
Randall, Richard D. ... Wichita, KS
Randall, Richard L. ... Indianapolis, IN
Randall, Richard P. ... Pasadena, CA
Randall, Robert D. ... Dearborn Heights, MI
Randall, Robert G. ... Rochester, NY
Randall, Robert G., Jr. ... Albany, NY
Randall, Robert K. ... Minneapolis, MN
Randall, Robert N. ... Mooresville, NC
Randall, Robert W. ... Anchorage, AK
Randall, Robert W. ... Houston, TX
Randall, Robt. L. ... San Jose, CA
Randall, Roger D. ... Bakersfield, CA
Randall, Roger H. ... Boston, MA
Randall, Ross S. ... Waterloo, IA
Randall, Russell S. ... Lewiston, ID
Randall, Ryan A. ... Dallas, TX
Randall, Ryan M. ... Albuquerque, NM
Randall, S. Brewster, II ... Columbus, OH
Randall, Samuel B. ... Columbus, OH
Randall, Shelley ... Lynn, MA
Randall, Stephen Patrick ... San Francisco, CA
Randall, Steven B. ... Chicago, IL
Randall, T. Keith ... Alliance, OH
Randall, Ted L. ... Kansas City, MO
Randall, Thomas William ... Westwood, NJ
Randall, Timothy J. ... Milwaukee, WI
Randall, Timothy L. ... Irvine, CA
Randall, Toni Michelle ... Richmond, VA
Randall, Toree S. ... Lansing, MI
Randall, Tracey Nicole ... Richmond, VA
Randall, Vanessa D ... Lafayette, LA
Randall, Vernellia R. ... Dayton, OH
Randall, Walter R., Jr. ... Kansas City, MO
Randall, Warren S. ... Hartford, CT
Randall, William B. ... St. Paul, MN
Randall, William C. ... Macon, GA
Randall, William H. ... Santa Ana, CA
Randall, William I. ... Framingham, MA
Randall, William O. ... Willsboro, NY
Randall, Wm. L. ... Milwaukee, WI
Randau, Charles E. ... Southfield, MI
Randazzo, Anthony J., Jr. ... Norwood, MA
Randazzo, Daniel, Law Office of
Birmingham, MI
Randazzo, Frank C. ... White Plains, NY
Randazzo, Gaspare Joseph
East Meadow, NY
Randazzo & Giffords ... New Hyde Park, NY
Randazzo, James A. ... White Plains, NY
Randazzo, Jeannie Morris
New Orleans, LA
Randazzo, Joseph L. ... Buffalo, NY
Randazzo, Joyce D. ... New Hyde Park, NY
Randazzo, Louis A.
Securities and Exchange Commission, Division of Market Regulation, GV
Randazzo, Mary E. ... Cleveland, OH
Randazzo, Matthew J., III
New Orleans, LA
Randazzo, Michele E. ... Boston, MA
Randazzo, Monica M. ... Los Angeles, CA
Randazzo, Ralph Michael ... Huntington, NY
Randazzo, Rose M. ... Philadelphia, PA
Randazzo, Samuel C. ... Columbus, OH
Randazzo, Sebastian ... New Hyde Park, NY
Randazzo, Sheryl L. ... Melville, NY
Randazzo, Susanna C. ... Philadelphia, PA
Randazzo, Thomas ... Detroit, MI
Randazzo, Thomas M. ... Cleveland, OH
Randel, James A. ... Westport, CT
Randel, Rick ... San Francisco, CA
Randell, Bradley F. ... Brick, NJ
Randell, Crandon H. ... Anchorage, AK
Randell, David F. ... Chicago, IL
Randell, David F. ... Austin, TX
Randell, Howard B. ... Chicago, IL
Randell, Linda L. ... New Haven, CT
Randell, Robert J. ... New York, NY
Randell, Terrence M. ... New York, NY
Randels, Ed L. ... Wichita, KS
Randels, Stephen M. ... Seattle, WA
Randerson, Roelif J. ... San Diego, CA
Randich, Robert A. ... West Hartford, CT
Randick & O'Dea ... Oakland, CA
Randick, Robert A., Jr. ... Oakland, CA
Randisi, Martin A. ... Smithtown, NY
Randle, Carver A. ... Indianola, MS
Randle, Craig A. ... Springfield, IL
Randle, David S. ... Boston, MA
Randle, Deamer, Zarr & Lee, A Professional Corporation ... Salt Lake City, UT
Randle, Donald C. ... La Mirada, CA
Randle, Ellen M. ... Springfield, MA
Randle, J. Grady ... Houston, TX
Randle, Janet R. ... Dallas, TX
Randle, Joe L. ... Dallas, TX
Randle, Ned W. ... Belleville, IL
St. Louis, MO
Randle, Raymond G., Jr. ... Houston, TX
Randle, Richard L. ... Jacksonville, FL
Randle, Robert ... Rensselaer, IN
Randle, Rodger A. ... Tulsa, OK
Randle, Russell V. ... Washington, DC
Randle, S.A. & Associates, P.C.
Houston, TX
Randle, Sarnie A., Jr. ... Houston, TX
Randle, Stephen R. ... Salt Lake City, UT
Randle, William M. ... Cleveland, OH
Randleman, R. Kirk ... Elkin, NC
Randleman, Richard N. ... Yadkinville, NC
Randleman, Richard N., P.A.
Yadkinville, NC
Randleman, Robert S. ... Racine, WI
Randles, Amy E. ... St. Louis, MO
Randles, Anthony V. ... San Clemente, CA
Randles, Billy R. ... Kansas City, MO
Randles, Carl A., Jr. ... Kalamazoo, MI
Randles, Don ... Las Vegas, NV
Randles, Guy A. ... Portland, OR
Randles, Michael D. ... Shelbyville, TN
Randles, Rebecca M. ... Kansas City, MO
Randles, Steven G. ... Zanesville, OH
Randlett, Jennifer Kathleen
San Francisco, CA
Randlett, Mark A. ... Lewiston, ME
Rand-Lewis, Suzanne E. ... Van Nuys, CA
Rando & Associates, P.C. ... Freehold, NJ
Levittown, NY
New York, NY
Rando, David A. ... Hopedale, MA
Rando, Robert J. ... Levittown, NY
New York, NY
Rando, Steven J. ... New Orleans, LA
Randol, Suzanne M. ... Sacramento, CA
Randol, Ward, Jr. ... Bloomfield Hills, MI
Randol, Willard C. ... Independence, MO
Randol, William L., Jr. ... Miami, FL
Randolph, A. Raymond
United States Court Of Appeals District Of Columbia Circuit, GV
Randolph, Adrian L. ... Sacramento, CA
Randolph, Alfred M., Jr.
Virginia Beach, VA
Randolph, Anne ... Honolulu, HI
Randolph, Boyd, Cherry and Vaughan
Chesterfield, VA
Richmond, VA
Randolph, Burleigh A. ... La Crosse, WI
Randolph, C. Carl, Jr. ... New York, NY
Randolph, Carole ... Chicago, IL
Randolph, Christopher F. ... Oyster Bay, NY
Randolph, Curtis ... Fort Pierce, FL
Randolph, D. Edward, Jr. ... Dallas, TX
Randolph, Daniel P. ... Cincinnati, OH
Randolph, David D. ... San Diego, CA
Randolph, Deborah A. ... Minneapolis, MN
Randolph, Deborah S. ... San Francisco, CA
Randolph, Denise L. ... Charlotte, NC
Randolph, Dolores A. ... Boston, MA
Randolph, Donald C. ... Santa Monica, CA
Randolph & Fischer ... Winston-Salem, NC
Randolph, George B., III ... Paoli, PA
Randolph, George Frederick ... Phoenix, AZ
Randolph, Grady L. ... Atlanta, GA
Randolph, James C. ... Lone Tree, CO
Randolph, James D.K.F. ... Salisbury, NC
Randolph, Jane Ellen ... Los Angeles, CA
Randolph, Jeffrey Bruce ... Montvale, NJ
Randolph, Jeremy R. ... Chehalis, WA
Randolph, Jerome C. ... Cincinnati, OH
Randolph, John C. ... West Palm Beach, FL
Randolph, John Clayton ... Little Rock, AR
Randolph, John L., Jr. ... Tulsa, OK
Randolph, John M. ... Phoenix, AZ
Randolph, John M., III ... Philadelphia, PA
Randolph, John N. ... Birmingham, AL
Randolph, John S., Jr. ... Radnor, PA
Randolph, John W., Jr.
West Palm Beach, FL
Randolph, Kenneth E. ... Houston, TX
Randolph, Kevin K. ... Riverside, CA
Randolph & Larsen, P.A. ... Stuart, FL
Randolph, LeRoy, Jr. ... Kansas City, KS
Randolph, Leslie J. ... Salt Lake City, UT
Randolph, Liane M. ... San Leandro, CA
Randolph, Lloyd H. ... Department of Justice, Civil Division, GV
Randolph, Lonnie M. ... East Chicago, IN
Randolph, Marc A. ... Richmond, VA
Randolph, Mark A. ... San Antonio, TX
Randolph, Mark E. ... Winston-Salem, NC
Randolph, Michael D. ... Fort Myers, FL
Randolph, Michael K. ... Hattiesburg, MS
Randolph, Patricia J. ... Bakersfield, CA
Randolph, Patrick A., Jr.
Kansas City, MO
Randolph, Peter J. ... Cincinnati, OH
Randolph, R. Jerry, Jr. ... Stuart, FL
Randolph, R. Layne ... Denver, CO
Randolph, Rebekah L.
Winston-Salem, NC
Randolph, Richard G. ... San Mateo, CA
Randolph, Robert B. ... St. Joseph, MO
Randolph, Robert C. ... Seattle, WA
Randolph, Robert D. ... Pittsburgh, PA
Randolph, Robert D., Jr. ... Chicago, IL
Randolph, Robert M. ... Fort Worth, TX
Randolph, Robert P. ... Austin, TX
Randolph, Robert R. ... Houston, TX
Randolph, Roosevelt ... Tallahassee, FL
Randolph, Sheila R. ... Fort Worth, TX
Randolph, Sheila S. ... Houston, TX
Randolph, Sheridan C. ... Cleveland, TN
Randolph, Suzanne Edgar
Pacific Palisades, CA
Randolph, Thomas H., Jr. ... Detroit, MI
Randolph, Thomas P. ... Dayton, OH
Randolph, Timothy G. ... Sparks, NV
Randolph, William
Department of Defense, GV
Randolph, William B. ... New York, NY
Randolph, William D. ... Coronado, CA
Randolph, William K. ... Dyersburg, TN
Randolph, William L. ... Macomb, IL
Randon, Rene L. ... Metairie, LA
Randour, Paul A. (IBA) ... New York, NY
Randow, Harry F. ... Alexandria, LA
Randow, Herman F. ... Dallas, TX
Rands, Dale G. ... Bloomfield Hills, MI
Rands, Douglas R. ... Reno, NV
Rands, Monica L. ... Redwood City, CA
Rands, South & Gardner ... Las Vegas, NV
Reno, NV
Rands, William J. ... Cincinnati, OH
Randt, Thomas P. ... Houston, TX
Rane, Andrew L. ... Chicago, IL
Rane, James W. ... Abbeville, AL
Rane, Tracy B. ... Los Angeles, CA
Ranellucci, Raymond M. ... Albany, NY
Ranen, Robert D. ... Dallas, TX
Ranew, Thomas C., Jr. ... Ocala, FL
Raney, Cara Jenkins ... Edmond, OK
Raney, Carla Hope ... Department of Justice, Criminal Division, GV
Raney, D. Raymond ... Glen Carbon, IL
Raney, Daryl G. ... Fayetteville, AR
Raney, Donald P. ... Searcy, AR
Raney, Greta F. ... San Bernardino, CA
Raney, Hollaman M. ... Memphis, TN
Raney, Jamie Forrest ... Santa Barbara, CA
Raney, Jeffrey L. ... Atlanta, GA
Raney, Jennifer J. ... Eugene, OR
Raney, Jonathan M. ... Portland, OR
Raney, Julian H., Jr. ... Roanoke, VA
Raney, Julie ... Sacramento, CA
Raney, Kenneth C., Jr. ... Dallas, TX
Raney, Kenneth E. ... Tyler, TX
Raney, Linn J. ... Cleveland, OH
Raney, Milbrey E. ... Austin, TX
Raney, Morris H. ... El Paso, TX
Raney, Nancy E. ... Newport Beach, CA
Raney, Paul A. ... Portland, OR
Raney, Penny L. ... Dallas, TX
Raney, Rhonda Gillespie
Daytona Beach, FL
Raney, Ronald E. ... Shreveport, LA
Raney, Roy E. ... Largo, FL
Raney, Steve E. ... El Paso, TX
Raney, Steve T. ... Nashville, TN
Raney, Thomas M. ... Lawrence, KS
Raney, William A., Jr. ... Wilmington, NC
Raney, William E. ... Kansas City, MO
Ranft, Mark L. ... Ukiah, CA
Ranftl, James R. ... Akron, OH
Rang, Kevin A. ... Southfield, MI
Rang, Paul D. ... Orlando, FL
Rangachar, Sumana S. ... Bronx, NY
Rangaswami, Viji ... Washington, DC
Range, James A. ... New Philadelphia, OH
Range, Jane A. ... Gainesville, GA
Range, Jason T. ... Huntington Woods, MI
Range, John Jay ... Washington, DC
Range, Ronald S., Jr. ... Johnson City, TN
Rangel, Charles B. ... New York, NY
Rangel, Diego R. ... Chicago, IL
Rangel, Irma ... Kingsville, TX
Rangel, Jennifer A. ... Dallas, TX
Rangel, Jennifer Lynn ... Austin, TX
Rangel, Joann M.O. ... Lodi, CA
Rangel, Jorge C. ... Corpus Christi, TX
Rangel, Jorge C., P.C., The Law Offices of
Corpus Christi, TX
Rangel, Rodrigo H. ... Longmont, CO
Rangel, Yvonne ... Houston, TX
Ranger Copeland & Willcox, P.A.
Brunswick, ME
Ranger, Edward M. ... Scottsdale, AZ
Ranger, Jennifer J. ... Northbrook, IL
Ranger, Orville T. ... Brunswick, ME
Ranger, Patti Woo ... San Diego, CA
Ranger, Richard J. ... Irvine, CA
Ranges, Dawn E. ... Bedford, OH
Ranghiasci, Eugene J. ... San Francisco, CA
Rangos, Jill E. ... Allison Park, PA
Ranheim, David A. ... Minneapolis, MN
Ranich, David K. ... East Chicago, IN
Merrillville, IN
Ranier, Drew, (Professional Law Corporation) ... Cameron, LA
Lake Charles, LA
Ranier, Edward M. ... Baltimore, MD
Ranier, Rosemary Motsay ... Timonium, MD
Ranier, Sarah R. ... New Orleans, LA
Raniere, Daniel A. ... St. Louis, MO
Raniere, William S. ... Chicago, IL
Ranieri, Alfred J. ... Bronx, NY
Ranieri, Anthony M. ... New York, NY
Ranieri, Caterina A. ... Syracuse, NY
Ranieri, Christopher M. ... Coral Springs, FL
Ranieri, David B. ... Columbus, GA
Ranieri, Gregory C. ... Holmdel, NJ
Ranieri, Joseph F. ... Parsippany, NJ
Ranieri, L. Eric ... Baltimore, MD
Ranieri, Margaret Cove ... Franklin, MA
Ranieri, Patricia A. ... Huntingdon Valley, PA
Ranieri, Richard S. ... Voorhees, NJ
Ranieri, Salvatore A. ... Garden City, NY
Ranieri, William F. ... New York, NY
Raniero, Andrew T. ... Buffalo, NY
Ranill, William Lee ... Ketchum, ID
Raniolo, Gary J. ... Tarrytown, NY
Ranis, Paul B. ... Fort Lauderdale, FL
Raniszeski, Lawrence F.
Bloomfield Hills, MI
Ranitz, John F. M., Jr. ... Savannah, GA
Ranitz, Mahoney, Coolidge & Mahoney, P.C.
Savannah, GA
Rank, Daryl G. ... Snoqualmie, WA
Rank, Deborah E. ... Houston, TX
Rank, Jerry D. ... Kansas City, MO
Rank, Jody S., (Mr.) ... Riverside, CA
Rank, John J. ... Paradise, CA
Rank, Kevin Jay ... Salem, OR
Rank, Kyle K. ... Lawrence, KS
Rank, Paula Winchester ... Fairfax, VA
Rank, Peter C. ... Los Angeles, CA
Rank, W. Barry, (P.C.) ... Princeton, NJ
Ranke, John M. ... Bloomfield Hills, MI

Rapoport, Bernard R. ...New York, NY
Rapoport, Christa Speight
Parsippany, NJ
Rapoport, David E. ...Chicago, IL
Rosemont, IL
Rapoport, David M. ...Philadelphia, PA
Rapoport, Ellen ...New York, NY
Rapoport, Erik ...San Francisco, CA
Rapoport, Frank M. ...Washington, DC
Philadelphia, PA
Rapoport, Gregg A. ...Los Angeles, CA
Rapoport, Jonathan I. ...Stamford, CT
Rapoport, Kenneth J. ...Cleveland, OH
Rapoport Law Offices, P.C. ...Chicago, IL
Rosemont, IL
Rapoport, Leonard ...Allentown, PA
Rapoport, Leonard A. ...Edina, MN
Rapoport, Lisa M. ...New York, NY
Rapoport, Lissa L. ...San Francisco, CA
Rapoport, Michelle Bardavid ...Atlanta, GA
Rapoport, Nancy B. ...Columbus, OH
Rapoport, Norman Mark ...Columbia, SC
Rapoport, Richard N. ...San Francisco, CA
Rapoport, Robert J. ...Syosset, NY
Rapoport, Russell H. ...Encino, CA
Rapoport, Sandra E. ...New York, NY
Rapoport, Spitz, Friedland & Courtney
Cleveland, OH
Rapoport, Steven C. ...Houston, TX
Rapoport, William R. ...San Mateo, CA
Rapore, Jonathan David ...Los Angeles, CA
Raposa, John F. ...Irving, TX
Raposo, Cynthia A. ...Washington, DC
Rapoza, Arthur H. ...East Falmouth, MA
Rapoza, Bridget K. ...Omaha, NE
Rapoza, Irene F. ...San Francisco, CA
Rapoza, Philip ...Boston, MA
Rapp, Bradley W. ...El Campo, TX
Rapp, Britanya E.
Corporation for National and Community Service, Office of the General Counsel, GV
Rapp, Christopher T. ...Phoenix, AZ
Rapp, David M. ...Wichita, KS
Rapp, David M. ...Norwell, MA
Rapp, Dieter K., & Associates
Mission Viejo, CA
Rapp, Donald J. ...Dayton, OH
Rapp, Edward C. ...Phoenix, AZ
Rapp, Erich P. ...Baton Rouge, LA
Rapp, F. Brian ...Santa Barbara, CA
Rapp, F. C. ...Louisville, KY
Rapp, Ferd J. ...Santa Barbara, CA
Rapp, Francis C., Jr. ...Pittsburgh, PA
Rapp, Geo. E. ...Madison, WI
Rapp, Gregory J. ...Grand Rapids, MI
Rapp, James A. ...Quincy, IL
Rapp, James S. ...Kenton, OH
Rapp, John ...Honolulu, HI
Rapp, John B. ...Kalamazoo, MI
Rapp, John P. ...Philadelphia, PA
Rapp, John W., Jr. ...Miami, FL
Rapp, John W., Jr. ...Lanark, IL
Rapp, Kathryn M. ...Department of Justice, Civil Rights Division, GV
Rapp, Keith ...Tulsa, OK
Rapp, Kenneth A. ...Bethlehem, PA
Harrisburg, PA
Rapp, Kiepen & Harman ...Pleasanton, CA
Rapp, Kristine A. ...Deerfield, IL
Rapp, Larry G. ...Wichita, KS
Rapp, Mark ...Greeley, CO
Rapp, Michael T. ...Alexandria, VA
Rapp, Patricia Palm ...Woodland Hills, CA
Rapp, Patricia Vitale ...Germantown, MD
Rapp, Paul C. ...Albany, NY
Rapp, Paul H. ...Silver Spring, MD
Rapp, Polly S. ...Phoenix, AZ
Rapp, Randall S. ...Chicago, IL
Rapp, Richard A., Jr. ...Hicksville, NY
Rapp, Robert A., Jr. ...San Antonio, TX
Rapp, Robert C. ...Marco Island, FL
Rapp, Robert D. ...Houston, TX
Rapp, Robert N. ...Cleveland, OH
Rapp, Roland G. ...Pleasanton, CA
Rapp, Ronald J. ...Rosemont, IL
Rapp, S. Todd ...Apple Valley, MN
Rapp, S. Todd, P.A. ...Apple Valley, MN
Rapp, Stephen A. ...West Palm Beach, FL
Rapp, Stephen J. ...Cedar Rapids, IA
Rapp, Steven M. ...Somers, NY
Rapp, Stuart W. ...Centerville, MA
Rapp, Susan H. ...Santa Rosa, CA
Rapp, Susan L. ...San Diego, CA
Rapp, Susan T. ...Detroit, MI
Rapp, Teresa Cohen ...Batavia, OH
Rapp, Thomas ...Philadelphia, PA
Rapp, Vincent G. ...Belleville, IL
Rapp, Virginia L. ...Torrance, CA
Rapp, W. C. ...Cincinnati, OH
Rapp, William D. ...Houston, TX
Rapp, William Joseph ...Cincinnati, OH
Rappa, Michael J. ...Merrillville, IN
Rappa, Michael J. ...Hackensack, NJ
Rappa, Nancy M.
Securities and Exchange Commission, Division of Investment Management, GV
Rappa, Salvatore ...New York, NY
Rappa, Thomas A., Jr. ...Woodsville, NH
Rappaport, Abe ...Fair Lawn, NJ
Rappaport, Abraham ...Boca Raton, FL
Rappaport, Andrew ...Glendale, CA
Rappaport, B. Howard ...Mamaroneck, NY
Rappaport, Bernard I. ...Miami, FL
Rappaport, Bret A. ...Chicago, IL
Rappaport, Brian C. ...New York, NY
Rappaport, Charles J. ...Melville, NY
Rappaport, Charles O. ...New York, NY
Rappaport, David M. ...Miami Lakes, FL
Rappaport, David R. ...New York, NY
Rappaport, Douglas A. ...New York, NY
Rappaport, Douglas Lee ...San Francisco, CA
Rappaport, Earle S. ...Chicago, IL
Rappaport, Edward ...Gloversville, NY
Rappaport, Edward J. ...Alpharetta, GA
Rappaport, Estee ...Boston, MA
Rappaport, Freeman & Pinta ...Boston, MA
Rappaport, Gail ...Santa Barbara, CA
Rappaport, Gary S. ...New York, NY
Rappaport, Howard S. ...New York, NY
Rappaport, Irving S. ...Palo Alto, CA
Rappaport, Jack ...Sunrise, FL
Rappaport, James W. ...Boston, MA
Rappaport, Jay ...Vienna, VA
Rappaport, Jay A. ...New York, NY
Rappaport, Jeffrey ...Ridgefield, NJ
Rappaport, Jennifer R. ...New York, NY
Rappaport, Jerome L. ...Boston, MA
Rappaport, Jerry ...Los Angeles, CA
Rappaport, Jonathan R. ...Seattle, WA
Rappaport, Jordan L. ...Boca Raton, FL
Rappaport, Kenneth S. ...Boca Raton, FL
Rappaport, Kenneth S., P.A.
Boca Raton, FL
Boynton Beach, FL
Coral Springs, FL
Rappaport, Lary A. ...Los Angeles, CA
Rappaport, Laurence J. ...Parsippany, NJ
Rappaport, Lester H. ...Rochester, NY
Rappaport, Linda E. ...New York, NY
Rappaport, Louis M. ...Philadelphia, PA
Rappaport, Mark L. ...Binghamton, NY
Rappaport, Meyer & Wolberg ...Chicago, IL
Rappaport, Michael D. ...Los Angeles, CA
Rappaport, Michael K. ...New York, NY
Rappaport, Nancy Shane
Philadelphia, PA
Rappaport, Nolan W. ...Department of Justice, Executive Office for Immigration Review, GV
Rappaport, Paul H. ...Ellicott City, MD
Rappaport, Paul M. ...Auburn Hills, MI
Rappaport & Rappaport ...Binghamton, NY
Rappaport, Richard A.
Salt Lake City, UT
Rappaport, Richard I. ...Portland, OR
Rappaport, Richard J. ...Chicago, IL
Rappaport, Richard V. ...Uniondale, NY
Rappaport, Richard Warren ...Miami, FL
Rappaport, Ronald H. ...Edgartown, MA
Rappaport, Samuel ...Philadelphia, PA
Rappaport, Sandra L. ...San Francisco, CA
Rappaport & Shaffer ...Philadelphia, PA
Rappaport, Sheila A. ...Denver, CO
Rappaport, Sheldon G. ...Forest Hills, NY
Rappaport, Stacey J. ...New York, NY
Rappaport, Stacey P. ...Florham Park, NJ
Rappaport, Steven ...Great Neck, NY
Rappaport, Steven F.
National Labor Relations Board, Office of Board Members, GV
Rappaport, Steven J. ...Boston, MA
Rappaport, Steven J. ...New York, NY
Rappaport, Stuart Jay ...New York, NY
Rappaport, Thomas J. ...Boston, MA
Rappaport, Victoria E. ...New Paltz, NY
Rappaport, William J. ...Flushing, NY
Rappard, Andres R. ...Las Vegas, NV
Rappard & Denue ...Las Vegas, NV
Rappard, Gary D. ...Lenexa, KS
Rappe, Curtis B. ...Los Angeles, CA
Rappe, David C. ...Coventry, CT
Rappe, Janet B. ...Suffern, NY
Rappel, Craig M. ...Melbourne, FL
Vero Beach, FL
Rappel, Marc W. ...Los Angeles, CA
Rappel, Michael B. ...Coral Springs, FL
Rappel & Rappel, P.A. ...Melbourne, FL
Vero Beach, FL
Rappel, Robert ...Melbourne, FL
Vero Beach, FL
Rappenecker, Stephen A. ...Gainesville, FL
Rappeport, Andrew H.
Bay Harbor Islands, FL
Rappeport, Andrew H., P.A.
Bay Harbor Islands, FL
Rappeport, David A. ...Bloomfield, NJ
Rappeport, Ira J. ...Los Angeles, CA
Rappeport, Jack J. ...Tucson, AZ
Rappin, Jeffrey C. ...Chicago, IL
Rappin, Steven R ...Chicago, IL
Rapping, Jonathan A. ...Washington, DC
Rappis, James G. ...Milwaukee, WI
Rappis, Jill M. ...Chicago, IL
Rappleye, Ann G. ...New York, NY
Rappleye, Diane M. ...Jackson, MI
Rappleye, Gregory J. ...Grand Haven, MI
Rappleye, Matthew W. ...Reading, PA
Rappleye & Rappleye ...Jackson, MI
Rappleye, Willard F. ...Jackson, MI
Rappleye, William G. ...Jackson, MI
Rappleye, Alan A. ...Prineville, OR
Rappleyea, Allan B., Jr.
Poughkeepsie, NY
Rappleyea, Allan E. ...Millbrook, NY
Poughkeepsie, NY
Rappleyea, Clarence D., Jr.
Binghamton, NY
Rappleyea, Kirsten A. ...Poughkeepsie, NY
Rappleyea, Tal G. ...Albany, NY
Rappo, Ronald A. ...New York, NY
Rappold, Bernadette M. ...Philadelphia, PA
Rappold, Charles E. ...New York, NY
Rappold, Richard W. ...Chicago, IL
Rappoport, Adi ...West Palm Beach, FL
Rappoport, Joel E. ...Washington, DC
Rappoport, Larry J. ...Wayne, PA
Rappoport, Lauren J. ...New York, NY
Rappoport, Lawrence A. ...Albany, NY
Rappoport, Lewis J. ...New York, NY
Rappoport, Margo ...New York, NY
Rappoport, Milton J. ...Longboat Key, FL
Rappoport, Ronald A. ...Somers, NY
Rappoport & Rosenberg, P.C.
Cherry Hill, NJ
Rappoport, Stephen M. ...East Providence, RI
Rappoport, Stephen S. ...Washington, DC
Rapport, Adele ...Detroit, MI
Rapport, Carmi ...Hudson, NY
Poughkeepsie, NY
Rapport, Daniel B. ...New York, NY
Rapport, David J. ...Ukiah, CA
Rapport, DeGiovanni & Caslowitz
East Providence, RI
Rapport, Meyers, Whitbeck, Shaw & Rodenhausen, LLP ...Albany, NY
Catskill, NY
Hudson, NY
Poughkeepsie, NY
Rapport, Sara ...Boston, MA
Rapprich, Francis X., III ...Orlando, FL
Rapprich, Kathryn Smith
Altamonte Springs, FL
Rapps, Dennis ...New York, NY
Rapps, William R. ...Jefferson City, MO
Rappuhn, Charlotte Houchins ...Nashville, TN
Rappuhn, Jeffrey G. ...Nashville, TN
Rapson, Ann G. ...Piedmont, CA
Rapson, David J. ...Oakland, CA
Rapson, Richard ...Minneapolis, MN
Rapson, Roxanne R. ...Palo Alto, CA
Rapson, William R. ...Denver, CO
Rapstine, Jackie A. ...Topeka, KS
Raptakis, Harry ...Mineola, NY
Raptis, Andrew, Jr. ...Charleston, WV
Raptis, Peggy C. ...Basking Ridge, NJ
Raptis, Sam L. ...Cambridge, OH
Raptis, Stephen T. ...Washington, DC
Rapuano, David A. ...Haddonfield, NJ
Rapuano, Robert A. ...New York, NY
Raquet, Bonnie E. ...Washington, DC
Raquet, Kevin F. ...Parsippany, NJ
Raquet, Steven K. ...Kokomo, IN
Rardin, Kevin Russell ...Memphis, TN
Rardin, Lia E. ...Dallas, TX
Rardin, Richard R. ...Denver, CO
Rardon, Larry L. ...Tampa, FL
Rarick, John R. ...St. Francisville, LA
Rarick, Philip J. ...Fairview Heights, IL
Raridan, Julie ...Sacramento, CA
Rariden, Nina ...Philadelphia, PA
Raridon, Michael W. ...Rockford, IL
Rarie, Robin Lynn ...Pittsburgh, PA
Rarig, Cynthia K. ...Pittsburgh, PA
Rarrick, C. Steven ...Topeka, KS
Rary, Warren Henry ...Atlanta, GA
Ras, Anthony S., P.C. ...Oak Brook, IL
Ras, Luis F. ...Millburn, NJ
New York, NY
Ras, Robert A. ...Oak Brook, IL
Rasa, Joseph M. ...Livingston, NJ
Rasak, Richard A. ...Torrance, CA
Rasak, Stephen C. ...Torrance, CA
Rasamny, Mary Kinnally ...Chappaqua, NY
Rasamny, Robert ...Bethel, CT
Rasansky, Jeffrey H. ...Dallas, TX
Rasansky, Jeffrey H., P.C. ...Dallas, TX
Rasansky, Jerald M. ...Dallas, TX
Rasband, James R. ...Provo, UT
Rasberry, Francis P., Jr. ...Raleigh, NC
Rasberry, John Quitman, Jr. ...Memphis, TN
Rascati, Ann E. ...Nantucket, MA
Rasch, Albert J., Jr. ...Costa Mesa, CA
Rasch, Bruce J. ...Battle Creek, MI
Rasch, Douglas W. ...Houston, TX
Rasch, Edward B. ...Los Angeles, CA
Rasch, Edward B., A Professional Corporation
Los Angeles, CA
Rasch, George B. ...Flint, MI
Rasch, Howard L. ...Beverly Hills, CA
La Quinta, CA
Rasch, Kevin S. ...Hartford, CT
Rasch, M. Stephen ...New York, NY
Rasch, Mark D. ...Washington, DC
Rasch, Michael H. ...Metairie, LA
Rasch and Morris ...Costa Mesa, CA
Rasch, Nancy D. ...San Francisco, CA
Rasch, Reginald M. ...New York, NY
Rasch, Robert M. ...Newport Beach, CA
Rasch, Robert W. ...Altamonte Springs, FL
Rasch, Robert W., P.A.
Altamonte Springs, FL
Orlando, FL
Rasch, Stephen C. ...Dallas, TX
Rasche, Charlotte M. ...Houston, TX
Rasche, Patrick W. ...St. Louis, MO
Rasche, Sandra K. ...Jasper, IN
Rasche, Simon W., Jr. ...Camanche, IA
Rasche, Stephen M. ...Portsmouth, NH
Rasche, William G. ...Madison, WI
Raschid, Imran M. ...Arlington, VA
Raschid, Michael I. ...Washington, DC
Raschke, Fred D. ...Galveston, TX
Raschke, Karen A. ...New York, NY
Raschke, Paul D. ...Baltimore, MD
Rascio, Anthony A. ...Eatontown, NJ
Rasco, Eduardo I. ...Aventura, FL
Rasco, Guy A. ...Miami, FL
Rasco, Larry O. ...San Marcos, TX
Rasco, Mark A. ...Talladega, AL
Rasco, Ramon E. ...Coral Gables, FL
Rasco, Reininger & Perez, P.A.
Coral Gables, FL
Rascoe, Christopher A. ...Atlanta, GA
Rascoe, Craig L. ...Richmond, VA
Rascoe, Donna R. ...Raleigh, NC
Rascoe, J. Peter, III ...Edenton, NC
Rascoe, Robert B. ...Winston-Salem, NC
Rascoe, Susan J. ...Dallas, TX
Rascoff, Jonathan C. ...Spokane, WA
Rascona, Nathan C. ...Somerset, PA
Rase, Leslie J. ...Phoenixville, PA
Rasenberger, Ann L. ...Baltimore, MD
Rasenberger, Mary E. ...New York, NY
Rasenberger, Raymond J.
Washington, DC
Rasetti, Fabrizio F.R. ...Muskegon, MI
Rasey, Randall ...New York, NY
Rash, Alan V. ...El Paso, TX
Rash, Anthony J. ...Pittsburgh, PA
Rash, Carol ...Los Angeles, CA
Rash, Chapman, Schreiber & Porter, L.L.P.
Austin, TX
Georgetown, TX
Rash, David C. ...Fort Lauderdale, FL
Rash, Debra L. ...Milwaukee, WI
Rash, Eugene F. ...Charlotte, NC
Rash, H. Stephen ...Miami, FL
Rash, James Dennis ...Charlotte, NC
Rash, Jason A. ...Philadelphia, PA
Rash & Katzen, P.A. ...Miami, FL
Rash, Ralph A. ...Austin, TX
Rash, Ralph R. ...Austin, TX
Rash, Robert ...Montgomery, AL
Rash, Robin E. ...Oak Brook, IL
Rash, Susan Taylor ...Asheville, NC
Rash, Todd A., Law Offices of
Riverside, CA
Rash, Wayne A. ...Santa Ana, CA
Rashak, John J. ...Whitehouse Station, NJ
Rashap, Arthur W. ...Mount Trempler, NY
Rashba, Malcolm L. ...Hamden, CT
Rashbaum, Gilbert ...Newburgh, NY
Rashbaum, Kenneth N. ...New York, NY
Rashbaum, Maurice, Jr. ...New York, NY
Rashbaum, Phillip ...St. Louis, MO
Rashby, Carolyn ...Oakland, CA
Rasheed, Ousama M. ...Albuquerque, NM
Rasher, Donald C. ...Montgomery, AL
Rasher, Howard Wm. ...Thornwood, NY
Rasher, Steven M. ...Elk Grove Village, IL
Rashes, Alan M. ...New York, NY
Rashes, Haran C. ...Okemos, MI
Rashid, Aurelia Donovan
Charlotte Amalie, St. Thomas, VI
Rashid, Aurelia Donovan, P.C.
Charlotte Amalie, St. Thomas, VI
Rashid, Carl, Jr. ...Detroit, MI
Grosse Pointe Farms, MI
Rashid, James J. ...Detroit, MI
Rashid, James M. ...Richfield, OH
Rashid, Judy A. ...Grosse Pointe Woods, MI
Rashid Law Firm, P.C. ...Fort Madison, IA
Rashid, Michael J. ...Fort Madison, IA
Rashid, Peter J. ...Toledo, OH
Rashid, Richard R. ...Lansing, MI
Rashid, Soraya N. ...Santa Clara, CA
Rashid, Vicki L. ...Department of Justice, Drug Enforcement Administration, GV
Rashke, John ...Madison, WI
Rashkin, Michael D. ...Saratoga, CA
Rashkind, Alan B. ...Norfolk, VA
Rashkind, Paul M. ...Miami, FL
Rashkis, Jerome ...Neponsit, NY
Rashkow, Bruce C. ...New York, NY
Rashley, A. O'Neil, Jr. ...Columbia, SC
Rashman, Lydia L. ...Hubbard Woods, IL
Rashman, Richard ...Los Angeles, CA
Rashti, Donna Kaye ...Dallas, TX
Rashti & Mitchell ...Dallas, TX
Rasich, Marc T. ...Los Angeles, CA
Rasile, Craig V. ...Miami, FL
Rasilewicz, Casimir E. ...Woodland Hills, CA
Rasin, Alexander P., III ...Chestertown, MD
Rasin, Geo. B., Jr. ...Chestertown, MD
Rasin, Gregory I. ...New York, NY
Rasin, Martha F. ...Annapolis, MD
Rasin, Wright & Wootton
Chestertown, MD
Rasines, Stephanie Probst
Santa Monica, CA
Rask, Kelly S. ...St. Paul, MN
Rask, Pamela A. ...New York, NY
Rask, Pamela P. ...Lihue, HI
Rask, Paul J. ...Portland, OR
Rask, Raymond M. ...Portland, OR
Rask, Robby H. ...Lihue, HI
Rask, Scott C. ...Parsons, KS
Rask, Thomas R., III ...Portland, OR
Raskas, Aron U. ...Baltimore, MD
Raskas, Daniel A. ...Washington, DC
Raskas, Jerome F. ...St. Louis, MO
Raskasky, Michael A. ...Tacoma, WA
Raskauskas, Joseph C. ...Bethany Beach, DE
Raske, Michael D. ...New York, NY
Raskin & Berman ...Providence, RI
Raskin, Bernard H. ...Omaha, NE
Raskin, Carol M. ...Louisville, KY
Raskin, Daniel E. ...Atlanta, GA
Raskin, Daniel E. ...Atlanta, GA
Raskin, David ...New York, NY
Raskin, David B. ...Washington, DC
Raskin, Debra L. ...New York, NY
Raskin, Ellen ...Larchmont, NY
Raskin, Fred B. ...Deerfield, IL
Raskin, Gary S. ...Los Angeles, CA
Raskin, Gerald ...Denver, CO
Raskin, Isabel Sara ...Chelsea, MA
Raskin, Jamin Ben ...Washington, DC
Raskin, Jane Serene ...Miami, FL
Raskin, Jeffrey S. ...Los Angeles, CA
San Francisco, CA

Rather, Hugh R. .... Milwaukee, WI
Rather, James B., III .... Melville, NY
Rather, James C., Jr. .... Lafayette, LA
Rather, Julius E. .... Lexington, KY
Rathert, Alfred J. .... Fenton, MO
Rathert, Fred C. .... Williston, ND
Rathert, John W. .... Waterloo, IA
Rathert, Kenneth A. .... Kalamazoo, MI
Rathert, Kenneth A., P.C. .... Kalamazoo, MI
Rathet, Brooks C. .... Atlanta, GA
Rathfon, Steven D. .... Oakland, CA
Rathgeb, Thomas D. ..... Department of Defense, Defense Commissary Agency, GV
Rathgeb, Thomas M. .... Houston, TX
Rathgeber & Associates .... Doylestown, PA
Rathgeber, David K. .... Chicago, IL
Rathgeber, Ellen .... Austin, TX
Rathgeber, Joanne Weil .... Doylestown, PA
Rathgeber, John R. .... Hartford, CT
Rathgeber, Julia J. .... Austin, TX
Rathhaus, Eric W. .... San Francisco, CA
Rathi, Vijay K. .... Brooklyn, NY
Rathie, Robert W. .... Monterey, CA
Rathje, Karen E. .... Lake Oswego, OR
Rathje, Kulp & Monaghan .... Chicago, IL
Rathje, Lena R. .... Lincoln, NE
Rathje & Rathje .... Lake Oswego, OR
Rathje, S. Louis .... Springfield, IL
Rathje, Theron L. .... Chicago, IL
Rathje, William John .... Lake Oswego, OR
Rathje, Woodward, Dyer & Burt
Wheaton, IL
Rathjen, Daniel Y. .... Dysart, IA
Tama, IA
Rathjen, Jon L. .... Walnut Creek, CA
Rathjen, Richard J. .... Wautoma, WI
Rathjen, Stephen Paul .... Hauppauge, NY
Rathjen, William E., III .... Highland Park, NJ
Rathke, Monica J. .... Greensboro, NC
Rathke, Paul C. .... Greenville, SC
Rathke, Robert W. .... Troy, MI
Rathke, Stephen C. .... Minneapolis, MN
Rathkopf, Clifford A., Jr. .... New York, NY
Rathkopf, Daren A. .... Melville, NY
Rathle, Frank R. .... Thibodaux, LA
Rathman, John G. .... Rumson, NJ
Rathman, Marcy S. .... Stamford, CT
Rathman, William E. .... Middletown, OH
Rathmann, Dennis T.
North Little Rock, AR
St. Louis, MO
Rathmann, Diane V. .... Dos Palos, CA
Rathmann & Francis
North Little Rock, AR
St. Louis, MO
Rathmel, John B. .... Overland Park, KS
Rathnau, Joseph N. .... Chicago, IL
Rathsack, Michael W. .... Chicago, IL
Rathvon, James P. .... Washington, DC
Rathwell, Lyle .... Houston, TX
Rathwell, Peter J. .... Phoenix, AZ
Ratican, Sari Lyn Heller .... Chicago, IL
Ratican, William A., Jr. .... Aurora, MO
Ratigan, Gerard J. .... Providence, RI
Ratigan, John J. .... Exeter, NH
Ratigan, John R. .... Department of State, Foreign Service Officers (Overseas), GV
Ratigan, Maura F. .... Philadelphia, PA
Ratiner, Edwin C. .... Miami, FL
Ratiner & Glinn, P.A. .... Miami, FL
Ratiner, Leigh S. .... Annapolis, MD
Ratiner, Robert J. .... Miami, FL
Ratino, John M. .... Washington, DC
Ratinoff, Eric J. .... Sacramento, CA
Ratinoff, Jeffrey M. .... San Jose, CA
Ratinoff, Joanne D. .... Los Angeles, CA
Ratinoff, Marisa S. .... Los Angeles, CA
Ratje, Randall J. .... Medford, NY
Ratke, Mark J. .... Milwaukee, WI
Ratkovsky, Rudolf .... Yuba City, CA
Ratkowitz, John .... Roseland, NJ
Ratkowski, Allen M. .... Milwaukee, WI
Ratley, Sharon Thames .... Macon, GA
Ratliff, Alan G. .... Houston, TX
Ratliff, Alice A. .... Durham, NC
Ratliff, Anthony B. .... Indianapolis, IN
Ratliff, B. Truman .... Cooper, TX
Ratliff, Barbara Kay .... Los Angeles, CA
Ratliff, Benjamin L. .... Fresno, CA
Ratliff, Carl T. .... Detroit, MI
Ratliff, Christopher T. .... Pikeville, KY
Ratliff, Darlene .... Charleston, WV
Ratliff, Donald M. (Mike)
Klamath Falls, OR
Ratliff, Edwards & De Hoyos
Ballinger, TX
Del Rio, TX
Ozona, TX
San Angelo, TX
Sonora, TX
Ratliff, Ernest E. .... Clinton, NC
Ratliff, Gerald R. .... San Angelo, TX
Ratliff, Jack .... Austin, TX
Ratliff, James B. .... Pikeville, KY
Ratliff, James K.V. .... Birmingham, AL
Ratliff, James R. .... Brooklyn, NY
Ratliff, Jeffrey S. .... Portland, OR
Ratliff, Joan S. .... Jackson, MS
Ratliff, John D. .... House of Representatives, Office of Legislative Counsel, GV
Ratliff, John M. .... Fort Lauderdale, FL
Ratliff, Kevin .... Tulsa, OK
Ratliff Law Offices, Chartered .... Boise, ID
Ratliff, Lee Roger .... Silsbee, TX
Ratliff, Leif C. .... Madisonville, KY
Ratliff, Louis M. (Mickey), Jr.
Lubbock, TX
Ratliff, Marianne Shimanek .... Norman, OK
Ratliff, Marilyn R. .... Evansville, IN
Ratliff, Michael V. .... Hattiesburg, MS
Ratliff, Pamela Sue .... Dallas, TX
Ratliff, Philip Q. .... Ashland, KY
Ratliff, Ray, Jr. .... Charleston, WV
Ratliff, Rayford A. .... Dumas, TX
Ratliff, Reeder E. .... Oklahoma City, OK
Ratliff, Remi .... Treasury Department, Office of the General Counsel, GV
Ratliff, Richard C. .... Sacramento, CA
Ratliff, Robert Lee, III .... Sanibel, FL
Ratliff, Robert Lee, III, P.A. .... Sanibel, FL
Ratliff, Samuel C. .... Houston, TX
Ratliff, Shannon H. .... Austin, TX
Houston, TX
Ratliff, Shannon H., II .... Washington, DC
Ratliff, Stephen H. .... Fairfax, VA
Ratliff, Susanne T. .... Birmingham, AL
Ratliff, Terry S. .... Boise, ID
Ratliff, Theresa H. .... Casa Grande, AZ
Ratliff, Thos. B. .... Robinson Creek, KY
Ratliff, Warren L. .... Nashville, TN
Ratliff & Wells .... Littlefield, TX
Lubbock, TX
Ratliff, Wesley W., Jr. .... Bloomington, IN
Ratliff & Whitney-Smith
Klamath Falls, OR
Ratliff, William A. .... Birmingham, AL
Ratliff, William D., III .... Fort Worth, TX
Ratliff-Connor, Lynise .... Kansas City, MO
Ratliff Morris, Tami .... Abilene, TX
Ratnaswamy, John P. .... Chicago, IL
Ratnavale, B. Lynn F. .... Washington, DC
Ratnayake, Ananda Everard L. Damian
Eagan, MN
Ratner, Adam .... Richmond, CA
Ratner, Adam K. .... San Diego, CA
Ratner, Allan .... Valley Forge, PA
Ratner, Allan .... McLean, VA
Ratner, Amy R. .... Boston, MA
Ratner, Anthony D. .... San Francisco, CA
Ratner, Bruce C. .... Brooklyn, NY
Ratner, Carolyn J. .... Denver, CO
Ratner, Charles A. .... Cleveland, OH
Ratner, Charles H. .... Miami, FL
Ratner, Cliff Warren .... Wichita, KS
Ratner, Daniel J. .... New York, NY
Ratner, Daniel S. .... Stamford, CT
New York, NY
Ratner, David L. .... San Francisco, CA
Ratner, David R. .... New York, NY
Ratner, David S. .... New York, NY
Ratner, Elizabeth .... Palo Alto, CA
Ratner, Gail R. .... Miami, FL
Ratner, Gerald .... Chicago, IL
Ratner, Hank J. .... Bethpage, NY
Ratner, Herman A. .... Colorado Springs, CO
Ratner, Howard .... Seattle, WA
Ratner, Howard, Inc., P.S. .... Seattle, WA
Ratner, Ian Peter .... New York, NY
Ratner, Ilana Horowitz .... Cleveland, OH
Ratner, Jane A. .... Atlanta, GA
Ratner, Jill H. .... Los Angeles, CA
Ratner, Joel I. .... Cleveland, OH
Ratner, Jonathan D. .... Bedminster, NJ
Ratner, Loren .... Garden City, NY
Ratner, Margaret L. .... New York, NY
Ratner, Mark S. .... Chicago, IL
Ratner, Marvin .... Battle Creek, MI
Ratner, Marvin L. .... Memphis, TN
Ratner, Michael .... New York, NY
Ratner, Michael S. .... Springfield, MA
Ratner, Michelle L. .... Flagstaff, AZ
Ratner, Morris A. .... San Francisco, CA
Ratner, Pamela Anne .... San Diego, CA
Ratner, Patricia E. .... Beverly, MA
Ratner, Patricia L. .... Princeton, NJ
Ratner, Payne H. .... Garfield, AR
Sarasota, FL
Ratner & Prestia, A Professional Corporation .... Wilmington, DE
Allentown, PA
Berwyn, PA
Philadelphia, PA
Valley Forge, PA
Ratner, Randall M., (P.C.) .... Dallas, TX
Ratner, Robert J. .... Jersey City, NJ
Ratner, Ryan S. .... Boca Raton, FL
Ratner, Scott E. .... New York, NY
Ratner & Sealand .... Memphis, TN
Ratner, Stephen L. .... New York, NY
Ratner, Steven Edward .... Cooperstown, NY
Ratner, Steven R. .... Austin, TX
Ratner, Stuart B. .... Stamford, CT
Ratner, Stuart B., P.C. .... Stamford, CT
Ratner, Susan B. .... New York, NY
Ratner, Todd .... Atlanta, GA
Ratner-Salzberg, Deborah C.
Washington, DC
Ratnesar, Mishthi Grace .... Metairie, LA
Ratnoff, Marian F., (Mrs.) .... Cleveland, OH
Ratoza Long, P.C. .... Portland, OR
Ratoza, Michael M. .... Portland, OR
Ratschko, Imke .... New York, NY
Ratskoff, Ellyce F. .... Rockville, MD
Rattan, James E. .... Columbus, OH
Rattan, Mark W. .... Chicago, IL
Shorewood, WI
Rattay, Thomas J. .... Roseland, NJ
Ratteree, Jane S. .... Charlotte, NC
Ratterman, David B. .... Louisville, KY
Ratterman, George W. .... Lakewood, CO
Rattermann, Paul D. .... Cincinnati, OH
Ratterree, Amy S. .... Belleville, IL
Ratterree, Donald E., Jr. .... Bartow, FL
Ratterree, John, II .... Atlanta, GA
Ratterree, R. Clay .... Savannah, GA
Rattet, Gary S. .... Los Angeles, CA
Rattet & Pasternak, LLP .... Harrison, NY
New York, NY
Scarsdale, NY
White Plains, NY
Rattet, Robert L. .... Harrison, NY
New York, NY
Rattey, Norman J. .... Auburn, ME
Rattigan, David H. .... Pottsville, PA
Rattigan, Ellen
Environmental Protection Agency, Office of Enforcement and Compliance Assurance, GV
Rattigan, John E., Jr. .... Boston, MA
Rattigan, Joseph A. .... Santa Rosa, CA
Rattigan, Margaret Fogerty
Farmington, CT
Rattikin, Jack, Jr. .... Fort Worth, TX
Rattikin, Jack, Jr., P.C., Law Offices of
Fort Worth, TX
Rattikin, Jeffrey A. .... Fort Worth, TX
Rattley, Donna Carrie .... Washington, DC
Rattley, Robin A. .... Newport News, VA
Rattliff, D. Brian .... Louisville, KY
Rattman, Joseph J. Hauser .... Stroudsburg, PA
Rattnar, David L. .... Washington, DC
Rattner, Andrea S. .... New York, NY
Rattner, Brian M. .... Spring Valley, NY
Rattner, Jeffrey E. .... Claremont, CA
Rattner, Jonathan E. .... Palo Alto, CA
Rattner, Mark S. .... Morristown, NJ
Rattner, Richard D. .... Birmingham, MI
Rattner, Ronald D. .... San Francisco, CA
Rattner, William E. .... Chicago, IL
Ratto, Anthony Gerald .... Oakland, CA
Ratto, John Russell .... Portland, OR
Rattoballi, Anthony J. .... Valley Stream, NY
Ratton, Michael T. .... Royal Oak, MI
Ratton, R. Robert, III .... Newport, AR
Ratton, Robert W., Jr. .... Memphis, TN
Ratton & Wangler .... Royal Oak, MI
Rattray, James B. .... Hampton, VA
Rattray, M. Thompson .... Washington, DC
Rattray, Tammie L. .... Tampa, FL
Ratts, Andrew W. .... Chicago, IL
Ratwik, Paul C. .... Minneapolis, MN
Ratwik, Roszak & Maloney, P.A.
Minneapolis, MN
Raty, Matthew H. .... Salt Lake City, UT
Ratych, Jurij W. .... New Brunswick, NJ
Ratz, Charles A. .... Atlanta, GA
Ratz, Richard W. .... Omaha, NE
Ratzan, Mycki L. .... Miami, FL
Ratzan, Stuart N. .... Miami, FL
Ratzburg, Frederick, II .... Shreveport, LA
Ratzel, James C. .... Brookfield, WI
Ratzel, Mary Lee .... Milwaukee, WI
Ratzel & Mathie LLC .... Brookfield, WI
Ratzenberger, Sheila A.
General Accounting Office, Office of the General Counsel, GV
Ratz Graham, Kathleen M. .... Irvine, CA
Ratzkin, Andrew S. .... New York, NY
Ratzkin, Jack L. .... Boynton Beach, FL
Ratzkoff, Philander S. .... Boston, MA
Ratzlaff, Amy K. .... Dallas, TX
Ratzlaff, Ben D. .... Elkhart, KS
Ratzlaff, Gary H. .... Lamar, MO
Ratzlaff, John A. .... Marianna, FL
Ratzlaff, Kurt W. .... Wichita, KS
Ratzlaff, Ruth E. .... Fresno, CA
Ratzlaff, Virginia H. .... Lawrence, KS
Ratzman, Dean F. .... Spokane, WA
Rau, Alan S. .... Austin, TX
Rau, Andrew D.H. .... West Chester, PA
Rau, C. Glennon .... Columbia, IL
Waterloo, IL
Rau, Charles W. .... Washington, DC
Rau, Christopher R. .... Arlington, VA
Rau & Cooper .... Red Bud, IL
Rau, Curtis A. .... San Francisco, CA
Rau, Daniel H. .... Cape Girardeau, MO
Rau, David P. .... Red Bud, IL
Rau, Edward J. .... Frisco, CO
Rau & Floyd, P.L.L.P. .... Minneapolis, MN
Rau, George H., Jr. .... Angleton, TX
Rau, Jack L. .... Carlsbad, CA
Rau, James P. .... New York, NY
Rau, James Thomas, Jr. .... Wilmington, DE
Rau, Jeanne Gorman .... Kansas City, KS
Rau, John C. .... Palm Beach, FL
Rau, John E. .... Columbus, OH
Rau, John H. .... Glen Oaks, NY
Rau, Judith A. .... Columbia, IL
Waterloo, IL
Rau, Julia L. .... Minneapolis, MN
Rau, Laurie D. .... Newport Beach, CA
Rau, Lee A. .... Washington, DC
Rau, Lisa Millett .... Philadelphia, PA
Rau, Littie E. .... Bloomfield, NJ
Rau, Mark E. .... Lakewood, CO
Rau, Marvin .... Kansas City, MO
Rau, Matthew W. .... Arlington, VA
Rau and Rau .... Columbia, IL
Waterloo, IL
Rau, Robert .... Minot, ND
Rau, Robert E. .... Honolulu, HI
Rau, Robert W. .... Los Angeles, CA
Rau, Ronald B. .... Yreka, CA
Rau, Sally J. .... Palo Alto, CA
Rau, Sally Millett .... Bellevue, NE
Rau, Steven E. .... Minneapolis, MN
Rau, Steven G. .... Fresno, CA
Raub, Andrea B. .... Walnut Creek, CA
Raub, Benj. D. .... Sarasota, FL
Raub, David W. .... Mill Valley, CA
San Francisco, CA
Raub, L. Donald, Jr. .... Palo Alto, CA
Raub, Michael E. .... Urbana, IL
Raub, Morris I. .... Scranton, PA
Raub, Paul T. .... Orinda, CA
Raubach, Thomas J. .... Lexington, MA
Rauber, Alan E. .... Decatur, GA
Rauber, David L. .... Visalia, CA
Rauber, Theresa C. .... Richardson, TX
Raubicheck, Charles J. .... New York, NY
Raubinger, Timothy J. .... Lansing, MI
Raubitschek, John H.
Department of Commerce, Office of the General Counsel, GV
Raubvogel, Amir H. .... Palo Alto, CA
Raubvogel, Andrew N. .... Boston, MA
Raucci, Andrew M. .... Chicago, IL
Raucci, Anthony L. .... New York, NY
Raucci, Francis J. .... Salt Lake City, UT
Rauch, Alfred, III .... Marlton, NJ
Philadelphia, PA
Rauch, Allan H. .... Des Moines, IA
Rauch, Allan N. .... Springfield, NJ
Rauch, Bradley E. .... Houston, TX
Rauch, David E. .... Phoenix, AZ
Rauch, David S. .... Los Angeles, CA
Rauch, Douglas Paul .... Wyomissing, PA
Rauch, George W. .... Chicago, IL
Rauch, Harold L. .... Farmington Hills, MI
Rauch, Henri .... Miami, FL
Rauch, Jack A. .... San Rafael, CA
Rauch, John G. .... Chicago, IL
Rauch, John O. .... Denver, CO
Rauch, Kevin D. .... Pittsburgh, PA
Rauch, Layni S. .... Millburn, NJ
Rauch, Lee B. .... Baltimore, MD
Rauch, Lisa K. .... Oakland, CA
Rauch, Lynn Rosner .... Philadelphia, PA
Rauch, Marc .... New York, NY
Rauch, Marilyn F. .... Little Rock, AR
Rauch, Michael A. .... Boston, MA
Rauch, Michael H. .... New York, NY
Rauch, Nick E. .... Eugene, OR
Rauch, Oscar C. .... Scottsdale, AZ
Rauch, Pamela M. .... West Palm Beach, FL
Rauch, Paul E. .... Arlington, VA
Rauch, Paul (Rick), III .... Indianapolis, IN
Rauch, R. Stewart, Jr. .... Bryn Mawr, PA
Rauch, Rhonda L. .... Encino, CA
Rauch, Samuel D., III ..... Department of Justice, Environment and Natural Resources Division, GV
Rauch, Stephen .... Palm Beach Gardens, FL
Rauch, Susan H. .... Stamford, CT
Rauch, T. Stewart .... Washington, DC
Rauch, Thomas C. .... Troy, MI
Rauch, Thomas G. .... Dayton, OH
Rauch & Van Voorhis .... Denver, CO
Rauch, W. Wyatt .... Petersburg, IN
Rauchberg, Ronald S. .... New York, NY
Rauchberg, Steven C. .... New York, NY
Raucher, Morris B. .... New York, NY
Raucher, Nicole Andraya .... Boston, MA
Raucher, Stephen L. .... Beverly Hills, CA
Raucher, Steven A. .... Hamden, CT
Rauchfuss, George W., Jr. .... Stamford, CT
Rauchfuss, R. E. "Russ" .... Casper, WY
Rauchholz, William F. .... Washington, DC
Rauchman, Judith L. .... Cincinnati, OH
Rauchway, Audrey B. .... St. Petersburg, FL
Rauchway, Jonathan W. .... New York, NY
Rauchwerger, Dean S. .... Chicago, IL
Raudabaugh, John N. .... Chicago, IL
Raudabaugh, Robert L. .... Villa Park, IL
Raudenbush, Eric M.
Federal Housing Finance Board, Office of General Counsel, GV
Raudonis, Valerie C. .... Nashua, NH
Raue, Philip B. .... Pelham Manor, NY
Rauen, Eugene B. .... Atherton, CA
Rauen, James A. .... Department of Commerce, Patent and Trademark Office, GV
Rauen, Janice M. .... Chicago, IL
Rauenhorst, Joseph J. .... Bethesda, MD
Rauer, Beth A. .... Charleston, WV
Rauer, James M. .... Dallas, TX
Rauer, Larry M. .... Cherry Hill, NJ
Rauer, Paul W. .... Bensalem, PA
Rauer, Suzanne .... Harrisburg, PA
Raufer, Colin M. .... Albuquerque, NM
Raufman, William Leonard .... Van Nuys, CA
Raugust, Mary C. .... Framingham, MA
Rauh, B. Michael .... Washington, DC
Rauh, Carl S. .... Washington, DC
Rauh, Charles E. .... Hutchinson, KS
Rauh, Conrad A. .... Telluride, CO
Rauh, Heidi Mallory .... Chicago, IL
Rauh, John R. .... Rio Grande, NJ
Rauh, Robert M. .... Tucson, AZ
Rauh, Sue N. .... Sylvania, OH
Rauh, Trudy D. .... Cincinnati, OH
Rauhut, Kathryn A. .... Livermore, CA
Rauhut, Stanley Eugene .... Houston, TX
Raukar, Robert M. .... Maple Grove, MN
Raukko, Julia M. .... Visalia, CA
Raul, Alan Charles .... Washington, DC
Raulerson, R. Kelly .... Albany, GA
Raulet, Paul P. .... Atlanta, GA
Rauls, Joseph T. .... Houston, TX
Rauls, Monique F. .... Alexandria, LA
Rauls, Stanley D. .... Little Rock, AR
Raulston, J. Christopher .... Little Rock, AR
Raulston, Jackson C. .... Kingsport, TN
Raulston, Keith R. .... Jackson, MS
Raulston Law Offices, P.C. .... Kingsport, TN
Rault, Gerard A. .... New Orleans, LA
Rault, Jos. M., Jr. .... New Orleans, LA
Raum, Alice C. .... Tallahassee, FL
Raum, Bernard A. .... Ellicott City, MD
Raum, Nora .... Arlington, VA
Raum, Robert S. .... New York, NY

Raum, Thomas C. ... Wichita, KS
Raum, Violet G. ... Washington, DC
Raun, Eric L.
Department Of Veterans Affairs, Office of the General Counsel, GV
Raun, Michael C. ... Wilton, CA
Rauner, Vincent J. ... Chicago, IL
Raunikar, F. Nils ... McAlester, OK
Raup, Calvin L. ... **Phoenix, AZ**
Tucson, AZ
Raup, James R. ... **Austin, TX**
Raup, Mitchell D. ... **Washington, DC**
Raup, Thomas C. ... Williamsport, PA
Raupp, Robert L. ... Hesperia, CA
Raupple, Kenneth B., (P.C.) ... Dallas, TX
Raus, George M., Jr. ... Syracuse, NY
Rausa, Bradley G. ... St. Charles, IL
Rausa, D. J. ... San Diego, CA
Rausch, A. Peter, Jr. ... San Francisco, CA
Stockton, CA
Rausch, Charles A. ... **York, PA**
Rausch, Christopher J. ... **St. Louis, MO**
Rausch, E. James ... San Antonio, TX
Rausch, Edward W., Jr. ... Hinckley, OH
Rausch, Edwin A., Jr. ... **Louisville, KY**
Rausch, Edwin A., Sr. ... Louisville, KY
Rausch, Eldred A. ... Tucson, AZ
Rausch, Fred W., Jr. ... Topeka, KS
Rausch, Frederick A. ... Evanston, IL
Rausch, James P. ... Bismarck, ND
Rausch, Jean L. ... Minneapolis, MN
Rausch, John F. ... Albany, NY
Rausch, John M. ... Rockville, MD
Rausch, Joseph W. ... Metairie, LA
Rausch, Julie A. ... Milwaukee, WI
Rausch Law Firm ... Waterloo, IA
Rausch Law Office, The ... Bismarck, ND
Rausch, Lawrence R. ... Jacksonville, FL
Rausch, Lynn M. ... Glen Allen, VA
Rausch, Martha W. ... **Wakefield, MA**
Rausch, Michael P. ... **Philadelphia, PA**
Rausch, Michael W. ... Tucson, AZ
Rausch, Raymond J. ... Milwaukee, WI
Rausch, Robert A. ... **Albany, NY**
Rausch, Robert L. ... Waterloo, IA
Rausch, Robert S. ... **Miami, FL**
McLean, VA
Rausch, Siobhan C. ... **Washington, DC**
Rausch, Sturm, Israel & Hornik, S.C.
Milwaukee, WI
Rausch, Tom E. ... **Crystal Lake, IL**
Rauschenbach, Kurt ... **Boston, MA**
Rauschenbach, Paul M. ... Belleville, IL
St. Louis, MO
Rauschenberger, F. Arthur, III ... Butler, PA
Rauschenberger, James T. ... **Atlanta, GA**
Rauschenburg, Lauren K. ... **Honolulu, HI**
Rauscher, Christopher L. ... Syracuse, NY
Rauscher, Claire J. ... **Charlotte, NC**
Rauscher, David J. ... **St. Louis, MO**
Rauscher, David J., P.C. ... **St. Louis, MO**
Rauscher, Edward A. ... Bellevue, WA
Rauscher, Ernest W. ... Springfield, MA
Rauscher, Kathleen L. ... **St. Louis, MO**
Rauschert, Donald R. ... Chicago, IL
Rauschert & Rauschert ... Chicago, IL
Rauschert, Robt. R. ... Sacramento, CA
Rauschl, Chris A. ... **Minneapolis, MN**
Rauschl, Rollin N. ... Victorville, CA
Rauseo, John P. ... Lynnfield, MA
Rauseo, Richard W. ... San Dimas, CA
Rauser, Paul C. ... **Washington, DC**
Rauser, Scott H. ... **St. Paul, MN**
Raush, Helene B. ... **Cherry Hill, NJ**
Raush, Tambra L. ... Wisconsin Rapids, WI
Raushenbush, Lorraine E.
San Francisco, CA
Raushenbush, Richard W.
San Francisco, CA
Raushenbush, Walter B. ... Coronado, CA
Rausher, Daniel E. ... Brooklyn, NY
Rausher, Judith A. ... Atlanta, GA
Rausher, Perry H. ... Woodland Hills, CA
Rauskolb, Fred W., III ... **New York, NY**
Rauss, Alan M. ... **Cleveland, OH**
Rauss, Dennis M. ... **Troy, MI**
Raust, Nelson A. ... **Manchester, NH**
Rautbort, Andrea L.
Farmington Hills, MI
Rautenstraus, Curt D. ... Louisville, CO
Rautenstraus & Joss, P.C. ... Louisville, CO
Rauterkus, Jerald L. ... **Omaha, NE**
Rauth, Paul A., (P.C.) ... **Omaha, NE**
Rauth, William R., III
Newport Beach, CA
Rauworth, Michael J. ... **Boston, MA**
Rauzi, David S. ... Kansas City, MO
Rauzi, Edwin D. ... **Honolulu, HI**
Seattle, WA
Rauzi, Harold R. ... **Cleveland, OH**
Rauzi, Robert L. ... **Mt. Vernon, OH**
Rauzin, Alan H. ... Miami, FL
Rava, Alfred G. ... **Houston, TX**
Rava, John A. ... **St. Louis, MO**
Rava, Joseph J. ... **New York, NY**
Raval, Abhilash M. ... Los Angeles, CA
Raval, Navnit R. ... Glenarm, MD
Ravalese, Theresa Fennell ... Newark, DE
Ravalli, Michael P. ... **Albany, NY**
Ravan, Howell C. ... Marietta, GA
Ravan, Joseph Scott ... Columbia, SC
Ravani, Ronald J. ... San Rafael, CA
Ravary, Ray R. ... Jerome, MI
Ravas, Andrea L. ... Oakland, CA
Ravas, Theodore E., Jr.
Equal Employment Opportunity Commission, Office of Legal Counsel, GV
Ravaschiere, Dominic ... **Toms River, NJ**
Ravaschiere, Rocco ... Eatontown, NJ
Ravazzini, Terry J. ... Emeryville, CA
Ravazzini, Terry J., A Professional Corporation
Emeryville, CA
Ravdel, Connie-Ann ... **Houston, TX**
Ravdin, Linda J. ... **Washington, DC**
Ravdin & Wofford, A Professional Corporation ... **Washington, DC**
Bethesda, MD
Fairfax, VA
Rave, Donald T. ... Locust Valley, NY
Rave, Donald T., Jr. ... Locust Valley, NY
Rave, Michael T. ... **Morristown, NJ**
Rave, Norman L., Jr. ... Department of Justice, Environment and Natural Resources Division, GV
Ravech, Barry ... Boston, MA
Ravech, Matthew J. ... **Boston, MA**
Ravech, Melvin ... Boston, MA
Ravech, Paul E. ... Boston, MA
Ravech, Roy & Ravech, P.C. ... Boston, MA
Ravech, Stuart D. ... Boston, MA
Raveh, Gil A. ... **New York, NY**
Ravel, Ann M. ... San Jose, CA
Ravel, J. Stephen ... **Austin, TX**
Ravel, Judith A. ... **Branford, CT**
Ravel, Judith A. ... **New Haven, CT**
Ravel, Roger C. ... Bedford Hills, NY
Ravella, Peter A., II ... Eugene, OR
Ravelle, James J. ... Slatington, PA
Ravellette, Lynne Trulock
Little Rock, AR
Ravelo, Keila D. ... **New York, NY**
Raven, Brett L. ... Santa Rosa, CA
Raven, Donald W. ... Kyle, TX
Raven, John W. ... Greenville, MI
Raven, Jonathan ... Okemos, MI
Raven, Kenneth B. ... New York, NY
Raven & Kirschner, P.C. ... **Tucson, AZ**
Raven, Mara L. ... Big Rapids, MI
Raven, Marc E. ... **Chicago, IL**
Raven, Mark B. ... **Tucson, AZ**
Raven, Mark D. ... Scottville, MI
Raven, Ricky A. ... **Houston, TX**
Raven, Robert D. ... **San Francisco, CA**
Raven, Ronald E. ... **Atlanta, GA**
Raven, Ronald E., P.C. ... **Atlanta, GA**
Raven, Teri Kessel ... **Phoenix, AZ**
Ravenburg, Ralph R. ... Austin, TX
Ravencraft, Mathew D. ... **Vienna, VA**
Ravenel, DuVal Cravens ... **Columbia, SC**
Ravenell, Kenneth W. ... **Baltimore, MD**
Ravenell, William H. ... Tallahassee, FL
Ravenelle, Robert B. ... **Portland, ME**
Raven-Hansen, Peter ... Washington, DC
Ravenhill, Robert H. ... Marshall, MO
Ravens, Gary E. ... Linneus, MO
Ravenscraft, Krista L. ... St. Charles, IL
Ravenscroft, Donald R. ... Rodman, NY
Ravenscroft, Sharon Elizabeth
Phoenix, AZ
Tucson, AZ
Raver, Paul C., Sr., Law Offices of
Fort Wayne, IN
Raver, William R. ... Cambria, CA
San Luis Obispo, CA
Raves, David ... Pittsburgh, PA
Ravesies, Carol S. ... **Brea, CA**
Ravesion, Louis S. ... Newark, NJ
Ravet, Gary K. ... La Jolla, CA
Ravetta, Michael G. ... St. Louis, MO
Ravetti Jaeger, Alessandra ... **New York, NY**
Ravich, David L. ... Rahway, NJ
Ravich, Evan S. ... **San Diego, CA**
Ravich, Koster, Tobin, Oleckna, Reitman & Greenstein, P.A. ... Rahway, NJ
Ravich, Marshall ... Lake Forest, IL
Ravich, Meyer, Kirkman, McGrath & Nauman, A Professional Association
Minneapolis, MN
Ravich, Paul H. ... **Minneapolis, MN**
Ravicz, Martina Kang ... Fairbanks, AK
Ravid, Cory M. ... San Francisco, CA
Ravid, Nadav ... **Los Angeles, CA**
Ravid, Ossie ... **Los Angeles, CA**
Ravikoff, Ronald B. ... **Miami, FL**
Ravin, Andrea ... Oak Park, IL
Ravin & Associates, LLC ... Houston, TX
Ravin, Carole B. ... **Roseland, NJ**
Ravin, David ... **Roseland, NJ**
Ravin, Greenberg & Marks, A Professional Corporation ... **Newark, NJ**
Roseland, NJ
Ravin, Irwin ... Homer, AK
Ravin, Michael L. ... Newark, NJ
Ravin, Nathan ... **Roseland, NJ**
Ravin, Richard L. ... **Roseland, NJ**
Ravin, Sarasohn, Cook, Baumgarten, Fisch & Rosen, A Professional Corporation
Newark, NJ
Roseland, NJ
West Orange, NJ
New York, NY
Ravin, Sean A. ... Rockville, MD
Ravin, Stephen B. ... **Roseland, NJ**
Ravin & Taylor, LLP ... **San Diego, CA**
Ravin, William W. ... **San Diego, CA**
Ravinal, Frank T. ... Boston, MA
Ravindra, Geetha ... Glen Allen, VA
Ravindranathan, Lekshmy ... Houston, TX
Ravine, Laura D. ... **San Diego, CA**
Ravinski, Catherine ... Miami, FL
Raviola, Patrick R. ... Jersey City, NJ
Raviola, Silvia ... San Jose, CA
Raviolo, John B. ... Grants Pass, OR
Raviotta, Dominick A. ... New Orleans, LA
Ravis, Raymond M. ... **Jacksonville, FL**
Ravis, Thomas P. ... Pittsburgh, PA
Ravitch, Beverly ... New York, NY
Ravitch, Ellen S. ... New York, NY
Ravitch, Frank Stuart ... Orlando, FL
Ravitch, Michael D. ... **Washington, DC**
Ravitz, Allyn ... Farmington Hills, MI
Ravitz, Amy L. ... North Haven, CT
Ravitz, Barbara W. ... **Beverly Hills, CA**
Ravitz, Gary ... **Chicago, IL**
Ravitz, Georgia C. ... Washington, DC
Ravitz, James R. ... **Chicago, IL**
Ravitz, Justin C. ... **Southfield, MI**
Ravitz, Lawrence ... Toms River, NJ
Ravitz, Lee G. ... Southfield, MI
Ravitz, Lynn G. ... Cherry Hill, NJ
Ravitz & Palles, P.C. ... **Chicago, IL**
Raviv, Gil A. ... **New York, NY**
Ravji, Aamer ... **Dallas, TX**
Ravkind, Lauren C. ... **Miami, FL**
Ravkind, Sidney L. ... Houston, TX
Ravkind, William M. ... Dallas, TX
Ravn, Michael E. ... **Merrill, WI**
Ravn, Thomas E. ... **Milwaukee, WI**
Ravnik, Diane M. ... Oakland, CA
Ravosa, Anthony W. ... Springfield, MA
Ravotti, Kathleen A. ... Denver, CO
Ravreby & Gibson ... **Carlsbad, CA**
Ravreby, Mark D. ... **Des Moines, IA**
Ravreby, Richard R. ... **Carlsbad, CA**
Rawdin, Scott M. ... **Dallas, TX**
Rawding, George T. ... Verona, NJ
Rawdon, Francis D. ... New York, NY
Rawdon, Richard M., Jr.
Georgetown, KY
Rawe, C. Maurice ... Sioux City, IA
Rawers, Brian A. ... San Diego, CA
Rawers, Kimberlee S. ... **San Diego, CA**
Rawert, Jennifer R. ... **Louisville, KY**
Rawich, Isabelle ... South Fallsburg, NY
Rawicz, John M. ... **Miami, FL**
Rawicz, Leonard ... **Washington, DC**
Rawitscher & Carnahan, L.L.P.
Houston, TX
Rawitscher, Jack J. ... Houston, TX
Rawitt, Peggy D. ... Westport, CT
Rawitz, Brett G. ... **Oak Brook, IL**
Rawitz, Gary D. ... **New York, NY**
Rawitz, Jeffrey M. ... Los Angeles, CA
Rawitz, Margaret J. ... **Anchorage, AK**
Rawitz, Sidney B. ... Chevy Chase, MD
Rawl, A. Victor ... North Charleston, SC
Rawl, A. Victor, Jr. ... **Columbia, SC**
Rawl, Helen M. ... Charleston, SC
Rawle & Henderson LLP ... **Marlton, NJ**
New York, NY
Philadelphia, PA
Rawle, Jeremy W. ... Draper, UT
Rawles, Douglas C. ... **Los Angeles, CA**
Rawles, Edward H. ... **Champaign, IL**
Rawles, Frederick D. ... Waukegan, IL
Rawles, Frederick D., P.C. ... Waukegan, IL
Rawles, Lee W. ... **Los Angeles, CA**
Rawles, Linda ... Mesa, AZ
Rawles, Margaret O'Donoghue ... Urbana, IL
Rawles, O'Byrne, Stanko & Kepley, P.C.
Champaign, IL
Danville, IL
Monticello, IL
Tuscola, IL
Urbana, IL
Rawles, Thomas V. ... Mesa, AZ
Rawley, James A., Jr. ... Albuquerque, NM
Rawlin, Ronald V. ... Cleveland, OH
Rawlings, Alice Leslie ... **Wichita, KS**
Rawlings, Andrea C. ... **Clarksville, TN**
Rawlings, Charles Scott ... **Cleveland, OH**
Rawlings, Charles Scott ... **Rocky River, OH**
Rawlings, Curtis R. ... **Las Vegas, NV**
Rawlings, David L. ... Columbia, MO
Rawlings, Douglas M. (IBA)
Los Angeles, CA
Rawlings, Dwayne S. ... Washington, DC
Rawlings, Edsel L. ... Lexington, KY
Rawlings, Geoffrey W. ... San Jose, CA
Rawlings, George C., Jr. ... Fredericksburg, VA
Rawlings, George R. ... Louisville, KY
Rawlings, Gregory Dee ... Denver, CO
Rawlings, Henry H., Jr. ... **Las Vegas, NV**
Rawlings, J. Steven ... Florence, KY
Rawlings, J. Thomas ... **Lexington, KY**
Rawlings, James D., II ... Bethlehem, PA
Rawlings, Jeffrey D. ... **Jackson, MS**
Rawlings, John P. ... Richmond, VA
Rawlings, Joyce ... Boston, MA
Rawlings, Linda ... Denver, CO
Rawlings, Nieland, Probasco, Killinger, Ellwanger, Jacobs & Mohrhauser
Sioux City, IA
Rawlings, Olson, Cannon, Gormley & Desruisseaux, A Professional Corporation
Las Vegas, NV
Rawlings, R. Scott ... **Salt Lake City, UT**
Rawlings, Raymond W. ... **Boston, MA**
Rawlings, Richard J. ... St. Cloud, MN
Rawlings, Sherry L. ... Greeley, CO
Rawlings, Steven G. ... **New York, NY**
Rawlings, Stuart L. ... Auburn, CA
Rawlings, Suzanne C. ... Santa Rosa, CA
Rawlings, Thomas Charles ... Atlanta, GA
Rawlings, William J. ... **Sioux City, IA**
Rawlings, William R.
Rancho Cucamonga, CA
Salt Lake City, UT
Rawlings & Wood ... Richmond, VA
Rawlins, Andrew E. ... **Washington, DC**
Rawlins, Charles E. ... **Thomasville, GA**
Rawlins, David D. ... Atlanta, GA
Rawlins, David D., P.C. ... Atlanta, GA
Rawlins, Donald R. ... Memphis, TN
Rawlins, Earl A. ... New York, NY
Rawlins, Elizabeth Dru
Treasury Department, Internal Revenue Service, GV
Rawlins, Elvin E. ... Sun Prairie, WI
Rawlins, Gary N. ... **New York, NY**
Rawlins, J. Anne ... Sacramento, CA
Rawlins, Mary M. ... Houston, TX
Rawlins, Michael D. ... **Las Vegas, NV**
Rawlins, Preston N., Jr. ... McRae, GA
Rawlins, Ralph T. ... Houston, TX
Rawlins, Randa ... **Kansas City, MO**
Rawlins, Robert E. ... Lexington, KY
Rawlins, Robert W. ... Satsuma, FL
Rawlins, Wiley H., Jr. ... Dallas, TX
Rawlinson, David A. ... Portland, OR
Rawlinson, Dennis P., P.C. ... **Portland, OR**
Rawlinson & Ewen, Inc. ... Burbank, CA
Rawlinson, Gary C. ... **Norman, OK**
Rawlinson, Johnnie B. ... Las Vegas, NV
Rawlinson, Joseph E. ... Burbank, CA
Rawlinson, Matthew ... **Chicago, IL**
Rawlinson, Matthew C. ... **Houston, TX**
Rawlinson, Melissa Lehane ... **Portland, OR**
Rawlinson, Michael R. ... New York, NY
Rawlinson, Rex J. ... Burbank, CA
Rawlinson, Terry Marie ... Holly Hill, FL
Rawls, B.J. ... Morgan City, LA
Rawls, Brewster S. ... **Richmond, VA**
Rawls, Brewster S., & Associate, P.C.
Richmond, VA
Rawls, Bruce A. ... **Birmingham, AL**
Rawls, Charles R. ... Washington, DC
Rawls, Charles R.
Department of Agriculture, Office of the General Counsel, GV
Rawls, David ... Little Rock, AR
Rawls, Dawn M. ... **New Orleans, LA**
Rawls, Deborah L. ... Virginia Beach, VA
Rawls & Dickinson, P.A. ... **Charlotte, NC**
Rawls, Eben T., III ... **Charlotte, NC**
Rawls, Frank M. ... Suffolk, VA
Rawls, James C. ... **Atlanta, GA**
Rawls, Jennifer L. ... Nashville, TN
Rawls, John C., III ... **Los Angeles, CA**
Rawls, John D. ... New Orleans, LA
Rawls, Joyce L. ... Atlanta, GA
Rawls, L. Richard ... **Irvine, CA**
Rawls, Leslie C. ... Charlotte, NC
Rawls, Lester L. ... **Portland, OR**
Rawls, Olga Maria Goizueta ... Atlanta, GA
Rawls, R. Steven ... **Tampa, FL**
Rawls, Raleigh R. ... Fort Lauderdale, FL
Rawls, Raytheon M. ... Atlanta, GA
Rawls, Thompson T., II ... **Atlanta, GA**
Rawls, W. Lee ... Washington, DC
Rawls, Walter C., Jr. ... Orange Park, FL
Rawls, William J. ... Indianapolis, IN
Rawls, William J., II ... **Atlanta, GA**
Rawn, Robert J. ... **Stamford, CT**
Rawnsley, Kathi A. ... Palo Alto, CA
Rawnsley, Marla Jayne
Daytona Beach, FL
Maitland, FL
Rawnsley, Terry L. ... Springfield, OH
Rawski, John ... Columbus, OH
Rawson, Chas. M. ... Houston, TX
Rawson, Christopher M. ... **Providence, RI**
Rawson, David A. ... Vista, CA
Rawson, David A. ... New York, NY
Rawson, David P ... New York, NY
Rawson, Donald S. ... Darien, IL
Rawson, E. Blaine ... **Salt Lake City, UT**
Rawson, Henry A. ... Okanogan, WA
Rawson, Hubert E. ("Buddy"), Jr.
Birmingham, AL
Rawson, Jennifer L. ... **Pittsburgh, PA**
Rawson, Jerold S. ... Northbrook, IL
Rawson, Joshua H. ... **New York, NY**
Rawson, Judith Harris ... Shaker Heights, OH
Rawson, M. Jean ... **Naples, FL**
Rawson, Michael R. ... Boston, MA
Rawson, M. Jean, P.A. ... **Naples, FL**
Rawson, Rachel L. ... **Cleveland, OH**
Rawson, Rebecca H. ... **New York, NY**
Rawson, Rebecca H., The Law Firm of
New York, NY
Rawson, Richard J. ... **Murray Hill, NJ**
Rawson, Richard M. ... **Seattle, WA**
Rawson, Robert G. ... Marietta, OH
Rawson, Robert H., Jr. ... **Cleveland, OH**
Rawson, Robert J. ... Washington, DC
Rawson, Vincent E. ... **Kansas City, MO**
Rawson, Warren ... Houston, TX
Rawson, William C., Jr. ... **Glendale, CA**
Rawson, William K. ... **Washington, DC**
Rawson, William L. ... **Chicago, IL**
Rawson, William R. ... Savannah, GA
Raxenberg, Jay D. ... Lawrence, MA
Raxter, M. Elizabeth ... **Honolulu, HI**
Raxter, Ronald D. ... **Raleigh, NC**
Ray, A. Patrick, III ... Birmingham, AL
Ray, Aaron E. ... Houston, TX
Ray & Adair, L.L.C. ... Phoenix, AZ
Prescott, AZ
Ray, Alexander V. ... **Tampa, FL**
Ray, Allen L. ... Chicago, IL
Ray, Allen L. ... Aynor, SC
Conway, SC
Ray & Alton, L.L.P. ... **Columbus, OH**
Ray, Alyson Ann ... **Denver, CO**
Ray, Amy Elizabeth ... Asheville, NC
Ray, Andrew M. ... **Washington, DC**
Ray, Andrew P. ... **Houston, TX**
Ray, Arne M. ... Houston, TX
Ray, Arthur E., Jr. ... Memphis, TN
Ray, Arthur F., II ... **Montgomery, AL**

Ray & Bagnal, Attorneys at Law, P.A.
Aynor, SC
Conway, SC
Ray, Barry ..... Harlingen, TX
Ray, Barry L. ..... Dayton, OH
Ray, Beth P. ..... Columbus, OH
Ray, Borden Martin ..... Tuscaloosa, AL
Ray, Borden Martin, Jr. ..... Tuscaloosa, AL
Ray, Brenda A. ..... Toledo, OH
Ray, Bruce A. ..... San Diego, CA
Ray, Bruce D. ..... Denver, CO
Ray, C. Fount ..... Brownsville, TX
Ray, C. Kenneth, II ..... Phoenix, AZ
Prescott, AZ
Ray, Carl L. ..... Houston, TX
Ray, Carla C. ..... Birmingham, AL
Ray, Carolyn B. ..... Tampa, FL
Ray, Carrold E. ..... Little Rock, AR
North Little Rock, AR
Ray, Cecil A., Jr. ..... Dallas, TX
Ray & Chandler ..... Copperas Cove, TX
Ray, Charles A., IV ..... Huntsville, AL
Ray, Charles A., Jr. ..... Washington, DC
Ray, Charles D. ..... Hartford, CT
Ray, Charles Edwin ..... Port St. Lucie, FL
Ray, Charles R. ..... Nashville, TN
Ray, Charles W., Jr. ..... Anchorage, AK
Ray, Charlotte K. ..... Baton Rouge, LA
Ray, Chas. P. ..... Los Osos, CA
Ray, Christine ..... Santa Barbara, CA
Ray, Christopher D. ..... Dallas, TX
Ray, Christopher L. ..... Savannah, GA
Ray, Christopher S. ..... Las Cruces, NM
Ray, C.L., Law Offices of ..... Austin, TX
Ray, Claudia E. ..... New York, NY
Ray & Cobb ..... Meridian, MS
Ray, Colleen A. ..... Anchorage, AK
Ray, Cristi M. ..... Austin, TX
Ray, Dale C., Jr. ..... Atlanta, GA
Ray, Daniel R. ..... Pittsburg, KS
Ray, David A. ..... Stevens Point, WI
Ray, David C. ..... Doylestown, PA
Philadelphia, PA
Ray, David C. ..... Huntington, WV
Ray, David K. ..... Atlanta, GA
Ray, David L. ..... Los Angeles, CA
Ray, David L. ..... Sacramento, CA
Ray, David L. ..... Wilmington, NC
Ray, David L., & Associates
Baton Rouge, LA
New Orleans, LA
Ray, David P. ..... Portland, ME
Ray, Diane B. ..... Minneapolis, MN
Ray, Donald H. ..... Fort Worth, TX
Ray, Donald J. ..... Tullahoma, TN
Ray, Donald R. ..... Norfolk, VA
Ray, Doug W. ..... Austin, TX
Ray, Douglas J. ..... New York, NY
Ray, E. Alston ..... Birmingham, AL
Ray, E. Garland ..... Huntington, WV
Ray, Eileen Frances
Department of Housing and Urban Development, Office of General Counsel, GV
Ray, Elissa V. ..... Dexter, MI
Ray, Elizabeth ..... Houston, TX
Ray, Ellen G. ..... Atlanta, GA
Ray, Ellen P. ..... Richmond, VA
Ray, Elmer P., III ..... Memphis, TN
Ray & Fleischer ..... Chicago, IL
Ray, Frank A. ..... Columbus, OH
Ray, Frank D. ..... Columbus, OH
Ray, Frank N. ..... Providence, RI
Ray, G. Scott, & Associates ..... Edmond, OK
Ray, Gallinaro & Strayhorne
Annandale, VA
Ray, Gary A. ..... Dallas, TX
Ray, Gary R. ..... Monterey, CA
Ray, Gayle W. ..... Buffalo, TX
Ray, George
Department of Housing and Urban Development, GV
Ray, George T., Jr. ..... Littleton, NH
Ray, Gerald K.
Department Of Health And Human Services, Social Security Administration, GV
Ray, Gilbert T. ..... Los Angeles, CA
Ray, Glenn R. ..... Newport Beach, CA
Ray & Glick, Ltd. ..... Libertyville, IL
Ray, Greg A. ..... Denver, CO
Ray, Gregory C. ..... Mattoon, IL
Ray, Gregory R. ..... Pittsburgh, PA
Ray, Hal R., Jr. ..... Fort Worth, TX
Ray, Harlan L. ..... Denver, CO
Ray, Harry B. ..... Chattanooga, TN
Ray, Harvey B. ..... Meridian, MS
Ray, Henry T. ..... Amarillo, TX
Ray, Herbert B. ..... Binghamton, NY
Ray, Herbert H., Jr. ..... Anchorage, AK
Ray, Herbert L. ..... Springdale, AR
Ray, Hillary J. ..... Miami, FL
Ray, Hugh M. ..... New York, NY
Houston, TX
Ray, Hugh M., III ..... Houston, TX
Ray, Ira S. ..... Louisville, KY
Ray & Isler, P.C. ..... Vienna, VA
Ray, J.A., II, P.C. ..... Pittsburgh, PA
Ray, J. Billie, Jr. ..... Birmingham, AL
Ray, J. Christopher ..... Sanford, FL
Ray, J. Kevin ..... Denver, CO
Ray, J. Mark ..... Atlanta, GA
Ray, J. Phillip ..... Houston, TX
Ray, J. Stevenson ..... Jackson, MS
Ray, J. Thomas ..... Little Rock, AR
Ray, J. William ..... Greenville, SC
Ray, Jack P. ..... Monterey, TN
Ray, James C. ..... Raleigh, NC
Ray, James Hugh ..... Tupelo, MS
Ray, James L. ..... Harrisburg, PA
Philadelphia, PA
Ray, James L. ..... Houston, TX
Ray, James P. ..... Hartford, CT
Ray, James S. ..... Washington, DC
Ray, Janet I. ..... Los Angeles, CA
Ray, Jared S. ..... Cleveland, OH
Ray, Jay Edward ..... Dallas, TX
Ray, Jeanne Cullinan ..... New York, NY
Ray, Jeff ..... El Paso, TX
Ray, Jefferson G., III (P.A.) ..... Mount Dora, FL
Ray, Jeffrey A. ..... Morgantown, WV
Ray, Jeffrey G. ..... Ocean City, MD
Ray, Jeffrey P. ..... Okemos, MI
Ray, Jeffrey P. ..... Kansas City, MO
Ray, Jeffrey P., P.C. ..... Okemos, MI
Ray, Jeffrey S. ..... Fairfax, VA
Ray, Jeffrey W. ..... Las Vegas, NV
Ray, Jennifer S., Law Office of
Houston, TX
Ray, Jennifer Smith ..... San Francisco, CA
Ray, Jerry C. ..... Sherman, TX
Ray, Jerry D. ..... Palo Pinto, TX
Ray, Jesse M. ..... Greenville, SC
Ray, JoAnne ..... Houston, TX
Ray, John ..... Miller Place, NY
Ray, John & Associates ..... Miller Place, NY
Ray, John D. ..... Salt Lake City, UT
Ray, John E. ..... La Plata, MD
Ray, John J. ..... Buffalo, NY
Ray, John J., III ..... Chicago, IL
Ray, John J., Jr. ..... Glens Falls, NY
Ray, John J., Jr. ..... Lake George, NY
Ray, John L. ..... Washington, DC
Ray, John L. ..... San Antonio, TX
Ray, John L. ..... Charleston, WV
Ray, John S. ..... Los Angeles, CA
Ray, John Warner, Jr. ..... Atlanta, GA
Ray, Jon R. ..... San Antonio, TX
Ray, Jonathan M. ..... Brookfield, WI
Ray, Joseph H. ..... Dallas, TX
Ray, Joseph Lane ..... Tabor City, NC
Ray, Joseph T. ..... Louisville, KY
Ray, Julius A., II ..... Pittsburgh, PA
Ray, Karla Pankratz ..... Greenwich, CT
Ray, Katherine D. ..... San Francisco, CA
Ray, Katherine Ella ..... Denver, CO
Ray, Kathryn D. ..... Department of Justice, Civil Division, GV
Ray, Keith P. ..... Dallas, TX
Ray, Kenneth G. ..... New York, NY
Ray, Kenneth P. ..... Utica, NY
Ray, Kenneth P., P.C. ..... Utica, NY
Ray, Kimberly Robinson
Oklahoma City, OK
Ray, Kristin L. ..... Louisville, KY
Ray, Larry E. ..... Washington, DC
Ray, Laura K. ..... Wilmington, DE
Ray, Laurie D. ..... Boston, MA
Ray, Lelia M. ..... Houma, LA
Ray, Lisa ..... Grand Rapids, MI
Ray, Loraine Anne ..... Chicago, IL
Ray, Louis F., Jr. ..... Pensacola, FL
Ray, M. Cecilia ..... Minneapolis, MN
Ray, Magan ..... Palo Alto, CA
Ray, Marshall R. ..... Brownsville, TX
Ray, Mary Beth Pendley ..... Washington, DC
Ray, Mary E. ..... Covington, KY
Ray, Mary Lou Ryan ..... Brownsville, TX
Ray, Matthew W. ..... Dallas, TX
Ray, Maureen E. ..... Austin, TX
Ray, McChristian & Jeans
Las Cruces, NM
El Paso, TX
Ray, Melanie A. ..... Columbus, OH
Ray, Michael B. ..... Washington, DC
Ray, Michael C. ..... Orange, CA
Ray, Michael D. ..... Crossett, AR
Ray, Michael E. ..... Atlanta, GA
Ray, Michael E. ..... Winston-Salem, NC
Ray, Michael S. ..... Washington, DC
Ray, Michael W. ..... Birmingham, AL
Ray, Michelle L. ..... Phoenix, AZ
Ray, Middleton P., Jr. ..... Little Rock, AR
Ray, Montfort S. ..... Blairsville, GA
Ray, Natasha R. ..... San Francisco, CA
Ray, Nathan A. ..... Akron, OH
Ray, Neal H. ..... Atlanta, GA
Ray, Nicholas M ..... Columbus, OH
Ray, Oliver & Ward, L.L.C. ..... Tuscaloosa, AL
Ray, Pamela A. ..... Denver, CO
Ray, Patricia ..... Longview, TX
Ray, Patricia R. ..... Boston, MA
Ray, Patrick A. ..... Phoenix, AZ
Ray, Patrick R., Jr ..... Atlanta, GA
Ray, Paul C. ..... Las Vegas, NV
Ray, Paula Marie ..... Denver, CO
Ray, Peter C. ..... Coral Gables, FL
Ray, Peter Richard
North Palm Beach, FL
Ray, Priscilla M. ..... Virginia Beach, VA
Ray, Quinney & Nebeker, A Professional Corporation ..... Albuquerque, NM
Provo, UT
Salt Lake City, UT
Ray, R. David ..... West Plains, MO
Ray, Rachel P. ..... Pensacola, FL
Ray, Ralph J., Jr. ..... Fort Lauderdale, FL
Ray, Randall G. ..... Dallas, TX
Ray, Raymond B. ..... Fort Lauderdale, FL
Ray, Renee ..... Louisville, KY
Ray, Richard Barton ..... Bradenton, FL
Ray, Richard J. ..... Fairbanks, AK
Ray, Richard L. ..... Canton, TX
Ray, Robert A., Law Offices of ..... Tyler, TX
Ray, Robert B. ..... Gainesville, FL
Ray, Robert B. ..... Knoxville, TN
Ray, Robert C. ..... Greenville, SC
Ray, Robert D. ..... Des Moines, IA
Ray, Robert E. ..... Greeley, CO
Ray, Robert E. ..... Lincoln, NE
Ray, Robert G. ..... Fayetteville, NC
Ray, Robert J. ..... Pittsburgh, PA
Ray, Robert N. ..... San Antonio, TX
Ray, Robert W. ..... Alexandria, VA
Ray, Robinson, Carle & Davies P.L.L.
Cleveland, OH
Ray, Robyn R. ..... Pottsville, PA
Ray, Rod A. ..... Lafayette, IN
Ray, Rodney A. ..... West Point, MS
Ray, Rodney Bruce ..... Tacoma, WA
Ray, Rodney D.
Federal Deposit Insurance Corporation, Liquidation Branch, GV
Ray, Roger ..... Geneseo, IL
Ray, Roger B. ..... Largo, FL
Ray, Ronald A. ..... Alexandria, VA
Ray, Ronald D. ..... Crestwood, KY
Ray, Ronald E. ..... Louisville, KY
Ray, Ronald O., Jr. ..... Tulsa, OK
Ray, Rosalind R. ..... Silver Spring, MD
Ray, Royce A., III ..... Mobile, AL
Ray, Russell S. ..... Montrose, CO
Ray, Russell W. ..... Annandale, VA
Ray, S. Lorrie ..... Denver, CO
Ray, S. Michele ..... New Orleans, LA
Ray, Sandra K. ..... Columbia, SC
Ray, Sarah Wimberly ..... Houston, TX
Ray, Scott A. ..... Atlanta, GA
Ray, Scott E. ..... Miami, FL
Ray, Sharon L. ..... Marianna, FL
Ray, Smith ..... Midland, TX
Ray, Sophia R. ..... Carlsbad, CA
Ray, Stephan M. ..... Los Angeles, CA
Ray, Stephanie L. ..... New York, NY
Ray, Stephen E. ..... Chicago, IL
Ray, Stephen W. ..... Tulsa, OK
Ray, Steve R. ..... Menlo Park, CA
Ray, Steven B. ..... Fort Collins, CO
Ray, Steven H. ..... Cincinnati, OH
Ray, Steven W. ..... Columbus, GA
Ray, Steven W. ..... Vienna, VA
Ray, Susan C. ..... Hartford, CT
Ray, Susan J. ..... Philadelphia, PA
Ray, Suzette L. ..... Austin, TX
Ray, T. Hulen ..... DeLand, FL
Ray, Theodore P. ..... Beaumont, TX
Ray, Thomas E. ..... Cardington, OH
Ray, Thomas E. ..... Chattanooga, TN
Ray, Thomas E., Co., Ltd. ..... Cardington, OH
Ray, Thomas J. ..... St. Louis, MO
Ray, Thomas J. ..... Carson City, NV
Ray, Thomas J., Jr. ..... Arnold, MO
Ray, Thomas L.
Department of Transportation, Office of the General Counsel, GV
Ray, Thomas L. ..... Farmington, MO
Ray, Thomas M. ..... San Francisco, CA
Ray, Thomas R. ..... Jacksonville, FL
Ray, Timothy B. ..... Gainesville, FL
Ray, Timothy P. ..... Livingston, NJ
Ray & Tipton ..... Opelika, AL
Ray, Todd L. ..... Dalton, GA
Ray, Van Cleave & Jackson, P.C.
Tullahoma, TN
Ray, W. Larry ..... Opelika, AL
Ray, Walter J. ..... Pennsville, NJ
Ray, William B. ..... Copperas Cove, TX
Ray, William C. ..... Greensboro, NC
Ray, William F. ..... Jackson, MS
Ray, William H. ..... Haltom City, TX
Ray, William M., II ..... Lawrenceville, GA
Ray, William N. ..... Birmingham, AL
Ray, William P. ..... Eugene, OR
Ray, William R. ..... Knoxville, TN
Ray, William Thomas ..... Mint Hill, NC
Ray, Wood & Fine, L.L.P. ..... Austin, TX
Longview, TX
Rosenberg, TX
Raya, Edgardo G. ..... Carolina, PR
Raya, Kevin M. ..... San Diego, CA
Raya, Simeon ..... Winchester, MA
Rayano, Janine M. ..... New York, NY
Rayback and Blanarik, Inc.
State College, PA
Rayback, Brian M. ..... Portland, ME
Rayback, James M. ..... State College, PA
Raybin, David L. ..... Nashville, TN
Raybin, Gregg A. ..... New York, NY
Raybin, Louis ..... Brooklyn, NY
Raybold, Donald E. ..... Waco, TX
Rayborn, David E. ..... Pocatello, ID
Rayborn, Maureen M. ..... Camden, NJ
Philadelphia, PA
Rayborn and Rayborn ..... Twin Falls, ID
Rayborn, Robert E. ..... Twin Falls, ID
Raybould, Patricia L. ..... Atlanta, GA
Raybould, Warren A. ..... Los Angeles, CA
Rayboun, Michael ..... Pensacola, FL
Raybuck, David W. ..... Columbus, OH
Raybuck, Julia Varrasse, Law Offices of
Philadelphia, PA
Rayburn, Beverly Kay ..... Columbia, TN
Rayburn, C. Richard, Jr. ..... Charlotte, NC
Rayburn, Clyde J., Jr. ..... Kansas City, MO
Rayburn, D. Lawrence ..... Tampa, FL
Rayburn, Douglass M. ..... Dallas, TX
Rayburn, James T. ..... Phoenix, AZ
Rayburn, Jill A. ..... Kingsport, TN
Rayburn, Kermit O. ..... Oklahoma City, OK
Rayburn, Madison S. ..... Houston, TX
Rayburn, Mark D. ..... Beaumont, TX
Rayburn, Mary-Anne S. ..... Portland, OR
Rayburn, Moon & Smith, P.A.
Charlotte, NC
Rayburn, Paige B. ..... Oxford, MS
Rayburn, Patrick M. ..... Atlanta, GA
Rayburn, Paul V. ..... Los Angeles, CA
Rayburn & Pierce ..... Oxford, MS
Rayburn, Ralph F. ..... Portland, OR
Rayburn, Robert John, III
Prairie Village, KS
Rayburn, Robert P. ..... Chattanooga, TN
Rayburn, Ross ..... Ingleside, TX
Rayburn, Scott M. ..... Oklahoma City, OK
Rayburn, S. T. ..... Oxford, MS
Rayburn, Wm. W. ..... Gadsden, AL
Raycraft, Laura A. ..... Placerville, CA
Raycraft, Terry L. ..... Montgomery, AL
Rayder, Helene Norcross ..... Little Rock, AR
Raydon, Gerald T.
Rancho Palos Verdes, CA
Raye, Jesse A ..... New York, NY
Raye, Kenneth M. ..... Barnhart, MO
Rayer, Catherine Chavez
Los Angeles, CA
Rayer, Frances P. ..... Philadelphia, PA
Rayer, Michael A. ..... St. Paul, MN
Rayer, Thomas A. ..... New Orleans, LA
Rayer, Thomas A., Jr. ..... New Orleans, LA
Rayes, Donna S. ..... Pleasanton, TX
Rayes, Douglas L. ..... Scottsdale, AZ
Raye-Wong, Catherine ..... Redwood City, CA
Raye-Wong, Catherine ..... San Carlos, CA
Rayfield, Donald R. ..... Princeton, IL
Rayfield, Jacqueline F. ..... New York, NY
Rayfield, John D. ..... Crystal City, MO
Rayford, Greg W. ..... Chicago, IL
Rayford, James E. ..... Memphis, TN
Rayford, Konrad J. ..... Chicago, IL
Raygor, Kent R. ..... Los Angeles, CA
Rayhill Bankert & Rayhill
New Hartford, NY
Rayhill, Brian J. ..... New York, NY
Rayhill, Ellen S. ..... New Hartford, NY
Rayhill, James W. ..... New York, NY
Rayhill, Peter M. ..... New Hartford, NY
Rayhill, Philip A. ..... New Hartford, NY
Rayhill, Philip Richard ..... Boise, ID
Rayis, James Y. ..... Atlanta, GA
Rayis, John D. ..... Chicago, IL
Raykher, Simon ..... New York, NY
Raykhinshteyn, Tamara Delane
Farmington Hills, MI
Rayl, Brian D. ..... Cadiz, OH
Rayl, Charles R. ..... Cottonwood Falls, KS
Rayl, Christopher J. ..... Pittsburgh, PA
Rayl and Fowler, Chartered
Cottonwood Falls, KS
Rayl, Laura R. ..... Temple, TX
Rayl, Randy L. ..... Pittsburgh, PA
Rayl, Rick E. ..... Irvine, CA
Rayl, Susan D. ..... Indianapolis, IN
Rayle, Brad A. ..... Bloomfield Hills, MI
Rayle & Matthews ..... Bowling Green, OH
Rayle, Max E. ..... Bowling Green, OH
Rayle, Merrick Scott ..... Chicago, IL
Rayle, Nathaniel
Pension Benefit Guaranty Corporation, Office of the General Counsel, GV
Raylesberg, Alan I. ..... New York, NY
Raylesberg, Caren Thea Coven
Chappaqua, NY
Rayll, John A., Jr. ..... Tulsa, OK
Raymaker, Mindy K. ..... Tallahassee, FL
Rayman, Arthur M. ..... Rockville, MD
Rayman, Emilie H. ..... Marina Del Rey, CA
Rayman & Hamlin ..... Kalamazoo, MI
Rayman, Robert C. ..... State College, PA
Rayman, S. Eric ..... New York, NY
Rayman, Steven L. ..... Calabasas, CA
Rayman, Steven L. ..... Kalamazoo, MI
Raymar, Donald ..... Kenilworth, NJ
Raymar, Irving ..... Flushing, NY
Raymar, Robert S. ..... Newark, NJ
Rayment, Brian J. ..... Tulsa, OK
Rayment, David W. ..... Concord, NH
Raymer, Brian Todd ..... Newport, OR
Raymer, Debra L. ..... Chicago, IL
Raymer, Edward E., Jr.
Winston-Salem, NC
Raymer, Gregory P. ..... San Diego, CA
Raymer, Joel L. ..... Cincinnati, OH
Raymer, Richard E. ..... Atlanta, GA
Memphis, TN
Nashville, TN
Raymer, Robert M. ..... San Francisco, CA
Raymer, William B. ..... Napoleon, MI
Raymon, Edward B. ..... Tuskegee, AL
Raymon, Elaine Lubel ..... Tuskegee, AL
Raymon, Gerald ..... Farmingdale, NY
Raymon, Hillel ..... Highland Park, NJ
Raymon and Raymon, L.L.C.
Tuskegee, AL
Raymond, Anne E. ..... New Orleans, LA
Raymond, Arthur F. ..... Hesperia, MI
Raymond, Aubrey L. ..... Syracuse, IN
Raymond, Bradley T.
Farmington Hills, MI
Raymond, Bruce H. ..... Hartford, CT
Raymond, Catherine O. ..... Philadelphia, PA
Raymond, Charles D. ..... Department of Labor, Office of the Solicitor, GV
Raymond, Charles E. ..... Wyandotte, MI
Raymond, Charles W. ..... Neligh, NE
Raymond, Cynthia J. ..... Wayne, PA
Raymond, Cyrus V. ..... Garnerville, NY
Raymond, Dana M. ..... New York, NY
Raymond, David ..... Mount Vernon, IL
Raymond, David B. ..... Overland Park, KS
Raymond, David J. ..... Richfield, MN
Raymond, David W. ..... Washington, DC
Raymond, Deborah L. ..... San Diego, CA
Raymond, Deborah L. ..... Solana Beach, CA

Raymond, Dina M. ....Boston, MA
Raymond, Dion-Cherie ....Los Angeles, CA
Raymond, Donald E. ....Kansas City, MO
Raymond, Dorothy A. ....Newton, MA
Raymond, Dorothy Gill ....Louisville, CO
Raymond, Douglas F. ....Scotia, NY
Raymond, Douglas J. ....Denver, CO
Raymond, Edward M. ....Clinton, WA
Raymond, Elam Jewett ....Tulsa, OK
Raymond, Elizabeth A. ....Chicago, IL
Raymond, F. Douglas ....Philadelphia, PA
Raymond & Feldman ....New York, NY
Raymond, Frank H. ....Citrus Heights, CA
Raymond, George L. ....Englewood, CO
Raymond, Gerald David ....Wampsville, NY
Raymond, Greer & Sassaman, P.C.
Phoenix, AZ
Raymond, J. Joseph ....St. Louis, MO
Raymond, J. Paul ....Clearwater, FL
Raymond, J. Todd ....Manalapan, NJ
Raymond, James F. ....Concord, NH
Raymond, Jan H. ....San Francisco, CA
Raymond, Jan S. ....Woodland, CA
Raymond, Jason ....Chicago, IL
Raymond, Jeanne-Marie S.
Washington, DC
Raymond, Joanie ....Frederick, MD
Raymond, John A. ....Tarzana, CA
Raymond, John D. ....San Francisco, CA
Raymond, John F. ....Seattle, WA
Raymond, John J., Jr. ....Boca Raton, FL
Naples, FL
Palm Beach Gardens, FL
Birmingham, MI
Raymond, John J., Sr. ....Boca Raton, FL
Naples, FL
Palm Beach Gardens, FL
Raymond, John W. ....Norge, VA
Raymond, Jonathan P. ....Boston, MA
Raymond, Jonathan S. ....New York, NY
Raymond, Joshua H. ....West Orange, NJ
Raymond, Katherine ....New York, NY
Raymond, Kevin M. ....Seattle, WA
Raymond, Laurie A. ....Portland, OR
Raymond, Laurier T., Jr. ....Lewiston, ME
Raymond Law Office ....Milwaukee, WI
Raymond, Lisa M. ....Plymouth, MA
Raymond, Lorraine ....Chattanooga, TN
Raymond, Louis F. ....Milwaukee, WI
Raymond, Louis K. ....Burbank, CA
Raymond, Mark E. ....West Palm Beach, FL
Raymond, Mark F. ....Miami, FL
West Palm Beach, FL
Raymond, Mark R. ....Chicago, IL
Raymond, Martha E. ....Seattle, WA
Raymond, Mary C. ....Buffalo, NY
Raymond, Mary, Law Office of ....Miami, FL
Raymond, Melvin L. ....St. Louis, MO
Raymond, Michael J. ....Phoenix, AZ
Raymond, Michael T. ....Farmington Hills, MI
Raymond, Mildred D. ....Kansas City, MO
Raymond, Patrick J. ....Binghamton, NY
Raymond, Paul W. ....Newport Beach, CA
Raymond, Perry M. ....Irving, TX
Raymond, Peter D. ....New York, NY
Raymond, Philip T., III ....Macon, GA
Raymond, Phillip C. ....Seattle, WA
Raymond & Prokop, P.C. ....Detroit, MI
Southfield, MI
Raymond, Raymond & Minton
Kansas City, MO
Raymond, Richard C. ....Greenwich, CT
New York, NY
Raymond, Richard L. ....Media, PA
Raymond, Robert ....Bronx, NY
Raymond, Robert C. ....Milwaukee, WI
Raymond, Robert G. ....Cleveland, OH
Raymond, Robert H., Jr. ....Harrisburg, PA
Raymond, Robert J. ....Department of Justice,
Criminal Division, GV
Raymond, Robert J. ....New York, NY
Raymond, Robert L. ....Little River, CA
Raymond, Robert L. ....Destrehan, LA
Raymond, Robert P. ....Ridgefield, CT
Raymond, Robert R. ....Kansas City, MO
Raymond, Robert S. ....Shutesbury, MA
Raymond, Spencer H. ....Chicago, IL
Raymond, Stephanie W. ....Farmington, CT
Raymond, Stephen G. ....Cherry Hill, NJ
Raymond, Stephen L. ....Rochester, NY
Raymond, Steven E. ....Shelbyville, MO
Raymond, Steven M. ....Bloomfield Hills, MI
Raymond, Steven P. ....New York, NY
Raymond, Sumner Low ....Essex, MA
Salem, MA
Raymond, Susan Dalton ....Macon, GA
Raymond, Suzanne ....Englewood, NJ
Raymond, Tim C. ....Florham Park, NJ
Raymond, Tobias J ....New York, NY
Raymond, Virginia M. ....Austin, TX
Raymond & Walsh, P.C.
Farmington Hills, MI
Raymond, William D. ....Woodland Hills, CA
Raymond, William M. ....Carson City, NV
Raymond, Wilson, Conway, Barr, Hahl & Jenkins, P.A. ....Daytona Beach, FL
Ormond Beach, FL
Raymond-Flood, Margaret ....Somerville, NJ
Raymondi, Daniel G. ....Quincy, MA
Raymondis, Stephen C. ....Milwaukee, WI
Raymos, Victor E. ....Interlachen, FL
Raynak, James A. ....Phoenix, AZ
Raynak, Janis Posner ....Phoenix, AZ
Raynal, Lazar Pol ....Chicago, IL
Raynaud, Kari L. ....Santa Ana, CA
Raymdon, Darra Lynn ....Scottsdale, AZ
Rayndon & Longfellow, P.C. ....Phoenix, AZ
Scottsdale, AZ
Tempe, AZ
Rayne, Ronald G. ....Salisbury, MD
Rayne, Steven T. ....Portland, OR
Rayne, Susan Dechant ....Worcester, MA
Rayne, Timothy F. ....West Chester, PA
Rayner, Daniel A. J. ....New York, NY
Rayner, Edward J. ....New York, NY
Rayner, Kim M. ....Chestnut Ridge, NY
Rayner, Peter D. ....Spokane, WA
Rayner, Ruth ....Dallas, TX
Rayner, Seymour ....Brooklyn, NY
Rayner, W. Whitaker ....Jackson, MS
Raynes, Alan S. ....Los Angeles, CA
Raynes, Arthur G. ....Philadelphia, PA
Raynes, Arthur L. ....Morristown, NJ
Raynes, Bonnie ....Norristown, PA
Raynes, Boris ....Palos Verdes Estates, CA
Raynes, Christopher P. ....Trenton, MO
Raynes, David A. ....Dallas, TX
Raynes, Evan A. ....Washington, DC
Raynes, Jeffrey S. ....San Bernardino, CA
Raynes, Matthew S. ....Bangor, ME
Raynes, McCarty, Binder, Ross & Mundy
Haddon Heights, NJ
Philadelphia, PA
Raynes, Robert S., Jr. ....Stuart, FL
Raynes, Scott E. ....Houston, TX
Raynes, Stephen E. ....Philadelphia, PA
Raynes, Thomas R. ....Gunnison, CO
Raynolds, Kelly B. ....Tacoma, WA
Raynolds, Ronald G. ....Tulsa, OK
Raynolds, William F., II ....Tulsa, OK
Raynor, Alan H. ....Dallas, TX
Raynor, Arnold ....Hawley, PA
Raynor, Charles P.
Department Of The Interior,
Office of the Solicitor, GV
Raynor, David F. ....Akron, OH
Raynor, Glenn C. ....Raleigh, NC
Raynor, Gordon R. ....Hamden, CT
Raynor, Harvey W., III ....Belhaven, NC
Raynor, Jeffrey S. ....Hobe Sound, FL
Juno Beach, FL
Raynor, Jerome H. ....Buffalo, NY
Raynor, John P. ....Omaha, NE
Raynor, Kenneth R. ....Charlotte, NC
Raynor Law Firm, P.A. ....Hobe Sound, FL
Juno Beach, FL
Jupiter, FL
Raynor, Mark E. ....Jacksonville, NC
Raynor, Nancy Kahl ....Philadelphia, PA
Raynor, Rensch & Pfeiffer ....Omaha, NE
Raynor, Robert G., Jr. ....New Bern, NC
Raynor, Shirley Pharr ....Warner Robins, GA
Raynor, Stephen J. ....Dallas, TX
Raynor, Stephen James, P.C. ....Dallas, TX
Raynor, Steven L. ....Charlottesville, VA
Raynor, Ted C. ....Beverly Hills, CA
Memphis, TN
Raynor, Theresa A. ....Denver, CO
Raynor, William J., Jr. ....Plainsboro, NJ
Raynovich, George, Jr. ....Pittsburgh, PA
Raynsford, Craig O. ....Department of Justice,
Immigration and Naturalization Service, GV
Raynsford, Kathleen J. ....Washington, DC
Raynsford, Rick L. ....Newport Beach, CA
Rayo, I. Peter ....Brooklyn, NY
Rayo, Mark J. ....Brooklyn, NY
Rayome, James P. ....Washington, DC
Rayon, Howard W. ....La Mesa, CA
Raysa, Richard G. ....Oak Park, IL
Raysa, Richard J. ....St. Charles, IL
Raysa & Skelton, P.C. ....Oak Park, IL
Raysa, William G. ....Oak Park, IL
Raysman, Richard ....New York, NY
Rayson, E. H. ....Knoxville, TN
Rayson, G. Scott ....Nashville, TN
Rayson, John B. ....Knoxville, TN
Rayson, John C. ....Fort Lauderdale, FL
Rayson, Ronald A. ....Knoxville, TN
Raysses, Kathryn G. ....Chicago, IL
Rayton, Michael R. ....Seattle, WA
Rayve, Brian Richard ....Salt Lake City, UT
Rayvis, Cynthia ....Los Angeles, CA
Rayvis, Myron J. ....Miami, FL
Ray-Yarletts, Jeanine S.
Research Triangle Park, NC
Rayzor, J. Newton ....Denton, TX
Raz, Donald J. ....Seattle, WA
Raz, Lawrence W. ....Washington, DC
Raz, Noam Y. ....Skokie, IL
Raza, Asim S. ....St. Louis, MO
Raza, Mark ....Rockville, MD
Raza, Saleem ....Topeka, KS
Razani, Sara Shirin ....Honolulu, HI
Razban, Kevin M. ....Orange, CA
Razi, Maziar ....Pasadena, CA
Razim, Edward A., III ....Dallas, TX
Razis, George J. ....Astoria, NY
Razis, Jack, II ....Grand Prairie, TX
Razman, Anita R. ....Jericho, NY
Raznick, Brian S. ....Detroit, MI
Raznick, Carol S. ....Denver, CO
Raznick, Fred S. ....Santa Fe, NM
Raznick, Linda Diamond ....Encino, CA
Raznick, Melvin M. ....Southfield, MI
Raznikov, Richard ....San Rafael, CA
Razo, Gregory P. ....Kodiak, AK
Razo, Jose H. ....Redwood City, CA
Razook, Bradley G. ....New York, NY
Razook, Richard J. ....Miami, FL
Razor, Kimberly L. ....Flemingsburg, KY
Razza, Michael S. ....Norwood, MA
Razzak, M. Amr I. ....New York, NY
Razzano, A. William ....Clifton, IL
Watseka, IL
Razzano, Frank C. ....Washington, DC
Razzano & Kinzer ....Clifton, IL
Piper City, IL
Watseka, IL
Razzano, Pasquale A. ....New York, NY
Razzano, Vincent J. ....Brea, CA
Razzolini, J. Claire ....Rochester, NY
R. Benjamin, Scott ....San Diego, CA
Rdzanek, Caroline E. ....Chicago, IL
Re, Andrea Geiger ....Boston, MA
Re, Daniel C. ....Bend, OR
Ré, Donald M. ....Los Angeles, CA
Re, James B. ....Boston, MA
Ré, Jennifer Godfrieda Parser
New York, NY
Re, John C. ....New York, NY
Re, Joseph R. ....Newport Beach, CA
Ré, Lawrence C. ....Great Neck, NY
Re, Margaret A. ....Neponsit, NY
Re, Matthew R. ....Sacramento, CA
Re, Michael G. ....St. Louis, MO
Re, Michael S. ....Garden City, NY
Re, Robert B. ....New York, NY
Re, Robert J. ....Morristown, NJ
Re, Robert V. ....Flushing, NY
Ré , Stephanie A. ....St. Louis, MO
Ré, Thomas C. ....New York, NY
Re, Victor M. ....Rockaway Park, NY
Rea, Anne E. ....Chicago, IL
Rea, Barbara S. ....Frankfort, KY
Rea, Bryce, Jr. ....Washington, DC
Rea, C. Marshall ....Houston, TX
Rea, Carroll Daniel ....Roanoke, VA
Rea, Charles A. ....Pittsburgh, PA
Rea, Charles R. ....Plano, IL
Rea, Charles W. ....Baton Rouge, LA
Rea, Cross & Auchincloss
Washington, DC
Rea, Cyrus Franklin, II ....San Antonio, TX
Rea, David P. ....Bloomfield Hills, MI
Rea, Donald A. ....Baltimore, MD
Rea, Dorothy Giberson ....Austin, TX
Rea, Henry E., Jr. ....Pittsburgh, PA
Rea, Herbert William ....New York, NY
Rea, James M. ....Clarkesville, GA
Rea, James M. ....Upper Marlboro, MD
Rea, James P. ....Birmingham, AL
Rea, Jeanne Marie ....Memphis, TN
Rea, Jeffrey C. ....Fort Worth, TX
Rea, Jeffrey J., Law Offices of
Westfield, NJ
New York, NY
Rea, Joette J. ....San Rafael, CA
Rea, John C. ....Scottsdale, AZ
Rea, John M. ....San Francisco, CA
Rea, John S. ....Cleveland, OH
Rea, Joseph L. ....New Brunswick, NJ
Rea, Kimberlea Shaw ....White Plains, NY
Rea, Loren G. ....Kansas City, MO
Rea, Lynda B. ....Ellijay, GA
Rea, Natalie B. ....New York, NY
Rea, Norman H. ....Pittsburgh, PA
Rea, Pam ....Houston, TX
Rea, Patricia K. ....Birmingham, AL
Rea, Patrick I. ....Alexandria, VA
Rea, Paul W. ....Lincoln, NE
Rea, Peter H. ....Branson, MO
Rea, R. Sam. ....Austin, TX
Rea, Rea & Lashinsky ....Hollidaysburg, PA
Rea, Richard H. ....Phoenix, AZ
Tucson, AZ
Rea, Richard H. ....Wilmington, DE
Rea, Robert C. ....Washington, DC
Rea, Robert P. ....Hollidaysburg, PA
Rea, Roger W. ....Phoenix, AZ
Rea, Russell R. ....Phoenix, AZ
Rea, Stanley M., Jr. ....St. Louis, MO
Rea, Susan P. ....Hollidaysburg, PA
Rea, Teresa Stanek ....Alexandria, VA
Rea, Traci S. ....Pittsburgh, PA
Rea, William C. ....Little Rock, AR
Rea, William J. ....Los Angeles, CA
Rea, William John, Jr. ....Los Angeles, CA
Reabuck, Karen M. ....Cherry Hill, NJ
Philadelphia, PA
Reabuck, Roy A. ....Allentown, PA
Reach & Associates, P.A. ....Greenville, SC
Reach, Charles H., III ....New York, NY
Reach, Diane Nicas ....New York, NY
Reach, Ian J. ....Ann Arbor, MI
Reach, James B. ....Florham Park, NJ
Reach, Ranney & Carpenter ....Ann Arbor, MI
Reach, Russell P. ....Greenville, SC
Read, Alice E. ....Milwaukee, WI
Read, Allen C. ....Saratoga Springs, NY
Read, Alten W. ....Hackettstown, NJ
Read, Arthur M., II ....North Scituate, RI
Read, Arthur N. ....Philadelphia, PA
Read, Benjamin H. ....Dallas, TX
Read, Betty ....Albuquerque, NM
Read, Bruce M. ....Kennebunk, ME
Read, Cameron, (P.C.) ....Boston, MA
Manchester, NH
Read, Carole L. ....Southampton, NY
Read, Charles C. ....Los Angeles, CA
Washington, DC
Read, Charles Gregory ....Jeffersonville, IN
Read, Christopher M. ....New York, NY
Read, Dale, Jr. ....Vancouver, WA
Read, Dale W. ....Vancouver, WA
Read, Daniel F. ....Durham, NC
Read, Daniel K. ....Abingdon, VA
Read, D'Ann ....Carlsbad, NM
Read, David ....Burbank, CA
Read, David B. ....San Angelo, TX
Read, David C. ....Los Angeles, CA
Read, David C. ....Chicago, IL
Read, David H. ....Winston-Salem, NC
Read, David M. ....Natchez, MS
Read, Deborah Zider ....Cleveland, OH
Read, Donald H. ....Berkeley, CA
Palo Alto, CA
Read, Donna L. Bice ....Dallas, TX
Read, Douglas J. ....Traverse City, MI
Read, E. Nelson ....Key West, FL
Read, Edgar M. ....Tucson, AZ
Read, Elizabeth A. ....Swarthmore, PA
Read, Elizabeth L. ....San Francisco, CA
Boston, MA
Read, Elizabeth R. ....Miami, FL
Read, Evelyn Foster ....Olympia, WA
Read, Frank T. ....Houston, TX
Read, Frederick W., III ....Greenfield, MA
Read, Frederick W., Jr.
Port Washington, NY
Read, George E. ....Oxford, MS
Read, Gregory C. ....San Francisco, CA
Read, Henry J., (A Professional Law Corporation) ....New Orleans, LA
Read, Howard J. ....Albany, NY
Read, J. Andrew ....Washington, DC
Read, J. Milton, Jr. ....Durham, NC
Read, James Kirby ....El Paso, TX
Read, James LeGrand ....Houston, TX
Read, James M.
Merit Systems Protection Board,
Office of Appeals Counsel, GV
Read, James W., Jr. ....Newport Beach, CA
Read, Jeffrey A. ....Springfield, IL
Read, Jerry ....Biloxi, MS
Read, Jo-Hanna G. ....Seattle, WA
Read, John R. ....Department of Justice,
Antitrust Division, GV
Read, John W. ....Cleveland, OH
Read, Jonathan P. ....Escondido, CA
Read, Karen A. ....Kansas City, MO
Read, Karen M. ....Valparaiso, IN
Read and Laniado, LLP ....Albany, NY
Read, Laura Elizabeth ....Redwood City, CA
Read, Lauri A. ....Detroit, MI
Read, Lisa A. ....Atlanta, GA
Read, Lynn Peterson ....Boston, MA
Read, Mary B. ....Milwaukee, WI
Read, Michael J. ....Boise, ID
Read, Michael K. ....Belleville, IL
Read, Michael O. ....New Orleans, LA
Read, Nicholas C. ....Boston, MA
Read, Nolan K. ....Corpus Christi, TX
Read, P. Michael ....Belleville, IL
Read, Peter S. ....Brooklyn, NY
Read, Randal Jason ....Newport Beach, CA
Read & Read ....Vancouver, WA
Read, Richard F. ....Los Angeles, CA
Read, Robert M. ....Westfield, NJ
Read, Robert O. ....Columbus, OH
Read, Robin A. ....Williamsport, PA
Read, Roger H. P. ....Boston, MA
Read, Russell S. ....Cambria, CA
Read, Sarah J. ....Chicago, IL
Read, Stan ....Raton, NM
Read, Susan B. ....Staunton, VA
Read, Thomas B. ....Cedar Rapids, IA
Read, Thomas L., III ....Memphis, TN
Read, Thomas W. ....Seattle, WA
Read, Timothy T. ....Charlottesville, VA
Read, Tod W. ....Washington, DC
Read, Verne R. ....Milwaukee, WI
Read, Walter N. ....Riverton, NJ
Read, William E. ....Louisville, KY
Read, William T. ....Madison, WI
Read, Winona T. ....Parksville, NY
Readdick, Terry L. ....Brunswick, GA
Reade, Arthur I., Jr. ....Nantucket, MA
Reade, Claire E. ....Washington, DC
Reade, Gerald L. ....Yankton, SD
Reade, Gullicksen, Hanley & Gifford, LLP
Nantucket, MA
Reade, John A., Jr. ....New York, NY
Reade, John E. ....Grants Pass, OR
Reade, Linda R. ....Des Moines, IA
Reade, Lynne, (Ms.) ....Fremont, CA
Reade, Randall Roger ....
Department of Labor, GV
Reade, Robert Christopher
Las Vegas, NV
Reade, Steven C. ....Hartford, CT
Reade, Steven G. ....Washington, DC
Reader, Anne-Marie ....Los Angeles, CA
Reader, Barbara ....Great Neck, NY
Reader, David I. ....Washington, DC
Reader, David J. ....Howell, MI
Reader, Donna L. ....Barre, VT
Reader, Grant A. ....Cypress, CA
Reader, Harold (Kip) ....Cleveland, OH
Reader, Jennifer Screen
Securities and Exchange Commission,
Division of Corporation Finance, GV
Reader, Joseph P. ....San Jose, CA
Reader, Marilyn S. ....Larchmont, NY
Reader, Paige Clark ....Atlanta, GA
Reader & Pierson ....Howell, MI
Reader & Ricelli ....Howell, MI
Reader, Russell B. ....Orlando, FL
Reader, Scot A. ....Calabasas, CA
Reader, Thomas W. ....New York, NY
Reader, W. Don, Jr. ....Canton, OH
Reader-Lenahan, Carol S. ....Brighton, MI
Readey, B. John, III ....Kansas City, MO
Readey, James A. ....Columbus, OH
Readey, Mary Lynn ....Dayton, OH
Readie, W. Allen ....Pittsburgh, PA
Reading, Alecia Anderson ....Kissimmee, FL
Reading, Douglas K. ....Ann Arbor, MI
Reading & Etter ....Ann Arbor, MI
Reading, J. Bruce ....Salt Lake City, UT
Reading, John W. ....Boston, MA

Reading, Mark A. .... Ann Arbor, MI
Reading, Sherry L. .... Chicago, IL
Readinger, Alan S. .... Reading, PA
Readler, Chad A. .... Columbus, OH
Readlinger, Donald R. .... Princeton, NJ
Readnour & Barone .... Rutland, VT
Readnour, Jon S. .... Rutland, VT
Ready, Apryl Lee .... Hattiesburg, MS
Ready & Associates .... Meridian, MS
Ready, Billy Ray .... Auburndale, FL
Ready, Charles Mark .... Piedmont, OK
Ready, Colleen M. .... Westmont, NJ
Ready, Daniel J., Jr. .... Oakland, CA
Ready, David T. .... South Bend, IN
Ready, Denise E. .... Albuquerque, NM
Ready, J. Damond .... Monticello, MS
Ready, John F. .... Monroe, MI
Ready, John T. .... San Diego, CA
Ready, Kenneth J. .... Mineola, NY
Ready, Kevin E. .... Santa Barbara, CA
Ready Law Firm .... Meridian, MS
Ready, M. Davis .... New Orleans, LA
Ready, Michael .... Raynham, MA
Ready, Michele E. .... Miami, FL
Ready, Paul F. .... San Luis Obispo, CA
Ready, Peggy E. .... St. Augustine, FL
Ready & Pontisakos, L.L.P.
Long Island City, NY
Mineola, NY
Ready, Richard Paul .... Mineola, NY
Ready, Robert D. .... Greeley, CO
Ready, Robert J. .... Chicago, IL
Ready, Sullivan & Ready, L.L.P.
Adrian, MI
Monroe, MI
Ready, Thomas D. .... Monroe, MI
Ready, William A., III .... Columbia, SC
Ready, William E. .... Meridian, MS
Ready, William E., Jr. .... Meridian, MS
Ready, William Judson .... Chapel Hill, NC
Ready-Luckman, Jane A. .... Scottsdale, AZ
Reagan, Barry J. .... Ventura, CA
Reagan, Bernard L. .... Marcellus, NY
Reagan, Bernida M. .... Berkeley, CA
Reagan, Brad Rock .... Austin, TX
Reagan Burrus Dierksen Lamon & Bluntzer
New Braunfels, TX
San Antonio, TX
Reagan, Carole E. .... Irvine, CA
Reagan, Charles E., Jr. .... Austin, TX
Reagan, Christopher .... Kennebunkport, ME
Reagan, David W. .... Austin, TX
Reagan, Denise C. .... San Francisco, CA
Reagan, Elaine W. .... Santa Ana, CA
Reagan, Gary Don .... Hobbs, NM
Reagan, Gary Don, P.A. .... Hobbs, NM
Reagan, Harry .... Philadelphia, PA
Reagan, J. C. .... New Braunfels, TX
Reagan, Jennifer R. .... Kansas City, MO
Reagan, John J. .... Cleveland, OH
Reagan, John S. .... Oklahoma City, OK
Reagan, Judith .... Dallas, TX
Reagan, Kathleen Agnes .... Braintree, MA
Reagan, Kelly L. .... West Palm Beach, FL
Reagan, Kinsey S. .... Washington, DC
Reagan, Lewis M. .... Great Bend, KS
Reagan, Margaret L. .... Long Beach, CA
Reagan, Margot Fisher .... South Bend, IN
Reagan, Mark B. .... Nashville, TN
Reagan, Mark E. .... San Francisco, CA
Reagan, Marni .... Mobile, AL
Reagan, Mary B. .... Austin, TX
Reagan & McLain .... Dallas, TX
Reagan, Michael E. .... Coeur d'Alene, ID
Reagan, Michael J. .... Phoenix, AZ
Reagan, Michael J. .... Belleville, IL
Reagan, Michael P. .... Boston, MA
Reagan, Michael T. .... Ottawa, IL
Reagan, Michelle A. .... Wichita, KS
Reagan, O. Walker, III .... Raleigh, NC
Reagan, Patrick A. .... Portland, OR
Reagan, Patrick H. .... San Antonio, TX
Reagan, Patrick M. .... Boston, MA
Reagan, Paul V. .... Chicago, IL
Reagan, R. Douglas .... Dodge City, KS
Reagan, Randall E. .... Knoxville, TN
Reagan, Randy .... Dallas, TX
Reagan, Robert J. .... Dallas, TX
Reagan, Robert M. .... New York, NY
Reagan, Robert Timothy ....
Federal Judicial Center, GV
Reagan, Ronald E. .... Papillion, NE
Reagan, Ronald R. .... Sevierville, TN
Reagan, Sean E. .... Midland, MI
Reagan, Sean P. .... Chester, VT
Reagan, Sheldon W. .... Kankakee, IL
Reagan, Tanya Doherty .... Hopewell, VA
Reagan, Thomas J. .... Portland, ME
Reagan, Willard M. .... Boca Raton, FL
Troy, MI
Reagan, William L., Jr. .... San Jose, CA
Reagan-Blood, Theresa .... Yorba Linda, CA
Reagen, Abby Lynn .... Chicago, IL
Reagen, Joseph P. .... Chicago, IL
Reager & Adler, P.C. .... Camp Hill, PA
Carlisle, PA
Harrisburg, PA
Reager, David W. .... Camp Hill, PA
Reager, Glenda N. .... Sacramento, CA
Reager, Kevin W. .... Sacramento, CA
Reagin, Arthur H. .... Armonk, NY
Reagin, Julie C. .... San Francisco, CA
Reagin, Ronald W. .... Los Angeles, CA
Reagin, Roy Daniel, Jr. .... Atlanta, GA
Reagle, John M. .... Columbia, SC
Reagle, Raymond E. .... Pittsburgh, PA
Reagler, Karen Baim .... Memphis, TN
Reagor, Dale E. .... Helena, MT
Reagor, Michael W. .... Englewood, CO
Reagor, Thomas D. .... Dallas, TX
Reagor, Vincent W. .... Nine Mile Falls, WA
Reagoso, Anthony D. .... Media, PA
Reagoso • Paul & Baer, Attorneys at Law, P.C.
Media, PA
Reahard, Carol M. .... Indianapolis, IN
Reak, Kevin P. .... Milwaukee, WI
Real, Alfred .... Santa Ana, CA
Real, Barbara M. .... Columbus, OH
Real, Catherine Williams .... Tampa, FL
Real, Catherine Williams, P.A.
Tampa, FL
Real, Christopher .... Torrance, CA
Real Estate Law Group, LLP .... Sausalito, CA
Real, Gary R. .... Birmingham, AL
Real, Hal .... Villanova, PA
Real, John J. .... San Pedro, CA
Real, Lilliana M. .... Miami, FL
Real, Manuel L. .... Los Angeles, CA
Real, Mark J. .... Columbus, OH
Real, Ralph A. .... Oakhurst, NJ
Realberg, Leo .... Bronx, NY
Reale, Bruce .... Bethel Park, PA
Reale, C. Anthony .... New York, NY
Reale, Debra Lynn .... Miami, FL
Reale & Fossee, P.C. .... Pittsburgh, PA
Reale, Frank C. .... Massillon, OH
Reale, John P. .... Atlanta, GA
Reale, Joseph J., Jr. .... Providence, RI
Reale, Jr., Joseph J., Ltd. .... Providence, RI
Reale, Lewis T. .... Cicero, NY
Reale, P. Edward .... East Hampton, NY
Riverhead, NY
Reale, Philip A. .... Glenville, WV
Reale, Samuel, Jr. .... Trenton, NJ
Reale, William A. .... Cleveland, OH
Reali, Janet L. .... Chicago, IL
Reali, John P. .... Jericho, NY
Reall, Christopher S. .... Dublin, OH
Reall, Elaine M. .... Northampton, MA
Reall, George F. .... Sedona, AZ
Reall, Kevin B. .... Providence, RI
Reals, John F. .... Wichita, KS
Reals & Weber .... Wichita, KS
Realuyo, Pompeyo R. .... New York, NY
Ream, Anne K. .... Palo Alto, CA
Ream, Carl J. .... Aurora, CO
Ream, Carl J., P.C. .... Aurora, CO
Ream, Christopher .... Palo Alto, CA
Ream, Dale J. .... Ottawa, KS
Ream, Darren .... Terrell, TX
Ream, David L. .... Houston, TX
Ream, David W. .... Department of Defense,
Defense Legal Services Agency, GV
Ream, Davidson .... Chicago, IL
Ream, Donald M., Jr. .... Indianapolis, IN
Ream, Jack F. .... York, PA
Ream, James D. .... San Luis Obispo, CA
Ream, James J. .... Las Vegas, NV
Ream, Juliet L. .... Santa Monica, CA
Ream, Lawrence R. .... Seattle, WA
Ream, Lea A. .... San Antonio, TX
Ream, M. David .... Alexandria, VA
Ream, Robert D. .... Atlanta, GA
Reaman, Susan J. Pristo
Treasury Department,
Internal Revenue Service, GV
Reamer, David C. .... Los Angeles, CA
Reamer, Greg N. .... Lutherville, MD
Reamer, Greg N., P.A. .... Lutherville, MD
Reamer, Howard G. .... Lutherville, MD
Reamer, Isabel Libby Crystal
Baltimore, MD
Reamer, Jodi B. .... New York, NY
Reamer, Richard R. .... Salisbury, NC
Reamer, Robert J. .... Torrance, CA
Reamer, Robert J., The Law Offices of, A
Professional Corporation .... Torrance, CA
Reamer, Walter P. .... York, PA
Reames, Jane E. .... Chicago, IL
Reames, Timothy P. .... Glendale, CA
Reamey, Gerald S. .... San Antonio, TX
Reamey, Kay L. .... San Antonio, TX
Reamon, Katherine .... Menlo Park, CA
Reamon, Martha E. .... Grand Rapids, MI
Reamon, William G., Jr. .... Grand Rapids, MI
Reamon, William G., P.C.
Grand Rapids, MI
Reamon, William G., Sr. .... Grand Rapids, MI
Reams, Anne Sprecher .... Evanston, IL
Reams, Bernard D., Jr. .... St. Louis, MO
Newark, NJ
Reams, Brooks, Schell, Gaston & Gottlieb, P.C.
Mobile, AL
Reams, Chanda Elizabeth .... Baton Rouge, LA
Reams, Charles F. .... Grand Junction, CO
Reams, Coff & Majors, P.C.
Grand Junction, CO
Reams, David A. .... Washington, DC
Reams, Frazier, Jr. .... Perrysburg, OH
Reams, Gerald B., Jr. .... Catlettsburg, KY
Reams, Gwendolyn Young
Equal Employment Opportunity
Commission,
Office of the General Counsel, GV
Reams, H. Scott .... Morristown, TN
Reams, Haywood L. .... Montgomery, AL
Reams, Hugh D. .... Richmond, VA
Reams, Hugh E. .... St. Petersburg, FL
Reams, Radford M. .... Longwood, FL
Reams, Robert P. .... Kansas City, MO
Reams, Stephen M. .... Atlanta, GA
Reams, Warren F. .... Grand Junction, CO
Reams, William D., Jr. .... Culpeper, VA
Reams-Martin, Cynthia L.
Kansas City, MO
Reamy, M. R.(Chip) .... Fredericksburg, VA
Rean, Susan Palmer .... Oklahoma City, OK
Reap, Belden R. .... Silver Spring, MD
Reap, Coleman R. .... Murray Hill, NJ
Reap, James B. .... White Plains, NY
Reap, John R., Jr. .... West Pittston, PA
Reap, Judith B. .... Lebanon, NJ
Reap, Michael H. .... West Paterson, NJ
Reap, Peter .... Riverwoods, IL
Reape, James P. .... Valencia, CA
Reape, James P., A Professional Law
Corporation .... Valencia, CA
Rear, Sherwin .... Lynbrook, NY
Reardan, Nancy B. .... Elk Grove, CA
Reardanz, Leslie E., III .... Bellingham, WA
Rearden, Jennifer H. .... New York, NY
Rearden, John B., Jr. .... Darien, CT
Rearden, John, Jr. .... Rockford, IL
Rearden, Sara B.
Merit Systems Protection Board,
Office of the General Counsel, GV
Rearden-Hamly, Julia .... New York, NY
Reardon, Allison E. .... Wilmington, DE
Reardon, Andrew F. .... Chicago, IL
Reardon, Barbara M. .... Glendale, CA
Reardon, Carl F. .... Creve Coeur, IL
Reardon, Carolyn A. .... Kalispell, MT
Reardon, Cecely A. .... Brockton, MA
Reardon, Charles C. .... Garden City, NY
Reardon, Christine A. .... Toledo, OH
Reardon, Daniel P., Jr. .... St. Louis, MO
Reardon, David A. .... Gloucester, MA
Reardon, Dennis A. .... Lewes, DE
Reardon, Dennis T. .... Newtown Square, PA
Reardon, Donna M. .... Brockton, MA
Reardon, Edward P. .... Worcester, MA
Reardon, Edward P., Jr. .... New York, NY
Reardon, Edward P., P.C. .... Worcester, MA
Reardon, Eileen A. .... New York, NY
Reardon, Frank E. .... Boston, MA
Scituate, MA
Providence, RI
Reardon, Gene F. .... Aspen, CO
Reardon, George M. .... Troy, MI
Reardon, Gerald E. .... Columbia, SC
Reardon, Gerard V. .... Denver, CO
Reardon Golinkin & Reed .... Chicago, IL
Reardon, Gregory .... Covington, LA
Metairie, LA
Reardon, Jacqueline M. .... Windsor, CT
Reardon, James D. .... New York, NY
Reardon, James G., Jr. .... Worcester, MA
Reardon, James J., Jr. .... Hartford, CT
Reardon, James N. .... Topeka, KS
Reardon, James P. .... Milwaukee, WI
Reardon, Janet C. .... Largo, FL
Reardon, Janet Macaulay .... New York, NY
Reardon, John .... Washington, DC
Reardon, John J. .... Boston, MA
Reardon, John T. .... Escanaba, MI
Reardon, John W. .... Glens Falls, NY
Reardon, Joseph A., III .... West Orange, NJ
Reardon, Joseph F. .... Kansas City, KS
Reardon, Joseph J. .... Barnstable, MA
Reardon, Judith N. .... Chocorua, NH
Reardon, Judy E. .... Manchester, NH
Reardon, Julie E. .... Worcester, MA
Reardon, Karen A. .... Chicago, IL
Reardon, Kathleen C. .... St. Louis, MO
Reardon, Kathleen P.
Department Of Veterans Affairs,
Board of Veterans Appeals, GV
Reardon, Kathleen Patricia .... Rochester, NY
Reardon Law Firm, The, P.C.
New London, CT
Norwich, CT
Westerly, RI
Reardon, Leigh A.
National Labor Relations Board,
Office of Board Members, GV
Columbus, OH
Reardon, Lesley A. .... Garden City, NY
Reardon, Lynne M. .... Chicago, IL
Reardon, Marc A. .... Boston, MA
Reardon, Mark F. .... Los Angeles, CA
Reardon, Mark L. .... Wilmington, DE
Reardon, Mark W. .... Seattle, WA
Reardon, Maureen P. .... Concord, CA
Reardon, Michael E. .... Liberty, MO
Reardon, Michael H.
Department of Housing and Urban
Development,
Office of General Counsel, GV
Reardon, Michael J. .... Southbury, CT
Waterbury, CT
Reardon, Michael J. .... Boise, ID
Reardon, Neil J. .... Hampstead, NH
Reardon, Patricia L. .... Hampstead, NH
Reardon, Patrick A. .... Fort Worth, TX
Reardon, Patrick G. .... Chicago, IL
Reardon, Patrick J. .... Santa Paula, CA
Reardon, Patrick J. .... Leavenworth, KS
Reardon, Paul A. .... Rye Brook, NY
Reardon & Reardon .... Boston, MA
Framingham, MA
Worcester, MA
Reardon, Rebecca Sue .... Oxford, OH
Reardon, Robert I., Jr. .... New London, CT
Reardon, Robert W. .... Atlanta, GA
Reardon, Roxane F. .... New York, NY
Reardon, Roy L., (P.C.) .... New York, NY
Reardon & Sclafani, P.C. .... Yonkers, NY
Reardon, Stephen G. .... Richmond, VA
Reardon, Susan Erburu .... Los Angeles, CA
Reardon, T. Michael .... Houston, TX
Reardon & Thoma .... Bronxville, NY
Reardon, Thomas M. .... Boston, MA
Reardon, Thomas M., III .... Shrewsbury, NJ
Reardon, Thomas W., Jr. .... Longview, TX
Reardon, Tim .... Helena, MT
Reardon, Timothy A. .... San Francisco, CA
Reardon, Timothy J. .... Springfield, IL
Reardon, Timothy J., III
Department of Justice,
Criminal Division, GV
Reardon, Timothy M. .... Youngstown, OH
Reardon, Timothy P. .... Milwaukee, WI
Reardon, Walter L., Jr., (P.A.)
Albuquerque, NM
Reardon, Walter T. .... Yonkers, NY
Reardon, William Frantz .... Hondo, TX
Reardon, William H. .... Pago Pago, TT
Reardon, William J. .... Pekin, IL
Reas, Wanda M. .... Maitland, FL
Reasbeck, James M. .... Fort Lauderdale, FL
Reaser, Dan R. .... Reno, NV
Reaser, Vernon N., Jr. .... Victoria, TX
Reaser, William J., Jr. .... Stroudsburg, PA
Reason, Roger D. .... Greenfield, IN
Reason, Sally C. .... Oak Ridge, TN
Reasoner, Barrett H. .... Houston, TX
Reasoner, C. Dean .... Washington, DC
Reasoner, Carroll J. .... Cedar Rapids, IA
Reasoner, Harry M. .... Houston, TX
Reasoner, Janet G. .... Cedar Rapids, IA
Reasoner, Paul A. .... Farmington Hills, MI
Reasoner, Stephen M. .... Little Rock, AR
Reasoner, Susan Hardig .... Houston, TX
Reasoner, W. Irl, III .... Columbus, OH
Reasonover, Carl R. .... Camden, SC
Reasonover, Charles K., (P.L.C.)
New Orleans, LA
Reasonover, Kirk .... New Orleans, LA
Reasor, Charles B., Jr. .... Nashville, TN
Reasor, Edward J. .... Anchorage, AK
Honolulu, HI
Reasor, Edward J., A Professional Corporation
Anchorage, AK
Reasor, Jackson E., Jr. .... Bluefield, VA
Reasor, Shannon .... Atoka, OK
Reat, Daniel J. .... Houston, TX
Reategui, Lisa J. .... Chicago, IL
Reath, George, Jr. .... Philadelphia, PA
Reath, Henry T. .... Philadelphia, PA
Reath, Patricia C. .... Fairfield, CT
Reaud Law Firm .... Beaumont, TX
Reaud, Morgan & Quinn .... Beaumont, TX
Reaud, Wayne A. .... Beaumont, TX
Reaugh, Dan .... Seattle, WA
Reaugh Fischnaller Oettinger Merker &
Luppert, P.S., A Prof. Serv. Corp.
Seattle, WA
Reaugh, Stephanie L. .... Dallas, TX
Reaume, Timothy G. .... Troy, MI
Reavely, R. Lynn .... San Diego, CA
Reavely, Sally A. .... Des Moines, IA
Reavely, Thomas S. .... Des Moines, IA
Reaven, Saul D. .... Akron, OH
Reaven, Sidney .... San Francisco, CA
Reaver, Kelly A. .... Towson, MD
Reaves, Asa E. .... Cerritos, CA
Reaves, Bobbie C. .... Manning, SC
Reaves, Craig C. .... Kansas City, MO
Reaves, Cynthia F. .... Washington, DC
Reaves, David M. .... Phoenix, AZ
Reaves, Dennis D. .... Stockton, MO
Reaves, Gary A. .... El Paso, TX
Reaves, George G. .... Florence, SC
Reaves, H. Frances .... Baltimore, MD
Reaves, J. Daniel .... Fairfax, VA
Reaves, James A. .... New York, NY
Reaves, James E., Jr. .... San Antonio, TX
Reaves, John C. .... Fayetteville, NC
Reaves, John Daniel .... Washington, DC
Reaves, John H. .... San Diego, CA
Reaves, John H., A P.C., Law Offices of
San Diego, CA
Reaves, Kimberly P. .... Charlotte, NC
Reaves, Lacy H. .... Raleigh, NC
Reaves Law Firm, P.C. .... Kansas City, MO
Reaves, Leonard "Holden" .... Charlotte, NC
Reaves, Martina E. .... Emeryville, CA
Reaves, Nanci W. .... Norfolk, VA
Reaves, Perry M. .... Katy, TX
Reaves, Randall R. .... Austin, TX
Reaves, Randolph P. .... Montgomery, AL
Reaves, Randolph P., P.C. .... Montgomery, AL
Reaves, Rhonda M. .... Los Angeles, CA
Reaves, Steven A. .... Oakland, CA
Reaves, Walter M., Jr. .... Waco, TX
West, TX
Reaves, William C.O., P.S.C.
Ashland, KY
Reaves, William C. O. .... Ashland, KY
Reaves & Yates .... New York, NY
Reavey, Christopher R. .... Northampton, MA
Reavey, Patrick G. .... Kansas City, MO
Reavey, Rosemary K. .... New Brunswick, NJ
Reavey, Sidney Ellis .... Springfield, MA
Reavey, William A., III .... San Diego, CA
Reavill, Jonathon T. .... Arlington, VA
Reavis, Anne Rivers .... Houston, TX
Reavis, David L. .... Charlotte, NC
Reavis, Don H. .... Amarillo, TX
Reavis, Edwin R. .... Tulsa, OK
Reavis, Gillis E. .... Seattle, WA
Reavis, H. Clay, Jr. .... Santa Ana, CA
Reavis, Helen D. .... Los Angeles, CA
New York, NY
Reavis, James O. .... Boston, MA
Providence, RI
Reavis, Randall W. .... Greensboro, NC
Reavley, Thomas M. .... Austin, TX
Reavley, Thomas W. .... Austin, TX
Reay, Rebecca W. .... Menomonee Falls, WI
Reay & Shaw .... San Marino, CA
Reb & Buchanio .... Lebanon, PA

Reb, Patrick M. ..... Lebanon, PA
Reba, Ronald W. ..... South River, NJ
Reba, Sheryl L. ..... New York, NY
Reback, Ariella Faye ..... New York, NY
Reback, David C. ..... Mount Vernon, NY
Reback, Forbes Robinson
Charlottesville, VA
Reback, Gary L. ..... Palo Alto, CA
Reback, Hulbert, McAndrews & Kjar, LLP
Manhattan Beach, CA
Reback, Joel A. ..... Newburgh, NY
Reback, Joyce E. ..... Washington, DC
Reback, Larry A. ..... San Francisco, CA
Reback & Potash ..... Mount Vernon, NY
Reback, Robert C. ..... Manhattan Beach, CA
Reback, Rochelle A. ..... Tampa, FL
Reback, Sanford B. ..... Los Angeles, CA
Reback, Sanford C. ..... Washington, DC
Reback, Shelley Wall ..... Reston, VA
Reback & Slayton ..... Charlottesville, VA
Reback, Steven C. ..... Trenton, NJ
Reback, Steven M. ..... Austin, TX
Rebagliati, Steve F. ..... Mountain View, CA
Rebak, Joseph L. ..... Miami, FL
West Palm Beach, FL
Rebalko, L. Anton ..... Coral Springs, FL
Rebane, John T. ..... St. Paul, MN
Rebane, Kai I. ..... New York, NY
Rebar, Beverly ..... Virginia Beach, VA
Rebar, Leroy M. ..... Detroit, MI
Rebarchak, James ..... Mobile, AL
Rebay, Alexandra ..... Stamford, CT
Rebbe, James M. ..... General Accounting Office,
Office of the General Counsel, GV
Rebbe, Laura K. W. ..... St. Louis, MO
Rebe, Sal ..... El Paso, TX
Rebeck, Gerald A. ..... Naperville, IL
Rebeck, Joseph P. ..... Long Beach, CA
Rebeck, Richard S. ..... New Brunswick, NJ
Rebeck, Susan J. ..... Great Falls, MT
Rebein, David J. ..... Dodge City, KS
Rebein, Joseph M. ..... Kansas City, MO
Rebein, Mark J. ..... Kansas City, MO
Rebein, Paul W. ..... Overland Park, KS
Rebein, Steven Richard ..... Lenexa, KS
Rebel, Thomas P. ..... Atlanta, GA
Rebelein, Dana Brandt ..... Minneapolis, MN
Rebell, Adele S. ..... Paramus, NJ
Rebell, Michael A. ..... New York, NY
Rebelo, Mary-Jo ..... Pittsburgh, PA
Reben, Howard T. ..... Portland, ME
Rebenack, Edward J. ..... New Brunswick, NJ
Rebensdorf, George O.
Rancho Santa Margarita, CA
Rebensdorf, John G. ..... Dallas, TX
Rebenstorf, Gary E. ..... Wichita, KS
Rebeor, Daniel E. ..... Chapel Hill, NC
Reber, Aaron J. ..... Columbus, OH
Reber, Brett A. ..... McPherson, KS
Reber, C. Bryant, P.C. ..... Denver, CO
Reber, David J. ..... Honolulu, HI
Reber, David J. ..... Houston, TX
Reber, Fay E. ..... St. George, UT
Reber, Frank K. ..... Marion, OH
Reber, Jill P. ..... Sausalito, CA
Reber, John C. ..... Orlando, FL
Reber, Joseph E. ..... Los Angeles, CA
Reber, Joseph E. ..... Marina Del Rey, CA
Reber, Lori B. ..... Thousand Oaks, CA
Reber, M. Kenetta ..... Los Angeles, CA
Reber, Robert D., Jr. ..... Harrisburg, PA
Reber, Robert R. ..... Reading, PA
Reber, W. Matthew ..... Philadelphia, PA
Reberkenny, Madeleine M. ..... Alexandria, VA
Rebernak, Kathee R. ..... Dallas, TX
Rebernik, Mark J. ..... New York, NY
Rebeschini, Robert G. ..... Grosse Ile, MI
Rebholz, Douglas J. ..... Milwaukee, WI
Rebholz, Paul E. ..... Milwaukee, WI
Rebholz, Rebecca Link ..... Dodgeville, WI
Rebholz & Rebholz, S.C. ..... Milwaukee, WI
Rebholz, Terry ..... Appleton, WI
Rebhuhn, Harry J. ..... Glendale, CA
Rebhun, Joyce Anne, (Miss) ..... Pittsburgh, PA
Rebish, Karen Jill ..... New York, NY
Rebish, Stuart T. ..... New York, NY
Reblitz, Howard F. ..... Washington, DC
Rebman, John R. ..... Irving, TX
Rebman, Joseph E. ..... St. Louis, MO
Rebman, Lawrence Gerard
Jefferson City, MO
Rebman Wagener & Linhares, P.C.
St. Louis, MO
Rebney, Bjorn Eric ..... Irvine, CA
Rebold, Peter M. ..... Cincinnati, OH
Rebolini, William B. ..... Central Islip, NY
Rebollo, Anthony E. ..... San Antonio, TX
Rebollo, Robert G. ..... Staten Island, NY
Rebollo Casalduc, Francisco
San Juan, PR
Rebone, Joseph W. ..... Irving, TX
Rebore, Bartholomew J. ..... Farmingdale, NY
Reboredo, Carlos J. ..... San Juan, PR
Rebori, Frank J. ..... Kansas City, MO
Reboso, Manuel A. ..... Miami, FL
Reboul, Brian ..... Metairie, LA
Reboul, John W. ..... New York, NY
Reboul, MacMurray, Hewitt, Maynard & Kristol ..... Los Angeles, CA
Washington, DC
New York, NY
Rebstock, Holly E. ..... Denver, CO
Rebstock, John W ..... Albuquerque, NM
Rebstock & Kelley, P.C. ..... Denver, CO
Rebstock, Robert F. ..... Santa Barbara, CA
Rebuck, David L. ..... Trenton, NJ
Rebuck, Monica L. ..... Harrisburg, PA
Rebull, Thomas J. ..... Miami, FL
Reby, Jacob W. ..... St. Louis, MO
Reby-Eidelman, Rachel G. ..... Clayton, MO
Recalde, Maria-Eugenia ..... Boston, MA
Recana, Mel Red ..... Los Angeles, CA
Recanati, Joyce J. ..... New York, NY
Recanzone, Mario G. ..... Fallon, NV
Recchia, Kevin V. ..... Rochester, NY
Recchia, Nancy J. Schucker
Federal Deposit Insurance Corporation,
Liquidation Branch, GV
Recchia, Peter L. ..... Lake Forest, CA
Recchie, Joseph J., Jr. ..... Columbus, OH
Recchio, Judith A. ..... San Jose, CA
Recchuite, Martin C. ..... Calabasas, CA
Recchuiti, Francis ..... Norristown, PA
Reccia, Maurice ..... New York, NY
Receski, Edward A. ..... Lexington, KY
Receveur, Richard L. ..... Louisville, KY
Rech, Johannes T., II ..... Montgomery, AL
Rech, Leana Morrell ..... The Woodlands, TX
Rech, Ola N. ..... New York, NY
Rech, Patricia ..... Woodbury, NY
Rech, Steven R. ..... Houston, TX
Rechel, Theodore J. ..... Tampa, FL
Rechen, Thomas J. ..... Hartford, CT
Rechenberg, Paul N. ..... St. Louis, MO
Rechenmacher, LeRoy L. ..... Naperville, IL
Recher, Bruce C. ..... Minneapolis, MN
Recher, Laura A. ..... Nashville, TN
Recher, Louis G. ..... Richmond, VA
Rechlicz, Richard A. ..... Menomonee Falls, WI
Rechlin, Charles F. ..... Los Angeles, CA
Rechlitz, Anthony J., II ..... Denver, CO
Rechlitz, Jennifer S. ..... Woodbury, MN
Rechner, Carl J. ..... Columbus, OH
Rechner, Hugh ..... Honesdale, PA
Rechnitzer, Martin A. ..... Burleson, TX
Rechs, Randall C. ..... San Diego, CA
Rechsteiner, Vera Ann ..... Washington, DC
Recht, Arthur J. ..... Weirton, WV
Recht, Arthur M. ..... Wheeling, WV
Recht, Charles H. ..... Hamilton, MT
Recht, Daniel N. ..... Denver, CO
Recht, Harris M. ..... Upper Saddle River, NJ
Recht, Hays & Hayes, P.L.L.P.
Hamilton, MT
Recht, Howard F. ..... Hamilton, MT
Recht, James C. ..... Castle Rock, CO
Recht, Leslie, (Ms.) ..... Chicago, IL
Recht, Milton R. ..... Mount Kisco, NY
Recht, Orville F. ..... Ojai, CA
Recht, Paul A. ..... Pittsburgh, PA
Recht & Pepin, A Professional Corporation
Denver, CO
Recht, Philip R. ..... Los Angeles, CA
Recht, Phillip E. ..... Milwaukee, WI
Recht & Recht, P.C. ..... Hamilton, MT
Recht, Ronald E. ..... Washington, DC
Recht, Ronald E., Chartered
Washington, DC
Recht, Samuel J. ..... Milwaukee, WI
Recht, William, Jr. ..... Upper Saddle River, NJ
Rechter, Sarah M. ..... Dallas, TX
Rechtin, George A. ..... Cleveland, OH
Rechtin, Michael D. ..... Chicago, IL
Rechtin, Michael D., Jr. ..... Chicago, IL
Rechtin, N. Clark ..... Louisville, KY
Rechtin, Tom ..... Wenatchee, WA
Rechtman, David B. ..... Atlanta, GA
Rechtoris, Kenneth E. ..... Chicago, IL
Rechtschaffen, Clifford L.
San Francisco, CA
Rechtschaffen, Joyce ..... United States Senate,
Senatorial Assistants, GV
Rechtschaffen, Scott D.
San Francisco, CA
Recicar, Thomas S. ..... Altamonte Springs, FL
Recile, George B. ..... Metairie, LA
Recine, Anthony F. ..... New York, NY
Recinella, Dale S. ..... Tallahassee, FL
Recinto, Jose R., Jr. ..... Washington, DC
Recio, Carlos M. ..... Washington, DC
Recio, Frances M.
Commodity Futures Trading Commission,
Division of Enforcement, GV
Recio, Robert A. ..... Hackensack, NJ
Reck, Belynda ..... Los Angeles, CA
Reck, Christopher M. ..... Rogers, AR
Reck, Gothard J., (P.C.) ..... New Orleans, LA
Reck, J. David ..... Ann Arbor, MI
Howell, MI
Reck, J. Rodney ..... Rocky Hill, CT
Reck, Joel M. ..... Boston, MA
Reck, Michael R. ..... Des Moines, IA
Reck, R. Randolph ..... Los Angeles, CA
Reck, Robert F., Jr. ..... Miami, FL
Reck, Robert H. ..... Mendota, IL
Reck, Stephen E. ..... Bridgeport, CT
Reck, Stephen M. ..... Westerly, RI
Recka & Joannes, S.C. ..... Green Bay, WI
Recka, Joseph M. ..... Green Bay, WI
Reckamp, Christopher J. ..... Northbrook, IL
Reckart, Timothy John ..... Tucson, AZ
Recke, John F. ..... Boston, MA
Recker, Brice O. ..... Columbus, OH
Recker, Catherine M. ..... Philadelphia, PA
Recker, David Charles
Department of Commerce,
Office of the General Counsel, GV
Recker, David H. ..... Indianapolis, IN
Recker, Deanna ..... Gilbert, AZ
Recker, Frank R., & Assoc. Co., LPA
Marco Island, FL
Cincinnati, OH
Recker, James M. ..... Bloomfield Hills, MI
Recker, James R., II ..... Indianapolis, IN
Recker, Roberta Sabin ..... Indianapolis, IN
Reckford, Ashley Richards ..... Richmond, VA
Reckler, Henry R. ..... Denver, CO
Reckler, Henry R., P.C. ..... Denver, CO
Reckler, Sherry .....
Department of Defense, GV
Reckler, Stanley R. ..... New York, NY
Reckless, Walter W. ..... Columbus, OH
Reckman, Mark S. ..... Cincinnati, OH
Reckman, Robert F. ..... Cincinnati, OH
Reckmeyer, Peter R. ..... Portsmouth, NH
Reckmeyer, Tracy Donner ..... Chicago, IL
Reckmeyer, Victor ..... Milwaukee, WI
Reckmeyer, W. Herbert ..... Hartford, CT
Recknaged, Joline M. ..... Seattle, WA
Recknagel, Robert R. ..... Long Beach, CA
Recknagel, Thomas M. ..... Chevy Chase, MD
Recknor, Ann Kathryn
Department Of Veterans Affairs,
Office of the Secretary, GV
Recknor, John F. ..... Lincoln, NE
Reckord, Sherril M. ..... Newark, NJ
Reckseen, Don M. ..... Northglenn, CO
Reckseit, Lucy W. ..... San Mateo, CA
Reckseit, Peter H. ..... New York, NY
Recktenwald, William E. ..... Chicago, IL
Recob, Jere ..... Atlanta, GA
Recoon, Eric Laurence ..... Buffalo, NY
Record, Caroline ..... Morristown, NJ
Record, Christopher S. ..... Nashville, TN
Record, J. William ..... Decatur, IL
Record, Richard F., Jr. ..... Mattoon, IL
Record, Rush H. ..... Houston, TX
Record, Stephen C. ..... Santa Barbara, CA
Record, Thomas M. ..... Augusta, ME
Record, Warren A. ..... Gulfport, MS
Recsetar, Ernie L. ..... Scottsdale, AZ
Rectanus, Daniel G. ..... Madison, WI
Rectenwald, David J. ..... Toledo, OH
Rectenwald, Edward F. ..... Louisville, KY
Rectenwald, Scott ..... Marshall, TX
Rector, Andrew C. ..... Fort Worth, TX
Rector, Baker R., (P.C.) ..... Dallas, TX
Rector, Brent D. ..... Grand Rapids, MI
Rector, Bruce A. ..... Lexington, KY
Rector, Charles ..... Lemoyne, PA
Rector, Daniel G. ..... Cincinnati, OH
Rector, Donald R. ..... Dallas, TX
Rector, Edwin ..... Alexandria, VA
Rector & Farry ..... Colorado Springs, CO
Rector, Harold C. ..... Clarendon, TX
Rector, James D. ..... Glasgow, MT
Rector, Jay M. ..... Wichita, KS
Rector, John M. ..... United States Senate,
Committee Legal Personnel, GV
Rector, Kenneth B. ..... Vicksburg, MS
Rector, L. Dan ..... Colorado Springs, CO
Rector, Larry J. ..... Clarksburg, WV
Rector Law Office, P.C. ..... Glasgow, MT
Rector, Leo W. ..... Colorado Springs, CO
Rector, Lloyd K. ..... Winston-Salem, NC
Rector, Mark E. ..... Lebanon, MO
Rector, Neil K. ..... Columbus, OH
Rector, Patricia L. ..... Hamilton, TX
Rector, Richard P. ..... Washington, DC
Rector, Roy James ..... Memphis, TN
Rector, Sharon S. ..... Austin, TX
Rector, Susan Darnell ..... Columbus, OH
Rector, Terry E. ..... Colorado Springs, CO
Rector, Thomas A. ..... San Diego, CA
Rector, Wendy M. ..... Phoenix, AZ
Rector, William B., Jr. ..... Richmond, VA
Rector, William P. ..... Moline, IL
Recupero, James R. ..... Canton, OH
Recupero, Joseph J. ..... Providence, RI
Recupero, Michael J. ..... San Francisco, CA
Recupero, Patricia Ryan ..... Providence, RI
Red, David L. ..... Irving, TX
Red Earth Environmental, Inc.
Oklahoma City, OK
Red Hot Law Group of Ashley LLC
Atlanta, GA
Red & Parker, L.L.P. ..... Houston, TX
Red, W. Scott, Jr. ..... Houston, TX
Reda & Associates, P.C. ..... Chicago, IL
Reda, David N. ..... Virginia Beach, VA
Reda, Douglas M. ..... Mineola, NY
Reda, Edward E. ..... Chicago, IL
Reda, Edward E., Jr. ..... Chicago, IL
Reda, Jennifer A. ..... New York, NY
Reda, Joseph A. ..... Bronx, NY
Reda, Louis Joseph ..... Bronx, NY
Reda, Ltd. ..... Chicago, IL
Reda, Michael ..... Edwardsville, IL
Reda, Michael L. ..... Melbourne, FL
Reda, Ralph R. ..... White Plains, NY
Reda, Robert S. ..... Chicago, IL
Redak, William, Jr. ..... Boulder, CO
Redamak, Mary E. ..... New Buffalo, MI
Redamak, Terry L. ..... New Buffalo, MI
Redano, Richard T. ..... Houston, TX
Redavid and Caranci ..... Springfield, PA
ReDavid, Walter T. ..... Springfield, PA
ReDavid Rack, Michelle
Virginia Beach, VA
Redbord, Glenn L. ..... Succasunna, NJ
Redbord, Robert P. ..... Boston, MA
Redburn, Chris R. ..... San Francisco, CA
Redburn, David T. ..... Golden Valley, MN
Redburn, Thomas E., Jr. ..... Roseland, NJ
Redcay, Ronald C. ..... Los Angeles, CA
Redchuk, Petra Ann ..... Syracuse, NY
Redd, Andrew W. ..... Montgomery, AL
Redd, Bruce C. ..... Derry, NM
Redd, Catharine A. ..... Prestonsburg, KY
Redd, Charles A. ..... St. Louis, MO
Redd, Christopher J. ..... Philadelphia, PA
Redd, David K. ..... Salt Lake City, UT
Redd, Donald A. ..... Rosemead, CA
Redd, Edward R. ..... Roxbury, MA
Redd, F. Bennion ..... Monticello, UT
Redd, H. Carter ..... Richmond, VA
Redd, Helen ..... Salt Lake City, UT
Redd, Jamus R., III ..... Hopkinsville, KY
Redd, Jeffrey N. ..... Tustin, CA
Redd, Joe P. ..... Stone Mountain, GA
Redd, Joseph T. ..... White Plains, NY
Redd, Kimberly C. ..... Southfield, MI
Redd, Lavinia L. ..... Fort Pierce, FL
Redd, Michael K. ..... Fort Smith, AR
Redd, W. Mitchell ..... Lake Charles, LA
Redd, William L. ..... Huntington, WV
Reddam, Grace O'Neil ..... Detroit, MI
Reddan, David M. ..... Minneapolis, MN
Reddan, John T. M. ..... Gaithersburg, MD
Reddeck, Larry G. ..... Lake City, SC
Reddel, David A. ..... Omaha, NE
Redden, Arthur J., Jr. ..... Hendersonville, NC
Redden, Brian R ..... Cincinnati, OH
Redden, Charles F. ..... Chicago, IL
Redden, Charles R. ..... Winston-Salem, NC
Redden, David ..... Newport News, VA
Redden, Donald M. ..... Portsmouth, NH
Redden, Edward T. ..... Anaheim, CA
Redden, James A. ..... Portland, OR
Redden, Joe W., Jr. ..... Houston, TX
Redden, John S. ..... Roseland, NJ
Redden, Kenneth A.
Environmental Protection Agency,
Office of the General Counsel, GV
Redden, Kenneth R. ..... Charlottesville, VA
Redden, L. Drew ..... Birmingham, AL
Redden, Michael A. ..... Portland, OR
Redden, Miller S., III ..... Rockville, MD
Redden, Mills & Clark ..... Birmingham, AL
Redden, Monroe M., Jr. ..... Hendersonville, NC
Redden, Randy C. ..... Millville, NJ
Redden, Roger D. ..... Baltimore, MD
Easton, MD
Redden, Vicki Thornton ..... Dallas, TX
Redden, Wm. A. ..... Green Valley, AZ
Redder, Bonnie A. ..... Buffalo, NY
Redder, Edward C. ..... Canton, OH
Redder, George W. ..... Kingston, NY
Reddick, Bonzo C. ..... Savannah, GA
Reddick, Brian David ..... Little Rock, AR
Reddick, Charles R. ..... Homerville, GA
Reddick, Charles R., P.C. ..... Homerville, GA
Reddick, C. N. Franklin, III
Los Angeles, CA
Reddick, Conrad R. ..... Wheaton, IL
Reddick, David G. ..... Conyers, GA
Reddick, Deborah L. ..... Hurst, TX
Reddick, Edward, Jr. ..... Springfield, GA
Reddick, Elaine M. ..... Wichita, KS
Reddick, Erica L. ..... Chicago, IL
Reddick, Ernest L., III ..... Tallahassee, FL
Reddick, Ernest N. ..... San Francisco, CA
Reddick, Grady K. ..... Sylvania, GA
Reddick, James H. ..... Gulf Breeze, FL
Reddick, Les V. ..... Dubuque, IA
Reddick, Marci A. ..... Indianapolis, IN
Reddick, Ryan D. ..... Beaver, OK
Hooker, OK
Reddick, Sarah J. ..... New York, NY
Reddick, Solomon ..... Baltimore, MD
Reddick, Thos. J. ..... Fort Lauderdale, FL
Reddick, Wayne D. ..... Salt Lake City, UT
Reddick-Hood, LaXavier Patrice
Atlanta, GA
Reddie, Scott M. ..... Fresno, CA
Reddig, Daniel J. ..... Braintree, MA
Reddig, Jeffrey J. ..... Department of Labor,
Employment Standards Administration, GV
Reddig, Michael ..... Flagstaff, AZ
Reddin, Evelyn ..... Bowling Green, OH
Reddin, George M. ..... Fort Morgan, CO
Reddin, Jane E. ..... Phoenix, AZ
Reddin, Jon N. ..... Milwaukee, WI
Reddin, Mark B. ..... Pemberville, OH
Reddin, Michele A. ..... Sarasota, FL
Reddin & Singer ..... Milwaukee, WI
Reddin, Thomas E. ..... Dallas, TX
Reddin, William J. ..... Milwaukee, WI
Reddin Eliou, Jennifer E. ..... New York, NY
Redding, Andrea Swanner ..... Portland, OR
Redding & Associates, P.C. ..... Houston, TX
Redding, Benjamin W. ..... Panama City, FL
Redding, Bloor ..... Camas, WA
Redding, Bobbie N. ..... Fayetteville, NC
Redding, Brian J. ..... Chicago, IL
Redding, Bryan S. ..... Indianapolis, IN
Redding, David G. ..... Asheville, NC
Redding, David P. ..... Goshen, IN
Redding, Earl L. ..... Portland, OR
Redding, Edward L. ..... Bethlehem, PA
Redding, Gene W. ..... Springfield, MO
Redding, George H., Jr. ..... Winnetka, IL
Redding, Gregory R. ..... Arlington, VA
Redding, H. Randall ..... Henderson, KY
Redding & Hyde ..... Chicago, IL
Redding, J. Christopher ..... Washington, DC
Redding, J. Howard ..... Asheboro, NC
Redding, James M. ..... Chicago, IL
Redding, James P. ..... Boston, MA
Providence, RI
Redding, John C. ..... El Cajon, CA
Redding, Jonathan W. ..... Oakland, CA
Redding, Joseph E. ..... West Allis, WI
Redding, Laura A. ..... Dover, DE
Redding, Louis L. ..... West Chester, PA
Redding, Marjorie C. ..... Asheville, NC
Redding, Martha M. ..... New York, NY
Redding, Robert C. ..... San Jose, CA
Redding, Robert E. ..... Bethesda, MD
Redding, Robert M. ..... Coronado, CA
Redding, Robert S. ..... Baltimore, MD
Redding, Robert Steven ..... Hagerstown, MD

Redding, Robert V. .... Jackson, TN
Redding, Robert W. .... Portland, OR
Redding, Scott J. .... Asheboro, NC
Redding, Shelagh K. .... Oakland, CA
Redding, Sherry A. .... Sapulpa, OK
Redding, Susan McMarlin .... McMurray, PA
Redding, Thomas E. .... Houston, TX
Reddinger, Jeanne Rae .... Little River, SC
Reddingius, R. P. .... Fallbrook, CA
Pasadena, CA
Reddington, Edward Charles
Copperas Cove, TX
Reddington, G. Joseph .... Chicago, IL
Reddington, Kevin J. .... Brockton, MA
Reddington, Linda .... Beech Grove, IN
Reddington, Raymond .... Jersey City, NJ
Reddington, Shawn P. .... Boston, MA
Reddington, Shoshan E. .... Chicago, IL
Reddington, Thomas J. .... New York, NY
Reddington, William A. .... Columbus, OH
Reddish, Albert T. .... Alliance, NE
Reddish, Carin S. .... Chicago, IL
Reddish, Gary E. .... Riverside, CA
Redditt, Frank Grey, Jr. .... Mobile, AL
Redditt, Mark L. .... Mobile, AL
Reddix-Smalls, Brenda Raye .... Florence, SC
Reddoch, James F., Jr. .... Tuscaloosa, AL
Reddoch, John B. .... Liberty, MO
Reddock, Angela J. .... Los Angeles, CA
Reddy, Barbara A. .... Roswell, NM
Reddy, Begley & McCormick
Washington, DC
Reddy, Brian .... Buffalo, NY
Reddy, C. Alan .... New York, NY
Reddy, Chas. S. .... Notre Dame, IN
Reddy, Christa Hoeher .... Wayne, NJ
Reddy, David M. .... Elkhorn, WI
Reddy, Donald M. .... Lake Orion, MI
Reddy, Harsha .... New York, NY
Reddy, Jaideep P. .... Palo Alto, CA
Reddy, James H. .... Chicago, IL
Reddy, Jayant A. .... Department of Labor, Office of the Solicitor, GV
Reddy, John J., Jr. .... Wayne, NJ
Reddy, John W. .... Mineola, NY
Reddy, K. Prabhaker .... Decatur, GA
Reddy, Kalpana B. .... Hunt Valley, MD
Reddy, Kim Ackourey .... Atlanta, GA
Reddy, K. Prabhaker, P.C. .... Decatur, GA
Reddy, L. Creighton .... Muskegon, MI
Reddy, Lakshmi .... Indianapolis, IN
Reddy, Michael V., Jr. .... New York, NY
Reddy, Narsimha M. .... Monroeville, PA
Reddy, Nina A. .... New York, NY
Reddy and Reddy .... Wayne, NJ
Reddy, Richard L. .... Washington, DC
Reddy, Robert J. .... Barnstable, MA
Reddy, Shaila .... El Centro, CA
Reddy, Shilpa S. .... Department of Justice, Office of Justice Programs, GV
Reddy, Thomas G. .... San Francisco, CA
Reddy, William J. .... Tucson, AZ
Reddy, William J.
Department Of Veterans Affairs, Board of Veterans Appeals, GV
Redeker, Henry K .... El Monte, CA
Redeker, James R. .... Overland Park, KS
Redeker, James R. .... Philadelphia, PA
Redeker, John E. .... Cleveland, OH
Redel, Charles L. .... La Crosse, WI
Redel, Dennis J. .... Jefferson City, MO
Redelberger, J. John, Jr. .... Crestwood, KY
Redell, Lisa T. .... Honolulu, HI
Redell, William L. .... Solvang, CA
Redell, William R. .... Tulsa, OK
Redemann, Linda G. .... Tulsa, OK
Redemann, Robert P. .... Tulsa, OK
Reden, Carol Lee .... Hicksville, NY
Reden, Robert J. .... Buffalo, NY
Redenbacher, Gary F. .... Santa Cruz, CA
Redenbaugh, Phil C. .... Storm Lake, IA
Redenbaugh, Phil C., P.C.
Storm Lake, IA
Redepenning, Charles W., Jr. .... Danvers, MA
Reder, Barry .... San Francisco, CA
Reder, Benjamin R. .... Los Angeles, CA
Reder, Henry I. .... Cleveland, OH
Reder, Kathleen V. E. .... Crystal Lake, IL
Reder, L. George .... Pittsfield, MA
Reder, Margo E.K. .... Waltham, MA
Reder, Randall O. .... Tampa, FL
Reder, Robert S. .... New York, NY
Redfearn, B. Wilson .... Wilmington, DE
Redfearn & Brown, A Professional Corporation .... Kansas City, MO
Stockton, MO
Redfearn, Douglas W. .... New Orleans, LA
Redfearn, James I. .... Chesterfield, SC
Redfearn, Kyle Lee .... Tallahassee, FL
Redfearn, Paul L. .... Kansas City, MO
Stockton, MO
Redfearn, Robert L. .... New Orleans, LA
Redfearn, Robert L., Jr.
New Orleans, LA
Redfern, C. E. .... Atlanta, GA
Redfern, Courtney E. .... New York, NY
Redfern, Declan P. .... New York, NY
Redfern, Donald B. .... Cedar Falls, IA
Redfern, E. Lee .... Atlanta, GA
Redfern, Jerry L. .... Springfield, MO
Redfern, LeRoy H. .... Cedar Falls, IA
Redfern, Mason, Dieter, Larsen & Moore, P.L.C. .... Cedar Falls, IA
Waterloo, IA
Redfern, Richard .... Jackson, MS
Redfield, Charles S. .... San Francisco, CA
Redfield, Christine Baddell .... San Jose, CA
Redfield, Christine F. .... Rochester, NY
Redfield, Douglas A. .... Keene, NH
Redfield, Jared .... Stevens Point, WI
Redfield, John H. .... Schaumburg, IL
Redfield, Joseph F.
Grosse Pointe Shores, MI
Redfield Law Offices, LLP
Stevens Point, WI
Redfield, Mary H. .... Sherman Oaks, CA
Redfield, Michael L. .... Seattle, WA
Redfield, Robin L. .... Washington, DC
Redfield, Sarah E. .... Concord, NH
Redfield, Susan T. .... Chicago, IL
Redfield, Walter C. .... New York, NY
Redford, Carroll M., III .... Lexington, KY
Redford, Carroll M., Jr. .... Glasgow, KY
Redford, David C. .... Houston, TX
Redford, Debra S. .... Seattle, WA
Redford, Hugh .... Boise, ID
Redford, James R. .... Grand Rapids, MI
Redford Law Office .... Glasgow, KY
Redford, Mack A. .... Boise, ID
Redford, Robert D. .... Los Angeles, CA
Redford, Susan M. .... Odessa, TX
Redford, Timothy R. .... Seattle, WA
Redford & Zillmer .... Milwaukee, WI
Redgate, Russell J. .... West Barnstable, MA
Redgrave, Arthur R. .... Boca Raton, FL
Redgrave, Jonathan M. .... Minneapolis, MN
Redhair, Jack .... Tucson, AZ
Redhair, Michael Scott .... Tucson, AZ
Redhair, Rex R. .... Kansas City, MO
Redic, Dennis J. .... Atlanta, GA
Redic, Geraldine M. .... Pittsburgh, PA
Redican, Laurence M. .... Syosset, NY
Redick, Glenn B. .... Columbus, OH
Redick, Jeffrey B. .... Oakbrook Terrace, IL
Redick, Thomas P. .... San Diego, CA
Redick, William P., Jr. .... Whites Creek, TN
Rediehs, Carol Ann .... Hinsdale, IL
Rediehs, Christopher R. .... St. Paul, MN
Canton, NY
Rediess-Hoosein, Brenda J. .... Newark, NJ
Rediger, Gregory G. .... Miller, SD
Rediger McHugh, LLP .... Sacramento, CA
Rediger, Michael E. .... Chicago, IL
Rediger, Richard K. .... Englewood, CO
Rediger, Robert L. .... Sacramento, CA
Redihan, Charles N., Jr. .... Providence, RI
Rediker, J. Michael .... Birmingham, AL
Rediker, Robert J. Carl .... Brooklyn, NY
Redinbo, Catherine A. .... Chicago, IL
Reding, Beverly L. .... Madison, WI
Reding, Curtis C., Jr. .... Montgomery, AL
Reding, James A. .... Stillwater, MN
Reding, James A., Jr. .... St. Paul, MN
Reding, James T. .... St. Louis, MO
Reding, John A. .... San Francisco, CA
Reding, John P. .... Fort Worth, TX
Reding, Nancy A. .... Chicago, IL
Reding & Pilney .... St. Paul, MN
Stillwater, MN
Reding, Rea & Cooper, P.C. .... Pittsburgh, PA
Reding, Warren S. .... Pittsburgh, PA
Reding-Brubaker, Tami J. .... Chicago, IL
Redinger, Craig T. .... Washington, DC
Redinger, Gary S. .... San Bernardino, CA
Redinger, Ivan L., Jr. .... Canton, OH
Redinger, Janice L. .... Charlottesville, VA
Redinger & Morris, L.L.P. .... Canton, OH
Redington, Edward S. .... New York, NY
Redington, Penelope Graves
Waxahachie, TX
Redington, Penny .... Austin, TX
Redington, Ted .... Dallas, TX
Waxahachie, TX
Redis, Robert M. .... White Plains, NY
Redisch, Elizabeth D. .... Tucker, GA
Redish, Gary S. .... Hackensack, NJ
Redish, Martin H. .... Chicago, IL
Redjaian, Babak .... Costa Mesa, CA
Redl, Frank E. .... Poughkeepsie, NY
Redland, Dorsey .... San Francisco, CA
Redle, David A. .... Akron, OH
Redle, Matthew F. .... Sheridan, WY
Redle, William D. .... Sheridan, WY
Redleaf, David A. .... Great Neck, NY
Redleaf, Diane L. .... Chicago, IL
Redler, Bettie G. .... New Orleans, LA
Redler, Craig S. .... St. Louis, MO
Redler, Robert .... St. Marys, KS
Redlich, Allen .... Albany, NY
Redlich, Catherine L. .... New York, NY
Redlich, James W. .... Springfield, IL
Redlich, Marc, Law Offices of
Boston, MA
Redlich, Norman .... New York, NY
Redlich, Richard J., Jr. .... Universal City, CA
Redlick, David E. .... Boston, MA
Redlinger, Lance J. .... Minneapolis, MN
Redlingshafer, Rex A., P.C.
Kansas City, MO
Redlitz, Gregory V. .... Los Angeles, CA
Redlus, Burt E. .... Miami, FL
Redlus, Burt E., P.A. .... Miami, FL
Redman, Alyson Leigh .... New York, NY
Redman, Anne M. .... Seattle, WA
Redman, Barbara J. .... Greensboro, NC
Redman, Bruce R. .... Bloomfield Hills, MI
Redman, Charles .... Los Angeles, CA
Redman, Cherie Diemer .... Birmingham, MI
Redman, Cherie Diemer, P.C.
Birmingham, MI
Redman, Clarence Owen .... Chicago, IL
Redman, Daniel K. .... Saratoga, CA
Redman, Debra Lynn Burkett
Charleston, SC
Redman, Eric .... Seattle, WA
Redman, Eric C. .... Indianapolis, IN
Redman, James E. .... Milwaukie, OR
Redman, James E. .... Portland, OR
Redman, James L. .... Plant City, FL
Redman, James O. .... Minneapolis, MN
Redman, Leon E. .... Taylor, MI
Redman, Lesley Ann .... Glenview, IL
Redman, Lipman .... Washington, DC
Redman, Manville .... Lawton, OK
Redman, Mark C. .... New York, NY
Redman, Mark William .... Dearborn, MI
Redman, Michael C. .... Tulsa, OK
Redman, Michael C. .... Olympia, WA
Redman, Patricia M. .... Charlotte, NC
Redman, Patrick D. .... Austin, TX
Redman, R. Michael .... Twin Falls, ID
Redman, Reagan S. .... Houston, TX
Redman, Renee Colette .... New York, NY
Redman, Scott D.H. .... Chicago, IL
Redman, Scott T. .... Pittsburgh, PA
Redman, Steven L. .... Fort Lauderdale, FL
Redman, Thomas G. .... Annapolis, MD
Redman, Timothy D. .... Cincinnati, OH
Redman, Toney J. .... Lincoln, NE
Redmann, David E., Jr. .... New Orleans, LA
Redmann, Denise C. .... New Orleans, LA
Redmann, Esther A. .... New Orleans, LA
Redmann, JoAnne S. .... Los Angeles, CA
Redmann, John W. .... New Orleans, LA
Redmann, Kristopher M.
New Orleans, LA
Redmann, Robert E. .... Metairie, LA
Redmaster, Christopher V.
Crawfordsville, IN
Redmiles, Brad Douglas .... Fort Morgan, CO
Redmiles, Mark A. .... Denver, CO
Redmon, Boykin & Braswell, L.L.P.
Alexandria, VA
Redmon, Gant .... Alexandria, VA
Redmon, Gary L. .... Las Vegas, NV
Redmon, Harry S., Jr. .... New Orleans, LA
Redmon, J. Shad .... Marianna, FL
Redmon, Jeffrey A. .... St. Paul, MN
Redmon, John A. .... New York, NY
Redmon, Joseph H. .... Redding, CA
Redmon, Joyann .... Stockton, CA
Redmon, Marsha .... Tampa, FL
Redmon, Marshall M. .... Baton Rouge, LA
Redmon, Michael .... Kansas City, KS
Redmon, Ronald L. .... Columbus, OH
Redmon, Thomas G., (Inc.)
Sacramento, CA
Redmond, Albert G. .... Galveston, TX
Redmond, Brendan T. .... Boston, MA
Redmond, Brian Harold .... Rochester, NY
Redmond, Burgin & Gutierrez, P.A.
Baltimore, MD
Upper Marlboro, MD
Redmond, Carla Rogers .... Chicago, IL
Redmond, Charles C. .... Cleveland, OH
Redmond, Charles D. .... Columbus, OH
Redmond, Christopher .... Islandia, NY
Redmond, Christopher J.
Overland Park, KS
Kansas City, MO
Redmond, Daniel M. .... Washington, DC
Redmond, David A. .... Dayton, OH
Redmond, David D. .... Richmond, VA
Redmond, David P. .... Mineola, NY
New York, NY
Smithtown, NY
Redmond, Donald W. .... Washington, DC
Redmond, Edward C. .... Painesville, OH
Redmond, E. J. .... Ravenna, OH
Redmond, Elizabeth G. .... Buffalo, NY
Redmond, Elizabeth Jane Shannahan
St. Louis, MO
Redmond, Elliott J. .... Baton Rouge, LA
Redmond, George F. .... Milwaukee, WI
Redmond, Gregg H. .... Rochester, NY
Redmond, Gregory M. .... Washington, DC
Redmond, Gregory S. .... Pittsburg, CA
Redmond, Hope S. .... St. Louis, MO
Redmond, Iris W. .... Richmond, VA
Redmond, James C. .... San Francisco, CA
Redmond, James M. .... Miami, FL
Redmond, James N. .... Highland Heights, OH
Redmond, James W. .... Sioux City, IA
Redmond, Jeanette .... New York, NY
Redmond, Jeanne Martinak
San Antonio, TX
Redmond, Jennifer G. .... San Francisco, CA
Redmond, Jerry D., Jr. .... Birmingham, AL
Redmond, Joan S. .... Columbus, GA
Redmond, John E. .... St. Louis, MO
Redmond, John F. .... Rochester, NY
Redmond, John M. .... Los Angeles, CA
Redmond, John R. .... Richmond, VA
Redmond, John T. .... Garden City, NY
Redmond and Jones .... Marietta, OH
Redmond, Joseph C., Jr. .... Washington, DC
Redmond, Kathleen M. .... Reading, MA
Redmond, Kernard Edward
Hartsville, SC
Redmond, Kimberly K. .... Hawthorne, NY
Redmond, Lawrence C., Jr. .... Chicago, IL
Redmond, Lawrence J. .... Parlin, NJ
Redmond, Lee R., Jr. .... Columbus, GA
Redmond, Leonard C., III .... Baltimore, MD
Redmond, Loretta A. .... New York, NY
Redmond, Machelle L. .... Tucker, GA
Redmond, Margaret Ann .... San Jose, CA
Redmond, Mark A. .... Sacramento, CA
Redmond, Maurice S. .... Dakota City, NE
Redmond & Nazar, L.L.P. .... Wichita, KS
Redmond & Parrinello .... Rochester, NY
Redmond, Patricia A. .... Miami, FL
Redmond, Paul J. .... Towson, MD
Redmond, Paul J. .... Scituate, MA
Redmond, Peter M. .... Bayside, NY
Redmond, Phillip H., Jr. .... Charlotte, NC
Redmond, Phoebe V. .... Brooklyn, NY
Redmond, P.J. .... West Chester, PA
Redmond, Pollio & Pittoni, P.C.
Garden City, NY
Redmond, R. Todd .... Kalamazoo, MI
Redmond, Richard A. .... Chicago, IL
Redmond, Richard M. .... Sacramento, CA
Redmond, Robert .... Fairfax, VA
Redmond, Robert .... Falls Church, VA
Redmond, Robert F., III
Kansas City, MO
Redmond, Robert F., Jr. .... Richmond, VA
Redmond, Robert W. .... Albany, NY
Redmond, Roger F. .... Marietta, OH
Parkersburg, WV
Redmond, Rosemary E. .... Dallas, TX
Redmond & Sapio .... Galveston, TX
Redmond, Stephen J. .... Boston, MA
Redmond, Susan Rachel .... Montgomery, AL
Redmond, Tara .... Trenton, NJ
Redmond, Terence A. .... San Francisco, CA
Redmond, Thomas Eugene .... Washington, DC
Redmond, Vance R. .... Bethesda, MD
Redmond, Velma A. .... Hershey, PA
Redmond and Walker .... Painesville, OH
Redmond, Wayne E. .... Woodland Hills, CA
Redmond, Wesley C. .... Birmingham, AL
Redmond, William A. .... Kalamazoo, MI
Redmond, William E. .... Albany, NY
Redmond, William W. .... Philadelphia, PA
Redner, James Burke .... Tallahassee, FL
Redner, Susan Mikes .... Stamford, CT
Rednick, Robert I. .... Port Chester, NY
Rednik, Debra H. .... Washington, DC
Rednor, Howard S. .... Trenton, NJ
Rednor, Joshua A. .... Lake Success, NY
Rednor, Neil M. .... Trenton, NJ
Redo, Frank Louis .... Woodstown, NJ
Redondo, Roberto .... New York, NY
Redos, Joyce L.
Department of Transportation, Federal Aviation Administration, GV
Redpath, Charles A., Jr. .... Englewood, CO
Redpath, James D.R. .... Scottsdale, AZ
Redpath, James R. .... Phoenix, AZ
Redpath, John S., Jr. .... New York, NY
Redpath, Randolph A. .... Greensboro, NC
Redrow, Allan R. .... Worcester, MA
Redshaw, Stephen A. .... Portland, OR
Redstone, David M. .... Tallahassee, FL
Redstone, Irene .... Vero Beach, FL
Redstone, Laura B. .... Denver, CO
Redstone, Marion O. .... Indianapolis, IN
Redstone, Michael G. .... Deerfield, IL
Redstone, Sumner M. .... Dedham, MA
Redula, Ludovico R. .... Salinas, CA
Reduto, James P. .... Mount Kisco, NY
Redvanly, Carolyn N. .... Atlanta, GA
Redway, H. Jonathan .... Alexandria, VA
Redway, John T. .... Middletown, CT
Redway, Linn Kaiser .... Washington, DC
Redwine & Associates .... Norman, OK
Redwine, Earnest, Jr. .... Atlanta, GA
Redwine, Glynis Wheeler .... Fort Worth, TX
Redwine, Jack T. .... Evanston, IL
Redwine, James M. .... Mt. Vernon, IN
Redwine, James M. .... Monroeville, PA
Redwine, Kathryn D. .... Denver, CO
Redwine, Mabary & Batchelor .... Sherman, TX
Redwine, Philip O. .... Raleigh, NC
Redwine, Philip O., P.A. .... Raleigh, NC
Redwine, Philip Warren .... Norman, OK
Redwine, R. Kevin .... Tulsa, OK
Redwine, Robert A. .... New Orleans, LA
Redwine, Robert R. .... Oklahoma City, OK
Redwine and Sherrill .... Riverside, CA
Santa Ana, CA
Redwine, Shirley R. .... Houston, TX
Redwine, Thomas A. .... Sherman, TX
Redwine, William R. .... Sandy Hook, KY
Redwing, Dennis J. .... Gastonia, NC
Redwood, Jason D. .... Treasury Department, Office of the Comptroller of the Currency, GV
Reeb, David P., Jr. .... Clovis, NM
Reeb, Robert L. .... Chicago, IL
Reeback, Robert T. .... Albuquerque, NM
Reebel, Walter F. .... Birmingham, MI
Reece, A. Douglas .... London, KY
Reece & Associates .... Washington, DC
Atlanta, GA
Reece and Baker, LLC .... Denver, CO
Reece, Carla T. .... Fort Lauderdale, FL
Reece, Carolyn C. .... Burbank, CA
Reece, Cathy L. .... Phoenix, AZ
Reece, Craig J. .... Phoenix, AZ
Reece, Daniel B., III .... Kingsport, TN
Reece, Daniel Boone, IV .... Charleston, SC
Reece, Daniel L. .... Scott Depot, WV
Reece, David B. .... Dallas, TX
Reece, Debra G. .... Coral Gables, FL
Reece, Donald B. .... Lake Forest, IL
Reece, D. W. .... El Paso, TX
Reece, Guy Lester, II .... Columbus, OH
Reece, James S. .... Minneapolis, MN
Reece, James W. .... Charlotte, NC
Reece, Janice M. .... General Accounting Office, Personnel Appeals Board, GV
Reece, Jason H. .... Charlotte, NC
Reece & Jensen, PLLC .... London, KY
Reece, Joe T. .... Denver, CO
Reece, John M. .... Stockton, CA
Reece, John M., A Professional Law Corporation .... Stockton, CA
Reece, John W. .... Akron, OH
Reece, Joseph D. .... Fayetteville, AR

Reece, Joseph L. ... Anchorage, AK
Reece, Kaden Parenicka ... Sacramento, CA
Reece, Laurence H., III ... Boston, MA
Reece, Lewis P. ... St. George, UT
Reece, Marilyn Cranley ... Portland, OR
Reece, Mary M. ... Goldsboro, NC
Reece, Matthew ... Washington, DC
Reece, Michael J. ... Smithfield, NC
Reece, Monte M. ... South Lake Tahoe, CA
Reece, Norman G., Jr. ... Pocatello, ID
Reece, Robert A. ... Oklahoma City, OK
Reece, Robert W. ... Ocala, FL
Reece, Sharon A. ... Albany, NY
Reece, Shelly Reneé ... Springfield, MO
Reece, Warren L. ... Mustang, OK
Reece, Wayne ... Washington, DC
Atlanta, GA
Reece, William A., II ... Dallas, TX
Reece, William H. ... Mobile, AL
Reece, William R., III ... Atlanta, GA
Reece, William T., Jr. ... San Antonio, TX
Reecer, Dena A. ... Snyder, TX
Reecer, Larry M. ... Albuquerque, NM
Reecher, Eric W. ... Bristol, VA
Reecht, Christopher Michael ... Olathe, KS
Reeck, Amy R. ... Fort Lauderdale, FL
Reed, Aaron J. ... Washington, DC
Reed, Adami & Kaiser, P.C. ... Brockton, MA
Reed, Alan J., Jr.
Securities and Exchange Commission,
Division of Market Regulation, GV
Reed, Alan L. ... Philadelphia, PA
Reed, Alan P. ... Penn Yan, NY
Reed, Alette E. ... Boston, MA
Reed, Alex P., Jr. ... New York, NY
Reed, Allen P. ... North Miami Beach, FL
Reed, Allen P., P.A. ... North Miami Beach, FL
Reed, Allen R. ... Long Grove, IL
Reed, Ancil M. ... Fort Belvoir, VA
Reed, Andrew ... Franklin, LA
Morgan City, LA
Reed, Angelique A. ... New Orleans, LA
Reed, Ann Lubinski ... Seymour, WI
Reed, Anne Willis ... Milwaukee, WI
Reed, Armstrong, Gorman, Coffey, Gilbert & Mudge, Professional Corporation
Belleville, IL
Edwardsville, IL
Springfield, IL
Reed & Associates ... Portola Valley, CA
Reed, Austin F. ... Glen Allen, VA
Reed, B. Thomas ... Norfolk, VA
Reed, Barbara A. ... Lewisburg, PA
Reed, Barry ... Boston, MA
Reed, Barry G. ... Minneapolis, MN
Reed, Barry, Jr. ... Boston, MA
Reed, Barry S. ... Washington, DC
Reed, Benjamin B. ... Washington, DC
Reed, Benjamin W. ... Helena, MT
Reed, Benjie S. ... Mexia, TX
Reed, Berton D. ... Melrose, MA
Reed, Betty Ann ... Modesto, CA
Reed, Bobby Lynn ... Groesbeck, TX
Reed, Bradley J. ... Cumberland, MD
Reed, Brian E. ... Lancaster, OH
Reed, Brian R.
Department of Transportation,
Federal Aviation Administration, GV
Reed & Brown LLP ... Pasadena, CA
Reed, Bruce A. ... Rosemead, CA
Reed, Bruce D. ... Philadelphia, PA
Reed, Bruce G. ... New Orleans, LA
Reed, Bruce M. ... Seattle, WA
Reed, Bryan V., Law Offices of
Chicago, IL
Reed, Candace A. ... Salem, OR
Reed, Carey J. ... Appleton, WI
Reed, Carl L., Co. (L.P.A.) ... Akron, OH
Reed, Carl T. ... Salt Lake City, UT
Reed, Carol V. ... Orinda, CA
Reed, Carole ... Houston, TX
Reed, Carolyn Ryan ... Newark, NJ
Reed, Carrera & McLain, L.L.P.
Edinburg, TX
Reed, Cathy R. ... Los Angeles, CA
Reed, Chad ... Houston, TX
Reed, Chad Kenneth ... Marietta, GA
Reed, Charles D. ... Washington, DC
New York, NY
Reed, Charles E. ... Fall River, MA
Reed, Charles E. ... Lancaster, OH
Reed, Charles Gordon ... Beaumont, TX
Reed, Charles J. ... Chicago, IL
Reed, Charles K. ... Atlanta, GA
Reed, Charles L. ... Fresno, CA
Reed, Charles L. ... Richmond, VA
Reed, Charles M. ... Houston, TX
Reed, Charles P. ... New Haven, CT
Reed, Charles R. ... San Jose, CA
Reed, Charles W., Jr. ... Montgomery, AL
Reed, Chatham H. ... Shreveport, LA
Reed, Christine Balbo ... Monterey, CA
Reed, Christopher H. ... Phoenix, AZ
Reed, Christopher K. ... Buffalo, NY
Reed, Christopher H., L.L.C., Law Office of
Phoenix, AZ
Reed, Christopher S. ... Maitland, FL
Reed, Clarence E. ... Cassville, MO
Reed, Clarence E. ... Houston, TX
Reed, Claude W. ... Louisville, KY
Reed, Clifton E. ... Ventura, CA
Reed, Cory J. ... Columbus, OH
Reed, Cynthia K. ... New York, NY
Reed, Cynthia S. ... Pawtucket, RI
Reed, D. Gary ... Louisville, KY
Reed, D. Roger ... Spokane, WA
Reed, Damon L. ... Waco, TX
Reed, Dan M. ... Fort Worth, TX

Reed, Dana A. ... Baltimore, MD
Reed, Dana W., (Mr.) ... Costa Mesa, CA
Los Angeles, CA
Reed, Daniel A. ... Riverside, CA
Reed, Daniel A. ... Aurora, IL
Reed, Daniel A. ... Baton Rouge, LA
Reed, Daniel E. ... Miami, FL
Reed, Darrel E., Jr. ... Houston, TX
Reed, David A.
Commodity Futures Trading Commission,
Division of Enforcement, GV
Reed, David A. ... Fort Lauderdale, FL
Reed, David A. ... St. Louis, MO
Reed, David A. ... Fairfax, VA
Reed, David C. ... Seattle, WA
Reed, David E. ... Bellevue, WA
Reed, David J. ... Roswell, GA
Reed, David L. ... San Carlos, CA
Reed, David Lee ... Princeton, NJ
Reed, David N. ... Dayton, OH
Reed, David N. ... Dallas, TX
Reed, David Q. ... Kansas City, MO
Reed, David R. ... Beverly Hills, CA
Reed, David R. ... St. Petersburg, FL
Reed, David R. ... Chicago, IL
Reed, David T. ... Cleveland, OH
Reed, David T. ... Marion, OH
Reed, David W. ... Davis, CA
Reed, David W. ... Woodland, CA
Reed & Davidson ... Costa Mesa, CA
Los Angeles, CA
Reed, Deborah E. ... Charleston, WV
Reed, Dena C. ... Washington, DC
Reed, Denis Y. ... Des Moines, IA
Reed, Derrick W. ... New York, NY
Reed, Devin J. ... Jacksonville, FL
Reed, Diana L. ... Pittsburgh, PA
Reed, Diane M. ... Newport Beach, CA
Reed, Dianne E. ... Portola Valley, CA
Reed, Dianne Tillman ... South Bend, IN
Reed, Donald J. ... Department of Commerce,
Office of the General Counsel, GV
Reed, Donald P. ... Naples, FL
Reed, Donald R. ... Sierra Madre, CA
Reed, Donna L. ... Sacramento, CA
Reed, Doris M. ... Tucson, AZ
Reed, Dottie W. ... Maryville, TN
Reed, Douglas J. ... Des Moines, IA
Reed, Douglas L. ... Milwaukee, WI
Reed, Dwight D. ... Opelousas, LA
Reed, E. Charles, Jr. ... Atlanta, GA
Reed & Earhart ... Warsaw, IN
Reed, Earl F., Jr. ... Jamesburg, NJ
Reed, Edward C., Jr. ... Reno, NV
Reed, Edward J. ... Washington, DC
Reed, Edward L. ... Danvers, MA
Reed, Edward T. (Ned) ... Carson City, NV
Reed, Elise A. ... Minneapolis, MN
Reed, Elise N. ... Bloomfield Hills, MI
Reed, Elizabeth E. ... San Diego, CA
Reed, Elizabeth J. ... Department of Justice,
Antitrust Division, GV
Reed, Elliott, Creech & Roth
San Jose, CA
Reed, Eric A. ... Salisbury, MD
Reed, Erin E. ... Baton Rouge, LA
Reed, Evan J. ... Akron, OH
Reed, Floyd J. ... New Orleans, LA
Reed, Frank J., Jr. ... Columbus, OH
Reed, Frederic C. ... Cheyenne, WY
Reed, Frederick G. ... Canandaigua, NY
Reed, Frederick R. ... Columbus, OH
Reed, Fredric D. ... Seattle, WA
Reed, Gardner ... Newport, KY
Reed, Gary K. ... Battle Creek, MI
Reed, George E. ... Bethesda, MD
Reed, George E., Jr. ... White Plains, NY
Reed, George L. ... Tallahassee, FL
Reed, Gerald S. ... Murphysboro, IL
Reed & Giesa, P.S. ... Coeur d'Alene, ID
Spokane, WA
Reed, Glen A. ... Atlanta, GA
Reed, Glenn A. ... San Antonio, TX
Reed, Glenn D. ... Covina, CA
Reed, Glenn E. ... Glendale, CA
Reed, Glenn W. ... Chicago, IL
Reed, Gloria Darty ... Jonesboro, GA
Reed, Gloria Darty, P.C. ... Jonesboro, GA
Reed, Greg ... Austin, TX
Reed, Gregg ... New York, NY
Reed, Gregory ... Baltimore, MD
Reed, Gregory A. ... Wilmington, DE
Reed, Gregory M. ... Murfreesboro, TN
Reed, Gregory R. ... Harrisburg, PA
Reed, Gretchen S. ... Beaver, PA
Reed, Hal C. ... Auburn, AL
Reed, Harold B. ... St. Johns, MI
Reed, Harold F., Jr. ... Beaver, PA
Reed, Harry L. ... Houston, TX
Reed, Harry W., Jr. ... Lebanon, PA
Reed, Harvey J. ... Baltimore, MD
Reed & Hatem ... Bel Air, MD
Reed, Heather ... Milwaukee, WI
Reed, Heller, Mansfield & Gross
Murphysboro, IL
Reed, Henry M., III ... Louisville, KY
Reed & Hickman, P.A. ... Maryville, TN
Reed & Hostage, P.C. ... Washington, DC
Reed, Howard F., Jr. ... Media, PA
Reed, Hugh D., Jr. ... Fairfield, TX
Reed, Irwin & Tilley, P.A.
Heber Springs, AR
Reed, J. Bradbury ... Nashville, TN
Reed, J. David ... Montrose, CO
Telluride, CO
Reed, J. David, P.C. ... Montrose, CO
Telluride, CO
Reed, J. Davis, III ... Virginia Beach, VA

Reed, J. George ... Cary, NC
Reed, J. Michael, (A Professional Corporation) ... San Diego, CA
Reed, J. William (Bill) ... Rockwall, TX
Reed, Jack W. ... Salt Lake City, UT
Reed, Jackson R. ... Sugar Land, TX
Reed, James ... Miami, OK
Reed, James A. ... Colorado Springs, CO
Reed, James A. ... Indianapolis, IN
Reed, James A. ... Austin, TX
Reed, James A., II ... Kansas City, MO
Reed, James A., Jr. ... Rochester, NY
Reed, James A., P.C.
Colorado Springs, CO
Reed, James A., P.C. ... Austin, TX
Reed, James B. ... Phoenix, AZ
Reed, James B. ... Elmira, NY
Reed, James C. ... Georgetown, DE
Reed, James C., Jr. ... San Antonio, TX
Reed, James D. ... Mission Viejo, CA
Reed, James D. ... Towson, MD
Reed, James D., A Professional Corporation,
Law Offices of ... Mission Viejo, CA
Reed, James E. ... Oakland, CA
Reed, James E. ... Orinda, CA
Reed, James E. ... Battle Creek, MI
Reed, James E. ... Spokane, WA
Reed, James K. ... Atlanta, GA
Reed, James K. ... Hagerstown, MD
Reed, James L. ... Chicago, IL
Reed, James L., Jr. ... Houston, TX
Reed, James M. ... Tampa, FL
Reed, James M. ... Tulsa, OK
Reed, James M., II ... Kansas City, MO
Reed, James R. ... Caro, MI
Reed, James Robert ... Crown Point, IN
Reed, James S. ... Los Angeles, CA
Reed, James S. ... Mammoth Lakes, CA
Reed, James T., Jr.
Huntington Beach, CA
Reed, James William ... Dallas, TX
Reed, James Y. "Bo" ... Knoxville, TN
Reed, Jan Stern ... Deerfield, IL
Reed, Janet E. ... Philadelphia, PA
Reed, Janet Lynn ... Chicago, IL
Reed, Janet Pittman ... Jacksonville, NC
Reed, Jas. C., Jr. ... Charleston, WV
Reed, Jas. W. ... Clay, WV
Reed, Jason C. ... Omaha, NE
Reed, Jason L. ... Salina, KS
Reed, Jason V. ... Lexington, KY
Reed, Jeffrey ... Pittsburgh, PA
Reed, Jeffrey A. ... Bowling Green, KY
Reed, Jeffrey B. ... Parkersburg, WV
Reed, Jeffrey L. ... Murfreesboro, TN
Reed, Jeffrey Lee ... Lima, OH
Reed, Jeffrey M. ... Indianapolis, IN
Reed, Jeffrey W. ... Minneapolis, MN
Reed, Jerry D. ... Charlotte, NC
Reed, Jerry, (Inc.) ... Tulsa, OK
Reed, Jill E. ... Columbus, OH
Reed, Joe B. ... Springdale, AR
Reed, Joel D. ... Akron, OH
Reed, Joel S. ... Dallas, TX
Reed, Johana A. ... Washington, DC
Reed, John A. ... Hartford, CT
Reed, John A. ... Joliet, IL
Reed, John A., Jr. ... Orlando, FL
Reed, John A., Ltd. ... Joliet, IL
Reed, John Alan ... Seattle, WA
Reed, John C. ... Jefferson City, MO
Reed, John C. ... Sharon, PA
Reed, John D. ... Department of Commerce,
Patent and Trademark Office, GV
Reed, John F., (A P.C.) ... Marina Del Rey, CA
Reed, John G. ... New York, NY
Reed, John H. ... Wheeling, WV
Reed, John H., III ... Hurricane, WV
Reed, John H., Jr. ... Hurricane, WV
Reed, John L. ... Fresno, CA
Reed, John L. ... Wilmington, DE
Reed, John M. ... Boston, MA
Reed, John M. ... Poughkeepsie, NY
Reed, John P. ... Hammond, IN
Reed, John P. ... Uhrichsville, OH
Reed, John S. ... Louisville, KY
Reed, John T. ... Paducah, KY
Reed, John T. ... Lancaster, PA
Reed, John W. ... La Jolla, CA
Reed, John W. ... Ann Arbor, MI
Reed, John W., Jr. ... Toledo, OH
Reed, John W., Law Offices of, A Prof. Corp.
La Jolla, CA
Reed, John Wilson ... New Orleans, LA
Reed, Jon A. ... Morgantown, WV
Reed, Jonathan C. ... Las Vegas, NV
Reed, Jonathan D. ... Knoxville, TN
Reed, Jonathan S. ... Hackensack, NJ
Reed, Joseph H. ... Medford, OK
Reed, Joseph H. ... Vermillion, SD
Reed, Joseph W. ... Knoxville, TN
Reed, Joy E. ... Uhrichsville, OH
Reed, Joyce G. ... Greenville, NC
Reed, Juden Justice ... San Francisco, CA
Reed, Julie L. ... Camas, WA
Reed, K. Karan ... Houston, TX
Reed, Karlen J. ... Boston, MA
Reed, Karyn K. ... Philadelphia, PA
Reed, Katherine ... Dallas, TX
Reed, Kathleen ... Treasury Department,
Internal Revenue Service, GV
Reed, Kathleen A. ... Detroit, MI
Reed, Keith A. ... Chicago, IL
Reed, Kelly K. ... Lansing, MI
Reed, Kendall C. ... Chatsworth, CA
Reed, Kenneth C. ... Flint, MI
Reed, Kenneth D. ... Hammond, IN
Reed, Kevin A. ... Austin, TX

Reed, Kevin Albert ... Cincinnati, OH
Reed, Kevin E. ... Memphis, TN
Reed, Kevin F. ... Washington, DC
Reed, Kevin S. ... Santa Monica, CA
Reed, Kim D. ... La Grange, IL
Reed, Kimberley Del Rio ... Detroit, MI
Reed, Kimberly ... Glenview, IL
Reed, Kimberly D. ... Chapel Hill, NC
Reed, Kristen S. ... Columbus, OH
Reed, Kristine H. ... Waynesfield, OH
Reed, Kyle A. ... New York, NY
Reed, L. Andrew, Jr. ... Akron, OH
Reed, Lane B. ... Meadville, MS
Reed, Larry A. ... St. Louis, MO
Reed, Larry E. ... Minneapolis, MN
Reed, Larry E. ... Fort Worth, TX
Reed, Laura A. ... San Francisco, CA
Reed, Laura K. ... Salem, VA
Reed, Laura L. ... Philadelphia, PA
Reed, Laura S. ... Indianapolis, IN
Reed Law Associates, P.C. ... Glenview, IL
Reed Law Firm, The, A P.C.
San Diego, CA
Reed, Leland ... Los Angeles, CA
Reed, Leo A., Jr. ... Norwell, MA
Reed, Leon ... Heber Springs, AR
Reed, Leslie E. ... Edinburg, TX
Reed, Leslie K.
Export-Import Bank of The United States,
Office of the General Counsel, GV
Reed, Leslie M. ... Boulder, CO
Reed, Linda B. ... Los Angeles, CA
Reed, Linda F. ... Dayton, OH
Reed, Lisa M. ... Houston, TX
Reed, Lisa S. ... Aberdeen, WA
Reed, Louis J. ... Sauk Rapids, MN
Reed, Lowell A., Jr. ... Philadelphia, PA
Reed, Loyd W. ... Glendale, CA
Reed, Luce, Tosh, Wolford & Douglass, A Professional Corporation ... Beaver, PA
Reed, Lucy F. ... New York, NY
Reed, Lynne Gavin ... Boston, MA
Reed, M. Ann ... Raleigh, NC
Reed, M. Kasim ... Atlanta, GA
Reed, Marcus G. ... Clinton, MO
Reed, Margaret G. ... Houston, TX
Reed, Margery N. ... Philadelphia, PA
Reed, Marjorie E. ... Fountain Valley, CA
Reed, Mark ... Hudson, IA
Reed, Mark L. ... Sullivan, IN
Reed, Mark N. ... Luray, VA
Reed, Mark S. ... Minneapolis, MN
Reed, Mark W. ... Fort Thomas, KY
Reed, Marlene Watts ... New York, NY
Reed, Martin S. ... Los Angeles, CA
Reed, Martine B. ... Amherst, MA
Reed, Mary ... Department of Justice,
Environment and Natural Resources
Division, GV
Reed, Mary Bennett ... Spokane, WA
Reed, Mary Helen ... Cody, WY
Reed, Mary Hutchings ... Chicago, IL
Reed, Mary Lynn ... Washington, DC
Baltimore, MD
Rockville, MD
Vienna, VA
Reed, Matthew R. ... Palo Alto, CA
Reed, Max E. ... Warsaw, IN
Reed, Mazanec & Wheeler ... Cleveland, OH
Reed McClure ... Seattle, WA
Reed, McGavock D.
Executive Office Of The President,
Office of Management and Budget, GV
Reed, Merner & Sabbath ... Cedar Falls, IA
Reed, Michael ... Austin, TX
Reed, Michael A. ... San Diego, CA
Reed, Michael A. ... Flossmoor, IL
Reed, Michael D. ... Olathe, KS
Reed, Michael D. ... Harrisburg, PA
Reed, Michael E. ... Orlando, FL
Reed, Michael E. ... Centralia, IL
Reed, Michael E. ... Chicago, IL
Reed, Michael G. ... Cincinnati, OH
Reed, Michael H. ... Philadelphia, PA
Reed, Michael J. ... Oakland, CA
Reed, Michael James ... Malvern, PA
Reed, Michael L. ... San Francisco, CA
Reed, Michael L. ... Alexandria, VA
Reed, Michael P., Law Offices of
Lubbock, TX
Reed, Michael R. ... Columbus, OH
Reed, Michael V. ... Portland, OR
Reed, Michael W. ... Warsaw, IN
Reed, Michele E. ... Montgomery, AL
Reed, Michele Lee ... Philadelphia, PA
Reed, Mickie ... Indio, CA
Reed, Nadine N. ... Clearwater, FL
Reed, Nancy M. ... Luray, VA
Reed, Natalie L. ... Washington, DC
Reed, Nathaniel J. ... Las Vegas, NV
Reed, Nathaniel J., Ltd. ... Las Vegas, NV
Reed, Neil A. ... Kingwood, WV
Reed, Norman Joseph ... Las Vegas, NV
Reed, Norman M. ... New York, NY
Reed, O'Reilly & Brett ... Boston, MA
Reed, Orville L., III ... Akron, OH
Reed, Oscar E., Jr. ... Lafayette, LA
Reed, Pamela J. ... San Francisco, CA
Walnut Creek, CA
Reed, Pat ... Dallas, TX
Reed, Patricia Ann ... Naperville, IL
Reed, Patrick C. ... New York, NY
Reed, Paul J., Jr. ... Towson, MD
Reed, Paul Lewis ... La Jolla, CA
Reed, Paula L. ... St. Louis, MO
Reed, Paula Whitson ... Nashville, TN
Reed, Philip C. ... Cheshire, CT
Reed, Phillip S. ... Chicago, IL

Reed, Pierce J. .... **Boston, MA**
Reed & Polito, P.S. .... Bellevue, WA
Reed & Pond, Ltd. .... Mound, MN
Reed, Presley R., Jr.
Federal Energy Regulatory Commission,
Office of the General Counsel, GV
Reed, R. Kenneth .... Baton Rouge, LA
Reed, R. Michael .... Charleston, WV
Reed, R. Phillip .... Springfield, IL
Reed, Randall B. .... Phoenix, AZ
Reed, Randall B. .... **Cheyenne, WY**
Reed, Randall C. .... Dallas, TX
Reed, Randall L. .... **Plattsburgh, NY**
Reed, Rayford E. .... Oakland, CA
Reed, Raymond C. .... Beverly Hills, CA
Reed, Raymond M. .... Smyrna, GA
Reed, Rebecca R. .... **Washington, DC**
Reed, Rebecca S. .... **Riverside, CA**
Reed & Reed .... New Orleans, LA
Poughkeepsie, NY
Dallas, TX
Reed & Reed .... Groesbeck, TX
Mexia, TX
Reed & Reed .... Hurricane, WV
Reed, Reed, Kelly & Poggi, P.A.
Glen Burnie, MD
Towson, MD
Reed & Reed, P.C. .... Luray, VA
Reed & Reed, P.C., Law Office of
Boulder, CO
Reed, Renee M. .... **New Haven, CT**
Reed, Rex H. .... **Springfield, VA**
Reed, Rex L. .... Warsaw, IN
Reed, Richard A. .... **Albany, NY**
Reed, Richard C. .... Accokeek, MD
Reed, Richard C. .... Bellevue, WA
Reed, Richard C., III .... **Austin, TX**
Reed, Richard D. .... **Kalamazoo, MI**
Reed, Richard D. .... Dallas, TX
Reed, Richard D. .... Seattle, WA
Reed, Richard E. .... Atlanta, GA
Reed, Richard G. .... **Scranton, PA**
Reed, Richard K. .... **Greenbelt, MD**
Reed, Richard L. .... Mobile, AL
Reed, Richard L. .... **San Antonio, TX**
Reed, Richard R. .... Las Vegas, NV
Reed, Richard R. .... **Murray Hill, NJ**
Reed, Richard T. .... **Baton Rouge, LA**
Reed, Richard W. .... Muncie, IN
Reed, Robert .... Beverly Hills, CA
Reed, Robert A. .... Greensboro, NC
Reed, Robert B. .... Boynton Beach, FL
Reed, Robert B. .... Flemington, NJ
Reed, Robert C. .... Cleveland, OH
Reed, Robert C. .... Beaver, PA
Reed, Robert D. .... Albany, NY
Reed, Robert D. .... **San Antonio, TX**
Reed, Robert E. .... Department of Defense,
Office of the General Counsel, GV
Reed, Robert E. .... Syracuse, IN
Reed, Robert E. .... Detroit, MI
Reed, Robert F. .... Cincinnati, OH
Reed, Robert G., Jr. .... Kenton, OH
Reed, Robert J. .... Gainesville, GA
Reed, Robert K. .... Philadelphia, PA
Reed, Robert L. .... Topeka, KS
Reed, Robert L. .... Brockton, MA
Reed, Robert L., P.A. .... Topeka, KS
Reed, Robert M. .... **Virginia Beach, VA**
Reed, Robert M., Jr. .... **Dallas, TX**
Reed, Robert P. .... **Camp Hill, PA**
Reed, Robert R. .... **New York, NY**
Reed, Robert W. .... Denver, CO
Reed, Robt. C., Jr. .... Madison, WI
Reed, Robt. R. .... Columbus, OH
Reed, Roger A. .... Hayti, MO
Reed, Roger H. .... **Edinburg, TX**
Reed, Roger W. .... Mound, MN
Reed, Rolon A., III .... **New York, NY**
Reed, Rolon W. .... Mount Dora, FL
Reed, Ronald A. .... Chico, CA
Reed, Ronald E. .... **Jacksonville, FL**
Reed, Ronald S. .... **Tampa, FL**
Reed, Ronald S., Jr. .... **St. Joseph, MO**
Reed, Ronald S., P.A. .... **Tampa, FL**
Reed, Roni .... **Los Angeles, CA**
Reed, Ronna S. .... **Irvine, CA**
Sacramento, CA
Santa Rosa, CA
Reed, Russell L. .... **Springfield, IL**
Reed, Ryan Clifford .... **Bowling Green, KY**
Reed, Sally A. .... Downers Grove, IL
Reed, Samuel L. .... **Muncie, IN**
Reed, Sarah L. .... Charlotte, MI
Reed and Scholl .... Flemington, NJ
Reed, Scott K. .... **New York, NY**
Reed, Scott L. .... **Orlando, FL**
Reed, Scott M. .... **Boulder, CO**
Reed, Scott M. .... Virginia Beach, VA
Reed, Scott O. .... **Chicago, IL**
Reed, Scott W. .... **Coeur d'Alene, ID**
Reed, Shane A. .... Central Point, OR
Reed, Shari .... Philadelphia, PA
Reed, Shawn L. .... **Wheeling, WV**
Reed, Shelley A. .... **Dayton, OH**
Reed, Sherman A. .... Oklahoma City, OK
Reed, Shirley .... Clarkston, GA
Reed Smith Hazel & Thomas LLP
Falls Church, VA
Leesburg, VA
McLean, VA
Richmond, VA
Reed Smith Shaw & McClay LLP
Washington, DC
Newark, NJ
Princeton, NJ
New York, NY
Harrisburg, PA
Philadelphia, PA
Pittsburgh, PA
Reed, Stanley F., Jr. .... **New York, NY**
Reed, Stanley J. .... **Bethesda, MD**
Reed, Stephanie A. .... **Miami, FL**
Reed, Stephanie R. .... Cleveland, OH
Reed, Stephen B. .... **Boston, MA**
Reed, Stephen C. .... Chico, CA
Reed, Stephen L. .... Oquawka, IL
Reed, Stephen W. .... **Pasadena, CA**
Reed, Steven .... **Washington, DC**
Reed, Steven A. .... Ann Arbor, MI
Reed, Steven A. .... **Philadelphia, PA**
Reed, Steven A., P.C., Law Offices
Ann Arbor, MI
Reed, Steven B. .... St. Helens, OR
Reed, Steven C. .... West Des Moines, IA
Reed, Steven C. .... Gallatin, MO
Reed, Steven G. .... Columbus, OH
Reed, Steven J. .... Parsippany, NJ
Reed, Steven L. .... **Phoenix, AZ**
Reed, Steven L. .... Department of the Army,
Office, Chief of Engineers/Headquarters,
U.S. Army Corps of Engineers, GV
Reed, Stover & O'Connor, P.C.
Kalamazoo, MI
Reed, Susan D. .... San Antonio, TX
Reed, Susan E. .... Indianapolis, IN
Reed, Susan F. .... Detroit, MI
Reed, Susan K. .... Oakland, NJ
Reed, Susanne K. .... Santa Rosa, CA
Reed, Sylvia Monique .... **Memphis, TN**
Reed, T. Michael .... **San Diego, CA**
Reed, T. Michael .... Hattiesburg, MS
Reed, Taylor .... **Riverton, WY**
Reed, Teresa G. Combs .... **Hazard, KY**
Reed, Terrance G. .... Washington, DC
Reed & Terry .... Sugar Land, TX
Reed, Terry D. .... Buckhannon, WV
Reed, Thomas .... **Lufkin, TX**
Reed, Thomas A. .... **Chicago, IL**
Reed, Thomas A. .... **Boston, MA**
Reed, Thomas A. .... Poughkeepsie, NY
Reed, Thomas C. .... Tucson, AZ
Reed, Thomas C. .... **Pittsburgh, PA**
Reed, Thomas F. .... **Los Angeles, CA**
Reed, Thomas Grady, III .... Pensacola, FL
Reed, Thomas Grady, III, P.A.
Pensacola, FL
Reed, Thomas H. .... Lancaster, PA
Reed, Thomas J. .... Wilmington, DE
Reed, Thomas J. .... Newton, NJ
Reed, Thomas J., Law Offices of
Chicago, IL
Reed, Thomas J. B. .... Boulder, CO
Reed, Thomas L. .... Claremont, CA
Reed, Thomas L. .... **Bluffton, SC**
Hilton Head Island, SC
Reed, Thomas L., Jr. .... Murfreesboro, TN
Reed, Thomas Louis .... Little Rock, AR
Reed, Thomas R. .... Milwaukee, WI
Reed, Thomas S. .... **Chicago, IL**
Reed, Timothy J. .... **Chicago, IL**
Reed, Timothy L. .... McMinnville, TN
Reed & Tisdale .... **Waco, TX**
Reed, Todd A. .... Austin, TX
Reed, Todd M. .... **Providence, RI**
Reed, Toni Scott .... **Dallas, TX**
Reed, Tracy Cotts .... **Oklahoma City, OK**
Reed, Tyrone E., & Associates
Cleveland, OH
Reed, Valerie .... Worcester, MA
Reed, Victor P. .... Mill Valley, CA
Reed, Virginia Jane .... **Atlanta, GA**
Reed, W. Brooks .... Youngstown, OH
Reed, W. Chad .... Houston, TX
Reed, W. Franklin .... **Pittsburgh, PA**
Reed, W. Phillip .... Maryville, TN
Reed, Wallace B. .... Weaverville, NC
Reed, Wallace C. .... **Los Angeles, CA**
Reed, Walter A. .... Reading, PA
Reed, Walter D. .... Vermillion, SD
Reed, Walter G. D. .... **Providence, RI**
Reed, Walter L. .... Dallas, TX
Reed Weitkamp Schell & Vice, PLLC
Louisville, KY
Reed, Wendy .... **Irvine, CA**
Reed, Wendy Cohen .... Bala Cynwyd, PA
Reed, Wendy N. .... **Washington, DC**
Reed, Wes .... Dallas, TX
Reed, William C. .... **Augusta, GA**
Reed, William E., II .... Steubenville, OH
Reed, William E., III .... **Boston, MA**
Reed, William F. .... Washington, DC
Reed, William H. .... **Bath, NY**
Reed, William H. .... Vancouver, WA
Reed, William J. .... Walnut Creek, CA
Reed, William L. .... San Diego, CA
Reed, William M. .... Denver, CO
Reed, William M. .... Lexington, KY
Reed, William N. .... England, AR
Reed, William N. .... **Jackson, MS**
Reed, William Townsend .... **Pascagoula, MS**
Reed, Winthrop B., III .... **St. Louis, MO**
Reed, Wm. C., Jr. .... Jackson, MS
Reed-Cobble .... Harrisburg, PA
Greeneville, TN
Reede, Barbara S. .... Forest Hills, NY
Reede, George E., Jr. .... **Baltimore, MD**
Reeder, Alton A., Jr. .... Lincolnton, NC
Reeder, Alvin S. .... Frankfort, KY
Reeder & Associates .... **Upland, CA**
Reeder & Boeh, Chartered .... Troy, KS
Reeder, Cathleen Marie Martin .... Topeka, KS
Reeder, Charles .... Mobile, AL
Reeder, Charles C. .... **Dallas, TX**
Reeder, Charles G. .... **Indianapolis, IN**
Reeder, Chris .... **Austin, TX**
Reeder, Christopher S. .... **Los Angeles, CA**
Reeder, Dennis James .... Majuro, TT
Reeder, Donald R. .... Powell, OH
Reeder, Donald V. .... Madras, OR
Reeder, Donald W. .... Ramsey, NJ
Reeder, F. Robert .... **Salt Lake City, UT**
Reeder, Frank G. .... **Chicago, IL**
Reeder, Harold C. .... **Cleveland, OH**
Reeder, Harvey Bruce .... Huntingdon, PA
Reeder, James A. .... **Washington, DC**
Reeder, James Arthur, Jr. .... **Houston, TX**
Reeder, Jeffrey T. .... New Orleans, LA
Reeder, Joe, Jr. .... Knox City, TX
Reeder, Joe R. .... **Washington, DC**
Reeder, Joel B. .... Medford, OR
Reeder, Joel B., P.C. .... Medford, OR
Reeder, John A. .... **Anchorage, AK**
Reeder, John B. .... Bryan, TX
Reeder, John W. .... Plano, TX
Reeder, Joseph K. .... **Charleston, WV**
Reeder and Karro .... Twisp, WA
Reeder, L. Martin, Jr.
West Palm Beach, FL
Reeder, Linda M. .... Fort Worth, TX
Reeder, Lloyd R. .... Hobart, OK
Reeder, Mary K. .... **Indianapolis, IN**
Reeder, Michael H. .... New City, NY
Reeder, Pamela J. .... Los Angeles, CA
Reeder, Patricia A. .... **Topeka, KS**
Reeder, Robert A. .... Troy, KS
Reeder, Robert H. .... **Upland, CA**
Reeder, Robert H. .... Evanston, IL
Reeder, Robert H. .... **Binghamton, NY**
Reeder, Robert R. .... **Philadelphia, PA**
Reeder, Robert W., III .... **New York, NY**
Reeder, Sarah Luce .... **Joplin, MO**
Reeder, Shackelford .... Midland, TX
Reeder, Shauna Joy .... New York, NY
Reeder & Shuman .... **Morgantown, WV**
Reeder, Thomas M. .... Miami, FL
Reeder, Thos. J. .... Medford, OR
Reeder, William H. .... Independence, KS
Reeder, William Thomas, Jr.
Washington, DC
Reedhead, William .... San Diego, CA
Reedich, Michael J. .... **Washington, DC**
Reedman, Lane C. .... **El Paso, TX**
Reed Murry, Victoria .... **Alexandria, LA**
Reed-Rolando, Dianna .... Turnersville, NJ
Reeds, Michael W. .... Walled Lake, MI
Reeds, Travis Michael .... Walled Lake, MI
Reed-Slaten, Dawn .... Anchorage, AK
Reed-Workman, C. .... Boston, MA
Reedy, Christopher J. .... **Leawood, KS**
Reedy, Daniel P. .... Chicago, IL
Reedy, David J. .... Scranton, PA
Reedy, Heather Rochelle .... **Brevard, NC**
Reedy, Jay E. .... **Arlington, TX**
Reedy, John R. .... Bakersfield, CA
Reedy, Joseph B., (P.C.) .... Council Bluffs, IA
Omaha, NE
Reedy, Kevin J. .... Los Angeles, CA
Reedy, L. Fred .... Fort Lauderdale, FL
Reedy, M. Kilburg .... **New York, NY**
Reedy, Mark R. .... Palo Alto, CA
Reedy, Michael .... **San Jose, CA**
Reedy, Patricia J. .... Department of Justice,
Criminal Division, GV
Reedy, Patrick Martin .... Denver, CO
Reedy, Randall D. .... Los Gatos, CA
Reedy, Richard L. .... Houston, TX
Reedy, Robert G. .... **Houston, TX**
Reedy, Sam M. .... Tupelo, MS
Reedy, William J. .... Atlanta, GA
Reedy, William W. .... Athens, TN
Reef, Norman S. .... Portland, ME
Reefe, John J., Jr. .... **Omaha, NE**
Reefer, Elizabeth Dross .... **Kansas City, MO**
Reeg, Jed D. .... **Kansas City, MO**
Reeg, Kurtis B. .... **St. Louis, MO**
Reegler, Sari Lynn .... Venice, FL
Reegler & Tornese, P.A. .... Venice, FL
Reehil, Paul .... Bloomfield Hills, MI
Reehill, William E. .... Florence, KY
Reehl, James R. .... Canonsburg, PA
Reek, Wendy Allyson .... **Cedar Knolls, NJ**
Reeker, Friedrich Arthur .... Minneapolis, MN
Reeks, F. John, Jr. .... **Shreveport, LA**
Reeks, Thomas E. .... Los Angeles, CA
Reeks, Warren G. .... River Ridge, LA
Reel, Anton E., III
Federal Election Commission,
Offices of the Commissioners, GV
Reel, Frederick U. .... Alexandria, VA
Reel, Jeffrey T. .... Belleville, IL
Reel, Jonathan R.
Federal Communications Commission,
Common Carrier Bureau, GV
Reel, Linda L. .... Jacksonville, FL
Reel, Raymond L. .... Marshalltown, IA
Reel, Stephen E. .... Oklahoma City, OK
Reely, Shane N. .... **Missoula, MT**
Reem, Jeffrey R. .... Flint, MI
Reemer, Ellis L. .... **New York, NY**
Reemes, C. Glenn .... St. Louis, MO
Reemes, Chalmous Glenn .... St. Louis, MO
Reems, Ronda R. .... Kansas City, MO
Reemsnyder, Bruce D. .... **Salt Lake City, UT**
Reemsnyder, Ronald D. .... **Atlanta, GA**
Reen, William J. .... Ottumwa, IA
Reenan, John J. .... **Dallas, TX**
Reenan, Lara L. .... **Dallas, TX**
Reens, Louis H. .... **Stamford, CT**
Reens, William C. .... **Grand Rapids, MI**
Reents, Mark R. .... **Tulsa, OK**
Reents, Scott T. .... St. Louis, MO
Reep, Cornelia .... Clarksburg, WV
Reep, Janine J. .... Juneau, AK
Reep, John D. .... St. Cloud, MN
Reep, Richard A. .... **Missoula, MT**
Reep, Richard L. .... El Paso, TX
Reep, Scott D. .... Benicia, CA
Reep, Spoon & Gordon, P.C. .... **Helena, MT**
Missoula, MT
Reers, Richard L. .... **New Hyde Park, NY**
New York, NY
Westbury, NY
Rees, Albert C., Jr. .... New Orleans, LA
Rees, Albert H., Jr. .... Lawrenceville, NJ
Rees, Amy E. .... **Palo Alto, CA**
Rees, Andrea .... Bronx, NY
Rees, Andrew Thomas .... Tulsa, OK
Rees & Associates, P.C. .... **Denver, CO**
Rees, Brian J. .... Zeeland, MI
Rees, Brian S. .... Phoenix, AZ
Rees, Broome & Diaz, P.C.
Washington, DC
Alexandria, VA
Fairfax, VA
Vienna, VA
Rees, Charles A. .... Baltimore, MD
Rees, Charles W., Jr. .... San Diego, CA
Rees, Cheryl M. .... Houston, TX
Rees, Daniel A., (L.L.C.) .... **Lafayette, LA**
Rees, David .... Jonesboro, AR
Rees, David Charles .... Washington, DC
Rees, David F. .... Indianapolis, IN
Rees, David F. .... **Portland, OR**
Rees, David K. .... **Denver, CO**
Rees, David M. .... Salt Lake City, UT
Rees, David S. .... Chicago, IL
Rees, David W. .... **Tucson, AZ**
Rees, Donald W. .... **San Diego, CA**
San Francisco, CA
Rees, Donley K. .... Gunnison, CO
Rees, Edmond H. .... Carlinville, IL
Rees, Elizabeth .... **Los Angeles, CA**
Rees, Eric M. .... Papillion, NE
Rees, Garrison C., Jr. .... Fairfield, CA
Rees, Grant C. .... Burlington, VT
Rees, Harry D. .... **Cleveland, OH**
Rees, James S., III .... Covington, LA
Rees, J.B. .... Fayetteville, WV
Rees, Jefferson C.V. .... **Bartlesville, OK**
Rees, John B. .... Chicago, IL
Rees, John B., Jr. .... Athens, GA
Rees, John E. .... Wichita, KS
Rees, John H. .... Treasury Department,
Bureau of Alcohol, Tobacco and Firearms,
GV
Rees, John H. .... **Salt Lake City, UT**
Rees, John W. .... Bloomfield Hills, MI
Rees, Jonathan T. .... **Washington, DC**
Rees, Judson M. .... Ashfield, MA
Rees, Kay Sibille .... Metairie, LA
Rees and Kincaid .... Lenexa, KS
Rees Law Firm .... Jonesboro, AR
West Memphis, AR
Rees, Lloyd Rodgers .... Coral Gables, FL
Rees, Lynn Modica .... River Forest, IL
Rees, Marcia .... Wilmington, DE
Rees, Mark .... Jonesboro, AR
Rees, Mark B. .... **Boston, MA**
Rees, Martha L. .... **Wilmington, DE**
Rees, Maura .... **Palo Alto, CA**
Rees, Merrifield B. .... **Lakewood, WA**
Rees, Michael B. .... Lecompton, KS
Rees, Michael J. .... Angleton, TX
Rees, Miryam Rosie .... **Chicago, IL**
Rees, Nancy L. .... Bremerton, WA
Rees, Natalie H. .... Towson, MD
Rees, Natalie H., The Law Office of, P.A.
Towson, MD
Rees, Patricia A. .... Hobart, IN
Rees, Paul Damian .... **New Orleans, LA**
Rees, Paul G., P.C. .... Tucson, AZ
Rees, Paul G., P.C., Law Offices
Tucson, AZ
Rees, R. Douglas .... **Chicago, IL**
Rees, R. Douglas .... **Dallas, TX**
Rees & Rees, LLP .... **Colorado City, TX**
Sweetwater, TX
Rees, Robert A. .... **Los Angeles, CA**
Rees, Robert B. .... Gretna, LA
Rees, Robert H. .... Kaysville, UT
Rees, Robert Palmer .... **Salt Lake City, UT**
Rees, Samuel T. .... **Los Angeles, CA**
Rees, Stephen D. .... **Sarasota, FL**
Rees, Stuart M. .... **Boston, MA**
Rees, Susan E. .... Department of Labor,
Office of the Solicitor, GV
Rees, Terry L. .... Lenexa, KS
Rees, Thomas D. .... **Norristown, PA**
Rees, Thomas J. .... Santa Ana, CA
Rees, Thomas L., Jr. .... **Sweetwater, TX**
Rees, Thomas M. .... Santa Cruz, CA
Rees, Thomas S. .... Washington, DC
Rees, T.L. .... **Colorado City, TX**
Sweetwater, TX
Rees, V. Lee Okarma .... Seattle, WA
Rees, Walter L. .... Glen Ellyn, IL
Rees, Warren D. .... Minneapolis, MN
Rees, William B. .... **Beverly Hills, CA**
Rees, William H. .... Duluth, MN
Rees, William J. .... **Franklin, MA**
Rees, William Joseph .... Columbus, OH
Rees, William T. .... Indianapolis, IN
Rees, Winship E. .... Lawrenceville, GA
Rees, Winship E., P.C. .... Lawrenceville, GA
Reese, A. Susan .... Cheyenne, WY
Reese, Algernon B., III .... Amenia, NY
Reese, Alicia Jo .... Daleville, AL
Reese, Andrew J. .... Santa Rosa, CA
Reese, B. Gail .... **Nashville, TN**
Reese, Baffney, Schrag & Frol, P.S.
Walla Walla, WA

Reese, Benjamin W., III ... San Jose, CA
Reese, Bernard P., Jr. ... Rockford, IL
Reese, Brian P. ... Rockford, IL
Reese, Bryan Powell ... Dallas, TX
Reese, C. Scott ... Newark, DE
Wilmington, DE
Reese, C. Thomas ... Lubbock, TX
Reese, Calvin W. ... Lutherville, MD
Reese and Carney, LLP ... Annapolis, MD
Baltimore, MD
Columbia, MD
Ellicott City, MD
Rockville, MD
Reese, Catharine C. ... De Funiak Springs, FL
Reese, Catherine M. ... Washington, DC
Reese, Catherine R. ... Indianapolis, IN
Reese, Cathy L. ... Wilmington, DE
Reese, Charles A. ... Columbia, MD
Reese, Charles Neville ... Daleville, AL
Reese, Charles W., Jr. ... Oakland, CA
Reese, Christopher J. ... Mount Lebanon, PA
Reese, Clay W. ... Atlanta, GA
Reese, Craig L. ... Dallas, TX
Reese, Curtis L. ... Olivia, MN
Reese, Cynthia E. ... Treasury Department, Bureau of the Public Debt, GV
Reese, Cynthia M. ... Treasury Department, Office of Regulations and Rulings, GV
Reese, Daniel G. ... Taylorville, IL
Reese, David C. ... Detroit, MI
Reese, David D., Jr. ... Canton, OH
Reese, David E. ... Santa Barbara, CA
Reese, David J. ... Redwood City, CA
Reese, David J. ... Reno, NV
Reese, Dennis R. ... Austin, TX
Reese, Dennis S. ... Portland, OR
Reese, Derrick B. ... Chicago, IL
Reese, Donald M. ... Seattle, WA
Reese, Elna ... Montgomery, AL
Reese, Flurnoy W. ... Dallas, TX
Reese, Foster, III ... Dallas, TX
Reese, Gary A. ... Fairfax, VA
Reese, Gary Stephen ... Rockford, IL
Reese, George B. ... Jamaica, NY
Reese, Gina ... Los Angeles, CA
Reese, Gregory S. ... Mobile, AL
Reese, Harlan M. ... San Diego, CA
Reese, Harry B. ... Kansas City, KS
Reese, Hirsch, Diamond & Kennedy
New Canaan, CT
Ridgefield, CT
Reese, Howard W. (Trey), III
Lawrenceville, GA
Reese, J. Don ... Abilene, TX
Reese, J. Dudley, IV ... Merion, PA
Reese, J. Gilbert ... Newark, OH
Reese, J. Richard ... Houston, TX
Reese, James D. ... Warren, MI
Reese, James L. ... Sterling, IL
Reese, James N. ... Los Angeles, CA
Reese, Janet Anne ... Oxnard, CA
Reese, Jason R. ... Indianapolis, IN
Reese, Jay M. ... Addison, IL
Reese, Jerry Alan ... Charlotte, NC
Reese, Jill E. ... Indianapolis, IN
Reese, Joel W. ... Dallas, TX
Reese, John ... Anchorage, AK
Reese, John E. ... Washington, DC
Reese, John H. ... Denver, CO
Reese, John M. ... Walla Walla, WA
Reese, John R. ... San Francisco, CA
Reese, John R. ... New Canaan, CT
Ridgefield, CT
Reese, John Thomas ... Nashville, TN
Reese, John W., Jr. ... Redding, CA
Reese, Joseph L., Jr. ... Birmingham, AL
Reese, Judith R. ... Wilmington, DE
Reese, Judith R. ... Chicago, IL
Reese, Julie A. ... Washington, DC
Reese, Kelly D. ... Mobile, AL
Reese, Kelly Susan ... Seattle, WA
Reese, Kenneth P. ... Indianapolis, IN
Reese, Kern A. ... New Orleans, LA
Reese, Kern A., & Associates, A Prof. Law Corp. ... New Orleans, LA
Reese, Kevin D. ... San Francisco, CA
Reese, Kevin W. ... Greenville, SC
Reese, Kirk D. ... Rhinelander, WI
Reese, Larry Bryan ... Houston, TX
Reese, Leanne J. ... Wilmington, DE
Reese, Leonard J., Jr. ... Austin, TX
Reese, Lindsey E., (Mr.) ... Taylorville, IL
Reese, Lucius E. ... Chicago, IL
Reese, M. Frances ... Manchester, CT
Reese, Mary Ann McCord ... Nashville, TN
Reese, Mary C. ... Annapolis, MD
Columbia, MD
Reese & Mathey ... Green River, WY
Reese, Melissa Proffitt ... Indianapolis, IN
Reese, Michael ... East Hartford, CT
Lebanon, NH
Woodstock, VT
Reese, Michael ... Seattle, WA
Reese, Michael E. ... Richboro, PA
Reese, Michael H. ... Cheyenne, WY
Reese, Michael K. ... Palm Harbor, FL
St. Petersburg, FL
Reese, Michael Thomas ... Fort Myers, FL
Reese, Morris M., Jr. ... San Angelo, TX
Reese, Nancy L. ... Sacramento, CA
Reese, Norman G. ... Ingleside, IL
Reese, Olan R. ... Cleveland, OH
Reese, Paul D. ... Los Angeles, CA
Reese, Paul Kipling ... Charleston, WV
Reese, Peter A. ... Buffalo, NY
Reese, Pyle, Drake & Meyer, P.L.L.
Newark, OH
Reese, Randall K. ... Rockford, IL

Reese, Raymond H. ... Cuero, TX
Reese, Rebecca ... Hobbs, NM
Reese, Rebecca Mei
Department of Commerce, Office of the General Counsel, GV
Reese & Reese ... Daleville, AL
Reese & Reese ... Rockford, IL
Reese & Reese ... Taylorville, IL
Reese, Richard T. ... Lima, OH
Reese, Robert H., Jr. ... Lancaster, PA
Reese, Robert J. ... Green River, WY
Reese, Robert M. ... Hershey, PA
Reese, Robin A. ... San Francisco, CA
Reese, Robin W. ... Salt Lake City, UT
Reese, Ross J. ... Philadelphia, PA
Reese, Sara Gaye ... St. Petersburg, FL
Reese, Sarah E. ... Philadelphia, PA
Reese, Scott Frederick ... Denver, CO
Reese, Serbin, Kovacs & Nypaver, L.L.P.
Altoona, PA
Martinsburg, PA
Reese, Smalley, Wiseman & Schweitzer, LLP
Redding, CA
Reese, Spencer ... Idaho Falls, ID
Reese, Stephanie L. ... Winston-Salem, NC
Reese, Stephen E. ... Denton, TX
Reese, Stephen E., P.C. ... Denton, TX
Reese, Steven A. ... Dallas, TX
Reese, Susan Elizabeth ... Portland, OR
Reese, Susan Elizabeth, P.C.
Portland, OR
Reese, Susan W. ... Huntington Station, NY
Reese, Tamee V. ... St. Louis, MO
Reese, Tamora L. ... California, PA
Reese, Thomas D. ... Palo Alto, CA
Reese, Thomas F. ... Casper, WY
Reese, Thomas H. ... Atlanta, GA
Reese, Thomas M. ... Altoona, PA
Martinsburg, PA
Reese, Thomas S. ... Fort Myers, FL
Reese, Timothy J. ... Lancaster, PA
Reese, Tom F., Jr. ... Garland, TX
Reese, W. Allen ... Greer, SC
Reese, Wade B. ... Houston, TX
Reese, William D. ... San Francisco, CA
Reese, William S. ... Coral Gables, FL
Reese-Gordon, Edith ... Chicago, IL
Reeser, Christopher M. ... Williamsport, PA
Reeser, Edwin B., III ... Los Angeles, CA
Reeser, Lori A. ... San Francisco, CA
Reeser, Michael S., P.A. ... Palm Harbor, FL
Reeser, Patricia P. ... Dedham, MA
Reeser, Ralph R., Jr. ... Wheaton, MD
Reeser, Robert B., III ... St. Louis, MO
Reeser, Robert B., Jr. ... Sedalia, MO
Reeser, Robert E. ... San Francisco, CA
Reeser, Rose Ann ... Austin, TX
Reeser, William B. ... Philadelphia, PA
Reesha, Edward J. ... Glendale, CA
Reesing, A. Glenn ... Tempe, AZ
Reesing, A. Glenn, P.C. ... Tempe, AZ
Rees-Jones, Trevor D. ... Dallas, TX
Rees-Jones, Trevor Wm. ... Dallas, TX
Reeslund, Michael E. ... Minneapolis, MN
Reesman, Ann Elizabeth ... Washington, DC
Reesman, Dale ... Boonville, MO
Reesman, David A. ... Washington, DC
Reesman, Sarah Kelley ... Columbia, MO
Reesor, John F. ... Louisville, KY
Reetz, C. Ryan ... Miami, FL
Reetz, Fox & Bartlett LLP
Santa Barbara, CA
Reetz, Margaret A. ... New York, NY
Reetz, Robert E., Jr. ... Austin, TX
Reetz, William H. ... Seattle, WA
Reeve, Arthur H. ... Englewood, NJ
Reeve & Associates ... Irvine, CA
Reeve, Benjamin ... Arlington, MA
Reeve, C. Allan ... Rockville Centre, NY
Reeve, Carol B. ... Houston, TX
Reeve, Donna R. ... New Orleans, LA
Reeve, Earl J. ... Orinda, CA
Reeve, Edward John ... Seattle, WA
Reeve, Elizabeth K. ... Seattle, WA
Reeve, Gary A. ... Dublin, OH
Reeve, Henry R. ... Denver, CO
Reeve, Jay D. ... Dallas, TX
Reeve Kearns PC ... Portland, OR
Reeve, Kenlon W. ... Ogden, UT
Reeve, Kevin S. ... Cincinnati, OH
Reeve, Mark P. ... Portland, OR
Reeve, Mary E. ... Cleveland, OH
Reeve, Oliver J. ... Waverly, IA
Reeve, Pamela A. ... Boonton, NJ
Reeve and Reeve ... Englewood, NJ
Reeve, Richard A. ... New Haven, CT
Reeve, Robert J. ... Unionville, CT
Reeve, Rosemary ... Seattle, WA
Reeve, Sally A. Steurer ... Bellevue, WA
Reeve, Thomas C. ... Denver, CO
Reeve, Tracy Pool ... Portland, OR
Reeve, William L. ... Savannah, GA
Reever, Robert W. ... Upland, CA
Reever, Shelley ... Boston, MA
Reevers, Stephanie R. ... Nashville, TN
Reeves, Adam A. ... New York, NY
Reeves, Alan L. ... Fremont, CA
Reeves, Allen G. ... Denver, CO
Reeves, Allen G., P.C. ... Denver, CO
Reeves, Allen S. ... Selma, AL
Reeves, Andrea Barton ... Hartford, CT
Reeves, Andrea Levitan
Newport Beach, CA
Reeves, Anne Moorman ... Daytona Beach, FL
Reeves, Archibald T., IV ... Mobile, AL
Reeves, Archie T., Jr. ... Selma, AL
Reeves, B. James ... Las Cruces, NM
Reeves, Barbara A. ... Rosemead, CA

Reeves, Ben C. ... Eufaula, AL
Reeves, Bernard C. ... Fairfield, TX
Reeves, Beth Ellen ... Lake Oswego, OR
Reeves, Beth Singletary ... Atlanta, GA
Reeves, Beverly G. ... Austin, TX
Reeves, B.J. ... Pembroke Pines, FL
Reeves, Blair ... San Antonio, TX
Reeves, Bradley C. ... Atlanta, GA
Reeves, Brian ... Bowling Green, KY
Reeves, Bruce C. ... Alameda, CA
Reeves, Bruce F. ... Sacramento, CA
Reeves, C. Fred ... Marietta, GA
Reeves, C. Lee ... Birmingham, AL
Reeves, Calvin B. ... Palmer, TX
Reeves, Cameron L. ... Lakeport, CA
Reeves, Carlton W. ... Jackson, MS
Reeves, Cary R. ... Warsaw, IN
Reeves, Catharine E. ... Department of Justice, Office of Attorney Personnel Management, GV
Reeves, Charles B., Jr. ... Baltimore, MD
Reeves, Charles H. ... Coquille, OR
Reeves, Charles R. ... Indianapolis, IN
Reeves, Charles W. ... Barrington, IL
Reeves, Chavez, Greenfield & Walker, P.A.
Deming, NM
Las Cruces, NM
Reeves, Christopher M. ... Bristol, CT
Reeves, Craig R. ... Carbondale, IL
Reeves, Dan L. ... Princeton, IN
Reeves, Daniel P. ... Yucaipa, CA
Reeves, Daniel S. ... Los Angeles, CA
Reeves, Danny C. ... Lexington, KY
Reeves, David A. ... Denver, CO
Reeves, David B. ... Los Angeles, CA
Reeves, David C. ... Sarasota, FL
Reeves, David R. ... Grayson, KY
Reeves, David W. ... Woodstock, VT
Reeves and Davis ... Pensacola, FL
Reeves, Dean A. ... Los Angeles, CA
Reeves, Dennis R. ... Lubbock, TX
Reeves, Don R. ... Longview, TX
Reeves, Dougal B., Jr. ... Scottsdale, AZ
Reeves, Dougal B., Jr., P.C. ... Scottsdale, AZ
Reeves, Douglas M. ... Philadelphia, PA
Reeves, Earl Leslie, Jr. ... Edmond, OK
Reeves, Edith M. ... Las Cruces, NM
Reeves, Edward J. ... Portland, OR
Reeves, Edward V. ... Philadelphia, PA
Reeves, Eric A. ... Chicago, IL
Reeves, Eric George ... Richmond, VA
Reeves, Eric Miller ... Raleigh, NC
Reeves, Ernest R. ... Horseshoe Bay, TX
Reeves, Ernest R., Jr. ... Chapel Hill, NC
Reeves, Eugene E. ... Caruthersville, MO
Reeves, Frederick T.
New Port Richey, FL
Reeves, G. Kathleen ... Eminence, MO
Reeves, G. Lawrence, Jr. ... Raleigh, NC
Reeves, Gary D. ... Troy, MI
Reeves, Gayle A. ... Vermilion, OH
Reeves, Glenna J. ... Tallahassee, FL
Reeves, Gregory A. ... Decatur, AL
Reeves, Gwendolyn D. ... Chicago, IL
Reeves, Harold ... Nashville, TN
Reeves, Harold S. ... Washington, DC
Reeves, Howell J. ... Philadelphia, PA
Reeves, J. William ... Rochester, NY
Reeves, Jack R. ... Spokane, WA
Reeves, James C., III ... Lynchburg, VA
Reeves, James E. ... Caruthersville, MO
Reeves, James E. ... Charleston, SC
Reeves, James J. ... Pensacola, FL
Reeves, James L. ... Columbus, OH
Reeves, James N. ... Anchorage, AK
Reeves, James R., Jr. ... Biloxi, MS
Reeves, Janice Church ... Lafayette, LA
Reeves, Jean B. ... Topeka, KS
Reeves, Jeffrey H. ... Irvine, CA
Reeves, Jeffrey W. ... Phoenix, AZ
Reeves, Jimmy D. ... West Jefferson, NC
Reeves, Joe B. ... Lawton, OK
Reeves, John A. ... Sacramento, CA
Reeves, John C. ... Harrisonburg, LA
Reeves, John D. ... Macon, GA
Reeves, John E. ... Urbana, IL
Reeves, John R. ... Jackson, MS
Reeves, John R. ... Oklahoma City, OK
Reeves & Jones, P.C. ... Lansing, MI
Reeves, Joseph A., Jr. ... Houston, TX
Reeves, Joseph S., III ... Nashville, TN
Reeves, Joseph W. ... Myrtle Beach, SC
Reeves, Judith L. ... Brea, CA
Reeves, Judith N. ... Staten Island, NY
Reeves, Julianne Simonin
Granada Hills, CA
Reeves, Kahn & Eder ... Portland, OR
Reeves & Karren, P.A. ... Bentonville, AR
Reeves, Kathryn A. ... Denver, CO
Reeves, Kay L. Gunderson ... Dallas, TX
Reeves, Ken ... Harrison, AR
Reeves, Kenneth W., III ... Phoenix, AZ
Reeves, Kim Ward ... Houston, TX
Reeves, Laura H. ... St. Louis, MO
Reeves, Leigh Lawson ... Atlanta, GA
Reeves, Leonard R. ... Latrobe, PA
Reeves, M. Lee ... Atlanta, GA
Reeves, Mae C. ... Lutherville, MD
Reeves, Mark Edward ... Hartford, CT
Reeves, Marsha Y. ... Washington, DC
Reeves, Martin W. ... Portland, OR
Reeves, Mary E. ... Seattle, WA
Reeves, Mary Elisa ... Philadelphia, PA
Reeves, Mary Morgan ... Raleigh, NC
Reeves, Matthew G. ... Houston, TX
Reeves, Meg ... Salem, OR
Reeves, Michael C. ... Charlotte, NC
Reeves, Michael S. ... Phoenix, AZ

Reeves, Michael S. ... Atlanta, GA
Reeves & Miller ... Casper, WY
Reeves, Monica Lynch ... Sacramento, CA
Reeves, Nancy L. ... Clinton, OH
Reeves, Pamela L. ... Knoxville, TN
Reeves, Penny L. ... Los Angeles, CA
Reeves, Philip A. ... Soldotna, AK
Reeves, Phillip E. ... Greenville, SC
Reeves, Ragan G. ... Washington, DC
Reeves, R. B. ... Mc Comb, MS
Reeves, Rebecca Morlock ... Watertown, SD
Reeves, Reginald R. ... Idaho Falls, ID
Reeves, Rex T. ... Hapeville, GA
Reeves, Rex T., Jr. ... Newport Beach, CA
Reeves, R. H., III ... Millen, GA
Reeves, Richard W. ... Tampa, FL
Reeves, R. L. ... Arcadia, CA
Reeves, Robert, & Associates, Law Offices of
Pasadena, CA
Reeves, Robert B. ... Los Angeles, CA
Reeves, Robert E. ... Lexington, KY
Reeves, Robert H. ... Americus, GA
Reeves, Robert J. ... Chester, SC
Columbia, SC
Lancaster, SC
Rock Hill, SC
Reeves, Robert K. ... Lafayette, LA
Houston, TX
Reeves, Robert L. ... Pasadena, CA
Reeves, Robert S. ... Swainsboro, GA
Reeves, Robert S. ... Jackson, MS
Reeves, Robert W. ... Stamford, CT
Reeves, Ron L. ... Dallas, TX
Reeves, Ronald K. ... Evergreen, CO
Reeves, Ross C. ... Norfolk, VA
Reeves, Samuel M. ... Bentonville, AR
Reeves, Seidler & Howell ... Alameda, CA
Reeves, Sharon Hurt ... Macon, GA
Reeves & Stewart, P.C. ... Camden, AL
Greensboro, AL
Marion, AL
Selma, AL
Reeves, Susan E. ... Anchorage, AK
Reeves, Susan K. ... Colorado Springs, CO
Reeves, Susan W. ... Birmingham, AL
Reeves, Thomas G. ... Augusta, ME
Reeves, Thomas R. ... Houston, TX
Reeves, Thomas W. ... Hendricks, MN
Reeves, Thos. M. ... Burlington, VT
Reeves, Timothy D. ... Lansing, MI
Reeves, Todd D. ... Monterey, CA
Reeves, Tom M.
Federal Deposit Insurance Corporation, Liquidation Branch, GV
Reeves, Tracy Enochs ... Sullivan, IN
Reeves, Troy A. ... North Canton, OH
Reeves, Vicki L. ... Tampa, FL
Reeves, Vivian M. ... Orlando, FL
Reeves, W. Boyd ... Mobile, AL
Reeves, W. Edward ... Caruthersville, MO
Reeves, Warren J. ... Englewood, CO
Reeves, Wayne E. ... Birmingham, AL
Reeves, Weston W. ... Casper, WY
Reeves, William A. ... Knoxville, TN
Reeves, William C. ... Jackson, MS
Reeves, William G. ... Tallahassee, FL
Reeves, William G ... Farmington, MO
Reeves, William T., Jr. ... Baton Rouge, LA
Reeve-Wilson, Gregory K. ... San Jose, CA
Refakis, P. Michael ... Fort Worth, TX
Referente, J. Anthony ... Houston, TX
Refermat, John T. ... Rochester, NY
Reff, Alisa H. ... Washington, DC
Reff Baivier Bermingham Zierdt & Lim, S.C. ... Oshkosh, WI
Reff, Herbert L. ... Studio City, CA
Reff, Russell J. ... Oshkosh, WI
Reffe, Paige E. ... Washington, DC
Reffkin, Alan D., Law Offices of
Arlington, VA
Reffner, Carol L. ... Fostoria, OH
Reffner, Craig Douglas
Federal Election Commission, Office of the General Counsel, GV
Reffner, Robert P. ... Akron, OH
Refinski-Knight, Bonnie J. ... New Bern, NC
Refior, Paul D. ... Warsaw, IN
Refior, Robert L., II ... Lansing, MI
Refkin, Martin N. ... Los Angeles, CA
Refling, Mark D. ... Bozeman, MT
Refo, Carter L. ... Mechanicsville, VA
Refo, Patricia Lee ... Phoenix, AZ
Refo & Tompkins ... Mechanicsville, VA
Refolo, Michael A. ... Baltimore, MD
Refowich, Mark S. ... Easton, PA
Refsell, Stephen T. ... Little Rock, AR
Refsin, Barry L. ... Philadelphia, PA
Refuerzo, Carl R. ... Fresno, CA
Refuerzo, Sharon M. ... Fresno, CA
Rega, Jennifer J. ... Indiana, PA
Rega, Patrick J. ... Donora, PA
Regal, Bruce ... New York, NY
Regal, Dorothea W. ... New York, NY
Regal, Edwin M. ... Akron, OH
Regal, Kelly L. ... Atlanta, GA
Regal, Robert B. ... South St. Paul, MN
Regal, Seymour I. ... Chicago, IL
Regalado, Amy J. ... Los Angeles, CA
Regalado, Eloisa ... Washington, DC
Regalado, Jose ... Matteson, IL
Regalado, P. Kim ... Sacramento, CA
Regalbuti, Mark ... Sacramento, CA
Regalia, Edmund L. ... Sacramento, CA
Walnut Creek, CA
Regalia, Michelle C. ... San Francisco, CA
Regan, Alison Genevieve ... Los Angeles, CA
Regan, Andrew W. ... New York, NY
Regan, Ann W. ... Boston, MA

Regan, Anne Patricia .... **New York, NY**
Regan, Anne-Marie B. .... **Boston, MA**
Regan Associates, Chartered
Washington, DC
Regan, Barbara H. .... **Philadelphia, PA**
Spring House, PA
Regan, Brian M. .... **El Segundo, CA**
Regan, Brian T. .... **Sacramento, CA**
Regan, Cabell J., P.A. .... Lumberton, NC
Regan, Cabell Jones .... Lumberton, NC
Regan & Cantwell .... **Charleston, SC**
Hilton Head Island, SC
Regan, Charles F., Jr. .... **Chicago, IL**
Regan, Christopher F. .... **Washington, DC**
Regan, Christopher F. .... **Orlando, FL**
Regan, Christopher J. .... **Wellston, OH**
Regan, Christopher T. .... Dover, NH
Regan, Colleen M. .... **Santa Monica, CA**
Regan, Cornelius E. .... New Orleans, LA
Regan, Craig B. .... Sacramento, CA
Regan, Deborah M. .... **Minneapolis, MN**
Regan, Deborah Mitchell .... Chicago, IL
Regan, Deidre Brennan .... **Boston, MA**
Regan, Denis G. .... Whitman, MA
Regan, Denis J. .... **Milwaukee, WI**
Regan, Dickerson .... Juneau, AK
Regan, Donald J. .... **Solana Beach, CA**
Regan, Donald J., P.C. .... **Solana Beach, CA**
Regan, Edw. J. .... Bronx, NY
Regan, Edward J. .... Providence, RI
Regan, Edward J. .... Fairfax, VA
Regan, Elizabeth G. .... New York, NY
Regan, Frances Eve .... New York, NY
Regan, Frances F. .... New York, NY
Regan, Frank J. .... La Mesa, CA
Regan, Franklin F., Jr. .... Flushing, NY
Regan, Geo. J. .... Whitestone, NY
Regan, Geoffrey A. .... Cranston, RI
Regan, George D. .... St. Pauls, NC
Regan, Halperin & Long, P.L.L.C.
Washington, DC
Upper Marlboro, MD
Fairfax, VA
Regan, Harold E. .... Tallahassee, FL
Regan, Harold R. .... Omaha, NE
Regan, J. Brendan .... **Minneapolis, MN**
Regan, J. Martin, Jr. .... **Memphis, TN**
Regan, James C. .... Glendale, CA
Regan, James I. .... Atlanta, GA
Regan, James J. .... **Washington, DC**
Regan, James J. .... Treasury Department, Financial Management Service, GV
Regan, James J. .... Omaha, NE
Regan, James J., Law Offices of
Los Angeles, CA
Regan, James J., Law Offices of
Redondo Beach, CA
Regan, James P. .... **Chicago, IL**
Regan, Jeffrey C. .... **Jacksonville, FL**
Regan, Jeremiah S. .... **Washington, DC**
Regan, John C. B., III .... Lumberton, NC
Regan, John D. .... Wakefield, RI
Regan, John E. .... Elgin, IL
Regan, John E. .... **Mankato, MN**
Regan, John E. .... Riverhead, NY
Regan, John F., Jr. .... Decatur, IL
Regan, John J. .... **Boston, MA**
Regan, John J. .... **Lynn, MA**
Regan, John J. .... Hempstead, NY
Regan, John M., Jr. .... Rochester, NY
Regan, John Manning .... Rochester, NY
Regan, John N. .... New York, NY
Regan, John P. .... **Stamford, CT**
Regan, John P. .... Lincoln, NE
Regan, John R. .... Farmington Hills, MI
Regan, John S. .... **Detroit, MI**
Regan, Joseph A. .... **Boston, MA**
Regan, Joseph A. .... **Rochester, NY**
Regan, Joseph D. .... **Lowell, MA**
Regan, Joseph F. .... New London, CT
Regan, Joseph G. .... Whitestone, NY
Regan, Joseph J., III .... Austin, TX
Regan, Judith M.
Department of the Air Force, Office of the Judge Advocate General, GV
Regan, Kathleen M. .... **Albuquerque, NM**
Regan, Kerry M. .... **Seattle, WA**
Regan, Kevin E. J. .... **Kansas City, MO**
Regan, Kevin M. .... **Springfield, NJ**
Regan & Kiely, LLP .... **Boston, MA**
Regan, Larry J. .... Lafayette, LA
Regan, Laura Partee .... **Washington, DC**
Regan Law Firm, The, L.L.C.
Kansas City, MO
Regan, Lawrence E. .... Irvington, NY
Regan, Lawrence F., Jr. .... **Rockville, MD**
Regan, Lawrence J. .... Buffalo, NY
East Amherst, NY
Regan, Lee Ann .... Burke, VA
Regan, M. Scott .... **Denver, CO**
Regan, Manasseh & Boshea, P.L.C.
Baton Rouge, LA
New Orleans, LA
Regan, Margaret M. .... Chicago, IL
Regan, Margaret M. .... New Boston, NH
Regan, Mark J. .... Lowell, MA
Regan, Mark W. .... Juneau, AK
Regan, Martin Edward, Jr.
Baton Rouge, LA
New Orleans, LA
Regan, Mary B. .... Maynard, MA
Regan, Marylou B. .... Centereach, NY
Regan, MaryNell .... **Milwaukee, WI**
Regan, Matthew C., III .... Boston, MA
Regan, Matthew D. .... **Anchorage, AK**
Regan, Matthew E. .... Medford, MA
Regan, Matthew T. .... **Chicago, IL**
Regan, Maureen T.
Department Of Veterans Affairs, Inspector General, GV
Regan & McGannon .... Wichita, KS
Regan, Michael D. .... **St. Louis, MO**
Regan, Michael J. .... Chicago, IL
Regan, Michael L. .... New London, CT
Regan, Michael P. .... Oregon City, OR
Regan, Michael P. .... **Danville, VA**
Regan, Michael P., P.C., Law Offices of
Danville, VA
Regan, Michelle S. .... **New York, NY**
Regan, Nancy .... Boston, MA
Regan, Nancy A. .... **Fair Oaks, CA**
Regan, Nancy, Law Offices
Fair Oaks, CA
Sacramento, CA
Regan, Patricia E. .... New Orleans, LA
Regan, Patrick J. .... Wichita, KS
Regan, Patrick M. .... **Washington, DC**
Upper Marlboro, MD
Fairfax, VA
Regan, Paul K. .... Washington, DC
Regan, Paul L. .... Wilmington, DE
Regan, Paul M. .... **Syracuse, NY**
Regan, Penelope A. .... Carlsbad, CA
Regan, Peter Brent .... **Newport, RI**
Regan, Peter J. .... Highland Park, IL
Regan & Post, L.L.P. .... Metairie, LA
Regan, R. Michael .... North Mankato, MN
Regan, Ramon S. .... **Detroit, MI**
Regan, Ray R. .... **Albuquerque, NM**
Regan, Raymond A. .... **Daytona Beach, FL**
Regan, Raymond P. .... Milford, NH
Regan & Regan .... Buffalo, NY
East Amherst, NY
Regan, Regan and Meyer .... **Mankato, MN**
Regan, Regina Kathleen .... Brooklyn, NY
Regan, Richard E. .... Metairie, LA
Regan, Richard E. .... Rochester, NY
Regan, Richard F.X. .... Weehawken, NJ
Regan, Richard J. .... Boston, MA
Regan, Richard R. .... **Bath, ME**
Regan, Richard T. .... Metairie, LA
Regan, Robert Francis .... **Mineola, NY**
Regan, Robert John .... **Chicago, IL**
Regan, Robert M. .... Mankato, MN
Regan, Robert T. .... **Westwood, NJ**
Regan, Robert T., A Professional Corporation .... **Westwood, NJ**
Regan, Roderick J. .... **San Antonio, TX**
Regan, Ruairi J. .... **New York, NY**
Regan, Scott D.
Department Of Veterans Affairs, Board of Veterans Appeals, GV
Regan, Sean E. .... **Middletown, NJ**
Regan, Sharon D. .... Pensacola, FL
Regan, Shawn Patrick .... New York, NY
Regan, Steven M. .... **Pittsburgh, PA**
Regan, Susan G. .... **Buffalo, NY**
Regan, Susan L. .... Hampstead, NH
Regan, Terri Conrad .... Albany, NY
Regan, Terri D. .... Jackson, MS
Regan, Thomas C. .... Peabody, MA
Regan, Thomas C. .... **Morristown, NJ**
Regan, Thomas J. .... **Hartford, CT**
Regan, Thomas J. .... **Chicago, IL**
Regan, Thomas K. .... Crowley, LA
Regan, Thomas M. .... **San Diego, CA**
Regan, Thomas M. .... **Bloomington, MN**
Regan, Thomas M. .... **Philadelphia, PA**
Regan, Thomas M. .... Elkins, WV
Regan, Timothy D., Jr. .... San Francisco, CA
Regan, Timothy W. .... **Minneapolis, MN**
Regan & Tueth .... Decatur, IL
Regan, Victor M. .... Mineola, NY
Regan & Vincent, PLC .... **Bloomington, MN**
Regan, William B. .... **Charleston, SC**
Regan, William Ben .... Magnolia, MS
Regan, William J. .... Buffalo, NY
East Amherst, NY
Regan, William J. .... New York, NY
Regan, William J. .... Sewanee, TN
Regan, William M. .... Bronxville, NY
Regan-Harrington, Tina .... New Bedford, MA
Regan-Henry, Susan .... White Plains, NY
Regante, Jedde V. .... **Key West, FL**
Regante, Mark L. .... **New York, NY**
Regar, Barry .... Indian Wells, CA
Regar, Barry, A Professional Law Corporation
Indian Wells, CA
Regard, Daniel L. .... New Iberia, LA
Regard, Joseph T., III .... Madisonville, LA
Metairie, LA
Regard, Joseph T., Ltd., A Prof. Law Corp.
Madisonville, LA
Metairie, LA
Regas, Beth H. .... **Washington, DC**
Regas, Frezados & Harp .... Chicago, IL
Regas, Gus R. .... Kankakee, IL
Regas, James A. .... Chicago, IL
Regas, Jennifer Hanselman .... Cleveland, OH
Regas, John S. .... Cleveland, OH
Regas, Michael G., II .... **Atlanta, GA**
Regas, Peter L. .... Chicago, IL
Regas, Sharon Szolosi .... **Cleveland, OH**
Regas, Steve G. .... Canton, OH
Regas, Suzanne .... Chicago, IL
Regas, William J. .... **Indianapolis, IN**
Regas, William T. .... Park Ridge, IL
Regazzini, Gregory .... Somerville, MA
Regberg, Neil S. .... Cincinnati, OH
Regehr, Preston C. .... **Salt Lake City, UT**
Regel, Kristin A. .... **Dallas, TX**
Regel, Walter W. .... **New York, NY**
Regelbrugge, Paul V. .... Detroit, MI
Regelin, Louise O. .... Genesee, ID
Regelin, Nancy P. .... **Rockville, MD**
Regelman, Dale F. .... Tucson, AZ
Regen, Barney B. .... **Dickson, TN**
Regen, Benjamin C. .... **Dickson, TN**
Regen, Claudia G. .... **Washington, DC**
Regen, Ezra J. .... **Sarasota, FL**
Regen, Mark J. .... **Reston, VA**
Regenass, Inga .... **Salt Lake City, UT**
Regenbogen, Adam .... Binghamton, NY
Regenbogen, Ellis A. .... **Dallas, TX**
Regenbogen, Howard W. .... Niles, IL
Regenbogen, Laurie B. .... Chicago, IL
Regenbogen, Mitchell .... Brooklyn, NY
Regenburgh, Richard, III .... Friendswood, TX
Regenfuss, Michael D. .... **Milwaukee, WI**
Regenogen, Brad Eric .... Hempstead, NY
Regenovich, Dean .... Highland, IN
Regensburg, Kenneth .... **New York, NY**
Regensdorf, Paul R. .... **Fort Lauderdale, FL**
Regenstreich, Bruce N. .... **Shrewsbury, NJ**
New York, NY
Regenstreich, Myron J. .... Youngstown, OH
Regenstreif, Herbert .... Mineola, NY
Regenstreif, Mitchell C.
Santa Monica, CA
Regent, Anh H. .... **Houston, TX**
Regenwether, Steven R. .... **Memphis, TN**
Reger, C. Michael .... Albany, NY
Reger, David W. .... **Florham Park, NJ**
Reger, Gary N. .... **Beaumont, TX**
Houston, TX
Reger, Gregory M. .... **New Albany, IN**
Reger, Jacob E. .... Buckhannon, WV
Reger, Jas. W. .... Billings, MT
Reger, Lisa Garcia .... New Albany, IN
Reger, Margaret .... Harrison, AR
Reger & Rizzo .... Wilmington, DE
Cherry Hill, NJ
King Of Prussia, PA
Philadelphia, PA
Reger, Robert J. .... **King Of Prussia, PA**
Reger, Robert J., Jr. .... **New York, NY**
Reger, Robert S. .... Hamden, CT
Reges, Mala J. .... Juneau, AK
Reges, Robert K., Jr. .... **Juneau, AK**
Regez, Rudolph F. .... Monroe, WI
Regez, Rudolph P. .... **Monroe, WI**
Reggiardo, Silvio, III .... **Sacramento, CA**
Reggie, Christopher E. .... San Rafael, CA
Reggie, Gregory F. .... Crowley, LA
Reggie, Paul Peter .... Lake Charles, LA
Reggie & Reggie .... Crowley, LA
Regier, Gregory P. .... **Irvine, CA**
Westlake Village, CA
Regier, Jarold W. .... **Pompano Beach, FL**
Regier, John R. .... **Boston, MA**
Regier, Kathryn A. .... Overland Park, KS
Regier, Michael J. .... Austin, TX
Regier, Wade V. .... **Portland, OR**
Regimbal, Maria S. .... Seattle, WA
Regimbal, Robert P. .... **Morristown, NJ**
Regina, Alfred E. .... Broad Brook, CT
Regina, Giovanni .... **Secaucus, NJ**
Reginelli, Amy R. .... Rockville, MD
Reginelli, Anthony, Jr. .... **Metairie, LA**
Reginelli, Arthur M. .... **Akron, OH**
Regini, Lisa A. .... Department of Justice, Federal Bureau of Investigation, GV
Regirer, Walter W. .... Richmond, VA
Regis, Ellin M. .... **Lake Success, NY**
Regis, George Edward .... New York, NY
Regis, M. Jacqueline .... **St. Paul, MN**
Register, Anthony L. .... Wilmington, NC
Register, Eric Louis .... **New Orleans, LA**
Register, G. June .... Fresno, CA
Register, J. Michael .... Homosassa, FL
Register, J. Willard .... Columbus, GA
Register, Joe Lee .... Lufkin, TX
Register, Penelope W. .... **Memphis, TN**
Register, Rob S. .... **Atlanta, GA**
Register, William R.
Department of Transportation, Office of the General Counsel, GV
Registrato, Joseph J. .... Tampa, FL
Registre, Rose May .... **New York, NY**
Regli, Robert .... Kealakekua, HI
Reglos, Rose Fe Reyes .... Los Angeles, CA
Regnante, Sterio & Osborne .... **Boston, MA**
Wakefield, MA
Regnante, Theodore .... **Wakefield, MA**
Regnante, Theodore C. .... **Wakefield, MA**
Regnault, Phillips M.
Englewood Cliffs, NJ
Regnell, Janet K. .... Salem, OR
Regner, Jeffrey A. .... **Baltimore, MD**
Regner, John H. .... Houston, TX
Regner, Raymond A., Jr. .... **Detroit, MI**
Regner, William D. .... **New York, NY**
Regnery, Alfred S. .... **Washington, DC**
Regnery, Ellen L. .... **North Palm Beach, FL**
Palm Beach, FL
Regnery, John W. .... **Kenosha, WI**
Regnery, Ronald N. .... **Richmond, VA**
Regnier, Andrea Christine .... Houston, TX
Regnier, Georgianna Pennington
Oxnard, CA
Regnier, Gerald A. .... Edina, MN
Regnier, James M. .... Helena, MT
Regnier, Joseph F. .... Detroit, MI
Regnier, Kingsley G. .... Fort Wayne, IN
Régnier, Marc (IBA) .... **Greenville, SC**
Regnier, Mari Yamamoto .... **Chicago, IL**
Regnier, Mark R. .... Tipton, IN
Regnier, Michael W. .... **Toledo, OH**
Regnier, Paul P., Jr. .... Houston, TX
Regnier, Pierre N. .... **St. Paul, MN**
Regnier, Richard A. .... **Oxnard, CA**
Regnier, Richard O. .... Tipton, IN
Regnier, Taylor, Curran & Eddy
Hartford, CT
Rego, Alfred R., Jr. .... **Bristol, RI**
Rego, Anson O. .... Waianae, HI
Rego, Cullen & Hagan Co., L.P.A.
Fairview Park, OH
Rego, John A. .... **Rockville, MD**
Rego, John A. .... **Cleveland, OH**
Rego, John G. .... **Bristol, RI**
Rego, John J. .... **Bristol, RI**
Rego, Linda S.
Federal Deposit Insurance Corporation, Corporate Affairs Section, GV
Rego, Lucian C. .... Fairview Park, OH
Rego, Matthew .... White Plains, NY
Rego & Rego .... **Bristol, RI**
Rego, Thomas M. .... Tallapoosa, GA
Regojo, Fernando .... Union City, NJ
Regoli, David A. .... New Kensington, PA
Regolo, Attilio M., Jr. .... Beverly Hills, CA
Regolo, Attilio M., Jr., A Professional Law Corp. .... Beverly Hills, CA
Regosin, Bernard .... Flushing, NY
Regosin, Edwards, Stone & Feder
New York, NY
Regot, Mary K. .... Jefferson City, MO
Regozin, Roy L. .... **New York, NY**
Regula, Maureen Duggan .... Hartford, CT
Regula, Ralph S. .... Canton, OH
Regula, Steven M. .... New Haven, CT
Regulatory Law Group, The, Philip J. Smith and Terri M. Lyndall, LLC .... **Atlanta, GA**
Reguli, Connie .... Nashville, TN
Regulinski, Michael C. .... Richmond, VA
Regulski, John J. .... Long Island City, NY
Regusis, Constantine .... Bronx, NY
Reh, Deanie J. .... Phoenix, AZ
Reh, Matthew J. .... **St. Louis, MO**
Reh, Thomas D. .... Warsaw, NY
Reha, John F. .... **Littleton, CO**
Rehak, Judith L. .... St. Paul, MN
Rehak, Linda J. .... Dayton, OH
Rehanek, Edw. W. .... Redwood City, CA
Rehard, Lisa K. .... Platte City, MO
Rehaste, Rita A. .... Orange, CA
Rehaut, Steven M. .... Los Angeles, CA
Rehberg & Albertson, P.S. .... **Bellevue, WA**
SeaTac, WA
Seattle, WA
Rehberg, Curt P. .... Crystal Lake, IL
Rehberg, James C. .... Macon, GA
Rehberg, Janice L. .... **Billings, MT**
Rehberg, Phil J. .... Seattle, WA
Rehberg, Robert A. .... Redding, CA
Rehbock, Ernest Z. .... Anchorage, AK
Rehbock, Jean L. .... McLean, VA
Rehbock & Rehbock .... Anchorage, AK
Rehbock, Richard A. .... Jericho, NY
Rehbock, Robert A. .... Anchorage, AK
Rehder, Alfred L. .... **Rockville, MD**
Rehe, David E. .... Rutherford, NJ
Rehe, Mark R. .... **Los Angeles, CA**
Reheard, Deborah A., Law Office
Eufaula, OK
Reher, Cathryn D. .... **Minneapolis, MN**
Reher, Robley C. .... Chino, CA
Reheuser, Michael E. .... **Washington, DC**
Fairfax, VA
Reheuser, Stephen Thomas .... Alameda, CA
Rehfeld, Barry .... San Francisco, CA
Rehfeld, Franklin C. .... St. Louis, MO
Rehfeld, Jeffrey K. .... **San Francisco, CA**
Rehfeldt, Frederick E. .... Fort Worth, TX
Rehfeldt, Richard A. .... Jackson, MS
Rehfeldt, Richard A., P.A. .... Jackson, MS
Rehfeldt, Stephen A. .... **Wheaton, IL**
Rehfuss, John W. .... **Albany, NY**
Rehfuss, Stephen J. .... **Albany, NY**
Rehg, Robert Franz .... New York, NY
Rehill, Michael F. .... **Westwood, NJ**
Rehkamp, C. Joseph .... New Bloomfield, PA
Rehkamp, Marlene V. .... New York, NY
Rehkop, C. Neil .... Los Angeles, CA
Rehkopf, Donald G., Jr. .... **Rochester, NY**
Rehlen, Pamela H. .... Castleton, VT
Rehler, Jan Edward .... **Corpus Christi, TX**
Rehler, Kristin .... Houston, TX
Rehling, Beth L. .... Cincinnati, OH
Rehling, Charles G. .... **Phoenix, AZ**
Rehling, William R. .... Chicago, IL
Rehm, Agigail M. .... **New York, NY**
Rehm, Arthur K. .... Clayton, MO
Rehm, Charles H. .... St. Louis, MO
Rehm, Elizabeth D. .... **Mobile, AL**
Rehm, Eric S. .... Burnsville, MN
Rehm, Joan L. .... Chicago, IL
Rehm, Joanna Lynn .... Los Angeles, CA
Rehm, John B. .... **Washington, DC**
Rehm Law Firm, A Professional Corporation
Lincoln, NE
Rehm, Linda S. .... Seattle, WA
Rehm, Martha Dugan .... Vail, CO
Rehm, Richard L. .... Portage, WI
Rehm, Rod .... **Lincoln, NE**
Rehm, Ronald L. .... **Wooster, OH**
Rehm and Stafford .... **Lake George, NY**
Rehm, T. Robert, Jr. .... **Washington, DC**
Rehm, Walter O., III .... **Lake George, NY**
Rehmann, Mary V. .... Springfield, IL
Rehmann, Steven E. .... Chesaning, MI
Rehme, Thomas F. .... **Cincinnati, OH**
Rehmeier, Randall L. .... Nebraska City, NE
Rehmel, Tera M. .... **Louisville, KY**
Rehmer, Fred R. .... Aurora, CO
Rehmet, Christopher .... **Fort Collins, CO**
Rehmet, Patrick G. .... Wimberley, TX
Rehmet, Vincent W. .... Houston, TX
Rehmeyer, Jeffrey L., II .... **York, PA**

Reid, Dale R. ....Marriottsville, MD
Reid, Dana M. ....Bellevue, WA
Reid Dandridge Rodriguez & Rouse, LLP
New York, NY
Reid, Danielle E. ....Rumson, NJ
Reid, Darla Davis ....Austin, TX
Reid, David C. ....Rochester, NY
Reid, David E. ....Kansas City, MO
Reid, David G. ....Brattleboro, VT
Reid, David P. ....Tulsa, OK
Reid, David R. ....Springfield, IL
Reid, David S. ....South Yarmouth, MA
Reid, David S. ....Fort Worth, TX
Reid, David W. ....Dayton, OH
Reid, Dawn L ....Topeka, KS
Reid, Deborah A.
Commission on Civil Rights,
Office of the General Counsel, GV
Reid, Deborah A. ....Mequon, WI
Reid, Deborah R. ....New York, NY
Reid, Dennis Michael ....Ashtabula, OH
Reid, Derek J. ....Doylestown, PA
Reid, Derrick M. ....Laguna Beach, CA
Reid, Don ....Gainesville, FL
Reid, Donald B. ....Athens, TN
Reid, Donald E. ....Wilmington, DE
Reid, Donald F. ....Norwalk, CT
Reid, Donald J. ....Tampa, FL
Reid, Donald J., Jr. ....Houston, TX
Reid, Donald W. ....Eastland, TX
Reid, Donna L. ....Los Angeles, CA
Reid, Dora E. ....Kansas City, MO
Reid, Douglas Dale, Jr. ....New Brighton, MN
Reid, Duncan P. ....Richmond, VA
Reid, E. Lewis, (P.C.) ....San Francisco, CA
Reid, E. Lowry, Jr. ....Columbus, GA
Reid, Edward C. ....Trabuco Canyon, CA
Reid, Edward O. ....Bradenton, FL
Reid, Edward S. ....New York, NY
Reid, Ellis E. ....Chicago, IL
Reid, Elsie L. ....Chevy Chase, MD
Reid, Eugenie C. ....St. Petersburg, FL
Reid, Eva Christine ....Kingfisher, OK
Reid, F. Barbara Gluck ....New York, NY
Reid, Felicia R. ....San Francisco, CA
Reid & Flowers, A Professional Corporation
Dallas, TX
Reid, Forrest ....Albany, OR
Reid, Forrest W. ....Washington, DC
Reid, Frank E. ....Houston, TX
Reid, G. Kelley, Jr. ....San Francisco, CA
Reid, G. Williams ....Sturtevant, WI
Reid, Garth O., Jr. ....Escondido, CA
Reid, Garth O., Jr., A Professional Law Corporation ....Escondido, CA
Reid, Gary L. ....Olympia, WA
Reid, Gavin A. ....Danville, VT
Reid, George B., Jr. ....Washington, DC
Reid, George C. ....Atlanta, GA
Reid, George R., II ....New York, NY
Reid, Geraldine Mery ....San Antonio, TX
Reid, Gertrude Armstrong ....Corinth, MS
Reid, Ghillaine A ....New York, NY
Reid, Glen G., Jr. ....Memphis, TN
Reid, Glenn J. ....Charlotte, NC
Reid, Graeme A. ....San Diego, CA
Reid, Gregory L. ....New York, NY
Reid, H. Collis, Jr. ....Louisville, KY
Reid, H. Richard ....Minneapolis, MN
Reid, Harland H., II ....Torrance, CA
Reid, Harry ....Las Vegas, NV
Reid, Harry G., III ....Deltona, FL
Reid, Harry G., III ....Sanford, FL
Reid & Hellyer, A Professional Corporation
Ontario, CA
Palm Springs, CA
Riverside, CA
San Bernardino, CA
Temecula, CA
Reid, Ilene G. ....Rockville, MD
Reid, Ira A. ....New York, NY
Reid, James E. ....Newark, NY
Syracuse, NY
Reid, James E., Jr. ....Harrisburg, PA
Reid, James G. ....Boise, ID
Reid, James G. ....Lexington, KY
Reid, James H., Jr. ....Bay Minette, AL
Reid, James J. ....Columbia, SC
Reid, James L. ....Milwaukee, WI
Reid, James M. ....Oklahoma City, OK
Reid, James P. ....Dallas, TX
Reid & James, P.C. ....Flint, MI
Reid, James Roland ....Brownsville, TN
Reid, James S. ....Washington, DC
Reid, James W. ....New York, NY
Reid, James W. ....Scranton, PA
Reid, Jan T. ....Tulsa, OK
Reid, Jane F. ....Sherman Oaks, CA
Reid, Jane R. ....Saratoga Springs, NY
Reid, Jas. S., Jr. ....Cleveland, OH
Reid, Jean Margo ....New York, NY
Reid, Jennifer Ellen ....Honolulu, HI
Reid, Jeremiah F., (A P.C.) ....Ramona, CA
Reid, Jim T. ....Kearney, MO
Reid, Joan A. ....Boulder, CO
Reid, Joan E., Mrs. ....Carson City, NV
Reid, John E. ....Fort Collins, CO
Reid, John F. ....Thousand Oaks, CA
Reid, John H. ....Los Angeles, CA
Reid, John H. ....Wausau, WI
Reid, John H., III ....Hartford, CT
Reid, John J. ....San Rafael, CA
Reid, John J. ....Hartford, CT
Reid, John J. ....Orlando, FL
Reid, John J. ....Waukegan, IL
Reid, John R., Jr. ....Orlando, FL
Reid, John T. ....Wichita, KS
Reid, Jon S. ....Omaha, NE

Reid, Joseph B. ....Herndon, VA
Reid, Joseph C. ....Baltimore, MD
Reid, Joseph C., P.A. ....Baltimore, MD
Reid, Joseph D. ....Lansing, MI
Reid, Joseph K., III ....Richmond, VA
Reid, Joseph M. ....Pleasant Hill, CA
Reid, Joseph S. ....Schererville, IN
Reid, Joseph S., Jr. ....Woodruff, SC
Reid, Justus W. ....West Palm Beach, FL
Reid, Kahlil ....New York, NY
Reid, Kathryn A. ....Portland, ME
Reid, Kathryn J. ....Westborough, MA
Reid, Kenneth H. ....Springfield, MO
Reid, Kenneth M. ....Troy, MI
Reid, Kevin B. ....Chicago, IL
Reid, Kevin C. ....Allentown, PA
Reid, Kevin James ....Chicago, IL
Reid, Kimberly A. ....Albany, GA
Reid, Kimberly M. ....Winter Park, FL
Reid, Kirkland E. ....Mobile, AL
Reid, L. Byron ....Fort Walton Beach, FL
Panama City, FL
Reid, Lawrence H., Jr. ....Garden City, NY
Reid, Lewis, Deese, Nance & Person, L.L.P.
Fayetteville, NC
Reid, Linda K. ....Pittsburgh, PA
Reid, Lisa Amato ....Cleveland, OH
Reid, Lisette M. ....Miami, FL
Reid, Lorine M. ....Dayton, OH
Reid, Lyle ....Nashville, TN
Reid, Lynn M. ....Chicago, IL
Reid, Lynne L. ....San Diego, CA
Reid, M. Catherine ....Orange, CA
Reid, M. David ....Xenia, OH
Reid, Malcolm D. ....Minneapolis, MN
Reid & Maniscalco ....Fairfield, CT
Reid, Marcus W. ....Anniston, AL
Reid, Marilyn J. ....Beavercreek, OH
Reid, Marion K. ....Edina, MN
Reid, Marland C. ....Fayetteville, NC
Reid, Mary Bruce ....Seattle, WA
Reid, Mary Catherine ....Orange, CA
Reid, Mary E. ....Bedford Heights, OH
Reid, Metzger, & Associates, P.A.
West Palm Beach, FL
Reid, Michael J. ....Colorado Springs, CO
Reid, Michael K. ....Portland, OR
Reid, Michael T. ....Chicago, IL
Reid, Michael Thomas ....Troy, MI
Reid & Morgan ....Atlanta, GA
Reid, N. Neville ....Chicago, IL
Reid, Nancy W. ....San Diego, CA
Reid, Neil D. ....San Rafael, CA
Reid, Neil Henry ....New York, NY
Reid, Nelson M. ....Columbus, OH
Reid, Nora A. ....San Francisco, CA
Reid, Norman S. ....Riverbank, CA
Reid, Patrick Scott ....Saratoga Springs, NY
Reid, Patrick T. ....Lansing, MI
Reid, Paul D. ....Lockport, NY
Reid, Paul H., Jr. ....Niagara Falls, NY
Reid, Paul T. ....Miami, FL
Reid, Penny Packard ....Dallas, TX
Reid, Peter H. ....Redwood City, CA
Reid, Philip A. ....Dayton, OH
Reid, Philip C. ....Milwaukee, WI
Reid, Philip H., Jr. ....Palm Beach, FL
Reid, R. Scott ....Fredericktown, MO
Reid, R. Thompson ....Ellicott City, MD
Reid, Ramon P. ....Toppenish, WA
Reid, Raymond A. ....Salem, OR
Reid and Reedy ....Athens, TN
Reid, Regina Benton ....Atlanta, GA
Reid & Reid ....San Jose, CA
Reid, Renee M. ....Tampa, FL
Reid, Rhonda Y. ....Detroit, MI
Reid, Richard A. ....Blytheville, AR
Reid, Richard A. ....Towson, MD
Reid, Richard G. ....Princeton, NJ
Reid, Richard J. ....East Lansing, MI
Reid, Richard J. ....Mount Olive, NJ
Reid, Richard L. ....Kansas City, KS
Reid and Riege, P.C. ....Hartford, CT
Lakeville, CT
West Hartford, CT
Woodbury, CT
Reid, Robert ....Dallas, TX
Reid, Robert C. ....Tallahassee, FL
Reid, Robert D. ....Wausau, WI
Reid, Robert J. ....Flint, MI
Reid, Robert J. ....Bronx, NY
Reid, Robert J. ....Cincinnati, OH
Reid, Robert Newton ....Washington, DC
Reid, Robert R., Jr. ....Birmingham, AL
Reid, Robert V. ....Warren, MI
Reid, Robert W. ....Eugene, OR
Reid & Rodgers, P.L.C. ....Brattleboro, VT
Reid, Roger H. ....Albany, OR
Reid, Roger J. ....Greenfield, MA
Reid, Ronald L. ....Atlanta, GA
Reid, Rory J. ....Las Vegas, NV
Reid, Russell J. ....Seattle, WA
Reid, Russell L., Jr. ....Dallas, TX
Reid, Rust E. ....Dallas, TX
Reid, Sally C. ....Boston, MA
Reid, Samuel F., Jr. ....Orangeburg, SC
Reid, Samuel R., III ....Dover, NH
Reid, Sarah L. ....New York, NY
Reid, Scott W. ....Durham, NC
Reid, Sharah A. ....Santa Ana, CA
Reid, Sheila A. ....San Francisco, CA
Reid, Spencer ....Albuquerque, NM
Reid, Stephen C., III ....Dallas, TX
Reid, Stephen J., Jr. ....Providence, RI
Reid, Stephen P. ....Los Angeles, CA
Reid, Steven ....Greene, NY
Reid, Steven J. ....Granbury, TX

Reid, Stewart D. ....Los Angeles, CA
Rancho Cucamonga, CA
Reid, Strickland & Gillette, L.L.P.
Anahuac, TX
Baytown, TX
Reid, Stuart A. ....Lake Forest, IL
Reid, Sue Titus ....Tallahassee, FL
Reid, Susan E. ....Atlanta, GA
Reid, Susan M. ....Palo Alto, CA
Reid, Susan M. ....San Francisco, CA
Reid, Suzann M. ....Bloomington, IL
Reid, Sylvia D. ....Hartford, CT
Reid, T. Dwight ....Mobile, AL
Reid, T. Dwight, P.C. ....Mobile, AL
Reid, T. Preston ....Greenville, SC
Reid, T. Robert ....Atlanta, GA
Reid, Tanis M. ....Fairfield, CT
Reid, Taylor S. ....Palo Alto, CA
Reid, Teresa ....Philadelphia, PA
Reid, Thomas D., Jr.
Department of State, GV
Reid, Thomas F. ....Pittsburgh, PA
Reid, Thomas G. ....Denver, CO
Reid, Thomas H. ....New York, NY
Reid, Thomas M. ....Denver, CO
Reid, Thomas M. ....Rochester, MI
Reid Thomas Marquez, P.C. ....Bronx, NY
Reid, Thomas P. ....Miami, FL
Reid, Thomas R., III ....Washington, DC
Reid, Timm W. ....Des Moines, IA
Reid, Timothy A. ....Issaquah, WA
Reid, Timothy T. ....Cleveland, OH
Reid, Trevor A. ....Bronx, NY
Reid, Victor L. ....Washington, DC
Reid, W. Joseph ....Jackson, MS
Winona, MS
Reid, Warren F. ....United States Senate,
Senatorial Assistants, GV
Reid, Warren G. ....Oakland, CA
Reid, William D. ....Springfield, IL
Reid, William E. ....Dallas, TX
Reid, William G. ....Pilot Mountain, NC
Reid, William G. ....Austin, TX
Reid, William M. ....East Hartford, CT
Reid, William Stuart ....Riverside, CA
Reid, William W. ....Los Angeles, CA
Reid, Wm. A. ....Great Falls, MT
Reid, Wm. W. ....Santa Barbara, CA
Reida, Frank J. ....Omaha, NE
Reida, Larry T. ....Waynesville, NC
Reida, Steven W. ....Bozeman, MT
Reidbord, Todd E. ....Pittsburgh, PA
Reidder, William A. ....Long Beach, CA
Reid-Dodick, John B. ....New York, NY
Reidel, Karl W. ....Hackensack, NJ
Reidel, Michael L. ....Greeley, CO
Reidel, Thomas G. ....Muscatine, IA
Reideler, Terrence E.
Federal Communications Commission,
Wireless Telecommunications Bureau, GV
Reidenbach, Frederick E. ....Milwaukee, WI
Reidenbach, J. Michael
San Francisco, CA
Reidenbach, Kenneth G., II ....Lancaster, PA
Reidenbach, Laura L. ....Redwood City, CA
Reidenbach, Scott R. ....Lancaster, PA
Reidenbach, Thomas R. ....Rockford, IL
Reidenberg & Barton, P.L.L.P.
Minneapolis, MN
Reidenberg, Joel R. ....New York, NY
Reidenberg, Louis M. ....Minneapolis, MN
Reidenberg, Seth J. ....Wilmington, DE
Reider, Alan E. ....Washington, DC
Reider & Brown, P.C. ....Muskegon, MI
Reider, D. Brian ....Ontario, CA
Reider, Helen Linda Dallas
Washington, DC
Reider, Jeffrey R. ....Bethesda, MD
Reider, Leslie ....New York, NY
Reider, Marvin W. ....Southfield, MI
Reider, Richard K. ....Muskegon, MI
Reider, Shirley A. ....St. Paul, MN
Reider, Victoria A. ....Mechanicsburg, PA
Reid-Green, Dawn Elicia ....Brooklyn, NY
Reidhead, Kelly Justin ....Phoenix, AZ
Reidich, Steven A. ....Duluth, GA
Reidinger, Martin K. ....Asheville, NC
Reidinger, Paul A. ....San Francisco, CA
Reidinger, Priscilla K. ....Burlington, VT
Reidinger, Tim ....New Albany, IN
Reidl, Paul W. ....Modesto, CA
Reid-Moore, Christina J. ....Phoenix, AZ
Reid-Peterson, Jacqueline ....Topeka, KS
Reid-Robinson, Natosha ....New York, NY
Reidy, Andrew M. ....Washington, DC
Reidy, Anne Marie ....Cleveland, OH
Reidy, Catherine Skahan ....Boston, MA
Reidy, Charles P., III ....Boston, MA
Reidy, Christine A. ....New York, NY
Reidy, Christine M. ....Chicago, IL
Reidy, Daniel E. ....Chicago, IL
Reidy, Daniel F. ....San Francisco, CA
Reidy, Daniel F., A Professional Corporation
San Francisco, CA
Reidy, Daniel J. ....Tucson, AZ
Reidy, Donna M. ....Worcester, MA
Reidy, Edward J. ....San Francisco, CA
Reidy, Edward J.
Office of Personnel Management, GV
Reidy, Edward P. ....Cranston, RI
Reidy, Gerald P. ....Danbury, CT
Reidy, Grace E.
Department of Transportation,
Federal Highway Administration, GV
Reidy, James J. ....Chicago, IL
Reidy, James J., Ltd. ....Chicago, IL
Reidy, James P. ....Concord, NH
Manchester, NH

Reidy, Jerome G. ....Cuyahoga Falls, OH
Reidy, John J. ....Chicago, IL
Reidy, John J., III ....Chicago, IL
Reidy, John J., Jr. ....Painesville, OH
Reidy, John S. ....Braintree, MA
Reidy, Joseph F. ....Baytown, TX
Reidy, Joseph M. ....Columbus, OH
Reidy, Kevin C. ....Boston, MA
Reidy, M. Bridget ....Chicago, IL
Reidy, Marilyn McCabe ....Chicago, IL
Reidy, Mary ....New York, NY
Reidy, Michael E. ....Denver, CO
Reidy, Michael J. ....Cleveland, OH
Reidy, Michael T. ....Kansas City, MO
Reidy, Patrick G. ....New York, NY
Reidy, Patrick J. ....Pittsburgh, PA
Reidy, Patrick M. ....Kansas City, MO
Reidy, Paul N. ....Chicago, IL
Reidy, Richard M. ....Albuquerque, NM
Reidy, Robert E. ....Hickory Hills, IL
Reidy, Robert G. ....White Plains, NY
Reidy, Thomas A. ....Newark, OH
Reidy, Thomas E. ....Rochester, NY
Reier, David J. ....Boston, MA
Reier, Richard C. ....Lincoln, NE
Reiersgord, Camilla L. ....Minneapolis, MN
Reiersgord Law Firm ....Minneapolis, MN
Reiersgord, Thomas E. ....Minneapolis, MN
Reierson, Karen ....Minneapolis, MN
Reierson, Kent ....Watford City, ND
Williston, ND
Reierson, Maynard ....Menasha, WI
Reif, Alison C. ....Boston, MA
Reif, Andrew ....Beverly Hills, CA
Reif, Burton ....Chicago, IL
Chicago, IL
Reif, David Joseph ....St. Louis, MO
Reif, Donald E., Jr. ....Hoisington, KS
Reif, Edward ....Philadelphia, PA
Reif, Eric P. ....Pittsburgh, PA
Reif, Frederick W. ....New York, NY
Reif and Gregory ....Minneapolis, MN
Reif, James M. ....New York, NY
Reif, Jerome P. ....Saginaw, MI
Reif, Jerome P., P.C. ....Saginaw, MI
Reif, John F. ....Tulsa, OK
Reif, Joseph A. ....Chicago, IL
Reif & Kendall ....Markesan, WI
Randolph, WI
Reif, Kevin A. ....Reston, VA
Reif, Lawrence H. ....New York, NY
Reif, Louis R. ....Buffalo, NY
Reif, R. Roger ....Canby, OR
Reif, Raymond R. ....Canby, OR
Reif, Robert D. ....Washington, DC
Alexandria, VA
Reif, Scott R. ....Markesan, WI
Reif, Thomas J. ....Alexandria, MN
Reif, Thomas S. ....Chicago, IL
Reif, Timothy M. ....Washington, DC
Reif, W. Michael ....Little Rock, AR
Reif, Wanda J. ....Washington, DC
Reifeis, Paul E. ....Carmel, IN
Reifel, Charles M. ....Washington, DC
Reifenberg, Arno ....Portland, OR
Reifenberg, Lisa D. ....New York, NY
Reifenberg, Robert L. ....Chicago, IL
Reifer, Avrum ....Chicago, IL
Reifer, Joseph R. ....Washington, DC
Reifer, Sol S. ....Dallas, TX
Reifers, S. Camille ....Memphis, TN
Reifersen, Bernard ....Brooklyn, NY
Reiferson, Drew S. ....Washington, DC
Reiff, Andrew L. ....Orlando, FL
Reiff, Andrew L., P.A. ....Orlando, FL
Reiff, David E. ....Tomahawk, WI
Reiff, Devon ....New York, NY
Reiff, Gary M. ....Denver, CO
Reiff, Helen H. ....Middlebury, VT
Reiff, Jeffrey M. ....Philadelphia, PA
Reiff, John K. ....Baltimore, MD
Reiff, John M. ....Wichita, KS
Reiff, Jonathan D. ....Oklahoma City, OK
Reiff, Laura F. ....Washington, DC
Reiff, Michelle G. ....Englewood, CO
Reiff, Morrissey & Bily, P.A.
Philadelphia, PA
Reiff, Neil P. ....Washington, DC
Reiff, Robert S. ....Miami, FL
Reiff, Robert S., P.A. ....Miami, FL
Reiff, Robt. ....Cicero, IL
Reiff, Steven N. ....Decatur, GA
Reiff, William C. ....Mount Desert, ME
Reiff, William R. ....Corpus Christi, TX
Reiffe, Solomon ....New York, NY
Reiffel, Jamie J. ....New York, NY
Reifin, Melvin H. ....Georgetown, OH
Reifler, Albert H. ....Oak Park, MI
Reifler, Elizabeth Ann, Law Offices of
Martinez, CA
Napa, CA
San Francisco, CA
Reifler, Elizabeth Ann, Law Offices of
San Rafael, CA
Reifler, Elizabeth Ann, Law Offices of
Sonoma, CA
Reifler, Margery Evans ....New York, NY
Reifler, Natt O. ....Orlando, FL
Reifler, Stewart ....New York, NY
Reifman & Altman ....Los Angeles, CA
Reifman, David L. ....Chicago, IL
Reifman, Irving P. ....Los Angeles, CA
Reifman, Steven W. ....Scottsdale, AZ
Farmington Hills, MI
Reifman, Suzanne D. ....Washington, DC
Reifschneider, Eric M. ....Palo Alto, CA

Reifsnyder, Daniel A. ....Department of State, Bureau of Oceans, International Environmental & Scientific Affairs, GV
Reifsteck, Edward R. ....Rochester, NY
Reifsteck, Kenneth D. ....Champaign, IL
Reifsteck, Reneé M. ....Chicago, IL
Reifsteck, William E. ....Mount Laurel, NJ
Reifurth, Lawrence M. ....Honolulu, HI
Reig, Linda Pissott ....Morristown, NJ
Reig, Neil H. ....Mount Kisco, NY
Reig, Richard S. ....Springfield, NJ
Reig, Shari C. ....New York, NY
Reigel, Ernest W. ....Charlotte, NC
Reigel, Gregory J. ....Hopkins, MN
Reigel, Julia ....Palo Alto, CA
Reigel, Stanley A. ....Kansas City, MO
Reigel, Susan J. ....Green Bay, WI
Reigert, M. James ....Issaquah, WA
Reighard, Steven W. ....Decatur, GA
Reighart, Charles M. ....Towson, MD
Reigner, Karen McLoughlin ....Atlanta, GA
Reigner, Roger S., Jr. ....Atlanta, GA
Reigstad, Marvin J. ....Hector, MN
Reigstad, Marvin J., P.A. ....Hector, MN
Reihart, Donald L. ....York, PA
Reiher, James C. ....Milwaukee, WI
Reihner, David C. ....Department of Commerce, Patent and Trademark Office, GV
Reihner, George A. ....Harrisburg, PA
Scranton, PA
Reihsen, Gerald J., III ....Dallas, TX
Reik, Jonathan F. ....Vernon, CT
Reik, Rose ....Cincinnati, OH
Reik, Willard J. ....Milwaukee, WI
Reiken, Paul D. ....Shingle Springs, CA
Reiken, Robyn L. ....Bloomfield, NJ
Reiken, Samuel N. ....Parsippany, NJ
New York, NY
Reil, Mary M. ....Cleveland, OH
Reiland, Earl D. ....Minneapolis, MN
Reiland, Hal P. ....Pleasanton, CA
Reiland, Karen S. ....Canton, OH
Reiland, Melinda P. ....Pleasanton, CA
Reiland & Reiland ....Pleasanton, CA
Reiland, Robert N. ....Clarendon Hills, IL
Reilender, Paul E., Jr. ....Frankfort, KY
Reilert, Robert ....Atlantic City, NJ
Reiley, Don C., III
Department of Commerce, Patent and Trademark Office, GV
Reiley, Eldon H. ....San Francisco, CA
Reiley, Julie L.
Commodity Futures Trading Commission, Division of Enforcement, GV
Reiley, Kathleen ....Madison, WI
Reiley, Kimberly A. ....San Francisco, CA
Reiley, R. Martin ....Bedford, PA
Reiley & Reiley ....Bedford, PA
Reiley, William C. ....Pottsville, PA
Reiling, Donald P. ....Albany, OR
Reiling, Donald P., P.C. ....Albany, OR
Reiling, Henry B. ....Boston, MA
Reiling, Richard B ....Dayton, OH
Reiling, Robert C., Jr. ....Lafayette, IN
Reiling, Ronald T. ....Cambridge, MA
Reiling, Teder & Schrier ....Lafayette, IN
Reilley, James W. ....Arlington Heights, IL
Reilley, John B. ....Walnut Creek, CA
Reilley, Martin T. ....Santa Rosa, CA
Reilley, Mary Eileen ....San Francisco, CA
Reilley, Robert J., Jr. ....King Of Prussia, PA
Reilley, Steven S. ....Houston, TX
Reilley, Susan M. ....Buffalo, NY
Reilley, Timothy R. ....Hurst, TX
Reilly, Aileen M. ....Washington, DC
Reilly, Aileen M. ....Orlando, FL
Reilly, Allison Louise ....Waterbury, CT
Reilly, Amy D. ....Dallas, TX
Reilly, Andrew J. ....Media, PA
Reilly, Andrew R. ....Haines City, FL
Reilly, Ann ....Fox Point, WI
Reilly, Anne Elizabeth Sarah
New York, NY
Reilly and Archer ....Toms River, NJ
Reilly, Archer E. ....Columbus, OH
Reilly, Arthur M. ....Ventura, CA
Reilly, Bernard J. ....Wilmington, DE
Reilly, Bernard M. ....Red Bank, NJ
Reilly, Bobbi ....Arlington, TX
Reilly, Brendan C. ....Albany, NY
Reilly, Brendan W. ....Sioux Falls, SD
Reilly, Brennan R. ....Vienna, VA
Reilly, Brent P. ....New York, NY
Reilly, Brian J. ....Raleigh, NC
Reilly, Brian M. ....New York, NY
Reilly, Brian P. ....Red Bank, NJ
Reilly, Carey B. ....Bridgeport, CT
Reilly, Carolyn L. ....San Diego, CA
Reilly, Charles F. ....Providence, RI
Reilly, Charles J. ....Providence, RI
Reilly, Charles P. ....Los Angeles, CA
Reilly, Charles T. ....McHenry, IL
Reilly, Charles V. ....New York, NY
Reilly, Christie N. ....Cincinnati, OH
Reilly, Christine M. ....Stuart, VA
Reilly, Conor D. ....New York, NY
Reilly, Craig C. ....Alexandria, VA
Reilly, D. Brennan ....Houston, TX
Reilly, D. Michael ....Seattle, WA
Reilly, Daniel G. ....Uniontown, PA
Reilly, Daniel M. ....Denver, CO
Reilly, David F. ....Wickford, RI
Reilly, David J. ....Montvale, NJ
Reilly, David J. ....Newark, NJ
Reilly, David J. ....New York, NY
Reilly, David M. ....Stamford, CT
Reilly, David Scott ....Newton, NC
Reilly, David T. ....Mineola, NY

Reilly, Denise D. ....Minneapolis, MN
Reilly, Dennis W. ....Santa Barbara, CA
Reilly, Dónal Eoin ....Boston, MA
Reilly, Donald R. ....Wakefield, MA
Reilly, Douglas L. ....Novato, CA
Reilly, Edgar Bourke ....Chicago, IL
Reilly, Edw. R., Jr. ....New York, NY
Reilly, Edward A. ....New York, NY
Reilly, Edward A., Jr. ....Hartford, CT
Reilly, Edward F. ....St. Louis, MO
Reilly, Edward G., Jr. ....Los Angeles, CA
Reilly, Edward M. ....Boston, MA
Reilly, Eileen A. ....Forty Fort, PA
Reilly, Eileen Anne ....Annapolis, MD
Reilly, Eileen Marquette
La Canada Flintridge, CA
Reilly, Elaine C. ....Wilmington, DE
Reilly, Elizabeth A. ....Akron, OH
Reilly, Ellen ....Englewood, CO
Reilly, Elsie M. ....Southampton, NY
Reilly, Erin R. ....Baltimore, MD
Reilly, Erline A. ....Penacook, NH
Reilly, Eugene A. ....Walpole, MA
Reilly, Francis L.O. ....Fairfield, CT
Reilly, Francis X. ....Barrington, IL
Reilly, Frank B., Jr. ....Newark, NJ
Reilly, Frank E. ....Pittsburgh, PA
Reilly, Frank M. ....Austin, TX
Reilly, Fred ....Haines City, FL
Reilly, George A. ....Darien, CT
Reilly, George F. ....Department of the Navy, Office of the Judge Advocate General, GV
Reilly, George F. ....Minneapolis, MN
Reilly, Gerald D. ....White Plains, NY
Reilly & Goodwin, A Professional Corporation
Vienna, VA
Reilly, Gregory B. ....Roseland, NJ
Reilly, Gregory B., III ....New York, NY
Reilly, G.T. (Tom) ....Dubuque, IA
Reilly, Heather Anne
Plymouth Meeting, PA
Reilly, Heather C. ....Boise, ID
Reilly, Helen Anne ....Massapequa, NY
Reilly, Howard S. ....Poughkeepsie, NY
Reilly, Hugh L. ....Fort Smith, AR
Reilly, J. Donald ....McLean, VA
Reilly, J. Stephen ....Albany, NY
Reilly, James A. ....Great Neck, NY
Reilly, James A. ....Houston, TX
Reilly, James B. ....Hauppauge, NY
Reilly, James C. ....Birmingham, AL
Reilly, James E. ....Boston, MA
Reilly, James H. ....Providence, RI
Reilly, James J. ....Detroit, MI
Reilly, James J. ....Troy, NY
Reilly, James M. ....Chicago, IL
Reilly, James M. ....Albany, NY
Reilly, James R. ....San Francisco, CA
Reilly, James R. ....Troy, NY
Reilly, James R., Jr. ....Irvine, CA
Reilly, James R., Jr. ....Chicago, IL
Reilly, James T. ....Mill Valley, CA
Reilly, James T. ....Washington, DC
Reilly, James T. ....Streator, IL
Reilly, James T. ....Lebanon, PA
Myerstown, PA
Reilly, Jay G. ....Boston, MA
Reilly, Jean ....New York, NY
Reilly, Jean-Marie ....Waukesha, WI
Reilly, Jeffrey M. ....San Diego, CA
Reilly, Jeffrey P. ....Towson, MD
Reilly, Jerrold B. ....Los Angeles, CA
Reilly, Jessica ....Miami, FL
Reilly, John A. ....Ocean Ridge, FL
Reilly, John B. ....Baltimore, MD
Reilly, John B. ....Warwick, RI
Reilly, John C. ....New York, NY
Reilly, John E. ....Denver, CO
Reilly, John E. ....Hicksville, NY
Reilly, John E. ....New Hyde Park, NY
Reilly, John F. ....Morristown, NJ
Reilly, John F. ....Hauppauge, NY
Reilly, John F. ....Philadelphia, PA
Reilly, John F. X. ....Media, PA
Reilly, John G. ....Houston, TX
Reilly, John H., Jr. ....New York, NY
Reilly, John J. ....Newark, NJ
Reilly, John J. ....Mineola, NY
Reilly, John J. ....New York, NY
Reilly, John J. ....Columbus, OH
Reilly, John Kevin ....New York, NY
Reilly, John M. ....Boston, MA
Reilly, John M. C. ....Torrance, CA
Reilly, John P. ....Marlborough, MA
Reilly, John P. ....Detroit, MI
Reilly, John P. ....Toms River, NJ
Reilly, John P. ....Greensboro, NC
Reilly, John Patrick ....Newark, NJ
Reilly, John R. ....Washington, DC
Reilly, John W. ....Honolulu, HI
Reilly, Joseph A., Jr. ....Houma, LA
Reilly, J. P., Jr. ....Cherry Hill, NJ
Reilly, Judith C. ....Northvale, NJ
Reilly, Judith M. ....New York, NY
Reilly, Karen ....New London, CT
Reilly, Karen E. ....Minneapolis, MN
Reilly, Katherine B. ....San Francisco, CA
Reilly, Kathleen A. ....Los Angeles, CA
Reilly, Kathleen C.
Pension Benefit Guaranty Corporation, Office of the General Counsel, GV
Reilly, Kathleen M. ....Buffalo, NY
Reilly, Kathleen M., Law Offices of
Kearny, NJ
Reilly, Kathleen McGeehin ....Washington, DC
Reilly, Kelly B. ....Milwaukee, WI
Reilly, Kenneth F. ....Montgomery, TX
Reilly, Kenneth J. ....Miami, FL

Reilly, Kevin A. ....New York, NY
Reilly, Kevin C. ....New York, NY
Reilly, Kevin F. ....Alexandria, VA
Reilly, Kevin M. ....Syracuse, NY
Reilly, Kevin Michael ....Washington, DC
Reilly, Kevin Olds ....Port Jefferson, NY
Reilly, Kevin V. ....Santa Fe, NM
Reilly, Kirk W. ....Minneapolis, MN
Reilly, Laura A. ....Washington, DC
Reilly, Laura B. ....Denver, CO
Reilly, Laura J. ....Englewood, CO
Reilly Law Associates, Inc.
Providence, RI
Reilly, Lawrence F. ....Greenwich, CT
Reilly, Lawrence F. ....Morristown, NJ
Reilly, Lawrence H. ....Darien, CT
Reilly, Like and Tenety ....Babylon, NY
Reilly, Lisa E. ....Pelham, NY
Reilly, Lisa W. ....Fort Lauderdale, FL
Reilly, Madelyn Anne ....Pittsburgh, PA
Reilly, Marcos ....Chicago, IL
Reilly, Margaret A. ....North Chelmsford, MA
Reilly, Margaret D. ....New York, NY
Reilly, Margaret T. ....San Francisco, CA
Reilly, Marie Sambor ....Philadelphia, PA
Reilly, Marie T. ....Columbia, SC
Reilly, Marina A. ....Norristown, PA
Reilly, Mark ....Pittsburgh, PA
Reilly, Mark C. ....Newtown, PA
Reilly, Mark E. ....Boston, MA
Reilly, Mary Ellen ....Collingswood, NJ
Philadelphia, PA
Reilly, Mary Jo ....Philadelphia, PA
Reilly, Mary T. ....New York, NY
Reilly, Maryanne ....Santa Fe, NM
Reilly, Matthew J. ....Washington, DC
Reilly, Maureen E. ....Philadelphia, PA
Reilly, Maureen E. ....Boston, MA
Reilly, Maureen Pulte ....Detroit, MI
Reilly, Michael ....Boston, MA
Reilly, Michael ....New York, NY
Reilly, Michael E. ....Buffalo, NY
Reilly, Michael F., Jr. ....Jersey City, NJ
Reilly, Michael G. ....Council Bluffs, IA
Reilly, Michael J. ....Hartford, CT
Reilly, Michael J. ....Troy, MI
Reilly, Michael James ....Lansing, MI
Reilly, Michael K. ....Wilmington, DE
Reilly, Michael T. ....Mineola, NY
Reilly, Michael W. ....Omaha, NE
Reilly, Michele Kozlowicz
Bloomfield Hills, MI
Reilly, Nancy Goering ....St. Paul, MN
Reilly, Ned P., (A Professional Corporation)
Santa Ana, CA
Reilly, Nina K. ....Houston, TX
Reilly, Oliver & Olsen, Ltd. ....Wickford, RI
Reilly, Patricia E. ....New Haven, CT
Reilly, Patricia F. ....Dallas, TX
Reilly, Patricia Mary ....Red Bank, NJ
Reilly, Patrick A. ....New York, NY
Reilly, Patrick D. ....Minneapolis, MN
Reilly, Patrick J. ....Seward, AK
Reilly, Patrick J. ....Las Vegas, NV
Reilly, Patrick J. ....Allentown, PA
Reilly, Patrick J. ....North Myrtle Beach, SC
Reilly, Patrick, Jr. ....Galveston, TX
Reilly, Patrick M. ....White Plains, NY
Reilly, Patrick V. ....Springfield, IL
Reilly, Patrick W.
Department of Transportation, Federal Transit Administration, GV
Reilly, Patty
Federal Labor Relations Authority, Office of the Chair, GV
Reilly, Paul A. ....Huntington Beach, CA
Reilly, Paul F. ....Mukwonago, WI
Waukesha, WI
Reilly, Paul H. ....Mount Vernon, WA
Reilly, Paul J. ....Chicago, IL
Reilly, Paul J. ....New York, NY
Reilly, Paulina M. ....Hyannis, MA
Reilly, Peter B. ....New Haven, CT
Reilly, Peter E. ....Clifton Park, NY
Reilly, Peter J. ....Phoenix, AZ
Reilly, Peter K. ....Treasury Department, Internal Revenue Service, GV
Reilly, Peter M. J. ....Islip, NY
Reilly, Peter M. J., Jr. ....Islip, NY
Reilly, Peter R. ....Washington, DC
Reilly, Peter R. ....Commission on Civil Rights, Office of the General Counsel, GV
Reilly, Petersen & Hannan, P.L.C.
Council Bluffs, IA
Reilly, Petrea Knudsen ....Seattle, WA
Reilly & Purcell, P.C. ....Denver, CO
Reilly, R. Stephen ....Albany, NY
Reilly, R. William ....Minneapolis, MN
Reilly & Reilly ....Southampton, NY
Reilly and Reilly, P.C. ....New Haven, CT
Reilly, Richard E. ....Harrisburg, PA
Reilly, Richard E. ....Milwaukee, WI
Reilly, Richard G., Jr. ....Syracuse, NY
Reilly, Richard J., Jr. ....New York, NY
Reilly, Richard M. ....Boston, MA
Reilly, Richard R. ....New York, NY
Reilly, Richard R. ....York, PA
Reilly, Robert J. D. ....New York, NY
Reilly, Robert R., Jr. ....Raleigh, NC
Reilly, Rosemary G. ....Palo Alto, CA
Reilly, Sally S. ....Birmingham, AL
Reilly, Sara S. ....Houston, TX
Reilly, Sean M. ....Washington, DC
Reilly, Sean M. ....Philadelphia, PA
Reilly, Shawn N. ....Mukwonago, WI
Waukesha, WI
Reilly, Shawn P. ....Abington, MA
Reilly, Sheila M. ....Chicago, IL

Reilly, Stephanie Nicoll ....Redmond, WA
Reilly, Stephen C. ....Tallahassee, FL
Reilly, Stephen C. ....Boston, MA
Reilly, Stephen M.
Department of Agriculture, Office of the General Counsel, GV
Reilly, Stephen M. ....Springfield, MA
Reilly, Stephen R. ....Louisville, KY
Reilly, Steven M. ....Lawrenceville, GA
Reilly, Stuart J. ....Phoenix, AZ
Reilly, Stuart J., P.C. ....Glendale, AZ
Phoenix, AZ
Scottsdale, AZ
Reilly, Susan B. ....Department of Justice, Civil Rights Division, GV
Reilly, Susann Reising
Securities and Exchange Commission, Division of Corporation Finance, GV
Reilly, Tara ....Redlands, CA
Reilly, Terence Patrick ....Boston, MA
Reilly, Terrance James ....Philadelphia, PA
Reilly, Terri A. ....Scottsdale, AZ
Aliso Viejo, CA
San Diego, CA
Westlake Village, CA
Reilly, Thomas A. ....Laguna Beach, CA
Reilly, Thomas E. ....Atlanta, GA
Reilly, Thomas E. ....Elmira, NY
Reilly, Thomas E. ....Pittsburgh, PA
Reilly, Thomas E., Jr. ....Boston, MA
Reilly, Thomas E., Jr. ....Allentown, PA
Reilly, Thomas F. ....Cambridge, MA
Reilly, Thomas F. ....Colonia, NJ
Philadelphia, PA
Reilly, Thomas G. ....Boston, MA
Reilly, Thomas H. ....Irvine, CA
Reilly, Thomas H. ....Los Angeles, CA
Reilly, Thomas J. ....Phoenix, AZ
Reilly, Thomas J. ....Des Moines, IA
Reilly, Thomas J., Jr. ....Providence, RI
Reilly, Thomas K. ....White Plains, NY
Reilly, Thomas P. ....Oakland, CA
Reilly, Thomas S. ....New York, NY
Reilly, Thomas W. ....Annandale, VA
Reilly, Tim ....St. Petersburg, FL
Reilly, Timothy A. ....Springfield, MA
Reilly, Timothy E. ....Colorado Springs, CO
Reilly, Timothy J. ....Latham, NY
Reilly, Timothy P. ....Cincinnati, OH
Reilly, Trudy P. ....Boston, MA
Reilly, Vincent E. ....Morristown, NJ
Reilly, Vincent F. ....Westmont, NJ
Philadelphia, PA
Reilly, Vincent J., Jr. ....Schenectady, NY
Reilly, Vincent P. ....Northbrook, IL
Reilly, Vincent P. ....Newtown Square, PA
Reilly, Virginia A. ....New York, NY
Reilly, William A., II ....Rockford, IL
Reilly, William B. ....San Francisco, CA
Reilly, William F. ....New York, NY
Reilly, William F. ....Waukesha, WI
Reilly, William F., Jr. ....Millville, NJ
Reilly, William G., Jr. ....Murray Hill, NJ
Reilly, William J. ....Mineola, NY
Reilly, William Leonard ....Ellijay, GA
Reilly, William Leonard, P.C. ....Ellijay, GA
Reilly, William P. ....New York, NY
Reilly, William T. ....Northville, MI
Reilly, William T. ....Newark, NJ
Reilly, Wm. B. ....Buffalo, NY
Reilly, Wolfson, Sheffey, Schrum and Lundberg
Lebanon, PA
Myerstown, PA
Reilly-Gruhn, Laurie K. ....Cedar Rapids, IA
Reilly-Shefcik, Patricia A. ....Hamilton, OH
Reily, David H. ....Los Angeles, CA
Reily, James ....Oceanside, NY
Reily & Jeffery LLP ....Los Angeles, CA
Reily, Patrick M. ....Destin, FL
Reim, Adrienne B. ....Marlton, NJ
Reim, Paul E. ....Lincoln City, OR
Reiman, Arvo ....New York, NY
Reiman & Bayaz, P.C. ....Denver, CO
Reiman, Cathy S. ....Naples, FL
Reiman, David L. ....Lake Butler, FL
Reiman, Donald L. ....Parma Heights, OH
Reiman, James A. ....Northbrook, IL
Reiman, Jeff ....Denver, CO
Reiman, Kelly ....Denver, CO
Reiman, Pamela S. ....Berkeley Springs, WV
Reiman, Richard J. ....New York, NY
Reiman, Robert K. ....Anchorage, AK
Reiman, Ronnie D. ....New York, NY
Reimann, Curt D. ....Tucson, AZ
Reimann, David W. ....Los Angeles, CA
Reimann, Eric L. ....Grand Island, NY
Reimann, Kathryn ....Monterey, CA
Reimann, Kathryn S. ....New York, NY
Reimann, Lee B. ....Lansing, MI
Reimann, Nancy Baldwin
Los Angeles, CA
Reimann, Nicole M. ....Philadelphia, PA
Reimann, Robert K. ....Boulder, CO
Reimche, Laura A. ....Sacramento, CA
Reimel, Miriam A. ....Bristol, PA
Reimel-Campbell, Susan Y. ....Carlsbad, CA
Reimer, B. LaVonne ....Portland, OR
Reimer, Bill M. ....San Antonio, TX
Reimer, Brian M.
United States Postal Service, Law Department, GV
Reimer, Charles R. ....Wichita, KS
Reimer, Craig E. ....Chicago, IL
Reimer, Daniel S. ....Denver, CO
Washington, DC
Reimer, David H. ....Hollywood, FL
Reimer, Dennis ....Twinsburg, OH
Reimer, Douglas M. ....Chicago, IL

Reimer, Drew A. ... Denver, CO
Reimer, Eric R. ... Los Angeles, CA
Reimer, Gary B. ... Colorado Springs, CO
Reimer, Juliana K. ... Oklahoma City, OK
Reimer, Leah M. ... Windsor, CT
Reimer, Lisa J. ... Hartford, CT
Reimer, Lohman & Reitz ... Denison, IA
Reimer, Mark S. ... Deerfield, IL
Reimer, Melissa L. ... Bellingham, WA
Reimer, Michael J. ... South Orange, NJ
Reimer, Nancy M. ... Boston, MA
Reimer, P. Renée ... Albuquerque, NM
Reimer, R. Galen ... Albuquerque, NM
Reimer, Richard H. ... New York, NY
Reimer, Rita Ann
Federal Election Commission, Office of the General Counsel, GV
Reimer, Robert A. ... Martinez, GA
Reimer, Robert C. ... Denison, IA
Reimer, Russell H. ... Albany, NY
Reimer, Susan M. ... Augusta, GA
Reimer, Troy A. ... Dallas, TX
Reimer, Warren L. ... Norfolk, NE
Reimer, Wendy Gerard ... Los Angeles, CA
Reimer, Wendy K. ... San Francisco, CA
Reimers, Alan G. ... Saginaw, MI
Reimers, Charles H. ... Chicago, IL
Reimers, Frank H. ... Montclair, NJ
Reimers, Wade A. ... Pierre, SD
Reimert, Gretchen C. ... Salinas, CA
Reimondo, Robert N. ... Crawfordsville, IN
Reimonenq, Simeon Bernard, Jr.
New Orleans, LA
Reimus, William S. ... Carlsbad, CA
Rein, Alan John ... White Plains, NY
Rein, Barry D. ... New York, NY
Rein, Bert W. ... Washington, DC
Rein, Catherine A. ... New York, NY
Rein, Cory D. ... Everett, WA
Rein, David L., Jr. ... Kansas City, MO
Rein, David M. J. ...
United States Court Of Appeals For The Federal Circuit, GV
New York, NY
Rein, Douglas J. ... San Diego, CA
Rein, Eric S. ... Chicago, IL
Rein, Frederick H. ... New York, NY
Rein, Gerald A. ... Moses Lake, WA
Spokane, WA
Rein, H. Lisa ... Seattle, WA
Rein, Irwin R., A Prof. Corp.
West Orange, NJ
Rein, Jan Ellen ... Sacramento, CA
Rein, Jeff ... Albuquerque, NM
Rein, Jill D. ... Chicago, IL
Rein, Kathleen W. ... Pratt, KS
Rein, Linda S. ... New York, NY
Rein, Martin L. ... New York, NY
Rein, Michael A. ... Modesto, CA
Rein, Paul L. ... Oakland, CA
Rein, Phillip A. ... Colorado Springs, CO
Rein & Rein ... Modesto, CA
Rein, Robert S. ... Los Angeles, CA
Rein, Ryan D. ... Seattle, WA
Rein, Samuel ... New York, NY
Rein, Scott J. ... Los Angeles, CA
Rein, Stanley M. ... Minneapolis, MN
Rein, Steven ... West Hills, CA
Rein, Teresa Vig ... Modesto, CA
Rein, Thomas D. ... Chicago, IL
Rein, William C. ... Topeka, KS
Reina, Brett M. ... Morristown, NJ
Reina, C. Douglas ... Bound Brook, NJ
Reina, Frank C. ... Rochester, NY
Reina, J. Joseph ... Dallas, TX
Reina, Joseph F. ... Lancaster, NY
Reina, Kevin R ... Brooklyn, NY
Reina, Lawrence J. ... New York, NY
Reina, Leonard P. ... Naples, FL
Reina, Richard P. ... Denham Springs, LA
Reinach, Alan J. ... Fillmore, CA
Reinach, Carolyn S. ... Great Neck, NY
Reinan, Jerome M. 'Jay' ... Denver, CO
Reinard, David J. ... Los Angeles, CA
Reinarts, Timothy J. ... Stockton, CA
Reinbach, Sheree D. ... New York, NY
Reinberg, Deborah B. ... Los Angeles, CA
Reinberg, Ronald I. ... Santa Cruz, CA
Reinbold, Eugene J. ... Pittsburgh, PA
Reinbold, Gary W. ... Chicago, IL
Reinbold, Rodney M. ... Okanogan, WA
Reinbolt, Jacob C. ... San Diego, CA
Reinbolt, Steven D. ... Toledo, OH
Reincke, Janet Woehl ... Norfolk, VA
Reincke, Julie Harrison ... Eaton Rapids, MI
Reindel, F. William ... New York, NY
Reindel, Roberta Berman ... Mamaroneck, NY
Reinders, Bruce E. ... Traer, IA
Reindl, Gayle A. ... Indianapolis, IN
Reindl, Kimberly S. ... Washington, DC
Reindollar, Michael W. ... Dallas, TX
Reine, Alton J., Jr. ... Baton Rouge, LA
Reine, Willard C. ... Jefferson City, MO
Reineck, William R., Sr. ... Baltimore, MD
Reinecke, Barbra ... Encino, CA
Reinecke & Daily ... Irvine, CA
Reinecke, David W. ... Madison, WI
Reinecke, Frederick M. ... Louisville, KY
Reinecke, Mark Gregory ... Bend, OR
Reinecke, Mike G. ... Milwaukee, WI
Reinecke, Petra M. ... San Francisco, CA
Reinecke, Thomas G. ... Irvine, CA
Reinecke, Wm. L. ... Lancaster, WI
Reineke & Associates, P.A. ... Tampa, FL
Reineke, Beth Gilmore ... Tampa, FL
Reineke, Juliana Webber ... Cleveland, OH
Reineke, Stephen L. ... Central Valley, NY
Reinemann, Michael R. ... Boston, MA

Reinen, Jeffrey W. ... New Milford, CT
Reiner, Alan J. ... Oklahoma City, OK
Reiner, Alissa S. ... New York, NY
Reiner, Andrew E. ... Los Angeles, CA
Reiner, Boccher & Pollak, P.C.
Morristown, NJ
Reiner and Bouffard ... Kittery, ME
Reiner, Bryan ... Los Angeles, CA
Reiner, Burton J. ... Washington, DC
Reiner, Christine S. ... Bloomfield Hills, MI
Reiner, Dale Vincent ... Atlanta, GA
Reiner, David B. ... Fairfax Station, VA
Reiner, Donald F. ... Centereach, NY
Reiner, Edward J. ... New York, NY
Reiner, Eliot M. ... Sacramento, CA
Reiner, Gary H. ... Kittery, ME
Reiner, Glenn A. ... New York, NY
Reiner, Howard M. ... Houston, TX
Reiner, Ira K. ... Los Angeles, CA
Reiner, Irving ... Windsor Locks, CT
Reiner, Jacqueline M. ... Richmond, VA
Reiner, Jan Allen ... New York, NY
Reiner, Jeffrey A. ... New York, NY
Reiner, Jeffrey L. ... Morristown, NJ
Reiner, John ... Los Angeles, CA
Reiner, John J. ... Los Angeles, CA
Reiner, John Paul ... New York, NY
Reiner, John Peter ... New York, NY
Reiner, Kevin L. ... New York, NY
Reiner, Lisa ... Brooklyn, NY
Reiner, Lori K. ... Haddon Heights, NJ
Philadelphia, PA
Reiner, Marc S. ... New York, NY
Reiner, Mary E. ... New York, NY
Reiner, Michael D. ... Farmington, CT
Reiner, Michael R. ... New York, NY
Reiner, Miles S. ... New York, NY
Reiner, Nancy B. ... Boston, MA
Reiner, Paul A. ... San Francisco, CA
Reiner, Paul A. ... New York, NY
Reiner, Reiner and Reiner, LLP
New York, NY
Reiner, Richard C. ... New Rochelle, NY
Reiner, Robert M. ... Washington, DC
Reiner, Russell ... Redding, CA
Reiner, Samuel B., II ... Miami, FL
Reiner, Simpson & Kennedy ... Redding, CA
Reiner, Stephen R. ... New York, NY
Reiner, Valentina ... Sacramento, CA
Reinerman, Margaret ... Portland, OR
Reiners, Jennifer ... Chicago, IL
Reiners, Paul R. ... Canton, OH
Reinert, Albert C. ... Saginaw, MI
Reinert, Anthony ... Miami, FL
Reinert, Anton Richard ... Boston, MA
Reinert, Bernard A. ... St. Louis, MO
Reinert, Cynthia ... Indianapolis, IN
Reinert, Dawn W. ... Omaha, NE
Reinert, James M. ... Kingston, PA
Reinert, James P. ... St. Louis, MO
Reinert, John E. ... Northbrook, IL
Reinert, Joseph A. ... Waterbury, VT
Reinert, Michael C. ... Saginaw, MI
Reinert, Michael L. ... New York, NY
Reinert, Peter E. ... Orlando, FL
Reinert and Reinert, P.C. ... Saginaw, MI
Reinert & Rourke, P.C. ... St. Louis, MO
Reinert, Thomas E., Jr. ... Washington, DC
Reinert, Trent D. ... Council Bluffs, IA
Reinertson, Robert J. ... Wausau, WI
Reines, Edward ... Menlo Park, CA
Reiness, Steven M. ... Washington, DC
Reiney, C. William ... Jacksonville, FL
Reinfeld, Albert I. ... South Orange, NJ
Reinfeld, Joel J. ... Ridgewood, NJ
Reinfeld, Lawrence A. ... Philadelphia, PA
Reinfranck, James D. ... Northbrook, IL
Reinfranck, Marcy Weaver
Northbrook, IL
Reinfurt, Susan ... Watervliet, NY
Reing, Steven H. ... New York, NY
Reingen, Marsha L. ... Tempe, AZ
Reinglass, Michelle A. ... Laguna Hills, CA
Reingold, Abraham ... Brooklyn, NY
Reingold, Arvin H. ... Chattanooga, TN
Reingold, Arvin H., P.C. ... Chattanooga, TN
Reingold, Barry J. ... Washington, DC
Reingold, Daniel ... Riverdale, NY
Reingold, Gordon A. ... Northbrook, IL
Reingold, Irwin ... New York, NY
Reingold, Jesse D. ... New York, NY
Reingold, Julia Ann ... North Hollywood, CA
Reingold, Mark S. ... Rochester, NY
Reingold, Marvin D. ... Bronx, NY
Larchmont, NY
Reingold, Melinda L. ... McLean, VA
Reingold, Paul D. ... Ann Arbor, MI
Reingold, Sara L. ... Northbrook, IL
Reingold, Steven C. ... Boston, MA
Reingold, Suzy A. ... New York, NY
Reinhalter, Mark A. ... Department of Labor, Office of the Solicitor, GV
Reinhard, Ann K. ... Columbus, OH
Reinhard & Barnett, P.C. ... Arlington, TX
Fort Worth, TX
Reinhard, Christine E. ... San Antonio, TX
Reinhard Co., Dean G., L.P.A.
Columbus, OH
Reinhard, Constance Whyte
Hoffman Estates, IL
Reinhard, David J. ... Rockford, IL
Reinhard, Dean G. ... Columbus, OH
Reinhard, Eric D. ... Farmington, MO
Reinhard, G. Douglas ... Cumberland, MD
Reinhard, James R. ... Hannibal, MO
New London, MO
Perry, MO
Reinhard, Jeffery P. ... St. Louis, MO

Reinhard, Kenneth E. ... New York, NY
Reinhard, Leland A. ... Arlington, TX
Reinhard, Rawn Howard ... Chicago, IL
Reinhard, Sanford N., (P.A.)
North Miami Beach, FL
Reinhard, Scott A. ... Park Falls, WI
Phillips, WI
Reinhard, Steven I. ... Raleigh, NC
Reinhard, Theodore ... Albany, NY
Reinhard, Walter G. ... Somerville, NJ
Reinhardsen, James S. ... Seattle, WA
Reinhardt & Anderson ... St. Paul, MN
Reinhardt, Andrew J. ... Richmond, VA
Reinhardt, Benjamin M., (A Prof. Law Corp.)
Palm Desert, CA
Reinhardt, Bob ... Tifton, GA
Reinhardt, Cathy A. ... Lawrence, KS
Reinhardt, Charles A., Jr. ... Durham, NC
Reinhardt, Charles H., Jr. ... Uniondale, NY
Reinhardt, Cheryl L. ... Overland Park, KS
Reinhardt, Christine ... New York, NY
Reinhardt, Craig R. ... Prospect, KY
Reinhardt, Daniel S. ... Atlanta, GA
Reinhardt, Denise ... Newark, NJ
Reinhardt, Edward B, Jr ... Albuquerque, NM
Reinhardt, Eileen ... Tampa, FL
Reinhardt, Elinor Karen ... New York, NY
Reinhardt, Eric C. ... Winter Garden, FL
Reinhardt, Erik J. ... Lapeer, MI
Reinhardt, George ... Grangeville, ID
Reinhardt, George R., Jr. ... Tifton, GA
Reinhardt, J. Alec ... Findlay, OH
Reinhardt, J. Randall ... Lexington, KY
Reinhardt, Jane C. ... Islandia, NY
Reinhardt, Jean Mary ... Cohoes, NY
Reinhardt, Joe A., III ... Maitland, FL
Reinhardt, John D. ... Fairfax, VA
Reinhardt, John R. ... Tifton, GA
Reinhardt, Joseph H. ... Boston, MA
Reinhardt, Julie A. ... Erlanger, KY
Reinhardt, LeRoy J. ... Kerman, CA
Reinhardt, Mark ... St. Paul, MN
Reinhardt, Mark A. ... Chicago, IL
Reinhardt, Mark W. ... Denver, CO
Reinhardt, Michael ... Akron, NY
Reinhardt, Michael J. ... New York, NY
Reinhardt, Michael R. ... Boston, MA
Reinhardt, Michael W. ... Seattle, WA
Reinhardt, Mona R. ... Great Falls, VA
Reinhardt, Morgan & Isaacs ... Lexington, KY
Reinhardt, Nancy ... San Bernardino, CA
Reinhardt, Paul H. ... Grand Rapids, MI
Reinhardt, Peter M. ... Menomonie, WI
Reinhardt, R. Craig ... Lexington, KY
Reinhardt, Randall E. ... Milwaukee, WI
Reinhardt, Robert L. ... El Paso, TX
Reinhardt, Sarah J. ... Albuquerque, NM
Reinhardt & Schachter, P.C. ... Newark, NJ
Reinhardt, Stephanie A. ... Great Falls, MT
Reinhardt, Stephen ... Los Angeles, CA
Reinhardt, Steven ... Southbury, CT
Reinhardt, Whitley, Wilmot & Summerlin, P.C. ... Tifton, GA
Reinhardt, William D, II ... Tifton, GA
Reinhardt, William H., Jr. ... Metairie, LA
Reinhardt, William H., Jr., A P.L.C.
Metairie, LA
New Orleans, LA
Reinhart, Andrew W. ... Pittsburgh, PA
Reinhart, Barbara O'Neill ... Stroudsburg, PA
Reinhart, Boerner, Van Deuren, Norris & Rieselbach, P.C. ... Denver, CO
Madison, WI
Milwaukee, WI
Reinhart, Douglas S. ... Baltimore, MD
Reinhart, Gail D.
Federal Labor Relations Authority, Authority Member Staff, GV
Reinhart, Harry R. ... Columbus, OH
Reinhart, James C. ... Portland, OR
Reinhart, John E. ... San Antonio, TX
Reinhart, John J. ... Detroit, MI
Reinhart, Joseph K. ... Pittsburgh, PA
Reinhart, Joseph L. ... Portland, OR
Reinhart, Lulita ... Medina, OH
Reinhart, Peter S. ... Red Bank, NJ
Reinhart, Richard P. ... Orlando, FL
Reinhart, Robert H. ... Cumberland, MD
Reinhart, Robert R., Jr. ... Minneapolis, MN
Reinhart, Tara Lee ... Washington, DC
Reinhart, William J. ... New York, NY
Reinhart, William M. ... Philadelphia, PA
Reinhartsen, Laurence J. ... Portland, ME
Reinharz, Alfred ... Baldwin, NY
Reinharz, Mark N. ... Mineola, NY
New York, NY
Reinharz & Nessel ... Baldwin, NY
Reinharz, Peter ... New York, NY
Reinheimer, Frank W. ... Port Clinton, OH
Reinheimer, James L. ... Port Clinton, OH
Reinheimer & Krug ... Toms River, NJ
Reinheimer, Kurt E. ... Toms River, NJ
Reinheimer, Linda S. ... Toms River, NJ
Reinheimer & Reinheimer ... Port Clinton, OH
Reinheitz, Amie S. ... New York, NY
Reinherdt, Elizabeth S. ... Boston, MA
Reinherz & Dunn ... Malden, MA
Reinherz, Robert N. ... Philadelphia, PA
Reinhold, Barbara A. ... Portage, WI
Reinhold, Charles ... Phoenix, AZ
Reinhold, Dennis J. ... Baltimore, MD
Reinhold, Kent T. ... Phoenix, AZ
Reinhold, Kristin R. ... Harrisburg, PA
Reinhold, Lawrence G.
Huntington Woods, MI
Reinhold, Lawrence James ... El Monte, CA
Reinhold, Marianne ... Los Angeles, CA
Reinhold, Melissa L. ... Los Angeles, CA

Reinhold, Rhonda L. ... Barrow, AK
Reinhold, Richard L. ... New York, NY
Reinhold, Robert J. ... St. Louis, MO
Reinholdt, Carolyn ... San Francisco, CA
Reinholdt, Richard T. ... Madison, WI
Reinholdtsen, Kelly ... Seattle, WA
Reinholm, Michael T. ... Birmingham, MI
Reinholtsen, Dale A. ... Eureka, CA
Reinholtsen, Dennis Craig ... Eureka, CA
Reinholtz, Jack R. ... Long Beach, CA
Reinicke, Eric D. ... Platteville, WI
Reinicke, Stephanie A., P.A. ... Sarasota, FL
Reinicke, Stephanie Ann ... Sarasota, FL
Reiniers, John B. ... Spring Hill, FL
Reinig, Timothy W. ... New York, NY
Reiniger, Douglas Haigh ... New York, NY
Reiniger, George C. ... Ossining, NY
Reinikka, Leo A. ... Beaverton, OR
Reining, Robert J. ... New York, NY
Reininga, J. Chris ... Indianapolis, IN
Reininger, Steven R. ... Coral Gables, FL
Reinis, Mitchell N. ... Los Angeles, CA
Reinis & Reinis ... Los Angeles, CA
Reinis, Richard G. ... Los Angeles, CA
Reinisch, Morris N. ... Danbury, CT
Reinisch, Steven R. ... Portland, OR
Reinish, Richard L., (P.C.) ... Chicago, IL
Reinjohn, Richard G. ... Los Angeles, CA
Reinjohn, Richard G., P.C.
Los Angeles, CA
Reinke, Alan M. ... San Francisco, CA
Reinke, Ann E. ... Milwaukee, WI
Reinke, Brent A. ... Los Angeles, CA
Reinke, Cecil E. ... Portland, OR
Reinke, Colleen J. ... Madison, WI
Reinke, Donald C. ... Oakland, CA
Reinke, Fred W. ... Washington, DC
Reinke, Jean M. ... Calabasas, CA
Reinke, Jennifer M. ... Pittsburgh, PA
Reinke, Joan Mary ... Evanston, IL
Reinke, John J. ... New York, NY
Reinke, Joseph J. ... Oklahoma City, OK
Reinke, Mark A. ... Littleton, CO
Reinke, Mark W. ... Chicago, IL
Reinke, Robert L. ... Richmond, IN
Reinke, Stefan M. ... Honolulu, HI
Reinke, Wayne F. ... Albany, NY
Reinke, William J. ... South Bend, IN
Reinken, Eric L. ... Stamford, CT
Reinken, Janis J. ... Austin, TX
Reinken, Patrick A. ... Minneapolis, MN
Reinken, W. Michael ... Spokane, WA
Reinker, Randall J. ... St. Louis, MO
Reinker, Robb F. ... Cleveland, OH
Reinker, Susan M. ... Cleveland, OH
Reinking, Teresa A. ... Kansas City, MO
Reinking, William H. ... Lisle, IL
Reinl, Raymond B. ... Furlong, PA
Reinlieb, Laurence ... New York, NY
Reinman, James L. ... Melbourne, FL
Reinman, John W. ... Jersey City, NJ
Reinman & Wattwood, A Professional Association ... Melbourne, FL
Reinmiller, Catherine A.
Kansas City, MO
Reinmiller, David H. ... Kansas City, MO
Reinmiller, Nathan R. ... Las Vegas, NV
Reinnoldt, Donald H. ... Carmichael, CA
Reino, Donald J. ... Lakewood, CA
Reino, Michael L. ... Santa Barbara, CA
Reinoehl, John H. ... Bath, MI
Reinoso, Bruce D. ... Buffalo, NY
Reinoso, Marybel ... West Palm Beach, FL
Reinowski, Leonard E. ... Mount Clemens, MI
Reinsch, Diane M. ... Moline, IL
Reinsch, Donald G. ... Salina, KS
Reinsch, Gayle S. ... Ponte Vedra Beach, FL
Reinsch, Heather L. ... St. Louis, MO
Reinsch, Lyle O. ... Phoenix, AZ
Reinsch, Margaret J. ... Augusta, ME
Reinsch, Mark A. ... Jacksonville, FL
Reinsch & Slattery, P.C. ... Louisville, NE
Plattsmouth, NE
Reinsch, William R. ... Louisville, NE
Plattsmouth, NE
Reinschmidt, David L. ... Sioux City, IA
Reinschreiber, M. Robert, Jr.
Cardiff-By-The-Sea, CA
Reinsdorf, Judith A. ... St. Louis, MO
Reinsel, Ronald E. ... Phoenix, AZ
Reinsel, Steven M. ... Pittsburgh, PA
Reinshagen, Kendra ... Chicago, IL
Reinsma, Thomas R. ... Grand Haven, MI
Reinsmith, R. William ... Hartford, CT
Reinstein, Alan L. ... Chicago, IL
Reinstein, Amy Melissa ... Brooklyn, NY
Reinstein, Arthur ... Chicago, IL
Reinstein & Calkins, A Professional Law Corporation ... Los Angeles, CA
Reinstein, Eric ... New York, NY
Reinstein, Ezra J. ... New York, NY
Reinstein, Howard ... Brighton, CO
Reinstein, Joel ... Boca Raton, FL
Reinstein, John ... Boston, MA
Reinstein, Lowell ... Los Angeles, CA
Reinstein, Paul J. ... Camp Springs, MD
Reinstein, Paul M. ... New York, NY
Reinstein, Philip T. ... Northbrook, IL
Reinstein, Richard A. ... New York, NY
Reinstein, Ronald S. ... Phoenix, AZ
Reinstein, Sanford M. ... Miami, FL
Reinstein & Sherman ... Northbrook, IL
Reinstein, Todd Russell, (P.C.)
Los Angeles, CA
Reinstine, Franklin ... Jacksonville, FL
Reinstine, Reinstine & Panken
Jacksonville, FL
Reinstra, L. R. ... New Richmond, WI

Reinstra, Mark L. ... **Palo Alto, CA**
Reinstra, Susan Pasquinelli ... **Palo Alto, CA**
Reinsurance Counsel, Law Corporation
Pasadena, CA
Reinthaler, Richard W. ... **New York, NY**
Reintjes, David C. ... **Fort Worth, TX**
Reintzel, Warren A. ... Philadelphia, PA
Reinwald, Arthur B. ... **Honolulu, HI**
Reinwald, Charles A. ... Scarsdale, NY
Reinwald, O'Connor & Playdon
Honolulu, HI
Reinwasser, Louis B. ... **Lansing, MI**
Reioux, Karen P. ... Eagan, MN
Reis, Alan B. ... New York, NY
Reis, Allen J. ... **Columbus, OH**
Reis, Artis I. Van Roekel, Ms.
Des Moines, IA
Reis, Barbara ... Coral Gables, FL
Reis, Brian H. ... New York, NY
Reis, Bryan J., (P.A.)
Hot Springs National Park, AR
Hot Springs Village, AR
Reis, C. Scott ... Baton Rouge, LA
Reis, Catherine H. ... Carmel, IN
Reis, Charles E., IV ... **St. Louis, MO**
Reis, Charles R. ... **Pittsburgh, PA**
Reis, Christopher ... **Rutland, VT**
Reis, Constance Shipe ... St. Louis, MO
Reis, David J. ... **San Francisco, CA**
Reis, David S. ... Chicago, IL
Reis, Dennis P. ... **Milwaukee, WI**
Reis, Donald J. ... Las Vegas, NV
Reis, Edward Joseph ... Oro Valley, AZ
Reis, Edwin J. ... Bethesda, MD
Reis, Eric G. ... **Dallas, TX**
Reis, Evelyn H. ... Teterboro, NJ
Reis, Frank L., Jr. ... Boston, MA
Reis, Gregory F. ... **Orlando, FL**
Reis, Harold F. ... Washington, DC
Reis, Herbert K. ... New York, NY
Reis, Janet D. ... Seattle, WA
Reis, Jason C. ... Austin, TX
Reis, Jeffrey W. ... Seattle, WA
Reis, John C. ... Carol Stream, IL
Reis, John W. ... **Charlotte, NC**
Reis, Karen A. ... **Washington, DC**
Reis, Karen M. ... Hackensack, NJ
Reis, Kevin J. ... **Columbus, OH**
Reis, Kimberlie C. ... San Francisco, CA
Reis, Mark W. ... **Cincinnati, OH**
Reis, Muriel Henle ... New York, NY
Reis, Paul G. ... **Indianapolis, IN**
Reis, Randolph J. ... **Manchester, NH**
Nashua, NH
Reis, Robert I. ... Amherst, NY
Reis, Robert K. ... **Rutland, VT**
Reis, Robert R. ... **Tulsa, OK**
Reis, Ronald ... New York, NY
Reis, Sean P. ... **Irvine, CA**
Reis, Sharon M. ... **Grand Forks, ND**
Reis, Steven E. ... Bay City, TX
Reis, Timothy C. ... **Atlanta, GA**
Reis, V. Peter, Jr. ... Torrington, CT
Reis, Werner A., M.D. ... Milwaukee, WI
Reisacher, Carl R. ... **Pittsburgh, PA**
Reisbaum, Emily E. ... **New York, NY**
Reisberg, Bernard D. ... Minneapolis, MN
Reisberg, Sol S. ... Brooklyn, NY
Reisberg, Steven H. ... **New York, NY**
Reisbick, William B. ... Bellevue, WA
Reisbig, Michael D. ... St. Paul, MN
Reisbord, Andrea E. ... **Minneapolis, MN**
Reisch, Alan M. ... **Boston, MA**
Reisch, Kevin J. ... **Irvine, CA**
Reisch, Lawrence W., Jr. ... Springfield, IL
Reisch, Randy J. ... New York, NY
Reisch, Randy J., P.C. ... New York, NY
Reisch, Richard J. ... Carle Place, NY
Reisch, Scott H. ... **Denver, CO**
Reisch, Steven A. ... Lisbon, OH
Reischauer, P. Amy ... **Seattle, WA**
Reische, Alan L. ... **Manchester, NH**
Reische, Kirk M. ... **New York, NY**
Reische, Richard W. ... Baltimore, MD
Reischel, Charles L. ... Washington, DC
Reischel, Chas. C. ... St. Paul, MN
Reischl, Susan R. ... **San Jose, CA**
Reischman, Owen A., Jr. ... Austin, TX
Reischmann, Catherine D. ... **Sanford, FL**
Reischmann, Charles F.
South Pasadena, FL
Reischmann, William E., Jr. ... **Sanford, FL**
Reischmann, William E., Sr.
South Pasadena, FL
Reisdorf, Bartholomew G. ... Fort Myers, FL
Reisdorf, R. Alex. ... Madison, WI
Reisdorff, Steven J. ... Crete, NE
Reise, Edward H. ... Menomonee Falls, WI
Reise, Jack ... **Boca Raton, FL**
Reiselt, Gordon W. ... Albuquerque, NM
Reiseman, Harvey I. ... Miami, FL
Reiseman, Harvey I., P.A. ... Miami, FL
Reiseman, Neil ... **Parsippany, NJ**
Reiseman Sharp Kelsey & Brown LLP
Morristown, NJ
Parsippany, NJ
Roseland, NJ
Reisen, Amy R. ... Millburn, NJ
Reisen, Patricia M. ... Dubuque, IA
Reisenauer, Elyse ... Peekskill, NY
Reisenauer, Keith W. ... Fargo, ND
Reisenfeld & Associates ... Cincinnati, OH
Reisenfeld, Bradley A. ... Cincinnati, OH
Reisenfeld, Kenneth B. ... **Washington, DC**
Reisenfeld, Sylvan P. ... Cincinnati, OH
Reisenfeld-Davis, Lesly Ann
Frankfort, KY
Reisenman, Debra J. ... Newburgh, NY

Reiser, Bert C. ... **Washington, DC**
Reiser, Carolyn S. ... **San Francisco, CA**
Reiser, Craig J. ... Springfield, IL
Reiser, Daniel C. ... **Boston, MA**
Reiser, David A. ... Washington, DC
Reiser, Deborah E. ... **Bethesda, MD**
Reiser, Debra S. ... New York, NY
Reiser, Donald J. ... San Juan, PR
Reiser, Dorian L. ... **Vernon, CT**
Reiser, Francis B. ... Kansas City, MO
Reiser, George Kott ... Toledo, OH
Reiser, George R. ... Toledo, OH
Reiser, Glenn R. ... Hackensack, NJ
Reiser & Grant, P.C. ... Boston, MA
Reiser, Harold L. ... **Salt Lake City, UT**
Reiser, James R. ... Richmond Hill, NY
Reiser, Jason M ... **Philadelphia, PA**
Reiser, Kenneth R. ... **Mineola, NY**
New York, NY
White Plains, NY
Reiser, Kristine Diane ... Diamond Bar, CA
Reiser, Law Office ... **Miami, FL**
Reiser, Michael J., Law Offices of
Walnut Creek, CA
Reiser, Murray P. ... Boston, MA
Reiser, Paul E. ... **Farmingdale, NY**
Reiser, Peter J. ... **New York, NY**
Reiser, Philip ... Charlottesville, VA
Reiser, Ralph G. ... Syosset, NY
Reiser, Randy Kass ... **New York, NY**
Reiser, Raymond A. ... **Miami, FL**
Reiser & Reiser ... Toledo, OH
Reiser, Richard E. ... Redding, CA
Reiser, Richard S. ... Omaha, NE
Reiser, Robert K. ... Brooklyn, NY
Reiser, Rosalind ... **Monroe, MI**
Reiser, Samuel J. ... New York, NY
Reiser, Stuart, P.C. ... **Hackensack, NJ**
Reiser, Thomas F. ... Carmel, CA
Reiser, Walter A., Jr. ... Edgefield, SC
Reiser, William L. ... Walnut Creek, CA
Reiserer, Kenneth H. ... Bellevue, WA
Reisert, Mary E. ... **New York, NY**
Reisert, Richard J. ... **New York, NY**
Reisert-Wehmueller, Mary Ann
Anderson, IN
Reisetter, Philip M. ... Iowa City, IA
Reise-Zwick, Randy ... Sylvan Lake, MI
Reisgen, Cyril H., Jr. ... Metairie, LA
Reish, Andrew F. ... Fairfax, VA
Reish, C. Frederick ... **Los Angeles, CA**
Reish, Loraine Bolton ... Ypsilanti, MI
Reish & Luftman, A Professional Corporation ... **Los Angeles, CA**
Reishman, James M. ... Charleston, WV
Reishtein, Allen T. ... Wilkes-Barre, PA
Reisig, Barry L. ... McLean, VA
Reisig, Edmund W., Jr. ... Monroe, MI
Reisig, Martin I. ... **Birmingham, MI**
Reisig, Norman W., Jr. ... Lacombe, LA
Reisig, Robert ... Department of Commerce, Patent and Trademark Office, GV
Reisine, Gary R. ... Marlborough, CT
Reising, Dan ... San Juan Capistrano, CA
Reising, Daniel K. ... **Portland, OR**
Reising, Ethington, Barnes, Kisselle, Learman & McCulloch, P.C.
Bay City, MI
Detroit, MI
Elk Rapids, MI
Flint, MI
Midland, MI
Saginaw, MI
Troy, MI
Reising, Gregory S. ... **Gary, IN**
Reising, H. William ... **Flint, MI**
Reising, Richard P. ... Decatur, IL
Reising, Sandra A. ... San Juan Capistrano, CA
Reisinger & Associates, Inc.
San Rafael, CA
Reisinger, Edwin J. ... Chicago, IL
Reisinger, Jay K. ... **Pittsburgh, PA**
Reisinger, Joseph C. ... **San Rafael, CA**
Reisinger, Joseph R. ... Wilkes-Barre, PA
Reisinger, Ralph M. ... **Grand Rapids, MI**
Reisinger, Robert ... **Long Beach, CA**
Reisinger, Timothy A. ... Dover, DE
Reiske, Peter F. ... Milwaukee, WI
Reiskin, Terri Steinhaus ... **Washington, DC**
Reiskind, Andrew S. ... **Greenwich, CT**
Reiskytl, Elizabeth McGraw
Minneapolis, MN
Reisler, Frances F. ... Peoria, IL
Reisler, Marc S. ... **New York, NY**
Reisler, Melvin ... New York, NY
Reisler, Steven A. ... **Seattle, WA**
Reisman & Abraham, P.A. ... Coral Gables, FL
Reisman, Abramson & Magro, P.C.
New York, NY
Reisman, Albert F. ... **New York, NY**
Reisman, Andrew E. ... **Shelton, CT**
Reisman, Andrew L. ... **Chicago, IL**
Reisman & Associates, P.A. ... Boca Raton, FL
Reisman, Bernard E. ... Palm Beach, FL
Reisman, Beth B. ... Staten Island, NY
Reisman, Carl H. ... Champaign, IL
Reisman, Carol Welborn
New Orleans, LA
Reisman, Cary S. ... Santa Monica, CA
Reisman, Charles P. ... Birmingham, MI
Reisman, Daniel N. ... **Philadelphia, PA**
Reisman, David L. ... **New Orleans, LA**
Reisman, David S. ... New York, NY
Reisman, Dennis Marc ... **Bayside, NY**
Reisman, Dennis Marc ... **Great Neck, NY**
Reisman, Donald S. ... Fort Pierce, FL

Reisman, Edward Steven
Department of Commerce, Office of the General Counsel, GV
Reisman, Eugene ... Yonkers, NY
Reisman, Glenn M. ... **Bridgeport, CT**
Reisman, Glenn M. ... **Shelton, CT**
Reisman, Gregg D. ... **Great Neck, NY**
Reisman, J. Michelle ... **Shelton, CT**
Reisman, James ... **New York, NY**
Reisman, Jason Eric ... **Philadelphia, PA**
Reisman, Jennifer Brooke ... Atlanta, GA
Reisman, Jerome ... **Garden City, NY**
Reisman, Jerome S. ... Coral Gables, FL
Reisman, Joanne ... Portland, OR
Reisman, Jonathan B. ... Boca Raton, FL
Reisman, Joseph B. ... **Miami, FL**
Reisman, Joseph M. ... **San Diego, CA**
Reisman, Joshua H. ... **Las Vegas, NV**
Reisman, Keith J. ... **Atlanta, GA**
Reisman, Kenneth P. ... Newton, MA
Reisman, Lawrence A. ... Trenton, NJ
Reisman, Lawrence M. ... New York, NY
Reisman, Louis A. ... **Los Angeles, CA**
Reisman, Marc E. ... Memphis, TN
Reisman, Marc S. ... **Pittsburgh, PA**
Reisman, Marvin ... New York, NY
Reisman, Maurice S. ... Farmington Hills, MI
Reisman, Nancy H. ... **New York, NY**
Reisman, Neal R. ... **McAllen, TX**
Reisman, Neil A. ... Chicago, IL
Reisman, Paul P. ... Mamaroneck, NY
Reisman, Peirez & Reisman, L.L.P.
Garden City, NY
Mineola, NY
New York, NY
Reisman, Richard A. ... Schenectady, NY
Reisman, Richard J. ... New York, NY
Reisman, Richard S. ... Laguna Beach, CA
Reisman, Samuel ... Beverly Hills, CA
Reisman, Seymour J. ... **Garden City, NY**
Reisman, Sharyl A. ... **New York, NY**
Reisman, Sheldon J. ... Fair Lawn, NJ
Reisman, Stanley J. ... Pittsburgh, PA
Reisman, Stephen H. ... **Miami, FL**
Reisman, Steven J. ... **New York, NY**
Reisman, Steven M. ... Rochelle Park, NJ
Reisman, Suzanne G. ... **Philadelphia, PA**
Reisman, William M. ... New Haven, CT
Reisner, Adam J. ... **Los Angeles, CA**
Reisner, Alan K. ... Hartford, CT
Reisner, Anna M. ... Croton-On-Hudson, NY
Reisner, Carl L. ... **New York, NY**
Reisner, Daniel ... **New York, NY**
Reisner, Dean F. ... **Grand Haven, MI**
Reisner, Donald J. ... Sacramento, CA
Reisner, Edward J. ... Madison, WI
Reisner, Edward M. ... **New York, NY**
Reisner, Jeffrey M. ... **Irvine, CA**
Reisner, John H., III ... Haddonfield, NJ
Reisner, Joseph J. ... St. Paul, MN
Reisner, Linda Carroll ... **St. Louis, MO**
Reisner, Lorin L. ... **New York, NY**
Reisner, Michael A. ... **New York, NY**
Reisner, Ralph ... Chicago, IL
Reisner, Ronald L. ... Newark, NJ
Reisner, Ronald Lee ... **Red Bank, NJ**
Reisner, Samuel L. ... Westbrook, CT
Reisner, Sarah C. Hardison ... **Nashville, TN**
Reisner, Susan Canter ... **Atlanta, GA**
Louisville, KY
Reisnour, James A. ... Jamestown, ND
Reiss, Adam B. ... Orlando, FL
Reiss, Adam J. ... **West Palm Beach, FL**
Reiss, Agnes A. ... Newark, NJ
Reiss, Albert J. ... Miami Beach, FL
Reiss, Allan D. ... **New York, NY**
Reiss, Allan S. ... **Miami, FL**
Reiss, Amy L. ... **New York, NY**
Reiss, Andrea ... Ardsley, NY
Reiss, Andrew H. ... Naples, FL
Reiss, Anthony E. ... Loveland, OH
Reiss, Barry A. ... Phoenix, AZ
Reiss, Benjamin L. ... **Miami, FL**
Reiss, Berit Amlie ... **Metairie, LA**
Reiss, Bonnie F. ... New York, NY
Reiss, Bonnie M. S. ... **North Brunswick, NJ**
Red Bank, NJ
Reiss, Brett M. ... Great Neck, NY
Reiss, Brian R. ... Newport Beach, CA
Reiss, Carmin C. ... Boston, MA
Reiss, Christina ... **Burlington, VT**
Reiss, Christopher D. ... **Denver, CO**
Reiss, Dan ... Freehold, NJ
Reiss, Daniel H. ... **Santa Monica, CA**
Reiss, David B. ... Connellsville, PA
Reiss, David J. ... **New York, NY**
Reiss, Deanna ... Staten Island, NY
Reiss, Debbie F. ... **Louisville, KY**
Reiss, Deborah A. ... **New York, NY**
Reiss, Dennis M. ... Wading River, NY
Reiss, Edward A. ... Pompton Lakes, NJ
Reiss, Elaine S. ... Brooklyn, NY
Reiss, Evelyn Ann ... Anadarko, OK
Reiss, Evelyn Ann, P.C. ... Anadarko, OK
Reiss, George ... New York, NY
Reiss, Guy A. ... **New York, NY**
Reiss, Hans F. ... New Canaan, CT
Reiss, Howard R. ... **New York, NY**
Reiss, Howard S. ... Orlando, FL
Reiss, Jacob ... Niles, IL
Reiss, James V. ... **Rancho Cucamonga, CA**
Reiss, John B. ... **Philadelphia, PA**
Reiss, John M. ... **New York, NY**
Reiss & Johnson ... **Rancho Cucamonga, CA**
San Bernardino, CA
Reiss, Jonathan J. ... **Malone, NY**
Reiss, Kenneth ... Bronx, NY

Reiss, Kenneth M. ... Department of Justice, Federal Bureau of Investigation, GV
Reiss, Lawrence J. ... White Plains, NY
Reiss, Leonard S. ... **New York, NY**
Reiss, Marlene S. ... **Miami, FL**
Reiss, Mary Elizabeth ... Redwood City, CA
Reiss, Michael ... **Seattle, WA**
Reiss, Nadine M. ... Reno, NV
Reiss, Pamela R. ... Jenkintown, PA
Reiss, Peter L. ... **San Diego, CA**
New York, NY
New Hope, PA
Reiss, Peter W. ... Scottsdale, AZ
Reiss, Philip S. ... **New York, NY**
Reiss, R. Rick ... Newport News, VA
Reiss & Reiss ... Orlando, FL
Reiss, Rena Hozore ... **Washington, DC**
Reiss, Richard D. ... New York, NY
Reiss, Samantha ... New York, NY
Reiss, Sandra B. ... **Birmingham, AL**
Reiss, Saul ... Beverly Hills, CA
Reiss, Seth M., (Atty. At Law, A Law Corp.)
Honolulu, HI
Reiss, Sharon M. ... **Philadelphia, PA**
Reiss, Sherri D. ... New York, NY
Reiss, Sidney H. ... Paterson, NJ
Reiss, Steven Alan ... **New York, NY**
Reiss, Steven M. ... Durham, NC
Reiss, Susan Jane ... New York, NY
Reiss, Susan R. ... **New York, NY**
Reiss, Tammy J. ... Southfield, MI
Reiss, Thomas E. ... Farmington Hills, MI
Reiss, William R. ... Houston, TX
Reissman, Ralph J. ... **Islandia, NY**
Reist, James T. ... **Albuquerque, NM**
Reist, Roger S. ... **Ephrata, PA**
Lancaster, PA
Lititz, PA
Quarryville, PA
Reister, Andrea G. ... **Washington, DC**
Reister, Elizabeth A. ... **Lancaster, PA**
Reister, Frederick T. ... Columbus, OH
Reister, John J. ... **Hamilton, OH**
Reister, Raymond A. ... **Minneapolis, MN**
Reister, Ruth Alkema ... Minneapolis, MN
Reisterer, Michael P. ... Kalamazoo, MI
Reistman, Maurice B. ... Lincoln Park, MI
Reistroffer, Douglas J. ... Chicago, IL
Reiswerg, Joseph J. ... **Indianapolis, IN**
Reisz, Bernard (Sonny), Law Offices of
Evansville, IN
Reisz, Cynthia Y. ... **Nashville, TN**
Reisz, Frederick S. ... **Los Angeles, CA**
Reisz, John P. ... **Louisville, KY**
Reisz, Lisa Pierce ... **Columbus, OH**
Reisz, Michael ... Los Angeles, CA
Reisz, Willard M. ... Los Angeles, CA
Reisz, Wm. Stephen ... **Louisville, KY**
Reit, Scott J. ... **Fort Lauderdale, FL**
Reitan, Milton W. ... Virginia, MN
Reitan, Peter J. ... **Pasadena, CA**
Reitano, Anthony J., Jr. ... **Warren, NJ**
Reitano, Christine ... **New Orleans, LA**
Reitano, John Peter ... **Mineola, NY**
Reitano, Jos. ... Memphis, TN
Reitenbach, Daniel ... **Middlebury, CT**
Reitenour, Steven L. ... **Minneapolis, MN**
Reiter, Allen G. ... **New York, NY**
Reiter, Arlene ... New Brunswick, NJ
Reiter, Arnold E. ... Mahwah, NJ
Reiter, Bernard A., (P.C.) ... Houston, TX
Reiter, Burton L. ... **Northfield, IL**
Reiter, Carol Conrad ... Wadsworth, OH
Reiter, Carol L. ... Boston, MA
Reiter, Catherine Coyne ... **Chicago, IL**
Reiter, Charles E., III ... **Chicago, IL**
Reiter, Charles Jay ... **New York, NY**
Reiter, Darlene L. ... **Sheridan, WY**
Reiter, David ... **Houston, TX**
Reiter, Dee Deese ... Jacksonville, FL
Reiter, Dennis O. ... **Bellefonte, PA**
State College, PA
Reiter, Diane Kronberg ... Livingston, NJ
Reiter, Donna Shader ... York, PA
Reiter, Edward ... Miami, FL
Reiter, Elisa M. ... Dallas, TX
Reiter, Ellen Rich ... Denver, CO
Reiter, Ellis D., Jr. ... **Los Angeles, CA**
Reiter, Fred A. ... Minneapolis, MN
Reiter, Garvin ... Albany, OR
Reiter, Gary C. ... Edina, MN
Reiter, Genise R., (A Professional Corporation) ... **Los Angeles, CA**
Reiter, Glenn M. ... **New York, NY**
Reiter, Gregory M. ... Chicago, IL
Reiter, Harvey L. ... **Washington, DC**
Reiter, Howard S. ... **West Hartford, CT**
Reiter, Jack ... McLean, VA
Reiter, Jack R. ... **Miami, FL**
Reiter, James A. ... **Detroit, MI**
Farmington Hills, MI
Reiter, Jennifer ... **Chicago, IL**
Reiter, Jesse M. ... Southfield, MI
Reiter, Jill Levy ... New York, NY
Reiter, Jill Soman ... **Miami, FL**
Reiter, Joann M. ... Seattle, WA
Reiter, John L. ... Denver, CO
Reiter, Joseph ... New City, NY
Reiter, Joseph H. ... Department of Defense, Armed Services Board of Contract Appeals, GV
Reiter, Joseph J., (P.A.)
West Palm Beach, FL
Reiter, Kenneth E. ... Marysville, OH
Reiter, Laura J. ... New York, NY
Reiter, Lisa L. ... Paramus, NJ
Reiter, Lohman D., II ... **Sumter, SC**
Reiter, Lohman D., II, LLC ... **Sumter, SC**

Reiter, Lucille Anderson ....**Houston, TX**
Reiter, Luis ....**Miami, FL**
Reiter, Marc J. ....**Pittsburgh, PA**
Reiter, Mark A. ....**Kansas City, MO**
Reiter, Mark N. ....**Dallas, TX**
Reiter, Marla ....Newport Beach, CA
Reiter, Maury B. ....**Cherry Hill, NJ**
Blue Bell, PA
Reiter, Michael A. ....**Chicago, IL**
Reiter, Michael J. ....Englewood, FL
Reiter, Michael P. ....Spring Hill, FL
Reiter, Michelle L. ....Morris Plains, NJ
Reiter, Mitchell B. ....**New York, NY**
Reiter, Neil S.
Department Of Veterans Affairs, Board of Veterans Appeals, GV
Reiter, Paul G. ....Rochester, NY
Reiter, Peter I. ....**New York, NY**
Reiter, Putnam W. ....Mexia, TX
Reiter, Richard E. ....Fayetteville, GA
Reiter, Robert D. ....**Oakland, CA**
Reiter, Robert E. ....Kansas City, MO
Reiter, Robert P. ....New York, NY
Reiter, Samuel Sheldon ....Tucson, AZ
Reiter, Scott E. ....**Miami, FL**
Reiter, Scott L.
United States Postal Service, Law Department, GV
Reiter, Sheldon ....**New York, NY**
Reiter, Stephen E. ....**San Diego, CA**
Reiter, Susan Fuhrer ....**Erie, PA**
Reiter, Susan K. ....Chicago, IL
Reiter, Susan M. ....Folsom, CA
Reiter, Thomas J., & Associates
St. Paul, MN
Reiter, Thomas M. ....**Jacksonville, FL**
Reiter, Thomas M. ....**Pittsburgh, PA**
Reiter, Walter A., III ....Annapolis, MD
Reiter, Walter A., Jr. ....Baltimore, MD
Reiter, William R., II ....**San Diego, CA**
Reith, Daniel I. ....**Monterey, CA**
Reith, Michael J. ....Atlanta, GA
Reith, Roger J. ....**Dallas, TX**
Reithal, Georgia J. ....Hoffman Estates, IL
Reithauser, Claudia G. ....**Bradenton, FL**
Reither, Fred W. ....Virginia, IL
Reither, Philip H. ....Santa Monica, CA
Reitinger, Philip R. ....Department of Justice, Criminal Division, GV
Reitknecht, Seymour ....New York, NY
Reitkopp, Edward B. ....**Cerritos, CA**
Reitkopp, Elizabeth A. ....**Bethesda, MD**
Reitkopp, Richard I. ....Rochester, NY
Reitkopp, Richard I., P.C. ....Rochester, NY
Reitler, Edward G. ....**New York, NY**
Reitler, Paul M. ....**Los Angeles, CA**
Reitmaier, Angela ....Washington, DC
Reitman, Daniel R. ....**Portland, OR**
Reitman, Edwin H. ....**Atlanta, GA**
Reitman, Gordon H. ....Agoura Hills, CA
Reitman, Jeffrey B. ....**Houston, TX**
Reitman, John P. ....**Los Angeles, CA**
Reitman, Jonathan W. ....Brunswick, ME
Reitman, M. Joseph, Jr. ....**Madison, GA**
Reitman, Marc A. ....Albuquerque, NM
Reitman, Michael R. ....Rahway, NJ
Reitman, Naran ....Palm Desert, CA
Reitman Parsonnet ....Newark, NJ
Reitman, R. Toni ....San Antonio, TX
Reitman, Robert S. ....Cleveland, OH
Reitman, Sheldon ....Chicago, IL
Reitman, Stanley H. ....**Anchorage, AK**
Reitmeier, George J. ....Knoxville, TN
Reitmeyer, Charles J. ....**Philadelphia, PA**
Reitmeyer, Mary ....**Pittsburgh, PA**
Reitmeyer, Mary, P.C. ....**Pittsburgh, PA**
Reitner, Barnet, (P.C.) ....San Luis Obispo, CA
Reitnour, George F. ....Spring City, PA
Reiton, Charles D. ....San Jose, CA
Reiton, Jerold A. ....**San Jose, CA**
Reitsch, Gerry A. ....**Longview, WA**
Reitsch & Weston, PLLC ....**Cathlamet, WA**
Kelso, WA
Longview, WA
Reitsema, David R. ....Englewood, CO
Reitsema, David R., P.C. ....Englewood, CO
Reitsma, Jan H. ....Boston, MA
Reittinger & Reittinger, L.L.P.
Eagle Bay, NY
Utica, NY
Reittinger, Richard J. ....**Eagle Bay, NY**
Utica, NY
Reittinger, Robert R. ....**Utica, NY**
Reitz and Chesley ....Brooklyn, NY
Reitz, Christopher M. ....**Kansas City, MO**
Reitz, Curtis R. ....Philadelphia, PA
Reitz, David W. ....**Erie, PA**
Reitz, Howard D., Jr. ....**Washington, DC**
Reitz, Howard W. ....Frankenmuth, MI
Reitz, James F. ....**Carmel, NY**
Reitz, James W., Jr. ....Palm Desert, CA
Reitz, John C. ....Iowa City, IA
Reitz, Kenneth W. ....Omaha, NE
Reitz, Kris F. ....**Columbia, IL**
Reitz, Kurt E. ....**Belleville, IL**
Reitz, Lois ....Syracuse, NY
Reitz, Marc H. ....**Syracuse, NY**
Reitz, Mark R. ....**Columbus, OH**
Reitz, Mark R. ....**Baraboo, WI**
Reitz, Mary L. ....**St. Louis, MO**
Reitz, Nathaniel J. ....Roseville, MN
Reitz, Norman E. ....Hayward, CA
Reitz, Peter W. ....**Denver, CO**
Reitz, Reed H. ....Denison, IA
Reitz, Ronald E. ....**Pittsburgh, PA**
Reitz, Sidney A. ....**Salina, KS**
Reitz, Thomas ....Brooklyn, NY
Reitz, Thomas L. ....**Columbus, OH**

Reitz, Thomas Richard ....Aurora, OH
Reitz, William L. ....**Akron, OH**
Reitzas, Lois B. ....Fall River, MA
Reitze, Arnold W., Jr. ....**Washington, DC**
Reitze, Glenn L. ....Library of Congress, Law Library, GV
Reitzel, J. Brooks, Jr. ....**High Point, NC**
Reitzell, William R., Jr. ....Worcester, MA
Reitzenstein, Henry A. ....**Los Angeles, CA**
Reitzes, Edward J. ....Overland Park, KS
Reitzes, Robin M. ....San Francisco, CA
Reitzfeld, Alan D. ....**New York, NY**
Reive, Christopher L. ....**Portland, OR**
Reiver, Joanna ....**Wilmington, DE**
Reivitz, Leon C. ....**Phoenix, AZ**
Reixach, Rene H., Jr. ....**Rochester, NY**
Reizen, Mark E. ....Southfield, MI
Reizen, Myla R. ....**Santa Barbara, CA**
Reizen, Richard S. ....**Chicago, IL**
Reizenstein, Philip L. ....Miami, FL
Reizes, David M. ....Virginia Beach, VA
Reizes, Leslie N. ....Waverly, NY
Reizfeld, Leonard C. ....New Haven, CT
Rezian, John L. ....**Fort Wayne, IN**
Reiziss, Jay
United States International Trade Commission, Office of the Commissioners, GV
Reizman, Neil M. ....Los Angeles, CA
Reizner, Robert B. ....**Ann Arbor, MI**
Reizner, Robin C. ....Niles, IL
Rejali, Fred M. ....Fairfax, VA
Rejan, Jeffrey N. ....**New York, NY**
Rejcek, Bet J. ....Irving, TX
Rejent, Joseph K. ....Hatboro, PA
Rejent, Robert J. ....Ridgefield, NJ
Rejent, Ronald P. ....Toledo, OH
Rejent-Lee, Denise L. ....Phoenix, AZ
Rejowski, Joseph A. ....Chicago, IL
Rejowski, Joseph A., P.C. ....Chicago, IL
Reju, Sandhya Susan ....**Richmond, VA**
ReKant, Kenneth N. ....Miami Beach, FL
Rekant, Scott E. ....Trenton, NJ
Rekant, Stuart B. ....New York, NY
Rekar, Pamela ....Naperville, IL
Rekart, Kirsten L. ....Washington, DC
Rekate, Mary Warren ....Scottsdale, AZ
Rekemeyer, Terri J. ....**Newton, IA**
Reker, Norbert M. ....St. Louis, MO
Reklaitis, Robert F. ....**Washington, DC**
Rekofke, Brian T. ....**Spokane, WA**
Rekoon, Barry G. ....**Santa Clara, CA**
Rekosh, Edwin B. ....New York, NY
Rekow, Kenneth E. ....**Seattle, WA**
Rekowski & Associates ....Collinsville, IL
Rekowski, John J. ....Collinsville, IL
Rekshan, William R., II ....Marquette, MI
Rekstis, Fredric T. ....Philadelphia, PA
Rekstis, Walter J., III ....**Cleveland, OH**
Rekte, V. Andre ....**San Bernardino, CA**
Relat, Emil J. ....Sacramento, CA
Relation, A. Joseph ....**Cincinnati, OH**
Relfe, Charles P. ....Birmingham, AL
Relfe, J. Massey, Jr. ....Birmingham, AL
Relfe, Mary Margaret ....**Birmingham, AL**
Relford, Guy A. ....Indianapolis, IN
Relias, John A. ....**Chicago, IL**
Relic, Grant D. ....Cleveland, OH
Relich, Kelly E. ....Tucson, AZ
Relich, Michael ....Pittsburgh, PA
Relich, Paul A. ....Tucson, AZ
Reliford, Julie ....**Kansas City, MO**
Religa, Stanley F. ....Asheville, NC
Relihan, Carol F. ....**Houston, TX**
Relihan, Charles F., Jr. ....Framingham, MA
Relihan, John J. ....Phoenix, AZ
Relihan, Julie C. ....**Chicago, IL**
Relihan, Relihan & Relihan
Smith Center, KS
Relihan, Terry E. ....Smith Center, KS
Relihan, Walter J., Jr. ....Ithaca, NY
Relin, Adam H. ....**Irvine, CA**
Relin, Goldstein and Crane, LLP
Rochester, NY
Relin, Leonard ....Rochester, NY
Relin, Milton M. ....Los Angeles, CA
Relkin, David H. ....**New York, NY**
Relkin, Donald B. ....**New York, NY**
Relkin, Ellen ....**South Orange, NJ**
New York, NY
Rella, Anthony J. ....Suffern, NY
Rella, Carl F. ....**Bangor, ME**
Rella, Dianne ....Suffern, NY
Rella, Dostie & Tucker, P.A. ....**Bangor, ME**
Rella, Gerarda M. ....White Plains, NY
Rellan, Benu ....**Huntington, WV**
Rellas, Chris S. ....Monrovia, CA
Reller, George R. ....Richmond, IN
Reller, Mendenhall, Kleinknecht & Milligan
Richmond, IN
Reller, Nancy S. ....San Jose, CA
Reller, William H. ....Richmond, IN
Relles, David D. ....Madison, WI
Relles, Eliot L. ....**New York, NY**
Relles, George ....Miamisburg, OH
Relles, Meeker & Borns ....Madison, WI
Rellick, Jennifer M. ....Chapel Hill, NC
Rellick, John R. ....Tappahannock, VA
Rellos, Anthony J. ....Herndon, VA
Relman, Craig W. ....Beachwood, OH
Relman, Craig W., Co., L.P.A.
Beachwood, OH
Relman, Harvey M. ....Beachwood, OH
Relman, John P. ....Washington, DC
Relock, Donald M. ....Anaheim, CA
Relph, Jerry O. ....**St. Cloud, MN**
Relph, Robert B. ....**Grand Rapids, MI**
Relphorde, Kevin B. ....Gary, IN

Relyea, Chester F. ....San Francisco, CA
Relyea, Jane P. ....**Burlingame, CA**
San Jose, CA
Relyea, Richard J., III ....Washington, DC
Relyea, Richard W. ....**Spokane, WA**
Relyea, Spencer C. ....**Dallas, TX**
Rem, Joseph P., Jr. ....Hackensack, NJ
Rem, Karen Kurland ....Hackensack, NJ
Rem, Kenneth M. ....Detroit, MI
Rem, Zeller and Associates, PC
Hackensack, NJ
Remaklus, Robert H. ....Cascade, ID
Remaklus, Robert H., P.A. ....Cascade, ID
Remaklus, Theodore R. ....**Cincinnati, OH**
Remar, Robert B. ....**Atlanta, GA**
Remark, Robert R. ....Fertile, MN
Rembar, Charles ....New York, NY
Rembar & Curtis ....New York, NY
Rembaum, George J. ....Chatsworth, CA
Rembe, Toni ....**San Francisco, CA**
Rembert, Michael D. ....Houston, TX
Rembert, Robert W. ....**Pullman, WA**
Rembert, William A., Jr. ....Dallas, TX
Rembisz, Eugene R. ....Tulsa, OK
Rembold, Michael Duane ....Littleton, CO
Rembold, Sabrina Mendoza ....Miami, FL
Rembold, Scott D. ....**Miami, FL**
Remboldt, Darwin R. ....Glendale, CA
Rembolt, James E. ....**Lincoln, NE**
Seward, NE
Rembolt Ludtke & Berger ....**Lincoln, NE**
Seward, NE
Rembrandt, Ann Brannon
Charleston, WV
Remcho, Johansen and Purcell
Sacramento, CA
San Francisco, CA
Remcho, Joseph ....**Sacramento, CA**
San Francisco, CA
Remedios, Marianne T. ....**Minneapolis, MN**
Remedios, Robert A. ....San Mateo, CA
Remeika, Diane H. ....Madison, WI
Remeika, James ....Lexington, MA
Remejes, Kristi M. ....Clinton Township, MI
Remele, Lewis A., Jr. ....**Minneapolis, MN**
Remelmeyer, Stanley E.
Redondo Beach, CA
Remels, Alyssa P. ....Houston, TX
Remels, Keith M. ....Houston, TX
Remencius, Leonard C. ....Rockford, IL
Remenick, James ....**Washington, DC**
Remennik, Marina ....**Palo Alto, CA**
Remensperger, D. Eric ....**Los Angeles, CA**
Remer, Daniel V. ....Ossining, NY
Remer, DiVincenzo & Griffith, A Professional Corporation ....**Newport Beach, CA**
Remer, Earl M. ....Pinckney, MI
Remer, Franklin I. ....**Newport Beach, CA**
Remer, Frederick R. ....Hayward, CA
Remer, Gary M. ....**Southfield, MI**
Remer, George R. ....Battle Creek, IA
Remer, Jodi C. ....**New York, NY**
Remer, Kersten G. ....Ada, OK
Remer, Patricia A. ....**Boston, MA**
Remer, Zatkin & Green, P.C. ....Pinckney, MI
Remerowski, Anita ....Boulder, CO
Remer-Smith, Carol Ann ....New York, NY
Remery, William R. ....Glendale, CA
Remes, Allen S. ....**Rancho Cucamonga, CA**
Remes, David H. ....**Washington, DC**
Remes, Emily R. ....**New York, NY**
Remes, Robert A. ....**Washington, DC**
Remick, Alex J. ....**Southfield, MI**
Remick, Bradley D. ....**Philadelphia, PA**
Remick, Franklin E. ....Forsyth, GA
Remick, Hillary L. ....**Philadelphia, PA**
Remick, Jeffrey S. ....Crookston, MN
Remick, Lani A. ....**San Francisco, CA**
Remick, Lloyd Zane ....**Philadelphia, PA**
Remick Martone, A Professional Corporation
Hammonton, NJ
Philadelphia, PA
Remick, Timothy ....**Willcox, AZ**
Remick, Timothy P. ....**Willcox, AZ**
Remigino, Meredith Gordon
New Haven, CT
Remijas, Hilary H. ....**Chicago, IL**
Remillard, Jane E. ....**Boston, MA**
Remillard, Joseph H. ....Watkinsville, GA
Remillard, L.J. (Bud), Jr. ....Middleboro, MA
Remillard, Mary Ann ....Lawrence, MA
Remillard, Paul ....Tallahassee, FL
ReMine, Gary B. ....Mantorville, MN
ReMine, William H., III ....**Denver, CO**
Reming, Joanne M. ....**San Francisco, CA**
Reminger & Reminger Co., L.P.A.
Cincinnati, OH
Cleveland, OH
Columbus, OH
Reminger, Richard T. ....Cleveland, OH
Remington, Ann ....Minneapolis, MN
Remington, Clark A. ....Brooklyn, NY
Remington, D. Dale ....Oklahoma City, OK
Remington, Eric J. ....**New Bern, NC**
Remington, Frank D. ....Madison, WI
Remington, Gifford, Williams & Colicchio, L.L.P. ....**Rochester, NY**
Remington, Güzidé Gigi ....**Pleasanton, CA**
Remington, James T. ....**New Richmond, WI**
Remington, Janna L. ....Boulder, CO
Remington, Jeffray & Hansen, A Professional Corporation ....**Arlington, TX**
Fort Worth, TX
Remington, Judith A. ....**New Richmond, WI**
Remington, Laura J. ....**San Francisco, CA**
Remington, Laurel A. ....**Los Angeles, CA**
Remington Law Offices
New Richmond, WI

Remington, Mark A. ....Dallas, TX
Remington, Michael D. ....**Blue Bell, PA**
Remington, Michael J. ....**Washington, DC**
Remington, Philipa M. ....**Dallas, TX**
Remington, Royce R. ....**Cleveland, OH**
Remington, Scott A. ....**Pensacola, FL**
Remington, Suzanne M. ....Rochester, MN
Remington, Thomas R., (P.C.)
St. Louis, MO
Remington, Thomas T. ....Shalimar, FL
Remington, William P. ....**Arlington, TX**
Remis, Marc Dvorak ....Sacramento, CA
Remis, Robert G. ....Orlando, FL
Remis, Sharon E. ....**St. Louis, MO**
Remis, Shepard M., (P.C.) ....**Boston, MA**
Remis, William Burton ....St. Louis, MO
Remke, Kathryn France ....Portola Valley, CA
Remland, Joel T. ....Orlando, FL
Remler, Albert N. ....**Atlanta, GA**
Remler, Jane E. ....Bronx, NY
Remler Law Group ....**Atlanta, GA**
Remley, Arthur P. ....**Neenah, WI**
Remley, Cynthia L. ....Clearwater, FL
Remley, David M. ....Cedar Rapids, IA
Remley, David M. ....**Cape Girardeau, MO**
Remley, Howard M. ....Anamosa, IA
Remley, Richard J. ....**San Francisco, CA**
Remley & Sensenbrenner, S.C.
Neenah, WI
Remley, Willems & McQuillen
Anamosa, IA
Remlinger, Patricia L. ....Springfield, NJ
Remlinger, Roger R.
Rancho Cucamonga, CA
Remly, Lynn L.
Federal Communications Commission, Office of Engineering & Technology, GV
Remm, Henry C., Jr. ....Lafayette, LA
Remme, Michael J. ....Arlington, TX
Remmel, Augustus C. ....Little Rock, AR
Remmel, Earl H. ....Oklahoma City, OK
Dallas, TX
Remmel, Lawrence ....**New York, NY**
Remmel, Ronald F. ....Mountain View, CA
Remmel, U. Charles, II ....**Portland, ME**
Remmell, Robert E. ....New Hartford, NY
Remmenga, Greg R. ....**Grand Junction, CO**
Remmenga, Merlin E. ....Houston, TX
Remmer, Richard H. ....Oakdale, NY
Remmer, Sharon ....**Boston, MA**
Remmers, Cynthia L. ....**Sacramento, CA**
Remmers, Donald H. ....Downers Grove, IL
Remmers, John M. ....**Waukesha, WI**
Remmers, Philip J. ....**Waukesha, WI**
Remmers, Richard D. ....Louisville, KY
Remmers, Richard F. ....Oklahoma City, OK
Remmert, George J. ....Arlington, MA
Remmert, James E. ....Austin, TX
Remmes, Michael J. ....Bloomington, IL
Remmler, Erik F. ....**New York, NY**
Remnitz, Martin A. ....**New York, NY**
Remo, Lorraine I. ....Albany, NY
Remondet, Michael J., Jr. ....**Lafayette, LA**
Remondini, David Joseph ....Indianapolis, IN
Remondino, Edmund M. ....**Stamford, CT**
Rempe, Anne R. ....**Chicago, IL**
Rempe, George A., III
Santa Barbara, CA
Rempe, James H. ....Gaithersburg, MD
Rempe, Marianne I. ....Harrisburg, PA
Rempe, Stephen M. R. ....Phoenix, AZ
Rempel, David J. ....**Kansas City, MO**
Rempel, Michelle R. ....**Kansas City, MO**
Rempel, William ....Brick, NJ
Rempert, Susan W. ....Indianapolis, IN
Remphrey, Emily I. ....**Philadelphia, PA**
Remphrey, William. E., Jr.
Philadelphia, PA
Rempis, James A. ....Arlington, MA
Rems, J. P. ....Santa Monica, CA
Rems, Ricky E. ....New York, NY
Remsberg, Stephen R. ....**New Orleans, LA**
Remsburg, Edward W. ....**Des Moines, IA**
Remsburg, F. Raine ....**Winston-Salem, NC**
Remsen, Alfred S., Jr. ....Silver Creek, NY
Remsen, John L. ....**West Palm Beach, FL**
Remshak, Jonathan M. ....**Hackensack, NJ**
Remsnyder, Donna S. ....St. Petersburg, FL
Remson, Kenneth A. ....**Los Angeles, CA**
Remson, Michael M. ....**Baton Rouge, LA**
Remter, Laurie G. ....Atlanta, GA
Remund, James W. ....Windom, MN
Remund, Rene J. ....**Chehalis, WA**
Remus, Edward W. ....**Chicago, IL**
Remus, Margarita R. ....Louisville, KY
Remus, Mark H. ....**Chicago, IL**
Remus, Nan A. ....**Minneapolis, MN**
Remus, Paul C. ....**Andover, MA**
Manchester, NH
Remuzzi, Stephen G., Jr. ....Rocky Point, NY
Remy, Carol E. ....**New York, NY**
Remy, Christine F. ....Gretna, LA
Remy, Christine Patterson ....Washington, DC
Remy, David L. ....Mansfield, OH
Remy, Donald Michael
Department of Justice, Civil Division, GV
Remy, Joanne T. ....Canton, MA
Remy, John M. ....**Washington, DC**
Remy, Michael Anthony ....**Miami, FL**
Remy, Michael Anthony, P.A. ....**Miami, FL**
Remy, Michael Helge ....**Sacramento, CA**
Remy, Raelynn Tibayan ....Washington, DC
Remy, Robert D. ....Houston, TX
Remy, Thomas and Moose, LLP
Sacramento, CA
Remy, William Thomas ....Cameron Park, CA
Remz, Sanford F. ....**Boston, MA**
Ren, Courtney F. ....**Indianapolis, IN**

Ren, Yunling ... New York, NY
Renaghan, Joseph F. ... Glen Cove, NY
Renahan, Kathryn R. ... Westmont, NJ
Renahan, William J. ... New York, NY
Renaker, Teresa ... Oakland, CA
Renaldo, Anthony J. ... Buffalo, NY
Renaldo, Keith N. ... Bangor, PA
Renaldo, Myers & Palumbo, P.C.
Buffalo, NY
Williamsville, NY
Renard, Bruce W. ... Tallahassee, FL
Renard, Henry F. ... West Bend, WI
Renard, James S. ... Dallas, TX
Renard, Sandra J. ... Detroit, MI
Renard, Susan R. ... Fort Lauderdale, FL
Renardo, Charissa I ... Los Angeles, CA
Renas, Stanford ... New York, NY
Renati, Charles G. ... San Francisco, CA
Renau, Donald I. ... Louisville, KY
Renaud, Ann L. ... East Brunswick, NJ
Renaud, Brian J. ... Bloomfield Hills, MI
Renaud, Brigette H. ... New York, NY
Renaud, Cook & Drury, P.A. ... Phoenix, AZ
Renaud, Elizabeth A. ... Trenton, NJ
Renaud, John W.
Department Of The Interior, National Park Service, GV
Renaud, Leonardo G. ... Miami, FL
Renaud, Matthew J. ... Chicago, IL
Renaud, Merrell B. ... McLean, VA
Renaud, Michael T. ... Boston, MA
Providence, RI
Renaud, Pedro J. ... Department of Agriculture, Food and Consumer Service, GV
Renaud, Raoul A. ... Sacramento, CA
Renaud, Robert F. ... Cranford, NJ
Renaud, Ronald K. ... Phoenix, AZ
Renaud, Thad W. ... Denver, CO
Renaudin, George W. ... Houston, TX
Renaudin, William V., Jr. ... Metairie, LA
Renauer, Albin J. ... Berkeley, CA
Renauld, David L. ... Worcester, MA
Renaut, Gilbert T. ... Department of Energy, Office of the General Counsel, GV
Renauto, Alfred T. ... White Plains, NY
Renbarger, Daniel ... Atlanta, GA
Renbarger, Grace Fisher
Round Rock, TX
Renbarger, Robert O. ... Austin, TX
Renbaum, Lawrence C. ... Washington, DC
Renberg, Charles L. ... Fresno, CA
Renberg, Dan ... United States Senate, Senatorial Assistants, GV
Renberg, Gregory D. ... Tulsa, OK
Renberg, Michael L. ... Fresno, CA
Rench, Elena Fletcher ... Cincinnati, OH
Rench, Frederick A. ... Clifton Park, NY
Rench, James L. ... Akron, OH
Rench, Stephen C. ... Denver, CO
Rencher, Guy B., II ... Portland, OR
Rencher, Guy B., II, P.C. ... Portland, OR
Rencher, Jaryl L. ... Salt Lake City, UT
Rencher, Ronald L. ... Salt Lake City, UT
Renchof, Sharon A. ... Chicago, IL
Renck, Gary M. ... Stamford, CT
Rencoret, Michelle R. ... Orlando, FL
Renda, Andrew J., Jr. ... Cedar Grove, NJ
Renda, Barbara L. ... Parsippany, NJ
Renda, Charles L. ... New Brunswick, NJ
Renda, Charles R. ... Sacramento, CA
Renda, Christine M. ... Providence, RI
Renda, Dominic P. ... Rancho Mirage, CA
Renda, Ernest A. ... Bridgewater, NJ
Renda, Ernest A., Attorney At Law, A Prof. Corp. ... Flemington, NJ
Renda, Ernest A., Attorney At Law, A Prof. Corp. ... New Brunswick, NJ
Bridgewater, NJ
Renda, James P. ... Buffalo, NY
Renda, John J. ... Poughkeepsie, NY
Renda, Michael O. ... Hawthorne, NJ
Renda, Pares & Pfalzgraf ... Buffalo, NY
Renda, Thomas A. ... Des Moines, IA
Renda, Thomas D. ... Baltimore, MD
Renda & Voynick ... Cedar Grove, NJ
Rendahl, David F. ... Visalia, CA
Rendahl, Nicole M. ... Seattle, WA
Rendahl, Roberta R. ... San Francisco, CA
Rendall, Donald J., Jr. ... Burlington, VT
Rendall, Robert V., Jr. ... Midland, TX
Rende and Baronti ... Rye, NY
Rende, Bruce E. ... Pittsburgh, PA
Rende, Joseph G. ... White Plains, NY
Rende, Kristina M. ... Rye, NY
Rende, Ryan & Downes, LLP
White Plains, NY
Rendeiro, Andrew S. ... Brooklyn, NY
Rendeiro, Gino J. ... New Orleans, LA
Rendeiro, James C., III ... Somers, NY
Rendeiro, Jill J. ... Hartford, CT
Rendeiro, Richard R. ... Hartford, CT
Rendell, Bradley E. ... Chicago, IL
Rendell, Marjorie O. ... Philadelphia, PA
Rendell, Steven K. ... Phoenix, AZ
Rendemonti, John J.
Point Pleasant Beach, NJ
Render, Ann C. ... Lexington, KY
Render, Edwin R. ... Louisville, KY
Render, John C. ... Indianapolis, IN
Render Kamas, L.C. ... Wichita, KS
Render, Kathryn Shemwell ... St. Louis, MO
Render, Leon M. ... Cincinnati, OH
Render, M. Dale ... Cincinnati, OH
Render, Patrick ... Omaha, NE
Render, Richard A. ... Wichita, KS
Render, Robert A. ... Louisville, KY
Renders, Arlana Gay ... Kailua-Kona, HI

Rendigs, Fry, Kiely & Dennis, L.L.P.
Lawrenceburg, IN
Covington, KY
Cincinnati, OH
Rendine, Danl. M. ... Philadelphia, PA
Rendish, Kimberly A.A. ... Tacoma, WA
Rendleman, Charles A. ... Columbia, SC
Rendleman, D. Scott ... Chicago, IL
Rendleman, Dennis A. ... Springfield, IL
Rendleman, Douglas R. ... Williamsburg, VA
Rendleman, James D. ... Springfield, VA
Rendleman, John S., III ... Carbondale, IL
Rendleman, Nancy S. ... Raleigh, NC
Rendlen, Albert L. ... Jefferson City, MO
Rendlen, Charles E., III ... Hannibal, MO
Rendlen, Charles E., Jr. ... Hannibal, MO
Rendlen Law Firm, The, P.C.
Hannibal, MO
Rendler, Devereaux ... Cupertino, CA
Rendler & Stevens, A Professional Corporation
Phoenix, AZ
Rendler, Terrie Seymour ... Phoenix, AZ
Rendo, Andrea Carapella ... New York, NY
Rendon, Carole Schwartz ... Cleveland, OH
Rendon, Josefina M. ... Houston, TX
Rendon, Patrick L. ... Long Beach, CA
Rendon, Ruben ... Houston, TX
Rendón, Santiago J., (P.C.) ... New York, NY
Rendón, Veronica E. ... White Plains, NY
Rendos, Thomas A. ... Minneapolis, MN
René, James M. ... Los Angeles, CA
Reneau, Andrew R. ... Milwaukee, WI
Reneau, Dale ... Oklahoma City, OK
Reneau, Peter J. ... Chicago, IL
Reneau, Robert B. ... Wetumpka, AL
Reneau, Roger ... Midwest City, OK
Reneau & Thornton ... Wetumpka, AL
Reneer, Jere ... Spanish Fork, UT
Renegar, Dona K. ... Lafayette, LA
Renegar, Gaile L.
Research Triangle Park, NC
Renegar, Gregg R. ... Oklahoma City, OK
Renegar, Joan A. ... Oklahoma City, OK
Renegar, O. Blanchard ... Oklahoma City, OK
Renehan, Alexa A. ... Silver Spring, MD
Renehan, Bryan ... Gaithersburg, MD
Renehan, Edward G. ... Jonesboro, GA
Renehan, Richard P. ... Waterbury, CT
Renehan, Richard W. ... Boston, MA
Renehan, Robert J. ... Staten Island, NY
Renehan, Thomas J., Jr. ... Philadelphia, PA
Reneker, D. Ronald ... Dallas, TX
Renella, John R. ... Trenton, NJ
Renert, Claudia B. ... San Francisco, CA
Renert, Douglas J. ... Redwood City, CA
Renetzky, Donald ... Van Nuys, CA
Renetzky, Lori A. ... Chicago, IL
Renetzky, Martin ... Lawndale, CA
Renetzky, Michael K. ... Chicago, IL
Reney, Donald P., Jr. ... Newington, CT
Renfer, Mary A. ... Honolulu, HI
Renfer, R. A., Jr. ... Raleigh, NC
Renfer, Susan Oliver ... Raleigh, NC
Renfert, Blaine ... Madison, WI
Renforth, James David, II ... Fort Worth, TX
Renfrew, Charles B. ... San Francisco, CA
Renfrew, Dwight H., Jr. ... Tarrytown, NY
Renfrew, James ... Oxford, MI
Renfrew, Yvonne M. ... Santa Monica, CA
Renfro & Associates, Law Corporation
Irvine, CA
Renfro, C. Brian ... Colorado Springs, CO
Renfro, J. Kevin ... Maryville, TN
Renfro, Julia Ann ... Cleveland, OH
Renfro, Julian C. ... Winter Park, FL
Renfro, Karen Yvonna ... New Albany, IN
Renfro, Kevin J. ... Louisville, KY
Renfro, L. Michael ... St. Joseph, MI
Renfro, Lesley Ann ... Trenton, MO
Renfro, Mike ... Austin, TX
Renfro, Phillip M. ... San Antonio, TX
Renfro, Robert L. ... Wheaton, IL
Renfro, Robert R. ... Portsmouth, NH
Renfro, Roger D. ... Irvine, CA
Renfro, Sally J. ... New York, NY
Renfro, Tom B. ... Fort Worth, TX
Renfro, Toni Cline ... Louisville, KY
Renfro, William L. ... Washington, DC
Renfro, William M., Jr. ... Kansas City, MO
Renfroe, Iona A. ... New Orleans, LA
Renfroe, James E. ... Jackson, MS
Renfroe, James Scott ... Chicago, IL
Renfroe, Judith A. ... Boulder, CO
Renfroe, Patricia M. ... Philadelphia, PA
Renfroe, Robert Randall ... Brandon, FL
Renfroe, Timothy R. ... Batesville, IN
Renfroe, Tracie J. ... Houston, TX
Renfrow, Bryan T. ... Springfield, MO
Renfrow & Frazier, P.L.L.C.
Mt. Crested Butte, CO
Renfrow, J. Royce ... Mt. Crested Butte, CO
Renfrow, James H., Jr. ... Dillon, SC
Renfrow, Kent E. ... Tulsa, OK
Renfrow, Robert P. ... St. Petersburg, FL
Renfrow, Robert R., III ... Fairburn, GA
Renga, Louis J. ... Santa Barbara, CA
Renge, Howard ... Fowler, CA
Renge, Lawson K. ... Fresno, CA
Rengel, D. Jeffery ... Sandusky, OH
Rengel, Michael T. ... Fergus Falls, MN
Rengel, Thomas C. ... St. Louis, MO
Renger, James D ... Boca Raton, FL
Renger, James D. ... New York, NY
Renger, John F., Jr. ... Charlotte, NC
Rengert, Joseph S. ... Harrisburg, PA
Rengifo, Ricardo ... Elmhurst, NY
Rengifo, Ricardo, P.C. ... Elmhurst, NY
Rengiil, Ernestine Kawai ... Koror, TT

Reni, Paul J. ... Lynnwood, WA
Reniche, Allan J. ... Coronado, CA
Renick, A. L. ... Beverly Hills, CA
Renick, C. John ... Roanoke, VA
Renick, Cecil Oren, Jr. ... San Marcos, TX
Renick, Clay D. ... San Diego, CA
Renick, Gary S. ... St. Cloud, MN
Renick, John B. ... St. Louis, MO
Renick, Kenneth H. ... Lake Worth, FL
Renick, Singer and Kamber
Lake Worth, FL
Renick, Stephen E. ... Homestead, FL
Renick, Steven J. ... Los Angeles, CA
Renier, Edith A. ... Morton Grove, IL
Renier, Elaine C. ... Chicago, IL
Renigar, James A. "Del" ... Washington, DC
Renihan, Joseph A. ... Grand Rapids, MI
Reninger, Nicole A. ... New York, NY
Renison, Brent W. ... Portland, OR
Renjilian, James ... Department of Energy, Office of the General Counsel, GV
Renk, Christopher J. ... Chicago, IL
Renk, Henry J. ... New York, NY
Renk, Richard J. ... Winona, MN
Renk, Richard J., Jr. ... St. Paul, MN
Renke, John K., II ... New Port Richey, FL
Renke, Kristine McKimson ... Detroit, MI
Renke, Robert P. ... Southfield, MI
Renkemeyer, Troy D. ... Kansas City, KS
Renken, Carl E. ... Charleston, SC
Renken, John O. ... Washington, DC
Ann Arbor, MI
Renken, Robert W. ... Los Angeles, CA
Renken, Sarai K. ... Cedar Rapids, IA
Renkens, Madeline A. ... Snohomish, WA
Renker, Thomas G. ... New York, NY
Renkert, Richard C. ... Cleveland, OH
Renkert-Thomas, Amelia S. ... Canton, OH
Renkes, Robert N. ... Tulsa, OK
Renkey, Albert Zuard ... Washington, DC
Renkey, Leslie E. ... Richmond, KY
Renkin, Richard M. ... San Diego, CA
Renkoff, Franklin D. ... New York, NY
Renkow, Peter M. ... Santa Rosa, CA
Renn, Cecilia F. ... Tallahassee, FL
Renn, Chad M. ... Wellington, KS
Renn, Donna E. ... Lisle, IL
Renn, Edward A. ... New Haven, CT
Renn & High, Chartered ... Lisle, IL
Renn, Lori A. ... Henderson, NC
Renn, Ralph ... Lisle, IL
Renn, Richard H. ... Albany, OR
Renn, Richard K. ... York, PA
Renn, Thomas M. ... Portland, OR
Renna, Gary S. ... Dallas, TX
Renna, Joseph P. ... Huntington Station, NY
Renna, Leonardo ... New York, NY
Renna, Maria S. ... Purchase, NY
Renna, Michael James ... Southampton, NY
Renne, Christine M. ... Houston, TX
Renne, Louise H. ... San Francisco, CA
Renne, Michael A. ... Columbus, OH
Renne, Paul A. ... San Francisco, CA
Renne, Virgil, Jr. ... Milwaukee, WI
Renneberg, George E. ... Conroe, TX
Renneburg, John P. ... Lutherville, MD
Rennecker, Jeffrey W. ... Washington, DC
Renneisen, G. Wayne ... Cherry Hill, NJ
Philadelphia, PA
Renneisen, Gordon W., Jr.
San Francisco, CA
Renneisen, Jay P. ... Walnut Creek, CA
Renneisen, John D. ... Washington, DC
Renneisen, John William ... Cheyenne, WY
Renneke, Gary A. ... Minneapolis, MN
Renneker, Robert H. ... Dallas, TX
Rennell, John M. ... Binghamton, NY
Rennell, Robert J. ... Ann Arbor, MI
Rennella, Cosme Ernest, (P.A.) ... Miami, FL
Renner, Arnold E. ... Salem, VA
Renner, Carol J. ... Round Rock, TX
Renner, Clarence E. ... Pratt, KS
Renner Clark Buckwalter & Voltz, P.C.
Coatesville, PA
Exton, PA
Wayne, PA
West Grove, PA
Renner, Curtis S. ... Washington, DC
Renner, Dale W. ... Haddonfield, NJ
Renner, Daniel R. ... Austin, TX
Renner, Darren P. ... Stamford, CT
Renner, Deborah ... New York, NY
Renner, Dianne M. ... Lafayette, IN
Renner, Edward H. ... St. Louis, MO
Renner, Frank R. ... Denver, CO
Renner, Franklin L. ... Peoria, IL
Renner, George C. ... Escanaba, MI
Renner, Jack L. ... Akron, OH
Renner, Jane ... San Diego, CA
Renner, Jas. E. ... Lakewood, CO
Renner, Jerome L. ... Steele, ND
Renner, Joe T. ... Dallas, TX
Renner, John F. ... Haddonfield, NJ
Renner, John J. ... Fort Myers, FL
Renner, John Robert ... Los Angeles, CA
Renner, John W. ... Cleveland, OH
Renner, Jonathan K. ... Sacramento, CA
Renner, Keith Eugene ... Auburn, KS
Renner, Kenner, Greive, Bobak, Taylor & Weber, A Legal Professional Association
Akron, OH
Canton, OH
Cleveland, OH
Westlake, OH
Youngstown, OH
Renner, Kenneth D. ... Portland, OR
Renner, Larry E. ... San Diego, CA
Renner, Mark S. ... San Jose, CA

Renner, Michael D. ... Wayne, PA
Renner, Michael J. ... Columbus, OH
Renner, Otto, Boisselle & Sklar, P.L.L.
Cleveland, OH
Renner, Patrice M. ... Livingston, NJ
Renner, Ray ... Lamesa, TX
Renner, Richard ... Dover, OH
Renner, Richard R. ... Riverside, CA
Renner, Richard W. ... Elgin, IL
Renner, Robert G. ... St. Paul, MN
Renner, Robert G., Jr. ... Minneapolis, MN
Renner, Robert K. ... Newport Beach, CA
Renner, S. Todd ... Pittsburgh, PA
Renner, Shawn D. ... Lincoln, NE
Renner, Snell & Schildknecht
Lamesa, TX
Renner, Tamara L. ... Elkhart, IN
Renner, Thomas J. ... Towson, MD
Renner, W. Karl ... Falls Church, VA
Renner, William D., II ... Coldwater, MI
Renner, William R. ... Lexington, KY
Rennert, Charles J. ... Miami, FL
Rennert, Jamie Palter ... Washington, DC
Rennert, Lynn M. ... San Jose, CA
Rennert, Richard L. ... Treasury Department, Office of Thrift Supervision, GV
Rennert, Sharon E.
Equal Employment Opportunity Commission, Office of Legal Counsel, GV
Rennert, Valerie L. ... Miami, FL
Rennett, Allen E. ... Los Angeles, CA
Rennett, Harold J,
Department of Housing and Urban Development, Office of General Counsel, GV
Renney, James W. ... Wakefield, VA
Rennick, Anne C. ... Wyoming, IL
Rennick, Charles H. ... Ruidoso, NM
Rennick, James A. ... Bradford, IL
Toulon, IL
Rennick, Kyme W. ... Columbus, OH
Rennick & Rennick ... Wyoming, IL
Rennick, Rennick & Rennick ... Bradford, IL
Toulon, IL
Rennick, Richard L., Jr. ... Covington, IN
Rennick, Robert H., Sr. ... Toulon, IL
Rennick, Robert Hamilton, Jr. ... Peoria, IL
Rennick, Sandra G. ... Fort Pierce, FL
Rennicke, James Jay ... Anoka, MN
Rennie, Aven ... East Amherst, NY
Rennie, Douglas W. ... Cincinnati, OH
Rennie, Frank F., IV ... Richmond, VA
Rennie, Heather E. ... Pittsburgh, PA
Rennie, Keith C. ... Polson, MT
Rennie, Kevin F. ... South Windsor, CT
Rennie, Kimberly S. ... Baltimore, MD
Rennie, Mary E. ... Sacramento, CA
Rennie, Paul R. ... Pittsburgh, PA
Rennie, Robert T. ... Pauls Valley, OK
Rennie, Sheldon K. ... Wilmington, DE
Rennillo, Irene Holyk ... Cleveland, OH
Renning, Tony J. ... Oshkosh, WI
Renninger, John H. ... Glendora, CA
Renninger, John S. ... Newtown, PA
Renno, Maureen ... Hinsdale, IL
Renno, William K. ... Anchorage, AK
Rennock, Michael J. W. ... New York, NY
Reno & Artura ... Lindenhurst, NY
Reno, Bogden & Ferber, Co., L.P.A.
Sandusky, OH
Reno & Cavanaugh, PLLC
Washington, DC
Baltimore, MD
Reno, David S. ... Fort Washington, PA
Reno, Douglas W. ... Omaha, NE
Reno, Duane W. ... San Francisco, CA
Reno, Gloria J. ... St. Louis, MO
Reno, James C., Jr. ... Rock Hill, SC
Reno, Janet ... Department of Justice, Office of the Attorney General, GV
Reno, John A. ... Lindenhurst, NY
Reno, Juliana ... Omaha, NE
Reno, Lawrence R. ... Denver, CO
Reno, Lee Ann ... Amarillo, TX
Reno, Lee P. ... Washington, DC
Reno, Michael J. ... Worcester, MA
Reno, Molly H. ... Ann Arbor, MI
Reno, Molly H., P.C. ... Ann Arbor, MI
Reno, Ottie W. ... Lucasville, OH
Reno, Richard H. ... Tulsa, OK
Reno, Robert B. ... Bala Cynwyd, PA
Reno, Robert Edward ... Kew Gardens, NY
Reno, Robert M. ... Sandusky, OH
Reno, Roger ... Rockford, IL
Reno, Russell Ronald, Jr., (P.C.)
Baltimore, MD
Reno, Scott G. ... Chicago, IL
Reno, Stephen E. ... Des Moines, IA
Reno, Tamara L. ... Dallas, TX
Reno, Valerie L. ... Philadelphia, PA
Reno, Vi Jean ... Seattle, WA
Reno, Zahm, Folgate, Lindberg & Powell
Rockford, IL
Renollet, Tamara S. ... Defiance, OH
Renouf, Katrina ... Washington, DC
Renouf & Polivy ... Washington, DC
Renovitch, Patricia A. ... Tallahassee, FL
Renquist, Arthur R. ... Coon Rapids, MN
Rens, Gerrit L. ... Orange City, IA
Rens, LaVerne G.
Equal Employment Opportunity Commission, Office of Legal Counsel, GV
Rensberry, Hicok & O'Hagan, P.C.
Cadillac, MI
Rensberry, Thomas R. ... Cadillac, MI
Rensch, Joseph R. ... Rancho Santa Fe, CA

Rensch, Patrick H. ....Marco Island, FL
Rensch, Richard J. ....Omaha, NE
Rensch, Steven R. ....Mesa, AZ
Rensch, Timothy J. ....Rapid City, SD
Rensch, Wm. ....Rapid City, SD
Renschler, Sharon ....Lodi, CA
Rensen, Carolyn A. ....Knoxville, TN
Rensen, Jules S. ....Knoxville, TN
Renshaw, Amy Soppel ....Columbus, OH
Renshaw, C. Kent ....Mount Vernon, IL
Renshaw, Charles C., II ....Escondido, CA
Renshaw, David L. ....Greenville, TX
Renshaw & Davis, L.L.P. ....Greenville, TX
Renshaw, Edward E. ....Carbondale, IL
Renshaw, Gail Gaus ....St. Louis, MO
Renshaw, Jean D. ....Philadelphia, PA
Renshaw, Jeffrey F ....Portland, OR
Renshaw, John C. ....Las Vegas, NV
Renshaw, Karen K. ....Ada, MN
Renshaw, Steven J. ....Los Angeles, CA
Renshaw, Terri L. ....Troy, MI
Rensin, Howard M. ....Hyattsville, MD
Rensin, Howard M., P.A. ....Hyattsville, MD
Rensin, Samuel Kallet ....Hyattsville, MD
Rensink, John L. ....Orange City, IA
Renstrom, Peter K. ....San Francisco, CA
Rensvold, Philip M. ....Olympia, WA
Renswick, Julien C. ....Brunswick, OH
Rent A Lawyer - By The Day
Washington, DC
Rentas-Pilutti, Rachael Teresa
Columbus, OH
Rentenbach, Paul R. ....Detroit, MI
Renteria, Douglas D. ....Austin, TX
Renteria, Hector A. ....Huntington Park, CA
Renteria, Joseph R.
Rancho Cucamonga, CA
Renteria-Platz, Norma ....San Antonio, TX
Rentfro, Daniel L. ....Brownsville, TX
Rentfro, Daniel L., Jr. ....Brownsville, TX
Rentfro, Faulk & Blakemore, P.C.
Brownsville, TX
Rentfro, William E. ....Boulder, CO
Rentfro, William L. ....Brownsville, TX
Rentfrow, Stacey A. ....Paw Paw, MI
Rentie, Andrea W. ....Dallas, TX
Rentiers, J. Kenneth ....Charleston, SC
Rentiers, Sally M. ....Columbia, SC
Rentmeester, Lois E. ....Madison, WI
Renton, Jeffrey B. ....Andover, MA
Renton, Susan L. ....Washington, DC
Renton, William James ....Los Angeles, CA
Rentrop, Gary R. ....Bloomfield Hills, MI
Rentrop, Haynes & Morrison, P.C.
Bloomfield Hills, MI
Rentsch, David J. ....Boston, MA
Rentschler, Judith J. ....Foster City, CA
Rentschler, Matthew J. ....Fort Wayne, IN
Rentschler, Susan M. ....Chicago, IL
Rentschler Tursi Guastamachio, LLP
Foster City, CA
Rentto, David A. ....San Diego, CA
Rentto, Robert L. ....San Diego, CA
Rentto, Robert L., Professional Law Corporation ....San Diego, CA
Rentz, Donald D. ....Albany, GA
Rentz, G. Stanley ....Waco, TX
Rentz, John K. ....Houston, TX
McAllen, TX
Rentz, Mary Catherine ....Detroit, MI
Rentz, Ronald H. ....Colquitt, GA
Rentz & Shepard ....Colquitt, GA
Rentz, Sheryl R. ....Voorhees, NJ
Wynnewood, PA
Rentz, William K. ....Salinas, CA
Rentz, William W. ....Beloit, WI
Rentzel, Christopher H. ....Dallas, TX
Rentzel, Rudolf P. ....San Rafael, CA
Rentzer, Gail E. ....Woodland Hills, CA
Rentzer, Nona ....Monterey Park, CA
Rentzer, Robert D. ....Encino, CA
Renuart, Cheridah V. ....Tallahassee, FL
Renuart, Elizabeth A. ....Washington, DC
Renville, Joseph Wm. ....Madison, WI
Renwand, Sandra Mackey ....Pittsburgh, PA
Renwand, Thomas William ....Pittsburgh, PA
Renwick, Daniel P. ....San Diego, CA
Renwick, Dianne Theresa ....Bronx, NY
Renwick, Edward S., (A Professional Corporation) ....Los Angeles, CA
Renwick, J. Roger ....Mansfield, OH
Renwick, John B. ....Sacramento, CA
Renwick, Karen Wedel ....Kansas City, MO
Renwick, Malcolm G. ....Arlington, TX
Renwick & Pierret, P.C. ....Arlington, TX
Fort Worth, TX
Renwick, Welsh & Burton ....Mansfield, OH
Reny, Charles E. ....Kingwood, TX
Reny, D. Michael ....Toledo, OH
Renyer, Kimberly W. ....Hays, KS
Renz, David W. ....Washington, DC
Renz, Eugene E., Jr. ....Media, PA
Renz, Eugene E., Jr., P.C. ....Media, PA
Renz, Greg W. ....Milwaukee, WI
Renz, James B. ....St. Louis, MO
Renz, Jeffrey C. ....Norcross, GA
Renz, Jeffrey T. ....Missoula, MT
Renz, Karen J. ....Cincinnati, OH
Renz, Phillip A. ....Fort Wayne, IN
Renz, Walter A. ....New York, NY
Renz, William T. ....Doylestown, PA
Renzi, Alexander R. ....Rochester, NY
Renzi, Anthony J., Jr. ....Washington, DC
Renzi, Constance Burnett ....Aurora, IL
Renzi, Eugene Raymond ....Watertown, NY
Renzi, Frank, Jr. ....La Canada Flintridge, CA
Renzi, George J. ....Madison, NJ
Renzi, John C. ....Joliet, IL
Renzi, Linda S. ....Department of Justice, Civil Division, GV
Renzi, Michael J. ....Joliet, IL
Renzi, Nicholas J. ....Jenkintown, PA
Renzi, Renee L. ....Watertown, NY
Renzi, Robert V. ....Watertown, NY
Renzi, Sharon M. ....Irvine, CA
Renzi, Stephanie B. N. ....Washington, DC
Renzi, Vincent D ....Washington, DC
Renzo, Anthony F. ....Des Moines, IA
Renzo, Joseph A. ....Des Moines, IA
Renzoni, George E. ....Seattle, WA
Renzulli, Christopher ....New York, NY
Renzulli, Dante W., Jr. ....Exton, PA
Renzulli, Jeffrey J. ....McLean, VA
Renzulli, John F. ....New York, NY
Renzulli, Judith Nichols ....Wilmington, DE
Renzulli, Lori Magliochetti
East Brunswick, NJ
Renzulli, Nora Drew ....Staten Island, NY
Renzulli & Rutherford ....Hackensack, NJ
New York, NY
Renzullo, Patsy M. ....Winsted, CT
Reoch, John J., Jr. ....Dallas, TX
Reosti, Ronald, & Associates, P.C.
Detroit, MI
Reosti, Ronald J. ....Detroit, MI
Reott, Raymond T. ....Chicago, IL
Repa, Barbara Kate ....Berkeley, CA
Repaci, Nicolette ....New York, NY
Repak, Michael J. ....New York, NY
Repaske, William A. ....New Iberia, LA
Repasky, Blaise A. ....Woodhaven, MI
Repasky, Blaise A., P.C. ....Woodhaven, MI
Repasky, Robert D. ....Madison, WI
Repasky, William T. ....Louisville, KY
Repass, Dale P. ....Dubuque, IA
Repass, David Michael ....Washington, DC
RePass, Frank M., III ....New Orleans, LA
Repass, James W. ....Houston, TX
Repass, M. Robin ....Knoxville, TN
Repass, Michael D. ....Toledo, OH
Repass, Thomas W. ....Birmingham, AL
Repasy, Christine Hayer ....Simsbury, CT
Repasy, Roberta D. ....San Diego, CA
Repath, Paul R. ....St. Johns, MI
Repay, Bridgett Jo ....Hammond, IN
Repay, Henry ....Elgin, IL
Repcheck, John J. ....Pittsburgh, PA
Repczynski, Thomas W. ....Arlington, VA
Repel, Robert J. ....Chicago, IL
Repella, S. Gary ....Steubenville, OH
Repenning, Betty J. ....Mokena, IL
Repenning, Dennis ....Covington, KY
Repenning, John E. ....Tempe, AZ
Reper, Ronald R. ....Houston, TX
Reperowitz, Deborah A. ....Roseland, NJ
Repetti, Elizabeth M. ....Winston-Salem, NC
Repetti, Frederick F. ....Falls Church, VA
Repetti, George L. ....Williston Park, NY
Repetti, James R. ....Boston, MA
Repetti, Joan H. ....Atlanta, GA
Repetti, Peter J. ....New York, NY
Repetti, Susan Leonard ....Boston, MA
Repetto, Augustine A., Jr. ....Linwood, NJ
Repetto, Augusto ....Washington, DC
Repetto, Bruce E. ....Montclair, NJ
Repetto, David M. ....Hackensack, NJ
Repetto, Maureen C. ....Media, PA
Rephan, Jack ....Norfolk, VA
Rephan, Jerry M.
Hot Springs National Park, AR
Rephen, Paul T. ....New York, NY
Repice, Nancy A. ....Worcester, MA
Repici, Anthony, Jr. ....Abington, PA
Repici, Dominic J. ....Fairfax, VA
Repicky, Thomas, Co., L.P.A.
Willoughby, OH
Repicky, Thomas G. ....Willoughby, OH
Repiso, Michael ....Miami, FL
Repka, David A. ....Washington, DC
Repka, Janet N. ....Department of Defense, Defense Legal Services Agency, GV
Repka, Janice J. ....York, PA
Repka, Michael J. ....Fairfield, NJ
Repke, Thomas E. ....McLean, VA
Repko, David V. ....Cleveland, OH
Repko, John F. ....Fayetteville, NY
Repko, Rita L. ....Novi, MI
Repko, Rodney J. ....Sayre, PA
Repkow, Karol Martin ....Sacramento, CA
Replansky, Warren S. ....Pine Plains, NY
Replin, Norman S. ....Aurora, CO
Replin, Ricki M. ....Tulsa, OK
Replin, Ricki M., P.C. ....Tulsa, OK
Replin, Stephen D. ....Denver, CO
Replogle, Daniel M., III ....Camden, NJ
Replogle, David ....San Francisco, CA
Replogle, David, A Prof. Corp., Law Offices of
San Francisco, CA
Replogle, Dee A., Jr. ....Oklahoma City, OK
Replogle, J. Marc ....Marietta, GA
Replogle, John ....Riverside, CA
Replogle, Ronald P. ....New York, NY
Replogle, Thomas J. ....Dayton, OH
Replogle, William H. ....Lake Oswego, OR
Repole, Michael E. ....Smithtown, NY
Repp, David M. ....Des Moines, IA
Repp, Gordon ....Waukegan, IL
Repp, G. P. ....Sacramento, CA
Repp, Marissa G. ....Washington, DC
Repp, Paul H. ....New York, NY
Repp, Rhonda L. ....Prescott, AZ
Repp, Richard A. ....Richmond, VA
Repp, Robert E. ....Portland, OR
Repp, Sheldon D. ....Washington, DC
Reppa, Jerome J. ....Munster, IN
Reppart, William C., Jr. ....Grove, OK
Reppe, Michael K. ....Denver, CO
Reppell, Thomas H. ....Grandview, MO
Reppen, Kyra E. ....New York, NY
Repper, George R. ....Washington, DC
Repper, Theodore, Jr. ....Middletown, OH
Reppert, Bruce E. ....Fairview Heights, IL
Reppert, Richard L. ....Cleveland, OH
Reppert, Sibley P., & Associates
Boston, MA
Reppeto, William M., III ....Boerne, TX
Reppeto, William M., Jr. Law Offices of
Dallas, TX
Reppetto, Gerald G. ....Los Angeles, CA
Reppucci, David K. ....Lowell, MA
Reppucci, Frank J., Jr. ....Parsippany, NJ
Reppucci, Victoria V. ....Lowell, MA
Reppy, William ....Santa Barbara, CA
Reppy, William A., Jr. ....Durham, NC
Repsher, William C.
Environmental Protection Agency, Office of Enforcement and Compliance Assurance, GV
Repsis, Helen T. ....Dallas, TX
Repsis, John S. ....Dallas, TX
Repsold, Nelson B. ....Vancouver, WA
Repucci, Michael J. ....Boulder, CO
Requa, David L. ....Springfield, IL
Requadt, Scott G. ....New York, NY
Requenez, Linda ....Dallas, TX
Rerat, Michael L ....Eden Prairie, MN
Reres, Matt ....Department of the Army, Office of the General Counsel, GV
Reres, Vincent ....New York, NY
Rering, Alexander J. ....Fort Lauderdale, FL
Rerko, A. Tereasa ....Greensburg, PA
Rerko, Cynthia Johnson ....Dallas, TX
Rerko, Frederick J. ....Dallas, TX
Rerucha, Cynthia L. ....Toledo, OH
Rerucha, Janice ....Laramie, WY
Resar, Jeremy L. ....Madison, WI
Resar, Kenneth R. ....Lorain, OH
Resavage, Todd P. ....Mobile, AL
Resch, Ann W. ....Anchorage, AK
Resch, Betty C. ....Lake Worth, FL
Resch, Diane M. ....Elkhorn, WI
Resch, Kurt M. ....Hackensack, NJ
Resch, Marilyn B. ....Casey, IL
Effingham, IL
Resch Polster Alpert & Berger LLP
Los Angeles, CA
Resch, Richard K. ....Fort Lauderdale, FL
Resch, Ronald M., (Professional Corporation) ....Los Angeles, CA
Resch, Timothy J. ....Portland, OR
Resch, Tracy W. ....Marshall, IL
Resch, William H., Jr. ....Philadelphia, PA
Reschke, Jennifer L. ....Wichita, KS
Reschke, Michael W. ....Chicago, IL
Reschly, Jason A. ....Kansas City, MO
Rescho, Richard F. ....San Francisco, CA
Rescia, Kara Schultz ....Springfield, MA
Rescigno, Peter J. ....Parsippany, NJ
Rescinio, Albert J. ....Oakhurst, NJ
Resciniti, Michael P. J. ....Manalapan, NJ
Resciniti, S. Edmund ....Brooklyn, NY
Rescorla, Richard C. ....Morristown, NJ
Reseburg, Walter J., Jr. ....Seattle, WA
Reseburg, William R. ....Seattle, WA
Reseburg, William R., P.S. ....Seattle, WA
Reseigh, John D. ....Southfield, MI
Resella, Dita ....College Station, TX
Resen, W. Patrick ....Walnut Creek, CA
Resendez, Carlos ....San Antonio, TX
Resendez, Gilbert ....Laguna Beach, CA
Resendez, Ignacio ....Idaho Falls, ID
Resendez, Jay A. ....Sacramento, CA
Resendez, Joel Cruz ....Corpus Christi, TX
Resendez, John R. ....Austin, TX
San Antonio, TX
Resendez, Linda Flores ....Corpus Christi, TX
Resendez, Victor A. "Tony", III
San Antonio, TX
Resendiz, Gustavo ....Boston, MA
Reser, Don C. ....San Antonio, TX
Reser, Don C., P.C. ....San Antonio, TX
Reser, Philip N. ....Knoxville, IA
Reser, Rebecca Jo ....San Antonio, TX
Reser, Yancey ....Walla Walla, WA
Reservitz, Andrew F. ....Brockton, MA
Reservitz, Edward L. ....Brockton, MA
Reservitz & Steinberg, P.C. ....Brockton, MA
Resetar, Janet F. ....Garland, TX
Resh, Dennis D. ....Los Angeles, CA
Resh, Harvey J. ....Waltham, MA
Resh, John A. ....Rockford, IL
Resh, Linda S. ....Chicago, IL
Resh, Ronald E. ....Chevy Chase, MD
Resha, Salem N., Jr. ....Birmingham, AL
Resheter, Daniel D., Jr. ....Milwaukee, WI
Resich, John J., Jr. ....San Pedro, CA
Resich, John J., Jr., A Professional Corporation ....San Pedro, CA
Resick, Hansen & Follis ....Bellingham, WA
Resick, Thomas J., (P.S.) ....Bellingham, WA
Resila, James Anthony ....Albany, NY
Resis, Michael ....Chicago, IL
Resis, Robert H. ....Chicago, IL
Resisa, Abraham ....Los Angeles, CA
Resk, Nancy A. ....Chicago, IL
Resk, Terry E. ....North Palm Beach, FL
Palm Beach, FL
Reske, James R. ....New York, NY
Resko, Michael John ....New York, NY
Resler, Edward C. ....Golden Valley, MN
Resler, Jeffrey A. ....Los Angeles, CA
Resler, Katherine A. ....Golden, CO
Resler, Mark L. ....Cincinnati, OH
Resley, Susan D. ....Palo Alto, CA
Resmini & Cantor, Ltd. ....Fall River, MA
Seekonk, MA
Providence, RI
Resmini, Ronald J. ....Fall River, MA
Seekonk, MA
Providence, RI
Resneck, William A. ....Oakland, CA
Resneck, William A. ....Orinda, CA
Resneck, William A. ....Walnut Creek, CA
Resnek, Barbara F. ....Newton, MA
Resnek & Fields ....Boston, MA
Newton, MA
Resnek, Frank M. ....Newton, MA
Resner, Peter C. ....Chicago, IL
Resney, Michael M. ....Calumet City, IL
Resnic, Beauregard, Waite and Driscoll
Holyoke, MA
Northampton, MA
Resnic, Burton S. ....Holyoke, MA
Resnic, Harold I. ....Springfield, MA
Resnick, Aaron R. ....Miami, FL
Resnick and Abraham, L.L.C.
Los Angeles, CA
Wilmington, DE
Washington, DC
Pembroke Pines, FL
Norcross, GA
Baltimore, MD
Burlington, NJ
Hicksville, NY
Charlotte, NC
Glen Mills, PA
Fairfax, VA
Resnick, Adam D. ....Washington, DC
Resnick, Alan N. ....New York, NY
Resnick, Alice Robie ....Columbus, OH
Resnick, Allan M. ....Deerfield, IL
Resnick, Alleck A. ....Baltimore, MD
Resnick, Allen S. ....Los Angeles, CA
Resnick & Associates ....Milwaukee, WI
Resnick, B. Stanley ....Baltimore, MD
Resnick, Barbara J. ....New York, NY
Resnick, Barnet, (Law Corporation)
Los Angeles, CA
Newport Beach, CA
Resnick, Barry A. ....Detroit, MI
Resnick, Barry A. ....Farmington Hills, MI
Resnick, Bernard Max ....Bala Cynwyd, PA
Resnick, Bruce M. ....Voorhees, NJ
Resnick Caffrey & Webster ....Warwick, RI
Resnick, Carlton R. ....Lincolnwood, IL
Resnick, Charles G. ....Cherry Hill, NJ
Resnick, Charles H. ....Lexington, MA
Resnick, Claudia ....Phoenix, AZ
Resnick, David A. ....Baltimore, MD
Resnick, David L. ....Madison, WI
Resnick, David S. ....Boston, MA
Resnick, Debra I. ....New York, NY
Resnick, Donald I. ....Chicago, IL
Resnick, Douglas W. ....Hopkinton, MA
Resnick, Douglas W., P.C. ....Hopkinton, MA
Resnick, Eddy R. ....Tampa, FL
Resnick, Edward ....Brooklyn, NY
Resnick, Edward S. ....Hollywood, FL
Resnick, Eidelberg & Jack, A Professional Association ....Baltimore, MD
Resnick, Elise ....Chicago, IL
Resnick, Ellen Beth ....New York, NY
Resnick, Elliott I. ....Cleveland, OH
Resnick, Elliott I., Co., L.P.A.
Cleveland, OH
Resnick, Eugene L. ....Chicago, IL
Resnick, Franklin D. ....Norcross, GA
Resnick, Gail W. ....Flushing, NY
Resnick, Gary A. ....Highland Park, IL
Resnick, Gerald A. ....New York, NY
Resnick, Gerald J. ....Springfield, NJ
Resnick & Gray ....Los Angeles, CA
Newport Beach, CA
Resnick, H. Nathan ....West Bloomfield, MI
Resnick, Harriette I. ....New York, NY
Resnick, Harris J. ....Jenkintown, PA
Resnick, Janet F. ....Milwaukee, WI
Resnick, Jason E. ....Orange, CA
Resnick, Jay A.
Pension Benefit Guaranty Corporation, Office of the General Counsel, GV
Resnick, Jeffrey ....Pennsauken, NJ
Resnick, Jeffrey B. ....Dallas, TX
Resnick, Jeffrey B., P.C. ....Dallas, TX
Resnick, Jeffrey L.
Christiansted, St. Croix, VI
Resnick, Joel E. ....Chicago, IL
Resnick, Johanna K. ....Bronx, NY
Resnick, John J. ....Orange, CA
Resnick, Joyce M. ....Hartford, CT
Resnick, Kalman D. ....Chicago, IL
Resnick, Kathleen M. ....Albany, NY
Resnick, Kenneth A. ....Morristown, NJ
Resnick, Kenneth S. ....Cincinnati, OH
Resnick, Lawrence R., (Professional Corporation) ....Los Angeles, CA
Resnick, Lois S. ....Shaker Heights, OH
Resnick, Marc L. ....Washington, DC
Resnick, Mark H. ....Beverly Hills, CA
Resnick, Mark S. ....Boston, MA
Resnick, Marvin, (S.C.) ....Milwaukee, WI
Resnick, Melvin L. ....Toledo, OH
Resnick, Melvyn E. ....Painesville, OH
Resnick, Michael ....Chicago, IL
Resnick, Michael L. ....Sarasota, FL
Resnick, Mitchell J. ....Phoenix, AZ
Resnick & Moss, P.C. ....Detroit, MI
West Bloomfield, MI
Resnick, Murray I. ....Wilmington, DE
Washington, DC
Baltimore, MD
Resnick, Myron J. ....Northbrook, IL

Revlett, Constance E. ....Calhoun, KY
Revness, Alissa L. ....Seattle, WA
Revness, Michael J. ....Cherry Hill, NJ
Wayne, PA
Revnew, Thomas R. ....Milwaukee, WI
Revo, Terrence ....Albuquerque, NM
Revord, Lisa Maria Carrizales ....Chicago, IL
Revord, Matthew ....Chicago, IL
Revord, Raoul D. ....Marquette, MI
Revta, George, Jr. ....Columbus, OH
Revuelta, Magdalena S. ....San Juan, PR
Revuelta, Noreen M. ....Port Washington, NY
Revvill, Jack Carson ....Fresno, CA
Revzen, Debra K. ....St. Paul, MN
Revzin, Bruce D. ....Boston, MA
Rew, Christine M. ....Chicago, IL
Rew, Lawrence B. ....Pendleton, OR
Rew, R. Kevin ....Atlanta, GA
Rew, Richard W., II ....Austin, TX
Rew, Vernon E., Jr. ....Fort Worth, TX
Rewald, Margaret M. ....Black River Falls, WI
Rewalt, Richard E. ....St. Clair Shores, MI
Rewalt, Sandra L. ....Bloomfield Hills, MI
Rewerts, Carl R. ....New Orleans, LA
Rewerts, Glendon E. ....Scott City, KS
Rewinski, Jon L. ....Los Angeles, CA
Rewoldt, Dana ....Slater, IA
Rex, Beth L. ....New York, NY
Rex, David C. ....Dallas, TX
Rex, Edgar H., Jr. ....Edina, MN
Rex, Gary L. ....Lincoln, NE
Rex, James L. ....Andrews, TX
Rex, Kevin E. ....Encino, CA
Rex, Leslie Van Natta ....Indianapolis, IN
Rex, Michael J. ....Bloomfield Hills, MI
Rex, Robert H. ....Boca Raton, FL
Rexach & Picó ....San Juan, PR
Rexach, Ralph J. ....San Juan, PR
Rexach-Benítez, Clotilde ....San Juan, PR
Rexach González, Denise M.
San Juan, PR
Rexach-Rexach, Magda Mariela
San Juan, PR
Rexer, Christian ....Chicago, IL
Rexer, Linda K. ....Lansing, MI
Rexford, Clisson S. ....Chicago, IL
Rexford, Gary W. ....Topeka, KS
Rexford, John C. ....Upton, MA
Rexford & Kilmartin, A Professional Corporation ....Newport, VT
Rexinger, Allan R. ....Washington, DC
Rexinger, Allen Robert ....Washington, DC
Rexon, Brian L. ....Los Angeles, CA
Rexon, Freedman, Klepetar & Hambleton, A Professional Corporation
Los Angeles, CA
Rexroad, David R. ....Buckhannon, WV
Rexroad, Lynne W., (Mrs.)
Buckhannon, WV
Rexroad & Rexroad ....Buckhannon, WV
Rexroat, Christopher L. ....Milwaukee, WI
Rexrode, David S. ....Tampa, FL
Rexrode, Robert R. ....Knoxville, TN
Rexroth, Lori A. ....Selinsgrove, PA
Rexroth, Melissa J. C. ....Binghamton, NY
Rey, Albert D. ....Miami, FL
Rey, Albert D., P.A. ....Miami, FL
Rey, Clifford F., The Law Office of
Wake Forest, NC
Rey, F. Cary ....Department Of The Interior, Office of Hearings & Appeals, GV
Rey, Javier A. ....Kingwood, TX
Rey, Jorge A. ....New York, NY
Rey, Joseph J., Jr. ....El Paso, TX
Rey, Kendra L. ....Dallas, TX
Rey, L. Ruby ....New York, NY
Rey, Oskar E. ....Seattle, WA
Seattle, WA
Rey, Richard Charles, II ....Los Angeles, CA
Rey-Bear, Daniel I. S. J.
Albuquerque, NM
Reybitz, Chester A. ....Bethlehem, PA
Reybitz, Ronald J. ....Allentown, PA
Reyburn, Mary J. ....Washington, DC
Rey-Cancio, María-Isabel ....San Juan, PR
Reycraft, George D. ....New York, NY
Reyelts, Steven L. ....Duluth, MN
Reyen, Keith ....San Francisco, CA
Reyer, Jamaes N., P.A. ....Boca Raton, FL
Reyer, James N. ....Boca Raton, FL
Reyer, Merswind C. ....Sacramento, CA
Reyering, William H. ....Cincinnati, OH
Reyes, Alma ....Houston, TX
Reyes, Angel L., III ....Dallas, TX
Reyes, Angel M. ....Miami, FL
Reyes, Antonio A. ....Visalia, CA
Reyes, Arcadio J. ....Washington, DC
Reyes, Arcadio J. ....Rockville, MD
Reyes, Arnold ....Austin, TX
Reyes & Associates, P.C. ....Dallas, TX
Reyes, Benjamin T., II ....Oakland, CA
Reyes, Brenda P. ....San Francisco, CA
Reyes, Carlos J., Jr. ....Boca Raton, FL
Fort Lauderdale, FL
Reyes, Carolyn Lenihan ....Coral Gables, FL
Reyes, David K. ....Gardena, CA
Reyes, Dolores ....El Paso, TX
Reyes, Dorothy B. ....Los Angeles, CA
Reyes, E. David ....Minneapolis, MN
Reyes, Edw. O. ....Lafayette, CA
Reyes, Elaine M. ....Newark, NJ
Reyes, Elena ....Fullerton, CA
Reyes, Eloise Gomez ....San Bernardino, CA
Reyes, Eric A. ....Port Charlotte, FL
Reyes, Eric A., P.A. ....Port Charlotte, FL
Reyes, Eric R. ....Fort Worth, TX
Harlingen, TX
Reyes, Faith Kalman ....Nashville, TN

Reyes, Frumencio, Jr. ....Houston, TX
Reyes, George M., (P.C.) ....Riverside, CA
Reyes, Hector I. ....El Paso, TX
Reyes, Israel U. ....Miami, FL
Reyes, Janet Bloom ....Los Angeles, CA
Reyes, Jason A. ....Boston, MA
Reyes, Jason D. ....Birmingham, MI
Reyes, Jerry S. ....Los Angeles, CA
Reyes, Jesse Salvador ....Boston, MA
Reyes, John L. ....Akron, OH
Reyes, Julio Cesar Perez ....Miami, FL
Reyes Law Firm, The, A Professional Corporation ....Austin, TX
Reyes, Lillian J. ....Tampa, FL
Reyes, Loretta D. Nelms ....San Diego, CA
Reyes, Lori E. ....Topeka, KS
Reyes, Lourdes Ivette ....New York, NY
Reyes, Lucy E. ....Boston, MA
Reyes, Manuel ....Chicago, IL
Reyes, Margaret Popp ....Omaha, NE
Reyes, Marizela ....Miami, FL
Reyes, Mary E. ....Dallas, TX
Reyes, Nancy H. ....San Antonio, TX
Reyes, Orlando Emilio ....Miami, FL
Reyes, Paul R. ....Laurel, MD
Reyes Peña & Santiago Romero
San Juan, PR
Reyes, Peter M., Jr. ....Minneapolis, MN
Reyes, Raul Alberto ....New York, NY
Reyes, Raul H. ....Pasadena, CA
Reyes, Ray J. ....Los Angeles, CA
Reyes & Regan, A Professional Corporation
Rochester, NY
Reyes, Ricardo A. ....Boca Raton, FL
Reyes, Richard R., Law Offices of
Pasadena, CA
Reyes, Rita A. ....Los Angeles, CA
Reyes, Robin A. ....Dedham, MA
Reyes, Rudolph ....San Francisco, CA
Reyes, Sam ....Abilene, TX
Reyes, Sara Garcia ....Miami, FL
Reyes, Sara L. ....Miami, FL
Reyes, Sean D. ....Salt Lake City, UT
Reyes, Victor I. ....Pueblo, CO
Reyes, Victor Tenorio ....Philadelphia, PA
Reyes, Yvette B. ....Miami, FL
Reyes, Yvonne ....Boston, MA
Reyes-Bibiloni, Pedro J. ....San Juan, PR
Reyes-Burke, John N.K. ....Honolulu, HI
Reyes-Castillo, A. Imelda ....Houston, TX
Reyes-Gavilan, Adelina ....New York, NY
Reyes-Gilestra, Alcides ....San Juan, PR
Reyes-Gilestra, Tristán ....San Juan, PR
Reyes Kopack, Laura ....Livonia, MI
Reyes-Lopez, Vivian ....San Juan, PR
Reyes Peña, Erasmo ....San Juan, PR
Reyes Perez, Melissa ....San Juan, PR
Reyes Robbins, Ann ....Fort Wayne, IN
Reyes-Vidal, Antonio ....San Antonio, TX
Reyes-Villanueva, Adriana I. ....Chicago, IL
Reyff, Robert R. ....Novato, CA
Reyher, Deborah M. ....Department of Justice, Environment and Natural Resources Division, GV
Reymann, Jonathan M.
San Francisco, CA
Reymann, Joseph ....San Dimas, CA
Reymann, Lara A. ....Salt Lake City, UT
Reymann, Lucille E. ....Charlotte, NC
Reymann, Patrick H. ....Akron, OH
Reymond, Leon J., III ....New Orleans, LA
Reymond, Leon J., Jr. ....New Orleans, LA
Rey-Moran, Monica A. ....Miami, FL
Reymore, Douglas E., Jr. ....Stuart, FL
Reyna, Armando L. ....Corpus Christi, TX
Reyna, Arthur C., Jr. ....San Antonio, TX
Reyna, Cheryl ....Waco, TX
Reyna, Felipe ....Waco, TX
Reyna, Jeffrey W. ....San Francisco, CA
Reyna, Jimmie V. ....Washington, DC
Reyna, Jose J. ....McAllen, TX
Reyna, Laura Salinas ....San Antonio, TX
Reyna, Mary E. ....Los Angeles, CA
Reyna, Michael ....San Antonio, TX
Reyna, Nelda C. ....Department of Justice, Civil Division, GV
Reyna & Reyna, P.C. ....Waco, TX
Reyna, Ricardo R. ....San Antonio, TX
Reyna, Rose Marie Guerra ....McAllen, TX
Reyna, Ruben F. ....Washington, DC
Reyna, Sarah Matson ....Long Beach, CA
Reynaga, Gilbert ....Sacramento, CA
Reynaga, Paul ....Sacramento, CA
Reynard & Associates, P.C. ....Denver, CO
Reynard, Charles G. ....Bloomington, IL
Reynard, David D., Jr. ....Beaumont, TX
Reynard, Ellen G. ....Beaumont, TX
Reynard, Jack P., Jr. ....Springfield, OH
Reynard, James A. ....Thousand Oaks, CA
Reynard, Paul J. ....Nashville, TN
Reynard, William F. ....Denver, CO
Reynardus, Jorge E. ....Miami, FL
Reynaud, Ann L. ....Houston, TX
Reynaud, Claude F., Jr. ....Baton Rouge, LA
Reynaud, Wilbur W. ....Lutcher, LA
Reynaud-Bills, Jeanne M. ....Winter Park, FL
Reynders, Thomas R. ....Department of State, Foreign Service Officers (Overseas), GV
Reynen, John D. ....Sacramento, CA
Reynen, John L. ....New York, NY
Reynen, John R., II ....Victorville, CA
Reyner, Alan J. ....Columbia, SC
Reyner, William S., Jr. ....Washington, DC
Reynerson, R. Jeffrey ....Springdale, AR
Reynes, Stephen A. ....Montpelier, VT
Reynier, Allebach & Reber, P.C.
Pottstown, PA
Reynier, Ronald H. ....Pottstown, PA

Reynier, Ronald H., Jr. ....Hood River, OR
Reynolds, A. David ....New York, NY
Reynolds, Aidan C. ....Baton Rouge, LA
Reynolds, Alicia C. ....Baltimore, MD
Reynolds, Allan S. ....Norfolk, VA
Reynolds, Allan S., Jr. ....Norfolk, VA
Reynolds, Amy K. ....Charlotte, NC
Reynolds, Amy Lou ....Athens, GA
Reynolds, Andrew J. ....Little Rock, AR
Reynolds, Andrew P.
United States Court Of Veterans Appeals, GV
Reynolds, Angela M. ....Detroit, MI
Reynolds, Anne B.
United States Postal Service, Law Department, GV
Reynolds, Anson D. ....Irvine, CA
Reynolds, B. Gerald ....Bloomington, IL
Reynolds, Babette Maria ....Charlotte, NC
Reynolds & Baker ....Chicago, IL
Reynolds, Barbara W. ....New Milford, CT
Reynolds, Barry G. ....Tulsa, OK
Reynolds, Ben L. ....Houston, TX
Reynolds, Benoni O. ....Winnsboro, SC
Reynolds, Bernard E. ....Moorhead, MN
Fargo, ND
Reynolds, Bill D. ....Fort Smith, AR
Reynolds, Bradley Kenneth ....Atlanta, GA
Reynolds, Brett A. ....Bowling Green, KY
Reynolds, Brett T. ....San Antonio, TX
Reynolds, Brian C. ....Los Angeles, CA
Reynolds, Brian E. ....Springfield, IL
Reynolds, Brian R. ....Denver, CO
Reynolds, Bruce A.
Department of Commerce, Patent and Trademark Office, GV
Reynolds, Bruce Elliott ....Keene, NH
Reynolds, Bruce M. ....Lexington, KY
Reynolds, Bruce W. ....McLean, VA
Reynolds, Bryan R. ....Owensboro, KY
Reynolds, Bryan W. ....St. Petersburg, FL
Reynolds, C. Michael ....Bowling Green, KY
Reynolds, C. Roderick ....Ames, IA
Reynolds, C. Timothy ....Dallas, TX
Reynolds, Cameron ....Bryan, TX
Reynolds, Candice A. ....Wichita, KS
Reynolds, Carl R. ....Rochester, NY
Reynolds, Carl V. ....Austin, TX
Reynolds, Carole L.
Federal Trade Commission, Bureau of Consumer Protection, GV
Reynolds, Carolyn M. ....Los Angeles, CA
Reynolds, Caronia, Gianelli & Hagney
Hauppauge, NY
Reynolds, Carroll Van ....Metter, GA
Reynolds, Catherine Ingram ....Marietta, OH
Reynolds, Catherine M. ....Jackson, MI
Reynolds, Catherine S. ....New York, NY
Reynolds, Cathy A. ....Sacramento, CA
Reynolds, Chad Frederick
Baton Rouge, LA
Reynolds, Charles C. ....Portland, OR
Reynolds, Charles (Chuck) G., Jr.
Lanett, AL
Reynolds, Charles E. ....Cincinnati, OH
Reynolds, Charles E., II ....Tampa, FL
Reynolds, Charles G., Sr.
Alexander City, AL
Reynolds, Charles L. ....Amarillo, TX
Reynolds, Charles P. ....Albuquerque, NM
Reynolds, Charles Patrick ....Austin, TX
Fort Worth, TX
Houston, TX
Reynolds, Charles W. ....Little Rock, AR
Reynolds, Charles W. ....Crookston, MN
Reynolds & Christiansen, P.C. ....Provo, UT
Reynolds, Christopher J.
Prince Frederick, MD
Reynolds, Christopher P. ....New York, NY
Reynolds, Clayton ....New York, NY
Reynolds, Clinton A. ....Riverside, CT
Reynolds & Conway, P.C.
Springfield, MO
Reynolds, Corinne K. ....Stockton, CA
Reynolds, Craig R. ....Wooster, OH
Reynolds, C. V. ....Prestonsburg, KY
Reynolds, Dallas T., III ....Knoxville, TN
Reynolds, Daniel D. ....Binghamton, NY
Reynolds, Daniel E. ....New York, NY
Reynolds, Daniel P. ....Trenton, NJ
Reynolds, Daniel S. ....De Kalb, IL
Reynolds, Danna D. ....Midland, TX
Reynolds, Darnall W. ....Oakland, CA
Reynolds, David C. ....New York, NY
Reynolds, David E., (P.C.)
Los Angeles, CA
Reynolds, David G. ....Albuquerque, NM
Reynolds, David H. ....Austin, TX
Reynolds, David J., Jr. ....St. Louis, MO
Reynolds, David L. ....Conway, AR
Reynolds, David L. ....New Haven, CT
Reynolds, David Reaves ....Raleigh, NC
Reynolds & Davis, L.L.C.
Kansas City, KS
Independence, MO
Kansas City, MO
Reynolds, Deborah R. ....Woodstock, NH
Reynolds, Dennis D. ....Seattle, WA
Reynolds, Dennis J. ....Leawood, KS
Reynolds, Dennis W. ....Longview, WA
Reynolds, Diane C. ....San Gabriel, CA
Reynolds, Diane D. ....Columbus, OH
Reynolds, Don L. ....Wooster, OH
Reynolds, Donald B., Jr. ....Washington, DC
Reynolds, Donald P. ....Chicago, IL
Reynolds, Donald R. ....Modesto, CA
Reynolds, Donald R. ....Raleigh, NC
Reynolds, Douglas C. ....Boston, MA

Reynolds, Douglas G. ....Penn Yan, NY
Reynolds, Douglas H., (P.A.)
Fort Lauderdale, FL
Reynolds, Douglas R. ....San Diego, CA
Reynolds, Douglas Ward ....Viera, FL
Reynolds, Duane L. ....Farmington Hills, MI
Reynolds, Dudley Cole ....Birmingham, AL
Reynolds, E. Thompson ....Trout Lake, WA
Reynolds, Earl Cyril ....Baton Rouge, LA
Reynolds, Edward B., Jr.
Charlotte Amalie, St. Thomas, VI
Reynolds, Edward C., Jr. ....Detroit, MI
Reynolds, Edward E. ....Metairie, LA
Reynolds, Edward F., Jr. ....Hartford, CT
Reynolds, Edward J. ....Leominster, MA
Reynolds, Edward Kim
Lexington Park, MD
Reynolds, Edward L. ....Branford, CT
Reynolds, Elizabeth D. ....Honolulu, HI
Reynolds, Ellsworth G. ....Pigeon, MI
Reynolds, Ernest (Skip), III
Fort Worth, TX
Reynolds, Eugene G. ....Morris Plains, NJ
Reynolds, Farmer & Warner, LLP
Columbus, OH
Reynolds, Floyd K. ....Standish, MI
Reynolds, Forker, Berkley, Suter & Rose
Hutchinson, KS
Reynolds, Francis T. ....Arlington, MA
Reynolds, Frank ....Toledo, OH
Reynolds, Frank Harrison ....Lansing, MI
Reynolds, Frank R., Jr. ....Chicago, IL
Reynolds, Franklin B., Jr. ....Washington, VA
Reynolds, Fred E., Jr. ....Houston, TX
Reynolds, Fred M. ....Pasadena, TX
Reynolds, Fred S., Jr. ....Rock Hill, SC
Reynolds, Frederick W., III ....Dallas, TX
Reynolds, G. Thomas, Jr. ....Skillman, NJ
Reynolds, Garry L. ....Pendleton, OR
Reynolds, Gary M. ....Smithville, TX
Reynolds, Gary S. ....Fair Oaks, CA
Reynolds, Gayle A. ....New Orleans, LA
Reynolds, George K., III ....Baltimore, MD
Reynolds, George R. ....Birmingham, AL
Reynolds, George S., III ....Tallahassee, FL
Reynolds, George T. ....Cherry Hill, NJ
Harrisburg, PA
King Of Prussia, PA
Reynolds, George W. ....Philadelphia, PA
Reynolds, Gerald A. ....Kansas City, MO
Reynolds, Glenn C. ....Madison, WI
Reynolds, Glenn Harlan ....Knoxville, TN
Reynolds, Glenn T.
Federal Communications Commission, Common Carrier Bureau, GV
Reynolds, Gordon D. ....Somerset, PA
Reynolds, Grant C. ....Potomac, MD
Reynolds, Gregory C. ....Glen Burnie, MD
Reynolds, Gregory S. ....Nashville, TN
Reynolds, Guy D. ....Baraboo, WI
Reynolds, Guy E. ....Jackson, CA
Reynolds, H. Don ....Phoenix, AZ
Reynolds, H. Gerald ....Tampa, FL
Reynolds, H. Newlin ....Hutchinson, KS
Reynolds, Hal F. ....Washington, DC
Reynolds, Hanson S. ....Boston, MA
Reynolds, Harold F. ....Naples, FL
Reynolds, Harriet T. ....Norfolk, VA
Reynolds, Harry M. ....Tehachapi, CA
Reynolds, Harry Rand ....Pittsburgh, PA
Reynolds, Heather ....Astoria, OR
Reynolds & Henehan ....Avon, NY
Reynolds, Henry F. ....Santa Monica, CA
Reynolds, Herrick & Kasdorf ....Madison, WI
Reynolds, Homer B., III ....Plano, TX
Sherman, TX
Reynolds, Horace H., III ....Omaha, NE
Reynolds, Horace H., IV ....Omaha, NE
Reynolds, Howard A. ....Watertown, MA
Reynolds, Hugh E., Jr. ....Indianapolis, IN
Reynolds, J. Allen, III ....Nashville, TN
Reynolds, J. Christopher ....Houston, TX
Reynolds, J. Steven ....West Palm Beach, FL
Reynolds, J. Steven ....Baldwin, NY
Reynolds, J. Terry, Jr. ....Mobile, AL
Reynolds, J. Thomas ....Avon, NY
Reynolds, Jackson B., III ....Columbus, OH
Reynolds, Jacqueline M. ....Norristown, PA
Reynolds, James A. ....Camarillo, CA
Reynolds, James D. ....Peoria, IL
Reynolds, James E. ....Los Altos, CA
Reynolds, James E. ....St. Louis, MO
Reynolds, James E., Jr. ....Albany, GA
Reynolds, James F. ....Edgartown, MA
Reynolds, James F., Jr. ....Quincy, MA
Reynolds, James G. ....Forest Grove, OR
Reynolds, James G. ....Fort Worth, TX
Reynolds, James H. ....Dubuque, IA
Reynolds, James J. ....San Diego, CA
Reynolds, James J. ....Danville, VA
Reynolds, James J., III ....Philadelphia, PA
Reynolds, James L. ....Los Angeles, CA
Reynolds, James P. ....Minneapolis, MN
Reynolds, James P. ....Helena, MT
Reynolds, James R. ....Kennett, MO
Reynolds, James R. ....Austin, TX
Reynolds, James S. ....Department of Justice, Criminal Division, GV
Reynolds, James T. ....Hauppauge, NY
Reynolds, James T. ....Dallas, TX
Reynolds, James W. ....Phoenix, AZ
Reynolds, James W. ....Fairfax, VA
Reynolds, Jason B. ....Oklahoma City, OK
Reynolds, Jay ....Boca Raton, FL
Reynolds, Jeanne M. ....Chicago, IL
Reynolds, Jefferson D. ....Santa Fe, NM
Reynolds, Jeffery P. ....Jackson, MS
Reynolds, Jeffery P., P.A. ....Jackson, MS

Reynolds, Jeffrey L. .... Indianapolis, IN
Reynolds, Jennifer L. .... Philadelphia, PA
Reynolds, Jennifer M. .... Clayton, MO
Reynolds, Jerry D. .... Idaho Falls, ID
Reynolds, Jerry L. .... Springfield, MO
Reynolds, Jerry L. .... Provo, UT
Reynolds, Jessica K. .... Syracuse, NY
Reynolds, Jim D. .... St. Petersburg, FL
Reynolds, Jimmie B., Jr. .... Jackson, MS
Reynolds, JoAnn B. .... Portland, OR
Reynolds, Joe Brett .... Oklahoma City, OK
Reynolds, Joe H. .... Houston, TX
Reynolds, Joe P. .... Austin, TX
Reynolds, Joe S. .... Mesa, AZ
Reynolds, Joel R. .... Los Angeles, CA
Reynolds, John A. .... Salina, KS
Reynolds, John B., III .... Washington, DC
Reynolds, John C. .... New Orleans, LA
Reynolds, John Edward .... Lexington, KY
Reynolds, John J. .... Chicago, IL
Reynolds, John M. .... Boston, MA
Reynolds, John M. .... St. Louis, MO
Reynolds, John M. .... Keene, NH
Reynolds, John M. .... McLean, VA
Reynolds, John N. .... Hamden, CT
Reynolds, John R. .... Nashville, TN
Reynolds, John Randolph .... Greenville, SC
Reynolds, John S. .... Philadelphia, PA
Reynolds, John T. .... Pontiac, MI
Reynolds, John W. .... Decatur, GA
Reynolds, John W. .... Silver City, NM
Reynolds, John W. .... Milwaukee, WI
Reynolds, Johnston, Hinton, Thomas &
Pepper, LLP .... Bowling Green, KY
Reynolds, Jon F., Jr. .... Phoenix, AZ
Reynolds, Jonathan P. .... Columbus, IN
Reynolds, Josann M. .... Cross Plains, WI
Reynolds, Joseph C. .... Asheville, NC
Reynolds, Joseph E. .... Lexington, MA
Reynolds, Joseph H. .... Washington, DC
Reynolds, Joseph K. .... Denver, CO
Reynolds, Joseph L., III .... Fort Myers, FL
Reynolds, Joseph M. .... Locust Valley, NY
Reynolds, Joshua E. .... Sarasota, FL
Reynolds, Joyce A. .... Detroit, MI
Reynolds, Julianne .... Washington, DC
Reynolds, K. Jeffrey .... Pensacola, FL
Reynolds, K. Scott .... Phoenix, AZ
Reynolds, Karen .... Bridgeport, CT
Reynolds, Katherine M. .... Manitowoc, WI
Reynolds, Kathleen .... Destin, FL
Reynolds, Kathleen .... Chicago, IL
Reynolds, Kathryn June Vaughan
Edmond, OK
Flower Mound, TX
Reynolds & Keinarth .... Smithville, TX
Reynolds, Kelly K. .... Sugar Land, TX
Reynolds & Kenline, L.L.P. .... Dubuque, IA
Reynolds, Kenneth A. .... Westbury, NY
Reynolds, Kenneth E. .... Los Angeles, CA
Reynolds, Kenneth P. .... Springfield, MO
Reynolds, Kent V. .... Pocatello, ID
Reynolds, Kevin M. .... Des Moines, IA
Reynolds, Kevin N. .... Hartford, CT
Reynolds, Kevin P. .... Auburn, MA
Reynolds, Kevin T. .... New York, NY
Reynolds, Kirk Mallory .... Arlington, VA
Reynolds, Kristina .... Washington, DC
Reynolds, L. George, Jr. .... Austin, TX
Reynolds, Larry C. .... Carson City, NV
Reynolds, Larry K. .... Riverside, CA
Reynolds, Laura L. .... Menlo Park, CA
Reynolds, Laura Susan .... Englewood, CO
Reynolds, Laurie E. .... San Francisco, CA
Reynolds Law Firm .... Baton Rouge, LA
Reynolds Law Firm, P.C. .... Lansing, MI
Reynolds' Law Firm, P.C. .... Silver City, NM
Reynolds Law Firm, The, P.A.
Fort Scott, KS
Iola, KS
Pittsburg, KS
Reynolds, Lawrence D.
Department of Labor,
Office of the Solicitor, GV
Reynolds, Lawrence S. .... Colts Neck, NJ
Reynolds, Lee J. .... Sequim, WA
Reynolds, Leo R. .... Lexington, MA
Reynolds, Leslie M. .... Wickliffe, OH
Reynolds, Leslie Reeve .... Bartlesville, OK
Reynolds, Linda S. .... Buffalo, NY
Reynolds, Lizanne
South San Francisco, CA
Reynolds, Lola Sullivan .... New York, NY
Reynolds, Lorena M. .... Ontario, OR
Reynolds, Lori D. .... New York, NY
Reynolds, Lucinda A. .... Columbus, OH
Reynolds, Lyman H., Jr.
West Palm Beach, FL
Reynolds, Lynn .... Birmingham, AL
Reynolds, Lynn M. .... Dayton, OH
Reynolds, M. Fletcher .... Dallas, TX
Reynolds, MacDaniel E. .... Portland, OR
Reynolds, Mack .... Hogansville, GA
Reynolds and Manning, P.A.
Prince Frederick, MD
Reynolds, Marc J. .... Miami, FL
Reynolds, Margaret B. .... San Francisco, CA
Reynolds, Margaret Elizabeth .... Scarsdale, NY
Reynolds, Marie A. .... West Palm Beach, FL
Reynolds, Marilee M. .... Orange, CA
Reynolds, Mark A. .... Dublin, OH
Reynolds, Mark F., II .... High Point, NC
Reynolds, Mark M. .... Cincinnati, OH
Reynolds, Mark Phillip .... Papillion, NE
Reynolds, Mark T. .... Providence, RI
Reynolds, Mary Kay .... Los Angeles, CA
Reynolds, Mary Lou .... Terre Haute, IN
Reynolds, Mary Louise Montague
Pickens, SC
Reynolds, MaryJane .... Washington, DC
Reynolds, Matthew
Truth or Consequences, NM
Reynolds, Matthias J. .... Manchester, NH
Reynolds, Max M. .... Washington, DC
Reynolds & McArthur .... Atlanta, GA
Macon, GA
Reynolds, McLaughlin, Josel & Reynolds
Norristown, PA
Reynolds, Meg M. .... Chicago, IL
Reynolds, Melinda L .... Cleveland, OH
Reynolds, Melissa J. .... Bangor, ME
Reynolds, Meredith B.
La Canada Flintridge, CA
Reynolds, Michael A. .... Orange, CA
Reynolds, Michael A. .... Southfield, MI
Reynolds, Michael B. .... Irvine, CA
Reynolds, Michael C. .... Concord, NH
Reynolds, Michael D .... Columbus, GA
Reynolds, Michael D. .... Salem, OR
Reynolds, Michael F. .... Lexington, KY
Reynolds, Michael J. .... Detroit, MI
Reynolds, Michael J. .... Auburn, WA
Reynolds, Michael K. .... Grand Rapids, MI
Reynolds, Michael M. .... Duncan, OK
Reynolds, Michael P. .... Rapid City, SD
Reynolds, Michael R. .... Oakland, CA
Reynolds, Michael T. .... Atlanta, GA
Reynolds, Michael T. .... Chicago, IL
Reynolds, Michael T. .... Erie, PA
Reynolds, Michael V. .... Royal Oak, MI
Reynolds, Michele A. .... Albuquerque, NM
Reynolds, Moira E. .... Providence, RI
Reynolds, Montie M., Law Office of
Pasadena, CA
Reynolds, Morgan .... Clanton, AL
Reynolds, Motl and Sherwood, PLLP
Helena, MT
Reynolds, Murphy & Associates, P.C.
Peoria, IL
Reynolds, Nancy F. .... Atlanta, GA
Reynolds, Nancy F. .... Roanoke, VA
Reynolds, Nancy L. .... Chicago, IL
Reynolds, Neal J.
United States International Trade
Commission,
Office of the General Counsel, GV
Reynolds, Neil V. .... Leadville, CO
Reynolds, Nicholas S. .... Washington, DC
Reynolds, Norman E.
Oklahoma City, OK
Reynolds, Norman T. .... Houston, TX
Reynolds, Osborne M., Jr. .... Norman, OK
Reynolds, Pamela Reardon
New Britain, CT
Reynolds, Parmele & Gold, P.C.
Springfield, MO
Reynolds, Patricia D. .... Liberty, MO
Reynolds, Patrick F. .... Beverly Hills, CA
Reynolds, Patrick Heith .... Norton, VA
Roanoke, VA
Reynolds, Patrick J. .... Department of Defense,
Defense Legal Services Agency, GV
Reynolds, Patrick J. .... Chicago, IL
Reynolds, Paul A. .... San Diego, CA
Reynolds, Paul B. .... Riverside, CA
Reynolds, Paul David .... Fayetteville, AR
Reynolds, Paul F. .... Helena, MT
Reynolds, Paul V. .... Providence, RI
Reynolds & Pendergrass, P.A. .... Raleigh, NC
Reynolds & Pennington, L.L.P.
Fort Worth, TX
Reynolds, Peter J. .... Mahopac, NY
Reynolds, Peter L. .... Charlotte, NC
Reynolds, Peter M. .... Irving, TX
Reynolds, Peter R. .... Hartford, CT
Reynolds, Philip L. .... Los Angeles, CA
Reynolds & Powers, A L.C.
Laguna Hills, CA
Reynolds, Price, Casas & Riley, LLP
Los Altos, CA
Reynolds, R. Louis .... Tulsa, OK
Reynolds, R. Monti .... Auburn, CA
Reynolds, Randall W. .... Pecos, TX
Reynolds, Ransom P., Jr. .... Elmira, NY
Reynolds, Rappaport & Kaplan LLP
Edgartown, MA
Reynolds, Ray A. .... Fayetteville, AR
Reynolds, Raymond J. .... Lansing, MI
Reynolds, Rexford M. .... Lodi, CA
Reynolds & Reynolds .... Clanton, AL
Reynolds & Reynolds .... Charleston, SC
Reynolds & Reynolds, Chartered
Boca Raton, FL
Reynolds, Reynolds & Hunt, P.C.
Savannah, TN
Reynolds & Reynolds, Law Offices of, Ltd.
Chicago, IL
Reynolds & Reynolds, P.C. .... Quincy, MA
Reynolds, Rhona E.F. .... Atlanta, GA
Reynolds, Rhonda Murphy
Oklahoma City, OK
Reynolds & Richard .... Wooster, OH
Reynolds, Richard F. .... Mount Clemens, MI
Reynolds, Richard H. .... Miami, FL
Reynolds, Richard J. .... Irvine, CA
Reynolds, Richard J. .... Littleton, CO
Reynolds, Richard J. .... Shreveport, LA
Reynolds, Richard J., III
San Antonio, TX
Reynolds, Richard L. .... Oakland, CA
Reynolds, Richard L. .... Covington, LA
New Orleans, LA
Reynolds, Richard L. .... Saugus, MA
Reynolds, Richard M. .... Hartford, CT
Reynolds, Richard R. .... Storrs, CT
Reynolds Richards .... New York, NY
Reynolds, Ridings, Vogt & Morgan
Oklahoma City, OK
Reynolds, Robert B. .... Benkelman, NE
Ogallala, NE
Reynolds, Robert B., (P.C.) .... Houston, TX
Reynolds, Robert C. .... Westborough, MA
Reynolds, Robert C., Jr. .... Atlanta, GA
Reynolds, Robert D. .... Montgomery, AL
Reynolds, Robert F. J. .... Baltimore, MD
Reynolds, Robert H. .... Peachtree City, GA
Reynolds, Robert H. .... Indianapolis, IN
Reynolds, Robert J. .... Dunnellon, FL
Ocala, FL
Reynolds, Robert J. .... Boston, MA
Reynolds, Robert J. .... Wooster, OH
Reynolds, Robert J., P.S. .... Yakima, WA
Reynolds, Robert L. .... Santa Rosa, CA
Reynolds, Robert N. .... Winter Park, FL
Reynolds, Robert N., Jr. .... New Britain, CT
Reynolds, Robert N., Professional Association
Winter Park, FL
Reynolds, Robert P. .... Huntsville, AL
Tuscaloosa, AL
Reynolds, Robert P., P.C. .... Decatur, AL
Huntsville, AL
Tuscaloosa, AL
Reynolds, Robert R., IV
West Palm Beach, FL
Reynolds, Robert S. .... Albany, NY
Reynolds, Robert W. .... Wichita, KS
Reynolds, Robin F. .... Dadeville, AL
Reynolds, Rodney J. .... Houston, TX
Reynolds, Roger B., Jr. .... Norristown, PA
Reynolds, Roger D. .... Los Angeles, CA
Reynolds, Roger L. .... Lexington, KY
Reynolds, Roger S. .... San Francisco, CA
Reynolds, Roland P. .... Newport Beach, CA
Reynolds, Ronald D. .... Los Angeles, CA
Reynolds, Ronald E. .... Birmingham, MI
Reynolds, Ronald H. .... Las Vegas, NV
Reynolds, Rose Marie .... Las Vegas, NV
Reynolds, Roy B., Jr. .... Columbia, SC
Reynolds, Rufus W. .... Greensboro, NC
Reynolds, Russell W. .... Fresno, CA
Reynolds, Ruthie G. .... Atlanta, GA
Reynolds, S. Scott .... Fairfield, CA
Napa, CA
Redlands, CA
Reynolds, Sallie Tiernan
Laguna Hills, CA
Reynolds, Samuel F., Jr. .... Pittsburgh, PA
Reynolds, Sandra .... Dallas, TX
Reynolds, Sandra L. .... Austin, TX
Reynolds, Sarah J. .... Cambridge, MA
Reynolds & Sayers .... Mobile, AL
Reynolds, Scott F. .... Martinsburg, WV
Reynolds, Scott H. .... Chicago, IL
Reynolds, Scott W. .... New York, NY
Reynolds, Sharon M. .... Hartford, CT
Reynolds, Sheila .... Topeka, KS
Reynolds, Sheila M. .... Milwaukee, WI
Reynolds, Shelley G. .... Gulf Breeze, FL
Reynolds, Sherman B. .... Miami, FL
Reynolds, Sheryl .... Kansas City, MO
Reynolds, Sibley G. .... Clanton, AL
Reynolds, Smith & Winters, P.C.
Norfolk, VA
Reynolds, Stacey E. .... Greenwich, CT
Reynolds, Stanley Q. .... Dickson, TN
Reynolds, Stephen .... Albany, NY
Reynolds, Stephen B. .... Hartford, CT
Reynolds, Stephen D. .... Portland, OR
Reynolds, Stephen E. .... Indianapolis, IN
Reynolds, Stephen H. .... Tampa, FL
Reynolds, Stephen M., Law Offices of
Sacramento, CA
Reynolds, Stephen R. .... Newark, NJ
Reynolds & Stowell, A Professional
Association .... Bradenton, FL
St. Petersburg, FL
Sarasota, FL
Reynolds, Stuart M., Jr. .... Dallas, TX
Reynolds, Sung Park .... Washington, DC
Reynolds, Susan Sheridan .... Ridgefield, CT
Reynolds, Suzanne .... Winston-Salem, NC
Reynolds, Suzanne S.
Bloomfield Hills, MI
Reynolds, Tamera M. .... New York, NY
Reynolds, Tara H. .... Dallas, TX
Reynolds, Ted R. .... Raleigh, NC
Reynolds, Terri Warren .... Dallas, TX
Reynolds, Thomas A. .... Oswego, NY
Reynolds, Thomas A. .... Memphis, TN
Reynolds, Thomas A., III .... Chicago, IL
Reynolds, Thomas A., Jr. .... Chicago, IL
Reynolds, Thomas B. .... Atlanta, GA
Reynolds, Thomas B. .... Absecon, NJ
Reynolds, Thomas C. .... Santa Clara, CA
Reynolds, Thomas E. .... Birmingham, AL
Reynolds, Thomas E. .... St. Petersburg, FL
Reynolds, Thomas F. .... Northfield, NJ
Reynolds, Thomas J. .... Chicago, IL
Reynolds, Thomas S. .... Sturgeon Bay, WI
Reynolds, Thomas S., II .... Indianapolis, IN
Reynolds, Thomas Todd .... Indianapolis, IN
Reynolds, Thurston H., II .... Montgomery, AL
Reynolds, Timothy F. .... Rockville, MD
Reynolds, Timothy G. .... New York, NY
Reynolds, Timothy J.
West Palm Beach, FL
Reynolds, Timothy R. .... Toledo, OH
Reynolds, Tina M. .... Washington, DC
Reynolds, Tina R. .... Washington, DC
Reynolds, Toinette Lobo .... Manassas, VA
Reynolds, Tracy L. .... Dallas, TX
Reynolds, Troy D. .... Lexington, KY
Reynolds & Underhill .... Charlotte, NC
Reynolds, Vanessa A.
Fort Lauderdale, FL
Reynolds, Vicki Rideout .... Jacksonville, FL
Reynolds, W. Carl, (P.C.) .... Atlanta, GA
Macon, GA
Reynolds, W. Joseph .... Dunnellon, FL
Ocala, FL
Reynolds, W. Nicholas .... Ashland, KY
Huntington, WV
Reynolds, Walter .... Dayton, OH
Reynolds, Warren F. .... Hobbs, NM
Reynolds, Warren F., P.A. .... Hobbs, NM
Reynolds, Wendy K. .... Modesto, CA
Reynolds, William A. .... Knoxville, TN
Reynolds, William B. .... Bronx, NY
Reynolds, William Bradford
Washington, DC
Reynolds, William Carl .... Indianapolis, IN
Reynolds, William D. .... Gainesville, FL
Reynolds, William E. .... Boston, MA
Reynolds, William E. .... Cherry Hill, NJ
Reynolds, William F. .... Schuylerville, NY
Reynolds, William F. .... Schuylerville, NY
Reynolds, William F., Jr. .... Washington, DC
Reynolds, William G., Jr. .... Richmond, VA
Reynolds, William H. .... Kansas City, MO
Reynolds, William H. .... Albany, NY
Reynolds, William J. .... Reading, PA
Reynolds, William Jay .... Savannah, TN
Reynolds, William L. .... Baltimore, MD
Reynolds, William M., Jr. .... Charleston, SC
Reynolds, William R. .... Bala Cynwyd, PA
Reynolds, William Roscoe
Martinsville, VA
Reynolds, William S. .... Buffalo, NY
Reynolds, Wilma E. .... Rochester, NY
Reynolds, W. J. (Jack) .... Savannah, TN
Reynolds, Zackery E. .... Fort Scott, KS
Reynolds Zellmer LLP .... Auburn, CA
Roseville, CA
Reynolds-Johnson, Lyn L.
San Juan Capistrano, CA
Reynoldson, Elisabeth S. .... Osceola, IA
Reynoldson, Robert W. .... Osceola, IA
Reynoldson, Van Werden, Lloyd &
Reynoldson, L.L.P. .... Osceola, IA
Reynoldson, W. Ward .... Osceola, IA
Reynolds-Quillin, Michika R.
Jonesboro, GA
Reynolds-Sewell, Cynthia K. .... Topeka, KS
Reynoso, Cruz .... Los Angeles, CA
Reynoso, Frank, A Law Corp.
Sacramento, CA
Reynvaan, Michael T. .... Seattle, WA
Reytblat, Julia .... New York, NY
Rez, Donald G. .... San Diego, CA
Reza, Elizabeth J. .... Boston, MA
Reza, Mark E. .... Kansas City, MO
Reza, Sadaf Mona .... Rockville, MD
Rezabek, Debra P. .... Long Grove, IL
Rezabek, James L. .... Chicago, IL
Rezac, John K. .... Atlanta, GA
Rezac, Marcia A. .... Omaha, NE
Newport, OR
Rezac, Rex A. .... Omaha, NE
Rezai, Shahin .... Washington, DC
Rezainia, Parvin .... Los Angeles, CA
Rezaizadeh, Amir .... Boston, MA
Rezanka, Thomas W. .... Palm Harbor, FL
Rezek, Richard A. .... Indianapolis, IN
Rezen, Randy L. .... Los Angeles, CA
Rezendes, Manuel M. .... Fall River, MA
Rezendes, Michael R. .... Quincy, MA
Rezendes & Trezise .... Quincy, MA
Rezentes, Stacy P. .... Honolulu, HI
Rezents, Stephanie A. .... Honolulu, HI
Rezet, Penny J. .... Philadelphia, PA
Rezneck, Daniel A. .... Washington, DC
Rezner, Barbara A. .... Hartford, CT
Rezner, Ray G. .... Chicago, IL
Reznicek, Clifford D. .... Davie, FL
Reznicek, Joseph R. .... Dallas, TX
Reznicek, Rebecca Colton .... Des Moines, IA
Reznicek, Stephen L. .... San Antonio, TX
Reznick, Allan E. .... New York, NY
Reznick, Bruce S. .... Brooklyn, NY
Reznick, Darrin M. .... Livingston, NJ
Reznick, Dennis M. .... Short Hills, NJ
Reznick, Felix B. .... New York, NY
Reznick, Harvey .... St. Louis, MO
Reznick, Michael E. .... Los Angeles, CA
Reznick, Morris M. .... Cleveland, OH
Reznick, Nina J. .... New York, NY
Reznick, Paul M. .... Pittsburgh, PA
Reznick, Robert P. .... Washington, DC
Reznick, Russell I. .... Brooklyn, NY
Reznick, Scott M. .... United States Senate,
Committee Legal Personnel, GV
Reznick, Seema .... Towson, MD
Reznicsek, Rick Monte .... Jacksonville, FL
Reznik, Benjamin M. .... Los Angeles, CA
Reznik, Bruce A. .... Washington, DC
Reznik, Mallary L. .... Los Angeles, CA
Rezvani, Shahin .... Los Angeles, CA
Rezvani, Tracy D. .... Washington, DC
Rezzemini, Harry B. .... Slingerlands, NY
Rezzo, Patrick G. C. .... San Diego, CA
Rezzonico, Ann Marie G.
Boynton Beach, FL
Rezzonico, Ann Marie G., P.A.
Boynton Beach, FL
Rhame, Harold Ellis, Jr. .... Fairfield, CT
Rhame, John M., III .... Portage, IN
Rhames, Michael R. .... Santa Monica, CA
Rhaney, Mahlon C., Jr. .... Marietta, GA
Rhasiatry, Cecelia M. .... Statesville, NC
Rhatican, James P. .... Roseland, NJ
Rhatican, Peter E. .... Mendham, NJ

Rhatican, Peter E., P.C. .... Mendham, NJ
Rhatican, Thomas M. .... Beaver Dam, WI
Rhatican, Tim B. .... Richardson, TX
Rhatigan, Brian H. .... Fairfax, VA
Rhatigan, Sarah Like .... Cambridge, MA
Rhatigan, Sean M. .... San Francisco, CA
Rhatigan, Timothy P. .... Chicago, IL
Rhea, Alan D. .... Carthage, MS
Rhea, Albert G., III .... Russellville, KY
Rhea, Andrew .... Pennsville, NJ
Rhea, Bill .... Dallas, TX
Rhea, Boyd & Rhea .... Anniston, AL
Gadsden, AL
Guntersville, AL
Rhea, Clarence F. .... Gadsden, AL
Rhea, Claude H., III .... Reston, VA
Rhea, Dan D. .... Knoxville, TN
Rhea, David E., Jr. .... Bellingham, WA
Rhea, Donald R. .... Gadsden, AL
Rhea, Elizabeth M. .... Chicago, IL
Rhea, Floyd W. .... Sneedville, TN
Rhea, Gordon C.
Christiansted, St. Croix, VI
Rhea, Howard F. .... Walnut Creek, CA
Rhea, Howard W. .... Sneedville, TN
Rhea, James Parker .... Tallahassee, FL
Rhea, John D. .... Rock Hill, SC
Rhea, Melissa .... Washington, DC
Rhea & Miller, P.C. .... Staunton, VA
Rhea, Richard A. .... Gadsden, AL
Rhea, Robert H.M. .... Memphis, TN
Rhea, Robert L. .... Staunton, VA
Rhea & Rodman, L.L.P. .... Austin, TX
Rhea, Todd Carleton .... Harrisonburg, VA
Rhea, William H., III .... Gadsden, AL
Rhea, William S., IV .... Austin, TX
Rhead, Robert J. .... Midland, MI
Rhead, Roland F. .... Grand Ledge, MI
Lansing, MI
Rheam, Daniel Jay .... Lewisburg, PA
Rheaume, Daniel J. .... Miami, FL
Rheaume, Mark W. .... Troy, MI
Rheaume, Warren J. .... Seattle, WA
Rheaume, William E. .... Lansing, MI
Rhebergen, Constance Gall .... Houston, TX
Rhee, Andrew D. .... Greenwich, CT
Rhee, Erik L. .... Englewood, CO
Rhee, Gloria Tanigawa .... Portland, OR
Rhee, Hansel H. .... Washington, DC
Rhee, Michael J. .... New York, NY
Rhee, Michelle H. .... Boston, MA
Rhee, Mina .... Department of Justice,
Civil Division, GV
Rhee, Robert E. .... Fort Wayne, IN
Rhee, Tae J. .... Portland, OR
Rheeling, Jeffrey S. .... Chicago, IL
Rheem, Uel .... New York, NY
Rhees, Carol A. .... Washington, DC
Rhees, Hopkins & Kreamer .... Phoenix, AZ
Rhees, Michael L. .... Phoenix, AZ
Rhein, Clyde K. .... Rocky River, OH
Rhein, David R. .... Des Moines, IA
Rhein, Eric M. .... Belleville, IL
Rheinberger, Francis J. .... Stillwater, MN
Rheinberger, Henry .... Oklahoma City, OK
Rheinberger, John H. .... Stillwater, MN
Rheinberger, John R. .... Stillwater, MN
Rheinberger, Jos. A. .... St. Paul, MN
Rheinberger & Rheinberger .... Stillwater, MN
Rheiner, Heather S. .... Washington, DC
Rheiner, William H. .... Philadelphia, PA
Rheingold, Bennett A. .... Torrance, CA
Rheingold, David B. .... New York, NY
Rheingold, Paul D. .... New York, NY
Rheingold, Valet, Rheingold & Shkolnik, P.C.
New York, NY
Rheinhardt, Jeffrey N. .... Ilion, NY
Rheinhardt, Sheree R. .... Trenton, NJ
Rheinheimer, Edward G. .... Bisbee, AZ
Rheinheimer, Jane A. .... Los Angeles, CA
Newport Beach, CA
San Diego, CA
Rheinheimer, Jean .... Santa Ana, CA
Rheinlander, Nathan B. .... New Braunfels, TX
Rheinlander, Robert E. .... Evansville, IN
Rheinscheld, John H. .... Big Spring, TX
Rheinstein, Bruce .... Woodbridge, VA
Rheinstein, Peter H.
Department Of Health And Human Services,
Food & Drug Administration, GV
Rheinstein, Thomas P. .... Rochester, NY
Rheintgen, Kathleen A. .... Chicago, IL
Rhem, David A. .... Grand Rapids, MI
Rhem, John F., Jr. .... Houston, TX
Rheney, J. Alan .... Jackson, TN
Rheney, T. David .... Greenville, SC
Rhetts, Peter Scott .... Marion, IN
Rheuban, Deborah R. .... Malibu, CA
Rheuban, Norman A. .... Canfield, OH
Rheuban & Palma .... Canfield, OH
Youngstown, OH
Rheuban, Steven Victor .... Los Angeles, CA
Rheuben, Sean .... New York, NY
Rheude, Gregory L., Jr. .... Canandaigua, NY
Rhew, Kathleen K. .... New York, NY
Rhew, Perry J. .... Kennett, MO
Rhiel, John V. .... Milwaukee, WI
Rhiel, Susan L. .... Columbus, OH
Rhieu, David M. .... New Haven, CT
Rhilinger, James E. .... Washington, DC
Rhim, J. Alexandra .... Los Angeles, CA
Rhim, Michael J. .... Atlanta, GA
Rhind, David S. .... Chicago, IL
Rhind, James T. .... Chicago, IL
Rhine, Alan .... Chicago, IL
Rhine, Arthur .... New York, NY
Rhine, Bertrand .... La Canada Flintridge, CA
Rhine, Ernest & Vargo .... Albion, IL
Mount Carmel, IL
Rhine, Frederick S. .... Chicago, IL
Rhine, Howard I. .... New York, NY
Rhine, James M. .... Santa Rosa, CA
Rhine, Jennie .... Berkeley, CA
Rhine, Joel R. .... Wilmington, NC
Rhine, John E. .... Mount Carmel, IL
Rhine, Michael A. .... Norfolk, VA
Rhine, Wayne .... Chicago, IL
Rhinehart, Kathleen M. .... Albuquerque, NM
Rhinehart, Randy E. .... Jamestown, NY
Rhinehart, Richard, and Associates
Sioux City, IA
Rhinehart, Richard S. .... Sioux City, IA
Rhinehart, Robert F. .... Syracuse, NY
Rhinelander, John B., (P.C.)
Washington, DC
Rhiner, Joel J. .... Chicago, IL
Rhinerson, David K. .... Owensboro, KY
Rhines, John H. .... Baltimore, MD
Rhines, Steven P. .... Dallas, TX
Rhines, William G. .... Wells, ME
Rhiney, Sean Lincoln .... Cincinnati, OH
Rho, Clara H. .... New York, NY
Rho, Jai H. .... Los Angeles, CA
Rho, Theresa .... Hempstead, NY
Rhoa, Albert J. .... Cleveland, OH
Rhoa, Follen & Rawlin Co., L.P.A.
Cleveland, OH
Rhoa, Joseph A. .... Bethesda, MD
Rhoa, Patrick J. .... Cleveland, OH
Rhoad, Kenneth R. .... Baltimore, MD
Rhoad, Robert D. .... Princeton, NJ
Rhoad, Robert T. .... Washington, DC
Rhoad, William D. .... Bamberg, SC
Rhoades, A. Christine .... Neosho, MO
Rhoades, Amy E. .... Detroit, MI
Rhoades, Brenda T. .... Dallas, TX
Rhoades, Bruce A. .... Fayetteville, AR
Rhoades, C.R., P.C. .... Neosho, MO
Rhoades, Clifford R. .... Avon Park, FL
Sebring, FL
Rhoades, Clifford R., P.A. .... Avon Park, FL
Sebring, FL
Rhoades, Corlene C. .... Chicago, IL
Rhoades, C. R. .... Neosho, MO
Pineville, MO
Rhoades, Dale W. .... Grand Rapids, MI
Rhoades, Dana .... Monticello, IL
Rhoades, Daniel .... Brewster, NY
Rhoades, David A. .... Raleigh, NC
Rhoades, Doug .... Lakeport, CA
Rhoades, Gary E. .... Portland, OR
Rhoades, Gary W. .... Redding, CA
Rhoades, Glenn E. .... Carlsbad, CA
Rhoades, J. Eric .... Rockville, MD
Rhoades, Jack S. .... Alexandria, VA
Rhoades, Jamese Lou .... Salem, OR
Rhoades, Jeffrey A. .... Lafayette, LA
Rhoades, Jerry D., Jr. .... Southern Pines, NC
Rhoades, Joel D. .... Dublin, OH
Rhoades, John A., Jr. .... St. Petersburg, FL
Rhoades, John S. .... Lafayette, CA
Rhoades, John S. .... San Diego, CA
Rhoades, Joseph J. .... Wilmington, DE
Rhoades, Kimberley Kelley .... Mt. Vernon, IN
Rhoades, Lyman .... Denver, CO
Rhoades, Mark L. .... Philadelphia, PA
Rhoades, Mary Jane .... Grand Rapids, MI
Rhoades, McKee, Boer, Goodrich & Titta
Grand Rapids, MI
Rhoades, Michael P. .... Chicago, IL
Rhoades, Nancy B. .... St. Petersburg, FL
Rhoades, Norma .... Brewster, NY
Rhoades, Quentin M. .... Missoula, MT
Rhoades, R. Scott .... Dallas, TX
Rhoades, Ralph R. .... San Francisco, CA
Rhoades, Randall R. .... Pittsburgh, PA
Rhoades & Rhoades .... St. Petersburg, FL
Rhoades & Rhoades, P.C. .... Brewster, NY
Rhoades, Robert F. .... Detroit, MI
Rhoades, Ron A., P.A. .... Hernando, FL
Rhoades, Ronald A. .... Hernando, FL
Rhoades, Rufus Von Thülen
Los Angeles, CA
Rhoades, Stephanie L. .... Anchorage, AK
Rhoades, Stephen D. .... Allentown, PA
Rhoades, Stephen J. .... Naperville, IL
Rhoades, Stephen J. .... Albuquerque, NM
Rhoads, Alexander R. .... Adel, IA
Rhoads, Ann E. .... Harrisburg, PA
Rhoads, Arthur L., Jr. .... Baltimore, MD
Rhoads, Bradley P. .... Madisonville, KY
Owensboro, KY
Rhoads, Carl L. .... Ecorse, MI
Rhoads, Carrie Aleen .... Washington, DC
Rhoads, Christopher L. .... Lexington, KY
Rhoads, Dale Zelony .... Boston, MA
Rhoads, Daniel L. .... Chevy Chase, MD
Rhoads, David L. .... Trenton, NJ
Rhoads, Dean B. .... Peoria, IL
Rhoads, Deborah L. .... San Leandro, CA
Rhoads, Donald L. .... New York, NY
Rhoads, Donald Perry .... Lake Arrowhead, CA
Rhoads, Donald Perry, A Professional
Corporation .... Lake Arrowhead, CA
Rhoads, Ed .... Waverly, OH
Rhoads, George R. .... Rogers, AR
Rhoads, Henry W. .... Harrisburg, PA
Rhoads, Howard S. .... Naples, FL
Rhoads, J. Mark .... San Diego, CA
Rhoads, James B. .... Atlanta, GA
Rhoads, James L. .... Anchorage, AK
Rhoads, Jerry P. .... Madisonville, KY
Rhoads, Johnnie Emberton, (Ms.)
Rogers, AR
Rhoads, Joseph .... Juno Beach, FL
Rhoads, Kathleen M. .... Sacramento, CA
Rhoads, Kaylee K. .... Fort Lauderdale, FL
Rhoads, Kimberly Ann .... Columbus, OH
Rhoads, Lynn E. .... Minneapolis, MN
Rhoads, Mark B. .... Richmond, VA
Rhoads, Nancy Glenn .... Philadelphia, PA
Rhoads, Paul K. .... Chicago, IL
Rhoads, Paula J. .... Naples, FL
Rhoads, Philip S. .... Washington, DC
Rhoads & Rhoads, P.S.C.
Madisonville, KY
Owensboro, KY
Rhoads, Richard E. .... Tallahassee, FL
Rhoads, Richard L. .... Santa Ana, CA
Rhoads, Robert G. .... Trenton, NJ
Rhoads, Robert K. .... Bentonville, AR
Rhoads & Sinon LLP .... Harrisburg, PA
Rhoads, Stephen G. .... Philadelphia, PA
Rhoads, Steven R. .... Greenbrae, CA
Rhoads, Terry W. .... Midland, TX
Rhoads, Thomas J. .... Long Beach, CA
Rhoads, Thomas M. .... Wichita, KS
Rhoads, Thomas M. .... Madisonville, KY
Rhoads-Reith, Kerry
Farmington Hills, MI
Rhoda, Stoudt & Bradley .... Birdsboro, PA
Fleetwood, PA
Kutztown, PA
Oley, PA
Pottsville, PA
Reading, PA
Rhoda, Timothy E. .... Oak Park, IL
Rhode, Christine M. .... Chicago, IL
Rhode, Deborah L. .... New York, NY
Rhode, Edward W. .... Sandusky, OH
Rhode, Edward W., III .... Sandusky, OH
Rhode, John B. .... Antigo, WI
Rhode, John P. .... Sacramento, CA
Rhode, Lisa M. .... Blue Bell, PA
Rhode, Randall E. .... Portage, WI
Rhode, Rebekah A. .... Springfield, IL
Rhode, Robert H. .... Peoria, IL
Rhode, Shari R. .... Carbondale, IL
Rhode, Susan C. .... Minneapolis, MN
Rhode, Tim R. .... Portage, WI
Rhodebeck, Larry .... Columbus, OH
Rhodeen, Penn .... New Haven, CT
Rhodehamel, David R. .... Columbus, OH
Rhoden, Aimee .... Sacramento, CA
Rhoden, Carolyn Carr .... Wilkes-Barre, PA
Rhoden, Garry J. .... Tampa, FL
Rhoden, Horace .... New York, NY
Rhoden, James C. .... Columbia, MS
Rhoden, Lacy, Downey & Colbert
Jackson, MS
Rhoden, Linda B. .... Tacoma, WA
Rhoden, Mary Beth .... Tacoma, WA
Rhoden, Thomas H. .... Jackson, MS
Rhoden, William G. .... Gaffney, SC
Rhodes, A. Alexander .... Tampa, FL
Rhodes, A. L. (Dusty) .... Abilene, TX
Rhodes, Alan R. .... Glens Falls, NY
Rhodes, Alice G. .... Ashland, KY
Arlington, VA
Rhodes, Amy Katharine .... New York, NY
Rhodes, Andrew J.
Federal Communications Commission,
Mass Media Bureau, GV
Rhodes, Ann Marie .... Iowa City, IA
Rhodes, Anne-Marie .... Chicago, IL
Rhodes, Ascolillo & Schuman
Westfield, MA
Rhodes, Aubrey C., Jr. .... Augusta, GA
Rhodes, Aubrey C., Jr., P.C. .... Augusta, GA
Rhodes, Avery England .... Oklahoma City, OK
Rhodes, Barry G. .... Brooklyn, NY
Rhodes, Bernard J. .... Kansas City, MO
Rhodes, Blake M. .... Denver, CO
Rhodes, Boyd L., Jr. .... Memphis, TN
Rhodes, Brian W. .... Los Angeles, CA
Rhodes, Byron Cole
Hot Springs National Park, AR
Rhodes, C. David .... Austin, TX
Rhodes, C. Harker, Jr. .... Chicago, IL
Rhodes, Carl A. .... Columbus, GA
Rhodes, Carol Bennett .... Fort Wayne, IN
Rhodes, Carroll E. .... Hazlehurst, MS
Rhodes, Carroll, Law Offices of
Hazlehurst, MS
Rhodes, Catherine L. .... Los Angeles, CA
Rhodes, Charles E. .... Cherry Hill, NJ
Rhodes, Charles R. .... Scottsboro, AL
Rhodes, Charles R., Jr. .... Myrtle Beach, SC
Rhodes, Charles Robert .... Greensboro, NC
Rhodes, Charles W. "Rocky" .... Austin, TX
Rhodes, Charmaine J. .... Austin, TX
Rhodes, Chris L., III .... Tulsa, OK
Rhodes, Christopher D. .... Conroe, TX
Rhodes, Christopher L. .... Austin, TX
Rhodes, Christopher P. .... Rutland, VT
Rhodes, Crawford Adams .... Eagle Pass, TX
Rhodes, Cynthia J. .... Newark, NJ
Rhodes, Dan C. .... Houston, TX
Rhodes, Daniel E. .... Battle Creek, MI
Rhodes, Daniel J. .... La Mirada, CA
Rhodes, Daniel M. .... Huntington Woods, MI
Rhodes, David A. .... Sacramento, CA
Rhodes, David A .... Washington, DC
Rhodes, David J. .... Erie, PA
Rhodes, David W. .... Houston, TX
Rhodes, Deborah E. .... Westborough, MA
Rhodes, Deborah L. .... Southfield, MI
Rhodes, Dennis A. .... Flint, MI
Rhodes, Dennis J. .... San Francisco, CA
Rhodes, Diana J. .... Fort Collins, CO
Cheyenne, WY
Rhodes, Diana J., P.C. .... Cheyenne, WY
Rhodes, Dinah Petree .... Huntsville, AL
Rhodes, Donald .... Bloomfield, MO
Rhodes, Donald H. .... Virginia Beach, VA
Rhodes, Donald W. .... Marco Island, FL
Rhodes, Douglas Keith .... El Cajon, CA
Rhodes, Dunbar and Lomax, Chartered
Annapolis, MD
Rhodes, Earl G. .... Grand Junction, CO
Rhodes, Edward F. .... Beverly, MA
Rhodes, Elizabeth .... Columbia, SC
Rhodes, Elizabeth W. .... New York, NY
Rhodes, Eugene E., Jr. .... Port Orange, FL
Rhodes, Fletcher F. .... Temple, TX
Rhodes, Frank J., Jr. .... Decatur, GA
Rhodes, Fred .... Houston, TX
Rhodes, Fred B. .... Anderson, SC
Rhodes, Frederick A., III .... Houston, TX
Rhodes, Gabrielle .... Kansas City, MO
Rhodes, Gary C. .... Salisbury, NC
Rhodes, Gary C. .... Oklahoma City, OK
Rhodes, Gene .... Oakland, CA
Rhodes, George F. .... Port Lavaca, TX
Rhodes, George Ross .... Pittsburgh, PA
Rhodes, Glenn W. .... Menlo Park, CA
Rhodes, Gregory H. .... Denver, CO
Rhodes, Harold J. .... Morgan City, LA
Rhodes, Harris C. .... Stanford, KY
Rhodes, Harry H., III .... Wilmington, DE
Rhodes, Harry S. .... Roanoke, VA
Rhodes, Harry W., III .... Houston, TX
Rhodes, Herbert B. .... Newport Beach, CA
Rhodes, Hieronymus, Jones, Tucker &
Gable, P.L.L.C. .... Oklahoma City, OK
Tulsa, OK
Rhodes, Horace G. .... Oklahoma City, OK
Rhodes, Howard W. .... Santa Ynez, CA
Rhodes, Howard W., Jr. .... Lynchburg, VA
Rhodes, J. Thomas, III .... Brownsville, TX
San Antonio, TX
Rhodes, James A. .... Wheeling, IL
Rhodes, James D. .... Anchorage, AK
Rhodes, James E. .... St. Louis, MO
Rhodes, James L. .... Chicago, IL
Rhodes, James M. .... New York, NY
Rhodes, James M., Jr. .... New York, NY
Rhodes, James R., III .... Little Rock, AR
Rhodes, James W. .... Oklahoma City, OK
Rhodes, Jane C. .... Kent, WA
Rhodes, Janice A. .... Milwaukee, WI
Rhodes, Jean .... Bridgeport, NE
Rhodes, Jefferson R. .... Alamogordo, NM
Rhodes, Jeffrey .... Washington, DC
Rhodes, Jeffrey K. .... Tulsa, OK
Rhodes, Jerome H. .... Woodland Hills, CA
Rhodes, Jerry S. .... Springfield, IL
Rhodes, Jeter E., Jr. .... Columbia, SC
Rhodes, J. G., Jr. .... Clarksburg, WV
Rhodes, John B. .... Reno, NV
Rhodes, John David .... Pittsburgh, PA
Rhodes, John H., Jr. .... Winter Garden, FL
Rhodes, John J. .... Washington, DC
Rhodes, John J. .... Westfield, MA
Rhodes, John J., III .... Washington, DC
Rhodes, Joseph A., Jr. .... Greenville, SC
Rhodes, Judith Dahlman
Westlake Village, CA
Rhodes, Karen .... Los Angeles, CA
Rhodes, Kathlyn A., The Law Offices of
Sacramento, CA
Rhodes, Keith S. .... Savannah, MO
Rhodes, Kenneth D. .... Houston, TX
Rhodes, Kenneth O. .... Pasadena, CA
Rhodes, Kevin D. .... Columbus, OH
Rhodes, Kevin H. .... Chicago, IL
Rhodes, Kimberly L. .... Norristown, PA
Rhodes, Kimberly N. .... Atlanta, GA
Rhodes, Kimberly Toomey .... Voorhees, NJ
Philadelphia, PA
Rhodes, Kirk D. .... Scotch Plains, NJ
Rhodes, Laura Kelsey .... Rockville, MD
Rhodes, Lee Ann .... Pittsburgh, PA
Rhodes, Linda Lewis .... Washington, DC
Rhodes, Lizabeth .... Los Angeles, CA
Rhodes, Lydia M. .... Shreveport, LA
Rhodes, Macel E. .... Charleston, WV
Rhodes, Margaret C. .... Washington, DC
Rhodes, Margaret M. .... Ames, IA
Rhodes, Margaret Smith "Sage"
Washington, DC
Rhodes, Mark .... Houma, LA
Rhodes, Mark A. .... New York, NY
Rhodes, Mark M. .... Albuquerque, NM
Rhodes, Mark S. .... Rochester, NY
Rhodes, Mark S. .... Philadelphia, PA
Rhodes, Mary Frances .... Silver Spring, MD
Rhodes, Mary Kathleen .... Oklahoma City, OK
Rhodes & Mason, P.L.L.C.
Greensboro, NC
Wilmington, NC
Rhodes, Michael D. .... Jackson, MS
Rhodes, Michael G. .... San Diego, CA
Rhodes, Michael H. .... Lansing, MI
Rhodes, Michael W. .... Kansas City, MO
Rhodes, Nancy D. .... Doylestown, PA
Rhodes, Naomi .... New York, NY
Rhodes, Nate .... Corpus Christi, TX
Rhodes, Osborne H. .... Walterboro, SC
Rhodes, Pamela E. .... San Francisco, CA
Rhodes, Paul M. .... Washington, DC
Rhodes, Paula McDonald .... Tampa, FL
Rhodes, Peter M. .... Haddonfield, NJ
Rhodes, Philip, Law Office of
Sacramento, CA
Rhodes, R. Gale, Jr. .... Red Bank, NJ
Rhodes, Ralph B. .... Denver, CO
Rhodes, Ralph B. .... Rocky Mount, VA
Rhodes, Randall L. .... Kansas City, MO
Rhodes, Raphael H. .... Jamaica, NY
Rhodes, Rebecca G. .... Oklahoma City, OK

Rhodes, Reginald A. ..... Dothan, AL
Rhodes, Rhonda ..... Miami, FL
Rhodes, Rhonda Alicia ..... Chicago, IL
Rhodes, Rhonda L. ..... Denver, CO
Rhodes, Rhoshunda R. ..... Shreveport, LA
Rhodes, Rhys D. ..... Paoli, IN
Rhodes, Richard F. ..... Osceola, AR
Rhodes, Richard H. ..... Spartanburg, SC
Rhodes, Richard P., Jr. ..... New York, NY
Rhodes, Richard R. ..... Arlington, VA
Rhodes, Richard S. ..... Chicago, IL
Rhodes, Richard W. ..... Saratoga, CA
Rhodes, Robert A. ..... Westport, CT
Rhodes, Robert C. ..... Columbia, SC
Rhodes, Robert C. ..... Columbia, SC
Rhodes, Robert L., Jr. ..... Washington, DC
Rhodes, Robert M. ..... Jacksonville, FL
Rhodes, Robin Neil ..... Beulaville, NC
Rhodes, Roger ..... Dallas, TX
Rhodes, Ronald E. ..... Portland, OR
Rhodes, Ross ..... Brooklyn, NY
Rhodes, Roy T. ..... Tallahassee, FL
Rhodes, Roy W., Jr. ..... Prescott, AZ
Rhodes & Salmon, P.C.
Albuquerque, NM
Rhodes, Sandra Lynn ..... Houston, TX
Rhodes, Sara Beth Fulford ..... Greenville, NC
Rhodes, Sarah Jackson
Oklahoma City, OK
Rhodes, Scott ..... Phoenix, AZ
Rhodes, Scott A. ..... Brentwood, TN
Rhodes, Scott M. ..... Oklahoma City, OK
Rhodes, Sharon L. ..... San Diego, CA
Rhodes, Sherry L. ..... Rockville, MD
Rhodes, Sonja H. ..... Santa Ana, CA
Rhodes, Stephen J. ..... Lansing, MI
Rhodes, Steven C. ..... Harrisonburg, VA
Rhodes, Steven W. ..... Detroit, MI
Rhodes, Susan E. ..... Gastonia, NC
Rhodes, Susan E., P.A. ..... Gastonia, NC
Rhodes, Susan T. ..... Miami, FL
Rhodes, T. Alan ..... Amarillo, TX
Rhodes, Terry G. ..... Mill Creek, WA
Rhodes, Terry L. ..... Irvine, CA
Rhodes, Theodore E. ..... Los Angeles, CA
Rhodes, Thomas E. ..... Orlando, FL
Rhodes, Thomas E., P.A. ..... Orlando, FL
Rhodes, Thomas F., Jr. ..... Port St. Lucie, FL
Rhodes, Thomas J. ..... Wilson, NC
Rhodes, Thomas W. ..... Atlanta, GA
Rhodes, Thurman H. ..... Upper Marlboro, MD
Rhodes, Timothy A. ..... New York, NY
Rhodes, Tina Y. ..... Cleveland, OH
Rhodes, Tom B. ..... Dallas, TX
Rhodes, Tonya M. ..... New Orleans, LA
Rhodes & Tucker ..... Marco Island, FL
Naples, FL
Rhodes, Velma M. ..... Santa Ynez, CA
Rhodes, Vincent A. ..... Honolulu, HI
Rhodes, Viola ..... Ruidoso, NM
Rhodes, W. Gregory ..... Pittsburgh, PA
Rhodes, Warner & Lomax, P.C.
Columbus, GA
Rhodes, Wilfrid E. ..... Elmira, NY
Rhodes, William C. ..... Philadelphia, PA
Rhodes, William E. ..... Colorado Springs, CO
Rhodes, William E. ..... Naples, FL
Rhodes, William H. ..... Arlington, VA
Rhodes, William S.
Agency for International Development, Other Offices of A.I.D., GV
Rhodes, Wm. J., Jr. ..... Franklin, VA
Rhodes-Devey, Michael ..... Slingerlands, NY
Rhodes-Ford, Berna L. ..... Columbus, OH
Rhodes-Miller, Rosemarie
Philadelphia, PA
Rhodes-Zittrer, Leigh Ann ..... Houston, TX
Rhodus, David M. ..... Atlanta, GA
Rhodus, G. Tomas ..... Dallas, TX
Rhodus, Linda Mohney ..... Lansing, MI
Rhody, John P., Jr. ..... Annapolis, MD
Rhomberg, Mary L. ..... Rochester, MN
Rhome, John O. ..... Sudbury, MA
Rhonan, Hilary A. ..... Los Angeles, CA
Rhone, James R. ..... New York, NY
Rhone, Traci L. ..... Wichita, KS
Rhorer, Alexis Rondell ..... San Francisco, CA
Rhorer, John R., Jr. ..... Lexington, KY
Rhorer, William G., Jr., Law Office of
Long Beach, CA
Rhoten, David A. ..... Salem, OR
Rhoten, J. Ray ..... Salem, OR
Rhoten, Lyneth A. ..... Omaha, NE
Rhough, Gene ..... Palo Alto, CA
Rhow, Ekwan E. ..... Los Angeles, CA
Rhudy, Robert J. ..... Baltimore, MD
Rhudy, Stephen C. ..... Durham, NC
Rhue, Bond E.
Department of Justice, GV
Rhue, Christopher Windly ..... Abingdon, VA
Rhulen, Harry W. ..... Monticello, NY
Rhum, Jaime N. ..... Chicago, IL
Rhymes, Jamie D. ..... Lafayette, LA
Rhymes, Ray L. ..... New Orleans, LA
Rhymes, Shawn Carney ..... Lafayette, LA
Rhynard, Russell L. ..... Alpena, MI
Rhyne, Charles E. ..... Denver, CO
Rhyne, J. Harris ..... Palmetto, FL
Rhyne, J. Harris, P.A. ..... Palmetto, FL
Rhyne, John G. ..... Wilmington, NC
Rhyne, John W., Jr. ..... La Fayette, GA
Rhyne, Johnathan L., Jr. ..... Lincolnton, NC
Rhyne, Karen A. ..... Newport Beach, CA
Rhyne, Katherine L. ..... Washington, DC
Rhyne, Laura C. ..... Colorado Springs, CO
Rhyne, Martha Cameron ..... Lincolnton, NC
Rhyne, Megan H. ..... Williamsburg, VA
Rhyne, Pegheen ..... Los Angeles, CA
Rhyne, Richard D. ..... Kansas City, MO
Rhyne, Sidney White ..... Washington, DC
Rhyne, Stephen K. ..... Charlotte, NC
Rhyne, Teresa J. ..... Riverside, CA
Rhyne, William S. ..... McLean, VA
Rhynes, Gloria F. ..... Oakland, CA
Rhynhart, Daniel E. ..... Philadelphia, PA
Rhynhart, Erich G. ..... Chicago, IL
Rhys, Adam W. ..... West Palm Beach, FL
Riach Gese PLLC ..... Lynnwood, WA
Seattle, WA
Riach, Ronald J. ..... Roseville, MN
Riad & Associates, P.C. ..... New York, NY
Riad, Maged F. ..... New York, NY
Riahei, Melissa M. ..... Chicago, IL
Rial, Edward A. ..... Brooklyn, NY
Rial, J. Hamilton, III ..... Austin, TX
Rial, LeAnn B. ..... Trenton, TN
Rian, Heidi M. ..... Honolulu, HI
Riancho, Juan Guillermo ..... Houston, TX
Riashi, Mark K. ..... Detroit, MI
Riave, Diane ..... Studio City, CA
Riave, Lionel L. ..... Fair Oaks, CA
Riback, Adam ..... Chicago, IL
Riback, Frank D. ..... Glencoe, IL
Riback, Jeffrey L. ..... New York, NY
Riback, Jeffrey N. ..... Vancouver, WA
Riback, Katherine Irwin
General Accounting Office, Office of the General Counsel, GV
Riback, Linda ..... Oakland, CA
Riback, Michael S. ..... San Leandro, CA
Riback, Rena S. ..... Jamaica, NY
Riback, Ronald H. ..... Troy, MI
Riback, Scott H. ..... General Accounting Office, Office of the General Counsel, GV
Riback, Stuart M. ..... New York, NY
Ribak, Abraham D. ..... San Antonio, TX
Ribak, David ..... Dedham, MA
Ribak, Jason ..... Dedham, MA
Ribak, Pamela B. ..... Greenwich, CT
Ribakoff, Alan P., (A Professional Corporation) ..... Santa Monica, CA
Ribakoff, Joseph ..... Long Beach, CA
Ribakove, Kevin D. ..... Forest Hills, NY
Ribakove, Richard D. ..... Hillside, NJ
Riband, Herbert S., Jr. ..... Philadelphia, PA
Ribando, Monique L. ..... New York, NY
Ribar, Peter A. ..... Kentfield, CA
Ribar, Tammy L. ..... Pittsburgh, PA
Ribarich, John M. ..... Los Angeles, CA
Ribarits, Eva M. ..... Worcester, MA
Ribarits, John M. ..... Lake Charles, LA
New Orleans, LA
Houston, TX
Ribas, Cynthia ..... Houston, TX
Ribas, Tamara M. ..... San Francisco, CA
Ribaudo, Anthony J. ..... Chicago, IL
Ribaudo, Guy G. ..... New York, NY
Ribble, Dan A. ..... Albuquerque, NM
Ribble, Donald G. ..... Cedar Rapids, IA
Ribble, Jack T., Jr. ..... Philadelphia, PA
Ribeiro, John J. ..... Riverhead, NY
Ribeiro, Robert R. ..... Minneapolis, MN
Ribeiro, Traci M. ..... Philadelphia, PA
Ribel, Frank A., Jr. ..... Arcadia, FL
Ribera, Joseph R. ..... Santa Clara, CA
Riberi, Gina Marie ..... Los Angeles, CA
Ribes, Sandra Bologna ..... Baton Rouge, LA
Ribes, Sandra Bologna, A.P.L.C.
Baton Rouge, LA
Ribet, Claudia ..... Los Angeles, CA
Ribezzo, Frank A., Jr. ..... West Warwick, RI
Ribiat, Jack ..... Southfield, MI
Ribiat, Steven M. ..... Detroit, MI
Ribich, Frank A. ..... Sheboygan, WI
Ribich, Lewis J. ..... Minneapolis, MN
Ribicoff, Abraham A. ..... New York, NY
Ribis, Nicholas L. ..... Morristown, NJ
Ribitwer, Debra N. ..... Birmingham, MI
Ribitwer, Debra N., & Associates, P.C.
Birmingham, MI
Detroit, MI
Mount Clemens, MI
Pontiac, MI
Ribitwer, Mitchell
Bloomfield Township, MI
Ribitwer & Sabbota
Bloomfield Township, MI
Detroit, MI
Ribka, Nicole J. ..... Atlanta, GA
Rible, Charles H. ..... San Mateo, CA
Rible, Morton ..... Mount Prospect, IL
Rible, Stephen V. ..... New York, NY
Rible, Tracey ..... Philadelphia, PA
Ribler, Lawrence S. ..... Miami, FL
Riblet, Douglas H. ..... Morrisville, PA
Riblet, Robin L. ..... Santa Barbara, CA
Ribley, Julie L. ..... Rushville, IN
Ribman, Elana Michelle ..... Sacramento, CA
Ribman, James W. ..... Dallas, TX
Ribner, Clifford N. ..... Tulsa, OK
Ribner, Paul ..... Philadelphia, PA
Ribner, Seth A. ..... Universal City, CA
Ribnick, Catherine A.
Federal Deposit Insurance Corporation, Liquidation Branch, GV
Ribnick, Jacqueline S. ..... Garden City, NY
Ribnick-Kleiman, Amelia ..... Houston, TX
Ribolow & Feinsod ..... Brooklyn, NY
Ribolow, Maurice H ..... Brooklyn, NY
Ribons, Michael P. ..... Woodland Hills, CA
Ribordy, Linda J. ..... Santa Cruz, CA
Ribstein, Larry E. ..... Arlington, VA
Ribstein, Rick A. ..... Brookings, SD
Ribyat, Wm. D., Jr. ..... Utica, NY
Ricapito, Jeffrey M. ..... Stamford, CT
Ricard, Donald Z. ..... St. Clair Shores, MI
Ricard, Donald Z., P.C. ..... St. Clair Shores, MI
Ricard, Kathryn A. ..... Washington, DC
Ricard, Melissa M. ..... Corpus Christi, TX
Ricard, Stephen A. ..... Seattle, WA
Ricard, Thomas W. ..... Detroit, MI
Ricardo, Henry J. ..... New York, NY
Ricardo, Jason J. ..... Tampa, FL
Ricardo, Mark E. ..... Washington, DC
Ricardo, Marta Galan ..... New York, NY
Ricardo, S. Preston ..... Dallas, TX
Ricardo Toro, José ..... San Juan, PR
Ricarte, Maria-Christina ..... New York, NY
Ricaurte, Eve K. ..... Toledo, OH
Ricca, Alan
National Labor Relations Board, Office of Board Members, GV
Ricca, Bettie N. ..... Treasury Department, Internal Revenue Service, GV
Ricca, Catherine A. ..... Chicago, IL
Ricca & Donnelly ..... Jericho, NY
Ricca, James C., Jr. ..... Jericho, NY
Ricca, Jas. C. ..... Woodhaven, NY
Ricca, John A. ..... Novato, CA
Ricca, John J., Jr. ..... New York, NY
Ricca, Karen Grace ..... Norristown, PA
Ricca, Mark A. ..... Jericho, NY
Ricca, Michele McCaul
Fort Lauderdale, FL
Ricca, Steven J. ..... Buffalo, NY
Riccardelli, Michael F. ..... Montclair, NJ
Riccardi, Gilda P. ..... New York, NY
Riccardi, Jennifer Danner
Washington, DC
Riccardi, John William ..... Charleston, WV
Riccardi & Lutz, PLLC ..... Charleston, WV
Riccardi, Mark R. ..... Washington, DC
Riccardi, Michael A. ..... Doylestown, PA
Riccardo, Alfred E. ..... Woodcliff Lake, NJ
Riccardo, R. Randall ..... Miami, FL
Riccardo, Vickie ..... New York, NY
Riccelli, Michael J. ..... Spokane, WA
Riccelli, Michael J., P.S. ..... Spokane, WA
Riccetti, Eugene L. ..... Houston, TX
Ricchetti, Eugene T. ..... Cleveland, OH
Ricchetti, Steven J. ..... Washington, DC
Ricchezza, Joseph A. ..... Marlton, NJ
Ricchini, Catherine T. ..... Cherry Hill, NJ
Ricchiuti, James ..... Phoenix, AZ
Ricchiuti, Joseph F. ..... Philadelphia, PA
Ricchiuto, Edward D. ..... New York, NY
Ricci, Adrian J. ..... Washington, DC
Ricci, Albert J. ..... Beverly, MA
Ricci, Alexander D. ..... Trevose, PA
Ricci, Arthur, III ..... Seekonk, MA
Providence, RI
Ricci, Arthur O. ..... Boston, MA
Ricci, Brian M. ..... Rocky Mount, NC
Ricci, Christopher P. ..... Wilmington, MA
Ricci, Dennis H. ..... Providence, RI
Ricci, Edward M. ..... West Palm Beach, FL
Ricci, Evelyn Brandt ..... Santa Barbara, CA
Ricci, Faye ..... New York, NY
Ricci, Frances ..... Bridgeport, CT
Ricci, Frank W. ..... Palm Beach Gardens, FL
Ricci, Frank W., P.A.
Palm Beach Gardens, FL
Ricci, George P. ..... Garden City, NY
Ricci, Gregory J. ..... Harrisburg, PA
Ricci, Gregory J. ..... Milwaukee, WI
Ricci, Hubbard, Leopold, Frankel & Farmer, P.A. ..... Boca Raton, FL
Palm Beach, FL
West Palm Beach, FL
Ricci, Hugo L., Jr. ..... Providence, RI
Ricci, Jack A. ..... New Orleans, LA
Ricci, Jane K. ..... Chattanooga, TN
Ricci, Joanne Maria ..... Lansing, MI
Ricci, John C. ..... Los Angeles, CA
Ricci, Jonathane M. ..... Newark, NJ
Ricci, Joseph A. ..... Harrisburg, PA
Ricci, Judith A. ..... New York, NY
Ricci, Linda ..... New York, NY
Ricci, Lori Ann ..... Rochester, NY
Ricci, Maria L. ..... Philadelphia, PA
Ricci, Michael V. ..... Whitestone, NY
Ricci, Michele A. ..... Farmington Hills, MI
Ricci, Patricia A. ..... Wauwatosa, WI
Ricci, Paula ..... Marshfield, MA
Ricci, Raymond E. ..... Cranston, RI
Ricci & Ricci ..... Providence, RI
Ricci, Richard F. ..... Roseland, NJ
Ricci, Richard J. ..... Eau Claire, WI
Ricci, Robert, Jr. ..... Saddle Brook, NJ
Ricci, Ronald J. ..... Pittsburgh, PA
Ricci, Stephen Anthony ..... New York, NY
Ricci, Susan D. ..... Worcester, MA
Ricci & Taneff ..... Harrisburg, PA
Ricci, Vincent A. ..... New York, NY
Ricci, Vincent L. ..... San Francisco, CA
Ricci, William J. ..... Mount Laurel, NJ
New York, NY
Philadelphia, PA
Ricciani, Jacqueline ..... Chester, NY
Ricciardella, Lynn E. ..... Towson, MD
Ricciardelli, Manfred F. ..... Livingston, NJ
Ricciardelli, Peter A. ..... Telluride, CO
Ricciardelli, Peter A., P.C., Law Office of
Telluride, CO
Ricciardelli, Renee C. ..... Trenton, NJ
Ricciardelli, Thomas P. ..... Dallas, TX
Ricciardi, Alfred W. ..... Phoenix, AZ
Ricciardi, Carl L. ..... Tomahawk, WI
Ricciardi, Charles A. ..... Brooklyn, NY
Ricciardi, Edward T. ..... Watertown, CT
Ricciardi, Francis M. ..... Ravenna, OH
Ricciardi, James P. ..... New York, NY
Ricciardi, John A. ..... Freehold, NJ
Ricciardi, Kathleen McCoy
Haddonfield, NJ
Ricciardi, Laura ..... Chicago, IL
Ricciardi, Lawrence R. ..... Armonk, NY
Ricciardi, Louis ..... New York, NY
Ricciardi, Louis C. ..... Philadelphia, PA
Ricciardi, Mark J. ..... Las Vegas, NV
Ricciardi, Martin J. ..... Albany, NY
Ricciardi, Matthew M. ..... New York, NY
Ricciardi & Paustian ..... Las Vegas, NV
Reno, NV
Ricciardi, Peter E. ..... Hamden, CT
Ricciardi, Susan C. ..... New York, NY
Ricciardi, Vincent F. ..... Worcester, MA
Ricciardi, Walter G. ..... New York, NY
Ricciardone, David ..... Worcester, MA
Ricciardone, Enza ..... Dallas, TX
Ricciardulli, Alex ..... Los Angeles, CA
Ricciardulli, Guy A. ..... San Diego, CA
Ricciardulli, Michael R. ..... Millburn, NJ
Riccio, Angela M. ..... Chicago, IL
Riccio, Arthur R., Jr. ..... East Haven, CT
Riccio, Charles A., Jr. ..... Golden, CO
Riccio, Eugene J. ..... Bridgeport, CT
Riccio, Frank J. ..... Bridgeport, CT
Riccio, Frank J. ..... Braintree, MA
Riccio, Frank J., P.C. ..... Braintree, MA
Riccio, John C., Law Office of
San Francisco, CA
Riccio, Joyce A. ..... Fairfield, CT
Riccio, Laura F. ..... Dedham, MA
Riccio, Laurie B. ..... Boston, MA
Riccio, Michael J. ..... Amsterdam, NY
Riccio, Ronald J. ..... Newark, NJ
Riccio, Willis H. ..... Boston, MA
Riccione, John M. ..... Chicago, IL
Riccio-Ryan, Jeanmarie A. ..... Bridgeport, CT
Riccio Wisner, Marie ..... New Orleans, LA
Riccitelli, William J. ..... Cranston, RI
Ricciuti, Janet G. ..... Alexandria, VA
Ricciuti, Louis F. ..... Decatur, GA
Ricciuti, Thomas G. ..... New York, NY
Ricci-Warren, Lauren E. ..... Hartsdale, NY
Ricco, Anthony L. ..... New York, NY
Ricco, Edward ..... Albuquerque, NM
Ricco, Felix A. ..... Minneapolis, MN
Ricco, Robert G. ..... New York, NY
Riccobene, Peter E. ..... Midland Park, NJ
Riccobono, Donna L. ..... Hicksville, NY
Riccobono, Joseph X. ..... New York, NY
Riccobono, Richard M. ..... Houston, TX
Riccobono, Xavier C. ..... New York, NY
Riccolo & Baker, P.C. ..... Cedar Rapids, IA
Riccolo, John L. ..... Cedar Rapids, IA
Rice & Adams ..... Jacksonville, AR
Rice, Alan J. ..... New York, NY
Rice and Amon ..... Suffern, NY
Rice, Amy Hallman ..... Minneapolis, MN
Rice, Amy L. ..... Los Angeles, CA
Rice, Andrea Lynn ..... Los Angeles, CA
Rice, Andrea Lynn, Law Offices of A Prof. Corp. ..... Los Angeles, CA
Rice, Andrew ..... Chicago, IL
Rice, Ann ..... West Des Moines, IA
Rice, Ann C. ..... Denver, CO
Rice, Ann E. ..... Pittsburgh, PA
Rice, Ann M. ..... Concord, NH
Rice, Anne C. ..... Houston, TX
Rice, Anne E. ..... Salt Lake City, UT
Rice, Anne Marshall ..... Laconia, NH
Rice, Arthur Halsey ..... Miami, FL
Rice & Associates ..... Houston, TX
Rice & Associates, L.C. ..... Scott Depot, WV
Rice, B. Stephen ..... Houston, TX
Rice, Barry T. ..... Edmond, OK
Rice, Bart O. ..... Colorado Springs, CO
Rice, Ben E. ..... Jacksonville, AR
Rice, Ben H., III ..... Houston, TX
Rice, Benjamin ..... Santa Cruz, CA
Rice, Benjamin R. ..... Huntsville, AL
Rice, Benjamin Z. ..... Pleasanton, CA
Rice, Bernadine ..... Orlando, FL
Rice, Bernard C. ..... Sikeston, MO
Rice, Bert W. ..... Atmore, AL
Rice, Bill ..... Eden Prairie, MN
Bordentown, NJ
Rice, Bonnie Beaman ..... Vandalia, OH
Rice, Boop & Storaska ..... Sunbury, PA
Rice, Bradley E. ..... Twin Falls, ID
Rice, Bradley F. ..... Albany, NY
Rice, Bradley H. ..... Fort Worth, TX
Rice, Brenda L. ..... Overland Park, KS
Rice, Brian E. ..... Chicago, IL
Rice, Brian F. ..... Minneapolis, MN
Rice, Bruce M. ..... Oxford, AL
Rice, C. Daniel ..... Jacksonville, FL
Rice, C. Patrick ..... Minneapolis, MN
Rice, Canice Timothy, Jr. ..... St. Louis, MO
Rice, Carlotta Wick ..... Princeton, NJ
Rice, Carole Comfort ..... Ocala, FL
Rice, Casey C. ..... Washington, DC
Rice, Cassandra L.
Environmental Protection Agency, Office of Enforcement and Compliance Assurance, GV
Rice, Charles A., Jr. ..... Spartanburg, SC
Rice, Charles B. ..... Homerville, GA
Rice, Charles E. ..... San Marcos, CA
Rice, Charles E. ..... South Bend, IN
Rice, Charles E. ..... Minneapolis, MN
Rice, Charles E., III ..... Wilmington, NC
Rice, Charles F. ..... Summit, NJ
Rice, Charles H. ..... Oxford, AL
Rice, Charles L., Jr. ..... New Orleans, LA
Rice, Charles M. ..... Atlanta, GA
Rice, Charles M. ..... St. Louis, MO
Rice, Charles M., Jr. ..... Weatogue, CT
Rice, Charles P. ..... South Bend, IN

Rice, Charles R. ... **San Francisco, CA**
Rice, Charles W. ... **Miami, FL**
Rice, Cheryl Gilley ... **Reston, VA**
Rice, Christine E. ... **Grand Rapids, MI**
Rice, Christopher K. ... **Montpelier, VT**
Rice, Clark D. ... **Cleveland, OH**
Rice, Clark H., Jr. ... Cincinnati, OH
Rice, Clarke B. ... Billings, MT
Rice, Claude L. ... **Overland Park, KS**
Rice, Clayton K., II ... **Las Vegas, NV**
Rice, Cleaveland J., Jr. ... Bethany, CT
Rice, Clifford J. ... Valparaiso, IN
Rice, Craig C. ... Chicago, IL
Rice, Cynthia Ciliotta ... Bronx, NY
Rice, Cynthia I. ... **Clearwater, FL**
Rice, Cynthia L. ... Santa Rosa, CA
Rice, Cynthia Westcott ... Hubbard, OH
Rice, Dale A. ... **San Francisco, CA**
Rice, Dale E. ... **Crestview, FL**
Rice, Dan M. ... New York, NY
Rice, Dana Lorne ... **Centre, AL**
Rice, Daniel ... Great Falls, MT
Rice, Daniel J. ... Oak Park, IL
Rice, Danton B. ... Wichita, KS
Rice, Darrel A. ... **Dallas, TX**
Rice, Darrel L. ... Toledo, OH
Rice, Darren W. ... Seattle, WA
Rice, Daryl L. ... **Washington, DC**
Rice, David A. ... Chestnut Hill, MA
Rice, David A ... Washington, PA
Rice, David C. ... Madison, WI
Rice, David Eugene ... **Baltimore, MD**
Rice, David G. ... Havre, MT
Rice, David J. ... **Tampa, FL**
Rice, David J. ... Chicago, IL
Rice, David J. ... Philadelphia, PA
Pottstown, PA
Rice, David J. ... **Eau Claire, WI**
Rice, David L. ... Englewood, CO
Rice, David L. ... Toledo, OH
Rice, David L. ... **Seattle, WA**
Rice, David Lee ... **Los Angeles, CA**
Rice, David Lee ... **Santa Monica, CA**
Rice, David M. ... Carle Place, NY
Rice, David Mullaney ... **San Francisco, CA**
Rice, Dawrence W., Jr. ... Fresno, CA
Rice, Daya Masada Laufer
Buckhannon, WV
Rice, Dean E., (P.C.) ... **Atlanta, GA**
Rice, Debra J. ... Fullerton, CA
Rice, Delbert L. ... Tulsa, OK
Rice, Denis T. ... **San Francisco, CA**
Rice, Derry S. ... Littleton, CO
Rice, Diane S. ... **San Francisco, CA**
Rice and Diedrichs, LLP ... **Cincinnati, OH**
Rice Dolan & Kershaw ... **Providence, RI**
Rice, Donald S. ... New York, NY
Rice, Donald W. ... Valparaiso, IN
Rice, Donna J. ... San Francisco, CA
Rice, Donnellda L. ... Washington, DC
Rice, Douglas A. ... **Oklahoma City, OK**
Rice, Douglas W. ... Miami, FL
Rice, E. Carew, III ... **Beaufort, SC**
Rice, Earl J. ... Van Wert, OH
Rice, Earle McGee ... **Anderson, SC**
Rice, Edith A. ... Rochester, NY
Rice, Edward G. ... Buffalo, NY
Rice, Edward H. ... **St. Louis, MO**
Rice, Edward J., Jr. ... **New Orleans, LA**
Rice, Edward W. ... Boise, ID
Rice & Edwards ... Mount Olive, NC
Rice, Edwin D. ... Catlettsburg, KY
Rice, Edwin G. ... **Tampa, FL**
Rice, Elaine S. ... Baytown, TX
Rice, Eldridge Eugene, Jr
Randallstown, MD
Rice, Elizabeth G. ... **Tampa, FL**
Rice, Elizabeth Jane ... Ottawa, IL
Rice, Elizabeth M. ... **Camarillo, CA**
Rice, Elizabeth M. ... Boston, MA
Rice, Elizabeth M. ... Houston, TX
Rice, Elizabeth T. ... Somerville, TN
Rice, Ellen C. ... **Washington, DC**
Rice, Ellen Lewis ... **Livingston, NJ**
Rice, Emily Gray ... **Manchester, NH**
Rice, Eugene C. ... Paintsville, KY
Rice, Evan B. ... Fargo, ND
Rice, Everett S. ... Clearwater, FL
Rice, Everhart & Baber ... **Richmond, VA**
Rice & Ewinger ... Aberdeen, SD
Rice, Fowler, Rodriguez, Kingsmill & Flint, L.L.P. ... **Miami, FL**
New Orleans, LA
Rice, Fowler, Rodriguez, Kingsmill & Flint, L.L.P. ... **Houston, TX**
Rice, Frank M. ... Topeka, KS
Rice, Fred E. ... Milwaukee, WI
Rice, Fred J., Jr. ... Washington, DC
Rice, Frederick W. ... Columbus, OH
Rice, Fredrick L. ... Jacksonville, FL
St. Augustine, FL
Rice, Fredrick L., P.A. ... St. Augustine, FL
Rice, G. Johnson, Jr. ... Raleigh, NC
Rice, G. Mark ... **Des Moines, IA**
Rice, Gail Brooks ... New Rochelle, NY
Rice, Garry Stephen ... **Charlotte, NC**
Rice, Gary ... **New York, NY**
Rice, Gary R. ... Dallas, TX
Rice, Gary R., P.C. ... Dallas, TX
Rice, Gay Lynn ... Columbus, OH
Rice, Geoffrey F. ... Clearwater, FL
Rice, Geoffrey I. ... Portland, ME
Rice, George A. ... **Chicago, IL**
Rice, George B. ... Aurora, CO
Rice, George E. ... **Montpelier, VT**
Rice, George E. ... Muskego, WI
Rice, George E. (Jed) ... **Boston, MA**
Rice, George F. ... Rockville Centre, NY
Rice, George J. ... Aberdeen, SD
Rice, George L., Jr. ... Memphis, TN
Rice, George Lawrence (Larry), III
Memphis, TN
Rice, Glenn A. ... **Chicago, IL**
Rice, Glenn B. ... **New York, NY**
Rice, Gloria K. ... **Montpelier, VT**
Rice, Gordon A. ... Madison, WI
Rice, Gretchen A. ... **Boston, MA**
Rice, Gudrun Jane ... Grand Junction, CO
Rice, Guy G. ... Independence, MO
Rice, H. Hamilton, III ... **Tampa, FL**
Rice, H. Hamilton, Jr. ... **Bradenton, FL**
Rice, Harold D. ... **Brookwood, AL**
Rice, Harry E. ... San Francisco, CA
Rice, Helen R. ... Kansas City, KS
Rice & Hendrickson ... **Harlan, KY**
Pineville, KY
Rice, Henry J. ... Englewood, CO
Rice, Herbert S. ... Montgomery, AL
Rice, Horace A. ... Houston, TX
Rice, Howard H. ... Montgomery, AL
Rice, Howard T. ... North Miami Beach, FL
Rice, Hugh D. ... **Oklahoma City, OK**
Rice, Hugh M. ... Weatogue, CT
Rice, Hugh T., Jr. ... **Myrtle Beach, SC**
Rice & Hundman, Ltd., A Professional Corporation ... **Wheaton, IL**
Rice, J. David ... **La Crosse, WI**
Sparta, WI
Rice, J. Dean ... San Diego, CA
Rice, J. Jeffrey ... **Fort Myers, FL**
Rice, James A. ... **Los Angeles, CA**
Rice, James A., Jr. ... **Atlanta, GA**
Rice, James A., Jr. ... **Helena, MT**
Rice, James B. ... Glenview, IL
Rice, James B., Jr., The Law Offices of
Sedalia, MO
Rice, James C. ... Alexandria, VA
Rice, James D. ... New York, NY
Rice, James E. ... **Southport, CT**
Rice, James E. ... Hammond, IN
Rice, James G. ... Eugene, OR
Rice, James H. ... Midwest City, OK
Rice, James K. ... **Cincinnati, OH**
Rice, James L., III ... **Houston, TX**
Rice, James M. ... Aurora, OR
Rice, James N. ... **Boston, MA**
Rice, James P. ... Manhasset, NY
Rice, James W. ... Sparta, WI
Rice, Jane E. ... Fayetteville, NY
Rice, Janet L. ... **Seattle, WA**
Rice, Janine L. ... **Ellicott City, MD**
Rice, Jann J. ... **Birmingham, AL**
Rice, Jason S. ... **Chicago, IL**
Rice, Jay Clinton ... **Cleveland, OH**
Rice, Jay J. ... **Livingston, NJ**
Rice, Jean Ellen ... Edgewater, MD
Rice, Jean Weaver ... Phoenix, AZ
Rice, Jennifer ... **Walnut Creek, CA**
Rice, Jerome S. ... **Minneapolis, MN**
Rice, Jim Ed ... Smithville, TN
Rice, Joe M. ... Smithville, TN
Rice, Joe Perry, III ... **Cape Girardeau, MO**
Rice, Joel W. ... **Chicago, IL**
Rice, John B. ... **Doylestown, PA**
Rice, John Carter ... **Albany, NY**
Rice, John D. ... Chanhassen, MN
Rice, John D. ... San Antonio, TX
Rice, John David ... Cincinnati, OH
Rice, John F. ... San Diego, CA
Rice, John G. ... **Lexington, KY**
Rice, John H. ... **Gulfport, MS**
Rice, John J. ... San Diego, CA
Rice, John J. ... Newport News, VA
Rice, John Joseph ... New York, NY
Rice, John K. ... Midvale, UT
Rice, John Lloyd ... **Washington, DC**
Rice, John M. ... Juneau, AK
Rice, John M. ... Phoenix, AZ
Rice, John P., III ... Mayville, NY
Rice, John P., Jr. ... Cleveland, OH
Rice, John R., Jr. ... Burlington, MA
Rice, John S. ... **Dallas, TX**
Rice, John Stuart ... San Diego, CA
Rice, John T. ... Chattanooga, TN
Rice, Jonathan P. ... **Springfield, MA**
Rice, Joseph F. ... **Charleston, SC**
Rice, Juanita L. ... Colorado Springs, CO
Rice, Judith Gail ... Tallahassee, FL
Rice, Julia A. ... Chicago, IL
Rice, Julian C. ... Fairbanks, AK
Rice, Juliana deHaan ... Boston, MA
Rice & Justice ... **Albany, NY**
Saratoga Springs, NY
Schenectady, NY
Troy, NY
Rice, Justin G. ... **San Antonio, TX**
Rice, Karen Lamoreaux ... Rochester, MI
Rice, Karl M. ... Woodbridge, VA
Rice, Kathleen S. ... **Washington, DC**
Rice, Kay J. ... **Denver, CO**
Rice & Keene ... Atlanta, GA
Rice & Kendig ... Shreveport, LA
Rice, Kenneth C. ... **Lynn, MA**
Rice, Kevin J.
General Services Administration, Office of the General Counsel, GV
Rice, Klaus C. ... Brooklyn, NY
Rice, Kollin L. ... Toledo, OH
Rice, Kristen Rebers ... **Minneapolis, MN**
Rice, Kristin L. ... Gettysburg, PA
Rice, L. Jeanette ... Upper Marlboro, MD
Rice, Lacy I., Jr. ... **Martinsburg, WV**
Rice, Laura A. ... Athens, GA
Rice Law Firm, The, L.L.C.
St. Louis, MO
Rice, Lawrence C. ... Vero Beach, FL
Rice, Lawrence W. ... Beloit, WI
Rice, Lenore DiStefano ... Short Hills, NJ
Rice, Leon L., III ... Atlanta, GA
Rice, Leonard S. ... **Minneapolis, MN**
Rice, LeRoy M. ... Richfield, MN
Rice, LeRoy W. ... San Francisco, CA
Rice, Linda Fermoyle, Law Office of
Woodland Hills, CA
Rice, Linda S. ... Ashland, KY
Rice, Lisa S. ... Houston, TX
Rice, Louis W., III ... Urbana, IL
Rice & Lund ... **Anderson, SC**
Rice, M. Barton, Jr. ... Athens, GA
Rice, M. Carl ... Shreveport, LA
Rice & MacDonald, P.A.
Myrtle Beach, SC
Rice, MacDougal ... **Manassas, VA**
Rice, Margaret M. ... Washington, DC
Rice, Margaret Susan ... **Houston, TX**
Rice, Marian C. ... **Garden City, NY**
Rice, Mark J., (A Professional Corporation)
San Rafael, CA
Rice, Martin Errol ... **St. Petersburg, FL**
Rice, Martin Errol, P.A. ... **Clearwater, FL**
St. Petersburg, FL
Tampa, FL
Rice, Marvin M. ... Atlanta, GA
Rice, Mary A. ... **Owatonna, MN**
St. Paul, MN
Rice, Mary C. ... **Annapolis, MD**
Baltimore, MD
Rice, Mary T. ... La Plata, MD
Rice, Matthew J. ... **Trenton, NJ**
West Orange, NJ
New York, NY
Rice, Maurice G., Jr. ... **Stevens Point, WI**
Rice, M. Barton, Jr., P.C. ... Athens, GA
Rice, Melissa B. ... Columbia, SC
Rice, Michael ... Albany, NY
Rice, Michael D. ... Cincinnati, OH
Rice, Michael Downey ... Old Saybrook, CT
Rice, Michael G. ... Rochester, NY
Rice, Michael J. ... **Manchester, CT**
Rice, Michael L. ... Hauppauge, NY
Rice, Michael Lyn ... **Dallas, TX**
Rice, Michael S., III ... Metairie, LA
Rice, Michael W. ... Hanover, PA
Rice, Michael W. ... Scott Depot, WV
Rice, Michelle A. ... **New York, NY**
Rice, Milton ... Stratford, CT
Rice, Mitchel T. ... **Salt Lake City, UT**
Rice, M. Susan, P.C. ... **Houston, TX**
Rice, Nancy G. ... Cincinnati, OH
Rice, Nancy M. ... Voorhees, NJ
Rice, Nancy R. ... **Boston, MA**
Rice, Nida Brinkis ... San Diego, CA
Rice, Owen, Jr. ... Tampa, FL
Rice, Patrick A. ... Westminster, CO
Rice, Patrick F. ... **New York, NY**
Rice, Patrick J. ... **Augusta, GA**
Aiken, SC
Rice, Paul D. ... **Cincinnati, OH**
Rice, Paul E. ... **Ann Arbor, MI**
Rice, Paul E., Jr. ... **Daytona Beach, FL**
Palm Coast, FL
Rice, Paul F. ... New Berlin, WI
Rice, Paul Jackson ... **Washington, DC**
Rice, Peter J., Jr. ... Greensboro, GA
Rice, Peter J., Jr., P.C. ... Greensboro, GA
Rice, Peter S. ... **Boston, MA**
Rice, Philip M. ... Sycamore, IL
Rice, Philip M. ... **Toledo, OH**
Rice, Randolf J. ... **San Jose, CA**
Rice, Raymond Brian ... Big Creek, KY
Rice, Rebecca A. ... **Rutland, VT**
Rice, Rebecca S. ... Topeka, KS
Rice, Reginald G. ... **Irvine, CA**
Rice, Reid, Broderick & Wattengel
Niagara Falls, NY
Rice & Rice ... Marietta, GA
Valparaiso, IN
Rice, Rice, Adams & Rice, P.C. ... Oxford, AL
Rice, Rice & Gilbert, P.C.
Bingham Farms, MI
Detroit, MI
Rice & Rice, P.C. ... Voorhees, NJ
Rice, Rice & Rice, P.C., Law offices of
Conroe, TX
Rice, Richard A. ... Phoenix, AZ
Rice, Richard A. ... Atlanta, GA
Rice, Richard A. ... South Bend, IN
Rice, Richard A., Jr. ... **Washington, DC**
Rice, Richard C. ... Laurel, MD
Rice, Richard E. ... **Alexandria, VA**
Rice, Richard F. ... Dayton, OH
Rice, Richard F. ... Madison, WI
Rice, Richard James ... Maryville, TN
Rice, Richard L. ... **Lincoln, NE**
Rice, Richard L., Jr. ... Birmingham, AL
Rice, Richard R. ... Encinitas, CA
Rice, Richard T. ... **Winston-Salem, NC**
Rice, Robert C. ... San Diego, CA
Rice, Robert C. ... Dallas, TX
Rice, Robert C. ... **Houston, TX**
Rice, Robert C. ... **Richmond, VA**
Rice, Robert E. ... Lexington, KY
Rice, Robert E. ... New York, NY
Rice, Robert H. ... Delmar, NY
Rice, Robert J. ... Pasadena, CA
Rice, Robert J. ... **Richmond, VA**
Rice, Robert L. ... Redondo Beach, CA
Rice, Robert Lawrence, V ... Conroe, TX
Rice, Robert M. ... **Cincinnati, OH**
Rice, Robert O. ... **Benton Harbor, MI**
Rice, Robert O. ... **Salt Lake City, UT**
Rice, Robert R. ... Washington, DC
Rice, Robert T. ... Mount Olive, NC
Rice, Robert T. ... **Angleton, TX**
Rice, Robin A. ... **Houston, TX**
Rice, Robin E. ... **Amarillo, TX**
Rice & Robinson, P.A. ... **Miami, FL**
Rice, Robt. E. ... Duncan, OK
Rice, Roger B. ... Naples, FL
Rice, Roger, (P.A.) ... Tavares, FL
Rice, Ronald A. ... **Atlanta, GA**
Rice, Ronald G., Jr. ... Miami, FL
Rice, Ronald J. ... Hubbard, OH
Rice, Ronald W. ... Quincy, MA
Rice, Ronald W. ... Southfield, MI
Rice Rose & Snell ... **Daytona Beach, FL**
Palm Coast, FL
Rice, S. Theis ... Dallas, TX
Rice, Saml. K. ... Orange, CA
Rice, Sanford A. ... Marietta, GA
Rice, Sarah A. ... **Rocky Mount, VA**
Rice, Saundra L. ... **Chicago, IL**
Rice, Sean J. ... Minneapolis, MN
Rice, Shawn G. ... **Milwaukee, WI**
Rice, Shirley G. ... Greenwood, MS
Rice, Shirley G., P.A. ... Greenwood, MS
Rice, Smith, Bursi, Veazey, Amundsen, Jewell & Armstrong, L.L.P.C.
Memphis, TN
Rice & Stallknecht, P.C. ... Woodbridge, VA
Rice, Stanley E. ... **Kansas City, MO**
Rice, Stephen C. ... **Lewiston, ID**
Rice, Stephen J. ... Grafton, ND
Rice, Stephen M. ... Kalamazoo, MI
Rice, Stephen M. ... **Las Vegas, NV**
Rice, Steven C. ... **Long Beach, CA**
Rice, Steven H. ... **Albany, NY**
Rice, Steven J. ... **New York, NY**
Rice, Steven P. ... **Irvine, CA**
Rice, Stewart N. ... **Corpus Christi, TX**
Rice, Stuart J. ... **Bingham Farms, MI**
Rice, Susan ... San Francisco, CA
Rice, Susan Braun ... Laguna Niguel, CA
Rice, T. Patrick ... **Wheaton, IL**
Rice, Tamyra ... Santa Cruz, CA
Rice, Ted W. ... Dayton, OH
Rice, Terence R. ... Atascadero, CA
Rice, Teresa E. ... Minneapolis, MN
Rice, Teresa McLoughlin
San Francisco, CA
Rice, Terre Ellen ... Knoxville, TN
Rice, Terry A., (Mr.) ... **Suffern, NY**
Rice, Terry D. ... Oakland, CA
Rice, Thomas ... **Washington, DC**
Rice, Thomas C. ... **New York, NY**
Rice, Thomas E., Jr. ... **Overland Park, KS**
Kansas City, MO
Rice, Thomas G. ... Albuquerque, NM
Rice, Thomas H. Speedy ... San Diego, CA
Rice, Thomas J. ... **New York, NY**
Rice, Thomas O. ... Brooklyn, NY
Melville, NY
Rice, Thomas Sullivan ... **Denver, CO**
Rice, Timothy G. ... Dayton, OH
Rice, Timothy J. ... Voorhees, NJ
Rice, T. R. ... **Denver, CO**
Rice, Tricia A. ... **Boston, MA**
Rice, V. Thomas ... Maunaloa, HI
Rice, Vaughan, Allen & Duncan
Angleton, TX
Rice, Vernon R. ... **Wilmington, DE**
Rice, Virginia G. ... **St. Louis, MO**
Rice, Volland & Taylor, P.C. ... Anchorage, AK
Rice, W. Brent ... **Lexington, KY**
Rice, W. Kenneth ... **Santa Maria, CA**
Rice, W. Mack ... Havelock, NC
Rice, Walter H. ... Dayton, OH
Rice, Warren W., Jr.
Department Of Veterans Affairs, Board of Veterans Appeals, GV
Rice, Wesley E. ... **Newport News, VA**
Rice, William A. ... Overland Park, KS
Rice, William A. ... **Harlan, KY**
Rice, William C., Jr. ... Normangee, TX
Rice, William E. ... Atlanta, GA
Rice, William Gregg ... Port Jervis, NY
Rice, William H. ... Montpelier, VT
Rice, William J., Jr. ... Houston, TX
Rice, William K. ... **Houston, TX**
Rice, William L., Jr. ... Marietta, GA
Rice, William M. ... **Decatur, IL**
Rice, William P., Jr. ... Ormond Beach, FL
Rice, William R. ... **Dublin, GA**
Vidalia, GA
Rice, Wilson A. ... Anchorage, AK
Rice & Winer, P.C. ... Chattanooga, TN
Rice, Winston Edward ... **New Orleans, LA**
Rice, Wm. Roy ... Charleston, WV
Rice, Zachariah A., Jr. ... **Cumming, GA**
Rice, Zel S., II ... Sparta, WI
Rice-Bartlett, Kathleen ... Salem, OH
Rice-Charouhis, Juliean Lynn ... **Miami, FL**
Rice-Kent, Mary K. ... Portland, OR
Ricelli, Michael L. ... Howell, MI
Rice Roque, Susana ... **Miami, FL**
Rich, A. Bruce ... Ripley, MS
Rich, A. Wayne ... Orlando, FL
Rich, Alan B. ... **Dallas, TX**
Rich, Alan J. ... Parsippany, NJ
Rich, Alan J. ... New York, NY
Rich, Alan S. ... **Carlsbad, CA**
Rich, Alan S., A Professional Law Corporation ... **Carlsbad, CA**
Rich, Allegra R. ... **Chicago, IL**
Rich, Andrew M. ... Hillsboro, OR
Rich, April ... Atlanta, GA
Rich & Archer, P.S.C. ... Louisville, KY
Rich, Archie L., II ... **Washington, DC**
Rich, Arnold G. ... Lansing, MI
Rich, Arnold I. ... **White Plains, NY**
Rich, Arthur D. ... Aiken, SC
Rich, Arthur W. "Buzz", P.A. ... **Aiken, SC**

Rich, Arthur W. "Buzz" ... **Aiken, SC**
Rich, Ashley Mooney ... Mobile, AL
Rich & Associates, LLC ... **Dallas, TX**
San Antonio, TX
Rich, Barry M. ... Boston, MA
Rich, Beckman ... **New Brunswick, NJ**
Rich, Bradford W. ... **San Antonio, TX**
Rich, Bradley P. ... **Salt Lake City, UT**
Rich, Brian A. ... Mobile, AL
Rich, Brian G. ... **Miami, FL**
Rich, Bruce A. ... **New York, NY**
Rich, Bruce A. ... **New York, NY**
Rich, Bruce G. ... Taunton, MA
Rich, Bruce M. ... Washington, DC
Rich, C. Edward ... Jacksonville, FL
Rich, Carol Ann ... **Cruz Bay, St. John, VI**
Charlotte Amalie, St. Thomas, VI
Rich, Carolyn S. ... Woodland Hills, CA
Rich, Casper ... Decatur, GA
Rich, Charles A. ... **Youngstown, OH**
Rich, Charles B. ... Hartford, CT
Rich, Charles B. ... **New York, NY**
Rich, Charles E. ... Memphis, TN
Rich, Charles Henry, III ... Englewood, CO
Rich, Charles L. ... Shelbyville, TN
Rich, Charles S. ... **New York, NY**
Rich, Cheryl I. ... Sherman Oaks, CA
Rich, Christopher Bowman
Salt Lake City, UT
Rich, Christopher C. ... Salem, MA
Rich, Christopher W. ... Portland, OR
Rich, Clara ... Detroit, MI
Rich, Claude D. ... **Dallas, TX**
Rich, Craig R. ... **Tulsa, OK**
Rich, D. Tate ... Nashville, TN
Rich, Daniel M. ... Norton, MA
Rich, David A. ... San Diego, CA
Rich, David A. ... **Boston, MA**
Rich, David B., III ... **Richmond, VA**
Rich, David H. ... **Boston, MA**
Rich, David L. ... Hawthorne, NY
Rich, David L. ... Hillsboro, OR
Rich, David M. ... **Denver, CO**
Rich, David S. ... **New York, NY**
Rich, David T. ... Boston, MA
Rich, Dawn M. ... **Springfield, MA**
Rich, Dean A. ... **Pinehurst, NC**
Rich, Diana G. ... **Sacramento, CA**
Rich, Dixon R., Jr. ... Pittsburgh, PA
Rich, Donald E. ... Glendale, CA
Rich, Edward J. ... Washington, DC
Rich, Elizabeth G. ... **Milwaukee, WI**
Rich, Elizabeth N. ... **Asheville, NC**
Rich, Elmer F. ... Rockwood, TN
Rich, Elwood M. ... Riverside, CA
Rich, Emily Platt ... Oakland, CA
Rich, Eric Arthur ... **Cleveland, OH**
Rich, F. Tyler ... Phoenix, AZ
Rich, Frederic C. ... **New York, NY**
Rich & Friedman ... Parsippany, NJ
Rich, Fuidge, Morris & Iverson, Inc.
Chico, CA
Colusa, CA
Marysville, CA
Nevada City, CA
Rich, Gary R ... Warren, OH
Rich, Genie ... **Roanoke, VA**
Rich, Geoffrey ... Altamonte Springs, FL
Rich, George B. ... Memphis, TN
Rich, George R. ... Hamburg, NY
Rich, Gloria T. ... Riverside, CA
Rich, Gregory Alan ... **St. Louis, MO**
Rich and Henderson, P.C. ... **Annapolis, MD**
Easton, MD
Rich, Herbert R. ... Nashville, TN
Rich, Ivan H., Jr. ... Louisville, KY
Rich, J. David ... Phoenix, AZ
Rich, J. Jeffery ... **Huntsville, AL**
Rich, J. Peter ... **Los Angeles, CA**
Rich, J. Steven ... **Washington, DC**
Rich, James A. ... **Cleveland, OH**
Rich, James B. ... Salem, OR
Rich, James B., III ... Falling Waters, WV
Rich, James E., Jr. ... Washington, DC
Rich, James E., Jr. ... Beverly, MA
Rich, James H., Jr. ... Ardmore, PA
Rich, James R. ... West Palm Beach, FL
Rich, Janet Lowry ... **Pittsburgh, PA**
Rich, Janet R. ... Los Angeles, CA
Rich, Jean Zoubek ... Bow, NH
Rich, Jeffrey ... New York, NY
Rich, Jeffrey A. ... **Sacramento, CA**
Rich, Jeffrey A. ... **Columbus, OH**
Rich, Jeffrey N. ... **New York, NY**
Rich, Jeffrey R. ... **Woodbridge, NJ**
Rich, Jeffrey T. ... **San Francisco, CA**
Rich, Jessica ... Federal Trade Commission,
Bureau of Consumer Protection, GV
Rich, Joan Ferrante ... Princeton, NJ
Rich, Joel C. ... Dixon, KY
Rich, Joel D. ... **Dallas, TX**
Rich, John C. ... Corvallis, OR
Rich, John D. ... Tampa, FL
Rich, John E., Jr. ... **Manchester, NH**
Rich, John G. ... **New York, NY**
Rich, John H., III ... **Portland, ME**
Rich, John L. ... Cypress, CA
Rich, John Townsend ... **Washington, DC**
Rich, Jonathan ... New York, NY
Rich, Jonathan A. ... Cleveland, OH
Rich, Jonathan D. ... **Orlando, FL**
Rich, Jonathan E. ... **Los Angeles, CA**
Rich, Jonathan M. ... **Washington, DC**
Rich, Jordan J. ... **Phoenix, AZ**
Rich, Joseph A., Jr. ... Lawrenceville, NJ
Rich, Joseph Curtis ... **Arlington, VA**
Rich, Joseph D. ... Department of Justice,
Civil Rights Division, GV
Rich, Joseph L. ... Gallup, NM
Rich, Joseph T., Jr. ... **Phoenix, AZ**
Rich, Joshua R. ... **Chicago, IL**
Rich, Julie A. ... **Minneapolis, MN**
Rich, Kenneth A. ... **Farmington Hills, MI**
Rich, Kimberly F. ... **Dallas, TX**
Rich, Lauren ... Cleveland, OH
Rich, Laurence J. ... Englewood, CO
Rich, Lawrence J. ... Cleveland, OH
Rich, Leo S. ... **Los Angeles, CA**
Rich, Lesley S. ... Somerset, MA
Rich, Linda G. ... Tampa, FL
Rich, Linda M. ... Cleveland, OH
Rich, Lisa Lenack ... Irvine, CA
Rich, Lloyd L. ... Denver, CO
Rich, Lonnie C. ... **Alexandria, VA**
Rich, Lynnette ... New York, NY
Rich, Marc L. ... New York, NY
Rich, Marcia R. ... **New York, NY**
Rich, Mark D. ... **Miami, FL**
Rich, Mark V. ... San Antonio, TX
Rich, Marshall H. ... Murrieta, CA
Rich, Marvin L. ... **Kansas City, MO**
Rich, May, Bilodeau & Flaherty, P.C.
Boston, MA
Rich, Melissa Saxe ... New York, NY
Rich, Melvin D. ... San Diego, CA
Rich, Michael B. ... Sacramento, CA
Rich, Michael D. ... **Phoenix, AZ**
Rich, Michael J. ... Wilmington, DE
Rich, Michael L. ... Arlington, MA
Rich, Michael L. ... **Morristown, NJ**
Rich, Millard R., Jr. ... Raleigh, NC
Rich, Miriam ... Indianapolis, IN
Rich & Nalefski ... Fairview Heights, IL
Rich, Nancy J. ... **Chicago, IL**
Rich, Nelson B. ... St. Louis, MO
Rich, Norman J. ... **Washington, DC**
Rich, Paul A. ... **Arlington, VA**
Rich, Paul D. ... **Dallas, TX**
San Antonio, TX
Rich, Paul S. ... Newton, MA
Rich, Peter G. ... Cape Elizabeth, ME
Rich, Peter R. ... Weirton, WV
Rich, Phillipe W. ... **Louisville, KY**
Rich, Pott, Wetherell, Foster & Miller
Cincinnati, OH
Rich, R. Bruce ... **New York, NY**
Rich, Randall B. ... Los Angeles, CA
Rich, Randall S. ... **Washington, DC**
Rich, Randi B. ... **Jackson, TN**
Rich, Randolph Gregory
Lawrenceville, GA
Rich, Randolph M. ... Marshall, IL
Rich, Richard P. ... Los Angeles, CA
Rich, Rita G. ... **Middletown, NY**
Rich, Robert ... San Francisco, CA
Rich, Robert A. ... **San Francisco, CA**
Rich, Robert A. ... Jamesburg, NJ
Rich, Robert Aubrey ... New York, NY
Rich, Robert E. ... **Newport Beach, CA**
Rich, Robert E. ... **Cincinnati, OH**
Rich, Robert F., Jr. ... **Fishkill, NY**
Rich, Robert M. ... Verona, NJ
Rich, Robert P. ... **Lafayette, CA**
Rich, Robert P. ... New York, NY
Rich, Robert S. ... **Denver, CO**
Rich, Ronald B., & Associates ... **Detroit, MI**
Rich, Ronald B., & Associates
Farmington Hills, MI
Rich, Sally K. ... Washington, DC
Rich, Sandra L. ... Columbus, OH
Rich, Sherri S. ... **Los Angeles, CA**
Rich & Smith, P.C. ... **Lawrenceville, GA**
Rich, Stephen P. ... Randolph, MA
Rich, Stevan C. ... Riverside, CA
Rich, Steven D. ... Charlotte, NC
Rich, Steven D. ... Sioux Falls, SD
Rich, Steven E. ... **Los Angeles, CA**
Rich, Steven M. ... **Los Angeles, CA**
Rich, Stuart I. ... **Hackensack, NJ**
New York, NY
Rich, Susan Elliott ... **Chattanooga, TN**
Rich, Sussman & Shipley, A Professional Corporation ... San Diego, CA
Rich, Thomas C. ... Fairview Heights, IL
Rich, Tracy L. ... **Springfield, MA**
Rich, Tracy S. ... **Burbank, CA**
Rich, Veto J. ... Pittsburgh, PA
Rich, Virginia Hourigan ... Morristown, NY
Rich, Walter ... Cooperstown, NY
Rich, Warren K. ... **Annapolis, MD**
Easton, MD
Rich, Wayne A. ... Williamsburg, VA
Rich, Wayne A., Jr. ... Chattanooga, TN
Rich, William D. ... Akron, OH
Rich, William H.B. ... **Lexington, KY**
Rich, William J. ... Topeka, KS
Rich, William M. ... **Atlanta, GA**
Richan, David S. ... **New York, NY**
Richard, Alan Sanders ... Tallahassee, FL
Richard, Andrea Leah ... **Cheyenne, WY**
Richard, Andrew L., III ... Miami, FL
Richard, Andrew L., Jr. ... Miami, FL
Richard, Ashley A. ... Colfax, LA
Richard, Barbara L. ... **Ocala, FL**
Richard, Barry ... **Tallahassee, FL**
Richard, Bennie L. ... **Greenville, MS**
Richard, Bert A., Jr. ... Oklahoma City, OK
Richard, Bridgette J. ... Baton Rouge, LA
Richard, Charles R. ... **Washington, DC**
Richard, Charles W. ... Lake Charles, LA
Richard, Chris ... Opelousas, LA
Richard, Clarence C., Jr. ... Princeton, NJ
Richard, Clark A. ... Gretna, LA
Richard, Cobb & Hall, P.C.
Las Cruces, NM
El Paso, TX
Richard, Dana F. ... **Arlington, VA**
Richard, David A. ... Santa Barbara, CA
Richard, Deborah A. ... Hoffman Estates, IL
Richard, Dell A. ... **Cedar Rapids, IA**
Richard, Dell A. ... **Iowa City, IA**
Richard, Dennis A. ... **Miami, FL**
Richard, Dennis L. ... **El Paso, TX**
Richard, Diana Gale ... **Washington, DC**
Richard, Don M. ... **Metairie, LA**
Richard, Donald J. ... Opelousas, LA
Richard, Douglas W. ... Collinsville, IL
Richard, Edward C. ... **Chicago, IL**
Richard, Eric L. ... Washington, DC
Richard, Eugene R. ... **Boston, MA**
Richard, George B. ... Marrero, LA
Richard, Graddy C. ... Lynchburg, TN
Richard, Gwen E. ... **Sugar Land, TX**
Richard, Herschel E., Jr. ... **Shreveport, LA**
Richard, Hillary ... **New York, NY**
Richard, Howard ... Media, PA
Richard, Howard M., (P.C.) ... **Chicago, IL**
Richard, James L. ... **Ocala, FL**
Richard, James L., P.A. ... **Ocala, FL**
Richard, James M. ... Wooster, OH
Richard, Jeffrey M. ... **Costa Mesa, CA**
Richard, Jennifer I. ... **Portland, ME**
Richard, Joan C. ... Fort Collins, CO
Richard, Joel Charles
Department of Transportation,
Maritime Administration, GV
Richard, John E. ... Gladstone, OR
Richard, John M. ... Anchorage, AK
Richard, John M. ... Boston, MA
Richard, Jonathan M. ... Sidney, OH
Richard, Katia M. ... Hopkinton, MA
Richard, Kenneth D. ... San Diego, CA
Richard, Kenneth J. ... Anaheim, CA
Richard, Kerry McLain ... **Bethesda, MD**
Richard, Lance P. ... Stuart, FL
Richard, Larry T. ... Rayne, LA
Richard, Lawrence R. ... Philadelphia, PA
Richard, Leonce A. ... **Phoenix, AZ**
Richard, Loretta R. ... **Boston, MA**
Richard, Lucy R. ... Edmonds, WA
Richard, Marcel A. ... Providence, RI
Richard, Mark ... Miami, FL
Richard, Mark M. ... Department of Justice,
Criminal Division, GV
Richard, Maurice M., (Ms) ... Anchorage, AK
Richard, Melvin J. ... **Miami, FL**
Richard, Molly Buck ... **Austin, TX**
Richard, Monte D. ... Santa Fe, NM
Richard, Oliver G., III ... Omaha, NE
Richard, Patrick J. ... **San Francisco, CA**
Richard, Patrick J. ... Lowell, MA
Richard, Patrick Ragan ... **Baton Rouge, LA**
Richard, Paul F. ... Fargo, ND
Richard, Paul J. ... Flagstaff, AZ
Richard, Penelope Quinn ... Cameron, LA
Richard, Peter J. ... Klamath Falls, OR
Richard, R. Paul
Equal Employment Opportunity
Commission,
Office of the Commissioners, GV
Richard, Ralph P. ... Fort Myers, FL
Richard, Reñee Tramble ... **Cleveland, OH**
Richard, Richard J. ... Spokane, WA
Richard and Richard, P.A. ... **Miami, FL**
Richard & Richard, P.A. ... Stuart, FL
Richard, Riley P. ... **Livonia, MI**
Richard, Robert S. ... **Montgomery, AL**
Richard, Ronald C. ... Lake Charles, LA
Richard, Rosemarie ... Stuart, FL
Richard, Roy W., Jr. ... San Antonio, TX
Richard, S. Joe ... Tulsa, OK
Richard, Sam T. ... **Dallas, TX**
Richard, Sandra S. ... Boston, MA
Richard, Scott H. ... **Bedford, TX**
Richard, Scott H. ... **Paris, TX**
Wichita Falls, TX
Richard, Serena H. ... New York, NY
Richard, Shawn J. ... **Thibodaux, LA**
Richard, Steven M. ... **Providence, RI**
Richard, Steven T. ... Metairie, LA
Richard, Thomas A. ... San Francisco, CA
Richard, Thomas M. ... **Mandeville, LA**
Metairie, LA
Richard, Timothy G. ... **Fargo, ND**
Richard, Toby B. ... **Boston, MA**
Richards ... **Miami, FL**
Richards, A. Shawn ... Fort Worth, TX
Richards, Alan E. ... **Vernon Hills, IL**
Richards, Alan Z. ... Garden City, NY
Richards, Allan M. ... Cedar Rapids, IA
Richards, Amy Kutt ... Dearborn, MI
Richards, Andrew D. ... **Frankenmuth, MI**
Saginaw, MI
Richards, Andrew L. ... **New York, NY**
Richards, Arthur V. ... Rye, NY
Richards, Ashby T., Jr. ... Wilmington, DE
Richards and Associates, A Legal Professional Association ... **Cincinnati, OH**
Richards & Associates, P.C. ... **Erie, PA**
Richards, Benjamin T., Jr. ... Darien, CT
Richards, Bernard, Jr. ... Chapel Hill, NC
Richards, Beverly J. ... Akron, OH
Richards, Bird & Kump, A Professional Corporation ... Salt Lake City, UT
Richards, Bradley J. ... **Houston, TX**
Richards, Brandt, Miller & Nelson, A Professional Corporation
Salt Lake City, UT
Richards, Brian F. ... **Chicago, IL**
Richards, Brian P. ... Warwick, RI
Richards, Bruce L. ... Salt Lake City, UT
Richards, Bruce S. ... **Atlanta, GA**
Richards, C. Wesley ... Seattle, WA
Richards, C. A. ... Hudson, WI
Richards, Carlyle E. ... Aberdeen, SD
Richards, Carlyle E., P.C. ... Aberdeen, SD
Richards, Carol T. ... Metairie, LA
Richards, Carver ... Virginia, MN
Richards, Channing O. ... **Charlotte, NC**
Richards, Charles E., Jr. ... New Orleans, LA
Richards, Charles Emery ... Red Oak, IA
Richards, Charles F., Jr. ... **Phoenix, AZ**
Richards, Charles F., Jr. ... **Wilmington, DE**
Richards, Charles H., Jr. ... Atlanta, GA
Richards, Charles L. ... **Warren, OH**
Richards, Charles M. ... Tucker, GA
Richards & Chemerinski
Los Angeles, CA
Richards, Cheryl S. ... **Chicago, IL**
Richards, Christine P. ... **Memphis, TN**
Richards, Clark H. ... **Spokane, WA**
Richards, Claude C. ... Orem, UT
Richards, Claudia Tennant ... Mattapoisett, MA
Richards & Connor ... **Tulsa, OK**
Richards, Cynthia D. ... San Francisco, CA
Richards, Cynthia R. ... New York, NY
Richards, Damon C. ... **Lubbock, TX**
Richards, Daniel A. ... **Cleveland, OH**
Richards, Daniel F., (Co., L.P.A.)
Eastlake, OH
Richards, Daniel R.
Federal Deposit Insurance Corporation,
Liquidation Branch, GV
Richards, Daniel Read ... **Austin, TX**
Richards, Darryl R. ... **Tampa, FL**
Richards, David A. J. ... New York, NY
Richards, David Alan ... New York, NY
Richards, David C. ... **Salt Lake City, UT**
Richards, David C. ... **Kenosha, WI**
Richards, David F. ... **Clovis, NM**
Richards, David G. ... **Atlanta, GA**
Richards, David J. ... **Chicago, IL**
Richards, David J., Jr. ... **Painesville, OH**
Richards, David L. ... Arroyo Grande, CA
Richards, David L. ... Troy, MI
Richards, David L. ... Greenland, NH
Richards, David L. ... **New York, NY**
Richards, David M. ... Austin, TX
Richards, David R. ... Santa Fe, NM
Richards, Dean B., Law Office of
Delafield, WI
Richards, Dean E. ... Indianapolis, IN
Richards, Deborah D. ... Albany, NY
Richards, Deirdre M. ... **Wilmington, DE**
Richards, Dennis W. ... Houston, TX
Richards & DeWitt, P.C. ... Troy, MI
Richards, Don J ... Santa Ana, CA
Richards, Don R. ... **Lubbock, TX**
Richards, Donald A. ... **Parsippany, NJ**
Richards, Donald K. ... Jackson, MS
Richards, Dorothy Regas ... **Cleveland, OH**
Richards, Douglas ... **Springfield, VT**
Richards, Douglas A. ... Washington, DC
Richards, Douglas B. ... Englewood, CO
Richards, Douglas C. ... Lockwood, MO
Richards, Douglas C., and Associates
Lockwood, MO
Richards, Douglas N. ... St. Louis, MO
Richards, Dwayne A. ... San Francisco, CA
Seattle, WA
Richards, E. Douglas ... **Lexington, KY**
Richards, Edward E., Jr. ... Oregon, MO
Richards, Edward P., III ... Kansas City, MO
Richards, Edward W. ... Nashua, NH
Richards, Edward W., & Associates, P.C.
Nashua, NH
Richards, Edwin J. ... **Santa Ana, CA**
Richards, Elizabeth A.
Oklahoma City, OK
Richards, Elizabeth B. ... San Francisco, CA
Richards, Elvige Cassard
New Orleans, LA
Richards, Eric A.S. ... **Los Angeles, CA**
Richards, Eric L. ... Reno, NV
Richards, Eric S. ... **Grand Rapids, MI**
Richards, Ernest L. ... Woodbury, TN
Richards, Ernest V., IV ... Gretna, LA
Richards, Evelyn W. ... Charleston, SC
Richards, Everett O. ... Chappell, NE
Richards, Floyd H. ... Dalhart, TX
Richards, Frederick F., III ... **Chicago, IL**
Richards, Frederick, III ... **Vienna, VA**
Richards, Frederick S., II ... Minneapolis, MN
Richards, Frederick W. ... Merritt Island, FL
Richards, G. John ... Troy, MO
Richards, G. William ... Aurora, IL
Richards, Gary C. ... Gainesville, FL
Richards, Gary R. ... **Spearfish, SD**
Richards, Gates T. ... Cincinnati, OH
Richards, G. B. ... Lansford, PA
Richards, Geoffrey A. ... **Chicago, IL**
Richards, George A. ... **Wausau, WI**
Richards, George H., II ... **New Haven, CT**
Richards, George L., III ... Natick, MA
Richards, George M. ... Midlothian, VA
Richards, George R. ... Miami, FL
Richards, George R., P.A. ... Miami, FL
Richards, Gilkey, Fite, Slaughter, Pratesi & Ward, P.A. ... **Clearwater, FL**
Port Richey, FL
Richards, Glenn S. ... **Washington, DC**
Richards, Gordon C. ... Las Vegas, NV
Richards, Gordon C., Professional Corporation, Ltd. ... Las Vegas, NV
Richards, Gregory A., Jr. ... **Tampa, FL**
Richards, Gregory B. ... **Memphis, TN**
Richards, Gregory K. ... **Hershey, PA**
Richards, H. Ames, Jr. ... Stamford, CT
Richards, H. Leroy ... Racine, WI
Richards, Helen M. ... Wilmington, DE
Richards, Henry S. ... Nashville, TN
Richards, Homer R. ... Canton, OH

Richards, Hood and Nies, P.C. Deadwood, SD; Spearfish, SD
Richards, Howard Curtis ...... Santa Barbara, CA
Richards, Howard N. ...... Austin, TX
Richards, Hugh Montgomery London, KY
Richards, Ira Neil ...... Philadelphia, PA
Richards, J. Douglas Commodity Futures Trading Commission, Office of the General Counsel, GV
Richards, J. Kent ...... Duluth, MN
Richards, J. Randall ...... Columbus, OH
Richards, Jack A. ...... Ogden, UT
Richards, Jack W. ...... Wayne, NJ
Richards, James B. ...... Goodland, IN
Richards, James G. ...... New York, NY
Richards, James H., P.C. ...... Wyoming, MI
Richards, James J. ...... Hammond, IN
Richards, James M. ...... Salt Lake City, UT
Richards, James R. ...... Boise, ID
Richards, James R. ...... Lynchburg, VA
Richards, Jana V. ...... Kansas City, MO
Richards, Janet Leach ...... Memphis, TN
Richards, Jason R. ...... San Francisco, CA
Richards, Jason W. ...... Cleveland, OH
Richards, Jeannette D. ...... Larkspur, CA
Richards, Jeff ...... Yuma, AZ
Richards, Jeffery C. ...... Poughkeepsie, NY
Richards, Jeffery C., P.C. ...... Poughkeepsie, NY
Richards, Jeffrey Iven ...... Austin, TX
Richards, Jeffrey J. ...... Denver, CO
Richards, Jeffrey P. ...... Douglasville, GA
Richards, Jeffrey W. ...... Chicago, IL
Richards, Jeremy V. ...... Los Angeles, CA
Richards, Jerome J. ...... Ogdensburg, NY
Richards, Jett ...... Plano, TX
Richards, Jim M. ...... Houston, TX
Richards, Joanne S. ...... Fort Lauderdale, FL
Richards, Joe B. ...... Eugene, OR
Richards, John ...... New York, NY
Richards, John A. ...... Washington, DC
Richards, John B. ...... Washington, DC
Treasury Department, Internal Revenue Service, GV
Richards, John E., (P.C.) ...... Dallas, TX
Richards, John F. ...... Lynchburg, VA
Richards, John G., III ...... Philadelphia, PA
Richards, John H. ...... Fort Lauderdale, FL
Richards, John H. ...... Hampden, ME
Richards, John H. ...... Glens Falls, NY
Richards, John H. ...... Paducah, TX
Richards, John T., II ...... Austin, TX
Richards, John T., III ...... Pittsburgh, PA
Richards, John T., Jr. ...... Pittsburgh, PA
Richards, John Thorpe ...... Alexandria, VA
Richards, John Thorpe, Jr. Washington, DC; Alexandria, VA
Richards, John W. ...... Sacramento, CA
Richards, John W. ...... Bloomington, IN
Richards, Jonathan A. ...... New York, NY
Richards, Jonathan W. Salt Lake City, UT
Richards, Joseph D. ...... Miami, FL
Richards, Joseph V., Jr. ...... Cleveland, OH
Richards, Julia Ellen ...... Costa Mesa, CA
Richards, Julian I. ...... Virginia Beach, VA
Richards, Karen E. ...... Fort Wayne, IN
Richards, Karen M. ...... Syracuse, NY
Richards, Karen Trevathan Baton Rouge, LA
Richards, Karin F. Federal Trade Commission, Bureau of Competition, GV
Richards, Kathleen R. ...... St. Louis, MO
Richards, Kathy ...... San Francisco, CA
Richards, Keith M. ...... Oakland, CA
Richards, Keith P. ...... Baton Rouge, LA
Richards, Keith P. ...... Metairie, LA
Richards & Kelly ...... Pittsburgh, PA
Richards, Kelly Merritt ...... Pensacola, FL
Richards, Kenneth M. ...... Columbus, OH
Richards, Kerry A. ...... Seattle, WA
Richards, Kevin M. ...... Lebanon, PA
Richards, Kevin M. ...... Houston, TX
Richards, Kimberly A. ...... Albuquerque, NM
Richards & Kinerk ...... San Francisco, CA; Seattle, WA
Richards, Kip D. ...... Kansas City, MO
Richards, Kristen A. ...... Overland Park, KS
Richards, Kurt T. ...... Staten Island, NY
Richards, Lance D. ...... Albuquerque, NM
Richards, Latta ...... Dyersburg, TN
Richards, Laura M. Commodity Futures Trading Commission, Office of the General Counsel, GV
Richards, Laurie J. ...... Los Angeles, CA
Richards, Lavern D., Jr. Farmers Branch, TX
Richards Law Firm, A Professional Law Corporation ...... Baton Rouge, LA
Richards Law Office ...... Red Oak, IA
Richards Law Office, P.C. ...... Phoenix, AZ
Richards, Lawrence ...... Boise, ID
Richards, Lawrence H. ...... Youngstown, OH
Richards, Layton & Finger, P.A. Wilmington, DE
Richards, Lee S., III ...... New York, NY
Richards, Linda J. ...... Arroyo Grande, CA
Richards, Lindsay & Martin, LLP Austin, TX
Richards, Lloyd D. ...... Montpelier, VT
Richards, Loren J. ...... Laramie, WY
Richards, Lori A. Securities and Exchange Commission, Office of Compliance Inspections and Examinations, GV
Richards, Lowell E. ...... Walnut Creek, CA
Richards, Lowell L., III ...... Boston, MA
Richards, Lynn E. ...... Conneaut, OH
Richards, Lynn S. ...... Salt Lake City, UT
Richards, Marc E. ...... New York, NY
Richards, Marc H. ...... Newport Beach, CA
Richards, Marc V. ...... Chicago, IL
Richards, Margie A. ...... Incline Village, NV
Richards, Mark A ...... Denver, CO
Richards, Mark J. ...... Indianapolis, IN
Richards, Mark S. ...... Dallas, TX
Richards, Markt ...... Cle Elum, WA
Richards, Martha L. ...... Minnetonka, MN
Richards, Martin B. ...... Richmond, VA
Richards, Mary Beth Federal Communications Commission, GV
Richards, Mary Lynne Church ...... Tampa, FL
Richards, Matthew D. ...... Dallas, TX
Richards, Matthew K. ...... Salt Lake City, UT
Richards, Matthew R. ...... Baton Rouge, LA
Richards, Maureen ...... Mahwah, NJ
Richards, Maureen E. ...... Warren, OH
Richards, Max C. ...... Tucson, AZ
Richards McGettigan Reilly & West, P.C. Alexandria, VA
Richards, Meg Goodman Research Triangle Park, NC
Richards, Megan ...... Middletown, OH
Richards, Melissa K. ...... Boulder, CO; Denver, CO
Richards, Melvin A., Jr. ...... Noblesville, IN
Richards & Merrill ...... Canton, OH
Richards, Michael ...... Portland, ME
Richards, Michael E. ...... South Gate, CA
Richards, Michael S. ...... Lakewood, CO
Richards, Misti DeLane ...... Creve Coeur, MO
Richards, Morgan W., Jr. ...... Boise, ID
Richards, Nancy Ann ...... Las Vegas, NM
Richards, Nancy R. ...... St. Louis, MO
Richards, Natalie K. ...... Louisville, KY
Richards, Norman B. ...... San Francisco, CA
Richards, Norman E. Farmington Hills, MI
Richards, Norman J. ...... East Falmouth, MA
Richards & Norrell ...... Lancaster, SC
Richards, Olive M ...... Oxnard, CA
Richards & O'Neil, LLP ...... Greenwich, CT; New York, NY
Richards, Opal D. ...... San Bernardino, CA
Richards, Patricia McCloskey Washington, DC
Richards, Patrick A. Farmington Hills, MI
Richards, Patti M. ...... Washington, DC
Richards, Paul ...... San Diego, CA
Richards, Paul A. ...... Reno, NV
Richards, Paul A., Ltd. ...... Reno, NV
Richards, Peter C., (A Professional Corporation) ...... Los Angeles, CA
Richards, Peter R. ...... West Trenton, NJ
Richards, Phil R. ...... Tulsa, OK
Richards, R. Andrew ...... Newark, NJ
Richards, R. Barrett ...... Dallas, TX
Richards, R. Jeffrey ...... Portland, OR
Richards, Ralph & Schwab, Chartered Chicago, IL; Vernon Hills, IL; Waukegan, IL
Richards, Ralph Wm. ...... Las Cruces, NM
Richards, Randall ...... Bronxville, NY
Richards, Randall J. ...... Woodbridge, NJ
Richards, Randall W. ...... Ogden, UT
Richards, Ray E, II ...... Oak Park, MI
Richards, Raymond A. ...... Baltimore, MD
Richards, Raymond R. ...... New York, NY
Richards, Raymond W. ...... Amarillo, TX
Richards, R. D., Jr. ...... Houston, TX
Richards, Rebecca L. ...... Denver, CO
Richards, Reed C. ...... Deadwood, SD
Richards, Reed M. ...... Salt Lake City, UT
Richards, Renee A. ...... San Francisco, CA
Richards, Richard ...... Washington, DC
Richards, Richard A. ...... Oxnard, CA
Richards, Richard E. ...... Lancaster, SC
Richards, Richard L. ...... Coral Gables, FL
Richards, Richard L. ...... Des Moines, IA
Richards & Richards ...... Chappell, NE; Deadwood, SD
Richards, Richards & Silverman Silver Spring, MD
Richards, R. L. ...... Dublin, OH
Richards, Robert E. ...... Atlanta, GA
Richards, Robert E. ...... Chicago, IL
Richards, Robert E. ...... Silver Spring, MD
Richards, Robert E., Jr. ...... Boston, MA
Richards, Robert H., III ...... Wilmington, DE
Richards, Robert J., Jr. ...... Boston, MA
Richards, Robert Keith ...... Woodstock, VA
Richards, Robert L. ...... Greenville, GA
Richards, Robert P., (A Law Corporation) Honolulu, HI
Richards, Robert R., Jr. National Labor Relations Board, Office of Board Members, GV
Richards, Robert W. ...... Kansas City, KS
Richards, Robt. E. ...... Chappell, NE
Richards, Rodney A. ...... Binghamton, NY
Richards, Rodney N. Tendai Morristown, NJ
Richards, Roger W. ...... Erie, PA
Richards, Ronald ...... Los Angeles, CA
Richards, Rosa Lee ...... Venetia, PA
Richards, Rosemarie ...... Philadelphia, PA
Richards, Rowland ...... Buffalo, NY
Richards, Russell B. ...... Atlanta, GA
Richards, Ruth L. ...... West Bloomfield, MI
Richards, R. W. (Ricky) ...... Jacksonville, TX
Richards, Ryan L. ...... Orem, UT
Richards, Sarah C. ...... New York, NY
Richards, Sarah M. ...... Boston, MA
Richards, Scott I. ...... Diamond Bar, CA
Richards, Shan F. ...... Plano, TX
Richards, Shannon ...... Napa, CA
Richards, Shannon ...... Houston, TX
Richards Spears Kibbe & Orbe Washington, DC; Bronx, NY; Brooklyn, NY; New York, NY; White Plains, NY; Yonkers, NY; Fairfax, VA
Richards, Stanley ...... Des Moines, IA
Richards, Stanley H. ...... Chicago, IL
Richards, Stanley K. ...... Atlanta, GA
Richards, Stephen D. ...... Menlo Park, CA
Richards, Stephen D. ...... Houston, TX
Richards, Stephen H. ...... New York, NY
Richards, Steven A. ...... Idaho Falls, ID
Richards, Steven E. ...... Burlington, VT
Richards, Steven L. ...... Chicago, IL
Richards, Steven L. ...... Troy, NY
Richards, Steven T. ...... Scottsdale, AZ
Richards, Stuart L. ...... Cincinnati, OH
Richards, Susan Ann ...... Washington, DC
Richards, Suzanne G. ...... Raleigh, NC
Richards, Suzanne K. ...... Columbus, OH
Richards, Suzanne V. ...... Washington, DC
Richards, Sybil V. ...... Knoxville, TN
Richards, Ted E. ...... San Francisco, CA
Richards, Thomas C. ...... Sacramento, CA
Richards, Thomas D. ...... Cincinnati, OH
Richards, Thomas G. ...... Everett, WA; Seattle, WA
Richards, Thomas G. ...... Redmond, WA
Richards, Thomas H. ...... Manchester, NH
Richards, Thomas S. ...... Pontiac, MI
Richards, Thomas S. ...... Rochester, NY
Richards, Thomas W. ...... Buffalo, MN
Richards, Timothy D. ...... Miami, FL
Richards, Timothy S. ...... Belleville, IL
Richards, Tina M. ...... Springfield, VA
Richards, Todd A. ...... Detroit, MI
Richards, Tom ...... Carrollton, OH
Richards, Van R., Jr. ...... Elgin, IL
Richards, Vernon L. ...... Sandy, OR
Richards, Veronica A. ...... Pittsburgh, PA
Richards, Virginia E. ...... Washington, DC
Richards, W. Michael ...... Memphis, TN
Richards, Wanda M. ...... Peapack, NJ
Richards, Ward D. ...... Savannah, GA
Richards, Watson and Gershon, Professional Corporation ...... Brea, CA; Los Angeles, CA; San Francisco, CA
Richards, Wayne M. West Palm Beach, FL
Richards, William A. ...... Phoenix, AZ
Richards, William J. ...... Detroit, MI
Richards, William J. ...... Milwaukee, WI
Richards, William L., Jr. Sugar Loaf Shores, FL
Richards, William Le Gro, Jr. Sugar Loaf Shores, FL
Richards, William R. ...... Pompano Beach, FL; Indianapolis, IN
Richards, William R., P.C. Pompano Beach, FL; Indianapolis, IN
Richards, William Ralph ...... Salt Lake City, UT
Richards, William S. ...... Oregon, MO
Richards, William S. ...... Salt Lake City, UT
Richards, Wm. Geo. ...... Austin, TX
Richards, Yale, (P.C.) ...... Omaha, NE
Richards-Brie, Rebecca M. ...... Mauston, WI
Richardson, A. Haynes, III ...... Little Rock, AR
Richardson, Aimee N. ...... New Haven, CT
Richardson, Albert S., Jr. ...... Erie, PA
Richardson, Alicia ...... Jacksonville, FL
Richardson, Allan Edward ...... Woodbury, NJ
Richardson, Althea F. ...... Monticello, NY
Richardson, Ambrose M., III New York, NY
Richardson, Ami Lynn Department Of Health And Human Services, Office of the General Counsel, GV
Richardson, Amie ...... Dallas, TX
Richardson, Andra V. ...... Bloomfield Hills, MI
Richardson, Andrew James Indianapolis, IN
Richardson, Andrew L. ...... Tulsa, OK
Richardson, Andrew N. ...... Charleston, WV
Richardson, Andrew S. ...... Providence, RI
Richardson, Andrew T., III Washington, DC; Richmond, VA
Richardson, Ann B. ...... Washington, DC
Richardson, Ann M. ...... San Francisco, CA
Richardson, Ann Marie ...... New York, NY
Richardson, Anne ...... Pasadena, CA
Richardson, Arthur L. B. ...... Pinehurst, NC
Richardson, Arthur W. ...... Bronxville, NY
Richardson & Associates ...... Los Angeles, CA; Santa Monica, CA
Richardson, Barbara P. ...... Honolulu, HI
Richardson, Barbara Palone West Palm Beach, FL
Richardson, Barrett R. ...... Portsmouth, VA
Richardson, Beth C. ...... Scarborough, ME
Richardson, Bettina J. ...... Houston, TX
Richardson, Betty H. ...... Boise, ID
Richardson, Beverly D. ...... McMinnville, OR
Richardson, Billy W. ...... Seattle, WA
Richardson, Bob, Law Firm, The Austin, TX
Richardson, Bobby H. ...... Glasgow, KY
Richardson, Bradley J. ...... Las Vegas, NV
Richardson, Brenda J. ...... Louisville, KY
Richardson, Bruce L. ...... Washington, DC
Richardson, Bruce L. ...... Baltimore, MD
Richardson, Bruce M. ...... Long Beach, CA
Richardson, Bruin S., III ...... Richmond, VA
Richardson, Bryan D. ...... Washington, DC
Richardson, Campbell ...... Portland, OR
Richardson, Carolyn S. ...... Sacramento, CA
Richardson, Carrie Lynn ...... Syracuse, NY
Richardson, Catherine A. ...... San Diego, CA
Richardson, Catherine Bax Washington, DC
Richardson, Celie Benton Winston-Salem, NC
Richardson, Chadwick R. Oklahoma City, OK
Richardson, Chadwick R. ...... Tulsa, OK
Richardson, Charles ...... Red Wing, MN
Richardson, Charles E., III Birmingham, AL
Richardson, Charles H. ...... Santa Ana, CA
Richardson, Charles H. ...... Columbia, SC
Richardson, Charles H., Jr. ...... Aurora, CO
Richardson, Charles L. ...... Tulsa, OK
Richardson, Charles O. ...... Red Wing, MN
Richardson, Charles T. ...... Indianapolis, IN
Richardson, Charles T. ...... Clute, TX
Richardson, Charles W. ...... San Bernardino, CA
Richardson & Chenggis ...... Atlanta, GA
Richardson, Chester A. ...... Chicago, IL
Richardson, Christa B. ...... Kansas City, MO
Richardson, Christine L. ...... Palo Alto, CA
Richardson, Christopher ...... Houston, TX
Richardson, Christopher J. Greensburg, PA; **Pittsburgh, PA**
Richardson, Christopher L. ...... Boulder, CO
Richardson, Christopher S., Chartered, Law Office of ...... Chevy Chase, MD
Richardson, Christopher S. Chevy Chase, MD
Richardson, Claiborne T., II ...... Manassas, VA
Richardson, Clare ...... Los Angeles, CA
Richardson, Clarence J., III ...... Jackson, MS
Richardson, Clark V. ...... Bronx, NY
Richardson, Clinton D. ...... Atlanta, GA
Richardson, Corinne Ann Washington, DC
Richardson, Corinne Louise ...... Clayton, MO
Richardson, Craig E. ...... Department of Justice, Drug Enforcement Administration, GV
Richardson, Craig V. ...... Denver, CO
Richardson, Curtis R. ...... Decatur, GA
Richardson, D. Brian ...... Monterey, VA
Richardson, D. Matthew ...... Los Angeles, CA
Richardson, Dana L. ...... Seattle, WA
Richardson, Daniel D. ...... Jacksonville, FL
Richardson, Daniel R., Law Offices of **San Francisco, CA**; San Jose, CA
Richardson, Daniell, Spear & Upton, P.C. Mobile, AL
Richardson, David B. ...... Scottsdale, AZ
Richardson, David B. ...... Bellevue, WA
Richardson, David B., A Professional Service Corporation ...... Bellevue, WA
Richardson, David G. ...... Kansas City, MO
Richardson, David Gregory **Glens Falls, NY**; Cincinnati, OH
Richardson, David James Sacramento, CA
Richardson, David John ...... Los Angeles, CA
Richardson, David K. ...... Miami, FL
Richardson, David L., II ...... Richmond, VA
Richardson, David L., P.C. ...... Tempe, AZ
Richardson, David M. ...... Gainesville, FL
Richardson, David M. ...... Chicago, IL
Richardson, David N. ...... Lapeer, MI
Richardson, David R. ...... New Orleans, LA
Richardson, David W. Department of Commerce, Office of the General Counsel, GV
Richardson, David William ...... Dallas, TX
Richardson & Davis ...... Bluefield, WV; Princeton, WV
Richardson, Dean E. Grosse Pointe Woods, MI
Richardson, Dean F. ...... Pittsburgh, PA
Richardson, Dean M. ...... Salem, OR
Richardson, Deann R. ...... Charlotte, NC
Richardson, Deborah ...... Austin, TX
Richardson, Deborah E. ...... Gainesville, GA
Richardson, Deborah S. ...... Baltimore, MD
Richardson & Decker ...... Sacramento, CA
Richardson, Dennis W. ...... Sacramento, CA
Richardson, Dion F. ...... Greenville, NC
Richardson, Don E. ...... Ocean City, MD; Salisbury, MD
Richardson, Don E., P.A., Law Office of Ocean City, MD; Salisbury, MD
Richardson, Donald B., Jr. ...... San Jose, CA
Richardson, Donald J. ...... Cleveland, OH
Richardson, Donald J. ...... Richmond, VA
Richardson, Donald S. ...... Portland, OR
Richardson, Donald V., III ...... Columbia, SC
Richardson, Douglas F. ...... Los Angeles, CA
Richardson, Douglas W. ...... Santa Ana, CA
Richardson, Edith A. ...... Bangor, ME
Richardson, Edmund F. ...... Phoenix, AZ
Richardson, Edward J. ...... Melbourne, FL
Richardson, Edward J. ...... Tampa, FL
Richardson, Edward J. South Weymouth, MA
Richardson, Edward T., Jr. South Portland, ME

Richardson, Edwin J. ... Tinley Park, IL
Richardson, Edwina G. ... Bronx, NY
Richardson, Elise M. ... Pasadena, CA
Richardson, Elizabeth Anne ... Hagåtña, GU
Richardson, Elizabeth L. ... Long Beach, CA
Richardson, Ellen J. ... Lansing, MI
Richardson, Elliot L. ... Washington, DC
Richardson, Elwood H., Jr. ... Hampton, VA
Richardson, Enos, Jr. ... Fredericksburg, VA
Richardson, Eric ... Cincinnati, OH
Richardson, Eric A. ... Atlanta, GA
Richardson, Eric A. ... Greensboro, NC
Richardson, Eric W. ... Santa Monica, CA
Richardson, Erick E., Jr. ... Los Angeles, CA
Richardson, Ernest C., III ... New Bern, NC
Richardson, Ernest Hampton ... Pratt, KS
Richardson, Ernie J. ... Poplar Bluff, MO
Richardson, Eugene K. ... Newport, OR
Richardson, Eugenia R.G. Anchorage, AK
Richardson, Florence M. ... Albany, NY
Richardson & Folise ... Seattle, WA
Richardson, Frank ... Ann Arbor, MI
Richardson, Frank E., III ... Waynesboro, PA
Richardson, Frank L. Jr. ... Martinsville, VA
Richardson, Frank P. ... Honolulu, HI
Richardson, Fred M. ... Atlanta, GA
Richardson, G. Grady, Jr. Wilmington, NC
Richardson, Gail ... New York, NY
Richardson, Gail W. ... Signal Hill, CA
Richardson, Gardner & Barrickman Glasgow, KY
Richardson, Gary B. ... Concord, NH
Richardson, Gary L. ... Tulsa, OK
Richardson, Genae M. ... Washington, DC
Richardson, Geoffrey P. ... New York, NY
Richardson, George B. ... Menlo Park, CA
Richardson, George E. ... Swampscott, MA
Richardson, George, III ... Bluefield, WV
Richardson, George, Jr. ... Fort Lauderdale, FL
Richardson, George O., III New York, NY
Richardson, George W. ... Butte, MT
Richardson, Gerald B. ... Santa Fe, NM
Richardson, Gerald D. ... Nashville, TN
Richardson, Gerald M. ... St. Louis, MO
Richardson, Gerald T. ... Lansing, MI
Richardson, Gex F. ... Fort Lauderdale, FL
Richardson, Glen S. ... Cleveland, OH
Richardson, Glenn E. ... New York, NY
Richardson, Glenn P. ... Richmond, VA
Richardson, Grant A. ... Bridgewater, VA
Richardson, Greg D. ... Washington, DC
Richardson, Greg J. ... San Francisco, CA
Richardson & Gresham, LLP Poplar Bluff, MO
Richardson, Groseclose, Wyly, Wise & Sauck, LLP ... Aberdeen, SD
Richardson, Guy H. ... Poplar Bluff, MO
Richardson, H. Albert, Jr. ... Seattle, WA
Richardson, H. Smith, III Santa Barbara, CA
Richardson, H. Tracy, III ... Beaumont, TX
Richardson & Harman LLP Los Angeles, CA Pasadena, CA
Richardson, Harrison L. ... Portland, ME
Richardson, Harry D. ... Boise, ID
Richardson, Helen H. ... Philadelphia, PA
Richardson, Henry B., Jr. ... Columbia, SC
Richardson, Henry J., III ... Washington, DC
Richardson, Herbert L. ... Lumberton, NC
Richardson, Herbert M., III ... Dublin, OH
Richardson, Herman F., Jr. ... Prosperity, SC
Richardson, Homer W. ... Brooklyn, NY
Richardson, Ian T. ... Eugene, OR
Richardson, J. Glenn ... Dallas, GA
Richardson, J. Jeff ... Tempe, AZ
Richardson, J. Jeff, P.C. ... Tempe, AZ
Richardson, J. Jeffery ... Dallas, TX
Richardson, J. Michael ... Minneapolis, MN
Richardson, J. Peter ... Bluefield, WV
Richardson, J. Thomas ... Seattle, WA
Richardson, Jack L., IV ... Louisville, KY
Richardson and James ... Sumter, SC
Richardson, James B. ... Beaverton, OR
Richardson, James B., Jr. ... Beaufort, SC
Richardson, James Bruce ... Atlanta, GA
Richardson, James Bruce, P.C. Atlanta, GA
Richardson, James C. ... Watchung, NJ
Richardson, James D. Treasury Department, GV
Richardson, James H. ... Huntsville, AL
Richardson, James H., Jr. ... Erie, PA
Richardson, James M. ... Audubon, IA
Richardson, James M. ... Austin, TX
Richardson, James P. ... Roseland, NJ
Richardson, James R. ... Chicago, IL
Richardson, James S., Sr. United States Court Of Appeals For The Armed Forces, GV
Richardson, James W. ... Tucson, AZ
Richardson, Jamie I. ... San Antonio, TX
Richardson, Jane ... San Francisco, CA
Richardson, Jane ... Paoli, PA
Richardson, Jane E. ... San Diego, CA
Richardson, Jane Jeffries, (Mrs.) Grand Island, NE
Richardson, Janet M. ... Los Angeles, CA
Richardson, Jared S. ... Dallas, TX
Richardson, Jason W. ... Sherman, TX
Richardson, Jeffrey D. ... Decatur, IL
Richardson, Jeffrey E. ... New Orleans, LA
Richardson, Jeffrey F. ... Warwick, RI
Richardson, Jeffrey L. ... Los Angeles, CA
Richardson, Jeffrey R. ... Tallahassee, FL
Richardson, Jeffrey S. ... Parma Heights, OH
Richardson, Jeremy David ... New York, NY
Richardson, Jerry A. ... Tulsa, OK
Richardson, Jesse J., Jr. ... Winchester, VA
Richardson, Jesse J., Jr., P.C. Winchester, VA
Richardson, J. L., III ... Louisville, KY
Richardson, J. M. ... Owingsville, KY
Richardson, Joan ... San Francisco, CA
Richardson, Joan Hamilton ... Newark, NJ
Richardson, Joanne A ... New York, NY
Richardson, Jody ... Austin, TX
Richardson, Joel W., Jr. ... Chattanooga, TN
Richardson, John ... Elkhart, KS
Richardson, John ... Bozeman, MT
Richardson, John A. ... Hazen, ND
Richardson, John C. ... Tucson, AZ
Richardson, John D. ... Mobile, AL
Richardson, John D. ... El Paso, TX
Richardson, John D. ... Houston, TX
Richardson, John Daniel ... Memphis, TN
Richardson, John F. ... Somerville, NJ
Richardson, John G. ... Denver, CO
Richardson, John G. ... Portland, ME
Richardson, John G. ... Rochester, NH
Richardson, John J. ... Marlton, NJ
Philadelphia, PA
Richardson, John J. ... Flushing, NY
Richardson, John J. ... New York, NY
Richardson, John, Jr. ... Washington, DC
Richardson, John L. ... Washington, DC
Richardson, John L. ... Chicago, IL
Richardson, John M. ... New York, NY
Richardson, John M. ... Clarksville, TN
Richardson, John M., Jr. ... Clarksville, TN
Richardson, John R. ... Orlando, FL
St. Petersburg, FL
Richardson, John R. ... Myrtle Beach, SC
Richardson, John S. ... Detroit, MI
Richardson, John S. ... Salem, OR
Richardson, John T. ... St. Paul, MN
Richardson, John W. ... Shelburne Falls, MA
Richardson, John W. ... Richmond, VA
Richardson, John W. ... Virginia Beach, VA
Richardson, John Y., Jr. ... Norfolk, VA
Richardson, Johnny K. Jefferson City, MO
Richardson, Jon N. ... San Jose, CA
Richardson, Jones & Esraelian Fresno, CA
Richardson, Joseph H. ... St. Petersburg, FL
Richardson, Joseph N. ... Dallas, TX
Richardson, Joseph P. ... Phoenix, AZ
Richardson, Judith L. ... El Segundo, CA
Richardson, Judith M. ... New York, NY
Richardson, Julia R. ... Washington, DC
Richardson, Julie Alyssa ... Beaumont, TX
Richardson, Julie H. ... Raleigh, NC
Richardson, Julieanna L. ... Chicago, IL
Richardson, Justin ... Concord, NH
Richardson, K. Danielle ... Kansas City, MO
Richardson, Kandace W. ... San Diego, CA
Richardson, Karen E. ... Buffalo, NY
Richardson, Karen M. ... Amarillo, TX
Richardson, Kathleen H. ... Havre, MT
Richardson, Kathy Machan ... Boston, MA
Richardson, Keith L. ... Atlanta, GA
Richardson, Keith L. ... Baton Rouge, LA
Richardson, Kelly G. ... Pasadena, CA
Richardson, Kemp A. ... Glendale, CA
Richardson, Kennedy P. ... Oakland, CA
Richardson, Kenneth E. Postal Rate Commission, Office of the Consumer Advocate, GV
Richardson, Kenneth J. ... Visalia, CA
Ottumwa, IA
Richardson, Kenneth R. Cape Girardeau, MO
Richardson, Kent R. ... Palo Alto, CA
Richardson, Kevin F. ... West Palm Beach, FL
Richardson, Kevin R. ... Puyallup, WA
Richardson, Kim Fallwell ... Freeport, TX
Richardson, Kim Y. ... Los Angeles, CA
Richardson, Kimberly A. ... Atlanta, GA
Richardson, Kristan L. ... Lansing, MI
Richardson, Lamar M. ... Covington, LA
Franklinton, LA
Richardson, Lamar M. ... Mandeville, LA
Richardson, Lance G. ... Centreville, MD
Richardson, Lange & Donovan ... Hazen, ND
Richardson, Larry T. ... Jackson, MS
Richardson, Lauren Nagel ... Gainesville, FL
Richardson Law Center, P.C. ... Detroit, MI
Richardson Law Firm ... Memphis, TN
Richardson Law Firm ... Sherman, TX
Richardson Law Office ... Austin, MN
Richardson Law Office ... Rochester, MN
Richardson, Lee D. ... Louisville, KY
Richardson, Lee G. ... Gainesboro, TN
Richardson, Lisa Hendricks ... Newark, NJ
Richardson, Lisa R. ... Savannah, GA
Richardson, Lita S. ... Beverly Hills, CA
Richardson, Lloyd C., Jr. ... Aberdeen, SD
Richardson, Lloyd Macauley Richmond, VA
Richardson, Lucy B. ... Frankfort, KY
Richardson, Lyne A. ... Newport Beach, CA
Richardson, Lynn Pride ... Dallas, TX
Richardson, M. Catherine ... Syracuse, NY
Richardson Mahon Casey & Rooney, LLP Los Angeles, CA New York, NY
Richardson, Margaret M. ... Los Angeles, CA
Richardson, Marian ... Houston, TX
Richardson, Marianne O'Laughlin Commodity Futures Trading Commission, Division of Enforcement, GV
Richardson, Mark A. ... Jefferson City, MO
Richardson, Mark E. ... Raleigh, NC
Richardson, Mark E., III Research Triangle Park, NC
Richardson, Mark J. ... Santa Monica, CA
Richardson, Mark L. ... Poplar Bluff, MO
Richardson, Mark Louis ... Charlotte, NC
Richardson, Mary Alice C. Rochester, MN
Richardson, Mary W. ... New York, NY
Richardson, MaryAnne Powers Mineola, NY
Richardson, Marzell L. ... Joliet, IL
Richardson, Matthew D. Poplar Bluff, MO
Richardson, Melody Z. ... Atlanta, GA
Richardson, Melody Z., P.C. ... Atlanta, GA
Richardson, Meredith L. ... Dracut, MA
Richardson, Michael ... Baltimore, MD
Richardson, Michael ... New York, NY
Richardson, Michael A. ... Hopkinsville, KY
Richardson, Michael D. ... Dallas, TX
Richardson, Michael E. ... Chattanooga, TN
Richardson, Michael E. ... Houston, TX
Richardson, Michael Gilles ... Northridge, CA
Richardson, Michael I. ... Chicago, IL
Richardson, Michael J. ... Rockville, MD
Richardson, Michael T. ... Lathrup Village, MI
Richardson, Michele Baker ... Chicago, IL
Richardson, Morris Wade Birmingham, AL
Richardson & Mortensen ... Safford, AZ
Richardson, N. Craig ... Lafayette, LA
Richardson, N. James ... San Diego, CA
Richardson, N. James, A.P.C. San Diego, CA
Richardson, Nancy A. ... Helena, MT
Richardson, Nancy H. ... New York, NY
Richardson, Nancy L. ... Gainesville, GA
Richardson, Nathan G., Jr. Port Angeles, WA
Richardson, Navada C. ... Big Flat, AR
Richardson, Neal A. ... Denver, CO
Richardson, Nicole A. ... Atlanta, GA
Richardson, Noel ... Boston, MA
Richardson, Nola M. ... Tamarac, FL
Richardson, Noll A. ... Bishop, CA
Richardson, O. Leonard, Jr. ... Charlotte, NC
Richardson, Ouderkirk & Hollen Newport, OR
Richardson, P. David, II ... Washington, DC
Richardson, Packard & Lambert Salt Lake City, UT
Richardson, Pamela Jean Newport Beach, CA
Richardson, Patricia Ann ... Vashon, WA
Richardson, Patricia M. ... Morganville, NJ
Richardson, Patrick E. ... Green City, MO
Richardson, Patrick J. ... East Brunswick, NJ
Richardson, Patrick J., P.C. East Brunswick, NJ
Richardson, Patrick M.K. San Francisco, CA
Richardson, Patrick W. ... Huntsville, AL
Richardson, Paul J. ... San Bruno, CA
Richardson, Paul J. ... Jackson, MS
Richardson, Paul K. ... Sacramento, CA
Richardson, Paul M. ... Cambridge, MA
Richardson, Peggy D. ... Jefferson City, MO
Richardson, Peter C. ... New York, NY
Richardson, Peter J. ... Boise, ID
Richardson, Peter K. ... Milwaukee, WI
Richardson, Philip ... Austin, MN
Richardson, Philip M. ... Columbia, TN
Richardson, Philip W. ... Webb City, MO
Richardson, Philip W. ... Olympia, WA
Richardson, Phyliss W. ... Atlanta, GA
Richardson, Pierce ... Pittsburgh, PA
Richardson, Plowden, Carpenter & Robinson, P.A. ... Columbia, SC
Myrtle Beach, SC
Richardson & Pullen, P.C. ... Fillmore, NY
Richardson, R. Nelson ... Graham, NC
Richardson, Rae ... Riverside, CA
Richardson, Ralph A. ... Bonita Springs, FL
Richardson, Ralph A. & Associates, P.A., Law Offices of ... Bonita Springs, FL
Richardson, Ralph H. ... Detroit, MI
Richardson, Ralph H. ... Plano, TX
Richardson, Randolf E. ... Wheeling, WV
Richardson, Randolph E., II ... Waterbury, CT
Richardson, Randolph M., III ... Roswell, NM
Richardson, Randolph T., III ... Lexington, KY
Richardson, Randy ... Columbus, OH
Richardson, Ray ... Greenfield, IN
Richardson, Rebecca A. ... Indianapolis, IN
Richardson, Rebecca C. ... Hyannis, MA
Richardson, Reginald ... Greensboro, AL
Richardson, Richard A. ... Covington, LA
Richardson, Richard L. New Port Richey, FL
Richardson and Richardson Red Wing, MN
Richardson & Richardson ... Butte, MT
Richardson & Richardson Parkersburg, WV
Richardson & Richardson, P.S.C. Louisville, KY
Richardson, Rick E. ... Corpus Christi, TX
Richardson, Rickey E. Corpus Christi, TX
Richardson, Robert A. ... New Haven, CT
Richardson, Robert A. ... Kahului, HI
Richardson, Robert C. ... Jackson, MS
Richardson, Robert C., Jr. ... Camilla, GA
Richardson, Robert E. ... Washington, DC
Richardson, Robert E. ... Smyrna, GA
Richardson, Robert E. ... Brooklyn, NY
Richardson, Robert E ... Lewisburg, WV
Richardson, Robert E., Jr. ... Sherman, TX
Richardson, Robert E. L. ... Norman, OK
Richardson, Robert E. L. ... Sherman, TX
Richardson, Robert G. ... Dallas, TX
Richardson, Robert H., Jr. ... Houston, TX
Richardson, Robert J. ... Louisville, KY
Richardson, Robert J. ... Spring Valley, WI
Richardson, Robert K. ... Fairfax, VA
Richardson, Robert L., Jr. ... Saginaw, MI
Richardson, Robert M. ... Warner Robins, GA
Richardson, Robert M. ... Bluefield, WV
Richardson, Robert N., Jr. ... Conway, SC
Richardson, Robert O. ... Bettendorf, IA
Richardson, Robert R. ... Seattle, WA
Richardson, Robert T. ... Department of Justice, Drug Enforcement Administration, GV
Richardson, Robert W. Walnut Creek, CA
Richardson, Robert W. Grand Rapids, MI
Richardson, Robin M. ... Department of Justice, Environment and Natural Resources Division, GV
Richardson, Rod L. ... Overland Park, KS
Richardson, Rodney C. ... Indianapolis, IN
Richardson, Rodney C. ... Fairfax, VA
Richardson, Roger W. ... Ridgewood, NJ
Richardson, Ronald E. ... Baltimore, MD
Richardson, Rosemary ... Salt Lake City, UT
Richardson & Rosenberg, L.L.C. Portsmouth, VA
Richardson, Ross M. ... Florham Park, NJ
Richardson, Ross Patrick ... Butte, MT
Richardson, Roy J. ... Dallas, TX
Richardson, Russell L. ... Irving, TX
Richardson, Sally M. ... Miami, FL
Richardson, Samac S. ... Brandon, MS
Richardson, Samuel L. ... Boston, MA
Richardson, Sandra L. Board of Governors Of The Federal Reserve System, Office of the General Counsel, GV
Richardson, Schuyler H., III Huntsville, AL
Richardson, Scott ... Austin, MN
Richardson, Scott A. ... Canton, OH
Richardson, Scott C. ... Alexandria, VA
Richardson, Scott E. ... Mesa, AZ
Richardson, Scott E. ... Boston, MA
Richardson, Scott E., P.C. ... Mesa, AZ
Richardson, Scott J. ... Phoenix, AZ
Richardson, Scott K. ... Simsbury, CT
Richardson, Scott N. West Palm Beach, FL
Richardson, Scott T. ... Indianapolis, IN
Richardson, Sean K. ... New York, NY
Richardson, Sharion H. ... Fulton, MS
Richardson, Sharon Nalbone ... Pottstown, PA
Richardson and Silverman ... Tempe, AZ
Richardson, Song ... Tacoma, WA
Richardson, Stephen A. ... Bloomfield, IA
Richardson, Stephen M. ... Wading River, NY
Richardson, Steven B. ... Denver, CO
Richardson, Steven J. ... Woodbury, NJ
Richardson, Susan Hearne ... Atlanta, GA
Richardson, Susan R. ... Midland, TX
Richardson, Susan S. ... Washington, DC
Richardson, T. Randolph ... New Orleans, LA
Richardson, Tammy L. ... Boston, MA
Richardson, Teresa G. ... Stockton, CA
Richardson, Terry B. ... Wilmington, NC
Richardson, Terry E., Jr. ... Barnwell, SC
Richardson, Thais L. ... Washington, DC
Richardson, Thomas A. ... Denver, CO
Richardson, Thomas C. ... Kalamazoo, MI
Richardson, Thomas D. ... Rome, GA
Richardson, Thomas D. ... Ann Arbor, MI
Richardson, Thomas E. ... Memphis, TN
Richardson, Thomas F. ... Macon, GA
Richardson, Thomas F. ... Liberal, KS
Richardson, Thomas L. ... Portland, ME
Richardson, Thomas W. ... Washington, DC
Richardson, Timothy D. ... Springfield, MO
Richardson, Timothy J. ... San Diego, CA
Richardson, Timothy M. Virginia Beach, VA
Richardson, Todd A. ... Indianapolis, IN
Richardson, Todd A. ... Omaha, NE
Richardson, Todd Council Daytona Beach, FL
Richardson, Todd Martin ... El Dorado, KS
Richardson, Todd S. ... Salt Lake City, UT
Richardson, Tony L. ... Los Angeles, CA
Richardson, Travis ... Chicago, IL
Richardson and Tyler, LLP ... Boston, MA
Richardson, V. Britt, Jr. ... Fairfax, VA
Richardson, Valerie Gail Poplar Bluff, MO
Richardson, Veta T. ... Washington, DC
Richardson, Vicki M. ... Washington, DC
Richardson, Victor R. ... Redding, CA
Richardson, Wallace A. ... Lincoln, NE
Richardson, Walter F., III ... Warwick, RI
Richardson & Ward ... Tulsa, OK
Richardson, Warren S. ... Washington, DC
Richardson, Wayne M. New Brunswick, NJ
Richardson, Whitman, Large & Badger, A Professional Corporation ... Bangor, ME
Portland, ME
Richardson, Wilbur Gene ... Rome, GA
Richardson, Wilford R. ... Safford, AZ
Richardson, Will J. ... Tallahassee, FL
Richardson, William A. ... Denver, CO
Richardson, William B ... Alexandria, VA
Richardson, William B. ... Parkersburg, WV
Richardson, William B., Jr. Parkersburg, WV

Richardson, William D. ....Petersburg, IN
Richardson, William D. ....Greenville, SC
Richardson, William F. ....Ann Arbor, MI
Richardson, William K. ....Honolulu, HI
Richardson, William K. ....Galesburg, IL
Richardson, William K. ....Kenosha, WI
Richardson, William L. ....Salem, OR
Richardson, William M. ....McLean, VA
Richmond, VA
Richardson, William O. ....Fayetteville, NC
Richardson, William R. ....Mesa, AZ
Richardson, William R., Jr.
Washington, DC
Richardson, William R., P.C. ....Mesa, AZ
Richardson, William S. ....Grand Junction, CO
Richardson, William S. ....Honolulu, HI
Richardson, William T. ....Minneapolis, MN
Richardson, William W., III
Providence Forge, VA
Richardson, Willie J. ....Richmond, VA
Richardson, Willis J., Jr. ....Savannah, GA
Richardson, W. W. Bob ....Austin, TX
Richardson, Yolonda C. ....New York, NY
Richardson-Harp, Wayne M.
New Orleans, LA
Richardson-Kott, Bonnie ....Portland, OR
Richardson-Pelliccioni, Lori S.
Los Angeles, CA
Richardson-Rohrer, Karen ....Atlanta, GA
Richard-Spencer, Julie ....Metairie, LA
Richards-Rutberg, Anne E. ....Sanford, FL
Richards-Stower, Nancy A. ....Concord, NH
Richards Wallace, Melissa ....Irvine, CA
Richards-Yellen, Leslie ....Malvern, PA
Richarme, Jas. O., Jr. ....New Orleans, LA
Richart, Christie L. ....Washington, DC
Richart Law Offices ....Joplin, MO
Richart, R. Scott ....Independence, MO
Richart, Robert W. ....Joplin, MO
Richart, Susan Leah ....Kansas City, MO
Richau, A. D. ....Bismarck, ND
Richaud, George J. ....New Orleans, LA
Richbook, Brent J. ....Galveston, TX
Richbourg, John S. ....Memphis, TN
Richbourg, Luke S. ....New York, NY
Richbourg, Robert B. ....Tifton, GA
Richbourg, Teresa Scardino ....Houston, TX
Richbourg, William B. ....Pensacola, FL
Richbourg, Winn ....Houston, TX
Richburg, Scott D. ....Jacksonville, FL
Richdale, David A. ....Seattle, WA
Riche, Kenneth L. ....Baton Rouge, LA
Riche & Wall, A Law Corporation
Baton Rouge, LA
Richebourg, J. Ron ....Mission Viejo, CA
Richeda, Russell L. ....San Francisco, CA
Richeimer, Gabriela A. ....Washington, DC
Richek, Stephen D. ....Chicago, IL
Richel, Stuart M. ....New York, NY
Richelew, Sarah Beth ....New York, NY
Richelieu, Carole R. ....Honolulu, HI
Richelieu, Elaine ....Watsonville, CA
Richelle, Marie-Pierre ....Atlanta, GA
Richelo, Morrissey & Toler, P.C.
Atlanta, GA
Richelo, Thomas ....Atlanta, GA
Richelson, Andrew M. ....Londonderry, NH
Richelson, Harvey ....Thousand Oaks, CA
Richelson, Mark P. ....Los Angeles, CA
Richelson, Stan L. ....Blue Bell, PA
Richenderfer, Linda ....Philadelphia, PA
Richens, Dana M. ....Atlanta, GA
Richenstein, Mindy R. ....New York, NY
Richenthal, Abrams & Moss ....New York, NY
Richenthal, Arthur ....New York, NY
Richenthal, Donald I. ....New York, NY
Richer, Alan B. ....Albany, NY
Richer, Arnold ....Salt Lake City, UT
Richer, Diane Shapiro ....Washington, DC
Richer, Donald A. ....Painesville, OH
Richer, Gerard P. ....Boston, MA
Richer, Joseph D. ....Casper, WY
Richer, Swan & Overholt, A Professional Corporation ....Salt Lake City, UT
Richerson, Bill W. ....Kansas City, MO
Richerson, Nancy L. ....Bardstown, KY
Richert, Allyn I. ....Fairfax, VA
Richert, Cara S. ....Ellington, CT
Richert, Clyde W., III ....Springfield, TN
Richert, Milton ....Denver, CO
Richert, Monica Marie ....Lincoln, NE
Richert, Paul ....Akron, OH
Richert, Peter A. ....Monroe, MI
Richert, Richard J. ....Kentfield, CA
Richert, Robert L. ....St. Paul, MN
Richert, Scott ....Sacramento, CA
Richert, Steven V. ....Pocatello, ID
Riches, John W., II ....Appleton, MN
Riches, Joseph H. ....Philadelphia, PA
Riches, Suzanne M. ....Boston, MA
Riches, Waine C. ....Salt Lake City, UT
Richeson, Cedric M. ....Chicago, IL
Richeson, Dallas P. ....Paradise Valley, AZ
Richeson, David B. ....Lakewood, CO
Richeson, Geroge ....St. Charles, IL
Richeson, Hugh A., Jr. ....Gainesville, FL
Richeson, J. David ....Fort Pierce, FL
West Palm Beach, FL
Richeson, J. David, & Associates, P.A.
Fort Pierce, FL
West Palm Beach, FL
Richeson, John L. ....Baldwin City, KS
Ottawa, KS
Richeson, McGready Lewis ....Dallas, TX
Richeson, Stuart G. ....New Orleans, LA
Richesson, Kirsten Ellen ....Dallas, TX
Richette, Lisa A. ....Philadelphia, PA
Richetti, Malissa A. ....Philadelphia, PA

Richey, Alan R. ....Round Rock, TX
Richey, Alice Carmichael ....Charlotte, NC
Richey, Amber L. ....Sturgis, SD
Richey, Anne W. ....Blanchard, OK
Richey, Benjamin H. ....Russellville, AL
Richey, Bill ....Beaumont, TX
Richey, Cassandra J. ....Pasadena, CA
Richey, Charles R., Jr. ....Hamilton, MA
Richey, Clinton G. ....Gilbert, AZ
Richey, Craig R. ....Pittsburg, KS
Richey, Danny P. ....Tulsa, OK
Richey, Darrell S. ....Indianapolis, IN
Richey, David S. ....Indianapolis, IN
Richey & Decker, LLP ....Tulsa, OK
Richey, Diane J. ....Los Angeles, CA
Richey, Elton B., Jr. ....Shreveport, LA
Richey & Fowler, P.A. ....Melbourne, FL
Richey, Gordon L. ....Fort Worth, TX
Richey, J. Martin ....Boston, MA
Richey, Jack A. ....Redmond, WA
Richey, James H. ....Melbourne, FL
Richey, James L. ....Birmingham, AL
Richey, Jason L. ....Pittsburgh, PA
Richey, Julie E. ....Girard, KS
Richey, Kathleen Stewart ....Baton Rouge, LA
Richey, Kaye, (Mrs.) ....Vallejo, CA
Richey, Keith D. ....Wichita, KS
Richey, Kenneth A. ....Austin, TX
Richey, Kent E. ....Minneapolis, MN
Richey, Kent R. ....New York, NY
Richey, Linda Bangs ....Warminster, PA
Richey, Lola Stradford ....Greenville, SC
Richey, Lon M. ....Morrison, IL
Richey, Mary Ellen ....San Francisco, CA
Richey, Merle U. ....Durham, NC
Richey, Mia S. ....San Diego, CA
Richey, Michael L. ....Cape Girardeau, MO
Richey, P. Jerome ....Pittsburgh, PA
Richey, Paula K. ....Minneapolis, MN
Richey, Rand D. ....Lebanon, IN
Richey & Richey ....Greenville, SC
Richey, R. K. ....Birmingham, AL
Richey, Rodney ....Greenville, SC
Richey, Ronald D. ....Rockville, MD
Richey, Stephen L. ....Cincinnati, OH
Richey, Stephen W. ....Jefferson City, MO
Lake Ozark, MO
Richey, Steven J. ....Leesburg, FL
Richey, Steven J., P.A. ....Leesburg, FL
Richey, Thomas B. ....Visalia, CA
Richey, Thomas S. ....Atlanta, GA
Richey, Trice Ragon ....Dallas, TX
Richey, Truitt A., Jr. ....San Francisco, CA
Richey, Walter ....St. Paul, MN
Richey, William A. ....Denver, CO
Richey, William L. ....Miami, FL
Palm City, FL
Richey, William L., P.A. ....Miami, FL
Palm City, FL
Richey, Win R. ....Sacramento, CA
Richey & Young, P.C. ....Austin, TX
Richford, Lisa M. ....Trenton, NJ
Richgels, Mary ....De Kalb, IL
Richheimer, David E. ....Branford, CT
Richichi, Joseph ....Stamford, CT
Richichi, Thomas ....Washington, DC
Richie, Boyd L. ....Graham, TX
Richie, Byron A. ....Shreveport, LA
Richie, C. Vernon ....Shreveport, LA
Richie, Carl S. ....Austin, TX
Richie, Christopher R. ....Fort Worth, TX
Richie, Crystal Renee ....Columbus, OH
Richie, David E. ....Eau Claire, WI
Richie, David R., II ....Reading, PA
Richie & Gueringer, P.C. ....Austin, TX
San Antonio, TX
Richie, Jennifer A. ....Dallas, TX
Richie, John A. ....Shreveport, LA
Richie, John P. ....Eau Claire, WI
Richie, Kenneth R. ....Orlando, FL
Richie, Laurel Fleming ....Shreveport, LA
Richie, Lillian Evans ....Shreveport, LA
Richie & Richie, L.L.P. ....Shreveport, LA
Richie, Scott A. ....Washington, DC
Richie, Sheldon E. ....Austin, TX
San Antonio, TX
Richie, Steven L. ....Oakland, CA
Richieri, Kenneth A. ....New York, NY
Richilano, John M. ....Denver, CO
Richilano & Ridley, P.C. ....Denver, CO
Richin, David A. ....Silver Spring, MD
Richin, David A., P.A. Law Offices
Washington, DC
Silver Spring, MD
Richins, Keith W. ....Redding, CA
Richins, Keith W., A Professional Corporation
Redding, CA
Richins, Kent A. ....Worland, WY
Richins, Nancy K. ....Carson City, NV
Richitelli, Edward Andre ....Rockville, MD
Richitt, Erwin P., Jr. ....Las Vegas, NV
Richlak, James D. ....Cleveland, OH
Richlan, Robert Thomas ....Springfield, NJ
Richland, Bruce I. ....Los Angeles, CA
Richland, Felipa Ruthe ....Los Angeles, CA
Richland, Kent L. ....Beverly Hills, CA
Richler, Paul A. ....Los Angeles, CA
Richley, M. A., Jr. ....Newport Beach, CA
Richley, Robert D. ....San Diego, CA
Richlin, Dean ....Boston, MA
Richlin, Margaret G. ....Columbia, MD
Richlin, Margaret G., P.A. ....Columbia, MD
Richlin, Stewart E. ....Los Angeles, CA
Richlin, W. Gar ....Baltimore, MD
Richling, Mitchell David ....New York, NY
Richling, Theodore L. ....Omaha, NE
Richman, Alan E. ....Denver, CO
Richman, Alvin ....Milwaukee, WI

Richman, Andrew D. ....New York, NY
Richman, Arlene B. ....Chicago, IL
Richman, Arlene C. ....Hollywood, FL
Richman & Associates ....Salt Lake City, UT
Richman, Barbara W. ....Salt Lake City, UT
Richman & Berenbaum, P.C.
Philadelphia, PA
Richman, Brian H. ....Cleveland, OH
Richman, Charles I. ....Philadelphia, PA
Richman, Daniel A. ....Chicago, IL
Richman, Daniel C. ....New York, NY
Richman, David ....Philadelphia, PA
Richman, David A. ....Washington, DC
Richman, David E. ....New York, NY
Uniondale, NY
Richman, David J. ....Denver, CO
Richman, David M. ....West Hartford, CT
Richman, David M. ....New York, NY
Richman, David S. ....Los Angeles, CA
Richman, Deifik, Lanier and Ross, P.A.
Naples, FL
Richman, Derek P. ....Atlanta, GA
Richman, Donna ....Chicago, IL
Richman, Donnaline ....Syracuse, NY
Richman, Dvorah A. ....Washington, DC
Richman, Edith Ruth ....Archer, FL
Richman, Edward S. ....Chicago, IL
Richman, Eric B. ....New York, NY
Richman, Evan Asher ....New York, NY
Richman & Ferren ....Haddonfield, NJ
Richman, Frederick A. ....Los Angeles, CA
Richman, Fredric N. ....Beverly Hills, CA
Richman, Gabriella F. ....Westbury, NY
Richman, Gail M. ....Marietta, GA
Richman, Gerald ....New York, NY
Richman, Gerald F. ....Miami, FL
Richman, Gerald L.
Federal Energy Regulatory Commission,
Office of the General Counsel, GV
Richman, Gerald M. ....Ellicott City, MD
Richman, Glen M. ....Salt Lake City, UT
Richman, Gordon B.
Research Triangle Park, NC
Richman Greer Weil Brumbaugh Mirabito & Christensen, P.A. ....Miami, FL
West Palm Beach, FL
Richman, Harold L. ....New York, NY
Richman, Harvey ....Coeur d'Alene, ID
Richman, Hershel J. ....Philadelphia, PA
Richman, Howard R. ....Reston, VA
Richman, Howard S.
Englewood Cliffs, NJ
New York, NY
Richman, Iris S. ....New York, NY
Richman, Irvin F. ....Chicago, IL
Richman, Irwin ....Silver Spring, MD
Richman, James A. ....San Francisco, CA
Richman, James A. ....Yakima, WA
Richman, James D. ....Los Angeles, CA
Richman, Jeff ....Washington, DC
Richman, Jeffrey L. ....Chicago, IL
Richman, Jeffrey L. ....New York, NY
Richman, Jerald F. ....Chicago, IL
Richman, Jerome B.
Upper Marlboro, MD
Richman, Jerome R. ....Chicago, IL
Richman, Jerome S. ....Miami, FL
Richman, Joan M. ....Chicago, IL
Richman, Joel Eser ....Paia, HI
Richman, John M. ....New York, NY
Richman, Jonathan E. ....New York, NY
Richman & Jones, P.C. ....Denver, CO
Richman, Judith Mendelson ....Edison, NJ
Richman, Judith Rubin ....New York, NY
Richman, Kathryn ....Denver, CO
Richman, Kay L.
Office of Government Ethics,
Office of General Counsel and Legal Policy,
GV
Richman, Kenneth H. ....Chicago, IL
Richman, Kenneth M. ....Beverly Hills, CA
Richman, Kenneth W., Jr. ....Naples, FL
Richman, Labe M. ....New York, NY
Richman, Labe M., Law Offices of
New York, NY
Richman, Laura D. ....Chicago, IL
Richman, Lawrence I. ....Chicago, IL
Richman, Lawrence, Mann, Chizever & Phillips, A Professional Corporation
Beverly Hills, CA
Los Angeles, CA
Richman, Lawrence W. ....Philadelphia, PA
Richman, Lester G. ....Solvang, CA
Richman, Lionel ....Los Angeles, CA
Richman, Louis J., Jr. ....Newport News, VA
Richman, Luna, Kichaven & Glushon
Los Angeles, CA
Richman, Marc H., Law Offices of
Dallas, TX
Richman, Marc P. ....Department of Justice,
Civil Division, GV
Richman, Mark J. ....Edison, NJ
Richman, Martin F. ....New York, NY
Richman, Mary ....New York, NY
Richman, Michael ....White Plains, NY
Richman, Michael A. ....New York, NY
Richman, Michael B. ....Washington, DC
Richman, Michael C. ....Philadelphia, PA
Richman, Michael D. ....Chicago, IL
Richman, Michael F. ....Salt Lake City, UT
Richman, Michael J. ....New York, NY
Richman, Michael P. ....New York, NY
Richman, Milton ....Boston, MA
Richman, Monica Blair ....Washington, DC
Richman, Morris L. ....Decatur, GA
Richman, Murray ....Bronx, NY
Richman, Murray, Law Offices of
Bronx, NY

Richman, Nancy E. ....Chevy Chase, MD
Richman, Neil ....Richmond, VA
Richman, Neil S.
Department Of Veterans Affairs,
Office of the General Counsel, GV
Richman, Paul J.
Department of Labor, GV
Richman, Peter A.
Federal Trade Commission,
Bureau of Competition, GV
Richman & Richman LLC
Salt Lake City, UT
Richman, Robert D. ....Minneapolis, MN
Richman, Roger B. ....Beverly Hills, CA
Richman, Ronald E. ....New York, NY
Richman, Ronald L. ....San Francisco, CA
Richman, S. Richard ....Fairborn, OH
Richman, Scott A. ....Orlando, FL
Richman, Scott G. ....Miami, FL
Richman, Sheldon ....Los Angeles, CA
Richman & Smith, LLP ....Washington, PA
Richman, Sonya Stern ....Philadelphia, PA
Richman, Stacey ....Bronx, NY
Richman, Stephanie ....Philadelphia, PA
Richman, Stephen C. ....Allentown, PA
Philadelphia, PA
Richman, Stephen D. ....Cleveland, OH
Richman, Stephen E. ....Phoenix, AZ
Richman, Stephen E. ....Milwaukee, WI
Richman, Stephen I. ....Washington, PA
Richman, Steven Howard ....New York, NY
Richman, Steven M. ....Princeton, NJ
Richman, Steven N. ....Los Angeles, CA
Richman, Susan Katz ....Mineola, NY
Richman, Terry M. ....Rochester, NY
Richman, Todd M. ....Washington, DC
Richman, William I. ....San Pedro, CA
Richman, William M. ....Toledo, OH
Richmand, Brian J. ....New York, NY
Richmond, Adam B. ....Chicago, IL
Richmond, Alice E. ....Boston, MA
Richmond, Allan E. ....Beaverton, OR
Richmond, Allen W. ....Bartlesville, OK
Richmond, Amy G. ....Greenville, SC
Richmond, Anna M. ....Buffalo, NY
Richmond, Anne S. ....Augusta, ME
Richmond, Anthony J. ....Menlo Park, CA
Richmond, Barbara Zicht ....Cambridge, MA
Richmond, Barry D. ....Baltimore, MD
Richmond, Beth Alpha ....Charlotte, NC
Richmond, Carolyn D. ....New York, NY
Richmond, Carolynn K. ....Philadelphia, PA
Richmond, Charles ....Indianapolis, IN
Richmond, Charles D. ....San Diego, CA
Richmond, Charles D. ....London, OH
Richmond, Christopher ....North Syracuse, NY
Richmond, D. Scott ....Owensboro, KY
Richmond, David W. ....Washington, DC
Richmond, Delmas R.
Lake San Marcos, CA
Richmond, Diana ....San Francisco, CA
Richmond, Diana, Law & Mediation Offices, A Professional Corporation
San Francisco, CA
Richmond, Donald J. ....Philadelphia, PA
Richmond, Douglas J. ....Medford, OR
Richmond, Douglas R. ....Olathe, KS
Kansas City, MO
Richmond, Edward L. ....Brookline, MA
Richmond and Fishburne, L.L.P.
Charlottesville, VA
Richmond, Frank J. ....Boston, MA
Richmond, Gail Levin ....Fort Lauderdale, FL
Richmond, Garth D. ....Washington, DC
Richmond, Hal ....Quincy, FL
Richmond, Harlee A. ....New York, NY
Richmond, Harold N. ....West Orange, NJ
Richmond, Harold S. ....Quincy, FL
Richmond, Henry C. T., III
Lexington, KY
Richmond, Hochron & Burns ....Red Bank, NJ
Woodbridge, NJ
Richmond, Howard E., Jr. ....Issaquah, WA
Richmond, James B. ....Durham, NC
Richmond, James G. ....Chicago, IL
Richmond, James L. ....Quincy, FL
Richmond, James L. ....Rowe, NM
Richmond, James P. ....De Witt, IA
Richmond, Janet A. ....Chicago, IL
Richmond, Janet M. ....Gold River, CA
Richmond, Janet M. ....Utica, NY
Richmond, Jeanette Camara ....Boston, MA
Richmond, Jeffrey A. ....Los Angeles, CA
Richmond, Jennifer L. ....Los Angeles, CA
Richmond, Joel C. ....Baltimore, MD
Richmond, John Cotton ....Roanoke, VA
Richmond, John J. ....San Francisco, CA
Richmond, John T., Jr. ....St. Louis, MO
Richmond, Jonathan E. ....New York, NY
Richmond, Joseph W., Jr.
Charlottesville, VA
Richmond, Judith Klein ....Washington, DC
Richmond, Julie A. ....Boston, MA
Richmond, Larry J. ....Phoenix, AZ
Richmond, Laurence K. ....Boston, MA
Richmond Law Office ....Beckley, WV
Lewisburg, WV
Richmond, Lawrence H.
Federal Deposit Insurance Corporation,
Appellate Litigation Section, GV
Richmond, Lionel ....Arlington, VA
Richmond, Lisbeth ....Jackson, MS
Richmond, Lyle L. ....Pago Pago, TT
Richmond, Marcy ....Danvers, MA
Richmond, Mariana ....Indianapolis, IN
Richmond, Mariana J. ....Rochester, MI
Richmond, Mark ....Frisco, CO
Richmond, Mark S. ....Chicago, IL

Ridberg, Press & Sherbill
Washington, DC
Bethesda, MD
Rockville, MD
Alexandria, VA
Arlington, VA
Riddel, Ann Ysleta ..... Austin, TX
Riddell, Baylor G. ..... San Francisco, CA
Riddell, James A. ..... Fort Worth, TX
Riddell, James W. ..... McLean, VA
Riddell, Jefferson F., (P.A.) ..... Sarasota, FL
Riddell, John R. ..... Newtown Square, PA
Riddell, Joseph M., III ..... Austin, TX
Riddell, Joy V. ..... Concord, NH
Riddell, Karen Stahel ..... Atlanta, GA
Riddell & Mancuso Co., L.P.A.
Gahanna, OH
Riddell, Michael T., (P.C.) ..... Riverside, CA
Riddell, Neill T. ..... Troy, MI
Riddell, Peter H. ..... Gahanna, OH
Riddell, Rebecca S. ..... Peoria, IL
Riddell, Richard H. ..... Seattle, WA
Riddell, Robert C. ..... Indianapolis, IN
Riddell, Robert C. ..... Hurst, TX
Riddell, Stephen W.
Federal Trade Commission, Bureau of Competition, GV
Riddell, Stephen W. ..... Atlanta, GA
Riddell, Tally D. ..... Quitman, MS
Riddell, Timothy T. ..... Frankfort, KY
Riddell Williams P.S. ..... Seattle, WA
Ridder, Bryan M. ..... Youngstown, OH
Ridder, Bryan M., Co., LPA
Youngstown, OH
Ridder, Constance M. ..... San Francisco, CA
Ridder, Daniel H., Jr. ..... Eugene, OR
Ridder, Lorrie K. ..... Memphis, TN
Ridder, Mark A. ..... Lakewood, CO
Ridder, Maura Troy ..... San Francisco, CA
Riddet, James D. ..... Santa Ana, CA
Riddett, Kenneth E. ..... Albany, NY
Riddick, Annita M. ..... Washington, DC
Riddick, Ben L. ..... Jackson, MS
Riddick, Catherine Lynn ..... Chicago, IL
Riddick, David A. ..... Jackson, TN
Riddick, Harry H. ..... Mobile, AL
Riddick, Harry S., Jr. ..... Department of Justice, Executive Office for Immigration Review, GV
Riddick, Jennifer A. ..... Atlanta, GA
Riddick, Johnny M., & Associates
Washington, DC
Riddick, Michael E. ..... Shreveport, LA
Riddick, Patricia Turner ..... Baton Rouge, LA
Riddick, Roger C. ..... Jackson, MS
Riddick, Shelia C. ..... Portsmouth, VA
Riddick, Stephen A. ..... Washington, DC
Riddick, Walter G. ..... Little Rock, AR
Riddick, Walter G., III ..... Little Rock, AR
Riddick, William H., III ..... Smithfield, VA
Riddick, William P. ..... San Antonio, TX
Riddick, Winston W., Sr. ..... Baton Rouge, LA
Riddle & Associates, P.C. ..... Sandy, UT
Riddle, Barbara M. ..... San Antonio, TX
Riddle & Baumgartner ..... Houston, TX
Riddle, C. Russell ..... Richardson, TX
Riddle, Carmalita M. ..... New York, NY
Riddle, Carol J. ..... Dallas, TX
Riddle, Catherine E.K. ..... Kansas City, MO
Riddle, Charles A., III ..... Marksville, LA
Riddle, Christopher A. ..... Orange, CA
Riddle, Clarine Nardi ..... Washington, DC
Riddle, Clayton L. ..... Milwaukee, WI
Riddle, Dale A. ..... Eugene, OR
Riddle, David A. ..... Pacific Grove, CA
Riddle, David L. ..... Las Vegas, NV
Riddle, Dean Arden ..... Dallas, TX
Riddle, Don R. ..... Houston, TX
Riddle, E. Donald ..... Palmer, MA
Riddle, Ervin A. ..... McLean, VA
Riddle, Eugene N. ..... Houston, TX
Riddle, Frank R. ..... Franklin, PA
Riddle, Gene A. ..... Goldsboro, NC
Kinston, NC
Riddle, Greg R. ..... San Francisco, CA
Riddle, Guy H. ..... Dallas, TX
Riddle, H. Wayne ..... Lexington, KY
Riddle, Hayley B. ..... Lafayette, LA
Riddle, J. Albert ..... Houston, TX
Riddle, James A. ..... San Francisco, CA
Riddle, Jeffrey Leon ..... Atlanta, GA
Riddle, Jesse L. ..... Sandy, UT
Riddle, John D. ..... Peoria, IL
Riddle, John E. ..... San Jose, CA
Riddle, John H. ..... San Francisco, CA
Riddle, John R. ..... Brooklyn, NY
Riddle, John R. ..... Dallas, TX
Riddle, Joseph M. ..... Boulder, CO
Riddle, Joseph M., P.C. ..... Boulder, CO
Riddle, Julie L. ..... El Dorado, KS
Riddle, June ..... Lunenburg, MA
Riddle, Kevin C. ..... Birmingham, MI
Riddle, Lance A. ..... Warrensburg, MO
Riddle, Laura Patricia ..... Boca Raton, FL
Miami, FL
Riddle Law Offices ..... Marksville, LA
Riddle, Leslie Kirkland ..... Columbia, SC
Riddle, Lynne ..... Santa Ana, CA
Riddle, Margaret L. ..... Columbia, SC
Riddle, Mark S. ..... Louisville, KY
Riddle, Mark S. ..... Canton, OH
Riddle, Mary L. ..... Atlanta, GA
Riddle, Melinda Paniagua ..... Naples, FL
Riddle, Michael E. ..... Birmingham, AL
Riddle, Michael H. ..... Papillion, NE
Riddle, Michael Lee ..... New Orleans, LA
Austin, TX
Dallas, TX
Riddle, Nancy Menard ..... Indianapolis, IN
Riddle, Norman C. ..... Asheville, NC
Riddle, P. Donovan ..... Tucson, AZ
Riddle, Pamela L. ..... Farmville, VA
Riddle, Patrick D. ..... Stockton, CA
Riddle, Patrick D., P.C., Law Offices of
Stockton, CA
Riddle, Paul N. ..... Department of Education, Office of the General Counsel, GV
Riddle, Peter E. ..... San Diego, CA
Riddle, R. Krannert ..... Savannah, GA
Riddle, Richard W. ..... Tulsa, OK
Riddle, Robert B. ..... Prince Frederick, MD
Riddle, Robert E. ..... Asheville, NC
Riddle, Robert E., P.A. ..... Asheville, NC
Riddle, Sabrina H. ..... Provincetown, MA
Riddle, Scott B. ..... Atlanta, GA
Riddle, Todd A. ..... Houston, TX
Riddle, Veryl L. ..... St. Louis, MO
Riddle, W. Stanley, Jr. ..... Kihei, HI
Riddle, Wanda P. ..... Chardon, OH
Riddle & White ..... Lunenburg, MA
Riddle & Williams, P.C. ..... Dallas, TX
Riddle & Wimbish, P.C. ..... Tulsa, OK
Riddles, Alvin J. ..... Scarsdale, NY
Riddles, Andrew M. ..... New York, NY
Riddles, Benjamin T., II ..... McLean, VA
Riddles, Darin Todd ..... Oklahoma City, OK
Riddles, Laurie Lynn ..... Richmond, VA
Riddlesperger, Anthony G. ..... Dallas, TX
Ridehalgh, Ronald L. ..... Beaverton, OR
Ridella, Gregory J. ..... Highland Park, MI
Ridella, James M. ..... Ann Arbor, MI
Riden, Joseph ..... La Grange Park, IL
Ridenbaugh, J. Donald ..... Annapolis, MD
Ridener, Laurel Peters ..... Pittsburgh, PA
Ridenhour, Janis C. ..... Charlotte, NC
Ridenhour, Monroe H., III ..... Charlotte, NC
Ridenhour, Patricia P. ..... Greensboro, NC
Ridenour, Brian K. ..... Lincoln, NE
Ridenour, Charles E. ..... Sweetwater, TN
Ridenour, David E. ..... Whittier, CA
Ridenour, Eric B. ..... Sylva, NC
Ridenour, Garland Q. ..... Helena, AR
Ridenour, Garland Q., P.A. ..... Helena, AR
Ridenour, Glen H., II ..... Philadelphia, PA
Ridenour, Michael D. ..... Hartford, CT
Ridenour, Patricia B. ..... Cimarron, KS
Ridenour, Philip D. ..... Cimarron, KS
Ridenour, Rex J. ..... Davenport, IA
Ridenour and Ridenour ..... Cimarron, KS
Ridenour, Ridenour & Fox ..... Clinton, TN
Ridenour, Robert N. ..... Los Angeles, CA
Ridenour, Roger L. ..... Clinton, TN
Ridenour, Ronald H. ..... Clinton, TN
Ridenour, Sally M. ..... Atlanta, GA
Ridenour, Swenson, Cleere & Evans, P.C.
Phoenix, AZ
Ridenour, William G. ..... Phoenix, AZ
Rideout, Anne M. ..... Springfield, MA
Rideout, Brenda Price ..... Oklahoma City, OK
Rideout, E. William ..... Salt Lake City, UT
Rideout, Joi Huckaby ..... New York, NY
Rideout, Joseph A. ..... Toledo, OH
Rideout, Laurence W., Jr. ..... Sacramento, CA
Rideout, Merle C., Jr. ..... Portland, ME
Rideout, Patricia L. ..... Toledo, OH
Rideout, Preston Davis, Jr. ..... Greenwood, MS
Rideout, Richard ..... Cheyenne, WY
Rideout, Richard, P.C. ..... Cheyenne, WY
Rideout, Robert H. ..... Boonville, IN
Rideout, Stephen Morris ..... Lansing, MI
Rideout, Teri L. ..... Tacoma, WA
Rider, Ann Sherwood ..... Pasadena, CA
Rider, Ann T. ..... Wichita, KS
Rider, Bennett, Egan & Arundel, LLP
Minneapolis, MN
Rider, Brian A. ..... Indianapolis, IN
Rider, Calvin D. ..... Wichita, KS
Rider, Carol M. ..... Gretna, LA
Rider, Cecile Evans ..... Jacksonville, FL
Rider, Charles P. ..... El Centro, CA
Rider, David L. ..... Newburgh, NY
Rider, Donald G.
Federal Deposit Insurance Corporation, Corporate Affairs Section, GV
Rider, Fred C. ..... Ellicottville, NY
Rider, G. William ..... Galveston, TX
Rider, Gary V. ..... Terre Haute, IN
Rider, George E. ..... Kansas City, MO
Rider, J. Allen, III ..... Columbus, OH
Rider, Jacqueline W. ..... Portland, ME
Rider, Jacquelyn L. ..... Mountain View, CA
Rider, James L. ..... Washington, DC
Fairfax, VA
Rider, Jeffrey C. ..... Delphi, IN
Rider, Joseph L. ..... Williamsport, PA
Rider, Julia J., (P.C.) ..... Los Angeles, CA
Rider, Kent M. ..... Austin, TX
Rider, Kevin V. ..... Wichita, KS
Rider, Kirk ..... Grand Junction, CO
Rider, Lawrence C. ..... Boulder, CO
Rider, Lynn M. ..... Prairie du Chien, WI
Rider, Martina A. ..... Encino, CA
Rider, Michael A. ..... Lake Placid, FL
Rider, Michael A., P.A. ..... Lake Placid, FL
Rider, Michelle F. ..... Nashville, TN
Rider, Pandora ..... Las Vegas, NV
Rider, Peter S. ..... Amherst, MA
Rider, R. Bruce ..... Norfolk, VA
Rider, Rebecca A. ..... Sarasota, FL
Rider, Robert E., Jr. ..... Washington, DC
Baltimore, MD
Rockville, MD
Vienna, VA
Rider, Robert F. ..... Roanoke, VA
Rider, Roger ..... Houston, TX
Rider, Ronald Thomas ..... Fort Pierce, FL
Rider, Stephen W. ..... New Orleans, LA
Rider, Stephen W. ..... Boston, MA
Rider, Steven R. ..... Aurora, CO
Rider, Stuart W., Jr. ..... Minneapolis, MN
Rider, Susan H. ..... Chicago, IL
Rider, Thomas, Cleaveland, Ferris & Eakin, P.C. ..... Roanoke, VA
Rider, Weiner, Frankel & Calhelha, P.C.
Goshen, NY
Newburgh, NY
Rider, William H. ..... Cleveland, OH
Rider, William (Tim) ..... Indianapolis, IN
Rider and Wilson ..... Galveston, TX
Rider & Woulf, P.C. ..... Aurora, CO
Ridge, Anita S. ..... Chicago, IL
Ridge, Carol Stever ..... North Wales, PA
Ridge, Christopher Jarvis ..... Spartanburg, SC
Ridge, Clarence A., Jr. ..... Knoxville, TN
Ridge, David C. ..... Bloomington, IL
Ridge, David G. ..... Erie, PA
Ridge, Denise ..... Honolulu, HI
Ridge, Donald ..... Waukegan, IL
Ridge, Donald L. ..... Los Angeles, CA
Ridge, Garth J. ..... Baton Rouge, LA
Ridge, George E. ..... Jacksonville, FL
Ridge, Holley & Morris ..... Graham, NC
Ridge & Isaacson, P.C. ..... Phoenix, AZ
Ridge, Janet Durholz ..... Washington, DC
Ridge, John ..... Norwalk, OH
Ridge, Kieran T. ..... Northbrook, IL
Ridge, Lisa C. ..... Sacramento, CA
Ridge, Martin J. ..... Portland, ME
Ridge, Paul Edward ..... Boca Raton, FL
Ridge, Paul H., (P.A.) ..... Graham, NC
Ridge, Raymond L. ..... Newport Beach, CA
Ridge, Ridge & Lindsay ..... Waukegan, IL
Ridge, Robert J. ..... Pittsburgh, PA
Ridge, Samuel B. ..... Chico, CA
Ridge, Scott G. ..... Waukegan, IL
Ridge, Warren C. ..... Phoenix, AZ
Ridgell, Dolores Owens ..... Crownsville, MD
Ridgell, Jason Christopher ..... Lutherville, MD
Ridgely & Hanley ..... Towson, MD
Ridgely, Henry duPont ..... Dover, DE
Ridgely, James H. ..... Towson, MD
Ridgeway, B. Luann ..... Smithville, MO
Ridgeway, Henry ..... San Antonio, TX
Ridgeway, Jack F. ..... San Antonio, TX
Ridgeway, James G. ..... Denver, CO
Ridgeway, Judith A. ..... Norman, OK
Ridgeway, Lori A.F. ..... Washington, DC
Rockville, MD
Ridgeway, Mary Jo ..... Miles City, MT
Ridgeway & McMeen ..... Murphysboro, IL
Ridgeway, Michael J. ..... Missoula, MT
Ridgeway, Paul A. ..... East Granby, CT
Ridgeway, Paul C. ..... Raleigh, NC
Ridgeway, Robert D., Sr.
Hot Springs National Park, AR
Ridgeway, Robert D., Sr., P.A.
Hot Springs National Park, AR
Ridgeway, Stephanie ..... Sacramento, CA
Ridgeway, Susan G. ..... Missoula, MT
Ridgeway, Teresa Ericsson ..... Portland, OR
Ridgeway, Tod ..... Newport Beach, CA
Ridgeway, William E., III ..... Hurst, TX
Ridgeway, William G. ..... Murphysboro, IL
Ridgill, Michael E. ..... Manning, SC
Ridgley, Robert L. ..... Portland, OR
Ridgley, Robert W. ..... Lancaster, CA
Ridgley, Sherry E. ..... Torrance, CA
Ridgley, Susan M. ..... Seattle, WA
Ridgley, Thomas B. ..... Cincinnati, OH
Ridgway, Brock G. ..... Houston, TX
Ridgway, Candace A. ..... Washington, DC
Ridgway, Catherine M. ..... Scarsdale, NY
Ridgway, Constance J. ..... Ellicott City, MD
Ridgway, C. R., Jr. ..... Jackson, MS
Ridgway, Curtis L.
Hot Springs National Park, AR
Ridgway, Deirdre K. ..... Seattle, WA
Ridgway, Delissa A. ..... New York, NY
Ridgway, Derek A. ..... San Francisco, CA
Ridgway, Dorothy Moseley
Tallahassee, FL
Ridgway and Griffin, Chartered
Bethesda, MD
Rockville, MD
Ridgway, John A. ..... Linwood, NJ
Ridgway, John A., III ..... Utica, NY
Ridgway, John E. ..... Cary, IL
Ridgway, Joseph J. ..... Maple Shade, NJ
Ridgway, Kirk T. ..... Overland Park, KS
Ridgway, Leslie Karas ..... Bowie, MD
Ridgway, Lynne M. ..... St. Cloud, MN
Ridgway, Maureen Abbott ..... Herald, CA
Ridgway, Michael C. ..... Rockville, MD
Ridgway, Michael E. ..... Yankton, SD
Ridgway, Michael S. ..... Maple Shade, NJ
Ridgway, Nancy E. ..... Dallas, TX
Ridgway, Nancy L. ..... Linwood, NJ
Ridgway, Richard C. ..... Rockville, MD
Ridgway, Richard D. ..... Ocala, FL
Ridgway, Richard L. ..... Jackson, MS
Ridgway & Ridgway ..... Linwood, NJ
Ridgway, Ridgway & Stayton
Maple Shade, NJ
Ridgway, Robert E. ..... Pendleton, OR
Ridgway, Robert E., Jr. ..... Hartwell, GA
Ridgway, Rushton H. ..... Bridgeton, NJ
Ridgway, Sheila C. ..... Seattle, WA
Ridgway, Spencer ..... Madison, NJ
Ridgway, Theodore S. ..... Linwood, NJ
Ridgway, Vicki Lynne ..... Elkton, KY
Ridgway, Whitman Hawley
Silver Spring, MD
Riding, Kenneth L. ..... Saratoga, CA
Ridinger, Patrick L. ..... Charlotte, NC
Ridinger, Willa J. ..... New Haven, CT
Ridings, Craig A. ..... Springfield, IL
Ridings, James A. ..... London, KY
Ridings, Joe B. ..... Baytown, TX
Ridings, Marcia Milby ..... London, KY
Ridings, William John, Jr.
Pompano Beach, FL
Ridini, Christopher J. ..... Centerport, NY
Ridini, Leonard M., Jr. ..... Garden City, NY
Melville, NY
Ridker, Susan K. ..... Chestnut Hill, MA
Ridl, David J. ..... Dickinson, ND
Ridl, David L. ..... New York, NY
Ridle, Robert A. ..... Oklahoma City, OK
Ridle, Teresa S. ..... Anchorage, AK
Ridlehoover, Kenneth R. ..... Pensacola, FL
Ridlehuber, Ted R. ..... Athens, GA
Ridler, Gregory L. ..... Youngstown, OH
Ridler, Jack R. ..... Dayton, OH
Ridless, Joshua A. ..... San Francisco, CA
Ridley, Andrew E. ..... Washington, DC
Ridley, Arthur K. ..... Milford, PA
Ridley, Barton Lance ..... Dallas, TX
Ridley, Bruce E. ..... Spokane, WA
Ridley, Charles B., Jr. ..... Rock Hill, SC
Ridley, Charles B., Jr., P.A. ..... Rock Hill, SC
Ridley, Christy ..... Bethesda, MD
Ridley, Clarence H. ..... Atlanta, GA
Ridley, Donald T. ..... Patterson, NY
Ridley, Earle D. ..... Binghamton, NY
Ridley, Eileen R. ..... San Francisco, CA
Ridley, Eleanor H. ..... Atlanta, GA
Ridley, Fred S. ..... Tampa, FL
Ridley, Hal R. ..... Orlando, FL
Ridley, Harry W., Jr. ..... Huntsville, TX
Ridley, James A., III ..... Knoxville, TN
Ridley, James I. ..... Fort Lauderdale, FL
Ridley, John A. ..... Newark, NJ
Ridley, Kerri A. ..... San Jose, CA
Ridley, Kevin L. ..... Chicago, IL
Ridley, Lori A. ..... Burbank, CA
Ridley, Michael P. ..... Irvine, CA
Ridley, Nathan H. ..... Nashville, TN
Ridley, Pamela Miller ..... Malibu, CA
Ridley, Patrick ..... Temple, TX
Ridley, Patrick L. ..... Denver, CO
Ridley, Paul E. ..... Dallas, TX
Ridley, Robert W., (A Professional Corporation) ..... Los Angeles, CA
Ridley, Roger H. ..... Riverside, CA
Ridley, Roslyn B. ..... Washington, DC
Ridley, Shawn M. ..... Redwood City, CA
Ridley, Tamela ..... San Diego, CA
Ridley, Terence M. ..... Denver, CO
Ridley, Timothy W. ..... Minneapolis, MN
Ridley, William H. ..... Belleville, MI
Ridling, Curtis C. ..... Santa Barbara, CA
Ridloff, Richard ..... Jericho, NY
Ridlon, Ian C. ..... Providence, RI
Ridlon, Ray W. ..... El Cajon, CA
Ridner, Jeffrey D. ..... Tullahoma, TN
Ridolfi, Friedman, Frank & Edelstein, A Prof. Corp. ..... Lawrenceville, NJ
Ridolfi, Kathleen M. ..... Santa Clara, CA
Ridolfi, Robert N. ..... Lawrenceville, NJ
Ridolfi, Sido L. ..... Lawrenceville, NJ
Ridolfo, James P., Jr. ..... Wethersfield, CT
Ridolfo, Phillip T., Jr.
West Palm Beach, FL
Ridolphi, Fred M., Jr. ..... Memphis, TN
Ridout, John T. ..... Houston, TX
Ridout, Josh S. ..... Los Angeles, CA
Ridout, Ross Norman ..... Searcy, AR
Ridout, William B. ..... Estherville, IA
Ridout, William D. ..... Tulsa, OK
Ridulfo, Michael P. ..... Corpus Christi, TX
Ridyard, Lori Forter ..... Exton, PA
Rie, Michael ..... Cleveland, OH
Riebandt & DeWald, Inc.
Arlington Heights, IL
Riebandt, James J. ..... Arlington Heights, IL
Riebe, Frank D. ..... Portland, OR
Riebe, Michael J. ..... Grafton, WI
Riebe, Radd L. ..... Cleveland, OH
Riebel, David L. ..... Clifton Park, NY
Riebel, Richard D. ..... Milwaukee, WI
Riebenack, F. Walter ..... Fort Wayne, IN
Riebesehl, Gregory A. ..... Garden City, NY
Riebesell, Gary R. ..... Bakersfield, CA
Riebesell, H. F., Jr. ..... Denver, CO
Riebling, Peter J. ..... Washington, DC
Riebling, Stephen J., Jr. ..... White Plains, NY
Riebman, Hyman I. ..... Des Plaines, IL
Rieboldt, Benton K. ..... Walnut Creek, CA
Riebschleger, Peter J. ..... Saginaw, MI
Riecan, George M. ..... Tacoma, WA
Riechel, Gerhard P. ..... Auburn Hills, MI
Riechelson, Kevin S. ..... Philadelphia, PA
Riechelson, Susan Silverman
Philadelphia, PA
Riechenbach, Seth T. ..... Columbus, OH
Riechert, Melinda Collins ..... Palo Alto, CA
Riechert, Melinda Shena ..... Belmont, CA
Riechert, Peter G. ..... Redwood City, CA
Riechmann, Michael J. ..... Santa Ana, CA
Rieck, Bruce F. ..... Austin, TX
Kerrville, TX
Rieck, Charles ..... Chicago, IL
Rieck, Charles H. ..... Huntington Beach, CA
Rieck and Crotty, A Professional Corporation ..... Chicago, IL
Rieck, Edward E. ..... Pittsburgh, PA
Rieck, Frederick C., Jr. ..... New York, NY
Rieck, John Jacob, Jr. ..... New York, NY
Rieck, Kim A. ..... Columbus, OH
Rieck, Thomas W. ..... Chicago, IL
Riecke, Charles Sanford ..... Fargo, ND
Riecke, Randall ..... Dallas, TX

Riethmiller, Lynn Kent .... Woodsfield, OH
Riethmiller, William C. .... Boca Raton, FL
Riethmiller, William C., P.A.
Boca Raton, FL
Riethmuller, Mark S. .... Washington, PA
Rietman, Mark W. .... Evansville, IN
Rietz, Dean K. .... Owatonna, MN
Rietz, Eric J. .... Chicago, IL
Rietz, James K. .... Naples, FL
Rietz, Jason P. .... Owatonna, MN
Rietz, Joel L. .... San Francisco, CA
Rietz, Larry J. .... Owatonna, MN
Rietz, Neal L. .... Owatonna, MN
Rietz, Rietz, Rietz & Worke .... Owatonna, MN
Rieves, Elton A., III .... Little Rock, AR
West Memphis, AR
Rieves, Elton A., IV .... Little Rock, AR
West Memphis, AR
Rieves, L. Michael .... Oklahoma City, OK
Rieves & Mayton .... Blytheville, AR
Forrest City, AR
Helena, AR
Jonesboro, AR
Little Rock, AR
Marianna, AR
West Memphis, AR
Wynne, AR
Rieveschl, David C. .... Washington, DC
Rievman, David M. .... New York, NY
Rievman, Joshua D. .... New York, NY
Riewald, David J. .... Portland, OR
Riewaldt, Martha L. .... Toledo, OH
Riewe, Brian E. .... Austin, TX
Riewe, Phyllis P. .... Melbourne, FL
Riewer, Nicholas A. .... Chicago, IL
Riexinger, Stephen P. .... Atlanta, GA
Riezman & Blitz, P.C. .... Jefferson City, MO
St. Louis, MO
Riezman, Eric N. .... Irvine, CA
Riezman, Richard M. .... St. Louis, MO
Riezman, Susan P. .... Santa Ana, CA
Rifaat, Julie A. .... Houston, TX
Rifai, Ali E. .... Long Beach, NY
Rifai, D'Ann Naylor .... Austin, TX
Rifai, Hamdi M. .... Newark, NJ
Rifai & Ramadan LLC .... Newark, NJ
Rifas, Earle V., (P.A.) .... Miami, FL
Rifas, Gaylen, (Mrs.) .... Miami, FL
Rifas, Harold M., (P.A.) .... South Miami, FL
Rife, Gary A. .... Oklahoma City, OK
Rife, Harry P. .... Kettering, OH
Rife, Jack M., Jr. .... Charleston, WV
Rife, Joan H. .... Toledo, OH
Rife, John .... Danville, AR
Rife, Kimberly D. .... Goshen, IN
Rife, Knute A. .... Goldendale, WA
Rife, Richard C. .... Orem, UT
Rife, Wayne T. .... College Station, TX
Rifenbark, Neil .... Los Angeles, CA
Rifenberg, R. Ramsey .... Encinitas, CA
Riff, I. Joel .... Mountain View, CA
Riff, Lawrence P. .... Los Angeles, CA
Riff, Liat .... Chicago, IL
Riff, Stephen H. Falla .... New York, NY
Riff, Todd G. .... Houston, TX
Riffaterre, Lee K. .... New York, NY
Riffaud, Marcelo L. .... New York, NY
Riffe, C. Keith .... Yakima, WA
Riffe, Gerald H. .... Beaver, OK
Riffe, H. Duane .... Broken Arrow, OK
Riffe, Lovice D. .... Colorado Springs, CO
Riffe, Richard .... Charleston, WV
Riffee, Charles A., II .... Charleston, WV
Riffel, Jerome D. .... Kansas City, MO
Riffel, Katresa J. .... Enid, OK
Riffel & King, P.L.C. .... Pocahontas, AR
Riffel, Kirby .... Pocahontas, AR
Riffel, Michael Craig .... Enid, OK
Riffel, Paul E. .... Tampa, FL
Riffel, Paul E., P.A. .... Tampa, FL
Riffel, Paul W. .... Waverly, IA
Riffenburgh, Ernest E. .... Riverside, CA
San Bernardino, CA
Riffer, Jeffrey K. .... Los Angeles, CA
Riffer, John I.
Federal Communications Commission, Office of the General Counsel, GV
Riffkin, Bernard .... Roslyn, NY
Riffkin, Linda A. .... New York, NY
Riffkin, Michael L. .... Rockville, MD
Riffkin, Mitchell S. .... Warwick, RI
Riffle, Charles M. .... Redwood City, CA
Riffle, H. Stanley .... Waukesha, WI
Riffle, John J. .... St. Louis, MO
Riffle, Paul G. .... Pinehurst, NC
Riffle, Robert A. .... Parkersburg, WV
Riffle, Robert M. .... Peoria, IL
Riffle, Timothy J. .... Indianapolis, IN
Riffner, Robert G. .... Schaumburg, IL
Rifici, Anthony M. .... Cleveland, OH
Rifino, Carl H. .... Somerville, NJ
Rifis, Jordan B. .... Oak Park, IL
Rifis, Jordan, P.C. .... Oak Park, IL
Rifka, Margaret Dillenburg
Washington, DC
Rifken, Ben .... Elgin, IL
Rifken, Frankel & Greenman, P.C.
Syracuse, NY
Rifken, Herold L. .... Wilmette, IL
Rifken, Jeff .... Elgin, IL
Rifken, Lawrence Eric .... McLean, VA
Rifken, Richard E. .... Syracuse, NY
Rifken, Sonja J.
Federal Communications Commission, Office of the General Counsel, GV
Rifkin, Alan M. .... New York, NY
Rifkin, Alan Mark .... Baltimore, MD
Rifkin, Andrew P. .... Marina Del Rey, CA
Rifkin, Arnold G. .... Short Hills, NJ
Rifkin & Associates, LLC .... Paoli, PA
Rifkin and Associates, P.A. .... Miami, FL
Orlando, FL
Rifkin, Avron C. .... Stuart, FL
Rifkin, B. Andrew .... Huntington Woods, MI
Rifkin, Bernard M. .... New York, NY
Rifkin, Bruce .... Seattle, WA
Rifkin, Dave
United States Tax Court, GV
Rifkin, David W. .... Salem, MA
Rifkin, Dori .... Salem, MA
Rifkin, Gillian Lee .... Birmingham, MI
Rifkin, Harry Martin .... Towson, MD
Rifkin, Hillary .... Buffalo, NY
Rifkin, Jessica R. .... Washington, DC
Rifkin, Judith .... New York, NY
Rifkin, Larry S. .... Miami, FL
Orlando, FL
Rifkin, Livingston, Levitan & Silver, LLC
Annapolis, MD
Baltimore, MD
Greenbelt, MD
Rifkin, Marjorie L., (Ms.) .... Washington, DC
Rifkin, Mark C. .... Paoli, PA
Rifkin, Martin S. .... Fort Wayne, IN
Rifkin, Michael .... Durham, NC
Rifkin, Paul L. .... Asheville, NC
Rifkin, Paul L., P.A. .... Asheville, NC
Rifkin, Richard .... Albany, NY
Rifkin, Robert A. .... Rye, NY
Rifkin, Robert S. .... Indianapolis, IN
Rifkin, Robert W. .... Washington, DC
Rifkin, Ronnie A. .... New York, NY
Rifkin, Ross N. .... Minneapolis, MN
Rifkin, Roy G. .... Los Angeles, CA
Rifkin, Ruth A. .... Philadelphia, PA
Rifkin, Stuart G. .... Denver, CO
Rifkin, William M. .... New York, NY
Rifkin, William T. .... Chicago, IL
Rifkind, Amy B. .... Washington, DC
Rifkind, David F. .... Washington, DC
Rifkind, David S. .... King Of Prussia, PA
Rifkind Law Firm .... Mill Valley, CA
Rifkind, Leonard A. .... Mill Valley, CA
Rifkind, Marc H. .... Washington, DC
Rifkind, Neil C. .... New York, NY
Rifkind, Nina L. .... New York, NY
Rifkind, Norman .... Chicago, IL
Rifkind, Richard D. .... Pleasanton, CA
Rifkind, Robert Gore, Law Offices of
Los Angeles, CA
Rifkind, Robert S. .... New York, NY
Rifkind, Steven A. .... Princeton Junction, NJ
Riga, Joseph F. .... Maple Shade, NJ
Rigal, Roberto, Jr. .... Miami, FL
Rigali, James F. .... Santa Maria, CA
Rigali, Joseph P. .... Concord, MA
Rigan, Susan K. .... Grand Rapids, MI
Rigano, Hayward M., II .... Tyler, TX
Rigano, James P. .... Melville, NY
Rigas, John N. .... Lancaster, PA
Rigas, Peter N. .... Grand Rapids, MI
Rigassio, Nancy M. .... Moorestown, NJ
Rigau, Marco A. .... San Juan, PR
Rigau, Marco A., Jr. .... San Juan, PR
Rigau & Rigau, Law Offices of .... Tampa, FL
Rigau, Roger V. .... Tampa, FL
Rigaux, Stephanie A. .... Washington, DC
Rigazio & Bertani .... Morris, IL
Rigazio, Mark W. .... Morris, IL
Rigberg, James S. .... Phoenix, AZ
Rigberg, Karen Tearston .... Torrance, CA
Rigberg, Saul A. .... Albany, NY
Rigby, Barry W. .... Orlando, FL
Rigby, Bradford L. .... Jackson, TN
Rigby, James .... Seattle, WA
Rigby, Jane A. .... Newark, NJ
Rigby, Jerry R. .... Rexburg, ID
Rigby, Jesse W. .... Pensacola, FL
Rigby, John J. .... Arlington, VA
Rigby, John M. .... Salem, SC
Rigby, Kenneth .... Shreveport, LA
Rigby, Kenneth Arthur .... New York, NY
Rigby, L. Gerald .... Philadelphia, PA
Rigby, Mitchell C. .... Madera, CA
Rigby, R. Glen .... Houston, TX
Rigby, Ray W. .... Rexburg, ID
Rigby, Ren Patrick, Jr. .... Houston, TX
Rigby, Robert E., Jr. .... Boston, MA
Rigby, Suzanne
Federal Deposit Insurance Corporation, GV
Rigby, Thatcher, Andrus, Rigby, Kam & Moeller, Chartered .... Rexburg, ID
Rigby, Thomas W.
Small Business Administration, Office of the General Counsel, GV
Rigby, Timothy .... Springfield, IL
Rigby, Todd A. .... Phoenix, AZ
Rigby, Twila Kay .... Oak Grove, MO
Rigby-Conyers, Kimberly A.
Fayetteville, NC
Rigdon, Fred W., Jr. .... Sylvester, GA
Rigdon, Fred W., Jr. .... Tifton, GA
Rigdon, H. A., Jr. .... Cocoa, FL
Orlando, FL
Rigdon, Harry J. .... Bryan, OH
Rigdon, Jay A. .... Warsaw, IN
Rigdon, Kendall Bradley .... Cocoa, FL
Orlando, FL
Rigdon, Michael D., (A Law Corp.)
Pasadena, CA
Rigdon, Muckerman, Alexander & Rigdon, P.A. .... Cocoa, FL
Orlando, FL
Rigdon, Patricia A. .... Pasadena, CA
Rigdon, Robert N. .... Santa Monica, CA
Rigdon, Thomas M. .... Newkirk, OK
Rigdon, William R., Jr. .... Moss, MS
Rigel, Joseph Reuben .... St. Louis, MO
Rigelhaupt, Bert .... Youngstown, OH
Rigelhaupt, James L., Jr. .... San Francisco, CA
Rigelhaupt, Peter D. .... Garden City, NY
Rigell, David R. .... West Palm Beach, FL
Rigell, Leal & Ring, P.A.
West Palm Beach, FL
Rigelman, Bruce D. .... Columbus, OH
Rigely, George A. .... San Antonio, TX
Rigely, George A., Attorney at Law, P.C.
San Antonio, TX
Riger, Brian D. .... Bethesda, MD
Rigero, Peter D. .... Uxbridge, MA
Rigg, Brian J. .... Columbus, OH
Rigg and Dean .... Newport Beach, CA
Rigg, Debra S. .... Maysville, KY
Rigg, Dermot .... Sugar Land, TX
Rigg, Dermot, P.C. .... Sugar Land, TX
Rigg, Douglas C. .... Berkeley, CA
Rigg, J. Keith .... Des Moines, IA
Rigg & Jackson-Rigg .... Maysville, KY
Rigg, Jennifer E. .... Lakewood, CO
Rigg Law Firm .... Maysville, KY
Rigg, Margaret S. .... San Francisco, CA
Rigg, Michael G. .... Hartford, CT
Rigg, Philip D. .... Houston, TX
Rigg, Robert R. .... Des Moines, IA
Rigg, Robert R., (Professional Corporation)
Newport Beach, CA
Rigg, Robert S. .... Chicago, IL
Rigg, Ronald L. .... Maysville, KY
Riggall, Kneave .... Pasadena, CA
Riggenbach, William V. .... Richmond, VA
Riggens, Bonita M. .... St. Petersburg, FL
Riggers, Rick J. W. .... Atlanta, GA
Riggert, David B. .... Bloomington, IL
Riggi, Dean A. .... Schenectady, NY
Riggin, George B., Jr. .... Annapolis, MD
Riggin, Matthew E. .... Tulsa, OK
Riggins, C. Allen .... Virginia Beach, VA
Riggins, David N. .... Shelbyville, IN
Riggins, Jay E. .... Corpus Christi, TX
Riggins, John R. .... Edgewater, NJ
Riggins, Phillip Tyler .... Atlanta, GA
Riggins, Sandra MacQuarrie .... Norcross, GA
Riggins, Thomas W. .... Grand Prairie, TX
Riggins, William G. .... Kansas City, MO
Riggins, William J. .... Milwaukee, WI
Riggins, William W., III
Silver Spring, MD
Riggio, Caroline A. .... New York, NY
Riggio, Christopher Charles
Palm Beach Gardens, FL
Riggio, Donald M. .... Stockton, CA
Riggio, Joseph V. .... Los Angeles, CA
Riggio, Michael V. .... Tacoma, WA
Riggio & Mitchell, P.A. .... Daytona Beach, FL
Riggio, Nicholas J., Sr. .... St. Louis, MO
Riggio, Robert J. .... Daytona Beach, FL
Riggiola, Loryn P. .... Newark, NJ
Riggle and Craven .... Chicago, IL
Riggle, Darren Blaine .... Portland, ME
Riggle, David A. .... Chicago, IL
Riggle, James A. .... Sault Ste. Marie, MI
Riggle, Jennifer S. .... Portland, ME
Riggle, Paul T. .... Flora, IL
Riggle, Raymond E., Jr. .... Sunnyvale, CA
Riggle, Ronald L. .... New Orleans, LA
Riggs, Abney, Neal, Turpen, Orbison & Lewis, A Professional Corporation
Denver, CO
Muskogee, OK
Oklahoma City, OK
Tulsa, OK
Riggs, Amanda M. .... Austin, TX
Riggs, Arthur J. .... Carrollton, TX
Riggs, Arthur L. .... Whittier, CA
Riggs, Becky J. .... Indianapolis, IN
Riggs, Benjamin F., Jr. .... York, PA
Riggs, Bradner C. .... Rockford, IL
Riggs, Brent D. .... Los Angeles, CA
Riggs, Burkeley N. .... Denver, CO
Riggs, Carole R. .... Houston, TX
Riggs, Charles E. .... Banning, CA
Riggs, Charles T., Jr. .... Chicago, IL
Riggs, Conrad A. .... Santa Monica, CA
Riggs, Dan B. .... Sheridan, WY
Riggs, David A. .... Boca Raton, FL
Riggs, David E. .... Kalamazoo, MI
Riggs, Elizabeth Ann .... El Cajon, CA
Riggs, Frank E., Jr. .... Atlanta, GA
Riggs, Frank P. .... Sun City Center, FL
Riggs, Frank W. .... Montgomery, AL
Riggs, Geoffrey G. .... Los Angeles, CA
Riggs, George C. .... Blaine, MN
Riggs, George E., Jr. .... Louisville, KY
Riggs, Gerald E. .... El Cerrito, CA
Riggs, Gregory L. .... Atlanta, GA
Riggs, Harry L., Jr. .... Cincinnati, OH
Riggs, Howell Roger, Jr. .... Huntsville, AL
Riggs, Jack A. .... Indianapolis, IN
Riggs, James H. .... Oakland, CA
Riggs, James R. .... Haddonfield, NJ
Riggs, Janet C. .... Irvine, CA
Riggs, Jas. S. .... Sun City, AZ
Riggs, Jeffrey A. .... Alexandria, LA
Riggs, Jennifer S. .... Austin, TX
Riggs, Jo Ann .... Seattle, WA
Riggs, Joann Cecil .... Adelphi, MD
Riggs, Joel W. .... Wichita, KS
Riggs, John C. .... High Point, NC
Riggs, John V. .... Las Vegas, NV
Riggs, Katherine R. .... New York, NY
Riggs, Kea W. .... Roswell, NM
Riggs, Kendrick R. .... Louisville, KY
Riggs, L. Alton, Jr. .... Mesa, AZ
Riggs, Lisa R. .... Tulsa, OK
Riggs, Louis W. .... Hannibal, MO
Riggs, M. David .... Tulsa, OK
Riggs, Marion S. .... Manning, SC
Riggs, Marshall T. .... Boulder, CO
Riggs, Mary Onie Ford .... Metairie, LA
Riggs, Matthew L. .... Mesa, AZ
Riggs, Michael L. .... Bartlesville, OK
Riggs, Natasha M. .... Beverly Hills, CA
Riggs & NeSmith, P.A. .... Montgomery, AL
Riggs, Orion .... Kansas City, MO
Riggs, Paul C. .... Mesa, AZ
Riggs, Paula F. .... New York, NY
Riggs, Peter .... White Plains, NY
Riggs, R. William .... Salem, OR
Riggs, Randall R. .... Indianapolis, IN
Riggs, Richard A. .... Oklahoma City, OK
Riggs & Riggs, Professional Association
Manning, SC
Riggs, Robert E. .... Orem, UT
Riggs, Robert M. .... New York, NY
Riggs, Robert R. .... Berkeley, CA
Cobb, CA
Riggs, Robin L. .... Salt Lake City, UT
Riggs, Robin R. .... Winder, GA
Riggs, Roger D. .... Mount Sterling, KY
Riggs, Roland W., III .... Marietta, OH
Riggs, Ronald T. .... Memphis, TN
Riggs, Russell H. .... Louisville, KY
Riggs, Sandra B. .... Big Stone Gap, VA
Riggs, Scott J. .... Minneapolis, MN
Riggs, Sidney S., III .... Columbia, SC
Riggs, Stephen J. .... Pasadena, CA
Riggs, Steve L. .... Little Rock, AR
Riggs, Susan J. .... Charleston, WV
Riggs, T. Sherman .... Shelbyville, KY
Riggs, T. H. .... Houston, TX
Riggs, Thomas J. .... Fresno, CA
Riggs, Thomas J. .... Wheaton, IL
Riggs, Thomas S. .... Charleston, WV
Riggs, Thomas S., III .... New York, NY
Riggs, Walter M. .... Manning, SC
Riggs, Warren G. .... Columbus, OH
Riggs, William F. .... Tulsa, OK
Riggs, William R. .... Indianapolis, IN
Riggs, Zennie L. .... Jacksonville, NC
Riggsbee, Leslie Shea .... Greenville, NC
Riggsbee, Lunday A. .... Pittsboro, NC
Riggsbee, Renee C. .... Raleigh, NC
Righeimer, Christine E. .... Wheaton, IL
Righeimer Martin & Cinquino, P.C.
Chicago, IL
Righi, Alan J. .... Pittsfield, MA
Right, Richard L. .... Phoenix, AZ
Right, Richard H. .... Denver, CO
Righter, Dale A. .... Charleston, IL
Righter, Joan M. .... Norristown, PA
Righter, Mark .... State College, PA
Righter, Michael A. .... El Rito, NM
Righter-Thornton, Anne H.
San Francisco, CA
Righthand, Scott D. .... San Francisco, CA
Righthand, Scott, P.C., Law Office of
San Francisco, CA
Rightmyer, Katherine A. .... Reading, PA
Rightmyer, Lee H. .... St. Petersburg, FL
Rightmyer, Robert D. .... Miami, FL
Rightnour, Donald .... Chantilly, VA
Rights, D. Michael .... Brewster, NY
Rights, Nancy S. .... Stamford, CT
Rightsell, William T., Jr. .... Greensboro, NC
Rigie, Lawrence .... White Plains, NY
Rigilano, Thomas A. .... New York, NY
Rigler, Douglas V. .... Washington, DC
Arlington, VA
Rigler, Earl Kenneth .... Kennett Square, PA
Rigler, James David .... Richmond, VA
Rigler, Jane .... Carlisle, PA
Rigler, Joseph W. .... Salem, MO
Rigler Law Firm, The, P.C. .... Alexandria, VA
Rigler, Lionel .... New Haven, CT
Rigler, Maeve T. .... Alexandria, VA
Rigler & Perna .... Kennett Square, PA
Rigler, Robert E. .... Alexandria, VA
Rigler, William .... Brooklyn, NY
Rigley, Kevin J. .... Santa Ana, CA
Rignanese, Cynthia Crofoot
Winter Haven, FL
Rigney, Anne .... Philadelphia, PA
Rigney, Heidi K. .... New York, NY
Rigney, John F. .... New York, NY
Rigney, Jon D., Law Offices of
San Diego, CA
Rigney, Michael E. .... Chicago, IL
Rigney, Robert B. .... Norfolk, VA
Williamsburg, VA
Rigney, Robert M. .... Berkeley, CA
Rigney, Roger T. .... Elizabethtown, KY
Rigo, Barbara Rittinger .... Philadelphia, PA
Rigo, Daniel J. .... Jacksonville, FL
Rigoglioso, Joseph P. .... Shelton, CT
Rigolio, Joseph M. .... North Haledon, NJ
New York, NY
Rigonan, Brian P. .... Chicago, IL
Rigone, Donald R. .... Greensburg, PA
Rigopoulos, Paul P. .... Boston, MA
Fitchburg, MA
Rigor, Bradley G. .... Bonita Springs, FL
Naples, FL
Syracuse, NY
Rigor, K. Tracy .... Louisville, KY
Rigos, Chris J. .... Seattle, WA
Rigot, Joseph M. .... Dayton, OH
Rigot, Linda M. .... Tallahassee, FL
Rigrish, James W. .... Akron, OH
Rigrish, Robert E. .... Miami, FL
Rigrod, Andrew C. .... Beverly Hills, CA
Rigrodsky, Marc A. .... Treasury Department, Office of the General Counsel, GV

Riley, Thomas K. ... Fulton, MO
Riley, Thomas P. ... San Francisco, CA
Riley, Thomas V. ... Waterbury, CT
Riley, Thos. J., Jr. ... Omaha, NE
Riley, Timothy C. ... Pasadena, CA
Riley, Timothy Clifford ... Channel Island, CA
Riley, Timothy D. ... Brownsville, TX
Houston, TX
Riley, Timothy G. ... San Diego, CA
Riley, Tom ... Cedar Rapids, IA
Iowa City, IA
Riley, Tom, Law Firm, P.L.C.
Cedar Rapids, IA
Iowa City, IA
Riley, Trey ... Huntsville, AL
Riley, Tyrone ... Toledo, OH
Riley, V. Alan ... Keyser, WV
Riley, V. Jan ... Houston, TX
Riley, Vincent J. ... Washington, DC
Riley, W. Edward, IV ... Richmond, VA
Riley, W. Kent ... Fort Worth, TX
Riley, Wallace D. ... Detroit, MI
Riley, Walters & Damaron, P.S.C.
Pikeville, KY
Riley, Wesley B., Jr. ... Montgomery, AL
Riley, William C. ... Lawton, OK
Riley, William D. ... Burlington, VT
Riley, William E. ... Chicago, IL
Riley, William F. ... Chatham, MA
Riley, William F. ... Natchez, MS
Riley, William F., Jr. ... Atlanta, GA
Riley, William J. ... Boston, MA
Riley, William J. ... Boonville, NY
Riley, William J., III ... Jennings, LA
Riley, William Jay ... Omaha, NE
Riley, William L. ... San Francisco, CA
Riley, William N. ... Indianapolis, IN
Riley, William S. ... Frankfort, KY
Riley, Yale Kelly Pat ... Brentwood, TN
Riley-Shoemaker, Sheryl Lynn
Minneapolis, MN
Riling, Burkhead & Nitcher
Lawrence, KS
Riling, Eugene C. ... Lawrence, KS
Riling, Michael E. ... Lawrence, KS
Riling, Timothy G. ... Lawrence, KS
Rilinger, Dennis R. ... Kansas City, MO
Rill, James F. ... Washington, DC
Rill, Peter P., Jr. ... Long Grove, IL
Rill, Thomas A. ... Syracuse, NY
Rill, W. Albert ... Naples, FL
Rilla, Alan J. ... Lee, MA
Rilley, Michael D. ... Columbus, OH
Rilley, Sue A. ... Cleveland, OH
Rillie, Robert J. ... Aledo, IL
Rilling, John E. ... Fargo, ND
Rillo, Christopher J. ... San Francisco, CA
Rillo, Troy J. ... Miami, FL
Rillstone, Douglas J. ... Tallahassee, FL
Rilo, Nora M. ... Miami, FL
Rim, Dianne Soomee ... Washington, DC
Rim, Peter W. ... McLean, VA
Rima, Robert A., The Law Office of
Austin, TX
Rimac, Joseph M., Jr. ... San Francisco, CA
San Francisco, CA
Rimac & Martin, A Professional Corporation
San Francisco, CA
Rimai, Marcia ... Milwaukee, WI
Rimar, Patrick G. ... Williamsville, NY
Rimas, A. Paul ... San Francisco, CA
Rimas, Vytas M. ... Minneapolis, MN
Rimbach, David ... Encino, CA
Rimbach, Louis ... Sherman Oaks, CA
Rimberg and Associates ... New York, NY
Rimberg, Robert ... New York, NY
Rimbey, Lori Lin ... Portland, OR
Rimedio, Jim ... Cincinnati, OH
Rimel, Jack J. ... Tustin, CA
Rimel, Jacquelyn D. ... Tustin, CA
Rimel and Rimel ... Tustin, CA
Rimel, Whitney ... Fresno, CA
Rimelspach, Ron L. ... Toledo, OH
Rimer, Alec A. ... Cheshire, CT
Rimer, Andrea L. ... Atlanta, GA
Rimer, Daniel N. ... Farmington Hills, MI
Rimer, Darren S. ... Laguna Hills, CA
Rimer, Edward S., Jr. ... Wilton, CT
Rimer, Neal M. ... Encino, CA
Rimerman, Fred ... San Fernando, CA
Rimerman, Randi-Sue
Department of Justice, Civil Division, GV
Rimes, Eugene B. ... Fort Lauderdale, FL
Rimes, John J., III ... Tallahassee, FL
Rimes, Stephen R. ... Houston, TX
Rimland, Edward ... Brooklyn, NY
Rimland, Jack P. ... Chicago, IL
Rimland, Sharon Katz ... Princeton, NJ
Rimler, Lee R. ... Charlotte, NC
Rimm, Harry H. ... Iselin, NJ
New York, NY
Rimm, Marvin N. ... Atlantic City, NJ
Rimm, William R. ... Alexandria, VA
Rimmel, Andrew A. ... St. Louis, MO
Rimmel, James E. ... Canfield, OH
Rimmel, James E., Co., L.P.A. ... Canfield, OH
Rimmele, John F. ... Warren, NJ
Rimmer, David H. ... Pensacola, FL
Rimmer, D. R. ... Treasury Department,
Office of Regulations and Rulings, GV
Rimmer, Kirk S. ... Sacramento, CA
Rimmer, Rawlings, MacInnis & Hedglin,
P.A. ... Jackson, MS
Rimmer, Rebecca S. ... Philadelphia, PA
Rimmer, Robert T. ... Hartford, CT
Rimmer, Stephen W. ... Jackson, MS
Rimmer, Thomas E. ... Selma, AL
Rimmer, William D. ... Wilmington, DE

Rimmler, Anne B. ... Buffalo, NY
Rimmler, Philipp L. ... Buffalo, NY
Rimokh, Jacques M. ... New York, NY
Rimon, Keren ... New York, NY
Rimon, Michael J. ... New York, NY
Rimsky, Neil T. ... White Plains, NY
Rimstidt, David L. ... Indianapolis, IN
Rinaca, James M. ... Richmond, VA
Rinaldi, Albert A., Jr. ... Seattle, WA
Rinaldi, Alexander J. ... Succasunna, NJ
Rinaldi, Andrea J. ... New York, NY
Rinaldi, Angelo Anthony ... Syracuse, NY
Rinaldi, Angelo J. ... Syracuse, NY
Rinaldi, Arthur J. ... Scranton, PA
Rinaldi & Associates ... Greenwich, CT
Rinaldi, Bruce ... Treasury Department,
Office of Thrift Supervision, GV
Rinaldi, Catherine A. ... Albany, NY
Rinaldi, Catherine Brennan ... Newark, NJ
Rinaldi, Charles J. ... Washington, DC
Rinaldi, David J. ... Santa Ana, CA
Rinaldi, David J. ... Scranton, PA
Rinaldi, Donald E. ... San Dimas, CA
Rinaldi, Donald J. ... Waterbury, CT
Rinaldi, Edward J. ... White Plains, NY
Rinaldi, Elaine M. ... Philadelphia, PA
Rinaldi, Ellis F. ... Greenwich, CT
Rinaldi, Emil A. ... Brighton, CO
Rinaldi, Frank ... Garden City, NY
Rinaldi, Frank ... New York, NY
Rinaldi, Frank R. ... New York, NY
Rinaldi, George H. ... Providence, RI
Rinaldi, Gina A. ... Hempstead, NY
Rinaldi, Herbert M. ... Roseland, NJ
Rinaldi, John A. ... Chester, NY
Rinaldi, John A. ... Pearl River, NY
Rinaldi, John E. ... Woodbridge, VA
Rinaldi, Joseph ... New York, NY
Rinaldi Law Office ... Syracuse, NY
Rinaldi, Linda A. ... Trenton, NJ
Rinaldi, Lisa J. ... New York, NY
Rinaldi, Lori A. ... Richmond, VA
Rinaldi, Matthew J. ... Oakland, CA
Rinaldi, M'Liss K. ... Providence, RI
Rinaldi, Ralph D. ... Fairfax, VA
Rinaldi, Raymond C. ... Scranton, PA
Rinaldi, Roscoe & Poveromo, P.C.
Scranton, PA
Rinaldi, Rose A. ... Greenwich, CT
Rinaldi, Steven D. ... Washington, DC
Rinaldi, Victor F. ... Fairfax, VA
Rinaldi, William J. ... Scranton, PA
Rinaldi, William J. ... Wilkes-Barre, PA
Rinaldi, Zipoli, Bruno, Agati and Lugauskas,
P.C. ... Waterbury, CT
Rinaldi-Dimitriou, Gail A. ... San Diego, CA
Rinaldo, Amy E. ... Farmington Hills, MI
Rinaldo, Anthony D., Jr. ... Elizabeth, NJ
Rinaldo, Catherine M. ... Tampa, FL
Rinaldo, Donald W. ... Union, NJ
Rinaldo, Elizabeth A.
Department of Justice, Civil Division, GV
Rinaldo, Matthew T. ... Elizabeth, NJ
Rinaldo, Richard F. ... Pittsburgh, PA
Rinaldo and Rinaldo, A Professional
Corporation ... Elizabeth, NJ
Rinaldo, Thomas N. ... Buffalo, NY
Rinaman, James C., III ... Jacksonville, FL
Rinaman, James C., Jr. ... Jacksonville, FL
Rinard, Jack C. ... Brandon, FL
Rinard, Marquin S., (P.A.) ... Cape Coral, FL
Rinard, Patrick W. ... Clearwater, FL
Rinardo, Joanne ... New Orleans, LA
Rinaudo, V. Charles ... Towson, MD
Rinck, James R. ... Grand Rapids, MI
Rincon, Carlos ... El Paso, TX
Rincon, Alberto V., Jr. ... Irving, TX
Rincones, Jesse E., III ... Amarillo, TX
Rind, Alison W. ... Washington, DC
Rind, Michael D. ... Baltimore, MD
Rindal, Ellen J. ... Bloomingdale, IL
Rindal, Ellen J., P.C. ... Bloomingdale, IL
Rinde, Irving S. ... Elmira, NY
Rinde, Jeffrey A. ... Atlanta, GA
New York, NY
Rinde, Jonathan E. ... Bala Cynwyd, PA
Rindels, Paula S. ... Minneapolis, MN
Rinden, Gerry M. ... Moline, IL
Des Moines, IA
Rinden, Paul A. ... Concord, NH
Rinden Professional Assn. ... Concord, NH
Rinder, Lawrence J. ... Chicago, IL
Rinder, Lewis ... Palm City, FL
Rinder, Lewis, P.A. ... Palm City, FL
Rinder, Sheila M. ... Phoenix, AZ
Rinderer, William P., Jr. ... Oklahoma City, OK
Rindfuss, James A. ... San Antonio, TX
Rindfuss, Julia Leedham ... Pittsfield, MA
Rindfusz, Robert D. ... Gresham, OR
Rindge, Samuel F. ... Monterey Park, CA
Rindge, Samuel H. ... Los Angeles, CA
Rindler, Alan B. ... Boston, MA
Rindler, Richard M. ... Washington, DC
Rindler, Sidney L. ... Lowell, MA
Rindlisbacher, Curtis D. ... Fresno, CA
Rindner, Gary M. ... New York, NY
Rindner, Howard C. ... Goshen, NY
Rindner, Karen C. ... Alexandria, VA
Rindner, Marc E. ... Washington, DC
Rindner, Marc W. ... Beverly Hills, CA
Rindner, Mark ... Anchorage, AK
Rindner, Steven E. ... Washington, DC
Rindone, Robert H. ... Atlanta, GA
Rindsberg, Jane E. ... Columbus, OH
Rindsberg, Martin E. ... Long Beach, NY
Rindsig, Steven J. ... Sioux Falls, SD
Rindskopf-Parker, Elizabeth ... Madison, WI
Rindt, Brian A. ... Smyrna, GA

Rindy, Dean A. ... West Fargo, ND
Rine, John A. ... Dade City, FL
Rinear, Richard J. ... Cincinnati, OH
Rinear, Robert L. ... Cincinnati, OH
Rinear, Robert T., Jr. ... West Babylon, NY
Rinearson, Judith ... New York, NY
Rineberg, Gail M. ... Chicago, IL
Rinebolt, Richard J. ... Findlay, OH
Rineer, Hugh V. ... Tulsa, OK
Rinegar, Roberta L. ... Casper, WY
Rinehardt, John J. ... Mansfield, OH
Rinehardt, John K. ... Mansfield, OH
Rinehart, Dana G. ... Columbus, OH
Rinehart, Edmon L. ... Montgomery, AL
Rinehart, Edwin O., Jr., (P.C.) ... Austin, TX
Rinehart, Francis E. ... New York, NY
Rinehart, Gary R., (P.C.) ... Piedmont, CA
Rinehart, Howarth, Rishel & Kopech
Columbus, OH
Rinehart, J. Kelley ... Silverdale, WA
Rinehart, James E. ... Chesapeake, VA
Rinehart, James P. ... Youngstown, OH
Rinehart, John D. ... Rock Hill, SC
Rinehart, John E., Jr. ... Seattle, WA
Rinehart, Karen ... Los Angeles, CA
Rinehart, Kathleen A. ... Milwaukee, WI
Rinehart, Keith L. ... Fort Lauderdale, FL
Rinehart, Kyle Bennett ... Portland, OR
Rinehart, Laurie A. ... Dublin, OH
Rinehart, Lisa A. ... Chicago, IL
Rinehart, Mark E. ... Salt Lake City, UT
Rinehart Matthews & Bruce, L.L.C.
Rock Hill, SC
Rinehart & Nugent ... Austin, TX
Rinehart, R. Dean ... El Reno, OK
Rinehart, Ralph W. ... Tampa, FL
Rinehart, Rinehart & Rinehart, P.C.
El Reno, OK
Rinehart, Robert L. ... Norco, CA
Rinehart, Roger ... El Reno, OK
Rinehart and Scaffidi ... Milwaukee, WI
Rinehart, Stephen G. ... New York, NY
Rinehart, Tandy B. ... Stafford, VA
Rinehart, Tara ... Washington, DC
Rinehart, Tina M. ... Los Angeles, CA
Rinehart, William A. ... Milwaukee, WI
Rinehart, William J. ... El Reno, OK
Rinella, Bernard B. ... Chicago, IL
Rinella, Joseph J. ... Fort Myers, FL
Rinella and Rinella, Ltd. ... Chicago, IL
Waukegan, IL
Wheaton, IL
Rinella, Vincent J., Jr. ... Eagleville, PA
Riner, James W. ... Jefferson City, MO
Riner, Steve N. ... Barker, TX
Riner, Turnbull & Walker, P.C.
Jefferson City, MO
Rinere, Joseph C., Jr. ... Rochester, NY
Rines, David A. ... Boston, MA
Rines, Robert H. ... Concord, NH
Rinesmith, Steven L. ... Honolulu, HI
Riney, Michael H. ... San Diego, CA
Riney, Stanley J. ... Wichita, KS
Riney, T. Richard ... Louisville, KY
Riney, Theodore J. ... Dallas, TX
Riney, Thomas C. ... Amarillo, TX
Rinfret & Knowling ... Millersburg, OH
Rinfret, Robert D. ... Millersburg, OH
Ring, Bart Ivan ... Woodland Hills, CA
Ring, Berton N. ... Chicago, IL
Ring, Beth Carole ... New York, NY
Ring, Bob L. ... Greeley, CO
Ring, Bruce A. ... Jefferson City, MO
Ring, Bruce E. ... Walnut Creek, CA
Ring, C. Nicholas ... Georgetown, OH
Ring, C. Terence ... Walnut Creek, CA
Ring, Carlyle C., Jr. ... Washington, DC
Ring, Christine S. ... San Francisco, CA
Ring, Christopher P. ... Patchogue, NY
Ring, Dan F. ... Lake Forest, IL
Ring, Daniel L. ... Chicago, IL
Ring, David A. ... Long Beach, CA
Ring, David D. ... San Francisco, CA
Ring, David L. ... Los Angeles, CA
Ring, David M. ... Los Angeles, CA
Ring, David W. ... Cambridge, WI
Ring, Diane M. ... Cambridge, MA
Ring, Douglas R., (A Professional
Corporation) ... Los Angeles, CA
Ring, Eileen ... Concord, CA
Ring, Elizabeth E. ... Washington, DC
Ring, Eric ... Bala Cynwyd, PA
Ring, Gerard D. ... Chicago, IL
Ring, Gerard W. ... Rochester, MN
Ring & Green ... Los Angeles, CA
Ring, Gregory A., Law Offices of
Bullhead City, AZ
Las Vegas, NV
Laughlin, NV
Ring, Gregory A., Law Offices of
Kingman, AZ
Laughlin, NV
Ring, Jack Samuel ... Chicago, IL
Ring, Jack Samuel, & Associates, Ltd.
Chicago, IL
Ring, James F. ... Boston, MA
Ring, Jeffery W. ... Portland, OR
Ring, Jeffrey B. ... St. Louis Park, MN
Ring, Joel S. ... Los Angeles, CA
Ring, John F. ... Washington, DC
Ring, John H. ... Friendswood, TX
Ring, John J. ... San Francisco, CA
Ring, Judith H. ... Philadelphia, PA
Ring, Karen A. ... Minnetonka, MN
Ring, Kathleen A. ... Chicago, IL
Ring, Kathleen Murphy ... Washington, DC
Ring, Laurence ... Beverly Hills, CA
Ring, Lawrence T. ... Roseville, CA

Ring, Liza G. ... San Francisco, CA
Ring, Lucile Wiley ... St. Louis, MO
Selah, WA
Ring, Michael A. ... Westmont, NJ
Ring, Michael J. ... West Palm Beach, FL
Ring, Michael J. ... Lexington, MA
Ring, Michael P. ... Santa Barbara, CA
Ring, Michael P. ... Atlanta, GA
Ring, Michael W. ... Los Angeles, CA
Ring, Millard A. ... Glen Cove, NY
Ring, Nancy Horwitz ... Baltimore, MD
Ring, Peter S. ... Los Angeles, CA
Ring, Renée E. ... New York, NY
Ring, Richard D., Law Offices of
Vista, CA
Ring, Richard R. ... Houston, TX
Ring, Robert A. ... Los Angeles, CA
Ring, Robert G. ... San Francisco, CA
Ring, Robt J. ... Denver, CO
Ring, Rodney D. ... Norman, OK
Ring, Ronald H. ... Rapid City, MI
Ring, Sanford B. ... Washington, DC
Ring, Scott S. ... Menlo Park, CA
Ring, Sharon Levine ... Palo Alto, CA
Ring, Sidney B. ... St. Louis, MO
Ring, Stephen D. ... Houston, TX
Ring, Stephen H. ... Rockville, MD
Ring, Steven J. ... Dayton, OH
Ring, Thomas E. ... Minneapolis, MN
Ring, Thomas J. ... Chicago, IL
Ring, Timothy J. ... New York, NY
Ring, Timothy P. ... White Plains, NY
Ring, Timothy R. ... Minneapolis, MN
Ring, William F., Jr. ... Deerfield Beach, FL
Ring, William P. ... Flagstaff, AZ
Ringe, Frederick L. ... Pocatello, ID
Ringe, Thomas B. K., III
Philadelphia, PA
Ringeisen, Wayne W. ... Pittsburgh, PA
Ringel, Andrew D. ... Denver, CO
Ringel, Benjamin O. ... New York, NY
Ringel, Claire Y. ... Mount Laurel, NJ
Ringel, Cynthia E. ... Newark, NJ
Ringel, Dean ... New York, NY
Ringel, Douglas E. ... New York, NY
Ringel, Fred B. ... New York, NY
Ringel, Fred M. ... Jacksonville, FL
Ringel, Jay B. ... New York, NY
Ringel, Jed ... Westport, CT
Ringel, Jordan E. ... New York, NY
Ringel Law Group, P.C. ... Needham, MA
Ringel, Malcolm H. ... St. Michaels, MD
Ringel, Malcolm H., P.C. ... St. Michaels, MD
Ringel, Maurice J. ... Needham, MA
Ringel, Melissa B. ... New York, NY
Ringel, Paul ... Brookline, MA
Ringel, Robert J. ... Cleveland, OH
Ringel, Ronald P. ... Coeur d'Alene, ID
Ringel, Stuart A. ... Chicago, IL
Ringel, Susannah Z. ... New York, NY
Ringel, Thomas ... Miami, FL
Ringel, Valerie D. ... New York, NY
Ringelberg, Jon H. ... Clare, MI
Ringelheim, Laura Beth ... New York, NY
Ringell, Richard H. ... Washington, DC
Ringelman, David J. ... Denver, CO
Ringelspaugh, Keith A. ... St. Petersburg, FL
Ringelspaugh, Keith A., P.A.
St. Petersburg, FL
Ringelstein, David B., II ... Birmingham, AL
Ringenbach, Laura A. ... Cincinnati, OH
Ringenberg, James E. ... Fort Collins, CO
Ringer, Bill D. ... Stockton, CA
Ringer & Bobo ... Brandon, MS
Florence, MS
Ringer, Charles E. ... Canton, OH
Salem, OH
Ringer, Darrell (Dan) ... Morgantown, WV
Ringer, David ... Florence, MS
Ringer, Edwin F. ... Minneapolis, MN
Ringer, Frank M. ... Oklahoma City, OK
Ringer, G. David ... Dallas, TX
Ringer, Geoffrey D. ... Orlando, FL
Ringer & Henry, P.A. ... Orlando, FL
Ringer, James M. ... New York, NY
Ringer, John Wm. ... Dexter, MO
Ringer, Jules J. ... New York, NY
Ringer, Rebecca S. ... Seattle, WA
Ringer, Robert J., Jr. ... Waterville, ME
Ringer, Steven
Commodity Futures Trading Commission,
Division of Enforcement, GV
Ringer, Thomas Mdodana ... Durham, NC
Ringer, Wayne ... Norfolk, VA
Ringer, William F. ... Kansas City, MO
Ringers, Andrew L. ... Orlando, FL
Ringers, Andrew L., Jr. ... Fort Myers, FL
Ringers, Annette Lynne ... Orlando, FL
Ringers, Thomas J. ... Laguna Beach, CA
Ringert Clark ... Hammett, ID
Boise, ID
Ringert, William F. ... Boise, ID
Hammett, ID
Ringes, Mark J. ... Somers, NY
Ringgenberg, Beth ... Madison, WI
Ringgenberg, Dennis R. ... Sioux City, IA
Ringgold, Kathryn E. ... San Francisco, CA
Ringgold, Wm. ... Manhattan Beach, CA
Ringham, William P. ... St. Paul, MN
Ringhand, Lori A. ... Madison, WI
Ringhausen, Jacklyn L. ... Atlanta, GA
Ringhausen, John C.
General Services Administration,
Office of Regional Counsel, GV
Ringhausen, Richard J. ... Jerseyville, IL
Ringhofer, Richard A. ... St. Louis, MO
Ringhoff, Stephen ... Modesto, CA
Ringholm, Sally ... Forest Grove, OR

Ringkamp, Stephen H. ..... St. Louis, MO
Ringland, Robert P. ..... Batavia, OH
Ringle, James W. ..... Buffalo, NY
Ringle, Leonard R. ..... Los Angeles, CA
Ringle, Phil H., Jr. ..... Oregon City, OR
Ringle, Richard ..... Newark, NJ
Ringle, Sharon J. ..... New York, NY
Ringle, Gary V. ..... Tempe, AZ
Ringler, Jerome L. ..... Santa Monica, CA
Ringler, Kim D. ..... Hackensack, NJ
Ringler, Leonard E. ..... Newport News, VA
Ringler, Michael S. ..... Palo Alto, CA
Ringler, Phyllis J. ..... Baltimore, MD
Ringler, Susan Moss ..... Baltimore, MD
Ringler, V. Lee ..... Augusta, GA
Ringo, Michelle A. ..... Silver Spring, MD
Ringo, Robert G. ..... Corvallis, OR
Ringo, Stuber, Ensor & Hadlock, P.C.
Corvallis, OR
Ringo, Wesley L. ..... St. Louis, MO
Ringold, A. F. ..... Oklahoma City, OK
Tulsa, OK
Ringold, David A. ..... New Haven, CT
Ringold, Leslie Beth ..... Los Angeles, CA
Ringold, Solie M. ..... Seattle, WA
Ringold, Steven M. ..... Seattle, WA
Ringquist, Judy P. ..... San Diego, CA
Ringquist, Randall Scott ..... Fairmont, MN
Ringrose, John G. ..... Utica, NY
Rings, Kevin A. ..... Parkersburg, WV
Rings, Randall ..... Cedar Rapids, IA
Ringsak, Marnell ..... Bismarck, ND
Ringsmuth, Peter D. ..... Fort Myers, FL
Ringsred, Karen J. ..... St. Paul, MN
Ringsred, Ted K. ..... St. Paul, MN
Ringstad, Kenneth P., Law Offices of
Fairbanks, AK
Ringstad, Todd C. ..... Irvine, CA
Ringstrom, Bruce N. ..... Moorhead, MN
Ringuet Daniels & Collier, A Professional Law Corporation ..... Jennings, LA
Lafayette, LA
Ringuet, Reginald J. ..... Jennings, LA
Lafayette, LA
Ringus, Kevin G. ..... Fircrest, WA
Ringus, Kevin G., P.S. ..... Fircrest, WA
Ringwald, Daniel Lawrence ..... St. Louis, MO
Ringwald, Rosemary L. ..... Los Angeles, CA
Ringwald, Siegfried C. ..... Artesia, CA
Ringwalt, Mary V. ..... New Bern, NC
Ringwood, David K. ..... Los Angeles, CA
Ringwood, H. Burt ..... Salt Lake City, UT
Ringwood, Irene L. ..... Washington, DC
Ringwood, Michael P. ..... Syracuse, NY
Ringwood, Richard S. ..... Binghamton, NY
Ringwood, Stephen B. ..... Orinda, CA
Rini, Alice Gertrude ..... Highland Heights, KY
Rini, Charles A., Jr. ..... Fairview Park, OH
Rini, Coran & Lancellotta, P.C.
Washington, DC
Rini, Donnell M. .....
United States Tax Court, GV
Rini, Gusty A. ..... Cleveland, OH
Rini, Joseph L. ..... New Haven, CT
Rini, Mary Ann O. ..... Cleveland, OH
Rini, Michele C. ..... Hillsboro, OR
Rini, Nicholas C. ..... Los Angeles, CA
Rini, Robert J. ..... Washington, DC
Rini, William T. ..... Cleveland, OH
Rinicella, Randy D. ..... Cleveland, OH
Rinier, Alton L. ..... Canton, OH
Rink, Andrew M. ..... Rock Island, IL
Rink, Donald E. ..... Howell, MI
Rink, Harold H. ..... Southbury, CT
Rink, Joseph J. ..... Philadelphia, PA
Rink, Lawrence J. ..... Granada Hills, CA
Rink, Les ..... Beaverton, OR
Rink, Paul E. ..... Rock Island, IL
Rink, Paul W. ..... Chicago, IL
Rink, Richard ..... Paradise Valley, AZ
Rink, Robert P. ..... Cleveland, OH
Rink, Thomas C. ..... Cincinnati, OH
Rink, Traci L. ..... Huntington Woods, MI
Rinka, Patrick K. ..... Orlando, FL
Rinke - Noonan ..... St. Cloud, MN
Rinke, O. Michael ..... Minneapolis, MN
Rinke, Orrin V. ..... St. Cloud, MN
Rinke, W. Joel ..... Little Rock, AR
Rinkel, Michael J. ..... Southfield, MI
Rinkenberger, Gwenn R. ..... Valparaiso, IN
Rinker, Andrew, Jr. ..... New Orleans, LA
Rinker, Belinda D. ..... Clay Center, NE
Rinker, Bruce G. ..... Cleveland, OH
Rinker, Dana R. ..... Fairfax, VA
Rinker Law Office ..... Clay Center, NE
Rinker, Lynn D. ..... Encino, CA
Rinkerman, Gary J. ..... Washington, DC
Rinko, Paul J. ..... Oneida, NY
Rinks, Kathleen Y. ..... Vernonia, OR
Rin-Laures, Li-Hsien ..... Chicago, IL
Rinn, Andrew J. ..... Carroll, IA
Rinn, Bart ..... Chicago, IL
Rinn, Christine Clements
Washington, DC
Rinn, Eugene P. ..... Walnut Creek, CA
Rinn, Gregory T. ..... Rockville Centre, NY
Rinn, Leslie C. ..... Tulsa, OK
Rinn, Louise A. ..... Omaha, NE
Rinn, Michael G. ..... Baltimore, MD
Rinn, Michael G. ..... Cockeysville, MD
Rinn, R. Scott ..... Cold Spring, MN
Rinn, Richard A. ..... Sandusky, MI
Rinne, Jeffrey M. ..... Kansas City, MO
Rinne, Mary Johns ..... Ann Arbor, MI
Rinne, Susan R. ..... Winston-Salem, NC
Rinner, Margaret E. ..... Martinez, CA
Rinner, Richard D. ..... Heathrow, FL
Rinner, Ronald R. ..... Largo, FL

Rinos, Dimitrios C., (A Professional Corporation) ..... Santa Ana, CA
Rinos, Shephard & Martin ..... Santa Ana, CA
Rinquest, Randall A. ..... Arvada, CO
Rinsky, Arthur C. ..... Palo Alto, CA
Rinsky, Joel C. ..... Livingston, NJ
Rinsler, Steven H ..... New York, NY
Rinta, Keith D. ..... Minneapolis, MN
Rintala, Pamela A. ..... Warren, OH
Rintala, Smoot, Jaenicke & Rees
Los Angeles, CA
Rintala, William T. ..... Los Angeles, CA
Rintamaki, John M. ..... Dearborn, MI
Rintelman, Donald B. ..... Milwaukee, WI
Rintels, Jonathan B., Jr. ..... Keswick, VA
Rintoul, David S. ..... West Hartford, CT
Rintoul, John W.
Research Triangle Park, NC
Rintoul, Liana Margaret ..... Chicago, IL
Rintoul, William Mallory ..... Old Lyme, CT
Rinzel, Daniel F. ..... Washington, DC
Fairfax, VA
Rinzler, James K. ..... New York, NY
Rinzler, Kenneth ..... Washington, DC
Rinzler, Milton S. ..... New York, NY
Rio, Linda M. ..... Hinsdale, IL
Rio, Robert ..... Clearwater, FL
Rio, S. Richard, Jr. ..... Alexandria, VA
Rio, Vincent J., III ..... Tallahassee, FL
Rioja, Amalia S. ..... Chicago, IL
Riojas, Antonio F., Jr. ..... Tucson, AZ
Riojas, David ..... Eagle Pass, TX
Riojas, Robert Eric ..... El Paso, TX
Riola, Jill Sarnoff ..... Cleveland, OH
Riolo, Andrew Manuel ..... Charlotte, NC
Riolo, Greg A. ..... White Plains, NY
Rion, James H., Jr. ..... Charleston, SC
Rion, James P. ..... Dayton, OH
Rion, James W. ..... Columbia, SC
Rion, John H. ..... Dayton, OH
Rion, Jon P. ..... Dayton, OH
Rion, Jon Paul ..... Dayton, OH
Rion, Rion & Rion, L.P.A. Inc.
Dayton, OH
Riondino, Marc A. ..... Camden, NJ
Riopel, Mark D. ..... Charlotte, NC
Riopelle, Brian C. ..... Richmond, VA
Riopelle, Christopher James ..... Detroit, MI
Riopelle, Roland G. ..... New York, NY
Riordan, Angela S. ..... Trumbull, CT
Riordan, Anne M. ..... Chicago, IL
Riordan, Beverly S. ..... Columbia, MO
Riordan, Brian J. ..... Chicago, IL
Riordan, Brian K. ..... Milwaukee, WI
Riordan, Christopher P. ..... Milwaukee, WI
Riordan, Cornelius F. ..... Chicago, IL
Riordan, Crivello, Carlson, Mentkowski & Steeves, S.C. ..... Milwaukee, WI
Riordan, Daniel T. ..... Department of Justice, Tax Division, GV
Riordan, Danielle H. ..... Glendale, AZ
Riordan, Dashiell & Donnelly, Ltd.
Chicago, IL
Riordan, David W. ..... Williamsburg, VA
Riordan, Deborah Truby ..... Little Rock, AR
Riordan, Denis J. ..... Bethel, CT
Riordan, Eileen B. ..... Baltimore, MD
Riordan, Eugene J. ..... Boulder, CO
Riordan, Eugene J. ..... New York, NY
Riordan, Henry J. ..... Department of Justice, Tax Division, GV
Riordan, Henry P. ..... New York, NY
Riordan, J. Michael ..... Florham Park, NJ
New York, NY
Riordan, James B. ..... Los Angeles, CA
Riordan, Joan M. ..... Denver, CO
Riordan, Joan Marie ..... Chicago, IL
Riordan, John ..... San Francisco, CA
Riordan, John B. ..... Mineola, NY
Riordan, John D. ..... Abington, MA
Riordan, John D. ..... Boston, MA
Riordan, John H., Jr. ..... Pittsburgh, PA
Riordan, John L., Jr. ..... Livingston, NJ
Riordan, John P., Jr. ..... Brockton, MA
Riordan, John Patrick ..... Greenville, SC
Riordan, Kevin B. ..... Toms River, NJ
Riordan, Kevin J. ..... Washington, DC
Riordan, Larson, Bruckert & Moore
Chicago, IL
Riordan, Lester E., III ..... Salem, MA
Riordan, Lori Molander ..... Bellevue, WA
Riordan, Mary J. ..... Chicago, IL
Riordan, Marybeth ..... New York, NY
Riordan, Matthew ..... New York, NY
Riordan, Maureen S. ..... Mineola, NY
Riordan & McKinzie, A Professional Law Corporation ..... Costa Mesa, CA
Los Angeles, CA
Westlake Village, CA
Riordan, Megan Kennedy ..... Southfield, MI
Riordan, Michael J. ..... Chicago, IL
Riordan, Michael Patrick ..... Beverly, MA
Riordan, Michael T. ..... Green Bay, WI
Riordan, Molly Bridget ..... Chicago, IL
Riordan, Nathan ..... Minneapolis, MN
Riordan, Noah W. ..... New York, NY
Riordan, P. James ..... Bridgehampton, NY
Riordan, Paul M. ..... Rochester, NY
Riordan, R. Patrick ..... Topeka, KS
Riordan, Ray J. ..... Madison, WI
Riordan, Retta M. ..... Kenilworth, NJ
Riordan, Richard J. ..... Los Angeles, CA
Riordan, Richard J. ..... Chicago, IL
Riordan & Robbins ..... Chicago, IL
Riordan, Robert A., Jr. ..... Springfield, MA
Riordan, Robert J. ..... Pleasanton, CA
Riordan, Robert J. ..... San Ramon, CA
Riordan, Robert P. ..... Atlanta, GA

Riordan, Robert W. ..... Pittsburgh, PA
Riordan, Sarah Steele ..... Toledo, OH
Riordan, Theodore F. ..... Boston, MA
Riordan, Thomas J. ..... Princeton, NJ
Riordan, Thomas J. ..... New Hartford, NY
Riordan, Thomas L. ..... Sacramento, CA
Riordan, Thomas M. ..... Los Angeles, CA
Riordan, Thomas P. ..... Chicago, IL
Riordan, Timothy J. ..... Chicago, IL
Riordan, Timothy P. ..... Rocky River, OH
Riordan, Timothy S. ..... Raleigh, NC
Riordan, William F. ..... Albuquerque, NM
Riordon, Judith Gibbons ..... College Park, MD
Riordon, Richard P. ..... Lexington, MI
Rios, Angela Fiorentino ..... San Diego, CA
Rios, Angelo ..... New York, NY
Rios, Arturo M. ..... St. Petersburg, FL
Rios & Bain, A Prof. Corp. ..... Houston, TX
Rios, Blaire Rose ..... Portland, OR
Rios, Daniel G. ..... McAllen, TX
Rios, Daniel P. ..... Sacramento, CA
Rios, David ..... Boston, MA
Rios, Delilah Knox, Attorney At Law
Diamond Bar, CA
Rios, Edgar G. ..... Vienna, VA
Rios, Edward E. ..... Pasadena, CA
Rios, George ..... San Jose, CA
Rios, Hernan, Jr. ..... San Juan, PR
Rios, Jason E. ..... Sacramento, CA
Rios, Javier Demetrio ..... San Jose, CA
Rios, Jerry L. ..... Houston, TX
Rios, Jose R. ..... New York, NY
Rios, Manuel Armando ..... San Diego, CA
Rios, Modesto ..... Indio, CA
Rios, Paul A. ..... Minneapolis, MN
Rios, Rafael ..... Oak Brook, IL
Rios, Rafael, III ..... Napa, CA
Rios, Ralph R. ..... El Monte, CA
Rios, Randall A. ..... Houston, TX
Rios, Raul, P.C., Law Offices of
San Antonio, TX
Rios, Rene Henry de los ..... Coral Gables, FL
Rios, Reuben R. ..... Dallas, TX
Rios, Ronald R. ..... Tustin, CA
Rios, Ruben ..... Dallas, TX
Rios, Santiago ..... Oak Brook, IL
Rios, Stacy M. ..... Madison, WI
Rios, Stephen M. ..... San Juan Capistrano, CA
Rios-Gautier, Carlos R., Law Offices of
San Juan, PR
Rios Marques, Arturo ..... Arecibo, PR
Rios Mendez, Amelio ..... San Juan, PR
Ríos Méndez, Edgar ..... San Juan, PR
Ríos-Ríos, José ..... San Juan, PR
Ríos-Rivera, Francisco ..... San Juan, PR
Rios Rosario, Luz M. ..... San Juan, PR
Rioth, Lenard ..... Colorado Springs, CO
Riotte, Christina L. ..... Greensboro, NC
Riotto, Sharon ..... Department of Justice, Executive Office for Immigration Review, GV
Riou, Pierre ..... Austin, TX
Rioux, Denise M. ..... New Haven, CT
Rioux, Michele L. ..... New Bedford, MA
Ripa, Glenn ..... New York, NY
Ripa, Samuel W. ..... Holyoke, MA
Ripani, Joseph A., Jr. ..... Citrus Heights, CA
Ripani, Michael N. ..... Chicago, IL
Ripani, Philip J. ..... Indianapolis, IN
Ripans, Jon M. ..... Atlanta, GA
Ripepe, Suzette D. ..... Grosse Pointe, MI
Riper, John S. ..... Seattle, WA
Riper, Joseph G. ..... Kennett Square, PA
Ripes, Michael J. ..... Chicago, IL
Ripin, Peter M. ..... New York, NY
Ripin, Robert A. ..... New York, NY
Ripka, Alan S., P.C. ..... New York, NY
Ripka, Alan Seth ..... New York, NY
Ripko, Cindy ..... Newark, OH
Ripley, Alfred Thomas ..... Durham, NC
Ripley, Arthur, Jr. ..... Pago Pago, TT
Ripley, Audrey Y. ..... Los Angeles, CA
Ripley, Barbara G. ..... Montpelier, VT
Ripley, Brenton M. ..... Kennewick, WA
Ripley, Brian A. ..... San Francisco, CA
Ripley, Earl M. ..... San Francisco, CA
Ripley, Edward L. ..... Houston, TX
Ripley, George W., II ..... Shelton, CT
Ripley, George W., III ..... Hartford, CT
Ripley, James H. ..... Sevierville, TN
Ripley, Jeanne M. ..... Baltimore, MD
Ripley, Joseph M., Jr. ..... Jacksonville, FL
Ripley, Joseph M., Jr., P.A. ..... Jacksonville, FL
Ripley, Judith G. ..... Indianapolis, IN
Ripley, Karen A. ..... Milwaukee, WI
Ripley, Larry D. ..... Boise, ID
Ripley, Lewis H., Jr. ..... Ebensburg, PA
Ripley, Marvin G. ..... Sterling, IL
Ripley, Michael E. ..... San Diego, CA
Ripley, Michael O. ..... Jacksboro, TN
Ripley, Richard A. ..... Washington, DC
Ripley, Robert F. ..... Newark, NJ
Ripley, Robert F., Jr. ..... Grafton, VA
Ripley, Ronald L. ..... Oklahoma City, OK
Ripley, Ronald S. ..... Tacoma, WA
Ripley, Scott R. ..... Watseka, IL
Ripley, Shirley M. ..... Baltimore, MD
Ripley, Terry Lensgraf
Oklahoma City, OK
Ripley, Thomas M. ..... Richland, MI
Ripoli, Christine M. ..... Schaumburg, IL
Riposanu, Ann M. ..... New York, NY
Riposanu, Pamfil A. ..... New York, NY
Riposta, Anthony J. ..... Hackensack, NJ
North Arlington, NJ
Riposta & Reilly, P.C. ..... North Arlington, NJ
Ripp, Amanda J. ..... Chicago, IL
Ripp, Marc Leonard ..... Florham Park, NJ

Ripp, Marvin P. ..... Madison, WI
Ripp, Melvin G., Jr. ..... Gretna, LA
Ripp, Michael H., Jr. ..... Austin, TX
Ripp, Michael P. ..... Phoenix, AZ
Ripp, Thomas R. ..... Wheat Ridge, CO
Ripp, Thomas R. ..... New York, NY
Ripp, William G. ..... Melville, NY
Rippa, Larissa A. ..... New York, NY
Rippa, Vincent ..... Purchase, NY
Rippamonti, Russell N. ..... Dallas, TX
Rippas, Walter J. ..... Lafayette, LA
Rippe, Hammell & Murphy ..... Caledonia, MN
La Crescent, MN
Spring Grove, MN
Rippe, John H. ..... Caledonia, MN
Rippe, Lawrence C. ..... Springfield, IL
Rippe, Robert D., Jr. ..... Irving, TX
Rippee, Stephanie M. ..... Jackson, MS
Rippel, David D. ..... Dallas, TX
Rippel, George E., Jr. ..... Baltimore, MD
Rippel, Paul B. ..... Idaho Falls, ID
Rippen, Eugene ..... Atascadero, CA
Ripper, Angela A. ..... Chattanooga, TN
Ripper, Daniel J. ..... Chattanooga, TN
Ripper, James F. ..... Rocky Hill, CT
Ripper, Joanne S. ..... Peoria, IL
Ripperger, Brian L. ..... St. Paul, MN
Ripperger, James ..... Pueblo, CO
Ripperger, Nancy L. ..... Jefferson City, MO
Ripperger, Rhonda L. McNutt
Oklahoma City, OK
Rippert, Stephan K. ..... New York, NY
Rippes, Carlos M. ..... Hialeah, FL
Rippetoe, Elizabeth L. ..... Charlotte, NC
Rippetoe, Gregory L. ..... Santa Ana, CA
Rippey, Edward Holden ..... Washington, DC
Rippey, Joseph S. ..... Rochester, NY
Rippey, Susan E. ..... Bryn Mawr, PA
Philadelphia, PA
Rippie, E. Glenn ..... Chicago, IL
Rippie, Eloise L. ..... Ames, IA
Rippin, Charles ..... Princeton, NJ
Rippin, Joseph P., III ..... Northbrook, IL
Ripple, Albert A. ..... Lathrup Village, MI
Ripple, John J. ..... Spokane, WA
Ripple, Kenneth F. ..... South Bend, IN
Ripple, Raymond M. ..... Wilmington, DE
Ripple, Richard C. ..... Carthage, IL
Rippley, John M. ..... Lakewood, CO
Rippley, P. Jaye ..... Casper, WY
Ripplinger, George, & Associates
Belleville, IL
St. Louis, MO
Ripplinger, George R., Jr. ..... Belleville, IL
Rippner, Schwartz & Carlin
Cleveland, OH
Rippo, Victor A. ..... Niagara Falls, NY
Rippon, Michelle ..... Asheville, NC
Rippon, Thomas R. ..... Mifflinburg, PA
Ripps, Judith A. ..... Boca Raton, FL
Ripps, Leonard ..... Englewood, CO
Rippy, Conrad M. ..... New York, NY
Rippy, Elizabeth P. ..... Austin, TX
Rippy, Felix O'Neill ..... Round Rock, TX
Rippy, G. Crawford, III ..... Albemarle, NC
Rippy, Jack ..... Corona Del Mar, CA
Rippy, John T. ..... Louisville, KY
Rippy, Lisa A. ..... Knoxville, TN
Rippy, Roger A. ..... Houston, TX
Rippy, Tina L. ..... Whittier, CA
Rippy & Whitlow, L.L.P.
Round Rock, TX
Rips, Martin A. ..... Los Angeles, CA
Rips, Matthew A. ..... Culver City, CA
Ripsom, David B. ..... Wilmington, DE
Ripsteen, Jack B. ..... Berkeley, CA
Ripstra, Steven E. ..... Jasper, IN
Ripton, James C. ..... Massapequa, NY
Ripullone, Shirley A. ..... New York, NY
Ripy, Thomas B. ..... Library of Congress, Congressional Research Service, GV
Riquelmy, Elaine ..... Houston, TX
RiRie, James A., Chtd. ..... Las Vegas, NV
RiRie & Kurth ..... Las Vegas, NV
Ririe, Verna B. ..... Washington, DC
Ris, Cynthia Nitz ..... Cincinnati, OH
Ris, David R. ..... Coquille, OR
Ris, Elena L. ..... Atlanta, GA
Ris, William K. ..... Denver, CO
Risacher, Martin E. ..... Noblesville, IN
Risavi, Diana Cook ..... Heathsville, VA
Risavy, Thomas William ..... Miami, FL
Risberg, John F. ..... Fenton, MO
Risberg, Perry A. ..... Hayward, WI
Risberg, Robert L., Jr. ..... Menlo Park, CA
Risbrough, Robert C. ..... Santa Ana, CA
RisCassi and Davis, P.C. ..... Hartford, CT
RisCassi, Louis ..... West Hartford, CT
RisCassi, Richard N. ..... Hartford, CT
Risch, Carl C. ..... Carlisle, PA
Risch, Charles J. ..... Chicago, IL
Risch, Daniel J. ..... Louisville, KY
Risch, Dennis S. ..... Cincinnati, OH
Risch, Goss & Insinger ..... Boise, ID
Nampa, ID
Risch, Jacqueline ..... New Bedford, MA
Risch, James E. ..... Boise, ID
Risch, James O. ..... Louisville, KY
Risch, Jeffrey A. ..... Tulsa, OK
Risch, Melvin ..... St. Louis, MO
Risch, Michael ..... Palo Alto, CA
Risch, Patrick J. ..... Tampa, FL
Risch, Robert C., Jr. ..... Milwaukee, WI
Risch, Robert D. ..... Indianapolis, IN
Risch, Robert N. ..... Wilmington, MA
Rischard, Denis P. ..... Edmond, OK
Rischitelli, D. Gary ..... Ellicott City, MD

Rischman, Suzanne Elaine
San Francisco, CA
Rischmiller, Knippel & Aronson
Minneapolis, MN
Rischmiller, Reid G. ... Minneapolis, MN
Risden, Arthur F. ... Haddonfield, NJ
Risdon, Ronald B. ... New York, NY
Risdon, William A., II ... Kalamazoo, MI
Riseberg, Michael D. ... Boston, MA
Riseberg, Richard J. ... Rockville, MD
Riseborough, George E. ... Waukegan, IL
Riseborough, John C. ... Spokane, WA
Risebrow, Albert E. ... Hauppauge, NY
Riseley, Nancy T. ... Kingston, NY
Riseley, Richard F. ... Kingston, NY
Riseley, Salzmann & Ball ... Kingston, NY
Riseling & Associates, A Professional
Corporation ... Bartlesville, OK
Tulsa, OK
Riseling, Jerry L. ... Columbus, OH
Riseling, Ted M. ... Bartlesville, OK
Tulsa, OK
Riselli, Michael J. ... Washington, DC
Riselli & Pressler, P.C. ... Washington, DC
Riseman, Carl M. ... Lapeer, MI
Riseman, Susan G. ... Boston, MA
Risen, Douglas M. ... Philadelphia, PA
Risenhoover, Jack, II ... Delray Beach, FL
Riser, Christopher M. ... Highlands, NC
Riser, Elizabeth Mayer ... Highlands, NC
Risey, Suzanne M. ... New Orleans, LA
Rish, Gibson & Jones, P.A. ... Port St. Joe, FL
Rish, William J. ... Port St. Joe, FL
Risha, Edward E. ... Rawlins, WY
Risha, Elizabeth ... El Segundo, CA
Rishe, Jerrold Elliot ... Northridge, CA
Rishe, Melvin ... Washington, DC
Rishe, Mitchell Elliott ... Santa Monica, CA
Rishel, George Fox ... Springfield, IL
Rishel, James R. ... Columbus, OH
Risher, Eldon Donald, III
Myrtle Beach, SC
Risher, Jeff C. ... Costa Mesa, CA
Risher, John R., Jr. ... Washington, DC
Risher, Julie Ann ... Burlington, NC
Rishling, Steve A. ... Juliaetta, ID
Rishoff, Louise C. ... Woodland Hills, CA
Rishoff, Stephen L. ... Lancaster, CA
Woodland Hills, CA
Rishoi, William M. ... Winter Park, FL
Rishor, Kurt S. ... Butler, PA
Cranberry Township, PA
Rishor Simone ... Butler, PA
Cranberry Township, PA
Rishty, Jacqueline ... Silver Spring, MD
Rishwain, Ben M. ... Lodi, CA
Rishwain, Brian A. ... Los Angeles, CA
Rishwain, David A. ... Stockton, CA
Rishwain and Hastings ... Stockton, CA
Rishwain, James M., Jr. ... Los Angeles, CA
Rishwain, Joseph T., Jr. ... Stockton, CA
Rishwain, Mark B. ... Stockton, CA
Rishwain, Michael T. ... Stockton, CA
Rishwain & Rishwain ... Stockton, CA
Rishwain, Robert J. ... Stockton, CA
Rishwain, Scott D. ... Stockton, CA
Rishwain, Victoria ... Los Angeles, CA
Risi & Assocs. ... Long Island City, NY
Risi, Domenico ... Long Beach, CA
Risi, John A. ... White Plains, NY
Risi, John M. ... Flushing, NY
Risi, Joseph J. ... Long Island City, NY
Risi, Joseph John ... Long Island City, NY
Risi, Mark A. ... Winter Park, FL
Risi, Mark A., P.A. ... Orlando, FL
Winter Park, FL
Risi, Walter ... Dover, NJ
Risik, Philip M. ... Potomac, MD
Risin, Clarence ... Knoxville, TN
Rising, Arnold Joseph, II ... Pine City, MN
Rising, Carol Smith ... Santa Fe, NM
Rising, Gail ... Minneapolis, MN
Rising, Jay B. ... Lansing, MI
Rising, Kent B. ... Dallas, TX
Rising, Mark F. ... Seattle, WA
Rising, Wendy Anne ... Wilmington, DE
Risinger, Bradley M. ... Raleigh, NC
Risinger, D. Michael ... Newark, NJ
Risinger, Marlin, Jr. ... Shreveport, LA
Risjord & James, P.C.
Overland Park, KS
Kansas City, MO
Risjord, John C. ... Overland Park, KS
Risk, Jayne Anderson ... Baltimore, MD
Philadelphia, PA
Risk, Mark A. ... Traverse City, MI
Risk, Mark D. ... New York, NY
Risk, Sharon C. ... Washington, DC
Riske & Arnold, P.C. ... Cheyenne, WY
Riske, Charles W. ... St. Louis, MO
Riske, Don W. ... Cheyenne, WY
Riskedahl, Burt L. ... Bismarck, ND
Risken, Patrick M. ... Spokane, WA
Risker, Frederick L., Jr. ... Stafford, TX
Riskin, Harry J. ... Morristown, NJ
Riskin, Ira D. ... Los Angeles, CA
Riskin & Joseph ... Passaic, NJ
Riskin, Leonard L. ... Columbia, MO
Riskin, Martin R. ... Incline Village, NV
Riskin, Michael E. ... Bethlehem, PA
Riskin, Milton B. ... Bethlehem, PA
Riskin, Philip W. ... Passaic, NJ
Riskin and Riskin ... Bethlehem, PA
Riskin, Stan ... Plantation, FL
Riskin, Steve R. ... Venice, CA
Riskind, Jay S. ... Chicago, IL
Riskind, Miriam J. ... Houston, TX
Riskind, Morris S. ... Eagle Pass, TX

Risko, Carla Heathershaw ... Blair, NE
Risko, Edward W. ... Detroit, MI
Risko, Joseph S. ... Omaha, NE
Risko, Mary Elizabeth ... Denver, CO
Risko, Michael P. ... Detroit, MI
Risko, Paul K. ... New York, NY
Riskowski, Patrick T. ... Omaha, NE
Risku, Daniel M. ... Durham, NC
Risler, Christopher T., P.C. ... St. Louis, MO
Risler, Christopher T. ... St. Louis, MO
Risler, William A. ... Albany, NY
Risley & Associates ... Costa Mesa, CA
Risley, David R. ... Atlanta, GA
Risley, David R. ... Lewiston, ID
Risley, John H. ... Houston, TX
Risley, Kevin F. ... Houston, TX
Risley, Lynn Plimpton ... Jackson, MS
Risley, Michael D. ... Louisville, KY
Risley, Miles ... Victoria, TX
Risley, Robert L. ... Costa Mesa, CA
Risley, Robert L. ... Pasadena, CA
Risley, Scott K. ... Prescott, AZ
Risley, Stephen R. ... Atlanta, GA
Risling, Mary J. ... Arcata, CA
Risman, Clifford J. ... Dallas, TX
Risman, Ina J. ... San Francisco, CA
Risman, Michael B. ... Buffalo, NY
Risman, Richard S. ... Albany, NY
Risman, Robert G. ... Cleveland, OH
Risman, Robt. R. ... Beachwood, OH
Risman, Wm. B. ... Cleveland, OH
Rismiller, Cynthia A. ... Omaha, NE
Rismiller, David, Jr. ... Kansas City, MO
Rismiller, Karen E. ... Pottsville, PA
Risner, Albert H., Jr. ... Dunkirk, MD
Risner, Gerald C. ... Chicago, IL
Risner, Gerald C., P.C. ... Chicago, IL
Risner & Graham ... Tucson, AZ
Risner, Michael T. ... Denver, CO
Risner, Paul E. ... Memphis, TN
Risner, Randy J. ... Fresno, CA
Risner, Rick L. ... Toledo, OH
Risner, William J. ... Tucson, AZ
Risnes, Danny L. ... St. Paul, MN
Riso, Eric J. ... Philadelphia, PA
Riso, Gerard A. ... New York, NY
Riso, Salvatore V. ... New York, NY
Risoldi, Carla V. ... Trenton, NJ
Langhorne, PA
New Hope, PA
Risoleo, Robert Samuel ... New York, NY
Risoli, Wayne A. ... Houston, TX
Rispo, Ronald A. ... Cleveland, OH
Rispoli, James J., Jr. ... New Brunswick, NJ
Rispoli, Robert L. ... Hartford, CT
Rispoli, Vincent S., Jr. ... Paterson, NJ
Rissberger, Patty T. ... Portland, OR
Risse, Annette M. ... Marietta, GA
Risse, Kisti Good ... Merrillville, IN
Risse, Richard H. ... Fairview Heights, IL
Risse, Walter ... Santa Rosa, CA
Risser, Fred A. ... Madison, WI
Risser, Patricia Z. ... Elm Grove, WI
Risser, Rita ... Santa Cruz, CA
Rissetto, Christopher L. ... Washington, DC
Rissetto, Harry A. ... Washington, DC
Rissi, Bruce P. ... Muskegon, MI
Rissier, J. Warren ... Los Angeles, CA
Rissland, Karl R. ... Streetsboro, OH
Rissler, Donald J. ... Riverton, WY
Rissler, Robert L.
Shenandoah Junction, WV
Rissling, R. Eric ... Sumter, SC
Rissman, Burton R., (P.C.) ... Chicago, IL
Rissman, Francine G. ... Chicago, IL
Rissman, Glenn M. ... Fort Lauderdale, FL
Rissman, Harold A. ... De Kalb, IL
Rissman, Jena E. ... Miami, FL
Rissman, John A. ... Boston, MA
Rissman, Lawrence E. ... Chicago, IL
Rissman, Michael P. ... Chicago, IL
Rissman, Steven A. ... Orlando, FL
Rissman, Steven B. ... New York, NY
Rissman, Steven E. ... Chicago, IL
Rissman, Stuart E. ... Encino, CA
Rissman, Thomas W. ... Chicago, IL
Rissman, Weisberg, Barrett, Hurt, Donahue & McLain, P.A. ... Orlando, FL
Tampa, FL
Vero Beach, FL
Rissmiller, Kent J. ... Worcester, MA
Risso, Ann M. ... Boston, MA
Risso, Jack E. ... San Jose, CA
Rist, Beth V. ... Loudonville, NY
Rist, Dianne E. ... Chicago, IL
Rist, John F., III ... Beckley, WV
Rist, Leslie V. ... Kansas City, MO
Rist, Michael D. ... Dallas, TX
Rist, Steven L. ... Kansas City, MO
Rist, William B. ... Beatrice, NE
Ristaino, David C. ... Fort Lauderdale, FL
Ristaino, Edward Louis ... Miami, FL
Ristaneo, Robert F. ... Lexington, KY
Ristanovic, Zorka ... Northbrook, IL
Ristas, L. James ... Hartford, CT
Ristau, Bruno A. ... Washington, DC
Ristau, Bruno A., P.L.L.C., Law Offices of
Washington, DC
Ristau, Emily Pettis ... Orange, CA
Ristau, Kenneth E., Jr. ... Irvine, CA
Ristau, Kevin T. ... Bethesda, MD
Ristau, Mark D. ... St. Paul, MN
Ristau, Mark M. ... Warren, PA
Ristau & McKeirnan ... Warren, PA
Ristau, Timothy P. ... Cleveland, OH
Ristig, Lynn E. ... Seattle, WA
Ristine, Barbara Buckley ... Carson City, NV
Ristine, Richard O. ... Crawfordsville, IN

Ristine, Thomas H. ... Indianapolis, IN
Ristino, Laurie Ann
Department of Agriculture,
Office of the General Counsel, GV
Ristkok, Tuuli-Ann ... New York, NY
Ristoff, David R. ... Tampa, FL
Ristow, Barbara L. ... Chicago, IL
Ristow, Philip C. ... Jefferson, WI
Ristuben, Karen R. ... Boston, MA
Ristvedt, Steven K., Law Offices of
Independence, IA
Ristvey, Michael, Jr. ... Hermitage, PA
Rita, Elizabeth R. ... Denver, CO
Rita, George T. ... Alexandria, VA
Rita, Matthew J. ... Denver, CO
Rita, William J. ... New York, NY
Ritardi, Steven F. ... Roseland, NJ
Ritch, Bevin G. ... Gainesville, FL
Ritch, Christine P. ... Westborough, MA
Ritch, Joe H. ... Huntsville, AL
Ritch, John B. ... Kissimmee, FL
Ritch, R. Franklin ... Gainesville, FL
Ritch, R. Franklin, P.A. ... Gainesville, FL
Ritch, Scott A. ... Providence, RI
Ritchel, Raymond B., Jr. ... Jamaica, NY
Ritcheson, Dollahite & Lauffer, A Professional Corporation ... Tyler, TX
Ritcheson, Scott A. ... Tyler, TX
Ritcheson, Steven W. ... Palo Alto, CA
Ritchey, Albert E. ... Birmingham, AL
Ritchey, Brian J. ... Birmingham, AL
Ritchey, C. Michael ... St. Petersburg, FL
Ritchey, Catherine E. ... Palo Alto, CA
Ritchey, Craig S. ... Palo Alto, CA
Ritchey, Daniel G. ... Blytheville, AR
Ritchey, David A. ... West Yellowstone, MT
Ritchey, David C. ... San Francisco, CA
Ritchey, Ferris S., III ... Birmingham, AL
Ritchey, Ferris S., Jr. ... Birmingham, AL
Ritchey Fisher Whitman & Klein, A Professional Corporation ... Palo Alto, CA
Ritchey, Gary H. ... Palo Alto, CA
Ritchey, George M. ... Birmingham, AL
Ritchey, Glenn A., Jr. ... Modesto, CA
Ritchey, Gregory S. ... Birmingham, AL
Ritchey, Harry L. ... St. Louis, MO
Ritchey, Jacob M. ... Canton, MS
Ritchey, James L. ... Sarasota, FL
Ritchey, James M. ... Sacramento, CA
Ritchey, James M. ... Santa Cruz, CA
Ritchey, Jed S. ... San Jose, CA
Ritchey, Joe B. ... Santa Cruz, CA
Ritchey, John J. ... Cleveland, OH
Ritchey, John L., III ... Santa Cruz, CA
Ritchey, Joseph T. ... Birmingham, AL
Ritchey, Katherine Salo
San Francisco, CA
Ritchey, Kevin L. ... Memphis, TN
Ritchey, Lewis E. ... Little Rock, AR
Ritchey, Michael G. ... Westminster, MD
Ritchey, Michael L. ... Portland, OR
Ritchey, Patrick W. ... Pittsburgh, PA
Ritchey & Ritchey, P.A. ... Birmingham, AL
Ritchey, Robert M. ... Montgomery, AL
Ritchey, Stephen S. ... Atlanta, GA
Ritchey, Steven M. ... St. Louis, MO
Ritchey-Andrews, Diane ... San Diego, CA
Ritchie, Alan S. ... Cleveland, OH
Ritchie, Albert ... Chicago, IL
Ritchie, Alexander B. ... Southfield, MI
Ritchie, Alice Saulnier ... Centreville, MD
Ritchie, Allen A. ... Mobile, AL
Ritchie, Ann Marie ... Philadelphia, PA
Ritchie, Barbara J. ... Juneau, AK
Ritchie, Bernard S., Jr. ... Louisville, KY
Ritchie, Brian T. ... Seattle, WA
Ritchie, Carol J. ... Santa Fe, NM
Ritchie, Carolyn ... Dallas, TX
Ritchie, Charles A., Jr. ... Lebanon, PA
Ritchie, Christopher D.
Fort Lauderdale, FL
Ritchie, Clinton H., Jr. ... Birmingham, AL
Ritchie, Corwin ... Storm Lake, IA
Ritchie, Craig A. ... Port Angeles, WA
Ritchie, Craig D. ... St. Joseph, MO
Ritchie, D. Alexander ... Dallas, TX
Ritchie, David A. ... Lake Charles, LA
Ritchie, David B. ... San Jose, CA
Ritchie, David J. ... Basking Ridge, NJ
Ritchie, David M. ... Los Angeles, CA
Ritchie, Diane ... San Jose, CA
Ritchie, Douglas V. ... Las Vegas, NV
Ritchie, Fels & Dillard, P.C.
Knoxville, TN
Ritchie, Frederick M. ... Southfield, MI
Ritchie, Gary L. ... San Diego, CA
Ritchie, George Faulkner, IV
Baltimore, MD
Ritchie & Glass ... Houston, TX
Ritchie, Graham A. ... Los Angeles, CA
Ritchie, Harold A. ... Duarte, CA
Ritchie, Henry G., Jr. ... Taft, TX
Ritchie, Herb H. ... Houston, TX
Ritchie, Hugh J. ... Los Angeles, CA
Ritchie, Jack ... Amarillo, TX
Ritchie, James B. ... Atlanta, GA
Ritchie, James B., A Professional Corporation ... Atlanta, GA
Ritchie, James C. ... Albuquerque, NM
Ritchie, James E. ... North Canton, OH
Ritchie, James H., Jr. ... Dinwiddie, VA
Ritchie, James R. ... San Francisco, CA
Ritchie, Jan M. ... Philadelphia, PA
Ritchie, Jeffrey ... Amana, IA
Ritchie, Jill E. ... Pittsburgh, PA
Ritchie, John A. ... Washington, DC
Ritchie, John E. ... San Francisco, CA
Ritchie, John, Jr. ... Richmond, VA

Ritchie, John M. ... Pekin, IL
Ritchie, John P. ... Mineral Wells, TX
Ritchie, John S. ... Twin Falls, ID
Ritchie, John W. ... New York, NY
Ritchie & Johnson, PLLC ... Knoxville, TN
Ritchie, K. Ellis ... Pryor, OK
Ritchie, Katherine W. ... Houston, TX
Ritchie, Kathryn L. ... Tampa, FL
Ritchie, Kellie Wingate ... St. Joseph, MO
Ritchie, K. Ellis, P.C. ... Pryor, OK
Ritchie, Kenneth A. ... Knoxville, TN
Ritchie, Kimberly S. ... Blacksburg, VA
Ritchie, Klinkert & McCallion ... Ontario, CA
Ritchie, Lorelei D. ... Los Angeles, CA
Ritchie, Mark H. ... Houston, TX
Ritchie, Matthew E. ... Abilene, TX
Ritchie, Meredith Emerson ... Maywood, IL
Ritchie, Michael E. ... Tacoma, WA
Ritchie, Michael Shields ... Hudson, NH
Ritchie, Morris, Jr. ... Lebanon, IN
Ritchie, Paul Scott ... Chicago, IL
Ritchie, Peggy J. ... Alameda, CA
Ritchie, Raymond E. ... Augusta, ME
Ritchie, Rebecca Thompson ... Buffalo, NY
Ritchie & Rediker, L.L.C.
Birmingham, AL
Ritchie, Richard G. ... Los Angeles, CA
Ritchie, Richard Jon ... San Diego, CA
Ritchie, Robert A. ... Litchfield Park, AZ
Ritchie, Robert J. ... Burlington, VT
Ritchie, Robert W. ... Amherst, MA
Ritchie, Robert W. ... Boston, MA
Ritchie, Robert W. ... Knoxville, TN
Ritchie, Rocky D. ... Bakersfield, CA
Ritchie, Roger A. ... Harrisonburg, VA
Staunton, VA
Winchester, VA
Ritchie, Roger A. "Skip", Jr.
Harrisonburg, VA
Staunton, VA
Winchester, VA
Ritchie, Roger, & Partners, P.L.C.
Harrisonburg, VA
Staunton, VA
Winchester, VA
Ritchie, Ronald A. ... Madison, WI
Ritchie, Ronald W. ... Naples, FL
Ritchie, Ronald W., P.A. ... Naples, FL
Ritchie, Scott A. ... St. Paul, MN
Ritchie, Stafford D., II ... Buffalo, NY
Ritchie, Stark ... Washington, DC
Ritchie, Stephen L. ... Chicago, IL
Ritchie & Strohmeyer, P.S.
Port Angeles, WA
Ritchie, Suzanne Cutts
San Francisco, CA
Ritchie, Thomas A. ... Birmingham, AL
Ritchie, Thomas A., Jr. ... Las Vegas, NV
Ritchie, Thomas B. ... Ontario, CA
Ritchie, Verl C. ... Salt Lake City, UT
Ritchie, Wayne A., II ... Knoxville, TN
Ritchie, Wesley G. ... Austin, TX
Ritchie, William B. ... Bar Harbor, ME
Ritchie, William J. ... Mary Esther, FL
Ritchie, William P. ... Chicago, IL
Ritchie, William R. ... Conyers, GA
Ritchie, Wilson S. ... Knoxville, TN
Ritchings, Jon M. ... Storrs, CT
Ritenour, Anthony L. ... Sebring, FL
Ritenour, David K. ... Sacramento, CA
Ritenour, Jennifer Morgan ... Atlanta, GA
Ritenour, Joe S. ... Leesburg, VA
Ritenour, Joe S., P.C. ... Leesburg, VA
Ritenour, John J., Jr. ... San Antonio, TX
Riter, Bruce D. ... Mountain View, CA
Riter, Charles D. ... Santa Fe, NM
Riter, Charles L. ... Rapid City, SD
Riter, George M. ... Philadelphia, PA
Riter, Mayer, Hofer, Wattier & Brown, L.L.P. ... Pierre, SD
Riter, Robert C., Jr. ... Pierre, SD
Ritger, Edward J. ... Random Lake, WI
Ritger, Mary Beth ... New York, NY
Rither, Alan C. ... Richland, WA
Ritholz, Andrew, Law Offices of
Los Angeles, CA
Ritkes, Daniel ... Santa Monica, CA
Ritland, James ... Black River Falls, WI
Ritner, George ... La Jolla, CA
Ritner, Rodney G. ... San Bernardino, CA
Ritner, Stephen F. ... Wayne, PA
Ritner, William B. ... Palm Desert, CA
Ritner, William F., (A Professional Corporation) ... Los Angeles, CA
San Bernardino, CA
Ritnour, Randall R. ... Lincoln, NE
Ritok, Joseph A., Jr. ... Detroit, MI
Ritondo, John T., Jr. ... Homewood, AL
Ritorto, Joseph P. ... New York, NY
Ritorto, Richard ... New York, NY
Ritrivi, Nicholas A. ... New York, NY
Ritsch, Malcolm E., Jr. ... Richmond, VA
Ritsch, Robert W. ... Tallahassee, FL
Ritschard, Jeffrey R. ... Sacramento, CA
Ritscher, Andrea Katz ... New York, NY
Ritscherle, Elizabeth M. ... Chicago, IL
Ritsema, Fred ... Denver, CO
Ritsema, George W. ... Canyon Lake, CA
Ritsema & Lyon, P.C.
Colorado Springs, CO
Denver, CO
Fort Collins, CO
Ritsema, Paul W. ... Auburn Hills, MI
Grand Rapids, MI
Ritsema, Scott A. ... Long Beach, CA
Ritsher, John A. ... Boston, MA
Ritsko, Janet D. ... Boston, MA
Ritson, John D. ... Hartford, CT

Rivera-Aspinall, Julián R. ... **San Juan, PR**
Rivera Barrera, Marissa ... San Juan, PR
Rivera-Carbone, Javier ... **San Juan, PR**
Rivera Carrasquillo, Dario ... **San Juan, PR**
Rivera-Carretero, Armando A.
Watertown, NY
Rivera-Cestero, Gaspar ... San Juan, PR
Rivera-Cestero & Marchand-Quintero
San Juan, PR
Rivera-Cruz, Victoria ... **Lawrenceville, NJ**
Rivera de Jesús, Donato ... **San Juan, PR**
Rivera-Delgado, Jesus M. ... San Juan, PR
Rivera-Figueroa, Wilfredo ... Fajardo, PR
Rivera-Fournier, Alberto ... San Juan, PR
Rivera-Fourquet, Gerardo J.
San Juan, PR
Rivera-Gonzalez, Juan M. ... **San Juan, PR**
Rivera González, Luis R. ... San Juan, PR
Rivera-Longchamps, Javier ... San Juan, PR
Rivera-Lozada, Eugenio ... Bayamon, PR
Rivera MacMurray, Patricia
San Juan, PR
Rivera-Marín Law Offices ... San Juan, PR
Rivera-Marín, Luis Gerardo ... San Juan, PR
Rivera-Matos, Pedro Mario ... San Juan, PR
Rivera-Mazziotta, Coralina (IBA)
Houston, TX
Rivera Méndez, Manuel ... **San Juan, PR**
Rivera-Millet, Domingo ... San Juan, PR
Rivera-Miranda, Thelma ... **San Juan, PR**
Rivera-Morales, J. Ramón ... **San Juan, PR**
Rivera-Ortiz, Andres ... Miami, FL
Rivera Ortiz, Mariluz ... **San Juan, PR**
Rivera-Padilla, Norma M. ... San Juan, PR
Riveira Rivera, Edgardo L. ... **San Juan, PR**
Rivera Rosa, Rafael A. ... **San Juan, PR**
Rivera-Rosa, Ruben ... **San Juan, PR**
Rivera Rosario, Rafael G. ... **San Juan, PR**
Rivera-Ruiz, Leonardo ... San Juan, PR
Rivera-Sanchez, Kim M. ... **Cleveland, OH**
Rivera-Santander, Elizabeth G.
Torrance, CA
Rivera-Scozzafava, Maria D. ... Worcester, MA
Rivera-Soto, Roberto A. ... Las Vegas, NV
Philadelphia, PA
Rivera-Torres, Loyda E. ... **San Juan, PR**
Rivera-Ulwick, Jennifer ... **Boston, MA**
Rivera-Vicente, Alejandrina
San Juan, PR
Rivera-Vicente, Carlos M. ... **San Juan, PR**
Rivera-Worley, Maria del Carmen
Del Rio, TX
Rivera-Zayas, Annette C. ... Chicago, IL
Rivero, Ana M. ... **Miami, FL**
Rivero, Andrés ... **Miami, FL**
Rivero, David R. ... Washington, DC
Rivero, Humberto ... Coral Gables, FL
Rivero, Ivonne Hernandez ... **Ponce, PR**
Rivero, Juan Agustín ... **San Juan, PR**
Rivero, Laura Thomas ... Miami, FL
Rivero, Mary Jo ... Pembroke Pines, FL
Rivero, Omar S. ... Houston, TX
Rivero, Oscar ... Miami, FL
Rivero, Pedro M., Jr. ... Miami Beach, FL
Rivero-Cervera, Rafael ... San Juan, PR
Riverol, Rene ... Jersey City, NJ
Riveron, Adis ... **Coral Gables, FL**
Riveros, Bettina Tweardy ... Wilmington, DE
Rivero-Vergne, Jose L. ... **San Juan, PR**
Rivers, Beck, Dalrymple & Ledet
Alexandria, LA
Rivers, Billy Jack ... Department of Justice, Executive Office for Immigration Review, GV
Rivers, Brian T. ... Dallas, TX
Rivers, Bruce M. ... Minneapolis, MN
Rivers & Burrell ... Anderson, SC
Rivers, Carol S. ... **Chicago, IL**
Rivers, Clarence "Chip", IV
Birmingham, AL
Rivers, Courtney ... **Tampa, FL**
Rivers, D. Adolphus ... Chicago, IL
Rivers, Dana R. ... Stockton, CA
Rivers, David H. ... Vernon, CT
Rivers, David J., II (Chartered)
Las Vegas, NV
Rivers, Diane L. ... **New Haven, CT**
Rivers, Donna ... San Pablo, CA
Rivers, Ernest W. ... Paducah, KY
Rivers, Faith R. ... Columbia, SC
Rivers, Felice D. ... **Tampa, FL**
Rivers, Geo. E. ... Department of Labor, Office of Secretary, GV
Rivers, Geoffrey A. ... Muncie, IN
Rivers, G. L. Buist, Jr. ... **Charleston, SC**
Rivers, Harry I., Jr. ... Easley, SC
Rivers, Herbert A. ... Marietta, GA
Rivers, J. Elaine ... **Atlanta, GA**
Rivers, Janeen L. ... **Miami, FL**
Rivers, John ... **Prospect Heights, IL**
Rivers, John C., III ... Anderson, SC
Rivers, John P. ... Brunswick, GA
Rivers, Joyce Mansfield ... Anchorage, AK
Rivers, Kathleen E. ... Hailey, ID
Rivers, L. Alan ... Carmel, IN
Rivers, L. Mendel, Jr.
Mount Pleasant, SC
Rivers, Larry W. ... **Alexandria, LA**
Rivers, Mari-Ann Gibbs ... San Rafael, CA
Rivers, R. Thayer, Jr. ... **Beaufort, SC**
Rivers, R. Thayer, Jr. ... **Ridgeland, SC**
Rivers, Richard R., (P.C.) ... Washington, DC
Rivers, Richel ... **Austin, TX**
Rivers, Robert Calvin ... Jacksonville, FL
Rivers, Robert Calvin, P.A. ... Jacksonville, FL
Rivers, Robert J., Jr. ... **Boston, MA**
Rivers, Robert P. ... Troy, NY
Rivers, Rodney W. ... **Provo, UT**

Rivers, Stephen F. ... Philadelphia, PA
Rivers, Steven A. ... **Los Angeles, CA**
Rivers, Susie V., Ms. ... Brooklyn, NY
Rivers, Timothy F. ... **Los Angeles, CA**
Rivers, W. Nelson ... Tampa, FL
Rivers, Walter E. ... Big Stone Gap, VA
Rivers, Walter E., A Professional Corporation
Big Stone Gap, VA
Rivers, Wesley D. ... Beaumont, TX
Rivers, William Jones, III ... Florence, SC
Rivers, William L. ... Amarillo, TX
Rivers, William L. ... **Dallas, TX**
Rivers, Wilson L. ... **Virginia Beach, VA**
Riverso, Pia Elena ... **Uniondale, NY**
Riverso, Vincent G. ... Scarsdale, NY
Rives, Ashley Hale ... Montgomery, AL
Rives, Carol A. ... Salem, OR
Rives, Don L. ... Austin, TX
Rives, George D. ... **Portland, OR**
Rives, Howard P. ... Clearwater, FL
Rives, Howard P., III ... Clearwater, FL
Rives, Huffaker, Littorno & Jenny
Pittsburg, CA
Rives, James A. ... **Montgomery, AL**
Rives, Marie Tami ... Clearwater, FL
Rives, Nicole Laccetti ... **Boston, MA**
Rives, Patricia Ann ... Columbus, MS
Rives & Peterson, A Professional Corporation ... **Birmingham, AL**
Rives & Rives, P.A. ... Clearwater, FL
Rives, Robert C., Jr. ... **Boston, MA**
Rives, Robert D. ... **Montgomery, AL**
Rives, Ronald P. ... Pittsburg, CA
Rives, Shauna Steiger ... Hanover, MA
Rives, Stephanie K. ... Lake Forest, IL
Rives, Sterling E., III ... Hanover, VA
Rives, Tony J. ... Louisville, KY
Rives, William ... Scarsdale, NY
Rivest, Joseph R. ... **Goshen, NY**
Rivest, Mark A. ... Department of the Army, Office of the General Counsel, GV
Rivet, Claude ... **Baton Rouge, LA**
Rivet, Claude, APLC ... **Baton Rouge, LA**
Rivet, David M. ... **Houston, TX**
Rivet, Diana W. ... Orangeburg, NY
Rivett, Robin L. ... Sacramento, CA
Rivette, David A. ... Santa Barbara, CA
Rivette, Dorothy J. ... Palo Alto, CA
Rivette, Francis P. ... Syracuse, NY
Rivette, Francis R. ... Syracuse, NY
Rivette & Rivette, P.C. ... Syracuse, NY
Rivetti, Daniel L. ... **Pittsburgh, PA**
Rivieccio, Rosemary ... New York, NY
Riviera, Daniel J. ... **Reno, NV**
Riviera, David J. ... Bakersfield, CA
Riviere, Camille D. ... **Coral Gables, FL**
Riviere, Christopher H. ... **Thibodaux, LA**
Riviere, Christopher H., A Professional Law Corporation ... **Franklin, LA**
Houma, LA
Napoleonville, LA
Thibodaux, LA
Riviere, Leslie C. ... Tampa, FL
Riviere, Mary Frances Waitz ... Houma, LA
Riviere, Roger W. ... **Phoenix, AZ**
Riviere, William J. ... **New Orleans, LA**
Riviezzo, Albert R. ... **Exton, PA**
Riviezzo, Charles D. ... **New York, NY**
Riviezzo, Dineen A. ... **New York, NY**
Rivin, Ira G., (P.C.) ... **Costa Mesa, CA**
Rivin, Jonathan ... **San Francisco, CA**
Rivin, Kenneth A. ... Los Angeles, CA
Rivitz, Richard S. ... **Cleveland, OH**
Rivitz, Robert N. ... New York, NY
Rivizzigno, Anthony P. ... Syracuse, NY
Rivkin, Bernard L. ... Chicago, IL
Rivkin, Bruce Charles ... New York, NY
Rivkin, David B. ... **Washington, DC**
Rivkin, David W. ... **New York, NY**
Rivkin, Deborah R. ... Annapolis, MD
Rivkin, Donald H. ... **New York, NY**
Rivkin, John L. ... **Uniondale, NY**
Rivkin, Larry A. ... Chicago, IL
Rivkin, Lawrence ... **New York, NY**
Rivkin, Leonard L., (P.C.) ... Uniondale, NY
Rivkin, Oleg ... **New York, NY**
Rivkin, Radler & Kremer ... **Chicago, IL**
Newark, NJ
Rivkin, Radler & Kremer LLP
Santa Rosa, CA
Rivkin, Radler & Kremer, LLP
Mineola, NY
Rivkin, Radler & Kremer LLP
New York, NY
Rivkin, Radler & Kremer, LLP
Riverhead, NY
Rivkin, Radler & Kremer LLP
Uniondale, NY
Rivkin, Robert S. ... San Francisco, CA
Rivkin, Robert S. ... **Chicago, IL**
Rivkin, Steven M. ... **Troy, MI**
Rivkin, Steven R. ... Washington, DC
Rivkin, V. David ... **New York, NY**
Rivkind, Brett A. ... **Miami, FL**
Rivkind, Leonard ... Miami, FL
Rivkind, Nina R. ... Berkeley, CA
Rivkind & Pedraza, P.A. ... **Miami, FL**
Rivkind, Ralph J. ... **Boston, MA**
Providence, RI
Rivkind, Shari A. ... North Haledon, NJ
Rivkind, Susan G. ... Springfield, NJ
Rivkis, Renee H. ... New York, NY
Rivlin, Catherine A. ... San Francisco, CA
Rivlin, Elisa M. ... **New York, NY**
Rivlin, Judith E. ... Washington, DC
Rivlin, Kenneth S. ... New York, NY
Rivlin, Lewis A. ... **Washington, DC**

Rivlin, Lewis A., P.C., Law Offices of
Washington, DC
Rivlin, Madeline J. ... **New York, NY**
Rivlin, Mark L. ... Coral Gables, FL
Rivlin, Rachel ... Boston, MA
Rivo, Michael D. ... San Diego, CA
Rivoir & Kiese, Ltd. ... Scottsdale, AZ
Rivoir, William H., III ... Scottsdale, AZ
Rivoire, Thomas Alexis ... Spring, TX
Rivoli, John J. ... Rochester, NY
Rivosecchi, Thomas D. ... **Indiana, PA**
Rivtta, Robert J. ... Shelbyville, IN
Rix, Brian G. ... Studio City, CA
Rix, Martha J. ... Brooklyn, NY
Rix, Nancy E. ... New Orleans, LA
Rix, Theo. R. ... Minneapolis, MN
Rixen, Jacqueline ... Austin, TX
Rixey, J. Barbour ... **Virginia Beach, VA**
Rixey, J. Barbour, P.C.
Virginia Beach, VA
Rixey, John F. ... Virginia Beach, VA
Rixey, John F., Jr. ... United States Senate, Committee Legal Personnel, GV
Rixner, Kelly Rae ... Charleston, WV
Rixon, Christopher J. ... **Hartford, CT**
New London, CT
Rixon, W. Blair ... Brentwood, CA
Rixse, James S. ... **Washington, DC**
Riz, Iona Rachel ... Philadelphia, PA
Rizek, Christopher S. ... **Washington, DC**
Rizer, Edward N. ... Dayton, OH
Rizer, Jo Jones ... Cincinnati, OH
Rizer, Michael P. ... Cincinnati, OH
Rizescu, Sandra ... **New York, NY**
Rizik, Christopher L. ... Bloomfield Hills, MI
Rizik, Mark E. ... **Grand Rapids, MI**
Rizika, Jeffrey A. ... **Roseland, NJ**
Rizio, Gregory G. ... Santa Ana, CA
Rizio & Hamilton ... Philadelphia, PA
Rizio, Laura M. ... Philadelphia, PA
Rizio, Raymond ... **Fairfield, CT**
Rizk, Fred E. ... **Des Moines, IA**
Rizk, Georgiana ... **Atlanta, GA**
Rizk, Michael K. ... Gaithersburg, MD
Rizk, Michael K., P.A. ... Gaithersburg, MD
Rizk, Richard ... Beaverton, OR
Rizk, Roger W. ... **Charlotte, NC**
Rizk, Roger W., P.A. ... **Charlotte, NC**
Rizley, Jerry W. ... **Woodward, OK**
Rizley, Robert S. ... **Tulsa, OK**
Rizo, John B., Sr. ... **Plano, TX**
Rizoli, Louis A. ... Boston, MA
Rizor, Barbara D. ... Lima, OH
Rizor, Minnard, Rizor & Golden Co., L.P.A.
Lima, OH
Rizor, Paul D. ... Lima, OH
Rizos, Susan Ellen ... Astoria, NY
Rizowy, Carlos Guillermo ... **Chicago, IL**
Rizvi, H. John ... **New York, NY**
Rizvi, Rebecca Elsie ... Alexandria, VA
Rizvi, Syed Saleem ... New York, NY
Rizza, Bernard R. ... **Pittsburgh, PA**
Rizza, Elaine Cribbs ... Washington, PA
Rizza, Kimberly L. ... Westport, CT
Rizzardi, Donald Ned ... Huntsville, AL
Rizzardi, John ... **Seattle, WA**
Rizzardi, Keith W. ... West Palm Beach, FL
Rizzi, Annette Caligiuri ... New York, NY
Rizzi, Brian R. ... Santa Ana, CA
Rizzi, Charles A. ... Bellmawr, NJ
Rizzi, Charles A., Jr. ... **Mount Laurel, NJ**
Rizzi, Daniel A. ... **Garden City, NY**
Rizzi, Dom J. ... **Chicago, IL**
Rizzi, Joseph A. ... **Hackensack, NJ**
Rizzi, Margaret Rhinelander
Washington, DC
Rizzi, Michael J. ... Greenville, NC
Rizzi, Patrick R. ... **Washington, DC**
Rizzi, Robert A. ... **Washington, DC**
Rizzi, Steven J. ... Chicago, IL
Rizzi, Steven Jay ... **New York, NY**
Rizzi, Steven T., Jr. ... **Austin, MN**
Rizzieri, Barbara A. ... Santa Cruz, CA
Rizzieri, L. Stephen ... Dallas, TX
Rizzo, Albert M., Law Offices of
New York, NY
Rizzo, Albert V. ... Kalamazoo, MI
Rizzo, Annette M. ... Philadelphia, PA
Rizzo, Anthony ... Camden, NJ
Rizzo, Anthony R. ... Saugus, MA
Rizzo, Barbara A. ... **Washington, PA**
Rizzo, Blake E. ... **Baton Rouge, LA**
Rizzo, Bruno M. ... **Burlington, WI**
Kenosha, WI
Rizzo, Carl A. ... **Hackensack, NJ**
Rizzo, Carl M. ... San Antonio, TX
Rizzo, Carol ... **Mineola, NY**
Rizzo, Cindy T. ... Boston, MA
Rizzo, Craig ... **Lake Success, NY**
Rizzo, Danielle L. ... **New York, NY**
Rizzo, David C. ... Syracuse, NY
Rizzo, David Gerald ... **New York, NY**
Rizzo, Deborah B. ... Iselin, NJ
Rizzo, Diana Ayella ... King Of Prussia, PA
Rizzo, Dominic S. ... Garden City, NY
Rizzo, Eugene J. ... **Poughkeepsie, NY**
Rizzo, Frank J., III ... **King Of Prussia, PA**
Rizzo, George J. ... **New Orleans, LA**
Rizzo, Guy C. ... Narragansett, RI
Rizzo, Guy T. ... Longwood, FL
Rizzo, James Augustine
North Tonawanda, NY
Rizzo, James G. ... **Washington, DC**
Rizzo, James J. ... Rochester, NY
Rizzo, John A. ... Central Intelligence Agency, Office of the General Counsel, GV
Rizzo, John A. ... Oradell, NJ
Rizzo, John J. ... Waukegan, IL

Rizzo, John J. ... **Newark, NJ**
Rizzo, John J., III ... **Traverse City, MI**
Rizzo, John L. ... Le Roy, NY
Rizzo, Joseph ... Pembroke Pines, FL
Rizzo, Joseph B. ... Rochester, NY
Rizzo, Joseph M. ... Brooklyn, NY
Rizzo, Joseph N., Jr. ... **New York, NY**
Rizzo, Joseph, P.A. ... Pembroke Pines, FL
Rizzo, Juliet T. ... **Baton Rouge, LA**
Rizzo, Karen ... Los Angeles, CA
Rizzo & Kelley ... **Poughkeepsie, NY**
Rizzo, Lawrence A. ... Pittsburgh, PA
Rizzo, Louis J. ... Pound Ridge, NY
Rizzo, Louis J., Jr. ... Wilmington, DE
Rizzo, Maria A. ... Boston, MA
Rizzo, Matthew Anthony ... **Fairfax, VA**
Rizzo, Michael C. ... **Schenectady, NY**
Rizzo, Michael J. ... Tualatin, OR
Rizzo, Michael R. ... **Los Angeles, CA**
Rizzo, Nicholas S.
Department of Commerce, Patent and Trademark Office, GV
Rizzo, Nicole L. ... Burlington, WI
Kenosha, WI
Rizzo, N. N. ... Niagara Falls, NY
Rizzo, Patricia L. ... Media, PA
Rizzo, Paul R. ... Warren, NJ
Rizzo, Paula C. ... Middlesex, NJ
Rizzo, Peter Bryson ... Cranston, RI
Rizzo, Peter C. ... New Orleans, LA
Rizzo, R. Daniel ... Dunn, NC
Rizzo, Ralph A. ... Belmont, CA
Rizzo, Richard C. ... **Philadelphia, PA**
Rizzo & Rizzo, P.C. ... Pound Ridge, NY
Rizzo, Robert J. ... Mineola, NY
Rizzo, Ronald S. ... **Chicago, IL**
Rizzo, Rudolph V. ... Painesville, OH
Rizzo, Sandra E. ... **Washington, DC**
Rizzo, Severin V. ... San Francisco, CA
Rizzo, Stephen J. ... **New York, NY**
Rizzo, Steven V. ... **Portland, OR**
Rizzo, Thomas A. ... Pound Ridge, NY
Rizzo, Thomas F. ... Sanibel, FL
Rizzo, Thomas M. ... **Washington, DC**
Rizzo, Thomas M. ... Grand Rapids, MI
Rizzo, Thomas M. ... Buffalo, NY
Rizzo & Vignali, S.C. ... Burlington, WI
Kenosha, WI
Rizzo, Virgil R. ... Fort Lauderdale, FL
Rizzo, William J. ... **New York, NY**
Rizzo, William O. ... **Boston, MA**
Rizzolo, M. Kristan ... **Washington, DC**
Rizzolo, Nicole D. ... Newark, NJ
Rizzolo, Stanley F. ... Somerville, NJ
Rizzolo, Vicky A. ... **Eden Prairie, MN**
Rizzotti, Anthony D. ... **Boston, MA**
Rizzotti, K. Jill ... **Boston, MA**
Rizzotto, Kathleen M. ... Santa Ana, CA
Rizzuti, Benedict E. ... Floral Park, NY
Rizzuto, Christopher A.
Department of Justice, Office of Justice Programs, GV
Rizzuto, Donald N. ... Manhasset, NY
Rizzuto, Frank P. ... Endwell, NY
Rizzuto, John F. ... Chicago, IL
Rizzuto, Louis R. ... Reading, PA
Rizzuto, Michael D. ... Lemont, PA
Rizzuto, Michael, P.A. ... Brick, NJ
Rizzuto, Michael R. ... Brick, NJ
Rizzuto, Philip J. ... Garden City, NY
Rizzutto, Thomas P. ... Endicott, NY
Rizzuto, Anne Marie ... **Newark, NJ**
RLM International, Ltd. ... **Novato, CA**
San Francisco, CA
Ro, Elena ... **San Francisco, CA**
Ro, Juli J. ... **Irvine, CA**
Ro, Lusanna J. ... **Denver, CO**
Ro, Nicholas H. ... **Houston, TX**
Roach, Adrienne J. ... **Cincinnati, OH**
Roach, Annette Fuller ... Lake Charles, LA
Roach, Arvid E., II ... **Washington, DC**
Roach, B. Randall ... Springboro, OH
Roach, Barry A. ... Lake Charles, LA
Roach Becker & Gallagher ... Louisville, KY
Roach, Brown, McCarthy & Gruber, P.C.
Buffalo, NY
Roach, Bruce E., Jr. ... **Tulsa, OK**
Roach, Camille M. ... Endicott, NY
Roach & Carpenter, P.C. ... **Boston, MA**
Roach, Catherine B. ... Seattle, WA
Roach, Charles A. ... **Minneapolis, MN**
Roach, Charles H. ... Fort Worth, TX
Roach, Charles W. ... Denver, CO
San Antonio, TX
Roach, Christine M. ... **Boston, MA**
Roach, Christopher L. ... Purchase, NY
Roach, Christopher T. ... **Portland, ME**
Roach, Cornelius, III ... Kansas City, MO
Roach, Daniel J. ... **Walla Walla, WA**
Roach, Daniel T. ... **Buffalo, NY**
Roach, Darren P. ... **Oakland, CA**
Roach, David A. ... **Kingston, NY**
Roach, David G. ... **Dayton, OH**
Enon, OH
Roach, David L. ... Tonawanda, NY
Roach, Dennis A., (A Professional Corporation)
Los Angeles, CA
Roach, Donald E. ... Brea, CA
Roach, Donald P. ... Portland, OR
Roach, Doris Ferrer ... Boston, MA
Roach, Douglas R. ... **Seattle, WA**
Roach, Edward G. ... Oakland, CA
Roach, Edward G. ... Bronx, NY
Roach, Eileen A. ... Boston, MA
Roach, Erika C. ... Indianapolis, IN
Roach, Francis T., Jr. ... Albany, NY
Roach, Garrett M. ... **Millersburg, OH**
Roach, Gary Byron ... Ventura, CA

Robbins, Gary E., P.C. ... **Flagstaff, AZ**
Robbins, Gary J. ... **New York, NY**
Robbins, Gary Lee ... Crocker, MO
Robbins, Gayle B. ... **Mayfield, KY**
Robbins, Gene E. ... **Frankfort, IN**
Robbins, Glenn B., Law Offices of ... **New York, NY**
Robbins, Glenn K. ... St. Louis, MO
Robbins, Glenn K., II ... **St. Louis, MO**
Robbins & Green, A Professional Association ... **Phoenix, AZ**
Robbins, Gregory ... New York, NY
Robbins, Gregory D. ... **Portsmouth, NH**
Robbins, Gregory M. ... Seattle, WA
Robbins, H. Franklin, Jr. ... Orlando, FL
Robbins, H. Franklin, Jr., P.A. ... Orlando, FL
Robbins, Harold J. ... Chicago, IL
Robbins & Holdaway, A Professional Corporation ... Chino, CA
Robbins, Holly M. ... **Minneapolis, MN**
Robbins, Howard S. ... Fairlawn, OH
Robbins, Howard Z. ... **New York, NY**
Robbins, Hugh R. ... Washington, DC
Robbins, Ira P. ... Washington, DC
Robbins, J. Lee ... **Greenwood, IN**
Robbins, J. Michael ... Kenai, AK
Robbins, Jack A., Jr. ... **Manassas, VA**
Robbins, Jack H. ... Dana Point, CA
Robbins, Jack W. ... Fort Washington, PA
Robbins, James A. ... **New York, NY**
Robbins, James A., Jr. ... Rome, GA
Robbins, James M. ... New York, NY
Robbins, James M. ... **Myrtle Beach, SC**
Robbins, James R. ... Fort Worth, TX
Robbins, James S. ... Boston, MA
Robbins, Jane Tishman ... Westwood, KS
Robbins, Janice E. ... **Raynham, MA**
Robbins, Jason S. ... **Fort Lauderdale, FL**
Robbins, Jeffery P. ... **Durango, CO**
Robbins, Jeffrey A. ... **Bloomfield Hills, MI**
Robbins, Jeffrey C. ... **Minneapolis, MN**
Robbins, Jeffrey D. ... **Evansville, IN**
Robbins, Jeffrey P.
Department Of Health And Human Services, Office of the General Counsel, GV
Robbins, Jeffrey S. ... **Boston, MA**
Robbins, Jenifer M. ... **Chicago, IL**
Robbins, Jerome ... New York, NY
Robbins, Jerome N. ... Chicago, IL
Robbins, Jill S. ... Pacific Palisades, CA
Robbins, Jim P., (P.C.) ... Boone, IA
Robbins, Joanne A. ... **Boston, MA**
Robbins, JoAnne Earls ... Los Angeles, CA
Robbins, Joel B. ... Phoenix, AZ
Robbins, Joel S. ... Prospect Park, PA
Robbins, John ... Birmingham, AL
Robbins, John B. ... Little Rock, AR
Robbins, Jon N. ... **San Ramon, CA**
Robbins, Jon Paul ... **New York, NY**
Robbins, Jonathan ... Denver, CO
Robbins, Jonathan D. ... **Washington, DC**
Robbins, Jonathan David ... Potomac, MD
Robbins, Jonathan S. ... **Fort Lauderdale, FL**
Robbins, Joseph C. ... **Boston, MA**
Robbins, Joseph K. ... St. Louis, MO
Robbins, Joseph K., P.C. ... St. Louis, MO
Robbins, Judith A. ... Walnut Creek, CA
Robbins, Julia S. ... New York, NY
Robbins, Kally K. ... Dallas, TX
Robbins, Kalyani ... **San Francisco, CA**
Robbins, Kathleen Rolston ... Houston, TX
Robbins & Keehn, A Professional Corporation ... **San Diego, CA**
Robbins, Keith D. ... **Hartford, CT**
Robbins, Kelly Jana ... **San Francisco, CA**
San Francisco, CA
Robbins, Kelly, Patterson & Tucker, A Legal Professional Assoc. ... **Cincinnati, OH**
Robbins, Kenneth C. ... Naperville, IL
Robbins, Kenneth M. ... Merced, CA
Robbins, Kenneth M. ... **Boston, MA**
Robbins, Kenneth S. ... **Honolulu, HI**
Robbins, Kent Harrison ... Miami Beach, FL
Robbins, Kevin F. ... Troy, MI
Robbins, Kimberley A. ... **Tampa, FL**
Robbins, Lance Jay ... Culver City, CA
Robbins, Larry E. ... **Raleigh, NC**
Robbins, Lauren Miller ... Houston, TX
Robbins, Laurence S. ... Chicago, IL
Robbins, Laurie S. ... Atlanta, GA
Robbins, Lawrence J. ... Miami, FL
Robbins, Lawrence S. ... **Washington, DC**
Robbins, Lee J. ... New York, NY
Robbins, Leonard ... **Hollywood, FL**
Robbins, Leonard J. ... New York, NY
Robbins, Linda Hansen ... Cedar Rapids, IA
Robbins, Lori A. ... **Lenox, MA**
Robbins, Lyle W. ... Macomb, IL
Robbins, Lynda J. ... Chelmsford, MA
Robbins, M. Kathleen ... Cincinnati, OH
Robbins, Malcolm J. ... Jersey City, NJ
Robbins, Manuel J. ... **Chicago, IL**
Robbins, Mara Lerner ... **Boca Raton, FL**
Robbins, Marianne Goldstein ... **Milwaukee, WI**
Robbins, Marjorie F. ... Bay Harbor Islands, FL
Robbins, Mark ... Los Angeles, CA
Robbins, Mark T. ... Indianapolis, IN
Robbins, Mark W. ... **Los Angeles, CA**
Robbins, Marvin N. ... Baltimore, MD
Robbins, Matthew R. ... **Milwaukee, WI**
Robbins, May & Rich, LLP ... **Pinehurst, NC**
Southern Pines, NC
Robbins & McLeod ... Gainesville, GA
Robbins, Melvin Lloyd ... Long Island City, NY
Robbins, Merrill W. ... Phoenix, AZ
Robbins, Merrill W., P.C. ... Phoenix, AZ
Robbins, Michael A. ... Beverly Hills, CA
Robbins, Michael A. ... Bedford, IN
Robbins, Michael A. ... Bloomfield Hills, MI
Robbins, Michael D. ... Chicago, IL
Robbins, Michael D. ... **Houston, TX**
Robbins, Michael D. ... San Antonio, TX
Robbins, Michael H. ... **Tampa, FL**
Robbins, Milton ... Miami Beach, FL
Robbins, Mindy Paige ... **Tampa, FL**
Robbins, Nicholas W. ... **Boston, MA**
Robbins, Nora Van Lahr ... Louisville, KY
Robbins, Norman ... Woodbridge, NJ
Robbins, Norman N. ... Bingham Farms, MI
Robbins, Orem O. ... Balsam Lake, WI
Robbins, Orrin R. ... Chapel Hill, NC
Robbins, O. W. ... Selby, SD
Robbins, Owsley & Wilkins ... Talladega, AL
Robbins Palmer & Allen LLP ... **Fairfield, CA**
Oakland, CA
San Francisco, CA
Walnut Creek, CA
Robbins, Pamela S. ... **Columbus, OH**
Robbins, Patrick D. ... San Francisco, CA
Robbins, Paul ... Oakland, CA
Robbins, Paul A. ... **Lufkin, TX**
Robbins, Paul J. ... St. George, UT
Robbins, Paul S. ... Long Beach, CA
Robbins, Peter ... Sherman Oaks, CA
Robbins, Peter R. ... **Washington, DC**
Robbins, Philip A. ... **Phoenix, AZ**
Robbins, Phillip Wayne ... **Pinehurst, NC**
Robbins, R. James, Jr. ... **Tampa, FL**
Robbins, Rachel F. ... **New York, NY**
Robbins, Randall E. ... **Wilmington, DE**
Robbins, Ray F., II ... Talladega, AL
Robbins, Reagen C. ... **Chicago, IL**
Robbins, Rebecca T. ... **Bloomington, IN**
Indianapolis, IN
Robbins & Reynolds, P.A. ... Miami, FL
Robbins & Rhodes, Attorneys At Law, A Law Corporation ... **Honolulu, HI**
Robbins, Richard A. ... Chicago, IL
Robbins, Richard A. ... **New York, NY**
Robbins, Richard C. ... **Van Nuys, CA**
Robbins, Richard C., A Professional Corporation ... **Van Nuys, CA**
Robbins, Richard E. ... **Chicago, IL**
Robbins, Richard L. ... **Atlanta, GA**
Robbins, Richard M. ... Clearwater, FL
Robbins & Robbins ... Dana Point, CA
Robbins & Robbins ... **Mayfield, KY**
Robbins & Robbins ... St. Louis, MO
Robbins & Robbins, Ltd. ... Chicago, IL
Robbins, Robert A. ... Miami, FL
Robbins, Robert B. ... Fresno, CA
Robbins, Robert B., (P.C.) ... **Washington, DC**
Robbins, Robert C., IV ... **Lewiston, ME**
Robbins, Robert E. ... **Grand Haven, MI**
Robbins, Robert E., P.C. ... **Grand Haven, MI**
Robbins, Robert H. ... Cleveland, TN
Robbins, Robert J., Jr. ... Lenoir, NC
Robbins, Robert R. ... Panama City Beach, FL
Robbins, Robert Thomas ... Los Angeles, CA
Robbins, Roberta E. ... Miami, FL
Robbins, Robt. L. ... Columbus, OH
Robbins, Robt. S. ... Philadelphia, PA
Robbins, Roger B. ... Santa Ana, CA
Robbins, Ron G. ... **Chicago, IL**
Robbins, Ronald E. ... **Columbia, SC**
Robbins, Ronnie Orzoff, (Mrs.) ... Chicago, IL
Robbins, Rose H. ... Pompano Beach, FL
Robbins, Ruthie H. ... Albuquerque, NM
Robbins, S. Sue ... **Ocala, FL**
Robbins, Salomon & Patt, Ltd. ... **Chicago, IL**
Glenview, IL
Robbins, Samara H. ... Fort Lauderdale, FL
Robbins, Sanford L. ... Canoga Park, CA
Robbins, Sara ... Brooklyn, NY
Robbins, Schwartz, Nicholas, Lifton & Taylor, Ltd. ... Chicago, IL
Robbins, Scott A. ... Poplar Bluff, MO
Robbins, Scott D. ... Kew Gardens, NY
Robbins, Scott M. ... **Knoxville, TN**
Morristown, TN
Robbins, Sean Leonard ... Shavertown, PA
Robbins, Sidney ... Miami, FL
Robbins, Spencer B. ... **Woodbridge, NJ**
Robbins, Stanley Wade ... Gainesville, GA
Robbins, Stephanie L. ... **Philadelphia, PA**
Robbins, Stephanie M. ... Edwardsville, IL
Robbins, Stephen ... **Sacramento, CA**
Robbins, Stephen A. ... Ada, MI
Robbins, Steven C. ... **Philadelphia, PA**
Robbins, Steven E. ... Jacksonville, FL
Robbins, Steven J. ... **San Diego, CA**
Robbins, Steven L. ... **West Palm Beach, FL**
Robbins, Stuart B. ... Newton, MA
Robbins, Stuart E. ... Boston, MA
Robbins, Susan I. ... **New York, NY**
Robbins, Susan M. ... **Sun City, AZ**
Robbins, Sy A. ... Hialeah, FL
Robbins, Tammy Schwitz ... Mineola, NY
Robbins, Timothy C. ... Everett, WA
Robbins, Timothy C., P.S. ... Everett, WA
Robbins, Tinker, Smith & Tinker ... **Wichita, KS**
Robbins, Tunkey, Ross, Amsel, Raben & Waxman, P.A. ... **Fort Lauderdale, FL**
Miami, FL
Robbins, Valerie ... Atlanta, GA
Robbins, Vernon E. ... Cambridge, MD
Robbins, Virginia C. ... **Syracuse, NY**
Robbins, Wayne Lindsey, Jr. ... **Nashville, TN**
Robbins, Wendy L. ... Miami, FL
Robbins, William A. ... Cavalier, ND
Robbins, William A. ... Pittsburgh, PA
Robbins, William C., III ... **Fairfield, CA**
Oakland, CA
Robbins, William D. ... White Plains, NY
Robbins, William E. ... Richardson, TX
Robbins, William H. ... **Greensburg, IN**
Robbins, William J. ... **New York, NY**
Robbins, William K., Jr. ... Houston, TX
Robbins, William N. ... **Atlanta, GA**
Robbins, William N., Attorney at Law, P.C. ... **Atlanta, GA**
Robbins, William R., Jr. ... Coral Gables, FL
Robbins, William S. ... **Baton Rouge, LA**
Robbins, William Sterling, Jr. ... **Kansas City, MO**
Robbins, William T. ... Tulsa, OK
Robbins-Kralapp, Mary K. ... **East Lansing, MI**
Robbinson, William H. ... Flat Rock, NC
Robbinson, William H., Jr. ... **Winter Park, FL**
Robbins-Ost, Harriet Beth ... Skokie, IL
Robbins-Penniman, Gus E. ... Columbus, OH
Robbins-Penniman, Sylvia B. ... Columbus, OH
Robbins-Shea, Theresa A. ... **Chicago, IL**
Robbio, Louis F. ... Cranston, RI
Robblee, Neil H. ... Seattle, WA
Robblee, Richard H. ... Seattle, WA
Robboy, Anita W. ... **Boston, MA**
Robe, Donna M. Calf ... Seattle, WA
Robe, Edward S. ... Athens, OH
Robe Law Offices ... Athens, OH
Robe, Lynette Berg ... Studio City, CA
Robe, Penny R. ... Plainview, TX
Robe, R. Chris ... **Wichita, KS**
Robe, Scott M. ... Athens, OH
Robeck, Mark R. ... **Austin, TX**
Robeck, Paul G. ... Portland, OR
Robedee, William Joseph ... Brooklyn, NY
Robein, Louis L., Jr. ... **Metairie, LA**
Robein, Urann & Lurye, A Professional Law Corporation ... **Metairie, LA**
New Orleans, LA
Robelen, Scott G. ... Oklahoma City, OK
Robelot, Walter A., II ... New Orleans, LA
Robenalt, James D. ... **Cleveland, OH**
Robenalt, Jeffrey L. ... Austin, TX
Robenalt, John A. ... **Bluffton, OH**
Lima, OH
Robenalt, John F. ... Osprey, FL
Robenalt & Robenalt ... **Osprey, FL**
Lima, OH
Robenalt, Robert M. ... **Columbus, OH**
Robenalt, Thomas D. ... **Cleveland, OH**
Robenhymer, Timothy J. ... **Providence, RI**
Roberg, LaVerne M. ... **Maquoketa, IA**
Roberg, Marilee ... **Chicago, IL**
Roberg, Richard M. ... Arlington Heights, IL
Roberge, Christopher S. ... Indianapolis, IN
Roberge, David J. ... Seattle, WA
Roberge, Donald C. ... Boca Raton, FL
Roberge, Elizabeth A. ... Indianapolis, IN
Roberge, Kathleen A. ... St. Paul, MN
Roberge, Kevin C. ... St. Paul, MN
Roberge, Kristi Stapf ... Hartford, CT
Roberge, Richard L. ... Mount Clemens, MI
Roberge, Stephanie Z. ... **New Haven, CT**
Roberge, Wilfrid F., Jr. ... **Oakland, CA**
Walnut Creek, CA
Roberge, William H., Jr. ... **Rockville, MD**
Robers, Gregory J. ... Houston, TX
Roberson, Antony D. ... Chapel Hill, NC
Roberson, Arletra Chantelle ... Chattanooga, TN
Roberson, Benjamin W. ... **Jackson, MS**
Roberson, Bruce H. ... **Tampa, FL**
Roberson, Cheryl A. ... **Jacksonville, FL**
Roberson, Dale C. ... Ellington, CT
Roberson, Dalton A. ... Detroit, MI
Roberson, David ... Savannah, GA
Roberson, Dean B. ... **Charlotte, NC**
Roberson, Derrick L. ... **Manhattan, KS**
Roberson, Don B. ... Kansas City, MO
Roberson, Donald E. ... Monterey, CA
Roberson, Douglas B. ... **Houston, TX**
Roberson, Eric M. ... **Chicago, IL**
Roberson, Eric N. ... **Dallas, TX**
Roberson, Frank F. ... Bethesda, MD
Roberson, Fred, Jr. ... Little Rock, AR
Roberson, G. Gale, Jr. ... **Chicago, IL**
Roberson, Gary F. ... Pittsburgh, PA
Roberson, Georgia Sullivan ... **Birmingham, AL**
Roberson, Haworth & Reese, P.L.L.C. ... **High Point, NC**
Roberson, Holly G. ... Anchorage, AK
Roberson, James K. ... Graham, NC
Roberson, James O., Jr. ... New York, NY
Roberson, Jamie P. ... San Francisco, CA
Roberson, Jerome L. ... Great Bend, KS
Roberson, Jessie C. ... Athens, OH
Roberson, John ... **Houston, TX**
Roberson, Keith P. ... **Peoria, IL**
Roberson, Kim A. ... **Atlanta, GA**
Roberson, Kippy ... La Grande, OR
Roberson & Kumiega, LLC ... Ellington, CT
Roberson Law Office ... **Tulsa, OK**
Roberson, Leslie Bruce ... Perryton, TX
Roberson, Linda ... **Madison, WI**
Roberson, Lloyd W. ... Yonkers, NY
Roberson, Lynn M. ... **Atlanta, GA**
Roberson, M. Richbourg ... **Columbia, SC**
Roberson, Michael J. ... New York, NY
Roberson, Michael Lee ... **Syracuse, NY**
Roberson, Nancy A. ... Dayton, OH
Roberson, Nathaniel ... Columbia, SC
Roberson, Pamela M. ... **Los Angeles, CA**
Roberson, Patrick A. ... **Baltimore, MD**
Roberson, Peggie Lewis ... Asheville, NC
Roberson, R. Lawrence ... **Tulsa, OK**
Roberson, Ralph K. ... DeLand, FL
Roberson, Rebecca Ann ... **Modesto, CA**
Roberson, Richard M. ... **Dallas, TX**
Roberson, Richardson & Deal ... Graham, NC
Roberson, Robert J. ... Yuma, AZ
Roberson, Robert L., Jr. ... Los Angeles, CA
Roberson, Robert S. ... **Lockport, NY**
Roberson, Russell P. ... Austin, TX
Roberson, Sam H. ... **Washington, DC**
Roberson & Shelley ... Yuma, AZ
Roberson, Sheri L. ... **Raleigh, NC**
Roberson, Stephen D. ... Thousand Oaks, CA
Roberson, Tena T. ... Chattanooga, TN
Roberson, Thomas M. ... Houston, TX
Roberson, Thomas Y., Jr. ... **New Orleans, LA**
Roberson, Victoria J. ... **Richmond, VA**
Roberson, Walter W. ... Okemah, OK
Roberson, William D. ... Wareham, MA
Robert, Alan J., & Associates ... Gonzales, LA
Robert, Ann P. ... Springfield, IL
Robert, Bruce P. ... St. Louis, MO
Robert, Cavett ... Phoenix, AZ
Robert, Charles R. ... Rockville Centre, NY
Robert, David G. ... Torrance, CA
Robert, Gary ... **Lahaina, HI**
Robert, Gary, Attorney at Law, A Law Corporation ... **Lahaina, HI**
Robert, Gary J. ... Valencia, CA
Robert, Jane A. ... **Baton Rouge, LA**
Robert, Janet M. ... Stillwater, MN
Robert, Jeffery P. ... Baton Rouge, LA
Robert, Joan Lensky ... Rockville Centre, NY
Robert, Lerner & Robert ... Rockville Centre, NY
Robert, Marc H. ... Albuquerque, NM
Robert, Marie A. ... **San Juan, PR**
Robert, Michelle D. ... New Orleans, LA
Robert, Michelle M. ... Augusta, ME
Robert & Miller ... **Louisville, KY**
Robert, Paul L. ... Hartford, CT
Robert, Pierre L. ... **Portland, OR**
Robert, Portia A. ... **Washington, DC**
Robert, R. Dieter ... Melville, NY
Robert, Rachel Katherine ... Naperville, IL
Robert, Randal J. ... **Baton Rouge, LA**
Robert, William J. ... Eugene, OR
Robertazzi, George J. ... Brooklyn, NY
Robertelli, John J. ... Hackensack, NJ
Robertelli, Vincent ... Bloomingdale, IL
Roberti, Angelo J. ... Milford, MA
Roberti, Anthony ... Jim Thorpe, PA
Roberti, Betsy G. ... Boston, MA
Roberti, Christopher D. ... **Washington, DC**
Roberti, John ... **New York, NY**
Roberti, Paul J. ... Providence, RI
Roberti, Samuel ... Durham, NC
Roberti, Stephen R. ... Chicago, IL
Roberti, Wittenberg, Holtkamp & Lauffer, P.A. ... Durham, NC
Robertie, George F. ... Los Angeles, CA
Robertie, James P. ... **Boston, MA**
Roberto, Carmen V. ... Akron, OH
Roberto, Cheryl ... Meadville, PA
Roberto, Douglas P. ... **Atlanta, GA**
Roberto, Joanna ... **White Plains, NY**
Roberto, Robert, Jr. ... Mineola, NY
Roberto, Susan E. ... **Yakima, WA**
Roberto, William A. ... **Glastonbury, CT**
Roberto, William A., LLC ... **Glastonbury, CT**
Robertory, Robert J. ... Fairfax Station, VA
Roberts, A. Michelle ... Austin, TX
Roberts, Abokhair & Mardula, LLC ... **Reston, VA**
Roberts, Adam D. ... **Stamford, CT**
Roberts, Alan K. ... New York, NY
Roberts, Albert P. ... **Poughkeepsie, NY**
Wappingers Falls, NY
Roberts, Allen B. ... **New York, NY**
Roberts, Allen G. ... Danville, VA
Roberts, Allen P. ... **Camden, AR**
Roberts, Allen P., P.A. ... **Camden, AR**
Roberts, Allison C. ... Portland, OR
Roberts, Alvin G. ... Portland, OR
Roberts, A. M. (Mike) ... Sun Lakes, AZ
Roberts, Amy Friend ... Swampscott, MA
Roberts, Amy J. ... **New York, NY**
Roberts, Amy T. ... Washington, DC
Roberts, Andrea Ford ... San Francisco, CA
Roberts, Andrea M. ... **Indianapolis, IN**
Roberts, Andrew S. ... Washington, DC
Roberts, Andrew Stephen ... Thousand Oaks, CA
Roberts, Andrew Stephen, P.C. ... Thousand Oaks, CA
Roberts, Angela Edwards ... Richmond, VA
Roberts, Anita U. ... Manlius, NY
Roberts, Anne B. ... Santa Monica, CA
Roberts, Arthur E. ... Groveland, FL
Roberts, Ashby & Parrish ... **Fredericksburg, VA**
Roberts & Associates ... **Nashville, TN**
Roberts, Aubrey L., Jr. ... Abilene, TX
Roberts, Austin L., Jr. ... Williamsburg, VA
Roberts, B. Edward ... Youngstown, OH
Roberts, Bana Burkett ... Oklahoma City, OK
Roberts, Barbara E. ... **Houston, TX**
Roberts, Barbara G. ... Minneapolis, MN

Roberts, Joseph B., III ... Gastonia, NC
Roberts, Joseph D., II ... Falls Church, VA
Roberts, Joseph E., Jr. ... Jackson, MS
Roberts, Joseph G. ... Noblesville, IN
Roberts, Joseph R. ... Tulsa, OK
Roberts, Joshua ... Springfield, MO
Roberts, Judith ... Whittier, CA
Roberts, Judith ... New York, NY
Roberts, Judith L. ... San Francisco, CA
Roberts, Judith L. ... Denver, CO
Roberts, Judy S. ... Nashville, TN
Roberts, Julia C. ... Albuquerque, NM
Roberts, Julia J. ... Visalia, CA
Roberts, Julie Ann ... San Francisco, CA
Roberts, June E. ... Needham, MA
Roberts, Justin A. ... Lafayette, CA
Roberts, Justin J. ... Washington, DC
Roberts, J. W. H. ... Greenville, NC
Roberts, K. David ... Oklahoma City, OK
Roberts, K. Steven ... New York, NY
Roberts, Karen K. ... Walnut Creek, CA
Roberts, Karen L. ... Oakland, CA
Roberts, Karen R. ... Tyler, TX
Roberts, Katherine ... Houston, TX
Roberts, Kathleen ... Salinas, CA
Roberts, Kathryn A. ... Southlake, TX
Roberts, Kathryn E. ... Allentown, PA
Roberts, Kathryn R. ... Merced, CA
Roberts, Kay ... Winfield, KS
Roberts, Keith ... Pascagoula, MS
Roberts, Keith ... Moonachie, NJ
Roberts, Keith E. (Chuck), Jr.
Wheaton, IL
Roberts, Keith E., Sr. ... Wheaton, IL
Roberts, Keith F. ... Tampa, FL
Roberts, Keith L.
Department of the Air Force, Office of the Judge Advocate General, GV
Roberts, Kelly P. ... Denver, CO
Roberts, Kelly P., P.C. ... Denver, CO
Roberts, Kelly Tice ... Frederick, OK
Roberts, Kenneth A. B., P.C. ... Denver, CO
Roberts, Kenneth A. B., Jr. ... Denver, CO
Roberts, Kenneth B. ... New York, NY
Roberts, Kenneth D. ... Newport, OR
Roberts, Kenneth E. ... Portland, OR
Roberts, Kenneth E., Jr. ... Portland, OR
Roberts, Kenneth G. ... New York, NY
Roberts, Kenneth L. ... Nashville, TN
Roberts, Kenneth L. ... Newport News, VA
Roberts, Kenneth M. ... Chicago, IL
Roberts, Kenneth M. ... Las Vegas, NV
Roberts, Kenneth N. ... San Francisco, CA
Roberts, Kenneth P. ... Woodland Hills, CA
Roberts, Kenneth P., A Professional Law Corporation ... Woodland Hills, CA
Roberts, Kenneth S. ... Irvine, CA
Roberts, Kenneth T. ... Indianapolis, IN
Roberts, Kevin A. ... Los Angeles, CA
Roberts, Kevin C. ... Hillsboro, MO
Roberts, Kevin P. ... Cincinnati, OH
Roberts, Kevin P. ... Cleveland, OH
Roberts, Kevin T. ... Cleveland, OH
Mentor, OH
Roberts, Kim Alan ... Dallas, TX
Roberts, Kimberly G. ... Pittsburgh, PA
Roberts, Kimberly J. ... Los Angeles, CA
Roberts, Kirby J. ... Junction, TX
Roberts, Kirkland T. ... Portland, OR
Roberts, Kyle Ann ... Palm Harbor, FL
Roberts, Landon ... Asheville, NC
Roberts, Larry A. ... Atlanta, GA
Roberts, Larry B., (P.A.) ... Miami, FL
Roberts, Larry E. ... Meridian, MS
Roberts, Larry J. ... Pasadena, CA
Roberts, Larry K. ... Newport Beach, CA
Roberts, Larry K., Inc.
Newport Beach, CA
Roberts, Larry L. ... Detroit, MI
Roberts, Larry L. ... Nashville, TN
Roberts, Larry M. ... Los Angeles, CA
Pasadena, CA
Roberts, Larry S. ... Lexington, KY
Roberts, Laura Eve
South San Francisco, CA
Roberts, Laura Hicks ... Coral Gables, FL
Roberts, Laurel L. ... Hermosa Beach, CA
Roberts, Lauren ... Washington, DC
Roberts, Lauren E. ... Kansas City, MO
Roberts, Laurin C. ... Lansing, MI
Roberts Law Firm, A Professional Association
West Palm Beach, FL
Roberts Law Firm, P.C. ... Peru, IN
Roberts Law Firm, The, P.A.
Little Rock, AR
Roberts Law Firm, The, P.A.
Charlotte, NC
Gastonia, NC
Shelby, NC
Roberts Law Office ... Grant, NE
Roberts & Law, P.A. ... Groveland, FL
Roberts, Lawrence ... Washington, DC
Roberts, Lawrence C. ... Plantation, FL
Roberts, Lawrence C., P.A. ... Plantation, FL
Roberts, Lawrence D. ... New York, NY
Roberts, Lawrence J. ... Miami, FL
Roberts, Lawrence J. ... Elkins Park, PA
Roberts, Lawrence W. ... Cordele, GA
Roberts, Lee H. ... Lock Haven, PA
Roberts, Lee Harriss ... Washington, DC
Roberts, LeGrande ... Ontario, CA
Roberts, Leslie Jean ... Bealeton, VA
Roberts, Leslie M. ... Portland, OR
Roberts, Lewis J. ... Glastonbury, CT
Roberts, Linda ... New York, NY
Roberts, Linda L. ... Yorba Linda, CA
Roberts, Lindsay E. ... Chicago, IL
Roberts, Lindsey Charles ... Dallas, TX

Roberts, Lisa A. ... Boston, MA
Roberts, Lisa C. ... San Jose, CA
Roberts, Lisa K. ... Palo Alto, CA
Roberts, Lisa R. ... Walnut Creek, CA
Roberts, Lisa Reid ... Griffin, GA
Roberts, Lisa Trueba ... Miami, FL
Roberts, Littleton W., Jr. ... Wayne, PA
Roberts, Lloyd M. ... New York, NY
Roberts, Lollie A. ... Prescott, AZ
Roberts, Lon E. ... Wausau, WI
Roberts, Loretta K. ... Tulsa, OK
Roberts, Lori L. ... Denver, CO
Roberts, Lori R. ... Oklahoma City, OK
Roberts & Lothrop ... Newport, OR
Roberts, Louis ... Laguna Hills, CA
Roberts, Louis C. ... New York, NY
Roberts, Lu Ann ... Savannah, GA
Roberts, Lucille C. ... Arlington, VA
Roberts, Lucille K. ... Department of Justice, United States Marshals Service, GV
Roberts, Lyle ... Washington, DC
Roberts, M. Keith ... Chattanooga, TN
Roberts, M. Kristina ... Kansas City, MO
Roberts, Manley W. ... Charlotte, NC
Roberts, Marc A. ... York, PA
Roberts, Margaret A.
National Aeronautics And Space Administration, Office of the General Counsel, GV
Roberts, Margot S. ... Jonesboro, GA
Roberts, Maria C. ... San Diego, CA
Roberts, Marjorie Rawls
Charlotte Amalie, St. Thomas, VI
Charlotte Amalie, St. Thomas, VI
Roberts, Mark ... Malvern, AR
Roberts, Mark ... Blue Springs, MO
Roberts, Mark ... Seattle, WA
Roberts, Mark A. ... Cedar Rapids, IA
Roberts, Mark A. ... Southfield, MI
Roberts, Mark C., II ... Dallas, TX
Roberts, Mark F. ... Springfield, OH
Roberts, Mark J. ... Indianapolis, IN
Roberts, Mark L. ... Natchitoches, LA
Roberts, Mark S. ... Farmington Hills, MI
Roberts, Mark Scott ... Fullerton, CA
Roberts, Mark Scott, and Associates, A Prof. Law Corp. ... Fullerton, CA
Roberts, Mark W. ... Boston, MA
Roberts, Mark W. ... Seattle, WA
Roberts, Markel & Folger, L.L.P.
Houston, TX
Roberts, Marty R. ... Solvang, CA
Roberts, Mary Agnes ... Columbus, OH
Roberts, Mary Ann ... Powell, OH
Roberts, Mary Ann ... Pauls Valley, OK
Roberts, Mary Colleen ... Chicago, IL
Roberts, Mary E. ... Seattle, WA
Roberts, Mary Kathryn ... Jackson, MS
Roberts, Mary Kathryn ... Trenton, NJ
Roberts, Mary Louise Horner
Richmond, VA
Roberts, Mary Maloney ... Oakland, CA
Roberts, Mary S. ... San Antonio, TX
Roberts, Matthew B. ... Columbia, SC
Roberts, Matthew D. ... Department of Justice, Office of the Solicitor General, GV
Roberts, Matthew F. ... Atlanta, GA
Roberts, Matthew F. ... Kirkland, WA
Roberts, Maureen C. ... La Crosse, WI
Roberts, Maurice A. ... Washington, DC
Roberts, Maxey J. (Miss) ... Mobile, AL
Roberts & McFarquhar, P.C.
Mount Vernon, NY
Roberts & McGivney ... Chicago, IL
Roberts, Melanie D. ... San Jose, CA
Roberts, Melissa J. ... Richmond, VA
Roberts, Melville N. ... El Monte, CA
Roberts, Melvin L. ... York, SC
Roberts & Mercanti, L.L.P. ... Princeton, NJ
Roberts, Miceli & Boileau ... Lock Haven, PA
Roberts, Michael A. ... Cincinnati, OH
Roberts, Michael B. ... Waco, TX
Roberts, Michael D. ... Enid, OK
Roberts, Michael D. ... Nashville, TN
Roberts, Michael E. ... Los Angeles, CA
Roberts, Michael E. ... North Charleston, SC
Roberts, Michael G. ... Washington, DC
Roberts, Michael G. ... Chicago, IL
Roberts, Michael G. ... Florence, SC
Roberts, Michael J. ... San Diego, CA
Roberts, Michael J. ... Washington, DC
Roberts, Michael J. ... Detroit, MI
Roberts, Michael J. ... Grand Rapids, MI
Roberts, Michael J. ... New York, NY
Roberts, Michael L. ... Gadsden, AL
Roberts, Michael L. ... Little Rock, AR
Roberts, Michael P. ... Bangor, ME
Roberts, Michael P. ... New York, NY
Roberts, Michael S. ... Chicago, IL
Roberts, Michael T. ... Ogden, UT
Roberts, Michael W. ... Los Angeles, CA
Roberts, Michael W. ... Cambridge, MA
Roberts, Michele A. ... Washington, DC
Roberts, Michelle E. ... Dallas, TX
Roberts, Mickey G. ... Duluth, GA
Roberts, Mike ... Memphis, TN
Roberts, Moira T. ... Washington, DC
Roberts, Monica Kay ... Stilwell, OK
Roberts, Monte B. ... El Paso, TX
Roberts & Morgan ... Riverside, CA
Roberts & Murphy ... Independence, IA
Roberts, N. David, Jr. ... Knoxville, TN
Roberts, N. Elizabeth ... Burbank, CA
Roberts, Nancy A. ... Omaha, NE
Roberts, Nancy Lynn ... Tulsa, OK
Roberts, Nancy Oliver ... Bowling Green, KY
Roberts, Nancy Sue ... Alameda, CA
Roberts, Nathan M. ... Lafayette, LA

Roberts, Neal A. ... Los Angeles, CA
Roberts, Neil E. ... Washington, DC
Roberts, Neil E. ... Lakewood, OH
Roberts & Newman, P.A. ... Newton, MA
Roberts, Nolte T. ... Jackson, MS
Roberts, Norman A., II ... New York, NY
Roberts, Norman L. ... Beverly Hills, CA
Roberts, Norman T. ... Key Biscayne, FL
Roberts, O. E. Jack ... Phoenix, AZ
Roberts, Owen ... Brookhaven, MS
Roberts, Owen Earl, Jr. ... Birmingham, AL
Roberts, Owen L. ... Austin, TX
Roberts, Pamela ... Cameron Park, CA
Roberts, Pamela G. ... Carson City, NV
Roberts, Pamela J. ... Columbia, SC
Roberts, Pamela Moseley ... Little Rock, AR
North Little Rock, AR
Roberts, Parish & Castleman, Ltd.
Decatur, IL
Roberts, Parks ... Winston-Salem, NC
Roberts, Patricia ... Winston-Salem, NC
Roberts, Patricia A. ... Hartford, CT
Roberts, Patricia A.
Environmental Protection Agency, Office of the General Counsel, GV
Roberts, Patricia A. ... Farmingdale, NJ
Roberts, Patricia A. ... New York, NY
Roberts, Patricia E. ... Bellevue, WA
Roberts, Patricia Erikson
Newport News, VA
Roberts, Patricia L. ... Atlanta, GA
Roberts, Patricia S. ... Indianapolis, IN
Roberts, Patricia S. ... Youngstown, OH
Roberts, Patrick J. ... Peru, IN
Roberts, Patrick K. ... Springfield, MO
Roberts, Patti R. ... Oakland, CA
Roberts, Paul ... Prescott, AZ
Roberts, Paul ... New York, NY
Roberts, Paul A. ... Santa Barbara, CA
Roberts, Paul A. ... Washington, DC
Roberts, Paul C. ... New York, NY
Roberts, Paul E. ... Denver, CO
Roberts, Paul G. ... Chicago, IL
Roberts, Paul G. ... Boston, MA
Roberts, Paul K. ... Warren, AR
Mesquite, TX
Roberts, Paul R., Jr. ... New Braunfels, TX
Roberts, Penny K. ... Portland, OR
Roberts, Perryman, Bomkamp & Meives, P.C. ... Belleville, IL
Clayton, MO
St. Louis, MO
Roberts, Peter D. ... New York, NY
Roberts, Peter J. ... Chicago, IL
Roberts, Peter W. ... Fairfax, VA
Roberts, Philip A., Jr. ... Chesterfield, VA
Roberts, Philip C. ... Fort Fairfield, ME
Roberts, Philip E. ... Lafayette, LA
Roberts, Philip H. ... Texas City, TX
Roberts, Philip J. ... Laramie, WY
Roberts, Philip M. ... Seattle, WA
Roberts, R. Bruce ... Anchorage, AK
Roberts, R. Kenney ... Portland, OR
Roberts, R. Kent ... Buffalo, NY
Roberts, R. Lee ... Boise, ID
Roberts, R. Lee, Jr. ... Chattanooga, TN
Roberts, R. Richard ... Drasco, AR
Roberts, R. Stephen ... Decatur, GA
Roberts, R. Thomas ... Jacksonville, FL
Roberts, Rainwater & Ingram, L.L.P.
Cordele, GA
Roberts, Ralph ... Jacksonville, FL
Roberts, Ralph P. ... Atlanta, GA
Roberts, Ralph, P.A. ... Jacksonville, FL
Roberts, Ralston P. ... Napa, CA
Roberts, Randal W. ... Albuquerque, NM
Roberts, Randall C. ... Ann Arbor, MI
Roberts, Randall E. ... Chicago, IL
Roberts, Randall E. ... Dallas, TX
Roberts, Randall L. ... Tyler, TX
Roberts, Randall S. ... Farmington, NM
Roberts, Randall S., P.C. ... Farmington, NM
Roberts, Randell C. ... Tyler, TX
Roberts, Randi J. ... New York, NY
Roberts, Raymond D. ... Philadelphia, PA
Roberts, Raymond E. ... Campbell, CA
Palo Alto, CA
Roberts, Raymond L. ... Newton, MA
Roberts, Raymond M. ... Lima, OH
Roberts, Raymond McCollough
Pittsburgh, PA
Roberts, Raymond R. ... Auburn, CA
Roberts, Reid B. ... Pittsburgh, PA
Roberts, Reid W. ... Stockton, CA
Roberts, Reinisch, Mackenzie, Healey & Wilson, P.C. ... Portland, OR
Seattle, WA
Roberts & Reiter, P.A. ... Jacksonville, FL
Roberts, Renee A. ... Bremerton, WA
Roberts, Renee J. ... New York, NY
Roberts, Rex G. ... Dallas, TX
Roberts, Rex H. ... Nashville, TN
Roberts & Reynolds, P.A.
West Palm Beach, FL
Roberts, Richard ... Mesa, AZ
Roberts, Richard A. ... Cheshire, CT
Roberts, Richard A. ... Mount Vernon, NY
Roberts, Richard C. ... Paducah, KY
Roberts, Richard C., III ... Jackson, MS
Roberts, Richard D. ... Denver, CO
Roberts, Richard D. ... Portland, OR
Roberts, Richard E. ... Schenectady, NY
Roberts, Richard E. ... Quitman, TX
Roberts, Richard H. ... Grant, NE
Roberts, Richard J. ... Kew Gardens, NY
Roberts, Richard J., Jr. ... Shamokin, PA
Roberts, Richard K. ... Ypsilanti, MI
Roberts, Richard L. ... San Bernardino, CA

Roberts, Richard L. ... Washington, DC
Roberts, Richard L. ... Olathe, KS
Roberts, Richard L., Sr. ... Toledo, OH
Roberts, Richard M. ... Washington, DC
Roberts, Richard M. ... West Orange, NJ
Roberts, Richard O. ... St. Louis, MO
Roberts, Richard P. ... Hartford, CT
Roberts, Richard P. ... Seattle, WA
Roberts, Richard R. ... Jackson, MS
Memphis, TN
Roberts, Richard S. ... Wheaton, MN
Roberts, Richard S. ... Princeton, NJ
Roberts, Richard S. ... Cincinnati, OH
Roberts, Richard W. ... Washington, DC
Roberts, Richard Y. ... Washington, DC
Roberts, Rita McCallister ... La Grange, GA
Roberts, Robb F. ... Portland, OR
Roberts, Robert A.
Environmental Protection Agency, Office of Enforcement and Compliance Assurance, GV
Roberts, Robert C. ... Salem, OH
Roberts, Robert E. ... New Castle, IN
Roberts, Robert H. ... Decatur, IL
Roberts, Robert, III ... Shreveport, LA
Roberts, Robert L. ... Denver, CO
Roberts, Robert L. ... Topeka, KS
Roberts, Robert L., Jr. ... Irving, TX
Roberts, Robert Thomas ... Jacksonville, FL
Roberts & Roberts ... Los Angeles, CA
Lowell, IN
Hauppauge, NY
Roberts & Roberts, A Professional Corporation ... Tyler, TX
Roberts, Roberts & Burcham, L.L.C.
Farmington, MO
Roberts & Roberts, L.L.P. ... Killeen, TX
Roberts & Roberts, P.C. ... Newport News, VA
Roberts, Roberts & Roberts
Nevada City, CA
Roberts, Robin K. ... Jacksonville, FL
Roberts, Rohn M. ... Eugene, OR
Roberts, Rokki F. ... Houston, TX
Roberts, Ronald ... Dallas, TX
Roberts, Ronald A. ... Tacoma, WA
Roberts, Ronald D. ... Southfield, MI
Roberts, Ronald L. ... Colorado Springs, CO
Roberts, Ronald L. ... Columbus, MS
Tupelo, MS
Roberts, Ronald L., P.C.
Colorado Springs, CO
Roberts, Ronald W. ... Grand Prairie, TX
Roberts, Ronna ... New York, NY
Roberts, Roscoe C. ... Richmond, VA
Roberts, Roscoe O., Jr. ... Huntsville, AL
Roberts, Rose & Bates, P.C.
Stamford, CT
Roberts, Rosemary G. ... Rush, NY
Roberts & Rowley, Ltd. ... Mesa, AZ
Roberts, Royce A. ... Seattle, WA
Roberts, Russell D. ... Austin, TX
Roberts, Russell H. ... Fredericksburg, VA
Roberts, Russell L. "Jack" ... Conway, AR
Roberts, Russell S. ... Jackson, MS
Roberts, Russell W. ... Rochester, NY
Roberts, St. Peter & Kuntz
San Bernardino, CA
Roberts & Salazar, L.L.P.
Key Biscayne, FL
Miami, FL
Roberts, Sam ... Broken Arrow, OK
Roberts, Sandra K., Law Offices of
Lufkin, TX
Roberts, Sandy A. ... Capitol Heights, MD
Roberts, Sanford ... Meredith, NH
Portsmouth, NH
Roberts, Sara E. ... Macon, GA
Roberts, Sarah Meeks ... Rochester, NY
Roberts, Scott A. ... Boston, MA
Roberts, Scott Alan ... Decatur, IL
Roberts, Scott C. ... Orlando, FL
Roberts, Scott M. ... Birmingham, AL
Roberts, Scott N. ... Groton, CT
Roberts, Scott R. ... Columbus, OH
Roberts, Scott R. ... Dallas, TX
Roberts, Scott W. ... Gastonia, NC
Roberts, Sean Alan ... Houston, TX
Roberts, Sean D. ... New York, NY
Roberts, Seth G. ... New York, NY
Roberts, Seymour, Jr. ... Fort Worth, TX
Roberts, Shaler S., III ... Florence, AL
Roberts, Shaun A. ... Dayton, OH
Roberts, Shawn J. ... Oklahoma City, OK
Roberts, Shea E. ... Atlanta, GA
Roberts, Shearl J. ... Dayton, OH
Roberts, Shelley D. ... Birmingham, MI
Roberts, Sheri ... Chicago, IL
Roberts, Sheridan & Kotel, A Professional Corporation ... New York, NY
Roberts, Sherrill P. ... Liberty, MO
Roberts, Shirleen A. ... Woodbridge, NJ
Roberts & Shirley ... Springvale, ME
Roberts, Sidney I. ... New York, NY
Roberts, Simon D. ... Alexandria, VA
Roberts, Simon & Even, Ltd. ... Inverness, IL
Roberts & Smaby, P.C. ... Dallas, TX
Roberts & Smith ... Lexington, KY
Roberts, Stanley L. ... Denver, CO
Roberts, Stephanie U.
Winston-Salem, NC
Roberts, Stephen A. ... Austin, TX
Roberts, Stephen B. ... Fresno, CA
Roberts, Stephen B. ... New York, NY
Roberts, Stephen D. ... Bozeman, MT
Roberts, Stephen H. ... Dover, NH
Roberts, Stephen M. ... Wellesley Hills, MA
Roberts, Stephen N. ... San Francisco, CA
Roberts, Stephen Thomas ... New York, NY

Robertson, Mark J. .... New York, NY
Robertson, Mark W. .... Los Angeles, CA
Robertson, Marvin E. .... St. Johns, MI
Robertson, Marvin H. .... Searcy, AR
Robertson, Mary .... Norman, OK
Robertson, Matthew H. .... Charlotte, NC
Robertson, Melissa A.
Securities and Exchange Commission, Division of Enforcement, GV
Robertson, Melissa Lanni
United States Court Of Appeals For The Federal Circuit, GV
Robertson, Michael L. .... Austin, TX
Robertson, Michelle F. .... Chapel Hill, NC
Robertson, Michelle M. .... Oklahoma City, OK
Robertson, M. Lee, Jr., P.A.
Mount Pleasant, SC
Robertson, Monagle & Eastaugh, A Professional Corporation
Anchorage, AK
Juneau, AK
Washington, DC
Arlington, VA
Robertson, Monica E. .... Toms River, NJ
Robertson, Morgan McNeel .... Marietta, GA
Robertson, Morris S. .... Dublin, GA
Robertson, Moura A.J.
Oklahoma City, OK
Tulsa, OK
Robertson, Murray J. .... Irvine, CA
Robertson, Ned S. .... Chicago, IL
Robertson, Neil .... Ashland City, TN
Robertson, Neil P. .... Miami, FL
West Palm Beach, FL
Robertson, Neil P. .... Lancaster, PA
Robertson, Norman M. .... Newark, NJ
Robertson, Pamela A. .... Greensboro, NC
Robertson, Pamela S. .... Palm Beach, FL
Robertson, Pat H. .... Austin, TX
Robertson, Patricia H. .... Austin, TX
Robertson, Patricia Quinn .... Franklin, TN
Robertson, Paul F. .... Encinitas, CA
Robertson, Paul J. .... Bethesda, MD
Robertson, Paul K. .... San Antonio, TX
Robertson, Paul M. .... Boston, MA
Robertson, Peter A. .... Daytona Beach, FL
Gainesville, FL
Maitland, FL
Robertson, Peter A., & Associates, P.A.
Gainesville, FL
Robertson, Peter D. .... Washington, DC
Robertson, Philip H. .... Wellesley, MA
Robertson, Phillip J. .... Crystal Lake, IL
Robertson, Phillip O. .... Altoona, PA
Robertson, Phillips & Webster
Redmond, WA
Robertson, R. Bruce .... Orange Beach, AL
Robertson, R. Eric .... Granite City, IL
Robertson & Railsback .... Dallas, TX
Robertson, Ralph B. .... Richmond, VA
Robertson, Ralph J., Jr. .... Carbondale, IL
Robertson, Randall .... Granite City, IL
Robertson, Randall E. .... Washington, DC
Robertson, Randolph C. .... Richmond, VA
Robertson, Raymond C. .... Staunton, VA
Robertson, Rebecca L. .... Houston, TX
Robertson, Reece B. .... Salt Lake City, UT
Robertson, Reginald .... West Memphis, AR
Robertson, Reuben B. .... Washington, DC
Robertson, Rhonda F.
Department of Labor, GV
Robertson, Richard H. .... Charlotte, NC
Robertson, Richard L. .... Charlotte, NC
Robertson, Richard L. .... Dallas, TX
Plano, TX
Robertson, Richard L., P.A. .... Charlotte, NC
Robertson, Richd. W. .... Santa Barbara, CA
Robertson, R. J., Jr. .... Carbondale, IL
Robertson, Rob .... Baltimore, MD
Robertson, Rob .... Columbia, MD
Robertson, Rob F.M. .... Oklahoma City, OK
Robertson, Rob V. .... Austin, TX
Robertson, Robert C. .... Medford, OR
Robertson, Robert N. .... Reno, NV
Robertson, Robert S. .... Morgan City, LA
Robertson, Robert Stafford .... Huntsville, AL
Robertson & Robertson .... La Porte City, IA
Robertson & Robertson .... Lincoln, NE
Robertson & Robertson, Attorneys, P.C.
Clifton, TX
Robertson, Rodger O. .... Baltimore, MD
Robertson, Rodney T. .... Boston, MA
Robertson, Roger E. .... Camarillo, CA
Robertson, Ronald E. .... Monroe, LA
Robertson, Roy R., Jr. .... Michigan City, IN
Robertson, Russell .... Charlottesville, VA
Robertson, Russell Brown .... Jasper, AL
Robertson, Ryan G. .... Tulsa, OK
Robertson, Sally Ireland .... Long Prairie, MN
Robertson, Samuel H., Jr. .... Houston, TX
Robertson, Sandra M. .... Ventura, CA
Robertson, Sarah E. .... Oakland, CA
Robertson, Scott C. .... Kannapolis, NC
Robertson, Scott L. .... Washington, DC
Robertson, Scott T. .... Lincoln, NE
Robertson, Stephen .... San Jose, CA
Robertson, Stephen W. .... Carmel, IN
Robertson, Steve .... Clifton, TX
Robertson, Steven E .... Lakewood, NJ
Robertson, Stewart M. .... New York, NY
Robertson, Stokes V., Jr. .... Jackson, MS
Robertson, Susan Ford .... Columbia, MO
Robertson, Susan L. .... New York, NY
Robertson, Susan R. .... Milwaukee, WI
Robertson, Ted Z. .... Dallas, TX
Robertson, Thomas .... Lansing, MI
Robertson, Thomas A. .... San Francisco, CA
Robertson, Thomas D. .... Newark, NJ

Robertson, Thomas D. .... Tulsa, OK
Robertson, Thomas E., Jr.
Fort Smith, AR
Waldron, AR
Robertson, Thomas H. .... Miami, FL
Robertson, Thomas H. .... Everett, WA
Robertson, Thomas M. .... Twin Falls, ID
Robertson, Tracey L.
Bloomfield Hills, MI
Robertson, Tracey M. .... Houston, TX
Robertson, Trudy H. .... Charleston, SC
Robertson, Vicki .... Oklahoma City, OK
Robertson, Victoria S. .... Suffolk, VA
Robertson, Vincent G. .... Georgetown, DE
Robertson, Vincent L. .... Moorestown, NJ
Robertson, W. Kent, Jr. .... Metairie, LA
Robertson, W. Marsh, (P.A.)
Greenville, SC
Robertson, W.R., III, P.C. .... Marietta, GA
Robertson & Walker, Attys, LLC
Canton, GA
Jasper, GA
Woodstock, GA
Robertson and Wall, P.C. .... Lilburn, GA
Robertson, Walter P. .... Junction City, KS
Robertson, Walter P., Chartered
Junction City, KS
Robertson, Wayman M., Jr. .... Oakland, CA
Robertson, William A., III .... St. Helena, CA
Robertson, William Craig, III
Lexington, KY
Robertson, William Dixon, III
Columbia, SC
Robertson, William E. .... Montgomery, AL
Robertson, William E., Jr. .... Sarasota, FL
Robertson, William F., III, (P.A.)
Greenville, SC
Robertson, William H. .... Clayton, AL
Robertson, William L. .... Indianapolis, IN
Robertson, William P. .... Somerville, NJ
Robertson, William S., III .... Wayne, NJ
Robertson, William Shore .... Warrenton, VA
Robertson, William W. .... Newark, NJ
Robertson & Williams, Inc.
Oklahoma City, OK
Robertson, Williams & McDonald, P.A.
Orlando, FL
Robertson, Wm. A. .... Houston, TX
Robertson, Worsham, Gregory & Giffin
Tullahoma, TN
Robertson, W.R., III .... Marietta, GA
Robertson, Yoshiko I. .... Irvine, CA
Robertson, Yvette
Department Of Veterans Affairs, Board of Veterans Appeals, GV
Robertson, Zeglen & Pidcock .... Akron, OH
Canton, OH
Robertson-Thissell, Nancy L.
Yorba Linda, CA
Roberts-Suskin, Catherine .... Montpelier, VT
Robertus, Carole A. .... Minneapolis, MN
Robés, J. Stephen .... Farmington Hills, MI
Robés & Kobliska, P.L.C.
Farmington Hills, MI
Robes, Robert J. .... Miami, FL
Robeson, J. Jay .... Springfield, IL
Robeson, James B. .... Manassas, VA
Robeson, Miriam E. .... Flora, IN
Robeson, Rebecca S. .... St. Louis, MO
Robeson, Renée M. .... Westfield, NJ
Robeson, Robeson & Van Doren
Manassas, VA
Robeson, Ruth W. .... Petaluma, CA
Robeson, Stuart H., Jr. .... Manassas, VA
Robey, Daniel L. .... Fairfax, VA
Robey, Edwin W. .... Washington, PA
Robey, Katharine C. .... Atlanta, GA
Robey, Peter E. .... Washington, DC
Robey, Richard M. .... Garfield Heights, OH
Robey, Ronald G. .... Atlanta, GA
Robey, Steve P. .... Providence, KY
Robey, Steven M. .... Bellingham, WA
Robey, William T., III .... Buena Vista, VA
Robeznieks, Paul A. .... Wilsonville, OR
Robfogel, Nathan J. .... Rochester, NY
Robfogel, Susan S. .... New York, NY
Rochester, NY
Robic, Michael P., II .... Pittsburgh, PA
Robichaud, Helen A. (IBA) **.... Boston, MA**
Robichaud, Kathleen L. .... Rensselaer, NY
Robichaud, Louise M. .... Kingston, NJ
Robichaud, Todd D. .... New York, NY
Robichaud, Yvette D. .... Las Vegas, NV
Robichaux, Craig J. .... Bogalusa, LA
Mandeville, LA
Robichaux, J. Van, Jr. .... Chalmette, LA
Robichaux, J. Van, Jr. .... New Orleans, LA
Robichaux, James H. .... Corpus Christi, TX
Robichaux, John F. .... Lake Charles, LA
Robichaux Mize & Wadsack, LLC
Lake Charles, LA
Robichaux, Rebecca N. .... Raceland, LA
Robicheaux, Carl W. .... Abbeville, LA
Robicsek, Susanne M. .... Charlotte, NC
Robida, J. Randolph .... Denver, CO
Robideaux, Jason W. .... Lafayette, LA
Robie, James R. .... Los Angeles, CA
Robie & Matthai, A Professional Corporation .... Los Angeles, CA
Robie, Ronald B. .... Sacramento, CA
Robie, Todd R. .... Sacramento, CA
Robillard, Donald F. .... Plano, TX
Robillard, Gail M. .... Torrance, CA
Robillard & Katz .... Los Angeles, CA
Torrance, CA
Robillard, Scott A. .... Boston, MA
Robilotti, Mark G. .... New York, NY
Robin, Alan J. .... San Francisco, CA

Robin, Alan J. .... Houston, TX
Robin, Albert .... New York, NY
Robin, Ansley J. .... Pittsburgh, PA
Robin, Barry A. .... Chicago, IL
Robin, Blecker & Daley .... New York, NY
Robin, Dan A., Jr. .... New Orleans, LA
Robin, Daniel K. .... Arlington Heights, IL
Robin, Daniel K., Ltd.
Arlington Heights, IL
Robin, Dennis R. .... Crofton, MD
Robin, Edward B. .... Encino, CA
Robin, Ellis Paul .... Los Angeles, CA
Robin, F. Philip .... Philadelphia, PA
Robin, Howard S. .... New York, NY
Robin, Howard S., Law Office of, P.C.
New York, NY
Robin, James G. .... Wayzata, MN
Robin, Jeffrey S. .... Beverly Hills, CA
Robin, Jeremy Todd .... Boston, MA
Robin, Joan Deasy .... San Francisco, CA
Robin, John M. .... Covington, LA
Robin, Kenneth .... Jonesboro, GA
Robin, Kenneth D. .... San Francisco, CA
Robin, Kenneth H. .... Prospect Heights, IL
Robin, Lonnie Hank .... Fort Worth, TX
Robin, Louis S. .... Longmeadow, MA
Robin, Marni Rae .... Brooklyn, NY
Robin, Miller & Tabis, A Prtn. incl. Prof. Corps. .... Chicago, IL
Robin, Nancy R.
Department Of Veterans Affairs, Board of Veterans Appeals, GV
Robin, Neil A. .... Chicago, IL
Robin, Paul .... New York, NY
Robin, Raymond L. .... Hollywood, FL
Robin, Renée Louise .... San Francisco, CA
Robin, Richard C. .... Chicago, IL
Robin, Robert M. .... Los Angeles, CA
Robin, Robert S., (P.C.) .... Chicago, IL
Robin, Sherwin P. .... Savannah, GA
Robin, Sherwin P., P.C. .... Savannah, GA
Robin, Sidney .... Chicago, IL
Robin, Susan K. .... Columbia, MD
Robin, T. Sydings, Jr. .... Birmingham, AL
Robin & Thompson, P.A. .... Wayzata, MN
Robin, Tracy J. .... Tampa, FL
Robin, Valerie B. .... Boston, MA
Robiner, Donald M. .... Cleveland, OH
Robiner, Mitchell C. .... Tampa, FL
Robiner, Susan M. .... Minneapolis, MN
Robinett, Bruce W. .... Bartlesville, OK
Robinett, Eileen Duffy .... Palo Alto, CA
Robinett, Erica B. .... Irvine, CA
Robinett, John D. .... Columbus, OH
Robinett, Mark W. .... Austin, TX
Robinett, Nancy M. .... Tucson, AZ
Robinett & Osmond .... Tulsa, OK
Robinett, Susan Markham .... Tulsa, OK
Robinett, Thomas A., Jr.
Overland Park, KS
Robinett, Thomas R. .... Gloucester, VA
Robinett, Timothy D. .... Los Angeles, CA
Robinett, Tracy W. .... Tulsa, OK
Robinette, Charles G. .... Morristown, TN
Robinette, Christopher J.
Charlottesville, VA
Robinette, Dugan & Jakubowski
Baltimore, MD
Robinette, Georgia A. .... Nashville, TN
Robinette, Gilbert H. .... Baltimore, MD
Charleston, WV
Robinette, James Harvey, II .... Hartville, MO
Robinette, Jeff S. .... McLean, VA
Robinette, Jeffery L. .... Morgantown, WV
Robinette, Joseph A. .... Cincinnati, OH
Robinette, Joseph A. .... Franklin, OH
Robinette, Kaye C. .... Eugene, OR
Robinette Law Office .... Morgantown, WV
Robinette, Mark B. .... Chesterfield, VA
Robinette, Renia L. .... Rogers, AR
Robinette, W. Theodore .... Indianapolis, IN
Robinette-May and Associates, Attorneys at Law, P.S.C. .... Pikeville, KY
Robinette-May, Pamela .... Pikeville, KY
Robinow, Lisa .... Ithaca, NY
Robinowitz, Charles .... Portland, OR
Robinowitz, Cohlan & Dubow
White Plains, NY
Robinowitz, Deborah A. .... Dallas, TX
Robinowitz, Kevin .... Dallas, TX
Houston, TX
Robinowitz, Marcialyn G. .... Tulsa, OK
Robinowitz, Seymour .... White Plains, NY
Robinowitz, Stuart .... New York, NY
Robins, Andrew B. .... Middletown, NJ
Robins, Andrew S. .... Fort Lauderdale, FL
Robins, Angela Iammatteo .... Armonk, NY
Robins, Ann .... Denver, CO
Robins & Associates .... Menlo Park, CA
Robins, Bernard J. .... New York, NY
Robins, Bill, III .... Houston, TX
Robins, Bruce .... New York, NY
Robins, Charles W. .... Boston, MA
Robins, Clayton I. .... West Hills, CA
Robins, Cloud, Greenwood & Lubel, L.L.P.
Beaumont, TX
Freeport, TX
Galveston, TX
Houston, TX
Victoria, TX
Robins, Corey J. .... Los Angeles, CA
Robins, Cory S. .... Fort Lauderdale, FL
Robins, Craig D. .... Westbury, NY
Robins, Cynthia A. .... Santa Monica, CA
Robins, David A. .... Jericho, NY
New York, NY
Robins, David M., (P.C.) .... Houston, TX
Robins, Dorothy M. .... San Francisco, CA

Robins, Eli .... New York, NY
Robins, Elizabeth S. .... New Orleans, LA
Robins, Fred .... New York, NY
Robins, Gina R. .... Miami Beach, FL
Robins, Gregory .... Los Angeles, CA
Robins, Harlan W. .... Columbus, OH
Robins, Harry .... New York, NY
Robins, Harvey E. .... Pittsburgh, PA
Robins, Irma J. .... Baltimore, MD
Robins, Irwin B. .... New York, NY
Robins, Jacquelyn .... Albuquerque, NM
Robins, Jeff P. .... Carrboro, NC
Robins, Jeffrey A. .... New York, NY
Robins, Jeffrey C. .... New York, NY
Robins, John B., IV .... Salisbury, MD
Robins, Johnson & Wade .... Salisbury, MD
Robins, Jon S. .... Philadelphia, PA
Robins, Kaplan, Miller & Ciresi
Chicago, IL
Robins, Kaplan, Miller & Ciresi L.L.P.
Costa Mesa, CA
Los Angeles, CA
Washington, DC
Atlanta, GA
Boston, MA
Minneapolis, MN
Robins, Kevin P. .... Oaks, PA
Robins, Kevin S. .... Houston, TX
Robins, Lawrence A., (P.C.) .... Chicago, IL
Robins, Lawrence R. .... Boston, MA
Providence, RI
Robins, Lena
Department Of Health And Human Services, Office of the General Counsel, GV
Robins, Lucy B. .... Baltimore, MD
Robins, Mark D. .... Boston, MA
Robins, Mark D. .... Detroit, MI
Robins, Martin B. .... Northbrook, IL
Robins, Mary Leslie .... Columbus, OH
Robins, Mathew .... Decatur, GA
Robins, Melvin L. .... Albuquerque, NM
Robins, Meredith E. .... Livingston, NJ
Robins, Michael J. Taichman
Philadelphia, PA
Robins, Michael L. .... Santa Monica, CA
Robins, Michelle S. .... Encino, CA
Robins, Pauline Y. .... Los Angeles, CA
Robins, Philip L. .... Treasury Department, Office of Regulations and Rulings, GV
Robins, Preston, Beckett, Graff & Gugle Co., L.P.A. .... Columbus, OH
Robins, Richard A. .... New York, NY
Robins, Richard B. .... Roseland, NJ
Robins, Richard C. .... El Paso, TX
Robins, Richard D. .... Los Angeles, CA
Robins, Robert .... Daytona Beach, FL
Robins, Roberta L. .... Menlo Park, CA
Robins, Ronald A., Jr. .... Columbus, OH
Robins, Rosetta B. .... Kansas City, MO
Robins, Scott .... Gaithersburg, MD
Robins, Sean .... Elkins Park, PA
Robins, Stanford .... St. Paul, MN
Robins, Steven A. .... Rockville, MD
McLean, VA
Robins, Thomas D. .... Asheboro, NC
Robins, Thomas G. .... San Antonio, TX
Robins, Thomas M., III .... Los Angeles, CA
Robins, W. Ronald .... Houston, TX
Robins, Warren S. .... Paramus, NJ
Robins, William M. .... Piscataway, NJ
Robins-Kaufman, Susan .... Denver, CO
Robins Liben, Fran R. .... Providence, RI
Robinson, A. Carl .... Muskogee, OK
Robinson, A. Douglas, Jr. .... Gastonia, NC
Robinson, A. Francis, Jr. .... New York, NY
Robinson, A. Jeffry, (P.A.) .... Miami, FL
Robinson, A. Stanley .... New York, NY
Robinson, Adam D. .... McLean, VA
Robinson, Alan B. .... Washington, DC
Greenbelt, MD
Robinson, Alan S. .... Pearl River, NY
Robinson, Albert S. .... Wellesley, MA
Robinson, Alfred B., Jr. .... Greenville, SC
Robinson, Allen Byron .... Hayward, CA
Robinson, Alma .... San Francisco, CA
Robinson, Amy .... New York, NY
Robinson, Amy E. .... Newark, NJ
Robinson, Amy Herter .... Schenectady, NY
Robinson, Andrea A. .... Thousand Oaks, CA
Robinson, Andrea J. .... Boston, MA
Robinson, Andrew B. .... Denver, CO
Robinson, Andrew S. .... Farmington, ME
Robinson, Angela P. .... Philadelphia, PA
Robinson, Ann Gallagher .... Cincinnati, OH
Robinson, Ann K. .... Farmington, ME
Robinson, Ann R. .... Augusta, ME
Robinson, Anne E. .... New York, NY
Robinson, Anthony J. .... Arcadia, CA
Robinson, Antonio D. .... Baton Rouge, LA
Robinson, Archie S. .... San Jose, CA
Robinson, Armand I. .... Washington, DC
Robinson, Arnold .... Millville, NJ
Robinson, Aron D. .... Chicago, IL
Robinson, Arthur C. .... Cicero, IL
Robinson, Arthur D. .... New York, NY
Robinson, Arthur S. .... Soldotna, AK
Robinson, Ashley T. .... Birmingham, AL
Robinson & Associates .... Lansing, MI
Robinson, Aubin Wade
West Palm Beach, FL
Robinson, Aubrey E., Jr.
United States District Court For The District Of Columbia, GV
Robinson, Audrey Denise .... Huntsville, AL
Robinson, Barbara M. .... Millbrae, CA
Robinson, Barbara Paul .... New York, NY
Robinson, Barclay, Jr. .... Hartford, CT

Robinson, Barnett, Jr. .... **Boca Raton, FL**
Coral Gables, FL
Robinson, Barnett, Jr., P.A.
Boca Raton, FL
Coral Gables, FL
Robinson, Barry K. .... **Washington, DC**
Robinson, Barry R. .... **Columbus, OH**
Robinson, Barton, McCarthy & Calloway, P.A. .... **Columbia, SC**
Robinson, Battle Rankin, (Ms.)
Georgetown, DE
Robinson, Beiswenger and Ehrhardt
Soldotna, AK
Robinson, Benjamin .... New York, NY
Robinson, Bernard J. .... San Rafael, CA
Robinson, Bert K., Law Offices of
Baton Rouge, LA
Robinson, Beth .... **Middlebury, VT**
Robinson, Bill D., Jr. .... Kansas City, KS
Robinson, Billy J. .... Dallas, TX
Robinson, Billy R. .... Bossier City, LA
Robinson, Blue & Wilson, L.L.P.
Belmont, NC
Gastonia, NC
Robinson, Bobby D. .... Vicksburg, MS
Robinson, Bonnie M. .... Larchmont, NY
Robinson, Bradshaw & Hinson, P.A.
Charlotte, NC
Rock Hill, SC
Robinson, Brenda .... Atlanta, GA
Robinson, Brent N. .... Mansfield, OH
Robinson, Brent T. .... **Rupert, ID**
Robinson, Brett A. .... **Springfield, MO**
Robinson, Brett H. .... Topeka, KS
Robinson, Brett W. .... **Laurel, MS**
Robinson, Brian D. .... **Washington, DC**
Robinson, Brian P. .... **Columbia, SC**
Robinson, Brian T. .... New York, NY
Robinson, Brian T. .... **Cleveland, OH**
Robinson, Brian W. .... **Boston, MA**
Robinson, Bridget R. .... **Austin, TX**
Robinson Brog Leinwand Greene Genovese & Gluck P.C. .... **New York, NY**
Robinson, Bruce E. .... South Hill, VA
Robinson, Bruce H. .... Wallace, NC
Robinson, Bruce M. .... **Baltimore, MD**
Robinson, Bruce W. .... **Lake City, FL**
Robinson, Bryant, III .... **Washington, DC**
Robinson, C. Arthur, II .... **Norfolk, VA**
Robinson, C. Frederick .... Mobile, AL
Robinson, Calcagnie & Robinson
Laguna Niguel, CA
Los Angeles, CA
Santa Ana, CA
Newport Beach, CA
San Diego, CA
Robinson, Calvin E. .... Omaha, NE
Robinson, Calvin S. .... **Kalispell, MT**
Robinson & Campbell .... **Irvine, CA**
Robinson, Cari S. .... White Plains, NY
Robinson, Carl C. .... Los Angeles, CA
Robinson, Carl Ray .... Bessemer, AL
Robinson, Carl Wade .... Bessemer, AL
Robinson, Carroll George .... Houston, TX
Robinson, Carter Alan .... Huntsville, AL
Robinson, Casey U. .... Caldwell, ID
Robinson, Catherine R. .... **Tampa, FL**
Robinson, Chad .... Rochester, NY
Robinson, Charles .... New Vernon, NJ
Robinson, Charles B. .... Lutz, FL
Robinson, Charles B. .... Sherman, TX
Robinson, Charles C. .... **Seattle, WA**
Robinson, Charles E. .... **Ashville, AL**
Robinson, Charles E., Jr. .... **Ashville, AL**
Robinson, Charles F. .... Menlo Park, CA
Robinson, Charles F., Jr. .... **Indianapolis, IN**
Robinson, Charles F., Law Office of
Clearwater, FL
Robinson, Charles Grigg .... **Huntsville, AL**
Robinson, Charles L. .... **Birmingham, AL**
Robinson, Charles M. .... Redwood City, CA
Robinson, Charles T. .... Mansfield, OH
Robinson, Charles W. .... Warrendale, PA
Robinson, Charlotte R. .... **Denver, CO**
Robinson, Christine A. .... Cheshire, CT
Robinson, Christopher D. .... **Brainerd, MN**
Robinson, Christopher D., (P.A.)
Fort Lauderdale, FL
Robinson, Christopher R. .... Cambridge, MD
Robinson & Chur .... **Honolulu, HI**
Robinson, Cindy L. .... **Denver, CO**
Robinson, Cindy Lori .... **Bridgeport, CT**
Robinson, Claire .... **Burbank, CA**
Robinson, Clarissa A. .... Liverpool, NY
Robinson, Clarissa R. .... Sacramento, CA
Robinson, Clark .... Evansville, IN
Robinson, Clarke C. .... Chicago, IL
Robinson, Claudia J. .... **Sacramento, CA**
Robinson, Clayton L. .... **Lexington, KY**
Robinson, Clifford A. .... Towson, MD
Robinson, Clifford O. .... Findlay, OH
Robinson & Cole & Craig LLP
Manchester, NH
Robinson & Cole LLP .... **Greenwich, CT**
Hartford, CT
Stamford, CT
Boston, MA
New York, NY
Robinson, Coleman Lee .... Pensacola, FL
Robinson, Colin W. .... Lyme, NH
Robinson, Collins H. .... St. Louis, MO
Robinson, Constance K.
Department of Justice,
Antitrust Division, GV
Robinson, Cooper Brett .... Tulsa, OK
Robinson, Cora-Jean Eaton
Northampton, MA
Robinson, Craig A. .... **Akron, OH**

Robinson, Craig D. .... Springfield, MA
Robinson Curley & Clayton, P.C.
Chicago, IL
Robinson, Cynthia A. .... Winchester, MA
Robinson, Cyril D. .... Carbondale, IL
Robinson, D. Clay .... **Columbia, SC**
Robinson, D. Taylor .... Birmingham, AL
Robinson, Dale W. .... Mesa, AZ
Robinson, Daniel A. .... **San Francisco, CA**
Robinson, Daniel A. .... **Exton, PA**
Robinson, Daniel C. .... Barboursville, WV
Robinson, Daniel K. .... Salem, OR
Robinson, Daniel L. .... Indianapolis, IN
Robinson, Daniel T., Jr. .... St. Louis, MO
Robinson, Darlene .... Oakland City, IN
Robinson, Daryl A. .... Atlanta, GA
Robinson, David .... Phoenix, AZ
Robinson, David A. .... **Irvine, CA**
Robinson, David A. .... **Los Angeles, CA**
Robinson, David A. .... San Francisco, CA
Robinson, David A. .... Springfield, MA
Robinson, David A. .... **New York, NY**
Robinson, David B. .... **Washington, DC**
Robinson, David B. .... **Fort Worth, TX**
Robinson, David C. .... **Simsbury, CT**
Robinson, David D. .... **Atlanta, GA**
Robinson, David D. .... **Indianapolis, IN**
Robinson, David E. .... Jacksonville, IL
Robinson, David Edward
West Conshohocken, PA
Robinson, David J. .... Akron, OH
Robinson, David, Jr. .... Washington, DC
Robinson, David K. .... Evansville, IN
Robinson, David K., Jr.
Coeur d'Alene, ID
Robinson, David K., (P.C.) .... **Pasadena, CA**
Robinson, David L. .... Ashland, MS
Robinson, David L. .... **Greensburg, PA**
Robinson, David M. .... **San Francisco, CA**
Robinson, David M. .... **Honolulu, HI**
Robinson, David P. .... Portland, ME
Robinson, David S., Jr. .... **Southfield, MI**
Robinson, David W. .... **Baton Rouge, LA**
Robinson, David W. .... White Bear Lake, MN
Robinson, David W. .... New York, NY
Robinson, David W. .... Bellingham, WA
Robinson, David W., II .... **Columbia, SC**
Robinson, Davis R. .... **Washington, DC**
Robinson, Dean .... Mount Juliet, TN
Robinson, Dean L. .... **Fairfax, VA**
Robinson, Dean M. .... **San Francisco, CA**
Robinson, Deborah .... Philadelphia, PA
Robinson, Deborah A.
United States District Court For The District
Of Columbia, GV
Robinson, Deborah J. .... **Pittsburgh, PA**
Robinson, Deborah L. .... **Baltimore, MD**
Robinson, Deborah L. .... Pittsburgh, PA
Robinson, Deborah Lea .... Towson, MD
Robinson, Deborah Lynn .... Upland, CA
Robinson, Deborah S. .... Phoenix, AZ
Robinson, Debra A. .... **Alpharetta, GA**
Robinson, Debra B. .... **Reno, NV**
Robinson, Debra F. .... Newark, NJ
Robinson, Deirdre M. .... **Boston, MA**
Robinson, Denis .... Van Nuys, CA
Robinson, Denis O. .... Manchester, NH
Robinson, Denise A. .... LaGrange, IN
Robinson, Derrick J. .... Hauppauge, NY
Robinson, Diamant & Brill, A Professional Corporation .... **Irvine, CA**
Los Angeles, CA
Robinson, Diana C. .... Irving, TX
Robinson, Di Lando & Whitaker, A Professional Law Corporation
Los Angeles, CA
San Francisco, CA
Robinson, Don W. .... **Burlingame, CA**
San Francisco, CA
Robinson, Donald A. .... **Newark, NJ**
Robinson, Donald C. .... **Butte, MT**
Robinson, Donald H. .... Louisville, KY
Robinson, Donald J. .... **New York, NY**
Robinson, Donald L. .... Tucson, AZ
Robinson, Donald L. .... Bloomington, IL
Macomb, IL
Peoria, IL
Quincy, IL
Rushville, IL
Springfield, IL
Robinson, Donald M. .... Jacksonville, FL
Robinson, Donald W. .... Detroit, MI
Robinson, Donna M. .... Martinsburg, WV
Robinson, Donnell L. .... Marine City, MI
Robinson Donovan Madden & Barry, P.C.
Northampton, MA
Springfield, MA
Robinson, Doris J. .... Payson, AZ
Robinson, Dorothy A. .... Marietta, GA
Robinson, Dorothy K. .... New Haven, CT
Robinson, Douglas E. .... **New York, NY**
Robinson, Douglas G. .... **Washington, DC**
Robinson, Douglas J. .... Camden, SC
Robinson, Douglas M. .... **Atlanta, GA**
Robinson, Douglas W.
Department of Commerce,
Patent and Trademark Office, GV
Robinson, Douglas W. .... **Kansas City, MO**
Robinson, Douglas W. .... **Arlington, VA**
Robinson, D.R. .... **Auburn, CA**
Robinson, Drew M. .... **Cleveland, TN**
Robinson and Dufault, P.C. .... Royal Oak, MI
Robinson, E. Barney, III .... **Jackson, MS**
Robinson, E. Glenn .... **Charleston, WV**
Robinson, E. Gordon .... Atlanta, GA
Robinson, E. Luckett, II .... **Mobile, AL**
Robinson, Edith A. .... Germantown, TN
Robinson, Edmund H. .... Cambridge, MA

Robinson, Edmundo .... Phoenix, AZ
Robinson, Edward E. .... **Harlingen, TX**
Robinson, Edward E. .... **Brookfield, WI**
Robinson, Edward L. .... **Buffalo, NY**
Robinson, Edward Murray .... Torrance, CA
Robinson, Edward O. .... **Pasadena, CA**
Robinson, Edward T., III .... Oyster Bay, NY
Robinson, Edwin T. .... Fort Thomas, KY
Robinson, Eileen .... Creston, CA
Robinson, Eileen C. .... Falls Church, VA
Robinson, Elaine B. .... **Piscataway, NJ**
Robinson, Elaine J. .... Louisville, KY
Robinson, Eldon M. .... Wilmington, DE
Robinson, Eliot William .... **Atlanta, GA**
Robinson, Elizabeth Harlow
Newburyport, MA
Robinson, Elizabeth J. .... **Rochester, NY**
Robinson, Elizabeth K. .... Austin, TX
Robinson, Ellen G. .... **Chicago, IL**
Robinson, Elliott .... Bethesda, MD
Robinson, Ellis F. .... **Toledo, OH**
Robinson, Emmett F. .... Burke, VA
Robinson, E. O., Jr. .... **Las Vegas, NV**
Robinson, E. R., III .... Lake Charles, LA
Robinson, Eric D. .... Orlando, FL
Robinson, Eric J. .... **McLean, VA**
Robinson, Eric L. .... **Salt Lake City, UT**
Robinson, Eric L. .... **Milwaukee, WI**
Robinson, Eric M. .... **New York, NY**
Robinson, Eric N. .... **Sacramento, CA**
Robinson, Eric Peter .... Kew Gardens, NY
Robinson, Eric S. .... **New York, NY**
Robinson, Erika L. .... **Washington, DC**
Baltimore, MD
Robinson, Eugene .... Dayton, OH
Robinson, Eugene .... **Tulsa, OK**
Robinson, Farida Moreau .... Kensington, MD
Robinson, Floyd I.
Federal Deposit Insurance Corporation,
Professional Liability Section, GV
Robinson, Forrest James, Jr. .... **Wichita, KS**
Robinson & Fotheringham .... **Amarillo, TX**
Robinson, Francis J. .... Philadelphia, PA
Robinson, Francis L. .... Ypsilanti, MI
Robinson, Frank E., II .... **Columbia, SC**
Robinson, Frank L. .... **Denver, CO**
Robinson, Frank S. .... Albany, NY
Robinson, Franklin E. .... Nekoosa, WI
Robinson, Franklin L., Jr. .... Pittsburgh, PA
Robinson, Frederick .... **Washington, DC**
Robinson, Frederick H. .... **Washington, DC**
Robinson, Frederick M. .... **Seattle, WA**
Robinson, Frederick W. .... Corpus Christi, TX
Robinson, Fredk. B. .... Indianapolis, IN
Robinson, Fredric W. .... Helena, MT
Robinson, G. Craig .... Wichita, KS
Robinson, Gail .... Frankfort, KY
Robinson, Gail A. .... Washington, DC
Robinson, Gale .... Nashville, TN
Robinson, Galen D. .... Minneapolis, MN
Robinson, Gary J. .... Tallahassee, FL
Robinson, Gary L. .... **Cedar Rapids, IA**
Robinson, Gary W. .... **Santa Barbara, CA**
Robinson, Gayle Lisa .... Towson, MD
Robinson, Genita C. .... **Chicago, IL**
Robinson, Geoffrey K. .... Miami, FL
Robinson, Geoffrey L. .... Walnut Creek, CA
Robinson, George D. .... **Anniston, AL**
Robinson, George H., Jr. .... **Lafayette, LA**
Robinson, George J. .... Webster, MA
Robinson, George M. .... Fairfield, TX
Robinson, Gerald H. .... **Portland, OR**
Robinson, Gerald J.
United States Postal Service,
Law Department, GV
Robinson, Gerald J. .... **New York, NY**
Robinson, Gerald J. .... Cincinnati, OH
Robinson, Gerald S. .... Carlisle, PA
Harrisburg, PA
Robinson and Geraldo, A Professional Corporation .... Washington, DC
Carlisle, PA
Harrisburg, PA
Robinson, Gerri Lyles .... Montgomery, AL
Robinson, Gillian A. .... **Houston, TX**
Robinson and Glavin .... Rochester, NY
Robinson, Glen O. .... Charlottesville, VA
Robinson, Glen S. .... Bakersfield, CA
Robinson, Glenn Arthur .... **Montpelier, VT**
Robinson, Glenn H. .... **Portland, ME**
Robinson & Glorisi .... **Somerville, NJ**
Robinson, Goldwyn J. .... Ellenton, FL
Robinson, Gray .... **Winston-Salem, NC**
Robinson, Gray .... Bristol, VA
Robinson & Grayson, P.A.
Wilmington, DE
Robinson, Gregory A. .... Phoenix, AZ
Robinson, Gregory C. .... Chagrin Falls, OH
Robinson, Gregory E. .... Irvine, CA
Robinson, Gregory N. .... **Pine Bluff, AR**
Robinson, Gregory P. .... **Annapolis, MD**
Robinson, Gregory P. .... Fayette, MO
Robinson, Gretel S. .... Birmingham, MI
Robinson, Grover C., III .... Pensacola, FL
Robinson, Guy D. .... **Fort Lauderdale, FL**
Robinson, H. Clay .... Little Rock, AR
Robinson, H. Jeffrey .... Akron, OH
Robinson, H. Murray .... Tulsa, OK
Robinson, Hank .... Louisville, KY
Robinson, Harold H., III .... **Santa Rosa, CA**
Robinson, Harold J. .... Royal Oak, MI
Robinson, Harold L.R. "Bob"
Oklahoma City, OK
Robinson, Harold M. .... Morganton, NC
Robinson, Harriet A. .... Washington, DC
Robinson, Harrison S. .... **Oakland, CA**
Robinson, Harry D., (P.A.)
West Palm Beach, FL

Robinson, Harry, III .... **Parsippany, NJ**
Robinson, Harry L. .... Cohoes, NY
Robinson, Heidi D. .... **Portland, OR**
Robinson, Helen .... Holly Springs, MS
Robinson, Henry A. .... Dover, KY
Robinson, Henry C. .... Youngstown, OH
Robinson, Henry H. .... **Fort Worth, TX**
Robinson, Herbert .... **New York, NY**
Robinson, Herman .... Baton Rouge, LA
Robinson, Hollis H. .... **New Orleans, LA**
Robinson, Holly L. .... Newark, NJ
Robinson & Hoover .... Oklahoma City, OK
Robinson, Horace B. B. .... **New York, NY**
Robinson, Howard L. .... Louisville, KY
Robinson, Howard M. .... Chicago, IL
Robinson, Hugh, Jr. .... Atlanta, GA
Robinson, Hugh M. .... **Okmulgee, OK**
Robinson, Ian .... **Salem, OH**
Robinson, Ira L. .... **Los Angeles, CA**
Robinson, Ira S. .... Albuquerque, NM
Robinson, Irl R. .... San Diego, CA
Robinson, Irwin Jay .... New York, NY
Robinson, Irwin Z. .... Manhasset, NY
Robinson, J. Craig .... Hutchinson, KS
Robinson, J. Howland .... Hackensack, NJ
New York, NY
Robinson, J. Kent .... **Rolla, MO**
Robinson, J. Mark .... New Albany, IN
Robinson, J. Mark .... **Baton Rouge, LA**
Robinson, J. Michael, Jr.
Baton Rouge, LA
Robinson, J. Neil .... **Charlotte, NC**
Robinson, J. Neil .... **Monroe, NC**
Robinson, J. Paul .... Knoxville, TN
Robinson, J. Randall .... **Oklahoma City, OK**
Robinson, J. Richard .... **Okemos, MI**
Robinson, J. Richard, P.C. .... **Lansing, MI**
Okemos, MI
Robinson, J. Russell, II .... Hagerstown, MD
Robinson, J. Russell, III .... Hagerstown, MD
Robinson, J. Scott .... Richmond, VA
Robinson, J. Terry .... Elyria, OH
Robinson, Jack .... Argonne, IL
Robinson, Jack D. .... **Denver, CO**
Robinson, Jack E., III .... Greenwich, CT
Robinson, Jack O. .... Boulder, CO
Robinson, Jack R. .... **Rockport, IN**
Robinson, Jack W., Jr. .... **Nashville, TN**
Robinson, Jack Wright, Sr. .... **Nashville, TN**
Robinson, Jackie .... **Dallas, TX**
Fort Worth, TX
Robinson, Jacob M. .... Wheeling, WV
Robinson & Jacobs .... Hyattsville, MD
Robinson, James A. .... Tulsa, OK
Robinson, James A. .... **Seattle, WA**
Robinson, James A. .... Seattle, WA
Robinson, James A., III .... Tallahassee, FL
Robinson, James A., Jr. .... Memphis, TN
Robinson, James B. .... Roswell, GA
Robinson, James B. .... Cincinnati, OH
Robinson, James C. .... **Orlando, FL**
Robinson, James C. .... **New York, NY**
Robinson, James D. .... **Los Angeles, CA**
Robinson, James D. .... Brighton, CO
Robinson, James D. .... **Fort Lauderdale, FL**
Robinson, James D. .... **Chattanooga, TN**
Robinson, James D. .... **Houston, TX**
Robinson, James D., P.A.
Fort Lauderdale, FL
Miami, FL
Robinson, James E. .... Smithtown, NY
Robinson, James E. .... **Philadelphia, PA**
Robinson, James F. .... **Irvine, CA**
Robinson, James F. .... Oklahoma City, OK
Robinson, James G. .... **Oxford, OH**
Robinson, James H. .... Suisun, CA
Robinson, James H., Jr .... Greensburg, PA
Robinson, James J. .... **Birmingham, AL**
Robinson, James J., Jr. .... **Chesterfield, MO**
Robinson, James K. .... Detroit, MI
Robinson, James K. .... Rochester, NY
Robinson, James Kenneth
Department Of Veterans Affairs,
Board of Contract Appeals, GV
Robinson, James L., Jr. .... Tucson, AZ
Robinson, James M. .... San Diego, CA
Santa Ana, CA
Robinson, James M. .... Ashland, KY
Robinson, James M. .... **Easley, SC**
Robinson, James Patrick, III .... **Austin, TX**
Robinson, James R. .... **Louisville, KY**
Robinson, James S. .... West Palm Beach, FL
Robinson, James S. .... Gary, IN
Robinson, James S. .... Houston, TX
Robinson, James S. .... Houston, TX
Robinson, James T. .... **Oklahoma City, OK**
Robinson, James V. .... Austin, TX
Robinson, James W. .... Newberry, MI
Robinson, James W. .... Broken Arrow, OK
Robinson, James W., P.C. .... Newberry, MI
Robinson, Jane I. .... Shrewsbury, MA
Robinson, Jane L. .... Honolulu, HI
Robinson, Janice Holman .... Chicago, IL
Robinson, Janice Sheryl .... Newark, NJ
Robinson, Janipher W. .... Richmond, VA
Robinson, Janipher W., Ltd. .... Richmond, VA
Robinson, Janis E. .... Bay City, TX
Robinson, Jason H. .... **Salt Lake City, UT**
Robinson, Jay .... **Burbank, CA**
Robinson, Jay D., Jr. .... **Indianapolis, IN**
Robinson, Jay N. .... **Philadelphia, PA**
Washington Crossing, PA
Robinson, Jay R. .... **Memphis, TN**
Robinson, Jayne S. .... **New York, NY**
Robinson, J. C. .... **Silver City, NM**
Robinson, Jeanne P. .... Santa Rosa, CA
Robinson, Jeffery P. .... **Seattle, WA**
Robinson, Jeffrey .... Salt Lake City, UT

Robinson, Jeffrey A. .... Irvine, CA
Robinson, Jeffrey A. .... Gig Harbor, WA
Robinson, Jeffrey C. .... Montgomery, AL
Robinson, Jeffrey D. .... Washington, DC
Robinson, Jeffrey L. .... Wauseon, OH
Robinson, Jennifer C. .... Denver, CO
Robinson, Jennifer J.
Fort Lauderdale, FL
Robinson, Jennifer L. .... Kansas City, MO
Robinson, Jennifer O. .... Hartford, CT
Robinson, Jennifer R. .... New York, NY
Robinson, Jeoffrey L. .... Newport Beach, CA
San Diego, CA
Robinson, Jerome W.
Federal Communications Commission, Mass Media Bureau, GV
Robinson, Jerry G. .... Charleston, SC
Robinson, Jerry H. .... San Francisco, CA
Robinson, Jerry L. .... Danbury, CT
Robinson, Jesse C. .... Lancaster, PA
Robinson, J. F. .... Fayetteville, AR
Robinson, J. F. Heaword, Jr. .... Scotia, NY
Robinson, Jill L. .... Redwood City, CA
Robinson, Jill R. .... Baltimore, MD
Robinson, Jimmy Don .... Wickliffe, KY
Robinson, Jimmy F., Jr. .... Roanoke, VA
Robinson, Joan E. .... Seattle, WA
Robinson, Joanna .... Austin, TX
Robinson, Joe T. .... Miami, FL
Robinson, Joel .... Warwick, RI
Robinson, Joel D.
Department of Housing and Urban Development, Office of General Counsel, GV
Robinson, Joel P., Jr., (P.C.) .... Jasper, AL
Robinson, John .... Washington, DC
Robinson, John A. .... Hutchinson, KS
Robinson, John B. .... Wheatland, WY
Robinson, John D. .... Orlando, FL
Robinson, John E. .... Decatur, GA
Robinson, John H. .... Notre Dame, IN
Robinson, John H. .... Austin, TX
Robinson, John H., III .... Glen Burnie, MD
Robinson, John J. .... San Diego, CA
Robinson, John J. .... Hartford, CT
Robinson, John J. .... Glenarm, MD
Robinson, John J., Jr. .... Harrisburg, PA
Robinson, John K. .... New York, NY
Robinson, John L. .... Arlington, TX
Robinson, John M. .... La Jolla, CA
Robinson, John M. .... Pebble Beach, CA
Robinson, John M.
Federal Energy Regulatory Commission, Office of the General Counsel, GV
Robinson, John M. .... Springhill, LA
Robinson, John M. .... Frederick, MD
Robinson, John M., Jr. .... Fort Smith, AR
Robinson, John R. .... St. Paul, MN
Robinson, John R. .... Rye, NY
Robinson, John R. .... Arlington, TX
Bedford, TX
Fort Worth, TX
Granbury, TX
Grand Prairie, TX
Irving, TX
Robinson, John R. .... Dallas, TX
Robinson, John S., Jr. .... Olympia, WA
Robinson, John T. .... Miami, FL
Robinson, John T. .... Decatur, IL
Robinson, John T. .... Selinsgrove, PA
Robinson, John V. .... Richmond, VA
Robinson, John W. .... Gretna, LA
Robinson, John W., III .... Jackson, MS
Robinson, John W., IV .... Tampa, FL
Robinson, John W., P.C. .... Gretna, LA
Robinson, Jon D. .... Sherman Oaks, CA
Robinson, Jon D. .... Decatur, IL
Robinson, Jon P. .... Fayetteville, AR
Robinson, Jon R. .... Jackson, MI
Robinson, Jonathan S. .... Trenton, NJ
Robinson, Joseph A. .... Irving, TX
Robinson, Joseph D. .... Miami, FL
Robinson, Joseph L. .... Pittsburgh, PA
Robinson, Joseph M. .... Oak Brook, IL
Robinson, Joseph R. .... New York, NY
Robinson, Joseph W. .... San Diego, CA
Robinson, Josephine Shaw .... Memphis, TN
Robinson, Joshua L. .... Luray, VA
Robinson, Judith L. ....
Department of Commerce, GV
Robinson, Judith S. .... Fort Washington, MD
Robinson, Judy L. .... Knoxville, TN
Robinson, Judy S. .... Greeneville, TN
Robinson, Julee .... Orange, CA
Robinson, Julia O. .... Boulder, CO
Robinson, Julia O., P.C. .... Boulder, CO
Robinson, Julie .... Topeka, KS
Robinson, Julie M. .... Palo Alto, CA
Robinson, Julius .... Beach Haven, NJ
Robinson, J. W. .... New York, NY
Robinson, J. W. .... Palestine, TX
Robinson, K. English .... San Diego, CA
Robinson, Karen .... New York, NY
Robinson, Karen L. .... Long Beach, CA
Robinson, Karen M. .... Washington, DC
Robinson, Kari S. .... Houston, TX
Robinson, Karl Edward .... Minneapolis, MN
St. Paul, MN
Robinson, Katharine H. .... New Haven, CT
Robinson, Katherine O. .... Chicago, IL
Robinson, Kathleen M. .... Portsmouth, NH
Robinson, Kathleen M., P.A.
Portsmouth, NH
Robinson, Keith A. .... Calabasas, CA
Robinson, Keith A. .... Denver, CO
Robinson, Keith A. .... Paw Paw, MI
Robinson, Keith T. .... Washington, DC
Robinson, Kelly Koepp .... Denver, CO

Robinson, Kendall .... Booneville, KY
Robinson, Kenneth B. .... Miami, FL
Robinson, Kenneth D. .... Boulder, CO
Robinson, Kenneth D., P.C. .... Boulder, CO
Robinson, Kenneth F. .... Cleveland, OH
Robinson, Kenneth G. .... Arlington, VA
Robinson, Kenneth G., Jr. .... Washington, DC
Robinson, Kenneth J. .... Bloomfield Hills, MI
Robinson, Kenneth Jerome .... Birmingham, AL
Robinson, Kenneth L. .... Danbury, CT
Robinson, Kenneth L., Jr. .... Greensboro, NC
Robinson, Kenneth M. .... Brooklyn, NY
Robinson, Kenneth Michael
Washington, DC
Robinson, Kenneth P. .... Huntington, NY
Robinson, Kenneth W. .... San Jose, CA
Robinson, Kenneth W., A P.C. .... San Jose, CA
Robinson, Kent S. .... Glendale, CA
Robinson, Kent W. .... Houston, TX
Robinson, Kerry .... Chesterland, OH
Robinson, Kerry G. .... Bellevue, WA
Robinson, Kevin D. .... Buffalo, NY
Robinson, Kevin M. .... Chicago, IL
Robinson, Kevin S. .... Yreka, CA
Robinson, Kim H. .... Sells, AZ
Robinson, Kim L. .... San Francisco, CA
Robinson, Kimberly J. .... Chicago, IL
Robinson, Kimberly L. .... Chicago, IL
Robinson, Kimberly M. .... Dallas, TX
Robinson, Kirk T. .... Watertown, NY
Robinson, Klyde .... Charleston, SC
Robinson & Kole .... Bellingham, WA
Robinson, Kriger & McCallum
Portland, ME
Robinson, Kurt .... Blaine, MN
Robinson, Kurt L. .... Torrance, CA
Robinson, Kurt, P.A. .... Blaine, MN
Robinson, L. Andrew .... Palmer, AK
Robinson, L. Ashley .... New York, NY
Robinson, L. Kent .... Louisville, KY
Robinson, L. Steven .... Warren, OH
Robinson, L. Vern .... Iowa City, IA
Robinson, Lance J. .... Kenner, LA
Robinson Lapidus & Livelli .... Newark, NJ
Robinson, Lara B. .... Atlanta, GA
Robinson, Laron D. .... Houston, TX
Robinson, Larry E. .... Los Angeles, CA
Robinson, Laura P. .... Altamonte Springs, FL
Robinson, Laura S. .... Martinez, CA
Robinson, Laura Schiele .... Birmingham, AL
Robinson, Laura W. .... Columbia, SC
Robinson, Lauren G. .... Chicago, IL
Robinson, Lauretta D. .... New York, NY
Robinson, Laurie Nicole .... New York, NY
Robinson Law Firm .... Abilene, TX
Robinson Law Firm .... Appleton, WI
Robinson Law Firm, P.A. .... Easley, SC
Robinson Law Firm, The
Washington, DC
Robinson Law Firm, The
Oklahoma City, OK
Tulsa, OK
Robinson Law Office, P.C.
Anchorage, AK
Palmer, AK
Wasilla, AK
Robinson Law Offices .... Louisville, KY
Robinson & Lawing, L.L.P.
Greensboro, NC
High Point, NC
Winston-Salem, NC
Robinson, Lawrence D. .... Irving, TX
Robinson, Lawrence J. .... Sarasota, FL
Robinson, Lawrence L. .... Philadelphia, PA
Robinson, Lawrence T. .... Gaithersburg, MD
Robinson, Layon F., II .... Bradenton, FL
Robinson, Lee M. .... Charleston, SC
Robinson, Leigh Meredith .... San Diego, CA
Robinson, Lena A. .... Lynn, MA
Robinson, Leon M. .... Boynton Beach, FL
Robinson, Leonardo D. .... Indianapolis, IN
Robinson, Leslie S. .... Greenville, NC
Robinson, Lewis J., Jr. .... Hartford, CT
Robinson, Linda .... San Antonio, TX
Robinson, Linda Brooks .... Sarasota, FL
Robinson, Linda J. .... Lawrenceville, NJ
Robinson, Linda S., Law Offices of
San Diego, CA
Robinson & Lipnickey Co., L.P.A.
Oxford, OH
Robinson, Lisa .... Washington, DC
Robinson, Lisa A. .... La Plata, MD
Robinson, Lisa A. .... Detroit, MI
Robinson, Lisa Bermingham .... Boston, MA
Robinson, Lisa Levine .... Bloomfield Hills, MI
Robinson, Lisa M. .... Washington, DC
Robinson, Lisa S. .... Minneapolis, MN
Robinson, Lloyd B. .... Seattle, WA
Robinson, Logan G. .... Auburn Hills, MI
Robinson, Loreen M. .... Cleveland, OH
Robinson, Loren T., Jr. .... Birmingham, MI
Robinson, Louis F., III .... Palm Beach, FL
Robinson, Louis F., Jr. .... La Crosse, WI
Robinson, Louisa Ashmead .... Philadelphia, PA
Robinson, Luke .... Philadelphia, PA
Robinson, Lynda C. .... Jackson, MS
Robinson, Lynn M. .... Las Vegas, NV
Robinson, Lyon & Springford LLP
Auburn, CA
Robinson, M. Gayle .... Grand Rapids, MI
Robinson, Mac E. .... Nashville, TN
Robinson, Mac E., Jr. .... Nashville, TN
Robinson, Malcolm .... Austin, TX
Robinson, Malcolm B., Jr. .... Metairie, LA
Robinson, Malcolm S. .... Dallas, TX
Robinson, Marc B. .... Stockton, CA
Robinson, Marcia .... Boston, MA
Robinson, Margaret M. .... Winder, GA

Robinson, Margaret M. .... Syracuse, NY
Robinson, Marguerite Maria Longoria
Tampa, FL
Robinson, Maria Theresa .... Chicago, IL
Robinson, Marietta S. .... Detroit, MI
Robinson, Mark A. .... Rockford, IL
Robinson, Mark A. .... Louisville, KY
Robinson, Mark A. .... Toledo, OH
Robinson, Mark A. .... Charleston, WV
Robinson, Mark B. .... New York, NY
Robinson, Mark E. .... Atlanta, GA
Robinson, Mark E. .... Boston, MA
Robinson, Mark E. .... Houston, TX
Robinson, Mark E. .... Janesville, WI
Robinson, Mark F. .... Provo, UT
Robinson, Mark P., Jr.
Newport Beach, CA
San Diego, CA
Robinson, Mark P., Law Offices of
Los Angeles, CA
Robinson, Marla Merhab .... Santa Ana, CA
Robinson, Marnia L. .... Norwalk, CT
Robinson, Martin F. .... Chicago, IL
Robinson, Martin S. .... Melrose, MA
Robinson, Marvin A. .... North Wales, PA
Robinson, Marvin S. .... New York, NY
Robinson, Mary Anna .... Houston, TX
Robinson, Mary Beth S. .... Chicago, IL
Robinson, Mary E. .... Oakland, CA
Robinson, Mary Lou .... Amarillo, TX
Robinson, Mary Lou .... Appleton, WI
Robinson, Mary T. .... Elgin, IL
Robinson, Matthew C. .... Indianapolis, IN
Robinson & McElwee LLP
Charleston, WV
Clarksburg, WV
Robinson, McFadden & Moore, P.C.
Columbia, SC
Robinson, Melinda C. .... Tigard, OR
Robinson, Melissa B. .... Houston, TX
Robinson, Melissa Mize .... Charleston, WV
Robinson, Melissa W. .... Roanoke, VA
Robinson, Melvin A. .... Chicago, IL
Robinson, Melvin, Jr. .... Atlanta, GA
Robinson, Michael A. .... Castle Rock, CO
Highlands Ranch, CO
Robinson, Michael A. .... Fort Lauderdale, FL
Robinson, Michael A. .... Memphis, TN
Robinson, Michael A., A Professional Association .... Fort Lauderdale, FL
Robinson, Michael A., P.C.
Castle Rock, CO
Highlands Ranch, CO
Robinson, Michael C. .... Hutchinson, KS
Robinson, Michael C. .... Portland, OR
Robinson, Michael C., Jr.
Los Angeles, CA
San Francisco, CA
Robinson, Michael D. .... Goddard, KS
Robinson, Michael E.
Department of Justice, Civil Division, GV
Robinson, Michael E. .... Dallas, TX
Robinson, Michael G. .... Los Angeles, CA
Robinson, Michael G. .... Chicago, IL
Robinson, Michael J. .... Detroit, MI
Robinson, Michael J. .... Seattle, WA
Robinson, Michael K. .... Eureka, CA
Robinson, Michael L. .... Grand Rapids, MI
Muskegon, MI
Robinson, Michael L. .... Winston-Salem, NC
Robinson, Michael M. .... Boston, MA
Robinson, Michael M. .... Tulsa, OK
Robinson, Michael P. .... Naples, NY
Robinson, Michael S. .... Los Angeles, CA
Robinson, Michael S. .... Pittsburgh, PA
Robinson, Michael T.
Department of Housing and Urban Development, Office of General Counsel, GV
Robinson, Michael W. .... Laguna Beach, CA
Robinson, Michael W. .... McLean, VA
Robinson, Michelle K. .... Columbus, OH
Robinson, Mike .... Benton, AR
Robinson, Mildred Wigfall
Charlottesville, VA
Robinson, Milton H.
Environmental Protection Agency, Office of Enforcement and Compliance Assurance, GV
Robinson, Mindi C. .... Montgomery, AL
Robinson, Miriam M. .... New York, NY
Robinson, Monica L. .... Huntington, WV
Robinson, Morris .... North Hollywood, CA
Robinson, Morris N. .... Wellesley, MA
Robinson, Muriel .... Nashville, TN
Robinson Murphy & McDonald
New York, NY
Robinson, Murray .... Pearland, TX
Robinson, Murray, Apple, Tindal & Wang, PLLC .... Reidsville, NC
Robinson, Myrtle C. .... Hyattsville, MD
Robinson, Nancy Hyder .... Greenville, SC
Robinson, Nancy J. .... Chicago, IL
Robinson, Neal J. .... Williamsburg, VA
Robinson, Ned .... Lafayette, CA
Robinson, Neil .... Folsom, CA
Robinson, Neil C., Jr. .... Charleston, SC
Robinson, Neil M. .... Treasury Department, Office of the Comptroller of the Currency, GV
Robinson, Neil M. .... Jamestown, NY
Robinson & Nelson .... Jasper, AL
Robinson, Nicholas A. .... White Plains, NY
Robinson, Nichole A. .... Chicago, IL
Robinson, Nicolas P. .... Pittsboro, NC
Robinson, Nila Jean .... Appleton, WI
Green Bay, WI
Robinson, Noel J. .... Sacramento, CA

Robinson, Norwood .... Winston-Salem, NC
Robinson, Oliver U. .... Bakersfield, CA
Robinson, Otto P., Jr. .... Scranton, PA
Robinson, Owen H. .... Troy, MO
Robinson, Owen M .... Jericho, NY
Robinson, Pall & Pall .... Upper Darby, PA
Robinson, Palmer .... Seattle, WA
Robinson, Palmer & Logan
Bakersfield, CA
Robinson, Pamela DeFanti .... Columbia, SC
Robinson, Pamela S. .... Alpharetta, GA
Atlanta, GA
Duluth, GA
Marietta, GA
Robinson, Patricia A. .... Lewisville, AR
Robinson, Patricia A.
Board of Governors Of The Federal Reserve System, Office of the General Counsel, GV
Robinson, Patricia S. .... Somerset, NJ
Robinson, Patrick A. .... Somerville, NJ
Robinson, Patrick A. .... Queens Village, NY
Robinson, Paul E. .... Novi, MI
Robinson, Paul E., (A Professional Corporation) .... San Diego, CA
Robinson, Paul F. .... New York, NY
Robinson, Paul F. .... Columbia, SC
Robinson, Paul H. .... Chicago, IL
Robinson, Paul Jules
North Miami Beach, FL
Robinson, Paul M. .... Fresno, CA
Robinson, Paul M. .... New York, NY
Robinson, Paul R. .... Hartington, NE
Robinson, Paul R. .... Pittsburgh, PA
Robinson, Paul W. .... Albuquerque, NM
Robinson, Paula .... Monterey, CA
Salinas, CA
Robinson, Paula S. .... Philadelphia, PA
Robinson & Pearman .... Los Angeles, CA
Robinson, Peggy M.H. .... Baton Rouge, LA
Robinson, Peggy M.H., P.L.C.
Baton Rouge, LA
Robinson, Penny .... Indianapolis, IN
Robinson, Percy E., III
Department of Commerce, Minority Business Development Agency, GV
Robinson, Perry D. .... Washington, DC
Robinson, Perry J. .... Yakima, WA
Robinson, Pete .... Columbus, GA
Robinson, Peter .... Santa Rosa, CA
Robinson, Peter A. .... Denver, CO
Robinson, Peter B. .... Lowell, MA
Robinson, Peter E. .... Denver, CO
Robinson, Peter L. .... Belmont, CA
Robinson, Peter R. .... Malibu, CA
Robinson, Peterson, Berk & Cross, LLP
Appleton, WI
Green Bay, WI
Robinson, Philip H. .... Sandpoint, ID
Robinson, Philip H., Jr. .... Bellevue, NE
Robinson, Phillip .... Austin, TX
Robinson, Phillip F. .... Cambridge, NY
Robinson, Phillip L. .... Washington, DC
Robinson, Phillip R. .... Nashville, TN
Robinson, Phyllis L. .... Hyden, KY
Robinson & Post, L.L.P. .... Dallas, TX
Robinson, Quintero & Lopez, P.C.
Silver City, NM
Robinson, R. Clark .... St. Petersburg, FL
Robinson, R. Michael .... St. Petersburg, FL
Robinson, R. Scott .... Torrance, CA
Robinson, R. Spencer, II .... Murray, UT
Robinson, R. Townsend ....
Administrative Office Of The United States Courts, GV
Robinson, Raleigh M., Jr. .... St. Louis, MO
Robinson, Ralph C., Jr. .... Columbia, SC
Robinson, Ralph D. .... Washington, DC
Herndon, VA
Robinson, Ralph L. .... Lafayette, IN
Robinson, Ralph N. .... Elmont, NY
Robinson, Ralph W. .... San Francisco, CA
Robinson, Randal D. .... Columbus, OH
Robinson, Randall B. .... Englewood, CO
Robinson, Randall P. .... Oklahoma City, OK
Robinson, Randall R. .... Shreveport, LA
Robinson, Randall W. .... Lewiston, ID
Robinson, Randy L. .... Sandy, UT
Robinson, Rappaport, Jampol, Aussenberg & Schleicher, L.L.P. .... Alpharetta, GA
Atlanta, GA
Cumming, GA
Roswell, GA
Robinson, Rauleigh D. .... Mandan, ND
Robinson, Rayfield & Schmidt
Crystal City, MO
Robinson, Raymond G. .... Bakersfield, CA
Robinson, Raymond L. .... New York, NY
Robinson, Reginald L. .... Washington, DC
Robinson, Rekasha A. .... New York, NY
Robinson, R. H. .... Missoula, MT
Robinson, Rice & Levy .... Ashland, KY
Robinson, Richard .... York, PA
Robinson, Richard A. .... Orlando, FL
Robinson, Richard A. .... Oklahoma City, OK
Robinson, Richard Allan .... Stamford, CT
Robinson, Richard B. .... Denver, CO
Robinson, Richard C. .... Hartford, CT
Robinson, Richard C. .... Seattle, WA
Robinson, Richard D. .... Orlando, FL
Robinson, Richard D. .... Fort Wayne, IN
Robinson, Richard E. .... Los Angeles, CA
Robinson, Richard H., Jr. .... Chapel Hill, NC
Robinson, Richard K. .... Dallas, TX
Robinson, Richard L. .... Florence, KY
Cincinnati, OH
Robinson, Richard L. .... Angleton, TX
Robinson, Richard M. .... Orlando, FL

Robles, Martin Roy ....South Pasadena, CA
Robles, Monica M. ....Los Angeles, CA
Robles, Rafael A. ....Spring Hill, FL
Robles, Richard R. ....Miami, FL
Robles, Richard R., P.A. ....Miami, FL
Robles, Robert R. ....Oklahoma City, OK
Robles, Ruben S. ....El Paso, TX
Robles, Valerie ....San Juan, PR
Robles, Victoria ....New York, NY
Robles, William A. ....San Francisco, CA
Robles-Abraham, Nector ....Fajardo, PR
Robles Diaz, Nelson ....San Juan, PR
Robles-Román, Carol A. ....New York, NY
Robling, Kenneth C. ....Washington, DC
Robling, Kevin R. ....Phoenix, AZ
Roblyer, Christopher B. ....Atlanta, GA
Roblyer, Michael R. ....Annapolis, MD
Robman, Louis ....Encino, CA
Robman & Seeley ....Encino, CA
Robnett, Ausey H., III ....Coeur d'Alene, ID
Robnett, Cary S. ....San Francisco, CA
Robnett, Harriet L. ....United States Senate, Committee Legal Personnel, GV
Robnett, Janet D. ....Coeur d'Alene, ID
Robnett, Lance V. ....Amarillo, TX
Robol, Richard T. ....Virginia Beach, VA
Robon, Marvin A. ....Toledo, OH
Roboostoff, Constantin V.
San Francisco, CA
Robosson, Gwendolyn M., (P.C.)
Iselin, NJ
Robotti, Dorene E. ....Rocky Hill, CT
Robottom, John S. ....Arlington, TX
Robrahn, Reese H. ....Waynesboro, VA
Robreno, Eduardo C. ....Philadelphia, PA
Robsahm, Reid L. ....Victorville, CA
Robshaw & Associates, P.C. ....Buffalo, NY
Robshaw, John P., Jr. ....Buffalo, NY
Robson, Arthur L. ....Fairbanks, AK
Robson, C. Mark ....Miami, FL
Robson, Charles B., Jr. ....Raleigh, NC
Robson, Charles L. V ....Mesa, AZ
Robson, Douglas J. ....Mason, MI
Robson, Douglas S. ....Chicago, IL
Robson Ferber Frost Chan & Essner, LLP
New York, NY
Robson, Jane Woodard ....New Orleans, LA
Robson, Jeanelle R. ....Lincoln, NE
Robson, John E. S. ....Las Vegas, NV
Salt Lake City, UT
Robson, John T., Jr. ....Tacoma, WA
Robson, Joyce E. ....Tacoma, WA
Robson, Karen M. ....New York, NY
Robson, Kevin K. ....Salt Lake City, UT
Robson, Mark E. ....Walnut Creek, CA
Robson, Martin C., III ....Dallas, TX
Robson, Michael D. ....Santa Cruz, CA
Robson, Morton S. ....New York, NY
Robson, Paul Louis ....Seattle, WA
Robson, Susan C. ....Marion, KS
Robson, Wayne D. ....Hemet, CA
Robson-Higgins, Yanna M. ....Cleveland, OH
Robuck, H.D., Jr., P.A. ....Leesburg, FL
Robuck, H. D., Jr., P.A. ....Tavares, FL
Robuck, H.D., Jr. ....Leesburg, FL
Robuck, Jo Keaton ....Dallas, TX
Robus, Marion T. ....San Francisco, CA
Robustelli, Dominick J. ....Mineola, NY
Robustelli, Dominick J. ....Mineola, NY
Monroe, NY
New York, NY
White Plains, NY
Robustelli, Dominick J. ....New York, NY
New York, NY
Robusto, Anthony R. ....Glendora, CA
Robusto, Michael A. ....Brooklyn Heights, OH
Robusto, Michael A. ....Virginia Beach, VA
Robutz, Mary E. ....Azusa, CA
Roby, Ahmad M. ....Pontiac, MI
Roby, Beverly R. ....Boston, MA
Roby, Bruce A. ....Topeka, KS
Roby, Daniel A. ....Anderson, IN
Fort Wayne, IN
Marion, IN
Roby, David A., Jr. ....Washington, DC
Roby, David Charles ....Detroit, MI
Roby, David M. ....Lyme, NH
Roby, E. Starkey, Jr. ....Kenbridge, VA
Roby & Hood ....Anderson, IN
Fort Wayne, IN
Marion, IN
Roby, James C., (P.C.) ....Watertown, SD
Roby, James J. ....Department of Justice, Justice Management Division, GV
Roby, John S. ....Mansfield, OH
Roby, Joseph J., Jr. ....Duluth, MN
Roby, Karen Wells, (P.C.) ....New Orleans, LA
Roby, Nicholas H. ....Des Moines, IA
Roby, Patrick M. ....Cedar Rapids, IA
Roby, Richard Eric ....San Francisco, CA
Roby, Robert J. ....Newport Beach, CA
Roby, Robert R. ....Dallas, TX
Roby, Robert S. ....Columbus, OH
Roby, Ronald H. ....Winter Park, FL
Roby, Ronald H., P.A. ....Winter Park, FL
Roby, Scott T. ....Louisville, KY
Roby, Steven B. ....Farmington Hills, MI
Roby, Surrenden Hill, (Mrs.) ....Austin, TX
Roby, William L. ....Stuart, FL
Robyn, Noel L. ....Clarkdale, AZ
Robyt, William J. ....Cambridge, MN
Roca, Angeles ....Philadelphia, PA
Roca, John M. ....Toledo, OH
Roca, Rafael J., (P.A.)
West Palm Beach, FL
Roca & Sharpe, P.A.
West Palm Beach, FL
Roca, William Joseph ....Wayne, NJ

Rocafort, Carmen J. ....San Juan, PR
Rocah, Miriam E. ....New York, NY
Rocamboli, Stephen C. ....New York, NY
Rocamora, Larry H. ....Durham, NC
Rocanelli, Andrea L. ....Wilmington, DE
Rocap, Donald E. ....Chicago, IL
Rocap, Edward ....Media, PA
Rocap, James E., III ....Washington, DC
Rocap, James E., Jr. ....Indianapolis, IN
Rocap, Richard A. ....Indianapolis, IN
Rocap, Witchger & Threlkeld
Indianapolis, IN
Rocca, Ahl & Pena ....Fort Lee, NJ
Rocca, Anthony J. ....Philadelphia, PA
Rocca, Brian C. ....Chicago, IL
Rocca, Glenn M. ....Fort Lee, NJ
Rocca, Gregory J. ....San Francisco, CA
Rocca, Joseph ....Albuquerque, NM
Rocca, Saverio M. ....Baltimore, MD
Roccaforte, Frank W. ....New Orleans, LA
Roccaforte & Rousselle ....New Orleans, LA
Roccamo, Anthony L. ....Forest Hills, NY
Roccanova, Bernard ....Chicago, IL
Roccanova, Gina M. ....San Francisco, CA
Roccanova, Johanna D. ....Emerson, NJ
Roccanova, Johanna D. ....Hackensack, NJ
Roccanova, Joseph T. ....Mineola, NY
Roccapriore, Marie C. ....Meriden, CT
Rocchi, Albino M. ....New York, NY
Rocchini, Richard A. ....Murray Hill, NJ
Rocchio, David M. ....Montpelier, VT
Rocchio, James A. ....Bloomfield Hills, MI
Rocchio, Patrick K. ....Coldwater, MI
Rocchio, Peter A. ....New York, NY
Rocchio, Peter P., Jr. ....Winter Park, FL
Rocci, Steven J. ....Philadelphia, PA
Roccia, Vincent J. ....Philadelphia, PA
Roccio, John P. ....Beverly, MA
Roccio, Thomas J. ....Lynn, MA
Rocco, Anthony M. ....Passaic, NJ
Rocco, Charles J. ....Newark, NJ
New York, NY
Rocco, Claire ....Delran, NJ
Philadelphia, PA
Rocco, David T. ....West Caldwell, NJ
Rocco, Dominick A. ....Westbury, NY
Rocco, Gerald A. ....Columbus, OH
Rocco, James A., III ....Cherry Hill, NJ
Philadelphia, PA
Rocco, Jennifer ....Carpinteria, CA
Rocco, John P. ....Milwaukee, WI
Rocco, Joseph D. ....Levittown, NY
Rocco, Joseph P. ....Phoenix, AZ
Rocco, Kenneth A. ....Cleveland, OH
Rocco, Matthew P., Law Office of
Carlsbad, CA
Rocco, Michaelangelo ....Kenmore, NY
Rocco, Patrick L. ....Newark, NJ
Rocco, Patrick R. ....Cleveland, OH
Rocco, Perry C. ....Chicago, IL
Rocco, Richard J. ....Levittown, NY
Rocco, Thomas J. ....Columbus, OH
Rocco, Victor J. ....New York, NY
Roccograndi, Anthony J. ....Washington, DC
Rocconi, Larry A., Jr. ....Clarksville, TN
Rocconi, Margo A. ....Los Angeles, CA
Roccosalvo, Felicia J. ....Brooklyn, NY
Roch, Carolyn D. ....Houston, TX
Roch, Jeanette R. ....Nashville, TN
Roch, Michael ....Denver, CO
Roch, William C. ....Garden City, NY
Rocha, Albert ....Boston, MA
Rocha, Armando M. ....San Antonio, TX
Rocha, Denise M. ....Milpitas, CA
Rocha, Elaine A. ....New York, NY
Rocha, Gilbert T. ....Barrington, RI
Rocha, Karen E. ....Kansas City, MO
Rocha, Nancy Gast ....Washington, DC
Rocha, Patricia K. ....Boston, MA
Providence, RI
Rocha, Patricia S. ....Nutley, NJ
Rocha, Richard A. ....Riverside, CA
Rocha, Richard J. ....New York, NY
Rocha, Robert F. ....San Jose, CA
Rocha, Roger C. ....Laredo, TX
Rocha, Stephen D. ....West Des Moines, IA
Rocha, Susan C. ....San Antonio, TX
Rocha, Thomas, Jr. ....San Antonio, TX
Rocha, Victor E. ....Miami, FL
Rocha, Victor M. ....Kansas City, MO
Rochau, Alvin A. G. ....Merrillville, IN
Rochau, Craig A. ....St. Joseph, MI
Roche, Alvis J. ....Lake Charles, LA
Roche, Brent O. ....Pocatello, ID
Roche, Brian D. ....Chicago, IL
Roche, Brien A. ....McLean, VA
Roche, Carens & DeGiacomo, A Professional Corporation ....Woburn, MA
Boston, MA
Roche, Cathy A. ....Napa, CA
Roche, Christopher A. ....Marco Island, FL
Roche, Christopher C. ....New York, NY
Roche, Clayton P. ....San Francisco, CA
Roche Corrigan McCoy & Bush
Albany, NY
Roche, David I. ....Chicago, IL
Roche, Diana Elaine ....Paoli, PA
Roche, Douglas D. ....Detroit, MI
Roche, Edward J., Jr. ....Boulder, CO
Roche, Francis J. ....Hudson, NY
Roche, Francis X. ....Boston, MA
Roche, Genevieve Harris ....New York, NY
Roche, Heifetz, Murphy & Wholley
Boston, MA
Roche & Holt, A Professional Corporation
Los Angeles, CA
Santa Monica, CA
Roche, J. Francis ....Manchester, NH

Roche, J. Patrick ....Maplewood, NJ
Roche, J. Vincent ....Philadelphia, PA
Roche, James A., Jr. ....Jennings, MO
Roche, James B. ....Tacoma, WA
Roche, James E. ....Boston, MA
Roche, James J. ....Chicago, IL
Roche, James L., III ....Baltimore, MD
Roche, James M. ....Chicago, IL
Roche, James M. ....Wheaton, IL
Roche, James T. ....Rockville, MD
Roche, Jean M., & Associates
Oak Lawn, IL
Roche, Jerome
Securities and Exchange Commission, Division of Market Regulation, GV
Roche, John J. ....Franklin, MA
Roche, John J. ....New York, NY
Roche, John J., & Associates ....Boston, MA
Roche, John J., & Associates
Cambridge, MA
Roche, John L. ....San Diego, CA
Roche, John M. ....Denver, CO
Roche, John M. ....Grosse Pointe, MI
Roche, John S. ....Lexington, KY
Roche, John T., Jr. ....North Vernon, IN
Roche, Kathleen M. ....Lakewood, CA
Roche, Kathryn Reyburn
White Plains, NY
Roche, Kenneth L., Jr. ....Houston, TX
Roche, Kent O. ....Salt Lake City, UT
Roche, Kevin M. ....Hartford, CT
Roche, Laura C. ....San Francisco, CA
Roche, Leo F., Jr. ....Boston, MA
Roche, M. Therese ....Boston, MA
Roche, Mark A. ....Lincolnshire, IL
Roche, Mary Engler ....Buffalo, NY
Roche, Mary-Lisa Favret ....Houston, TX
Roche, Maurice R. ....New York, NY
Roche, Megan M. ....Cleveland, OH
Roche, Michael B. ....Chicago, IL
Roche, Michael B. ....Silver Spring, MD
Roche, Michael F. ....St. Louis, MO
Roche, Michael J. ....Denver, CO
Roche, Michael P. ....Chicago, IL
Roche, Michael P. ....Boston, MA
Roche, Michael W. ....Sturbridge, MA
Roche, Michael W. ....Secaucus, NJ
Roche and Murphy ....Franklin, MA
Roche, Neil J. ....Franklin, MA
Roche, Pamela Weidman ....Canaan, CT
Roche, Patricia Ellen ....Succasunna, NJ
Roche, Patrick F. ....Melbourne, FL
Roche, Patrick F. ....Cleveland, OH
Roche, Patrick J. ....Virginia, MN
Roche, Patrick R. ....Cleveland, OH
Roche, Paul D. ....Boston, MA
Roche, Paul G. ....Washington, DC
Roche, Philip J. ....Painted Post, NY
Roche, Raquel R. ....Holtville, CA
Roche, Raymond T. ....East Orange, NJ
Roche, Richard Andrew ....West Orange, NJ
Roche, Richard T. ....Milwaukee, WI
Roche, Robert B. ....Minneapolis, MN
Roche, Robert J. ....Los Angeles, CA
Roche, Robert J. ....Seattle, WA
Roche, Robert P. ....Albany, NY
Roche, Sandra L. ....Greeley, CO
Roche, Sean ....Boston, MA
Roche, Stephen G. ....Boston, MA
Roche, Stewart J. ....Hart, MI
Roche, Susan Lynn ....Dearborn, MI
Roche, Susan M. ....Bronx, NY
Roche, Terence S. ....Bethesda, MD
Roche, Thomas E. ....Chicago, IL
Roche, Thomas F. ....Chicago, IL
Roche, Thomas G. ....San Diego, CA
Roche, Thomas H. ....New York, NY
Roche, Thomas J. ....Boston, MA
Roche, Thomas K. ....Syosset, NY
Roche, Thomas M. ....Houston, TX
Roche, Thomas S. ....Sacramento, CA
Roche, Vincent E. ....West Hartford, CT
Roche, Wilbank J. ....Santa Monica, CA
Roche, William E. ....Overland Park, KS
Roche, William G. ....Atlanta, GA
Roche, William J. ....Dallas, TX
Roche, William J., Jr. ....Arlington, VA
Rocheford, David R., Jr. ....Southborough, MA
Rocheford, Lawrence M. ....St. Paul, MN
Rocheford, Paul J. ....Minneapolis, MN
Rochefort, John M. ....Los Angeles, CA
Rochefort, Lawrence P.
West Palm Beach, FL
Rocheleau, Dale A. ....Burlington, VT
Montpelier, VT
Rocheleau, Dean A. ....Southfield, MI
Rocheleau, Lisa M. ....San Antonio, TX
Rocheleau, William, Jr. ....Lewiston, ME
Rochell, Lawrence H. ....Highland Park, IL
Rochelle, Ann M. ....Casper, WY
Rochelle, Cary G. ....Texarkana, TX
Rochelle, Dudley C. ....Atlanta, GA
Rochelle Hutcheson & Murphy LLP
Dallas, TX
Rochelle, Jack P. ....Austin, TX
Fort Worth, TX
Houston, TX
Rochelle, James M., III ....Irmo, SC
Rochelle, Jeffrey A. ....San Antonio, TX
Rochelle, Jeffrey A., P.C., Law Offices of
San Antonio, TX
Rochelle, Jerry A. ....Texarkana, AR
Rochelle, Joseph B. ....Albuquerque, NM
Rochelle, L. Raquel ....Peoria, IL
Rochelle, Mark D. ....San Diego, CA
Rochelle, Martha Peak ....Austin, TX
Rochelle, Martin C. ....Austin, TX

Rochelle, McCulloch & Aulds
Lebanon, TN
Rochelle, Michael R. ....Dallas, TX
Rochelle, Patricia Linehan ....Dallas, TX
Rochelle, Robert ....Lebanon, TN
Rochelle, Robert D. ....San Diego, CA
Rochelle, Vernon H. ....Kinston, NC
Rochelle, Victor C. ....Normal, IL
Rochelle, William J., III ....New York, NY
Rocher, Rafael G. ....San Juan, PR
Rochester, John E. ....Ashland, AL
Rochester, Richard R. ....Northbrook, IL
Rochester, RoxAnne L. ....Chicago, IL
Rochester, Terrell B. ....Florence, AL
Rochester, William ....San Francisco, CA
Rochester, Wong, Shepard & Johnson, A Professional Corporation
San Francisco, CA
Rochester Young, Valarie J. ....Columbia, SC
Rochestie, Gary A. ....Bensalem, PA
Philadelphia, PA
Rochette, Edward C., III ....Lake Oswego, OR
Rochez, Nicholas ....New York, NY
Rochford & Associates ....Peoria, IL
Rochford, Cynthia S. ....Victor, NY
Rochford, James M. ....Peoria, IL
Rochford, James T. ....Mineola, NY
Rochford, John C. ....Nashville, TN
Rochford, John T., III ....Nashville, TN
Rochford, Mary K. ....Chicago, IL
Rochford, Rebecca S. ....Nashville, TN
Rochford, Richard D., Jr. ....Rochester, NY
Rochford, Robert E. ....Hackensack, NJ
Rochford, Robert G. ....Lake City, MN
Plainview, MN
Rochkind, Deborah M. ....Dulles, VA
Rochkind, Jonathan S. ....Fairfax, VA
Rochkind, Louis P. ....Detroit, MI
Rochkind, Mark H. ....Caldwell, NJ
Rochkind, Rosalind ....Detroit, MI
Rochkind, Steven H. ....New York, NY
Rochlen, Bradley S. ....Chicago, IL
Rochlin, Carole H. ....Oakland, CA
Rochlin, David M. ....Denver, CO
Rochlin, David S. ....Minneapolis, MN
Rochlin, Judith ....Los Angeles, CA
Rochlin, Karen E. ....Miami, FL
Rochlin, Mordecai ....New York, NY
Rochlin, Paul R ....Baltimore, MD
Rochlin, Settleman & Dobres, P.A.
Baltimore, MD
Rochlis, Steven M.
Department of Transportation, Federal Highway Administration, GV
Rochlitz, Imre ....New York, NY
Rochman, David S. ....Millville, NJ
Rochman, Harvey ....Los Angeles, CA
Rochman, Irwin ....New York, NY
Rochman, Jeri L. ....Los Angeles, CA
Rochman, Michael J. ....Lafayette, CA
Rochman, Morton ....Los Angeles, CA
Rochman, Platzer, Fallick & Sternheim
New York, NY
Rochman, Richard E. ....San Francisco, CA
Rochna, Paul G. ....Houston, TX
Rochon, Jennifer L. ....New York, NY
Rochon, Mark ....Washington, DC
Rochow, K. W. James ....Harrisburg, PA
Rochvarg, Arnold ....Baltimore, MD
Rochwarg, Leah A. ....Boston, MA
Providence, RI
Rochwarger, Jonathan ....New York, NY
Rochyby, Jack R. ....Woodburn, IN
Rocissano, Maria B. ....Manhasset, NY
Rock, Allison ....Providence, RI
Rock, Allison A. ....San Carlos, CA
Rock, Andrea W. ....Philadelphia, PA
Rock, Andrew Peter ....Orlando, FL
Rock, Angela K. ....Las Vegas, NV
Rock & Borgelt, P.C.
Dearborn Heights, MI
Detroit, MI
Rock, Bradley E. ....Smithtown, NY
Rock, Bradley J. ....Palo Alto, CA
Rock, C. Russell ....San Francisco, CA
Rock, Calvin C. ....Eastpointe, MI
Rock, Cecily W. ....
Joint Committees And Commissions, GV
Rock, Charles M. ....Peoria, IL
Rock, Charles N. ....White Plains, NY
Rock, Corinne A. ....Springfield, MA
Rock, Daniel L. ....Omaha, NE
Rock, Daniel P. ....New Port Richey, FL
Rock, Danny F. ....Hodgenville, KY
Rock, David F. ....Vail, CO
Atlanta, GA
Rock, Douglas J. ....Ontario, OR
Rock, Edward B. ....Philadelphia, PA
Rock, Erick H. ....Atlanta, GA
Rock, Fusco, Reynolds, Crowe & Garvey, Ltd.
Chicago, IL
Rock, Gerald J. ....Albany, NY
Rock, Gordon M., Jr. ....Olathe, KS
Rock, Harold L. ....Omaha, NE
Rock, Howard J. ....Waltham, MA
Rock, J. Robert ....Dearborn Heights, MI
Rock, James M. ....Boston, MA
Rock, James P. ....Cheshire, CT
Rock, Jason H. ....Rockford, IL
Rock, Jeffrey B. ....Peoria, IL
Rock, Jeffrey S.
Department of Housing and Urban Development, Office of General Counsel, GV
Rock, Jerome F. ....Oak Park, MI
Rock, John A. ....Rock Island, IL
Rock, Kenneth Isom ....Golden, CO
Rock & Leitz, P.C. ....Atlanta, GA

Roderman, Glenn R., P.A.
Fort Lauderdale, FL
Rodery, Patrick W. ... Mountain Grove, MO
Rodery, Rick M. ... Piggott, AR
Rodes, Clifton W. ... Houston, TX
Rodes, David B. ... Pittsburgh, PA
Rodes, Leonard A. ... New York, NY
Rodes, Nelson D., Jr. ... Danville, KY
Rodes, Robert E., Jr. ... Notre Dame, IN
Rodewald, Jeffrey P. ... Chicago, IL
Rodewald, John E. ... Chicago, IL
Rodewald, Roderick A.
San Luis Obispo, CA
Rodewald-Fout, April J. ... Reno, NV
Rodey, Dickason, Sloan, Akin & Robb, P.A.
Albuquerque, NM
Santa Fe, NM
Rodey, Ray H. ... Albuquerque, NM
Santa Fe, NM
Rodez, Miguel A. ... Miami, FL
Rodger, Bruce E. ... Media, PA
Rodger, Lester R., Jr. ... Marysville, OH
Rodger, Richard G. ... Olympia, WA
Rodger, Wallace G. ... Springfield, MA
Rodgers, Allan G. ... Boston, MA
Rodgers, Amy N. ... Houston, TX
Rodgers, Anne Marie ... Houston, TX
Rodgers, Bettie A. ... Shorewood, WI
Rodgers, Beverly ... Midwest City, OK
Rodgers, Bobby D. ... Loomis, CA
Rodgers, Bonita G. ... Knoxville, TN
Rodgers, Brett N. ... Grand Rapids, MI
Rodgers, Bruce M. ... Tampa, FL
Rodgers, Carrie Ann ... Denver, CO
Rodgers, Charles ... Hackensack, NJ
Rodgers, Cherie L. ... Santa Monica, CA
Rodgers, Christopher S. ... Birmingham, AL
Rodgers, Cindy L. ... Orlando, FL
Rodgers, Clifford A. ... Knoxville, TN
Rodgers and Co., L.P.A. ... Cleveland, OH
Rodgers and Cullis, P.C. ... Greensburg, PA
Rodgers, C.W. (Quincy) ... Washington, DC
Rodgers, Damian M. ... Toledo, OH
Rodgers, Daniel C. ... New York, NY
Rodgers, Daniel G. ... Anchorage, AK
Rodgers, Daniel J. ... Oil City, PA
Rodgers, Danny P. ... Hope, AR
Rodgers, David A. ... Corning, CA
Rodgers, David D. ... Phoenix, AZ
Rodgers, David E. ... Knoxville, TN
Oak Ridge, TN
Rodgers, David R. ... Boston, MA
Rodgers, Dennis C. ... Washington, DC
Rodgers, Derick J. ... San Antonio, TX
Rodgers & Deutsch ... Bellevue, WA
Rodgers, Dwight G., Jr. ... Greensboro, NC
Rodgers, Edward ... West Palm Beach, FL
Rodgers, Edward J., III ... Canon City, CO
Rodgers, Elizabeth A. ... Boston, MA
Rodgers, Elizabeth Lindley
Mount Shasta, CA
Rodgers, Elma Elizabeth ... Knoxville, TN
Rodgers, Frank C. ... San Antonio, TX
Rodgers, Frederic B. ... Golden, CO
Rodgers, G. Dennis ... Oakland, CA
Rodgers, G. Saxon ... Olympia, WA
Rodgers, Gary L. ... Englewood, CO
Rodgers, George H. ... Mesa, AZ
Rodgers & Greenfeld ... Los Angeles, CA
Rodgers, Gregg ... Seattle, WA
Rodgers, Gregory P. ... Los Angeles, CA
Rodgers, Hazlett M., Jr. ... Wellsburg, WV
Rodgers, Heidi M. ... Hanalei, HI
Rodgers, Horace J. ... Southfield, MI
Rodgers, J. Christopher ... Washington, DC
Rodgers, J. Daniel ... Fort Worth, TX
Rodgers, J. Mark ... West Palm Beach, FL
Rodgers, J. Neal ... Charlotte, NC
Rodgers, James A. ... Williamsburg, VA
Rodgers, James H. ... New York, NY
Rodgers, James J. ... Philadelphia, PA
Rodgers, James Louis, Jr. ... Eldorado, IL
Rodgers, James M. ... Brattleboro, VT
Rodgers, James R. ... Blackwell, OK
Rodgers, James R. ... Paris, TX
Rodgers, James W., Jr. ... Holdenville, OK
Rodgers, Janice E. ... Chicago, IL
Rodgers, Janice M. ... Department of Justice, Justice Management Division, GV
Rodgers, Jason ... Dallas, TX
Rodgers, J. B., Jr. ... Zellwood, FL
Rodgers, Jeffrey A. ... Columbus, OH
Rodgers, Jeffrey S. ... Lewisburg, WV
Rodgers, Jimmy D., II ... Wichita Falls, TX
Rodgers, Jimmy F., Jr. ... Chattanooga, TN
Rodgers, John Allan ... Washington, PA
Rodgers, John B. ... Washington, DC
Rodgers, John D. ... Albany, NY
Rodgers, John E. ... Nashville, TN
Rodgers, John E., Jr. ... Nashville, TN
Rodgers, John F. ... Alexandria, VA
Rodgers, John H. ... Dallas, TX
Rodgers, John Jeffrey ... Oklahoma City, OK
Rodgers, John P. ... Wilkes-Barre, PA
Rodgers, John Q. ... Hermosa Beach, CA
Rodgers, John S. ... New York, NY
Rodgers, John W. ... Orlando, FL
Rodgers, John W. ... Murfreesboro, TN
Rodgers, Joseph J. ... Wildwood, NJ
Rodgers, Joseph J., Chartered
Wildwood, NJ
Rodgers, Joseph P. ... Cleveland, OH
Rodgers, Karma S. ... Milwaukee, WI
Rodgers, Katherine J. ... Kansas City, MO
Rodgers, Kathryn J. ... New York, NY
Rodgers, Kelly S. ... Austin, TX
Rodgers, Kenneth M. ... Philadelphia, PA
Rodgers, Kerry ... New York, NY

Rodgers, Kevin D. ... Raleigh, NC
Rodgers & Kiser ... Martinsburg, WV
Rodgers, Lance R. ... Chicago, IL
Rodgers, Lawrence B. ... Miami, FL
Rodgers, Lawrence B., P.A. ... Miami, FL
Rodgers, Linda R. ... Worcester, MA
Rodgers, Lori B. ... Cincinnati, OH
Rodgers, Lynn C. ... Springfield, MO
Rodgers, M. Casey ... Pensacola, FL
Rodgers, Marcia J. ... Kansas City, MO
Rodgers, Marcia L. ... Englewood, CO
Rodgers, Mark C. ... Buffalo, NY
Rodgers, Mark L. ... Bemidji, MN
Rodgers, Mark L. ... Allentown, PA
Rodgers, Mary Anne ... San Jose, CA
Rodgers, Menard & Coppola, LLP
Buffalo, NY
Rodgers, Michael A. ... Coshocton, OH
Rodgers, Michael E. ... Morristown, NJ
Rodgers, Michael S. ... Atlanta, GA
Rodgers, Michelle ... Oklahoma City, OK
Rodgers, Miller & McLain, P.C.
Bryan, TX
College Station, TX
Rodgers & Morgenstein ... Southfield, MI
Rodgers, Patricia A. ... Greensburg, PA
Rodgers, Patrick L. ... Merrick, NY
Rodgers, Paul ... Washington, DC
Rodgers, Paul B., III ... Columbia, SC
Rodgers, Perfilio, Heiman & Sewinsky, P.C.
Sharon, PA
Rodgers, Peter H. ... Washington, DC
Rodgers, Peter T. ... Rochester, NY
Rodgers, Philip E., Jr. ... Traverse City, MI
Rodgers, R. Neil ... Orange, CA
Rodgers, R. Terrance ... Charleston, WV
Rodgers, Ralph E. ... Knoxville, TN
Rodgers, Ricardo J. (Rick) ... Duncan, OK
Rodgers, Richard A. ... Orlando, FL
Rodgers, Richard L. ... Canajoharie, NY
Rodgers, Richard M. ... Ambler, PA
Rodgers, Richard T. ... Buies Creek, NC
Rodgers, Richd. W. ... Winter Park, FL
Rodgers, Rick, Law Firm ... Duncan, OK
Rodgers, Robert S. ... Lubbock, TX
Rodgers, Robert V. ... Birmingham, AL
Rodgers & Rodgers ... Atlanta, GA
Rodgers, Ronald F. ... Durham, NH
Rodgers, Ronald L., Jr. ... Los Angeles, CA
Rodgers, S. Michael ... Bellevue, WA
Rodgers, Samuel L. ... Pittsburgh, PA
Rodgers, Scott D. ... Somerville, NJ
Rodgers, Scott T. ... Denver, CO
Rodgers, Scott W. ... Phoenix, AZ
Rodgers, Sean D. ... New York, NY
Rodgers, Sharon L. ... Graniteville, SC
Rodgers, Sharon S. ... Houston, TX
Rodgers, Stanley C. ... Mount Pleasant, SC
Rodgers, Stephen J. ... Wilmington, DE
Rodgers, Steven R. ... Phoenix, AZ
Rodgers, Susan Carson ... Canton, OH
Salem, OH
Rodgers, Susan M. ... Baltimore, MD
Rodgers, Susan P. ... Traverse City, MI
Rodgers, Thomas H. ... Troy, OH
Rodgers, Thomas J. ... Old Lyme, CT
Rodgers, Thomas Paul ... San Francisco, CA
Rodgers, Timothy A. ... Pine Brook, NJ
Rodgers, Timothy R. ... Monroe, NC
Rodgers, Tommy Rea ... Dallas, TX
Rodgers, Victor A. ... Los Angeles, CA
Rodgers, W. Ralph, Jr. ... Albany, GA
Rodgers, W. Stanley ... Huntsville, AL
Rodgers, W. Stephen ... Bryan, TX
Rodgers, Walter A. ... Atlanta, GA
Rodgers, Walter A. ... Cleveland, OH
Rodgers, Walter M. ... Atlanta, GA
Rodgers, Wayne ... Kingwood, TX
Rodgers, W.F. "Rick" ... Sacramento, CA
Rodgers, William F. L. ... Newtown, CT
Rodgers, William J. ... Washington, DC
Rodgers, William, Jr. ... Carrollton, TX
Rodgers, William R. ... Boston, MA
Rodgers, W. S., Jr. ... Tampa, FL
Rodgers-Leahy, Paulette E. ... San Diego, CA
Rodgers-Waire, Cynthia E.
Baltimore, MD
Rodgman, Paul A. ... Kinston, NC
Rodgon, Maris M. ... New York, NY
Rodgríguez-Amadeo, Nitzia Michelle
San Juan, PR
Rodham & Fine, P.A.
Fort Lauderdale, FL
Rodham, Hugh ... Fort Lauderdale, FL
Rodham, Steven M. ... Knoxville, TN
Rodi, David M. ... Houston, TX
Rodi, Michael Anthony ... New York, NY
Rodi, Pollock, Pettker, Galbraith & Cahill, A Law Corporation ... Los Angeles, CA
Rodi, Sharon R. ... New Orleans, LA
Rodi, Stephen B. ... Metairie, LA
Rodi, Thomas J. ... New Orleans, LA
Rodia, John M. ... Hartford, CT
Rodibaugh, Robert K. ... South Bend, IN
Rodich, Gary R. ... Oak Park, CA
Rodich, Lorraine E. ... San Jose, CA
Rodich, Norman J. ... Irvine, CA
Rodick, Frank D. ... Weymouth, MA
Rodick, S. Bennet ... Arlington Heights, IL
Rodie, Andrew ... Prospect Heights, IL
Rodie and Connolly ... Stratford, CT
Rodie, Wilfred J., Sr. ... Stratford, CT
Rodieck, Kelly R. ... Minneapolis, MN
Rodier, Alan G. ... San Francisco, CA
Rodier, Christopher P. ... New York, NY
Rodier, William I., Jr. ... New York, NY
Rodiger, Georgiana G. ... Los Angeles, CA
Rodiger, William B. ... Santa Ana, CA

Rodihan, Ian A. ... Seattle, WA
Rodihan & Keane ... Seattle, WA
Rodin, Carl O. ... Portage, IN
Rodin, Carl S. ... Queens Village, NY
Rodin, Curt N. ... Chicago, IL
Rodin, Dana F. ... Boston, MA
Rodin, Ellen E. ... Oakland, CA
Rodin, James A. ... Minneapolis, MN
Rodin, Mike ... Englewood, CO
Rodin, Richard S. ... Washington, DC
Rodin, Rita A. ... New York, NY
Rodin, Sherwin A. ... Norwalk, CT
Rodin, W. Victor ... Washington, DC
Rodino, Joy ... Paterson, NJ
Rodino, Peter W., III ... Montclair, NJ
Rodino, Peter W., Jr. ... Newark, NJ
Rodino, Samuel J. ... Elkhart, IN
Rodio & Brown, Ltd. ... Providence, RI
Rodio, James H. ... Falls Church, VA
Rodio, Joseph J. ... Providence, RI
Rodio, Mark L. ... Cleveland, OH
Rodio, Stephen A. ... Providence, RI
Rodio & Ursillo, Ltd. ... Providence, RI
Rodis, Rodel E. ... San Francisco, CA
Rodis, Theodore G. ... Austin, TX
Rodis, William Reeve ... San Antonio, TX
Roditti, Esther C. ... New York, NY
Rodkey, F. Stanley ... Lena, IL
Rodkey, Joseph F., Jr. ... Pittsburgh, PA
Rodkey, Randall C. ... Johnstown, PA
Rodli, Beskar, Boles & Krueger, S.C.
Prescott, WI
River Falls, WI
Rodli, Keith ... River Falls, WI
Rodli, Lauren Thor
La Canada Flintridge, CA
Rodman, Allen ... Malden, MA
Rodman, Allen, P.C. ... Malden, MA
Rodman, Andrew L. ... Boston, MA
Rodman, Bernard ... Lynn, MA
Rodman, Catherine A. ... Oceanside, CA
Rodman, Charles B. ... White Plains, NY
Rodman, Charles F. ... Miami, FL
Rodman, Cheryl ... Los Angeles, CA
Rodman, Daniel S. ... Irvine, CA
Rodman, Edward N. ... Washington, NC
Rodman, Holscher, Francisco & Peck, P.A.
Washington, NC
Rodman, James A. ... Austin, TX
Rodman, Jay Hilyard ... Naples, FL
Rodman, Jeffrey S. ... Boston, MA
Rodman, John D. ... Middleburg Heights, OH
Rodman, John R. ... Denver, CO
Rodman, John S. ... Boston, MA
Rodman, Jordan A. ... Santa Rosa, CA
Rodman, Keith ... Eugene, OR
Rodman, Kenneth B. ... Westlake Village, CA
Rodman, Kevin D. ... Jackson, CA
Rodman, Kimberly Lee ... Versailles, KY
Rodman, Lawrence B. ... New York, NY
Rodman, Lee ... Colorado Springs, CO
Rodman, Leroy E. ... New York, NY
Rodman, Lesli Eisinger ... Westfield, NJ
Rodman, Martha J. ... Eugene, OR
Rodman, Mimi L. ... Chicago, IL
Rodman, Patrice M. ... Warren, NJ
Rodman, Philip L. ... White Plains, NY
Rodman, Richard B., (P.C.)
New York, NY
Rodman, Richard L. ... Manchester, NH
Rodman and Rodman, LLP
White Plains, NY
Rodman, Ronald David ... Sunrise, FL
Rodman, Rosemarie ... Pearl River, NY
Rodman & Ross-Shannon ... Denver, CO
Rodman, Stephen J. ... Chelmsford, MA
Rodman, Thomas E. ... Odessa, TX
Rodman, Thomas Edward, Jr. ... Austin, TX
Rodman, Todd ... Worcester, MA
Rodman, William B. ... Riverdale, NY
Rodman, Yale D. ... Rockville, MD
Rodne, Jay R. ... Carson City, NV
Seattle, WA
Rodner, Jeffrey S. ... Bronxville, NY
Rodner, Judith E. ... West Orange, NJ
Rodner, Seth L. ... Department of Justice, Antitrust Division, GV
Rodner, Stephen B. ... New York, NY
Rodness, Roger A. ... Clarkfield, MN
Rodney, Amy ... Santa Rosa, CA
Rodney, Bordenave, Boykin, Bennette & Boyle ... Metairie, LA
New Orleans, LA
Rodney, Burton ... Princeton, NJ
Rodney, Donna Marie ... Washington, DC
Rodney, Glenn ... Ossining, NY
Rodney, John C. ... Pittsburgh, PA
Rodney, Laraine ... Pittsburgh, PA
Rodney, Leonard ... Great Neck, NY
Rodney, Mindy S. ... Miami, FL
Rodney, Mindy S., P.A. ... Miami, FL
Rodney, Morgan R. ... Covina, CA
Rodney, Richard J. ... Mound, MN
Rodney, Richard J., P.A. ... Mound, MN
Rodney, Roy J., Jr. ... New Orleans, LA
Rodney, Wayne A. ... Bethesda, MD
Philadelphia, PA
Rodnick, Amie ... Austin, TX
Rodnick, Randy C. ... Warren, MI
Rodnick & Unger, P.C. ... Warren, MI
Rodnite, Andrew J., Jr. ... Clearwater, FL
Rodnite, Andrew John ... Tampa, FL
Rodnite, Peter Martin ... Tallahassee, FL
Rodock, John N. ... Washington, DC
Rodocker, Peter B. ... Columbus, OH
Rodolakis, Alex M. ... Boston, MA
Rodolakis, James M. ... Springfield, MA
Rodolakis, Mano ... Springfield, MA

Rodolakis, Stephan M. ... Worcester, MA
Rodolf, Sandra F. ... Tulsa, OK
Rodolf, Stephen J. ... Tulsa, OK
Rodolf & Todd ... Tulsa, OK
Rodolff, Barry L. ... Orange, CA
Rodolph, Don ... Clinton, OK
Taloga, OK
Rodoni, Catherine A. ... Santa Cruz, CA
Rodophele, Robert P. ... Boston, MA
Rodos, Bradley S. ... Philadelphia, PA
Rodos, Gerald J., (P.C.) ... Philadelphia, PA
Rodos, Stephen ... Philadelphia, PA
Rodosevich, Denise ... Rocky Hill, CT
Rodov, Valentina ... Redondo Beach, CA
Rodovich, Andrew P. ... Hammond, IN
Rodowsky, Lawrence F. ... Baltimore, MD
Rodrick, Richard J. ... Franklin Lakes, NJ
Rodrick, Robert M. ... Memphis, TN
Rodrick, Scott S. ... Long Beach, CA
Rodrigue, Edward A., Jr., (A Law Corporation) ... New Orleans, LA
Rodrigue, Jon P. ... San Diego, CA
Rodrigue, Julian J. ... Covington, LA
Rodrigue, Julian J., Jr. ... Covington, LA
Rodrigue, Julie E. ... New Orleans, LA
Rodrigue, Linda G. ... Baton Rouge, LA
Rodrigue, Monica C. ... Baton Rouge, LA
Rodrigue, Peirre E. ... Northampton, MA
Rodrigue, Robert P. ... Boston, MA
Rodrigue & Rodrigue ... Covington, LA
Rodrigues, Alan J. ... Los Angeles, CA
Rodrigues, Albert J. ... Seaford, NY
Rodrigues, Andrew J. ... Bethlehem, PA
Rodrigues, Carl R. ... Portland, OR
Rodrigues, Cecil A. ... Trenton, NJ
Rodrigues, Daryl A. ... Spokane, WA
Rodrigues, Eliza M. ... San Francisco, CA
Rodrigues, Gene E. ... Rosemead, CA
Rodrigues, Robert W. ... Washington, DC
Rodrigues-Miranda, Luis G. ... San Juan, PR
Rodriguez, Aaron M. ... Bloomington, MN
Rodriguez, Adolfo R., Jr. ... Dallas, TX
Rodriguez, Agnes Milagros ... Washington, DC
Rodríguez, Agustín E. ... Richmond, VA
Rodriguez, Albert L. ... San Antonio, TX
Rodriguez, Albert M. ... New York, NY
Rodriguez, Albert R. ... Los Angeles, CA
Rodriguez, Alberto A. ... Miami, FL
Rodriguez, Alonso J. ... Oklahoma City, OK
Rodriguez, Alonzo T. ... Sinton, TX
Rodriguez, Ambarina A. ... Miami, FL
Rodriguez, Ana Quincoces ... Miami, FL
Rodriguez, Anabel ... Cambridge, MA
Rodriguez & Angelo, P.A.
Fort Lauderdale, FL
Miami, FL
Rodriguez, Anita M. ... Quincy, IL
Rodriguez, Anne Marie ... Miami, FL
Rodriguez, Anthony ... Boston, MA
Rodriguez, Anthony C., Law Office of
Oakland, CA
Rodriguez, Anthony E. ... Los Angeles, CA
Rodriguez, Anthony J., Jr.
Kew Gardens, NY
Rodriguez, Antonio H. ... Los Angeles, CA
Rodrĭguez, Antonio I. Hernández
San Juan, PR
Rodriguez, Antonio J. ... New Orleans, LA
Rodríguez, Antonio J. ... San Juan, PR
Rodriguez, Ariel ... Alexandria, VA
Rodriguez, Ariel A. ... Jersey City, NJ
Rodriguez, Armando O. ... Fresno, CA
Rodriguez, Armando V. ... Houston, TX
Rodriguez & Aronson, P.A. ... Miami, FL
Rodriguez, Arturo ... Douglas, AK
Rodriguez, B. Vincent ... Lexington, KY
Rodriguez, Barbara Equen ... Boston, MA
Rodriguez, Beth M. ... Chicago, IL
Rodriguez, Blanca I. ... New York, NY
Rodriguez, Bob ... Houston, TX
Rodriguez, Brenda R. ... Fairfax, VA
Rodriguez, Brian D. ... Riverview, MI
Rodriguez, Carlos ... Los Angeles, CA
Rodriguez, Carlos ... Rochester, NY
Rodriguez, Carlos A. ... Fort Lauderdale, FL
Rodriguez, Carlos A. ... Tampa, FL
Rodriguez, Carlos A. ... New York, NY
Rodriguez, Carlos, & Associates
Washington, DC
Rodriguez, Carlos Domingo Grillasca
Ponce, PR
Rodriguez, Carlos G. ... Washington, DC
Rodriguez, Carmen ... Miami, FL
Rodriguez, Carmen I. ... Stoughton, MA
Rodriguez, Carmen M. ... Lafayette, LA
Rodriguez, Carmen, P.A. ... Miami, FL
Rodriguez, Carol H. ... Detroit, MI
Rodriguez, Carolyn ... New York, NY
Rodriguez, Catherine B. ... Orlando, FL
Rodriguez, Catherine M.
Fort Lauderdale, FL
Rodriguez, Celeste Jo ... Tampa, FL
Rodriguez, Celso C. ... Corpus Christi, TX
Rodriguez, Cheryl Ann, Law Offices of
Bridgeport, CT
Rodriguez, Colvin & Chaney, L.L.P.
Brownsville, TX
Harlingen, TX
McAllen, TX
Rodriguez, Connie ... New York, NY
Rodriguez, Cristina Espinosa
Houston, TX
Rodriguez, Cynthia A. ... Fairfield, CA
Rodriguez, Cyril A. ... New York, NY
Rodriguez, D. Anthony
Walnut Creek, CA
Rodriguez, Dale M. ... Dallas, TX
Rodriguez, Daniel ... Bakersfield, CA

Roe, Kathryn A. .... Chicago, IL
Roe, Kenneth Dale .... Dallas, TX
Roe, Kevin G. .... Syracuse, NY
Roe & Kramer, LLP .... New York, NY
Roe Law Firm .... Palm Beach, FL
Minneapolis, MN
Roe, Leslie H. .... San Diego, CA
Roe, Mallon and Tess .... Rochelle, IL
Roe, Mark J. .... New York, NY
Roe, Mark K. .... Everett, WA
Roe, Maura .... San Francisco, CA
Roe, Michael A. .... Tampa, FL
Roe, Michael F. .... Naperville, IL
Roe, Michael F. .... Rhinelander, WI
Roe, Michael S. .... Cincinnati, OH
Roe, Michael V. .... Vancouver, WA
Roe, Patricia B. .... Toms River, NJ
Roe, Patricia M. Green .... San Jose, CA
Roe, R. Thomas .... Palm Beach, FL
Minneapolis, MN
Roe, Rebecca J. .... Seattle, WA
Roe, Richard L. .... Washington, DC
Roe, Richard N. .... Olathe, KS
Roe, Richard W. .... Vancouver, WA
Roe, Robert H. .... San Diego, CA
Roe, Robert W. .... St. Paul, MN
Roe, Roger R., Jr. .... Minneapolis, MN
Roe, Stephen C. .... Elmira, NY
Roe, Stephen J. .... Alexandria, VA
Roe, Susan .... Los Angeles, CA
Roe, Tamara L. .... Seattle, WA
Roe, Thomas A. .... Minneapolis, MN
Roe, Thomas W., Jr. .... Fincastle, VA
Roe, Troy D. .... Irvine, CA
Roe, Wallace, Esteve, Taroff & Taitz, LLP
Patchogue, NY
Roe, William A. .... Belle Chasse, LA
Roe, William H. .... Oneonta, AL
Roeb, Craig A. .... Los Angeles, CA
Roeback, Linda Marie .... Naples, FL
Chicago, IL
Roebel, Jack E. .... Fort Wayne, IN
Roeber, Kenneth T. .... Richmond, VA
Roeber, Leonard W. .... Forked River, NJ
Roeber & Stonehill .... Forked River, NJ
Roeberg, David .... Wilmington, DE
Roeberg, Kenneth J. .... Blue Bell, PA
Roeberg, Moore & Associates, P.A.
Wilmington, DE
Roebig, Thomas D., Jr. .... Palm Harbor, FL
Roebke, Harry G. .... Bowling Green, OH
Roebuck, A. Scott .... Bessemer, AL
Hoover, AL
Roebuck, Arthur R., Jr. .... Wellington, FL
Roebuck, J. Michael .... New York, NY
Roebuck, M. Lloyd .... Mobile, AL
Roebuck, Marie T. .... Providence, RI
Roebuck, Michael .... Houston, TX
Roebuck, Michael C. .... Kotzebue, AK
Roebuck, Randolph L. .... Fort Wayne, IN
Roebuck, Raymond L. .... Jacksonville, FL
Roebuck, Sidney O., Jr. .... Birmingham, AL
Roebuck, Thomas P., Jr. .... Beaumont, TX
Roebuck, Thurman M.
Equal Employment Opportunity Commission,
Office of Federal Operations, GV
Roeca, Arthur F. .... Honolulu, HI
Roeca, Douglas R. .... Cameron Park, CA
Roeca, Jodie D. .... Honolulu, HI
Roeca, Louie & Hiraoka .... Honolulu, HI
Roeca, Russell S. .... San Francisco, CA
Roeck, George Edward .... Staten Island, NY
Roeckell, Elizabeth V. .... Bronx, NY
Roecker, R. Paul .... Orlando, FL
Roeckl, Eric A. .... Hicksville, NY
Roeckl, Margaret E. .... Berkeley, CA
Roecklein, Laura S. .... Washington, DC
Roecks, Craig R. .... Las Vegas, NV
Roedder, William C., Jr. .... Mobile, AL
Roedel, John K., Jr. .... St. Louis, MO
Roedel, Larry M. .... Baton Rouge, LA
New Orleans, LA
Roedel, Parsons, Koch, Frost, Balhoff & McCollister, A Law Corporation
Baton Rouge, LA
New Orleans, LA
Roeder, Alan C. .... Farmington Hills, MI
Roeder, Alan W. .... Walker, MN
Roeder and Associates, P.C.
Washington, DC
McLean, VA
Roeder, Craig A. .... Washington, DC
Roeder, Douglas Robert .... Mount Wolf, PA
Roeder, E. Curtis .... Minneapolis, MN
Roeder, Eric .... Torrance, CA
Roeder, Erick J. .... Kansas City, MO
Roeder, George E., III .... Morgantown, WV
Roeder, James L. .... Auburn, CA
Roeder, Kim H. .... Atlanta, GA
Roeder, Mark A. .... Manchester, IA
Roeder, Mark V. .... Palo Alto, CA
Roeder, Martin A. .... New York, NY
Roeder, Mary Alice .... Sandusky, OH
Roeder, Michael L. .... Bettendorf, IA
Roeder, Michael L. .... Madison, WI
Roeder, Miles .... San Francisco, CA
Cambridge, MA
Roeder, Paul H. .... Palo Alto, CA
Roeder, Randolph C. .... San Francisco, CA
Roeder, Richard D. .... Boston, MA
Roeder, Richard W. .... Titusville, PA
Roeder, Robert E. .... North Platte, NE
Roeder, Robert H. .... McKinney, TX
Roeder & Rothschild .... Titusville, PA
Roeder, Steven G. .... San Diego, CA
Roeder, Steven J. .... Chicago, IL
Roeder, Susan .... San Jose, CA

Roeder, William F., Jr. .... McLean, VA
Roeder, William V. .... Philadelphia, PA
Roedersheimer, Charles J. .... Columbus, OH
Roediger, Joan M. .... Plymouth Meeting, PA
Roediger, Joseph H. .... Phoenix, AZ
Roediger, Linda Louise .... St. Louis, MO
Roedler, George R., Jr. .... St. Paul, MN
Roeger, Deborah L. .... Dublin, OH
Roeger, Walker, Cassel & Holko
Allentown, PA
Perkasie, PA
Roeger, William C., Jr. .... Perkasie, PA
Roegge, Bradford J. .... Minneapolis, MN
Roegge, James F. .... Minneapolis, MN
Roegge, Jeannette O. .... Minneapolis, MN
Roegge, L. Roland .... Grand Rapids, MI
Roegner, Nicholas M. .... Washington, DC
Roeh, Kenneth J. .... Hammond, IN
Roehl, Arlene T. .... Long Lake, MN
Roehl, Carl F., Jr. .... Bellingham, WA
Roehl, Cynthia .... Laguna Hills, CA
Roehl, Jerrald J. .... Albuquerque, NM
Roehl, Joseph M. .... Miami, FL
Roehl, Karen S. .... Oshkosh, WI
Roehl Law Firm, P.C. .... Albuquerque, NM
Roehl, Rex A. .... Chicago, IL
Roehl & Roehl, P.S. .... Bellingham, WA
Roehl, William P. .... Bellingham, WA
Roehler, R. Stephen .... Los Angeles, CA
Roehling, Jerald E. .... Princeton, NJ
Roehlk, Thomas M. .... Orlando, FL
Roehm, John F., III .... Dallas, TX
Roehm, Marie L. .... San Francisco, CA
Roehm, Matthew E. .... Raleigh, NC
Roehm, Susan E. .... Houston, TX
Roehn, Thomas J. .... Tampa, FL
Roehnert, Henrick A. .... Albuquerque, NM
Roehr, Benjamin N. .... Bellevue, WA
Roehr, Nancy L. .... Minneapolis, MN
Roehr, Ronald K. .... Watertown, SD
Roehr, Thomas L. .... Sacramento, CA
Roehrdanz, Charles .... Bloomington, MN
Roehrdanz, George M. .... Minneapolis, MN
Roehrdanz, James W. .... Indianapolis, IN
Roehrenbeck, David C. .... Fairfax, VA
Roehrick, Hulting, Blumberg, Kirlin & Krull, P.C. .... Des Moines, IA
Roehrick, John P. .... Des Moines, IA
Roehrig, August E., Jr. .... Syracuse, NY
Roehrig, Christopher J. .... Kamuela, HI
Roehrig, Michael G. .... Monroe, MI
Roehrig, Roehrig, Wilson & Hara .... Hilo, HI
Kamuela, HI
Roehrig, Stanley H. .... Hilo, HI
Roehrig, William Bryan, III .... Gallatin, TN
Roehrig, William Bryan, III., P.C.
Gallatin, TN
Roehrs, Christopher S. .... New York, NY
Roelandt, Raymond R. .... Crestwood, KY
Roelke, Donald P. .... Phoenix, AZ
Roelke, Mark S. .... Vallejo, CA
Roelke, Norman L. .... Fort Wayne, IN
Roell, Wayne A. .... Rockport, IN
Roelle, Robert H. .... Columbus, OH
Roeller, Robert K. .... Cincinnati, OH
Roeller, Roeller & Jameson .... Cincinnati, OH
Roellgen, J. David .... Vincennes, IN
Roellig, Kristen .... Burlingame, CA
Roellig, Mark D. .... Denver, CO
Roellke, Jon Randall .... Washington, DC
Roelofs, Gene A. .... St. Louis, MO
Roelofs, Jeffrey L. .... Boston, MA
Roelofs, Richard P. .... New York, NY
Roelofs, Stacey E. .... Minneapolis, MN
Roels, Bernard U. .... De Pere, WI
Roels, John M. .... Grand Rapids, MI
Roels, Keidatz & Parent .... De Pere, WI
Roels, Robert J. .... Oshkosh, WI
Roels, Starla K. .... Portland, OR
Roemer, Albert L. .... Montgomery, AL
Roemer, Arthur C. .... St. Paul, MN
Roemer, Charles .... South Bend, IN
Roemer, Charliene .... Biloxi, MS
Roemer, Daniel J. .... San Francisco, CA
Roemer, David F. .... Miami, FL
Roemer, Edward G. .... Albany, NY
Roemer, Eleanor K. .... New Orleans, LA
Roemer, Elizabeth K. .... San Francisco, CA
Roemer, Harnik & Nethery, LLP
Indian Wells, CA
Palm Springs, CA
Roemer, H. C. .... Winston-Salem, NC
Roemer, Henry C., III
Winston-Salem, NC
Roemer, James W., Jr. .... Albany, NY
Roemer, Janice H. .... Davenport, IA
Roemer, John J. .... Worcester, MA
Roemer, Mary C. .... Atlanta, GA
Roemer, Mary P. .... Montgomery, AL
Roemer and Mintz .... Elkhart, IN
South Bend, IN
Roemer, Richard I. .... Indian Wells, CA
Roemer, Robert B. .... Palm Beach, FL
Roemer & Roemer .... Montgomery, AL
Roemer, Terry .... San Francisco, CA
Roemer, Victoria Lane .... Winston-Salem, NC
Roemer, Wallens & Mineaux, LLP
Albany, NY
Roemer, Wellington F., III .... Toledo, OH
Roemer, William C. .... Fort Collins, CO
Roemer, William Stayton .... Drexel Hill, PA
Roemerman, William H.
Cedar Rapids, IA
Roemershauser, Ryan J. .... Metairie, LA
Roemersma, Brian A. .... Phillipsburg, NJ
Roemig, Martin .... Amana, IA
Roemmelt & Pager .... Loudonville, NY
Roemmelt, R. Charles .... Loudonville, NY

Roen, Craig M. .... Minneapolis, MN
Roen, Hal .... Orlando, FL
Roen, James P. E. .... Coral Gables, FL
Roen, Stephen A. .... New York, NY
Roenigk, Patricia L. .... State College, PA
Roenisch, Cynthia C. .... San Francisco, CA
Roepe, R. Frederick .... Milwaukee, WI
Roeper, Dean E. .... San Diego, CA
Roeper, Kristin A. .... Milwaukee, WI
Roepke, Stephen A. .... Findlay, OH
Roepke, Thomas C. .... El Paso, TX
Roepsch, Edward J. .... Milwaukee, WI
Roer, David M., P.C. .... Chandler, AZ
Roer, Kathleen M. .... Long Lake, MN
Roer, Patricia Lang .... New York, NY
Roer, Ricki .... New York, NY
Roerden, Thomas P. .... Syracuse, NY
Roerig, Jeffrey D. .... Brownsville, TX
Roerig, Oliveira & Fisher, L.L.P.
Brownsville, TX
McAllen, TX
Roers, David S. .... Tacoma, WA
Roers, Rolland H. .... Minneapolis, MN
Roerty, Gerard J., Jr. .... Richmond, VA
Roes, Geo. David .... Annandale, MN
Roes, Larsen& Kiernan, P.A.
Annandale, MN
Roesch, Barbara A. .... Geneva, NY
Roesch, Brian D. .... Renton, WA
Roesch, Charles M. .... Cincinnati, OH
Roesch, Donald G. .... San Mateo, CA
Roesch, Ellen S. .... Albany, NY
Roesch, George F., III .... Middletown, NY
Roesch, Laura .... Panama City, FL
Roesch, Lynda E. .... Cincinnati, OH
Roesch, Max E. .... Giddings, TX
Roesch, Paul R., Jr. .... Longview, WA
Roesch, Richard R. .... Lansing, MI
Roesch, Robert J., Jr. .... Staten Island, NY
Roesch & Schaberg .... Saline, MI
Roesch, Stanton G. .... Saline, MI
Roescher, Waldo F., Sr. .... Decatur, GA
Roeschlaub, Ronald C. .... Glendale, CA
Roesel, Elizabeth M. .... Washington, DC
Roesel, Erwin J. .... St. Louis, MO
Roesel, James L. .... Chicago, IL
Roesel, Richard .... Washington, DC
Roesel & Scher, A Prof. Corp.
St. Louis, MO
Roesen, Lawrence P. .... Newport News, VA
Roeser, Allan D. .... Chalfont, PA
Roeser, Anne L. .... Duluth, MN
Roeser, Carlton R. .... Pontiac, MI
Roeser, Jack L. .... Colorado Springs, CO
Roeser, Ronald O. .... Elgin, IL
Roesink, Bonnie Smith .... Craig, CO
Roeske-Fernandez, Lara K. .... Tampa, FL
Roesler, Bruce H. E. .... Pitman, NJ
Roesler, J. Reed .... Peoria, IL
Roesler, John B. .... Denver, CO
Roesler, Judith A. .... Evansville, IN
Roesler, Kenneth W. .... Sherman, TX
Roesler, Oscar R. .... Pleasanton, CA
Roesler, Robert C. .... Burlington, VT
Roesler, Robert J. .... Tulsa, OK
Roesler & Roesler .... Pitman, NJ
Roesler, Whittlesey, Meekins & Amidon
Burlington, VT
Roesmann, Matej .... Euclid, OH
Roesner, David B. .... Muncie, IN
Roess, Dean M. .... Santa Ana, CA
Roess, Martin J. .... St. Petersburg Beach, FL
Roess, Paul L. .... Portland, OR
Roessel, Faith R. .... Washington, DC
Roessel, Theodore B. .... Casanova, VA
Roesser, Eugene F. .... Potomac, MD
Roesser, John J. .... New York, NY
Roesser, Joseph C. .... Wheaton, MD
Roesser, Tom E. .... Honolulu, HI
Roessing, Charles T. .... Paoli, PA
Roessler, Kirk W. .... Cleveland, OH
Roessler, P. Dee .... Melissa, TX
Roessler, Richard M. .... Belleville, IL
St. Louis, MO
Roessler, Russell V. .... San Jose, CA
Roessmann, Anita M. .... Helena, MT
Roessner, Joel J.
Federal Election Commission,
Office of the General Counsel, GV
Roessner, Karl A. .... New York, NY
Roess-Smith Crivello, Julie A.
New Port Richey, FL
Roest, Peter R. .... Houston, TX
Roesti, Frederick C. .... San Francisco, CA
Roetcisoender & Tannesen .... Seattle, WA
Roetcisoender, William R. .... Seattle, WA
Roethe, Jeffrey T. .... Edgerton, WI
Milton, WI
Roethe, Krohn, Pope & McCarthy, LLP
Edgerton, WI
Milton, WI
Roethel, John Edward .... Las Vegas, NV
Roethele, John T. .... Denham Springs, LA
Roethele, John T., A P.L.C.
Denham Springs, LA
Roether, Robert H. .... Novi, MI
Roethler, Wayne .... Longview, WA
Roets, Gary L. .... Portage, WI
Roets Law Office .... Portage, WI
Roets-Dorband, Patricia Ann .... Skokie, IL
Roetter, Frederick A. .... Indianapolis, IN
Roetter, Theresa L. .... Madison, WI
Roettger, C. Edward, Jr. .... Suffolk, VA
Roettger, Garry J. .... Livingston, NJ
Roettger, Kathryn N. .... Florham Park, NJ
Roettger, Norman C., Jr.
Fort Lauderdale, FL
Roettgers, David J. .... Milwaukee, WI

Roetzel & Andress, A Legal Professional Association .... Bonita Springs, FL
Fort Myers, FL
Naples, FL
Akron, OH
Cincinnati, OH
Cleveland, OH
Columbus, OH
Toledo, OH
Roetzel, Danny Nile .... Department of Justice,
Tax Division, GV
Roever, Geoffrey P. .... Waltham, MA
Roewe, Michael P. .... Chehalis, WA
Rofes, Peter K. .... Milwaukee, WI
Roff, J. Hugh, Jr. .... Houston, TX
Roff, Michael B. .... Quincy, CA
Roffe, Andrew S. .... New York, NY
Roffé, Saul .... New York, NY
Roffer, Michael H. .... New York, NY
Roffers, Juley M. .... Tulsa, OK
Roffino, L. Michael .... Miami, FL
Roffino, L. Michael, P.A. .... Miami, FL
Roffman, Allan R. .... Madison, GA
Roffman, Allen H. .... Randolph, MA
Roffman, Charles S. .... Punta Gorda, FL
Roffman, Ian D. .... Chicago, IL
Roffman, I. L. .... Marblehead, MA
Roffman, Rachel M. .... Brighton, MA
Roffmann, M. Andrew .... Kansas City, MO
Roffwarg, Aaron P. .... Houston, TX
Rofman, Gregory Lee .... New York, NY
Rofoli, Roberta L. .... Irvine, CA
Rofrano, Christian A. .... New York, NY
Rog, Kathlyne M. .... Niles, IL
Rogachevsky, Barbara J. .... Sandusky, OH
Rogaczewski, Gregory J. .... Greenfield, WI
Rogak, Joyce Lipton .... Uniondale, NY
Rogak, Lawrence N. .... Oceanside, NY
Rogal, Aaron .... Bronx, NY
Rogal, Bert L. .... Beverly Hills, CA
Rogal, Helen R. .... Chicago, IL
Rogal, Ira A. .... La Grange, IL
Rogal, Michael J. .... Miami, FL
Rogala, Donald J. .... Erie, PA
Rogala, Frances F. .... Beverly Hills, CA
Rogalin, Edward N. .... Eagan, MN
Rogaliner, Susan W. .... St. Charles, IL
Rogalski, Alan T. .... Southfield, MI
Rogalski, Eleanore A. .... Cherry Hill, NJ
Rogalski, Marilyn Komosa
Department Of Veterans Affairs,
Office of the General Counsel, GV
Rogalski, Martin L. .... Jenison, MI
Rogalski, Robert J. .... Wheeling, WV
Rogalsky, Marni .... West Palm Beach, FL
Rogan, Christopher L. .... Washington, DC
Vienna, VA
Rogan, Daniel P. .... Minneapolis, MN
Rogan, Edward G. .... San Francisco, CA
Rogan, Edward T. .... Hackensack, NJ
New City, NY
Rogan & Faugno .... Hackensack, NJ
New City, NY
Rogan Guida & Orenstein .... New York, NY
White Plains, NY
Rogan, J. James .... Danville, KY
Rogan, James E. .... Pasadena, CA
Rogan, Jeffrey P. .... White Plains, NY
Rogan, Kathleen T. .... Sacramento, CA
Rogan, Kevin J. .... Dallas, TX
Rogan, Mary Goode .... Burbank, CA
Rogan, Mary T. .... New York, NY
Rogan, Michael J. .... Cleveland, OH
Rogan, Michael P. .... Washington, DC
Rogan, Neal P. .... Bridgeport, CT
Rogan, Patrick G. .... Los Angeles, CA
Rogan, Patrick M. .... Scranton, PA
Rogan, Richard A. .... San Francisco, CA
Rogan, Robert .... Greenville, NC
Rogan, Sherman .... Boston, MA
Rogan, Terry A. .... San Francisco, CA
Rogan, Thomas F. .... Salt Lake City, UT
Rogan, Tom H. .... Rogersville, TN
Rogan & Welch .... Greeneville, TN
Rogart, Mark Edward .... Verona, NJ
Rogas, KeithR. .... Austin, TX
Rogaski, Anne M. .... Palo Alto, CA
Rogaski, Chester A., Jr. .... Vallejo, CA
Rogaski, Michael E. .... San Diego, CA
Rogatinsky, Iris Sara .... Miami, FL
Rogatnick, Howard M. .... New York, NY
Roge, Bret A. .... Milwaukee, WI
Roge, Paul E. .... North Chicago, IL
Rogel, David H. .... Miami, FL
Rogel, Todd S. .... Fuquay-Varina, NC
Rogell, Diane Kosh .... Bethesda, MD
Rogells, F. Onell .... Sarasota, FL
Rogelstad, Otto E., Jr. .... Boston, MA
Rogen, Richard D. .... Los Angeles, CA
Rogeness, Dean A. .... Springfield, MA
Rogensues, Roy W. .... Clinton Township, MI
Roger, David J. J. .... Las Vegas, NV
Roger, Douglas C., Jr. .... Media, PA
Roger, Kent M. .... San Francisco, CA
Roger, Michael B. .... Oakland, CA
Roger, Norman J. .... Redwood City, CA
Roger, Robin .... New York, NY
Roger, Scott & Helmer LLP
Redwood City, CA
Roger, Thomas H. .... Longmeadow, MA
Rogero, David M. .... Miami, FL
Rogers, Alan T. .... Birmingham, AL
Rogers, Alex E. .... Washington, DC
Rogers, Alexander H. .... San Diego, CA
Rogers, Alexander L. .... Indianapolis, IN
Rogers, Alfred J. .... Phoenix, AZ
Rogers, Alfred M., Jr. .... Chicago, IL
Rogers, Allan H, ... Alpine, NJ

Rogers, Kimberly S. ..... **Miami, FL**
Rogers, King W. ..... **Memphis, TN**
Rogers, Kristine M. ..... **Salt Lake City, UT**
Rogers, Kristine O. ..... Portland, OR
Rogers, Kurt M. ..... **New York, NY**
Rogers, L. Kirk ..... Tallahassee, FL
Rogers, L. Lawton, III ..... **Alexandria, VA**
Rogers, Lance J. ..... Charlottesville, VA
Rogers, Larry E. ..... Monticello, KY
Rogers, Larry R. ..... **Chicago, IL**
Rogers, Larry R., Jr. ..... **Chicago, IL**
Rogers, Larry V. ..... Saipan, TT
Rogers, Laughlin, Nunnally, Hood & Crum
Greeneville, TN
Rogers, Laura ..... **Phoenix, AZ**
Rogers, Laura L. ..... San Diego, CA
Rogers, Laura L. ..... **St. Louis, MO**
Rogers, Laurence S. ..... **New York, NY**
Rogers, LaVelle & Dapelo ..... Holtsville, NY
Rogers Law Firm ..... **Columbia, MO**
Rogers Law Firm, The ..... **Las Vegas, NV**
Rogers Law Offices, PLLC ..... Norman, OK
Rogers, Lawrence B. ..... Troy, MI
Rogers, Lee C. ..... Durham, NC
Rogers, Lee M., Jr. ..... **Roswell, NM**
Rogers, Leo P. ..... Williamsburg, VA
Rogers, Leonard D. ..... Wise, VA
Rogers, Leonard D., P.C. ..... Wise, VA
Rogers, Leslie S. ..... Indianapolis, IN
Rogers, Leslie T. ..... San Francisco, CA
Rogers, Lester M. ..... Miami, FL
Rogers, Lila E. ..... **Burbank, CA**
Rogers, Linda B. ..... **Greensboro, NC**
Rogers, Linda Weeks ..... Columbia, SC
Rogers, Lisa Y. ..... West Palm Beach, FL
Rogers, Lloyd E. ..... Cynthiana, KY
Rogers, Lon B. ..... Lexington, KY
Rogers, Lore A. ..... Whitmore Lake, MI
Rogers, Lore A., P.C., Law Firm of
Whitmore Lake, MI
Rogers, Louis J. ..... **Richmond, VA**
Rogers, Lucas ..... **Boston, MA**
Rogers, Lynette ..... **Conway, SC**
Rogers, Lynn C. ..... Norman, OK
Oklahoma City, OK
Rogers, M. Lynn ..... **Oak Ridge, TN**
Rogers, Malcolm T. ..... **Monticello, MS**
Rogers, Mara H. ..... **New York, NY**
Rogers, Marilyn A. ..... **San Francisco, CA**
Rogers, Marilyn C. ..... Utica, OH
Rogers, Marilyn L. ..... Encinitas, CA
Rogers, Marjorie A. ..... **Albuquerque, NM**
Rogers, Marjorie M. ..... **Marietta, GA**
Rogers, Mark Alan ..... **Little Rock, AR**
Rogers, Mark F. ..... **Bethesda, MD**
Rogers, Mark J. ..... **San Francisco, CA**
Rogers, Mark J. ..... **Plattsburgh, NY**
Rogers, Mark J. ..... Milwaukee, WI
Rogers, Mark M. ..... New York, NY
Rogers, Mark N. ..... Phoenix, AZ
Rogers, Mark W. ..... Department of Justice,
Civil Division, GV
Rogers, Marsha Lee ..... Tulsa, OK
Rogers, Martha Purcell ..... **Washington, DC**
Rogers, Marvin ..... Ransom Canyon, TX
Rogers, Marvin L. ..... **Charlotte, NC**
Rogers, Mary B. ..... **Morristown, NJ**
Rogers, Mary Belle ..... Houston, TX
Rogers, Mary Ellen Welch ..... **Boston, MA**
Rogers, Mary L. ..... **Visalia, CA**
Rogers, Mary T. ..... Boston, MA
Rogers, Matthew R. ..... **Los Angeles, CA**
Rogers, Matthew S. ..... **Hackensack, NJ**
Rogers, Maureen A. ..... Summit, NJ
Rogers, Maurice ..... Birmingham, AL
Rogers, Max E. ..... Blackwell, OK
Rogers & McCranie ..... **Douglas, GA**
Ocilla, GA
Rogers, Melanie Dale McDaniel
Mullins, SC
Rogers, Melissa ..... Washington, DC
Rogers, Melissa B. ..... Washington, DC
Rogers & Melody ..... Keyser, WV
Rogers, Michael B. ..... New York, NY
Rogers, Michael C. ..... **San Diego, CA**
Rogers, Michael D. ..... **Anniston, AL**
Rogers, Michael Dean ..... El Cajon, CA
Rogers, Michael F. ..... **Blue Bell, PA**
Rogers, Michael F. ..... **Houston, TX**
Rogers, Michael G. ..... Chicago, IL
Rogers, Michael G. ..... Chicago, IL
Rogers, Michael J. ..... Somerville, NJ
Rogers, Michael J ..... Cleburne, TX
Rogers, Michael L. ..... North Vernon, IN
Rogers, Michael R. ..... **Beverly Hills, CA**
Rogers, Michael S. ..... **Seattle, WA**
Rogers, Michael T. ..... **New York, NY**
Rogers & Moore ..... Gallatin, TN
Rogers, Moore & Rogers ..... **Baltimore, MD**
Rogers & More ..... **Washington, DC**
Rogers, Morlan Ty ..... **New York, NY**
Rogers, Morris & Ziegler
Fort Lauderdale, FL
Rogers, Mortimer A. ..... Howell, NJ
Rogers & Munnerlyn ..... Bennettsville, SC
Rogers, Murphey ..... **Ocilla, GA**
Rogers, N. Daniel, Jr. ..... Birmingham, AL
Rogers, N. Pendleton ..... **Richmond, VA**
Rogers, Nancy Bainbridge ..... **Seattle, WA**
Rogers, Nancy Hardin ..... Columbus, OH
Rogers, Nancy M. ..... Parker, CO
Rogers, Nancy Newton ..... **Richmond, VA**
Rogers, Nancy Scott ..... **Atlanta, GA**
Rogers, Nolan H. ..... Baltimore, MD
Rogers, Norene M. ..... Conshohocken, PA
Rogers, Norman E., Jr.
New Hartford, CT
Rogers, Norman R. ..... **Dallas, TX**

Rogers, Noyes W. ..... Columbus, NE
Rogers, Oby T. ..... Collins, MS
Rogers, Page & Associates ..... Norristown, PA
Rogers, Patrick A. ..... **Providence, RI**
Rogers, Patrick J. ..... Rancho Cucamonga, CA
Rogers, Patrick J. ..... **Albuquerque, NM**
Rogers, Patrick J. ..... **Dallas, TX**
Rogers, Patrick P. ..... Austin, TX
Rogers, Patrick Wayne ..... **Jackson, TN**
Rogers, Paul E. ..... **Jackson, MS**
Rogers, Paul G. ..... **Washington, DC**
Rogers, Paul J. ..... Anchorville, MI
Rogers, Paul R. ..... **San Francisco, CA**
Rogers, Paul R. ..... Springfield, MA
Rogers, Paul V. ..... **Washington, DC**
Rogers, Paula T. ..... Concord, NH
Rogers, Peggy J. ..... Franklin, WI
Rogers, Perry C. ..... **Las Vegas, NV**
Rogers, Peter ..... Boulder, CO
Rogers, Peter A. ..... Neenah, WI
Rogers, Peter F. ..... Philadelphia, PA
Rogers, Peter J. ..... Portland, ME
Rogers, Philip ..... Mineola, NY
Rogers, Philip J. ..... **St. Petersburg, FL**
Rogers, Philip W. ..... Holtsville, NY
Rogers, Phillip C. ..... Grand Rapids, MI
Rogers, Phyllis Ann ..... Friendswood, TX
Rogers & Pucher ..... Rochester, NY
Rogers & Puckhaber ..... Concord, NH
Rogers, R. Allen ..... Austin, TX
Rogers, R. Anthony ..... Department of Justice,
Environment and Natural Resources
Division, GV
Rogers, R. Gregg ..... Louisville, MS
Rogers, R. Merritt ..... **Birmingham, AL**
Rogers, R. Michael ..... Waco, TX
Rogers, Ramona Francesconi ..... Ashland, OH
Rogers, Randall F. ..... **Marietta, GA**
Rogers, Randall L. ..... Tyler, TX
Rogers, Randolph A. ..... Lancaster, CA
Rogers, Randy ..... **San Francisco, CA**
Rogers, Randy C. ..... Tempe, AZ
Rogers, Randy George ..... Athens, TN
Rogers, Rayford P., Jr. ..... Tifton, GA
Rogers, R. E., Jr. ..... Little Rock, AR
Rogers & Ready ..... **Monticello, MS**
Rogers, Rebecca C. ..... **Charlotte, NC**
Rogers, Regina J. ..... Houston, TX
Rogers, Reginald J. ..... Washington, DC
Rogers, Reginald J., P.C. ..... Washington, DC
Rogers, Rex R. ..... **Houston, TX**
Rogers, Rhonda K. ..... Austin, TX
Rogers, Rhonda L. ..... Plantation, FL
Rogers, Richard A., Jr. ..... **Raleigh, NC**
Rogers, Richard B. ..... **Washington, DC**
Rogers, Richard D. ..... Topeka, KS
Rogers, Richard D. ..... Casper, WY
Rogers, Richard D., Jr. ..... Stuart, VA
Rogers, Richard G. ..... **Dallas, TX**
Rogers, Richard H. ..... Dayton, OH
Rogers, Richard J. ..... Towson, MD
Rogers, Richard J. ..... **Hawthorne, NY**
Rogers, Richard L. ..... Tallahassee, FL
Rogers, Richard L., (P.A.) ..... Titusville, FL
Rogers, Richard M. ..... San Francisco, CA
Rogers, Richard M. ..... Department of Justice,
Office of Professional Responsibility, GV
Rogers, Richard M. ..... Portland, OR
Rogers, Richard P. ..... Wilkes-Barre, PA
Rogers, Richard W. ..... Middlebury, IN
Rogers, Richard W. ..... Norristown, PA
Rogers, Richard W., III, Law Offices of
Corpus Christi, TX
Rogers, Rick L. ..... North Chicago, IL
Rogers, R. M. ..... Marion, OH
Rogers, Robert A. ..... Van Nuys, CA
Rogers, Robert B. ..... **Kansas City, MO**
Rogers, Robert B. ..... Trenton, NJ
Rogers, Robert C., Jr. ..... Fort Lauderdale, FL
Rogers, Robert E. ..... Phoenix, AZ
Rogers, Robert F. ..... Naples, FL
Rogers, Robert F. ..... Burlington, NJ
Rogers, Robert H. ..... Dallas, TX
Rogers, Robert H., Jr. ..... San Pedro, CA
Rogers, Robert I. "Bob", Jr.
Russellville, AL
Rogers, Robert J. ..... Toledo, OH
Rogers, Robert K. ..... **Phoenix, AZ**
Rogers, Robert L. ..... Greenville, SC
Rogers, Robert L., Jr. ..... **Hattiesburg, MS**
Rogers, Robert M. ..... Springfield, IL
Rogers, Robert O. ..... **West Palm Beach, FL**
Rogers, Robert P. ..... Chetek, WI
Rogers, Robert Ranger ..... Sheridan, WY
Rogers, Robert Warren ..... New York, NY
Rogers, Robin N. ..... **El Segundo, CA**
Rogers, Robin Phelan ..... Dexter, MO
Rogers, Robyn A. ..... Riverside, CA
Rogers, Robyn Steiner ..... **New York, NY**
Rogers and Rogers ..... Wellington, KS
Rogers & Rogers ..... Florence, SC
Rogers & Rogers, P.C. ..... **Marion, IN**
Rogers, Romney C. ..... **Fort Lauderdale, FL**
Rogers, Ronald R. ..... **Raleigh, NC**
Rogers, Ronald W. ..... **Atlanta, GA**
Rogers, Rosemary Myles
Oklahoma City, OK
Rogers, Roslyn ..... Ontario, CA
Rogers, Russell J. ..... **Atlanta, GA**
Rogers, Ruth ..... New York, NY
Rogers, S. Emory ..... **West Palm Beach, FL**
Rogers, S. Mills, III ..... Marietta, GA
Rogers, S. Taggart ..... Fremont, CA
Rogers, Sandra J. ..... **Phoenix, AZ**
Rogers, Sanford ..... Beverly Hills, CA
Rogers, Sara S. "Sally" ..... **Columbia, SC**
Rogers, Sarah Greden ..... **Palo Alto, CA**
Rogers & Schlesinger, P.C. ..... New City, NY

Rogers & Scott ..... Murfreesboro, TN
Rogers, Scott A. ..... **Huntsville, AL**
Rogers, Scott D. ..... **San Francisco, CA**
Rogers, Scott J. ..... **Council Bluffs, IA**
Rogers, Scott L. ..... **Miami, FL**
Rogers, Sean C. ..... **Morrow, GA**
Rogers, Sean J. ..... Rockville, MD
Rogers & Shadek ..... **Incline Village, NV**
Rogers, Sharon K. ..... Pittsburgh, PA
Rogers, Sharyn G. ..... **Buffalo, NY**
Rogers, Shawn ..... Overland Park, KS
Kansas City, MO
Rogers, Sheadyn R. ..... **Dallas, TX**
Rogers & Sheffield, LLP
Santa Barbara, CA
Rogers, Shelby R. ..... **Houston, TX**
Rogers, Shelley ..... **Houston, TX**
Rogers, Sherilyn M. ..... Denver, CO
Rogers, Sherman ..... Tulare, CA
Rogers, Sherman, A Professional Corporation
Tulare, CA
Rogers, Sherry H. ..... **Seattle, WA**
Rogers, Sheryl ..... **Durango, CO**
Rogers, Shireen Banki ..... **Irvine, CA**
Rogers, Si Randall ..... Arlington, TX
Rogers & Smith ..... Burlington, NJ
Rogers, Smith & Rogers ..... Fort Atkinson, WI
Rogers, Stanley ..... Los Angeles, CA
Rogers, Stephan B. ..... **San Antonio, TX**
Rogers, Stephanie B. ..... Miami, FL
Rogers, Stephen C. ..... **Washington, DC**
Rogers, Stephen D. ..... **Milwaukee, WI**
Rogers, Stephen H. ..... **Las Vegas, NV**
Rogers, Stephen J. ..... Stuart, FL
Rogers, Stephen J. ..... Scarsdale, NY
Rogers, Stephen M. ..... Hartford, CT
Rogers, Steve ..... Los Angeles, CA
Rogers, Steven B. ..... Anchorage, AK
Rogers, Steven E. ..... Dallas, TX
Rogers, Steven F. ..... Milford, CT
Rogers, Steven G. ..... **New York, NY**
Rogers, Steven Glen ..... Ocala, FL
Rogers, Steven M. ..... **Los Angeles, CA**
Rogers, Steven M. ..... Arlington Heights, IL
Rogers, Steven S. ..... Jersey City, NJ
Rogers, Steven W. ..... Fredonia, KS
Rogers, Stillman D. ..... Keene, NH
Rogers, Sumner H. ..... **Boston, MA**
Rogers, Susan ..... **Birmingham, AL**
Rogers, Susan Bernhardt
Fort Lauderdale, FL
Rogers, Susan K. ..... Blandinsville, IL
Rogers, Susan R. ..... Naperville, IL
Rogers, Susan R. K. ..... Milledgeville, GA
Rogers, Susan Windle ..... West Chester, PA
Rogers, Suzanne B.
Department Of Health And Human Services,
GV
Rogers, Suzanne E. ..... Sacramento, CA
Rogers, Suzanne M. ..... Denver, CO
Rogers, Sydney Michael, Jr. ..... Larchmont, NY
Rogers, T. Pollard ..... **Fort Worth, TX**
Rogers, Tad S. ..... **Denver, CO**
Rogers, Tami Walker ..... Austin, TX
Rogers, Terry ..... Boulder, CO
Rogers, Terry Ann ..... Portland, OR
Rogers, Terry C. ..... **Traverse City, MI**
Rogers, Terry L. ..... Lutz, FL
Rogers, Terry L. ..... Lincoln, NE
Rogers, Terry L. Law Firm of, P.C.
Lincoln, NE
Rogers, Theodore O. ..... West Chester, PA
Rogers, Theodore O., Jr. ..... **New York, NY**
Rogers, Thomas C. ..... Oakland, CA
Rogers, Thomas C. ..... **Philadelphia, PA**
Rogers, Thomas DeWitt, III
Charleston, SC
Rogers, Thomas E., III ..... Florence, SC
Rogers, Thomas E., Jr. ..... Florence, SC
Rogers, Thomas F. ..... Swampscott, MA
Rogers, Thomas H., III ..... **Marietta, GA**
Rogers, Thomas H., III, P.C. ..... **Canton, GA**
Cartersville, GA
Marietta, GA
Rogers, Thomas H., Jr. ..... **Athens, GA**
Rogers, Thomas J. ..... Cincinnati, OH
Rogers, Thomas J., Jr. ..... Greenbelt, MD
Rogers, Thomas L. ..... South Fulton, TN
Rogers, Thomas M. ..... **Phoenix, AZ**
Rogers, Thomas M., III ..... **Denver, CO**
Rogers, Thomas P. ..... **Norristown, PA**
Rogers, Thomas R.
Altamonte Springs, FL
Rogers, Thomas T. ..... **Austin, TX**
Rogers, Thomas W. ..... Ruston, LA
Rogers, Thomasina V.
Occupational Safety and Health Review
Commission,
Office of the Chairman, GV
Rogers, Timothy F. ..... Columbia, SC
Rogers, Timothy G. ..... **Kenilworth, NJ**
Rogers, Timothy J. ..... Jericho, NY
Rogers, Timothy J. ..... Pittsburgh, PA
Rogers, Timothy J. ..... Bellevue, WA
Rogers, Timothy W. ..... **Rosemead, CA**
Rogers, Todd W. ..... **Fort Collins, CO**
Rogers, Tommy B. ..... Collins, MS
Rogers, Towers, Bailey, Jones & Gay, P.A.
Jacksonville, FL
St. Augustine, FL
Tallahassee, FL
Rogers Townsend & Thomas, PC
Columbia, SC
Rogers, Travis Leamon ..... Somerset, KY
Rogers, Velda H. ..... Salem, OR
Rogers, Vicki F. ..... Chicago, IL
Rogers, Victor J., (P.C.) ..... Austin, TX
Rogers, Virgil E. ..... Dallas, TX

Rogers, W. Charles, III ..... **Baltimore, MD**
Rogers, W. David, Jr., (P.A.) ..... **Orlando, FL**
Rogers, W. Glenn, Jr. ..... Camden, SC
Rogers, W. Jane ..... **Boston, MA**
Rogers, W. Sherman ..... Washington, DC
Rogers, W. Timothy ..... Knoxville, TN
Rogers & Walker LLC
New Hartford, CT
Rogers, Wallace N. ..... Louisville, KY
Rogers, Wallett Bancroft
Federal Communications Commission,
Common Carrier Bureau, GV
Rogers, Walter C. ..... Phoenix, AZ
Rogers, Walter D. ..... Martinez, CA
Rogers, Walter E., Sr. ..... Naples, FL
Rogers, Walter F., Jr. ..... **Jacksonville, FL**
Rogers, Walter M. ..... **Chicago, IL**
Rogers, Walter R., Jr. ..... **Raleigh, NC**
Rogers, Walter S. C. ..... Miami, FL
Rogers, Walter T. ..... Meridian, MS
Rogers, Warren K., Jr. ..... **Jackson, MS**
Rogers, Wayne ..... Milledgeville, GA
Rogers, Wayne L. ..... Honolulu, HI
Annapolis, MD
Rogers, W. E., III ..... Hopkinsville, KY
Rogers & Weatherwax, P.C. ..... Jackson, MI
Rogers & Wells ..... **New York, NY**
Rogers, W. H. ..... Moulton, AL
Rogers & Whalen, P.A. ..... **Phoenix, AZ**
Rogers & Whitley, L.L.P. ..... **Austin, TX**
Rogers, Willard B., Jr. ..... Aurora, CO
Rogers, William A. ..... Bennettsville, SC
Rogers, William A., III ..... **Denver, CO**
Rogers, William A., Jr. ..... **Dayton, OH**
Rogers, William A., Jr. ..... **Austin, TX**
Rogers, William B. ..... Oklahoma City, OK
Rogers, William B., Jr. ..... Bennettsville, SC
Rogers, William C., Jr.
San Francisco, CA
Rogers, William C., Jr. ..... **Baltimore, MD**
Rogers, William C., (P.C.) ..... **Boston, MA**
Rogers, William D. ..... **Washington, DC**
Rogers, William D. ..... **New York, NY**
Rogers, William E. ..... Austin, TX
Rogers, William F. ..... **Burbank, CA**
Rogers, William F. ..... St. Louis, MO
Rogers, William G. ..... Washington, DC
Rogers, William H. ..... Dallas, TX
Rogers, William H. ..... Fort Atkinson, WI
Rogers, William J. ..... Novato, CA
Rogers, William J. ..... **Chicago, IL**
Rogers, William J., Sr. ..... Staunton, VA
Rogers, William James ..... **Pittsburgh, PA**
Rogers, William K. ..... **Santa Barbara, CA**
Rogers, William K. ..... Kingsport, TN
Rogers, William K., Jr. ..... Childersburg, AL
Rogers, William L. ..... Naples, FL
Rogers, William L., Jr. ..... **Gainesville, GA**
Rogers, William N. ..... Rockville, MD
Rogers, William P. ..... **Washington, DC**
New York, NY
Rogers, William P., Jr. ..... **New York, NY**
Rogers, William S. ..... **Hartford, CT**
Rogers, William S., Jr. ..... **Atlanta, GA**
Rogers, William S., Jr. ..... **Worcester, MA**
Rogers, Wilson D., III ..... **Boston, MA**
Rogers, Wilson D., Jr. ..... **Boston, MA**
Rogers, Wilson D., Jr. P.C., Law Offices of
Boston, MA
Rogers & Wright, P.C. ..... **Dallas, TX**
Rogers & Wughalter ..... Bronx, NY
Rogers, Yale I. ..... Phoenix, AZ
Rogers, Yandell, Jr. ..... Houston, TX
Rogers, Yolande B. ..... Chicago, IL
Rogers, Young, Wollstein & Hughes, L.L.C.
Anniston, AL
Rogers, Yvette M. ..... Brookhaven, PA
Rogers, Yvonne Gonzalez
San Francisco, CA
Rogers-Goodstein, Alyce ..... **New York, NY**
Rogerson, Christine H. ..... **Richmond, VA**
Rogerson, Christopher Alan ..... Kinston, NC
Rogerson, Clinton ..... Moundsville, WV
Rogerson, Elise Streicher ..... **San Diego, CA**
Rogerson, James F. ..... **Wilson, NC**
Rogerson, John T., III ..... **Jacksonville, FL**
Rogerson, John T., Jr. ..... Hammondsport, NY
Rogerson, Kent Bradley
San Francisco, CA
Rogerson, Kristi ..... **Doylestown, PA**
Philadelphia, PA
Rogerson, Lex A., Jr. ..... **Lexington, SC**
Rogerson, Thomas D. ..... Philadelphia, PA
Rogerson, William G. ..... **Boston, MA**
Rogers Parsons, A. Elaine ..... Wethersfield, CT
Rogg, Kasey Alan ..... **Wichita, KS**
Rogg, Katherine L. ..... Dillon, CO
Rogg, Ronald H. ..... Wichita, KS
Rogg, Brian T. ..... Milwaukee, WI
Rogge, C. Frederick, III ..... **New York, NY**
Rogge, Carl F., Jr. ..... New York, NY
Rogge, Gretchen ..... **Cleveland, OH**
Rogge, Hendrick ..... **Miami, FL**
Rogge, Joel J. ..... Ipswich, MA
Rogge, Kathleen L. ..... Mandeville, LA
Rogge, Stephan A. ..... La Crosse, WI
Rogge, Theodore C. ..... Tacoma, WA
Roggeman, Chad M. ..... Edina, MN
Roggeman, John J. ..... Mishawaka, IN
Roggen, Felice ..... **Washington, DC**
Roggenbaum, Frances R. ..... **Harrisburg, PA**
Roggenbaum, Peter M. ..... **Birmingham, MI**
Roggenkamp, David C. ..... Alexandria, OH
Roggenkamp, Richard D. ..... New Albany, OH
Roggensack, Margaret E.
Washington, DC
Roggensack, Rolland R. ..... Lancaster, WI
Roggeveen, Dirk Gardiner ..... Washington, DC

Roland, Lynn M. ..... New York, NY
Roland, Marcus A. ..... Lexington, KY
Roland, Maureen Weise ..... San Rafael, CA
Roland, Paul G. ..... Indianapolis, IN
Roland, R. William ..... Tallahassee, FL
Roland, Richard R. ..... Bellevue, WA
Roland, Robert E. ..... Canton, OH
Roland, Robert L. ..... Baton Rouge, LA
Roland & Schlegel, P.C. ..... Pottsville, PA
Reading, PA
Roland, Stephen P. ..... New York, NY
Roland, Steven D. ..... San Francisco, CA
Roland, Tanya L. ..... Oklahoma City, OK
Roland, Thomas F. ..... Gulph Mills, PA
Roland, Thomas L. ..... Pittsburgh, PA
Roland, Thomas V. ..... Berkeley, CA
Roland, Ty G ..... Cape Coral, FL
Roland, William "Bo" ..... Jackson, MS
Roland, Yvette D. ..... Los Angeles, CA
Rolando, Carole L. ..... Spokane, WA
Rolando, Elizabeth M. ..... Los Angeles, CA
Rolando, Margaret A. ..... Miami, FL
Rolapp, Todd J. ..... Nashville, TN
Rolater, John R., Jr. ..... Dallas, TX
Rolbin, Jonathan M. ..... San Francisco, CA
Rold, Cynthia L. ..... Littleton, CO
Rold, William J. ..... New York, NY
Roldan, Alberto S. ..... Sacramento, CA
Roldan, Jonathan M. ..... Hacienda Heights, CA
Roldan, Marc A. ..... Lee's Summit, MO
Roldan, Marco A. ..... Kansas City, MO
Roldan, Rex J. ..... Woodbury, NJ
Roldan Figueroa, Pedro ..... Caguas, PR
Roldan-Gonzalez, Israel ..... Aguadilla, PR
Role, Gerald A. ..... Department of Justice,
Tax Division, GV
Rolef, Steven Allen ..... Silver Spring, MD
Rolefson, Jon R. ..... Pleasanton, CA
Rolek, Jill Southworth ..... Des Moines, IA
Rolek, Robert W ..... Chicago, IL
Roleke, Christine M ..... Middle Village, NY
Rolen, Gregory J. ..... San Francisco, CA
Rolen, Patrick T. ..... Oklahoma City, OK
Rolenc, Michael S. ..... Chicago, IL
Roles, Alan W. ..... Louisville, KY
Roles, Forrest H. ..... Charleston, WV
Rolewick, David F. ..... Wheaton, IL
Rolewick & Gutzke, P.C. ..... Wheaton, IL
Rolewicz, Peter C. ..... Chicago, IL
Rolewicz, Tricia L. ..... Charlotte, NC
Roley, Robert W. ..... Portland, OR
Roley, Ryan R. ..... Anchorage, AK
Rolf, A. William ..... Southfield, MI
Rolf, Alice J. ..... Springfield, IL
Rolf, Carol ..... Cleveland, OH
Rolf, Carol A. ..... Amherst, NH
Rolf, David A. ..... Springfield, IL
Rolf, Dennis A. ..... Concordia, MO
Rolf, Devon A. ..... Kansas City, MO
Rolf, Donald H., Jr. ..... Cincinnati, OH
Rolf, Michael L. ..... Muskegon, MI
Rolf, Ramon F., Jr. ..... Midland, MI
Rolf, Rebecca L. ..... Kansas City, MO
Rolf, Theodore D. ..... San Diego, CA
Rolf, Troy A. ..... Washington, DC
Rolfe, Bennett, A Professional Corporation
Camarillo, CA
Rolfe, Brian H. ..... Southfield, MI
Rolfe, Carol A. ..... New York, NY
Rolfe, Craig A. ..... Kalamazoo, MI
Rolfe, David S. ..... Parker, CO
Rolfe, Donald H. ..... Los Angeles, CA
Rolfe, Harold E. ..... Park Ridge, NJ
Rolfe, James A. ..... Dallas, TX
Rolfe, James D. ..... Seattle, WA
Rolfe, John McKain, Jr. ..... Nashville, TN
Rolfe, Jonathan P. ..... Washington, DC
Rolfe, Lawrence C. ..... Jacksonville, FL
Rolfe, Randall C. ..... West Chester, PA
Rolfe, Robert A. ..... Lamoni, IA
Rolfe, Robert M. ..... New York, NY
Richmond, VA
Rolfe, Robin A. ..... New York, NY
Rolfe, Ronald S. ..... New York, NY
Rolfe, Stuart T. ..... Seattle, WA
Rolfe, William C. ..... Sacramento, CA
Rolfes, A. James ..... Sarasota, FL
Rolfes, Andrew J. ..... Philadelphia, PA
Rolfes, Garvey, Walker & Robbins
Batesville, IN
Greensburg, IN
Rolfes, Gary J. ..... Clinton, IA
Rolfes, James A. ..... Chicago, IL
Rolfes, James W., Sr. ..... London, OH
Rolfes, Jerome F. ..... Cincinnati, OH
Rolfs, Craig A. ..... Menominee, MI
Rolfs, Debra L. Haselow ..... Milwaukee, WI
Rolfs, Emile C., III ..... Baton Rouge, LA
Rolfs, Jacqueline R. ..... Minneapolis, MN
Rolfs, Leland E. ..... Topeka, KS
Rolfs, Pamela A. ..... Jefferson City, MO
Rolfs, Richmond B. ..... St. Paul, MN
Rolfson, Calvin N. ..... Bismarck, ND
Rolfson Schulz Lervick & Geiermann, P.C.
Bismarck, ND
Rolfsrud, Stephen P. ..... Minneapolis, MN
Rolfstad, John ..... United States Senate,
Senatorial Assistants, GV
Rolfstad, Patricia Ashton ..... Topeka, KS
Rolfstad, Telmar E. ..... Williston, ND
Rolig, Jeffrey E. ..... Twin Falls, ID
Rolig, John E. ..... St. Paul, MN
Rolig & Peterson, L.L.P. ..... Boise, ID
Twin Falls, ID
Rolin, Christopher ..... Los Angeles, CA
Roling, David A. ..... Annapolis, MD
Baltimore, MD
Roling, Michael S. ..... Des Moines, IA

Rolinger, Mark S. ..... Cedar Falls, IA
Rolinski, Sylvia J. ..... Silver Spring, MD
Rolinski, William F. ..... Gaylord, MI
Rolison, Elmond T., Jr. ..... Mobile, AL
Rolison, Jay P., Jr. ..... Poughkeepsie, NY
Rolitsky, Sandra G. ..... Cleveland, OH
Rolker, John G. ..... Baltimore, MD
Rolker, John G. ..... Towson, MD
Roll, David A. ..... Fairfax, VA
Roll, David L. ..... Washington, DC
Roll, Donald L ..... North Haven, CT
Roll, Harry ..... Attleboro, MA
Roll, Joan M. ..... Bala Cynwyd, PA
Roll, John McCarthy ..... Tucson, AZ
Roll, Kenneth R. ..... Painesville, OH
Roll, Michael E. ..... Chicago, IL
Roll, Nicholas J. ..... Berwick, PA
Roll, Patricia H. ..... Dayton, OH
Roll, Randolph E. ..... Houston, TX
Roll, Raymond F., Jr. ..... Alden, NY
Buffalo, NY
East Aurora, NY
Roll, Richard D. ..... Los Angeles, CA
Roll, Rick W. ..... Tillamook, OR
Roll, Robert D. ..... Atlanta, GA
Roll, Sally A. ..... Short Hills, NJ
Roll, Stewart D. ..... Cleveland, OH
Roll, Thomas R. ..... Lewisville, TX
Roll, William D., Jr. ..... Point Pleasant, WV
Roll, William J. F., III ..... New York, NY
Rolla, Adrienne M. ..... Deer Park, NY
Rolla, Dudley B. ..... Mayfield Heights, OH
Rolla, Joseph J., Jr.
Department of Commerce,
Patent and Trademark Office, GV
Rolla, Louis A ..... Wallingford, CT
Rolla, Mario F. ..... Deer Park, NY
Rolla, Peter M. ..... Deer Park, NY
Rolland, James L. ..... Olympia, WA
Seattle, WA
Rolland, Michael S. ..... Houston, TX
Rolland, O'Malley, Williams & Wyckoff, P.S.
Olympia, WA
Seattle, WA
Rollberg, Owen M. ..... Granite City, IL
Rolle, Alexander F. ..... Denver, CO
Rolle, Anthony A. ..... Miami, FL
Rolle, Breeland, Ryan & Landau, P.C.
Dallas, TX
Rolle, Christopher D., (P.A.) ..... Orlando, FL
Rolle, James B., III ..... Phoenix, AZ
Rolle, Jonathan P. ..... Las Vegas, NV
Rolle, Larry ..... Dallas, TX
Rolle, Lisa M. ..... Bronxville, NY
Rolle, Tanya L. ..... New York, NY
Rolle, Wade M. ..... Jacksonville, FL
Rollema, Melvin T. ..... Albany, OR
Roller and Allensworth, L.L.P.
Austin, TX
Roller, Barbara Rose ..... North Hollywood, CA
Roller & Bauer, PLLC ..... Washington, DC
Roller, Douglas P. ..... St. Louis, MO
Roller, Elmer L. ..... Bloomfield Hills, MI
Roller, Frederic ..... Philadelphia, PA
Roller, Jan L. ..... Cleveland, OH
Roller, Joan M. ..... Department of Labor,
Office of the Solicitor, GV
Roller, Jos. J. ..... Tacoma, WA
Roller, Larry L. ..... Chesapeake, WV
Roller, Mindy Kapner ..... Brooklyn, NY
Roller, Moffett B. ..... Washington, DC
Roller, Richard M. ..... Davenport, IA
Roller, Robert M. ..... Austin, TX
Roller, Stanley ..... Fairfax, VA
Roller, Steve R. ..... McMinnville, TN
Roller, Steven L. ..... Bakersfield, CA
Roller, Vernon, Powers & Larson, Inc., P.S.
Tacoma, WA
Rolleri, Ronald J. ..... New York, NY
Rollert, E. David ..... Traverse City, MI
Rollert and MacNeal ..... Traverse City, MI
Rolleston, Christopher L. ..... Kansas City, MO
Rolleston, Moreton, Jr. ..... Atlanta, GA
Rollett, Michael H. ..... San Clemente, CA
Rolley, Donald B. ..... Topeka, KS
Rolley, Melanie Ann ..... Madisonville, KY
Rollin, Arthur S. ..... Chicago, IL
Rollin, Claude A.
Federal Deposit Insurance Corporation,
Regulation and Legislation Section, GV
Rollin, Harold L. ..... Visalia, CA
Rollin, Kenneth B. ..... Deerfield, IL
Rollin, Lawrence S., P.C. ..... Tucson, AZ
Rollin, Steven P.
Environmental Protection Agency,
Office of Enforcement and Compliance
Assurance, GV
Rolling, E. Jane ..... New Orleans, LA
Rolling, Garland R. ..... Metairie, LA
Rolling, J. Mark ..... Hammond, LA
Rolling, Jane M. ..... Waukesha, WI
Rolling, Laurie E. ..... Metairie, LA
Rolling, Perrilloux & Sledge
Hammond, LA
Rollinger, Robert S. ..... Bingham Farms, MI
Rollinger, Robert S., P.C.
Bingham Farms, MI
Rollings & Associates, P.C.
St. Charles, MO
Rollings, Cynthia ..... New York, NY
Rollings, Dale L. ..... St. Charles, MO
Rollings, Harvey ..... Cape Coral, FL
Rollings, Jeffrey M. ..... New York, NY
Rollings, Kym Catoe ..... Chesterfield, SC
Rollings, Pamela E. ..... Pittsburgh, PA
Rollings, Richard L., Jr. ..... Ozark, MO
Rolling-Tarbox, Marie R. ..... Davenport, IA
Rollins, Adam Lincoln ..... Monrovia, CA

Rollins, Alton D. ..... Arlington, VA
Rollins, Anne-Herbert ..... Frederick, MD
Rollins, B. Keith ..... Douglasville, GA
Rollins, Barbara B. ..... Abilene, TX
Rollins, Brooke Leslie ..... Dallas, TX
Rollins, Carl P. ..... Dalton, GA
Rollins, Caroline Von Malottke
Campobello, SC
Rollins & Combs ..... Collinsville, OK
Rollins, Cynthia L. De Reamer
Louisville, KY
Rollins, D. Keith ..... Waco, TX
Rollins, David L. ..... Nashville, TN
Rollins, David W. ..... Ocean City, NJ
Rollins, Edward D. E., III ..... Elkton, MD
Rollins, Edward D. E., Jr. ..... Elkton, MD
Rollins, Elaine G. ..... Houston, TX
Rollins, Fowlkes, Jacoby & Kaplan
Boston, MA
Rollins, Gene A. ..... Claymont, DE
Rollins, Herbert L. ..... Frederick, MD
Rollins and Ives, P.A. ..... Camden, AR
Rollins, J. Andrew ..... Chicago, IL
Rollins, James E., Jr. ..... Atlanta, GA
Rollins, James H. ..... Atlanta, GA
Rollins, James Scott ..... Hartford, CT
Rollins, Jamie T. ..... Washington, DC
Rollins, Jeffrey R. ..... West Palm Beach, FL
Rollins, John A. ..... Charleston, WV
Rollins, John F. ..... Chicago, IL
Rollins, John M. ..... Greer, SC
Rollins, John M., Jr. ..... Greer, SC
Rollins, John M., Jr., P.C. ..... Greer, SC
Rollins, John S. ..... Kansas City, MO
Rollins, John W. ..... Manchester, TN
Rollins, Joseph G. ..... Houston, TX
Rollins, Kendric V. ..... Los Angeles, CA
Rollins, Luther J., Jr. ..... St. Louis, MO
Rollins, M. Glynn, Jr. ..... Roanoke Rapids, NC
Rollins, M. Metrinko ..... Wilmington, DE
Rollins, Martin Dominic ..... Spokane, WA
Rollins, Martin H. ..... Bronx, NY
Rollins, Marvin R. ..... West Bloomfield, MI
Rollins, Michael F. ..... Tucson, AZ
Rollins, Norman D. ..... Nashville, TN
Rollins, O. Randolph ..... Martinsville, VA
Rollins, Pamela L. ..... New York, NY
Rollins, Paul B. ..... Greenville, SC
Rollins, Philip A. ..... Barnstable, MA
Rollins, Phyllis B. ..... Roanoke Rapids, NC
Rollins, Prabha Raja ..... Washington, DC
Rollins, Raleigh W., Jr. ..... Thomasville, GA
Rollins, Raymond Lee ..... Arlington, VA
Rollins and Rollins ..... Roanoke Rapids, NC
Rollins, Rollins & Fox ..... Chestnut Hill, MA
Rollins, Ronald L. ..... Minneapolis, MN
Rollins, Scott C. ..... San Diego, CA
Rollins, Smalkin, Richards & Mackie, L.L.C.
Baltimore, MD
Rollins, Steven J. ..... Manitowoc, WI
Rollins, Steven M. ..... Harrisburg, PA
Rollins, Susan E. ..... Chicago, IL
Rollins, Thomas M. ..... United States Senate,
Committee Legal Personnel, GV
Rollins, Timothy J. ..... Rockford, IL
Rollins, Traci H., (P.A.)
West Palm Beach, FL
Rollins, V. Benton ..... Camden, AR
Rollins, Victoria Radd ..... Washington, DC
Rollins, Wilbur C. ..... South Miami, FL
Rollins, William R. ..... Boston, MA
Rollinson, David C. ..... Syracuse, NY
Rollinson, Gary ..... Soquel, CA
Rollinson, Kristine ..... Houston, TX
Rollinson, Mark ..... Washington, DC
Rollinson, Mark ..... Leesburg, VA
Rollison, Gerardo Roy ..... Toledo, OH
Rollison, James P. ..... Lexington, SC
Rollison, Karen B. ..... Greenville, SC
Rollison, Kent A. ..... Indianapolis, IN
Rollison, Kristen K. ..... Indianapolis, IN
Rollison, Lawrie F. ..... Woodbridge, VA
Rollison, Sherri T. ..... Tucson, AZ
Tallahassee, FL
Rollman, Fredric A. ..... Los Angeles, CA
Rollman, Jeffrey M. ..... Cincinnati, OH
Rollman, Richard M. ..... Tucson, AZ
Rollman, Sarah O. ..... Potomac, MD
Rollman, Tony E. ..... Asheville, NC
Rollnick & Linden, P.A.
Coral Gables, FL
Miami, FL
Rollnick, Neil Steven ..... Coral Gables, FL
Rollo, Anthony ..... New Orleans, LA
Rollo, David M. ..... San Jose, CA
Rollo, Edmund J. ..... Morgantown, WV
Rollo & Harter ..... Huntington, IN
Rollo, Herbert D. ..... Huntington, IN
Rollo, Marc A. ..... Haddonfield, NJ
Rollo, Sharon S. ..... Chatsworth, CA
Rollo, Vincent P., Jr. ..... Taunton, MA
Rollock, Alysa Christmas ..... Bloomington, IN
Rollock, Phillip T. ..... New York, NY
Rollocks, Mildred V. Rucker ..... Cleveland, OH
Rolloff, Aaron A. ..... St. Paul, MN
Rollolazo, Llorente E. ..... Thousand Oaks, CA
Rollow, J. Douglas, III ..... Philadelphia, PA
Rollow, William E. ..... Falls Church, VA
Rolls, Jack M., Jr. ..... Honolulu, HI
Rolls, James E. ..... Buffalo, NY
Rolls Kohn & Associates, LLP
Buffalo, NY
Rolls, Randall J. ..... Frederick, MD
Rollston, Henderson, Rasmussen & Crabb
South Lake Tahoe, CA
Rollston, Kenneth C., (P.C.)
South Lake Tahoe, CA
Rollwagen, James R. ..... St. Paul, MN

Rollyson, James H. ..... East Brunswick, NJ
Rollyson, Mikel M. ..... New York, NY
Rolnick, Alan H. ..... Miami, FL
Rolnick, Alan L. ..... Atlanta, GA
Rolnick, Bernard ..... New York, NY
Rolnick, David M. ..... Elkhorn, WI
Rolnick, Gary ..... Brooklyn, NY
Rolnick, Harriet M. ..... Los Angeles, CA
Rolnick, Jonathan C. ..... Oakland, CA
Rolnick, Lawrence M. ..... Roseland, NJ
Rolnick & Reger ..... Hamden, CT
Rolnick, Robert L., III ..... Sugar Land, TX
Rolnick, Ronald G. ..... Los Angeles, CA
Rolnick, Steven R. ..... Hamden, CT
Rolnicki, Joseph M. ..... St. Louis, MO
Rolnicki, Rolf J. ..... Santa Ana, CA
Rolnik, Mark D. ..... New York, NY
Roloff, Christine A. ..... Sacramento, CA
Roloff, David ..... Cleveland, OH
Roloff, David, Co., L.P.A. ..... Cleveland, OH
Roloff, Earl J. ..... Hanover Park, IL
Roloff, Larry R. ..... Eugene, OR
Roloff, Melvin L. ..... Houston, TX
Roloff, Ross D. ..... Chicago, IL
Roloff, Scott W. ..... Dallas, TX
Roloff, W. Kevin ..... Anoka, MN
Rolon, Eleoterio, Jr. ..... Brooklyn, NY
Rolon, Millicent L. ..... Los Angeles, CA
Rolón, Rachael M. ..... Dallas, TX
Rolph, Beth Rutherford ..... Salem, OR
Rolph, Charles F., III ..... Indianapolis, IN
Rolph, Charles W. ..... Flemingsburg, KY
Rolph, John W. ..... Department of the Navy,
Office of the Judge Advocate General, GV
Rolph, Katherine A. ..... Washington, DC
Rolsch, Steven E. ..... Lake City, MN
Rochester, MN
Rolshouse, James E. ..... Minneapolis, MN
Rolsma, Carl B. ..... Middleton, WI
Rolstad, Dennis G. ..... San Francisco, CA
Rolston, Arthur L., (A Professional Law
Corporation) ..... Los Angeles, CA
Rolston, Berne ..... Santa Monica, CA
Rolston, Berne, A Professional Corporation
Santa Monica, CA
Rolston, Bradley P. ..... New York, NY
Rolston, G. Drew ..... Logan, OH
Rolston & Hamill ..... Oklahoma City, OK
Rolston, Joe S., III ..... Oklahoma City, OK
Rolston, Joe S., IV ..... Las Vegas, NV
Rolston, Kenneth E. ..... Houston, TX
Rolston, Kimberly D. ..... Las Vegas, NV
Rolston, Morris ..... Mount Pleasant, TX
Rolston, Robert ..... Point Clear, AL
Rolston, Robert ..... Mount Pleasant, TX
Rolston, Shirley D. ..... Oklahoma City, OK
Roltburg, Igor ..... Morristown, NJ
Roltsch-Anoll, H. Jan ..... Falls Church, VA
Rolwes, Edward J. ..... Chicago, IL
Rolwing, Richard M. ..... Columbus, OH
Rom, Alan Jay ..... Boston, MA
Rom, Barbara ..... Detroit, MI
Rom, Frederick W. ..... Raleigh, NC
Rom, Judith R. ..... New York, NY
Rom, Katherine E. ..... Minneapolis, MN
Rom, Louis ..... Lexington, KY
Rom, Marcia L. Howell ..... Anchorage, AK
Rom, Rebecca L. ..... Minneapolis, MN
Rom, Roger B. ..... Anchorage, AK
Roma, Mary K.
United States Postal Service,
Law Department, GV
Roma, Patricia ..... Half Moon Bay, CA
Roma, Patrick J. ..... Palisades Park, NJ
Roma, Thomas E., Jr. ..... Louisville, KY
Romadka, Gontrum & Hennegan, P.A.
Baltimore, MD
Romadka, Robert J. ..... Baltimore, MD
Romag, James J. ..... St. Charles, IL
Romagna, Robert A. ..... Miami, FL
Romagna, Robert A., P.A. ..... Miami, FL
Romagnoli, Joseph J. ..... New York, NY
Romagosa, Mary Shirer ..... Lafayette, LA
Romaguera, Frank J., IV ..... Metairie, LA
Romaguera, Luis ..... Miami, FL
Romaguera, Raul ..... North Palm Beach, FL
Romain, George G. ..... Los Angeles, CA
Romain, Julie A. ..... Grafton, WV
Romain, Kuck & Egerer, P.C. ..... Detroit, MI
Mount Clemens, MI
Pontiac, MI
Southfield, MI
Romain, Michael ..... Lenexa, KS
Romain, Myra Jones ..... Vineyard Haven, MA
Romain, Paul R. ..... Portland, OR
Romain, Rene Y.
Securities and Exchange Commission,
Division of Investment Management, GV
Romain, Robert M. ..... Valley Forge, PA
Romaine, Alfred R., III ..... Kaplan, LA
Romaine, Barbara Jean ..... Garden City, NY
Romaine, Carol Grey ..... Riverside, CT
Romaine, Christopher D. ..... Wilmington, DE
Romaine, Daniel A. ..... Cleveland, OH
Romaine, Douglas P. ..... Lexington, KY
Romaine, Howard M. ..... Nashville, TN
Romaine, Jeffrey V., (P.C.) ..... Phoenix, AZ
Romaine, Judith B. M. ..... New York, NY
Romaine, V. Seeley ..... Brick, NJ
Montclair, NJ
Romaine, William A. ..... Visalia, CA
Romajas, Suzanne J. ..... New York, NY
Romaker, Charles P. ..... Chicago, IL
Romaker, John L. ..... La Jolla, CA
Roman, A. Michelle ..... Atlanta, GA
Roman, Allen R. ..... Tallahassee, FL
Roman, Andrew M. ..... Pittsburgh, PA
Roman, Antonino B., III ..... New York, NY

Romero, Craig P. ... Houston, TX
Romero, Dave, Jr. ... Las Vegas, NM
Romero, Dennis C. ... Taos, NM
Romero, Donna S. Waters
Fort Lauderdale, FL
Romero, Edward ... Walnut Creek, CA
Romero, Edwin ... Youngstown, OH
Romero, Eliu E. ... Taos, NM
Romero, Elsie ... Miami, FL
Romero, Enrique ... Los Angeles, CA
Romero, E.O. Rick ... Dallas, TX
Romero, Ernesto A. ... Milwaukee, WI
Romero, Ernesto J. ... Albuquerque, NM
Romero, Eugenio C. ... San Juan, PR
Romero, Francisco L. ... Cheyenne, WY
Romero, Freddie J. ... Roswell, NM
Romero, Frederic L. ... Auburn, IN
Romero, Frederick A. ... Los Angeles, CA
Romero, Geoffrey R. ... Albuquerque, NM
Romero, George E. ... San Francisco, CA
Romero, Glenn D. ... Harlingen, TX
McAllen, TX
Romero, Gregory A. ... New York, NY
Romero, H. Troy ... Bellevue, WA
Romero, Jacqueline A. ... Belle Chasse, LA
Romero, Jacqueline C. ... Roseland, NJ
Romero, Jason L. ... Denver, CO
Romero, Jeff ... Albuquerque, NM
Romero, Jerome ... Salt Lake City, UT
Romero, Jessica ... Miami, FL
Romero, Joanne Nielsen ... Monterey Park, CA
Romero, Joe M., Jr. ... Albuquerque, NM
Romero, John J., Jr. ... Albuquerque, NM
Romero, Jorge ... Washington, DC
Romero, Joseph L. ... Albuquerque, NM
Romero, Julia A. ... Phoenix, AZ
Romero, Julia E. ... Roseland, NJ
Romero, L. Louise ... Boulder, CO
Romero, Laura P. ... San Jose, CA
Romero Law Firm ... Albuquerque, NM
Romero, Leo M. ... Albuquerque, NM
Romero, Mario ... Orlando, FL
Romero, Mario S. ... Washington, DC
Romero, Martha E. ... Whittier, CA
Romero, Michael E. ... Denver, CO
Romero, Michael M. ... Las Cruces, NM
Romero, Michelle Anne ... Boston, MA
Romero, Molly Moore ... Omaha, NE
Romero, Parr, & Associates ... Lewisville, TX
Romero, Philip P. ... Dallas, TX
Romero, Phillip E. ... Lewisville, TX
Romero, Ramona E. ... Wilmington, DE
Romero, Raquel ... Elizabeth, NJ
Romero, Raul J., III ... Fairfax, VA
Romero, Raymond G. ... Chicago, IL
Romero, Reynold E. ... Santa Fe, NM
Romero, Richard J. B. ... Albuquerque, NM
Romero, Richard R. ... Long Beach, CA
Romero, Richard Thomas
Treasury Department,
Office of Regulations and Rulings, GV
Romero, Robert J. ... San Francisco, CA
Romero, Robert M. ... Welsh, LA
Romero, Robert R., Jr ... Coeur d'Alene, ID
Romero, Ronald L. ... Normal, IL
Romero, Ross L., Jr. ... Salt Lake City, UT
Romero, Rupal Naik ... Atlanta, GA
Romero, Stephen M. ... El Monte, CA
Romero, T. Robert ... Rockville, MD
Romero, Thomas C. ... Martinez, CA
Romero, Tobin J. ... Washington, DC
Romero, Victor C. ... Carlisle, PA
Romero, Victor M. ... Baton Rouge, LA
Romero, Virginia G. ... Houston, TX
Romero, William Troy ... Denver, CO
Romero-Wirth, Carol ... Santa Fe, NM
Romeu, Frank A., Jr. ... Riverside, CA
Romeu, Xavier E. ... New York, NY
Romey, Daniel ... Calabasas, CA
Romey, John H. ... Bluffton, OH
Lima, OH
Romey, Michael G. ... Los Angeles, CA
Romey, Steven A. ... Lima, OH
Romey and Vandemark ... Bluffton, OH
Lima, OH
Romeyn, Jonathan W. ... Pacific Grove, CA
Romeyn, Thomas A. ... Los Angeles, CA
Romfh, Nancy A. ... West Palm Beach, FL
Romfo, Darla M. ... Washington, DC
Romich, Keith B. ... Atlanta, GA
Romich, Kelly M. ... Atlanta, GA
Romick, Chase ... New York, NY
Romick, Ina S. H. ... Columbus, OH
Romick, Jason M. ... Chicago, IL
Romick, Marci L. ... Dallas, TX
Romig, Frederick ... Wappingers Falls, NY
Romig, Jeffrey L. ... Department of Justice,
Executive Office for Immigration Review,
GV
Romig, Marvin A. ... Oshkosh, NE
Romig, Melissa A. ... Columbus, OH
Romig, Michael ... Tulsa, OK
Romine, Carol Jean ... Noblesville, IN
Romine, David E. ... Philadelphia, PA
Romine, Leslie Moore ... Greenbelt, MD
Romine, Mary B. ... Okmulgee, OK
Romine, Melissa Brook ... Houston, TX
Romine, Richard ... Upper Marlboro, MD
Romine, Stephen L. ... Omaha, NE
Romine, Stephen R. ... Chesterfield, VA
Virginia Beach, VA
Romine, Wesley ... Montgomery, AL
Romines, Elizabeth J. ... St. Louis, MO
Romines, Kenneth M. ... St. Louis, MO
Romines, Ron ... Palo Alto, CA
Romines, Stephen H. ... Mountain Grove, MO
Rominger, Anna S. ... Crown Point, IN
Rominger, Charles S., Jr. ... Grand Rapids, MI
Rominger, M. Kyle ... Springfield, IL
Rominger, Richard A. ... Savannah, GA
Romino, D. J., II ... Fairmont, WV
Romino, Dominick J. ... Fairmont, WV
Romino & Romino ... Fairmont, WV
Rominski, Joseph R. ... Waukegan, IL
Romita, Carla L. ... Harrison, NY
Romita, Michael N. ... Department of Justice,
Environment and Natural Resources
Division, GV
Romito, Charles J. ... Cornwall, PA
Romito, Joseph A. ... Richmond, VA
Romito, Karen E. ... Boston, MA
Brewster, MA
Rom-Jensen, Stacy Gail ... New York, NY
Romley, Arthur E. ... Phoenix, AZ
Romley, David ... Burbank, CA
Romley, Elias M. ... Phoenix, AZ
Romley, Joe M. ... Phoenix, AZ
Romley, Joe M., P.C. ... Phoenix, AZ
Romley, Joseph D. ... Denver, CO
Romley, Lori E. ... San Francisco, CA
Romley, Richard M. ... Phoenix, AZ
Romm, Barry M. ... Washington, DC
Romm, David C. ... Washington, DC
Romm, Jacquelyn ... Eugene, OR
Romm, Michael R. ... Pompano Beach, FL
Romm, William H., Jr. ... Currituck, NC
Rommel, A. Ross, Jr. ... Houston, TX
Rommel, John M. ... Washington, DC
Rommel, Kurt C. ... McLean, VA
Rommel, Sean F. ... Texarkana, TX
Rommelmann, Douglas W. ... Houston, TX
Rommelmann, Nancy L. ... Houston, TX
Rommes, Isadore F., Jr. ... Perry, FL
Romness, Mark D. ... Charleston, SC
Romney, Brenda ... Washington, DC
Romney, David S. ... San Diego, CA
Romney, David T. ... Pasadena, CA
Romney, G. Scott ... Detroit, MI
Romney, George J. ... Salt Lake City, UT
Romney, Keith B., Jr. ... Salt Lake City, UT
Romney, Lisa Gretta ... Salt Lake City, UT
Romney, Mark W. ... Dallas, TX
Fort Worth, TX
Romney, Nelson & Cassity
Salt Lake City, UT
Romney, Norman D. ... Washington, DC
Romney, Phillip H. ... Santa Paula, CA
Romney, Richard B. ... New York, NY
Romney, Walter A., Jr.
Salt Lake City, UT
Romo, Anthony Lawrence
Albuquerque, NM
Romo & Associates, A Professional Corporation
Albuquerque, NM
Romo, Gina M. ... Dallas, TX
Romo, James C. ... Cerritos, CA
Romo, Jose Simon ... Albuquerque, NM
Romo, Les ... Georgetown, TX
Romo, Peter E., III ... San Francisco, CA
Romo, Peter E., Jr. ... San Francisco, CA
Romo, Richard R. ... Albuquerque, NM
Romoff, Joyce ... Philadelphia, PA
Romoff, Spencer J. ... New York, NY
Romond, Anne M. ... Oshkosh, WI
Romosca, Kevin C. ... Greenville, SC
Romoser, W. David ... Milwaukee, WI
Romotsky, Maxwell ... Waltham, MA
Romp, Thomas L. ... Vermilion, OH
Rompage, Henry F. ... Kansas City, KS
Rompf, John H., Jr. ... Winchester, KY
Rompola, Randolph R. ... South Bend, IN
Rompon, John P. ... Chicago, IL
Romriell, Brian J. ... Salt Lake City, UT
Romsa, Matthew H. ... Cheyenne, WY
Romsdahl, Randall J. ... Wayzata, MN
Romshek, Andrew P. ... Omaha, NE
Romski, Gerard J. ... New York, NY
Romundson, Donald L. ... Green Bay, WI
Romundstad, John E. ... Long Beach, CA
Romweber, Anthony A. ... Batesville, IN
Versailles, IN
Romweber, Richard J. ... Akron, OH
Romweber, Robert B. ... Akron, OH
Romweber & Romweber ... Akron, OH
Romyn, David C. ... Los Angeles, CA
Romza, John J. ... Pittsburgh, PA
Romza-Kutz, Diane J. ... Chicago, IL
Romzek, James E. ... Southfield, MI
Romzick, Vernon C. ... Sarasota, FL
Ron, Manuel D. ... New York, NY
Rona, Michael ... New York, NY
Róna, Patrick N.Z. ... New York, NY
Ronai, Kim V. ... Portland, OR
Ronai, Stephen E. ... New Haven, CT
Ronald, Carl Adam ... Pittsburgh, PA
Ronald, David G. ... Minneapolis, MN
Ronald, David W. ... Phoenix, AZ
Ronald, Keith E. ... Towson, MD
Ronald, Lauren M. ... Omaha, NE
Ronald, Marilla J. ... San Jose, CA
Ronald, Seymour J. ... Wheaton, MD
Ronaldson, Don A. ... Santa Ana, CA
Ronaldson, Glenn C. ... Chicago, IL
Ronallo, Amy L. ... Pittsburgh, PA
Ronalter, William J. ... Hartford, CT
Ronan, Anne M. ... Walnut Creek, CA
Ronan, Anne M. ... Tenafly, NJ
Ronan, Christopher P. ... Garden City, NY
Ronan, Daniel S. ... Bellerose, NY
Ronan, Edward S. ... Lynnfield, MA
Ronan, Emmet J. ... Mesa, AZ
Ronan & Firestone, PLC ... Phoenix, AZ
Ronan, Gail E. ... Atlanta, GA
Ronan, Gregory E. ... New York, NY
Ronan & Holmes, A Professional Corporation
Boston, MA
Salem, MA
Ronan, J. Patrick ... Milwaukee, WI
Ronan, James J. ... Boston, MA
Ronan, James M., Jr. ... Tinton Falls, NJ
Ronan, Jay Patrick ... Pontiac, MI
Ronan, Jeanne M. ... Chicago, IL
Ronan, John ... Rockaway Park, NY
Ronan, John H. ... Boston, MA
Ronan, John J. ... New Haven, CT
Ronan, John T. ... Boston, MA
Salem, MA
Ronan, Joseph E., Jr. ... San Jose, CA
Ronan, Joseph E., Jr. ... Philadelphia, PA
Ronan, Kenneth J. ... Boca Raton, FL
Ronan, Martin W., Jr. ... New York, NY
Ronan, Michael D. ... Chattanooga, TN
Ronan, Michael P. ... Danbury, CT
Ronan, Patrick E. ... Rockville, MD
Ronan, Peter W. ... Farmington Hills, MI
Ronan, Riley & Dever, P.C. ... Lynnfield, MA
Ronan, Segal & Harrington ... Salem, MA
Ronan, Timothy D. ... Phoenix, AZ
Ronan, Timothy G. ... Stamford, CT
Ronan, Tuzzio & Giannone, P.A.
Tinton Falls, NJ
Ronan, William P., III ... Overland Park, KS
Ronay, J. Richard ... Dunkirk, MD
Ronay, Peter E. ... Pasadena, CA
Ronayne, Amy M. ... Howell, MI
Ronayne, Colleen V. ... Sylvan Lake, MI
Ronayne, Donald A. ... Stevensville, MD
Ronayne, Hackeling & Rolla ... Deer Park, NY
Ronayne, John A. ... Brooklyn, NY
Ronayne, John J., III ... Detroit, MI
Ronayne, John T. ... Boston, MA
Ronayne, Michael O. ... Aberdeen, SD
Ronayne, Patricia M. ... Haddon Heights, NJ
Ronayne, Robert M. ... Aberdeen, SD
Ronayne and Wein ... Aberdeen, SD
Ronbeck, Jeffrey S. ... Minnetonka, MN
Ronca, Daniel G. ... Norristown, PA
Ronca, James A. ... Mount Holly, NJ
Ronca, James R. ... Harrisburg, PA
Ronca, John A., Jr. ... San Luis Obispo, CA
Santa Maria, CA
Ronca, John J., Jr. ... Livingston, NJ
Ronca & Kennedy, A Professional Law Corporation ... San Luis Obispo, CA
Santa Maria, CA
Ronca, McDonald & Hanley
Livingston, NJ
Morristown, NJ
Newark, NJ
New York, NY
Ronca, Stephen Christopher
San Luis Obispo, CA
Ronca, Theodore J. ... New York, NY
Ronca, Theodore P. ... New York, NY
Roncaioli, Rosemary ... Arlington, VA
Roncalio, Teno ... Cheyenne, WY
Roncalli, Anthony M. ... New York, NY
Roncallo, Angelo D. ... Uniondale, NY
Ronce, Thomas M. ... Newport Beach, CA
Ronchetto, Maria ... Los Angeles, CA
Roncke, Barbara S. ... Brookfield, WI
Ronco, Leonard D. ... Newark, NJ
Roncone, John L., III ... Leominster, MA
Roncone, John L., Jr. ... Leominster, MA
Roncone, John M. ... Springfield, IL
Roncone & Roncone ... Leominster, MA
Ronda, Scott M. ... Clifton Park, NY
Ronda-Del Toro, Eric R. ... San Juan, PR
Rondeau, Charles R. ... Beverly Hills, CA
New York, NY
Rondeau, Eugene M. ... Toms River, NJ
Rondeau, George C., Jr. ... Seattle, WA
Rondeau & Homampour ... Los Angeles, CA
Beverly Hills, CA
New York, NY
Rondeau, J C. ... Stevens, PA
Rondeau, Joseph Edward ... Plymouth, MA
Rondeau, Katherine M. ... Naples, FL
Rondeau, Mark A. ... Great Bend, KS
Rondeau, Patrick E. ... North Adams, MA
Rondeau, Patrick J. ... Boston, MA
Rondeau, Pierre G. ... Woonsocket, RI
Rondeau, Thomas ... Las Vegas, NV
Rondelli, Charles J. ... Tucson, AZ
Rondepierre, Edmond F. ... Stamford, CT
Ronder, Charles S. ... Kingston, NY
Ronder, Robert A. ... Kingston, NY
Ronder, Robert A., P.C. ... Kingston, NY
Rondolino, Anthony ... St. Petersburg, FL
Rondon, Brian D. ... San Jose, CA
Rondon, Edania C. ... Union City, NJ
Rondon, Mauricio ... Houston, TX
Rondoni, Francis J. ... Plymouth, MN
Rondoni, MacMillan & Schneider, Ltd.
Plymouth, MN
Rondos, A. Wm. ... Shelton, CT
Rondos, Steven T. ... Brooklyn, NY
Mineola, NY
New York, NY
Rondy, James A. ... Akron, OH
Rone, David B. ... Burbank, CA
Rone, Frank L., II ... Vineland, NJ
Rone, Gerald J., Jr. ... Wapakoneta, OH
Rone, Wm. E., Jr. ... Columbia, SC
Ronecker, Jerry K. ... St. Louis, MO
Ronemus & Heath Co., L.P.A.
Springfield, OH
Ronemus, Michael B. ... New York, NY
Ronemus, Thor G. ... Springfield, OH
Rones, Clifford I. ...
Department of Justice, GV
Rones, Henry L. ... New York, NY
Rones, Joseph P. ... Newburgh, NY
Rones, Kenneth S. ... New City, NY
Rones, Stephanie K. ... Baltimore, MD
Rones, Steven Z. ... New York, NY
Rones, Victor K. ... South Miami, FL
Roney, Ben E., Jr. ... Rocky Mount, NC
Roney, Buffy Lyn ... Los Angeles, CA
Roney, Charles F.
General Accounting Office,
Office of the General Counsel, GV
Roney, Christine A. ... Los Angeles, CA
Roney, Christopher H. ... Augusta, ME
Roney, Deirdre ... Albany, NY
Roney, Donald E. ... Wilmington, DE
Roney, Edward M. ... Peoria, AZ
Roney, Edward M., III ... Schaumburg, IL
Roney, Frank C., Jr. ... Washington, PA
Roney, Gerard F. ... San Jose, CA
Roney, Gregory Peele ... Greenville, NC
Roney, Jennifer A. ... New York, NY
Roney, John A. ... Honolulu, HI
Roney, John H. ... Los Angeles, CA
Roney, John M. ... Providence, RI
Roney & Labinger ... Providence, RI
Roney, Michael B. ... Louisville, KY
Roney, Paul H. ... St. Petersburg, FL
Roney, Paula B. ... Department of Agriculture,
Farm Service Agency, GV
Roney, Richard T. ... Murfreesboro, TN
Roney, Scott Allen ... Decatur, IL
Roney, Susan C. ... Buffalo, NY
Roney, Teresa M. ... Syracuse, NY
Rong, Mao ... Washington, DC
Ronge, John R. ... Los Angeles, CA
Rongey, Robert W., II ... Granite City, IL
Ronhovde, Kent M. ... Library of Congress,
Congressional Research Service, GV
Ronick, H. Robert, (P.C.) ... Atlanta, GA
Roniger, Timothy T., (P.C.)
New Orleans, LA
Ronin, Andrea H. ... Bedford, NY
Ronin, Herbert A. ... Lincoln, NE
Ronin, Michael D. ... Chicago, IL
Roningen, Robert N. ... Duluth, MN
Ronis, Catherine Kane ... Washington, DC
Ronis, Jan Edward ... San Diego, CA
Ronis, John George ... San Diego, CA
Ronis & Ronis ... San Diego, CA
Ronish, Donald E. ... Lewistown, MT
Roniss, Allen ... Chicago, IL
Ronk, Alice L. ... Department of Justice,
Tax Division, GV
Ronk, Cheryl L. ... Saginaw, MI
Ronk, James M. ... Mt. Vernon, OH
Ronk, Stephen E. ... Los Angeles, CA
Ronka, Robert I. ... Calabasas, CA
Ronkin, Joel B. ... Boca Raton, FL
Ronkowski, Edward E., Jr. ... Chicago, IL
Ronn, David L. ... Houston, TX
Ronnau, Frederick J. ... Lincoln City, OR
Ronne, Robert R. ... El Segundo, CA
Ronneau, Suzanne W. ... Cincinnati, OH
Ronneberg, Norman J., Jr.
San Francisco, CA
Ronnel, Jennifer Averbuch
Little Rock, AR
Ronnell, Anne J. ... Washington, DC
Ronnen, Dan ... New York, NY
Ronner, Amy D. ... Miami, FL
Ronning, James W. ... Minneapolis, MN
Ronning, Julia A. ... Chicago, IL
Ronning, Lawrence M. ... Parkersburg, WV
Ronning, Mark Allen ... Salem, OR
Ronning, Palmer & Titus
Parkersburg, WV
Ronning, Richard L. ... Willmar, MN
Ronning, Royal N., Jr. ... Piscataway, NJ
Ronnow, D. Williams, (P.C.)
St. George, UT
Ronnow, Kurt S. ... Bakersfield, CA
Ronnow, Lorin D. ... Salt Lake City, UT
Ronquillo, Allan L. ... Mandeville, LA
Ronquillo, Carol A. ... San Diego, CA
Ronquillo, David G. ... San Diego, CA
Ronquillo Law Firm, The, P.C.
Dallas, TX
Ronquillo, Marcos G. ... Dallas, TX
Ronquillo & Orderica, L.L.P.
San Diego, CA
Rons, Pamela A. ... Washington, DC
Rons, R. Happy ... Hagåtña, GU
Ronshausen, Roland, Jr. ... Coral Springs, FL
Ronsick, Laura Diane ... Overland Park, KS
Ronson, Alan B. ... Chicago, IL
Ronson, Cindy Birnbaum ... New York, NY
Ronson, Joseph ... New York, NY
Ronstadt, Carlos D. ... Phoenix, AZ
Ronyak, David M. ... Richfield, OH
Ronzetti, Thomas A. Tucker ... Miami, FL
Ronzio, Frank E. ... Los Angeles, CA
Ronzio, Judith A. ... St. Louis, MO
Roob, Richard ... Montvale, NJ
Rood, Alicia C. ... Buffalo, NY
Rood, Amy B. ... Jamaica, NY
Rood & Associates, P.C. ... Fairport, NY
Rood, Bruce A. ... Norway, ME
Rood, Clay B. ... Tampa, FL
Rood, David R. ... Jackson, MI
Rood, Donald C. ... Garnerville, NY
Rood, Gary W. ... Fairport, NY
Rood, Jennifer ... Manchester, NH
Rood, Jill K. ... Boulder, CO
Rood, John W., III ... Phoenix, AZ
Rood, Leslie L. ... Atlantic Beach, FL
Rood & Mills, L.C. ... Huntington, WV
Rood, Morgan Roger ... Fort Lauderdale, FL
Rood, Norman E. ... Huntington, WV
Rood, Penelope Anne ... Fairfax, VA

Rood, Ralph E. ... Columbus, MS
Rood, Steven ... Oakland, CA
Rood, William A. ... Lexington, KY
Roodhouse, Linda C. ... Oakland, CA
Roodman, David A. ... St. Louis, MO
Roodman, Sheldon H. ... Chicago, IL
Roodman, Stephanie B. ... Chicago, IL
Rood-Ojalvo, Jan E. ... Haddonfield, NJ
Roof, C. Joseph ... Columbia, SC
Roof, Carl J. ... Cincinnati, OH
Roof, Jay B. ... Port Orchard, WA
Roof, Jennifer M. ... Washington, DC
Roof, John L. ... Kenton, OH
Roof, Martha A. ... Santa Ana, CA
Roof, R. Michael ... Carmichael, CA
Roof, Stephen L. ... Miami, FL
Roof, Thomas A. ... Kenton, OH
Roof, Vernon D. C. ... Ridgway, PA
Roofian, Michael ... Los Angeles, CA
Roohi, Azeen H. ... New York, NY
Rook, Chad Carlton ... Dallas, TX
Rook, David E. ... Slingerlands, NY
Rook, Edward ... Delmar, NY
Rook, James E. ... Columbus, OH
Rook, Richard T. ... Sheldonville, MA
Rook, Robert N. ... Brookline, MA
Rook, Roger N. ... Milwaukie, OR
Rooke, Ben G. ... Harrisburg, PA
Rooke, Eugene O. ... Denver, CO
Rooke, Kermit V. ... Richmond, VA
Rooke, Michael R. ... Houston, TX
Rooke, Thomas John ... Springfield, MA
Rooke-Ley, Michael M. ... Fort Lauderdale, FL
Rooker, Andrew D. ... Dallas, TX
Rooker, Bruce R. ... Oklahoma City, OK
Rooker, C. Keith ... Henderson, NV
Rooker, David ... Waltham, MA
Rooker, D. B., III ... Houston, TX
Rooker, Dennis S. ... Charlottesville, VA
Rooker, Dennis S., P.C. ... Charlottesville, VA
Rooker & Gibson ... Henderson, NV
Las Vegas, NV
Rooker, John C. ... Salt Lake City, UT
Rooker, Marvin P. ... Warrenton, NC
Rookes, Kathryn A. ... Silver Spring, MD
Rookhuyzen, Lawrence S.
San Bernardino, CA
Rooklidge, William C.
Newport Beach, CA
Rooks, Cyril E. ... Westbury, NY
Rooks, David M., III ... Chapel Hill, NC
Rooks, Edith F. ... Carrollton, GA
Rooks, Gwendolyn ... Memphis, TN
Rooks, Harold R. ... Seattle, WA
Rooks, J. Taylor ... Baton Rouge, LA
Rooks, James E., Jr. ... Washington, DC
Rooks, John N. ... Morris, IL
Rooks, Marvin E. ... Orlando, FL
Rooks, Pitts and Poust ... Chicago, IL
Joliet, IL
Lisle, IL
Winnetka, IL
Rooks, Timothy J. ... West Palm Beach, FL
Rooks, Wayne D. ... New York, NY
Rooks, Weyman E. ... Carrollton, GA
Roomberg, Lila G. ... Philadelphia, PA
Roomberg, Mark T. ... Midland, TX
Roome, Anne H. ... New York, NY
Roome, Katherine D. ... New York, NY
Roome, Ronald L. ... Bend, OR
Roonan, Gregory D. ... Denville, NJ
Roonan, Randall K. ... Denville, NJ
Roond, Estelle J. ... Brooklyn, NY
Rooney, Arthur J., II ... Philadelphia, PA
Pittsburgh, PA
Rooney, Arthur P. ... Charleston, WV
Rooney, Becky Toevs ... Minneapolis, MN
Rooney, Bernard J. ... New York, NY
Rooney, Bethel Ann ... Southport, CT
Rooney, Carol M. ... Tampa, FL
Rooney, Celia A. ... Philadelphia, PA
Rooney, Charles A., Jr. ... Verona, NJ
Rooney, Charles, Jr. ... Topeka, KS
Rooney, Chas. C. ... Buffalo, NY
Rooney, Christopher ... New Haven, CT
Rooney, Christopher S. ... New York, NY
Rooney, Covette
Occupational Safety and Health Review Commission, Administrative Law Judges, GV
Rooney, Daniel G. ... Los Angeles, CA
Rooney, Daniel P. ... Winter Haven, FL
Rooney, David A. ... Alamosa, CO
Rooney, Dean M. ... Painesville, OH
Rooney, Diane Janofsky ... New York, NY
Rooney, Donald R., Jr. ... Pittsburgh, PA
Rooney, Donna L., Law Firm of
Hollywood, FL
Rooney, Edward F. ... Minneapolis, MN
Rooney, Edward J. ... New City, NY
Rooney, Edward J., Jr. ... New York, NY
Rooney, Edward S., Jr. ... Boston, MA
Rooney, F. Sean ... Mineola, NY
New York, NY
White Plains, NY
Rooney, Frederick Price ... Bethlehem, PA
Rooney, Gavin J. ... Roseland, NJ
Rooney, George W. ... Akron, OH
Rooney, George W., Jr. ... Akron, OH
Cleveland, OH
Rooney, Gerard P. ... Danbury, CT
Rooney, J. Garry ... Melbourne, FL
Rooney, J. Kevin ... Upper Saddle River, NJ
Rooney, J. Michael ... Punta Gorda, FL
Rooney, James A. ... Chicago, IL
Rooney, James A. ... Rochester, MN
Rooney, James Byron ... Mount Clemens, MI
Rooney, James C., Jr. ... Chicago, IL
Rooney, James F. ... Woodhaven, NY
Rooney, James J. ... Boston, MA
Rooney, James M. ... Peoria, IL
Rooney, James P. ... Palmer, MA
Rooney, James T. ... Carmel, NY
Rooney, James W. ... Arlington, VA
Rooney, Jaye E. ... Department of Justice, Tax Division, GV
Rooney, Jeffrey J. ... Walnut Creek, CA
Rooney, JoAnn ... Hull, MA
Rooney, John E. ... Chicago, IL
Rooney, John E. ... Tulsa, OK
Rooney, John E., Jr. ... Tulsa, OK
Rooney, John F. ... Key West, FL
Rooney, John F., III ... Boston, MA
Rooney, John G. ... Rockledge, FL
Rooney, John H., Jr. ... Miami, FL
Rooney, John J. ... Cheyenne, WY
Rooney, John James ... North Olmsted, OH
Rooney, John L. ... Minneapolis, MN
Rooney, John L., Jr. ... St. Louis, MO
Rooney, John P. ... Lansing, MI
Rooney, John P. ... New York, NY
Rooney, John T. ... Washington, DC
Rooney, Karen A. ... Los Angeles, CA
Rooney, Kathryn K. ... Staten Island, NY
Rooney, Keith E. ... Marina Del Rey, CA
Rooney, Kevin ... New York, NY
Rooney, Kevin F. ... San Francisco, CA
Rooney, Kevin G. ... Cincinnati, OH
Rooney, Kevin M. ... Silver Spring, MD
Rooney, Kevin P. ... Fresno, CA
Rooney, Kimberly Ptak ... Cicero, IL
Rooney, Kristie Ann ... St. Louis, MO
Rooney, Kristin E. ... Chicago, IL
Rooney, L. Francis, III ... Houston, TX
Rooney, Lee Ann ... Charlotte, NC
Rooney, Lynn C. ... Cambridge, MA
Rooney, Marjorie Weinberg
Staten Island, NY
Rooney, Mark B. ... Mount Horeb, WI
Rooney, Martin J. ... Boston, MA
Rooney, Mary F. ... Westchester, IL
Rooney, Mary Massman ... Dallas, TX
Rooney, Matthew A. ... Chicago, IL
Rooney, Michael J. ... Dallas, TX
Rooney, Michael M. ... Fresno, CA
Rooney, Michael R. ... Scottsdale, AZ
Rooney, Michael T. ... Cherry Hill, NJ
Philadelphia, PA
Rooney, Nancy M. ... Department of Labor, Office of the Solicitor, GV
Rooney, Neil E. ... Littleton, CO
Rooney & Neilson ... St. Paul, MN
Rooney, Patricia A. ... Chicago, IL
Rooney, Patricia A. ... Melville, NY
Rooney, Patrick A. ... Detroit, MI
Southfield, MI
Rooney, Patrick D. ... New York, NY
Rooney, Patrick J. ... Minneapolis, MN
Rooney, Patrick J., Jr.
West Palm Beach, FL
Rooney, Paul C. ... New York, NY
Rooney, Paul K. ... New York, NY
Rooney, Paul K., P.C. ... New York, NY
Rooney, Paul P. ... New York, NY
Rooney, Peter F. ... Glen Cove, NY
Rooney, Philip L. ... Findlay, OH
Rooney, Randi Shanley
Arlington Heights, IL
Rooney, Rita M. ... Boston, MA
Rooney, Robert D. ... Houston, TX
Rooney, Robert G. ... Kansas City, MO
Rooney, Robert W., Jr. ... Chicago, IL
Rooney, Robert W., Jr., Chartered
Chicago, IL
Rooney, Robert W., Sr. ... Chicago, IL
Rooney, Ronald N. ... San Francisco, CA
Rooney, Scott W. ... Detroit, MI
Rooney, Stephen G. ... New York, NY
Rooney, Steven P. ... Metairie, LA
Rooney, Susan M. ... Wilkes-Barre, PA
Rooney, Terence L. ... Salt Lake City, UT
Rooney, Teresa J. ... Clearwater, FL
Rooney, Thomas D. ... Cleveland, OH
Rooney, Thomas J. ... St. Paul, MN
Rooney, Thomas J. ... Pewaukee, WI
Rooney, Timothy F. ... Glen Cove, NY
Rooney, Timothy J. ... Chicago, IL
Rooney, Timothy J., Jr. ... White Plains, NY
Rooney, Wayne M. ... Haleiwa, HI
Rooney, William E. ... Holyoke, MA
Rooney, William H. ... New York, NY
Rooney, William J., Jr. ... Andover, MA
Roop, Carl W. ... Beckley, WV
Roop, David E., Jr. ... Vienna, VA
Roop, John D., Jr. ... Indianapolis, IN
Roop, Kevin James ... La Crosse, WI
Roop Law Office, PLLC ... Beckley, WV
Roop, Paul W., II ... Beckley, WV
Roop, Susan R. ... Trenton, NJ
Roopnarine, Colin M. ... Tallahassee, FL
Roorda, Hess ... Rock Rapids, IA
Roos, Armand L. ... Shreveport, LA
Roos, Armand W., Jr. ... Shreveport, LA
Roos, Bert L. ... Phoenix, AZ
Roos, Bert L., P.C. ... Phoenix, AZ
Roos, Carlotta J. ... Miami, FL
Roos, Charles L. ... Challis, ID
Roos, Cohen & Long, P.C. ... Denver, CO
Roos & Frazier, L.L.P. ... Shreveport, LA
Roos, Gretchen Louise ... Pittsburgh, PA
Roos, Gwenn ... Boston, MA
Roos, J. James ... Baltimore, MD
Roos, Jahn Marie ... Lansdale, PA
Roos, John V. ... Palo Alto, CA
Roos, Kenneth A. ... Blue Bell, PA
Roos, Leonard M. ... Los Angeles, CA
Roos, Leslie J. ... Denver, CO
Roos, Lloyd I. ... Elmsford, NY
Roos, Martin I. ... San Antonio, TX
Roos, Miriam G. ... Randolph, MA
Roos, Norman H. ... Hartford, CT
Roos, Peter D. ... San Francisco, CA
Roos, Raal H. ... Denton, TX
Roos, Randall A. ... Sioux Center, IA
Roos, Richard J. ... Boston, MA
Roos, Robert C., Jr. ... Chicago, IL
Roos, Robert F. ... Phoenix, AZ
Roos, Roberta M. ... White Plains, NY
Roos, Ronald R. ... Department of Justice, Criminal Division, GV
Roos, Shelley ... Northridge, CA
Roos, Sigmund J. ... Boston, MA
Roos, Stephen H. ... Seattle, WA
Roos, Susan H. ... San Francisco, CA
Roos, William A., IV ... New York, NY
Roosa, Benjamin P., Jr. ... Beacon, NY
Roosa, David ... South New Berlin, NY
Roosa, Elizabeth A. ... Beacon, NY
Roosa, Gary S. ... Waterbury, CT
Roosa, James K. ... Cleveland, OH
Roosa, John D. ... Midland, TX
Roosa, Kenneth S. ... Anchorage, AK
Roosa, Richard V.S. ... Cape Coral, FL
Roosa & Roosa ... Beacon, NY
Roosa, Steven B. ... Westmont, NJ
Roosa, Sutton, Burandt & Adamski
Cape Coral, FL
Roosaare, K. Jaak ... Bogota, NJ
Roos-Collins, Margit ... Berkeley, CA
Roose, Birmingham & Lavender
Oberlin, OH
Roose, B. J. ... Capistrano Beach, CA
Roose, Eric N. ... Honolulu, HI
Roose, J. Earle ... Goshen, IN
Roose, Kirk B. ... Oberlin, OH
Roose, Richard G. ... Asheboro, NC
Roose, Stanley V. ... Garden City, MI
Roosen, Richard G. ... Troy, MI
Roosenberg, Richard J. ... Kalamazoo, MI
Roosevelt & Arfa, LLP ... New York, NY
White Plains, NY
Roosevelt, Christopher D. ... New York, NY
White Plains, NY
Roosevelt, Emily ... Salt Lake City, UT
Roosevelt, Greg E. ... Edwardsville, IL
Roosevelt, Haven C. ... New York, NY
White Plains, NY
Roosevelt, James M. ... Cleveland, OH
Roosevelt, Kermit
Supreme Court Of The United States, GV
Roosevelt, Kermit, Jr. ... Washington, DC
Roosevelt, Kimberly Clark ... New York, NY
Roosevelt, Michael A. ... San Francisco, CA
Roosevelt, Ruth Barrons ... New York, NY
Roosevelt, Simon C. ... New York, NY
Roosje, Harry A. ... Costa Mesa, CA
Roosjen, Maja M. ... Manitowoc, WI
Roossien, Dennis L., Jr. ... Dallas, TX
Roossien, Peter M. ... Houston, TX
Roost & Daugirda ... Eugene, OR
Roost, Eric R.-T. ... Eugene, OR
Roosth, Sam ... Tyler, TX
Roosth, Steven C. ... Tyler, TX
Root, Allan P. ... Weaverville, NC
Root, Allen F. ... Middleton, WI
Root, Arnold S. ... Los Angeles, CA
Root, Benj. ... New York, NY
Root, Bennett W., Jr. ... Huntington Beach, CA
Root, Carole A. Z. ... Everett, MA
Root, Caroline G. ... Richmond, VA
Root, Charles W. ... Huntington, NY
Root, Chas. M. ... Walnut Creek, CA
Root, Colleen Campbell ... Houston, TX
Root, Darren E. ... Topeka, KS
Root, David A. ... Columbia, SC
Root, David F. ... Atlanta, GA
Root, Duane G. ... Akron, NY
Root, Duane G., P.C. ... Akron, NY
Root, Frank M. ... Centerville, OH
Root, Fred C. ... Missoula, MT
Root, George L., Jr. ... San Diego, CA
Root, Gregory Brian ... Barrington, IL
Root & Harris ... Encinitas, CA
Root, Harry H., III ... Tampa, FL
Root, Harry L. ... San Clemente, CA
Root, Henry W. ... Santa Monica, CA
Root, J. Andrew ... Xenia, OH
Root, James G. ... Burbank, CA
Root, Jennifer ... San Diego, CA
Root, John A. ... Largo, FL
Root, John B. ... Altamonte Springs, FL
Root, John Frick ... New York, NY
Root, John H. ... Warwick, RI
Root, Jonathan S. ... Boca Raton, FL
Root, Joseph E. ... Phillips, WI
Root, Kapsy W., (Mrs.) ... Walnut Creek, CA
Root, Karen L. ... Decatur, IL
Root, Kathryn Smith ... Portland, OR
Root, Lawrence C. ... Big Rapids, MI
Root, Lawrence H. ... Georgetown, CA
Root, Leonard P. ... Las Vegas, NV
Root, Linda A. ... Joshua Tree, CA
Root, Louise Critz ... Weaverville, NC
Root, Mary Ann ... Irving, TX
Root, Matthew I. ... Buffalo, NY
Root, Michael G. ... Denver, CO
Root, Nancy Ann ... Washington, DC
Root, Oren ... New York, NY
Root, Palmer G. ... Minneapolis, MN
Root, Peter E. ... San Francisco, CA
Root, Robert A. ... Miami, FL
Root & Root, P.L.L.C. ... Asheville, NC
Weaverville, NC
Root, Sally Ann ... Sterling Heights, MI
Root & Schindler, P.C. ... Denver, CO
Root, Sherwin F. ... Irwindale, CA
Root, Simon C. ... Minneapolis, MN
Root, Stephen G., (P.C.) ... Encinitas, CA
Root, Stuart D. ... Livingston Manor, NY
Root, Thomas B. ... Topeka, KS
Root, Thomas E. ... Denver, CO
Root, Thomas F., III ... Hollywood, FL
Root, Thomas L. ... Council Bluffs, IA
Root, Thomas M. ... Groves, TX
Root, Tinley & Sondag ... Council Bluffs, IA
Omaha, NE
Root, Walter H. ... Irvine, CA
Rooten, Allan C. ... San Diego, CA
Rootenberg, Sharyn Michele ... Brooklyn, NY
Rootes, David R. ... Grandview, MO
Rooth, Barry D. ... Merrillville, IN
Rooth, Gilbert J. ... Seminole, FL
Rooth, Michael J. ... Hamburg, NY
Rooth, Robert S. ... New Orleans, LA
Rooth & Rooth ... Seminole, FL
Rooth, Susan A. ... Seminole, FL
Rooth, Walter L. ... Hamburg, NY
Roots, Judy M. ... Lincoln, NE
Roots, Kelvin L. ... Terre Haute, IN
Roou, Tammy M. ... Milwaukee, WI
Roover, Charles A. ... Boston, MA
Roover, Melissa ... Washington, DC
Rooy, Paul S. ... Daytona Beach, FL
Roozekrans, Michael A. ... Spokane, WA
Ropchock, Mark A. ... Akron, OH
Rope, Herbert M., (P.C.) ... Kansas City, MO
Ropelewski, Irene K. ... Clifton Park, NY
Ropelewski, James L.
Department of Justice, Bureau of Prisons, GV
Roper, Angela M. ... Totowa, NJ
Roper, Barandes & Fertel, LLP
New York, NY
Roper Bauer, P.C. ... Holland, MI
Roper, Beverlee J. ... Kansas City, MO
Roper, Brent D. ... Topeka, KS
Roper, C. Todd ... Siler City, NC
Roper & Cobb ... Boulder, CO
Roper, Dana W. ... Lincoln, NE
Roper, Daniel M. ... Rome, GA
Roper, Donald E. ... Houston, TX
Roper, Donovan A.
Altamonte Springs, FL
Roper, Donovan A., P.A., Law Offices of
Altamonte Springs, FL
Orlando, FL
Winter Park, FL
Roper, E. Dean ... Amarillo, TX
Roper, Edward (Ted) L. ... Phoenix, AZ
Roper, Elizabeth G. ... St. Louis, MO
Roper, Ellen S. ... Columbia, MO
Roper, Eric R. ... New York, NY
Roper & Folino ... Los Angeles, CA
Roper, George H. ... Houston, TX
Roper, Glade F. ... Porterville, CA
Roper, Glena J. ... Porterville, CA
Roper, Gregory D. ... San Diego, CA
Roper, Harry J. ... Chicago, IL
Arlington, VA
Roper, Helen M., (Mrs.) ... Miami, FL
Roper, J. David, P.C. ... Augusta, GA
Roper, James D. ... Port Orchard, WA
Roper, James L. ... Los Angeles, CA
Roper, James M. ... Columbus, OH
Roper, Janine Nesbit ... Pasadena, CA
Roper, John D. ... Wichita, KS
Roper, John J. ... South Bend, IN
Roper, John M. ... Biloxi, MS
Roper, John W. ... Boulder, CO
Roper, John W. ... Columbus, GA
Roper, Joseph J. ... Kansas City, MO
Roper, Julie L. ... Chicago, IL
Roper, Karen Sanchez ... Greenville, SC
Roper, Kenneth Scott ... Greenville, SC
Roper, Lauree ... Lawrence, KS
Roper Law Firm, LLC ... Greenville, SC
Roper, Margene ... Tallahassee, FL
Roper, Mary E. ... Baton Rouge, LA
Roper, MaryCatherine ... Philadelphia, PA
Roper & McPherson ... Columbus, GA
Roper, Michael E. ... Fort Worth, TX
Roper, Michael J. ... Orlando, FL
Roper, Milard King ... Floral Park, NY
Roper, Pamela F. ... Atlanta, GA
Roper & Quigg ... Washington, DC
Chicago, IL
Arlington, VA
Roper, Richard L., (P.A.) ... Warren, AR
Roper, Robert L., Jr. ... Columbia, MO
Roper, Robert St. John ... Evergreen, CO
Roper, Sandra E. ... Brooklyn, NY
Roper, Sharon L. ... San Jose, CA
Roper, Steve ... Lufkin, TX
Roper, Steven C. ... Chicago, IL
Roper, Teresa Schiele
Altamonte Springs, FL
Roper, Theodore J. ... Los Angeles, CA
Roper, Thomas B. ... Rock Hill, SC
Roper, Tiffany L. ... Georgetown, TX
Roper, Tom S. ... Birmingham, AL
Roper, W. Lee, II ... Greenwood, SC
Roper, Walter D. ... Dallas, TX
Roper, Walter J. ... Holland, MI
Roper, Wayne A. ... Raleigh, NC
Roper, Wayne J. ... Milwaukee, WI
Roper, William E. ... Middlebury, VT
Roper-Barnett, Melissa A. ... New York, NY
Ropers, Majeski, Kohn & Bentley, A Professional Corporation
Los Angeles, CA
Redwood City, CA
San Francisco, CA

Ropers, Majeski, Kohn & Bentley, A Professional Corporation—Continued
San Jose, CA
New York, NY
Ropers, Mark .... **Larkspur, CA**
Ropers, Michael .... **San Jose, CA**
Ropes, Austin T., Jr. .... Salem, MA
Ropes & Gray .... **Washington, DC**
Boston, MA
Providence, RI
Ropes, Lawrence G., Jr. .... Coral Gables, FL
Ropiequet, John L. .... **Chicago, IL**
Ropos, Truman J. .... Miami, FL
Ropp, E. P. Barlow .... Glasgow, KY
Ropp, James B. .... Wilmington, DE
Roppé, Bradley R. .... **San Diego, CA**
Roppe, Laura H. .... **San Diego, CA**
Roppel, Mark .... **New York, NY**
Ropple, Lisa M. .... **Boston, MA**
Roppolo, Rita .... Department of Labor, Office of the Solicitor, GV
Roppolo, Stephen J. .... **New Orleans, LA**
Rops, Mia C. .... Oklahoma City, OK
Ropski, Gary M. .... **Chicago, IL**
Roque, Carmen .... Miami, FL
Roque, Francisco A. .... Lincolnshire, IL
Roque, Gerald W. .... Foxboro, MA
Roque, Gilbert A. .... Woodland, CA
Roque, Raul .... Tampa, FL
Roque, Steven V. .... Department of Justice, United States Marshals Service, GV
Roque, Susan C. .... New York, NY
Roque, Victor A. .... **Pittsburgh, PA**
Roquemore, David W., Jr. .... **Orlando, FL**
Roquemore, Kelvin L. .... **Dallas, TX**
Roquemore, Lisa A. .... **Costa Mesa, CA**
Roquemore, Perry C., Jr. .... Montgomery, AL
Roquemore, Pringle & Moore, Inc.
Los Angeles, CA
Roquemore, Thomas L. .... **Los Angeles, CA**
Roques, Claire A. .... Slidell, LA
Roques, Jeanne B. .... **New Orleans, LA**
Roquet, Warren A. .... Houston, TX
Roraback, Andrew W. .... **Torrington, CT**
Roraback, Catherine G. .... Canaan, CT
Roraback, Charles E. .... **Torrington, CT**
Roraback, Charles W. .... **Torrington, CT**
Roraback, John K. .... McPherson, KS
Roraback, Margaret P. .... **Torrington, CT**
Roraback & Roraback .... **Torrington, CT**
Roragen, Kevin J. .... **Lansing, MI**
Rorapaugh, M. Brooks .... Columbus, OH
Rorem, Bradley J. .... **Seattle, WA**
Rorem, John A. .... Gig Harbor, WA
Rorem, Mark O. .... **San Francisco, CA**
Rorer, Kathryn E. .... **Washington, DC**
Rorer, Sara Simrall .... **Cincinnati, OH**
Rores, John T. .... San Jose, CA
Rorex, Barry W. .... McIntosh, FL
Rorick, Alan G. .... Waite Hill, OH
Rorick, Dennis Lynn .... Wolcottville, IN
Rorick, Horton C. .... Toledo, OH
Rorick, Michael H. .... **Seattle, WA**
Rorie, Frank Daniel .... **Redondo Beach, CA**
Rorie, Ivey .... Winston-Salem, NC
Rorie, Tom D. .... Nacogdoches, TX
Rorie, Wendell H. .... **Hopkinsville, KY**
Rorie, William E. .... Los Angeles, CA
Rorimer, Louis .... **Cleveland, OH**
Rork, Christopher N. .... Billings, MT
Rork, Daniel Scott .... Salisbury, MO
Rork, Galyn Johnson .... Colorado Springs, CO
Rork, Matthew S. .... **Los Angeles, CA**
Rork, William K. .... Topeka, KS
Rork, William M. .... San Antonio, TX
Rorke, Lorraine .... San Francisco, CA
Rorrer, George T., III .... Louisville, KY
Rorschach, Donald J. .... Irving, TX
Rorschach, Jill Stewart .... Dallas, TX
Rorschach, Richard G. .... Kilgore, TX
Rorty, Bruce Vail .... **Irvine, CA**
Rorty, Jay .... San Francisco, CA
Ros, Joseph Henry .... **Jackson, MS**
Rosa, Alan A. .... Torrington, CT
Rosa, Andrew K. .... Washington, DC
Rosa, Bruno A. .... Toledo, OH
Rosa, Frederick C. .... Far Rockaway, NY
Rosa, Gary A. .... Margaretville, NY
Rosa, Jill Dahlmann .... Department of Justice, Civil Division, GV
Rosa, Joseph A. .... **Kansas City, MO**
Rosa, Joseph F. .... Assonet, MA
Rosa, Joseph, Jr. .... Lyndhurst, NJ
Rosa, Lawrence M. .... West Windsor, NJ
Rosa, Leonard P. .... **Hackensack, NJ**
Rosa, Magda I. .... San Juan, PR
Rosa, Melinda L. .... Dublin, OH
Rosa, Nicholas W. .... Waterbury, CT
Rosá, Randall W. .... Lodi, CA
Rosa, Raymond J. .... West Springfield, MA
Rosa, Richard M. .... Hackensack, NJ
Rosa, William .... **Raynham, MA**
Rosa, William E. .... **New York, NY**
Rosaaen, Marc .... San Francisco, CA
Rosack, Charlene P. .... **San Francisco, CA**
Rosacker, J. Warren .... Portland, OR
Rosacker, John Jay .... Topeka, KS
Rosa Di Sant, Rudolph .... New York, NY
Rosado, A. Ninoska .... Malden, MA
Rosado, Christopher .... Mineola, NY
Rosado, David R. .... El Paso, TX
Rosado, Justino .... New Haven, CT
Rosado, Louis .... Buffalo, NY
Rosado, Mary V. .... New York, NY
Rosado, Raul, Jr. .... Cincinnati, OH
Rosado, Vivian .... Miami, FL
Rosado-Domenech, Samuel .... **San Juan, PR**
Rosado-Linera, Ramón A. .... San Juan, PR
Rosado-Marrero, Rafael A. .... **San Juan, PR**
Rosado-Perez, Erik A. .... San Juan, PR
Rosado-Rivera, Ernesto .... Newark, NJ
Rosado Vila, Ramon .... Guaynabo, PR
Rosales, Benjamin .... Boston, MA
Nantucket, MA
Rosales, David Ray .... **Albuquerque, NM**
Rosales, Denise M. .... **San Francisco, CA**
Rosales, Lisa M. .... Boston, MA
Rosales, Mara E. .... San Francisco, CA
Rosales, Olivia .... Los Angeles, CA
Rosales, Ramon, Jr. .... Mission, TX
Rosales, Richard A. .... El Segundo, CA
Rosales & Rosales .... Boston, MA
Rosales, Stephen B. .... Boston, MA
Rosales, Ulrico S. .... **Palo Alto, CA**
Rosa Marcano, Juan .... Las Piedras, PR
Rosamilia & Brungard .... Lock Haven, PA
Rosamilia, Charles R., Jr. .... Lock Haven, PA
Rosamond, Ariel Townsend
Orangeburg, SC
Rosamond, Cecil H. .... Dallas, TX
Rosamond, Geoffrey Curran
Franklin Lakes, NJ
Rosamond, Jeffrey M. .... Jackson, MS
Rosamond, Mary Frances Lindquist
New Orleans, LA
Rosamond, Samuel M., III .... Metairie, LA
Rosan, Felice B. .... New York, NY
Rosan, Jonathan S. .... Rosemont, PA
Rosan, Richard A. .... Georgetown, MD
Rosan, Robert J. .... New York, NY
Rosan & Rosan, P.C. .... New York, NY
Rosan, Shellie D. .... **Hartford, CT**
Rosand, Eric A. .... Department of State, Office of the Legal Adviser, GV
Rosander, C. Stephen .... Universal City, CA
Rosander, Sheryl J. .... **Bridgeport, CT**
Rosandic, Anton M. .... Irvine, CA
Rosandich, Steven James .... New York, NY
Rosanelli, Carol Egan .... Mill Valley, CA
Rosanelli, Donald S. .... Newark, NJ
Rosania, John S. .... **Hartford, CT**
Rosania, Joseph G. .... **Denver, CO**
Rosano, Michele P. .... **Worcester, MA**
Rosansky, Steve G. .... Irvine, CA
Rosanswank, Jeffrey J. .... Cape Girardeau, MO
Rosard, Steven J. .... Wayne, PA
Rosario, Charles .... New York, NY
Rosario, David Gomez .... **San Juan, PR**
Rosario, Dexter B. .... Los Angeles, CA
Rosario, Enrique .... Philadelphia, PA
Rosario, Mariano, Jr. .... Jacksonville, FL
Rosario, Richard H. .... Towson, MD
Rosario, Richard R. .... Marengo, IL
Rosario, Serena .... Brooklyn, NY
Rosario Martinez, Thomas J. .... Vega Baja, PR
Rosario-Vega, César R. .... **San Juan, PR**
Rosas, Eloise .... Department of Justice, Washington, D.C. District Office, GV
Rosas, James D. .... **Chicago, IL**
Rosas, Jeffrey J .... Eugene, OR
Rosas, Mauro .... El Paso, TX
Rosas, Richard M. .... Monterey Park, CA
Rosas, Tomas .... El Paso, TX
Rosasco, Richard J. .... Jamestown, CA
Rosasco, Stephen J. .... Baltimore, MD
Rosasco, Troy Gordon .... Islandia, NY
Rosa-Tedla, Andrea .... Sacramento, CA
Rosati, Anthony D. .... West Bloomfield, MI
Rosati Associates, P.C. .... West Bloomfield, MI
Rosati, Carol A. .... Farmington Hills, MI
Rosati, Claire .... Chicago, IL
Rosati, Elaine .... West Bloomfield, MI
Rosati, Giacomo G. .... Trenton, NJ
Rosati, Jack R. .... **Columbus, OH**
Rosati, James J. .... San Francisco, CA
Rosati, John J. .... Santa Monica, CA
Rosati, Juste A. .... Dearborn, MI
Rosati, Kristen B. .... **Phoenix, AZ**
Rosati, Marc D. .... **Redwood City, CA**
Rosati, Mario M. .... **Palo Alto, CA**
Rosati, Michael E. .... Farmington Hills, MI
Rosati, Michelle A. .... **McLean, VA**
Rosati, Pavan L. .... **San Francisco, CA**
Rosati, Richard M. .... **New York, NY**
Rosati, Robert J. .... **Fresno, CA**
Rosati, Robert T. .... Stratford, CT
Rosati, Thomas J. .... Stratford, CT
Rosato, James R., Jr. .... Valley Forge, PA
Rosato, Jennifer L. .... Brooklyn, NY
Rosato, Joseph S. .... **New York, NY**
Rosato, M. Paige Freeman .... **Covington, LA**
Rosato, Peter A. .... **Columbus, OH**
Rosato, Peter P. .... White Plains, NY
Rosato, Ralph L. .... North Hollywood, CA
Rosato & Samuels, A Professional Corporation
North Hollywood, CA
Rosato, Vincent L. .... Brooklyn, NY
Rosbe, Judith W. .... Marion, MA
Rosberg, Jack A. .... **Minneapolis, MN**
Rosberger, Richard E. .... **New York, NY**
Rosborough, Amy R. .... Taylorville, IL
Rosborough, Joseph R. .... Moline, IL
Rosborough, Michael J. .... Viroqua, WI
Rosborough, Susan L. .... **Northbrook, IL**
Rosbrook, William B. .... Syracuse, NY
Rosbrugh, Lori Wiggins .... **Wilmington, NC**
Rosburg, Susan K. .... Omaha, NE
Rosbury, Susan A. .... Ashburnham, MA
Roscetti, James C. .... Niagara Falls, NY
Rosch & Burke .... Ballston Spa, NY
Rosch, Gary D. .... Bethesda, MD
Rosch, Gilbert .... Granite City, IL
Rosch, J. Thomas .... **San Francisco, CA**
Rosch, Renee A. .... Ballston Spa, NY
Rosch & Ross .... **Houston, TX**
Rosch, William G., III (Professional Corporation) .... **Houston, TX**
Roscha, Nicholas .... **Concord, CA**
Rosche, Richard J. .... Buffalo, NY
Roschelle, Andrea L. .... **New York, NY**
Roscher & Associates, P.C. .... Bethesda, MD
Roscher, David K. .... **Camden, NJ**
Philadelphia, PA
Roscher, Laurence .... Bethesda, MD
Roscher, Stephen Renn .... Towson, MD
Roschke, Andrea H. .... **Milwaukee, WI**
Roschke, Kin Ming .... Bryan, TX
Roschko, David M. .... Tarzana, CA
Roschko, Myron .... Tarzana, CA
Roschko, Myron, A Prof. Law Corp.
Tarzana, CA
Roschwalb, Jerold .... Washington, DC
Roscich, Carolyn S. .... Naperville, IL
Roscich, John V. .... Naperville, IL
Roscich & Roscich .... Naperville, IL
Roscio, Richard V.
Equal Employment Opportunity Commission, Office of Legal Counsel, GV
Roscioli, Tara Ann .... **Newark, NJ**
Roscoe, Dana Ryan .... Dedham, MA
Roscoe, Dvosha G. .... Houston, TX
Roscoe, Edwin A. .... New Haven, CT
Roscoe, Francis W., II .... **Scranton, PA**
Roscoe, George Dennis .... Cleveland, OH
Roscoe, James S. .... Waldorf, MD
Roscoe, Jerry P. .... Washington, DC
Roscoe, Lisa Le Grow .... Washington, DC
Roscoe, Nancy T. .... San Francisco, CA
Roscoe, Roy J. .... Pittsburgh, PA
Roscoe, Stephanie A .... Springfield, MA
Roscoe, William P., III .... Sacramento, CA
Roscoe, William P., III, Attorney at Law
Sacramento, CA
Roscopf, Charles B. .... **Helena, AR**
Roscopf, Charles David .... **Helena, AR**
Roscopf & Roscopf, P.A. .... **Helena, AR**
Roscow, John F., III .... **Gainesville, FL**
Roscow, John F., IV .... **Gainesville, FL**
Roscow, John Frederick, IV .... Gainesville, FL
Rosdeitcher, Sidney S. .... **New York, NY**
Rosden, Peter E. .... Charlottesville, VA
Rosdil, William J. .... Kailua-Kona, HI
Rose, A. Hewitt .... **Washington, DC**
Rose, Aaron A. .... Brooklyn Park, MN
Rose, Adam D. .... **Portland, OR**
Rose, Alan B. .... **West Palm Beach, FL**
Rose, Alan C. .... **Los Angeles, CA**
Rose, Alan D. .... **Boston, MA**
Rose, Alan D., Jr. .... **Boston, MA**
Rose, Albert S. .... **St. Louis, MO**
Rose, Alex J. .... El Segundo, CA
Rose, Alex J. .... **Seattle, WA**
Rose, Alex W. .... Frankfort, KY
Rose, Alfred O. .... **Boston, MA**
Rose, Allen G. .... Springfield, MO
Rose, Allen M. .... **New York, NY**
Rose, Allison .... **Los Angeles, CA**
Rose, Andre .... **Charlotte, NC**
Rose, Andrew .... Sewickley, PA
Rose, Andrew C. .... Fort Lauderdale, FL
Rose, Andrew C. .... **Albany, NY**
Rose, Anne Preston .... Richmond, VA
Rose, Anthony J. .... **Indianapolis, IN**
Rose, Arthur .... Hackensack, NJ
Rose, Arthur R. .... **Baltimore, MD**
Rose, Arthur S. .... **Newport Beach, CA**
Rose, Ashley S. .... Glen Ellyn, IL
Rose & Associates .... **Boston, MA**
Rose & Atkinson .... **Charleston, WV**
Rose, B. Derek .... **St. Louis, MO**
Rose, Barbara A. .... **Nashville, TN**
Rose, Barbara M. .... Richmond, VA
Rose, Barry A. .... Sherman Oaks, CA
Rose, Barry A. .... Evanston, IL
Rose, Barry F. .... Tallahassee, FL
Rose, Barry Ira .... **Pago Pago, TT**
Rose, Benjamin .... **Philadelphia, PA**
Rose, Bernard F. .... **San Jose, CA**
Rose, Bert L. .... **Columbus, OH**
Rose, Beth S. .... **Newark, NJ**
New York, NY
Rose & Bevelheimer, P.C. .... Westland, MI
Rose, Beverly M. .... Akron, OH
Rose, Billy .... Los Angeles, CA
Rose & Boxer .... New York, NY
Rose, Brad D. .... **New York, NY**
Rose, Brad Lee .... **Boulder, CO**
Rose, Bradley M. .... **Los Angeles, CA**
Rose, Brent A. .... St. Petersburg, FL
Rose, Brent D. .... Salt Lake City, UT
Rose, Brian T. .... Philadelphia, PA
Rose, Bruce J. .... **Charlotte, NC**
Rose, Bruce R. .... Cleveland, OH
Rose, Burton A. .... Philadelphia, PA
Rose, C. Alex .... **Louisville, KY**
Rose, C. Kimball .... Scottsdale, AZ
Rose, C. Michael .... **Athens, GA**
Rose, C. Tanner, Jr. .... **New York, NY**
Rose, Calvin S. .... **Tarzana, CA**
Rose, Carey Christine .... **Burlington, VT**
Rose, Carl P. .... United States Senate, Committee Legal Personnel, GV
Rose, Carol Ann .... Bedford, PA
Rose, Carol L. .... Los Angeles, CA
Rose, Carol V. .... **Boston, MA**
Rose, Catherine .... Pueblo, CO
Rose, Charles D. .... Rancho Cordova, CA
Rose, Charles G. .... Galena, IL
Rose, Charles G., III .... Fayetteville, NC
Rose, Charles Jon .... Thornton, CO
Rose, Charles P. .... Columbus, GA
Rose, Charles P. .... **Chicago, IL**
Rose, Charles P., Jr. .... Washington, DC
Rose, Charles P., Jr. .... **Hinesville, GA**
Rose, Charles T. .... Scottsdale, AZ
Rose, Cheryl A. .... Denver, CO
Rose, Cheryl E. .... Rockville, MD
Rose, Cheryl T.
Environmental Protection Agency, Office of Administrative Law Judges, GV
Rose, Chip .... Santa Cruz, CA
Rose, Christopher A. .... **Palo Alto, CA**
Rose, Christopher A. .... **New York, NY**
Rose, Christopher W. .... Palmer, AK
Rose, Christopher W. .... **Kenosha, WI**
Rose, Cirina A. K. .... **Los Angeles, CA**
Rose, Clark M. .... Cleveland, OH
Rose, Claudia J. .... **St. Paul, MN**
Rose, Clayton W. .... Dublin, OH
Rose, Collin A. .... **Houston, TX**
Rose, Crawford A., Jr. .... Waverly, AL
Rose, Crystal K., (A Law Corporation)
Honolulu, HI
Rose, Curtis G. .... **Corvallis, OR**
Rose, Cynthia S. .... Indianapolis, IN
Rose, D. Brent .... **Salt Lake City, UT**
Rose, Dale R. .... **Dallas, TX**
Rose, Dan M. .... **Lexington, KY**
Rose, Dana A. .... **Cleveland, OH**
Rose, Daniel A. .... Columbus, OH
Rose, Daniel E. .... Dunwoody, GA
Rose, Daniel H. .... San Francisco, CA
Rose, Daniel J. .... **Portland, ME**
Rose, Daniel O. .... **New York, NY**
Rose, Danny .... Hazard, KY
Rose, David A. .... **New York, NY**
Rose, David Alan .... **Houston, TX**
Rose, David C. .... New York, NY
Rose, David E. .... Dublin, OH
Rose, David H. .... San Francisco, CA
Rose, David L. .... **Phoenix, AZ**
Rose, David L. .... **Washington, DC**
Rose, David L. .... Newton, IA
Rose, David L. .... **Rahway, NJ**
Rose, David M. .... **Redwood City, CA**
Rose, David P. (Dade) .... **Salt Lake City, UT**
Rose, David V. .... **Los Angeles, CA**
Rose, Deana E. .... **Washington, DC**
Rose, Deborah A. .... **Edison, NJ**
Lawrenceville, NJ
Rose, Deborah A., A Prof. Corp.
Lawrenceville, NJ
Edison, NJ
Rose, Debra .... West Palm Beach, FL
Rose & De Fuccio .... Hackensack, NJ
Rose, Denise McIntyre .... Mountain View, CA
Rose, Dennis C. .... Nags Head, NC
Rose, Dennis E. .... **Belleville, IL**
Rose, Dennis R. .... **Cleveland, OH**
Rose, Diane L. .... **Lexington, KY**
Rose, Diane L. .... **New York, NY**
Rose & Dobyns .... Wilmington, OH
Blanchester, OH
Rose, Donald G. .... Dublin, OH
Rose, Donald M. .... **Rosemont, IL**
Rose, Donald McG. .... **Cincinnati, OH**
Rose, Donald R. .... **Lexington, KY**
Rose, Donald S. .... Miami, FL
Rose, Donald W. .... **New York, NY**
Rose, Douglas J. .... Woonsocket, RI
Rose, Douglas W. .... Brookfield, WI
Rose, Edith S. .... Princeton, NJ
Rose, Edward E., III .... Fairfax, VA
Rose, Edward J. .... Little Falls, NY
Rose, Edward L. .... Woodbury, NY
Rose & Eklund .... Montague, MI
Rose, Elaine Taylor .... Seattle, WA
Rose, Elihu I. .... **Lake Success, NY**
Rose, Elihu I., P.C. .... **Lake Success, NY**
Rose, Elisabeth H. .... **Fairmont, WV**
Rose, Elise .... Anchorage, AK
Rose, Elizabeth .... **New York, NY**
Rose, Elizabeth .... **Houston, TX**
Rose, Elizabeth G. .... Haverhill, MA
Rose, Ellen .... **Miami, FL**
Rose, Eric C. .... **Piscataway, NJ**
Rose, Eric S. .... Syracuse, NY
Rose, Erin .... **Anchorage, AK**
Rose, Evans, Jr. .... **Pittsburgh, PA**
Rose, Farris V. .... Van Horn, TX
Rose & Figura .... Anchorage, AK
Rose, Filmore E. .... **San Francisco, CA**
Rose, Flavio .... **Los Angeles, CA**
Rose, Frank H. .... Mount Laurel, NJ
Rose, Frank J., Jr. .... **New Philadelphia, OH**
Rose, Frank W. .... **San Angelo, TX**
Rose, Frederick W. .... **Rumson, NJ**
Summit, NJ
Rose, Gary M. .... Newtown, PA
Rose, Gary T. .... Brighton, MI
Rose, Gene C. .... Ontario, OR
Rose, George B. .... Rockville, MD
Rose, George L. .... Chicago, IL
Rose, George Peter .... Tacoma, WA
Rose, Geraldine H. .... Boonville, CA
Rose, Gerard A. .... **Carmel, CA**
Rose, Gerry B. .... Tallahassee, FL
Rose, Glenn B. .... **Nashville, TN**
Rose, Gordon J. .... Beverly Hills, CA
Rose, Gordon J. .... **Atlanta, GA**
Rose, Gordon L. .... Blanchester, OH
Wilmington, OH
Rose, Gordon S. .... Yellowtail, MT
Rose, Graham S. .... Rockville Centre, NY
Rose, Greg I. .... Baltimore, MD
York, PA
Rose, Henry .... **Washington, DC**
Rose, Henry G. .... Chicago, IL
Rose, Henry S. .... Los Angeles, CA
Rose, Herbert B. .... New York, NY

Rose, Herbert C. ... Washington, DC
Rose, Herbert S. ... Miami, FL
Rose, Herschel H., III ... Charleston, WV
Rose & Hildebrand, P.C. ... Phoenix, AZ
Rose, Howard A. ... Aventura, FL
Rose, Howard L. ... Hallandale Beach, FL
Bethesda, MD
Rose, Howard V. ... Austin, TX
Rose, Hugh, III ... Modesto, CA
Rose, I. Nelson ... Costa Mesa, CA
Rose Immigration Law Firm ... Nashville, TN
Rose, J. Scott ... San Antonio, TX
Rose, J. William, Jr. ... Birmingham, AL
Rose, Jack A. ... Fullerton, CA
Rose, Jacob A. ... West Palm Beach, FL
Rose, James A. ... East Meadow, NY
Rose, James C. ... Farmington Hills, MI
Rose, James E. ... Houston, TX
Rose, James E., Jr. ... Orlando, FL
Rose, James F. ... Lexington, KY
Rose, James L.
National Labor Relations Board,
Division of Administrative Law Judges, GV
Rose, James L. ... Daytona Beach, FL
Rose, James M. ... Montague, MI
Rose, James M. ... White Plains, NY
Rose, James M., Jr. ... Washington, DC
Rose, James R. ... St. Helena, CA
Rose, James V. ... Columbus, OH
Rose, James W. ... San Jose, CA
Rose, James W. ... Dallas, TX
Rose, James W., Jr. ... Dallas, TX
Rose, Jane A. ... Tallahassee, FL
Rose, Jane A. ... Dallas, TX
Rose, Janet K. ... Santa Fe, NM
Rose, Janet T., (Ms.) ... Cincinnati, OH
Rose, Jason J. ... Dallas, TX
Rose, Jason S. ... Troy, MI
Rose, Jason W. ... Itasca, IL
Rose, Jay ... Boston, MA
Rose, Jay A. ... Woodland Hills, CA
Rose, Jay R. ... Milford, PA
Rose, Jeff L. ... Austin, TX
Rose, Jeffery L. ... Sacramento, CA
Rose, Jeffrey B. ... Chicago, IL
Rose, Jeffrey M. ... New York, NY
Rose, Jeffrey W. ... Newport Beach, CA
Rose, Jennifer ... Independence, MO
Rose, Jennifer Gabler ... New York, NY
Rose, Jennifer Martin ... Sherman Oaks, CA
Rose, Jennifer R. ... Overland Park, KS
Rose, Jerold A. ... Van Nuys, CA
Rose, Jerome Cornelious ... Birmingham, AL
Rose, Jerome J. ... Bayonne, NJ
Rose, Jerry E. ... Fayetteville, AR
Rose, Jim, III ... Fayetteville, AR
Rose, Jo Ann ... Reston, VA
Rose, Joan A. ... Morgantown, WV
Rose, Joanne M. ... Coral Gables, FL
Rose, Joanne W. ... New York, NY
Rose, Joe Lee ... Abilene, TX
Rose, John C. ... Houston, TX
Rose, John, Jr. ... Farmington, CT
Rose, John K. ... Cincinnati, OH
Rose, John R. ... Asheville, NC
Rose, John W. ... Cincinnati, OH
Rose, Jonathan ... Tempe, AZ
Rose, Jonathan C. ... Washington, DC
Rose, Jonathan G. ... Washington, DC
Rose, Jonathan H. ... Secaucus, NJ
Rose, Jonathan P. ... Miami, FL
Rose & Joneson, A Professional Corporation
Pago Pago, TT
Rose, Jordan P. ... San Francisco, CA
Rose, Jos. E. ... Louisville, KY
Rose, Joseph A. ... Clearwater, FL
Rose, Joseph B., III ... Cleveland, OH
Rose, Joseph J. ... Santa Monica, CA
Rose, Joshua N. ... Washington, DC
Rose, Judith L. ... Chicago, IL
Rose, Julia B. ... Santa Fe, NM
Rose, Julie ... Oakland, CA
Rose, Julie G. ... Minneapolis, MN
Rose, Karen E. ... Arlington, VA
Rose, Karen M. ... Williamsburg, VA
Rose, Kathleen ... Houston, TX
Rose, Kathryn H. ... Modesto, CA
Rose, Kathy Lynne Herbert
Greenwich, CT
New York, NY
Rose, Keith B. ... Albany, NY
Rose, Kelly Brunetti ... Houston, TX
Rose, Kenneth D. ... Anna, IL
Rose, Kenneth J. ... San Diego, CA
Rose, Kenneth Lowell ... Passaic, NJ
Rose, Kenneth S. ... New York, NY
Rose, Kenton R. ... Lincolnshire, IL
Rose, Kevin H. ... San Francisco, CA
Rose, Kevin L. ... Ventura, CA
Rose, Kevin M. ... Harrisonburg, VA
Rose, Kim M. ... Mt. Vernon, OH
Rose, Kirk A. ... Hoffman Estates, IL
Rose, Klein & Marias ... Long Beach, CA
Los Angeles, CA
Ontario, CA
San Diego, CA
Santa Ana, CA
Ventura, CA
Rose, Lance J. ... Forest Hills, NY
Rose, Laura, & Associates, Law Offices of
Martinsburg, WV
Rose, Laurence F. ... Mansfield, MA
Rose, Laurence M. ... Coral Gables, FL
Rose Law Firm, A Professional Association
Little Rock, AR
Rose, Lawrence D. ... Beverly Hills, CA
Rose, Lawrence G. ... New York, NY

Rose, Lawrence H. ... Great Neck, NY
Rose, Lawrence J. ... San Francisco, CA
Rose, Lawrence J. ... Stoughton, MA
Rose, Lawrence N. ... Los Angeles, CA
Rose, Lawrence W. ... New York, NY
Rose, Leo, III ... Atlanta, GA
Rose, Leon H. ... Pennsauken, NJ
Rose, Leonard ... Waltham, MA
Rose, Leonard B. ... Kansas City, MO
Rose, Leroy C. ... Garden City, KS
Rose, Leslie ... Palm Beach, FL
Rose, Lewis ... Washington, DC
Rose, Lilia Conzuelo ... Mountain View, CA
Rose, Linda ... Nashville, TN
Rose, Lisa ... Newark, NJ
Rose, Lois C. ... Silver Spring, MD
Rose, Lori L. ... Everett, MA
Rose, Louis W. ... Santa Fe, NM
Rose, Lyle D. ... Auburn, CA
Rose, Lynden ... West Palm Beach, FL
Rose, M. Fred ... Mill Valley, CA
Rose, M. Zev ... Pennsauken, NJ
Rose, Manuel Costa, Jr. ... Pittsburg, CA
Rose, Marcey P. ... Charlotte, NC
Rose, Marci ... Key West, FL
Rose, Maria S. ... New York, NY
Rose, Marilyn G. ... Jacksonville, FL
Rose, Mark A. ... Peoria, IL
Rose, Mark E. ... Dayton, OH
Rose, Mark H. ... Greenwich, CT
Rose, Mark H. ... Toledo, OH
Rose, Mark I. ... Beverly Hills, CA
Rose, Mark J., Law Offices of
Chicago, IL
Rose, Mark R. ... Little Falls, NY
Rose, Marsha E. ... Houston, TX
Rose, Marta ... Philadelphia, PA
Rose, Martha A. ... Lancaster, OH
Rose, Martin E. ... Dallas, TX
Rose, Marvin H. ... Cedarhurst, NY
Rose, Mary B. ... Palo Alto, CA
Rose, Mary Ellen ... Overland Park, KS
Rose, Mary H. ... Los Angeles, CA
Rose, Mary Jo ... Dayton, OH
Rose, Marya J. ... Chicago, IL
Rose, Matthew T. ... Montvale, NJ
Rose, Maurice A. ... Farmington Hills, MI
Rose, Megan M. ... Boston, MA
Rose, Melodie R. ... Minneapolis, MN
Rose, Merle B. ... Indianapolis, IN
Rose, Meyer H. ... Tucker, GA
Rose, Michael ... St. Albans, VT
Rose, Michael A. ... Rochester, NY
Rose, Michael Benjamin ... Cleveland, OH
Rose, Michael C. ... Jefferson City, MO
Rose, Michael D. ... Cincinnati, OH
Rose, Michael D. ... Columbus, OH
Rose, Michael G. ... Plainview, NY
Rose, Michael I. ... Miami, FL
Rose, Michael I., P.A. ... Miami, FL
Rose, Michael J. ... Hartford, CT
Rose, Michael K. ... Beaumont, TX
Rose, Michael Paul ... Chicago, IL
Rose, Michael T. ... Summerville, SC
Rose, Michel Marie ... New York, NY
Rose, Michele E. ... Palo Alto, CA
Rose, Milton C. ... New York, NY
Rose, Mitchell D. ... Chicago, IL
Rose and Mitchell, P.A. ... Annapolis, MD
Rose, Mona L. ... Santa Barbara, CA
Rose, Morgan E. ... Pomona, CA
Rose, Munns, Fout and Chin ... Coronado, CA
Rose, Nancy A. ... New York, NY
Rose, Nancy Ileen ... Clearwater, FL
Rose, Nancy L. ... Treasury Department,
Internal Revenue Service, GV
Rose, Natasha ... Scarsdale, NY
Rose, Nathaniel B. ... Phoenix, AZ
Rose, Neal P. ... Sherrill, NY
Rose, Neil L. ... Virginia Beach, VA
Rose & Nelson ... Overland Park, KS
Rose, Nevin A. ... Westland, MI
Rose, Nissel A. ... Anchorage, AK
Rose, Norman ... Fort Lauderdale, FL
Rose, Norman D., (Inc.) ... Beverly Hills, CA
Rose, Ovid ... Kensington, CA
Rose Padden & Petty, L.C.
Clarksburg, WV
Fairmont, WV
Morgantown, WV
Rose, Patricia S. ... Seattle, WA
Rose, Patrick ... Calabasas, CA
Rose, Patrick A. ... Las Vegas, NV
Rose, Patrick Levine ... Lansing, MI
Rose, Paul A. ... Los Angeles, CA
Rose, Paul A. ... Akron, OH
Rose, Paul G. ... Tulsa, OK
Rose, Paul M. ... San Francisco, CA
Rose, Paula ... Philadelphia, PA
Rose, Peter A. ... Fort Lauderdale, FL
Rose, Peter A. ... New York, NY
Rose, Peter G. ... San Francisco, CA
Rose, Philip H. ... McArthur, OH
Rose, Phillip R. ... Woodland Hills, CA
Rose, Portia N. Toynes ... Treasury Department,
Internal Revenue Service, GV
Rose, R. Mark ... Sacramento, CA
Rose, Ralph, Jr. ... Montague, MI
Rose, Rand, Orcutt, Cauley, Blake & Ellis,
P.A. ... Wilson, NC
Rose, Randall E. ... Tulsa, OK
Rose, Randall Garry ... Rockville, MD
Rose, Ray, O'Connor, Manning & McCauley,
P.A. ... Fayetteville, NC
Rose, Raymond C. ... Peoria, IL
Rose, Raymond C., II ... Charlestown, MA
Rose, Raymond K. ... Tulsa, OK
Rose, Reid A. ... Los Angeles, CA

Rose, Richard B. ... Denver, CO
Rose, Richard C. ... Kingsville, OH
Rose, Richard C., Jr. ... Cleveland, OH
Rose, Richard Christopher
Chattanooga, TN
Rose, Richard D. ... Pittsburgh, PA
Rose, Richard E. ... Kansas City, MO
Rose, Richard J. ... Rocky Mount, NC
Rose, Richard L. (IBA) ... Stamford, CT
Rose, Richard L. ... Houston, TX
Rose, Rick L. ... Salt Lake City, UT
Rose, Robert A. ... Indianapolis, IN
Rose, Robert Allen ... Palm Springs, CA
Rose, Robert D. ... San Diego, CA
Rose, Robert E. ... Carson City, NV
Rose, Robert E. ... Bartlett, TN
Rose, Robert E. ... Memphis, TN
Rose, Robert Edmund ... San Diego, CA
Rose, Robert G. ... Morristown, NJ
Rose, Robert G. ... Johnstown, PA
Rose, Robert J. ... Pasadena, CA
Rose, Robert J., Sr. ... Beaumont, TX
Rose, Robert L. ... Philadelphia, PA
Rose, Robert Lee ... Winchester, KY
Rose, Robert M. C. ... Tallahassee, FL
Rose, Robert P. ... Austin, TX
Rose, Robert R., III ... Cheyenne, WY
Rose, Robert S. ... Los Angeles, CA
Rose, Robert S. ... Binghamton, NY
Rose, Ronald ... Mentor, OH
Rose, Ronald B. ... Wichita, KS
Rose, Ronald D. ... Brooklyn, NY
Rose, Ronald F. ... Lansing, MI
Rose, Ronald L. ... Bloomfield Hills, MI
Rose, Ronald W. ... Irvine, CA
Rose, Ronald W. ... San Jose, CA
Rose & Rose ... Washington, DC
Rose & Rose ... Bayonne, NJ
Rose & Rose ... Kenosha, WI
Rose & Rose, P.A. ... Fort Lauderdale, FL
Rose & Rose, P.A. ... West Palm Beach, FL
Rose & Rose, P.C. ... Cheyenne, WY
Rose, Roxi J. ... Weymouth, MA
Rose, Rudolph L. ... Baltimore, MD
Rose, Ruth C. ... Los Angeles, CA
Rose, Sam L. ... Cleveland, OH
Rose, Sara L. ... Lancaster, OH
Rose, Schmidt, Hasley & DiSalle, P.C.
Pittsburgh, PA
Washington, PA
Rose, Scott ... New York, NY
Rose, Scott A. ... Phoenix, AZ
Rose, Scott A. ... Pulaski, VA
Rose, Scott L. ... Glendora, CA
Rose, Scott M. ... Sanford, FL
Rose, Scott P. ... Frederick, MD
Rose, Scott S. ... New York, NY
Rose, Sean P., Law Office of ... Reno, NV
Rose, Senders and Bovarnick
Portland, OR
Rose, Seymour M. ... Walnut Creek, CA
Rose, Sharon ... West Palm Beach, FL
Rose, Sharon M. ... Evanston, WY
Rose, Sharren B. ... Green Bay, WI
Rose, Shaun Michael ... Washington, DC
Rose, Short & Hollon ... Beattyville, KY
Rose, Short & Pitt ... Ashland, KY
Rose, Sidney R. ... Los Angeles, CA
Rose, Simon L. ... Camarillo, CA
Rose, Spencer M. ... Miami Beach, FL
Rose, Stanley F. ... Naples, FL
Rose, Stephen ... New Orleans, LA
Rose, Stephen ... Taos, NM
Rose, Stephen D. ... Los Angeles, CA
Rose, Stephen D. ... Bellevue, WA
Rose, Stephen K. ... Sausalito, CA
Rose, Stephen S. ... Bayonne, NJ
Rose, Steven C. ... Kingsport, TN
Rose, Steven D. ... Springfield, MA
Rose, Steven J. ... Schaumburg, IL
Rose, Steven J. ... Raleigh, NC
Rose, Steven K. ... Carrollton, TX
Rose, Steven M. ... Portland, OR
Rose, Stewart ... Albuquerque, NM
Rose, Sundstrom & Bentley, LLP
Tallahassee, FL
Rose, Susan G. ... Oakland, CA
Rose, Susanne Dye ... Brighton, MI
Rose, Sydney A. ... Bayonne, NJ
Rose, Sylvia Woody ... Newport News, VA
Rose, Tania B. ... Berkeley, CA
Rose, Terrence ... New York, NY
Rose, Terry W. ... Kenosha, WI
Rose, Thomas A.
Federal Deposit Insurance Corporation,
Liquidation Branch, GV
Rose, Thomas H., Jr. ... Stony Creek, VA
Rose, Thomas M. ... Xenia, OH
Rose, Thomas M. ... Milwaukee, WI
Rose, Thomas N. ... Little Rock, AR
Rose, Thomas P. ... Jefferson City, MO
Rose, Thomas S. ... Houston, TX
Rose, Timothy F. ... Cleveland, OH
Rose, Todd A. ... Memphis, TN
Rose, Todd E. ... Richmond, VA
Rose, Trish ... Hutchinson, KS
Rose, Valerie Scott ... Los Angeles, CA
Rose & Vanwinkle, P.A. ... Fayetteville, AR
Rose, Verlinda C. ... San Rafael, CA
Rose • Walker, L.L.P. ... Dallas, TX
Rose, Walter T., Jr. ... Cocoa Beach, FL
Rose, Warren M.
Department of Transportation,
Maritime Administration, GV
Rose and Weller ... Cocoa Beach, FL
Rose, William L. ... Williamsburg, KY
Rose, William M. ... Roseville, CA
Rose, William N. ... San Jose, CA

Rose, William P. ... New York, NY
Rose, William Porter ... Lynnfield, MA
Rose, William S. ... Austin, TX
Rose, William S., Jr.
Hilton Head Island, SC
Rose, William S., Jr. ... Knoxville, TN
Rose, William W. ... Syracuse, NY
Rose, Willie L. ... Mc Comb, MS
Rose, Wm. O. ... Woodland, CA
Roseberg, John B. ... Rockford, IL
Roseberry, Darwin N. ... Morrisville, PA
Roseberry, David E. ... Lexington, KY
Roseberry & Lanctot ... Morrisville, PA
Roseberry, Michael R. ... Pittsfield, IL
Roseberry, Robert C. ... Greensboro, AL
Roseberry, Robert H. ... Milford, IA
Roseberry, Stanley L. ... Flossmoor, IL
Roseboro, Anthony M. ... Columbus, OH
Roseborough, Kathleen ... Chicago, IL
Roseborough, Larry C. ... Richardson, TX
Roseborough, Teresa Wynn ... Atlanta, GA
Rosebrock, Charles A. ... Boston, MA
Rosebrock, Elizabeth Ashley ... Orange, CA
Rosebrook, L. W. ... Des Moines, IA
Rosebrough, Christina A. ... Akron, OH
Rosebrough, H. D., P.C. ... Farmington, NM
Rosebrough, Haskell D. ... Farmington, NM
Rosebrough & Howe, A Professional
Corporation ... Gallup, NM
Rosebrough, Robert F. ... Gallup, NM
Rosebush, Windy L. ... Boston, MA
Rosecan, Mortimer A. ... St. Louis, MO
Rosecrance, Barbara B.
Pacific Palisades, CA
Rosedahl, David E. ... San Francisco, CA
Rosedale, Herbert L. ... New York, NY
Rosedale, Miles R. ... Azusa, CA
Rosedale, Peter K. ... Providence, RI
Rosedale, Thomas B. ... Boston, MA
Roseen, Kathryn L. ... Woodridge, IL
Rose-Epstein, Bari E. ... Philadelphia, PA
Rosefielde, Alan P. ... New York, NY
Rosefielde-Keller, Cindy S. ... Raleigh, NC
Rosefsky, Katherine P. ... McLean, VA
Rosefsky, Steven M. ... New York, NY
Rosegarten, Peter A. ... Great Neck, NY
Rosegay, Margaret N. ... San Francisco, CA
Rosehill, Adrian W. ... Honolulu, HI
Rosehill, Ambrose J. ... Honolulu, HI
Rose-Hughes, Michelle M. ... Denver, CO
Rosekrans, Bruce A. ... Shortsville, NY
Rosekrans, Fred A. ... Greene, NY
Rosekrans, John C. ... Greene, NY
Rosekrans, Scott William ... Coldspring, TX
Rosel, Steven D. ... Topeka, KS
Roseland, Jill A. ... Virginia Beach, VA
Roselinsky, Myra ... Orange, CA
Roselius, Jason E. ... Oklahoma City, OK
Rosell, Jeffrey S. ... Santa Cruz, CA
Rosell, Jill ... White Plains, NY
Rosell, Kurt F. ... New York, NY
Rosell, Timothy J. ... Hornell, NY
Rosella, Michael R. ... New York, NY
Rosella, Ralph A. ... Melville, NY
Roselle, Andrew W. ... Shrub Oak, NY
Roselle, George C., III ... Jersey City, NJ
Roselle, James E. ... Chicago, IL
Roselle, Louise M. ... Cincinnati, OH
Roselle, Mary-Beth Chadwick
Chicago, IL
Roselli, Carol Ann ... Westfield, NJ
Roselli, Catherine L. ... Fort Lauderdale, FL
Roselli, Francesco ... Oak Brook, IL
Roselli, Frederick D. ... South River, NJ
Roselli, John T. ... Chicago, IL
Roselli, Karen E. ... West Palm Beach, FL
Roselli, Philip J. ... Denver, CO
Roselli, Richard J. ... Fort Lauderdale, FL
Roselli, Robert M. ... Fort Lauderdale, FL
Roselli, Robert M., P.A., Law Offices of
Fort Lauderdale, FL
Rosellini, Albert D. ... Seattle, WA
Rosellini, Ildo L. ... Belmont, CA
Rosellini, Kenneth J. ... Livingston, NJ
Rosellini, Philip E. ... Bellingham, WA
Rosellini & Ward ... Belmont, CA
Rosello, Roland A. ... Tampa, FL
Rosely, H. C., (P.C.) ... Mount Clemens, MI
Roseman, Abbott I. C. ... Silver Spring, MD
Roseman, Abigail L. ... Georgetown, CA
Roseman, Alan S. ... New York, NY
Roseman, Arnold D. ... Scarsdale, NY
Roseman, Barry D. ... Denver, CO
Roseman, Barry L. ... Atlanta, GA
Roseman, Bernard ... Ambler, PA
Roseman, Charles S., & Associates, Law
Offices of ... San Diego, CA
Roseman, Christina Gill ... Detroit, MI
Roseman, David B., Law Offices of
San Francisco, CA
Roseman, David C. ... Washington, DC
Roseman, David M. ... Boston, MA
Roseman, Donald B. ... Houston, TX
Roseman, Frederick K. ... Springfield, VA
Roseman, Gilbert ... Melville, NY
Roseman, Howard ... Melville, NY
Roseman, Howard A. ... Hartford, CT
Roseman, James D. ... Cleveland, OH
Roseman, Jodyne ... San Diego, CA
Roseman, Jordan L. ... Dallas, TX
Roseman, Joshua S. ... Dallas, TX
Roseman, Joyce A. ... Los Angeles, CA
Roseman & Kazmierski, LLC
Denver, CO
Roseman, Kenneth M. ... Wilmington, DE
Roseman, Lawrence S. ... Valley Stream, NY
Roseman, Leslie R. ... Newport Beach, CA
Roseman, Mark A. ... Hollywood, FL

Roseman, Mark E. .... Orange, CA
Roseman, Matthew G. .... Melville, NY
Mineola, NY
Roseman, Mindy Jane .... New York, NY
Roseman, Robert A. .... New York, NY
Roseman, Robert D. .... Washington, DC
Roseman, Robert M. .... Philadelphia, PA
Roseman, Ronald L. .... Seattle, WA
Roseman Roseman & Feldman
Melville, NY
Roseman, Stephen .... Newton, NJ
Roseman, Steven .... Long Beach, CA
Roseman, Steven A. .... Englewood, CO
Roseman, Steven A., Law Offices of
Los Angeles, CA
Rosemann, Martin L. .... Olathe, KS
Kansas City, MO
Rosemarin, Carey S. .... Chicago, IL
Rosemark, Daniel S. .... Lowell, MA
Rosemark, Jennifer F. .... Minneapolis, MN
Rosemary, Nancy J. .... Plainfield, IN
Rosemary, Ralph .... Plainfield, IN
Rosemary & Rosemary .... Plainfield, IN
Rosemblat, Raphael A. .... Los Angeles, CA
Roseme, Sharon Day .... Sacramento, CA
Rosemergy, James Jonathan
St. Louis, MO
Rosemeyer, Donna Cox .... Northbrook, IL
Rosemeyer, Jon M. .... Dayton, OH
Rosemeyer, Mary Ellen .... Chicago, IL
Rosemond, Edward Delane .... Columbia, SC
Rosemond, Ernest E. .... Washington, DC
Rosemond, G. Erick .... San Antonio, TX
Rosemond, St. Julien P., Jr. .... Miami, FL
Rosemond, W. Thomas, Jr. .... Chicago, IL
Rosemurgy, Robert S. .... Escanaba, MI
Rosen, A. Eric .... Framingham, MA
Rosen, Aaron .... Granada Hills, CA
Rosen, Adam J. .... New York, NY
Rosen, Adam L. .... Garden City, NY
New York, NY
Rosen, Adam W. .... Burbank, CA
Rosen, Alan .... Chicago, IL
Rosen, Alan L. .... Los Angeles, CA
Rosen, Alan M. .... Philadelphia, PA
Rosen, Alfred H. .... Palm Beach, FL
Rosen, Allan J. .... Southport, CT
Rosen, Allan S. .... Pembroke Pines, FL
Rosen, Allard J. .... Cleveland, OH
Rosen, Amy .... San Diego, CA
Rosen, Amy .... Basking Ridge, NJ
Rosen, Andrea .... West Sacramento, CA
Rosen, Andrew M. .... Boulder, CO
Rosen, Andrew M. .... Philadelphia, PA
Rosen, Andrew S. .... New York, NY
Rosen, Andrew S. .... Syosset, NY
Rosen, Ann K.
Research Triangle Park, NC
Rosen, Ann M. .... Stamford, CT
Rosen, Anna Anello .... San Francisco, CA
Rosen, Arlene B. .... Brooklyn, NY
Rosen, Arlene M. .... San Francisco, CA
Rosen, Arnold A. .... Chicago, IL
Rosen, Arnold L. .... Encino, CA
Rosen, Arthur L. .... Troy, NY
Rosen, Arthur R. .... New York, NY
Rosen, Arthur S. .... Liberty Corner, NJ
Rosen, Arvin E. .... Baltimore, MD
Rosen & Associates .... Los Angeles, CA
Rosen & Associates .... Denver, CO
Rosen & Avigliano, P.A. .... Randolph, NJ
Rosen, Avrum J., Law Offices of
Huntington, NY
Rosen, Barbara .... Greenwich, CT
Rosen, Barbara J. .... New York, NY
Rosen, Barbara Kulick .... Aventura, FL
Rosen, Barry A., Law Offices of
Cherry Hill, NJ
Lafayette Hill, PA
Rosen, Barry A., Law Offices of
Norristown, PA
Philadelphia, PA
Rosen, Barry F. .... Baltimore, MD
Rosen, Barry M. .... Dallas, TX
Rosen, Barry S. .... Chicago, IL
Rosen, Bernard .... New York, NY
Rosen, Bernard A. .... Miami Beach, FL
Rosen, Bernard I. .... Akron, OH
Rosen, Beth I. .... Bayside, NY
Rosen, Beth J. .... New York, NY
Rosen, Beth L. .... New Haven, CT
Rosen, Bien & Asaro .... San Francisco, CA
Rosen, Billie A. .... Phoenix, AZ
Rosen, Bonnie .... Orange, CA
Rosen, Bradley C. .... Rochester, NY
Rosen, Brenda H. .... Boca Raton, FL
Rosen, Brian S. .... New York, NY
Rosen, Bruce D. .... West Caldwell, NJ
Rosen, Bruce Daniel .... Dana Point, CA
Rosen, Bruce G. .... Washington, DC
Rosen, Bruce J. .... Madison, WI
Rosen, Bruce S. .... San Diego, CA
Rosen, Bruce S. .... Chatham, NJ
Toms River, NJ
Rosen, Bruce T. .... Oil City, PA
Rosen, Bryna A. .... Randolph, MA
Rosen, Burt .... New York, NY
Rosen, Burt E. .... United States Senate,
Senatorial Assistants, GV
Rosen, Calvin R. .... Fairfield, NJ
Rosen, Candace J. .... Washington, DC
Rosen, Carl S. .... Boca Raton, FL
Rosen, Carol L. .... Pittsburgh, PA
Rosen, Caroline .... Savannah, GA
Rosen, Caryn .... New York, NY
Rosen, Catherine P. .... San Francisco, CA
Rosen, Cathryn .... Philadelphia, PA

Rosen, Charlene A.
Department of Agriculture,
Office of the General Counsel, GV
Rosen, Charles A. .... Newark, NJ
Rosen, Charles A. .... Roseland, NJ
New York, NY
Rosen, Charles F. .... Laguna Niguel, CA
Rosen, Charles H. .... Port Jefferson, NY
Rosen, Charles, II .... New Orleans, LA
Rosen, Charles M. .... New York, NY
Rosen, Charlotte Rothenberg
Washington, DC
Rosen, Claire I. .... Chicago, IL
Rosen, Cook, Sledge, Davis, Cade & Shattuck, P.A. .... Eutaw, AL
Greensboro, AL
Tuscaloosa, AL
Vance, AL
Rosen, Courtney A. .... Chicago, IL
Rosen, Dainow & Jacobs .... New York, NY
Rosen, Daisy .... Department of Justice,
Executive Office for Immigration Review,
GV
Rosen, Dan .... New Orleans, LA
Rosen, Dana .... New York, NY
Rosen, Dana Adler .... Norfolk, VA
Rosen, Daniel A. .... New York, NY
Rosen, Daniel Elias .... New York, NY
Rosen, Daniel, (Law Corporation)
Orange, CA
Rosen, Daniel M. .... Newark, CA
Rosen, Daniel N. .... St. Paul, MN
Rosen, Danielle Leigh
Fort Lauderdale, FL
Rosen, Darrell .... Denver, CO
Rosen, David .... Brooklyn, NY
Rosen, David A. .... New York, NY
Rosen, David A. .... New York, NY
Rosen, David B. .... Honolulu, HI
Rosen, David B. .... New York, NY
Rosen, David B. .... Mesquite, TX
Rosen, David E. .... Santa Monica, CA
Rosen, David I. .... Fort Lee, NJ
New York, NY
Rosen, David J. .... New York, NY
Rosen, David K. .... Phoenix, AZ
Rosen, David L. .... Los Angeles, CA
Rosen, David L. .... Washington, DC
Rosen, David M. .... Natick, MA
Rosen, David M. .... St. Louis, MO
Rosen, David N. .... New Haven, CT
Rosen, David N. .... Philadelphia, PA
Rosen, David Neal .... Phoenix, AZ
Rosen, David Neal, Ltd. .... Phoenix, AZ
Rosen, David S. .... Los Angeles, CA
Rosen, David S. .... Framingham, MA
Rosen, David S. .... New York, NY
Rosen, Dayan R. .... New York, NY
Rosen, Dean A. .... United States Senate,
Senatorial Assistants, GV
Rosen, Deborah A. .... Salem, NH
Rosen, Deborah N. .... Winnetka, IL
Rosen, Debra J.
Department of Transportation,
Office of the General Counsel, GV
Rosen, Debra S. .... Haddonfield, NJ
Rosen & De Martino .... Washington, DC
Rosen, Dennis A. .... Tucson, AZ
Rosen, Dennis C. .... Buffalo, NY
Rosen, Dianne L. .... Colchester, VT
Rosen & Dolan, P.C. .... New Haven, CT
Rosen, Donald A. .... Salinas, CA
Rosen, Donald B. .... Beverly Hills, CA
Rosen, Donna .... Hauppauge, NY
Rosen, Donna A. .... Albany, NY
Rosen, Dorothea-Maria
Massapequa Park, NY
Rosen, E. David .... Miami, FL
Rosen, Edith S. .... Hartford, CT
Rosen, Edw. I. .... Skokie, IL
Rosen, Edward J. .... New York, NY
Rosen, Edward L .... Mineola, NY
Rosen, Edward Roy .... Freehold, NJ
Rosen, Edward S. .... Fort Lee, NJ
Rosen, Einbinder & Dunn, P.C.
New York, NY
Rosen, Elaine S. .... Los Angeles, CA
Rosen, Elisa P. .... Washington, DC
Rosen, Elizabeth Melinda .... New York, NY
Rosen, Ellen L. .... New York, NY
Rosen, Ellen Resinski .... Los Angeles, CA
Rosen, Ellen R.Z. .... Los Angeles, CA
Rosen, Ellen Sisson .... Horsham, PA
Rosen, Eric A. .... New York, NY
Westbury, NY
Rosen, Eric D.
Department of Justice, GV
Rosen, Eric S. .... Topeka, KS
Rosen, Errol M. .... Miami Beach, FL
Rosen, Etan Emanuel .... Sacramento, CA
Rosen, Evan E. .... Golden Valley, MN
Rosen, Evan M. .... Hollywood, FL
Rosen, Evan S. .... Middlesex, NJ
Rosen, Eve Cutler .... Cincinnati, OH
Rosen, Eve Wagner .... Fort Lauderdale, FL
Rosen, Eve Wagner, P.A.
Fort Lauderdale, FL
Rosen, Felicia Lebewohl .... New York, NY
Rosen, Frank P. .... West Hills, CA
Rosen, Gary A. .... Rockville, MD
Rosen, Gary A. .... Philadelphia, PA
Rosen, Gary A., Chartered .... Rockville, MD
Rosen, Gary C. .... Fort Lauderdale, FL
West Palm Beach, FL
Rosen, Gary M. .... New York, NY
Rosen, Gary M. .... Akron, OH
Rosen, Gene S. .... North Miami Beach, FL
Rosen, George M. .... Long Beach, CA

Rosen, Gerald E. .... Detroit, MI
Rosen, Gerald L. .... New York, NY
Rosen, Gerald P. .... Roswell, GA
Rosen, Gerald S. .... Southampton, NJ
Rosen, Glenn M. .... Fountain Valley, CA
Rosen, Goodstein & Hagood, LLC
Charleston, SC
Moncks Corner, SC
Summerville, SC
Rosen, Gordon .... Tuscaloosa, AL
Rosen, Greenhut, Catuogno & Low
Springfield, MA
Rosen, Gregg M. .... Pittsburgh, PA
Rosen, Gwynn S. .... Minneapolis, MN
Rosen, H. Morton .... Baltimore, MD
Rosen, Harold .... Miami Beach, FL
Rosen, Harold .... Chicago, IL
Rosen, Harold .... Philadelphia, PA
Rosen, Harold E. .... New York, NY
Rosen, Harold I. .... Potomac, MD
Rosen, Harold, Law Office of
Washington, DC
Potomac, MD
Rosen, Harriet B. .... New York, NY
Rosen, Harris M. .... Houston, TX
Rosen, Harris Roy .... Philadelphia, PA
Rosen, Harry M. .... Weston, FL
Rosen, Harvey .... New York, NY
Rosen, Harvey D. .... New York, NY
Rosen, Harvey H., (P.C.) .... Los Angeles, CA
Rosen, Heather E. .... Moorestown, NJ
Philadelphia, PA
Rosen, Helen Grundstein .... Bethesda, MD
Rosen, Helene Cohen .... Boca Raton, FL
Rosen, Henry .... San Diego, CA
Rosen, Henry M. .... Boston, MA
Rosen, Herbert R. .... Stoughton, MA
Rosen, Howard D. .... Miami, FL
Rosen, Howard I. .... Boston, MA
Rosen, Howard J. .... Fort Lauderdale, FL
Rosen, Howard M. .... River Edge, NJ
New York, NY
Rosen, Howard M. .... Girard, OH
Rosen, Howard S. .... Woodland Hills, CA
Rosen, Howard Z. .... Los Angeles, CA
Rosen, Irving E. .... Downey, CA
Rosen, Irving H. .... Cincinnati, OH
Rosen, Irwin .... Chicago, IL
Rosen, Isadore A. .... Library of Congress,
Copyright Office, GV
Rosen, J. Philip .... New York, NY
Rosen, Jack .... Secaucus, NJ
Rosen, Jack .... Cincinnati, OH
Rosen, Jack I. .... Sherman Oaks, CA
Rosen, Jack W. .... Chicago, IL
Rosen, James D. .... Chicago, IL
Rosen, James D. .... Philadelphia, PA
Rosen, Janet .... Kinderhook, NY
Rosen, Janet S. .... Clifton, NJ
Rosen, Jay M. .... Atlanta, GA
Rosen, Jay M. .... New York, NY
Rosen, Jay W. .... Garden City, NY
Rosen, Jeff D. .... Philadelphia, PA
Rosen, Jeff W. .... Norfolk, VA
Virginia Beach, VA
Rosen, Jeffrey A. .... San Francisco, CA
Rosen, Jeffrey A. .... Washington, DC
Rosen, Jeffrey A. .... New York, NY
Rosen, Jeffrey B. .... Department of Education,
Office of the General Counsel, GV
Rosen, Jeffrey B. .... Kansas City, MO
Rosen, Jeffrey B. .... New York, NY
Rosen, Jeffrey J. .... Washington, DC
New York, NY
Rosen, Jeffrey L. .... Schererville, IN
Rosen, Jeffrey M. .... Washington, DC
Rosen, Jeffrey S. .... San Francisco, CA
San Francisco, CA
Rosen, Jeffrey S. .... Washington, DC
New York, NY
Rosen, Jeffrey Tod
Equal Employment Opportunity
Commission,
Office of Legal Counsel, GV
Rosen, Jerald I. .... Longwood, FL
Rosen, Jeremy Noam .... Miami, FL
Rosen, Jerome A. .... Willimantic, CT
Rosen, Jerrold B. .... Salt Lake City, UT
Rosen, Jerrold D. .... St. Louis, MO
Rosen, Jess L. .... Atlanta, GA
Rosen, Jesse N. .... Glendale, CA
Rosen, Jillian .... New York, NY
Rosen, Joanne Lembert
Santa Monica, CA
Rosen, Joel .... Salem, MA
Rosen, Joel B. .... Camden, NJ
Rosen, Joel D. .... Princeton, NJ
Rosen, Joel D., Law Offices of
Philadelphia, PA
Rosen, Joel D., Law Office of
Plymouth Meeting, PA
Rosen, Joel M. .... Morristown, NJ
New York, NY
Rosen, Joel S. .... Philadelphia, PA
Rosen, Jon Howard .... Seattle, WA
Rosen, Jonathan .... Boston, MA
Rosen, Jonathan M. .... Garden City, NY
Rosen, Jonathan P. .... New York, NY
Rosen, Joseph .... Los Angeles, CA
Rosen, Joseph F. .... Miami, FL
Rosen, Joseph S. .... Boston, MA
Rosen, Joshua H. .... Sarasota, FL
Rosen, Joshua L. .... Los Angeles, CA
Rosen, Joshua N. .... Mount Vernon, IL
Rosen, Judith M. .... Huntington, NY
Rosen, Judith S. .... San Francisco, CA
Rosen, Jules S. .... Miami, FL
Rosen, Julia Hoffert .... Southfield, MI

Rosen, Julie L. .... New York, NY
Rosen, Julie Leamon .... Denver, CO
Rosen, Karen Z. .... Miami, FL
Rosen, Keith M. .... Philadelphia, PA
Rosen, Kenneth A. .... Roseland, NJ
Rosen, Kenneth Jay .... New York, NY
Rosen, Kenneth L. .... Bloomfield Hills, MI
Rosen, Kenneth M.
Securities and Exchange Commission,
Office of the General Counsel, GV
Rosen, Kevin S. .... Los Angeles, CA
Rosen & Kreiling, P.A. .... Weston, FL
Rosen, Lance S. .... Cherry Hill, NJ
Bethlehem, PA
Blue Bell, PA
Bristol, PA
Feasterville, PA
North East, PA
Philadelphia, PA
Rosen, Lance S. .... Seattle, WA
Rosen, Larry J. .... Albany, NY
Rosen, Laurence Matthew .... New York, NY
Rosen Law Firm .... Collinsville, IL
Rosen Law Firm, The .... Portland, OR
Rosen, Lawrence .... Princeton, NJ
Rosen, Lawrence A. .... Chicago, IL
Rosen, Lawrence E. .... Redwood City, CA
Rosen, Lawrence N. .... Miami, FL
Rosen, Lawrence S. .... New York, NY
Rosen, Lee E. .... San Francisco, CA
Rosen, Lee S. .... Raleigh, NC
Rosen, Leff .... Hempstead, NY
Rosen, Leon .... New York, NY
Rosen, Leon D. .... Los Angeles, CA
Rosen, Leonard D. .... Hollywood, FL
Rosen, Leonard G. .... New York, NY
Rosen, Leonard M. .... New York, NY
Rosen, Leslie B. .... Studio City, CA
Rosen, Leslie J. .... Chicago, IL
Rosen, Lester .... Chicago, IL
Rosen, Lester .... Hempstead, NY
Rosen, Lester S. .... Novato, CA
Rosen, Linda F. .... Philadelphia, PA
Rosen, Lisa Alpert .... Washington, DC
Rosen & Livingston .... New York, NY
Rosen, Lloyd C. .... Merrick, NY
Rosen, Lois N. .... White Plains, NY
Rosen, Lorri Staal .... New York, NY
Rosen, Louis A. .... Freehold, NJ
Rosen, Louis C. .... Cherry Hill, NJ
Rosen, Louis E. .... Chicago, IL
Rosen, Louis L. .... Columbia, SC
Rosen & Lovell, P.C. .... Southfield, MI
Rosen, Luane .... Phoenix, AZ
Rosen, Lucile L. .... San Francisco, CA
Rosen & Lundeen LLP .... New Orleans, LA
Rosen, Marc .... Boston, MA
Rosen, Marc I. .... Catlettsburg, KY
Rosen, Marc Seldin .... Baltimore, MD
Rosen, Marcia Ann .... Rancho Santa Fe, CA
Rosen, Marian S. .... Houston, TX
Rosen, Mark A. .... Washington, DC
Rosen, Mark A. .... Frankfort, KY
Rosen, Mark A. .... Boston, MA
Rosen, Mark A. .... Morristown, NJ
Rosen, Mark A., & Associates
Boston, MA
Rosen, Mark E. .... Department of the Navy,
Office of the Judge Advocate General, GV
Rosen, Mark I. .... Simsbury, CT
Rosen, Mark J. .... Bridgeport, CT
Rosen, Mark J. .... Philadelphia, PA
Rosen, Mark Jay .... Auburn, ME
Rosen, Mark L. .... Miami, FL
Rosen, Mark L., P.A. .... Miami, FL
Rosen, Mark R. .... Philadelphia, PA
Rosen, Mark S. .... Hollywood, FL
Rosen, Mark S. .... Mountainside, NJ
Rosen, Marsha C. .... Miami, FL
Rosen, Marshall H. .... Brooklyn, NY
Rosen, Martin .... New York, NY
Rosen, Martin .... Plainview, NY
Rosen, Martin A. .... Sarasota, FL
Rosen, Martin E. .... Los Angeles, CA
Rosen, Martin J. .... White Plains, NY
Rosen, Martin J., P.C. .... White Plains, NY
Rosen, Marvin N. .... New York, NY
Rosen, Marvin S. .... Miami, FL
Rosen, Marvin S. .... West Palm Beach, FL
Rosen, Mary Pat .... Detroit, MI
Rosen, Mary W. .... Washington, DC
Rosen, Matthew .... New York, NY
Rosen, Matthew .... Lebanon, OH
Rosen, Matthew A. .... New York, NY
Rosen, Melvin .... North Miami Beach, FL
Rosen, Mervin Z. .... Baltimore, MD
Rosen, Meyer .... Georgetown, SC
Rosen, Michael .... New York, NY
Rosen, Michael A. .... Miami, FL
Rosen, Michael B. .... Boston, MA
Rosen, Michael B. .... Wellesley, MA
Rosen, Michael Dana .... Andover, MA
Rosen, Michael E. .... Albany, NY
Rosen, Michael H. .... Tampa, FL
Rosen, Michael J. .... Treasury Department,
Bureau of Alcohol, Tobacco and Firearms,
GV
Rosen, Michael J. .... Miami, FL
Rosen, Michael J. .... Chicago, IL
Rosen, Michael J. .... Bristol, PA
Rosen, Michael J., P.A. .... Miami, FL
Rosen, Michael L. .... Tallahassee, FL
Rosen, Michael L. .... Boston, MA
Rosen, Michael L. .... St. Louis, MO
Rosen, Michael N. .... New York, NY
Rosen, Michael N. .... Seattle, WA
Rosen, Michael S. .... Wellesley, MA
Rosen, Michael W. .... New York, NY

Rosen, Mildred Pafundi ... New York, NY
Rosen, Miriam R. ... Detroit, MI
Rosen, Mitch ... Los Angeles, CA
Rosen, Mitchell H. ... Palo Alto, CA
Rosen, Mitchell S. ... Atlanta, GA
Rosen, Morris ... South Bend, IN
Rosen, Morris D. ... Charleston, SC
Rosen, Morton ... Santa Monica, CA
Rosen, Morton H. ... New York, NY
Rosen, Myron S. ... New York, NY
Rosen, N. Hilton ... New York, NY
Rosen, N. Hilton, P.C. ... New York, NY
Rosen, Naomi S. ... Davis, CA
Rosen, Nathan Aaron ... New York, NY
Rosen, Nathan D. ... North Tonawanda, NY
Rosen, Nathan M. ... Plano, TX
Rosen, Nathan M., P.C. ... Plano, TX
Rosen, Neal A. ... Boston, MA
Rosen, Neal B. ... Chicago, IL
Rosen, Neil R. ... Pittsburgh, PA
Rosen, Neil S. ... Toms River, NJ
Rosen & Newey, P.C. ... Houston, TX
Rosen, Nina J. ... Boston, MA
Rosen, Norman E. ... Princeton, NJ
New York, NY
Rosen, Norman G. ... Ukiah, CA
Rosen, Norman H. ... Livingston, NJ
Rosen, Norman J. ... Rego Park, NY
Rosen, Norman N. ... El Paso, TX
Rosen, Norman S. ... Skokie, IL
Rosen & Osborne, P.A. ... Tampa, FL
Rosen, Paul A. ... Southfield, MI
Rosen, Paul B. ... Houston, TX
Rosen, Paul M. ... Briarcliff Manor, NY
Rosen, Paul R. ... Moorestown, NJ
Philadelphia, PA
Rosen, Perry M. ... Denver, CO
Washington, DC
Rosen, Peter ... Randolph, NJ
Rosen, Peter K. ... Los Angeles, CA
Rosen, Peter Stephen ... Nashville, TN
Rosen, Philip A. ... Forest Hills, NY
Rosen, Philip B. ... New York, NY
Rosen, Philip S. ... Short Hills, NJ
Rosen, Phillip A. ... Washington, DC
Rosen, Phillip L. ... Beverly Hills, CA
Rosen, Preminger & Bloom ... Bronx, NY
Brooklyn, NY
New York, NY
White Plains, NY
Rosen, Rachel Rodriguez ... Houston, TX
Rosen, Randie Beth ... New York, NY
Rosen, Raymond M. ... Baltimore, MD
Rosen & Reade, LLP ... Greenwich, CT
West Palm Beach, FL
New York, NY
Rosen, Reid A. ... New York, NY
Rosen, Rena C.B. ... Lafayette, CA
Rosen, Reuben ... San Diego, CA
Rosen, Richard ... Salinas, CA
Rosen, Richard A. ... New York, NY
Rosen, Richard C. ... New York, NY
Rosen, Richard D. ... Department of the Army, Office of the Judge Advocate General, GV
Rosen, Richard D. ... Pittsburgh, PA
Rosen, Richard F. ... Tucson, AZ
Rosen, Richard L. ... Washington, DC
Rosen, Richard L. ... New York, NY
Rosen, Richard N. ... Little Rock, AR
Rosen, Richard P. ... Denver, CO
Rosen, Richard P., P.C. ... Denver, CO
Rosen, Richard S. ... Chicago, IL
Rosen, Richard S. ... Charleston, SC
Rosen, Richard T. ... Poughkeepsie, NY
Rosen, Rick E. ... Collinsville, IL
Rosen, Risë E. ... Mineola, NY
Rosen, Robert ... Wilmington, DE
Rosen, Robert A. ... Department of Justice, Tax Division, GV
Rosen, Robert A. ... Executive Office Of The President, GV
Rosen, Robert B. ... Chicago, IL
Rosen, Robert B. ... Englewood, NJ
Newark, NJ
Rosen, Robert C. ... Los Angeles, CA
Rosen, Robert G. ... Lansdale, PA
Rosen, Robert J. ... New Milford, CT
Rosen, Robert L. ... Dallas, TX
Rosen, Robert Lawrence ... New York, NY
Rosen, Robert M. ... Washington, DC
Rosen, Robert M. ... Boston, MA
Rosen, Robert M. ... Springfield, MA
Rosen, Robert M. ... Hempstead, NY
Rosen, Robert M. ... Monticello, NY
Rosen, Robert N. ... Charleston, SC
Rosen, Robert T., (P.A.) ... Orlando, FL
Rosen, Robin L. ... Beverly Hills, CA
Rosen, Robin P. ... Federal Trade Commission, Bureau of Consumer Protection, GV
Rosen, Roger J. ... Los Angeles, CA
Rosen, Roger M. ... Los Angeles, CA
Rosen, Rona J. ... Philadelphia, PA
Rosen, Ronald ... Hollywood, FL
Rosen, Ronald B. ... West Long Branch, NJ
Rosen, Ronald D. ... Beverly Hills, CA
Rosen, Ronald I. ... Philadelphia, PA
Rosen, Ronald M. ... Los Angeles, CA
Rosen, Ronald S. ... Los Angeles, CA
Rosen & Rosen ... St. Paul, MN
Rosen and Rosen ... Georgetown, SC
Rosen, Rosen & Bloom ... Oil City, PA
Rosen & Rosen, LLP ... Monticello, NY
Rosen & Rosen, P.A.
Fort Lauderdale, FL
Hollywood, FL
Miami, FL
Rosen & Rosen, P.C. ... Philadelphia, PA
Rosen, Russell W. ... New York, NY
Rosen, Ruth W. ... San Rafael, CA
Rosen, S. Alan, (A Professional Corporation)
Los Angeles, CA
Rosen, Sam ... Towson, MD
Rosen, Sam ... Euless, TX
Fort Worth, TX
Rosen, Samuel D. ... New York, NY
Rosen, Samuel K. ... New York, NY
Rosen, Samuel R. ... Nashville, IN
Rosen, Samuel R. ... New York, NY
Rosen, Sanford Jay ... San Francisco, CA
Rosen, Sanford P. ... New York, NY
Rosen, Sanford P., & Associates, P.C.
New York, NY
Rosen, Sarah K. ... San Diego, CA
Rosen, Scott D. ... Hartford, CT
Rosen, Scott M. ... Department of Justice, Immigration and Naturalization Service, GV
Rosen, Seth L. ... New York, NY
Rosen, Seth M. ... Los Angeles, CA
Rosen & Shapiro ... Sarasota, FL
Rosen, Sheldon M. ... Westbury, NY
Rosen, Sheldon M. ... Toledo, OH
Rosen, Shelley L. ... Santa Monica, CA
Rosen, Sidney ... New York, NY
Rosen, Sidney M. ... Phoenix, AZ
Rosen, Simon Jeffrey ... Philadelphia, PA
Rosen & Slome, LLP ... Garden City, NY
New York, NY
Rosen, Sol ... Washington, DC
Rosen, Stacy Yolish ... New York, NY
Rosen, Stanley A. ... Albany, NY
Rosen, Stanley I. ... San Diego, CA
Rosen, Stanley I. ... Roseland, NJ
Rosen, Stanley L., (A P.C.) ... Dana Point, CA
Rosen, Stanton T. ... St. Louis Park, MN
Rosen, Stephan C. ... New York, NY
Rosen, Stephanie C. ... Morristown, NJ
Rosen, Stephen ... Oakland, CA
Rosen, Stephen D. ... New York, NY
Rosen, Stephen H. ... Coral Gables, FL
Rosen, Stephen H. ... Glen Ridge, NJ
Rosen, Stephen J. ... Washington, DC
Rosen, Stephen L. ... San Francisco, CA
Rosen, Stephen L. ... Tampa, FL
Rosen, Steven ... Washington, DC
Rosen, Steven ... College Park, MD
Rosen, Steven A. ... New York, NY
Rosen, Steven C. ... Atlanta, GA
Rosen, Steven H. ... New York, NY
Rosen, Steven J. ... Springfield, IL
Rosen, Steven M. ... Encinitas, CA
Rosen, Steven M. ... Miami, FL
Rosen, Steven M. ... Baltimore, MD
Rosen, Steven M. ... Seattle, WA
Rosen, Steven O. ... Portland, OR
Rosen, Steven Rocket ... Sugar Land, TX
Rosen, Stuart ... New York, NY
Rosen, Stuart ... New York, NY
Rosen, Stuart D. ... Hartford, CT
Rosen, Stuart I. ... New York, NY
Rosen, Stuart J. ... Torrance, CA
Rosen, Stuart M. ... New York, NY
Rosen, Sue-Ann ... Chicago, IL
Rosen, Susan Corner ... Charleston, SC
Rosen, Suzanne K. ... Fort Worth, TX
Rosen & Swikes ... Miami Beach, FL
Rosen, Ted D. ... New York, NY
Rosen, Ted M. ... Trenton, NJ
West Orange, NJ
Great Neck, NY
New York, NY
Rosen, Terri L. ... Atlanta, GA
Rosen & Tetelman ... New York, NY
Rosen, Theodore W. ... Denver, CO
Rosen, Theodore W., P.C. ... Denver, CO
Rosen, Thomas E. ... Dallas, TX
Rosen, Tobin ... Tucson, AZ
Rosen, Victor D. ... Oakland, CA
Rosen, Walter K. ... Glendale, CA
Rosen, Warren H. ... Fort Lauderdale, FL
Rosen, Wendi R. ... Miami, FL
Rosen, Wendy Michelle ... Doylestown, PA
Rosen, William C. ... Monticello, NY
Rosen, William E. ... Fresh Meadows, NY
Rosen, William S. ... St. Paul, MN
Rosen, William W. ... New Orleans, LA
Rosen, Yasinow & Roberts ... Buffalo, NY
Rosenacker, Frank B. ... Cincinnati, OH
Rosenacker, Frank B. Co., L.P.A.
Cincinnati, OH
Rosenak, Alan W. ... Overland Park, KS
Rosenak, Charles B. ... Tesuque, NM
Rosenak, Mary Jan ... Madison, WI
Rosenau, Angela K. ... San Diego, CA
Rosenau, Gareth W.
Department of Transportation, Federal Railroad Administration, GV
Rosenau, Ira A. ... Philadelphia, PA
Rosenau, Kenneth H. ... Washington, DC
Rosenau, Lee H. ... Philadelphia, PA
Rosenau & Rosenau ... Washington, DC
Rosenau, Susan Hansen ... Washington, DC
Rosenauer, Cecilia Lee ... Reno, NV
Rosenauer, David B. ... New York, NY
Rosenauer, Michael A. ... Reno, NV
Rosenauer, Michael A., Ltd. ... Reno, NV
Rosenbach, Anne ... Massapequa, NY
Rosenbach, Dean J. ... North Palm Beach, FL
Rosenbach, Philip ... Florham Park, NJ
Rosenbach, Robert J. ... San Antonio, TX
Rosenbalm, Wheeler A. ... Knoxville, TN
Rosenbauer, Wm. A. ... Union City, NJ
Rosenbaum, Alan ... Peabody, MA
Rosenbaum, Alan D., (P.C.) ... Lawton, OK
Rosenbaum, Alvin ... Waterbury, CT
Rosenbaum, Andrew H.
Spring Valley, NY
Rosenbaum, Arthur R. ... New York, NY
Spring Valley, NY
White Plains, NY
Rosenbaum, Ary D. ... Syosset, NY
Rosenbaum, Barbara M. ... Lexington, KY
Rosenbaum, Barry A. ... Santa Monica, CA
Rosenbaum, Barry M. ... Southfield, MI
Rosenbaum, Ben, III ... McLean, VA
Rosenbaum, Beverly Block
New Rochelle, NY
Rosenbaum, Bloom, Meyerson, Galinsky, Weiner & Cirino, P.C. ... Detroit, MI
Rosenbaum, Bruce ... New York, NY
Rosenbaum, C. Fred ... Washington, DC
Rosenbaum, Carol P. ... St. Louis, MO
Rosenbaum, Cindy Yost ... Katonah, NY
Rosenbaum, Cory J. ... New York, NY
Rosenbaum, Dan A. ... New York, NY
Rosenbaum, Dan L. ... New York, NY
Rosenbaum, Daniel B. ... Washington, DC
Rosenbaum, Daniel S.
West Palm Beach, FL
Rosenbaum, David B. ... Phoenix, AZ
Rosenbaum, David B. ... New York, NY
Rosenbaum, David E. ... Glendale, CA
Rosenbaum, David G. ... Chicago, IL
Rosenbaum, David Ira ... Cherry Hill, NJ
Philadelphia, PA
Rosenbaum, David S. ... Los Angeles, CA
Rosenbaum, David S. ... Redwood City, CA
Rosenbaum, Debra B. ... Summit, NJ
Rosenbaum, Diane H. ... Slingerlands, NY
Rosenbaum, Edward ... Southfield, MI
Rosenbaum, Elizabeth A. ... Sioux City, IA
Rosenbaum, Elliott M. ... Valley Stream, NY
Rosenbaum, Eric C. ... Kew Gardens, NY
Rosenbaum, Faye Pous ... Birmingham, AL
Rosenbaum, Gary B. ... Los Angeles, CA
Rosenbaum, George D. ... New York, NY
Rosenbaum, Glen A. ... Houston, TX
Rosenbaum, Greg A. ... Bethesda, MD
Rosenbaum, Harold ... Brooklyn, NY
Rosenbaum, Henry J. ... Saginaw, MI
Rosenbaum, Jack ... Glendale, CA
Rosenbaum, Jacob I. ... Cleveland, OH
Rosenbaum, Jacob P. ... New York, NY
Rosenbaum, James Edward ... Milton, MA
Rosenbaum, James M. ... Minneapolis, MN
Rosenbaum, James R. ... Des Moines, IA
Rosenbaum, Jay D. ... Boston, MA
Rosenbaum, Jeffrey M. ... Albany, NY
Rosenbaum, Jeremy A. ... Cleveland, OH
Rosenbaum, Jessica T. ... Washington, DC
Rosenbaum, Jody B. ... Chicago, IL
Rosenbaum, John A. ... Santa Ana, CA
Rosenbaum, John E. ... Palo Alto, CA
Rosenbaum, Jonathan E. ... Elyria, OH
Rosenbaum, Joseph I. ... New York, NY
Rosenbaum, Joseph L. ... Lexington, KY
Rosenbaum, Joseph S. ... Miami, FL
Rosenbaum, Joseph S., P.A. ... Miami, FL
Rosenbaum, Judith Ann ... Chicago, IL
Rosenbaum, Keith A. ... Irvine, CA
Rosenbaum, Lee K. ... Colorado Springs, CO
Rosenbaum, Lee K., & Associates
Colorado Springs, CO
Rosenbaum, Lee N. ... Beverly Hills, CA
Rosenbaum, Leonard S. ... New York, NY
Rosenbaum, Lester ... Yorktown Heights, NY
Rosenbaum, Lois Omenn ... Portland, OR
Rosenbaum, Marcia F. ... Clementon, NJ
Philadelphia, PA
Rosenbaum, Marcy C. ... New York, NY
Rosenbaum, Margaret A. ... Miami, FL
Rosenbaum, Marilyn Brown
Minneapolis, MN
Rosenbaum, Mark A. ... Anchorage, AK
Rosenbaum, Mark A. ... New York, NY
Rosenbaum, Mark J. ... Los Angeles, CA
Rosenbaum, Mark R. ... Chicago, IL
Rosenbaum, Martin M. ... New York, NY
Rosenbaum, Martin R. ... Minneapolis, MN
Rosenbaum, Marty Ira ... Albany, NY
Rosenbaum, Matthew A. ... Rochester, NY
Rosenbaum, Melissa G. ... Dallas, TX
Rosenbaum, Michael A. ... Atlanta, GA
Rosenbaum, Michael D. ... Chicago, IL
Rosenbaum, Michael F. ... New York, NY
Rosenbaum, Michael J. ... Miami, FL
Rosenbaum, Michael L. ... Portland, OR
Rosenbaum, Michael M. ... Short Hills, NJ
New York, NY
Rosenbaum, Mortimer ... San Diego, CA
Rosenbaum, Morton I. ... Cincinnati, OH
Rosenbaum, Murray S. ... Chicago, IL
Rosenbaum, N. Rosie ... Chicago, IL
Rosenbaum, Neal A. ... Newport News, VA
Rosenbaum, Neil ... Washington, DC
Rosenbaum, Neil J. ... San Francisco, CA
Rosenbaum, Norman S. ... New York, NY
Rosenbaum, Norman V. ... Clayton, MO
Rosenbaum, Paul A. ... Lansing, MI
Rosenbaum, Paul R. ... Los Angeles, CA
Rosenbaum, Paul W. ... San Antonio, TX
Rosenbaum, Phyllis S. ... Nashville, TN
Rosenbaum, Richard A.
Fort Lauderdale, FL
New York, NY
Rosenbaum, Richard G. ... New York, NY
Rosenbaum, Richard L.
Fort Lauderdale, FL
Rosenbaum, Richard M. ... New York, NY
Rosenbaum, Robert A. ... Minneapolis, MN
Rosenbaum, Robert D. ... Washington, DC
Rosenbaum, Robert F. ... Beachwood, OH
Rosenbaum, Robert F., Co., L.P.A.
Beachwood, OH
Rosenbaum, Robert H. ... Riverdale, MD
Rosenbaum, Robert Leslie ... Lexington, KY
Rosenbaum, Robin S. ... Fort Lauderdale, FL
Rosenbaum, Ronald L., Law Offices of
San Juan, PR
Rosenbaum, Ronald S. ... St. Paul, MN
Rosenbaum & Rosenbaum
Yorktown Heights, NY
Rosenbaum & Rosenbaum, P.S.C.
Lexington, KY
Rosenbaum, S. Wayne ... San Diego, CA
Rosenbaum, Sally ... Yorktown Heights, NY
Rosenbaum, Scott H. ... Los Angeles, CA
Rosenbaum, Sheldon A. ... Danbury, CT
Rosenbaum, Sidney J., IV ... Danville, VA
Rosenbaum, Solomon ... San Diego, CA
Rosenbaum, Stanton D. ... Denver, CO
Rosenbaum, Stephan L. ... New York, NY
Rosenbaum, Stephen A. ... San Francisco, CA
Rosenbaum, Stephen A. ... Newburyport, MA
Rosenbaum, Stephen N. ... Baltimore, MD
Rosenbaum, Steven E. ... Portland, OR
Rosenbaum, Steven H.
Department of Justice, Civil Rights Division, GV
Rosenbaum, Steven I. ... Providence, RI
Rosenbaum, Steven J. ... Washington, DC
Rosenbaum, Sylvan H. ... Roslyn Heights, NY
Rosenbaum, Thane N. ... New York, NY
Rosenbaum, Warren B. ... Rochester, NY
Rosenbaum, William ... Madison, WI
Rosenbaum, William T. ... Indianapolis, IN
Rosenbaum, Zachary D. ... Morristown, NJ
Rosenbaum-Steele, Mandy
East Brunswick, NJ
Suffern, NY
Rosenbaum-Werner, Hope E.
New York, NY
Rosenberg, A. Irving ... Union, NJ
Rosenberg, Abraham ... Atlantic City, NJ
Rosenberg, Adam D. ... Southfield, MI
Rosenberg, Adam S. ... New York, NY
Rosenberg, Alan ... Haddonfield, NJ
Rosenberg, Alan ... Brooklyn, NY
Rosenberg, Alan G. ... Washington, DC
Rosenberg, Alan I. ... Media, PA
Rosenberg, Alan M. ... Melbourne, FL
Rosenberg, Alan N. ... Philadelphia, PA
Rosenberg, Alan P., P.C. ... West Hartford, CT
Rosenberg, Alan S. ... Fort Lauderdale, FL
Rosenberg, Alan S. ... New York, NY
Rosenberg, Albert ... Vincennes, IN
Rosenberg, Alexander ... Santa Monica, CA
Rosenberg, Alexander P. ... New York, NY
Rosenberg, Alfred A. ... Brooklyn, NY
Rosenberg, Alicia G. ... Los Angeles, CA
Rosenberg, Allen I. ... Philadelphia, PA
Rosenberg, Allen P. ... Arlington, VA
Rosenberg, Allison Beth ... Stamford, CT
Rosenberg, Amy Kidd ... Fort Collins, CO
Rosenberg, Amy Lynn ... Boston, MA
Rosenberg, Andrew I. ... Miami, FL
Rosenberg, Andrew L. ... New York, NY
Rosenberg, Andrew M. ... Washington, DC
Rosenberg, Andrew N. ... New York, NY
Rosenberg, Anne M. ... Minneapolis, MN
Rosenberg, Arlene Boxerman ... Chicago, IL
Rosenberg, Armand J. ... New York, NY
Rosenberg, Arnold S. ... San Francisco, CA
Rosenberg, Arthur E. ... New York, NY
Rosenberg, Arthur G. ... Bethesda, MD
Rosenberg, Arthur H., P.C.
Lake Success, NY
Rosenberg, Arthur J. ... Miami, FL
Rosenberg, Arthur M. ... New York, NY
Rosenberg, Arthur R.
Fort Lauderdale, FL
Rosenberg and Associates ... Houston, TX
Rosenberg, B. Robert ... Rochester, NY
Rosenberg, Barbara E. ... New York, NY
Rosenberg, Barbara E. ... Dallas, TX
Rosenberg, Barrie ... New York, NY
Rosenberg, Barry E. ... Newport Beach, CA
Rosenberg, Benjamin ... Baltimore, MD
Rosenberg, Benjamin ... New York, NY
Rosenberg, Benjamin E. ... New York, NY
Rosenberg, Bernard L. ... Cincinnati, OH
Rosenberg, Brenda P. ... Hackensack, NJ
Rosenberg, Brent D. ... Des Moines, IA
Rosenberg, Bruce M. ... Vista, CA
Rosenberg, Bruce R. ... Hackensack, NJ
Rosenberg, Bruce S. ... Boca Raton, FL
Rosenberg, Bruce S., P.A.
Boca Raton, FL
Rosenberg, Bryan D. ... Raleigh, NC
Rosenberg, Burton I. ... Beverly Hills, CA
Rosenberg, Burton S. ... Woodbridge, CT
Rosenberg, Burton X. ... Chicago, IL
Rosenberg Calica & Birney LLP
Garden City, NY
Rosenberg, Carol Ann ... West Hartford, CT
Rosenberg, Carolyn Hope ... Chicago, IL
Rosenberg, Charles ... Los Angeles, CA
Rosenberg, Charles B. ... Los Angeles, CA
Rosenberg, Charles H. ... New York, NY
Rosenberg, Charles H. ... New York, NY
Rosenberg, Charles M. ... Cleveland, OH
Rosenberg, Charles P. ... Norfolk, VA
Rosenberg, Chas. ... New York, NY
Rosenberg, Cheryl K. ... Houston, TX
Rosenberg, Chester G. ... Atlanta, GA
Rosenberg, Craig M. ... Washington, DC
Rosenberg, Cynthia Beth ... Baltimore, MD
Rosenberg, Cynthia Stanger ... Pittsburgh, PA
Rosenberg, Daniel A. ... Des Moines, IA
Rosenberg, Daniel A. ... Springfield, NJ
Rosenberg, Daniel B. ... New York, NY

Rosenberg, Daniel L.
Colorado Springs, CO
Rosenberg, Daniel S. ... Vista, CA
Rosenberg, Darren B. ... San Francisco, CA
Rosenberg, David ... New York, NY
Rosenberg, David A. ... Washington, DC
Rosenberg, David A. ... Sarasota, FL
Rosenberg, David A. ... Baltimore, MD
Rosenberg, David A. ... New Brunswick, NJ
Rosenberg, David A. ... Richmond, VA
Rosenberg, David B. ... Southfield, MI
Rosenberg, David B. ... New York, NY
Rosenberg, David H ... Harrisburg, PA
Lancaster, PA
Rosenberg, David H. ... Dallas, TX
Rosenberg, David H., P.C. ... Dallas, TX
Rosenberg, David I. ... Garden City, NY
Rosenberg, David J. ... Pittsburgh, PA
Rosenberg, David, Law Offices of
Davis, CA
Rosenberg, David M. ... Blue Ridge, GA
Rosenberg, David M. ... New York, NY
Rosenberg, David M. ... Dallas, TX
Rosenberg, David R. ... Santa Ana, CA
Rosenberg, David S. ... Los Angeles, CA
Rosenberg, David W. ... Lisle, IL
Rosenberg, David W. ... Boston, MA
Rosenberg, David W., P.C. ... Lisle, IL
Rosenberg & Davis ... Carlsbad, NM
Rosenberg, Deanne Silk ... Randolph, MA
Rosenberg, Debra Goetz ... Bethpage, NY
Rosenberg, Debra L. Goetz ... Bethpage, NY
Rosenberg, Diane S. ... Bethesda, MD
Rosenberg, Don L. ... Bloomfield Hills, MI
Rosenberg, Donald ... Oakland, CA
Rosenberg, Donald B. ... New York, NY
Rosenberg, Donald C. ... Hartford, CT
Rosenberg, Donald J. ... White Plains, NY
Rosenberg, Donald S. ... Miami, FL
Rosenberg, Douglas H. ... Seattle, WA
Rosenberg, Edward A. ... Los Angeles, CA
Rosenberg, Edwin M. ... Los Angeles, CA
Rosenberg, Ellen ... Worcester, MA
Rosenberg, Ellen P. ... Towson, MD
Rosenberg, Ellen P., P.A. ... Towson, MD
Rosenberg, Elliot E. ... Norwell, MA
Rosenberg, Elliott ... West Hartford, CT
Rosenberg, Eric D. ... Cooper City, FL
Rosenberg, Eric D., P.A. ... Cooper City, FL
Fort Lauderdale, FL
Rosenberg, Eric F. ... Riverdale, MD
Rosenberg, Eric P. ... New York, NY
Rosenberg, Erwin ... Miami Beach, FL
Rosenberg, Esta M.
Department of Transportation, Office of the General Counsel, GV
Rosenberg & Estis, P.C. ... New York, NY
Rosenberg, Eugene N. ... San Francisco, CA
Rosenberg, Ezra D. ... Princeton, NJ
Rosenberg, Faye R. ... Atlanta, GA
Rosenberg & Fenchel ... Pittsburgh, PA
Rosenberg, Florence Pessah ... Calabasas, CA
Rosenberg & Fortuna, LLP
Garden City, NY
Mineola, NY
Riverhead, NY
Rosenberg, Frank S. ... Washington, DC
Rosenberg, Fred E. ... Yorktown Heights, NY
Rosenberg, Freedman & Goldstein
Newton, MA
Rosenberg, Frieda Unger ... Merrick, NY
Rosenberg, Gary A. ... Boston, MA
Rosenberg, Gary D. ... Florham Park, NJ
Rosenberg, Gary E. ... Walnut Creek, CA
Rosenberg, Gary E. ... Forest Hills, NY
Rosenberg, Gary E., P.C. ... Forest Hills, NY
Rosenberg, Gary I. ... Miami, FL
Rosenberg, Gary M. ... New York, NY
Rosenberg, Geanne Perlman ... Scarsdale, NY
Rosenberg, George ... West Palm Beach, FL
Rosenberg, George ... Great Neck, NY
Rosenberg, George M. ... Los Angeles, CA
Rosenberg, Gerald A. ... New York, NY
Rosenberg, Gerald B. ... Palo Alto, CA
Rosenberg, Gerald N. ... Chicago, IL
Rosenberg, Gerald P. ... Melville, NY
Rosenberg, Gerard H. ... Staten Island, NY
Rosenberg, Gilbert S. ... Madison, WI
Rosenberg, Gina M. J. ... New York, NY
Rosenberg, Glen C. ... New York, NY
Rosenberg & Gluck, LLP
Port Jefferson, NY
Rosenberg & Goldstein, A Professional Corporation ... Atlantic City, NJ
Egg Harbor Township, NJ
Northfield, NJ
Rosenberg, Gregg M. ... Houston, TX
Rosenberg, H. James ... Van Nuys, CA
Rosenberg, Harriet B. ... Boca Raton, FL
Rosenberg, Harry ... New Orleans, LA
Rosenberg, Harry B. ... Chicago, IL
Rosenberg, Harry B., Jr. ... Chicago, IL
Merrillville, IN
Rosenberg, Helen K. ... White Plains, NY
Rosenberg, Herbert ... New York, NY
Rosenberg, Herbert B. ... Chicago, IL
Rosenberg, Herfel, Stethem & Bender, LLP
Covington, KY
Cincinnati, OH
Rosenberg, Hilary B. ... Morristown, NJ
Rosenberg, Hiram ... Monroe, CT
Rosenberg, Howard I.
Greenwood Village, CO
Rosenberg, Howard S. ... Westbury, NY
Rosenberg, Howell K. ... Philadelphia, PA
Rosenberg, Hyman L. ... Silver Spring, MD
Rosenberg, Ian ... New York, NY

Rosenberg, Ira A. ... Newark, NJ
New York, NY
Rosenberg, Irene M. ... Houston, TX
Rosenberg, J. David ... Cincinnati, OH
Rosenberg, J. Mitchell ... New York, NY
Rosenberg, Jack ... Los Angeles, CA
Rosenberg, Jack H. ... Suffern, NY
Rosenberg, James E. ... Crystal Lake, IL
Rosenberg, James F. ... Miami, FL
Rosenberg, James F. ... Pittsburgh, PA
Rosenberg, James G. ... Philadelphia, PA
Rosenberg, James L. ... Los Angeles, CA
Rosenberg, James R. ... Baltimore, MD
Rosenberg, James T. ... Willingboro, NJ
Rosenberg, Jamie C. ... New York, NY
Rosenberg, Jason ... North Andover, MA
Rosenberg, Jason A. ... Newton, MA
Rosenberg, Jay A. ... New York, NY
Rosenberg, Jay A. ... Cincinnati, OH
Rosenberg, Jay M. ... Addison, TX
Rosenberg, Jeffrey J. ... Union, NJ
Rosenberg, Jeffrey P. ... San Jose, CA
Rosenberg, Jeffrey R. ... Chicago, IL
Rosenberg, Jeffrey R. ... Houston, TX
Rosenberg, Jeffrey S. ... Pembroke Pines, FL
Rosenberg, Jeffrey S. ... Atlanta, GA
Rosenberg, Jennifer P. ... Washington, DC
Rosenberg, Jennifer S. ... Walnut Creek, CA
Rosenberg, Jeremy D. ... Minneapolis, MN
Rosenberg, Jerome I. ... New York, NY
Rosenberg, Jerome R. ... New York, NY
Rosenberg, Jill Daitch ... Roseland, NJ
Rosenberg, Jill L. ... New York, NY
Rosenberg, Jodi L. ... Woodbridge, NJ
Rosenberg, Joel
Federal Communications Commission, Mass Media Bureau, GV
Rosenberg, Joel R. ... Cherry Hill, NJ
Rosenberg, John B. ... Alexandria, VA
Rosenberg, John D. ... Dallas, TX
Rosenberg, John J. ... Boston, MA
Rosenberg, John K. ... Topeka, KS
Rosenberg, John M. ... Prestonsburg, KY
Rosenberg, John P. ... Woodland Hills, CA
Rosenberg, John W. ... San Rafael, CA
Rosenberg, Jon S. ... Orlando, FL
Rosenberg, Jonah ... Chicago, IL
Rosenberg, Jonathan ... New York, NY
Rosenberg, Jonathan S.
Universal City, CA
Rosenberg, Joseph ... Rockville, MD
Rosenberg, Joseph B. ... New York, NY
Rosenberg, Joseph F. ... Nashville, TN
Rosenberg, Joseph S. ... New York, NY
Rosenberg, Joyce R. ... Kansas City, MO
Rosenberg, Judith ... Stamford, CT
Rosenberg, Judith A. ... San Francisco, CA
Rosenberg, Judith M. ... San Francisco, CA
Rosenberg, Judith M. ... Washington, DC
Rosenberg, Jules H. ... Smithtown, NY
Rosenberg, Karen B. ... Hyannis, MA
Rosenberg, Karen Krisher ... Columbus, OH
Rosenberg, Karen L. ... Chicago, IL
Rosenberg, Karen L. ... Manchester, NH
Rosenberg, Karen Schneider
Kansas City, MO
Rosenberg, Katherine B. ... New York, NY
Rosenberg, Keith A. ... Washington, DC
Rockville, MD
Towson, MD
Rosenberg, Keith A., L.L.C.
Washington, DC
Baltimore, MD
Rockville, MD
Towson, MD
Rosenberg, Kenneth F. ... Worcester, MA
Rosenberg, Kenneth I. ... Philadelphia, PA
Rosenberg, Kenneth W.
Department of Justice, Tax Division, GV
Rosenberg, Kermit A. ... Washington, DC
Rosenberg & Kirby ... Toms River, NJ
Rosenberg, Klein & Bilker
Ellicott City, MD
Rosenberg & Koffman ... Los Angeles, CA
Rosenberg, L. Stuart ... Madison, WI
Rosenberg, Lauren S. ... Miami, FL
Rosenberg Law Firm, The
Des Moines, IA
Rosenberg, Lawrence ... New York, NY
Rosenberg, Lawrence ... Houston, TX
Rosenberg, Lawrence B. ... Baltimore, MD
Rosenberg, Lawrence B., P.A.
Baltimore, MD
Rosenberg, Lawrence D.
Woodland Hills, CA
Rosenberg, Lawrence D. ... Washington, DC
Rosenberg, Lawrence Scott ... Van Nuys, CA
Rosenberg, Lee ... Garden City, NY
Rosenberg, Lee Marcy
West Palm Beach, FL
Rosenberg, Leonard A. ... San Francisco, CA
Rosenberg, Leonard B. ... Houston, TX
Rosenberg, Leonard L.
San Francisco, CA
Washington, DC
Miami, FL
Atlanta, GA
Chicago, IL
Riverdale, MD
New York, NY
Rosenberg, Leonard M. ... Great Neck, NY
Rosenberg, Leonard X. ... Chicago, IL
Rosenberg, Lewis ... New York, NY
Rosenberg & Liebentritt, P.C.
Chicago, IL
Rosenberg, Lindsay J. ... Scarsdale, NY
Rosenberg & Link ... Sacramento, CA
Rosenberg, Lloyd C. ... Plymouth, MA

Rosenberg, Loren ... Roseland, NJ
New York, NY
Rosenberg, Lory D. ... Department of Justice, Executive Office for Immigration Review, GV
Rosenberg, Louis ... Indianapolis, IN
Rosenberg, Louis T., (P.C.) ... San Antonio, TX
Rosenberg, Marc D. ... New York, NY
Rosenberg, Marc S. ... New York, NY
Rosenberg, Margot ... San Francisco, CA
Rosenberg, Marian ... New York, NY
Rosenberg, Marianne ... New York, NY
Rosenberg, Marilyn ... Mountain View, CA
Rosenberg, Mark ... Patchogue, NY
Rosenberg, Mark David ... Beverly Hills, CA
Rosenberg, Mark F. ... New York, NY
Rosenberg, Mark I. ... Los Angeles, CA
Rosenberg, Mark J. ... New York, NY
Rosenberg, Mark L. ... Jacksonville, FL
Rosenberg, Mark L. ... Bethesda, MD
Rosenberg, Mark S. ... Los Angeles, CA
Rosenberg, Mark S. ... West Chester, PA
Rosenberg, Marla ... Philadelphia, PA
Rosenberg, Marshall E. ... Woodland Hills, CA
Rosenberg, Marshall G. ... Houston, TX
Rosenberg, Marshall L. ... New York, NY
Rosenberg, Marshall L.
Rockville Centre, NY
Rosenberg, Marshall L., P.C. ... New York, NY
Rosenberg, Martha ... Walnut Creek, CA
Rosenberg, Martha A. ... Lexington, KY
Rosenberg, Martin A. ... Chapel Hill, NC
Rosenberg, Marvin ... Washington, DC
Arlington, VA
Rosenberg, Marvin ... Great Neck, NY
Rosenberg, Marvin ... Jackson Heights, NY
Rosenberg, Marvin ... Cincinnati, OH
Rosenberg, Marvin B. ... Westport, CT
Rosenberg, Marvin J. ... Houston, TX
Rosenberg, Matthew A. ... St. Louis, MO
Rosenberg, Matthew L. ... Chicago, IL
Rosenberg, Maurice ... New York, NY
Rosenberg, Max D. ... Bismarck, ND
Rosenberg, Max D., P.C. ... Bismarck, ND
Rosenberg, Meira ... Stamford, CT
Rosenberg, Melvin ... Pittsburgh, PA
Rosenberg, Merwin S. ... Chicago, IL
Rosenberg, Meryl Berger
Washington, DC
Rosenberg, Meryl Berger ... Potomac, MD
Rosenberg, Michael ... Denver, CO
Rosenberg, Michael ... Miami, FL
Rosenberg, Michael ... New York, NY
Rosenberg, Michael ... White Plains, NY
Rosenberg, Michael ... Portsmouth, VA
Rosenberg, Michael A. ... New York, NY
Rosenberg, Michael A. ... New York, NY
Rosenberg, Michael B. ... Burlington, VT
Rosenberg, Michael D. ... Cambridge, MA
Rosenberg, Michael D. ... Milwaukee, WI
Rosenberg, Michael G. ... Albuquerque, NM
Rosenberg, Michael G., & Associates, P.C.
Albuquerque, NM
Rosenberg, Michael L. ... Trenton, NJ
Rosenberg, Michael Steven
Philadelphia, PA
Rosenberg, Michael T. ... Washington, DC
Rosenberg, Michael W. ... Warren, OH
Rosenberg, Michelle B. ... Boston, MA
Rosenberg, Michelle F. ... Hingham, MA
Rosenberg, Milton L. ... New York, NY
Rosenberg, Miriam A. ... Riverdale, MD
Rosenberg, Morris H. ... Seattle, WA
Rosenberg, Morton ... Library of Congress, Congressional Research Service, GV
Rosenberg, Morton J. ... Ellicott City, MD
Rosenberg, Musso & Weiner, LLP
Brooklyn, NY
Rosenberg, Nachman ... Atlanta, GA
Rosenberg, Nathan L. ... Indian Wells, CA
Rosenberg, Neal E. ... Marlton, NJ
Rosenberg, Neal L. ... New York, NY
Rosenberg, Ned M. ... East Orange, NJ
Fairfield, NJ
Rosenberg, Neil ... Columbus, OH
Rosenberg, Noah D. ... Beverly Hills, CA
Rosenberg & Parker, LLC ... Bethesda, MD
Rosenberg, Patricia E. ... Chatham, NJ
Rosenberg, Patricia G. ... San Francisco, CA
Rosenberg, Patricia S. ... Hartford, CT
Rosenberg, Paul D. ... Short Hills, NJ
Rosenberg, Paul E. ... Camp Springs, MD
Rosenberg, Paul F. ... Roseland, NJ
Rosenberg, Paul H. ... Des Moines, IA
Rosenberg, Paul I. ... Livingston, NJ
Rosenberg, Paul L. ... Boston, MA
Rosenberg, Paul M. ... Baltimore, MD
Rosenberg, Paul M. ... Durham, NC
Rosenberg, Paul S. ... Hollywood, FL
Rosenberg, Paul W. ... Cherry Hill, NJ
Rosenberg, Penny J. ... New York, NY
Rosenberg, Peter ... West Conshohocken, PA
Rosenberg, Peter D. ... New York, NY
Rosenberg, Peter D. ... Syracuse, NY
Rosenberg, Peter L. ... New York, NY
Rosenberg, Peter N. ... Boston, MA
Rosenberg, Philip ... Albany, NY
Rosenberg, Phillip G. ... Southfield, MI
Rosenberg, Priscilla Elliott ... Melbourne, FL
Rosenberg Proutt Funk & Greenberg, LLP
Baltimore, MD
Rosenberg, Randi I. ... New York, NY
Rosenberg, Raymond ... Des Moines, IA
Rosenberg, Reisman & Stein, LLP
Miami, FL
Rosenberg, Richard ... Department of State, Foreign Service Officers (Overseas), GV
Rosenberg, Richard ... New York, NY

Rosenberg, Richard A. ... DeLand, FL
Rosenberg, Richard A. ... North Brunswick, NJ
Rosenberg, Richard Allen ... Encino, CA
Rosenberg, Richard E. ... Royal Oak, MI
Rosenberg, Richard E. ... Janesville, WI
Rosenberg, Richard H. ... New York, NY
Rosenberg, Richard Harris
New York, NY
Rosenberg, Richard I. ... Northfield, NJ
Rosenberg, Richard K. ... Englewood, CO
Rosenberg, Richard M. ... San Francisco, CA
Rosenberg, Richard M. ... Chicago, IL
Rosenberg, Richard M. ... New York, NY
Rosenberg, Richard S. ... Universal City, CA
Rosenberg, Richard W. ... Garden City, NY
Rosenberg, Robert ... Oakland, CA
Rosenberg, Robert ... New York, NY
Rosenberg, Robert ... New York, NY
Rosenberg, Robert A. ... Fort Lauderdale, FL
Rosenberg, Robert A. ... New York, NY
Rosenberg, Robert D. ... Washington, DC
Rosenberg, Robert E. ... Springfield, NJ
Rosenberg, Robert E. ... Akron, OH
Rosenberg, Robert E. ... El Paso, TX
Rosenberg, Robert I. ... Beverly Hills, CA
Rosenberg, Robert J. ... New York, NY
Rosenberg, Robert M. ... New Orleans, LA
Rosenberg, Robert M. ... Houston, TX
Rosenberg, Robert Merrill
Minneapolis, MN
Rosenberg, Robert Merrill, P.A.
Minneapolis, MN
Rosenberg, Robert W. ... Toms River, NJ
Rosenberg, Robin E. ... New York, NY
White Plains, NY
Rosenberg, Robin L. ... Tampa, FL
Rosenberg, Robin L. ... Edison, NJ
Rosenberg, Robin Lee
West Palm Beach, FL
Rosenberg, Robin Meyer ... Houston, TX
Rosenberg, Roger M., Law Offices of
Hicksville, NY
Rosenberg, Ronald G. ... Los Angeles, CA
Rosenberg, Ronald J. ... Garden City, NY
Rosenberg, Rosalind
National Labor Relations Board, Office of Board Members, GV
Rosenberg & Rosenberg ... Marlton, NJ
Rosenberg & Rosenberg
Jackson Heights, NY
New York, NY
Rosenberg, Rosenberg & Calabrese
Florham Park, NJ
Rosenberg & Rosenberg, P.C.
Springfield, NJ
Rosenberg, Ross A. ... Miami, FL
Rosenberg, Ruth ... New York, NY
Rosenberg, Ruth Borsuk ... Washington, DC
Rosenberg & Ryan ... Norwell, MA
Rosenberg, Sally A. ... Washington, DC
Rosenberg & Saloman, A Professional Corporation ... Elizabeth, NJ
New Brunswick, NJ
Somerville, NJ
Rosenberg, Sam ... Parsippany, NJ
Rosenberg, Samantha ... Baltimore, MD
Rosenberg, Samuel ... West Orange, NJ
Rosenberg, Samuel ... New York, NY
Rosenberg, Samuel L. ... Spring Valley, NY
Rosenberg, Sanford L. ... Hartford, CT
Rosenberg, Sarah Ruth ... Portland, OR
Rosenberg & Schapiro, A Professional Corporation ... Boston, MA
Rosenberg, Scott A. ... Newark, NJ
Rosenberg, Scott A. ... Garden City, NY
Rosenberg, Scott D. ... Chicago, IL
Rosenberg, Scott F. ... Miami, FL
Rosenberg, Scott Ray ... Gastonia, NC
Rosenberg, Seth L. ... New York, NY
Rosenberg, Sewak, Pizzi & Bell, P.C.
Washington, PA
Rosenberg, Seymour ... New York, NY
Rosenberg, Seymour I. ... Muskegon, MI
Rosenberg, Seymour, P.C. ... Muskegon, MI
Rosenberg, Seymour S. ... Memphis, TN
Rosenberg, Shannon & Fayne, LLP
Riverdale, MD
Rosenberg, Sheldon ... Scranton, PA
Rosenberg, Sheli Z. ... Chicago, IL
Rosenberg, Sid M. ... Sacramento, CA
Rosenberg, Sol, (P.A.) ... Clifton, NJ
Rosenberg, S. R. ... Beverly Hills, CA
Rosenberg, Stacey B. ... Livingston, NJ
Rosenberg, Staci A. ... New Orleans, LA
Rosenberg, Stacy Kellner ... New York, NY
Rosenberg, Stanford H. ... Ingomar, PA
Rosenberg, Stanley ... New York, NY
Rosenberg, Stanley D. ... San Antonio, TX
Rosenberg, Stephen ... New York, NY
Rosenberg, Stephen D. ... Boston, MA
Rosenberg, Stephen J. ... Eureka, CA
Rosenberg, Stephen M. ... New York, NY
Rosenberg, Steven ... New York, NY
Rosenberg, Steven A. ... Treasury Department, Office of Thrift Supervision, GV
Rosenberg, Steven E. ... Poughkeepsie, NY
Rosenberg, Steven G. ... Alameda, CA
Rosenberg, Steven J. ... Mill Valley, CA
Rosenberg, Steven J. ... Chicago, IL
Rosenberg, Steven J., P.C. ... Chicago, IL
Rosenberg, Steven L. ... Alexandria, VA
Rosenberg, Steven M. ... New Brunswick, NJ
Rosenberg, Stewart ... Liberty, NY
Rosenberg, Sumner C. ... Atlanta, GA
Rosenberg, Susan ... Milwaukee, WI
Rosenberg, Susan H. ... Chicago, IL
Rosenberg, Susanne E. ... New York, NY
Rosenberg, SusanW. ... Towson, MD

Rosenberg, Ted M. ... Marlton, NJ
Rosenberg, Ted M. ... Port Jefferson, NY
Rosenberg, Terrence E. ... Miami Beach, FL
Rosenberg, Thomas L. ... White Plains, NY
Rosenberg, Thomas L. ... Columbus, OH
Rosenberg, Thomas M. ... Honolulu, HI
Rosenberg, Toby ... New York, NY
Rosenberg, Todd D. ... Washington, DC
Rosenberg, Todd O. ... Cleveland, OH
Rosenberg, Victor ... Springfield, MA
Rosenberg, Victor J. ... Bethesda, MD
Rosenberg, Vigiletti & McCrandall, P.C.
Grand Blanc, MI
Rosenberg, W. Scott ... Nashville, TN
Rosenberg & Watson ... Alexandria, VA
Rosenberg, William B. ... Somerville, NJ
Rosenberg, William H. ... Los Angeles, CA
Rosenberg, William J. ... Clifton, NJ
Rosenberg, William L. ... Nashville, TN
Rosenberg, William S. ... Las Vegas, NV
Rosenberger, Amy L. ... Philadelphia, PA
Rosenberger, Bryan D. ... Pittsburgh, PA
Rosenberger, Charles M. ... Jacksonville, FL
Rosenberger, David M.
Bloomfield Hills, MI
Rosenberger, Ernst H. ... New York, NY
Rosenberger, Francine J. ... Washington, DC
Rosenberger, Francis C.
United States Senate,
Committee Legal Personnel, GV
Rosenberger, George G., Jr. ... Salem, NJ
Rosenberger, Hermann, II
Philadelphia, PA
Rosenberger, J. Gorman, Jr. ... Lynchburg, VA
Rosenberger, James J. ... Seattle, WA
Rosenberger, James R. ... Las Vegas, NV
Rosenberger, John C. ... Columbus, OH
Rosenberger, John H. ... Linwood, NJ
Rosenberger, Lisa K. ... Vevay, IN
Rosenberger, M. Gervase ... New York, NY
Rosenberger, Matthew G.
Philadelphia, PA
Rosenberger, Michael ... Seattle, WA
Rosenberger, Moira B. ... Philadelphia, PA
Rosenberger, Patrick J. ... Avon, CT
Rosenberger, Paul D. ... Long Beach, CA
Rosenberger, Paul R. ... Cleveland, OH
Rosenberger, Richard A. ... Souderton, PA
Rosenberger, Robert N. ... Waverly, OH
Rosenberger, Rodman M.
Philadelphia, PA
Rosenberger, Roger N. ... Berwyn, PA
Rosenberger, Sharon ... Atlanta, GA
Rosenberger, Wm., Jr. ... Lynchburg, VA
Rosenberger-Smolen, Rebecca M.
Philadelphia, PA
Rosenberg-Wohl, David M.
San Francisco, CA
Rosenberg-Wohl, Katherine
San Francisco, CA
Rosenberry, Katharine ... San Diego, CA
Rosenberry, Melody A. ... Washington, DC
Rosenberry, Richard ... Caldwell, ID
Rosenberry, William K. ... Arlington, TX
Rosenbilt, Joel L. ... Salem, OR
Rosenblad, Eric J. ... Pittsburg, KS
Rosenblad, Milton A. ... Rochester, MN
Rosenblad, Robert A. ... Rochester, MN
Rosenbladt, Gregg R. ... Mason City, IA
Rosenblat, Alan ... Washington, DC
Rosenblat, Stephen ... Chicago, IL
Rosenblatt, Alan E. ... Virginia Beach, VA
Rosenblatt, Alan G. ... New City, NY
Rosenblatt, Albert M. ... Poughkeepsie, NY
Rosenblatt, Allan L. ... Morristown, NJ
Rosenblatt, Andrew ... New York, NY
Rosenblatt, Andrew B. ... Miami, FL
Rosenblatt, Arnold ... Manchester, NH
Rosenblatt, Brett ... Los Angeles, CA
Rosenblatt, Burton ... Phoenix, AZ
Rosenblatt, Carolyn L. ... San Rafael, CA
Rosenblatt, Cynthia S. ... Minneapolis, MN
Rosenblatt, David A. ... Miami, FL
Rosenblatt, David P. ... Boston, MA
Rosenblatt, David R. ... Skokie, IL
Rosenblatt, Edward M. ... Southington, CT
Rosenblatt, Erica W. ... San Francisco, CA
Rosenblatt, Gerald F. ... Santa Monica, CA
Rosenblatt, Glenn T. ... Sherman Oaks, CA
Rosenblatt, Gregory S. ... New Haven, CT
Rosenblatt, H. M., P.A. ... Gainesville, FL
Rosenblatt, Harold J. ... New York, NY
Rosenblatt, Harry J. ... New York, NY
Rosenblatt, Howard C. ... Beverly Hills, CA
Rosenblatt, Howard M. ... Gainesville, FL
Rosenblatt, Howard T. ... Washington, DC
Rosenblatt, Ira H. ... Encino, CA
Rosenblatt, Ira L. ... Roseland, NJ
Rosenblatt, Irwin M. ... Boynton Beach, FL
Rosenblatt, James D. ... San Antonio, TX
Rosenblatt, Jaqueline B. ... Tacoma, WA
Rosenblatt, Jeffrey ... Lewiston, ME
Rosenblatt, Jennifer M. ... Long Beach, CA
Rosenblatt, Jerome C. ... Mc Comb, MS
Rosenblatt, Jerrold H. ... Hillsborough, CA
Rosenblatt, Joel David ... Miami, FL
Rosenblatt, Joel I. ... Melbourne, FL
Rosenblatt, John P. ... Farmingdale, NY
Rosenblatt, Josef E. ... Baltimore, MD
Rosenblatt, Judith L. ... Virginia Beach, VA
Rosenblatt, Katherine A. ... San Jose, CA
Rosenblatt, Keith J. ... Roseland, NJ
New York, NY
Rosenblatt, Kenneth S. ... San Jose, CA
Rosenblatt Law Firm, The ... Miami, FL
Rosenblatt, Lawrence W. ... New York, NY
Rosenblatt, Leon M. ... West Hartford, CT
Rosenblatt, Leonard A. ... Beverly Hills, CA
Rosenblatt, Leonard Reed ... Scotch Plains, NJ
Rosenblatt, Lois M. ... Far Rockaway, NY
Rosenblatt, Lorie A. ... Bingham Farms, MI
Rosenblatt, Martin J. ... New York, NY
Rosenblatt, Martin S. ... Boston, MA
Rosenblatt, Matthew A. ... Aberdeen, MD
Rosenblatt, Meryl S. ... New York, NY
Rosenblatt, Michael B. ... New York, NY
New York, NY
Rosenblatt, Nathaniel M. ... Bangor, ME
Rosenblatt, Patricia ... Bayonne, NJ
Rosenblatt, Paul G. ... Phoenix, AZ
Rosenblatt, Paul M. ... Atlanta, GA
Rosenblatt, Peter R. ... Washington, DC
Rosenblatt, Philip R. ... Boston, MA
Rosenblatt, Philip S. ... San Jose, CA
Rosenblatt, Phillip (IBA) ... Chicago, IL
Rosenblatt, Rand E. ... Camden, NJ
Rosenblatt & Redano, P.C. ... Houston, TX
Rosenblatt, Richard ... Englewood, CO
Rosenblatt, Richard B. ... Baltimore, MD
Rosenblatt, Richard B. ... Rockville, MD
Rosenblatt, Richard G. ... Philadelphia, PA
Rosenblatt, Richard J. ... Omaha, NE
Rosenblatt, Robert ... White Plains, NY
Rosenblatt, Robert Alan ... Miami, FL
Rosenblatt, Robert T. ... Brooklyn, NY
Rosenblatt, Scott H. ... New York, NY
Rosenblatt & Sheffy, L.L.P.
Southington, CT
Rosenblatt, Sidney L. ... Newington, CT
Rosenblatt, Stanley L. ... Fort Wayne, IN
Rosenblatt, Stanley M. ... Miami, FL
Rosenblatt, Stanley M., Professional Association ... Miami, FL
Rosenblatt, Stephanie ... New York, NY
Rosenblatt, Stephen M. ... Alexandria, VA
Rosenblatt, Stephen W. ... Jackson, MS
Rosenblatt, Steve ... Philadelphia, PA
Rosenblatt, Susan ... Miami, FL
Rosenblatt, Tzipporah R. ... New York, NY
Rosenblatt, Victor E. ... Scarsdale, NY
Rosenblatt, Warren B. ... Fort Wayne, IN
Rosenblatt, William M. ... Camden, NJ
Rosenblatt, William W. ... New York, NY
Rosenblit, Joel L. ... Salem, OR
Rosenblit, Joseph C., Law Offices of
San Juan Capistrano, CA
Rosenblit, Mark S. ... West Hartford, CT
Rosenblit, Steven H. ... Beverly Hills, CA
Huntington Park, CA
Los Angeles, CA
Rosenblith, Robert M. ... Jersey City, NJ
Rosenblithe & Slagle ... Massillon, OH
Rosenblitt, Richard W. ... Philadelphia, PA
Rosenblood, Kenneth L. ... Los Angeles, CA
Rosenbloom, Alan B. ... New York, NY
Rosenbloom, Allan M. ... New York, NY
Rosenbloom, Alvin D. ... Encino, CA
Los Angeles, CA
Rosenbloom, Amy ... New York, NY
Rosenbloom, Anita S. ... New York, NY
Rosenbloom, Bernard ... El Paso, TX
Rosenbloom, Betsy Ann ... Woodbridge, NJ
Rosenbloom, Brian S. ... Reston, VA
Rosenbloom, Carl ... Albany, NY
Rosenbloom, Carol S. ... Pittsburgh, PA
Rosenbloom, Daniel ... New York, NY
Rosenbloom, David S. ... Chicago, IL
Rosenbloom, Deborah D. ... Bethesda, MD
Rosenbloom, Elizabeth B. ... Chicago, IL
Rosenbloom, Eric J. ... Northbrook, IL
Rosenbloom, H. David ... Washington, DC
Rosenbloom & Hofflich ... New York, NY
Rosenbloom, Jack A. ... Livingston, NJ
Rosenbloom, James B. ... Chicago, IL
Rosenbloom, James P. ... Kansas City, MO
Rosenbloom, Jay A. ... Northbrook, IL
Rosenbloom, Jeffrey A. ... Rochester, NY
Rosenbloom, Jerald ... New York, NY
Rosenbloom, Joel ... Washington, DC
Rosenbloom, John W. ... Rockford, IL
Rosenbloom, Jonathan B. ... New York, NY
Rosenbloom, Jonathan L. ... Encino, CA
Los Angeles, CA
Rosenbloom, Judith L. ... Santa Ana, CA
Rosenbloom, Lawrence A. ... New York, NY
Rosenbloom, Lewis S. ... Chicago, IL
Rosenbloom, Louis S. ... Philadelphia, PA
Rosenbloom, Martin S. ... Tamarac, FL
Rosenbloom, Martin S., P.A. ... Tamarac, FL
Rosenbloom, Michael A. ... Rochester, NY
Rosenbloom, Milton M. ... New York, NY
Rosenbloom, Morey S. ... Philadelphia, PA
Rosenbloom, Nancy ... New York, NY
Rosenbloom, Neal M. ... New York, NY
Rosenbloom, Noah S. ... New Ulm, MN
Rosenbloom, Norma F. ... Ocean Township, NJ
Rosenbloom, Oscar A. ... Cupertino, CA
Rosenbloom, Peter C. ... Seal Beach, CA
Rosenbloom, Richard D. ... Rochester, NY
Rosenbloom, Robert A. ... Bound Brook, NJ
Rosenbloom, Robert A. ... New York, NY
Rosenbloom, Robert H. ... Decatur, GA
Rosenbloom & Rosenbloom, LLP
Encino, CA
Los Angeles, CA
Rosenbloom, Samuel M. ... New York, NY
Rosenbloom, Sandra Moschel ... Evanston, IL
Rosenbloom, Sanford M.
Philadelphia, PA
Rosenbloom, Thomas A. ... Boston, MA
Rosenbloum, Alan H. ... Gulf Breeze, FL
Rosenbloum, Louis K. ... Pensacola, FL
Rosenbloum, Louis K., P.A.
Pensacola, FL
Rosenbloum, Robert A. ... Atlanta, GA
Rosenblueth, Jeffrey ... New York, NY
Rosenblum, A. Arthur ... Charleston, SC
Rosenblum, Alan ... Alexandria, VA
Rosenblum & Anders, P.C. ... Stroudsburg, PA
Rosenblum, Andrea R. ... New York, NY
Rosenblum, Andrew I.
Rockville Centre, NY
Rosenblum, Anne M. ... Delmar, NY
Rosenblum, Arthur ... Chicago, IL
Rosenblum, Bernard ... Albuquerque, NM
Rosenblum, Bernard M. ... Nashville, TN
Rosenblum, Betsy D. ... New York, NY
Rosenblum, Bruce ... Culver City, CA
Rosenblum, Bruce A. ... Washington, DC
Rosenblum, Bruce E. ... Washington, DC
Rosenblum, Carl D. ... New Orleans, LA
Rosenblum, Charles B. ... Merrick, NY
Rosenblum, Dai ... Butler, PA
Rosenblum, Daniel M. ... New York, NY
Rosenblum, Daniel W. ... Chicago, IL
Rosenblum, Darren ... New York, NY
Rosenblum, David ... Alexandria, VA
Rosenblum, David A. ... Los Angeles, CA
Rosenblum, David A. ... Chicago, IL
Rosenblum, David J. ... Garden City, NY
Rosenblum, David M. ... Murray Hill, NJ
Rosenblum, Donn D. ... Youngstown, OH
Rosenblum, Edward G. ... Teaneck, NJ
Rosenblum, Elisha S. ... Chicago, IL
Rosenblum, Ellen E. ... Washington, DC
Rosenblum, Ellen F. ... Portland, OR
Rosenblum, Elyse ... Washington, DC
Rosenblum, Eric S. ... Levittown, NY
Rosenblum, Everett A. ... Merrick, NY
Rosenblum & Filan, L.L.C.
Greenwich, CT
New Haven, CT
Stamford, CT
New York, NY
White Plains, NY
Rosenblum, G. David ... Bala Cynwyd, PA
Philadelphia, PA
Rosenblum, Gary M. ... New York, NY
Rosenblum, Gene H. ... St. Paul, MN
Rosenblum, Glenn F. ... Cherry Hill, NJ
Philadelphia, PA
Rosenblum, Gloria M. ... East Islip, NY
Rosenblum, Goldenhersh, Silverstein & Zafft, P.C. ... Belleville, IL
Clayton, MO
Columbia, MO
St. Louis, MO
Rosenblum, Grant A. ... Sacramento, CA
Rosenblum, H. Robert ... Cocoa Beach, FL
Rosenblum, H. William ... Somers, NY
Rosenblum, Helen J. ... Riverhead, NY
Southold, NY
Rosenblum, Herbert S. ... Alexandria, VA
Rosenblum, Herbert S., A Professional Corporation ... Alexandria, VA
Rosenblum, Howard E. ... Chicago, IL
Rosenblum, Howard S. ... Boston, MA
Rosenblum, James B. ... Stamford, CT
New York, NY
White Plains, NY
Rosenblum, Jay D. ... Albuquerque, NM
Rosenblum, Jay Macey ... Kansas City, MO
Rosenblum, Jeffrey A. ... O'Fallon, MO
Rosenblum, Jeffrey M. ... Great Neck, NY
Rockville Centre, NY
Rosenblum, Jeffrey M., P.C.
Great Neck, NY
Rockville Centre, NY
Rosenblum, Jeffrey S. ... Philadelphia, PA
Rosenblum, Jeffrey S. ... Memphis, TN
Rosenblum, Jerald E. ... San Francisco, CA
San Jose, CA
Rosenblum, Jeremy T. ... Philadelphia, PA
Rosenblum, Jerold ... Philadelphia, PA
Rosenblum, Jerome J. ... Bridgeport, CT
Rosenblum, Jerome M. ... Hollywood, FL
Rosenblum, Judith Keene ... Denver, CO
Rosenblum, Kathleen G. ... San Antonio, TX
Rosenblum, Kenneth A. ... Huntington, NY
Rosenblum, Kenneth A. ... New York, NY
Rosenblum, Kenneth I. ... Santa Monica, CA
Rosenblum & Lamb ... Saugerties, NY
Rosenblum, Lauren J. ... New York, NY
Rosenblum, Lisa ... New York, NY
Rosenblum, Mandy C. ... Philadelphia, PA
Rosenblum, Marc J.
Equal Employment Opportunity
Commission,
Office of the General Counsel, GV
Rosenblum, Mark A. ... Hartford, CT
Rosenblum, Mark C. ... Washington, DC
Rosenblum, Mark J. ... Seattle, WA
Rosenblum, Matthew ... Hauppauge, NY
Rosenblum, Michael ... Albany, NY
Rosenblum, Michael A. ... Oakland, CA
Rosenblum, Michael C. ... Norfolk, VA
Rosenblum, Michael F. ... Chicago, IL
Rosenblum, Michael J. ... Madison, WI
Rosenblum, Michael S. ... Los Angeles, CA
Rosenblum, Monte I. ... Prairie Village, KS
Rosenblum, Morris ... Saugerties, NY
Rosenblum, N. Scott ... St. Louis, MO
Rosenblum, Norman ... Scottsdale, AZ
Rosenblum, Norman J. ... Paterson, NJ
Rosenblum & Oliver, P.A. ... Hollywood, FL
Rosenblum, Parish & Isaacs, Professional Corporation ... San Francisco, CA
San Jose, CA
Rosenblum, Paul A. ... Chicago, IL
Rosenblum, Paul W. ... La Grange, KY
Rosenblum, Peter M. ... Boston, MA
Rosenblum, Randy ... Miami, FL
Rosenblum & Reisman, P.C. ... Memphis, TN
Rosenblum, Richard G.
Fort Lauderdale, FL
Rosenblum, Richard H. ... New York, NY
Rosenblum, Richard J. ... Chicago, IL
Rosenblum, Richard K. ... New York, NY
Rosenblum, Richard S. ... Somerville, NJ
Rosenblum, Ricky H. ... San Antonio, TX
Rosenblum, Robert ... Los Angeles, CA
Rosenblum, Robert ... Savannah, GA
Rosenblum, Robert H. ... Washington, DC
Rosenblum, Robert M. ... Stroudsburg, PA
Rosenblum, Roberta A. ... Philadelphia, PA
Rosenblum, Ronald ... Chicago, IL
Rosenblum, Ronan, Kessler & Sarachan
Albany, NY
Rosenblum & Rosenblum, L.L.C.
Alexandria, VA
Fairfax, VA
Rosenblum, Sanford ... Albany, NY
Rosenblum, Sarah Carlin ... Chicago, IL
Rosenblum, Schwartz & Rogers, L.L.C.
St. Louis, MO
Rosenblum, Scott S. ... New York, NY
Rosenblum, Shari L. ... New York, NY
Rosenblum, Sondra ... Mineola, NY
Rosenblum, Stanley M. ... Belleville, IL
Columbia, MO
St. Louis, MO
Rosenblum, Steven A. ... New York, NY
Rosenblum, Stewart G. ... New York, NY
Rosenblum, Stewart I. ... Central Islip, NY
East Stroudsburg, PA
Rosenblum, Stuart ... New York, NY
Rosenblum, Susan Landis ... Annapolis, MD
Rosenblum, Terry M. ... Hollywood, FL
Rosenblum, Thomas F. ... Jacksonville, FL
Rosenblum & Vandenberg ... Chicago, IL
Rosenblum, Victor G. ... Chicago, IL
Rosenblum, William F., Jr. ... New York, NY
Rosenblum, Wolf & Lloyd, A Professional Corporation ... Hackensack, NJ
Jersey City, NJ
Newark, NJ
Teaneck, NJ
Rosenblume, Theodore M. ... Seattle, WA
Rosenblume, Theodore M., & Associates, P.S.
Seattle, WA
Rosenblut, Joanna R. ... New York, NY
Rosenbluth, Alan W. ... New York, NY
Rosenbluth, Ellen P. ... San Ramon, CA
Rosenbluth, Emery H., Jr. ... Orlando, FL
Rosenbluth, Harold S. ... Philadelphia, PA
Rosenbluth, James E. ... Hartford, CT
Rosenbluth, Jerrell P. ... Atlanta, GA
Rosenbluth, Jonathan H. ... South Orange, NJ
Rosenbluth, Lawrence ... New York, NY
Rosenbluth, Lee M. ... Philadelphia, PA
Rosenbluth, Lewis E. ... Coconut Creek, FL
Rosenbluth, Valerie S. ... Doylestown, PA
Rosenblutt, David K. ... High Point, NC
Rosenbohm, Kay F. Graves ... Rock Port, MO
Rosenbower, Albert V. ... Minneapolis, MN
Rosenburgh, Lisa ... New York, NY
Rosenburgh, Martin J. ... New York, NY
Rosenbush, Mark ... San Francisco, CA
Rosenbush, Robert C. ... Memphis, TN
Rosencrance, Done ... Wilbraham, MA
Rosencrans, Suzanne ... Los Angeles, CA
Rosencrans, Todd W. ... Seattle, WA
Rosencrantz, Jeffrey K. ... Cedar Rapids, IA
Rosencrantz, Mark ... Las Vegas, NV
Rosencrantz, Robin A. ... Seattle, WA
Rosencranz, D. ... Boston, MA
Rosencranz & Dailey ... Boston, MA
Rosencranz, James ... Boston, MA
Rosencranz, Linda ... Chicago, IL
Rosendahl, Craig A. ... Hopkins, MN
Rosendahl, David E. ... Fort Wayne, IN
Rosendahl, John A. ... Tacoma, WA
Rosendahl, Roger W. ... New York, NY
Rosendale, J. King ... Shaker Heights, OH
Rosendale, John C. ... Salinas, CA
Rosendin, David W. ... Ketchikan, AK
Rosendin, Joanne ... Oakland, CA
Rosendo, Kim S. ... Newcastle, ME
Rosendorf, David L. ... Miami, FL
Rosendorf, Donald F. ... Department of Justice,
Environment and Natural Resources
Division, GV
Rosendorf, Martin W. ... Silver Spring, MD
Rosene, Haugrud & Staab, Chartered
St. Paul, MN
Rosene, Kenneth T. ... Guadalupe, CA
Rosene, Peter M. ... St. Paul, MN
Rosene, Robert B. ... Los Angeles, CA
Rosener, Douglas G. ... Austin, TX
Rosener, James D. ... Cherry Hill, NJ
Berwyn, PA
Rosener, Ronald D. ... Dallas, TX
Rosenfarb, Heidi ... New York, NY
Rosenfeld, Aaron J. ... Asbury Park, NJ
Rosenfeld, Aaron P. ... Columbus, OH
Rosenfeld, Alan M. ... Forest Hills, NY
Rosenfeld, Alexander M. ... Miami, FL
Rosenfeld, Andrew M. ... Torrance, CA
Rosenfeld, Arnold R. ... Boston, MA
Rosenfeld, Arthur B. ... Oakland, CA
Rosenfeld, Arthur F. ... Department of Labor,
Office of the Solicitor, GV
Rosenfeld & Associates ... Boston, MA
Rosenfeld, Barbara ... Encino, CA
Rosenfeld, Betty ... Los Angeles, CA
Rosenfeld, Brian D. ... Stamford, CT
Rosenfeld, Dana B.
Federal Trade Commission,
Bureau of Consumer Protection, GV
Rosenfeld, Daniel ... New York, NY
Rosenfeld, Daniel E. ... Boston, MA

Rosenfeld, Daniel F. ....Manalapan, NJ
Rosenfeld, David A. ....Oakland, CA
Rosenfeld, David J ....Downers Grove, IL
Rosenfeld, David Ross ....Alexandria, VA
Rosenfeld, David Ross, P.C.
Alexandria, VA
Rosenfeld, Debby R. ....Hewlett, NY
Rosenfeld, Donald M. ....Berea, OH
Rosenfeld, Douglas E. ....Washington, DC
Rosenfeld, E.A. ....Las Vegas, NV
Rosenfeld, Elizabeth ....Encino, CA
Rosenfeld, Elizabeth M. ....Buffalo, NY
Rosenfeld, Eric ....New York, NY
Rosenfeld, Eric D. ....New York, NY
Rosenfeld, Frank A. ....Department of Justice, Civil Division, GV
Rosenfeld, Fred M. ....Alexandria, LA
Rosenfeld, Frederick H. ....Phoenix, AZ
Rosenfeld, Gary M. ....Costa Mesa, CA
Rosenfeld, Grover & Frang, P.C.
Jackson, MI
Rosenfeld, Harold E. ....Miami, FL
Rosenfeld, Howard H. ....Chicago, IL
Rosenfeld, Irving ....Ventura, CA
Rosenfeld, Irving, A Professional Corp.
Ventura, CA
Rosenfeld, Jack E. ....Weehawken, NJ
Rosenfeld, James E. ....New York, NY
Rosenfeld, James S. ....Detroit, MI
Rosenfeld, Jay H. ....Philadelphia, PA
Rosenfeld, Jeff ....State College, PA
Rosenfeld, Jeffrey ....Fairfax, VA
Rosenfeld, Jeffrey A. ....Los Angeles, CA
Rosenfeld, Jeffrey S. ....Baltimore, MD
Rosenfeld, Jennifer W. ....Redwood City, CA
Rosenfeld, Jo Anne ....Jackson, MI
Rosenfeld, John H. ....Portland, OR
Rosenfeld, Jonathan D. ....Boston, MA
Rosenfeld, Joseph L. ....Allentown, PA
rosenfeld, Joshua E. ....Palo Alto, CA
Rosenfeld, Kenneth Neal ....New York, NY
Rosenfeld, Larry ....Babylon, NY
Rosenfeld, Lawrence J. ....Phoenix, AZ
Rosenfeld, Lee David ....Philadelphia, PA
Rosenfeld, Leonard J. ....Gwynedd, PA
Rosenfeld, Lori J. ....Bronxville, NY
Rosenfeld, Lorraine ....Oceanside, CA
Rosenfeld, Madelon M ....New York, NY
Rosenfeld, Marc S. ....Westport, CT
Rosenfeld, Maria S. ....Sacramento, CA
Rosenfeld, Mark L. ....New York, NY
Rosenfeld, Martin ....Chicago, IL
Rosenfeld, Meyer & Susman, LLP
Beverly Hills, CA
Los Angeles, CA
Rosenfeld, Michael ....Beverly Hills, CA
Rosenfeld, Michael ....Burbank, CA
Rosenfeld, Michael J. ....Commack, NY
Rosenfeld, Michel ....New York, NY
Rosenfeld, Mitchell B., (P.C.)
Washington, DC
Rosenfeld, Mitchell J. ....Norwalk, CT
Rosenfeld, Mitchell S. ....Lafayette, CA
Rosenfeld, Morton M. ....Los Angeles, CA
Rosenfeld, Nancy Bryn ....San Diego, CA
Rosenfeld, Nancy J. ....Washington, DC
Rosenfeld, Nancy P. ....New York, NY
Rosenfeld, Neal D. ....Chicago, IL
Rosenfeld, Phillip B. ....Dallas, TX
Rosenfeld, Phillip Charles ....Bronx, NY
Rosenfeld, Richard M.
Securities and Exchange Commission, Division of Enforcement, GV
Rosenfeld, Richard Z. ....Jackson, MI
Rosenfeld, Robert A. ....San Francisco, CA
Rosenfeld, Robert A. ....New York, NY
Rosenfeld, Robert C. ....South Bend, IN
Rosenfeld, Robert C. ....Madison Heights, MI
Rosenfeld, Robert C. ....Solon, OH
Rosenfeld, Robert H. ....Wheeling, IL
Rosenfeld, Robert L., Jr. ....St. Louis, MO
Rosenfeld, Robert M. ....Farmington, CT
Rosenfeld, Robert M. ....Greenville, SC
Rosenfeld, Robert S. ....Dorset, VT
Rosenfeld, Robert T. (Buzz) ....Cleveland, OH
Rosenfeld, Roger C. ....Westport, CT
Rosenfeld, Ronald ....Northfield, IL
Rosenfeld, Ronald A. ....Beverly Hills, CA
Rosenfeld, Ronald A. ....Cleveland, OH
Rosenfeld, Rotenberg, Hafron & Shapiro
Chicago, IL
Schaumburg, IL
Rosenfeld, S. Stephen ....Boston, MA
Rosenfeld, Sandi ....Flushing, NY
Rosenfeld and Shearer, P.C. ....Fairfax, VA
Rosenfeld, Sheldon S. ....Northbrook, IL
Rosenfeld, Shelli ....San Francisco, CA
Rosenfeld, Shimon A. ....New York, NY
Rosenfeld & Stein, P.A. ....Miami, FL
Rosenfeld, Stephen J. ....Chicago, IL
Rosenfeld, Steven B. ....New York, NY
Rosenfeld, Steven E. ....Atlantic City, NJ
Rosenfeld, Steven E., P.C., Law Offices of
New York, NY
Rosenfeld, Steven Eric ....New York, NY
Rosenfeld, Steven H. ....New York, NY
Rosenfeld, Susan C. ....New York, NY
Rosenfeld, Susan P. ....Coral Gables, FL
Rosenfeld, Tab K. ....New York, NY
Rosenfeld, Thomas P. ....St. Louis, MO
Rosenfeld, Warren S., (P.C.)
Washington, DC
Rosenfeld, William ....Rockville Centre, NY
Rosenfeld, Wolff, Aronson, Kurland & Klein, A Professional Corporation
Los Angeles, CA
Rosenfelder, Michael J.
Whitehouse Station, NJ

Rosenfeldt, Paul W. ....Fond du Lac, WI
Rosenfeldt, Philip R. ....Philadelphia, PA
Rosenfeldt, Stuart A. ....Hollywood, FL
Rosenfelt, Barlow & Borg, P.A.
Albuquerque, NM
Gallup, NM
Shiprock, NM
Rosenfelt, Benj. ....Paterson, NJ
Rosenfelt, Daniel M. ....Albuquerque, NM
Shiprock, NM
Rosenfelt, Donald A. ....West Palm Beach, FL
Rosenfelt, Frank E. ....Los Angeles, CA
Rosenfelt, Philip H.
Department of Education, Office of the General Counsel, GV
Rosenfield, Alan L. ....Westborough, MA
Rosenfield, Alan S. ....Valencia, CA
Rosenfield, Andrew M. ....Chicago, IL
Rosenfield, Barnett I. ....Minneapolis, MN
Rosenfield, Bruce A. ....Philadelphia, PA
Rosenfield, Coleman R.
Palm Beach Gardens, FL
Rosenfield, Harry N. ....Washington, DC
Rosenfield, Harvey J. ....Santa Monica, CA
Rosenfield, Howard M. ....Avon, CT
Rosenfield, J. David ....Laguna Niguel, CA
Rosenfield, Jeffrey L. ....Plano, TX
Rosenfield, Joseph L. ....Dallas, TX
Rosenfield, Kaplan & Halperin ....Chicago, IL
Rosenfield, Kim E. ....Birmingham, AL
Rosenfield, Mark J. ....Fort Worth, TX
Rosenfield, Maurice ....Chicago, IL
Rosenfield, Michael L. ....Los Angeles, CA
Rosenfield, Mittenthal & Shieder .....Dallas, TX
Rosenfield, Neal G. ....Chicago, IL
Rosenfield, Paul W. ....Orange, CA
Rosenfield, Robert H. ....Los Angeles, CA
Rosenfield, Ronald L. ....Cleveland, OH
Rosenfield, Roslyne E. ....West Hartford, CT
Rosenfield, Sheldon ....Encino, CA
Rosenfield, Stephen N. ....Palo Alto, CA
Rosenfield, Susan Stone ....Phoenix, AZ
Rosengard, David A. ....Boston, MA
Rosengard, Lee A. ....Philadelphia, PA
Rosengard & McDonagh ....Boston, MA
Rosengarden, Eugene A.
United States International Trade Commission, Office of Tariff Affairs & Trade Agreements, GV
Rosengart, Oliver A. ....New York, NY
Rosengarten, Amy J. ....Cambridge, MA
Rosengarten, Howard ....New York, NY
Rosengarten, Howard, P.C. ....New York, NY
Rosengarten, Jerome ....Memphis, TN
Rosengarten, Marvin ....Lauderdale Lakes, FL
Rosengarten, Norman M. ....Philadelphia, PA
Rosengarten, Paul Jay ....Lincolnwood, IL
Rosengarten, Roger N. ....Kew Gardens, NY
Rosengarten, Ronald D. ....Calabasas, CA
Rosengarten, Ronald M. ....Miami, FL
Rosengarten, Solomon ....Brooklyn, NY
Rosengarten, Susanne B. ....White Plains, NY
Rosengren, David E. ....Hartford, CT
Rosengren, John C. ....Itasca, IL
Rosengren, Kenneth ....Phoenix, AZ
Rosengren, Lisa J. ....Los Angeles, CA
Rosengren, Paul G. ....Washington, DC
Rosengren, William R. ....St. Paul, MN
Rosenhagen, Thomas H. ....Kalamazoo, MI
Rosenhauer, James J. ....Washington, DC
Rosenhaus, Ruth H. ....New York, NY
Rosenheck, Doron ....Mineola, NY
Rosenheck, Manford ....Elmira, NY
Rosenheim, Gustav A. ....Boise, ID
Rosenheim, Margaret K. ....Chicago, IL
Rosenheim, Mitchell S. ....San Antonio, TX
Rosenhoch, Howard S. ....Buffalo, NY
Rosenhoffer, Chris ....Batavia, OH
Rosenhoffer, Gary A. ....Batavia, OH
Rosenhoffer, Nichols & Schwartz
Batavia, OH
Rosenhouse, Howard ....North Brunswick, NJ
Rosenhouse, Michael A. ....Rochester, NY
Rosenhouse, Nathan ....Kendall Park, NJ
Rosenhouse, Nathan, P.C. ....Kendall Park, NJ
Rosenkoetter, Claudia R. ....Sarasota, FL
Rosenkrans, Carol Mary ....Clifton, NJ
Rosenkrantz, Arthur B. ....New York, NY
Rosenkrantz, Dena Cohen ....Richmond, VA
Rosenkrantz, Edmund R. ....New York, NY
Rosenkrantz, Gayle Nin
San Francisco, CA
Rosenkrantz, Jennifer ....Garden City, NY
Rosenkrantz, Steven J. ....Department of State, Office of the Secretary, GV
Rosenkranz, Andrew L. ....Tampa, FL
Rosenkranz, Georgiana ....Los Angeles, CA
Rosenkranz, Jack M. ....Tampa, FL
Rosenkranz, Jack M., P.A. ....Tampa, FL
Rosenkranz, Jacob ....West Caldwell, NJ
Rosenkranz, Paul B. ....Brooklyn, NY
Rosenkranz, Richard I. ....Brooklyn, NY
Rosenkranz, Ronald ....Newburgh, NY
Rosenkranz, Stanley W. ....Tampa, FL
Rosenlieb, Jay L. ....Bakersfield, CA
Rosenlund, Lisa H. ....San Francisco, CA
Rosenlund, Paul S. ....San Francisco, CA
Rosenlund, Scott Alan ....Olympia Fields, IL
Rosenman, Andrew S. ....Chicago, IL
Rosenman & Colin LLP ......Washington, DC
Newark, NJ
New York, NY
Charlotte, NC
Rosenman, Ellen J. ....Great Neck, NY
Rosenman, Jaime F. ....Philadelphia, PA
Rosenman, Louis ....Washington, DC
Rosenman, Mark B. ....New York, NY

Rosenman, Michael H. ....New York, NY
Rosenman, Robert ....New York, NY
Rosenman, Robert O. ....Chicago, IL
Rosenman, Shari Cohen
Santa Monica, CA
Rosenman, Shep ....Los Angeles, CA
Rosenman, Stephen J. ....Menlo Park, CA
Rosenman, Stephen J. ....Seattle, WA
Rosenmeier, Anderson & Vogel
Little Falls, MN
Rosen-Moy, Carol L. ....Pittsburgh, PA
Rosenmund, Baio & Morrow ....Oxnard, CA
Rosenmund, Frederick ....Oxnard, CA
Rosenn, Harold ....Wilkes-Barre, PA
Rosenn, Jenkins & Greenwald, L.L.P.
Hazleton, PA
Wilkes-Barre, PA
Rosenn, Jonathan R. ....Miami, FL
Rosenn, Keith S. ....Coral Gables, FL
Rosenn, Max ....Wilkes-Barre, PA
Rosenoer, Jonathan ....San Francisco, CA
Rosenow, Beverly J. ....Auburn, WA
Rosenow, Jack G. ....Tacoma, WA
Rosenow, James ....Milwaukee, WI
Rosenow, James F. ....Milwaukee, WI
Rosenow, Manfred ....Miami, FL
Rosenow, Scott Edward ....Washington, DC
Rosenquest, John B., III ....Providence, RI
Rosenquest, Nils C. ....San Francisco, CA
Rosenquist, Carl E. ....Santa Ana, CA
Rosenquist, James W. ....Oakland, CA
Rosenquist, John E. ....Chicago, IL
Rosenrauch, Sheila S. ....Newburgh, NY
Rosenson, Arthur E. ....Chicago, IL
Rosenson, S. David ....Los Angeles, CA
Rosenson, Valerie T. ....Albany, NY
Rosenstadt, William S. ....New York, NY
Rosensteel, Amy Orr ....Hollidaysburg, PA
Rosensteel & Beckmann LLC
New York, NY
Rosensteel, Edward M. ....New York, NY
Rosensteel, Harry W. ....Pittsburgh, PA
Rosensteel, Thomas E. ....St. Charles, IL
Rosenstein, Alfred ....New York, NY
Rosenstein, Andrew B. ....Washington, DC
Rosenstein, Arnold ....Albany, NY
Rosenstein, Arthur ....San Diego, CA
Rosenstein, Arthur ....Cedarhurst, NY
Rosenstein, Arthur H. ....Rochester, NY
Rosenstein Associates ....Philadelphia, PA
Rosenstein & Barnes ....Bridgeport, CT
Fairfield, CT
Rosenstein, Barney ....Sarasota, FL
Rosenstein, Bill D. ....Tyler, TX
Rosenstein, Brian D. ....New York, NY
Rosenstein, Bruce D.
National Labor Relations Board, Division of Administrative Law Judges, GV
Rosenstein & Buess ....Chicago, IL
Rosenstein, Charles B. ....Albany, NY
Rosenstein, Craig A. ....Hyattsville, MD
Rosenstein, Daniel N. ....Washington, DC
Rosenstein, David D. ....Chicago, IL
Rosenstein, David Evan ....New York, NY
Rosenstein, Elinor C. ....Minneapolis, MN
Rosenstein, Elinor C., P.A.
Minneapolis, MN
Rosenstein, Eric M. ....Hingham, MA
Rosenstein, Fist & Ringold, A Professional Corporation .... Oklahoma City, OK
Tulsa, OK
Rosenstein, Gayle E. ....Dallas, TX
Rosenstein, Gerald ....Bakersfield, CA
Rosenstein, Harold ....New York, NY
Rosenstein, Herbert ....White Plains, NY
Rosenstein, Howard F. ....Ellicott City, MD
Rosenstein, Ira G. ....New York, NY
Rosenstein, Irwin B. ....Pasadena, CA
Rosenstein, James A. ....Philadelphia, PA
Rosenstein, Jane E. ....Seattle, WA
Rosenstein, Jeffrey P. ....New York, NY
Rosenstein, Joel S. ....Denver, CO
Rosenstein, Jonathan L. ....Cincinnati, OH
Rosenstein, Joshua ....Bellevue, WA
Rosenstein, Larry D. ....Los Angeles, CA
Rosenstein, Larry M. ....Washington, DC
Rosenstein, Leonard ....Short Hills, NJ
Rosenstein, Leslie A. ....North Woodmere, NY
Rosenstein, Mace J. ....Washington, DC
Rosenstein & Magistrali ....Winsted, CT
Rosenstein, Martin G. ....Chicago, IL
Rosenstein, Matthew A. ....Corpus Christi, TX
Rosenstein & McKenna ....Middletown, NY
Rosenstein, Michael H. ....Beverly Hills, CA
Rosenstein, Michael P. ....New York, NY
Rosenstein, Monte J. ....Middletown, NY
Rosenstein, Neil M. ....Houston, TX
Rosenstein, Paul S. ....Oakland, CA
Rosenstein, Paula S. ....San Diego, CA
Rosenstein, Richard S. ....Boston, MA
Rosenstein, Richard S., The Law Offices of
Chicago, IL
Rosenstein, Richard T. ....Glendale, CA
Rosenstein, Robert B. ....Temecula, CA
Rosenstein, Rod J. ....Greenbelt, MD
Rosenstein, Ronald I. ....Norristown, PA
Rosenstein, Ronald S. ....Winsted, CT
Rosenstein, Samuel ....Minneapolis, MN
Rosenstein, Sheila K. ....Fairfield, CT
Rosenstein, Tony P. ....Houston, TX
Rosenstein, Walter S. ....Purchase, NY
Rosenstein, Wilson & Dean, P.L.C.
San Diego, CA
Rosenstengel, Jon E. ....Belleville, IL
Rosenstengel, Nancy J. ....St. Louis, MO
Rosenstiel, Jeffrey S. ....Cincinnati, OH
Rosenstock, Allison C. ....San Diego, CA
Rosenstock, Dennis I. ....Encino, CA

Rosenstock, Donald M. ....Valley Center, CA
Rosenstock, E. Michael
Rockville Centre, NY
Rosenstock, Howard J. ....Washington, DC
Rosenstock, Jerome ....New York, NY
Rosenstock, Joan L. ....New York, NY
Rosenstock, Lawrence David ....Detroit, MI
Rosenstock, Lawrence G. ....Cambridge, MA
Rosenstock, Lawrence M. ....New York, NY
Rosenstock, Louis A., III
Colonial Heights, VA
Rosenstock, Louis J. ....Brooklyn, NY
Rosenstock, Robert ....Department of State, U.S. Mission to the United Nations, GV
Rosenstone, Howard ....Bay Shore, NY
Rosenstrach, Joann C. ....New Rochelle, NY
Rosenstrauch, Lawrence S. ....Columbus, GA
Rosenstroch, David E. ....Brooklyn, NY
Rosenstrock, Jeffrey S. ....New York, NY
Rosenstrock, Philip ....Chicago, IL
Rosensweet, Stuart ....Bronx, NY
Rosensweig, Carol ....Cambridge, MA
Rosensweig, David Z. ....New York, NY
Rosensweig, Dorothy ....New York, NY
Rosensweig, Gary S. ....Montclair, NJ
Trenton, NJ
Rosensweig, Judah E. ....New York, NY
Rosenswieg, Neal Gary ....Miami, FL
Rosensweig, Richard J. ....Boston, MA
Rosensweig, Robert L. ....Hartford, CT
Rosensweig, Ronald A. ....Waldwick, NJ
Rosensweig, William ....Beverly Hills, CA
Rosental, Burton E. ....Boston, MA
Rosenthal, Alan ....Miami, FL
Rosenthal, Alan ....Syracuse, NY
Rosenthal, Alan B. ....Syracuse, NY
Rosenthal, Alan B. ....Pittsburgh, PA
Rosenthal, Alan D. ....Houston, TX
Rosenthal, Alan S. ....Aventura, FL
Rosenthal, Albert J. ....New York, NY
Rosenthal, Alex P. ....Hollywood, FL
Rosenthal, Alina R. ....Bronx, NY
Rosenthal, Alisa Michelle ....Beverly, MA
Rosenthal, Allan M. ....Los Angeles, CA
Rosenthal, Allen ....Brooklyn, NY
Hicksville, NY
Rosenthal, Allen & Smith, LLP
Encino, CA
Los Angeles, CA
Rosenthal, Alvin M. ....Houston, TX
Rosenthal, Alvin M., & Associates, P.A.
Houston, TX
Rosenthal, Amir ....Middlebury, CT
Rosenthal, Amy L. ....Lansdale, PA
Rosenthal, Andrea ....San Francisco, CA
Rosenthal, Anita ....Phoenix, AZ
Rosenthal, Ann ....Department of Labor, Office of the Solicitor, GV
Rosenthal, Ann J. ....Van Nuys, CA
Rosenthal, Anne S. ....Newton, MA
Rosenthal, Anton H. ....West Chester, PA
Rosenthal, Ari J. ....Chicago, IL
Rosenthal, Arla G. ....Chicago, IL
Rosenthal, Arnold S. ....Department of Justice, Environment and Natural Resources Division, GV
Rosenthal & Associates ....Durham, NC
Rosenthal, Barbara S. ....Cleveland, OH
Rosenthal, Barry C.
Department of State, GV
Rosenthal, Barry J. ....Rockville, MD
Rosenthal, Barry P. ....Washington, DC
Rosenthal, Benjamin ....Portland, OR
Rosenthal, Benjamin F.
Bloomfield Hills, MI
Rosenthal, Bernard J. ....New York, NY
Rosenthal, Bernice J. ....New York, NY
Rosenthal, Beth Mandel ....Philadelphia, PA
Rosenthal, Betsy R. ....Pacific Palisades, CA
Rosenthal, Blair A. ....Denver, CO
Rosenthal, Bob B. ....Boston, MA
Rosenthal, Brent D. ....Columbus, OH
Rosenthal, Brent M. ....Dallas, TX
Rosenthal, Brett ....Sacramento, CA
Rosenthal, Brian ....Little Rock, AR
Rosenthal, Brian D. ....Philadelphia, PA
Rosenthal, Bruce A. ....Miami, FL
Rosenthal, Bruce C. ....Wilkes-Barre, PA
Rosenthal, Bruce E. ....New York, NY
Rosenthal, Bruce R. ....Clifton Park, NY
Rosenthal, Burton E. ....Boston, MA
Rosenthal, Carol E. ....New York, NY
Rosenthal, Chandra Triplett .....Washington, DC
Rosenthal, Charles ....Los Angeles, CA
Rosenthal, Craig L. ....St. Louis, MO
Rosenthal & Curry ....East Meadow, NY
Rosenthal, Dale Susan ....Bethesda, MD
Rosenthal, Dan
Executive Office Of The President, GV
Rosenthal, Daniel B. ....New York, NY
Rosenthal, Daniel G. ....Cincinnati, OH
Rosenthal, Daniel L. ....Portland, ME
Rosenthal, Daniel L. ....Richmond, VA
Rosenthal, Daniel P. ....Massapequa, NY
Rosenthal, David ....Miami, FL
Rosenthal, David A. ....Oakland, CA
Rosenthal, David A. ....Lafayette, IN
Rosenthal, David B. ....New York, NY
Rosenthal, David E. ....Buffalo, NY
Rosenthal, David L. ....Farmington Hills, MI
Rosenthal, David L., P.C.
Farmington Hills, MI
Rosenthal, David M. ....Durham, NC
Rosenthal, David R. ....Roanoke, VA
Rosenthal, David S. ....Phoenix, AZ
Rosenthal, David S. ....Boston, MA
Rosenthal, David S. ....New York, NY
Rosenthal, David S. ....Cincinnati, OH

Rosenthal, David S., P.C. .... Phoenix, AZ
Rosenthal, Deborah .... Los Angeles, CA
Rosenthal, Deborah B. .... Clinton, NJ
Rosenthal, Deborah G. .... Murray Hill, NJ
Rosenthal, Deborah M. .... Costa Mesa, CA
Rosenthal, Dohn M., (P.C.) .... Scottsdale, AZ
Rosenthal, Donald L. .... Washington, DC
Rosenthal, Donald L. .... New York, NY
Rosenthal, Dorene Cadoff
Treasury Department, Office of Thrift Supervision, GV
Rosenthal, Douglas .... New York, NY
Rosenthal, Douglas E. .... Washington, DC
Rosenthal & Drimer .... Syracuse, NY
Rosenthal & Druyan .... New York, NY
Rosenthal, Edward .... Miami, FL
Rosenthal, Edward B. .... Wilmington, DE
Rosenthal, Edward F. .... West Hartford, CT
Rosenthal, Edward H. .... New York, NY
Rosenthal, Edward M. .... New Britain, CT
Rosenthal, Edward M. .... East Meadow, NY
Rosenthal, Edward S. .... Los Angeles, CA
Rosenthal, Edward S. .... Alexandria, VA
Rosenthal, Elden M. .... Portland, OR
Rosenthal, Eleanor .... San Francisco, CA
Rosenthal, Ellen B. .... Detroit, MI
Rosenthal, Ellen J. .... New York, NY
Rosenthal, Eric David .... Washington, DC
Rosenthal, Eric S. .... Detroit, MI
Rosenthal, Fred J. .... Beverly Hills, CA
Rosenthal, Fred R. .... Great Neck, NY
New York, NY
Rosenthal, Gabriel S. .... Seattle, WA
Rosenthal and Ganister .... West Chester, PA
Rosenthal, Gary H. .... Mentor, OH
Rosenthal, Gary L. .... Houston, TX
Rosenthal, Gary P. .... New York, NY
Rosenthal, Gerald A.
West Palm Beach, FL
Rosenthal, Gil B.
Agency for International Development, Other Offices of A.I.D., GV
Rosenthal, Gilbert .... Baltimore, MD
Rosenthal, Glenn H. .... Chicago, IL
Rosenthal & Goldhaber, P.C.
Farmingdale, NY
Rosenthal & Greene, P.C. .... Portland, OR
Rosenthal, Greg H. .... West Palm Beach, FL
Rosenthal, Gregory A. .... Phoenix, AZ
Rosenthal, Greives & O'Bryan
Lafayette, IN
Rosenthal, Harold .... Philadelphia, PA
Rosenthal, Harold, & Associates, P.C.
Philadelphia, PA
Rosenthal, Harold J. .... San Francisco, CA
Rosenthal, Harold J. .... Albany, NY
Rosenthal, Harold J. .... New York, NY
Rosenthal, Harold L. .... Mineola, NY
Rosenthal, Harry .... Philadelphia, PA
Rosenthal, Harry J. .... Natchez, MS
Rosenthal, Henry C., Jr. .... Omaha, NE
Rosenthal, Henry L., Jr. .... Winchester, KY
Rosenthal, Herbert A. .... Washington, DC
Rosenthal, Herbert A., Chartered
Washington, DC
Rosenthal, Herbert M. .... Millbrae, CA
Rosenthal, Herman B. .... Baltimore, MD
Columbia, MD
Rosenthal & Herman, P.C. .... New York, NY
Rosenthal, Howard A. .... Philadelphia, PA
Rosenthal, Howard L. .... Kansas City, MO
Rosenthal, Ian D. .... Mobile, AL
Rosenthal, Ilene G. .... Washington, DC
Rosenthal, Irene G. .... Santa Monica, CA
Rosenthal, Irvin A. .... New York, NY
Rosenthal, Irvin H. .... New York, NY
Rosenthal, Irwin M. .... New York, NY
Rosenthal, Irwin P. .... Trenton, NJ
Rosenthal, James A. .... Sioux City, IA
Rosenthal, James A. .... New York, NY
Rosenthal, James B. .... Cleveland, OH
Rosenthal, James M. .... Washington, DC
Rosenthal, Jan Carol .... West Hartford, CT
Rosenthal, Jane E. .... Kansas City, KS
Rosenthal, Janis B. .... Columbus, OH
Rosenthal, Janis C. .... Albany, NY
Rosenthal, Jason A. .... Orlando, FL
Rosenthal, Jason M. .... Chicago, IL
Rosenthal, Jason O. B. .... Inwood, NY
Rosenthal, Jay A. .... Washington, DC
Rosenthal, Jay F. .... Boise, ID
Rosenthal, Jay N. .... Amherst, NY
Buffalo, NY
Rosenthal, Jay P. .... Phoenix, AZ
Rosenthal, Jeffrey A. .... New York, NY
Rosenthal, Jeffrey M. .... Princeton, NJ
Rosenthal, Jerod A. .... New York, NY
Rosenthal, Jerome R. .... Brooklyn, NY
Rosenthal, Jerrold P. .... East Meadow, NY
Rosenthal, Jerry .... New York, NY
Rosenthal, Joanne Miller .... Owings Mills, MD
Rosenthal, Joel B. .... Boston, MA
Rosenthal, Joel H. .... Brookfield, WI
Rosenthal, John J. .... Washington, DC
Rosenthal, John L. .... Los Angeles, CA
Rosenthal, John M. .... San Francisco, CA
Rosenthal, Jonathan H. .... Miami, FL
Rosenthal, Jonathan S. .... Baltimore, MD
Rosenthal, Jonathan S., P.C.
Baltimore, MD
Rosenthal, Joseph A. .... Hartford, CT
New Haven, CT
Rosenthal, Joseph A. .... Wilmington, DE
Rosenthal, Joseph F.
Consumer Product Safety Commission, Office of the General Counsel, GV
Rosenthal, Joseph M. .... Treasury Department, Internal Revenue Service, GV
Rosenthal, Joseph M. .... Huntington, NY
Rosenthal, Joseph S. .... St. Ann, MO
Rosenthal, Joseph S. .... New York, NY
Rosenthal, Joshua A. .... Sherman Oaks, CA
Rosenthal, Joyce E. .... Royal Oak, MI
Rosenthal Judell & Uchima
New York, NY
Rosenthal, Judith L. .... Miami, FL
Rosenthal, J. W. .... Washington, DC
Rosenthal, Karen A. .... Washington, DC
Rosenthal, Karen Beth .... New York, NY
Rosenthal, Kate .... Syracuse, NY
Rosenthal, Kathy N. .... Elmsford, NY
Rosenthal, Kathy N., P.C. .... Elmsford, NY
Rosenthal, Kaufman & Ries, P.A.
Baltimore, MD
Rosenthal, Kenneth .... New Haven, CT
Rosenthal, Kenneth W.
San Francisco, CA
Rosenthal, Kerry E., (Mr.) .... Aventura, FL
Rosenthal, Kimberly A. .... Washington, DC
Rosenthal, L. Kenneth .... Chino Hills, CA
Rosenthal, Larry S. .... Kingman, AZ
Rosenthal, Lauren S. .... Chicago, IL
Rosenthal Law Firm, The, P.C.
New York, NY
Rosenthal, Lawrence .... New York, NY
Rosenthal, Lawrence D. .... Washington, DC
Rosenthal, Lawrence G. .... Hartford, CT
Rosenthal, Lee .... Pittsburgh, PA
Rosenthal, Lee C. .... San Francisco, CA
Rosenthal, Lee S. .... Columbus, OH
Rosenthal, Leonard H. .... Natchez, MS
Rosenthal, Leonard L. .... Albany, NY
Rosenthal, Leslie Dannin .... South Orange, NJ
Rosenthal, Lewell .... Larchmont, NY
Rosenthal, Linda K. .... Washington, DC
Rosenthal, Lisa .... New York, NY
Rosenthal, Lisa D.
Federal Trade Commission, Bureau of Consumer Protection, GV
Rosenthal, Louis J. .... Baltimore, MD
Rosenthal, Louis R. .... Brooklyn, NY
Rosenthal, Lynn D. .... Fort Lauderdale, FL
Rosenthal, Marc B. .... Pittsburgh, PA
Rosenthal, Marc E. .... Chicago, IL
Rosenthal, Marci A. R. .... Washington, DC
Rosenthal, Margaret .... Los Angeles, CA
Rosenthal, Margo Beth .... Troy, MI
Rosenthal, Marjorie Lynne .... Manhasset, NY
Rosenthal, Mark A. .... Hartford, CT
Rosenthal, Mark C. .... Boston, MA
Rosenthal, Mark H. .... San Francisco, CA
San Francisco, CA
Rosenthal, Mark M. .... Los Angeles, CA
Rosenthal, Marshall W. .... Woodbury, NY
Rosenthal, Martin E. .... Chicago, IL
Rosenthal, Martin R. .... Boston, MA
Rosenthal, Martin S. .... Chevy Chase, MD
Rosenthal, Martin S. .... Columbus, OH
Rosenthal, Marvin .... Plainview, NY
Rosenthal, Marvin J. .... Rochester, NY
Rosenthal, Marvin R. .... Los Angeles, CA
Rosenthal, Mary Beth .... Washington, DC
Rosenthal, Melvin E. .... Woodside, NY
Rosenthal, Meredith Anne .... Boston, MA
Rosenthal, Meyer L. .... Morristown, NJ
Rosenthal, Michael .... Honolulu, HI
Rosenthal, Michael .... Sandpoint, ID
Rosenthal, Michael A. .... Dallas, TX
Rosenthal, Michael B. .... Cheyenne, WY
Rosenthal, Michael D. .... Chicago, IL
Rosenthal, Michael H. .... Philadelphia, PA
Rosenthal, Michael J.
Department of Justice, Tax Division, GV
Rosenthal, Michael L. .... Washington, DC
Rosenthal, Michael S. .... Atlanta, GA
Rosenthal, Michael T. .... Los Angeles, CA
Rosenthal, Monhait, Gross & Goddess, P.A.
Wilmington, DE
Rosenthal, Morton D. .... Tarzana, CA
Rosenthal, Murphey, Coblentz & Janega
Chicago, IL
Rosenthal, Murray, Esq. .... Bronx, NY
Rosenthal, Neal R. .... West Hills, CA
Rosenthal, Norbert N. .... Chicago, IL
Rosenthal, Norbert N., & Associates, Ltd.
Chicago, IL
Rosenthal, Norman L. .... Woodbury, NY
Rosenthal, Norman S. .... Clifton, NJ
Rosenthal, Norton .... Dallas, TX
Rosenthal, Oren .... Washington, DC
Rosenthal & Osha, L.L.P. .... Houston, TX
Rosenthal, Pamela M. .... Hollywood, CA
Rosenthal, Pat Booher .... Youngstown, OH
Rosenthal, Paul C. .... San Francisco, CA
Rosenthal, Paul C. .... Washington, DC
Rosenthal, Paul E. .... Orlando, FL
Rosenthal, Paul E. .... New York, NY
Rosenthal, Paula .... Berkeley, CA
Rosenthal, Peggy B. .... New York, NY
Rosenthal, Peter D. .... Palo Alto, CA
Rosenthal, Peter F. .... Philadelphia, PA
Rosenthal, Peter H. .... Indianapolis, IN
Rosenthal, Peter H. .... Boston, MA
Rosenthal, Peter M. .... Chicago, IL
Rosenthal, Philip J. .... Washington, DC
Rosenthal, Philip J. .... New York, NY
Rosenthal, Phillip B. .... Philadelphia, PA
Rosenthal, Phillip I. .... Lincolnwood, IL
Rosenthal & Popp .... Trenton, NJ
Rosenthal & Press, P.C. .... Woodbury, NY
Rosenthal, Randi L. .... New York, NY
Rosenthal, Reynolds, Mateer & Shaffer, P.C.
Dallas, TX
Rosenthal, Rhoda .... Santa Barbara, CA
Rosenthal, Rich & Costle, LLP
Washington, DC
Alexandria, VA
Fairfax, VA
Rosenthal, Richard A., Jr. .... Barrington, IL
Rosenthal, Richard D. .... Baltimore, MD
Rosenthal, Richard D. .... Wayne, NJ
Rosenthal, Richard H. .... San Francisco, CA
Rosenthal, Richard L. .... Totowa, NJ
Rosenthal, Richard M. .... Encino, CA
Rosenthal, Richard M. .... Santa Monica, CA
Rosenthal, Richard M. .... New York, NY
Rosenthal, Richard M. .... Pittsburgh, PA
Rosenthal, Richard R. .... Birmingham, AL
Rosenthal, Richard R., P.C.
Birmingham, AL
Rosenthal, Richard S. .... St. Louis, MO
Rosenthal, Richard W. .... New York, NY
Rosenthal, Risa .... Los Angeles, CA
Rosenthal, Robert .... Garden City, NY
Rosenthal, Robert .... New York, NY
Rosenthal, Robert .... Portland, OR
Rosenthal, Robert A. .... San Antonio, TX
Rosenthal, Robert D. .... Jericho, NY
Rosenthal, Robert E. .... Monterey, CA
Rosenthal, Robert E. .... Philadelphia, PA
Rosenthal, Robert F. .... North Hollywood, CA
Rosenthal, Robert F. .... Denver, CO
Rosenthal, Robert L. .... Las Vegas, NV
Rosenthal, Robert L. .... New York, NY
Rosenthal, Robert M. .... Los Angeles, CA
Rosenthal, Robert, P.C. .... Portland, OR
Rosenthal, Robert S. .... Hartford, CT
Rosenthal, Robert S. .... St. Louis, MO
Rosenthal, Roger C. .... Washington, DC
Rosenthal & Rosenthal .... Natchez, MS
Philadelphia, PA
Rosenthal Rosenthal Rasco Stok Denberg
Aventura, FL
Rosenthal, Ruby Leppo .... Michigan City, IN
Rosenthal, Russell .... Miami, FL
Rosenthal, Russell H. .... Columbus, OH
Rosenthal, S. David .... Sacramento, CA
Rosenthal, Samuel .... Washington, DC
Rosenthal, Sandra .... Sudbury, MA
Rosenthal, Sandra J. .... Beachwood, OH
Rosenthal, Sanford .... Southfield, MI
Rosenthal and Schanfield, Professional Corporation .... Chicago, IL
Rosenthal, Scot D. .... Newark, NJ
Rosenthal, Scott S. .... Cleveland, OH
Rosenthal, Shari L. .... Los Angeles, CA
Rosenthal, Sharon Traci .... New York, NY
Rosenthal, Shawn M. .... New York, NY
Rosenthal, Sheldon .... San Francisco, CA
Rosenthal, Sheldon M. .... Springfield, MA
Rosenthal, Sheldon R. .... Miami, FL
Rosenthal, Sidney .... Spokane, WA
Rosenthal, Siegel, Muenkel & Maloney, LLP
Amherst, NY
Buffalo, NY
Rosenthal, Simon M. .... San Francisco, CA
Rosenthal, Sol .... Los Angeles, CA
Rosenthal & Stark .... Indianapolis, IN
Rosenthal, Stephen B. .... Tamarac, FL
Rosenthal, Stephen D. .... Richmond, VA
Rosenthal, Stephen L. .... Dallas, TX
Rosenthal, Stephen N. .... Miami, FL
Rosenthal, Steven .... New York, NY
Rosenthal, Steven Louis .... Mineola, NY
Rosenthal, Steven M. .... New York, NY
Rosenthal, Steven P. .... Boston, MA
Rosenthal, Steven R. .... Coral Springs, FL
Rosenthal, Steven S. .... San Francisco, CA
Rosenthal, Steven S. .... Washington, DC
Rosenthal, Stuart A. .... Great Neck, NY
Rosenthal, Stuart L. .... Boston, MA
Rosenthal, Stuart M. .... Beverly Hills, CA
Rosenthal, Stuart P. .... Washington, DC
Rosenthal, Stuart S. .... Pompano Beach, FL
Rosenthal, Stuart S., P.A.
Pompano Beach, FL
Rosenthal, Sue D. .... Houston, TX
Rosenthal, Susan G. .... New York, NY
Rosenthal, Thomas S. .... New York, NY
Rosenthal, Thorn .... New York, NY
Rosenthal, Todd A.
Commodity Futures Trading Commission, Office of Proceedings, GV
Rosenthal, Trent L. .... Houston, TX
Rosenthal, Wayne P. .... Miami, FL
Rosenthal and Weisberg, P.C.
Norristown, PA
Philadelphia, PA
Rosenthal & Weissman, P.A.
West Palm Beach, FL
Rosenthal, William .... St. Joseph, MO
Rosenthal, William E. .... Windsor Locks, CT
Rosenthal, William J. .... Baltimore, MD
Rosenthal, William P. .... Chicago, IL
Rosenthal & Zimmerman
Costa Mesa, CA
Rosenthal-Goldsmith, Dayna Renee
Bethesda, MD
Rosentrater, Gary L. .... Denver, CO
Rosentreter, John D. .... Wichita Falls, TX
Rosenvold, Robert E. .... West Fargo, ND
Rosenwald, Jay N. .... Tarzana, CA
Rosenwald, Lawrence S. .... Philadelphia, PA
Rosenwald, Lawrence S., P.C.
Philadelphia, PA
Wynnewood, PA
Rosenwald, Peter .... Cincinnati, OH
Rosenwald, Peter B., II .... Baltimore, MD
Rosenwald, Robert F., Jr. .... Miami, FL
Rosenwald, Sharon B. .... Milford, OH
Rosenwasser, Arnold R. .... New York, NY
Rosenwasser, Arnold R., P.C.
New York, NY
Rosenwasser, Fern .... Fort Lauderdale, FL
Rosenwasser, Lisa G. .... Glendale, CA
Rosenwasser, Marc R. .... Pittsburgh, PA
Rosenwasser, Mike .... New York, NY
Rosenwasser, Robert D. .... Somerset, NJ
Rosenwasser, Ronald N. .... Boca Raton, FL
Rosenwasser, Steven J. .... Los Angeles, CA
Rosenwasser, Steven Jason .... Atlanta, GA
Rosenwasser, Stewart A., P.C. .... Walden, NY
Rosenwater, Bruce S.
West Palm Beach, FL
Rosenwater, Bruce S., & Associates, P.A.
Boca Raton, FL
West Palm Beach, FL
Rosenwein & Oberholtzer .... Chicago, IL
Rosenwein, Thomas D. .... Chicago, IL
Rosenwinkel, Julie A. .... Hammond, IN
Rosenzweig, Alexander .... Lexington, SC
Rosenzweig, Andrew E. .... Phoenix, AZ
Rosenzweig, Anne J. .... San Jose, CA
Rosenzweig, Barry A. .... Edina, MN
Rosenzweig, Burke .... Phoenix, AZ
Rosenzweig, Charles L. .... Secaucus, NJ
Rosenzweig, Charles L. .... New York, NY
Rosenzweig, Darryl B. .... Chicago, IL
Rosenzweig, David A. .... New York, NY
Rosenzweig, David L. .... Cleveland, OH
Rosenzweig, David M. .... Los Angeles, CA
Rosenzweig, David S. .... Boston, MA
Rosenzweig, Dena J. .... Atlanta, GA
Rosenzweig, Elias .... New York, NY
Rosenzweig, Ellen P. .... Brooklyn, NY
Rosenzweig, Ellis B. .... Chicago, IL
Rosenzweig, Eric Jon .... Palo Alto, CA
Rosenzweig, Fagan & Sheehan
New Britain, CT
Rosenzweig, Francine .... Boston, MA
Rosenzweig, Gary K. .... Corona, CA
Rosenzweig, George C. .... Newnan, GA
Rosenzweig, Harlan J. .... Stamford, CT
Rosenzweig, Harvey A. .... Atlanta, GA
Rosenzweig, Ira J. .... New Orleans, LA
Rosenzweig, Irving .... New York, NY
Rosenzweig, Irwin N. .... Philadelphia, PA
Rosenzweig, Israel .... New Britain, CT
Rosenzweig, Jeff .... Little Rock, AR
Rosenzweig, Joan Huddy
Department of Labor, Office of Secretary, GV
Rosenzweig, Jodi Sydell
Florham Park, NJ
Rosenzweig, Jones & MacNabb, P.C.
Newnan, GA
Peachtree City, GA
Rosenzweig, Joseph A. .... Tamarac, FL
Rosenzweig, Joseph I. .... New York, NY
Rosenzweig, Kenneth M. .... Chicago, IL
Rosenzweig, Laurie S. .... Rutland, VT
Rosenzweig Law Office, P.A. .... Edina, MN
Rosenzweig, Lawrence R., (P.C.)
Santa Monica, CA
Rosenzweig, Linda E. .... Kansas City, MO
Rosenzweig, Lisa Renee .... Brooklyn, NY
Rosenzweig, Loren Callan
Chestnut Hill, MA
Rosenzweig, M. Claire .... New Orleans, LA
Rosenzweig, Michael .... Atlanta, GA
Rosenzweig, Mitchell S. .... Cherry Hill, NJ
Rosenzweig, Paula .... Coral Gables, FL
Rosenzweig, Peter Ryan .... Philadelphia, PA
Rosenzweig, Philip S. .... Trenton, NJ
Rosenzweig, Richard A.
Staten Island, NY
Rosenzweig, Richard L. .... Pittsburgh, PA
Rosenzweig & Rosenzweig .... Pittsburgh, PA
Rosenzweig, Sidney A. .... Washington, DC
Rosenzweig, Stefan M. .... San Francisco, CA
Rosenzweig, Steven Z. .... New York, NY
Rosenzweig, Susanne Kaufmann
Newark, NJ
New York, NY
Rosenzweig, Theodore B. .... New York, NY
Rosenzweig, Victor M. .... New York, NY
Rosepink & Estes, P.L.L.C.
Scottsdale, AZ
Rosepink, Robert J. .... Scottsdale, AZ
Rosequist, David K. .... Las Vegas, NV
Rosequist, Ronald V. .... Oakland, CA
Roser, Christopher P. .... Cincinnati, OH
Roser, Samuel J. .... St. Johns, AZ
Rosero, Linda Cassone, Esq.
Kew Gardens, NY
Roses, Steven M. .... Brooklyn, NY
Roseta, Richard A. .... Eugene, OR
Rose-Tappert, Jill W. .... Denver, CO
Rosett, Arthur I. .... Los Angeles, CA
Rosett, Richard L. .... Santa Monica, CA
Rosett, Wendy S. .... Shaker Heights, OH
Rosette, Christopher J. .... Chicago, IL
Rosette, Kristina .... Washington, DC
Rosette, Robert A. .... Washington, DC
Omaha, NE
Rosetti, George, Jr. .... Gulfport, MS
Rosetti, Jerry J. .... Gulfport, MS
Rosetti, Kimberly S. .... Gulfport, MS
Rosetto, Bruce C. .... Boca Raton, FL
Roseveare, Christine D. .... Dallas, TX
Rosewarne, Philip J. .... Ann Arbor, MI
Rosewater, Robert D. .... Cleveland, OH
Rosfeld, Roydell S. .... Silver Spring, MD
Rosh, Jessica A. .... New York, NY
Rosh, Joseph P. .... Hauppauge, NY
Rosh, Kenneth I. .... New York, NY
Rosh, Meyer .... New York, NY
Rosh, Robert H. .... White Plains, NY
Rosha, Cathlene L. .... Los Angeles, CA

Rosha, Darrin M. ....St. Paul, MN
Roshak, Anthony B. ....Flint, MI
Roshala, Danielle L. ....Los Angeles, CA
Roshanali, Dabeer M. ....Chicago, IL
Roshanian, Tamineh ....Washington, DC
Roshan-Zamir, Perry ....Santa Monica, CA
Roshar, Michael L. ....Milwaukee, WI
Roshia, Marylou K. ....Buffalo, NY
Roshka Heyman & DeWulf, PLC
Phoenix, AZ
Roshka, Paul J., Jr. ....Phoenix, AZ
Roshkind, Robin Bogen
West Palm Beach, FL
Roshkoff, Marla G. ....Philadelphia, PA
Roshkoff, Robert L. ....Philadelphia, PA
Rosholt, John A. ....Twin Falls, ID
Rosholt, John C. ....Minneapolis, MN
Rosholt, Robertson & Tucker, Chartered
Boise, ID
Twin Falls, ID
Rosholt, Stephen ....Minneapolis, MN
Roshuk, Alex T. ....Brooklyn, NY
Rosi Law Offices, P.C. ....Traverse City, MI
Rosi, Philip R. ....Traverse City, MI
Rosi, Robert L. ....Tampa, FL
Rosiak, Richard J. ....Downey, CA
Rosic, Edward A., Jr. ....Washington, DC
Rosic, George S. ....Deerfield, IL
Rosie, Frank J. ....Humble, TX
Rosie, John F. ....Fairbanks, AK
Rosiek-Cardin, Mary E. ....Crete, IL
Rosiello, Michael ....Indianapolis, IN
Rosiello, Thomas A. ....Chicago, IL
Rosien, Scott ....San Francisco, CA
Rosier, Jeffrey P. ....New York, NY
Rosier, Jeffrey S. ....San Antonio, TX
Rosier, Joseph A. ....Lake Mary, FL
Rosier, Phyllis M. ....Starke, FL
Rosier, Phyllis M., P.A. ....Starke, FL
Rosier, Richard M. ....New York, NY
Rosik, Lynn ....Salem, OR
Rosillo, Albert P. ....Miami, FL
Rosillo, Robert A. ....West Palm Beach, FL
Rosin, A. Robert ....San Mateo, CA
Rosin, Benjamin J. ....New York, NY
Rosin, David I. ....Huntington Woods, MI
Rosin & Elperin, A Professional Corporation
Los Angeles, CA
Rosin, Eric M. ....Los Angeles, CA
Rosin, Gary S. ....Houston, TX
Rosin, George H. ....Akron, OH
Rosin, Jeffrey M. ....Boston, MA
New York, NY
Rosin, Marcus A. ....Sarasota, FL
Rosin, Marla Jo ....Tampa, FL
Rosin, Matthew L. ....Philadelphia, PA
Rosin, Nat ....Escondido, CA
Rosin & Reiniger ....New York, NY
Rosin, Richard E. ....Mount Clemens, MI
Rosin, Richard E. ....Philadelphia, PA
Rosin, Richard M. ....Los Angeles, CA
Rosin, Robert A. ....Chicago, IL
Rosin, Robert A. ....Philadelphia, PA
Rosin, Robert P. ....Sarasota, FL
Rosin, Stephen V. ....Clermont, FL
Rosin, Stephen V., Law Firm, Chartered, The
Clermont, FL
Rosin, William L. ....Bloomfield Hills, MI
Rosinek, Jeffrey ....Miami, FL
Rosing, Heather L. ....Los Angeles, CA
San Diego, CA
Rosing, Robert J. ....Louisville, KY
Rosing, Sheldon ....Chicago, IL
Rosing, Smith, Ericksen, Zeit & Stanczak, Ltd.
Waukegan, IL
Rosing, William G. ....Waukegan, IL
Rosingana, Raphael L. ....San Bruno, CA
Rosini, Anthony J. ....Shamokin, PA
Rosini, James E. ....New York, NY
Rosini, James J. ....Shamokin, PA
Rosini, Matthew M. ....Pittsburgh, PA
Rosini, Neil J. ....New York, NY
Rosini, Robert J. ....Hockessin, DE
Rosino, John E. ....Sandusky, OH
Rosinski, Douglas J. ....Washington, DC
Rosinski, John P. ....Madison, WI
Rosinski, Marcella L. ....Hamburg, NY
Rosinski, Thomas H. ....Hamburg, NY
Rosinsky, Timothy P. ....Huntington, WV
Rosintoski, Lawrence J. ....Charleston, SC
Rosinus, David A. ....New York, NY
Rosiny, Allen P. ....New York, NY
Rosiny, Frank R. ....New York, NY
Rosiny & Rosiny ....New York, NY
Roska, A. Kay ....Dallas, TX
Roska, John ....Mattoon, IL
Roskam, Peter J. ....Wheaton, IL
Roske, Henry ....New York, NY
Roske, Randall J. ....Las Vegas, NV
Roske, Susan Deems ....Las Vegas, NV
Roskelley, Rick D. ....Las Vegas, NV
Rosken, Brad ....Garden City, NY
Roskens, Lisa Y. ....Omaha, NE
Roskens, William E. ....Omaha, NE
Rosker, Benjamin H.
La Canada Flintridge, CA
Roskey, Colin Thomas ....Washington, DC
Roski-Amendola, Reon ....Los Angeles, CA
Roskin, Howard E. ....Miami, FL
Roskin, Howard E., P.A. ....Miami, FL
Roskin and Leeds ....St. Louis, MO
Roskin, Preston E. ....St. Louis, MO
Roskin, William A. ....New York, NY
Roskind, Frank D. ....Cheverly, MD
Roskoff, Daniel ....New York, NY
Roskoph Associates, Professional Corporation
Palo Alto, CA
Roskoph, Paul H. ....Palo Alto, CA
Roskoph, Robert K. ....Palo Alto, CA
Roskopp, Frederick J. ....Mount Clemens, MI
Roskos, David M. ....Trenton, NJ
Roskos, Joseph W.
Department of Commerce,
Patent and Trademark Office, GV
Roskos, Joseph W. ....King Of Prussia, PA
Roskovensky, Vincent J., II ....Uniontown, PA
Roskovich, Robert J. ....Virginia Beach, VA
Rosky, Burton S. ....Beverly Hills, CA
Rosky, Dianne L. ....New York, NY
Roslansky, John W. ....Wellesley, MA
Rosler, Craig N. ....Birmingham, AL
Rosler, Debra B. ....Menlo Park, CA
Rosler, Russell R. ....Columbus, OH
Roslin, Martin ....Colorado Springs, CO
Roslokken, Daniel W. ....Midland Park, NJ
Rosloniec, James J. ....Grand Rapids, MI
Roslund, Bryan ....Rockville, MD
Roslund, James T. ....Alma, MI
Roslyn, Barbara D. ....New York, NY
Rosman, Adam L. ....Washington, DC
Rosman, Barbara Goldberg
Cleveland, OH
Rosman, Barbara Goldberg
South Euclid, OH
Rosman, Brian P. ....Boston, MA
Rosman, David M. ....Los Angeles, CA
Rosman, Donna ....Miami, FL
Rosman & Germain LLP
Los Angeles, CA
Rosman, Jay B. ....Fort Myers, FL
Rosman, Judith A. ....St. Louis, MO
Rosman, Lewis ....Philadelphia, PA
Rosman, Marvin A. ....Richmond, VA
Rosman, Michael E. ....Washington, DC
Rosman, Richard D. ....Encino, CA
Rosman, Robert D. ....Southfield, MI
Rosman, Stephen L. ....Council Bluffs, IA
Rosman, Warren ....Cleveland, OH
Rosmann, David J. ....Los Angeles, CA
Rosmarin, John G. ....Hamilton, OH
Rosmarin, Noah R. ....Boston, MA
Rosmarin, R. Scott ....North Caldwell, NJ
Rosmarin, Sam ....Spring Valley, NY
Rosmarin, Shurl ....Chicago, IL
Rosmarin, Susan G. ....Newark, NJ
New York, NY
Rosmarin, Yvonne W. ....Arlington, MA
Rosmini, Maria S. ....Philadelphia, PA
Rosnack, Rebecca L. ....Austin, TX
Rosnell, Tara M. ....Cincinnati, OH
Rosner, Abraham J. ....Washington, DC
Rosner, Alan E. ....Jacksonville, FL
Rosner, Andrew ....Carle Place, NY
Rosner, Arthur J. ....New York, NY
Rosner and Associates Co., L.P.A.
Cleveland, OH
Rosner, Bernat ....San Ramon, CA
Rosner, Beth J. ....Chicago, IL
Rosner, Bonnie Rentschler ....Hollywood, FL
Rosner, Brian ....New York, NY
Rosner, Cary G. ....New York, NY
Rosner, Corinne B. ....Fort Lauderdale, FL
Rosner, Corinne B., P.A.
Fort Lauderdale, FL
Rosner, Daniel E. ....Philadelphia, PA
Rosner, David L., (A Professional Law Corporation) ....Los Angeles, CA
Rosner, David N. ....Hollywood, FL
Rosner, David S. ....New York, NY
Rosner, Douglas B. ....Boston, MA
Rosner, Earl M. ....Santa Fe, NM
Rosner, Ellen S. ....Jacksonville, FL
Rosner, Eugene ....Clark, NJ
Rosner & Grayson, P.C. ....Philadelphia, PA
Rosner, Hallen ....San Diego, CA
Rosner, Helen B. ....Neptune, NJ
Rosner, Irving ....Painesville, OH
Rosner, James F. ....Towson, MD
Rosner, Jay R. ....New York, NY
Rosner, Jodi C. ....San Francisco, CA
Rosner, John L. ....Tallahassee, FL
Rosner, Jonathan L. ....Westport, CT
New York, NY
Rosner, Julie E. ....Lincolnwood, IL
Rosner, Kimberly R. ....Tempe, AZ
Rosner & Law ....San Diego, CA
Rosner, Leonard Allen ....Rochester, NY
Rosner, Lisa Miner ....Cincinnati, OH
Rosner, Louis ....Woodbury, NJ
Philadelphia, PA
Rosner, Louis J. ....Merchantville, NJ
Rosner, Marian Probst ....New York, NY
Rosner, Martin B. ....Brooklyn, NY
Rosner, Mary Winward ....Las Cruces, NM
Rosner, Michael J. ....Akron, OH
Rosner Murray & Tucker LLP
Westport, CT
New York, NY
Rosner, Myron ....Woodbridge, NJ
Rosner & Nocera ....Monmouth Junction, NJ
New York, NY
Rosner, Norma J. ....Houston, TX
Rosner, Norman H. ....Atlanta, GA
Rosner, Owens & Nunziato, L.L.P.
Los Angeles, CA
Rosner, Randy G. ....Monmouth Junction, NJ
New York, NY
Rosner, Richard A. ....Cleveland, OH
Rosner, Robert E. ....West Bloomfield, MI
Rosner, Saml. M. ....Miami Beach, FL
Rosner, Seth ....Greenfield Center, NY
New York, NY
Rosner & Simon, P.A. ....Hollywood, FL
Rosner, William R. ....Cleveland, OH
Rosnick, Harold L. ....Bridgeport, CT
Rosnik, Robert R. ....Denver, CO
Rosof, Alan H. ....New York, NY
Rosof, Benjamin J. ....New York, NY
Rosof, Eric ....New York, NY
Rosoff, David M. ....Harrison, NY
Rosoff, Howard L., (P.C.) ....Los Angeles, CA
Rosoff, Joan C. ....Philadelphia, PA
Rosoff, Michael H. ....New York, NY
Rosoff, Noah P. ....New York, NY
Rosoff, Robert J. ....Berkeley, CA
Rosoff & Rosoff ....New York, NY
Rosoff, Schiffres & Barta ....Los Angeles, CA
Rosoff, Sidney D. ....New York, NY
Rosoff, Thelma ....New York, NY
Rosoff, William G. ....Treasury Department,
Office of Regulations and Rulings, GV
Rosoff, William L. ....New York, NY
Rosolio, Charles E. ....Baltimore, MD
Towson, MD
Rosove, Debra L. ....Los Angeles, CA
Rosow, Malcolm B. ....Roslyn Heights, NY
Rosow, Richard F. ....Minneapolis, MN
Rosow, Stanley M. ....Yountville, CA
Rosow, Stuart L. ....New York, NY
Rospars, William
Department of Transportation,
U. S. Coast Guard, GV
Rosplock, Perez & Ezzone ....Willoughby, OH
Rosplock, Robert S. ....Willoughby, OH
Ross, A. Joseph ....Boston, MA
Ross, A. Richard ....Roseland, NJ
Ross, A. Scott ....Nashville, TN
Ross, A. A. Jack, IV ....San Antonio, TX
Ross, Abbe L. ....Boston, MA
Ross, Abraham ....Floral Park, NY
Ross, Adam ....Los Angeles, CA
Grand Prairie, TX
Ross, Adam B. ....Grand Prairie, TX
Ross, Adam D. ....Washington, DC
Ross, Aimee Dicker ....New York, NY
Ross, Al ....Beverly Hills, CA
Ross, Alan ....Plainview, NY
Ross, Alan B. ....Tulsa, OK
Ross, Alan D. ....Encino, CA
Ross, Alan D., Law Corporation
Encino, CA
Ross, Alan G. ....Irvine, CA
Ross, Alan G. ....Cleveland, OH
Ross, Alan H. ....Philadelphia, PA
Ross, Alan J. ....Cleveland, OH
Ross, Alan, Jr. ....Los Angeles, CA
Ross, Alan L. ....Rochester, NY
Ross, Alan S. ....Miami, FL
Ross, Albert C. ....Arlington, TX
Ross, Albert M. ....Kansas City, KS
Ross, Alexa R. ....Atlanta, GA
Ross, Alexander C. ....Department of Justice,
Civil Rights Division, GV
Ross, Alexander J. ....Hurricane, WV
Ross, Alexander M. ....Buckhannon, WV
Ross, Alexandra ....San Francisco, CA
Ross, Alfred J., Jr. ....New York, NY
Ross, Allan ....Melville, NY
Ross, Allen ....New York, NY
Ross, Allen N. ....New York, NY
Ross, Allison ....New York, NY
Ross, Allison J. ....New York, NY
Ross, Allyne R. ....Brooklyn, NY
Ross, Alvin L. ....Omaha, NE
Ross, Andrea E.L. ....Pasadena, CA
Ross, Andrew ....Walnut Creek, CA
Ross, Andrew ....New York, NY
Ross, Andrew D. ....Chicago Heights, IL
Ross, Andrew M. ....New York, NY
Ross, Andrew P. ....New York, NY
Ross, Andrew R. ....West Palm Beach, FL
Ross, Angela T. ....Grand Rapids, MI
Ross, Anne E. ....Dayton, OH
Ross, Anne Elizabeth ....Madison, WI
Ross, Annette Z. P. ....Venice, FL
Westfield, MA
Ross, Anthony F. ....Cheyenne, WY
Ross, Anthony G, III ....Pittsburgh, PA
Ross, Anthony J. ....Roslindale, MA
Ross, Anthony J. ....Pittsburgh, PA
Ross, Arnold J. ....New York, NY
Ross, Art ....Honolulu, HI
Ross, Arthur D. ....Great Neck, NY
Ross & Associates ....Miami, FL
Ross & Associates, P.A. ....Brandon, FL
Tampa, FL
Temple Terrace, FL
Wesley Chapel, FL
Ross, Audrey Ann ....Fresno, CA
Ross, August ....Omaha, NE
Ross, Autry W. ....Houston, TX
Ross, B. Schlessinger ....Newport, RI
Ross, Banks, May, Cron & Cavin, P.C.
Houston, TX
Ross, Barbara Ava ....Kew Gardens Hills, NY
Ross, Barbara D. ....Mount Vernon, NY
Ross, Barbara E. ....Taylor, MI
Ross, Barbara K. ....Pittsburgh, PA
Ross, Barbara M. ....Minneapolis, MN
Ross & Barlow ....Savannah, TN
Ross, Barry A. ....Long Beach, CA
Ross, Barry C. ....New York, NY
Ross, Barry L. ....Minneapolis, MN
Ross, Ben B. ....Thomson, GA
Ross, Bennett L. ....Atlanta, GA
Ross, Bert A. ....Indiana, PA
Ross, Bert T. ....Sterling Heights, MI
Ross, Beth A. ....Vail, CO
Ross, Beth A. ....Great Neck, NY
Ross, Beth Anne ....Seattle, WA
Ross, Beverly D. ....Washington, DC
Ross, Beverly Jean ....Miami, FL
Ross, Bill E. ....Blytheville, AR
Ross & Block, P.C. ....Chicago, IL
Ross, Bonnie M. ....San Jose, CA
Ross, Bonnie Mae ....Solon, OH
Ross, Bradford ....Washington, DC
Ross, Bradley D. ....Los Angeles, CA
Ross, Brendan J. ....Washington, DC
Ross, Brett A. ....Birmingham, AL
Ross, Brian ....Hayward, CA
Ross, Brian A. ....Los Angeles, CA
Ross, Brian L. ....New York, NY
Ross, Brian M. ....Tampa, FL
Ross, Brittain & Schonberg Co., L.P.A.
Cleveland, OH
Ross, Bruce A. ....Raleigh, NC
Ross, Bruce S. ....Los Angeles, CA
Ross & Brunner ....Indianapolis, IN
Ross, Burt L. ....Englewood, NJ
Ross, Burton G. ....Minneapolis, MN
Ross, Burton R. ....New York, NY
Ross, C. Lewis ....San Francisco, CA
Ross, C. Randolph ....Philadelphia, PA
Ross, C. Thomas ....Winston-Salem, NC
Ross, C. Todd ....Albany, GA
Ross, Carl W. ....Monroe, WI
Monticello, WI
Ross, Carol Fein ....New York, NY
Ross, Carol Motyka ....Norwalk, CT
Ross, Carroll L. ....Athens, TN
Ross, Carter J. ....Columbia, MO
Ross, Cary A. ....Westlake Village, CA
Ross, Cary Alan, A Professional Corporation
Westlake Village, CA
Ross, Catherine A. ....Lawrenceville, NJ
Ross, Cecil H. ....Nashville, TN
Ross, Cecile I. ....West Palm Beach, FL
Ross, Chad A. ....Columbus, OH
Ross, Charles A. ....New York, NY
Ross, Charles E. ....Jackson, MS
Ross, Charles G. ....Pittsburgh, PA
Ross, Charles N. ....St. Davids, PA
Ross, Charles W. ....St. Petersburg, FL
Ross, Chester M. ....New York, NY
Ross, Chris ....Ada, OK
Ross, Christina Bieniek ....New York, NY
Ross, Christine ....Monmouth, IL
Ross, Christopher J. ....Pensacola, FL
Ross, Christopher T. W. ....Buffalo, NY
Ross, Clifford C. ....Park City, UT
Ross, Clifford J. ....Manchester, NH
Ross & Cohen, LLP ....New York, NY
Ross & Connor, L.L.P. ....Austin, TX
Ross, Curlee ....Los Angeles, CA
Ross, Curtis B. ....Chicago, IL
Ross, Cye E. ....New York, NY
Ross, Cynthia Ann ....Fort Myers, FL
Ross, Dale ....Fort Lauderdale, FL
Ross, Dale Yamada ....Kailua-Kona, HI
Ross, Dalton Roberts ....Shreveport, LA
Ross, Daniel ....New York, NY
Ross, Daniel A. ....New York, NY
Ross, Daniel B. ....Austin, TX
Ross, Daniel C. ....Patchogue, NY
Ross, Daniel D. ....Palm Beach, FL
Ross, Daniel F.
Federal Deposit Insurance Corporation,
Trial Litigation Section, GV
Ross, Daniel J. ....Malibu, CA
Ross, Daniel J. ....Kansas City, MO
Ross, Daniel J. ....New York, NY
Ross, Daniel M. ....Chevy Chase, MD
Ross, Daniel R. ....Lake Success, NY
Ross, Daniel R. ....Philadelphia, PA
Ross, Daniel S. ....Middleburgh, NY
Ross, Danny R. ....Houston, TX
Ross, Darlene Y. ....Ashland, KY
Ross, Darrell S. ....Cranston, RI
Ross, Darren A. ....New York, NY
Ross, Darryl ....Santa Ana, CA
Ross, David ....Baltimore, MD
Ross, David ....Cleveland, OH
Ross, David ....Newkirk, OK
Ross, David A. ....Las Vegas, NV
Ross, David A. ....New York, NY
Ross, David Bennet ....New York, NY
Ross, David E. ....Washington, DC
Ross, David E. ....New York, NY
Ross, David E. ....Cincinnati, OH
Ross, David E., II ....Salt Lake City, UT
Ross, David Eric ....Westport, CT
Ross, David F. ....Bellevue, WA
Ross, David G. ....Atlanta, GA
Ross, David G. ....Washington, NJ
Ross, David G. ....Rochester, NY
Ross, David Gray ....Upper Marlboro, MD
Ross, David H. ....Santa Cruz, CA
Ross, David H. ....Flushing, NY
Ross, David J.
Executive Office Of The President,
Office of the U.S. Trade Representative, GV
Ross, David J. ....Evansville, WI
Ross, David Jonathan ....Salem, OR
Ross, David K. ....Stockton, CA
Ross, David K. ....New Ulm, MN
Ross, David L. ....Miami, FL
Ross, David L. ....Richmond, VA
Ross, David M. ....Washington, DC
Ross, David M. ....Anderson, SC
Ross, David M. ....Addison, TX
Ross, David P. ....Kansas City, MO
Ross, David R. ....Los Angeles, CA
Ross, David S. ....Northampton, MA
Ross, David S. ....Houston, TX
Ross, David T. ....Arlington, TX
Ross, David W. ....Pittsburgh, PA
Ross, David W. ....San Antonio, TX
Ross, Dawn M. ....Pensacola, FL
Ross, Dawn Marie ....Santa Rosa, CA
Ross, Dawn Patrice ....Los Angeles, CA

Ross, Nicole L. ... Long Beach, CA
Caledonia, MI
Ross, Nina J. ... Mamaroneck, NY
Ross, Norman C. ... Gloucester, MA
Ross, Norman I. ... Paterson, NJ
Ross & Norton, PLLP ... Chaska, MN
Ross & O'Brien, P.C. ... Colorado Springs, CO
Ross, Otho B. ... New York, NY
New York, NY
Ross, Pamela Homer
Greenwood Village, CO
Ross, Patrick ... Los Angeles, CA
Ross, Patrick A. ... Horse Cave, KY
Ross, Patrick G. ... Anchorage, AK
Ross, Paul B. ... New York, NY
Ross, Paul D. ... Lexington, KY
Ross, Paul E. ... Chaska, MN
Ross, Paul L., Jr. ... Boston, MA
Ross, Paul M. ... East Lansing, MI
Ross, Paul M., P.C. ... East Lansing, MI
Ross, Paul R. ... Henderson, NC
Ross, Paul W. ... Hackensack, NJ
Ross, Paulette E. ... Buffalo, NY
Ross, Peggy M. ... Santa Clarita, CA
Ross, Peter A. ... Albuquerque, NM
Ross, Peter B. ... Chicago, IL
Ross, Peter D. ... Washington, DC
Ross, Peter E. ... Lincolnshire, IL
Ross, Peter G. ... Chicago, IL
Ross, Peter M. ... Ipswich, MA
Ross, Peter W. ... Beverly Hills, CA
Ross, Philip A. ... East Orange, NJ
Ross, Philip A. ... Newkirk, OK
Ross, Philip J.
Environmental Protection Agency, Office of the General Counsel, GV
Ross, Philip L. ... San Francisco, CA
Ross, Philip M. ... Castroville, TX
Ross, Philip S. ... New York, NY
Ross and Powell ... Riverdale, MD
Ross, R. Christina
General Services Administration, Office of Regional Counsel, GV
Ross, R. Ian ... North Las Vegas, NV
Ross, R. Mitchell ... Clarksville, TN
Ross, R. Oliver ... Phoenix, AZ
Ross, Rakhael ... Chicago, IL
Ross, Ralph ... Minneapolis, MN
Ross, Ralph L. ... Dallas, TX
Ross, Ralph L. ... Dallas, TX
Ross, Ralph W. ... Canton, OH
Ross, Randy ... Fort Collins, CO
Ross, Randy Ellen
Rancho Palos Verdes, CA
Ross, Raymond F. ... Westport, CT
Ross, Rebecca L. ... Washington, DC
Ross, Renee S. ... Washington, DC
Ross, Rhonda L. ... Bloomfield Hills, MI
Ross, Ricci C. ... Alexandria, LA
Ross, Richard ... Gaithersburg, MD
Greenbelt, MD
Ross, Richard A. ... Minneapolis, MN
Ross, Richard A. ... Carle Place, NY
Ross, Richard A. ... Mount Vernon, NY
Ross, Richard C. ... Mount Vernon, NY
Ross, Richard C. ... Sebring, OH
Ross, Richard C., Co., L.P.A. ... Sebring, OH
Ross, Richard D. ... Topeka, KS
Ross, Richard D. ... Falls Church, VA
Ross, Richard E. ... Venice, CA
Ross, Richard F. ... Phoenix, AZ
Ross, Richard G. ... Bridgeport, CT
Ross, Richard G. ... Cleveland, OH
Ross, Richard H. ... Sacramento, CA
Ross, Richard L. ... Chesterfield, MO
Ross, Richard L. ... McConnelsville, OH
Ross, Richard M. ... Sacramento, CA
Ross, Richard R. ... Los Angeles, CA
Ross, Richard R. ... St. Louis, MO
Ross, Richard S. ... Fort Lauderdale, FL
Ross, Richard S. ... Pittsburgh, PA
Ross, Richard S. ... Ridgefield, WA
Ross, Richard W. ... Chicago, IL
Ross, Richard W. ... Columbus, OH
Ross, Rita A. ... Irvine, CA
Ross, Rita Wiles
Federal Deposit Insurance Corporation, Corporate Affairs Section, GV
Ross, Robert ... Philadelphia, PA
Ross, Robert A. ... Los Angeles, CA
Ross, Robert A. ... Huntington, NY
Ross, Robert A. ... Kew Gardens, NY
Ross, Robert A. ... Cleveland, OH
Ross, Robert A., Jr. ... Sturgeon Bay, WI
Ross, Robert B. ... New York, NY
Ross, Robert B. ... Midland, TX
Ross, Robert C. ... Jupiter, FL
Ross, Robert C. ... New York, NY
Ross, Robert D. ... Little Rock, AR
Ross, Robert D. ... Dayton, OH
Ross, Robert E. ... Iowa City, IA
Ross, Robert I.
Department of Transportation, Office of the General Counsel, GV
Ross, Robert J. ... Inverness, IL
Ross, Robert L. ... Columbia, MO
Ross, Robert L. ... Lawton, OK
Ross, Robert M. ... Los Angeles, CA
Ross, Robert M. ... Philadelphia, PA
Ross, Robert M. ... Fairfax, VA
Ross, Robert N., Jr. (Professional Corporation) ... Houston, TX
Ross, Robert P. ... Palm Beach Gardens, FL
Ross, Robert P. ... Louisville, KY
Ross, Robert R. ... Little Rock, AR
Ross, Robert R. ... Trenton, NJ
Ross, Robert R. ... Southampton, NY
Ross, Robert S. ... Chicago, IL
Ross, Robert S. ... Shenandoah, IA
Ross, Robert S., Jr. ... Washington, DC
Ross, Robert S., Jr. ... Dover, NH
Ross, Robert Tayloe ... Richmond, VA
Ross, Robert W. ... San Diego, CA
Ross, Roberta L. ... Indianapolis, IN
Ross & Rockwell ... Boston, MA
Ross, Roger F., II ... San Francisco, CA
Ross, Roger L. ... Buffalo, NY
Ross, Roger M. ... New York, NY
Ross, Roger S. ... Anaheim, CA
Ross, Ronald ... Rolling Hills Estates, CA
Ross, Ronald D. ... Randolph Center, VT
Ross, Ronald F. ... Albuquerque, NM
Ross, Ronald J. ... Youngstown, OH
Ross, Ronald R. ... Washington, DC
Ross, Rosalind Maron ... Pittsburgh, PA
Ross, Rosemary ... Bethesda, MD
Ross Rosenblatt, Ltd. ... Minneapolis, MN
Ross & Ross ... Springfield, MA
Ross & Ross ... Lawrence, NY
Ross & Ross ... Dayton, OH
Ross, Ross & Flavin ... Springfield, MA
Ross & Ross, P.C. ... Westport, CT
Ross, Ross & Santini, L.L.C.
Cheyenne, WY
Ross, Roy F. ... Pawtucket, RI
Ross, Roy S. ... Philadelphia, PA
Ross & Rubino ... Westmont, NJ
Ross, Ryan C. ... Sioux City, IA
Ross, S. Blair ... Miami, FL
Ross, S. K., & Assoc., P.C.
Los Angeles, CA
Ross, S. Margaux ... Los Angeles, CA
Ross, Sacks & Glazier LLP
Los Angeles, CA
Ross, Samantha Evans ... Washington, DC
Ross, Samuel F., Jr. ... East St. Louis, IL
Ross, Samuel P. ... New York, NY
Ross, Sander B. ... New York, NY
Ross, Sandra D. ... Indian Rocks Beach, FL
Ross, Sandra Hendrickson ... Birmingham, AL
Ross, Sanford R. ... New York, NY
Ross, Sarah P. ... Winston-Salem, NC
Ross, Sari Stabler ... Los Angeles, CA
Ross, Schroeder & Romatzke ... Kearney, NE
Ross, Scott ... Maryville, MO
Ross, Scott A. ... San Jose, CA
Ross, Scott A. ... Denver, CO
Ross, Scott Hunter ... La Jolla, CA
Ross, Scott N. ... Minneapolis, MN
Ross, Seth H. ... Lawrence, NY
Ross, Sharryn E. ... Boston, MA
Ross, Sheldon E. ... Corona Del Mar, CA
Ross, Sheri E. ... Los Angeles, CA
Ross, Sherman A. ... Houston, TX
Ross, Simone ... Washington, DC
Ross, Stacy L. ... Richmond, VA
Ross, Stanford G. ... Washington, DC
Ross, Stanley ... Flushing, NY
Roslyn, NY
Ross, Stanley D. ... Columbus, OH
Ross, Stefan ... Smithfield, RI
Ross, Stephan J. ... Tampa, FL
Ross, Stephanie Dawn ... Lexington, KY
Ross, Stephanie Scanlan ... San Francisco, CA
Ross, Stephen ... Burbank, CA
Ross, Stephen F. ... United States Senate, Committee Legal Personnel, GV
Ross, Stephen H. ... Atlanta, GA
Ross, Stephen I. ... Harwich, MA
Ross, Stephen M. ... Cross River, NY
Ross, Stephen R. ... Washington, DC
Ross, Stephen S. ... Victoria, TX
Ross, Sterling L., Jr. ... Mill Valley, CA
Ross, Steven A. ... Los Angeles, CA
Ross, Steven A. ... Boston, MA
Ross, Steven B. ... New York, NY
Ross, Steven E. ... Dallas, TX
Ross, Steven H. ... Glencoe, IL
Ross, Steven J. ... Washington, DC
Ross, Steven J. ... Atlanta, GA
Ross, Steven K. ... New York, NY
Ross, Steven L. ... Minneapolis, MN
Ross, Steven N. ... Seattle, WA
Ross, Steven O. ... Chicago, IL
Ross, Steven P. ... Detroit, MI
Ross, Steven R. ... Washington, DC
Ross, Steven U. ... Los Angeles, CA
Ross, Stuart Philip ... Washington, DC
Ross, Suchoff, Egert, Hankin, Maidenbaum & Mazel, P.C. ... New York, NY
Ross, Susan B. ... Washington, DC
Ross, Susan Julia ... Phoenix, AZ
Ross, Susan Kohn ... Los Angeles, CA
Ross, Susan Linda ... New York, NY
Ross, Susan Margaret Smith ... Chicago, IL
Ross, Susanne J. ... Mount Clemens, MI
Ross, Suzanne C. ... Pittsburgh, PA
Ross, Suzanne W. ... Houston, TX
Ross & Taylor ... Houston, TX
Ross, Taylor J. ... Orlando, FL
Ross, Ted A. ... Austin, TX
Ross, Terence P. ... Washington, DC
Ross, Terri L. ... New York, NY
Ross, Terry ... Long Beach, CA
Ross, Terry Ann ... Chicago, IL
Ross, Terry D. ... San Diego, CA
Ross, Terry Levich ... Beverly Hills, CA
Ross, Thomas ... South Royalton, VT
Ross, Thomas E. ... Harrisburg, PA
Ross, Thomas G. ... Des Moines, IA
Ross, Thomas G. ... Riverdale, MD
Ross, Thomas I. ... Chicago, IL
Ross, Thomas James, II ... Warrenton, VA
Ross, Thomas M. ... Brooklyn, NY
Ross, Thomas P. ... McLean, VA
Ross, Thomas Prescott, Jr. ... Bowie, MD
Ross, Thomas R., II ... Elkins, WV
Ross, Thomas T. ... Orlando, FL
Ross, Thomas W. ... Greensboro, NC
Ross & Tilghman ... Miami, FL
Ross, Timothy W. ... Miami, FL
Ross, Tina M. ... Dallas, TX
Ross, Tom T., Jr. ... Clarksdale, MS
Ross & Toner, P.C. ... Roslindale, MA
Ross, Trini E. ... Buffalo, NY
Ross, Tyler B. ... Louisville, KY
Ross, Valerie Ellen ... Washington, DC
Ross, Valerie Michael ... Turlock, CA
Ross, Verna J. ... Oakland, CA
Ross, Victoria M. ... San Diego, CA
Ross, Vincent A. ... Cheyenne, WY
Ross, Vivian ... Oak Brook, IL
Ross, W. Barrett ... Glendale, CA
Ross, W. David ... Jackson, MS
Ross, W. Wayne ... Macon, GA
Ross, Wallace & Hammond, P.C.
Thomson, GA
Ross, Walter H. ... Clifton, KS
Ross, Warren R. ... Punta Gorda, FL
Ross, Wayne Anthony ... Anchorage, AK
Ross, Wendi L. ... Sacramento, CA
Ross, Wilford H. ... Department of Defense, Defense Legal Services Agency, GV
Ross, William ... Mount Clemens, MI
Ross, William D. ... Los Angeles, CA
Palo Alto, CA
Ross, William D. ... Gloucester, MA
Ross, William D., A Prof. Corp., Law Offices of ... Los Angeles, CA
Palo Alto, CA
Ross, William F. ... Wooster, OH
Ross, William G. ... Bethlehem, PA
Ross, William G. ... Seattle, WA
Ross, William G., Jr. ... Greensboro, NC
Raleigh, NC
Ross, William George ... New York, NY
Ross, William H. ... Columbus, OH
Ross, William J. ... Kearney, NE
Ross, William J. ... Oklahoma City, OK
Ross, William L., Jr.
New Smyrna Beach, FL
Ross, William L. S. ... Cleveland, OH
Ross, William M. ... Santa Monica, CA
Ross, William R. ... Littleton, CO
Ross Williamson Loitz, PLLC ... Seattle, WA
Ross, Yan ... Santa Fe, NM
Ross, Yolanda L.
Securities and Exchange Commission, Division of Enforcement, GV
Rossa, Joseph W. ... Chicago, IL
Rossa, Thomas J. ... Salt Lake City, UT
Rossabi, Amiel J. ... Greensboro, NC
Rossabi, Amy ... New York, NY
Rossander, Jeff ... Stillwater, OK
Rossanese, Maurino J., Jr. ... Norristown, PA
Rossano, GinaMarie ... Phoenix, AZ
Rossano, Louis A. ... Garden City, NY
Rossano, Mosé, Hirschhorn & Corleto, P.C.
Garden City, NY
Rossano, Robert A. ... Miami, FL
Rossano, Robert A., P.A. ... Miami, FL
Rossbach Brennan, P.C. ... Missoula, MT
Rossbach, John A. ... Santa Barbara, CA
Rossbach, Laur. B., Jr. ... New York, NY
Rossbach, William A. ... Missoula, MT
Rossbacher & Associates ... Los Angeles, CA
Rossbacher, Henry H. ... Los Angeles, CA
Rossback, Kathryn McDuff ... Tuscaloosa, AL
Ross-Bennett, Vivian E. ... Orangeburg, SC
Rosscup & Kragh, P.C. ... Polson, MT
Rosscup, Shawn E. ... Polson, MT
Rosse, Cindi ... San Jose, CA
Rosse, Diane ... Boston, MA
Rosse, Gregory S. ... San Francisco, CA
Rosse, Jennifer ... Dallas, TX
Rosse, Melissa T. ... Stamford, CT
Ross-Edwards, Yvette D.
Frederiksted, St. Croix, VI
Rosseel, James W. ... Worcester, MA
Rosseel-Jones, Mary L. ... Highland Park, MI
Rosse Fowler, Sharon L. ... Seattle, WA
Rossein, Merrick T. ... Flushing, NY
Rosseland, Thomas ... Atlanta, GA
Rossell, Craig N. ... Pasadena, CA
Rossell, Marc M. ... New York, NY
Rossell, Nancy R. ... Key West, FL
Rossell, Thomas C. ... Northfield, NJ
Rosselli, Charles ... Great Neck, NY
Rossello, Juan O. ... Boston, MA
Rossello & Rabell ... San Juan, PR
Rossello-Rentas, Antonio ... San Juan, PR
Rossello Reyes, Jose R. ... Manati, PR
Rosselot, Alan T. ... Atlanta, GA
Rosselot, David E., (P.C.) ... Kokomo, IN
Rossen, Howard M. ... Pepper Pike, OH
Rossen, Joel M. ... Cleveland, OH
Rossen, Jordan ... Mineola, NY
Rossen, Leslie E.
National Labor Relations Board, Office of Board Members, GV
Rossen, Paula Carton ... Attleboro, MA
Rosser, Alan Comstock ... Cincinnati, OH
Rosser, Aubrey J., Jr. ... Altavista, VA
Rosser, C. B., Jr. ... Richmond, VA
Rosser, Charles D. ... Tuscumbia, AL
Rosser, Christopher R. ... Philadelphia, PA
Rosser, Daniel P. ... Birmingham, AL
Rosser, David B. ... Burbank, CA
Rosser, Derrick E. ... Richmond, VA
Rosser, Emmett V., Jr. ... Perry, OK
Rosser, Forrest W. ... Cedar Rapids, IA
Rosser, Gerald E., P.A. ... Fort Lauderdale, FL
Rosser, Janis L. ... Roswell, GA
Rosser, Janis L., P.C. ... Roswell, GA
Rosser, Malcolm E., IV ... Tulsa, OK
Rosser, Mark A. ... Knoxville, TN
Sevierville, TN
Rosser, Matthew C. ... Washington, DC
Rosser, Mildred ... Atlanta, GA
Rosser, Randye W. ... Montgomery, AL
Rosser, Richard G. ... Somerville, TN
Rosser, Richard L. ... Department of the Navy, Office of the Judge Advocate General, GV
Rosser, Thomas E. ... Baltimore, MD
Rosser, Thomas J. ... Oxford, MS
Rosset, Jerome H. ... Media, PA
Rossetter, F. Thomas ... Jacksonville, FL
Rossetti, Andrew J. ... Cherry Hill, NJ
Rossetti, Armand John, Jr. ... Boston, MA
Rossetti, Christopher J. ... Avon, CT
Rossetti, Fernande ... Albany, NY
Rossetti, Frank, III ... Mineola, NY
Rossetti, Frederick A. ... Bronx, NY
Rossetti, John D. ... Rock Springs, WY
Rossetti, John J., Jr. ... Washington, DC
Rossetti, Joseph ... San Diego, CA
Rossetti, Kenneth J. ... Andover, MA
Rossetti, Leonard R. ... Pennsauken, NJ
Rossetti, Mario J. ... Buffalo, NY
Rossetti, Michael Anthony ... Arlington, TX
Rossetti, Patricia ... Middleton, MA
Rossetti, Patrick Anthony
Garden Grove, CA
Rossetti, Philip P. ... Boston, MA
Rossetti, Rudolph J. ... Camden, NJ
Rossetti, Victor A. ... Buffalo, NY
Rossetti, Victoria Ann ... Waukegan, IL
Rossettie, Mary Ann ... Manchester, CT
Rossettie, Richard P. ... Corning, NY
Rossettie, Rossettie & Martino ... Corning, NY
Rossettie, Stephen V. ... Corning, NY
Rossetto, A. W. ... Great Neck, NY
Rossheim, Anne M. ... Rockville, MD
Rosshirt, John L. ... Austin, TX
Rossi, Alan D. ... Spokane, WA
Rossi, Allan J. ... Harrisburg, PA
Rossi, Angela M. ... Irvine, CA
Rossi, Anna M. ... San Francisco, CA
Rossi, Anne Marie ... San Mateo, CA
Rossi, Anthony G. ... Warren, OH
Rossi, Anthony G., III ... Warren, OH
Rossi, Anthony J. ... Los Angeles, CA
Rossi, Anthony J. ... Philadelphia, PA
Rossi, Anthony R. ... Chicago, IL
Rossi, Arthur J., Jr. ... San Antonio, TX
Rossi & Associates ... Reston, VA
Rossi, Assunta ... Cleveland, OH
Rossi, Barry, Corrado, Grassi & Radell, P.C.
Wildwood, NJ
Rossi, Ben, Jr. ... Orlando, FL
Rossi, Bret R. ... Sacramento, CA
Rossi, Catherine ... Monson, MA
Rossi, Charles J. ... Laguna Beach, CA
Rossi, Christine M. ... Detroit, MI
Rossi, Christine N. ... Brick, NJ
Rossi, Christopher A. ... Berwyn, PA
Rossi, Collins C. ... Metairie, LA
Rossi, Cox, Kiker & Inderwish, P.C.
Lincoln, NE
Aurora, CO
Denver, CO
Rossi, Craig ... Englewood, CO
Rossi, Daniel ... Oakland, CA
Rossi, Daniel L. ... Youngstown, OH
Rossi, David V. ... New York, NY
Rossi, Dean C. ... Burlingame, CA
Rossi, Dominic ... Niles, IL
Rossi, Dominic J. ... Philadelphia, PA
Rossi, Donald M. ... Brewster, NY
Rossi, Douglas A. ... Aurora, CO
Rossi, Douglas D. ... Santa Barbara, CA
Rossi, E. Jeffrey ... Youngstown, OH
Rossi, Emil M. ... Syracuse, NY
Rossi, Eugene J. ... Department of Justice, Tax Division, GV
Rossi, Faith Glickman ... Boston, MA
Rossi, Faust F. ... Ithaca, NY
Rossi, Francis S. ... New York, NY
Rossi, Frederic J. ... Little Falls, NJ
Rossi, Gary A. ... Bloomfield Hills, MI
Rossi, Giancarlo ... West Haven, CT
Rossi, Glenn J. ... Cleveland, MS
Rossi, Gregg A. ... Youngstown, OH
Rossi, Gregory T. ... Cleveland, OH
Rossi, Gustave J. ... Reno, NV
Rossi, Harry L. ... Doylestown, PA
Rossi, I. John ... West Des Moines, IA
Rossi, J. Joseph ... Grand Rapids, MI
Rossi, James A. ... Washington, DC
Rossi, Jennifer R. ... New York, NY
Rossi, Joanne ... Wilmington, DE
Rossi, John B., Jr. ... Philadelphia, PA
Rossi, John C. ... Auburn, NY
Rossi, John F. ... Boston, MA
Rossi, John J. ... Aurora, CO
Rossi, Joseph ... Newton, MA
Rossi, Kent D. ... Owatonna, MN
Rossi, Laurence J. ... Andover, MA
Rossi Law Offices, Ltd. ... Bridgeport, CT
Braintree, MA
East Providence, RI
Rossi, Lisa Mammone ... Glen Head, NY
Rossi, Lorraine ... Boston, MA
Rossi, M. Anthony ... Sioux City, IA
Rossi, Marc A. ... Reston, VA
Rossi, Margaret Surowka ... Albany, NY
Rossi, Marianne C. ... Redwood City, CA
Rossi & Maricle, A Professional Corporation
Denver, CO
Rossi, Mark A. ... Seattle, WA
Rossi, Mark F. ... Pekin, IL
Rossi, Mary Ann ... Exton, PA

Roth, David C. ....Detroit, MI
Roth, David E. ....Birmingham, AL
Roth, David H.O. ....San Antonio, TX
Roth, David I. ....Massapequa, NY
Roth, David J., II ....Cape Girardeau, MO
Roth, David L. ....Oakland, CA
Roth, David M. ....Farmington, CT
Roth, David M. ....Louisville, KY
Roth, David M. ....Salem, OR
Roth, David, P.C. ....Beverly Hills, CA
Roth, David R. ....Houston, TX
Roth, David S., Law Offices of
Seattle, WA
Roth, Dean and Kohn, P.C. ....Southfield, MI
Roth, Debra A. ....New York, NY
Roth, Debra J. ....Los Angeles, CA
Roth, Debra L. ....Washington, DC
Roth, Deena Godshall ....Washington, DC
Roth, Dennis ....Garden City, NY
Roth, Dennis A. ....Cleveland, OH
Roth, Derek V. ....Los Angeles, CA
Roth, Diane C. ....Riverside, CA
Roth, Donald H. ....Kansas City, MO
Roth, Donald M. ....Syracuse, NY
Roth, Donna ....Houston, TX
Roth, Doris E. ....Melville, NY
Roth and Duncan, P.A.
West Palm Beach, FL
Roth, Edw. I. ....Palm Beach, FL
Roth, Edward M. ....St. Louis, MO
Roth, Edward M. ....New York, NY
Roth, Edwards & Smith, P.A.
Maitland, FL
Orlando, FL
Roth, Elizabeth ....Mountain View, CA
Roth, Elizabeth A. ....Salem, MA
Roth, Elizabeth Diven ....Winnetka, IL
Roth, Ellen Carlstein ....Iselin, NJ
Roth, Ellyn S.
Commodity Futures Trading Commission, Office of the General Counsel, GV
Roth, Eric D. ....New York, NY
Roth, Eric J. ....Spokane, WA
Roth, Eric M. ....New York, NY
Roth, Eric M. ....New York, NY
Roth, Eric S. ....Miami, FL
Roth, Eugene ....Wilkes-Barre, PA
Roth, Evan J. ....Washington, DC
Roth, F. Joel ....Santa Fe, NM
Roth Foley Bryant & Cooper, PLLC
Clarksville, IN
Jeffersonville, IN
New Albany, IN
Louisville, KY
Roth, Frank A. ....Philadelphia, PA
Roth, Fred ....St. Louis, MO
Roth, Fred, P.C. ....St. Louis, MO
Roth, Fred W., Jr. ....Grand Prairie, TX
Roth, Frederick E. ....Naperville, IL
Roth, Fredric E., Jr. ....Auburn Hills, MI
Roth, Fredric J. ....New York, NY
Roth, Gabrielle S. ....Washington, DC
Roth, Gail P. ....Lafayette Hill, PA
Roth, Gary B. ....New Orleans, LA
Roth, Gary D. ....New York, NY
Roth, Gary E. ....Scotch Plains, NJ
Roth, Gary F. ....New York, NY
Roth, Gary S. ....Victorville, CA
Roth, George F. ....Milwaukee, WI
Roth, George G. ....Rochester, NY
Roth, George J. ....Sacramento, CA
Roth, Gerald ....Carle Place, NY
Roth, Gerald I. ....Allentown, PA
Roth, Gerald J. ....Rye Brook, NY
Roth, Glenn L. ....Freeman, SD
Olivet, SD
Roth, Glenn T., Jr. ....Easton, PA
Roth & Goldman, A Professional Association
Los Angeles, CA
Torrance, CA
Roth, Gregg ....Great Neck, NY
Roth, Gregory A. ....Thousand Oaks, CA
Roth, Gregory J. ....Rochester Hills, MI
Roth, Gregory L. ....La Palma, CA
Roth, Hadden, Law Offices of
San Rafael, CA
Roth, Harry D. ....Davis, CA
Roth, Harry M. ....Philadelphia, PA
Roth, Harvey A. ....Chicago, IL
Roth, Heidi M. ....Miami, FL
Roth, Heidi M., P.A. ....Miami, FL
Roth, Herbert J. ....New York, NY
Roth, Herbert L. ....Los Angeles, CA
Roth, H. I. ....Los Angeles, CA
Roth, Holly A. ....Washington, DC
Roth, Howard W. ....Albany, NY
Roth, Howard W., III ....Norfolk, VA
Roth, Irving A. ....Drexel Hill, PA
Roth, Irwin ....New York, NY
Roth, Irwin F. ....New York, NY
Roth, James A. ....Chicago, IL
Roth, James A. ....New York, NY
Roth, James Anthony ....Oklahoma City, OK
Roth, James F. ....Lafayette, IN
Roth, James J. ....Dubuque, IA
Roth, James M. ....San Diego, CA
Roth, James R. ....Wichita, KS
Roth, James Robert ....San Francisco, CA
Roth, James V. ....Minneapolis, MN
Minneapolis, MN
Roth, Jane R. ....Wilmington, DE
Roth, Jason M. ....Rochester, NY
Roth, Jay D. ....Los Angeles, CA
Roth, Jay Mark ....Atlanta, GA
Roth, Jeanne M. ....Arlington, VA
Roth, Jeff A. ....Wichita, KS
Roth, Jeffrey ....Springfield, NJ
Roth, Jeffrey A. ....Washington, DC
Roth, Jeffrey C. ....Coral Gables, FL
Roth, Jeffrey C., P.A. ....Coral Gables, FL
Roth, Jeffrey H. ....New York, NY
Roth, Jeffrey L. ....Huntsville, AL
Roth, Jeffrey P. ....Upper Sandusky, OH
Roth, Jeffrey R. ....Miami, FL
Roth, Jeffrey R. ....Moorefield, WV
Roth, Jeffrey S. ....St. Louis, MO
Roth, Jeffrey S. ....Lakewood, NJ
Roth, Jennifer C. ....Topeka, KS
Roth, Jeremy A. ....San Diego, CA
Roth, Jerome C. ....San Francisco, CA
Roth, Jessica Ann ....Newark, NJ
Roth, Joel G. ....Great Falls, MT
Roth, Joel H. ....New York, NY
Roth, Joel L. ....Boca Raton, FL
Roth, John A. ....McHenry, IL
Roth, John A. ....Latrobe, PA
Roth, John C. ....Joliet, IL
Roth, John E. ....Redlands, CA
Roth, John E. ....San Bernardino, CA
Roth, John Henry ....Freehold, NJ
Roth, John M. ....Minneapolis, MN
Roth, John P. ....Rockville, MD
Roth, John R. ....Detroit, MI
Roth, John T. ....Treasury Department, Departmental Offices, GV
Roth, John W., Jr. ....Chicago, IL
Roth, Jonathan H. ....Summit, NJ
Roth, Jonathan P. ....Beverly Hills, CA
Roth, Joseph N. ....El Paso, TX
Roth, Joshua ....New York, NY
Roth, Joyce T. ....Dallas, TX
Roth, Judith K. ....Manhattan, KS
Roth, Judith Shulman ....New York, NY
Roth, Karin N.
Commodity Futures Trading Commission, Division of Enforcement, GV
Roth, Katalin E. ....Bethesda, MD
Roth, Katherine Langley ....Asheville, NC
Roth, Kathleen E. ....Cleveland, OH
Roth, Kenneth A. ....Northville, MI
Roth, Kenneth D. ....Cherry Hill, NJ
Roth, Kenneth M. ....Lansing, MI
Roth, Kenneth T. ....New York, NY
Roth, Kent A. ....Great Bend, KS
Roth, Kristine A. ....Treasury Department, Internal Revenue Service, GV
Roth, L. Jeffrey ....New York, NY
Roth, Lad J. ....Cleveland, OH
Roth, Larry M. ....Maitland, FL
Roth, Larry R. ....Allentown, PA
Roth Law Office ....Storm Lake, IA
Roth Law Offices ....Granite City, IL
Roth, Lawrence H. ....New York, NY
Roth, Lawrence J. ....New York, NY
Roth, Lawrence W. ....Wilkes-Barre, PA
Roth, Leah L. ....Pittsburgh, PA
Roth, Lee B. ....Flemington, NJ
Roth, Leo A., Jr. ....Washington, DC
Rockville, MD
Fairfax, VA
Roth, Leon A. ....Miami, FL
Roth, Leonard S. ....Houston, TX
Roth, Leonard S., P.C., The Law Offices of
Houston, TX
Roth, Leonardo A. ....Miami, FL
Roth, Lilli Siegel ....New York, NY
Roth, Linda G. ....New York, NY
Roth, Linda Singer ....New York, NY
Roth, Lisa ....Harrisburg, PA
Roth, Lisa B. ....Boca Raton, FL
Roth, Lissa S. ....New York, NY
Roth, Lorenz H. ....Fort Myers, FL
Roth, Lori ....Pittsburgh, PA
Roth, Luis M. ....New York, NY
Roth, Marc S. ....Chicago, IL
Roth, Marc S. ....New York, NY
Roth, Marcie G. ....New York, NY
Roth, Marguerite R. ....Sacramento, CA
Roth, Mark Bradley ....Westbury, NY
Roth, Mark S. ....Los Angeles, CA
Roth, Mark S. ....Hollywood, FL
Roth, Mark W. ....Scottsdale, AZ
Roth, Martin G. ....Phoenix, AZ
Roth, Martin L. ....Miami, FL
Roth, Martin, (P.A.) ....Miami, FL
Roth, Mary Alice ....San Francisco, CA
Roth, Mary Helen ....St. Louis, MO
Roth, Matthew ....Denver, CO
Roth, Matthew Aaron ....Pontiac, MI
Roth, Melvyn K. ....Melville, NY
Roth, Michael ....New York, NY
Roth, Michael A. ....New York, NY
Roth, Michael B. ....Trenton, NJ
Roth, Michael D. ....Scottsdale, AZ
Roth, Michael Dundon, Law Offices of
Los Angeles, CA
Roth, Michael H. ....New York, NY
Roth, Michael H. ....Scranton, PA
Roth, Michael J. ....Highland Park, IL
Roth, Michael J. ....Skokie, IL
Roth, Michael J. ....Grand Rapids, MI
Roth, Michael J. ....Akron, OH
Roth, Michael J. ....Sheboygan, WI
Roth, Michael M. ....Chicago, IL
Roth, Michelle L. ....New York, NY
Roth, Mildred ....Chevy Chase, MD
Roth, Mindy Michaels ....Paramus, NJ
Roth, Mitchel W. ....North Miami Beach, FL
Roth, Mitchell I. ....Riverside, CA
Roth, Mitchell N. ....Vienna, VA
Roth, Mitchell S. ....Chicago, IL
Roth, Mollie D. ....New York, NY
Roth, Monica A. ....Chicago, IL
Roth, Murray ....New York, NY
Roth, Nathaniel H. ....Lakewood, NJ
Roth, Neal A. ....Boca Raton, FL
Miami, FL
Sarasota, FL
Roth, Neil J. ....Cincinnati, OH
Roth, Nelson E. ....Ithaca, NY
Roth, Nicholas B. ....Decatur, AL
Roth, Nicole A. ....Chicago, IL
Roth, Nora E. ....Denver, CO
Roth, Norma ....Cambridge, MA
Roth, Pamela A. ....Department of Justice, Civil Division, GV
Roth, Patricia O. ....Washington, DC
Roth, Paul ....Woodland Hills, CA
Roth, Paul N. ....New York, NY
Roth, Peter ....Springfield, MA
Roth, Peter C.L.
Pension Benefit Guaranty Corporation, Office of the General Counsel, GV
Roth, Peter J. ....Los Angeles, CA
Roth, Phillip J. ....Portland, OR
Roth, Rachel A. ....Buffalo, NY
Roth, Randall C. ....New Orleans, LA
Roth, Randall D. ....Palo Alto, CA
Roth, Randall W. ....Honolulu, HI
Roth, Randi I. ....St. Paul, MN
Roth, Raoul Y. ....Encino, CA
Roth, Rashell ....Kansas City, MO
Roth, Raymond B. ....Charlotte, NC
Roth, Renee R. ....New York, NY
Roth, Richard ....Clifton, NJ
Roth, Richard A. ....St. Louis, MO
Roth, Richard A. ....New York, NY
Roth, Richard D. ....Riverside, CA
Roth, Richard F. ....Southfield, MI
Roth, Richard G. ....Edinburg, TX
Roth, Richard G., P.C. ....Edinburg, TX
Roth, Richard H. ....Pompano Beach, FL
Roth, Richard H., P.A.
Pompano Beach, FL
Roth, Richard M. ....New York, NY
Roth, Richard S. ....Houston, TX
Roth, Robert ....Brooklyn, NY
Roth, Robert A. ....Los Angeles, CA
Roth, Robert A. ....Pacific Palisades, CA
Roth, Robert A. ....Chicago, IL
Roth, Robert A. ....Crystal Lake, IL
Roth, Robert B. ....Sacramento, CA
Roth, Robert C., Jr. ....Denver, CO
Roth, Robert E. ....Grayville, IL
Roth, Robert H. ....Orlando, FL
Roth, Robert J. ....Wichita, KS
Roth, Robert J. ....Toms River, NJ
Roth, Robert J. ....Charlotte, NC
Roth, Robert L. ....Washington, DC
Roth, Robert L. ....Miami, FL
Roth, Robert L., P.A. ....Miami, FL
Roth, Robert P. ....Bloomfield Hills, MI
Roth, Robert R. ....Galena, IL
Roth, Robert S. ....South Gate, CA
Roth, Robert T. ....Salem, OR
Roth, Robert W. ....Monticello, IN
Roth, Robert W. ....Milwaukee, WI
Roth, Robyn L. ....Beverly Hills, CA
Roth, Roger R. ....Punta Gorda, FL
Chagrin Falls, OH
Roth, Rolf & Goffman Co., L.P.A.
Cleveland, OH
Roth, Ronald A. ....Granite City, IL
Roth, Ronald J. ....Cleveland, OH
Roth, Ronald L. ....Miami, FL
Roth, Ronald M. ....Palo Alto, CA
Roth, Rosemarie S. ....Miami, FL
Roth, Rosemarie S., P.A. ....Miami, FL
Roth, Roslyn Zisie ....Garden City, NY
Roth & Roth, P.A. ....Lakewood, NJ
Roth & Roth, P.C. ....Flagstaff, AZ
Phoenix, AZ
Scottsdale, AZ
Tucson, AZ
Roth, Rousso & Benjamin, P.A. ....Miami, FL
Roth, Roy Paul ....Milwaukee, WI
Roth, Ruth Becker ....Arcadia, CA
Roth, Ruth Schorr ....White Plains, NY
Roth, Sandra R. ....Albany, NY
Roth, Sandra Z. ....Hinsdale, IL
Roth, Sandy L. ....San Francisco, CA
Roth, Sanford ....Southfield, MI
Roth, Saul ....Mineola, NY
Roth, Sharon F. ....Los Angeles, CA
Roth, Sharon R. ....Denver, CO
Roth, Simon, Jr. ....Hays, KS
Roth, Stacey P. ....Princeton, NJ
Roth, Stefanie H. ....New York, NY
Roth, Stephan J. ....Springfield, IL
Roth, Stephen E. ....Washington, DC
Roth, Stephen E. ....Knoxville, TN
Roth, Stephen F. ....Westfield, NJ
Roth, Stephen H. ....Hackensack, NJ
Roth, Stephen L. ....Salt Lake City, UT
Roth, Steven ....Philadelphia, PA
Roth, Steven D. ....New York, NY
Roth, Steven H. ....San Francisco, CA
Roth, Steven I. ....Harrisburg, PA
Roth, Steven J. ....San Jose, CA
Roth, Steven J. ....Dallas, TX
Roth, Steven M. ....Thousand Oaks, CA
Roth, Steven M. ....Washington, DC
Roth, Steven M. ....North Miami Beach, FL
Roth, Steven M. ....Westmoreland, KS
Roth, Steven P. ....Wilkes-Barre, PA
Roth, Steven T. ....Storm Lake, IA
Roth, Steven W. ....Rochester, MN
Roth, Stuart ....Mobile, AL
Roth, Stuart M. ....West Hartford, CT
Roth, Stuart N. ....Norwalk, CT
Roth, Susan Nance ....Chattanooga, TN
Roth, Susan R. ....Minneapolis, MN
Roth, Suzan E. ....Atlanta, GA
Roth, Sylvia Diana ....Los Angeles, CA
Roth, Terry E. ....Harrisburg, PA
Roth, Thomas D. ....Denver, CO
Washington, DC
Roth, Thomas G. ....Newark, NJ
Roth, Thomas J. ....Benton Harbor, MI
Roth, Thomas M., III ....Winston-Salem, NC
Roth, Timothy J. ....Los Angeles, CA
Roth, Timothy Patrick ....Cleveland, OH
Roth, Urban L. ....Butte, MT
Roth, Van Amberg, Rogers, Ortiz, Fairbanks & Yepa, LLP ....Albuquerque, NM
Santa Fe, NM
Roth, Virgil L. ....Los Angeles, CA
Roth, W. Norman ....Los Angeles, CA
Roth, Walter ....Chicago, IL
Roth, Warren J. ....Mineola, NY
New York, NY
White Plains, NY
Roth, Wayne M. ....New York, NY
Roth, William ....Garden City, NY
Roth, William D. ....Winter Haven, FL
Roth, William D., P.A. ....Winter Haven, FL
Roth, William H. ....New York, NY
Roth, William J., Jr. ....Akron, OH
Roth, William M. ....Yonkers, NY
Roth, William Mark ....Los Angeles, CA
Roth, William N. ....Dallas, TX
Roth, Wm. V., Jr. ....Wilmington, DE
Roth, Zipkin, Cove and Roth
North Miami Beach, FL
Roth/LiPuma, LLC ....Naperville, IL
Rothaar, Marvin E. ....Columbus, OH
Rothacker, Robert D. ....Milwaukee, WI
Rothal, Max ....Akron, OH
Rothandler, Stephen ....Washington, DC
Rothans, Steven J. ....Los Angeles, CA
Rothans, Tim C. ....San Diego, CA
Rothauge, Renée E. ....Portland, OR
Rothauser, Eric H. ....Hartford, CT
Rothbard, Alan T. ....Forest Hills, NY
Rothbard, Burton ....Syosset, NY
Rothbard, Herbert ....Bayside, NY
Rothbard, Jeffrey M. ....Newark, NJ
Rothbard, Leo ....Lauderhill, FL
Rothbard, Rothbard, Kohn & Kellar
Newark, NJ
Rothbard, William I. ....Los Angeles, CA
Rothbardt, Marlene Schwartz ....Chicago, IL
Rothbardt, Patricia A. ....New York, NY
Rothbart, Anna Ruiz ....Palo Alto, CA
Rothbart, David D. ....Mineola, NY
Rothbart, Gary B. ....Northbrook, IL
Rothbart, Herbert I. ....Chicago, IL
Rothbart, Heyman ....New York, NY
Rothbart, James Edmond ....Los Angeles, CA
Rothbart, Lawrence N. ....Brooklyn, NY
Rothbart, Ronni M. ....New York, NY
Rothbaum, Arnold ....New York, NY
Rothbaum, Bernard J.
Oklahoma City, OK
Rothbaum, Julian J. ....Tulsa, OK
Rothbaum, Sandra Lazarus
Indianapolis, IN
Rothbaum, Victoria C. ....Lexington, MA
Rothbell, Sheldon B. ....East Setauket, NY
Rothberg, Barry ....Washington, DC
Rothberg, David A. ....Woodland Hills, CA
Rothberg, Debra L. ....New York, NY
Rothberg, DL, & Associates, P.C.
New York, NY
Rothberg, Edward L. ....Houston, TX
Rothberg, Eric P. ....Bensalem, PA
Rothberg & Federman, P.C.
West Collingswood, NJ
Bensalem, PA
Rothberg, Harvey J. ....Stamford, CT
Rothberg, Karen S. ....Santa Barbara, CA
Rothberg, Lawrence ....Brooklyn, NY
Rothberg & Logan ....Fort Wayne, IN
Rothberg, Louis K. ....Department of the Army, Army Materiel Command, GV
Rothberg, Michael D. ....Washington, DC
Rothberg, Myron B. ....Encino, CA
Rothberg, Naomi ....Newark, NJ
Rothberg, Peter W. ....New York, NY
Rothberg, Richard S. ....New York, NY
Rothberg, Robert ....Boston, MA
Rothberg, Robert N. ....Miami, FL
Rothberg, Russell ....Kew Gardens, NY
Rothberg, Steven D. ....Philadelphia, PA
Rothberg, Steven S. ....New York, NY
Rothberg, Victor ....Plainview, NY
Rothberg, William ....Brooklyn, NY
Rothberg, William ....New York, NY
Rothberger, Gary ....Boston, MA
Rothberger, Mark G. ....Chattanooga, TN
Rothblatt, Emma Alden ....Coral Gables, FL
Rothblatt, Jon G. ....New York, NY
Rothblatt, Martine A. ....Washington, DC
Rothblatt, Steven D. ....South Orange, NJ
Rothbloom, Marvin E. ....Atlanta, GA
Rothblum, Lisa S. ....New York, NY
Rothburd, Craig E. ....Tampa, FL
Rothchild, Caran L. ....Fort Lauderdale, FL
Rothchild, Eugene M. ....Cincinnati, OH
Rothchild, Jane A. ....West Hartford, CT
Rothchild, John ....Federal Trade Commission, Bureau of Consumer Protection, GV
Rothchild, Morlee A. ....Cleveland, OH
Rothchild, Sander N. ....New York, NY
Rothe, Barbara R. ....Milwaukee, WI
Rothe, Christine M. ....Austin, TX
Rothe, Courand N., Jr. ....San Antonio, TX
Rothe, Edward J. ....Hingham, MA
Rothe, Edward W. ....Chicago, IL
Rothe, Mark A. ....Arlington, VA
Rothe, Robert J. ....Hondo, TX

Rothschild, Marjorie Ulman
Nuclear Regulatory Commission, Office of the General Counsel, GV
Rothschild, Martin J. ....Syracuse, NY
Rothschild, Maury ....Savannah, GA
Rothschild, Michael ....Sacramento, CA
Rothschild, Morgan & Brown
Phenix City, AL
Columbus, GA
Rothschild, Paul H. ....Springfield, MA
Rothschild, Philip E. ....Fort Lauderdale, FL
Rothschild, Philip R. ....Akron, NY
Rothschild, Randall S. ....Los Angeles, CA
Rothschild, Randall S. ....New York, NY
Rothschild, Richard K.
Hoffman Estates, IL
Rothschild, Rivkah ....New York, NY
Rothschild, Ronald J. ....Fort Lauderdale, FL
Rothschild, Roxanne L. ....St. Paul, MN
Rothschild, S. Zane ....Los Angeles, CA
Rothschild, Sandra ....Durham, NC
Rothschild, Shelly ....Los Angeles, CA
Rothschild, Shira B. ....New York, NY
Rothschild, Sidney F. ....New Orleans, LA
Rothschild, Stephen A. ....Toledo, OH
Rothschild, Stephen D. ....Los Angeles, CA
Rothschild, Steven B., P.C.
Spring Valley, NY
Rothschild, Steven J. ....Wilmington, DE
Rothschild, Susan B. ....New York, NY
Rothschild, Tamera Ochs ....Titusville, PA
Rothschild, Thomas N. ....Brooklyn, NY
Rothschild, Tina ....Lake St. Louis, MO
Rothschild, Toby J. ....Long Beach, CA
Rothschild, Walter S. ....New York, NY
Rothschild, Walter W. ....Waterloo, IA
Rothschild, William G. ....Atlanta, GA
Rothschild, William L. ....Atlanta, GA
Rothschild, Wishek & Sands
Sacramento, CA
Rothschild-Groves, Amy B. ....Charleston, SC
Rothschild-Rippe, Judith H.
New Haven, CT
Rothseid, Andrew N. ....Wilmington, DE
Rothstadt, Garry S. ....Parsippany, NJ
Rothstein, Alan ....Commack, NY
Rothstein, Alan R. ....Daly City, CA
Sun Valley, CA
Rothstein, Amy ....New York, NY
Rothstein, Amy L. ....Washington, DC
Rothstein, Andrew David ....Cambridge, MA
Rothstein, Andrew G. ....New York, NY
Rothstein, Andrew M. ....Elmira, NY
Rothstein & Associates, P.A. ....Bethesda, MD
Rothstein, Barbara A. ....Chicago, IL
Rothstein, Barbara Jacobs ....Seattle, WA
Rothstein, Benjamin ....East Patchogue, NY
Rothstein, Beverly I. ....Rockville, MD
Rothstein, Bruce E. ....Dallas, TX
Rothstein, Charles J. ....Minneapolis, MN
Rothstein, Chester ....New York, NY
Rothstein, David ....Boston, MA
Rothstein, David Alan ....Miami, FL
Rothstein, David E. ....Columbia, SC
Rothstein, David I. ....Milwaukee, WI
Rothstein, Debra ....Cincinnati, OH
Rothstein, Denise Jill ....New York, NY
Rothstein, Donatelli, Hughes, Dahlstrom, Cron & Schoenburg, LLP ....Phoenix, AZ
Rothstein, Donatelli, Hughes, Dahlstrom & Schoenburg, LLP ....Albuquerque, NM
Santa Fe, NM
Rothstein, Edward M. ....Lakewood, NJ
Rothstein, Ellen ....New York, NY
Rothstein, Elliot ....New York, NY
Rothstein, Eric ....Livingston, NJ
New York, NY
Rothstein, Erlich & Rothstein
Southfield, MI
Rothstein, Esther R. ....Chicago, IL
Rothstein, Gary D. ....San Francisco, CA
Rothstein, Gary S. ....New York, NY
Rothstein, George J.
Department of Defense, GV
Rothstein, Glen A. ....Beverly Hills, CA
Rothstein, Gregory F. ....Milwaukee, WI
Rothstein, Harold M. ....Melville, NY
Rothstein, Herman ....Commerce City, CO
Rothstein, Irving ....New York, NY
Rothstein, J. Adam ....Detroit, MI
Rothstein, Jacquelynn B. ....Milwaukee, WI
Rothstein, Jay L. ....Southfield, MI
Rothstein, Jeffrey S. ....Chicago, IL
Rothstein, Jesse ....New York, NY
Rothstein, Jessica Lynn ....New York, NY
Rothstein, John A. ....Millburn, NJ
Rothstein, John A. ....Milwaukee, WI
Rothstein, Jonathan A. ....Chicago, IL
Rothstein, Julie M. ....Atlanta, GA
Rothstein, Julius ....Fairfax, VA
Rothstein, Karbel & Wallace, P.C.
Detroit, MI
Southfield, MI
Rothstein, Kenneth G. ....Rockville Centre, NY
Rothstein, Larry A. ....Los Angeles, CA
Rothstein, Larry A. ....Woodland Hills, CA
Rothstein, Larry J. ....San Francisco, CA
Rothstein, Laurence Ira ....Neptune, NJ
Rothstein, Laurence L. ....Brooklyn, NY
Rothstein, Lawrence R. ....Southfield, MI
Rothstein, Lazarus ....Miami, FL
Rothstein, Lisa A. ....Chicago, IL
Rothstein, Mandell, Strohm, Must & Gertner, A Professional Corporation
Lakewood, NJ
Rothstein, Martin L. ....New York, NY
Rothstein, Michael D. ....Chicago, IL
Rothstein, Michael F. ....Madison, WI
Rothstein, Michael I ....Chicago, IL
Rothstein, Mortimer M. ....New York, NY
Rothstein, Nathaniel ....Southbury, CT
Rothstein, Paul F. ....Washington, DC
Rothstein, Paul M. ....Annapolis, MD
Rothstein, Paul S. ....Gainesville, FL
Rothstein, Rachel Joy ....Vienna, VA
Rothstein, Randall M. ....Bethesda, MD
Rothstein, Richard I. ....Norwich, CT
Rothstein, Robert A. ....Lakewood, NJ
Rothstein, Robert G. ....Atlanta, GA
Rothstein, Robert G. ....Alexandria, VA
Rothstein, Robert Michael ....Chicago, IL
Rothstein, Robert R. ....Santa Fe, NM
Rothstein, Ronald M. ....Southfield, MI
Rothstein, Ronald Y. ....Chicago, IL
Rothstein, Scott H. ....Hartford, CT
Rothstein, Scott W. ....Hollywood, FL
Rothstein, Seymour ....Chicago, IL
Rothstein, Simon D. ....Jacksonville, FL
Rothstein, Steven H.
North Miami Beach, FL
Rothstein, Steven M. ....Cincinnati, OH
Rothstein, Sydney ....New York, NY
Rothstein, Thomas ....Minneapolis, MN
Rothstein, Thomas D. ....Pasadena, CA
Rothstein & Weinstein ....Melville, NY
Rothstein, Wendy A. ....New York, NY
Rothstein, Wendy G. ....Lansdale, PA
Rothstein, William I. ....Nogales, AZ
Rothstein & Zuckerman, P.C. ....Millburn, NJ
Roth-Toll, Patricia ....Woodland Hills, CA
Roth Warnecke, Diana ....Dallas, TX
Rothwax, Harold J. ....New York, NY
Rothweiler, Beatrice A. ....Minneapolis, MN
Rothweiler, Kenneth M. ....Philadelphia, PA
Rothwell, Albert F.
Westhampton Beach, NY
Rothwell, Catherine A. ....Seattle, WA
Rothwell, David J. ....Washington, DC
Rothwell, Denise ....Oxnard, CA
Rothwell, Donald E. ....Columbia, SC
Rothwell, Figg, Ernst & Kurz, A Professional Corporation ....Washington, DC
Omaha, NE
Rothwell, G. Franklin ....Washington, DC
Rothwell, George C. ....Altadena, CA
Rothwell, Gregory R. ....Baltimore, MD
Rothwell, James C. ....San Diego, CA
Rothwell, James T. ....New York, NY
Rothwell, Patrick N. ....Seattle, WA
Rothwell, Peter Sutherland
South Hackensack, NJ
Rothwell, Ralph K., Jr. ....Baltimore, MD
Rothwell, Robert J. ....Washington, DC
Rothwell, Susan P. ....New York, NY
Rothwell, Suzanne E. ....Washington, DC
Rothwell, Thomas H. ....Orinda, CA
Roti, Richard E. ....Charlotte, NC
Roti, Ruth A ....Renton, WA
Roti, Scott L. ....Orlando, FL
Roti, Stephen L. ....New York, NY
Roti, Thomas D. ....Northlake, IL
Rotker, Karyn L. ....Milwaukee, WI
Rotker, Laurel S. ....New York, NY
Rotker, Michael A. ....Washington, DC
Rotker, Seymour ....Kew Gardens, NY
Rotkis, Susan M. ....Arlington, VA
Rotko, Michael J. ....Philadelphia, PA
Rotko, Thomas C. ....New York, NY
Rotkofska, Randall L. ....Detroit, MI
Rotman, Arline S. ....Worcester, MA
Rotman, Arnold J. ....Palm Springs, CA
Rotman, David ....Concord, NH
Rotman, Harvey A. ....Okanogan, WA
Rotman, Jerry F. ....Minneapolis, MN
Rotman, Lewis J. ....Minneapolis, MN
Rotman, Medansky & Elovitz, Ltd.
Chicago, IL
Rotman, Michael H. ....Chicago, IL
Rotman, Orin S. ....Chicago, IL
Rotman, Pamela F. ....Springfield, IL
Rotman, Phillip A., II ....Cincinnati, OH
Rotman, Steven B. ....Boston, MA
Rotmil, Robert L. ....New York, NY
Rotner, Glen L. ....Upland, CA
Rotner, Philip R. ....New York, NY
Rotole, Jaunarajs, Blanchard & Lumbye
Denver, CO
Parker, CO
Rotole, John F. ....Denver, CO
Parker, CO
Rotole, Richard J. ....Denver, CO
Rotolo, John P. ....Key West, FL
Rotolo, John P., P.A. ....Key West, FL
Rotolo, Joseph A. ....Cleveland, OH
Rotolo, Joseph J. ....Hackensack, NJ
Rotolo, P. Cliff ....Palisades Park, NJ
Rotolo, Peter J., III ....New Orleans, LA
Rotolo, Peter S. ....Palisades Park, NJ
Rotolo & Rotolo ....Palisades Park, NJ
Rotolo, Victor A. ....Lebanon, NJ
Rotolo, Victor A., P.A., Law Offices of
Audubon, NJ
Flemington, NJ
Lebanon, NJ
Rotondi, Anthony ....Troy, NY
Rotondi, Liana P. ....Worcester, MA
Rotondi, Samuel ....Burlington, MA
Rotondo, David J. ....Attleboro, MA
Rotondo, Eric P. ....Columbus, OH
Rotondo, James H. ....Hartford, CT
Rotramble, Brenda B. ....Deer Park, TX
Rotroff, Ann S. ....Marietta, GA
Rotruck, Sandra E. ....Santa Fe, NM
Rotskoff, Peter L. ....Springfield, IL
Rotstein, Andrew D. ....New York, NY
Rotstein, Harold B. ....Chicago, IL
Rotstein, Rachel Anne ....New York, NY
Rotstein, Robert H. ....Los Angeles, CA
Rotsten, Michael ....Encino, CA
Rotsztain, Diego ....New York, NY
Rott, David H. ....Missoula, MT
Rott, Michael Ian ....San Diego, CA
Rottaris, Albert ....Niagara Falls, NY
Rottaris, John K. ....Buffalo, NY
Rottenberg, Alan W. ....Boston, MA
Rottenberg, Erika F. ....Milpitas, CA
Rottenberg, Julie B. ....Washington, DC
Rottenberg, Mark M. ....Hackensack, NJ
New York, NY
Rottenstreich, Dan ....New York, NY
Rottenstreich, Stacie ....New York, NY
Rotter, Andrew S. ....Los Angeles, CA
Rotter, David A. ....Milwaukee, WI
Rotter, Emanuel N. ....Milwaukee, WI
Rotter, Gregory C. ....Indian River, MI
Rotter, Harriet B. ....Franklin, MI
Rotter, Harriet B., P.C. ....Franklin, MI
Rotter, Irving L. ....New York, NY
Rotter, Kenneth B. ....Newark, NJ
Rotter, Merton N. ....Milwaukee, WI
Rotter, Russell J. ....Secaucus, NJ
Rotter, Scott M. ....Baltimore, MD
Rotthoff, Eleanor ....Austin, TX
Rotticci, Thomas E. ....San Francisco, CA
Rottier, Catherine M. ....Madison, WI
Rottier, Daniel A. ....Madison, WI
Rottier, Kenneth F. ....Seymour, WI
Rottier, Nancy M. ....Madison, WI
Rottier, Stuart R. ....Wausau, WI
Rottinghaus, Daniel L. ....San Francisco, CA
Rottinghaus, Thomas J. ....Cincinnati, OH
Rottinghaus, Tom ....Kansas City, MO
Rottkamp & Flacks ....Trenton, NJ
Rottkamp, Robert B., Jr. ....Trenton, NJ
Rottler, Christopher D. ....Granbury, TX
Rottler, Terry R. ....Ste. Genevieve, MO
Rottler, Terry R., P.C.
Ste. Genevieve, MO
Rottman & Associates, A Professional Law Corporation ....Los Angeles, CA
Rottman, Daniel S. ....Denver, CO
Rottman, Linda M. ....Los Angeles, CA
Rottman, Robert B. ....Denver, CO
Rottman, S. Leonard ....Baltimore, MD
Rottman, Steven J. ....Los Angeles, CA
Rottner, Jack H. ....Chicago, IL
Rottner, Joel J. ....Hartford, CT
Rotto, Howard F. ....Valley Stream, NY
Rottschaefer, John R. ....Riverside, CA
Rottschaefer, William F., Jr. ....St. Paul, MN
Rottunda, Larry ....Bloomington, IL
Rotunda, Gerald S. ....Hackensack, NJ
Rotunda, Marcia A. ....Urbana, IL
Rotunda, Ronald D. ....Champaign, IL
Rotundo, John J. ....Sherman Oaks, CA
Rotundo, Michael J. ....Fort Lauderdale, FL
Rotunno, Anthony M. ....Flemington, NJ
Rotunno, John W. ....Chicago, IL
Rotunno, Mary L. ....Fort Smith, AR
Rotunno, Michael C. ....Miami, FL
Rotunno, Norma C. ....Treasury Department, Internal Revenue Service, GV
Rotunno, Steven J. ....Chicago, IL
Rotwein, Abe A. ....Jackson, MS
Rotwein, Abraham ....New York, NY
Rotwein, Geoffrey ....San Francisco, CA
Rotwein, Jos. ....Washington, DC
Rotwitt, Jeffrey B. ....Philadelphia, PA
Roty, Maragret Mehall ....Ann Arbor, MI
Rotz, Jay H.
Treasury Department, GV
Rotz, Linda S. ....Glen Allen, VA
Rotz, Rhiman A. ....Gary, IN
Rotz, Richard B. ....Cherry Hill, NJ
Rotzien, William A. ....West Des Moines, IA
Roualet, Nancy J. ....Bloomfield Hills, MI
Roualet, Nancy J., P.C.
Bloomfield Hills, MI
Roubanes, Barbara A. ....Columbus, OH
Roubenes, Jerry G. ....Akron, OH
Roubic, Melissa R. ....Windham, OH
Roubicek, Chris, P.S. ....Castle Rock, WA
Roubicek, Christopher J.
Castle Rock, WA
Roubicek, Frank ....Creighton, NE
Roubideaux, Ramon A. ....Rapid City, SD
Roubideaux, Teresa K. ....Yuma, CO
Roubik, Linda M. ....Seattle, WA
Rouch, Kevin C. ....Columbus, OH
Rouchell, John A. ....New Orleans, LA
Rouchell, Lisa M. ....Thibodaux, LA
Rouco, Richard Paul ....Birmingham, AL
Rouda, David L. ....San Francisco, CA
Rouda, Feder & Tietjen
San Francisco, CA
Rouda, Gail Victoria ....San Francisco, CA
Rouda, Harley E., Jr. ....Columbus, OH
Rouda, Ronald H. ....San Francisco, CA
Roude, Carl L. ....Cypress, CA
Roudebush, George S. ....St. Louis, MO
Roudebush, Kathryn J. ....Fort Wayne, IN
Rouder, Wendy P. ....Oakland, CA
Roudiez, Cecelia T. ....Arlington, VA
Roue, John M. ....Crookston, MN
Rouen, Deborah B. ....New Orleans, LA
Rouff, George A. ....Yuma, AZ
Rouff, Stephen J. ....Yuma, AZ
Rougeau, Butler & Largay ....Hyannis, MA
Rougeau, Gregory A. ....San Francisco, CA
Rougeau, Reuvan N. ....Lake Charles, LA
Rougeau, Richard N. ....Hyannis, MA
Rougeau, Vincent D. ....Chicago, IL
Rougelot, Robert E. ....New Orleans, LA
Rougeou, Francis A., Jr. ....Baton Rouge, LA
Rougeux, Debra C. ....Buffalo, NY
Roughen, Patrick F. ....Arlington, VA
Roughgarden, Frederick ....Hawthorne, NJ
Roughley, Shane ....Fort Smith, AR
Roughsedge, Robert J. ....Boston, MA
Roughton, Michael D. ....Des Moines, IA
Rouhana, Anna M. ....Youngstown, OH
Rouhandeh, James P. ....New York, NY
Rouhandeh, Jeffrey A. ....Woodstock, IL
Rouillard, Claire W. ....Concord, NH
Rouillard, Mark R. ....Rochester, NH
Rouillard, Rebecca Ann ....Portland, OR
Rouille, David W. ....Boston, MA
Rouin, Carole C. ....Long Beach, CA
Roulan, Michael J. ....Geneva, NY
Rouland, J. Thomas ....McLean, VA
Roule, Arthur L. ....La Porte, IN
Roule, Arthur L., Jr. ....La Porte, IN
Rouleau, Mark A. ....Rockford, IL
Rouleau, Robert H. ....Boston, MA
Roules, Daniel F. ....Cleveland, OH
Roulhac, Derick J. ....Fort Lauderdale, FL
Roulhac, Derick J., P.A.
Fort Lauderdale, FL
Roulhac, Joseph Milton ....Murrells Inlet, SC
Roulhac, Roy Lee ....Detroit, MI
Roullard, Geoffrey D. ....Carson City, NV
Roulo, Barbara A. ....Detroit, MI
Roulston, David C. ....Wilmington, DE
Roulston, David R. ....Greenfield, MA
Roulston, Laurie Laidlaw ....Cleveland, OH
Roult, Neil J. ....Hollywood, FL
Roumbos, Peter S. ....Pensacola, FL
Roumeliotis, Chrisoula I. ....Springfield, VT
Roumeliotis, George I. ....Springfield, MA
Roumell, George T., Jr. ....Detroit, MI
Roumell, Michael T. ....Chicago, IL
Roumell, Thomas ....Northville, MI
Rounaghi, Robin Hayward ....Costa Mesa, CA
Round, Deborah R. ....Denver, CO
Round, Edmund ....Cleveland, OH
Round, John K. ....Dallas, TX
Round, Lauren H. ....Florham Park, NJ
Rounds, Bernard J. ....Athens, GA
Rounds, Charles E., Jr. ....Boston, MA
Rounds, Christopher B. ....Vancouver, WA
Rounds, John K. ....Palmdale, CA
Rounds, Mary J. ....Tulsa, OK
Rounds, Michael D. ....Las Vegas, NV
Reno, NV
Rounds, Philard L., Jr. ....Tulsa, OK
Rounds, Stephen E. ....Denver, CO
Rounds, Thomas M. ....Windsor, VT
Rounds, Thomas M., P.C. ....Windsor, VT
Rounds, Wendy S. ....Miami, FL
Rounds, William D. ....Taunton, MA
Roundtree, Dovey J., (Mrs.)
Washington, DC
Roundtree, Knox, Hunter & Parker
Washington, DC
Roundtree, Lynda T. ....Bartlett, IL
Roundtree, Robert E., Jr. ....Gainesville, FL
Roundtree, Robert, II ....Tallahassee, FL
Roundtree, William H. ....Cocoa, FL
Roundy, Catherine A. ....San Francisco, CA
Roundy, Dale K. ....Coupeville, WA
Roundy, Vicki Stueve ....Dover, NH
Rouner, Robert L. ....Clear Lake Shores, TX
Rounick, Jack A. ....Norristown, PA
Rounsavall, David S. ....Greenville, MS
Rounsavall, George Hunt, Jr.
Louisville, KY
Rounsaville, Guy, Jr. ....San Francisco, CA
Rounsaville, John, Jr. ....Washington, DC
Rounsaville, Keith E. ....Tampa, FL
Rounsaville, Royce ....Miami, FL
Rounsborg, William K. ....Denver, CO
Rounsley, James J. ....Warren, OH
Rountree, Allen D. ....Tyler, TX
Rountree, Asa ....Birmingham, AL
Rountree, Billy J. ....Victoria, TX
Rountree, Cadle & McNeely, P.C.
Swainsboro, GA
Rountree, Charles S., III ....Tarboro, NC
Rountree, Cox, Guin & Achee
Shreveport, LA
Rountree, David J. M. ....New York, NY
Rountree, Ernest V. ....Tyler, TX
Rountree, George, III ....Wilmington, NC
Rountree, George M. ....Brunswick, GA
Rountree, George M., & Associates, P.C.
Brunswick, GA
Saint Simons Island, GA
Rountree, Gordon E. ....Shreveport, LA
Rountree, James A. ....Monroe, LA
Rountree, James S. ....Beverly Hills, CA
Rountree, Kimberly Dyslin ....Atlanta, GA
Rountree & Kithcart, L.L.P.
Harlingen, TX
Rountree, L. Clarke ....Fresno, CA
Rountree, Michael D. ....Los Angeles, CA
Rountree, Michael W. ....Montgomery, AL
Rountree, Neal ....Akron, OH
Rountree, Patricia M. ....Houston, TX
Rountree, Robert ....Dallas, TX
Rountree, Robert B. ....Atlanta, GA
Rountree, Robert B. ....South Bend, IN
Rountree, Robert W. ....Citrus Heights, CA
Rountree & Seagle, L.L.P.
Wilmington, NC
Rountree, Tamara N. ....Department of Justice, Environment and Natural Resources Division, GV
Rountree, Timothy Bura ....Brooklyn, NY
Rountree, W. E. ....Swainsboro, GA
Rountree, William C., III ....Harlingen, TX
Rountry, Robert J. ....Mineola, NY

Rowe, Bobby, Law Offices, P.S.C. Prestonsburg, KY
Rowe, Brenda ... Fort Worth, TX
Rowe, Brett B. ... San Antonio, TX
Rowe, Brian F. ... Los Angeles, CA
Rowe, Bruce K. ... Renton, WA
Rowe, Burrel ... Livingston, TX
Rowe, C. Edward, Jr. ... Exeter, NH
Rowe, Charles B. ... Courtland, VA
Rowe, Charles E. ... San Diego, CA
Rowe, Charles L. ... Chicago, IL
Rowe, Charles R. ... Homestead, FL
Rowe, Charles Warren ... Enterprise, AL
Rowe, Clyde C. ... Bethesda, MD
Rowe, David A. ... West Palm Beach, FL
Rowe, David E. ... Westlake Village, CA
Rowe, David M. ... Franklin, TN
Rowe, David P. ... Miami, FL
Rowe, David W. ... Lincoln, NE
Rowe, Debra A. ... Fort Myers, FL
Rowe, Dee ... Minneapolis, MN
Rowe, Del B. ... Bountiful, UT
Rowe, Dibbon M. ... Seminole, TX
Rowe, Donald A. ... Cleveland, OH
Rowe, Donald C. ... New York, NY
Rowe, Donald M. ... Bedford, VA
Rowe, Dorothy Parker ... Grove, OK
Rowe, Douglas E. ... Mineola, NY
Rowe, Douglas E. ... Rochester, NY
Rowe, Edward C. ... El Paso, TX
Rowe, Edward T., Jr. ... Lower Burrell, PA
Rowe, Elizabeth A. ... Boston, MA
Rowe, Eric C. ... Washington, DC
Rowe, Evelyn F. ... Washington, DC
Rowe, Foltz & Martin, P.C. ... Atlanta, GA
Rowe, Frederick M. ... Washington, DC
Rowe, Fredk. H. ... Jacksonville, IL
Rowe, G. Russell ... Austin, TX
Rowe, G. Steven ... Portland, ME
Rowe, Gary A. ... Grand Rapids, MI
Rowe, Gayle K. ... Portland, OR
Rowe, George, Jr. ... New York, NY
Rowe, George W. ... Richmond, VA
Rowe, Gerard P. ... Portland, OR
Rowe, Gordon A., Jr. ... Louisville, KY
Rowe, Gordon H., III ... South Fork, CO Albuquerque, NM
Rowe, Gordon H., Jr. ... South Fork, CO Albuquerque, NM
Rowe, Gordon H., Jr. ... Dallas, TX
Rowe, Greg A. ... Philadelphia, PA
Rowe & Hales, LLP ... Carson City, NV Minden, NV
Rowe & Hamilton ... Indianapolis, IN
Rowe, Harry J. ... San Francisco, CA
Rowe & Hawkins, LLC ... Jasonville, IN
Rowe, Helen ... San Diego, CA
Rowe, H. Y. ... El Dorado, AR
Rowe, J. David ... Austin, TX
Rowe, Jack D. ... Kansas City, MO
Rowe, James A. ... Largo, FL
Rowe, James C. ... St. Petersburg, FL
Rowe, James E., Jr. ... Aurora, CO
Rowe, James F. ... Yardley, PA
Rowe, James F., II ... Philadelphia, PA
Rowe, James Gary ... Asheville, NC
Rowe, James H., III ... Washington, DC
Rowe, James J. ... Lewisburg, WV
Rowe, James L. ... Indianapolis, IN
Rowe, James L. ... Flint, MI
Rowe, James Merek, (P.A.) Hot Springs National Park, AR Hot Springs Village, AR
Rowe, James S. ... Chicago, IL
Rowe, Jane G. ... Oklahoma City, OK
Rowe, Jean Elting ... Smithtown, NY
Rowe, Jennifer C. ... Lakewood, CO
Rowe, Jill B. ... San Francisco, CA
Rowe, Joan Allen ... New Haven, CT
Rowe, Jody R. ... Moline, IL
Rowe, Joe A. ... Albion, IN Kendallville, IN
Rowe, John S. ... Jasonville, IN
Rowe, Jonathan D. ... Ann Arbor, MI
Rowe, Joseph V., Jr. ... Philadelphia, PA
Rowe, Katherine F. ... Jacksonville, FL
Rowe, Kathryn M. ... Annapolis, MD
Rowe, Keith A. ... Livingston, LA
Rowe, Kelly, & Associates Minneapolis, MN St. Paul, MN
Rowe, Kenneth C. ... Minneapolis, MN
Rowe, Keven M. ... Salt Lake City, UT
Rowe, Kevin ... New York, NY
Rowe, Kim G. ... Reno, NV
Rowe, Kirsten ... Washington, DC
Rowe, Kirsten Lindquist Altamonte Springs, FL
Rowe, Kristin C. ... Albany, NY
Rowe, L. Abraham, Jr. ... Jackson, MS
Rowe, Larry J. ... Boston, MA
Rowe, Larry L. ... Charleston, WV
Rowe, Larry W. ... Macon, GA
Rowe, Laur & Associates ... Albion, IN Kendallville, IN
Rowe, Laura B. ... Houston, TX
Rowe Law Firm, The, P.C. Albuquerque, NM
Rowe Law Offices, P.C. ... Ann Arbor, MI
Rowe, Lawrence J. ... Boston, MA
Rowe, Lenford A. ... New York, NY
Rowe, Lloyd B. ... Carson City, NV
Rowe, Margaret ... New York, NY
Rowe, Margaret Mc ... Kansas City, MO
Rowe, Marie Rost ... Kemah, TX
Rowe, Martin K. ... Baldwin, NY
Rowe, Mary C. ... Tucson, AZ
Rowe, Mary Patricia ... St. Paul, MN
Rowe, Matthew D. ... Wausau, WI
Rowe, Max L. ... Paris, IL Springfield, IL
Rowe, Michael A. ... New York, NY
Rowe, Michael D. ... Department of Justice, Environment and Natural Resources Division, GV
Rowe, Michael E. ... Fresno, CA
Rowe, Michael Smiley ... Minden, NV
Rowe, Nancy L. ... Washington, DC
Rowe, Nansi I. ... Detroit, MI
Rowe, Neil J. ... Rochester, NY
Rowe, Neil M.B. ... Montgomery, AL
Rowe, Norman P. ... Indianapolis, IN
Rowe, O. Brenton ... St. George, UT
Rowe, Patricia S. ... Scottsdale, AZ
Rowe, Paul A. ... Irvine, CA
Rowe, Paul A. ... Woodbridge, NJ
Rowe, Paul C. ... New York, NY
Rowe, Paul D., Jr. ... Exton, PA
Rowe, Paul K. ... New York, NY
Rowe, Peter W. ... Norfolk, VA
Rowe, R. Damon ... Dallas, TX
Rowe, R. Kent ... South Bend, IN
Rowe, R. Kent, III ... South Bend, IN
Rowe, R. Lee, III ... Jacksonville, FL
Rowe, R. Leonard, Jr. ... Charlotte, NC
Rowe, Rachael A. ... Cincinnati, OH
Rowe, Randall K. ... Chicago, IL
Rowe, Randell H., III ... Bunnell, FL
Rowe, Randell H., Jr. ... Madison, FL
Rowe, Raymond T. ... Troy, MI
Rowe, Raymond T., P.C. ... Troy, MI
Rowe, Richard E. ... Charleston, WV Ripley, WV
Rowe, Richard H. ... Washington, DC
Rowe, Robert C. ... Oakland, CA
Rowe, Robert C. ... Missoula, MT
Rowe, Robert D. ... Washington, DC
Rowe, Robert E. ... Lafayette, LA
Rowe, Robert E., A Law Corporation Lafayette, LA
Rowe, Robert F., Jr. ... Overland Park, KS
Rowe, Robert G., III ... Washington, DC
Rowe, Robert K. ... Bonnieville, KY
Rowe, Robert L., Jr. ... Jacksonville, FL
Rowe, Robert P. ... Atlanta, GA
Rowe, Robt. S. ... Elmhurst, IL
Rowe, Roger D. ... Little Rock, AR
Rowe & Rowe ... Elkhart, IN South Bend, IN
Rowe and Rowe, P.A. ... Jacksonville, FL
Rowe, Royce Glenn, Jr. ... Chicago, IL
Rowe, Russell M. ... Las Vegas, NV
Rowe, Russell P. ... Denver, CO
Rowe, Russell William, II ... Denver, CO
Rowe, S. Dagnal ... Huntsville, AL
Rowe, Samuel T. ... Livingston, LA
Rowe, Scott P. ... Orlando, FL
Rowe, Shirley V. ... League City, TX
Rowe, Stacey-Ann M. ... Miami, FL
Rowe, Stephen A. ... Birmingham, AL
Rowe, Stephen Jackson ... Birmingham, AL
Rowe, Sterling E. ... Marblehead, MA
Rowe, Steven A. ... Rocky Mount, NC
Rowe, Steven D. ... Sarasota, FL
Rowe, Steven D. ... Columbus, OH
Rowe, Steven P. ... Dundee, MI
Rowe, Stewart F., Jr. ... Fort Worth, TX
Rowe, Susan N. ... St. Louis, MO
Rowe, Terry L. ... Lafayette, LA
Rowe, Thomas D., Jr. ... Durham, NC
Rowe, Thomas Dean ... Arcata, CA
Rowe, Thomas L. ... Chesterfield, VA
Rowe, Thomas R. ... Fairfield, CT
Rowe, Timothy ... Indianapolis, IN
Rowe, Timothy E. ... Reno, NV
Rowe, W. Bayless ... El Dorado, AR
Rowe, Walter P. ... Douglasville, GA
Rowe, Warren, & Associate, Attys. at Law, P.A. ... Elba, AL Enterprise, AL
Rowe, William C., Jr. ... Baton Rouge, LA
Rowe, William L. S. ... McLean, VA Richmond, VA
Rowe, William P., III ... Duluth, GA
Rowe, William P., III, P.C. ... Atlanta, GA Duluth, GA Lawrenceville, GA
Rowedder, Deanes L. ... Kennesaw, GA
Rowek, Michael A. ... Wayne, NJ
Rowekamp, Leonard G. ... Covington, KY
Rowe-Linn, Peggy ... West Palm Beach, FL
Rowe-Linn, Peggy, P.A. West Palm Beach, FL
Rowell, A. Hoyt, III ... Charleston, SC
Rowell, Ansley E. ... Birmingham, AL
Rowell, Anthony A. ... Atlanta, GA
Rowell, Charles W., IV ... Augusta, GA
Rowell, David L. ... Fresno, CA
Rowell, Frank M., Jr. ... Tulsa, OK
Rowell, Gary L. ... Treasury Department, Federal Law Enforcement Training Center, GV
Rowell, James A. ... New Orleans, LA
Rowell, Jeffrey E. ... Birmingham, AL
Rowell, John D. ... Los Angeles, CA Los Angeles, CA
Rowell, June K. ... Birmingham, AL
Rowell, Lewis S. ... Greensboro, NC
Rowell, Nathan D. ... Knoxville, TN
Rowell, Steven F. ... New Haven, CT
Rowell, Susan E. ... Conway, SC
Rowell, William B. ... San Francisco, CA
Rowell, Wilma S. ... New York, NY
Rowells, Timothy L. ... Chicago, IL
Rowels, L. Victoria ... Chicago, IL
Rowen, Andrew S. ... New York, NY
Rowen, Brendan J. ... Wauwatosa, WI
Rowen, Eric V. ... Los Angeles, CA
Rowen, Francis A., Jr. ... Fairfax, VA
Rowen, Gary M. ... Warren, NJ
Rowen, Hilary N. ... San Francisco, CA
Rowen, J. Thomas ... Omaha, NE
Rowen, James S. ... Jersey City, NJ
Rowen, Kenneth H. ... Van Nuys, CA
Rowen, Lyle D. ... Chicago, IL
Rowen, Marvin D. ... Van Nuys, CA
Rowen, Mary Helen ... New York, NY
Rowen, Nancy L. ... Phoenix, AZ
Rowen, Russell F. ... San Francisco, CA
Rowen, Sharon L. ... Atlanta, GA
Rowen, Theodore M. ... Toledo, OH
Rowerdink, William H., III ... Quincy, MA
Rowett, Robert M. ... Mountain Home, ID
Rowin, Barbara S. ... Larchmont, NY New York, NY
Rowin, Daniel A. ... Chicago, IL
Rowin, Gerald J. ... Bloomfield Hills, MI
Rowin, Marc ... New York, NY
Rowin & Sparrow ... Bloomfield Hills, MI
Rowings, John W. ... Indianapolis, IN
Rowings, Linda R. ... Indianapolis, IN
Rowland, Adam B. ... New York, NY
Rowland & Andrews ... Siler City, NC
Rowland, Annelva ... Austin, TX
Rowland, Barbara ... Washington, DC
Rowland, Bertram I. ... Palo Alto, CA
Rowland, Brent ... Bartlesville, OK
Rowland, Brent A. ... Marion, OH
Rowland, Carole A. ... Fulton, NY
Rowland, Carolyn A. ... Atlanta, GA
Rowland, Celia Elaine ... San Francisco, CA
Rowland, Charles M., II ... Xenia, OH
Rowland, Cynthia R. ... San Francisco, CA
Rowland, D. Stanley ... San Francisco, CA
Rowland, Dan ... Prestonsburg, KY
Rowland, David A. ... Tampa, FL
Rowland, David J. ... Chicago, IL
Rowland, David J. ... New York, NY
Rowland, David P. ... Bartlesville, OK
Rowland, Dawn L. ... Bloomington, IN
Rowland, Donald F. ... Topeka, KS
Rowland & Doyle ... Muncie, IN
Rowland, Doyle A. ... Kalamazoo, MI
Rowland, Elizabeth Ann ... Knoxville, TN
Rowland, Fauniel D. ... Fort Worth, TX
Rowland & Franceschini ... San Rafael, CA
Rowland, Frank C. ... Chicago, IL
Rowland, Frederick C. ... Metairie, LA
Rowland, Gary ... Claremore, OK
Rowland, Gershom C. ... Tacoma, WA
Rowland, Guy M. ... Memphis, TN
Rowland, Herbert M., Jr. San Francisco, CA
Rowland, Hodges ... Wrightsville, GA
Rowland, Hugh, Jr. ... New York, NY
Rowland, James H. ... New York, NY
Rowland, James H., Jr. ... Harrisburg, PA
Rowland, James L. ... Reston, VA
Rowland, James T. ... Blythe, CA
Rowland, James W. ... Troy, MI
Rowland, Janet M. ... Bedford, TX
Rowland, Joan K. ... Kansas City, MO
Rowland, Joe W. ... Wrightsville, GA
Rowland, John A. ... Redwood City, CA
Rowland, John C. ... St. Paul, MN
Rowland, John D. ... Racine, WI
Rowland, John H. ... Nashville, TN
Rowland, John M. Environmental Protection Agency, Office of the General Counsel, GV
Rowland, John M. ... Rye, NY
Rowland, Juliana ... Jacksonville, FL
Rowland, Karen C. ... Dallas, TX
Rowland, L. Ross ... Muncie, IN
Rowland, Landon H. ... Kansas City, MO
Rowland, Lee W. ... Lexington, KY
Rowland, Lloyd A. ... Bartlesville, OK
Rowland, Lloyd A., Jr. ... San Diego, CA
Rowland, Lori L. Pruitt ... Atlanta, GA
Rowland, Marcia ... Minnetonka, MN
Rowland, Mark A. ... San Diego, CA
Rowland, Mark A. ... Seattle, WA
Rowland, Mark C. ... Anchorage, AK
Rowland, Mark D. ... Palo Alto, CA
Rowland, Maureen L. ... Towson, MD
Rowland, Melanie J. ... Seattle, WA
Rowland and Mertensotto, P.A. St. Paul, MN
Rowland, Michael A. ... Benton, IL
Rowland, Michael C., Jr. ... Siler City, NC
Rowland, Michael J. ... Denville, NJ
Rowland, Milton G. ... Spokane, WA
Rowland, Patti L ... Helena, MT
Rowland & Petroff ... New York, NY
Rowland, Richard E. ... Sherman, TX
Rowland, Richd. W. ... Akron, OH
Rowland, Rita ... San Dimas, CA
Rowland, Robert C. ... Tucson, AZ
Rowland, Robert D. ... Edwardsville, IL
Rowland, Robert E., (A Law Corporation) Kahului, HI
Rowland, Robin ... Federal Judicial Center, GV
Rowland, Roger D. ... Baton Rouge, LA
Rowland, Ronald D. ... Eureka, CA
Rowland, Ronald L. ... Columbus, OH
Rowland & Rowland ... Bartlesville, OK
Rowland & Rowland, P.C. ... Knoxville, TN
Rowland, Sam E. ... Bryan, TX
Rowland, Sam E., Law Offices of, A Professional Corporation ... Bryan, TX
Rowland, Scott R. ... Tulsa, OK
Rowland, Stephen N. ... Wallisville, TX
Rowland, Steven R. ... Newark, NJ
Rowland, Suzan S. ... San Ramon, CA
Rowland, Terry A. ... Long Beach, CA
Rowland, Thomas W. ... Greenwich, CT
Rowland, Walter Speed ... Wilmington, DE
Rowland, William A. ... Burbank, CA
Rowland, William B., Jr. ... San Francisco, CA
Rowland, William Baxter ... Atlanta, GA
Rowland, William C. ... Alexandria, VA
Rowland, William M., III ... Orlando, FL
Rowland, William M., Jr. (P.A.) Orlando, FL
Rowland, Woodford G. ... San Rafael, CA
Rowlands, Donald E., II ... North Platte, NE
Rowlands, Elizabeth M. ... Santa Rosa, CA
Rowlands, Helen L. ... Wilmington, OH
Rowlands, Hopkin T., Jr. ... Wilkes-Barre, PA
Rowlands, Hubert L. ... Kansas City, MO
Rowlands Law Firm, The ... Albany, NY
Rowlands, Richard E. ... Albany, NY
Rowlee, Wayne E. ... LaBelle, FL
Rowlenson, Richard C. ... Greensboro, NC
Rowles, James P. ... Houston, TX
Rowles, Karen W. ... Atlanta, GA
Rowles, Michael G. ... San Diego, CA
Rowles, Steven G. ... San Diego, CA
Rowles-Stokes, Cheryl Ann ... Denver, CO
Rowlett, Beverly A. ... Little Rock, AR
Rowlett, Catherine J. ... Irvine, CA
Rowlett, G. Andrew ... Nashville, TN
Rowlett, John R. ... Dallas, TX
Rowlett, Margaret F. ... Greensboro, NC
Rowlett, Robert D. ... Newport Beach, CA
Rowlett, Sherry ... Madison, MS
Rowlett, William D. ... Dallas, TX
Rowlette, Mark A. ... Beaverton, OR
Rowlette, Roger L. ... Minneapolis, MN
Rowley, Ace E. ... Kansas City, MO
Rowley, Alison R. ... Santa Rosa, CA
Rowley, Anne Environmental Protection Agency, Office of the General Counsel, GV
Rowley, Bowen & O'Quinn, P.A. Tucumcari, NM
Rowley, Carl L. ... St. Louis, MO
Rowley, Charles S., Jr. Fort Lauderdale, FL
Rowley, Christian J. ... Boston, MA
Rowley, Christopher R. ... Dallas, TX
Rowley, Daniel A. ... Houston, TX
Rowley, David C. ... Albany, NY
Rowley, Diane L. ... Thousand Oaks, CA
Rowley, Don F ... Verplanck, NY
Rowley, Forrest, O'Donnell & Beaumont, P.C. ... Albany, NY
Rowley, George Hardy ... Greenville, PA
Rowley, Glenn A. ... Irvine, CA
Rowley, Glenn H. ... Chatham, MA
Rowley, Horace P., III ... Covington, LA
Rowley, James A. ... Green Lake, WI
Rowley, John C. ... Ithaca, NY
Rowley, John F. ... Chalmette, LA
Rowley, John H. ... Austin, TX
Rowley, John P., III ... Falls Church, VA
Rowley, Kathleen H. ... Houston, TX
Rowley, Kathleen M. ... St. Louis, MO
Rowley, Keith A. ... Jackson, MS
Rowley, Kyle M. ... Houston, TX
Rowley Law Firm, P.C. ... Clovis, NM
Rowley, Lisa J. ... Richmond, VA
Rowley, Marilyn A. ... Hoffman Estates, IL
Rowley, Mark A. ... Seattle, WA
Rowley, Marshall G. ... Wilmette, IL
Rowley, Martin K. ... Albany, NY
Rowley, Marty L. ... Amarillo, TX
Rowley, Maureen K. ... Philadelphia, PA
Rowley, Michael J. ... Philadelphia, PA
Rowley, Michael Stephen ... St. Paul, MN
Rowley, Mitchell D. ... Lincoln, NE
Rowley, Nathan D. ... San Rafael, CA
Rowley, Paul S. ... Mesa, AZ
Rowley, Richard C. ... Chicago, IL
Rowley, Richard F., II ... Clovis, NM
Rowley, Richard F., III ... Albuquerque, NM
Rowley, Richard R. ... Albany, NY
Rowley, Robert R. ... Spokane, WA
Rowley, Robert W. ... Toledo, OH
Rowley, Ronald E. ... Oneonta, NY
Rowley, Shane T. ... New York, NY
Rowley, Smith, Lewis & Dohanich Ambridge, PA
Rowley, Stephen J. ... Oakdale, MN
Rowley, Stephen P. ... Billerica, MA
Rowley, Susan C. ... Lubbock, TX
Rowley, Susan E. ... Wilmington, DE
Rowley, Timothy J. ... Pottsville, PA Reading, PA
Rowley, Vincent C. ... Pinellas Park, FL
Rowley, Wallace, Keck, Karson & St. John Greenville, PA
Rowley & Watts ... Washington, DC
Rowley, William F., III ... New York, NY
Rowley, William J., Jr. ... Bohemia, NY
Rowling, Hugh William, Jr. ... Atlanta, GA
Rowling, Lisa Gill ... Atlanta, GA
Rowling, Robert J. ... Port Huron, MI
Rowling, Streeter & Partipilo, P.C. Port Huron, MI
Rowlinson, David W. ... Moreland Hills, OH
Rowlinson, Harry G. ... Hurst, TX
Rownd, David M. ... Chicago, IL
Rownd, James H. ... Cleveland, OH
Rowney, Randy R. ... Houston, TX
Rowniewski, Wesley S. ... Newark, NJ
Rowntree, John M. ... Oklahoma City, OK
Rowntree, John M., Jr. Oklahoma City, OK
Rowny, Michael J. ... United States Senate, Committee Legal Personnel, GV

Rozmarin, George C. .... Omaha, NE
Rozmiarek, Edward J. .... Boston, MA
Rozmus, Scott V. .... Chicago, IL
Rozner, Irwin D. .... Des Plaines, IL
Rozner, Joel D. .... Baltimore, MD
Greenbelt, MD
Rozner, Maurice .... Woodland Hills, CA
Roznowski, Bruce W. .... Hampton, NJ
Roznowski, Thomas W. .... Green Bay, WI
Roznoy, Richard T. .... East Granby, CT
Rozof, Phyllis G. .... Detroit, MI
Rozos, Nicholas H. .... New York, NY
Rozran, Alfred .... Milwaukee, WI
Rozran, Jack L. .... Chicago, IL
Rozsa, Thomas I. .... Encino, CA
Rozwaski, David B. .... North Haven, CT
Rozwood, Benjamin .... Los Angeles, CA
Rozycki, Andrew G. .... Minnetonka, MN
Rozycki, Anthony T., III .... Roseville, MN
Rozycki, Carla J. .... Chicago, IL
Rozycki, Kent A. .... Traverse City, MI
Rozynko, Alisande M. .... Palo Alto, CA
Rozza, Denise Furiano .... Kings Park, NY
Rozza, Michael S. .... Huntington, NY
Rozzell, Scott E. .... Houston, TX
Rozzelle, David G. .... San Francisco, CA
Rozzi, James W. .... Naples, FL
Rozzi, Santa C. .... Mineola, NY
Rozzo, Bonny B. .... New York, NY
Rua, Christine E. .... Hartford, CT
Rua, M. Jane .... Cleveland, OH
Rua, Salvatore M. .... Tonawanda, NY
Ruan, Carlos Cristobal .... Chula Vista, CA
Ruan, Jeffrey J. .... New York, NY
Ruane, Edward P. .... New Brunswick, NJ
Ruane, James J. .... Bridgeport, CT
Ruane, James P. .... Brooklyn, NY
Ruane, James Peter .... Wichita, KS
Ruane, Joseph P. .... Shippensburg, PA
Ruane, Kevin J. .... Philadelphia, PA
Ruane, Martin J. .... San Francisco, CA
Ruane, Martin T., Jr. .... San Rafael, CA
Ruane, Michael J. .... Washington, DC
Ruane, Richard E. .... Rosemont, PA
Ruane, Thomas D. .... New York, NY
Ruane, William J. .... Madison, NJ
Ruark, Barbara E. .... Winston-Salem, NC
Ruark, Bruce W. .... Salisbury, MD
Ruark, Darrell K. .... Flemingsburg, KY
Ruark, Davis R. .... Salisbury, MD
Ruark, Eugene H. .... Chicago, IL
Ruark, J. D. .... Morganfield, KY
Ruark, John D. .... Chicago, IL
Ruark, Michael P. .... Bellevue, WA
Ruark, Patricia S. .... Atlanta, GA
Ruaro, Randall P. .... Ketchikan, AK
Rubach, Stanford M. .... Plymouth, MI
Rubacha, Edward .... Phoenix, AZ
Ruback, Alan S. .... Fort Lauderdale, FL
Ruback, Chad M. .... Dallas, TX
Ruback, R. Barry .... Atlanta, GA
Ruback, Robert I. .... New York, NY
Ruback, Steven W. .... Canton, MA
Rubacky, Joseph F., Jr. .... Hackensack, NJ
Rubadue, David W. .... Columbus, OH
Rubaii, Jawdet I. .... Clearwater, FL
Rubaii, Jawdet I., P.A. .... Clearwater, FL
Rubal & Hamm .... Houston, TX
Rubal, Mark A. .... Houston, TX
Rubalcava, Avra O. .... Boulder, CO
Rubalcava, Dominick W. .... Santa Monica, CA
Rubalcava, Sharon F. .... Los Angeles, CA
Rubano, Charles F., Jr. .... Flushing, NY
Rubano, Danielle .... Chicago, IL
Rubano, Louis Mark .... New Haven, CT
Rubano, Matthew F., Law Office of
Madison, CT
Rubanoff, Dian R. .... Portland, OR
Rubanowitz, Daniel B. .... Los Angeles, CA
Rubanowitz, Shalom .... Beverly Hills, CA
Rubard, Gary A. .... Temple Hills, MD
Rubarts, Barry .... Sherman, TX
Rubarts, Bobby M. .... Dallas, TX
Rubas, Joseph E. .... Chicago, IL
Rubas, Wendy L. .... Chicago, IL
Rubashkin, Martin .... Summit, NJ
Rubaum, David J. .... Los Angeles, CA
Rubaum, Lawrence S .... Los Angeles, CA
Rubay, Donnell M. .... Fairfield, CA
Rubbelke, Bruce R. .... Chaska, MN
Rubbert, Thomas E. .... Pasadena, CA
Rubbert, Thomas E., A Prof. Corp., Law Offices of .... Pasadena, CA
Rubbert, William R. .... Wilmington, DE
Rubbinaccio, Michael M. .... Butler, NJ
Rubbright, Kendra L. .... Minneapolis, MN
Rube, Melvin K. .... Fresno, CA
Rube, Neil A. .... Syracuse, NY
Rubel, Charles M. .... Encino, CA
Rubel, Dacia A. .... Boston, MA
Rubel, Douglas A. .... Bethesda, MD
Rubel, Ellen A. .... Bethesda, MD
Rubel, Eric A. .... Washington, DC
Rubel, Gregory A. .... Encino, CA
Rubel, Hewitt L. .... Forest Hills, NY
Rubel, Ilana Simone .... Chicago, IL
Rubel, Jeffery S. .... Kalamazoo, MI
Rubel, Jeffrey Andre .... Prospect Heights, IL
Rubel, Joseph Charles .... Winter Park, FL
Rubel, Joseph Charles, P.A. .... Winter Park, FL
Rubel, Kimberly K. .... Chicago, IL
Rubel, Michael A. .... Beverly Hills, CA
Rubel, Ralph .... Merrick, NY
Rubel, Scott M. .... Palm Springs, CA
Rubel, Steven .... Rockville Centre, NY
Rubel, Suz .... Pacific Palisades, CA
Rubel, Walter P. .... Salt Lake City, UT
Rubell, Paul .... Mineola, NY

Rubelmann, Donna A. .... Hermosa Beach, CA
Ruben, Alan M. .... Cleveland, OH
Ruben, Ann A. .... Philadelphia, PA
Ruben, Audrey H. .... Mission Viejo, CA
Ruben, Bradley N. .... New York, NY
Ruben, Charles E. .... Los Angeles, CA
Ruben, Dan .... Midlothian, VA
Ruben, David L. .... Ellicott City, MD
Ruben, David N. .... Los Angeles, CA
Ruben, Dennis L. .... Scottsdale, AZ
Ruben, Diane Daskal .... New Haven, CT
Ruben, Don .... Columbus, OH
Ruben, Francisco J. .... Washington, DC
Ruben, Gary N. .... Chicago, IL
Ruben, Harvey .... San Diego, CA
Ruben, Herbert E. .... Rye Brook, NY
Ruben, Jeffrey M. .... Bala Cynwyd, PA
Ruben, Joel D. .... Los Angeles, CA
Ruben, Johnson & Morgan, P.C.
Hartford, CT
Ruben & Jones LLP .... Los Angeles, CA
Ruben & Justman .... Los Angeles, CA
Ruben, Kaplan & Rosen .... Skokie, IL
Ruben, Laurie Gluck .... Freehold, NJ
Ruben Law Firm, The .... San Francisco, CA
Ruben, Leon .... Nashville, TN
Ruben, Marshall S. .... Hartford, CT
Ruben, Michael P. .... New York, NY
Ruben, Micheline R. .... Los Angeles, CA
Ruben, Nicholas E. .... Narberth, PA
Ruben, Philip E. .... Northfield, IL
Ruben, Richard C. .... Harrisburg, PA
Ruben, Richard G. .... Purchase, NY
Ruben, Richard S. .... Costa Mesa, CA
Ruben, Robert J. .... Mission Viejo, CA
Ruben, Robert M. .... Santa Ana, CA
Ruben, Stephen B. .... San Francisco, CA
Ruben, Stephen D. .... Landover, MD
Ruben, Steven A. .... Los Angeles, CA
Ruben, Steven J. .... Los Angeles, CA
Rubendall, Charles W., II .... Harrisburg, PA
Rubendall, Robert L. .... Halifax, PA
Rubendall, William M. .... Concord, CA
Rubenfaer, Karen .... Southfield, MI
Rubenfaer, Rachel Lynn .... Southfield, MI
Rubenfeld, Abby R. .... Nashville, TN
Rubenfeld, Eric P. .... New York, NY
Rubenfeld, Herbert, (P.C.) .... Melville, NY
Rubenfeld, Leonard .... Peekskill, NY
Rubenfeld, Leslie R. .... New York, NY
Rubenfeld, Louis .... White Plains, NY
Rubenfeld, Paul .... Kew Gardens, NY
Rubenfeld, Robert A. .... New Providence, NJ
New York, NY
Rubenfeld, Stanley I. .... New York, NY
Rubenfire, Mark D. .... Detroit, MI
Rubenoff, Richard P. .... Atlanta, GA
Rubens, Alan L. .... Spokane, WA
Rubens, Arnold E. .... Glencoe, IL
Rubens, Brad A. .... Philadelphia, PA
Rubens, David N. .... Spokane, WA
Rubens, David N., P.S. .... Spokane, WA
Rubens, Eileen Driscoll .... Los Angeles, CA
Rubens, Gregory J. .... San Carlos, CA
Rubens, Jack .... Rochester, NY
Rubens, Jack H. .... Los Angeles, CA
Rubens, James I. .... Boston, MA
Rubens, James Jay .... Santa Monica, CA
Rubens, James L. .... Chicago, IL
Rubens, Jane C. .... New York, NY
Rubens, Jason H. .... Chicago, IL
Rubens, Jonathan Tiger
San Francisco, CA
Rubens, Kent J. .... West Memphis, AR
Rubens, Raymond B. .... Bridgeport, CT
Rubens, Raymond D. .... Philadelphia, PA
Rubenstein, Alan B. .... Boston, MA
Rubenstein, Alan D. .... Succasunna, NJ
Rubenstein, Alan J. .... Chicago, IL
Rubenstein, Alan M. .... Doylestown, PA
Rubenstein, Alan S. .... Stamford, CT
Rubenstein, Alec .... Chicago, IL
Rubenstein, Alex .... Shreveport, LA
Rubenstein, Allan B. .... New Haven, CT
Rubenstein, Allen I. .... New York, NY
Rubenstein, Andrea F. .... Minneapolis, MN
Rubenstein, Andrew E. .... Houston, TX
Rubenstein, Anne Magrath
Belvedere-Tiburon, CA
Rubenstein, Arthur .... Hempstead, NY
Rubenstein, Arthur Lee .... Lake Success, NY
Rubenstein, Arthur M. .... Baltimore, MD
Rubenstein, Barry .... Eugene, OR
Rubenstein, Barry J. .... Boston, MA
Rubenstein, Benjamin
Yorktown Heights, NY
Rubenstein, Bernard W. .... Baltimore, MD
Rubenstein, Brian H. .... New York, NY
Rubenstein, Bruce M. .... Yonkers, NY
Rubenstein, Carl J. ....
Department Of Health And Human Services, GV
Rubenstein, Charles A. .... Cincinnati, OH
Rubenstein, Charles D. .... New York, NY
Rubenstein, Charles H.
Fort Lauderdale, FL
Rubenstein, Clifford T. .... Carmel, IN
Rubenstein & Cohen .... New York, NY
Rubenstein, Corey B. .... Chicago, IL
Rubenstein • Crowson, L.L.P. .... Houston, TX
Rubenstein, Daniel H.
Securities and Exchange Commission, Division of Enforcement, GV
Rubenstein, David A. .... Chicago, IL
Rubenstein, David A. .... New York, NY
Rubenstein, David M. .... Washington, DC
Rubenstein, David M., P.C. .... Washington, DC
Rubenstein, David S. .... New York, NY

Rubenstein, Debra J. .... Middletown, NJ
Rubenstein, Donald .... San Francisco, CA
Rubenstein, Donald P. .... San Francisco, CA
Rubenstein, Edward J.
Securities and Exchange Commission, Division of Investment Management, GV
Rubenstein, Edward M. .... Sugar Land, TX
Rubenstein, Eli .... Boston, MA
Rubenstein, Enid
Department of Transportation, National Highway Traffic Safety Administration, GV
Rubenstein, Eric C. .... Mineola, NY
Rubenstein, Ernest .... New York, NY
Rubenstein, Erwin A. .... Southfield, MI
Rubenstein, F. Thomas .... Morgantown, WV
Rubenstein & Finnie .... Bridgeport, CT
Rubenstein, Gary S. .... Nashville, TN
Rubenstein, Geo. .... North Miami Beach, FL
Rubenstein, Gilbert Y. .... Flint, MI
Rubenstein & Green, L.L.C.
Bridgeport, CT
Stamford, CT
Westport, CT
Rubenstein, Gregg A. .... Boston, MA
Rubenstein, Harry M. .... Morgantown, WV
Rubenstein, Harvey Bernard
Wilmington, DE
Rubenstein, Helen G. .... St. Paul, MN
Rubenstein, Herbert F. .... Broad Axe, PA
Rubenstein, Herbert R. .... Washington, DC
Rubenstein, Howard A. .... Guilderland, NY
Rubenstein, Howard A., (P.A.)
Baltimore, MD
Rubenstein, Howard D. .... Baltimore, MD
Rubenstein, Howard J. .... New York, NY
Rubenstein, Hy David .... Washington, DC
Rubenstein, Hyman B. .... Baltimore, MD
Rubenstein, I. H. .... Chicago, IL
Rubenstein, Ilana B. .... Los Angeles, CA
Rubenstein, Isaacs & Xenos, Professional Corporation .... Detroit, MI
Southfield, MI
Rubenstein, Jack C. .... Cincinnati, OH
Rubenstein, James A. .... Minneapolis, MN
Rubenstein, Jay .... Hackensack, NJ
Rubenstein, Jeffrey C. .... Chicago, IL
Rubenstein, Jeremy N. .... Washington, DC
Rubenstein, Jerome M. .... St. Louis, MO
Rubenstein, Joshua L. .... New Orleans, LA
Rubenstein, Joshua S. .... Newark, NJ
New York, NY
Rubenstein, Keith .... New York, NY
Rubenstein, Keith A. .... Bridgeport, CT
Rubenstein, Kenneth .... East Williston, NY
Rubenstein, Kenneth .... New York, NY
Rubenstein, Kenneth A. .... New York, NY
Rubenstein, Kenneth J. .... Dallas, TX
Rubenstein, Kenneth J., P.C. .... Dallas, TX
Rubenstein, Lawrence D. .... Edison, NJ
Rubenstein, Lawrence H.
San Antonio, TX
Rubenstein, Lee Alan .... New York, NY
Rubenstein, Leonard H. .... New Orleans, LA
Rubenstein, Leonard S. .... Washington, DC
Rubenstein, Lisa E. .... Pleasant Valley, NY
Rubenstein, Lori Sue .... Roseburg, OR
Rubenstein, Louis .... Cincinnati, OH
Rubenstein, Marc A. .... Boston, MA
Rubenstein, Mark A. .... Westport, CT
Rubenstein, Mark H. .... Pittsburgh, PA
Rubenstein, Martin G. .... Philadelphia, PA
Rubenstein, Martin J. .... Staten Island, NY
Rubenstein, Michael .... San Francisco, CA
Rubenstein, Michael .... Hackensack, NJ
Rubenstein, Michael .... Houston, TX
Rubenstein, Michael A.
Oklahoma City, OK
Rubenstein, Michael D. .... New Orleans, LA
Rubenstein, Michael I. .... Rochester, NY
Rubenstein, Michael J. .... San Jose, CA
Rubenstein, Michael S. .... Baltimore, MD
Rubenstein, Mitchell .... Boca Raton, FL
Rubenstein, Mitchell .... Bethesda, MD
Rubenstein, Morris .... Brooklyn, NY
Rubenstein, Morton C. .... Glenview, IL
Rubenstein, Neil J. .... San Francisco, CA
Rubenstein, Nicole R. .... Tampa, FL
Rubenstein, Norman L. .... Chicago, IL
Rubenstein, Novak, Einbund & Pavlik, LLP
Cleveland, OH
Rubenstein, Pamela .... Ridgewood, NJ
Rubenstein, Paul D. .... Los Angeles, CA
Rubenstein, Philip H. .... Carnegie, PA
Rubenstein, Randall .... Seattle, WA
Rubenstein, Richard B. .... Livingston, NJ
Rubenstein, Richard H. .... New York, NY
Rubenstein, Richard M. .... Louisville, KY
Rubenstein, Richard W. .... Columbus, OH
Rubenstein, Robert C. .... Chicago, IL
Rubenstein, Robert H. .... Gaithersburg, MD
Rubenstein, Robert J. .... Minneapolis, MN
Rubenstein, Robert, Law Offices of
Miami, FL
Rubenstein, Ronald A. .... Richmond, CA
Rubenstein, Ronald A. .... Walnut Creek, CA
Rubenstein, Ronald M. .... Cleveland, OH
Rubenstein, Roni .... New York, NY
Rubenstein, Rudolph, Meyerson, Blake & Strull, P.A. .... Oakland, NJ
Rubenstein, Samuel G. .... Washington, DC
Rubenstein, Sanford A. .... Brooklyn, NY
Rubenstein, Sarah W. .... St. Louis, MO
Rubenstein, Seth, (P.C.) .... Brooklyn, NY
Rubenstein & Silvers, P.A. .... Boca Raton, FL

Rubenstein, Stephen R.
Treasury Department, Bureau of Alcohol, Tobacco and Firearms, GV
Rubenstein, Steven M. .... Beverly Hills, CA
Rubenstein, Steven R. .... Oakland, NJ
Rubenstein, Susan, Law Offices of
San Francisco, CA
Rubenstein & Thurman, A Legal Prof. Assn.
Cincinnati, OH
Rubenstein, Todd Barrett .... New York, NY
Rubenstein, Todd Corey .... Valley Stream, NY
Rubenstein, Todd David
Santa Monica, CA
Rubenstein, Walter .... Santa Rosa, CA
Rubenstein, William B. .... Los Angeles, CA
Rubenstein, William M. .... Hartford, CT
Rubenstein, William S. .... New York, NY
Rubenstone, Edward H. .... Bensalem, PA
Rubenzahl, David J. .... St. Louis, MO
Rubenzer, Sallie Leigh .... West Bend, WI
Rubeo, Mark A., Jr .... Albany, NY
Rubeo, Stephen Vincient .... Yonkers, NY
Ruberg, Charles S. .... Tallahassee, FL
Ruberg, Donald J. .... Covington, KY
Ruberg, Michael K. .... Covington, KY
Ruberg, Robert E. .... Covington, KY
Ruberry, Edward F. .... Chicago, IL
Ruberry, Patrick J. .... Chicago, IL
Des Plaines, IL
Ruberry, William J. .... Department of Defense, Armed Services Board of Contract Appeals, GV
Rubert, Ellen Blumberg .... Grayslake, IL
Rubert, H. C., Jr. .... Kansas City, MO
Rubert, Mary Catherine .... Baiting Hollow, NY
Rubert, Soledad .... Brooklyn, NY
Ruberti, E. Michael .... Albany, NY
Ruberti, Girvin & Ferlazzo, P.C.
Albany, NY
Ruberto, A. J. .... North Adams, MA
Ruberto, Anthony J., Jr. .... North Adams, MA
Ruberto, John A., Jr. .... Fort Lauderdale, FL
Ruberto, Michael J. .... Boston, MA
Rubery, Paul T. .... Palmyra, NY
Rubes, Stephen A. .... Council Bluffs, IA
Rubesh, Karl G., II .... Chicago, IL
Rubey, C. Bonnie .... Houston, TX
Rubi, Kathryn E. .... Monroe, NC
Rubi, Pete M. .... Tucson, AZ
Rubianes-Collazo, Wanda .... San Juan, PR
Rubick, Steven J. .... Indianapolis, IN
Rubick, Wade D. .... Indianapolis, IN
Rubiera, Celestino P. .... Fort Pierce, FL
Rubillo, Thomas J. .... Georgetown, SC
Rubin, A. Barry .... Leawood, KS
Rubin, A. Michael .... Wayne, NJ
Rubin, A. Ronald .... Baltimore, MD
Rubin, Aimee Feuer .... New York, NY
Rubin, Alan .... Los Angeles, CA
Rubin, Alan .... Hackensack, NJ
Rubin, Alan M. .... New York, NY
Rubin, Alan M. .... Uniondale, NY
Rubin, Alan Marc .... New York, NY
Rubin, Albert A. .... Rockville Centre, NY
Rubin, Albert G. .... Skokie, IL
Rubin, Albert G., & Associates, Ltd.
Skokie, IL
Rubin, Alex .... Hallandale Beach, FL
Rubin, Alfred P. .... Medford, MA
Rubin, Alice Fisher .... Brooklyn, NY
Rubin, Alix R. .... Roseland, NJ
Rubin, Allan .... Hawthorne, NY
Rubin, Allan M. .... Fort Lauderdale, FL
Rubin, Allen .... Worcester, MA
Rubin, Allen W. .... Philadelphia, PA
Rubin, Allison Epstein .... Baltimore, MD
Rubin, Amy Michelle
Department of Justice, Civil Division, GV
Rubin, Amy S. .... West Palm Beach, FL
Rubin, Andrea B. .... San Francisco, CA
Rubin, Andrea J. .... Woodland Hills, CA
Rubin, Andrea Kanter .... Beachwood, OH
Rubin, Andrew .... Bloomfield, NJ
Rubin, Andrew A. .... White Plains, NY
Rubin, Andrew Ellis .... Washington, DC
Rubin, Andrew S. .... Miami, FL
Rubin, Ann .... Livingston, NJ
Rubin, Ann Harris .... New Haven, CT
Rubin, Ann R. .... Elizabeth, NJ
Rubin, Arnold .... Hialeah, FL
Rubin, Arnold E. .... Media, PA
Rubin, Arnold G. .... Chicago, IL
Rubin, Arnold G., Ltd. .... Chicago, IL
Rubin, Arthur D. .... Jacksonville, FL
Rubin, Arthur E. .... Tulsa, OK
Rubin, Asher .... San Francisco, CA
Rubin, Asher M. .... Baltimore, MD
Rubin & Associates, P.C. .... Paoli, PA
Philadelphia, PA
Rubin, Audrey H. .... Chicago, IL
Rubin, Audrey P. .... New York, NY
Rubin, Bailin, Ortoli, Mayer, Baker & Fry LLP .... New York, NY
Rubin, Barbara C. .... Fort Lauderdale, FL
Rubin, Barry .... Great Neck, NY
Rubin, Barry S. .... Beverly Hills, CA
Rubin, Benjamin M. .... Palo Alto, CA
Rubin, Beth L. .... Blue Bell, PA
Rubin, Beth S. .... Chicago, IL
Rubin, Blake D. .... Washington, DC
Rubin, Brian L. .... Washington, DC
Rubin, Brian N. .... Buffalo Grove, IL
Rubin, Bruce A., P.C. .... Portland, OR
Rubin, Bruce Brian .... Troy, NY
Rubin, Bruce J. .... New York, NY
Rubin, Burton J. .... Alexandria, VA
Rubin, Burton R., (P.C.) .... New York, NY

Rubin, Byron H. .... Dallas, TX
Rubin, Carl M. .... Oakland, CA
Rubin, Carol L. .... Baltimore, MD
Rubin, Carol S. .... Rockville, MD
Rubin, Caroline C. .... Ambler, PA
Rubin, Carolyn .... New York, NY
Rubin, Charles D. .... Boca Raton, FL
Rubin, Charles E. .... Overland Park, KS
Rubin, Charles G. .... Beverly Hills, CA
Rubin, Charles T. .... New York, NY
Rubin & Connelly .... Paterson, NJ
Wayne, NJ
Rubin, Conrad P. .... New York, NY
Rubin, Corey A. .... Washington, DC
Rubin, Curt M. .... New York, NY
Rubin, Cynthia B. .... New York, NY
Rubin, Cynthia Lu .... Los Angeles, CA
Rubin, Dale M. .... Los Angeles, CA
Rubin, Damon .... Los Angeles, CA
Rubin, Daniel .... Flushing, NY
Rubin, Daniel .... Dallas, TX
Rubin, Daniel R. .... Santa Fe, NM
Rubin, Daniel R. .... Columbus, OH
Rubin, Daniel S. .... New York, NY
Rubin, Daryl K. .... Toledo, OH
Rubin, David (IBA) .... New Hyde Park, NY
Rubin, David .... Reston, VA
Rubin, David A. .... Phoenix, AZ
Rubin, David A. .... Schaumburg, IL
Rubin, David A. .... New York, NY
Rubin, David B. .... Washington, DC
Rubin, David B. .... Metuchen, NJ
Rubin, David B., P.C. .... Metuchen, NJ
New Brunswick, NJ
Rubin, David H.
United States Postal Service, Law Department, GV
Rubin, David H. .... St. Louis, MO
Rubin, David J. .... Boston, MA
Providence, RI
Rubin, David L. .... Boston, MA
Rubin, David M. .... Chicago, IL
Rubin, David M. .... New York, NY
Rubin, David Neal .... Philadelphia, PA
Rubin, David S. .... Baton Rouge, LA
Rubin, David S. .... Boston, MA
Rubin, David S. J. .... Hauppauge, NY
Rubin, David W. .... Stamford, CT
Rubin, Deborah L. .... Boynton Beach, FL
Rubin, Deborah L. .... Southfield, MI
Rubin, Deborah S. .... Southfield, MI
Rubin, Debra L. .... Lake Success, NY
Rubin, Debra M. .... Coral Gables, FL
Rubin, Debra O. .... Miami, FL
Rubin, Denise D. .... Briarcliff Manor, NY
Rubin, Derrick A. .... Great Neck, NY
Rubin, Diane .... Boston, MA
Rubin, Donald H. .... Santa Ana, CA
Rubin, Donald T. .... Chicago, IL
Rubin, Dora B. .... Miami, FL
Rubin & Dornbaum .... Newark, NJ
Rubin, E. Leonard .... Chicago, IL
Rubin, Eagan & Kane, LLP
Beverly Hills, CA
San Francisco, CA
Rubin, Edward .... New York, NY
Rubin, Edward .... Lansdale, PA
Rubin, Edward D. .... Lafayette, LA
Rubin, Edward L. .... Berkeley, CA
Rubin, Edward M. .... Northbrook, IL
Rubin, Edwin R. .... Newark, NJ
Rubin, Edwin S. .... Roseland, NJ
Rubin, Ehrlich & Buckley, A Professional Corporation .... Princeton, NJ
Rubin & Eldrich, P.C. .... New Haven, CT
Rubin, Elisabeth S. .... Rockville, MD
Rubin, Ellen J. .... Boston, MA
Rubin, Elliot M. .... Brooklyn, NY
Rubin, Ellis S. .... Miami, FL
Rubin, Emily Beth .... Washington, DC
Rubin, Eric H. .... Washington, DC
Rubin, Eric M., (P.C.) .... Washington, DC
Rubin, Erika B. .... Washington, DC
Rubin, Erwin .... Chicago, IL
Rubin, Eugene L. .... Worcester, MA
Rubin, Eugene S. .... New York, NY
Rubin, Frank A. .... Amarillo, TX
Rubin, Frank D. .... Encino, CA
Rubin, Frank J. .... Piscataway, NJ
Rubin, Fred P. .... Great Neck, NY
Rubin, G. David .... Los Angeles, CA
Rubin, Gail P. .... New York, NY
Rubin, Gary I. .... Washington, DC
Rubin, Gary L. .... New York, NY
Rubin, Gene L. .... North Hollywood, CA
Rubin, George A. .... Indianapolis, IN
Rubin, Gerald H. .... Irving, TX
Rubin, Gerald, (P.C.) .... Totowa, NJ
Rubin, Gilbert V. .... Baltimore, MD
Rubin, Glen D. .... Atlanta, GA
Rubin, Glickman and Steinberg, P.C. A Professional Corporation
Doylestown, PA
Lansdale, PA
Norristown, PA
Rubin & Gold .... New York, NY
Rubin, Gregory S. .... Paoli, PA
Rubin & Gugenheim, P.C. .... Dallas, TX
Rubin, Guy B. .... Stuart, FL
Rubin, Harold H. .... Lafayette Hill, PA
Rubin, Harold J. .... Phippsburg, ME
Rubin, Harry .... Washington, DC
Rubin, Harry A. .... Haddon Heights, NJ
Philadelphia, PA
Rubin, Harry J. .... Harrisburg, PA
York, PA
Rubin, Hay & Gould, P.C.
Framingham, MA

Rubin & Hays .... Louisville, KY
Rubin, Helen .... Woodbury, NY
Rubin, Herbert .... New York, NY
Rubin, Howard .... Boston, MA
Rubin, Howard .... Portland, OR
Rubin, Howard C. .... Dallas, TX
Rubin, Howard I. .... Philadelphia, PA
Rubin, Howard I. .... McLean, VA
Rubin, Howard J. .... Minneapolis, MN
Rubin, Howard J. .... New York, NY
Rubin, Howard M. .... Los Angeles, CA
Rubin, Howard M. .... Chicago, IL
Rubin, Howard M. .... New York, NY
Rubin, Howard R. .... Washington, DC
Rubin, Hyman S., Jr. .... Columbia, SC
Rubin, Ira .... Dayton, OH
Rubin, Ira E. .... Chicago, IL
Rubin, Ira S. .... Eugene, OR
Rubin, Irving I. M. .... Los Angeles, CA
Rubin, Irving W. .... New Brunswick, NJ
Rubin, Irwin N. .... White Plains, NY
Rubin, Irwin S. .... Lansdale, PA
Rubin, Isaac .... Brooklyn, NY
Rubin, Isadore .... Whippany, NJ
Rubin, Israel .... New York, NY
Rubin, Ivan B. .... Brooklyn, NY
Rubin, Jack .... Farmington, CT
Rubin, Jack B. .... Pikesville, MD
Rubin, Jaime Fredrick
Truth or Consequences, NM
Rubin, James E. .... Washington, DC
Rubin, James I. .... Chicago, IL
Rubin, James S.
Federal Communications Commission, Wireless Telecommunications Bureau, GV
Rubin, James S. .... Santa Fe, NM
Rubin, James W .... Department of Justice, Environment and Natural Resources Division, GV
Rubin, Jamie .... New York, NY
Rubin, Jane Gregory .... New York, NY
Rubin, Janice E. .... Library of Congress, Congressional Research Service, GV
Rubin, Janice Lavernia .... Miami, FL
Rubin, Jason L. .... Chicago, IL
Rubin, Jay T. .... Ventura, CA
Rubin, Jay Y. .... Indiana, PA
Rubin, Jeanne C. .... Tehachapi, CA
Rubin, Jeanne M. .... Denver, CO
Rubin, Jeannie M. .... Columbia, SC
Rubin, Jeff E. .... Miami, FL
Rubin, Jeff H. .... Oakland, CA
Rubin, Jeffrey B .... Newton, MA
Rubin, Jeffrey D. .... Irvine, CA
Rubin, Jeffrey K. .... Anchorage, AK
Rubin, Jeffrey M. .... Atlanta, GA
Rubin, Jeffrey M. .... Manchester, NH
Rubin, Jeffrey M. .... New York, NY
Rubin, Jeffrey O. .... Evanston, IL
Rubin, Jeffrey W. .... Rockville, MD
Rubin, Jeffrey W. .... New York, NY
Rubin, Jennifer A. .... Los Angeles, CA
Rubin, Jennifer B. .... Stamford, CT
Rubin, Jennifer S. .... Harrisburg, PA
Rubin, Jerome L. .... Seattle, WA
Rubin, Jerome S. .... New York, NY
Rubin, Jesse R. .... New York, NY
Rubin, Jessica S. .... Stamford, CT
Rubin, Jill Bishop
Pension Benefit Guaranty Corporation, Office of the General Counsel, GV
Rubin, Joanne .... Toledo, OH
Rubin, Joel B. .... New York, NY
Rubin, Joel D. .... Chicago, IL
Rubin, Joel R., Law Offices of
Santa Rosa, CA
Rubin, John H. .... Briarcliff Manor, NY
Rubin, Jonathan .... Lake Success, NY
Rubin, Jonathan L. .... Palm Beach, FL
Rubin, Jonathan L., P.A. .... Palm Beach, FL
Rubin, Jonathan R. .... Miami, FL
Rubin, Jonathan S. .... New York, NY
Rubin, Jon-David .... Sacramento, CA
Rubin, Joseph .... Hartford, CT
Rubin, Joseph .... Sarasota, FL
Rubin, Joseph .... New York, NY
Rubin, Joseph D. .... Fresno, CA
Rubin, Joseph F. .... South Bend, IN
Rubin, Joseph H. .... Dunwoody, GA
Rubin, Joseph L. .... San Diego, CA
Rubin, Joseph S. .... St. Louis, MO
Rubin, Joshua N. .... New York, NY
Rubin, Joshua P. .... New York, NY
Rubin, Joyce C. .... Denver, CO
Rubin, Julian .... Cincinnati, OH
Rubin, Julie A. Stewart .... Garden City, NY
Rubin, Julie H. .... Beverly Hills, CA
Rubin, Julie L. .... Philadelphia, PA
Rubin, Julie P. .... Chicago, IL
Rubin, Julie R. .... Baltimore, MD
Rubin, Kaplan & Associates, A Professional Corporation .... New Brunswick, NJ
Piscataway, NJ
Rubin, Karen E. .... Cleveland, OH
Rubin, Katz, Salazar, Alley & Rouse, A Professional Corporation .... Santa Fe, NM
Rubin, Kay F. .... Alameda, CA
Rubin, Kenneth A. .... Washington, DC
Rubin, Kenneth A. .... Hollywood, FL
Rubin, Kenneth B. .... New Haven, CT
Rubin, Kenneth D. .... Princeton, NJ
Rubin, Kenneth J. .... Philadelphia, PA
Rubin, Kenneth M. .... West Palm Beach, FL
Rubin, Kenneth S. .... Tamarac, FL
Rubin, Kerry Pyle .... Washington, DC
Rubin, Kidney, Myer & DeWolfe .... Barre, VT
Rubin, Kim M. .... Boston, MA
Rubin, L. Anthony .... Los Angeles, CA

Rubin, Lael R. .... Los Angeles, CA
Rubin, Laura H. .... New York, NY
Rubin, Laurence D. .... Santa Monica, CA
Rubin, Laurence K. .... Buffalo, NY
Rubin, Laurie F. .... Boston, MA
Rubin, Laurine M. .... Albertson, NY
Rubin, Lawrence C. .... Chicago, IL
Rubin, Lawrence E. .... Silver Spring, MD
Rubin, Lawrence J. .... New York, NY
Rubin, Lawrence M. .... Buffalo, NY
Rubin, Lawrence S. .... Media, PA
Rubin, Lee H. .... Washington, DC
Rubin, Leonard .... Highland Park, IL
Rubin, Leonard .... Wyncote, PA
Rubin, Leonard G. .... Palm Beach, FL
Rubin, Leonard J. .... Washington, DC
Rubin, Leslie A. .... Brooklyn, NY
Rubin, Lester W. .... New York, NY
Rubin & Levin, P.C. .... Indianapolis, IN
Rubin, Lewis A. .... New York, NY
Rubin & Licatesi, P.C. .... Garden City, NY
Rubin, Linda Brown .... Irving, TX
Rubin, Lois C. .... New York, NY
Rubin, Lois E. .... Newport Beach, CA
Rubin, Lois S. .... Buffalo, NY
Rubin, Lori S. .... New York, NY
Rubin, Lowell M. .... Brooklyn, NY
Rubin, Marc A. .... Miami, FL
Rubin, Marc H. .... New York, NY
Rubin, Marc W. .... Cincinnati, OH
Rubin, Marci .... San Francisco, CA
Rubin, Mark B. .... Bronx, NY
Rubin, Mark D. .... Tucson, AZ
Rubin, Mark D. .... Detroit, MI
Rubin, Mark E. .... Richmond, VA
Rubin, Mark J. .... Denver, CO
Rubin, Mark R. .... Miami, FL
Rubin, Mark R. .... Miami Beach, FL
Rubin, Mark S. .... Chicago, IL
Rubin, Mark S. .... Duluth, MN
Rubin, Mark S. .... St. Louis, MO
Rubin, Mark S. .... Dallas, TX
Rubin, Mark Scott .... Fort Walton Beach, FL
Rubin, Mark Stuart
Federal Communications Commission, Office of Legislative and Intergovernmental Affairs, GV
Rubin, Marla B. .... New York, NY
Rubin, Marshall L. .... Encino, CA
Rubin, Martin H., (P.C.) .... Atlanta, GA
Rubin, Martin J. .... Chicago, IL
Rubin, Martin J., Law Offices of
Dallas, TX
Rubin, Martin, (P.C.) .... Eatontown, NJ
Rubin, Matt E. .... Houston, TX
Rubin, Maxwell A. .... Great Neck, NY
Rubin, Melvin .... Narberth, PA
Rubin, Melvin A. .... Coral Gables, FL
Rubin, Melvyn R. .... Sunrise, FL
Rubin, Merek S. .... Framingham, MA
Milford, MA
Rubin, Merrill Neil .... New York, NY
Rubin, M. H. .... Chicago, IL
Rubin, Michael .... San Francisco, CA
Rubin, Michael .... Providence, RI
Rubin, Michael .... Fairfield, CA
Napa, CA
Rubin, Michael A.
Treasury Department, GV
Rubin, Michael A. .... Coral Gables, FL
Rubin, Michael A. .... New York, NY
Rubin, Michael A., P.A. .... Coral Gables, FL
Rubin, Michael D. .... Costa Mesa, CA
Rubin, Michael D. .... Philadelphia, PA
Rubin, Michael E. .... Braintree, MA
Rubin, Michael F. .... New York, NY
Rubin, Michael H. .... Baton Rouge, LA
Rubin, Michael J. .... Bowie, MD
Rubin, Michael L. .... Phoenix, AZ
Prescott, AZ
Rubin, Michael R.
Department of Commerce, Office of the General Counsel, GV
Rubin, Michael S. .... Phoenix, AZ
Rubin, Michael S. .... Cupertino, CA
Rubin, Michael S. .... Livingston, NJ
Rubin, Miles J., Law Offices of
Los Angeles, CA
Rubin, Miles L. .... New York, NY
Rubin, Miriam R. .... Somerset, NJ
Rubin, Mitchell D. .... Basking Ridge, NJ
Rubin, Mitchell Jay .... Tallahassee, FL
Rubin, Mitchell S. .... Phoenix, AZ
Rubin & Monahan, Chtd. .... Rockville, MD
Rubin, Mori Pam .... Los Angeles, CA
Rubin, Morris D. .... Bangor, ME
Rubin & Moss .... Santa Monica, CA
Rubin, Myer .... Detroit, MI
Rubin, Myron L. .... Denver, CO
Rubin, Nancy .... Miami, FL
Rubin, Nancy G. .... San Francisco, CA
Rubin, Nancy G. .... Washington, DC
Rubin, Neal A. .... Palo Alto, CA
Rubin, Norman .... Woodmere, NY
Rubin, Norman A. .... Los Angeles, CA
Rubin, Paul .... San Francisco, CA
Rubin, Paul .... Bordentown, NJ
Mount Holly, NJ
Robbinsville, NJ
Rubin, Paul A. .... Princeton, NJ
New York, NY
Rubin, Paul D. .... Washington, DC
Rubin, Paul L. .... Bristol, CT
Rubin, Penny .... Albany, NY
Rubin, Peter D. .... Santa Rosa, CA
Rubin, Peter G. .... Rockville Centre, NY
Rubin, Peter J. .... Washington, DC
Rubin, Peter J. .... Portland, ME

Rubin, Peter M. .... Baltimore, MD
Rubin, Peter M. .... Carle Place, NY
Rubin, Philip H. .... Great Neck, NY
Rubin, Philip L. .... Atlanta, GA
Rubin, Quinn, Moss & Patterson, P.C.
Philadelphia, PA
Rubin, Rand S. .... Los Angeles, CA
Rubin, Randi Lynne .... Philadelphia, PA
Rubin, Remey J. .... Chicago, IL
Rubin, Renee .... San Francisco, CA
Rubin, Renee M. .... Los Angeles, CA
Rubin, Rhesa C. .... Palo Alto, CA
Rubin, Richard .... Washington, DC
Rubin, Richard .... Baltimore, MD
Rubin, Richard A. .... Atlanta, GA
Rubin, Richard A. .... New York, NY
Rubin, Richard A. .... Philadelphia, PA
Rubin, Richard E. .... New York, NY
Rubin, Richard H. .... Basking Ridge, NJ
Rubin, Richard H. .... Garden City, NY
Rubin, Richard I. .... Barre, VT
Rubin, Richard J. .... Phoenix, AZ
Rubin, Richard J. .... Chicago, IL
Rubin, Richard J. .... Santa Fe, NM
Rubin, Richard J. .... Harrison, NY
Rubin, Richard J., P.C. .... Phoenix, AZ
Rubin, Richard P. .... Hartford, CT
Rubin, Rick J. .... Denver, CO
Rubin, Robert .... Farmington Hills, MI
Rubin, Robert A. .... New York, NY
Rubin, Robert B. .... Birmingham, AL
Rubin, Robert C. .... Chicago, IL
Rubin, Robert D. .... Miami, FL
Rubin, Robert F. .... Santa Monica, CA
Rubin, Robert G. .... Atlanta, GA
Rubin, Robert H. .... Westport, CT
Rubin, Robert I., Law Offices of
Fort Lauderdale, FL
Rubin, Robert J. .... Rockport, ME
Rubin, Robert M. .... Cherry Hill, NJ
Rubin, Robert Marc .... Greenville, NC
Rubin, Robert R. .... Sacramento, CA
Rubin, Robert S. .... Los Angeles, CA
Rubin, Robert S. .... Cincinnati, OH
Rubin, Robert W. .... Universal City, CA
Rubin, Roberta L. .... Boston, MA
Rubin, Rochelle .... Philadelphia, PA
Rubin, Roger A. .... Chicago, IL
Rubin, Roger R. .... San Francisco, CA
Rubin, Ronald B. .... Rockville, MD
Rubin, Ronald G. .... Voorhees, NJ
Rubin, Ronald M. .... Denver, CO
Rubin, Ronit .... New York, NY
Rubin, Rose Luttan .... New York, NY
Rubin, Ross N. .... Chicago, IL
Rubin & Rothman .... Islandia, NY
Rubin & Rubin .... Los Angeles, CA
Rubin & Rubin .... Miami, FL
Stuart, FL
Rubin & Rubin .... Worcester, MA
Rubin & Rubin .... Haddon Heights, NJ
Philadelphia, PA
Rubin, Rubin & Di Paola .... New York, NY
Rubin & Rubin, P.A. .... Miami, FL
Rubin & Rubin, P.C. .... Washington, DC
Silver Spring, MD
Rubin and Rudman LLP .... Boston, MA
Rubin, Russell M. .... Los Angeles, CA
Rubin, Ruthlyn B. .... Trenton, NJ
Rubin, S. Richard .... Boise, ID
Rubin, Samuel .... Thompson, ND
Rubin, Samuel D. .... Flushing, NY
Rubin, Samuel K. .... Hempstead, NY
Rubin, Scott D. .... Mineola, NY
Rubin, Scott L., (P.A.) .... Miami, FL
Rubin, Scott L.H. .... Norristown, PA
Rubin, Scott N. .... Newark, NJ
Rubin, Seth Ian .... Mineola, NY
Rubin, Seymour J. .... Washington, DC
Rubin, Shapiro & Weisse .... Philadelphia, PA
Rubin, Sharon Sirota .... Baltimore, MD
Rubin, Sheila .... Baltimore, MD
Rubin, Sheila, P.A., Law Offices of
Baltimore, MD
Rubin, Sheldon .... Beverly Hills, CA
San Francisco, CA
Rubin, Sheldon J. .... Toledo, OH
Rubin, Sherle .... Farmington Hills, MI
Rubin, Sidney .... St. Louis, MO
Rubin, Stanford K., (A P.C.)
Los Angeles, CA
Rubin, Stanley R. .... Canton, OH
Rubin, Stephen .... Washington, DC
Rubin, Stephen B. .... Oak Park, IL
Rubin, Stephen M. .... Tucson, AZ
Rubin, Stephen M. .... Fort Lauderdale, FL
Rubin, Stephen W. .... New York, NY
Rubin, Steve .... Northbrook, IL
Rubin, Steven .... Tarrytown, NY
Rubin, Steven C. .... Oakhurst, NJ
Rubin, Steven D. .... Los Angeles, CA
Rubin, Steven D. .... Boca Raton, FL
Rubin, Steven D. .... Miami, FL
Rubin, Steven D. .... Houston, TX
Rubin, Steven E. .... Minneapolis, MN
Rubin, Steven G. .... Mineola, NY
Rubin, Steven H. .... Atlanta, GA
Rubin, Steven H. .... King Of Prussia, PA
Rubin, Steven L. .... San Diego, CA
Rubin, Steven M. .... Beverly Hills, CA
Rubin, Steven M. .... Worcester, MA
Rubin, Steven M. .... Minneapolis, MN
Rubin, Steven M. .... Philadelphia, PA
Rubin, Steven R. .... New York, NY
Rubin, Stewart A. .... Santa Monica, CA
Rubin, Stuart D. .... Brooklyn, NY
Rubin, Susan J. .... Rockville, MD
Rubin, Susan J., P.A. .... Rockville, MD

Rubin, Thai Edan ... Greenwich, CT
Rubin, Thea F. ... Edwardsville, IL
Rubin, Thomas C. ... Redmond, WA
Rubin, Todd M. ... Hauppauge, NY
Rubin, Todd M. ... Raleigh, NC
Rubin, Victor R. ... Jericho, NY
Rubin, Walter I. ... Cincinnati, OH
Rubin, Warren ... Philadelphia, PA
Rubin, Wayne M. ... White Plains, NY
Rubin & Wildau ... Atlanta, GA
Rubin, William ... New York, NY
Rubin, William A. ... Havertown, PA
Rubin, William J. ... Baltimore, MD
Rubin, William L. ... Tucson, AZ
Rubin, Winston, Diercks, Harris & Cooke, L.L.P. ... Washington, DC
Rubin, Winter, Rapoport & Hall
Atlanta, GA
Rubin, Zick ... Boston, MA
Rubinas, Wayne L. ... Tallahassee, FL
Rubinate, Frank J. ... Philadelphia, PA
RubinBaum LLP ... Iselin, NJ
Short Hills, NJ
New York, NY
Rubinberg, Michael ... Brooklyn, NY
Rubinchik, Harvey L. ... Plantation, FL
Rubinchik, Harvey L., P.A.
Fort Lauderdale, FL
Plantation, FL
Rubinchik, Scott David
Pembroke Pines, FL
Rubin-Collins, Lee ... Boston, MA
Rubin-de-Cervens, Andrea ... East Islip, NY
Rubine, Allen P. ... Providence, RI
Rubine, Marilyn Carol ... Mineola, NY
Rubine, Robert S. ... Mineola, NY
Rubine & Rubine, P.L.L.C. ... Mineola, NY
Rubin-Elbaz, Betty ... Beverly Hills, CA
Rubinelli, Joseph O. ... Chicago, IL
Rubinelli, Joseph O., Jr. ... Chicago, IL
Rubinelli, Mark J. ... St. Louis, MO
Rubiner, Arthur J. ... West Bloomfield, MI
Rubiner, Mark M., Law Office of
Tucson, AZ
Rubinett, Arthur E. ... Dallas, TX
Rubinett, Gordon M. ... Austin, TX
Rubinfeld, Alyce Ann ... Los Angeles, CA
Rubinfeld, Amy L. ... Los Angeles, CA
Rubinfeld, Gail N. ... Berkeley, CA
Rubinfeld, Ira B. ... Salt Lake City, UT
Rubinfeld, Paige F. ... Newport Beach, CA
Rubinfeld, Teena ... New York, NY
Rubinfeld and Wertenteil ... New York, NY
Rubinfier, Jon B. ... Encino, CA
Rubinger, Bruce ... Minneapolis, MN
Rubinger, Hedy Silver ... Atlanta, GA
Rubinger, James C. ... Washington, DC
Rubinger, Jeffrey L. ... New York, NY
Rubinger, Karen L. ... Stockton, CA
Rubinger, Kenneth L. ... Stockton, CA
Rubinger, Michael E. ... Atlanta, GA
Rubinger, Robert ... New York, NY
Rubinger & Rubinger ... Stockton, CA
Rubin-Howton, Vicki
San Juan Capistrano, CA
Rubini, D. Laurence ... Philadelphia, PA
Rubini, Jonathan B. ... Anchorage, AK
Rubini, Suzanne ... Atlanta, GA
Rubin-Ness, Rochelle ... Edina, MN
Rubino, Carl J. ... New Rochelle, NY
Rubino, Carl J., Jr. ... Elizabethtown, NY
Rubino, Carmine ... New York, NY
Rubino & Crosmer ... Munster, IN
Rubino, Daniel D. ... New York, NY
Rubino, David L. ... Rockville, MD
Rubino, Douglas F. ... Newport Beach, CA
Rubino, Eric N. ... Newtown Square, PA
Rubino, Frank J. ... New York, NY
Rubino, Gary Michael ... Mount Vernon, NY
Rubino, Gennaro ... Jersey City, NJ
Rubino, James M. ... Stamford, CT
Rubino, John A., III ... Columbus, IN
Rubino, Joseph D. ... Columbus, OH
Rubino, Joseph R. ... Millburn, NJ
Rubino, Louis A. ... Boulder, CO
Rubino, Louis G. ... Westmont, NJ
Rubino, Louis J., Jr. ... Potomac, MD
Rubino, Michael A., Jr. ... Stamford, CT
Rubino, Michael C. ... Las Vegas, NV
Rubino, Michael J. ... Irvine, CA
Rubino, Michael J. ... Berkeley Heights, NJ
Rubino, Michael R., Jr. ... Spring Lake, NJ
Rubino, Nancy S. ... Kalamazoo, MI
Rubino, Nicholas J., Jr. ... Maitland, FL
Rubino, Raymond C. ... West Orange, NJ
Rubino, Renee A. ... Secaucus, NJ
Rubino, Richard D. ... Washington, DC
Rubino, Richard L. ... Brookline Village, MA
Rubino, Stephen C. ... Westmont, NJ
Rubino, Steven C. ... Boca Raton, FL
Rubino, Terrence M. ... Munster, IN
Rubino, Thomas W. ... Princeton, NJ
Rubino, Victor J. ... New York, NY
Rubino, Vincent ... Marshalls Creek, PA
Stroudsburg, PA
Rubino, Vincent J., Jr. ... Secaucus, NJ
Rubinoff, Arnold E. ... Atlanta, GA
Rubinoff, David B. ... Oakland, CA
Rubinoff, Edward G. ... Miami, FL
Rubinoff, Edward L., (P.C.)
Washington, DC
Rubinoff, Greg B. ... Lodi, CA
Rubinoff, Harry J. ... Phoenix, AZ
Rubinoff, Harry W. ... Chicago, IL
Rubinoff, Mark R. ... Pittsburgh, PA
Rubinoff, Mike R. ... Greensburg, PA
Rubinoff, N. Arthur ... Chicago, IL
Rubinoff, Norman J. ... Toledo, OH

Rubinoff, Stephanie Susan ... Oakland, CA
Rubinovitz, Susan M. ... Millersville, MD
Rubinow, Carlyle M. ... Silver Spring, MD
Rubinow, Jay E. ... Manchester, CT
Rubinow, Laurence P. ... Manchester, CT
Rubinow, Nicola E. ... Hartford, CT
Rubinowitz, Ben B. ... New York, NY
Rubinowitz, Jay B. ... New York, NY
Rubinowitz, Leonard S. ... Chicago, IL
Rubinowitz, Michael ... Carle Place, NY
Rubinroit, Howard J. ... Los Angeles, CA
Rubins, Harlan W. ... Columbus, OH
Rubins, Joshua M. ... New York, NY
Rubins, Kase, Rubins, Cambiano & Bryant, A Professional Corporation
Kansas City, MO
Rubins, Richard A. ... Kansas City, MO
Rubins, Stephen S. ... Wildwood, NJ
Rubins, Suzanne C. ... Boston, MA
Rubinshteyn, Steve A. ... New York, NY
Rubinsky, Abraham I. ... Houston, TX
Rubinsky, David E. ... New York, NY
Rubinsky, Joshua P. ... Philadelphia, PA
Rubinsky, Melanie A. ... Houston, TX
Rubinson, Adolph A. ... Chicago, IL
Rubinson, Alan M. ... Philadelphia, PA
Rubinson, Elaine ... Shelton, CT
Rubinson, Gene Z. ... Washington, DC
Rubinson, Robert J. ... Baltimore, MD
Rubinson, Seth Ian ... Boston, MA
Rubinstein, Aaron ... New York, NY
Rubinstein, Alan F. ... Morris Plains, NJ
Rubinstein, Alan J. ... Fort Myers, FL
Rubinstein, Alan J. ... New York, NY
Rubinstein, Alfred ... Hicksville, NY
Rubinstein, Arnold E. ... New York, NY
Rubinstein, Asher ... New York, NY
Rubinstein, Carl E. ... Brookline, MA
Rubinstein, Caryn M. ... Florham Park, NJ
Princeton, NJ
Rubinstein, Clara E. ... Chicago, IL
Rubinstein, Danielle ... New York, NY
Rubinstein, David P. ... Elmsford, NY
Rubinstein, Edward ... Clifton, NJ
Rubinstein, Edward M. ... Anaheim, CA
Rubinstein, Frederic A. ... New York, NY
Rubinstein, H. Jonathan ... Millburn, NJ
Rubinstein, Heidi ... New York, NY
Rubinstein, Holly Mills ... Palo Alto, CA
Rubinstein & Holz, P.A. ... Fort Myers, FL
Rubinstein, Ira S. ... Redmond, WA
Rubinstein, Jack ... Mineola, NY
Rubinstein, Javier H. ... Chicago, IL
Rubinstein, Jay H. ... New Haven, CT
Rubinstein, Jeffrey D. ... Miami, FL
Rubinstein, Joel L. ... New York, NY
Rubinstein, Joel S. ... Washington, DC
Rubinstein, Julius L. ... Van Nuys, CA
Rubinstein, Karl L. ... Los Angeles, CA
Rubinstein, Kenneth ... New York, NY
Rubinstein, Kenneth ... New York, NY
Rubinstein, Kenneth J. ... New York, NY
Rubinstein, Leif I. ... Lake Ronkonkoma, NY
Rubinstein, Marc H. ... Las Vegas, NV
Rubinstein, Mark S. ... Denver, CO
Rubinstein, Marvin ... New York, NY
Rubinstein, Michael Lee ... Tampa, FL
Rubinstein, Mitchell H. ... New York, NY
Rubinstein & Perry, A Professional Corporation ... Los Angeles, CA
Rubinstein, Phyllis M. ... Richmond, VA
Rubinstein, Reed D. ... Hartford, CT
Southport, CT
Rubinstein, Richard E. ... Cleveland, OH
Rubinstein, Robert ... Fort Lauderdale, FL
Rubinstein, Robert J. ... New York, NY
Rubinstein, Robert W. ... Princeton, NJ
Rubinstein, Sheila B. ... Monarch Beach, CA
Rubinstein, Sherwin R. ... Chicago, IL
Lincolnwood, IL
Rubinstein, Sidney E. ... New York, NY
Rubinstein, Steven I. ... Buffalo, NY
Rubinstein, Steven M. ... Mount Pleasant, SC
Rubinstein, Steven S. ... Alpharetta, GA
Rubinstein, Todd M. ... New York, NY
Rubinstein, Vadim J. ... New York, NY
Rubinstein, Walter D. ... Baltimore, MD
Rubinton, David S. ... Little Neck, NY
Rubinton, Jeffrey A. ... Fort Lauderdale, FL
Rubinton, Joel J. ... Brooklyn, NY
Rubinton, Noel ... New York, NY
Rubinton, Peter D. ... Huntington, NY
Rubio, Alex ... Miami, FL
Rubio, Fermin A. ... Albuquerque, NM
Rubio, H. Frank ... Miami Shores, FL
Rubio, H. Frank, P.A. ... Miami Shores, FL
Rubio, Jane ... Houston, TX
Rubio, Lionel Enrique ... Orlando, FL
Rubio, Lisa Tobin ... Miami, FL
Rubio, Marco A. ... Miami, FL
Rubio, Maria L. ... Miami, FL
Rubio, Martha Elena ... Department of Justice, Civil Division, GV
Rubio, Miguel Eugenio
Export-Import Bank of The United States, Office of the General Counsel, GV
Rubio, Rafael, Sr. ... Baton Rouge, LA
Rubio-Campos, Francisco A. ... Chicago, IL
Rubiola, Charles A., Jr. ... San Antonio, TX
Rubis, Gregory J. ... Washington, DC
Rubish, Renee C. ... Mankato, MN
Rubitschun, John S. ... Lansing, MI
Rubke, Mark E. ... Oakland, CA
Ruble and Bozarth ... Taloga, OK
Ruble, Charles H. ... San Antonio, TX
Ruble, Jay R. ... Morristown, NJ
Ruble, Joseph T. ... Englewood, CO
Ruble, Lisa A. ... Chicago, IL

Ruble, Marcella L. ... Los Angeles, CA
Chicago, IL
Ruble, Matthew B. ... Frederick, MD
Ruble, R. J. ... New York, NY
Ruble, Steven P. ... Milaca, MN
Ruble, Tammy Stafford ... Richmond, VA
Ruble, Tom J. ... Taloga, OK
Rublee, George
Agency for International Development, Other Offices of A.I.D., GV
Rublee, Laura Chandler ... Florence, SC
Rubler, Leila J. ... New York, NY
Rubley, C. Ronald ... Philadelphia, PA
Rublin, Arthur ... New York, NY
Rublin, Burt M. ... Philadelphia, PA
Rublin, Joel S. ... New York, NY
Rubloff, Gilbert W. ... Boca Raton, FL
Rubloff & Jacobs, L.L.C.
Gaithersburg, MD
Rockville, MD
Rubloff, Ronald A. ... Gaithersburg, MD
Rubman, Scott A. ... Roslyn, NY
Rubner & Kutner, P.C. ... Denver, CO
Rubner, Paul D. ... Denver, CO
Rubner-Frandsen, Nancy A.
Philadelphia, PA
Rubnitz, Jeffrey W. ... Savannah, GA
Rubnitz, Jeffrey W., P.C., Law Office of
Savannah, GA
Rubock, Daniel B. ... New York, NY
Rubocki, Melanie G. ... Chicago, IL
Rubolino, Jmaes R., Jr. ... Doylestown, PA
Rubottom, John W. ... Austin, TX
Rubow, John C. ... Chanute, KS
Rubow & Mikulka ... Chanute, KS
Ruboy, George M. ... Norwood, MA
Rubrich, John S. ... Hartford, CT
Rubright, Charles R. ... Indianapolis, IN
Rubright, Domalakes, Troy & Miller
Frackville, PA
Schuylkill Haven, PA
Rubright, Harry A. ... Schuylkill Haven, PA
Rubright, James A. ... Birmingham, AL
Rubright, Scott E. ... Red Bluff, CA
Rubright, Susan R. ... Somerville, NJ
Rubright, Wilbur H. ... Frackville, PA
Rubstello, Greg A. ... Seattle, WA
Rubtchinsky, Ira P. ... Albany, NY
Ruby, Alexandra M. ... Irvine, CA
Ruby, Allen, (L.C.) ... San Jose, CA
Ruby, Arlin F. ... Richmond, VA
Ruby, Barbara C. ... Greensboro, NC
Ruby, Cecilia Preciado ... San Diego, CA
Ruby, Charles S. ... Harrison, NY
Ruby, David R. ... Richmond, VA
Ruby, Debra S. ... Houston, TX
Ruby, Edward L. ... Birmingham, MI
Ruby, Frederic J. ... Southfield, MI
Ruby, Frederick C. ... Portland, OR
Ruby, George D. ... Sun City, AZ
Ruby, Jack E. ... Charlotte, NC
Ruby, Jay C. ... New Orleans, LA
Ruby, Jill M. ... Chicago, IL
Ruby, Joan ... New York, NY
Ruby, John H. ... Louisville, KY
Ruby, Joseph L. ... Washington, DC
Ruby, Kevin A. ... Alexandria, VA
Ruby, Lauren S. ... Chicago, IL
Ruby, Marguerite R. ... Richmond, VA
Ruby, Mark H. ... Boston, MA
Ruby, Matthew P. ... Los Gatos, CA
Ruby, Paul J., II ... Naples, FL
Ruby, Richard F. ... New Buffalo, MI
Ruby, Richard G. ... New Bedford, MA
Ruby, Richard P. ... Edmonds, WA
Ruby, Robert A. ... Oakland, CA
Ruby, Russell ... Muskogee, OK
Ruby, Samuel H. ... San Francisco, CA
Ruby, Sarajane C. ... Atlanta, GA
Ruby & Schofield ... San Jose, CA
Ruby, Scott W. ... Phoenix, AZ
Ruby, Stanley L. ... Cincinnati, OH
Ruby, Stephanie L. ... Palo Alto, CA
Ruby, Steven N. ... Los Angeles, CA
Ruby, Sydney L. ... Southfield, MI
Ruby, Thomas B. ... San Jose, CA
Ruby, Thomas O. ... Columbus, OH
Ruby, Veronica ... Oakland, CA
Ruby, William S. ... Rochester, NY
Rucci, Burnham, Carta & Edelberg, LLP
Darien, CT
New Canaan, CT
Stamford, CT
Rucci, David J. ... Darien, CT
Rucci, Gerard R. ... New London, CT
Rucci, Joseph J., Jr. ... Darien, CT
Stamford, CT
Rucci, Paul L. ... Philadelphia, PA
Rucci, Robert S. ... San Diego, CA
Ruccia, Diane J. ... Newark, NJ
Ruccolo, Laura D. ... Cherry Hill, NJ
Ruccolo, Nat ... Peabody, MA
Ruch, Cheri J. ... Wilson, NC
Ruch, Edward D., Jr. ... Sykesville, MD
Ruch, Joseph J., Jr. ... Washington, DC
Ruch, Larry G. ... Phoenix, AZ
Ruch, Lawrence S. ... Burbank, CA
Ruch, Lisa Dorio ... Princeton, NJ
Ruch, Louis J. ... Philadelphia, PA
Ruch, Shipon & Skarbek, P.C.
Philadelphia, PA
Ruch, Stacy C. ... Philadelphia, PA
Ruch, Susan Gwin ... Winston-Salem, NC
Rucha, Paul ... Augusta, ME
Ruchala, Heidi K. Brauer ... Buffalo, NY
Ruchala, Joseph F. ... Hempstead, NY
Ruchandani, Nandita P. ... Fairfield, CT
Ruchefsky, Steven B. ... New York, NY

Ruchelman Law Firm, The
New York, NY
Ruchelman, Stanley C. ... New York, NY
Ruchim, Mitchell B. ... Northbrook, IL
Ruchman, Marshall D. ... Dayton, OH
Rucigay, Emil J. ... Ridgewood, NY
Rucigay, John D. ... Ridgewood, NY
Rucigay & Rucigay ... Ridgewood, NY
Rucinski, Keith L. ... Akron, OH
Rucinski, Randy C. ... Buffalo, NY
Rucinski, Thomas E. ... Hammond, IN
Rucinski, Virginia Maroulakos
Piscataway, NJ
Ruck, Andrew J. ... Philadelphia, PA
Ruck, Charles K. ... Costa Mesa, CA
Ruck, David E. ... New York, NY
Ruck, J. Douglas ... Bowling Green, OH
Pemberville, OH
Ruck, Jack E. ... Louisville, KY
Ruck, John C. ... Muskegon, MI
Ruck, Mary Kay ... Irvine, CA
Ruck, Wilson, Helline & Brockman
Louisville, KY
Rucka, N. Michael ... Salinas, CA
Rucka, O'Boyle & Lombardo ... Salinas, CA
Ruckdaschel, John G. ... Minneapolis, MN
Ruckdaschel-Haley, Kim
Minneapolis, MN
Ruckdeschel, Jonathan ... Baltimore, MD
Rückel & Collegen ... Atlanta, GA
Ruckel, H. Anthony ... Denver, CO
Ruckel, Laurie S. ... New York, NY
Ruckelshaus, Catherine K.
San Francisco, CA
Ruckelshaus, Gary J. ... Newark, NJ
Ruckelshaus, John C. ... Indianapolis, IN
Ruckelshaus, Roland, Kautzman & Hasbrook ... Indianapolis, IN
Ruckenbrod, Richd. ... Salt Lake City, UT
Rucker, A. A. ... Bedford, VA
Rucker, Alan L. ... Dallas, TX
Rucker, Ann Gaylor ... St. Louis, MO
Rucker, Charles B., Jr. ... Chattanooga, TN
Rucker, Cynthia C. ... Santa Rosa, CA
Rucker, David B. ... Richmond, VA
Rucker, Denman A. ... Arlington, VA
Rucker, Donna ... Norfolk, VA
Rucker, Donna W. ... Silver Spring, MD
Rucker, Douglas P., Jr. ... Richmond, VA
Rucker, Edgar F. ... Tucson, AZ
Rucker, Edward A. ... Santa Monica, CA
Rucker, Edward B. ... Kansas City, MO
Rucker, Edward B., P.C. ... Kansas City, MO
Rucker, Eric J. ... Minneapolis, MN
Rucker, Eric K. ... Topeka, KS
Rucker, Fillenwarth & Panszi, Professional Association ... Indianapolis, IN
Rucker, Fred ... Los Angeles, CA
Rucker, Fred T., III ... Jackson, MS
Rucker, Guy W. ... Addison, TX
Rucker, Harold V. ... San Diego, CA
Rucker, Jacqueline ... Los Angeles, CA
Rucker, James J. ... Orange, CA
Rucker, James R., Jr. ... Denver, CO
Rucker, Jamie C. ... New York, NY
Rucker, Jeannette M. ... Bronx, NY
Rucker, Jeffrey Keith ... Media, PA
Rucker, Jerry D. ... Dallas, TX
Rucker, John M. ... Newberry, SC
Rucker, John R. ... Murfreesboro, TN
Rucker, John R., Jr. ... Murfreesboro, TN
Rucker, Kathleen Ann Troy ... Fort Worth, TX
Rucker, Kenneth W. ... Nashville, TN
Rucker, Kevin M. ... Kansas City, MO
Rucker, Kim K. W. ... Chicago, IL
Rucker, M. Pierce, II ... Richmond, VA
Rucker, Mark D. ... Lexington, KY
Rucker, Molly P. ... Indianapolis, IN
Rucker, R.D. ... Dallas, TX
Rucker, Richard W. ... Murfreesboro, TN
Rucker, Richmond W. ... Winston-Salem, NC
Rucker, Robert W. ... Dallas, TX
Rucker, Ronald E. ... St. Louis, MO
Rucker and Rucker, P.C.
Murfreesboro, TN
Rucker, Shelley D. ... Chattanooga, TN
Rucker, Sheryl A. ... Huntington, WV
Rucker, Steven M. ... New York, NY
Rucker, Thomas A. ... Norfolk, VA
Virginia Beach, VA
Rucker, Thomas J. ... Winston-Salem, NC
Rucker, Truman B., Jr. ... Tulsa, OK
Rucker, Truman B., P.C., Law Office of
Tulsa, OK
Rucker, Walter J. ... Gainesville, GA
Ruckert, Edward M. ... Washington, DC
Ruckle, James S., Jr. ... Baltimore, MD
Ruckman, Deirdre B. ... Dallas, TX
Ruckman, Norris E. ... Wilmington, DE
Ruckman, Robert F. ... Dallas, TX
Ruckman, Shelley J. ... Dearborn, MI
Ruckman, Timothy R. ... Summersville, WV
Ruckoldt, Charmaine Guffa
Wonder Lake, IL
Ruckriegle, W. Terry ... Breckenridge, CO
Rucks, Edward L. ... Memphis, TN
Rucksdashel, R. Neil ... Bellevue, WA
Rucoba, Reginald ... San Diego, CA
Rud, Angela L. ... Minneapolis, MN
Rud, Roxanne ... Ocala, FL
Rud, Victor ... Ridgefield Park, NJ
Ruda, Heather McNamara
West Palm Beach, FL
Ruda, Howard ... New York, NY
Ruda, Jacques S. ... Denver, CO
Ruda, Joseph A. ... Atwood, KS
Ruda, Mark B. ... Chicago, IL
Ruda, Richard ... Washington, DC

Rudacille, Raymond S. ....Baltimore, MD
Rudalevige, Suzanne ....Bolton, CT
Rudansky, Daniel ....Sag Harbor, NY
Rudas, Melissa P. ....Bethlehem, PA
Rudasill, A. J., Law Office of ......Clinton, IL
Rudasill, Mary C. ....Carbondale, IL
Rudasill, Michael L. ....Spartanburg, SC
Rudasill, Michael L., P.A.
Spartanburg, SC
Rudasill & Spence ....Clinton, IL
Rudasill, Thomas J. ....Clinton, IL
Rudavsky, Dahlia ....Boston, MA
Rudawski, Jerome M. ....Roseville, MN
Rudawsky, Larry W. ....Wooster, OH
Rudbach, Karl K. ....Great Falls, MT
Rudberg, Joe A. ....Dallas, TX
Rudd, A. E. ....Garden City, KS
Rudd, Aubrey G. ....Miami, FL
Rudd, Brenda ....Austin, TX
Rudd, Charlie L.
Hot Springs National Park, AR
Rudd, Christopher L. ....Los Angeles, CA
Rudd, David R. ....South Orange, NJ
Rudd, David R. ....Salt Lake City, UT
Rudd, Dwight G. ....Williamsburg, VA
Rudd, Edward J. ....Brooksville, KY
Rudd, Eldon ....Scottsdale, AZ
Rudd, Ellen R. ....Louisville, KY
Rudd, G. Lee ....Draper, UT
Rudd, J. Gordon ....Xenia, OH
Rudd, J. Marie ....New Orleans, LA
Rudd, James D. ....Boca Raton, FL
Fort Lauderdale, FL
Miami, FL
Rudd, James L. ....Neenah, WI
Rudd, James T. ....Grand Prairie, TX
Rudd, Jim D. ....Austin, TX
Rudd, John A. ....Tallahassee, FL
Rudd, John S. ....Portland, ME
Rudd, Jonathan H. ....Harrisburg, PA
Rudd, Kenneth C. ....Bronx, NY
Rudd, Kenneth E. ....St. Louis, MO
Rudd, Lawrence ....Pasadena, CA
Rudd, Lee ....Salt Lake City, UT
Rudd, Mark S. ....New York, NY
Rudd, Matthew H. ....Oakland, NJ
Rudd, McDonough and Feeley
Westmont, NJ
Rudd, Michael P. ....Miami, FL
Palm Beach, FL
Rudd, Michael Patrick
Klamath Falls, OR
Rudd, Myron S. ....Cincinnati, OH
Rudd, Philip Randolph ....Phoenix, AZ
Rudd and Poss ....South Orange, NJ
Rudd, Ralph Corlies ....State College, PA
Rudd, Roy H., Jr. ....Bayside, NY
Rudd and Rudd ....Austin, TX
Rudd & Schumacher ....Brooksville, KY
Rudd, Silverberg, Zaharieff & Orlins Co., L.P.A. ....Xenia, OH
Rudd, Stephen S. ....Cupertino, CA
Rudd, William M. ....Cumberland, MD
Ruddell, Brian W. ....Peoria, IL
Ruddell, Gary H. ....Visalia, CA
Ruddell, Hornburg, Cochran, Stanton, Smith & Gulla, LLP ....Visalia, CA
Ruddell, J. Preston ....Glastonbury, CT
Ruddell, Jane ....Radnor, PA
Rudden, Dennis J. ....Daytona Beach, FL
Rudden, Monica ....San Rafael, CA
Rudden, Paul J. ....Syosset, NY
Rudden, R. Julia F. ....Seattle, WA
Rudder, Deborah K. ....Corpus Christi, TX
Rudder, Mark Thomas ....Eureka, MO
St. Louis, MO
Washington, MO
Rudder, Richard D. ....New York, NY
Rudder, Robert R., Jr. ....Montgomery, AL
Rudder, Verner R., Jr. ....Northfield, OH
Rudderham, Lawrence R. ....Chester, PA
Rudderow, Daniel T. ....Costa Mesa, CA
Rudderow, Robin ....San Francisco, CA
Rudder-Taylor, Marva M. ....Stamford, CT
Ruddick, Elizabeth ....Philadelphia, PA
Ruddick, Elizabeth Michelle
Gloucester, MA
Ruddick, James M. ....Yuba City, CA
Ruddick, Pamela A. ....St. Paul, MN
Ruddick, Peter V. ....Olathe, KS
Ruddick, Stephen Richard ....Aurora, CO
Ruddick, Steven L. ....Kansas City, KS
Ruddock, Eldonna M. ....Lansing, MI
Ruddock & Innes, P.A. ....Bedford, NH
Ruddock, Robert R. ....Boston, MA
Ruddock, Steven B. ....Bedford, NH
Ruddock, W. Parker ....Indiana, PA
Rudduck, John W. ....Wilmington, OH
Ruddy, Betty L. ....Mercer Island, WA
Ruddy, Bradley, Kolkhorst & Reges, A Professional Corporation ....Juneau, AK
Ruddy, C. John ....Aurora, IL
Ruddy, Catherine Hunt ......Los Angeles, CA
Ruddy, Clarence J. ....Aurora, IL
Ruddy, David D. ....Newark, NJ
Ruddy, Francis S. ....Department of State, Foreign Service Officers (Overseas), GV
Ruddy, Frank ....Washington, DC
Ruddy, James J. ....New York, NY
Ruddy, James W. ....Seattle, WA
Ruddy, Joan Marie ....New York, NY
Ruddy, John R. ....Chicago, IL
Ruddy, Kevin J. ....Riverside, CA
Ruddy Law Firm, The ....Fairfax, VA
Ruddy, Margaret E. ....Boca Raton, FL
Ruddy, Mary ....Mineola, NY
Ruddy & Muir, LLP ....Washington, DC
Ruddy, Philip C. ....Aurora, IL
Ruddy, Richard John, Jr. ....Fairfax, VA
Ruddy, Robert ....Glendale, CO
Ruddy, Roberta E. ....New York, NY
Ruddy, Sara H. ....Berkeley, CA
Ruddy, Timothy F. ....Cape Girardeau, MO
Ruddy & Varga ....Aurora, IL
Ruddy, William G. ....Juneau, AK
Rude, Alisa L. ....Fort Wayne, IN
Rude, Arthur M. ....Muskegon, MI
Rude, Brian W. ....Minneapolis, MN
Rude, C. Edwin, Jr. ....Tallahassee, FL
Rude, Dan J. ....Coeur d'Alene, ID
Rude, David J. ....San Jose, CA
Rude, Harris E. ....Bradenton, FL
Rude, James W. ....Minneapolis, MN
Rude, Jeffrey Paul ....Fargo, ND
Rudebock, David Thomas ....Canton, OH
Rudebusch, Alice A. ....Racine, WI
Rudebusch, Thomas L. ....Washington, DC
Rudebusch, Verne ....Dallas, TX
Rudeen, Bruce W. ....Honolulu, HI
Rudeen, Karen T. ....Trenton, NJ
Rudel, Jack N. ....Phoenix, AZ
Rudel, Lewis C. ....East Tawas, MI
Rudell, Edwin ....Howard Beach, NY
Rudell, Joel M. (IBA) **............New York, NY**
Rudell, Michael I. ....New York, NY
Rudell, Phedra R. ....Bernardsville, NJ
Rudell, William B. ....Los Angeles, CA
Rudelman, Uri ....Miami, FL
Rudeloff, Richard E. ....Beeville, TX
Rudeloff & Stansell ....San Antonio, TX
Rudeloff, Walter F. ....San Antonio, TX
Ruden, Audrey F. ....New York, NY
Ruden & Cramer, P.C. ....New York, NY
Ruden, Elaine J. ....Freehold, NJ
Ruden, Elise A ....Los Angeles, CA
Ruden, Linda Marie ....Council Bluffs, IA
Ruden, McClosky, Smith, Schuster & Russell, P.A. ....Fort Lauderdale, FL
Miami, FL
Naples, FL
St. Petersburg, FL
Sarasota, FL
Tallahassee, FL
Tampa, FL
West Palm Beach, FL
Ruden, Morton R. ....Westport, CT
Ruden, Paul M. ....Alexandria, VA
Ruden, Peter L. ....Hauppauge, NY
Ruden, Sanford I. ....New York, NY
Ruden, Thomas A. ....New York, NY
Rudenick, Catherine A. ....Minneapolis, MN
Rudenko, Dawn L. ....New York, NY
Rudenstine, David M ....New York, NY
Ruder and Associates ....Chicago, IL
Ruder, Clifford C. ....Dallas, TX
Ruder, David S. ....Chicago, IL
Ruder, Eric ....New York, NY
Ruder, Jay S. ....Haddonfield, NJ
Philadelphia, PA
Ruder, Joseph B. ....San Francisco, CA
Ruder, Julie B. ....Chicago, IL
Ruder, Lawrence T. ....Chicago, IL
Ruder, Susan M. ....Highland Park, IL
Ruder, Ware & Michler, S.C.
Wausau, WI
Ruderman, Alan ....Chattanooga, TN
Ruderman, Barry L. ....San Diego, CA
Ruderman, Barry M. ....New York, NY
Ruderman, Daniel H. ....Lowell, MA
Ruderman, Eric P. ....Denver, CO
Ruderman, Esther Zapata
West Palm Beach, FL
Ruderman & Glickman, P.C. ......Springfield, NJ
Ruderman, Horace A.
Rancho Palos Verdes, CA
Ruderman, Jay ....Lynnfield, MA
Ruderman, Jeffrey C. ....White Plains, NY
Ruderman, Jerold R. ....White Plains, NY
Ruderman, Jerome M. ....Boca Raton, FL
Ruderman, Joel W. ....Silver Spring, MD
Ruderman, Judy L. ....Westwood, NJ
Ruderman, Marc S. ....West Palm Beach, FL
Ruderman, Mark S. ....Springfield, NJ
Ruderman, Michael A. ....Boulder, CO
Ruderman, Robyn ....Brooklyn, NY
Ruderman, Terry Jane ....White Plains, NY
Rudert, Evan C. ....Erie, PA
Rudert, William J. M. ....Vienna, IL
Rudes, Terrence R. ....Port Clinton, OH
Rudewicz, Frank E. ....Hartford, CT
Rudewicz, Michael T. ....Miami, FL
Rudey, Samuel R. ....New York, NY
Rudge, Andrew W. ....Washington, DC
Rudge, Howard J. ....Wilmington, DE
Rudgers, David E. ....East Lansing, MI
Rudgers, Sarah B.
Federal Labor Relations Authority, Authority Member Staff, GV
Rudges, Seymour C. ....New York, NY
Rudibaugh, C. Scott ....Hemet, CA
Temecula, CA
Rudibaugh, Jerry ....Phoenix, AZ
Rudicell, Michael J. ....Pensacola, FL
Rudich, David ....Los Angeles, CA
Rudich, Fran L. ....New York, NY
Rudich, Keith B. ....Treasury Department, Office of Regulations and Rulings, GV
Rudich, Kevin ....San Jose, CA
Rudich, Roger D., (Ltd.) ....Chicago, IL
Rudich, Sharon ....New York, NY
Rudicil, Michael T. ....Louisville, KY
Rudick, Brian Scott ....Pittsburgh, PA
Rudick, Elliot M. ....New York, NY
Rudick Platt Glatt & Getz, A Professional Corporation ....San Diego, CA
Rudick, Richard S. ....New York, NY
Rudick, Stuart M. ....Southfield, MI
Rudie, Jonathan B. ....Baltimore, MD
Rudig, Robert H. ....Cincinnati, OH
Rudiger, David S. ....Norfolk, VA
Rudin and Alder ....Los Angeles, CA
Rudin, Frederick S. ....Great Neck, NY
Rudin & Herzog ....Canton, MA
Rudin, Irving L. ....Canton, MA
Rudin, Jeffrey ....Bedford, MA
Rudin, Jessica B. ....San Francisco, CA
Rudin, Joel B. ....New York, NY
Rudin, Michael B. ....Rochester, NY
Rudin, Milton A. ....Los Angeles, CA
Rudin, Mitchell E. ....New York, NY
Rudin, Richard L. ....Parsippany, NJ
Rudin, Scott H. ....Chicago, IL
Rudin, Sheila H. ....Chicago, IL
Rudin, Stanley R. ....Syracuse, NY
Rudin, Steven ....Miami, FL
Rudin, Steven, P.A. ....Miami, FL
Rudinger, Jennifer I ....Anchorage, AK
Rudinski, Michael J. ....Williamsport, PA
Rudisill, Ann L. ....Portland, ME
Rudisill, Bryan S. ....Evansville, IN
Rudisill, Bynum Griffin ....Charlotte, NC
Rudisill, Cathy M. ....Raleigh, NC
Rudisill, Guthrie, Nonemaker, Guthrie & Yingst
Hanover, PA
Rudisill, J. Richardson, Jr. ....Hickory, NC
Rudisill, J. Richardson, Jr., Law Firm of
Hickory, NC
Rudisill, Justus C. ....Raleigh, NC
Rudisill, Kenneth M., Jr. ....Phoenix, AZ
Rudisill, R. Mack, Jr.
Altamonte Springs, FL
Rudisill, Stephen G. ....Chicago, IL
Rudisill, Steven M. ....Rock Hill, SC
Ruditz, George R. ....Woodmere, NY
Rudnitzky, Howard A. ....Brooklyn, NY
Rudkin, Bob ....Edmond, OK
Rudkin, Rodger R. ....Overland Park, KS
Rudkin, Sven C. ....Burbank, CA
Rudland, Regan Leigh ....Louisville, KY
Rudland, William P. ....Cleveland, OH
Rudlin, D. Alan ....Richmond, VA
Rudloff, Daniel B. ....Bowling Green, KY
Rudloff, G. Edward, Jr. ....San Francisco, CA
Rudloff, Randil J. ....Warren, OH
Rudloff & Rudloff ....Bowling Green, KY
Rudloff, William J. ....Bowling Green, KY
Rudman, Anne B. ....New York, NY
Rudman, Barry M. ....Beverly Hills, CA
Rudman, Bruce David ....Los Angeles, CA
Rudman, Ephraim Z. ....New York, NY
Rudman, Gerald E. ....Bangor, ME
Rudman, Gilbert W. ....Philadelphia, PA
Rudman, Jamie ....Los Angeles, CA
Rudman, Jeffrey A. ....Beverly Hills, CA
Rudman, Jeffrey B. ....Boston, MA
Rudman, Jerry I. ....Chicago, IL
Rudman, Jody L. ....Dallas, TX
Rudman, Laurence D. ....Metairie, LA
Rudman, Leslie P. ....Sands Point, NY
Rudman, Mara E. ....Washington, DC
Rudman, Martin ....Joliet, IL
Rudman, Michael A. ....Fall River, MA
Rudman, Michael A., Law Offices of P.C.
Fall River, MA
Rudman, Michael P. ....Sands Point, NY
Rudman, Nicole ....Chicago, IL
Rudman, Norman G. ....Los Angeles, CA
Rudman, Paul L. ....Bangor, ME
Rudman, Perry ....Joliet, IL
Rudman, Rhonda A. ....Pittsburgh, PA
Rudman, Rhonda Lee
Bainbridge Island, WA
Rudman, Richard D. ....Boston, MA
Rudman, Samuel H. ....New York, NY
Rudman, Samuel K. ....Portland, ME
Rudman, Silvia C. Fioo ....Fall River, MA
Rudman, Stanley H. ....Boston, MA
Rudman, Stephen D. ....Elkins Park, PA
Rudman, Stephen T. ....Tiburon, CA
Rudman, Susan R. ....Doylestown, PA
Rudman, T. Britt ....Beverly Hills, CA
Rudman, Tony J. ....Salt Lake City, UT
Rudman, Warren B. ....Washington, DC
New York, NY
Rudman & Winchell, LLC ....Bangor, ME
Rudman, Zachary S. ....Kansas City, MO
Rudmann, Max ....Boca Raton, FL
Rudnansky, Richard R. ....Santa Rosa, CA
Rudnansky & Varner ....Santa Rosa, CA
Rudner, Mark A. ....Bay Shore, NY
Rudner, Robert E. ....Patchogue, NY
Rudner, Steven M. ....Phoenix, AZ
Dallas, TX
Rudnick, Addonizio, Pappa & Comer, P.C.
Hazlet, NJ
Rudnick, Alan A. ....Richmond, VA
Rudnick, Amy G. ....Washington, DC
Rudnick, Ben H. ....Los Angeles, CA
Rudnick, Brian M. ....Philadelphia, PA
Rudnick, Brumbaugh & Rohrer
Greenville, OH
Rudnick, Charles S. ....New York, NY
Rudnick, Claire ....Beverly Hills, CA
Rudnick, Constance L., (P.C.)
Boston, MA
Rudnick, Dana M. ....Los Angeles, CA
Rudnick, Daniel L., Law Office of
Bakersfield, CA
Rudnick, Elizabeth Sarah ......Baltimore, MD
Rudnick, Holly L. ....Dallas, TX
Rudnick, Howard ....New York, NY
Rudnick, Irene K. ....Aiken, SC
Rudnick, Jeffrey L. ....Philadelphia, PA
Rudnick, Jody Ann ....Forest Hills, NY
Rudnick, Joel M. ....Washington, DC
Rudnick, Jonathan ....Hazlet, NJ
Rudnick, Jordan M. ....Chicago, IL
Rudnick, Karen J. ....Ephrata, PA
Rudnick, Lawrence A. ....Summit, NJ
Rudnick, Lawrence H. ....Philadelphia, PA
Rudnick, Leslie H. ....Boston, MA
Rudnick, Lewis G. ....Chicago, IL
Rudnick, Linda J. ....Portland, OR
Rudnick, Lori Beth ....Boston, MA
Rudnick, M. Jack ....Skaneateles, NY
Rudnick, Martin M. ....Hazlet, NJ
Rudnick, Marvin L. ....Pasadena, CA
Rudnick, Morris ....Aiken, SC
Rudnick, Paul D. ....Chicago, IL
Rudnick, Philip ....Bakersfield, CA
Rudnick, Philip E. ....Norton, MA
Rudnick, Rebecca S. ....Bloomington, IN
Rudnick, Rhoda L. ....Stamford, CT
Rudnick, Robert A. ....Washington, DC
Rudnick, Robert J. ....Colorado Springs, CO
Rudnick & Rudnick ....Aiken, SC
Rudnick, Scott D. ....Greenville, OH
Rudnick, Sharon A. ....Eugene, OR
Rudnick Sheps ....New York, NY
Rudnick, Stuart W. ....Los Angeles, CA
Rudnick, William A. ....Chicago, IL
Rudnick & Wolfe ....Chicago, IL
Baltimore, MD
Rudnicki, Andrew M. P. ....Los Angeles, CA
Rudnicki, James W. ....Arlington, TX
Rudnicki, Paul E. ....West Seneca, NY
Rudnik, Eugene J., Jr. ....Oak Brook, IL
Rudnik, Robert J. ....Chicago, IL
Rudnik, Thomas H. ....Villa Park, IL
Rudnik, Wendy S. ....Longmont, CO
Rudnik, William J. ....Clinton, NJ
Rudnikas, Elias B. ....Miami, FL
Rudnit, Phyllis Miriam ....Glenview, IL
Rudnitsky, Edward ....Watertown, MA
Rudnitsky & Hackman, L.L.P.
Selinsgrove, PA
Rudnitsky, Marvin J. ....Selinsgrove, PA
Rudnitsky, Steven J. ....New York, NY
Rudnitsky, Taras Stefan ....Brighton, MI
Rudo, Saul E. ....Chicago, IL
Rudock, Robert J. ....Miami, FL
Rudof, Joel ....Pacific Palisades, CA
Rudoff, Abigail L. ....Chicago, IL
Rudoff, Howard S. ....Westminster, CA
Rudoff, Mark R. ....Chicago, IL
Rudoff, Sheldon ....New York, NY
Rudoff, Surie ....New York, NY
Rudofski, Kenneth J. ....Lisle, IL
Rudofsky, Barry S. ....Forest Hills, NY
Rudofsky, Edward S., (P.C.)
New York, NY
Rudofsky, Jack L. ....Encino, CA
Rudofsky, Jane E. ....Los Angeles, CA
Rudofsky & Meo ....Encino, CA
Rudofsky, Steven Z. ....New York, NY
Rudoler, Stuart D. ....Philadelphia, PA
Rudolf, David S. ....Chapel Hill, NC
Rudolf, Donald R., II ....Carlsbad, CA
Rudolf, Gary L. ....Fort Lauderdale, FL
Rudolf, Heinz M., Jr. ....Belleville, IL
Rudolf, Joseph C. ....Philadelphia, PA
Rudolf, Keith J. ....Orange Park, FL
Rudolf & Maher, P.A. ....Chapel Hill, NC
Rudolf, Nanette J. ....Fort Lauderdale, FL
Rudolf, Richard G. ....New York, NY
Rudolf, Steven G. ....Indianapolis, IN
Rudolph, Amelia Toy ....Atlanta, GA
Rudolph, Andrew J. ....Philadelphia, PA
Rudolph, Anne M. ....Eureka, CA
Rudolph, Barbara R. ....Washington, DC
Rudolph & Beer, L.L.P. ....New York, NY
Rudolph, Blaine O. ....Beresford, SD
Rudolph, Carl Wm. ....Geneva, IL
Rudolph, Catherine L. ....Bedford, MA
Rudolph, Daniel A. ....Bethesda, MD
Rudolph, David L. ....Chicago, IL
Rudolph, David M. ....Memphis, TN
Rudolph, Dorian, Goldstein, Rochestie, Wisniewski & Taylor, P.C. ......Bensalem, PA
Philadelphia, PA
Rudolph, Edward ....Bensalem, PA
Philadelphia, PA
Rudolph, Eric B. ....Atlanta, GA
Rudolph, Eugene A. ....Woodland Hills, CA
Rudolph, Fine, Porter & Johnson LLP
Carmi, IL
Evansville, IN
Vincennes, IN
Rudolph, Francis R. ....Portland, OR
Rudolph, Gary B. ....San Diego, CA
Rudolph, George C. ....Irvine, CA
Rudolph, Gilbert L. ....Phoenix, AZ
Rudolph, Glenn Phillip ....Cincinnati, OH
Rudolph, Howard M.
West Palm Beach, FL
Rudolph, Isidore J. ....Kings Park, NY
Rudolph, Jack M. ....Clarksville, TN
Rudolph, James Bradley ....San Diego, CA
Rudolph, James L. ....Boston, MA
Marblehead, MA
Swampscott, MA
Rudolph, Jason S. ....Miami, FL
Rudolph, Jeffrey P. ....Stamford, CT
Rudolph, Jennifer L. ....Akron, OH
Rudolph, John A., Jr. ....Tallahassee, FL
Rudolph, John B. ....Washington, DC
Rudolph, Jonathan D. ....Fort Lee, NJ
Rudolph, Joseph A. ....Philadelphia, PA
Rudolph, Karin ....New York, NY
Rudolph, Kenneth W. ....White Plains, NY
Rudolph, Kimberly A. ....Philadelphia, PA
Rudolph & Kroner ....Georgetown, MA

Rudolph, L. Michael .... New York, NY
Rudolph, Laurence H. .... New York, NY
Rudolph, Lawrence
National Science Foundation, Office of the General Counsel, GV
Rudolph, L. Michael, P.C. .... New York, NY
Rudolph, Marilyn .... Northridge, CA
Rudolph, Mark E. .... Thiensville, WI
Rudolph, Mark J. .... Charleston, WV
Rudolph, Marshall S. .... Bridgeport, CA
Rudolph, Martha E. .... Lakewood, CO
Rudolph, Martha Jane .... Goleta, CA
Rudolph, Melinda P. .... Philadelphia, PA
Rudolph, Michael C. .... Oakland, NJ
Rudolph, Michael D. .... Jacksonville, FL
Rudolph, Michael E., Law Offices of
Appleton, WI
Rudolph, Nancy J. .... White Plains, NY
Rudolph, Patrick J. .... Bronx, NY
Rudolph, Paul B. .... Scottsdale, AZ
Rudolph, Paul N. .... Nashville, TN
Rudolph, Phillip Howard .... Oak Brook, IL
Rudolph, R. D., Jr. .... Washington, DC
Rudolph, Richard B. .... Santa Ana, CA
Rudolph, Richard J. .... Cleveland, OH
Rudolph, Robert J. .... Indianapolis, IN
Rudolph, Robert P. .... Georgetown, MA
Rudolph, Ronald .... New York, NY
Rudolph, Ronald W. .... Miami, FL
Rudolph, Ross E. .... Evansville, IN
Rudolph, Ross, Fendley, Hogan, Moyer & Sykes, P.L.L.C. .... Clarksville, TN
Rudolph & Rudolph .... Scottsdale, AZ
Rudolph, Russell W. .... Hammond, LA
Rudolph, Samuel B. .... Hayward, CA
Rudolph, Sarah L. .... Wausau, WI
Rudolph, Stephen A. .... Sea Girt, NJ
Rudolph, Stephen Bert .... Riverwoods, IL
Rudolph, Steven P. .... Folsom, CA
Rudolph, Theodore .... Cleveland, OH
Rudolph, Timothy L. .... Glen Rose, TX
Rudolph, Trudy F. .... Tucson, AZ
Rudolph, Wallace M. .... Orlando, FL
Rudolph, William D. .... New York, NY
Rudolph, William H. .... Hillsboro, WI
Rudorfer, Joseph .... West Hills, CA
Rudov, David K. .... Pittsburgh, PA
Rudov & Stein, P.C. .... Pittsburgh, PA
Rudovsky, David .... Philadelphia, PA
Rudow, David B., (P.A.) .... Baltimore, MD
Rudow, Marc S. .... Asheville, NC
Rudow, William M. .... Baltimore, MD
Rudoy, Bruce F. .... Pittsburgh, PA
Rudoy, Herbert L., Ltd. .... Chicago, IL
Rudoy, Martin Stuart .... Los Angeles, CA
Rud-Pentz, Ada .... Los Angeles, CA
Rudquist, Barbara J. .... Zimmerman, MN
Rudquist, John B. .... Stockton, CA
Rudser, Donald K. .... Jasper, FL
Rudser, James C. .... Boston, MA
Rudser, Mary M. .... Oakland, CA
Rudstein, David S. .... Chicago, IL
Rudstrom, Kenneth R. .... Memphis, TN
Rudwall, David F. .... Dayton, OH
Rudy, Abraham M. .... Beverly Hills, CA
Rudy, Allen C., Jr. .... Dallas, TX
Rudy & Associates, P.C. .... Aspen, CO
Vail, CO
Rudy, Beverly D. .... Houston, TX
Rudy, Beverly J. .... Washington, DC
Rudy, Bryan C. .... Austin, TX
Rudy, Charles S. .... Southfield, MI
Rudy, Christopher G. .... San Jose, CA
Rudy, Christopher John .... Port Huron, MI
Rudy, Cynthia A. .... North Palm Beach, FL
Rudy, Daniel W. .... South Bend, IN
Rudy, Daron Allen .... Oklahoma City, OK
Rudy, David W. .... Walnut Creek, CA
Rudy, Donald M. .... North Olmsted, OH
Rudy, Elmer C. .... Rockford, IL
Rudy, Exelrod, Zieff & True, L.L.P.
San Francisco, CA
Rudy, Floyd D. .... Cloquet, MN
Rudy, Gassert, Yetka, Doran & Pritchett, P.A.
Cloquet, MN
Rudy, George F. .... Tyler, TX
Rudy, Herbert E. .... Orange Village, OH
Rudy, J. Frank, Jr. .... Nashville, TN
Rudy, James F. X. .... Trenton, NJ
Rudy, John A. .... New York, NY
Rudy, John F., II .... Tampa, FL
Rudy, Lisa Anne .... Frederick, MD
Rudy, Mark M. .... Los Angeles, CA
Rudy, Mark S., (A Professional Corporation)
San Francisco, CA
Rudy, Mark T. .... Cleveland, OH
Rudy, Mary Catherine .... San Francisco, CA
Rudy, Mary Frances .... Nashville, TN
Rudy, Michael D. .... Honolulu, HI
Rudy, Michael H. .... White Plains, NY
Rudy & Mikula .... Chesterfield, VA
Richmond, VA
Rudy, Oliver D. .... Chesterfield, VA
Rudy, Peter Harris .... Aspen, CO
Vail, CO
Rudy, Robert J., Jr. .... Whippany, NJ
Rudy, Robert John, III .... Verona, NJ
Rudy, Robert T. .... Minneapolis, MN
Rudy, Sidney .... San Francisco, CA
Rudy, Susan K. .... Department of Justice, Civil Division, GV
Rudy, Timothy D. .... Cleveland, OH
Rudy, William A. .... Kansas City, MO
Rudzewicz, Alan C. .... Bloomfield Hills, MI
Rudzin, Abby F. .... Chicago, IL
Rudzinski, Eugene A. .... Buffalo, NY
Rue, Bart A. .... Fort Worth, TX
Rue, David H. .... Nashville, TN
Rue, Elizabeth G. .... New York, NY
Rue, J. Alexander .... Atlanta, GA
Rue, John D .... Port Orange, FL
Rue, John P., II .... Salisbury, MD
Rue, Jonathan L. .... Atlanta, GA
Rue, Mark J. .... Colorado Springs, CO
Rue, Nancy B. .... Department of Justice, Civil Rights Division, GV
Rue, Patricia D. .... Juno Beach, FL
Rue, Robert Emmet .... Ship Bottom, NJ
Rue, Stephen, & Associates, L.L.C.
Gretna, LA
Kenner, LA
New Orleans, LA
Rue, Stephen R., & Associates .... Gretna, LA
Kenner, LA
New Orleans, LA
Rue, Thomas S. .... Mobile, AL
Rue & Ziffra, P.A. .... Daytona Beach, FL
Port Orange, FL
Rueb, Gregory D. .... Martinez, CA
Rueb & Karl .... Burnsville, MN
Rueb, Mary W. .... Oklahoma City, OK
Rueb, Terry H. .... Burnsville, MN
Ruebel, Alfred L. .... Dallas, TX
Ruebel, Jeffrey Clay .... Denver, CO
Ruebel, Richard J. .... Cincinnati, OH
Ruebhausen, Oscar M. .... New York, NY
Rueble, Jeffrey S. .... Grand Rapids, MI
Ruebner, Ralph .... Chicago, IL
Ruebsamen, Carol A. .... Pensacola, FL
Ruebush, Susan L. .... San Francisco, CA
Ruechel, Joel H. .... Holbrook, AZ
Rueckel, Gail A. .... Garden City, NY
Rueckert, Morgan P. .... Hartford, CT
Rueckert, Thomas E. .... Glenview, IL
Rueckhaus, Michael M. .... Albuquerque, NM
Rueda, John J. .... Sacramento, CA
Ruedig, Michael D. .... Concord, NH
Ruediger, David L. .... Boston, MA
Ruediger, George J. .... Green Bay, WI
Ruedisueli, John L. .... Troy, MI
Ruedlin, David E. .... Schaumburg, IL
Ruedy, Donald E. .... Rosemount, MN
Rueff, Christine S. .... Detroit, MI
Rueff, David A., Jr. .... Jackson, MS
Rueff, Larry A. .... Southfield, MI
Rueff & Schreiner .... Morgantown, KY
Rueff, William E., Jr. .... Morgantown, KY
Rueger, Barbara J. .... Visalia, CA
Rueger, James M. .... Cincinnati, OH
Rueger, Thomas C. .... Elburn, IL
Rueggeberg, Robert C. .... Concord, NH
Ruegger, Arthur H. .... New York, NY
Ruegger, MaryAnn Schlegel
Indianapolis, IN
Ruegger, Philip T., III .... New York, NY
Ruegger, Robert E. .... Raleigh, NC
Ruegsegger, Douglas P. .... Denver, CO
Ruegsegger, Ervan D. .... Boyne City, MI
Ruegsegger, Gregory A. .... Lakewood, CO
Ruegsegger, Martin C. .... Charlotte, NC
Ruegsegger Thomas, LLC
Colorado Springs, CO
Denver, CO
Rueh, Mark W. .... New York, NY
Ruehl, Charles A. .... Department of Commerce, Patent and Trademark Office, GV
Ruehl, Robert F. .... Doylestown, PA
Ruehl, Theodore S. .... Princeton, NJ
Ruehle, Linda Alsid .... Minnetonka, MN
Ruehle, Walter Hammele .... Rochester, NY
Ruehlman, Robert P. .... Cincinnati, OH
Ruehlmann, Eugene P. .... Cincinnati, OH
Ruehlmann, Gregory A. .... Cincinnati, OH
Ruehlmann, Mark J. .... Cincinnati, OH
Ruehmann, Albert C., III .... Richfield, OH
Ruehmann, Stephen C. .... Sacramento, CA
Ruel, Debra C. .... Hartford, CT
Ruel, Dennis P. .... San Francisco, CA
Ruel, Linda S. .... Chicago, IL
Rueli-Rilla, Laura .... Lee, MA
Ruelo, Roberto R. .... Tampa, FL
Ruemenapp, Harold A. .... Detroit, MI
Ruemenapp, John A. .... Bingham Farms, MI
Ruemenapp, Raymond V. .... Roseville, MI
Ruemmele, Henry G. .... Grand Forks, ND
Ruemmele, Jane C. H. .... Indianapolis, IN
Ruemmler, Kathryn H. .... Washington, DC
Ruenitz, John S. .... Rochester, MN
Ruenzel, Juliana M. .... Green Bay, WI
Ruer, Elisa Mia .... Brookfield, WI
Ruesch, A. Robert .... Portland, ME
Ruesch, Gary M. .... Milwaukee, WI
Ruesch, Jack E. .... Council Bluffs, IA
Ruesch, Janet .... Denver, CO
Ruescher, Mary Lou A. .... Mineola, NY
Ruescher, Robert A. .... New York, NY
Rueseler, John M. .... Houston, TX
Ruesink, Charles A. .... Austin, TX
Ruess, Brian Knight .... Portland, OR
Ruest, Pamela A. .... State College, PA
Ruestow, Edward A. .... Glen Cove, NY
Rueter, Brice F. .... Wauneta, NE
Rueter, Carl C. .... Pittsburgh, PA
Rueter, Elizabeth Ryan .... Casa Grande, AZ
Rueter, Gary A. .... McMinnville, OR
Rueter, Loren D. .... Bloomington, IN
Rueter, Matthew C. .... New York, NY
Rueter, Matthew C., P.C. .... New York, NY
Rueter, Thomas J. .... Philadelphia, PA
Rueth, Joseph E. .... Dayton, OH
Ruettinger, William C. .... San Francisco, CA
Ruetz, David P. .... Milwaukee, WI
Ruetz, Todd L. .... Carmel, IN
Rue Wittstein, Jane .... New York, NY
Ruez, Dawn Marie .... St. Louis, MO
Ruf, Alan Francis .... Fort Lauderdale, FL
Ruf & Basquill .... New York, NY
Ruf, Catherine Thomas .... Bloomington, IN
Ruf, Ernst Hermann .... Concord, OH
Ruf, James A., Jr. .... New York, NY
Ruf, John F. .... Pewaukee, WI
Ruf, Kevin F. .... Los Angeles, CA
Rufe, John J. .... Doylestown, PA
Rufenacht, Dale W. .... Amarillo, TX
Rufenacht, Joel S. .... Plymouth, MI
Rufer, Stephen F. .... Fergus Falls, MN
Ruff, Arlen M. .... Mandan, ND
Ruff and Bell .... Paris, IL
Ruff, Berry, Tillett & MacNeill
Charlotte, NC
Ruff, Betsy L. .... Gainesville, FL
Ruff, Bond, Cobb, Wade & Bethune, L.L.P.
Charlotte, NC
Ruff, Brian S. .... Salem, OR
Ruff, Charles F.C. .... Washington, DC
Ruff & Cohen, P.A. .... Gainesville, FL
Ruff, Deborah Schavey .... Chicago, IL
Ruff, Donald E. .... Paris, IL
Ruff, Edward B., III .... Chicago, IL
Ruff, Ellen T. .... Charlotte, NC
Ruff, Eric S. .... Gainesville, FL
Ruff, Erin J. .... Salem, OR
Ruff, Gary .... Massapequa, NY
Ruff, Gary Kay .... Dallas, TX
Ruff, George Gamble, Jr. .... Birmingham, AL
Ruff, Harley D. .... Beaufort, SC
Ruff, Jacquelynn ....
Federal Communications Commission, GV
Ruff, James Ira .... Leesville, SC
Ruff, Joan R. .... Houston, TX
Ruff, John D. .... Chevy Chase, MD
Ruff, Joseph W. .... San Diego, CA
Ruff, Karen Plumer .... Columbia, MD
Ruff, Katherine L. .... Denver, CO
Ruff, Larry Lee .... Atlanta, GA
Ruff, Leslie F. .... New York, NY
Ruff, Marilyn K. .... Thousand Oaks, CA
Ruff, Mark H. .... Winter Park, FL
Ruff, Matthew J. .... Bakersfield, CA
Ruff, Nisley & Lindemeier .... North Platte, NE
Ruff, Norma Carr .... Tampa, FL
Ruff, Randolph E. .... Chicago, IL
Ruff, Raymond L. .... Rochester, NY
Ruff, Rex R. .... Marietta, GA
Ruff, Ronald A. .... North Platte, NE
Ruff, Sara J. .... Minneapolis, MN
Ruff, Stephen L., Jr. .... Chicago, IL
Ruff, Thomas C. .... Charlotte, NC
Ruff, Thomas C., Jr. .... Charlotte, NC
Ruff, Weidenaar & Reidy, Ltd.
Chicago, IL
Ruffa, Gregory J. .... Westport, CT
Ruffa & Ruffa .... New York, NY
Ruffa, William P., Sr. .... New York, NY
Ruffa, William Peter, Jr. .... New York, NY
Ruffalo, Daniel L. .... Rochester, MN
Ruffalo, John, Jr. .... Hilton Head Island, SC
Ruffalo, Sandra S. .... Milwaukee, WI
Ruffalo, Steven M. .... Chicago, IL
Wheaton, IL
Ruffatto, Peter M. .... Seattle, WA
Ruffatto, Steven P. .... Billings, MT
Ruffee, Richard E. .... Hartford, CT
Ruffenach, Laurie A. .... Trenton, NJ
Ruffenach, Michael R. .... Bemidji, MN
Ruffennach, C. Gregory .... Denver, CO
Ruffennach, C. James .... Pittsburgh, PA
Ruffennach & Lochner .... Pittsburgh, PA
Ruffeno, Tracy Cruse .... Houston, TX
Ruffer, Anne B. .... Syracuse, NY
Ruffer, Galya B. .... Merion, PA
Ruffer, Lowell L. .... Skokie, IL
Ruffer, William C. .... New York, NY
Ruffier, Cheryl L. .... La Jolla, CA
Ruffier, John Daniel .... Orlando, FL
Ruffier, William E. .... Orlando, FL
Ruffin, Bruce E. .... Detroit, MI
Ruffin, C. Bradley, Jr. .... Surfside Beach, SC
Ruffin, C. Bradley, Jr., P.C. .... Conway, SC
Surfside Beach, SC
Ruffin, Charles L. .... Macon, GA
Ruffin, Charles L. .... Warner Robins, GA
Ruffin, Edmund S., III .... Pittsburgh, PA
Ruffin, Edmund S., Jr. .... Menlo Park, CA
Ruffin, Edna A. .... Rutherfordton, NC
Ruffin, F. Eugene .... Jackson, MS
Ruffin, Fayth A. .... East Orange, NJ
Ruffin, Fayth A., P.C. .... East Orange, NJ
Ruffin, John H., Jr. .... Atlanta, GA
Ruffin, Joseph Luis .... Oklahoma City, OK
Ruffin, Joseph Luis, P.C.
Oklahoma City, OK
Ruffin, Louie F. .... Hattiesburg, MS
Ruffin, Robert D. .... Norfolk, VA
Ruffin, Sandra C. .... Miami, FL
Ruffin, Sean P. .... Columbus, OH
Ruffin, Sidney M. .... Pittsburgh, PA
Ruffin, Stacy S. .... Laurel, MS
Ruffin, Thomas, III .... Fort Lauderdale, FL
Ruffin, Thomas T., Jr. .... Washington, DC
Ruffin, William H., Jr. .... Haverford, PA
Ruffin, William R. .... Bay Springs, MS
Ruffine, Louisa S. .... New York, NY
Ruffinengo, Piero G. .... Cleveland, OH
Ruffing, Elizabeth J. .... Denver, CO
Ruffing, Gregory J. .... Franklin Lakes, NJ
Ruffing, Rourke .... Golden, CO
Ruffing, Vickie B. .... Milan, OH
Ruffini, Nina .... New York, NY
Ruffino, Andrew A. .... New York, NY
Ruffino, Joseph W. .... Hopewell Junction, NY
Ruffino, Stephen F. .... New York, NY
Ruffley, Mary Jane .... Detroit, MI
Rufflo, Suzanne M. .... Los Angeles, CA
Ruffner, Ben F. .... Camarillo, CA
Ruffner, Charles L. .... Miami, FL
Ruffner, Charles L., P.A. .... Miami, FL
Ruffner, Ernest L. .... Alexandria, VA
Ruffner, J. David, II .... Dayton, OH
Ruffner, Jay S. .... Phoenix, AZ
Ruffner, Joseph R. .... Rancho Mirage, CA
Ruffner, Keith C., II .... Akron, OH
Ruffner, Malissa .... Baltimore, MD
Ruffner, Robert J. .... St. Louis, MO
Ruffner, Sarah Wright .... Birmingham, AL
Ruffo, David A. .... Albany, NY
Ruffo, Edward A. .... New York, NY
Ruffo, Judith H. .... Lincoln, NE
Ruffolo, Anthony J., Jr. .... Los Angeles, CA
Ruffolo, Hercules E. .... Somers, NY
Ruffolo, John M. .... Dayton, OH
Ruffolo, Mary .... Hoffman Estates, IL
Ruffolo, Samuel J. .... Chicago, IL
Ruffolo, Stone, Dressel & Lipowicz
Dayton, OH
Ruffra, Robin A. .... Los Angeles, CA
Rufien, Paul C. .... Denver, CO
Rufkahr, Michael J. .... Washington, DC
Rufner, Richard K. .... Denver, CO
Rufo, Danny Tom .... Sunnyvale, CA
Rufo, Dino F. .... Sacramento, CA
Rufo, Loreto P. .... Wilmington, DE
Rufo, Mark MacLean .... Nashua, NH
Rufo, Nanette Ferguson .... Sacramento, CA
Rufo, Paul Alan .... Boston, MA
Rufo, Robert C. .... Brighton, MA
Rufo, Sergio .... Hagåtña, GU
Rufolo, Jeffrey W. .... Chattanooga, TN
Rufolo, Laura Beth .... Chattanooga, TN
Rufolo, Pasquale J. .... Florham Park, NJ
Rufty, Alfred J. .... New Orleans, LA
Rufus-Isaacs, Alexander G.
Beverly Hills, CA
Ruga, Barbara A. .... Grand Rapids, MI
Grand Rapids, MI
Ruga, Jonathan M. .... Salt Lake City, UT
Rugai, Ado L. .... Evergreen Park, IL
Rugani, Alexander E. .... New York, NY
Rugani, Frank L. .... Newport Beach, CA
Ruge, Corwin S., Jr. .... Wright City, MO
Ruge, Daniel T. .... Department of Energy, Office of the General Counsel, GV
Ruge, Deborah Shore .... West Berlin, NJ
Ruge, Mark H. .... Washington, DC
Ruge, Thomas R. .... Indianapolis, IN
Rugel, Gerald S. .... Reston, VA
Rugeley & Bosworth, P.C. .... Cleburne, TX
Glen Rose, TX
Rugeley, Edward W., Jr. .... Charleston, WV
Rugeley, Henry L., III .... Wichita Falls, TX
Rugeley, Lane E. .... Cleburne, TX
Glen Rose, TX
Rugeley, William M. .... San Marcos, TX
Rugen, Michael L. .... San Francisco, CA
Rugendorf, Alan .... Chicago, IL
Rugendorf, David Scott .... Los Angeles, CA
Ruger, James C. .... Boulder, CO
Ruger, James R. .... New York, NY
Ruger, James W. .... Cincinnati, OH
Ruger, Michael C. .... Washington, DC
Ruger, Richard M. .... Los Angeles, CA
Ruger, Theodore W. .... Washington, DC
Ruger, William G. .... Watkins Glen, NY
Rugg, Allen S. .... Washington, DC
Rugg, Anne L. Vignovic .... Lanham, MD
Rugg, Betty .... Baldwin, NY
Rugg, Joseph W. N. .... Tampa, FL
Rugg, Thomas F. .... Beaumont, TX
Rugg, William F. .... Indianapolis, IN
Rugg, William F. .... St. Albans, VT
Rugge, Dale R. .... Albuquerque, NM
Ruggeri, James P. .... Washington, DC
Ruggeri, Philip P. .... Sterling Heights, MI
Ruggeri, Richard E. .... White Plains, NY
Ruggeri, Robert A. .... Cleveland, OH
Ruggeri, Robert E. .... Albany, NY
Ruggeri, Robert H. .... Moab, UT
Ruggeri and Ruggeri .... Greenfield, MA
Ruggeri, Sebastian J. .... Greenfield, MA
Ruggerio, Cynthia .... Haddonfield, NJ
Ruggero, John J. .... Philadelphia, PA
Ruggero, Rebecca G. .... Sacramento, CA
Ruggier, Duane J., II .... Charleston, WV
Ruggieri, Andrea M. .... Washington, DC
Ruggieri, Bernard J., (P.C.)
New York, NY
Ruggieri, Brandon M. .... Danvers, MA
Ruggieri, Ellen V. ....
United States Tax Court, GV
Ruggieri, Francis R. .... Modesto, CA
Ruggieri, James A. .... Providence, RI
Ruggieri, John G.F. .... Mansfield, MA
Ruggieri, Joseph A. .... Ventnor City, NJ
Ruggieri, Michael A. .... Ventnor City, NJ
Ruggieri, Michael J. .... Cleveland, OH
Ruggieri, Richard R. .... San Rafael, CA
Ruggieri, Robert W. .... Red Bank, NJ
Ruggieri, Thomas J. .... Philadelphia, PA
Ruggierio, William S. .... Old Bridge, NJ
Ruggiero, Anthony J. .... Hingham, MA
Ruggiero, Anthony J. .... Staten Island, NY
Ruggiero, Anthony J., Jr. .... Rocky Mount, NC
Ruggiero, Attillio P. .... Redwood City, CA
Ruggiero, Carl A. .... New York, NY
Ruggiero, Charles N. J. .... Stamford, CT
Ruggiero, Christopher A.
Philadelphia, PA
Ruggiero, Daniel P. .... Portsmouth, OH
Ruggiero & Duberstein Glenn
Fort Lauderdale, FL
Ruggiero & Haas .... Portsmouth, OH
Ruggiero, James A. .... Providence, RI

Rundle, Richard G. ......Pineville, WV
Rundle, Sandi Jo ......Dallas, TX
Rundle-Borowski, Cheryl ......Island Heights, NJ
Rundles, Janice K. ......Concord, NH
Rundlet, Megan Paris ......Denver, CO
Rundlet, Peter ......Washington, DC
Rundlett, Ellsworth T., III ......Portland, ME
Rundorff, William J. ......Hermitage, PA
Rundquist, Arthur Wm. ......Minneapolis, MN
Rundquist, David E. ......Homestead, FL
Rundquist, David E., Jr. ......Pittsburgh, PA
Rundquist, Karen ......Miami, FL
Rundquist, Timothy A ......Bremerton, WA
Rundstrom, Robert A. ......Sacramento, CA
Rundstrom, William E. ......Oakland, CA
Rundus, Carolyn J. ......Greeley, CO
Rune, Michael Jay, II ......Miami, FL
Runeborg, Robert M. ......Somerville, NJ
Runes, Kenneth A. ......Palatine, IL
Runes, Paul ......Calabasas, CA
Runey, Joseph F. ......Charleston, SC
Runfola, John M. ......San Francisco, CA
Runfola, Ross J. ......Albany, NY
Runfola, Ross L. ......Buffalo, NY
Runfola, Ross T. ......Buffalo, NY
Runft, John L. ......Boise, ID
Rungaitis, Matthew R. ......Glendale, CA
Runge, Barbara Kay ......Houston, TX
Runge, Carrie L. ......Kennewick, WA
Runge, Christianne Y. ......Bismarck, ND
Runge, Dale K. ......Los Angeles, CA
Runge, Eric K. ......Boston, MA
Runge, Frederick W., Jr. ......Baltimore, MD
Runge, Grace Dana ......McKinney, TX
Runge, Gregory Ian ......Bismarck, ND
Runge, H. Carl, Jr. ......Collinsville, IL
Greenville, IL
Runge, H. Carl, Jr., Ltd., Law Offices of
Collinsville, IL
Greenville, IL
Runge, John Byron ......Grand Prairie, TX
Runge, Louis T., Jr. ......Columbia, SC
Runge, Luanne Lambert ......Greenville, SC
Runge, Patrick R. ......Omaha, NE
Runge, Ronald E. ......Sioux City, IA
Runge, Steven M. ......Franklin, OH
Runion, Courtney Lee ......Arlington, VA
Runion, Daniel M. ......Topeka, KS
Runion, Joyce A. ......St. Petersburg, FL
Runion, Kenneth D. ......Delmar, NY
Runion, Shelley Ann ......Kansas City, MO
Runk, Daniel B. ......Cincinnati, OH
Runk, Thomas A. ......Los Angeles, CA
Runke, David W. ......Milwaukee, WI
Runkel, Ansay & Haggenjos, S.C.
Port Washington, WI
Runkel, Christopher M.
National Archives And Records
Administration,
General Counsel Staff, GV
Runkel, John F., Jr. ......San Francisco, CA
Runkel, Matthew W. ......Seattle, WA
Runkel, Paul D. ......Port Washington, WI
Runkel, Philip S. ......Charlotte, NC
Runkel, Ross R. ......Salem, OR
Runkle, Peter W. ......Richmond, VA
Runkle, Richard F. ......Santa Monica, CA
Runkle, Roger A. ......Cameron Park, CA
Runkle, Ronald A. ......Grayslake, IL
Runkle, Walter D. ......Windermere, FL
Runne, Andres ......New York, NY
Runne, Herbert R. ......New York, NY
Runne, Jeanne K. ......Philadelphia, PA
Runne, Juhan ......Haddonfield, NJ
Runnells, John E., III ......Summit, NJ
Runnells, Kent B. ......Brandon, FL
Runnells, Mary M. ......Bloomington, IN
Runnells, Rick ......Little Rock, AR
Runnels, Bruce R. ......Chester, NJ
Runnels, Charles W. ......Greenwood, IN
Runnels, Davage J., III ......Destin, FL
Runnels, David G. ......Houston, TX
Runnels, Dee Ann ......Rock Island, IL
Runnels, Gail R. ......Oklahoma City, OK
Tulsa, OK
Runnels, George D. ......Magee, MS
Runnels, John H. ......Baton Rouge, LA
Runnels, Lawrence A. ......Madison, AL
Runnels, Mark L. ......Klamath Falls, OR
Runnels, Michael ......Beverly Hills, CA
Runnels, Susan L. ......Jackson, MS
Runnels, Therese M. ......Houston, TX
Runnels, Thomas Doyle ......Newark, DE
Runnels, Tramuel L. ......Bowling Green, KY
Runner, Brenda J. ......Louisville, KY
Runner, David ......Salem, OR
Runner, E. Michael ......Louisville, KY
Runner, Edwin C. ......Kingwood, WV
Runner, George F. ......Toledo, OH
Runner, John F. ......Fresno, CA
Runner, Raymond A. ......Toledo, OH
Runner & Runner ......Toledo, OH
Runnerstrom, Lars R. ......Golden, CO
Runnette, Deirdre L. ......Seattle, WA
Runnfeldt, Gail P. ......Seattle, WA
Running, Andrew R. ......Chicago, IL
Running & Gerlach ......Duluth, MN
Running, Jon R., P.C. ......Tulsa, OK
Running, Michael P. ......San Diego, CA
Running, Michael P., Jr. ......San Diego, CA
Running, Steven J. ......Duluth, MN
Running, Wise, Ford and Phillips, P.L.C.
Traverse City, MI
Runnion, David A. ......Atlanta, GA
Runnion, Hilary ......Emeryville, CA
Runnion, Jack C. ......Emeryville, CA
Runnymede Brown, Karen E. ......Portland, OR
Runowicz, Michael E. ......New Haven, CT

Runquist, Lisa A. ......Los Angeles, CA
Runquist & Zybach, LLP
Los Angeles, CA
Runser, C. Allan ......Van Wert, OH
Runstad, Judith M. ......Seattle, WA
Runstadler, George H., III ......Troy, MI
Runstein, Robin M. ......Portland, OR
Runstein, Ted E. ......Portland, OR
Runsvold, James M. ......Caldwell, ID
Runte, Jennifer M. ......Sacramento, CA
Runte, John A. ......Los Banos, CA
Palo Alto, CA
Runtz, David W. ......New York, NY
Runyan, C. Alan ......Hampton, SC
Runyan, Charles W. ......Douglasville, GA
Runyan, Chuck ......Phoenix, AZ
Runyan, Cindy LoCicero
St. Petersburg, FL
Runyan, Cody H. ......Driggs, ID
Runyan, David H. ......St. Petersburg, FL
Runyan, Douglas K. ......New Haven, IN
Runyan, Harley L. ......Fort Wayne, IN
Runyan, Jeffrey L. ......Ashland, OH
Runyan, Jessica Eve ......Austin, TX
Runyan, John E. ......Salt Lake City, UT
Runyan, John G. ......Thomasville, GA
Runyan, John R., Jr. ......Detroit, MI
Runyan, Michael H. ......Seattle, WA
Runyan, Norman E. ......Tyrone, NM
Runyan, R. Bradley ......Washington, DC
Runyan, Richard V. ......Dayton, OH
Runyan & Runyan ......St. Petersburg, FL
Runyan, Thomas B. ......Columbus, OH
Runyan, Wm. A. ......Oberlin, OH
Runyeon, William W. ......Reading, PA
Runyon, Brett L. ......Fresno, CA
Runyon, Elmer E. ......Springvale, ME
Runyon, Frank J. ......Clarksville, TN
Erin, TN
Runyon, Frank J., III ......Clarksville, TN
Runyon, James C. ......St. Petersburg, FL
Runyon, James T. ......Tomahawk, WI
Runyon, John P. ......Pikeville, KY
Runyon, Judith A. ......Riverside, CA
Runyon, Keith L. ......Louisville, KY
Runyon, L. Phillips, III ......Peterborough, NH
Runyon, Michael E. ......Tampa, FL
Runyon, Raymond F. ......Clarksville, TN
Runyon, Robt. E. ......Dunellen, NJ
Runyon and Runyon, PLLC
Clarksville, TN
Erin, TN
Runyon, William L., Jr. ......Charleston, SC
Runyons, J. Rodney ......Orlando, FL
Runzheimer, James D. ......Arlington, TX
Runzi, Michael J. ......St. Louis, MO
Runzler, Kurt William ......Portland, OR
Ruocchio, John H. ......Raleigh, NC
Ruocco, Davide R. ......Minneapolis, MN
Ruocco, Nicole D. ......Orlando, FL
Ruoff, Carl ......Rochester, NY
Ruoff, James A. ......Houston, TX
Ruohomaki, Dale D. ......Dearborn, MI
Ruohonen, Richard Arthur ......Minneapolis, MN
Ruonala, Arnold W. ......Portland, OR
Ruonala, Kenneth R. ......Cloquet, MN
Ruotolo, Robert ......Dallas, TX
Ruotolo, William J. ......Westwood, MA
Rupar, Daniel J. ......Wausau, WI
Rupard, Paul L. ......Pasadena, CA
Rupcich, Richard J. ......Valparaiso, IN
Rupe, Alan L. ......Wichita, KS
Rupe, Andee L. ......Cincinnati, OH
Rupe, Gregory L. ......Richmond, VA
Rupe, Manuel R. ......Kalamazoo, MI
Rupe, Michael C. ......Covington, KY
Rupert, Anton J. ......Oklahoma City, OK
Rupert, C. Bradley ......Boulder, CO
Rupert, Cynthia ......Tampa, FL
Rupert, Donald W. ......Chicago, IL
Rupert, Douglas S. ......Chicago, IL
Rupert, Frederick E. ......Tacoma, WA
Rupert, Gregory J. ......Vienna, VA
Rupert, Jeffrey G. ......Columbus, OH
Rupert, John E. ......Lakewood, OH
Rupert, Kurt M. ......Oklahoma City, OK
Rupert, Loren I. ......Stockton, CA
Rupert, Marcia Austin ......Oklahoma City, OK
Rupert, Peter L. ......Slingerlands, NY
Rupert, Wayne W. ......Cary, NC
Rupinski, Robert F. ......Mount Holly, NJ
Rupiper, Karla R. ......Omaha, NE
Rupiper, Lindsay A. ......Leawood, KS
Rupke, John E. ......Brookfield, WI
Rupkey, Joseph S. ......Milwaukee, WI
Ruple, Dawn Nine, P.C. ......Harrisonburg, VA
Ruple, Dawn Wine ......Harrisonburg, VA
Ruple, Jeffrey W. ......Dayton, OH
Rupley, Jerry T. ......Detroit, MI
Rupley, Ralph C., Jr. ......Houston, TX
Rupli, Danny C. ......Silver Spring, MD
Rupnarain, Trevor K. ......Richmond Hill, NY
Rupnarain, Trevor K., P.C.
Richmond Hill, NY
Ruport, David O., Jr. ......Pinole, CA
Ruport, Scott H. ......Akron, OH
Ruport, Scott H., Co., L.P.A. ......Akron, OH
Rupp, Anthony F. ......Overland Park, KS
Kansas City, MO
Rupp, Brian A. ......Department of Commerce, Patent and Trademark Office, GV
Las Vegas, NV
Rupp, Brian C. ......Chicago, IL
Rupp, Daniel R. ......Columbus, OH
Rupp, David P., Jr. ......Archbold, OH
Rupp, Donald M. ......Edina, MN
Rupp, Edson S. ......Birmingham, MI

Rupp, Ehrlich, Foley & Serwer
Birmingham, MI
Detroit, MI
Pontiac, MI
Troy, MI
Rupp, Gerald E. ......New York, NY
Rupp, H. Marc ......Los Angeles, CA
Rupp, James D. ......Kansas City, KS
Rupp, James M. ......Everett, WA
Rupp, Jeff D. ......Department of Transportation, Office of the General Counsel, GV
Rupp, John A. ......Chicago, IL
Rupp, John A. ......Richmond, VA
Rupp, John Peter ......Washington, DC
Rupp, Kevin J. ......Minneapolis, MN
Rupp, Lynne Ann ......Durham, NC
Rupp, Margaret A. ......Lebanon, OH
Rupp, Mary C. ......San Francisco, CA
Rupp, Mary Foote
National Credit Union Administration,
Office of General Counsel, GV
Rupp, Megan E. ......Washington, DC
Rupp, Nancy McCartney
Laguna Niguel, CA
Rupp, Nelson W., Jr. ......Rockville, MD
Rupp, Paul E., Jr ......Boston, MA
Rupp, Paul V. ......Arvada, CO
Rupp, R. Anthony, III ......Buffalo, NY
Rupp, Robert C. ......Indianapolis, IN
Rupp, Robert E. ......Annapolis, MD
Rupp, Robert K. ......Columbus, OH
Rupp, Sherry L. ......Elmhurst, IL
Rupp, Stephen V., (A Professional Corporation) ......Costa Mesa, CA
San Diego, CA
Rupp, Stephen W. ......Salt Lake City, UT
Rupp & Tenhoeve ......Hackensack, NJ
Rupp, Teresa M. ......Department of Commerce, Patent and Trademark Office, GV
Rupp, Theodore L. ......Post Falls, ID
Rupp, Timothy R. ......Costa Mesa, CA
Rupp, William F. ......Hackensack, NJ
Ruppar, Peter G. ......Buffalo, NY
Ruppe, Arthur M. ......Fayetteville, NC
Ruppe, Erik ......San Francisco, CA
Ruppe, Robert T. ......San Francisco, CA
Ruppel, Charles W. ......Daytona Beach, FL
Ruppel, Dennis G. ......Clearwater, FL
Tampa, FL
Ruppel, Jennifer C. ......Binghamton, NY
Ruppel, Lawrence M. ......Pittsburgh, PA
Ruppel, Richd. W. ......Cumberland, WI
Ruppel, Timothy E. ......Jacksonville, IL
Ruppelt, Ronna F. ......Mayfield Village, OH
Ruppelt, Susan M. ......Mequon, WI
Ruppersberger, Timmy F. ......Towson, MD
Ruppert, Bronson & Smith Co., L.P.A.
Franklin, OH
Lebanon, OH
Springboro, OH
Ruppert, Douglas D. ......Iowa City, IA
Ruppert, James D. ......Franklin, OH
Springboro, OH
Ruppert, John L. ......Denver, CO
Ruppert, Joseph W. ......Pueblo, CO
Ruppert, Mark R. ......Cincinnati, OH
Ruppert, Raymond C.
Department of the Army,
Office of the Judge Advocate General, GV
Ruppert, Rebecca S. ......Cleveland, OH
Ruppert, Ronald W. ......Franklin, OH
Springboro, OH
Ruppert, Rupert E. ......Franklin, OH
Springboro, OH
Ruppert, Scott J. ......Minneapolis, MN
Rupprecht, Richard C. ......Beloit, WI
Rupprecht, Charles J. ......East Brunswick, NJ
Rupprecht, Donald W. ......Naples, FL
Rupprecht, Michael W. ......San Ramon, CA
Rupprecht, Philip R. (IBA) **......Phoenix, AZ**
Ruprecht, G. Steven ......Kansas City, MO
Ruprecht, Harry R. ......Pittsburgh, PA
Ruprecht, John J. ......Fort Bragg, CA
Ruprecht, Richard N. ......Bethesda, MD
Ruprich, Jeffrey S. ......Detroit, MI
Rupright, Christopher J.
San Francisco, CA
Rupright, Pamela G. H. ......Oakland, CA
Rupright, Verne E., Law Office of
Wasilla, AK
Ruran, Dani Noam ......Providence, RI
Rurka, Linda ......Mahwah, NJ
Rus, Miliband & Smith ......Irvine, CA
Orange, CA
Rus, Ronald ......Irvine, CA
Rus, Thomas R. ......Baltimore, MD
Rusak, Steven E. ......Department of Justice, Environment and Natural Resources Division, GV
Rusboldt, Thomas B. ......Manitowoc, WI
Rusca, Rodney ......Fresno, CA
Rusch, Alfred E. T.
Securities and Exchange Commission,
Division of Enforcement, GV
Rusch, Arthur L. ......Vermillion, SD
Rusch, Daniel C. ......Saginaw, MI
Rusch, David W. ......Mandeville, LA
Rusch, David W., A Prof. Corp.
Mandeville, LA
Rusch, James F. ......Whittier, CA
Rusch, John S. ......Sioux City, IA
Rusch, Jonathan J. ......Department of Justice, Criminal Division, GV
Rusch, Kenneth E. ......Milwaukee, WI
Rusch, Mark J. ......McKinney, TX
Rusch, Randall Gregory ......Wilmington, NC
Rusch, Renee M. ......Driftwood, TX
Rusch, Robert ......Medford, WI

Rusch, Robert K. ......Madison, WI
Rusch, Shelly Jean ......Kenosha, WI
Rusch, Thomas M. ......Medford, WI
Rusch, Virginia A. ......Anchorage, AK
Rusch, Wayne H. ......Washington, DC
Rusch, Wesley ......New York, NY
Ruschak, Melinda L. ......Cleveland, OH
Ruschau, Lehman & Hobbs
Miamisburg, OH
Ruschau, Pamela J. ......Chicago, IL
Ruschau, Steve J. ......Miamisburg, OH
Rusche, Edmund W., Jr.
Woodland Hills, CA
Rusche, Joseph F. ......Cincinnati, OH
Rusche, Mark C. ......Atlanta, GA
Ruschel, Brian G. ......Cleveland, OH
Ruschel, Rebecca J. ......Bartow, FL
Ruschell, Stephen M. ......Lexington, KY
Ruscher, Robert P. ......Raleigh, NC
Ruschin, Timothy ......San Jose, CA
Ruschke, David Palmer
United States Court Of Appeals For The
Federal Circuit, GV
Ruschky, Eric Wm. ......Columbia, SC
Ruschman, Richard C. ......Dallas, TX
Ruschmann, Herbert F. ......New York, NY
Ruschmann, Paul G. ......Ann Arbor, MI
Rusciano, Anthony J. ......Bloomfield Hills, MI
Rusciano, Carol Huddleston ......Houston, TX
Rusciano, Charles D. ......Houston, TX
Ruscica, Diana Marie ......Philadelphia, PA
Ruscick, Carolus ......Alpine, NJ
Ruscitti, Donna M. ......Columbus, OH
Ruscitti, Giovanni M. ......Boulder, CO
Ruscitti, Leslee C. ......Milwaukee, WI
Rusconi, Carla Haunz ......Cincinnati, OH
Rusconi, Foster, Thomas & Wilson, A
Professional Corporation ......Morgan Hill, CA
Rusconi, Joseph C. ......Oakland, CA
Rusconi, Robin L. ......Kansas City, MO
Rusconi, Steven A. ......Boston, MA
Ruscus, Stephen E. ......Washington, DC
Rusczyk, Scott E. ......New York, NY
Rusden, John W. ......Kirkland, WA
Ruse, Charles K., Jr. ......Ocala, FL
Ruse, Steven D. ......Overland Park, KS
Kansas City, MO
Ruse, William E. ......Findlay, OH
Rusek, Christopher J. ......Louisville, KY
Rusek, Peter K. ......Waco, TX
Rusek, Randy R. ......Helena, MT
Ruselowski, Ann ......Topeka, KS
Ruselowski, Ann ......Topeka, KS
Rusen, Charles, Jr. ......Florham Park, NJ
Rusen, Michele ......Parkersburg, WV
Rusen, Paul E. ......Florham Park, NJ
Ruser, Kevin L. ......Lincoln, NE
Rusert, Scott M. ......Minneapolis, MN
Rush, Albert F. ......Santa Ana, CA
Rush, Amy E. ......Kansas City, MO
Rush, Andrea N. ......Santa Clara, CA
Rush, Andrew P. ......San Francisco, CA
Rush, Annette ......Kokomo, IN
Rush, Barbara Ann ......Southfield, MI
Rush, Bradley A. ......Washington, DC
Rush, Brian P. ......Tampa, FL
Rush, Caleb A. ......Vallejo, CA
Rush, Carter C. ......Austin, TX
Rush, Charles G. ......Fair Oaks, CA
Rush, Christiana M. ......St. Louis, MO
Rush, Coy J., Jr. ......Paris, AR
Rush, Curt Stefan ......Port Washington, NY
Rush, Cyril B., Jr. ......Columbia, SC
Rush, D. Todd ......Cincinnati, OH
Rush, Daniel T. ......Kennebunk, ME
Rush, Daryl P. ......Cleveland, OH
Rush, Daryn ......Philadelphia, PA
Rush, David H. ......Chico, CA
Rush, David L. ......Paris, AR
Rush, David P. ......Springfield, MO
Rush, Deborah K. ......St. Louis, MO
Rush, Deborah N. ......Chadds Ford, PA
Rush, Debra Featherston ......Worland, WY
Rush, Douglas K. ......St. Louis, MO
Rush, Dwight M. ......Honolulu, HI
Rush, Erin Archer ......Addison, TX
Rush, Ethan M. ......St. Louis, MO
Rush, Fletcher G. ......Orlando, FL
Rush, Fred ......Troy, MO
Rush, Freddie S. ......Vicksburg, MS
Rush, Glenn K. ......Woodland Hills, CA
Rush & Gransee, L.C. ......San Antonio, TX
Rush, Hannula, Harkins & Kyler
Tacoma, WA
Rush, Henri F. ......Department of Transportation, Surface Transportation Board, GV
Rush, Hilary Mason ......New York, NY
Rush, J. Avery, Jr. ......Amarillo, TX
Rush, James J., Jr. ......Glastonbury, CT
Rush, James K. ......Orlando, FL
Rush, James M. ......Odessa, TX
Rush, Jason Bruce ......Belleville, IL
Rush, Jason L. ......Covington, LA
Rush, Jason M. ......Denver, CO
Rush, Jeffery R. ......Cincinnati, OH
Rush, Jeffrey, Jr. ......Department of Agriculture, Office of Inspector General, GV
Rush, John Charles ......Raleigh, NC
Rush, John H. ......Eden, NC
Rush, John L. ......Pine Bluff, AR
Rush, John M. ......Weston, WV
Rush, Judy Taylor ......Daytona Beach, FL
Rush, Kenneth G., (L.P.A.)
Springfield, OH
Rush, Kenneth R. ......Oakdale, LA
Rush, Kenneth R. ......Hackensack, NJ
Rush, Laura ......Tallahassee, FL
Rush Law Office ......Worland, WY

Rush, Linda C. .... Camarillo, CA
Rush, Linda D. .... Parsippany, NJ
Rush, Lorena R. .... Bangor, ME
Rush, Marian B. .... Tampa, FL
Rush, Mark A. .... Pittsburgh, PA
Rush, Marshall, Reber and Jones, P.A.
Daytona Beach, FL
DeLand, FL
Kissimmee, FL
Orlando, FL
Sanford, FL
Titusville, FL
Rush, Mary Ann .... Waterbury, CT
Rush, Mary Jeanette .... Lafayette, LA
Rush, Michael D. .... Columbia City, IN
Rush, Michael J. .... Washington, DC
Rush, Michael L. .... Dallas, TX
Rush, Michael L., P.C., Law Office of
Dallas, TX
Rush Moore Craven Sutton Morry & Beh
Honolulu, HI
Wailuku, HI
Rush, Nancy C. .... Dallas, TX
Rush, Neelema .... Indianapolis, IN
Rush, Peter G. .... Chicago, IL
Rush, Philip A. .... Portland, OR
Rush, Philip H. .... Philadelphia, PA
Rush, Randolph J. .... Winter Park, FL
Rush, Renee Berliner .... New York, NY
Rush, Richard E. .... New York, NY
Rush, Richard E. .... Pittsburgh, PA
Rush, Richard E., Jr. .... Novato, CA
Rush, Richd. O. .... Baton Rouge, LA
Rush, Robert Alan .... Grove, OK
Vinita, OK
Rush, Robert F., (P.A.) .... Charlotte, NC
Rush, Robert L .... New York, NY
Rush, Robert L. .... San Antonio, TX
Rush, Robert P. .... Salida, CO
Rush, Robert R. .... Cedar Rapids, IA
Rush & Rush .... Salida, CO
Rush, Rush & Calogero .... Lafayette, LA
Rush, Rush and Cook .... Fort Smith, AR
Paris, AR
Rush, Scott R. .... Cleveland, OH
Rush & Seiken, P.C. .... Philadelphia, PA
Rush, Sharon E. .... Chicago, IL
Rush, Stephen K. .... Nashville, TN
Rush, Steven G. .... Bloomington, MN
Rush, Thomas J. .... Minneapolis, MN
Rush, Thomas Michael .... Fairfax, VA
Rush, Thomas P. .... Bethlehem, CT
Rush, Tonda F. .... Nashville, TN
Rush, Versel .... Wichita Falls, TX
Rush, Warren D. .... Lafayette, LA
Rush, Wayne F. .... Columbia, SC
Rush, William B. .... Bridgeport, CT
Rush, William J. .... Tacoma, WA
Rush, William R. .... Mount Pleasant, MI
Rushakoff, Susan C. .... San Francisco, CA
Rushall, Bruce J. .... Carlsbad, CA
Rushall & McGeever, A Professional Law Corporation .... Carlsbad, CA
San Diego, CA
Rushbrook, Sandra C. .... Stamford, CT
Rushbrooke, Joseph P. .... Roanoke, VA
Rushd, Shaheen .... New York, NY
Rushdoony, Jonathan H.
Treasury Department,
Office of the Comptroller of the Currency, GV
Rushe, R. Robert .... Annandale, VA
Rushefsky, Cynthia A. .... Springfield, MO
Rushefsky, Norman .... Rochester, NY
Rusher, Ashley S. .... Roswell, GA
Rusher, Derwood H. .... Salem, VA
Rusher, Derwood H., II .... Atlanta, GA
Rusher, James T. .... Boone, NC
Rusher, James W. .... Tulsa, OK
Rusher, Mary Nash Kelly .... Raleigh, NC
Rusher, Robert H. .... Chicago, IL
Rusher, William G., Jr. .... Savannah, GA
Rushevics, Maris .... Plover, WI
Rushfeldt, Alan L., (A Professional Corporation) .... Sherman Oaks, CA
Rushfeldt, Shelley & Drake LLP
Los Angeles, CA
Sherman Oaks, CA
Rushfelt, Gerald L. .... Kansas City, KS
Rushfield, Mark C. .... Edison, NJ
Rushford & Bonotto, LLP
Sacramento, CA
Rushford, Donald L. .... Rutland, VT
Rushford, Francis G. .... Los Angeles, CA
Rushford, James W. .... Sacramento, CA
Rushford, John H. .... Pittsburgh, PA
Rushford, Robert H. .... Burlington, VT
Rushforth, Brent N. .... Washington, DC
Rushforth Firm, The, Ltd. .... Las Vegas, NV
Rushforth, Layne T. .... Las Vegas, NV
Rushforth, Marjorie .... Pomona, CA
Rushiddin, Candace L. .... Los Angeles, CA
Rushin, Mark A. .... San Francisco, CA
Rushing, Allen I. .... Lexington, KY
Rushing, Charles E. .... Department of State,
Foreign Service Officers (Overseas), GV
Rushing, Conrad L. .... San Jose, CA
Rushing, Cynthia G. .... La Jolla, CA
Rushing, David C. .... St. Louis, MO
Rushing, Dennis Lowell, Law Office of
Ashville, AL
Rushing, Don G. .... San Diego, CA
Rushing, Don S. .... Lancaster, SC
Rushing, Elizabeth .... Princeton, NJ
Rushing, Ernest L. .... Olympia, WA
Rushing, Geoffrey C. .... San Francisco, CA
Rushing, George B. .... Augusta, GA
Rushing and Griffith, P.C. .... Lancaster, SC
Newberry, SC
Rushing & Guice .... Biloxi, MS
Gulfport, MS
Hattiesburg, MS
Jackson, MS
Pascagoula, MS
Rushing, Jack D. .... Dallas, TX
Rushing, James K. .... Dallas, TX
Rushing, Janet L. .... Galveston, TX
Rushing, Joy .... Independence, MO
Rushing, Linda Welte .... Austin, TX
Rushing, Lyions & Anderson .... Modesto, CA
Rushing, Michael T. .... Yazoo City, MS
Rushing, Michael W. .... Atlanta, GA
Rushing, Robert W., Jr. .... Florence, SC
Rushing, Stephen O. .... Clearwater, FL
Rushing, Stephen T. .... Statesboro, GA
Rushing, Susan K. .... New York, NY
Rushing, Terri A. .... Atlanta, GA
Rushing, Terryl K. .... Jackson, MS
Rushkoff, Bennett .... Baltimore, MD
Rush-Lloyd, Harold .... Philadelphia, PA
Rushman, Michael J. .... Phoenix, AZ
Rush-Masuret, Laurie .... Bernardsville, NJ
Rush-Masuret, Laurie, P.A.
Bernardsville, NJ
Rushmer, Gary H. .... Orlando, FL
Rush-Milstead, Sheryl .... Wilmington, DE
Rushmore, Mason, Marcus & Crocker
Delhi, NY
Stamford, NY
Rushton, Allen D. .... Birmingham, AL
Rushton, Ann .... Los Angeles, CA
Rushton, Audrey G. .... Boston, MA
Rushton, James C., III .... Florence, SC
Rushton, Jane .... New York, NY
Rushton, Janice G. .... Troy, MI
Rushton, Kathy Ouzts .... Saluda, SC
Rushton, Kenneth A. .... Lehi, UT
Rushton, Lisa K. .... Washington, DC
Rushton, Stakely, Johnston & Garrett, P.A.
Auburn, AL
Clayton, AL
Greenville, AL
Hayneville, AL
Montgomery, AL
Opelika, AL
Prattville, AL
Selma, AL
Troy, AL
Tuskegee, AL
Union Springs, AL
Wetumpka, AL
Rushton, Terre Lee .... Louisville, CO
Rushworth, Emily Charlotte Alexandra
Sugar Land, TX
Rushworth, Kim R. .... Chesterland, OH
Rusignola, Carmen C. .... Newark, NJ
Rusignola, Joseph R. .... Maplewood, NJ
Rusignola, Robert A. .... Short Hills, NJ
Rusin, Bron J. .... Winnetka, IL
Rusin, F. David .... Buffalo, NY
Rusin, John B. .... Chicago, IL
Rusin, Mark P. .... Chicago, IL
Rusin, Michael E. .... Chicago, IL
Rusin Patton Maciorowski & Friedman, Ltd.
Champaign, IL
Chicago, IL
Urbana, IL
Rusin, Thomas D. .... Winnetka, IL
Rusina, Frederick C. .... Portland, OR
Rusinak, Ronald P. .... Johnstown, PA
Rusinek, Walter E. .... Phoenix, AZ
Rusing, Gary M. .... Bellingham, WA
Rusing, Herbert J. .... Grosse Pointe Woods, MI
Rusing & Lopez, P.L.L.C. .... Tucson, AZ
Rusing, Michael J. "Mick" .... Tucson, AZ
Rusing & Platte, A Ptshp. of Prof. Corp.
Bellingham, WA
Rusinowitz, Louis M. .... Melville, NY
Rusis, Robert .... Warren, NJ
Rusitzky & Russell .... New Bedford, MA
Rusk, Carroll Guy, Jr. .... Olympia, WA
Rusk, Daniel J. .... Kingston, NY
Marlboro, NY
Rusk, George A. .... Buffalo, NY
Lancaster, NY
Rusk, George, Jr. .... Kingston, NY
Marlboro, NY
Rusk, J. Craig .... Seattle, WA
Rusk, Jeff E. .... Austin, TX
Rusk, John G. .... Kingston, NY
Rusk, L. Giles .... Nacogdoches, TX
Rusk, L. Giles, A Professional Corporation
Nacogdoches, TX
Rusk, Michelle K.
Federal Trade Commission,
Bureau of Consumer Protection, GV
Rusk, Overton & Sobecki .... Washington, IN
Rusk, Pamela D. .... Kingston, NY
Rusk, Richard C. .... Washington, IN
Rusk, Roberta L. .... Roseville, CA
Rusk, Wadlin, Heppner & Martuscello, LLP
Kingston, NY
Marlboro, NY
Rusk, Willard W., Jr. .... Cortez, CO
Ruskamp, Todd W. .... Kansas City, MO
Ruskan, Ronald J. .... Lorain, OH
Ruskaup, Larry D. .... Rossville, GA
Ruskay, Shira .... New York, NY
Ruskell, Jean M. .... Atlanta, GA
Ruskell, Richard C. .... Suwanee, GA
Ruskey, John A. .... Los Angeles, CA
Ruskin, Alvin R. .... White Plains, NY
Ruskin, Andrew .... New York, NY
Ruskin, Barbara A. .... New York, NY
Ruskin, Bradley I. .... New York, NY
Ruskin, David B. .... Anchorage, AK
Ruskin, David S. .... Chicago, IL
Ruskin, David Wm. .... Southfield, MI
Ruskin, Debbie Sinclair .... Omaha, NE
Ruskin, Elliott E. .... Merrick, NY
Ruskin, Howard M. .... Northbrook, IL
Ruskin, John J. .... New Orleans, LA
Ruskin, Jonathan S. .... Department of the Navy,
Office of the Judge Advocate General, GV
Ruskin, Laurie M. .... Boston, MA
Ruskin, Lea .... Mineola, NY
Ruskin, Lloyd L. .... Miami Beach, FL
Ruskin, Marcia B. .... Port Ludlow, WA
Ruskin, Marcia S. .... New York, NY
Ruskin, Melvyn B. .... Mineola, NY
Ruskin & Molenda .... Anchorage, AK
Ruskin, Moscou, Evans & Faltischek, P.C.
Hauppauge, NY
Mineola, NY
New Rochelle, NY
New York, NY
Ruskin, Nancy I. .... New York, NY
Ruskin, Neil S. .... Brooklyn, NY
Ruskin, Paul J. .... Douglaston, NY
Ruskin, Rachel L. .... Atlanta, GA
Ruskin, Rachel Suzanne .... Brooklyn, NY
Ruskin, Robert H.
Christiansted, St. Croix, VI
Ruskin, Robert K., (P.C.) .... New York, NY
Ruskin, Stephen A. .... Waterbury, CT
Ruskin, Steven A. .... New York, NY
Ruskin, Steven M. .... Los Angeles, CA
Ruskowski, Carl J. .... Schenectady, NY
Ruskus, Geniveve Joan .... Los Angeles, CA
Ruskusky, John T. .... Chicago, IL
Rusky, Arnold N. .... Madison, WI
Ruslander, Betsy R. .... Albany, NY
Ruslander, Julian .... Pittsburgh, PA
Ruslander, Robert K. .... Albany, NY
Ruslander, S. Lee, II .... Parkesburg, PA
West Chester, PA
Rusley, Eric W. .... Phoenix, AZ
Rusman, Jared M. .... New York, NY
Rusmisel, Stephen R. .... New York, NY
Rusnack, Denise .... Belleville, IL
Rusnak, Albert, Jr. .... Bloomington, MN
Rusnak, Anthony Andrew .... La Jolla, CA
Rusnak, Anthony F. .... Skokie, IL
Rusnak, Cyndi Moss .... Houston, TX
Rusnak, David L. .... Atlanta, GA
Rusnak, Joseph P. .... Nashville, TN
Rusnak, Michael J. .... Indianapolis, IN
Rusnak, Susan E. .... Cleveland, OH
Rusnica, John F. .... Albany, NY
Rusoff, David M. .... Helena, MT
Rusoff, David T. .... Chicago, IL
Rusoff, Lester R. .... Missoula, MT
Russ, Abraham .... Massapequa, NY
Russ, Adam H. .... New York, NY
Russ, Albert B., Jr. .... Jacksonville, FL
Russ, Alexander J. .... Orchard Park, NY
Russ, Allen, (P.A.) .... East Brunswick, NJ
Russ, Arthur A., Jr. .... Buffalo, NY
Russ, August & Kabat, A Professional Corporation .... Los Angeles, CA
Russ, Barbara A. .... Duluth, MN
Russ, Brian .... Irvine, CA
Russ, Bryan F., Jr. .... Hearne, TX
Russ, Carol G. .... Greensburg, PA
Russ, Cary, (Mr.) .... Morton Grove, IL
Russ, Charles P., III .... Kula, HI
Russ, Christopher J. .... Cleveland, OH
Russ, Daniel C. .... Tacoma, WA
Russ, David J. .... Tallahassee, FL
Russ, Denis A. .... Miami Beach, FL
Russ, Devon Woodward .... Hoboken, NJ
Russ, Donald J., Jr. .... Chicago, IL
Russ, D. P., Jr. .... Fayetteville, NC
Russ, Edmond J. .... Gardena, CA
Russ, George H. .... Leesburg, FL
Russ, H. Gene .... Fayetteville, NC
Russ, Hugh M., III .... Buffalo, NY
Russ, James F., Jr. .... Downers Grove, IL
Russ, James M. .... Orlando, FL
Russ, James M., P.A., Law Offices of
Orlando, FL
Russ, Jay E. .... Massapequa, NY
Russ, Jeffrey A. .... New York, NY
Russ, Joel B. .... Augusta, ME
Russ, John E., III .... Charlotte, NC
Russ, Larry C. .... Los Angeles, CA
Russ, Lawrence E. .... New York, NY
Russ, Linda E. .... Massapequa, NY
Russ, Lisa A. .... Eureka, CA
Russ, Lisa M. LaValle .... Mineola, NY
Russ, Margaret Riddle .... Fayetteville, NC
Russ, Michael C. .... Atlanta, GA
Russ, Michael M. .... Chicago, IL
Russ, Peter S. .... Pittsburgh, PA
Russ, Philip R. .... Norman, OK
Amarillo, TX
Russ, Robert .... Nashville, TN
Russ, Roberta R. .... Detroit, MI
Russ & Russ .... Massapequa, NY
Russ, Scott M. .... Atlantic City, NJ
Russ, Sharon Portnof .... New York, NY
Russ, Wilbur J. .... Oakland, CA
Russ, Worth, Cheatwood & Hancox
Fayetteville, NC
Russak, Irene S. .... New York, NY
Russak, Jack M. .... Brooklyn, NY
Russak, Kenneth N. .... Los Angeles, CA
Russak, Robert M. .... Woodland Hills, CA
Russakis, Jacqueline L. .... Fort Pierce, FL
Russakoff, Edward L. .... Pittsburgh, PA
Russakow, Mark L. .... Pasadena, CA
Russart, Michael P. .... Milwaukee, WI
Russe, Laurence P., II .... Fairfax, VA
Russe, R. D. .... Fort Worth, TX
Russek, Carol R. .... Richmond, VA
Russell, A. David .... West Redding, CT
Russell, Adrian Oakes .... Jackson, MS
Russell, Albert J. .... Grand Rapids, MI
Russell & Alegria .... Brownsville, TX
Russell, Alford J. .... Fort Worth, TX
Russell, Allen D. .... Houston, TX
Russell, Allen S., Jr. .... Overland Park, KS
Russell, Allen S., Jr. .... Kansas City, MO
Russell, Andrew G. .... New York, NY
Russell, Andrew J. .... Louisville, KY
Russell, Andrew S. .... Overland Park, KS
Russell, Angela W. .... Washington, DC
Russell, Angus M. .... Hanover, NH
Russell, Anne L. .... Nashville, TN
Russell, Anne M. .... San Luis Obispo, CA
Russell, Anson H. .... Elyria, OH
Russell, Anthony R. .... Newport Beach, CA
Russell, Antonette P. .... Miami, FL
Russell, Arthur .... New York, NY
Russell, Barbara M. .... San Francisco, CA
Russell, Barry .... Los Angeles, CA
Russell, Barry A. .... Des Moines, IA
Russell & Batchelor .... Grand Rapids, MI
Russell, Benjamin A. .... Central Square, NY
Russell, Bernard J. .... Towson, MD
Russell, Bernard L. .... Seattle, WA
Russell, Bertrand, Jr. .... Phoenix, AZ
Russell, Beverly J. .... Kensington, CA
Russell, Bill W. .... Victoria, TX
Russell, Bill W., P.C. .... Victoria, TX
Russell, Bonnie E. .... Augusta, ME
Russell, Bradley S. .... Overland Park, KS
Russell, Brenda A. .... Jacksonville, FL
Russell, Brian D. .... Hartford, CT
Russell, Brian F. .... Austin, TX
Russell, Brian P. .... Lawrence, KS
Russell, Brian P. .... Seattle, WA
Russell, Brock D. .... Millville, NJ
Russell, Brown, Bickel & Breckenridge
Nevada, MO
Russell, Bruce J. .... San Francisco, CA
Russell, Bruce S. .... Miami, FL
Russell, Bruce T. .... Department of Justice,
Tax Division, GV
Russell, Byron R. .... Richardson, TX
Russell, C. David .... Reno, NV
Russell, C. Edward, Jr. .... Norfolk, VA
Russell, C. Joseph .... Indianapolis, IN
Russell, C. Mario .... New York, NY
Russell, Carlton E. .... Long Beach, CA
Russell, Carol E. .... New York, NY
Russell, Carolyn .... Phoenix, AZ
Russell & Carowitz .... Grand Rapids, MI
Russell, Carroll .... Blackshear, GA
Russell, Caryl L. .... San Mateo, CA
Russell, Chadwick W. .... Jackson, MS
Russell, Charles A. .... Concord, NH
Russell, Charles A., III .... Newark, NJ
Russell, Charles B. .... Wichita Falls, TX
Russell, Charles E. .... Pensacola, FL
Russell, Charles M. .... Indianapolis, IN
Russell, Charles M., P.C. .... Indianapolis, IN
Russell, Charles S. .... Richmond, VA
Russell, Charles S., Jr.
Charlotte Amalie, St. Thomas, VI
Russell, Charles W. .... Rochester, NY
Russell, Chas. B. .... Greenwich, NY
Russell, Chas. E., Jr. .... Wellington, KS
Russell, Cheryl A. .... Logan, UT
Russell, Cheryll .... Seattle, WA
Russell, Christina M. .... New York, NY
Russell, Christopher .... Indianapolis, IN
Russell, Christopher C. .... Columbus, OH
Russell, Christopher E. .... Newport Beach, CA
Russell, Christopher L. .... Sacramento, CA
Russell, Clark P. .... New York, NY
Russell, Clayton B. .... Denver, CO
Russell, Clement F. .... Acton, MA
Russell, Cliff G. .... Southampton, PA
Russell, Constance C. .... Atlanta, GA
Russell, Corinne Griffin .... Raleigh, NC
Russell, Craig H. .... San Diego, CA
Russell, Craig Hamson .... Boulder, CO
Russell, Craig P.
Department Of Veterans Affairs,
Board of Veterans Appeals, GV
Russell, Craig R., Sr. .... Fullerton, CA
Russell, Craig V. .... Lancaster, PA
Russell, Cramer Anderson "Andy"
Kansas City, MO
Russell, Crystal A. .... Mesa, AZ
Russell, Cynthia Jay .... New York, NY
Russell, D. Andee .... Fort Worth, TX
Russell, D. Craig, III .... Pittsburgh, PA
Russell, D. Lynn .... Decatur, GA
Russell, Dale C. .... Deer Park, WA
Russell, Dale G. .... Hattiesburg, MS
Russell, Dale L. .... Deer Park, WA
Russell, Dallas B. .... Silver Spring, MD
Russell, Dan M., Jr. .... Gulfport, MS
Russell, Daniel Eric .... Portland, OR
Russell, Daniel J. .... Roselle Park, NJ
Russell, Daniel K. .... Princeton, IL
Russell, Daniel Lindsay .... Springfield, MA
Russell, Daniel P. .... Fresno, CA
Russell, Darris L. .... Greenville, KY
Russell, David A. .... Coral Gables, FL
Russell, David A. .... Tulsa, OK
Russell, David B. .... Daytona Beach, FL
Russell, David B. .... Des Moines, IA
Russell, David B. .... Cleveland, OH
Russell, David B. .... La Crosse, WI
Russell, David E. .... Sacramento, CA
Russell, David E. .... New Bedford, MA
Russell, David G. .... Atlanta, GA
Russell, David J. .... Seattle, WA

Russell, David L. ..... Middlesex, NJ
Russell, David L. ..... Newburgh, NY
Russell, David L. ..... Oklahoma City, OK
Russell, David M. ..... Amarillo, TX
Russell, David P. ..... Stamford, CT
Russell, David P. ..... Edgemont, SD
Russell, David S. ..... Pasadena, CA
Russell, David T. ..... Falls Church, VA
Russell, David W. ..... Liberty, MO
Russell, David Williams ..... Indianapolis, IN
Russell, Dean W. ..... Atlanta, GA
Russell, Deborah Moreland
Richmond, VA
Russell, Dennis K. ..... Metairie, LA
Russell, Dennis L. ..... Holmen, WI
Russell, Diane E. ..... San Ramon, CA
Russell, Diane F. ..... Silverdale, WA
Russell, Diane M.
Christiansted, St. Croix, VI
Russell, Dianne C. ..... Rochester, NY
Russell, Donald B. ..... Nevada, MO
Russell, Donald J. ..... Department of Justice,
Antitrust Division, GV
Russell, Donald R. ..... Indianapolis, IN
Russell, Donna Jean ..... Minneapolis, MN
Russell, Donna L. ..... Boston, MA
Russell, Dorothy J. ..... Orlando, FL
Russell, Dorothy Miller ..... Los Angeles, CA
Russell, Douglas S. ..... Iowa City, IA
Russell, E. Lanny ..... Jacksonville, FL
Russell, E. Macey ..... Boston, MA
Russell, Edward ..... Walnut Creek, CA
Russell, Edward C. ..... Bangor, ME
Russell, Edward P. ..... Minneapolis, MN
Russell, Edward W. ..... Bridgeport, CT
Russell, Edwin F. ..... Brooklyn, NY
Russell, Edwin G., Jr. ..... Atlanta, GA
Russell, Elaine M. ..... Marietta, GA
Russell, Elizabeth A. ..... Department of Justice,
Civil Division, GV
Russell, Elizabeth A. ..... Boston, MA
Russell, Elizabeth G. ..... Indianapolis, IN
Russell, Elizabeth H. ..... Albany, NY
Russell, English, Scoma & Beneke, P.C.
Princeton, IL
Russell, Erich J. ..... Bloomington, MN
Russell, Erin L. ..... Charlotte, NC
Russell, Ermea J. ..... Jackson, MS
Russell, Eva C. ..... San Francisco, CA
Russell, F. Alton ..... Raleigh, NC
Russell, Faye H. ..... San Diego, CA
Russell, Floyd, III
Department of the Air Force,
Office of the Judge Advocate General, GV
Russell, Frances W. ..... Virginia Beach, VA
Russell, Francis G., Jr. ..... St. Louis, MO
Russell, Francis J. ..... Worcester, MA
Russell, Frank A. ..... Tupelo, MS
Russell, Frank E. ..... Phoenix, AZ
Russell, Frank F. ..... Malden, MA
Russell, Frank S. ..... West Islip, NY
Russell, Franklin L. ..... Shelbyville, TN
Russell, Franklin T. ..... Syracuse, NY
Russell, Frederick L. ..... Charlottesville, VA
Russell, Frederick M. ..... Dallas, TX
Russell, G. Darrell ..... Towson, MD
Russell, Gail L. ..... Plainfield, NJ
Russell, Gaylon Brent ..... Duncan, OK
Russell, Geoffrey E. ..... San Francisco, CA
Russell, George G. ..... Merrill, WI
Russell, George L., Jr. ..... Baltimore, MD
Russell, Gerald K. ..... Rawlins, WY
Russell, Gerald V. ..... Littleton, CO
Russell, Geraldine Koeneke ..... Stamford, CT
New York, NY
Russell, Geraldine S. ..... La Mesa, CA
Russell, Gilda Tuomi ..... Boston, MA
Russell, Glover A., Jr. ..... Jackson, MS
Russell, Gordon B. ..... Dallas, TX
Russell, Gordon L. ..... Cambria, CA
Russell, Grady M. ..... Pasadena, CA
Russell, Gregory D. ..... Columbus, OH
Russell, Gregory D. ..... Columbus, OH
Russell, Gregory L. ..... St. Louis Park, MN
Russell, Gregory L. ..... Bellevue, WA
Russell, Gregory W. ..... Kalamazoo, MI
Russell, Grover, Jr. ..... Center, TX
Russell, H. Warren ..... Tucson, AZ
Russell, Hamilton E., III ..... Greenville, SC
Russell, Hancock, Jeffries & Gaston, LLP
Los Angeles, CA
Pasadena, CA
Russell, Harker E. ..... Wichita, KS
Russell, Harold S. ..... Washington, DC
Russell, Harrison F. ..... Gunnison, CO
Russell, Heather A. ..... New York, NY
Russell, Heffner & Morrison
Frederick, MD
Russell, Henry ..... Towson, MD
Russell & Herrera, P.C. ..... Decatur, GA
Russell, Holiday Hunt
Fort Lauderdale, FL
Russell & Hollan, P.C. ..... San Antonio, TX
Russell, Hollis F. ..... New York, NY
Russell, Howard M. ..... Boston, MA
Russell, Howard P. ..... Portland, OR
Russell, Hugh E. ..... Milwaukee, WI
Russell, Irma S. ..... Memphis, TN
Russell, Irwin E. ..... Beverly Hills, CA
Russell, J. Keith ..... Houston, TX
Russell, J. Kenneth
Research Triangle Park, NC
Russell, J. MacDonald, Jr. ..... Greenville, AL
Russell, J. Michael ..... Burlington, MA
Russell, J. Michael ..... Dallas, TX
Russell, J. Robert ..... Clarksburg, WV
Russell, J. Shepherd, III (P.A.)
Little Rock, AR

Russell, J. William ..... Asheville, NC
Russell, Jack K. ..... The Woodlands, TX
Russell, Jacque Lyn ..... Golden, CO
Russell, James A. ..... Morgantown, WV
Russell, James B., Jr. ..... Long Beach, CA
Russell, James D. ..... St. Louis, MO
Russell, James F. ..... Cleveland, OH
Russell, James F. ..... Memphis, TN
Russell, James H. ..... Chicago, IL
Russell, James H. ..... Golden Valley, MN
Russell, James H. ..... Belton, TX
Russell, James J. ..... Tulsa, OK
Russell, James L. ..... Coral Gables, FL
Russell, James M. ..... Washington, DC
Russell, James M. ..... Reading, PA
Russell, James T. ..... Carson City, NV
Russell, James T. ..... Houston, TX
Russell, Jan ..... Chicago, IL
Russell, Janice A. ..... Mountain City, TN
Russell, Janice D. ..... Olathe, KS
Russell, Janice L. ..... Miami, FL
Russell, Jas. T. ..... Clearwater, FL
Russell, Jason D. ..... Los Angeles, CA
Russell, Jay C. ..... San Francisco, CA
Russell, Jeffrey A. ..... Fresno, CA
Russell, Jeffrey J. ..... Pittsburgh, PA
Russell, Jeffrey M. ..... Kansas City, MO
Russell, Jeffrey P. ..... Gaithersburg, MD
Russell, Jeffrey R. ..... Norfolk, VA
Russell, Jeffrey S. ..... Sarasota, FL
Venice, FL
Russell, Jeffrey S. ..... St. Louis, MO
Russell, Jeffrey T. ..... Harrisburg, PA
Russell, Jennifer ..... Telluride, CO
Russell, Jennifer Lynn ..... Philadelphia, PA
Russell, Jerry T. ..... Dallas, TX
Russell, Jim G. ..... Salem, OR
Russell, Joan Topping ..... Birmingham, MI
Russell, Joann M. ..... San Francisco, CA
Russell, JoAnn P. ..... Atlanta, GA
Russell, Joe E. ..... Dallas, TX
Russell, Joe W., Jr. ..... Falmouth, MA
Russell, Joel S. ..... Northampton, MA
Russell, John A., III ..... Aliceville, AL
Russell, John A., III ..... Carrollton, AL
Eutaw, AL
Russell, John B. ..... Baltimore, MD
Russell, John B. ..... Richmond, VA
Russell, John B., Jr ..... Richmond, VA
Russell, John C. ..... Pasadena, CA
Russell, John D. ..... Atherton, CA
Russell, John D. ..... Tampa, FL
Russell, John D. ..... Salt Lake City, UT
Russell, John E. ..... Frederick, MD
Russell, John E. ..... St. Louis, MO
Russell, John E. ..... Richmond, VA
Russell, John H. ..... San Francisco, CA
Russell, John H. ..... Linthicum, MD
Russell, John J. ..... Billings, MT
Russell, John Kenneth ..... San Diego, CA
Russell, John L. ..... Houston, TX
Russell, John M. ..... Memphis, TN
Russell, John M., II ..... Great Bend, KS
Russell, John M., Jr. ..... Revere, MA
Russell, John R. ..... South Holland, IL
Russell, John S., Jr. ..... New York, NY
Russell, John T. ..... Cape Coral, FL
Russell, John V., (P.A.) ..... Fort Lauderdale, FL
Russell, John W. ..... Carlinville, IL
Russell, John W. ..... New York, NY
Russell, John W. ..... Midlothian, VA
Russell, John W., Jr. ..... Wagoner, OK
Russell, Johnnie H. ..... Dallas, TX
Russell, Jonathan J. ..... Allentown, PA
Doylestown, PA
Stroudsburg, PA
Russell, Joseph B. ..... New York, NY
Russell, Joseph J. ..... Cape Girardeau, MO
Russell, Joseph L. ..... Birmingham, AL
Russell, Joseph M. ..... Chicago, IL
Russell, Joseph P. ..... Monterey, CA
Russell, Joseph P. ..... Evanston, IL
Russell, Joseph W. ..... San Francisco, CA
Russell, Joseph W. ..... Syracuse, NY
Russell, Joseph W. ..... San Antonio, TX
Russell, Joyce M. ..... Bowling Green, KY
Russell, Joyce Newman ..... Atlanta, GA
Russell, Judith B. ..... Houston, TX
Russell, Julie A. ..... Indianapolis, IN
Russell, Julie Bednarz ..... Worcester, MA
Russell, K. Gail ..... Louisville, KY
Russell, Karen A. ..... Portland, OR
Russell, Karen D. ..... Morristown, NJ
Russell, Karen Drury ..... San Jose, CA
Russell, Karen F. ..... Chesterfield, VA
Russell, Karen L. ..... Anchorage, AK
Russell, Kathleen ..... Indianapolis, IN
Russell, Kathleen A. ..... Chicago, IL
Russell, Kathleen Angela ..... Rego Park, NY
Russell, Kathleen Flynn ..... Baltimore, MD
Russell, Kathleen M. ..... Boston, MA
Russell, Kathryn A. ..... Salem, OR
Russell & Kazan ..... San Francisco, CA
Russell, Kenneth C., Jr.
Huntingdon Valley, PA
Russell, Kenneth J. ..... Boca Raton, FL
Russell, Kenneth L., Jr. ..... Whitefield, NH
Russell, Kenneth P. ..... Salem, OR
Russell, Kenneth R. ..... North Brunswick, NJ
Russell, Kenneth R., Jr. ..... Abingdon, VA
Bristol, VA
Russell, Kent A. ..... San Francisco, CA
Russell, Kent A. ..... Metairie, LA
Russell, Kerry E. ..... Austin, TX
Georgetown, TX
Russell, Kerry L. ..... Tyler, TX
Russell, Kevin A. ..... Chicago, IL
Russell, Kevin J. ..... Roseland, NJ

Russell, Kevin K. ..... Department of Justice,
Civil Rights Division, GV
Russell, Kevin L. ..... Portland, OR
Russell, Kimberly G. ..... San Francisco, CA
Russell, Kimberly L. ..... Cherry Hill, NJ
Blue Bell, PA
Russell, Kimberly P. ..... Pittsford, NY
Russell & King, P.A. ..... Asheville, NC
Russell, Krafft & Gruber, LLP
Ephrata, PA
Lancaster, PA
Willow Street, PA
York, PA
Russell, Kristen Gaven ..... New York, NY
Russell, Kristi Bynum
Oklahoma City, OK
Russell, Kyle E. ..... Columbia, MO
Russell, L. Michael ..... El Segundo, CA
Russell, Lance A. ..... San Francisco, CA
Russell, Laura Broughton ..... Raleigh, NC
Russell, Laurence B. ..... Baltimore, MD
Russell Law Firm ..... Central Square, NY
Russell Law Offices ..... Miami, FL
Russell Law Offices, P.A. ..... Kissimmee, FL
Orlando, FL
Sanford, FL
Russell, Lawrence A. ..... Austin, TX
Russell, Lawrence C. ..... New York, NY
Russell, Lawrence F. ..... Walnut Creek, CA
Russell, Lee H. ..... Northlake, IL
Russell, Lee M. (Russ), Jr.
Montgomery, AL
Russell, Leeolin V. ..... Houston, TX
Russell, Leon R. ..... Dallas, TX
Russell & Leonard, P.L.L.C.
Wichita Falls, TX
Russell, Linda C. ..... Portland, ME
Russell, Lingley & Silver, P.A. ..... Bangor, ME
Russell, Lisa A. ..... Oklahoma City, OK
Russell, Lisa S. ..... Kansas City, MO
Russell, Lloyd G. ..... Irving, TX
Russell, Loren H., (P.C.) ..... Pasadena, CA
Russell, Lori D. ..... Bellevue, WA
Russell, Louis B. ..... New Bedford, MA
Russell & Lueckenbach ..... Greenville, MS
Russell, Lyle D., Jr. ..... Troy, MI
Russell, Lynda A. ..... Redondo Beach, CA
Russell, Lynda J. ..... Tucson, AZ
Russell, Lynda K. ..... Center, TX
Russell, M. Frank ..... San Antonio, TX
Russell, M. George ..... Santa Barbara, CA
Russell, M. Reid ..... Salt Lake City, UT
Russell, Madeline Brady ..... Jackson, NJ
Russell, Margaret A. ..... Minneapolis, MN
Russell, Margaret J. ..... Alamosa, CO
Russell, Margaret R. ..... Anchorage, AK
Russell, Margaret S. ..... Columbus, OH
Russell, Marie Boyce ..... Atlanta, GA
Russell, Mark C. ..... Sugar Hill, NH
Russell, Mark C., P.C. ..... Littleton, NH
Sugar Hill, NH
Russell, Mark D. ..... Marion, OH
Russell, Mark T. ..... West Harwich, MA
Russell, Mark W. ..... Las Vegas, NV
Russell, Mark W. ..... New York, NY
Russell, Mary A. ..... Lafayette, IN
Russell, Mary Beth ..... Tampa, FL
Russell, Mary L. ..... San Diego, CA
Russell, Mary L. ..... Cherry Hill, NJ
Wynnewood, PA
Russell, Mary Rhodes ..... St. Louis, MO
Russell, Maura I. ..... New York, NY
Russell, Maurice L., II ..... Independence, OR
Russell, Maynard B. ..... Chicago, IL
Russell, McIntyre, Hilligoss & Welke
Kokomo, IN
Russell, Melanie J. ..... Department of Justice,
Office of Professional Responsibility, GV
Russell, Melinda L. ..... Morgantown, WV
Russell, Melody A. ..... Irvine, CA
Russell, Meredith E. ..... New London, CT
Russell, Michael ..... Dayton, OH
Russell, Michael D. ..... Bakersfield, CA
Russell, Michael D.
Department of Transportation,
U. S. Coast Guard, GV
Russell, Michael D. ..... Troy, MI
Russell, Michael J. ..... Grand Junction, CO
Russell, Michael K. ..... Dallas, TX
Russell, Michael S. ..... Palo Alto, CA
Russell, Michael S. ..... North Canton, OH
Russell, Michael T. ..... Allen Park, MI
Russell, Michael T. ..... Shelburne, VT
Russell, Michelle A. ..... Riverside, MO
Russell & Mirkovich ..... Long Beach, CA
Los Angeles, CA
Russell, Mitchell E. ..... Blue Bell, PA
Russell and Moltzen ..... Palo Alto, CA
Russell, N. Douglas ..... Millville, NJ
Russell, Norman L., A Professional Corporation
Oklahoma City, OK
Russell, Owen M. ..... Ruidoso, NM
Russell, P. Rupert ..... San Francisco, CA
Russell, P. Scott, IV ..... Jacksonville, FL
Russell, P. Stephen, III ..... Portland, OR
Russell, P. Vaughan ..... Selma, AL
Russell, Pamela A. ..... Parsippany, NJ
Russell, Pamela C. ..... Wicomico Church, VA
Russell, Pamela J. ..... Library of Congress,
Congressional Relations Office, GV
Russell, Pamela Peterson ..... San Francisco, CA
Russell, Patience M. ..... Atlanta, GA
Russell, Patricia J. ..... New York, NY
Russell, Patrick ..... Miami, FL
Russell, Patrick ..... Brownsville, TX
Russell, Patrick J. ..... Denver, CO
Russell, Patrick J., P.C. ..... Denver, CO
Russell, Patti E. ..... Franklin Lakes, NJ

Russell, Paul A. ..... Columbus, OH
Russell, Paul E. ..... Chatsworth, CA
Russell, Paul E. ..... Allentown, PA
Russell, Paul F. ..... Chicago, IL
Russell, Paul K. ..... Livingston, NJ
Russell, Peter A. ..... Cleveland, OH
Russell, Philip D. ..... Greenwich, CT
Russell, Philip, P.C. ..... Greenwich, CT
Stamford, CT
Russell, Philip W. ..... Austin, TX
Russell, Phillip B. ..... Atlanta, GA
Russell & Pitts, P.L.L.C. ..... Seattle, WA
Russell, Plummer and Rutherford, P.C.
Wakefield, MA
Russell, Polly E. ..... Anniston, AL
Russell, Quita ..... Longview, TX
Russell, R. Bruce, Sr. ..... Clayton, GA
Russell, R. Jerry ..... Broomfield, CO
Russell, R. Scott ..... Plainfield, IL
Russell, Ralph T., Jr. ..... Chicago, IL
Russell, Ralph W. ..... Oklahoma City, OK
Russell, Randall D., Sr. ..... Macon, GA
Russell, Randi Davis ..... Tyler, TX
Russell, Ray B. ..... Valley View, TX
Russell, Raymond G. ..... Jackson, MS
Russell, Raymond W. ..... Asheville, NC
Russell, Reed L. ..... Washington, DC
Russell, Regan S. ..... New Albany, MS
Russell, Reid ..... Raleigh, NC
Russell, R. G. ..... Arlington, TX
Russell, Rhett R. ..... Tupelo, MS
Russell, Richard A. ..... Ocean City, NJ
Russell, Richard A. ..... Syracuse, NY
Russell, Richard A. ..... Pittsburgh, PA
Russell, Richard A., A Professional
Corporation ..... Ocean City, NJ
Russell, Richard B. ..... Tremont, PA
Russell, Richard B., Jr. ..... Winder, GA
Russell, Richard F. ..... New York, NY
Russell, Richard F. ..... Nashville, TN
Russell, Richard L. ..... Kokomo, IN
Russell, Richard L. ..... New York, NY
Russell, Richard L., Jr. ..... Los Angeles, CA
Russell, Richard M. ..... Falmouth, MA
Russell, Richard R. ..... Kirkwood, MO
Russell, Richard S. ..... Boca Raton, FL
Russell, Richard Wesley ..... Castroville, TX
Russell, Riley R. ..... Foster City, CA
Russell, Robert A. ..... New York, NY
Russell, Robert A. ..... Portland, OR
Russell, Robert B. ..... Clinton, MA
Russell, Robert C. ..... Vancouver, WA
Russell, Robert C., Jr. ..... Archer City, TX
Wichita Falls, TX
Russell, Robert F. ..... Princeton, IL
Russell, Robert G. ..... Detroit, MI
Russell, Robert G. ..... Sedalia, MO
Russell, Robert G. ..... Chattanooga, TN
Russell, Robert G., Jr. ..... San Diego, CA
Las Vegas, NV
Russell, Robert Henry, III ..... Boston, MA
Russell, Robert Homer, II ..... Englewood, CO
Russell, Robert J., Jr. ..... Montgomery, AL
Russell, Robert L., III ..... Fergus Falls, MN
Russell, Robert M., Jr. ..... Boston, MA
Russell, Robert R. ..... Melbourne, FL
Russell, Robert R. ..... Merrill, WI
Russell, Robert T. ..... Palo Alto, CA
Russell, Robert T. ..... Roswell, GA
Russell, Robert T., P.C. ..... Roswell, GA
Russell, Robert W.
Federal Deposit Insurance Corporation,
Criminal Restitution, GV
Russell, Robert W. ..... Sedalia, MO
Russell, Robie G. ..... Seattle, WA
Russell, Robin ..... Houston, TX
Russell, Rodney Laird ..... Orlando, FL
Russell, Roger T. ..... Belvidere, IL
Russell, Roger V. ..... Lynbrook, NY
Russell, Ronald E.
Frederiksted, St. Croix, VI
Russell, Ronald G. ..... Washington, DC
Russell, Ronald G. ..... Salt Lake City, UT
Russell, Ronald L. ..... Alliance, OH
Russell, Ronald T. ..... Gulfport, MS
Russell, Ronald W. ..... Montgomery, AL
Russell, Rosanna S. ..... San Francisco, CA
Russell, Rossi A. ..... Los Angeles, CA
Russell & Russell ..... Millville, NJ
Russell and Russell, A Professional Law
Corporation ..... San Francisco, CA
Russell & Russell, P.C. ..... Falls Church, VA
Russell, Ryan T. ..... San Francisco, CA
Russell, S. Layne ..... Christiansburg, VA
Russell, Sallie C. ..... Laguna Hills, CA
Russell, Sam W. ..... Mount Pleasant, TX
Russell, Samuel B. ..... Reading, PA
Russell, Samuel L. ..... Bessemer, AL
Russell, Samuel T. ..... Huntsville, AL
Russell, Sara J. ..... Oakland, CA
Russell, Scott ..... Oceanside, NY
Russell, Scott David ..... Chicago, IL
Russell, Sera H., III ..... Lafayette, LA
Russell, Sharon D. ..... Fayetteville, AR
Russell, Shauna D. ..... Department of Defense,
Office of the General Counsel, GV
Russell, Shawn R. ..... Akron, OH
Brook Park, OH
Russell, Shelley D. ..... Portland, OR
Russell, Stacy B. ..... Fulton, MS
Russell, Stacy Stanley ..... Houston, TX
Russell, Stanley D. ..... Clifton Park, NY
Russell, Stell, Smith & McLocklin, P.C.
Lawrenceville, GA
Winder, GA
Russell, Stephanie E. ..... Kansas City, MO
Russell, Stephen B. ..... Fort Myers, FL
Russell, Stephen Joseph ..... Plainview, TX

Russell, Stephen M. ... Winston-Salem, NC
Russell, Stephen S. ... York, PA
Russell, Stephen T. ... Portland, ME
Russell, Steve ... San Antonio, TX
Russell, Steven A. ... Lincoln, NE
Russell, Steven L. ... Dallas, TX
Russell, Steven T. ... Seattle, WA
Russell, Stoychoff & Hankus, P.C. ... Troy, MI
Russell, Straub & Kyle ... Decatur, AL
Russell, Sue Ellen ... Falls Church, VA
Russell, Susan ... Hoffman Estates, IL
Russell, Susan A. ... Portland, OR
Russell, Susan B. ... Washington, DC
Russell, Susan Glenn ... Albany, NY
Russell, Susan H. ... Annapolis, MD
Russell, Suzanne M. ... Chicago, IL
Russell, T. Hans ... Townshend, VT
Russell, T. Newton ... Fresno, CA
Russell, Tamara E. ... Portland, OR
Russell, Tanya H. ... San Francisco, CA
Russell, Terence L. ... Troy, MI
Russell, Terrence ... Fort Lauderdale, FL
Russell & Tesche ... Anchorage, AK
Russell, Theodore A. ... Beverly Hills, CA
Russell, Theodore A. ... San Francisco, CA
Russell, Theodore W. ... Pasadena, CA
Russell, Thomas A. ... Long Beach, CA
Russell, Thomas A. ... Bangor, ME
Russell, Thomas B. ... Paducah, KY
Russell, Thomas B. ... Lynnwood, WA
Russell, Thomas G. ... Jerseyville, IL
Russell, Thomas Hunter ... Los Angeles, CA
Russell, Thomas J. ... Chicago, IL
Russell, Thomas J. ... Chicago, IL
Russell, Thomas J. ... Media, PA
Russell, Thomas K.
San Juan Capistrano, CA
Russell, Thomas O., III ... Los Angeles, CA
Russell, Thomas R. ... Memphis, TN
Russell, Timothy C. ... Philadelphia, PA
Russell & Tlusty ... Abbotsford, WI
Merrill, WI
Russell, Turner, Laird & Jones, L.L.P.
Dallas, TX
Fort Worth, TX
Irving, TX
Russell, V. Eric ... Lafayette, CA
Russell, Valerie L. ... Palo Alto, CA
Russell, Van Priest ... Apalachicola, FL
Russell, Vernon A. ... Concord, NC
Russell, Vickie ... Wailuku, HI
Russell, Vickie L. ... Johnston, IA
Russell, Victor W. ... Chicago, IL
Russell, W. Bryant ... Houston, TX
Russell, W. Clyde ... Greeneville, TN
Russell, W. Kevin ... Port Charlotte, FL
Russell, W. Ryan ... Oklahoma City, OK
Russell & Walker LLP ... San Francisco, CA
Russell, Walter B., Jr. ... Avondale Estates, GA
Russell, Walter J. ... Grand Rapids, MI
Russell, Wayne ... Wilburton, OK
Russell, Wendell P., Jr. ... Fairfax, VA
Russell, Wendi K. ... Los Angeles, CA
Russell, Wesley G., Jr. ... Richmond, VA
Russell, Wilderson, O'Hayre & Dawson, P.C.
Gunnison, CO
Russell, Wiley F. ... Vienna, VA
Russell, Willa M. ... Clearwater, FL
Russell, William B., Jr. ... Portland, OR
Russell, William D., Jr. ... Gadsden, AL
Russell, William E. ... Chicago, IL
Russell, William E. ... Keeseville, NY
Russell, William E., Jr. ... Memphis, TN
Russell, William F. ... Ransom Canyon, TX
Russell, William H. ... San Francisco, CA
Russell, William H. ... San Mateo, CA
Russell, William H. ... Lenoir City, TN
Russell, William J. ... Kellogg, ID
Russell, William J., Jr. ... Daphne, AL
Russell, William L., Jr. ... Little Silver, NJ
Russell, William M. ... Fort Worth, TX
Russell, William M., Jr. ... Tuskegee, AL
Russell, William P. ... Montpelier, VT
Russell, William R. ... Palo Alto, CA
Russell, William S. ... Shelbyville, TN
Russell, William T. ... Chicago, IL
Russell, William T. ... Brighton, MI
Russell, William T., Jr. ... New York, NY
Russell, William W. ... Houston, TX
Russell, Wm. Greg ... Fort Worth, TX
Irving, TX
Russell, Wm. T., Jr. ... Towson, MD
Russell, Wondie ... San Francisco, CA
Russell & Wootten, P.C.
Mount Pleasant, TX
Russell-Albach, Cynthia L. ... Washington, DC
Russell-Brown, Sherrie L. ... New York, NY
Russell-Einhorn, Malcolm L.
Washington, DC
Russell-Einhorn, Michele K. ... Bethesda, MD
Russell-Forrester, Nancy H. ... Baltimore, MD
Russell-Hunter, Janet W.
Securities and Exchange Commission,
Division of Market Regulation, GV
Russell-Hunter, Peregrine D.
Department of Defense,
Defense Legal Services Agency, GV
Russello, Alexandra Hines ... New York, NY
Russello, Gerald J. ... New York, NY
Russello, Lucille D. ... North Arlington, NJ
Russello, Mark M. ... North Arlington, NJ
Russell-Schafer, Ruth ... Austin, TX
Russell-Simpler, Elizabeth A. ... Chicago, IL
Russert, Timothy J. ... United States Senate,
Senatorial Assistants, GV
Russeth, Richard Q. ... Ardsley, NY
Russett, Steven P. ... Minneapolis, MN
Russey, Edward W., III ... Irvine, CA

Russi, Andrea L. ... Los Angeles, CA
Russi, Patrick K. ... Rochester, NY
Russian, Hrant H. ... Wellesley, MA
Russian, Stephen T. ... Lexington, MA
Russian, Thomas P. ... Summit, IL
Russian-Ukrainian Legal Group, P.A.
Washington, DC
Russick, James C. ... Tampa, FL
Russiello, William D. ... Hackensack, NJ
Russillo, Craig G. ... Portland, OR
Russin, Andrea F. ... Miami Beach, FL
Russin, Basil G. ... Wilkes-Barre, PA
Russin, Jill L. ... Philadelphia, PA
Russin, Jonathan ... Washington, DC
New York, NY
Russin, Peter D. ... Miami, FL
Russin, Richard J. ... Woodland Hills, CA
Russin, Rodion ... Cleveland, OH
Russin, Vecchi & Berg LLP
New York, NY
Russin & Vecchi L.L.P. ... Washington, DC
Russis, Vasili D. ... Northbrook, IL
Russler, Nicole Q. ... Knoxville, TN
Russler, Thomas C. ... New York, NY
Russman, David P. ... Boston, MA
Russman, Joel D. ... Denver, CO
Russman, Matthew D. ... New York, NY
Russman, Richard L. ... Exeter, NH
Russman, Richard L. ... Aberdeen, SD
Russman, Sandra Lee ... Atlanta, GA
Russo, Alan ... New York, NY
Russo, Albert ... Red Bank, NJ
Russo, Alfonse R. ... Teaneck, NJ
Russo, Alfred A., Jr. ... Johnston, RI
Russo, Andrew F. ... Ocala, FL
Tampa, FL
Russo, Angela E. ... South Bend, IN
Russo, Aniella ... Hauppauge, NY
Russo, Anne Marie ... Brooklyn, NY
Russo, Anthony ... Los Angeles, CA
Russo, Anthony A. ... Seattle, WA
Russo, Anthony E. ... Union, NJ
Russo, Anthony F. ... New York, NY
Russo, Anthony F., Jr. ... Latham, NY
Russo, Anthony J. ... Stamford, CT
Russo, Anthony J. ... Tampa, FL
Russo, Anthony J. ... New Orleans, LA
Russo, Anthony J., Jr. ... Baton Rouge, LA
Russo, Anthony J., Jr. ... Scarsdale, NY
Russo, Anthony L. ... Oak Brook, IL
Russo, Anthony L. ... Totowa, NJ
Russo, Anthony L., Jr. ... Oak Brook, IL
Russo, Anthony T. ... Stockton, CA
Russo Appellate Firm, P.A. ... Miami, FL
Russo, Arleen D. ... Lakeport, CA
Russo, Arthur J. ... Phillipsburg, NJ
Russo & Baker, P.A. ... Coral Gables, FL
Russo, Basil M. ... Parma, OH
Russo, Benjamin D. ... Patchogue, NY
Russo, Bianca A. ... New York, NY
Russo & Burke ... New York, NY
Russo, C. Anthony ... Washington, DC
Russo, Carl ... Northampton, MA
Russo, Carl L. ... Chicago, IL
Russo, Charles C. ... Hauppauge, NY
Russo, Christine M. ... Plantation, FL
Russo, Christopher J., Jr. ... Annapolis, MD
Russo, Christopher L. ... Cranston, RI
Russo, Colleen M. ... St. Petersburg, FL
Russo, Cox & Russo, P.C. ... Tucson, AZ
Russo, Craig A. ... Boston, MA
Russo, Cynthia Marques ... Newark, NJ
Russo, Cynthia Selin ... Fitchburg, MA
Russo, D. Nicholas ... New York, NY
Russo, Daniel J. ... Vallejo, CA
Russo, Daniel L., Jr. ... New York, NY
Russo, Daniel P. ... New Haven, CT
Russo, David C. ... Teaneck, NJ
Russo, David S. ... Charleston, WV
Russo, Deborah S. ... Hartford, CT
Russo, Denean M. ... Providence, RI
Russo, Dennis W. ... New York, NY
Russo, Dianne H. ... Houston, TX
Russo, Don ... Miami, FL
Russo, Donald ... Vancouver, WA
Russo, Donald P. ... Bethlehem, PA
Russo, Donna ... Hackensack, NJ
Russo, Donna M. ... Summit, NJ
Russo, Dorcas A. ... Medina, OH
Russo, Edmund Peter ... Coral Gables, FL
Russo, Edwin Fortune ... Parkland, FL
Russo, Elizabeth DuBois ... Weatogue, CT
Russo, Elizabeth K. ... Miami, FL
Russo, Eric J. ... Sayville, NY
Russo, Ernest W. ... Phillipsburg, NJ
Russo, Fox & Karl ... Hauppauge, NY
Russo, Frances ... Staten Island, NY
Russo, Frank D. ... Oakland, CA
Russo, Frank D. ... Rome, NY
Russo, Frank J. ... Stuart, FL
Russo, Frank J., III ... Richmond, VA
Russo, Frank K. ... Clearwater, FL
St. Petersburg, FL
Russo, Frank, The Law Offices of
Clearwater, FL
St. Petersburg, FL
Russo, Frank W. ... South Windsor, CT
Russo, Frederick ... Marina Del Rey, CA
Russo, Frederick J. ... Staten Island, NY
Russo & Galgano ... White Plains, NY
Russo, Gary ... West Palm Beach, FL
Russo, Gary J. ... Lafayette, LA
Russo, George F. ... Richmond Hill, NY
Russo, Giacchino J. ... White Plains, NY
Russo & Graham ... Seattle, WA
Russo & Hale LLP ... Palo Alto, CA
Russo & Heffernan, P.A. ... Key West, FL
Miami, FL

Russo, J. Scott ... Irvine, CA
Russo, Jack ... Palo Alto, CA
Russo, Jack G. ... Mineola, NY
Russo, James ... East Providence, RI
Russo, James A. ... Hackensack, NJ
Russo, James F., Jr. ... Rockledge, FL
Russo, Jerry J. ... Harrisburg, PA
Russo, Joan ... New York, NY
Russo, John ... Albuquerque, NM
Russo, John A. ... Oakland, CA
Russo, John F. ... Ridgewood, NJ
Russo, John F. ... Toms River, NJ
Russo, John J. ... Los Angeles, CA
Russo, John J. ... Fairview Park, OH
Russo, John J. ... Kaukauna, WI
Russo, John M. ... North Haven, CT
Russo, John S. ... San Diego, CA
Russo, Jolie A. ... Portland, OR
Russo, Jonathan J. ... New York, NY
Russo, Joseph ... San Diego, CA
Russo, Joseph A. ... Hackensack, NJ
Russo, Joseph A., Jr. ... White Plains, NY
Russo, Joseph C. ... Department of Justice,
Civil Rights Division, GV
Russo, Joseph C. ... Tampa, FL
Russo, Joseph C., Jr. ... Arlington, VA
Russo, Joseph J., Jr. ... Fairfax, VA
Russo, Joseph, Jr. ... Galveston, TX
Russo, Josephine ... New York, NY
Russo, Karen C. ... Syracuse, NY
Russo, Kathleen M. ... Washington, DC
Russo, Kathryn J. ... Woodbury, NY
Russo, Kathy Baird ... New York, NY
Russo, Keane, Sokoloff & Toner, LLP
New York, NY
Russo, Kenneth B. ... Kew Gardens, NY
Russo, Kenneth E. ... Providence, RI
Russo, Kevin F. ... Thiells, NY
Russo & Kieck ... Hackensack, NJ
Russo, Laura A. ... Woodland Hills, CA
Russo, Laura L. ... Coral Gables, FL
Russo, Lawrence, III ... Shreveport, LA
Russo, Lee Ann ... Chicago, IL
Russo, Lesley A. ... Charleston, WV
Russo, Leslie Hayes ... Baltimore, MD
Russo, Linda A ... Hartford, CT
Russo, Linda Nuss ... New Orleans, LA
Russo, Lori M. ... New York, NY
Russo, Louis A. ... New York, NY
Russo, Louis J. ... Brooklyn, NY
Russo, Louis J. ... Buffalo, NY
Russo, Louis P. ... Jefferson, LA
Russo & Lowry LLP ... Los Angeles, CA
Russo, Lucio F. ... Staten Island, NY
Russo, Maria T ... Farmingdale, NY
Russo, Marian H. ... Patchogue, NY
Russo, Marianne Manning ... Bronxville, NY
Russo, Martin P. ... Cortlandt Manor, NY
New York, NY
Russo, Mary Meyer ... Buffalo, NY
Russo, Matthew J. ... Denver, CO
Russo, Michael ... New York, NY
Russo, Michael A. ... White Plains, NY
Russo, Michael D., III ... Fairfield, NJ
Russo, Michael J. ... Cleveland, OH
Russo, Michael J. ... Cleveland, OH
Russo, Michael L. ... Roswell, GA
Russo, Michael N., Jr. ... Baltimore, MD
Russo, Michelle ... Garden City, NY
Russo, Michelle S. ... Baldwin, NY
Russo, Nancy ... Phillipsburg, NJ
Russo, Nancy M. ... Cleveland, OH
Russo, Nicholas C. ... White Plains, NY
Russo, Nicholas F. ... Mineola, NY
Russo, Pasqualino ... Brooklyn, NY
Russo, Patricia A. ... Trenton, NJ
Russo, Paul E. ... Chicago, IL
Russo, Paul J. ... Cranston, RI
Russo, Peter M. ... Rochester, NY
Russo, Philip A. ... Hauppauge, NY
Russo, Philip L. ... Virginia Beach, VA
Russo, Philip L., Jr. ... Virginia Beach, VA
Russo & Prince, Law Offices of
Fairfield, CA
Russo, R. Anthony ... Plantation, FL
Russo, R. Vincent ... Tallahassee, FL
Russo, Ralph D. ... Findlay, OH
Russo, Raphael M. ... New York, NY
Russo, Rex E. ... Coral Gables, FL
Russo, Richard ... Wheaton, IL
Russo, Richard ... Phillipsburg, NJ
Russo, Richard A. ... Wilkes-Barre, PA
Russo, Richard Michael ... Denver, CO
Russo, Robert ... San Antonio, TX
Russo, Robert A. ... Middletown, NJ
Russo, Robert D. ... Boston, MA
Russo, Robert J. ... Morris, IL
Russo, Robert John ... Los Angeles, CA
Russo, Robert V. ... Providence, RI
Russo, Robert W. ... New York, NY
Russo, Ron ... Los Angeles, CA
Russo, Ronald G. ... New York, NY
Russo, Ronald J. ... Tampa, FL
Russo, Ronald R. ... Wilmington, DE
Russo, Roy R. ... Washington, DC
Russo, Rudolph P. ... Hopewell Junction, NY
Poughkeepsie, NY
Russo, Russell ... Tucson, AZ
Russo & Russo, Ltd. ... Oak Brook, IL
Teaneck, NJ
Russo, Russo & Russo ... Phillipsburg, NJ
Russo, Salvatore J. ... New York, NY
Russo, Salvatore S. ... Brooklyn, NY
Russo, Samuel M. ... Marlboro, NJ
Russo, Santo F. ... New York, NY
Russo, Scamardella & D'Amato, P.C.
New York, NY
Staten Island, NY

Russo, Severin A. ... Pittsburgh, PA
Russo, Stephanie Ann ... Boca Raton, FL
Russo, Stephen A. ... Forest Hills, NY
Russo, Stephen M. ... Ridgewood, NJ
Russo, Steven ... Tucson, AZ
Russo, Steven ... New York, NY
White Plains, NY
Russo, Steven Benito ... Hollister, CA
Russo, Steven C. ... New York, NY
Russo, Steven P. ... Toms River, NJ
Russo, Steven W. ... Greenwich, CT
Russo, Susan C. ... Paramus, NJ
Russo, Susan Schneider ... Aurora, IL
Russo, Terence A. ... Mineola, NY
Russo, Theresa M. ... Franklin Lakes, NJ
Russo, Thomas ... New York, NY
Russo, Thomas A. ... New York, NY
Russo, Thomas A. ... Florence, SC
Russo, Thomas J. ... Staten Island, NY
Russo, Thomas M. ... New York, NY
Russo, Thomas M., III ... Pennington, NJ
Russo, Thomas W. ... Bronx, NY
Russo, Thomas W. ... New York, NY
Russo, Toni Ann ... Lodi, NJ
Russo, Tumulty & Nester ... Jersey City, NJ
Russo, Victor A. ... Los Angeles, CA
Russo, Vincent J. ... Orange, CA
Russo, Vincent J. ... Islandia, NY
Westbury, NY
Russo, Vincent J., & Associates, P.C.
Islandia, NY
Mineola, NY
Westbury, NY
Russo, Vincent M. ... Waterbury, CT
Russo, Vincent M. ... Newark, NJ
Russo, W. Mark ... Boston, MA
Providence, RI
Russo, Walsh & Walsh ... Johnstown, NY
Russo, William F. ... Cincinnati, OH
Russo, William J. ... New York, NY
Russo-DiStaulo, Francesca ... Miami, FL
Russo-Doyle, Sara L. ... St. Joseph, MI
Russomanno & Borrello, P.A. ... Miami, FL
Russomanno, Herman J. ... Miami, FL
Russon, Leonard H. ... Salt Lake City, UT
Russonello, William J. ... Staten Island, NY
Russoniello, Joseph P. ... San Francisco, CA
Russoniello, Paul J. ... Cherry Hill, NJ
Russoniello, Savino J., Jr. ... West Orange, NJ
Russotti, Philip ... New York, NY
Russotto, David S. ... Virginia Beach, VA
Russotto, Patricia M. ... Department of Justice,
Civil Division, GV
Russow, Thomas P. ... Monroe, MI
Russu, Julius L. ... Dearborn, MI
Russum, John C., Jr. ... Los Angeles, CA
Russum, W. Lance ... Alameda, CA
Russwurm, Rick L. ... Dumas, TX
Rust, Adrian ... Jacksonville, FL
Rust, Armenis, Schwartz, Lamb & Bills, A Professional Corporation
Sacramento, CA
San Francisco, CA
Rust, Benjamin D. ... Tallahassee, FL
Rust, Benjamin D., P.A. ... Tallahassee, FL
Rust, Charles R. ... Tampa, FL
Cleveland, OH
Rust, D. Michael ... Sacramento, CA
Rust, Dana L. ... Richmond, VA
Rust, Daniel L. ... Crookston, MN
Rust, Jefferson I. ... Oklahoma City, OK
Rust, John B. ... Stratford, CT
Rust, John G. ... Toledo, OH
Rust, John H., Jr. ... Fairfax, VA
Rust, John H., Sr. ... Fairfax, VA
Rust, Joseph C. (IBA) ... Salt Lake City, UT
Rust, Kai-Oliver ... New York, NY
Rust, Lloyd G., Jr. ... Wharton, TX
Rust, Mark E. ... Chicago, IL
Rust, Mary E. ... Cincinnati, OH
Rust, Mary L. ... Cincinnati, OH
Rust, Melissa K. ... Conway, AR
Rust, Michael G. ... Pittsburgh, PA
Rust, Michael J. ... Atlanta, GA
Rust, Neil W. ... Los Angeles, CA
Rust, Rachel L. ... Charlottesville, VA
Rust, Richard A. ... Portland, OR
Rust, Richard N. ... Beverly Hills, CA
Rust, Richd. S., Jr. ... Cincinnati, OH
Rust, Robert E. ... New Orleans, LA
Rust, Robert W. ... Coral Gables, FL
Rust, Ronald A. ... Reston, VA
Rust, Shannon ... Newport Beach, CA
Rust, Sharp M. ... Philadelphia, PA
West Conshohocken, PA
Rust, William C., Jr. ... San Francisco, CA
Rustad, Gerald ... Williston, ND
Rustad, Jeannine ... Washington, DC
Rustad, Michael ... Boston, MA
Rustad, Roger A. ... West Allis, WI
Rustam, William R. ... Houston, TX
Rustand, Kay ... Los Angeles, CA
Rustay, Allen H. ... Houston, TX
Rustay, George A. ... Houston, TX
Ruster, Catherine L. ... Rochester, NY
Ruster, Deborah A. ... Lakeland, FL
Lake Wales, FL
Winter Haven, FL
Ruster, Gregory M. ... Lakeland, FL
Rusterholz, Theophil ... St. Paul, MN
Rusthoven, Jeffery Harold ... Dallas, TX
Rusthoven, Peter J. ... Indianapolis, IN
Rustia, Lois Sanders ... Pittsfield, MA
Rustigian, Darrel R. ... Fresno, CA
Rustigian, Darrel R., A Professional Corporation ... Fresno, CA
Rustigian, Lloyd A. G. ... Johnston, RI
Rustik, James A. ... Chicago, IL

Rustin, Charles L. ... Milwaukee, WI
Rustin, Peter B. ... Redondo Beach, CA
Rustin, William D. ... Wichita, KS
Rustmann, Daniel R. W. ... Detroit, MI
Rustomjee, Naomi ... San Francisco, CA
Ruston, Donald A. ... Costa Mesa, CA
Ruston, Paul A. ... Denver, CO
Rust-Tierney, Diann ... Washington, DC
Rustum, Michael J. ... Washington, DC
Rustum, William M. ... New York, NY
Rusu, Robert N., Jr. ... Canfield, OH
Ruswick, Frank J. ... Brookfield, WI
Ruswick, Richard P. ... Ithaca, NY
Rusyn, Daria H. ... Cleveland, OH
Rusyn, Paul F. ... Bellevue, WA
Ruszak, John A. ... Long Beach, CA
Ruszczyk, Paul ... Cheshire, CT
Ruszczyk, Peter T. ... Buffalo, NY
Ruta, Joseph A. ... New York, NY
Ruta, Melanie Males ... Orlando, FL
Ruta, R. Steven ... Orlando, FL
Rutala, Donna Renfrow ... Raleigh, NC
Rutan, Edwin P., II ... Basking Ridge, NJ
Rutan, Kenneth A. ... San Diego, CA
Rutan, Kenneth D. ... Tucker, GA
Rutan, Kenneth D., P.C. ... Tucker, GA
Rutan & Tucker, LLP ... Costa Mesa, CA
Los Angeles, CA
Newport Beach, CA
Santa Ana, CA
Rutberg, Fredric D. ... Great Barrington, MA
Rutberg, Joseph
Nuclear Regulatory Commission, Office of the General Counsel, GV
Rutberg, Martin P. ... Poughkeepsie, NY
Rutberg, Michael B. ... West Covina, CA
Rutberg, Susan ... San Francisco, CA
Rutchick, Harold L. ... Scottsdale, AZ
Rutchik, David H. ... Tysons Corner, VA
Rutchik, Gregory Alan ... Palo Alto, CA
Rutchik, Martin M. ... Norwich, CT
Rutchow, William ... Nashville, TN
Rutcofsky, Barry S. ... New York, NY
Rute, Kay Y. ... Topeka, KS
Rute, Lawrence R. ... Topeka, KS
Rutecki, Mark, & Associates, P.A.
Orlando, FL
Rutecki, Mark C. ... Orlando, FL
Rutecki, Robert J. ... Boston, MA
Rutenbar, Marsha L. ... Waxahachie, TX
Rutenbeck, Blaine A. ... Denver, CO
Rutenberg, Alan D. ... Washington, DC
Rutenberg, John K. ... Myrtle Beach, SC
Rutenberg, Michael J. ... Haverford, PA
Rutenberg, Sara J. ... Universal City, CA
Rutens, Andrew J. ... Mobile, AL
Ruter, Gerald C. ... Baltimore, MD
Rutgers, Gerritt A. ... Redwood City, CA
Rutgers, Robert C., Jr. ... Grand Rapids, MI
Ruth, Agnes L. ... San Diego, CA
Ruth, Anna Holmes ... Ashland, KY
Ruth, Bryce C., Jr. ... White House, TN
Ruth, Carolyn J. ... San Rafael, CA
Ruth, Celinas ... Sedona, AZ
Ruth, David P. ... San Diego, CA
Ruth, Dennis R. ... Granite City, IL
Ruth, Douglas L. ... Owatonna, MN
Ruth, Elyse ... Los Angeles, CA
Ruth, Frederick A. ... United States Senate, Senatorial Assistants, GV
Ruth, H. Steve ... Atlanta, GA
Ruth, Henry S., Jr. ... Tucson, AZ
Ruth, Hilton L., III ... Kannapolis, NC
Ruth, James C. ... Houston, TX
Ruth, James M. ... Sturgeon Bay, WI
Ruth, John A. ... Jefferson City, MO
Ruth, John H., III ... San Francisco, CA
Ruth, Joseph E. ... Vineland, NJ
Ruth, Kristin H. ... Raleigh, NC
Ruth, Larry L. ... Lincoln, NE
Ruth, Laura Jeanne ... Austin, TX
Houston, TX
Ruth, Lawrence A. ... Conshohocken, PA
Ruth, Lisa L. ... Sacramento, CA
Ruth & MacNeille, Professional Association
Beaufort, SC
Bluffton, SC
Hilton Head Island, SC
Ruth, Margaret Anne ... Washington, DC
Ruth, McCarthy & Coleman, P.C.
Chattanooga, TN
Ruth & Mueller Law Firm ... Lincoln, NE
Ruth, Patrick A. ... Nashville, TN
Ruth, R. Scott ... Chattanooga, TN
Ruth, Richard L. ... Jacksonville, FL
Ruth, Richard R., Jr. ... Chattanooga, TN
Ruth, Richard T. ... Erie, PA
Ruth, Robert W. ... Houston, TX
Ruth, Ronald W. ... Boston, MA
Ruth, Schreiner & Long ... Owatonna, MN
Ruth, Scott A. ... Hanover, PA
Ruth, Sharon A. ... San Francisco, CA
Ruth, Sharon Neil ... Gainesville, FL
Ruth, Stephen W. ... Davenport, IA
Ruth, Steven C. ... St. Petersburg, FL
Ruth, Steven R. ... Walnut Creek, CA
Ruth, Susan D.
Treasury Department, GV
Ruth, Thomas J. ... Flint, MI
Ruth, Thomas L., Jr. ... Tucson, AZ
Ruth, Timothy M. ... Naperville, IL
Ruth, Timothy P. ... Hallam, PA
York, PA
Ruth, Vicky K. ... Jefferson City, MO
Ruth, William A. ... Hilton Head Island, SC
Ruthazer, Maureen L. ... Haverhill, MA
Ruthberg, Miles N. ... Los Angeles, CA
Ruthenbeck, Arthur W. ... Sacramento, CA

Ruthenberg, Joan ... Indianapolis, IN
Ruthenberg, Kenneth W., Jr.
Gold River, CA
Ruthenberg, Kirk R. ... Washington, DC
Ruthenberg, Sidney M. ... New York, NY
Ruther, Brent ... Burlington, IA
Ruther, Ronald W. ... Santa Ana, CA
Ruther, Scott ... Shawnee, KS
Rutherford, Albert G., II ... Honesdale, PA
Rutherford, Ann H. ... Chico, CA
Rutherford, Arda S. ... Dewey, AZ
Rutherford, Boyd K. ... Baltimore, MD
Rutherford, Bradley J. ... Marshalltown, IA
Rutherford, Charles E. ... Boca Raton, FL
West Palm Beach, FL
Rutherford, Charles R.
Bloomfield Hills, MI
Rutherford, Connie M. ... Oakland, CA
Rutherford, Crystal Grace ... Seattle, WA
Rutherford, Daniel R. ... San Antonio, TX
Rutherford, David A. ... Atlanta, GA
Rutherford, David C., (P.C.) ... Nashville, TN
Rutherford, David L. ... Ridgewood, NJ
Rutherford, David S. ... New York, NY
Rutherford, DeMarco, White & Soloman
Nashville, TN
Rutherford, Douglas M. ... Minneapolis, MN
Rutherford, Elizabeth M. ... Cincinnati, OH
Rutherford, Floyd R., II ... Augusta, ME
Rutherford, Gaynor K. ... Wakefield, MA
Rutherford, Glen B. ... Knoxville, TN
Rutherford, J. Todd ... Columbia, SC
Rutherford, Jay K. ... Fort Worth, TX
Rutherford, Jenice L. ... Reading, PA
Rutherford, Joan N. ... Tacoma, WA
Rutherford, John C. ... Dallas, TX
Rutherford, Julia ... Kingman, AZ
Rutherford, Kari L. ... Redlands, CA
Rutherford, Kenneth A. ... Jackson, MS
Rutherford, Kevin D.
Bloomfield Hills, MI
Rutherford, Launa K. ... Orlando, FL
Rutherford Law Office ... Marshalltown, IA
Rutherford Law Offices ... Springfield, IL
Rutherford, Leigh A. ... Batesville, MS
Hernando, MS
Rutherford, Leland R. ... Mt. Vernon, OH
Rutherford, Linda L. ... Dallas, TX
Rutherford, Lisa H. ... Madison, WI
Rutherford, Luanne ... Walnut Creek, CA
Rutherford, M. Jacqueline ... Conyers, GA
Rutherford, Marjorie M. ... Raleigh, NC
Rutherford, Mark C. ... Westlake Village, CA
Rutherford, Mark W. ... Indianapolis, IN
Rutherford, Mary J. ... Morristown, TN
Rutherford, Michael C. ... Elkhorn, WI
Rutherford, Michael Peter ... Denver, CO
Rutherford, Mulhall & Wargo, Professional Association ... Boca Raton, FL
West Palm Beach, FL
Rutherford, Nikkee E. ... Beaumont, TX
Rutherford, Palmer S., Jr. ... Norfolk, VA
Rutherford, Paul A. ... Nashville, TN
Rutherford, Raymond S., Jr. ... Houston, TX
Rutherford, Rebecca T. ... Dallas, TX
Rutherford, Richard Stephen ... Nampa, ID
Rutherford, Richard W. ... Raleigh, NC
Rutherford, Robert H., Jr.
Birmingham, AL
Rutherford, Robert W. ... Nashville, TN
Rutherford, Roger L. ... Springfield, IL
Rutherford, Roger W. ... Norton, VA
Rutherford, S. Morton, III ... Tulsa, OK
Rutherford, Samuel C. ... Chelan, WA
Wenatchee, WA
Rutherford, Samuel W. ... Knoxville, TN
Rutherford, Shan S. ... Austin, TX
Rutherford, Sherri K. ... Chillicothe, OH
Rutherford, Sherrie N. ... Houston, TX
Rutherford, Steve K.
Sulphur Springs, TX
Rutherford, Susan L. ... Atlanta, GA
Rutherford, Susan S. ... Hackensack, NJ
Rutherford, Syzzette B. ... New York, NY
Rutherford, Terrance G. ... Atlantic, IA
Rutherford, Thomas ... Albuquerque, NM
Rutherford, Thomas M., Jr. ... Tustin, CA
Rutherford, Thomas S. ... Tampa, FL
Rutherford, Timothy C. ... San Diego, CA
Rutherford, Tonya
Federal Communications Commission, Common Carrier Bureau, GV
Rutherford, W. Fain ... Roanoke, VA
Rutherford, William F. ... Norfolk, VA
Rutherford, William L. ... Peoria, IL
Rutherfurd, Guy G. ... New York, NY
Rutherfurd, Robert S. ... Santa Rosa, CA
Rutherfurd, Winthrop, Jr. ... New York, NY
Rutherglen, George A. ... Charlottesville, VA
Ruthford, William C. ... Bellevue, WA
Ruth-Heffelbower, Duane F. ... Fresno, CA
Ruthig & Leonard ... Cortland, NY
Ruthig, Russell E. ... Cortland, NY
Ruthizer, Jeffrey ... New York, NY
Ruthizer, Theodore ... New York, NY
Ruthman, Maureen ... Delray Beach, FL
Ruthmeyer, Bernard A. ... St. Louis, MO
Ruthrauff & Armbrust, P.C.
Cherry Hill, NJ
Philadelphia, PA
Ruthrauff, Wilbur Bourne
Philadelphia, PA
Ruthruff, Jerry A. ... Honolulu, HI
Ruthven, Cotton ... University, MS
Ruti, John M. ... Mount Kisco, NY
Rutigliano, Emilia I ... New York, NY
Rutigliano, Joseph E. ... Cleveland, OH
Rution, Joseph A. ... Santa Barbara, CA

Rutkey, Jenifer Powers ... Glenville, NY
Rutkin, Alan S. ... Uniondale, NY
Rutkin, Arnold H. ... Greenwich, CT
Westport, CT
Rutkin, David S., Law Office of
Bridgeport, CT
Monroe, CT
Rutkin, Norman K. ... Miami, FL
Rutkin and Oldham, L.L.C
Greenwich, CT
Westport, CT
Rutkoff, Alan S. ... Chicago, IL
Rutkoske, Eric A. ... New York, NY
Rutkovsky, Julius ... Brooklyn, NY
Rutkowski, Anthony R. ... Chicago, IL
Des Plaines, IL
Rutkowski, Arthur D. ... Evansville, IN
Rutkowski, Chad A. ... Westmont, NJ
Rutkowski, David S. ... Washington, DC
Rutkowski, Donna Alaimo ... Buffalo, NY
Rutkowski, James ... Oakland, CA
Rutkowski, Joanne C. ... Washington, DC
New York, NY
Rutkowski, Lawrence ... New York, NY
Rutkowski, Mary Hollie ... Sacramento, CA
Rutkowski, Max A. ... Levittown, PA
Rutkowski, Michael R. ... Dartmouth, MA
Rutkowski, Renee S. ... Arlington, VA
Rutkowski, Rheba ... Boston, MA
Rutkowski, Robert W.
Brooklyn Heights, OH
Rutkowski & Rutkowski, Law Offices of
Levittown, PA
Rutkowski, Stanley E. ... Lawrenceville, NJ
Rutkowski, Stanley W. ... Levittown, PA
Rutkowski, Thomas J. ... Michigan City, IN
Rutland, Anne Solomon ... Rochester, NY
Rutland & Braswell, L.L.C.
Union Springs, AL
Rutland, D. Lee ... Annapolis, MD
Baltimore, MD
Rutland, Fairy Davenport ... Austin, TX
Rutland, J. Brian ... Albany, GA
Rutland, John D. ... Beaumont, TX
Rutland, John W., Jr. ... Dallas, TX
Rutland, L. Cooper, Jr.
Union Springs, AL
Rutland, Leonard, Jr. ... Stuart, FL
Rutland, Lori L. ... St. Petersburg, FL
Rutland, Lori L., P.A. ... St. Petersburg, FL
Rutland, Louis C. ... Union Springs, AL
Rutland, Michael Alan ... Eufaula, AL
Rutland, Nancy E. ... St. Petersburg, FL
Rutland, Roy ... Waco, TX
Rutledge, Alvin A. ... Detroit, MI
Rutledge, Anthony R. ... White Plains, NY
Rutledge, Arthur D. ... Los Angeles, CA
Rutledge, Brad S. ... Lansing, MI
Rutledge, Brian S. ... Las Vegas, NV
Rutledge, Corinne E. ... Cheyenne, WY
Rutledge, Dane Keller ... New York, NY
Rutledge, David W. ... Santa Ana, CA
Rutledge, David W. ... Clarkston, GA
Rutledge, Dean B. ... Winston-Salem, NC
Rutledge, Debra ... Baton Rouge, LA
Rutledge, Donald T. ... Johns Island, SC
Rutledge, Donna B. ... New Orleans, LA
Rutledge, Donnie W., II ... Springdale, AR
Rutledge, E. Preston ... Washington, DC
Rutledge, Earl, Law Offices of, A Prof. Corp.
Hurst, TX
Rutledge, Ecenia, Purnell & Hoffman, P.A.
Tallahassee, FL
Rutledge, Evans S. ... Abilene, TX
Rutledge, Frederic B. ... Seattle, WA
Rutledge, Friday, Safrit & Smith
Kannapolis, NC
Rutledge, Gary L. ... St. Louis, MO
Rutledge, Gary R. ... Tallahassee, FL
Rutledge, Gerald L. ... Pittsburgh, PA
Rutledge, Glen R., II ... Williamson, WV
Rutledge, Irvine H. ... Hagerstown, MD
Rutledge, Ivan C. ... Macon, GA
Rutledge, J. Carlyle ... Kannapolis, NC
Rutledge, J. Kent ... Cheyenne, WY
Rutledge, James A. ... Columbus, OH
Rutledge, James B., III ... Baltimore, MD
Rutledge, James V. ... Roscommon, MI
Rutledge, Janice E. ... Iowa City, IA
Rutledge, Jeffrey Merrell ... Savannah, GA
Rutledge, Jerry ... Walnut Cove, NC
Rutledge, John F. ... Columbus, OH
Rutledge, John F. ... Arlington, VA
Rutledge, John R. ... Baltimore, MD
Rutledge, Jonathan M. ... San Francisco, CA
Rutledge, Keith ... Batesville, AR
Rutledge Law Office ... New Albany, MS
Rutledge, Lois V. ... Beavercreek, OH
Rutledge, Loren D. ... Austin, TX
Rutledge, Manion, Rabaut, Terry & Thomas, P.C. ... Detroit, MI
Rutledge, Mark A. ... Deerfield Beach, FL
Rutledge, Marybeth W. ... Dayton, OH
Rutledge, Michael J. ... Department of Labor, Office of the Solicitor, GV
Rutledge, Paul F. ... Wellesley Hills, MA
Rutledge, Paul P. ... Metairie, LA
Rutledge, Paul V. ... Boston, MA
Rutledge, Peter A. ... Greenville, SC
Rutledge, R. Michael ... Houston, TX
Rutledge, Ralph M. ... Gastonia, NC
Rutledge, Randall ... Fort Lauderdale, FL
Rutledge, Richard B. ... Kew Gardens, NY
Rutledge, Richard C., III ... Houston, TX
Rutledge, Robert B. ... Portland, OR
Rutledge, Robert M. ... Abilene, TX
Rutledge, Roger K. ... Memphis, TN
Rutledge, Russell C. ... Memphis, TN

Rutledge & Rutledge ... Abilene, TX
Rutledge & Rutledge, P.C. ... Memphis, TN
Rutledge, Sally A. ... Birmingham, MI
Rutledge, Shell L. ... Atlanta, GA
Rutledge, Thomas A. ... Carlsbad, NM
Rutledge, Thomas A. ... Austin, TX
Rutledge, Thomas E. ... Louisville, KY
Rutledge, Tommy C. ... De Quincy, LA
Rutledge, Virginia S. ... Treasury Department, Office of the Comptroller of the Currency, GV
Rutledge, W. Thomas, Jr. ... Charleston, SC
Rutledge, Walter S. ... Dallas, TX
Rutledge, Wiley B. ... New Haven, CT
Rutledge, William E. ... Tulsa, OK
Rutledge, William K. ... Abilene, TX
Rutledge, William M. ... Warren, MI
Rutledge, William O., III ... New Albany, MS
Rutledge-Parisi, Allison ... New York, NY
Rutley, Dean Wayne ... Washington, DC
Atlanta, GA
Rutley, Jonathan C. ... Dedham, MA
Rutlin, Ronald J. ... Wausau, WI
Rutman, Donald L. ... St. Paul, MN
Rutman, Gerald E. ... Golden Valley, MN
Rutman, Gregory L. ... Avon Lake, OH
Rutman, Herbert A. ... New York, NY
Rutman, Hyman L. ... Hauppauge, NY
Rutman, Keith H. ... San Diego, CA
Rutman, Rick J. ... New York, NY
Rutman, Wayne D. ... Philadelphia, PA
Rutnik, Christopher P., Law Office of
Albany, NY
Rutnik, Daniel J. ... Albany, NY
Rutnik, Douglas P. ... Albany, NY
Rutnik, Gregory A. ... Albany, NY
Rutnik, Kirsten E. ... New York, NY
Rutrich, Elena S. ... Newton, NJ
Rutschow, Robert F. ... Charlottesville, VA
Rutsky, Scott K. ... New York, NY
Rutson, Victoria J.
Department of Transportation, Surface Transportation Board, GV
Rutstein, David W. ... Washington, DC
Rutstein, Joel Scott ... Treasury Department, Internal Revenue Service, GV
Rutstein, Leonard David ... Chicago, IL
Rutstein, Louis M. ... Memphis, TN
Rutstein, Neal D. ... Chicago, IL
Rutstein, Steven M. ... Hartford, CT
Rutstein, Susan R. ... Boston, MA
Rutt, David N. ... Georgetown, DE
Milford, DE
Rutt, Ellen Keane ... Hartford, CT
Rutt, J. Steven ... Washington, DC
Rutt, Robert G. ... Fairfield, IA
Rutta, Jas. M. ... Columbus, TX
Rutta, Michelle B. ... New York, NY
Ruttan, John A. ... San Antonio, TX
Rutten, James C. ... Los Angeles, CA
Rutten, Randy J. ... El Centro, CA
Rutten, Thomas E. ... Devils Lake, ND
Rutten, Thomas H. ... Phoenix, AZ
Rutten, Timothy M. ... Washington, DC
Ruttenberg, A. Fred ... Cherry Hill, NJ
Ruttenberg, Adam J. ... Boston, MA
Ruttenberg, Alison L. ... Boulder, CO
Ruttenberg, Barnett P., (P.C.) ... Chicago, IL
Ruttenberg, Bernard ... Los Angeles, CA
Ruttenberg, Brenda H. ... Los Angeles, CA
Ruttenberg, Bruce R. ... Providence, RI
Ruttenberg, Charles B. ... Washington, DC
Ruttenberg, Daniel H. ... Vienna, VA
Ruttenberg, David A. ... New York, NY
Ruttenberg, David C. ... Chicago, IL
Ruttenberg, David H. ... Providence, RI
Ruttenberg, David W. ... Chicago, IL
Ruttenberg, Edward A. ... Los Angeles, CA
Ruttenberg, Frank Z. ... San Antonio, TX
Ruttenberg, Fred S. ... Evanston, IL
Ruttenberg, Gary M. ... Los Angeles, CA
Ruttenberg, Hattie ... Washington, DC
Ruttenberg, Joan Ellen ... Newton, MA
Ruttenberg, Kenneth G. ... Los Angeles, CA
Ruttenberg, Marvin H. ... Rolling Meadows, IL
Ruttenberg, Neil H. ... Fairfax, VA
Ruttenberg, Pilar ... Department of Agriculture, Office of the General Counsel, GV
Ruttenberg & Ruttenberg ... Chicago, IL
Ruttenberg, Valerie H. ... Minneapolis, MN
Ruttenberg, Victoria A.
General Services Administration, Office of the General Counsel, GV
Ruttencutter, Eric A. ... St. Louis, MO
Rutter, C. Arthur, III ... Norfolk, VA
Rutter, C. Arthur, Jr. ... Norfolk, VA
Rutter, Carol A. ... St. Louis, MO
Rutter, David A. ... Nashville, TN
Rutter & DiPiero ... Philadelphia, PA
Rutter, Donna M. ... San Francisco, CA
Rutter, Gorham, Jr. (P.A.) ... Longwood, FL
Rutter, Hobbs & Davidoff, Incorporated
Los Angeles, CA
Rutter, J. Edgar T., II ... Newport Beach, CA
Rutter, James L. ... Columbia, MO
Rutter, Kent ... Houston, TX
Rutter, Marion Ty ... Clovis, NM
Rutter, Mark D. ... Long Beach, CA
Rutter, Mark H. ... Research Triangle Park, NC
Rutter, Marshall A. ... Los Angeles, CA
Rutter, Michael K. ... New Brunswick, NJ
Rutter, Mitchell Brent ... Bayside, NY
Rutter, Neil K. ... New Haven, CT
Rutter, Paul S. ... Santa Monica, CA
Rutter, Peter J. ... Tyler, TX
Rutter, R. William, Jr.
West Palm Beach, FL
Rutter, Robert C. ... St. Louis, MO

Rutter, Robert P. ... Cleveland, OH
Rutter, Thomas B. ... Philadelphia, PA
Rutter, Walsh, Mills & Rutter ... Norfolk, VA
Rutter, William A. ... Encino, CA
Rutterer, Paul J. M. ... St. Louis, MO
Ruttinger, George D. ... Washington, DC
Ruttle, David L. ... Joliet, IL
Ruttle, J. Michael ... Newtown, PA
Ruttle, Timothy M. ... Cincinnati, OH
Ruttman, Danielle D. ... Brooklyn, NY
Ruttman, David C. ... Tulsa, OK
Ruttman, Lawrence A. ... Brookline, MA
Ruttum, Paul T. ... Denver, CO
Rutty-Bowen, Diron E. ... Bronx, NY
Rutyna, Edward J. ... Fountain Valley, CA
Rutz, Allen L. ... Columbus, OH
Rutz, David M. ... Sacramento, CA
Rutz, J. Nicole ... Springfield, IL
Rutz, John R. ... Port Angeles, WA
Rutz, Suzan L. ... Fort Wayne, IN
Rutzen, Douglas B. ... Washington, DC
Rutzen, Gregory J. ... Milwaukee, WI
Rutzick, Adam Paul ... St. Paul, MN
Rutzick, Mark C. ... Portland, OR
Rutzick, Steven R. ... St. Paul, MN
Rutzick, William ... Seattle, WA
Rutzky, Sally ... Ann Arbor, MI
Ruud, Brenda Temke ... Bloomington, IL
Ruud, Eric T. ... Bloomington, IL
Ruud, F. Douglas ... Seattle, WA
Ruud, Glenn F. ... Rock Island, IL
Ruud, Judith Kish ... Boise, ID
Ruud, Peter J. ... Milwaukee, WI
Ruud, Robert R. ... Moline, IL
Ruud, Ronald C. ... Riverside, CA
Ruud, Russell W. ... Albuquerque, NM
Ruud, Scovil & Marsh ... Rock Island, IL
Ruud, Thomas G. ... Rockford, IL
Ruuska, Paul Jon ... Seattle, WA
Ruvalcaba, Ralaina J. ... Tacoma, WA
Ruvell, Nathaniel S. ... New York, NY
Ruvelson, Alan K., Jr. ... St. Paul, MN
Ruvelson & Kautzer, Chartered
St. Paul, MN
Ruvin, Harvey, (P.A.) ... Miami Beach, FL
Ruvinsky, Philip H. ... Washington, DC
Ruvoldt, Harold J., Jr. ... New York, NY
Ruvolo, Anthony D. ... Washington, DC
Ruvolo, Peter H., III ... Danbury, CT
Ruwe, Bradley N. ... Cincinnati, OH
Ruwe, Joseph ... Cincinnati, OH
Ruwe, Robert P. ...
United States Tax Court, GV
Ruwe, Thomas J. ... Cincinnati, OH
Ruxin, Paul T. ... Chicago, IL
Ruxin, Robert H. ... Concord, MA
Ruyak, Edw. G. ... Bethlehem, PA
Ruyak, Matthew D. ... Sacramento, CA
Ruyak, Robert F. ... Washington, DC
Ruybalid, Francisco E., IV ... Trinidad, CO
Ruybalid, Victor R. ... Santa Fe, NM
Ruygrok, Ellynn ... La Crescenta, CA
Ruyle, C. E. ... Neosho, MO
Ruyle, David C. ... Santa Fe, NM
Ruyle, David J. ... San Diego, CA
Ruyle, J. Philip ... Toledo, OH
Ruyle, James B. ... Portland, OR
Ruyle, Jennifer L. ... St. Louis, MO
Ruyle, Nancy L. ... Carlinville, IL
Ruyle, Stephen W. ... Defiance, OH
Ruys de Perez, Charles A. ... Boston, MA
Ruysser, Bernard J. ... Kansas City, KS
Ruzek, Peter R. ... Hartford, CT
Ruzi, Seth H. ... Wayne, NJ
Ruzic, Karen A. ... Chicago, IL
Ruzich, Nancy M. ... New York, NY
Ruzich, Richard T. ... Department of Justice,
Civil Division, GV
Ruzicho, Andrew J. ... Columbus, OH
Ruzicho, Andrew J. ... Dallas, TX
Ruzicka, Edward ... Lenexa, KS
Ruzicka, Gregory V. ... Newport Beach, CA
Ruzicka, Irvin L. ... St. Louis, MO
Ruzicka, Jeffrey A. ... San Diego, CA
Ruzicka, Jill ... St. Paul, MN
Ruzicka, Snyder & Wallace
Newport Beach, CA
Ruzicka, Thomas E. ... Olathe, KS
Ruzics, Ivan Z. ... Burbank, CA
Ruzin, Irene ... Van Nuys, CA
Ruzinsky, Bruce J. ... Houston, TX
Ruzow, Daniel A. ... Albany, NY
Ruzow, Lawrence A. ... Window Rock, AZ
Ruzow, Theodore M. ... Willsboro, NY
Ruzumna, Daniel S. ... Washington, DC
Ruzumna, David ... Seattle, WA
Ruzzier, Antoinette Leone ... Hartford, CT
Ruzzo, Edward J. ... Marion, OH
Ruzzo, Loreto J. ... New York, NY
Nashville, TN
Ruzzo, Patrick J. ... Houston, TX
Ruzzo, William ... Kingston, PA
Ryal, James T., Jr. ... Humboldt, TN
Ryall, Jacqueline Bley ... Beaumont, TX
Ryall, Judy ... Beaumont, TX
Ryals, Davyne Anita ... Colorado Springs, CO
Ryals, J. Lenn ... Montgomery, AL
Ryals, James W. ... Hollywood, CA
Ryals, Kent ... Vinita, OK
Ryals, Marshall J. ... Metairie, LA
Ryals, Robert E. ... Colorado Springs, CO
Ryals, Robinson & Saffo, P.C.
Wilmington, NC
Ryals, Sara O'Shields ... Bakersfield, CA
Ryals, Scott G. ... Fort Pierce, FL
Ryals & Soffer, P.C. ... St. Louis, MO
Ryals, Stephen M. ... St. Louis, MO
Ryals, William D. ... Roswell, GA

Ryan, Adam B. ... Redding, CA
Ryan, Agnes C. ... Chicago, IL
Ryan, Aline C. ... Crofton, MD
Ryan, Allan A., Jr. ... Cambridge, MA
Ryan, Allen L. ... Warren, OH
Ryan, Allison Ansell ... Ocean Township, NJ
Ryan, Allison M. ... Atlanta, GA
Ryan, Andrada & Lifter, A Professional Corporation ... Oakland, CA
Ryan, Andrew C. ... Windsor, CT
Ryan, Andrew D. ... Minneapolis, MN
Ryan, Andrew D. ... St. Louis, MO
Ryan, Andrew J. ... New York, NY
Ryan, Andrew J. ... Sodus, NY
Ryan, Andria Lure ... Atlanta, GA
Ryan, Ann ... New Brunswick, NJ
New York, NY
Ryan, Ann Powell ... Leawood, KS
Ryan, Anne G. ... Rochester, NY
Ryan, Anne M. ... Cleveland, OH
Ryan, Anne M. Kenney ... Media, PA
Ryan, Anne S. ... Department of Justice,
Environment and Natural Resources
Division, GV
Ryan, Anthony G. ... Islamorada, FL
Ryan, Anthony J. ... Philadelphia, PA
Ryan, Anthony W. ... Baltimore, MD
Ryan, Archie J. ... Dania, FL
Ryan, Arnold Jerome, Jr. ... Williamson, WV
Ryan, Atherton B. ... Vernon, CT
Ryan, Barbara ... Phoenix, AZ
Ryan, Barbara A. ... Jersey City, NJ
New York, NY
Ryan, Barry E., (P.S.) ... Spokane, WA
Ryan, Barry M. ... Springfield, MA
Ryan, Barry T. ... San Diego, CA
Ryan, Bennett, Radloff, Koester & O'Brien
Charleston, IL
Effingham, IL
Marshall, IL
Mattoon, IL
Paris, IL
Shelbyville, IL
Ryan, Bernard ... Olympia, WA
Ryan, Bernard A., Jr. ... Harrisburg, PA
Ryan & Bijak ... Oak Forest, IL
Ryan, Boudreau & Kirkpatrick
South Hadley, MA
Ryan, Brenda R. ... Denver, CO
Ryan, Brendan ... St. Louis, MO
Ryan, Brendan P. ... New York, NY
Ryan, Brent W. ... Austin, TX
Ryan, Brown, McDonnell, Berger Gibbons & LaRocca, LLP ... Cherry Hill, NJ
Philadelphia, PA
Ryan, Brown & Ryan ... Latham, NY
Mechanicville, NY
Ryan, Bruce D. ... Washington, DC
Ryan, Burton T. ... Hempstead, NY
Ryan, Burton T., Jr. ... Garden City, NY
Ryan, C. Jean ... San Francisco, CA
Ryan, Carl E. ... El Paso, TX
Ryan, Carla G. ... Tucson, AZ
Ryan, Carolyn M. ... Boston, MA
Ryan, Catherine S. ... Pittsburgh, PA
Ryan, Catherine Verdery ... Augusta, GA
Ryan, Cathy Kaman ... Rochester, NY
Ryan, C. E. ... Galion, OH
Ryan, Charles A. ... Gardena, CA
Ryan, Charles C. ... Anaheim, CA
Ryan, Charles D., Jr. ... Springfield, MA
Ryan, Charles E. ... New York, NY
Ryan, Charles F. ... Midland Park, NJ
Ryan, Charles H. ... Monroe, LA
Ryan, Charles J., Jr. ... Chicago, IL
Ryan, Charles P. ... Alexandria, VA
Ryan, Charles R. ... Houma, LA
Ryan, Charles S. ... Stony Brook, NY
Ryan, Charles T. ... Homewood, IL
Ryan, Charles V. ... Springfield, MA
Ryan, Charles W., III ... Washington, DC
Ryan, Cheryl Feik ... Washington, DC
Ryan, Christine C. ... Washington, DC
Ryan, Christopher J. ... Dania, FL
Ryan, Christopher P. ... Peoria, IL
Ryan, Christopher P. ... Quincy, MA
Ryan, Christopher R.
Securities and Exchange Commission,
Office of Compliance Inspections and
Examinations, GV
Ryan, Claudia A. ... Albany, NY
Ryan, Clifford C. ... New York, NY
Ryan, Conway T. ... Chandler, AZ
Ryan, Corinne W. ... Columbus, OH
Ryan, Cornelius O'Brien ... Houston, TX
Ryan & Coté ... Midland Park, NJ
Ryan, Coughlin & Betke, L.L.P.
Boston, MA
Ryan, Craig A. ... Lafayette, LA
Ryan, Cynthia D. ... New York, NY
Ryan, Cynthia R. ... Department of Justice,
Drug Enforcement Administration, GV
Ryan, D. Jay ... Phoenix, AZ
Ryan, D. Jean ... Miami, FL
Ryan, D. Kevin ... Louisville, KY
Ryan, Dan ... Houston, TX
Ryan, Dan G. ... Benicia, CA
Ryan, Dan G. ... Concord, CA
Ryan, Dan G. ... Fairfield, CA
Martinez, CA
Walnut Creek, CA
Ryan, Dana L. ... Dallas, TX
Ryan, Dana Michael ... Milton, WA
Ryan, Daniel A. ... Milwaukee, WI
Ryan, Daniel B. ... Middletown, CT
Ryan, Daniel D. ... Brookfield, WI
Ryan, Daniel E., III ... Stamford, CT
Ryan, Daniel E., Jr. ... Stamford, CT

Ryan, Daniel F. ... Columbus, OH
Ryan, Daniel F., III
Plymouth Meeting, PA
Ryan, Daniel H. ... Glens Falls, NY
Ryan, Daniel J. ... Annapolis, MD
Ryan, Daniel J. ... St. Paul, MN
Ryan, Daniel J. ... Kansas City, MO
Ryan, Daniel J. ... Philadelphia, PA
Ryan, Daniel J., Jr. ... Philadelphia, PA
Ryan, Daniel K. ... Chicago, IL
Ryan, Daniel P. ... Redford, MI
Ryan, Daniel P. ... La Crosse, WI
Ryan, Daniel T. ... St. Louis, MO
Ryan, David A. ... Foley, AL
Ryan, David A., Jr. ... Waterbury, CT
Ryan, David B. ... Milwaukee, WI
Ryan, David C. ... Department of Justice,
Office of Intelligence Policy and Review,
GV
Ryan, David E. ... Kalamazoo, MI
Ryan, David F. ... Chicago, IL
Ryan, David F. ... New York, NY
Ryan, David F. ... Pittsburgh, PA
Ryan, David H. ... Pasadena, CA
Ryan, David J. ... Chicago, IL
Ryan, David J. ... Danville, IL
Ryan, David J. ... Indianapolis, IN
Ryan, David J. ... Portland, OR
Ryan, David K. ... Battle Creek, MI
Ryan, David L. ... Topeka, KS
Ryan, David M. ... Garden City, NY
Ryan, David Thomas ... Hartford, CT
Ryan, David W. ... Vista, CA
Ryan, Dawn C. ... Brooklyn, NY
Ryan, Deborah Cappozzo ... Dallas, TX
Ryan, Deborah L. ... Dallas, TX
Ryan, Denise ... Charlottesville, VA
Ryan, Denise G. ... Bethlehem, PA
Ryan, Dennis J. ... Bartlesville, OK
Ryan, Dennis M. ... Framingham, MA
Ryan, Dennis M. ... Minneapolis, MN
Ryan, Dennis M. ... Richmond, VA
Ryan, Dennis Neil ... Dallas, TX
Ryan, Dennis P., Jr. ... Libertyville, IL
Ryan, Dennis P., Sr. ... Libertyville, IL
Ryan, Dennis W. ... Woodland Hills, CA
Ryan, Diana Deyo ... Rochester, NY
Ryan, Diana J. ... Rapid City, SD
Ryan, Diane ... Westwood, MA
Ryan, Donald F. ... Brainerd, MN
Ryan, Donald I. ... Brainerd, MN
Ryan, Donald J. ... West Chicago, IL
Ryan, Donald P. ... San Francisco, CA
Ryan, Donald P. ... New York, NY
Ryan, Donald P. ... Cranston, RI
Ryan, Donald S. ... Little Rock, AR
Ryan, Donald S. ... Cherry Hill, NJ
Ryan, Donna H. ... Boston, MA
Ryan, Donna L. ... Santa Rosa, CA
Ryan, Dorsey ... Fort Smith, AR
Ryan, Douglas N. ... Indianapolis, IN
Ryan & Drewniak, P.A. ... Annapolis, MD
Ryan, Dudley ... St. Paul, MN
Ryan, E. Christopher ... Los Angeles, CA
Ryan, E. Joseph, Jr. ... Miami, FL
Ryan, Earle V. ... Toluca, IL
Ryan, Edw. L., Jr. ... Norfolk, VA
Ryan, Edward A. ... Sacramento, CA
Ryan, Edward A. ... Washington, DC
Ryan, Edward A. ... Basking Ridge, NJ
Ryan, Edward A., Jr. ... Boston, MA
Ryan, Edward F. ... Boca Raton, FL
Chicago, IL
Ryan, Edward F. ... Newark, NJ
Ryan, Edward F. X., Jr. ... Larchmont, NY
Ryan, Edward J. ... North Brunswick, NJ
Ryan, Edward J., Jr. ... South Hadley, MA
Ryan, Edward P. ... Albany, NY
Ryan, Edward P., Jr. ... Fitchburg, MA
Ryan, Edward V. ... Florham Park, NJ
Ryan, Edwin L., Jr. ... Dayton, OH
Ryan, Eileen ... New York, NY
Ryan, Eileen Mary ... Syracuse, NY
Ryan, Elaine A. ... Phoenix, AZ
Ryan, Elissa M. ... Portland, OR
Ryan, Elizabeth ... Oakland, CA
Ryan, Elizabeth ... Washington, DC
Ryan, Elizabeth ... Boston, MA
Ryan, Elizabeth A. ... Trenton, NJ
Ryan, Elizabeth B. ... Berkeley, CA
Ryan, Elizabeth E. ... Duncan, OK
Ryan, Elizabeth Haecker
New Orleans, LA
Ryan, Elizabeth K. ... Longmont, CO
Ryan, Elizabeth Turney ... Nashville, TN
Ryan, Ellen M. ... Seattle, WA
Ryan, Ellen Seery ... Rockville, MD
Ryan, Emily M. ... Media, PA
Ryan, Emmett W. ... Towson, MD
Ryan, Emmie Mary Glynn ... Brooklyn, NY
Ryan, Emory & Ryan, LLP ... Paoli, PA
Ryan, Eric D. ... San Francisco, CA
Ryan, Eric D. ... Dallas, TX
Ryan, Eric D., P.C., Law Offices of
Dallas, TX
Ryan, Erin E. ... Chicago, IL
Ryan, Fay E. ... West Palm Beach, FL
Ryan, Frances E. ... Philadelphia, PA
Ryan, Frances V. ... Philadelphia, PA
Ryan, Francis J. ... East Moline, IL
Ryan, Francis J., Jr.
Westhampton Beach, NY
Ryan, Francis M. ... Onida, SD
Ryan, Francis W., IV ... New York, NY
Ryan, Francis X. ... Cherry Hill, NJ
Ryan, Frank E. ... Greenbelt, MD
Ryan, Frank J. ... Oak Forest, IL
Ryan, Frederick J., Jr. ... Washington, DC

Ryan, G. Thomas ... Tacoma, WA
Ryan and Gannon ... Florham Park, NJ
Morristown, NJ
Newark, NJ
Ryan, Gary L. ... New Orleans, LA
Ryan, Gary P. ... Santa Ana, CA
Ryan, Geo. B. ... Louisville, KY
Ryan, Geoffrey W. ... Washington, DC
Ryan, George L. ... New York, NY
White Plains, NY
Ryan, Gerald B. ... Huntington, NY
Mineola, NY
New York, NY
Smithtown, NY
Ryan, Gerald F. ... Houston, TX
Ryan, Gerald P. ... Branford, CT
Ryan, Gerald R. ... Brookeville, MD
Ryan, Gerard J. ... Millis, MA
Ryan, Gerard K., Jr. ... Mineola, NY
Ryan, Gordon D. ... Oklahoma City, OK
Ryan, Gordon G. ... Montauk, NY
Ryan, Greg J. ... San Diego, CA
Ryan & Gregory ... Louisville, KY
Ryan, Gregory J. ... New York, NY
Ryan, Gregory J. ... Edmond, OK
Ryan, Gregory L. ... Grand Junction, CO
Ryan, Gregory L. ... Urbana, IL
Ryan, Gregory R. ... Los Angeles, CA
Ryan & Grinde, Ltd. ... Rochester, MN
St. Charles, MN
Ryan, Guy P. ... Toms River, NJ
Ryan, H. Alfred ... Philadelphia, PA
Ryan, H. Eugene ... Mansfield, OH
Ryan, Harold M. ... St. Clair Shores, MI
Ryan, Harry R., III ... Rutland, VT
Ryan, Heather ... Boulder, CO
Ryan, Heather M. ... New York, NY
Ryan, Helen B. ... Honolulu, HI
Ryan, Helen F. ... Middletown, CT
Ryan & Henderson, P.C. ... Carle Place, NY
Ryan, Henry G., III ... Oklahoma City, OK
Ryan, Howard C. ... Chicago, IL
Ryan, Howard C., Jr. ... Ottawa, IL
Ryan, Hugh H. ... Lee's Summit, MO
Ryan, Irving A. ... Berea, OH
Ryan, Isaac H. ... New Orleans, LA
Ryan, J. Brennan ... Atlanta, GA
Ryan, J. Colleen Ward ... Bakersfield, CA
Ryan, J. Dennis ... Edmond, OK
Ryan, J. Kelly ... Department of Justice,
Immigration and Naturalization Service, GV
Ryan, J. Kelly ... Fort Worth, TX
Ryan, J. Michael ... Exton, PA
Ryan, J. Patrick, (P.C.) ... San Antonio, TX
Ryan, J. Richard ... New York, NY
Ryan, J. Rodney, Jr. ... Baton Rouge, LA
Ryan, James A. ... Phoenix, AZ
Ryan, James B. ... San Diego, CA
Ryan, James D. ... North Palm Beach, FL
Ryan, James D. ... Kalamazoo, MI
Ryan, James David, Jr. ... St. Louis, MO
Ryan, James E. ... New York, NY
Ryan, James E. ... Silverdale, WA
Ryan, James E., Jr. ... Richmond, VA
Ryan, James F. ... Metairie, LA
Ryan, James F. ... Boston, MA
Ryan, James F. ... Jersey City, NJ
Ryan, James F. ... Rochester, NY
Ryan, James F. ... Philadelphia, PA
Wayne, PA
Ryan, James F., Jr. ... Jersey City, NJ
Ryan, James G. ... Minneapolis, MN
Ryan, James G. ... Garden City, NY
Ryan, James Gregory ... Columbus, OH
Ryan, James H. ... North Palm Beach, FL
Ryan, James H. ... Chicago, IL
Ryan, James, III ... New Orleans, LA
Ryan, James J. ... Pasadena, CA
Ryan, James J. ... Minneapolis, MN
Ryan, James J. ... Ossining, NY
Ryan, James J. ... Voorheesville, NY
Ryan, James J. ... Cincinnati, OH
Ryan, James J. ... Cincinnati, OH
Ryan, James L. ... Rockville, MD
Ryan, James L. ... Detroit, MI
Ryan, James L. ... Derry, NH
Ryan, James M. ... Milwaukee, WI
Ryan, James M. Scott ... Tulsa, OK
Ryan, James P. ... Los Angeles, CA
Ryan, James P. ... Opelousas, LA
Ryan, James P. ... Plymouth, MI
Ryan, James P., Jr. ... Rochester, MN
St. Charles, MN
Ryan, James P. A. ... Washington, DC
Ryan, James R. ... Tulsa, OK
Ryan, James Richard ... Fairfax, VA
Ryan, James S., III ... Dallas, TX
Ryan, James T. ... Woodbury, CT
Ryan, James T. ... Rolling Meadows, IL
Ryan, James T., Jr. ... Parsippany, NJ
Ryan, James V. ... Boston, MA
Ryan, James V. ... New York, NY
Ryan, James W. ... Hillside, IL
Ryan, James W. ... Providence, RI
Ryan, James W. ... Houston, TX
Ryan, James W., III ... Albany, NY
Ryan, James W., (P.C.) ... Phoenix, AZ
Ryan, Jamie M. ... San Diego, CA
Ryan, Jamieson, Morris & Ryan
Kalamazoo, MI
Ryan, Jane Craddock ... Elgin, IL
Ryan, Jane I. ... Washington, DC
Ryan, Jay T. ... Washington, DC
Ryan, Jaye ... Los Angeles, CA
Ryan, Jean A. ... Bonita Springs, FL
Naples, FL
Ryan, Jeanne Ward ... Narberth, PA
Ryan, Jeffrey F. ... San Jose, CA

Ryan, Jeffrey Michael ....Redwood City, CA
Ryan, Jeffrey S. ....Breckenridge, CO
Ryan, Jeffrey W. ....Dallas, TX
Ryan, Jennifer M. ....Towson, MD
Ryan, Jeremy William ....Philadelphia, PA
Ryan, Jerri A. ....Pittsburgh, PA
Ryan, Jerry ....Mena, AR
Ryan, Jerry W. ....Washington, DC
Ryan, Jessica A. ....Atlanta, GA
Ryan, Jessica A. ....Seattle, WA
Ryan, Jill W. ....Boston, MA
Ryan, Joan Rosenberg ....Norwell, MA
Ryan, Joanne M. ....Cheshire, CT
Ryan, John A. ....Watertown, MA
Ryan, John A. ....Philadelphia, PA
Ryan, John C. ....Carbondale, IL
Ryan, John C. ....Frankfort, KY
Ryan, John C. ....New York, NY
Ryan, John C. ....Philadelphia, PA
Ryan, John Clemens ....Chicago, IL
Ryan, John D. ....Chicago, IL
Ryan, John D. ....Somers, NY
Ryan, John D. ....Cleveland, OH
Ryan, John D. ....Portland, OR
Ryan, John D. ....Dulles, VA
Ryan, John D., P.C. ....Portland, OR
Ryan, John E. ....Sacramento, CA
Ryan, John E. ....Santa Ana, CA
Ryan, John E. ....Naples, FL
Ryan, John E. ....Lexington, MA
Ryan, John E. ....Floral Park, NY
Ryan, John E. ....Philadelphia, PA
Ryan, John E. ....Fairfax, VA
Ryan, John F. ....Brooklyn, NY
Ryan, John F. ....New York, NY
Ryan, John F. ....White Plains, NY
Ryan, John F. ....Houston, TX
Ryan, John F. ....Springfield, VA
Ryan, John G. ....Phoenix, AZ
Ryan, John G. ....Palo Alto, CA
Ryan, John G. ....Boston, MA
Ryan, John G. ....Houston, TX
Ryan, John H. ....New Orleans, LA
Ryan, John J. ....Santa Ana, CA
Ryan, John J. ....Annapolis, MD
Ryan, John J. ....Hampton, NH
Ryan, John J. ....Red Bank, NJ
Ryan, John J. ....Albertson, NY
Ryan, John J. ....Brooklyn, NY
Ryan, John J., Jr. ....Boston, MA
Ryan, John J., Jr. ....West Orange, NJ
Ryan, John J., Jr. ....Elmira, NY
Ryan, John J., Jr. ....Memphis, TN
Ryan, John J., Law Offices of
Norwalk, CT
Ryan, John J., Law Offices of
Stamford, CT
Ryan, John Joseph ....Kent, WA
Ryan, John L. ....Los Angeles, CA
Ryan, John L. ....Mineola, NY
Ryan, John M. ....Washington, DC
Ryan, John M. ....Lincolnshire, IL
Ryan, John M. ....Omaha, NE
Ryan, John M. ....Kew Gardens, NY
Ryan, John M. ....New York, NY
Ryan, John M. ....Norfolk, VA
Ryan, John P. ....Indianapolis, IN
Ryan, John P. ....Indianapolis, IN
Ryan, John P. ....Boston, MA
Ryan, John P. ....Lansing, MI
Ryan, John P. ....Middleburg, VA
Ryan, John P., Jr. ....Grandview, MO
Ryan, John Phillip ....Milwaukee, WI
Ryan, John R. ....Punta Gorda, FL
Ryan, John R. ....Wayne, MI
Ryan, John R. ....Clearfield, PA
Ryan, John T. ....Phoenix, AZ
Ryan, John T. ....Tucson, AZ
San Mateo, CA
Ryan, John T. ....East Rockaway, NY
Ryan, John T., Jr. ....Homer, NY
Ryan, John T., Jr. ....New York, NY
Ryan, John V. ....Pittsburgh, PA
Ryan, John W. ....Washington, DC
Ryan, Jos. E. ....Columbus, OH
Ryan, Joseph ....Washington, DC
Atlanta, GA
Ryan, Joseph A. ....Honolulu, HI
Ryan, Joseph A. ....Paoli, PA
Ryan, Joseph B. ....Locust Valley, NY
Ryan, Joseph D. ....Chicago, IL
Ryan, Joseph D. ....Eagan, MN
Ryan, Joseph D., Jr. ....Oakland, CA
Ryan, Joseph E., Jr. ....Columbus, OH
Ryan, Joseph F. ....Boston, MA
Ryan, Joseph F. ....Boston, MA
Ryan, Joseph F. ....Salem, MA
Ryan, Joseph J., Sr. ....Chateaugay, NY
Ryan, Joseph M. ....New York, NY
Ryan, Joseph M. F., Jr. ....Bethesda, MD
Ryan, Joseph P. ....Larkspur, CA
Ryan, Joseph P. ....Paoli, PA
Ryan, Joseph T. ....Jersey City, NJ
Ryan, Joseph T. ....Vermilion, OH
Ryan, Joseph W. ....Aitkin, MN
Ryan, Joseph W. ....Houston, TX
Ryan, Joseph W., Jr. ....Uniondale, NY
Ryan, Joseph W., Jr. ....Columbus, OH
Ryan, Joseph W., Jr., P.C. ....Uniondale, NY
Ryan, Joy ....Department of Justice,
Environment and Natural Resources
Division, GV
Ryan, Joy-Elan M. ....Washington, DC
Ryan, Juan J. ....New Providence, NJ
Ryan, Julia Court ....Washington, DC
Ryan, Julianna ....New York, NY
Ryan, Karel Brown ....Clintwood, VA
Ryan, Karen P. ....New York, NY
Ryan, Kari J. ....Orlando, FL
Ryan, Karin M. ....Washington, DC
Fairfax, VA
Ryan, Karl T. ....Indianapolis, IN
Ryan, Kate Moriarty ....Los Angeles, CA
Ryan, Katharine M. ....Philadelphia, PA
Ryan, Kathleen ....San Francisco, CA
Ryan, Kathleen ....Waukegan, IL
Ryan, Kathleen A. ....Providence, RI
Ryan, Kathleen Anne ....Raleigh, NC
Ryan, Kathleen C. ....Department of Justice,
Civil Rights Division, GV
Ryan, Kathleen C.
Board of Governors Of The Federal Reserve
System,
Division of Consumer and Community
Affairs, GV
Ryan, Kathleen K. ....Harrisburg, PA
Ryan, Kathleen M. ....Washington, DC
Ryan, Kathleen M. ....Peoria, IL
Ryan, Kathleen M. ....Troy, NY
Ryan, Keith P. ....McKinney, TX
Ryan, Kelly A. ....West Sacramento, CA
Ryan, Kelly A. ....Roseland, NJ
Ryan, Kelly G. ....Kansas City, MO
Ryan, Kelly J. ....Salt Lake City, UT
Ryan, Kelly Thomas ....Winter Park, FL
Ryan, Kenneth E. ....Washington, DC
Ryan, Kenneth E. ....Passaic, NJ
Ryan, Kenneth J., Jr. ....New York, NY
Ryan, Kent B. ....New Orleans, LA
Ryan, Kerry T. ....Boston, MA
Ryan, Kevin A. ....Omaha, NE
Ryan, Kevin D. ....Washington, DC
Ryan, Kevin G. ....Roswell, GA
Ryan, Kevin G. ....White Plains, NY
Ryan, Kevin J. ....Chicago, IL
Ryan, Kevin J. ....New York, NY
Ryan, Kevin J. ....Cincinnati, OH
Ryan, Kevin J. ....West Chester, PA
Ryan, Kevin K. ....Plattsburgh, NY
Ryan, Kevin M. ....Chicago, IL
Ryan, Kevin M. ....New York, NY
Ryan, Kevin M. ....New York, NY
Ryan, Kevin Michael ....New York, NY
Ryan, Kevin P. ....Reno, NV
Ryan, Kevin P., (A P.C.) ....Santa Rosa, CA
Ryan, Kevin W. ....Charlottesville, VA
Richmond, VA
Ryan, Kim E. ....Huntington, NY
Ryan, Kimberlie K. ....Denver, CO
Ryan, Kimberly K. ....Wellesley, MA
Ryan, Kristine V. ....Newark, NJ
Ryan Kromholz & Manion, S.C.
Brookfield, WI
Milwaukee, WI
Ryan, L. Peter ....San Francisco, CA
Ryan, L. Thomas, Jr. ....Huntsville, AL
Ryan, Laura A. ....Cincinnati, OH
Ryan, Laura D. ....Chicago, IL
Ryan, Laura G. ....San Francisco, CA
Ryan, Laurence K. ....Columbus, OH
Ryan Law Firm ....New Orleans, LA
Ryan Law Firm, The, L.L.C. ....Denver, CO
Ryan, Lehan J. ....St. Paul, MN
Ryan, Leigh P. ....New York, NY
Ryan, Leo, Jr. ....Towson, MD
Ryan, Linda A. ....Santa Rosa, CA
Ryan, Linda Cowell ....Somerville, NJ
Ryan, Linda M. ....New York, NY
Ryan, Lisa F. ....Washington, DC
Ryan, Lisa M. ....New York, NY
Ryan, Lois B. ....Libertyville, IL
Ryan, Lois B., Ltd., Law Office of
Libertyville, IL
Ryan, Louis Farthing ....Norfolk, VA
Ryan, Luke P. ....San Diego, CA
Ryan, Lynn M. ....New York, NY
Ryan, M. Andrea ....Morris Plains, NJ
Ryan, M. Frances ....Philadelphia, PA
Ryan, M. Kevin ....Richfield, OH
Ryan, Margaret E. ....Grand Rapids, MI
Ryan, Margaret (Peggy) J. ....Springfield, IL
Ryan, Margaret W. ....Woodland Hills, CA
Ryan, Marguerite L.
Department Of Health And Human Services,
Social Security Administration, GV
Ryan, Marian T. ....Cambridge, MA
Ryan, Marianne E. ....New York, NY
Ryan, Marie G. ....Bronx, NY
Ryan, Marilee A. ....Portland, ME
Ryan, Mark ....Norristown, PA
Ryan, Mark D. ....Bay Minette, AL
Ryan, Mark F. ....Palo Alto, CA
Ryan, Mark R. ....Dallas, TX
Ryan, Mark W. ....Washington, DC
Ryan, Mark X. ....Hartford, CT
Ryan and Marks ....Jacksonville, FL
Ryan Marks Johnson Todd & Broder
Las Vegas, NV
Ryan, Marsha G. ....Carbondale, IL
Ryan, Martin F. ....Tucson, AZ
Ryan, Martin H. ....Jackson, CA
Ryan, Martin L. ....Pittsburgh, PA
Ryan, Martin P. ....Chicago, IL
Ryan, Mary Ann ....Laurel, MD
Ryan, Mary B. ....Plantsville, CT
Ryan, Mary Beth
Federal Labor Relations Authority,
Authority Member Staff, GV
Ryan, Mary D. ....Rockville, MD
Ryan, Mary E. ....New York, NY
Ryan, Mary E., Law Offices of
Baltimore, MD
Ryan, Mary Grace ....Treasury Department,
Bureau of Alcohol, Tobacco and Firearms,
GV
Ryan, Mary Jane ....Waterbury, CT
Ryan, Mary Jaques ....Loris, SC
Ryan, Mary Judge ....Tucson, AZ
Ryan, Mary K. ....Boston, MA
Ryan, Mary Katharine ....River Forest, IL
Ryan, Mary Lee ....Beverly Hills, CA
Ryan, Mary Margaret ....Emeryville, CA
San Francisco, CA
Ryan, Maryanne ....Boston, MA
Ryan & Mason, L.L.P. ....Fairfield, CT
Locust Valley, NY
Ryan, Matthew C. ....Dallas, TX
Ryan, Matthew J. ....Media, PA
Ryan, Matthew J., Jr. ....Springfield, MA
Ryan, Matthew K. ....New York, NY
Ryan, Matthew Owen ....Portland, OR
Ryan, Matthew P. ....Marion, IN
Ryan, Matthew T. ....Binghamton, NY
Ryan, Matthew W. ....Albany, NY
Ryan, Maureen ....New York, NY
Ryan, Maureen E. ....Seattle, WA
Ryan, Maurice J. ....Kansas City, KS
Ryan, Maurice W. ....Staten Island, NY
Ryan, Maury A. ....Providence, RI
Ryan, Maxine S. ....Fort Lauderdale, FL
Ryan, Melissa M. ....Portland, OR
Ryan, Melissa McKenney
United States Court Of Appeals District Of
Columbia Circuit, GV
Ryan, Melvyn M. ....Bellevue, WA
Ryan, Michael A. ....Orlando, FL
Ryan, Michael B. ....Harrington Park, NJ
Ryan, Michael C. ....Hartford, CT
Ryan, Michael C. ....New York, NY
Ryan, Michael D. ....Los Angeles, CA
Ryan, Michael D. ....Stamford, CT
Ryan, Michael D. ....Mattoon, IL
Ryan, Michael E. ....New York, NY
Ryan, Michael F. ....Aitkin, MN
Ryan, Michael F. ....Albany, NY
Ryan, Michael F. ....Columbus, OH
Ryan, Michael G. ....Chicago, IL
Ryan, Michael H. ....Dallas, TX
Ryan, Michael J. ....Phoenix, AZ
Ryan, Michael J. ....Los Angeles, CA
Ryan, Michael J. ....Fort Lauderdale, FL
Ryan, Michael J. ....Juno Beach, FL
Ryan, Michael J. ....Troy, MI
Ryan, Michael J. ....Las Vegas, NV
Ryan, Michael J. ....Goffstown, NH
Ryan, Michael J. ....Buffalo, NY
Ryan, Michael J. ....New York, NY
Ryan, Michael J. ....Milwaukee, WI
Ryan, Michael J., Jr. ....Washington, DC
Ryan, Michael J., Jr. ....New Brunswick, NJ
Ryan, Michael James ....Concord, CA
Ryan, Michael L. ....New York, NY
Ryan, Michael P. ....Springfield, MA
Ryan, Michael P. ....Suffern, NY
Ryan, Michael P. ....Portland, OR
Ryan, Michael S. ....St. Paul, MN
Ryan, Michael S. ....Oklahoma City, OK
Ryan, Michael T. ....Stamford, CT
Ryan, Michael T. ....North Andover, MA
Ryan, Michael T. ....St. Clair Shores, MI
Ryan, Michael T. ....Buffalo, NY
Ryan, Michael W. ....Clay Center, KS
Ryan, Michael W., Jr. ....Bowie, MD
Ryan, Michaela ....Chicago, IL
Ryan, Michelle A. ....Portland, OR
Ryan, Michelle (Micky) ....Portland, OR
Ryan, Miles F., III
Department of Commerce,
Office of the General Counsel, GV
Ryan, Miles F., Jr. ....Lakewood, OH
Ryan, Molly Anne ....St. Louis, MO
Ryan, Moore, Cook & Hunter
Frankfort, IN
Ryan, Nancie ....Oakland, CA
Ryan, Nancy ....New York, NY
Ryan, Nancy C. ....Philadelphia, PA
Ryan, Nancy J. ....Honolulu, HI
Ryan, Nancy O. ....Philadelphia, PA
Ryan, Nancy R. ....Shawnee, KS
Ryan, Nicholas J. ....West Palm Beach, FL
Ryan, Nicola J. ....New York, NY
Ryan, Nicole M. ....San Francisco, CA
Ryan, Norman A. ....San Diego, CA
Las Vegas, NV
Ryan, Orlando & Smallacombe, LLP
Albany, NY
Ryan, Oscar J. ....Blackstone, MA
Ryan, Paige C. ....St. Louis, MO
Ryan, Pamela L. ....Rochester, NY
Ryan, Patricia A. ....Chicago, IL
Ryan, Patricia A ....Omaha, NE
Ryan, Patricia B. ....Elmsford, NY
Ryan, Patricia D. ....Arlington, VA
Ryan, Patricia G. ....Riverside, CA
San Diego, CA
Ryan, Patrick C. ....Oklahoma City, OK
Ryan, Patrick D. ....Mount Clemens, MI
Ryan, Patrick E. ....House of Representatives,
Committee on Veterans Affairs, GV
Ryan, Patrick J. ....Chicago, IL
Ryan, Patrick J. ....New York, NY
Ryan, Patrick John ....Camden, NJ
Ryan, Patrick Louis ....Trenton, NJ
Ryan, Patrick M. ....Fullerton, CA
Ryan, Patrick M. ....Englewood, CO
Ryan, Patrick M. ....St. Paul, MN
Ryan, Patrick M. ....Oklahoma City, OK
Ryan, Patrick M. ....Fort Worth, TX
Ryan, Patrick M. ....Milwaukee, WI
Ryan, Patrick N. ....Marion, IN
Ryan, Patrick T. ....Mentor, OH
Ryan, Patrick T. ....Philadelphia, PA
Ryan, Patrick W. ....Keene, NH
Ryan, Patrick W. ....Seattle, WA
Ryan, Paul E. ....Taunton, MA
Ryan, Paul F. ....Boston, MA
Ryan, Paul G. ....Stamford, CT
White Plains, NY
Ryan, Paul J. ....Cambridge, MA
Ryan, Paul J. ....Lock Haven, PA
Ryan, Paul L. ....Schenectady, NY
Ryan, Paul M. ....Sacramento, CA
Ryan, Paul M., Jr. ....Los Angeles, CA
Ryan, Paul T. ....Atlanta, GA
Ryan, Paul T. ....Missoula, MT
Ryan, Paula Aileen ....New York, NY
Ryan, Paula G. A. ....New York, NY
Ryan, Paula Terese ....Philadelphia, PA
Ryan, Perry T. ....Frankfort, KY
Ryan & Peryer ....Plattsburgh, NY
Ryan, Peter M. ....Darien, CT
Ryan, Peter M. ....Philadelphia, PA
Ryan, Peter W. ....Iron Mountain, MI
Ryan, Peter W., P.C. ....Iron Mountain, MI
Florence, WI
Ryan, Philip A. ....Moorestown, NJ
Philadelphia, PA
Ryan, Philip D. ....Oklahoma City, OK
Ryan, Philip J. ....Waukegan, IL
Ryan, Philip J. ....Springfield, MA
Ryan, Philip Scott ....Mendocino, CA
Ryan, Phillip J. ....Clarkston, MI
Ryan, Phillips, Utrecht & MacKinnon
Washington, DC
Ryan, Phyllis P. ....Pittsfield, MA
Springfield, MA
Ryan, Porter K. ....Houston, TX
Ryan, Priscilla E. ....Chicago, IL
Ryan, R.R., P.C. ....Billings, MT
Ryan, R. Steven ....Fowler, IN
Kentland, IN
Ryan, R. Todd ....St. Charles, MO
Ryan, R. A. ....Cincinnati, OH
Ryan, Rae M. ....Cincinnati, OH
Ryan, Ralph R. ....Pawtucket, RI
Ryan, Randy G. ....Detroit, MI
Ryan, Raymond J. ....Newark, NJ
Ryan, Raymond J., Jr. ....Saginaw, MI
Ryan, Reade H., Jr. ....New York, NY
Ryan, Rebecca A. ....Kansas City, MO
Ryan, Rhonda Colbert ....Austin, TX
Ryan, Ricardo M. ....Mobile, AL
Ryan, Richard A. ....Fresno, CA
Ryan, Richard D. ....Syracuse, NY
Ryan, Richard J. ....Los Angeles, CA
Ryan, Richard J. ....Roseville, CA
Ryan, Richard J. ....Oak Forest, IL
Ryan, Richard J. ....Hackensack, NJ
Ryan, Richard L. ....Chicago, IL
Ryan, Richard P. ....Wallingford, CT
Ryan, Richard R. ....Shelton, CT
Ryan, Richard R. ....Chicago, IL
Ryan, Richard T. ....Chicago, IL
Ryan, Richd. J. ....Cedar Rapids, IA
Ryan, Roach & Ryan, P.C. ....Kingston, NY
Ryan, Robert ....Beverly Hills, CA
Ryan, Robert C. ....San Diego, CA
Ryan, Robert C. ....Hoffman Estates, IL
Reno, NV
Ryan, Robert D. ....Phoenix, AZ
Ryan, Robert D. ....Boston, MA
Ryan, Robert D. ....White Plains, NY
Ryan, Robert E. ....Alton, IL
Ryan, Robert E. ....Cleveland, OH
Ryan, Robert Emmett ....Roseland, NJ
Ryan, Robert J. ....San Francisco, CA
Ryan, Robert J. ....Winnetka, IL
Ryan, Robert J. ....Baltimore, MD
Ryan, Robert J. ....Boston, MA
Ryan, Robert J. ....Milton, MA
Ryan, Robert K. ....Frankfort, IN
Ryan, Robert K., Jr. ....Frankfort, IN
Ryan, Robert L., Jr. ....Carle Place, NY
Ryan, Robert N. ....New Orleans, LA
Ryan, Robert P. ....Billings, MT
Ryan, Robert S. ....Lexington, KY
Ryan, Robert S. ....Minneapolis, MN
Ryan, Robert S. ....Columbus, OH
Ryan, Robert T., Jr. ....Seguin, TX
Ryan, Robyn Lynne ....Nashville, TN
Ryan, Rodney A. ....Bellevue, WA
Ryan, Rodney J. ....Des Moines, IA
Ryan, Rodney J., P.C. ....Des Moines, IA
Ryan, Roger Edward ....Springfield, IL
Ryan, Roibin J. ....Muskegon, MI
Ryan, Ronald J. ....Madison, WI
Ryan, Ronald W. ....Tucson, AZ
Ryan, Ronald W. ....Kalamazoo, MI
Ryan, Rory C. ....Orlando, FL
Ryan, Rosa Amaral ....Exton, PA
Ryan, Rosemary A. ....Liberty Corner, NJ
Ryan, Roxann M. ....Des Moines, IA
Ryan & Rumsey ....Homer, NY
Ryan, Russell G.
Securities and Exchange Commission,
Division of Enforcement, GV
Ryan, Russell Jay, Jr. ....Indianapolis, IN
Ryan, Russell K. ....Fresno, CA
Ryan, Russell, Ogden & Seltzer LLP
Harrisburg, PA
Reading, PA
Ryan & Ryan ....Honolulu, HI
Ryan & Ryan ....Marion, IN
Ryan & Ryan ....Kalamazoo, MI
Ryan & Ryan ....Aitkin, MN
Ryan and Ryan ....New York, NY
Ryan & Ryan ....Columbus, OH
Williamson, WV
Ryan & Ryan, Attorneys At Law, A Prof. Assn. ....Jupiter, FL
North Palm Beach, FL
Palm Beach Gardens, FL

Rynders, James A. ....Greendale, WI
Rynders, Perrin ....Grand Rapids, MI
Ryneal, F. Steve ....Riverside, CA
Ryneal, Fred H. ....Riverside, CA
Ryneal & Ryneal, A Law Corporation
Riverside, CA
Rynearson, Arthur J. ....United States Senate, Office of the Legislative Counsel, GV
Rynearson, Max D. ....Indianapolis, IN
Rynearson, Sam P. ....St. Louis, MO
Rynearson, Scott J. ....Jacksonville, FL
Rynecki, Scott ....Brooklyn, NY
Rynecki, Steven B. ....Milwaukee, WI
Ryner, Elizabeth A. ....San Diego, CA
Rynerson, S. Diane ....Portland, OR
Rynes, Michael J. ....Madison, WI
Ryniec, Tracey S. ....San Francisco, CA
Ryniker, Margaret R. ....Syracuse, NY
Ryniker, Robert J. ....Houston, TX
Ryning, Jason D. ....Seattle, WA
Rynkar, Robert D. ....Mineola, NY
Rynkiewicz, John P. ....Washington, DC
Columbia, MD
Rynkiewicz, Walter P. ....Milwaukee, WI
Rynkowski, David Joseph ....Troy, NY
Rynn & Janowsky ....Newport Beach, CA
Rynn, Patricia J. ....Newport Beach, CA
Rynning, Lawrence K. ....Chicago, IL
Rynor, Jeffrey A. ....Miami, FL
Ryntz, Amy L. ....Southfield, MI
Ryo, Emily ....Washington, DC
Ryon, H. Perry ....Conifer, CO
Denver, CO
Ryon, Joan E. ....Rockville, MD
Ryon, Mortimer ....Dobbs Ferry, NY
Ryp, Norman C. ....New York, NY
Rypinski, Richard G. ....Oakland, CA
Ryplansky, Cristina M. ....McLean, VA
Rypma, Curtis D. ....Grand Rapids, MI
Rypma, Jacqueline Stetson ....Des Moines, IA
Rys, John L. ....St. Paul, MN
Rys, Laura M. ....Milford, NJ
Rysavy, Charles F. ....Newark, NJ
Rysavy, Don L. ....Bismarck, ND
Rysavy, Donald E. ....Austin, MN
Ryscavage, Mark P. ....Baltimore, MD
Rysdyk, Edith C. ....Allentown, PA
Ryser, David G. ....Milwaukee, WI
Ryser, Philip P. ....Dublin, OH
Ryser, Shannon J. ....St. Louis, MO
Ryskamp, Kenneth L. ......West Palm Beach, FL
Ryskamp, Patrick W. ....Sarasota, FL
Ryskamp, Randall M. ....Treasury Department, Office of the Comptroller of the Currency, GV
Ryske, Paul R. ....South Barrington, IL
Ryskoski, Scott J. ....St. Paul, MN
Rysman, Peter H. ....Key West, FL
Rysted, Karl M. ....Moore, OK
Rystrom, Clayton A., Jr. ....Pearcy, AR
Rystrom, Nancy A. ....Minneapolis, MN
Ryter, William J. ....Boston, MA
Ryterski, Louise Rose ....St. Louis, MO
Ryther, James P. ....Chicago, IL
Ryther, Paul M. ....East Bloomfield, NY
Ryther, Scott R. ....Salt Lake City, UT
Rytlewski, Jeff R. ....Lafayette, LA
New Orleans, LA
Rytting, James ....Houston, TX
Rytting, Paul D. ....Salt Lake City, UT
Ryu, Bobby J. ....Los Angeles, CA
Ryu, Donna M. ....San Francisco, CA
Ryu, Francis ....Los Angeles, CA
Ryu, Regina P. ....New York, NY
Ryu, Tammy Chung ....Los Angeles, CA
Ryu, Thomas J. ....Beverly Hills, CA
Ryva, Jeffrey A. ....Peoria, IL
Rywak, Walter Z. ....Chicago, IL
Rywalski, Robert F. ....Fairlawn, OH
Rywant, Alvarez, Jones, Russo & Guyton
Clearwater, FL
Gainesville, FL
St. Petersburg, FL
Brooksville, FL
Inverness, FL
Leesburg, FL
Ocala, FL
Tampa, FL
Rywant, Michael S. ....Ocala, FL
Tampa, FL
Rywick, Robert ....New York, NY
Rywkin, Robert ....New York, NY
Ryza, Willis S. ....Olympia Fields, IL
Ryzen, Elisabeth ....Palo Alto, CA
Ryzewic, Michelle ....Newburyport, MA
Rzeczkowski, Henry F. ....Milwaukee, WI
Rzepecki, David S. ....Erie, PA
Rzepezynski, Gregg M. ....Chicago, IL
Rzepiennik, H. Andrew ....Denver, CO
Rzepka, Thomas J. ....Rochester, NY
Rzepski, Elaine M. ....Bryn Mawr, PA
Rzonca, Lynn E. ....Chicago, IL
Rzucidlo, Eugene C. ....New York, NY
Rzycki, Wladek ....Chicago, IL
Rzymek, Michael ....Columbus, OH

S. L. Epstein, Law Office of ....Wilmette, IL
Saab, George J. ....Buffalo, NY
Saab, Joseph R. ....Buffalo, NY
Saab, Louis M. ....Lowell, MA
Saab, Thomas J. ....Lowell, MA
Saabneh, Salah A. ....New York, NY
Saacke, Charles F., (P.C.) ....Torrance, CA
Saacke, William C. ....Long Beach, CA
Saad, Elias J. ....Mobile, AL
Saad, Henry W. ....Southfield, MI
Saad, James A. ....Columbus, OH
Saad, Leon J. ....San Diego, CA
Saad, Martin L. ....Washington, DC
Saad, Michael D. ....Columbus, OH
Saad, Tarek F.M. ....Denver, CO
Saada, John M., Jr. ....Cleveland, OH
Saadah, Alex Katherine ....Oklahoma City, OK
Saadat, David A. ....St. Louis, MO
Saadat, Mahshid D.
Department of Commerce, Patent and Trademark Office, GV
Saadeh, Catherine M.
Securities and Exchange Commission, Division of Investment Management, GV
Saadeh, Laura L. ....Irvine, CA
Saadeh, Nicole T. ....Los Angeles, CA
Saadi, Edward T. ....Youngstown, OH
Saadi, Joseph M. ....Youngstown, OH
Saady, Claire ....Tampa, FL
Saady & Saxe ....Tampa, FL
Saaf, Adele Matsumi ....Bloomington, IL
Saafir, Carlin Talib ....Philadelphia, PA
Saager, Irvin R. ....Elm Grove, WI
Saah, Andrea V. Imredy ....Blue Bell, PA
Saakvitne, Nicholas L.
Marina Del Rey, CA
Saakvitne, Nicholas L., A Law Corporation
Los Angeles, CA
Marina Del Rey, CA
Santa Monica, CA
Saal, Edward G., Jr. ....Gueydan, LA
Saal, I. P., Jr. ....Gueydan, LA
Saal, Jennifer S. ....North Bergen, NJ
Saal and Saal ....Gueydan, LA
Saalfeld, Griggs, Gorsuch, Alexander & Emerick, P.C. ....Salem, OR
Saalfeld, Harold M. ....Chicago, IL
Saalfeld, James R. ....Grand Rapids, MI
Saalfeld, Robert J. ....Salem, OR
Saalfield, Albrecht ....Concord, MA
Saalfield, Coulson, Shad & Jay, P.A.
Jacksonville, FL
Saalfield, Janet H. ....Sausalito, CA
Saalfield, John R. ....Jacksonville, FL
Saalfield, Shannon C. ....Dallas, TX
Saalman, Gary J. ....Columbus, OH
Saam, Kristen T. ....Chicago, IL
Saame, Philipp O. ....Deerfield, IL
Saande, Colleen J. ....Las Vegas, NV
Saar, David A. ....Titusville, NJ
Saar, Douglas A. ....Spokane, WA
Saar, Peter ....Baltimore, MD
Saari, Charles L. ....Caldwell, ID
Saari, Claudia S. ....Decatur, GA
Saari, Clyde W. ....Osceola, WI
Saari, David J. ....Washington, DC
Saari, John W. ....Rhinelander, WI
Saari, Leonard M. ....White Plains, NY
Saari, Peter A. ....Washington, DC
Saari, Peter J. ....Hampton, NH
Saari, Roy A. ....Mammoth Lakes, CA
Saarinen, Lynn E. ....Houston, TX
Saas, J. Richard ....Bethesda, MD
Saas, Richard T. ....Washington, DC
Saasto, Ernest O. ....Lindenhurst, NY
Saasto, Robert ....Brooklyn, NY
Saat, Regina C. ....New York, NY
Saathoff, Denise L. ....Fort Collins, CO
Saathoff, Dwight D. ....Orlando, FL
Saathoff Law Office, P.C. ....Fort Collins, CO
Saathoff, Scott K. ....Fort Collins, CO
Saatjian, Raymond G. ....Sacramento, CA
Saavedra, Claudia I. ....Minneapolis, MN
Saavedra, Damaso W.
Fort Lauderdale, FL
Saavedra, Jose A. ....Miami, FL
Saavedra & Pelosi ....Fort Lauderdale, FL
Saavedra, Richard A., Jr. ....Springfield, IL
Saavedra, Sheryl L. ....Roswell, NM
Saba, David W., Law Offices of
Berwick, PA
Kingston, PA
Saba, David W., Law Offices of
Wilkes-Barre, PA
Saba, Gary M. ....Phoenix, AZ
Saba, George E., Jr. ....Kingston, PA
Saba, Joseph A., Jr. ....Utica, NY
Saba, Joseph P. ....Washington, DC
Saba, Michele A. ....San Francisco, CA
Baltimore, MD
Saba, Olivier D. ....New York, NY
Saba, Paul ....Tucson, AZ
Saba, Paul T. ....Cincinnati, OH
Saba, Peter A. ....Cincinnati, OH
Saba, Peter B. ....Washington, DC
Saba, Philip M., II ....Boston, MA
Saba, Regina Baluyot ....Cincinnati, OH
Saba, Richard D., Law Offices of
Sarasota, FL
Saba, Ruth Hakaim ....Cleveland, OH
Saba, William A. ....Sarasota, FL
Saba, William M. ....Greenwich, CT
Sabadie, Francisca A. ....Scarsdale, NY
Sabadish, Joseph S. ....Harrisburg, PA
Sabados, Bruce M. ....New York, NY
Sabag, Cathy D. ....Los Angeles, CA
Sabag, Tina M. ....Dakota City, NE
Sabagh, Denyse ....Washington, DC
Sabagh, Mitchell J. ....Port St. Lucie, FL
Sabag-Hodne, Tina Marie ....Sioux City, IA
Sabah, Daniel L. ....Encino, CA
Sabaitis, Catherine P. ....Brockton, MA
Sabaitis, Frank T. ....Los Angeles, CA
Sabaitis, James T. ....Spring Lake, NJ
Sabaj, Mary E. ....Mason, MI
Sabalis, Patricia M. ....Burlington, VT
Sabalot, Richard A. ....Baton Rouge, LA
Saban, Cheryl R. ....New York, NY
Sabanosh, John A. ....Bridgeport, CT
Sabarese, Sharon Ann ....Rootstown, OH
Sabarra, Nancy ....New York, NY
Sabarsky, Martin A. ....Los Angeles, CA
Sabat, Richard J. ....Philadelphia, PA
Sabatasse, H. James ....Northridge, CA
Sabatelli, Anthony D. ....Rahway, NJ
Sabatello, Mary L. ....River Forest, IL
Sabatello, Michael J., IV
West Palm Beach, FL
Sabath, Kenneth M. ....Honolulu, HI
Sabath, Mark K. ....Columbus, OH
Sabath, Michael S. ....Chicago, IL
Sabath, Robert P. ....San Jose, CA
Sabath & Truong ....San Jose, CA
Sabatina, John Patrick, Jr. ....Philadelphia, PA
Sabatine, Jeffrey P. ....Bedford Heights, OH
Sabatine, Nicholas R., III ....Wind Gap, PA
Sabatine, Paul L. ....Palo Alto, CA
Sabatini, Albert, Jr. ....Ada, MI
Sabatini, Alex R. ....Bethesda, MD
Sabatini and Associates ....Hartford, CT
Newington, CT
Wethersfield, CT
Sabatini & Associates, L.L.P.
New York, NY
Sabatini, Carolyn A. ....Westwood, MA
Sabatini, Catherine Gibbons
Los Angeles, CA
Sabatini, David P. ....Chicago, IL
Sabatini, Donald S. ....Philadelphia, PA
Sabatini, Frank C. ....Topeka, KS
Sabatini, Frederick A. ....Logansport, IN
Sabatini, Jack B. ....Huntsville, AL
Sabatini, James V. ....Newington, CT
Sabatini, John R. ....Los Angeles, CA
Sabatini, Randy S. ....Atlanta, GA
Sabatini, Richard J. ....New York, NY
Sabatini, Vincent F. ....Newington, CT
Sabatino, Alessandro ....Columbus, OH
Sabatino, Charles P. ....Washington, DC
Sabatino, Frank C. ....Philadelphia, PA
Sabatino, Jack M. ....Newark, NJ
Sabatino, James R. ....Bay Harbor Islands, FL
Sabatino, Lawrence J. ....Bethesda, MD
Sabatino, Louis A. ....Miami, FL
Sabatino, Paul, II ....Huntington Station, NY
Sabatino, Ralph M. C. ....Brooklyn, NY
Sabatino & Spindel ....Bay Harbor Islands, FL
Sabatino, Thomas J., Jr. ....Deerfield, IL
Sabatiuk, Lynne
Department Of Veterans Affairs, Veterans Benefits Administration, GV
Sabato, Leonard S. ....Philadelphia, PA
Sabatt, Charles M. ....West Yarmouth, MA
Sabbadini, Steven C. ....Woodland, CA
Sabbadini, Steven C., A Professional Law Corporation ....Davis, CA
Woodland, CA
Sabbah, Mark S. ....Riverside, CA
Sabban, Ariel Joseph ....San Diego, CA
Sabban, Nina Madden ....Los Angeles, CA
Sabbath, Dennis M. ....Las Vegas, NV
Sabbath, Dennis M., & Associates, Chartered, The Law Firm of
Las Vegas, NV
Sabbath, George E. ....Riverdale, NJ
Sabbath, John W. ....Cedar Falls, IA
Sabbath, Michael D. ....Macon, GA
Sabbatini, Mildred L ....Memphis, TN
Sabbatini, Robert L. ....Memphis, TN
Sabbatino, Francesca A. ....New York, NY
Sabbert, Richard D. ....St. Charles, MO
Sabbey, Norman C. ....Boston, MA
Sabbia, Anthony C. ....Chicago, IL
Sabbota, Jerome
Bloomfield Township, MI
Sabbs, Patrick S. ....Springfield, MA
Sabec, Margo Harlan ....Casper, WY
Sabel, Bradley Kent ....New York, NY
Sabel, Celeste W. ....Montgomery, AL
Sabel, Charles R. ....New York, NY
Sabel, David G. ....New York, NY
Sabel, Dawn M. ....Fond du Lac, WI
Sabel, John ....Morristown, NJ
Sabel, John D. ....Bridgewater, NJ
Sabel, M. Wayne ....Montgomery, AL
Sabel, Mark ....Montgomery, AL
Sabel, Myra Baker ....Montgomery, AL
Sabel, Robert H. ....Winter Haven, FL
Sabel, Robert M. ....Newport, RI
Sabel & Sabel, P.C. ....Montgomery, AL
Sabel, Sharon M. ....Fort Lauderdale, FL
Sabel, Trudi Baltz ....Los Angeles, CA
Sabele, Glenn ....Brooklyn, NY
Sabella, Anthony J. ....Memphis, TN
Sabella, Candance M. ....Tampa, FL
Sabella, Edward V. ....Springfield, MA
Sabella, James J. ....New York, NY
Sabella, Thomas, Jr. ....Tampa, FL
Sabella, Vincent A. ....Mineola, NY
Sabelli, Martin Antonio ....San Francisco, CA
Sabelli, Veronica ....Waterbury, CT
Sabellico, Thomas M. ....Farmingdale, NY
Saber, Bruce D. ....New York, NY
Saber, Charles W. ....Washington, DC
Saber, Christina ....New York, NY
Saber, Lee ....Houston, TX
Saber, Michael P. ....Raleigh, NC
Saber, Rashid Lee ....Houston, TX
Saber, Steven S. ....Hollywood, FL
Saber-Assad, April L. ....Fall River, MA
Saber-Assad & Assad ....Fall River, MA
Saberg, Marge ....San Diego, CA
Sabers, Richard W. ....Sioux Falls, SD
Sabers, Robert E. ....Dubuque, IA
Sabers, Susan M. ....Sioux Falls, SD
Sabersky, Cynthia ....Chico, CA
Saberson, Roger G. ....Delray Beach, FL
Saberson, Roger G., P.A. ....Delray Beach, FL
Sabes, Charles H. ....San Jose, CA
Sabesin, Marcia L. ....Chicago, IL
Sabet, Shahla S. ....Rancho Cucamonga, CA
Sabett, Marina Lolley ....Baltimore, MD
Sabett, Randy V. ....Herndon, VA
Sabetta, Andrew D. ....Derby, CT
Sabetta, Andrew, Jr. ....Derby, CT
Sabetta, John C. ....New York, NY
Sabetta, Paul M. ....New Haven, CT
Sabetta & Sabetta ....Derby, CT
Sabetti, Daniel P. ....Allentown, PA
Sabetti, Staci Ann ....Easton, PA
Sabety, Ted ....New York, NY
Sabey, Andrew ....Walnut Creek, CA
Sabey, Erin Ruddy ....Walnut Creek, CA
Sabey, Mark L. ....Denver, CO
Sabey, Melvin B. ....Denver, CO
Sabey, Scott R. ....Salt Lake City, UT
Sabga, George M., Jr. ....Vista, CA
Sabghir, Jonathan M. ....Tamarac, FL
Sabghir, Jonathan, P.A. ....Tamarac, FL
Sabgir, Kristin J. ....Columbus, OH
Sabharwal & Associates ....New York, NY
Sabharwal, Keeto H. ....New York, NY
Sabharwal, Rohit ....New York, NY
Sabia & Hartley, LLC ....Hartford, CT
Sabia, Randall J. ....Hartford, CT
Sabian, Andrea ....Staten Island, NY
Sabian, Michael A. ....Denver, CO
Sabich-Robison, Katharine
Los Angeles, CA
Sabido, Robert E. ....Portland, OR
Sabih, David S. ....Pacific Grove, CA
Sabik, John L. ....Clayton, NY
Sabilia, Elizabeth A. ....New London, CT
Sabin, Arthur J. ....Chicago, IL
Sabin, Bermant & Gould LLP
New York, NY
Sabin, Brainard S. ....Tallahassee, FL
Sabin, Conrad B. ....West Hempstead, NY
Sabin, David R. ....Grayling, MI
Sabin, David R., P.C. ....Grayling, MI
Sabin, Deborah A. ....Albany, NY
Sabin, Edward N. ....Los Angeles, CA
Sabin, James N. ....Corpus Christi, TX
Sabin, Jay I. ....New York, NY
Sabin, Jeffrey S. ....New York, NY
Sabin, Jonathan B. ....Williamstown, MA
Sabin, Marsha A. ....Treasury Department, Internal Revenue Service, GV
Sabin, Neil R. ....Salt Lake City, UT
Sabin, Nettie F. ....Chicago, IL
Sabin, Norman E. ....Chattanooga, TN
Sabin, Paul ....Chicago, IL
Sabin, Robert E. ....Roswell, NM
Sabin, Robert J. ....Arlington Heights, IL
Sabin, Robert J., Jr. ....Arlington Heights, IL
Sabin, Robt. R. ....La Junta, CO
Sabin & Sabin ....Williamstown, MA
Sabin & Sabin ....West Hempstead, NY
Sabin, Scott A. ....Springfield, IL
Sabin, Thomas R. ....Kirkland, WA
Sabin, William C. ....Rockville, MD
Sabin, William C., Jr. ....Treasury Department, Internal Revenue Service, GV
Sabin, Wm. I. ....Williamstown, MA
Sabina, James M. ....Anderson, IN
Sabine, Glenn ....El Cajon, CA
Sabine, Harry D. ....Crossville, TN
Sabine, Harry D., P.C. ....Crossville, TN
Sabine, J. David ....Youngstown, OH
Sabine, Karen ....New York, NY
Sabini, Robert C. ....Ross, CA
Sabino, Anthony J. ....Bethpage, NY
Sabino, Anthony Michael ....Mineola, NY
Sabino, Evelyn M. ....Philadelphia, PA
Sabino, Francis V. ....Pittsburgh, PA
Sabino, Jamie Ann ....Cambridge, MA
Sabino, Mary Jane C. ....Mineola, NY
Sabino & Sabino, P.C. ....Mineola, NY
Sabino, Thomas W. ....Roseland, NJ
Sabino, William ....Wayne, NJ
Sabins, Jany ....Westfield, NJ
Sabis, Ramona Miller ....Gainesville, FL
Sabiston, E. Paul ....Marietta, GA
Sabiston, Michael A. ....Troy, NC
Sabitoni, Armand E. ....Providence, RI
Sabl, John J. ....Carmel, IN
Sablack, Michael A. ....Mayfield Village, OH
Sablak, Laurie J. ....Simsbury, CT
Sable, Alan K. ....Pittsburgh, PA
Sable, Allan D. ....Dallas, TX
Sable, Amy E. ....Pittsburgh, PA
Sable, D. Stella ....Fort Myers, FL
Sable, Deborah ....Marina Del Rey, CA
Sable, Edward Todd ....Birmingham, MI
Sable, Jesse C., (P.C.) ....New York, NY
Sable, Joel N. ....Hartford, CT
Sable, John D. ....Stamford, CT
Sable, Joshua M. ....Los Angeles, CA
Sable, Kenneth L. ....Harrisburg, PA
Sable, Linda G. ....Boston, MA
Sable, Louise B. ....Birmingham, MI
Sable, Martin J., Law Offices of
Irvine, CA
Sable, Marvin E. ....Beachwood, OH
Sable, Michael H. ....Pittsburgh, PA
Sable, Pusateri, Rosen, Gordon & Adams, LLC ....Pittsburgh, PA
Sable, Richard J. ....Sterling Heights, MI
Sable, Robert G. ....Pittsburgh, PA
Sable, Theresa E. ....Mayfield Heights, OH
Sableman, Mark ....St. Louis, MO
Sablich, Christopher G. ....Chicago, IL
Sablich, Joseph F. ....Lansing, MI
Sabloff, Matthew B. ....New York, NY
Sablone, Francis R., Jr. ....Old Saybrook, CT

Sablone, Jonathan ... Boston, MA
Sablone, Kathleen M. ... Boston, MA
Sablosky, Ann H. ... Bethesda, MD
Sablove, Herbert J. ... Trenton, NJ
Sablowsky, Steven L. ... Pittsburgh, PA
Sabludowsky, Meyer ... New Orleans, LA
Sabludowsky, Stephen M. ... Metairie, LA
Sabo, Aberdeen H. ... Independence, OH
Sabo, Albert F. ... Philadelphia, PA
Sabo, Alex J. ... Miami, FL
Sabo, Alvin O. ... Albany, NY
Sabo & Associates ... Grand Blanc, MI
Sabo, Charles M., P.C. ... Tempe, AZ
Sabo, Frank, Jr. ... Houston, TX
Sabo, Gerard E. ... Los Angeles, CA
Sabo & Green, A Professional Corporation
Calabasas, CA
Cathedral City, CA
Los Angeles, CA
San Bernardino, CA
Sabo, Gregory K. ... Los Angeles, CA
Sabo, Helen A. ... Poway, CA
Sabo, Jill W. ... Pittsburgh, PA
Sabo, John B. ... Warrendale, PA
Sabo, John D. ... Buckhannon, WV
Sabo, John E. ... Belleville, IL
Sabo, John W., III ... Colorado Springs, CO
Sabo, Joshua A. ... Albany, NY
Sabo, Katherine ... Sacramento, CA
Sabo, Kenneth B. ... Los Alamitos, CA
Sabo, Kenneth B., A Professional Corporation
Los Alamitos, CA
Sabo, Melanie ... Washington, DC
Sabo, Michael G. ... Philadelphia, PA
Sabo, Roger L. ... Columbus, OH
Sabo, Ronald W. ... Grand Blanc, MI
Sabo, Sean M. ... Mesa, AZ
Sabo, Stacey ... New York, NY
Sabo, Susan J. ... Ann Arbor, MI
Sabo, Thomas I. ... Gallatin Gateway, MT
Sabo, Timothy J. ... Calabasas, CA
San Bernardino, CA
Sabo, Werner A. ... Chicago, IL
Sabo, William D. ... Essex Junction, VT
Sabo & Zahn ... Chicago, IL
Saboe, James O. ... Minneapolis, MN
Sabol, Andrew B. ... Buffalo, NY
Sabol, Carolyn A. ... Department of Justice,
Bureau of Prisons, GV
Sabol & Fisher ... Lima, OH
Sabol, Garry Albert ... Columbus, OH
Sabol, JoAnn ... Olympia, WA
Sabol, John A. ... Lima, OH
Sabol, Lori Stein ... Lafayette, IN
Sabol, Patricia A. ... Wilmington, DE
Sabol, Sherry E. ... Department of Justice,
Federal Bureau of Investigation, GV
Sabol, Suzanne Kay ... Columbus, OH
Sabol, Thomas A. ... Philadelphia, PA
Sabom, Robert T. ... Houston, TX
Sabongui, Amgad Michael ... New York, NY
Sabonis, J. Peter, Jr. ... Boston, MA
Saboorian, Mohammad Patrick
Beverly Hills, CA
Sabora, Marilyn G. ... Skokie, IL
Sabot, David A. ... Fort Lauderdale, FL
Sabourin, Anne Gerry ... Mount Olive, NJ
Sabourin & Associates ... Farmington, MI
Sabourin, Debra S.
Federal Communications Commission,
Common Carrier Bureau, GV
Sabourin, Dennis H. ... Montclair, NJ
Sabourin, John J., Jr. ... McLean, VA
Sabourin, Robert A. ... Ridgefield Park, NJ
Sabourin, Rodney W. ... Farmington, MI
Sabourin, Sandra J. ... Syracuse, NY
Sabourin, William ... San Clemente, CA
Sabra & Aspden, Professional Association
Somerset, MA
Sabra, Richard B. ... Hollywood, FL
Sabra, Steven P. ... Somerset, MA
Sabraw, Bonnie Lewman ... Hayward, CA
Sabraw, Ronald M. ... Hayward, CA
Sabreen, Susan Ellen Berger
White Plains, NY
Sabrin, Amy R. ... Washington, DC
Sabshon, Frances ... Dallas, TX
Sabshon, Mitchell A. ... New York, NY
Sabuco, Roy A. ... Joliet, IL
Saca, Diana M. ... Palo Alto, CA
San Francisco, CA
Sacasas, René ... Miami, FL
Sacavage, Robert B. ... Mount Carmel, PA
Sacca, Gerald Stephen ... Lockport, NY
Sacca, James R. ... Atlanta, GA
Sacca, Joseph N. ... New York, NY
Sacca, Justin I. ... Huntington, NY
Sacca and Sacca ... Lockport, NY
Sacca, Stephen A. ... Lockport, NY
Sacca, Thomas C. ... Troy, NY
Saccany, John C. ... Cleveland, OH
Saccheri, James L. ... Fresno, CA
Sacchetta & Baldino ... Media, PA
Norristown, PA
Sacchetta, Linda Vacca ... Bala Cynwyd, PA
Sacchetta, Susan J. ... Paoli, PA
Sacchetta, Thomas F. ... Norristown, PA
Sacchetti, Joyce M. ... San Rafael, CA
Sacchetti, Robert F. ... Lawrence, MA
Sacchetti, Vincent M. ... Boston, MA
Sacchotti, Robert F. ... Lawrence, MA
Sacco, Andrea E. ... Westfield, NJ
New York, NY
Sacco, Anthony H. ... San Jose, CA
Sacco, Daniel C. ... Boston, MA
Sacco, Dena T. ... Department of Justice,
Office of Policy Development, GV
Sacco, Gary A. ... Wheeling, WV
Sacco, George F. ... Staten Island, NY
Sacco, Henry J., Jr. ... Westfield, NJ
Sacco, James A. ... Binghamton, NY
Sacco, James S. ... Chapel Hill, NC
Sacco, Joel F. ... Cleveland, OH
Sacco, John M. ... Las Vegas, NV
Sacco, Joseph G. ... Kenmore, NY
Sacco, Kristin Sacco ... Toledo, OH
Sacco, M. Susan ... Orlando, FL
Sacco, Madonna A. ... Bridgeport, CT
Sacco, Marci L. ... Morristown, NJ
Sacco, Michael ... Boston, MA
Sacco, Paul F. ... Yonkers, NY
Sacco, Paul W. ... Greeley, CO
Sacco, Robert C. ... Holyoke, MA
Sacco, Robert J. ... West Palm Beach, FL
Sacco, Rudolph A. ... Pittsfield, MA
Sacco, Russell N. ... Lake Oswego, OR
Sacco, Thomas N. ... Windsor, CT
Sacco, Todd A. ... Pittsburgh, PA
Saccocci, Donna Lee
Department of Defense,
Defense Legal Services Agency, GV
Saccoccia, Steven W. ... Atlanta, GA
Saccoccio & Lopez ... Haleiwa, HI
Saccoccio, Louis J. ... Washington, DC
Saccoccio, Louis J. ... Kingston, RI
Saccoccio, Marie Elena ... Cheyenne, WY
Saccoccio, Paul ... Haleiwa, HI
Saccocio, John R. ... Albany, NY
Saccocio, Patrick J. ... Schenectady, NY
Saccocio, Richard M. ... Fort Lauderdale, FL
Saccogna, Patrick J. ... Cleveland, OH
Saccoman, Charles J. ... Kingston, NY
Saccoman, John L. ... Las Vegas, NV
Saccoman, Joseph D. ... Kingston, NY
Saccomandi, Angela ... Media, PA
Saccomandi, Frank J., III ... Hartford, CT
Saccomando, Vincent George ... Buffalo, NY
Saccomano, Joseph A., Jr.
White Plains, NY
Saccone, Dianne M. ... Syosset, NY
Saccone, Girolamo M. ... New York, NY
Saccone, Joseph A., Jr. ... Chicago, IL
Sacerich, Thomas J. ... Mentor, OH
Sacha, Alfred N. ... Chicago, IL
Sacha, Barbara A. ... East Chicago, IN
Sacha, John F. ... Atlanta, GA
Sacha, Laura J ... Cleveland, OH
Sacha, Mark A. ... Cheektowaga, NY
Sachanowicz, Leslie J.A. ... Austin, TX
Sachar, Bruce N. ... Lynn, MA
Sachar, Leonard S. ... Elizabeth, NJ
Sachar, Libby E. ... South Plainfield, NJ
Sachar, Mark D. ... Irvine, CA
Sachar, Surinder ... Arlington, VA
Sachar, Vincent J. ... Rose Bud, AR
Sacharin, Kirkscey & Flexsenhar
Memphis, TN
Sacharoff, Adam K. ... Chicago, IL
Sacharoff, Laurent A. ... New York, NY
Sacharow, Steven B. ... Cherry Hill, NJ
Sachat, Marilyn R. ... Chicago, IL
Sachdev, Amit K. ... Washington, DC
Sachdeva, Gurjeev K. ... Palo Alto, CA
Sachdeva, Neelu ... Houston, TX
Sacheli, Concettina M. ... New York, NY
Sacheli, Tina ... New York, NY
Sachen, Michael J. ... West Allis, WI
Sacher, Andrew N. ... New York, NY
Sacher, Barton S. ... Miami, FL
Sacher, Charles P., (P.A.) ... Coral Gables, FL
Sacher, Charles S. ... Coral Gables, FL
Sacher, James P. ... Houston, TX
Sacher, Jeffery W. ... Miami, FL
Sacher, John W. ... Celina, OH
Sacher, Joseph A. ... Miami, FL
Sacher, Michael S. ... Celina, OH
Sacher, Paul A. ... Washington, DC
Department of Commerce,
Patent and Trademark Office, GV
Sacher, Steven J. ... Washington, DC
Sacher Zelman Paul Beiley & Van Sant, P.A.
Fort Lauderdale, FL
Miami, FL
West Palm Beach, FL
Sachitano, Nancy A. ... Bethesda, MD
Sachner, S. Peter ... New Haven, CT
Sachner, Stephen P. ... Cheshire, CT
Sachnik, Gregory J. ... Chattanooga, TN
Sachnoff, Lee F. ... Denver, CO
Sachnoff, Lowell E. ... Chicago, IL
Sachnoff, Scott D. ... Chicago, IL
Sachnoff & Weaver, Ltd. ... Chicago, IL
Sachrison, Eric W. ... Phoenix, AZ
Tucson, AZ
Costa Mesa, CA
San Diego, CA
Sachrison, Melinda J.
Cardiff-By-The-Sea, CA
Sachs, Aaron Wm. ... Springfield, MO
Sachs, Adam ... Los Angeles, CA
San Francisco, CA
Sachs, Alan A. ... St. Louis, MO
Sachs, Alan L. ... Las Vegas, NV
Sachs, Alan Richard, P.A. ... Baltimore, MD
Towson, MD
Sachs, Alan Richard "Rick"
Baltimore, MD
Sachs, Amy M. ... Boston, MA
Sachs, Andrea ... New York, NY
Sachs, Andrew ... Oklahoma City, OK
Sachs, Andrew M. ... Chicago, IL
Sachs, Arthur S. ... North Haven, CT
Sachs & Associates ... San Diego, CA
Sachs, Benjamin I. ... Denver, CO
Sachs, Bernard J. ... Baltimore, MD
Sachs, Betti J. ... New York, NY
Sachs, Brown & Proto, LLC
North Haven, CT
Sachs, Byron ... Dallas, TX
Sachs, Carolyn C. ... Mendota, MN
Sachs, Caryn P. ... San Francisco, CA
Sachs, Charles H. ... Bayonne, NJ
Sachs, Christopher R. ... Waukegan, IL
Sachs, Coleman R.
Department of Transportation,
National Highway Traffic Safety
Administration, GV
Sachs, David ... New York, NY
Sachs, David E. ... Metuchen, NJ
Sachs, David H. ... Chicago, IL
Sachs, Delaney, Maretz & Zemetis
New Haven, CT
Sachs, Douglas A. ... Orlando, FL
Sachs & Drake ... Morton Grove, IL
Sachs, Edgar F. ... New York, NY
Sachs, Edward E. ... Santa Barbara, CA
Sachs, Elizabeth R. ... Washington, DC
Sachs, Elka ... Boston, MA
Sachs, Eric ... Bellmore, NY
Sachs, Eric D. ... Miami, FL
Sachs, Ernest P. ... Norwich, VT
Sachs, Franklin M. ... Newark, NJ
New York, NY
Sachs, Gary B. ... Carle Place, NY
Sachs, George M. ... Libertyville, IL
Sachs, Gerald M. ... Chicago, IL
Sachs, Gregory J. ... Branford, CT
Sachs & Hansen, L.L.C. ... Waynesville, MO
Sachs, Heidi L. ... Seattle, WA
Sachs, Herbert ... Bellmore, NY
Sachs, Herbert L. ... Union City, NJ
Sachs & Hess, P.C. ... Hammond, IN
Sachs, Howard B. ... Great Neck, NY
Sachs, Howard F. ... Kansas City, MO
Sachs, Hunington ... Seattle, WA
Sachs, Jack ... New York, NY
Sachs, Jane C. ... St. Joseph, MO
Sachs, Jane E. ... New York, NY
Sachs, Jeffrey H. ... Denver, CO
Sachs, Jeffrey M. ... North Haven, CT
Sachs, Jeffrey M. ... Burlington, MA
Sachs, Jeffrey W. ... Aurora, IL
Sachs, Jeffry A. ... Norfolk, VA
Sachs, Jennifer Franco ... Chelsea, MA
Sachs, Jennifer L. ... Stamford, CT
Sachs, Jeremy ... Fort Wayne, IN
Sachs, Joel ... Los Angeles, CA
Sachs, Joel H. ... Rye, NY
White Plains, NY
Sachs, John F. ... San Luis Obispo, CA
Sachs, John F., A Professional Law Corporation
San Luis Obispo, CA
Sachs, John L. ... Washington, DC
Sachs, John R., Jr. ... New York, NY
Sachs, Jonathan E. ... Newark, NJ
Sachs, Jonathan M. ... Boston, MA
Sachs, Joshua ... Chicago, IL
Sachs, Joshua ... Morton Grove, IL
Sachs, Joshua M. ... Newark, NJ
Sachs, Kalman A. ... New Haven, CT
Sachs, Kamhi & Kushner, P.C.
Carle Place, NY
Sachs, Keith L. ... Boston, MA
Sachs, Lawrence B. ... East Brunswick, NJ
Sachs, Lawrence E. ... Pittsburgh, PA
Sachs, Lee H. ... Cincinnati, OH
Sachs, Lee N. ... Towson, MD
Sachs, Leonard B. ... Norfolk, VA
Sachs, Leonard W. ... Peoria, IL
Sachs, Lester G., Law Offices
San Jose, CA
Sachs, Lisa Kimberly ... New York, NY
Sachs, Maitlin, Fleming, Greene, Wilson &
Marotte ... Morristown, NJ
Newark, NJ
Paterson, NJ
West Orange, NJ
Sachs, Marc I. ... Tampa, FL
Sachs, Maria L. ... New York, NY
Sachs, Maria Lorts ... Boca Raton, FL
Sachs, Marshall L. ... Watsonville, CA
Sachs, Martin ... Robbinsville, NJ
Sachs, Martin H. ... Department of Justice,
Washington, D.C. District Office, GV
Sachs, Marvin A. ... West Orange, NJ
Sachs, Mel A. ... New York, NY
Sachs, Michael A. ... San Bernardino, CA
Sachs, Michael B. ... San Diego, CA
Sachs, Michael B. ... Chicago, IL
Sachs, Michael C. ... Chicago, IL
Sachs, Michael J. ... Santa Ana, CA
Sachs, Michael M., (Professional Corporation)
Encino, CA
Sachs, Michael S. ... New Windsor, NY
Sachs, Ned R. ... New York, NY
Sachs, Olivia J., Mrs. ... New Rochelle, NY
Sachs, Patricia S. ... New York, NY
Sachs, Peter A. ... West Palm Beach, FL
Sachs, Peter S. ... Boca Raton, FL
Sachs, Peter W. ... Holmdel, NJ
Sachs, Philip Heller ... Baltimore, MD
Sachs, Philip M. ... Santa Cruz, CA
Sachs, Phillip B. ... St. Louis, MO
Sachs, Ralph Gordon ... Troy, MI
Sachs, Rebecca Levy ... Newark, NJ
Sachs, Richard A. ... Fort Lauderdale, FL
Sachs, Richard A., Jr. ... Mequon, WI
Sachs, Richard F. ... Golden Valley, MN
Sachs, Richard J. ... San Diego, CA
Sachs, Robert A. ... Sea Girt, NJ
Sachs, Robert H. ... Louisville, KY
Sachs, Robert K. ... Cincinnati, OH
Sachs, Robert L., Jr. ... Philadelphia, PA
Sachs, Robert R. ... Palo Alto, CA
Sachs, Roger M. ... New York, NY
Sachs, Russell M. ... New York, NY
Sachs, Samuel L. ... East Windsor, NJ
Sachs, Sax & Klein, P.A. ... Boca Raton, FL
Sachs, Sheila K. ... Baltimore, MD
Sachs, Sidney S. ... Chevy Chase, MD
Sachs, Spector, Glasser & Waxman, P.C.
New York, NY
Sachs, Stacey Beth ... Falls Church, VA
Sachs, Stephen B. ... Jackson, NJ
Sachs, Stephen H. ... Washington, DC
Sachs, Susan ... Fairfax, VA
Sachs, Susan D. ... Northampton, MA
Sachs, Susan Valerie ... Washington, DC
Sachs, Tana Rori ... Fort Lauderdale, FL
Sachs, Teresa Ficken ... Philadelphia, PA
Sachs, Terry L. ... Danbury, CT
Sachs, Theodore ... Detroit, MI
Sachs, Valerie Gentile ... Cleveland, OH
Sachs, Waldman, O'Hare, Helveston, Bogas &
McIntosh, P.C. ... Detroit, MI
Flint, MI
Lansing, MI
Pontiac, MI
Sachs, Wayne ... Los Angeles, CA
Sachs & Werdine, P.A. ... Tampa, FL
Sachs, William R. ... Waynesville, MO
Sachse, Douglas T. ... Towson, MD
Sachse, Harry R. ... Washington, DC
Sachse, James & Lopardo ... Fallbrook, CA
Sachse, Jeffrey E. ... Chicago, IL
Sachse, Kimberly L. ... Pittsburgh, PA
Sachse, Mark J. ... Kansas City, KS
Sachse, Robert G. ... Tulsa, OK
Sachse, Thomas H. ... Ottawa, KS
Sachse, Victor A., III ... Baton Rouge, LA
Sachse, William R., Jr. ... Milwaukee, WI
Sachsel, Allen Huberth ... Fairfax, VA
Sachs-Hyman, Robin L. ... Miami, FL
Sachter, Margaret Hardy ... New York, NY
Sachtjen, Peter D. ... Wake Forest, NC
Sachtleben, Cynthia B. ... St. Louis, MO
Sachtleben, Earl H. ... Red Bud, IL
Sachtleben, Scott A. ... Belleville, IL
St. Louis, MO
Sachtleben-Green, Sue ... Wood River, IL
Sacilotto, Kara M. ... Washington, DC
Sacino Bertolino & Hallissy, A Professional
Corporation ... Sacramento, CA
Sacino, Christine ... San Francisco, CA
Sacino, D. F. ... Glendale, CA
Sacramento, CA
Sacirbey, Muhamed ... Staten Island, NY
Sack, Alan M. ... Syosset, NY
Sack & Associates, P.C. ... McLean, VA
Sack, Barry D. ... Hudson, NY
Sack, Bernard ... Laguna Hills, CA
Sack, Dana ... Oakland, CA
Sack, David J. ... New York, NY
Sack, Diane L. ... New York, NY
Sack, Edward J. ... New York, NY
Sack, Emily J. ... New York, NY
Sack, Gary B. ... Palm Bay, FL
Sack, Gerald S. ... West Hartford, CT
Sack, Henry ... Encino, CA
Sack, Irwin S. ... Woodmere, NY
Sack, James M. ... McLean, VA
Sack, Jane M. ... Oakbrook Terrace, IL
Sack, Jennifer B. ... New York, NY
Sack, Jonathan S. ... Brooklyn, NY
Sack, Jonathan Scott ... New York, NY
Sack, Joseph A. ... New York, NY
Sack, Judith M. ... Encino, CA
Sack, Laura ... New York, NY
Sack, Margaret P. ... Portland, ME
Sack, Mark J. ... Cleveland Heights, OH
Sack, Martin, Jr. ... Jacksonville, FL
Sack, Miller and Rosendin, LLP
Oakland, CA
San Francisco, CA
Sack, Nathaniel ... Chicago, IL
Sack, Nelson J. ... Media, PA
Sack, Nelson J., P.C. ... Media, PA
Sack, Peter J. ... New York, NY
Sack, Polly Grunfeld ... Cleveland, OH
Sack, Rebecca A. ... Miami, FL
Sack, Robert ... Morro Bay, CA
Sack, Robert ... New York, NY
Sack, Robert D. ... New York, NY
Sack & Sack ... New York, NY
Sack, Saul J. ... Coral Gables, FL
Sack, Spector & Karsten, LLP
West Hartford, CT
Sack, Steven J. ... Boston, MA
Sack, Steven Mitchell ... New York, NY
Sack, Sylvan H. ... Baltimore, MD
Sack, Sylvan H., P.A. ... Baltimore, MD
Sack, William D. ... Franklin, MA
Sacker, John E., Jr. ... Atlanta, GA
Sackerman, Pamela J. ... New York, NY
Sacket, James ... Schoharie, NY
Sackett, Barry Shaw ... St. Paul, MN
Sackett, Bruce A. ... Glendale, CA
Sackett, Christine A. ... Rochester, NY
Sackett, Christopher R. ... Des Moines, IA
Sackett, Elizabeth C. ... Boston, MA
Sackett, G. Robert ... Perry, IA
Sackett, Gary G. ... Salt Lake City, UT
Sackett, Gary L. ... Mount Pleasant, MI
Sackett, Harry E., Jr. ... Hacienda Heights, CA
Sackett, Henry M., III ... Lynchburg, VA
Sackett, Howard A. ... Hilton Head Island, SC
Sackett, Jennifer J. ... Wheaton, IL
Sackett, Jody V. ... Rumson, NJ
Sackett, Mark H. ... Basalt, CO
Sackett, Peter A. ... Cleveland, OH
Sackett, Peter Campbell ... Lynchburg, VA
Sackett, Richard A. ... San Diego, CA

Sackett, Robert W. ....**Milford, IA**
Sackett, Robert W. ....**Spencer, IA**
Sackett, Rosemary Shaw ....Okoboji, IA
Sackett, Schuyler W. ....Boston, MA
Sackett, Shelley A.
Greenwood Village, CO
Sackey, Larry A. ....Claremont, CA
Sackheim, Andrew F. ....**Sacramento, CA**
Sackheim, Gilbert M. ....Boulder, CO
Sackheim, Michael S. ....**New York, NY**
Sackin, Erwin R. ....Overland Park, KS
Sackin, Eugene M. ....Kansas City, MO
Sackl, Darrell L. ....Los Angeles, CA
Sackler, Arthur B. ....**Washington, DC**
Sackler, Craig A. ....Fort Lauderdale, FL
Sackler, Seymour S. ....Maynard, MA
Sackman, J. David ....Los Angeles, CA
Sackman, Julie I. ....Los Angeles, CA
Sackman, Kenneth J. ....Los Angeles, CA
Sackman, Steven W. ....Englewood, CO
Sackmann, Jeremy P. ....**Chicago, IL**
Sackmann, John P. ....Warrenville, IL
Sackmann Law Office ....Othello, WA
Sackmann, Milton P. ....Ritzville, WA
Sackmann, Pamela J. ....New York, NY
Sackmann, Steven H. ....Othello, WA
Sackmann, Thomas F. ....Spokane, WA
Sackmann, William A. ....Findlay, OH
Sackmary, Risa I. ....**New York, NY**
Sackrider, Gary S. ....Salem, MA
Sackrider, Gregg R. ....Chicago, IL
Sackrin, Alan D. ....Hallandale Beach, FL
Sackrin, Cindy D. ....Hallandale Beach, FL
Sacks, Alan D. ....**New York, NY**
Sacks, Albrecht, Copeland, Herzog & Sacks
Kankakee, IL
Sacks, Alexander ....Bay Shore, NY
Sacks, Allan
Federal Communications Commission,
Office of the General Counsel, GV
Sacks, Andrew B. ....Hoffman Estates, IL
Round Rock, TX
Sacks, Andrew B. ....**Philadelphia, PA**
Sacks, Andrew M. ....**Norfolk, VA**
Sacks & Associates ....White Plains, NY
Sacks & Associates ....Houston, TX
Sacks, Avram L. ....Riverwoods, IL
Sacks, Barbara B. ....Hartford, CT
Sacks, Barbara M. ....St. Louis, MO
Sacks, Barry H. ....**San Francisco, CA**
Sacks, Belinda Jeri Mason ....Calabasas, CA
Sacks, Bernard L. ....**New York, NY**
Sacks, Bernard R. ....Lynnfield, MA
Sacks, Bernstein & Greenspan
Garden City, NY
Sacks, Brad R. ....White Plains, NY
Sacks, Bradley A. ....New York, NY
Sacks, Carol S. ....Forest Hills, NY
Sacks & Chapin, P.C. ....**Washington, DC**
Sacks, David A. ....**Washington, DC**
Sacks, David A. ....**Atlantic City, NJ**
Sacks, David B. ....Jacksonville, FL
Sacks, David G. ....Springfield, MA
Sacks, David J. ....Houston, TX
Sacks, Deborah A. ....Mamaroneck, NY
Sacks, Debra G. ....Holliston, MA
Sacks, Diana L. ....Harrisburg, PA
Sacks, Diane ....**Scottsdale, AZ**
Sacks, Edward ....New York, NY
Sacks, Edward M. ....Brighton, MA
Sacks, Edward S. ....Wynnewood, PA
Sacks, Eric A. ....**Chicago, IL**
Sacks, Eric D. ....**New York, NY**
Sacks, Frank ....Baltimore, MD
Sacks, Gary T. ....**St. Louis, MO**
Sacks, Gordon W. ....Buffalo, NY
Sacks, Harley M. ....**Northampton, MA**
Sacks, Harry P. ....**New York, NY**
Sacks, Howard D. ....San Diego, CA
San Pedro, CA
Sacks, Howard R. ....Hartford, CT
Sacks, Ira S. ....**New York, NY**
Sacks, Ivan A. ....**New York, NY**
Sacks, Jack ....**Boca Raton, FL**
Sacks, Jack, Dr., P.A., Law Office of
Boca Raton, FL
Sacks, Jaqueline L. ....Cambridge, MA
Sacks, Jay B. ....San Diego, CA
Sacks, Jeanne L. ....**Cumming, GA**
Sacks, Jeffrey W. ....**Boston, MA**
Sacks, Jeremy D. ....**Portland, OR**
Sacks, Joel D. ....Manzanita, OR
Sacks, Joshua ....**Atlanta, GA**
Columbus, GA
Sacks, Judy A. ....**Kankakee, IL**
Sacks, Judy Bruckner ....Woodmere, NY
Sacks, Katharine B. ....**Bridgeport, CT**
Hartford, CT
Sacks, Kenneth ....Council Bluffs, IA
Sacks, Kenneth N. ....**New York, NY**
Sacks & Kolken ....Buffalo, NY
Sacks, Laura A. ....New York, NY
Sacks, Lauren ....New York, NY
Sacks, Lawrence J. ....**New York, NY**
Sacks, Lee ....Santa Monica, CA
Sacks, Leonard A. ....**Washington, DC**
Sacks, Leonard F. ....**Kankakee, IL**
Sacks, Leonard M. ....Granada Hills, CA
Sacks, Lester ....Floral Park, NY
Sacks, Linda Susan ....Westbury, NY
Sacks, Lois R. ....Rockville, MD
Sacks, Luanne ....**San Francisco, CA**
Sacks, Marcus B. ....Oceanside, CA
Sacks & Margulies, P.C. ....Rockville, MD
Sacks, Mark A. ....Santa Ana, CA
Sacks, Marleen L. ....**Pleasanton, CA**
Sacks, Marvin, (Ltd.) ....Chicago, IL
Sacks, Mason J. ....**Los Gatos, CA**
Sacks, Mason J., Inc., A Prof. Law Corp.
Los Gatos, CA
San Jose, CA
Sacks, Melvyn Douglas ....Los Angeles, CA
Sacks, Michael ....Bryn Mawr, PA
Sacks, Michael B. ....Parsippany, NJ
Sacks, Michael J. ....Chicago, IL
Sacks, Michael Joseph ....Venice, CA
Sacks, Michael Wm. ....**Washington, DC**
Sacks, Milton ....Philadelphia, PA
Sacks, Monika Holzer, (Ms.)
Ann Arbor, MI
Sacks, Montgomery, Pastore & Levine, P.C.
Westport, CT
Sacks Montgomery, P.C. ....**New York, NY**
Sacks, Morton A. ....**Baltimore, MD**
Sacks, Murray D. ....**Washington, DC**
Sacks, Myra W. ....Harrisburg, PA
Sacks, N. Scott ....Department of Justice,
Antitrust Division, GV
Sacks, Paul R. ....Bala Cynwyd, PA
Sacks, Peter W. ....Boston, MA
Sacks, Rand Evan ....Washington, DC
Sacks, Renee ....New York, NY
Sacks, Richard A. ....Dallas, TX
Sacks, Richard B. ....Poughkeepsie, NY
Sacks, Rivera & Zolonz ....**Beverly Hills, CA**
Culver City, CA
Los Angeles, CA
Rancho Cucamonga, CA
Santa Monica, CA
Torrance, CA
Sacks, Robert A. ....**Los Angeles, CA**
Sacks, Robert A. ....Portland, OR
Sacks, Robert L. ....New York, NY
Sacks, Robert N. ....**Los Angeles, CA**
Sacks, Robert N. ....**Chicago, IL**
Sacks, Rudolph B., Jr. ....Santa Fe, NM
Sacks, Russell A. ....Window Rock, AZ
Sacks, Ruth E. ....New York, NY
Sacks & Sacks, A Professional Corporation
Hampton, VA
Norfolk, VA
Portsmouth, VA
Virginia Beach, VA
Sacks, Samuel ....Beverly Hills, CA
Sacks, Selig D. ....**New York, NY**
Sacks, Seymour ....Phoenix, AZ
Scottsdale, AZ
Sacks & Smith, L.L.C. ....**New Orleans, LA**
Sacks, Spencer Paul ....San Francisco, CA
Sacks, Stanley ....**Boston, MA**
Sacks, Stanley E. ....**Norfolk, VA**
Sacks, Stefan Eric ....Los Angeles, CA
Sacks, Stephen Andrew ....New York, NY
Sacks, Stephen M. ....**Washington, DC**
Sacks, Steven B. ....**San Francisco, CA**
Sacks, Steven J.
Department of Housing and Urban
Development,
Office of General Counsel, GV
Sacks, Stewart J. ....Chesapeake, VA
Sacks, Stuart ....Bronx, NY
Sacks, Stuart S. ....**Harrisburg, PA**
Sacks, Susan Brickerd ....Highland Park, IL
Sacks Tierney P.A. ....Phoenix, AZ
Scottsdale, AZ
Sacks, Warren S. ....White Plains, NY
Sacks, Weston, Smolinsky & Albert
Philadelphia, PA
Sacks, William ....New York, NY
Sacks, Zachary H., (P.C.)
Culver City, CA
Sacks & Zweig, A Professional Corporation
Santa Monica, CA
Sacksteder, Elizabeth M. ....New York, NY
Sacksteder, Michael J. ....**Palo Alto, CA**
Sackstein, Ellen ....Garden City, NY
Sackstein, Eric A. ....Port Jefferson, NY
Sackstein, Harvey A. ....Garden City, NY
Sackstein, Mark H. ....Garden City, NY
Sackstein, Sackstein and Sackstein
Garden City, NY
Sacks-Wilner, James E. ....Trenton, NJ
Sacks-Wilner, Joan L., Law Offices of
Lawrenceville, NJ
Sacks-Wilner, Steven L. ....Skillman, NJ
Sacman, Marcial Eugenio
San Bernardino, CA
Sacoff, Robert W. ....**Chicago, IL**
Sacoman, James R. ....Omaha, NE
Sacon, Jennifer P. ....Chicago, IL
Sacopulos, Gus ....**Terre Haute, IN**
Sacopulos, Johnson, Carter & Sacopulos
Terre Haute, IN
Sacopulos, Michael J. ....**Terre Haute, IN**
Sacopulos, Peter J. ....**Terre Haute, IN**
Sacorafas, Nick ....Encinitas, CA
SáCouto, Susana L. ....Washington, DC
Sacra, Constance H. ....Tucson, AZ
Sacra, J. Ryan ....**Tulsa, OK**
Sacramone, Frank, Jr. ....Orange, CT
Sacripanti, Peter J. ....**New York, NY**
Saczawa, Matthew P. ....Scottsdale, AZ
Sada, Gary E. ....Mount Laguna, CA
Sadacca, Stephen S. ....Dallas, TX
Sadacca, Todd Adam ....Miami, FL
Sadagopan, Usha ....**Pittsburgh, PA**
Sadaka, Thomas A. ....Orlando, FL
Sadaoka, Robert R. ....**Honolulu, HI**
Sadauskas, Renée M. ....Granville, OH
Sadayasu, Chris J. ....**Honolulu, HI**
Sadberry, Anthony J. ....**Houston, TX**
Sadd, George J. ....Cleveland, OH
Sadd, James N. ....**Atlanta, GA**
Sadd, Mark A. ....**Charleston, WV**
Sadd, Steven S. ....Los Angeles, CA
Sadd, William W. ....Round Hill, VA
Sadden, Mohummed ....South Sioux City, NE
Saddler, Bryan P.
Department of Housing and Urban
Development,
Office of the Inspector General, GV
Saddler, H. McConnell ....Elyria, OH
Saddler, Obie, Jr. ....**Waterloo, IA**
Sade, David A. ....Charleston, WV
Sade, Norman G. ....**Short Hills, NJ**
New York, NY
Sadecky, Layden C. ....Beaver, PA
Sadeghi, Farnaz ....**Boston, MA**
Sadeghi, Leila ....**Costa Mesa, CA**
Sadeghi, Reza ....San Bernardino, CA
Sadeghian, Christopher K. ....Palo Alto, CA
Sadeghian, Holly H. ....**Washington, DC**
Sadeghi-Nejad, Fatemeh ....**New York, NY**
Sadeghi-Nejad, Fati ....New York, NY
Sadek, William ....Derby, CT
Saden, George A. ....Bridgeport, CT
Sader & Albertine, P.A. ....Fort Lauderdale, FL
Sader, Elisa D. ....Chicago, IL
Sader & Garvin LLC ....**Kansas City, MO**
Sader, Laura E. ....**Ann Arbor, MI**
Sader, Neil S. ....**Kansas City, MO**
Sader, Robert L. ....Fort Lauderdale, FL
Sader, Robert M. ....Reno, NV
Sadewater, Brent E. ....Chicago, IL
Sadicario, Steven ....New York, NY
Sadick, Craig S. ....Washington, DC
Sadick, David J. ....Seattle, WA
Sadick, J. L., P.C. ....Houston, TX
Sadick, J. L. ....Houston, TX
Sadick, Mary Heim ....Stafford, VA
Sadigh, James K. ....Beverly Hills, CA
Sadighian, Joseph A. ....Midlothian, VA
Sadighpour, Kourosh ....Beverly Hills, CA
Sadik-Khan, Janette ....Washington, DC
Sadilek, Dennis ....Burr Ridge, IL
Sadin, Arthur ....**Friendswood, TX**
Sadin, Shelley R. ....**Bridgeport, CT**
Sadin, Stephen C. ....**Chicago, IL**
Sadinsky, Lisa A. ....East Rochester, NY
Sadinsky, Susan H. ....Buffalo, NY
Sadis & Goldberg LLC ....**New York, NY**
Sadis, Jack M. ....**New York, NY**
Sadjadi, Shirley ....Elgin, IL
Sadlak, Charlotte A. ....St. Paul, MN
Sadlek, Lawrence A., Jr. ....Mount Carmel, IL
Sadler, Alex E. ....Department of Justice,
Tax Division, GV
Sadler & Associates, P.C. ....Atlanta, GA
Sadler, Benjamin ....Torrance, CA
Sadler, Benjamin L., III ....**Columbia, SC**
Sadler, Bruce P. ....Windsor, CA
Sadler, Carole P. ....New York, NY
Sadler, Christopher ....Denver, CO
Sadler, Constance A. ....**Washington, DC**
Sadler, Derry D. ....Denver, CO
Sadler, Elizabeth Utsey ....**Tuscaloosa, AL**
Sadler, Gareth W. ....San Francisco, CA
Sadler, Gary Leonard ....Old Hickory, TN
Sadler, H. Brenner ....**Alexandria, LA**
Sadler, Henry L., III ....Norfolk, VA
Sadler, J. Pat ....Atlanta, GA
Sadler, James F. ....Dallas, TX
Sadler, James L. ....**Modesto, CA**
Sadler, James P. ....**Dallas, TX**
Sadler, Jeffrey H. ....**Tacoma, WA**
Sadler, John M. ....**Williamsburg, VA**
Sadler, Judith Batson ....**Houston, TX**
Sadler, Karen Tall ....**Modesto, CA**
Sadler, Kevin M. ....**Austin, TX**
Sadler, Lance R. ....Spokane, WA
Sadler, Leon Y., IV ....**Tuscaloosa, AL**
Sadler, Lisa L. ....Columbus, OH
Sadler, Lloyd W. ....Salt Lake City, UT
Sadler, Louise T. ....Tallahassee, FL
Sadler, Luther F., Jr. ....**Jacksonville, FL**
Sadler, L. Y., Jr. ....Camden, AL
Sadler, Martin R. ....**Houston, TX**
Sadler, Nancy D. ....Beaufort, SC
Sadler, Patricia Lynn ....Baltimore, MD
Sadler, Paul L. ....**Henderson, TX**
Sadler, R. Russell ....Ellicott City, MD
Sadler, Ranson & Bordis
Ocean Springs, MS
Sadler, Richard L. ....**Portland, OR**
Sadler, Richard T. ....Pepper Pike, OH
Sadler, Robert M. ....Department of Commerce,
Office of the General Counsel, GV
Sadler, Rodger A. ....**Chicago, IL**
Sadler, Roger A. ....**New York, NY**
Sadler, Stephen T. ....Boston, MA
Sadler, Stuart R. ....Wintergreen, VA
Sadler, Sullivan & Sharp, P.C.
Birmingham, AL
Sadler, Susan J. ....**Bloomfield Hills, MI**
Sadler & Swan ....Norfolk, VA
Sadler, Thomas C. ....**Los Angeles, CA**
Sadler, Thomas C., Jr. ....**Allentown, PA**
Sadler, Thomas W. ....Chicago, IL
Sadler, Timothy ....**Washington, DC**
Sadler, Walter R. ....**Los Angeles, CA**
Sadler, William J. ....Lewisburg, WV
Princeton, WV
Sadler, William L. ....Los Angeles, CA
Sadlo, Henry B. ....Louisville, KY
Sadlo, Timothy S. (Todd) ....Portland, OR
Sadlock, Richard A. ....Harrisburg, PA
Sadlon, Holly J. ....**Los Angeles, CA**
Sadlowski, Dennis A. ....New York, NY
Sadlowski, Jeffrey R. ....**Cleveland, OH**
Sado, Diane L. ....Kingshill, St. Thomas, VI
Sado, John J. ....Department of Transportation,
Surface Transportation Board, GV
Sadock, James, Jr. ....Boca Raton, FL
Sadoff, B.J. ....**Arlington, VA**
Sadoff, David ....Department of Justice,
Civil Division, GV
Sadoff, David A.
Central Intelligence Agency,
Office of the General Counsel, GV
Sadoff, Harold ....Minneapolis, MN
Sadoff, Michael B. ....**Chicago, IL**
Sadoff, Richard Alan ....Covington, KY
Sadoff, Ronald B. ....Milwaukee, WI
Sadofski, Joseph E. ....New Brunswick, NJ
Sadoskas, Gail G. ....Corpus Christi, TX
Sadosuk, Kimberly A. ....Fairfax, VA
Sadoun, Kathy Kranitz ....St. Joseph, MO
Sadow, Eric S. ....Charlotte, NC
Sadow, Helen ....New York, NY
Sadow, Joseph ....New York, NY
Sadow, Mark D. ....**St. Louis, MO**
Sadow, Michael S., (P.C.)
Washington, DC
Sadow, Richard ....Miami, FL
Sadow, Sharon ....New York, NY
Sadow, Steven H. ....**Atlanta, GA**
Sadow, Steven H., P.C. ....**Atlanta, GA**
Sadow, Susan J. ....Atlanta, GA
Sadowitz, March ....**Boston, MA**
Sadowski, Anthony ....**Itasca, IL**
Sadowski, Daniel J. ....Anoka, MN
Sadowski, Donald L., Jr. ....Schaumburg, IL
Sadowski, Donald L., P.C. ....Schaumburg, IL
Sadowski, Elizabeth A. ....Rochester, MI
Sadowski, Francis W. ....Chicopee, MA
Sadowski, James D. ....**Washington, DC**
Sadowski, Jatha B. ....Jefferson City, MO
Sadowski, Jeffrey A. ....**Bloomfield Hills, MI**
Sadowski, Joseph J. ....Endicott, NY
Sadowski, L. Marcene ....Edmonds, WA
Sadowski, Marilyn E. ....Hackensack, NJ
Sadowski, Mark V. ....Mahwah, NJ
Sadowski, Mary Anne ....Northport, NY
Sadowski, Peter T. ....Santa Barbara, CA
St. Louis, MO
Sadowski, Richard H. ....Norwood, MA
Sadowski, Robert A. ....Kew Gardens, NY
Sadowski, Robert W. ....New York, NY
Sadowski, Ronald W. ....Oak Brook, IL
Sadowski, Stephen M. ....**Sylvania, OH**
Sadowsky, Donald A.
Environmental Protection Agency,
Office of the General Counsel, GV
Sadowsky, Edward ....New York, NY
Sadowsky, Edward L. ....**New York, NY**
Sadowsky, Gersten ....Silver Spring, MD
Sadowsky, Richard L. ....New York, NY
Sadowsky, Shelley ....**Washington, DC**
Sadowsky, Stephen B. ....**Los Angeles, CA**
Sadowsky, Timothy A. ....**Bowman, ND**
Sadowsky and Wild, Law Offices, P.C.
Bowman, ND
Sadr, Kasra ....San Diego, CA
Sadtler, Randolph W. ....Tavernier, FL
Sadugor, Irving ....Beachwood, OH
Sadur, Irving ....New York, NY
Sadur, Marvin P. ....Washington, DC
Sadur, Stanley S. ....San Francisco, CA
Sadwick, David B. ....**Los Angeles, CA**
Sadwin, Sue Matney ....Cherry Hill, NJ
Sadwith, John Alan ....Denver, CO
Sady, Stephen Reese ....Portland, OR
Saeed, Faiza J. ....**New York, NY**
Saef, Scott E. ....**Chicago, IL**
Saefke, Fred E., Jr. ....Bismarck, ND
Saeger, Susan L. ....San Antonio, TX
Saegert, Angenend & Augustine, P.C.
Austin, TX
Georgetown, TX
Saegert, Ann M. ....**Dallas, TX**
Saegert, Jerry C. ....**Austin, TX**
Saegh, Sheila ....**New York, NY**
Saeki, Rika ....**Chicago, IL**
Saeks, Allen I., (P.A.) ....**Minneapolis, MN**
Saeks, Jerrold N. ....Northbrook, IL
Saeli, Joseph F., Jr. ....Buffalo, NY
Saeli, Mary-Jo V. ....New York, NY
Saelinger, Gina M. ....**Cincinnati, OH**
Saelinger, Robert R. ....**Florence, KY**
Cincinnati, OH
Saeltzer, Douglas S. ....**San Francisco, CA**
Saeltzer, Eugene W. ....Sacramento, CA
Saenger, Gary P. ....Pine City, MN
Saenger, George W. ....**Asheville, NC**
Saenz, Alexandra Prentice ....Houston, TX
Saenz, Alfredo N., Jr. ....San Antonio, TX
Sáenz, Alvin N. ....Houston, TX
Saenz, Angel L. ....Las Cruces, NM
Saenz, Brenda I. ....Pontiac, MI
Saenz, Carla M. ....**Brownsville, TX**
McAllen, TX
Saenz, Ciria Sylvia ....San Antonio, TX
Saenz, David ....Edinburg, TX
Saenz, David R. ....San Francisco, CA
Saenz, E. Luis ....San Jose, CA
Saenz, Edgar A. ....**Los Angeles, CA**
Saenz, Gary D. ....San Bernardino, CA
Saenz, Gracie Guzman ....**Houston, TX**
Saenz, Graciela Lee ....Edinburg, TX
Saenz, Hector X. ....**San Antonio, TX**
Saenz, Jaime A. ....**Brownsville, TX**
Saenz, Kathleen T. ....**Los Angeles, CA**
Saenz, Martha ....Bethesda, MD
Saenz, Otila ....Abilene, TX
Saenz, Paul B. ....**Houston, TX**
Saenz, Paul C. ....**Laredo, TX**
Saenz, Pete, Jr. ....**Laredo, TX**
Saenz, Ralph ....Lawton, OK
Saenz, Thomas A. ....Los Angeles, CA
Saer, E. Harold, Jr. ....New Orleans, LA
Saer, Kevin F. ....**New York, NY**

Saetre, Gaylord A. ....Long Prairie, MN
Saetre, Gaylord A. ....Perham, MN
Saetre, Homer A. ....Moorhead, MN
Saetre, Warren A. ....Thief River Falls, MN
Saetta, Stacy Lee ....Soquel, CA
Saevig, Roger A. ....Santa Ana, CA
Saevitz, Daniel S. ....Needham, MA
Saewert, Ilse Masselink
Grand Rapids, MI
Saewitz, Michael L. ....Huntington, NY
Saez, Carolina M. ....Library of Congress, Copyright Office, GV
Saez, Ketty A. ....Boston, MA
Saez, León, Urdaneta, Calzadilla & Perez-Burelli ....Miami, FL
Sáez, Pedro P. ....Miami, FL
Saf, Ronald V. ....Des Moines, IA
Safa, Lamis Ali ....Myrtle Beach, SC
Safaie, Majid ....Los Angeles, CA
Safanda, Carl F. ....St. Charles, IL
Safanda Law Firm ....St. Charles, IL
Safanda, Roy A. ....St. Charles, IL
Safar, Jay ....New York, NY
Safar, Joseph C. ....Pittsburgh, PA
Safarian, Rose ....Fresno, CA
Safavi, Elizabeth Linville ....Winchester, KY
Safavian, David H. ....Alexandria, VA
Safavian, Jennifer M.
House of Representatives, Committee Legal Personnel, GV
Safdari, Yusuf H. ....Lake Forest, IL
Safechuck, Barbara Z. ....Santa Monica, CA
Safenowitz, Howard B. ....Burbank, CA
Safer, Adam J. ....New York, NY
Safer, David I. ....Miami, FL
Safer, David M. ....Oakland, CA
Safer, David R. ....New York, NY
Safer, Eliot J. ....Jacksonville, FL
Safer, Elissa J. ....Denver, CO
Safer, Fredrick J. ....Milwaukee, WI
Safer, Jay G. ....New York, NY
Safer, Jerome T. ....Milwaukee, WI
Safer & Lensky Law Firm ....Milwaukee, WI
Safer, Ronald S. ....Chicago, IL
Safer, Shelley J. ....Madison, WI
Saferstein, Harvey I. ....Los Angeles, CA
Saferstein, Jeffrey D. ....New York, NY
Saferstein, Melvin A. ....Sandusky, OH
Saff, Jeffrey M. ....Baltimore, MD
Saffa, Ronald J. ....Tulsa, OK
Saffan, Howard S. ....Manhasset, NY
Saffari, Karen Youree ....Wagoner, OK
Saffarian, Jayne L. ....Berkeley, CA
Saffell, J. Robert ....Versailles, KY
Saffell, James W. ....Boulder, CO
Saffell, James W. ....Denver, CO
Saffelle, Robert N. ....Richmond, VA
Saffels, Dale E. ....Topeka, KS
Saffer, Charles F.W. ....Charleston, WV
Saffer, David E. ....Louisville, KY
Saffer, Ian L. ....Denver, CO
Saffer, Jennifer L. ....New York, NY
Saffer, Judith M. ....New York, NY
Saffer, Martin V. ....Marlinton, WV
Saffer, Michael A. ....Roseland, NJ
Saffer, Michael D. ....New Haven, CT
Saffer, Sherry M. ....Los Angeles, CA
Saffer, Walter ....Otis, MA
Morristown, NJ
Saffern, David H. ....Washington, DC
Saffery, Edmund K. ....Honolulu, HI
Saffi, Joseph A. ....Danbury, CT
Saffian, James M. ....Portland, ME
Saffioti, Joseph M. ....Newburgh, NY
Saffir, Cynthia R. ....Los Angeles, CA
Saffner, Ronald ....New York, NY
Saffo, Anthony A. ....Wilmington, NC
Saffo, Paul L., III ....Menlo Park, CA
Saffold, Shirley Strickland ....Cleveland, OH
Safford, A. Thomas S. ....New York, NY
Safford, Beverly ....St. Clair Shores, MI
Safford, Carrie M. ....Washington, DC
Safford, Frederick B., Jr. ....Harbor City, CA
Safford, Howard I. ....Springfield, MA
Safford, Jerry F. ....Bowling Green, KY
Safford, John M. ....Manchester, NH
Safford, Kenneth W. ....St. Paul, MN
Safford & Lanphear ....Bowling Green, KY
Safford, Patricia ....Kentfield, CA
Safford, Ralph R. ....Bloomfield Hills, MI
Detroit, MI
Safford, Robert C. ....Los Angeles, CA
Safford, Scott ....Nashville, TN
Safford, West, Tornow & Jaeger
Chillicothe, IL
Peoria, IL
Saffouri, Hassan M. ....Minneapolis, MN
Saffouri, Hussein M. ....San Francisco, CA
Saffran, Dennis J. ....New York, NY
Saffran, Kenneth S. ....Jenkintown, PA
Saffren & Weinberg ....Jenkintown, PA
Saffron, Clifford R. ....New York, NY
Saffron, Ronald J. ....Blairsville, PA
Saffron, Samuel ....Clifton, NJ
Safi, Deborah Cavazos ....Houston, TX
Safi, Deborah Cavazos, A Prof. Corp., Law Offices of ....Houston, TX
Safi, George F. ....Houston, TX
Safi, S. Anthony ....El Paso, TX
Safian, Janet H. ....Department of Agriculture, Office of the General Counsel, GV
Safier, Kerry D. ....Boca Raton, FL
Safier, Richard M. ....Sugar Land, TX
Safier, Seth ....San Francisco, CA
Safine, Stuart A. ....Concord, CA
Safion, Stacy J. ....Newport Beach, CA
Safir, Alan P. ....New York, NY
Safir, Arthur S. ....Trenton, NJ
Safir, Benjamin ....San Francisco, CA
Safir, Peter O. ....Washington, DC
Safirstein, Peter G.A. ....New York, NY
Safko, Fred A. ....Van Nuys, CA
Safley, James R. ....Minneapolis, MN
Safley, Robin C. ....Tallahassee, FL
Safley, Thomas G. ....Indianapolis, IN
Safley, Wm. Michael ....Nashville, TN
Safon, Brad J. ....Torrance, CA
Safon, David Michael, (P.C.)
New York, NY
Safon, Todd L. ....Seattle, WA
Safora, Isabel R. ....Seattle, WA
Safos, Robert P. ....Warren, OH
Safran, Alan P. ....Malden, MA
Safran, Andrew N. ....Columbia, SC
Safran, Barbara J. ....Southfield, MI
Safran, Dana S. ....New York, NY
Safran, David S. ....McLean, VA
Safran, Edward B. ....New York, NY
Safran, Efrat ....New York, NY
Safran, Hubert M. ....Denver, CO
Safran, Jonathan S. ....Milwaukee, WI
Safran, Karen H. ....Novi, MI
Safran, Kenneth J., P.C. ....Howell, MI
Safran, Kenneth Jay ....Howell, MI
Safran, Lawrence ....New York, NY
Safran, Leslie C. ....Philadelphia, PA
Safran, Paul, Jr. ....Palm Beach, FL
Safran, Perry R. ....Raleigh, NC
Safran, Raymond ....Delray Beach, FL
Safranek, Richard J. ....Washington, DC
Safranek, Robert J. ....Limon, CO
Safranek, Stephen J. ....Chicago, IL
Safranko, Stephen A. ....Albany, NY
Safrath, Richard W., Jr. ....Hauppauge, NY
Safreed, Christopher G. ....Owensboro, KY
Safren, Ronald B. ....Milwaukee, WI
Safreno, D. Casey ....Pleasanton, CA
Safriet, Barbara J. ....New Haven, CT
Safrin, Allen ....Cranford, NJ
Safrin & Associates ....Indianapolis, IN
Safrin, Franklin A. ....Indianapolis, IN
Safrin, Ronald A. ....Indianapolis, IN
Safrin, Sabrina ....Department of State, Office of the Legal Adviser, GV
Safrit, Walter M., II ....Kannapolis, NC
Safro, Bella ....Lafayette, LA
New Orleans, LA
Beaumont, TX
Safro, Bruce L. ....Hackensack, NJ
Safro, LeRoy D. ....Union City, NJ
Safron, Elwood P. ....Punta Gorda, FL
Safron, Linda H. ....New York, NY
Safron, Robert M. ....New York, NY
Safronoff, Holly B. ....Detroit, MI
Saft, David ....Monterey Park, CA
Saft, Stephen J. ....Southport, CT
Saft, Stuart M. ....New York, NY
Saftig, Leslie Silva ....University Park, PA
Saftler, Laurence B., Law Offices of
New York, NY
Safty, Mark D. ....Denver, CO
Safwat, Adam G. ....Palo Alto, CA
Safyurtlu, John A. ....San Francisco, CA
Sagal, David Lewis ....Burbank, CA
Sagal, Lanny M. ....New York, NY
Sagal, Roger F. ....Denver, CO
Sagal, Stuart Lee ....Towson, MD
Sagalow, Teresa Burns ....New York, NY
Sagalow, Ty R ....New York, NY
Sagalyn, Jeffrey B. ....Chicopee, MA
Sagan, B. Adam ....Bensalem, PA
Sagan & Greenberg, P.C. ....Bensalem, PA
Sagan, Jean S. ....Anchorage, AK
Sagan, John R. ....Chicago, IL
Sagan, Kenneth R. ....Lexington, KY
Sagan, Mark A. ....Tinton Falls, NJ
Sagan, Michael P. ....Reston, VA
Sagan, Nicholas R. ....Lakewood, OH
Sagan, Paul P. ....Los Angeles, CA
Sagan, Rachel L. ....Irvine, CA
Saganich, John M. ....Cleveland, OH
Saganich, Suzanne K. ....Cleveland, OH
Sagapolutele, Aitofele T. ....Pago Pago, TT
Sagar, Alka Khosla ....Los Angeles, CA
Sagar, Barbara H. ....Wynnewood, PA
Sagar, Michael C. ....Laguna Beach, CA
Sagara, Kevin C. ....San Diego, CA
Sagardia Sanchez, Jorge ....San Juan, PR
Sagarin, J. Daniel ....Milford, CT
Sagartz, Andrew P. ....Chicago, IL
Cincinnati, OH
Sagaser, Franson & Jones, A Professional Corporation ....Fresno, CA
Sagaser, Howard A. ....Fresno, CA
Sagaser, John W. ....Augusta, ME
Sagaser, Teresa I. ....Margate, FL
Sagat, Kenneth A. ....New York, NY
Sagatelian, Marguerite ....New York, NY
Sagatelyan, Levon ....Foster City, CA
Sagawa, Shirley S. ....United States Senate, Committee Legal Personnel, GV
Sage, Al ....Ridgeland, MS
Sage, Andrea L. ....New York, NY
Sage, Arthur P. ....New York, NY
Sage, Brad Douglas ....New York, NY
Sage, Bruce J. ....Lake Orion, MI
Sage and Burks, P.C. ....Las Cruces, NM
Sage, C. Scott ....Ocean Shores, WA
Sage, Candace L. ....Indianapolis, IN
Sage, Charles A. ....Houston, TX
Sage, Charles E. ....West Lafayette, IN
Sage, Cynthia L. ....St. Petersburg, FL
Sage, David L. ....Louisville, KY
Sage, David W. ....Denver, CO
Sage, Dennis K. ....Wauwatosa, WI
Sage, Doyle L. ....Howard, SD
Sage, G. Patrick ....Kalamazoo, MI
Sage, Gerald Redmond ....Tampa, FL
Sage, Hugh ....Portland, OR
Sage, Jack D. ....Grand Rapids, MI
Sage, James A. ....Duluth, MN
Sage, John A. ....Fresno, CA
Sage, John H. ....Louisville, KY
Sage, Justin L. ....Indianapolis, IN
Sage, Larry G. ....Sparks, NV
Sage, Lyle P. ....Howard, SD
Sage, Malcolm ....New York, NY
Sage, Marcia ....Washington, DC
Sage, Michael J. ....New York, NY
Sage, Michael J. ....Hamilton, OH
Sage, Norman J. ....Tucson, AZ
Sage, Paul ....Carle Place, NY
Sage, Paul, P.C. ....Carle Place, NY
Sage, Paula Jan ....Shawnee, OK
Sage, Ray O. ....Las Cruces, NM
Sage, Richard D. ....Miami, FL
Sage, Robert E. ....Farmington, MI
Sage, Robert S. ....Woodland Hills, CA
Sage, Robin D. ....Longview, TX
Sage, Roger ....Madison, WI
Sage, Ronald W. ....Freehold, NJ
Sage, Ronald W., P.A. ....Freehold, NJ
Sage, Russell R. ....Charlotte, NC
Sage, S. Scott ....Phillipsburg, KS
Sage & Sage ....Howard, SD
Sage & Sage Law Offices ....Phillipsburg, KS
Sage, Stephen M. ....Ambler, PA
Sage, Stephen Nicholas ....St. Paul, MN
Sage, Stephen S. ....Phillipsburg, KS
Sage, Victoria M. ....Cleveland, OH
Sage, William B. ....Huntington Beach, CA
Sage, William M. ....New York, NY
Sage, Zona ....Oakland, CA
Sagebiel, Dennis H. ....Seguin, TX
Sagedy, Deborah C. ....Virginia Beach, VA
Sagel, Bruce ....Philadelphia, PA
Sagendorph, Samuel L. ....Blue Bell, PA
Sager, Adam J. ....Pottstown, PA
Sager, Audrey M. ....Forest Hills, NY
Sager, Barbara L. ....Dayton, OH
Sager, Bert ....Miami, FL
Sager, Carol L. ....Tucson, AZ
Sager, Daniel D. ....Riverside, CA
Sager, Daniel I. ....Pottstown, PA
Sager, David S. ....Morristown, NJ
Sager, Deborah J. ....Los Angeles, CA
Sager, Edmond S. ....Nederland, CO
Sager, Edward A. ....Berwyn, PA
Sager, Elizabeth A. ....Houston, TX
Sager, Frederick N., Jr. ....Atlanta, GA
Sager, Glenn E. ....Nashville, TN
Sager, Gregory W. ....Ukiah, CA
Sager & Hardt, P.C. ....Richmond, VA
Sager, Heather M. ....San Francisco, CA
Sager, James S. ....Rolling Meadows, IL
Sager, Jerome I. ....New York, NY
Sager, John F. ....Lansing, IL
Sager, John W. ....Cleveland, OH
Sager, Jonathan W. ....Syracuse, NY
Sager, Karen Goldberg ....Brooklyn, NY
Sager, Kelli L. ....Los Angeles, CA
Sager, Laura ....New York, NY
Sager, Laurence J. ....Marysville, CA
Sager, Lawrence S. ....Pottstown, PA
Sager, Leonard R. ....Palm Springs, CA
Sager, Linda L. ....San Diego, CA
Sager, Lorraine R. ....Ossipee, NH
Sager, Madeline D. ....Ukiah, CA
Sager, Marcel A. ....Brooklyn, NY
Sager, Margaret E.W. ....Philadelphia, PA
West Conshohocken, PA
Sager, Marilyn T. ....New York, NY
Sager, Marilynn ....Cambridge, MA
Sager, Melvin S. ....Encinitas, CA
Sager, Michelene T. ....Detroit, MI
Sager, Michelene T., P.C. ....Detroit, MI
Sager, Pamela H. ....Hopkinton, MA
Sager & Pavlick, S.C. ....Fond du Lac, WI
Sager, Rex E. ....Akron, OH
Sager, Richard D. ....Ossipee, NH
Sager, Roderick C. ....Fayetteville, NY
Sager, Rodney ....Richmond, VA
Sager & Sager ....Hopkinton, MA
Sager & Sager Associates ....Pottstown, PA
Reading, PA
West Chester, PA
Sager, Sally A. ....Charlotte, NC
Sager, Sally A. ....Charlotte, NC
Sager, Sheldon M. ....Cleveland, OH
Sager, Stanley C. ....Albuquerque, NM
Sager, Stephen M. ....Cincinnati, OH
Sager, Steven P. ....Fond du Lac, WI
Sager, Steven T. ....San Francisco, CA
Sager, Steven T. ....Hopkinton, MA
Sager, Thomas L. ....Wilmington, DE
Sagerholm, A. Denise
Fort Lauderdale, FL
Sagerman, Eric E. ....Los Angeles, CA
Sagers, Christopher L. ....Washington, DC
Sagers, John M. ....Cedar Rapids, IA
Sages, Patrick M. ....Florham Park, NJ
Saggau, Michael F. ....Detroit, MI
Saggese, Alfred E., Jr. ....Boston, MA
Saggese, Mary Ann Fuchs
Indianapolis, IN
Saggese, Nicholas P. ....Los Angeles, CA
Saggio, Charles ....Cedarburg, WI
Saggio, David R. ....Milwaukee, WI
Saggio, Joseph A. ....Westlake, OH
Saghatelian, Tommi R. ....Bakersfield, CA
Sagheb, S. Shane ....Encino, CA
Sagheb, Sohaila ....Woodland Hills, CA
Saginar, Edwin M. ....Norcross, GA
Saginario, Carmen, Jr. ....Trenton, NJ
Saginaw, Jane N. ....Dallas, TX
Saginaw, John Corr ....Santa Ana, CA
Saginaw, Robert B. ....Arlington, VA
Sagle, Tracy E. ....Fresno, CA
Saglimben, Michael J. ....Olean, NY
Saglio, Joan L. ....Plainville, CT
Saglioccolo, Gaetano ....Toledo, OH
Sagmeister, Laura M. ....San Francisco, CA
Sagnor, Art L., III ....West Chester, PA
Sago, Brett A. ....Raleigh, NC
Sago, James E. ....Fairmont, WV
Sagoff, Kendra H.
Environmental Protection Agency, Office of the General Counsel, GV
Sagona, Beau ....Metairie, LA
Sagona-Lynch, Marian ....York, ME
Concord, NH
Sagor, Elliot G. ....New York, NY
Sagoskin, Arthur R. ....Newtown, PA
Sagot, Jennings & Sigmond
Philadelphia, PA
Sagot, Leonard M. ....Jupiter, FL
Sagot, Neil ....Philadelphia, PA
Sagotsky, Samuel S. ....Freehold, NJ
Sagrillo Hammond & Dineen, LLC
Denver, CO
Sagrillo, Robert L. ....Denver, CO
Sagstuen, Warren R. ....Minneapolis, MN
Sagsveen, Murray G. ....Bismarck, ND
Saguil, Karla E. ....Washington, DC
Sagun, Stanley J., Jr. ....Columbus, OH
Sagurton, Edwin C. ....Rahway, NJ
Saguto, Leslie ....San Rafael, CA
Sagy, Rony ....San Francisco, CA
Saha, Matthew W. ....New York, NY
Saha, Sunil K. ....Providence, RI
Sahady, Entin & Entin, P.C. ....Fall River, MA
Sahady, Michael ....Fall River, MA
Sahady, Paul M. ....Fall River, MA
Sahagian, Mary Anne ....Chelmsford, MA
Sahagian, Neal H. ....Boston, MA
Sahagian, Phillip M. ....Thousand Oaks, CA
Sahagian, Richard G. ....Providence, RI
Sahagian, Susan L. ....Orlando, FL
Sahaj, Frank P. ....Westfield, NJ
Sahakian, Curtis E. ....Naperville, IL
Sahakian, James W. ....Cambridge, MA
Sahakian, Stephanie A. ....Sacramento, CA
Sahakian, Suzanne ....Detroit, MI
Saham, Scott H. ....San Diego, CA
Sahami, Malek M. ....McLean, VA
Sahami, Sohaila ....Santa Ana, CA
Sahandy, Sheida R. ....Miami, FL
Sahar, Nadim ....Madison, WI
Sahara, Ralph ....Honolulu, HI
Saharack, Paul T. ....Chicago, IL
Saharovich, Alex ....Memphis, TN
Sahatjian, Elizabeth R. ....Boston, MA
Sahatjian, Laurie Crick ....Washington, DC
Sahebjami, Dara ....Washington, DC
Saheed, Christopher ....Bourne, MA
Sahgal, Rohit ....Chicago, IL
Sahhar, John F. ....Vista, CA
Sahid, Joseph R. ....New York, NY
Sahin, Daniel F. ....Clarksburg, NJ
Sahin, Daniel F., P.C. ....Clarksburg, NJ
Sahkul, Sven J. ....Arlington, VA
Sahl, Daniel Michael ....Westport, CT
Sahl, Eric H. D. ....Denver, CO
Sahl, Nels T. ....St. Anthony, ID
Sahlaney, Michael W. ....Johnstown, PA
Sahlberg, John T. ....Boise, ID
Sahlfeld, Linden C. ....Cincinnati, OH
Sahli & Padovani ....Hammonton, NJ
Sahli, Richard C. ....Columbus, OH
Sahli, Ronald W. ....Hammonton, NJ
Sahlin, Russell Charles ....Santa Ana, CA
Sahlman, Scott A. ....Phoenix, AZ
Sahloff, Kurt W. ....Ottawa, OH
Sahlsten, Greg W. ....Orlando, FL
Sahlsten, Greg W., P.A. ....Orlando, FL
Sahlstrom, Craig ....Rockford, IL
Sahlstrom & Dugdale ....Eugene, OR
Sahlstrom, E. B. ....Eugene, OR
Sahm, Russell R. H. ....Amarillo, TX
Sahm, S. Cary ....Portland, OR
Sahn, Brian R. ....Melville, NY
Mineola, NY
Sahn, John G. ....Peoria, IL
Sahn, Michael H. ....Garden City, NY
Sahn, Michael, PLLC ....Garden City, NY
Sahn, Victor A. ....Los Angeles, CA
Sahner, Todd M. ....Livingston, NJ
Sahni, Gurvinder ....New York, NY
Sahota, Angela ....Indianapolis, IN
Sahovey, Paul J. ....Boston, MA
Sahr, David R. ....Washington, DC
Sahr, Evelyn D. ....Washington, DC
Sahr, Kunert & Tambornino
Minneapolis, MN
Sahr, R. Lawrence ....Hudson, OH
Sahr, Roger T. ....Minneapolis, MN
Sahradnik, John C. ....Toms River, NJ
Saia, Christopher Hahn ....Miami, FL
Saia, David ....Bryn Mawr, PA
Saia, Dominick Michael ....Boulder, CO
Saia, Doreen Unis ....Washington, DC
Albany, NY
Saia, Frank J. ....Baton Rouge, LA
Saia, Frank R. ....Springfield, MA
Saia, Joseph J. ....Peachtree City, GA
Saia, Meinken & Associates
Peachtree City, GA
Saia, Nancy W. ....Buffalo, NY
Saia, Stephen V. ....Boston, MA
Saia, Timothy K. ....Livingston, NJ
Saibeni, Theodore A. ....Glendale, CA
Saiber, Samuel S. ....Newark, NJ

Saiber Schlesinger Satz & Goldstein, LLC
Newark, NJ
Saibert, Frank J. .... **Chicago, IL**
Saichek, B. Shana .... **Seattle, WA**
Saichek, David A. .... **Milwaukee, WI**
Saichek & Hertel, S.C. .... **Milwaukee, WI**
Saichek, Lawrence A. .... Miami, FL
Said, Mark C. .... **Newport Beach, CA**
Said, Mary Staples .... Arlington, VA
Said, Naima M. .... Columbia, MD
Saida, Eric .... **Miami, FL**
Saidara, Frank .... **Los Angeles, CA**
Saide, Steven A. .... **New York, NY**
Saidel, Daniel H. .... Philadelphia, PA
Saidel, Jonathan .... **Philadelphia, PA**
Saidel, Joseph .... Albany, NY
Saidel, Marc L. .... Yorktown Heights, NY
Saidel, Scott F. .... Carefree, AZ
Saidel, Susan W. .... Camden, NJ
Saideman, Sanford .... New York, NY
Saidenberg, Lynn .... **New York, NY**
Saidi, Mohammad F. .... Largo, MD
Saidi, Rola .... **Dallas, TX**
Saidian, Susan G. .... Wichita, KS
Saidian, Susan Swayze .... Wichita, KS
Saidis, Robert C. .... Carlisle, PA
Saidis, Shuff & Masland .... Camp Hill, PA
Carlisle, PA
SAIDMAN DesignLaw Group
Washington, DC
Silver Spring, MD
Saidman, Gary K. .... **Atlanta, GA**
Saidman, Perry J. .... **Washington, DC**
Silver Spring, MD
Saied, Robert M. .... Lubbock, TX
Saied, William R. .... Oklahoma City, OK
Saieg, Julie .... **Jacksonville, FL**
Saielli, Roberta M. .... **Chicago, IL**
Saier, Frank P. .... **Gainesville, FL**
Saiers, K. Peter .... Stockton, CA
Saieva, Frances M. .... Brooklyn, NY
Saieva and Rousselle, P.A. .... **Tampa, FL**
Saieva, Thomas .... **Tampa, FL**
Saievetz, Meyer .... Chelsea, MA
Saiewitz, Arthur H. .... New York, NY
Saifee, Salim Kutub .... **Pittsburgh, PA**
Saifer, Michelle Oyler .... **Los Angeles, CA**
Saiger, Neil R. .... Syracuse, NY
Saigh, Jennifer Phipps .... Du Quoin, IL
Saijwani, Vinaya .... **Princeton, NJ**
Saiki, Curtis .... **Honolulu, HI**
Saiki, Eric H. .... **Los Angeles, CA**
Saikin, Linda K. .... **Houston, TX**
Saikley, Garrison & Colombo, Ltd.
Danville, IL
Saikley, Gilbert H. .... **Danville, IL**
Saile, George O., Jr. .... Poughkeepsie, NY
Saile, James J. .... Philadelphia, PA
Saile, John C., Jr. .... **Bridgewater, NJ**
Saile, Michael J. .... Langhorne, PA
Sailer, Camille Elizabeth .... Maple Glen, PA
Sailer, Dennis H. .... Whiting, NJ
Sailer, Francis J. .... **Washington, DC**
Sailer, Henry P. .... Washington, DC
Sailer, Jacqueline .... **New York, NY**
Sailer, John R. .... Queen Anne, MD
Sailer, Randolph C., II .... Chicago, IL
Sailer, Robert O. .... **Redmond, WA**
Sailer, Rosemarie .... **New York, NY**
Sailer, Steven H. .... **Newtown, PA**
Sailer, Victoria .... Providence, RI
Sailer, William B. .... San Diego, CA
Sailers, Andre' D. .... Atlanta, GA
Sailing, Roberta L. .... **Springfield, MA**
Saillant, Kimberly M. .... **Boston, MA**
Sailon, Ronald .... Henderson, NV
Sailor, Peter T. .... Philadelphia, PA
Sailstad, Charles A. .... Toledo, OH
Saiman, Martin S. .... **New York, NY**
Saimre, Monika E. .... **Virginia Beach, VA**
Sain, Cynthia Michelle .... **Charlotte, NC**
Sain, Donald Lee, Jr. .... Charlotte, NC
Sain, Edward R. .... Toms River, NJ
Sain, Efrain .... **Dallas, TX**
Sain, George R. .... Reynoldsburg, OH
Sain, Kevin T. .... **Idabel, OK**
Sain, Robert M. .... Norris, TN
Sainburg, Robert P. .... Glendale, CA
Saindon, Elizabeth A. .... **Washington, DC**
Saindon, Elizabeth H. .... **Washington, DC**
Saindon, Gregory E. .... Ellis, KS
Saindon, Gregory E., P.A. .... Ellis, KS
Saindon, Kelly A. .... Chicago, IL
Saindon, Phillip, Sr. .... Nashville, TN
Saindon, Steven R. .... San Antonio, TX
Saine, Christian D. .... **Cleveland, OH**
Saine, David L. .... Bakersfield, CA
Saine, Jennifer L. .... **New York, NY**
Saines, Dorit .... Los Angeles, CA
Saines, Richard M. .... **Chicago, IL**
Saines, W. Gus .... **St. Clairsville, OH**
Wheeling, WV
Sai-Ngarm, Sukum .... Sacramento, CA
Sai-Ngarm, Sukum, P.C. .... Sacramento, CA
Saini, Tina K. .... **Philadelphia, PA**
Sainick & Coté .... Newport Beach, CA
Sainick, Frederick B. .... Newport Beach, CA
Sainsbury, Lori Anne .... Brighton, MA
Sainsbury, Patrick .... Seattle, WA
Sainsbury, Sterling B. .... Provo, UT
St. Amand, Michael D. .... **Atlanta, GA**
St. Amant, Alexis A., II .... Baton Rouge, LA
St. Amant, Joseph L. S. .... New Orleans, LA
St. Amant, Owen Bennett
New Orleans, LA
St. Amant, Penrose C. .... Gonzales, LA
St. Amant & St. Amant .... Gonzales, LA
St. Amant, Stephen J. .... Lansing, MI

St. Amour, Paul A. A. .... Boston, MA
St. Amour, Susan .... Berkeley, CA
St. Andre, John J., Jr. .... Framingham, MA
St. André, Michael J. .... **Boston, MA**
St. Angelo, Denise C. .... Carmel, CA
St. Angelo, Gregory J. .... New Orleans, LA
St. Angelo, Mark .... San Jose, CA
St. Antoine, Theodore J. .... Ann Arbor, MI
St. Arnauld, Gregory G. .... **Kalamazoo, MI**
St. Arnold, Jack R. .... **Dunedin, FL**
St. Arnold & Stearns, Chartered
Dunedin, FL
St. Bernard, Terry Rae .... Los Angeles, CA
Saint, Camilla R. .... Estes Park, CO
Saint & Carmichael, P.C. .... Bloomington, IL
Pekin, IL
St. Charles, Kean .... Rancho Mirage, CA
St. Charles, Michael N. .... **Chattanooga, TN**
St. Charles, Suanne C. .... **Boston, MA**
St. Charles, Wendy R.
West Palm Beach, FL
St.Clair, Amber .... Wichita, KS
St. clair, Amber Lee .... Wichita, KS
St. Clair, Barbara J. .... Dallas, TX
St. Clair, Basil S. .... Fort Worth, TX
St. Clair, Beverly J. .... **Toledo, OH**
St. Clair, Carol L. .... **Houston, TX**
St. Clair, Clifford M. .... Columbus, OH
St. Clair, David A. .... **Newport Beach, CA**
St. Clair, Donald D. .... Toledo, OH
St. Clair, Duncan R., III .... Norfolk, VA
St. Clair, Elizabeth .... New York, NY
St. Clair, Gilbert C. .... Boise, ID
St. Clair, Grace Greer
Hermosa Beach, CA
St. Clair, Gregory J. .... **New York, NY**
St. Clair, Greschler & Woodford, P.C.
Boulder, CO
St. Clair, Hal K. .... Clifton Forge, VA
Lexington, VA
St. Clair, J. Gregory .... **Chicago, IL**
St. Clair, J. Wm. .... **Huntington, WV**
St. Clair, Jack F. .... Springfield, MA
St. Clair, James D., (P.C.) .... **Boston, MA**
St. Clair, James E. .... Colchester, CT
St. Clair, James P. .... **Virginia Beach, VA**
St. Clair, James W. .... **Huntington, WV**
St. Clair, Jay D. .... **Birmingham, AL**
St. Clair, John A. .... **Denver, CO**
St. Clair, John D. .... San Francisco, CA
St. Clair, John F. .... Springfield, MA
St. Clair, John G. .... **Idaho Falls, ID**
St. Clair and Levine .... **Charleston, WV**
Huntington, WV
St. Clair, Margaret N. .... Wellesley, MA
St. Clair & Markey .... Fort Worth, TX
St. Clair, McFetridge, Griffin & Legernes, A Professional Corporation
San Francisco, CA
St. Clair, Michael L. .... East Brunswick, NJ
St. Clair & Miller, P.C. .... Norfolk, VA
St. Clair, Richard P. .... **Santa Monica, CA**
St. Clair, Richard T., (Chartered)
Idaho Falls, ID
St. Clair, Robert B. .... Columbus, OH
St. Clair, Robert D. .... Martinsville, IN
St. Clair, Robert J. .... Tucson, AZ
St. Clair, Robert W. .... **Lubbock, TX**
St. Clair, Scott A. .... Boulder, CO
St. Clair, Shawn P. .... **Austin, TX**
St. Clair, Talmage H. .... Indianapolis, IN
St. Clair, Timothy D. .... **Columbia, SC**
St. Clair & Wilson .... Clifton Forge, VA
Lexington, VA
St. Claire, Diane D. .... Grand Rapids, MI
St. Claire, Frank A., (P.C.) .... **Dallas, TX**
St. Clare, Francine .... New York, NY
St. Cyr, Gregory V. .... Dedham, MA
St. Cyr, John F. .... Orleans, MA
St. Denis, Donald W. .... **Jacksonville, FL**
St. Denis, Michael J. .... **Los Angeles, CA**
St. Denis, Richard A. .... Boulder, CO
St. Denis, Susan M. .... **Los Angeles, CA**
St. Dizier, Paul .... Baton Rouge, LA
Saint, Gale W. .... Bloomington, IL
St. George, M. Jeffrey .... Coral Gables, FL
St. George, Matthew C., Jr. .... San Pedro, CA
St. George, Melinda Lee .... Santee, CA
St. George, Michael E. .... Tempe, AZ
St. George, Michael E., P.C., Law Offices of
Tempe, AZ
St. George, Nicholas J. .... Newport News, VA
St. George, Robert J. .... Rochester, NY
St. George & Tejera .... Coral Gables, FL
St. George, William R. .... San Diego, CA
St. Germain, Constance Ann .... Fairfax, VA
St. Germain, Tonia P. .... Bloomington, IN
St. Helaire, Theresa A. .... Bennington, VT
St. Hilaire, Brian D. .... Glen Ellyn, IL
St. Hilaire, Gerald E. .... Boston, MA
St. Hilaire, Ricardo A. .... Laconia, NH
St. Hilaire, Sheila B. .... Worcester, MA
St. Hilaire, Stephen V. .... Newark, NJ
St. Hill & Associates, P.C.
Philadelphia, PA
St. Hill, Jennifer W. .... **Philadelphia, PA**
St Jacques, Deborah M. .... Sarasota, FL
St. Jacques, Michele M. .... Albany, NY
St. Jacques, Robert G. .... **Cincinnati, OH**
St. James, Bonnie .... San Francisco, CA
St. James, Brian R. .... **St. Louis, MO**
St. James, Brion L. .... Sacramento, CA
St. James, Dana J. .... Maynard, MA
St. James & Dougal .... Florence, MA
St. James, Kim Marie .... West Palm Beach, FL
St. James, Michael .... **San Francisco, CA**
San Jose, CA
St. James, Michelle R. .... Malden, MA

St. James, William .... Florence, MA
St. Jean, Deborah .... **Washington, DC**
St. Jeanos, Christopher J. .... **New York, NY**
St. Jeanos, John C. .... **New York, NY**
St. Joan, Jacqueline .... Denver, CO
St. John, Bowling & Lawrence
Charlottesville, VA
St. John, Christine C. .... **New Orleans, LA**
St. John, Christopher .... Augusta, ME
St. John, Christopher J. .... Greenville, PA
St. John & Curtin, L.L.C. .... **Rochester, NY**
St. John, David .... **West Palm Beach, FL**
St. John, David A. .... Santa Barbara, CA
St. John, Dicker, Caplan, Krivok & Core, P.A. .... **Boca Raton, FL**
Stuart, FL
West Palm Beach, FL
St. John, Edmund R., III .... Adams, MA
St. John, Edmund R., Jr. .... Adams, MA
St. John, Eric M. .... Long Beach, CA
St. John, Finis E., IV .... **Cullman, AL**
St. John, Francis X. .... Trenton, NJ
St. John, Frank W. .... Meriden, CT
St. John, Gaynor L. .... **Cullman, AL**
St. John, George R. .... **Charlottesville, VA**
St. John, Gerard J. .... **Philadelphia, PA**
St. John, Gregory G. .... **Waterbury, CT**
St. John, Gregory, III .... **Miami, FL**
St. John, Gregory J. .... Chicago, IL
St. John, Hayden B. .... Topeka, KS
St. John, Heather .... **New York, NY**
St. John, Howard C., and Associates
Kingston, NY
St. John, J. Berry, Jr. .... **New Orleans, LA**
St. John, J. Delene .... Oceanside, CA
St. John, J. Warren .... Fort Worth, TX
St. John, James B., III .... **Washington, DC**
St. John, Jerome M. .... **New York, NY**
St. John, John .... San Francisco, CA
St. John, John R. .... **Torrance, CA**
St. John, Juliet G. .... **Cullman, AL**
St. John, Kane .... Marietta, GA
St. John, Kathleen J. .... **Cleveland, OH**
St. John, Keith Christopher .... Albany, NY
St. John Law Office .... San Francisco, CA
St. John, Leon, III .... West Palm Beach, FL
St. John, Mary C. .... **Pasadena, CA**
St. John, Michael E. .... San Antonio, TX
St. John, Newton D., Jr. .... Chatsworth, GA
St. John, Orson L. .... **Greenwich, CT**
St. John, Pamela J. .... **San Antonio, TX**
St. John, Pamela R. .... Pawtucket, RI
St. John, Park & Scott .... **Greenwich, CT**
St. John, Peggy Dean .... **Alexandria, LA**
St. John, Richard A. .... Santa Maria, CA
St. John, Richard C. .... **Los Angeles, CA**
St. John, Richard J. .... **Spokane, WA**
St. John, Robert M. .... **Albuquerque, NM**
St. John, Ronald R. .... **Los Angeles, CA**
St. John & St. John, L.L.C. .... **Cullman, AL**
Decatur, AL
St. John, Scappini, Lombard & Stevens
Waterbury, CT
St. John, Stephanie Roberts .... Victorville, CA
St. John, Stephen C. .... Chesapeake, VA
St. John, Terrence P. .... **New York, NY**
St. John, Thomas F. .... **Trumbull, CT**
St. John, Thomas W. .... **Milwaukee, WI**
St. John, Thomas W., Jr.
Birmingham, AL
St. John, Wallace, Brennan & Folan LLP
Los Angeles, CA
Torrance, CA
St. John & Wayne, L.L.C. .... **Newark, NJ**
New York, NY
St. John, Wendy .... **San Diego, CA**
St. John, William J., Jr. .... Waterbury, CT
St. John-Zegel, Cynthia .... Los Angeles, CA
St. Julian, Andrea R. .... San Diego, CA
St. Julien, Mtumishi .... New Orleans, LA
St. Landau, Norman .... Princeton, NJ
St. Landau, Norman, P.C. .... Princeton, NJ
St. Laurent, Ann .... **Washington, DC**
St. Lawrence, Franklin R. .... Chicago, IL
St. Lawrence, George F. .... Lehigh Acres, FL
St. Ledger-Roty, Judith .... **Washington, DC**
St. Leger, Michael Gerard .... Syracuse, NY
St. Leger, Robert E. .... Rocky River, OH
Saint, Lerinda R. .... **Winston-Salem, NC**
St. Lifer, Elizabeth A. .... **New York, NY**
St. Louis, David J. .... Fresno, CA
St. Louis, David J., Inc., A Professional Corporation .... Fresno, CA
St. Louis, Gary M. .... Portland, OR
St. Louis, Joseph P., P.L.L.C. .... **Nogales, AZ**
St. Louis, Joseph P., P.L.L.C. .... **Tucson, AZ**
St. Louis & Martinez, P.A.
Coral Gables, FL
Miami, FL
St. Louis, Roland R., Jr.
Coral Gables, FL
St. Marie, Paul R. .... **Elyria, OH**
St. Marie, Ronald M. .... **Los Angeles, CA**
St. Marie, St. Marie & Couch Co., L.P.A.
Elyria, OH
St. Marie, Scott D. .... **New York, NY**
St. Marie, Thomas A. .... **Elyria, OH**
St. Martin, Andrée M. .... **Washington, DC**
St. Martin, Christopher J. .... **Houma, LA**
St. Martin, James R. .... Gate City, VA
St. Martin, Louis J. .... Houma, LA
St. Martin, Mahoney & Associates, A Professional Law Corporation .... Houma, LA
St. Martin, Michael X. .... **Houma, LA**
St. Martin, Steven P. .... **Houma, LA**
St. Martin, Victor C. .... San Rafael, CA
St. Martin & Williams, A Professional Law Corporation .... **Houma, LA**

St. Mary, Michele T. .... **Washington, DC**
St. Mary, Randall L. .... Everett, WA
St. Omer, Denise .... Kansas City, MO
St. Onge, Anita M. .... Cape Elizabeth, ME
St. Onge, Edward F. .... **Providence, RI**
St. Onge, Eric M. .... **Lansing, MI**
St. Onge, Joseph E. .... **Scarsdale, NY**
St. Onge, Kathleen A. .... **Hartford, CT**
St.Onge, Kevin M. .... Westfield, NJ
St. Onge, Ronald J. .... **New Haven, CT**
Stamford, CT
St. Onge Steward Johnston & Reens, LLC
Bridgeport, CT
Danbury, CT
Fairfield, CT
Greenwich, CT
Hartford, CT
New Haven, CT
Norwalk, CT
Stamford, CT
New York, NY
St. Onge, Walter J., III .... **Boston, MA**
St. Onge, William H. .... **Putnam, CT**
St. Ores, Sheryl A. .... Milwaukee, WI
St. Ours, Gerard D. .... Baltimore, MD
St. Ours, Gregory T. .... **Harrisonburg, VA**
St. Paul, Alexandra .... Bradenton, FL
St. Pé, Kenneth D. .... Lafayette, LA
St. Pe, Philippi P. .... Metairie, LA
St. Peter, David A. .... San Bernardino, CA
St. Peter, Don C. .... Missoula, MT
St. Peter, George M. .... **Fond du Lac, WI**
St. Peter, John A. .... **Fond du Lac, WI**
St. Peter Law Group, The .... **Alameda, CA**
St. Peter Law Group, The
San Francisco, CA
St. Peter Law Offices, P.A.
Minneapolis, MN
St. Peter, Linda Osorio .... Missoula, MT
St. Peter, Mary
Environmental Protection Agency, Office of Enforcement and Compliance Assurance, GV
St. Peter, Michael .... **San Francisco, CA**
St. Peter, Nicholas M. .... **Winfield, KS**
St. Peter, Patricia .... **Minneapolis, MN**
St. Peter, Peter L. .... **Minneapolis, MN**
St. Peter & Warren, P.C. .... Missoula, MT
St. Peter-Griffith, Ann M. .... **Augusta, ME**
St. Peters, Robert B. .... Alton, IL
St. Phillip, Peter D., Jr. .... **White Plains, NY**
St. Pierre, Catherine S. .... **Baton Rouge, LA**
St. Pierre, Duane .... Chicago, IL
St. Pierre, Emile R. .... Destrehan, LA
St. Pierre, Kraig Stephen .... Los Angeles, CA
St. Pierre, Michael A. .... **Warwick, RI**
St. Pierre, Michelle M. .... **Denver, CO**
St. Pierre, Robt. A. .... Manchester, NH
St. Pierre, Roderick A. .... Shrewsbury, MA
St. Pierre, Suzanne .... **New York, NY**
St. Pierre, Thomas G. .... **Columbus, OH**
St. Pierre-Kumar, Jeanine M.
Los Angeles, CA
St. Raymond, Perry F. .... **New Orleans, LA**
Saint, Robert E. .... Indianapolis, IN
St. Romain, Clare M. .... Metairie, LA
St. Romain, Jude .... Galliano, LA
St. Romain, Phillip W. .... Lake Charles, LA
St. Sauver, Barbara .... Wailuku, HI
St. Sauver, Beverly K. .... Eugene, OR
St. Sauveur, Jeffrey A. .... Providence, RI
St. Sauveur, Kimberly A. .... Boston, MA
St. Thomas, Suzanne S. .... Salem, OR
St. Ville, Thomas J. .... **Baltimore, MD**
St. Vincent, Roger L. .... **Washington, DC**
St. Vincent Vogl, Kathryn .... Charlotte, NC
St. Vrain, Robert D. .... St. Louis, MO
St. Yves, Kenneth R. .... Aberdeen, WA
Saint-Amand, Thompson & Brown, P.A.
Gaffney, SC
Saint Andre, Barbara J. .... **Boston, MA**
Saint-Antoine, Paul Hewit
Philadelphia, PA
Saint-Antoine, Susan M. .... **Philadelphia, PA**
Saint-Aubin Chartered, A Professional Law Corporation .... **Reno, NV**
Saint-Aubin, Robert F. .... **Reno, NV**
Saint Clair, J. Wesley .... Seattle, WA
Sainten, Kim V. .... Mountain View, CA
Saint-Evans, Angus .... Orland, CA
Saintil, Diane Helene .... Rockville, MD
Saint James, Patricia A. .... **Boston, MA**
Saint-Louis, Layn M. .... **Washington, DC**
Saint-Louis, Rudolph A.
Department of Transportation, Surface Transportation Board, GV
Saint Martin, Manuel L. .... Los Angeles, CA
Saint-Paul, Nancy .... Galveston, TX
Saints, Sheldon S. .... Wilmington, DE
Saintsing, Byron L. .... **Raleigh, NC**
Saintsing, George W. .... Thomasville, NC
Saintsing, James R. .... **Greensboro, NC**
Saint-Veltri, Joseph .... Denver, CO
Sainz, Marco A., Jr. .... Miami, FL
Sainz, Raymond R. .... Westminster, CO
Saiontz, Donald S. .... Baltimore, MD
Saiontz & Kirk, P.A. .... Baltimore, MD
Sais, Julianne .... Wellington, FL
Sais, Yvette Janine .... Farmington, NM
Saison, Tania M. .... **New York, NY**
Sait, Mohammed F. .... Washington, DC
Saiter, Mark R. .... **Dallas, TX**
Saiter Connolly, Cynthia .... **Austin, TX**
Saitlin, Sheldon I. .... Chicago, IL
Saito, Billy M. .... Kansas City, MO
Saito, Dennis K. .... Honolulu, HI
Saito, Jacquilyn E. .... Lake Oswego, OR
Saito, Janice Hee .... Honolulu, HI

Sale, Hillary A. .... Iowa City, IA
Sale, James P. .... Atlanta, GA
Sale, Jerret E. .... Seattle, WA
Sale, John G. .... Grand Rapids, MI
Sale, Jon A. .... Fort Lauderdale, FL
Miami, FL
Sale, Kelly McIntosh .... Panama City, FL
Sale & Kuehne, P.A. .... Fort Lauderdale, FL
Miami, FL
Sale, Llewellyn, III .... St. Louis, MO
Sale, Nell Graham .... Wilmington, DE
Sale, Robert .... Hempstead, NY
Sale, Robert D. .... Panama City, FL
Sale, Stephen .... Washington, DC
Washington, DC
Sale, Thomas, Jr. .... Panama City, FL
Saleeby & Cox, P.A. .... Florence, SC
Hartsville, SC
Saleeby, Dudley, Jr. .... Florence, SC
Saleeby, Edward E. .... Florence, SC
Hartsville, SC
Saleeby, Edward E., Jr. .... Florence, SC
Hartsville, SC
Saleeby, Emmette J. .... Spartanburg, SC
Saleeby, James M. .... Florence, SC
Saleeby, James M., Jr. .... Florence, SC
Saleeby, Nadim .... Miami, FL
Saleeby & Ransier, P.A. .... Palm Beach, FL
Saleeby, Reinette .... St. Louis, MO
Saleem, Omar .... Myrtle Beach, SC
Saleh, Alex N. .... Detroit, MI
Saleh, Anis N. .... Miami, FL
Saleh, David J. .... Batavia, NY
Saleh, John .... Lamesa, TX
Saleh, Joseph V. .... New York, NY
Saleh, Omar S. .... Houston, TX
Saleh, Sam .... Lamesa, TX
Saleh, Saraab A. .... Stamford, CT
Salehi, Dan .... Washington, DC
Salehi, Maria S. .... San Jose, CA
Salehi, Nader Hossain .... Washington, DC
Salehi, Susan J. .... Ventura, CA
Salehieh, Shawn S. .... San Francisco, CA
Salek, Ann E. .... Cleveland, OH
Salek, Elise H. .... Concord, NH
Salek, Frederick J. .... Ridgefield Park, NJ
Salek, Keith .... Lake Worth, FL
Salek, Sima R. .... Tarzana, CA
Salem, Albert, and Associates, P.A.
Tampa, FL
Salem, Albert M., III .... Tampa, FL
Salem, Albert M., Jr. .... Tampa, FL
Salem, Carol .... Salt Lake City, UT
Salem, D.L., Law Offices of .... San Diego, CA
Salem, Donald L. .... San Diego, CA
Salem, George R., (P.C.) .... Washington, DC
Salem, George T., Jr. .... Providence, RI
Salem, Irving .... New York, NY
Salem, Isaac .... New York, NY
Salem Law Offices .... Norman, OK
Salem, Linda Margolies .... Los Angeles, CA
Salem, Lucien S. .... San Francisco, CA
Salem, Marjorie N. .... Miami, FL
Salem, Michael J. .... Department of Justice,
Tax Division, GV
Salem, Micheal C. .... Norman, OK
Salem, Nadeem S. .... Toledo, OH
Salem, Nadia .... Park Ridge, IL
Salem, Richard J. (IBA) **........ Tampa, FL**
Salem, Richard P. .... Leicester, MA
Salem, Robert S. .... Toledo, OH
Salem, Saxon & Nielsen, Professional Association .... Orlando, FL
Tallahassee, FL
Tampa, FL
Salem, Stephen G. .... Long Beach, CA
Saleman, Michael N. .... Austin, TX
Saleme, Anthony J., Jr. .... St. Martinville, LA
Saleme, Pedro E. .... Lynn, MA
Salemi, Constance M.
Federal Trade Commission,
Bureau of Competition, GV
Salemi, Dominick J.
Department of Commerce,
Patent and Trademark Office, GV
Salemi, John .... Newark, NJ
Salemi, John B. .... Anchorage, AK
Salemme-Riccio, Cynthia M. .... Easton, CT
Salen, Abe G. .... Rancho Santa Margarita, CA
Salen, Elizabeth J. .... Brooklyn, NY
Salen, Roger L. .... Alexandria, VA
Salen, Susan Richards .... Vienna, VA
Salen, William O. .... Seattle, WA
Salend, Michael W. .... Las Vegas, NV
Salenfriend, Randy S. .... San Francisco, CA
Salenger, Marvin .... Commack, NY
Salenko, Bruce E. .... Sacramento, CA
Salenko, Cathy Deubel .... Sacramento, CA
Salens & Salens, P.C. .... Bad Axe, MI
Salens, Tami Woodworth .... Bad Axe, MI
Salens, Walter J. .... Bad Axe, MI
Salentine, David M. .... San Francisco, CA
Saler, Alan G. .... Los Angeles, CA
Saler, Anthony David
Commodity Futures Trading Commission,
Executive Staff, GV
Saler, H. B. .... Philadelphia, PA
Saler, Lawrence D. .... Calistoga, CA
Salera, Albert J. .... San Francisco, CA
Salerni, Lisa M. .... Simsbury, CT
Salerno, Alexander M. .... Berwyn, IL
Salerno, Anthony J. .... Chicago, IL
Salerno, Anthony M. .... Worcester, MA
Salerno, Barbara A. .... Reno, NV
Salerno, Charles A., Sr. .... Tallahassee, FL
Salerno & Dassoff .... Los Angeles, CA
Salerno, Dennis, & Assoc. .... Jersey City, NJ
Salerno, Dennis M. .... Jersey City, NJ
Salerno, Donna L. .... Newark, NJ
Salerno, Francis H. .... Bridgeport, CT
Salerno, George A. .... Norridge, IL
Salerno, George D. .... New York, NY
Salerno, Gerald R. .... Hackensack, NJ
Salerno, Heidi T. .... Oakland, CA
Salerno, James G. .... Fort Lauderdale, FL
Salerno, James J. .... New York, NY
Salerno, James J., Jr. .... Lexington, VA
Salerno, Jason E. .... Bloomington, IN
Salerno, John P. .... Huntington Station, NY
Salerno, Laure .... New York, NY
Salerno, Lauren Ruder .... St. Paul, MN
Salerno, Mark A. .... Brimfield, OH
Salerno, Nicholas B. .... San Diego, CA
Las Vegas, NV
Salerno, Paul R., Jr. .... Los Angeles, CA
Salerno, Peter C. .... New York, NY
Salerno, Ralph J. .... Roseland, NJ
Salerno, Robert A. .... Washington, DC
Salerno, Rocco V., Jr. .... Eastchester, NY
Salerno, Scott M. .... Rockford, IL
Salerno, Terrence J., (P.C.) .... Omaha, NE
Salerno, Thomas J. .... Phoenix, AZ
Salerno, Tricia N. .... Scottsdale, AZ
Salerno, Victor E., III .... New York, NY
Salerno, Victor M. .... Los Angeles, CA
Salerno, Vincent F. .... Mount Clemens, MI
Salerno, Vincent F., P.C.
Mount Clemens, MI
Sales, Bruce D. .... Tucson, AZ
Sales, Bruce H. .... Westfield, NJ
Sales, Charlene K. .... Northbrook, IL
Sales, David J. .... West Palm Beach, FL
Sales, Gary N. .... Canton, OH
Sales, Goodloe & Golden .... Atlanta, GA
Sales, Goodloe, Golden & Blakemore
Chicago, IL
Sales, James B. .... Houston, TX
Sales, James J. .... Indianapolis, IN
Sales, Jimmy R. .... Oklahoma City, OK
Sales, Joseph E. .... Somerville, NJ
Sales, Juanita B. .... Huntsville, AL
Sales, Kathleen M. .... Miami, FL
Sales, Kenneth L. .... Louisville, KY
Sales, Mark K. .... Dallas, TX
Sales, Michael .... Lubbock, TX
Sales, Michael W. .... El Segundo, CA
Sales, Michele M. .... Seattle, WA
Sales, Milton S. .... Rochester, NY
Sales, Norman B. .... Richmond, VA
Sales, Raymond A. .... Atlanta, GA
Sales, Raymond L. .... Louisville, KY
Sales, Raymond M. .... New York, NY
Sales, Ronald .... West Palm Beach, FL
Sales, Ronald, P.A. .... West Palm Beach, FL
Sales, Sassoon .... Los Angeles, CA
Sales, Sassoon, A Professional Corporation
Los Angeles, CA
Sales, Travis James .... Houston, TX
Sales, Walter Lapp .... Louisville, KY
Salese, Anthony .... Westport, CT
Salese, Armand .... Tucson, AZ
Salese, Canio J. .... Fishkill, NY
Salese & McCarthy, P.C. .... Tucson, AZ
Salesin, Dianne B. .... San Francisco, CA
Salesin, Jeremy Rothman .... San Rafael, CA
Salesin, Lowell D. .... Southfield, MI
Saleson, Stephan G. .... Riverside, CA
Saletta, John M. .... Chicago, IL
Saletta, John S. .... Franklin Park, IL
Saletta, Richard J. .... Boston, MA
Salewski, Richard W. .... Damariscotta, ME
Salfi, Dominick J. .... Altamonte Springs, FL
Salfi, Dominick J., P.A., Law Offices of
Altamonte Springs, FL
Orlando, FL
Salfrank, Linda J. .... Kansas City, MO
Salg, Heather A. .... Englewood, CO
Salgado & Associates .... Washington, DC
Salgado, Isabelle M. .... San Ramon, CA
Salgado, Jason T. .... Tampa, FL
Salgado, John .... Tampa, FL
Salgado, Luis F. .... Washington, DC
Salgado, Luis Fred .... Canovanas, PR
Salgado, Mario A. .... San Francisco, CA
Salgado, Pamela H. .... Seattle, WA
Salgado, R. Anthony .... Washington, DC
Salgado, Ralph F. .... Philadelphia, PA
Salgado, Richard P. .... Boulder, CO
Denver, CO
Salgado, Susana T. .... El Centro, CA
Salgado, Tanya A. .... Philadelphia, PA
Salgado, Vincent A.
National Aeronautics And Space
Administration,
Office of the General Counsel, GV
Salgado, William H. .... Jackson Heights, NY
Salgh, Jonathan W. .... Worley, ID
Salgo, Michael .... Westbury, NY
Salgo, Peter E. .... Brookline, MA
Salguero, Sally Ann .... Wichita, KS
Salhab, Joseph .... Houston, TX
Salhab, Melissa .... Austin, TX
Salhaney, Michael P. .... Pontiac, MI
Salhanick, Beverly .... Las Vegas, NV
Salhanick, Beverly, A Professional Corporation .... Las Vegas, NV
Salhanick, Brenda Crane .... Dallas, TX
Salhus, Jennifer E.
Department of Transportation,
National Highway Traffic Safety
Administration, GV
Salhus, Knute J. .... New York, NY
Salhus, Victoria D. .... Bethpage, NY
Saliba, Andrew Jason .... Marietta, GA
Saliba & Company, P.C. .... Wytheville, VA
Saliba, Dale C. .... Arlington, VA
Saliba, David G. .... Boston, MA
Saliba, David J. .... Boston, MA
Saliba, David S. .... Wytheville, VA
Saliba, Franklin A. .... Montgomery, AL
Saliba, George M. .... Valdosta, GA
Saliba, Michael G. .... Long Beach, CA
Saliba, Raja N. .... Washington, DC
Saliba, Richard J. .... Vero Beach, FL
Saliba, Rita S. .... Portland, ME
Saliba, Robert G. .... Morristown, NJ
Saliba & Saliba .... Boston, MA
Saliba, William H. .... Mobile, AL
Salibello, Salvatore .... Morristown, NJ
Salibello, Salvatore, A Professional Corporation
Morristown, NJ
Salibra, Lawrence A., II
Mayfield Heights, OH
Salica, William J. .... Sherman Oaks, CA
Salichs, Helen A. .... San Juan, PR
Salichs Pou, Juan C. .... San Juan, PR
Salierno, John V. .... Middle Village, NY
Saligman-Stein, Gale .... Philadelphia, PA
Salii, Carlos H. .... Koror, TT
Salik, Jacob P. .... White Plains, NY
Salim, Abdullah .... Beltsville, MD
Salim, Abdullah, P.C. .... Beltsville, MD
Salim, Edward N. .... Cleveland, OH
Salim, Frederick E. .... Flint, MI
Salim, Hollander, Esper & Nolfi
Cleveland, OH
Salim, Michael D. .... Dallas, TX
Salim, Sheikh .... New York, NY
Salim, William G., Jr.
Fort Lauderdale, FL
Saliman, Andrew A. .... Pueblo, CO
Saliman, Brian L. .... Washington, DC
Saliman, Lisa A. .... San Francisco, CA
Saliman, Mark Enger .... Denver, CO
Saliman, S. Gerald .... New York, NY
Salimando, Scott J. .... Smithtown, NY
Salimbene, Franklyn P. .... Boston, MA
Salimbene, John M. .... Columbus, OH
Salimi, Wasim B. .... New York, NY
Salin, Janis B. .... Los Angeles, CA
Salin, William N. .... Fort Wayne, IN
Salina, Martin L. .... Spokane, WA
Salina, Sanger & Gauper .... Spokane, WA
Salinardi, Michele L. .... New York, NY
Salinas, Arturo T. .... Los Angeles, CA
Salinas, E. D. .... Laredo, TX
Salinas, Felix E. .... Houston, TX
Salinas, Gregory B. .... Austin, TX
Salinas, Janice Roybal .... Austin, TX
Salinas, Javier G. .... Houston, TX
Salinas, Marco A. .... Eagle Pass, TX
Salinas, Michael R. .... San Antonio, TX
Salinas, Octavio, II .... Laredo, TX
Salinas, Paula J. .... Austin, TX
Salinas, Raúl F. .... Los Angeles, CA
Salinas, Richard S. .... Fresno, CA
Salinas, Sandra I. .... Newport Beach, CA
Salinas, Santiago .... Fort Worth, TX
Salinas, Sharon A. .... Chicago, IL
Salinas, Vada A. .... Dallas, TX
Salinas, Vilsen .... Fort Worth, TX
Salinas, Vincent A. .... Cincinnati, OH
Salinas Ender, Elma T. .... Laredo, TX
Salinas-Gonzalez, Yvonne .... Laredo, TX
Saline, Matthew A. .... Camden, NJ
Saling, Alison T. .... Morristown, NJ
Saling, Daniel R. .... San Marcos, CA
Saling, John A. .... West Chester, PA
Saling & Litvin .... West Chester, PA
Salinger, Ann J. .... Cincinnati, OH
Salinger, Daniel I. .... Elk Grove, CA
Salinger, Deborah Falk .... Troy, MI
Salinger, Debra R. .... Chicago, IL
Salinger, Jana O. .... Houston, TX
Salinger, Jeffrey L. .... Boston, MA
Salinger, Kenneth W. .... Boston, MA
Salinger, Lillian D. .... Santa Monica, CA
Salinger, Lynne K. .... New York, NY
Salinger, Robert M. .... Stevens Point, WI
Salinger, Ronald D. .... Staten Island, NY
Salinger, Stephen M. .... Washington, DC
Salinger, Thomas S., (P.C.)
Costa Mesa, CA
Salinitro, Barbara .... Bronx, NY
Salins, Mary Josephine
Treasury Department, GV
Salins, Sidney .... San Diego, CA
Salins, Stuart M. .... Chicago, IL
Salinsky, David J. .... Webster, TX
Salinsky, Robert A. .... Los Angeles, CA
Salis, Adam R. .... Costa Mesa, CA
Salis & Lefari .... New York, NY
Salis, Marc I. .... New York, NY
Salis, Monica I., (P.A.)
Fort Lauderdale, FL
Salisbury, Anne B. .... Raleigh, NC
Salisbury, Anne W. .... New York, NY
Salisbury, Barry K. .... Frederick, MD
Salisbury, Carl A. .... Clark, NJ
Salisbury, Daryle .... Novi, MI
Salisbury, David E. .... Salt Lake City, UT
Salisbury, David W. .... Cleveland, OH
Salisbury, Debra M. .... Sarasota, FL
Salisbury, Debra M., P.A., Law Office of
Sarasota, FL
Salisbury, Don R. .... Santa Ana, CA
Salisbury, Elizabeth W. .... Lakewood, OH
Salisbury, Erwin A. .... Sun City Center, FL
Salisbury, Eugene W. .... Buffalo, NY
Salisbury, George A. .... Cleveland, OH
Salisbury, Gordon James .... Santa Cruz, CA
Salisbury, Harold W. .... Tulsa, OK
Salisbury, Howard G., Jr.
Charleston, WV
Salisbury, J. Alexander .... Charlotte, NC
Salisbury, Jeffrey L. .... Rockford, IL
Salisbury, Jeffrey S. .... Eugene, OR
Salisbury, Jennifer .... Dallas, TX
Salisbury, John G.
Department of Transportation,
Maritime Administration, GV
Salisbury, John P. .... Clatskanie, OR
Salisbury, Kenneth R. .... Sacramento, CA
Salisbury, Kevin .... Marietta, GA
Salisbury, Kevin M. .... Morristown, NJ
Salisbury, Kimberly L.
Charlotte Amalie, St. Thomas, VI
Salisbury, Lawrence J. .... San Diego, CA
Salisbury, Lee W. .... Pasadena, CA
Salisbury, Linda .... Chicago, IL
Salisbury, Lisa G. .... Newport Beach, CA
Salisbury, Lois .... San Francisco, CA
Salisbury, Mark A. .... Beaver, OH
Salisbury, Mason D. .... Charleston, SC
Salisbury & McLister .... Frederick, MD
Salisbury, Michael J. .... Hillsboro, OR
Salisbury & Olsen .... Clatskanie, OR
Salisbury, Patrick P. .... New York, NY
Salisbury, Paul M. .... Westlake Village, CA
Salisbury, R. Keith .... Poughkeepsie, NY
Salisbury, Richard E. .... Orlando, FL
Salisbury, Robert D. .... Santa Ana, CA
Salisbury, Robert L. .... Portland, OR
Salisbury & Ryan LLP .... New York, NY
Salisbury, S. Ann .... Santa Ana, CA
Salisbury, Stephen R. .... Raleigh, NC
Salisbury, Susan D. .... Rosemead, CA
Salisbury, Terry B.
St. Petersburg Beach, FL
Salisbury, Thomas Eugene .... Tonkawa, OK
Salisbury, Tod P. .... Frederick, MD
Salisbury, Tracy L. .... San Francisco, CA
Salisbury, William J. .... Boston, MA
Salisbury, Wm. Craig .... West Palm Beach, FL
Salisch, Victoria J. .... Fresno, CA
Salisian, Myron H. .... Pasadena, CA
Salit, Gary S. .... Skokie, IL
Salit, Lauren C. .... New York, NY
Salit, Scott L. .... Metuchen, NJ
Salita, Allan P. .... Minneapolis, MN
Salita, Brian R. .... Minneapolis, MN
Salita, Matthew L. .... Chicago, IL
Salita, Wayne J. .... Minnetonka, MN
Salitan, Victor .... Spencerport, NY
Saliterman, Gail J. .... San Francisco, CA
Saliterman, Richard A. .... Minneapolis, MN
Saliterman & Siefferman, P.C.
Minneapolis, MN
Salitrero, Hector E. .... Tustin, CA
Salituro, Joseph .... Kenosha, WI
Salivar, David C. .... St. Louis, MO
Salivar & Harms .... St. Louis, MO
Salivia Janer, Emilio .... San Juan, PR
Saliwanchik, David Roman
Gainesville, FL
Saliwanchik, Lloyd & Saliwanchik
Gainesville, FL
Orlando, FL
Hamilton, MT
Salk, Bruce A. .... Northbrook, IL
Salk, Howard A. .... Barrington, IL
Salk, James A. .... Ithaca, NY
Salka, Fern Topas .... Los Angeles, CA
Salkeld, Mark W. .... Oak Brook, IL
Wheaton, IL
Salkeld, Pamela G. .... New York, NY
Salken, Barbara C. .... White Plains, NY
Salker, Kelly Kay .... Sioux City, IA
Salkield, G. Lawrence .... Seattle, WA
Salkin, Avram .... Beverly Hills, CA
Salkin, Barry L. .... New York, NY
Salkin, Gerald B. .... Manchester Center, VT
Salkin, James S. .... Baltimore, MD
Salkin, Jeanette M. .... Sacramento, CA
Salkin, Mark Jay .... Culver City, CA
Salkin, Patricia E. .... Albany, NY
Salkin, Philip .... Lansdale, PA
Salkin, Richard E. .... Hackensack, NJ
Salkin & Shockett, P.A. .... Baltimore, MD
Salkin, Sidney .... Sarasota, FL
Salkin, Sonya L. .... Gainesville, FL
Plantation, FL
Salko, Heather A. .... Philadelphia, PA
Salko, Joseph R. .... Baltimore, MD
Salkow, Alan M., (A Professional Corporation) .... Beverly Hills, CA
Salkowski, Albert S. .... Kingsville, MD
Salkowski, Robert F. .... Miami, FL
Salky, Irvin M. .... Memphis, TN
Salky, Mark A. .... Miami, FL
Salky, Randall P. .... Memphis, TN
Salky, Steven M. .... Washington, DC
Sall, Caltagirone & Coleman
Poughkeepsie, NY
Sall, David B. .... Poughkeepsie, NY
Sall, Frederick W. .... Miami, FL
Sall, Millie Aponte .... Houston, TX
Sall, Mimi L. .... Fort Lauderdale, FL
Sall, Robert K. .... Laguna Beach, CA
Sall & Smolowitz, A Professional Corporation .... Laguna Beach, CA
Salla, John N. .... Philadelphia, PA
Sallach, Wayne N. .... Detroit, MI
Salladay, G. Lance .... Boise, ID
Salladay & Harrigfeld .... Boise, ID
Salladin, Anne W. .... Treasury Department,
Office of the General Counsel, GV
Salladin, Richard C. .... San Francisco, CA
Sallah, Dean J. .... Holtsville, NY
Sallah, Donald R. .... Holtsville, NY
Sallah, James D. .... St. Petersburg, FL
Salland, Jos. E. .... St. Paul, MN

Sallander, Robert L., Jr. **Walnut Creek, CA**
Sallans, James W. ... Austin, TX
Sallas, John B. ... Crockett, TX
Sallas, John B., P.C. ... Crockett, TX
Sallas, Linda Ann ... North Hollywood, CA
Sallato, Maria T. ... Miami, FL
Sallay, Christopher L. ... New York, NY
Sallay, Tibor, (P.C.) ... New York, NY
Sallaz, Dennis J. ... Boise, ID
Sallaz Law Offices, Chtd. ... Boise, ID
Sallberg, Leslie S. Federal Deposit Insurance Corporation, Liquidation Branch, GV
Salle, Alan J. ... Menomonee Falls, WI
Sallé, Charles M. ... Virginia Beach, VA
Salle, Frank E. ... Tulsa, OK
Salle, Jerome M. ... Detroit, MI
Salle, Marc A. ... Kansas City, MO
Sallee, Frank F. ... Kansas City, MO
Sallee, Gary D. ... Indianapolis, IN
Sallee, Jerry S. ... Cincinnati, OH
Sallee, Joseph L., Jr. ... Cincinnati, OH
Sallee, Philip A. ... Bloomington, IN
Sallee, Richard E. ... Indianapolis, IN
Sallee, Robb K. ... Savannah, GA
Sallee, Stacy E. ... Austin, TX
Sallee, V. James ... Covington, KY
Sallen, Alvin C. ... Southfield, MI
Sallen, David U. ... Fort Madison, IA
Sallen, Philip M. ... Southfield, MI
Sallen, Steven D. ... Southfield, MI
Sallenger, Thomas R. ... Wilson, NC
Saller, Catherine Miller ... Stafford, VA
Saller, H. Andrew, Jr. ... Tacoma, WA
Sallerson, Dawn A. ... Belleville, IL
Sallerson, Samuel I. ... Chicago, IL
Sallerson, Steven R. ... St. Louis, MO
Salles, James E. ... Washington, DC
Salles, Stuart ... New York, NY
Salley & Associates ... Covington, LA **Metairie, LA**
Salley, Cecily S. ... Covington, LA
Salley, Charles W. ... Shreveport, LA
Salley, David P. ... New Orleans, LA
Salley, Edward M., Jr. ... Garden City, NY
Salley, Feinberg, Hames & Hintze, P.A. **Orlando, FL**
Salley, Fred E. ... Covington, LA **Metairie, LA**
Salley, George H., III ... Colorado Springs, CO
Salley, J. Paul ... Shreveport, LA
Salley, Jack R. ... Slidell, LA
Salley, James L. ... Kent, WA
Salley, James O. ... New Iberia, LA
Salley, Julian B., Jr. ... Aiken, SC
Salley Law Firm, The ... Covington, LA **New Orleans, LA**
Salley, Lourie A. ... Lexington, SC
Salley, Patrick P. ... Detroit, MI
Salley, Robert B. ... Los Angeles, CA
Salley, Ronald E. ... Brooklyn, NY
Salley, Ronald M. ... Orangeburg, SC
Salley, Sandra S. ... Metairie, LA
Salley, Stephen G. ... Orlando, FL
Salley, Thomas R., III ... Reston, VA
Salley, Timothy D. ... Houston, TX
Salley, Walter S. ... Shreveport, LA
Salling-Davies, Kelly Jo ... Palisade, CO
Sallinger, Alfred ... Dallas, TX
Sallinger, Barry J. ... Lafayette, LA
Sallinger, Barry J., A Professional Law Corporation ... Lafayette, LA
Sallinger, Don M. ... Dallas, TX
Sallinger, Janis ... Somerville, MA
Sallings, Deborah Ruth ... Little Rock, AR
Sallings, Jerry J. ... Little Rock, AR
Salliotte, Raymond H., III Dearborn Heights, MI
Sallit, Joanne ... Norristown, PA
Sallmann, Laura A. ... Peoria, IL
Sallop, Linda J. ... Boston, MA
Salloum, Kaleel G., Jr. ... Gulfport, MS
Salloum, Michael G. ... Worcester, MA
Salloum, Raymond J. ... Detroit, MI
Salloum, Richard P. ... Gulfport, MS
Salloway, Irving ... Boston, MA
Sallquist & Drummond, P.C. ... Phoenix, AZ
Sallquist, Richard L. ... Phoenix, AZ
Salls, Sherry K. ... Murrieta, CA
Sallus, Gerald M. ... Culver City, CA
Sallus, Marc L. ... Los Angeles, CA
Sallusti & Gray ... Oklahoma City, OK
Sallusti, Ralph A. ... Oklahoma City, OK
Sallwasser and McCain ... La Porte, IN
Sallwasser, Thomas D. ... La Porte, IN
Sallwasser, U. Albert ... Norfolk, VA
Sally & Fitch ... Boston, MA **Providence, RI**
Sally, Francis J. ... Boston, MA
Sally, Ronald O. ... Los Angeles, CA
Salm, Donald L. ... Madison, WI
Salma, Riyad Robert ... San Mateo, CA
Salmaggi, Michael Herman **Newport Beach, CA**
Salman, Barry ... Bronx, NY
Salman, Robert R. ... New York, NY
Salman, Steven L. ... Coral Gables, FL
Salman, Suzanne A. ... New York, NY
Salmanowitz, John M. ... San Francisco, CA
Salmanson, Irwin R. ... Austin, TX
Salmanson, Michael J. ... Philadelphia, PA
Salmanson, Michael J., P.C. **Philadelphia, PA**
Salmanson, Smith, L.L.P. ... Austin, TX
Salmas & Braun ... Los Angeles, CA
Salmas, George C. ... Los Angeles, CA
Salmas, Kathleen M. ... Los Angeles, CA
Salmen, Cynthia L. ... Los Angeles, CA
Salmen, Gerald G., Law Offices of **Cincinnati, OH**
Salmen, Richard C. ... Minneapolis, MN
Salmen, T. Jay ... Minneapolis, MN
Salmeron, Barbara Doolittle ... Kenilworth, IL
Salmi, Christine M. ... Boise, ID
Salmi, Rod O. ... Phoenix, AZ
Salmon, Andrew E. ... Spokane, WA
Salmon, Andrew M. ... St. Louis, MO
Salmon, Arthur L. ... New York, NY
Salmon, Beverly B. ... Baltimore, MD
Salmon, Bradley J. ... Evansville, IN
Salmon, Carl S., Jr. ... Amsterdam, NY
Salmon, David D. ... San Francisco, CA
Salmon, David J. ... Lake Worth, FL
Salmon, Denis R. ... Palo Alto, CA
Salmon, Donna A. ... Grand Junction, CO
Salmon, Elizabeth E. ... Madison, WI
Salmon, Emigdio J. ... Bartlesville, OK
Salmon, F. Larry ... Rome, GA
Salmon, J. Anthony ... Birmingham, AL
Salmon, J. Quint ... Beaver, PA
Salmon, J. Thaddeus ... Montgomery, AL
Salmon, James F. ... Amsterdam, NY
Salmon, James P. ... Upper Marlboro, MD
Salmon, Jeffrey W. ... Chicago, IL
Salmon, John E. ... Philadelphia, PA
Salmon, John F. ... Morristown, NJ
Salmon, John G. ... Breckenridge, CO **Englewood, CO**
Salmon, John J. ... Washington, DC
Salmon, John W. ... Miami, FL
Salmon, Keith H. ... Warner Robins, GA
Salmon, Kenneth L. ... Pittsburgh, PA
Salmon, Lampert & Clor, Professional Corporation ... Breckenridge, CO **Denver, CO** **Englewood, CO**
Salmon, Larry D. ... Dallas, TX
Salmon, Lewis & Weldon, P.L.C. **Phoenix, AZ**
Salmon, Marlin B. ... Tonawanda, NY
Salmon, MaryBeth Pfeiler ... Dubuque, IA
Salmon, Michael C. ... Torrance, PA
Salmon, Michael H. ... Miami, FL
Salmon, Michael J. ... Gulf Shores, AL
Salmon, Michael J., P.C. ... Gulf Shores, AL
Salmon, Milton S. ... Princeton, NJ
Salmon and Nostrand ... Bellows Falls, VT
Salmon, Pauline Marie ... Central Islip, NY
Salmon, Peter J. ... San Diego, CA
Salmon, Raymond J. ... Clinton, MA
Salmon, Rebecca K. ... Aurora, NE
Salmon, Riney B., II ... Phoenix, AZ
Salmon, Robert E. ... Minneapolis, MN
Salmon & Russell ... Morristown, NJ Roselle Park, NJ
Salmon, Salmon & Goodman Amsterdam, NY
Salmon, Samuel M. ... Long Beach, CA
Salmon, Scott A. ... Phoenix, AZ
Salmon, Sheila C. ... Washington, DC
Salmon, Steven B. ... Kansas City, MO
Salmon, Thomas P. ... Bellows Falls, VT
Salmon, Tracey L. ... Brooklyn, NY
Salmon, Vivian R. ... Vineland, NJ
Salmon, William B. ... Gainesville, FL
Salmon, William C. ... Albuquerque, NM
Salmon, William R. ... Bensalem, PA
Salmon, Wilma H. ... New Orleans, LA
Salmon, Zachary C. ... Manakin-Sabot, VA
Salmond, Andrew W. ... Long Beach, CA
Salmond, Kathryn B. ... Irvine, CA
Salmond, William G. ... College Park, MD
Salmond, William J. ... Raritan, NJ
Salmons, Carlton G. ... Des Moines, IA
Salmons, Cynthia M. ... Charleston, WV
Salmons, David B. ... Washington, DC
Salmons, Emily Morris ... Media, PA
Salmons, Harold I., III ... Wilmington, DE
Salmons, Lisa A. ... New York, NY
Salmonson, David P. ... Woodland Hills, CA
Salmonson, Scott T. ... Islandia, NY
Salmony, Lawrence D. ... Eugene, OR
Salmore, Evan R. ... Woodbridge, NJ
Salna, Vytas P. ... Portage, WI
Salnick, Michael ... West Palm Beach, FL
Salniker, David J. ... Oakland, CA
Salny, Redbord & Rinaldi ... Succasunna, NJ
Salo, Ann Distler ... Atlanta, GA
Salo, Earl Environmental Protection Agency, Office of the General Counsel, GV
Salo, James D. ... Lodi, CA
Salo & Walker ... Atlanta, GA
Saloga, James E. ... Naperville, IL
Salom, Don Eric ... San Diego, CA
Salom, Pedro G., IV ... Wallingford, PA
Saloman, Josef G. ... New Brunswick, NJ
Saloman, Mark Andrew ... Roseland, NJ **New York, NY**
Saloman, Ronald D. J. ... Burlington, MA
Salome, Roy D. ... El Paso, TX
Salometo, Peter J. M. ... New York, NY
Salomon, Allen M. ... Milwaukee, WI
Salomon, Barbara ... Denver, CO
Salomon, Chester B. ... New York, NY
Salomon, Claude E. ... Roseland, NJ
Salomon, Claudia T. ... Phoenix, AZ
Salomon, Craig N. ... Hampton, NH
Salomon, Daniel J. ... Agoura Hills, CA
Salomon, Darrell J. ... San Francisco, CA
Salomon, Edward H. ... Vauxhall, NJ
Salomon, Edward S. ... Chicago, IL
Salomon, F. L., II ... Pensacola, FL
Salomon, Garry R. ... Teaneck, NJ
Salomon, Gizella E. ... Houston, TX
Salomon Green & Ostrow, P.C. **New York, NY**
Salomon, J. Eugene, Jr. (A Professional Corporation) ... Los Angeles, CA
Salomon, Joseph N. ... New York, NY
Salomon, Kanner, Damian & Rodriguez, P.A. **Miami, FL**
Salomon, Kenneth D. ... Washington, DC
Salomon, Lavalle ... Monroe, LA
Salomon, Lavalle, A Professional Law Corporation ... Monroe, LA
Salomon, Lawrence Charles ... Boca Raton, FL
Salomon, Lorna ... Miami, FL
Salomon, Manfred F., (P.A.) ... Paterson, NJ
Salomon, Mercedes ... Los Angeles, CA
Salomon, Mittelberg & Nicosia, P.A. **Coral Springs, FL** **Fort Lauderdale, FL**
Salomon & Nebling ... Hampton, NH
Salomon, Peter E. ... Miami, FL
Salomon, Philippe M. ... New York, NY
Salomon, Rene I. ... Baton Rouge, LA
Salomon, Richard B. ... New York, NY
Salomon, Robert B. ... Woodside, CA
Salomon, Robert J. ... Sterling, VA
Salomon, Scott Alan ... Coral Springs, FL
Salomon, Sheila M. ... San Francisco, CA
Salomon, Warren M. ... Miami, FL
Salomone, Geno D. ... Riverview, MI
Salomone, Janine M. ... Wilmington, DE
Salomone, Kenneth L. ... Sunrise, FL
Salomone, Michael J., (P.A.) ... Sunrise, FL
Salomone, Peter P. ... Woodland Hills, CA
Salomone, Rapp & Ferko Woodland Hills, CA
Salomone, Rosemary C. ... Jamaica, NY
Salomone, William G. ... Sarasota, FL
Salon, Christine Lynne ... Pittsburgh, PA
Salon, Joel ... New York, NY
Salon, Jonathan ... Boston, MA
Salon, Karen W. ... Boston, MA
Salon, Leo ... New York, NY
Salon, Marrow, Dyckman & Newman **Fort Lauderdale, FL** **Hackensack, NJ** **New York, NY**
Salon, Richard L. ... Des Plaines, IL
Salon, Stephen M. ... Boston, MA
Salonen, Eric P. ... Washington, DC
Salony, James M. ... Lilly, PA
Saloom, Douglas J. ... Lafayette, LA
Saloom, Gregory J. ... Lafayette, LA
Saloom, Kaliste J., III ... Lafayette, LA
Saloom, Kaliste J., Jr. ... Lafayette, LA
Saloom & Saloom ... Lafayette, LA
Salopek, John F. ... Aliquippa, PA
Salorio, Susan Cochrane ... New York, NY
Saloschin, Robert L. ... Bethesda, MD
Salot, Susan E. ... Irvine, CA
Salotti, Christopher P. Department Of The Interior, Office of the Solicitor, GV
Salovaara, Kaarina ... Chicago, IL
Salovesh, Charles E. ... Brea, CA
Salovin, Allan ... West Palm Beach, FL
Salowitz, Charles B. ... Chicago, IL
Salpeter, Alan N. ... Chicago, IL
Salpietra, Richard ... San Diego, CA
Salpietro, Frank G. ... Pittsburgh, PA
Salpius & Partner ... Pasadena, CA
Sals, Terrence A. ... Hickory Hills, IL
Salsberg, Brian S. ... New York, NY
Salsberg, John ... Boston, MA
Salsberg, Mark R. ... Uniondale, NY
Salsberg, Richard M. ... Morristown, NJ
Salsbery, David A. ... Mankato, MN
Salsbery & Druckman ... Charleston, WV
Salsbery, H. F. ... Charleston, WV
Salsbery, Thomas E. ... Des Moines, IA
Salsburg, Amy J. ... Fort Lauderdale, FL
Salsburg, Daniel R. Commodity Futures Trading Commission, Division of Enforcement, GV
Salsburg, Richard M. ... West Orange, NJ
Salsbury, Alan M. ... Norfolk, VA
Salsbury, Douglas B. ... Eureka, MO
Salsbury, Mark D. ... Houston, TX
Salsbury, Michael H. ... Washington, DC
Salsbury, Patrick M. ... Topeka, KS
Salsbury, Scott ... Akron, OH
Salsbury, Stuart Marshall ... Baltimore, MD
Salsbury, Sue Ellen ... Akron, OH
Salseda, Gerald C. ... Los Angeles, CA
Salsich, Peter W., III ... St. Louis, MO
Salsich, Peter W., Jr. ... St. Louis, MO
Salsieder, Michael W. ... Milwaukee, WI
Salsky, Don H. ... Califon, NJ
Salstone, Sande L. ... Downers Grove, IL
Salt, Albert E. ... Melrose, MA
Salt & Don ... Melrose, MA
Salt, Kelly J. ... San Diego, CA
Salt, Patrick R. ... Colorado Springs, CO
Salt, Sidney S. ... Peabody, MA
Salta, Romeo J. ... New York, NY
Saltalamachia, Joyce Diane ... New York, NY
Saltamachia & Baker ... Baton Rouge, LA
Saltamachia, Darrell J. ... Baton Rouge, LA
Saltarelli, Arthur J. ... Boulder, CO
Saltarelli, Douglas C. ... St. Petersburg, FL
Saltarelli, Gabriel ... New York, NY
Saltarelli, Gerald G. ... Chicago, IL
Saltarelli, John M. ... Austin, TX **Fort Worth, TX** Houston, TX
Saltarelli, Joseph J. ... New York, NY
Saltarelli Law Corporation **Newport Beach, CA**
Saltarelli, Mark E. ... Tonawanda, NY
Saltarelli, Thomas R. ... Newport Beach, CA
Salter, Amanda C. ... Atlanta, GA
Salter, Andrew H., P.C. ... Seattle, WA
Salter, Ben ... Hollywood, FL
Salter, Charles W. ... Vista, CA
Salter, Charlotte ... Austin, TX
Salter, Christopher M. ... Washington, DC
Salter, Dianne S. ... Philadelphia, PA
Salter, Elliot A. ... Providence, RI
Salter, Eric B. ... Los Angeles, CA
Salter, Erin M. ... Los Angeles, CA
Salter, Feiber, Yenser, Murphy & Hutson, P.A. ... Gainesville, FL
Salter, Frank M. ... Birmingham, AL
Salter, Frank T., Jr. ... Lake Charles, LA
Salter, George A. ... New York, NY
Salter, James D. ... Gainesville, FL
Salter, James H. ... Sunnyvale, CA
Salter, James W., III ... Rockville, MD
Salter, James W., III, P.A. ... Rockville, MD
Salter, Janice A. ... Los Angeles, CA
Salter, John F. ... Albany, GA
Salter, John L. ... Los Angeles, CA
Salter, Kelly L. ... Redding, CA
Salter, Kerrean L. ... Jacksonville, FL
Salter, Kevin T. ... New York, NY
Salter, Lee W. ... Redding, CA
Salter, Leon M. ... Los Angeles, CA
Salter, Leonard M. ... Boston, MA
Salter, Lester H. ... Providence, RI
Salter, M. Brad ... St. Petersburg, FL
Salter, Mark Edward ... Sioux Falls, SD
Salter, Maureen Annette ... New York, NY
Salter McGowan Swartz & Sylvia, Incorporated ... Providence, RI
Salter & Michaelson ... Providence, RI
Salter, Paul V. ... Palm Beach Gardens, FL
Salter, Randall G. ... Sherman Oaks, CA
Salter, Richard J. ... Elgin, IL
Salter, Robert F. ... Gatesville, TX
Salter, Robert S. ... Providence, RI
Salter, Ronald L. ... Medford, OR
Salter, Rubin, Jr. ... Tucson, AZ
Salter, Sarah ... Boston, MA
Salter, Scott M. ... Birmingham, AL
Salter, Shawn C. ... Boston, MA
Salter, Streete & Hale, A Professional Law Corporation ... Lake Charles, LA
Salter, Theodore, Jr. ... Atlanta, GA
Salter, Theodore, Jr., & Associates, P.C. **Atlanta, GA**
Salter, Timothy E. ... San Diego, CA
Salter, Timothy W. ... Modesto, CA
Salter, Vance E. ... Miami, FL
Salter, W. Dean ... Denver, CO
Salter, William E., III ... Columbia, SC
Salter, Wilmer L. ... Vidalia, GA
Salter, Zoanne A. ... Walnut Creek, CA
Salter-Ferris, Heidi ... Ann Arbor, MI
Salters, Leonard A. ... Rockville, MD
Saltiel, David M. ... Chicago, IL
Saltiel, David M. ... Boston, MA
Saltiel, Jeffrey ... Brooklyn, NY
Saltiel, Steven J. ... New York, NY
Saltman, Alan I. ... Washington, DC
Saltman, David A. ... East Windsor, NJ
Saltman, Eve T. ... San Rafael, CA
Saltman & Stevens ... Fairfax, VA **Washington, DC**
Saltman, Stuart I. ... Raleigh, NC
Saltmarsh, Kathryn ... Springfield, IL
Saltmarsh, Sara E., Law Offices of **Austin, TX**
Salton, Catherine A. ... Cupertino, CA
Salton, Marc H. ... New Port Richey, FL
Salton, Peter D. ... Ithaca, NY
Saltonstall, Stephen L. ... Bennington, VT
Saltonstall, Stephen L. ... Manchester, VT
Saltoun, André M. ... Palo Alto, CA
Saltoun, Diane L. ... Chicago, IL
Saltser, Michael J. ... New York, NY
Saltsgaver, V. Rand ... Orlando, FL
Saltsman, Daniel L., Jr. ... Webster, FL
Saltsman, Gary D. ... Department of Justice, Executive Office for Immigration Review, GV
Saltsman, George S. ... Seminole, FL
Saltsman, Glenn A. ... Farmington Hills, MI
Saltsman, Jane D. ... Beverly Hills, CA
Saltsman, Jay R. ... Playa Del Rey, CA
Saltsman, John K. ... Carrollton, OH
Saltsman, John W., Jr. ... Bardstown, KY
Saltsman, Ralph B. ... Playa Del Rey, CA
Saltsman, Richard H. ... Washington, DC
Saltsman, Robert P. ... Winter Park, FL
Saltsman, Robert P., P.A. ... Winter Park, FL
Saltsman, Ronald G. ... Phoenix, AZ
Saltsman & Willett ... Bardstown, KY
Saltsman, William H. ... New York, NY
Saltus, Brian R. ... Boise, ID
Saltus, Cheryl A. ... Dana Point, CA
Saltveit, Noreen K. ... Portland, OR
Saltz, Albert M. ... Philadelphia, PA
Saltz, Beverly I. ... Santa Fe, NM
Saltz, Brian K. ... Farmingdale, NY
Saltz, Camille E. ... Lafayette, LA
Saltz, Daniella ... Dearborn, MI
Saltz, Harvey A. ... Sherman Oaks, CA
Saltz, Irwin J. ... Chicago, IL
Saltz, Jeffrey S. ... Philadelphia, PA
Saltz, Jeffrey S., P.C., Law Office of **Philadelphia, PA**
Saltz, Jeffrey T. ... Chicago, IL
Saltz, Leonard H. ... New York, NY
Saltz, Mongeluzzi, Barrett & Bendesky, P.C. Cherry Hill, NJ **Philadelphia, PA**
Saltz, Sidney G. ... Chicago, IL

Saltz, Stephen T. ... **Philadelphia, PA**
Saltz, Susan ... Huntington, NY
Saltz, Veronica W. ... **Cherry Hill, NJ**
Philadelphia, PA
Saltzberg, Gerald B. ... Chicago, IL
Saltzberg, Lee ... **Towson, MD**
Saltzberg, Robert A. ... **San Francisco, CA**
Saltzburg, Damon G. ... **Los Angeles, CA**
Saltzburg, David A. ... **Philadelphia, PA**
Saltzburg, Henley L. ... **Los Angeles, CA**
Saltzburg, Joel ... Encino, CA
Saltzburg, Michael ... **Philadelphia, PA**
West Chester, PA
Saltzburg, Ray & Bergman, LLP
Los Angeles, CA
Saltzen, Paul H. ... Cameron Park, CA
Saltzer, Bruce ... Pasadena, CA
Saltzgiver, Laurie A. ... **Harrisburg, PA**
Saltzman, Abraham ... Valley Stream, NY
Saltzman, Alan H. ... Detroit, MI
Saltzman, Amy ... Bronx, NY
Saltzman, Andrea ... **San Leandro, CA**
Saltzman, Barbara E. ... Shaker Heights, OH
Saltzman, Barbara R. ... Northridge, CA
Saltzman, Barry N. ... **New York, NY**
Saltzman, Beth H. ... Lynnfield, MA
Saltzman, Bonnie E. ... Denver, CO
Saltzman, Carol Lipton ... **Herndon, VA**
Saltzman Chetkof & Rosenberg, LLP
Garden City, NY
Saltzman, Daniel ... Somerville, MA
Saltzman, David A. ... Austin, TX
Saltzman, David H. ... **New York, NY**
Saltzman, David L. ... Baltimore, MD
Saltzman, David S. ... Washington, DC
Saltzman, Deborah J. ... **Los Angeles, CA**
Saltzman, Deborah L. ... **New York, NY**
Saltzman, Donald Lawrence
Los Angeles, CA
Saltzman, Eric F. ... New York, NY
Saltzman, Eric T. ... Foster City, CA
Saltzman, Gordon ... New Castle, DE
Saltzman, Irving ... Flushing, NY
Saltzman, Jay A. ... **Chicago, IL**
Saltzman, Jay P. ... **New York, NY**
Saltzman, Jeffrey H. ... San Francisco, CA
Saltzman, Joan ... **Philadelphia, PA**
Saltzman & Johnson, Law Corporation
San Francisco, CA
Saltzman, Judith C. ... Boston, MA
Saltzman, Kathleen D. ... **Sioux City, IA**
Saltzman, Kenneth B. ... Bronx, NY
Saltzman, Kerry Evan ... **Chicago, IL**
Saltzman, Kevin M. ... **Omaha, NE**
Saltzman, Lee S. ... **New York, NY**
Saltzman, Lysa M. ... **San Diego, CA**
Saltzman, Mark Elliott ... Canoga Park, CA
Saltzman, Martin W. ... Phoenix, AZ
Saltzman, Matthew D. ... **Las Vegas, NV**
Saltzman & McNaught ... Stoneham, MA
Saltzman, Michael I. ... **New York, NY**
Saltzman, Michael S. ... Cherry Hill, NJ
Philadelphia, PA
Saltzman, Neil S. ... **New City, NY**
Saltzman, Oren D. ... **Ellicott City, MD**
Saltzman, Paul ... Greenwich, CT
Saltzman, Paul ... **Boston, MA**
Saltzman, Paul B. ... Dallas, TX
Saltzman, Penelope W. ... Washington, DC
Saltzman, Richard M. ... Parsippany, NJ
Saltzman, Robert ... Cherry Hill, NJ
Saltzman, Robert J. ... Bronx, NY
Saltzman, Robert J. ... Brooklyn, NY
Saltzman, Robert M. ... Los Angeles, CA
Saltzman, Robert M. ... Stoneham, MA
Saltzman, Selig A. ... **Boston, MA**
Saltzman, Stanley D. ... **Santa Ana, CA**
Woodland Hills, CA
Saltzman, Stephen A. ... **New York, NY**
Saltzman, Stephen L. ... **Los Angeles, CA**
Saltzman, Stephen L., (P.C.)
New Haven, CT
Saltzman, Steven I. ... Chicago, IL
Saltzman, Stuart ... Tamarac, FL
Saltzman, Susan P. ... **Southfield, MI**
Saltzman, Todd Y. ... Chicago, IL
Saltzman, William B. ... Garden City, NY
Saltzman, William H. ... Fort Lee, NJ
Saltzmann, Eric George ... Anderson, IN
Saltzstein, Arthur ... Milwaukee, WI
Saltzstein, Robert A. ... Washington, DC
Saltzstein, Robert A. and Guy Martin, Law Office of ... Washington, DC
Saltzstein, Robert M. ... Lake Success, NY
Saltzstein, Robert S. ... Chicago, IL
Saltzstein, Susan L. ... **New York, NY**
Saluan, Andrew J. ... Naples, FL
Saluja, Amit ... **Washington, DC**
Salup-Schmidt, Linda ... **Miami, FL**
Saluri, Joseph B. ... **Des Moines, IA**
New York, NY
Salus, Babette P. ... **Springfield, IL**
Salus, Joseph W., II ... Chevy Chase, MD
Salus, Richard A. ... **Irvine, CA**
Salus, Robert R. ... Oak Forest, IL
Salus, Samuel W., II ... Norristown, PA
Salus, Stanley M. ... **Washington, DC**
Vienna, VA
Salus, Therese I. ... Washington, DC
Salus, Thomas D. ... **Berwyn, PA**
Salusky, Monica R. ... Walnut Creek, CA
Salussolia & Associates ... Miami, FL
Salussolia, Piero ... Miami, FL
Salustro, Larry ... Chicago, IL
Salute, Darren P. ... Beverly Hills, CA
Salute, Eugene M. ... Encino, CA
Salute, Gregory J. ... **Los Angeles, CA**
Saluti, Gerald M., Jr. ... Hackensack, NJ

Salutz, Lawrence V. ... Manitowoc, WI
Salutz & Salutz ... Manitowoc, WI
Salutz, Timothy M. ... Manitowoc, WI
Salva, Dianne M.
National Credit Union Administration, Office of General Counsel, GV
Salva, Laurence J. ... **New York, NY**
Salvacion, Mark I. ... **Philadelphia, PA**
Salvador, Julio Cesar, Jr ... **Jacksonville, FL**
Salvador, Vernon W. ... Albuquerque, NM
Salvadore, Guido R. ... **Providence, RI**
Salvadore, Janice ... **Burlington, MA**
Salvadore, Joseph C. ... Providence, RI
Salvadore, Mal A. ... **Providence, RI**
Salvadore, Marisa M. ... **Providence, RI**
Salvadore & Salvadore ... **Providence, RI**
Salvage, Andrew L. ... **Fort Lauderdale, FL**
Salvage, Andrew L., P.A.
Fort Lauderdale, FL
Salvage, James N., Jr. ... Hauppauge, NY
Salvage, Paul R. ... **Springfield, MA**
Salvaggio, David F. ... Morristown, NJ
Salvagio, Dennis L. ... Orlando, FL
Salvagio, Peter L. ... Philadelphia, PA
Salvagione, Carol A. ... **San Francisco, CA**
Salvagni, A. Michael ... Bozeman, MT
Salvagni, Brian C. ... Westlake, OH
Salvagno, Elizabeth A. ... **Syracuse, NY**
Salvagno, Olivier ... **Woodbridge, NJ**
Salvan, Sherwood A. ... New York, NY
Salvant, Wayne F. ... Fort Worth, TX
Salvas, Adam R. ... **Oakland, CA**
Salva-Sandoval, Nereida M.
San Juan, PR
Salvati, Carol Ann ... Phoenix, AZ
Salvati, Frank A. ... Woodbury, NJ
Salvati, Mark J. ... Woburn, MA
Salvati, Rodney L. ... Mount Kisco, NY
Salvati, Stephen J. ... Morristown, NJ
Salvati, Steve J. ... Pembroke Pines, FL
Salvatierra, Estella H.
Federal Communications Commission, Mass Media Bureau, GV
Salvatierra, Mark M. ... **Santa Monica, CA**
Salvato, Frank ... Alexandria, VA
Salvato, Gregory M. ... **Los Angeles, CA**
Salvato, Lawrence A. ... New York, NY
Salvato, Mark A. ... Houston, TX
Salvatore, Albert N. ... **Cleveland, OH**
Salvatore, Anthony ... East Setauket, NY
Salvatore, Anthony M. ... **Oak Hill, WV**
Salvatore, David A. ... Providence, RI
Salvatore, David M. ... New York, NY
Salvatore, Jack ... Glendale, AZ
Salvatore, John R. ... Hagerstown, MD
Salvatore, Joseph J. ... **Melville, NY**
Salvatore, Lara E. ... **Boston, MA**
Salvatore, Lynn M. ... Tallahassee, FL
Salvatore, Paul ... **New York, NY**
Salvatore, Richard A. ... **Reno, NV**
Salvatore, Ronald A. ... West Point, NY
Salvatore, Susan M. ... **Tampa, FL**
Salvatore, Timothy L. ... **Lancaster, PA**
York, PA
Salvatore, Vincent D., Jr. ... **Washington, DC**
Salvatori, Dominic D. ... Pittsburgh, PA
Salvatori, Leo J. ... **Naples, FL**
Salvaty, Benjamin B., (P.C.)
Los Angeles, CA
Salvaty, Paul ... **Los Angeles, CA**
Salvaty, Paul B. ... Oakland, CA
Salvay, Craig L. ... Kansas City, MO
Salve, Patrick J. ... Hartford, CT
Salven, Valerie L. ... Frankfort, KY
Salvesen, Douglas W. ... **Boston, MA**
Salveson, Elizabeth S. ... **San Francisco, CA**
Salveson, Erik T. ... **Minneapolis, MN**
Salveson, Kent Erwin
San Juan Capistrano, CA
Salveson, Michael N. ... **McLean, VA**
Salvest, John J. ... Kearny, NJ
Salveter, Theodore C., III ... Springfield, MO
Salvetti, Donald N ... Apopka, FL
Salvetti, Susan ... **New York, NY**
Salvi, Albert J., & Associates ... Wauconda, IL
Waukegan, IL
Wheaton, IL
Salvi, Albert S. ... Lake Zurich, IL
Salvi, Joseph V. ... Lake Zurich, IL
Salvi, Michael J. ... Lake Zurich, IL
Salvi, Patrick A. ... **Chicago, IL**
Waukegan, IL
Salvi & Roskam ... Wheaton, IL
Salvi, Salvi & Wifler, P.C. ... Lake Zurich, IL
Salvi, Sara Luca ... **White Plains, NY**
Salvi & Schostok, P.C. ... **Chicago, IL**
Waukegan, IL
Salvi, Vincent P. ... Portland, OR
Salvia, Margherita ... Darien, CT
Salvia, Robert F. ... Sleepy Hollow, NY
Salvidio, Anthony J., II ... Worcester, MA
Salvidio, Donna Toman ... **Worcester, MA**
Salvin, Arthur H. ... Wilton, CT
Salvin, Darren Marcus ... **Los Angeles, CA**
Salvin, David J. ... **Irvine, CA**
Salvin, David J. ... **Laguna Hills, CA**
Salvin, David J. ... **Mission Viejo, CA**
Newport Beach, CA
Salvin & Salvin ... Wilton, CT
Salvini, Barbara J. ... **Santa Ana, CA**
Salvino, Anthony P. ... **Allentown, PA**
Salvino, Paul Michael ... Albany, NY
Salvito, Kirsten ... Santa Barbara, CA
Salvo, Alice A. ... **Los Angeles, CA**
Salvo, Alice A. ... **Tarzana, CA**
Salvo, Cindy D. ... **New York, NY**

Salvo, Deren, Schenck & Lauterbach, P.C.
Earling, IA
Harlan, IA
Salvo, Deren Schenck & Lauterbach, P.C.
Logan, IA
Salvo, Deren, Schenck & Lauterbach, P.C.
Panama, IA
Walnut, IA
Woodbine, IA
Salvo, Donna Marie ... New York, NY
Salvo, Edward J., Jr. ... Schenectady, NY
Salvo, Elaine E. ... Buffalo, NY
Salvo, J. C. ... **Harlan, IA**
Salvo, Joseph A. ... Douglaston, NY
Salvo, Joseph P. ... New York, NY
Salvo, Lori Miller ... Plainsboro, NJ
Salvo, Louis R. ... New York, NY
Salvo, Michael C. ... **New York, NY**
Salvo, Natale A. ... Jackson, MS
Salvo, Russell and Fichter ... Blue Bell, PA
Salvo, S. Kemble ... Millville, NJ
Salvo, Santo J. ... Millville, NJ
Salvo, Stephen A. ... Blue Bell, PA
Salvucci, Dina Lee ... Minden, NV
Salvucci, John T. ... **Philadelphia, PA**
Salvucci, Stephen J. ... **Costa Mesa, CA**
Salvucci, Susan D. (Johnson)
Bakersfield, CA
Salwen, Estelita J. ... Forest Hills, NY
Salwen, Jack B. ... **New York, NY**
Salwen, Joan C. ... Scarsdale, NY
Salwen, Richard ... Round Rock, TX
Salwen, Robert J. ... New York, NY
Salwin, Lester N. ... Washington, DC
Salwin, Marjorie B. ... Washington, DC
Salwowski, Brian D. ... Indianapolis, IN
Saly, Matthew J. ... **Los Angeles, CA**
Salyards, Janine ... Boston, MA
Salyards, Michael L. ... Dallas, TX
Salyars, A. W. ... Lubbock, TX
Salyer, B. R., P.S.C. ... Morehead, KY
Salyer, Buddy R. ... Morehead, KY
Salyer, Christopher T. ... Fayetteville, NC
Salyer, David P. ... **Galveston, TX**
Salyer, David R. ... **Dayton, OH**
Salyer, Jack E. ... Lakewood, CO
Salyer, James D. ... **Houston, TX**
Salyer, James E. ... Lawrence, KS
Salyer, James Patrick ... McArthur, OH
Salyer, Jerry L. ... Oklahoma City, OK
Salyer, John Clark, III ... Sterling, VA
Salyer, Kathleen M. ... Miami, FL
Salyer, Kathryn P. ... **Portland, OR**
Salyer, Richard D. ... Downey, CA
Salyer, Robert M. ... **Elko, NV**
Salyer, Shannon E. ... Corpus Christi, TX
Salyer, Shawn Renee ... Virginia Beach, VA
Salyer, Susan Ballard ... **Cincinnati, OH**
Salyer, Timothy J. ... **Irvine, CA**
Salyers, Alix Magid ... Chicago, IL
Salyers, Donnie W. ... Abingdon, VA
Salyers, Douglas D. ... **Atlanta, GA**
Salyers & Eiteljorg ... Indianapolis, IN
Salyers, Helana A. ... **Cincinnati, OH**
Salyers, Nancy Sidote ... Chicago, IL
Salyers, Paul A. ... **Troy, MI**
Salyers, Paul A., P.C. ... **Troy, MI**
Salyers, Robert J. ... Indianapolis, IN
Salys, Casimer K. ... Austin, TX
Salz, Constance E. ... **Pasadena, CA**
Salz, Frank ... **Pasadena, CA**
Salz, Mark S. ... Los Angeles, CA
Salz, Marlo Deborah ... **New York, NY**
Salz, Richard F. ... New York, NY
Salz, Rubin R. ... Brooklyn, NY
Salz & Salz ... **Los Angeles, CA**
Pasadena, CA
Salza, Peter J. ... Milwaukee, WI
Salzano, Joseph V. ... **New York, NY**
Salzano, Loretta ... **Atlanta, GA**
Salzano, Sergio ... Las Vegas, NV
Salzarulo, Anthony J. ... Rocky Hill, CT
Salzarulo, Lori ... **Seattle, WA**
Salzberg, Arthur J. ... **McLean, VA**
Salzberg, Arthur J., & Associates, P.C.
McLean, VA
Salzberg, Fredric E. ... New York, NY
Salzberg, Harry E. ... Madison, WI
Salzberg, Jerry M. ... Chicago, IL
Salzberg, Karl I. ... Beloit, WI
Salzberg, Kenneth C. ... St. Paul, MN
Salzberg, Lisa P. ... New York, NY
Salzberg, Marc E. ... Denver, CO
Salzberg, Mark A. ... **West Palm Beach, FL**
Salzberg, Mark Daniel ... **New York, NY**
Salzberg, Mark S. ... **Los Angeles, CA**
Salzberg, Robert L. ... New York, NY
Salzberger, Paul L. ... Dallas, TX
Salzberger, Paul L., A Professional Corporation
Dallas, TX
Salzburg, Bruce A. ... **Cheyenne, WY**
Salzburg, Milton ... North Port, FL
Salzeider, John A. ... **Chicago, IL**
Salzer, Bret R. ... **New York, NY**
Salzer, Craig M. ... **Milwaukee, WI**
Salzer, Douglas ... **New Orleans, LA**
Salzer, Jeffrey D ... **Rockville, MD**
Salzer, Karl F. ... **Rochester, NY**
Salzer, Kathleen A. ... **Chicago, IL**
Salzer, Robert C. ... Brookfield, WI
Salzer, Robert D. ... Rockville, MD
Salzer, Theodore D. ... Superior, WI
Salzer, Thomas ... **Clinton, NJ**
Salzer, William T. ... **Philadelphia, PA**
Salzetta, Paul L. ... **Chicago, IL**
Salzhandler, Henry J. ... Houston, TX
Salzillo, Benjamin ... **Washington, DC**
Salzl, Lorrie L. ... **Minneapolis, MN**

Salzler, Mark J. ... Columbus, OH
Salzman, Alan C. ... New York, NY
Salzman, Amelia Stuart ... Washington, DC
Salzman, Andrew J. ... **Clearwater, FL**
Salzman, Anthony J. ... **Gainesville, FL**
Salzman, Barbara J. ... Hicksville, NY
Salzman, Barbara J., P.C. ... Hicksville, NY
Salzman, Barry A. ... **New York, NY**
Salzman, Barry M. ... **Clearwater, FL**
Salzman, Barry M. ... **St. Petersburg, FL**
Salzman, Barry M. ... **Tampa, FL**
Salzman, Bonnie Stotsky ... Richmond, VA
Salzman, Charles C. ... New York, NY
Salzman, David B. ... Bedford, NH
Salzman, David B. ... **Pittsburgh, PA**
Salzman, Donald P. ... Rockville, MD
Salzman, Elena E. ... **New York, NY**
Salzman, Gary I. ... Miami, FL
Salzman, Gary S. ... **Orlando, FL**
Salzman, Gerald H.
Department of Housing and Urban Development, Office of General Counsel, GV
Salzman, Hollis L. ... **New York, NY**
Salzman, Ira ... New York, NY
Salzman, Ira M. ... **Anaheim, CA**
Los Angeles, CA
Newport Beach, CA
Palm Springs, CA
Salzman, Ira M. ... **Pasadena, CA**
Salzman, Ira M. ... **Santa Ana, CA**
Ventura, CA
Salzman, James G. ... **New York, NY**
Salzman, James John ... **Chicago, IL**
Salzman, Janet B. ... **Miami, FL**
Salzman, Janice Greenberg ... Baltimore, MD
Salzman, Jaya ... Oakland, CA
Salzman, Jennifer A. ... **Los Angeles, CA**
Salzman, Jerrold E. ... **Chicago, IL**
Salzman, Joan R. ... New York, NY
Salzman, Julie B. ... **New York, NY**
Salzman, Kirstin Pace ... **Kansas City, MO**
Salzman, Leo ... Brooklyn, NY
Salzman, Leo C. ... **Harlingen, TX**
Salzman, Leslie Fran ... New York, NY
Salzman & Levy ... **Binghamton, NY**
Salzman, Louis ... Baltimore, MD
Salzman, Margery E. ... Fort Lee, NJ
Salzman, Marilyn J. ... Great Neck, NY
Salzman, Martha L. ... **Buffalo, NY**
Salzman, Martin J., (Ltd.) ... Chicago, IL
Salzman, Martin R. ... **Atlanta, GA**
Salzman, Martin W. ... **Chicago, IL**
Salzman, Matthew J. ... **Kansas City, MO**
Salzman, Mervyn A. ... Rochester, NY
Salzman, Michael E. ... **New York, NY**
Salzman, Michael R. ... **Pittsburgh, PA**
Salzman, Nancy Miller ... **Santa Ana, CA**
Salzman, Richard ... Brooklyn, NY
Salzman, Richard A. ... **Washington, DC**
Salzman, Richard B. ... **Miami, FL**
Salzman, Richard Glenn ... Dania, FL
Salzman, Robert ... Utica, NY
Salzman, Robert S. ... **Binghamton, NY**
Salzman, Sidney J. ... Rochester, NY
Salzman, Stanley P., (P.C.) ... Great Neck, NY
Salzman, Stephen J. ... Santa Barbara, CA
Salzman, Steven A. ... Chicago, IL
Salzman, Steven L. ... **New York, NY**
Port Washington, NY
Salzmann, Carl A. ... Bloomington, IN
Salzmann, L. John ... Kingston, NY
Salzmann, Michael A. ... Monterey Park, CA
Salzmann, William T. ... **Los Angeles, CA**
Salzsieder, Edward J. ... Oshkosh, WI
Salzsieder, Karl Ray ... Longview, WA
Salzstein, Ernest F. ... Delray Beach, FL
Sam, David ... Salt Lake City, UT
Sam, Jennifer J. ... San Francisco, CA
Sam, Kenneth G. ... **Seattle, WA**
Sama, Lillian ... Irwindale, CA
Sama, Ronald J. ... Lakewood, NJ
Sama, Vincent A. ... New York, NY
Samaan, Peter S. ... **New York, NY**
Samad, Stanley A. ... Akron, OH
Samad-Salameh, Alia ... **San Francisco, CA**
Samaha, Adam M. ... **Minneapolis, MN**
Samaha, Charles M. ... St. Petersburg, FL
Samaha, Cynthia M. ... Cape Coral, FL
Samaha, Edward G.
Rancho Cucamonga, CA
Samaha, George T., III ... Little River, SC
Samaha Grogin, LLP ... Pasadena, CA
Samaha, John N. ... Baton Rouge, LA
Samaha, Lawrence H. ... Tampa, FL
Samaha, Mari Ann ... Boston, MA
Samaha & Simpson, LLC ... Little River, SC
Samaha, Stephen U. ... **Littleton, NH**
Samaha, Steven M. ... **Tampa, FL**
Samaha, Thomas J. ... Pasadena, CA
Samaha, Unwar J. ... Littleton, NH
Samaha & Vaughan, P.A. ... **Littleton, NH**
Samakow, Paul A. ... Wheaton, MD
Samalin, Edwin ... Yorktown Heights, NY
Samalot Rodríguez, Yammir ... San Juan, PR
Saman, Robert M. ... **Palo Alto, CA**
Samani, Ann E. ... Lexington, KY
Samanie, Barnes & Allen ... Houma, LA
Samanie, Michael J. ... Houma, LA
Samaniego, Christa ... San Antonio, TX
Samaniego, Jesus E. ... **El Paso, TX**
Samanoglu, Murat L. ... Lodi, NJ
Samanowitz, Ronald A. ... Great Neck, NY
Samansky, Allan J. ... Columbus, OH
Samansky, Deborah H. ... Hempstead, NY
Samansky, J. Leonard ... Mineola, NY
Samansky, Scott D. ... East Hanover, NJ
Samara, Noah A. ... Washington, DC

Samaras, Harrie R. .... Alexandria, VA
Samaraweera, Rohan J. .... Washington, DC
Samarco, David T. .... Van Nuys, CA
Samarel, Jaime S. .... Spring Valley, NY
Samarghachian, Haroutioun H.
Los Angeles, CA
Samargya, Milan "Bo"
New Port Richey, FL
Samarias, Joseph J. .... Washington, DC
Samarin, Paul W. .... Long Beach, CA
Samarkos, Charles A. .... Clearwater, FL
Samaro, Samuel J. .... Hackensack, NJ
Samartin, Robert .... Tampa, FL
Samartin, Robert A., P.A. .... Tampa, FL
Samay, Christian E. .... Newark, NJ
Samay, Scott R. .... New York, NY
Samay, Wolf A. .... Morristown, NJ
Samay, Z. Lance, (P.C.) .... Morristown, NJ
Samber, Alan W. .... Sterling, CO
Samber, David M. .... Roslyn, NY
Samber, Judith E. .... Wellsville, NY
Samberg, Alfred M. .... New York, NY
Samberg, Amy M. .... Tucson, AZ
Samberg, Gilbert A. .... New York, NY
Samberg, Jeffrey M. .... Rockville Centre, NY
Samberg, John M. .... Pasadena, CA
Samberg, Peter .... White Plains, NY
Samberson, C. Gene .... Lovington, NM
Sambol, Charles M. .... Oroville, CA
Sambol, Lori E. .... Marina Del Rey, CA
Sambol, Mary Lee Gill .... Eaton, OH
Sambol, Stephen B. .... Winter Park, FL
Sambolin, David .... Philadelphia, PA
Samboni, Aldo A. .... Seattle, WA
Samborn, Hope Viner .... Chicago, IL
Samborn, James A. .... Detroit, MI
Samborsky, Mercedes C. .... Joppa, MD
Sambrano-Soracco, Andrea Antonio
Boston, MA
Sambroak, Robert A., Jr. .... Erie, PA
Sambur, Robin A. .... Bay Shore, NY
Sambursky, Neil L. .... Jersey City, NJ
New York, NY
Samdal, Richard A. .... Grand Rapids, MI
Same, Robert G. .... Appleton, WI
Sameiro, Manuel B., Jr. .... New Brunswick, NJ
Sameiro, Susan Dimler .... Newark, NJ
Samek & Associates .... Boston, MA
Samek, Carol K. .... Los Angeles, CA
Samek, Kolleen K. .... Des Moines, IA
Samek & McMillan, P.C. .... Rockville, MD
Samek, Peter L. .... Boston, MA
Samek, Richard P. .... Fort Wayne, IN
Samek, Roger C. .... Rockville, MD
Samel, Barbara J. .... Albany, NY
Samel, Charles H. .... Los Angeles, CA
Samel, David M. .... New York, NY
Samel, Dorothy .... New York, NY
Samel, Ellen Donsky .... Philadelphia, PA
Samel, Jeffrey .... New York, NY
Samel, Jeffrey, & Partners .... Bronx, NY
Brooklyn, NY
New York, NY
White Plains, NY
Samel, Jonathan .... Lansdale, PA
Samellas, Christopher G. .... Greenville, SC
Samels, George .... Department of Energy,
Office of the General Counsel, GV
Samels, James E. .... Framingham, MA
Samels, Stephen C. .... Minneapolis, MN
Samelson, Allen .... San Francisco, CA
Samelson, Kirk S. .... Colorado Springs, CO
Samelson & Knickerbocker .... Des Plaines, IL
Samelson, Lawrence D. .... Truckee, CA
Samelson, Linda M. .... Bloomfield Hills, MI
Samelson, Norman E. .... Des Plaines, IL
Samelson, Samuel L. .... Goldsboro, NC
Samelstein, Barney .... Syracuse, NY
Samen, Jonathan L. .... Boston, MA
Samenfeld, Lisa A. .... New York, NY
Samenga, Alfred F. .... Mineola, NY
Samenga, Frank A. .... Seaford, NY
Samenga, Loretta F. .... Levittown, NY
Samero, Marcia E. .... Philadelphia, PA
Sames, Jay R. .... Peacham, VT
Sames, Richard E. .... Laredo, TX
Sameshima, Beverly Wee .... Honolulu, HI
Sameshima, Douglas J. .... Lahaina, HI
Sameshima, Douglas J. .... Wailuku, HI
Samet, Andrew B. .... Morristown, NJ
Samet, Carol L. .... Houston, TX
Samet, Dee-Dee .... Tucson, AZ
Samet, Dee-Dee, P.C. .... Tucson, AZ
Samet, Jack I. .... Los Angeles, CA
Samet, Jan H. .... High Point, NC
Samet, Joseph .... New York, NY
Samet, Joyce S. .... Brookline, MA
Samet, Leo .... Silver Spring, MD
Samet, Melissa A. .... San Francisco, CA
Samet, Naomi F. .... Baltimore, MD
Samet, Richard S. .... Richmond, VA
Samet, Robert G. .... Rockville, MD
Samet & Samet .... Baltimore, MD
Samet, Walter L. .... Baltimore, MD
Sameth, Ellen M. .... Houston, TX
Sameth, Patricia A. .... Houston, TX
Sameth, Paul N. .... Baltimore, MD
Samford, A. Morris, Jr. .... Carthage, TX
Samford, Denson, Horsley & Pettey
Opelika, AL
Samford & DePaola, P.C. .... Montgomery, AL
Samford, John S. P. .... Birmingham, AL
Samford, Michael L. .... Houston, TX
Samford, Thomas D., IV .... Montgomery, AL
Samford, Thomas Drake, III .... Auburn, AL
Samford, Vonda J. .... Virginia Beach, VA
Samford, William J., Jr. .... Montgomery, AL
Samford, Yetta G., Jr. .... Opelika, AL

Samia, John R. .... Boston, MA
Samide, Steven A. .... New York, NY
Samiere, Carolyn A. .... San Francisco, CA
Samii, Roxanne E. .... Cambridge, MA
Samii, Salimé .... San Francisco, CA
Samila, Mark S. .... Evansville, IN
Samiljan, Katriana L. .... Seattle, WA
Samiljan, Nancy B. .... Boston, MA
Samilow, Gary B. .... New York, NY
Samilson, Lori A. .... Turnersville, NJ
Samimi & Murphy .... New City, NY
Samimi, Sandra .... New City, NY
Samini, Babak .... Newport Beach, CA
Samini, Keyvan .... Costa Mesa, CA
Saminski, Karen .... Jersey City, NJ
Saminsky, Robert L. .... Hauppauge, NY
New York, NY
Samios, Gus D. .... New York, NY
New York, NY
Samios, Mary Lynn .... Santa Cruz, CA
Samios-Uy, Herminio S. .... Baltimore, MD
Samis, Michael J. .... Deerfield, IL
Samis, Scot E. .... St. Petersburg, FL
Samit, Audrey J. .... Boston, MA
Samito, Christian G. .... Boston, MA
Samkange, Stanlake J. T. M. .... Bethesda, MD
Samlan, Alan B. .... Miami, FL
Chicago, IL
Samley, Matthew C. .... Lancaster, PA
Samlin, Scott D. .... Montvale, NJ
Samloff, Harold .... Rochester, NY
Samm, E. Selena .... Boston, MA
Sammarco, Anthony .... Wheaton, IL
Sammarco, Cynthia K. .... New Haven, CT
Sammarco, Leslie A. .... Chicago, IL
Sammarco, Maria-Rose .... Maywood, NJ
Sammarco, Vincent T.
Pembroke Pines, FL
Sammartano, Anthony .... White Plains, NY
Sammartano, Linda J. .... New York, NY
Sammartano, Sandra F. .... East Providence, RI
Sammartino, Catherine A. .... Providence, RI
Sammartino, Nicole .... Newport Beach, CA
Sammer, Frank J. .... Orlando, FL
Sammeth, Russell W., III .... Edisto Island, SC
Sammeth, Traci A. .... Seattle, WA
Sammi, P. Anthony .... New York, NY
Sammis, H. Wade .... Sacramento, CA
Sammis, Ian M. .... San Rafael, CA
Sammis, Jason D. .... Jacksonville, FL
Sammis, Richard C. .... New York, NY
Sammis, Robert J. .... Greenbrae, CA
Sammis, Robert L. .... Cerritos, CA
Sammis, William, Jr. .... New York, NY
Sammon, Albert C. .... Cleveland, OH
Sammon & Bolmeyer Co., L.P.A.
Cleveland, OH
Sammon, Elaine R. .... Uniondale, NY
Sammon, James P. .... Cleveland, OH
Sammon, John C. .... Decatur, GA
Sammon, John D. .... Cleveland, OH
Sammon, John K.
Federal Energy Regulatory Commission,
Office of Administrative Litigation, GV
Sammon, Karen Elizabeth
New Hartford, NY
Sammon, Leslie C. .... Boston, MA
Sammond, David T. .... Sacramento, CA
Sammond, John S. .... West Palm Beach, FL
Sammons, Angela W. .... Warner Robins, GA
Sammons, Anthony .... Memphis, TN
Sammons, Barry E. .... Milwaukee, WI
Sammons, C. David .... Orangeburg, NY
Sammons, Charles E. .... Miami, FL
Sammons, Daniel J. .... Tucson, AZ
Sammons, Darrell E. .... Pikeville, KY
Sammons, Diane Elizabeth .... Livingston, NJ
Sammons, Donald .... Huntington, WV
Sammons, Donald E. .... Mission Viejo, CA
Sammons, Gary S. .... Cincinnati, OH
Sammons, George M. .... Kentland, IN
Sammons, J. Kirkland .... Houston, TX
Sammons, Jack Lee .... Macon, GA
Sammons, Jeffery D. .... Columbus, OH
Sammons & Johnson, Co., L.P.A.
Columbus, OH
Sammons, Julie Anne .... Atlanta, GA
Sammons, Lee .... Tyler, TX
Sammons, Lloyd F. .... Arlington, VA
Sammons, Lucien R., Jr. .... West Union, WV
Sammons, Martin Z., Jr. .... Tyler, TX
Sammons, Mary Kathryn .... Houston, TX
Sammons, Melinda G. .... La Salle, IL
Sammons & Parker, A Professional
Corporation .... Longview, TX
Tyler, TX
Sammons, Randall M. .... Tucson, AZ
Sammons, Robert O. .... Winter Haven, FL
Sammons & Smith, P.L.L.C. .... Arlington, VA
Sammons, William C. .... Baltimore, MD
Sammons, William F. .... Morocco, IN
Sammons, Winn L. .... Phoenix, AZ
Samms, Gary M. .... Philadelphia, PA
Samms, Gregory Antonio .... Miami, FL
Samms, Maya C. .... Omaha, NE
Samms, Richard O. .... Norcross, GA
Samms, Ronnie .... Houston, TX
Sammut, Charles P. .... San Francisco, CA
Sammut, Norman A. .... Garden City, NY
Samnick, Jonathan Evan .... New York, NY
Samnick, Norman K. .... New York, NY
Samnick, Robert L. .... Garden City, NY
Samnick, Stephen E. .... West Caldwell, NJ
Samodovitz, Arthur J. .... Endicott, NY
Samofal, Alexander W.
Department of Agriculture,
Office of the General Counsel, GV
Samoff & Benton, PLLC .... Kingston, NY

Samoff, Jay L. .... Kingston, NY
Samol, Robert J. .... Wheeling, WV
Samole & Berger, P.A. .... Hollywood, FL
Miami, FL
Samole, Myron M. .... Hollywood, FL
Miami, FL
Samolewicz, Steven E. .... Northampton, MA
Samolis, Frank R. .... Washington, DC
Samols, Selma W. .... Silver Spring, MD
Samoluk, Thomas E. .... Boston, MA
Samolyk, Jennifer .... Providence, RI
Samonsky, Louis (Chuck) .... Ventura, CA
Samor, Alexander W. .... Southport, CT
Samora, Gwen J. .... Houston, TX
Samora, R. Eli .... San Jose, CA
Samorajczyk, Edward J., Jr.
Hartford, CT
Samorajczyk, Lisa A.
Department Of Veterans Affairs,
Board of Veterans Appeals, GV
Samorajczyk, Stanley J., (P.C.)
Washington, DC
Samore, Edward F. .... Sioux City, IA
Samore, Eric L. .... Chicago, IL
Samore, John F. Moon .... Albuquerque, NM
Samosiuk, Steven W. .... Bloomfield Hills, MI
Samost, Stephen D. .... Berlin, NJ
Samotny, Marc Z. .... Chicago, IL
Samouce, Robert C. .... Naples, FL
Samour, Carlos A., Jr. .... Littleton, CO
Samouris, Phillip C. .... San Diego, CA
Samovar, Kerry R. .... Los Angeles, CA
Samovar, Phillip G. .... Santa Monica, CA
Samowitz, Cary Brian .... New York, NY
Samowitz, Lee A. .... Bridgeport, CT
Samp, Edward J., Jr. .... Boston, MA
Samp, Frederick .... Bangor, ME
Samp Law Offices .... Sioux Falls, SD
Samp, Rollyn H. .... Sioux Falls, SD
Sampair, Patrick S. .... Phoenix, AZ
Sampang, Jocelyn M. .... Cincinnati, OH
Sampas, George J. .... New York, NY
Sampas, George P. .... Miami Beach, FL
Sampath, Elizabeth D. .... Philadelphia, PA
Sampedro, David .... Miami, FL
Sampel, James J. .... Staten Island, NY
Sampel & Nalley .... Staten Island, NY
Sampels, Merlyn D. .... Dallas, TX
Sampen, Don R. .... Chicago, IL
Samper, Ferd .... Indianapolis, IN
Samper, Hawkins, Atz & Reid
Indianapolis, IN
Samper, Ricardo G. .... La Grange, GA
Sampinos, Nick .... Price, UT
Sample, Beth A. .... El Cajon, CA
Sample & Birch .... Fresno, CA
Sample, Bryan L. .... Dallas, TX
Sample, Gregory W. .... Portland, ME
Sample, John .... Washington, DC
Sample, Julie A. N. .... Overland Park, KS
Sample, Karen N. .... Los Angeles, CA
Sample, Michael J. .... Washington, DC
Sample, Michael L. .... Boulder, CO
Sample, Molly McGuire .... Houston, TX
Sample, René L. .... Fresno, CA
Sample, Ronald F. .... Bishop, CA
Sample, Susan Virginia .... Houston, TX
Sample, Wallace .... Fort Pierce, FL
Sample, William S. .... Madison, WI
Samples, Colleen M. .... Birmingham, AL
Samples, Daniel H. .... Wheeling, WV
Samples, Frank P. .... Bakersfield, CA
Samples, Hoyt O. .... Chattanooga, TN
Samples, James M. .... Minneapolis, MN
Samples, Jennings & Pineda, PLLC
Chattanooga, TN
Samples, Kenneth H. .... Chicago, IL
Samples, Mitzi P. .... Chattanooga, TN
Samples, S. Shay .... Birmingham, AL
Samples, Warren K. .... Hoover, AL
Samplin, Caren L. .... Wantagh, NY
Sampliner, Gary H. .... Washington, DC
Sampliner, Thomas A. .... Cleveland, OH
Sampo, Kristen L. .... Fort Lauderdale, FL
Sampo, Peter L. .... Miami, FL
Sampo, Virginia Herrero .... Coral Gables, FL
Sampoli, L. Patricia .... Atlantic City, NJ
Pleasantville, NJ
Sampras, Chris C. .... Morton Grove, IL
Sampsel, Charles F. .... Bristol, PA
Langhorne, PA
Sampsell, David H. .... Minneapolis, MN
Sampson, Alan G. .... Beaumont, TX
Sampson, April Woodard .... Columbia, SC
Sampson, Arthur F., III .... Washington, DC
Sampson & Associates, P.C.
Lakewood, CO
Sampson & Associates, P.C. .... Boston, MA
Sampson, Bryan D. .... San Diego, CA
Sampson, Carolyn L. .... Lakewood, CO
Sampson, Charles P. .... Salt Lake City, UT
Sampson, Christine M. .... Houston, TX
Sampson, Craig S. .... Newport, RI
Sampson, Craig W. .... Charlottesville, VA
Sampson, Curry & Hummel
Central City, NE
Sampson, D. Kyle .... Salt Lake City, UT
Sampson, David A. .... Auburn, CA
Sampson, David C. .... Los Angeles, CA
Sampson, David F. .... Las Vegas, NV
Sampson, David S. .... Albany, NY
Sampson, DeMetris Aquilla .... Dallas, TX
Sampson, Donald J. .... Greenville, SC
Sampson, Donald R. .... Central City, NE
Sampson, Ellen G. .... Minneapolis, MN
Sampson, Erie F. .... Washington, DC
Sampson Firm, The, P.C. .... Omaha, NE

Sampson, Frederick D. R.
Kew Gardens, NY
Sampson, George W. .... Seattle, WA
Sampson, Gerald S. .... Stockton, CA
Sampson, Gregory W. .... Dallas, TX
Sampson, Herbert M., III .... Omaha, NE
Sampson, J. David .... Buffalo, NY
Rochester, NY
Sampson, J. John .... Story, WY
Sampson, Jean A. .... New York, NY
Sampson, John J. .... Austin, TX
Sampson, John L. .... Lancaster, PA
Sampson, John P. .... Ogden, UT
Sampson, Jonathan D. .... New York, NY
Sampson, Karen Elizabeth
Department of Justice,
Antitrust Division, GV
Sampson, Karen L. .... Montgomery, AL
Sampson, Karoline .... St. Paul, MN
Sampson, Keith T. .... San Francisco, CA
Sampson, Kellis W. .... Sherman, TX
Sampson, Kevin M. .... Vancouver, WA
Sampson, Kirk .... Cincinnati, OH
Sampson, Larry B. .... Raleigh, NC
Sampson, Linda A. .... Irvine, CA
Sampson, Linda C. .... San Rafael, CA
Sampson, Linnwood D. .... Spokane, WA
Sampson, M. Olene .... Matthews, NC
Sampson, Mark J. .... Andover, MA
Sampson, Matthew J. .... Chicago, IL
Sampson, Michael L. .... Dallas, TX
Sampson, Michael P. .... Washington, DC
Sampson, Michael P. .... Orlando, FL
Sampson, Michael P. .... Minneapolis, MN
Sampson, M. Olene, P.A. .... Matthews, NC
Sampson, Patrick J. .... Riverside, CA
Sampson, Phillip L., Jr. .... Houston, TX
Sampson, Raymond H. .... Albany, NY
Sampson, Richard I. .... Seattle, WA
Sampson, Richard L., Jr. .... Boston, MA
Sampson, Richard T. .... Washington, DC
Sampson, Rita M. .... Department of Justice,
Federal Bureau of Investigation, GV
Sampson, Robert W. .... Olympia, WA
Sampson, Roberta J. .... Philadelphia, PA
Sampson, Roger S. .... San Francisco, CA
Sampson, Russell E., Jr. .... Braintree, MA
Sampson, Sherri A. Braden
Washington, DC
Sampson, Sue Scott .... Richmond, VA
Sampson, Susan S. .... Boston, MA
Sampson, Thomas A., Jr. .... Mercer, PA
Sampson, Thomas G. .... Atlanta, GA
Sampson, Thomas G., II .... Atlanta, GA
Sampson, Timothy S. .... Arlington, VA
Sampson, Tonya L. .... Houston, TX
Sampson, Walter W., Jr. .... Portage, IN
Sampson, William A., II & Associates
Los Angeles, CA
Sampson, William A., II & Associates
Pacific Palisades, CA
Sampson, William Andrew .... Dayton, OH
Sampson, William E.
Department Of Veterans Affairs,
Board of Veterans Appeals, GV
Sampson, William R. .... Overland Park, KS
Sampson, William W. .... Malibu, CA
Sampson A., Patricia .... New York, NY
Samra, Jeanette M. .... Secaucus, NJ
Samra, Joseph S., Jr. .... Shrewsbury, MA
Samra, Ravinder .... El Centro, CA
Samrick, Phillip R. .... San Francisco, CA
Sams, Cathy R. .... St. Paul, MN
Sams, Celia M. .... Garland, TX
Rockwall, TX
Sams, Celia M. .... Rowlett, TX
Sams, Charles A. .... West Linn, OR
Sams, Charles M. .... New Smyrna Beach, FL
Sams, David A. .... West Jefferson, OH
Sams, Duane E. .... Boston, MA
Sams, Garvis L., Jr. .... Marietta, GA
Sams, Gary M. .... Decatur, GA
Sams, Gary P. .... Tallahassee, FL
Sams, H. William, Jr. .... Augusta, GA
Sams, Henry Brian .... Atlanta, GA
Sams & Hollon .... Coral Gables, FL
Sams & Hollon .... Jacksonville, FL
Sams, J. David .... Department of Commerce,
Patent and Trademark Office, GV
Sams, James F. .... Washington, DC
Sams, Jane Lamberti .... Atlanta, GA
Sams, Jeffrey B. .... Columbus, OH
Sams, Joe O., Jr. .... Columbus, MS
Sams, John G. .... Irving, TX
Sams, Jonathan D. .... Mason, OH
Sams, Joseph D. .... Cherry Hill, NJ
Sams, L. Wayne .... Charlotte, NC
Sams & Larkin, LLP .... Marietta, GA
Sams, Laurie B. .... Sarasota, FL
Sams, Lewis O. .... Coushatta, LA
Sams, L. F., Jr. .... Columbus, MS
Jackson, MS
Tupelo, MS
Sams, Lisa G. .... Treasury Department,
Internal Revenue Service, GV
Sams & Lister, P.A. .... Coral Gables, FL
Fort Lauderdale, FL
Miami, FL
West Palm Beach, FL
Sams, Louise S. .... Atlanta, GA
Sams, Marion A. .... Marietta, GA
Sams, Mary Margaret .... Aberdeen, MS
Sams, Michael P. .... Boston, MA
Sams, Murray, Jr. .... Coral Gables, FL
Jacksonville, FL
Miami, FL
Sams, Paul Steven .... Indianapolis, IN
Sams, Robert A. .... Riverside, CA

Sams, Robert A. ... Punta Gorda, FL
Sams, Robin Malone ... Midland, TX
Sams, Rufus D., III ... Macon, GA
Sams and Sams ... Beaufort, SC
Sams, Stanley M. ... Greenville, NC
New Bern, NC
Sams, Talbird Reeve ... Beaufort, SC
Sams, W. Fletcher ... Fayetteville, GA
Sams, W. Toland ... Beaufort, SC
Sams, Warren N., III ... Atlanta, GA
Sams, William H. ... San Diego, CA
Samsa, Mary K. ... Chicago, IL
Samsel, Amy E. ... Boston, MA
Samsel, Christine A. ... Los Angeles, CA
Samsel, David A. ... Ashland, OH
Samsel, Edward C. ... Columbus, OH
Samsel, Jennifer N. ... Boston, MA
Samsel, Tammy ... Los Angeles, CA
Samsil, D. M. ... Birmingham, AL
Samsky, Scott B. ... Oxnard, CA
Samson, Alexander M., Jr.
Bridgewater, NJ
Samson, Allen L. ... Milwaukee, WI
Samson, Andrew ... Roseland, NJ
Samson, Anthony D. ... San Diego, CA
Samson and Brown, P.C. ... Longmont, CO
Samson, Bruce B. ... Portland, OR
Samson, David ... Roseland, NJ
Samson, Deborah L. ... Smithfield, RI
Samson, Donald M. ... Belleville, IL
Samson, Douglas C. ... Arlington, VA
Samson, Edward S. ... New York, NY
Samson, Elizabeth A. ... Portland, OR
Samson, Emil ... Mayfield, KY
Samson, Eugene G. ... Summit, NJ
Samson, Gary D. ... Los Angeles, CA
Samson, Harvey G. ... Appleton, WI
Samson, Howard ... Vernon Hills, IL
Samson, Hugh W. ... Lynn, MA
Samson, Ivor E. ... San Francisco, CA
Samson, James G. ... New York, NY
Samson, Jane M. ... Irvine, CA
Samson, Jo Ann ... Concord, NH
Samson, Joel B. ... St. Louis, MO
Samson, John E. ... Blair, NE
Samson, Joseph M. ... Franklin, MA
Samson, Judith Ann ... Minneapolis, MN
Samson, Katharine Malley ... Gulfport, MS
Samson, Kendra E. ... Nashville, TN
Samson, Kenneth P. ... Livingston, NJ
Samson, Lawrence A.
North Hollywood, CA
Samson, Linda H. ... Wayne, NJ
Samson, Marc. L. ... Los Angeles, CA
Samson, Mark D. ... Phoenix, AZ
Samson, Martin H. ... New York, NY
Samson, Michael E. ... Castleton, VT
Samson, Paul M. ... Dayton, OH
Samson, Paul S. ... Boston, MA
Samson, Peter ... Philadelphia, PA
Samson, Richard E. ... Longmont, CO
Samson, Richard J. ... Missoula, MT
Samson, Richard L. ... Chicago, IL
Samson, Richard S. ... New York, NY
Samson, Robert T. ... Smithtown, NY
Samson, Roland F., III ... Gulfport, MS
Samson, Russell L. ... Des Moines, IA
Samson, Sandra Ansley ... Tallahassee, FL
Samson, Timothy T. ... Houston, TX
Samson, Wayne H. ... Montvale, NJ
Samster, James P. ... Milwaukee, WI
Samtani, Lavesh ... Palo Alto, CA
Chicago, IL
Samter, Nadine S ... Seattle, WA
Samton, Zachary E. ... New York, NY
Samuel, Amanda Cynthia ... New York, NY
Samuel, Arthur F. ... Richmond, VA
Samuel, Arthur R. ... Louisville, KY
Samuel and Ballard, A Professional Corporation
Philadelphia, PA
Samuel, Carl R. ... Fair Oaks, CA
Samuel, Charles E. ... Treasury Department, Internal Revenue Service, GV
Samuel, Charles R. ... Chattanooga, TN
Samuel, Cynthia A. ... New Orleans, LA
Samuel, Deborah P. ... Department of Justice, Civil Division, GV
Samuel, Denise L. ... Hartford, CT
Samuel, Donald F. ... Atlanta, GA
Samuel, Dwight M. ... Sacramento, CA
Samuel, Dwight M., P.C. ... Sacramento, CA
Samuel, Giordano Carmen ... New York, NY
Samuel, Gregory R. ... Dallas, TX
Samuel, Ilene D. ... Garden City, NY
Samuel, Jane Durkin ... Lexington, KY
Samuel, Jean ... Fair Oaks, CA
Samuel, Jeanne J. ... Department of State, Foreign Service Officers (Overseas), GV
Samuel, Jordan M. ... Arlington, VA
Samuel, Joseph S. ... Sacramento, CA
Samuel, Larry ... New Orleans, LA
Samuel, Linda L. ... Oklahoma City, OK
Samuel, Linda M. ... Department of Justice, Criminal Division, GV
Samuel, Louis ... Encino, CA
Samuel, Marcy B. ... Columbus, OH
Samuel, Mathias W. ... Minneapolis, MN
Samuel, Michael E. ... Hollywood, FL
Samuel, Percy M. ... Elmont, NY
Samuel, Peter F. ... Fair Oaks, CA
Samuel, Pustilnik & Marks, PLLC
Richmond, VA
Samuel, Ralph David ... Philadelphia, PA
Samuel, Ralph D. & Co., A Professional Corporation ... Philadelphia, PA
Samuel, Raphael ... New York, NY
Samuel, Reuben ... New York, NY
Samuel, Richard I. ... Roseland, NJ
New York, NY
Samuel, Robert F. ... Fair Oaks, CA
Samuel, Robert L., Jr. ... Virginia Beach, VA
Samuel, Robin J. ... Los Angeles, CA
Samuel, Sally ... Owings Mills, MD
Samuel, Shafie & Samuel ... Fair Oaks, CA
Samuel, Sofia ... Morristown, NJ
Samuel, Steven A. ... King Of Prussia, PA
Samuel, Steven B. ... Lake Success, NY
Samuel, Thomas L. ... Baltimore, MD
Samuel, Vini E. ... Aberdeen, WA
Samuel, Wayne G. ... Beverly Hills, CA
Samuel & Weininger ... Lake Success, NY
Samuel, Wendy B. ... Washington, DC
Samuelian, Anna E. ... Edgemont, PA
Samuelian, Karl M. ... Los Angeles, CA
Samuels, Adam D. ... Los Angeles, CA
Samuels, Allan C. ... New York, NY
Samuels, Allen H. ... Fort Plain, NY
Samuels, Allen R. ... Treasure Island, FL
Samuels, Anchel S. ... Savannah, GA
Samuels, Arnold ... Newark, NJ
Samuels, Arthur M. ... Winnetka, IL
Samuels, Barbara A. ... Castlewood, VA
Samuels, Barbara L. ... Brooklyn, NY
Samuels, Benford L., Jr. ... Jacksonville, FL
Samuels, Brian Jay ... Fort Lauderdale, FL
Samuels, Brian M. ... Denver, CO
Samuels, Bruce ... Metuchen, NJ
Samuels, Bruce E. ... Phoenix, AZ
Samuels, Burrel ... Utica, NY
Samuels, Calla B. ... Harrisburg, PA
Samuels, Cary S. ... North Hollywood, CA
Samuels, Charles Alan ... Washington, DC
Samuels, Charles E. ... Richmond, VA
Samuels, Charles J. ... Fairfax, VA
Samuels, Colin M. ... Salem, OR
Samuels, Craig E. ... Chicago, IL
Samuels, David G. ... New York, NY
Samuels, David L. ... Woodside, CA
Samuels, David M. ... Los Angeles, CA
Samuels, Deborah A. ... Orlando, FL
Samuels, Donald B. ... Hollywood, CA
Samuels, Donald L. ... Denver, CO
Samuels, Dorothy J. ... New York, NY
Samuels, Edward B. ... New York, NY
Samuels, Eleanor R. ... Houston, TX
Samuels, Ellen J. ... Dayton, OH
Samuels, Elliot M. ... Chicago, IL
Samuels, Emerson ... Pittsburgh, PA
Samuels, Eugene Paul ... Miami, FL
Samuels, Frederick N. ... Washington, DC
Rockville, MD
Samuels, Gary A. ... Newark, DE
Samuels, Gary C. ... Spring Valley, NY
Samuels, Gauthier & Stevens LLP
Boston, MA
Samuels, George H.
Department Of Health And Human Services, Social Security Administration, GV
Samuels, Gloria ... Johnson City, TN
Samuels, Harris J. ... Utica, NY
Samuels, Harvey M. ... Columbus, OH
Samuels, Henry B. ... Chicago, IL
Samuels, Herbert N. ... Irvine, CA
Samuels, Howard J. ... Hauppauge, NY
Samuels, I. Stephen ... Boston, MA
Samuels, Jack D. ... Los Angeles, CA
Samuels, Jacqueline ... New York, NY
Samuels, James A. ... Cleveland, OH
Samuels, James R. ... Big Rapids, MI
Samuels, Janet L. ... New York, NY
Samuels, Jay ... Princeton, NJ
Samuels, Jeanne M. ... New York, NY
Samuels, Jeffrey A. ... New York, NY
Samuels, Jeffrey B. ... New York, NY
Samuels, Jeffrey C. ... Marietta, GA
Samuels, Jeffrey M. ... Alexandria, VA
Samuels, Jeffrey P. ... Agoura Hills, CA
Samuels, Jocelyn F.
Equal Employment Opportunity Commission, Office of Legal Counsel, GV
Samuels, Jody R. ... New York, NY
Samuels, Joel G. ... Los Angeles, CA
Samuels, John M. ... Fairfield, CT
Samuels, Jonathan J. ... Kenilworth, NJ
Samuels, Kenneth B. ... Fort Worth, TX
Samuels, Kristine W. ... Santa Monica, CA
Samuels, Kyle R. ... Seattle, WA
Samuels, Lawrence C. ... Encino, CA
Samuels, Lawrence R. ... Chicago, IL
Samuels, Leonard K.
Fort Lauderdale, FL
Samuels, Leonard Michael ... Los Angeles, CA
Samuels, Leslie B. ... New York, NY
Samuels, Linda B. ... Fairfax, VA
Samuels, Lisa A. ... Atlanta, GA
Samuels, Lynn ... Atlanta, GA
Samuels, Lynn F. ... Morristown, NJ
New York, NY
Samuels, M. Dee ... San Francisco, CA
Samuels, Marcia B. ... Pembroke Pines, FL
Samuels, Margaret Ann ... Columbus, OH
Samuels, Marianne R. ... New Orleans, LA
Samuels, Mark A. ... Los Angeles, CA
Samuels, Martin ... Miami, FL
Samuels, Michael A. ... New York, NY
Samuels, Michael D. ... Arlington Heights, IL
Samuels, Michael J. ... Miami, FL
Samuels, Michael S. ... Phoenix, AZ
Samuels, Michael W. ... Los Angeles, CA
Samuels, Miller, Schroeder, Jackson & Sly
Arthur, IL
Chicago, IL
Decatur, IL
Samuels, Nancy B.
La Canada Flintridge, CA
Samuels and Northrop Co., LPA
Columbus, OH
Samuels, Paul E. ... Largo, FL
Samuels, Paul H., Law Offices of, P.C.
Los Angeles, CA
Samuels, Paul N. ... New York, NY
Samuels, Peter G. ... New York, NY
Samuels, Rachel L. ... Hudson, NY
Samuels, Randy ... Florham Park, NJ
Samuels, Richard A. ... Manchester, NH
Samuels, Robert A. ... St. Louis, MO
Samuels, Robert C. ... Hartford, CT
Samuels, Robert E. ... Northbrook, IL
Samuels, Roberta N. ... Livingston, NJ
Samuels, Ronald S. ... Chicago, IL
Samuels, S. Zachary, (P.C.)
Los Angeles, CA
Samuels, Sam ... Lido Beach, NY
Samuels and Samuels ... Utica, NY
Samuels, Sandor E. ... Calabasas, CA
Samuels, Scott Alan ... Boston, MA
Samuels & Shawn ... San Francisco, CA
Samuels, Shellie L. ... Valencia, CA
Samuels, Shepard H. ... New Orleans, LA
Samuels, Sherwin L. ... Los Angeles, CA
Samuels, Sidney P. ... Sausalito, CA
Samuels, Simonetti ... Chicago, IL
Samuels, Stanley L. ... Norfolk, VA
Samuels, Stanley M. ... Portland, OR
Samuels & Steel, LLP ... Irvine, CA
Samuels, Stephen L. ... Department of Justice, Environment and Natural Resources Division, GV
Samuels, Stephen P. ... Columbus, OH
Samuels, Steven B. ... Blue Bell, PA
Samuels, Steven G. ... Chicago, IL
Samuels, Sue Rose ... Miami, FL
Samuels, Suzanne Uttaro ... Yardley, PA
Samuels, Suzette M. ... Detroit, MI
Samuels, Sylvia S. ... San Mateo, CA
Samuels, Taylor W., Jr. ... Louisville, KY
Samuels, Valerie C. ... Boston, MA
Samuels, William J. ... Phoenix, AZ
Samuels, William S., Jr. ... Orinda, CA
Samuels, William S., Jr., Inc. ... Orinda, CA
Samuels Yoelin Kantor Seymour & Spinrad LLP ... Portland, OR
Samuelsen, David J. ... Oakland, CA
Samuelsen, David R. ... Boise, ID
Samuelsen, Douglas G. ... New Ulm, MN
Samuelsen, Gonzalez, Valenzuela & Sorkow
Glendale, CA
San Pedro, CA
Samuelsen, Gordon ... Alamo, TX
Samuelsen, James ... Milwaukee, WI
Samuelsen, Norman R. ... San Pedro, CA
Samuelsen, Robert Erling, II
Minnetonka, MN
Samuelson, Anne K. ... Los Angeles, CA
Samuelson & Associates, P.C. ... Houston, TX
Samuelson, Bryan M. ... Houston, TX
Samuelson, C. Lois ... Oak Park, IL
Samuelson, C. Ransom, II
Los Angeles, CA
Samuelson, Charles ... New York, NY
Samuelson, Charles M. ... Pender, NE
Samuelson, Christian C. ... Houston, TX
Samuelson, Derrick W. ... San Diego, CA
Samuelson, Diana ... Sebastopol, CA
Samuelson, Don S. ... Lake Villa, IL
Samuelson, Douglas A. ... Houston, TX
Samuelson, Elliot D. ... Garden City, NY
Samuelson, Jaki K. ... Des Moines, IA
Samuelson, Jerome C. ... Minneapolis, MN
Samuelson, Joan I. ... Los Angeles, CA
Samuelson, John R. ... Jamestown, NY
Samuelson, Joseph ... Belleville, IL
Samuelson, Kathryn L. ... Des Plaines, IL
Samuelson, Kenneth L. ... Washington, DC
Samuelson, Lawrence J. ... Washington, DC
St. Louis, MO
Samuelson, Lee ... New York, NY
Samuelson, M. Eugene ... Santa Rosa, CA
Samuelson, Matthew A. ... Denver, CO
Samuelson, Matthew Carl
Bennington, VT
Samuelson, Michael L. ... St. Cloud, MN
Samuelson, Mitchell ... Costa Mesa, CA
Samuelson, Pamela ... Pittsburgh, PA
Samuelson, Paul W. ... Boise, ID
Samuelson, Peter G. ... San Jose, CA
Samuelson, Peter J. ... Santa Barbara, CA
Samuelson Rieger & Yovino, LLP
Garden City, NY
Mineola, NY
Samuelson, Ronald K. ... Pender, NE
Samuelson, Scott A. ... Seattle, WA
Samuelson, Stephanie L. ... Phoenix, AZ
Samuelson, Susan L. ... Seattle, WA
Samuelson, Susan Stobaugh ... Boston, MA
Samuelson, Wayne P. ... Williamsport, PA
Samuelson, Wendy B. ... Garden City, NY
Samuely, Giselle M. ... New York, NY
Samulon, Eliot R. ... Pasadena, CA
Samus, Natasha ... New York, NY
Samway, Michael ... Miami, FL
Samwick, Matthew D. ... Portland, OR
Samy, Sharadchandra A. ... New York, NY
Sanabria, Christina ... New York, NY
Sanabria, Diana ... New York, NY
Sanabria, Eufemio ... Los Angeles, CA
Sanagavarapu, Sapna ... New York, NY
San Agustin, Donna Marie ... Los Angeles, CA
Sananes-Katz, Julie ... Johnstown, PA
Sanberg, Kathleen H. ... Minneapolis, MN
Sanberg, Lora K. ... Chicago, IL
Sanborn, Barry P. ... Walpole, MA
Sanborn, Brandon, Duvall & Valentine Co., L.P.A. ... Columbus, OH
Sanborn, Bruce E. ... Dearborn, MI
Sanborn, Carol Prenatt
Pacific Palisades, CA
Sanborn, Clairenne ... Garland, TX
Sanborn, Clifford W. (Sandy)
Panama City, FL
Sanborn, David W. ... Springfield, MA
Sanborn, Douglas G. ... Parsippany, NJ
Sanborn, Elizabeth M. ... Cleveland, OH
Sanborn & Grayson ... St. Paul, MN
Sanborn, Jacques A. ... Chalmette, LA
Sanborn, James B. ... Woodland Hills, CA
Sanborn, Jeffrey A. ... Richmond, VA
Sanborn, John E. ... Janesville, WI
Sanborn, Kathryn W. ... Richmond, VA
Sanborn, Kenneth N. ... Washington, MI
Sanborn, Kurt Douglas ... Brooklyn, MI
Sanborn, Marlene E. ... Stockton, CA
Sanborn, McCleary H., III
Santa Barbara, CA
Sanborn and Mills ... Wichita, KS
Sanborn, Nancy L. ... New York, NY
Sanborn, Richard ... Mulvane, KS
Wichita, KS
Sanborn, Richard B. ... Brunswick, ME
Sanborn, Robert C. ... Elma, NY
Sanborn, Robert S. ... Elma, NY
Sanborn, Roger L. ... Santa Rosa, CA
Sanborn, Steven K. ... Raleigh, NC
Sanborn, Von E. ... Manchester, NH
Sanborn, Warren L. ... Long Beach, CA
Sanborne, Marilyn C. ... Philadelphia, PA
Sanbrook, George A. ... Palo Alto, CA
Sanbrook, John ... Marysville, CA
Sances, Martin Ross ... San Francisco, CA
Sanchas, Raymond N. ... Pittsburgh, PA
Sanchelima & Associates, P.A. ... Miami, FL
Sanchelima, Jesus ... Miami, FL
Sánchez Acosta & Rosado-Perez
San Juan, PR
Sanchez, Agustin ... Union City, NJ
Sanchez, Albert A., Jr. ... Sarasota, FL
Sanchez, Alberto B. ... Portland, OR
Sanchez, Alexander ... Bronx, NY
Sanchez, Alexandra J. ... Miami, FL
Sanchez, Alexandro M. ... Miami, FL
Sanchez, Alfonso G. ... Santa Fe, NM
Sanchez, Alfonso G., P.A. ... Santa Fe, NM
Sanchez, Alfonso P. ... Cleveland, OH
Sanchez, Alfred, Jr. ... Los Angeles, CA
Sanchez, Alfred M. ... Albuquerque, NM
Sanchez, Aloyma M. ... Miami, FL
Sanchez, Alphonse, III ... Northridge, CA
Sanchez & Amador, LLP
Los Angeles, CA
Sanchez, Amelia D. ... San Diego, CA
Sanchez, Andrew M. ... Albuquerque, NM
Sanchez, Angela M. ... Chicago, IL
Sanchez, Angela Marie ... San Antonio, TX
Sanchez, Anthony F. ... Miami, FL
Sanchez, Anthony F., P.A. ... Miami, FL
Sanchez, Anthony G. ... Pittsburgh, PA
Sanchez, Anthony M. ... Rapid City, SD
Sanchez, Antonio R., Jr. ... Laredo, TX
Sanchez, Armando J. ... Bronx, NY
Sanchez, Arturo D. ... Los Angeles, CA
Sanchez, Barbara A. ... Belen, NM
Sanchez, Benjamin C. ... San Francisco, CA
Sanchez, Benjamin, Jr. ... San Diego, CA
Sanchez, Benjamin K. ... Houston, TX
Sanchez, Bertha P. ... Fort Lauderdale, FL
Sanchez, Carl R. ... San Diego, CA
Sanchez Castaño, Sanchez Rivera, & Associates ... San Juan, PR
Sanchez, D. Jean ... Lima, OH
Sanchez, Daniel E. ... Stamford, CT
Sanchez, Daniel F. ... Los Angeles, CA
Sanchez & Daniels ... Bloomington, IL
Chicago, IL
Wheaton, IL
Sanchez, Daniels & Fitch ... Boston, MA
Sanchez, Dave A. ... San Francisco, CA
Sanchez, David ... Los Angeles, CA
Sanchez, David V. ... Buffalo, NY
Sanchez, Deanna L. ... Denver, CO
Sanchez, Deborah L. ... South Pasadena, CA
Sanchez, Dennis M., (P.C.)
Brownsville, TX
Sanchez, Dennis T. ... Taos, NM
Sánchez de Varona, Raúl J., P.A.
Coral Gables, FL
Sanchez, Dorothy C. ... Albuquerque, NM
Sanchez, Douglas P. ... San Juan, PR
Sanchez, Douglas V. ... Hackensack, NJ
Sanchez, Eduardo B.
Englewood Cliffs, NJ
Sanchez, Eduardo I. ... Miami, FL
Sanchez, Elizabeth Biemer
St. Petersburg, FL
Sanchez, Elmer ... Orlando, FL
Sanchez, Emil J. ... New York, NY
Sanchez, Enedina Pilar ... Astoria, NY
Sanchez, Ernest E. ... Pasadena, CA
Sanchez, Ernest T. ... Washington, DC
Sanchez, Ernesto ... Coral Gables, FL
Sanchez, Ernesto G. ... Boise, ID
Sanchez, Ernesto, P.A. ... Coral Gables, FL
Sanchez, Esteban F. ... Springfield, IL
Sanchez, Felipe B. ... San Juan, PR
Sanchez, Felix ... Yonkers, NY
Sanchez, Francisco R. ... Torrance, CA
Sanchez, Frank E. ... New York, NY
Sanchez, Gabriel M. ... Miami, FL
Sanchez, Gabriel M., P.A. ... Miami, FL
Sanchez, George I. ... Palm Harbor, FL

Sanchez, Geraldine G. .... Portland, ME
Sanchez, Gloria Slominski .... Las Vegas, NV
Sanchez, Gordon D. .... Denver, CO
Sanchez, Gregoria .... New York, NY
Sanchez, H. Daniel .... Los Angeles, CA
Sanchez, Hazel A. .... Metairie, LA
Sanchez, Heidi P. .... St. Petersburg, FL
Sanchez, Henry, Jr. .... Rockville, MD
Sanchez, Henry L. .... Beverly Hills, CA
Sanchez, Henry V. .... Houston, TX
Sanchez, Idelsi C. .... Miami, FL
Sanchez, Ignacio E. .... Miami, FL
Sanchez, Israel I. .... Miami, FL
Sanchez, Israel M., Jr. .... Boston, MA
Sanchez, Jaime .... El Paso, TX
Sanchez, James C. .... Salinas, CA
Sanchez, James J. .... Fresno, CA
Sanchez, James L. .... Los Lunas, NM
Sanchez, Janette L. .... Miami, FL
Sanchez, Jeffrey .... Chicago, IL
Sanchez, Jennifer Tomlin
San Francisco, CA
Sanchez, Jerry G. .... Dallas, TX
Sanchez, Jesse M., JR .... San Antonio, TX
Sanchez, Jesusa .... Alice, TX
Sanchez, John .... Reno, NV
Sanchez, John E. .... Fort Lauderdale, FL
Sanchez, Jose F. .... Los Angeles, CA
Sanchez, Jose L. .... Redmond, WA
Sanchez, Jose Manuel .... Miami, FL
Sanchez, Joseph .... Denver, CO
Sanchez, Joseph M. .... Garden City, NY
Sánchez, Joyce K. .... Colorado Springs, CO
Sanchez, Juan Antonio .... Fort Myers, FL
Sanchez, Julian A. .... Tampa, FL
Sanchez, Julio .... Elizabeth, NJ
Sanchez, Karla G. .... New York, NY
Sanchez, Kerri L. .... Albuquerque, NM
Sanchez, Kimberly M.O. .... Houston, TX
Sanchez Law Firm .... Washington, DC
Sanchez Law Firm .... Houston, TX
Sanchez, Leopoldo G. .... Whittier, CA
Sanchez, Lilly Ann .... Washington, DC
Sanchez, Linda .... Houston, TX
Sanchez, Linda Q. .... Albuquerque, NM
Sanchez, Linda T. .... Orange, CA
Sanchez, Lou .... Los Angeles, CA
Sanchez, Loura K. .... Wheat Ridge, CO
Sanchez, Luis P. .... Folsom, CA
Sanchez, Luis R. .... Elizabeth, NJ
Sanchez, Manuel A., Jr. .... Bronx, NY
Sanchez, Manuel "Manny"
Bloomington, IL
Chicago, IL
Wheaton, IL
Sanchez, Manuel P. .... Elizabeth, NJ
Sanchez, Manuel R. .... New City, NY
Sanchez, Marc A. .... Cleveland, OH
Sanchez, Marcel P., Jr.
Department of Transportation, Research and Special Programs Administration, GV
Sanchez, Marcela M. .... New York, NY
Sanchez, Maria C. .... St. Louis, MO
Sanchez, Maria S. .... Austin, TX
Sanchez, Mark J. .... Vero Beach, FL
Sánchez, Mark Terrence .... Hobbs, NM
Sanchez, Maurice .... Irvine, CA
Los Angeles, CA
Sanchez, Maya .... San Diego, CA
Sanchez, Michael Eloy .... Rio Rancho, NM
Sanchez, Michael Patrick .... Gallup, NM
Sanchez, Michael S. .... Los Lunas, NM
Sanchez, Michele A. .... Brownsville, TX
Sanchez, Millicent N. .... Beverly Hills, CA
Sanchez, Miriam A. .... Los Angeles, CA
Sanchez, Moses M. (Moe) .... Houston, TX
Sanchez, Moses Moe, P.C. .... Houston, TX
Sanchez, Nicholas A. .... Los Angeles, CA
Sanchez, Nilo J., Jr. .... Tampa, FL
Sanchez, Olga Jonas .... San Francisco, CA
Sanchez, Oscar A. .... Miami, FL
Sanchez, Oscar E. .... Pembroke Pines, FL
Sanchez, Paulson, Mitchell & Laurie, A Professional Service Corporation
Bremerton, WA
Sanchez, Peter P. .... Moorestown, NJ
Sanchez, Philip A. .... Ardsley, NY
Sanchez, Philip J., IV .... Monroeville, AL
Sanchez, R. Michael .... Denver, CO
Sanchez, Rachelle C. .... Stockton, CA
Sánchez, Raúl M. .... New York, NY
Sanchez, Raymond G. .... Albuquerque, NM
Sanchez, Rebecca Rowland
San Antonio, TX
Sanchez, Ricky R. .... San Diego, CA
Sanchez, Robert .... Hialeah, FL
Sanchez, Robert C. .... St. Petersburg, FL
Sanchez, Robert D. .... Palo Alto, CA
Sanchez, Robert F. .... Las Vegas, NM
San-Chez, Robert H. .... San Rafael, CA
Sanchez, Robert J. .... San Jose, CA
Sanchez, Robert L. .... Waldwick, NJ
Sanchez, Ronald L. .... North Platte, NE
Sanchez, Ross C. .... Albuquerque, NM
Sanchez, Royner Caballero .... Pasadena, CA
Sanchez, Rozier E. .... Albuquerque, NM
Sanchez, R. P. (Bob) .... McAllen, TX
Sanchez, Ruben F. .... Encino, CA
Sanchez, Ruthanne G. .... Watertown, NY
Sanchez, Sam B. .... Taos, NM
Sanchez, Sandra Anne .... Denver, CO
Sanchez, Sharon Louise .... Santa Ana, CA
Sanchez, Steven W. .... San Diego, CA
Sanchez, Susan Barrington .... Houston, TX
Sanchez, Suzanna O. .... Dallas, TX
Sanchez, Terence M. .... Pasadena, CA
Sánchez, Teresa Gayle .... McKinney, TX
Sanchez, Terry E. .... Los Angeles, CA
Sanchez, Tony F., III .... Las Vegas, NV
Sanchez, Vincent A. .... Chicago, IL
Sanchez, Vincent J. .... Buffalo, NY
Sanchez, Walter M. .... Lake Charles, LA
Sanchez, Whittington, Janis & Zabarte, L.L.P. .... Brownsville, TX
Sanchez, William A. .... Los Lunas, NM
Sanchez, William J. .... Coral Gables, FL
Sanchez, William J., P.A. .... Coral Gables, FL
Sanchez, Willis Robert .... Houston, TX
Sanchez, Willow J. .... New York, NY
Sanchez, Zenaida .... Alice, TX
Sánchez-Aballí, Rafael J. .... Miami, FL
Sánchez Acosta, José .... San Juan, PR
Sánchez-Alvarez, Jose A. .... San Juan, PR
Sanchez-Arroyo, Miriam Waleska
San Juan, PR
Sánchez-Betances, Luis .... San Juan, PR
Sánchez-Betances & Sifre, PSC
San Juan, PR
Sánchez-Caso, Luis H. .... San Juan, PR
Sanchez-Castro, Jose C. .... San Juan, PR
Sanchez-Cooper, Martha Lucia .... Topeka, KS
Sánchez de Varona, Raúl J.
Coral Gables, FL
Sanchez-Figueroa, Norma I. .... Hartford, CT
Sanchez-Galarraga, Jorge .... Coral Gables, FL
Sanchez-Galarraga, Jorge, P.A.
Coral Gables, FL
Sanchez-Gronlier, Jose R. .... Coral Gables, FL
Sanchez-Hayes, Lorraine .... Atlanta, GA
Sanchez Hernandez, Rafael .... San Juan, PR
Sanchez-Ledo, Ivonne S. .... Miami, FL
Sanchez-Marte, Lourdes .... Eugene, OR
Sanchez-Masi, Linda Reed .... Lincoln, NE
Sanchez-Medina, Roland, Jr. .... Miami, FL
Sanchez Pizarro, Felix E. .... San Juan, PR
Sanchez-Ramos, Roberto J. .... Pasadena, CA
Sanchez Rivera, Benicio .... San Juan, PR
Sanchez-Ruiz, Amaury .... San Juan, PR
Sanchez-Solivan, Jose E. .... San Juan, PR
Sanchez-Vélez, José J. .... San Juan, PR
Sanchy, Jerome J. .... Torrington, CT
Sancilio, Michele Ann .... Marion, VA
Sancimino, Mary G. .... San Francisco, CA
Sancinito, Louis S. .... Trenton, NJ
San Clemente, Alphonse P. .... Fitchburg, MA
Worcester, MA
Sanclemente, Frank .... Randolph, MA
Sand, David B. .... Minneapolis, MN
Sand, Fred W. .... Washington, DC
Sand, Gibbs, Marcu, Smilk & Sherman
Broomall, PA
Sand, James C. .... Seattle, WA
Sand Law Office .... Bozeman, MT
Sand, Leonard B. .... New York, NY
Sand, Michael .... Canton, OH
Sand, Michael P. .... Bozeman, MT
Sand, Norman A. .... West Palm Beach, FL
Sand, Percy H. .... Broomall, PA
Sand, Peter .... Philadelphia, PA
Sand, Richard M. .... Philadelphia, PA
Sand, Richard W. .... Warsaw, IN
Sand, Robert A. .... Moorestown, NJ
Sand, Robert H. .... Morristown, NJ
Sand, Robert L. .... Montpelier, VT
Sand, Rosellen M. .... Bismarck, ND
Sand and Saidel, P.C. .... Philadelphia, PA
Sand, Scott G. .... San Diego, CA
Sand & Sebolt, A Legal Professional Association .... Canton, OH
Sand, Stephen J. .... Arlington, VA
Sand, Steven S. .... Woodbury, NJ
Sand, Thomas C., P.C. .... Portland, OR
Sanda, Constance S. .... Westlake, OH
Sanda, Timothy J. .... St. Paul, MN
Sandack, Arthur F. .... Salt Lake City, UT
Sandack, Roger D. .... Salt Lake City, UT
Sandack, Ronald L. .... Chicago, IL
Sandacz, Beverly A. .... Cleveland, OH
Sandage, Charles E., Jr. .... Independence, MO
Sandage, Douglas S., (P.C.) .... Houston, TX
Sandage, John Byron .... Department of State, Office of the Legal Adviser, GV
Sandage, Lance D. .... Independence, MO
Sandage, Lawrence H. .... Independence, MO
Sandager & Cuneo, L.L.P.
Albuquerque, NM
Sandager, John T. .... Albuquerque, NM
Sandahl, Bruce E. .... Hastings, NE
Sandahl, M. Todd .... Nashville, TN
Sandahl, Suzanne M. .... Minneapolis, MN
Sandak Friedman Hennesey & Greco, LLP
Bridgeport, CT
Fairfield, CT
Greenwich, CT
Norwalk, CT
Sandak Friedman Hennessey & Greco, LLP
Stamford, CT
Sandak, Jay H. .... Stamford, CT
Sandak, Lawrence R. .... New York, NY
Sandala, Maria A. .... Pittsburgh, PA
Sandall, Kenneth W. .... Los Gatos, CA
Sandalls, Helen M. .... Washington, DC
Sandalow, Terrance .... Ann Arbor, MI
Sandals, Alan M. .... Philadelphia, PA
Sandals, Barry S. .... San Francisco, CA
Sandals, Langer & Taylor, LLP
Philadelphia, PA
Sandars, Paul A., III .... Roseland, NJ
Rochester, NY
Sandau, Roger A. .... Santa Ana, CA
Sandbach, David F., Jr. .... Valdosta, GA
Sandbach, David F., Jr., P.C. .... Valdosta, GA
Sandbach, Robert F. .... Ventura, CA
Sandback, Birnbaum & Michelen
Mineola, NY
Sandback, William A. .... Mineola, NY
Sandbaken, Mark G. .... Salt Lake City, UT
Sandberg, Alicia K. .... White Plains, NY
Sandberg, Arne Blough .... San Leandro, CA
Sandberg, B. David .... Cambridge, MA
Sandberg, Carolyn M. .... Minneapolis, MN
Sandberg, Christopher K.
Minneapolis, MN
Sandberg, Craig M. .... Roseville, CA
Sandberg, Cynthia L. .... Ben Lomond, CA
Sandberg, Daniel H. .... Sacramento, CA
Sandberg, Daniel H., A Prof. Corp., Law Offices of .... Sacramento, CA
Sandberg, Daniel M. .... Birmingham, MI
Sandberg, David .... Forest Lake, MN
Sandberg, David Nils .... Hampton, NH
Sandberg, Douglas R. .... Atlanta, GA
Sandberg, Earle C. .... Totowa, NJ
Sandberg, Elisabet K. .... Columbus, OH
Sandberg, J. Ronald .... Houston, TX
Sandberg, James P. .... Owatonna, MN
Sandberg, Jeffrey R. .... Dallas, TX
Sandberg, Jennifer B. .... Atlanta, GA
Sandberg, John A. .... West Hartford, CT
Sandberg, John H. .... Denver, CO
Sandberg, John S. .... Belleville, IL
St. Louis, MO
Sandberg, Kevin C. .... Ellington, CT
Sandberg, Marc L. .... St. Louis, MO
Sandberg, Mark A., (P.C.)
Anchorage, AK
Sandberg, Neal L. .... Miami, FL
Sandberg, Ole R. .... Los Angeles, CA
Sandberg, Peter C. .... Rochester, MN
Sandberg, Phoenix & von Gontard, A Professional Corporation .... Belleville, IL
St. Louis, MO
Sandberg, Richard J. .... Wheaton, IL
Sandberg, Robt. L. .... Akron, OH
Sandberg, Scott C. .... Salt Lake City, UT
Sandberg, Simone Marie .... Wahpeton, ND
Sandberg, Stevan A. .... New York, NY
Sandberg, Susan E. .... Chicago, IL
Sandberg, Theodore .... Sault Ste. Marie, MI
Sandberg, Theresa A. .... Palm Harbor, FL
Sandberg, Victoria A. .... Minneapolis, MN
Sandberg, Wuestenfeld & Corey
Anchorage, AK
Sandblom, Gary P. .... Boulder, CO
Sandblom, Gary P., P.C., Law Offices of
Boulder, CO
Sandblom, Steven K. .... Humboldt, IA
Sandborn, Marilyn Drivas .... Tampa, FL
Sandbote, Louis J. .... Dallas, TX
Sandbote, Louis J., P.C. .... Dallas, TX
Sandbower & Gabler, P.A.
Baltimore, MD
Sandbower, John E., III .... Baltimore, MD
Sandcork, Robert R. .... St. Louis, MO
Sande, Brian H. .... New Richmond, WI
Sande, C. Ken .... Billings, MT
Sande, Christian M. .... Minneapolis, MN
Sande, John P., III .... Las Vegas, NV
Reno, NV
Sande, Kermit A. .... Department of Defense, Defense Legal Services Agency, GV
Sande, Margaret J. .... Royal Oak, MI
Sande, Michael E. .... Brooklyn, NY
Sande, Steven C. .... Lewistown, MT
Sandeen, Searle R. .... Stillwater, MN
Sandeen, Sharon K. .... Sacramento, CA
Sandeen, Winston E. .... Scottsdale, AZ
Sandefer, Debra D. .... Houston, TX
Sandefer, Jim McDonald
Mountain Brook, AL
Sandefer, Larry .... Clearwater, FL
Sandefer, Larry, P.A. .... Clearwater, FL
St. Petersburg, FL
Sandefer, Richard Ellis .... Oneonta, AL
Pinson, AL
Sandefer, Sandefer & Francis, P.C.
Mountain Brook, AL
Oneonta, AL
Pinson, AL
Sandefer, Virgil K. .... Mountain Brook, AL
Sandefur, David L. .... Jackson, MS
Sandefur, Gregory C. .... Texarkana, TX
Sandefur, Jerry D. .... Elk Grove, CA
Sandefur, Rebecca .... St. Petersburg, FL
Sandel, Charles P. .... San Francisco, CA
Sandel, David E., Jr. .... Philadelphia, PA
Sandel, Jerry A. .... Huntsville, TX
Sandel, Kevin S. .... Copley, OH
Sandel, Larry W. .... Tulsa, OK
Sandel, Martin L. .... Cleveland, OH
Sandel, Wantland L., Jr. .... Chicago, IL
Sandelands, David B., Jr.
Los Angeles, CA
Sandelands, William C. .... New York, NY
Sandelin, D. Scott .... Camano, WA
Sandelin, Paul J. .... Pequot Lakes, MN
Sandelin & Sandelin .... Camano, WA
Sandell, Charles W. .... Seattle, WA
Sandell, Daniel G. .... Madison, WI
Sandell, David W. .... Seattle, WA
Sandell, David W., P.S. .... Seattle, WA
Sandell, Jerry .... Silverton, CO
Sandell, Joseph R. .... Spokane, WA
Sandell & Young, Inc. .... Fresno, CA
Sandelman, Raymond L. .... Chico, CA
Sandelmann, Frank .... Los Angeles, CA
Sandels, Stephen C. .... Chicago, IL
Sandeman, Sonja E. .... San Francisco, CA
Sandeman, Teri A. .... Davenport, IA
Sanden, Carolyn A. .... Lake Stevens, WA
Sanden, David R. .... Lincoln, NE
Sanden, Gerald A. Vander .... Cedar Rapids, IA
Sanden, James M. .... Fargo, ND
Sanden, Jennifer H. .... Sacramento, CA
Sanden, Minut A. .... Conroe, TX
Sandenaw, Carrillo & Piazza, P.C.
Las Cruces, NM
Sandenaw, Thomas A., Jr.
Las Cruces, NM
Sander, David C. .... Austin, TX
Sander, David J. .... Warrington, PA
Sander, Donald A. .... Eastham, MA
Sander, Dorothy L. .... Racine, WI
Sander, Frank E. A. .... Cambridge, MA
Sander, Frank J., III .... Cuyahoga Falls, OH
Sander, George F., Jr. .... Baltimore, MD
Sander, Harvey S. .... New York, NY
Sander, James K. .... Minneapolis, MN
Sander, James M. .... Pittsburgh, PA
Sander, John F. .... St. Louis, MO
Sander, John L. .... Kenilworth, NJ
Sander Law Offices P.C. .... Austin, TX
Sander, Lori Anne .... Oklahoma City, OK
Sander, Malvin G., III .... Honolulu, HI
Sander, Mark R. .... Voorhees, NJ
Sander, Nancy Ann .... Austin, TX
Sander, Nancy L. .... Palm Springs, CA
Toledo, OH
Sander, Nancy N. .... Morton Grove, IL
Sander, Paul B. .... Dallas, TX
Sander, Richard G. .... Denver, CO
Sander, Richard G., Jr. .... Chicago, IL
Sander, Richard W. .... Cleveland, OH
Sander, Robert J. .... Harrisburg, PA
Sander, Ronni .... Pound Ridge, NY
Sander, Sabrina .... Los Angeles, CA
Sander, Thomas G. .... Miami, FL
Sander, Timothy .... New York, NY
Sander, Timothy George .... Miami, FL
Sandercock, Colin G. .... Washington, DC
Sandercock, John P. .... New York, NY
Sandercock, Margaret B. .... New York, NY
Sanderfer, Steve E. .... Dallas, TX
Sanderford, David M. .... Avon, CT
Sanderford, John R., III .... Kansas City, MO
Sanderford, Paul H. .... Arlington, TX
Sanderlin, James L. .... Richmond, VA
Sanderlin, William W. .... Falls Church, VA
Sanderman, Philip H. .... Medford, NY
Sanders, A. Powell .... Fort Smith, AR
Sanders, Alain L. .... New York, NY
Sanders, Alan A. .... Philadelphia, PA
Sanders, Alan J. .... Melville, NY
Sanders, Alan M. .... Freeport, NY
Sanders, Alison A. .... Los Angeles, CA
Sanders, Allen H. .... Seattle, WA
Sanders, Amy Stewart .... El Paso, TX
Sanders & Anderson .... Marysville, CA
Sanders, Andra D. .... New York, NY
Sanders, Andre Keith .... Atlanta, GA
Sanders, Andrew .... New York, NY
Sanders, Andrew Jonas .... New York, NY
Sanders, Andrew T., Jr. .... Richmond, VA
Sanders, Anika K. .... Washington, DC
Sanders, Anita F. .... Oklahoma City, OK
Sanders, Ann Morgan .... Charlotte, NC
Sanders, Anne C. .... Jackson, MS
Sanders, Annette .... Windsor, CT
Sanders, Anthony L. .... Waverly, TN
Sanders, Archie, III .... Memphis, TN
Sanders, Arthur .... White Plains, NY
Sanders & Associates, P.C. .... Tulsa, OK
Sanders, Austin, Swope & Flanigan
Bluefield, WV
Princeton, WV
Welch, WV
Sanders, Barbara Spohrer .... Apalachicola, FL
Sanders, Barefoot .... Dallas, TX
Sanders, Barnet, Goldman, Simons & Mosk, A Professional Corporation
Los Angeles, CA
Sanders, Barrett .... Mount Dora, FL
Sanders, Barry A. .... Los Angeles, CA
Sanders, Barry R. .... Phoenix, AZ
Sanders, Betty R. .... Atascadero, CA
Sanders, Billy J. .... Beaumont, TX
Sanders, Bluford B., Jr. .... El Paso, TX
Sanders, Bobby F. .... Greenup, IL
Sanders, Bobby L. .... Canton, TX
Sanders, Branch .... Rye, NH
Sanders, Brenda K. .... Detroit, MI
Sanders, Brent .... Seattle, WA
Sanders, Bret A. .... Tulsa, OK
Sanders, Brian C. .... Fort Walton Beach, FL
Sanders, Brian C., P.A.
Fort Walton Beach, FL
Sanders, Brigham "Buddy" .... Houston, TX
Sanders, Bruce .... Silver Spring, MD
Sanders, Bruce A. .... Virginia Beach, VA
Sanders, Bruin, Coll & Worley, P.A.
Carlsbad, NM
Hobbs, NM
Lovington, NM
Roswell, NM
Sanders, Bryan H. .... Elyria, OH
Sanders, B. W. .... Arkadelphia, AR
Sanders, C. Dylan .... Boston, MA
Sanders, C. Wilton .... Atlanta, GA
Sanders, Carl E. .... Atlanta, GA
Sanders, Carl N. .... Bronx, NY
Sanders, Carlton E. .... Corydon, IN
Sanders, Carmel W. .... Savannah, GA
Sanders, Caroline W. .... Yuma, AZ
Sanders, Carolyn Holstein .... Columbia, SC
Sanders, Catherine D. .... Chicago, IL
Sanders, Cecil C. .... Lancaster, KY
Sanders, Charlene M. .... Green Bay, WI
Sanders, Charles E. .... Spartanburg, SC
Sanders, Charles E., Jr. .... Jasper, AL
Sanders, Charles J. .... Miami, FL
Sanders, Charles J. .... New York, NY

Sanders, Charles J. ... New York, NY
Sanders, Charles M., Jr. ... Vero Beach, FL
Sanders, Charles W., Jr. ... Marysville, CA
Sanders, Chase J. ... Washington, DC
Sanders, Christopher C. ... Charlotte, NC
Sanders, Christopher D. ... Garden City, KS
Sanders, Christopher M. ... Sacramento, CA
Sanders, C. J. ... Spring, TX
Sanders, Clarence R., Jr.
Commodity Futures Trading Commission, Division of Trading and Markets, GV
Sanders, Claudia Jane ... Chicago, IL
Sanders, Clayton R., Jr. ... Cincinnati, OH
Sanders, Clifford E. ... Kingsport, TN
Sanders, Collins & Rehaste ... Orange, CA
Sanders, Conkright & Warren, LLP
Overland Park, KS
Sanders, Conkright & Warren LLP
Kansas City, MO
Sanders, Conrad W. ... Scottsdale, AZ
Sanders, Corey M. ... Conway, SC
Sanders, Crochet & Chism, L.L.P.
Lake Charles, LA
Sanders, Curtis B. ... Aspen, CO
Sanders, Cynthia L. ... Omaha, NE
Sanders, D. Billye ... Nashville, TN
Sanders, D. Blaine ... Charlotte, NC
Sanders, Dale Edwin ... Alexandria, VA
Sanders, Dale R. ... Fort Lauderdale, FL
Sanders, Dan C. ... Kansas City, MO
Sanders, Daniel R. ... Seattle, WA
Sanders, David A. ... Greenwich, CT
Sanders, David C. ... Baton Rouge, LA
Lafayette, LA
New Orleans, LA
Austin, TX
Sanders, David D. ... Evansville, IN
Sanders, David E. ... Milpitas, CA
Sanders, David H. ... Tulsa, OK
Sanders, David H. ... Martinsburg, WV
Sanders, David H., Jr. ... Tulsa, OK
Sanders, David L. ... San Bernardino, CA
Sanders, David L. ... Columbus, MS
Sanders, David M. ... Carmichael, CA
Sanders, David M. ... Knoxville, TN
Sanders, David M. ... Milwaukee, WI
Sanders, David P. ... Washington, DC
New York, NY
Sanders, David P. ... Chicago, IL
Sanders, David R. ... Baltimore, MD
Sanders, David Seth ... Washington, DC
Sanders, Dean A. ... Wichita Falls, TX
Sanders, Deborah Michelle
San Francisco, CA
Sanders, Deirdre E. ... Lexington, MA
Sanders, Denise L. ... Bridgewater, NJ
Sanders, Dennis C. ... Thomson, GA
Sanders, Dennis E. ... Leucadia, CA
Sanders, Devon ... Philadelphia, PA
Sanders, Diana M. ... Raceland, LA
Sanders, Don H. ... Roseburg, OR
Sanders, Donald E. ... San Marcos, TX
Sanders, Donald G. ... Columbia, MO
Sanders, Doris I. ... Crawfordville, FL
Sanders, Dorothy G. ... Sharon, MA
Sanders, Douglas B. ... Chicago, IL
Sanders, Douglas W. ... San Antonio, TX
Sanders, Douglas W., Jr. ... Poteau, OK
Sanders, Doyle D. ... Des Moines, IA
Johnston, IA
Sanders, E. Frederick ... Augusta, GA
Sanders, E. Leon ... Birmingham, AL
Sanders, E. Scott ... Greenville, SC
Sanders, E. Scott, LLC ... Greenville, SC
Sanders, Earl A.
Office of Personnel Management, Compensation Division, GV
Sanders, Edward ... Los Angeles, CA
Sanders, Edward ... Lexington, MS
Sanders, Edwin P. B. ... DeLand, FL
Sanders, Elaine ... Oklahoma City, OK
Sanders, Elizabeth A. ... Chicago, IL
Sanders, Elzie S., (Mr.) ... Gainesville, FL
Sanders, Eric L. ... Beverly Hills, CA
Sanders, Eric T. ... Anchorage, AK
Sanders, F. Michael ... Fort Worth, TX
Sanders, Frank E. ... Houston, TX
Sanders, Fredric M. ... New York, NY
Sanders, Gary A. ... Washington, DC
Sanders, Gary D. ... El Paso, TX
Sanders, Gary L. ... Ocala, FL
Sanders, Gary L. ... Southfield, MI
Sanders, Gary W. ... Orange, CA
Sanders, Gayle S. ... New York, NY
Sanders, Geoffrey W. ... Houston, TX
Sanders, George B., Jr. ... Worcester, MA
Sanders, George M. ... Chicago, IL
Sanders, Gerald J. ... San Francisco, CA
Sanders, Glenda ... Costa Mesa, CA
Sanders, Grant D. ... Des Moines, IA
Sanders, Gregory J. ... Salt Lake City, UT
Sanders, Gregory W. ... Irvine, CA
Sanders, Gutman & Brodie, P.C.
Brooklyn, NY
Sanders, H. David ... Kansas City, MO
Sanders, H. Gibert, III ... Greenville, SC
Sanders, H. Kendrick ... Fairfax, VA
Sanders, Hal L., Jr., (P.C.) ... Austin, TX
Sanders, Harold Barefoot, Jr. ... Dallas, TX
Sanders, Harvey G., Jr. ... Greenville, SC
Sanders, Harvey P. ... Amherst, NY
Sanders, Haugen & Sears, P.C.
Newnan, GA
Sanders, Helaine E. ... Amherst, NY
Sanders, Henry ... Selma, AL
Sanders, Henry E. ... Madison, WI
Sanders, Henry T. ... Chicago, IL
Sanders, Henry V. ... Louisville, KY

Sanders, Herbert A. ... Detroit, MI
Sanders, Howard M. ... Columbus, OH
Sanders, Howard R. ... New York, NY
Sanders, Hugh A. ... Newport Beach, CA
Sanders, H. W. ... Wichita Falls, TX
Sanders, Ira Allen ... Denver, CO
Sanders, Ira S. ... Little Neck, NY
Sanders, J. Bradley ... New Albany, IN
Sanders, J. Christopher ... Louisville, KY
Sanders, J. Lawrence ... Marion, IL
Sanders, J. Stanley ... Los Angeles, CA
Sanders, Jack L. ... Orchard Park, NY
Sanders, Jack M., Jr. ... Marshall, TX
Sanders, Jack M., Jr., P.C. ... Marshall, TX
Sanders, Jacquelyn D. ... Dublin, GA
Sanders, Jaime M. W. ... Portland, OR
Sanders, James ... Seattle, WA
Sanders, James E. ... Fairway, KS
Sanders, James E. ... Warren, OH
Sanders, James E. B. ... Atlanta, GA
Sanders, James F. ... St. Louis, MO
Sanders, James F. ... Nashville, TN
Sanders, James F., Jr. ... Orange, CA
Sanders, James G. ... Montclair, NJ
Sanders, James L. ... Los Angeles, CA
Sanders, James L. ... Overland Park, KS
Sanders, James L. ... St. Louis, MO
Sanders, James L., II ... Birmingham, AL
Sanders, James M.
Commodity Futures Trading Commission, Division of Enforcement, GV
Sanders, James M. ... Atlanta, GA
Sanders, James S. ... Lancaster, KY
Sanders, James W. ... Rochester, NY
Sanders, Janet L. ... Waltham, MA
Sanders, Janet Lee ... Grandview, MO
Sanders, Janney E. ... Toccoa, GA
Sanders, Jason D. ... Phoenix, AZ
Sanders, Jay D. ... Los Angeles, CA
Sanders, Jay Edwin
Hot Springs National Park, AR
Sanders, Jay M. ... Gainesville, FL
Sanders, Jay P. ... San Francisco, CA
Sanders, J. E.
Hot Springs National Park, AR
Sanders, Jeff ... New York, NY
Sanders, Jeffrey M. ... Covington, KY
Sanders, Jennifer L. ... Portland, ME
Sanders, Jennifer T. ... San Francisco, CA
Sanders, Jenny L. ... Lexington, KY
Sanders, Jerry C. ... Houston, TX
Sanders, Jerry D. ... Columbus, GA
Sanders, Joel S. ... San Francisco, CA
Sanders, John ... Altamonte Springs, FL
Sanders, John ... Uniondale, NY
Sanders, John A. ... Orlando, FL
Sanders, John A. ... Green Bay, WI
Sanders, John Burke ... Covington, LA
Sanders, John C. ... Anoka, MN
Sanders, John E. ... Eureka, KS
Sanders, John E., Jr. ... Johnson City, TN
Sanders, John L. ... Chapel Hill, NC
Sanders, John L. ... San Antonio, TX
Sanders, John M. ... San Diego, CA
Sanders, John M. ... Houston, TX
Sanders, John M. ... Lubbock, TX
Sanders, John T., IV ... Houston, TX
Sanders, John W. ... Marion, IL
Sanders, Johnnie M. ... Carson, CA
Sanders & Johnson, P.L.L.C. ... Detroit, MI
Sanders, Jonathan Scott ... Miami, FL
Sanders, Jos. H. ... Chicago, IL
Sanders, Joseph ... Houston, TX
Sanders, Joseph M., Jr. ... Bluefield, WV
Sanders, Joseph P. ... Beaumont, TX
Sanders, Judith B. ... Columbus, OH
Sanders, Karen J. ... East Hartford, CT
Sanders, Kathryn A. ... Los Angeles, CA
Sanders, Keith A. ... Anchorage, AK
Sanders, Kelvin G. ... New Orleans, LA
Sanders, Kenneth J. ... Grand Rapids, MI
Sanders, Kevin L. ... Johnstown, PA
Sanders, Kevin S. ... Jacksonville, FL
Sanders, Kevin S., P.A. ... Jacksonville, FL
Sanders, Kimberly Elaine ... Tucker, GA
Sanders, Kimberly J. ... New Orleans, LA
Sanders, Kristi Kay ... Bartlesville, OK
Sanders, Kristi Lee ... Golden, CO
Sanders, Kyle W. ... Houston, TX
Sanders, L. Gray ... Tampa, FL
Sanders, L. Norman
Upper Marlboro, MD
Sanders, Larry ... Grand Haven, MI
Sanders, Laurie A. ... San Francisco, CA
Sanders, Lawrence I. ... Beechhurst, NY
Sanders, LeAnn ... Las Vegas, NV
Reno, NV
Sanders, Lisa Smith
Upper Marlboro, MD
Sanders, Lloyd A. ... Wellesley, MA
Sanders, Lora B. ... Phoenix, AZ
Sanders, Louis W. ... White Plains, NY
Sanders, Lynn ... Austin, TX
Sanders, Lynwood ... Orange, TX
Sanders, M. Bradford ... Cincinnati, OH
Sanders, M. Franklin ... Spartanburg, SC
Sanders, Madge O'Brien ... Chicago, IL
Sanders, Margaret D. ... Des Moines, IA
Sanders, Margaret E. ... Atlanta, GA
Sanders, Maria DelPizzo ... Milwaukee, WI
Sanders, Mark A. ... Houston, TX
Sanders, Mark A. ... Milwaukee, WI
Sanders, Mark E. ... Milwaukee, WI
Sanders, Mark G. ... Seattle, WA
Sanders, Mark I. ... Atlanta, GA
Sanders, Mark R. ... St. Louis, MO
Sanders, Martin S., III ... Winnfield, LA
Sanders, Mary H. ... Charleston, WV

Sanders, Mary McDermott ... Des Moines, IA
Sanders, Mary Roby ... Towson, MD
Sanders, Maureen A. ... Albuquerque, NM
Sanders & McDermott, P.L.L.C.
Concord, NH
Hampton, NH
Waterville Valley, NH
Sanders, McEwan, Martinez, Luff & Dukes, P.A. ... Orlando, FL
Sanders, Melinda M. ... St. Cloud, MN
Sanders, Michael ... Los Angeles, CA
Sanders, Michael ... Morris Plains, NJ
Sanders, Michael C. ... Houston, TX
Sanders, Michael D. ... Lansing, MI
Sanders, Michael E.
Hot Springs National Park, AR
Sanders, Michael I. ... Washington, DC
Sanders, Michael L. ... St. Charles, IL
Sanders, Michael P. ... Elizabeth City, NC
Sanders, Michael R. E. ... Seattle, WA
Sanders, Michael W. ... Houston, TX
Sanders, Michele M. ... Rockford, IL
Sanders, Mike C. ... Monroe, LA
Sanders & Millette ... Charlotte, NC
Sanders, Monica C. ... Daytona Beach, FL
Sanders, Muriel ... Bronx, NY
Sanders, Nanette D. ... Irvine, CA
Sanders, Natalie Kay ... Greensboro, NC
Sanders, Nathan D. ... Portland, OR
Sanders, Neal A. ... Washington, DC
Butler, PA
Sanders, Neal I. ... Eureka, CA
Sanders, Neal I., Law Office of ... Eureka, CA
Sanders, Neil H., II ... Tampa, FL
Sanders, Nissa Mykleby ... San Antonio, TX
Sanders, Norman O. ... Kansas City, MO
Sanders, P. Alan ... Orange, TX
Sanders, Patrick G. ... St. Louis, MO
Sanders, Patrick J. ... Metairie, LA
Sanders, Patrick J. ... New Orleans, LA
Sanders, Patrick M. ... St. Louis, MO
Sanders, Paul H. ... Nashville, TN
Sanders, Paula G. ... Harrisburg, PA
Sanders, Perry R., Jr. ... Lake Charles, LA
Sanders, Peter M. ... Stamford, CT
Sanders, Phyllis L. ... Mineola, NY
Sanders, R. Carter, Jr. ... Washington, DC
Sanders, Rance M. ... Birmingham, AL
Sanders, Raymond J. ... Chicago, IL
Sanders, Rebecca A. ... Olathe, KS
Sanders, Rhonda Wood ... Bowie, MD
Sanders, Richard ... Palm Harbor, FL
Sanders, Richard B. ... Phoenix, AZ
Sanders, Richard B. ... Houston, TX
Sanders, Richard B. ... Bellevue, WA
Sanders, Richard C. ... Detroit, MI
Sanders, Richard D. ... Morristown, NJ
Sanders, Richard H. ... Chicago, IL
Sanders, Richard S. ... Boston, MA
Sanders, R. J. ... Moweaqua, IL
Sanders, Robert A. ... Santa Cruz, CA
Sanders, Robert A. ... Schenectady, NY
Sanders, Robert A., Jr. ... DeLand, FL
Sanders, Robert B. ... Cleveland, OH
Sanders, Robert C. ... Baltimore, MD
Sanders, Robert C. ... Liberty, MO
Sanders, Robert E. ... Covington, KY
Sanders, Robert E., and Associates, P.S.C.
Covington, KY
Cincinnati, OH
Sanders, Robert G. ... Charlotte, NC
Sanders, Robert H. ... Glendale, CA
Sanders, Robert I. ... Portland, OR
Sanders, Robert J. ... Forsyth, MO
Sanders, Robert L. ... Walnut Creek, CA
Sanders, Robert L., Professional Law Corporation ... Walnut Creek, CA
Sanders, Robert M. ... Reynoldsburg, OH
Sanders, Robert R. ... Amarillo, TX
Sanders, Robert T., III ... Elkhart, IN
Sanders, Robin Lynn ... Pacoima, CA
Sanders, Roger E. ... McLean, VA
Sanders, Roger J. ... Denver, CO
Sanders, Ronald M. ... New York, NY
Sanders, Rose M. ... Selma, AL
Sanders, Roy Gene ... Little Rock, AR
Sanders, Russell J., III ... Shelbyville, IN
Sanders, Russell R. ... Pittsburgh, PA
Sanders, Ruth Armfield
Securities and Exchange Commission, Division of Investment Management, GV
Sanders, Sallie Jones ... Cameron, LA
Sanders, Salvador ... Los Angeles, CA
Sanders & Sanders ... Marion, IL
Sanders & Sanders ... Lancaster, KY
Sanders & Sanders ... Greenbelt, MD
La Plata, MD
Lexington Park, MD
Upper Marlboro, MD
Sanders & Sanders ... Amherst, NY
Sanders & Sanders ... Canton, TX
Sanders, Sanders & Block, P.C.
Mineola, NY
Sanders & Sanders, L.L.P. ... Orange, TX
Sanders & Sanders, P.C. ... Tulsa, OK
Sanders, Sanders & Sullivan ... Poteau, OK
Sanders, Sandra ... Arcadia, FL
Sanders, Sandra K. ... Phoenix, AZ
Sanders, Sandra L. ... Little Rock, AR
Sanders, Sandra R. ... Somers, NY
Sanders, Sara Jade ... Miami, FL
Sanders, Schnabel, Brandenburg & Zimmerman, P.C. ... Washington, DC
Rockville, MD
Fairfax, VA
Sanders, Scott C. ... Houston, TX
Sanders, Scott L. ... Charlotte, MI

Sanders, Sheila Mathis
Research Triangle Park, NC
Sanders, Sheldon J. ... Garden City, NY
Sanders, Sheva J. ... Minneapolis, MN
Sanders, Silvia R. ... Orlando, FL
Sanders, Simpson, Fletcher & Smith, L.C.
Kansas City, MO
Sanders & Solomon ... Melville, NY
Sanders, Stanley A. ... Brooklyn, NY
Sanders, Stanley J. ... Mineola, NY
Sanders, Stephen C. ... Frankfort, KY
Sanders, Steven A. ... Hackensack, NJ
New York, NY
Sanders, Steven C. ... Washington, DC
Sanders, Steven G. ... Chatham, NJ
Sanders, Steven K. ... Albuquerque, NM
Sanders, Steven L. ... Bakersfield, CA
Sanders, Steven L. ... Kansas City, KS
Sanders, Steven P. ... Belleville, IL
St. Louis, MO
Sanders, Steven R. ... Hollister, CA
Sanders, Steven T. ... Secaucus, NJ
Sanders, Stuart L. ... Ridgewood, NJ
Sanders, Susan E. ... Denver, CO
Sanders, Susan L. ... Washington, DC
Sanders, Susan Leigh ... Arlington, TX
Sanders, Suzan R. ... Wichita Falls, TX
Sanders, Sylvia ... Gaylord, MI
Sanders, Ted H. ... Mountain Home, AR
Sanders, Teresa M. ... Westlake Village, CA
Sanders, Terrill W. ... Birmingham, AL
Sanders, Theodore A. ... La Follette, TN
Sanders, Thomas ... Sterling, IL
Sanders, Thomas C. ... Dallas, GA
Sanders, Thomas E. ... San Antonio, TX
Sanders, Thomas J. ... Elkhart, IN
Sanders, Thomas O., IV ... Charleston, SC
Sanders, Thomas P. ... Minneapolis, MN
Sanders, Thomas Trigg ... Florissant, MO
Sanders, Thomas W. ... Lake Charles, LA
Sanders, Thomas W., A Professional Law Corporation ... Lake Charles, LA
Sanders, Thomas W., Jr.
Lake Charles, LA
Sanders, Tiffany A. ... Minneapolis, MN
Sanders, Timothy E. ... Evansville, IN
Sanders, Todd F. ... Fairfax, VA
Sanders, Tristan W. ... Orlando, FL
Sanders, Valerie S. ... Las Vegas, NV
Sanders, Vance A. ... Juneau, AK
Sanders, Victor D. ... Merced, CA
Sanders, Virginia DeCarlo ... Idabel, OK
Sanders, W. Kirk ... Winston-Salem, NC
Sanders, Walt A.
Consumer Product Safety Commission, Chairmans Office, GV
Sanders, Walter H., Jr. ... Fairfax, SC
Sanders, Walter H., Jr., P.A. ... Fairfax, SC
Sanders, Walter W. (Buck)
The Woodlands, TX
Sanders, Wardell ... Trenton, NJ
Sanders & Westbrook, P.C.
Albuquerque, NM
Sanders, Wilfred L., Jr. ... Concord, NH
Hampton, NH
Sanders, William C. ... Thomasville, GA
Sanders, William D. ... Pompano Beach, FL
Sanders, William D. ... West Orange, NJ
New York, NY
Sanders, William H. ... Anchorage, AK
Sanders, William H. ... Jena, LA
Sanders, William H., II ... Princeton, WV
Sanders, William H., III ... Princeton, WV
Sanders, William H., Jr.
Overland Park, KS
Kansas City, MO
Sanders, William H., Sr.
Kansas City, MO
Sanders, William J. ... Kansas City, MO
Sanders, William R., Jr. ... Charleston, MS
Sanders, William S. ... Oklahoma City, OK
Sanders, Yeomans & Goodwin, LLP
Seattle, WA
Sanders, Yolanda M. ... San Francisco, CA
SandersBakerpc ... Amarillo, TX
Sanders-Castro, Judith A.
San Antonio, TX
Sanders-Clardy, Thelma E. ... Dallas, TX
Sanders-Cochran, Rachel
Montgomery, AL
Sanders-Demott, Jill ... White Plains, NY
Sandersen, Gerard L. ... Yakima, WA
Sanders-Mazzarella, Judy A.
San Marcos, CA
Sanderson, Adwoa Ayo ... New York, NY
Sanderson, Alfred L., Jr. ... Sacramento, CA
Sanderson, Alfred T. ... Woodbury, NJ
Sanderson, Brenda Harvey ... Knoxville, TN
Sanderson, Brian R. ... Fairfax, VA
Sanderson, Brian W. ... Pascagoula, MS
Sanderson, C. Ted, Jr. ... Jackson, MS
Sanderson, Catherine ... Atlanta, GA
Sanderson, Cynthia E. ... Paducah, KY
Sanderson, Dale E. ... Iowa City, IA
Sanderson, David ... Portsmouth, NH
Sanderson, David S. ... Boulder, CO
Sanderson, David V. ... Phoenix, AZ
Sanderson, Dennis L. ... Afton, WY
Sanderson, Donald L. ... Hillsdale, MI
Sanderson, Donald R. ... Bernardsville, NJ
Sanderson, Douglas J. ... Fairfax, VA
Sanderson and Dudley ... Portsmouth, NH
Sanderson, Emily E. ... New York, NY
Sanderson, Eric D. ... Denver, CO
Sanderson, Everett H. ... Beaumont, TX
Sanderson, Forrest L., III ... Bastrop, TX
Sanderson, Gail L. ... Wilder, VT

Sanderson, Garrett, III San Francisco, CA
Sanderson, Gregory A. ... Marietta, GA
Sanderson, Gretchen L. ... Evergreen, CO
Sanderson, Gretchen L., P.C. ... Evergreen, CO
Sanderson, Harold D. ... Amarillo, TX
Sanderson, Harold R. ... McLean, VA
Sanderson, Harry N., Jr. Windsor Locks, CT
Sanderson, Hebern "Sandy" W., Jr. Clinton, NC
Sanderson, J. Richard ... Dallas, TX
Sanderson, James A. ... Salem, OR
Sanderson, James E. ... Holland, MI
Sanderson, James E., Jr. ... Richmond, VA
Sanderson, James T. ... Bolivar, TN
Sanderson, James T. 'Jim, & Associates, A Professional Corporation ... Bolivar, TN
Sanderson, James W. ... Denver, CO
Sanderson, Jessica H. ... San Diego, CA
Sanderson, John O. ... Emporia, KS
Sanderson, John P. ... Blakely, PA
Sanderson, Kari L. ... Chicago, IL
Sanderson, Kathryn A. ... Natick, MA
Sanderson, Keith ... Monmouth, IL
Sanderson, Linda J. ... Hadley, MA
Sanderson, Lisa A. ... El Cajon, CA
Sanderson, M. Melinda ... St. Louis, MO
Sanderson, Mandee ... Westlake Village, CA
Sanderson, Mark O. ... Kansas City, MO
Sanderson, Michael G. ... Toledo, OH
Sanderson, Michael K. ... Dallas, TX
Sanderson, Myron E. ... Jackson, MI
Sanderson, Patrick J. ... Richmond, VA
Sanderson, R. Bruce ... Akron, OH
Sanderson, Rex F. ... Houston, MS
Sanderson, Rhea D. ... Dallas, TX
Sanderson, Richard H. ... Williamsburg, MI
Sanderson, Richard L., Jr. Ann Arbor, MI
Sanderson, Richard R. ... Woodland Hills, CA
Sanderson, Richard S. ... Natick, MA
Sanderson, Ridout & Martens Estherville, IA
Sanderson, Robert F. ... Lamar, CO
Sanderson, Robert L. ... Milwaukee, WI
Sanderson, Robert S. ... St. Louis, MO
Sanderson & Rotroff, L.L.P. Marietta, GA
Sanderson & Sanderson ... Bernardsville, NJ
Sanderson, Stuart A. ... Denver, CO
Sanderson, W. Everett ... Port Arthur, TX
Sanderson, W. Merrill ... Albany, NY
Sanderson, W. B. ... Wayne, PA
Sanderson, William B., Jr ... Bryn Mawr, PA
Sanderson, William F., Jr. ... Dallas, TX
Sanderson, William J. ... Estherville, IA
Sanderson, William S. ... Irvine, CA
Sanderson, William W., Jr. ... Huntsville, AL
Sanderson, Wm. H. ... Port Angeles, WA
Sanderson-Burke, Elizabeth J. ... Seattle, WA
Sanders-Zinser, Mary Lu ... St. Louis, MO
Sandfield, Robert E. ... Houston, TX
Sandford, Dean ... New York, NY
Sandford, H. Neal ... Boston, MA
Sandford, Harold R. ... Fair Lawn, NJ
Sandford, Irene W. ... Armonk, NY
Sandford, Jill Ellen ... New York, NY
Sandford, Jules ... Monrovia, CA
Sandford, Michael L., (P.C.) Santa Barbara, CA
Sandford, Sara P. ... Seattle, WA
Sandfort, Randall J. ... Wausau, WI
Sandfry, Marilyn A. ... Radford, VA
Sandgren, Clyde D. ... Provo, UT
Sandgren, Gilbert R. ... Green Bay, WI
Sandgren, Michael Eric San Francisco, CA
Sandground, Barondess, West & New, P.C. Rockville, MD Fairfax, VA Vienna, VA
Sandground, Evelyn H. ... Vienna, VA
Sandground, Mark B., Jr. Washington, DC
Sandground, Mark B., Sr. ... Vienna, VA
Sandgrund, Amy ... New York, NY
Sandgrund, David M ... New York, NY
Sandgrund, Ronald M. ... Denver, CO
Sandhaus, Ronald E. ... Overland Park, KS Kansas City, MO
Sandhaus, Stuart H. ... Laguna Niguel, CA
Sandholm, Alvine & Ruud ... Moline, IL
Sandhop, Garland, Jr. ... Victoria, TX
Sandhop, John R., (P.C.) ... Baytown, TX
Sandhouse, Charles H. ... Sterling, CO
Sandhu, Papu ... Department of Justice, GV
Sandhu, Sukhbinder K. ... Cerritos, CA
Sandick, Bennett C. ... Naples, FL
Sandick, Harry ... New York, NY
Sandidge, Jon R. ... San Antonio, TX
Sandidge, Ridley M., Jr. ... Louisville, KY
Sandidge, Russell L. ... Huntsville, AL
Sandidge, Susan J. ... Dallas, TX
Sandifer, Connie Cooke ... Los Angeles, CA
Sandifer, Courtney Byron ... Washington, DC
Sandifer, Homer V. ... Lexington, SC
Sandifer, J. Edward ... Indianapolis, IN
Sandifer, James E. ... Indianapolis, IN
Sandifer, Jawn A. ... New York, NY
Sandifer, John Wells ... Atlanta, GA
Sandifer Law Office ... Allen, TX McKinney, TX
Sandifer, Robert D. ... Raymore, MO
Sandifer, Samuel J. ... Monroe City, MO
Sandifer & Sandifer, P.C. ... Indianapolis, IN
Sandifer, T. Mark ... Tifton, GA
Sandifer, T. Randall ... Allen, TX
Sandiford, Stanley S. ... St. Paul, MN
Sandilands, T. Malcolm ... Boston, MA
Sandilos, Charles P. ... Cherry Hill, NJ
Sandilos, Robert J. ... Houston, TX
Sandin, Alissa G. ... Newport Beach, CA Omaha, NE
Sandin, Carl O. ... Houston, TX
Sandin, John R. ... Herndon, VA
Sandine, Julie K. ... Nashville, TN
Sandish, Linda A. ... Chandler, AZ
Sandison, Ian L. ... Honolulu, HI
Sandison, James D. ... Sacramento, CA
Sanditen, Edward S. ... Aspen, CO
Sanditen, Scott A. ... Tulsa, OK
Sandkuhler, Kevin M. ... Stafford, VA
Sandkuhler, Monica S. ... Fort Wayne, IN
Sandkuhler, Robert J. ... Lancaster, PA
Sandle, Sharon A. ... Hobbs, NM
Sandler Ahern & McConaughy, PLLC Seattle, WA
Sandler, Alan G. ... Cleveland, OH
Sandler, Alan M. ... Coral Gables, FL
Sandler, Andrew L. ... Washington, DC
Sandler, Andrew R. ... Baltimore, MD
Sandler, Balkin, Hellman, Weinstein & Witten, P.C. ... Kansas City, MO
Sandler, Benjamin ... Andover, MA
Sandler, Betty Moore ... Woodbridge, VA
Sandler, Bradford J. ... Philadelphia, PA
Sandler, Bradley A. ... St. Louis, MO
Sandler, Bryan N. ... Phoenix, AZ
Sandler, Cary L. ... Philadelphia, PA
Sandler, Charles E. ... Washington, DC
Sandler, Charles R. ... Williamsville, NY
Sandler, David B. ... Louisville, KY
Sandler, David M. ... Kalispell, MT
Sandler, David N. ... San Francisco, CA
Sandler, Debbie D. ... Louisville, KY
Sandler, Debbie Rodman Philadelphia, PA
Sandler, Deborah Jo ... Walnut Creek, CA
Sandler, Donald M. ... Washington, DC
Sandler, George J. ... Flushing, NY
Sandler, Gilbert ... Oradell, NJ
Sandler, Gilbert Lee ... San Francisco, CA Washington, DC Miami, FL Atlanta, GA Chicago, IL New York, NY
Sandler, Glen S. ... San Bernardino, CA
Sandler, Goldstein & Mara, P.C. Hartford, CT
Sandler, Guy E. ... Vallejo, CA
Sandler, H. Richard ... South Bend, IN
Sandler, Howard B. ... Fort Wayne, IN
Sandler, Howard E. ... Lake Forest, CA
Sandler, Irving ... Elmira, NY
Sandler, Irwin E. ... Beverly Hills, CA
Sandler, Irwin L. ... Denver, CO
Sandler, Irwin L., P.C. ... Denver, CO
Sandler, James E. ... Boston, MA
Sandler, James G. ... San Diego, CA
Sandler, James P. ... Hartford, CT
Sandler, Jeffrey R. ... Chicago, IL
Sandler, Jeffrey S. ... Hollywood, FL
Sandler, John R. ... Fairfax, CA
Sandler, Jon L. ... Ellicott City, MD
Sandler, Joseph E. ... Washington, DC
Sandler, Judy M. ... New York, NY
Sandler, Kaylene Wright Ellicott City, MD
Sandler, Kenneth S., (P.A.) ... Hollywood, FL
Sandler, Krista M. ... San Diego, CA
Sandler & Laramee ... Gloucester, MA
Sandler, Leonard A. ... Centreville, MD
Sandler, Lewis H. ... Dallas, TX
Sandler, Lewis S. ... New York, NY
Sandler, Linda Blum ... Carle Place, NY
Sandler, Marc N. ... Gloucester, MA
Sandler & Marchesini, P.C. ... Philadelphia, PA
Sandler, Martin L. ... Miami, FL
Sandler, Merle H. ... Marina Del Rey, CA
Sandler, Michael B. ... Boston, MA
Sandler, Michael D. ... Seattle, WA
Sandler, Michael P. ... Ontario, CA Walnut Creek, CA
Sandler, Mitchell H. ... Chicago, IL
Sandler, Myron ... Hollywood, FL
Sandler, Neil F. ... Fort Wayne, IN
Sandler, Olga ... New York, NY
Sandler, Paul ... New York, NY
Sandler, Paul Mark ... Baltimore, MD
Sandler, Paul N. ... Philadelphia, PA
Sandler, Philip W. ... Chicago, IL
Sandler, Raymond C. ... Los Angeles, CA
Sandler & Reiff, P.C. ... Washington, DC
Sandler, Richard A. ... Washington, DC
Sandler, Richard Jay ... New York, NY
Sandler, Richard L. ... Chicago, IL
Sandler, Richard M. ... Roseland, NJ
Sandler, Richard V. ... Los Angeles, CA
Sandler, Risa D. ... Department of Labor, Office of the Solicitor, GV
Sandler, Robert A. ... Los Angeles, CA
Sandler, Robert E. ... Uniondale, NY
Sandler, Robert J. ... Detroit, MI
Sandler, Robert M. ... Bethesda, MD
Sandler, Robert N. ... New York, NY Philadelphia, PA
Sandler, Robin Bruce ... Branford, CT
Sandler, Robin Bruce, P.C. ... Branford, CT
Sandler, Robt. G. ... Des Moines, IA
Sandler, Rolnick & Morse ... Los Angeles, CA
Sandler, Rona H. ... San Francisco, CA
Sandler, Ronald A. ... Chicago, IL
Sandler, Ronald F. ... Falls Church, VA
Sandler and Rosen, LLP ... Los Angeles, CA
Sandler, Ross ... New York, NY
Sandler, Scott M. ... Miami, FL
Sandler, Sharon Jill ... Los Angeles, CA
Sandler, Sheldon N. ... Wilmington, DE
Sandler, Sheldon P. ... Kansas City, MO
Sandler, Stephen P. ... Chicago, IL
Sandler, Steven ... Calabasas, CA
Sandler, Susan ... Tampa, FL
Sandler, Susan F. ... New York, NY
Sandler, Susan J. ... Houston, TX
Sandler, Theodore H. ... Atlanta, GA
Sandler, Theodore L. ... Southport, CT
Sandler, Travis & Rosenberg and Glad & Ferguson, P.C. ... San Francisco, CA
Sandler, Travis & Rosenberg, P.A. Washington, DC Miami, FL Atlanta, GA Chicago, IL
Baltimore, MD
New York, NY
Sandler, Tucker ... Los Angeles, CA
Sandler, Will Burt ... New York, NY
Sandler, Winifred A. ... Boston, MA
Sandler, Woodrow J. ... New York, NY
Sandles, Norman L. ... Bingham Farms, MI
Sandlin, Albert L., Jr. ... Atlanta, GA
Sandlin, Ava M. ... Los Angeles, CA
Sandlin, Billy G. ... Jacksonville, NC
Sandlin & Buckner ... Marshall, TX
Sandlin, Dana C. ... Louisville, KY
Sandlin, J. Oliver ... Austin, TX
Sandlin, J. Wescoat ... Charleston, SC
Sandlin, J. Wescoat, Mediation & Conflict Management ... Charleston, SC
Sandlin, Jimmy ... Florence, AL
Sandlin, Joe F. ... Anahuac, TX
Sandlin, Mark J. ... New Albany, IN Louisville, KY
Sandlin, Mary Jo ... Houston, TX
Sandlin, Max A., Jr. ... Marshall, TX
Sandlin, N. Bennett ... Austin, TX
Sandlin, Paul Marc ... Huntsville, AL
Sandlin, R. Forney ... Muskogee, OK
Sandling, Craig F. ... Austin, TX
Sandlow, Lisa I. ... Chicago, IL
Sandman, Alison P. ... Sacramento, CA
Sandman, Andrew K. ... Raleigh, NC
Sandman, Cary ... Tucson, AZ
Sandman, Charles W., III Cape May Court House, NJ
Sandman, Dan D. ... Pittsburgh, PA
Sandman, Irvin W. ... Seattle, WA
Sandman, James H. ... Newburyport, MA
Sandman, James J. ... Washington, DC
Sandman, Jamie L. ... Philadelphia, PA
Sandman, Jeffrey I. ... Englewood, CO
Sandman, Jeffrey M. ... Washington, DC
Sandman, Levy & Petrich ... Chicago, IL
Sandman, Marc L. ... New York, NY
Sandman, Michael G. ... Raleigh, NC
Sandman, Paul W. ... Natick, MA
Sandman, Richard E. ... Atlantic City, NJ
Sandman, Richard M. ... Malden, MA
Sandman, Robert S. ... Atlantic City, NJ
Sandman, Sheldon J. ... Chicago, IL
Sandmann, Peter B. ... Mill Valley, CA **San Francisco, CA**
Sandmeier, Pamela J. ... Sound Beach, NY
Sandmeyer, Bruce G. ... Erie, PA
Sandmeyer, Gregory J. ... Boise, ID
Sandmire, Michael J. ... Portland, OR
Sandner, James R. ... New York, NY
Sandner, John F. ... Chicago, IL
Sandner, Lisa A. ... Dayton, OH
Sandner, Michael W. ... Dayton, OH
Sandnes, James T. ... New York, NY
Sandness, Lawrence K. ... Quincy, IL
Sandness, Paul K. ... Bismarck, ND
Sando, Frank J. ... Department of the Army, Office of the General Counsel, GV
Sando, Gregory A. ... Jackson, MI
Sando, Jack C. ... Bethesda, MD
Sando, John M. ... Tucson, AZ
Sando, T. Parker ... Albuquerque, NM
Sandoe, Anthony B. ... Boston, MA
Sandoe, Kenneth C. ... Myerstown, PA
Sandok, Craig D. ... Minneapolis, MN
Sandoloski, Lee R. ... San Antonio, TX
Sandomire, Hazel ... Garrison, NY
Sandomire, Richard C. ... Denver, CO
Sandomirsky, Gregory A. ... Boston, MA
Sandona, Ray ... Los Angeles, CA
Sandonato, Gina C. ... Boston, MA
Sandonato, Michael P. ... New York, NY
Sandone, Joseph M., Jr. ... Westmont, NJ
Sandone, Kathleen M. ... Camden, NJ Philadelphia, PA
Sandone, Steven A. ... Glenolden, PA
Sandor, David L. ... Long Beach, CA
Sandor, Geraldine G. ... Irvine, CA
Sandor, Lawrence P. ... Washington, DC
Sandor, Richard J., Jr. ... Pawling, NY
Sandor, Russell A. ... Portland, OR
Sandor III, Frank J. ... Akron, OH
Sandorse, Michael ... Melrose, MA
Sandoval, Antonio Z. ... Gardena, CA
Sandoval, Brian E. ... Reno, NV
Sandoval, Carlos M. ... Waldorf, MD
Sandoval, Catherine J.K. ... Sacramento, CA
Sandoval, Charles F. ... McKinney, TX
Sandoval, Cynthia S. ... San Francisco, CA
Sandoval, David ... Glenwood Springs, CO
Sandoval, Dennis M. ... Torrance, CA
Sandoval, Diana V. ... Newport Beach, CA
Sandoval, Eduardo South San Francisco, CA
Sandoval, Elizabeth ... McAllen, TX
Sandoval, Frank D. ... San Antonio, TX
Sandoval, Gabriel A. ... Sunnyvale, CA
Sandoval, J. Robert ... Peoria, IL
Sandoval, Jan Catherine ... Kansas City, MO
Sandoval, Jimmy ... Laredo, TX
Sandoval, Jose ... Torrance, CA
Sandoval, Jose A. ... Espanola, NM
Sandoval, José I. ... Torrance, CA
Sandoval, Joseph, Jr. ... San Francisco, CA
Sandoval, Karl A. ... San Diego, CA
Sandoval & Keng ... Waldorf, MD
Sandoval Law Office ... Reno, NV
Sandoval, Matty M. ... San Diego, CA
Sandoval, Michael R. ... Portland, OR
Sandoval, Omar ... Orange, CA
Sandoval, P. Joseph ... San Francisco, CA
Sandoval, Pete ... Houston, TX
Sandoval, Quilichini, Oliver, Medina, Salamone & Gorbea ... San Juan, PR
Sandoval, Robert J. ... Glendale, CA
Sandoval & St. Clair, P.L.C. ... Tucson, AZ
Sandoval, Scot G. ... Burbank, CA
Sandoval, Steven G. ... Tucson, AZ
Sandoval, Susan Beecher West Sacramento, CA
Sandoval, Trina ... New York, NY
Sandoval-Alemañy, Raymond ... San Juan, PR
Sandow, Bernard S. ... Van Nuys, CA
Sandow, Dean T. ... Portland, OR
Sandow, Garrett H. ... Blackfoot, ID
Sandow, Richard ... Pittsburgh, PA
Sandow, Robert A. ... Live Oak, FL
Sandow, Sidney A. ... Pembroke Pines, FL
Sandoz, John H. ... Los Angeles, CA
Sandoz, Jonathan H. ... New Orleans, LA
Sandoz, Lawrence B., III ... Opelousas, LA
Sandoz, Lawrence B., Jr. ... Opelousas, LA
Sandoz & Sandoz, A Professional Law Corporation ... Opelousas, LA
Sandoz, W. Simmons, (P.C.) ... Opelousas, LA
Sandoz, William C. ... Opelousas, LA
Sandoz, William C., and W. Simmons Sandoz, Law Firm of ... Opelousas, LA
Sandquist, Allan H. ... Riverside, CA
Sandquist, Christopher E. ... Mankato, MN
Sandquist, Elroy C., Jr. ... Chicago, IL
Sandquist, Jeffrey A. ... Phoenix, AZ
Sandquist, John A. ... Eureka, CA
Sandquist, Ronda L. ... Denver, CO
Sandquist, Ronnetta Fagan ... Dallas, TX
Sandquist, Susan J ... Raleigh, NC
Sandquist, Thomas P. ... Rockford, IL
Sandre, John R. ... West Des Moines, IA
Sandri, Joseph M., Jr. ... Washington, DC
Sandridge, Hala Ayoub ... Tampa, FL
Sandridge, Mark E. ... Dickinson, TX
Sandridge, W. P., Jr. ... Winston-Salem, NC
Sandrock, Peter F., Jr. ... Corvallis, OR
Sandrock, Scott P. ... Canton, OH
Sandrok, Richard W., (Ltd.) ... Lisle, IL
Sandroni, Andrew D. ... St. Louis, MO
Sandronsky, Vera ... Sacramento, CA
Sandros, Tanya M. ... Library of Congress, Copyright Office, GV
Sandry, Paul A. ... Kalispell, MT
Sands, Ada P. ... Beverly Hills, CA
Sands, Alexander H., III ... Boston, MA
Sands, Alexander P., III ... Raleigh, NC
Sands Anderson Marks & Miller, A Professional Corporation ... Radford, VA Richmond, VA
Sands, April J. ... Federal Election Commission, Office of the General Counsel, GV
Sands, Barbara ... New York, NY
Sands, Beverly R. ... Santa Monica, CA
Sands, Bobby W. ... Columbia, TN
Sands, Bradley E. ... Medford, OR
Sands, Bruce E. ... West Palm Beach, FL
Sands, Carol J. ... Trenton, NJ
Sands, Catherine S. ... Dillon, MT
Sands, Charles E. ... West Roxbury, MA
Sands, Charles T. ... Coral Gables, FL
Sands, Christian E. ... Peru, IN
Sands, Darry Gene ... Kansas City, MO
Sands, David A. ... Tucson, AZ
Sands, David H. ... Los Angeles, CA
Sands, Donald G. ... Holton, KS
Sands, Donald J. ... Los Angeles, CA
Sands, Donna V. ... Summerville, SC
Sands, Douglas C. ... San Francisco, CA
Sands, Douglas K. ... Stuart, FL
Sands, Edward I. ... Los Angeles, CA
Sands, Edward P. ... Rifle, CO
Sands, Elizabeth W. ... Boston, MA
Sands, Eugene P. ... Los Angeles, CA
Sands, Fredericka ... Miami, FL
Sands, George ... Fort Lauderdale, FL
Sands, George L., Jr. ... Anderson, SC
Sands, George L., Jr., P.A. ... Anderson, SC
Sands & Halpern ... Santa Monica, CA
Sands, Holli K. ... Philadelphia, PA
Sands, J. Keith M. ... Jacksonville, FL
Sands, Jack E. ... Billings, MT
Sands, Jeffrey H. ... Princeton, NJ
Sands, Jeffrey K. ... Department of Justice, Environment and Natural Resources Division, GV
Baltimore, MD
Sands, Jennifer K. ... Wenatchee, WA
Sands, Jesse L. ... New York, NY
Sands, John C. ... Chicago, IL
Sands, John E. ... Roseland, NJ
Sands, John F. ... Cleveland, OH
Sands, Jon F. ... Denver, CO
Sands, Jon M. ... Phoenix, AZ
Sands, Joseph W. ... New York, NY
Sands, Judith Davies ... New York, NY

Sands, Karen .... Albuquerque, NM
Sands, Kenneth E., Jr. .... Fleetwood, PA
Reading, PA
Sands, Kenneth E., Jr., P.C. .... Fleetwood, PA
Reading, PA
Sands, Kenton V., Law Office of
Orlando, FL
Sands, Kimberly .... Daytona Beach, FL
DeLand, FL
Sands, Larry .... Daytona Beach, FL
DeLand, FL
Sands, Lawrence D. .... Columbia, TN
Sands, Leonard A. .... Miami, FL
Sands, Marc L. .... San Diego, CA
Sands, Merrell Frank, III .... Key West, FL
Sands, Michael A. .... Palo Alto, CA
Sands, Michael S. .... Sacramento, CA
Sands & Michaud .... Peru, IN
Sands, Morris H. .... Santa Monica, CA
Sands, Morton H. .... Youngstown, OH
Sands & Moskowitz, P.A. .... Miami, FL
Sands Narwitz Leonard & Lerner, Professional Corporation
Los Angeles, CA
Sands, Norman .... Scottsdale, AZ
Sands, O. Jackson, III .... Boston, MA
Sands, Paul T., Jr. .... Chicago, IL
Sands, Philip .... Garden City, NY
Sands, Rachel .... Boston, MA
Sands, Richard E. .... Jamaica, NY
Sands, Richard J. .... St. Paul, MN
Sands, Robert H. .... Edwardsville, IL
Sands, Robert J. .... New York, NY
Sands, Robert O. .... Atlanta, GA
Sands, Robert S. .... Canandaigua, NY
Sands, Robert-John H. .... Bethesda, MD
Sands, Ronald L., The Law Office of
Fort Worth, TX
Sands, Serafina .... San Francisco, CA
Sands, Steven L. .... Daytona Beach, FL
DeLand, FL
Sands, Thomas A. .... New Orleans, LA
Sands, Timothy C. .... Houston, TX
Sands, Traci L. .... Pittsburgh, PA
Sands, W. Louis .... Albany, GA
Sands, White & Sands, P.A.
Daytona Beach, FL
DeLand, FL
Orlando, FL
Sands, William S., Jr. .... Alexandria, VA
Sandsmark, James D. .... Fargo, ND
Sandson, Mark H. .... Atlantic City, NJ
Sandstead, Morris W., Jr. .... Boulder, CO
Sandstedt, J. Erik .... Newark, NJ
Sandstrom, Dale V. .... Bismarck, ND
Sandstrom, Douglas J. .... Gresham, OR
Sandstrom, Douglas J., P.C. .... Gresham, OR
Sandstrom, Gail Dunn .... Hilo, HI
Sandstrom, Harry N. .... Des Moines, IA
Sandstrom, Mark Roy .... Washington, DC
Sandstrom, Theodore F. .... Wilmington, DE
Sandstrom, Thomas J. .... Eden Prairie, MN
Sandstrum, Michael A. .... Orange, CA
Sandul, Michael L. .... Odenton, MD
Sandulli, Joseph G. .... Boston, MA
Sanduski, Jos. S. .... Omaha, NE
Sandusky, Cynthia .... Plano, TX
Sandusky, James E. .... Meridian, MS
Sandusky, Kathleen .... Austin, TX
Sandusky, Robert Ralph, III .... Bronx, NY
Sandusky, Shelley J. .... Menlo Park, CA
Sandusky, Steven .... Chicago, IL
Sandusky, W. Scott .... York, PA
Sandven, Themia E. .... Denver, CO
Sandven, Themia E., Professional Corporation
Denver, CO
Sandvick, Carol A. .... Houston, TX
Sandvick, Clinton M. .... San Diego, CA
Sandvick, Frederick .... San Diego, CA
Sandvig, Douglas A. .... Houston, TX
Sandvik, Carl N. .... Walnut Creek, CA
Sandvik, Kenneth A. .... Two Harbors, MN
Sandvold, Juliana C. .... Saipan, TT
Sandvos, Jay .... Boston, MA
Sandvoss & Lentz .... Ravenna, OH
Sandvoss, Norman W. .... Ravenna, OH
Sandweg, Gerard K., Jr. .... St. Louis, MO
Sandweg, William H., III .... Phoenix, AZ
Sandweiss, David L., (Ltd.) .... Phoenix, AZ
Sandweiss, Jerome W. .... St. Louis, MO
Sandweiss, Kathi Mann .... Phoenix, AZ
Sandwisch, Michael W. .... Port Clinton, OH
Sandy, Alan M. .... Troy, MI
Sandy, Carl J. .... Lafayette, IN
Sandy, Carolyn Smith .... Birmingham, MI
Sandy, Joan Phillips .... Waterville, ME
Sandy, John .... Bloomington, IL
Sandy, John P. M. .... Georgetown, DE
Sandy Law Firm .... Spirit Lake, IA
Sandy, Lyman G. .... Albuquerque, NM
Sandy, Mathew S. .... Lafayette, IN
Sandy, Pamela A. .... Amsterdam, NY
Sandy, Robert C. .... Sussex, NJ
Sandy, Robert E., Jr. .... Waterville, ME
Sandy, Shannon L. .... Spirit Lake, IA
Sandza, Elizabeth Barry .... Washington, DC
Sanek, Kenneth E. .... Irving, TX
Saner, Robert J., II .... Washington, DC
Sanes, Frank, Jr. .... Los Angeles, CA
Sanes, Gail .... Los Angeles, CA
Sanes, Noah H. .... Los Angeles, CA
Sanes, Scott A., Law Offices of
Houston, TX
Sanet, John A. ....
Office of Personnel Management, GV
Sanet, Morton J. .... Miami, FL
Sanetti, Stephen L. .... Southport, CT
Sanevich, Bella L. F. .... New York, NY

San Felipe, Clemente J.
South San Francisco, CA
San Fellipo, John R. .... Portland, OR
Sanfield, Joel A. .... Detroit, MI
St. Clair Shores, MI
Sanfilipo, Cheryl Lynne .... Washington, DC
San Filipo, Thos. .... Rochester, NY
San Filippo, Augustin J., P.C.
New York, NY
Sanfilippo, Christine Green
Sacramento, CA
SanFilippo, Joseph A. .... New Haven, CT
Sanfilippo, Joseph C. .... Fairfield, CT
San Filippo, Michael A. .... San Diego, CA
San Filippo, Michael J.
Altamonte Springs, FL
San Filippo, Michael J., P.A.
Altamonte Springs, FL
San Filippo, N. Paul .... Naples, FL
San Filippo, Nicholas, IV .... Roseland, NJ
San Filippo, Philip E. .... Red Bank, NJ
Sanfilippo, Salvatore T. .... Commack, NY
Sanfilippo, Shannon S. .... Philadelphia, PA
Sanfilippo, T. Anthony .... Los Angeles, CA
Sanford, Alma F. .... Falls Church, VA
Sanford Amerling & Associates
Christiansted, St. Croix, VI
Charlotte Amalie, St. Thomas, VI
Sanford, Amy Marie .... Nashville, TN
Sanford, Ann Marks .... Minneapolis, MN
Sanford & Associates .... Baton Rouge, LA
Sanford, Barbara J. .... Delta, CO
Sanford, Brian P. .... Richardson, TX
Sanford, Bruce W. .... Washington, DC
Sanford, Calvin Garner, Jr. .... Atlanta, GA
Sanford, Chapman L. .... Baton Rouge, LA
Sanford, Charles H. .... Columbia, SC
Sanford, David T. .... Newport Beach, CA
Sanford, David W. .... Washington, DC
Sanford, Dianne H. .... Washington, DC
Sanford, Donald E., Jr. .... Buffalo, NY
Sanford, Eric .... New York, NY
Sanford, Frank L. .... Silver Spring, MD
Sanford, Gene .... Florence, OR
Sanford, Gordon Urban "Sandy", III
Jackson, MS
Sanford & Harmssen .... San Jose, CA
Santa Cruz, CA
Sanford Holshouser Law Firm PLLC, The
Washington, DC
Cary, NC
Pinehurst, NC
Raleigh, NC
Research Triangle Park, NC
Southern Pines, NC
Sanford, James G. .... Reno, NV
Sanford, Jay H. .... Columbus, OH
Sanford, Jeannine C. .... Washington, DC
Sanford, Jeb C. .... McLean, VA
Sanford, Jeffry L. .... Baton Rouge, LA
Sanford, Jerome R. .... Muskegon, MI
Sanford, Jill R. .... Denver, CO
Sanford, Joanne .... Raleigh, NC
Sanford, John J. .... Camden, ME
Sanford, John L., Jr. .... Ocean City, MD
Sanford, Jon R. .... Russellville, AR
Sanford, Keith R. .... Holcomb, NY
Sanford, Kelly N. .... Lafayette, LA
Sanford, Kimberly Ann .... Los Angeles, CA
Sanford, Kuhl & Perkins .... Austin, TX
Houston, TX
Sanford, L. Bentley .... Houston, TX
Sanford, Larry E. .... Evergreen, CO
Sanford, Laura A. .... Bedford, MA
Sanford Law Offices, The .... Reno, NV
Sanford, Marion, Jr., P.C. .... Austin, TX
Sanford, Mark D. .... Kalamazoo, MI
Sanford, Mark S. .... Carlsbad, NM
Sanford, Michael J.
Christiansted, St. Croix, VI
Sanford, Nicholas A. .... Santa Barbara, CA
Sanford, Paul .... Federal Election Commission,
Office of the General Counsel, GV
Sanford, Paul M. .... Providence, RI
Sanford, Paul P. .... Jacksonville, FL
Tallahassee, FL
Sanford, Paul S. .... Aptos, CA
Sanford, Peter L. .... San Jose, CA
Santa Cruz, CA
Sanford, Peter L., A Professional Law
Corporation .... Santa Cruz, CA
Sanford, Philip W. .... Seattle, WA
Sanford, R. Jerome .... Gainesville, FL
Sanford, Raymond F. .... Tulsa, OK
Sanford, Rebecca B. .... St. Joseph, MI
Sanford, Richard M. .... San Francisco, CA
Sanford, Robert D. .... San Francisco, CA
Sanford, Robert Preston .... Unionville, CT
Sanford, Robt. R. .... Sherman, TX
Sanford, Roy L. .... Minneapolis, MN
Sanford, Russell B. .... Fort Collins, CO
Sanford, Samuel C. .... Syracuse, NY
Sanford, Sara (Taye) H. .... Denver, CO
Sanford, Scott R. .... St. Joseph, MI
Sanford, Stephen D.
West Palm Beach, FL
Sanford, Steven W. .... Sioux Falls, SD
Sanford & Stiritz .... Russellville, AR
Sanford, Suzanne Langford
Washington, DC
Sanford, Thomas C. .... Los Angeles, CA
Sanford, Thomas F. .... Los Angeles, CA
Sanford, Thomas G. .... Gridley, CA
Sanford, Thomas M. .... New York, NY
Sanford, Thomas W. .... Jackson, MS
Sanford, Timothy B.
Mammoth Lakes, CA
Sanford, Valerius .... Nashville, TN

Sanford, Vernon T., Jr. .... San Antonio, TX
Sanford, W. Russell .... South Bend, IN
Sanford, William C., Jr. .... Reno, NV
Sanford-Wachtel, Timothy D.
Rancho Cucamonga, CA
San Diego, CA
Sang, Allen C. .... Deerfield Beach, FL
Orlando, FL
Stuart, FL
Sang, Lewis M. .... Palm Beach, FL
Sang, Marie F. .... San Jose, CA
Sang, Peter B. .... Ellsworth, ME
Sang, Peter B., P.A. .... Ellsworth, ME
Sanga, Arjun S. .... Kansas City, MO
Sangani, Parthiv R. .... San Francisco, CA
Sange, Leon S. .... St. Helena, CA
Sangeorge, Andrew J. .... West Caldwell, NJ
Sanger, Alexander Campbell .... New York, NY
Sanger, Brendan J. .... Litchfield, MI
Sanger, Carol .... New York, NY
Sanger, Charles S. .... Nashville, TN
Sanger, Diane
Securities and Exchange Commission,
Office of the General Counsel, GV
Sanger, Floyd C., Jr. .... Downey, CA
Sanger, Gail .... New York, NY
Sanger, Gail .... Pittsburgh, PA
Sanger, Herbert S., Jr. .... Knoxville, TN
Sanger, Herbert Warren .... Knoxville, TN
Sanger, Howard L., Law Offices of
Palm Springs, CA
Sanger, John M. .... San Francisco, CA
Sanger, Jordon T. .... Englewood, CO
Sanger, Julian D. .... Richmond, VA
Sanger, Karen Ogren .... Delano, MN
Sanger, Ladd .... Dallas, TX
Sanger, Laura Jeanne .... Houston, TX
Sanger, Laurence S. .... Dallas, TX
Sanger, Matthew K. .... Spokane, WA
Sanger, Michael D. .... Milwaukee, WI
Sanger, Michael Kent .... Bel Air, MD
Sanger & Olson, A Law Corporation
San Francisco, CA
Sanger, Reggie David .... Fort Lauderdale, FL
Sanger, Reggie David, P.A.
Fort Lauderdale, FL
Sanger, Richard C. .... Canton, CT
Sanger, Robert M. .... Santa Barbara, CA
Sanger & Sanger .... Milwaukee, WI
Sanger, Scott H. .... Taos, NM
Sanger, Scott H., Attorney at Law, P.C.
Taos, NM
Sanger, Susan L., LLC .... Denver, CO
Sanger, Susan M. .... Minneapolis, MN
Sanger & Swysen .... Santa Barbara, CA
Sanger, Warren J. .... New York, NY
SanGermain, Lyzette .... Maitland, FL
Sangerman, Harry M. .... Chicago, IL
Sangerman, Jay J. .... Boca Raton, FL
Clifton, NJ
New York, NY
Sanghavi, Bina .... Chicago, IL
Sanghavi, Nehal .... New York, NY
Sanghvi, Rasik S. .... Plainview, NY
San Giacomo, Henry L. .... Newark, NJ
Sangiamo, Dino S. .... Baltimore, MD
Sangillo, Paul A. .... Newark, NJ
Sanginario, Carol Mary .... New York, NY
Sanginario, Gary P. .... Boston, MA
Sangiorgi, Salvatore F. .... Brooklyn, NY
Sangiorgio, James V. .... St. James, NY
SanGiovanni, Paul L. .... Orlando, FL
Sangiuliano, Barbara Ann .... Scotch Plains, NJ
Sangmeister, George E. .... Frankfort, IL
Joliet, IL
Sangmeister, Sarah Tong .... Long Beach, CA
Sangree, Suzanne .... New York, NY
Sangster, Aimee F. .... Chesterfield, VA
Sangster, Claudia B. .... Malibu, CA
Sangster, Edward P. .... San Francisco, CA
Sangster, Jeffrey M. .... Detroit, MI
Sangster, Kimberly A. .... Chicago, IL
Sangster, Sarah Mack .... Novato, CA
Sanguinet, Gary J. .... St. Louis, MO
Sanguinetti, Elise .... Walnut Creek, CA
Sanguinetti, Margot .... San Diego, CA
Sanguinetti, Raymond J. .... Chicago, IL
Sanguinetti, Richard B. .... San Jose, CA
Sanguino, Stephen, Jr. .... Miami, FL
Sanhueza, Rebecca .... San Francisco, CA
Sani, Babak Sadegh .... San Francisco, CA
Sani, Barmak S. .... San Jose, CA
Sani & Barnhouse .... New Philadelphia, OH
Sani, Eli .... Houston, TX
Sani, Suresh L. .... Long Island City, NY
Sanislo, Audrey L. .... St. Paul, MN
Sanislo, Bacevice & Associates Co., L.P.A.
Cleveland, OH
Sanislo, Kevin R. .... Akron, OH
Sanislo, Linda Anne .... New York, NY
Sanislo, Paul S. .... Cleveland, OH
Sanjenis, Michael L. .... New York, NY
San Jose, Jon A. .... Long Beach, CA
San Juan, Del C. .... Los Angeles, CA
San Juan, Eric A.
United States Tax Court, GV
San Juan, Julie C. .... Los Angeles, CA
San Juan, Manuel .... San Juan, PR
Sanjurjo, Damaris E. .... Holly Hill, FL
Sank, Arnold M. .... Calabasas, CA
Sank, Mark A. .... Stamford, CT
Sankaran, Annapoorni R. .... Boston, MA
Sankaran, Sri K. .... Minneapolis, MN
Sankary, Dana Dumas .... Walnut Creek, CA
Sankary, Jerry H. .... Cardiff-By-The-Sea, CA
Sankary, Morris .... Del Mar, CA
Sankary, Myer J. .... Sherman Oaks, CA
Sankary & Sankary .... Del Mar, CA

Sankary, Wanda Y. .... San Diego, CA
Sankbeil, William A. .... Bloomfield Hills, MI
Detroit, MI
Sankel, Arlene Kalish .... Miami, FL
Sankel, Joel S. .... New York, NY
Sankel, Skurman & McCartin
New York, NY
Sanker, George J. .... Boston, MA
Sanker, Mary F. .... Cincinnati, OH
Sanker, Robert G. .... Cincinnati, OH
Sankey, Jeffrey M. .... Boston, MA
Sankey & Luck, L.L.P .... Dallas, TX
Houston, TX
Sankey, Thomas W. .... Houston, TX
Sankiewicz, Thea Marie .... Las Vegas, NV
Sankin, Alan R. .... San Jose, CA
Sankin, Julius .... Delray Beach, FL
Sankin, Kenneth L. .... New York, NY
Sanko, Rhonda H. .... Bloomfield Hills, MI
Sankovitch & Menz .... New York, NY
Sankovitch, Natasha .... San Francisco, CA
Sankovitch, Nina .... New York, NY
Sankovitz, Richard J. .... Milwaukee, WI
Sanks, Julius F. .... Cincinnati, OH
Sanks, Terry M. .... Orlando, FL
Sanman, Grace-Taylor, (Miss)
New York, NY
San Martin, Frank J.
Department of Transportation,
Federal Aviation Administration, GV
San Miguel, Abe .... San Antonio, TX
San Miguel, Alejandro R. .... New York, NY
San Miguel, Eduardo G. .... Las Vegas, NV
San Miguel, Eduardo G., Chartered
Las Vegas, NV
Sanmiguel, Ruben D. .... Maywood, IL
San Miguel-Casteleiro, Jorge L.
San Juan, PR
Sann, Alexander .... New York, NY
Sann & Howe .... New York, NY
Sann, John .... New York, NY
Sann, Ronald B. .... Department of Education,
Office of the General Counsel, GV
Sanne, Christian E. .... Glendale, CA
Sanneman, William C. .... Garden City, NY
Sannen, Marcelle B. .... Oregon City, OR
Sanner, Cecil R. .... Hackberry, LA
Lake Charles, LA
Sanner, David L. .... Newport Beach, CA
Sanner, John E. .... Decatur, IL
Sanner, Jon R. .... St. Louis, MO
Sanner, Margaret L. .... Las Vegas, NV
Sanner, Michael R. .... Lexington, KY
Sanner, Paul J. .... San Francisco, CA
Sanner, Royce N. .... Minneapolis, MN
Sanner, Thomas E. .... Minneapolis, MN
Sanner, Timothy K. .... Orange, VA
Sannes, Brenda K. .... Los Angeles, CA
Sannes, Joel E. .... Phoenix, AZ
Sannes, Jon K. .... Long Prairie, MN
Sannes, Victor E. .... Washington, DC
Sannicandro, Ronald W. .... New York, NY
Sannicandro, Thomas V. .... Ashland, MA
Sanning, Elizabeth M. .... Worcester, MA
Sanning, Matthew T. .... Florence, KY
Sanning, Stacey S. .... Florence, KY
Sannitti, Anthony F. .... East Hanover, NJ
Sano, Bryan Karl .... Honolulu, HI
Sano, Curtis L. .... Washington, DC
Sano, Jeannine Y. .... Palo Alto, CA
Sano, Joseph M. .... Lynn, MA
Sano, Joseph S. .... Boston, MA
Sano, Kazuhiko .... San Francisco, CA
Sanoba, Gregory A. .... Lakeland, FL
Sanoba, Karie L. .... Lakeland, FL
Sanoba & Sanoba, P.A. .... Lakeland, FL
Sanocki, Edward J., Jr. .... New York, NY
Sanocki, Newman & Turret .... New York, NY
Sanoff, Meyer K. .... Scarsdale, NY
Sanoff, Robert S. .... Boston, MA
Sanoff, Stanford .... La Quinta, CA
Sanoian, Joanne .... Fresno, CA
Sanoian, Paul Vaughn .... Los Angeles, CA
Sanok, Jeffrey D. .... Washington, DC
Sanok, Scott A. .... Boca Raton, FL
Sanok, Scott A., P.A. .... Boca Raton, FL
Sanom, Laura A. .... Dayton, OH
Sanom, Samuel T. .... Detroit, MI
Mount Clemens, MI
Sanow, Nancy J.
Securities and Exchange Commission,
Division of Market Regulation, GV
Sanowski, Deborah A. .... Hermosa Beach, CA
San Pedro, Juan .... New York, NY
Sanpei, Edward M. .... Honolulu, HI
Sanpei, Julie L. .... Las Vegas, NV
Sanphilip, William J. .... Monroe, MI
Sanpietro, J. Scott .... New York, NY
San Pietro, Richard .... La Jolla, CA
Sanregret, Robert A. .... Tustin, CA
Sans, Henri L., Jr. .... Gardner, MA
Sans, Roger .... Woodland, CA
Sansalone, Antonio M. .... Cincinnati, OH
Sansalone, Kevin V. .... Fairmont, WV
Sansalone, Monica A. .... Cleveland, OH
Sansberry, Dickmann, Freeman & Builta
Anderson, IN
Sansbury, Amy Zeldin .... Cincinnati, OH
Sansbury, Catherine R. .... New York, NY
Sansbury, John A., Jr. .... Maurice, LA
Sansbury, John T. .... Boca Raton, FL
Sanseverino, Raymond A. .... New York, NY
Sansevero, Michael, Jr. .... New York, NY
Sansing, Charles M. .... Canadian, TX
Sansing, Jennifer L. .... Los Angeles, CA
Sansing, Perry .... Jackson, MS
Sansiper, Beth A. .... Chicago, IL
Sansom, B. Stephen .... Florala, AL

Sansom, Ernest S. .... Freeport, TX
Sansom, Ted L. .... Rockwall, TX
Sanson, Charles H. .... Northville, MI
Sanson, Michael A. .... Cleveland, OH
Sanson, Paul D. .... Hartford, CT
Sanson, Ralph .... Aptos, CA
Sanson, Rudolph J., Jr. .... Stanhope, NJ
Sansone, A. J. .... Cincinnati, OH
Sansone, Alexander V. .... Mineola, NY
Mineola, NY
New York, NY
White Plains, NY
Sansone, Annette M. .... Buffalo, NY
Sansone, Charles F. .... Tampa, FL
Sansone, James J. .... Lockport, NY
Sansone, Joel S. .... Pittsburgh, PA
Sansone, John J. .... San Diego, CA
Sansone, John M. .... New York, NY
Sansone, Jos. A. .... Greensboro, NC
Sansone, Leslie A. .... Sierra Vista, AZ
Sansone, Lisa J. .... Baltimore, MD
Sansone, Nicholas J. .... Cherry Hill, NJ
Philadelphia, PA
Sansone, P. Leigh .... Birmingham, AL
Sansone, Samuel W. .... New York, NY
Sansone, Thomas J. .... New Haven, CT
Sansone, Timothy C. .... St. Louis, MO
Sansonetti, Jos. P. .... Akron, OH
Sansonetti, Thomas L., (P.C.)
Cheyenne, WY
Sansonetti, Vincent .... Chicago, IL
Sansonia, Caravita .... West Palm Beach, FL
Sansoucy, Andre A. .... Boston, MA
Sansoucy, Paul M. .... Syracuse, NY
Sans Souci, Andrew L. .... St. Louis, MO
Sanstead, Jonathan P. .... Bismarck, ND
Sansted, Douglas R. .... Westport, CT
Sant, Geetha R. .... St. Louis, MO
Sant, John T. .... St. Louis, MO
Sant, John Talbot, Jr.(P.C.) .... Belleville, IL
St. Louis, MO
Sant, Matthew .... Newport Beach, CA
Sant, Raymond S. .... Cato, NY
Sant, Robert J. .... Rochester, NY
Sant, Thomas R. .... Bath, OH
Santa, Donald F., Jr. .... Louisville, KY
Santa, Kevin J. .... Cleveland, OH
Santa, Martin M. .... Lincoln, MA
Santa, Sue .... Daytona Beach, FL
Santa Anna, Aaron
Department of Housing and Urban Development, Office of General Counsel, GV
Santa Barbara, Jennifer R.
Charlotte Amalie, St. Thomas, VI
Santa Barbara, Kathy M.
Martinsburg, WV
Santa Barbara, Michael S. .... Martinsburg, WV
Santacroce, Anthony F. .... Orange, CT
Santacroce, Loretta .... Department of Labor, Office of Secretary, GV
Santacroce, Marie V. .... Mount Olive, NJ
Santacroce, Mary Ann .... Hartford, CT
Santa Cruz, Bruce R. .... Lafayette, LA
Santa Cruz, Rudolfo .... Houston, TX
Santa Cruz, Susan Judlin
New Orleans, LA
Santaella Conde, Francisco C. .... San Juan, PR
Santagata, Jules W., Jr. .... Great Neck, NY
Santagata, Marie G. .... Mineola, NY
Santagata, Mark P. .... Stamford, CT
Santagata, Michael W. .... Stamford, CT
Santagata, Scott R. .... Irvine, CA
Santaguida, Joseph C. .... Philadelphia, PA
Santalone, James .... New York, NY
Santalone, John J., Jr. .... New York, NY
Santa Lucia, John S. .... Chicago, IL
Santa Lucia, Robert A. .... Clearwater, FL
Santa Lucia & Thomas, P.A.
Clearwater, FL
SantaMaria, Amy L. .... Mount Laurel, NJ
Santa Maria, Carmen .... Harrisburg, PA
SantaMaria, Carmen J. .... Portland, OR
Santamaria, Christopher Rene
Royal Palm Beach, FL
Santa Maria, Diana .... Fort Lauderdale, FL
Santa Maria, Diana, P.A., Law Offices of
Fort Lauderdale, FL
Miami, FL
West Palm Beach, FL
Santamaria, Erin B. .... Haddonfield, NJ
Philadelphia, PA
Santa Maria, Michael E. .... Dallas, TX
Santa Maria, Philip J. .... Frederick, MD
Gaithersburg, MD
Santa Maria, Victoria .... Walnut Creek, CA
Santa Maria & Weiss, Chartered
Frederick, MD
Gaithersburg, MD
Santamarina, Maria E. .... Miami, FL
Santamauro, Paul D. .... South Weymouth, MA
Sant'Ambrogio, Paul .... Bloomfield, NJ
Santamour, Gretchen M. .... Philadelphia, PA
Santana, Anthony M. .... Sacramento, CA
Santana, Arturo, Jr. .... Los Angeles, CA
Santana, Carmen .... Los Angeles, CA
Santana, Christine E. .... Miami, FL
Santana, Christine E., P.A. .... Miami, FL
Santana, Dawn C. .... White Plains, NY
Santana Fay & Bratt, P.S.C. .... Lexington, KY
Santana, Francis X. .... Miami, FL
Santana, Gloria de los Angeles Reyes
Austin, TX
Santana, Jorge Raul Ojeda
San Antonio, TX
Santana, Joseph C. .... Saratoga, CA
Santana, Joshua E. .... Lexington, KY
Santana, Laila Morcos .... Costa Mesa, CA
Santana, M. Teresa .... Chula Vista, CA
Santana, Maria D. .... Orlando, FL
Santana, Mark R. .... Phoenix, AZ
Santana, Monica S. .... Tallahassee, FL
Santana, Nancy C. .... El Paso, TX
Santana, Penny .... Bronx, NY
Santana, Peter J. .... Bloomfield, NJ
Santana, Susan I. .... San Diego, CA
Santana Aparicio, Roberto .... San Juan, PR
Santana-Mejias, Mildred L. .... San Juan, PR
Santana Oyola, Hector .... Bayamon, PR
Santanasto, Susan M. .... Woodbury, NJ
Santander, Robert S. .... White Plains, NY
Santangelo, Anne Marie .... New York, NY
Santangelo, Anthony A. .... East Meadow, NY
Santangelo, Benvenuto & Slattery
Manhasset, NY
Santangelo, Beth E. .... Denver, CO
Santangelo, Betty .... New York, NY
Santangelo, Carl G. .... Fort Lauderdale, FL
Santangelo, Carl G., P.A.
Fort Lauderdale, FL
Sant'Angelo, Celeste M. .... New York, NY
Santangelo, Dino R. .... Boston, MA
Santangelo, Francis R. .... Harrison, NY
Santangelo, Francis X. .... New York, NY
Santangelo, Frank J. .... Boston, MA
Santangelo, George L. .... New York, NY
Santangelo, Geraldine D. .... Brooklyn, NY
Santangelo, Jerry M. .... Chicago, IL
Santangelo, John N. .... Waltham, MA
Santangelo, Jon A. .... St. Louis, MO
Santangelo, Joseph T., Jr.
Richmond Hill, NY
Santangelo Law Offices, P.C.
Fort Collins, CO
Santangelo, Louis G. .... White Plains, NY
Santangelo, Luke .... Fort Collins, CO
Santangelo, Mark S. .... Pottstown, PA
Santangelo, Marsha F. .... Philadelphia, PA
Santangelo, Matthew S. .... Pennsburg, PA
Santangelo, Michael G. .... White Plains, NY
Santangelo, Michael L. .... New York, NY
Santangelo, Nicholas R. .... New York, NY
Santangelo, Robert P. .... Toms River, NJ
Santangelo, Santangelo & Cohen
New York, NY
Santangelo, Stephen A. .... Columbus, OH
Santangelo, Vincent .... Manhasset, NY
Santaniello, Alfred T. .... Norwalk, CT
Santaniello, Andrew J. .... Asheville, NC
Santaniello, Angelo G. .... New London, CT
Santaniello, Carmine R. .... Providence, RI
Santaniello, Carmino J., Jr. .... Hartford, CT
Santaniello, Cheryl Ann .... Haddonfield, NJ
Santaniello, Daniel J.
Fort Lauderdale, FL
Santaniello, Joseph J. .... Charlotte, NC
Santaniello, Joseph M. .... Burbank, CA
Santaniello, Julie A. .... Methuen, MA
Santaniello, Michael A. .... New York, NY
Santaniello, Michael C. .... Wildwood Crest, NJ
Santaniello, Posnik & Basile, P.C.
Springfield, MA
Santaniello, Robert M. .... Springfield, MA
Santapietro, Lisa .... Morristown, NJ
Santarella, Joseph M., Jr. .... Littleton, CO
Santarella Law Office, LLC .... Littleton, CO
Santarelli, Bryan A. .... Bellevue, WA
Santarelli, Donald E. .... Washington, DC
Santarelli, Frederick P. .... Blue Bell, PA
Harrisburg, PA
Santarelli, Gianna M. .... Philadelphia, PA
Santarelli, R. A. .... Gunnison, CO
Santarelli, Raymond J. .... Blue Bell, PA
Santarelli, Michael .... Fairport, NY
Santa-Romana, Mark V. .... El Centro, CA
Santarone, Joseph J., Jr. .... Norristown, PA
Santarpia, Sabatino C. .... Buffalo, NY
Santarpio, H. Edward .... Boston, MA
Santarsiero, Christopher G. .... Waterbury, CT
Santarsiero, Daniel M. .... Freehold, NJ
Santarsiero, Steven J. .... Newark, NJ
Santarsiero, Veronica R. .... Palm Beach, FL
Santa-Sánchez, Pedro J. .... San Juan, PR
Santasiere, Alfred G., Jr. .... Newton, NJ
Santa Teresa, Jose Emmanuel I.
Yonkers, NY
Santee, Dale W. .... San Diego, CA
Santee, Jack H. .... Bixby, OK
Tulsa, OK
Santee, John C. .... Prospect Heights, IL
Santee, Richard E., Jr. .... Bethlehem, PA
Santee, T. Daniel, II .... Abilene, TX
Santella, Gary D. .... Chicago, IL
Santellani, Lianne L. .... Columbus, OH
Santelle, James L. .... Milwaukee, WI
Santelle, Patricia B. .... Philadelphia, PA
Santello, Deborah M. .... Boston, MA
Santema, Steven R. .... Chicago, IL
Santemma and Deutsch, LLP
Mineola, NY
Santemma, Jon Noel .... Mineola, NY
Santemma, Suzanne .... Mineola, NY
Santen & Hughes, A Legal Professional Association .... Covington, KY
Cincinnati, OH
Santen, John .... Cincinnati, OH
Santen, William E. .... Cincinnati, OH
Santen, William E., Jr. .... Cincinnati, OH
Santer, Pamela Zhulkie .... Minneapolis, MN
Santer, Thomas F. .... Parkersburg, WV
Santerelli, Susan M. .... San Francisco, CA
Santerre, John P. .... Barron, WI
Santerre, Scott R. .... Scottsdale, AZ
Santerre & Vande Krol, Ltd. .... Phoenix, AZ
Scottsdale, AZ
Santeufemia, Michael N. .... Southfield, MI
Santeusanio, David J. .... Portland, ME
Santeusanio, Iginio .... Lynnfield, MA
Santez, David L. .... Dayton, OH
Santi, David R. .... San Rafael, CA
Santi, David W. .... Atlanta, GA
Santi, Emilio B. .... Waukegan, IL
Santi, Richard G. .... Des Moines, IA
Santiago, Alberto Omar Jimenez
San Juan, PR
Santiago, Beatriz .... Chicago, IL
Santiago, Carlos R. .... Fishers, NY
Santiago, Daniel V. .... Chicago, IL
Santiago, Fernando .... Rochester, NY
Santiago, Gregory N. .... Los Angeles, CA
Santiago, Hector L. .... Richmond Hill, NY
Santiago, Israel .... Mineola, NY
Santiago, José J. .... San Juan, PR
Santiago, Jose R. .... Clifton, NJ
Santiago, Julie .... Albany, NY
Santiago, Louis A. .... Portland, OR
Santiago, Lourdes .... Toledo, OH
Santiago, Lourdes I., (Ms) .... Jersey City, NJ
Santiago, Miguel A. .... Bronx, NY
Santiago, Nancy .... Yonkers, NY
Santiago, Nilsa .... New York, NY
Santiago, Osvaldo .... Ponce, PR
Santiago, Rafael A. .... Hartford, CT
Santiago, Ruth .... San Juan, PR
Santiago, Simon J. .... Washington, DC
Vienna, VA
Santiago, Stephen P. .... Miami, FL
Santiago, Victor G. .... Port Charlotte, FL
Santiago-Acevedo, Brunilda R.
San Juan, PR
Santiago-Acevedo, Eduardo A.
San Juan, PR
Santiago-Camacho, Ineabelle
San Juan, PR
Santiago-Ducos, Maura .... San Juan, PR
Santiago-Loperena, Laura I.
San Juan, PR
Santiago Marrero, Jesus .... San Juan, PR
Santiago Martinez, Jose A. .... San Juan, PR
Santiago-Ramos, María .... San Juan, PR
Santiago-Ramos, Marta .... San Juan, PR
Santiago-Ríos, Pedro A. .... San Juan, PR
Santiago Rivera, Miguel A. .... San Juan, PR
Santiago-Rivera, Pedro .... San Juan, PR
Santiago-Romero, Basilio .... San Juan, PR
Santiago Romero, Héctor A. .... San Juan, PR
Santiago-Rosa, Rafael M. .... San Juan, PR
Santiago-Sarkis, Carlos P. .... San Juan, PR
Santiago-Sastre, William .... San Juan, PR
Santiago Semidey, J. .... San Juan, PR
Santiago-Torres, Blanca I.
Department of Commerce, Patent and Trademark Office, GV
Santiago-Vazquez, Monica A.
San Juan, PR
Santiago-Vélez, Pedro A. .... San Juan, PR
Santiago Zayas, Yasmín M. .... San Juan, PR
Santiello, Carmino J. .... Hartford, CT
Santiesteban, H. Tati .... Austin, TX
El Paso, TX
Santiglia, Lori L. .... Fairfield, NJ
Santillan, Edgardo D. .... Beaver, PA
Santillana, Louis, Jr. .... Hallandale Beach, FL
Santillanes, Janet .... Albuquerque, NM
Santilli, Desiree M. .... North Kingstown, RI
Santilli, Elizabeth P. .... Providence, RI
Santilli, Frank A. .... Chicago, IL
Santilli, Mario, Jr. .... Pittsburgh, PA
Santilli, Paul T. .... Columbus, OH
Santilli, Sharon A. .... Providence, RI
Santillo, Keith R. .... Brooklyn, NY
Santillo, Stephen .... Lafayette, LA
Santin, Peter G. .... Phoenix, AZ
Las Vegas, NV
Santin, Poli, Ball & Sims, P.L.C.
Phoenix, AZ
Las Vegas, NV
Santini, Anthony M. .... New York, NY
Santini, Dennis P. .... Fairfax, VA
Santini, George .... Cheyenne, WY
Santini, James D. .... Alexandria, VA
Santini, John A. .... Harwinton, CT
Santini, Raphael J. .... Baltimore, MD
Santini, Raphael J., P.A. .... Baltimore, MD
Santini, Sean R. .... Miami, FL
Santin-Lerner, Lynnette M.
New York, NY
Santino, Richard Paul .... Concord, MA
Santino, Wendi E. .... San Diego, CA
Santire, Stanley P. .... Houston, TX
Santirocco, Laura A. .... Hartford, CT
Santis, Elizabeth D. .... Chicago, IL
Santisi, Frank J. .... Boston, MA
Santisi, Leonard J. .... New York, NY
Santisi, Michael J. .... Denver, CO
Santisteban, Marina R. .... Bakersfield, CA
Santivasci, Michael A. .... Philadelphia, PA
Santner, James M .... Staten Island, NY
Santo, Donna C., Law Offices of
Ventura, CA
Santo, Eric C. .... Singer Island, FL
Santo, Francis J. .... Los Angeles, CA
Santo, Fred M. .... New York, NY
Santo, Henry E. .... Evergreen, CO
Santo, James M. .... Clearwater, FL
Santo, Jess P. .... Warren, MI
Santo, Mark V. .... Wickliffe, OH
Santo, Michael A. .... Mineola, NY
Santo, Michael C. .... Grand Junction, CO
Santo, Ronald J. .... Detroit, MI
Santo, Samuel B., Jr. .... Roseland, NJ
Santo, Stephen S. .... New York, NY
Santo, William R. .... Wayland, MA
Santochi, Fitzer & Gable .... Glendale, CA
Irvine, CA
Santochi, Victor W. .... Glendale, CA
Santohigashi, Betty J. .... San Diego, CA
Santola, Daniel R. .... Albany, NY
Santola, Stacy A. .... Orange, NJ
Santola, Stephen A. .... Westfield, NJ
Santoli, Dennis R. .... Vienna, VA
Santoli, Joseph R .... Clifton, NJ
Santoli, Joseph R. .... New York, NY
Santoli, Paul .... Plainview, NY
Santoliquido, Joseph C. .... Elizabeth, NJ
Santomartino, Martha Lewis
Department of Commerce, Patent and Trademark Office, GV
Santomas, Ann M. .... Virginia Beach, VA
Santomassimo, Christopher M.
Roseland, NJ
Santomenna, Robert C. .... Portland, ME
Santona, Gloria .... Oak Brook, IL
Santone, Karl L. .... Charlottesville, VA
Santone, Thomas J. .... Pittsburgh, PA
Santoni, Cynthia L. .... McLean, VA
Santoni, Jane P. .... Baltimore, MD
Santoni, Roland J. .... Omaha, NE
Santopadre, Tina Crawford
New Orleans, LA
Santopietro, Albert R. .... Springfield, MA
Santopietro, George L. .... Providence, RI
Santora, Frank M. .... Pompton Lakes, NJ
Santora, Hugo G. .... Treasury Department, Departmental Offices, GV
Santora, John .... Great Neck, NY
Santora, Joseph J. .... New York, NY
Santora, Leslie A. .... Union, NJ
Santora, Richard Ernest
New Orleans, LA
Santora, Robert J. .... Troy, MI
Santora, Rocco T. .... Hammonton, NJ
Santora, Ronald V. .... Wilkes-Barre, PA
Santora, Thomas M. .... Chicago, IL
Santore, Anthony C. .... Hightstown, NJ
Santore, Dennis A. .... Torrington, CT
Santore, Francis X. .... Greeneville, TN
Santore, Francis X., Jr. .... Greeneville, TN
Santore & Santore .... Greeneville, TN
Santorelli, Albert J. .... Washington, DC
Santorelli, Joseph A. .... Brooklyn, NY
Santori, David J. .... Chicago, IL
Santori, Gino F. .... Northfield, NJ
Santori, Margaret N. .... Pittsburgh, PA
Santori, Peter W. .... Vallejo, CA
Santoro, A. William .... Manhasset, NY
Santoro, Alfred D., Jr. .... Parsippany, NJ
Santoro, Angela M. .... New York, NY
Santoro, Anne R. .... East Lyme, CT
Santoro, Anthony D. .... Waterbury, CT
Santoro, Anthony M., Jr. .... Livingston, NJ
Santoro, August J. .... Frankfort, IL
Santoro, Barbara A. .... Woodcliff Lake, NJ
Santoro, Christopher A. .... Wolfeboro, NH
Santoro, Christopher N. .... Philadelphia, PA
Santoro, David M. .... New York, NY
Santoro, Denyse J. .... New York, NY
Santoro, Edward J., Jr. .... South Plainfield, NJ
Santoro, Ernest D. .... Rochester, NY
Santoro, Frank A. .... South Plainfield, NJ
Santoro, Frank C. .... Los Angeles, CA
Santoro, Frank H. .... Hartford, CT
Santoro, Frank J. .... Portsmouth, VA
Santoro, Glenn A. .... Hartford, CT
Santoro, Gregory C. .... Harrisburg, PA
Santoro, Joseph G. .... Fort Lauderdale, FL
Santoro, Joseph J. .... Cleveland, OH
Santoro, Maria A. .... Tallahassee, FL
Santoro, Michael A. .... Los Angeles, CA
Santoro, Nicholas J. .... Las Vegas, NV
Santoro, Pamela Ann .... Philadelphia, PA
Santoro & Reinsel, LLC .... Pittsburgh, PA
Santoro, Rosemarie .... Kew Gardens, NY
Santoro, Salvatore A. .... Stamford, CT
Santoro, Stephen M. .... White Plains, NY
Santoro, Steven S. .... Pittsburgh, PA
Santoro, Susan E. .... Rockville Centre, NY
Santoro, William A. .... Manhasset, NY
Santos, Adela P. .... San Antonio, TX
Santos, Alberto G. .... Newark, NJ
Santos, Angel A. .... Pasadena, CA
Santos, Arthur J., Jr. .... Lowell, MA
Santos & Baez .... Mayaguez, PR
Santos, Carlos A. .... Naugatuck, CT
Santos, Carlos M. .... Hartford, CT
Santos, Daniel J. .... Atlanta, GA
Santos, Daniel P. .... Salem, OR
Santos Del Valle, Law Offices
San Juan, PR
Santos, Dutton, Lynott & Henry, P.A.
Tampa, FL
Santos, Elizabeth A. .... Pittsburgh, PA
Santos, Enrique .... Plano, TX
Santos, Eric W. .... Wheeling, WV
Santos, F. Robert .... Tampa, FL
Santos, Herb, Jr., The Law Firm of
Reno, NV
Santos, Herbert J. .... Reno, NV
Santos, Herbert J., Ltd. .... Reno, NV
Santos, Hubert J. .... Hartford, CT
Santos, Jaime E., Jr. .... San Juan, PR
Santos, Joel A. .... Reno, NV
Santos, Jose L. .... New York, NY
Santos, Jose ("Tony") A., Jr., (P.A.)
Miami, FL
Santos, Jose "Tony", Jr. .... Miami, FL
Santos, Joseph A. .... Farmington, CT
Santos, Laura L. .... Los Angeles, CA
Santos, Luis Roberto .... Mayaguez, PR
Santos, Marc J. .... Taunton, MA
Santos, Margarita D. .... Cleveland, OH

Santos, María I. .... San Juan, PR
Santos, Mauro C. .... Miami, FL
Santos, Melecio M. .... San Francisco, CA
Santos, Peter A. .... Pittsburgh, PA
Santos, Ralph G. .... Dallas, TX
Santos, Reydel .... Miami, FL
Santos, Roland M. .... Harrisonburg, VA
Santos, Rui M. .... Newark, NJ
Santos & Seeley, P.C. .... Hartford, CT
Santos, Vanessa A. .... Washington, DC
Santos, Victor M. .... Staunton, VA
Santos, Virna L. .... Fresno, CA
Santos, Zara J. .... San Francisco, CA
Santos-Alvarez, Brunilda .... Carolina, PR
Santos-Caballero, Lillian .... Washington, DC
Santos Del Valle, Rafael A. .... San Juan, PR
Santos-Gonzales, Laura C. .... San Antonio, TX
Santos Mimoso, José Javier .... San Juan, PR
Santospirito, John A. .... Long Island City, NY
Santos-Prats, Antonio J. .... San Juan, PR
Santos-Toledo, Rafael .... San Juan, PR
Santosuosso, Cara L. .... Cleveland, OH
Santosuosso, Joseph .... Clifton, NJ
Santow, Michael L. .... Brooklyn, NY
Santowasso, Nicholas L. .... Woodbridge, NJ
Santry, Aine M. .... New York, NY
Santry, Frank J. .... Tallahassee, FL
Santry & Macdonald .... Danvers, MA
Santry, Phyllis Ann .... New York, NY
Santry, Shelley Montgomery .... Louisville, KY
Santschi, Francis G. .... Chicago, IL
Santucci, Anthony H. .... Santa Clara, CA
Santucci, Danny C. .... Costa Mesa, CA
Santucci, Ettore A., (P.C.) .... Boston, MA
Santucci, Fred T. .... Jamaica, NY
Santucci, Fred T., Jr. .... Lake Success, NY
Santucci, James A. .... Chicago, IL
Santucci, James A. .... Federal Way, WA
Santucci, John J. .... Richmond Hill, NY
Santucci, John P. .... Waterbury, CT
Santucci, John P., P.C. .... Waterbury, CT
Santucci, Joseph E., Jr. .... Washington, DC
Santucci, Lisa S. .... Tallahassee, FL
Santucci, Maria C. .... East Brunswick, NJ
Santucci, Michael A. .... Fort Lauderdale, FL
Santucci, Michael I. .... Fort Lauderdale, FL
Santucci, Michael I., P.A.
Fort Lauderdale, FL
Santucci, Michele A. .... Troy, NY
Santucci, Ronald .... San Diego, CA
Santucci, Ronald R. .... Morristown, NJ
Santucci, Teresa .... Hempstead, NY
Santucci, Thomas J. .... Richmond Hill, NY
Santulli, James V. .... Paramus, NJ
Santurbane, Kimberly A. .... Dexter, MI
Santurri, Thomas R. .... Pensacola, FL
Santurri, Thomas R., P.A. .... Pensacola, FL
Santwier, Dennis Rickard .... Pasadena, CA
Santwier, Rickard .... Los Angeles, CA
Santwier, Rickard .... Pasadena, CA
Santy, Frank G. .... Enfield, CT
Sanua, David .... New York, NY
Sanville, Stephen M. .... Las Vegas, NV
Sanvordeker, Shilpa D. .... Los Angeles, CA
Sanz, Cristina P. .... Medford, OR
Sanz, Parris J. .... San Francisco, CA
Sanza, Mark D. .... Albany, NY
Sanzalone, Lisa .... Westfield, NJ
Sanzari, Leah P. .... New York, NY
Sanzaro, Karen M. .... Bethesda, MD
Sanzo, Frank A. .... Montebello, CA
Sanzo, Judi M. .... Solana Beach, CA
Sanzo, Kathleen M. .... Washington, DC
Sanzo, Michael A. .... Washington, DC
Sanzo, Paul S. .... Denver, CO
Sanzo, Robert L. .... Mount Laurel, NJ
Philadelphia, PA
Sanzone & Baker, P.C. .... Lynchburg, VA
Richmond, VA
Roanoke, VA
Sanzone, Christopher W. .... Boston, MA
Sanzone, Joseph A. .... Lynchburg, VA
Sanzone, Vincent A. .... Middletown, OH
Sanzone, Vincent James, Jr. .... Elizabeth, NJ
Sanzone, Virginia R. .... Denver, CO
Sanz-Rexach, Gabriel R. .... Washington, DC
SaoBento, Augusto W. .... East Providence, RI
Saotome, Chigusa .... Sacramento, CA
Sapadin, David .... Haddonfield, NJ
Sapadin, Lawrence M. .... New York, NY
Sapakie, Carol H. .... Mount Laurel, NJ
Sapakoff, Gregory G. .... Denver, CO
Sapala, Donald J. .... Chattanooga, TN
Sapala, Michael F. .... Detroit, MI
Sapanai, Elizabeth .... Stinson Beach, CA
Sapanara, Denise D. .... New York, NY
Saparilas, Nicholas Timothy .... Raleigh, NC
Saparoff, Peter M. .... Boston, MA
Sapcoe, Lisa A. .... Kansas City, MO
Saper, Gus A. .... Houston, TX
Saper, Jaclyn D. .... Chicago, IL
Saper, Jeffrey B. .... Marlton, NJ
Saper, Jeffrey D. .... Palo Alto, CA
Saper, Michael S. .... Chicago, IL
Saper, Michael S., & Associates, P.C.
Chicago, IL
Saper, Ronald A., (P.C.) .... Phoenix, AZ
Saper, Vernon P. .... Grand Rapids, MI
Saperman, Dylan .... New York, NY
Sapero, Robert Allen .... Baltimore, MD
Sapero & Sapero .... Baltimore, MD
Sapers, Carl M. .... Boston, MA
Sapers, Cristine M. .... New York, NY
Saperstein, Alan .... Brooklyn, NY
Saperstein, Allen H. .... Bronx, NY
Saperstein, Charles .... New York, NY
Saperstein, Clare F. .... New York, NY
Saperstein, David M. .... Detroit, MI
Saperstein, Drew F. .... Southfield, MI
Saperstein, Edward .... Great Falls, VA
Saperstein, Gerald .... Auburn, NY
Saperstein, Gerald W. .... Chicago, IL
Saperstein, Goldstein, Demchak & Baller, A Professional Corporation .... Oakland, CA
Saperstein, Guy T. .... Oakland, CA
Saperstein, Herschel J.
Salt Lake City, UT
Saperstein, Ira B. .... Southfield, MI
Saperstein, Israel .... Los Angeles, CA
Saperstein, Jennifer Beth .... Bronx, NY
Saperstein, Jonathan .... Washington, DC
Saperstein, Karen D. L. .... New York, NY
Saperstein, Lanier .... New York, NY
Saperstein, Marc C. .... Teaneck, NJ
New York, NY
Saperstein, Mark L. .... Brookline, MA
Saperstein, Martin I. .... Garden City, NY
Saperstein, Melvyn D. .... Southfield, MI
Saperstein, Nathan .... New York, NY
Saperstein, Nathaniel .... New York, NY
Saperstein, Robert A. .... New York, NY
Saperstein, Robert J. .... Santa Barbara, CA
Saperstein, Robert M. .... Stamford, CT
Saperstein, Scott .... Fort Lauderdale, FL
Saperston & Day, P.C. .... Amherst, NY
Buffalo, NY
Niagara Falls, NY
Rochester, NY
Syracuse, NY
Saperston, Lee R. .... New York, NY
Saperton, Patricia Santemma
Mineola, NY
Saph, Hale P., III .... Lighthouse Point, FL
Saph, Val A., (P.C.) .... Marine City, MI
Sapherstein, Michael B. .... New York, NY
Saphier and Heller, Law Corporation
Los Angeles, CA
Saphier, Michael D. .... Los Angeles, CA
Saphier, Michael S. .... Los Angeles, CA
Saphier, Rein & Walden .... Los Angeles, CA
Saphire, Daniel .... Washington, DC
Saphire, David A. .... Dayton, OH
Saphire, Gerald .... Sharon, MA
Saphire, Roberta Waterman, (Mrs.)
Sharon, MA
Saphire & Saphire .... Sharon, MA
Saphire-Bernstein, Leonard D.
Chicago, IL
Saphire-Bernstein, Leonard D. .... Skokie, IL
Saphos, Charles S. .... Columbia, MD
Sapienza, Charles D. .... Manasquan, NJ
Sapienza, Charles P., Jr. .... Ellwood City, PA
New Castle, PA
Sapienza, David J. .... Santa Monica, CA
Sapienza, James L. .... Palmyra, NY
Sapienza, John T., Jr. .... Treasury Department, Internal Revenue Service, GV
Sapienza & Kocher .... Palmyra, NY
Sapienza, Michael .... New York, NY
Sapienza, Stephen L. .... New York, NY
Sapienza, Stephen P. .... Bunnell, FL
Sapier, Jacques .... San Diego, CA
Sapin, Craig P. .... San Diego, CA
Sapin, David R. .... Washington, DC
Sapin, Marc E. .... Jersey City, NJ
Sapinski, Richard J. .... Newark, NJ
Sapinski, Sigismund L., Jr. .... Hartford, CT
Sapinsley, Thomas S. .... Cincinnati, OH
Sapio, George N. .... Washington, DC
Sapio, Jos. A. .... Brooklyn, NY
Sapio, Peter J., Jr. .... Galveston, TX
Sapir, Diane C. .... Bethesda, MD
Sapir, Donald L. .... White Plains, NY
Sapir, Eddie L. .... New Orleans, LA
Sapir, Eric J. .... Hartford, CT
Newark, NJ
New York, NY
Sapir & Frumkin, LLP .... White Plains, NY
Sapir, Genevieve D.
National Archives And Records Administration, General Counsel Staff, GV
Sapir, George R. .... Walton Hills, OH
Sapir, Isidore .... West Palm Beach, FL
Sapir, Jeffrey L. .... White Plains, NY
Sapir, Judith S. ....
Overseas Private Investment Corporation, GV
Sapir, M. Richard .... West Palm Beach, FL
Sapir, Michael L., (P.C.) .... Rockville, MD
Sapir, Robert E. .... Melville, NY
Sapira, Lee E. .... Reading, PA
Sapire, Dennis H. .... Los Angeles, CA
Sapire, Gregory Philip .... Houston, TX
Sapirman, Louis A. .... Princeton, NJ
New York, NY
Sapiro, Andrew B. .... Miami, FL
Sapiro, David M. .... East Brunswick, NJ
Sapiro & Gottlieb .... East Brunswick, NJ
Sapiro, Jeffrey D. .... Lake Oswego, OR
Sapiro, Jerome .... San Francisco, CA
Sapiro, Jerome, Jr. .... San Francisco, CA
Sapiro Law Firm, The .... San Francisco, CA
Sapiro, Miriam .... Department of State, Office of the Legal Adviser, GV
Sapiro, Stanley M. .... Laguna Niguel, CA
Sapiro, Todd S. .... Washington, DC
Sapirstein, Jonathan C. .... Springfield, MA
Sapirstein, Rhoda L. .... Berkeley, CA
Sapirstein & Sapirstein, P.C.
Greenfield, MA
Pittsfield, MA
Springfield, MA
Sapirstein, Tani E. .... Springfield, MA
Sapodin, Josh .... Atlantic Beach, NY
Sapon, Andrew .... New York, NY
Saponara, Ann .... San Jose, CA
Saponara, Michael A. .... Philadelphia, PA
Saponaro, Frank P., Jr. .... Potomac, MD
Sapone, Brian P. .... Omaha, NE
Sapone, Mary Ann .... Los Angeles, CA
Sapone & Smith, P.C. .... Omaha, NE
Sapone, William J. .... New York, NY
Sapora, John A. .... Jacksonville, FL
Saporito, Frank .... Chicago, IL
Saporito, Gina M. .... Washington, DC
Vienna, VA
Saporito, Jerry L. .... New Orleans, LA
Saporito, Joseph F. .... Pittston, PA
Saporito, Joseph F., Jr. .... Pittston, PA
Saporito, Michael R. .... Winter Park, FL
Saporito & Saporito .... Pittston, PA
Saporito & Sledge, L.L.C.
New Orleans, LA
Saporito, Steven A. .... Brooklyn, NY
Saporta, Lionel R. .... New York, NY
Saposhnik, Thalia .... Bronx, NY
Saposnik, Gary H. .... Chicago, IL
Sapp, Annmarie Tornello
Fort Lauderdale, FL
Sapp, Conwell F. .... Columbia, MD
Sapp, David A. .... Pensacola, FL
Sapp, David A. .... Atlanta, GA
Sapp, David A., P.A. .... Pensacola, FL
Sapp, David C., II .... Gainesville, FL
Sapp, David C., Jr. .... New York, NY
Sapp, David R. .... Austin, TX
Sapp, David W. .... Kenansville, NC
Sapp, Ernestine S. .... Tuskegee, AL
Sapp, F. Rebecca .... Kansas City, MO
Sapp, Gay N. .... Austin, TX
Sapp, Gregory V. .... Savannah, GA
Sapp, H. P. .... Panama City, FL
Sapp, J. C. .... Keystone Heights, FL
Sapp, John Lewis .... Atlanta, GA
Sapp, John Mark .... Oneonta, AL
Sapp, John R. .... Milwaukee, WI
Sapp, Joseph D. .... Columbia, SC
Sapp, Judith .... Portland, ME
Sapp, Karen E. .... Houston, TX
Sapp, Kimberly L. .... Lake Placid, FL
Sebring, FL
Sapp, Mast & Stroud .... Winston-Salem, NC
Sapp, Michael K. .... Jacksonville, FL
Sapp, Richard H., III .... Atlanta, GA
Sapp, Richard J. .... Des Moines, IA
Sapp, Richard S. .... Winston-Salem, NC
Sapp, Richd. H., Jr. .... Dalton, GA
Sapp, Robert A., Jr. .... Cullman, AL
Sapp, Robert H. .... Winston-Salem, NC
Sapp, Robt. A. .... Cullman, AL
Sapp & Sapp .... Cullman, AL
Sapp, Sapp & White, P.C. .... Austin, TX
Sapp, Stephen L. .... Dallas, TX
Sapp, Susan Kubert .... Lincoln, NE
Sapp, Vincent D. .... Fort Myers, FL
Sapp, Walter W. .... Houston, TX
Sapp, Warren H. .... Kansas City, KS
Sapp, William H., Jr. .... Roanoke, VA
Sapp, William W. .... Atlanta, GA
Sapp, Wm. H. .... Panama City, FL
Sappanos, Donald L. .... Lansing, MI
Sappé, David F. .... Huntington, NY
Sappe, Robert R. .... Fishkill, NY
Sappenfield, Ann Elizabeth .... Chantilly, VA
Sappenfield, Eric L. .... Southaven, MS
Sappenfield, Keith M., II .... Tulsa, OK
Sapper, Arthur G. .... Washington, DC
Sapper, Charles B. .... Modesto, CA
Pleasanton, CA
Sapper, Charles B. .... San Ramon, CA
Sapper, Charles B. .... Walnut Creek, CA
Sappern, Yale W. .... New Haven, CT
Sapperstein, Benjamin .... Baltimore, MD
Sapperstein, Scott A. .... Austin, TX
Sappett, Joseph S. .... Hudson, MA
Sappington, Bryn A. .... Dallas, TX
Sappington, G. Mark .... Kansas City, MO
Sappington, John A. .... Vista, CA
Sappington, Nancy M. .... St. Louis, MO
Sappington, Warren A. .... Decatur, IL
Sapriel, Daniella .... Los Angeles, CA
Sapronov, Walter .... Atlanta, GA
Sapru, Tara .... New York, NY
Sapse, Alfred Theodore .... Santa Monica, CA
Sapsin, Jason W. .... Burlington, IA
Sapsin, Michelle A. .... Burlington, IA
Sapunor, John M. .... Sacramento, CA
Sapunor, Peter A .... Sacramento, CA
Sapunor, Thomas L., Jr. .... Sacramento, CA
Sapurstein, Bertram A. .... Miami, FL
Sapurstein & Bloch, P.A. .... Miami, FL
Saputelli, Gregory D. .... Haddonfield, NJ
Saputo, Peter T. .... Walnut Creek, CA
Saqqal, Paul T. .... New York, NY
Saqui, Michael C. .... Fresno, CA
Sar, David W. .... Greensboro, NC
Sar, Jeffrey A. .... Sioux City, IA
Sar, Robert A. .... Raleigh, NC
Sara, Charles S. .... Madison, WI
Sara, J. Michael .... Miami Springs, FL
Sarabia, Antonio R. .... Chicago, IL
Sarabia, Antonio R., II
Rolling Hills Estates, CA
Sarabia, Ariana N. .... Spokane, WA
Sarabia, Richard .... Grand Prairie, TX
Sarabia, Richard, The, Law Firm, P.C.
Grand Prairie, TX
Saracco, Gail C. .... Chicago, IL
Saracco, Louis A., Jr. .... Fairfield, CT
Saracco, William V. .... Chicago, IL
Saraceni, Paul M. .... San Francisco, CA
Saraceno, David A. .... Coeur d'Alene, ID
Saraceno, Kent R. .... Golden, CO
Sarachan, Gary R. .... St. Louis, MO
Sarachan, George L. .... Albany, NY
Sarachan, Ronald A. .... Philadelphia, PA
Saracino, Alessandro .... New York, NY
Saracino, Christopher J.
Mount Laurel, NJ
Saracino, David P. .... Newark, NY
Saracino, Nancy J. .... Sacramento, CA
Saracino, Samuel F. .... Redmond, WA
Saracino, William .... Totowa, NJ
Saracoff, Norman .... Neillsville, WI
Saracusa, Lynda L. .... Andover, MA
Sarad, Nicolai J. .... New York, NY
Sarados, George S. .... Stoughton, MA
Saraf, Irene Baslow .... Seattle, WA
Saraf, Richard T. .... Buffalo, NY
Sarafa, Christa .... Detroit, MI
Sarafa, Derek J. .... Chicago, IL
Sarafa, Haithem K. .... Farmington Hills, MI
Sarafa, Haithem K., P.C.
Farmington Hills, MI
Sarafa, Joseph D. .... Southfield, MI
Sarafa, Karim Y. .... West Bloomfield, MI
Sarafa, Karim Y., P.C. .... West Bloomfield, MI
Sarafan, Richard J. .... Miami, FL
Sarafian, Robert K. .... Ridgefield Park, NJ
Sarafin, James A. .... Anchorage, AK
Sarafiny, James C. .... Hartford, WI
Sarafoglu, Alexander T. .... Miami, FL
Sarafopoulos, John .... Los Angeles, CA
Saraga, Robert S. .... Boca Raton, FL
Saragas, Antony L. .... Harlan, KY
Sarah, Laura S. .... Boston, MA
Sarahan, Paul C. .... Austin, TX
Sarai, Baldev S. .... St. Louis, MO
Sarajian, Renee .... Philadelphia, PA
Sarajian, Richard H. .... New City, NY
Sarak, Cynthia Marie .... Woodland Hills, CA
Sarakatsannis, Thomas J. .... New York, NY
Sarakin, Lizabeth .... Hackensack, NJ
Sarakin, Lloyd B. .... Park Ridge, NJ
Saralino, Mark D. .... Cleveland, OH
Sarama, Kenneth F. .... Hammond, LA
Saran, Atul .... Washington, DC
Saran, Melinda R. .... Buffalo, NY
Saran, Roopal Mehta .... Washington, DC
Arlington Heights, IL
Sarancik, Karen L. .... Bend, OR
Sarandis, Nicholas P. .... Westbury, NY
Sarandis, William S. .... Decatur, GA
Sarandos, Dena C. .... Salt Lake City, UT
Sarandos, Dolores K. .... Tacoma, WA
Saranec, A. Henry .... Midland, TX
Saranecki, Todd M. .... Chicago, IL
Saranello, Joseph A. .... Houston, TX
Saranow, Mitchell H. .... Chicago, IL
Sarant, Jeremy V. .... Portland, OR
Sarantes, Mary Papadopoulos
Los Angeles, CA
Sarantopoulos, Dorothy M. .... New York, NY
Sarantopoulos, Nicholas G. .... Danielson, CT
Sarantopoulos, Stephanie D.
Minneapolis, MN
Sarantos, Anastasia M. .... Lowell, MA
Sarantos, Marianthi Chicklis
Newburyport, MA
Sarasek, Peter A. .... Chicago, IL
Sarasin, Joanne A. .... Chicago, IL
Sarasin, Ronald A. .... Alexandria, VA
Sarasky, Arnold L. .... Coral Springs, FL
Sarasohn, Peter R. .... Roseland, NJ
Sarason, Ernest L., Jr. .... Boston, MA
Sarason, Scott M. .... Miami, FL
Saravay, Adam N. .... Newark, NJ
Saravia, Alma L. .... Cherry Hill, NJ
Saraydarian, Arjuna T., (Mr.) .... Blythe, CA
Sarazen, Linda J. .... Charlotte, NC
Sarazin, Mary E. .... St. Paul, MN
Sarb, Thomas P. .... Grand Rapids, MI
Sarbacher, Harold J. .... Washington, DC
Sarbacker, Steven J. .... Sioux Falls, SD
Sarbanes, Dina E. .... Towson, MD
Sarbanes, John P. .... Baltimore, MD
Sarbaugh, Bruce W. .... Boulder, CO
Sarber, L. Johnson, III .... Jacksonville, FL
Sarber, Robert L. .... Newark, NJ
Sarbin, Hershel B. .... Bedford, NY
Sarbo, Jerry, (P.A.) .... Tampa, FL
Sarcevich & Epsha, PLC .... Royal Oak, MI
Sarcevich, Rod N. .... Royal Oak, MI
Sarchet, Bruce J. .... Sacramento, CA
Stockton, CA
Sarchio, Christina Guerola
Washington, DC
Sarchio, John J. .... New York, NY
Sarcinella, Joseph A. .... New York, NY
Sarcona, Richard John .... Jamaica, NY
Sarcone, C. Robert .... Bloomfield, NJ
Sarcone, Francis X. .... Los Angeles, CA
Sarcone, James V., Jr. .... Des Moines, IA
Sarcone, James V., Sr. .... Des Moines, IA
Sarcone, John A., III .... New York, NY
Sarcone, John P. .... Des Moines, IA
Sarcone, Stephanie G. .... Des Moines, IA
Sard, Barbara .... Boston, MA
Sard, Michael .... Atlanta, GA
Sarda, Peter J. .... Raleigh, NC
Sardam, William W. .... Irvine, CA
Sardano, Richard J. .... Liverpool, NY
Sardar, John J. .... St. Louis, MO
Sardelis, Nicholas P. .... Sarasota, FL
Sardell, William .... Englewood, NJ
Sardella, Albert M. .... Coatesville, PA
Sardella, Alfred .... York, PA
Sardella, Dennis J. .... Boston, MA
Sardella, William J. .... Syracuse, NY
Sardelli, Joseph J. .... Smithtown, NY
Sardelli, Lawrence A. .... Chadwicks, NY

Sardina-Cardona, Blanca E. .... San Juan, PR
Sardiñas, Alina .... Miami Beach, FL
Sardinia, Lisa M. .... Forest Grove, OR
Sardino, J. Richard .... Syracuse, NY
Sardino & Paquette .... Syracuse, NY
Sardino, Patrick B. .... Syracuse, NY
Sardo, Rose Marie .... Newark, NJ
Sarduy, George A. .... Miami, FL
Sare & Cherry .... South Lake Tahoe, CA
Sare, Dale L. .... South Lake Tahoe, CA
Sare, John P. .... New York, NY
Sareen, Tina .... Yorba Linda, CA
Saremi, Deborah K. .... Springfield, MA
Sarenpa, Mark B. .... Minneapolis, MN
Sares, Mark A. .... Westminster, CO
Saret, Larry L. .... Chicago, IL
Saret, Lewis J. .... Washington, DC
Saretsky, Barry G. .... New York, NY
Saretsky, Gary M. .... Bloomfield Hills, MI
Saretsky, Judith Share .... Birmingham, MI
Saretsky Katz Dranoff & Glass, L.L.P.
New York, NY
Sarezky, Laurence .... Westport, CT
Sarfan, Edward I. .... Newport News, VA
Sarfan, Leon R. .... Newport News, VA
Sarfan, Mayer A. .... Newport News, VA
Sarfan & Nachman .... Newport News, VA
Sarfatis, Brandi Wickline .... Dallas, TX
Sarfatis, Robert .... Irving, TX
Sarfatti, Steven .... Washington, DC
Sarfaty, Joseph .... Los Angeles, CA
Sarfaty, Valerie J. .... San Francisco, CA
Sarff, Jon G. .... Mankato, MN
Sarfoh, Eugene N. .... Albany, NY
Sargalski, Dianne .... Meriden, CT
Sargeant, Bernadette .... Department of Justice, Office of Professional Responsibility, GV
Sargeant, Christina Peterson .... Phoenix, AZ
Sargeant, Daniel L. .... West Bend, WI
Sargeant, Ernest J. .... Boston, MA
Sargeant & Friedman, P.C. .... Vienna, VA
Sargeant, Harry A., Jr. .... Fremont, OH
Sargeant, Jonathon L. .... Kinston, NC
Sargeant, Kimball J.P., Law Office of
Davis, CA
Sargeant, Leonard, III .... Williamsburg, VA
Sargeant, Richard T. .... Columbus, OH
Toledo, OH
Sargeant, William H. .... Arlington, TX
Sargeant, William H. .... Fort Worth, TX
Sargeant, William L. .... Vienna, VA
Sargeant, William P., III .... Phoenix, AZ
Sargent, Ann M. .... Chatham, NJ
Sargent, Anne Gresham .... Athens, AL
Sargent, Anne-Marie E. .... Seattle, WA
Sargent, Barbara S. .... Boston, MA
Sargent, C. Forbes, III .... Boston, MA
Sargent, Cathleen M. .... Burbank, CA
Sargent, Clint .... Sioux Falls, SD
Sargent, Craig A. .... Glendale, CO
Sargent, David J. .... Boston, MA
Sargent, David L. .... Dallas, TX
Sargent, David R. .... Pittsburgh, PA
Sargent, Dean R. .... Seattle, WA
Sargent, Dennis J., Jr. .... Wilmington, DE
Sargent, Devon J. .... New York, NY
Sargent, Dolores S. .... Danville, CA
Sargent, Edward J. .... Chesapeake, VA
Sargent, Gary A. .... Salt Lake City, UT
Sargent, Gordon .... Albuquerque, NM
Sargent, Gordon W. .... Austin, TX
Sargent, Hale C. .... Westport, CT
New York, NY
Sargent, Hugh A. A. .... Philadelphia, PA
Sargent, Jack D. .... El Paso, TX
Sargent, James C. .... Charlottesville, VA
Sargent, James C., Jr. .... West Chester, PA
Sargent, James F. T., Jr. .... Greenwood, IN
Sargent, James W. .... Dallas, TX
Houston, TX
Sargent, John E., Jr. .... Oklahoma City, OK
Sargent, Johnny V., Jr. .... Ridgeland, MS
Sargent, Jon W. .... Rockville, MD
Sargent, Joseph P. .... Bridgeport, CT
Sargent, Karen C. .... Dallas, TX
Sargent, Linda C. .... Whitehouse Station, NJ
Sargent, Louisa B. .... Springfield, NJ
Sargent, Lynn S. .... Cleveland, OH
Sargent, Margie M. .... San Francisco, CA
Sargent, Mark S. .... Springfield, IL
Sargent, Mark T.L. .... New York, NY
Sargent, Maxwell L. .... Detroit, MI
Sargent & Meier .... Greenwood, IN
Sargent, Murray, Jr. .... Westport, CT
New York, NY
Sargent & Myers, LLP .... Syracuse, NY
Sargent, Nicholas J. .... Buffalo, NY
Sargent, Nicole A. .... Houston, TX
Sargent, Pamela A. .... Richmond, VA
Sargent, Patricia Gail .... Houston, TX
Sargent, Patrick C. .... Dallas, TX
Sargent, Ralph W., Jr. .... Worcester, MA
Sargent, Richard A. .... Laurel, MD
Sargent, Richard C. .... Morrisville, VT
Sargent, Richard H. .... Syracuse, NY
Sargent, S. Scott .... Huntsville, AL
Sargent, Sally Larson .... Chicago, IL
Sargent, Sarah J. .... Topeka, KS
Sargent, Shelton E. .... Fort Smith, AR
Sargent, Stephen M. .... Salt Lake City, UT
Sargent, Susan T. .... Oakland, CA
Sargent, Waldo .... Houston, TX
Sargent, Walter H. .... Colorado Springs, CO
Sargent, Walter H., A Professional Corporation .... Colorado Springs, CO
Sargent & White .... Morrisville, VT
Sargent, William D. .... Detroit, MI
Sargente, Alfred J. .... Morristown, NJ
Sargenti, Gregory A. .... Santa Ana, CA
Sargentich, Lewis D. .... Cambridge, MA
Sargert, Janet L. .... Pittsburgh, PA
Sargetis, John S. .... Rancho Cordova, CA
Sargis, Kevin M. .... Lexington, MA
Sargis, Marc W. .... Lincolnwood, IL
Sargis, Mark R. .... Chicago, IL
Sargis, Ronald H. .... Sacramento, CA
Sargis, Scott A. .... Boston, MA
Sargisson, Duane Thomas .... Worcester, MA
Sargoy, Kenneth J. .... Los Angeles, CA
Sargoy, Stein, Rosen & Shapiro
New York, NY
Sargrad-Terry, Gita .... Burbank, CA
Sarguis, Francis .... Santa Barbara, CA
Sargus, Edmund A., Jr. .... Columbus, OH
Sargus, Jennifer L. .... St. Clairsville, OH
Sarhad, Ronald D. .... Turlock, CA
Sari, Robert B. .... Harrisburg, PA
Saria, Robert J. .... Norwalk, CA
Saria, Sarah Namnama .... Sacramento, CA
Sarian, Ara J .... Belmont, MA
Sarian, Ronald N. .... Los Angeles, CA
Saridakis, Anthony A. .... Rockville, MD
Sarikas, John M. .... Tucson, AZ
Sarikas, Thomas E. .... Chicago, IL
Sarin, Garish .... Los Angeles, CA
Sarin, Melvin .... Sharon, MA
Sarin, Neil Roy .... Baltimore, MD
Sarin, Sujata .... Fairfax, VA
Saringer, John R. .... Abilene, TX
Sario, Markku A., (Mr.) .... Klamath Falls, OR
Sariol, Frank R. .... Santa Ana, CA
Sariol, Maria D. .... Coral Gables, FL
Saripkin, Mark A. .... Memphis, TN
Saris, Elena Marie .... Los Angeles, CA
Saris, Emanuel F. .... New York, NY
Saris, Patti B. .... Boston, MA
Sarisky, David S. .... Los Angeles, CA
Sarisky, Thomas J.
Federal Deposit Insurance Corporation, GV
Sarisohn, Bernard .... Commack, NY
Sarisohn, Floyd .... Commack, NY
Sarisohn, Sarisohn, Carner, LeBow, Braun & Shiebler .... Commack, NY
Sarisohn, Steven L. .... Commack, NY
Sarjeant, John A. .... Rancho Palos Verdes, CA
Sarka, Rosemary .... Santa Cruz, CA
Sarkar, George A. .... New York, NY
Sarkar, Neil S. .... Elyria, OH
Sarkar, Rumu
Agency for International Development, Office of the General Counsel, GV
Sarke, Dena M. .... Boston, MA
Sarkees, Marie T. .... Philadelphia, PA
Sarkela, Margaret A. .... New York, NY
Sarkesian, Peter J. .... Birmingham, MI
Sarkessian, Juliet M. .... Asheville, NC
Sarkin, Allan J. .... Encino, CA
Sarkin, Barbara E. .... Philadelphia, PA
Sarkin, Jeremy J. .... Pittsfield, MA
Sarkinen, Anne L. .... Chicago, IL
Sarkis, Anthony J. .... Los Angeles, CA
Sarkis, Frederick .... Merritt Island, FL
Sarkis, George R. .... Akron, OH
Sarkis, Roberta Kyselka
Mount Clemens, MI
Sarkisian, Alan H. .... Torrance, CA
Sarkisian, Albert E. .... Providence, RI
Sarkisian, Barry P. .... Hoboken, NJ
Sarkisian, Charles .... St. Louis, MO
Sarkisian, Debra N. .... Worcester, MA
Sarkisian, Edward, Jr. .... Fresno, CA
Sarkisian & Fleming .... Portage, IN
Sarkisian & Florio .... Hoboken, NJ
Sarkisian, Gregory J. .... Portage, IN
Sarkisian, Jack N. .... Woburn, MA
Sarkisian, Pamela Rose .... New York, NY
Sarkisian, Philip V. .... Oakland, CA
Sarkisian, Ruben N. .... Glendale, CA
Sarkisian, Ruben N. .... Glendale, CA
Sarkisian, Thomas A. .... Lafayette, CA
Sarkisian & Woods .... Woburn, MA
Sarkis-Rozeboom, Kristine E.
San Antonio, TX
Sarkissian, Ivan A. .... Denver, CO
Sarko, Lynn Lincoln, (Mr.) .... Seattle, WA
Sarko, Michele Y.F. .... Department of Justice, Civil Division, GV
Sarkos, Peter M. .... Atlantic City, NJ
Sarkozi, Beverly Shuldiner .... Fort Lee, NJ
Sarkozi, Paul D. .... New York, NY
Sarkozy, Jennifer J. .... Oakland, CA
Sarles, Burton B. .... Buffalo, NY
Sarles, Dave .... Houston, TX
Sarles & Frey .... Buffalo, NY
Sarles, Gary D. .... Dallas, TX
Sarles, Jeffrey W. .... Chicago, IL
Sarles, Neil R. .... Seattle, WA
Sarles & Ouimet, L.L.P. .... Chicago, IL
Dallas, TX
Sarles, Shannon Brady .... New York, NY
Sarley, Bernard J. .... Chicago, IL
Sarli, Anthony J., Jr. .... Schaumburg, IL
Sarli, Michael G. .... Providence, RI
Sarlo, Jim D. .... Astoria, NY
Sarlo, Gary P. .... Morganville, NJ
Sarlson, Katherine Graham
Cleveland, OH
Sarlson, Mark L. .... Akron, OH
Cleveland, OH
Sarma, Ann .... Sacramento, CA
Sarmiento, Ellen Ann .... Los Angeles, CA
Sarmiento, John C. .... San Francisco, CA
Sarmiento, Juliette Topacio
San Francisco, CA
Sarmiento, Vincent F. .... Irvine, CA
Sarmiento Knowlton, Janette
Los Angeles, CA
Sarmont, Richard L. .... Antioch, IL
Sarmov, Kalina .... Hudson, FL
Sarna & Associates, P.C. .... New York, NY
Sarna, Cheryl L.S. .... Palos Heights, IL
Sarna, Dominic .... Brooklyn, NY
Melville, NY
Sarna, Ira M. .... Bridgeport, CT
Sarna, James A. .... New York, NY
Sarna, Mark .... Englewood, NJ
Sarna, Richard F. .... Chicago, IL
Sarna, Shirley F. .... New York, NY
Sarnacki, David C. .... Grand Rapids, MI
Sarnacki, Henry E. .... Mount Clemens, MI
Sarnacki, Michael T. .... Holyoke, MA
Sarnacki, Randolph E. .... Hamburg, NY
Sarnat, Barry Marc .... Glenview, IL
Sarne, Andrew J. .... Houston, TX
Sarnecka-Crouch, Bozena
Library of Congress, Law Library, GV
Sarnecky, James M. .... San Diego, CA
Las Vegas, NV
Sarnell, Matthew F. .... Merrick, NY
Sarner & Associates, A Professional Corporation .... Haddonfield, NJ
Philadelphia, PA
Sarner, Craig Lawrence .... Fairfax, VA
Sarner, Eric J. .... New York, NY
Sarner, Eric S. .... New York, NY
Sarner, Harold L. .... St. Louis, MO
Sarner, Joshua .... Haddonfield, NJ
Philadelphia, PA
Sarner, Leonard .... Philadelphia, PA
Sarner, Richard A., Law Offices of
Stamford, CT
New York, NY
Sarnese, Regina M. .... Garden City, NY
Sarney & Pierson, P.C. .... Denver, CO
Sarney, Saul R. .... Denver, CO
Sarni, Kimberly J. .... Santa Ana, CA
Sarno, Angelo .... Roseland, NJ
Sarno, Anthony M. .... Kearny, NJ
Sarno, Cynthia N. .... Los Angeles, CA
Sarno, Daniel A., Jr.
Department of Labor, GV
Sarno, Glenn R. .... New York, NY
Sarno, Gregory G. .... San Francisco, CA
Sarno, Lindafel Lynnette .... New York, NY
Sarno, Paul .... New York, NY
Sarno, Robert A., (A Professional Corporation)
Los Angeles, CA
Sarno, Ronald A. .... Newark, NJ
Sarnoff, Alan J. .... Woodbury, NY
Sarnoff & Baccash .... Chicago, IL
Sarnoff & Bayer .... Miami, FL
Sarnoff, Joshua D. .... Washington, DC
Sarnoff, Kenneth R. .... Chicago, IL
Sarnoff, Laurence M. .... Los Angeles, CA
Sarnoff, Marc David .... Miami, FL
Sarnoff, Merton .... Stamford, CT
Sarnoff, Norman .... Baldwin, NY
Sarnoff, Robert M. .... Chicago, IL
Sarnoff, Stuart M. .... New York, NY
Sarnoski, Dorene R. .... Minneapolis, MN
Sarnoski, Stephen R. .... South Windsor, CT
Sarnowski, David F. .... Carson City, NV
Saro, Bridget .... Montclair, NJ
Sarofeen, Michael J. .... Syracuse, NY
Saroian, Stephen A. .... Calabasas, CA
Saroians, Vahan .... Los Angeles, CA
Sarokhan, Nancy E. .... Northampton, MA
Sarokin, H. Lee .... Roseland, NJ
Sarokin, Rebecca .... Corte Madera, CA
Saron, William K. .... St. Petersburg, FL
Saronson, Matthew D. .... New York, NY
Saros, John .... Akron, OH
Sarosdy, Randall L. .... Washington, DC
Sarosiek, James J. .... Neenah, WI
Saroukhanioff, Ninos .... Los Angeles, CA
Sarow, Robert D. .... Bay City, MI
Sarowitz, Lawrence S. .... Cherry Hill, NJ
New York, NY
Philadelphia, PA
Saroyan, Cyril M. .... Daly City, CA
Sarp, Paulette Steffes .... Phoenix, AZ
Sarpong, Awo A. .... Silver Spring, MD
Sarpy, A. Lester .... Metairie, LA
Sarpy, Christopher A. .... Metairie, LA
Sarpy, Henry L. .... New Orleans, LA
Sarpy, John Robert
Department of Labor, GV
Sarpy, Leon .... New Orleans, LA
Sarpy, R. Henry, Jr. .... New Orleans, LA
Sarra, James A. .... Torrance, CA
Sarra, Laurel .... Torrance, CA
Sarra, Martha Cutright .... Cincinnati, OH
Sarrafian, Vahe H. .... Palo Alto, CA
Sarraga, Jose F. .... San Juan, PR
Sarrail, James A. .... San Francisco, CA
Sarrail, Karen A. .... San Mateo, CA
Sarrail, Lynch & Hall .... San Francisco, CA
Sarraille, William A. .... Washington, DC
Sarra-Meyer, Heather G. .... Jacksonville, FL
Sarran, Sandra D. .... Canyon Lake, TX
Sarrantonio, Barbara A. .... Hartford, CT
Sarrao, Michael J. .... Irvine, CA
Sarrat, Alfred Ambrose, Jr.
New Orleans, LA
Sarrat, Donald M., Jr. .... Marrero, LA
Sarratori, Frank C. .... Troy, NY
Sarratt & Clarke, The Legal Clinic of
Greenville, SC
Sarratt, James C. .... Greenville, SC
Sarratt, John L. .... Raleigh, NC
Sarratt, Victor S. .... Gaffney, SC
Sarrazin, Anna .... Oakland, CA
Sarrazin, Robbin T. .... Memphis, TN
Sarrel, Kenneth A. .... New York, NY
Sarrell, Warren G., Jr. .... Heflin, AL
Sarret, Erin D. .... San Francisco, CA
Sarrett, Ben .... Austin, TX
Sarrett, Saul P. .... New York, NY
Sarrey, Michael P. .... Columbus, OH
Sarringhaus, Kurt G. .... Oberlin, OH
Sarris, Charles A. .... Schenectady, NY
Sarris, Christina M. .... Washington, DC
Sarris, Nicholas Michael .... Arlington, VA
Sarris, Phillip J. .... Birmingham, AL
Sarro, Anita F. .... Springfield, MA
Sarro, Christopher A.
Yorktown Heights, NY
Sarro, Dale M. .... Washington, DC
Sarro, Frank P., Law Office of
San Francisco, CA
Sarro, Lloyd A. .... Baltimore, MD
Sarro, Mark J. .... Valhalla, NY
Sarro, Thomas P. .... Alexandria, VA
Sarron, Julia R. .... Chicago, IL
Sarrouf, Camille F., Jr. .... Boston, MA
Sarrouf, Camille Francis .... Boston, MA
Sarrouf, Daneil Marie .... Pittsfield, MA
Sarrouf, Tarricone & Flemming
Boston, MA
Sarsano, Anthony F. .... Union City, NJ
Sarsany, Dennis M., (P.C.) .... Chicago, IL
Sarsen, Cynthia .... Louisville, KY
Sarsfield, James B. .... Washington, DC
Sarsfield, John J. .... Salinas, CA
Sarsfield, Patrick D., II .... Charlotte, NC
Sarsfield, Timothy J. .... St. Louis, MO
Sarsgard, William R. .... Fort Worth, TX
Sarshik, Barbara
Federal Deposit Insurance Corporation, Appellate Litigation Section, GV
Sarskas, S. Edward .... Milwaukee, WI
Sarsten, Taya K. .... Boston, MA
Sartain, C. Lenton .... Baton Rouge, LA
Sartain, Charles W. .... Dallas, TX
Sartain, J. Edward .... Abilene, TX
Fort Worth, TX
Sartain, James P., Jr. .... Chattanooga, TN
Sartain, Joe B., Jr. .... Gainesville, GA
Sartain, John B., Jr. .... Austin, TX
Sartain, Julianne .... Irvine, CA
Sartain, Larry O. .... Gainesville, GA
Sartain Law Offices .... Gainesville, GA
Sartain, Perry M. .... Gainesville, GA
Sartain, Phillip B. .... Gainesville, GA
Sartain, Thomas H. .... Central Islip, NY
Sarte, Gerald E. .... San Diego, CA
Sarter, Alvin J. .... New York, NY
Sarthou, Cynthia M. .... Seattle, WA
Sarti, Edward R. .... San Francisco, CA
Sarti, Janine .... Tacoma, WA
Sartin, J. Scott .... Columbia, LA
Sartin, John M., Jr. .... New Orleans, LA
Sartin, Larry J. .... Tallahassee, FL
Sartin, Linda Diane .... Dallas, TX
Sartin, Peter A. T. .... Dallas, TX
Sartin, Robert B. .... Tulsa, OK
Sartin, Robert V. .... Lexington, KY
Sartin, Scott M. .... Oklahoma City, OK
Sartini, James J. .... Ashtabula, OH
Sartini Law Firm .... Ashtabula, OH
Sartini, Thomas L. .... Ashtabula, OH
Sartip, Michael H. .... Myrtle Beach, SC
Sarto, Charlene M. .... Chicago, IL
Sarto, Joseph M. .... Prattville, AL
Sartoga, John .... Fair Lawn, NJ
Sartoga, Susan G. .... Jersey City, NJ
Sartoga, Thomas J. .... Fair Lawn, NJ
Sartor, Clara Moss .... Monroe, LA
Sartor, Colette .... Culver City, CA
Sartor, Daniel Ryan, Jr. .... Monroe, LA
Sartor, F. Williams, Jr. .... Monroe, LA
Sartore, John T. .... Burlington, VT
Sartorelli, Joseph C. .... Crystal Falls, MI
Sartori, Anthony C. .... Little Falls, NJ
Sartori, Bruce J. .... Hackensack, NJ
Sartori, Duane P. .... Petaluma, CA
Sartori, Lee A. .... Bloomfield Hills, MI
Sartori, Michael A. .... Washington, DC
Sartori, Michael C. .... San Antonio, TX
Sartori, Paul A. .... Elmira, NY
Sartorio, Dion J. .... Chicago, IL
Sartorio, Lynda G. .... New York, NY
White Plains, NY
Sartorio, Steven M. .... Raleigh, NC
Sartoris, Martha W. .... Monticello, MN
Sartorius, Arthur G., III .... Jacksonville, FL
Sartorius, Peter S. .... Philadelphia, PA
Sartorius, Sharon C. .... Culver City, CA
Sartory, Thomas J. .... Boston, MA
Sartwelle, Thomas P. .... Houston, TX
Sarubbi, Dante J. .... Audubon, NJ
Sarubbi, Janis Jean Wilson
White Plains, NY
Sarubbi, Joanne M. .... West Orange, NJ
Sarubbi, Melissa .... New York, NY
Sarubbi & Sarubbi .... Audubon, NJ
Sarubbi, Vincent P. .... Audubon, NJ
Sarudis, Sandra H. .... Cleveland, OH
Sarumida, Hiroshi .... New York, NY
Sarup, Raj Prem .... Los Angeles, CA
Saruski, Ana Morel .... Miami, FL
Sarussi, Steven J. .... Chicago, IL
Saruwatari, Kenneth K. .... Honolulu, HI
Sarvadi, David G. .... Washington, DC
Sarvas, Alan David .... Santa Ana, CA
Sarver, J. William .... Bedford, PA
Sarver, Larry T. .... Green Bay, WI
Sarver, Lisa A. .... Omaha, NE
Sarver, Marnie K. .... Washington, DC
Sarver, Martin .... Fairfield, NJ
Sarver, Richard E. .... New Orleans, LA

Sarver, Todd L. ... **Columbus, OH**
Sarver, William R. ... Warren, MI
Sarvis, Aubrey L. ... United States Senate, Senatorial Assistants, GV
Sarvis & Herrmann, P.C. **Bingham Farms, MI**
Sarvis, J. Steven ... **Bingham Farms, MI**
Sarvis, Norman G. ... Southfield, MI
Sarwal, Andy D. ... **Dallas, TX**
Sarwal, Melanie P. ... **Dallas, TX**
Sarwate, Sanjiv D. ... **Chicago, IL**
Sarzin, Evan ... **New York, NY**
Sarzin, Evan, P.C., Law Offices of **New York, NY**
Sarzynski, Edward J. ... **Binghamton, NY**
Sasada, Tamao ... New York, NY
Sasadu, Brian J. ... **Atlanta, GA**
Sasadu, Chester J., Jr. **Fort Lauderdale, FL**
Sasaki, Alvin T. ... Honolulu, HI
Sasaki & Brown, A Professional Corporation **Los Angeles, CA**
Sasaki, Carolyn A. ... Marysville, CA
Sasaki, Edwin Y. ... Kailua, HI
Sasaki, J. K. ... San Francisco, CA
Sasaki, John S. ... **Los Angeles, CA**
Sasaki, John Y. ... **Palo Alto, CA**
Sasaki, Joshua M. F. ... **Portland, OR**
Sasaki, Judith M. ... **Los Angeles, CA**
Sasaki, Laralyn M. ... Columbus, OH
Sasaki, Laura J. ... Honolulu, HI
Sasaki, Richard S. ... Honolulu, HI
Sasaki, Stephanie T. ... **Los Angeles, CA**
Sasaki-Baxley, Linda A. ... **Cupertino, CA**
Sasala, Kathleen M. ... **Cleveland, OH**
Sasala, Stephen N.J. ... Newark, NJ
Sasamori, Norman Cousins Marina Del Rey, CA
Sasamoto, Nancy E. ... **Chicago, IL**
Sasanow, Terri Feinstein ... New York, NY
Saseen, Jos. O. ... Savannah, GA
Saseen, Sandra M. ... Halifax, VA
Sasek, Gerald F. ... Livonia, MI
Sasfai, Beth M. ... **New York, NY**
Sash, Alan E. ... **Uniondale, NY**
Sash, Sharon M. ... **New York, NY**
Sashihara, Craig T. ... **Morristown, NJ**
Sasine, Joan Bollen ... **Atlanta, GA**
Sasine, Stephen J. ... **Dunwoody, GA**
Sasinoski, Kevin Gerard ... Pittsburgh, PA
Sasinowski, Frank J. ... **Washington, DC**
Saskor, Ludwig A. ... **New York, NY**
Saslaw, Alan B. ... Miami, FL
Saslaw, Alan B., P.A. ... Miami, FL
Saslaw, Dianne Capps ... Dallas, TX
Saslaw, Edward D. ... New York, NY
Saslaw, Gary R. ... Aventura, FL
Saslaw, Gary R., P.A. ... Aventura, FL
Saslaw, Michael A. ... **Dallas, TX**
Saslaw, Susan R. ... New York, NY
Sasloff, Robert M. ... **New York, NY**
Saslow, David M. ... Detroit, MI
Saslow, Edward ... Los Angeles, CA
Saslow, Everett B., Jr. ... **Greensboro, NC**
Saslow, Julie Anna ... **Washington, DC**
Saslow, Richard P. ... Southfield, MI
Saslow, Sharon ... **San Diego, CA**
Sasman, Lin Cheney ... Boston, MA
Sasnauskas, Kathleen M. ... Yardley, PA
Sasnett, Edward C. ... Rockville, MD
Sasnett, William B., Jr. ... Joshua Tree, CA
Sasnett-Stauffer, Gail E. ... St. Petersburg, FL
Saso, Diana M. ... **Palo Alto, CA**
Sass, Cynthia, Law Offices of ... **Tampa, FL**
Sass, David W. ... **New York, NY**
Sass, Frederick, Jr. ... Gaithersburg, MD
Sass, James C. ... Toledo, OH
Sass, John F. ... Golden, CO
Sass, Kenneth J. ... Toledo, OH
Sass, Lara M. ... **New York, NY**
Sass, Laurence J. ... New York, NY
Sass, Lorrie A. ... Chardon, OH
Sass, Maria P. ... Minneapolis, MN
Sass, Nancy S. ... Chicago, IL
Sass, Paul L. ... Brooklyn, NY
Sass, Robert P. ... **St. Louis, MO**
Sass, Stephen J. ... Burbank, CA
Sass, Steven D. ... Baltimore, MD
Sassak, Mark D. ... **Troy, MI**
Sassalos, S. Paul ... **Seattle, WA**
Sassaman, John C., Jr United States Court Of Appeals For The Federal Circuit, GV
Sassaman, Randy L. ... **Phoenix, AZ**
Sassaman, Shawn M. ... **Blue Bell, PA**
Sassan, Anthony J. ... **Oak Brook, IL** **Wheaton, IL**
Sassan, Dennis D. ... Oakbrook Terrace, IL
Sassani, Kathleen C. ... Syracuse, NY
Sassano, James F. ... Stony Brook, NY
Sassano, James L. ... **Cleveland, OH**
Sassano, M. Elizabeth ... **Deerfield, IL**
Sassano, Michelle ... Pasadena, CA
Sasscer, Clagett & Bucher **Upper Marlboro, MD**
Sasse, Cynthia A. ... Painesville, OH
Sasse, Daniel A. ... **Washington, DC** Kansas City, MO
Sasse Wood, Joyce, Law Offices of **Oakland, CA** **Walnut Creek, CA**
Sasseen, David ... San Jose, CA
Sassen, Douglas E. ... Newark, OH
Sassenhausen, Amy ... Rochester, NY
Sasser, Cestero & Sasser, P.A. **Boca Raton, FL** **West Palm Beach, FL**
Sasser, Charles McBrayer ... **Charlotte, NC**
Sasser, D. Carol ... **Virginia Beach, VA**
Sasser, David ... **Boise, ID**
Sasser, David C. ... **Brooksville, FL** **Spring Hill, FL**
Sasser, Debra A. Smith ... Raleigh, NC
Sasser, Donald J. ... **West Palm Beach, FL**
Sasser, Douglas B. ... Whiteville, NC
Sasser, Duffy A., II ... Stamford, CT
Sasser, J. Gray ... **Houston, TX**
Sasser, James T. ... **Gadsden, AL**
Sasser, Jeanine B. ... **Jacksonville, FL**
Sasser, Jeanine B. ... **Orange Park, FL**
Sasser, Jonathan D. ... **Raleigh, NC**
Sasser, Justin J. ... **Upper Marlboro, MD**
Sasser, Linda G. ... Tampa, FL
Sasser, M. Michael ... **Boise, ID**
Sasser, Meenu T. ... **West Palm Beach, FL**
Sasser, Michael D. ... San Francisco, CA
Sasser, N. Lee, Jr. ... Orlando, FL
Sasser, Phillip D. ... Conway, SC
Sasser, Phillip, Jr ... **Spotsylvania, VA**
Sasser, Robert E. ... **Montgomery, AL**
Sasser, Robert H., III ... **Raleigh, NC**
Sasser, Roy E. ... **Metairie, LA**
Sasser, Steven C. ... **Decatur, AL**
Sasser, Suzanne K. ... **Baton Rouge, LA**
Sasser, Thomas E., III ... Blakely, GA
Sasser, Thomas J. ... **West Palm Beach, FL**
Sasser, Weathers & Slate, P.C. **Decatur, AL** **Huntsville, AL**
Sasser and Weber, P.A. ... Orlando, FL
Sasser, William F., III ... **St. Louis, MO**
Sasseville, David L. ... **Minneapolis, MN**
Sasseville, Katherine E. ... Fergus Falls, MN
Sasse Wood, Joyce, Law Offices of **Lafayette, CA**
Sassi, Richard M. ... Miami, FL
Sassi, William A., Jr. ... Glastonbury, CT
Sassin, Lynn B. ... **Baltimore, MD**
Sasso, Andrew B. ... **Clearwater, FL**
Sasso & Bodolay, P.A. ... **Clearwater, FL**
Sasso, Cassandra G. ... **Denver, CO**
Sasso, David A. ... **Philadelphia, PA**
Sasso, Ernest, Law Offices of ... Blue Bell, PA
Sasso, Gary L. ... **St. Petersburg, FL**
Sasso, Kelly J. ... Wilmington, DE
Sasso, M. Daniel ... Cape Coral, FL
Sasso, M. Daniel, P.A. ... Cape Coral, FL
Sasso, Michael C. ... **Orlando, FL**
Sasso, Michael P ... Carle Place, NY
Sasso, Michael P. ... Schenectady, NY
Sasso, Michael P., P.C. ... Schenectady, NY
Sasso, Peter J., Jr. ... Greenville, SC
Sasso, Phil ... San Francisco, CA
Sasso, Phillip D. ... **San Francisco, CA**
Sasso, Richard M. ... Warren, NJ
Sasso, Theodore S. ... Wallington, NJ
Sasso, Vic J. ... Dallas, TX
Sasso, Warren F., Jr. ... **New Haven, CT**
Sasso, William R. ... **Philadelphia, PA**
Sassoe, Albert L., Jr. ... **Los Angeles, CA**
Sasson, Alysa Susan ... Larchmont, NY
Sasson, Esther Kaufman ... **New York, NY**
Sasson, Howard S. ... Springfield, MA
Sasson, Jaclyn ... Syosset, NY
Sasson, Moshe ... **New York, NY**
Sasson, Shai ... Lawrence, NY
Sassone, Arthur J. ... Red Bluff, CA
Sassone, Lawrence D. ... Santa Ana, CA
Sassone, Martha E. ... Gretna, LA
Sassone, Robert J. ... Norwood, NY
Sassoon, André G. ... New York, NY
Sassoon, Lewis A. ... **Boston, MA**
Sassoon, Phillip M. ... Miami, FL
Sassoon, Salomon R. ... **New York, NY**
Sassover, Moshe J. ... Santa Fe Springs, CA
Sassower, Herman ... **New York, NY**
Sassower, Mitchell J. ... New York, NY
Sastow, Gary S. ... **Manhasset, NY** **New York, NY**
Sastre, Cesar A. ... **Miami, FL**
Sastre, Michael A. ... Miami, FL
Sastri, Venki M. ... Daytona Beach, FL
Sasz, William L. ... **Colorado Springs, CO**
Sata, Yuriko K. ... Auburn, WA
Satagaj, John S. ... Washington, DC
Satagaj, Joseph S., Jr. ... Dallas, TX
Satalic, John M. ... **Chicago, IL**
Satalino, Frank A. ... **Irvine, CA**
Sataloff, Joanne S. ... Cape Elizabeth, ME
Satava, Martin R. ... Memphis, TN
Satava, Susan E. ... Athens, OH
Satchell, Harold C., Jr. ... Hollywood, FL
Satchell, Kwame K. ... **Houston, TX**
Satchell, Robert B. ... Pacific, MO
Satchell, William H. ... **Washington, DC** **New York, NY**
Satcher, John N. ... Heidelberg, MS
Satcher, Milton B., III ... Atlanta, GA
Sateary, Thomas J. ... **Summit, NJ**
Satel, James E. ... San Antonio, TX
Satenberg, Andrew L. ... **Los Angeles, CA**
Sater, Gregory J. ... Los Angeles, CA
Sater, Nazli G. ... **Birmingham, MI**
Sater, Rex H. ... Santa Rosa, CA
Saternus, Christopher M. Hoffman Estates, IL
Sather, Arvid A. ... Madison, WI
Sather & Associates, P.C. ... Portland, OR
Sather, Byerly & Holloway, LLP **Portland, OR**
Sather, David S. ... Denver, CO
Sather, Deborah L. ... **Portland, OR**
Sather, John S. ... Portland, OR
Sather, Katrina T. ... **Boise, ID**
Sather, Kelly L. ... Pacific Palisades, CA
Sather, Robert A. ... Milwaukee, WI
Sather, Stephen W. ... **Austin, TX**
Sathre, Constance J. Department of Commerce, National Oceanic and Atmospheric Administration, GV
Sathre, Jeanne L. ... Marshall, IL
Sathy, Anup ... **Chicago, IL**
Satin, Adam R. ... **Boston, MA**
Satin, Kenneth A. ... **Los Angeles, CA**
Satin, Kenneth A. ... **Newport Beach, CA**
Satin, Kenneth A. ... **Riverside, CA**
Satin, Lisa Anne ... Lexington, KY
Satin, Max J. ... Chicago, IL
Satin, Michael N. ... Colorado Springs, CO
Satin, Michelle A. ... New York, NY
Satin, Richard G. ... Hauppauge, NY
Satina, Donald M. ... Pittsburgh, PA
Satine, Barry R. ... **New York, NY**
Satine, Roy A. ... New York, NY
Satinsky, Alex ... **Philadelphia, PA**
Satinsky, Barnett ... **Philadelphia, PA**
Satinsky, Martin J. ... Philadelphia, PA
Satisky, Howard P. ... **Raleigh, NC**
Satisky, Keith A. ... **Raleigh, NC**
Satisky, Sheldon S. ... **Baltimore, MD**
Satisky & Silverstein, L.L.P. ... **Raleigh, NC**
Satkiewicz, Jeremy J. ... **New York, NY**
Satkin, Stephen A. ... Scotch Plains, NJ
Satkowski, Susan Ellyn ... **Philadelphia, PA**
Satler, Susan A. ... Boca Raton, FL
Satler, Susan A., P.A. ... Boca Raton, FL
Satlin, Kenneth B. ... Alexandria, VA
Satloff, Martin ... Brooklyn, NY
Satlow, Barry ... Boulder, CO
Satnick, David M. ... **New York, NY**
Sato, Charlotte P. ... Sacramento, CA
Sato, Dana Kiyomi Nalani ... **Honolulu, HI**
Sato, Earl T. ... **Honolulu, HI**
Sato, Edwin K. ... **Seattle, WA**
Sato, Emily C. ... **Seattle, WA**
Sato, Gerald Masahiro ... Westlake Village, CA
Sato, Glen Y. ... Fremont, CA
Sato, Glenn K. ... **Honolulu, HI**
Sato, Greg Yoshiaki ... **Palo Alto, CA**
Sato, Gregory M. ... **Honolulu, HI**
Sato, Keiichi ... **Honolulu, HI**
Sato, Linda ... San Francisco, CA
Sato, Ned Y. ... **Seattle, WA**
Sato, Norman K. ... San Jose, CA
Sato, P. Miyoko ... **Boston, MA**
Sato, Paul H. ... Honolulu, HI
Sato, Robert J. ... **Anchorage, AK**
Sato, Roger J. ... Sacramento, CA
Sato, Taitt ... **San Francisco, CA**
Sato, Vincent B. ... Los Angeles, CA
Sato, Wayne T. ... New York, NY
Sato, Wilbur I. ... Torrance, CA
Satola, James W. ... **Cleveland, OH**
Satorius, Daniel M. ... **Minneapolis, MN**
Satorius, John A. ... **Minneapolis, MN**
Satoskar, Shilpa S. ... **Washington, DC**
Satovsky, Abraham ... Southfield, MI
Satow, Clayton L. ... Maynard, MA
Satow, Michael S. ... New York, NY
Satra, Janice S. ... Lincoln, NE
Satran, Edward S. ... Brooklyn, NY
Satran, Jerome R. ... San Diego, CA
Satran, Jill ... Olympia, WA
Satran & Marino, P.C. ... Boston, MA
Satran, Neal E. ... Boston, MA
Satre, Philip G. ... Memphis, TN
Satriale, Gloria M. ... Downingtown, PA
Satriale, Louis R., Jr. ... **New York, NY**
Satriana, Daniel R., Jr. ... **Denver, CO**
Satris, Michael ... Bolinas, CA
Satrom, James D. ... **Tulsa, OK**
Satrom, Thomas L. ... **Cambridge, MN**
Satta, Frank ... Alexandria, VA
Sattari, Caroline A. ... Cape St. Claire, MD
Sattely, James X. ... Hackensack, NJ
Sattely, James X., Jr. ... Paramus, NJ
Sattely, Maris Catherine ... Ridgewood, NJ
Satten, Kenneth E. ... **Washington, DC**
Satter, Beyer & Bertram ... Collinsville, IL Pontiac, IL
Satter & Connor ... Syracuse, NY
Satter, Cynthia A. ... Manchester, NH
Satter, Edwin C., III Department Of Health And Human Services, Social Security Administration, GV
Satter, John G. ... Pontiac, IL
Satter, Lisa A. ... **Los Angeles, CA**
Satter, Mimi C. ... Syracuse, NY
Satter, Muneer A. ... New York, NY
Satter, Raymond N. ... Denver, CO
Satter, Robert ... Hartford, CT
Satter, Rodney J. ... Prairie du Chien, WI
Satter, Susan L. ... Chicago, IL
Satterberg, Richard A. ... Seattle, WA
Satterberg, William R., Jr. ... Fairbanks, AK
Satterfield, Andreas N., Jr. ... **Greenville, SC**
Satterfield, Bonnie S. ... **Coral Springs, FL**
Satterfield, Bonnie S., P.A. **Coral Springs, FL** **Fort Lauderdale, FL**
Satterfield, Dixie R. ... Bowling Green, KY
Satterfield, Grey W., Jr. ... Oklahoma City, OK
Satterfield, Guy R. ... Little Rock, AR
Satterfield and Harmon ... Bowling Green, KY
Satterfield, James E. ... **Washington, DC**
Satterfield, James L. ... Princeton, WV
Satterfield, Janette Lowry ... El Dorado, KS
Satterfield, John L. ... Akron, OH
Satterfield, L. Kendall ... **Washington, DC**
Satterfield Law Firm ... Little Rock, AR
Satterfield, Lee A. ... **Washington, DC**
Satterfield, Lisa ... Frederick, MD
Satterfield, Lori J.M. **Glenwood Springs, CO**
Satterfield, Pamela S. ... Washington, DC
Satterfield, Peggy C. ... Liberty, TX
Satterfield, Richard W. ... North Platte, NE
Satterfield, T. Michael ... **Wilmington, NC**
Satterfield, William H. ... **Birmingham, AL**
Satterlee, Donald W. ... Portola Valley, CA
Satterlee, Karen Boring ... **Parsippany, NJ**
Satterlee, Richard D. ... Simi Valley, CA
Satterlee, Robert J. ... Syracuse, NY
Satterlee Stephens Burke & Burke LLP **Summit, NJ** **New York, NY**
Satterlee, Terry J., (Ms.) **Kansas City, MO**
Satterlee, William F., III ... **Valparaiso, IN**
Satterlund, Lisa Louise ... Seattle, WA
Satterly, Kenneth R. ... Houston, TX
Satterthwaite, Henry F. ... Trenton, NJ
Satterthwaite, Janet F. ... **Washington, DC**
Satterthwaite, Janet J. ... Moorestown, NJ
Satterthwaite, Margaret A. ... Madison, WI
Satterthwaite & Satterthwaite ... Trenton, NJ
Satterwhite, Allison A. ... Charlotte, NC
Satterwhite, Brandon N. ... **Dallas, TX**
Satterwhite, Charles F. ... Owenton, KY
Satterwhite, Darvin E. ... Goochland, VA
Satterwhite, Gordon A. ... Mobile, AL
Satterwhite, Harry V. ... **Mobile, AL**
Satterwhite, Jill K. ... **Pensacola, FL**
Satterwhite, Kimberly A. ... **Richmond, VA**
Satterwhite, Lillian R. ... Houston, TX
Satterwhite, Melissa Federal Deposit Insurance Corporation, Professional Liability Section, GV
Satterwhite, Michael E. ... **Henderson, NC**
Satterwhite, Rodney A. ... **Richmond, VA**
Satterwhite, Rodney W. ... **Midland, TX**
Satterwhite, Roy F., III ... Atlanta, GA
Satterwhite, Terry F. **Colorado Springs, CO**
Satterwhite, Thomas H. ... Mesquite, TX
Satterwhite, Wayne R. ... Birmingham, AL
Sattes, F. Lyle ... Charleston, WV
Satti, C. Robert, Sr. ... New London, CT
Sattin, Bruce M. ... Bordentown, NJ
Sattin, Cheryl ... **West Conshohocken, PA**
Sattin, Jerry P. ... **Newark, NJ**
Sattin, Robert U. ... **Hartford, CT**
Sattinger, Jack M. ... **Burbank, CA**
Sattinger, Loren R. ... Somerset, NJ
Sattler, Adam B. ... New York, NY
Sattler, Albert J., Jr. ... Peekskill, NY
Sattler, Barbara C. ... Tucson, AZ
Sattler, Brian R. ... **Marshall, MN**
Sattler, Bruce W. ... **Denver, CO**
Sattler, Claudine R. ... Albuquerque, NM
Sattler, David Alan ... **Arlington, VA**
Sattler, Erica B. ... New York, NY
Sattler, James M. ... Honolulu, HI
Sattler, John J. ... Tomahawk, WI
Sattler, Joseph, Jr. ... **Hyannis, MA**
Sattler, Leonard S. ... Arlington, VA
Sattler, Lisa R. ... **Menlo Park, CA**
Sattler, Melvin ... Encino, CA
Sattler, Robert J. ... Detroit, MI
Sattler, Rosanna ... **Boston, MA**
Sattler, Thomas C. ... **Lincoln, NE**
Sattler, Todd A. ... **Minneapolis, MN**
Satto, Joseph A. ... **New York, NY**
Satty, Andrea N. ... **New York, NY**
Satula, Anthony E., Jr. ... **New York, NY**
Satullo, Nicholas D. ... Cleveland, OH
Satuloff, Wendy C. ... Irvine, CA
Saturley, Ellen E. ... **Boston, MA**
Saturley, Thomas W. ... Portland, ME
Saturley, William C. ... **Manchester, NH**
Saturn, Rachel B. ... **Suffern, NY**
Saturnelli, Anne E. ... **Boston, MA**
Saturno, Teresa J. ... Woodbury, NY
Satyendra, Indira ... New York, NY
Satyr, Alan ... **Chicago, IL**
Satz, Brian M. ... **New York, NY**
Satz, Cathy S. ... Stamford, CT
Satz, David J. ... **Newark, NJ**
Satz, David M., Jr. ... **Newark, NJ**
Satz, Harold L. ... **St. Louis, MO**
Satz, Joseph R. ... San Diego, CA
Satz & Kirshon, P.C. ... **Poughkeepsie, NY**
Satz, Mark D. ... Indianapolis, IN
Satz, Michael B. ... **Chicago, IL**
Satz, Michael J. ... Fort Lauderdale, FL
Satz, Perry ... **Poughkeepsie, NY**
Satz, Richard B. ... Oakland, CA
Satz, Steven F. ... **North Brunswick, NJ**
Satz, Steven L. ... **Costa Mesa, CA**
Satzberg, Burton ... Philadelphia, PA
Satzman, Barry ... Beverly Hills, CA
Satzman, Richard E. ... Sherman Oaks, CA
Saub, Victor ... Houston, TX
Sauber, Anthony F. ... Universal City, CA
Sauber, Joseph P., Jr. ... **St. Charles, IL**
Sauber, Karl A. ... St. Louis, MO
Sauber, Pamela G. ... Washington, DC
Sauber, Richard A. ... **Washington, DC**
Sauberman, Oren ... **New York, NY**
Saubert, R. Wayne ... Radford, VA
Sauby, Shane ... Beverly Hills, CA
Sauceda, Jesse B. ... Denver, CO
Sauceda, Shannon Breaux ... Houston, TX
Saucedo, Christopher ... Albuquerque, NM
Saucedo & Corsiglia, A Law Corporation **San Jose, CA**
Saucedo, Norman W. ... **San Jose, CA**
Saucedo, Renée M. ... San Francisco, CA
Saucedo, Silvia ... **Los Angeles, CA**
Saucedo, Valeriano ... **Visalia, CA**

Saucer, S. Ann ..... Dallas, TX
Saucier, Ben L. ..... Ocean Springs, MS
Saucier, Brian D. ..... Chicago, IL
Saucier, Michael E. ..... Portland, ME
Saucier, Peter S. ..... Baltimore, MD
Saucier, Susan ..... Boston, MA
Saucillo, Rudolph ..... Houston, TX
Sauck, William K., Jr. ..... Aberdeen, SD
Saucy, Paul E. ..... Salem, OR
Saude, Fernanda A. ..... Merced, CA
Saudek, Mark S. ..... Baltimore, MD
Saudek, Richard H. ..... Montpelier, VT
Saudek, Robert E. ..... Atlanta, GA
Sauder, Lisa M. ..... Harrisburg, PA
Sauder, Phillip Paul ..... Orange, CA
Sauder, Randall J. ..... Marietta, GA
Sauder, Scot ..... Owings Mills, MD
Saue, Jacqueline Marie ..... Washington, DC
Saue, Lucinda Larsen ..... Spokane, WA
Sauer, Alfred H. ..... Roselle Park, NJ
Sauer, Anthony W. ..... Fredericksburg, TX
Sauer, Becker, Flanagan & Lynch, Ltd.
La Crosse, WI
Sauer, Bradford B. ..... Richmond, VA
Sauer, Brian J. ..... Mineola, NY
Sauer, David A. ..... New Britain, CT
Sauer, Devin A. ..... St. Louis, MO
Sauer, Diane M. ..... Willimantic, CT
Sauer, Donna M. ..... Henderson, KY
Sauer, Dorothy C. ..... Peosta, IA
Flower Mound, TX
Sauer, Edward W. ..... Washington, DC
Sauer, Elisabeth R. ..... Kansas City, MO
Sauer, Elisabeth R., P.C.
Kansas City, MO
Sauer, Francis A. ..... Baltimore, MD
Sauer, Franklin W. ..... Independence, IA
Sauer, Frederick A. ..... Kalamazoo, MI
Sauer, George D. ..... Marietta, OH
Sauer, George H., Jr. ..... Houston, TX
Sauer, George H., Jr., P.C. ..... Houston, TX
Sauer, Gerald L. ..... Los Angeles, CA
Sauer, Gordon E. ..... Fredericksburg, TX
Sauer, Henry A., Jr. ..... Houston, TX
Sauer, J. Michael ..... Indianapolis, IN
Sauer, Jane E. ..... Anchorage, AK
Sauer, Jeanne M. ..... Pittsburgh, PA
Sauer, Jeffrey C. ..... Louisville, KY
Sauer, Jeffrey F. ..... Douglas, AK
Sauer, Jeffrey T. ..... Pensacola, FL
Sauer, John A. ..... North Hollywood, CA
Sauer, Jonathan B. ..... St. Joseph, MI
Sauer, Kirke D. ..... Wausau, WI
Sauer, Kristen K. ..... New York, NY
Sauer, Kurt M. ..... Austin, TX
Sauer, Larry ..... Austin, TX
Sauer, Larry S. ..... Columbus, OH
Sauer, Linda A. ..... Phoenix, AZ
Sauer, Lisa S. ..... Chicago, IL
Sauer, Margaret L. ..... Kansas City, MO
Sauer, Mark A. ..... Wausau, WI
Sauer, McKinley Hobart, III
Cleveland, OH
Sauer, Melvin J., Jr. ..... Hays, KS
Sauer, Michael B. ..... Towson, MD
Sauer, Michael J. ..... Saginaw, MI
Sauer, Norman A., Jr. ..... San Francisco, CA
Sauer, Norman G. ..... Republic, WA
Sauer, Raymon ..... Boca Raton, FL
Sauer, Richard C.
Securities and Exchange Commission,
Division of Enforcement, GV
Sauer, Richard H. ..... New York, NY
Sauer, Richard H. ..... Redmond, WA
Sauer, Rick P. ..... Canon City, CO
Sauer, Robert F. ..... Key West, FL
Sauer, Robert K. ..... White Plains, NY
Sauer, Roger P. ..... Roseland, NJ
Sauer, Russell F., Jr. ..... Los Angeles, CA
Sauer, S. Jack ..... Chicago, IL
Sauer, Stephan Lars ..... Santa Ana, CA
Sauer, Terri L. ..... Albuquerque, NM
Sauer & Wagner LLP ..... Los Angeles, CA
Sauer, William J. ..... La Crosse, WI
Sauer, William N., Jr.
Cardiff-By-The-Sea, CA
Sauer, William R. ..... Berkley, MI
Sauerberg, Eric M., (P.A.)
North Palm Beach, FL
Sauerburger, David P. ..... St. Louis, MO
Sauerhaft, Bernard J. ..... Oceanside, NY
Sauermilch, Thomas ..... New York, NY
Sauers, C. Brian ..... La Porte, IN
Sauers, David A. ..... San Francisco, CA
Sauers, William D. ..... Menlo Park, CA
Sauer-Swensson, Barbara
Newport Beach, CA
Sauerteig, Paul J. ..... Fort Wayne, IN
Sauerteig, Paul O. ..... Fort Wayne, IN
Sauerwein, Joseph C. ..... Upper Marlboro, MD
Sauerwein, William L. ..... St. Louis, MO
Sauerwein, William L., P.C. ..... St. Louis, MO
Sauey, Jeffrey L. ..... Ocala, FL
Saufer, Isaac A. ..... New York, NY
Saufley, Jeffrey O. ..... Colorado Springs, CO
Saufley, Leigh Ingalls ..... Portland, ME
Saufley, Shelton M., III ..... Richmond, KY
Saufley, William E. ..... Portland, ME
Saul, Alana ..... New York, NY
Saul, Bentley M. ..... Philadelphia, PA
Saul, Bruce H. ..... Baltimore, MD
Saul, Charles H. ..... Philadelphia, PA
Pittsburgh, PA
Saul, Daniel J. ..... Atlantic City, NJ
Saul, David J. ..... Palo Alto, CA
Saul, Diane A. ..... San Diego, CA
Saul, Ewing, Remick & Saul LLP
Wilmington, DE
Princeton, NJ
New York, NY
Berwyn, PA
Harrisburg, PA
Philadelphia, PA
Saul, Ewing, Weinberg & Green
Baltimore, MD
Saul, Gary A. ..... Miami, FL
Saul, H. Carol ..... Atlanta, GA
Saul, Harold A. ..... Fort Lauderdale, FL
Saul, Irving I. ..... Dayton, OH
Saul, James R. ..... Danville, VA
Saul, Jason A. ..... Chicago, IL
Saul, Jeffrey A. ..... Saginaw, MI
Saul, Jonathan A. ..... Sacramento, CA
Saul, Karen E. ..... Portland, OR
Saul, Lewis J. ..... Washington, DC
Saul, Lewis J., P.C. ..... Washington, DC
Saul, Louis ..... Augusta, GA
Saul, Louis, P.C. ..... Augusta, GA
Saul, Lynn Elaine ..... Sells, AZ
Saul, Michael H. ..... Marietta, GA
Saul, Milton H. F. ..... Baltimore, MD
Saul, Myra L. ..... New York, NY
Saul, Nancy ..... Atlanta, GA
Saul, Ralph S. ..... Philadelphia, PA
Saul, Rhonda R. ..... West Point, MS
Saul, Richard J. ..... Denver, CO
Saul, Richard M.
Department Of Health And Human Services,
Office of Community Services, GV
Saul, Robert M. ..... Atlanta, GA
Saul, Roland ..... Hereford, TX
Saul, William E. ..... San Francisco, CA
Sauleda, Lisette M. ..... Miami, FL
Sauler, Max A. ..... Encino, CA
Saulino, Anthony J., Jr. ..... Birmingham, MI
Saulino, John E. ..... Fall River, MA
Saulino, Mark ..... New York, NY
Saulino & Silvia, P.C. ..... Fall River, MA
Saulino, Steven Michael ..... Wilmington, DE
Saulitis, Andrew P. ..... New York, NY
Saulitis, Andrew P., P.C., Law Offices of
New York, NY
Saull, Ellis M. ..... King Of Prussia, PA
Saulnier, Andrée M. ..... Boston, MA
Saulnier, Brian F. ..... Pittsburgh, PA
Saulnier, George S. ..... Media, PA
Saulnier, Victoria A. ..... Dallas, TX
Saul-Olson, Randi ..... Dinuba, CA
Visalia, CA
Saulque, Richard E. ..... Sacramento, CA
Sauls, Daniel C. ..... Washington, DC
Sauls, Jonathan Chad ..... Durham, NC
Sauls, Karen A. ..... St. Louis, MO
Sauls, N. Sanders ..... Tallahassee, FL
Sauls, Randall M. ..... Goldsboro, NC
Sauls & Semeta ..... San Diego, CA
Sauls, Shawn V. ..... Cherry Hill, NJ
Philadelphia, PA
Sauls, Thomas P. ..... Edgar Springs, MO
Sauls, W. Lewis ..... Whiteville, NC
Sauls, William Harvey ..... San Diego, CA
Saulsberry, Belinda T. ..... Houston, TX
Saulsberry, Charles R. ..... St. Louis, MO
Saulsberry, Karen A. ..... Atlanta, GA
Saulsbury, Frances ..... Baltimore, MD
Saulsbury, James Thomas ..... Seattle, WA
Saulson, Saul R. ..... Scottsdale, AZ
Saum, Gregory A. ..... Greenwich, CT
Saum, Heather L. ..... Jackson, MS
Saum, Hugh H., III ..... Houston, TX
Saum, Scott J. ..... Toledo, OH
Saums, Harry W. ..... Wichita, KS
Saunders, Adrienne Faye ..... New York, NY
Saunders, Albert D., Jr. ..... Warwick, RI
Saunders, Alexander I. ..... Roanoke, VA
Saunders, Alfred C. ..... Albany, NY
Saunders, Alfred Lagran ..... Tallahassee, FL
Saunders, Allyson G. ..... Los Angeles, CA
Saunders, Alonzo D., II ..... Boston, MA
Saunders, Amos C. ..... Paterson, NJ
Saunders, Andrea Dawn ..... Washington, DC
Saunders, Anne L. ..... Williamsport, PA
Saunders, Anne-Marie ..... Los Angeles, CA
Saunders, Arpiar G., Jr. ..... Concord, NH
Saunders, Avram J. S. ..... Boulder, CO
Saunders, B. Anthony ..... Nashville, TN
Saunders, Barney R. ..... Park City, UT
Saunders, Benjamin B. ..... Metairie, LA
Saunders, Brad K. ..... Miami, FL
Saunders, Brent A. ..... Gallipolis, OH
Saunders, Bruce J. ..... Westbrook, ME
Saunders, Bryan L. ..... Newport News, VA
Saunders, Burt L. ..... Naples, FL
Saunders, C. Daniel ..... Centreville, MD
Saunders, C. Daniel ..... Chestertown, MD
Saunders, C. Stephen ..... Austin, TX
Saunders, Calvin C. ..... New York, NY
Saunders, Carl A. ..... Fort Madison, IA
Saunders & Carroll, LLP
Rockingham, NC
Saunders Cary & Patterson
Chesterfield, VA
Richmond, VA
Saunders, Charles A. ..... Houston, TX
Saunders, Charles, Jr. ..... Dublin, OH
Saunders, Charles L., Jr. ..... Corrales, NM
Saunders, Charles P. ..... Denton, TX
Saunders, Charles W., Jr. ..... Greensboro, NC
Saunders, Chas. ..... Columbus, OH
Saunders, Chase B. ..... Charlotte, NC
Saunders, Christine R. ..... San Francisco, CA
Saunders, Cope, Olson and Yoffy
Newport News, VA
Saunders, Craig A. ..... Fort Lee, NJ
New York, NY
Saunders, Daniel A. ..... Los Angeles, CA
Saunders, Darcy Ann ..... Trenton, NJ
Saunders, Darrell L. ..... Corbin, KY
Saunders, Darren W. ..... New York, NY
Saunders, David A. ..... Chicago, IL
Saunders, David L. ..... Goshen, IN
Saunders, David R. ..... Corona, CA
Saunders, David R. ..... New York, NY
Saunders, Dawnmarie I. ..... San Diego, CA
Saunders, Derek W. ..... Austin, TX
Saunders, Diane M. ..... Boston, MA
Saunders, Dickson M. ..... Tulsa, OK
Saunders, Don W. ..... San Antonio, TX
Saunders, Donald L. ..... Houston, TX
Saunders, Douglas L. ..... Oakland, CA
Saunders, Dwight L. ..... Matthews, NC
Saunders, E. Sue ..... Reno, NV
Saunders, Edward H. ..... Atlanta, GA
Saunders, Elizabeth E. ..... Charleston, SC
Saunders, Elizabeth M. ..... Palo Alto, CA
Saunders, Elizabeth Tauro ..... Cambridge, MA
Saunders, Ellen M. ..... Great Neck, NY
Saunders, Eric F. ..... Portland, ME
Saunders, Ethel S. ..... Philadelphia, PA
Saunders, Evelyn L. ..... Park City, UT
Saunders, F. Eric ..... San Jose, CA
Saunders, Frank, Jr. ..... Overland Park, KS
Kansas City, MO
Saunders, Frank K. ..... Roanoke, VA
Saunders, Frederick F., Jr. ..... Atlanta, GA
Saunders, Gary A. ..... New York, NY
Saunders, George L., Jr. ..... Chicago, IL
Saunders, Gerald D., (P.C.) ..... Waterford, MI
Saunders, Gordon F. ..... Lexington, VA
Saunders, Gregory E. ..... Ada, OK
Saunders, Gwenn ..... New York, NY
Saunders, Harry D. ..... Atlanta, GA
Saunders, Henri M. ..... Baton Rouge, LA
Saunders, Holly L. ..... Charlotte, NC
Saunders, Howard F., III ..... Amarillo, TX
Saunders, Hubbard T., IV ..... Jackson, MS
Saunders, Humphrey & Johnson, LLP
Fort Madison, IA
Saunders, J. Brantley ..... Dallas, TX
Saunders, James D. ..... Shaker Heights, OH
Saunders, James E. ..... Tulsa, OK
Saunders, James F. ..... Los Angeles, CA
Saunders, James, III ..... Miami, FL
Saunders, James M. ..... McLean, VA
Saunders, James S. ..... New York, NY
Saunders, Janet ..... Davis, CA
Saunders, Jason Alan ..... Cypress, CA
Saunders, Jeffrey A. ..... Indianapolis, IN
Saunders, Jeffrey B. ..... New City, NY
Saunders, Jeffrey N. ..... Minneapolis, MN
Saunders, Jeffrey W. ..... Richmond, VA
Saunders, Jennifer K. ..... Santa Monica, CA
Saunders, Jennifer McKeone
Washington, DC
Saunders, Jennifer Upham
Los Angeles, CA
Saunders, Jenny Lee ..... Lakewood, CO
Saunders, Joanne H. ..... Chicago, IL
Saunders, John ..... Ville Platte, LA
Saunders, John C., Jr. ..... New Orleans, LA
Saunders, John D. ..... Atlanta, GA
Saunders, John K. ..... San Antonio, TX
Saunders, Jon C. ..... Willmar, MN
Saunders, Joseph A. ..... South Pasadena, CA
Saunders, Joseph A., P.C.
South Pasadena, CA
Saunders, Joseph E. F. ..... Utica, NY
Saunders, Joseph H. ..... Bradenton, FL
Pinellas Park, FL
Saunders, Kathy J. ..... Bloomington, IN
Lawrence, KS
Saunders, Keith ..... Cedar Falls, IA
Saunders, Keith J. ..... Enola, PA
Plymouth, PA
Saunders, Keith W. ..... Dallas, TX
Saunders, Kelly A. ..... Department of Education,
Office for Civil Rights, GV
Saunders, Kenneth G. ..... Cleveland, OH
Saunders, Kenneth L. ..... Columbus, OH
Saunders, Kevin J., (P.C.) ..... Atlanta, GA
Saunders, Kevin W. ..... Norman, OK
Saunders, Lara A. ..... Newport Beach, CA
Saunders, Larry L. ..... Louisville, KY
Saunders, Larry L., & Associates, P.S.C.
Louisville, KY
Saunders, Laurie A. ..... Santa Clara, CA
Saunders, LaVerne Rolle ..... Chicago, IL
Saunders Law Firm, P.A. ..... Jackson, MS
Saunders, Lee S. ..... Somerville, TN
Saunders, Lisa Watts ..... Atlanta, GA
Saunders, Lonnie B. ..... Spirit Lake, IA
Saunders, Louis N., Jr. ..... San Diego, CA
Saunders, Lynne Faith
Oklahoma City, OK
Saunders, M. Brent ..... Danville, VA
Saunders, M. Katherine ..... Tulsa, OK
Saunders, Marcus Brent ..... Danville, VA
Saunders, Margot Freeman ..... Washington, DC
Saunders, Mark A. ..... New York, NY
Saunders, Mark A. ..... Burlington, VT
Saunders, Mark R. ..... Fort Lauderdale, FL
Saunders, Martin J. ..... Pittsburgh, PA
Saunders, Mary Jane ..... Washington, DC
Saunders, Matthew J. ..... Los Angeles, CA
Saunders, Maud, (Miss) ..... Atlanta, GA
Saunders, Melissa L. ..... Chapel Hill, NC
Saunders, Melvin A. ..... New York, NY
Saunders, Michael A. ..... San Diego, CA
Saunders, Michael B. ..... Seattle, WA
Saunders, Michael D. ..... Watertown, NY
Saunders, Michael F. ..... Kansas City, MO
Saunders, Michael K. ..... Orlando, FL
Saunders, Michael Young ..... Houston, TX
Saunders, Michelle R. ..... Prince Frederick, MD
Saunders & Monroe ..... Chicago, IL
Saunders, Morris R. ..... Chicago, IL
Saunders, Myra K. ..... Los Angeles, CA
Saunders, N. Leslie, Jr. ..... Richmond, VA
Saunders, Nancy Mayfield
Los Angeles, CA
Saunders & Norval ..... Austin, TX
Saunders, O'Neal ..... Columbus, OH
Saunders, Pamela H.
Federal Deposit Insurance Corporation, GV
Saunders, Pamela R. ..... Minneapolis, MN
Saunders, Patti J. ..... Anchorage, AK
Saunders, Paul C. ..... New York, NY
Saunders, Paul G., II ..... Richmond, VA
Saunders, Paula S. ..... Tallahassee, FL
Saunders, Peggy McDaniel
Morganton, NC
Saunders, Philip A. ..... Cleveland, OH
Saunders, Preston H., (P.C.) ..... Boston, MA
Saunders, Ralph J., Jr. ..... Pittsburgh, PA
Saunders, Raymond A. ..... Winter Park, FL
Saunders, Raymond E. ..... Chicago, IL
Saunders, Ready & Luckman ..... Chicago, IL
Saunders, Rebecca L. ..... Chicago, IL
Saunders, Reginald P. ..... Hayward, CA
Saunders, Rhonda B. ..... Los Angeles, CA
Saunders, Richard A. ..... Norfolk, VA
Saunders, Richard A. ..... Vancouver, WA
Saunders, Richard P. ..... Totowa, NJ
Saunders, Richard R., Jr. ..... Leesburg, VA
Saunders, Robert H. ..... New York, NY
Saunders, Robert L. ..... Bradford, PA
Saunders, Robert Lee ..... Salisbury, NC
Saunders, Robert M. ..... Miami, FL
Saunders, Robert M. ..... New York, NY
Saunders, Robert M. ..... Newport News, VA
Saunders, Robert M., P.A. ..... Miami, FL
Saunders, Robert R. ..... Orlando, FL
Saunders, Robert S. ..... Wilmington, DE
Saunders, Robert W. ..... Greensboro, NC
Raleigh, NC
Saunders, Ron ..... Tallahassee, FL
Saunders, Russell H. ..... Louisville, KY
Saunders, Sanford M., Jr.
Washington, DC
Saunders, Sarah M. ..... Richmond, VA
Saunders & Saunders ..... Park City, UT
Saunders, Schmidt & Echols, P.C. ..... Tyler, TX
Saunders & Schmieler ..... Washington, DC
Baltimore, MD
Greenbelt, MD
Rockville, MD
Silver Spring, MD
Arlington, VA
Richmond, VA
Saunders, Sharon Michelle
Spring Valley, NY
Saunders, Stacey B. ..... Houston, TX
Saunders, Stella ..... Albuquerque, NM
Saunders, Stephen D. ..... Elkader, IA
Saunders, Stephen W. ..... Scranton, PA
Saunders, Steven G. ..... Boston, MA
Saunders, Stuart T., Jr. ..... Philadelphia, PA
Saunders, Suzanne ..... Denver, CO
Saunders, Suzanne N. ..... Jackson, MS
Saunders, Terry Rose, Law Offices of
Chicago, IL
Saunders, Thomas C. ..... Bartow, FL
Saunders, Thomas J. ..... Montgomery, AL
Saunders, Thomas J. ..... Baltimore, MD
Saunders, Thomas M. ..... Boston, MA
Saunders, Timothy K., Jr. ..... New York, NY
Saunders, T. J., Jr. ..... San Antonio, TX
Saunders, V. Denise ..... Corvallis, OR
Saunders, Virginia C. ..... Newark, NJ
Saunders, W. Reece, Jr. ..... Rockingham, NC
Saunders, Ward B. ..... Oakland, CA
Saunders, Whitney G. ..... Suffolk, VA
Saunders, Willard H. ..... Centreville, VA
Fairfax, VA
Saunders, William Bradford ..... Vista, CA
Saunders, William D. ..... Ellicott City, MD
Saunders, William Lee, Jr. ..... Washington, DC
Saunders, William W. ..... Honolulu, HI
Saunders, William W., Jr. ..... Honolulu, HI
Saunders, Wm. Charles ..... Camden, NJ
Saunders, Wyatt ..... Laurens, SC
Saunderson, Christina M. ..... Springfield, IL
Saunderson, Robert F. ..... Riverhead, NY
Saundry, Susan L. ..... Cheshire, CT
Saunier, Stanley M., III ..... Lexington, KY
Saunier, Stanley M., Jr. ..... Lexington, KY
Sauntry, John P., Jr. ..... Department of Justice,
Antitrust Division, GV
Sauntry, June Ann ..... Atlanta, GA
Sauntry, Michael J. ..... St. Paul, MN
Sauntry, Susan S. ..... Washington, DC
Saupe, A. William ..... Anchorage, AK
Saupé, Joan M. ..... Walnut Creek, CA
Saur, John A. ..... Houston, TX
Saur, John K. ..... Laguna Beach, CA
Saur, Karl W. ..... Boston, MA
Saur and Saur ..... Oelwein, IA
Saur and Saur ..... Houston, TX
Saur, Suzanne M. ..... Houston, TX
Saur, Thomas W. ..... Dearborn, MI
Saur, W. Wayne ..... Oelwein, IA
Saur, Walter L. ..... Oelwein, IA
Saurack, Walter A. ..... New York, NY
Saurbier, Marc D. ..... St. Clair Shores, MI
Saurbier, Scott A. ..... Detroit, MI
St. Clair Shores, MI

Saurbier, Siegan & Sanfield, P.C.
Detroit, MI
Mount Clemens, MI
Pontiac, MI
St. Clair Shores, MI
Saurborn, Henry L., Jr. ....New York, NY
Saurer, Beth A. ....San Diego, CA
Sauriol, Thomas R. ....Tacoma, WA
Saurman, Elizabeth A. ....Wilmington, DE
Saurman, Jan A. ....Lakewood, OH
Sauro, Brenda M. ....Denver, CO
Sauro, Frank ....Springfield, NJ
Sauro, Robert A. ....Atlanta, GA
Sause, John W., Jr. ....Centreville, MD
Sause, Richard ....Rocky Point, NY
Sauseda, J. E., Jr. ....Amarillo, TX
Sausen, George E. ....Pine City, MN
Sauser, Frank ....Rock Island, IL
Sauser, Robert W. ....Chattanooga, TN
Sausjord, Ingrid R. ....United States Senate, Senatorial Assistants, GV
Sausser, Gordon F. ....Los Angeles, CA
Sausser, John C. ....Findlay, OH
Sausser, Mark C. ....Indianapolis, IN
Sausto, Joseph A. ....Leeds, NY
Sautebin, Bruce L. ....Greenwood, WI
Sautebin Law Office ....Greenwood, WI
Sautel, Daniel L. ....Pittsburgh, PA
Sauter, Dennis C. ....Charleston, WV
Sauter, Douglas G. ....Coon Rapids, MN
Sauter, Eric J. ....New York, NY
Sauter, George V. ....Mansfield, OH
Sauter, Gwen ....Bellevue, WA
Sauter Hohenberger & Beddow
Mansfield, OH
Sauter, James E. ....Ann Arbor, MI
Sauter, James J. ....St. Louis, MO
Sauter, James P. ....New York, NY
Sauter, Jean U., (Mrs.) ....Mansfield, OH
Sauter, Jeffrey L. ....Charlotte, MI
Sauter, John L. ....Columbus, OH
Sauter, Julie ....Eaton, CO
Sauter, Kenneth R. ....Morristown, NJ
Sauter, Kurt T. ....Cocoa Beach, FL
Sauter, Lawrence J. ....Lansing, MI
Sauter, Matthew J. ....St. Louis, MO
Sauter, Michael ....Morenci, MI
Sauter, Patrick J. ....Minneapolis, MN
Sauter, Rachel K. ....Minneapolis, MN
Sauter, Robert W. ....Columbus, OH
Sauter, Stephanie Ann ....Chicago, IL
Sauthoff, Harry, Jr. ....Sauk City, WI
Sautter, Joan Mendelson ....San Francisco, CA
Sautter, Peter, Jr. ....Miami, FL
Sauvain, Edward M. ....Greenville, SC
Sauvain, Timothy W. ....Cleveland, OH
Sauve, Gerald A. ....Buffalo Grove, IL
Sauve, Mary K. ....Glendale, CA
Sauvey, David R. ....Evansville, IN
Sauvey, Marian Weilert ....Evansville, IN
Sauviac, Donald A., Jr. ....New Orleans, LA
Sava, George S. ....New York, NY
Sava, Matthew J. ....New York, NY
Sava, Michael F. ....Westlake, OH
Sava, Stacey ....Fort Lee, NJ
Savad, Paul ....Nanuet, NY
Savadove, Frederick M. ....Jenkintown, PA
Savadove, Lionel ....Bensalem, PA
Savadove, Sylvan H. ....Philadelphia, PA
Savadow, Mark I. ....
Administrative Office Of The United States Courts, GV
Savadow, Victor H. ....Baltimore, MD
Savage, Andrew J., III ....Charleston, SC
Savage, Andrew M. ....Chicago, IL
Savage, Andrew T. ....Boston, MA
Savage, Anthony ....Seattle, WA
Savage, Arthur V. ....New York, NY
Savage, Barry E. ....Toledo, OH
Savage, Bernard G. ....Staten Island, NY
Savage, Bob E. ....Tishomingo, OK
Savage, Bonnie A. ....Dallas, TX
Savage, Brent J. ....Savannah, GA
Savage, Bryan F. ....Wheaton, IL
Savage, Carroll J. ....Washington, DC
Savage, Charles D. ....Tampa, FL
Savage, Charles D., P.A. ....Tampa, FL
Savage, Charles F. ....Denver, CO
Savage, Charles W., III ....San Francisco, CA
Savage, Christine M. ....Dallas, TX
Savage, Christopher R. ....Costa Mesa, CA
Savage, Christopher R. ....Newport Beach, CA
Savage, Christopher W. ....Washington, DC
Savage, Craig D. ....North Miami Beach, FL
Savage, Cynthia Ann ....Denver, CO
Savage, Dale G. ....Tulsa, OK
Savage, Daryl DaVinci ....Falls Church, VA
Savage, David A. ....Austin, TX
Savage, David F. ....Palo Alto, CA
Savage, David L. ....Charleston, SC
Savage, David W. ....Pullman, WA
Savage, Deirdre Walsh ....Boston, MA
Savage, Desiree Ann ....Sacramento, CA
Savage, Diane ....Sidney, MT
Savage, Diane Wilkins ....Palo Alto, CA
Savage, Donna Parker ....Gastonia, NC
Savage, E. Scott ....Salt Lake City, UT
Savage, Edward Turney ....New York, NY
Savage, Elizabeth ....Denver, CO
Savage, Elizabeth A. ....Las Vegas, NV
Savage, Eric A. ....Newark, NJ
Savage, Frederick G. ....Baltimore, MD
Savage, Garmer & Elliott, P.S.C.
Lexington, KY
Savage, George F. ....Green Bay, WI
Savage, George S. ....Miami, FL
Savage, Gina R. ....Dallas, TX
Savage & Godfrey ....Apex, NC

Savage, Gordon H. ....Dayton, OH
Savage, Greg ....Houston, TX
Savage, Greggory J. ....Salt Lake City, UT
Savage, Harold M., Jr. ....Bloomfield, NJ
Savage, Harry A. ....House of Representatives, Office of Legislative Counsel, GV
Savage, Henry E. ....Worley, ID
Savage, Herndon & Turner, P.C.
Hinesville, GA
Savannah, GA
Savage, J. Diane ....Anoka, MN
Savage, J. Michael ....Birmingham, AL
Savage, James C. ....Rockville, MD
Savage, James C., III ....Watertown, MA
Savage, James D. ....Long Beach, CA
Savage, James F. ....Kansas City, KS
Savage, James J. ....Newark, NJ
Savage, James S. ....Chesterton, IN
Savage, James S., III ....Columbus, OH
Savage, Jana H. ....Pasadena, CA
Savage, Jana T. ....Redding, CA
Savage, Janet A. ....Denver, CO
Savage, Janet M. ....Los Angeles, CA
Savage, Jeffrey A. ....Trenton, NJ
Savage, Jennifer A. ....Cleveland, OH
Savage, Joe C. ....Lexington, KY
Savage, John ....Fort Myers, FL
Savage, John C. ....Manitowoc, WI
Savage, John J., Jr. ....Cheshire, CT
Savage, John M. ....Greenville, NC
Savage, John M. ....Toledo, OH
Savage, John P. ....Milwaukee, WI
Savage, John S. ....Hartford, CT
Hartsdale, NY
Savage, John W. ....Rifle, CO
Savage, John W., P.C. ....Rifle, CO
Savage, John William ....Portland, OR
Savage, Jonathan D. ....St. Louis, MO
Savage, Jonathan N. ....Providence, RI
Savage, Jos. L., Jr. ....Fredericksburg, VA
Savage, Joseph F., III ....Hartford, CT
Savage, Joseph F., Jr. ....Boston, MA
Savage, Joseph P. ....Washington, DC
Savage, Judith Colenback ....Providence, RI
Savage, Julia S. ....Warrenton, VA
Savage, Julian ....Chevy Chase, MD
Savage, Julie D. ....New Orleans, LA
Savage, Justin A. ....Washington, DC
Savage, Katherine D. ....Rockville, MD
Savage, Kay Webb ....Birmingham, AL
Savage, Kenneth W. ....Bloomfield Hills, MI
Grand Rapids, MI
Savage, Kim K. ....Los Angeles, CA
Savage, Krim, Simons & Jones, LLC
Gainesville, FL
Ocala, FL
Savage, Laurence A. ....Seattle, WA
Savage, Leigh H. ....St. Clair Shores, MI
Savage, Lesley W ....Goffstown, NH
Savage, Lilla Ann ....Mont Belvieu, TX
Savage, Lois ....Phoenix, AZ
Savage, Louis D. ....Portland, OR
Savage, Lucia C. ....Oakland, CA
Savage, Malcolm Brooks, Jr.
Washington, DC
Savage, Malcolm Mauirice
Oklahoma City, OK
Savage, Margaret K. ....Minneapolis, MN
Savage, Mark ....San Francisco, CA
Savage, Mark Joseph ....Cleveland, OH
Savage, Mary C. ....Baltimore, MD
Savage, Mary Lou ....Milwaukee, WI
Savage, Meeka ....Baltimore, MD
Savage, Michael D. ....New York, NY
Savage, Michael E. ....Sherman, TX
Savage, Michael G.
Research Triangle Park, NC
Savage, Michael T. ....Dallas, TX
Savage, Milton S., Jr. ....Philadelphia, PA
Savage, Morris W. ....Jasper, AL
Savage, Nancy D. ....Las Vegas, NV
Savage, Nancy V. ....Portland, ME
Savage, O'Donnell, McNulty & Affeldt
Tulsa, OK
Savage, Pamela E. ....Jacksonville, FL
Savage, Paul A. ....Concord, NH
Savage, Paul C. ....Miami, FL
Savage, Peter J. ....Wilkes-Barre, PA
Savage, Philip L. (Larry)
Oklahoma City, OK
Savage, Philip M., III ....Riverside, CA
San Bernardino, CA
Savage, Philip M., IV ....Riverside, CA
San Bernardino, CA
Savage, Phyllis ....Danbury, CT
Savage, Ralph ....Arco, ID
Savage, Ralph M. ....Schenectady, NY
Savage, Richard H. ....Brooklyn, NY
Savage, Rita D. ....Franktown, CO
Savage, Robert J. ....Sidney, MT
Savage, Robert J. ....East Hampton, NY
Savage, Robert L., Jr. ....Apex, NC
Savage, Robert Scott ....Tulsa, OK
Savage, Robert W. ....Piscataway, NJ
Savage, Royall and Sheheen, L.L.P.
Bishopville, SC
Camden, SC
Savage, Russell Thomas ....New York, NY
Savage, Sally P. ....Pullman, WA
Savage, Sandra J. ....San Jose, CA
Savage, Sara Beth ....New York, NY
Savage & Savage ....Bloomfield, NJ
Savage & Savage, P.A. ....Charleston, SC
Moncks Corner, SC
St. George, SC
Summerville, SC
Savage, Shannon ....Houston, TX
Savage, Sharon L. ....San Antonio, TX

Savage, Stacey A. ....Salem, NH
Savage, Stephen J. ....Washington, DC
Savage, Stephen M. ....Phoenix, AZ
Savage, Stewart W. ....Fort Myers, FL
Savage, Stuart E. ....Pittsburgh, PA
Savage, Susan J. ....Austin, TX
Savage, T. Gardner ....Dallas, TX
Savage, Terry E. ....Imperial, NE
Savage, Theodore J. ....Annandale, NJ
Savage, Thomas I. ....Palo Alto, CA
Savage, Thomas J. ....Lambertville, NJ
Savage, Thomas R. ....Milwaukee, WI
Savage, Thomas W. ....Key Largo, FL
Savage, Thomas Y. ....Fredericksburg, VA
Savage, Timothy J. ....Philadelphia, PA
Savage, Timothy J., P.C. ....Philadelphia, PA
Savage, Toy D., Jr. ....Norfolk, VA
Savage, Wallace H. ....Dallas, TX
Savage, Walter A. ....Parma, OH
Savage, Warren Tobin, IV ....Raleigh, NC
Savage & Wiedt ....Pittsburgh, PA
Savage, William E., II ....Lexington, KY
Savage, William H., Jr. ....Barceloneta, PR
Savage, William M. ....Fairfax, VA
Savage, William R. ....Portland, ME
Savage, William R. ....Marble Falls, TX
Savage, William R., III ....Suffolk, VA
Savage, Woodson J., Jr. ....Bolivar, TN
Savageau, Nancy ....Farmington Hills, MI
Savaglio, Michael T. ....Milwaukee, WI
Savaiano, Anthony A. ....Loves Park, IL
Savaiano, Dominick W. ....Chicago, IL
Savakes, Wendy Marie ....Rosemount, MN
Savakis, Alexander J. ....Warren, OH
Saval, Paul L. ....Owings Mills, MD
Savala, Rudy L. ....Fresno, CA
Savalan, Thomas L. ....Akron, OH
Savan, Cheryl ....Canton, OH
Savan, Jakki L. ....Denver, CO
Savanis, Irene ....Chicago, IL
Savant, Chalone R. ....Austin, TX
Savant, Kristen Ieyoub ....Dallas, TX
Savanyu, Jean M. ....New York, NY
Savar, Barbara ....Philadelphia, PA
Savar, Jonathan S. ....New York, NY
Savar, Ronnie R. ....Davie, FL
Savar, Stephen ....Lafayette Hill, PA
Savard, David M. ....Taylor, MI
Savard, Glenn L. ....Los Angeles, CA
Savard, Jane ....Seattle, WA
Savaree, Jean B. ....San Carlos, CA
Savarese, Andrea C. ....Lake Success, NY
Savarese, Anthony P., Jr. ....Garden City, NY
Savarese, Deborah A. ....Dallas, TX
Savarese, Glenn ....Livingston, NJ
Savarese, J. Todd ....Doylestown, PA
Savarese, John F. ....New York, NY
Savarese, Paul J. ....Brooklyn, NY
Savarese, Peter A. ....West Palm Beach, FL
Savarese, Ralph J. ....Washington, DC
Savarese, Stephen C. ....Chelsea, MA
Savarese, Stephen L. ....Newtown, CT
Savarino, William F. ....Washington, DC
Savarise, Jeffrey A. ....Louisville, KY
Cincinnati, OH
Savarise, René Remek ....Louisville, KY
Savary, Johnson S. ....Sarasota, FL
Savary, Johnson S., Jr. ....Sarasota, FL
Savas, Madeline Rizzo ....Westwood, NJ
Savas, Theodore Peter ....Mason City, IA
Savasito, Edward A. ....West Chester, PA
Savasta, Natale "Neil" G. ....Cherry Hill, NJ
Clifton, NJ
Savastano, Anthony ....Hackensack, NJ
Savastano, Anthony C. ....New Bedford, MA
Savastano, Francis M. ....Manhasset, NY
Savasten, David H. ....Berkeley Springs, WV
Savasuk, Michael X. ....Portland, ME
Savate, Rose D. ....Encino, CA
Savatta, Don ....Brooklyn, NY
Save, Eric ....Houston, TX
Savedge, O. Eugene ....Mount Pleasant, SC
Savee, Timothy J. ....Newport, OR
Saveikis Burrow, Lisa K.
Silver Spring, MD
Savel, Andrew M. ....Birmingham, MI
Savel, Mary Beth ....Tucson, AZ
Savela, Eila E. ....Minneapolis, MN
Savela, Susan K. ....Reno, NV
Savelkoul, Donald C. ....Fridley, MN
Savelkoul, Donald W. ....Albert Lea, MN
Savelkoul, Henry J. ....Albert Lea, MN
Savelkoul, Richard J. ....Minneapolis, MN
Savell, Edward L. ....Atlanta, GA
Savell, Lawrence E. ....New York, NY
Savell, Polly C. ....New York, NY
Savell, Richard D. ....Fairbanks, AK
Savell & Williams, L.L.P. ....Atlanta, GA
Savella, Donna Marie ....Cranston, RI
Savelson, Donald W. ....New York, NY
Savelson, Robert S. ....New York, NY
Savely, Carl D. ....Reno, NV
Savenko, Melissa Loughridge
Richmond, VA
Saver, John Gregory ....New York, NY
Saver, Matthew H. ....Los Angeles, CA
Savereide, Paul B. ....Wayzata, MN
Saveri, Guido ....San Francisco, CA
Saveri, Joseph R. ....San Francisco, CA
Saveri Law Group, Inc.
San Francisco, CA
Saveri, Lisa M. ....San Francisco, CA
Saveri, R. Alexander ....San Francisco, CA
Saverin, Kenneth A. ....Westport, CT
Saverino, Domenico ....Palm Bay, FL
Saverino, Michael V. ....Phoenix, AZ

Saverson, Ester, Jr.
Securities and Exchange Commission, Office of International Affairs, GV
Savery, Barbara Jane ....Pleasanton, CA
Savery, Donald J. ....Boston, MA
Savery, Rex T., Jr. ....Chapel Hill, NC
Saveth, Henry ....Washington, DC
Savett Frutkin Podell & Ryan, P.C.
Philadelphia, PA
Savett, Michael S. ....Cherry Hill, NJ
Savett, Sherrie Raiken ....Philadelphia, PA
Savett, Stuart H. ....Philadelphia, PA
Saviano, Anthony T. ....Cranbury, NJ
Saviano, Edward S. ....New York, NY
Saviano, Timothy J. ....Milwaukee, WI
Saviano & Tobias, P.C. ....New York, NY
Savich, Marya ....Chicago, IL
Savich, Matt ....Novi, MI
Savich, Rudolph Wm. ....Bloomington, IN
Savickas, Stephen A. ....Grand Rapids, MI
Savidge, Keith A. ....Cleveland, OH
Savidge, Paul J. ....Whitehouse Station, NJ
Saviers, Allen Boyd ....Sapulpa, OK
Saviers, John D. ....Denver, CO
Saviers, William P., Jr. ....Clarksburg, WV
Saviet, Annette Colston ....New City, NY
Saviet, Elwyn ....Elmwood Park, NJ
Saviet, Richard D. ....Department of Defense, Defense Legal Services Agency, GV
Savignac, Raymond J. ....Dade City, FL
Savignac, Thomas A. ....Brookfield, WI
Savikas, Victor G. ....Los Angeles, CA
Savill, Nirja N. ....Hartford, CT
Savill, Robert A. ....Orlando, FL
Saville, Daniel V. ....Wichita, KS
Saville and Davis, PLLC ....Romney, WV
Saville, Derric ....Maple Grove, MN
Saville, James A. ....Queens Village, NY
Saville, James A., Jr. ....Jersey City, NJ
New York, NY
Saville, John W. E. ....Dallas, TX
Saville, Kevin ....Minneapolis, MN
Saville, Kevin H. ....Wheaton, IL
Saville Law Firm ....Maple Grove, MN
Saville, Richard L., Jr. ....St. Louis, MO
Saville, Robert J. ....New York, NY
Saville, Royce B. ....Romney, WV
Saville, Sandra K. ....Anchorage, AK
Saville, Yvonne Takvorian
Wilmington, DE
Savin, Adina L. ....Los Angeles, CA
Savin, Bernard ....Highland Park, IL
Savin & Bursk ....Granada Hills, CA
Savin, George J., Jr. ....Granada Hills, CA
Savin, Harris B. ....Philadelphia, PA
Savin, James R. ....New York, NY
Savin, Kenneth P. ....Northport, NY
Savin, Mark D. ....Minneapolis, MN
Savina, James J. ....Dallas, TX
Savina, Leslie J. ....Redmond, WA
Savinar, Tim ....San Francisco, CA
Savinell, Alvin J. ....Steubenville, OH
Savini, Gina M. ....Chicago, IL
Savinis, Janice M. ....Pittsburgh, PA
Savino, Angela M. Alexander
Columbus, OH
Savino, Angelo G. ....New York, NY
Savino, Carmine, Jr. ....Lyndhurst, NJ
Savino, Daniel J., Jr. ....New York, NY
Savino, Elizabeth Martin ....Buffalo, NY
Savino, Ellen N. ....Uniondale, NY
Savino, George O. ....Lyndhurst, NJ
Savino, Louis T., Jr. ....Philadelphia, PA
Savino, Mona B. ....Los Angeles, CA
Savino, Nicholas L. ....Brooklyn, NY
Savino, Richard J. ....Glen Rock, NJ
Savino, Robert Louis ....New York, NY
Savino, William F. ....Buffalo, NY
Savino, William M. ....Uniondale, NY
Savinski, Sharon Ann ....
Administrative Office Of The United States Courts, GV
Savio, Charles J. ....Port Richey, FL
Savio, James P. ....Absecon, NJ
Savio, John A., III ....Atlanta, GA
Savio, Maria A. ....New York, NY
Savio, Reynolds & Drake ....Absecon, NJ
Saviola, Georgia Tatsios ....Los Angeles, CA
Savir, Mika Z.
Federal Communications Commission, Common Carrier Bureau, GV
Savis, Niloo ....Los Angeles, CA
Savit, Glenn F. ....New York, NY
Savit, Jeffrey K. ....Needham, MA
Savit, Lester J. ....Chicago, IL
Savit, Mark N. ....Washington, DC
Savitch, Emmanuel ....San Diego, CA
Savitch, Jonathan ....Alexandria, VA
Savitch, Jordan B. ....Wayne, PA
Savitch, Leon ....Oxnard, CA
Savitch, Rhonda L. ....Fairfield, CA
Napa, CA
Savits, Glen D. ....West Orange, NJ
Savits, Joel M. ....Washington, DC
Baltimore, MD
Rockville, MD
Savitski, Peter A. ....Rockford, IL
Savitsky, Gerald S. ....Washington, DC
Savitsky, Jeffrey C. ....Indianapolis, IN
Savitsky, Michael T. ....Philadelphia, PA
Scranton, PA
Savitsky, Robert ....Rockville Centre, NY
Savitsky, Thomas R. ....Princeton, NJ
Savitt, Beverly B. ....Belvedere-Tiburon, CA
Savitt, Charles ....Hopkins, MN
Savitt, David N. ....Philadelphia, PA
Savitt, Ephraim, Law Offices of
New York, NY

Savitt, Harvey B. ... Commack, NY
Savitt, Herbert S. ... Ansonia, CT
Savitt, James P. ... Seattle, WA
Savitt, Joel A. ... North Miami Beach, FL
Savitt, Joel A., P.A. ... North Miami Beach, FL
Savitt, Linda C. Miller
Sherman Oaks, CA
Savitt, Lisa J. ... Washington, DC
Savitt, Nancy L. ... Paramus, NJ
New York, NY
Savitt, Richard P. ... Ansonia, CT
Savitt, Richard S. ... Miami, FL
Savitt, Robert E. ... Los Angeles, CA
Savitt, William ... Armonk, NY
Savitz, Andrew W. ... Boston, MA
Savitz, Bennett R. ... Boston, MA
Savitz, Burton D. ... New York, NY
Savitz, David Barry ... Denver, CO
Savitz, Edward O. ... Tampa, FL
Savitz, James E. ... Gaithersburg, MD
Potomac, MD
Savitz, Joseph J. ... Wilkes-Barre, PA
Savitz, Michael J. ... Boston, MA
Savitz, Nita Jagoda ... Flushing, NY
Savitz, Richard E. ... San Diego, CA
Savitz, Sidney R. ... Orlando, FL
Savitz, Stephen T. ... Columbia, SC
Savitz, Stuart M. ... Chicago, IL
Savitzky, Martin F. ... Maple Glen, PA
Savitzky, Martin F. ... Philadelphia, PA
Savkar, Sonya ... Department of Education, Office of the General Counsel, GV
Savkar, Sunil William ... New York, NY
Savlov, David B. ... Syracuse, NY
Savlov, Jeffrey H. ... Winter Park, FL
Savner, David A. ... Falls Church, VA
Savnik, Gerard R. ... Cranford, NJ
Savo, William B. ... Somerville, NJ
Savoca, John B. ... Boston, MA
Savoca, Joseph E. ... Lancaster, PA
Savoca, Susan ... Trenton, NJ
Savoca, Thomas-Joseph, II ... Venice, CA
Savoian, H. Raymond ... Torrance, CA
Savoiardo, Maurizio, III ... New York, NY
Savoie, Catherine J. ... Boston, MA
Savoie, D. Kent ... Sulphur, LA
Savoie, Damien ... New Orleans, LA
Savoie, Deborah Johnston ... Birmingham, MI
Savoie, Felix H., Jr. ... Napoleonville, LA
Savoie, Harold L. ... Lafayette, LA
Savoie, Herman M., Jr. ... Alexandria, LA
Savoie, M. Damien ... New Orleans, LA
Savoie, Nancy M. ... Norwood, MA
Savoie, Ronald J. ... Baton Rouge, LA
Savoie, Rusty J. ... New Orleans, LA
Savoie, Thomas R. ... Rye Brook, NY
Savola, L.H. Steven ... Miami Lakes, FL
Savoldi, Frank P. ... Youngstown, OH
Savon, Thomas M. ... Philadelphia, PA
Savona, Frank V. ... Parsippany, NJ
Savona, Joseph F. X. ... New York, NY
Savona & Scully ... New York, NY
Savone, Dino ... Yonkers, NY
Savoni, Charles F. ... Costa Mesa, CA
Savopoulos, Savvas P. ... Potomac, MD
Savopoulos, Savvas P., P.C. ... Potomac, MD
Savor, Kathleen M. ... Fort Lauderdale, FL
Savord, George Hugh, (A Professional Law Corporation) ... Cave Junction, OR
Savory, Russell W. ... Memphis, TN
Savoth, John E. ... Brick, NJ
Savoth, Paul G. ... West Long Branch, NJ
Savoth, Thomas Charles ... Bedminster, NJ
Savoy, Bilancini, Flanagan & Kenneally
Elyria, OH
Savoy, Damon J. ... Treasury Department, Office of the Comptroller of the Currency, GV
Savoy, Jerome J. ... Elyria, OH
Savoy, John E. ... Phoenix, AZ
Savoy, Kristin D. ... Newark, NJ
Savoy, Richard E. ... Burlington, MA
Savoy, Richard L. ... Lake Charles, LA
Savoy, Robert ... Trevose, PA
Savoy, Wade J. ... Pittsburgh, PA
Savoye, April A. ... Saddle Brook, NJ
New York, NY
Savoye, Herbert Fitzhugh, Jr.
Bergenfield, NJ
Savoy-Lewis, April ... Atlanta, GA
Savrann, Richard A. ... Boston, MA
Savrann, Russell C. ... Braintree, MA
Savre, Beth A. ... Minneapolis, MN
Savre, Michael R. ... Glencoe, MN
Savren, Clifford ... Cleveland, OH
Savren, Joy B. ... Cleveland, OH
Savrick, Mitchell D. ... Austin, TX
Savrin & Berson ... New York, NY
Savrin, Daniel S. ... Boston, MA
Savrin, Janet A. ... New York, NY
Savrin, Louis ... New York, NY
Savrin, Philip Wade ... Atlanta, GA
Savrnoch, John T. ... Fresno, CA
Savryn, Karl ... New York, NY
Savu, David M., P.C. ... Ishpeming, MI
Savva, John L. ... Los Angeles, CA
Savvaides, Anastasios T. ... Stamford, CT
Sawa, Takatoshi ... Rochester, NY
Sawada, Suzanne R. ... Chicago, IL
Sawall, Eugene R. ... Milwaukee, WI
Sawamura, James K. ... San Francisco, CA
Sawamura, Michael A. ... Sacramento, CA
Sawan, Dennis P. ... Toledo, OH
Sawan, Edmund M. ... Akron, OH
Sawan & Farris ... Akron, OH
Sawasaki, Isa Crystal ... Ventura, CA
Sawatzke, Roger L. ... Council Bluffs, IA
Sawatzky, Gerald ... Wichita, KS
Sawaya, Alfred ... Southfield, MI
Sawaya, Dianne L. ... Denver, CO
Sawaya, Donald ... Salt Lake City, UT
Sawaya, George ... Brooklyn, NY
Sawaya, Michael G. ... Denver, CO
Sawaya, Michael S. ... Mineola, NY
New York, NY
White Plains, NY
Sawaya, Nathan John ... New York, NY
Sawaya, Rose, Roberts & Sawaya, P.C.
Denver, CO
Sawaya, Thomas D. ... Ocala, FL
Sawch, William B. ... Norwalk, CT
Sawchak, Matthew W. ... Raleigh, NC
Sawchik, Paul ... San Diego, CA
Sawchuck, Ann M. ... Pittsburgh, PA
Sawchuk, Edward Steven ... Bayside, NY
Sawczuk, Maria Aprile ... Wilmington, DE
Sawdayi, Devin ... Los Angeles, CA
Sawdei, Milan A. ... Orange, CA
Sawdey, Richard M. ... Chicago, IL
Sawdey, Robert W. ... Grand Rapids, MI
Sawers, Daniel T. ... Buffalo, NY
Sawers, J. Kemp ... Dallas, TX
Sawers, Kathryn R. ... Dallas, TX
Sawers, Tim ... Buffalo, NY
Sawertailo, Larysa ... Rochester Hills, MI
Sawh, Sally N. ... Miami, FL
Sawhill, Walter A. ... Haysville, KS
Sawhney, Pamela Ettema ... Detroit, MI
Sawhook, Celeste ... Corpus Christi, TX
Sawi, Tarek ... Department of Justice, Civil Division, GV
Sawicki, Daniel ... Royal Oak, MI
Sawicki, George J. ... Redwood City, CA
Sawicki, James ... New York, NY
Sawicki, Janice M. ... Media, PA
Sawicki, John S. ... Secaucus, NJ
Sawicki, K. Michael ... Buffalo, NY
Sawicki, Michael A. ... Southfield, MI
Sawicki, Michael G. ... Dallas, TX
Sawicki, Michael P. ... Hunt Valley, MD
Sawicki, Myron ... Ukiah, CA
Sawicki, Neese & Phelps, P.A.
St. Paul, MN
Woodbury, MN
Sawicki, Neil J. ... Wyandotte, MI
Sawicki, Stephen C. ... Orlando, FL
Sawicki, Theodore J. ... Atlanta, GA
Sawicki, Walter E., Jr. ... Woodbury, MN
Sawicki, Zbigniew Peter ... Minneapolis, MN
Sawicky, Michael E. ... Warren, MI
Sawicz, James P. ... New York, NY
Sawilowsky, Jay M. ... Augusta, GA
Sawilowsky, Jay M., P.C. ... Augusta, GA
Sawin, Deborah A. ... Waltham, MA
Sawin, Richard A., Jr. ... Boston, MA
Sawislak, Richard S. ... Chicago, IL
Sawitsky, Heather B. ... Wellesley, MA
Sawitsky, Kitt ... Boston, MA
Sawka, Alison M. ... Flint, MI
Sawkar, Suhasini S. ... Los Angeles, CA
Sawkiewicz, Kathleen ... Duxbury, MA
Sawko & Burroughs, L.L.P. ... Denton, TX
Sawko, Gregory J. ... Denton, TX
Sawko, Victor J. ... Chicago, IL
Sawran, James C. ... Fort Lauderdale, FL
West Palm Beach, FL
Sawransky, Howard Craig ... New York, NY
Sawtell, Michelle Dillon ... Seattle, WA
Sawtell, Stephen M. ... Omaha, NE
Sawtell, W. Anthony ... Santa Fe, NM
Sawtell, William A., Jr. ... Santa Fe, NM
Sawtelle, Barry Wayne ... Reading, PA
Sawtelle, Gary W. ... Fountain Valley, CA
Sawtelle, Henry G. ... New York, NY
Sawtelle, James G. ... Des Moines, IA
Sawtelle, Susan D. ... Washington, DC
Sawusch, Bonnie Y. ... Kalamazoo, MI
Sawyer, A. Curtis, Jr. ... Sacramento, CA
Sawyer, Adrian J. ... San Francisco, CA
Sawyer, Akin & Herron, P.A.
Wilmington, DE
Sawyer, Andrew H. ... Sacramento, CA
Sawyer & Associates ... Palo Alto, CA
Sawyer, Ava M. ... Reston, VA
Sawyer, Barney Wade ... Paris, TX
Sawyer, Barrie ... Tampa, FL
Sawyer, Brian A. ... Rutland, VT
Sawyer, Bruce D. ... Lincoln, RI
Sawyer, C. David, Jr. ... Saluda, SC
Sawyer, Carolyn H. ... Orlando, FL
Sawyer, Charles F. ... Minneapolis, MN
Sawyer, Charles L. ... Buffalo, NY
Sawyer, Chas. M. T., II ... Fort Payne, AL
Sawyer, Christopher Glenn ... Atlanta, GA
Sawyer, Christy ... Nashville, TN
Sawyer, Clarence E., Jr. ... Northford, CT
Sawyer, Dale B. ... Federal Way, WA
Sawyer, Dana P. ... Houston, TX
Sawyer, Daniel D. ... Kansas City, MO
Sawyer, Daniel W. ... Charlotte, NC
Sawyer, David ... Pass Christian, MS
Sawyer, David A. ... Maitland, FL
Sawyer, David A. ... Birmingham, MI
Sawyer, David F. ... Troy, MI
Sawyer, David H. ... Grand Rapids, MI
Sawyer, David T. ... White Springs, FL
Sawyer, Davis, Halpern & Demetri
Garden City, NY
Sawyer, Deborah A. ... Fort Pierce, FL
Sawyer, Dianne L. ... Portland, OR
Sawyer, Donald A. ... Harrisburg, PA
Sawyer, Edward ... Cincinnati, OH
Sawyer, Edward E. ... Miami, FL
Sawyer, Edwin A. ... Decatur, GA
Sawyer, Eric C. ... Los Angeles, CA
Sawyer, Erica ... Newark, NJ
Sawyer, Erin ... San Francisco, CA
Sawyer, Francis A. ... Kansas City, MO
Sawyer, Frederic A. ... Walnut Creek, CA
Sawyer, Frederick G. ... High Point, NC
Sawyer, Gale & Laughlin, L.L.P. ... Hazlet, NJ
Sawyer, Gary W. ... Lakeland, FL
Tampa, FL
Sawyer, George P. ... Torrington, WY
Sawyer & Glancy, PLLC ... Lexington, KY
Sawyer, H. Dan ... Shreveport, LA
Sawyer, H. Kimbrell, III ... Ringgold, GA
Sawyer, H. Murray, Jr. ... Wilmington, DE
Sawyer, Harold S. ... Grand Rapids, MI
Sawyer, Harold Z. ... Chicago, IL
Sawyer, Harry M., Jr. ... Lakeland, FL
Sawyer, Herbert H. ... Portland, ME
Sawyer, Herman M., Jr. ... Arlington, VA
Sawyer, Irene ... Bartlesville, OK
Sawyer, J. Anthony ... Dayton, OH
Sawyer, J. Neal ... Kansas City, MO
Sawyer, James ... Garden City, NY
Sawyer, James B., II ... Shelton, WA
Sawyer, James F.B. ... Los Angeles, CA
Sawyer, James L. ... Chicago, IL
Sawyer, J. E., Jr. ... Enterprise, AL
Sawyer, Jerry K. ... Fort Worth, TX
Sawyer, Joe J. ... Austin, TX
Sawyer, Joel T. ... Fort Worth, TX
Sawyer, John C.
General Services Administration, Office of the General Counsel, GV
Sawyer, John C. ... Atlanta, GA
Sawyer, John Charles, Jr ... Jacksonville, FL
Sawyer, John D. ... Vienna, VA
Sawyer, John H. ... Santa Ana, CA
Sawyer, John N. ... Beaver, PA
Sawyer, John P., Jr. ... Boston, MA
Sawyer, John R. ... Pensacola, FL
Sawyer, John Randy ... Princeton, NJ
Sawyer, John S. ... Lexington, KY
Sawyer, John W. ... Gorham, ME
North Windham, ME
Sawyer & Johni, P.A. ... Tampa, FL
Sawyer, Jon D. ... Denver, CO
Sawyer, Joseph A., Jr. ... Palo Alto, CA
Sawyer, Joseph F., Jr. ... Worcester, MA
Sawyer, Joy Hendrix ... Ringgold, GA
Sawyer, J. P. ... Jasper, AL
Sawyer, K. David ... Birmingham, AL
Sawyer, Karen Korff ... Gulfport, MS
Sawyer, Karl S., Jr. ... Charlotte, NC
Sawyer, Katherine Ann ... New York, NY
Sawyer, K. David, L.L.C.
Birmingham, AL
Sawyer, Keary W. ... Grand Rapids, MI
Sawyer, Kenneth I. ... Fort Lauderdale, FL
Sawyer, Kim Sherrie ... Boston, MA
Sawyer, Laura W. ... Brunswick, GA
Sawyer, Laurence K. ... Santa Rosa, CA
Sawyer Law Group ... Bradenton, FL
Lakeland, FL
Tampa, FL
Sawyer, Lawrence R.
North Windham, ME
Sawyer, L. E., Jr. ... Midland, TX
Sawyer, Leonard E. ... Plymouth, NH
Sawyer, Loren L. ... Medford, OR
Sawyer, Marvin Thomas ... Rialto, CA
Sawyer, Meredith A. ... San Francisco, CA
Sawyer, Michael Dennis ... Leesburg, VA
Sawyer, Michael J. ... Quincy, MA
Sawyer, M.O. (Mick) ... Edinburg, TX
Sawyer & Myerberg ... Lexington Park, MD
Sawyer, Paul ... New York, NY
Sawyer, Paul E., III ... Fort Lauderdale, FL
Sawyer, Paula Schaeffer ... Baltimore, MD
Sawyer, Preston, Jr. ... Lynchburg, VA
Sawyer, R. Scott ... Boston, MA
Sawyer, Raymond T. ... Cleveland, OH
Sawyer, Rebecca ... San Francisco, CA
Sawyer, Robert E. ... Los Angeles, CA
Sawyer, Robert K., Jr. ... Randolph, MA
Sawyer, Robert M. ... Ventura, CA
Sawyer, Roberta F. ... Rockland, MA
Sawyer, Roderick T. ... Chicago, IL
Sawyer, Sam ... Tullahoma, TN
Sawyer, Sandra ... Medford, OR
Sawyer & Sawyer ... Ringgold, GA
Sawyer & Sawyer ... Grand Rapids, MI
Sawyer, Sawyer & Minott, P.A.
Gorham, ME
North Windham, ME
Portland, ME
Sawyer & Sawyer, P.A. ... Orlando, FL
Sawyer, Scott R. ... Seattle, WA
Sawyer, Sean J. ... Fairmont, WV
Sawyer, Sewell A. ... Winona, MN
Sawyer, Sheila W. ... Boston, MA
Sawyer, Sherri Hayes ... San Francisco, CA
Sawyer, Sidney I. ... Hazlet, NJ
Sawyer, Staci L. ... Providence, RI
Sawyer, Stephanie M. ... Philadelphia, PA
Sawyer, Stephen D. ... Long Beach, CA
Sawyer, Stephen G. ... Mount Carmel, IL
Sawyer, Stephen P. ... Bentonville, AR
Sawyer, Stephen P. ... Chicago, IL
Sawyer, Stephen W. ... Racine, WI
Sawyer, Susan ... New York, NY
Sawyer, Terrence V. ... Spokane, WA
Sawyer, Theodore D. ... Columbus, OH
Sawyer, Thomas E. ... Hood River, OR
Sawyer, Thomas G. ... Orlando, FL
Sawyer, Thomas G. ... Troy, MI
Sawyer, Thomas H. W. ... Chicago, IL
Sawyer, Thomas J. ... Department of Justice, Tax Division, GV
Sawyer, Thomas J. ... McLean, VA
Sawyer, Thomas R. ... Stuart, FL
Sawyer, Tom Y. ... Plant City, FL
Sawyer, V. Mishaune ... Chicago, IL
Sawyer, W. Whitney ... Mount Clemens, MI
Sawyer, W. Whitney, P.C.
Mount Clemens, MI
Sawyer, Walter W., III ... Lexington Park, MD
Sawyer & Warren ... Torrington, WY
Sawyer, Wendell H. ... Greensboro, NC
Sawyer, Wilbert L., Jr. ... Richmond, VA
Sawyer, William C. ... Boston, MA
Sawyer, William Kent ... New York, NY
Sawyer, William M. ... Frankfort, KY
Sawyer, William P. ... Montgomery, AL
Sawyer, William R. ... Mobile, AL
Sawyer-Knoll, Jo Anne ... San Diego, CA
Sawyers, Al B. ... New York, NY
Sawyers, E. Wayne ... Dublin, VA
Sawyers, Gary W. ... Fresno, CA
Sawyers, Gary W., Law Offices of
Fresno, CA
Sawyers, J. Michael ... Baltimore, MD
Sawyers, Jacqueline S. ... Covington, KY
Sawyers, John T. ... New York, NY
Sawyers, William R. ... San Francisco, CA
Sawyer-Sinclair, Holli J. ... Newfield, ME
Sawyier, Calvin P. ... Chicago, IL
Sawyier, David R. ... Chicago, IL
Sawyier, Michael T. ... Chicago, IL
Sawyier, Stephen K. ... New York, NY
Sawyko, Leon T. ... Rochester, NY
Sax, Anne H. ... Woodland Hills, CA
Sax, Barry M. ... Department of Defense, Defense Legal Services Agency, GV
Sax, Carl A. ... New York, NY
Sax, Carol A. C. ... Reading, MA
Sax, Eugene E. ... Los Angeles, CA
Sax, Helen Spigel ... Philadelphia, PA
Sax, Hilary H. ... Los Angeles, CA
Sax, James G. ... Metairie, LA
Sax, Jason M. ... Chicago, IL
Sax, Jeffrey F. ... Los Angeles, CA
Sax, Jerome M. ... Chicago, IL
Sax, Jodi L. ... Los Angeles, CA
Sax, Joseph L. ... Berkeley, CA
Sax, Laura Eames ... Los Angeles, CA
Sax, Leonard B. ... Olympia Fields, IL
Sax, M. Beth ... Troy, MI
Sax, Mark L. ... Houston, TX
Sax, Paul J. ... San Francisco, CA
Sax, Richard Lee ... Carlsbad, CA
Sax, Richard P. ... Santa Rosa, CA
Sax, Shawn K. ... Oakland, CA
Sax, Spencer M. ... Boca Raton, FL
Sax, Thomas F. ... Chicago, IL
Sax, Ward L. ... Seattle, WA
Sax, William L. ... Miami, FL
Sax & Willinger, P.A. ... Miami, FL
Saxbe, Charles Rockwell ... Columbus, OH
Saxbe, William B. ... Columbus, OH
Saxby, Edward F., Jr. ... Portland, ME
Saxby, Kent P. ... Kalispell, MT
Saxby, Kevin M. ... Anchorage, AK
Saxe, Alan J. ... Burbank, CA
Saxe, Allan R. (Bob) ... San Jose, CA
Saxe, Bernhard D. ... Washington, DC
Saxe, Bertram M. ... Atlantic City, NJ
Saxe, Bret ...
Administrative Office Of The United States Courts, GV
Saxe, Charlene Anne ... Columbus, OH
Saxe, Daniel L. ... Tampa, FL
Saxe, David B. ... New York, NY
Saxe, Deborah C. ... Los Angeles, CA
Saxe, Edward A. ... Boston, MA
Saxe Eustace & Vita P.C. ... New Haven, CT
Saxe, Harriet A. ... Houston, TX
Saxe, Harriet K. ... New York, NY
Saxe, Ira M. ... New York, NY
Saxe, Janine M. ... McLean, VA
Saxe, Jon S. ... Boulder, CO
Saxe, Judith A. ... Boston, MA
Saxe, Karen A. ... Woodbridge, CT
Saxe, Keith E. ... Department of Justice, Environment and Natural Resources Division, GV
Saxe, Lawrence C. ... Flint, MI
Saxe, R. Daniel, Jr. ... White Plains, NY
Saxe, Richard B. ... Midland, TX
Saxe, Richard H. ... Newark, NJ
Saxe, Stephen A. ... Washington, DC
Saxe, Steven L. ... San Francisco, CA
Saxe, Thomas L. ... Grand Rapids, MI
Saxe, Tracy Alan ... New Haven, CT
Saxe, W. Bruce ... Albion, IL
Saxena, Maya ... Boca Raton, FL
Saxenian, James R. ... Washington, DC
Saxenian, Stephen ... Park Ridge, NJ
Saxer Anderson Wolinsky & Sunshine PC
Plattsburgh, NY
Burlington, VT
Montpelier, VT
Richmond, VT
Saxer, Christopher P.
Fort Walton Beach, FL
Saxer, Christopher P., P.A.
Fort Walton Beach, FL
Saxer, Philip D. ... Burlington, VT
Saxer, Robert H. ... Swanton, OH
Saxer, Robert Pierce ... Bridgeview, IL
Saxer, Shelley Ross ... Malibu, CA
Saxer, Thomas M. ... Akron, OH
Saxhaug, Vernon D. ... Virginia, MN
Saxl, Michael V. ... Augusta, ME
Saxl, Richard H. ... Westport, CT
Saxl, Sherman J. ... New York, NY
Saxl, Stephen L. ... New York, NY
Saxman, Anna E. ... Burlington, VT
Saxman, Ron W. ... Los Angeles, CA

Saxman, Suzanne L. ... **Chicago, IL**
Saxner, Morris ... Chicago, IL
Saxon, Alexa Constance ... Portland, OR
Saxon, Anne Danza ... Columbus, OH
Saxon, Barry, Gardner & Kincannon, A Professional Corporation
Newport Beach, CA
Riverside, CA
San Diego, CA
Saxon, Benjamin Y. ... Melbourne, FL
Saxon, Bernice S. ... **Orlando, FL**
Tampa, FL
Saxon, Charles S. ... Ann Arbor, MI
Saxon, Charlotte M. ... **San Francisco, CA**
Saxon, David P., II ... Fort Smith, AR
Saxon, Donald R. ... **Concord, NH**
Saxon, Janet D. ... Washington, DC
Saxon, Jerome A. ... Libertyville, IL
Saxon, John D. ... **Birmingham, AL**
Saxon, John D., P.C. ... **Birmingham, AL**
Saxon, John J., Sr. ... Akron, OH
Saxon, Kenneth W. ... Portland, OR
Saxon, Kyle R. ... **Miami, FL**
Saxon, Mark A. ... **Newport Beach, CA**
San Diego, CA
Saxon, Marquoit, Bertoni & Todd
Portland, OR
Saxon, Peter ... **New York, NY**
Saxon, Robert S. ... Brooklyn, NY
Saxon, Sean G. ... **Washington, DC**
Saxon, Stephen M. ... **Washington, DC**
Saxon, Victoria J. ... **Buffalo, NY**
Saxowsky, David M. ... Fargo, ND
Saxtein, Henry S. ... Riverhead, NY
Saxton & Ayres ... **West Memphis, AR**
Saxton, Bradley ... Laramie, WY
Saxton, Bradley M. ... **Orlando, FL**
Saxton, Charles, & Associates
Longmont, CO
Saxton, Charles D. ... **Longmont, CO**
Saxton, Harold E. ... Ridgefield, CT
Saxton, James M., (P.A.) ... **Little Rock, AR**
Saxton, James W. ... **Lancaster, PA**
Saxton, Jay S. ... Rogers, AR
Saxton, Jonathan F. ... Baltimore, MD
Saxton, Jonathan P. ... **Cincinnati, OH**
Saxton, Karen L. ... **York, PA**
Saxton, Kathleen E. ... Dayton, OH
Saxton, R. Clinton ... **West Memphis, AR**
Saxton, Richard N., Jr. ... Lock Haven, PA
Saxton, Robert J. ... Wall Township, NJ
Saxton, Ronald L. ... **Portland, OR**
Saxton, Steven P. ... **Sacramento, CA**
Saxton, William M. ... **Detroit, MI**
Saxum, Gregory A. ... Rochester, NY
Say, Alexander M. ... **Louisville, KY**
Say, Margaret Tish Hall ... Louisville, KY
Saya, James M. ... **Hartford, CT**
Sayad & Biren, A Professional Corporation
San Francisco, CA
Sayad, E.W. Gentry ... **St. Louis, MO**
Sayad, Pamela M. ... **San Francisco, CA**
Sayad, Stephen S. ... **San Francisco, CA**
Sayad, William Y., Jr. ... Miami, FL
Sayah, Max ... New York, NY
Sayas, David A. ... Wauwatosa, WI
Saybe, Ellis G. ... Alexandria, LA
Saybolt, Thomas L. ... **Dearborn, MI**
Saydack, Roger M. ... **Eugene, OR**
Saydah, Michael F. ... San Diego, CA
Saye, John B. ... **Monroe, LA**
Sayed, Linda B. ... **Wilmington, NC**
Sayed, Mark A. ... **Long Beach, CA**
Sayed, Mona A. ... Port Huron, MI
Sayeedi, Nicholas R. ... **Littleton, CO**
Sayeg, Raymond, Jr. ... **Boston, MA**
Sayeg, Thomas J. ... **Bend, OR**
Sayegh, Andrew W. ... Yonkers, NY
Sayegh, Joseph ... Atlantic City, NJ
Sayegh, Joseph S. ... Yonkers, NY
Sayegh, Miriam H. ... Wilton, CT
Sayegh, Nader J. ... Scarsdale, NY
Sayegh & Sayegh ... Yonkers, NY
Sayegh, William ... San Dimas, CA
Sayegh, William G. ... Carmel, NY
Sayen, Joanne Vails ... Cypress, CA
Sayen, Margaret Wise ... Richland, MI
Sayenga, Jill C.
United States Court Of Appeals District Of Columbia Circuit, GV
Sayer, Andrew Fenning ... Los Angeles, CA
Sayer, Darell ... Portsmouth, VA
Sayer, Floyd ... Los Angeles, CA
Sayer, Floyd, Professional Corporationn
Los Angeles, CA
Sayer, H. Bartlett, Jr. ... San Diego, CA
Sayer, James A., Jr. ... Salem, NH
Sayer, James L. ... Fort Myers, FL
Sayer, Jeri L. ... Clark, NJ
Sayer, John W. ... Minneapolis, MN
Sayer, Michael Easton ... Irvine, CA
Sayer, Michelle M. ... **Los Angeles, CA**
Sayer, Regan & Thayer ... **Newport, RI**
Sayer, Richard N. ... **Newport, RI**
Sayer, Ron L. ... Salem, OR
Sayer, Thomas P., Jr. ... San Diego, CA
Sayers, Daniel G. ... Mobile, AL
Sayers, Donald D. ... **Salisbury, NC**
Sayers, Gretchen G. ... Kansas City, MO
Sayers, Michael M. ... **St. Louis, MO**
Sayers, Randall W. ... **St. Paul, MN**
Sayers, Rebeca A. ... Lutz, FL
Ballwin, MO
Sayers, Richard R. ... **Roanoke, VA**
Sayers, Robert H. ... Scranton, PA
Sayers, Sharon Kelly ... **Rochester, NY**
Sayers, Stephen M. ... **McLean, VA**
Sayers, Steven M. ... Woods Hole, MA
Sayers, Tonya L. ... **Hilton Head Island, SC**
Sayers, William D. ... Livingston, NJ
Sayers, William J. ... **Santa Monica, CA**
Sayes, James Melton ... **Little Rock, AR**
Sayet, Bart A. ... **Norwich, CT**
Sayet and Seder ... **Norwich, CT**
Sayetta, Howard E. ... Syosset, NY
Sayetta, Stacey ... **New York, NY**
Sayfie, Justin J. ... Miami, FL
Sayfie, Nicole S. ... **Miami, FL**
Sayfie, Robert J. ... **Grand Rapids, MI**
Sayid, Robin S. ... Bloomfield, NJ
Saykanic, John V. ... Clifton, NJ
Sayko, Andrew F., Jr. ... Summit, NJ
Sayko, Tami Davis ... College Station, TX
Sayle & Dennis ... Memphis, TN
Sayle, Harry E., III ... Memphis, TN
Sayle, Julia Robbins ... Memphis, TN
Sayle, Raymond H. ... Memphis, TN
Sayle & Sayle ... Memphis, TN
Sayler, Charles Keith ... **Topeka, KS**
Sayler, John Liston ... Cleveland, OH
Sayler, Lee B. ... Jupiter, FL
Sayler, Linda C. ... San Francisco, CA
Sayler, Michael M. ... Haverhill, MA
Sayler, Richard H. ... **Cleveland, OH**
Sayler, Robert N. ... **Washington, DC**
Sayler, Scott W. ... **Kansas City, MO**
Sayler, Steven C. ... **La Jolla, CA**
Sayles, Cathy A. ... Liberty, MO
Sayles, Crystal D. ... **Washington, DC**
Sayles, Elda G., (Mrs.) ... Kensington, CA
Sayles & Evans ... **Elmira, NY**
Sayles, Judith M. ... **Syracuse, NY**
Sayles, Julia L. ... Washington, DC
Sayles & Lidji, A Professional Corporation
Dallas, TX
Sayles, Michael J. ... **Cincinnati, OH**
Sayles, Richard A. ... **Dallas, TX**
Saylin, Brian G. ... **Orange, CA**
Saylin, Gregory M. ... **Costa Mesa, CA**
Saylor, Alice C. ... Washington, DC
Saylor, Andrew L. ... **Lancaster, PA**
Saylor, Bruce A. ... **Leesburg, FL**
Saylor, C. Murray, Jr. ... **Atlanta, GA**
Saylor, Charles H. ... **Sunbury, PA**
Saylor, Connie B. ... **Dallas, TX**
Saylor, Daniel S. ... **Detroit, MI**
Saylor, David J. ... **Washington, DC**
Saylor, F. Dennis, IV ... **Boston, MA**
Saylor, George V., III ... Grand Rapids, MI
Manistee, MI
Saylor, Ginevra M. ... Harrisburg, PA
Saylor, Jacquelyn Harmon ... **Atlanta, GA**
Saylor, Jett Gray ... **Baton Rouge, LA**
Saylor, John F. ... Stratford, CT
Saylor, John M. ... Troy, MI
Saylor, Kent ... Sabetha, KS
Saylor, Larry J. ... **Detroit, MI**
Saylor Law Firm, The, LLP ... **Atlanta, GA**
Saylor, Lyle R. ... Columbus, OH
Saylor, M. Daniel ... Claremont, CA
Saylor, Marsha M. ... Cambridge, MA
Saylor, Pamela H. ... Leesburg, FL
Saylor, Robert L. ... West Palm Beach, FL
Saylor, Ronald L. ... Williamsburg, IA
Saylor, Susan M. ... Los Angeles, CA
Saylor, Thomas G. ... Harrisburg, PA
Saylor, Timothy B. ... Canton, OH
Saymon, Bertram B. ... Leicester, MA
Sayner, Peter Bowne ... La Crosse, WI
Sayour, Joy ... **New York, NY**
Sayovitz, Sidney A. ... **Morristown, NJ**
Saypoff, Jess M. ... New York, NY
Saypol, Bruce P. ... Rockville, MD
Saypol, Natasha ... **Denver, CO**
Sayre, C. Franklin ... **Houston, TX**
Sayre, C. Michael ... Denver, CO
Sayre, Candice E. ... **Houston, TX**
Sayre, Charles L. ... Seattle, WA
Sayre, Claudia G. ... Washington, DC
Sayre, David A. ... Washington, DC
Sayre, David L. ... Cherokee, IA
Sayre, Eugene G. ... **Little Rock, AR**
Sayre, Federico Castelan ... **Los Angeles, CA**
Sayre, Federico Castelan
Newport Beach, CA
Sayre, Federico Castelan ... **Santa Ana, CA**
Sayre, Floyd M., III ... **Beckley, WV**
Sayre, George E. ... San Francisco, CA
Sayre, Greg C. ... Rochester, NY
Sayre, Grover C., III ... **Minneapolis, MN**
Sayre, Harry R. ... Trinidad, CO
Sayre, James L. ... Des Moines, IA
Sayre, James L., P.C. ... Des Moines, IA
Sayre, Jeffrey M. ... **Seattle, WA**
Sayre, Jeremy R. ... **Cleveland, OH**
Sayre, Jill Poses ... General Accounting Office, Office of the General Counsel, GV
Sayre, John D. ... **Cleveland, OH**
Sayre, John M. ... **Denver, CO**
Sayre, John M. ... Franklin, IN
Sayre, John M., III ... **Richmond, IN**
Sayre, Julian R. ... Tucson, AZ
Sayre, Karen L. ... **Spokane, WA**
Sayre Law Offices ... **Seattle, WA**
Sayre, Mark D. ... **Los Angeles, CA**
Sayre, Matt ... **Seattle, WA**
Sayre, Maurice M. ... **Cleveland, OH**
Sayre, Meredith M. ... **Hagåtña, GU**
Sayre, Michael B. ... **San Diego, CA**
Sayre, Patricia M. ... San Diego, CA
Sayre, Patricia M., P.C. ... San Diego, CA
Sayre, Peter B. ... Newark, NJ
Sayre, Richard L. ... **Spokane, WA**
Sayre, Robert B. ... Beckley, WV
Sayre, Robert D. ... **Philadelphia, PA**
Sayre, Robert J. ... **Lexington, MA**
Sayre, Robert M. ... Washington, DC
Sayre, Robert Q., Jr. ... **Charleston, WV**
Sayre, Robert W. ... **Philadelphia, PA**
Sayre, Russell S. ... **Cincinnati, OH**
Sayre & Sayre, P.S. ... **Spokane, WA**
Sayre, Scott E. ... **Phoenix, AZ**
Sayre, Stephen D. ... **Chicago, IL**
Sayre, Thomas H. ... Front Royal, VA
Sayre, Truman, Jr. ... Charleston, WV
Sayre Wittgraf & Meloy ... Cherokee, IA
Saytanides, Anthony M. ... New York, NY
Sayvetz, Ann ... Oak Brook, IL
Sayward, David W. ... **Salem, NH**
Sayward, Suzanne R. ... Westwood, MA
Saywell, John ... Burlington, VT
Sayyed, Bilal ... **Washington, DC**
Sazama, Gerald F. ... Chippewa Falls, WI
Sazant, Larry S., P.A. ... Miami, FL
Sazdanoff, Catherine A. ... North Chicago, IL
Sazdanoff, Michael L. ... Chicago, IL
Sazer, Gary N. ... Great Neck, NY
Sazzman, Ellen J. ... Treasury Department, Office of Thrift Supervision, GV
Sbandi, Francis T. ... Media, PA
Sbanotto, Dennis ... **Fort Smith, AR**
Sbanotto, Dennis, P.C. ... **Fort Smith, AR**
Sbar, Jonathan B. ... **Tampa, FL**
Sbar, Jonathan I. ... Menominee, MI
Sbar, Marian H. ... **Tampa, FL**
Sbar, Pamela S. ... **Denver, CO**
Sbar, Phillip E. ... Clementon, NJ
Philadelphia, PA
Sbar, Tamlyn ... **Tampa, FL**
Sbaratta, Philip W. ... **New York, NY**
Sbaratta, Richard M. ... **Atlanta, GA**
Sbaratta, Rosemarie ... Boston, MA
Sbaratta, Rosemarie, P.C., Law Offices of
Boston, MA
Sbarbaro, Jan B. ... Englewood, CO
Sbarbaro, John A. ... **Denver, CO**
Sbarbaro, John L., III ... West Chester, PA
Sbarbaro, Kelley L. ... **Los Angeles, CA**
Sbarbaro, Philip L. ... **Washington, DC**
Sbarbati, J. V. ... Niagara Falls, NY
Sbardellati, Robert G. ... **San Diego, CA**
Sbarge, Arnold ... West Hartford, CT
Sbarra, Anthony J., Jr. ... Easton, MA
Sbarra, Kristin A. ... **Washington, DC**
Boston, MA
Sbertoli, Dennis M. ... La Grange Park, IL
Sbertoli, Douglas L. ... **Richmond, VA**
Sbertoli, Thomas L. ... Libertyville, IL
Sbiroli, Joseph J. ... Flushing, NY
Sblendorio, Mark ... **Roseland, NJ**
Sblendorio, Sblend A. ... San Jose, CA
Sbrana, Lisa B. ... Bronx, NY
Sbrega, Dennis C. ... **Portland, ME**
Sbriglio, Karen E. ... Stratford, CT
Sbrocchi, Domenic P. ... Bangor, PA
Stroudsburg, PA
Sbrogna, Ralph F. ... **Worcester, MA**
Sbrollini, Jay P. ... Yorktown Heights, NY
Scacchetti, David J. ... Cincinnati, OH
Scacchetti, Marcia G. ... Cincinnati, OH
Scacchitti, Edmund J. ... **Scranton, PA**
Scaccia, Angelo M. ... Boston, MA
Scaccia, Dante M. ... Syracuse, NY
Scaccia, Donna M. ... **Rochester, NY**
Scaccia, John J. ... Dayton, OH
Scaccia, Nicholas C. ... Portland, ME
Scaccia, Tiziana M. ... **New Canaan, CT**
Scadden, Hamilton & Ryan ... **Oakland, CA**
San Francisco, CA
Scadden, James G. ... **San Francisco, CA**
Scadina, Mark R. ... San Jose, CA
Scadron, S. Michael ... Department of Justice, Civil Division, GV
Scadron, Terri Jane ... Department of Justice, Civil Division, GV
Scaduto, Dana Stevens ... **Harrisburg, PA**
Scaduto, James A. ... New York, NY
Scaduto, John ... **Garden City, NY**
Scaduto, Joseph ... Nutley, NJ
Scaduto, Karen Marie ... Bellmore, NY
Scaduto, Patricia M. ... **Midland, MI**
Scafe, Jennifer L. ... **San Francisco, CA**
Scafetta, Joseph, Jr. ... **Arlington, VA**
Scaff, Kenneth N., Jr. ... Jasper, FL
Scaffidi, John M. ... Milwaukee, WI
Scaffidi, Philip ... **Buffalo, NY**
Scaffidi, Roy F. ... New York, NY
Scafide, John A., Jr. ... Bay St. Louis, MS
Scafidi, Nicholas J. ... Philadelphia, PA
Scafidi, Stephen A. ... Leesburg, VA
Scafuri, Allison L. ... Franklin, MI
Scafuri, Frank A. ... La Grange, IL
Scafuri, Robert J. ... Troy, MI
Scafuro, Albert O. ... Allendale, NJ
Scafuro and Gianni, A Professional Corporation
Allendale, NJ
Scaggs, David J. ... **Philadelphia, PA**
Scaggs, Howard I., Jr. ... Timonium, MD
Scaggs, James L. ... Ocala, FL
Scaggs, John H. ... Madill, OK
Scaggs, Monte L. ... Colorado Springs, CO
Scaggs, R. Judson, Jr. ... **Wilmington, DE**
Scaglione, Cynthia M. ... Dallas, TX
Scaglione, David D. ... Willsboro, NY
Scaglione, Gregory C. ... **Omaha, NE**
Scaglione, Michael J. ... **Miami, FL**
Scaglione, Peter, Jr. ... Tampa, FL
Scaglione, Vincent, Jr. ... **Pittsburgh, PA**
Scagluso, Frank S. ... Smithtown, NY
Scagnelli, Janet L. ... **Philadelphia, PA**
Scagnelli, John M. ... Newark, NJ
Scagnetti, Carole M. ... San Francisco, CA
Scahill, James N. ... Indianapolis, IN
Scahill, John P. ... Cincinnati, OH
Scahill, Michael F. ... **Omaha, NE**
Scaia, Joan M. ... Milwaukee, WI
Scaife, William M., Jr. ... Fredericksburg, VA
Scaife, William O., Jr. ... Jacksonville, FL
Scal, Carol Lee Tepf ... Hempstead, NY
Scala, Gerald P. ... West Orange, NJ
Scala, Hugo R. ... Vero Beach, FL
Scala, Hugo R., Jr. ... **Chicago, IL**
Scala, James R. ... Essex, CT
Scala, Jerry A. ... Hackensack, NJ
Scala, M. Katherine ... Detroit, MI
Scala, Michael A. ... Warren, OH
Scala, Vincent David ... New York, NY
Scalabrini, Gary Edward
Los Angeles, CA
Scalard, Joanne M. ... **New York, NY**
Scaldaferri, Ezio ... **New York, NY**
Scaldara, John A. ... Baltimore, MD
Scaldara & Potler LLP ... Baltimore, MD
Scalera, Ciro A. ... San Francisco, CA
Scalera, David C. ... Florham Park, NJ
Scalera, Dominic John "Jack", III
West Palm Beach, FL
Scalera, Frank M. ... **Uniondale, NY**
Scalera, Mary Ellen ... **Livingston, NJ**
Scalera, Nicholas ... Florham Park, NJ
Scalera, Ralph F. ... **Pittsburgh, PA**
Scales, Ann C. ... Albuquerque, NM
Scales, Anne H. ... Los Angeles, CA
Scales, Archibald H., II ... Winston-Salem, NC
Scales, Archibald H., III
Winston-Salem, NC
Scales, Brenda Claudette
Charlotte Amalie, St. Thomas, VI
Scales, C. Ray, Jr. ... Jackson, MS
Scales, Camille G. ... Huntsville, AL
Scales, Cinda L. ... Martinsburg, WV
Scales, Clarence R. ... Jackson, MS
Scales, Donald J. ... **Winston-Salem, NC**
Scales, Donald L. ... Astoria, OR
Scales, E. Rhusha, (Mr.) ... Detroit, MI
Scales, Earl L. ... Weirsdale, FL
Scales, Edwin A., III ... Lakeland, FL
Scales, Gary V. ... Phoenix, AZ
Scales, James F. ... **Grand Rapids, MI**
Scales, John B. ... Boonville, IN
Scales, John K.
Agency for International Development, Office of the General Counsel, GV
Scales, John N. ... Greensburg, PA
Scales, Juliette W. ... Atlanta, GA
Scales, Kemp C. ... Titusville, PA
Scales, Leigh S. ... **Jacksonville, FL**
Scales, Michael L. ... **Martinsburg, WV**
Scales and Murray ... Greensburg, PA
Scales, Patricia G. ... **Winston-Salem, NC**
Scales, Robert P. ... Chicago, IL
Scales, Rolland T. ... Dallas, TX
Scales, Symone B. ... Seattle, WA
Scales, William D. ... Muskogee, OK
Scales, Wissner & Krantz ... Boonville, IN
Scalese, Anthony V. ... **Fort Lauderdale, FL**
Scalesse, Charles P. ... Branford, CT
Scaletta, Anthony J. ... **Orlando, FL**
Scaletta, Melissa S. ... **Orlando, FL**
Scaletta, Phillip J., Jr. ... Lafayette, IN
Scaletta, Phillip R., III ... **Indianapolis, IN**
Scaletty, Richard P. ... Independence, MO
Scalf, Lawrence G. ... Dallas, TX
Scalf & O'Halloran ... Portland, OR
Scalf, William D. ... Portland, OR
Scali, Christian J. ... **Los Angeles, CA**
Scali, Joseph G. ... **Middletown, NY**
Scali, Lois J. ... **Los Angeles, CA**
Scalia, Ann Marie ... Newark, NJ
Scalia, Antonin
Supreme Court Of The United States, GV
Scalia, Eugene ... **Washington, DC**
Scalia, John F. ... **San Francisco, CA**
Scalia, Joseph A., II ... Baltimore, MD
Scalia, Joseph W., Law Offices of
Gold River, CA
Scalia, Joseph W., Law Offices of
Sacramento, CA
Scalia, William C. ... Randolph, NJ
Scalici, Matt Paul ... Birmingham, AL
Scalione, Robert S. ... **Syracuse, NY**
Scalise, Amy C. ... **Chicago, IL**
Scalise, Carl G. ... Herkimer, NY
Scalise, Charles L. ... **Orlando, FL**
Scalise, David G. ... San Francisco, CA
Scalise, Deborah A. ... New York, NY
Scalise, Domenic J. ... North Andover, MA
Scalise, Eugene, Jr. ... Portland, CT
Scalise, Eugene, Jr., P.C. ... Portland, CT
Scalise, James J., (P.C.) ... New Britain, CT
Scalise, Joseph M. ... **Fairfield, CA**
Napa, CA
Scalise, Joseph R. ... New Britain, CT
Scalise, Lawrence F. ... **Des Moines, IA**
Scalise, Leah F. ... Birmingham, AL
Scalise, Marian Williams ... **Columbia, SC**
Myrtle Beach, SC
Scalise, Mark N. ... Davidson, NC
Scalise, Michael F. ... **Buffalo, NY**
Scalise, Nancy M. ... Pittsburgh, PA
Scalise, Richard C. ... Vienna, VA
Scalise, Richard C., & Associates
Vienna, VA
Scalise, Richard K. ... Waltham, MA
Scalise, Robert A. ... New Britain, CT
Scalise, Robert A. ... New Britain, CT
Scalise-Qubrasi, Celeste E. ... San Antonio, TX
Scalisi, James M. ... Brooklyn, NY
Scalisi, Jenifer Marie ... Buffalo, NY
Scalisi, Peter W. ... **Riverside, CA**
Scaliti, John J. ... Hackensack, NJ

Scall, Lester N. .... Treasury Department, Office of the Comptroller of the Currency, GV
Scallan, C. Catherine .... New York, NY
Scallan, Kathleen O. .... Chicago, IL
Scallan, Stephen D. .... Chicago, IL
Scallen, Eileen A. .... San Francisco, CA
Scallen, Julie A. .... Boston, MA
Scallen, Michael D. .... Grosse Pointe Park, MI
Scallen, Michael D., P.C. Grosse Pointe Park, MI
Scallen, Stephen B. .... Minneapolis, MN
Scallen, Thomas K. .... Minneapolis, MN
Scallen, Thomas P. .... Detroit, MI
Scallen, Timothy J. .... Minneapolis, MN
Scallet, Edward A. .... Washington, DC
Scallet, Leslie J. .... Washington, DC
Scalley, Ford G. .... Salt Lake City, UT
Scalley & Reading, A Professional Corporation .... Salt Lake City, UT
Scallion, James R. .... Hazleton, PA
Scallon, Edwin T. .... Taunton, MA
Scallon, Garth L. .... Carmichael, CA
Scallon, Gregory E. .... Madison, WI
Scallon, Hugh J. .... Dana Point, CA
Scallon, Mark W. .... Ellendale, ND
Scally, Erin L. .... Department of Justice, Executive Office for Immigration Review, GV
Scally, John J., Jr. .... Newark, NJ
Scally, Lawrence D. .... Upperco, MD
Scally, Scally and McMahon, P.A. Upperco, MD
Scalo, Joseph F. .... Orlando, FL
Scalo, Richard S. .... Bridgeport, CT
Scalone, Laurie J. .... San Diego, CA
Scalora, Anthony J. .... Sacramento, CA
Scalora, Nella M. .... New York, NY
Scalpone, Lisa R. .... Chicago, IL
Scalvino, Pauline C. .... Malvern, PA
Scalza, Debra B. .... New York, NY
Scalzi, John, Jr. .... Melville, NY
Scalzo, Cherry and Geudtner .... Toledo, OH
Scalzo, Christine R. .... Utica, NY
Scalzo, John R. .... Omaha, NE
Scalzo, Joseph R., Jr. .... Toledo, OH
Scalzo, Michael J. .... Oak Brook, IL
Scalzo, Michael S. .... Toledo, OH
Scalzo, Peter A. .... Bethel, CT
Waterbury, CT
Scalzo, Susan M. .... Chicago, IL
Scalzo, Victoria .... New York, NY
Scamardella, Robert J. .... Staten Island, NY
Scamardi, Joseph A. .... Houston, TX
Scambia, Diego .... New York, NY
Scamby, James T. .... Boston, MA
Scamell, Vincent A., Jr. .... Scranton, PA
Scaminaci, Andrés .... New York, NY
Scammel, H. Glenn House of Representatives, Committee Legal Personnel, GV
Scammon, Denise A. .... Phoenix, AZ
Scammon, Kristen S. .... Washington, DC
Scammons, Linda A. .... Springfield, MA
Scampini, Herman P., Jr. San Francisco, CA
Scampini, Lois J. .... San Mateo, CA
Scampini, Mortara & Harris San Francisco, CA
Scancarella, Dana J. .... Florham Park, NJ
Scancarella, Joseph F. .... Paterson, NJ
Scancarelli, Adrienne Hofmann White Plains, NY
Scancarelli, Eugene L. .... Mount Vernon, NY
Scancarelli, Janine L. .... Los Angeles, CA
San Francisco, CA
Scancarelli, Lawrence M. San Francisco, CA
Scandaglia, Gregory J. .... Chicago, IL
Scandariato, Peter A. .... North Bergen, NJ
Scandariato, Peter J. .... Englewood Cliffs, NJ
Scandirito, James A. .... Mount Clemens, MI
Scandone, Robert .... Philadelphia, PA
Scandura, Steven P. .... Beverly Hills, CA
Scandurra, Robert A. .... Barnstable, MA
Scandurro, Dewey M. .... New Orleans, LA
Scandurro, Dominick, Jr. .... Belle Chasse, LA
Scandurro & Layrisson, L.L.C.
Belle Chasse, LA
New Orleans, LA
Ponchatoula, LA
Scandurro, Stephen O. .... New Orleans, LA
Scandurro, Timothy D. .... New Orleans, LA
Scandy, Kelly Carbetta .... Cincinnati, OH
Scanelli, John A. .... Norfolk, VA
Scanes, Michael L. .... Waco, TX
Scanga, David M. .... Grand Junction, CO
Scanga, Frank A. .... New York, NY
Scangarella, Feeney & Dixon Pompton Plains, NJ
Scangarella, Frank .... Pompton Plains, NJ
Scaniffe, Shelli Dawn Department of Education, Office of the General Counsel, GV
Scanio, Frank J., III .... Refugio, TX
Scanio, Frank J., Jr. .... Refugio, TX
Scanio, Michael .... San Marcos, TX
Scanio, Salvatore .... Washington, DC
Scanio & Scanio, A Professional Corporation San Marcos, TX
Scanio, Stephen E. .... Refugio, TX
Scanio, Teer, Cox & Steele .... Refugio, TX
Scanio, Vincent J., Jr. .... San Marcos, TX
Scanlan, Alfred L., Jr. .... Baltimore, MD
Scanlan, Buckle & Young, P.C. Austin, TX
Scanlan, Charles F., and John J. Schiffner Spokane, WA
Scanlan, Christopher J. .... Dallas, TX
Scanlan, Edmund J. .... Chicago, IL
Scanlan, Edmund J., Ltd., Law Offices of Chicago, IL
Springfield, IL
Wheaton, IL
Scanlan, Elizabeth Baker .... Charlotte, NC
Scanlan, Elizabeth J. .... Miami, FL
Scanlan, Emmett A., Jr. .... Kansas City, MO
Scanlan, Francis A. .... Bryn Mawr, PA
Scanlan, Francis X. .... Bryn Mawr, PA
Scanlan, Genevieve M. .... Chicago, IL
Scanlan, James E. .... Boise, ID
Scanlan, James P. .... Washington, DC
Scanlan, Janice .... Bakersfield, CA
Scanlan, Jerome N. Equal Employment Opportunity Commission, Office of the General Counsel, GV
Scanlan, John J. .... Hinckley, MN
Scanlan, John M. .... Austin, TX
Austin, TX
Scanlan, Joseph A., Jr. .... San Jose, CA
Scanlan, Kathleen R. .... San Francisco, CA
Scanlan, Kevin J. .... Boise, ID
Scanlan, Kevin P. .... New York, NY
Scanlan, Lisa Federal Communications Commission, Mass Media Bureau, GV
Scanlan, M. Kay .... Baltimore, MD
Scanlan, Marilyn K. .... Houston, TX
Scanlan, Mary Ellen .... Denver, CO
Scanlan, Melissa A. .... Seattle, WA
Scanlan, Paul E. .... Harrisburg, PA
Scanlan, Richard S. .... White Plains, NY
Scanlan, Robert I. .... Tallahassee, FL
Scanlan, Robert J. .... Tampa, FL
Scanlan, Rosen & Shar, LLC Baltimore, MD
Scanlan and Scanlan, A Professional Corporation .... Bryn Mawr, PA
Scanlan, Sharon A. .... White Plains, NY
Scanlan, Sheila M. .... Herndon, VA
Scanlan, Suzanne O'N. .... Brooklyn, NY
Scanlan, Terence J. .... Seattle, WA
Scanlan, Thomas C. .... Fairfax, VA
Scanlan, William E. .... Kansas City, MO
Scanlan, William, Jr. .... San Antonio, TX
Scanlin, Elizabeth .... New York, NY
Scanlin, Steven F. .... Boise, ID
Scanlin, William R. .... Bethesda, MD
Scanlon, Alice Kelley .... Rockville, MD
Scanlon, Andrew J. .... Providence, RI
Scanlon, Anthony D. .... Media, PA
Springfield, PA
Scanlon, Brian J. .... Union, NJ
Scanlon, Charles R. .... North Little Rock, AR
Scanlon, Christopher .... New York, NY
Scanlon, Christopher G. .... Indianapolis, IN
Scanlon & Co., L.P.A. .... Akron, OH
Cleveland, OH
Scanlon, Cornelius J. .... Hartford, CT
Scanlon, Cynthia H. .... Sacramento, CA
Scanlon, D. Justine .... Bennington, VT
Scanlon & Danaher .... Endicott, NY
Scanlon, Daniel, Jr. .... Watertown, NY
Scanlon, David W. .... Litchfield Park, AZ
Scanlon, Eileen M. .... New York, NY
Scanlon, Elaine M. .... Shelton, CT
Scanlon, Elizabeth A. .... Montvale, NJ
Scanlon, Francis J. .... Nashville, TN
Scanlon & Gearinger Co., L.P.A. Akron, OH
Scanlon, Gregory M. .... San Francisco, CA
Scanlon, Howley, Scanlon & Doherty Scranton, PA
Scanlon, Jack M. .... Helena, MT
Scanlon, James .... Yuba City, CA
Scanlon, James A. .... Waltham, MA
Scanlon, James E. .... Chicago, IL
Scanlon, James J. .... Boston, MA
Scanlon, James M. .... Chicago, IL
Scanlon, James M. .... Scranton, PA
Scanlon, James W. .... Scranton, PA
Scanlon, Jerome W., Jr. .... San Antonio, TX
Scanlon, John B. .... Washington, DC
Scanlon, John C. .... Cincinnati, OH
Scanlon, John J., III .... St. Paul, MN
Scanlon, John M. .... Binghamton, NY
Scanlon, John P. .... Chicago, IL
Scanlon, John R. .... New Haven, CT
Scanlon, John T. .... Akron, OH
Scanlon, John W. .... Hayward, CA
Scanlon, Joseph .... Oakland, CA
Scanlon, Karen D. .... Indianapolis, IN
Scanlon, Katherine A. .... Hartford, CT
Scanlon, Kathleen M. .... Haworth, NJ
Scanlon, Kathryn R. .... Maitland, FL
Scanlon, Kerry Alan .... Washington, DC
Scanlon, Kevin P. .... Boston, MA
Scanlon, Laura L. .... New York, NY
Scanlon, Laura M. .... Newtown Square, PA
Scanlon, Lawrence J. .... Boca Raton, FL
Akron, OH
Scanlon, Lawrence J., P.A. Boca Raton, FL
West Palm Beach, FL
Scanlon, Lawrence R., III .... Chicago, IL
Scanlon, Lewis and Williamson East Stroudsburg, PA
Scanlon, Lorna S. .... Toms River, NJ
Scanlon, Mary A. .... McKinney, TX
Scanlon, Mary Gay .... Philadelphia, PA
Scanlon, Mary Jane .... South Euclid, OH
Scanlon, Maura E. .... Akron, OH
Scanlon, Michael C. .... Akron, OH
Scanlon, Michael C., Jr. San Francisco, CA
Scanlon, Michael J. .... Washington, DC
Scanlon, Michael L. .... Dallas, TX
Scanlon, Michael T. .... Sarasota, FL
Scanlon, Michael T. .... Indianapolis, IN
Scanlon, Nancy E. .... New York, NY
Scanlon, Pat H. .... Jackson, MS
Scanlon, Patricia M. .... Westlake, OH
Scanlon, Patrick .... Dover, DE
Scanlon, Patrick M. .... Washington, DC
Scanlon, Patrick R. .... Portland, ME
Scanlon, Paul D. .... Manassas, VA
Scanlon, Peter J. .... Erie, PA
Scanlon, Raymond C. .... Elmhurst, NY
Scanlon, Robert A. .... Portland, OR
Scanlon, Robert C. .... Spokane, WA
Scanlon, Robert P. .... Rockville, MD
Scanlon, Sessums, Parker & Dallas, P.L.L.C. Jackson, MS
Scanlon, Sheila Weis .... Pittsburgh, PA
Scanlon, Stephen D. .... Cleveland, OH
Scanlon, Susan J. .... Pittsford, NY
Scanlon, Tara A. .... Washington, DC
Scanlon, Terence E. .... Akron, OH
Scanlon, Thomas D. .... Orlando, FL
Scanlon, Thomas J. .... Cleveland, OH
Scanlon, Thomas M. .... Indianapolis, IN
Scanlon, Timothy F. .... Akron, OH
Scanlon, Timothy G. .... Bakersfield, CA
Scanlon, Walter Michael .... Lawrence, MA
Scanlon, William J. .... Westfield, MA
Scanlon, William J. .... Endicott, NY
Scanlon, William J. .... Madison, WI
Scanlon-Carey, Mary .... Springfield, MA
Scann, Susan Williams .... Las Vegas, NV
Scanna, Karen .... New York, NY
Scannapieco, John M. .... Nashville, TN
Scannapieco, Michael A. .... Cherry Hill, NJ
Scannell, Courtney L. .... Largo, MD
Scannell, David G. .... New Canaan, CT
Scannell, Francis J. .... Boston, MA
Scannell, J. Gordon, Jr. .... Auburn, ME
Scannell, Jeremiah J. .... Coos Bay, OR
Scannell, Jerry .... Grants Pass, OR
Scannell, Joan P. .... Morristown, NJ
Scannell, Joanna E. .... Dedham, MA
Scannell, John C. .... Rahway, NJ
Scannell, John W. .... New York, NY
Scannell, Katherine P. .... St. Louis, MO
Scannell, Merrill H. .... Mineola, NY
Scannell, Paul W. .... New Bedford, MA
Scannell, Raymond F. .... Richmond, VA
Scannell, Robert E. .... New York, NY
Scannell, Scarlett A. .... Worcester, MA
Scannell, Susannah P. .... Medford, MA
Scannell, Terry .... Beaverton, OR
Scannell, Theresa M. .... Dubuque, IA
Scannell, Thomas J. .... Worcester, MA
Scannell, Timothy C. .... Manchester, NH
Scannell, William E. .... Plymouth, MA
Scannell, William F. .... Worcester, MA
Scannell, William F., (Ltd.) .... Blue Island, IL
Scannell, William R. .... Lanham, MD
Scannicchio, Regina A. .... Chicago, IL
Scano, Paul F. .... Staten Island, NY
Scantalides, Peter G. .... Cambridge, MA
Scantlebury, Joseph .... Department of Labor, Office of the Solicitor, GV
Scantlebury, Phillip A. .... Bluefield, WV
Scantling, James G. .... Hartford, CT
Boston, MA
Scaparotti, Linda M., Law Offices of
Oakland, CA
San Francisco, CA
Scapellati, Daniel P. .... Hartford, CT
Scapellato, James E. .... Atlanta, GA
Scapelliti, Stephen .... Farmington Hills, MI
Scaperlanda, Michael A. .... Norman, OK
Scapicchio, Frank A. .... Long Island City, NY
Scapicchio, Paul J. .... Boston, MA
Scapicchio, Rosemary C. .... Boston, MA
Scapoli, Thomas .... Bedford, NY
Scappaticci, Nancy J. .... River Edge, NJ
Scappini, Richard J. .... Waterbury, CT
Scarafile, Michael C. .... Charleston, SC
Scarafone, Albert J., Jr. Plymouth Meeting, PA
Scaraggi, Michael T. .... Roseland, NJ
Scaraglino, Pietrina .... New York, NY
Scaramastra, Donald B. .... Seattle, WA
Scaramella, Adam .... Philadelphia, PA
Scaramella, Carlo .... Cherry Hill, NJ
Scaramella & Hoofnagle .... Cherry Hill, NJ
Scaramella, Mario .... Mount Laurel, NJ
Scaramella, Michael S. .... Cherry Hill, NJ
Scaramozza, James M. .... Wethersfield, CT
Scarano, Damon .... Boston, MA
Scarano, Linda C. .... Boston, MA
Scarano, R. Michael, Jr. .... San Diego, CA
Scarano, Richard F. .... New Bedford, MA
Scarano, Victor R. .... Houston, TX
Scarantino, James R. .... Albuquerque, NM
Scarantino, Nicholas J. .... Binghamton, NY
Scarbary, Otis L. .... Macon, GA
Scarberry, Mark Stephen .... Malibu, CA
Scarboro, Edward W., Jr. .... Raleigh, NC
Scarboro, James E. .... Denver, CO
Scarborough, Amy .... Bedford, MA
Scarborough, Boyd .... Portsmouth, VA
Scarborough, Brad R. .... Houston, TX
Scarborough, C. Joseph .... Pensacola, FL
Scarborough, C. Joseph, P.A. .... Pensacola, FL
Scarborough, Charles .... Abilene, TX
Scarborough, Charles Wylie Washington, DC
Scarborough, Claude M., Jr. Columbia, SC
Scarborough, Davis .... Abilene, TX
Scarborough, Dewitt Talmadge, III Pinehurst, NC
Scarborough, Frank .... Abilene, TX
Scarborough, Homer M., Jr. .... Macon, GA
Scarborough, Jane L. .... Boston, MA
Scarborough, John L. .... Elkton, MD
Scarborough, John M. .... Forest Hill, MD
Scarborough, Joseph T., Jr. .... Tallassee, AL
Scarborough, J.R. .... Chattanooga, TN
Scarborough, June D. .... Philadelphia, PA
Scarborough, Karen .... Fairfax, VA
Scarborough, Keith A. .... United States Senate, Senatorial Assistants, GV
Scarborough, Kenneth L. .... Honolulu, HI
Scarborough, Kirby .... Montpelier, VT
Scarborough, Lawrence G. .... Phoenix, AZ
Scarborough, Mark A. .... Meridian, MS
Scarborough, Matthew C. .... Brooksville, FL
Tampa, FL
Scarborough, Maxine .... North, SC
Scarborough, Mikell R. .... Charleston, SC
Scarborough, Paul .... Novato, CA
Scarborough, Rebecca A. .... Shrewsbury, NJ
Scarborough, Robert H. .... New York, NY
Scarborough, Ryan Thomas .... Honolulu, HI
Scarborough, Stephen R. .... New York, NY
Scarborough, Susan J. .... St. Paul, MN
Scarborough, Tarpley & Fouts, P.C. Abilene, TX
Scarborough, Terry .... Austin, TX
Scarborough, Theodore R. .... Chicago, IL
Scarborough, Tommy R. .... Dothan, AL
Scarborough, Truman G., Jr. .... Titusville, FL
Scarborough, Walter E. .... Riverside, CA
Scarborough, William E., Jr. .... Portland, OR
Scarborough, William G. .... Philadelphia, PA
Scarbrough, James E. .... Concord, NC
Scarbrough, James E. .... Cleveland, OH
Scarbrough, Jerry .... Killeen, TX
Scarbrough, Wayne E. .... Bronx, NY
Scarce, Max H. .... Pauls Valley, OK
Scarce, Stephen E. .... Richmond, VA
Scarcella, Anthony J. .... New York, NY
White Plains, NY
Scarcella, Anthony J., & Associates, P.C. New York, NY
White Plains, NY
Scarcella, Louis A. .... Garden City, NY
Scarcella, Russell B. .... Hoboken, NJ
New York, NY
Scarcelli, Susan K. S. .... Tampa, FL
Scarcello, Mark F. .... Buffalo, NY
Scarcello, Paul J., Jr. .... Southfield, MI
Scarcliff, Katherine J. .... Spokane, WA
Scardato, Michael A. .... Charleston, SC
Scardigno, Luke .... Kew Gardens, NY
Scardilli, Frank J. .... New York, NY
Scardino, Donald .... Kew Gardens, NY
Scardino, Kimberly Anne .... Rye Brook, NY
Scardino, Paula .... New York, NY
Scardino, P. J. .... Fairport, NY
Scardino, R. A. .... Houston, TX
Scardino, Theresa C. Fort Washington, PA
Scarduzio, Thomas A., Jr. .... Phoenix, AZ
Scarff, James E. .... San Francisco, CA
Scarff, Stuart W. .... Mercer Island, WA
Scarff, William N., Jr. .... Fullerton, CA
Scarfone, Anthony C. .... Golden Valley, MN
Scarfone & Geen, P.C. .... Grosse Pointe, MI
Scarfone, Nicholas A. .... Syracuse, NY
Scarfone, Richard R. .... St. Clair Shores, MI
Scarfone, Robert J. .... Grosse Pointe, MI
Scarglato, Joseph .... New York, NY
Scari, William A., Jr. .... Berwyn, PA
Scariano, Anthony G. .... Chicago, IL
Chicago Heights, IL
Scariano, Ellch, Himes, Sraga and Petrarca, Chartered .... Chicago, IL
Chicago Heights, IL
Scariati, Rosemary .... New York, NY
Scaricamazza, Angelo L. .... Philadelphia, PA
Scaricamazza, Angelo L., Jr. Philadelphia, PA
Scarinci, Donald .... Secaucus, NJ
Scarinci & Hollenbeck, LLC Jersey City, NJ
Secaucus, NJ
Scaring, Stephen P. .... Garden City, NY
Scaring, Stephen P., P.C. Garden City, NY
Scaringe, Christopher M. .... Albany, NY
Scaringelli, Lawrence F. .... Scottsdale, AZ
Scarino, Robert H. .... Boston, MA
Scarinzi, Angelo P. .... Mineola, NY
Scarito, Salvatore R. .... Longwood, FL
Scarlata, Barbara G. .... Media, PA
Scarlata, Charles F. .... Pittsburgh, PA
Scarlata, James V. .... Newark, NJ
Scarlatelli, Adam W. .... Phillipsburg, NJ
Scarlati, Frank S., Jr. Oakbrook Terrace, IL
Scarlati, Steven R., Jr. .... Chicago, IL
Scarlato, Angela E. .... New York, NY
Scarlato, Paul J. .... Philadelphia, PA
Scarlett, Charles E. .... Boca Raton, FL
Scarlett & Croll, P.A. .... Baltimore, MD
Scarlett, Darrell L. .... Murfreesboro, TN
Smyrna, TN
Scarlett, Donald W. .... Orlando, FL
Scarlett, Donald W., Jr. .... Bradenton, FL
Scarlett, Donald W., P.A. .... Orlando, FL
Sanford, FL
Scarlett, Dorothy K. .... Wilmington, DE
Scarlett, Gregory B. .... Los Angeles, CA
Scarlett, John D. .... Winston-Salem, NC
Scarlett, Joseph A., III .... DeLand, FL
Scarlett, Michael A. .... Oakland, CA

Scarlett, Robert B. ....**Baltimore, MD**
Scarlett, Robert E. ....Sacramento, CA
Scarlett, Robert R. ....**Honolulu, HI**
Scarlett, Stanley L. ....**Long Beach, CA**
Scarlett, Stephen G. ....**Brunswick, GA**
Scarlett, Teri Elaine ....Monterey, CA
Scarlett, Thomas ....**Washington, DC**
Scarlett, William J., (Of Counsel)
Kennett Square, PA
Scarlett, Zane M. ....Knoxville, TN
Scarlett-Johnson, Rana A. ....**Omaha, NE**
Scarlott, Kerry T. ....**Manchester, NH**
Scarminach, Charles A. ....Bluffton, SC
Hilton Head Island, SC
Scarmoutsos, Manuel P. ....Memphis, TN
Scarmozzino, James M. ....**Fort Myers, FL**
Scarnavack, Alan M. ....Chicago, IL
Scaro, Robert C. ....**Norfolk, VA**
Scarola, John ....**West Palm Beach, FL**
Scarola, Michael S. ....Elmwood Park, NJ
Scarola & Reavis ....**New York, NY**
Scarola, Richard J.J. ....**Los Angeles, CA**
New York, NY
Scarola, Susan M. ....Freehold, NJ
Scarp, Bradley P. ....**Seattle, WA**
Scarpa, Carmine J. ....Jersey City, NJ
Scarpa, Chrisotpher C. ....**Philadelphia, PA**
Scarpa, John A., Jr. ....Kew Gardens, NY
Scarpati, Susan Jeanne ....Fort Salonga, NY
Scarpato, Peter A. ....Wilmington, DE
Scarpato, Raymond A., Jr ....Philadelphia, PA
Scarpelli, Craig M. ....Chicago, IL
Scarpelli, Frank J. ....Dundee, IL
Scarpelli, Nate F. ....**Chicago, IL**
Scarpelli, Nicholas J. ....Chicago, IL
Scarpelli, Nicholas P., Jr. ....**Seattle, WA**
Scarpelli, Scott V. ....**Chicago, IL**
Scarpelli, William B. ....**Boston, MA**
Scarpellino, Philip A. ....New Haven, CT
Scarpellino, Tina ....Los Angeles, CA
Scarpello & Alling, Ltd. A Professional Corporation ....**Carson City, NV**
Las Vegas, NV
Reno, NV
Stateline, NV
Scarpello, Fred V. ....**Carson City, NV**
Scarpello, Jeffrey P. ....**Philadelphia, PA**
Scarpello, Joseph R. ....Garden Grove, CA
Scarpetti, Mary Elizabeth ....Burlingame, CA
Scarpino, John H. ....San Francisco, CA
Scarpino, Paul, Jr. ....Scituate, MA
Scarpitti, William F., Jr. ....Erie, PA
Scarpone, David John ....**Steubenville, OH**
Scarpone, James A. ....**Newark, NJ**
Scarpone, LaRue & Associates
Steubenville, OH
Scarpone, Robert H. ....Flanders, NJ
Scarpulla, Francis O. ....San Francisco, CA
Scarpulla, Stephen V. ....San Francisco, CA
Scarr, Amy F. ....Madison, WI
Scarr, Anthony E. ....Oakland, CA
Scarr, Karen P. ....**Redwood City, CA**
Scarr, Marshal A. ....**San Diego, CA**
Scarr, Thomas E. ....**Huntington, WV**
Scarrillo, Dana M. ....Newark, NJ
Scarritt, Richard W. ....**Kansas City, MO**
Scarritt, Thomas P., Jr. ....**Tampa, FL**
Scarr-Konel, Laurel B. ....**New York, NY**
Scarrow, James W. ....**Washington, DC**
Scarry, Brian T. ....**Miami, FL**
Scarry, Donald M. ....Mount Laurel, NJ
Scarry, Leo T ....Plymouth, MA
Scarsella, Vincent L. ....Buffalo, NY
Scarsi, Mark C. ....**Los Angeles, CA**
Scartelli, Melissa A. ....**Wilkes-Barre, PA**
Scartezina, Paul F. ....Tucson, AZ
Scarth, Bill R. ....Claremore, OK
Scarth & Rahmeier ....Claremore, OK
Scartz, Ted Matthew ....**Atlanta, GA**
Scartz, Thomas Edward ....Woodbridge, VA
Scarvie, Thomas G. ....**San Francisco, CA**
Scarzafava, Gary A. ....**Houston, TX**
Scarzafava, John F. ....**Oneonta, NY**
Scarzafava Law Office, The ....**Oneonta, NY**
Scarzafava, Nettie J. ....Cooperstown, NY
Scase, Christie ....Des Moines, IA
Scatchard, William B., Jr.
Mount Laurel, NJ
Scatena, Patrice C. ....**Santa Clara, CA**
Scatena, Renee J. ....Phoenix, AZ
Scatena, Rex ....San Francisco, CA
Scatenato & Alleva ....New York, NY
Scatenato, Amy ....New York, NY
Scates, J. C. Tim ....**Denver, CO**
Scates, Jennifer Ann ....Austin, TX
Scattarella, David L. ....Minneapolis, MN
Scatterday, George H. ....Bethesda, MD
Scattergood, Richard C. ....**Minneapolis, MN**
Scattergood, Thomas J. ....Mount Laurel, NJ
Scattoloni, Rosann ....Columbus, IN
Scatton, Barry R. ....Bedford, PA
Scaturro, Angelo F. ....Catskill, NY
Scaturro, Frank J. ....**New York, NY**
Scaturro, Michael ....**Uniondale, NY**
Scavazzo, Stephen D. ....Washington, DC
Scavdis, Antonios C. ....Ravenna, OH
Scavetta, Joseph F., Jr. ....**Washington, DC**
Scavitti, Pasquale A., III ....Cranston, RI
Scavo, James J. ....**Atlanta, GA**
Scavo, James M. ....Chicago, IL
Scavone, Arthur A. ....**New York, NY**
Scavone, Daniel J. ....Princeton, NJ
Scavone, Nicholas P., Jr. ....**Detroit, MI**
Scavone, Thomas G. ....**Chicago, IL**
Scavongelli, Anthony M. ....Boston, MA
Scavron, Robert L. ....Silver City, NM
Scavuzzo, Bruce D. ....New York, NY
Scavuzzo & Hart ....Mineola, NY
Scavuzzo, Julius J. ....Mineola, NY
Scavuzzo, Stephen ....Vienna, VA
Scaz, Kenneth A. ....**Tampa, FL**
Scearce, Bobby D. ....Dayton, OH
Scearce, Camden Ballard, Jr.
Chattanooga, TN
Scearce, Donald E. ....**Honolulu, HI**
Scearce, Kenneth R ....Seattle, WA
Scearce, Michael A. ....**Kansas City, MO**
Sceery, Jody M. ....East Greenwich, RI
Sceglio, Ronald F. ....Santa Ana, CA
Scelfo, Tammy B. ....**Lafayette, LA**
Scelsi, Joel A. ....Endicott, NY
Scena, Michael T. ....Denver, CO
Scena, Michael T., Ltd., P.C. ....Denver, CO
Scenna, Derrick A. ....**Red Bank, NJ**
Whiting, NJ
Scent, William E. ....**Paducah, KY**
Sceper, Duane H. ....San Diego, CA
Scerba, David R. ....Wilmington, DE
Scerbak, Adrienne A. ....**New York, NY**
Scerbo, Frank A. ....Rochester Hills, MI
Scerbo, Otto J. ....**Jersey City, NJ**
Millburn, NJ
Scerbo, Robert J. ....**Hackensack, NJ**
Scerni, Alfred R., Jr. ....**Mount Laurel, NJ**
Pleasantville, NJ
Scerra, Louis J., Jr. ....**Boston, MA**
Scesa, Steven ....**Chicago, IL**
Sceusa, Peter P. ....New York, NY
Sceusi, Louis S. ....Morristown, NJ
Rockaway, NJ
Sceviour, Timothy P. ....Norfolk, VA
Schaab, Arnold J. ....**New York, NY**
Schaab, Shannon Marieke ....Chicago, IL
Schaack, Daniel P. ....**Phoenix, AZ**
Schaack, R. Bard ....Mayville, NY
Schaack Whipple Clark Nelson Polowy, P.C.
Fredonia, NY
Mayville, NY
Schaad, Anne P. ....Augusta, ME
Schaad, Robert D. ....Louisville, KY
Schaaf, Bonita A. ....Michigan City, IN
Schaaf, Charles E. ....Los Angeles, CA
Schaaf, David W. ....**New York, NY**
Schaaf, Donald R., Jr. ....Jerseyville, IL
Schaaf, Douglas A. ....**Costa Mesa, CA**
Schaaf, Gary E. ....**Paducah, KY**
Schaaf, Gary M. ....**St. Petersburg, FL**
Schaaf, Gregg ....Cumberland, MD
Schaaf, Gregory R. ....Lexington, KY
Schaaf & Hodges ....**Marietta, GA**
Schaaf, Homer D. ....**New York, NY**
Schaaf, Kathleen E. ....New York, NY
Schaaf, K. C. ....**Newport Beach, CA**
Schaaf, Kristi Saladino ....**Paducah, KY**
Schaaf, Margaret L. ....**Seattle, WA**
Schaaf, Michael L. ....**Marietta, GA**
Schaaf, Peter G. ....Erie, PA
Schaaf, Robert M. ....Newark, NJ
Schaaf, Terry R. ....Lincoln, NE
Schaaf, Will J. ....**Erie, PA**
Schaaf, William J. ....**Erie, PA**
Schaaff, Harold J., Jr. ....**New York, NY**
Schaaff, Lesley-Anne
Environmental Protection Agency, Program Office Attorneys, GV
Schaafsma, James E. ....Ann Arbor, MI
Schaafsma, Marjorie B. ....Evanston, IL
Schaafsma, Paul E. ....**Chicago, IL**
Schaal, Aaron ....Denver, CO
Schaal, Deborah Kall ....Rochester, NY
Schaal, Ernest ....**Mill Valley, CA**
Schaal, John Eric ....**Chicago, IL**
Schaal, Marie ....Denver, CO
Schaal, Nadine ....**Orlando, FL**
Schaal, Randy J. ....Sherrill, NY
Schaal, Steven D. ....Dakota Dunes, SD
Schaal, Thomas E. ....San Rafael, CA
Schaal, William W. ....**Costa Mesa, CA**
La Jolla, CA
Schaalman, Michael H. ....**Milwaukee, WI**
Schaan, John J. ....Milwaukee, WI
Schaap, Dan L. ....**Amarillo, TX**
Schaap, Marcie E. ....**Salt Lake City, UT**
Schaap, Michelle A. ....**Roseland, NJ**
Schaap, Paula R. ....New York, NY
Schaap, Robert J. ....**Los Angeles, CA**
Woodland Hills, CA
Schaap, Robert J., A Professional Corporation ....**Los Angeles, CA**
Woodland Hills, CA
Schaap, Ryan D. ....**Westlake Village, CA**
Schaar, Donald F. ....Phoenix, AZ
Schaar, Jill A. ....**Houston, TX**
Schaar, Marvin B. ....Chicago, IL
Schaar-Mecklenberg, Cynthia ....Fargo, ND
Schaars, Steven ....**Washington, DC**
Schab & Barnett, P.A.
Bethany Beach, DE
Georgetown, DE
Lewes, DE
Schab, Thomas J. ....Chicago, IL
Schab, William ....**Georgetown, DE**
Lewes, DE
Schabacker, Christine M. ....Anchorage, AK
Schabacker, Mark M., (P.A.) ....**Tampa, FL**
Schabacker Simmons & Dunlap
Tampa, FL
Schabel, Donald A. ....Indianapolis, IN
Schabell, Gregory N. ....Florence, KY
Schaber, Andrew J. ....Bay Shore, NY
Schaber, Gordon D. ....Sacramento, CA
Schaber, John F. ....**Deming, NM**
Lordsburg, NM
Schaber, John F., P.A. ....**Deming, NM**
Lordsburg, NM
Schaberg, Courtney M. ....**Los Angeles, CA**
Schaberg, Jill A. ....**East Lansing, MI**
Schaberg, John I. ....Belleville, IL
St. Louis, MO
Schaberg, Peter C. ....Saline, MI
Schaberg, Richard A. ....**Washington, DC**
Schaberg, Robert E. ....**San Francisco, CA**
Schaberg, Terry H. ....Greenwood, IN
Schabes, Alan E. ....**Cleveland, OH**
Schabes, Sarah V. ....**Baltimore, MD**
Schabes, Stuart M. ....**Baltimore, MD**
Schabler, William M. ....Indianapolis, IN
Schablik, Noel E. ....**Parsippany, NJ**
Schablik, Noel E., P.A. ....**Morristown, NJ**
Parsippany, NJ
Schach, David Thomas ....**Minneapolis, MN**
Schach, Martha E. ....Kansas City, MO
Schacher, David B. ....New York, NY
Schacherl, Anne W. ....Madison, WI
Schachleiter, Kenneth T. ....Cincinnati, OH
Schachman, Robert B. ....Bloomfield, NJ
Schachman, Ronald H. ....Bloomfield, NJ
Schachne, Susan D. ....New York, NY
Schachner, Elizabeth M. ....**Atlanta, GA**
Schachner, Elliot M. ....Brooklyn, NY
Schachner, Jack E. ....White Plains, NY
Schachner, Larry ....Bronx, NY
Schachner, Mark ....**Glens Falls, NY**
Schachner, Stewart B. ....Staten Island, NY
Schachner Chanen, Jill E. ....**Chicago, IL**
Schacht, Alexei ....New York, NY
Schacht, Brad W. ....**Denver, CO**
Schacht, Christa Manzi ....New York, NY
Schacht, Clay Walter ....**Orlando, FL**
Schacht, Diana L. ....Washington, DC
Schacht, Donald W. ....Walla Walla, WA
Schacht, Herman D. ....Beaver Dam, WI
Schacht & Hicks ....Mount Vernon, WA
Schacht, James E. ....Milwaukee, WI
Schacht, James S. ....Tacoma, WA
Schacht, Kurt N. ....Madison, WI
Schacht, Laura J. ....**Duluth, MN**
Schacht, Maryann S. ....Beaver Dam, WI
Schacht & McElroy ....Providence, RI
Schacht, Michael R. ....**Bellingham, WA**
Schacht, Raymond H. ....New York, NY
Schacht, Richard F. ....Mount Vernon, WA
Schacht, Robert M. ....Providence, RI
Schacht, Ronald S. ....**New York, NY**
Schacht & Schacht ....Beaver Dam, WI
Schacht, William C. ....Rochester, MN
Schachte, Stephen T. ....Charleston, SC
Schachte, William L., Jr. ....**Washington, DC**
Schachtel, Debra S. ....**New York, NY**
Schachtel, Gerstley, Levine & Koplin, P.C.
Boca Raton, FL
Haddonfield, NJ
Philadelphia, PA
Schachtel, Neal ....Ardmore, PA
Schachter, Alesa M. ....**Sacramento, CA**
Schachter, Bonnie J. ....Stow, MA
Schachter, Cary Ira ....**Amarillo, TX**
Dallas, TX
Schachter, Charles I. ....**Rochester, NY**
Schachter, David ....Miami Beach, FL
Schachter, David ....Philadelphia, PA
Schachter, David M. ....Santa Monica, CA
Schachter, David N. ....**Denver, CO**
Schachter, David R. ....Briarcliff Manor, NY
Schachter, Diane A. ....Boston, MA
Schachter, Edward A. ....Kew Gardens, NY
Schachter, Howard ....Princeton, NJ
Schachter, Jerome ....Skokie, IL
Schachter, Kenneth R. ....**New York, NY**
Schachter, Kristoff, Orenstein & Berkowitz, L.L.P. ....**Menlo Park, CA**
Sacramento, CA
San Francisco, CA
Santa Clara, CA
Schachter, L. Michael ....Great Neck, NY
Schachter, Leigh R. ....**New York, NY**
Schachter, Leon J. ....Department of Defense, Defense Legal Services Agency, GV
Schachter, Madeleine ....**New York, NY**
Schachter, Michael S. ....Chicago, IL
Schachter, Milton H. ....Valley Stream, NY
Schachter, Morris ....Santa Rosa, CA
Schachter, Oscar H. ....New York, NY
Schachter, Patti Michelle ....Akron, OH
Schachter, Paul ....Newark, NJ
Schachter, Paul J. ....**Fort Mitchell, KY**
Schachter, Paul J., & Associates, P.S.C.
Covington, KY
Fort Mitchell, KY
Schachter, Richard J. ....**Somerville, NJ**
Schachter, Robert A. ....**New York, NY**
Schachter, Robert B. ....Torrance, CA
Schachter, Robert C. ....**Woodbridge, NJ**
Schachter, Robert S. ....**New York, NY**
Schachter, Robin A. ....**Seattle, WA**
Schachter, Robin M. ....**Los Angeles, CA**
Schachter, Samuel ....Lincolnwood, IL
Schachter, Scott A. ....Department of Justice, Environment and Natural Resources Division, GV
Schachter, Stanley I. ....New York, NY
Schachter, Trombadore, Offen, Stanton & Pavics, A Professional Corporation
Elizabeth, NJ
Flemington, NJ
Morristown, NJ
Newark, NJ
New Brunswick, NJ
Somerville, NJ
Trenton, NJ
Schachter, Victor ....**San Francisco, CA**
Schachterle, David L. ....Denver, CO
Schachterle, John C. ....**Des Moines, IA**
Schachtili, Richard J. ....**Palo Alto, CA**
Schachtman, Nathan A. ....**Cherry Hill, NJ**
Schachtman, Samuel ....Chicago, IL
Schachtner, Jeanette ....Santa Monica, CA
Schack, Alexander M. ....San Diego, CA
Schack, Arthur M. ....New York, NY
Schack, Catherine Light ....Tustin, CA
Schack, David P., (A Professional Corporation) ....**Los Angeles, CA**
Schack, Diana Davis ....Troy, MI
Schack, Larry ....Stuart, FL
Schack, Louis W. ....**Philadelphia, PA**
Schack, Michael L. ....Fullerton, CA
Schack, Robert E. ....**Miami, FL**
Schack, Susan ....Longmeadow, MA
Schack, Wendy G. ....East Williston, NY
Schackman, Walter M. ....**New York, NY**
Schackmann, Terry W. ....**Kansas City, MO**
Schackner, Harlan E. ....West Orange, NJ
Schackow, Gerald D. ....Gainesville, FL
Schackow, Lynn M. ....Gainesville, FL
Schackow, Mercadante & Mitchell, P.A.
Gainesville, FL
Schacter, Alan ....**New York, NY**
Schacter, David M. ....Burbank, CA
Schacter, Ira J. ....**New York, NY**
Schacter, Jane S. ....Madison, WI
Schacter, Janice Lynn ....New York, NY
Schacter, Kenneth I. ....**New York, NY**
Schacter, Stacey J. ....**Cincinnati, OH**
Schacter, Steven J. ....Long Beach, NY
Schad, Buda, Cook, LLC ....Cincinnati, OH
Schad, Jeffrey L. ....**Grand Rapids, MI**
Schad, Jerome D. ....**Buffalo, NY**
Schad, Kevin M. ....Cincinnati, OH
Schad, Larry J. ....**New Albany, IN**
Schad, Lawrence W. ....**Chicago, IL**
Schad, Matthew J. ....**New Albany, IN**
Schad, Matthew O. ....Department of Justice, Antitrust Division, GV
Schad, Michael A. ....**Salinas, CA**
Schad, Mildred K. ....Parma Heights, OH
Schad & Schad ....**New Albany, IN**
Schad, Steven P. ....**Washington, DC**
Schad, Tennyson ....**New York, NY**
Schad, William O. ....Glendale, CA
Schade, Dewey D. ....Scottsdale, AZ
Schade & Edwards, P.C. ....Philadelphia, PA
Schade, Emil A.G.M. ....Maynard, MA
Schade, George A., Jr. ....Phoenix, AZ
Schade, Malcolm R. ....**New York, NY**
Schade, Richard M. ....**Augusta, ME**
Schade, Rudolf G., Jr. ....**Chicago, IL**
Schade, Terrence J. ....Philadelphia, PA
Schade, William M. ....**New Ulm, MN**
Schadel, James R. ....**Pittsburgh, PA**
Schadel, Kelly L. ....**Detroit, MI**
Schaden, Erin Elizabeth ....**Washington, DC**
Schaden & Flohr ....**Washington, DC**
Schaden, Kathleen M. ....**Broomfield, CO**
Troy, MI
Schaden, Katzman, Lampert & McClune
Broomfield, CO
Denver, CO
Detroit, MI
Troy, MI
Schaden, Richard F. ....**Broomfield, CO**
Troy, MI
Schader, Charles R. ....New York, NY
Schader, Robert K. ....Boulder, CO
Schading, Elizabeth A. ....**Minneapolis, MN**
Schadl, John E. ....**King Of Prussia, PA**
Schadle, Richard Taylor ....**Pittsburgh, PA**
Schadle, William J. ....Des Moines, IA
Schadler, B. Holly ....**Washington, DC**
Schadler-Chang, Nancy J. ....Loveland, OH
Schadlich, Stephen H. ....**Oakland, CA**
Schadrack, Mark A. ....Laguna Niguel, CA
Schadt, Barbara S. ....Westport, CT
Schadt, Frederick W. V., Jr.
Jeffersonville, NY
Schadt, Gordon F. ....Anchorage, AK
Schadt & Schadt ....Jeffersonville, NY
Schadt, Stuart Alan ....**Towson, MD**
Schadt, Willard J. ....Port Jervis, NY
Schaeber, Mark Andrew ....Syracuse, NY
Schaeberle, Timothy M. ....Corning, NY
Schaech, L. Michael ....Baltimore, MD
Schaecher, Gina L. ....**Omaha, NE**
Schaecher, Gregory C. ....**Omaha, NE**
Schaecher, Susan M. ....**Denver, CO**
Schaechter, N. Jack ....New York, NY
Schaechterle, Kathleen ....**Anchorage, AK**
Schaedle, Michael B. ....**Philadelphia, PA**
Schaedler, Phillip A. ....Kalamazoo, MI
Schaedler, Richard J. ....**Bethlehem, PA**
Schaedtler, Stephen Mark ....Patchogue, NY
Schaefbauer, Mary E. ....Sioux Falls, SD
Schaefer, Alan P. ....Amherst, NY
Schaefer, Alexander H. ....**Washington, DC**
Schaefer, Allison J. ....Warren, NJ
Schaefer, Andrew J. ....**Chicago, IL**
Schaefer, Anne M. ....Traverse City, MI
Schaefer, Anneliese M. ....St. Louis, MO
Schaefer, Arthur P. ....Portland, ME
Schaefer and Associates, Ltd. ....Denver, CO
Schaefer, Barbara Baumann
Cincinnati, OH
Schaefer, Barbara W. ....Bethlehem, PA
Schaefer, Barry ....Teutopolis, IL
Schaefer, Carol S ....Columbus, OH
Schaefer, Charles H. ....**Catskill, NY**
Schaefer, Charles R. ....**Cleveland, OH**
Schaefer, Chris A., Law Office of
San Rafael, CA
Schaefer, Christian J. ....Cincinnati, OH
Schaefer, Christine R. ....Simsbury, CT
Schaefer, Claudia L. ....Cincinnati, OH
Schaefer, Clyde M. ....**New York, NY**

Schaefer, Daniel R. ...Hartford, CT
Schaefer, David A. ...Woodland Hills, CA
Schaefer, David A. ...Cleveland, OH
Schaefer, David R., (P.C.) ...New Haven, CT
Schaefer, David S. ...New York, NY
Schaefer, David T. ...Louisville, KY
Schaefer, Debra Geis ...Toledo, OH
Schaefer, Dennis L. ...Hollywood, FL
Schaefer, Don Henry ...Oakland, CA
Schaefer, Donald W. ...Decatur, GA
Schaefer, Donavon D. ...Cherokee, IA
Schaefer, Edmund, III ...Lynchburg, VA
Schaefer, Edward H. ...Cleveland, OH
Schaefer, Edward N. ...Walnut Creek, CA
Schaefer, Edwin M. ...St. Louis, MO
Schaefer, Elmer A. ...Wilmington, NC
Schaefer, Elmer J. ...Williamsburg, VA
Schaefer, Elwyn F. ...Denver, CO
Schaefer, Elwyn F. & Associates, P.C.
Denver, CO
Schaefer, Frederic L. ...San Francisco, CA
Schaefer, Gene E. ...Middletown, OH
Schaefer, George E., Jr. ...Batavia, NY
Schaefer, George F. ...Gainesville, FL
Schaefer, Georgette A. ...New York, NY
Schaefer, Gerard F. ...Northampton, MA
Schaefer, Gregory J. ...Minneapolis, MN
Schaefer, Gregory J. ...St. Paul, MN
Schaefer, Howard G. ...Pasadena, CA
Schaefer, Hugh V. ...Denver, CO
Schaefer, Ira J. ...New York, NY
Tarrytown, NY
Schaefer, J. Michael ...Las Vegas, NV
Schaefer, James E. ...Eden Prairie, MN
Schaefer, James E. ...Omaha, NE
Schaefer, James E. ...Toledo, OH
Schaefer, James H. ...Eau Claire, WI
Schaefer, James J. ...Cincinnati, OH
Schaefer, James R. ...Wichita, KS
Schaefer, James R. ...Cincinnati, OH
Schaefer, Jane H. ...San Antonio, TX
Schaefer, Jay Dee ...Laramie, WY
Schaefer, Jeffrey R. ...Cincinnati, OH
Schaefer, Jennifer A. ...Baltimore, MD
Schaefer, Jeri S. ...Newark, NJ
Schaefer, Jerome C. ...Washington, DC
Schaefer, Jerrold C. ...San Francisco, CA
Schaefer, Jerry I. ...Vista, CA
Schaefer, Joanne M. ...Rockland, MA
Schaefer, Joel B. ...Denver, CO
Schaefer, Joel B. ...Lakewood, CO
Schaefer, Joen M. ...Phoenix, AZ
Schaefer, John ...Clearwater, FL
Schaefer, John ...St. Petersburg, FL
Schaefer, John C. ...Denver, CO
Schaefer, John E. ...Clearwater, FL
Schaefer, John E., Jr. ...Mineola, NY
Schaefer, John F. ...Birmingham, MI
Schaefer, John F., The Law Firm of
Birmingham, MI
Schaefer, John N. ...Oklahoma City, OK
Schaefer, John P. ...Rochester, NY
Schaefer, John W. ...Belleville, IL
Schaefer, Jon P. ...Shelby, OH
Schaefer, Jonathan P. ...Chicago, IL
Schaefer, Karen ...Rochester, NY
Schaefer, Karen L. ...Monticello, NY
Schaefer, Kathryn ...Los Angeles, CA
Schaefer, Kenneth R. ...Basking Ridge, NJ
Schaefer, Kenneth R. ...Somerville, NJ
Schaefer & Kunz, P.C. ...Mattapoisett, MA
Schaefer, Kurt U. ...Jefferson City, MO
Schaefer, Laura G. ...San Diego, CA
Schaefer, Lawrence H. ...San Jose, CA
Schaefer, Lawrence H. ...Albany, NY
Schaefer, Lawrence P. ...Minneapolis, MN
Schaefer, Lily M. ...Merrillville, IN
Valparaiso, IN
Schaefer, Linda M. ...Rockville, MD
Schaefer, Lorene F. ...Atlanta, GA
Schaefer, Marci C. ...Alpharetta, GA
Schaefer, Margaret S. ...Meridian, ID
Schaefer, Maria Theresa "Tish"
Denver, CO
Schaefer, Mark ...Washington, DC
Schaefer, Mark E. ...New York, NY
Schaefer, Mark John ...Buffalo, NY
Schaefer, Martin ...Boston, MA
Schaefer, Matthew J. ...Fort Lauderdale, FL
Schaefer, Matthew P. ...Boston, MA
Schaefer, Michael ...Indianapolis, IN
Schaefer, Michael C. ...Denver, CO
Schaefer, Michael J. ...Irvine, CA
Schaefer, Michael J. ...Hagerstown, MD
Schaefer, Michael J. ...Mount Clemens, MI
Schaefer, Michael P. ...Bethel Park, PA
Schaefer, Michael R. ...San Bernardino, CA
Schaefer, Michael V. ...Denver, CO
Schaefer, Michael W. ...Chicago, IL
Schaefer, Nancy ...Chicago, IL
Schaefer, Nicholas E. ...Concord, CA
Schaefer, Nick F. ...Appleton, WI
Schaefer, Nina M. ...Richmond, TX
Schaefer, Pamela H. ...Milwaukee, WI
Schaefer, Pamela J. ...Boston, MA
Schaefer, Patrick M. ...Albuquerque, NM
Schaefer, Paul N. ...Longwood, FL
Schaefer, Paula R. H. ...Kansas City, MO
Schaefer, Peter C. ...Syracuse, NY
Schaefer, Peter J. ...Milwaukee, WI
Schaefer, Peter L. ...Oak Brook, IL
Schaefer, Philip D. ...Kalamazoo, MI
Schaefer, Philip E. ...Ontario, CA
Schaefer, Philip S. ...Columbus, OH
Schaefer, Philip W. ...White Plains, NY
Schaefer, Randy J. ...Huntington, NY
Schaefer, Richard P. ...Mattapoisett, MA
Schaefer, Richard W. ...Clayton, MO
Schaefer, Robert A., Jr. ...Millburn, NJ
New York, NY
Schaefer, Robert Bruce ...Reynoldsburg, OH
Schaefer, Robert M. ...Vancouver, WA
Schaefer, Robert W. ...Green Bay, WI
Schaefer, Sheila E. ...Los Angeles, CA
Schaefer & Smith ...Vista, CA
Schaefer, Stanley ...New York, NY
Schaefer, Stephen A. ...Maumee, OH
Schaefer, Stephen L. ...Austin, TX
Schaefer, Stephen L., P.C. ...Austin, TX
Schaefer, Stephen M. ...Washington, DC
Schaefer, Stephen R. ...Minneapolis, MN
Schaefer, Stephen R. ...Seattle, WA
Schaefer, Steven A. ...Bradenton, FL
Schaefer, Steven C. ...Minneapolis, MN
Schaefer, Susan G. ...Beverly Hills, CA
Schaefer, Susan Peters ...Chicago, IL
Schaefer, T. Dillon ...San Diego, CA
Schaefer, Theresa Rittinger ...Columbus, OH
Schaefer, Thomas H. ...Minneapolis, MN
Schaefer, Thomas L. ...Marietta, GA
Schaefer, Tina M. ...Jefferson City, MO
Schaefer, Wayne J. ...East Meadow, NY
Schaefer, William C. ...Troy, MI
Schaefer, William Dee ...Chicago, IL
Schaefer, William Donald ...Baltimore, MD
Schaefer, William E. ...Philadelphia, PA
Schaefer, William G. ...Baltimore, MD
Schaefer, Wirth & Wirth ...St. Petersburg, FL
Schaefermeier, Martin ...Washington, DC
Schaefers, John E. ...Seattle, WA
Schaefers, Robin A. ...Palo Alto, CA
Schaeff, B. Joseph ...Dayton, OH
Schaeffer, Alan B. ...Dayton, OH
Schaeffer, Alan J. ...Washington, DC
Schaeffer, Andrea W. ...West Chester, PA
Schaeffer, Andrew J. ...New York, NY
Schaeffer, Andrew L. ...Wilmington, DE
Schaeffer, Beth W. ...Dayton, OH
Schaeffer, Bruce E. ...Palo Alto, CA
Schaeffer, Bruce S. ...New York, NY
Schaeffer, Charles G. ...Clarkton, MO
Schaeffer, Daniel J. ...Chicago, IL
Schaeffer, David L. ...Baltimore, MD
Schaeffer, David L. ...New York, NY
Schaeffer, David N. ...Atlanta, GA
Schaeffer, Donald M. ...Jericho, NY
Schaeffer, Donna McCabe ...Annapolis, MD
Schaeffer, Earl G. ...Cincinnati, OH
Schaeffer, Edwin F., Jr. ...Lexington, KY
Schaeffer, Elliot L. ...New York, NY
Schaeffer, Eric Jon ...Cincinnati, OH
Schaeffer, Eric V.
Environmental Protection Agency,
Office of Enforcement and Compliance
Assurance, GV
Schaeffer, Forrest G., Jr. ...Reading, PA
Schaeffer, George H., III ...New York, NY
Schaeffer, Glen ...New York, NY
Schaeffer, Hazel Sweet ...Chattanooga, TN
Schaeffer, Herbert D. ...Clayton, MO
Schaeffer, J. Thomas ...Marshall, MI
Schaeffer, James C. ...San Diego, CA
Schaeffer, James F., Jr. ...Memphis, TN
Schaeffer, James F. (Tim), Sr. ...Eads, TN
Schaeffer, Janae L. ...Kansas City, MO
Schaeffer, John C., Jr. ...Mineola, NY
Schaeffer, John E. ...San Francisco, CA
Schaeffer, John H. ...Phoenix, AZ
Schaeffer, John N., III ...Doylestown, PA
Schaeffer, Judith E. ...Washington, DC
Schaeffer, Karren T. ...Irvine, CA
Schaeffer, Kevin M. ...Annapolis, MD
Schaeffer, Lance C. ...La Jolla, CA
Schaeffer Law Offices ...Memphis, TN
Schaeffer, Lawrence ...Mineola, NY
Schaeffer, Louis B. ...Phoenix, AZ
Schaeffer, Margaret G. ...Farmington Hills, MI
Schaeffer, Marjorie R. ...New York, NY
Schaeffer, Mark ...Los Angeles, CA
Schaeffer, Marlena ...Rye Brook, NY
Schaeffer, Marlowe R. ...Edgemont, PA
Schaeffer, Matthew T. ...Columbus, OH
Schaeffer, Meyer & MacKenzie
Marshall, MI
Schaeffer, Michael N. ...Columbus, OH
Schaeffer, Paul J. ...Department of Justice,
Environment and Natural Resources
Division, GV
Schaeffer, Paul Michael ...Hollywood, CA
Schaeffer, Peter J. ...New York, NY
Schaeffer, Peter M. ...Riverside, CA
Schaeffer, Philip H. ...New York, NY
Schaeffer, Richard B. ...Kew Gardens, NY
Schaeffer, Richard J. ...New York, NY
Schaeffer, Ronald J. ...Lufkin, TX
Schaeffer, Sandra ...Newport Beach, CA
Schaeffer, Stephanie L. ...Rochester, NY
Schaeffer, Stephen J. ...Jersey City, NJ
Schaeffer, Stephen L. ...Sioux City, IA
Schaeffer, Susan F. ...St. Petersburg, FL
Schaeffer, Suzanne R. ...Department of Justice,
Environment and Natural Resources
Division, GV
Schaeffer, T. Evan ...St. Louis, MO
Schaeffer, Virginia K. ...Corvallis, OR
Schaeffer, William B., Jr. ...Houston, TX
Schaeffer, William E. ...Yerington, NV
Schaeffer & Zapson LLP
Long Beach, NY
New York, NY
Schaeffner, Sean P. ...New York, NY
Schaefgen, John R., Jr. ...Washington, DC
Schaefle, William J. ...Glen Ellyn, IL
Schaefler, Alfred ...Pound Ridge, NY
Schaefler, Margaret ...Islandia, NY
Schael, Courtney A. ...Roseland, NJ
Schaen, Richard J. ...Cincinnati, OH
Schaengold, Gary C. ...Dayton, OH
Schaengold, Michael J. ...Washington, DC
Schaengold, Sol ...Cincinnati, OH
Schaenman, Leslie ...New York, NY
Schaeper, W. Christopher ...Houston, TX
Schaeperklaus, Rae Ellen ...Cincinnati, OH
Schaeperkoetter, Carl E. ...Jefferson City, MO
Schaeperkoetter, Jeffrey W. ...Owensville, MO
Schaer, Angela D. ...Boise, ID
Schaer, Gregory S. ...Red Bank, NJ
Schaer, Theodore M. ...Cherry Hill, NJ
Jersey City, NJ
Philadelphia, PA
Schaerf, Carl J. ...New York, NY
Schaerf, Howard ...New York, NY
Schaerf, Jonathan ...Livingston, NJ
New York, NY
Schaerges, Allen ...Detroit, MI
Schaerli, John A. ...Geneva, IL
Schaerr, Gene C. ...Washington, DC
Schaertel, Arthur T., (A Professional Corporation) ...Claremont, CA
San Francisco, CA
Schaetzel, Roy ...Naples, FL
Schaetzel, Stephen M. ...Atlanta, GA
Schaetzke, Wallace ...Milwaukee, WI
Schaevitz, Barry S. ...New York, NY
Schaewe, Catherine C. ...Binghamton, NY
Schafer, Alan B. ...Minneapolis, MN
Schafer, Arnold ...Bloomfield Hills, MI
Schafer, Bernard Karl ...Mount Olive, NJ
Schafer, Brenda L. ...Southborough, MA
Schafer, Brian M. ...Chicago, IL
Schafer, Brooke A. ...Seattle, WA
Schafer, Bruce L. ...Lake Oswego, OR
Schafer, C. Allison Brown ...Raleigh, NC
Schafer, C. Ben ...Denver, CO
Schafer, Carolyn ...Washington, DC
Schafer, Catherine H. ...Trenton, NJ
Schafer, Christine S.
Grosse Pointe Farms, MI
Schafer, Cynthia C. ...Cleveland, OH
Schafer, Cynthia J. ...Houston, TX
Schafer, Dale C. ...Cool, CA
Schafer, David E. ...Trenton, NJ
Schafer, David P. ...San Antonio, TX
Schafer, Dennis G. ...Montgomery City, MO
Schafer, Douglas A. ...Tacoma, WA
Schafer, Elsbeth D. ...Topeka, KS
Schafer, George M. ...Springfield, IL
Schafer, Gerald S. ...Greensboro, NC
Schafer, Gerard T. "Roger"
Virginia Beach, VA
Schafer, Gerry A. ...Plattsburgh, NY
Schafer, Harry R. ...Miami, FL
Schafer, Henry T. ...Seattle, WA
Schafer, Ilene Isaacman ...Philadelphia, PA
Schafer, James A. ...Muncie, IN
Schafer, Janice Oakes ...Seattle, WA
Schafer, Jeffrey A. ...San Francisco, CA
Schafer, John A., Jr. ...Baltimore, MD
Schafer, John H. ...Washington, DC
Schafer, John P. ...Los Angeles, CA
Schafer, Judy D. ...Washington, DC
Schafer, Julie A. ...Columbus, OH
Schafer, Kay Alley ...Morehead, KY
Schafer, Keith ...Hollywood, FL
Schafer, Kenneth C. ...Youngstown, OH
Schafer, Larry C. ...Phoenix, AZ
Schafer, Lee P. ...Deerfield, IL
Schafer, Lee W. ...St. Petersburg, FL
Schafer, M. Kathryn ...Washington, DC
Schafer, Mark ...Lonoke, AR
Schafer, Michael A. ...Louisville, KY
Schafer, Michael A. ...Troy, MI
Schafer, Michael W. ...Jupiter, FL
Buffalo, NY
Schafer, Michele M. ...Washington, DC
Schafer, Michelle M. ...Carbondale, IL
Schafer, Patricia K. ...Tacoma, WA
Schafer, Paul Jason ...Marion, IL
Schafer, Philip M. ...Crescent City, CA
Schafer, Richard A. ...Houston, TX
Schafer, Richard E.
Department of Commerce,
Patent and Trademark Office, GV
Schafer, Richard L. ...Shelby Township, MI
Schafer, Robert M. ...Pawnee City, NE
Schafer & Rooke, L.L.C. ...Denver, CO
Schafer & Russo ...Virginia Beach, VA
Schafer, Sam E. ...Wheeling, WV
Schafer & Schafer ...New Orleans, LA
Schafer, Scott D. ...Boston, MA
Schafer, Scott T. ...Escondido, CA
Schafer, Seymour J. ...Pittsburgh, PA
Schafer, Stephen G. ...Detroit, MI
Schafer, Steven H., & Associates
Boston, MA
Schafer, Stuart E. ...Bingham Farms, MI
Schafer, Susan N. ...Helena, MT
Schafer, T. Gregory ...New Orleans, LA
Schafer, Ted L. ...Austin, TX
Schafer, Terrence J. ...Newport Beach, CA
Schafer, Thomas E., III ...New Orleans, LA
Schafer, Timothy G. ...New Orleans, LA
Schafer, Timothy J. ...Irvine, CA
Denver, CO
Schafer, Timothy S. ...Merrillville, IN
Schafer, Todd A. ...Bloomfield Hills, MI
Schafer, Victoria E. ...Uniontown, OH
Schafer, Walter L., Jr. ...Clearwater, FL
Schafer, Walter L., Jr., P.A. ...Clearwater, FL
Schafer and Weiner, P.C.
Birmingham, MI
Bloomfield Hills, MI
Detroit, MI
Schafer, William G. ...Augusta, GA
Schafer, William J., III ...Phoenix, AZ
Schafer-Lewers, Therese ...Chicago, IL
Schafersman, Bernard T. ...Fremont, NE
Schafersman, Gary A. ...Overland Park, KS
Schaff, David ...Santa Monica, CA
Schaff, David
National Labor Relations Board,
Office of Board Members, GV
Schaff, Ethan N. ...Brighton, MA
Schaff, Gary M. ...Lancaster, NY
Schaff, John A. ...Flemington, NJ
Schaff, Kristine M. ...Omaha, NE
Schaff, Michael D. ...Cherry Hill, NJ
Philadelphia, PA
Schaff, Michael F. ...Woodbridge, NJ
Schaff, Michael J.B. ...St. Cloud, MN
Schaff, Tonja D. ...Great Falls, MT
Schaff, Valentine A., III ...Mandeville, LA
Schaffel, Eugene ...West Caldwell, NJ
New York, NY
Schaffel, Neil ...Coral Springs, FL
Schaffer, A. Frederick, Jr. ...Phoenix, AZ
Schaffer, A. Frederick, Jr., A Professional Corporation ...Phoenix, AZ
Schaffer, Alexandra M. ...St. Paul, MN
Schaffer, Andrew E. ...Alexandria, LA
Schaffer, Arthur D. ...Washington, DC
Schaffer, Barbara Janet ...New York, NY
Schaffer & Baumer ...Los Angeles, CA
Schaffer, Becky S. ...Miami, FL
Schaffer, Benson ...Pomona, CA
Schaffer, Beverly Bassett ...Fayetteville, AR
Schaffer, Brett Michael ...Baltimore, MD
Schaffer, Brian A. ...Washington, DC
Schaffer, Brian J. ...Philadelphia, PA
Schaffer & Cabell, P.C. ...Norfolk, VA
Richmond, VA
Schaffer, Charles E. ...Philadelphia, PA
Schaffer, Christopher E. ...Hunt Valley, MD
Schaffer, Clifford L. ...Los Angeles, CA
Schaffer, Daniel C. ...Boston, MA
Schaffer, David I. ...Mineola, NY
Schaffer, David L. ...Beverly Hills, CA
Schaffer, David N. ...Naperville, IL
Schaffer, David P. ...New York, NY
Schaffer, David R. ...Washington, DC
Schaffer, David S., Jr. ...Chicago, IL
Schaffer, Donald L. ...Evanston, IL
Schaffer, Doris ...Los Angeles, CA
Schaffer, Earl G. ...Severna Park, MD
Schaffer, Edith C. ...San Francisco, CA
Schaffer, Edmund S. ...Los Angeles, CA
Schaffer, Edward M. ...Carmel, NY
Schaffer, Eric A. ...Pittsburgh, PA
Schaffer, Eugene ...Freeport, NY
Schaffer, Frederick P. ...New York, NY
Schaffer, Gail M. ...Vermilion, OH
Schaffer, George W. ...St. Louis, MO
Schaffer, Gregory Paul ...Washington, DC
Schaffer, Grier D. ...Columbus, OH
Schaffer, H. Cy, (A Prof. Corp.)
Beverly Hills, CA
Schaffer & Henley ...Houston, TX
Schaffer, Henry M. ...Chicago, IL
Schaffer, Hyman L. ...New York, NY
Schaffer, Jeffrey D. ...Philadelphia, PA
Schaffer, Jeffrey K. ...Wellesley, MA
Schaffer, Jeffrey L. ...San Francisco, CA
Schaffer, Jennifer D. ...Athens, OH
Schaffer, Jerry R. ...Santa Ana, CA
Schaffer, JoAnn Weiss ...Houston, TX
Schaffer, John F. ...Houston, TX
Schaffer, Kent A. ...Houston, TX
Schaffer, Kirk ...San Francisco, CA
Schaffer, Lane A. ...New Orleans, LA
Schaffer, Larry A. ...Independence, MO
Schaffer, Laura A. ...New York, NY
Schaffer & Lax, A Professional Corporation
Los Angeles, CA
Schaffer, Lee Ann ...Akron, OH
Schaffer, Linda H. ...Erlanger, KY
Schaffer, Marguerite M. ...Bernardsville, NJ
Schaffer, Maria Lynn ...Phoenix, AZ
Schaffer, Mark B. ...Houston, TX
Schaffer, Mark C. ...Toledo, OH
Schaffer, Mark L., (P.C.) ...Washington, DC
Schaffer, Martin L., III ...Treasury Department,
Internal Revenue Service, GV
Schaffer, Martin P. ...Rockville, MD
Schaffer, Mary C. ...Wheeling, WV
Schaffer, McIntosh & Effertz
Independence, MO
Kansas City, MO
Schaffer, Michael J. ...Mineola, NY
Schaffer, Michael J. ...Sioux Falls, SD
Schaffer, Michael V. ...Vermilion, OH
Schaffer, Michelle I. ...Portland, ME
Boston, MA
Schaffer, Murray ...Mineola, NY
Schaffer, Natalie A. ...Buffalo, NY
Schaffer, Paul M. ...Bethlehem, PA
Schaffer, Peter J. ...Denver, CO
Schaffer, Peter K. ...Oklahoma City, OK
Schaffer, Randy ...Houston, TX
Schaffer, Richard B. ...Bala Cynwyd, PA
Schaffer, Richard W. ...Norfolk, VA
Richmond, VA
Schaffer, Robert ...New York, NY
Schaffer, Robert D. ...New York, NY
Schaffer, Robert E. ...Atlanta, GA
Schaffer, Robert G. ...Phoenix, AZ
Schaffer, Robert H S. ...Flint, MI
Schaffer, Robert J. ...Coral Gables, FL
Schaffer, Robert J. ...Miami, FL
Schaffer, Robert K. ...Houston, TX
Schaffer, Robert L. ...Los Angeles, CA
Schaffer, S. Andrew ...New York, NY
Schaffer, Scott A. ...Portland, OR

Schaffer, Scott L. .... Burlington, VT
Schaffer, Scott R. .... New York, NY
Schaffer, Stephen N. .... Norwalk, CT
Schaffer, Steven C. .... Washington, DC
Schaffer, Steven G. .... Atlanta, GA
Schaffer, Steven J. .... Florham Park, NJ
Schaffer, Stuart F. .... Houston, TX
Schaffer, Susan Gayle .... Atlanta, GA
Schaffer, Susan M. .... St. Paul, MN
Schaffer, Sylvan J. .... Mineola, NY
Mineola, NY
Schaffer, Thomas A. .... Salt Lake City, UT
Schaffer, Tony L. .... San Antonio, TX
Schaffer, Wendy H. .... Bloomington, IL
Schaffer, William Gray .... Portland, ME
Schaffert, Judith R. .... Phoenix, AZ
Schaffhausen, Paul J. .... Oak Brook, IL
Schaffhauser, Elizabeth J. .... Fairbanks, AK
Schaffield, Michael T. .... Islandia, NY
Schaffner, Ariel .... Chicago, IL
Schaffner, Charles H. .... Covington, KY
Schaffner, Clark F. .... Alden, NY
Schaffner, Corina N. .... Woodstock, VT
Schaffner, Daniel K. .... Clearwater, FL
Schaffner, David K.
New Philadelphia, OH
Schaffner, Georgia A. .... Hartford, CT
Schaffner, Harry .... Geneva, IL
Schaffner, Howard .... Chicago, IL
Schaffner, Jefferson N. .... Montgomery, OH
Schaffner, Jeffery O. .... Columbus, OH
Schaffner, Jennifer A. .... Detroit, MI
Schaffner, Lawrence S.
Federal Communications Commission,
Office of the General Counsel, GV
Schaffner, Mark S. .... Chicago, IL
Schaffner, Mary E. .... Louisville, KY
Schaffner, Mary Martin .... Nashville, TN
Schaffner, Melinda Reece .... Santa Ana, CA
Schaffner, Michael, & Assoc., P.C.
Chicago, IL
Schaffner, Rosanne K. .... Washington, CT
Schaffner, Theodore W. .... Schaumburg, IL
Schaffner & Van Der Snick, P.C.
Geneva, IL
St. Charles, IL
Schaffnit & Fletcher .... Gainesville, FL
Schaffnit, Gilbert A. .... Gainesville, FL
Schaffran, Andrew J. .... New York, NY
Schaffrath, Kurt A. .... Medina, OH
Schaffrick, Susan B. .... Simsbury, CT
Schaffroth, Lonnie D., Jr. .... Tempe, AZ
Schaffzin, Bethann P. .... Philadelphia, PA
Schaffzin, Edmund A. .... Los Angeles, CA
New York, NY
Schaffzin, Jonathan A. .... New York, NY
Schafle & Cotter .... Philadelphia, PA
Schafle, Joseph J., Jr. .... Philadelphia, PA
Schafler, Norman L. .... Los Angeles, CA
Schafler, Seth B. .... New York, NY
Schafran, Lynn Hecht .... New York, NY
Schafrann, Jay H. .... New York, NY
Schafrann, Jonathan B. .... New York, NY
Schafrick, Frederick C. .... Washington, DC
Schafstall, Richard D. .... Cincinnati, OH
Schafstall, Robert D. .... Franklin, IN
Schafstall, Robert H. .... Franklin, IN
Schager, Richard J., Jr. .... New York, NY
Schagrin Associates .... Washington, DC
Schagrin, Martin A. .... Wilmington, DE
Schagrin, Roger B. .... Washington, DC
Schaham, Gali .... Palo Alto, CA
Schai, Randall B. .... San Francisco, CA
Schaible, Charles M. .... San Francisco, CA
Schaible, Grace Berg .... Fairbanks, AK
Schaible, John C. .... Madisonville, KY
Schaible, Wayne A. .... Philadelphia, PA
Schaible-Jardine, Anne M. .... Bronx, NY
Schaibley, John R., III .... Indianapolis, IN
Schaich, Norman V. .... Black Mountain, NC
Schaich, W. Al .... San Antonio, TX
Schaider, Joel R. .... Chicago, IL
Schaier, Arthur G. .... Waterbury, CT
Schaier, Neil .... Mineola, NY
Schaier, Susan P. .... New York, NY
Schaier, Tribbitt & Schaier .... New York, NY
Schaikewitz, Steven .... Atlanta, GA
Schaiman, David S. .... New York, NY
Schaiman, Steven L. .... Redwood City, CA
Schain, Burney, Ross & Citron, Ltd.
Chicago, IL
Schain, Douglas Steven .... Brooklyn, NY
Schain, Jerome S. .... Chicago, IL
Schain, Linda .... Chicago, IL
Schain, Steven M. .... Philadelphia, PA
Schainbaum, Martin A.
San Francisco, CA
Schainbaum, Martin A., A Professional Law Corporation .... San Francisco, CA
Schainholz, Jay D. .... Cliffside Park, NJ
Schainker, William A. .... Chevy Chase, MD
Schainost, Jeanie L. .... Wichita, KS
Schair, Fern .... New York, NY
Schair, Stanley, (P.C.) .... New York, NY
Schair, Stephanie L. .... Stinnett, TX
Schairbaum, Daniel J. .... Chicago, IL
Schairbaum, Sarah Ryan .... Chicago, IL
Schairer, Patricia Reilly .... Islandia, NY
Schaitkin, Keith L. .... New York, NY
Schaitkin, Mark R. .... Troy, MI
Schaitman, Leonard .... Department of Justice,
Civil Division, GV
Schakel, Linda B. .... Washington, DC
Schaldach, Robert R. .... Sacramento, CA
Schaldenbrand, Cynthia B. .... Tustin, CA
Schalekamp, William A. .... Kansas City, MO
Schalestock, Peter K. .... Seattle, WA

Schalet, Lizabeth .... Jericho, NY
New York, NY
Schalge, Marilyn G. .... Denver, CO
Schalick, Walton O., Jr. .... Stamford, CT
Schalk, Charles Z. .... Somerville, NJ
Schalk, David E. .... Bloomington, IN
Schalk, Peter B. .... New York, NY
Schalk, Robert P. .... Santa Cruz, CA
Schalk, Stephen L. .... Davenport, IA
Schalkle, Barry L. .... St. Paul, MN
Schall, Alan M. .... Toledo, OH
Schall, Alvin A. ....
United States Court Of Appeals For The
Federal Circuit, GV
Schall, Boudreau & Gore, Incorporated
San Diego, CA
Schall, Edward W. .... New York, NY
Schall, Ellen K.
Federal Energy Regulatory Commission,
Office of the General Counsel, GV
Schall, Eric D. .... Warren, NJ
Schall, Gary K. .... Springfield, IL
Schall, Irene B. .... New Bedford, MA
Schall, James A. .... Storm Lake, IA
Schall, James M. .... Mc Connellsburg, PA
Schall, Jason Martin .... Houston, TX
Schall, Jeffrey .... New York, NY
Schall, Jenifer J. .... Department of Defense,
Defense Legal Services Agency, GV
Schall, Jennifer J. .... Joliet, IL
Schall, Kim M. .... San Diego, CA
Schall, Loren B. .... Fort Collins, CO
Schall, MiAnne .... Quincy, MA
Schall, Pamela Ann .... Andover, MA
Schall, Richard M. .... Cherry Hill, NJ
Northfield, NJ
Schall, Robert Wayne .... Philadelphia, PA
Schall, Todd A. .... Uniondale, NY
Schallau, Al .... Torrance, CA
Schaller, Barry R. .... Hartford, CT
Schaller, Campbell & Untied .... Newark, OH
Schaller, Charles E. .... Neenah, WI
Schaller, Charles R., Jr. .... Annapolis, MD
Schaller, Cynthia L. .... Chicago, IL
Schaller, Cyril D. .... Sun Lakes, AZ
Schaller, Douglas G. .... Eugene, OR
Schaller, Edward F., Jr. .... Olympia, WA
Schaller, Gordon A. .... Irvine, CA
Schaller & Gorski, L.L.P. .... Annapolis, MD
Schaller, Gregory D. .... Garden City, KS
Schaller, J. Scott .... San Diego, CA
Schaller, James M. .... Newark, OH
Schaller, James P. .... Washington, DC
Baltimore, MD
Rockville, MD
Vienna, VA
Schaller, Joel L. .... Florham Park, NJ
Schaller, John C. .... Chico, CA
Schaller, John H. .... Greenfield, WI
Schaller, Joseph N. .... Baltimore, MD
Schaller, Kenneth John .... Sacramento, CA
Schaller, Madeleine B. .... Washington, DC
Schaller, Michael J. .... Chicago, IL
Schaller, Michael J. .... St. Louis, MO
Schaller, Robert M. .... Severna Park, MD
Schaller, Robert V., & Associates
Hinsdale, IL
Schaller, Stephen E. .... Newark, OH
Schaller, William Lynch .... Chicago, IL
Schallert, Edwin G. .... New York, NY
Schallert, Mark .... San Francisco, CA
Schallert, Russell C. .... Mequon, WI
Schalles, George W., III .... Houston, TX
Schallhorn, J. Scott .... Little Rock, AR
Schalliol, Charles E. .... San Diego, CA
Schally, Timothy G. .... Milwaukee, WI
Schalmo, William E. .... Brookfield, WI
Schalow, Thomas R. .... Los Angeles, CA
Schaltegger, Eric H. .... Downers Grove, IL
Schaltegger, Herbert M.
Murfreesboro, TN
Schaltenbrand, Rebecca K. .... Dayton, OH
Schalter, John J., Law Office of
Sterling Heights, MI
Scham, Lee S. .... Houston, TX
Schamban, H. Nicole .... Albuquerque, NM
Schamber, Norman A. .... Alexandria, MN
Schamberger, Barbara A. .... Charleston, WV
Schamberger, Hermann M., Jr.
Villa Park, IL
Schamest, Joanne .... Washington, DC
Schamis, Jeffrey B. .... Chicago, IL
Schamus, Julian J. .... Reseda, CA
Schanbacher, David C. .... York, PA
Schanbacher, Nan Waksman
Merion Station, PA
Schanbacher, Walter W. .... Philadelphia, PA
Schanback, Jeffrey E. .... New York, NY
Schanck, Peter C. .... Clayton, MI
Schanck, William G., Jr. .... Red Bank, NJ
Schancupp, Arnold .... Fairfield, NJ
Schancupp, David E. .... New Haven, CT
Schancupp, Jennifer L. .... New Haven, CT
Schancupp, Peter J. .... New York, NY
Schandel, Phillip D. .... Canton, OH
Schander, F. Earl .... Dallas, TX
Schandlbauer, Nikolaus F.
Washington, DC
Schandler, Brad I. .... Miami Beach, FL
Schandler, Heidi L.
Equal Employment Opportunity
Commission,
Office of Federal Operations, GV
Schandler, Robert A. .... Hackensack, NJ
Schane, Durham .... Atlanta, GA
Schaneman, Jacqueline M .... Lincoln, NE
Schaner, Carol Peskoe .... Irvine, CA
Schaner, Dean J. .... Houston, TX

Schaner, Kenneth I. .... Washington, DC
Schaner, Lawrence S. .... Chicago, IL
Schanerman, Richard L. .... Miami, FL
Schaneville & Baringer, L.L.C.
Baton Rouge, LA
Schaneville, Dan D. .... Baton Rouge, LA
Schanfield, Karen G. .... Minneapolis, MN
Schang, Scott E. .... Washington, DC
Schank, H. John, II .... Newark, NJ
Schank, Jerry B. .... Houston, TX
Schank, Laura J. .... Toledo, OH
Schank, Martin J. .... Webster, NY
Schank, Roy M. .... Kaysville, UT
Schank, Thomas J. .... Toledo, OH
Schanker, Charles K. .... Wheaton, MD
Schanker, Darin L. .... Denver, CO
Schanker, David R. .... Indianapolis, IN
Schanker & Hochberg .... Huntington, NY
Schanker, Steven M. .... Huntington, NY
Schanker, Steven R. .... Kansas City, MO
Schankman, Benjamin M. .... Floral Park, NY
Schanks, Scott A. .... Chicago, IL
Schanlaber & Reed, A Professional Corporation .... Aurora, IL
Schanlaber, William C. .... Aurora, IL
Schannauer, Ashley C. .... Pittsburgh, PA
Schanne, Francis J. .... Wilmington, DE
Schannen, Richard H. .... Lynnfield, MA
Schanno, Joseph F. .... Ocean City, MD
Schano, Sarah K. .... Pittsburgh, PA
Schantz, Andrew V. .... Allentown, PA
Schantz, Hale .... Weston, FL
Schantz, Jeffrey A. .... New York, NY
Schantz, Jennifer Ellen .... New York, NY
Schantz, John L. .... Stowe, VT
Schantz, Laura L. .... Aloha, OR
Schantz Law Offices .... Allentown, PA
Schantz, Lawrence M. .... Miami, FL
Schantz, Matthew R. .... Indianapolis, IN
Schantz, Reid P. .... Santa Cruz, CA
Schantz, Robert M. .... Rochester, NY
Schantz, Roger L. .... Columbus, OH
Schantz, Stewart T. .... Highland, NY
Kingston, NY
Schantz, Stewart T. .... Poughkeepsie, NY
Schantz, William E. .... Allentown, PA
Schantz, William F. .... Wichita, KS
Schantz, William T. .... Portland, OR
Schantz, Wilmer S. .... McLean, VA
Schantz, Wilmer S., P.C. .... McLean, VA
Schanz, Daniel R. .... Salem, OR
Schanz, Gary W. .... Binghamton, NY
Schanz, Jeffrey E. ....
Department of Justice, GV
Schanz, William L. .... Irvine, CA
Schanzenbach, Robyn .... Oakland, CA
Schanzer, David H. .... Department of Defense,
Office of the General Counsel, GV
Schanzer, Kenneth D. .... New York, NY
Schanzer, Kimberly .... New York, NY
Schanzer, Robert M. .... New York, NY
Schanzle-Haskins, Thomas P., III
Springfield, IL
Schapanski, Stephen J. .... Fort Collins, CO
Schaper, Carlos E., Law Office
Brewster, NE
Schaper, Carlos E., Law Office
Broken Bow, NE
Schaper, Carlos E., Law Office
Burwell, NE
Taylor, NE
Thedford, NE
Schaper, John S. .... Phoenix, AZ
Schaper, Joseph A. .... St. Louis, MO
Schaper, Joseph R. .... Pittsburgh, PA
Schaper, Philip, Jr. .... Bowling Green, MO
Schaper, Reed E. .... Los Angeles, CA
Schaper, Todd .... Liberty Corner, NJ
Schaperkotter, John D. .... St. Louis, MO
Schaphorst, William K. .... Des Moines, IA
Schapira, Carol A. .... Seattle, WA
Schapira, Jeffry A. .... Manchester, NH
Schapira, Joel Richard .... Washington, DC
Schapira, Leonard L., Law Office of
Hermosa Beach, CA
Schapiro, Andrew H. .... New York, NY
Schapiro, Donald .... New York, NY
Schapiro, Gary A. .... Baltimore, MD
Schapiro, John H. .... Philadelphia, PA
Schapiro, Jules W. .... Brooklyn, NY
Schapiro, Karen M. .... Milwaukee, WI
Schapiro, Larry P. .... Sacramento, CA
Schapiro, Lawrence A. .... Sherman Oaks, CA
Schapiro, Lori Grumet .... Binghamton, NY
Schapiro, Louis A. .... New York, NY
Schapiro, Mark Edward .... Pomona, CA
Schapiro, Mary L. .... Washington, DC
Schapiro and Reich .... Lindenhurst, NY
Schapiro, Richard M. .... New York, NY
Schapiro, Robert A. .... Washington, DC
Schapiro, Robert D. .... New York, NY
Schapiro, Robert H. .... Baltimore, MD
Schapiro, S. A. .... Milwaukee, WI
Schapiro, Saul A. .... Boston, MA
Schapiro, Seth L. .... New York, NY
Schapiro, Sheldon M. .... Fort Lauderdale, FL
Schapiro, Stanley J. .... Towson, MD
Schapiro, Steven M. .... Lindenhurst, NY
Schapiro, Susan Freeman .... Hamilton, NY
Schapiro • Thorn, Inc. .... San Francisco, CA
Schapiro, William I. .... Buffalo, NY
Schapiro, Wisan & Krassner, P.C.
New York, NY
Schapker, Dennis R. .... Kansas City, MO
Schapker, Leonard J. .... Overland Park, KS
Schapler, Robert H. .... Middletown, RI
Schaplow, Terry F. .... Bozeman, MT
Schapp, Jonathan .... Buffalo, NY

Schappals, Julia A. .... Costa Mesa, CA
Schappaugh, Gary L. .... Garland, TX
Schappe, Michael G. .... O'Fallon, MO
Schappert, Jos. M. .... Muskegon, MI
Schappert, Leonard D. .... Ramona, CA
Schappert, Michael J. .... Rockford, IL
Schaps, James A. .... St. Paul, MN
Schaps, Joel P. .... Palos Park, IL
Schaps & Kluver, P.A. .... Litchfield, MN
Schaps, Robert D. .... Litchfield, MN
Schaps, Ronald T. .... Seattle, WA
Schar, Brian A. .... Irvine, CA
Schar, Stephen L. .... Chicago, IL
Scharaga, Ira M. .... Brooklyn, NY
Scharar, Robert W. .... Houston, TX
Scharbach, Linda K. .... Hobart, IN
Schard, Robin C. .... Cape May, NJ
Schardein, John M. .... Louisville, KY
Schardt, Elke Gordon .... Santa Clarita, CA
Schardt, James E. .... Richmond, VA
Schardt, Magdalena .... Trenton, NJ
Schare, Allan L. .... Los Angeles, CA
Scharer, Ronald J. .... Marion, OH
Scharf, Alan F. .... Tampa, FL
Scharf, Alan Z. .... New York, NY
Scharf, Benjamin H. .... Santa Cruz, CA
Scharf, David P. .... Hoffman Estates, IL
Scharf, Eric J. .... Burlingame, CA
Scharf, Erik W. .... Miami, FL
Minneapolis, MN
Scharf, Frank D. .... New York, NY
Scharf, Fred E. .... New York, NY
New York, NY
Scharf, Heino W. .... Greensboro, NC
Scharf, Herbert L. .... Woodmere, NY
Scharf, Irene .... North Dartmouth, MA
Scharf, Irwin L. .... New City, NY
Scharf, James A. .... San Francisco, CA
Scharf, Jared J. .... White Plains, NY
Scharf, Jeffrey D. .... Pasadena, CA
Scharf, Leslie D. .... Tampa, FL
Scharf, Leslie H. .... East Meadow, NY
Scharf, Marvin K. .... Brooklyn, NY
Scharf, Michael .... Boston, MA
Scharf, Paul S. .... White Plains, NY
Scharf, Rebecca L. .... Bronx, NY
Scharf, Robert B. .... Fort Lauderdale, FL
Scharf, Robert B., P.A. .... Fort Lauderdale, FL
Scharf, Robert D. .... Coral Springs, FL
Scharf, Robert Lee .... Tarzana, CA
Scharf, Ron .... New York, NY
Scharf, Roy H. .... Branford, CT
Scharf, Scott H. .... Cleveland, OH
Scharf, Shawn D. .... Salem, OH
Scharf, Stephanie A. .... Chicago, IL
Scharf, Stephen .... Los Angeles, CA
Scharf, Stephen L. .... Cleveland, OH
Scharf, Susan D. .... Englewood Cliffs, NJ
New York, NY
Scharf, William H. .... Charleston, WV
Scharf, Y. David .... New York, NY
Scharfeld, Leonard B. .... Cleveland, OH
Scharfen, Jeffrey C. .... Santa Rosa, CA
Scharfenberg, Edward .... New York, NY
Scharfenberg, S. Andrew, Jr .... Mobile, AL
Scharfenberg, Theodore M.
East Hampton, NY
Scharfenberger, Edward B. .... Forest Hills, NY
Scharfenberger, Edward P. .... Warwick, NY
Scharfenberger, James D. .... Warwick, NY
Scharfenberger, Kurt A. .... Louisville, KY
Scharfenberg-Ferrarone, Karen .... Barre, MA
Scharfer, James A. .... Los Angeles, CA
Scharff, Alex J. .... San Antonio, TX
Scharff, Audrey L. .... Seattle, WA
Scharff, Daniel W. .... Cincinnati, OH
Scharff, Jeffory J., Law Office of
Sacramento, CA
Scharff, Jeffrey S. .... Washington, DC
Scharff, Joel G. .... Springfield, NJ
Scharff, Jonathan E. .... Memphis, TN
Scharff, Lee W. .... New Orleans, LA
Scharff, Martin .... Dayton, OH
Scharff, Nancy Philion .... Haddonfield, NJ
Scharff, Paula Christine, Law Office of
Jeffersonville, PA
Scharfman, B. Leslie .... Hialeah, FL
Scharfman, Ian .... Houston, TX
Scharfstein, Dax .... New York, NY
Scharfstein, Joel .... New York, NY
Scharfy, Veronica L. .... Maumee, OH
Scharf-Zeldes, Barbara E. .... San Antonio, TX
Scharg, Donald H. .... Bloomfield Hills, MI
Detroit, MI
Scharg, Henry M. .... Warren, MI
Scharg, Sheldon M. .... Farmington Hills, MI
Schargorodski, Joyce M .... Fairfax, VA
Scharin, Allison R. .... New York, NY
Scharine, Cheryl A. .... Madison, WI
Scharlach, Alan M. .... Oakland, CA
Scharlach, David A. .... Rancho Murieta, CA
Scharlacken, Lorna J. .... New York, NY
Scharlat, Richard I. .... Roseland, NJ
Scharlau, Chas. E., Jr. .... Fayetteville, AR
Scharlau, Greg S. .... Fayetteville, AR
Scharlin, David Michael .... Hollywood, FL
Scharlin, Howard R. .... Miami, FL
Pittsburgh, PA
Scharmach, Sheryl L. .... Arlington, VA
Scharman, Clifford J. .... Washington, DC
Scharmen, George .... San Antonio, TX
Scharmer, Neal R. .... Cedar Rapids, IA
Scharmett, Gary Paul .... Philadelphia, PA
Scharmett, Steven W. .... Leominster, MA
Scharnberg, Charles J. .... Oklahoma City, OK
Scharnberg, Sarah L. .... Denison, TX
Scharnberg, Steven K. .... Des Moines, IA

Scharnberger, Laurence M.
Woodland Hills, CA
Scharnhorst, Todd A. ... Overland Park, KS
Scharnikow, William T. ... Yakima, WA
Scharoff, Smith, Murray and Nannini
West Springfield, MA
Scharon, John V., Jr. ... Cleveland, OH
Scharpf, Marjorie J. ... Evansville, IN
Scharpf, Michael J. ... Livingston, NJ
Scharrenberg, Mary L. ... San Jose, CA
Scharrer, Richard C. ... Dayton, OH
Scharstein, Harry E. ... Charleston, SC
Scharton, Barbara L. ... Fresno, CA
Schartz, Elizabeth A. ... Dallas, TX
Schartz, Robert M. ... Omaha, NE
Scharuda, Victoria ... Atlanta, GA
Schassler, Steven G. ... Albany, NY
Schatken, Steven N.
Department of Education,
Office of the General Counsel, GV
Schatteman, Sally A. ... Newport, KY
Schatten, Alexis ... Palo Alto, CA
Schatten, Arthur L. ... Summit, NJ
Schatten, David J. ... New York, NY
Schatten, Kenneth H., Law Offices of
Atlanta, GA
Schatten and Locker ... Summit, NJ
Schatten, Marc L. ... Memphis, TN
Schatten, Phyllis E. ... Royal Oak, MI
Schatten, Rachel N. ... New York, NY
Schattenfield, Scott W. ... Charlotte, NC
Schattenfield, Thomas ... Washington, DC
Schattenstein, David C. ... Allentown, PA
Schattinger, John J., III ... Auburn, NY
Schattman, Michael D.
Small Business Administration,
Office of the General Counsel, GV
Schattman, Nathan ... Fort Worth, TX
Schattner, Ann D. ... Hauppauge, NY
Schattner, Lawrence H.
Treasury Department,
Internal Revenue Service, GV
Schattner, Rochelle D. ... Dix Hills, NY
Schattnik, Daniel R. ... East Alton, IL
Schatz, Allen E. ... Milwaukee, WI
Schatz, Andrew M. ... Hartford, CT
Schatz, Arthur H. ... Bloomfield, CT
Schatz, Barbara A. ... New York, NY
Schatz, Barry A., (P.C.) ... Chicago, IL
Lake Forest, IL
Schatz, Daniel J. ... Providence, RI
Schatz, Diana R. Maurer ... Denver, CO
Schatz, Donald ... Putnam Valley, NY
Schatz, Gerald S. ... Wheaton, MD
Schatz, Gordon B. ... Washington, DC
Schatz, Gregory M. ... Omaha, NE
Schatz, Howard R. ... New York, NY
Schatz, Jacob J. ... San Francisco, CA
Schatz, James E. ... Minneapolis, MN
Schatz, Jerry A. ... Memphis, TN
Schatz, John ... San Jose, CA
Schatz, John D. ... Boston, MA
Schatz, Joseph L. ... San Francisco, CA
Schatz, Julie Pearlman ... Ardsley, NY
Schatz, Kathleen A. ... Charlestown, MA
Schatz, Katrin U. ... Dallas, TX
Schatz, Kenneth A. ... Waterbury, VT
Schatz, Larry H. ... New York, NY
Schatz, Louis B. ... Hartford, CT
Schatz, Marilyn B. ... New York, NY
Schatz, Marshal Z. ... Buffalo, NY
Schatz, Marvin P. ... Fairview Park, OH
Schatz, Monte L. ... Omaha, NE
Schatz, Nathan A. ... West Hartford, CT
Schatz & Nobel, P.C. ... Hartford, CT
Schatz, Norman L. ... Milwaukee, WI
Schatz, Patricia Ann ... Nutley, NJ
Schatz, Philip Ransom ... New York, NY
Schatz, Randee S. ... Palm Beach, FL
Schatz, Richard A. ... New London, CT
Schatz, Richard E. ... Miami, FL
Schatz, Robert B. B. ... Philadelphia, PA
Schatz, Robert F. ... West Hartford, CT
Schatz, Robert W. ... Marion, IN
Schatz, Russell W., Jr. ... Los Angeles, CA
Schatz, S. Michael ... Hartford, CT
Schatz & Schatz, Ribicoff & Kotkin
Hartford, CT
Stamford, CT
Schatz, Stephen M. ... Atlanta, GA
Schatz, Steven D. ... Tustin, CA
Schatz, Steven M. ... Palo Alto, CA
Schatz, Steven R. ... Oklahoma City, OK
Schatz, Stuart J. ... Norristown, PA
Schatz, Thomas A. ... Washington, DC
Schatz, Walter B. ... West Hartford, CT
Schatz, William B. ... Cleveland, OH
Schatzel, Thomas E. ... Los Gatos, CA
Schatzel, Thomas E., Law Offices of, A Prof.
Corporation ... Los Gatos, CA
Schatzki, George ... Hartford, CT
Schatzki, Ralph D. ... West Hartford, CT
Schatzle, Chad J. ... Miami, FL
Schatzman, Arnold D. ... Miami, FL
Schatzman, Jeffrey N. ... Miami, FL
Schatzman, Larry O. ... Miami, FL
Schatzman, Larry O., A Professional
Association ... Miami, FL
Schatzman, Linley ... Miami, FL
Schatzman, Richard ... Princeton, NJ
Schatzman, Robert A. ... Miami, FL
Schatzman and Schatzman, P.A. ... Miami, FL
Schatzman, Staci ... Miami, FL
Schatzow, Michael ... Washington, DC
Baltimore, MD
Schatzow, Steven ... Washington, DC
Schau, Andrew D. ... New York, NY
Schau, Jan F. ... Encino, CA
Schau, John M. ... El Cajon, CA
Schau, Jordan R. ... Kalamazoo, MI
Schaub, C. Robert ... Huntington, WV
Schaub, Charles E., Jr. ... Boston, MA
Providence, RI
Schaub, Charles R. ... Toledo, OH
Schaub, Frank ... Highlands, NC
Schaub, Harry Carl ... Philadelphia, PA
Schaub, Jeffrey L. ... New York, NY
Schaub, Jeffrey R. ... San Antonio, TX
Schaub, Jerome C. ... Pittsburgh, PA
Schaub, John P. ... San Jose, CA
Schaub, Kristin ... Irvine, CA
Schaub Law Offices, L.C.
Huntington, WV
Schaub, Nancy ... Bellaire, MI
Schaub, Paul B. ... Sidney, NE
Schaub, Peter M. ... Eden Prairie, MN
Schaub, Raymond C. ... West Nyack, NY
Schaub, Robert D. ... Wilkes-Barre, PA
Schaub, Robert R. ... Chamberlain, SD
Schaub, Scott J. ... Lincoln City, OR
Schaub, Victor T. ... Arcata, CA
Schaub, William C., Jr. ... Detroit, MI
Schaub, William D. ... Portland, OR
Schaubhut & Gill ... Austin, TX
Schaubhut, Larry Paul, Jr. ... Austin, TX
Schaubhut, Lawrence P. ... Austin, TX
Schauble, Albert J. ... Colfax, WA
Pullman, WA
St. John, WA
Schauble, John J.
Federal Communications Commission,
Wireless Telecommunications Bureau, GV
Schauble, Wayne L. ... Lewiston, MN
Schauble Pickett, Edith ... Birmingham, AL
Schauble-Ruff, Linda ... Colfax, WA
Pullman, WA
Schauder, Dawn ... New York, NY
Schauder, Edward H. ... New York, NY
Schauder, Edward Hal ... New York, NY
Schauder, Yael R. ... Redwood City, CA
Schauer, Andrew M. ... Denver, CO
Schauer, Cory B. ... Boston, MA
Schauer, David E. ... Winthrop, MN
Schauer, Frederick F. ... Cambridge, MA
Schauer, G. Don ... Corpus Christi, TX
Schauer, Hilbert ... Parker, CO
Schauer, Jason ... San Diego, CA
Schauer, John S. ... Chicago, IL
Schauer, Lillian R. ... Port Orchard, WA
Schauer, Nancy R. ... Culver City, CA
Schauer, Neil R. ... Boston, MA
Schauer, Patrick J. ... Glen Ellyn, IL
Schauer, Randall C. ... West Chester, PA
Schauer, Richard ... Los Angeles, CA
Schauer, Richard J. ... Battle Ground, WA
Schauer, Robert F. ... Ontario, CA
Schauer & Schauer ... Boston, MA
Schauer, Simank & Ledbetter, A Professional
Corporation ... Corpus Christi, TX
Schauer, Teresa Lee ... Alexandria, VA
Schauer, Tone T. ... Denver, CO
Schauer, Wilbert E., Jr. ... Elm Grove, WI
Schauer, William A. ... Ridgewood, NY
Schauer, William J. ... Ridgewood, NY
Schauerman, Anne M. ... Oak Park, CA
Schauermann, Craig F. ... Vancouver, WA
Schauermann & Thayer ... Vancouver, WA
Schauf, Carolyn J. ... Downey, CA
Schauf, Lawrence E. ... San Diego, CA
Schauf, Susan M. ... Tucson, AZ
Schauf, Susan M., Ltd. ... Tucson, AZ
Schaufel, Jarrett L. ... San Antonio, TX
Schaufel, Jarrett L., P.C. ... San Antonio, TX
Schaufelberger, Patrick F. ... Greenville, IL
Vandalia, IL
Schaufelberger, Thomas S.
Washington, DC
Schaufeld, Robert M. ... Great Neck, NY
Schauffert, Richard C. ... Fort Lauderdale, FL
Schauffler, Phyllis ... St. Louis, MO
Schaukowitch, Carl ... Washington, DC
Schaul, Cheryl Kehoe ... Chicago, IL
Schaul, Louis R. ... Cleveland, OH
Schaul, Robert F. ... Flemington, NJ
Schaul, Terrence Leigh ... Chicago, IL
Schaulat, Ronald A. ... Oklahoma City, OK
Schaul-Yoder, Richard R. ... Boston, MA
Schaum, Jacob ... Brooklyn, NY
Schaum, Mark A. ... Boca Raton, FL
Schaum, Martin ... Garden City, NY
Schaum, P. Andrew ... Philadelphia, PA
Schaum & Wiener, Law Offices of
Garden City, NY
Schaumann, David ... York, PA
Schaumann, Dennis M. ... St. Louis, MO
Schaumann, Niels B. ... St. Paul, MN
Schaumann, Robert W. ... Minneapolis, MN
Schaumber, Peter Carey ... Washington, DC
Schaumberg, Edward G., II ... Denver, CO
Schaumberg, Peter J.
Department Of The Interior,
Office of the Solicitor, GV
Schaumberg, Tom M. ... Washington, DC
Schaumberger, Debra ... New York, NY
Schaumberger, Norman H. ... Tappan, NY
Schaumburg, Seth H. ... New Orleans, LA
Schauner, David M. ... Topeka, KS
Schaupp, Melvin R. ... Mora, MN
Schaus, Barbara A. ... Buffalo, NY
Schaus, John G. ... Mesa, AZ
Schaus, Margaret E. ... Moraga, CA
Schaus, Maynard C. ... Buffalo, NY
Schaus, Richard M. ... Buffalo, NY
Schaus, Robert ... Naples, FL
Schaus & Schaus ... Buffalo, NY
Schauseil, Joseph B. ... Rochester, NY
Schaut, Donald D. ... Santa Rosa, CA
Schaut, Donald D., A Professional Corporation
Santa Rosa, CA
Schaut, Jos. W. ... Cleveland, OH
Schaut, Vicki ... Janesville, WI
Schavey, Kimberly A. ... Albuquerque, NM
Schavey, Kimberly A., P.C.
Albuquerque, NM
Schavone, Peter Anthony ... New London, CT
Schavrien, Joel H. ... Farmington Hills, MI
Schay, Alvin ... Little Rock, AR
Schaye, Jenifer ... Baton Rouge, LA
Schaye, Natman ... Tucson, AZ
Schayes, Jeanne B. ... New York, NY
Scheaf, O. Judson, III ... Columbus, OH
Schear, Abe J. ... Atlanta, GA
Schear, Andrea Seychett
Huntington Station, NY
Schear, Barry L. ... San Diego, CA
Schear, Kathi L. ... Columbus, OH
Schear, Stephen ... Oakland, CA
Scheb, John M. ... Sarasota, FL
Scheb, Robert P. ... Sarasota, FL
Schebaum, William H. ... Oneonta, NY
Schebel, Jodi M. ... Detroit, MI
Schebler, Thomas G., (P.C.) ... Davenport, IA
Schebler & Wine ... Davenport, IA
Schechet, David A. ... Los Angeles, CA
Schechner, David ... West Orange, NJ
Schechner, Mark S. ... Miami, FL
Schechner, P. Sheridan ... New York, NY
Schechner, Richard ... Ridgewood, NY
Schechner, Stephen H., Law Offices of
Millburn, NJ
Schechner, Stephen H., Law Offices of
Newark, NJ
Schechner and Targan, A Professional
Corporation ... West Orange, NJ
Schecht, Neil S. ... Tampa, FL
Schechter, Arlene H. ... New York, NY
Schechter, Arthur L. ... Houston, TX
Schechter & Associates ... Northbrook, IL
Schechter, Audrey Hildes ... Tampa, FL
Schechter, Benay H. ... Chicago, IL
Schechter, Bruce Lee ... Orange, CA
Schechter & Brucker, P.C. ... New York, NY
Schechter, Clifford ... Poway, CA
Schechter, Dan O.
Department Of Veterans Affairs,
Board of Veterans Appeals, GV
Schechter, Dan S. ... Los Angeles, CA
Schechter, Daniel P. ... New York, NY
Schechter, Daniel R. ... New York, NY
Schechter, David A. ... Providence, RI
Schechter, Dayle Anne ... La Crosse, WI
Schechter, Deborah ... New York, NY
Schechter, Donald L. ... Great Neck, NY
Schechter, Donald R. ... Kew Gardens, NY
Schechter, Donald R., P.C.
Kew Gardens, NY
Schechter, Dorothy L. ... Ojai, CA
Schechter, Dov S. ... New York, NY
Schechter, Erika Schafer ... Chicago, IL
Schechter, Gary ... Springfield, IL
Schechter, Harriet J. ... Boston, MA
Schechter, Harry L. ... Los Angeles, CA
Schechter, Harvey ... New York, NY
Schechter, Howard ... New York, NY
Schechter, Howard R.
West Los Angeles, CA
Schechter, Israel ... New York, NY
Schechter, Jay Eli ... Miami, FL
Schechter, Jeanne E. ... Modesto, CA
Schechter, Jeffrey H. ... Hackensack, NJ
Schechter, Jeffrey S. ... St. Louis, MO
Schechter, Jerome R.
Fort Lauderdale, FL
Schechter, Jerome R., P.A.
Fort Lauderdale, FL
Schechter, Joel A. ... Chicago, IL
Schechter, Joel B. ... Buffalo, NY
Schechter, Joel H. ... Stamford, CT
Naples, FL
Schechter, Jonathan ... New York, NY
Schechter, Jonathan A. ... New York, NY
Schechter, Jonathan D. ... Buffalo, NY
Schechter, Judy ... Goodlettsville, TN
Schechter, Julie S. ... Stamford, CT
Schechter, Kimberly A. ... East Amherst, NY
Schechter Law Firm, The, P.C.
Clayton, MO
St. Louis, MO
Schechter, Linda ... New York, NY
Schechter, Loren ... New York, NY
Schechter, Lori A. ... San Francisco, CA
Schechter, Marc D. ... Yorktown Heights, NY
Schechter, Marc S. ... San Diego, CA
Schechter, Marilyn M. ... New York, NY
Schechter, Mark C. ... Washington, DC
Schechter, Mark J. ... Chicago, IL
Schechter & Marshall, L.L.P. ... Houston, TX
Schechter, Martin David ... New York, NY
Schechter, Marvin E. ... New York, NY
Schechter, Marvin L. ... Jericho, NY
Schechter & Mathis ... La Crosse, WI
Schechter, Michael L. ... St. Louis, MO
Schechter, Michael R. ... Minneapolis, MN
Schechter, Minda R. ... Los Angeles, CA
Schechter, Neil J. ... Baltimore, MD
Schechter & Nimkoff, LLP ... New York, NY
Schechter, Pamela A. ... New York, NY
Schechter, Paul B. ... Newark, CA
Schechter, Peter C. ... New York, NY
Schechter, Richard M., (P.C.) ... Houston, TX
Schechter, Robert J. ... New York, NY
Schechter, Robert M. ... Piscataway, NJ
Schechter, Robin ... New York, NY
Schechter, Roger C. ... Los Angeles, CA
Roseland, NJ
New York, NY
Schechter, Roger E. ... Washington, DC
Schechter, Ronald A. ... Washington, DC
Schechter, Roy J. ... Cleveland, OH
Schechter, Scott A. ... New York, NY
Schechter, Selwyn ... Newark, NJ
Schechter, Stanley ... St. Louis, MO
Schechter, Steven C. ... Fair Lawn, NJ
Schechter, Stewart F. ... Northbrook, IL
Schechter, Stuart ... San Diego, CA
Schechter, Stuart A. ... Hollywood, FL
Schechter, Susan ... Washington, DC
Schechter, Susan ... St. Petersburg, FL
Schechter, Susan Alfred
Bingham Farms, MI
Schechter, Susan E. ... Hartford, CT
Schechter, Theodore S. ... St. Louis, MO
Schechter, Thomas L. ... Ojai, CA
Schechter, Wendy J. ... New York, NY
Schechterman, Jill L. ... New York, NY
Schechter Rakowski, Kara I.
New York, NY
Schechtman, Craig B. ... San Diego, CA
Schechtman, Ellen Rae ... Chicago, IL
Schechtman, Florence B. ... Chicago, IL
Schechtman, Larry A. ... Chicago, IL
Schechtman, Melvin A. ... Schaumburg, IL
Schechtman, Morrisa, Law Office of
Las Vegas, NV
Schechtman, Ronald H. ... Carroll, IA
Schechtman, Steven I. ... Newburgh, NY
Schechtman, Steven L. ... Minneapolis, MN
Scheck, Barry Charles ... New York, NY
Scheck, Edgar E. ... Orange, CA
Scheck, Frank F. ... New York, NY
Scheck, Frederick L., III ... Carey, OH
Upper Sandusky, OH
Scheck, Howard A.
Securities and Exchange Commission,
Division of Enforcement, GV
Scheck, Jacqueline M. ... Los Angeles, CA
Scheck, James H. ... Philadelphia, PA
Scheck, Laurie A. ... Upper Sandusky, OH
Scheck, Marion E. ... Great Neck, NY
Scheck, Martha ... Santa Barbara, CA
Scheck, Paul J. ... Miami, FL
Orlando, FL
Scheck, Stephanie N. ... Wichita, KS
Scheck, Stephen A. ... Irvine, CA
Scheck, Thomas B. ... Chicago, IL
Scheckel, Rosalie C. ... West Orange, NJ
Schecker, David A. ... Boston, MA
Schecker, Laurence H.
Federal Communications Commission,
Office of the General Counsel, GV
Scheckman, Howard B. ... Oakland, CA
Scheckman, Steven R. ... New Orleans, LA
Scheckner, Donna R. ... North Woodmere, NY
Scheckner, Dori-Ellen ... Brooklyn, NY
Scheckner, Kimberly H. ... Boston, MA
Scheckowitz, Bruce Evan ... New York, NY
Schecter, Adam H. ... Irvine, CA
Schecter, Adina ... New York, NY
Schecter, Alvin J. ... Brooklyn, NY
Schecter, Benjamin S. ... Louisville, KY
Schecter, Carole ... Chicago, IL
Schecter, Daniel Scott ... Los Angeles, CA
Schecter, Jay E. ... Miami, FL
Schecter, Jeffrey S. ... Garden City, NY
Schecter, Jennifer G. ... New York, NY
Schecter, Jennifer K. ... New York, NY
Schecter, Manny W. ... Yorktown Heights, NY
Schecter, Mardi J. ... New York, NY
Schecter, Mark S. ... Fort Lauderdale, FL
Schecter, Martha Jean ... Binghamton, NY
Schecter, Michael D. ... Washington, DC
Schecter, Mitchell P. ... Spring Valley, NY
Schecter, Pamela Jacobs ... Thiells, NY
Schecter, Paul A. ... Washington, DC
Schecter, Roger A. ... Nashville, TN
Schecter, Ronald G. ... West Orange, NJ
Schecter, Sheldon D. ... Cleveland, OH
Schecter, Stephen M. ... New York, NY
Schecter, William Lawrence
South Salem, NY
Schectman, Bart T. ... Scarsdale, NY
Schectman, Herbert A. ... Greenwich, CT
Schectman, Susan M. ... Pacifica, CA
Schector, Irwin B. ... Totowa, NJ
Schedler, Dale G. ... Kansas City, MO
Schedler, John W., Law Office of
Everett, WA
Seattle, WA
Schedler, John W., Law Office of
Snohomish, WA
Schedler, Karl W. ... Columbus, OH
Schedler, Mark D. ... Seattle, WA
Schedler, Martin ... Portland, OR
Schedler, Martin, P.C. ... Portland, OR
Scheef, C. John, III ... Dallas, TX
Scheef & Stone, L.L.P. ... Dallas, TX
Scheehle, Dorothy L. ... Fountain Hills, AZ
Scheehle, J. Scott ... Phoenix, AZ
Scheehle Law Firm, P.L.C.
Fountain Hills, AZ
Phoenix, AZ
Scheehle, Mark V. ... Fountain Hills, AZ
Scheel, Christine A. ... Chicago, IL
Scheel, Douglas W. ... St. Paul, MN
Scheele, Carol Ann ... Frankfort, KY
Scheele, Kathleen A. ... Brattleboro, VT
Scheele, Scott A. ... Department of Justice,
Antitrust Division, GV
Scheele, Stephen E. ... Highland, IN
Scheeler, Charles ... Towson, MD
Scheeler, Charles P. ... Baltimore, MD

Scheeler, Mary Katherine ... Towson, MD
Scheeler & Scheeler ... Towson, MD
Scheels, John M. ... Orange, CA
Scheer, Alan Dean ... Ithaca, NY
Scheer, Alan I. ... Bridgeport, CT
Hartford, CT
Scheer, Anne G. ... Concord, NH
Scheer, Anthony G. ... Charlotte, NC
Scheer, Barry S. ... Boston, MA
Scheer, Craig M. ... Washington, DC
Scheer, David A. ... Newark, NY
Scheer, George M., Jr. ... Atlanta, GA
Scheer, Green & Burke, Co., L.P.A.
Toledo, OH
Scheer, Harold ... Toledo, OH
Scheer, Jackson, Cohen & Schoenberg LLC
Atlanta, GA
Scheer, James A. ... Chicago, IL
Scheer, James J. ... Celina, OH
Scheer, Jeffrey B. ... Syracuse, NY
Scheer, Jerry A. ... Costa Mesa, CA
Scheer, Joel M. ... Easton, PA
Scheer, Keith ... Chicago, IL
Scheer, Kenneth L. ... Poughkeepsie, NY
Scheer, L. George ... Sunny Isles Beach, FL
Scheer, Lloyd K. ... Chicago, IL
Scheer, M. Richard ... Scotch Plains, NJ
Scheer, Marc R. ... Manchester, NH
Scheer, Marilyn S. ... Los Angeles, CA
Scheer, Mark J. ... Miami, FL
Scheer, Mark P. ... Seattle, WA
Scheer, Michael A. ... Fort Wayne, IN
Scheer, Michael J. ... New York, NY
Scheer, Randy P. ... Springfield, MO
Scheer, Richard A. ... New York, NY
Scheer, Spencer Paul ... Woodland Hills, CA
Scheer, Steven E. ... Savannah, GA
Scheer, Susan W. ... Morristown, NJ
Scheer, Thomas F. ... Milwaukee, WI
Scheerer, Ian V. ... Minneapolis, MN
Scheerer, Paul J. ... Minneapolis, MN
Scheerer, Stephen Neill
Incline Village, NV
Scheerer, Thomas M. ... Los Angeles, CA
Scheer-Mayer, Paula L. ... Brookline, MA
Scheetz, Lawrence R. ... Richboro, PA
Scheetz, Stanley D. ... Medina, OH
Scheetz, Stanley D., Co., L.P.A.
Medina, OH
Schefcik, Sandra I. ... Rochester, MI
Schefer, Alison J. ... Hollywood, FL
West Palm Beach, FL
Schefers, Steven H. ... Hawthorne, NJ
Scheff, Eileen R. ... Detroit, MI
Scheff, Lisa ... San Francisco, CA
Scheff, Richard L. ... Philadelphia, PA
Scheff, Robert ... New York, NY
Scheff, S. Leonard ... Tucson, AZ
Scheff, Simon ... Boston, MA
Scheffe, Michael S. ... Houston, TX
Scheffee, Elizabeth J. ... Portland, ME
Scheffel, Carrie L. ... Ocala, FL
Scheffel, Evan ... Los Angeles, CA
Scheffel, John C. ... Tarrytown, NY
Scheffel, John F. ... New York, NY
Scheffel, Mark H. ... Denver, CO
Scheffel, Thomas N., & Associates, P.C.
Denver, CO
Scheffel, Thomas Norman ... Denver, CO
Scheffer, David J.
Department of State, GV
Scheffer, Mark S. ... Philadelphia, PA
Scheffer, Mark T. ... Madison, WI
Scheffer, Robert P. ... Lockport, NY
Scheffer, Scott K. ... Eagan, MN
Scheffey, James D. ... Pottstown, PA
Scheffey, Merl H. ... Dallas, TX
Scheffey, Thomas B. ... Hartford, CT
Scheffing, Robert A. ... Irvine, CA
Scheffler, Allan J. ... Mount Kisco, NY
Scheffler, Eric R. ... New York, NY
Scheffler, Hans M. ... Salt Lake City, UT
Scheffler, Henry E. ... Maywood, IL
Scheffler, King & Bender, L.L.P.
Mount Kisco, NY
Scheffler, Lenor A. ... Minneapolis, MN
Scheffler, Mark D. ... Larchmont, NY
Scheffler, Richard J. ... Madison, CT
Scheffler, Stuart Jay ... Norristown, PA
Scheffler, William L., & Associates
Westport, CT
Scheffres, Alan J. ... Chicago, IL
Schefft, Karl D. ... Cedarburg, WI
Scheffy, Brackett L. ... Warner, NH
Scheffy, Robert W., Jr. ... Baton Rouge, LA
Scheflen, John W. ... Newark, DE
Scheflow, Douglas J. ... Elgin, IL
Scheflow, Richard S. ... Elgin, IL
Scheflow & Rydell ... Elgin, IL
Schefman, Bryan L. ... Troy, MI
Schefman, Leslie C. ... Troy, MI
Schefrin, Aram R. ... Providence, RI
Schefsky, Gary J. ... San Francisco, CA
Schefsky, Lynn A. ... Midland, MI
Schefstad, Steven R. ... Atlanta, GA
Schefter, Robert J. ... York, PA
Schefter, Walter L., Jr. ... Lacey, WA
Scheg, Kathleen E. ... Hyattsville, MD
Schegi, Nathan L. ... San Francisco, CA
Schehl, Joanne ... Washington, DC
Schehr, Curtis Lorin ... Fairfax, VA
Schehr, Kevin ... Versailles, MO
Schehr, Thomas Michael ... Detroit, MI
Schei, Lawrence A. ... Sacramento, CA
Schei, Pendergast & Collins
Sacramento, CA
Scheib, Elizabeth Mary ... Boca Raton, FL
Scheib, Hilda ... San Francisco, CA
Scheib, Jacqueline ... Hartford, CT
Scheib, John ... Washington, DC
Scheib, Julie A. ... Lafayette, LA
Scheib, Michael B. ... York, PA
Scheib, Paul M. ... New York, NY
Scheibal, Edward J. ... Fords, NJ
Scheibe, Benjamin D. ... Beverly Hills, CA
Scheibe, Frederick A. ... Berkeley Heights, NJ
Scheibe, Phillip F. ... Glen Burnie, MD
Scheibe, Robert H. ... New York, NY
Scheibel, E. Scott ... Fort Atkinson, WI
Scheibel, Elizabeth D. ... Northampton, MA
Scheibel, James R. ... Oak Lawn, IL
Scheibel, Kenneth M., Jr.
Federal Communications Commission,
Mass Media Bureau, GV
Scheibeler, James N. ... Danielson, CT
Scheibeler, John P. ... New York, NY
Scheibenberger, Kenneth R. ... Fort Wayne, IN
Scheiberling, Rogan & Maney
Albany, NY
Scheible, Eric D. ... Detroit, MI
Scheible, Mary L. ... Thermopolis, WY
Scheibler, Edward G., Jr. ... New York, NY
Scheibli, Michael A. ... Redding, CA
Scheibmeir, Mark C. ... Chehalis, WA
Scheibner, Catharine M. ... Monument, CO
Scheibner, M. Kathleen ... Little Rock, AR
Scheich, Goldsmith & Dreishpoon, P.C.
Hicksville, NY
Richmond Hill, NY
Scheich, John F. ... Hicksville, NY
Richmond Hill, NY
Scheich, Richard A. ... Toledo, OH
Scheichet, David I. ... New York, NY
Scheichet & Davis, P.C. ... New York, NY
Scheichet, Steven ... New York, NY
Scheid, Arthur M. ... McLean, VA
Scheid, Brian T. ... Narrows, VA
Scheid, Catherine C. ... Houston, TX
Scheid, John H. ... Chicago, IL
Scheid, John H. ... Chicago, IL
Scheid, Katherine Ann ... Warren, OH
Scheid, Peter L. ... Center Line, MI
Scheid, R. Daniel ... Denver, CO
Scheid, Robert E. ... Palo Alto, CA
Scheid, Susan E. J. ... Bronx, NY
Scheid, William D. ... Denver, CO
Scheid, William D., P.C. ... Denver, CO
Scheidegger, Kent S. ... Sacramento, CA
Scheidel, Rolf H. ... Toledo, OH
Scheideler, Joe ... Denver, CO
Scheideler & Pittam ... Denver, CO
Scheideman, Edward S. ... Washington, DC
Scheideman, James A. ... Portsmouth, VA
Scheidemantel, Paul E. ... Detroit, MI
Scheidemantle, David R. ... Los Angeles, CA
Scheidenhelm, Richard J. ... Boulder, CO
Scheider, James P., Jr.
Hilton Head Island, SC
Scheider, Robert F., Jr. ... Austin, TX
Scheider, Roy E. ... Chester, NJ
Scheider, Wayne Alfred ... Perrysburg, OH
Scheiderer, Judith M. ... Mandeville, LA
Columbus, OH
Scheiderich, William J. W. ... Beaverton, OR
Scheiderman, Patricia J. ... San Diego, CA
Scheiderman, Patricia J., P.C.
San Diego, CA
Scheiding, Philip H. ... Pittsburgh, PA
Scheidler, John B. ... Plainfield, IN
Scheidler, Sam F. ... Des Moines, IA
Scheidlinger, Jay ... New York, NY
Scheidlinger, Robert S. ... New York, NY
Scheidt, Andrea Harris ... New York, NY
Scheidt, Bruce A. ... Sacramento, CA
Scheidt, Charles E. ... New York, NY
Scheidt, Donna L. ... Chicago, IL
Scheidt, Douglas J.
Securities and Exchange Commission,
Division of Investment Management, GV
Scheidt, Jill M. ... Reading, PA
Scheidt, Kathleen Marie Sheil
Indianapolis, IN
Scheidt, Richard C. ... Oak Lawn, IL
Scheier, Henry ... Boca Raton, FL
Scheier, James M. ... Helena, MT
Scheier, Judith S. ... New York, NY
Scheier, Karyn Faith ... Boston, MA
Scheier, Michael L. ... Cincinnati, OH
Scheier, Saul ... Hastings-On-Hudson, NY
Scheifly, John E. ... Los Angeles, CA
Scheige, Steven S.
Occupational Safety and Health Review
Commission,
Office of the General Counsel, GV
Scheihing, Michaela D.
Daytona Beach, FL
Scheihing, Robert F. ... San Antonio, TX
Scheil, William H., Jr. ... Rockville, VA
Scheiman, Eugene R. ... New York, NY
Scheimer, Patti R. ... Pittsburgh, PA
Schein, Alvin S. ... New York, NY
Schein, Cynthia Dersh ... Long Beach, CA
Schein, Daniel B. ... Santa Clarita, CA
Schein, David D., Law Offices of
Houston, TX
Schein, Harvey A. ... Dallas, TX
Schein, Jill Fleischman ... Houston, TX
Schein, Mark D. ... New York, NY
Schein, Marvin H. ... Baltimore, MD
Schein, Michael L. ... New York, NY
Schein, Michael T. ... Seattle, WA
Schein, Robert S. ... Indianapolis, IN
Scheinbart, Jonathan R.
National Labor Relations Board,
Office of Board Members, GV
Scheinbaum, Alan C. ... Highland Park, IL
Scheinbaum, Robert K. ... Roseland, NJ
Scheinberg, Barry ... Newington, CT
Scheinberg, Bruce J. ... Miami Beach, FL
Scheinberg, Finno & Schwartz
Brooklyn, NY
Scheinberg, Michael E. ... Los Angeles, CA
Scheinberg, Michael O. ... Austin, TX
Scheinberg, Ronald ... New York, NY
Scheinberg, Schneps, De Petris & De Petris
Riverhead, NY
Scheinberg, Shepard M. ... Riverhead, NY
Scheinberg, Sidney H. ... Dallas, TX
Scheinberg, William ... Brooklyn, NY
Scheinblum, Howard ... West Hartford, CT
Scheinblum, Mark D. ... Orlando, FL
Scheindlin, Lewis A. ... Trenton, NJ
Scheindlin, Shira A. ... New York, NY
Scheine, Edward Robert ... Woodbury, NY
Scheine, Fusco, Brandenstein & Rada, P.C.
Woodbury, NY
Scheine, Jeffrey D. ... New York, NY
Scheiner, Alan H. ... New York, NY
Scheiner, Alec ... Washington, DC
Scheiner, Arthur ... Washington, DC
Scheiner, Barbara J. ... New York, NY
Scheiner, Burton S. ... Arlington, VA
Scheiner, Craig Ian ... Tallahassee, FL
Scheiner, Eric C. ... Chicago, IL
Scheiner, Howard ... West Palm Beach, FL
Scheiner, Julian ... Los Angeles, CA
Scheiner, Karen R. ... Haddonfield, NJ
Scheiner, Leslie H. ... Department of Labor,
Office of Secretary, GV
Scheiner, Richard W. ... Baltimore, MD
Scheiner, Rina ... New York, NY
Scheiner, Stanley R.
Federal Communications Commission,
Office of the General Counsel, GV
Scheiner, Suzanne R. ... San Francisco, CA
Scheiner, Terry E. ... Port Washington, NY
Scheiner, William ... Brooklyn, NY
Scheinert, Joel L. ... Nanuet, NY
Scheineson, Cathy Zeman
Washington, DC
Scheineson, Marc J. ... Washington, DC
Scheinfeld, David ... New York, NY
Scheinfeld, Fredric ... Mineola, NY
Scheinfeld, Noah S. ... New York, NY
Scheinfeld, Robert C. ... New York, NY
Scheinfeld, Steven G. ... New York, NY
Scheinfeldt, Jerry K. ... Simsbury, CT
Scheinfeldt, Steven C. ... Miami, FL
Scheinfield, Jay C. ... Lansdowne, PA
Scheingart, Roy C. ... Oakland, CA
Scheingold, Amy J.
Department of Labor, GV
Scheingross, Alex B. ... San Diego, CA
Scheinholtz, Leonard L. ... Pittsburgh, PA
Scheinholtz, Stuart D. ... San Francisco, CA
Scheinin, Steven J. ... Aberdeen, MD
Towson, MD
Scheininger, Michael G. ... Washington, DC
Scheininger, Pamela B. ... New York, NY
Scheinkman, Alan D. ... White Plains, NY
Scheinkman, James J. ... Irvine, CA
Scheinman, A. Daniel ... San Jose, CA
Scheinman, Cynthia Robin ... Los Angeles, CA
Scheinman, Douglas M. ... Valley Stream, NY
Scheinman, Graham M. ... New York, NY
Scheinman, Jessica E. ... Manchester, NH
Scheinman, Ronald L. ... Los Angeles, CA
Scheinman, Stanley B. ... Weston, CT
Scheinman, Steven H. ... New York, NY
Scheinman, Sydney E. ... Miami, FL
Scheinman, Tom ... New York, NY
Scheinmann, Ian R. ... Newark, NJ
Scheinthal, Alan R. ... Houston, TX
Scheinthal, Scott L. ... Houston, TX
Scheinz, Jennifer L. ... Helena, MT
Scheirer, Alexander ... New Haven, CT
Scheirer & Geller ... New Haven, CT
Scheirman, John R. ... Topeka, KS
Scheithauer, Chris C. ... Irvine, CA
Scheitler & Elio, P.C. ... Denver, CO
Scheitler, Frank I. ... Denver, CO
Scheiwe, Kenneth ... Wilmette, IL
Scheiwe, Steven D. ... Carlsbad, CA
Schekter, Leon ... New York, NY
Schekter Rishty Goldstein & Blumenthal
P.C. ... New York, NY
Schelberg, Charles B. ... Baltimore, MD
Schelberg, Jane S. ... Detroit, MI
Schelberg, Kenneth J. ... Beverly Hills, CA
Schelberg, Neal S. ... New York, NY
Schelberg & Ross LLP ... Beverly Hills, CA
Schelble, Jeffrey E. ... Milwaukee, WI
Scheld, Charles J. ... Bronx, NY
Scheldrup, Chris J. ... Cedar Rapids, IA
Scheldrup, Linda J. ... Portland, OR
Scheler, Brad Eric ... New York, NY
Scheley, L. Theodore, III ... Menlo Park, CA
Scheley, P. Christian ... Menlo Park, CA
Schelhaas, Ryan T. ... Cheyenne, WY
Schelin, Richard W. ... Denver, CO
Schelin, Sheryl Sisk ... Conway, SC
Schelin, Telisa W. ... Dallas, TX
Schelkopf, J. Bruce ... Chester Springs, PA
Schelkopf, J. Bruce, P.C.
Chester Springs, PA
Schell, Albert J., Jr. ... Philadelphia, PA
Schell, Ann Duggins ... Louisville, KY
Schell, Beene, Vaughan & Quillin, L.L.P.
Dallas, TX
Schell, Braxton ... Greensboro, NC
Schell Bray Aycock Abel & Livingston
P.L.L.C. ... Asheboro, NC
Burlington, NC
Greensboro, NC
High Point, NC
Reidsville, NC
Thomasville, NC
Winston-Salem, NC
Schell, Bridget Ann ... Wichita, KS
Schell, David N., Jr. (P.C.)
New Orleans, LA
Schell, David Stanford ... Fairfax, VA
Schell & Delamer LLP ... Los Angeles, CA
Schell, Elizabeth A. ... Roanoke, VA
Schell, Elizabeth Salzer ... New Orleans, LA
Schell, Eric F. ... Fairfax, VA
Schell, George A. ... Van Nuys, CA
Schell, George A. ... Rochester, NY
Schell, George A., Jr. ... Rochester, NY
Schell, Ivan J., (P.S.C.) ... Louisville, KY
Schell, J. Michael ... New York, NY
Schell, James A. ... Philadelphia, PA
Schell, James M. ... New York, NY
Schell, James W. ... Fort Worth, TX
Schell, John R. ... San Diego, CA
Schell, Kathleen Kearney ... Jeffersonville, IN
Schell, Kelly A. ... Chicago, IL
Schell, Kent Alan ... Tulsa, OK
Schell, L. Otto ... Portland, OR
Schell, Lawrence H. ... Sandusky, OH
Vermilion, OH
Schell, Leigh Ann ... New Orleans, LA
Schell, Marcella J. ... Philadelphia, PA
Schell, Mark E. ... Tulsa, OK
Schell, Merrill S. ... Louisville, KY
Schell, Michael W. ... Watertown, NY
Schell, Nancy A. ... Cincinnati, OH
Schell, P. Edward ... Franklin, TN
Schell, Pamela J. ... Honolulu, HI
Schell, Renée ... Southampton, NY
Schell, Richard ... Chicago, IL
Schell, Richard ... San Juan, PR
Schell, Richard A. ... Beaumont, TX
Schell, Richard D. ... Harlingen, TX
Schell, Richard K. ... Charlotte, NC
Schell, Robert ... Brownsville, TX
Schell, Roger D. ... Bottineau, ND
Schell, Rosemary ... Treasury Department,
Internal Revenue Service, GV
Schell, Ross S. ... Eastman, GA
Schell, Russell W. ... Dallas, TX
Schell, Sherrie V. ... Riverside, CA
Schell, Sidney H. ... Mobile, AL
Schell, Steven D. ... New York, NY
Schell, Steven R. ... Portland, OR
Schell, Theodore H. ... Lockport, NY
Schell, Thomas J. ... New York, NY
Schell, Thomas T. ... Toledo, OH
Schell, W. Braxton, Jr. ... Birmingham, AL
Schell, William M. ... Denver, CO
Schellberg, Timothy M. ... Tacoma, WA
Schellenberg & Associates, P.C.
Birmingham, MI
Schellenberg, Carl B. ... Des Plaines, IL
Schellenberg, David N. ... Peoria, IL
Schellenberg, John A. ... Peoria, IL
Schellenberg, Robert W., Jr.
Grand Rapids, MI
Schellenberg, Thomas L. ... Birmingham, MI
Scheller, Arthur M., III ... Chicago, IL
Scheller, Emil ... Montclair, NJ
Scheller, James C., Jr. ... Sunnyvale, CA
Scheller, John C. ... Madison, WI
Scheller, Karen M. ... Philadelphia, PA
Scheller, Michael J. ... Eagan, MN
Scheller, Stephen J. ... Waukegan, IL
Schellerup, Mark B. ... San Jose, CA
Schellgell, Frederick J. ... Milwaukee, WI
Schellhaas, Kimberly M. ... Columbus, OH
Schellhammer, Edw. R. ... Johnstown, PA
Schellhammer, Richard E. ... Dallas, TX
Schellhammer, Therese A. ... Poplar Bluff, MO
Schellhardt, Donald Joseph ... Waterbury, CT
Schellhas, Gretchen S. ... Minneapolis, MN
Schellhas, Heidi S. ... Minneapolis, MN
Schellhase, Adam R. ... Philadelphia, PA
Schellhase, David R. ... Santa Clara, CA
Schellhase, Gary R. ... Livonia, MI
Schellie, Peter D. ... Washington, DC
Schellin, Eric P. ... Arlington, VA
Schellin, Winfrid ... Cedar Rapids, IA
Schelling & Cotter, P.A. ... Naples, FL
Schelling, George C. ... Bangor, ME
Schelling, Jeffrey S. ... Naples, FL
Schelling, Robbie ... Riverside, CA
Schellinger & Associates ... Brookfield, WI
Schellinger & Doyle, S.C. ... Milwaukee, WI
Schellinger, Jacqueline Davids
Milwaukee, WI
Schellinger, Laurie L. ... Chicago, IL
Schellinger, Neal C. ... Brookfield, WI
Schellinger, Susan G. ... Milwaukee, WI
Schellpfeffer, Harvey H. ... Mayville, WI
Schellpfeffer, John M. ... Merrill, WI
Schellpfeffer, Walter R. ... Beaver Dam, WI
Schelly, Ralph M. ... Chicago, IL
Schelp, W. R. ... Lexington, MO
Schels, Donald Robert ... Fair Lawn, NJ
Schelstraete, Paul ... Crete, NE
Schelstraete, Peter H. ... Tempe, AZ
Scheltema, Chester W., Jr. ... Seattle, WA
Scheltema, James R. J. ... Washington, DC
Schelthoff, John W. ... Oak Park, IL
Schelwat, Kristin N. ... Milwaukee, WI
Schelwat, Timothy W. ... Brookfield, WI
Schelz, Stephen J. ... Stamford, CT
Schelzi, Michael J. ... Wakefield, MA
Scheman, L. Ronald ... Washington, DC
Schemanski, Glen L. ... Cherry Hill, NJ
Schemanski, Lee-Alan ... Cherry Hill, NJ
Schembari, Elaine E.G. ... Scituate, MA
Schembari, John E. ... Omaha, NE

Schember, Daniel M. .... Washington, DC
Schember, Steven G. .... Tampa, FL
Schembera, William A. .... Menomonie, WI
Schember-Lang, Jennifer L. .... Honolulu, HI
Schembra, Joseph C. .... Rochester, NY
Schembs, Robert A. .... Indianapolis, IN
Schemel, Edward F. .... Chattanooga, TN
Schemel, LeCroy-Schemel, P.C.
Chattanooga, TN
Schemel, William C. .... Woodland, CA
Schemenauer, Kelly W. .... Kansas City, MO
Schemer, Jack M. .... Jacksonville, FL
Schemery, Mary C. .... Williamsport, PA
Schemery Zicolello .... Williamsport, PA
Scheminger & McCrimlisk .... New York, NY
Scheminske, Bradley R. .... Lake Oswego, OR
Scheminske, Lyons & Bussman, LLP
Lake Oswego, OR
Schemm, Jennifer R. .... La Grande, OR
Schemm, John M., Jr. .... Chicago, IL
Schemm, Kearn C., Jr. .... Nutley, NJ
Schemm, Neil C. .... Atlanta, GA
Schemmel, Carla Tolbert .... Des Moines, IA
Schemmel, Jeffrey W. .... Minneapolis, MN
Schemmel, Judd T. .... Madison, WI
Schemmel, Luke W. .... Boston, MA
Schemmel, Mark A. .... Milwaukee, WI
Schemmel, Matthew L. .... Madison, WI
Schemmel, William T. .... Indianapolis, IN
Schempf, Bryan H. .... Newport News, VA
Schempp, Dale A. .... Springfield, IL
Schempp, Lawrence J. .... Philadelphia, PA
Schempp, Theodore L. .... Miami, FL
Schenberg, David L. .... St. Louis, MO
Schenberg, Sanford L. .... Maplewood, MO
Schenck, Adam M. .... New York, NY
Schenck, Benjamin R. .... Lee, MA
Schenck, Brett A. .... Marysville, OH
Schenck, Charles N., III .... New Haven, CT
Schenck, Daniel W. .... Somers, NY
Schenck, David Allen .... Fairfax, VA
Schenck, David J. .... Dallas, TX
Schenck, Donald A. .... Cincinnati, OH
Schenck, Douglas A. .... Los Angeles, CA
Schenck & Edelman .... Los Angeles, CA
Schenck, Edward A. .... Pittsburgh, PA
Schenck, Elizabeth .... Syracuse, NY
Schenck, Francis Carl .... Atlanta, GA
Schenck, Jack M. .... Indianapolis, IN
Schenck, James S., IV .... Raleigh, NC
Schenck, John D. .... Los Angeles, CA
Schenck, Keith M. .... Dade City, FL
Inverness, FL
Schenck, Kirk E. .... Los Angeles, CA
Schenck, Leslie Reade .... Seattle, WA
Schenck, Lucas D .... Seattle, WA
Schenck, Margaret T. .... Castlewood, VA
Schenck, Martin .... Loudonville, NY
Schenck, Matthew J. .... San Francisco, CA
Schenck, Moss K. .... New York, NY
Schenck, Peter F. .... Philadelphia, PA
Schenck, Price, Smith & King
New York, NY
Morristown, NJ
Newark, NJ
Schenck, Richard C. .... Harlan, IA
Walnut, IA
Schenck, Ronald D. .... Enterprise, OR
Schenck, William F. .... Xenia, OH
Schenck, William J. .... Butler, PA
Schencker, Richard L. .... Deerfield, IL
Schendel & Callahan .... Fairbanks, AK
Schendel, Kelly L. .... St. Paul, MN
Schendel, Mary L. .... Portland, ME
Schendel, N. Jean .... Fort Wayne, IN
Schendel, Paul .... Benzonia, MI
Schendel, Robert T. .... Kansas City, MO
Schendel, Ward C. .... St. Paul, MN
Schendel, William B. .... Fairbanks, AK
Schenden, James M. .... Lake Orion, MI
Schendle, James M., (P.C.) .... Dallas, TX
Schendt, Thomas G. .... Washington, DC
Schendzielos & Associates, LLC, The Law Firm of .... Denver, CO
Schendzielos, Daniel J. .... Denver, CO
Scheneck, Carol A. .... Randolph, NJ
Schenendorf, Jack L.
House of Representatives,
Committee Legal Personnel, GV
Schenerman, Brad S. .... Newark, NJ
Schenewerk, Joyce L. .... New Orleans, LA
Schenfeld, Deborah L. .... Kew Gardens, NY
Schengrund, Karin-Ann .... Chicago, IL
Schening, Judith A. .... Dallas, TX
Schenk, Alan S. .... Detroit, MI
Schenk, Annes, Brookman & Tepper, Ltd.
Chicago, IL
Schenk, Boncher and Prasher, P.C.
Caledonia, MI
Grand Rapids, MI
Schenk, Claire M. .... St. Louis, MO
Schenk, Cletus C. .... Wichita Falls, TX
Schenk, Cyndi .... Wichita Falls, TX
Schenk, David R. .... Chicago, IL
Schenk, Deborah H. .... Brooklyn, NY
Schenk, Duffy, Quinn, McNamara, Phelan, Carey and Ford, Ltd. .... Bolingbrook, IL
Joliet, IL
Naperville, IL
Schenk, Erich .... Houston, TX
Schenk, Erika Z. .... St. Louis, MO
Schenk, Frederick .... San Diego, CA
Schenk, Gary P. .... Grand Rapids, MI
Schenk, Gerald L. .... Chicago, IL
Schenk, Harry .... Beverly Hills, CA
Schenk, Harry O. .... Los Angeles, CA
Schenk, Jeffrey A. .... Cleveland, OH
Schenk, Jennifer L. .... Charlotte, NC
Schenk, John G. .... Cincinnati, OH
Schenk, John R. .... Glenwood Springs, CO
Schenk, Joseph A. .... Phoenix, AZ
Schenk, Joseph H. M., Jr. .... Martinsville, VA
Schenk, Kenneth A. .... Fort Wayne, IN
Schenk, Kerst & deWinter
Glenwood Springs, CO
Schenk, Larry W. .... Longview, TX
Schenk, Lynn A. .... San Diego, CA
Schenk, Marianna F. .... Hartford, CT
Philadelphia, PA
Schenk, Marion H. .... Chicago, IL
Schenk, Marvin J. .... Phoenix, AZ
Schenk, Mary Ann .... Cincinnati, OH
Schenk, Matthew Aaron .... Detroit, MI
Schenk, Michael J. .... Topeka, KS
Schenk, Michael L. .... Raleigh, NC
Schenk, Robert H. .... Joliet, IL
Schenk, Robert P. .... Philadelphia, PA
Schenk, Sarah A. .... Sarasota, FL
Schenk & Schenk .... Wichita Falls, TX
Schenk, Stefanie I. .... Chicago, IL
Schenk, Todd S. .... Chicago, IL
Schenk, Victor J. .... Baltimore, MD
Schenkar, Richard .... Mercer Island, WA
Schenkein, Pamela E. .... Denver, CO
Schenkein, William F. .... Denver, CO
Schenkel & Donaldson, A Professional Corporation .... Lynchburg, VA
Schenkel, Evan B. .... Woodland Hills, CA
Schenkel, Evan B., A Prof. Corp.
Woodland Hills, CA
Schenkel, Gregory Louis
Hilton Head Island, SC
Schenkel, James P. .... San Francisco, CA
Schenkel, Kent D. .... Wilmington, NC
Schenkel, Lisa L. .... Lynchburg, VA
Schenkel, Louis I. .... New York, NY
Schenkel, Mario W. .... Greenville, SC
Schenkel, Mario W. .... Spartanburg, SC
Schenkel, Norbert J., Jr. .... Fort Wayne, IN
Schenkel, Timothy B. .... Cincinnati, OH
Schenkel Tirpak & Kowalczyk
Fort Wayne, IN
Schenkelberg, Thomas J.
Kansas City, MO
Schenkel-Savitt, Susan .... New York, NY
Schenkemeyer, C. Donald, Jr.
Punxsutawney, PA
Schenken, Christopher .... Atlanta, GA
Schenken, Kathleen M. .... Alpharetta, GA
Schenken, Thomas Parker .... Omaha, NE
Schenkenberg, Philip R. .... St. Paul, MN
Schenker, Arlene Rosenfeld .... Pittsford, NY
Schenker, Carl R., Jr. .... Washington, DC
Schenker, Catherine .... New York, NY
Schenker, Cecil, (P.C.) .... San Antonio, TX
Schenker, Cindy P. .... New York, NY
Schenker, Harold G. .... Miami, FL
Schenker, Martin S. .... San Francisco, CA
Schenker, Michael S. .... Hartford, CT
Schenker, Nathan M. .... Kennett Square, PA
Schenker, Paul G. .... New York, NY
Schenkerman, Jodine L. .... White Plains, NY
Schenker, Sidney I. .... Chicago, IL
Schenkkan, Dirk M. .... San Francisco, CA
Schenkkan, Judith Lynn .... San Francisco, CA
Schenkkan, Pete .... Austin, TX
Schenkler, Bernard .... Roseland, NJ
Schenkman, Eugene .... Bridgewater, NJ
Schenkman, Gerald B. .... Lawrenceville, NJ
Schenkman, Mark A. .... Encino, CA
Schenkman, Michael L. .... Beverly Hills, CA
Schenkman, Russell U. .... Princeton, NJ
Schennum, Vicki L.
Huntington Beach, CA
Schenof, Anne R.
Federal Trade Commission,
Bureau of Competition, GV
Schenof, Barry R. .... Washington, DC
Schenone, Bart J. .... Hayward, CA
Schenone, Christine M. .... San Francisco, CA
Schenone, Matthew A. .... San Diego, CA
Schenone & Peck .... Hayward, CA
Schentur, Raymond E. .... Garfield Heights, OH
Schenz, Gregory R. .... Los Angeles, CA
Schepens, Anne-Claire .... New York, NY
Scheper, David C. .... Los Angeles, CA
Scheper, Gregory J. .... Covington, KY
Scheper, J. Scott .... San Diego, CA
Scheper, James H. .... Fairfield, OH
Schepers, Frank M. .... Omaha, NE
Schepers, James K. .... Grand Rapids, MI
Schepers, Jean .... Department of Defense, Armed Services Board of Contract Appeals, GV
Schepers, Paul G. .... Kansas City, MO
Schepis, Anthony J. .... Bronx, NY
Schepis, Steven C. .... Bronx, NY
Schepisi, Holly T. .... New York, NY
Schepisi, John A. .... Englewood Cliffs, NJ
Schepisi & McLaughlin, P.A., A Professional Corporation .... Englewood Cliffs, NJ
Hackensack, NJ
Schepker, Anita L. .... Hartford, CT
Schepler, Wendi R. .... Palo Alto, CA
Schepp, Carol Robinson .... New York, NY
Schepp, Edward C. .... Syracuse, NY
Schepp, Edward C., P.C. .... Syracuse, NY
Schepp, Janice L., & Associates
St. Louis, MO
Schepp, Louis Jon .... New York, NY
Scheppers, Ruth Clement .... Northridge, CA
Schepps, Lee M. .... Dallas, TX
Schepps, Mark H. .... Cherry Hill, NJ
Philadelphia, PA
Schepps, Mitchell D. .... West Palm Beach, FL
Schepps, Sara Zoe .... White Plains, NY
Schepps, Scott A. .... Houston, TX
Schepps, Solomon J. .... New York, NY
Schepps, Victoria Hayward .... Stoughton, MA
Scher, Alan B. .... Colmar, PA
Scher, Andrew William .... New York, NY
Scher, Ann Koto .... New York, NY
Scher, Anne G. .... Richmond, VA
Scher, Arnold I. .... Miami, FL
Scher & Bassett .... Sunnyvale, CA
Scher, Brian T. .... West Palm Beach, FL
Scher, Brian T. .... McLean, VA
Scher, Bruce M., P.C. .... Garden City, NY
Scher, Charles B. .... Richmond, VA
Scher, Dana J. .... New York, NY
Scher, David J. .... Great Neck, NY
Scher, David L. .... Sunnyvale, CA
Scher, Davida Shapiro .... New York, NY
Scher, Donald T. .... Scottsdale, AZ
Scher, Edward E. .... Richmond, VA
Scher, Edward M. .... Albany, NY
Scher, Elliot .... Millburn, NJ
Scher, Eric D. .... New York, NY
Scher, Eric S. .... Philadelphia, PA
Plymouth Meeting, PA
Scher, Gerald .... Washington, DC
Scher, Gerald H. .... Sunnyvale, CA
Scher, Gregory B. .... Los Angeles, CA
Scher, Howard D. .... Philadelphia, PA
Scher, Howard S. .... Department of Justice, Civil Division, GV
Scher, Irving, (P.C.) .... New York, NY
Scher, Isaac (Zeke) .... Denver, CO
Scher, Isadore .... St. Louis, MO
Scher, Jack .... Waldwick, NJ
Scher, Jefferson F. .... Palo Alto, CA
Scher, Jonathan L .... Carle Place, NY
Scher, Lauren Neufeld .... Livingston, NJ
Scher, Lee T. .... Stamford, CT
Scher, Leslie E. .... Garberville, CA
Sunnyvale, CA
Scher, Linda Rose .... Portland, OR
Scher, Mark Waclaw .... New York, NY
Scher, Martin H., Law Offices of
Carle Place, NY
New York, NY
Scher, Meyer .... Sunnyvale, CA
Scher, Meyer H. .... Millburn, NJ
Scher, Michael .... New York, NY
Scher, Michael H. .... New York, NY
Scher, Michael S. .... Baltimore, MD
Scher, Michael S. .... New York, NY
Scher, Milton .... Ridgewood, NY
Scher, Norman A. .... Richmond, VA
Scher, Peter L.
Executive Office Of The President,
Office of the U.S. Trade Representative, GV
Scher, Robert A. .... Great Neck, NY
Scher, Robert A. .... New York, NY
Scher, Robert E. .... Boynton Beach, FL
Scher, Robert E. .... Baltimore, MD
Scher, Robin J. .... Palm Beach Gardens, FL
Scher, Scott A. .... Dallas, TX
Scher, Scott R. .... Seattle, WA
Scher, Stanley J. .... New York, NY
Scher, Stephanie R. .... Los Angeles, CA
Scher, Steven L. .... Trenton, NJ
Scher, William B., Jr. .... Washington, DC
Scher, William G. .... Hackensack, NJ
New York, NY
Scher, William J.
Federal Communications Commission,
Mass Media Bureau, GV
Scherach, Michael J. .... Lorain, OH
Scheraga, Ronald G. .... Bethesda, MD
Scherago, Michael A. .... Los Angeles, CA
Scheraldi, Susan F. .... New York, NY
Scherb, Cynthia W. .... Kansas City, MO
Scherb, Esther R. .... Washington, DC
Scherb, Joan B. .... Commack, NY
Scherb, Louis H. .... Glenview, IL
Scherb, Richard A., (P.C.) .... Phoenix, AZ
Scherba, Richard .... Dallas, TX
Scherback, William J. .... Dallas, TX
Scherban, Jack S. .... Stamford, CT
Scherban, Ronald M. .... New Haven, CT
Scherban, Ronald M., P.C. .... New Haven, CT
Scherbarth, Jann E. .... Houston, TX
Scherbarth, John C. .... Lansing, MI
Scherbel, Paul R. .... Coshocton, OH
Scher-Bernbach, Allison .... New York, NY
Scherby, Michael L. .... Hackensack, NJ
Scherby, Stephanie H. .... New York, NY
Scherck, Randall F. .... St. Louis, MO
Scherck, Roger L. .... Belleville, IL
Schere, Leslie Alan .... Miami, FL
Schere, Leslie Alan, P.A. .... Miami, FL
Schere, Madelyn P. .... Miami, FL
Scherer, Bradford & Lyster
Los Angeles, CA
Scherer, C. Michael .... Richmond, TX
Scherer, Candyce Humphrey .... Metairie, LA
Scherer, Charles H. .... New York, NY
Scherer, Chris A. .... San Antonio, TX
Scherer, Diana .... Newport Beach, CA
Scherer, Donald F. .... Troy, MI
Scherer, Donald S. .... San Francisco, CA
Scherer, Douglas D. .... New York, NY
Scherer, Edward P. .... Hartford, CT
Scherer, Everett M. .... Morristown, NJ
Scherer, Fred L., Jr. .... Bell City, MO
Scherer, Howard B. .... Philadelphia, PA
Scherer, J. Peter .... Bloomfield Hills, MI
Scherer, Jack F. .... New York, NY
Scherer, Janice K. .... Woodbridge, NJ
Scherer, John H. .... St. Cloud, MN
Scherer, John K. .... Cold Spring, NY
Scherer, John P., II .... Department of Defense, Defense Commissary Agency, GV
Scherer, John Payne .... Beckley, WV
Scherer, Jonathan L. .... Washington, DC
Scherer, Joseph A. .... San Francisco, CA
Scherer, Kenneth E. .... Mount Clemens, MI
Scherer, Kenneth J.
North Palm Beach, FL
Scherer, Larry J. .... Lincoln, NE
Scherer, Lawrence E. .... Mineola, NY
Scherer, Lawrence J. .... Garden City, NY
Scherer, Leah .... New York, NY
Scherer, M. Mardsen .... Brooklyn, NY
Scherer, M. William .... New York, NY
Scherer, Mark A. .... Indianapolis, IN
Scherer, Mark R. .... Omaha, NE
Scherer, Mary Ann .... Fort Lauderdale, FL
Scherer, Michael A. .... Carlisle, PA
Scherer, Micki A., (Ms.) .... Brooklyn, NY
Scherer, Nancy N. .... Austin, TX
Scherer, Nancy S. .... New York, NY
Scherer, Paul .... Richmond, TX
Scherer, Paul C. .... St. Petersburg, FL
Scherer, Richard S. .... Minneapolis, MN
Scherer, Robert C. .... New York, NY
Scherer, Robert G. .... Louisville, KY
Scherer, Robert P. .... Austin, TX
Scherer, Robert T. .... New York, NY
Scherer, Roger H. .... Brooklyn Park, MN
Scherer, Sally H. .... Raleigh, NC
Scherer, Sandra O. .... New Berlin, WI
Scherer & Scherer .... Austin, TX
Scherer, Stephen E. .... Los Angeles, CA
Scherer, Steven J. .... Cincinnati, OH
Scherer, Stuart A. .... Louisville, KY
Scherer, Thomas C. .... Indianapolis, IN
Scherer, Thomas J. .... New York, NY
Scherer, William M. .... San Francisco, CA
Scherer, William N., Jr. .... Glen Burnie, MD
Scherer, William N., Sr. .... Glen Burnie, MD
Scherer, William R., III
Fort Lauderdale, FL
Scherer, William R., Jr., (P.A.)
Fort Lauderdale, FL
Miami, FL
Scherf, Davis & Gedgoudas
Birmingham, AL
Scherf, John G., IV .... Birmingham, AL
Scherf, Paul Wm. .... Andalusia, AL
Scherff, John Matthew .... Chillicothe, OH
Scherff, Scott Alan .... Canton, OH
Scherffius, Andrew M. .... Atlanta, GA
Scherffius, Andrew M., P.C. .... Atlanta, GA
Scherk, Robert M. .... San Diego, CA
Scherkenbach, Colleen A. .... Phoenix, AZ
Scherkenbach, Frank A. .... Milwaukee, WI
Scherkenbach, Frank E. .... Menlo Park, CA
Scherkenbach, Joseph R. .... Virginia, MN
Scherker, Elliot H. .... Miami, FL
Scherl, David A. .... New York, NY
Scherl, Ina .... New York, NY
Scherl, Jodi B. .... Saddle Brook, NJ
Scherlacher, John P. .... Los Angeles, CA
Scherle, Timothy A. .... Sioux City, IA
Scherle, William D. .... Des Moines, IA
Scherlen, Eileen E. .... San Antonio, TX
Scherlinck, Jeanne M. .... Detroit, MI
Scherline, Jay A. .... Allentown, PA
Scherling & Associates, P.C.
New York, NY
Scherling, Bruce D. .... New York, NY
Scherling, James S. .... Livingston, NJ
Scherling, John Bailie .... San Diego, CA
Scherling, Richard E., Jr. .... Pensacola, FL
Scherling, Robert .... Livingston, NJ
Scherlis, Edwin L. .... Philadelphia, PA
Scherma, Frederick M. .... Atlanta, GA
Scherman, Paul I. .... Hialeah, FL
Scherman, Paul I., P.A. .... Hialeah, FL
Scherman, William S. .... Washington, DC
Schermann, Rachel Thurston .... St. Cloud, MN
Schermer, Amy K. .... Columbus, OH
Schermer, Barry S. .... St. Louis, MO
Schermer, Beth J. .... Phoenix, AZ
Schermer, Cooper & Associates, P.C.
Cherry Hill, NJ
Philadelphia, PA
Schermer, Daniel W. .... Minneapolis, MN
Schermer, David W. .... Oregon City, OR
Schermer, Gregory P. .... Davenport, IA
Schermer, J. Leonard .... St. Louis, MO
Schermer, James .... Seattle, WA
Schermer, Kathy W. .... Bradenton, FL
Schermer, Leland P. .... Pittsburgh, PA
Schermer, Linda Joyce .... Beverly Hills, CA
Schermer, Marsha Rockey .... Columbus, OH
Schermer, Oscar S. .... Cherry Hill, NJ
Philadelphia, PA
Schermer, Richard N. .... Aventura, FL
Schermer, Robert C. .... Bradenton, FL
Schermer, Rodney L. .... Grand Haven, MI
Schermer, Sam .... Beverly Hills, CA
Schermer, Sam, A Professional Corp.
Beverly Hills, CA
Schermer, Wendy .... Philadelphia, PA
Schermerhorn, Gregory Robert
Birmingham, MI
Schermerhorn, James R. .... New York, NY
Schermerhorn, Jill Melius .... Needham, MA
Schermerhorn, Lee R. .... Portland, OR
Schermerhorn, Scot .... Billings, MT
Schermerhorn, Scott E. .... Scranton, PA
Schermerhorn, Scott E. .... Stroudsburg, PA
Wilkes-Barre, PA
Schermerhorn, Susan S. .... Boulder, CO
Schermerhorn, Thomas A. .... Woodstock, IL
Schermer-Kleinkopf, Victoria
Monterey, CA
Schermetzler, James P. .... Gillette, WY
Scherner, Benjamin .... Groveport, OH

Scherner, Hans .... **Columbus, OH**
Delaware, OH
Scherner, Hanson & Cornwell, LLC
Columbus, OH
Delaware, OH
Lima, OH
Mansfield, OH
Marion, OH
Scherr, Albert .... Concord, NH
Scherr, Barbara J. (Roberts)
Bingham Farms, MI
Scherr, Cole & Murphy .... Baltimore, MD
Glen Burnie, MD
Scherr, Daniel H. .... **Columbia, MD**
Scherr, Dorothy DuBose .... Fort Worth, TX
Scherr, Dorothy DuBose, P.C.
Fort Worth, TX
Scherr, H. Robert .... Baltimore, MD
Glen Burnie, MD
Scherr, Heidi Hornung .... **Lincoln, NE**
Scherr, Herbert H. .... Baltimore, MD
Scherr, James F. .... El Paso, TX
Scherr, Jason R. .... **Baltimore, MD**
Scherr, Jeffrey H. .... **Baltimore, MD**
Scherr, Judith E. .... San Francisco, CA
Scherr, Kandace L. .... **Lutherville, MD**
Scherr & Legate .... El Paso, TX
Scherr, Leslie .... Washington, DC
Scherr, Paige D. .... **Denton, TX**
Scherr, Peter L. .... Rockville, MD
Scherr, René Mario .... **Dallas, TX**
Scherr, S. Jacob .... Washington, DC
Scherr, Scott J. .... **Bryan, TX**
Scherr, Scott R. .... Owings Mills, MD
Scherr, Stanley .... Baltimore, MD
Scherr, Stephanie L. .... **New York, NY**
Scherr, Stephen A. .... Hastings, NE
Scherr, Stephen J. .... San Francisco, CA
Scherr, Stephen M. .... New York, NY
Scherr, Werner E. .... **Milwaukee, WI**
Scherr, Werner Erich .... **Milwaukee, WI**
Scherrer, Frederick W. .... **St. Louis, MO**
Scherrer, Richard B., (P.C.)
St. Louis, MO
Scherrer, Robert .... **Houston, TX**
Scherrer, Stephen T. .... **Chicago, IL**
Scherrer, Terrence M. .... Columbus, OH
Scherry, Richard J. .... Oklahoma City, OK
Scherschel, Mary M. .... Geneva, IL
Scherschel, Mathew S. .... Fort Wayne, IN
Scherschel, Thomas P. .... **Geneva, IL**
Scherschligt, Michael V. .... St. Paul, MN
Schertler, David .... **Washington, DC**
Schertz, Bonnie .... New York, NY
Schertz, David J. ...... Department of Commerce, Patent and Trademark Office, GV
Schertz, Lynne S. .... Roseland, NJ
Schertz, Philip R. .... Wayne, NJ
Schertz, Ronald B. .... **Peoria, IL**
Schertzer, Ivan A.
North Miami Beach, FL
Scherubel, Ronald L. .... **Cordova, TN**
Scherz, Carl C. .... **Dallas, TX**
Scherz, Dorr .... Austin, TX
Scherz, Michael D. .... New York, NY
Scherzer, Donald S. .... **Cleveland, OH**
Scherzer, Grant .... Dallas, TX
Scherzer, James David .... Kansas City, MO
Scherzer, Jeffrey .... Rochester, NY
Scherzer, Judith V. .... **New York, NY**
Scherzer, Mark P. .... New York, NY
Scherzer, Robert T. .... **Portland, OR**
Scherzer, Stephen G. .... **Los Angeles, CA**
Newport Beach, CA
Scherzer, Steven D. .... **Atlantic City, NJ**
Scheschuk, Peter A. .... Ridgewood, NJ
Scheske, Eric J. .... **Sturgis, MI**
Scheske, Jack J. .... **Duncanville, TX**
Scheske, James J. .... **Austin, TX**
Scheske, Robert B. .... Gonzales, TX
Schess, Nancy B. .... **New York, NY**
Schessler, Cheralyn E. .... **Washington, DC**
Schessler, John .... Ontario, CA
Schessler, Michael J. .... **Charleston, WV**
Schestopol, B. Michael .... **Seattle, WA**
Schetelich, Stephen .... Rockville, MD
Schetelich, Thomas J. .... **Baltimore, MD**
Schetina, Elizabeth D. .... Glendale, CA
Schetina, Gregory D. .... **Los Angeles, CA**
Schetman, Richard M. .... **New York, NY**
Schetroma, Russell L. .... **Meadville, PA**
Schetselaar, Janet Zarbock .... **Provo, UT**
Schettenhelm, Karl W., Jr. .... **Southfield, MI**
Schetter, Carl F. .... Napa, CA
Schetter, Mary Ellen E.
Mount Laurel, NJ
Schettewi, Jennifer Bastian
Washington, DC
Schettini, Diane C. T. .... Richmond, VA
Schettini, Patrick A., Jr.
South Yarmouth, MA
Schettino, John L. .... Oradell, NJ
Schettino, Joseph E., Jr. .... North Haven, CT
Schettino, Joseph V. .... Babylon, NY
Schettler, Charles C., Jr. .... Lansing, MI
Scheu, Ralph G. .... Chicago, IL
Scheu, William E. .... **Jacksonville, FL**
Scheuer, Edna V. .... **Cincinnati, OH**
Scheuer, G. Joseph .... Atlanta, GA
Scheuer, Jill C. .... **New York, NY**
Scheuer, Keith, Law Offices of
Los Angeles, CA
Scheuer, Ralph H. .... **Santa Fe, NM**
Scheuer, Richard J., Jr. .... Larchmont, NY
Scheuer, Thomas .... **Wilton, CT**
Scheuer, Yost & Patterson, A Professional Corporation .... **Santa Fe, NM**
Taos, NM

Scheuerle, James R. .... **Muskegon, MI**
Scheuerle, John R. .... Grand Haven, MI
Scheuerle, Robert J. .... Grand Haven, MI
Scheüerle, Stephen A. .... **Philadelphia, PA**
Scheuerle & Zitta .... Grand Haven, MI
Scheuerlein, Paul H. .... **Chicago, IL**
Scheuerman, Elizabeth C. .... Summit, NJ
Scheuerman, Jack J.
Colorado Springs, CO
Scheuerman, Karl E. .... New York, NY
Scheuerman, Karl M. .... Tallahassee, FL
Scheuerman, Kurt E. .... **San Diego, CA**
Scheuerman, Kurt E. .... Salem, OR
Scheuerman, Linda C. .... **Detroit, MI**
Scheuerman, Paul T. .... Washington, DC
Baltimore, MD
Scheuerman, Thomas J. .... St. Paul, MN
Scheuermann, Arthel J., (Miss)
New Orleans, LA
Scheuermann, Arthur P. .... **Albany, NY**
Scheuermann, Barbara Rusin .... **Albany, NY**
Scheuermann, Dan M. .... Baton Rouge, LA
Scheuermann, Edward W. .... **New York, NY**
Scheuermann, James E. .... **Pittsburgh, PA**
Scheuermann, Jane C. .... Metairie, LA
Scheuermann, John E. .... Washington, DC
Scheuermann, Mayra .... **Metairie, LA**
Scheuermann, Michael F. .... Mobile, AL
Scheuermann, Ronald J. .... New York, NY
Scheuermann, Wayne H. .... New Orleans, LA
Scheufele, R. Wayne .... Baltimore, MD
Scheufler, Alan W. .... **Cleveland, OH**
Scheufler, Rick J. .... Great Bend, KS
Scheuler, Richard .... Red Bluff, CA
Scheuneman, Christine A.
Los Angeles, CA
Scheunemann, Edw. J. .... Denver, CO
Scheurer, Kirsten .... **Woodbridge, NJ**
Scheurer, Philip C. .... **Washington, DC**
Scheurer, Richard J. .... **Lakewood, CO**
Scheurer, Terence Christian .... New York, NY
Scheurer Wiggin & Hardy .... New York, NY
Scheurer, William C. .... Lindenhurst, IL
Scheurer, William H., Jr. .... Smithtown, NY
Scheurich, Anne M. .... Evergreen Park, IL
Scheurich, G. Michael .... **Rockford, IL**
Scheurich & Greene .... New Orleans, LA
Scheurich, Michael R. .... **Phoenix, AZ**
Scheurich, Owen M. .... **Dallas, TX**
Scheurich, Paul A. .... **Beaumont, TX**
Scheurich, Rita W. .... Chicago, IL
Scheurich, Valentine K., III
New Orleans, LA
Scheuritzel, C. Paul .... **Philadelphia, PA**
Scheutzow, Susan O. .... **Cleveland, OH**
Scheve, Gerald B. .... Houston, TX
Scheve, Stephen E. .... **Houston, TX**
Scheve, Thomas J. .... Cincinnati, OH
Schewatz, Mary .... Thousand Oaks, CA
Schewe, Bruce V. .... **New Orleans, LA**
Schewe, Christopher Paul .... Alexandria, VA
Schewe, Edward C. .... **San Diego, CA**
Schewe, Joseph A. .... Detroit, MI
Schewe, William J. .... **Fairfax, VA**
Schewel, Michael J. .... **Richmond, VA**
Schexnaildre-Tyrrell, Charon
Baton Rouge, LA
Schexnayder, Chad L. .... **Phoenix, AZ**
Schexnayder, Martin S. .... **Houston, TX**
Schexnayder, Myra C. .... **Houston, TX**
Schexnayder, Thomas F. .... New Orleans, LA
Schexnayder, Valerie T. .... **Metairie, LA**
Schexnaydre, David J. .... **Covington, LA**
Schey, Peter A. .... Los Angeles, CA
Schey, Piller, Alspaugh & Wong, P.C.
Longmont, CO
Schey, Richard W. .... **Morristown, NJ**
Schey, Robert .... **Chicago, IL**
Schey, Robert, & Associates, P.C.
Chicago, IL
Schey, Walter M. .... San Francisco, CA
Schey, Walter M., A Professional Corporation
San Francisco, CA
Schey, William P. .... Clifton, NJ
Scheyer, Daniel .... **New York, NY**
Scheyer & Jellenik .... Smithtown, NY
Scheyer, Lawrence W. .... New York, NY
Scheyer, Richard I. .... Smithtown, NY
Scheyer, William J., Jr. .... Simi Valley, CA
Scheynost, Scott F. .... Louisville, KY
Schiada & Caballero .... Santa Fe Springs, CA
Schiada, James .... Santa Fe Springs, CA
Schiada, Paul .... **Los Angeles, CA**
Schiaffo, Thomas C. .... Hartford, CT
Schian, Dale C. .... **Phoenix, AZ**
Schian Walker, P.L.C. .... **Phoenix, AZ**
Schiano, Charles A., Jr. .... Rochester, NY
Schiano, Christopher A. .... Rochester, NY
Schiano, Francis S. .... Corona, NY
Schiano, Jane M. .... Islandia, NY
Schiano, Michael D. .... **New York, NY**
Schiano, Michael P. .... Rochester, NY
Schiano, Vincent A. .... New York, NY
Schiappa, Joseph P. .... East Brunswick, NJ
Schiappa, Matthew Austin
Morristown, NJ
Schiappa, Susan M. .... **Providence, RI**
Schiaroli, Francis P. .... Stamford, CT
Schiave, Anne Hamblin .... **Chicago, IL**
Schiavelli, Alan E. .... **Arlington, VA**
Schiavelli, George P. .... Los Angeles, CA
Schiavenza, James M. .... Sacramento, CA
Schiavetta, Daniel M., Jr. .... **New York, NY**
Schiavetti, Anthony L. .... New York, NY
Schiavetti, Geisler, Corgan, De Vito, Gabriele & Nicholson .... New York, NY
Schiavo, A. Mary ....
Department of Transportation, GV

Schiavo, Frank L. .... Winter Park, FL
Schiavo, J. Barry .... San Luis Obispo, CA
Schiavo, Mary F. .... **Los Angeles, CA**
Washington, DC
Schiavo, Michael Joseph .... Staten Island, NY
Schiavo, Pasco L. .... **Hazleton, PA**
Schiavo, Thomas J. .... Ledgewood, NJ
Schiavone, Ann Michelle .... Louisville, KY
Schiavone, David L. .... **Chicago, IL**
Schiavone, Domenico .... Woonsocket, RI
Schiavone, Frank Joseph .... Hamilton, OH
Schiavone, Joseph J. .... **Short Hills, NJ**
New York, NY
Schiavone, Leonard D. .... **Youngstown, OH**
Schiavone, Louis J. .... **Celina, OH**
Schiavone, Michael .... **Savannah, GA**
Schiavone, Michael .... **Buffalo, NY**
Schiavone, Michael J. .... **New York, NY**
Schiavone, Nancy E. .... **Chicago, IL**
Schiavone, Randall S.
San Bernardino, CA
Schiavone-Centeno, Elizabeth A.
San Juan, PR
Schiavoni, Joseph .... Youngstown, OH
Schiavoni, Louis .... Youngstown, OH
Schiavoni, Robert J. .... Martinsburg, WV
Schiavoni, Schiavoni & Bush Co., L.P.A.
Youngstown, OH
Schiavoni, Tancred V., III .... **New York, NY**
Schiavoni, Thomas F. .... Lynn, MA
Schiavoni, Timothy J. .... Haverhill, MA
Schibani, Albert J. .... Annandale, VA
Schibel, Robert L. .... **Los Angeles, CA**
Schibel, Robert L., A Professional Corporation .... **Los Angeles, CA**
Schibell & Mennie, L.L.C., Law Offices of
Ocean Township, NJ
Schibell, Richard D. .... Ocean Township, NJ
Schibley, James V. .... Fort Wayne, IN
Schibly, Michael P. .... **San Francisco, CA**
Schichtel, Kay L. .... **Chicago, IL**
Schichtel, Mark Anthony .... **New York, NY**
Schick, Alan .... **Washington, DC**
Schick, Beth S. .... Winter Park, FL
Schick, David A. .... New York, NY
Schick, David C. .... Dallas, TX
Schick, David L. .... **Orlando, FL**
Schick, Elizabeth Rose .... **Dallas, TX**
Schick, Gregory C. .... **San Francisco, CA**
Schick, James R. .... Springfield, IL
Schick, Jennifer .... **Chicago, IL**
Schick, John C. .... Stockton, CA
Schick, John J. .... Boynton Beach, FL
Schick, John K. .... Lansing, MI
Schick, John-Paul .... **Durham, NC**
Schick, Joseph S. .... **New York, NY**
Schick, Mariann E. .... **Philadelphia, PA**
Schick, Patricia .... Laramie, WY
Schick, Paul E. .... **Chicago, IL**
Schick, Robert J. .... **Waldorf, MD**
Schick, Robert M. .... **Houston, TX**
Schick, Sandor E. .... **New York, NY**
Schick, Sharon Hyman .... **Washington, DC**
Schick, Susan R. .... **New York, NY**
Schick, Thomas E. .... Arlington, VA
Schick, William Gerald .... **Rock Island, IL**
Schick, Wm. J., Jr. .... Covington, KY
Schickel, Candila Coutts .... Mason City, IA
Schickel, John J. .... **Jacksonville, FL**
Schickel, Norbert H., III .... Dryden, NY
Schicker, David .... Monterey Park, CA
Schicker, Richard J. .... Omaha, NE
Schickler, Arnold S. .... **New York, NY**
Schickler, Howard .... **New York, NY**
Schickler, Howard M. .... **New York, NY**
Schickler, Ronald S. .... Aurora, OH
Schickler & Schickler, L.L.P.
New York, NY
Schickler, Sloan .... **New York, NY**
Schickli, Scott E. .... **Portland, OR**
Schickli, Warren D. .... **Lexington, KY**
Schickli, Wright H. .... San Francisco, CA
Schickman, Mark Isaac
San Francisco, CA
Schidlow, Connie M. .... **Punta Gorda, FL**
Schieb, Scott A. .... **Sarasota, FL**
Schiebelhut, Robert K.
San Luis Obispo, CA
Schieber, David .... Medford, OR
Schieber, Evan R. .... **New York, NY**
Schieber, Judith A. .... **Chicago, IL**
Schieber, Keith J. .... St. Joseph, MO
Schieber, Kurt G. .... Cape Coral, FL
Schieber, Michelle L. .... Macon, GA
Schieber, Paul H. .... **Philadelphia, PA**
Schieber, Robert M. .... Kansas City, MO
Schieble, Daniel M. .... **Virginia Beach, VA**
Schieble, Mark T. .... **San Francisco, CA**
Schiebler, Alisa A. .... Phoenix, AZ
Schieck, David M. .... Las Vegas, NV
Schied, Suzanne C. .... Lincoln, NE
Schiedel, Charles M. .... Springfield, IL
Schiedler-Brown, Jean M. .... Seattle, WA
Schief, William R. .... Washington, DC
Schiefelbein, Chad A. .... **Chicago, IL**
Schiefelbein, Lester W., Jr. .... **Sunnyvale, CA**
Sunnyvale, CA
Schiefelbein, Robert G. .... Eden Prairie, MN
Schieferdecker, Eric .... Bemidji, MN
Schieferstein, David R. .... Eaton, CO
Schieffelin, Thomas L., Jr. .... **Orlando, FL**
Schieffelin, William O. .... Reston, VA
Schieffer, Joseph H. .... Oakland, CA
Schieffer, Richard J. .... **Minneapolis, MN**
Schieffer, Todd A. .... **Overland Park, KS**
Schieffler, Daniel K. .... West Helena, AR
Schieffler, Edward H. .... West Helena, AR
Schieffler, Eugene L. .... West Helena, AR

Schieffler Law Firm .... West Helena, AR
Schiek, John H. .... Crandon, WI
Rhinelander, WI
Schieken, William Nathan
Minneapolis, MN
Schield, Brian E. .... **Los Angeles, CA**
Schieler, Jean Marie .... **New York, NY**
Schielfelbein, Jerome J. .... **Austin, TX**
Schielke, Kent J. .... Plainfield, IL
Schiels, Thomas B. .... New York, NY
Schieman, Gordon E. .... Englewood, CO
Schieman, Nancy Eileen .... Cleveland, OH
Schieman, William F., III .... Port Huron, MI
Schiemann, Don A. .... **Detroit, MI**
Schienberg, Carin S. .... Vancouver, WA
Schienberg, Marvin B. .... Chicago, IL
Schienberg, Randy M. .... **Los Angeles, CA**
Schienke, Frederick H. .... Mount Clemens, MI
Schienke, Staugaard and Hearsch, P.C., Law Offices of .... Mount Clemens, MI
Schier, Carl F. .... **Troy, MI**
Schier, Deneweth & Parfitt, P.C.
Detroit, MI
Troy, MI
Schiera, Roger J. .... Jamaica, NY
Schierberl, Alice A. .... Portsmouth, NH
Schierberl, William L. .... New York, NY
Schierer, Carrie L. .... **St. Louis, MO**
Schierer, Paul D. .... **Laramie, WY**
Schierhorn, Nancy S. .... Anchorage, AK
Schiering, John H. .... Carmel, IN
Schierl, Paul J. .... Green Bay, WI
Schierling, Tanya Marie .... Rockville, MD
Schierloh, Anne P. .... Southfield, MI
Schiern, Stephanie J. .... **Los Angeles, CA**
Schiesel, David .... Tucson, AZ
Schiesel, Dolores R. .... Kent, CT
Schiesel, Steven Glen .... **New York, NY**
Schiesl, Andrew R. .... **Milwaukee, WI**
Schiess, Frederick E. .... Balsam, NC
Schiess, Ronald G. .... Salt Lake City, UT
Schiesser, Charles W. .... Austin, TX
Schiessl, Carl J. .... **Hartford, CT**
Schiessle, Michael .... Park Ridge, IL
Schiesswohl, Cynthia R. S. .... New Castle, IN
Schietroma, Paul H. .... New York, NY
Schiever, Carey J. .... **Libertyville, IL**
Schiever, Carey J., Ltd. .... **Libertyville, IL**
Schiewe, Jon A. .... Kings Beach, CA
Schifani, Ruth M. .... **Albuquerque, NM**
Schifano, Larry .... **Rice Lake, WI**
Schifeling, Barbara L. .... **Buffalo, NY**
Schifeling, Iris B. .... Buffalo, NY
Schiferl, Kevin C. .... **Indianapolis, IN**
Schiff, Abby-Gayle .... Philadelphia, PA
Schiff, Andrew J. .... **New York, NY**
Schiff, Andrew O. .... Philadelphia, PA
Schiff, Anthony Hunter .... Los Angeles, CA
Schiff, Arthur L. .... **New York, NY**
Schiff & Bernstein, A Professional Corporation
Los Angeles, CA
Schiff, Carl C., II .... Winnetka, CA
Schiff, Carolyn Traister .... **New York, NY**
Schiff, Cathy R. .... Irvine, CA
Schiff, Cathy R., P.C., Law offices of
Irvine, CA
Schiff, Charles M. .... St. Cloud, MN
Schiff, Daniel C. .... West Long Branch, NJ
Schiff, Daniel F. .... **New York, NY**
Schiff, David Brian .... **New York, NY**
Schiff, David S. T. .... New York, NY
Schiff, Debra Ann .... San Francisco, CA
Schiff & Dickson, Co., L.L.C.
Cleveland, OH
Schiff, Edward F. .... **Washington, DC**
Schiff, Edward H. .... Santa Barbara, CA
Schiff, Edward L. .... **New York, NY**
Schiff, Elizabeth York .... Cincinnati, OH
Schiff, Elliot R. .... Chicago, IL
Schiff, Gary S. .... **Birmingham, AL**
Schiff, Gerald H. .... Opelousas, LA
Schiff, Gordon J. .... **Tampa, FL**
Schiff, Gunther H. .... Beverly Hills, CA
Schiff, Gunther H., A Professional Corporation
Beverly Hills, CA
Schiff Hardin & Waite .... **Washington, DC**
Chicago, IL
Merrillville, IN
Schiff, Herbert S. .... **Colorado Springs, CO**
Schiff, Howard .... **New York, NY**
Schiff, Howard Lee .... **East Hartford, CT**
Schiff, Howard Lee, P.C., Law Offices
East Hartford, CT
Hartford, CT
Augusta, ME
Worcester, MA
Lebanon, NH
Providence, RI
Woodstock, VT
Schiff, Howard P. .... West Long Branch, NJ
Schiff & Hulbert .... **Chicago, IL**
Schiff, Jack B. .... St. Louis, MO
Schiff, James M. .... **Miami, FL**
Schiff, James M., P.A. .... **Miami, FL**
Schiff, Jamieson M. .... **Providence, RI**
Schiff, Janet S. .... Chicago, IL
Schiff, Janis B. .... **Washington, DC**
Schiff, Jay M. .... Chicago, IL
Schiff, Jeffrey R. .... Brooklyn, NY
Schiff, Jo Ann R. .... Monterey Park, CA
Schiff, Joel .... Indianapolis, IN
Schiff, Joel P. .... **Los Angeles, CA**
Schiff, John D. .... Indianapolis, IN
Schiff, Jonathan E. .... St. Bernard, OH
Schiff, Jordan Evan .... New York, NY
Schiff, Laurence J. .... **Detroit, MI**
Schiff, Laurie .... Santa Ana, CA

Schiff Law Corporation, APLC
Opelousas, LA
Schiff, Leslie J. ..... Opelousas, LA
Schiff, Lorin A. ..... Encino, CA
Schiff, Louis H. ..... Deerfield Beach, FL
Schiff, Mark H. ..... Chicago, IL
Schiff, Marshall S. ..... Hawthorne, NY
Schiff, Martin, Jr. ..... Clayton, MO
Schiff, Marvin E. ..... Carle Place, NY
Schiff, Marvin Evan, P.C., Law Offices of
Carle Place, NY
Schiff, Marvin H. ..... Cleveland, OH
Schiff, Mary Lee ..... Evansville, IN
Schiff, Matthew B. ..... Chicago, IL
Schiff, Michael J., (P.C.) ..... Los Angeles, CA
Schiff, Michael S. ..... Columbus, OH
Schiff, Michael S. ..... Philadelphia, PA
Schiff, Patricia Foisie ..... Winnetka, IL
Schiff, Patsy K. ..... Sacramento, CA
Schiff, Peter H. ..... Albany, NY
Schiff, Philip D. ..... Bethesda, MD
Schiff, Richard B. ..... Washington, DC
Schiff, Robert F. ..... Washington, DC
Schiff, Robert N. ..... San Francisco, CA
Schiff, Robin ..... New York, NY
Schiff, Ronald D. ..... Riverdale, MD
Schiff, Scott A. ..... Los Angeles, CA
Schiff, Scott Wilson ..... Columbus, OH
Schiff & Shelton ..... Santa Ana, CA
Schiff, Shoshana ..... West Orange, NJ
Schiff, Steven ..... Harrison, NY
Schiff, Steven H. ..... Rockville, MD
Schiff, Steven H. ..... Albuquerque, NM
Schiff, Sue Ann L. ..... San Francisco, CA
Schiff, Susan E. ..... Palo Alto, CA
Schiff, Susan W. ..... Pueblo, CO
Schiff, Teresa H. ..... Tampa, FL
Schiff, Terry ..... Chicago, IL
Schiff, Thomas E. ..... Los Angeles, CA
Schiff, Thomas R. ..... Dayton, OH
Schiff, Wm. Michael ..... Evansville, IN
Schiffer, Adam P. ..... Houston, TX
Schiffer, Carl E. ..... Rye, NY
Schiffer, Daniel L. ..... Detroit, MI
Schiffer, Daniel Q. ..... Murrieta, CA
Schiffer, Douglas J. ..... Marina Del Rey, CA
Schiffer, Edward E. ..... San Francisco, CA
Schiffer, Elizabeth G. ..... Houston, TX
Schiffer, Eric M. ..... Irvine, CA
Schiffer, Kelly Klumok ..... Atlanta, GA
Schiffer, Larry P. ..... New York, NY
Schiffer, Lois J. ..... Department of Justice,
Environment and Natural Resources
Division, GV
Schiffer, Michael C. ..... Irvine, CA
Schiffer, Michael David ..... Baltimore, MD
Schiffer, Michele J. ..... New York, NY
Schiffer, Nancy J. ..... Detroit, MI
Schiffer, Spencer F. ..... Aspen, CO
Schiffer, Spencer F., P.C. ..... Aspen, CO
Schiffer, Stuart E. ..... Department of Justice,
Civil Division, GV
Schiffer, Vivienne Rosalie (Lie)
Houston, TX
Schiffer, W. Patrick ..... Phoenix, AZ
Schifferdecker, Jack W., Jr. ..... Portland, OR
Schifferli, Jay R. ..... Stamford, CT
Schifferman, Reed P. ..... Seattle, WA
Schifferman, Robert P.
La Canada Flintridge, CA
Schiffhauer, John R. ..... Santa Clara, CA
Schiffhauer, Wayne D. ..... Buffalo, NY
Schiffhouer, Joseph L. ..... Memphis, TN
Schiffler, Geralyn A. ..... Buffalo, NY
Schiffler, Kenneth A. ..... Everett, WA
Schiffli, Gary A. ..... Indianapolis, IN
Schiffmacher, Cullen, Farrell & Limmer
Great Neck, NY
Schiffmacher, Mark D. ..... Los Angeles, CA
Schiffmacher, Todd M. ..... Buffalo, NY
Schiffmacher, Weinstein, Boldt & Racine, Professional Corporation
Los Angeles, CA
Schiffman, Adam R.
North Miami Beach, FL
Schiffman, Adelia T. ..... Greensboro, NC
Schiffman, Alan M. ..... Phoenix, AZ
Schiffman, Arielle N. ..... New York, NY
Schiffman, Berger, Abraham, Kaufman & Ritter, P.C. ..... Hackensack, NJ
Schiffman, Candace S. ..... Houston, TX
Schiffman, Carl R. ..... Pittsburgh, PA
Schiffman, Carole ..... New York, NY
Schiffman, Dana I. ..... San Diego, CA
Schiffman, Daniel ..... New York, NY
Schiffman, David M. ..... Chicago, IL
Schiffman, Doyle L. ..... Roseburg, OR
Schiffman & Frank ..... New York, NY
Schiffman, Gene N. ..... Hackensack, NJ
Schiffman, Harve Jay
Rancho Cucamonga, CA
Schiffman, Henry N. ..... Washington, DC
Schiffman, Howard ..... Washington, DC
Schiffman, Howard S. ..... Brooklyn, NY
Schiffman Hozier, P.C. ..... Phoenix, AZ
Schiffman, Jack B. ..... Phoenix, AZ
Schiffman, Jay ..... New York, NY
Schiffman, Joel A. ..... Chatsworth, CA
Schiffman, Jordan D. ..... New York, NY
Schiffman, Lance P. ..... Metairie, LA
Schiffman, Lisa A. ..... Dallas, TX
Schiffman, Mark E. ..... Irvine, CA
Irvine, CA
Schiffman, Michael S. ..... Chicago, IL
Schiffman, Philip ..... Washingtonville, NY
Schiffman, Richard W., Jr. ..... Atlanta, GA
Schiffman, Robyn M. ..... Evergreen, CO
Schiffman, Ronald M. ..... Garden City, NY
Schiffman, Ronald P. ..... Tolovana Park, OR
Schiffman, Roni ..... Pittsburgh, PA
Schiffman, Samuel A. ..... Charlotte, NC
Schiffman, Sheldon ..... Watchung, NJ
Schiffman, Steven J. ..... Harrisburg, PA
Schiffman, Steven M. ..... Brooklyn, NY
Schiffman, Todd K.
Securities and Exchange Commission,
Division of Corporation Finance, GV
Schiffman, William T. ..... Spring Valley, NY
Schiffman & Wojdowski ..... Pittsburgh, PA
Schiffmann, Richard F. ..... Barnstable, MA
Schiffmiller, Martin W. ..... New York, NY
Schiffner, Glenn D. ..... Colby, KS
Schiffner, John J. ..... Spokane, WA
Schiffres, H. Steven, (P.C.) ..... Los Angeles, CA
Schiffres, Michael E. ..... Long Island City, NY
Schiffrin, Albert W. ..... Philadelphia, PA
Schiffrin, Craig & Barroway, LLP
Buffalo Grove, IL
Bala Cynwyd, PA
Schiffrin, David W. ..... Seattle, WA
Schiffrin, Jon Alan ..... Arlington, VA
Schiffrin, Michael ..... Miami, FL
Schiffrin, Michael, & Associates, P.A.
Miami, FL
Schiffrin Olson Schlemlein & Hopkins, P.L.L.C. ..... Seattle, WA
Schiffrin, Richard S. ..... Buffalo Grove, IL
Bala Cynwyd, PA
Schifino & Fleischer, P.A. ..... Tampa, FL
Schifino, John A. ..... Tampa, FL
Schifino, Paul G. ..... Los Angeles, CA
Schifino, Sara Anne ..... Miami, FL
Tampa, FL
Schifino, William J. ..... Tampa, FL
Schifino, William J., Jr. ..... Tampa, FL
Schifko, Robert F. ..... Cleveland, OH
Schifman, Kenneth A. ..... Kansas City, MO
Schifone, Richard M. ..... Somerville, MA
Schifrin, Alvin J. ..... Mill Valley, CA
Schifrin, Andrew D. ..... New York, NY
Schifrin, Kristi A. ..... Seattle, WA
Schifrin, Mark E. ..... Bethesda, MD
Schifrin, Paula S. ..... New York, NY
Schifsky, Peter E. ..... Minneapolis, MN
Schiftan, Lynne G. ..... Greensboro, NC
Schifter, Carol R. ..... Rockville, MD
Schifter, Karen E. ..... Rockville, MD
Schifter, Richard P. ..... Washington, DC
Schigur, Ronald P. ..... Detroit, MI
Schij, Gabriel Israel ..... Seal Beach, CA
Schijman, Elizabeth Alixandre
New York, NY
Schikora, Rosemary G. ..... Detroit, MI
Schikora, William R. ..... Detroit, MI
Schilawski, Michael F. ..... Cary, NC
Schilcher, M.L., P.A. ..... Tampa, FL
Schilcher, Monika L. ..... Tampa, FL
Schild, Donald L. ..... Grinnell, IA
Schild, Kenneth R. ..... Santa Monica, CA
Schild, Kitty ..... El Paso, TX
Schild, Marvin ..... Maggie Valley, NC
Schild, Peter ..... Boulder, CO
Schild, Raymond D. ..... Boise, ID
Schild, Robert M. ..... Fairport, NY
Schildberg, Scott G. ..... Jacksonville, FL
Schilder, Joseph W. ..... Sunbury, OH
Schilder, Madeline L. ..... Beverly Hills, CA
Schildge, Heather A. ..... Department of State,
Office of the Legal Adviser, GV
Schildhammer, Ann Reinhard
Atlanta, GA
Schildhaus, Aaron ..... Washington, DC
Schildhause, Sol ..... Washington, DC
Schildhorn, Gary M. ..... Philadelphia, PA
Schildhouse, Mark B. ..... Akron, OH
Schildiner, Andrew D. ..... Roseland, NJ
Schildknecht, Carter Tinsley ..... Lamesa, TX
Schildknecht, Henry ..... Louisville, KY
Schildkraut, Bruce S. ..... Chatsworth, CA
Schildkraut, Lance Aaron ..... Newark, NJ
Schildkraut, Marc G. ..... Washington, DC
Schildkraut, Mark J. ..... New York, NY
Schildkraut, Peter J. ..... Washington, DC
Schildman, William S. ..... Jacksonville, IL
Schildnecht, C. William, Jr. ..... Pittsburgh, PA
Schildt, James M. ..... Quakertown, PA
Schildt, Steven ..... Philadelphia, PA
Schildt, William McClure
Hagerstown, MD
Schilian, Gerald ..... New Brunswick, NJ
Schilit, Menachem ..... Encino, CA
Schilke, Neil W. ..... Fremont, NE
Schilke, Steven R. ..... Neenah, WI
Schilken, Bruce A. ..... Englewood, CO
Schilken Kautt & Kindschuh, P.C.
Englewood, CO
Schilken, Michael C. ..... Omaha, NE
Schill, Charles F. ..... Washington, DC
Schill, Frederick H. ..... Paradise, CA
Schill, Gilbert E., Jr. ..... Richmond, VA
Schill, Gus A., Jr. ..... Houston, TX
Schill, Katherine W. ..... Milwaukee, WI
Schill, Lawrence C. ..... Pensacola, FL
Schill, Mary Ellen ..... Wausau, WI
Schill, Mary M. ..... Houston, TX
Schill, Susan C. ..... Wisconsin Rapids, WI
Schill, Todd Arthur ..... Grosse Pointe Park, MI
Schill, William T. ..... Cleveland, OH
Schillace, Gregory H. ..... Clarksburg, WV
Schillaci, Andrea ..... Buffalo, NY
Schillaci, Michael ..... Culver City, CA
Schillaci, Theresa Ann ..... Albany, NY
Schillawski, Paul ..... Atlanta, GA
Schillawski, Philip C. ..... Cleveland, OH
Schilleci, Vincent J., Jr. ..... Bessemer, AL
Schiller, Arthur J. ..... Northbrook, IL
Schiller, Arthur M. ..... Silver Spring, MD
Schiller & Associates, P.C. ..... New York, NY
Schiller, Baerbel E. ..... Kansas City, KS
Schiller, Bennett J., III ..... Chester, SC
Columbia, SC
Lancaster, SC
Rock Hill, SC
Schiller, Berle M. ..... Bala Cynwyd, PA
Schiller, Blanche E. ..... Albany, NY
Schiller, Bryan ..... San Antonio, TX
Schiller, Carol M. ..... Raleigh, NC
Schiller, Craig ..... New York, NY
Schiller, David A. ..... Rockville, MD
Schiller, David A. ..... Dallas, TX
Schiller, David I. ..... Dallas, TX
Schiller, David J. ..... Norristown, PA
Schiller, David M. ..... Stuart, FL
Schiller, Dawn D. ..... Chicago, IL
Schiller, Derek E. ..... Chicago, IL
Schiller, Donald C. ..... Chicago, IL
Schiller, Donald H.
Kennedy Space Center, FL
Schiller, Du Canto and Fleck ..... Chicago, IL
Lake Forest, IL
Wheaton, IL
Schiller, Edwin G. ..... Nampa, ID
Schiller, Eric M. ..... Chicago, IL
Schiller, Erika B. ..... Vienna, VA
Schiller, Eugene F., Jr. ..... Bloomington, IL
Schiller, Francis E. ..... Jersey City, NJ
New York, NY
Schiller, Frank A. ..... Raleigh, NC
Schiller, Frank E. ..... Montclair, NJ
Schiller, Fred ..... Las Cruces, NM
Schiller & Gerber ..... New York, NY
Schiller, Gideon H. ..... St. Louis, MO
Schiller, Gillian B. ..... Worcester, MA
Schiller, Glenn M. ..... Canton, OH
Schiller, Gregory B. ..... Bridgeport, CT
Schiller, Gregory E. ..... Chicago, IL
Schiller, Gregory J. ..... Monona, IA
Schiller, H. Paul ..... New York, NY
Schiller, Heidi A. ..... Boston, MA
Schiller, Howard B. ..... Willimantic, CT
Schiller, James A. ..... Nampa, ID
Schiller, James J. ..... Cleveland, OH
Schiller, James J., & Associates
Cleveland, OH
Schiller, Jay A., Jr. ..... Chicago, IL
Schiller, Jeffrey E. ..... Chicago, IL
Schiller, John E. ..... Cleveland, OH
Schiller, Jonathan D. ..... Washington, DC
Armonk, NY
Schiller, Joseph A. ..... Pensacola, FL
Schiller, Keith ..... Walnut Creek, CA
Schiller, L. Kip ..... Gainesville, TX
Schiller, Laura J. ..... Philadelphia, PA
Schiller, Lawrence F. ..... Detroit, MI
Schiller, Lee E. ..... Englewood, CO
Schiller, Lenore, (P.A.) ..... Miami, FL
Schiller, Lewis A. ..... Rockville, MD
Schiller, Lisa M. ..... Miami, FL
Schiller, M. Sharon ..... Cleveland, OH
Schiller, Marc Stuart
Fort Lauderdale, FL
Schiller, Marvin ..... Cary, NC
Schiller, Marvin ..... Raleigh, NC
Schiller, Marvin
Research Triangle Park, NC
Schiller, Mary Ann ..... Orange, CA
Schiller, Mary B. ..... Fredonia, NY
Jamestown, NY
Schiller, Melvin D. ..... Coral Gables, FL
Schiller, Michael I. ..... Redondo Beach, CA
Schiller, Miranda S. ..... New York, NY
Schiller, Osbourn & Barnes
Louisville, KY
Schiller, Pamela M. ..... Pittsburgh, PA
Schiller, Patricia ..... Washington, DC
Schiller, Peter N. ..... Sands Point, NY
Schiller, Philip J., & Assoc., P.C.
Chicago, IL
Schiller, P.L.L.C. ..... Dallas, TX
Schiller, Rebecca F. ..... St. Paul, MN
Schiller, Richard C. ..... Universal City, CA
Schiller, Richard D. ..... Oswego, IL
Schiller, Richard D., P.C. ..... Aurora, IL
Oswego, IL
Yorkville, IL
Schiller, Richard P. ..... Louisville, KY
Schiller, Robert J. ..... Boston, MA
Schiller, Ronald P. ..... Philadelphia, PA
Schiller, Royal A. ..... Salem, OH
Schiller, Sabrina Scharf
Pacific Palisades, CA
Schiller, Samuel J. ..... Tulsa, OK
Schiller & Schiller, Chartered ..... Nampa, ID
Schiller, Scott Y. ..... Chicago, IL
Schiller, Sidney S. ..... Chicago, IL
Schiller, Stephen A. ..... Chicago, IL
Schiller, Steven L. ..... Newport, KY
Schiller, Suzanne I. ..... Philadelphia, PA
Schiller, Teresa B. ..... Wilmington, DE
New York, NY
Schiller, Thomas P. ..... Cleveland, OH
Schiller, Vyzas, Squeo & Hartnett, A Professional Corporation ..... Jersey City, NJ
Schiller, Wanda M. ..... Harrisburg, PA
Schiller, William B. ..... Chicago, IL
Schiller, William M. ..... Atlanta, GA
Schiller-Lunde, Marsha L. ..... Temple, TX
Schillerstrom, Robert J. ..... Naperville, IL
Schillesci, Mary E. ..... New Orleans, LA
Schilli, David M. ..... Charlotte, NC
Schillie, Jon D. ..... Joplin, MO
Schilling, April R. ..... Bloomington, IN
Schilling, Christopher J. ..... Palm Beach, FL
Schilling, Debra S. ..... Seattle, WA
Schilling, Diane Lufkin ..... Albany, NY
Schilling, E. Thomas ..... Milwaukee, WI
Schilling, Edwin C., III, P.C. ..... Denver, CO
Schilling, Edwin C., Jr. ..... Amite, LA
Schilling, Edwin, III ..... Denver, CO
Schilling, George T. ..... Palm City, FL
Schilling, Glenn L. ..... Louisville, KY
Schilling, Gretchen M. Widdig ..... Tulsa, OK
Schilling, J. Baxter ..... Louisville, KY
Schilling, James G. ..... Dubuque, IA
Schilling, Jennifer L. ..... Chicago, IL
Schilling, Jill R. ..... Eau Claire, WI
Schilling, John F. ..... Los Angeles, CA
Schilling, John Leslie ..... Oregon City, OR
Schilling, John M. ..... Richmond, VA
Schilling, John R. ..... Newport Beach, CA
Schilling, John R., A Professional Corporation ..... Newport Beach, CA
Schilling, Joseph M. ..... San Diego, CA
Schilling, Kathryn M. ..... Blue Bell, PA
Schilling, Laura K. ..... Atlanta, GA
Schilling, Lawrence W. ..... New York, NY
Schilling, Linda ..... Costa Mesa, CA
Schilling, Mark W. ..... Tulsa, OK
Schilling, Michael ..... Laramie, WY
Schilling, Michael J. ..... Burlington, IA
Schilling, Michael L., Jr. ..... Abbeville, LA
Schilling, Michael, Law Firm of, The
Laramie, WY
Schilling, Nancy Ann ..... Galion, OH
Schilling, Patrick G. ..... Phillips, WI
Schilling, Rebecca G.
Fort Lauderdale, FL
Schilling, Richard D. ..... Cincinnati, OH
Schilling, Richard M. ..... Rockford, IL
Schilling, Richard R., Jr. ..... New York, NY
Schilling, Robert J. ..... Boston, MA
Schilling, Ron ..... Lewiston, ID
Schilling, Ronald D. ..... Cincinnati, OH
Schilling, Ronald F. ..... Pontiac, MI
Schilling, Sue Belevich ..... Syosset, NY
Schilling, Theodore A. ..... Centerville, MA
Schilling, W. Dennis ..... Birmingham, AL
Schilling, William H. ..... Amelia, OH
Schillinger, Bryan J. ..... Houston, TX
Schillinger & Finsterwald, LLP
New York, NY
Schillinger, Lawrence R. ..... Albany, NY
Schillinger, Lee H. ..... Hollywood, FL
Schillinger, Patrick ..... Green Bay, WI
Schillinger, Paul ..... Bloomington, IL
Schillinger, Peter ..... New York, NY
Schillinger, Randi ..... Newark, NJ
Schillinger, Wilbur ..... St. Joseph, MI
Schillings, Scott R. ..... Wichita, KS
Schilmeister, Lawrence D. ..... Mansfield, MA
Schilmoeller, Jane E. ..... Kansas City, MO
Schilmoeller, John Maurice ..... St. Louis, MO
Schilp, Susan M. Day
North Brunswick, NJ
Schilpp, E. Allen ..... Buies Creek, NC
Schilpp, J. Walter ..... Philadelphia, PA
Schilt, Bernerd E. ..... Denver, CO
Schilt, E. Nathan ..... Redlands, CA
Schiltz, Christine P. ..... Wilmington, DE
Schiltz, David W. ..... Kenosha, WI
Schiltz, Eugene J ..... Chicago, IL
Schiltz, Jane Ann ..... Milwaukee, WI
Schiltz, Mikkie R. ..... Bloomington, IL
Schiltz, Ronald L. ..... Gilroy, CA
Schiltz, Scott E. ..... Clearwater, FL
Schiltz, Todd ..... Wilmington, DE
Schilz, Harold L. ..... Fredericksburg, VA
Schimaneck, Anthony P. ..... Lancaster, PA
Schimaneck, Frank E. ..... San Francisco, CA
Schimanski, James R. ..... Cincinnati, OH
Schimanski, Robert G. ..... Spokane, WA
Schimanski, Scott A.
Oakbrook Terrace, IL
Schimberg, A. Bruce ..... Chicago, IL
Schimberg, Michael J. ..... Dallas, TX
Schimberg, Timothy P. ..... Denver, CO
Schimbor, Patricia Shuler ..... Orinda, CA
Schimek, Joanne M. ..... San Diego, CA
Schimek, Michael David ..... Houston, TX
Schimek, Terry E. ..... New York, NY
Schimel, Martin ..... New York, NY
Schimel, Richard E. ..... Bethesda, MD
Schimel, Ronald S. ..... Columbia, MD
Schimelfenig, Marianne ..... Moraga, CA
Schimelman, Stuart M. ..... New London, CT
Schimer, Maria R. ..... Rootstown, OH
Schimers, Bo ..... Southgate, MI
Schimizzi, Richard W. ..... Greensburg, PA
Schimkat, Helga C. ..... Santa Fe, NM
Schimkat, K. Renee ..... Miami, FL
Schimley, Paul F. ..... Los Angeles, CA
Schimmel, Alan I. ..... Sherman Oaks, CA
Schimmel, Albert W., III ..... Albuquerque, NM
Schimmel, David ..... Amherst, MA
Schimmel, George M. ..... Milwaukee, WI
Schimmel, George R. ..... Milwaukee, WI
Schimmel, Hillshafer & Loewenthal, A Professional Law Corporation
Los Angeles, CA
Santa Barbara, CA
Sherman Oaks, CA
Ventura, CA
Schimmel, Jennifer Brooke ..... Dallas, TX
Schimmel, Joseph Barry ..... Miami, FL
Schimmel, Judith Brown ..... Harrisburg, PA
Schimmel, Lana ..... New York, NY
Schimmel, Miriam Leigh
Los Angeles, CA
Schimmel, Morton ..... White Plains, NY
Schimmel, Nancy L. ..... Chicago, IL
Schimmel, Paul ..... Commack, NY
Schimmel, Raymond M. ..... San Diego, CA

Schimmel, Robert L. ... Miami, FL
Schimmel, Seth M. ... Tampa, FL
Schimmel, William G. ... Detroit, MI
Schimmelbusch, Erik S. ... Portland, OR
Schimmelpfennig, Jerel C. ... Fargo, ND
Schimmelpfennig, Randy E. ... Orlando, FL
Schimmels, Sarah Sullivan ... Richmond, VA
Schimmenti & Berberian ... El Segundo, CA
Schimmenti, John J. ... El Segundo, CA
Schimmerling, Thomas E.
Binghamton, NY
Delhi, NY
Schimming, Brian B. ... Washington, DC
Schimpf, Carey T. ... Shreveport, LA
Schimpf, Jerome L. ... Cincinnati, OH
Schimpf, Richard J. ... Cincinnati, OH
Schimpf, Robert M. ... Albany, NY
Schimpf, Thomas F. ... Lansing, MI
Schimpff, Kirsten M. ... Washington, DC
Schinasi, David ... Westfield, NJ
Schindel, Aaron J. ... New York, NY
Schindel, Andrew M. ... New York, NY
Schindel, Caren Z. ... Framingham, MA
Schindel, Carolyn K. ... New York, NY
Schindel, Donald ... Mamaroneck, NY
Schindel, Donald M. ... Chicago, IL
Schindel, Farman & Lipsius
New York, NY
Schindel, Matthew G. ... St. Petersburg, FL
Schindel, Matthew R. ... Dallas, TX
Schindel, Ronnie M. ... New York, NY
Schindel, Stephen F. ... New York, NY
Schindelar, John F. ... Hiawassee, GA
Schindele, Michael L. ... Boise, ID
Schindeler, Vincent E. ... Fort Lauderdale, FL
Schindeler, Vincent E., P.A.
Fort Lauderdale, FL
Schinder, Barry S. ... Hollywood, FL
Schinder, Jeremy Alan ... Miami, FL
Schinderman, Ivan ... New York, NY
Schindhelm, Steven M. ... Milwaukee, WI
Schindler, Ann ... Seattle, WA
Schindler, Barry J. ... New York, NY
Schindler, Barry M. ... New York, NY
Schindler, Brent W. ... Pittsburg, CA
Schindler, Charles S. ... Oklahoma City, OK
Schindler, Christopher A.
Washington, DC
Schindler Cohen & Hochman LLP
New York, NY
Schindler, Devin S. ... Grand Rapids, MI
Schindler, Edwin D. ... Coram, NY
Schindler, Eric J. ... Irvine, CA
Schindler, Gary ... Hermosa Beach, CA
Schindler, George A. ... Troy, NY
Schindler, Greg S. ... Westport, CT
Schindler, Hadley Blake ... St. Louis, MO
Schindler, Janice Amy ... West Caldwell, NJ
Schindler, Jerome R. ... Columbus, OH
Schindler, Joanna L. ... Sterling, VA
Schindler, John E. ... Price, UT
Schindler, John W., Jr. ... Mishawaka, IN
Schindler, Jonathan S. ... Boston, MA
Schindler, Joseph H. ... New York, NY
Schindler, Joseph I. ... Boston, MA
Schindler, Joshua M. ... St. Louis, MO
Schindler, Loren B. ... Garden City, NY
Schindler, Marc A. ... Baltimore, MD
Schindler, Mark A. ... Ottawa, IL
Schindler, Merrye P. ... New York, NY
Schindler & Meyer, Professional Corporation
San Francisco, CA
Schindler and Olson ... Mishawaka, IN
South Bend, IN
Schindler, Ozzie A. ... Miami, FL
Schindler, Paul D. ... New York, NY
Schindler, Paul M. ... New York, NY
Schindler, R. Ray ... Louisville, KY
Schindler, Ralph J. ... West Des Moines, IA
Schindler, Ralph J., Jr. ... Chicago, IL
Schindler, Richard A. ... San Francisco, CA
Schindler, Roger J. ... Miami, FL
Schindler, Roland R., II ... Indianapolis, IN
Schindler, Ronald I. ... Denver, CO
Schindler, Rose M. ... Los Angeles, CA
Schindler, Russell A. ... Kingston, NY
Schindler, Stanley H. ... Rockville Centre, NY
Schindler, Stella Speiser ... New York, NY
Schindler, Stephen S. ... New York, NY
Schindler, Steven E. ... Rutland, VT
Schindler, Steven R. ... New York, NY
Schindler, Thomas J. ... Duluth, MN
Schindler, Thomas K. ... West Chester, PA
Schindler, Victor R. ... Houston, TX
Schine, Julianelle & Antonucci, P.C.
Orange, CT
Westport, CT
Schineller, Elena Marie ... Boston, MA
Schiner, Curt J. ... New York, NY
Schingle, Michael J. ... Fort Morgan, CO
Schink, David F. ... Chicago, IL
Schink, James H., (P.C.) ... Chicago, IL
Schinman, H. Lawrence ... Paterson, NJ
Schinner, Michael G. ... San Francisco, CA
Schinnerer, Lisa M. ... Studio City, CA
Schinstock, Christopher W.
Alexandria, VA
Fairfax, VA
Schinzel, Dorothy A. ... Sutton, NE
Schiopota, Eugene ... Cleveland, OH
Schioppi, Joseph C. ... Flushing, NY
Schioppo, Richard A. ... New York, NY
Schiowitz, Martin ... New York, NY
Schipani, Cindy A. ... Ann Arbor, MI
Schipfer, Daniel C., Jr. ... Greenville, OH
Schippel, Bahar A.
United States Tax Court, GV
Schippel, John E. ... Chicago, IL

Schipper, Agnes M. ... Rochester, MN
Schipper, James L. ... Grand Rapids, MI
Schipper, Randall S. ... Holland, MI
Schipper, Sharla A. ... Fremont, MI
Schippers, David P. ... Chicago, IL
Schippers, John F. ... Hartford, WI
Schippers, Thomas, M. ... Waukegan, IL
Schipske, Gerrie ... Long Beach, CA
Schipske, Timothy J. ... Marlton, NJ
Schira, David Michael ... Columbus, OH
Schira, Diana R. ... Marathon, WI
Schira, Jacques D. ... Des Moines, IA
Schira, Jacques D., P.C. ... Des Moines, IA
Schira, Jeffrey S. ... Fort Worth, TX
Schirado, Jon D. ... St. Paul, MN
Schirado Law Office, P.A. ... St. Paul, MN
Schiraldi, Benedict A. ... Madison, CT
Schiraldi, Lori Ann ... Somerset, NJ
Schiraldi, Richard J. ... Youngstown, OH
Schiralli, Beth S. ... Irvine, CA
Schiralli, Nicholas J. ... Crown Point, IN
Schirard, Joseph P. ... Garland, TX
Schirber Law Offices, P.C. ... Papillion, NE
Schirber, Michael N. ... Papillion, NE
Schirch, Jane M. ... Concord, NH
Schirger, John J. ... Omaha, NE
Schirger, Monteleone & Hampilos
Rockford, IL
Schirger, William E. ... Rockford, IL
Schirle, K. Clark ... Chicago, IL
Schirle, Stephen L. ... San Francisco, CA
Schirm, Barry R. ... Los Angeles, CA
Schirman, Thomas R., Jr. ... De Witt, IA
Schirmeister, Charles F. ... New York, NY
Schirmer, Albert W. ... Cincinnati, OH
Schirmer, Dean Wayne ... Sacramento, CA
Schirmer, Drew W. ... Melville, NY
Schirmer, Fisher & Peterson ... Oak Park, IL
Schirmer & Hrdlicka ... Saugerties, NY
Schirmer, Keith R. ... Walnut Creek, CA
Schirmer, Mark J. ... Memphis, TN
Schirmer, Robert P. ... Saugerties, NY
Schirmer, Robin L. ... Oak Park, IL
Schirmer, Suter & Gaw ... Moberly, MO
Schirmer, Wayne E. ... Moberly, MO
Schirn, Robert ... Los Angeles, CA
Schiro, Anthony W. ... Milwaukee, WI
Schiro, Christine B. ... Boulder, CO
Schiro, Debra W. ... Tampa, FL
Schiro, Frank J. ... Milwaukee, WI
Schiro, Frank Joseph, Law Office of Ltd.
Milwaukee, WI
Schiro, Frank P., III ... New Orleans, LA
Schiro, Gasper J. ... New Orleans, LA
Schiro, Gregory W. ... Winston-Salem, NC
Schiro, Jeffrey J. ... Bedford, NY
Schiro, Lawrence T. ... Yonkers, NY
Schiro, Nicholas M. ... Danville, IL
Schiro, Richard B. ... Dallas, TX
Schiron, Peter Thomas ... Breckenridge, CO
Schirott, James R. ... Itasca, IL
Schirrmeister Ajamie, LLP ... Houston, TX
McAllen, TX
Schirrmeister, Andrew C., III
Houston, TX
McAllen, TX
Schirrmeister, Olivia T. ... Houston, TX
Schirtzer, Richard A. ... Los Angeles, CA
Schirtzer, Ronald M. ... Orlando, FL
Schisano, Richard ... New Windsor, NY
Schisano, Salvatore ... Newburgh, NY
Schisgall, Laura J. ... New York, NY
Schisler, Harold T., II ... Cincinnati, OH
Schisler, Richard C. ... Poughkeepsie, NY
Schisler, Richard T. ... Portsmouth, OH
Schisler, Scott A. ... Bay City, MI
Schisler, Charles E. ... Amesbury, MA
Schissel, Luke J. ... Greenwood, MS
Schissel, Michael D. ... New York, NY
Schissell, Gerald Z. ... Glendale, CA
Schissler, E. Denise ... Santa Rosa, CA
Schissler, Gerald J. ... Houston, TX
Schissler, Richard P., III ... Houston, TX
Schittina, Mark A. ... Burlington, VT
Schiveley, Mark ... Medford, OR
Schivera, Robert W. ... Savannah, GA
Schivley, G. Gregory ... Troy, MI
Schivo, Ronald D. ... San Francisco, CA
Schivone, Kenneth G. ... St. Paul, MN
Schiwetz, Stephen H. ... Corpus Christi, TX
Schiwetz, Theodore F., Jr. ... Kerrville, TX
Schizer, Hazel G. ... New York, NY
Schizer & Schizer ... New York, NY
Schizer, Zevie B. ... New York, NY
Schklair, Barry E. ... Portland, ME
Schklar, Edwin J. ... Atlanta, GA
Schkolnick, Richard S. ... West Orange, NJ
Schlaak, Ann L. ... Burbank, CA
Schlabs, Glenn H. ... Colorado Springs, CO
Schlachet, Jaye M. ... Cleveland, OH
Schlachet, Mark ... Cleveland, OH
Schlachman, Belsky & Weiner, P.A.
Baltimore, MD
Easton, MD
Towson, MD
Upper Marlboro, MD
Schlachman, Sidney ... Baltimore, MD
Schlachtenhaufen, Mary R. ... Houston, TX
Schlachter, David ... Commack, NY
Schlachter, David D. ... Denver, CO
Schlachter, Douglas J. ... Houston, TX
Schlachter, Ewald O. ... Oakland, CA
Schlachter, Margaret A. ... Springfield, MO
Schlachter & Mauro ... Commack, NY
Floral Park, NY
Mineola, NY
Riverhead, NY
Schlack, Carl J., Jr. ... Honolulu, HI

Schlack, David A. ... Chicago, IL
Schlack, Michael D. ... Kalamazoo, MI
Schlackman, David E. ... Detroit, MI
Schlackman, Marvin I. ... Long Beach, CA
Schlacks, Harrison & Cox, P.L.L.C.
The Woodlands, TX
Schlacks, Stephen M. ... The Woodlands, TX
Schlact, S. Alan ... Marietta, GA
Schlacter, Jed R. ... New York, NY
Schlade, Terry M. ... Chicago, IL
Schladt, William H. ... Gaithersburg, MD
Schlaefer, Cindy V. ... New York, NY
Schlaefer, Leo F. ... West Bend, WI
Schlaegel, E. Lee, Jr. ... Madison, WV
Schlaeppi, Yvonne E. ... Boston, MA
Schlafer, Dale L. ... Chicago, IL
Schlafer, Douglas J. ... San Francisco, CA
Schlaff, Barbara E. ... Baltimore, MD
Schlaff, Elizabeth ... New Britain, CT
Schlaff, John A. ... Los Angeles, CA
Schlaff, Robin ... Chappaqua, NY
Schlafly, John F. ... Alton, IL
Schlafly, Michael G. ... Houston, TX
Schlafly, Phyllis, (Mrs.) ... St. Louis, MO
Schlafly, Robert F. ... St. Louis, MO
Schlafly, Thomas F. ... St. Louis, MO
Schlafman, Gerald E. ... Fairborn, OH
Schlafman, Gerald E., Co., L.P.A.
Fairborn, OH
Schlag, Rebecca A. ... Cleveland, OH
Schlag, René C. ... Woodbridge, NJ
Schlagel, Alden E. ... St. Paul, MN
Schlagel, Damore & Gordon, LLC
Olathe, KS
Schlagel, George J. ... Olathe, KS
Schlagel, Gilbert J. ... St. Paul, MN
Schlagel, Legler & Nelson ... St. Paul, MN
Schlagel, Rodney L. ... Albuquerque, NM
Schlager, Charles E., Jr. ... Hackensack, NJ
Schlager, Ron ... Sherman Oaks, CA
Schlageter, Breier & Bryce, Co., L.P.A.
Oregon, OH
Toledo, OH
Schlageter, John J. ... Toledo, OH
Schlageter, John J., III ... Toledo, OH
Schlageter, John J., Jr. ... Toledo, OH
Schlageter, Thomas G. ... Oregon, OH
Toledo, OH
Schlageter, Thomas J.
Equal Employment Opportunity Commission,
Office of Legal Counsel, GV
Schlaich, Carl R. ... Bel Air, MD
Schlaich & Thompson, Chartered
Bel Air, MD
Schlaier, Gustav J. ... Clifton, NJ
Schlaifer, Alan N. ... Bethesda, MD
Schlaifer, Alan N., P.C. ... Bethesda, MD
Schlaifer, David A. ... Tampa, FL
Schlaifer, Jane P. ... Department of Energy,
Office of the General Counsel, GV
Schlaifer, Richard M. ... Marlton, NJ
Schlaikjer, Paul F. ... Princeton, MA
Schlain, Barbara E. ... New York, NY
Schlak, Douglas W. ... New Lenox, IL
Schlak, Douglas W. & Associates
New Lenox, IL
Schlak, Gregory Alan ... Houston, TX
Schlake, Jonathon T. ... Galesburg, IL
Schlake, Richard J. ... Park Ridge, IL
Schlake, Thomas T. ... Park Ridge, IL
Schlam, Eric Arthur ... Arlington, VA
Schlam, Paul E. ... Columbus, GA
Schlam, Peter R. ... New York, NY
Schlam Stone & Dolan ... New York, NY
Schlamp, Philip L. ... Sanford, NC
Schlang, Alan L. ... Auburn Hills, MI
Schlang, David ... New York, NY
Schlang, Setha ... Los Angeles, CA
Schlangel, Leonard J. ... New Rochelle, NY
Schlanger, Arnold G. ... New York, NY
Schlanger, Craig P. ... Syracuse, NY
Schlanger, David A. ... Chicago, IL
Schlanger, Eugene A. ... New York, NY
Schlanger, Herbert P. ... Atlanta, GA
Schlanger, Herbert P., P.C., Law Offices of
Atlanta, GA
Schlanger, Jeffrey R. ... New York, NY
Schlanger, John ... Van Nuys, CA
Schlanger, Lee D., (P.C.) ... Houston, TX
Schlanger, Margo ... Cambridge, MA
Schlanger, Michael A. ... Washington, DC
Schlanger, Michael, Law Offices of
White Plains, NY
Schlanger, Mills, Mayer & Silver, L.L.P.
Houston, TX
Schlanger, Phoebe ... Washington, DC
Schlanger, Robert A. ... Dallas, TX
Schlanger, Robert M. ... Fairview, NJ
Orangeburg, NY
Schlansker, Howard I., Jr. ... Norwell, MA
Schlant, Mark J. ... Buffalo, NY
Schlapach, David L. ... Atlanta, GA
Schlapak, Stephen D. ... Kenilworth, NJ
Schlapak, William J., Jr. ... Trenton, NJ
Schlapik, Jerome ... New York, NY
Schlapkohl, Thomas P. ... Des Moines, IA
Schlapkohl, Thomas P., P.C.
Des Moines, IA
Schlapprizzi, Donald L. ... St. Louis, MO
Schlapprizzi, Donald L., P.C.
St. Louis, MO
Schlarman, Lori A. ... Covington, KY
Schlatter, Augustus T. ... Incline Village, NV
Schlatter, Thomas Weissinger ... Nashville, TN
Schlather & Birch ... Cooperstown, NY
Schlather, Raymond M. ... Ithaca, NY
Schlather, Robert B. ... Cooperstown, NY

Schlather, Stephen ... Houston, TX
Schlatner, Adam J. ... New York, NY
Schlatter, Donald A. ... Toledo, OH
Schlatter, Edward A. ... Newport Beach, CA
Schlatter, LauraSue ... St. Paul, MN
Schlatter, O. Edward ... Salida, CO
Schlatter, Regina M. ... Costa Mesa, CA
Schlatter, Robert L. ... Columbus, OH
Schlattman, Robert W.
General Services Administration,
Office of the General Counsel, GV
Schlattmann, Kristen J. ... Cheyenne, WY
Schlau, Philip ... New York, NY
Schlau, Stephanie A. ... Houston, TX
Schlauch, Bambi J. ... Riverside, CA
Schlauch, Paul J. ... Greenwood Village, CO
Schlaudecker, David G. ... Toledo, OH
Schlauger, Rod ... Rapid City, SD
Schlax, Donald R. ... Melrose Park, IL
Schlax, Gregory J. ... Jacksonville, FL
Schlax, James A. ... Mandan, ND
Schlax, Michael G. ... Las Vegas, NV
Schlax, Peter M. ... Waukegan, IL
Schlax, Thomas P. ... Temecula, CA
Schlaybaugh, Rex E., Jr.
Bloomfield Hills, MI
Schleben, Mark E. ... Clearwater, FL
Schlech, Katherine A.
Department of Justice,
Antitrust Division, GV
Schlecht, James C. ... Fort Worth, TX
Schlecht, James M. ... Palm Springs, CA
Schlecht, Karl P. ... Los Angeles, CA
Schlecht, Shevlin & Shoenberger, A Law Corporation ... Palm Springs, CA
Schlecht, William R. ... San Antonio, TX
Schlechter, Alvin E. ... Niceville, FL
Schlechter, Amanda Parks
West Palm Beach, FL
Schlechter, Mark A. ... Bath, NY
Schleck, Mark T. ... Seattle, WA
Schleck, Mark T., P.S. ... Seattle, WA
Schlecker, Carolyn R. ... Wilmington, DE
Schlecker, David M. ... New York, NY
Schlecte, William M. ... Ann Arbor, MI
Jackson, MI
Southfield, MI
Schlecte, William M., & Associates, P.C.
Ann Arbor, MI
Jackson, MI
Southfield, MI
Schleder, John G. ... Chicago, IL
Schledwitz & Beaty ... Memphis, TN
Schledwitz, Karl A. ... Memphis, TN
Schlee, David R. ... Kansas City, MO
Schlee, Huber, McMullen & Krause, LLP
Kansas City, MO
Schlee, Teresa M. ... Department of Commerce,
Office of the Inspector General, GV
Schlee, William N. ... Kalamazoo, MI
Schleef, Joan E. ... Grand Rapids, MI
Schleer, Jorgen E. ... Redmond, WA
Schlefer, Mark P. ... Washington, DC
Schlegal, Julia Weston ... Eagan, MN
Schlegel, Beth J. ... New York, NY
Schlegel, Bruce F. ... Fayetteville, AR
Schlegel, Dick R. ... Ottumwa, IA
Schlegel, E. Bernard ... Philadelphia, PA
Schlegel, Frank G. ... Menlo Park, CA
Schlegel, Fred E. ... Indianapolis, IN
Schlegel & Jarman ... Salem, OR
Schlegel, Jeffrey A. ... Houston, TX
Schlegel, John H. ... Buffalo, NY
Schlegel, Leanne ... Martinez, CA
Schlegel, Matthew W. ... Southfield, MI
Schlegel, Maya Nicollier ... Houston, TX
Schlegel, Ralph H. ... Salem, OR
Schlegel, Raymond C. ... Reading, PA
Schlegel, Richard J. ... Los Angeles, CA
Schlegel, Richard P. ... Washington, DC
Schlegel, Richard R., II ... Ottumwa, IA
Schlegel, Richard S. ... Philadelphia, PA
Schlegel, Robert G. ... Washington, IA
Schlegel, Stephen J. ... Chicago, IL
New York, NY
Schlegel, Tamera D. ... Denver, CO
Schlegel, Walter H. ... Beltsville, MD
Schlegelmilch, John Paul ... Yerington, NV
Schleh, Robert C. ... Sacramento, CA
Schlehofer, Frank J. ... Anchorage, AK
Schlehuber, Clarence H. ... Carlsbad, CA
Schlehuber, Thomas E. ... Peoria, IL
Schlei, Mark ... Milwaukee, WI
Schleich, Gerald L. ... Lincoln, NE
Schleich, Michael L. ... Omaha, NE
Schleich, Thomas G. ... Lincoln, NE
Schleicher, Brian Leonard
Alpharetta, GA
Schleicher, Charles P. ... Kansas City, MO
Schleicher, David R. ... Waco, TX
Schleicher, Douglas F. ... Philadelphia, PA
Schleicher, Edward M. ... La Mesa, CA
Schleicher, Estelle A. ... Sacramento, CA
Schleicher, Henry E. ... Philadelphia, PA
Schleicher, Kevin R. ... Ingleside, TX
Schleicher, Kristofer R. ... Atlanta, GA
Schleicher, Leah A. ... Morristown, NJ
New York, NY
Schleicher, Lynn S. ... Morrisville, PA
Schleicher, Steven J. ... Kansas City, MO
Schleicher, Tara J. ... Portland, OR
Schleicher, William M. ... Park Ridge, NJ
Schleiden, Jeanine ... Harrisburg, PA
Schleider, Andrew R. ... New York, NY
Schleider & Associates ... Houston, TX
Schleider, Ben H., Jr. ... Houston, TX
Schleider, Edgar T. ... Brooklyn, NY
Schleider, Edwina C. ... Syracuse, NY

Schleier, Bradley H. ....Phoenix, AZ
Schleier & Brown, P.C. ....Kilgore, TX
Schleier, Jellison & Schleier, P.C.
Phoenix, AZ
Schleier, R. G. (Bob) ....Kilgore, TX
Schleier, R. G. (Rob), Jr. ....Kilgore, TX
Schleier, Thomas G. ....San Francisco, CA
Schleier, Tod F. ....Phoenix, AZ
Schleifer, Andrea M. ....Chicago, IL
Schleifer, Andrea M., & Associates, P.C.
Chicago, IL
Schleifer, Charles J. ....Philadelphia, PA
Schleifer, Ervin ....Hartsdale, NY
Schleifer, John H. ....Benton, WI
Schleifer, Nancy F. ....Miami, FL
Schleifer, Rebecca A. ....Belle Glade, FL
Schleifer, Richard W. ....Newark, NJ
Schleiff, Henry S. ....New York, NY
Schleifman, Jack ....Williston Park, NY
Schleifman, Paul S. ....Washington, DC
Schleifstein, Ellen Barbara ....Roseland, NJ
Schleifstein, Scott A. ....New York, NY
Schleifstein, Todd L. ....New York, NY
Schleig, Lisa Anne ....Philadelphia, PA
Schleimer, G. N. ....Cleveland, OH
Schleimer, Joseph D. ....Beverly Hills, CA
Schleimer, Karen B. ....New York, NY
Schleimer, Walter F. ....New York, NY
Schlein, Carol L. ....Montclair, NJ
Schlein, Daniel A. ....Newark, NJ
Schlein, Mark H. ....Tallahassee, FL
Schlein, Robert C. ....San Diego, CA
Schlein, Robert M. ....Boston, MA
Schlein, Stanley Kalmon ....New York, NY
Schlein, Steven ....Venice, CA
Schleinat, Lynn Warren ....Dallas, TX
Schleindl, Cynthia M. ....San Diego, CA
Schleiter, John R. ....Chicago, IL
Schlem, Stuart P. ....Manalapan, NJ
Schlemlein, Garth A. ....Seattle, WA
Schlemmer, Arthur H. ....Cincinnati, OH
Schlemmer, Carla K. ....Barrington, IL
Schlemmer, Dennis R. ....Chicago, IL
Schlemmer, Milton W., Law Office of
Bodega Bay, CA
Schlemmer, Robert C. ....Dayton, OH
Schlemmer, Robert N. ....Troy, OH
Schlemmer, Roy R., Jr.
Yorktown Heights, NY
Schlender, E. Lee, Chartered ....Hailey, ID
Schlender, Greg H. ....Boulder, CO
Schlender, James H. ....Hayward, WI
Schlender, Kevin V. ....York, NE
Schlender Law Firm, P.C. ....Boulder, CO
Schlener, Susan C. ....Woburn, MA
Schlenger, Jacques T., (P.C.)
Baltimore, MD
Schlenger, Kirsten ....San Francisco, CA
Schlenger, Robert P. ....Baltimore, MD
Schlenker, Dennis B. ....Albany, NY
Schlenker, Jeanette V. ....Houston, TX
Schlenker, Jonathan S. ....Birmingham, AL
Schlenker, Kendall O. ....Albuquerque, NM
Schlenker, Laura R. ....Dallas, TX
Schlenker, Mark F. ....Indianola, IA
Schlenker, Thomas M. ....Houston, TX
Houston, TX
Schlenker & Urrea L.L.P.
Albuquerque, NM
Schlenker, Wesley E. ....Richardson, TX
Schlenkert, Arthur W. ....Fort Lauderdale, FL
Schleppenbach, Gene ....Washington, DC
Schlepphorst, Kathryn Rose ....San Jose, CA
Schleppi, W. Joseph ....Columbus, OH
Schleppy, Marian Patchen ....Pittsburgh, PA
Schleppy-Tanner, Elizabeth M. ....Bristol, RI
Schler, Michael L. ....New York, NY
Schlereth, Ernest M. ....Anchorage, AK
Schlerf, Jeffrey M. ....Wilmington, DE
Schles, David ....Charleston, WV
Schlesinger, Aaron Charles
River Edge, NJ
Schlesinger, Adam ....New York, NY
Schlesinger, Alan J. ....Newton, MA
Schlesinger, Alan M. ....Basking Ridge, NJ
Schlesinger, Alan M. ....New York, NY
Schlesinger, Alan R. ....Shelton, CT
Schlesinger, Alexandra W. ....New York, NY
Schlesinger, Alvin ....New York, NY
Schlesinger, Anthony D. ....New York, NY
Schlesinger, Arnold ....Beverly Hills, CA
Schlesinger & Barbara, LLC ....Shelton, CT
Schlesinger, Benjamin
National Labor Relations Board,
Division of Administrative Law Judges, GV
Schlesinger, Beverly ....New York, NY
Schlesinger and Buchbinder, LLP
Newton, MA
Schlesinger, Claude A. ....New Orleans, LA
Schlesinger, Clifford D. ....Philadelphia, PA
Schlesinger, David A. ....New York, NY
Schlesinger, Diane L. ....Los Angeles, CA
Schlesinger, Don Kenneth ....Las Vegas, NV
Schlesinger, Edward S. ....New York, NY
Schlesinger, Edward S., P.C., Law Offices of
New York, NY
Schlesinger, Edwin O. ....Metairie, LA
Schlesinger, Fred H. ....Cedar Knolls, NJ
Schlesinger, Gary L. ....Libertyville, IL
Schlesinger, Gary L. ....Waukegan, IL
Schlesinger, George S. ....Fayetteville, NY
Schlesinger, Glenn N. ....New York, NY
Schlesinger, Guy W. ....Mount Carmel, PA
Shamokin, PA
Schlesinger, Harvey E. ....Jacksonville, FL
Schlesinger, Howard G. ....Edison, NJ
Schlesinger, James A. ....Farmington, MI
Schlesinger, Jan M. ....Mount Holly, NJ
Schlesinger, Jarrod S. ....White Plains, NY
Schlesinger, Jeffrey ....Crown Point, IN
Schlesinger, Joanna ....Philadelphia, PA
Schlesinger, John C. ....Miami, FL
Schlesinger, Kenneth ....New York, NY
Schlesinger, Kenneth S. ....Rosemont, IL
Schlesinger, Leonard ....Boston, MA
Schlesinger, Leslye M. ....New City, NY
Schlesinger, Lewis ....North Hollywood, CA
Schlesinger, M. Jean ....Washington, DC
Schlesinger, Marie M. ....New Orleans, LA
Schlesinger, Mark I. ....New York, NY
Schlesinger, Matthew J. ....Washington, DC
Schlesinger, Merideth ....New York, NY
Schlesinger, Michael ....New York, NY
Schlesinger, Michael A. ....Washington, DC
Schlesinger, Michael D. ....Chicago, IL
Schlesinger, Michael J. ....Miami, FL
Schlesinger, Michael N. ....Washington, DC
Schlesinger, Michael S. ....Miami, FL
Schlesinger, Michael S. ....New York, NY
Schlesinger, Milton A. ....Hattiesburg, MS
Schlesinger, Norman E. ....Newark, NJ
Schlesinger, P. Jeffrey ....Crown Point, IN
Schlesinger, Patrick ....Oakland, CA
Schlesinger, Patrick J. ....Chula Vista, CA
Schlesinger, Philip S. ....New York, NY
Schlesinger, Richard C. ....Burbank, CA
Schlesinger, Robert A. ....Palm Springs, CA
Schlesinger, Robert A., A Law Corporation
Palm Springs, CA
Schlesinger, Robert N. ....St. Paul, MN
Schlesinger, Robert N., P.A. ....St. Paul, MN
Schlesinger, Samuel ....Chicago, IL
Schlesinger, Sanford J. ....New York, NY
Schlesinger, Scott P. ....Fort Lauderdale, FL
Schlesinger, Sharon J. ....Boston, MA
Schlesinger, Shawn W. ....Cleveland, OH
Schlesinger, Sheldon J.
Fort Lauderdale, FL
Schlesinger, Sheldon J., P.A.
Fort Lauderdale, FL
Schlesinger, Stanley ....New York, NY
Schlesinger, Steven H.
Department of Justice,
Criminal Division, GV
Schlesinger, Steven R. ....Garden City, NY
Schlesinger, Stuart A. ....New York, NY
Schlesinger & Sussman ....Clifton, NJ
New York, NY
Schlesinger, Thomas J. ....Wellesley, MA
Schlesinger, Thomas R. (Tim)
St. Louis, MO
Schlesinger, Victoria A. ....Washington, DC
Schless, Adam L. ....Washington, DC
Schless, Eric H. ....Philadelphia, PA
Schless, Michael ....Newington, CT
Schless, Michael J. ....Austin, TX
Schlessel, Peter H. ....Burbank, CA
Schlesser, Melvyn ....Miami Beach, FL
Schlessinger, Albert ....Philadelphia, PA
Schlessinger, Daniel I. ....Chicago, IL
Schlessinger, Michael R. ....Chicago, IL
Schletker, Steven C. ....Covington, KY
Schletter, Delia N. ....San Francisco, CA
Schleunes, Anna F. ....Charlotte, NC
Schleuning, Elizabeth A. ....Portland, OR
Schleupner, Michael N., Jr. ....Baltimore, MD
Schleusner, Clifford E. ....Billings, MT
Schleuss, Christine S. ....Anchorage, AK
Schleuter, Johanna A. ....Los Alamitos, CA
Schley, Christian ....Houston, TX
Schley, Joseph H., Jr. ....Laguna Park, TX
Schley & Look, LLP ....Santa Barbara, CA
Schley, Michael D. ....Santa Barbara, CA
Schley, Michael W. ....Minneapolis, MN
Schley, Mitchell A. ....Los Angeles, CA
Schley, Scott H. ....Jersey City, NJ
Schley, William W. ....Denver, CO
Schleyer, Glen T. ....New York, NY
Schlezinger, Eric C. ....Palo Alto, CA
Schlich, Shaun R. ....Sea Bright, NJ
Schlicher, John W. ....Palo Alto, CA
Schlicher, Mary A. ....Waterloo, IA
Schlicher, Sarah J. ....Kansas City, MO
Schlicht, Gregory S. ....Kansas City, MO
Schlicht, Jane C. ....Milwaukee, WI
Schlichte & Johnstone, P.C. ....Gloucester, MA
Schlichte, Miles J. ....Gloucester, MA
Schlichte, Ray A., Jr. ....Hollywood, FL
Schlichter, Bogard & Denton ....Swansea, IL
St. Louis, MO
Schlichter, Eric ....Houston, TX
Schlichter, Jerome J. ....Swansea, IL
St. Louis, MO
Schlichter, Kurt A. ....Manhattan Beach, CA
Schlichting, Daniel J. ....Madison, WI
Schlichting, James D.
Federal Communications Commission,
Wireless Telecommunications Bureau, GV
Schlichting, James J. ....Albert Lea, MN
Schlichting, John K. ....San Diego, CA
Schlichting, Julia A. ....Roseland, NJ
Schlichting, Melissa A. ....Billings, MT
Schlichting, William H. ....St. Paul, MN
Schlichtmann, Jan R., (Mr.) ....Andover, MA
Schlichtmann, Jill ....San Francisco, CA
Schlick, Austin C. ....Washington, DC
Philadelphia, PA
Schlick, Fred ....Vashon, WA
Schlick, Robert M. ....North Olmsted, OH
Schlick, Susan L. ....Kenosha, WI
Schlicker, Wilfred E. ....Bellevue, WA
Schlickman, Eugene F.
Arlington Heights, IL
Schlickman, J. Andrew ....Chicago, IL
Schlickman, Stephen E. ....Chicago, IL
Schlicksup, Harold A. ....Peoria, IL
Schlidt, Andrew J., III ....Milwaukee, WI
Schlie, John Henry ....Denver, CO
Schlie, John Henry, P.C. ....Denver, CO
Schliebner, Joan R. ....Fayetteville, AR
Schliebs, Charles A. ....Pittsburgh, PA
Schliem, Richard H., III
Farmington Hills, MI
Schlieman, Albert H. ....Grand Prairie, TX
Schliemann, Walter C. ....Santa Fe, NM
Schlienger, Kent L. ....Madison, WI
Schlier, Carl E. ....Arlington, VA
Schlies, Christopher P. ....Pleasanton, CA
Schliesmann, John L. ....Milwaukee, WI
Schliesser, Peter C. O. ....New York, NY
Schliessmann, Donald J., Jr. ....Norcross, GA
Schlifka, Michael J. ....Roswell, GA
Schlifke, Bernard A. ....Chicago, IL
Schlifke, James S. ....Chicago, IL
Schlifke, Robert A. ....South Bend, IN
Schlifkin, Lewis W. ....Chicago, IL
Schlifkin, Robert S. ....Los Angeles, CA
Schlim, Albert William ....Newport News, VA
Schlimbach, William ....Edison, NJ
New York, NY
Schlimgen, John A. ....Sioux Falls, SD
Schlindra, Marie A. ....Walnut Creek, CA
Schlindwein, Eileen K. ....Trenton, NJ
Schlindwein, Paul C., II ....Wausau, WI
Schlinger, Alexander P. ....Kew Gardens, NY
Schlinger, Robin E. ....Walnut Creek, CA
Schlink, Theodore A., III ....San Francisco, CA
Schlinke, Bennett ....Edmond, OK
Schlinker, John C. ....Lansing, MI
Schlinkert, William J. ....San Francisco, CA
Schlinsog, Allen C., Jr. ....Milwaukee, WI
Schlintz, Gerald H. ....Pinole, CA
Schlissel, Burton L. ....Treasury Department,
Office of Regulations and Rulings, GV
Schlissel, Elliot S. ....Lynbrook, NY
Schlissel, Lois Carter ....Mineola, NY
Schlissel, Philip G. ....Fort Lauderdale, FL
Schlissel, Scott J. ....Danvers, MA
Schlissel, Stephen W. ....Mineola, NY
Schlitt, Albert J. ....North Manchester, IN
Schlitt, Irving ....Hartsdale, NY
Schlitt, Jeffrey D. ....Houston, TX
Schlitt, Kenneth L. ....Orlando, FL
Schlitt, Lyn M.
United States International Trade
Commission,
Office of the General Counsel, GV
Schlitter, Stanley A. ....Chicago, IL
Schlittner, Lisa G. ....Oakland, CA
Schlitz, David M. ....Alexandria, VA
Schlitz, Paul R., Jr. ....Baltimore, MD
Hagerstown, MD
Schlitz, Steven V. ....Eau Claire, WI
Schloat, Janet K. ....White Plains, NY
Schlobohm, Dean A. ....San Francisco, CA
Schlobohm, Michael B. ....Richardson, TX
Schloegel, Jennifer Thompson ....Atlanta, GA
Schloemer, Alderson, Spella & Muehlbauer,
S.C. ....West Bend, WI
Schloemer, Douglas B. ....Newport, KY
Schloemer, Jeffrey S. ....Cincinnati, OH
Schloendorn, Daniel ....New York, NY
Schloerb, John M. ....Chicago, IL
Schloerb, Robert G. ....Chicago, IL
Schloesser, Warren H. ....Honesdale, PA
Schloff, Kay D. ....Detroit, MI
Schloff, Michael D. ....Bloomfield Hills, MI
Schlom, Barry R. ....Beverly Hills, CA
Schlom, John S. ....Waupun, WI
Schlomann, Christine L. ....Kansas City, MO
Schlomann • McClelland, P.C.
Kansas City, MO
Schlomy, Keren ....Boston, MA
Schloneger, Mark R. ....Cincinnati, OH
Schlonsky, Michael A. ....Columbus, OH
Schlorf, Daniel K. ....Chicago, IL
Schlorff, Robert W., II ....Fort Lauderdale, FL
Schlorff, Russell E. ....Houston, TX
Schlosberg, David I. ....Miami, FL
Schlosberg, Herbert B. ....Sherman Oaks, CA
Schlosberg, Hubert M. ....Washington, DC
Schlosberg, Joey ....Miami, FL
Schlosberg, Michael G. ....Marietta, GA
Schlosberg, Myra J. ....Atlanta, GA
Schlosberg, Phillip ....North Hollywood, CA
Schlosberg, Phillip, A Professional
Corporation ....North Hollywood, CA
Schloss, Barbara A. ....New York, NY
Schloss, Bruce M. ....New York, NY
Schloss, Craig A. ....San Diego, CA
Schloss, Daniel I. ....New York, NY
Schloss, David M. ....Washington, DC
Schloss, David M. ....Philadelphia, PA
Schloss, Eric Neal ....Baltimore, MD
Schloss, Eugene M., Jr. ....Huntingdon, PA
Schloss, Howard H. ....Rockville, MD
Schloss, Irving S. ....Madison, CT
New Haven, CT
Schloss, Jack ....Pearl River, NY
Schloss, Jamie R. ....Los Angeles, CA
Schloss, Lawrence J. ....Mount Clemens, MI
Schloss, Leonora M. ....Los Angeles, CA
Schloss, Marnie L. ....Chicago, IL
Schloss, Martin E. ....New York, NY
Schloss, Michael A. ....Department of Labor,
Office of the Solicitor, GV
Schloss, Michael P. ....Phoenix, AZ
Schloss, Milton J. ....Cincinnati, OH
Schloss, Peter M. ....Liberty, MO
Schloss, Richard H. ....Bingham Farms, MI
Schloss, Stuart A., Jr. ....Cincinnati, OH
Schloss, Timothy T. ....Strawberry Point, IA
Schloss, William K. ....Northbrook, IL
Schlossberg, Albert ....Oakhurst, NJ
Schlossberg & Associates, P.A.
Greenbelt, MD
Hagerstown, MD
Schlossberg & Associates, P.C.
Bryn Mawr, PA
Schlossberg, Brett A. ....Bryn Mawr, PA
Schlossberg, David ....Chicago, IL
Schlossberg, David L. ....Roseland, NJ
Schlossberg, Ellen G., (P.C.) ....Atlanta, GA
Schlossberg, George R. ....Washington, DC
Schlossberg, Goodwin ....Greenbelt, MD
Schlossberg, Jack ....New York, NY
Schlossberg, Jason Blacher ....Seal Beach, CA
Schlossberg, Jeffrey M. ....Mineola, NY
Schlossberg, Joel ....Westport, CT
Schlossberg, Jules ....New York, NY
Schlossberg, Laurie A.
Winston-Salem, NC
Schlossberg, Mark A. ....Hartford, CT
Schlossberg, Michael J. ....Morristown, NJ
Schlossberg, Morton J. ....Great Neck, NY
Schlossberg, Robert L. ....Chicago, IL
Schlossberg, Robert S. ....Washington, DC
Schlossberg, Roger ....Greenbelt, MD
Hagerstown, MD
Schlossberg, Ruth Alderman ....Chicago, IL
Schlossberg & Siegel ....New York, NY
Schlossberg, Stephen I. ....Washington, DC
Schlossberg, Todd D. ....Burlington, VT
Schlossberg, Todd D., P.C.
Burlington, VT
Schlosser, Amy S., (P.A.) ....Boca Raton, FL
Schlosser, Andrew J. ....Austin, TX
Schlosser, Bernard A. ....Bloomingdale, IL
Schlosser, Bernard A., P.C.
Bloomingdale, IL
Schlosser, Bryon R. ....Topeka, KS
Schlosser, C. William, Jr. ....Denver, CO
Schlosser, Caroline G.
Department Of Veterans Affairs,
Board of Veterans Appeals, GV
Schlosser, Chalmer R. ....Indianapolis, IN
Schlosser, Elliot M. ....Hampton, VA
Schlosser, E. S., Jr. ....Greensboro, NC
Schlosser, F. Joseph ....Milwaukee, WI
Schlosser, Frederick J. ....Springfield, IL
Schlosser, Herbert S. ....New York, NY
Schlosser, J. Philip ....Reseda, CA
Schlosser, Jacob A. ....Columbus, OH
Schlosser, James D. ....Bismarck, ND
Schlosser, Jay W. ....Minneapolis, MN
Schlosser, John A. ....Bakersfield, CA
Schlosser, John D. ....Plymouth, IN
Schlosser, John H. ....Milwaukee, WI
Schlosser, John M. ....Phoenix, AZ
Schlosser, Joseph T. ....Kirkland, WA
Schlosser, Karin A. ....New York, NY
Schlosser, Kevin ....Mineola, NY
Schlosser, Lisa M. ....Erie, PA
Schlosser, Marvin E. ....Mount Holly, NJ
Schlosser, Michael A. ....Greensboro, NC
Schlosser & Neill ....Greensboro, NC
Schlosser, Paula M. P. ....Brockton, MA
Schlosser, R. Jeffrey ....Covington, KY
Schlosser, Richard A. ....Tampa, FL
Schlosser, Robert H. ....Phoenix, AZ
Schlosser, Robert H. ....New York, NY
Staten Island, NY
Schlosser, Ronald A. ....Phoenix, AZ
Schlosser & Schlosser ....Indianapolis, IN
Schlosser, Thomas P. ....Seattle, WA
Schlosser, Wayne W. ....Hudson, WI
Schlosser, William L. ....Indianapolis, IN
Schlossman, Robert S. ....Menlo Park, CA
Schlossman, William A., Jr. ....Fargo, ND
Schlosstein, Gary B. ....Alma, WI
Schlosstein, Jennifer B. ....Bellevue, WA
Schlosstein, John P. ....Warren, MA
Schlosstein, Mark F. ....Warren, MA
Schlosstein, Tobie Lozman ....Warren, MA
Schlotfeldt, Albert F. ....Vancouver, WA
Schloth, Gerard E. ....Jacksonville, FL
Schlothauer & Collins ....Los Angeles, CA
Schlothauer, Thomas L. ....Los Angeles, CA
Schlotman, Edward A. ....Los Angeles, CA
Schlotman, James T. ....Cincinnati, OH
Schlott, Mary C. ....Arlington Heights, IL
Schlott, Mary C., P.C. ....Arlington Heights, IL
Schlotter, Charles J. ....Los Angeles, CA
Schlotter, John D. ....Atlanta, GA
Schlotterbeck, John D. ....Los Angeles, CA
Schlotterbeck, Walter A. ....Bellevue, WA
Schlotterer, Amy ....Detroit, MI
Schlotterer, Bradley J. ....New Orleans, LA
Schlotthauer, Karen A. ....Minneapolis, MN
Schlotthauer, William G.
New Orleans, LA
Schlottman, Eldridge E. ....Santa Barbara, CA
Schlottman, Judi M. ....Mount Clemens, MI
Schlottman, Richard E. ....Los Angeles, CA
Schlottman & Wagner, P.C.
Mount Clemens, MI
Schlotz, Donald E. ....San Francisco, CA
Schlotzhauer, Thomas F. ....Houston, TX
Schlotzhauer, Thomas F., P.C. ....Houston, TX
Schlow, Marian Wossum, (P.A.)
Orlando, FL
Schlozman, Bradley J. ....Washington, DC
Kansas City, KS
Schluchter, Shari R. ....Bemidji, MN
Schluckebier, David P. ....San Francisco, CA
Schluckebier, Regina M. ....Philadelphia, PA
Schlue, Larry D. ....Belle Plaine, IA
Keystone, IA
Schluederberg, Peter Q. ....La Jolla, CA
Schluender, Kevin David ....Minneapolis, MN
Schluentz, Thomas G. ....Farmington Hills, MI
Schluesche, Todd W. ....Monroe, WI

Schlueter, Albert M. .... **St. Louis, MO**
Schlueter & Associates, P.C. .... **Denver, CO**
Schlueter, C. Grant .... **New Orleans, LA**
Schlueter, Charles D. .... Rockford, IL
Schlueter, Daniel H. .... **Atlanta, GA**
Schlueter, Daniel J. .... Cincinnati, OH
Schlueter, David A. .... San Antonio, TX
Schlueter, David R. .... Elk Grove Village, IL
Schlueter, Ecklund, Olson, Barrett & Mayfield
Rockford, IL
Schlueter, Haywood, Bick & Kistner, P.C.
St. Louis, MO
Schlueter, Henry F. .... **Denver, CO**
Schlueter, James W. .... West Union, OH
Schlueter, Jill Marie .... St. Louis, MO
Schlueter, John J. .... St. Louis, MO
Schlueter, Jon R. .... Grand Terrace, CA
Schlueter, Linda L. .... San Antonio, TX
Schlueter, Mahoney & Ross, P.C.
Denver, CO
Schlueter Mandel & Mandel .... St. Louis, MO
Schlueter, Melvin L. .... Rockford, IL
Schlueter, Michael A. .... **Denver, CO**
Schlueter, Peter B. .... San Bernardino, CA
Schlueter, Richard R. .... Conyers, GA
Schlueter, Susan J. .... **Sacramento, CA**
Schlumberger, Charles L. .... **Little Rock, AR**
Schlumberger, Pierre M., (A Prof. Corp.)
New Braunfels, TX
Schlunk, Herwig J. .... Wichita, KS
Schlur, Anthony J. .... **New York, NY**
Schlussel, Bruce M. .... Detroit, MI
Schlussel, Ira W. .... Livonia, MI
Schlussel, Mark E. .... **Detroit, MI**
Schlussel, Mark W. .... **New York, NY**
Schlussel, Steven M. .... **Great Neck, NY**
Schlusser & Reiver, P.A. .... **Wilmington, DE**
Schlusser, Robert E. .... **Wilmington, DE**
Schlussler, Jennifer Ross .... **Miami, FL**
Schluter, Dawn M. .... **Troy, MI**
Schluter, Kathleen Hyland
Milwaukee, WI
Schluter, Leslie L. .... **Denver, CO**
Schluter, Richard F. .... **Williamsport, PA**
Schlutow, Melissa A. .... **Fort Lauderdale, FL**
Schlyen, Gary .... Paterson, NJ
Schlyen, Jenifer L. .... New York, NY
Schlyer & Associates, P.C. .... Schererville, IN
Schlyer, Donald E. .... Schererville, IN
Schma, William G. .... Kalamazoo, MI
Schmachtenberg & Associates .... **Miami, FL**
Schmachtenberg, Lee C. .... **Miami, FL**
Schmad, Wayne A. .... Shingletown, CA
Schmadeka, Larry R. .... **Los Angeles, CA**
Schmadeke, Charles R. .... Springfield, IL
Schmaeling, Dan E. .... Montgomery, AL
Schmaeling, Daniel T. .... Redlands, CA
Santa Ana, CA
Schmahl, Michael C .... Lewiston, NY
Schmähl, Robin A. .... **Atlanta, GA**
Schmahmann, David R. .... **Boston, MA**
Schmal, Richard R. .... Phoenix, AZ
Schmal, Timothy J. .... **Santa Cruz, CA**
Schmalbeck, Richard L. .... Durham, NC
Schmalberger, Donna J. .... Denver, CO
Schmalenberger, Allan L. .... Dickinson, ND
Schmaler, Eric J. .... New York, NY
Schmall, Deborah J. .... **San Francisco, CA**
Schmall, Joseph E. .... **Cedar Rapids, IA**
Schmall, Lorraine A. .... De Kalb, IL
Schmall, Steven Todd .... Chicago, IL
Schmalle, Robert C. .... **Fresno, CA**
Schmaltz, Christopher A. .... **Phoenix, AZ**
Schmaltz, David .... **Minneapolis, MN**
Schmalz, Arthur E. .... **McLean, VA**
Schmalz, Eric .... Palatine, IL
Schmalz, Karl B. .... **Irving, TX**
Schmalz, Kurt L. .... **Beverly Hills, CA**
Schmalz, Peter N. .... **Rutland, VT**
Schmalz, Richard L. .... New York, NY
Schmalz, Robert L. .... **San Francisco, CA**
Schmalz, Robert N. .... **New Haven, CT**
Schmalz, Terry C. .... **Yakima, WA**
Schmalzbach, Kenneth R.
Treasury Department,
Office of the General Counsel, GV
Schmalzer, Robert L. .... Highlands Ranch, CO
Schmalzl, Mary W. .... Cincinnati, OH
Schmalzl, Richard G. .... **Cincinnati, OH**
Schmalzl, William A. .... **Chicago, IL**
Schmandt, Alexander G.
Environmental Protection Agency,
Office of the General Counsel, GV
Schmandt, Phillip H. .... **Austin, TX**
Schmarak, Barry J. .... Broadview, IL
Schmarak, Barry J., P.C. .... Broadview, IL
Schmarak, Bradley S. .... **Chicago, IL**
Schmarkey, John C. .... Birmingham, AL
Schmauder, Arthur R. .... **Florham Park, NJ**
Schmauder, Craig R.
Department of the Army,
Office, Chief of Engineers/Headquarters,
U.S. Army Corps of Engineers, GV
Schmauss, Karen R. Ferrera
Rancho Cucamonga, CA
Schmechel, David J. .... Milwaukee, WI
Schmechel, Marjorie A. .... Eugene, OR
Schmeck, Paula A. .... Pittsburgh, PA
Schmeckpeper, James E. .... Minneapolis, MN
Schmeckpeper, Jeff .... **Milwaukee, WI**
Schmedemann, Deborah A. .... St. Paul, MN
Schmedes, Susan M. .... Washington, DC
Schmeding, Paul D. .... Honolulu, HI
Schmedlen, Daniel G., Jr. .... **Charlotte, NC**
Schmedlen, George W. .... **Cleveland, OH**
Schmedlen, Michael J. .... Lansing, MI
Schmedt, Kelly Jo .... **Tampa, FL**
Schmeelcke, Kristen E. .... **Washington, DC**

Schmeelk, John B. .... Atlanta, GA
Schmeer, Michael H. .... **Portland, OR**
Schmehl, James W. .... Fort Collins, CO
Schmehl, John W. .... **Philadelphia, PA**
Schmehl, Peter W. .... Reading, PA
Schmehr, Frank L. .... Santa Ana, CA
Schmeichel, Kenneth R. .... **Cleveland, OH**
Schmeiderman, Maria S. .... Chicago, IL
Schmeidler, Mark F. .... Quinter, KS
Schmeidler, Richard L. .... Brooklyn, NY
Schmeiser, A. Russell .... Iowa City, IA
Schmeiser, Albert L. .... **Mesa, AZ**
Latham, NY
Schmeiser, Larry W. .... Limon, CO
Schmeiser, Olsen & Watts .... **Mesa, AZ**
Phoenix, AZ
Overland Park, KS
Latham, NY
Schmeisser, Christopher W. .... Hartford, CT
Schmeisser, William C., Jr. .... Potomac, MD
Schmeits, Alan J. .... Baker City, OR
Schmeling, Todd J. .... **Green Bay, WI**
Schmelkin, Martin L. .... **New York, NY**
Schmell, Herbert L., (P.C.) .... New York, NY
Schmelling, William H. .... Chicago, IL
Schmelter, Gerry C. .... **San Diego, CA**
Schmelter, Jay T. .... Denver, CO
Schmelter, Joseph C. .... **Baltimore, MD**
McLean, VA
Schmelter, Lee J. .... Sacramento, CA
Schmeltz, Andrew H., Jr.
Broken Arrow, OK
Schmeltz, Vincent P., III
Overland Park, KS
Schmeltzer, Aptaker & Shepard, P.C.
Los Angeles, CA
Washington, DC
Schmeltzer, David .... **Washington, DC**
Schmeltzer, Edward .... **Washington, DC**
Schmeltzer, Howard M.
Department of Housing and Urban
Development,
Office of General Counsel, GV
Schmeltzer, John Emile, III
New York, NY
Schmeltzer, Kathryn R. .... **Washington, DC**
Schmeltzer, Kurt M. .... Los Angeles, CA
Schmeltzer, Norman B. .... Irvine, CA
Schmelz, Ronie M. .... Los Angeles, CA
Schmelz, Stephanie T. .... **Washington, DC**
Schmelzer, Anne E. .... Brooklyn, NY
Schmelzer & Associates .... Cleveland, OH
Schmelzer, Charles J., III
Kansas City, MO
Schmelzer, D. Edwin .... **Washington, DC**
Schmelzer, F. Robert .... **Flint, MI**
Schmelzer, Gerald R. .... Indian Wells, CA
Schmelzer, Henry L. P. .... Boston, MA
Schmelzer, John D.
Equal Employment Opportunity
Commission,
Office of Federal Operations, GV
Schmelzer Law Firm, The, L.C.
Kansas City, MO
Schmelzer, Michael J. .... **Boston, MA**
Schmelzer, Nathaniel L. .... San Francisco, CA
Schmelzer, Pamela J. .... **Madison, WI**
Schmelzer, Rachel D. .... **Cleveland, OH**
Schmelzer, Thomas .... Cleveland, OH
Schmelzer, Troy M. .... **La Jolla, CA**
Schmelzle and Kroeger .... **Freeport, IL**
Stockton, IL
Schmelzle, Robert J. .... **Freeport, IL**
Schmelzle, Stephen S. .... **Freeport, IL**
Stockton, IL
Schmelzle, Theodore J. .... St. Paul, MN
Schmenk, Christiane W. .... Marysville, OH
Schmenk, Gerald E. .... Springfield, OH
Schmenk, Joseph N. .... Defiance, OH
Schmenk, Spencer & Hasselbach
Springfield, OH
Schmer, David R. .... Overland Park, KS
Schmerber, Donald E. .... Cincinnati, OH
Schmerberg, Fred R. .... Saline, MI
Schmerer-Haacke, Susan A. .... Roseburg, OR
Schmerfeld, Gail L. .... Rockville, MD
Schmerge, Peter J. .... **White Plains, NY**
Schmergel, George .... **Rochester, NY**
Schmerin, H. David .... Los Angeles, CA
Schmerin, Howard .... Houston, TX
Schmerin, Stephen M. .... Pittsburgh, PA
Schmerl, Peter G. .... **Green Valley, AZ**
Schmerler, Charles D. .... **New York, NY**
Schmerler, David .... New York, NY
Schmerler, Marci P. .... **Atlanta, GA**
Schmerler, Willie .... Austin, TX
Schmerling, Jonathan M. .... **Pittsburgh, PA**
Schmerling, Michael A. .... **Morristown, NJ**
Schmertz, David M. .... Salt Lake City, UT
Schmertz, Eric J. .... New York, NY
Schmertz, Herman .... **New York, NY**
Schmertz, Howard M. .... **New York, NY**
Schmertz, John R., Jr. .... Washington, DC
Schmerzler, Andrew J. .... **Beverly Hills, CA**
Schmesser, Tobin J. .... Glassboro, NJ
Schmett, Kim D. .... Des Moines, IA
Schmetterer, Jack B. .... Chicago, IL
Schmetterer, Kenneth L. .... **Chicago, IL**
Schmick Law Offices, P.C. .... **Ann Arbor, MI**
Schmick, Raynold A. .... **Ann Arbor, MI**
Schmicker, Robert D. .... **New York, NY**
Schmickle, Jason .... **Rochester, MN**
Schmid, Alexander L. .... **Danville, CA**
Schmid, Allan C. .... Saginaw, MI
Schmid, Andrew J. .... Minneapolis, MN
Schmid, Arthur E. S. .... St. Louis, MO
Schmid, Brandon Scott C. .... **Seattle, WA**
Schmid, Caitlin .... **Palo Alto, CA**

Schmid, Colleen M. .... Blaine, MN
Schmid, Connor F. .... Minneapolis, MN
Schmid, David J. .... Anchorage, AK
Schmid, Donald E., Jr. .... Sleepy Eye, MN
Schmid, Donald P. .... Phoenix, AZ
Schmid, Frear Stephen .... San Francisco, CA
Schmid, Gayanne K. .... Salt Lake City, UT
Schmid, Gregory C. .... Saginaw, MI
Schmid, Harry L., Jr. .... Sacramento, CA
Schmid, Jack T., Jr. .... New Orleans, LA
Schmid, John H., Jr. .... **Madison, WI**
Schmid, John L. .... Houston, TX
Schmid, John S. .... **Washington, DC**
Schmid, John U., Jr. .... **Milwaukee, WI**
Schmid, Jones & Meadows, PLLC
Knoxville, TN
Schmid, Kathryn M. .... Saginaw, MI
Schmid, Kevin J. .... Fort Worth, TX
Schmid, Kim M. .... **Minneapolis, MN**
Schmid, Laurel J. .... Millersburg, OH
Schmid Law Office, P.L.L.C. .... Saginaw, MI
Schmid, Lloyd A., Jr. .... Dover, DE
Schmid, Mark R. .... **Kansas City, MO**
Schmid, Marvin G. .... Omaha, NE
Schmid, Mary F. .... **Indianapolis, IN**
Schmid, Michael D. .... Atlanta, GA
Schmid, Minor J. .... Berkeley, CA
Schmid, Otto, Jr. .... San Jose, CA
Schmid, Patricia E. .... **Salt Lake City, UT**
Schmid, R. Culver .... **Knoxville, TN**
Schmid, Robert A. .... **Palo Alto, CA**
Schmid, Robert L. .... Salt Lake City, UT
Schmid & Roswold, P.C.
Overland Park, KS
Kansas City, MO
Schmid, Stephen H. .... Redwood City, CA
Schmid, Steven Lawrence .... Jacksonville, FL
Schmid, Susan H. .... Los Angeles, CA
Schmid, Timothy J. .... Shawano, WI
Schmid & Voiles .... Los Angeles, CA
Orange, CA
Schmid, William J. .... Cincinnati, OH
Schmid, William T. .... Elm Grove, WI
Schmid, Wm. Randall .... Fullerton, CA
Schmider, Ernest L. .... Newport Beach, CA
Schmid-Frazee, Carol .... **Rosemead, CA**
Schmidhauser, Paul A. .... Irvine, CA
Schmidley, Eugenia M. .... **Cleveland, OH**
Schmidli, James D. .... Deepwater, MO
Schmidlin, Alan T. .... Howard Beach, NY
Schmidlin, Randall R. .... Flint, MI
Schmidlin, Raymond J.
Mayfield Heights, OH
Schmidlin, Raymond J., Jr. .... Cleveland, OH
Schmidlin, Robert .... Albany, NY
Schmidly, Stephen S., (P.A.) .... Asheboro, NC
Schmidt, A. J. D. .... Rockville, MD
Schmidt, Alan W. .... Chicago, IL
Schmidt, Alexander H. .... New York, NY
Schmidt, Alexander T. .... Staten Island, NY
Schmidt, Alfred .... New York, NY
Schmidt, Alice M. .... Madison, WI
Schmidt, Amy K. .... **Springfield, IL**
Schmidt, Andrew W. .... Wausau, WI
Schmidt, Angelle E. .... Baton Rouge, LA
Schmidt, Anne B. .... **St. Louis, MO**
Schmidt, Anthony J. .... Bay Shore, NY
Schmidt, Arthur D. .... Bayside, NY
Schmidt, Arthur W. .... **Oklahoma City, OK**
Schmidt, Barbara .... Bartlesville, OK
Schmidt, Barbara A.
Commodity Futures Trading Commission,
Division of Enforcement, GV
Schmidt, Barbara J. .... Green Brook, NJ
Schmidt, Barbara Jean .... Gary, IN
Schmidt, Benno C. .... New York, NY
Schmidt & Botter .... Northampton, MA
Schmidt, Bradford Paul .... **Menlo Park, CA**
Schmidt, Bradley J. .... **Willmar, MN**
Schmidt, Brian H. .... **Kansas City, MO**
Schmidt, Bruce C. .... **Winsted, CT**
Schmidt, Bruce K. .... Oshkosh, WI
Schmidt, Bruce R. .... Buffalo, NY
Schmidt, C. Gregory .... **Cincinnati, OH**
Schmidt, C. Gregory, Co., L.P.A.
Cincinnati, OH
Schmidt, C. Jeffers, Jr. .... Lancaster, VA
Schmidt, C. Thomas .... **Houston, TX**
Schmidt, Carl A. .... Newark, NY
Schmidt, Carol A. .... Modesto, CA
Schmidt, Carolyn .... Detroit, MI
Schmidt, Catherine Grevers
New York, NY
Schmidt, Catherine Paige .... **Baytown, TX**
Schmidt, Cecil C. .... **Minneapolis, MN**
Schmidt, Charles A. .... San Antonio, TX
Schmidt, Charles E. .... **Carbondale, IL**
Schmidt, Charles E. .... Newark, NJ
New York, NY
Schmidt, Charles E., Jr. .... **Harrisburg, PA**
Schmidt, Charles J. .... La Mesa, CA
Schmidt, Charles M. .... St. Louis, MO
Schmidt, Charles T. .... **Boston, MA**
Schmidt, Charles W., III
New Orleans, LA
Schmidt, Chris E. .... Houston, TX
Schmidt, Christopher J. .... **Temecula, CA**
Schmidt, C. J., III .... **Cincinnati, OH**
Schmidt, C. L. Mike .... **Dallas, TX**
Schmidt, Cletus J. .... Bismarck, ND
Schmidt, Cletus V. .... Santa Ana, CA
Schmidt, Dale G. .... Cincinnati, OH
Schmidt, Dale R. .... Alexandria, VA
Schmidt, Daniel E., IV .... New York, NY
Schmidt, Daniel L. .... **Peoria, IL**
Schmidt, Daniela .... **Deerfield, IL**
Schmidt, Darling & Erwin .... Wauwatosa, WI
Schmidt, David E. .... Chicago, IL

Schmidt, David F. .... Martinez, CA
Schmidt, David F. .... **Chicago, IL**
Schmidt, David G. .... **Cleveland, OH**
Schmidt, David H. .... **New York, NY**
Schmidt, David I. .... Brooklyn, NY
Schmidt, David R. .... **Chicago, IL**
Schmidt, David R. .... Dayton, OH
Kettering, OH
Schmidt, David W. .... **Delray Beach, FL**
Schmidt, David W. .... **Kenilworth, NJ**
Schmidt & Davis, P.C. .... San Antonio, TX
Schmidt, Dawn M. .... Massena, NY
Schmidt, Dean M. .... San Francisco, CA
Schmidt, Debra J. .... **Albany, NY**
Schmidt, Dennis R. .... Austin, TX
Schmidt, Derek L. .... United States Senate,
Senatorial Assistants, GV
Schmidt, Diana M. .... **St. Louis, MO**
Schmidt, Diana V. .... Roswell, GA
Schmidt, Don F. .... Louisville, KY
Schmidt, Don M. .... **Kalamazoo, MI**
Schmidt, Donal R., Jr. .... **Dallas, TX**
Schmidt, Donald R. .... **Tampa, FL**
Schmidt, Donald W. .... San Diego, CA
Schmidt, Donna M. .... **Wichita, KS**
Oklahoma City, OK
Schmidt, Douglas E. .... **Santa Barbara, CA**
Schmidt, Douglas E. .... Minneapolis, MN
Schmidt, Douglas E., & Associates, P.A.
Minneapolis, MN
Schmidt, Douglas J. .... **Kansas City, MO**
Schmidt, Douglas M. .... **New Orleans, LA**
Schmidt, Douglas M., A P.L.C.
New Orleans, LA
Schmidt, Douglas R. .... San Francisco, CA
Schmidt, Earl W. .... Shawano, WI
Schmidt, E. C., II .... Houston, TX
Schmidt, Edmund F. .... Hartford, CT
Schmidt, Edmund J., III .... **Harahan, LA**
Schmidt, Edmund J., III .... **Jefferson, LA**
Schmidt, Edmund J., Jr. .... New Orleans, LA
Schmidt, Edward C. .... **Pittsburgh, PA**
Schmidt, Edward R. .... **Indianapolis, IN**
Schmidt, Edwin M. .... San Antonio, TX
Schmidt, Elizabeth F. .... Alexandria, VA
Schmidt, Elizabeth L. .... **Blue Bell, PA**
Schmidt, Elizabeth M. .... Williamsburg, VA
Schmidt, Elizabeth R. .... Pittsburgh, PA
Schmidt, Ellen Ann .... Fort Smith, AR
Schmidt, Ellen W. .... Andover, MA
Schmidt, Eric J. .... Belvedere-Tiburon, CA
Schmidt, Eric M. .... New York, NY
Schmidt, Eric W. .... Albuquerque, NM
Schmidt, Erik A. .... **Fairfield, CT**
Schmidt, Ernest H. .... Naples, FL
Schmidt, Ernest W. .... Palo Alto, CA
Schmidt, Ethan W. .... **Pierre, SD**
Rapid City, SD
Schmidt, F. Evans .... **New Orleans, LA**
Schmidt Firm, The .... **Dallas, TX**
Fort Worth, TX
Schmidt & Fleming .... **Peoria, IL**
Schmidt, Frederick Clarence .... Killeen, TX
Schmidt, Frederick Daniel, Jr
New York, NY
Schmidt, Frederick E. .... **New York, NY**
Schmidt, Frederick H. .... Silver Spring, MD
Schmidt, Frederick L. .... **Green Bay, WI**
Schmidt, Frederick W., Jr.
Cape May Court House, NJ
Schmidt, G. Booker .... Tampa, FL
Schmidt, G. Booker, P.A. .... Tampa, FL
Schmidt, G. Charles .... Shelton, WA
Schmidt, Gary .... California, MO
Schmidt, Gary B. .... Montclair, NJ
Schmidt, Gary E. .... **East Peoria, IL**
Peoria, IL
Schmidt, Gary P. .... **Melrose Park, IL**
Schmidt, G. C., Jr. .... Fort Benton, MT
Schmidt, Geoffrey L. .... **Overland Park, KS**
Schmidt, George A. .... Boardman, OH
Schmidt, George W., II .... Hattiesburg, MS
Schmidt, Georgeann .... Jersey City, NJ
Schmidt, Gerald .... Billings, MT
Schmidt, Gerald G., Jr. .... Wauwatosa, WI
Schmidt, Gerald W. .... Fredericksburg, TX
Schmidt, Gilbert & Jungers .... Big Sandy, MT
Fort Benton, MT
Schmidt, Gloria D. .... Eugene, OR
Schmidt, Glorida D., P.C. .... Eugene, OR
Schmidt, Gordon W. .... **Pittsburgh, PA**
Schmidt, Grace & Duncan
Stevens Point, WI
Wisconsin Rapids, WI
Schmidt, Gregory A. .... **Springfield, MA**
Schmidt, Gregory E. .... **Grand Rapids, MI**
Schmidt, Gregory J. .... St. Paul, MN
Schmidt, Gregory J., P.A., Law Offices
St. Paul, MN
Schmidt, Gregory L. .... Glendale, AZ
Schmidt, Gregory M. .... Washington, DC
Schmidt, Gretchen E. .... Kansas City, MO
Schmidt, H. Joachim .... St. Paul, MN
Schmidt, H. Lee .... Oklahoma City, OK
Schmidt, Harlan A. .... Spearfish, SD
Schmidt, Harold .... Mason, TX
Schmidt, Harold L., (A Law Corp.)
Santa Ana, CA
Schmidt, Harold R. .... Mason, TX
Schmidt, Henry .... Redding, CA
Schmidt, Henry W. .... Lockport, NY
Schmidt, Hopkins & Sandman
Cape May Court House, NJ
Schmidt, Howard J. .... Sayreville, NJ
Schmidt, Howard L. .... Oklahoma City, OK
Schmidt Hubbell, L.L.P. .... Clovis, CA
Schmidt, Hugo C. .... Tyler, TX
Schmidt, Isgrigg & Anderson .... **Pontiac, MI**

Schmitt, Kenneth K. ....Belleville, IL
Schmitt, Kimberly A. ....Menlo Park, CA
Schmitt & Koppelman, S.C. ....Merrill, WI
Schmitt, L. Eugene ....Leeds, AL
Schmitt, Laura Denise-Marie
Sioux City, IA
Schmitt, Lois J. ....Norcross, GA
Schmitt, Louis C., Jr. ....Hollidaysburg, PA
Schmitt, Mark C. ....Phoenix, AZ
Schmitt, Mark S. ....Milwaukee, WI
Schmitt, Marshall John ....Chicago, IL
Schmitt, Marvin J. ....Apollo Beach, FL
Schmitt, Mary A. ....Kansas City, MO
Schmitt, Mary E. ....Everett, WA
Schmitt, Michael A. ....Los Angeles, CA
Schmitt, Michael D. ....Rochester, NY
Schmitt, Michael J. ....Paintsville, KY
Schmitt, Michael K. ....Hiawatha, KS
Schmitt, Nicholas L. ....Buffalo, NY
Schmitt, Paul C. ....North Palm Beach, FL
Schmitt, Peggy F. ....North Kansas City, MO
Schmitt, Phillip E., Jr. ....Birmingham, MI
Schmitt, Randall K. ....Honolulu, HI
Schmitt, Rebecca J. ....Omaha, NE
Schmitt, Rebecca K. ....San Diego, CA
Schmitt, Reed S. ....Evansville, IN
Schmitt, Robert E. ....Kingman, AZ
Prescott, AZ
Yuma, AZ
Schmitt, Robert F. ....Dayton, OH
Schmitt, Robert G. ....Goleta, CA
Schmitt, Robert J., Jr. ....Hackensack, NJ
Schmitt, Robert R. ....Roseville, CA
Schmitt, Roger R. ....St. Cloud, MN
Schmitt, Ross A. ....Redondo Beach, CA
Schmitt, Ruth Ann ....Chicago, IL
Schmitt, Schneck, Fisher Smyth & Herrod, P.L.C. ....Carefree, AZ
Phoenix, AZ
Schmitt, Steven F. ....Tallassee, AL
Schmitt, Susan M. ....New Brunswick, NJ
Schmitt, Suzanne B. ....New York, NY
Schmitt, Terry B. ....Lincoln, NE
Schmitt, Thomas O. ....Pittsburgh, PA
Schmitt, Thomas P. ....Boca Raton, FL
Schmitt, Thomas W. ....Marengo, IL
Schmitt, Timothy J. ....Denver, CO
Schmitt, Vernon N. ....Leeds, AL
Schmitt, W. Allen ....Boca Raton, FL
Schmitt, W. A. ....Utica, NY
Schmitt, Wendy J. ....Santa Ana, CA
Schmitt, Wilfred J. ....Arcadia, CA
Schmitt, William A. ....Belleville, IL
Schmitt, William P. ....Utica, NY
Schmitter, Charles H. ....New York, NY
Schmitter, Patrick C. ....New York, NY
Schmittgens, Eugene P., Jr. ......St. Louis, MO
Schmittinger, Harold ....Dover, DE
Rehoboth Beach, DE
Wilmington, DE
Schmittinger, John J. ....Dover, DE
Rehoboth Beach, DE
Wilmington, DE
Schmittinger & Rodriguez, Professional Association ....Dover, DE
Odessa, DE
Rehoboth Beach, DE
Wilmington, DE
Schmittinger, Walt F. ....Dover, DE
Schmitz, Adrienne V. ....Wellington, FL
Schmitz, Alan J. ....Denver, CO
Schmitz, Ann Marie S. ....Charlotte, NC
Schmitz, Anne ....Sacramento, CA
Schmitz, Anthony J. ....Chicago, IL
Schmitz & Associates, P.C. ....Denver, CO
Schmitz, Cathy Howe ....Williston, ND
Schmitz, Charles A. ....Department of State, Foreign Service Officers (Overseas), GV
Schmitz, Craig M. ....Menlo Park, CA
Schmitz, David F. ....Bloomington, MN
Schmitz, David F., P.A. ....Bloomington, MN
Schmitz, Dennis R. ....Torrance, CA
Schmitz, Dieter A. ....Chicago, IL
Schmitz, Don W. ....Bridgewater, NJ
Schmitz, Elizabeth S. ....Columbus, OH
Schmitz & Evans, LLC ....Houston, TX
Schmitz, Fidel ....Torrance, CA
Schmitz, Francis D. ....Milwaukee, WI
Schmitz, Frank B. ....Portland, OR
Schmitz, Guy A. ....St. Louis, MO
Schmitz, John P. ....Washington, DC
Schmitz, John W., (P.A.) ....Miami, FL
Schmitz, Joseph E. ....Washington, DC
Schmitz, Joseph P. ....Cleveland, OH
Schmitz, Karl M., III ....Tampa, FL
Schmitz, Karl M., III, P.A. ....Tampa, FL
Schmitz, Kopman, Schreiber & Kaveney, P.C. ....St. Louis, MO
Schmitz Law Office, P.C. ....Williston, ND
Schmitz, Michael D. ....Lake Forest, IL
Schmitz, Moench & Schmidt, A Professional Corporation ....Bismarck, ND
Schmitz & Ophaug ....Northfield, MN
Schmitz, Orell D. ....Bismarck, ND
Schmitz, Patrick J. ....Columbus, OH
Schmitz, Paul L. ....Denver, CO
Schmitz, Paula ....Austin, TX
Schmitz, Peggy J. ....Wooster, OH
Schmitz, Peter J. ....Northfield, MN
Schmitz, Randall F. ....Green Bay, WI
Schmitz, Raymond F. ....Rochester, MN
Schmitz, Raymond P., Jr. ....Chicago, IL
Schmitz, Richard ....Pana, IL
Schmitz, Richard P. ....Prescott, AZ
Schmitz, Rita F. ....Tucson, AZ
Schmitz, Robert A. ....St. Paul, MN
Schmitz, Robert J. ....Minneapolis, MN
Schmitz, Stuart E. ....St. Paul, MN

Schmitz, Suzanne J. ....Carbondale, IL
Schmitz, Thomas Francis ....Syracuse, NY
Schmitz, Thomas J. ....Spearfish, SD
Schmitz, Thomas M. ....Cleveland, OH
Schmitz, Wilfried P. ....Houston, TX
Schmitz, William F. ....Cleveland, OH
Schmitz, William J. ....Monroe, WI
Schmitz, William James .....Minneapolis, MN
Schmitz, William M. ....Boulder, CO
Schmitzer, Martin E. ....Dover, OH
Schmitzer, Thomas G. ....Waukesha, WI
Schmocker, John B. ....Long Beach, CA
Schmoke, Kurt L. ....Baltimore, MD
Schmoker, Jane Anne ....Dallas, TX
Schmoker, Richard C. ....Minneapolis, MN
Schmolder, Carl J. ....Ferris, TX
Schmolesky, John M. ....San Antonio, TX
Schmolka, Andrew F. ....New York, NY
Schmolka, Leo L. ....New York, NY
Schmolke, Robert H. ....Baton Rouge, LA
Schmolke, Robert H., A Professional Law Corporation ....Baton Rouge, LA
Schmoll, Alan R. ....Mount Laurel, NJ
Schmoll, Brooke D. ....Marlton, NJ
Schmoll, Edward Wilson ....Tampa, FL
Schmoll, Frederick L., III ....Flint, MI
Schmoll, Jon F. ....Merrillville, IN
Schmoll, Lester J., Jr.
Department of Justice, Antitrust Division, GV
Schmoll, Robert J., Jr. ....Fort Wayne, IN
Schmoller, Eberhard G. H. ....Palo Alto, CA
Schmollinger, Mark S. ....Toledo, OH
Schmonsees, William ....Palo Alto, CA
Schmookler, Scott L. ....Chicago, IL
Schmor, Douglass H. ....Medford, OR
Schmoyer, Jeffrey P. ....Pittsburgh, PA
Schmoyer, Marjorie A. ....Sarasota, FL
Schmoyer, Shannon B. ....Dallas, TX
Schmuck, Barbara L. ....Philadelphia, PA
Schmuck, H. W. ....Canton, OH
Schmuck, John P. ....Denver, CO
Schmuckal, Tim J. ....Chicago, IL
Schmucker, Chad C. ....Jackson, MI
Schmucker, Rebecca ....Chicago, IL
Schmucker, Ronald C.
South Burlington, VT
Schmucki, Ross F. ....Wilmington, DE
Schmudde, David A. ....New York, NY
Schmudde, Lee G. ....Lake Buena Vista, FL
Schmude, Richard W. ....Tomball, TX
Schmudlach, Deborah J. ....Des Moines, IA
Schmuhl, Thomas R. ....Philadelphia, PA
Schmuhl, William J., Jr. ....Bristol, IN
Schmuki, Steven D. ....Milwaukee, WI
Schmukler, Eli H. ....Madison, WI
Schmukler, Martin L. ....New York, NY
Schmukler, Martin L., P.C.
New York, NY
Schmukler, Nelson W. ....Brooklyn, NY
Schmukler, Robert ....New York, NY
Schmukler & St. Clare ....New York, NY
Schmukler, Sidney ....Gainesville, FL
Schmulbach, G. Barry ....Lawton, OK
Schmulewitz, Leah ....Washington, DC
Schmults, Edward C. ....Stamford, CT
Schmus, Geo. A. ....Brookfield, WI
Schmus, William G. ....Milwaukee, WI
Schmutte, Nicholas Glenn ....Danville, IN
Schmutter, Daniel L. ....Paramus, NJ
Schmutter, David ....Oceanside, NY
Schmutter, Steven ....New York, NY
Schmutz, Andrew P. ....Philadelphia, PA
Schmutz, Arthur W. ....Los Angeles, CA
Schmutz, Chris L. ....Salt Lake City, UT
Schmutz, Chris L., P.C.
Salt Lake City, UT
Schmutz, Christina Jepson
Salt Lake City, UT
Schmutz, Evan A. ....Provo, UT
Schmutz, J. Stephen ....Charleston, SC
Schmutz, John F. ....Irving, TX
Schmutz, Thomas A. ....Washington, DC
Schmutzer, Alfred C., Jr. ....Sevierville, TN
Schmutzer, J. Edgar ....Greeneville, TN
Schmaar, Mitchell ....Southfield, MI
Schnaare, Stanley D. ....Hillsboro, MO
Schnabel, Christine A. ....Washington, DC
Schnabel, Danl. ....Rolling Hills, CA
Schnabel, David H. ....New York, NY
Schnabel, Donald E. ....Merrill, WI
Schnabel, E. Eugene ....Denver, CO
Schnabel, Edith J. C.
National Labor Relations Board, Office of the General Counsel, GV
Schnabel, Eileen Pius ....New York, NY
Schnabel, Eric L. ....Wilmington, DE
Philadelphia, PA
Schnabel, Joseph H. ....Brooklyn, NY
Schnabel, Kelly J. ....New York, NY
Schnabel, Laurence H. ....Los Angeles, CA
Schnabel, Lisa Marie ....New York, NY
Schnabel, Marta-Ann ....New Orleans, LA
Schnabel, Martin B. ....Brooklyn, NY
Schnabel, Pamela May ....El Segundo, CA
Schnabel, Philip H. ....Goshen, NY
Schnabel, Robert V. ....Washington, DC
Schnabel-Bray, Mary A. ....Salem, OR
Schnabl, Leonard F. ....Mayville, WI
Schnabl, Marco E. ....New York, NY
Schnably, Stephen J. ....Coral Gables, FL
Schnack, Andrew C., III ....Quincy, IL
Schnack, Andrew C., Jr. ....Quincy, IL
Schnack, Barbara Lynch ....Houston, TX
Schnack, Harold C. ....Honolulu, HI
Schnack, J. Jay ....Walnut Creek, CA
Schnack, Katherine Romano ....Chicago, IL
Schnack, Kent R. ....Quincy, IL

Schnack, Loren E. ....Quincy, IL
Schnack, Robert J. ....Gold River, CA
Schnack, Ronald L. ....Amana, IA
Schnack, Schnack & Cashman ....Quincy, IL
Schnack, Steven O. ....Chicago, IL
Schnacke, Donald P. ....Topeka, KS
Schnacke, J. Gregory ....United States Senate, Senatorial Assistants, GV
Schnacke, John Gregory ....Denver, CO
Schnacke, June Borina ....Hillsborough, CA
Schnackel, John ....Clearwater, FL
Schnader Harrison Segal & Lewis LLP
San Francisco, CA
Washington, DC
Atlanta, GA
Cherry Hill, NJ
New York, NY
Harrisburg, PA
Norristown, PA
Philadelphia, PA
Pittsburgh, PA
Washington, PA
Schnadig, Richard H. ....Chicago, IL
Schnag, Frank James ....West Dundee, IL
Schnaid, Stacy Norene ....Beverly Hills, CA
Schnaider, Guillermo W. ....Los Angeles, CA
Schnaier, Stuart J. ....Hackensack, NJ
Schnake, Jeffrey H. ....Bloomington, IL
Schnake, Paul W. ....Silverthorne, CO
Schnake, Richard L. ....Springfield, MO
Schnal, Richard M. ....Monterey, CA
Schnall, Alfred S. ....New York, NY
Schnall, Bella ....Philadelphia, PA
Schnall, David ....New York, NY
Schnall, Flora ....New York, NY
Schnall, Ilene ....Miami, FL
Schnall, Marc J. ....San Antonio, TX
Schnall, Margaret F. ....Norfolk, VA
Schnall, Matthew D. ....Boston, MA
Schnall, Renée Faye ....Miami Beach, FL
Schnall, Rosemary R. ....Paoli, PA
Schnaper, Kenneth ....Stamford, CT
Schnapf, David ....San Francisco, CA
Schnapf, Lawrence P. ....New York, NY
Schnapp, Daniel E. ....New York, NY
Schnapp, Douglas ....New York, NY
Schnapp, Elliot ....New York, NY
Schnapp, Fulton, Fall, Silvey & Reid, L.L.C.
Fredericktown, MO
Schnapp, Lawrence P. ....Los Angeles, CA
Schnapp & Levy ....Brooklyn, NY
Schnapp, Mark P. ....Miami, FL
Schnapp, Robert ....New York, NY
Schnapp, Roger H. ....Newport Beach, CA
Schnapp, Roger H., A Professional Corporation ....Newport Beach, CA
Schnapp, Stanley ....Brooklyn, NY
Schnapper, Eric ....Seattle, WA
Schnare, James H., II
North Palm Beach, FL
Palm Beach, FL
Schnare, Rhonda K.
Executive Office Of The President, Office of the U.S. Trade Representative, GV
Schnarr, Christine N. ....New York, NY
Schnarr, Kristine Elmlund ....Granger, IN
Schnars, Richard T. ....Uniontown, OH
Schnaubelt, Catherine L. ....Houston, TX
Schnaufer, John C. ....White Plains, NY
Schnautz, Stephen P. ....Bellevue, WA
Schnayer, Jerold B. ....Chicago, IL
Schnayerson, Philip A. ....Hayward, CA
Schnebel, Debra J. ....Chicago, IL
Schnebelen & Detring ....Farmington, MO
Schnebelen, Phyllis P. ....Farmington, MO
Schneberg, William G. ....Ventura, CA
Schneble, Alfred Wm., III ....Dayton, OH
Schneble, Alfred Wm., III Co., L.P.A.
Dayton, OH
Schnebly, Tura ....DeLand, FL
Schneck, Arthur M. ....New York, NY
Schneck, David M. ....San Jose, CA
Schneck, Eric E. ....Morristown, NJ
New York, NY
Schneck, Jeffrey M. ....Phoenix, AZ
Schneck, Karen E. ....Boston, MA
Schneck, Margaret M. ....San Jose, CA
Schneck, Matthew A. ....New York, NY
Spring Valley, NY
Schneck, Michael ....New York, NY
Schneck, Michael I. ....Roseland, NJ
Schneck, Paul D. ....Minneapolis, MN
Schneck, Sidney H. ....New York, NY
Schneck & Smyth, P.C. ....Phoenix, AZ
Schneck, Steven Paul ....Chicago, IL
Schneck, Stuart B. ....Piedmont, CA
Schneck, Thomas, Law Office of
San Jose, CA
Schneck Weltman & Hashmall LLP
New York, NY
Schneck, William C. ....New York, NY
Schneck, William W. ....Briarcliff Manor, NY
Schnedar, William J. ....Roswell, NM
Schnedler, Steven C. ....Asheville, NC
Schnee, Carl ....Wilmington, DE
Schnee, Craig ....St. Petersburg, FL
Schnee, Daniel J. ....Detroit, MI
Schnee, Douglas B. ....Cleveland, OH
Schnee, Howard A. ....Woodland Hills, CA
Schnee, Martin ....New City, NY
Schneebalg, Simon ....New York, NY
Schneebaum, Steven M. ....Washington, DC
Schneebeck, Douglas G.
Albuquerque, NM
Schneebeck, Harold N. ....Des Moines, IA
Schneebeck, Richard, (P.C.)
Cheyenne, WY
Schneebeck, Robert W. ....Milford, OH

Schneeberg, Sara
Environmental Protection Agency, Office of the General Counsel, GV
Schneeberg, William A. ....Garland, TX
Schneeberger, Ed ....Glendale, CA
Schneeberger, Edward Paul ....Downey, CA
Schneekloth, M. Roger ....Alliance, NE
Schneeman, Pamela G. ....Indianapolis, IN
Schneer, Stephen B. ....New York, NY
Schneer, Stephen B., LLC ....New York, NY
Schneeweis, Gerald P. ....San Diego, CA
Schneeweiss, Jonathan ....San Diego, CA
Schneeweiss, Samuel ....New York, NY
Schnegg, Patricia M. ....Los Angeles, CA
Schneid, David J. ....West Palm Beach, FL
Schneid, Thomas D. ....Richmond, KY
Schneidau, Gretchen Ott ....Phoenix, AZ
Schneidau Ruiz, Lauri J. ....Houston, TX
Schneider, A. Groh ....Hatboro, PA
Schneider, Adam ....Philadelphia, PA
Schneider, Al L. ....Jacksonville, FL
Schneider, Alan B. ....Aventura, FL
Schneider, Alan J.
Federal Communications Commission, Mass Media Bureau, GV
Schneider, Alan J. ....Arlington, VA
Schneider, Alan K. ....Los Angeles, CA
Schneider, Alan L. ....Portland, OR
Schneider, Alan Marc ....Raleigh, NC
Schneider, Albert E. R., III ....Cleveland, OH
Schneider, Alexander ....Portland, OR
Schneider, Alfred R. ....Garrison, NY
Schneider, Alison M. ....Washington, DC
Schneider, Amy L. ....Winston-Salem, NC
Schneider, Amy M. ....Albany, NY
Schneider, Andrea ....San Diego, CA
Schneider, Andrew ....San Francisco, CA
Schneider, Andrew F. ....Langhorne, PA
Schneider, Andrew J. ....Branford, CT
Schneider, Andy ....Washington, DC
Schneider, Angela Lobb ....Hampton, VA
Schneider, Ann C. ....Los Angeles, CA
Schneider, Ann M. ....New York, NY
Schneider, Ann Makela ....Tulsa, OK
Schneider, Anne Jeffrey ....Sacramento, CA
Schneider, Anne K., (Mrs.) .....Oregon City, OR
Schneider, Arnold C. ....Chicago, IL
Schneider, Arthur ....Hagerstown, MD
Schneider, Barbara ....West Chester, PA
Schneider, Barbara A. ....Albuquerque, NM
Schneider, Barbara J. ....Atlanta, GA
Schneider, Barbara T. ....Portland, ME
Schneider, Barry C. ....Phoenix, AZ
Schneider, Bernadette ....San Francisco, CA
Schneider, Bernard ....New York, NY
Schneider, Bernard D. ....Boynton Beach, FL
Schneider, Bernard E. ....Irvine, CA
Schneider, Bernard G. ....New York, NY
Schneider, Beth H. ....Phoenix, AZ
Schneider, Bonnie Gullatt ....Elkton, MD
Schneider, Brandon J. ....Fort Wayne, IN
Schneider, Brian C. ....Madison, WI
Schneider, Bruce H. ....New York, NY
Schneider, Bruce S. ....Murray Hill, NJ
Schneider, Bryan A. ....Chicago, IL
Schneider, C. Randall ....San Jose, CA
Schneider, Caitlin A. ....San Francisco, CA
Schneider, Carl W. ....Philadelphia, PA
Schneider, Carol A. ....Los Angeles, CA
Schneider, Caspar Carl, Jr.
New York, NY
Schneider, Catherine T. ....Providence, RI
Schneider, Ceil ....Palm Beach Gardens, FL
Schneider, Charles A. ....Washington, DC
Schneider, Charles A. ....Columbus, OH
Schneider, Charles A. ....State College, PA
Schneider, Charles E.
Rancho Cucamonga, CA
Schneider, Charles E. ....Fond du Lac, WI
Schneider, Charles F. ....Shalimar, FL
Schneider, Charles J. ....Livonia, MI
Schneider, Charles J., P.C. ....Livonia, MI
Schneider, Chris A. ....Fresno, CA
Schneider, Christine N. ....Atlanta, GA
Schneider, Christopher B. ....Chicago, IL
Schneider, Christopher D.
Kansas City, MO
Schneider, Christopher L. ....Kansas City, KS
Schneider, Clifford E. ....Peoria, IL
Schneider, Conrad ....Brunswick, ME
Schneider, Curt T. ....Coffeyville, KS
Schneider, Cynthia G. ....Washington, DC
Schneider, Dale A. ....Southfield, MI
Schneider, Dan W. ....Chicago, IL
Schneider, Daniel H. ....Huntington, CT
Schneider, Daniel H. ....New York, NY
Schneider, Daniel J. ....Los Gatos, CA
Schneider, Daniel M. ....De Kalb, IL
Schneider, Daniel M ....Boston, MA
Schneider, Daniel Steven
Department of Justice, Criminal Division, GV
Schneider, David ....New York, NY
Schneider, David A. ....Treasury Department, Internal Revenue Service, GV
Schneider, David A. ....Covington, KY
Schneider, David A. ....Midlothian, VA
Schneider, David Alan ....Chicago, IL
Schneider, David B. ....Oklahoma City, OK
Schneider, David K. ....San Diego, CA
Schneider, David L. ....Fort Smith, AR
Schneider, David M. ....Chicago, IL
Schneider, David M. ....Mayfield Village, OH
Schneider, David P. ....Florham Park, NJ
Schneider, David R. ....Munster, IN
Schneider, David R. ....Houston, TX
Schneider, David W. ....New Haven, CT

Schneider, Stephen J. .... Fresno, CA
Schneider, Stephen J. .... Los Gatos, CA
Schneider, Stephen J. .... Washington, DC
Schneider, Steven .... Spokane, WA
Schneider, Steven A. .... Los Angeles, CA
Schneider, Steven A. .... Pasadena, CA
Schneider, Steven A. .... Cedarhurst, NY
Schneider, Steven C. .... Fargo, ND
Schneider, Steven D. .... Chicago, IL
Schneider, Steven M., (A Professional Corporation) .... Los Angeles, CA
Schneider, Steven P. .... Detroit, MI
Schneider, Steven R. .... San Ramon, CA
Schneider, Steven R. .... Treasury Department, Internal Revenue Service, GV
Schneider, Steven W. .... Duluth, MN
Schneider, Stuart I. .... Los Angeles, CA
Schneider, Stuart L. .... Englewood, NJ
Schneider, Susan B. .... Chicago, IL
Schneider, Susan J. .... Denver, CO
Schneider, Susan K. .... Portland, OR
Schneider, Susan L. .... Department of Justice, Environment and Natural Resources Division, GV
Schneider, Susan R. .... Staten Island, NY
Schneider & Tammi .... Milwaukee, WI
Schneider, Taylor .... Los Angeles, CA
Schneider, Teresa Letson .... Houston, TX
Schneider, Terry Moldoff
Fort Lauderdale, FL
Schneider, Theodore G., Jr.
Rancho Cucamonga, CA
Schneider, Theodore J. .... Cincinnati, OH
Schneider, Thomas .... Berkeley, CA
Schneider, Thomas .... Van Nuys, CA
Schneider, Thomas A. .... Fort Washington, PA
Schneider, Thomas J. .... Washington, DC
Schneider, Thomas J. .... Mandan, ND
Schneider, Thomas M. .... Bloomington, IL
Schneider, Thomas M. .... Columbia, MO
Schneider, Timothy E. .... Covington, KY
Schneider, Tina .... Portland, ME
Schneider, Tobi Leanna .... Waterville, ME
Schneider, Todd J. .... Chicago, IL
Schneider, Todd M. .... San Francisco, CA
Schneider, Troy Ron .... Manitowoc, WI
Schneider, Vern H. .... St. Louis, MO
Schneider, Vivian L., Law Offices of
San Francisco, CA
Schneider, W. Daniel .... Albuquerque, NM
Schneider & Walsh, P.C. .... Boston, MA
Schneider, Walter Brian
Fort Lauderdale, FL
Schneider, Walter R. .... San Francisco, CA
Schneider, Warren A. .... Department of Justice, Civil Division, GV
Schneider, Warren A. .... New York, NY
Schneider & Warren, LLP
Beverly Hills, CA
Schneider, Wayne .... Albany, NY
Schneider, Wendy .... Los Angeles, CA
Schneider, Wilbur H. .... Catonsville, MD
Schneider, Wilfred J., Jr. .... Irvine, CA
Schneider, William F. .... Lynchburg, VA
Schneider, William H. .... Columbus, OH
Schneider, William J. .... Hazleton, PA
Schneider, William J., Jr. .... Burbank, CA
Schneider, William Paul .... Rochester, MN
Schneider, William R., Jr. .... Austin, TX
Schneider, Willys H. .... New York, NY
Schneider, Wm. J. .... Milwaukee, WI
Schneider, Wolfgang G. .... Dearborn, MI
Schneider, Zachary .... Kenilworth, NJ
Schneiderman, Andrew A. .... Commerce, CA
Schneiderman, Arthur F. .... Palo Alto, CA
Schneiderman, Barry A. .... Fairfax, VA
Schneiderman, Daniel .... Washington, DC
Schneiderman, David .... Milton, MA
Schneiderman, Diane .... Cincinnati, OH
Schneiderman, Edward D. .... Milwaukee, WI
Schneiderman, Eric T. .... New York, NY
Schneiderman, F. Brian .... Norfolk, VA
Schneiderman, Henry S.
Treasury Department, Internal Revenue Service, GV
Schneiderman, Irwin .... New York, NY
Schneiderman, Joseph .... Kew Gardens, NY
Schneiderman, Karen L. .... Norfolk, VA
Schneiderman, Lenore .... Rockville, MD
Schneiderman, Martin D.
Washington, DC
Schneiderman, Michael .... Chicago, IL
Schneiderman, Nancy T. .... Bethlehem, PA
Schneiderman, Nathan J. .... Newton, MA
Schneiderman, Paul .... New York, NY
Schneiderman, Peter L. .... San Francisco, CA
Schneiderman, Peter M.
Farmington Hills, MI
Schneiderman, Peter M., & Associates, P.C.
Farmington Hills, MI
Schneiderman, Scot .... Boston, MA
Schneiderman, Seth E. .... Miami, FL
Schneiderman, Stan B. .... Akron, OH
Schneiderman, Steven D. .... Chicago, IL
Schneiderman, Susan .... New York, NY
Schneiderman, Ted .... Akron, OH
Schneiders, Anne E. .... Washington, DC
Schneiders, Nancy L. .... Milwaukee, WI
Schneiders, Paul A. .... Canton, MA
Schneider-Truog, Keely .... Atlanta, GA
Schneider-Vogel, Merri .... Houston, TX
Schneiderwind, Barry J. .... Midland, TX
Schneider-Zena, Stephanie B. .... Roseland, NJ
Schneidewind, Eric J. .... Lansing, MI
Schneidler, Jon G. .... Seattle, WA
Schneidman, Edward J. .... Chicago, IL
Schneidman, Jeff .... Phoenix, AZ
Schneidman, Leonard .... Boston, MA
Schneidman, Sam .... Quincy, IL
Schneier, Alan N. .... Valley Stream, NY
Schneier, Alan S. .... Short Hills, NJ
Schneier, Bernard .... Akron, OH
Schneier, David L. .... Bethesda, MD
Schneier, Jamie B. .... Cleveland, OH
Schneier, Kenneth C. .... New York, NY
Schneier, Marc M. .... Wynnewood, PA
Schneier, Murray D. .... New York, NY
Schneier, Paul R. .... Red Bank, NJ
Schneier, Roger .... New York, NY
Schneier, Sharon L. .... New York, NY
Schneiger, Thomas M. .... Portland, OR
Schneikart, William Michael
St. Petersburg, FL
Schneir, Eleanor .... Venice, CA
Schneirov, Allan B. .... Philadelphia, PA
Schneirov, Allison R. .... New York, NY
Schnelker, Carrie L. .... Issaquah, WA
Schnell, Anthony L. .... Louisville, KY
Schnell, Brian B. .... Minneapolis, MN
Schnell, Carlton B. .... Cleveland, OH
Schnell, David R. .... Tonawanda, NY
Schnell, Gordon .... New York, NY
Schnell, Gordon W. .... Dickinson, ND
Schnell, James M. .... Fairfield, OH
Schnell, Jay John .... Denver, CO
Schnell, Kevin L. .... Kansas City, MO
Schnell, Laura S. .... New York, NY
Schnell, Melissa A. .... Atlanta, GA
Schnell, Molly O'Meara .... Rock Island, IL
Schnell, Patricia A. .... San Diego, CA
Schnell, Paul T. .... New York, NY
Schnell, Randi Engel .... Atlanta, GA
Schnell, Richard E. .... Tonawanda, NY
Schnell, Richard L. .... Mandan, ND
Schnell, Richards, Brown & Freeman, P.C.
Elgin, IL
Schnell, Robert H. .... Chapel Hill, NC
Schnell, Robert L., Jr. .... Minneapolis, MN
Schnell, Ronald H. .... St. Petersburg, FL
Schnell, Ronald H., P.A. .... St. Petersburg, FL
Schnell & Saltarelli .... Tonawanda, NY
Schnell, Sherry E. .... San Diego, CA
Schnell, Terry L. .... Pittsburgh, PA
Schnell, Theodore N., Jr. .... Elgin, IL
Schnell, Todd W. .... Minneapolis, MN
Schnellbacher, John J. .... Houston, TX
Schnelle, Keith M. .... Sidney, OH
Schnelle, Timothy J. .... Dearborn, MI
Schnellenberger, Thomas F., Jr.
Indianapolis, IN
Schneller, Barbara A. .... West Chester, PA
Schneller, Douglas J. .... New York, NY
Schneller, Gerard B. .... Wood River, IL
Schneller, John, IV .... Houston, TX
Schneller, John W. .... Washington, DC
Schneller, Marina V. .... Washington, DC
Schneller, Regina E. .... Westfield, NJ
Schneller, William F. .... Holly Springs, MS
Schnelling, Anthony H. N. .... New York, NY
Schnelwar, Philip G. .... Bronx, NY
Schnelz, Gene .... Pontiac, MI
Schnelz, Kurt E. .... Birmingham, MI
Detroit, MI
Schnelz, Wells, Monaghan & Wells, P.C.
Birmingham, MI
Detroit, MI
Troy, MI
Schnelzer, Ann T. .... Torrington, WY
Schnepf, Susan L. .... San Diego, CA
Schnepp, Charles M., Jr.
Garden City, NY
Schnepp, Eric R. .... Wauwatosa, WI
Schnepp, Wm. R. .... Milwaukee, WI
Schnepper, Barbara E. .... Miami, FL
Schnepper, Jeff A. .... Cherry Hill, NJ
Schnepper, R. Cory .... Miami, FL
Schneps, Barry C. .... Flushing, NY
Schneps, Murray B. .... Riverhead, NY
Schneps, Robert L. .... Manhasset, NY
Schner, Larry E. .... Boca Raton, FL
Schnessel, Benjamin S. .... Carbondale, PA
Schnetke, Julia E. .... Framingham, MA
Schnettler, Thomas P. .... Minneapolis, MN
Schnetz, Karl J. .... New Castle, CA
Schnetzler, Greta W. .... San Francisco, CA
Schnetzler & Herring, A Professional Corporation .... Oklahoma City, OK
Schnetzler, Martin K. .... Oklahoma City, OK
Schnetzler, Nancy J. .... Oklahoma City, OK
Schneur, Eugene .... New York, NY
Schneyer, Gene S. .... Melrose Park, PA
Schneyer, Kathleen S. .... Tucson, AZ
Schneyer, Kenneth .... Providence, RI
Schneyer, Olin A. .... San Gabriel, CA
Schneyer, Richard E. .... New York, NY
Schnibben, Jeffrey C. .... Mattoon, IL
Schnider, Charles S. .... Overland Park, KS
Schnider, David A. .... San Francisco, CA
Schnider, Frederick M. .... Oakland, CA
Schnider, Martin L., Jr.
Silver Spring, MD
Schnider, Robert A. .... Sherman Oaks, CA
Schnider, Wm. M. .... Kansas City, MO
Schnidman, Frank .... Coral Gables, FL
Schnidman, John .... Farmington, CT
Schnidrig, Veronica M. .... Clackamas, OR
Schnieder, George L. .... Fairfield, NJ
Schniederjan, Jay Lucas .... Oklahoma City, OK
Schniederjon, Frank H. .... Effingham, IL
Schniederjon, Weber & Jarrett
Effingham, IL
Schnieders, Robert H. .... Oak Grove, MO
Schnier, Andrew M. .... New York, NY
Schnier, Steven V. .... San Francisco, CA
Schnippel, Ernest P. .... Indianapolis, IN
Schnipper, Daniel R. .... New York, NY
Schnipper, Don M.
Hot Springs National Park, AR
Schnipper, Michael .... Bristol, CT
Schnippert, Regis J. .... Pittsburgh, PA
Schnirch, Peter M. .... Santa Ana, CA
Schnirman, Alan J. .... Linden, NJ
Schnirman & Charney .... Linden, NJ
Schnitker, Clay A. .... Madison, FL
Schnitker, John P. .... Department of Justice, Civil Division, GV
Schnitker, Kirk A. .... Minneapolis, MN
Schnitkey, Alan David .... Wichita, KS
Schnitkey, Mark D. .... Napoleon, OH
Schnitter, Joseph M. .... Buffalo, NY
Schnittgrund, Gary D. .... Santa Clarita, CA
Schnittke & Smith .... New Lexington, OH
Schnittke, Steven P. .... New Lexington, OH
Schnittman, Barry .... Melville, NY
Schnittman, Eric Alan .... New York, NY
Schnittman, Michael S. .... Rochester, NY
Schnittman & Schnittman .... Melville, NY
Schnittman, Steven N. .... Melville, NY
Schnitz, Robert C. .... Chicago, IL
Schnitz, Robert V. .... Newport Beach, CA
Schnitzer, Alan D. .... New York, NY
Schnitzer, Alan M. .... Los Angeles, CA
Schnitzer, Boaz M. .... New York, NY
Schnitzer, Dori .... Portland, OR
Schnitzer, Elliot M. .... Chevy Chase, MD
Schnitzer, Erwin C. .... Warren, NJ
Schnitzer, Gary E. .... Las Vegas, NV
Schnitzer, Harvie Ruth .... Fresno, CA
Schnitzer, Herbert .... Palatine, IL
Schnitzer, Howard B. .... New York, NY
Schnitzer, Iris Taymore .... Boston, MA
Schnitzer, Joseph M. .... Baltimore, MD
Schnitzer, Leonard .... Westbury, NY
Schnitzer, Mark C. .... San Bernardino, CA
Schnitzer, Martin J. .... Los Angeles, CA
Schnitzer, Maxine C. .... Fairfax, VA
Schnitzer, Michael A. .... Chicago, IL
Schnitzer, Richard D. .... Dallas, TX
Schnitzer & Segall, LLC .... Baltimore, MD
Schnitzer, Stephen .... Livingston, NJ
Schnitzer, Stephen, P.A. .... Livingston, NJ
Schnitzer, Steven C. .... Washington, DC
Schnitzer, Susan F. .... San Francisco, CA
Schnitzler, Thomas P. .... White Plains, NY
Schnizler, Robert W. .... Jamestown, NY
Schnobrich, John H. .... Redwood Falls, MN
Schnobrich, Roger W. .... Minneapolis, MN
Schnock, John K. .... Brooklyn, NY
Schnoebelen, Carroll Michael
Studio City, CA
Schnoebelen, Jodi C. .... Escondido, CA
Schnoll, Alan .... Philadelphia, PA
Pottsville, PA
Schnoll, Jack M. .... South Orange, NJ
Schnoll, Kenneth B. .... San Francisco, CA
Schnoll, Melanie C. .... New York, NY
Schnoll, Steven R. .... Milwaukee, WI
Schnoor, William J., Jr. .... Boston, MA
Schnopp, Stefan K. .... Cleveland, OH
Schnorbach, Philip T. .... Dallas, TX
Schnorbus, Walter W. .... Staten Island, NY
Schnorf, Brandon G., Jr. .... Toledo, OH
Schnorf, David M. .... Toledo, OH
Schnorf & Ferguson .... Toledo, OH
Schnorf & Schnorf Co., L.P.A., A Professional Corporation .... Toledo, OH
Schnorr, David E. .... Indianapolis, IN
Schnorr, Donna L. .... Fort Myers, FL
Schnorr, Good & Scahill .... Indianapolis, IN
Schnorr, Jimmie J. .... Bethany, OK
Schnorr, Jimmie J., P.C. .... Bethany, OK
Schnorr, John O. .... Milwaukee, WI
Schnorr, Mary Frances A. .... New York, NY
Schnorr, Thomas G. .... Boston, MA
Schnorrenberg, David M.
Washington, DC
Schnose, Paul A. .... Washington, DC
Schnuck, Terry E. .... St. Louis, MO
Schnupp, Karen S. .... Knoxville, TN
Schnur, Bradley D. .... New York, NY
Schnur, Jacob J. .... Inverness, IL
Schnur, Kenneth D. .... San Francisco, CA
Schnur, Margo .... New York, NY
Schnur, Morris J. .... Fort Lauderdale, FL
Schnur, Peter .... New York, NY
Schnur, Robert A. .... Milwaukee, WI
Schnur, Thomas E. .... Chicago, IL
Schnurbusch, Kevin P. .... St. Louis, MO
Schnure, Victoria K. .... New York, NY
Schnurer, Eric B. .... West Chester, PA
Schnurmacher, Eric P. .... Oakland, CA
Schnurmacher, Eric P., A Prof. Corp., Law Offices of .... Oakland, CA
Schnurman, Alan J. .... New York, NY
Schnurman, Daniel J. .... Houston, TX
Schnurpfeil, Eric W. .... San Francisco, CA
Schnurr, Elyssa M. .... Houston, TX
Schnurr, Jeremy M. .... Buffalo, NY
Schnurr, Jerry L., III .... Fort Dodge, IA
Schnurr, Mary Jankousky .... Chicago, IL
Schnurr, Michelle Darquea .... Hicksville, NY
Schnurr, Richard A. .... Chicago, IL
Schnurr, William A. .... Haddon Heights, NJ
Schnurrer, Rudolph G. .... La Crosse, WI
Schnyder, Clayton P., Jr. .... New Orleans, LA
Schnyder, Cornelia .... Washington, DC
Schoaf, Thomas L. .... Litchfield Park, AZ
Schobel, Diana Magazine .... Rockville, MD
Schobel, James E. .... St. Louis, MO
Schobel, Kathleen P. .... New York, NY
Schobel, Donna J. .... Tempe, AZ
Schober, Gary M. .... Buffalo, NY
New York, NY
Schober, George C. .... Colchester, CT
Schober, George C., P.C. .... Colchester, CT
Schober, George P. .... Cincinnati, OH
Schober, James M. .... Dallas, TX
Schober, John C. .... New Berlin, WI
Schober, John J. .... Buffalo, NY
Fredonia, NY
Schober, John L., Jr. .... Shreveport, LA
Schober, Leroy E. .... Enfield, CT
Schober & Radtke .... New Berlin, WI
Schober, Reynolds, Antee& Lafargue
Shreveport, LA
Schober & Schober, S.C. .... Dousman, WI
New Berlin, WI
Oconomowoc, WI
Schober, T. Michael .... New Berlin, WI
Schober, Thomas G. .... Dousman, WI
New Berlin, WI
Oconomowoc, WI
Schober, Thomas L. .... Green Bay, WI
Schober & Ulatowski, S.C.
Green Bay, WI
Schobert, Jeffrey E. .... Canton, OH
Schoborg, Jeffrey R. .... Tulsa, OK
Schoborg, Terri J. King .... Covington, KY
Schoby, Maurice .... Cleveland, OH
Schoch, Alexander C. .... Brecksville, OH
Schoch, Arch K., IV .... High Point, NC
Schoch, Edward D. .... Los Angeles, CA
Schoch, H. Pamela .... Dallas, TX
Schoch, Peter B. .... Boston, MA
Schoch & Woodruff, L.L.P.
Greensboro, NC
High Point, NC
Schochet, Brian .... New York, NY
Schochet, Harvey S. .... San Francisco, CA
Schochet, Howard S. .... New York, NY
Schochet, Ira A. .... New York, NY
Schochet, K. Barry .... Washington, DC
Schochet, K. Barry, P.C. .... Washington, DC
Schochet, Sherman .... Camarillo, CA
Schochet, William A. .... Dallas, TX
Schochor, Federico and Staton, P.A.
Washington, DC
Baltimore, MD
Rockville, MD
Towson, MD
Upper Marlboro, MD
Schochor, Jonathan .... Washington, DC
Baltimore, MD
Schoch V, Arch K. .... High Point, NC
Schock, Charles C. .... Mesa, AZ
Schock, Dawn M. .... Long Beach, CA
Schock, Edward J. .... Philadelphia, PA
Schock, Erich J. .... Allentown, PA
Schock, Jacqueline M. .... Los Angeles, CA
Schock, John P. .... Glendale, CA
Schock, Margaret .... Glendale, CA
Schock, Marnie S. .... Pittsburgh, PA
Schock & Schock, A Law Corporation
Glendale, CA
Schock, W. Bevis .... St. Louis, MO
Schockemoehl, Gwen M. .... Richmond, VA
Schocket, Eve .... Tucson, AZ
Schockett, Eleanor Levingston .... Miami, FL
Schockling, Scott David .... Columbus, OH
Schockman, Douglas J. .... Columbus, OH
Schockner, Leslie T. .... Milwaukie, OR
Schodde, Gregory C. .... Chicago, IL
Schodde, Melanie .... San Bernardino, CA
Schodde, Stephen C. .... West Des Moines, IA
Schoder, C. Anthony, Jr. .... Daytona Beach, FL
Schoder, Laurie A. .... Denver, CO
Schoder, Wendell L. .... Battle Creek, MI
Schoditsch, Richard E. .... Shalimar, FL
Schodowski, Karen Hiyama .... Detroit, MI
Schodowski, Thomas M. .... Good Hope, LA
Schoeberl, Joseph W. .... Carthage, MO
Schoeberl, Kevin E. .... Cresco, IA
Schoeberle, Stephen M. .... Morganton, NC
Schoeberlein, William A., III
Baltimore, MD
Schoeberlein, William E. .... Baltimore, MD
Schoeberlein, William F. .... Denver, CO
Schoech, Charles F. .... Palm Beach, FL
Schoeck, Brian J. .... Charlotte, NC
Schoeck, Kristen I.
Department of Commerce, GV
Schoede, Edw. C. .... Rock Island, IL
Schoedel, Elizabeth L. .... Spokane, WA
Schoedel, Phyllis Dolvin .... Spokane, WA
Schoedinger, Daniel H. .... Columbus, OH
Schoeffel, Amy .... Milwaukee, WI
Schoeffel, Jon M. .... Racine, WI
Schoeffel, Joseph Scott .... Irvine, CA
Schoeffel, Samantha S. .... Katy, TX
Schoeffler, Andrew P. .... Washington, DC
Schoeggl, David M. .... Seattle, WA
Schoel, Jerry W. .... Birmingham, AL
Schoel, Ogle, Liles and Upshaw, LLP
Birmingham, AL
Schoel, William P. .... Seattle, WA
Schoelch, Lawrence F. .... Tucson, AZ
Schoell, Joseph C. .... Wilmington, DE
Schoell, Roger R. .... Marshalltown, IA
Schoeller, Mark .... Clear Lake, IA
Schoeller, Mark B. .... Philadelphia, PA
Schoellerman, Jack L. .... Irvine, CA
Schoellkopf, Joseph J., Jr. .... Buffalo, NY
Schoellkopf, Thomas J. .... Buffalo, NY
Schoellkopf, William C. .... Buffalo, NY
Schoellkopff, Ernest W. .... Roseland, NJ
Schoem, Alan H.
Consumer Product Safety Commission, Office of Compliance, GV
Schoemaker, Charles, Jr. .... Encino, CA
Schoemaker, Donald K. .... Belleville, IL
Schoemaker, Linda A. .... Seattle, WA
Schoemaker, Richard C. .... Pittsburgh, PA

Schoemaker, Roger C. ....Grand Rapids, MI
Schoeman, Michael E. ....New York, NY
Schoeman, Stephen ....Scotch Plains, NJ
Schoeman, Updike & Kaufman, LLP
New York, NY
Schoemann, Peter A. ....Tampa, FL
Schoemann, Rudolph R. ....New Orleans, LA
Schoemer, Carl J. ....Brighton, MI
Schoen, Alan P. ....Scranton, PA
Schoen, Andrew J. ....New York, NY
Schoen, Carol M. ....Northfield, MN
Schoen, Constance B. ....Oxford, MI
Schoen, David ....Teaneck, NJ
Schoen, David C. ....Little Rock, AR
Schoen, Dennis T. ....Chicago, IL
Schoen, Dennis T., P.C., Law Offices
Chicago, IL
Schoen, Douglas A. ....Portland, OR
Schoen, Edward A., III ....Texarkana, TX
Schoen, Edward J., Jr. ....Palos Hills, IL
Schoen, Elizabeth Swinton ....Atlanta, GA
Schoen, George F. ....New York, NY
Schoen, George W. ....Miami, FL
Schoen & Getlan ....New York, NY
Schoen, Gregg L. ....Portland, OR
Schoen, Harry P., P.A. ....Hastings, MN
Schoen, Jeffrey A. ....Tempe, AZ
Schoen, Jeffrey A., P.C., Law Offices of
Phoenix, AZ
Tempe, AZ
Schoen, Jeffrey D. ....Covington, LA
Schoen, Kenneth A. ....Parsippany, NJ
New York, NY
Schoen, Laurence A. ....Boston, MA
Schoen, Lawrence C. ....New York, NY
Schoen, Lee J. ....Chicago, IL
Schoen, Linda Lee ....Geneva, IL
Schoen, Lindsay Mara ....New York, NY
Schoen, Lucille L. ....Beverly Hills, CA
Schoen, Mark W. ....Baton Rouge, LA
Schoen, Michael D. ....Dallas, TX
Schoen, Neal W. ....Albany, NY
Schoen, Patrick J. ....Milwaukee, WI
Schoen, Robert David ....Atlanta, GA
Schoen, Rodric B. ....Lubbock, TX
Schoen, Scott J. ....Boston, MA
Schoen & Smith, Ltd. ....Chicago, IL
Schoen, Stanley R. ....Santa Monica, CA
Schoen, Stevan J. ....Albuquerque, NM
Placitas, NM
Schoen, Stevan J., P.A. ....Albuquerque, NM
Placitas, NM
Schoen, Victor ....Hartford, CT
Schoen, William R. ....Novato, CA
Schoenauer, Kenneth F. ....Clinton, IA
Schoenauer Law Offices, P.C. ....Clinton, IA
Schoenbach, Lawrence H. ....New York, NY
Schoenbach, Marci C. ....Scotch Plains, NJ
Schoenbaechler, Edward L.
Louisville, KY
Schoenbauer, Laura J. ....Minneapolis, MN
Schoenbaum, Alan ....San Antonio, TX
Schoenbaum, Curphy & Scanlan, P.C.
San Antonio, TX
Schoenbaum, Edward J. ....Springfield, IL
Schoenbaum, Erin L. ....Santa Ana, CA
Schoenbaum, Ronald J.
Newport Beach, CA
Schoenbaum, Stanley ....San Antonio, TX
Schoenbaum, Sylvia B. ....Brookline, MA
Schoenbaum, Thomas J. ....Atlanta, GA
Schoenbeck, Albert E. ....St. Louis, MO
Schoenbeck, Donna L. ....Wilmington, DE
Schoenbeck, Lee ....Webster, SD
Schoenbeck, Patricia Martin
Webster Groves, MO
Schoenbeck & Schoenbeck, P.A.
Wilmington, DE
Schoenbeck, Stephen M. ....St. Louis, MO
Schoenberg & Associates ....Bala Cynwyd, PA
Schoenberg & Associates ....Burlington, VT
Schoenberg, Bernard J. ....San Francisco, CA
Schoenberg, Bonnie Barr ....Chicago, IL
Schoenberg, Bruce A. ....New York, NY
Schoenberg, Claude I. ....Bala Cynwyd, PA
Schoenberg, Clifford H. ....New York, NY
Schoenberg, David P. ....Atlanta, GA
Schoenberg, David W. ....Chicago, IL
Schoenberg, Debra R. ....Burlington, VT
Schoenberg, Douglas K. ....Summit, NJ
Schoenberg, E. Randol ....Los Angeles, CA
Schoenberg, Fisher, Newman & Rosenberg, Ltd. ....Chicago, IL
Schoenberg, Franklyn ....Cherry Hill, NJ
Princeton, NJ
Schoenberg, Herbert M. ....Tarzana, CA
Schoenberg, Karen ....Staten Island, NY
Schoenberg, Kenneth A. ....Downingtown, PA
Schoenberg, M. Eric ....Philadelphia, PA
Schoenberg, Patricia Romano
Bala Cynwyd, PA
Schoenberg, Renee M. ....Chicago, IL
Schoenberg, Richard Barry ....Goshen, NY
Schoenberg, Robert J. ....Morristown, NJ
Schoenberg, Ronald L. ....Mineola, NY
Schoenberg, Ronald R. ....Los Angeles, CA
Schoenberg, Steven C. ....Livonia, MI
Schoenberg, Todd & Kerbleski, Ltd.
San Francisco, CA
Schoenberger, Bruce S. ....Toledo, OH
Schoenberger, Herman B. ....Buras, LA
Schoenberger, Holman C. ....Baltimore, MD
Schoenberger, Ilan S. ....Spring Valley, NY
Schoenberger, James A., Jr. ....Irvine, CA
Schoenberger, Kevin C. ....New Orleans, LA
Schoenberger, Lincoln F. ....Shelton, CT
Schoenberger, Loren C.
Upper Sandusky, OH

Schoenberger, Maurice E. ....East Lansing, MI
Schoenberger, Maurice E., P.C.
East Lansing, MI
Schoenberger, Paul M. ....Garden City, NY
Schoenberger, Rhoda F. ....Spring Valley, NY
Schoenberger, Richard H.
San Francisco, CA
Schoenberger & Schoenberger
Spring Valley, NY
Schoenberger, Stuart J. ....North Bellmore, NY
Schoenblum, Eugene I. ....New York, NY
Schoenblum, Jeffrey A. ....Nashville, TN
Schoenbohm, Michael P. ....Appleton, WI
Schoenbohm, Richard B. ....Appleton, WI
Schoenbohm & Schoenbohm, S.C.
Appleton, WI
Schoenborn, Brian J. ....St. Cloud, MN
Schoenborn, Daniel L. ....Buffalo, NY
Schoenborn, Dru Hanna ....Warren, PA
Schoenborn, Eric D. ....Philadelphia, PA
Schoenborn, John W. ....Pagosa Springs, CO
Schoenbrod, David S. ....New York, NY
Schoenbrod, James T. ....Davie, FL
Schoenbrun, Gary L. ....New York, NY
Schoenbrun, Larry L. ....Dallas, TX
Schoenbrun, Ronald M. ....Tyler, TX
Schoenburg, Patrick S. ....Los Angeles, CA
Schoenburg, Peter ....Albuquerque, NM
Schoenburg, Stuart B. ....Department of Justice, Environment and Natural Resources Division, GV
Schoendorf, Joseph F., Jr. ....Milwaukee, WI
Schoendorf & Schoendorf ....Milwaukee, WI
Schoendorf, Thomas J. ....Milwaukee, WI
Schoene, Byrd & Palmer, P.A. ....Maitland, FL
Schoene, John S. ....Maitland, FL
Schoene, Kathleen S. ....St. Louis, MO
Schoene, Ralph F. ....White Plains, NY
Schoenebaum, Steven C. ....Des Moines, IA
Schoeneberg, Wayne T. ....O'Fallon, MO
Schoeneberger, Carl A. ....Chicago, IL
Schoeneberger, Keith Philip ....Chicago, IL
Schoenecker, David J. ....Minneapolis, MN
Schoenecker, Marc ....Irving, TX
Schoenecker, Robert E. ....Milwaukee, WI
Schoeneman, Andrea J. ....San Francisco, CA
Schoeneman, Donald C. ....Timonium, MD
Schoeneman, Jenna Lynn ....Des Plaines, IL
Schoeneman, Robt. F. ....Aplington, IA
Schoenenberger, Thomas R.
Oklahoma City, OK
Tulsa, OK
Schoener, George F., Jr. ....Philadelphia, PA
Schoener, George F., Jr., P.C.
Philadelphia, PA
Schoener, James F. ....Sarasota, FL
Schoener, James M. ....Troy, MI
Schoener, Jane M. ....Allentown, PA
Philadelphia, PA
Schoener & Kascavage, P.C.
Allentown, PA
Philadelphia, PA
Schoener, Mark R. ....Seattle, WA
Schoener, Wm. L. ....Albany, CA
Schoenewald, Michael A. ....Akron, OH
Schoenewolf, Walter W. ....Brick, NJ
Schoenewolf, Walter W., P.A. ....Brick, NJ
Schoenfarber, Jay A. ....New York, NY
Schoenfeld & Abilheira, P.C.
Shrewsbury, NJ
New York, NY
Schoenfeld, Andrew L. ....Jersey City, NJ
Schoenfeld, Barbara Braun ....Providence, RI
Schoenfeld, Benjamin N. ....Ottsville, PA
Schoenfeld, Brad L. ....Alpharetta, GA
Schoenfeld, Craig A. ....Baltimore, MD
Schoenfeld, D. Michael ....Sacramento, CA
Schoenfeld, David E. ....Chicago, IL
Schoenfeld, David M. ....Gaithersburg, MD
Schoenfeld, Donald A. ....Milwaukee, WI
Schoenfeld, Eric B. ....Shrewsbury, NJ
New York, NY
Schoenfeld, Eric S. ....New York, NY
Schoenfeld, Glenn E. ....New York, NY
Schoenfeld, Harris ....Melville, NY
Schoenfeld, Henry ....Washington, DC
Schoenfeld, Henry ....New York, NY
Schoenfeld, Howard A. ....Milwaukee, WI
Schoenfeld, Howard B. ....Milwaukee, WI
Schoenfeld, Howard K. ....Jamaica, NY
Schoenfeld, Irving ....San Mateo, CA
Schoenfeld, Jason A. ....New Orleans, LA
Schoenfeld, John A. ....Chicago, IL
Schoenfeld, Julie Selene ....Boulder, CO
Schoenfeld, Karey A. ....Vancouver, WA
Schoenfeld, Laura G. ....Peekskill, NY
Schoenfeld, Lawrence R. ....New York, NY
Schoenfeld, Lowell S. ....Fort Myers, FL
Schoenfeld, Lyn B. ....Media, PA
Schoenfeld, Marc ....New York, NY
Schoenfeld, Marcus ....Villanova, PA
Schoenfeld, Martin ....New York, NY
Schoenfeld, Michael P. ....Melville, NY
Schoenfeld, Norman P. ....Roslyn, NY
Schoenfeld, Otto B. ....New Orleans, LA
Schoenfeld, Pamela ....New York, NY
Schoenfeld, Peter N. ....Universal City, CA
Schoenfeld, Robert Morlas
New Orleans, LA
Schoenfeld, Roger L. ....Bensenville, IL
Schoenfeld, Roy Matthew ....Boston, MA
Schoenfeld, Sage L. ....New York, NY
Schoenfeld, Sam ....Boston, MA
Schoenfeld & Schoenfeld ....Melville, NY
Schoenfeld, Scott R. ....Washington, DC
Schoenfeld, Stephen H. ....Madison, WI
Schoenfeld, Steven R. ....New York, NY
Schoenfeld, Stuart H. ....Lake Success, NY

Schoenfeld, Susan R. ....New York, NY
Schoenfeld, Thomas R. ....Covington, KY
Cincinnati, OH
Schoenfeld & Yonek, P.C. ....Vancouver, WA
Schoenfelder, Peg A. ....Hayward, CA
Schoenfelder, Robert Philip ....Sacramento, CA
Schoenfield, Eli D. ....New York, NY
Schoenfield, James R. ....Los Angeles, CA
Schoenfield, James R., A Professional Corporation ....Los Angeles, CA
Schoenfield, Mark K. ....Chicago, IL
Schoenfield, Nichol M. ....Cleveland, OH
Schoenfield, Rick M. ....Chicago, IL
Schoenfield, Swartzman & Massin
Chicago, IL
Schoengold & Sporn, P.C. ....New York, NY
Schoengood, Elizabeth ....Monroe, CT
Schoenhaar, Mary McGrath ....Baltimore, MD
Schoenhals, Jack L. ....Salt Lake City, UT
Schoenhaus, Todd A. ....Philadelphia, PA
Schoenheit, Thomas E. ....Charlotte, NC
Schoenherr, Craig S., Sr.
Sterling Heights, MI
Schoenherr, Jeffrey T. ....Chatsworth, CA
Schoenherr-Warnez, Florence
Center Line, MI
Schoenholtz, Andrew I. ....Bethesda, MD
Schoenholz, William ....Los Angeles, CA
Schoenhorn, Jon L. ....Hartford, CT
Schoeni, K. Roger ....Cincinnati, OH
Schoenig, Rachel R. Watkins
Davenport, IA
Muscatine, IA
Schoenig, Richd. A. ....Marysville, CA
Schoenig, Susan L. ....Sacramento, CA
Schoenike, Jonathan K. ....Boardman, OH
Schoening, Kari C. ....Palo Alto, CA
Schoening, Kelleene Guilfoyle
Covington, KY
Schoening, Mary D. ....Cleveland, OH
Schoening, Michael A. ....Indianapolis, IN
Schoeninger, Carl J. ....Southfield, MI
Schoeninger, Danielle Wenner
Philadelphia, PA
Schoeninger, Terrence T. ....Chesterfield, MO
Schoenith, Antonia ....Warren, MI
Schoenlaub, Paul E. ....St. Joseph, MO
Schoenle, Paul D. ....Warsaw, IN
Schoenleber, Michael W. ....Los Angeles, CA
Schoenling, Lynne K. ....Columbus, OH
Schoenman, Edward M. ....New York, NY
Schoenmarklin, Susan L. ....Dublin, OH
Schoenmeyer, Joel M. ....Chicago, IL
Schoenmeyer, Ruth A. ....Oak Brook, IL
Schoenstadt, Richard G. ....Chicago, IL
Schoenstedt, Richard C. ....Joliet, IL
Schoenstedt, Richard Carl ....Joliet, IL
Schoenstein, Richard C. ....New York, NY
Schoenthaler, David E. ....Davenport, IA
Schoenthaler, Lauren K. ....Menlo Park, CA
Schoenthaler, Peter F. ....Atlanta, GA
Schoenthaler, Roberg, Bartelt & Kahler
Maquoketa, IA
Schoenwald, Bruce A. ....Fargo, ND
Schoenwald, David J. ....Melville, NY
Schoenwald, Donald L. ....Syracuse, NY
Schoenwald, Lawrence J., P.C.
Denver, CO
Schoenwald, Maurice L. ....Longboat Key, FL
Schoenwald, Sanger & Kudla, LLC
Denver, CO
Schoenwald & Schoenwald, P.C.
Melville, NY
Schoenwald, Scott M. ....Las Vegas, NV
Schoenwald, Sidney K. ....Rochester, NY
Schoenwalder, Timothy G.
Tallahassee, FL
Schoenwetter, Charles J.
Minneapolis, MN
St. Paul, MN
Schoenwetter, Sara ....New York, NY
Schoep, Linda ....Appleton, MN
Schoep, Nancy E. ....Albany, NY
Schoepfer, Joseph O. ....Atlanta, GA
Schoepfer, Martin W. ....New London, CT
Schoepfle, Anne M. ....Southfield, MI
Schoepflin, Frederick W. ....Seattle, WA
Schoepflin, Robert Reath ....Smithtown, NY
Schoepke, Amy M. ....Madison, WI
Schoeppe, Michele M. ....Columbus, OH
Schoeppel, James ....Fairview, OK
Schoeppel, Kevin A. ....Jacksonville, FL
Schoepperle, Richard K. ....Buffalo, NY
Schoeppey, Bryan ....Dallas, TX
Schoeppey, Christina R. ....Kansas City, MO
Schoeppl & Burke, P.A. ....Boca Raton, FL
Schoeppl, Carl F. ....Boca Raton, FL
Schoeppler, Timothy J. ....Madison, WI
Schoeppner, Cynthia W. ....Pittsburgh, PA
Schoeps, Ira S. ....Nyack, NY
Schoeps, Robin J. ....Washington, DC
Schoeps and Specht ....Nyack, NY
Schoer, Gary ....Syosset, NY
Schoer, Jack L. ....Aiken, SC
Schoessler, James M. ....Minneapolis, MN
Schoessler, Michael A.
Department Of The Interior, GV
Schoessow, Carl E. ....Fredericksburg, TX
Schoessow, Cristol N. ....Fredericksburg, TX
Schoettelkotte, William H. ....Newport, KY
Schoettinger, Douglas B. ....Midland, MI
Schoettle, Ekkehard ....Des Plaines, IL
Schoettle, Ferdinand P. ....Minneapolis, MN
Schoettle, Raymond J. ....Indianapolis, IN
Schoettle, Susan P. ....Sarasota, FL
Schoettle, Thomas J., Jr. ....San Diego, CA
Schoettler, James A., Jr. ....Bethesda, MD
Schoettler, John H. ....Palm Springs, CA

Schoettler, R. William, Jr.
Manhattan Beach, CA
Schoettly, Elizabeth H. ....Evanston, IL
Schoettmer, Sara A. ....Cincinnati, OH
Schoettmer, Stephen C. ....Dallas, TX
Schoetz, Kenneth A. ....Buffalo, NY
Schoewe, Philip Gregory ....Lubbock, TX
Schoewe, Timothy R. ....Milwaukee, WI
Schoewe, William M.
Colorado Springs, CO
Schofel, Linda A. ....Roseland, NJ
Schofer, Arthur J. ....Deerfield Beach, FL
Schofer, Joseph L.
Department of Commerce, Patent and Trademark Office, GV
Schoff, Dennis L. ....Fort Wayne, IN
Schoff, H. Keith ....Madison, WI
Schoff, James A. ....Cleveland, OH
Schoff, Paul J. ....Allentown, PA
Schoff, Tara C. ....Portsmouth, NH
Schoff & Wolstein Co., L.P.A.
Cleveland, OH
Schoffelman, Todd Richard ....St. Paul, MN
Schoffstall & Focht, P.C. ....Allentown, PA
Bethlehem, PA
Orefield, PA
Schoffstall, Sally L. ....Orefield, PA
Schofield, Ann E. ....New York, NY
Schofield, Anna M. ....Boulder, CO
Schofield, Anthony W. ....Provo, UT
Schofield & Associates ....Las Vegas, NV
Schofield, Bradford H. ....Belmont, MA
Schofield, Charles T. ....Pasadena, CA
Schofield, Dale H. (Hal) ....Portland, OR
Schofield, Dane C. ....Billings, MT
Schofield, Daniel L. ....Department of Justice, Federal Bureau of Investigation, GV
Schofield, Donald F. ....Amarillo, TX
Schofield, Duane E. ....Veradale, WA
Schofield, E. Victoria ....Rock Springs, WY
Schofield, Eileen M. ....New York, NY
Schofield, Glen W., (L.C.) ....San Jose, CA
Schofield, John D. ....Tyler, TX
Schofield, John P. ....New York, NY
Schofield, Kenneth E. ....Menomonie, WI
Schofield, Lorna G. ....New York, NY
Schofield, Louis F. ....Walnut Creek, CA
Schofield, Martin P. ....Tulsa, OK
Schofield, Mary Anne ....New York, NY
Schofield, Michael J. ....Washington, DC
Schofield, Michael J. ....Pensacola, FL
Schofield, P. Allen ....Bradenton, FL
Schofield, Paul F., (P.C.) ....Chicago, IL
Schofield, Paul H. ....Las Vegas, NV
Schofield, Paul Kevin ....New York, NY
Schofield, R. Scott ....Colorado Springs, CO
Schofield, Robert M. ....Raleigh, NC
Schofield & Schiller, Law Offices
Walnut Creek, CA
Schofield, Schofield & Cosgrove
New York, NY
Schofield & Spencer, P.A. ....Bradenton, FL
Schofield, Stephen J. ....Philadelphia, PA
Schofield, Thomas D. ....Walnut Creek, CA
Schofield, Thomas E. ....Buffalo, NY
Schofield, Tilden R. ....Sebring, FL
Schofield, Timothy J. ....Rochester, NY
Schofield & Wade, P.A. ....Pensacola, FL
Schofield, William W., Jr.
San Francisco, CA
Schofner, Keith A. ....Bloomfield Hills, MI
Schofner, Theodore R. ....Largo, FL
Tampa, FL
Schofner, Theodore R., P.A.
Clearwater, FL
Largo, FL
St. Petersburg, FL
Tampa, FL
Schohl, Albert W. ....Warren, MI
Schohl, Joseph ....Deerfield, IL
Schohn, Joseph L. ....Cambridge, MA
Schoifet, Edward ....New Brunswick, NJ
Schoifet, Edward, A Professional Corporation ....New Brunswick, NJ
Schoknecht, Kim T. ....San Francisco, CA
Schol, Sondra D. ....St. Louis, MO
Scholand, Margaret M. ....Chicago, IL
Scholar, Ronald J. ....Sacramento, CA
Scholar, Sam D. ....Falls Church, VA
Scholar, Sandra Kaye
Office of Personnel Management, Compensation Division, GV
Schold, Donald K. ....Naples, FL
Schold, John D. ....St. Louis, MO
Scholder, Paul A. ....New Haven, CT
Scholder, Paul A., Attorney at Law, P.C.
New Haven, CT
Schole, Allen ....New York, NY
Scholefield, Pamela J. ....Santee, CA
Scholer, Randal J. ....Cedar Rapids, IA
Scholer, Steven A. ....Omaha, NE
Scholes, Donald L. ....Nashville, TN
Scholes, Richard A. ....Montpelier, VT
Scholes, Steven S. ....Chicago, IL
Scholfield, Jack P. ....Mercer Island, WA
Scholhamer, Kristen E. ....Hartford, CT
Scholick, Gary P. ....San Rafael, CA
Scholin, Margo S. ....Houston, TX
Scholl, Amy F. ....Madison, WI
Scholl, Charles E. ....Grand Rapids, MI
Scholl, Chester B., Jr. ....Sharon, PA
Scholl, David A. ....Philadelphia, PA
Scholl, David B.
Federal Deposit Insurance Corporation, Office of Personnel Management, GV
Scholl, Debra S. ....Miami, FL
Scholl, Dennis, (P.A.) ....Coral Gables, FL
Scholl, Donald E. ....Tarpon Springs, FL

Scholl, Donald F., Jr. ... Flemington, NJ
Scholl, Glenn L. ... Farmington, CT
Scholl & Hamlin, P.C. ... Ilion, NY
Scholl, Harvey Jay ... Boca Raton, FL
Scholl, Jacob A. ... Seattle, WA
Scholl, Jane S. ... Hartford, CT
Scholl, Janet C. ... Pittsburgh, PA
Scholl, John D. ... Worthington, MN
Scholl, Judith T. ... Bronx, NY
Scholl, Lawrence E. ... Cincinnati, OH
Scholl, Linda D. ... Memphis, TN
Scholl, Marc Frazier ... New York, NY
Scholl, Marcie M. ... Columbus, OH
Scholl, Marlin F. ... Detroit, MI
Scholl, Mary Biacsi ... Cleveland, OH
Scholl, Melissa S. ... Greensburg, IN
Scholl, Robert P. ... Westport, CT
Scholl, Ronald F. ... Monterey, CA
Scholl, Roy W., III ... Birmingham, AL
Scholl, Roy W., III, P.C. ... Birmingham, AL
Scholl, Stefan J. ... Petoskey, MI
Scholl, Stephen G. ... Houston, TX
Scholl, Steven M. ... Chicago, IL
Scholl, Steven S. ... Albuquerque, NM
Scholl & Stieg ... Detroit, MI
Scholl, Verne C. ... Carlsbad, CA
Scholl, Wendy Anne ... Los Angeles, CA
Scholl, William F. ... Elm Grove, WI
Scholl, William V., Jr. ... Elizabeth, PA
Schollaert, Robert C. ... Chambersburg, PA
Schollander, Wendell L. ... Winston-Salem, NC
Schollars, D. Robert
North Kansas City, MO
Schollars, Rhoda E. ... Tucson, AZ
Scholle & Beisel, Ltd. ... Minneapolis, MN
Scholle, Mark ... Minneapolis, MN
Scholle, Paul R. ... Terre Haute, IN
Scholle, Stephen G. ... Minneapolis, MN
Schollenberger, Julia ... Los Angeles, CA
Scholler, Thomas P. ... Grand Rapids, MI
Scholles, James R. ... Cincinnati, OH
Scholles, Jeffrey J. ... Cincinnati, OH
Scholles & Scholles ... Cincinnati, OH
Scholley, Susan E. ... Zephyr Cove, NV
Schollian, Jerry ... Baltimore, MD
Westminster, MD
Scholly, Robert E. ... Rockville Centre, NY
Scholnick, Helaine A. ... Chicago, IL
Scholnick, John N. ... Chicago, IL
Scholnick, Lauren I. ... Salt Lake City, UT
Scholnick, Leonard ... Brooklyn, NY
Scholnick, Melvyn P. ... Miami, FL
Scholnick, Seymour A. ... Los Angeles, CA
Scholnik, Louis N., (P.A.)
Fort Lauderdale, FL
Scholom, Jacob ... Baltimore, MD
Scholte, Gordon D.
San Juan Capistrano, CA
Scholten and Fant, A Professional Corporation ... Grand Haven, MI
Grand Rapids, MI
Holland, MI
Scholten, Harvey L. ... Grand Haven, MI
Scholten, Maarten R. (IBA) ... New York, NY
Scholtens, Jay ... Jonesboro, AR
Scholtes, Michael E. ... Oakland, CA
Scholtes, William E. ... Baltimore, MD
Scholtz, Charles E. ... Louisville, KY
Scholtz, Jill Slipper ... Minneapolis, MN
Scholtz, Kenneth P. ... Los Angeles, CA
Scholtz, Nina E. ... Los Angeles, CA
Scholtz, Otto R. ... Palo Alto, CA
Scholz, Alan W. ... Pacifica, CA
Scholz, Birte Susanne ... Redwood City, CA
Scholz, Calvin W. ... Rockport, TX
Scholz, Charles A. ... Quincy, IL
Scholz, Charles W. ... San Antonio, TX
Scholz, Christopher G. ... Quincy, IL
Scholz, David A. ... Chicago, IL
Scholz, Elizabeth A. ... Scottsdale, AZ
Scholz, Fred J. ... Fremont, CA
Scholz, Heidi K. ... La Jolla, CA
San Jose, CA
Scholz, Joseph R. ... Newark, NJ
Scholz, Loos, Palmer, Siebers & Duesterhaus
Quincy, IL
Scholz, Louis A. ... Sykesville, MD
Scholz, Melissa Auchard ... Madison, WI
Scholz, Richard L. ... Bullhead City, AZ
Scholz, Robert D. ... Portland, OR
Scholz, Robert F. ... Baltimore, MD
Scholz, Robert W. ... Atlanta, GA
Scholz, Wesley S. ... Department of State, Bureau of Economic and Business Affairs, GV
Scholze, Richard ... Burlington, WI
Schomaker, Richard C. ... Pittsburgh, PA
Schomber, Philip R. ... Beloit, WI
Schomber, Scott R. ... Miami, FL
Schomburg, Glen C. ... St. Louis, MO
Schomburg, James B. ... Hartford, CT
Schomburg, John S. ... Minneapolis, MN
Schomburg, John S., P.A. ... Minneapolis, MN
Schomburger, John L. ... McKinney, TX
Schomer, Alvin R. ... Haddonfield, NJ
Schomer, Fred K. ... Fremont, MI
Schomer, Janet E. ... New York, NY
Schomer, John B. ... Akron, OH
Schomer, John H. ... Jackson, MI
Schomer, Kerry L. ... Carson City, NV
Schomer, Morton W. ... Washington, DC
Schomer, Scott P. ... Los Angeles, CA
Schomig, Jeffrey P. ... Baltimore, MD
Schomisch, John T., Jr. ... Appleton, WI
Schommer, Nicholas G., (P.A.) ... Sebring, FL
Schomp, Bonnie J. ... Oklahoma City, OK
Schon, Alan W. ... Hampton, VA
Schon, David F. ... Washington, DC
Schon, Jack ... Southfield, MI
Schon, Steven E. ... San Francisco, CA
Schonauer, Kimberly A. ... Philadelphia, PA
Schonberg, Bruce A. ... Goshen, NY
Schonberg, Edward R. ... Detroit, MI
Schonberg, Evelyn P. ... Cleveland, OH
Schonberg, Michael E. ... Dallas, TX
Schonberg, William E. ... Cleveland, OH
Schonberger, Anita Beth ... Boca Raton, FL
Schonberger, Arne Carl ... El Paso, TX
Schonberger, Eugene ... Fairfax, VA
Schonberger, Lawrence M. ... Fairfax, VA
Schonberger, Mark ... New York, NY
Schonbrun, Benjamin ... Venice, CA
Schonbrun & Desimone, LLP ... Venice, CA
Schonbrun, Harvey A. ... Tampa, FL
Schonbrun, Harvey, P.A. ... Tampa, FL
Schonbrun, Scott E. ... Clayton, MO
Schonbuch, Michael N. ... Los Angeles, CA
Schondebare, James A. ... Ronkonkoma, NY
Schondel, Matthew A. ... Santa Rosa, CA
Schondorf, Eric Lowell
New Hyde Park, NY
Schone, Larry T. ... Delray Beach, FL
Schonekas, Russell J. ... New Orleans, LA
Schoneman, William A. ... Murray Hill, NJ
Schonenberg, Frederick G., Jr.
Wynantskill, NY
Schonfeld, Alan H. ... San Diego, CA
Schonfeld, Arthur D. ... North Hollywood, CA
Schonfeld, Daniel ... Tucson, AZ
Schonfeld, David S. ... Fullerton, CA
Schonfeld, Joel ... New York, NY
Schonfeld, Joshua L. ... McLean, VA
Schonfeld, Mark ... Boston, MA
Schonfeld, Mark K. ... New York, NY
Schonfeld, Neely ... Washington, DC
Schonfeld, Richard A. ... Las Vegas, NV
Schonfeld, Robert L. ... Garden City, NY
Schonfeld, Victoria E. ... New York, NY
Schonfeld & Weinstein, LLP ... New York, NY
Schonhaut, Neal L. ... Princeton, NJ
Schonholtz, Margot B. ... New York, NY
Schoninger, Samuel F.
Colorado Springs, CO
Schonland, Rodney C. ... Boston, MA
Schonman, Gary P.
Federal Communications Commission, Wireless Telecommunications Bureau, GV
Schons, Larry H. ... Eugene, OR
Schons, Larry H., P.C. ... Eugene, OR
Schonthaler, Gary K. ... Erie, PA
Schonwald, Gary A. ... New York, NY
Schonwald, George D. ... Parsippany, NJ
Schonwald & Iskra ... Parsippany, NJ
Schoo, Henry J. ... Louisville, KY
Schoof, Gary J. ... La Porte, IN
Schoof, Szilagyi & Davis ... La Porte, IN
Schooff, George T. ... Troy, MI
Schooh, Frederick C. ... Columbus, OH
Schook, Nancy J. ... Louisville, KY
Schoolcraft, Alan L. ... Universal City, TX
Schoolcraft, David A. ... Lansing, MI
Schoolcraft, David G. ... Seattle, WA
Schoolcraft, David W. ... Glastonbury, CT
Schoolcraft, Kenneth G., Jr.
Anchorage, AK
Schoolenberg, David ... Grand Rapids, MI
Schooler, David A. ... Minneapolis, MN
Schooler, David R.
House of Representatives, Committee Legal Personnel, GV
Schooler, Don A. ... Oklahoma City, OK
Schooler, Jane L. ... San Diego, CA
Schooler, John T. ... Los Angeles, CA
Schooler, Lionel M. ... Houston, TX
Schooler, Michael S. ... Washington, DC
Schooler, Richard H. ... San Francisco, CA
Schooler, Scott H. ... Cleveland, OH
Schooler, Steven J. ... Madison, WI
Schooler, Stewart ... San Antonio, TX
Schooley, Elizabeth W. ... Pittsburgh, PA
Schooley, J. Bradley ... Indianapolis, IN
Schooley, Kimberly Y. ... Boston, MA
Schooley, R. William ... Ann Arbor, MI
Schooley, Renee E. ... Belleville, IL
Schooley, Sarah E. ... Amherst, MA
Schooley, Sharon K. ... Tulsa, OK
Schooley, Steven R. ... Orlando, FL
Schooley, Thomas E. ... Granite City, IL
Schooley, Timothy Michael ... Sacramento, CA
Schooley, Vern D. ... Long Beach, CA
Schooley, Virginia G. ... Chicago, IL
Schooley, William W. ... Belleville, IL
Schooley, William W. ... Granite City, IL
Schooley, William W., III ... Granite City, IL
Schooley, Wilson Adam ... La Mesa, CA
Schoolfield, Allen P., Jr. ... Dallas, TX
Schoolfield, Bruce W., Jr. ... Houston, TX
Schoolfield, Jas. W. ... Dallas, TX
Schooling, John W. ... Chico, CA
Schooling, Roy L. ... Edmond, OK
Schooling, Russell F. ... La Mirada, CA
Schoolman, Richard ... Brooklyn, NY
Schoolmaster, James H.
Bloomfield Hills, MI
Schools, Scott N. ... Charleston, SC
Schools, Shelly W. ... Washington, DC
Schools, Terrene M. ... San Diego, CA
Schoon, Cris A. ... Colorado Springs, CO
Schoon, Cris A., P.C. ... Colorado Springs, CO
Schoon, Eugene A. ... Chicago, IL
Schoon, Peter E., Jr. ... Loveland, CO
Schoone, Adrian P. ... Racine, WI
Schoone, Fortune, Leuck, Kelley & Pitts, S.C. ... Racine, WI
Schooner, Heidi M. ... Washington, DC
Schoonhoven, Ray J. ... Chicago, IL
Schoonmaker, Duane D. ... Rochester, NY
Schoonmaker & Friedberg, LLP
Schenectady, NY
Schoonmaker, George & Colin, P.C.
Darien, CT
Greenwich, CT
New Canaan, CT
Stamford, CT
Schoonmaker, George W. ... Seattle, WA
Schoonmaker, Jan ... House of Representatives, Congressional Assistants, GV
Schoonmaker, John R. ... Lansing, MI
Schoonmaker, Karen Ann ... Brookville, NY
Schoonmaker, Linda C. ... Houston, TX
Schoonmaker, Lisa K. ... Schenectady, NY
Schoonmaker, Meyressa H.
Winston-Salem, NC
Schoonmaker, Neill W., Jr. ... Ware, MA
Schoonmaker, Peter W. ... Chicago, IL
Schoonmaker, Samuel V., III
Greenwich, CT
Schoonmaker, Samuel V., IV
Greenwich, CT
Schoonmaker & Schoonmaker ... Ware, MA
Schoonover, Alice D. ... Brookfield, WI
Schoonover, Dale J. ... Minneapolis, MN
Schoonover, Donald R. ... Kansas City, MO
Schoonover, Jack R. ... Lakeland, FL
Schoonover, Jacquelyn K.
Minneapolis, MN
Schoonover, John E. ... Cleveland, OH
Schoonover, John H. ... Minneapolis, MN
Schoonover, Kristen Leigh ... Dallas, TX
Schoonover, Linda D. ... Longwood, FL
Schoonover, Linda D., P.A. ... Longwood, FL
Orlando, FL
Schoonover, Martha J. ... Washington, DC
Schoonover, Mary E. ... Lexington, KY
Schoonover, Paul D., (P.C.) ... Dallas, TX
Schoonover, Steven L. ... Minden, LA
Schoonover, Steven T. ... San Rafael, CA
Schoonveld, Eric P. ... Chicago, IL
Schoop, Devlin J. ... Chicago, IL
Schoor, Charles D. ... Los Angeles, CA
Schoorl, Arie G. ... Sacramento, CA
Schoor-Rube, Daniel ... New York, NY
Schoor-Rube, Patricia A. ... Stamford, CT
New York, NY
Schoos, Geoffrey A. ... Seekonk, MA
Schop & Pleskow, LLP ... Buffalo, NY
Erie, PA
Schop, Stephen J. ... Buffalo, NY
Schopf, Gregory E. ... San Francisco, CA
Schopf, Joshua N. ... Washington, DC
Schopf, Simeon M. ... Washington, DC
Schopf & Weiss ... Chicago, IL
Schopf, William G. ... Chicago, IL
Schopick, Daniel F. ... Bridgeport, CT
Schopler, Andrew G. ... Chapel Hill, NC
Schopmeyer, G. Michael ... Evansville, IN
Schopp, David C. ... Buffalo, NY
Schopp, N. Richard ... Port St. Lucie, FL
Schopp, N. Richard, P.A. ... Port St. Lucie, FL
Schopper, Mary A. ... Indianapolis, IN
Schoppert, Jeffrey S. ... San Rafael, CA
Schoppmann, Michael J. ... Bridgewater, NJ
Schor, Jeffrey D. ... Los Angeles, CA
Schor, Kenneth M.
Department of Commerce, Patent and Trademark Office, GV
Schor, Laurence ... Washington, DC
Schor, Michael ... New York, NY
Schor, Neil D. ... Youngstown, OH
Schor, Renee S. ... San Diego, CA
Schor, Robert H. ... New York, NY
Schor, Robert M. ... West Hartford, CT
Schor, Susan L. ... Washington, DC
Schor, William ... New York, NY
Schore, Niles ... Drexel Hill, PA
Schoren, James A. ... Norwalk, OH
Schorer, Joseph U. ... Woodstock, IL
Schorlemer, Suzanne E. ... San Antonio, TX
Schorling, Douglas D. ... Fresno, CA
Schorling, William H. ... Cherry Hill, NJ
Philadelphia, PA
Schorman, Robert H., Jr. ... Los Angeles, CA
Schorn, Frank J. ... New York, NY
Schorn, Harold F., II. ... Newton, KS
Schorn, John F. ... Treasury Department, Office of the General Counsel, GV
Schornack-Smith, Judith Ann ... Detroit, MI
Schornak, Donald G. ... Xenia, OH
Schornhorst, F. Thomas ... Bloomington, IN
Schornstein, Jay M. ... Portland, OR
Schornstein, Sherri L. ... Washington, DC
Schorpp, Edward L. ... Carlisle, PA
Schorr, Adam Wilder ... Los Angeles, CA
Schorr, Alan ... Marlton, NJ
Schorr, Alan H., P.C. & Associates
Marlton, NJ
Schorr, Amy B. ... New York, NY
Schorr, Andrew Daru ... Tucson, AZ
Schorr, Andrew W. ... New York, NY
Schorr, Brian D. ... Lyndhurst, OH
Schorr, Brian L. ... New York, NY
Schorr, Charles A. ... Omaha, NE
Schorr, David K. ... Washington, DC
Schorr, David L. ... Compton, CA
Schorr, Edward T. ... Honolulu, HI
Schorr, Eleanor D. ... Tucson, AZ
Schorr, Elisa Cullen ... New York, NY
Schorr, Elizabeth L. ... New York, NY
Schorr, Gary H. ... Federal Trade Commission, Bureau of Competition, GV
Schorr, Gerald J. ... Bala Cynwyd, PA
Philadelphia, PA
Schorr, Gerard J. ... Houston, TX
Schorr, Gloria P. ... Long Beach, CA
Schorr, Jon M. ... Seattle, WA
Schorr, Jonathan M. ... New York, NY
Schorr, Lawrence ... Hawaiian Gardens, CA
Schorr, Lawrence J. ... Binghamton, NY
Schorr, Lewis D. ... Tucson, AZ
Schorr, Mark B., (P.A.) ... Fort Lauderdale, FL
Schorr, Mark D. ... Trenton, NJ
Schorr, Mark M. ... Lincoln, NE
Schorr, Matthew S. ... Springfield, NJ
Schorr, Max ... Palm Beach, FL
Schorr, Nanette H. ... Bronx, NY
Schorr, Naomi ... New York, NY
Schorr, Neil ... Newark, NJ
Schorr, Saml. A. ... New York, NY
Schorr, S. L. ... Tucson, AZ
Schorr, Stephen A. ... Fort Lauderdale, FL
Schorr, Steven ... San Diego, CA
Schorr, Thomas E. ... Princeton, NJ
Schorre, Al W., Jr. ... Midland, TX
Schorr-Miller, Jill ... Atlantic City, NJ
Schorsch, Daniel ... Waynesboro, VA
Schorsch, John B., Jr. ... Dallas, TX
Schorsch, Martin B. ... Norridge, IL
Schorsch, Walter B. ... White Plains, NY
Schorsch Jones, Linda ... Waynesboro, VA
Schortgen, Steven G. ... Dallas, TX
Schory, Earl A., II ... Salem, OH
Schoshinski, Robert S. ... Washington, DC
Schoshinski, Terence W. ... Santa Monica, CA
Schossberger, Steven F. ... Boise, ID
Schostag, Alan D. ... Roseville, CA
Schostak, David W. ... Southfield, MI
Schostek, Rick ... Marysville, OH
Schostok, Michael P. ... Waukegan, IL
Schostok, Stephen J. ... Park Ridge, IL
Schoth, Karl W., Law Offices of
Glendora, CA
Schoth, Karl W., Law Offices of
Los Angeles, CA
Schotland, Marvin I. ... Los Angeles, CA
Schotland, Roy A. ... Washington, DC
Schotland, Sara D. ... Washington, DC
Schotsky, Arnold M. ... Melville, NY
Schott, Albert J. ... Stillwater, OK
Schott, Anne R. ... Washington, DC
Schott, Carolyn W. ... Kalamazoo, MI
Schott, Clifford J. ... Lakeland, FL
Schott, Cynthia ... Madison, WI
Schott, David R. ... London, KY
Schott, David R. ... Medford, OR
Schott, David R., P.S.C. ... London, KY
Schott, Dietmar E. ... San Diego, CA
Schott, Donald K. ... Madison, WI
Schott, Donald L. ... Cincinnati, OH
Schott, Elizabeth A. ... New Albany, IN
Schott, Elizabeth P. ... St. Louis, MO
Schott, Frank William ... Hillside, NJ
Schott, Frederic M. ... Orlando, FL
Schott, Frederic M., P.A. ... Orlando, FL
Schott, George E. ... Elmira, NY
Schott, Grace Mercer ... Los Gatos, CA
Schott, Gregory F. ... Sterling, IL
Schott, Gretchen ... Washington, DC
Schott, Helen L. ... Madison, WI
Schott, Howard M. ... Boston, MA
Schott, Jeana Sciarappa
Redondo Beach, CA
Schott, Jennifer ... San Francisco, CA
Schott, Jennifer Kaplan ... Chicago, IL
Schott, John F. ... Akron, OH
Schott, Joshua H ... New York, NY
Schott, Judy Cannella ... Covington, LA
Schott, L. Grace Mercer ... Los Gatos, CA
Schott, Lawrence D. ... Hallandale Beach, FL
Schott, Lee A. ... Des Moines, IA
Schott, Lewis M. ... Palm Beach, FL
Schott, Louis G. ... New Orleans, LA
Schott, Martin A. ... Baton Rouge, LA
Schott, Mary Monica ... Council Bluffs, IA
Schott, Max J., II ... Minneapolis, MN
Schott, Max James ... Des Moines, IA
Schott, Michelle M. ... Livingston, NJ
Schott, Nancy L. ... Dearborn, MI
Schott, Nash W. ... Alexandria, VA
Schott, Newton B., Jr. ... Stamford, CT
Schott, Patk. M. ... New Orleans, LA
Schott, Patrick J. ... Brookfield, WI
Schott, Robert H. ... Stuart, FL
Schott, Robert H., P.A. ... Stuart, FL
Schott, Ronald J. ... Short Hills, NJ
Schott, Stephen ... Menlo Park, CA
Schott, Stephen C. ... Washington, DC
Schott, Stephen M. ... St. Louis, MO
Schott, Stephen P. ... New Orleans, LA
Schott, Steven M. ... Alpharetta, GA
Schott, William R. ... Franklin, MI
Schotte, Jack P. ... Corte Madera, CA
Schottelkotte, Michael R. ... Delta, CO
Schottenfeld, David J. ... Plantation, FL
Schottenfeld, David J., P.A. ... Plantation, FL
Schottenstein, Diane ... New York, NY
Schottenstein, Edwin E. ... Louisville, KY
Columbus, OH
Schottenstein, James M. ... Columbus, OH
Schottenstein, James M., Co. L.P.A.
Columbus, OH
Schottenstein, Tamara L. ... San Francisco, CA
Schottenstein, Zox & Dunn, A Legal Professional Association ... Cincinnati, OH
Cleveland, OH
Columbus, OH
Schott Ferguson, Amy ... Cincinnati, OH
Schottky, Andrew R., Jr. ... Sacramento, CA
Schottland, Manning, Rosen & Caliendo, A Professional Association ... Freehold, NJ
Schottland, Michael D. ... Freehold, NJ
Schottle, Melody L. ... Schaumburg, IL
Schottmiller, Thomas C. ... Wayne, NJ

Schotz, Edward M. ... Hackensack, NJ
Schou, Norman ... Treasury Department, Office of Thrift Supervision, GV
Schouboe, Lee M. ... Portland, OR
Schouest, Brett W. ... San Antonio, TX
Schouest, John L. ... Houston, TX
Schoulson, Jay C. ... Long Island City, NY
Schoumacher, Bruce H. ... Chicago, IL
Schouman, Daniel J. M. ... Walled Lake, MI
Schourup, Serena M. ... Seattle, WA
Schouten, Dick A. ... Beaverton, OR
Schouten, Mark J. ... Sioux Center, IA
Schouten, Nicholas, Jr. ... San Bernardino, CA
Schouten, Paul R. ... Orland Park, IL
Schouten, Richard F ... Chicago, IL
Waukesha, WI
Schouten, Ronald ... Boston, MA
Schouten, Thomas W. ... Wyoming, MI
Schouvieller, Mary ... St. Paul, MN
Schouweiler, Bart M. ... Reno, NV
Schouweiler, Robert L. ... Carson City, NV
Schovajsa, Christina K. ... Houston, TX
Schovajsa, Henry J. ... La Grange, TX
Schovajsa, Wm. H. ... La Grange, TX
Schovanec, Philip A. ... Oklahoma City, OK
Schovanec, Sandra Leah
Oklahoma City, OK
Schovee, John R. ... Pittsford, NY
Schoville & Arnell L.L.P. ... San Diego, CA
Schoville, Dennis A. ... San Diego, CA
Schow, Don R. ... Salt Lake City, UT
Schow, Horace, II ... Tallahassee, FL
Schow, John B. ... Garland, TX
Schow, Lynn-Anne M. ... New York, NY
Schow, O.E., IV ... Knoxville, TN
Schowalter, Deborah ... Atlanta, GA
Schowalter & Edwards, S.C. ... West Bend, WI
Schowalter, Ronald O. ... St. Louis, MO
Schowalter, Thomas A. ... Milwaukee, WI
Schowalter, Timm W. ... St. Louis, MO
Schoyer, David K. ... Pittsburgh, PA
Schpero, Gary S. ... New York, NY
Schpok, Terry M., (P.C.) ... Dallas, TX
Schraa, David J. ... New York, NY
Schrack, Jennifer R. ... Los Angeles, CA
Schrack, William D., III ... Dillsburg, PA
Schrad, Dana G. ... Richmond, VA
Schrade & Heinrichs ... Delmar, NY
Schrade, Karl H. ... Delmar, NY
Schrade, Mary Jo ... Atlanta, GA
Schrade, Richard D.C., Jr.
Stockbridge, GA
Schrader, Alfred E. ... Akron, OH
Schrader, Andrew G. ... North Bangor, NY
Schrader, Brett A. ... Houston, TX
Schrader, Brian E. ... New York, NY
Schrader, Bruce R., II ... Akron, OH
Schrader Byrd & Companion, PLLC
Martins Ferry, OH
Steubenville, OH
Weirton, WV
Wheeling, WV
Schrader, Charles D. ... Toledo, OH
Schrader, Charles R. ... Portland, OR
Schrader, Charley J., Jr. ... Houma, LA
Schrader, Chris A. ... Lakeview, OH
Schrader, Craig V. ... Des Moines, IA
Schrader, Daniel P. ... Monterey, CA
Schrader, David L. ... Los Angeles, CA
Schrader, David L. ... Dade City, FL
Schrader, David Louis ... St. Louis, MO
Schrader, David Scott ... Little Rock, AR
Schrader, Dennis L. ... Georgetown, DE
Schrader, Dieter J. ... Huntsville, AL
Schrader, Douglas K. ... Annapolis, MD
Baltimore, MD
Schrader, Earl H., Jr. ... Kansas City, MO
Schrader, George D. ... Montgomery, AL
Schrader, Gerald L.
General Services Administration, Office of the General Counsel, GV
Schrader, Howard S. ... New York, NY
Schrader, Jerome G. ... Dade City, FL
Schrader, John P. ... Lexington, KY
Schrader, Johnson, Auvil & Brock, P.A.
Dade City, FL
Schrader, Kathleen B. ... Milwaukee, WI
Schrader, Kurt D. ... Binghamton, NY
Schrader, Leo W. ... Clearwater, FL
Schrader, Linda McMullen ... Tallahassee, FL
Schrader, Lynn R. ... Lexington, KY
Schrader, Mark G. ... Belleville, IL
Schrader, Michael E. ... Portland, OR
Schrader, Michael F. ... Coral Gables, FL
Schrader, Michael Steven ... Plymouth, MN
Schrader, Norman E. ... Rochester, NY
Schrader, Phyllis G. ... San Diego, CA
Schrader, Robert E., III ... Jacksonville, FL
Schrader, Robert G. ... Fort Lauderdale, FL
Schrader, Robert V. ... Ann Arbor, MI
Schrader, Robert W. ... Cheyenne, WY
Schrader, Russell W. ... San Francisco, CA
Schrader, Scott ... New York, NY
Schrader, Stacey B. ... Pacific Grove, CA
Schrader, Stephen J. ... Palo Alto, CA
Schrader, Steven C. ... Decorah, IA
Schrader, Thomas C. ... Cleveland, OH
Schrader, Thomas T. ... Lancaster, WI
Schrader, Tony ... Austin, TX
Schrader, Vanessa V. ... Eagan, MN
Schrader, Wayne A. ... Washington, DC
Schrading, Roger ... Philadelphia, PA
Schraeder, Darren L. ... Dallas, TX
Schraeder, Ivan L. ... Ballwin, MO
Schraeder, Joan M. ... Boston, MA
Schraeder, Terry E. ... Houston, TX
Schraer, George L. ... San Diego, CA
Schraeter, Paul E. ... Atlantic Beach, NY

Schraf, James R. ... Washington, DC
Silver Spring, MD
Schraff, Christopher R. ... Columbus, OH
Schraff, Paul A. ... Honolulu, HI
Schraffenberger, Mark D. ... Cincinnati, OH
Schraft, Jane ... Bloomington, MN
Schraft, John E. ... Birdsboro, PA
Schrag and Baum ... Berkeley, CA
Schrag, Donald E. ... Wichita, KS
Schrag, Edward A., Jr. ... Columbus, OH
Schrag, Frederic D. ... Berkeley, CA
Schrag, Gary M. ... Walla Walla, WA
Schrag, Minna ... New York, NY
Schrag, Naomi J. ... New York, NY
Schrag, Philip G. ... Washington, DC
Schrag, Raymond V. J. ... New York, NY
Schrag, Susan R. ... Wichita, KS
Schrag, Thomas F. ... Berkeley, CA
Schrag, William H. ... New York, NY
Schrage, Elliot J. ... New York, NY
Schrage, Leon ... Brooklyn, NY
Schrage, Louise R. ... Pittsburgh, PA
Schrage, Marjala, Kaiser & Welter
Eau Claire, WI
Schrage, Mitchell R. ... New York, NY
Schrage, Mitchell R., & Associates, PLLC
New York, NY
Schrage, Robert Alan ... Westport, CT
Schrage, Russell E. ... Des Moines, IA
Schrage, Stephen R. ... Eau Claire, WI
Schrage, Steven P. ... Washington, DC
Schrager, Allen E. ... South Bend, IN
Schrager, Amy ... New York, NY
Schrager, Barry ... Upper Montclair, NJ
Schrager, Carol A. ... New York, NY
Schrager, David L. ... Cedarhurst, NY
Schrager, Edward F. ... Indianapolis, IN
Schrager, Gerald N., (P.C.) ... New York, NY
Schrager, Harley D. ... Omaha, NE
Schrager, Julie Sarah ... Boston, MA
Schrager, Leonard Jay ... Chicago, IL
Schrager, Richard S. ... Rockville, MD
Schrager, S. Robert ... New York, NY
Schrager, Samuel L. ... Storrs, CT
Schrager & Schrager ... Cedarhurst, NY
Schrager, Sylvia T. ... Annandale, VA
Schragger, Andrew J. ... Lawrenceville, NJ
Schragger, Bruce M. ... Trenton, NJ
Schragger, Frederic J. ... Lawrenceville, NJ
Schragger, Henry C. ... Trenton, NJ
Schragger, James A. ... Trenton, NJ
Schragger, Lavine & Nagy
Lawrenceville, NJ
New Brunswick, NJ
Princeton, NJ
Trenton, NJ
West Trenton, NJ
Woodbridge, NJ
Schragger, Richard C. ... Washington, DC
Schragin, Howard Todd ... New York, NY
Schraibman, Sandra M.
Department of Justice, Civil Division, GV
Schraidt, James A. ... Chicago, IL
Schraier, Mark Z. ... St. Louis, MO
Schram, Anthony B. ... San Antonio, TX
Schram, Behan and Behan ... Okemos, MI
Schram, Bradley J. ... Bloomfield Hills, MI
Schram, Brenda A. ... Houston, TX
Schram, David B. ... New York, NY
Schram, Deborah C. ... Dayton, OH
Schram, Deborah C. ... Xenia, OH
Schram, Earl, Jr. ... Hudson, NY
Schram, Ivy V. ... Pittsburgh, PA
Schram, Jason ... Chicago, IL
Schram, Kevin M. ... Beaver Dam, WI
Schram, Leonard ... Glencoe, IL
Schram, Marc B. ... Hazlet, NJ
Schram, Peter S. ... New York, NY
Schram, Robert D. ... Miami, FL
Schram, Ronald B. ... Boston, MA
Schram, Ronald Y. ... Gainesville, FL
Schram, Ross L., III ... Chattanooga, TN
Schram, Stephen A. ... San Francisco, CA
Schram, Steven H. ... Washington, DC
Schram, Thomas H. ... Bloomfield Hills, MI
Schram, W. Neal ... La Jolla, CA
Schram, Walter S. ... Southfield, MI
Schrama, Martin P. ... Freehold, NJ
Schrameck, Marilyn Kay
Oklahoma City, OK
Schramel, Ronald J. ... Windom, MN
Schraml, Laurie A. ... Sarasota, FL
Schramm, Ann T. ... New Orleans, LA
Schramm, Cynthia L. ... Chicago, IL
Schramm, Damon E. ... Minneapolis, MN
Schramm, Daniel R. ... St. Louis, MO
Schramm, David ... Pittsburgh, PA
Schramm, Dean A. ... St. Louis, MO
Schramm, Donald L. ... Chicago, IL
Schramm, Erik Alan ... St. Clairsville, OH
Schramm, Harold B. ... Bridgewater, CT
Schramm, Harvey J. ... St. Louis, MO
Schramm, Howard M., Jr. ... Mobile, AL
Schramm, I. C. ... Syracuse, NY
Schramm, John J., Jr. ... Winston-Salem, NC
Schramm, Julie ... Boston, MA
Schramm, Kenneth R. ... Oregon City, OR
Schramm, LeRoy H. ... Helena, MT
Schramm, LoRetta Cummings ... Bayville, NY
Schramm, Marilyn J. ... Battle Creek, MI
Schramm, Mark A. ... Chicago, IL
Schramm, Paul H. ... St. Louis, MO
Schramm & Pines, L.L.C. ... Clayton, MO
St. Louis, MO
Schramm, Richard D. ... San Jose, CA
Schramm, Robert J. ... Perry, FL
Schramm, Susan ... Boston, MA
Schramm, Virginia M. ... San Antonio, TX

Schramm, William H. ... St. Louis, MO
Schramm, William J. ... Troy, MI
Schranck, Frederick H. ... Dover, DE
Schranck, Timothy O. ... St. Louis, MO
Schrand, James R. ... Covington, KY
Schrandt, Judith D. ... Albuquerque, NM
Schrandt, Stephanie A.
San Francisco, CA
Schrang, Michael Scott ... Atlanta, GA
Houston, TX
Schranghamer, Daniel F. ... Philadelphia, PA
Schrank, Charles E. ... Chicago, IL
Schrank, Edward A., (P.A.) ... Longwood, FL
Schrank, Fredk. ... St. James, NY
Schrank & Harrington ... St. James, NY
Schrank, Herbert ... New York, NY
Schrank, Raymond E., II ... Milwaukee, WI
Schrank, Robert M. ... Eugene, OR
Schrank, Stephen C. ... Newport Beach, CA
Schrank, William J. ... Phoenix, AZ
Schrant, Nancy Lankenau ... Boulder, CO
Schrant, Thomas M. ... Denver, CO
Schrantz, Nathan L. ... New Orleans, LA
Schrantz, R. Douglas ... Rogers, AR
Schranze, Bernard W. ... Bridgewater, MA
Schratwieser, Diane Beaudry
Federal Energy Regulatory Commission, Office of the General Counsel, GV
Schratwieser, Hugh C.
Department of Commerce, National Oceanic and Atmospheric Administration, GV
Schratwieser, John C. ... New Orleans, LA
Schratwieser, Mary K. ... Houston, TX
Schratz, James P. ... Glen Ellen, CA
Schraub, Billie B. ... Seguin, TX
Schraub & Company, Chtd., A Prof. Law Corp. ... McLean, VA
Washington, DC
Schraub, Frederick D. ... Austin, TX
San Antonio, TX
Schraub, J. Jonathan ... McLean, VA
Schraud, Gloria ... Concord, NH
Schraudner & Hillier ... Bozeman, MT
Schraudner, Leanne M. ... Bozeman, MT
Schrauff, Christopher W. ... Austin, TX
Schraufnagel, John C. ... Omaha, NE
Schrauth, William L. ... Utica, NY
Schraver, David M. ... Rochester, NY
Schraw, Thomas M. ... Boyne City, MI
Schrawyer, Lewis M. ... Colville, WA
Schrebler, Roland M. ... Baltimore, MD
Schreck, Andrew Z. ... Houston, TX
Schreck, Cheryl L. ... Los Angeles, CA
Schreck, David L. ... San Francisco, CA
Schreck, Frank A. ... Las Vegas, NV
Reno, NV
Schreck, Frederick R. ... Newark, NJ
Schreck, George C. ... Portland, OR
Schreck, Gordon D. ... Charleston, SC
Schreck, Ira ... New York, NY
Schreck, Jeffrey C. ... Providence, RI
Schreck, Jennifer K. ... Denver, CO
Schreck, John Wm. ... Wayne, PA
Schreck Law Associates ... Wayne, PA
Schreck, Mark I. ... New York, NY
Schreck Morris ... Las Vegas, NV
Reno, NV
Schreck, Myron ... Moscow, ID
Schreck, Nelse T. ... Albuquerque, NM
Schreck, Patricia A. ... Wayne, PA
Schreck, Raymond C. ... Los Angeles, CA
Schreck, Richard A. ... Cleveland Heights, OH
Schreck, Robert A., Jr. ... Chicago, IL
Schreck, Robert J. ... Buffalo, NY
Schreck Rose & Dapello ... New York, NY
Schreckengast, Lovern & Helm
Indianapolis, IN
Schreckengast, William O. ... Indianapolis, IN
Schreckengaust, Samuel A., Jr.
Harrisburg, PA
Schreckinger, Stephen P. ... New York, NY
Schreckinger, Steven L. ... Boston, MA
Schreckinger, Wendy B. ... Newark, NJ
Schreder, Carleen L. ... Chicago, IL
Schreder, Ellen M. ... Brooklyn Center, MN
Schreeder, Charles L., III ... Atlanta, GA
Schreeder, Lauren B. ... Chicago, IL
Schreeder, Wheeler & Flint, LLP
Atlanta, GA
Schreer, Andrew ... Wood Dale, IL
Schreffler & Associates ... New York, NY
White Plains, NY
Schreffler, Kenneth E. ... Bensalem, PA
Schreffler, Kenneth E., P.C., Law Offices of
Bensalem, PA
Schreffler, Neil F. ... New York, NY
Schreger, Elaine C. ... New York, NY
Schreger, Ira A. ... New York, NY
Schreibeis, George D. ... Columbus, OH
Schreiber, Ainslee Ann ... New York, NY
West Nyack, NY
Schreiber, Alan H. ... Fort Lauderdale, FL
Schreiber, Allison P. ... St. Louis, MO
Schreiber & Associates, P.C. ... Boston, MA
Danvers, MA
Dracut, MA
Lake Success, NY
Schreiber, Avram H. ... New York, NY
Schreiber, B. David ... New York, NY
Schreiber, Berthold H. ... Harwood Heights, IL
Schreiber, Bradley A. ... Belle Fourche, SD
Rapid City, SD
Schreiber, Bradley J. ... Rockford, IL
Schreiber, Brian C. ... Pittsburgh, PA
Schreiber, Burton S. ... Rochester, NY
Schreiber, Carey D. ... New York, NY
Schreiber, Catherine Dorn ... Riverside, CA

Schreiber, Charles J., Jr. ... Tallahassee, FL
Schreiber, Christina A.
San Francisco, CA
Schreiber, Cynthia N. ... Roslyn Estates, NY
Schreiber, Dale A. ... New York, NY
Schreiber, Darryl S. ... Hollywood, FL
Schreiber, David E., P.C. ... Bethesda, MD
Schreiber, David L. ... Essex, NY
Schreiber, David L. ... Tarrytown, NY
Schreiber, David L. ... Harrisburg, PA
Schreiber, Deborah L. ... Waltham, MA
Schreiber, Denise Foster ... Winona, MS
Schreiber, Donald E. ... Sunnyvale, CA
Schreiber, Donald E., A Professional Corporation ... Sunnyvale, CA
Schreiber, Douglas K. ... Encino, CA
Schreiber, Edward R. ... Newark, NJ
Schreiber, Edwin C. ... Los Angeles, CA
Schreiber, Eliot B. ... Northbrook, IL
Schreiber, Elliot J. ... New York, NY
Schreiber, Eric A. ... Los Angeles, CA
Schreiber, Erika L. ... Los Angeles, CA
Schreiber, Eugene H. ... Baltimore, MD
Schreiber, Frances P. ... New York, NY
Schreiber & Friedman, P.C. ... Linwood, NJ
Schreiber, Gary E. ... Huntington Beach, CA
Schreiber, Gay R. ... Chicago, IL
Schreiber, George J. ... Troy, MI
Schreiber, George J. ... North Wales, PA
Schreiber & Grier, P.C. ... Troy, MI
Schreiber, Herbert G. ... Danville, CA
Schreiber, Howard E. ... Dallas, TX
Schreiber, Ira L. ... Cranston, RI
Schreiber, Irving ... New York, NY
Schreiber, Jack R. ... Des Moines, IA
Schreiber, James P., (A Professional Corporation) ... Beverly Hills, CA
Schreiber & Jarstad ... Wabasha, MN
Schreiber, Jeanette Carpenter
New Haven, CT
Schreiber, Jeffrey ... East Brunswick, NJ
New York, NY
Schreiber, Jeffrey A. ... Danvers, MA
Dracut, MA
Lake Success, NY
Schreiber, Jeffrey D. ... Kingwood, TX
Schreiber, Jessica ... Port Angeles, WA
Schreiber, John T., Law Offices of
Walnut Creek, CA
Schreiber, Joseph Allen ... Birmingham, AL
Schreiber, Joseph P. ... Chicago, IL
Schreiber, Julian D. ... Chicago, IL
Schreiber, Karen L. ... Minneapolis, MN
Schreiber, Katherine L. ... Upper Darby, PA
Schreiber, Kenneth A. ... Cranston, RI
Schreiber, Kenneth J. ... Kew Gardens, NY
Schreiber, Kurt G. ... Nashville, TN
Schreiber, Lee A. ... Fort Myers, FL
Schreiber, Lenore ... Fresno, CA
Schreiber, Leonard I. ... New York, NY
Schreiber, Margaret H. ... Orlando, FL
Schreiber, Mark ... Encino, CA
Schreiber, Mark ... Los Angeles, CA
Schreiber, Mark B. ... Austin, TX
Schreiber, Mark E. ... Boston, MA
Schreiber, Mark P. ... San Francisco, CA
Schreiber, Martin J. ... Milwaukee, WI
Schreiber, Martin J., Law Firm
Milwaukee, WI
Schreiber, Marvin ... Pittsburgh, PA
Schreiber, Marvin Z.
Department Of Health And Human Services, GV
Schreiber, Matthew D. (IBA) ... Sunnyvale, CA
Schreiber, Mayo, Jr. ... New York, NY
Schreiber, Michael H. ... Linwood, NJ
Schreiber, Michael S. ... New York, NY
Schreiber, Myron N. ... Chicago, IL
Schreiber, Palmer Kress ... Philadelphia, PA
Schreiber, Paul ... Orland Park, IL
Schreiber, Paul R. ... Orland Park, IL
Schreiber, Paul S. ... New York, NY
Schreiber, Philip M. ... New York, NY
Schreiber, Philippe S. E. ... New York, NY
Schreiber, Phillip Michael ... Chicago, IL
Schreiber, Richard B. ... Orinda, CA
Schreiber, Richard D. ... St. Louis, MO
Schreiber, Richard J. ... Chicago, IL
Schreiber, Richard M. ... Red Wing, MN
Schreiber, Robert A. ... Miami, FL
Schreiber, Robert E., Jr. ... Milwaukee, WI
Schreiber, Robert P. ... Morristown, NJ
Schreiber, Roberta A. ... Middleton, MA
North Reading, MA
Schreiber, Rodd M. ... Chicago, IL
Schreiber, Ronald ... Chicago, IL
Schreiber, Rudolf L. ... Washington, DC
Schreiber, Ryan A. ... West Caldwell, NJ
Schreiber, Sally A. ... Dallas, TX
Schreiber, Sally P. ... Philadelphia, PA
Schreiber, Sanford D. ... Baltimore, MD
Schreiber & Schreiber ... Cranston, RI
Schreiber & Schreiber, Inc.
Los Angeles, CA
Schreiber, Scott B. ... Washington, DC
Schreiber, Scott N. ... Chicago, IL
Schreiber, Scott R. ... Las Vegas, NV
Schreiber, Scott T. ... Chicago, IL
Schreiber, Sidney M. ... Morristown, NJ
Schreiber, Sol ... New York, NY
Schreiber, Stephen D.
Pension Benefit Guaranty Corporation, Office of the General Counsel, GV
Schreiber, Stephen J. ... New York, NY
Schreiber, Stephen R. ... Plano, TX
Schreiber, Steven H. ... Cincinnati, OH
Schreiber, Susan ... Chicago, IL
Schreiber, Svetlana J. ... Cleveland, OH

Schreiber, Tera H. ....Seattle, WA
Schreiber, Vernon L. ....Vancouver, WA
Schreiber, Warren N. ....West Springfield, MA
Schreiber, W. E. ....Whitefish, MT
Schreiber, William B. ....New York, NY
Schreiber, William M. ....Red Bank, NJ
Schreiber, William R. ....Palo Alto, CA
Schreiberg, Frances C. ....Oakland, CA
Schreiberg, Sheldon L. ....Washington, DC
Schreiber II, Martin H. ....Baltimore, MD
Schreiber-Murray, Beth V. ....Chicago, IL
Schreiber-Parkhill, Sheila T. ....Tucson, AZ
Schreibersdorf, Lisa ....Brooklyn, NY
Schreibman, Barbara H. Fort Lauderdale, FL
Schreibman, Barry Martin ....Syracuse, NY
Schreibman, Eric M. ....Cleveland, OH
Schreibman, Isaac S. ....Woodbury, NY
Schreibman, Julian D. ....Washington, DC
Schreibman, Ted M. ....Pittsburgh, PA
Schreibstein, Jerome ....San Francisco, CA
Schreibstein, Richard B. ....Baltimore, MD
Schreier, Andrew M. ....New York, NY
Schreier, Arthur M. ....White Plains, NY
Schreier, Connie J. ....Eureka, MT
Schreier, David M. ....New York, NY
Schreier, Douglas B. ....Los Angeles, CA
Schreier, Gordon J. ....Pittsburgh, PA
Schreier, Holly J. ....Dallas, TX
Schreier, James M. ....Chicago, IL
Schreier, James S. ....Los Angeles, CA
Schreier, Jay B. ....Royal Oak, MI
Schreier, Jean E. ....New York, NY
Schreier, Jeffrey B. ....New York, NY
Schreier, Joel S. ....Chicago, IL
Schreier, Jordan S. ....Ann Arbor, MI
Schreier, Karen E. ....Sioux Falls, SD
Schreier & Kelley ....Eureka, MT
Schreier, Konrad F., III ......Los Angeles, CA
Schreier, Sherwin ....Royal Oak, MI
Schreier, Theodore R. ....New York, NY
Schreier, W. Terrance ....Kansas City, MO
Schreifels, LeRoy J. ....Brooklyn Park, MN
Schreifels, Roseann T. ....Minneapolis, MN
Schreiman, J. Leonard ....Southfield, MI
Schreimann, Daniel W. ....Dallas, TX
Schreimann, Duane E. Jefferson City, MO
Schrein, Patricia L. ....Washington, DC
Schreiner, C. Bryson ....Pittsburgh, PA
Schreiner, C. Mark ....Flagstaff, AZ
Schreiner, David E. ....Cleveland, OH
Schreiner, Eric J. ....Paoli, PA
Schreiner, James E. ....Schererville, IN
Schreiner, Joanne M. ....Cincinnati, OH
Schreiner, Lance D., P.C. ....Bismarck, ND
Schreiner, Laura Ann Bloomfield Hills, MI
Schreiner & Malloy, P.C. ....Schererville, IN
Schreiner, Michael W. ....Denver, CO
Schreiner, Robt. D. ....Ortonville, MN
Schreiner, Robt. E. ....Denver, CO
Schreiner, Scott L. ....Owatonna, MN
Schreiner, Stephen L. ....San Diego, CA
Schreiner, Stephen T. ....Washington, DC
Schreiner, Steven P. ....Los Angeles, CA
Schreiner, Steven T. ....Washington, DC
Schreiner, Thomas E. ....Westlake, OH
Schreiner, Urban J. ....Los Angeles, CA
Schreiner, William A., Jr. New Orleans, LA
Schreiner, William Edward Morgantown, KY
Schreiter, James G. ....Florham Park, NJ
Schreiter, Larry R. ....Kent, WA
Schrekinger, Frederick W. ....Golden, CO
Schrekinger, Frederick W. ....Lakewood, CO
Schremp, Pamela S. ....Cleveland, OH
Schrempf, James E. ....Alton, IL
Schrempp, Albert F. ....Oklahoma City, OK
Schrenk, Edward L. ....San Antonio, TX
Schrenk, Michael L. ....Seattle, WA
Schrenk, Roger L. ....Minneapolis, MN
Schrenk, William J., Jr. ....New York, NY
Schrepfer, John J. A. ....Manchester, NH
Schrepfer, Katherine Hilton ....Chicago, IL
Schrepfer & Paradis ....Manchester, NH
Schrepferman, Richard L. ....Denver, CO
Schreppler, John J., II ....Wilmington, DE
Schrero, Elizabeth D. ....New York, NY
Schreter, Lisa A. ....Atlanta, GA
Schretter, Judith D. ....Department of Justice, Criminal Division, GV
Schreuder, Ellen G. ....Warren, MI
Schreuer, Elisabeth ....Boston, MA
Schreur, Richard G. ....Portage, MI
Schreurs, Cynthia L. ....Burlingame, CA
Schreurs, Kate M. ....Santa Ana, CA
Schreve, Lawrence Bernard ....Houston, TX
Schrey, Stephen G. ....San Francisco, CA
Schreyer, Dean M. ....Woodland Hills, CA
Schreyer, Frederic E. ....Portland, OR
Schreyer, Frederick J. ....Averill Park, NY
Schreyer, Leslie John ....New York, NY
Schreyer, Walter K. ....Westwood, NJ
Schriar, Seymour ....Chicago, IL
Schriber, Arthur B. ....Mesa, AZ
Schriber, Kenneth L. ....Dayton, OH
Schriber, Wendy J. ....New York, NY
Schrick, Darrell L. ....Sunnyvale, CA
Schricker, David E. ....Redwood City, CA
Schricker, David E., Law Offices of, A Prof. Corp. ....Redwood City, CA
Schrider, John E. ....Cincinnati, OH
Schrieberg, Henry J. ....Richmond, VA
Schriefer, Carole C. ....Fort Collins, CO
Schriefer, Debra K. ....Houston, TX
Schriefer, George J. ....Pinellas Park, FL
Schrieffer, Paul K. ....West Covina, CA
Schriemer, James A. ....Ann Arbor, MI
Schrier and Balin ....Boston, MA
Schrier, Harvey Mitchell ....Salinas, CA
Schrier, James R. ....Lafayette, IN
Schrier, John C. ....Muskegon, MI
Schrier, Lori E. ....Miami, FL
Schrier, Lynn E. ....Stow, OH
Schrier, Martin T. ....Miami, FL
Schrier, Michael J. Office Of Special Counsel, GV
Schrier, Morris M. ....New York, NY
Schrier, Paul E. ....San Francisco, CA
Schrier, Paul K. ....Miami, FL
Schrier, Richard E. ....Garden City, NY
Schrier, Stephen D. ....Haddonfield, NJ
Schrier, Steven M ....Silver Spring, MD
Schrier, Stuart T. ....Boston, MA
Schrier-Polak, Carol ....Arlington, VA
Schrier-Rape, Deborah Lynn ....Dallas, TX
Schriever, Andrew P ....New York, NY
Schrils, Frederick S. ....Tampa, FL
Schrimp, Angela L. ....Sacramento, CA
Schrimp, Roger M. ....Modesto, CA Oakdale, CA
Schrimpf, Bruce D. ....Milwaukee, WI
Schrimpf, Stephen P. ....Edwardsville, IL
Schrimpf, Thomas R. ....Milwaukee, WI
Schrimpf, William W., Sr. ....Pittsburgh, PA
Schrimsher, B. Scott ....Charlotte, NC
Schrimsher, Frank L. ....Charlotte, NC
Schrimsher, Jack H. ....Kansas City, MO
Schrimshire, James B. ....Huntsville, AL
Schrinar, Howard ....Cheyenne, WY
Schriner, Bonnie M.J. ....Denver, CO
Schrinsky, Jacob L. ....Milwaukee, WI
Schriver, Elizabeth ....Alexandria, VA
Schriver, John T., III ....Chicago, IL
Schriver, Sandra S. ....Van Buren, AR
Schriver, Steven P. Pension Benefit Guaranty Corporation, Office of the General Counsel, GV
Schrock, Alan M. ....Pontiac, IL
Schrock, David E. ....Mason City, IA
Schrock, John Vernon ....Joliet, IL
Schrock, Lisa E.Douglass .....Springfield, MO
Schrock, Norma J. ....Washington, DC
Schrock, Ray C. ....Chicago, IL
Schrock, Sheri Gronhovd ....Phoenix, AZ
Schrock, Stephen B. ....Atlanta, GA
Schrock, Sterling W. ....St. Joseph, MI
Schrock, W. Fletcher McMurry Paducah, KY
Schrock, Wesley D. ....Anderson, IN
Schrode, Kristi Elaine ....Washington, DC
Schroder, Andrew J., III ....White Plains, NY
Schroder, Barry C. ....Grand Rapids, MI
Schröder, Ginger D. ....Buffalo, NY
Schroder, Jack Spalding, Jr. ....Atlanta, GA
Schroder, John C., Jr. ....Oroville, CA
Schroder, Karie E. ....Los Angeles, CA
Schroder, Katherine L. Federal Communications Commission, Common Carrier Bureau, GV
Schroder, Kirk T. ....Richmond, VA
Schroder Law Offices, P.C. Grand Rapids, MI
Schroder, Michael H. ....Atlanta, GA
Schroder, Michael T. ....Garden City, NY
Schroder Partners LC ....Atlanta, GA
Schroder, Paul Steel ....Blacksburg, VA
Schroder, R. Curtis ....West Chester, PA
Schroder, Regina J. ....Sacramento, CA
Schroder, Robert J. ....Covington, KY
Schroder, Robert Lanzon ....Troy, MI
Schroder, Sherrie A. ....Fort Worth, TX
Schroder, Wilfrid A. ....Crestview Hills, KY
Schroder, William H., Jr. ....Atlanta, GA
Schrodt, David I. ....Chicago, IL Grand Rapids, MI
Schroeck and Associates, P.C. ....Erie, PA
Schroeck, Bonnie ....Teaneck, NJ
Schroeck, Felicia R. ....Erie, PA
Schroeck, George M. ....Erie, PA
Schroeder, Alan C. ....Boone, IA
Schroeder, Alfred A. ....San Antonio, TX
Schroeder, Alfred G. ....Madison, KS
Schroeder & Anderson ....Mason City, IA
Schroeder, Anthony D. ....Columbus, OH
Schroeder, Asher E. ....Maquoketa, IA
Schroeder, Beth Ackerman Los Angeles, CA
Schroeder, Bill E. ....Los Angeles, CA
Schroeder, Bradford L. ....Green River, WY
Schroeder, Bradley P. ....Des Moines, IA
Schroeder, Brett ....Kansas City, MO
Schroeder, Brian F. ....Minneapolis, MN
Schroeder, Bruce E. ....Kenosha, WI
Schroeder, Bruce L. ....Seattle, WA
Schroeder, Carl F. ....Wheaton, IL
Schroeder, Carl F., Ltd. ....Wheaton, IL
Schroeder, Carolyn A. ....Geneva, IL
Schroeder, Catherine A. ....St. Louis, MO
Schroeder, Catherine A. ....St. Louis, MO
Schroeder, Charles F. ....Birmingham, MI
Schroeder, Charles F. ....Milwaukee, WI
Schroeder, Christopher H. ....Durham, NC
Schroeder, Clifton P. ....Denver, CO
Schroeder, Clinton A. ....Minneapolis, MN
Schroeder, Clyde A. ....Ottawa, OH
Schroeder, D. Renee ....Rockford, IL
Schroeder, Daniel J. ....Stockton, CA
Schroeder, Danny L., Jr. ....Peoria, IL
Schroeder, David A. ....Erie, PA Pittsburgh, PA
Schroeder, David E. ....Chicago, IL
Schroeder, David E. ....Springfield, MO
Schroeder, David T. ....Grand Island, NE
Schroeder, Debra L. ....Fort Wayne, IN
Schroeder, DeGraw, Kendall, Mayhall, DeGraw & Dickerson ....Marshall, MI
Schroeder, Delilah Seroussi Treasury Department, Internal Revenue Service, GV Baltimore, MD
Schroeder, Denise Groves ......Baton Rouge, LA
Schroeder, Donald E. ....Oklahoma City, OK
Schroeder, Donald R. ....Tucson, AZ
Schroeder, Donald R. ....Madison, WI
Schroeder, Donald W. ....Philadelphia, PA
Schroeder, Douglas J. ....Troy, MI
Schroeder, Douglas W. ....Santa Ana, CA
Schroeder, Duane W. ....Wayne, NE
Schroeder, E. Wayne ....Decatur, IL
Schroeder, Edmund R. ....New York, NY
Schroeder, Edward ....San Antonio, TX
Schroeder, Edward C., Jr. ....Berkeley, CA
Schroeder, Edward H. ....Northbrook, IL
Schroeder, Edward J. ....San Diego, CA
Schroeder, Edward P. ....Ronkonkoma, NY
Schroeder, Edwin M. ....Tallahassee, FL
Schroeder, Elaine D. ....Scarsdale, NY
Schroeder, Eric M. ....West Sacramento, CA
Schroeder, Eric M. ....New Orleans, LA
Schroeder, Eric P. ....Atlanta, GA
Schroeder, Ernest R. ....Pascagoula, MS
Schroeder, Everett J. ....Minneapolis, MN
Schroeder, Franceska O. ....Washington, DC
Schroeder, Francis X. ....Hempstead, NY
Schroeder, Frederick A. ....Yuba City, CA
Schroeder, Frederick S. ....Sacramento, CA
Schroeder, Gary J. ....Gonzales, TX
Schroeder, George L. ....Monterey, CA
Schroeder, Gerald A. ....Department of Justice, Office of Intelligence Policy and Review, GV
Schroeder, Gerald F. ....Boise, ID
Schroeder, Gilbert J. ....Chicago, IL
Schroeder, Gilliat G. ....Media, PA
Schroeder, Glenn C. ....Seattle, WA
Schroeder, Gregory W. ....Jefferson City, MO
Schroeder, Gregory Z. ....Atlanta, GA Decatur, GA
Schroeder Group, The, Attorneys at Law, S.C. ....Waukesha, WI
Schroeder, H. Kenneth, Jr. ....Buffalo, NY
Schroeder, Harry A. ....Chicago Heights, IL
Schroeder, Helene D. Commodity Futures Trading Commission, Division of Trading and Markets, GV
Schroeder, Herman F. ....Ballwin, MO
Schroeder, Herman M. ....New Orleans, LA
Schroeder, J. Conrad ....Playa Del Rey, CA
Schroeder, J. Michael ....New York, NY
Schroeder, Jack Barr ....New York, NY
Schroeder, James A. ....Neptune, NJ
Schroeder, James C. ....Chicago, IL
Schroeder, James C. ....New York, NY
Schroeder, James W. ....Washington, DC
Schroeder, Jan M. ....Milwaukee, WI
Schroeder, Jane E. ....Herndon, VA
Schroeder, Jeanne L. ....New York, NY
Schroeder, Jeannie L. ....Minneapolis, MN
Schroeder, Jeffery Alan ....Toledo, OH
Schroeder, Jeffery T. ....Lincoln, NE
Schroeder, Jeffrey J. ....Denver, CO
Schroeder, Jeffrey P. ....Miami, FL
Schroeder, Jerome B. ....Findlay, OH
Schroeder, Jill Gradwohl ....Lincoln, NE
Schroeder, Joan M. ....Minneapolis, MN
Schroeder, John ....Brea, CA
Schroeder, John E. ....Sigourney, IA
Schroeder, John G. ....San Jose, CA
Schroeder, John L. ....Geneva, IL
Schroeder, John N. ....Reno, NV
Schroeder, John T. ....Boise, ID
Schroeder, John Walter ....Santa Clara, CA
Schroeder, Jon S. ....Curtis, NE
Schroeder, Joseph C. ....Ottawa, OH
Schroeder, Joseph E. ....Marshall, MI
Schroeder, Joseph R. ....Marshall, IL
Schroeder, Katherine J. ....Portland, OR
Schroeder, Kathryn L. ....Denver, CO
Schroeder, Keith A. ....Jackson, MI
Schroeder, Kent A. ....Kearney, NE
Schroeder, Kent C. ....Brighton, CO
Schroeder, Kim R. ....Hugoton, KS
Schroeder, Kimberly B. ....Findlay, OH
Schroeder, Kurt Allan Federal Communications Commission, Common Carrier Bureau, GV
Schroeder, Kurt S. ....Belleville, IL
Schroeder, Lana Woolsey ....Columbia, MO
Schroeder & Larche, P.A. Boca Raton, FL
Schroeder, Laura A. ....Portland, OR
Schroeder Law Office ....Charles City, IA
Schroeder Law Offices ....Portland, OR
Schroeder, Lee J. ....Department of Commerce, Patent and Trademark Office, GV
Schroeder, Leila O. ....Baton Rouge, LA
Schroeder, Lexie D'Ann ....San Jose, CA
Schroeder & Lezamiz, Law Offices, L.L.P. Boise, ID
Schroeder, Lloyd F. (Fred) ....Metairie, LA
Schroeder, Lori M. ....Austin, TX
Schroeder, Lori N. ....Monterey Park, CA
Schroeder, Louis R. ....Chicago, IL
Schroeder, M. Richard ....New Orleans, LA
Schroeder & Mandel, PA ....St. Paul, MN
Schroeder, Margaret S. San Francisco, CA
Schroeder, Mark A. ....Brodhead, WI Janesville, WI
Schroeder, Mark E. ....Hamden, CT
Schroeder, Mark F. ....Cary, IL
Schroeder, Mark G. ....St. Paul, MN
Schroeder, Mark W. ....Chicago, IL
Schroeder, Mary Beth ....Toms River, NJ
Schroeder, Mary Bruntrager ....St. Louis, MO
Schröeder, Mary E. ....Oxnard, CA
Schroeder, Mary M. ....Phoenix, AZ
Schroeder, Mary Margaret ....Springfield, MA
Schroeder, Mary T. ....Mascoutah, IL
Schroeder, Matthew A. ....Union, MO
Schroeder, Matthew J. ....Dallas, TX
Schroeder, Maundrell, Barbiere & Powers Cincinnati, OH
Schroeder, McLetchie & Clough Ossipee, NH
Schroeder, Megan DeLamar Commodity Futures Trading Commission, Executive Staff, GV
Schroeder, Meryl T. ....Mascoutah, IL
Schroeder, Michael A. ....Boca Raton, FL
Schroeder, Michael A. ....Rocky River, OH
Schroeder, Michael J. ....Carrollton, TX
Schroeder, Michael J., (P.C.) Santa Ana, CA
Schroeder, Michael J., P.C. Carrollton, TX
Schroeder, Michele ....New York, NY
Schroeder, Michele D. ....San Jose, CA
Schroeder, Michele S. ....Rockford, IL
Schroeder, Milton R. ....Tempe, AZ
Schroeder, Nancy A.J. ....Kerrville, TX
Schroeder, Nancy M. ....Des Plaines, IL
Schroeder, Neil Thomas ....Hillsboro, IL
Schroeder, Norman J. ....White Plains, NY
Schroeder, Norman L., II Lake Worth, FL
Schroeder, Norman L., II, P.A. Lake Worth, FL
Schroeder, Oliver, Jr. ....Cleveland, OH
Schroeder, Otto H. ....Spring, TX
Schroeder, Patrick M. ....Sioux Falls, SD
Schroeder, Paul B. ....Oakland, CA
Schroeder, Paul J., Jr. ....Little Rock, AR
Schroeder, Paul W. ....Chicago, IL
Schroeder, Peter A. ....Indianapolis, IN
Schroeder, Peter V. ....Dallas, TX
Schroeder, R. Glenn ....Syosset, NY
Schroeder, Raymond F., Jr. ....El Cajon, CA
Schroeder, Raymond R. ....Greenville, SC
Schroeder, Reinhold ....South Bend, IN
Schroeder, Richard J. ....St. Paul, MN
Schroeder, Richard J. ....Seattle, WA
Schroeder, Richard J. ....Spokane, WA
Schroeder, Richard W. ....La Crosse, WI
Schroeder, Rick A. ....Agoura Hills, CA
Schroeder, Robert A. ....Los Angeles, CA
Schroeder, Robert F. ....Atlanta, GA
Schroeder, Robert H. ....Ossipee, NH
Schroeder, Robert J. ....Seattle, WA
Schroeder, Robert J. ....Appleton, WI
Schroeder, Robert R. ....Waukesha, WI
Schröeder, Robert W. ....Oxnard, CA
Schroeder, Robert W., & Associates Milwaukee, WI
Schroeder, Robert W., III ....Little Rock, AR
Schroeder, Roger M. ....Los Angeles, CA
Schroeder, Roland G. ....Washington, DC
Schroeder, Russell H., Jr. ....Charles City, IA
Schroeder, Sara ....Davenport, IA
Schroeder & Schroeder ....Boone, IA
Schroeder, Schroeder & Connolly Mascoutah, IL
Schroeder, Schroeder & O'Malley Ottawa, OH
Schroeder, Scott E. ....Duluth, GA
Schroeder, Scott H. ....Milwaukee, WI
Schroeder, Scott L. ....Janesville, WI
Schroeder, Sharon A. ....New Braunfels, TX
Schroeder & Siegfried, P.A. Minneapolis, MN
Schroeder, Stanley G. ....St. Louis, MO
Schroeder, Stephanie Ann ....Los Angeles, CA
Schroeder, Stephen Christopher St. Petersburg, FL
Schroeder, Steven D. ....Kentfield, CA
Schroeder, Steven F. ....Dulles, VA
Schroeder, Stuart R. ....Waukesha, WI
Schroeder, Susan J. ....Springfield, IL
Schroeder, Tami L. ....Minneapolis, MN
Schroeder, Theodore ....Pittsburgh, PA
Schroeder, Theodore J. ....Reno, NV
Schroeder, Thomas A. ....Janesville, WI
Schroeder, Thomas D. Winston-Salem, NC
Schroeder, Thomas E. ....Charlotte, NC
Schroeder, Thomas M. ....Chicago, IL
Schroeder, Thomas P. ....Detroit Lakes, MN
Schroeder, Thomas S. ....Minneapolis, MN
Schroeder, Tricia L. ....Orange, CA
Schroeder, Tyrus ....San Antonio, TX
Schroeder, Van A. ....Bellevue, NE
Schroeder, W. Alan ....Boise, ID
Schroeder, W. Jack ....Evansville, IN
Schroeder, W. Jack, P.C. ....Evansville, IN
Schroeder, Walter A., (P.C.) ....Houston, TX
Schroeder, Walter C. ....Mason City, IA
Schroeder Walthall Neville L.L.P. Houston, TX
Schroeder, Wayne B. ....Denver, CO
Schroeder, Wesley J. ....San Jose, CA
Schroeder, William A. ....Carbondale, IL
Schroeder, William A. ....Rhinelander, WI
Schroeder, William A., III ....New Orleans, LA
Schroeder, William B. ....Rockville, MD
Schroeder, William D., Jr. ....Quakertown, PA
Schroeder, William E. ....New York, NY
Schroeder, William F. ....Jamison, PA
Schroeder, William F., P.C., Sullivan & Powell Vale, OR

Schroeder, William F., (P.C.) ... Vale, OR
Schroeder, William H., Jr. ... Lockhart, TX
Schroeder, William J. ... Spokane, WA
Schroeder, William J., III ... St. Cloud, MN
Schroeder, William L. ... New Braunfels, TX
Schroeder, William P. ... Cincinnati, OH
Schroeder, William W. ... Burlington, VT
Schroeder de Orr, Yvonne ... Anaheim, CA
Schroeder-McCarty, DeDra ... Charles City, IA
Schroeder-Tabary, Karen ... Dallas, TX
Schroedter, Gregory J. ... Chicago, IL
Schroedter, Thomas P. ... Tulsa, OK
Schroeher, Katherine J. ... New Brunswick, NJ
Schroepfer, Kate Turshen ... Denver, CO
Schroepfer, Laurence J. ... Wilmington, DE
Schroepfer, Stephanie M. ... Houston, TX
Schroeppel, Douglas A. ... Buffalo, MN
Schroeppel and Schroeppel ... Buffalo, MN
Schroeppel, Timothy ... Buffalo, MN
Schroer, Charles E. ... Cincinnati, OH
Schroer, Dianna ... Florence, KY
Schroer, Donald A. ... Falls Church, VA
Schroer, Edmund A. ... Merrillville, IN
Schroer, Gene E. ... Topeka, KS
Schroer, Holly A. ... Union, MO
Schroer, Janet M. ... Portland, OR
Schroer, Jeffrey S. ... Corona, CA
Schroer, Jonathan ... Raleigh, NC
Schroer, Kenneth W. ... Panama City, FL
Schroer, Lee C.
Environmental Protection Agency, Office of the General Counsel, GV
Schroer, Michael ... Ann Arbor, MI
Schroer, Randall W. ... Overland Park, KS
Kansas City, MO
Schroer, Rebecca J. ... Tarzana, CA
Schroer, Rice, P.A. ... Topeka, KS
Schroer, Sharon M. ... Washington, DC
Schroer, Steven C. ... Chicago, IL
Schroer, Timothy L. ... Charlottesville, VA
Schroering, Edwin A., Jr. ... Louisville, KY
Schroeter, Goldmark & Bender, P.S.
Seattle, WA
Schroeter, Leonard W. ... Seattle, WA
Schroeter, Mary J. ... Long Beach, CA
Schroeter, Peter W. ... Saco, ME
Schroeter & Sloan, L.L.P. ... Houston, TX
Schroeter, Thomas F. ... Bakersfield, CA
Schroeter, Thomas G. ... Houston, TX
Schrof, Crystal ... Oak Ridge, TN
Schroff, Christine C. Schwartzkopf
Lincoln, NE
Schroff, James P. ... New York, NY
Schroff, Rebecca Lee Tomlinson
Torrance, CA
Schroff, Richard J. ... Niagara Falls, NY
Schroffner, Ingrid C. ... Boston, MA
Schroll, Edward ... Miami, FL
Schroll, James R. ... Arlington, VA
Schroll, Stephanie Anastasi ... Miami, FL
Schron, Dean ... Pittsburgh, PA
Schron, Jack H., Jr. ... Cleveland, OH
Schrope, Brian R., (P.C.) ... Caro, MI
Schropp, Buell & Elligett, Professional Association ... Tampa, FL
Schropp, Charles P. ... Tampa, FL
Schropp, James A. ... Long Beach, CA
Schropp, James H. ... Washington, DC
Schropp, Mark R. ... Hesperia, MI
Schropp, Russell P. ... Fort Myers, FL
Schropp, Tobin A. ... Omaha, NE
Schrot, John J., Jr. ... Birmingham, MI
Schrot, William C. ... Westmont, NJ
Schrotel, Betty F. ... Cincinnati, OH
Schrotel, Stanley R. ... Cincinnati, OH
Schrotenboer, Jerrold E. ... Grand Rapids, MI
Schrotenboer, Jon J. ... Grand Rapids, MI
Schrotenboer, Ronald B. ... Palo Alto, CA
Schroth, Allan ... Los Angeles, CA
Schroth, Andrew B. ... New York, NY
Schroth, David J. ... Trenton, NJ
Schroth, Deborah A. ... Jacksonville, FL
Schroth, John H. ... Green Bay, WI
Schroth, Kevin R. J. ... Hackensack, NJ
Schroth, Peter W. ... Glastonbury, CT
Schroth, Robert A. ... Benicia, CA
Schroth, Steven Neil ... San Diego, CA
Schroy, Paul H. ... Beaverton, OR
Schroyer, Charles P. ... Pierre, SD
Schruefer, John A., Jr. ... Baltimore, MD
Schruhl, Robert A. ... Palmdale, CA
Schrum, Betty-Jane ... Chicago, IL
Schrum, Loren A. ... Lebanon, PA
Schrum, Scott E. ... Seattle, WA
Schrumpf, Charles ... Sulphur, LA
Schrumpf, David W. ... Detroit, MI
Schrumpf, Oliver "Jackson" ... Sulphur, LA
Schrumpf and Schrumpf, P.L.C.
Sulphur, LA
Schrumpf, Stephen E. ... Shelbyville, IN
Schrunk, Irene A. ... Sioux City, IA
Schrunk, Michael D. ... Portland, OR
Schrup, Sarah ... Chicago, IL
Schrupp, Kenneth S. ... Nashville, TN
Schrupp, Mark K. ... Detroit, MI
Schruth, Susan E. ... Atlanta, GA
Schryber, John W. ... Washington, DC
Schryver, David G. ... Washington, DC
Schryver, Karen S. ... San Quentin, CA
Schryver, M. W., Chartered ... Naples, FL
Schryver, Paul C. ... Naples, FL
Schtokal, Jean G. ... Lansing, MI
Schtul, Marc Howard ... Denver, CO
Schu, Brian C. ... Hornell, NY
Schu, Michael E. ... Philadelphia, PA
Schub, Howard W. ... New York, NY
Schub, Michael A. ... Garrison, NY
Schub, Moshe ... Chicago, IL
Schuback, Marc G. ... Mahwah, NJ
Schubart, G. Lawrence ... Tucson, AZ
Schubb, Kenneth D. ... Austin, TX
Schube, Peter H. ... Los Angeles, CA
Schubel, Barbara E. ... Orange, CA
Schubel, David C. ... Medina, NY
Schubel, Jeffrey A. ... Battle Creek, MI
Schubel, Scott L. ... Hagerstown, MD
Schuber, Chas. L. ... Chicago, IL
Schuber, John, Jr. ... Charlotte, NC
Schuber, William P. ... Hackensack, NJ
Schubert, Anne Orrison ... San Antonio, TX
Schubert, Arline F. ... Grand Forks, ND
Schubert, Arthur C. ... Clinton, CT
Schubert, Bellwoar, Cahill & Quinn, A Professional Corporation
Haddon Township, NJ
Philadelphia, PA
Schubert, Christine L. ... Philadelphia, PA
Schubert, Christopher H. ... Doylestown, PA
Schubert, David J., (P.C.) ... Dallas, TX
Schubert, Donald M. ... Richmond, VA
Schubert, Edward S. ... Sunrise, FL
Schubert, Frederick T., II ... Richmond, VA
Schubert, Gail D. ... Los Angeles, CA
Sacramento, CA
Schubert, Gail R. ... Anchorage, AK
Schubert, James J. ... Columbus, OH
Schubert, Jane M. ... Houston, TX
Schubert, Jeffrey ... Houston, TX
Schubert, Jonathan P. ... Phoenix, AZ
Schubert, Joseph B. ... San Francisco, CA
Schubert, Joseph E. ... Milwaukee, WI
Schubert, Kenneth L., III ... Portland, OR
Schubert, Kenneth L., Jr. ... Seattle, WA
Schubert, Margareth ... Chicago, IL
Schubert, Mark D. ... Appleton, WI
Schubert, Melissa A. ... Chicago, IL
Schubert, Melvin ... Warwick, NY
Schubert, Michael H. ... Muskegon, MI
Schubert, P. Terence ... San Luis Obispo, CA
Schubert, Paul F. ... Alexandria, VA
Schubert, Paul R. ... Columbus, OH
Schubert, Rebecca E. ... St. Louis, MO
Schubert & Reed LLP ... San Francisco, CA
Schubert, Richard F. ... Washington, DC
Schubert, Richard J. ... Pittsburgh, PA
Schubert, Richard W. ... Los Angeles, CA
Schubert, R. L. ... Indianapolis, IN
Schubert, Robert C. ... San Francisco, CA
Schubert, S. Terry ... Department of Justice, Criminal Division, GV
Schubert, Samuel A. ... Panama City, FL
Schubert, Thomas E. ... Warren, OH
Schubert, Victor J. ... Irvine, CA
Schubert, Virginia S. ... Minneapolis, MN
Schubert, William C. ... Goleta, CA
Schubert, William D. ... Texarkana, TX
Schubin, Joseph A. ... Brooklyn, NY
Schubin, Milton J. ... New York, NY
Schubin, Myra, (Mrs.) ... White Plains, NY
Schubiner, S. David ... Southfield, MI
Schubiner, Scott Randall ... Troy, MI
Schubiner, Steven P. ... Troy, MI
Schubkegel, Alfred L., Jr. ... Kalamazoo, MI
Schuble, Frank L. ... Dallas, TX
Schuble, Kevin J. ... Houston, TX
Schubot, Gail A. ... Houston, TX
Schuch, Daniel A. ... Manhattan Beach, CA
Schuch, Paul W. ... Cincinnati, OH
Schuch, Robert S. ... Wausau, WI
Schuchard, Robert L. ... Los Angeles, CA
Schuchardt, Elliott J. ... Washington, DC
Schuchardt, Robert G. ... San Francisco, CA
Schuchart, Fred M. ... Spokane, WA
Schuchat, Cook & Werner ... St. Louis, MO
Schuchat, Frank J ... Denver, CO
Schuchat, Michael A. ... Washington, DC
Schuchinski, Luis ... Englewood Cliffs, NJ
Schuchman, Alan D. ... Denver, CO
Schuchman, Alan, Law Offices of
Los Angeles, CA
Schuchman, Frederick E., III
Midland, MI
Schuchman, Jerry ... Abington, PA
Schuchman, Lisa E. ... Seattle, WA
Schuchman & McDonald ... Seattle, WA
Schuchman, Peter F., Jr. ... Reading, PA
Schuchman, Roy S. ... New York, NY
Schuchman, William R. ... Torrance, CA
Schuchmann, John J. ... Toledo, OH
Schucht, Larry D. ... Salem, OR
Schuck, Ben A., III ... Santa Paula, CA
Schuck, Dennis H. ... Glendale, CA
Schuck, Donald Lockhart ... New York, NY
Schuck, Edwin G., Jr. (IBA)
Los Angeles, CA
Los Angeles, CA
Schuck, Frederick J. ... Camden, NJ
Schuck, Gregory L. ... Birmingham, AL
Schuck, John Frederick ... San Jose, CA
Schuck, Kenneth P. ... Muncie, IN
Schuck & McCormmach, P.S. ... Seattle, WA
Schuck, Robert D. ... Columbus, OH
Schuck, Robert Eben ... Findlay, OH
Schuck, Robert S. ... Seattle, WA
Schuck, Thomas R. ... Cincinnati, OH
Schuck, William ... Wallingford, CT
Schuck, William B. ... Columbus, OH
Schucker, Robert V. ... Imperial Beach, CA
Schuckers, Daniel R. ... Harrisburg, PA
Schuckit, Robert J. ... Indianapolis, IN
Schuckman, Robert A. ... Chicago, IL
Schuckman, William A. ... Stockton, CA
Schuckmann, Frank ... Pittsburgh, PA
Schuda, Daniel R. ... Charleston, WV
Schuda & Jones pllc ... Charleston, WV
Schuda, Katherine Tallman ... Palo Alto, CA
Schudel, Paul M. ... Lincoln, NE
Schudel, Teresa M. ... Fairfax, VA
McLean, VA
Schuder, Raymond F. ... Gainesville, GA
Schudson, Charles B. ... Milwaukee, WI
Schueftan, Oliver ... Rockville, MD
Reston, VA
Schuele, Therese M. ... Kansas City, MO
Schueler, J. Carroll ... Kenmore, WA
Schueler, Jas. L. ... Grosse Pointe, MI
Schueler, Jeffrey J.
Department Of Veterans Affairs, Board of Veterans Appeals, GV
Schueler, Kathryn Stegall ... Houston, TX
Schueler, Ken D. ... Rochester, MN
Schueler, Lawrence W. ... Roselle, IL
Schueler, Matthew J. ... Chicago, IL
Schueler, Sister Veronica ... Lowell, MI
Schueler, Stephen G. ... Sea Girt, NJ
Schueler, Stephen W. ... Houston, TX
Schueler, Veronica ... Lowell, MI
Schuelke, C. Brooks ... Austin, TX
Schuelke, Henry F., III ... Washington, DC
Schuelke, John H. ... Gallup, NM
Schuelke, Katherine E. ... San Jose, CA
Schueller, Christopher ... Rochester, NY
Schueller, Joan B. ... Milbank, SD
Schueller, Michael J. ... Milwaukee, WI
Schueller, Thomas G. ... New York, NY
Schuenemeyer, Judith A. ... Wilmington, DE
Schueppert, David G. ... Bemidji, MN
Schueppert, Karen S. ... Bemidji, MN
Schueppert, Mark C. ... Boston, MA
Schueppert, Stephanie R. ... Chicago, IL
Schuerch, Timothy A. ... Kotzebue, AK
Schuerenberg, Charles E. ... Mesquite, TX
Schuerenberg & Grimes, A Professional Corporation ... Mesquite, TX
Schuerger, William J. ... Dallas, TX
Schuering, Christopher D. ... Chicago, IL
Schuering, Daniel P. ... Springfield, IL
Schuering, Donald R. ... Quincy, IL
Schuering, Koratsky & Kerley, P.C.
Springfield, IL
Schuering, Leo H., Jr. ... Sacramento, CA
Schuering, Leo H., Sr. ... Sacramento, CA
Schuering, Mark A. ... Quincy, IL
Schuering Zimmerman & Scully, LLP
Sacramento, CA
Schuerman, Charles ... Colville, WA
Schuerman, Kelley & Craig, Law Offices
Batesville, IN
Versailles, IN
Schuerman, Kimberly ... Memphis, TN
Schuerman, Robert E. ... Columbus, OH
Schuermann, Eleanor C. ... San Jose, CA
Schuermann, Richard W., Jr.
Columbus, OH
Schuesler, Stephen F. ... Lansing, MI
Schuessler, Cindy S. ... Florence, AL
Schuessler, Delores C. ... Mason, OH
Schuessler, John S. ... Azusa, CA
Schuessler, Kenneth J. ... Belleville, IL
Schuessler & Sandlin ... Florence, AL
Schuessler, Thomas A. ... Beaver Dam, WI
Mayville, WI
Schuett, W. Murray, Law Offices of
Dallas, TX
Schuett, Clay Christopher ... Columbus, GA
Schuett, Laura E. ... Milwaukee, WI
Schuett, Linda M. ... Annapolis, MD
Schuett, Marjorie H. ... Madison, WI
Schuett, Stephen D. ... Bakersfield, CA
Schuette, Brian L. ... Bowling Green, KY
Schuette, Charles A. ... Miami, FL
Schuette, David A. ... Chicago, IL
Schuette, Debra S. ... Western Springs, IL
Schuette, James M., and Associates
Washington, DC
Schuette, James M., Jr. ... Washington, DC
Schuette, Jason G. ... Mansfield, TX
Schuette, June B. ... Wilmington, DE
Schuette, Mary K. ... New York, NY
Schuette, Mary L. ... Hartford, WI
Schuette, Maureen Nelson ... Edwardsville, IL
Schuette, Michael ... Chicago, IL
Schuette, P. Michael ... Breese, IL
Schuette, Paul W. ... Cleveland, OH
Schuette, Richard F. ... Wilmington, DE
Schuette, William D. ... Lansing, MI
Schuette, William L., Jr.
Baton Rouge, LA
Schuettpelz, Carl ... Cedar Rapids, IA
Schuetz, Christine L. ... Treasury Department, Financial Crimes Enforcement Network, GV
Schuetz, G. Gregory ... Bloomfield Hills, MI
Schuetz, Reinhold P. ... Port Orchard, WA
Schuetz, Rolf C., Jr. ... Clifton, NJ
Schuetz, Samuel ... Hiawatha, KS
Schuetz, William D. ... San Francisco, CA
Schuetze, Charles F. ... Anchorage, AK
Schuetze, Damon A. ... Las Vegas, NV
Schuetze, Julie Mathews ... Washington, DC
Schuetze, Mark M. ... Buffalo, NY
Schuetze, Robert A. ... Denver, CO
Schuetze, Steven M. ... Pasadena, CA
Schuetzeberg, Jerome H. ... Lubbock, TX
Schuffrin, Gina ... Van Nuys, CA
Schufreider, Charles J. ... Los Angeles, CA
Schug, Lynn M. ... Washington, DC
Schug, Otto F. ... Columbus, IN
Schug, Willis E. ... Quarryville, PA
Schugmann, Roberta E. ... Encinitas, CA
Schuh, Andrew C. ... Woodland Hills, CA
Schuh, Arthur J. ... Cincinnati, OH
Schuh, Arthur L., Jr. ... Appleton, WI
Schuh, Carl A. ... St. Petersburg, FL
Schuh, Charles E. ... St. Petersburg, FL
Schuh, Daniel B. ... St. Petersburg, FL
Schuh & Goldberg, LLP ... Cincinnati, OH
Schuh, James A. ... Boston, MA
Schuh, John A. ... Cincinnati, OH
Schuh, Lisa A. ... Denver, CO
Schuh, Maurice R. ... St. Petersburg, FL
Schuh, Michael W. ... St. Louis, MO
Schuh, N. Fraser, III ... Aventura, FL
Schuh, Robert A. ... Syracuse, NY
Schuh, Robin F. ... New York, NY
Schuh and Schuh ... St. Petersburg, FL
Schuh, Stephen J. ... Cincinnati, OH
Schuh, Steven ... Boston, MA
Schuh, Terry A. ... Sumner, WA
Schuh, William A. ... Scottsdale, AZ
Schuham, Aaron David
Department of Justice, Civil Rights Division, GV
Schuhmacher, Curtis W. ... Chicago, IL
Schuhmacher, Halford George
Marathon, FL
Schuhmacher, Robert E. ... Raleigh, NC
Schuhmann, Barbara L. ... Fairbanks, AK
Schuhmann, George S. ... Louisville, KY
Schuhmann, Nancy ... Arlington, VA
Schuhmann, Thomas M. ... Louisville, KY
Schuit, Michael J. ... Trenton, NJ
Schuitmaker, Cooper & Schuitmaker, P.C.
Kalamazoo, MI
Paw Paw, MI
South Haven, MI
Schuitmaker, Harold ... Paw Paw, MI
Schuitmaker, Tonya L. ... Paw Paw, MI
Schuk, Camellia Kuo ... Irvine, CA
Schukei, Clint L. ... Norfolk, NE
Schukei, Gordon W. ... Cheyenne, WY
Schuknecht, Barbara H. ... Seattle, WA
Schuknecht, Cynthia ... Charles City, IA
Schuknecht, Ronald A. ... Traverse City, MI
Schukoske, Jane E. ... Baltimore, MD
Schukraft, Stephen J. ... Media, PA
Schul, David D. ... Hamilton, OH
Schul, Scott E. ... Portland, ME
Schulak, Donald ... Kensington, CA
Schulaner, Norman ... Newark, NJ
Schular, Karen ... Allentown, PA
Schulberg, Arnold L. ... Hurricane, WV
Schulberg, Howard J. ... Pittsburgh, PA
Schulberg, June S. ... Pittsburgh, PA
Schulberg, Robin E. ... Shreveport, LA
Schulcz, Fred E. ... Los Angeles, CA
Schulcz, Mary C. Torbeck ... Cincinnati, OH
Schuldenfrei, A. Finley ... Baltimore, MD
Schuldenfrei, Harvey I. ... New York, NY
Schulder, Dan A. ... Harrisburg, PA
Schulder, David ... New York, NY
Schulder, Diane B. ... New York, NY
Schulder, Elliott ... Washington, DC
Schulder, Jacob J. ... Atlantic Beach, NY
Schulder, William ... Florham Park, NJ
Schuldiner, Rachael A. ... New York, NY
Schuldiner, Sharon ... New York, NY
Schuldiner, Stanley I. ... Norristown, PA
Schuldiner-Schor, Lori ... Millburn, NJ
Schuldinger, Henry Joseph ... Vienna, VA
Schuldinger, Moshe ... Washington, DC
Schuldt, Eric J. ... New York, NY
Schuldt, Nicholas J., III ... Barnegat, NJ
Schuldt, Nicholas J, III ... Ship Bottom, NJ
Schule, Flora M. ... Tempe, AZ
Schule, John J., III ... Springfield, VA
Schule, Nelson E., Jr. ... Buffalo, NY
Schule, Ronald C. ... Smithtown, NY
Schulenburg, Eric ... Madison, WI
Schulenburg, John A. ... Scottsdale, AZ
Schulenburg & Politan, P.L.C.
Phoenix, AZ
Scottsdale, AZ
Schuler, Albert J. ... Cherry Hill, NJ
Schuler, Alison K., (P.A.)
Albuquerque, NM
Schuler, Arlene R. ... Newton, MA
Schuler & Associates ... Costa Mesa, CA
Schuler, Bradley W. ... Coral Springs, FL
Schuler, Carl Scott ... Jacksonville, FL
Schuler, Cynthia A. ... Toledo, OH
Schuler, Galen G. ... Seattle, WA
Schuler, Gary E. ... Princeton, NJ
Schuler, Gregory G. ... Chicago, IL
Schuler & Halvorson, P.A.
West Palm Beach, FL
Schuler, Henry R., Jr. ... Fort Lauderdale, FL
Schuler, Jack M. ... Los Angeles, CA
Schuler, John D. ... Tulsa, OK
Schuler, John H. ... Wooster, OH
Schuler, John W. ... Millersburg, OH
Schuler, Joseph E. ... Washington, DC
Schuler, Judson C. ... Millersburg, OH
Schuler, Kenneth G. ... Chicago, IL
Schuler, Laura P.
Department Of Health And Human Services, Office of the General Counsel, GV
Bethesda, MD
Schuler, Lawrence D. ... New Brunswick, NJ
Schuler, Louis E. ... Clear Lake, IA
Schuler, Lynda ... Washington, DC
Schuler, Mark A. ... Des Moines, WA
Schuler, Messersmith & Daly
Albuquerque, NM
Schuler, Paul G. ... Loves Park, IL
Schuler, Peter L. ... Louisville, KY
Schuler, Raymond F. ... Costa Mesa, CA
Schuler, Richard D.
West Palm Beach, FL
Schuler, Richard P. ... Batavia, OH
Schuler, Robert A. ... Tucson, AZ
Schuler, Robert Carl ... Columbus, OH
Schuler, Robert D. ... Birmingham, MI

Schuler, Robert G. ... **Columbus, OH**
Schuler, Ronald W. ... **Pittsburgh, PA**
Schuler, Scott David ... San Antonio, TX
Schuler, Thomas P. ... Springfield, MA
Schuler, Timothy C. ... Seminole, FL
Schuler, W. Lance ... **Houston, TX**
Schuler, Walter E. ... **Memphis, TN**
Schuler, William F. ... **Wellesley, MA**
Schuler, William P. ... Chalmette, LA
Schuley, Phillip H. ... **Newton, KS**
Schulgasser, David S. ... Buffalo, NY
Schulgasser, Henry W. ... Scottsdale, AZ
Schulgasser, Leon I. ... Brooklyn, NY
Schulgen, Edward V. ... Philadelphia, PA
Schulhof, Amy L. ... New York, NY
Schulhof, H. Tuck ... Indianapolis, IN
Schulhof, Jonathan ... New York, NY
Schulhof, Robert P. ... Carbondale, IL
Schulhof, Thomas B. ... New York, NY
Schulhofer, Ellen ... **Las Vegas, NV**
Reno, NV
Schulhofer, S. Jason ... **Las Vegas, NV**
Schulhofer, Sanford B., Jr. (A P.C.)
Woodland Hills, CA
Schuling, Mark R. ... **Des Moines, IA**
Schulingkamp, David P. ... New Orleans, LA
Schulist, Kimberly Borah ... **San Rafael, CA**
Schulke, Gerald J. ... The Woodlands, TX
Schulke, J. Kim ... **Great Falls, MT**
Schulke, Kurt P. ... Las Vegas, NV
Schulken, Linda M. ... **Chico, CA**
Schulkens, Michael L. ... Newport, KY
Schulkin, Alan W. ... Seattle, WA
Schulkin, Jeffrey A. ... **Chicago, IL**
Schulkin, Vicki L.
Department Of Health And Human Services, Office of the General Counsel, GV
Schulkind, Laura J. ... **Emeryville, CA**
San Francisco, CA
Schull, E. Gunner ... **Honolulu, HI**
Schull, E. Gunner, Jr. ... Honolulu, HI
Schull, Lisa M. ... **San Francisco, CA**
Schulle, Wallis E. ... North Palm Beach, FL
Schuller, Annemarie ... Gainesville, FL
Schuller, David M. ... **New York, NY**
Schuller, Earl ... Los Angeles, CA
Schuller, Edward L. ... Chicago, IL
Schuller, Elizabeth Gerken ... Defiance, OH
Schuller, Gallit ... New York, NY
Schuller, Henri ... Encino, CA
Schuller, James L. ... Toledo, OH
Schuller, Kevin C. ... Milwaukee, WI
Schuller, Lars E. ... **Knoxville, TN**
Schuller, Mirjam ... **Dallas, TX**
Schuller, Randy P. ... Greenville, MO
Schuller, Robert W. ... **Kansas City, MO**
Schuller, Stephen ... **Tulsa, OK**
Schuller, Walter ... Hamtramck, MI
Schullian, Theodore R ... Springfield, IL
Schully, O. Foerster, III ... **New Orleans, LA**
Schully, Roberts, Slattery, Jaubert & Marino, A Professional Law Corporation
Metairie, LA
New Orleans, LA
Schulman, Alan ... Cincinnati, OH
Schulman, Allen, Jr. ... **Columbus, OH**
Schulman, Allen L. ... Baltimore, MD
Schulman, Alvin H. ... **New York, NY**
Schulman, Amy W. ... **New York, NY**
Schulman, Ann W. ... **New York, NY**
Schulman, B. Aaron ... **Alexandria, VA**
Schulman, Barry A. ... Beverly Hills, CA
Schulman, Bernard ... New York, NY
Schulman, Bertram F. ... Woodmere, NY
Schulman, Beth-Ann
Altamonte Springs, FL
Schulman, Brian ... **Phoenix, AZ**
Schulman, Brian J. ... **Phoenix, AZ**
Schulman, Carole Chipchin ... Potomac, MD
Schulman, Charles E. ... Woodmere, NY
Schulman, Charles Eric ... Boston, MA
Schulman, Charles P. ... **Chicago, IL**
Schulman, Clifford A. ... **Miami, FL**
Schulman, Dan J. ... **New York, NY**
Schulman, Danny G. ... Marietta, GA
Schulman, David A. ... Salisbury, NC
Schulman, David A. ... Austin, TX
Schulman, David B., (P.C.) ... **Chicago, IL**
Schulman, David H. ... Fullerton, CA
Schulman, David I. ... Los Angeles, CA
Schulman, David L. ... South Windsor, CT
Schulman, David M. ... **Woodbridge, NJ**
Schulman, David S. ... **San Diego, CA**
Schulman, Dean B. ... Columbus, OH
Schulman, Debra S. ... Springfield, NJ
New York, NY
Schulman, Edward H. ... Sacramento, CA
Schulman, Edwin R. ... Rochester, NY
Schulman, Eli C. ... New York, NY
Schulman, Elizabeth ... San Diego, CA
Schulman, Eric L. ... **Chicago, IL**
Schulman, Ethan P. ... **San Francisco, CA**
Schulman, Fredrick A. ... **New York, NY**
Schulman, George A. ... Glendale, CA
Schulman, George E., (A Professional Corporation) ... **Los Angeles, CA**
Schulman, Gregory M. ... **San Diego, CA**
Las Vegas, NV
Schulman & Grode, LLP ... **Las Vegas, NV**
Schulman, Harry ... Highland Park, IL
Schulman, Howard ... Millbrook, NY
Schulman, Howard A. ... Cleveland, OH
Schulman, Howard J. ... **Baltimore, MD**
Schulman, Illise M. ... Alameda, CA
Schulman, Ira M. ... **New York, NY**
Schulman, Irwin ... San Francisco, CA
Schulman, J. Brin ... **Beverly Hills, CA**
Schulman, J. Brin ... **Los Angeles, CA**
Schulman, Jack M. ... Cleveland, OH
Schulman, Jack N. ... New York, NY
Schulman, Jami L. ... Phoenix, AZ
Schulman, Janie F. ... **Los Angeles, CA**
Schulman, Jed N. ... West Hartford, CT
Schulman, Jeffrey ... **Chicago, IL**
Schulman, Jeffrey D. ... New York, NY
Schulman, Jeffrey Scott ... New York, NY
Schulman, Jeremy W. ... **New York, NY**
Schulman, Jerry A. ... Oakbrook Terrace, IL
Schulman, Joanne ... San Francisco, CA
Schulman, John A. ... **Burbank, CA**
Schulman, Joseph R. ... Washington, DC
Schulman, Joshua A. ... New York, NY
Schulman, Judith F. ... Denver, CO
Schulman, Julian Alan ... **Hackensack, NJ**
Suffern, NY
Schulman & Kaufman, LLC
Baltimore, MD
Towson, MD
Schulman, Kenneth A. ... **New York, NY**
Schulman, Lawrence J. ... Denver, CO
Schulman, LeRoy and Bennett, P.C.
Nashville, TN
Schulman, Lori S. ... Department of Commerce, Patent and Trademark Office, GV
Schulman, Louis ... Tampa, FL
Schulman, Marc S. ... Chicago, IL
Schulman, Margaret B. ... Washington, DC
Schulman, Mark L. ... Highland Park, IL
Schulman, Mark L. ... Monticello, NY
Schulman, Mark N. ... East Syracuse, NY
Schulman, Marshall M. ... **Costa Mesa, CA**
Schulman & McMillan, Incorporated
Costa Mesa, CA
Schulman, Melvyn J. ... San Diego, CA
Schulman, Michael ... **Irvine, CA**
Schulman, Michael D. ... **Los Angeles, CA**
Thousand Oaks, CA
Schulman, Michael E. ... New York, NY
Schulman, Michael R. ... **Dallas, TX**
Schulman, Michael T. ... **Los Angeles, CA**
Las Vegas, NV
Schulman, Michelle E. ... New York, NY
Schulman & Miller ... Beverly Hills, CA
Schulman, Mortimer J. ... New York, NY
Schulman, Myron ... Woodside, NY
Schulman, Phillip L. ... **Washington, DC**
Schulman, Richard A. ... Beverly Hills, CA
Schulman, Richard A. ... **San Diego, CA**
Schulman, Richard A. ... **Chattanooga, TN**
Schulman, Richard J. ... **New York, NY**
Schulman, Richard S.
National Credit Union Administration, Office of General Counsel, GV
Schulman, Robert A. ... San Antonio, TX
Schulman, Robert B. ... **Baltimore, MD**
Schulman, Robert D. ... New City, NY
Schulman, Robert E. ... Topeka, KS
Schulman, Robert M. ... **McLean, VA**
Schulman, Robert P. ... New Hyde Park, NY
Schulman, Robert S. ... **Los Angeles, CA**
Schulman, Ronnie E. ... Silver Spring, MD
Schulman & Schulman, A P.C.
San Diego, CA
Schulman, Schulman & Meros, L.P.A.
Cleveland, OH
Schulman, Schulman & Schulman
Woodmere, NY
Schulman, Sheldon C. ... Vineland, NJ
Schulman, Stephanie F. ... **New York, NY**
Schulman, Stephen Amadeus
Sacramento, CA
Schulman, Stephen B. ... New York, NY
Schulman, Stephen H. ... Detroit, MI
Schulman, Steven A. ... Palo Alto, CA
Schulman, Steven B. ... Encinitas, CA
Schulman, Steven G. ... Brooklyn, NY
Schulman, Steven G. ... **New York, NY**
Schulman, Steven H. ... **Washington, DC**
Schulman, Sydney T. ... Springfield, MA
Schulman, Thomas L. ... Santa Ana, CA
Schulman, Todd S. ... **New York, NY**
Schulman, Treem, Kaminkow & Gilden, P.A.
Baltimore, MD
Schulman, Walheim & Heidelberg Inc.
San Antonio, TX
Schulman, Yisroel Y ... New York, NY
Schulmeister, David ... **Honolulu, HI**
Schulmeisters, Janis G.
Department of Justice, Civil Division, GV
Schulner, Keith A. ... Camarillo, CA
Schulner, Lawrence M. ... Camarillo, CA
Schulner, L. M., & Associates
Camarillo, CA
Schulsohn, Richard A. ... New York, NY
Schulson, Andrew J. ... **Great Neck, NY**
Schulson, David H. ... Hollywood, FL
Schulson, Hyman A. ... New York, NY
Schulson, Stephen S. ... Chicago, IL
Schulson, Susan B. ... Chicago, IL
Schulstad, Paul M. ... Willmar, MN
Schulstad, Tara L. ... **Indianapolis, IN**
Schult, Frederick W. ... Huntington, NY
Schult, Thomas P. ... **Kansas City, MO**
Schulte, Anderson, Downes & Aronson, P.C.
Hillsboro, OR
Oregon City, OR
Portland, OR
Vancouver, WA
Schulte, Bernard J. ... Norwich, NY
Schulte, Bernard M. ... **Washington, DC**
Schulte, Beth La Vae
Fort Lauderdale, FL
Schulte & Bisbing ... **Miami, FL**
Schulte, Bruce J. ... Chicago, IL
Schulte, Charles A. ... Sac City, IA
Schulte, Christian Joseph ... Fort Morgan, CO
Schulte, Christopher J. ... **Tampa, FL**
Schulte, Christopher J. ... **Minneapolis, MN**
Schulte, Conly J. ... **Washington, DC**
Omaha, NE
Schulte, Dale L. ... **Kansas City, MO**
Schulte, Daniel C. ... Overland Park, KS
Schulte, Daniel C. ... **St. Paul, MN**
Schulte, Daniel J. ... **Detroit, MI**
Schulte, Deborah C. ... Cincinnati, OH
Schulte, Deborah R. ... Roseville, CA
Schulte, Diane G. ... Ellicott City, MD
Schulte, Duane J. ... Waterloo, IA
Schulte & Enget, P.C., Law Offices of
Stanley, ND
Schulte, Frances K. ... Portland, OR
Schulte, Gerald F. ... Riverside, CA
Schulte, Gerard J., Jr. ... Chicago, IL
Schulte and Graven Law Firm, P.C.
Early, IA
Sac City, IA
Schulte, J. Bryan ... **Burlington, IA**
Schulte, J. Timothy ... **Orlando, FL**
Schulte, James H. ... Dover, NH
Schulte, Jeffrey L. ... **Atlanta, GA**
Schulte, John A. ... Sac City, IA
Schulte, John H. ... **Miami, FL**
Schulte, John, Law Office ... **Missoula, MT**
Schulte, Joseph M. ... Covington, KY
Schulte, Karen Louise ... Cincinnati, OH
Schulte, Kathaleen B. ... Columbus, OH
Schulte, Kathleen B. ... Old Greenwich, CT
Schulte, Kendrick & Associates
Covington, KY
Schulte, Kurt D. ... **Oneonta, NY**
Schulte, Leonard E. ... Tallahassee, FL
Schulte, Mark J. ... Chicago, IL
Schulte, Mark J. ... **Syracuse, NY**
Schulte, Michael J. ... **Covington, KY**
Schulte & Mundt ... Newark Valley, NY
Schulte, Paul I. ... Kingfisher, OK
Schulte, Paul J. ... **St. Louis, MO**
Schulte, Quentin R. ... Stanley, ND
Schulte, Richard John ... **Ada, MI**
Schulte, Richard W. ... Miamisburg, OH
Schulte, Robert C. ... Lawton, OK
Schulte, Robert D. ... Baltimore, MD
Schulte Roth & Zabel LLP
New York, NY
Schulte, Sharon E. ... Jefferson City, MO
Schulte, Sherry L. ... **Cedar Rapids, IA**
Schulte, Stacy L. ... Colorado Springs, CO
Schulte, Stephen C. ... **Chicago, IL**
Schulte, Stephen J. ... **New York, NY**
Schulte, Tamara Joy
Greenwood Village, CO
Schulte, Thomas E. ... Indianapolis, IN
Schulte, Thomas J. ... Jupiter, FL
Schulte, Thomas J., Jr. ... **Tallahassee, FL**
Schulte, Thomas J., P.A. ... Jupiter, FL
Schulte, Thomas K. ... **New York, NY**
Schulte, Timothy M. ... **Denver, CO**
Schulte, Timothy R. ... Louisville, CO
Schulte, Valerie ... **Washington, DC**
Schulte, Werner H. ... St. Petersburg, FL
Schulte, William F. ... **Portland, OR**
Schulte-Dempsey, Catherine A.
Jefferson City, MO
Schulteis, Henry ... **Apple Valley, MN**
Schulteis, Henry J. ... **Topeka, KS**
Schulten, Jacqueline E. ... Chattanooga, TN
Schulten, Richard H. ... Louisville, KY
Schulten, Thomas ... **Portland, ME**
Schulten Ward & Turner, LLP
Atlanta, GA
Schulten, Wm. Scott ... **Atlanta, GA**
Schultes, Lisa M. ... **Kansas City, MO**
Schultess, LeRoy K. ... **LaGrange, IN**
Schultheis, Albert F. ... New York, NY
Schultheis, Alexandra ... San Francisco, CA
Schultheis, Andrew J. ... **Palo Alto, CA**
Schultheis, John A. ... Spokane, WA
Schultheis, Karen A. ... Burlington, KY
Schultheis, Mark A. ... **Des Moines, IA**
Schultheis, Nicole ... **Baltimore, MD**
Schultheis, Patrick J. ... **Kirkland, WA**
Schultheis, Richard E. ... Ephrata, WA
Schultheis, Richard L. ... Indianapolis, IN
Schultheis, Richard L., P.C. ... Indianapolis, IN
Schultheis & Tabler ... Ephrata, WA
Schultheis & Walton, P.A. ... **Baltimore, MD**
Schultheiss, Mark W. ... Fort Collins, CO
Schulthess, Stephen J. ... Bedford, NH
Schulthies, Randall D. ... Pocatello, ID
Schulthies, Valerie ... **Palo Alto, CA**
Schultis, Lawrence A. ... **Washington, DC**
Schultz, Adam J. ... **Syracuse, NY**
Harrisburg, PA
Schultz, Alexander ... West Palm Beach, FL
Schultz, Alfred C. ... Bismarck, ND
Schultz, Allen H. ... Berrien Center, MI
Schultz, Andrew B. ... **Lake Success, NY**
Schultz, Andrew C. ... Boston, MA
Schultz, Andrew E. ... **New York, NY**
Schultz, Andrew G. ... **Chicago, IL**
Schultz, Andrew G. ... **Albuquerque, NM**
Schultz, Andrew, (P.C.) ... **Atlanta, GA**
Schultz, Anne R. ... Miami, FL
Schultz, Arthur W. ... **Long Beach, CA**
Schultz, Audrey L. ... Beverly Hills, CA
Schultz, Barbara E. ... **Boston, MA**
Schultz, Barry A. ... Evanston, IL
Schultz, Barry J. ... **San Diego, CA**
Schultz, Bruce A. ... **Madison, WI**
Schultz, Bryan D. ... Chicago, IL
Schultz, Bryan S. ... **Milwaukee, WI**
Schultz, C. Gregory ... **Princeton, NJ**
Schultz & Carey ... Seattle, WA
Schultz, Carl B. ... **Harrisburg, PA**
Schultz, Carl T., III ... Houston, TX
Schultz, Carol Regina ... Washington, DC
Schultz, Caroline Mouallem
Philadelphia, PA
Schultz, Carolyn S. ... **Houston, TX**
Schultz, Charles J. ... **Chicago, IL**
Schultz, Charles T. ... Riverside, CA
Schultz, Chester Gitt ... Gettysburg, PA
Schultz, Chris J. ... Jackson, TN
Schultz, Christie ... Santa Maria, CA
Schultz, Christopher G.
Farmington Hills, MI
Schultz, Christopher S. ... **Boston, MA**
Schultz, Claire ... Stamford, CT
Schultz, Cort R. ... **San Francisco, CA**
Schultz, Curt A. ... Foster City, CA
Schultz, Cynthia B. ... Department of Justice, Civil Division, GV
Schultz, Daniel E., Law Offices of
Washington, DC
Rockville, MD
Schultz, Daniel J. ... **Los Angeles, CA**
Schultz, David ... Sacramento, CA
Schultz, David E. ... Madison, WI
Schultz, David J. ... Oshkosh, WI
Schultz, David Keith ... **Los Angeles, CA**
Schultz, David L. ... Caledonia, MN
Schultz, David M. ... West Palm Beach, FL
Schultz, David M. ... **Chicago, IL**
Schultz, David N. ... **Beverly Hills, CA**
Schultz, David R. ... **Reston, VA**
Schultz, David T. ... **Minneapolis, MN**
Schultz, David V. ... Chicago, IL
Schultz, Davis A. ... **Philadelphia, PA**
Schultz, Dean M. ... New York, NY
Schultz, Debra ... Irvine, CA
Schultz, Dennis B. ... **Detroit, MI**
Schultz, Donald ... Chicago, IL
Schultz, Donald C. ... **Norfolk, VA**
Schultz, Donald E. ... **Madison, WI**
Schultz, Donald I., (P.C.) ... **Cheyenne, WY**
Schultz, Douglas R. ... **Eugene, OR**
Schultz, Duane Wm. ... **Grants Pass, OR**
Schultz, Edward F., Jr. ... Albany, OR
Schultz, Edward J. ... White Plains, NY
Schultz, Elizabeth A. ... Columbus, OH
Schultz, Emily A. ... **Wayne, NJ**
Schultz, Enid H. ... Great Neck, NY
Schultz, Eric B. ... Minneapolis, MN
Schultz, Eric W. ... Buffalo, NY
Schultz, Erich Y. ... **Tampa, FL**
Schultz, Erika J. ... Albany, NY
Schultz, Evan P. ... Washington, DC
Schultz, Farner & Perrin, L.L.P.
Houston, TX
Schultz, Frank H. ... Lexington, KY
Schultz, Frederick D. ... Livonia, MI
Schultz, Frederick W. ... **Bloomington, IN**
Schultz, G. Robert ... St. Petersburg, FL
Schultz, Gary ... McMinnville, OR
Schultz, Gary D. ... Helena, MT
Schultz, Gene P. ... St. Louis, MO
Schultz, George J. ... Chula Vista, CA
Schultz, George "Russ" ... **Dallas, TX**
Schultz, Gerald D. ... Hamilton, MT
Schultz, Gerald O. ... Garden City, KS
Schultz, Gordon N. ... Boston, MA
Schultz and Green ... Primghar, IA
Schultz, Gregg Thaddeus ... **Houston, TX**
Schultz, Gregory B. ... Caledonia, MN
Schultz, Gregory C. ... Trenton, NJ
Schultz, Gregory Carl ... Minneapolis, MN
Schultz, Gregory G. ... Oldsmar, FL
Schultz, Gregory G. ... **Atlanta, GA**
Schultz, Gregory G. ... **Missoula, MT**
Schultz, Gregory S. ... **Newport, RI**
Schultz, Gregory T. ... **Detroit, MI**
Schultz, Harold W. ... St. Paul, MN
Schultz, Harold W., II ... Minneapolis, MN
Schultz, Heiko Kai ... **Los Angeles, CA**
Schultz, Helena ... Brush, CO
Schultz, Henry R. ... Green Bay, WI
Schultz, Herbert F. ... Rock Island, IL
Schultz, Herbert F., Sr. ... Rock Island, IL
Schultz, Herbert L. ... Lawrence, MA
Schultz, Hilary S. ... Boston, MA
Schultz, Hubert H. ... Sanborn, IA
Schultz, Hyman S. ... Houston, TX
Schultz, Ira J. ... **Arlington, VA**
Schultz, Irving ... Roseland, NJ
Schultz, J. Bruce ... Sapulpa, OK
Schultz, Jack ... Syracuse, NY
Schultz, Jack M. ... **Detroit, MI**
Schultz, Jack M. ... **Southfield, MI**
Schultz, Jacob D. ... **Los Angeles, CA**
Schultz, James A. ... Houston, MN
Schultz, James C. ... Washington, DC
Schultz, James C. ... Smithtown, NY
Schultz, James C., P.C. ... Smithtown, NY
Schultz, James D., Jr. ... Buffalo, NY
Schultz, James H. ... Rock Island, IL
Schultz, James K. ... **Chicago, IL**
Schultz, James R. ... **Albany, NY**
Schultz, James S. ... Yankton, SD
Schultz, James W. ... Chicago, IL
Schultz, Janet L. ... Anoka, MN
Schultz, Jason R. ... **Atlanta, GA**
Schultz, Jay L. ... St. Joseph, MI
Schultz, Jeffrey A. ... Detroit, MI
Schultz, Jeffrey B. ... Baltimore, MD
Schultz, Jeffrey L. ... **New York, NY**
Schultz, Jeffrey P. ... **New York, NY**
Schultz, Jerold M. ... Los Angeles, CA
Schultz, JerylLavay ... Bellaire, TX
Schultz, Jill K. ... **Rochester, NY**
Schultz, Joel R. ... Los Angeles, CA
Schultz, John A. ... New York, NY
Schultz, John E. ... Manitowish Waters, WI

Schumaecker, Michael P. ......New York, NY
Schumaier & Bartlett, P.C. ......St. Louis, MO
Schumaier, Steven G. ......St. Louis, MO
Schumaker & Bernstein ......Oregon City, OR
Schumaker, David G. ......Ventura, CA
Schumaker, Kenneth B. ......Newark, OH
Schumaker, Kenneth I. ......San Jose, CA
Schumaker, Larry M. ......Kansas City, MO
Schumaker, Robert S. ......St. Petersburg, FL
Tampa, FL
Schumaker, Stephen A. ......Springfield, OH
Schumaker, William E. ......Oregon City, OR
Schuman, Adam H. ......New York, NY
Schuman, Alan L. ......Hartford, CT
Schuman, Allan M. ......San Francisco, CA
Schuman, Andrea L. ......New York, NY
Schuman, August F. ......Bassett, NE
Schuman, Barton L. ......Los Angeles, CA
Schuman, Brett ......San Francisco, CA
Schuman & Butz, P.C. ......Toms River, NJ
Tuckerton, NJ
Schuman, Carl ......Butte, NE
Schuman, Carl J. ......Hartford, CT
Schuman, Carole Miner ......Newton, MA
Schuman, David ......Huntington, NY
Schuman, David ......Eugene, OR
Schuman, David J. ......Jersey City, NJ
Schuman, David S.
National Aeronautics And Space Administration, Goddard Space Flight Center, GV
Schuman, Deborah H. ......Maplewood, NJ
Schuman, Dennis A. ......New York, NY
Schuman, Eliot M ......White Plains, NY
Schuman, Gary ......Chicago, IL
Schuman, H. Mitchell ......Brooklyn, NY
Schuman, Harold A. ......Toms River, NJ
Schuman, Howard F. ......Cleveland, OH
Schuman, Ilyse W. ......Chicago, IL
Schuman, Jack ......Indianapolis, IN
Schuman, Jeanne ......New York, NY
Schuman, Jeanne M. ......Martinez, CA
Schuman, Jennifer A. ......La Jolla, CA
Schuman, Jill Evantash ......Elkins Park, PA
Schuman, John D. ......Columbus, OH
Schuman, John G. ......Northbrook, IL
Schuman, Jonathan D.
West Palm Beach, FL
Schuman, Jonathan R. ......Bethesda, MD
Schuman, Joseph ......Chicago, IL
Schuman, Joseph ......Westbury, NY
Schuman, Kane, Felts & Everngam, Chartered
Bethesda, MD
Schuman, Keith A. ......New York, NY
Schuman, Kenneth A. ......Bedford, OH
Schuman, Kerry Scott ......Princeton, NJ
Elkins Park, PA
Schuman, Leo M. ......Portland, OR
Schuman, Marian M. ......Long Island City, NY
Schuman, Mark A. ......New York, NY
Schuman, Mark D. ......Minneapolis, MN
Schuman, Michael D. ......Milwaukee, WI
Schuman & Pieper ......Milwaukee, WI
Schuman, Raymond J. ......Treasury Department, Internal Revenue Service, GV
Schuman, Rita H. ......San Francisco, CA
Schuman, Robert L. ......Rockford, IL
Schuman, Sheldon P. ......Bethesda, MD
Schuman, Stanton ......Chicago, IL
Schuman, Steven A. ......Beverly Hills, CA
Schuman, Stuart H. ......Philadelphia, PA
Schuman, Susan J. ......Chicago, IL
Schuman, Thomas R. ......Palatine, IL
Schuman, William P. ......Chicago, IL
Schuman, Wm. E. ......Ellicott City, MD
Schumann, Alexa M. ......Albany, NY
Schumann, Alfred W. ......Fairfax, VA
Schumann, Anthony L. ......Chicago, IL
Schumann, Arnold K. ......Jefferson, WI
Schumann, Belle Brotemarkle
Daytona Beach, FL
Schumann, Beth E.S.
Department of Labor, GV
Schumann, Bryan G. ......Chicago, IL
Schumann, David A. ......Janesville, WI
Schumann, Denise L. ......Fort Lauderdale, FL
Schumann, Edward L. ......Tustin, CA
Schumann, Elena Freshman
Los Angeles, CA
Schumann, Eric M. ......Pittsburgh, PA
Schumann, Gary N. ......Austin, TX
Schumann, George Monroe
Pittsburgh, PA
Wheeling, WV
Schumann, Glen E. ......Minneapolis, MN
Schumann, Hanlon, Doherty, McCrossin & Paolino ......Jersey City, NJ
New York, NY
Schumann, James J. ......San Diego, CA
Schumann, John A. ......Department of Justice, Civil Division, GV
Schumann, Lewis R. ......Rockville, MD
Schumann, Michael ......Portland, OR
Schumann, Michael D. ......Minneapolis, MN
Schumann, O. William ......Southfield, MI
Schumann, Paul A. ......San Francisco, CA
Schumann, Ralph J. ......Elk Grove Village, IL
Schumann, Raymond L. ......Fort Myers, FL
Schumann, Reno O. ......New Braunfels, TX
Schumann, Roger Neal ......New York, NY
Schumann, Ronald Gary ......Beavercreek, OH
Schumann, Roxy M. ......Galesburg, IL
Schumann, Tam Nomoto ......Santa Ana, CA
Schumann, Timothy J. ......Milwaukee, WI
Schumann, W. Christian
Department of Labor, Office of the Solicitor, GV
Schumann, William M. ......Westerville, OH

Schumb, Christopher, Law Offices of
San Jose, CA
Schumb, Joseph G., Jr. ......Santa Cruz, CA
Schumeister, David N. ......New York, NY
Schumeister, Steven A. ......Minneapolis, MN
Schumell, Donna Gardner ......Milwaukee, WI
Schumer, Allison F ......Montclair, NJ
Schumer, Charles E. ......Brooklyn, NY
Schumer, Jayne B. ......Garden City, NY
Schumer, Julie ......Orinda, CA
Schumer, Lee Susan ......New York, NY
Schumer, Robert B. ......New York, NY
Schuminsky, Lisa S. ......New York, NY
Schumm, Brooke, III ......Baltimore, MD
Schumm, Gilbert C. ......Northbrook, IL
Schumm, Jerry ......Bellingham, WA
Schumm, Sherry W. ......Phoenix, AZ
Schumm, Stephen L. ......Los Angeles, CA
Schummer, Walter ......Vernon Hills, IL
Schummer, Walter, Law Offices of, P.C.
Vernon Hills, IL
Schumock, Mark F. ......Lakewood, WA
Schumpert, J. Bruce, Jr. ......Walhalla, SC
Schumsky, Shari ......Santa Fe, NM
Schunck, Phyllis B. ......Austin, TX
Schundler, Peter O. ......New York, NY
Schunk, Catherine M. ......Albany, NY
Schunk, Eric H. ......Los Angeles, CA
Schunk, George M. ......Helena, MT
Schunk, Joli M. ......Campbell, CA
Schunk, Philip W. ......New Paltz, NY
Schunk, Richard A. ......Tallmadge, OH
Schunk, Wm. J. ......Kenmore, NY
Schupack, Jeffrey James ......Jersey City, NJ
Schupack, Stephen W. ......Springfield, MA
Schupak, Donald ......New York, NY
Schupak, Sidney ......Washington, DC
Schupak, Terri Lynn ......Martinez, CA
Schupansky, Robert C. ......Pittsburgh, PA
Schupansky, Susan P. ......Pittsburgh, PA
Schupbach, Arthur C. ......Garden City, NY
Schupbach, Cortlan R., Jr. ......Ponca City, OK
Schupbach, Rebecca F. ......Louisville, KY
Schupbach, Williams & Pavone, LLP
Garden City, NY
Schupler, Robert J. ......Los Angeles, CA
Schupp, Anastasia Luka ......Chicago, IL
Schupp, Benjamin O., (P.C.)
New Orleans, LA
Schupp, Bruce D. ......Las Vegas, NV
Schupp, Edmund J. ......Albany, NY
Schupp, H. Herbert ......Columbus, OH
Schupp, James L., Jr. ......New Orleans, LA
Schupp, Jason M. ......Towson, MD
Schupp, John R. ......New Orleans, LA
Schupp, Timothy R. ......Minneapolis, MN
Schuppener, Kathryn M. ......Elkins, WV
Schuppenhauer, John A. ......Canandaigua, NY
Schupper, John D. ......Roseland, NJ
Schuppert, Kenneth M., Jr. ......Decatur, AL
Schuppert, Lynn Belt ......Decatur, AL
Schur, Barbara E. ......Plano, TX
Schur, Dara L. ......Oakland, CA
Schur, Douglas A. ......Thousand Oaks, CA
Schur, Gerald S. ......Chicago, IL
Schur, Jerome ......Chicago, IL
Schur and McAuliffe ......Mayfield, NY
Schur, Robert ......New York, NY
Schur, Robert E. ......Half Moon Bay, CA
Schur, Robert E. ......Miami, FL
Miami, FL
Schur, Ronald R., Jr. ......Mayfield, NY
Schur, Steven M. ......Madison, WI
Schur, Thomas P. ......Plano, TX
Schur, Warren M. ......Boston, MA
Schur, William G. ......Chicago, IL
Schur, William M. ......San Antonio, TX
Schure, Alexander H. ......Campbell, CA
Schure, Richard J. ......Rockville Centre, NY
Schureman, Frakes & Glass, PLC
Detroit, MI
Harbor Springs, MI
Schureman, Jeptha W. ......Detroit, MI
Schurfranz, Peggy G. ......Bradenton, FL
Schurger, Eric D. ......Pensacola, FL
Schurger, Frederick A. ......Decatur, IN
Schurger, Severin H. ......Decatur, IN
Schurger, Zurcher & Harvey, P.C.
Decatur, IN
Schurgin, Leon M. ......Southfield, MI
Schurgin, Stanley M. ......Boston, MA
Schurgin, William P. ......Chicago, IL
Schurig, Elizabeth Morgan ......Austin, TX
Schurin, Marilyn C. ......Mineola, NY
Schuring, Dale A. ......Vicksburg, MI
Schurke, Marvin L. ......Olympia, WA
Schurkman, Steven A. ......Rye, NY
White Plains, NY
Schurlknight, John L. ......Florence, SC
Schurman, C. E. ......Fort Worth, TX
Schurman, Dennis W. ......Detroit Lakes, MN
Schurman, James R. ......Kansas City, MO
Schurman, Juana M. ......Redwood City, CA
Schurman, Linda S. ......Chicago, IL
Schurman, Paul R. ......Louisville, KY
Schurman, Rosemary B. ......Kirkland, WA
Schurman, Valerie K. ......Seal Beach, CA
Schurman, William S.
Steamboat Springs, CO
Schurmann, Anna M. ......Escondido, CA
Schurr, Carolyn ......Melville, NY
Schurr, Donald A. ......Toledo, OH
Schurr, Frederick S. ......Brooklyn, NY
Schurr, John B. ......Frisco, CO
Schurr, Kenneth B. ......Miami, FL
Schurr, M. Randolph ......Prescott, AZ
Schurr, Michael H. ......Chestnut Ridge, NY
Schurr, Patrick J. ......Dallas, TX

Schurr, Steven C. ......Chicago, IL
Schurr, Stuart G. ......Fort Lauderdale, FL
Schurr, Thomas R. ......Oklahoma City, OK
Schurr, Victor ......Bronx, NY
Mount Vernon, NY
Schurrer, Gary R. ......Stillwater, MN
Schurter, Neill ......Rantoul, IL
Schurtman, William ......New York, NY
Schurtz-Leon, M. Frances ......Carteret, NJ
Schurz, James M. ......San Francisco, CA
Schussler, Don W. ......Yakima, WA
Schussler, Edward G. ......Oak Lawn, IL
Schussler, Jane H. ......York, PA
Schussman, Barbara J.
Walnut Creek, CA
Schustal, Randy C., (Ms.) ......Brooklyn, NY
Schuster, Alan G. ......Highland Park, IL
Schuster, Andrew H. ......Fort Lauderdale, FL
Miami, FL
Schuster, Arnold P. ......San Francisco, CA
Schuster, Barry C. ......Lebanon, NH
Schuster, Bernard ......Rochester, NY
Schuster, Carl ......Fort Lauderdale, FL
Schuster, Carl ......San Juan, PR
Schuster, Carl E. ......Bloomfield Hills, MI
Schuster, Catherine L. ......Towson, MD
Schuster, Charles A. ......Pensacola, FL
Schuster, Christian E. ......Pittsburgh, PA
Schuster, Clifford Nelson ......Costa Mesa, CA
Schuster, Debra K. ......St. Louis, MO
Schuster, Donald E. ......Farmington Hills, MI
Schuster, E. Elaine ......Oklahoma City, OK
Schuster, E. Elaine, P.C.
Oklahoma City, OK
Schuster, Edward D. ......Fort Lauderdale, FL
Schuster, Elizabeth R. ......Albany, NY
Schuster, Eric S. ......Baltimore, MD
Schuster, Eugene ......Great Neck, NY
Schuster, Eugene G. ......Richland, WA
Schuster, Fredric H. ......Falls Church, VA
Schuster, Gary ......Sturgeon Bay, WI
Schuster, Gary M. ......New York, NY
Schuster, Gerard M. ......Wolf Point, MT
Schuster, Gregory L. ......Dallas, TX
Schuster, J. Stephen ......Marietta, GA
Schuster, James ......Southfield, MI
Schuster, James ......Cincinnati, OH
Schuster, James Kemp ......Amarillo, TX
Schuster, Jeanne M. ......Boston, MA
Schuster, Jeannine A. ......Pittsburgh, PA
Schuster, Jeffrey S. ......Milwaukee, WI
Schuster, Jennifer R. ......Newark, NJ
Schuster, Jeremy G. ......Los Angeles, CA
Schuster, Jerry W. ......Great Falls, MT
Schuster, John J. ......New York, NY
Schuster, John P. ......Madison, WI
Schuster, John S. ......Los Angeles, CA
Schuster, Kenneth R. ......Media, PA
Schuster, Kurt M. ......Waukesha, WI
Schuster, Lance J. ......Idaho Falls, ID
Schuster, Larry G. ......Great Falls, MT
Schuster, Linda B. ......Beachwood, OH
Schuster & Mader ......Madison, WI
Schuster, Mark ......Elgin, IL
Schuster, Michael ......Washington, DC
Schuster, Michael J. ......Guttenberg, IA
Schuster & Mick ......Guttenberg, IA
Schuster, Mitchell ......New York, NY
Schuster, Monis ......Detroit, MI
Schuster, Nancy C. ......Cleveland, OH
Schuster, Naomi H. ......Palos Heights, IL
Schuster, Neil M. ......Miami Beach, FL
Schuster, Neil S. ......Miami, FL
Schuster, Patricia S. ......Washington, DC
Schuster, Paul F. ......Dallas, TX
Schuster, Philip A. ......Northbrook, IL
Schuster, Philip F., II ......Portland, OR
Schuster, Richard C. ......Worthington, OH
Schuster, Richard D. ......Columbus, OH
Schuster, Richard L. ......Cincinnati, OH
Schuster, Richard L. ......West Chester, PA
Schuster, Robert J. ......Los Angeles, CA
Schuster, Robert P. ......Jackson, WY
Schuster, Robert R. ......Bethlehem, PA
Schuster, Roderic E. ......Fargo, ND
Schuster, Saundra D. ......Columbus, OH
Schuster, Shannon B. ......Dallas, TX
Schuster & Simmons Co., A Legal Professional Association ......Cleveland, OH
Schuster, Stephen B. ......Canoga Park, CA
Schuster, Stephen F. ......Louisville, KY
Schuster, Stephen M. ......Oak Brook, IL
Schuster, Stephen M., Jr. ......Herndon, VA
Schuster, Stephen P. ......Kansas City, MO
Schuster, Stephen W. ......Corpus Christi, TX
Schuster, Steven J. ......Boise, ID
Schuster, Steven V. ......Hackensack, NJ
Schuster, Steven W. ......New York, NY
Schuster, Theodore G. ......St. Charles, IL
Schuster Usera Aguiló & Santiago
San Juan, PR
Schuster, Walter W. ......Anaheim, CA
Schuster, Wheeler, Buttrey & Wing, P.A.
Lebanon, NH
Schuster, William D. ......Santa Ana, CA
Schuster, William P. ......Waukesha, WI
Schut, Wade H. ......Des Moines, IA
Schuth, Catherine Elizabeth ......Rensselaer, NY
Schutjer, Bradley A. ......Harrisburg, PA
Schutjer, James W. ......St. Paul, MN
Schutjer, Kristen L. ......San Francisco, CA
Schutt, Andrew J. ......Atlanta, GA
Schutt, Darrin R. ......Cape Coral, FL
Schutt, Dennis R., (P.A.) ......Jacksonville, FL
Schutt, E. Major ......North Muskegon, MI
Schutt, Humphries & Becker
Jacksonville, FL
Schutt, Kenneth W., Jr. ......Scottsdale, AZ

Schutt, Kenneth W., Jr., P.C., Law Offices of
Scottsdale, AZ
Schutt, Kimberly Baird ......Fort Collins, CO
Schutt, Melissa Lang ......Fremont, NE
Schutt, Michael P. ......Virginia Beach, VA
Schutt, Roderick ......New York, NY
Schutt, Rose Marie C. ......Ridgewood, NJ
Schutt, Stephen C. ......Anacortes, WA
Schutt, Thomas R. ......Chicago, IL
Schutt, Walter E. ......Wilmington, OH
Schutt, William E. ......Boulder City, NV
Schutt, William F. ......Richmond, VA
Schuttauf, Erich E. ......Kissimmee, FL
Schutte, Charles A., Jr. ......Baton Rouge, LA
Schutte, Frederick J., IV ......Jacksonville, FL
Schutte, Michael J. ......Cincinnati, OH
Schutte, Sandra E. Pechter ......Hilo, HI
Schutte, Scott T. ......Chicago, IL
Schutte, Stephen E. ......Springfield, OH
Schutte, Stephen K. ......Denver, CO
Schutte, William M. ......Kansas City, MO
Schutter, David C., & Associates
Honolulu, HI
Las Vegas, NV
Schutter, Kraig M. ......Saginaw, MI
Schutter, Laurin W. ......Kansas City, MO
Schutter, Stephen M. ......Kansas City, MO
Schuttish, Thomas R. ......San Francisco, CA
Schuttler, Holly Davidson ......Boca Raton, FL
Schutts, Raymond W. ......Bothell, WA
Schutty, John F., III ......New York, NY
Schutz, Andrew C. ......Irvine, CA
Schutz, Donald J. ......St. Petersburg, FL
Schutz, Frederick W. ......Midwest City, OK
Schutz, Henry A., III ......Fairfax, VA
Schutz, Henry A., III ......Fairfax, VA
Schutz, John F. ......West Palm Beach, FL
Schutz, Kevin P. ......Phoenix, AZ
Schutz & Markin ......Armonk, NY
Schutz, Matthew R. ......Three Bridges, NJ
Schutz, Otto W. ......Cleveland, OH
Schutz, Raymond M. ......Aberdeen, SD
Schutz, Robert N. ......Long Beach, NY
Schutz, Ronald J. ......Minneapolis, MN
Schutz, Sandra A. ......San Francisco, CA
Schutz, Scott M. ......Los Angeles, CA
Schutz, Sidney ......Armonk, NY
Schutz, Sigmund D. ......Portland, ME
Schutz, Tim ......Colorado Springs, CO
Schutza, James L. ......Dallas, TX
Schutza, Jerry L. ......Houston, TX
Schutza, John M. ......Corpus Christi, TX
Schutzbank, Eric ......Lowell, MA
Schutzer, George J. ......Washington, DC
Schutzer, Philip M. ......Coral Gables, FL
Schutzman, Edward I. ......Burlingame, CA
Schutzman, Keith ......Yonkers, NY
Schutzman, Lee A. ......Detroit, MI
Schutzman, Max F. ......New York, NY
Schutzman, Scott ......Santa Ana, CA
Schutzman, Steven J. ......New York, NY
Schutzman, Thomas J. ......Covington, KY
Schutzman & Valentine ......Irvington, NJ
Schuur, Morden P. ......Portage, MI
Schuur, Pamela M. ......San Jose, CA
Schuur, Peter F.G. ......New York, NY
Schuur, Robert G. ......New York, NY
Schuurman, Jan Marie ......Melbourne, FL
Schuurman, Willem G. ......Austin, TX
Schuver, Mark S. ......Belleville, IL
Schuwerk, Brown & Arbeiter ......Chester, IL
Schuwerk, William A. ......Chester, IL
Schuwerk, William A., Jr. ......Chester, IL
Schuyler, Anne R. ......Bethesda, MD
Schuyler, Billie W. C. ......Anderson, IN
Schuyler, Charles W. ......Missoula, MT
Schuyler, Christopher J. ......New York, NY
Schuyler, Daniel M. ......Chicago, IL
Schuyler, G. Michael ......Denver, CO
Schuyler, Jason A. ......Denver, CO
Schuyler, John B., Jr. ......Dewey, AZ
Schuyler, John Dave ......Aptos, CA
Schuyler, Marc P. ......Palo Alto, CA
Schuyler, Marilyn L. ......Alameda, CA
Schuyler, Nina L. ......San Francisco, CA
Schuyler Professional Corporation
Anderson, IN
Schuyler, Rob R., A Professional Corporation
Los Angeles, CA
Schuyler, Roche & Zwirner, a professional corporation ......Chicago, IL
Evanston, IL
Schuyler, Shanell M. ......Pompano Beach, FL
Schuyler, Stephen B. ......Denver, CO
Schuyler, Stephen W. ......Anderson, IN
Schuyler, William E., Jr. ......Bethesda, MD
Schuyler, William E., Jr., P.C.
Bethesda, MD
Schvimmer, Theodore A. ......Trenton, NJ
Schwaab, Richard L. ......Washington, DC
Milwaukee, WI
Schwaab, Thos. ......Nashotah, WI
Schwab, Andrew L. ......New York, NY
Schwab, Anna Katherine ......Chapel Hill, NC
Schwab, Anne Marie ......Westmont, NJ
Schwab, Anne T. ......New York, NY
Schwab, Anne Tyson ......Swarthmore, PA
Schwab, Arthur J. ......Pittsburgh, PA
Schwab, Barbara A. ......Secaucus, NJ
Schwab & Bauer, P.C. ......Fairbury, NE
Schwab, Bruce W. ......San Francisco, CA
Schwab, Carl E. ......Chicago, IL
Schwab, Carl Tracy ......Houma, LA
Schwab, Carol A. ......Culver City, CA
Schwab, Carol A. ......Raleigh, NC
Schwab, Carol M. ......Department of State, Office of the Legal Adviser, GV
Schwab, Charles A. ......Palo Alto, CA

Schwab, Charles L. ... Greenville, SC
Schwab, Charlotte ... Glendale, CA
Schwab, Danna E. ... Metairie, LA
Schwab, David A. ... Memphis, TN
Schwab, David E., II ... New York, NY
Schwab, David J. ... Vernon Hills, IL
Schwab, David M. ... Houston, TX
Schwab, Diane N. ... Philadelphia, PA
Schwab, Donald J. ... River Falls, WI
Schwab, Donna Garbarino
Baton Rouge, LA
Schwab, Donna Garbarino, A Professional Corporation ... Baton Rouge, LA
Schwab, Douglas A. ... Phoenix, AZ
Schwab, Douglas B. ... Los Angeles, CA
Schwab, Douglas M. ... San Francisco, CA
Schwab, Dwight L. ... Tigard, OR
Schwab, E. Curtis, Jr. ... Christiansburg, VA
Schwab, Edward H., III ... Kendalia, TX
Schwab, Eileen Caulfield ... New York, NY
Schwab, Eric ... Sacramento, CA
Schwab, Eric R. ... Woodbridge, NJ
Schwab, Evan L. ... Seattle, WA
Schwab, Fred ... Indianapolis, IN
Schwab, G. Joe ... Brewster, WA
Chelan, WA
Ellensburg, WA
Kennewick, WA
Moses Lake, WA
Wenatchee, WA
Schwab, Gary S. ... Springfield, IL
Schwab, George B. ... New York, NY
Schwab, George M. ... San Francisco, CA
Schwab, Gregory B. ... Columbus, OH
Schwab, Gregory G. ... Pittsburgh, PA
Schwab, Gregory J. ... Houma, LA
Schwab & Hardcastle ... Farmington, UT
Schwab, Harold Lee ... New York, NY
Schwab, Harry W. ... Akron, OH
Schwab, Helen Lorraine ... Encino, CA
Schwab, Herbert M. ... Cannon Beach, OR
Schwab, Howard J. ... San Fernando, CA
Schwab, James E. ... New York, NY
Schwab, James H. ... New York, NY
Schwab, Jeffrey ... Moses Lake, WA
Schwab, Jeffrey A. ... New York, NY
Schwab, Jerry H. ... Houma, LA
Schwab, Joan M. ... Newark, NJ
Schwab, John ... Baton Rouge, LA
Schwab, John H., Jr. ... Chicago, IL
Schwab, John J. ... New York, NY
Schwab, Jolie ... New York, NY
Schwab, Joseph E. ... Fremont, CA
Schwab, Joseph F., Jr. ... San Rafael, CA
Schwab, Karin E. ... Sacramento, CA
Schwab, Kelly J. ... Oshkosh, WI
Schwab, Kenneth L. ... Denver, CO
Schwab, Lawrence M., (Inc.)
Palo Alto, CA
Schwab, Manuel R. ... Binghamton, NY
Schwab, Martin A. ... Syracuse, NY
Schwab, Mary Ellen ... Wynnewood, PA
Schwab, Michael E. ... Yakima, WA
Schwab, Michael J. ... New York, NY
Schwab, Michael L. ... Farmington, UT
Schwab, Mikel W. ... Hagåtña, GU
Schwab, Mildred A. ... Portland, OR
Schwab, Nelson, Jr. ... Cincinnati, OH
Schwab, Norma W. ... Ithaca, NY
Schwab, Norman K.
Department Of The Interior, Office of Hearings & Appeals, GV
Schwab, Paul J. ... Southfield, MI
Schwab, Paul J., III ... Towson, MD
Schwab, Peter M. ... Mountain View, CA
Schwab, Philip E., Jr. ... Santa Ana, CA
Schwab, Priscilla Anne ... Department of Labor, Office of Secretary, GV
Schwab & Radcliffe, L.L.P.
Galveston, TX
Houston, TX
Schwab, Richard B. ... Cleveland, OH
Schwab, Richard J. ... Los Angeles, CA
Schwab, Robert ... Plano, TX
Schwab, Robert H., Jr. ... Atherton, CA
Schwab, Robert J. ... Madison, WI
Schwab, Robert L. ... New Haven, CT
Schwab, Ronald L. ... Fairbury, NE
Schwab, S. Scott ... Toledo, OH
Schwab & Schwab ... Houma, LA
Schwab, Solan ... New York, NY
Schwab, Stephen W. ... Chicago, IL
Schwab, Steven C. ... Indianapolis, IN
Schwab, Steven Franklin ... Chicago, IL
Schwab, Steven R. ... Albert Lea, MN
Schwab, Stewart Jon ... Ithaca, NY
Schwab, Susan E. ... Harrisburg, PA
Schwab, Susan Elizabeth ... Nashville, TN
Schwab, Taylor Townsend ... Galveston, TX
Schwab, Terrance W. ... New York, NY
Schwab, Thomas E. ... New Orleans, LA
Schwab, Thomas J. ... Holyoke, MA
Schwab, Torene L.M. ... Sacramento, CA
Schwab, Van A. ... Chicago, IL
Schwab & Walter ... Baton Rouge, LA
Schwab, William G., & Associates
Hazleton, PA
Schwab, William G., & Associates
Lehighton, PA
Schwab, William G., & Associates
Pottsville, PA
Stroudsburg, PA
Wilkes-Barre, PA
Schwaba, Thomas P. ... Menominee, MI
Marinette, WI
Schwabach, Aaron ... San Diego, CA
Schwabacher, Christopher C.
New York, NY
Schwabauer, D. Stephen ... Stockton, CA
Schwabe, Audrey Kotar ... Succasunna, NJ
Schwabe, Charles L. ... Mangum, OK
Schwabe, Clara G. ... Brooklyn, NY
Schwabe, G. Blaine, III
Oklahoma City, OK
Schwabe, John B., II ... Columbia, MO
Schwabe, John L. ... Portland, OR
Schwabe, Peter M. ... Cameron Park, CA
Schwabe, Richard R. ... Vista, CA
Schwabe, Williamson & Wyatt
Washington, DC
Seattle, WA
Vancouver, WA
Bend, OR
Portland, OR
Schwabedissen, Elizabeth M. ... Miami, FL
Schwabenland, Edward J.
Philadelphia, PA
Wayne, PA
Schwabenland and Ryan, P.C.
Philadelphia, PA
Wayne, PA
Schwaber, Jeffrey M. ... Rockville, MD
Falls Church, VA
Schwaber, Steven A., Law Offices of
San Marino, CA
Schwabinger, Jules ... Farmingdale, NY
Schwab-Radcliffe, Suzanne ... Galveston, TX
Schwach, Diane Musarra ... Buffalo, NY
Schwach, Lawrence R. ... Buffalo, NY
Schwach, Paula L. ... Kansas City, MO
Schwachter, Joseph A. ... San Francisco, CA
Schwade, Joseph A. ... Columbus, OH
Schwadel, Blaine Z. ... New York, NY
Schwadron, Aliza B., (Ms.) ... New York, NY
Schwadron, David Marc ... Philadelphia, PA
Schwadron, Richard M. ... Woodmere, NY
Schwadron, Steven C.
House of Representatives, Congressional Assistants, GV
Schwaeber, Lois ... Hempstead, NY
Schwaeble, Henry A. ... Houston, TX
Schwaemle, Judy ... Madison, WI
Schwager, Bradley J. ... Montgomery, IL
Schwager, Charles S. ... Houston, TX
Schwager, David E. ... Wilkes-Barre, PA
Schwager, Greg L. ... Des Moines, IA
Schwager, Linda H. ... Oakland, NJ
Schwager, Michael L. ... Libertyville, IL
Schwager, Pamela H. ... New York, NY
Schwager, Phillips & Cunningham, LLC
Louisville, KY
Schwager, Richard A. ... Columbus, OH
Schwager, Sheila R. ... Boise, ID
Schwager, Stephen A. ... Louisville, KY
Schwager, Stuart A. ... Bethesda, MD
Schwahn, George B. ... Madison, WI
Schwahn, Phyllis Lathrope ... Madison, WI
Schwaibold, Gerhard ... Harrisburg, PA
Schwaiger, Susan R. ... New York, NY
Schwait, Allen L. ... Baltimore, MD
Schwait, Carl B. ... Gainesville, FL
Schwake, Curtis H. ... Corpus Christi, TX
Schwalb, Brian L. ... Washington, DC
Schwalb, Burton A. ... Washington, DC
Schwalb, Donnenfeld & Sarfatti, A Professional Corporation
Washington, DC
Schwalb, Efrem T. ... New York, NY
Schwalb, Harris Lee ... Vienna, VA
Schwalb, John D. ... Nashville, TN
Schwalb, Natan ... Omaha, NE
Schwalb, Philip Glen Justin ... Atlanta, GA
Schwalbach, Dina M. ... Agoura Hills, CA
Schwalbach, Joseph C. ... San Diego, CA
Schwalbe, Alan L. ... Cherry Hill, NJ
Schwalbe, James E. ... New York, NY
Schwalbe, Richard B. ... Jacksonville, FL
Schwalbe, Tracey L. ... Monroe, WI
New Glarus, WI
Schwall & Becker ... Hillsdale, NJ
New City, NY
Schwall, Craig L. ... Atlanta, GA
Schwall, DeFord R. ... Wauseon, OH
Schwall, Emory A. ... Atlanta, GA
Schwall, Emory, Law Offices ... Atlanta, GA
Schwall, Leonard H. ... New City, NY
Schwall, Thomas D. ... Steamboat Springs, CO
Schwall, William G. ... Chattanooga, TN
Schwall, William G., P.C. ... Chattanooga, TN
Schwallie, David F. ... Cincinnati, OH
Schwallie, Dennis G. ... Columbus, OH
Schwallie, Mark T. ... Worcester, MA
Schwalm, Charles F. ... Burlingame, CA
Schwalm, David L. ... Bethlehem, PA
Harrisburg, PA
Schwam, Andrew ... Moscow, ID
Schwam, Barbara Banks
Mount Kisco, NY
Schwam, Bernard R. ... Encino, CA
Schwam, Brian D. ... Milwaukee, WI
Schwam Law Firm ... Moscow, ID
Schwam, Marilyn ... Moscow, ID
Schwam, Martin B. ... Livingston, NJ
Schwamb & Stabile, Inc. ... Orange, CA
Schwambach, John ... El Paso, TX
Schwamberger, Catherine S. ... Burnsville, MN
Schwamberger, Leo J., (Ltd.) ... La Salle, IL
Schwamkrug, Arno H. ... Baytown, TX
Schwamm, Albiston and Higgins, P.L.L.C.
Knoxville, TN
Schwamm, Lois C. ... New Orleans, LA
Schwamm, Michael D. ... New York, NY
Schwamm, Richard B. ... Orlando, FL
Schwamm, Virginia A. ... Knoxville, TN
Schwan, Henry M. ... Norfolk, VA
Schwan, Joy M. ... Rockville, MD
Schwan, Kristine E. ... Dallas, TX
Schwan, Mark D. ... Sioux Falls, SD
Schwanbeck & Present ... Tucson, AZ
Schwanbeck, Victor R. ... Tucson, AZ
Schwanbeck, Wm. J. ... Chicago, IL
Schwander, L. Howard, III ... Little Rock, AR
Schwandt, Craig A. ... Bellevue, WA
Schwandt, Daniel E. ... Fargo, ND
Schwandt, Gregory R. ... Great Falls, MT
Schwane, Steven J. ... Hartford, CT
Schwaneberg, Robert W. ... Trenton, NJ
Schwaninger, Robert H., Jr. ... Washington, DC
Schwanke, K. Dale ... Great Falls, MT
Schwanke, Marianne K.
Federal Trade Commission, Bureau of Consumer Protection, GV
Schwantes, Rita M. ... Boston, MA
Schwantes, Travis ... Racine, WI
Schwanz, Elizabeth F. ... Charlotte, NC
Schwappach, Harold R. ... La Grange, IL
Schwappach, Karl G. ... Minneapolis, MN
Schwappach, Kathleen R. ... Chicago, IL
Schwappach, Nancy S. ... Los Angeles, CA
Schwarb, Bruce A. ... Cincinnati, OH
Schwarb, F. Allan ... Winter Haven, FL
Schwarcz, Andrew L. ... Nashville, TN
Schwarcz, David R. ... Los Angeles, CA
Schwarcz, Gary ... Farmington Hills, MI
Schwarcz, Steven L. ... Washington, DC
Schwarcz, Susan K. ... Chapel Hill, NC
Schwarcz & Yoshino ... Los Angeles, CA
Schware, Rudolph ... Denver, CO
Schwarm, Richard P. ... Lake Mills, IA
Schwarm, Steve A. ... Topeka, KS
Schwart, C. Jay ... Columbus, OH
Schwart Law Offices ... Columbus, OH
Schwart, Omar A. ... Washington C. H., OH
Schwarte, David A. ... Fort Worth, TX
Schwarte, Joseph G. ... Eugene, OR
Schwarte, Lisa D. ... San Diego, CA
Schwartz, A. Duane ... Louisville, KY
Schwartz, Abel Jack ... Hewlett, NY
Schwartz, Abraham M. ... Baltimore, MD
Schwartz, Adam P. ... Tampa, FL
Schwartz, Adam R. ... Morristown, NJ
Schwartz, Adam J. ... Seattle, WA
Schwartz, Aileen R. ... Philadelphia, PA
Schwartz, A. J., Jr. ... Wichita, KS
Schwartz, Alan ... New Haven, CT
Schwartz, Alan ... Media, PA
Philadelphia, PA
Schwartz, Alan C. ... Grand Rapids, MI
Schwartz, Alan E. ... Aspen, CO
Schwartz, Alan E. ... Detroit, MI
Schwartz, Alan G. ... New Haven, CT
Schwartz, Alan G. ... New York, NY
Schwartz, Alan J. ... Garden City, NY
Schwartz, Alan Jay ... West Bloomfield, MI
Schwartz, Alan M. ... Columbia, MD
Schwartz, Alan R. ... Miami, FL
Schwartz, Alan R. ... New York, NY
Schwartz, Alan Stuart ... Detroit, MI
Schwartz, Alan U. ... Los Angeles, CA
Schwartz, Alana ... New York, NY
Schwartz, Albert ... Chicago, IL
Schwartz & Aldouby, P.A. ... Baltimore, MD
Schwartz, Alexander H. ... Westport, CT
Schwartz, Alice P.I. ... Philadelphia, PA
Schwartz, Allan C. ... New York, NY
Schwartz, Allan H. ... Boca Raton, FL
Schwartz, Allan L. ... Rochester, NY
Schwartz, Allen ... Detroit, MI
Schwartz, Allen ... Cincinnati, OH
Schwartz, Allen B. ... Boston, MA
Schwartz, Allen D. ... Chicago, IL
Schwartz, Allen E. ... Knoxville, TN
Schwartz, Allen G. ... New York, NY
Schwartz, Allen H. ... Scotts Valley, CA
Schwartz, Allen H. ... Richboro, PA
Schwartz, Allen L. ... Farmington Hills, MI
Schwartz, Allen M. ... New York, NY
Schwartz, Allen N. ... Chicago, IL
Schwartz, Allen R. ... Fort Collins, CO
Schwartz, Alvin M. ... New York, NY
Schwartz, Amitai ... San Francisco, CA
Schwartz, Amy ... Phoenix, AZ
Schwartz, Amy I. ... New York, NY
Schwartz, Amy L. ... New York, NY
Schwartz, Andre A. ... Telluride, CO
Schwartz, Andrea B. ... Roseland, NJ
Schwartz, Andrew ... Long Island City, NY
Schwartz, Andrew C. ... Walnut Creek, CA
Schwartz, Andrew D. ... Oklahoma City, OK
Schwartz, Andrew H. ... San Francisco, CA
Schwartz, Andrew H. ... Brockton, MA
Schwartz, Andrew N. ... Philadelphia, PA
Schwartz, Andrew R. ... Chicago, IL
Schwartz, Andrew W. ... San Francisco, CA
Schwartz, Andrew W. ... Newark, NJ
Schwartz, Andrew Z. ... Boston, MA
Schwartz, Anita ... Stratford, NJ
Schwartz, Ann Marie ... Seattle, WA
Schwartz, Anna R. ... Lake Success, NY
Schwartz, Anne L. ... Austin, TX
Schwartz, Ansel M. ... Pittsburgh, PA
Schwartz, Anthony E. ... Norwalk, CT
Schwartz, A. R. ... Houston, TX
Schwartz, Armond G. ... Hallettsville, TX
Schwartz, Arnold M. ... Chicago, IL
Schwartz, Arnold W. ... Los Angeles, CA
Schwartz, Aron M. ... Woodbridge, NJ
Schwartz, Arthur ... San Francisco, CA
Schwartz, Arthur ... Washington, DC
Schwartz, Arthur B. ... New York, NY
Schwartz, Arthur Edward ... Alexandria, VA
Schwartz, Arthur Jay ... Atlanta, GA
Schwartz, Arthur L. ... Rye Brook, NY
Schwartz, Arthur M. ... Denver, CO
Schwartz, Arthur M., P.C. ... Denver, CO
Schwartz, Arthur Z. ... New York, NY
Schwartz, Aryeh David ... Phoenix, AZ
Schwartz, Asher W. ... Washington, DC
New York, NY
Schwartz, Audra L. ... Hackensack, NJ
Schwartz, Audra Lee ... Hillside, NJ
Schwartz, Avraham ... Goshen, NY
Schwartz & Awad ... Owego, NY
Schwartz & Ballen ... Washington, DC
Schwartz, Barbara A. ... Iowa City, IA
Schwartz, Barbara A. ... New York, NY
Schwartz, Barbara D. ... Miami, FL
Schwartz, Barkin & Mitchell
Elizabeth, NJ
Union, NJ
Schwartz, Barney B. ... Syracuse, NY
Schwartz, Barry ... Rancho Palos Verdes, CA
Schwartz, Barry A. ... Denver, CO
Schwartz, Barry L. ... Merrick, NY
Schwartz, Barry M. ... Hackensack, NJ
Schwartz, Barry P. ... New York, NY
Schwartz, Barry S. ... New York, NY
Schwartz, Bart M. ... New York, NY
Schwartz, Bart R. ... Nashville, TN
Schwartz, Belinda G. ... New York, NY
Schwartz, Benjamin D. ... Chicago, IL
Schwartz, Benjamin S. ... Miami, FL
Schwartz, Bennett S. ... St. Joseph, MI
Schwartz, Berle L. ... Highland Park, IL
Schwartz, Bernard ... Tulsa, OK
Schwartz, Bernard J. ... Riverside, CA
Schwartz, Bernard M. ... Akron, OH
Schwartz, Beth Gail ... New York, NY
Schwartz, Beth P. ... Brooklyn, NY
Schwartz, Beverly Minette ... Bryn Mawr, PA
Schwartz & Blackman ... Cherry Hill, NJ
Philadelphia, PA
Schwartz, Blaine S. ... Buffalo, NY
Schwartz, Bob M. ... Glendale, CA
Schwartz, Bon, Walker & Studer, LLC
Casper, WY
Schwartz, Bradley D. ... Los Angeles, CA
Schwartz, Bradley D. ... Rockville, MD
Schwartz, Bradley D., P.A. ... Rockville, MD
Schwartz, Brandi C. ... Gulfport, MS
Schwartz, Brenda Keen ... Houston, TX
Schwartz, Brenda Keen, P.C.
Houston, TX
Schwartz, Brenda S. ... Canton, OH
Schwartz & Brennan, P.C. ... Andover, MA
Schwartz, Brett R. ... New York, NY
Schwartz, Brian D. ... Scotch Plains, NJ
Schwartz, Brian S. ... New York, NY
Schwartz & Browne ... New Orleans, LA
Schwartz, Bruce Edward
Beverly Hills, CA
Schwartz, Bruce H. ... Santa Rosa, CA
Schwartz, Bruce H. ... White Plains, NY
Schwartz, Bruce H., P.C. ... Santa Rosa, CA
Schwartz, Bruce M. ... Bala Cynwyd, PA
Schwartz, Bruce S. ... Miami Beach, FL
Schwartz, Bruce S., P.A. ... Miami Beach, FL
Schwartz, Bryan A. ... Washington, DC
Schwartz, Bryan I. ... Chicago, IL
Schwartz, Burton H. ... Farmington Hills, MI
Schwartz, C. Harold ... Newtown, CT
Schwartz, Carl F. ... New York, NY
Schwartz, Carl Ian ... New York, NY
Schwartz, Carl J. ... Pasadena, TX
Schwartz, Carl J., Jr. ... Penn Yan, NY
Schwartz, Carl R. ... Milwaukee, WI
Schwartz, Carol A. ... Treasury Department, Internal Revenue Service, GV
Schwartz, Carol B. ... Burlingame, CA
Schwartz, Carol V. ... New York, NY
Schwartz, Carolyn Karp ... New York, NY
Schwartz, Caryn Canner ... Miami, FL
Schwartz & Cera LLP ... San Francisco, CA
Newton, MA
Schwartz, Charles ... Walpole, MA
Schwartz, Charles A. ... Kensington, MD
Schwartz, Charles H. ... Culver City, CA
Schwartz, Charles I. ... Oakland, CA
Schwartz, Charles, Jr. ... New Orleans, LA
Schwartz, Charles M. ... Dallas, TX
Schwartz, Charles W. ... Houston, TX
Schwartz, Chas. P., Jr. ... Chicago, IL
Schwartz, Cheryl B. ... Philadelphia, PA
Schwartz, Cheryl R. ... Jackson, WY
Schwartz, Chester P. ... Denver, CO
Schwartz, Christopher "Kip"
Washington, DC
Schwartz, Cindy D. ... Denver, CO
Schwartz, Clarin S. ... Somerset, NJ
Schwartz, Clifford ... New York, NY
Schwartz, Cooper, Greenberger & Krauss, Chartered ... Chicago, IL
Schwartz, Cooper, Kolb & Gaynor
Chicago, IL
Schwartz, Craig M. ... Baltimore, MD
Schwartz, Craig S. ... Troy, MI
Schwartz, Cresence C. ... Troy, MI
Schwartz, Curtis W. ... Santa Fe, NM
Schwartz, Cynthia L. ... Spokane, WA
Schwartz, Dale M. ... Atlanta, GA
Schwartz, Dan T. ... Louisville, KY
Schwartz, Dana Schindler
Fort Lauderdale, FL
Schwartz, Daniel A. ... Hartford, CT
Schwartz, Daniel A. ... Roseland, NJ
Schwartz, Daniel B. ... New York, NY
Schwartz, Daniel C. ... Washington, DC
Schwartz, Daniel J. ... Chicago, IL
Schwartz, Daniel J. ... St. Louis, MO
Schwartz, Daniel L. ... Stamford, CT
Schwartz, Daniel L. ... Las Vegas, NV
Schwartz, Daniel M. ... New York, NY

Schwartz, Daniel S. .... **Miami, FL**
Schwartz, Darren A. .... **Tallahassee, FL**
Schwartz, David .... Floral Park, NY
Schwartz, David .... **New York, NY**
Schwartz, David A. .... Chicago, IL
Schwartz, David A. .... Newton, MA
Schwartz, David A. .... St. Paul, MN
Schwartz, David A. .... Asbury Park, NJ
Schwartz, David A. .... New York, NY
Schwartz, David A. .... **New York, NY**
Schwartz, David A. .... Kimberton, PA
Schwartz, David A. (Chip) .... Birmingham, AL
Schwartz, David B.
National Labor Relations Board, Office of Board Members, GV
Schwartz, David B. .... Allentown, PA
Schwartz, David C. .... **Orlando, FL**
Schwartz, David C., P.A. .... **Orlando, FL**
Schwartz, David Craig .... Washington, DC
Schwartz, David E. .... **Tampa, FL**
Schwartz, David E. .... **Chicago, IL**
Schwartz, David E. .... **New York, NY**
Schwartz, David F. .... San Diego, CA
Schwartz, David G. .... **New York, NY**
Schwartz, David G. .... **Fairfax, VA**
Schwartz, David H. .... **New York, NY**
Schwartz, David H., Law Offices of
San Francisco, CA
Schwartz, David J. .... **New York, NY**
Schwartz, David J. .... **New York, NY**
Schwartz, David J. .... Madison, WI
Schwartz, David L. .... **Washington, DC**
Schwartz, David L. .... **Chicago, IL**
Schwartz, David L. .... Pittsburgh, PA
Schwartz, David M. .... **Washington, DC**
Schwartz, David M. .... Washington, DC
Schwartz, David M. .... Baltimore, MD
Schwartz, David M. .... Portsmouth, NH
Schwartz, David M. .... New York, NY
Schwartz, David P. .... **Los Angeles, CA**
Schwartz, David P. .... **Thousand Oaks, CA**
Ventura, CA
Schwartz, David P. .... Las Vegas, NV
Schwartz, David P., Law Office of
Oxnard, CA
Schwartz, David R. .... **Mesa, AZ**
Schwartz, David R. .... West Palm Beach, FL
Schwartz, David R. .... Philadelphia, PA
Schwartz, David S. .... Los Angeles, CA
Schwartz, David S. .... Westlake Village, CA
Schwartz, David Scott .... **Washington, DC**
Schwartz, David Scott .... Floral Park, NY
Schwartz, Davida .... Norwell, MA
Schwartz, Dayla B. .... Independence, MO
Schwartz, Dean M. .... **Philadelphia, PA**
Schwartz, Debbra Wood .... Oakland, CA
Schwartz, Deborah .... **New York, NY**
Schwartz, Deborah A. .... **New York, NY**
Schwartz, Deborah R. .... New York, NY
Schwartz, Deborah R. .... Cleveland, OH
Schwartz, Debra E. .... Atlanta, GA
Schwartz, Dennis .... McKinney, TX
Schwartz, Dennis A. .... Sherman Oaks, CA
Schwartz, Dennis L. .... Carlinville, IL
Schwartz, Dennis S. .... Mission, KS
Schwartz, Derek A. .... **Miami, FL**
Schwartz, Diane .... Cleveland, OH
Schwartz, Diane .... Portland, OR
Schwartz, Don .... Oneonta, NY
Schwartz, Don T. .... Rosenberg, TX
Schwartz, Donald .... Camden, NJ
Schwartz, Donald .... Westbury, NY
Schwartz, Donald C. .... Aptos, CA
Schwartz, Donald C. .... Valley Stream, NY
Schwartz, Donald Jay .... Melville, NY
Mineola, NY
Schwartz, Donald L. .... **Chicago, IL**
Schwartz, Donna Lavista .... Florham Park, NJ
Schwartz, Douglas Hill .... Indianapolis, IN
Cincinnati, OH
Schwartz, Douglas R. .... **San Francisco, CA**
Schwartz, Douglas S. .... **Roseland, NJ**
Schwartz, Douglas W. .... **Los Angeles, CA**
Schwartz & Earp .... El Paso, TX
Schwartz, Edward A. .... Maynard, MA
Schwartz, Edward B. .... **Washington, DC**
Schwartz, Edward C. .... Treasury Department, Internal Revenue Service, GV
Schwartz, Edward D. .... San Jose, CA
Schwartz, Edward J. .... San Diego, CA
Schwartz, Edward L. .... Weston, MA
Schwartz, Edward N. .... Florham Park, NJ
Schwartz, Edward R. .... **Pasadena, CA**
Schwartz, Edward S. .... Miami, FL
Schwartz, Edward W. .... **Chicago, IL**
Schwartz, Edwin A.D. .... **Harrisburg, PA**
Schwartz, Edwin L. .... New York, NY
Schwartz, Edwin S. .... **Atlanta, GA**
Schwartz & Eichelbaum, P.C. .... **Austin, TX**
Plano, TX
San Antonio, TX
Schwartz, Elaine J. .... Hollywood, FL
Schwartz, Elaine M. .... Anoka, MN
Schwartz, Eleanor R.
Department Of The Interior, Bureau of Land Management, GV
Schwartz, Elisa .... Santa Maria, CA
Schwartz, Elisheva I. .... Racine, WI
Schwartz, Elissa .... New York, NY
Schwartz, Elissa Koopmans
Birmingham, MI
Schwartz, Elizabeth .... **Portland, OR**
Schwartz, Elizabeth A. .... Westborough, MA
Schwartz, Elizabeth F. .... Miami Beach, FL
Schwartz, Elizabeth J. .... **New York, NY**
Schwartz, Elizabeth R. .... Ann Arbor, MI
Schwartz, Ellen Tracy .... New York, NY
Schwartz, Elliot G. .... Valley Stream, NY

Schwartz and Ellis, Ltd. .... **Arlington, VA**
Fairfax, VA
Falls Church, VA
Schwartz, Eric .... Beverly Hills, CA
Schwartz, Eric A. .... New York, NY
Schwartz, Eric D. .... **Wilmington, DE**
Schwartz, Eric D. .... Pittsburgh, PA
Schwartz, Eric I. .... **New York, NY**
Schwartz, Eric J. .... **Washington, DC**
Schwartz, Eric R. .... Fort Lauderdale, FL
Schwartz, Eric W. .... **Norfolk, VA**
Schwartz, Erich T.
Securities and Exchange Commission, Division of Enforcement, GV
Schwartz, Esther Joy .... Chicago, IL
Schwartz, Eugene A. .... New York, NY
Schwartz, Eugene J. .... New York, NY
Schwartz, Eugene M. .... Santa Ana, CA
Schwartz, Eugene M. .... Treasury Department, Office of Thrift Supervision, GV
Schwartz, Evan S. .... **Garden City, NY**
Schwartz, Ferdinand M. .... New York, NY
Schwartz, Foster .... Woodbury, NY
Schwartz, Francine J. .... Daytona Beach, FL
Chicago, IL
Schwartz, Francis .... Los Angeles, CA
Schwartz, Frank .... Miami, FL
Schwartz, Frank .... **Philadelphia, PA**
Schwartz, Frank J. .... Liberal, KS
Schwartz, Franklin R. .... Brooklyn, NY
Schwartz, Fred A. .... **Sacramento, CA**
San Francisco, CA
Schwartz, Frederic S. .... Oklahoma City, OK
Schwartz, Frederick L. .... **Chicago, IL**
Schwartz, Frederick S. .... Encino, CA
Schwartz & Freeman .... **Chicago, IL**
Schwartz, Gabriel B. .... **New York, NY**
Schwartz, Garry B. .... **Miami, FL**
Schwartz, Garry B., P.A.
Coral Gables, FL
Miami, FL
Schwartz, Gary Allen .... New York, NY
Schwartz, Gary D. .... **Monterey, CA**
Schwartz, Gary H. .... Chicago, IL
Schwartz, Gary M. .... East Brunswick, NJ
Schwartz, Gary N. .... **Sherman Oaks, CA**
Schwartz, Gary R. .... **Rockville Centre, NY**
Schwartz, Geo. .... Pittsburgh, PA
Schwartz, Geoffrey B. .... **Tallahassee, FL**
Schwartz, George .... Woodland Hills, CA
Schwartz, Gerald A. .... New York, NY
Schwartz, Gerald B. .... **New York, NY**
Schwartz, Gerald K. .... Miami, FL
Miami, FL
Schwartz, Gertrude .... Brooklyn, NY
Schwartz, Gertrude M. .... Mount Kisco, NY
Schwartz, Gilbert T. .... **Washington, DC**
Schwartz, Glen H., (A Law Corp.)
Encino, CA
Schwartz, Glenn A. .... Chicago, IL
Schwartz, Glenn J., (Co., L.P.A.)
Girard, OH
Schwartz, Glenn P. .... Chicago, IL
Schwartz, Glenn R. .... Westbury, NY
Schwartz & Gnewuch, Ltd. .... Anoka, MN
Schwartz, Gold, Cohen, Zakarin & Kotler, P.A.
Boca Raton, FL
Schwartz, Grant C. .... North Prairie, WI
Schwartz & Greenberg .... New York, NY
Schwartz, Gregg R. .... **Miami, FL**
Schwartz, Gregg R., P.A., Law Offices of
Miami, FL
Schwartz, Gregory .... Mayfield Village, OH
Schwartz, Gregory J. .... **Washington, DC**
Schwartz, Gregory J. .... **Somerville, NJ**
Schwartz, Gregory J., A Professional Corporation .... **Washington, DC**
Schwartz & Grodofsky .... **Mineola, NY**
Schwartz, H. David .... **New York, NY**
Schwartz, H. Jeffrey .... **Cleveland, OH**
Schwartz, Harold Alan, Jr.
Chattanooga, TN
Schwartz, Harold D. .... Los Angeles, CA
Schwartz, Harold M. .... Brooklyn, NY
Schwartz, Harry .... Philadelphia, PA
Schwartz, Harry K. .... Rockville, MD
Schwartz, Harry S. .... Cincinnati, OH
Schwartz, Harvey .... Chicago, IL
Schwartz, Harvey .... **New York, NY**
Schwartz, Harvey A. .... **Boston, MA**
Schwartz, Helaine
Securities and Exchange Commission, Division of Enforcement, GV
Schwartz, Helen .... **San Antonio, TX**
Schwartz, Helen Iris .... **Miami, FL**
Schwartz, Helene J. .... Tallahassee, FL
Schwartz, Henry C. .... Philadelphia, PA
Schwartz, Henry E. .... **Baltimore, MD**
Schwartz, Henry R. .... New York, NY
Schwartz, Herbert A. .... Garberville, CA
Schwartz, Herbert F. .... **New York, NY**
Schwartz, Herbert T. .... **Houston, TX**
Schwartz, Herman .... United States Senate, Committee Legal Personnel, GV
Schwartz, Herman .... Dallas, TX
Schwartz, Hilda G. .... New York, NY
Schwartz, Howard .... Fair Lawn, NJ
Schwartz, Howard .... **Union, NJ**
Schwartz, Howard A. .... Rockaway Beach, NY
Schwartz, Howard D.
Fort Lauderdale, FL
Schwartz, Howard J. .... **Morristown, NJ**
New York, NY
Schwartz, Howard K. .... West Bloomfield, MI
Schwartz, Howard L. .... Piedmont, CA
Schwartz, Howard L. .... New York, NY
Schwartz, Howard M. .... **Cincinnati, OH**

Schwartz, Howard N.
Department Of Veterans Affairs, Board of Veterans Appeals, GV
Schwartz, Howard N. .... Chicago, IL
Schwartz, Howard N. .... Yakima, WA
Schwartz, Howard S. .... Washington, DC
Schwartz, Howard S. .... **Baltimore, MD**
Schwartz Hunter, P.C. .... Randolph, NJ
Schwartz, I. Michael .... New York, NY
Schwartz, Ian R. .... **San Francisco, CA**
Schwartz, Inbar .... **New York, NY**
Schwartz, Ira M. .... **Phoenix, AZ**
Schwartz, Ira S. .... Smithtown, NY
Schwartz, Iris N. .... Secaucus, NJ
Schwartz, Irving .... Bristol, CT
Schwartz, Irving .... New York, NY
Schwartz, Irving .... Milwaukee, WI
Schwartz, Irving A. .... Utica, NY
Schwartz, Irwin B. .... **Boston, MA**
Schwartz, Irwin H. .... New York, NY
Schwartz, Irwin H. .... Seattle, WA
Schwartz, Iurie A. .... **Alexandria, VA**
Schwartz, J. Michael .... **Minneapolis, MN**
Schwartz, J. Terry .... **Santa Barbara, CA**
Schwartz, Jack .... Baltimore, MD
Schwartz, Jack A. .... Rock Island, IL
Schwartz, Jack B. .... **Portland, OR**
Schwartz, Jack L. .... Los Angeles, CA
Schwartz, Jackie J. .... New York, NY
Schwartz, Jacob N. .... **Rockville Centre, NY**
Schwartz, Jaimie Paul .... **Portland, ME**
Schwartz & Jalkanen, P.C. .... **Detroit, MI**
Southfield, MI
Schwartz, James E. .... **New York, NY**
Schwartz, James E. .... **New York, NY**
Schwartz, James G., Law Offices of
Pleasanton, CA
Schwartz, James J. .... Pittsburgh, PA
Schwartz, James Jules .... **Atlanta, GA**
Schwartz, James K. .... **Boston, MA**
Schwartz, James L. .... Chicago, IL
Schwartz, James, (P.A.) .... Clearwater, FL
Schwartz, James Richard
Los Angeles, CA
Schwartz, James Stewart .... Alexandria, VA
Schwartz, James W. .... **Philadelphia, PA**
Schwartz, Jamie Brooke .... **Chicago, IL**
Schwartz, Janet Haynes .... Atlanta, GA
Schwartz & Janzen, LLP .... Los Angeles, CA
Schwartz, Jason C. .... **Washington, DC**
Schwartz, Jason J. .... **Indianapolis, IN**
Schwartz, Jay A. .... **Coral Springs, FL**
Schwartz, Jay B. .... Rahway, NJ
Schwartz, Jay D., (P.A.) .... Aventura, FL
Schwartz, Jay R. .... Tenafly, NJ
Schwartz, Jeff .... **Westmont, NJ**
Schwartz, Jeff E. .... **Washington, DC**
Schwartz, Jeffrey .... Carle Place, NY
Schwartz, Jeffrey A. .... **New Orleans, LA**
Schwartz, Jeffrey A. .... Nanuet, NY
Schwartz, Jeffrey B.
Monmouth Junction, NJ
Schwartz, Jeffrey B. .... **Albany, NY**
Schwartz, Jeffrey C. .... Philadelphia, PA
Schwartz, Jeffrey D. .... **Sherman Oaks, CA**
Schwartz, Jeffrey G. .... Vernon, CT
Schwartz, Jeffrey H. .... Tucson, AZ
Schwartz, Jeffrey H. .... New York, NY
Schwartz, Jeffrey I. .... **New York, NY**
Schwartz, Jeffrey J. .... **Charlotte, NC**
Schwartz, Jeffrey L. .... **Metuchen, NJ**
Schwartz, Jeffrey L. .... **Garden City, NY**
Schwartz, Jeffrey L. .... **New York, NY**
Schwartz, Jeffrey M. .... **Chicago, IL**
Schwartz, Jeffrey M. .... **Great Neck, NY**
Schwartz, Jeffrey M. .... New York, NY
Schwartz, Jeffrey M. .... **New York, NY**
Schwartz, Jeffrey N. .... Fort Lauderdale, FL
Schwartz, Jeffrey N. .... **New York, NY**
Schwartz, Jeffrey R.
Securities and Exchange Commission, Division of Market Regulation, GV
Schwartz, Jeffrey S. .... Batavia, OH
Schwartz, Jeffrey T. .... New York, NY
Schwartz, Jeffry R. .... **Janesville, WI**
Schwartz, Jennifer E. .... **New York, NY**
Schwartz, Jennifer E. .... **Cleveland, OH**
Schwartz, Jennifer Lee .... **New York, NY**
Schwartz, Jennifer Lynn .... Phoenix, AZ
Schwartz, Jennifer M. .... **Kansas City, MO**
Schwartz, Jeremy I. .... Department of Justice, Criminal Division, GV
Schwartz, Jerome M. .... **Detroit, MI**
Schwartz, Jerome M. .... New York, NY
Schwartz, Jerome W. .... Irvine, CA
Schwartz, Jerry H. .... Memphis, TN
Schwartz, Jesse B. .... **New York, NY**
Schwartz, Jesse Y. .... Bay Shore, NY
Schwartz, J. I. Milton .... Pierre, SD
Schwartz, Jill .... Fort Lauderdale, FL
Schwartz, Jill A. .... **Los Angeles, CA**
Schwartz, Jill S. .... **Winter Park, FL**
Schwartz, Jill S. .... Germantown, MD
Schwartz, Jill S., & Associates, P.A.
Orlando, FL
Winter Park, FL
Schwartz, Joan Weinman .... **Voorhees, NJ**
Schwartz, Joanne C. .... **Santa Ana, CA**
Schwartz, Jodi J. .... **New York, NY**
Schwartz, Jodi L. .... **New York, NY**
Schwartz, Jodi W. .... Plantation, FL
Schwartz, Joel A. .... Southfield, MI
Schwartz, Joel D. .... **Santa Monica, CA**
Schwartz, Joel D. .... **Washington, DC**
Schwartz, Joel G. .... San Jose, CA
Schwartz, Joel H. .... Boston, MA
Schwartz, Joel H., P.C. .... Boston, MA
Schwartz, Joel J. .... **St. Louis, MO**

Schwartz, Joel L. .... **Atlantic City, NJ**
Schwartz, Joel L. .... Columbus, OH
Schwartz, John .... **New York, NY**
Schwartz, John A. .... El Paso, TX
Schwartz, John B. .... **Chicago, IL**
Schwartz, John B., & Associates
Chicago, IL
Schwartz, John D. .... Chicago, IL
Schwartz, John E.
Cape May Court House, NJ
Schwartz, John G. .... Redwood City, CA
Schwartz, John K. .... **Austin, TX**
Schwartz, John L. .... Massillon, OH
Schwartz, John M. .... Titusville, FL
Schwartz, John M. .... **New York, NY**
Schwartz, John M. .... **New York, NY**
Schwartz, John N. .... **Dallas, TX**
Schwartz, John R. .... **Jersey City, NJ**
Millburn, NJ
Schwartz, John R. .... Rochester, NY
Schwartz, John S. .... **Miami, FL**
Schwartz, John W. .... Costa Mesa, CA
Schwartz, Jonathan .... Marina Del Rey, CA
Schwartz, Jonathan .... **New York, NY**
Schwartz, Jonathan B. .... Department of State, Office of the Legal Adviser, GV
Schwartz, Jonathan D. .... Department of Justice, Office of the Deputy Attorney General, GV
Schwartz, Jonathan D., Jr. .... **El Paso, TX**
Schwartz, Jonathan H. .... Phoenix, AZ
Schwartz, Jonathan M. .... **San Jose, CA**
Schwartz, Joni Beth .... New York, NY
Schwartz, Jordan M.
Department of Commerce, Patent and Trademark Office, GV
Schwartz, Jordan M. .... **New York, NY**
Schwartz, Jordana G. .... **Washington, DC**
Schwartz, Jos. X. .... Cincinnati, OH
Schwartz, Joseph A., III .... Annapolis, MD
Baltimore, MD
Schwartz, Joseph L. .... **Hollywood, FL**
Schwartz, Joseph L. .... **Morristown, NJ**
Schwartz, Joseph M. .... Houston, TX
Schwartz, Joshua I. .... Washington, DC
Schwartz, Joy S. .... New York, NY
Schwartz, Judith S. .... West Collingswood, NJ
Schwartz, Julia Plucker .... **Omaha, NE**
Schwartz, Julie C. .... Treasury Department, Internal Revenue Service, GV
Schwartz, Julie Lynne .... Brooklyn, NY
Schwartz, Julie M. .... **Miami, FL**
Schwartz, Julie R. .... **Atlanta, GA**
Schwartz Junell Campbell & Oathout, L.L.P.
Houston, TX
Schwartz, Justin .... Los Angeles, CA
Schwartz, Justin D. .... Oakland, CA
Schwartz & Kalinowski, L.L.P.
Rosenberg, TX
Schwartz, Karen .... **Thousand Oaks, CA**
Schwartz, Karen K. .... **Washington, DC**
Schwartz, Karen S. .... Montpelier, VT
Schwartz, Karin S. .... **New York, NY**
Schwartz, Karl, III .... Virginia Beach, VA
Schwartz, Kathleen Freeman
Southampton, NY
Schwartz, Kay Bittner .... **Bethesda, MD**
Hyattsville, MD
Schwartz, Kay Lyn .... **Dallas, TX**
Schwartz, Keira Lynne .... **Washington, DC**
Rockville, MD
Fairfax, VA
Schwartz, Keith M. .... **Washington, DC**
Schwartz, Kenneth B. .... Garden City, NY
Schwartz, Kenneth D. .... **Cleveland, OH**
Schwartz, Kenneth H.
Department of Transportation, Surface Transportation Board, GV
Schwartz, Kenneth J. .... **Boca Raton, FL**
Miami, FL
Schwartz, Kenneth L. .... Woodland Hills, CA
Schwartz, Kenneth L. .... **Washington, DC**
Schwartz, Kenneth L. .... **New York, NY**
Schwartz, Kenneth M. .... Beverly Hills, CA
Schwartz, Kenneth M. .... Latham, NY
Schwartz, Kenneth R. .... **Savannah, GA**
Schwartz, Kenneth R. .... **Clayton, MO**
Schwartz, Kevin .... Phoenix, AZ
Schwartz, Kimberly Leigh .... Atlanta, GA
Schwartz, Kobb & Scheinert .... **Nanuet, NY**
Schwartz, Kove J. .... Newington, CT
Schwartz, Krista S. .... **Chicago, IL**
Schwartz Kuck & Associates LLP
Atlanta, GA
Schwartz, Kurt Nathan .... Cambridge, MA
Schwartz, L. Bradley .... Chicago, IL
Schwartz, L. Michael .... Overland Park, KS
Schwartz, Lanny A. .... New York, NY
Schwartz, LaRee S. .... Santa Barbara, CA
Schwartz, Larry A. .... **Los Angeles, CA**
Schwartz, Larry C. .... Pueblo, CO
Schwartz, Larry E. .... Colorado Springs, CO
Schwartz, Larry H. .... El Paso, TX
Schwartz, Larry J. .... **New City, NY**
Schwartz, Larry R. .... Arkansas City, KS
Schwartz, Larry W. .... **Boston, MA**
Schwartz, Laura B. .... **New York, NY**
Schwartz, Laura E. .... **Denver, CO**
Schwartz, Laurence Allen .... Miami, FL
Schwartz, Laurence M. .... **West Bend, WI**
Schwartz, Laurens R. .... New York, NY
Schwartz Law Firm, P.C. .... Pueblo, CO
Schwartz Law Offices, P.C. .... Bondville, VT
Schwartz, Lawrence .... Merrick, NY
Schwartz, Lawrence .... Pittsburgh, PA
Schwartz, Lawrence H. .... Washington, DC
Schwartz, Lawrence I. .... Los Angeles, CA
Schwartz, Lawrence J. .... Melville, NY
Schwartz, Lawrence J. .... Montgomeryville, PA

Schwartz, Lawrence M. ... Fair Lawn, NJ
Schwartz, Lawrence S., (P.C.) ... Florham Park, NJ
Schwartz, Lawrence Y. ... Chicago, IL
Schwartz, Lawrence Y., Ltd. ... Chicago, IL
Schwartz, Lee A. ... Garden City, NY
Schwartz, Lee A. ... Philadelphia, PA
Schwartz, Lee J. ... Chicago, IL
Schwartz, Lee S. ... New York, NY
Schwartz, Leonard ... New York, NY
Schwartz, Leonard ... New York, NY
Schwartz, Leonard ... New York, NY
Schwartz, Leonard B. ... Southfield, MI
Schwartz, Leonard E. ... Florham Park, NJ
Princeton, NJ
Schwartz, Leonard J. ... Austin, TX
Schwartz, Leonard M. ... Birmingham, AL
Schwartz, Leonard M. ... Baltimore, MD
Schwartz, Leonard T. ... Williamstown, NJ
Schwartz, Leslie B. ... Englewood, CO
Schwartz, Lester ... San Francisco, CA
Schwartz, Lester P. ... Nanuet, NY
Schwartz, Lester S. ... Charleston, SC
Schwartz Levin & Milano, LLP ... New York, NY
Schwartz, Lew ... Minneapolis, MN
Schwartz, Lewis D., (P.C.) ... Fort Worth, TX
Schwartz, Lewis G. ... Stamford, CT
Schwartz, Lewis M. ... New York, NY
Schwartz, Linda C. ... Minneapolis, MN
Schwartz, Linda D. ... Bethesda, MD
Schwartz, Lisa A. ... Framingham, MA
Schwartz, Lisa B. ... New York, NY
Schwartz, Lisa E. ... New York, NY
Schwartz, Lisa R. ... New York, NY
Schwartz, Lisa R. ... Philadelphia, PA
Schwartz, Lloyd A. ... San Diego, CA
Schwartz, Lois Siegel
Merit Systems Protection Board, Office of Appeals Counsel, GV
Schwartz, Lonny M. ... New York, NY
Schwartz, Lori A. ... New York, NY
Schwartz, Louis ... Washington, DC
Schwartz, Louis B. ... San Francisco, CA
Schwartz, Louis C. ... Atlanta, GA
Schwartz, Louis S. ... Philadelphia, PA
Schwartz, Lynne M. ... Tucson, AZ
Schwartz, Madeline E. ... Philadelphia, PA
Schwartz, Manes & Ruby, A Legal Professional Association ... Cincinnati, OH
Schwartz, Marc ... Brooklyn, NY
Schwartz, Marc ... Media, PA
Schwartz, Marc A. ... East Brunswick, NJ
Schwartz, Marc E. ... Fort Lauderdale, FL
Schwartz, Marc H. ... Chicago, IL
Schwartz, Marc S. ... Southfield, MI
Schwartz, Marc S. ... Portland, OR
Schwartz, Marchmont J. ... Concord, CA
Schwartz, Marchmont J. ... Walnut Creek, CA
Schwartz, Marcus F. ... Hallettsville, TX
Schwartz, Margaret A. ... New York, NY
Schwartz, Maria E.
Nuclear Regulatory Commission, Office of the General Counsel, GV
Schwartz, Mark ... New York, NY
Schwartz, Mark ... Austin, TX
Schwartz, Mark A. ... Sarasota, FL
Schwartz, Mark B. ... Cleveland, OH
Schwartz, Mark D. ... Mechanicsburg, PA
Schwartz, Mark E. ... Houston, TX
Schwartz, Mark G. ... Atlantic City, NJ
Schwartz, Mark H. ... Purchase, NY
Schwartz, Mark I. ... Washington, DC
Schwartz, Mark J. ... San Jose, CA
Schwartz, Mark J. ... Washington, DC
Schwartz, Mark Kelley ... Pontiac, MI
Schwartz, Mark O. ... St. Paul, MN
Schwartz, Mark R. ... Los Angeles, CA
Schwartz, Mark S. ... Department of Energy, Office of the General Counsel, GV
Schwartz, Marlene F. ... New York, NY
Schwartz, Marlene R. ... Los Angeles, CA
Schwartz, Marshall L. ... Plymouth Meeting, PA
Schwartz, Marshall N. ... Encino, CA
Schwartz, Martin A. ... New York, NY
Schwartz, Martin A., (P.A.) ... Miami, FL
Schwartz, Martin B. ... Tampa, FL
Schwartz, Martin B. Immigration and Civil Law, Law Offices of, P.A. ... Tampa, FL
Schwartz, Martin J. ... Hollywood, FL
Schwartz, Martin J. ... New York, NY
Schwartz, Martin S. ... Los Angeles, CA
Schwartz, Martin V. ... New York, NY
Schwartz, Marty J. ... Chicago, IL
Schwartz, Marty J., P.C. ... Chicago, IL
Schwartz, Marvin ... New York, NY
Schwartz, Marvin L. ... New York, NY
Schwartz, Marvin L. ... Spring Valley, NY
Schwartz, Marvin O. ... Bethlehem, PA
Schwartz, Marvin S. ... Cleveland, OH
Schwartz, Mary Lynne ... Arlington, VA
Schwartz, Matthew D. ... Washington, DC
Schwartz, Matthew F. ... New York, NY
Schwartz, Matthew F. ... Pittsburgh, PA
Schwartz, Matthew Howard ... Los Angeles, CA
Schwartz, Matthew L. ... Washington, DC
Schwartz, Maurice ... Newburyport, MA
Schwartz, Maurice P. ... Walnut Creek, CA
Schwartz, Max H. ... New Haven, CT
Schwartz, Max H. ... Lexington, KY
Schwartz, Max J. ... New York, NY
Schwartz, McLeod, DuRant & Jordan ... Sumter, SC
Schwartz, Melissa A. ... Syosset, NY
Schwartz, Melissa A. ... Philadelphia, PA
Schwartz, Melissa Cales ... Atlanta, GA
Schwartz, Melissa Margaret ... Baltimore, MD
Schwartz, Melissa R. ... Denver, CO
Schwartz, Melvin ... North Palm Beach, FL
Schwartz, Melvin C. ... Brooklyn, NY
Schwartz, Melvin R. ... Southfield, MI
Schwartz, Merrill J. ... Oakland, CA
Schwartz, Merton L. ... Los Angeles, CA
Schwartz & Metz, P.A. ... Annapolis, MD
Baltimore, MD
Schwartz, Meyer ... Spring Valley, NY
Schwartz, Michael ... Ventura, CA
Schwartz, Michael A. ... Washington, DC
Schwartz, Michael A. ... New York, NY
Schwartz, Michael A. ... New York, NY
Schwartz, Michael A. ... New York, NY
Schwartz, Michael A. ... Philadelphia, PA
Schwartz, Michael Alan ... Southfield, MI
Schwartz, Michael B. ... Rockville, MD
Schwartz, Michael B. ... Salem, NH
Schwartz, Michael D. ... Ventura, CA
Schwartz, Michael D. ... Mount Clemens, MI
Schwartz, Michael D. ... Minneapolis, MN
Schwartz, Michael D. ... New York, NY
Schwartz, Michael E. ... Beverly Hills, CA
Schwartz, Michael E. ... Tacoma, WA
Schwartz, Michael F. ... New York, NY
Schwartz, Michael G. ... Palo Alto, CA
Schwartz, Michael G. ... Cincinnati, OH
Schwartz, Michael I. ... Tallahassee, FL
Schwartz, Michael J. ... Woodland Hills, CA
Schwartz, Michael J. ... Miami, FL
Schwartz, Michael L. ... Chicago, IL
Schwartz, Michael N. ... Chicago, IL
Schwartz, Michael R. ... Media, PA
Schwartz, Michael S. ... Springfield, NJ
Schwartz, Michael S. ... Cincinnati, OH
Schwartz, Michael S. ... Providence, RI
Schwartz, Michael W. ... New York, NY
Schwartz, Michele P. ... New York, NY
Schwartz, Michelle Leighton ... San Francisco, CA
Schwartz, Milton ... Boston, MA
Schwartz, Milton ... New York, NY
Schwartz, Milton ... Houston, TX
Schwartz, Milton L. ... St. Louis, MO
Schwartz, Mindi I. ... New York, NY
Schwartz, Mindy Ellis ... Philadelphia, PA
Schwartz, Mitchell N. ... Parsippany, NJ
Schwartz, Monica K. ... Charleston, WV
Schwartz, Mordecai T. ... New York, NY
Schwartz, Murray ... New York, NY
Schwartz, Murray D. ... Mineola, NY
Schwartz, Murray L. ... Pacific Palisades, CA
Schwartz, Murray M. ... Wilmington, DE
Schwartz, Mychal ... Seattle, WA
Schwartz, Nancee S. ... San Diego, CA
Schwartz, Nancy ... New York, NY
Schwartz, Nathan ... Pittsburgh, PA
Schwartz, Nathan A. ... Boca Raton, FL
Schwartz, Neil D. ... Encino, CA
Schwartz, Neil F. ... Encino, CA
Schwartz, Neil S. ... New York, NY
Schwartz, Newton B., Sr. ... Houston, TX
Schwartz, Niki Z. ... Cleveland, OH
Schwartz & Niles ... Glen Burnie, MD
Schwartz, Norman A. ... Carlsbad, CA
Schwartz, Norman C. ... Saugerties, NY
Schwartz, Norman L. ... Sarasota, FL
Schwartz and Nystrom, LLC ... Boston, MA
Schwartz, Page & Harding, L.L.P. ... Houston, TX
Schwartz, Pamela S. ... Methuen, MA
Schwartz, Patricia Bartley ... Wilmington, DE
Schwartz, Patricia Gorner ... Los Angeles, CA
Schwartz, Patrick D. ... Prospect Heights, IL
Schwartz, Paul ... McLean, VA
Schwartz, Paul A. ... Passaic, NJ
Schwartz, Paul D. ... Charleston, SC
Schwartz, Paul D., (P.C.) ... Boston, MA
Schwartz, Paul H. ... Charlottesville, VA
Schwartz, Paul K. ... Milwaukee, WI
Schwartz, Paul M. ... Berkeley, CA
Schwartz, Paul M. ... Southfield, MI
Schwartz, Paula L. ... Fort Lauderdale, FL
Schwartz & Perry ... New York, NY
Schwartz, Peter ... Los Angeles, CA
Schwartz, Peter ... Hartford, CT
Schwartz, Peter A. ... Newark, NJ
Schwartz, Peter A. ... New York, NY
Schwartz, Peter A. ... New York, NY
Schwartz, Peter C. ... Hartford, CT
Schwartz, Peter E. ... Boston, MA
Schwartz, Peter H. ... Washington, DC
Schwartz, Peter J. ... East Brunswick, NJ
Schwartz, Peter J. ... Middletown, OH
Schwartz, Peter L. ... Southfield, MI
Schwartz, Peter M. ... Los Angeles, CA
Schwartz, Peter R. ... New York, NY
Schwartz, Philip ... Arlington, VA
Schwartz, Philip B. ... Miami, FL
Schwartz, Philip K. ... Fort Lauderdale, FL
Schwartz, Philip L. ... Fort Lauderdale, FL
Schwartz, Philip L., P.A. ... Fort Lauderdale, FL
Schwartz, Philip M. ... Washington, DC
Schwartz, Phillip L. ... Washington, DC
Schwartz, Phyllis A. ... New York, NY
Schwartz & Posnock ... Asbury Park, NJ
Schwartz & Powell ... Ventura, CA
Schwartz, R. Monroe ... Atlanta, GA
Schwartz, Rachael E. ... Washington, DC
Schwartz, Rachel ... New York, NY
Schwartz, Ralph A. ... Las Vegas, NV
Schwartz, Ramon, Jr. ... Sumter, SC
Schwartz, Rand P. ... Massapequa Park, NY
Schwartz, Randall R. ... Burr Ridge, IL
Schwartz, Rebecca Joy ... Kansas City, MO
Schwartz, Renee ... New York, NY
Schwartz, Renee S. P. ... Albertson, NY
Schwartz, Renee Stencel ... Macon, GA
Schwartz, Revan R. ... Inwood, NY
Schwartz, Rhea S.
Federal Deposit Insurance Corporation, Trial Litigation Section, GV
Schwartz, Rhonda E. ... New York, NY
Schwartz, Rhonda J. ... St. Paul, MN
Schwartz, Richard ... Raleigh, NC
Schwartz, Richard ... Alexandria, VA
Schwartz, Richard A. ... Woodland Hills, CA
Schwartz, Richard A. ... Boca Raton, FL
Schwartz, Richard A. ... Daytona Beach, FL
Schwartz, Richard A. ... New Albany, IN
Louisville, KY
Schwartz, Richard A. ... Amite, LA
Schwartz, Richard A. ... New York, NY
Schwartz, Richard A. ... Dayton, OH
Schwartz, Richard A. ... Houston, TX
Schwartz, Richard, & Associates, Ltd. ... St. Louis, MO
Schwartz, Richard B. ... Jackson, MS
Schwartz, Richard B. ... Mineola, NY
Schwartz, Richard B. ... Philadelphia, PA
Schwartz, Richard E. ... Agoura Hills, CA
Schwartz, Richard E. ... Washington, DC
Schwartz, Richard E. ... St. Louis, MO
Schwartz, Richard G. ... New York, NY
Schwartz, Richard H. ... Palo Alto, CA
Schwartz, Richard H. ... Newark, NJ
Schwartz, Richard Hart ... Salem, MA
Schwartz, Richard J. ... Matawan, NJ
Schwartz, Richard L. ... Washington, DC
Schwartz, Richard L. ... Dallas, TX
Schwartz, Richard M.
Federal Deposit Insurance Corporation, Professional Liability Section, GV
Schwartz, Richard M. ... Parsippany, NJ
Schwartz, Richard M. ... New York, NY
Schwartz, Richard M. ... New York, NY
Schwartz, Richard M. ... New York, NY
Schwartz, Richard M. ... Owego, NY
Schwartz, Richard M. ... Cincinnati, OH
Schwartz, Richard N. ... Austintown, OH
Schwartz, Richard O. ... Long Beach, CA
Schwartz, Richard P. ... Boston, MA
Schwartz, Richard S. ... Merrick, NY
Schwartz, Richard Todd ... Owings Mills, MD
Schwartz, Richard W. ... Cleveland, OH
Schwartz, Rick L. ... Calabasas, CA
Schwartz & Riddle, P.A. ... Boca Raton, FL
Miami, FL
Schwartz, Robert ... Arlington Heights, IL
Schwartz, Robert ... Flushing, NY
Schwartz, Robert ... Hopewell Junction, NY
Schwartz, Robert A. ... Los Angeles, CA
Schwartz, Robert A. ... North Hollywood, CA
Schwartz, Robert A. ... San Francisco, CA
Schwartz, Robert A. ... Morristown, NJ
Princeton, NJ
Schwartz, Robert A. ... West Trenton, NJ
Schwartz, Robert A. ... Mineola, NY
Schwartz, Robert A. ... New York, NY
Schwartz, Robert A. ... Rochester, NY
Schwartz, Robert A. ... Houston, TX
Schwartz, Robert C. ... Atlanta, GA
Schwartz, Robert D. ... Los Angeles, CA
Schwartz, Robert D. ... Boca Raton, FL
Schwartz, Robert D. ... Minneapolis, MN
Schwartz, Robert E. ... Pennsauken, NJ
Schwartz, Robert F. ... Boston, MA
Schwartz, Robert G. ... Phoenix, AZ
Schwartz, Robert G., Jr. ... Bedford, MA
Schwartz, Robert H. ... Southfield, MI
Schwartz, Robert Hill ... New York, NY
Schwartz, Robert Hunt ... Fort Lauderdale, FL
Schwartz, Robert I. ... Ventura, CA
Schwartz, Robert J. ... Beverly Hills, CA
Schwartz, Robert J. ... Southfield, MI
Schwartz, Robert J. ... Harrisburg, PA
Schwartz, Robert L. ... Phoenix, AZ
Schwartz, Robert L. ... Bloomfield Hills, MI
Schwartz, Robert L. ... Detroit, MI
Schwartz, Robert L. ... Albuquerque, NM
Schwartz, Robert L. ... New York, NY
Schwartz, Robert L. ... Cincinnati, OH
Schwartz, Robert M. ... Los Angeles, CA
Schwartz, Robert M. ... Delray Beach, FL
Schwartz, Robert M. ... Hollywood, FL
Schwartz, Robert M. ... Miami, FL
Schwartz, Robert M. ... Boston, MA
Schwartz, Robert M. ... Jamesburg, NJ
Schwartz, Robert M. ... North Caldwell, NJ
Schwartz, Robert M. ... Philadelphia, PA
Schwartz, Robert M., P.A. ... Miami, FL
Schwartz, Robert P. ... St. Louis Park, MN
Schwartz, Robert P. ... New York, NY
Schwartz, Robert R. ... New York, NY
Schwartz, Robert S. ... Washington, DC
Schwartz, Robert S. ... Department of Defense, Office of the General Counsel, GV
Schwartz, Robert S. ... West Palm Beach, FL
Schwartz, Robert S. ... Newark, NJ
Schwartz, Robert S. ... Westfield, NJ
Schwartz, Robert S. ... Garden City, NY
Schwartz, Robert S. ... Columbus, OH
Schwartz, Robert T. ... Biloxi, MS
Schwartz, Robert W. ... Carbondale, IL
Mercedes, TX
Schwartz, Roberta S. ... Bridgeport, CT
Schwartz, Robin C. ... Randolph, NJ
Schwartz, Robt. N. ... New York, NY
Schwartz, Roger A. ... Phoenix, AZ
Schwartz, Roger A. ... Washington, DC
Schwartz, Roger G. ... New York, NY
Schwartz, Ronald ... Pueblo, CO
Schwartz, Ronald ... Hackensack, NJ
Schwartz, Ronald A. ... New York, NY
Schwartz, Ronald B. ... Newport Beach, CA
Schwartz, Ronald B. ... Chicago, IL
Schwartz, Ronald B. ... Chesterfield, MO
Schwartz, Ronald B., A Professional Corporation ... Newport Beach, CA
Schwartz, Ronald J. ... Jamaica, NY
Schwartz, Ronald M. ... Stamford, CT
Schwartz, Rose H. ... New York, NY
Schwartz, Ross J. ... San Diego, CA
Schwartz, Ross T., (P.C.) ... Encino, CA
Schwartz, Roy J. ... New York, NY
Schwartz, Ruben ... New York, NY
Schwartz, Russell J. ... Charlotte, NC
Schwartz, Russell P., Law Offices of ... Worcester, MA
Schwartz, Ruth R ... Florham Park, NJ
Schwartz, S. Emily ... Scottsdale, AZ
Schwartz & Salomon, P.C. ... New York, NY
Schwartz, Sam ... New York, NY
Schwartz, Samuel ... Matawan, NJ
Schwartz, Samuel A. ... Chicago, IL
Schwartz, Sara Goldsmith ... Andover, MA
Schwartz, Sarah Barone ... San Francisco, CA
Schwartz, Saul ... Coconut Creek, FL
Schwartz, Saul ... Detroit, MI
Schwartz, Saul E. ... Baltimore, MD
Schwartz, Saul Y.
Federal Deposit Insurance Corporation, Corporate Affairs Section, GV
Schwartz, Schlussel & Luckman ... Great Neck, NY
Schwartz & Schwartz ... Matawan, NJ
Valley Stream, NY
Cincinnati, OH
Schwartz & Schwartz ... Media, PA
Schwartz & Schwartz ... Hallettsville, TX
Schwartz & Schwartz, P.A. ... Portland, ME
Schwartz, Scott D. ... Sacramento, CA
Schwartz, Scott E. ... Treasury Department, Office of Thrift Supervision, GV
Schwartz, Scott J. ... Hattiesburg, MS
Schwartz, Scott M. ... Norwalk, CA
Schwartz, Scott M. ... Farmington, CT
Schwartz, Scott M. ... Buffalo, NY
Schwartz, Scott M. ... Staten Island, NY
Schwartz, Seth J. ... Oakland, CA
Schwartz, Seth J. ... Philadelphia, PA
Schwartz, Seth M. ... New York, NY
Schwartz, Seymour ... New York, NY
Schwartz, Sharon Lee ... Roseburg, OR
Schwartz, Shaw & Griffith ... Boston, MA
Schwartz & Shaw, P.L.L.C. ... Raleigh, NC
Schwartz, Sheila ... Ann Arbor, MI
Schwartz, Sheila F.G. ... Needham, MA
Schwartz, Sheldon ... Buffalo Grove, IL
Schwartz, Sheldon ... New York, NY
Schwartz, Shelley G. ... New York, NY
Schwartz, Sheri M. ... Los Angeles, CA
Schwartz, Sherry B. ... Philadelphia, PA
Schwartz, Sheryl Joy ... Alexandria, VA
Schwartz, Sheryl M. ... Warren, NJ
Schwartz, Shirley B. ... New York, NY
Schwartz, Sidney ... Nanuet, NY
Schwartz, Sidney A. ... New York, NY
Schwartz & Silverstein, LLP ... Montvale, NJ
New City, NY
New York, NY
Schwartz Simon Edelstein Celso & Kessler ... Florham Park, NJ
Morristown, NJ
Newark, NJ
West Orange, NJ
Schwartz, Sol ... Wilmington, DE
Schwartz, Sol ... East Northport, NY
Schwartz, Sondra R. ... Fort Lauderdale, FL
Schwartz, Spencer W. ... Chicago, IL
Schwartz, Stacey L. ... Cherry Hill, NJ
Philadelphia, PA
Schwartz, Stacey L. ... New York, NY
Schwartz, Stanley ... Roseland, NJ
Schwartz, Stanley D. ... Chicago, IL
Schwartz, Stanley D. ... Arlington, VA
Schwartz, Stanley E. ... Grass Valley, CA
Schwartz, Stanley G. ... Cleveland, OH
Schwartz, Stanley H. ... Denver, CO
Schwartz, Stanley M.
Occupational Safety and Health Review Commission, Administrative Law Judges, GV
Schwartz, Stanley M. ... Spokane, WA
Schwartz, Stanley S. ... Southfield, MI
Schwartz, Stefani C ... Florham Park, NJ
Schwartz, Stefanie L. ... Syracuse, NY
Schwartz, Steinsapir, Dohrmann & Sommers, LLP ... Los Angeles, CA
Pittsburgh, PA
Schwartz, Stephanie D. ... Kew Gardens, NY
Schwartz, Stephanie L. ... St. Paul, MN
Schwartz, Stephanie R. ... New York, NY
Schwartz, Stephen ... New York, NY
Schwartz, Stephen H. ... Glen Burnie, MD
Schwartz, Stephen H. ... New York, NY
Schwartz, Stephen J. ... Portland, ME
Schwartz, Stephen J. ... Yonkers, NY
Schwartz, Stephen Jay ... Ann Arbor, MI
Schwartz, Stephen L. ... Los Angeles, CA
Schwartz, Stephen M. ... Los Angeles, CA
Schwartz, Stephen M. ... Charleston, WV
Schwartz, Steve R. ... Pasadena, CA
Schwartz, Steven ... Dover, DE
Schwartz, Steven ... Chicago, IL
Schwartz, Steven ... Boston, MA
Schwartz, Steven A. ... New Bedford, MA
Schwartz, Steven A. ... New York, NY

Schwartz, Steven A. ....Haverford, PA
Schwartz, Steven Brian
Plymouth Meeting, PA
Schwartz, Steven C. ....New York, NY
Schwartz, Steven F. ....Washington, DC
Schwartz, Steven G. ....Boca Raton, FL
Schwartz, Steven G. ....Rochester, NY
Schwartz, Steven H. ....Los Angeles, CA
Schwartz, Steven H. ....Southfield, MI
Schwartz, Steven H. ....St. Louis, MO
Schwartz, Steven H. ....Philadelphia, PA
Schwartz, Steven J. ....Los Angeles, CA
Schwartz, Steven J. ....Washington, DC
Schwartz, Steven J. ....Northampton, MA
Schwartz, Steven J. ....Springfield, MA
Schwartz, Steven J. ....Southfield, MI
Schwartz, Steven J. ....Cuyahoga Falls, OH
Schwartz, Steven L. ....Southfield, MI
Schwartz, Steven M. ....New York, NY
Schwartz, Steven M. ....New York, NY
Schwartz, Steven N. ....San Diego, CA
Schwartz, Steven, P.A. ....Dover, DE
Schwartz, Stewart J. ....Los Angeles, CA
Schwartz, Stuart A. ....Norfolk, VA
Schwartz, Stuart A. ....Madison, WI
Schwartz, Stuart D. ....New York, NY
Schwartz, Stuart G. ....New York, NY
Schwartz, Stuart I. ....Laurel, MD
Schwartz, Stuart J. ....Rancho Cucamonga, CA
Schwartz, Stuart M. ....New York, NY
Schwartz, Stuart R. ....Chicago, IL
Schwartz, Stuart R. ....El Paso, TX
Schwartz, Sue Simpson ....Manvel, TX
Schwartz, Susan Abbott ....Dallas, TX
Schwartz, Susan E. ....San Francisco, CA
Schwartz, Susan E. ....Chicago, IL
Schwartz, Susan G. ....Portland, ME
Schwartz, Susan J. ....Chicago, IL
Schwartz, Susan J. ....Chicago, IL
Schwartz, Susan J. ....New York, NY
Schwartz, Susan Jill ....Atlanta, GA
Schwartz, Susette M. ....Wichita, KS
Schwartz, Suzanne ....Austin, TX
Schwartz, Suzanne W.
Fort Lauderdale, FL
Schwartz, Ted G. ....Department of Justice, Federal Bureau of Investigation, GV
Schwartz, Terence B. ....New York, NY
Schwartz, Teresa M. ....Washington, DC
Schwartz, Teri F. ....Pomona, CA
Schwartz, Terrence S. ....Miami, FL
Schwartz, Terry Ferraro ....Atlanta, GA
Schwartz, Tessa J. ....San Francisco, CA
Schwartz, Theodore A. ....Montclair, NJ
Trenton, NJ
Schwartz, Theodore A. ....Philadelphia, PA
Schwartz, Theodore F. ....San Francisco, CA
Santa Monica, CA
Clayton, MO
Schwartz, Theodore F. ....St. Louis, MO
Schwartz, Thomas ....Miami, FL
Schwartz, Thomas E. ....Hattiesburg, MS
Schwartz, Thomas E. ....St. Louis, MO
Schwartz, Thomas E. ....State College, PA
Schwartz, Thomas J. ....Ann Arbor, MI
Schwartz, Tiberio ....New York, NY
Schwartz, Timothy P. ....Bethesda, MD
Schwartz, Timothy R.
South San Francisco, CA
Schwartz, Tobia, Stanziale, Becker, Rosensweig & Sedita, A Professional Association
Montclair, NJ
Trenton, NJ
Schwartz, Tobiane ....New York, NY
Schwartz, Todd E. ....Atlanta, GA
Schwartz, Todd R. ....Miami, FL
Schwartz, Tofte & Nielsen, Ltd. ....Racine, WI
Schwartz & Ussach ....New Bedford, MA
Schwartz, Victor B. ....Providence, RI
Schwartz, Victor E. ....Washington, DC
Schwartz, Victor L. ....Santa Fe, NM
Schwartz, Victoria ....Rosemead, CA
Schwartz, Victoria A. ....Secaucus, NJ
Schwartz, Victoria Winkler
Los Angeles, CA
Schwartz, Vivian L. ....San Diego, CA
Schwartz, Wallace L. ....New York, NY
Schwartz, Walter M. ....Yonkers, NY
Schwartz, Walter S. ....Detroit, MI
Schwartz, Warren & Ramirez
Columbus, OH
Schwartz, Warren S. ....Miami, FL
Schwartz, Wayne H. ....Fort Lauderdale, FL
Schwartz, Wayne S. ....San Diego, CA
Schwartz & Weinrieb ....Arlington, VA
Schwartz Weiss Steckler Hoffman & Hade, P.C.
New York, NY
Schwartz, Weldon H. ....Grand Rapids, MI
Schwartz, Wendy H. ....New York, NY
Schwartz, Wendy Helene ....Washington, DC
Rockville, MD
Fairfax, VA
Schwartz, William ....Kearny, NJ
Schwartz, William ....New York, NY
Schwartz, William A. ....Philadelphia, PA
Schwartz, William B. ....New Orleans, LA
Schwartz, William B. ....Bondville, VT
Schwartz, William C. ....Pittsburgh, PA
Schwartz, William E. ....Boston, MA
Schwartz, William G. ....Murphysboro, IL
Schwartz, William G. ....Philadelphia, PA
Schwartz, William H. ....Los Angeles, CA
Schwartz, William I. ....San Francisco, CA
Schwartz, William J. ....Newark, NJ
Schwartz, William J. ....New York, NY
Schwartz, William J., Jr. ....San Diego, CA
Schwartz, William K. ....Charleston, WV
Schwartz, William M. ....Department of Energy, Office of Hearings and Appeals, GV
Schwartz, William P. ....Jackson, WY
Schwartz, William Scott ....Chicago, IL
Schwartz, William T. ....Casper, WY
Schwartz Willis, LLC ....Somerville, NJ
Schwartz, Wisot & Wilson, LLP
Beverly Hills, CA
Los Angeles, CA
Schwartz, Woods & Miller
Washington, DC
Schwartz & Zuckert ....New York, NY
Schwartzapfel, Langley ....Santa Cruz, CA
Schwartzapfel, Steven J. ....Huntington, NY
Schwartzbach, M. Gerald ....Mill Valley, CA
Schwartzbach, Marc P. ....Westfield, NJ
Schwartzbach, Saul M. ....Bethesda, MD
Schwartzbard, Gail I. ....Phoenix, AZ
Schwartzbard, Michael H. ....Cedar Grove, NJ
Schwartzbard, Richard L. ....Washington, DC
Schwartzbauer, Paula ....Minneapolis, MN
Schwartzbauer, Robert A.
Minneapolis, MN
Schwartzbaum, Barbara Carole
New York, NY
Schwartzbaum, David M. ....New York, NY
Schwartzberg, Alan L. ....Baton Rouge, LA
Schwartzberg, Barnett & Cohen
Chicago, IL
Schwartzberg, Brad J. ....New York, NY
Schwartzberg, Charles W. ....Elizabeth, NJ
Schwartzberg, David A. ....Garden City, NY
Schwartzberg, H. Lee, Jr.
Philadelphia, PA
Schwartzberg, Harris R. ....White Plains, NY
Schwartzberg, Harvey ....Elizabeth, NJ
Schwartzberg, Hugh J. ....Chicago, IL
Schwartzberg, Julie B.
Fort Lauderdale, FL
Schwartzberg, Louis J. ....New York, NY
Schwartzberg, Martin A.
Garden City, NY
Schwartzberg, Michael ....New York, NY
Schwartzberg, Michael Scott
St. Petersburg, FL
Schwartzberg, Murray B. ....Tenafly, NJ
Schwartzberg, Ora, (Ms) ....Saranac Lake, NY
Schwartzberg, Paul K. ....New York, NY
Schwartzberg, Raymond B. ....New York, NY
Schwartzberg, Richard ....Santa Ana, CA
Schwartzberg, Scot A. ....Houston, TX
Schwartzberg, Sherman D. ....Atlanta, GA
Schwartzberg, Sol E. ....Larchmont, NY
Schwartzberg, Stephanie M.
Philadelphia, PA
Schwartzburt, Norman ....Oak Lawn, IL
Schwartz-Carney, Sandra L. ....Waltham, MA
Schwartze, David A. ....Vienna, MO
Schwartze, Erich W., III ....Waco, TX
Schwartze, James E. ....Overland Park, KS
Schwartze, Richard J. ....St. Louis, MO
Schwartze, Terry Daley ....Vienna, MO
Schwartzel, C. Boone ....Houston, TX
Schwartzenburg, John Walter Van
Houston, TX
Schwartzer, Geraldine H. ....Las Vegas, NV
Schwartzer, Lenard E. ....Beverly Hills, CA
Las Vegas, NV
Schwartzer, Richard D ....Bay Shore, NY
Schwartzfield, Sidney M. ....Minneapolis, MN
Schwartzkopf, Carol Teague ....New York, NY
Schwartz-Leeper, David A. ....New York, NY
Schwartzman, Alan M. ....Boise, ID
Schwartzman, Amy ....New York, NY
Schwartzman, Andrea J. ....New York, NY
Schwartzman, Andrew Jay ....Washington, DC
Schwartzman, Annette ....Wantagh, NY
Schwartzman, Benjamin A. ....Seattle, WA
Schwartzman, Charles ....Highland Park, NJ
Schwartzman, Daniel A. ....New York, NY
Schwartzman, Denise Davis
Haverford, PA
Schwartzman, Emmet J. ....Miami, FL
Schwartzman, Eric A. ....Wilmington, DE
Schwartzman, Eric J. ....New York, NY
Schwartzman, Eva ....Libertyville, IL
Schwartzman, Everett H. ....Torrance, CA
Schwartzman, Frank A. ....Rochester, NY
Schwartzman, Frederick ....New York, NY
Schwartzman Garelik Walker Kapiloff & Troy, P.C. ....Stamford, CT
Boca Raton, FL
New York, NY
Schwartzman, Herbert D. ....Jamaica, NY
Schwartzman, Herman ....New York, NY
Schwartzman, Howard K. ....Allendale, NJ
Schwartzman, Jack ....Los Angeles, CA
Schwartzman, Jack A. ....Palo Alto, CA
Schwartzman, James ....New York, NY
Schwartzman, James C. ....Philadelphia, PA
Schwartzman, James C., & Associates, P.C.
Philadelphia, PA
Schwartzman, Jerome M.
Treasury Department, Internal Revenue Service, GV
Schwartzman, Jonathan B. ....Garden City, NY
Schwartzman, Julia ....Palo Alto, CA
Schwartzman, Mark A., (P.C.)
San Antonio, TX
Schwartzman, Melvin I. ....New Orleans, LA
Schwartzman, Mitchel ....San Antonio, TX
Schwartzman, Richard W. ....Washington, DC
Schwartzman, Robert M. ....Baltimore, MD
Schwartzman, Robin Berman
Chevy Chase, MD
Schwartzman, Ronald N. ....New York, NY
Schwartzman, Russell S. ....San Diego, CA
Schwartzman, S. Howard ....Highland Park, NJ
Schwartzman and Schwartzman
Highland Park, NJ
Schwartzman, Steven Bruce ....Towson, MD
Schwartzman, Wayne A. ....Marengo, IL
Schwartzmann, Martha ....Sacramento, CA
Schwartzreich, Sidney ....Harrison, NY
Schwartzreich, Steven S. ....Great Neck, NY
Schwartzstein, Arthur M. ....McLean, VA
Schwartzstein, Arthur M., P.C. ....McLean, VA
Schwartzstein, Linda A. ....Arlington, VA
Schwartz-Weinstock, Nancy A.
New York, NY
Schwary, Mitchell L., Jr. ....Santa Ana, CA
Schwarz, Alan F. ....Summit, NJ
Schwarz, Aloys K. ....Bloomfield Hills, MI
Schwarz, Aloys K., P.C., Law Office of
Bloomfield Hills, MI
Schwarz & Associates, P.C. ....Olivette, MO
Schwarz, Barry P. ....Atlanta, GA
Schwarz, Benedict, II ....Dundee, IL
Schwarz, Benjamin K. ....Washington, DC
Schwarz, Bernard A. ....Union City, NJ
Schwarz, Bradley K. ....Costa Mesa, CA
Schwarz, C. Fred, Jr. ....Boynton Beach, FL
Schwarz, Carl A., Jr. ....Garden City, NY
Schwarz, Carl W. ....Washington, DC
Schwarz, Daniel L. ....Billings, MT
Schwarz, Daniel P. ....Exeter, NH
Schwarz, Daniel R. ....Palo Alto, CA
Schwarz, David A. ....Los Angeles, CA
Schwarz, David H. ....Madison, WI
Schwarz, David M. ....Washington, DC
Schwarz, David M. ....New York, NY
Schwarz, Deborah Ballins ....Pasadena, CA
Schwarz, Deborah Glass ....Federal Mediation and Conciliation Service, GV
Schwarz & DeMarco, LLP
Garden City, NY
Schwarz, Douglas A. ....Cincinnati, OH
Schwarz, Earle J. ....Memphis, TN
Schwarz, Edward H., Jr. ....Lanham, MD
Schwarz, Elton H. ....Jensen Beach, FL
Schwarz, Eric F. ....Rock Island, IL
Schwarz, Eric T. ....Springerville, AZ
Schwarz, Erika R. ....New Orleans, LA
Schwarz, Frederick A.O., Jr.
New York, NY
Schwarz, Frederick D. ....San Francisco, CA
Schwarz, Frederick E. ....Englewood, CO
Schwarz, George ....Fresh Meadows, NY
Schwarz, George E.
Hastings-On-Hudson, NY
Schwarz, Helfried J. ....New York, NY
Schwarz, Jacob ....San Francisco, CA
Schwarz, James ....Daytona Beach, FL
Schwarz, James H. ....Indianapolis, IN
Schwarz, James N. ....Washington, DC
Schwarz, Jeff ....Milwaukee, WI
Schwarz, Jeffrey A. ....Washington, DC
Schwarz, Jeffrey A. ....Miami, FL
Schwarz, Jeffrey C. ....Chicago, IL
Schwarz, Jeffrey W. ....Denver, CO
Schwarz, Jerrold W. ....Pickerington, OH
Schwarz, Jerry L. ....Burlington, VT
Schwarz, Joel M. ....Binghamton, NY
Schwarz, John D., Jr. ....Chico, CA
Schwarz, John E. ....Washington, DC
Schwarz, John E. ....Minneapolis, MN
Schwarz, John M., Jr. ....Suffern, NY
Schwarz, Jonathan L. ....New York, NY
Schwarz, Joseph K. ....New York, NY
Schwarz, Julius R. ....New York, NY
Schwarz, Kahle & Keller, P.A.
Port Charlotte, FL
Punta Gorda, FL
Schwarz, Kenneth G. ....New York, NY
Schwarz, Kent L. ....Morristown, NJ
Schwarz, Kristina ....Kew Gardens, NY
Schwarz, Kurt A. ....Dallas, TX
Schwarz, Leigh E. ....Portland, OR
Schwarz, Lori Samet ....New York, NY
Woodbury, NY
Schwarz, Marcey Femling ....Billings, MT
Schwarz, Mark ....Watchung, NJ
Schwarz, Mark ....New York, NY
Schwarz, Mark L. ....Chicago, IL
Schwarz, Melbert, Jr. ....Houston, TX
Schwarz, Michael ....New York, NY
Schwarz, Michael B. ....San Francisco, CA
Schwarz, Michael H. ....Las Vegas, NV
Schwarz, Michael J. ....Atlanta, GA
Schwarz, Michael J., Law Offices of
Baltimore, MD
Towson, MD
Schwarz, Michelle ....Las Vegas, NV
Schwarz, Norah Ascoli
Department of Justice, Civil Division, GV
Schwarz, Norman K. ....Miami, FL
Schwarz, Paul A. ....Princeton, NJ
Schwarz, Paul E. ....Cincinnati, OH
Schwarz, Peter ....San Francisco, CA
Schwarz, Peter ....Tallahassee, FL
Schwarz, Peter C. ....White Plains, NY
Schwarz, Raimonde ....New York, NY
Schwarz, Ralph ....Westport, CT
Schwarz, Ralph J., Jr. ....New York, NY
Schwarz, Robert J. ....Chicago, IL
Schwarz, Robert L. ....McAllen, TX
Schwarz, Robert O. ....Miami, FL
Schwarz, Robert R. ....Olivette, MO
Schwarz, Rodney A. ....Santa Rosa, CA
Schwarz, Roger J. ....New York, NY
Schwarz, S. Bernard ....Newark, NJ
Schwarz, Scott J. ....Westmont, NJ
Philadelphia, PA
Schwarz, Self, White, Cooper & McDonald
Jerseyville, IL
Schwarz, Sidney M. ....Chula Vista, CA
Schwarz, Stanley M. ....Philadelphia, PA
Schwarz, Stephen ....San Francisco, CA
Schwarz, Stephen deH.
Port Charlotte, FL
Schwarz, Stephen G. ....Rochester, NY
Schwarz, Stephen W. ....New York, NY
Schwarz, Steven G. ....Bronx, NY
Schwarz, Susan E. ....West Palm Beach, FL
Schwarz, Suzanne M. ....Houston, TX
McAllen, TX
Schwarz, Suzanne M., P.C., Law Offices of
McAllen, TX
Schwarz, Thomas J. ....New York, NY
Schwarz, Thomas R. ....St. Louis, MO
Schwarz, Todd ....Albuquerque, NM
Schwarz, Todd A. ....Devils Lake, ND
Schwarz, William E. ....Wauwatosa, WI
Schwarz, William P. ....Riverview, FL
Schwarz, William W. ....Des Moines, IA
Schwarzbach, Glenn D. ....San Jose, CA
Schwarzbach, Marshall J. ....Chicago, IL
Schwarzbach, Robert T. ....El Paso, TX
Schwarzbach, Robert T., P.C. ....El Paso, TX
Schwarzbart, Robert M.
National Labor Relations Board, Division of Administrative Law Judges, GV
Schwarzberg & Kittrell ....New York, NY
Schwarzberg, Steven L.
West Palm Beach, FL
Schwarze, Carl F. ....Detroit, MI
Schwarze, Frederick B. ....Detroit, MI
Schwarze, Priscilla L. ....Detroit, MI
Schwarze, William W. ....Philadelphia, PA
Schwarzell, Michael L. ....London, OH
Schwarzenbach, Peter M. ....Dallas, TX
Schwarzenbart, Paul W. ....Madison, WI
Schwarzenberg, Joseph A. ....New York, NY
Schwarzer, Franklin J. ....Syracuse, NY
Schwarzer, Mary Esther ....Manchester, NH
Schwarzer, William W ....San Francisco, CA
Schwarzfeld, Ganfer & Shore, LLP
New York, NY
Schwarzfeld, Neal ....New York, NY
Schwarzkopf, Kurt I. ....St. Paul, MN
Schwarzkopf, Louis ....Miami Beach, FL
Schwarzkopf, Nancy E.
Port Washington, NY
Schwarzkopf, Peter B.
Department of Transportation, Office of the General Counsel, GV
Schwarzkopf, Robert A. ....Churdan, IA
Jefferson, IA
Schwarzkopf, Ronald Craig ....Sacramento, CA
Schwarzman, Christine Hearst
New York, NY
Schwarzmann, Michael D.
Los Angeles, CA
Schwarzmann, Sandra M.
Los Angeles, CA
Schwarzmann, Valorie G. ....Columbus, OH
Schwarzschild, Glen-David ....Cherry Hill, NJ
Schwarzschild, Hannah ....Philadelphia, PA
Schwarzschild, Jane L. ....Richmond, VA
Schwarzschild, Patricia M. ....Richmond, VA
Schwarzschild, William H., III
Richmond, VA
Schwarzstein, Richard J. (IBA)
Newport Beach, CA
Schwarzwaelder, Arthur L.
Pittsburgh, PA
Schwarzwald, Melvin S. ....Cleveland, OH
Schwarzwald & Rock, L.P.A.
Cleveland, OH
Schwarzwalder, Brian A. ....Seattle, WA
Schwarz-Zik, Jessica E. ....Dallas, TX
Schwasinger, Rodney W. ....Bozeman, MT
Schwass, Earl R. ....Newport, RI
Schway & Cowle, Ltd. ....Burnsville, MN
Schway, Eugene J. ....St. Paul, MN
Schway, Robert N. ....Burnsville, MN
Schway, Thomas B. ....St. Paul, MN
Schwebach, M. Joanne ....Orlando, FL
Schwebel, Abbot B. ....Vernon, CT
Schwebel, Goetz & Sieben, P.A.
Minneapolis, MN
St. Paul, MN
Schwebel, James R. ....Minneapolis, MN
Schwebel, M. Mac ....White Plains, NY
Schwebel, Nancy A. ....Delmar, NY
Schwebel, Paul R. M. ....Indianapolis, IN
Schwebel & Tarpey, P.C. ....Vernon, CT
Schweber, Izenson & Anderson, LLP
Atlanta, GA
Schweber, Matthew S. ....New York, NY
Schweber, Scott A. ....Atlanta, GA
Schweber, Scott M. ....New York, NY
Schweber, Todd A. ....Atlanta, GA
Schwebke, Mark William F ....Tulsa, OK
Schwebs, Monica A. ....Department of Justice, Environment and Natural Resources Division, GV
Schwebs, Robin Blain ....Claremont, CA
Schwechter, Arnold ....Chicago, IL
Schwechter, Melvin S. ....Washington, DC
Schwed, Alejandro ....New York, NY
Schwed, Douglas E. ....Kirkland, WA
Schwed, Kathryn S. ....Newark, NJ
Schwed, Lloyd R. ....West Palm Beach, FL
Schwed, Mariano ....New York, NY
Schwed, Michael J. ....Kew Gardens, NY
Schwed, Nathan ....New York, NY
Schwed, P. Gregory ....New York, NY
Schwed, Richard F. ....New York, NY
Schwed, Robert A. ....New York, NY
Schwed, Roger E. ....New York, NY
Schwed, Stephen W.
West Palm Beach, FL

Scibilia & McCuin, P.C. .... Berlin, CT
Hartford, CT
Scibilia, Suzanne M. .... Berlin, CT
Scibinico, Michael J., II .... Elkton, MD
Scicchitano, Anthony R. .... Lititz, PA
Scichili, Thomas P. .... Steamboat Springs, CO
Scidmore, Patricia N. .... Tustin, CA
Scidmore, S. Bruce .... Wheaton, IL
Scidurlo, Lisa Marie .... Philadelphia, PA
Scienski, Larry E. .... Paramus, NJ
Scieszinski, Annette J. .... Albia, IA
Scieszinski, D. Brian .... Des Moines, IA
Scieszinski, David L. .... Wilton, IA
Scieszinski, John J. .... Des Moines, IA
Scieszka, James A. .... Birmingham, MI
Scifo, Francis H. .... New York, NY
Scifo, Joann M. .... Mineola, NY
Scifo, Paul C. .... Franklin Square, NY
Scifres, C. Grigsby .... Virginia Beach, VA
Scifres, Dennis R. .... Fort Worth, TX
Scifres, Thomas E. .... Indianapolis, IN
Sciglimpaglia, Robert, Jr. .... Stamford, CT
Scileppi, James G., III .... Los Angeles, CA
Scileppi, Jeremy J. .... Poughkeepsie, NY
Scilley, Heather A. .... Houston, TX
Scillieri, David .... Elmwood Park, NJ
Scillieri, John A. .... Santa Monica, CA
Scillieri, Peter .... Waterford, CT
Scillieri, Salvatore R. .... Elmwood Park, NJ
Scime, Anthony J. .... Buffalo, NY
Scime, James T. .... Buffalo, NY
Scime, Joseph A. .... Williamsville, NY
Scimeca, James A. .... Oklahoma City, OK
Scimeca, Karen A. .... Sanford, FL
Scimeca, Lisa Sigall .... Marlton, NJ
Scimeca, Mark D. .... Orlando, FL
Scimeca, Michael .... Palo Alto, CA
Scimeca, Richard R. .... Austin, TX
Scimeca, S. A. (Tim), P.A., Law Offices of
Wichita, KS
Scimeca, S. A. (Tim) .... Wichita, KS
Scimia, Joseph M. .... Indianapolis, IN
Scimone, Richard S. .... Waltham, MA
Scimonelli, Paul M. .... Hartford, CT
Scinta, Arthur L. .... New York, NY
Scinta, Denis A. .... Buffalo, NY
Scinta, Joseph J., Jr. .... Buffalo, NY
Scinta, Michael C. .... Depew, NY
Scinta & Rinaldo .... Buffalo, NY
Scinto, Blaise A.
Federal Communications Commission,
Common Carrier Bureau, GV
Scinto, Frank J. .... Waterbury, CT
Scinto, Joseph F. .... Rockville, MD
Scinto, Lawrence F. .... New York, NY
Scinto, Michael L. .... Farmington, CT
Scinto, Michael R. .... Washington, DC
Scinto, Shelly A. .... Chicago, IL
Sciocchetti, Nancy .... Albany, NY
Sciocchetti, Paul V. .... Schenectady, NY
Sciolino, Anthony J. .... Rochester, NY
Sciolino, Leonard M. .... Vero Beach, FL
Sciolino, Nino R. .... Buffalo, NY
Sciolla, Anthony J., Jr. .... Elkins Park, PA
Sciolla, Gregory E. .... Moorestown, NJ
Philadelphia, PA
Sciolla, Guy R. .... Philadelphia, PA
Sciolto, Vito L. .... Cranston, RI
Scionti, Joseph J. .... Kokomo, IN
Scionti, Kevin L. .... Indianapolis, IN
Scionti, Michael J. .... Tampa, FL
Sciorra, Nicholas E. .... New York, NY
Sciortino & Albanese, Esqs. .... Goshen, NY
Sciortino, John .... Rochester, NY
Sciortino, John J. .... Fresno, CA
Sciortino, Michael A. .... Council Bluffs, IA
Sciortino, Richard J. .... Chicago, IL
Sciortino, Sandra B. .... Goshen, NY
Sciortino, Steven Domenic .... Macedonia, OH
Sciortino Vannier & Rater
Council Bluffs, IA
Sciota, Mark J. .... Southington, CT
Sciotti, Christopher R. .... St. Clair Shores, MI
Sciotti, Glen J. .... Cranston, RI
Sciotti, Michael J. .... Syracuse, NY
Scipione, John E. .... Denver, CO
Scipione, Richard S. .... Boston, MA
Scipioni, Mark L. .... St. Paul, MN
Sciretta, Antonia M. .... New York, NY
Sciria, Patricia A. .... Auburn, NY
Scirica, Anthony J. .... Philadelphia, PA
Sciro, Frank J., Jr. .... Paterson, NJ
Scirocco, Robert A. .... Budd Lake, NJ
Scirto, Thomas W. .... Lockport, NY
Medina, NY
Sciscente, Marybeth P. .... Garden City, NY
Sciscento, Joseph .... Las Vegas, NV
Sciscoe, Marc W. .... Indianapolis, IN
Scislowski, Richard J. .... Cleveland, OH
Scism, D. Reed .... Indianapolis, IN
Sciullo, Dan A. .... Denver, CO
Sciullo and Goodyear, P.C. .... Pittsburgh, PA
Sciullo, Joanne E. .... Philadelphia, PA
Sciullo, John J. .... Pittsburgh, PA
Sciullo, Lisa J. .... Washington, PA
Sciullo, Samuel R. .... Pittsburgh, PA
Sciurba, Dennis V. .... New York, NY
Sciuto, Anthony J. .... Hackensack, NJ
Sciuto, Cynthia A. .... St. Louis, MO
Sciuto, Linda A. .... New York, NY
Sciuto-Reidel, AnnMarie .... Newark, NJ
Skalor, Robert D. .... Santa Fe, NM
Sckerl, Carolyn M. .... Houston, TX
Sclafane, Salvatore .... Bayonne, NJ
Sclafani, Accursio P. .... New York, NY
Sclafani, Anthony .... Santa Monica, CA
Sclafani, Aurelius J. .... Sayville, NY
Sclafani, Karen C. .... Garden City, NY
Sclafani, Leonard A. .... New York, NY
Sclafani, Mario A. .... South Salem, NY
Sclafani, Mary Jane .... New York, NY
Sclafani, Michael V. .... Yonkers, NY
Sclafani, Rita Berry .... Fort Lauderdale, FL
Sclafani, Salvador H. .... Hackensack, NJ
Sclafani, Thomas D. .... Fort Lauderdale, FL
Sclafani, Thomas D., P.A.
Fort Lauderdale, FL
Sclafani, Vincent M. .... Yonkers, NY
Sclafanirhee, Jeannie H
Department of Justice,
Office of Policy Development, GV
Sclar, Alan .... New York, NY
Sclar, Andrew P. .... San Francisco, CA
Sclar, Bradley K. .... Bridgewater, NJ
Sclar, Diana S. .... Newark, NJ
Sclar, Douglass F. .... Florham Park, NJ
Sclar, Jennifer .... New York, NY
Sclar, Lee J. .... Maplewood, NJ
Sclarow, Marshall H. .... Lakewood, CO
Sclater, Hoskins M. .... Roanoke, VA
Sclawy, Mary P. .... Troy, MI
Scobbo, Nicholas J., Jr. .... Boston, MA
Scobee, H. Evans .... Baton Rouge, LA
Scobel, Bradley .... Birmingham, MI
Scobey, Alfredda .... Atlanta, GA
Scobey, John Nelson .... Eagan, MN
Scobey, Julia M. .... Oklahoma City, OK
Scobey, M. Kirk, Jr. .... Nashville, TN
Scobie & Morlang, L.L.C. .... Denver, CO
Scobie, Patrick .... Denver, CO
Scobie, Timothy F. .... Chippewa Falls, WI
Scoble, Andrew M. .... San Francisco, CA
Scoblionko, Mark H. .... Allentown, PA
Scoblionko, Scoblionko, Muir, Bartholomew & Melman, A Professional Corporation
Allentown, PA
Scoby, Jill A. .... Sunnyvale, CA
Scoby, Terry W. .... Boulder, CO
Scocca, Joseph E. .... Philadelphia, PA
Scoccia, Linda .... Everett, WA
Scoccimaro, Ralph O. .... Albany, GA
Scoco, Priscilla Rellas .... North Chicago, IL
Scodeller, Raymond L. .... Lansing, MI
Scodeller, Raymond L., P.C. .... Lansing, MI
Scoff, Paul Allen .... Houston, TX
Scoffield, Kelly H. .... Houston, TX
Scoffield, Lindy H. .... Sacramento, CA
Scofield, Bryan D. .... Lafayette, LA
Scofield, Christine A .... Syracuse, NY
Scofield, David W. .... Salt Lake City, UT
Scofield, Denise U. .... Houston, TX
Scofield, Douglas H. .... Birmingham, AL
Scofield, Douglas W. .... Chicago, IL
Scofield, E. Clayton, III .... Atlanta, GA
Scofield, Edward .... New York, NY
Scofield, Edward R. .... Bridgeport, CT
Scofield, Eileen M. G. .... Atlanta, GA
Scofield, Frank E. .... Austin, TX
Scofield, Frank L. .... Austin, TX
Scofield, George W. .... San Antonio, TX
Scofield, Gerard, Veron, Singletary & Pohorelsky, A Professional Law Corporation .... Lake Charles, LA
Scofield, John B. .... Lake Charles, LA
Scofield, John B. .... Houston, TX
Scofield, Joseph Trent .... Birmingham, AL
Scofield, Lars O. .... Atlanta, GA
Scofield, Lawrence F., Jr. .... Boston, MA
Scofield, Louis M. .... Beaumont, TX
Scofield, Melanie L. .... Richardson, TX
Scofield, Michael S., Law Offices of
Charlotte, NC
Scofield, Milton N. .... New York, NY
Scofield, Ralph F. .... Fairfield, CT
Scofield, Robert E. .... Tacoma, WA
Scofield, Robert G. .... Woodland, CA
Scofield, Sarah .... New York, NY
Scofield & Scofield, P.C. .... Austin, TX
Scofield, Scott J. .... Lake Charles, LA
Scofield, Stephen D. .... Dyersburg, TN
Scofield, Teresa Bauer .... Bath, NY
Scofield, Thomas M. .... Leawood, KS
Scofield, Tyler J. .... Houston, TX
Scofield, William A., Jr. .... Boston, MA
Scoggin, Andrew J. .... Boise, ID
Scoggin, Guy B. .... New Orleans, LA
Scoggin, Paul R. .... Minneapolis, MN
Scoggin, Robert L. .... Jekyll Island, GA
Scoggin, Sally A. .... St. Paul, MN
Scoggin, Sean W. .... Cheyenne, WY
Scoggin, William Guin .... Cary, NC
Scoggins, Al .... Waxahachie, TX
Scoggins, Carolyn Sue .... Santa Paula, CA
Scoggins, Connie .... Phoenix, AZ
Scoggins, Daniel L. .... Smyrna, GA
Scoggins, David R. .... Mesquite, TX
Scoggins, Donald L. .... Santa Monica, CA
Scoggins, Donald R. .... Dallas, TX
Scoggins & Goodman, P.C. .... Atlanta, GA
Scoggins, Gregg A. .... Richmond, VA
Scoggins, Harold B., III .... Portland, OR
Scoggins, James R., Jr. .... Frisco, TX
Scoggins, Linda G. .... Oklahoma City, OK
Scoggins, Mark C. .... Columbia, IL
Scoggins, Merritt E., Jr. .... Stockbridge, GA
Scoggins, P. Keith, Jr. .... Kaneville, IL
Scoggins, Randall B. .... Atlanta, GA
Scoggins, Robert D. .... Dallas, TX
Scoggins, Samuel M. .... Cincinnati, OH
Scogin, Hugh T., Jr. .... New York, NY
Scogin, Mark A. .... Tuscaloosa, AL
Scogin, Robert .... Kermit, TX
Scogland, William L. .... Chicago, IL
Scognamiglio, Patrick J., (P.C.)
New York, NY
Scognamillo, Lisa A. .... New York, NY
Scognamillo, Tina .... Mineola, NY
New York, NY
White Plains, NY
Scola, Anthony J. .... Worcester, MA
Scola, Christina M. .... Boston, MA
Scola, Daniel A., Jr. .... Parsippany, NJ
Scola, Jacqueline Hogan .... Miami, FL
Scola, James F. .... Worcester, MA
Scola, John E. .... Worcester, MA
Scola, Kelly L. .... Rochester Hills, MI
Scola, Laurie .... Novato, CA
Scola, Marc M. .... Allamuchy, NJ
Scola, Marc M., A Professional Corporation
Allamuchy, NJ
Scola, Matthew J. .... West Orange, NJ
Scola, Nicholas R. .... Plainfield, CT
Scola, Ralph J. .... Cleveland, OH
Scola, Richard J. .... Montvale, NJ
Scolamiero, Peter M. .... Albany, NY
Scolari, Brevetti, Goldsmith & Weiss, P.C.
New York, NY
Scolari, Lisa .... New York, NY
Scolari, Steven A. .... Malvern, PA
Scolaro, Richard S. .... Syracuse, NY
Scolaro, Shulman, Cohen, Lawler & Burstein, P.C. .... Syracuse, NY
Scolaro, Vincent .... Elmwood Park, NJ
Scoler, Elana K. .... Boca Raton, FL
Scoler, Galligan, Schless & Griffith, L.L.C.
Newington, CT
Scoler, Jerome A. .... Newington, CT
Scolieri, Joseph J., III .... Jackson, CA
Scoles, Anthony J. .... New York, NY
Scoles, Eugene F. .... Champaign, IL
Scoles, John F. .... Fillmore, CA
Scoles, Jon Stuart .... Mason City, IA
Scoles, Patricia McCombs
San Luis Obispo, CA
Scolforo, Leo J. .... Manassas, VA
Scoliard, Lewis A. .... Providence, RI
Scoliard, Sheldon R. .... Cranston, RI
Scoliere, Michael E. .... Columbus, OH
Scolieri, Philip J. .... Cranberry Township, PA
Pittsburgh, PA
Scolinos, Christopher .... Chino, CA
Scolinos, Harry F. .... Pasadena, CA
Scoll, David L. .... Los Angeles, CA
Scoll, David M. .... Newton, MA
Scoll, Geraldine R. .... Boston, MA
Scoll, Jonathan P. .... Minneapolis, MN
Scollan, Francis N. .... Los Angeles, CA
Scollan, Joseph C. .... Auburn, NY
Scollan, Paul F. .... Hicksville, NY
Scollan Weinstein Cannucciari Carbonaro & McKeon .... Auburn, NY
Scollar, Allison .... New York, NY
Scollar, Samuel L. .... Staten Island, NY
Scollard, Rosemary E. .... Cincinnati, OH
Scollins, Joan E. .... Osterville, MA
Scollo, John P. .... Bloomingdale, NJ
Scolney, Peter N. .... Los Angeles, CA
Scolnic, David M. .... Cherry Hill, NJ
Philadelphia, PA
Scolnick, Judith .... Englewood, NJ
Scolnick, Melvin J. .... Stamford, CT
Scolnick, Meyer .... New York, NY
Scolnick, Robin Cohen .... Feasterville, PA
Scolnick, Stephen M. .... Boston, MA
Scolnik, Maxim .... Gaithersburg, MD
Scolnik, Samuel .... Kensington, MD
Scoloveno, Rosann .... Verona, NJ
Scolton, Bruce S. .... Jamestown, NY
Scoma, Paul M. .... Princeton, IL
Sconiers, Lester G. .... Niagara Falls, NY
Sconiers, Rose H. .... Buffalo, NY
Sconion, Betty Stemley .... Pikesville, MD
Sconyers, Alison A. .... Modesto, CA
Sconyers, Anthony B. .... Rock Island, IL
Sconyers, J. Michael .... Litchfield, CT
Sharon, CT
Waterbury, CT
Sconyers, Jeffrey M. .... Seattle, WA
Sconzo, James M. .... Hartford, CT
Scooler, Kate E. .... Bronx, NY
Scooler, Noah .... New York, NY
Scoon, Cecile M. .... Panama City, FL
Scoon, Darwin D. .... Madison, WI
Scoones, Beatrice H. .... Cedar Hill, TX
Scoonover, Mary J. .... Sacramento, CA
Scoopmire, Sean A. .... Columbia, SC
Scopa, Jason R. .... Saugus, MA
Scopac, Mari-Jo F. .... Stamford, CT
Scopas, Stephen S. .... Flushing, NY
Scope, Alfred S. .... White Plains, NY
Scopel, Rand E. .... Bridgeton, MO
Scopelitis, Alki E. .... Indianapolis, IN
Scopelitis, Garvin, Light & Hanson, P.C.
Chicago, IL
Indianapolis, IN
Scopelitis, Michael P. .... South Bend, IN
Scopetta, Mercedes E. .... Miami, FL
Scopp, Kathleen H. .... New York, NY
Scopp, Leland S. .... New York, NY
Scoppetta, Nicholas .... New York, NY
Scoptur, Christina M. .... Milwaukee, WI
Scoptur, Paul J. .... Milwaukee, WI
Scoratow & Dudik .... Pittsburgh, PA
Scoratow, Martin M. .... Pittsburgh, PA
Scorce, John M. .... Washington, DC
Scorcia, Henry J. .... Brooklyn, NY
Scordato, Caridad Pineiro .... New York, NY
Scordato, Joseph P. .... New York, NY
Scordato, Marin R. .... Los Angeles, CA
Scordino, Joseph F., Jr. .... Endicott, NY
Scordo, Jack C. .... Watertown, NY
Scordo, John P. .... Morristown, NJ
Scoresby & Ellsworth, P.L.C. .... Mesa, AZ
Scoresby, J. Kyle .... Mesa, AZ
Scorese, Joseph P. .... Hackensack, NJ
Scorese, Patrick E. .... Saddle River, NJ
Scorey, Stephen D. .... Birmingham, AL
Scorgie, John G. .... Pueblo, CO
Scornik, Esteban .... Orlando, FL
Scorpion, Mark J. .... Pittsburgh, PA
Scorsone, Ernesto M. .... Lexington, KY
Scorsone, Francesca .... New York, NY
Scorsone, Joseph L. .... Saginaw, MI
Scorsone, Joseph Samuel .... Saginaw, MI
Scorsone & Ransdell .... Lexington, KY
Scorsone, Vincent .... Saginaw, MI
Scorza, Edwin D. .... Kensington, MD
Scorzari & Scorzari, P.C. .... Huntington, NY
Scorzari, William A. .... Huntington, NY
Scorzari, William A., Jr. .... Huntington, NY
Scorziell, Julie Miller
San Bernardino, CA
Scorziello, Melody Leavenworth
Westerly, RI
Scotch, Barry M. .... Manchester, NH
Scotch & Zalinsky .... Manchester, NH
Scotchel, John C., Jr. .... Morgantown, WV
Scotellaro, John P. .... Chicago, IL
Scotese, Robert A., Jr. .... Philadelphia, PA
Scotese, Robert A., P.C., Law Offices of
Philadelphia, PA
Scotillo, Anthony J. .... Chicago, IL
Scotland, Arthur G. .... Sacramento, CA
Scotland, Glenn F. .... Newark, NJ
Scotland, Paula .... Mission Viejo, CA
Scotney, Cheryl S. .... Columbus, OH
Scott, A. Hugh, (P.C.) .... Boston, MA
Scott, A. Irving, Jr. .... Sacramento, CA
Scott, A. Jay .... Bethany, IL
Scott, A. Joseph, III .... Albany, NY
Scott, A. Timothy .... Glendale, CA
Scott, Adele Taylor .... New York, NY
Scott, Alan .... New York, NY
Scott, Alan M. .... Portland, OR
Scott, Alan R. .... Portland, OR
Scott, Albin P. .... Covington, LA
Scott, Alexis Z. .... Cincinnati, OH
Scott, Alfred L. .... New York, NY
Scott, Alison .... New York, NY
Scott & Allen, A Professional Association
Oklahoma City, OK
Scott, Allen C. D., II .... St. Augustine, FL
Scott, Allen L. .... Mount Holly, NJ
Scott, Amanda B. .... Atlanta, GA
Scott, Ami G. .... Detroit, MI
Scott, Anderson B. .... Atlanta, GA
Scott, Andrew B. .... West Caldwell, NJ
Scott, Andrew F. .... Missoula, MT
Scott, Andrew P. .... Chicago, IL
Scott, Andrew R. .... Garden City, NY
Scott, Angela M. .... Sacramento, CA
Scott, Ann Victoria .... Chesapeake Beach, MD
Scott, Anne O'Laughlin .... Chicago, IL
Scott, Anoush Koroghlian .... Albany, NY
Scott, Anthony D. .... Redondo Beach, CA
Scott, Armando V. .... Orangevale, CA
Scott, Arnold D. .... Boston, MA
Scott, Arnold D., Jr. .... Boston, MA
Scott & Associates .... Sevierville, TN
Scott & Associates, P.C. .... Denver, CO
Scott, Audrey M. .... Memphis, TN
Scott, Barbara A. .... San Francisco, CA
Scott, Barry R. .... San Francisco, CA
Scott, Bert .... New York, NY
Scott, Betsy Sue .... Treasury Department,
Departmental Offices, GV
Scott, Bette-Jo .... Berlin, NH
Scott, Brian D. .... Seattle, WA
Scott, Brian J. .... Lake Oswego, OR
Scott, Bruce A. .... Metairie, LA
Scott, Bryan D. .... Macon, GA
Scott, Bryan W. .... Houston, TX
Scott, Burton A. .... Reno, NV
Scott, C. Brent, (A P.C.) .... San Clemente, CA
Scott, C. Dan .... Sevierville, TN
Scott, C. Dukes .... Columbia, SC
Scott, C. Thomas .... Houston, TX
Scott, Candace R. .... Morristown, NJ
Scott, Carol A. .... Miami, FL
Scott, Carol Wild .... Atlanta, GA
Scott, Caroline .... Austin, TX
Scott, Catherine A. .... Syracuse, NY
Scott, Catherine W. .... Norwich, VT
Scott, Cecil C. .... Brooklyn, NY
Scott, Celeste M. .... San Francisco, CA
Scott, Charles A. .... Beverly Hills, CA
Scott, Charles D. .... St. Petersburg, FL
Scott, Charles D. .... Louisville, KY
Scott, Charles F. .... Waukegan, IL
Scott, Charles L. .... Elkton, MD
Scott, Charles L., Jr. .... Elkton, MD
Scott, Charles M. .... Fort Payne, AL
Scott, Charles M., Attorney, P.A.
Fort Payne, AL
Scott, Charles R. .... Shreveport, LA
Scott, Charles T., Jr. .... San Diego, CA
Scott, Charlie Ann .... Sarasota, FL
Scott, Charlotte B. .... Paducah, KY
Scott, Cheryl A. .... Bronx, NY
Scott, Christian Steven .... San Diego, CA
Scott, Christine Mabe .... Chattanooga, TN
Scott, Christopher Bryan .... Carrollton, GA
Scott, Christopher D.
West Palm Beach, FL
Scott, Christopher R. .... Austin, TX
Scott, Christy .... Hartford, CT
Scott, Cindy S. .... Morgantown, WV
Scott, Clarence W., Jr. .... Pell City, AL
Scott, Clay C., Jr. .... Dallas, TX
Scott, Clayton M. .... Anoka, MN
Scott, Cleve M. .... Morristown, NJ
Scott, Clifford .... Columbia, SC

Scott, Clifford R. ....New York, NY
Scott, Clyde W. ....Grosse Pointe, MI
Scott, Colin E. ....Charlotte, NC
Scott, Courtney E. ....New York, NY
Scott, Craig C. ....Germantown, MD
Scott, Craig E. ....North Miami Beach, FL
Scott, Craig H. ....Berkeley, CA
Scott, Craig L. ....Sacramento, CA
Scott, Craig M. ....Providence, RI
Scott, Craig P. ....Columbus, OH
Scott, Cristi E. ....Nashville, TN
Scott, Curtis, Jr. ....Lakewood, OH
Scott, Cynthia L. ....Chicago, IL
Scott, Cynthia Rixey ....Denver, CO
Scott, Daltan & Van Lear, L.L.P. Fredericksburg, VA
Stafford, VA
Scott, Dana ....Knoxville, TN
Scott, Dana L., Jr. ....Washington, DC
Bethesda, MD
Fairfax, VA
Scott, Daniel E. ....Sarasota, FL
Scott, Daniel E. ....Joplin, MO
Scott, Daniel E., P.A. ....Sarasota, FL
Scott, Daniel L. ....St. Paul, MN
Scott, Daniel M. ....Minneapolis, MN
Scott, Darrel J. ....Amarillo, TX
Scott, Darrell J. ....Santa Rosa, CA
Scott, Darrell W. ....Spokane, WA
Scott, Daryl E. ....Anderson, IN
Scott, David ....New York, NY
Scott, David A. ....Fort Wayne, IN
Scott, David A. ....Spencer, IA
Scott, David A. ....Columbus, OH
Scott, David A. ....Pittsburgh, PA
Scott, David A. ....Dallas, TX
Scott, David A. ....Casper, WY
Scott, David B. ....Nashville, TN
Scott, David D. ....San Francisco, CA
Scott, David H. ....Independence, KS
Scott, David H. ....Nashville, TN
Scott, David H., Jr. ....Independence, KS
Scott, David J. ....Denver, CO
Scott, David J. ....Midland, MI
Scott, David L. ....Long Beach, CA
Scott, David M. ....Miami, FL
Scott, David M. ....Columbus, OH
Scott, David P. ....St. Louis, MO
Scott, David R. ....Colchester, CT
Scott, David R. ....New Brunswick, NJ
Scott, David R. ....Tulsa, OK
Scott, David S. ....Baltimore, MD
Scott, David T. ....Paoli, PA
Scott, David T. ....Perryton, TX
Scott, David T., P.C. ....Perryton, TX
Scott, David V. ....New Albany, IN
Scott, Dawna F. ....Portland, OR
Scott, Deanna K. ....Springfield, MO
Scott, Deborah Chisholm ....Tucson, AZ
Scott, Deborah R. ....Phoenix, AZ
Scott, Denasha A. ....Milwaukee, WI
Scott, Dennis J. ....Bethesda, MD
Scott, Dennis L. ....Oklahoma City, OK
Scott, Dennis P. ....San Francisco, CA
Scott, Dennis R. ....Firebaugh, CA
Scott, Dennis R. ....Newport, WA
Scott, Dennis S. ....Boston, MA
Scott, Denny F. ....Treasure Island, FL
Scott, Derek P. ....Dallas, TX
Scott, Diana P. ....Los Angeles, CA
Scott, Diane Adair ....Tallahassee, FL
Scott & Dominy Co., L.P.A. ....Columbus, OH
Delaware, OH
Scott, Don L. ....Liberal, KS
Scott, Don McCarty ....Ventura, CA
Scott, Donald A. ....Philadelphia, PA
Scott, Donald E. ....Denver, CO
Chicago, IL
Scott, Donald G. ....Kansas City, MO
Scott, Donald K. ....Dayton, OH
Scott, Donna A. ....Sunnyvale, CA
Scott, Donna A. ....Murfreesboro, TN
Scott, Donna Marie ....Sanford, FL
Scott, Doris P. ....Elkton, MD
Scott, Douglas ....Richmond, VA
Scott, Douglas A. ....Claremont, CA
Scott, Douglas D. ....Denver, CO
Scott, Douglas E. ....San Diego, CA
Scott, Douglas P. ....Rockford, IL
Scott, Douglas W. ....Bellevue, WA
Scott, Douglass & McConnico, L.L.P.
Austin, TX
Scott, Doyle C. ....Oklahoma City, OK
Scott, D. R. ....Knoxville, TN
Scott, Drew J. ....Chicago, IL
Scott, Dueward H., Jr. ....Clifton Forge, VA
Scott, Duncan ....Albuquerque, NM
Scott, E. Danny, (P.A.)
West Columbia, SC
Scott, E. John ....Santa Monica, CA
Scott, Earl L. ....New York, NY
Scott, Earnest W. ....Abilene, TX
Scott, Eddie E. ....Livermore, CA
Scott, Edmund M. ....Redwood City, CA
Scott, Edward A., III ....Schaumburg, IL
Scott, Edward A., Jr. ....South Holland, IL
Scott, Edward B., II ....San Ramon, CA
Scott, Edward L. ....Ocala, FL
Scott, Edward R. ....Santa Barbara, CA
Scott, Edward R., Jr. ....Amarillo, TX
Scott, Edward S. ....New York, NY
Scott, Edward W., IV ....Cupertino, CA
Scott, Edwin C. ....New Orleans, LA
Scott, Edwin D. ....New York, NY
Scott, Edwin W. ....New York, NY
Scott, Elizabeth A. ....Los Angeles, CA
Scott, Elizabeth Davenport ....Raleigh, NC
Scott, Elizabeth E. ....Houston, TX
Scott, Elizabeth Shumaker
Charlottesville, VA
Scott, Elizabeth V. ....Richmond, VA
Scott, Elizabeth W. ....San Francisco, CA
Scott, Ellen Kittredge ....Berwyn, PA
Scott, Elmer J. ....Worland, WY
Scott, Emily (Scherr) ....Omaha, NE
Scott, E. P. ....Louisville, KY
Scott, Eric L. ....Dallas, TX
Scott, Eric R. ....Oakland, CA
Scott, Eric S. ....Tallahassee, FL
Scott, Erin M. ....San Jose, CA
Scott, Ernestine V. Reeves ....Decatur, GA
Scott, Errol G. ....Everett, WA
Scott, Eve K. ....Fort Wayne, IN
Scott, F. Lindsey, Law Office of
Dallas, TX
Scott, F. Lindsey, Law Office of
Karnes City, TX
Scott, F. Linsey, Law Office of
Richardson, TX
Scott, F. Wayne ....Boulder, CO
Scott & Fenderson, P.A.
St. Petersburg, FL
Scott, Ferris A., P.A., Law Offices of
Miami, FL
Scott, Fitzhugh, III ....Aspen, CO
Scott & Forrest ....New Albany, IN
Scott, Francis E. ....Los Angeles, CA
Scott, Frank L. ....Port St. Lucie, FL
Scott, Frazier G. ....West Hartford, CT
Scott, Fred ....Indianapolis, IN
Scott, Fred Douglas ....Indianapolis, IN
Scott, Frederic R. ....Canton, OH
Scott, G. Albert ....Canton, IL
Scott, G. Harrison ....New Orleans, LA
Scott, G. Judson, Jr. ....Pleasanton, CA
Scott, Gail B.
Commodity Futures Trading Commission, Office of the General Counsel, GV
Scott, Gail P. ....Department of State, Foreign Service Officers (Overseas), GV
Scott, Gary R. ....Cheyenne, WY
Scott & Gentges ....Tulsa, OK
Scott, Geoffrey P. ....Worthington, OH
Scott, Geoffrey R. ....Carlisle, PA
Scott, George F. ....Junction City, KS
Scott, George M. ....Key West, FL
Scott, George M. ....Charleston, WV
Scott, George W., III ....Department of Labor, Office of the Solicitor, GV
Scott, George W., Jr. ....Greenwich, CT
Scott, Georgiana R. ....Boulder, CO
Scott, Gerald W., P.A. ....Wichita, KS
Scott, Gerard C. ....Wichita, KS
Scott, Gordon B. ....Havana, FL
Scott, Gordon H. S. ....Augusta, ME
Bangor, ME
Scott, Grant J. ....Raleigh, NC
Scott, Gregory A. ....United States Senate, Office of the Legislative Counsel, GV
Scott, Gregory A. ....Springfield, IL
Scott, Gregory B. ....Columbus, OH
Scott, Gregory J. ....Jefferson City, MO
Scott, Gregory L. ....West Palm Beach, FL
Scott, Gregory L. ....Yakima, WA
Scott, Gregory M. ....Washington, DC
Scott, Gregory S. ....Cleveland, OH
Scott, Gregory T. ....Dayton, OH
Scott & Guess, Chartered ....Kansas City, KS
Scott, H. Al ....Montgomery, AL
Scott, H. E., & Associates, P.A.
Vero Beach, FL
Scott, H. Pearce ....Valdosta, GA
Scott, Hal J. ....Jonesville, LA
Scott, Hal S. ....Cambridge, MA
Scott, Hardie ....Philadelphia, PA
Scott, Harris, Bryan, Barra & Jorgensen, Professional Association
Palm Beach Gardens, FL
West Palm Beach, FL
Scott, Harry W. ....Decatur, IN
Scott, Helen E. ....Vero Beach, FL
Scott, Helen S. ....New York, NY
Scott, Henry ....New York, NY
Scott, Hope H. ....Philadelphia, PA
Scott, Howard B. ....Logan, IA
Scott, Howard F. ....Miami, FL
Scott, Howard I. ....Pittsburgh, PA
Scott, Howard T. ....Athens, GA
Scott and Hoyt ....Walkill, NY
Scott, Hugh L., Jr. ....San Antonio, TX
Scott, Hugh N. ....Washington, DC
Scott, Hulse, Marshall, Feuille, Finger & Thurmond, P.C. ....El Paso, TX
Scott, Ian ....New York, NY
Scott, Isaac A., Jr. ....Little Rock, AR
Scott, Isabelle ....Washington, DC
Scott, Ivan M., Jr. ....Dallas, TX
Scott, J. Brian ....Rocky Mount, NC
Scott, J. Clinton ....Boca Raton, FL
Vero Beach, FL
Scott, J. Donald ....Columbia, SC
Scott, J. Gregory ....Decatur, IL
Scott, J. Katherine ....Providence, RI
Scott, J. Munford, Jr. ....Florence, SC
Scott, J. Norris B. ....New Orleans, LA
Scott, J. Thomas ....Plano, TX
Scott, J. Timothy ....Los Angeles, CA
Scott, Jacalyn D ....Houston, TX
Scott, Jack D. ....Salt Lake City, UT
Scott, Jack R. ....Philadelphia, PA
Scott, Jacqueline ....Bossier City, LA
Scott, Jacqueline D. ....Grand Rapids, MI
Scott, Jacques W. ....Bethany, IL
Scott & Jahn ....Florence, KY
Scott, James ....Knoxville, TN
Scott, James A. ....Fort Lauderdale, FL
Scott, James A. ....Albany, NY
Scott, James A., Jr. ....Palm Coast, FL
Scott, James A., Jr., P.A. ....Palm Coast, FL
Scott, James C. ....Cleveland, OH
Scott, James D. ....Rock Valley, IA
Scott, James E. ....Danville, CA
Scott, James E. ....Washington, DC
Scott, James F. H. ....Washington, DC
Scott, James G. ....United States Senate, Office of the Legislative Counsel, GV
Scott, James H. ....Jackson, TN
Scott, James H., Jr. ....Kansas City, KS
Scott, James J. ....Washington, DC
Scott, James J. ....St. Louis, MO
Scott, James K. ....Knoxville, TN
Oak Ridge, TN
Scott, James L., II ....Grand Rapids, MI
Scott, James M. ....Montgomery, AL
Scott, James M. ....Pawleys Island, SC
Scott, James M., III ....Princeton, NJ
Philadelphia, PA
Scott, James Morgan, Jr. ....Sugar Land, TX
Scott, James Pembrook ....Crownsville, MD
Scott, James R. ....Mineola, NY
Scott, James R. ....Cambridge, OH
Scott, James R. ....Milwaukee, WI
Scott, James S. ....Oakland, CA
Scott, James S. ....Yakima, WA
Scott, James S., Sr. ....New York, NY
Scott, James W., Jr. ....Philadelphia, PA
Scott, Jamie D. ....Cincinnati, OH
Scott, Jane Elizabeth ....Albany, NY
Scott, Janice G. ....Tallahassee, FL
Scott, Janis L. ....Victoria, TX
Scott, Jas. H. ....Dallas, TX
Scott, Jas. Walter, Jr. ....San Francisco, CA
Scott, Jason ....Woodbury, CT
Scott, Jason C. ....Milan, TN
Scott, Jason D. ....Pocatello, ID
Scott, Jason H. ....Charleston, WV
Scott, Jean ....St. Louis, MO
Scott, Jean M. ....St. Louis, MO
Scott, Jeanette S. ....Athens, GA
Scott, Jeanne E. ....Springfield, IL
Scott, Jeanne Schulte ....McLean, VA
Scott, Jeff E. ....Los Angeles, CA
Scott, Jeffery J. ....Platteville, WI
Scott, Jeffery Michael ....Tallahassee, FL
Scott, Jeffrey B. ....Albany, NY
Scott, Jeffrey G. ....San Diego, CA
Scott, Jeffrey J. ....Denver, CO
Scott, Jeffrey L. ....Houston, TX
Scott, Jeffrey P. ....Edina, MN
Scott, Jeffrey T. ....New York, NY
Scott, Jennifer A. ....Stockton, CA
Scott, Jeremiah R., Jr. ....Eureka, CA
Scott & Jernigan, P.C. ....Florence, SC
Scott, Jerry ....Murfreesboro, TN
Scott, Jill Baran ....Glendale, CA
Scott, Jim D. ....La Crosse, WI
Scott, Jo Ann
Federal Energy Regulatory Commission, Office of the General Counsel, GV
Scott, Joan C. ....Lewistown, IL
Scott, Joe H. ....Casper, WY
Scott, Joel D. ....Los Angeles, CA
Scott, Joel M. ....Humble, TX
Scott, John A. ....Palo Alto, CA
Scott, John A. ....Traverse City, MI
Scott, John A. ....Fairmont, WV
Scott, John A., P.C. ....Traverse City, MI
Scott, John B., Jr. ....Montgomery, AL
Scott, John B., P.C. ....Laramie, WY
Scott, John C. ....Denver, CO
Scott, John C. ....Cincinnati, OH
Scott, John C. ....Big Cove Tannery, PA
Scott, John D. ....Minneapolis, MN
Scott, John E. S. ....Detroit, MI
Scott, John F. ....Bethesda, MD
Scott, John F. ....Amarillo, TX
Scott, John F., Jr. ....St. Paul, MN
Scott, John Gregory ....Denver, CO
Scott, John H. ....Los Angeles, CA
Scott, John H., Jr. ....Pittsburgh, PA
Scott, John Houston ....San Francisco, CA
Scott, John J. ....Long Grove, IL
Scott, John J. ....Hodgenville, KY
Scott, John J. ....Scranton, PA
Scott, John J., Jr. ....Prince Frederick, MD
Scott, John J., Jr. ....Philadelphia, PA
Scott, John L. ....Branford, FL
Scott, John L. ....Enid, OK
Scott, John M. ....Phoenix, AZ
Scott, John M. ....Little Rock, AR
Scott, John M. ....New York, NY
Scott, John N. ....Vicksburg, MI
Scott, John N. ....Toledo, OH
Scott, John P. ....Tulsa, OK
Scott, John P. ....Houston, TX
Scott, John P., Jr. ....Birmingham, AL
Scott, John R. ....Bentonville, AR
Scott, John R. ....Morristown, NJ
Scott, John R. ....Morristown, NJ
Scott, John R. ....Cleveland, OH
Scott, John R. ....Dallas, TX
Scott, John T. ....Anderson, IN
Scott, John T. ....Monroe, LA
Scott, John T. ....West Monroe, LA
Scott, John T., III ....Washington, DC
Scott, John W. ....Birmingham, AL
Scott, John W. ....Department of Justice, Criminal Division, GV
Scott, John W. ....Alexandria, LA
Scott, John W. ....Albany, NY
Scott, John W., Jr. ....Fredericksburg, VA
Scott, Johnda Denise ....Dumfries, VA
Scott, Johnson & Johnson, LLP
Santa Maria, CA
Scott, Jonathan C. ....Melville, NY
Scott, Jonathan Glenn ....Rocky Mount, VA
Scott, Jonathan O. ....Mountain View, CA
Scott, Jonathan P. ....Washington, DC
Scott, Jos. P. ....San Antonio, TX
Scott, Joseph B. ....Washington, DC
Scott, Joseph C. ....Redwood City, CA
Scott, Joseph E. ....Columbus, OH
Delaware, OH
Scott, Joseph M. ....Linwood, NJ
Scott, Joseph M., Jr. ....Lexington, KY
Scott, Joseph W. ....Morristown, NJ
Scott, Judi ....New York, NY
Scott, Judith ....Hampton, VA
Scott, Judith A. ....Washington, DC
Scott, Judith H. ....Cambridge, MD
Scott, Judith I. ....Westerly, RI
Scott, Judy L. ....New Brunswick, NJ
Scott, Juli Christine ....Burbank, CA
Scott, Kandis ....Santa Clara, CA
Scott, Karen Gaughan ....Buffalo, NY
Scott, Kathleen A. ....New York, NY
Scott, Kathleen N. ....Richmond, VA
Scott, Kathryn I. ....Houston, TX
Scott & Kea ....Murfreesboro, TN
Scott, Keely Yoes ....Baton Rouge, LA
Scott, Keith A. ....Atlanta, GA
Scott, Keith A. ....Columbus, OH
Scott, Keldon K. ....Lansing, MI
Scott, Kelleen McGinnis ....Washington, DC
Scott, Kelly C. ....Milwaukee, WI
Scott, Kelly O. ....Beverly Hills, CA
Scott, Kendrick L. ....Lake Bluff, IL
Scott, Kenneth ....Philadelphia, PA
Scott, Kenneth E. ....Palo Alto, CA
Scott, Kenneth E. ....Fairmont, MN
Scott, Kenneth L. ....Denver, CO
Scott, Kenneth M. ....Flint, MI
Scott, Kenneth Mark ....Jackson Heights, NY
Scott, Kenneth W. ....Florence, KY
Scott, Kent B. ....Salt Lake City, UT
Scott, KeriAnn ....Anchorage, AK
Scott, Kerry L. ....Minneapolis, MN
Scott, Kevin B. ....Detroit, MI
Scott, Kevin B. ....Philadelphia, PA
Scott, Kevin G. ....Quincy, MA
Scott, Kevin M. ....Harrisburg, PA
Scott & Kienzle, P.A. ....Albuquerque, NM
Scott, Kimberlee ....Charlotte, NC
Scott, Kimberly Jardim ....Philadelphia, PA
Scott, Kimble Hale ....Akron, OH
Scott, Kirby A. ....Louisville, KY
Scott, Kristina R. ....Decatur, GA
Scott & Kroner, A Professional Corporation
Charlottesville, VA
Scott, Kyle Joseph ....Newport Beach, CA
Scott, L. Joe ....Poplar Bluff, MO
Scott, Lael French ....New York, NY
Scott, Larry A. ....Buffalo, NY
Scott, Larry D. ....Boise, ID
Scott, Larry E. ....Fort Collins, CO
Scott, Larry Frank ....Haddonfield, NJ
Scott, Larry R. ....Niles, IL
Scott, Laura A. ....Evansville, IN
Scott, Laura M. ....Department of Justice, Antitrust Division, GV
Scott, Laura M. ....Boston, MA
Scott, Laura S. ....Salt Lake City, UT
Scott, Laurence D. ....Honolulu, HI
Scott, Laurence K. ....Santa Maria, CA
Scott, Laurence T. ....Washington, DC
Rockville, MD
Scott Law Firm, P.C. ....Columbia, SC
Scott Law Firm, Professional Corporation
Columbia, MO
Scott Law Firm, The ....Hollywood, FL
Scott Law Offices ....Pipestone, MN
Scott Law Offices ....Missoula, MT
Scott, Lawrence ....Washington, DC
Scott, Lawrence E. ....Austin, TX
Scott, Lawrence J. ....Charlotte, NC
Scott, Lawrence L. ....Tampa, FL
Scott, Lawrence M. ....Sterling Heights, MI
Scott, Lawrence R. ....Oklahoma City, OK
Scott, Lawton W. ....Marietta, GA
Scott, Leonard A. ....Atlanta, GA
Scott, Leonard L. ....Little Rock, AR
Scott, Leonard Wayne ....San Antonio, TX
Scott, Leroy H., Jr. ....Shreveport, LA
Scott, Leroy H., Jr., A Prof. Law Corp.
Shreveport, LA
Scott, Leslie ....Ridgeland, MS
Scott, Leslie C. ....Jacksonville, FL
Scott, Lewis K. ....Portland, OR
Scott, Linda K. ....Mesa, AZ
Scott, Lindal L. ....New York, NY
Scott, Lindsey ....Baton Rouge, LA
Scott, Linzy O., III ....Atlanta, GA
Scott, Lisa D. ....Bellevue, WA
Scott, Lisa, Law Offices of ....Chicago, IL
Scott, L. Joe, & Daniel T. Moore
Poplar Bluff, MO
Scott, Lorinda ....Miami, FL
Scott, Lorrie D. ....Seattle, WA
Scott and Lutz ....High Point, NC
Kernersville, NC
Scott, Lynn A. ....Jamaica, NY
Scott, Lynn Rossi ....Dallas, TX
Fort Worth, TX
Scott, Lynn S. ....Atlanta, GA
Scott, M. Bruce ....Decatur, IN
Scott, M. Randall ....Atlanta, GA
Scott, Mackey, III ....Columbia, SC
Scott, Madalyn Carol ....Memphis, TN
Scott, Malcolm H. ....Eugene, OR
Scott, Marcia A. ....Tulsa, OK
Scott, Marcia J. ....Auburn, NE
Scott, Margo ....New York, NY

Scott, Maria Mancini ..... Boston, MA
Scott, Mark A. ..... Atlanta, GA
Scott, Mark A. ..... Kokomo, IN
Scott, Mark B. ..... San Rafael, CA
Scott, Mark C. ..... Reading, PA
Scott, Mark C., Jr. ..... Las Vegas, NV
Scott, Mark E. ..... New Haven, CT
Scott, Mark E. ..... Bridgeville, PA
Scott, Mark E. ..... Norristown, PA
Philadelphia, PA
Scott, Mark E. ..... Houston, TX
Scott, Mark J. ..... Morrow, GA
Scott, Mark M. ..... Irvine, CA
Scott, Mark S. ..... Miami, FL
Scott, Mark S. ..... Boston, MA
Scott, Mark S. ..... Grand Rapids, MI
Scott, Marlesa ..... Department of the Air Force, Office of the Judge Advocate General, GV
Scott, Marshall T. ..... Chicago, IL
Scott, Martha Buell ..... San Francisco, CA
Scott, Martin R. ..... New York, NY
Scott, Mary B. ..... San Diego, CA
Scott, Mary Davies ..... Little Rock, AR
Scott, Mary Kay ..... Chicago, IL
Scott, Mary L. ..... Dallas, TX
Scott, Mary Thomas ..... Buffalo, NY
Scott, Maryjane Thomas ..... Buffalo, NY
Scott, Matney William ..... Houston, TX
Scott, Matthew Henry ..... Fort Smith, AR
Scott, Matthew R. ..... Dallas, TX
Scott, Maureen E. ..... Garden City, NY
Scott & Mayo, A Professional Corporation
Houston, TX
Scott, McCurtain ..... Stigler, OK
Scott & McGlasson ..... Topeka, KS
Scott, McGregor W. ..... Martinez, CA
Scott, Melvin ..... Colchester, CT
New London, CT
Scott, Michael ..... Washington, DC
Scott, Michael B. ..... Sherman Oaks, CA
Scott, Michael D. ..... Menlo Park, CA
Scott, Michael D. ..... West Lafayette, IN
Scott, Michael D. ..... Pittsburgh, PA
Scott, Michael E. ..... Boston, MA
Scott, Michael E. ..... Burlington, MA
Providence, RI
Scott, Michael G. ..... Boston, MA
Scott, Michael J. ..... Anoka, MN
Scott, Michael J. ..... Londonderry, NH
Scott, Michael J. ..... Cleveland, OH
Scott, Michael J. ..... Tigard, OR
Scott, Michael K. ..... Milwaukee, WI
Scott, Michael P. ..... Healdsburg, CA
Scott, Michael R. ..... Seattle, WA
Scott, Michael T. ..... Philadelphia, PA
Scott, Michael W. ..... Great Falls, VA
Scott, Michelle A. ..... Arlington, VA
Scott, Michelle P. ..... Newark, NJ
Scott, Milton B. ..... Alamo, CA
Scott, Mona H. ..... Pontiac, MI
Scott, Myrl R. ..... Los Angeles, CA
Scott, Nadine L. ..... Oceanside, CA
Scott, Nancy Lee Ebert ..... Raleigh, NC
Scott & Narcisi ..... Philadelphia, PA
Scott, Nauman S. ..... Alexandria, LA
Scott, Neal C. ..... Atlanta, GA
Scott, Neale ..... Los Angeles, CA
Scott, Neil W. ..... Sarasota, FL
Scott, Nichols & Matteucci, A Professional Law Corporation ..... Stockton, CA
Scott, Nikki Parrish ..... Fort Payne, AL
Scott & Norman ..... Albany, OR
Scott, Norman ..... Philadelphia, PA
Scott, Norman J. ..... Stockton, CA
Scott, Obyrietta Gammett ..... Chicago, IL
Scott, Oswald J. ..... Houston, TX
Scott, O. V., Jr. ..... Lubbock, TX
Scott, P. Mars ..... Missoula, MT
Scott, P. Mars, P.C. ..... Missoula, MT
Scott, Paige ..... Cambridge, MA
Scott, Pamela D. ..... Anchorage, AK
Scott, Pamela F. ..... Topeka, KS
Scott, Pamela J. ..... Wilmington, DE
Scott, Pamela R. ..... Montgomery, AL
Scott, Patrice M. ..... Plymouth, NH
Scott, Patricia A. ..... Chicago, IL
Scott, Patricia F. ..... Laurie, MO
Scott, Patricia J. ..... Pittsburgh, PA
Scott, Patrick F. ..... Washington, DC
Scott, Patrick L. ..... Sacramento, CA
Scott, Patrick R. ..... Bradenton, FL
Scott, Patrick S. ..... Fort Lauderdale, FL
Scott, Patrick S., & Associates, P.A.
Fort Lauderdale, FL
Scott, Patti A. ..... Wayne, NJ
Scott, Paul ..... Columbus, OH
Scott, Paul A. ..... Oklahoma City, OK
Scott, Paul A. ..... Manassas, VA
Springfield, VA
Scott, Paul A., P.C. ..... Oklahoma City, OK
Scott, Paul B. ..... Vernon, TX
Scott, Paul, Co., L.P.A. ..... Columbus, OH
Scott, Paul D. ..... San Francisco, CA
Scott, Paul E. ..... Denver, CO
Scott, Paul, Jr. ..... Columbus, OH
Scott, Paul L. ..... North Little Rock, AR
Scott, Paul O. ..... Columbus, OH
Scott, Paul R. ..... Batesville, MS
Hernando, MS
Scott, Paul R. ..... New York, NY
Scott, Paul T. ..... Fredericksburg, VA
Scott, Paul W. ..... Denver, CO
Scott, Peggy A. ..... Dublin, OH
Scott, Peter B. ..... Lakewood, CO
Scott, Peter B., P.C. ..... Lakewood, CO
Scott, Peter C. ..... Concord, NH
Portsmouth, NH
Scott, Peter P. ..... Denver, CO
Scott, Peter T. ..... Springfield, MA
Scott, Phillip D. ..... Lexington, KY
Scott, Phillip R. ..... Hicksville, NY
Scott, Phillip R. ..... Waurika, OK
Scott, Preston T. ..... Washington, DC
Scott, Quarterman & Wells ..... Athens, GA
Scott, Quinlan & Hecht ..... Topeka, KS
Scott, R. Carter, III ..... Richmond, VA
Scott, R. Craig ..... Newport Beach, CA
Scott, R. Douglas ..... Dallas, TX
Scott, R. Gordon ..... Providence, RI
Scott, R. Stephen ..... Springfield, IL
Scott, R. Tod ..... Milwaukee, WI
Thiensville, WI
Scott, Rachel C. ..... San Francisco, CA
Scott, Ralph D. ..... Yakima, WA
Scott, Randall ..... Grand Prairie, TX
Scott, Randall K. ..... Sacramento, CA
Scott, Randall L. ..... Laurel, MD
Scott, Randall W. ..... Alexandria, VA
Scott, Randolph ..... Dallas, TX
Scott, Randolph A. ..... Allentown, PA
Warrington, PA
Scott, Randolph, Associates, A Professional Corporation ..... Allentown, PA
Doylestown, PA
Warrington, PA
Scott, Randolph E. ..... Durango, CO
Scott, Ray Harold ..... Clarion, PA
Scott, Ray J. ..... Boulder Creek, CA
Scott, Raymond C., Jr. ..... Garden City, NY
Scott, Raymond E. ..... Bloomfield Hills, MI
Scott, Raymond H. ..... Medford, WI
Scott, Reece A. ..... Bartlesville, OK
Scott, Richard ..... Los Angeles, CA
Scott, Richard ..... Austin, TX
Scott, Richard B. ..... Buffalo, NY
West Seneca, NY
Scott, Richard E. ..... Paris, IL
Scott, Richard F. ..... Fort Lauderdale, FL
Scott, Richard J. ..... Salt Lake City, UT
Scott, Richard M. ..... Lamar, MO
Scott, Richard N. ..... Malibu, CA
Scott, Richard S. ..... Santa Rosa, CA
Scott, Richard S. ..... Athens, GA
Scott, Richard S. ..... Pittsburgh, PA
Sewickley, PA
Scott, Richard W. ..... Houston, TX
Scott, Rider ..... Dallas, TX
Scott, Robb A. ..... San Francisco, CA
Scott, Robert A. ..... San Marino, CA
Scott, Robert A. ..... Watertown, CT
Scott, Robert A. ..... Baltimore, MD
Scott, Robert A. ..... Horsham, PA
Scott, Robert B. ..... Indianapolis, IN
Scott, Robert C. ..... Hartford, CT
Scott, Robert C. ..... Fort Lauderdale, FL
Scott, Robert C. ..... San Antonio, TX
Scott, Robert D. ..... Milwaukee, WI
Scott, Robert E. ..... Corona, CA
Scott, Robert E. ..... Buffalo, NY
Scott, Robert E. ..... Austin, TX
Scott, Robert E., Jr. ..... Baltimore, MD
Scott, Robert G. ..... Lenexa, KS
Scott, Robert G., Jr. ..... Washington, DC
Scott, Robert H. ..... Anoka, MN
Scott, Robert H. ..... Albuquerque, NM
Scott, Robert H., Jr. ..... Joplin, MO
Scott, Robert J. ..... High Point, NC
Kernersville, NC
Scott, Robert J. ..... Pawnee, OK
Scott, Robert J., Jr. ..... Walnut Creek, CA
Scott, Robert K. ..... Newport Beach, CA
San Francisco, CA
Scott, Robert K. ..... Chicago, IL
Scott, Robert K., A Prof. Corp., The Law Offices of ..... Newport Beach, CA
San Francisco, CA
Scott, Robert Kent ..... Dillon, CO
Scott, Robert L. ..... Carlsbad, CA
Scott, Robert L. ..... Woodland Hills, CA
Scott, Robert L. ..... Bradenton, FL
Scott, Robert L. ..... Albuquerque, NM
Scott, Robert L. ..... Greensboro, NC
Scott, Robert L. ..... Greenville, TX
Scott, Robert L., II ..... Alexandria, VA
Scott, Robert L., P.C. ..... Albuquerque, NM
Scott, Robert M. ..... Toledo, OH
Scott, Robert M. ..... Toledo, OH
Scott, Robert P., Jr. ..... Houston, TX
Scott, Robert R. ..... Katy, TX
Scott, Robert T. ..... West Palm Beach, FL
Scott, Robert T. ..... New Brunswick, NJ
Scott, Robert T. ..... Albany, OR
Scott, Robert W. ..... Fullerton, CA
Scott, Robert W. ..... Bloomfield Hills, MI
Scott, Robert W. ..... Grand Rapids, MI
Scott, Robert W. ..... Trenton, NJ
Scott, Robert W. ..... Toledo, OH
Scott, Robert W. ..... Philadelphia, PA
Scott, Robert W. ..... Fairfax, VA
Scott, Robert W., II ..... Toms River, NJ
Scott, Robert W., Jr. ..... Peoria, IL
Scott, Roberta Lee ..... New York, NY
Scott, Robin L. ..... Snohomish, WA
Scott, Robt. F. ..... Springfield, IL
Scott, Robt. G. ..... Rock Island, IL
Scott, Robt. G. ..... Terrell, TX
Scott, Rodney A. ..... Decatur, IL
Scott, Rodney L. ..... New Albany, IN
Scott, Rodney M. ..... Murfreesboro, TN
Scott, Roger C. ..... Buffalo, NY
Scott, Roger R. ..... Tulsa, OK
Scott, Romaine S., Jr. ..... Birmingham, AL
Scott, Ronald ..... Houston, TX
Scott, Ronald C. ..... Villanova, PA
Scott, Ronald C. ..... Columbia, SC
Scott, Ronald L. ..... Houston, TX
Scott, Ronald T. ..... Hartford, CT
Scott, Rosemary ..... Grand Rapids, MI
Scott, Ross R. ..... New York, NY
Scott, Royce George ..... Baytown, TX
Scott, Ruben H. ..... Glendale, CA
Scott, Rufus S. ..... Houston, TX
Scott, Russell C. ..... Austin, TX
Scott, Russell Charles ..... New Albany, IN
Scott, Russell D. ..... King City, CA
Scott, Russell D. ..... New York, NY
Scott, Russell K. ..... Belleville, IL
Scott, Ryan L. ..... Columbia, SC
Scott, S. Dell ..... Encino, CA
Scott, S. Kennon ..... Annapolis, MD
Scott, S. Kennon ..... Baltimore, MD
Scott, Sally E. ..... Albuquerque, NM
Scott, Sally J. ..... Chicago, IL
Scott, Samuel E. ..... Jackson, MS
Scott, Samuel J. ..... United States Senate, Committee Legal Personnel, GV
Scott, Sandra ..... Carlisle, MA
Scott, Sandra Davidson ..... Columbia, MO
Scott, Sandra L. ..... New York, NY
Scott, Sanford M. ..... Las Vegas, NV
Scott, Sarah E. ..... Boise, ID
Scott & Scott ..... Anderson, IN
Scott & Scott ..... Bel Air, MD
Chestertown, MD
Elkton, MD
Scott and Scott ..... Jackson, MS
Scott & Scott ..... New York, NY
Scott & Scott ..... Yakima, WA
Scott & Scott, A Professional Corporation
Springfield, IL
Scott, Scott, Robinson & Pavlich
Eureka, CA
Scott, Scriven & Wahoff LLP
Columbus, OH
Scott, Sean D. K. ..... Clearwater, FL
Scott, Sean W. ..... Largo, FL
Scott, Sharon H. ..... Stillwater, OK
Scott, Sharon L. ..... Boston, MA
Scott, Sharon M. ..... Minneapolis, MN
Scott, Shawn D. ..... Atlanta, GA
Scott, Shay S. ..... Portland, OR
Scott, Shelledy & Luhm, P.C. ..... Worland, WY
Scott, Shelly K. Hunt ..... Indio, CA
Scott, Sherry Lynn ..... Houston, TX
Scott, Sherry R. ..... Phoenix, AZ
Scott, Spencer ..... Irvine, CA
Scott, Stephanie Leigh ..... Washington, DC
Scott, Stephen A. ..... San Jose, CA
Scott, Stephen A. ..... Gainesville, FL
Scott, Stephen H. ..... Phoenix, AZ
Scott, Stephen L. ..... New Orleans, LA
Scott, Stephen R. ..... New York, NY
Scott, Stephen W. ..... Dubuque, IA
Scott, Sterling C. ..... Washington, DC
Scott, Steve ..... Columbia, MO
Scott, Steven ..... Hobbs, NM
Scott, Steven G. ..... Seattle, WA
Scott, Steven J. ..... Portland, ME
Scott, Steven John ..... Washington, DC
Scott, Steven R. ..... Oklahoma City, OK
Scott, Stewart M. ..... New York, NY
Scott, Stuart E. ..... Cleveland, OH
Scott, Susan ..... Hackensack, NJ
Scott, Susan C. ..... Houston, TX
Scott, Susan D. ..... Shreveport, LA
Scott, Susan Devlin ..... Doylestown, PA
Scott, Susan K. ..... Boston, MA
Scott, Susan K. Brown ..... Charleston, WV
Scott, Susan R. ..... Indianapolis, IN
Scott, Susan Tracey ..... Salem, OR
Scott, Suzanne R. ..... Portland, ME
Scott, Suzanne R. ..... Edinburg, TX
Scott, Sylvia A. ..... Newark, NJ
Scott, Sylvia Marie ..... Los Angeles, CA
Scott, T. Arthur, Jr. ..... Johnson City, TN
Kingsport, TN
Scott, Tabor ..... Amarillo, TX
Scott, Tacita A. Mikel ..... Atlanta, GA
Scott, Tamar Graham ..... Oklahoma City, OK
Scott, Tamla Tymus ..... Charlotte, NC
Scott, Tanya D. ..... Rosemead, CA
Scott, Tanya L. ..... Albuquerque, NM
Scott, Tara Leigh ..... Miami, FL
Scott, Terence M. ..... Clifton, NJ
Scott, Teresa A. ..... Treasury Department, Office of Thrift Supervision, GV
Scott, Terrence V. ..... Los Angeles, CA
Scott, Terry J. ..... Chula Vista, CA
Scott, Thane D. ..... Boston, MA
Scott, Theodore Ben ..... Buffalo, MO
Scott, Theodore R. ..... San Diego, CA
Scott, Theodore R. ..... Chicago, IL
Scott, Thomas C. ..... Indianapolis, IN
Scott, Thomas C. ..... Nashville, TN
Scott, Thomas E. ..... Miami, FL
Scott, Thomas E. ..... Miami, FL
Scott, Thomas G. ..... Golden, CO
Scott, Thomas J. ..... Blue Bell, PA
Scott, Thomas J., Jr. ..... Washington, DC
Scott, Thomas M. ..... Eagan, MN
Scott, Thomas P., III ..... Washington, DC
Scott, Thomas R. ..... Dillon, MT
Scott, Thomas R., Jr. ..... Grundy, VA
Scott, Thomas S., Jr. ..... Knoxville, TN
Scott, Thomas W. ..... Harrisburg, PA
Scott, Thomas W. ..... Oshkosh, WI
Scott, Tiffany T. ..... Metairie, LA
Scott, Timothy A. ..... Chicago, IL
Scott, Timothy E. ..... Kingsport, TN
Scott, Timothy H. ..... New Orleans, LA
Scott, Timothy J. ..... Baldwin, WI
New Richmond, WI
Scott, Timothy L. ..... Houston, TX
Scott, Timothy S. ..... Chicago, IL
Scott, Timothy T. ..... Palo Alto, CA
Scott, Todd A. ..... Perry, IA
Scott, Tokerud & McCarty
Great Falls, MT
Scott, Tom ..... Hays, KS
Scott, Tom ..... Midland, TX
Scott, Tom B., III ..... Jackson, MS
Scott, Tom B., Jr. ..... Jackson, MS
Scott, Tony A. ..... Oklahoma City, OK
Scott, Trina J. ..... Joplin, MO
Scott, Turner C. ..... Newport, RI
Scott, V. Katie Gilliam ..... Harlan, KY
Scott, Vanessa A. Simmons
Birmingham, AL
Scott, Victor Shane ..... Jefferson City, MO
Scott, Virginia K. ..... Swarthmore, PA
Scott, W. Andrew ..... Atlanta, GA
Scott, W. Grant, II ..... Pittsburgh, PA
Scott, W. James, Jr. ..... Irvine, CA
Scott, W. Jeffrey ..... Grayson, KY
Scott, W. Jeffrey, PSC ..... Ashland, KY
Grayson, KY
Scott, W. Michael ..... Houston, TX
Scott, W. Patrick ..... West Chester, PA
Scott, W. Roger ..... Los Angeles, CA
Scott, W. Steed ..... Atlanta, GA
Scott, W. Stephen ..... Stockton, CA
Scott, W. Stephen ..... Charlottesville, VA
Scott, W. Stuart ..... Nashville, TN
Scott, W. Thornton ..... Lexington, KY
Scott, W. Wade W. ..... Wilmington, DE
Scott & Wallace ..... Syracuse, NY
Scott, Wallace H., III ..... Austin, TX
Scott, Wallace H., Jr. ..... Austin, TX
Scott, Walter ..... Glendale, CA
Scott, Walter ..... New York, NY
Scott, Walter C. ..... Savannah, GA
Scott, Walter F. ..... Laramie, WY
Scott, Walter J. ..... Trenton, NJ
Scott, Walter J. ..... Grand Prairie, TX
Scott, Walter J., Jr. ..... Dallas, TX
Scott, Walter N., Jr. ..... Topeka, KS
Scott, Ward D. ..... Asheville, NC
Scott, Wendy A. ..... Buffalo, NY
Scott, Wesley William ..... St. Cloud, MN
Scott & Whitehead ..... Newport Beach, CA
Scott, Will T. ..... Pikeville, KY
Scott, William A. ..... Charleston, SC
Scott, William A., Jr. ..... Birmingham, AL
Scott, William Arbor ..... Little Rock, AR
Scott, William C. ..... Albuquerque, NM
Scott, William C. ..... Portland, OR
Scott, William Clement, IV
Charlottesville, VA
Scott, William D. ..... Sacramento, CA
Scott, William D. ..... Buffalo, NY
Scott, William E. ..... Cullowhee, NC
Scott, William E. ..... Fairless Hills, PA
Scott, William E., III ..... Baton Rouge, LA
Scott, William G. ..... Portsmouth, NH
Scott, William G. ..... Canandaigua, NY
Scott, William G., III ..... Tampa, FL
Scott, William J. ..... Jacksonville, FL
Scott, William J. ..... Rockville, MD
Scott, William J., Jr. ..... Wheaton, IL
Scott, William J., Jr. ..... West Chester, PA
Scott, William L., Jr. ..... Fairfax, VA
Scott, William L., Jr., P.C. ..... Fairfax, VA
Scott, William M. ..... Great Falls, MT
Scott, William M., IV ..... Los Angeles, CA
Scott, William O., Jr. ..... Susanville, CA
Scott, William P. ..... Pipestone, MN
Scott, William P. ..... Camden, NJ
Philadelphia, PA
Scott, William P. ..... Milwaukee, WI
Scott, William P., S.C. ..... Milwaukee, WI
Scott, William R. ..... Stuart, FL
Scott, William R. ..... Rantoul, IL
Scott, William Sumner ..... Hollywood, FL
Scott, William W. ..... Washington, DC
Scott, William W., III ..... Pittsburgh, PA
Scott, William W., Jr. ..... Pittsburgh, PA
Scott, William Z. ..... Bethlehem, PA
Scott & Williams, P.A. ..... Sarasota, FL
Scott, Winfield W. ..... Dallas, TX
Scott, Wm. Rowlett ..... Memphis, TN
Scott, Yava D. ..... Houston, TX
Scott, Yvonne E. ..... Aurora, CO
Scott, Zaldwaynaka L. ..... Chicago, IL
Scott, Zane B. ..... Big Stone Gap, VA
Scott-Bennett, Michelle E. ..... Gretna, LA
Scott-Brier, Barbara ..... Portland, OR
Scott-Buzzi, Patricia ..... Lawrenceville, NJ
Scott-Clayton, Patricia A.
Pension Benefit Guaranty Corporation, Office of the General Counsel, GV
Scotten, Donald M. ..... Los Angeles, CA
Scott-Henderson, Angela D. ..... Park Ridge, NJ
Scott-Howe, Carolyn E. ..... Belchertown, MA
Scotti, Carole L. ..... Lewisburg, WV
Scotti, Christopher M. ..... Minneapolis, MN
Scotti, Daniel B. ..... New York, NY
Scotti, David A., Law Offices of
Pittsburgh, PA
Scotti, Gavin W. ..... New York, NY
Scotti & Gerl ..... Lewisburg, WV
Scotti, Joel P. ..... Eugene, OR
Scotti, Michael J., III ..... Chicago, IL
Scotti, Michelle S. ..... Florham Park, NJ
Scotti, Neil A. ..... Beverly Hills, CA
Scotti, Richard F. ..... Las Vegas, NV
Scotti, Robert F. ..... Portland, OR
Scotti, Stacey Lynne ..... Utica, NY
Scotti, Steven Mark ..... New York, NY
Scott-Kakures, Megan ..... Rosemead, CA
Scott-McLaughlin, Randolph M.
White Plains, NY
Scott-Morgenthaler, Tina M. ..... Lakewood, CO

Scotto, Anthony T. ... Garden City, NY
Scotto, Francine ... New York, NY
Scotto, Francis A. ... Brooklyn, NY
Scotto, Georgoulis, Dockery & Scotto
New York, NY
Scotto, Michele F. ... New York, NY
Scotto, Paul J. ... New York, NY
Scotto, Raphael F. ... New York, NY
Scotto, Vincent J., III ... San Mateo, CA
Scott Ryan, Cheryl A. ... Dallas, TX
Scott-Sedley, Penny J. ... Philadelphia, PA
Scott-Smith, Kent I. ... Hartford, CT
Scott-Thomas, Deborah
Department of Education,
Office for Civil Rights, GV
Scott Witner, Kristine ... Doylestown, OH
Scoufos, Harry ... Sallisaw, OK
Scoufos, Harry, P.C., Law Offices of
Sallisaw, OK
Scoufos, Larry J. ... Santa Rosa, CA
Scoular, Dean J. ... St. Louis, MO
Scoular, Robert F. ... Los Angeles, CA
Scouller, Kimberly A. ... Largo, FL
Scoulos, Gary M. ... Pittsburgh, PA
Scoumperdis, Kristopher ... Portland, OR
Scourby, Nicholas ... Garden City, NY
Scourby, Nicholas ... New York, NY
Scouten, James W. ... Baltimore, MD
Scouten, John D. ... Toledo, OH
Scouton, Susan R. ... Los Angeles, CA
Scoutt, Jerrold, Jr. ... Washington, DC
Scova, Sarah ... Greenwich, CT
Scovel, Al ... Rapid City, SD
Scovel, Emert, Heasty & Chubb
Independence, KS
Scovel Law Office ... Rapid City, SD
Scovel, Robert K. ... Independence, KS
Scovel, Thomas R. ... White Plains, NY
Scovell, Frederic N., III ... Chicago, IL
Scovell, Robert J. ... Kingston, PA
Scovic, Stephen A. ... Wilmington, DE
Scovil, Douglas C. ... Rock Island, IL
Scovil, Geoffrey D. ... Albuquerque, NM
Scovill, H. William ... Sarasota, FL
Scovill, H. William, P.A., Law Offices of
Sarasota, FL
Scovill, Kim Robert ... Rochester, NY
Scovill, W. Bartlett ... Sarasota, FL
Scoville & Cessna ... London, KY
Scoville, Donald L. ... El Centro, CA
Scoville, George S. ... Springhill, TN
Scoville, Harmon G. ... Monarch Beach, CA
Scoville, Jack M., Jr. ... Georgetown, SC
Scoville, Jack M., Jr. ... Myrtle Beach, SC
Scoville, James C. ... New York, NY
Scoville, Joseph ... Chicago, IL
Scoville, Joseph G. ... Grand Rapids, MI
Scoville, Laurence M., Jr. ... Detroit, MI
Scoville, Mary E. ... Miami, FL
Scoville, Nancy C. ... London, KY
Scoville, Selden S. ... Leland, MI
Scoville, Tamara V. ... Washington, DC
Scoville, Thomas H. ... Rockford, IL
Scoville, Vernon E., III ... Independence, MO
Scoville, Warren N. ... London, KY
Scow, Aaron A. ... Dallas, TX
Scow, Steven R. ... Las Vegas, NV
Scow, Steven R., A Prof. Law Corp.
Las Vegas, NV
Scowcroft, Jerome C. ... Seattle, WA
Scowcroft, Karen ... Livingston, NJ
Scowcroft, Roger K. ... Salt Lake City, UT
Scoyen, Edward C. ... Palo Alto, CA
Scozio, John D. ... Pittsburgh, PA
Scozzafava, Mary Rose ... Boston, MA
Scrabis, Richard J. ... Key West, FL
Scrafford, J. Bruce ... Austin, TX
Scraggin, Gordon A. ... Tacoma, WA
Scramstad, Barbara E. ... Oakland, CA
Scrantom, Timothy D. ... Charleston, SC
Scrantom, W. G., Jr. ... Columbus, GA
Scrantom, William G., III ... Columbus, GA
Scranton, David F. ... Malvern, PA
Scranton, Drasan R. ... Los Angeles, CA
Scranton, Everett M. ... Grosse Pointe, MI
Scranton, Kenneth E., Ltd. ... Chicago, IL
Scranton, Michael ... Concord, CA
Scranton, Nancy M. ... Fremont, OH
Scranton & Solze ... Fremont, OH
Screen, Christopher T. ... New Orleans, LA
Screen, Donald P. ... Cleveland, OH
Screen, J. Patrick, Jr. ... Baton Rouge, LA
Screen, Patricia A. ... Cleveland, OH
Screen, Timothy M. ... Baton Rouge, LA
Screeton, Jack T. ... Santa Ana, CA
Scrementi, Anthony C. ... Chicago Heights, IL
Scremin, Anthony J. ... Miami, FL
Scremin, Anthony J., P.A. ... Miami, FL
Screnar, James J. ... Bozeman, MT
Screnci, Stephen W. ... Boca Raton, FL
Screnock, Evelyn J. ... Baraboo, WI
Screnock, Joseph J. ... Baraboo, WI
Screnock, Paul Steven, Law Office
Adams, WI
Screven, James O. ... Birmingham, AL
Screws, Euel A., Jr. ... Montgomery, AL
Screwvala, Erach F. ... New York, NY
Scribner, Alan F. ... Contoocook, NH
Scribner, Douglas G. ... Atlanta, GA
Scribner, Fred C., III ... Brookline, MA
Scribner, Hall & Thompson, LLP
Washington, DC
Scribner, John E. ... Washington, DC
Scribner, Linda ... Bentonville, AR
Scribner, Mark H. ... Burlington, VT
Scribner, Peter R. ... Rochester, NY
Scribner, Richard O. ... New York, NY
Scribner, Robert H. ... Fresno, CA
Scribner, Robert J. ... New York, NY
Scribner, Thomas E. ... Boston, MA
Scribner, Thomas J. ... Provo, UT
Scribner, Tom ... Walla Walla, WA
Scricca, Anna M. ... Northport, NY
Scriggins, L. P. ... Baltimore, MD
Scrimale, Richard E. ... Syracuse, NY
Scrimenti, Belinda Jayne ... Washington, DC
Scrimshire, Edward E. ... Malvern, AR
Scripp, John ... Milwaukee, WI
Scripter, Richard W. ... Honolulu, HI
Scripture, Jeffrey W. ... Indianapolis, IN
Scritsmier, Gary L. ... North Platte, NE
Scriven, Bradley A. ... Denver, CO
Scriven, Donald C. ... Columbus, OH
Scriven, John G. ... Midland, MI
Scriven, Lansing C. ... Tampa, FL
Scrivens, Kathleen M. ... Cincinnati, OH
Scrivens, Scott L. ... Cleveland, OH
Scrivner, Alan L. ... St. Louis, MO
Scrivner, Anne C. ... Chicago, IL
Scrivner, Chaland B. ... Redding, CA
Scrivner, James R. ... Ada, OK
Scrivner, Jill Hollingshead ... Sausalito, CA
Scrivner, Regina Marie ... New Albany, IN
Scrivner, Roger M. ... Belleville, IL
Scrivner, Thomas W. ... Milwaukee, WI
Scrivner, Wes L. ... Boise, ID
Scrivo, Florence Amato ... Totowa, NJ
Scrivo, Robert C. ... Roseland, NJ
Scrivo, Thomas P. ... Morristown, NJ
Scro, David A. ... Melville, NY
Scro, Lisa Fortunato ... Melville, NY
Scro, Salvatore G. ... Liverpool, NY
Scro & Scro ... Melville, NY
Scrobell, Daniel D. ... Minocqua, WI
Scroble, Melanie J. ... Hackensack, NJ
Scrocca, Renee E. ... Vineland, NJ
Scrocco, George L. ... Pearl River, NY
Scrodanus, Rose Marie S. ... Albany, NY
Scrofano, Sal G. ... Cincinnati, OH
Scroggie, Robin R. ... Los Angeles, CA
Scroggin, Don G. ... McLean, VA
Scroggin, John J., & Associates
Atlanta, GA
Cumming, GA
Scroggin, John J., & Associates
Roswell, GA
Scroggin, Pari K. ... Scottsdale, AZ
Scroggin, Steven ... Las Vegas, NV
Scroggins, Frances E. ... Conway, AR
Scroggins, Frank W., (P.C.) ... Atlanta, GA
Scroggins, James Jerome ... East Tallassee, AL
Scroggins, Jerry M., Jr. ... Houston, TX
Scroggins, Joan E. ... Caldwell, TX
Scroggins, Lawrence R. ... Caldwell, TX
Scroggins, Leon G., II ... Dallas, TX
Scroggins, Leon G., Sr. ... Granite City, IL
Scroggins, M. E., Jr. ... Afton, MN
Scroggins, R. Daniel ... Tulsa, OK
Scroggins, Robert C. ... Cincinnati, OH
Scroggins & Scroggins ... Caldwell, TX
Scroggins, Shemeika M. ... Omaha, NE
Scroggins & Williamson ... Atlanta, GA
Scroggs, Larry K. ... Collierville, TN
Scroggs & Rogers ... Collierville, TN
Scrogham, Kenneth L. ... Fort Wayne, IN
Scroghan, James S. ... Louisville, KY
Scrogin, Julia ... Yuba City, CA
Scrogin, Sue E. ... Worcester, MA
Scroope, Henry J., Jr. ... Fort Lauderdale, FL
Scruby, Frank M. ... Orange Park, FL
Scruby, Mark H. ... Green Cove Springs, FL
Scrudato, Paul A. ... New York, NY
Scrudder, Henry E., Jr. ... Atlanta, GA
Scrudders, Eric Scott ... West Palm Beach, FL
Scruggs & Carmichael, P.A.
Gainesville, FL
Scruggs, Charles H. ... Kokomo, IN
Scruggs, Charles H., III ... Tampa, FL
Scruggs, Charles L. ... El Paso, TX
Scruggs, David C. ... Memphis, TN
Scruggs, Frank P. ... Fort Lauderdale, FL
Miami, FL
Scruggs, G. Christopher ... Brownsville, TN
Scruggs, G. Dana, Law Offices of
Santa Cruz, CA
Scruggs, George L., Jr. ... Richmond, VA
Scruggs, Harry U., Jr. ... Memphis, TN
Scruggs, Horace Simon ... Gulfport, MS
Scruggs, J. Richard ... Portland, OR
Scruggs, Jan Craig ... Annapolis, MD
Scruggs, John A. ... Denver, CO
Scruggs, John P. ... Memphis, TN
Scruggs, John W., Jr. ... Maitland, FL
Scruggs, Jordan, Dodd & Dodd
Fort Payne, AL
Scruggs, Laura J. ... Bridgeton, NJ
Scruggs & Leverton, A Professional
Corporation ... El Paso, TX
Scruggs, Mark ... Nashville, TN
Scruggs, Mark A. ... Durham, NC
Scruggs, Mark C. ... Nashville, TN
Scruggs, Michael P. ... Seattle, WA
Scruggs, Millette, Bozeman & Dent, P.A.
Biloxi, MS
Jackson, MS
Pascagoula, MS
Scruggs, Philip G. ... Los Angeles, CA
Scruggs, Richard F. ... Pascagoula, MS
Scruggs, Robert C. ... Houston, TX
Scruggs, Robert L. ... Nashville, TN
Scruggs, Samuel D. ... Salt Lake City, UT
Scruggs, Sue Ellen ... Chattanooga, TN
Scruggs, Thomas H. ... Jackson, MS
Scruggs, William D., Jr. ... Fort Payne, AL
Scrupski, Mary E. ... Red Bank, NJ
Scrutchins, Arthur D.
Federal Communications Commission,
Mass Media Bureau, GV
Scruton, Denise R. ... New York, NY
Scruton, John W. ... Louisville, KY
Scruton, Joseph ... Bellevue, NE
Scruton, Kathleen A. ... Boston, MA
Scruton, Michele P. ... Chicago, IL
Scrutton, Suzanne J. ... Columbus, OH
Scuba, Audrey A. ... Kent, OH
Scuba, Richard J. ... Rancho Santa Fe, CA
Scucci, Ann T. ... Rockaway, NJ
Scuccimarra, Thomas H. ... Peekskill, NY
Scudder, C. Edward, Jr. ... Nashville, TN
Scudder, Charles I., Law Office of
Omaha, NE
Scudder, Charles S. K. ... Philadelphia, PA
Scudder, Daniel ... Hartford, CT
Scudder, Earl H. ... Lincoln, NE
Scudder & Esler Co., L.P.A. ... Dayton, OH
Scudder, Henry J. ... Bath, NY
Scudder, Joyce W. ... Hyannis, MA
Scudder, Laura L. ... Department of the Navy,
Office of the Judge Advocate General, GV
Scudder Law Firm, P.C. ... Lincoln, NE
Scudder, Mark A. ... Lincoln, NE
Scudder, Mark S. ... Dallas, TX
Scudder, Samuel A. ... Zebulon, NC
Scudder, Steven C. ... Dayton, OH
Scudder, Thad ... Kelso, WA
Scudder, Theodore T. ... Chicago, IL
Scudellari, Carla W. ... San Jose, CA
Scudellari, Deirdre ... Trenton, NJ
Scudellari, Richard ... Palo Alto, CA
Scudere, Frank T. ... New York, NY
Scuderi & Childs ... Marco Island, FL
Scuderi, Jon ... Naples, FL
Scuderi, Joseph W. ... Hagåtña, GU
Scuderi, Peter B. ... Philadelphia, PA
Scuderi, Peter J. ... Philadelphia, PA
Scuderi, Robert S. ... Sherman Oaks, CA
Scuderi, Salvatore C. ... Marco Island, FL
Scuderi, Stephen P. ... Springfield, MA
Scuderi, Susan M. ... De Witt, NY
Scudi, Morgan J.C. ... Detroit, MI
Scudiere, Debra Hodges
Morgantown, WV
Scudieri, David G. ... New York, NY
Scudiero, Joseph B. ... San Pedro, CA
Scukanec, John A. ... Anchorage, AK
Sculco, Thomas Warren ... Orlando, FL
Scull, David L. ... Washington, DC
Scull, David L. ... Bethesda, MD
Scull, James A. ... San Francisco, CA
Scull, John M. ... Columbus, OH
Scull, Kenneth C. ... Phoenix, AZ
Scull, Nancy T. ... San Diego, CA
Scull, Peter B. ... Lakewood, CO
Scull, Timothy B. ... Denver, CO
Scullary, James J. ... Pittsfield, MA
Scullen, Anne M. ... Chicago, IL
Scullen, Michael T. ... Troy, MI
Scullen, Peter R. ... Detroit, MI
Scullen, Sara Purtell ... Milwaukee, WI
Sculley, Jeffrey S.
Department of Agriculture,
Office of the General Counsel, GV
Sculley, Lynn ... Brooklyn, NY
Sculley, Michael P. ... Huntington, NY
Sculley, Paul D. ... Houston, TX
Sculli, Karen ... New York, NY
Scullin, Daniel J. ... Galveston, TX
Scullin, Frederick J., Jr. ... Syracuse, NY
Scullin, Michael E. ... Philadelphia, PA
Scullin, Robert P. ... Washington, DC
Scullin, Sharon M. ... Reading, PA
Scullion, Jennifer R. ... New York, NY
Scullion, Kevin ... Calumet City, IL
Scullion, Tara Waller ... Marietta, GA
Scully, Charles P., II ... San Francisco, CA
Scully, Charles R. ... St. Petersburg, FL
Scully, Craig M. ... New York, NY
Scully, Cynthia R. ... Bakersfield, CA
Scully, Daniel J. ... Long Beach, CA
Scully, Daniel J., Jr. ... Detroit, MI
Scully, Daniel R. ... Springfield, MA
Scully, David J. ... Waterbury, CT
Scully, David M. ... Fort Lauderdale, FL
Scully & Delaney ... Cleveland, OH
Scully, Donald S. ... Clawson, MI
Plymouth, MI
Scully, Edward F. ... Unionville, CT
Scully, Edward W. ... Bronx, NY
Scully, Elizabeth A ... Washington, DC
Scully, Erik V. ... Pittsburgh, PA
Scully, George F., Jr. ... Flossmoor, IL
Scully & Glass ... Winchester, VA
Scully, Glendalee ... Sacramento, CA
Scully, J. Michael ... Springfield, MA
Scully, Jack W. ... Standish, MI
Scully, James T. ... Hartford, CT
Scully, Janice Hansen ... Sacramento, CA
Scully, Jason ... Palo Alto, CA
Scully, Jean T. J. ... New York, NY
Scully, Jennifer L. ... Seattle, WA
Scully, Jerome J. ... Lee, MA
Scully, Joanne R. ... Palo Alto, CA
Scully, John A. ... Dallas, TX
Scully, John C. ... Springfield, VA
Scully, John F. ... Hartford, CT
Scully, John F. ... Garden City, NY
Scully, John F. ... New York, NY
Scully, John T. ... Hartford, CT
Scully, Judith A. M. ... Morgantown, WV
Scully, Katharine W. ... Washington, DC
Scully, Kathryn ... New York, NY
Scully, Keith ... Bellevue, WA
Scully, Lawrence B. ... Cleveland, OH
Scully, Leonard T. ... New York, NY
Scully, Lisa M. ... Brooklyn, NY
Scully, Marcia ... Los Angeles, CA
Scully, Margaret M. ... Wexford, PA
Scully, Marla L. ... Hamilton, OH
Scully, Martin, Jr. ... Treasury Department,
Internal Revenue Service, GV
Scully, Maureen ... Liberty, MO
Scully, Michael F. ... Minneapolis, MN
Scully, Michael R. ... Hackensack, NJ
Scully, Miles D. ... San Diego, CA
Scully, Nicksa, Martin & Reeve, LLP
Unionville, CT
Scully, O'Brien & McDermott
Rochester, NY
Scully, Patrice ... Chicago, IL
Scully, Patrick E. ... Unionville, CT
Scully, Patrick J. ... Portland, ME
Scully, Patrick R. ... Colorado Springs, CO
Scully, Peter B. ... Sun Valley, ID
Scully, Raymond F. ... Washington, DC
Scully, Richard A. ... Washington, DC
Scully, Richard A.
National Labor Relations Board,
Division of Administrative Law Judges, GV
Scully, Richard T. ... Garrison, NY
Scully, Robert E., Jr. ... Vienna, VA
Scully, Robin E., II ... Independence, MO
Scully, Roger Tehan, II ... Rockville, MD
Scully, Scott, Murphy & Presser, A
Professional Corporation
Garden City, NY
Mineola, NY
New York, NY
Riverhead, NY
Scully, Scott W. ... North Yarmouth, ME
Scully & Scully, LLP ... Pittsburgh, PA
Scully, Susan C. ... Buffalo, NY
Scully, Thomas ... West Haven, CT
Scully, Thomas G. ... Santa Ana, CA
Scully, Thomas J. ... San Pedro, CA
Scully, Thomas S. ... Erie, PA
Scully, Vincent C. A. ... Pittsburgh, PA
Scully, William E., Jr. ... Daphne, AL
Scully, William F., Jr. ... Cleveland, OH
Scully, William F., Jr. Co., L.P.A.
Cleveland, OH
Scully, William J. ... Hartford, CT
Scully, William S., Jr. ... Manhattan Beach, CA
Scully & Yenior ... Standish, MI
Sculnick, David H. ... New York, NY
Scult, Ellen Borkum ... Wellesley, MA
Scult, Morton M. ... Phoenix, AZ
Scumaci, Robert G. ... Buffalo, NY
Scungio, Americo M. ... Westerly, RI
Scungio, Benjamin M. ... Providence, RI
Scungio, John A. ... Providence, RI
Scunziano, Nicholas P. ... Brooklyn, NY
Scuorzo, Linda M. ... Florham Park, NJ
Scupholm, T. Gordon, II
Birmingham, MI
Scupi, Richard J. ... Chevy Chase, MD
Scura, John R. ... Dansville, NY
Scurfield, Robert M. ... Wichita, KS
Scurfield, Scott A. ... Somerset, PA
Scuri, Anita L. ... Sacramento, CA
Scurko, Laura ... Morristown, NJ
Scurlock, D. P., III ... Butler, AL
Scurlock, Jeff R. ... Kansas City, MO
Scurlock, John E. ... Kansas City, MO
Scurlock, Lloyd ... Fort Worth, TX
Scurlock, Mary C. ... Portland, OR
Scuro, James V. ... Ocean City, NJ
Scurrah, Robert G., Law Offices of
Tustin, CA
Scurry, John C., Jr. ... Greenwood, SC
Scurti, Adam E. ... Steubenville, OH
Scurti, Jason A. ... New York, NY
Scurti, Mark F. ... Baltimore, MD
Scurti Lowe, Kimberly ... Newark, NJ
Scussel, Michael G. ... Little Rock, AR
Scutari, Kenneth A. ... Short Hills, NJ
Scutch, Frank M., III ... Fort Lauderdale, FL
Scutchfield, Alex L. ... Lexington, KY
Scutchfield, Jennifer Schwartz ... Lebanon, KY
Scutella, Frank J. ... Erie, PA
Scuteri, Jeffrey T. ... Salem, MA
Scuteri, Sergio I. ... Bellmawr, NJ
Scutiere, Donald J. ... Salem, MA
Scutieri, Joseph A. ... White Plains, NY
Scutt, Robert C. ... Rochester, NY
Scutt, Gilbert J. ... Somerdale, NJ
Philadelphia, PA
Scutti, Jim ... Boca Raton, FL
Scutti, Jim, P.A. ... Boca Raton, FL
Scutti, Thomas A. ... San Diego, CA
Scyoc, David R. ... Pomona, CA
Scyphers & Austin, P.C. ... Abingdon, VA
Scyphers, David L. ... Abingdon, VA
Sczudlo, Paul A. ... Los Angeles, CA
Sczudlo, Walter ... Fairbanks, AK
Sczudlo, Walter J. ... Alexandria, VA
Szcygelski, Ralph Jon ... Manitowoc, WI
Sdao, Frederick J. ... Houston, TX
Sea, Francis Asokwu ... East Orange, NJ
Seab, R. Scott ... Colorado Springs, CO
Seaba, Lynn Collins ... Goldfield, IA
Seabaugh, Alan Thomas ... Shreveport, LA
Seabaugh, Paul W. ... Kennett, MO
Seabaugh, Paula D. ... St. Louis, MO
Seabaugh, Scot J. ... St. Louis, MO
Seabaugh, Scott ... San Jose, CA
Seabaugh, William F. ... St. Louis, MO
Seaberg, Arthur W. ... St. Paul, MN
Seaberg, Diane M. ... San Diego, CA
Seaberry, James J., Jr. ... Chicago, IL
Seaberry, Virgil T., Jr. ... Eastland, TX
Seablom, Scott F. ... Seattle, WA

Seaboard Law Group .... Malibu, CA
Seabold, John S. .... Memphis, TN
Seabolt, Billy Joe, Jr. .... Washington, DC
Seabolt, Carolyn A. .... Atlanta, GA
Seabolt, Charles F. .... Lynchburg, VA
Seabolt, D. Grant, Jr. .... Dallas, TX
Seabolt, Duane C. .... Honolulu, HI
Seabolt, Lee M. .... Baltimore, MD
Seabolt, Michael L. .... Honolulu, HI
Seabolt, Richard L. .... San Francisco, CA
Seabolt, Robert D. .... Richmond, VA
Seabolt, Scott T. .... Detroit, MI
Seaborg, Dorothy A. W. .... Joliet, IL
Seaborg, Priscilla .... Portland, OR
Seaborn, Katherine M. .... Dallas, TX
Seaborn, Linda P. .... San Francisco, CA
Seaborn, Stuart J. .... San Francisco, CA
Seaborne, Ellen .... Flagstaff, AZ
Seaborne, Ellen, P.C. .... Flagstaff, AZ
Seaborne, John K. .... Los Angeles, CA
Seabourne, George P. .... Thomaston, CT
Seabridge, William B. .... Folsom, CA
Seabright, David W. .... Chicago, IL
Seabrook, John B. .... Swampscott, MA
Seabrook, Juliette T. .... Charleston, SC
Seabrook, Robyn N. .... Richmond, VA
Seabrook, Susan E. .... Treasury Department, Internal Revenue Service, GV
Seaburg, Jean .... Northfield, MN
Seaburg-Brackett, Marcella M. Rochester, NY
Seabury & Brown .... Springfield, MA
Seabury, Chester C. .... Phoenix, AZ
Seabury, Jason D. .... Columbus, OH
Seabury, Leland B. .... Springfield, MA
Seabury, Suellen E. .... Lowell, MA
Seabury, Susan H. .... Atlanta, GA
Seacat, Carol Ann .... Okmulgee, OK
Seacat, Dennis F. .... Okmulgee, OK
Seach, Raymond T. .... Indianapolis, IN
Seach, Stephen A. .... West Hazleton, PA
Seacord, Pierre .... Orlando, FL
Seacord, Young, Young & Rosenstrach New Rochelle, NY
Seacrest, Gary L. .... Atlanta, GA
Seacrest & Kalkowski, Law Offices of, P.C. Lincoln, NE
Seacrest, Karesh, Tate & Bicknese, LLP Atlanta, GA
Seacrest, Kent .... Lincoln, NE
Seacrest, William A. .... Tallahassee, FL
Seacrist, Susan M. .... Cleveland, OH
Seadale, Vincent G. .... Cheshire, CT
Seado, Paul .... Bismarck, ND
Seafer, Mindi .... Camden, NJ
Seaford, Hurley N. .... Tampa, FL
Seaford, Raymond N. .... Tampa, FL
Seaford, Rodney W. .... Charlotte, NC
Seaford, Susan R. .... Tampa, FL
Seagears, Murray W. .... Fairfax, VA
Seager, Cheryl T. .... Dallas, TX
Seager, Edward R. .... Rutland, VT
Seager, Edward R., P.C., Law Offices of Rutland, VT
Seager, Elizabeth .... St. Louis, MO
Seager, Glenn M. .... Minneapolis, MN
Seager, Sarah L. .... Washington, DC
Seager, William .... Riverside, CA
Seagle, Catherine A. .... Chicago, IL
Seagle, Deborah Smith .... Dothan, AL
Seagle, J. Harold .... Wilmington, NC
Seagle, J. Mark .... Wilmington, NC
Seagle, Joseph E. .... Asheville, NC
Seagle, Victor R. .... Tulsa, OK
Seago, John E. .... Baton Rouge, LA
Seago, John V. .... Covington, LA
Seago, Randal .... Sylva, NC
Seagrave, Norman P. .... Concord, NH
Seagraves, Charles H., Jr. Grants Pass, OR
Seagraves, Lucian Earl, III .... Roswell, GA
Seagriff, Michael .... Canastota, NY
Seagroves, Corrie R. .... Rocky Mount, NC
Seagull, Keith A. .... Pomona, CA
Seagull, Lewis M. .... Westfield, NJ
Seah, Susan Lee K. .... Chicago, IL
Seaha, Thomas J. .... Manassas, VA
Seaholm, Reidar H. .... Cleveland, OH
Seahorn, Susan K. .... Carrboro, NC
Seaks, G. Henry .... Boulder, CO
Seal, Benjamin H., II .... Los Angeles, CA
Seal, Catherine A. .... Colorado Springs, CO
Seal, Christine M. .... Richmond, IN
Seal, David W. .... Long Beach, CA
Seal, Gregory L. .... Salt Lake City, UT
Seal, James A. .... Treasury Department, Office of Regulations and Rulings, GV
Seal, James L. .... Beverly Hills, CA
Seal, Jimmy L. .... Chattanooga, TN
Seal & Kennedy, P.C. .... Salt Lake City, UT
Seal, Lee, Branch, Brown & Briese Bogalusa, LA
Seal, Melody K. .... Mesa, AZ
Seal, Sharon E. .... Plano, TX
Seal, Spencer .... Santa Barbara, CA
Seal, Welton O., Jr. .... Raleigh, NC
Sealand, Joyce H. .... Memphis, TN
Sealander, Colleen Tove Federal Election Commission, Office of the General Counsel, GV
SEALAW Hawaii .... Honolulu, HI
Kamuela, HI
Lihue, HI
Sealby, Robert W. .... Wenatchee, WA
Seale, Albert J. .... Mobile, AL
Seale, C. Stevens .... Washington, DC
Seale Daigle & Ross, L.L.C. Baton Rouge, LA
Covington, LA
Hammond, LA
Seale, Erin K. .... Washington, DC
Seale, Gary Robert .... Birmingham, AL
Seale, H. Kyle .... San Antonio, TX
Seale, James H., III .... Greensboro, AL
Seale, James R. .... Montgomery, AL
Seale, John H. .... Jasper, TX
Seale, John S. .... Jasper, TX
Seale, John T. .... Monroe, LA
Seale, Marsal & Seale .... Mobile, AL
Seale, Michael D. .... Victoria, TX
Seale & Murrell .... Memphis, TN
Seale, Ned D. .... Gualala, CA
Seale, Robert M. .... Livingston, AL
Seale, Ronald A. .... Baton Rouge, LA
Seale, Sandia Suzanne .... Oklahoma City, OK
Seale, Smith, Zuber & Barnette Baton Rouge, LA
Seale, Stover, Coffield & Bisbey .... Jasper, TX
Seale, T. Jay, III .... Hammond, LA
Seale, Thomas F., Jr. .... Livingston, AL
Seale, William B. .... Memphis, TN
Seale, William R. .... Knoxville, TN
Morristown, TN
Seales, Frank, Jr. Department of Transportation, National Highway Traffic Safety Administration, GV
Sealey, Gail P. .... Newport News, VA
Sealey, Patrick L. .... Sioux City, IA
Sealey, Reginald M. Department of Transportation, U. S. Coast Guard, GV
Sealey, Shermane Townsend .... Waterford, MI
Seall, Stephen A. .... South Bend, IN
Sealls, Kenneth E. .... Washington, DC
Sealove, Allison D. .... New York, NY
Sealove, Morton J. .... New York, NY
Seals, Carla M. .... New York, NY
Seals, David B. .... Sacramento, CA
Seals, E. Earl .... La Grange, GA
Seals, James H. .... Fort Myers, FL
Seals, John D., III .... Roseland, NJ
Seals Law Firm, P.A. .... Marion, SC
Seals, Linda .... Santa Barbara, CA
Seals, Linda L. .... Anaheim, CA
Seals, Paul .... Austin, TX
Seals, Philbert E. .... Anaheim, CA
Seals, Ralph E., Jr. .... Enid, OK
Seals, Sidney R. .... Oneida, TN
Seals & Tenenbaum .... Anaheim, CA
Seals, Thomas C. .... Solon, OH
Seals, William E., Jr. .... Washington, DC
Seals, William H., Jr. .... Marion, SC
Seals, Yolanda Y. .... Stamford, CT
Sealy, Albert H. .... Dayton, OH
Sealy, Earl W. (Rusty) .... Austin, TX
Sealy, Michael S. .... Montgomery, AL
Seam, Anu .... Department of Justice, Antitrust Division, GV
Seaman, Alexander .... Verona, NJ
Seaman, Allan M. .... Pittsburgh, PA
Seaman, Allen R. .... Lake Worth, FL
Seaman, Andrew W., Jr. .... San Antonio, TX
Seaman and Ashley .... New York, NY
Seaman, Carol M. .... Bloomington, IN
Seaman, Charles H. .... San Francisco, CA
Seaman, Charles W. .... Natchitoches, LA
Seaman, Christopher A. .... Campbell, CA
Seaman and Clark .... New Brunswick, NJ
Perth Amboy, NJ
Seaman, Colin L. .... Middlebury, VT
Seaman, Daniel E. .... Lockport, NY
Seaman, David E. .... Lockport, NY
Seaman, David P. .... New York, NY
Seaman, David V. .... McLean, VA
Seaman, Dennis .... Cleveland, OH
Seaman, Dennis, & Associates Co., L.P.A. Cleveland, OH
Seaman, Drew F. .... St. Joseph, MI
Seaman, Elizabeth Hobson .... Encino, CA
Seaman, Elizabeth P. .... Boston, MA
Seaman, Garry D. .... Kalispell, MT
Seaman and Giometti, Professional Corporation .... Denver, CO
Seaman, J. Tad .... New Windsor, NY
Seaman, Jack E. .... Nashville, TN
Seaman, James G. .... Pittsburgh, PA
Seaman, James J. .... Secaucus, NJ
Seaman, James J. .... Albany, NY
Seaman, James M. .... Kansas City, MO
Seaman, J. C., Jr. .... Ruston, LA
Seaman, Jeffrey C. .... Cincinnati, OH
Seaman, Jeffrey R. .... New York, NY
Seaman, Jerome .... Baltimore, MD
Seaman, John Gates .... Corpus Christi, TX
Seaman, John N. .... East Lansing, MI
Seaman, John N., Jr. .... Traverse City, MI
Seaman, Joseph J. .... Philadelphia, PA
Seaman, Karen L. .... San Francisco, CA
Seaman, Kevin A. .... Stony Brook, NY
Seaman, Laurance B. .... Clearfield, PA
Seaman, Leonard R. .... San Luis Obispo, CA
Seaman, Louis David San Bernardino, CA
Seaman, Martha L. .... Scottsdale, AZ
Seaman, Noel W. .... San Francisco, CA
Seaman, P. Watson .... New York, NY
Seaman, Peggy J. .... Lakewood, CO
Seaman, Penny Quinn .... New Haven, CT
Seaman, Perry J. .... Elkton, MD
Seaman, Rebecca Martin .... Salt Point, NY
Seaman, Richard F. T. .... Cleveland, OH
Seaman, Robert D. .... Department of Defense, Defense Legal Services Agency, GV
Seaman, Robert E., III .... Northvale, NJ
Seaman, Robert L. .... New York, NY
Seaman, Scott M. .... Chicago, IL
Seaman & Seaman .... Corpus Christi, TX
Seaman & Seaman, A Law Corporation Gold River, CA
Sacramento, CA
Seaman, Stephen H. .... Corpus Christi, TX
Seaman, Thomas G. .... New York, NY
Seaman, Thomas J. .... Denver, CO
Seaman, Wareham C., Jr. .... Gold River, CA
Seamands, Michael C. .... St. Louis, MO
Seamands, Rebecca J. .... Indianapolis, IN
Seamans, Janette L. .... Avon Park, FL
Seamans, Kenneth W. .... Montrose, PA
Seamans, Peter B. .... Boston, MA
Seamans, Richard C. .... Seal Beach, CA
Seamans, Sandra L. .... Mesa, AZ
Seamans, Susan G. .... Oklahoma City, OK
Seamon, Gregory P. .... St. Paul, MN
Seamon, Janice L. .... Miami, FL
Seamon, John .... Tucson, AZ
Seamon, Theodore I. .... Washington, DC
Seamon, William P. .... Albany, NY
Seamons, Justin R. .... Twin Falls, ID
Seamons, Quinton F. .... Phoenix, AZ
Seamster, Don N. .... Abilene, TX
Seamster, Mark E. .... Hammond, LA
Seamster, Michael S. .... Abilene, TX
Seanor, J.W. .... Lexington, KY
Seanor, Stacey .... Washington, DC
Seapy, Marjorie A. .... Claremont, CA
Seaquist, Gwen E. .... Ithaca, NY
Sear, John D. .... Minneapolis, MN
Sear, Morey L. .... New Orleans, LA
Sear, Thomas H. .... New York, NY
Sear, Timothy J. .... Overland Park, KS
Searby, Bruce Hamilton .... Los Angeles, CA
Searby, Edmund W. .... Cleveland, OH
Searchinger, Timothy D. .... Washington, DC
Searcy, Ann H. .... Dalton, GA
Searcy, Christian D., Sr. West Palm Beach, FL
Searcy, David Joe .... Los Angeles, CA
Searcy Denney Scarola Barnhart & Shipley, Professional Association West Palm Beach, FL
Searcy, E. Dale .... Dayton, OH
Searcy, Earl R. .... Louisville, KY
Searcy, Edgar B. .... Indianapolis, IN
Searcy & Gandy, P.C. .... College Station, TX
Searcy, Gary W. .... Virginia Beach, VA
Searcy, Harley A. .... Los Angeles, CA
Searcy, Henry M. .... St. Augustine, FL
Searcy, Hollis L. .... Louisville, KY
Searcy, Jack C., III .... Houston, TX
Searcy, Jason R. .... Longview, TX
Searcy, Jason R., P.C. .... Longview, TX
Searcy, Kathy W. .... Little Rock, AR
Searcy, Lawrence S., Jr. .... Alexandria, LA
Searcy, Lum D. .... Opelika, AL
Searcy, Margie Tyler .... Birmingham, AL
Searcy, Marshall M. .... Los Angeles, CA
Searcy, Marshall M., Jr. .... Fort Worth, TX
Searcy, Philip E. .... Kernersville, NC
Winston-Salem, NC
Searcy, Roland M., Jr. .... College Station, TX
Searcy, Stanley A. .... Jeffersontown, KY
Searcy, Stephen D. .... Columbia, SC
Searcy, Tricia J. .... Los Angeles, CA
Searcy, William N. .... Savannah, GA
Searer, Francis A. .... Lewistown, PA
Searer, James M., P.C. .... Muskegon, MI
Searer, Timothy S. .... Lewistown, PA
Searfoss, Jesse D. .... Reading, PA
Searight, Murland W. .... Columbia Falls, MT
Searight, William H., III .... Dallas, TX
Searing, Adam S. G. .... Raleigh, NC
Searing, Daniel A. .... Department of Justice, Civil Rights Division, GV
Searing, Richelle E. .... Danbury, CT
Searing, Stephanie M. .... Bellevue, WA
Searl, Cathy L. (Youssi) .... Batavia, IL
Searl, Christine Pamela .... New York, NY
Searl, J. Scott .... Omaha, NE
Searle, Andrew C. .... Clinton, IA
Searle, Dean A. .... Marshall, TX
Searle, Duane M. .... Lemoyne, PA
Searle, Elizabeth B. .... Lafayette, IN
Searle, Geo. H. .... Salt Lake City, UT
Searle, H. Reed .... Santa Cruz, CA
Searle, Jennifer R. .... Boston, MA
Searle, Peter J. .... Brea, CA
Searle, Robert M. .... Houston, TX
Searle, Theodore A. .... Jamestown, NY
Searle, William F., III .... Knoxville, TN
Searleman, Bruce E. .... Boston, MA
Searles, David A. .... Philadelphia, PA
Searles, Mary Beth .... Denver, CO
Searles, Paul W. .... Dallas, TX
Searles, Richard W. .... Englewood, CO
Searles, Robert L., Jr. .... Minneapolis, MN
Searles, Sidney Z. .... Tucson, AZ
Searles, Eileen H. .... St. Louis, MO
Searls, James C. .... Minneapolis, MN
Searls, Julie A. .... Lancaster, OH
Searls, Steven D. .... Rochester, NY
Searns, Jason Edward .... Denver, CO
Sears, Andrew F. .... Overland Park, KS
Sears, Anthony A., Law Offices of Glendora, CA
Sears, Anthony Allison .... Glendora, CA
Sears, Barbara A. .... Silver Spring, MD
Sears, Benjamin R. .... Nashville, TN
Sears, Boyd M., Jr. .... West Point, VA
Sears, Bronwyn P. .... Chicago, IL
Sears, C. Bradford, Jr. .... Newnan, GA
Sears, C. Robin .... Sherman, TX
Sears, Charles B. .... San Luis Obispo, CA
Sears, Christopher S. .... Indianapolis, IN
Sears, Clifford R. .... Ephrata, WA
Sears, Craig F. .... Los Angeles, CA
Sears, Curtis R. .... Greeley, CO
Sears, Daniel J. .... Denver, CO
Sears, Daniel J., P.C. .... Denver, CO
Sears, David .... Manchester, NH
Sears, David A. .... Pleasant Valley, NY
Sears, Dennis S. .... Provo, UT
Sears, Don W. .... Boulder, CO
Sears, Donald J. .... North Brunswick, NJ
Sears, Donald R., Jr. .... Albuquerque, NM
Sears, Douglas A. .... Sacramento, CA
Sears, Douglas W. .... Tewksbury, MA
Sears, Edward B. .... Washington, DC
Sears, Edward L. .... Portland, OR
Sears, Elizabeth (Sally) .... Tucson, AZ
Sears, Eric M. .... New York, NY
Sears, Franklin R. .... Fort Worth, TX
Sears, George A. .... San Francisco, CA
Sears, George W., Jr. .... Moultrie, GA
Sears, H. Beth .... Ravenswood, WV
Sears, H. Christopher .... Greensboro, NC
Sears, Harry L. .... Denville, NJ
Sears, Hubert I., Jr. .... Winter Park, FL
Sears, James D. .... Mobile, AL
Sears, James L. .... Alexandria, VA
Sears, James M. .... Danvers, MA
Sears, James W. .... Orlando, FL
Sears, Jeannie G. .... Los Angeles, CA
Sears, Jesse W. .... Phoenix, AZ
Sears, John D., Jr. .... Bucyrus, OH
Sears, John E. .... Sunnyvale, CA
Sears, John H. .... San Francisco, CA
Sears, John J. .... Cape Elizabeth, ME
Sears, John M. .... Prescott, AZ
Sears, John M., P.C. .... Prescott, AZ
Sears, John P. .... Washington, DC
Sears, John P., Law Firm of Washington, DC
Sears, John Robert .... Jefferson City, MO
Sears, John T. .... Amarillo, TX
Sears, John W. .... Boston, MA
Sears, Jonathan .... Los Angeles, CA
Sears, Julia A. .... Cincinnati, OH
Sears, Kathrin E. .... Palo Alto, CA
Sears, Kelley D. .... Kansas City, MO
Sears, Kyle R. .... Houston, TX
Sears, Kyle R., P.C .... Houston, TX
Sears, Lance M. .... Colorado Springs, CO
Denver, CO
Sears, Laurie Page .... Treasury Department, Office of the Comptroller of the Currency, GV
Sears Law Offices, P.C. .... Lander, WY
Sears, Linda L. .... Augusta, ME
Sears, Lois A. .... St. Petersburg, FL
Sears & Manuel, P.A. .... Orlando, FL
Sears, Margie Ann .... Pensacola, FL
Sears, Mariann .... Houston, TX
Sears, Mark W. .... Greenwood, IN
Sears, Marvin .... Los Angeles, CA
Sears, Mary A. .... St. Louis, MO
Sears, Mary Ann .... Atlanta, GA
Sears, Mary Helen .... Washington, DC
Sears, M.H., The, Law Firm Washington, DC
Sears, Michael D. .... Munster, IN
Sears, Michael E. .... Palo Alto, CA
Sears, Michael J. .... San Francisco, CA
Sears, Michael K. .... Olathe, KS
Sears, Mitzi L. .... Opelika, AL
Sears, Nicholas N. .... Atlanta, GA
Sears, Pamela M. .... San Diego, CA
Sears & Parker .... Fort Worth, TX
Sears, Peter A. .... Wayne, PA
Sears, Philip B. .... Oklahoma City, OK
Sears, Richard Collier .... San Francisco, CA
Sears, Ross A. .... Missouri City, TX
Sears, Ross A., II .... Houston, TX
Sears, Roy W. .... Chicago, IL
Sears, Ruth A. .... St. Louis, MO
Dallas, TX
Sears, Samuel P., Jr. .... Boston, MA
Sears, Stephen H. .... Tampa, FL
Sears, Steven .... Tustin, CA
Sears, Steven R. .... Montevallo, AL
Sears, Susan C. .... Lexington, KY
Sears & Swanson, P.C. Colorado Springs, CO
Denver, CO
Sears, Sweeney & Marcickiewicz Denville, NJ
Sears, Terry H. .... Houston, TX
Sears, Thomas M., Jr. .... Greenville, SC
Sears, Todd Christopher .... Fort Smith, AR
Sears, Van Dyke & Associates, L.L.P. Auburn, AL
Opelika, AL
Phenix City, AL
Sears, Walt, Jr. .... Mount Vernon, TX
Sears, Walter J., III .... Birmingham, AL
Sears, William J. .... Tulsa, OK
Sears, William T. .... Los Angeles, CA
Sears-Collins, Leah Jeanette .... Atlanta, GA
Sears-Ewald, Dolores .... Troy, MI
Searson, Gregory W. .... Omaha, NE
Searson, W. Bradford .... Asheville, NC
Seas, Robert J., Jr. (P.C.) Washington, DC
Sease, Edmund J. .... Des Moines, IA
Omaha, NE
Sease, John M. .... Candler, NC
Sease, Randall G. .... Hartley, IA
Seasly, Steven E. .... Cleveland, OH
Season, James H. .... New York, NY
Seasonwein, Milton B. .... Scarsdale, NY

Sedwick, Edwin S., Law Office of Jeffersonville, IN
Sedwick, Edwin S., Law Office of New Albany, IN
Sedwick, Helen M. .... San Francisco, CA
Sedwick, John W. .... Anchorage, AK
Sedwick, Thomas S. .... Carlisle, PA
See, Andrew .... Kansas City, MO
See, C. F., III .... Louisa, KY
See, Clyde M., Jr. .... Moorefield, WV
See, Daniel .... Sandusky, OH
See, Diane Elizabeth .... Gainesville, FL
See, Edgar T. .... Westport, CT
See, Edmund M. .... Hartford, CT
See, Harold F., Jr. .... Tuscaloosa, AL
See, J. Fletcher, III .... Little Rock, AR
See, Karen M. .... Kansas City, MO
See, Milo J., Jr. .... Decatur, IL
See, Robert F., Jr. .... Dallas, TX
See & See .... Louisa, KY
Seebach, Alice A. .... Los Angeles, CA
Seebach, Barton L. .... Los Angeles, CA
Seebach, Daisy F. ...... Whitehouse Station, NJ
Seebach, Mary Jane M. .... Calabasas, CA
Seebach & Seebach .... Los Angeles, CA
Seebald, Carla McKitten .... Fairfax, VA
Seebald, Craig P. .... Washington, DC
Seeber, Bowkley & Zelante Morristown, NJ
Dover, NJ
Seeber, Brian R. .... Washington, DC
Seeber, Edward P. .... Harrisburg, PA
Seeber, Joe .... Honolulu, HI
Seeber, John S. .... Wichita, KS
Seeber, Joseph G. .... Washington, DC
Seeber, Kurt A. .... Greensboro, NC
Seeber, Philip J. .... New Orleans, LA
Seeber, Robt. A. .... Olympia, WA
Seeber, Ronald G. .... Winston-Salem, NC
Seeber, Roxanne C. .... Kalamazoo, MI
Seeber, William V., III .... Chauvin, LA
Seeberger, Charles W., Jr. .... Bensalem, PA
Seeberger, David M. .... Dallas, TX
Seeberger, Kathryn A. .... Wamego, KS
Seeberger, Matthew P. .... Los Angeles, CA
Seeberger & Siegel, L.L.P. .... Dallas, TX
Seeberger, Sue S. .... Dayton, OH
Seeberger, Terrence L. .... Canton, OH
Seeberger, Theresa J. .... Cedar Rapids, IA
Seebode, Julia E. .... Van Nuys, CA
Seebohm, John M. .... Denver, CO
Seeborg, Richard G. .... Palo Alto, CA
Seeburg, Noel M., Jr. .... Beaufort, SC
Seeburger, Jeffrey S. .... Dallas, TX
Seeburger, Stefanie Bauer .... Dallas, TX
Seeck, Vicki L. .... Davenport, IA
Seecof, Benjamin R. .... San Diego, CA
Seed and Berry LLP .... Seattle, WA
Seed, David H. .... Cleveland, OH
Columbus, OH
Seed, Harris W. .... Santa Barbara, CA
Seed, Mackall & Cole LLP Santa Barbara, CA
Seed, Peter H. .... St. Paul, MN
Seed, Richard W. .... Seattle, WA
Seed, William H. .... Gilford, NH
Seedall, Scott R. .... Idaho Falls, ID
Seedall, Sharon Stidley .... Gilbert, AZ
Seeder, Marshall .... Chicago, IL
Seeder, Robert D. .... Springfield, IL
Seedner, Maria J. .... San Diego, CA
Seedorf, James M. .... Anchorage, AK
Seedorf, Marc .... Bronx, NY
Seedorf, Roger L. .... Yuma, CO
Seeds, Melinda Gayle .... Newark, OH
Seeds, Robert G., Jr. .... Lake Forest, IL
Seeds, Robert Glenn .... Walnut Creek, CA
Seefeld, Amy J. .... Philadelphia, PA
Seefeld, Kim A. .... Santa Barbara, CA
Seefeld, Rodney D. .... Baraboo, WI
Seefer, Christopher Paul San Francisco, CA
Seefried, Robert A. .... Boulder, CO
Seefried, Robert A., P.C. .... Boulder, CO
Seegal, John F. .... San Francisco, CA
Seegal, Norma Ann .... Miami, FL
Seegars, Gerald C. Department of Commerce, Patent and Trademark Office, GV
Seegel, Lipshutz & Wilchins, P.C. Boston, MA
Wellesley, MA
Seegel, Richard L. .... Wellesley, MA
Seeger, Carol .... Gillette, WY
Seeger, Charles M., III .... Washington, DC
Seeger, Christopher A. .... Westfield, NJ
New York, NY
Seeger, David J. .... Buffalo, NY
Seeger, Edwin H. .... Washington, DC
Seeger & Forbes .... Lafayette, IN
Seeger, Israel G. .... White Plains, NY
Seeger, Jay T. .... Lafayette, IN
Seeger, Kenneth M. .... Oakland, CA
Seeger, Laureen McGurk .... Atlanta, GA
Seeger, Mark L. .... St. Paul, MN
Seeger, Martin L., IV .... Santa Rosa, CA
Seeger, Nevin A. .... Denver, CO
Seeger, Peter Markus .... Pleasanton, CA
Seeger Potter Richardson Luxton & Brooks, L.L.P. .... Washington, DC
Seeger, Richard T. .... Fort Wayne, IN
Seeger, Ronald L. .... Rochester, MN
Seeger & Seeger .... White Plains, NY
Seeger, Stephen M. .... Washington, DC
Seeger, Steven C. .... Chicago, IL
Seeger Weiss LLP .... Westfield, NJ
New York, NY
Seeger, William E. .... White Plains, NY

Seegers, Carolyn B. .... Harvard, IL
Seegers, Harvey F. .... Boston, MA
Seegers, James D. .... Houston, TX
Seegers, James W. .... Miami, FL
Orlando, FL
Seegers, Joseph W. .... Boone, NC
Seegers, Joseph W. .... Newland, NC
Seegers, Lori C. .... New York, NY
Seegert, Neal .... Whitefish Bay, WI
Seegert, Walter P. .... Buffalo, NY
Seegmiller, Clark .... Las Vegas, NV
Seegmiller, Douglas, Law Offices Albuquerque, NM
Seegmiller, W. West .... Sacramento, CA
Seegull, Larry Robert .... Baltimore, MD
Seehafer, Erwin C. .... Augusta, WI
Seehafer, Michele D. .... Minneapolis, MN
Seehafer, William R. .... Minneapolis, MN
Seeherman, Ellen J. Department of Commerce, Patent and Trademark Office, GV
Seehorn, Charles H. .... Oak Ridge, TN
Seehousen, John J. .... Langhorne, PA
Seehusen, Paul G. .... Culver City, CA
Seek, Robert J. .... Eldon, MO
Seeker, Thomas K. .... Akron, OH
Seekford, William E. .... Towson, MD
Seekings, Michael S. .... Charleston, SC
Seel, Betsy Anne .... Boston, MA
Seel, Donald H. .... Bloomington, MN
Seel, Gellert A., (P.C.) .... Detroit, MI
Seel, Karl P. .... Bozeman, MT
Seel, Magan C., FLLC .... Jackson, WY
Seel, Megan C. .... Jackson, WY
Seel, Rebecca Warren .... Augusta, ME
Seel, Steven H. .... Pittsburgh, PA
Seel, Theodore G. .... Victoria, TX
Seel, Thomas R. .... Covington, KY
Seelagy, Scott K. .... South Orange, NJ
Seelaus, Anne Kai .... Media, PA
Seele, Paul J. .... St. Louis, MO
Seele, Stephen E. .... St. Louis, MO
Seele, William H. .... Houston, TX
Seelen, Christopher M. .... Eau Claire, WI
Seelen, Joyce .... Denver, CO
Seelen, Joyce, & Associates .... Denver, CO
Seelen, Mary Jean M. .... New York, NY
Seelenfreund, Robert A. .... Elizabeth, NJ
Seeler, Evelyn H. .... New York, NY
Seeler, Marcia Drake .... Cambridge, MA
Seelert, John E. .... New Canaan, CT
Seeley & Berglass .... New Haven, CT
Southport, CT
Seeley, Bruce A. .... New Orleans, LA
Houston, TX
Seeley, Cindy L. .... San Jose, CA
Seeley, David J. .... Vancouver, WA
Seeley, David O. .... Salt Lake City, UT
Seeley, Donald W., Jr. .... Dallas, TX
Seeley, Dwight C. .... Louisville, CO
Seeley, Earlon L., Jr. .... North Adams, MA
Springfield, MA
Seeley, Elizabeth C. .... Westport, CT
New York, NY
Seeley, George W. .... Belmont, MA
Seeley, Glenn J. .... Cleveland, OH
Seeley, Gregory B. .... St. Petersburg, FL
Seeley, Gregory D. .... Cleveland, OH
Seeley, Hope C. .... Hartford, CT
Seeley, James F. .... Albany, NY
Seeley, James J. .... Bridgeton, NJ
Seeley, James N. .... Syracuse, NY
Seeley, James W. .... Spartanburg, SC
Seeley & Jones, P.A. .... Bridgeton, NJ
Seeley, Kathy C. .... Helena, MT
Seeley Legal Services, Inc. Minneapolis, MN
Seeley, Linda J. .... San Rafael, CA
Seeley, Mark Robert .... Dayton, OH
Seeley, Mark V. .... Santa Clara, CA
Seeley, Matthew K. .... Cleveland, OH
Seeley, Morgan B. .... Bainbridge Island, WA
Seeley, Paul B. .... Huntsville, AL
Seeley, Paul M. .... Skokie, IL
Seeley, Richard H. .... Sun City West, AZ
Seeley, Robert H. .... Lancaster, OH
Seeley, Robert L. .... Stuart, FL
Seeley, Robert L. .... Dayton, OH
Seeley, Robert L., & Associates .... Dayton, OH
Seeley, Robin J. .... San Francisco, CA
Seeley, Ronald J. .... Encino, CA
Seeley, Roxann D. .... Fairfax, VA
Seeley, Savidge and Ebert, A Legal Professional Association .... Cleveland, OH
Seeley, Sharon A. .... Department of Justice, Civil Rights Division, GV
Seeley, Terrence P. .... Goshen, NY
Seeley, Therese S. .... Wheaton, IL
Seeley, Thomas J., Jr. .... Erwin, TN
Seeley, W. Parker, Jr. .... Southport, CT
Seeley, William S. .... Minneapolis, MN
Seelhoff, Scott A. .... Beaufort, SC
Seelicke, Douglas H. .... San Diego, CA
Seelicke, William H. .... Lancaster, CA
Seelie & Doolittle .... Jacksonville, FL
Seelie, Jane T. .... Cleveland, OH
Seelie, John F. .... Cleveland, OH
Seelie, Michael E. .... Jacksonville, FL
Seelig, Carol A. .... New York, NY
Seelig, Cossé, Frischhertz & Poulliard New Orleans, LA
Seelig, David H. .... New Orleans, LA
Seelig, Elsa .... San Jose, CA
Seelig, George Gregory .... Morgantown, KY
Seelig, Jack L. .... Trenton, NJ
Seelig, Mark J. .... Los Angeles, CA
New York, NY
Seelig, Melanie J. .... Seattle, WA

Seelig, Robert L. .... Portland, OR
Seelig, Todd B. .... Philadelphia, PA
Seeliger, Jeannie .... Jersey City, NJ
Seeligson, Catherine .... San Francisco, CA
Seeligson, Henry .... Dallas, TX
Seeligson, Jordan, DeLoof & Hopper Ann Arbor, MI
Seeligson, Leslie R. .... Ann Arbor, MI
Seeling, Stephen S. .... Columbia, SC
Seelman, Frederick G., Jr. .... Bethesda, MD
Seelman, Richard L. .... New Orleans, LA
Seelman, Robert G. .... Milwaukee, WI
Seelman, Todd R. .... Denver, CO
Seely, Anne Wells .... New York, NY
Seely, Claxton B. .... San Antonio, TX
Seely, David G. .... Wichita, KS
Seely, Donald R. .... Youngstown, OH
Seely, Hall .... Newport Beach, CA
Seely, James G. .... San Francisco, CA
Seely, James T. .... Tacoma, WA
Seely, Jamey S. .... Houston, TX
Seely, John J. .... Chicago, IL
Seely, Kevin A. .... Hagåtña, GU
Seely, Kimberly A. .... Seattle, WA
Seely, Olin T. .... Alexandria, LA
Seely, Patrick L., Jr. .... Albany, NY
Seely, Philip E. .... Homewood, IL
Seely, Richard Dennis .... Irvine, CA
Seely, Robert F. .... Chicago, IL
Seely & Russell .... Newport Beach, CA
Seely, William R. .... St. Louis, MO
Seelye, Susan Heather .... Bremerton, WA
Tacoma, WA
Seeman, Fred L. .... New York, NY
Seeman, James W. .... Manchester, NH
Seeman, Jay W. .... New York, NY
Seeman, Leslie C. .... Dulles, VA
Seeman, Paul D. .... Berkeley, CA
Seeman, Stanley S. .... Los Angeles, CA
Seemann, Charles F., III New Orleans, LA
Seemann, Charles F., Jr., (P.L.C.) New Orleans, LA
Seemann, Ernest Albright Cape Coral, FL
Seemann, G. Frederick .... Lafayette, LA
Seemann, Jerry L. .... Huntsville, AL
Seemann & Schutt, P.A., Law Offices of Cape Coral, FL
Fort Myers, FL
Seemar, Frank A. .... Lancaster, PA
Seemar, Melinda F. .... Virginia Beach, VA
Seemiller, Susan M. .... Oxnard, CA
Seenath, Andrew A. .... Miami, FL
Seener, Michelle Silver .... New York, NY
Seener & Seener .... New York, NY
Seener, Steven .... New York, NY
Seep, Ralph V. .... House of Representatives, Office of Law Revision Counsel, GV
Seer, Ethan .... New York, NY
Seerden, Robert J. .... Corpus Christi, TX
Seerden, William F. .... Victoria, TX
Seering, James R. .... Reedsburg, WI
Seeronen, John R. .... Portland, OR
Seerveld, Christopher P. .... Denver, CO
Seery, Brian J. .... Los Angeles, CA
Seery, Catherine S. .... Washington, DC
Seery & Cox .... West Des Moines, IA
Seery, D. Scott .... Chesapeake, VA
Seery, James P., Jr. .... Garden City, NY
Seery, James T. .... New York, NY
Seery, Robert W. .... West Des Moines, IA
Seery, S. Andrews .... Thomasville, GA
Seery, Trudi A. .... New York, NY
Sees, John T. .... Huntington, IN
Seese, Harry P. .... Covina, CA
Seese, Michael D. .... Miami, FL
Seese, William D. .... Bluffton, IN
Ossian, IN
Seesel, Ellen .... St. Paul, MN
Seesel, Emily F. .... St. Paul, MN
Seesel, John H. .... Federal Trade Commission, Offices of Commissioners, GV
Seeser, Randall M. .... Alexandria, LA
Seeskin, Morris A. .... Oak Park, IL
Seethaler, Anthony A., Jr. .... Pittsburgh, PA
Seethoff, John A. .... Seattle, WA
Seevak, Sheldon .... New York, NY
Seevers, Gerald W. .... Williamsport, PA
Seevers, James S., Jr. .... Richmond, VA
Seevers, Tiffany L. .... Omaha, NE
Seewald, Alan .... Amherst, MA
Seewald, Amanda M. .... Cleveland, OH
Seewald, Collins & Jankowski, P.C. Amherst, MA
Seewald, J. Gary .... Cleveland, OH
Seewald, Jeffrey R. .... Charlotte, NC
Seewald, John R., Jr. .... Washington, DC
Seewald, Kathy M. .... Pittsburgh, PA
Seewald, Randal R. .... San Antonio, TX
Seewald, Robert A. .... Pittsburgh, PA
Seewald, Robert G. .... Bronx, NY
Seewald, Scott E. .... Washington, DC
Seewer, David W. .... Louisville, KY
Seezen, Michael James .... Columbia, SC
Sefcovic, Henry J. .... Bay City, MI
Sefcovic, Paul F. .... Columbus, OH
Seferi, Edmond .... New York, NY
Seferian, Anthony V. .... Los Angeles, CA
Seferian, Daniel B. .... Boston, MA
Seferian, Edw. G. .... Watertown, MA
Seferian, Robert R. .... Hilton Head Island, SC
Seferian, Suzanne C. .... Princeton, NJ
Seff, Daniel A. .... Burlington, VT
Seff, James M. .... San Francisco, CA
Seff, Mark A. .... Hollywood, FL
Seff, Richard M. .... Topanga, CA
Seff, Robert M. .... Sioux City, IA

Seffer, Shari .... Mountainside, NJ
Seffinger, Mark L. .... New York, NY
Sefkow, Gwen M. .... St. Cloud, MN
Sefkow, Robert J. .... Fergus Falls, MN
Seflin, Gary Stewart .... Media, PA
Sefret, Shawn J. .... Baltimore, MD
Sefrna, Ronald B. .... Tyler, TX
Seftel, Frank A. .... San Francisco, CA
Seftel, Suzanne .... Vienna, VA
Seftenberg, Stephen L. West Palm Beach, FL
Chicago, IL
Seftenberg, Stephen L., P.A. West Palm Beach, FL
Sefton, John T. .... Jacksonville, FL
Sefton, Keith Thomas Department of the Navy, Office of the Judge Advocate General, GV
Sefton, Kevin D. .... Sterling, IL
Sefton, Patrick Ladd Wheeler Montgomery, AL
Sefton, Scott M. .... Houston, TX
Sefton, Stephen B. .... Paso Robles, CA
Sega, A. Christopher .... Washington, DC
Segadelli, J. Drew .... Falmouth, MA
Segal, Adam P. .... Las Vegas, NV
Segal, Alan E. .... Minneapolis, MN
Segal, Alan F. .... Chicago, IL
Segal, Alan H. .... Braintree, MA
Segal, Alice .... Department of Justice, Executive Office for Immigration Review, GV
Segal, Allen J. .... Plainville, CT
Segal, Allen J. .... Bryan, TX
Segal, Allen J., P.C. .... Bryan, TX
Segal, Andrew J. .... Huntsville, AL
Segal, Anne L. .... New York, NY
Segal, Arlene .... Walnut Creek, CA
Segal, Barry A. .... Littleton, CO
Segal, Barry B. .... Patchogue, NY
Segal, Barry D. General Services Administration, Office of the General Counsel, GV
Segal, Benjamin H. .... New York, NY
Segal, Benjamin J. .... New York, NY
Segal, Bernard I. .... Los Angeles, CA
Segal, Bernard I., A Professional Corporation Los Angeles, CA
Segal, Bernard L. .... San Francisco, CA
Segal, Bernard, (P.C.) .... New Rochelle, NY
Segal, Betsy J. .... New York, NY
Segal, Bruce L. .... Bloomfield Hills, MI
Segal, Bryan .... Chicago, IL
Segal, Charles W. .... Garden City, NY
Segal, Cheryl L. .... Chicago, IL
Segal, Clement .... New York, NY
Segal, Cynthia E. Department of Defense, GV
Segal, Daniel .... Philadelphia, PA
Segal, Daniel N. .... Bethesda, MD
Segal, David A. .... Irvine, CA
Segal, David C. .... New York, NY
Segal, David F. .... New York, NY
Segal, David Lyle .... Philadelphia, PA
Segal, David M. .... Columbus, OH
Segal, David R. .... St. Louis, MO
Segal, Dawn A. .... Horsham, PA
Segal, Debbie L. .... Canton, MA
Segal, Deborah G. .... Washington, DC
Segal, Debra A. .... Atlanta, GA
Segal, Diana R. .... Chicago, IL
Segal, Donald .... Chicago, IL
Segal, Donald E. .... Washington, DC
Segal, Donald P. .... Albany, NY
Segal, Donald W. .... Chicago, IL
Segal, Donna .... New York, NY
Segal, Douglas S. .... Boston, MA
Segal, Dveera .... Chester, PA
Segal, Earl L. .... Washington, DC
Segal, Edan Dawn .... New York, NY
Segal, Edwin .... Marlton, NJ
Segal, Eleanor T. .... Philadelphia, PA
Segal, Eleanor T., & Associates Philadelphia, PA
Segal, Elizabeth Grant .... New York, NY
Segal, Ellen C. .... Potomac, MD
Segal, Elmer R. .... Chicago, IL
Segal, Eric .... Philadelphia, PA
Segal, Faith D. .... Newton, MA
Segal, Frederick L. .... Pittsburgh, PA
Segal, Gary L. .... Rockville, MD
Segal, Gary P. .... Chicago, IL
Segal, Gerald S. .... Philadelphia, PA
Segal, Glen R. .... Orange, CA
Segal, Gregory A. .... New York, NY
Segal, Harold .... Milwaukee, WI
Segal, Harry .... Philadelphia, PA
Segal, Herbert L. .... Indianapolis, IN
Louisville, KY
Segal, Howard B. .... Philadelphia, PA
Segal, Howard W. .... New York, NY
Segal, Hyman B. .... Newton, MA
Segal, Irving R. .... Philadelphia, PA
Segal, Isenberg, Sales, Stewart, Cutler & Tillman .... Louisville, KY
Segal, Jack .... New York, NY
Segal, Jack K. .... Flint, MI
Segal, Jacob S. .... Salem, MA
Segal, Jacqueline G. .... Norristown, PA
Segal, Jay .... Los Angeles, CA
Segal, Jay A. .... New York, NY
Segal, Jeffrey A. .... Parsippany, NJ
Segal, Jeffrey B. .... Louisville, KY
Segal, Jeffrey C. .... Los Angeles, CA
Segal, Jeffrey D. .... Los Angeles, CA
Segal, Jeffrey D. .... Atlanta, GA
Segal, Jeffrey D., A Professional Corporation Los Angeles, CA

Segal, Jeffrey H. .... Tiburon, CA
Segal, Jeffrey P. .... Garden City, NY
Segal, Jennifer Mann .... Treasury Department, Bureau of Alcohol, Tobacco and Firearms, GV
Segal, Jerald .... Brooklyn, NY
Segal, Jerome A. .... Beverly, MA
Segal, Jerome J. .... St. Paul, MN
Segal, John L., (A Professional Corporation) Los Angeles, CA
Segal, Jonathan A. .... Philadelphia, PA
Segal, Jonathan W. .... Miami, FL
Segal, Joseph F. .... New London, CT
Segal, Joseph T. .... Richmond, VA
Segal, Julie Ann .... Washington, DC
Segal, Kenneth C. .... Cincinnati, OH
Segal, Kenneth R. .... Boca Raton, FL
Segal & Kirby .... Sacramento, CA
Segal & Laska, LLC .... Plainville, CT
Segal, Laura L. .... New York, NY
Segal, Lauren Gage .... Redwood City, CA
Segal, Lawrence .... Beverly Hills, CA
Segal, Lawrence .... Los Angeles, CA
Segal, Leonard A. .... Jericho, NY
Segal, Leonard B. .... Minneapolis, MN
Segal, Lester E. .... Tampa, FL
Segal, Lewis .... Hartford, CT
Segal, Lisa P. .... New York, NY
Segal, Lloyd M. .... Los Angeles, CA
Segal, Malcolm S. .... Sacramento, CA
Segal, Marilyn K. .... Petaluma, CA
Segal, Mark .... Las Vegas, NV
Segal, Mark A. .... Decatur, GA
Segal, Mark A. .... Chicago, IL
Segal, Mark B. .... West Chester, PA
Segal, Mark Evan .... Merion, PA
Segal, Mark S. .... New York, NY
Segal, Mark Z. .... Trenton, NJ
Segal, Marshall B. .... Chicago, IL
Segal, Marshall D. .... Chicago, IL
Segal, Martin E., (P.A.) .... Coral Gables, FL
Segal, Martin N. .... Los Angeles, CA
Segal, Marvin B. .... New York, NY
Segal, Marvin E. .... Mineola, NY
Segal, Matthew D. .... Department of Justice, Antitrust Division, GV
Segal, Max M. .... South Orange, NJ
Segal McCambridge Singer & Mahoney, Ltd. Chicago, IL
Ann Arbor, MI
Segal & McMahan, Chartered, A Prof. Corp. Las Vegas, NV
Segal, Melvyn L. .... San Jose, CA
Segal, Michael J. .... New York, NY
Segal, Michelle C. .... Fort Collins, CO
Segal, Mike, (P.A.) .... Miami, FL
Segal, Milton .... Los Angeles, CA
Segal, Mitchell S., Law Offices of Great Neck, NY
Segal, Norman I. .... Miami, FL
Segal, Norman R. .... Philadelphia, PA
Segal, Paulette .... New York, NY
Segal, Peter J. .... Chicago, IL
Segal, Peter W. .... Washington, DC
Segal, Philip A. .... San Francisco, CA
Segal, Phyllis N. Federal Labor Relations Authority, Office of the Chair, GV
Segal, Randy S. .... Reston, VA
Segal, Richard .... Las Vegas, NV
Segal, Richard A. .... Phoenix, AZ
Segal, Richard E., & Associates Detroit, MI
Segal, Richard E., & Associates West Bloomfield, MI
Segal, Richard G. .... Jeffersonville, IN
Louisville, KY
Segal, Richard M. .... San Diego, CA
Segal, Richard M. .... Philadelphia, PA
Segal, Robert D. .... Chicago, IL
Segal, Robert Edward .... New York, NY
Segal, Robert I. .... Medford, NJ
Segal, Robert M. .... Philadelphia, PA
Segal, Robt. M. .... Boston, MA
Segal, Roger G. .... Salt Lake City, UT
Segal, Roitman & Coleman .... Boston, MA
Segal, Ronald .... Norristown, PA
Segal, Ronald D. .... Boston, MA
Segal, Ronald Ian .... Lynn, MA
Segal, Rory .... Aurora, CO
Segal & Roston .... Minneapolis, MN
Segal, Ruth .... Los Angeles, CA
Segal, Scott D. .... New York, NY
Segal, Scott H. .... Washington, DC
Segal, Scott S. .... Charleston, WV
Segal & Segal .... Chicago, IL
Segal and Shanks .... Jeffersonville, IN
Louisville, KY
Segal & Soifer, LLP .... Albuquerque, NM
Segal, Stanford A. .... Pittsburgh, PA
Segal, Stanley B. .... Albany, NY
Segal, Steven A. .... New York, NY
Segal, Steven A. .... Philadelphia, PA
Segal, Steven E. .... Denver, CO
Segal, Steven E. .... Houston, TX
Segal, Susan L. .... Minneapolis, MN
Segal, Susan Plimpton .... Phoenix, AZ
Segal, Sylvain .... Albuquerque, NM
Segal, Tamara Brock .... Dallas, TX
Segal, Terry Philip .... Boston, MA
Segal & Tesser, LLP .... New York, NY
Segal, Theodore D. .... Washington, DC
Baltimore, MD
Segal, Thomas J. .... Treasury Department, Office of Thrift Supervision, GV
Segal, Tracy Tatnall .... Chicago, IL
Segal, Vincent D. .... Atlantic City, NJ
Segal, Wayne S. .... Bloomfield Hills, MI
Segal, William .... Frederick, MD
Segal, William J. .... Aventura, FL
Segal, William J., P.A. .... Aventura, FL
Segal, Wolf, Berk, Gaines & Liss Philadelphia, PA
Segalas, Steven M. .... Paramus, NJ
New York, NY
Segale, Victor J. .... Rutland, VT
Segalini, Mark R. .... Boston, MA
Segalini & Neville .... Waltham, MA
Segalini, Roland, Jr. .... Waltham, MA
Segalini, Stephanie A. .... Orlando, FL
Segall, Andrew G. .... Baltimore, MD
Segall, Anthony R. .... Pasadena, CA
Segall, Arthur A. .... New York, NY
Segall, Avram B. .... Clifton, NJ
Segall, Barry S. .... Morganville, NJ
Segall, Brian F. .... Laguna Beach, CA
Segall, David M. .... St. Louis, MO
Segall, Eric J. .... Department of Justice, GV
Segall, Eric Stuart .... Los Angeles, CA
Segall, Frank A. .... Boston, MA
Segall, Harold A. .... New York, NY
Segall, Harold L. .... Washington, DC
Segall, Jeffrey B. .... Chicago, IL
Segall, Joel Edward .... Baltimore, MD
Segall, John B. .... San Mateo, CA
Segall, Karin .... New York, NY
Segall, Larry M. .... Tampa, FL
Segall, Leo .... Evanston, IL
Segall, Lewis Nathan .... Boston, MA
Segall, Mamie S. .... Minneapolis, MN
Segall, Mark B. .... New York, NY
Segall, Mark E. .... New York, NY
Segall, Matthew J. .... Palm Desert, CA
Segall, Maurice K. .... Stamford, CT
Segall, Norman S. .... Miami, FL
Segall, Robert D. .... Montgomery, AL
Segall, Scott E. .... El Paso, TX
Segall, Stephen L. .... Tampa, FL
Segall, Stephen L. .... New York, NY
Segall, Steven A. .... Brooklyn, NY
Segall, Steven L. .... White Plains, NY
Segall, Steven M. .... Lakewood, CO
Segall, Wendy E. .... Los Angeles, CA
Segall & Wieder .... Palm Desert, CA
Segall, Wynn H. .... Washington, DC
Segalla, Jody Mackenzie Arlington Heights, IL
Segalla, Thomas F. .... Buffalo, NY
Segalman, Marc J. .... New York, NY
Segalman, Teresa L. .... New York, NY
Segaloff, James H. .... New Haven, CT
Segan, Lawrence M. .... New York, NY
Segan, Leon .... New York, NY
Segan, Nemerov & Singer, P.C. New York, NY
Segan, Robert J. .... Annandale, VA
Segan, Saul H. .... Merchantville, NJ
Philadelphia, PA
Seganish, W. Michael .... Towson, MD
Segar, Geoffrey .... Indianapolis, IN
Segar, Robert L. .... Flint, MI
Segar & Sciortino .... Rochester, NY
Segar, Stephen A. .... Rochester, NY
Segar, Susan Pecoraro .... Washington, DC
Segarnick, Kenneth C. .... Philadelphia, PA
Segarra, Miguel A. .... Willimantic, CT
Segarra, Ninfa .... Brooklyn, NY
Segarra Vázquez, Manuel A. San Juan, PR
Segars, Ann M. .... Department of Justice, United States Marshals Service, GV
Segars, Darryl Keenan .... Troy, MI
Segars, Elizabeth Brown .... Booneville, MS
Segars, James R., Jr. .... Bishopville, SC
Segars, James W. .... Annandale, VA
Segars, Joyce A .... Austin, TX
Segars, Mark T. .... Iuka, MS
Segatto, Bernard G., III .... Springfield, IL
Segatto, Randall W. .... Springfield, IL
Segaul, John D. .... Sunrise, FL
Segebarth, Kim T. .... Cleveland Heights, OH
Segebarth, Stephen A. .... Muncie, IN
Segedy, Alan G. .... Akron, OH
Segedy, Ronald J. .... Brooklyn, NY
Segel, Alvin G. .... Los Angeles, CA
Segel, Amy .... Portland, OR
Segel, Benjamin B. .... Columbus, OH
Segel, Eric W. .... Washington, DC
Rockville, MD
Segel, Goldman & Mazzotta, P.C. Albany, NY
Segel, Jackie L. .... Boston, MA
Segel, James .... Boston, MA
Segel, Karen J. .... Beverly Hills, CA
Segel, Kenneth B. .... Albany, NY
Segel, Lisa S. .... Silver Spring, MD
Segel, Lisa Stearman, P.C. Silver Spring, MD
Segel, M Nelson .... Las Vegas, NV
Segel, M Nelson, Chartered, A Prof. Corp. Las Vegas, NV
Segel, Ronald .... Albuquerque, NM
Segel, Scott J. .... New York, NY
Segel, Sheldon .... Miami, FL
Segelbaum, Charles D. .... Minneapolis, MN
Segelbaum, Robert S. .... Phoenix, AZ
Segelberg, Janelle E. .... Denver, CO
Segelin, Bernard .... Los Angeles, CA
Segelken, Edward M. .... Columbus, OH
Segell, Hyam .... Santa Fe, NM
Segell, Jeffry A. .... Oklahoma City, OK
Segelman, Mark D. .... San Francisco, CA
Segen, Leon S. .... New York, NY
Segen, Leon S., P.C., Law Offices of New York, NY
Segenreich, George R., (Ltd.) Highland Park, IL
Seger, Kimberley Hall Corpus Christi, TX
Seger, Randolph L. .... Indianapolis, IN
Seger, Rick .... Cedar Rapids, IA
Seger, Thomas M. .... Cleveland, OH
Segerblom, Richard S. .... Las Vegas, NV
Segerdahl, James R. .... Pittsburgh, PA
Segerman, Charles Alan Upper Marlboro, MD
Segers, Jennifer Devereaux Birmingham, AL
Segers, Joseph William, III .... Dallas, TX
Segers, Timothy John .... Birmingham, AL
Segerson, Thomas P. .... New London, NH
Segerstrom, Kate Powell .... Sonora, CA
Segesta, Benedict .... Eastpointe, MI
Seget, Alan D. .... New York, NY
Seggebruch, Eric .... New York, NY
Seggerman, Anne B. .... Boston, MA
Seggio-Ball, Josephine .... Buffalo, NY
Seghers, Edward C., Jr. .... Baton Rouge, LA
Seghetti, David M. .... Chicago, IL
Seghetti, Michael R. .... Peoria, IL
Seghezzi, Alan R. .... Boston, MA
Segina, Zoran J. .... Los Angeles, CA
Segler, Judith M. .... Chicago, IL
Segler, Kathy Elaine .... Dadeville, AL
Segler, Michael D. .... Yukon, OK
Seglias, Edward .... Philadelphia, PA
Seglin, Steven G. .... Lincoln, NE
Seglund, Bruce R. .... Walled Lake, MI
Segmiller, Kathleen A. .... Pittsburgh, PA
Sego, Randy L. .... Denver, CO
Segor, Joseph C. .... Miami, FL
Segore-Freshman, Nancy .... Westport, CT
Segota, Denis .... Princeton, NJ
Segota, Jami .... Princeton, NJ
Segovia, Andrew .... Detroit, MI
Segovia, Herman H. .... San Antonio, TX
Segovia, Victor A. .... San Francisco, CA
Segovis, Elizabeth Wilson .... McKinney, TX
Segrato, Glen D. .... Austin, TX
Segrato, Joseph L. .... McAllen, TX
Segraves, Darryl B. .... Atlanta, GA
Segraves, J. Ed .... Decatur, GA
Segre, David J. .... Palo Alto, CA
Segré, Nina .... Philadelphia, PA
Segrest, Christopher M. College Station, TX
Segrest, D. Broward .... Montgomery, AL
Segrest, David H. .... Dallas, TX
Segrest, Eugene F. .... Dallas, TX
Segrest, Jere C. .... Dothan, AL
Segrest, John W. .... Waco, TX
Segrest, Noreen .... Tampa, FL
Segrest, Philip D., Jr. .... Chicago, IL
Segrest, Philip R. .... McGregor, TX
Segrest, Thomas L. .... Columbus, MS
Segreti, A. Mark, Jr. .... Dayton, OH
Segreti, Judith Dillon .... New York, NY
Segreti, Leonard (Len) .... Englewood, CO
Segreto, Antoinette Francesca New York, NY
Segreto, James V. .... Haledon, NJ
Segreto, John F. .... Haledon, NJ
Segreto & Segreto .... Haledon, NJ
Segretti, Donald .... Costa Mesa, CA
Segretti, Pitman & Erdbacher .... Salinas, CA
Segrist, Samuel W. .... Scottsbluff, NE
Segue, Taylor C., III .... Detroit, MI
Segui, Phillip W., Jr. .... Charleston, SC
Seguin, D. Peter .... Hudson, WI
Seguin, Gregory N. .... Irvine, CA
Seguin, James P. .... Groveport, OH
Seguin, Robert S. .... Milltown, NJ
Seguin, Robert S., P.C. .... Milltown, NJ
Seguin, Suzanne J. .... New Bedford, MA
Seguine, Thomas Edward .... Olympia, WA
Seguljic, Richard M. .... Plainville, CT
Segur, Robert W. .... Punta Gorda, FL
Segura, Ana I. .... Miami, FL
Segura, Hector H., Jr. .... Houston, TX
Segura, Jacob N. .... Beverly Hills, CA
Segura, James W. .... Greenville, SC
Segura, Patricia .... Houston, TX
Segura, Robert L. .... New Iberia, LA
Segura, Steve R. .... Los Angeles, CA
Segura, Susan C. .... Alexandria, LA
Segura, Victor H. .... Houston, TX
Segure, Celeste Thomas .... Brooklyn, NY
Seguritan, Reuben S. .... New York, NY
Segurola, Jorge (IBA) .... **San Juan, PR**
Segurola & Montalvo .... San Juan, PR
Segurola de Diego, Aldo .... San Juan, PR
Seha, Ann M. .... St. Paul, MN
Seham, Lee .... New York, NY
Seham, Martin C. .... New York, NY
Seham Seham Meltz & Petersen, LLP New York, NY
Seher, Alan R. .... San Francisco, CA
Seher, Ralph A. .... Milwaukee, WI
Seher & Seher .... Milwaukee, WI
Sehestedt, Michael W. .... Missoula, MT
Seheult, Malcolm .... Loma Linda, CA
Sehgal, Mona .... New York, NY
Sehgal, Zarrar .... New York, NY
Sehl, Barbara Anne .... Rochester, MN
Sehl, Jean K. .... Syracuse, NY
Sehlin, Jennifer C. .... Oak Harbor, WA
Sehlinger, Adolph J., III .... Louisville, KY
Sehr, Michael J. .... Chicago, IL
Sehr, Robert J. .... Walnut Creek, CA
Sehr, Robert J., A Professional Corporation Walnut Creek, CA
Sehrt-Green, Elaine A. .... Potomac, MD
Seib, John A., Jr. (P.C.) .... Dallas, TX
Seib, Jonathan E. .... Olympia, WA
Seib, Karl E., Jr. .... New York, NY
Seib, Kimberly M. .... New York, NY
Seib Law Firm, The, A Professional Corporation .... Dallas, TX
Seib, Michael J. .... Lewiston, ID
Seib, Philip M. .... Dallas, TX
Seibel, Amy R. .... Milwaukee, WI
Seibel, Anne Marie .... Birmingham, AL
Seibel, Brian D. .... Walnut Creek, CA
Seibel, Cathy .... New York, NY
Seibel, Daniel D. .... Milwaukee, WI
Seibel, David G. .... Boston, MA
Seibel & Eckenrode, P.C. .... St. Louis, MO
Seibel, Gerald J. .... Morris, MN
Seibel, John L. .... Bethesda, MD
Arlington, VA
Seibel, John N. .... Chicago, IL
Seibel, Kathleen M. .... Ithaca, NY
Seibel, Kenneth F. .... Cincinnati, OH
Seibel, Michael H. .... Austin, MN
Seibel, Michael J. .... Albuquerque, NM
Seibel, Peter R. .... Defiance, OH
Seibel, Richard D. .... Pasadena, CA
Seibel, Robert A. .... New York, NY
Seibel, Robert C. .... St. Louis, MO
Seibel, Robert F. .... Ithaca, NY
Seibel, Scott K. .... Cincinnati, OH
Seibel, Stacey L. .... Hays, KS
Seibel, Susan J. .... New York, NY
Seibel, Ted D. .... Harvey, ND
Seibel, William N., Jr. .... St. Charles, MO
Seibels, John P., Jr. .... Charleston, SC
Seiber, Christopher J. .... Irvine, CA
Seiber, Neta Frazier .... Opp, AL
Seiberling, John F. .... Akron, OH
Seibert, Arthur .... Lake Worth, FL
Seibert, Charles A., III .... Albuquerque, NM
Seibert, Dawn M. .... Plymouth, VT
Seibert, Edward F. .... Towson, MD
Seibert, Gregory L. .... Raleigh, NC
Seibert, Hal F. .... Concord, CA
Seibert, Harry W., Jr. .... Ballston Spa, NY
Seibert, Henry E., IV .... Cleveland, OH
Seibert, J. Oakley .... Martinsburg, WV
Seibert, J. Rix .... Akron, OH
Seibert, James E. .... Wheeling, WV
Seibert, Janice B. .... Wheeling, WV
Seibert, Jay L. .... Lowell, MA
Seibert, Jeffrey H. .... Baltimore, MD
Seibert, John C. .... Durango, CO
Seibert, John E. .... Saratoga, CA
Seibert, J. W., III .... Vidalia, LA
Seibert & Kasserman, L.C. Wheeling, WV
Seibert, Kevin M. .... Stockton, CA
Seibert, Kurt J. .... San Jose, CA
Seibert, Maribeth Wilt .... Harrisburg, PA
Seibert, Mark E. .... Cleveland, OH
Seibert, R. John .... Honolulu, HI
Seibert, Richard F. .... Dallas, TX
Seibert, Robert J. .... Mount Clemens, MI
Seibert, Robert L. .... Austin, TX
Seibert, Robert M. .... Lansdowne, PA
Seibert, Roger H. .... Pinckneyville, IL
Seibert, Sara A. .... Boulder, CO
Seibert, Steven D. .... Tulsa, OK
Seibert, Steven M. .... Tallahassee, FL
Seibert, Troy J. .... Minneapolis, MN
Seibert, William C. .... St. Louis, MO
Seiberth, Alexander M. .... Woodland, CA
Seibly, J. Thomas .... Lodi, CA
Seibly, Jennifer Sarah .... Palo Alto, CA
Seibly, W. Timothy .... Clarkston, WA
Seibold, Charles P. .... Madison, WI
Seibold, Gregory P. .... Madison, WI
Seibold, JoAnne Eichelberger Jacksonville, FL
Seich, John S. .... Cleveland, OH
Seichter, John J. .... Chantilly, VA
Seick, Steven A. .... San Diego, CA
Seid, David A. National Labor Relations Board, Office of the General Counsel, GV
Seid, David M. .... Ketchikan, AK
Seid, Elaine M. .... San Jose, CA
Seid, Gerald P. .... Princeton, NJ
Seid, Gerald P. .... Skillman, NJ
Seid, Leonora Cheryl .... New York, NY
Seid, Marcine Anne .... San Jose, CA
Seid, Richard A. .... Department of Labor, Office of the Solicitor, GV
Seid, Richard A. .... Detroit, MI
Seid, Scott A. .... Madison, WI
Seidberg, Daniel R. .... Syracuse, NY
Seidberg, Kenneth W. .... Phoenix, AZ
Seide, David Z. .... Los Angeles, CA
Seide, George N. .... Beverly Hills, CA
Seide, Harold .... Jersey City, NJ
Seide, Lonnie K. .... Orange, CA
Seide, Richard L. .... Newport Beach, CA
Seide, Robert G. .... Boston, MA
Seide, Rochelle K. .... New York, NY
Seidel, Adam L. .... Dallas, TX
Seidel, Allan D. .... Trenton, MO
Seidel, Amy C. .... Minneapolis, MN
Seidel, Anne I. .... Seattle, WA
Seidel, Arthur H. .... Philadelphia, PA
Seidel, Arthur W. .... New York, NY
Seidel, Baker & Tilghman, P.A. Salisbury, MD
Seidel, Barry G. .... Miami, FL
Seidel, Barry G., P.A. .... Miami, FL
Seidel, Barry N. .... New York, NY
Seidel, Barry S .... Forest Hills, NY
Seidel, Brad E. .... Dallas, TX

Seidel, Catherine W.
Federal Communications Commission, Wireless Telecommunications Bureau, GV
Seidel, Donna L. ....Pittsburgh, PA
Seidel, Esther J. ....New Braunfels, TX
Seidel, Eugene A. ....Mobile, AL
Seidel, Eugene A. ....Baltimore, MD
Seidel, Eugene A., P.A. ....Baltimore, MD
Seidel, Fanned, Jr. ....Lafayette, LA
Seidel, Frank J. ....San Francisco, CA
Seidel, George H., Jr. ....Glendale, CA
Seidel, Gerhard E. ....Lake Forest, IL
Seidel, Gonda, Lavorgna & Monaco, P.C.
Philadelphia, PA
Seidel, Harold M. ....Morristown, NJ
Seidel, Holly ....Cleveland, OH
Seidel, John D. ....Wheat Ridge, CO
Seidel, John E. ....Pacific Grove, CA
Seidel, John H. ....Phoenix, AZ
Seidel, Joseph L. ....Washington, DC
Seidel, Joseph L. ....Silver Spring, MD
Seidel, Joseph S. ....Roseland, NJ
Seidel, Joseph S., A Professional Corporation
Roseland, NJ
Seidel, Kathy L. ....Denver, CO
Seidel, Laura L. ....Atlanta, GA
Seidel, Lester B. ....Bethesda, MD
Seidel, Mark E. ....Roseland, NJ
Seidel, Martin L. ....New York, NY
Seidel, Maureen ....Albany, NY
Seidel, Michael G. ....Harker Heights, TX
Seidel, Norman ....Easton, PA
Seidel, Paul J. ....San Jose, CA
Seidel, Raymond M. ....Norristown, PA
Seidel, Rebecca S. ....Boston, MA
Seidel, Richard B. ....Strafford, PA
Seidel, Richard S. ....Philadelphia, PA
Seidel, Robert C. ....Seattle, WA
Seidel, Robert J., Jr. ....Norfolk, VA
Seidel, Robert Raymond ....Chapel Hill, NC
Seidel, Robert W., Jr. ....Columbia, MD
Seidel, Ronald J. ....Barnstable, MA
Seidel, Ronnie D. ....Philadelphia, PA
Seidel, Samuel B. ....New York, NY
Seidel, Scott M. ....Dallas, TX
Seidel, Selvyn ....New York, NY
Seidel, Sheldon B. ....Salisbury, MD
Seidel, Stephen A. ....Philadelphia, PA
Seidel, Stephen D. ....San Antonio, TX
Seidel, Stephen M. ....Portland, OR
Seidel, Stuart P. ....Treasury Department, Office of Regulations and Rulings, GV
Seidel, Sylvia B. ....San Jose, CA
Seidel, W. Michael ....Chicago, IL
Seidel, Walter T. ....Roswell, GA
Seidel, Warren A. ....Department of Defense, Defense Commissary Agency, GV
Seidel, William J. ....Richmond, VA
Seidel, Yarvin & Mervis, LLC
Bethesda, MD
Seidell, Seth T. ....Southfield, MI
Seidelson, David E. ....Washington, DC
Seidelson, Mark D. ....Arlington, VA
Seideman, Evan S. ....Stamford, CT
Seideman, Peter ....Port Washington, NY
Seideman, Richard A. ....Salem, OR
Seideman, Stephen A. ....Los Angeles, CA
Seidemann, Joel J. ....New York, NY
Seidemann, Mark J. ....San Francisco, CA
Seiden, Adam ....Mount Vernon, NY
Seiden, Alder, Rothman, Petosa & Matthewman, P.A. ....Boca Raton, FL
Miami, FL
West Palm Beach, FL
Seiden, Andrew ....Boca Raton, FL
Seiden, Daniel L. ....Endicott, NY
Seiden, David T. ....New York, NY
Seiden, Elliott M. ....Washington, DC
Seiden, Francine ....Cedarhurst, NY
Seiden, Glenn ....Chicago, IL
Seiden, Harold ....Palm Beach, FL
Seiden, Henry A. ....West Palm Beach, FL
Seiden, Herbert R. ....Sherman Oaks, CA
Seiden, Jan K. ....Miami, FL
Seiden, Jay G. ....New York, NY
Seiden, Katherine H. ....Forest Hills, NY
Seiden, Mark ....Miami, FL
Seiden, Mark ....New York, NY
Seiden, Mark, P.A. ....Miami, FL
Seiden, Mark R. ....New York, NY
Seiden, Marla Aronson ....Fort Lauderdale, FL
Seiden, Matthew J. ....Washington, DC
Seiden & Merkle, A Law Corporation
Woodland Hills, CA
Seiden, Peter ....Garden City, NY
White Plains, NY
Seiden, Peter G. ....New York, NY
Seiden, Richard F. ....Los Angeles, CA
Seiden, Richard, P.A. ....Baltimore, MD
Seiden, Robert W. ....New York, NY
Seiden & Schein, P.C. ....New York, NY
Seiden, Scott J. ....Woodland Hills, CA
Seiden, Sheryl J. ....New York, NY
Seiden, Steven A. ....Bellflower, CA
Seiden, Steven Eric ....New York, NY
Seiden, Steven J. ....Carle Place, NY
Seiden, Todd Hudson ....Mount Clemens, MI
Seidenberg, Faith A. ....Syracuse, NY
Seidenberg, Frederick S. ....Hampton, NH
Seidenberg, Harold A. ....Nyack, NY
Seidenberg, Kenneth ....Dallas, TX
Seidenberg, Laurie B. ....Laramie, WY
Seidenberg, Peter A. ....Irvine, CA
Seidenberg, Robert A. ....New York, NY
Seidenberg, Robert A. ....Yonkers, NY
Seidenberg & Strunk ....Syracuse, NY
Seidenfaden, Jann ....Fort Thomas, KY
Seidenfeld, Glenn K. ....Chicago, IL
Seidenfeld, Marc ....San Francisco, CA
Seidenfeld, Mark B. ....Albany, NY
Seidenfeld, Mark, P.C. ....New York, NY
Seidenfeld, Mark S. ....New York, NY
Seidenfeld, Mark S. ....New York, NY
Seidenfeld, Norman ....New York, NY
Seidenman, David S. ....Baltimore, MD
Seidenman, Herbert ....Bethesda, MD
Seidenman, Jerome J. ....Baltimore, MD
Seidenman, Jerome J., P.A.
Baltimore, MD
Seidenstein, Chas. E. ....Larchmont, NY
Seidenstein, Roy
Environmental Protection Agency, Program Office Attorneys, GV
Seidensticker, Anna M. ....Columbus, OH
Seidensticker, James P., Jr.
Indianapolis, IN
Seidensticker, John W. ....Columbus, OH
Seidensticker, Keiter & Baughman, P.C.
York, PA
Seidensticker, Kirk W. ....Hermosa Beach, CA
Seidensticker & San Filippo ....Naples, FL
Seidensticker, Wayde P. ....York, PA
Seidensticker, Wayde P., Jr. ....Naples, FL
Seidenstock, Paul H. ....Brooklyn, NY
Seidenstricker, Paul W. ....Milwaukee, WI
Seidenwar, Michael F. ....New York, NY
Seidenwurm, Richard L., (P.C.)
San Diego, CA
Seidenwurm, Robert S. ....Portland, OR
Seider, Anne Gale ....Philadelphia, PA
Seider, Dennis J., Law Offices of
Los Angeles, CA
Seider, Harold ....Great Neck, NY
Seider, Mitchell A. ....Houston, TX
Seider, Rona ....Rockville Centre, NY
Seider, William M. ....Sarasota, FL
Seiderman, Carol Riordan ....Hollywood, FL
Seiders, Joseph R. ....Philadelphia, PA
Seidita, Lawrence J. ....Youngstown, OH
Seidl & Chicchelly ....Marion, IA
Seidl, David ....Baltimore, MD
Seidl, Gerald D. ....Cedar Rapids, IA
Seidl, Jane P. ....Berlin, CT
Seidl, M. Rebecca ....Omaha, NE
Seidl, Mark A., (S.C.) ....Wausau, WI
Seidl, Mark J. ....Marion, IA
Seidl, Mary K. ....Wausau, WI
Seidl, Michael R. ....Wilmington, DE
Seidl, Michael R. ....Portland, OR
Seidl, Phillip D. ....Marion, IA
Seidl & Rizzo ....Portland, OR
Seidl, Sarah Curtis ....Washington, DC
Seidleck, Michelle Lee ....Baltimore, MD
Seidlein, Geoffrey H. ....Lansing, MI
Seidler, Arthur R. ....Corona, CA
Seidler, Bernard ....Brooklyn, NY
Seidler, Bernard A. ....Nyack, NY
Seidler, Charles J., Jr. ....New York, NY
Seidler, David R. ....Fort Worth, TX
Seidler, Felix A. ....Alameda, CA
Seidler, Ira M. ....St. Petersburg, FL
Seidler, Irving J. ....Schaumburg, IL
Seidler, Jennifer Anne ....Chicago, IL
Seidler, Kurt A. ....Corona, CA
Seidler, Kurt A., Law Offices ....Corona, CA
Seidler, Marc P. ....Chicago, IL
Seidler, Martin W. ....San Antonio, TX
Seidler & McErlean ....Chicago, IL
Seidler, Nancy C. ....Irvine, CA
Seidler, Patrick M. ....Mill Valley, CA
Seidler & Seidler, P.C. ....Omaha, NE
Seidler, Sharon Y. ....Chicago, IL
Seidler, William E. ....Omaha, NE
Seidler, William E., Jr. ....Omaha, NE
Seidlin, Larry S. ....Fort Lauderdale, FL
Seidlits, Curtis L., Jr. ....Sherman, TX
Seidlitz, John E., Jr. ....Great Falls, MT
Seidman, A. Jeffrey ....Chicago, IL
Seidman, Amy ....New York, NY
Seidman, Andrew P. ....New York, NY
Seidman, Anna M. ....Vienna, VA
Seidman & Associates, P.C.
Washington, DC
Vienna, VA
Seidman, Bernard H. ....New York, NY
Seidman, Brian William ....New York, NY
Seidman, Bruce A. ....Rutherford, NJ
Seidman, Christopher ....Grand Junction, CO
Seidman, Danny B. ....Waldorf, MD
Seidman, David ....Department of Justice, Antitrust Division, GV
Seidman, David ....East St. Louis, IL
Seidman, David S. ....Rocky Hill, CT
Seidman, Debra E. ....New York, NY
Seidman, Dorine R. ....Gaithersburg, MD
Seidman, Douglass J. ....New York, NY
Seidman, Evelyn H. ....New York, NY
Seidman, Ilene B. ....Cambridge, MA
Seidman, Irving P. ....New York, NY
Seidman, Jessica M. ....Fairfield, NJ
Carle Place, NY
Seidman, Joseph M. ....East Hampton, NY
Seidman, L. William ....Washington, DC
Seidman, Lawrence R. ....Baltimore, MD
Seidman, Leon B. ....New York, NY
Seidman, Lisa Ness ....Morristown, NJ
Seidman, Lon J. ....New York, NY
Seidman, Lorne H. ....Las Vegas, NV
Seidman, Maiman, Morenstein & Kimler
New York, NY
Seidman, Marc B.
National Labor Relations Board, Office of Board Members, GV
Seidman, Marshall J. ....Fort Myers, FL
Seidman, Marvin B. ....Miami, FL
Seidman, Michael A. ....Margate City, NJ
Seidman, Michael L. ....Bakersfield, CA
Seidman, Mildred L. ....Department of Justice, Tax Division, GV
Seidman, Mitchell B. ....Roseland, NJ
Seidman, Paul J. ....Vienna, VA
Seidman, Paula-Jane ....New York, NY
Seidman, Peter E. ....New York, NY
Seidman, Phillip K. ....Memphis, TN
Seidman, Rachel E. ....Chicago, IL
Seidman, Richard H. ....West Hartford, CT
Seidman, Ricki L. ....Department of Justice, Office of the Associate Attorney General, GV
Seidman, Sara F. ....Washington, DC
Seidman, Scott G. ....Portland, OR
Seidman, Silverman & Seidman, P.C.
New York, NY
Seidman, Stephanie L. ....La Jolla, CA
Seidman, Steven A. ....New York, NY
Seidman, Steven J. ....Chicago, IL
Seidman, Susan E. ....Glenview, IL
Seidman, Thomas L. ....Santa Ana, CA
Seidman, Vanessa Rae ....New York, NY
Seidman-Brownlee, Mary A.
South Orange, NJ
Seidner, Arthur J. ....Bensalem, PA
Philadelphia, PA
Seidner, Arthur J., P.C. ....Bensalem, PA
Philadelphia, PA
Seidner, Leslie Kremer ....Newport Beach, CA
Seidner, Mordechai ....Los Angeles, CA
Seidner, Randi M. ....Jericho, NY
Seidner, Stephen ....Babylon, NY
Seidscher, Seymour ....San Francisco, CA
Seidt, Arthur M. ....Bronx, NY
Seidule, Gloria ....Stuart, FL
Seielstad, Andrea M. ....Crownpoint, NM
Seier, A. J. ....Cape Girardeau, MO
Seier, Claiborne P. ....Birmingham, AL
Seieroe, Warren C. ....Chicago, IL
Seif, Alan Barton ....North Miami Beach, FL
Seif, Allan M. ....New York, NY
Seif, David D. ....Waverly, OH
Seif, Evan D. ....Miami, FL
Seif, Karl J.
Federal Deposit Insurance Corporation, Compliance and Enforcement Section, GV
Seif, Margaret K. ....Bedford, MA
Seif, Mark A. ....Newport Beach, CA
Seif, Steven J. ....New York, NY
Seife, Alan ....New York, NY
White Plains, NY
Seife, Howard ....New York, NY
Seifel, Donald R., Jr. ....Hartford, CT
Seifen, Matthew R. ....Irvine, CA
Seifer, Amy D. ....Boston, MA
Seifer & Associates, Law Offices of
San Diego, CA
Temecula, CA
Seifer, Daniel J. ....Portland, OR
Seifer, David Marc ....Miami, FL
Seifer, Melissa ....San Diego, CA
Temecula, CA
Seifer, Monroe ....San Francisco, CA
Seifer, Murken, Despina & James, A Law Corporation ....San Francisco, CA
Seifer, Yeats & Mills, LLP ....Portland, OR
Seiferheld, Kevin H. ....Southfield, MI
Seifert, Alan L.
Commodity Futures Trading Commission, Division of Trading and Markets, GV
Seifert, Ann L. ....Seattle, WA
Seifert, Arthur G. ....Philadelphia, PA
Seifert, Arthur J. ....Corvallis, MT
Seifert, Brit K. ....Stamford, CT
Seifert, Charlene M. DeBolt ....Dallas, TX
Seifert, Charles J. ....Helena, MT
Seifert, Christie A. ....Indianapolis, IN
Seifert, Conrad Ost ....Old Lyme, CT
Seifert, Edward W. ....Pittsburgh, PA
Seifert, Francis T. ....Sterling, MA
Seifert, Frederick D. ....Morton Grove, IL
Seifert, Henry L. ....Salem, OR
Seifert, James J. ....Bloomington, MN
Seifert, John D. ....Wheaton, IL
Seifert, Karen L. ....Oshkosh, WI
Seifert, Linda J. ....Suisun, CA
Seifert, Lisa Ellen ....Olympia, WA
Seifert, Lisa Mans ....Tulsa, OK
Seifert, Luke M. ....St. Cloud, MN
Seifert, Luke M. ....St. Cloud, MN
Seifert, Luke M., Ltd. ....St. Cloud, MN
Seifert, Mark G.
Federal Communications Commission, Common Carrier Bureau, GV
Seifert, Martin E. ....Fort Wayne, IN
Seifert, Michael V. ....Rochester, MN
Seifert, Miller & Slusher, P.A.
Orlando, FL
Seifert, Norbert M. ....Los Angeles, CA
Seifert, Patricia Hummel ....Dallas, TX
Seifert, Patricia L. ....Cleveland, OH
Seifert, Paul R. ....Milwaukee, WI
Seifert, R. Scott ....Addison, TX
Seifert, Rachel A. ....Brentwood, TN
Seifert, Randolph J. ....Pound Ridge, NY
Seifert, Ronald H. ....Newport, OR
Seifert, Scott P. ....Orlando, FL
Seifert, Stephen A. ....Appleton, WI
Seifert, Thomas L. ....New York, NY
Seifert, Thomas L., P.C. ....New York, NY
Seifert, Thomas V. ....Minneapolis, MN
Seifert, Timothy D. ....St. Louis, MO
Seifert-Benyak, Janet ....Bethesda, MD
Seiferth, Robert A. ....Williamsport, PA
Seiff, David W. ....San Jose, CA
Seiff, Eric A. ....New York, NY
Seiff Kretz & Maffeo ....New York, NY
Seiffert, Alan F. ....Los Angeles, CA
Seiffert and Frisch ....North Brunswick, NJ
Seiffert, James C. ....Louisville, KY
Seiffert, Margaret Kramer ....Louisville, KY
Seiffert, Perry B. ....Bethesda, MD
Seiffert, Terry L. ....Billings, MT
Seiffert, William C. ....Citrus Heights, CA
Seifman, Barry A. ....Farmington Hills, MI
Seifman, Barry A., P.C.
Farmington Hills, MI
Seifman, Jeffrey ....Chicago, IL
Seifman, Michelle G. ....Chicago, IL
Seifman, Richard M. ....Washington, DC
Seifried, Kent W. ....Newport, KY
Seifter, Lowell A. ....Syracuse, NY
Seigel, Anita Rose ....Los Angeles, CA
Seigel, Benjamin S. ....Los Angeles, CA
Seigel, Brian Robert ....St. Louis, MO
Seigel, Charles A. ....St. Louis, MO
Seigel, Charles A., III ....St. Louis, MO
Seigel, Charles J. ....New York, NY
Seigel, Christopher D. ....Indianapolis, IN
Seigel, Daniel J. ....Phoenix, AZ
Seigel, Darren D. ....Tarzana, CA
Seigel, Evan M. ....Washington, DC
Seigel, Frank R. ....Atlanta, GA
Seigel, Gerri ....New York, NY
Seigel, I. Steven ....Baltimore, MD
Cumberland, MD
Towson, MD
Seigel, Jacqueline A. ....New Haven, CT
Seigel, Jan K. ....Ridgewood, NJ
Seigel, Jane Ann ....Indianapolis, IN
Seigel, Jeffrey A. ....Hempstead, NY
Seigel, Jessica A.
Federal Energy Regulatory Commission, Office of the General Counsel, GV
Seigel, Karen S. ....Los Angeles, CA
Seigel, Mark D. ....Los Angeles, CA
Seigel, Mark D. ....Clayton, MO
Seigel, Mark L. ....Atlanta, GA
Seigel, Martin H. ....Staten Island, NY
Seigel & Mongiardo, P.C. ....Ridgewood, NJ
Seigel, Robert Lewis ....New York, NY
Seigel, Robert S. ....St. Louis, MO
Seigel, Samuel E. ....New York, NY
Seigel, Stephen P., (P.C.) ....Springfield, MO
Seigel, Steven ....Hackensack, NJ
Seigel, Stuart E. ....New York, NY
Seigel, Tully & Furrer ....Baltimore, MD
Cumberland, MD
Towson, MD
Seigel & Wolff, P.C. ....St. Louis, MO
Seiger, Mark B. ....Hartford, CT
Seiger, Robert C., III ....Cherry Hill, NJ
Philadelphia, PA
Seiger, Robert C., Jr. ....Evesham, NJ
Philadelphia, PA
Seigerman, Ellen M. ....Clifton, NJ
Seigfreid, Bingham, Levy, Selzer & Gee, A Professional Corporation
Kansas City, MO
Seigfreid, James T. ....Kansas City, MO
Seigfreid, James T., Jr. ....Kansas City, MO
Seigfreid, Jerome W. ....Naples, FL
Seigfreid Law Firm, The, L.L.C.
Mexico, MO
Seigfreid, Mary Patrick ....Mexico, MO
Seigfreid, Paul A. ....Mexico, MO
Seighman, Susan M. ....Harrisburg, PA
Seiglar-Stein, Victoria A. ....Friendswood, TX
Seigle, Harry J. ....Elgin, IL
Seigle, James L. ....Fayetteville, GA
Seigle, James L., P.C. ....Fayetteville, GA
Seigle, Jon David ....Aspen, CO
Seigle, Laura A. ....Los Angeles, CA
Seigle, Marc S. ....Boston, MA
Seigle, Meredith L. ....Southampton, PA
Seigle, Robt. L. ....Southampton, PA
Seigle, Susan M. ....West Palm Beach, FL
Seigler, Darrell K. ....Ottawa, IL
Seigler, Darrell K., Ltd. ....Ottawa, IL
Seigler, Earle & Ellsworth ....Columbia, SC
Seigler, J. Douglas ....Columbia, SC
Seigler, Joseph M., Jr. ....Rome, GA
Seigler, Michael ....Marietta, GA
Seigler, William J., III ....Atlanta, GA
Seigneur, Cliff R. ....Sheridan, WY
Seijas, Alan R. ....Rahway, NJ
Seijas, Joseph ....Bronx, NY
Seikaly, Christopher M. ....Southfield, MI
Seikel, David P. ....Houston, TX
Seikel, Harold H. ....Garden City, NY
Seikel, Louis A., Jr. ....Akron, OH
Seikel, Oliver E. ....Bratenahl, OH
Seiken, Eric A. ....San Diego, CA
Seiken, Jeffry M. ....Philadelphia, PA
Seiken, Roger A. ....Washington, DC
Seil, David G. ....New Lenox, IL
Seiland and Jednorski, P.A. ....Towson, MD
Seiland, John O. ....Towson, MD
Seiler, David Alan ....Miami, FL
Seiler, Dolores J. ....Hialeah, FL
Seiler, Donald W., Jr. ....Vienna, VA
Seiler Epstein Ziegler & Applegate, LLP
San Francisco, CA
Seiler, Eric ....New York, NY
Seiler, Frank W. ....Savannah, GA
Seiler, I. Leonard ....Orangeburg, NY
Seiler, James E. ....Creve Coeur, MO
Seiler, James E. ....New York, NY
Seiler, Jerry R. ....San Diego, CA
Seiler, John C. ....Prescott, AZ
Seiler, John P. ....Fort Lauderdale, FL
Seiler, Joseph L., III ....New York, NY
Seiler, Kenna M. ....Conroe, TX
Seiler, Lester R. ....Hastings, NE
Seiler, Margaret Gordon ....Richmond, VA

Seiler, Michael T. ... Conroe, TX
Seiler, Parker & Moncrief, P.C.
Hastings, NE
Seiler, Paul D. ... Irving, TX
Seiler, Paul F. ... Dallas, TX
Seiler, Randolph J. ... Pierre, SD
Seiler, Robert E. ... Jefferson City, MO
Seiler, Scott C. ... New Orleans, LA
Seiler, Scott J. ... Minneapolis, MN
Seiler, Seymour A. ... Hialeah, FL
Seiler, Shannon E. ... Lafayette, LA
Seiler, Stacie A. ... Cincinnati, OH
Seiler, Stephen R. ... New York, NY
Seiler, Steven D. ... San Francisco, CA
Seiler, Steven J. ... Duluth, MN
Seiler, Thomas W. ... Provo, UT
Seiler, Victor P. ... Minneapolis, MN
Seiler, Vincent K. ... Jackson, TN
Seiler, William H., Jr. ... McPherson, KS
Seiler, William J. ... Fresno, CA
Seiler, William Martin ... Memphis, TN
Seiler, Yee & Epstein, LLP
San Francisco, CA
Seilers, Harold W. ... Winter Haven, FL
Seilheimer, Edwin J. ... Granbury, TX
Seilheimer, Lisa K. ... Washington, DC
Seiling, Brad William ... Los Angeles, CA
Seiling, Valerie A. ... Hartford, CT
Seiller, Bill V. ... Louisville, KY
Seiller, Handmaker & Blevins, P.S.C.
Lexington, KY
Seiller & Handmaker, LLP
New Albany, IN
Louisville, KY
Seiller, John A. ... Ketchum, ID
Seils, William G. ... Lafox, IL
Seim, Richard ... San Jose, CA
Seimetz, Karen G. ... Chicago, IL
Seims, Alan G. ... Pasadena, CA
Sein, Ramona J. ... McLean, VA
Seine, Anthony D. ... Los Angeles, CA
Seines, Robert M. ... Spokane, WA
Seines, Robert M., P.S. ... Spokane, WA
Seinfeld, Dennis G. ... Tacoma, WA
Seinfeld, Kurt ... New York, NY
Seinfeld, Lester ... Tacoma, WA
Seiniger, Julie Marsh ... Boise, ID
Seiniger Law Offices, P.A. ... Boise, ID
Seiniger, William Breck, Jr. ... Boise, ID
Seink, Daniel P. ... Warren, OH
Seipel, John H. ... Fairfax, VA
Seiple, Andrew L. ... Seattle, WA
Seiple, Stephen B. ... Columbus, OH
Seiple, Stephen W. ... Springfield, IL
Seipp, David J. ... Boston, MA
Seipp, Flick & Kissane, P.A.
Fort Lauderdale, FL
Miami, FL
Seipp, Gerald P. ... Buffalo, NY
Seipp, John C., Jr. ... Miami, FL
Seipp, John Charles ... Salisbury, MD
Seirmarco, James Jay ... New York, NY
Seise, Ruben D. ... New York, NY
Seiselmeyer, Howard W. ... San Diego, CA
Seiser, Gary C. ... San Diego, CA
Seiser, Joyce Ann ... Milwaukee, WI
Seiser, M. D. ... Ames, IA
Seita, Alex Y. ... Honolulu, HI
Seitanakis, Nicholas J. ... Pittsburgh, PA
Seitas, Patricia A. ... San Diego, CA
Seitchik, Jay L. ... Bradenton, FL
Seitchik, Joseph B. ... Philadelphia, PA
Seitel, Andrew H. ... Minneapolis, MN
Seitel, Ian S., (P.A.) ... Fort Lauderdale, FL
Seitel, Owen ... San Francisco, CA
Seitel, Stanley ... New York, NY
Seitelman, Mark E., Law Offices
New York, NY
Seiter, Kevin R., Law Offices of
Kailua-Kona, HI
Seiter Law Firm ... Mexico, NY
Seiter, Lawrence J. ... Mobile, AL
Seiter, Norman W., Jr. ... Mexico, NY
Seiter, Patrick D. ... Baton Rouge, LA
Seiter, William J. ... Simi Valley, CA
Seith, Alex R. ... Chicago, IL
Seitl, Wayne F. ... Sarasota, FL
Seitlin, Janet S. ... Miami, FL
Seitlin, Jodi ... Inverness, FL
Seitman, John M. ... Del Mar, CA
Seiton, Brenda J. ... Atlanta, GA
Seitsinger, Daniel W. ... Oklahoma City, OK
Seitsinger, Mark Wendell
Oklahoma City, OK
Seitsinger, R. Mark ... Weymouth, MA
Seitter, David C. ... Kansas City, MO
Seitter, Robert P. ... White Plains, NY
Seitter, Scott E. ... Kansas City, MO
Seitz, Charles R. ... Cleveland, OH
Seitz, C. J. ... Wilmington, DE
Seitz, Collins J., Jr. ... Wilmington, DE
Seitz, Daniel B. ... Indianapolis, IN
Seitz, Daniel W., (P.C.) ... Roseburg, OR
Seitz, David M. ... Monroeville, PA
Seitz, Donald F. ... Buffalo, NY
Seitz, Douglas H. ... Baltimore, MD
Seitz, Douglas W. ... Phoenix, AZ
Seitz, Eric A. ... Honolulu, HI
Seitz, Eric A., A Law Corporation
Honolulu, HI
Seitz, Friedrich W. ... Los Angeles, CA
Seitz, Gary Francis ... Camden, NJ
Philadelphia, PA
Seitz, George H., III ... Wilmington, DE
Seitz, Gregory ... New York, NY
Seitz, Harry J. ... Monroe, MI
Seitz, Henry L. ... Stephenson, MI
Seitz, Howard G. ... New York, NY
White Plains, NY
Seitz, J. Barton ... Washington, DC
Seitz, Jack M. ... Allentown, PA
Seitz, James W. ... Detroit, MI
Seitz, Joan G. ... Roseburg, OR
Seitz, John T. ... Des Moines, IA
Seitz, Jon S. ... San Luis Obispo, CA
Seitz, Julie L. ... Cincinnati, OH
Seitz, Julie R. ... Highland, NY
Seitz, Kenneth P. ... Clearfield, PA
Seitz, K. G. ... Cincinnati, OH
Seitz, Marie ... Florham Park, NJ
Seitz, Mark Tyler ... Nashville, TN
Seitz, Michael K. ... Milwaukee, WI
Seitz, Michael W. ... San Luis Obispo, CA
Seitz, Patricia A. ... Miami, FL
Seitz, Peter A. ... Christiansburg, VA
Seitz, Raymond H. ... Buffalo, NY
Seitz, Reynolds C. ... Milwaukee, WI
Seitz, Rick ... Los Angeles, CA
Seitz, Stacie R. ... Grand Rapids, MI
Seitz, Sue Luettjohann ... Des Moines, IA
Seitz, Van Ogtrop & Green, P.A.
Wilmington, DE
Seitz, Virginia A. ... Washington, DC
Seitz, William F. ... Fort Lauderdale, FL
Seitz, William F., P.A. ... Fort Lauderdale, FL
Seitz, William H. ... Daytona Beach, FL
New Smyrna Beach, FL
Seitz, William J. ... Chicago, IL
Seitz, William J., III ... Cincinnati, OH
Seitz, William R. ... New York, NY
Seitzinger, Habib, Allen & Randazzo
Philadelphia, PA
Seitzinger, Kent B. ... Roseville, CA
Seitzinger, Mark P. ... Toledo, OH
Seitzinger, Michael D. ... Augusta, ME
Seitzinger, Michael V. ... Library of Congress, Congressional Research Service, GV
Seitzinger, Wilbur H., Jr. ... Philadelphia, PA
Seitzinger & Wilkens ... Roseville, CA
Seitzman, Howard S. ... Austin, TX
Seitzman, Markell ... Sterling Heights, MI
Seiver, Dinah ... Rockville, MD
Raleigh, NC
Seiver, John D. ... Washington, DC
Seiverling, Mary Benefield ... Harrisburg, PA
Seiwell, Robert T. ... Media, PA
Seiwert, Andrew P. ... Indianapolis, IN
Seiwert, Lawrence P. ... Park Ridge, IL
Seixas, Olga V. ... New York, NY
Seka, J. Georg ... San Francisco, CA
Seka, Mark A. ... Menlo Park, CA
Seka, Peter M. ... Washington, DC
Sekaloff, Dennis K. ... New York, NY
Sekaly, Walter M., (P.C.) ... Beaumont, TX
Sekaly-Loukas, Kevin ... Beaumont, TX
Sekany, D. J. ... Sacramento, CA
Sekas & Buzzetti, L.L.C.
Englewood Cliffs, NJ
Sekas, Nicholas G. ... Englewood Cliffs, NJ
Sekelick, Peter W. ... Fairfield, CA
Sekellick, William A. ... Clifton Park, NY
Sekellick, William A., P.C. ... Albany, NY
Clifton Park, NY
Seketa, Gregory J. ... Indianapolis, IN
Sekharan, Raja Narayanswami ... Webster, NY
Sekhri, Neil H. ... San Francisco, CA
Seki, Hoken S. ... Chicago, IL
Seki, James H. ... Honolulu, HI
Seki, Sherrie Thomas ... Honolulu, HI
Sekich, Dominick ... Denver, CO
Sekiguchi, Cathy Lee ... Honolulu, HI
Sekimura, Gerald T. ... San Francisco, CA
San Jose, CA
Sekits, Matthew J. ... Seattle, WA
Sekiya, Gerald Y. ... Honolulu, HI
Sekiya, Kellie M. N. ... Honolulu, HI
Seko, Joni D. ... Salt Lake City, UT
Seksay, Edward H. ... Boston, MA
Sekul, Hornsby, Tisdale & Baker
Biloxi, MS
Sekula & Graziano, P.A. ... Paterson, NJ
Sekula, J. Wm. ... North Canton, OH
Sekula, Jerome D. ... Treasury Department, Internal Revenue Service, GV
Sekula, Joseph G. ... Paterson, NJ
Sekula, Mary Lou ... Canton, OH
Sekula, Raymond F. ... Pittsburgh, PA
Sekuler, Scott H. ... Coral Springs, FL
Sekuler, Susan N. ... Concord, MA
Sekulow, Jay Alan ... Virginia Beach, VA
Sekulski, Richard Z. ... New York, NY
Selagy, F. Randall ... Kennett Square, PA
Selagy, F. Randall, P.C. ... Kennett Square, PA
Selaiden, Geo. ... Elm Grove, WI
Selak, Robert A. ... Cincinnati, OH
Selan, Fred ... Los Angeles, CA
Selan, Harold ... Orinda, CA
Selan, Lisa Faye ... Hidden Hills, CA
Selan, Robert E. ... Calabasas, CA
Selan, Steven M. ... Chicago, IL
Selander, Arthur F. ... Dallas, TX
Selander, Bryan G. ... Rockford, IL
Selander, Kenneth J. ... Seattle, WA
Selander, Larry ... Chicago, IL
Selander & Reese ... Olivia, MN
Selander, Robert R. ... Oregon City, OR
Selander, Ronald D. ... Olivia, MN
Selander, Stephen E. ... Detroit, MI
Selanders, Jay N. ... Birmingham, MI
Kansas City, MO
Selassie, Alemante G. ... Williamsburg, VA
Selassie, Joyce E. Haile ... Lawrence, KS
Selati, Romy A. ... San Diego, CA
Selawsky, John ... River Edge, NJ
Selbach, James F., (P.C.) ... Syracuse, NY
Selbach, Jeffrey P. ... West Palm Beach, FL
Selbach, Scott C. ... Syracuse, NY
Selbak, John J. ... Los Angeles, CA
Selbe, Steven D. ... Houston, TX
Selber, Bernard S. ... Los Angeles, CA
Selber, Leonard A. ... Jacksonville, FL
Selber, Marilyn G. ... Jacksonville, FL
Selber, Philip ... Jacksonville, FL
Selber & Selber, P.A. ... Jacksonville, FL
Selberg, Barbara J. ... Seattle, WA
Selberg, Janice K. ... Detroit, MI
Selbin, Jeffrey ... Berkeley, CA
Selbin, Jonathan D. ... San Francisco, CA
Selbo, Gregory B. ... Fargo, ND
Selbst, Linda G. ... Boca Raton, FL
Selbst, Stephen B. ... New York, NY
Selby, Anne C. ... Fairmount, IN
Selby, Beverly S. ... Charleston, WV
Selby, Bonnie J. ... Goodland, KS
Selby, C. Bradley ... Wilmington, NC
Selby, Carrie A. ... Tacoma, WA
Selby, Charles W. ... Bartlesville, OK
Selby, Connor, Maddux & Janer, L.L.P.
Bartlesville, OK
Selby, David J. ... Omaha, NE
Selby, David L., II ... Birmingham, AL
Selby, Dennis M. ... Mequon, WI
Selby, Donald E. ... Jacksonville, FL
Selby, Donald E., Jr. ... Charlottesville, VA
Selby, Douglass P. ... Atlanta, GA
Selby, Earl Nicholas ... Palo Alto, CA
Selby, Elizabeth
Research Triangle Park, NC
Selby, Eric H. ... Grosse Ile, MI
Selby, George W., Jr. ... Schaumburg, IL
Selby, Herbert Spencer ... Newton, IA
Selby, James M. ... Anaheim, CA
Selby, Janet Strand ... Seattle, WA
Selby, Jennifer J. ... Hattiesburg, MS
Selby, Jennifer Loope ... Troy, MI
Selby, Joseph D. ... Cheyenne, WY
Selby, Judith A. ... Baltimore, MD
Selby, Kevin Lee ... Neosho, MO
Selby, Leland C. ... Greenwich, CT
Selby, Louis L. ... Norco, CA
Selby, Manton L., II ... San Francisco, CA
Selby, Matt Alan ... Kimberling City, MO
Selby & Miller ... Fairmount, IN
Selby, Myra C. ... Indianapolis, IN
Selby, Paul D. ... Hamburg, AR
Selby, Ralph I. ... Bay City, MI
Selby, Richard N., II ... Youngstown, OH
Selby, Robert M. ... Everett, MA
Selby, Russell M. ... New York, NY
Selby, Ruth Koerber ... Brooklyn, NY
Selby, S. Richard ... Milwaukee, WI
Selby, Scott A. ... San Francisco, CA
Selby, Steve ... Austin, TX
Selby, Steven J. ... New York, NY
Selby, Steven L. ... Kelso, WA
Selby, Steven W. ... Alton, IL
Selby, Terence R. ... Chicago, IL
Selby, Terri Taylor ... Berlin, MD
Selby, Timothy P. ... New York, NY
Selby, Todd J. ... Indianapolis, IN
Selby, Traci M. ... San Diego, CA
Selby, Updegraff, Smith & Holwerda
Newton, IA
Selby, William R. ... Portland, OR
Selcer, David M. ... Columbus, OH
Selcer, Susan Pierce ... Columbus, OH
Selchick, Jeffrey M. ... Albany, NY
Selcov, Jay A. ... New York, NY
Selcov, Robert ... New Paltz, NY
Seld, Arthur I. ... Seneca Falls, NY
Selde, William H. ... Omaha, NE
Seldeen, Bruce A. ... Fullerton, CA
Seldeen, Elizabeth E. ... Indio, CA
Seldeen, Richard ... Camarillo, CA
Selden, A. Inge, III ... Birmingham, AL
Selden, Andrew C. ... Minneapolis, MN
Selden, Bard E., Jr. ... Tunica, MS
Selden, Barton S. ... San Francisco, CA
Selden, Brian G. ... Columbus, OH
Selden, David A. ... Phoenix, AZ
Selden, Deborah ... Houston, TX
Selden, Elizabeth Paige ... Richmond, VA
Selden, George L. ... New York, NY
Selden, Jack W. ... Birmingham, AL
Washington, DC
Selden, Jill B. ... Dix Hills, NY
Selden, Jules B. ... Braintree, MA
Selden Law Firm ... San Diego, CA
Selden Law Offices ... Beckley, WV
Selden, Lynch & Hopper ... Las Vegas, NV
Selden, Lynde, II ... San Diego, CA
Las Vegas, NV
Selden, Rush A. ... Houston, TX
Selden, Stanley I ... Beckley, WV
Selden, Stephen J. ... Bethlehem, PA
Selden, Thomas Lawson ... Birmingham, AL
Selders, Keila M. ... Indianapolis, IN
Seldin, Alex E. ... Exton, PA
Seldin, Barry A. ... Englewood, CO
Seldin, Craig ... Dallas, TX
Seldin, Ian Eric ... West Palm Beach, FL
Seldin, Irving P. ... Philadelphia, PA
Seldin, Jodi A. ... Miami, FL
Seldin, Keith A. ... Jupiter, FL
Seldin, Keith A., & Associates, P.A.
Jupiter, FL
Seldin, Marc I. ... Treasury Department, Financial Management Service, GV
Seldin, Richard ... General Accounting Office, Office of the General Counsel, GV
Seldin, Stephen ... New York, NY
Seldin, Theodore M. ... Omaha, NE
Seldin, William S. ... Ithaca, NY
Seldman, Ariana N. ... Palo Alto, CA
Seldman, Norman ... San Clemente, CA
Seldomridge, Robert D. ... Wellington, FL
Seldon, Robert A. ... Santa Monica, CA
Seldon, Robert C. ... Washington, DC
Seldon & Scillieri, LLP
Santa Monica, CA
Seldowitz, Steven R. ... Dallas, TX
Seleb, Bruce K. ... Tucson, AZ
Selecky, John R. ... Bloomfield Hills, MI
Selecman, Marsha L. K. ... Knoxville, TN
SeLegue, Roger ... Los Angeles, CA
SeLegue, Sean M. ... San Francisco, CA
Selem, Stacey Lynn ... Edison, NJ
Seleman, Fred ... Cleveland, OH
Seleman, Stephen J. ... Rochester, NY
Selenberg, Carl J. ... Metairie, LA
Selenberg, Roland R. ... Metairie, LA
Selendy, Jennifer M. H. ... New York, NY
Selenkow, Albert E. ... Baltimore, MD
Selent, John E. ... Louisville, KY
Selep, Joseph W. ... Pittsburgh, PA
Selert, Whitney J. ... Reno, NV
Selesko, John D. ... Southfield, MI
Selesky, Peter J. ... New Brunswick, NJ
Selesner, Leonard H. ... Millburn, NJ
Selesner, Leonard H., P.A. ... Millburn, NJ
Selesny, Abraham ... Bingham Farms, MI
Seletos, Louis T. ... Phoenix, AZ
Seletz, Edward M. ... Wynnewood, PA
Seletz, James Jay ... Scottsdale, AZ
Seletzky, Dimitri ... Washington, DC
Selevan, Jack S. ... Jacksonville, FL
Seley, Dennis G. ... Sacramento, CA
Seley, Peter E. ... Washington, DC
Seleyo, Brian J. ... Media, PA
Self, Andrew C. ... Hopkinsville, KY
Self & Bhamre ... Newport Beach, CA
Self, Bruce A. ... Aurora, IL
Self, Bruce A., & Associates, Ltd.
Aurora, IL
Self, Charles C., III ... Abilene, TX
Self, Charles H., Jr. ... Birmingham, AL
Self, Daniel P., Jr. ... Meridian, MS
Self, David A. ... San Ramon, CA
Self, David C., II ... Port St. Lucie, FL
West Palm Beach, FL
Self, Dolan D., Jr. ... Jackson, MS
Self, Earle B. ... Huntsville, AL
Self, Eben Cowles ... Orlando, FL
Self, Edward L. ... Plainview, TX
Self, Floyd R. ... Tallahassee, FL
Self, Giddens & Lees, Inc.
Oklahoma City, OK
Self, Gilbert P. ... Florence, AL
Self, Glaser & Davis, LLP ... Atlanta, GA
Marietta, GA
Roswell, GA
Self, Glen D. ... Plano, TX
Self, Henry (Hank) H., Jr. ... Florence, AL
Self & Holloway, L.L.P. ... Plainview, TX
Self, J. Philip ... Atlanta, GA
Self, Jacob & Kieronski, LLP
Meridian, MS
Self, James F., Jr. ... Oklahoma City, OK
Self, James F., Jr., & Assocs., Inc., The Law Office of ... Oklahoma City, OK
Self, Janet A. ... Cincinnati, OH
Self, Jerome C. ... Houston, TX
Self, Joseph C. ... Fort Smith, AR
Self, Judy H. ... Memphis, TN
Self & Kronenberg ... Huntsville, AL
Self, Laurie C. ... Washington, DC
Self Law Firm ... Fort Smith, AR
Self, Melinda R. ... Lafayette, CA
Self, Michael C. ... Newport Beach, CA
Self, Michael W. ... Columbia, SC
Sumter, SC
Self Mullins P.C. ... Phenix City, AL
Columbus, GA
Hamilton, GA
Self, Parker ... Shreveport, LA
Self, Randall E. ... Fayetteville, TN
Self, Robert E. ... San Diego, CA
Self, Robert J. ... Bakersfield, CA
Self, Ronald G. ... San Clemente, CA
Self, Ronald W. ... Columbus, GA
Self & Self ... Florence, AL
Tuscumbia, AL
Self, Shannon T. ... Oklahoma City, OK
Self, Sharon Anderson ... Wichita, KS
Self, Sheryl Anne L. ... Dallas, TX
Self, Steven M. ... Vancouver, WA
Self, Thomas A. ... Leesville, LA
Self, Thomas C. ... Dallas, TX
Self, Tiffany A. ... Dallas, TX
Self, Tilman E., III ... Macon, GA
Self, William J., II ... Macon, GA
Self, William King, Jr. ... Memphis, TN
Selfe, Edward M. ... Birmingham, AL
Selfe, Loura A. ... Lancaster, PA
Selfe, Roger L. ... Washington, DC
Selfon, Bruce I. ... Washington, DC
Selfridge, Calvin ... Chicago, IL
Selfridge, Caroline G. ... Santa Clara, CA
Selfridge, Gordon P. ... West Palm Beach, FL
Selfridge, Lance A. ... Los Angeles, CA
Selfridge, Richard J., Jr. ... Virginia Beach, VA
Selfridge, Ruth Nicole ... Tallahassee, FL
Selgrade, Edward L. ... Burlington, MA
Selgrath, Ronald J. ... Los Angeles, CA
Seliber, Sherrie ... San Francisco, CA
Selich, Judith N. ... Newport, OR
Selick, Jerome D. ... Rockville, MD
Selig, Amy Chaisson ... Houston, TX
Selig, Barry F. ... Bethesda, MD
Selig, Benjamin E. ... Stony Point, NY
Selig, David B. ... Chicago, IL

Selig, Edward I. ....Boston, MA
Selig, Edwin ....New York, NY
Selig & Hrabcak Co., L.P.A.
Worthington, OH
Selig, Joel L. ....Laramie, WY
Selig, John S. ....Little Rock, AR
Selig, Linda A. ....Sacramento, CA
Selig, Maria Elena ....Amityville, NY
Selig, Marilyn B. ....New York, NY
Selig, Michelle ....New York, NY
Selig, Raymond G. ....Amityville, NY
Selig, Renee J. ....St. Louis, MO
Selig, Robert A., & Associates
Boca Raton, FL
Selig, Stephen F. ....New York, NY
Seliga, Susan R. ....Cleveland, OH
Seliga, Thomas W. ....Pittsburgh, PA
Seliger, Brooke P. ....Boston, MA
Worcester, MA
Seliger, Carole E. ....San Francisco, CA
Seliger, David ....Cherry Hill, NJ
Seliger, Irwin ....New Hyde Park, NY
Seliger, Steven L. ....Tallahassee, FL
Seligman, Brad ....Berkeley, CA
Seligman, Carrie ....Dorchester, MA
Seligman, Craig S. ....Los Angeles, CA
Seligman, David A. ....North Caldwell, NJ
Seligman, David R. ....Chicago, IL
Seligman, Deborah S. ....Albuquerque, NM
Seligman, Delice F. ....Kingston, NY
New York, NY
Seligman, Frederick ....Kingston, NY
New York, NY
Seligman, Guy J. ....Fort Lauderdale, FL
Seligman, Guy J., P.A. ....Fort Lauderdale, FL
Seligman, Harold ....Bay Shore, NY
Seligman, Harold ....Houston, TX
Seligman, Howard L. ....Stockton, CA
Seligman, Hyatt E. ....Los Angeles, CA
Seligman, Jill I. ....Roswell, GA
Seligman, Joel ....Tucson, AZ
Seligman, John P. ....New York, NY
Seligman, John Schyler ....Miami, FL
Seligman, Joseph L., Jr. ....Stinson Beach, CA
Seligman, Judith R. ....Los Angeles, CA
Seligman, Manuel ....Los Angeles, CA
Seligman, Marc A. ....Los Angeles, CA
Seligman, Milton S. ....Albuquerque, NM
Seligman, Naomi A. ....Fort Lauderdale, FL
Seligman, Nicole K. ....Washington, DC
Seligman, Phil ....Department of Justice,
Civil Division, GV
Seligman, Raymond J. ....Schenectady, NY
Seligman, Richard M., (P.C.) ....Chicago, IL
Seligman, Robert J. ....New York, NY
Seligman, Robert Z. ....Los Angeles, CA
Seligman & Seligman ....Kingston, NY
New York, NY
Seligman, Shelly W. ....Bay Shore, NY
Seligman, Sidney D. ....Livingston, NJ
Seligman, Stephanie J. ....New York, NY
Seligman, Steven L. ....Hartford, CT
Seligman, Steven T. ....Sacramento, CA
Seligman, Terri J. ....New York, NY
Seligman & Willett, Inc. ....Stockton, CA
Seligman, William C. ....New York, NY
Seligmann, Eugene D. ....Seattle, WA
Seligmann, Paul F. ....Seattle, WA
Seligmann, Terry Jean ....Fayetteville, AR
Seligmann, William A. ....Los Angeles, CA
Seligmann, William R. ....Los Gatos, CA
Seligsohn, Henry N. ....Los Angeles, CA
Seligsohn, Irwin B. ....West Orange, NJ
Seligsohn, Walter I. ....Croton-On-Hudson, NY
Seligson, Aaron ....New York, NY
Seligson, Alan G. ....Eugene, OR
Seligson, Alexander W. ....New York, NY
Seligson, Damon M. ....Boston, MA
Seligson, Garry R. ....New York, NY
Seligson, Marla L. ....New Haven, CT
Seligson, Paul Y. ....Naples, FL
Seligson, Robert A. ....Piedmont, CA
Seligson, Rothman & Rothman
New York, NY
Seligson, Thomas F. ....Pittsburgh, PA
Selik, Joel Gary ....Kernville, CA
San Francisco, CA
Solana Beach, CA
Selik, Richard M. ....Farmington Hills, MI
Selikoff, Arthur ....Harrisburg, PA
Selikoff & Cohen, P.A. ....Mount Laurel, NJ
Selikoff, Joel S. ....Mount Laurel, NJ
Selim, Karen Wilson ....Lubbock, TX
Selimos, Dean J. ....North Hollywood, CA
Selimos, Vasiliki Billie ....Willow Springs, IL
Selin, Audrey E. ....Chicago, IL
Selin, Catherine Joyce ....New York, NY
Selin, M. Christina ....New Rochelle, NY
Selin, Paul E. ....Champaign, IL
Selin, Paul M. ....Milwaukee, WI
Selin, Todd S. ....Lansing, MI
Seline, Steven W. ....Omaha, NE
Selinfreund, Michael H. ....Denver, CO
Selinger, Brenda L. ....Dickinson, ND
Selinger, Bruce A. ....Dickinson, ND
Selinger, Carl M. ....Morgantown, WV
Selinger, Gary I. ....New York, NY
Selinger, Jerry R. ....Dallas, TX
Selinger, John S. ....Central Valley, NY
Selinger, Joseph J., Jr. ....Hartford, CT
New London, CT
Selinger, Loretta Hersh ....Los Angeles, CA
Selinger, Mark ....New York, NY
Selinger, Maurice A., III ....Portland, ME
Selinger, Morris L. ....Department of Labor,
Pension and Welfare Benefits, GV
Selinger, Neil L. ....White Plains, NY
Selingo, David J. ....Allentown, PA

Selinker, Phyllis ....Everett, WA
Selinsky, William J. ....Farmington Hills, MI
Selip, Mitchell ....Syosset, NY
Selis, Paula Lillian ....Seattle, WA
Selis, Scott A. ....Ormond Beach, FL
Selit, Max ....Elmhurst, NY
Selitto, Paul M. ....Denville, NJ
Selitto, Ralph W., Jr. ....Edison, NJ
Selivra, Anatole Alexander ....Ventura, CA
Selix, S. Russell, Jr. ....Sacramento, CA
Selk, Nancy ....El Cerrito, CA
Selk, Robert ....Madison, WI
Selk, Sharon E. ....Providence, RI
Selke, Donald A., Jr. ....Redding, CA
Selken, Thomas Lynn ....Fort Collins, CO
Selker, Diane E. ....White Plains, NY
Selker, Eugene I. ....Cleveland, OH
Selker & Furber, L.L.C. ....Cleveland, OH
Selkin, Albert C. ....Norfolk, VA
Selkirk, Alexander M., Jr. ....Woodbury, NY
Selko, Robert W. ....Pittsburgh, PA
Selkow, Andrew J. ....Cherry Hill, NJ
Selkowitz, Ira C. ....Denver, CO
Selkowitz, Larry B. ....Harrisburg, PA
Selkowitz, Leonard ....South Miami, FL
Selkowitz, Stanley I. ....Pleasant Hills, PA
Sell, Charles G. ....Nashville, TN
Sell, Charles H., II ....Troy, OH
West Milton, OH
Sell, Charles J. ....Parsons, KS
Sell, Charles W. ....Orlando, FL
Sell, Christine Mahn ....Chattanooga, TN
Sell, Clay ....Amarillo, TX
Sell, Daniel E. ....Scarsdale, NY
Sell, David L. ....Denver, CO
Sell, Donald M. ....St. Paul, MN
Sell, Dwain E. ....Plymouth, MN
Sell, Edward S., III ....Macon, GA
Sell, E. S., Jr. ....Macon, GA
Sell, Garland D. ....Amarillo, TX
Sell, Gregory J. ....Milwaukee, WI
Sell and Griffin, A Professional Corporation
Amarillo, TX
Sell, Howard William ....Tulsa, OK
Sell, James C. ....Englewood, CO
Sell, James E. ....San Francisco, CA
Sell, James S. ....Norristown, PA
Philadelphia, PA
Sell, Janet W. ....Mesa, AZ
Sell, Jeffrey Scott ....Chicago, IL
Sell, Jeffrey Z. ....Houston, TX
Sell, Jon R. ....Colorado Springs, CO
Sell, K. Christine Mahn ....Chattanooga, TN
Sell, Linda G. ....Akron, OH
Sell, Lisette ....Des Moines, IA
Sell & Melton, L.L.P. ....Atlanta, GA
Macon, GA
Sell, Michael D. ....Kansas City, MO
Sell, Neil I. ....Minneapolis, MN
Sell, Richard K. ....Milwaukee, WI
Sell, Robert J. ....Chicago, IL
Sell, Sharon Marie ....Massillon, OH
Sell, Timothy L. ....Seattle, WA
Sell, Timothy S. ....Sidney, OH
Sell, W. Edward ....Pittsburgh, PA
Sella, Carmel B. ....Los Angeles, CA
Sella, Uri ....New York, NY
Sellani, Roseann ....Bridgeton, NJ
Sellar, Alastair J. ....Roseland, NJ
Sellar, Charles B. P. ....Leesburg, FL
Sellar, Hazard, Fitzgerald, McNeely, Alm & Manning, A Professional Law Corporation
Walnut Creek, CA
Sellar Richardson, P.C. ....Newark, NJ
Roseland, NJ
Sellar, Rudd ....Walnut Creek, CA
Sellar, Sewell, Russ, Saylor & Johnson, P.A.
Leesburg, FL
Sellards, Robert M. ....San Francisco, CA
Sellaro, Eugene J. ....Morgantown, WV
Sellaro, Joseph M. ....Charleston, WV
Sellarole, Victor C. ....Hackensack, NJ
Sellars, James D., Law Offices of
Long Beach, CA
Sellars, Johnnie D. ....Dandridge, TN
Sellars, Jon K. ....Houston, TX
Sellars, Kim W. ....Los Angeles, CA
Sellars, Marion & Bachi, P.A.
West Palm Beach, FL
Sellars, Michael ....Olympia, WA
Sellars, Rick ....Little Rock, AR
Sellars, Robert L. ....West Palm Beach, FL
Sellars, Terry ....Lexington, KY
Sellars, Victor C. G. ....Emory, TX
Sellay, William T. ....Hartford, CT
Sellberg, Jeffrey B. ....Huntington Beach, CA
Selle, Elaine W. ....New Orleans, LA
Selle, James M. ....Kansas City, MO
Selle, Michael J. ....Charlotte, NC
Selle, Richard L. ....New York, NY
Selle, William J. ....Annapolis, MD
Greenbelt, MD
Selleck, Elizabeth K. ....Seattle, WA
Selleck, Joann ....San Diego, CA
Selleck, Lea Ellen ....Topeka, KS
Selleck, Nathaniel ....Hartford, CT
Selleck, Tom ....Angleton, TX
Sellei, Gabrielle J. ....Cherry Hill, NJ
Philadelphia, PA
Sellek, Mercedes Maria ....Coral Gables, FL
Sellen, Keith L. ....Lena, WI
Seller, Allan B. ....Treasury Department,
Internal Revenue Service, GV
Seller, Charles H. ....Detroit, MI
Sellergren, David C. ....Minneapolis, MN
Sellers, Abe ....Marietta, OH
Sellers, Andrea F. ....Kansas City, MO
Sellers, Andrew ....Jackson, TN

Sellers, Andrew P., Jr. ....Baton Rouge, LA
Sellers, Angela C. ....Columbus, GA
Sellers, Angela C. ....Tucson, AZ
Sellers, April E. ....Indianapolis, IN
Sellers, Arlene K. ....Santa Monica, CA
Sellers, Atkinson & Jose, P.C. ....Atlanta, GA
Marietta, GA
Woodstock, GA
Sellers, Barbara J. ....Columbus, OH
Sellers, Barbara S. ....St. Paul, MN
Sellers, Ben A., Jr. ....Panama City, FL
Sellers, Bradley A. ....Kansas City, MO
Sellers, C. Brandon, III ....Greenville, AL
Sellers, Cameron ....Menlo Park, CA
Sellers, Carey A. ....Charlotte, NC
Sellers, Caridad S. ....Gainesville, FL
Sellers, Carolyn Cook ....White Plains, NY
Sellers, Cathy Miller ....Tallahassee, FL
Sellers, Cheryl A. ....Bethesda, MD
Sellers, Clyde H. ....Omaha, NE
Sellers, Cynthia N. ....Nashville, TN
Sellers, David Lee ....Pensacola, FL
Sellers, Dorothy D. ....Honolulu, HI
Sellers, Dylan Karl ....Los Angeles, CA
Sellers, E. Brian ....Knoxville, TN
Sellers, Edith J. ....Memphis, TN
Sellers, Eldon ....Napa, CA
Sellers, Elizabeth M. ....Washington, DC
Sellers, Eric T. ....Tempe, AZ
Sellers, Ernest A. ....Live Oak, FL
Sellers, Ernest A., Jr. ....Live Oak, FL
Sellers, Ewing Thomas ....Murfreesboro, TN
Sellers, Gary ....Akron, OH
Sellers, Gary L. ....New York, NY
Sellers, Gene M. ....Birmingham, AL
Sellers, Gene T. ....Tallahassee, FL
Sellers, Gerald P. ....Baltimore, MD
Sellers, H. Donald ....Greenville, SC
Sellers, Herschel V., III ....St. Louis, MO
Sellers, Hinshaw, Ayers, Dortch, Honeycutt & Lyons, P.A. ....Charlotte, NC
Sellers, Holly Taylor ....Madison, CT
Sellers, J. Grant ....Jackson, MS
Sellers, Jack B. ....Sapulpa, OK
Sellers, Jack B., Law Associates, Inc.
Sapulpa, OK
Sellers & Jacobs ....Vancouver, WA
Sellers, Jacqueline H. ....Detroit, MI
Sellers, James L. ....Vancouver, WA
Sellers, Jane Whitt ....Richmond, VA
Sellers, Jefferson D. ....Tulsa, OK
Sellers, Jeffrey A. ....Buffalo, NY
Sellers, Jeffrey L. ....Phoenix, AZ
Sellers, Jennifer J. ....Omaha, NE
Sellers, Jere D. ....Overland Park, KS
Sellers, John A. ....Birmingham, MI
Sellers, John H. ....Menlo Park, CA
Sellers, Joseph M. ....Washington, DC
Sellers, Kathleen M. ....Buffalo, NY
Sellers, Keith F. ....Tulsa, OK
Sellers, Kimberlee ....St. George, UT
Sellers, Lawrence E., Jr. ....Tallahassee, FL
Sellers, Lee ....Wichita Falls, TX
Sellers, Linda A. ....Yakima, WA
Sellers, Lori A. ....Tallahassee, FL
Sellers, Lori J. ....Kansas City, MO
Sellers, M. Lee ....Cincinnati, OH
Sellers, Marc K. ....Portland, OR
Sellers, Marilyn R. S. ....Seattle, WA
Sellers, Mark R. ....New York, NY
Sellers, Marshall ....Louisville, KY
Sellers, Melissa Scanlan ....Baltimore, MD
Sellers, Michael E. ....Knoxville, TN
Sellers, Michael L. ....Atlanta, GA
Sellers, Michael M. ....West Des Moines, IA
Sellers, Michael T. ....Newtown, PA
Sellers, Mortimer ....Baltimore, MD
Sellers, Nancy S. ....Murfreesboro, TN
Sellers, Pamela C. ....Los Angeles, CA
Sellers, Pamela Heflin ....Richmond, VA
Sellers, Penny D. ....Richmond, VA
Sellers, Philip L. ....Montgomery, AL
Sellers & Prevatt ....Live Oak, FL
Sellers, R. Kent ....Kansas City, MO
Sellers, Randal H. ....Birmingham, AL
Sellers, Randy ....Cleveland, TN
Sellers, Robert D. ....Towson, MD
Sellers, Robert D., & Associates, P.A.
Towson, MD
Sellers, Robin Stone ....New York, NY
Sellers, Roger C. ....Abbeville, LA
Sellers, Sandra A. ....McLean, VA
Sellers, Sebie Gibbs ....Demopolis, AL
Sellers, Shelba D. ....Thomasville, GA
Sellers, Steven E. ....Tallahassee, FL
Sellers, Steven M. ....Rocky Hill, CT
Sellers, Terryl A. ....New York, NY
Sellers, Thomas G. ....Northridge, CA
Sellers, Thomas G. ....Athol Springs, NY
Sellers, Timothy G. ....Charlotte, NC
Sellers, Tonia C. ....Atlanta, GA
Sellers, Veronica M. ....Kansas City, MO
Sellers, W. C. (Bill), Inc. ....Sapulpa, OK
Sellers, W. Scott ....Dalton, GA
Sellers, W. C. (Bill) ....Sapulpa, OK
Sellers, W. C. (Bill), Jr. ....Sapulpa, OK
Sellers, William B. ....Montgomery, AL
Sellers, William T. ....Murfreesboro, TN
Sellers, William T., Jr. ....Murfreesboro, TN
Sellers, William W. ....Kansas City, MO
Selles, Terry L. ....Grand Rapids, MI
Sellier, Bertrand C. ....New York, NY
Sellinger, Barbara A. ....Newark, NJ
Sellinger, David E. ....Washington, DC
Sellinger, John J. ....Silver Spring, MD
Sellinger, John J. ....Philadelphia, PA

Sellinger, Philip R. ....Atlantic City, NJ
Newark, NJ
New York, NY
Sellinger, William ....Clifton, NJ
Sellingsloh, Hulda Knipling ....Crowley, TX
Sellingsloh, John S. ....Houston, TX
Sellins, W. John ....Cincinnati, OH
Sellitti, James J. ....Weirton, WV
Sellitti, Joseph Andrew ....Cherry Hill, NJ
Philadelphia, PA
Sellitti, Nogay & McCune ....Weirton, WV
Sellitto, Anthony M., Jr. ....Toms River, NJ
Sellman, Alvin ....Baltimore, MD
Sellman, David S. ....Baltimore, MD
Sellman, David S., P.A. ....Baltimore, MD
Sellman, John R. ....Mountain Home, ID
Sellman, Richard I. ....Avon, CT
East Hartford, CT
Sellman, Richard K. ....Hibbing, MN
Sellmer, Stephen M. ....Fishers, IN
Sellnau, George A. ....Houston, TX
Sellner, James J., Jr. ....Minneapolis, MN
Sellner, JoAnne Zoff ....St. Paul, MN
Sellner, John P. ....Clara City, MN
Montevideo, MN
Sello, Judy ....Basking Ridge, NJ
Sells, Bruce F. ....Dearborn, MI
Sells, Derek S. ....New York, NY
Sells, Edward (Ted) C. ....Evergreen, CO
Sells, James K. ....Silverdale, WA
Sells, John ....Olympia, WA
Sells, Larry E. ....Kansas City, MO
Sells, Marcia L. ....New York, NY
Sells, Martin A. ....St. Helens, OR
Sells, Scott A. ....Woodland Park, CO
Sells, Scott L. ....Denver, CO
Sells, William Lothian, Jr. ....South Bend, WA
Sellstrom, Dawn E. ....Chicago, IL
Sellstrom, John L. ....Jamestown, NY
Sellstrom, John L., P.C. ....Jamestown, NY
Sellstrom, Joy ....Chicago, IL
Sellstrom, Stephen E. ....Jamestown, NY
Sellung, Elizabeth Abrams ....Los Angeles, CA
Sellwood, Scott M. ....San Francisco, CA
Selman & Associates, P.C. ....Tulsa, OK
Selman • Breitman ....Los Angeles, CA
San Diego, CA
San Francisco, CA
Santa Ana, CA
Selman, Burton M. ....Los Angeles, CA
Selman & Camp ....McAllen, TX
Selman, F. Ben, Jr. ....Waco, TX
Selman, Jack A. ....Austin, TX
Selman, Jackson W. ....Jacksonville, AL
Selman, James D., III ....McAllen, TX
Selman, James Larkin, II
New Orleans, LA
Selman, Jeffrey C. ....San Francisco, CA
Selman, Jerry K. ....Jasper, AL
Selman, John B. ....Washington, DC
Austin, TX
Selman Munson & Lerner, P.C.
Austin, TX
Selman, Neil ....Los Angeles, CA
Selman, Robert B. ....Phoenix, AZ
Selman, Robert B., Ltd. ....Phoenix, AZ
Selman, Roland W., III ....San Francisco, CA
Selman, Russell B. ....Chicago, IL
Selman & Selman ....Jasper, AL
Selman, Thomas K. ....Jasper, AL
Selman, Thomas M. ....Washington, DC
Selman, William B. ....Tulsa, OK
Selman, William G. ....Minneapolis, MN
Selmann, Marja E. ....Anchorage, AK
Selmer, David R. ....Chicago, IL
Selmer Law Firm, P.A. ....Golden Valley, MN
Selmer, Scott E. ....Golden Valley, MN
Selmi, William, Jr. ....Okeechobee, FL
Selmi, William, Jr., Chartered
Okeechobee, FL
Selmo, Laurel A. ....Carmel, CA
Selmonsky, Penny Beth ....Buffalo, NY
Selmore, Kimberly A. ....Jacksonville, FL
Selna, James V. ....Fullerton, CA
Selna, Leland R., Jr. ....San Francisco, CA
Selna, Steven M. ....San Francisco, CA
Selner, Glaser, Komen, Berger & Galganski, P.C. ....St. Louis, MO
Selner, Norman A. ....St. Louis, MO
Selner, Paul A. ....Fort Worth, TX
Selnick, Donna S. ....Long Beach, CA
Selnick, R. Bruce ....Cincinnati, OH
Selod, Roshan Zaman ....Dallas, TX
Selover, Linda B. ....Annapolis, MD
Selover, R. Edwin ....Newark, NJ
Selover, Steven L. ....Universal City, CA
Selph, Douglas D. ....Atlanta, GA
Selph, Francis Moises ....Raton, NM
Selph, Harry H., II ....Oklahoma City, OK
Selph, Jeanne Byrum ....Cape Charles, VA
Selph Law Firm ....Raton, NM
Selph, Steven L. ....Bartow, FL
Selph, Victoria E. ....La Plata, MD
Selph, William F., III ....Jackson, MS
Selph, William F., Jr. ....Mc Comb, MS
Selsberg, Steven R. ....Houston, TX
Selsberg, William ....Stamford, CT
Selser, Jeffrey T. ....Rockville, MD
Selser, John E., III ....Hackensack, NJ
Selser, John R. ....Readfield, ME
Selser, Robert C., (P.A.) ....Hillsdale, NJ
Selsie, Andrew ....Phoenix, AZ
Selski, Berl H. ....Mission Viejo, CA
Selski, Sturgeon & Wehbe, A Professional Law Corporation ....Mission Viejo, CA
Selsky, Ira B. ....New York, NY
Selsor, Fred S. ....Kansas City, MO
Selsor, L. Grant ....Menominee, MI

Selsor, Robert J. ... St. Louis, MO
Seltenrich, Jennifer Rende ... Boston, MA
Selter, Eric Jay ... Encino, CA
Selter, Mary F. ... St. Petersburg, FL
Selter, Michael H. ... Washington, DC
Selter, Monica L. ... Washington, DC
Selterman, Kenneth ... New York, NY
Selters, J. Benjamin, III ... Pomona, CA
Selters, John B., Jr. ... Pomona, CA
Selters & Selters ... Pomona, CA
Selth, James R. ... Pasadena, CA
Seltman, Lee R. ... Los Angeles, CA
Seltun, Victoria L. ... Eau Claire, WI
Seltz, George G. ... Minneapolis, MN
Seltz, Joel ... Minneapolis, MN
Seltz, Lewis H. ... Minneapolis, MN
Seltz & Seltz ... Minneapolis, MN
Seltz, Thomas P., (A Professional Corporation) ... Los Angeles, CA
Seltz, William ... Minneapolis, MN
Seltzberg, Berton ... New York, NY
Seltzer, Abr. ... Whitestone, NY
Seltzer, Adolph D. ... New York, NY
Seltzer, Alan Michael ... Reading, PA
Seltzer, Arthur H. ... Miami, FL
Seltzer, Barry S. ... Fort Lauderdale, FL
Seltzer, Bradley M. ... Washington, DC
Seltzer, Brian Michael ... Mineola, NY
Seltzer, Brian P. ... St. Louis, MO
Seltzer, Brian T. ... San Diego, CA
Seltzer Caplan McMahon & Vitek, A Professional Corporation ... San Diego, CA
Seltzer, Carl L. ... University City, MO
Seltzer, Charles W. ... Midland, TX
Seltzer & Cody ... Oakland, CA
Seltzer, David A. ... Bethesda, MD
Seltzer, David M. ... Jenkintown, PA
Seltzer, David R. ... Palo Alto, CA
Seltzer, David S. ... Fairfield, CA
Seltzer, Diane A., Law Firm of ... Washington, DC
Seltzer, Donald M. ... Charlotte, NC
Seltzer, E. Manning ... Washington, DC
Seltzer, Edward D. ... Charlotte, NC
Seltzer, Eric H. ... Greenwich, CT
New York, NY
Seltzer, Eric S. ... Weehawken, NJ
Seltzer, Eugene S. ... Berkeley, CA
Seltzer, Francesca E. ... Narberth, PA
Seltzer, Garry ... St. Louis, MO
Seltzer, Garry, L.C. ... St. Louis, MO
Seltzer, George L. ... Margate City, NJ
Seltzer, George S. ... Plainsboro, NJ
Seltzer, Harold G. ... Brooklyn, NY
Seltzer, Ira ... Los Angeles, CA
Seltzer, Irving ... Hollidaysburg, PA
Seltzer, Jack ... Forest Hills, NY
Seltzer, James Jay ... Emeryville, CA
Seltzer, James Jay ... Los Angeles, CA
Monterey, CA
Oakland, CA
Sacramento, CA
San Francisco, CA
Seltzer, Jay S. ... Woodbury, NY
Seltzer, Jeffrey L. ... Hempstead, NY
Seltzer, Joan D. ... San Francisco, CA
Seltzer, Joel C. ... Union, NJ
Seltzer, John R. ... New Castle, PA
Seltzer, Keith B. ... Fort Lauderdale, FL
Seltzer, Kenneth A. ... Rahway, NJ
Seltzer Law Group ... San Francisco, CA
Seltzer, Lisa N. ... Washington, DC
Seltzer, Madeleine E. ... Los Angeles, CA
Seltzer, Marc ... Tucson, AZ
Seltzer, Marc I. ... Beverly Hills, CA
Seltzer, Marc M. ... Los Angeles, CA
Seltzer, Margaret A. ... San Francisco, CA
Seltzer, Marian Keidan ... Bloomfield Hills, MI
Seltzer, Marjorie S. ... Boca Raton, FL
Seltzer, Mark D. ... Boston, MA
Seltzer, Mark D. ... Philadelphia, PA
Seltzer, Mark F. ... Philadelphia, PA
Seltzer, Mark F., P.C. ... Philadelphia, PA
Seltzer, Martin S. ... Columbus, OH
Seltzer, Maryann ... Los Angeles, CA
Seltzer, Michael Elliot ... New York, NY
Seltzer, Miriam A. ... Trenton, NJ
Seltzer, Norman T. ... San Diego, CA
Seltzer, Phillip E. ... Troy, MI
Seltzer, Regina ... Riverhead, NY
Seltzer, Richard A. ... Oakland, CA
Seltzer, Richard C. ... New York, NY
Seltzer, Richard C. ... Houston, TX
Seltzer, Richard K. ... Los Angeles, CA
Seltzer, Richard M. ... New York, NY
Seltzer, Richard S. ... Radnor, PA
Seltzer, Robert A. ... Chicago, IL
Seltzer, Robin F. ... East Meadow, NY
Seltzer, Sally H. ... Fort Lauderdale, FL
Seltzer, Sol M. ... Boca Raton, FL
Seltzer, Stephen ... Jericho, NY
Seltzer, Steven P. ... New York, NY
Seltzer Sussman & Habermann LLP ... Jericho, NY
Seltzer, Tammy ... Washington, DC
Seltzer, Theodore ... New York, NY
Seltzer, Wm. R. ... Midland, TX
Selva, Lance H. ... Murfreesboro, TN
Selvaggi, Michael S. ... Hackettstown, NJ
Morristown, NJ
Trenton, NJ
Selvaggio, Andrea W. ... Washington, DC
Selvaggio, Anthony T. ... Rochester, NY
Selvaggio, Nick A. ... Columbus, OH
Selvaggio, Raymond A. ... Huntington, NY
Selver, Paul D. ... New York, NY
Selver, Tara ... San Pedro, CA
Selverne, Mandelbaum & Mintz, LLP ... New York, NY
Selverne, Michael ... New York, NY
Selvers, Jerome M. ... Freehold, NJ
Selvey, L. Sanford, II ... Billings, MT
Selvidge, Andrea ... Irvine, CA
Selvidge, Barry E. ... Mango, FL
Selvidge, Becca A. ... New Orleans, LA
Selvidge, Mark F. ... Oklahoma City, OK
Selvidge, Robert C. ... San Francisco, CA
Selvidge, Susan P. ... Wichita, KS
Selvig, Jettie Pierce ... San Francisco, CA
Selvig, Kenneth J. ... West Palm Beach, FL
Selvig, Victor E. ... Riverside, CA
Selvin, Brian R. ... Hackensack, NJ
Selvin, Dinah M. ... Maplewood, NJ
Selvin, Gary R. ... Oakland, CA
Selvin, Jared M. ... New York, NY
Selvin, Peter S. ... Los Angeles, CA
Selvin & Weiner & Weinberger LLP ... Los Angeles, CA
Selvo, Gerald V. ... Los Angeles, CA
Selwa, Frank ... Detroit, MI
Selway, Gary F. ... Greensburg, PA
Selwitz, L. Jay ... San Francisco, CA
Selwocki, Edwin Henry, Jr ... Lincoln Park, MI
Selwood, Clifford B., Jr. ... Plantation, FL
Selwood, Pierce T. ... Los Angeles, CA
Selwyn, Douglas M. ... Houston, TX
Selwyn, Herbert E. ... Encino, CA
Selwyn, Marc ... Montecito, CA
Selwyn, Mark Daniel ... Boston, MA
Selwyn, Robert D. ... Tuscaloosa, AL
Selya, Bruce M. ... Providence, RI
Selya, Robert P. ... New York, NY
Selz, Bryan K. ... Rustburg, VA
Selz, Mark H. ... Dallas, TX
Selz, Shirley A. ... Corpus Christi, TX
Selz, Thomas D. ... New York, NY
Selzer, Donald E. ... New York, NY
Selzer, Donald W. "Tad", Jr. ... Minneapolis, MN
Selzer, Ealy, Hemphill & Blasdel, LLP ... Palm Springs, CA
Selzer, Herbert M. ... New York, NY
Selzer, Jack R. ... Kansas City, MO
Selzer, James O. ... Kansas City, MO
Selzer, Jeanne G. ... Dallas, TX
Selzer, John A. ... Scottsbluff, NE
Selzer, Joseph M. ... Newark, NJ
Selzer, Josh ... Prairie Village, KS
Selzer, Laura L. ... Detroit, MI
Selzer, Nancy ... New Orleans, LA
Selzer, Paul T. ... Palm Springs, CA
Selzer, Robert S. ... Bethesda, MD
Selzer, Steven Michael ... Rockville, MD
Selzer, Steven R. ... Silver Spring, MD
Selzer, Susan Weiss ... Los Angeles, CA
Selzer, Terry A. ... Brooklyn, NY
Selznick, David R. ... White Plains, NY
Selznick, Gail Johnson ... Philadelphia, PA
Selznick, Helene ... Yonkers, NY
Selznick, Loren F. ... New York, NY
Semaan, John P. ... Dearborn Heights, MI
Semack, Mary H. ... New York, NY
Semack, Michael J. ... New York, NY
Seman, Eileen P. ... Boston, MA
Seman, Gayle E. ... Andover, MA
Seman, Karl C. ... Garden City, NY
Seman, Lawrence A. ... Cleveland, OH
Seman, Robert J. ... South Amboy, NJ
Semanchik, David A. ... Toms River, NJ
Semanchik, Mark ... Frackville, PA
Pottsville, PA
Semancik, Anthony P. ... New York, NY
Semancik, Caroline Hopkins ... Bethesda, MD
Semanek, Karen L. ... Houston, TX
Semanko, Gregory J. ... Minneapolis, MN
Semanko, Gregory J., P.A. ... Minneapolis, MN
Semanko, Norman M. ... Twin Falls, ID
Semanoff, Harold ... Jenkintown, PA
Semanoff, Ormsby & Greenberg, LLP ... Jenkintown, PA
Semanoff, Ormsby & Greenberg, LLP ... Philadelphia, PA
Semansky, Lisa Swan ... Great Falls, MT
Semarjian, Charles Armen ... Clinton Township, MI
Semarjian, Charles Armen, P.C. ... Clinton Township, MI
Semasek, Gerald ... Harrisburg, PA
Semasek, Joseph P. ... McAdoo, PA
Semaya, Francine L. ... New York, NY
Semaya, Robert J. ... New York, NY
Semaya, Ted G. ... New York, NY
Sembenini, Robyn Mary-Anuhea ... Burlingame, CA
Sember, Ada A. ... Sun Valley, CA
Sember, Rebecca ... Pittsburgh, PA
Sembos, Sophia ... Long Island City, NY
Semegen, Patrick W. ... King Of Prussia, PA
Semeister, Joanne ... Philadelphia, PA
Semel, Amy ... New York, NY
Semel, Betty M. ... New York, NY
Semel, Daniel M. ... New York, NY
Semel, Gabrielle ... New York, NY
Semel, Hilary ... New York, NY
Semel, Irwin David ... Maplewood, NJ
Semel, Martin I. ... Jericho, NY
New York, NY
Semel, Martin J. ... New York, NY
Semel & Patrusky ... Jericho, NY
New York, NY
Semel, Peter M. ... Baltimore, MD
Semel, Richard S. ... Hackensack, NJ
Semel, Scott N. ... Needham, MA
Semel, Theresa M. ... Iowa City, IA
Semelroth, Timothy S. ... Cedar Rapids, IA
Semelsberger, David J. ... San Diego, CA
Semenek, Scott A. ... Chicago, IL
Semeniuk, Catherine M. ... Sunrise, FL
Semenoff, Mark N. ... Denver, CO
Semensohn, Robert E. ... Garden City, NY
Semento, Lawrence J. ... Eustis, FL
Summerfield, FL
Semento & Swigert ... Eustis, FL
Summerfield, FL
Semenza, Lawrence J. ... Las Vegas, NV
Semer, Barry E. ... Chicago, IL
Semer, Jerry ... Fremont, OH
Semer, Scott L. ... New York, NY
Semerad, Mark F. ... Omaha, NE
Semeraro, Mark J. ... Wayne, NJ
Semeraro, Richard A. ... New York, NY
Semeraro, Steven ... Department of Justice, Antitrust Division, GV
Semerdjian, Dick A. ... San Diego, CA
Semerdjian, Steve A. ... New York, NY
Semerjian, Evan Y. ... Boston, MA
Semerjian, Evan Y., P.C. ... Boston, MA
Semerjian, Lisa A. ... Philadelphia, PA
Semerling, Joseph A. ... Chicago, IL
Semerly, Charles G. ... Chicago, IL
Semes, Michael J. ... Harrisburg, PA
Semet, Barry N. ... Miami, FL
Semet, Lickstein, Morgenstern, Berger, Brooke & Gordon, P.A. ... Miami, FL
Semeta, Richard K. ... Newport Beach, CA
Semetis, Arthur J. ... New York, NY
Semian, Stephen W. ... New York, NY
Semidey Garcia, Lolita J. ... San Juan, PR
Semien, Ralph M. ... Los Angeles, CA
Semilof, Bonnie J. ... Washington, DC
Seminara, Alisa K. ... New York, NY
Seminara, Caniglia, McCarthy & Sacoman ... Omaha, NE
Seminara, Joseph F. ... New York, NY
Seminara, Louis A. ... Omaha, NE
Seminara, Robert J. ... Bronx, NY
Seminatore, Kenneth F. ... Cleveland, OH
Seminer, Andrea G. ... Gold River, CA
Semion, John W. ... Menlo Park, CA
Semionow, Raina ... New York, NY
Semisch, Donald A. ... Willow Grove, PA
Semisch, Douglas R. ... Omaha, NE
Semisch, Mark R. ... Willow Grove, PA
Semisch, Scot W. ... Willow Grove, PA
Semisch and Semisch ... Willow Grove, PA
Semivan, Andrew J. ... Southfield, MI
Semke, Karen G. ... San Jose, CA
Semko, Eugene M. ... El Paso, TX
Semko & Minor, P.C. ... El Paso, TX
Semler & Associates, P.C. ... Denver, CO
Semler, Elizabeth ... Portland, OR
Semler, H. Michael ... Department of Justice, Environment and Natural Resources Division, GV
Semler, J. Dennis ... Tulsa, OK
Semler, John K., Jr. ... Camden, NJ
Philadelphia, PA
Semler & Pritzker ... Washington, DC
Semler, R. Parker ... Denver, CO
Semler, Robert C., (P.C.) ... Atlanta, GA
Semler, Ronald J. ... Indianapolis, IN
Semler, Steven R. ... Washington, DC
Semler, Susan A. ... Hackensack, NJ
Semmel, Amy ... Los Angeles, CA
Semmel, Herbert ... Los Angeles, CA
Semmelhack, Charles A. ... Chicago, IL
Semmelhack, Tricia Thomas ... Buffalo, NY
Semmelman, Andrew A. ... Lake Forest, IL
Semmelman, Andrew T. ... Wilmington, DE
Semmelman & Bertucci, Ltd. ... Lake Forest, IL
Semmelman, David A. ... Lake Forest, IL
Semmelman, Jacques ... New York, NY
Semmelman, Karen L. ... York, PA
Semmens, Daniel P. ... Portland, OR
Semmens, Michael P. ... Sacramento, CA
Semmer, Robert F. ... San Diego, CA
Semmes, Bowen & Semmes, A Professional Corporation ... Washington, DC
Baltimore, MD
Hagerstown, MD
Salisbury, MD
Towson, MD
McLean, VA
Semmes, David H. ... Flint Hill, VA
Semmes, Francis B. ... Atlanta, GA
Semmes, John Gibson ... Washington, DC
Semmes, John Gibson ... Potomac, MD
Semmes, Raphael ... Chevy Chase, MD
Semmes, Sara C. ... Anniston, AL
Semmes, Thomas M. ... Anniston, AL
Semmler, Albert K. ... Bloomington, IL
Semmler, Carl D. ... Greensboro, NC
Semo, Joseph ... Washington, DC
Semo, Judith Jurin ... Washington, DC
Semon, Jonathan Andrew ... New York, NY
Semon, Joseph V., (P.C.) ... Richardson, TX
Semon & Mondshein ... Woodbury, NY
Semon, Richard A. ... Santa Monica, CA
Semon, Robert V. ... Hampton, VA
Semon, Sigmund S. ... Woodbury, NY
Semonche, John E. ... Durham, NC
Semones, Christopher F. ... San Jose, CA
Semonian, Edward, Jr. ... Alexandria, VA
Semonite, Sally R. ... Iselin, NJ
New York, NY
Semonoff, Ellen Miriam ... Cambridge, MA
Semons, Charles W. ... Dallas, TX
Semons, William A. ... Columbus, OH
Semos, Demetrios P. ... Philadelphia, PA
Semotiuk, Andriy J. ... Los Angeles, CA
Sempeles, Leigh Anne ... Miamisburg, OH
Sempert, David H. ... Boston, MA
Sempf, Timothy T. ... Amery, WI
Semple, David ... Union, NJ
Semple, E. Michael ... Buffalo, NY
Semple, James W. ... Wilmington, DE
Semple, John F. ... Trenton, NJ
Semple, Kathleen M. ... Fairfield, OH
Semple, Lloyd A. ... Detroit, MI
Semple, Martin ... Denver, CO
Semple, Miller & Mooney, P.C. ... Denver, CO
Semple, Paul C. ... Concord, NH
Semple, Richard J. ... Boston, MA
Semple, T. Darrington, Jr. ... New York, NY
Sempliner, Myron ... Berkley, MI
Sempliner, Thomas and Boak ... Detroit, MI
Plymouth, MI
Semplonius, Reneé K. ... Pontiac, MI
Semprebon, Christin L. ... Springfield, VT
Semprevivo, Philip C., Jr. ... New York, NY
Semrad, Robert James, Jr. ... Chicago, IL
Semro, Geoffrey D. ... Los Angeles, CA
Semrod, T. Joseph ... Princeton, NJ
Semsch, Kinzle Lee ... Springfield, MO
Semsker, Richard H. ... Washington, DC
Semski, Lawrence ... Biloxi, MS
Semtner, Bernard L., III ... Oklahoma City, OK
Semuels, Joel M. ... Boston, MA
Sen, Amitabha ... Oakland, CA
Sen, Amitabha, Law Offices of ... Oakland, CA
Sen, Dev R. ... New York, NY
Sen, Merle ... Kaneohe, HI
Sen, Natasha ... San Francisco, CA
Sen, Rupa ... Stamford, CT
Sen, Sudakshina ... New York, NY
Sena, Barbara A. ... Fresno, CA
Sena, Cheryl A. ... San Francisco, CA
Sena, Claude S. ... Santa Fe, NM
Sena, F. Stanley ... Portland, OR
Sena, Francesca M. ... New York, NY
Sena, Jeffery L. ... Garden City, NY
Sena, Joseph A., Jr. ... New York, NY
Sena, Joseph A., Jr. ... White Plains, NY
Sena, Joseph J., Jr. ... Piscataway, NJ
Sena, Louis T. ... Coral Gables, FL
Sena, Michael B. ... Upper Saddle River, NJ
New York, NY
Sena, Robynn ... Albuquerque, NM
Sena, Staychia R. ... Costa Mesa, CA
Senac, Jean E., Jr. ... New Orleans, LA
Senaga, Gary K. ... Honolulu, HI
Senak, Mark N. ... Chicago, IL
Senal, James F. ... San Francisco, CA
Senander, Robert M. ... Department of the Air Force, Office of the Judge Advocate General, GV
Senape, James V., Jr. ... Freeland, PA
Senator, Stuart N. ... Los Angeles, CA
Senatore, Charles V. ... Miami, FL
Sencak, John L. ... Pittsburgh, PA
Sencer, Joel ... Gainesville, FL
Sencer, Nicholas M. ... Portland, OR
Sencer, Robert D. ... Torrance, CA
Sencer, Stephen D. ... Atlanta, GA
Senchak, Marlisa L. ... Washington, DC
Sencindiver, Michael V. ... Riverton, NJ
Senda, Trudy K. ... Lihue, HI
Sendak, Rominger & Stanko ... Crown Point, IN
Sendak, Theodore L. ... Crown Point, IN
Sendak, Timothy R. ... Crown Point, IN
Sendar, Michael D. ... Washington, DC
Sendek, Bruce L. ... Detroit, MI
Sendek, Carole Ann ... Royal Oak, MI
Sendek, Kristine L. ... Washington, DC
Sendek, Martin J. ... Department Of Veterans Affairs, Office of the General Counsel, GV
Sendelbach, Karen S. ... Ann Arbor, MI
Sender, Darin Ann ... Phoenix, AZ
Sender, Harvey ... Denver, CO
Sender, Jane Nothmann ... Boston, MA
Sender, Jennifer M. ... Chicago, IL
Sender, Marianne P. ... South Orange, NJ
Sender, R. Scott ... Oak Forest, IL
Sender, Stuart D. ... New York, NY
Sender & Wasserman, P.C. ... Denver, CO
Senderowitz, Stephen J. ... Chicago, IL
Senders, Richard D. ... Portland, OR
Senders, Roger S. ... Los Angeles, CA
Sendik, J. Richard ... Milwaukee, WI
Sendler, Robert B. ... Juno Beach, FL
Sendor, Benjamin B. ... Durham, NC
Sendor, Tracy M. ... Buffalo, NY
Sendowski, Michael H. ... Los Angeles, CA
Sendra, Maria ... San Diego, CA
Sendroff & Associates, P.C. ... New York, NY
Sendroff, Mark D. ... New York, NY
Sendrovitz, Howard M. ... New York, NY
Sendrow, Susan G. ... Phoenix, AZ
Sendrow, W. Mark ... Phoenix, AZ
Sendry, Douglas J. ... Ravenna, OH
Sendukas, Ronny ... Los Angeles, CA
Sendyk, Karen B. ... New York, NY
Sendziak, Jeffrey C. ... Buffalo, NY
Sendziak, Steven J., Jr. ... Chicago, IL
Sendziak, Walter T. ... Buffalo, NY
Seneca, Anthony J. ... Washington, PA
Seneca, Debbie O'Dell ... Washington, PA
Seneca, Mark W. ... Menlo Park, CA
Seneca, Van C. ... Lake Charles, LA
Senecal, Barbara M. ... Boston, MA
Senecal, Ernest ... Springfield, MA
Senecal, H. Jess ... Pasadena, CA

Senecal, Richard P. .... Atchison, KS
Leavenworth, KS
Senecal, Scott C. .... New York, NY
Senecal, Theodore F. .... Dublin, OH
Senechal, Alice R. .... Grand Forks, ND
Senechal, Jack S. .... Plainsboro, NJ
Senechalle, Robert E., Jr. .... Forest Park, IL
Seneczko, Alan E. .... Milwaukee, WI
Seneczko, John P. .... Calumet City, IL
Seneczko Law Offices, S.C.
Milwaukee, WI
Seneczko, Stacey L. .... Waukegan, IL
Seneff, Gregory E., Sr. .... Nashville, TN
Seneker, Carl J. (Kim), II
San Francisco, CA
Seneker, Mark .... Boulder, CO
Denver, CO
Senen, Sanford .... Pasadena, CA
Sener, Charles G.
Department Of Veterans Affairs,
Board of Veterans Appeals, GV
Sener, Martin C. .... Chicago, IL
Senerius, Gordon A. .... Anderson, SC
Senerote, Leonard A. .... Dallas, TX
Senesac, Sara J. .... Birmingham, AL
Senescu, Gerald J. .... Skokie, IL
Senescu, James D. .... Spokane, WA
Senescu, Stuart .... Highland Park, IL
Senesky, Kurt G. .... Morristown, NJ
Senet, Theodore L. .... Los Angeles, CA
Senette, Thomas C. .... Franklin, LA
Senezhak, Diana M. .... New York, NY
Senf, Chester G., Jr. .... Orlando, FL
Senff, Linda Caster .... Aurora, NE
Senff, Mark D. .... Columbus, OH
Senft, Janet M. .... Mendham, NJ
Senft, John L. .... Hanover, PA
York, PA
Senft, Lavere C. .... York, PA
Senft, Mitchell F. .... Cortlandt Manor, NY
Senft, Scott J. .... Dania, FL
Senft, William W. .... Washington, DC
Senftle, Patrick G. .... Washington, DC
Senftleben, Richard A. .... Columbia, MD
Senftner, Gloria M. .... Roseville, CA
Seng, Lauren M. .... Irvine, CA
Seng, Michael J. .... Fresno, CA
Seng, Michael P. .... Chicago, IL
Seng, Robert A. .... Minneapolis, MN
Senger, Bernard G., Jr. .... Somerville, NJ
Senger, Charles J. .... Lansing, MI
Senger, Dave F. .... Minneapolis, MN
Senger, James D. .... Washington, DC
Senger, Jeffrey M. .... Department of Justice,
Civil Rights Division, GV
Senger, Sara G. .... McKinleyville, CA
Senger, Theodore P. .... San Francisco, CA
Senger, Thomas L. .... Hoboken, NJ
Senger, William Nolan .... Somerville, NJ
Senghas, Robert E. .... Burlington, VT
Senghor, Sharon White .... New York, NY
Senglaub, Leslie M. .... Buffalo, NY
Rochester, NY
Sengstack, Warren G. .... Prince Frederick, MD
Sengstock, James W. .... West Allis, WI
SenGupta, P. Moni .... Washington, DC
Senhauser, William B. .... Toledo, OH
Senica, John L. .... Chicago, IL
Senical, John J., Jr. .... Orlando, FL
Senich, Charles F. .... Cheshire, CT
Senich, George A. .... New York, NY
Senich, Jack .... Cheshire, CT
Senich, Kevin J. M. .... Cleveland, OH
Senie, Alan H. .... Westport, CT
Senie, Allyson L. .... Department of Commerce,
Office of the General Counsel, GV
Senie, Christopher G. .... Westport, CT
Senie, Kathryn C. .... Norwalk, CT
Senie, Stephen R. .... New York, NY
Senie, Stock & LaChance, P.C.
Westport, CT
Senio, Paul P. .... Seattle, WA
Senio, Ronald M. .... New York, NY
Senior, Brett W. .... Conshohocken, PA
Senior, Christopher Glenn .... Manhasset, NY
Senior, David A. .... Los Angeles, CA
Senior, Howard B., III .... Miami, FL
Senior, James R. .... North Reading, MA
Senior, Julian G. .... Indianapolis, IN
Senior, Justin Michael .... Boca Raton, FL
Senior, M. Victoria Pangonis
Conshohocken, PA
Senior, Mark M. .... Los Angeles, CA
Senior, Milnor H., (P.C.) .... Evergreen, CO
Senior, Norman A. .... New York, NY
Senior, Rona E. .... New York, NY
Senior, Steven T. .... Morristown, NJ
Senior, Teresa R. .... Santa Monica, CA
Senk, Neil J. .... Highland Park, IL
Senkbeil, Donna J. .... Augusta, ME
Senkbeil, Martha L. .... New York, NY
Senkel, David P. .... Hillsboro, MO
Senkel, Tara Lyn .... New York, NY
Senker, Linda E. .... Horsham, PA
Senker, Richard C. .... Norristown, PA
Senkfor, Burton Mark .... Beverly Hills, CA
Senko, Ronald J. .... Woodville, MS
Senkow, Allan A. .... Van Nuys, CA
Senkowski, R. Michael .... Washington, DC
Senkus, Mary E. .... Minneapolis, MN
Senn, Charles L. .... Toledo, OH
Senn, Charles S. .... Thorp, WI
Senn, Craig R. .... Atlanta, GA
Senn, David F. .... Dickinson, ND
Senn, John E. .... Granville, OH
Senn, Kenneth A. .... LaVeta, CO
Senn, Kevin J. .... San Francisco, CA
Senn, Laurence V., Jr. .... New York, NY
Senn Lewis & Visciano, P.C. .... Denver, CO
Senn, Lisa R. .... Newberry, SC
Senn, M. Brooks .... Louisville, KY
Senn, M. Thurman .... Louisville, KY
Senn, Mara V.J. .... Washington, DC
Senn, Mark A. .... Denver, CO
Senn Palumbo Meulemans, LLP
Irvine, CA
San Diego, CA
San Francisco, CA
Reno, NV
Senn, Sandra J. .... Charleston, SC
Senn, Stephen R. .... Lakeland, FL
Lake Wales, FL
Winter Haven, FL
Senna, James P. .... Olympia, WA
Senna, Joseph J. .... Winchester, MA
Senna, Rocco F. .... Newark, NJ
Senne, Terry A. H. .... Oakland, CA
Senneff, Donald G. .... Des Moines, IA
Senneff Kelly, A Professional Corporation
Santa Rosa, CA
Senneff, Michael D. .... Santa Rosa, CA
Senneff, Thomas C. .... Iowa City, IA
Senneff, Thomas H., Law Offices of
Fulton, IL
Sennello, Carol Anne .... Chicago, IL
Sennello, Julie A. .... Chicago, IL
Sennello, Robert E. .... Elizabeth, NJ
Sennello, Shereen A. .... Bridgewater, NJ
Senner, Gary .... Chicago, IL
Senner, Geo. F., Jr. .... Lukeville, AZ
Senner, Sandra .... Gretna, LA
Sennet, Charles J. .... Chicago, IL
Sennett & Duncan .... Broken Bow, NE
Sennett, James A. .... Twinsburg, OH
Sennett, James C. .... Cleveland, OH
Sennett, John O. .... Broken Bow, NE
Sennett, Jonathan Ross .... New York, NY
Sennett, Mari Ann Connolly
New York, NY
Sennett, Michael .... Chicago, IL
Sennett, Nancy J. .... Milwaukee, WI
Sennett, Nancy M. .... Erie, PA
Sennett, Peter H. .... Department of the Navy,
Office of the Judge Advocate General, GV
Sennett, Richard S. .... Northbrook, IL
Sennett, Sandra .... Laguna Hills, CA
Sennett, T. Scott .... Ashland, KY
Sennett, Thomas E. .... Cherry Hill, NJ
Paoli, PA
Philadelphia, PA
Sennett, Timothy M. .... Erie, PA
Sennett, William C. .... Erie, PA
Sennett, William L., III .... Miamisburg, OH
Senney, Jeffrey S. .... Dayton, OH
Senniger, Powers, Leavitt & Roedel
St. Louis, MO
Senning, John L. .... Essex, CT
Senning & Rieder .... Essex, CT
Sennott, Andrea L. .... Exeter, NH
Sennott, John R., Jr. .... Cambridge, MA
Sennott, Justine McWilliams
Riverwoods, IL
Seno, John J. .... Chicago, IL
Senofaub, Leslie M. .... Rochester, NY
Senoff, David S. .... Philadelphia, PA
Senoff, Ira M. .... Somerville, NJ
Senopoulos, Peter A. .... Boston, MA
Senor, Robert .... Summerland Key, FL
Sens, John D. .... Minneapolis, MN
Sens, Joseph H.
Department of Housing and Urban
Development, GV
Sens, Rachel Ann .... Washington, DC
Sensabaugh, Don R., Jr. .... Charleston, WV
Sensale, Jo-Ann R. .... Bridgeport, CT
Westport, CT
Sensale, Joseph J. .... New Haven, CT
Sensale, Michele D. .... Farmington, CT
Sensale, Robert B. .... New York, NY
Sensale, Robert N. .... New Haven, CT
Sensale & Sensale .... New Haven, CT
Sensenbrenner, E. Paige .... New Orleans, LA
Sensenbrenner, Eric B. .... Washington, DC
Sensenbrenner, F. James, Jr. .... Brookfield, WI
Sensenbrenner, F. Joseph .... Neenah, WI
Sensenbrenner, F. Joseph, Jr. .... Madison, WI
Senseney, David A. .... Denver, CO
Senseney, Hilda A. .... Palo Alto, CA
Sensenich, Ila Jeanne .... Pittsburgh, PA
Sensenich, Jan M.
White River Junction, VT
Sensenig, Christine R.
West Palm Beach, FL
Sensenig, David J. .... Richmond, VA
Sensenig, Lana Smith .... Atlanta, GA
Senser, Karen L. .... Philadelphia, PA
Sensing, Benjamin M. .... Nashville, TN
Senske, Eric J. .... Dallas, TX
Senske, Kurt M. .... Austin, TX
Sensky, Robert S. .... Hazleton, PA
Sensky, Shawn A. .... New Castle, PA
Sensney, Maloy .... Prosser, WA
Sensny, John S. .... Garden City, NY
Sensoli, J. Albert .... Dearborn, MI
Sensoli, J. Albert, P.C. .... Dearborn, MI
Sensor, Michael L. .... Wilmington, DE
Senstad, Allen .... Alexandria, MN
Sentance, Michael J. .... Concord, MA
Sentell, C. Sherburne, Jr. .... Minden, LA
Sentell, Charles E. .... Jackson, MS
Sentell, Hutton W. .... Shreveport, LA
Sentell, R. Perry, III .... Augusta, GA
Sentell, Sherburne .... Minden, LA
Sentelle, David B.
United States Court Of Appeals District Of
Columbia Circuit, GV
Senter and Bowden .... Everett, WA
Senter, Caren A. .... Hartford, CT
Senter, David A. .... Greensboro, NC
Senter, Donald A. .... Everett, WA
Senter Goldfarb & Rice, L.L.C.
Denver, CO
Senter, Jack .... Fuquay-Varina, NC
Senter, James D., III .... Humboldt, TN
Senter, James Larry .... Louisburg, NC
Senter, Jas. C., Jr. .... New Orleans, LA
Senter, Jeff .... Austin, TX
Senter, Jeff, P.C., The Law Offices of
Austin, TX
Senter, Julian F. .... Laverock, PA
Senter, Kathryn Hibbs .... Madisonville, KY
Senter, Lyonel T., Jr. .... Aberdeen, MS
Senter, Mark S. .... Metairie, LA
Senter, Meredith S., Jr. .... Washington, DC
Senter, Richard H.
Grosse Pointe Woods, MI
Senter & Stephenson .... Fuquay-Varina, NC
Senter, Susan Hoffstein .... McLean, VA
Senter, Thomas C. .... Woodbridge, NJ
Senter, William L. .... Fayetteville, NC
Senter, William Lee .... Denver, CO
Senterfitt, Barry R. .... Austin, TX
Senterfitt, Childress & Shook .... San Saba, TX
Senterfitt, Diane B. .... Austin, TX
Senterfitt, Donald T. .... Orlando, FL
Senterfitt, Jack H. .... Atlanta, GA
Senterfitt, Reuben .... San Saba, TX
Senterfitt, Sarah Payne .... Austin, TX
Sentilles, Edward A., Jr. .... New Orleans, LA
Sentilles, Irwin F., III .... Dallas, TX
Sentilles, Shawn David .... Belle Chasse, LA
Sentivan, Jennifer R. .... Roseland, NJ
Senti-Willis, Anne E. .... San Jose, CA
Sentler, Steven M. .... Boston, MA
Sentman, Frederick J. .... Libertyville, IL
Sentman, Ronald G. .... Indianapolis, IN
Sentner, Fred J. .... Canonsburg, PA
Sentner, James J., Jr. .... Houston, TX
Sentner, Kevin A. .... Lady Lake, FL
Sentner, Kevin A., P.A. .... Lady Lake, FL
Sentner, Robert C. .... New York, NY
Senton, Robert E. .... Tallahassee, FL
Senton, Robert E., P.A. .... Tallahassee, FL
Sents, Steven A. .... Columbus Junction, IA
Senturia, Harris A. .... Cleveland, OH
Senty, Richard D. .... St. Petersburg, FL
Sentz, Barbara A. .... Columbus, OH
Sentz, John A., Jr. .... Columbus, OH
Sentz, Lester C. .... Milwaukee, WI
Senungetuk, Vivian .... Anchorage, AK
Carmichael, CA
Senuty, Peter J. .... Glendale, CA
Senville, Wayne M. .... Burlington, VT
Senyk, George R.
Department Of Veterans Affairs,
Board of Veterans Appeals, GV
Senyk, Waldemar B. .... Fergus Falls, MN
Senzel, Alyssa T. .... Washington, DC
Senzel, Bruce D. .... New York, NY
Senzel, David S.
Federal Communications Commission,
Office of the General Counsel, GV
Senzel, Martin L. .... New York, NY
Senzer, Paul H. .... Mineola, NY
Senzer, Richard Adam .... New York, NY
Senzer, Robert Owen .... New York, NY
Senzer, Stephanie G. .... Uniondale, NY
Senzon, Leonard J. .... New York, NY
Seo, David H. .... Los Angeles, CA
Seo, Howard H. .... Los Angeles, CA
Seo, Ik Hyun .... Chicago, IL
Seo, Sungjean .... New York, NY
Seo, Susan .... New York, NY
Seo, Timothy K. .... Houston, TX
Seoh, Thomas C. .... Baltimore, MD
Seone, Richard F. .... Los Angeles, CA
Sepaniak, Stephen .... Morristown, NJ
Sepanik, Damian V. .... Chicago, IL
Separ, Sharon .... Treasury Department,
Bureau of Alcohol, Tobacco and Firearms,
GV
Separk, W. Allen .... Canton, GA
Cartersville, GA
Separk, W. Allen .... Marietta, GA
Sepassi, Steven M. .... Encino, CA
Sepcich, Michael S. .... New Orleans, LA
Sepe, Alfonso C. .... North Bay Village, FL
Sepe, Dino G. .... Tacoma, WA
Sepe, Lisa K. .... Westminster, CA
Sepe, Robert J. .... Riverside, CA
Sepeda, Joe F. .... Corpus Christi, TX
Sepehri, John .... Dallas, TX
Sepenuk, Norman .... Portland, OR
Sepenuk, Norman, P.C. .... Portland, OR
Sepesi, Jeffrey A. .... Chicago, IL
Sepesy, Joseph G. .... Midland, MI
Sephton, Gregory B. .... New York, NY
Sepic, Douglas S. .... Connellsville, PA
Sepikas, Joseph P. .... Granada Hills, CA
Sepiol, Christina .... Chicago, IL
Sepkowitz, Irv .... Los Angeles, CA
Sepkowitz, Jerome S. .... Oklahoma City, OK
Sepkowitz, Joanna S. .... Oklahoma City, OK
Seplak, Mark J. .... Chicago, IL
Sepler, Harvey J. .... Miami, FL
Sepler, Richard M. .... Miami, FL
Seplow, Ira F. .... Brooklyn, NY
Seplow, Michael D. .... Venice, CA
Seplow, Philip A. .... Phoenix, AZ
Seplowe, Jonathan .... Jackson Heights, NY
Seplowitz, Betty .... Scarsdale, NY
Seplowitz, Rena C. .... Huntington, NY
Seplowitz, Terry F. .... New York, NY
Seplowitz, William S. .... New York, NY
Seps, Donald J. .... Daytona Beach, FL
Sept, Marcia Kay Good .... Billings, MT
Septembre, E. Thomas .... Miami Shores, FL
Septimus, Judah I. .... Brooklyn, NY
Septimus, Susan S. .... Houston, TX
Septowski, Charles D. .... River Rouge, MI
Sepucha, Robert C., Jr. .... Menlo Park, CA
Sepulvado-Ramos, Lee .... San Juan, PR
Sepulveda, Aristides .... Bronx, NY
Sepulveda, Carlos M. .... El Paso, TX
Sepulveda, Cheryl L. .... Chicago, IL
Sepulveda, Eloy .... Fort Worth, TX
Sepulveda, Irving .... Bronx, NY
Sepulveda, Jaime E. .... Mayaguez, PR
Sepulveda, Jose G. .... Miami, FL
Sepulveda & Sepulveda .... Bronx, NY
Sepulveda-Hambor, Silvia
Department of Justice,
Environment and Natural Resources
Division, GV
Sequeda-Torres, Vicente A. .... San Juan, PR
Sequeira, Manuel A., Jr. .... Mahopac, NY
Sequeira, Monisha M. .... San Francisco, CA
Sequeira, Patrick J. .... Los Angeles, CA
Sequeira, Paul D. .... Martinez, CA
Sequeira, Richard F. .... Redwood City, CA
Sequeira, Rodolfo .... San Juan, PR
Sequin, Jane M. .... Marinette, WI
Ser, Julius .... Coral Gables, FL
Ser, Lillian A. .... Fort Lauderdale, FL
Seraden, Rick .... Foster City, CA
Seradzky, Edward S. .... Bloomfield, NJ
Serafano, Donald B. .... Laguna Hills, CA
Serafin, Catherine J. .... Washington, DC
Serafin, Henry A., II .... Houston, TX
Serafin, Kenneth J. .... Harrisburg, PA
Serafin, Robert E. .... Westmont, IL
Serafin, Russell B. .... Houston, TX
Serafine, Mary Louise .... Los Angeles, CA
Serafini, Cynthia A. St. Onge
West Hartford, CT
Serafini, Evelina M. .... Los Angeles, CA
Serafini, John R. .... Salem, MA
Serafini, John R., Jr. .... Salem, MA
Serafini, Joseph J. .... Wayne, NJ
Serafini, Joseph L. .... Boston, MA
Serafini, Linda A. .... Boston, MA
Serafini, Lisa J. .... Merced, CA
Serafini, Louis J. .... Wayne, NJ
Serafini, Phillip S. .... Southfield, MI
Serafini, Purdy, DiNardo & Wells
Quincy, MA
Serafini, Richard A. .... Department of Justice,
Criminal Division, GV
Serafini, Serafini, Darling & Correnti, L.L.P.
Salem, MA
Serafini-Smith, Beth A. .... Merrillville, IN
Serafino, Barbara Gomes .... Staten Island, NY
Serafino, James .... New York, NY
Serafino, John A. .... Rutland, VT
Seraile, Janette L. .... New York, NY
Seran, Alonzo B. .... Minneapolis, MN
Serangeli, William B. .... Des Moines, IA
Serano, Andrew .... Orlando, FL
Seraphin, Leonard J. .... St. Charles, IL
Seraphin, Scott L. .... St. Charles, IL
Seraphin & Seraphin, Ltd. .... St. Charles, IL
Serapion, Margarita .... San Juan, PR
Serata, Daniel E. .... Union City, NJ
Serata, Samuel J. .... Bridgeton, NJ
Seratti, Donald V. .... San Jose, CA
Seravalli, Mary Ellen .... Sterling, VA
Seraydar, June C. .... Boston, MA
Seraydarian, Paul .... El Segundo, CA
Serazin & Deery .... Elyria, OH
Serazin, Scott F. .... Elyria, OH
Serbagi, Christopher .... New York, NY
Serbalik, Val M. .... Mechanicville, NY
Serban, Daniel E. .... Fort Wayne, IN
Serban, Eugene .... New York, NY
Serbanic, Christine L. .... Philadelphia, PA
Serbaroli, Francis J. .... New York, NY
Serber, Daniel J. .... Miami, FL
Serber, Konschak & Jaquett LLP
Atlantic City, NJ
Ocean City, NJ
Serber, Marcie A. .... New York, NY
Serber, Peter M. .... Potomac, MD
Serber, Seymour .... Brooklyn, NY
Serber, William R. .... Ocean City, NJ
Serbes, Filiz A. .... Treasury Department,
Internal Revenue Service, GV
Serbia, George W., III .... Santa Ana, CA
Serbin, David J. .... Washington, DC
Serbin, Ellen R. .... Long Beach, CA
Serbin, Howard .... Santa Ana, CA
Serbin, Jonathan P. .... New York, NY
Serbin, Neal D. .... Santa Barbara, CA
Serbin, Richard M. .... Altoona, PA
Serbin, Richard S. .... West Trenton, NJ
Serbin, Todd A. .... Miami, FL
Serbinowski, Paul A. .... Cleveland, OH
Serblin, Forrest D. .... Peoria, IL
Serby, Alan E. .... Atlanta, GA
Serby, Anne M. .... Long Beach, NY
Sercarz, Maurice H. .... New York, NY
Sercevich, Roa Rado .... Royal Oak, MI
Serchuk, Ivan .... White Plains, NY
Serchuk & Zelermyer, LLP
New York, NY
White Plains, NY
Serck, Duane L. .... Peoria, IL
Serck, Steven L. .... Des Moines, IA
Sercombe, Timothy J. .... Portland, OR
Sercovich, Terry W. .... Belle Chasse, LA
Sercovich, Valeria M. .... New Orleans, LA
Serdahely, Douglas J. .... Anchorage, AK
Serdar, George R. .... Minneapolis, MN

Sessions, Jefferson B., III .... Mobile, AL
Sessions, John T. .... Seattle, WA
Sessions, Mark G. .... San Antonio, TX
Sessions, O. Thomas .... South Windsor, CT
Sessions, Peter S. .... Los Angeles, CA
Sessions, Rex L. .... Chicago, IL
Sessions & Sessions, LLP
San Antonio, TX
Sessions, Steven E. .... Albuquerque, NM
Sessions, Susan W. .... Dallas, TX
Sessions, Thomas Scott .... Whiteville, NC
Sessions, Vernon K. .... Denver, CO
Sessions, William C., III .... Memphis, TN
Sessions, William K., III .... Burlington, VT
Sessions, William Lewis .... San Antonio, TX
Sessions, William Steele .... San Antonio, TX
Sessions-Cooley, Robin .... Cheyenne, WY
Sessler, Albert L., Jr. .... Kettering, OH
Sessler, Cashton L. .... Seattle, WA
Sessler, Cashton L., P.S. .... Seattle, WA
Sessler, James N. .... Laconia, NH
Sessler, Jennifer .... New York, NY
Sessler, Joshua Brian .... New York, NY
Sessler, Linda Rowland .... Atlanta, GA
Sessler, Paul .... New York, NY
Sessoms, A. Kelly, III .... Biloxi, MS
Pascagoula, MS
Sessoms & Associates, P.A. .... Durham, NC
Sessoms, B. M. .... Durham, NC
Sessoms, D. Edison .... Bay Pines, FL
Sessoms, Faison T., Jr. .... Minneapolis, MN
Sessoms, Lawrence R. .... Detroit, MI
Sessoms, Philip C. .... Williamsburg, VA
Sessoms, Stuart M., Jr. .... Durham, NC
Sessoms, Toni L. .... Mount Pleasant, MI
Sessoms, Toni L., P.C. .... Mount Pleasant, MI
Sessoms, William H., Jr. .... Whiteville, NC
Sessums, Craig R. .... Jackson, MS
Sessums, David M. .... Vicksburg, MS
Sessums, Mark A. .... Bartow, FL
Sessums, Mason & Black, P.A.
Tampa, FL
Sessums, Robert B. .... Jackson, MS
Sessums, Stephen W. .... Tampa, FL
Sessums, T. Terrell .... Tampa, FL
Sestak, Christine Irish .... Dallas, TX
Sestak, John G., Jr. .... Phoenix, AZ
Sestak, Regina M. .... Pittsburgh, PA
Sestak, Richard J. .... Los Angeles, CA
Sestak, William G. .... New Port Richey, FL
Sestanovich, Thomas R. .... Los Angeles, CA
Sestero, Robert F., Jr. .... Spokane, WA
Sesti, Robert A. .... New York, NY
Sestifo, Donna M. .... Red Bank, NJ
Sesto, Melinda L. .... San Francisco, CA
Sestric, Anthony J. .... St. Louis, MO
Sestric Law Firm, The .... St. Louis, MO
Sestric, Philip M. .... Ballwin, MO
Seta, Lesli R. .... Atlanta, GA
Setaro, Christopher C. .... Danbury, CT
Setaro, Mark S. .... Trenton, NJ
Setaro, Renu M. .... Richmond, VA
Setchel, Jerry A. .... Tampa, FL
Setchell, Donald E. .... Wichita, KS
Setchell, Larry .... Seattle, WA
Setchen, Jason A. .... Coral Gables, FL
Setel, Eugene M. .... Buffalo, NY
Setel, Susan W. .... Buffalo, NY
Seten, Kimberly Houser .... Kansas City, MO
Seter, Kim J. .... Greenwood Village, CO
Setera, Gerald V. .... Orange, CA
Seth, Donald F. .... Sonoma, CA
Seth Intellectual Property Law Offices
Denver, CO
Seth, J. Cabot .... Sumter, SC
Seth, Lynn S. .... Charlotte, NC
Seth, Rashmi .... New York, NY
Seth, Sandeep .... Denver, CO
Sethi, Akash D. .... Dallas, TX
Sethi, Dev K. .... Tucson, AZ
Sethi, Neil K. .... Columbus, OH
Sethi-Gulati, Rama .... Carmichael, CA
Sethna, Farhad B. .... Akron, OH
Sethness, Clifford D. .... Seattle, WA
Sethuraman, Anand .... Los Angeles, CA
Setley, Michael A. .... Reading, PA
Setliff, C. Stephen .... Richmond, VA
Setliff, Carter A. .... Conyers, GA
Setlik, Stanley J., Jr. .... North Tonawanda, NY
Setlin, Howard A. .... Miami, FL
Setlock, Edw. J. .... Farmington Hills, MI
Setlow, M. Greg .... Mesa, AZ
Setnes, Ann M. .... Minneapolis, MN
Setness, Jeffrey B. .... Stockton, CA
Setnor, Nikki M. .... Miami, FL
Seto, Fred .... San Francisco, CA
Seto, Karen B. .... Los Angeles, CA
Seto, Larissa M. .... Pleasanton, CA
Seto, Raymond J. .... Torrance, CA
Seto, Robert M.M.
Department of Agriculture,
Board of Contract Appeals, GV
Seto, Shuilun .... Boston, MA
Seto, Stephen C. .... Los Angeles, CA
Seto, Theodore P. .... Los Angeles, CA
Seton, Charles B. .... Larchmont, NY
Seton, Kent E. .... Los Angeles, CA
Setrakian, Berge .... New York, NY
Setrakian, Deborah A. .... Fresno, CA
Setrakian, Philip S. .... Fresno, CA
Setren, Janice Morrison .... Baltimore, MD
Setright, John C. .... Syracuse, NY
Setright & Longstreet, L.L.P.
Syracuse, NY
Setser, Henry R. .... Kansas City, MO
Setser, Jennifer A. .... Weatherford, TX
Setser, Tamra Wilson .... Kansas City, MO

Sett, David .... Department of Transportation,
Federal Highway Administration, GV
Settana, Daniel R., Jr. .... Columbia, SC
Settanni, Andrea M. .... Washington, DC
Settano, Marianne .... Roseville, MN
Sette Bonadies, P.C. .... Hamden, CT
Sette, Fred David .... Hamden, CT
Sette, Joseph Michael, Law Office of
Dublin, CA
Sette, Joseph Michael, Law Office of
Oakland, CA
Stockton, CA
Sette, Louis F. .... Ramsey, NJ
Settecase, Elissa .... New York, NY
Settelmayer, Daniel K. .... Los Angeles, CA
Settembrini, Joel, Jr. .... Jacksonville, FL
Setter, David F. .... Dubuque, IA
Setter, David M. .... Denver, CO
Setter, H. Jay .... Wichita, KS
Setter, Mary L. .... Minneapolis, MN
Setter, Michael J. .... Boulder, CO
Setterberg, Richard A. .... Cincinnati, OH
Setterberg, Richard A., Co., L.P.A., A Legal
Prof. Assn. .... Cincinnati, OH
Setterholm, Jean G. .... Madison, WI
Setterington, Stephanie Rae
Grand Rapids, MI
Setterlund, Jack E. .... Duluth, MN
Setterlund, Timothy A. .... Boca Raton, FL
Settineri, John F. .... New York, NY
Settlage, Steven P. .... Richmond, VA
Settle, Benjamin H. .... Shelton, WA
Settle, Bill .... Muskogee, OK
Settle, Candice A. .... Van Buren, AR
Settle, Charles Walsh, Jr. .... Arlington, TX
Settle, Elizabeth W. .... Charleston, SC
Settle, Eric L. .... Blue Bell, PA
Settle, Harold P. .... Roanoke, VA
Settle, Jane H. .... Department of Agriculture,
Office of the General Counsel, GV
Settle, John D. (Jay), Jr. .... Dallas, TX
Settle, John E., Jr. .... Bossier City, LA
Settle, John M. .... Larned, KS
Settle, John W. .... Fort Smith, AR
Settle & Johnson P.L.L.C. .... Shelton, WA
Settle, Joseph E., III .... Chattanooga, TN
Settle, Landrum and Brook
Fort Gibson, OK
Muskogee, OK
Settle, Lee W. .... Mebane, NC
Settle, Lisa A. .... Muskogee, OK
Settle, Marci Guttentag .... New York, NY
Settle, Norbert L. .... Phoenix, AZ
Settle, Norval D.
Department Of Health And Human Services,
GV
Settle, Peveril O., III .... Dallas, TX
Settle & Pou, P.C. .... Dallas, TX
Settle, R. Daniel, Jr. .... Fort Worth, TX
Settle, Richard L. .... Seattle, WA
Settle, Stuart W., Jr. .... Richmond, VA
Settle, Susan M. .... Caseyville, IL
Settle, Timothy E. .... Denver, CO
Settle, W. Sydnor .... New York, NY
Settle, W. Vincent, III .... Waycross, GA
Settle, William H. .... Atlanta, GA
Settleman, Irving .... Baltimore, MD
Settlemire, Amy C. .... Fort Myers, FL
Settlemire, R. Craig .... Chester, CA
Settlemire, Roger M. .... Quincy, CA
Settlemyer, A. Frank, III .... Atlanta, GA
Settlemyer, Carl H., III .... Washington, DC
Settlemyer, Steve B. .... Morganton, NC
Settlemyer, William B. .... Charleston, SC
Settler, Richard D. .... Miami, FL
Settles, Barry S. .... Frankfort, KY
Settles, G. Patrick .... Coral Gables, FL
Settles, Jennifer M. .... Phoenix, AZ
Settles, Robert S. .... Antlers, OK
Settles, Ty R. .... Seaside, OR
Settles, William R. .... Omaha, NE
Setton, Eliane R. .... Palo Alto, CA
Setton, Ronit .... New York, NY
Setty, Nagendra .... Atlanta, GA
Setty-Rosevear, Ann .... Vancouver, WA
Setum, Ted R. .... Cudahy, WI
Setwyn, Eugene J. .... Reedsburg, WI
Setzen, Joel A. .... Naperville, IL
Setzer, Beth R. .... Statesville, NC
Setzer, Donna .... Dallas, TX
Setzer, Jon L. .... Nashville, TN
Setzer, Joseph E., Jr. .... Goldsboro, NC
Setzer, Theodore D. .... Phoenix, AZ
Setzer, Wilfred A. .... Rocky Point, NY
Setzke, Raymond W. .... Boise, ID
Setzler, David M. W. .... St. Augustine, FL
Setzler, Edward A. .... Kansas City, MO
Setzler, Nikki G., (P.A.)
West Columbia, SC
Setzler & Scott, P.A. .... Columbia, SC
West Columbia, SC
Seu, Carlton W. M. .... Seattle, WA
Seu, Cynthia Unwin .... Seattle, WA
Seu, Melissa W.L. .... Honolulu, HI
Seubert, Anthony J. .... New York, NY
Seubert, Daniel K. .... Palo Alto, CA
Seubert, Patrick G. .... Neenah, WI
Seubert, Suzanne I. .... Wilmington, DE
Seubert, Timothy T. .... Houston, TX
Seuch, William M. .... Boston, MA
Seuer, Diana R. .... Marlton, NJ
Seufer, Howard E., Jr. .... Parkersburg, WV
Seuferer, Lawrence S. .... Sun Prairie, WI
Seufert, Christopher J. .... Franklin, NH
Seufert, Kenneth A. .... Farmington, MO
Seulean, David P. A. .... Medford, OR
Seung, Stephen K. .... New York, NY
Seuringer, Diana S. .... Astoria, NY

Seurynck, John P. .... Lansing, MI
Seus, Thomas E. .... Philadelphia, PA
Seusy, Paul Bennett .... Nashville, TN
Seuthe, Kathy B. .... Encino, CA
Seutter, Denise .... Bronxville, NY
Sevack, Milton .... Holmdel, NJ
Sevald, Mark D. .... Grand Rapids, MI
Sevarino, Angelo Paul .... Windsor, CT
Sevart, Daniel J. .... Wichita, KS
Sevart, Mark A. .... Derby, KS
Sevart & Sevart .... Wichita, KS
Sevart, Shoko K. .... Wichita, KS
Sevastianos, Noel A. .... St. Louis, MO
Sevcik, Beatrice E. .... New York, NY
Sevcik, Richard L. .... Chicago, IL
Sevcik, Wilma A. .... Cleveland, OH
Sève, Paul R. .... Dallas, TX
Sevekow, Frederick M., Jr. .... Oakland, CA
Sevel, Adam J. .... Baltimore, MD
Sevel, Bernard J. .... Baltimore, MD
Sevel & Sevel, P.A. .... Baltimore, MD
Sevell, Robert D. .... Los Angeles, CA
Sevely, Cynthia A. .... San Jose, CA
Sevely, Vincent C. .... Palo Alto, CA
Sevem, James C. .... St. Louis, MO
Sevener, Kent L. .... New York, NY
Sevenich, Robert J. .... Minneapolis, MN
Sevenish Law Firm, P.C. .... Indianapolis, IN
Sevenish, Randall R. .... Indianapolis, IN
Sever, Daniel C. .... Chehalis, WA
Sever, Dennis A. .... Phoenix, AZ
Sever, Frank, Jr. .... Washington, DC
Sever, Jay Russell .... New Orleans, LA
Sever, Mark J., Jr. .... Philadelphia, PA
Severa, Jos. J. .... Cedar Rapids, IA
Severaid, Ronald H. .... Sacramento, CA
Severance, A. Dale .... Brooklyn, NY
Severance, Burko & Spalter, P.C.
Brooklyn, NY
Severance, Carol M. .... Playa Del Rey, CA
Severance, David S. .... Kezar Falls, ME
Severance, David S., P.A. .... Kezar Falls, ME
Severance, Gregory S. .... Columbus, OH
Severance, Janna R. .... Minneapolis, MN
Severance, Karen B. .... Greenbelt, MD
Severance, Laurence J. .... Seattle, WA
Severance, Phyllis G. .... Burlington, VT
Severance, Sharon K. .... Midland, MI
Severance, Susan C. .... Lafayette, LA
Severance, Thomas L. .... Oceanside, CA
Severe, John T. .... Stillwater, OK
Severens, Eugene .... Walthill, NE
Severin, Gretchen R. .... Anoka, MN
Severin, Linda C. .... Seattle, WA
Severin, Matthew Joseph .... Omaha, NE
Severin, Ringsak & Morrow .... Bismarck, ND
Severin, Steven L. .... Fort Washington, PA
Severin, Thomas R. .... Omaha, NE
Severin, Tim B. .... Santa Ana, CA
Severin, William C. .... Bismarck, ND
Severing, Raymond Leo .... Woodstock, NY
Severini, Carl T. .... Pittsburgh, PA
Severino, John R. .... Baltimore, MD
Severino, Michael R. .... Baltimore, MD
Severinsen, Robert .... Great Meadows, NJ
Severinson, Neil M. .... Cheyenne, WY
Severn, David A. .... Frederick, MD
Severn & O'Connor, P.A. .... Frederick, MD
Severn Jackson, Karen E. .... Troy, MI
Severns Associates .... Indianapolis, IN
Severns, Michael G. .... Denver, CO
Severns, Scott R. .... Indianapolis, IN
Severns, Teresa S. .... Texarkana, TX
Severns, Thomas R. .... Las Vegas, NV
Severns, William C. .... Columbus, OH
Severns, William L. .... Deadwood, SD
Severo, Michael V. .... Los Angeles, CA
Severo, Michael V., A Prof. Corp., Law Offices
of .... Los Angeles, CA
Severovich, Thomas G. .... Cleveland, OH
Severs, Charles A., III .... New York, NY
Severs, Drew H. .... Canton, OH
Severs, Dwight W. .... Titusville, FL
Severs, Eric R. .... Oberlin, OH
Severs, Eric R., Co., L.P.A. .... Oberlin, OH
Severs, Mark B. .... Hanover, NH
Severs, Nancie G. .... Hanover, NH
Severson, Craig Browning .... Kansas City, MO
Severson, Dania M. .... Reno, NV
Severson, Deborah A. .... San Luis Obispo, CA
Severson, Donald S. .... Chicago, IL
Severson, Eric W. .... Topeka, KS
Severson, Gary A. .... Houlton, ME
Severson, Glen A. .... Sioux Falls, SD
Severson, Hand & Nelson, P.A.
Houlton, ME
Severson, Jack O. .... Carlsbad, CA
Severson, James .... San Francisco, CA
Severson, Jerry .... El Paso, TX
Severson, John M. .... Tequesta, FL
West Palm Beach, FL
Severson, Kim A. .... Minneapolis, MN
Severson, Larry S. .... Apple Valley, MN
Severson, Lawrence L. .... Fremont, CA
Severson, Mary L. .... Gainesville, GA
Severson, Nancy J. .... Wheat Ridge, CO
Severson, Robert Conrad .... Madison, WI
Severson, Robert K. .... Hallock, MN
Severson, Robert M. .... Denver, CO
Severson, Sarah B. .... San Antonio, TX
Severson, Sarah Kerr .... Chicago, IL
Severson, Sheldon, Dougherty & Molenda,
P.A. .... Apple Valley, MN
Minneapolis, MN
St. Paul, MN
Severson, Steven L. .... Minneapolis, MN

Severson & Werson, A Professional
Corporation .... Irvine, CA
San Francisco, CA
Severson, William C. .... Seattle, WA
Severt, John .... Rockville, MD
Severt, Katherine Kemp .... Troy, OH
Severt, Todd D. .... Troy, OH
Severtson, Tamara Kettner .... Louisville, KY
Severud, Stephen N. .... Newark, NJ
Severy, Bonita L. .... Irvine, CA
Severy, Karen L. .... New York, NY
Severy, Richard B. .... San Francisco, CA
Severyn, Donna Montano .... Southfield, MI
Severyn, Henry J. .... Tucson, AZ
Severyn, Michael J. .... Detroit, MI
Severyn, Thomas J. .... Flint, MI
Sevey, Jack C. .... Sacramento, CA
Sevey, James M. .... San Mateo, CA
Sevey, Jeffrey .... Sacramento, CA
Sevick, James J. .... Sausalito, CA
Sevier, Amy White .... Indianapolis, IN
Sevier, Charles A. .... Memphis, TN
Sevier, Charles B. .... Irvine, CA
Sevier, Elliot K. .... Auburn, CA
Placerville, CA
Sevier, Elliot K. .... Sacramento, CA
Sevier, Ernest Y. .... San Francisco, CA
Sevier, Francis-Aloysius Charles .... Miami, FL
Sevier, Gail R. .... Memphis, TN
Sevier, Henry C., Jr. .... Tallulah, LA
Sevier, Kirby .... Birmingham, AL
Sevier Law Firm, P.C. .... Memphis, TN
Sevier, Yerger & Bishop .... Tallulah, LA
Sevigny, Mark A. .... Santa Ana, CA
Sevila, Robert E. .... Leesburg, VA
Sevila, Saunders, Huddleston & White
Warrenton, VA
Leesburg, VA
Sevilla, Charles M. .... San Diego, CA
Sevilla, Exequiel Ricardo, Jr. .... Fairfax, VA
Sevilla, Leticia T. .... Vienna, VA
Sevilla, Stanley .... Pacific Palisades, CA
Sevilla, Stanley, A Prof. Law Corp.
Pacific Palisades, CA
Seville, Marci Beth .... San Francisco, CA
Seville, Michael W. .... Anchorage, AK
Seville-Jones, Sandra A. .... Los Angeles, CA
Sevin, Kelley A. .... New Orleans, LA
Sevin, Norman M. .... Coral Gables, FL
Sevin, Richard L. .... Sherman Oaks, CA
Sevinsky, James A. .... Schenectady, NY
Sevrin, Richard M. .... Ocean Township, NJ
Sevush, Ralph .... New York, NY
Sevy, Jerry .... Atlanta, GA
Sew, Arlene L. .... Towson, MD
Sewak, George R. .... Washington, PA
Sewak, Stephanie M. .... Washington, PA
Sewalk, Karen M. .... Columbus, OH
Sewall, Arthur F. .... Salem, NJ
Sewall, Frank B. .... Little Rock, AR
Sewall, Frederick L. .... Needham, MA
Sewall, Geo. O., Jr. .... Ellwood City, PA
Sewall, Grace C. .... Cincinnati, OH
Sewall, Mark V. .... Appleton, WI
Sewall, William D. .... San Mateo, CA
Seward, Ann M. .... St. Louis, MO
Seward, Ann M., & Associates, P.C.
St. Louis, MO
Seward, Bernard L., Jr. .... Department of State,
Office of the Legal Adviser, GV
Seward, David R. .... Gloversville, NY
Seward, Edward C., III .... Chicago, IL
Seward, George C. .... New York, NY
Seward, Gordon B. .... Akron, OH
Seward, J. Wesley .... Naples, FL
Seward, Jon M. .... Department of Justice,
Civil Rights Division, GV
Seward & Kissel LLP .... Washington, DC
New York, NY
Seward, Larry E. .... Tulsa, OK
Seward, Lewis M. .... Bay City, MI
Seward, Matthew A. .... Detroit, MI
Seward, Michael R. .... Miami, FL
Seward, Perry .... Taunton, MA
Seward, Peter G. .... Bay City, MI
Seward, Renata .... Chicago, IL
Seward, Robert S. .... Rockville Centre, NY
Seward & Seward .... Rockville Centre, NY
Seward, Steven T. .... Seattle, WA
Seward, T. Joseph .... Livonia, MI
Seward, Tally & Piggott, P.C.
Bay City, MI
Seward, Wade A. .... Cheshire, CT
Seward, William E. .... Rockville Centre, NY
Sewards, Frederick A. .... Columbus, OH
Sewell & Anderson .... Dallas, TX
Sewell and Associates .... Jeffersonville, IN
Louisville, KY
Sewell, Ben G. .... Houston, TX
Sewell, Bernadette D. .... Boston, MA
Sewell, Bruce .... Tahlequah, OK
Sewell, Cameron Dee, (P.C.) .... Dallas, TX
Sewell, Catherine M. .... Louisville, KY
Sewell, Charles T. .... Belvidere, IL
Sewell, Cindy K. .... Topeka, KS
Sewell, Craig J. .... Allegan, MI
Sewell, David J. .... Austin, TX
Sewell, Doris Kerr .... Birmingham, AL
Sewell and Forbis .... Decatur, TX
Sewell, Frank R. .... Oklahoma City, OK
Sewell, G. Bruce .... Wagoner, OK
Sewell, George Q. .... Norcross, GA
Sewell, Gerald L. .... Houston, TX
Sewell, Gerald L., P.C. .... Houston, TX
Sewell, Harry B., Jr. .... Kensington, MD
Sewell, Harry B., Jr., Chartered
Kensington, MD
Sewell, Henry F., Jr. .... Atlanta, GA

Sewell, J. Banks, III ... Birmingham, AL
Sewell, J. Harold ... Fort Worth, TX
Sewell, J. Roger ... Melrose Park, IL
Sewell, Jeffrey M. ... Birmingham, AL
Sewell, Jerry T. ... Newport Beach, CA
Sewell, John L. ... Orlando, FL
Sewell, John M. ... Margate City, NJ
Sewell, John R., Law Offices of ... Dallas, TX
Sewell, John T. ... Hood River, OR
Sewell, Joseph S. F. ... Utica, NY
Sewell, Kay D. ... Oklahoma City, OK
Sewell, Kevin L. ... Dallas, TX
Sewell & Krueger ... Sacramento, CA
Sewell, Larry M., (P.C.) ... St. Louis, MO
Sewell, Laurie Rusk ... Stuart, FL
Sewell, Lowell L. ... San Antonio, TX
Sewell, Margaret A. ... Chicago, IL
Sewell, Mark S. ... Sacramento, CA
Sewell, Martha L. ... Raleigh, NC
Sewell, Michael ... Fort Worth, TX
Sewell, P. Jefferson ... Tucker, GA
Sewell, Paul C. ... Dallas, TX
Sewell, Peter J. ... Louisville, KY
Sewell, Randall L. ... Oklahoma City, OK
Sewell, Raymond K., Jr. ... Birmingham, MI
Sewell, R. J. "Jim", Jr. ... Helena, MT
Sewell, Scott W. ... Oklahoma City, OK
Sewell, Sheila J. ... Oklahoma City, OK
Sewell, Stephen G. ... Leesburg, FL
Sewell, Steven H. ... Westbury, NY
Sewell, Steven H., P.C. ... Westbury, NY
Sewell, Susan E. ... Orlando, FL
Sewell, Ted L. ... Houston, TX
Sewell, Terri A. ... New York, NY
Sewell, Travis Taylor ... Portland, OR
Sewell, V. Lawrence ... Plano, TX
Sewell, Valerie K. ... Chicago, IL
Sewell, W. Curtis ... Alexandria, VA
Sewell, W. Hill ... Birmingham, AL
Sewell, William H. ... Kingsville, MD
Sewell, Wm. H., II ... Maysville, KY
Sewell-Wood, Jean E. ... New Albany, IN
Seweryn, Nancy ... Philadelphia, PA
Sewinsky, Henry E. ... Sharon, PA
Sewitch, Nicholas F. ... New Brunswick, NJ
Sewright, Michael W. ... Anchorage, AK
Sexauer, Edward J. ... Department of Labor, Office of the Solicitor, GV
Sexauer, Scott R. ... Springfield, VA
Sexauer, Stephen J. ... St. Louis, MO
Sexe, Sara R. ... Great Falls, MT
Sexner, Mitchell Scott ... Arlington Heights, IL
Sexsmith, James S. ... Ann Arbor, MI
Sexsmith, Jillian D. ... New York, NY
Sexter, Allan S. ... New York, NY
Sexter, Deborah R. ... New York, NY
Sexter, Halley F. ... Washington, DC
Sexter, Reed P. ... Washington, DC
Sexter & Warmflash, P.C. ... New York, NY
Sexton, Ashley E. ... Atlanta, GA
Sexton, Ben ... Abilene, KS
Sexton, Benjamin Joeseph ... Abilene, KS
Sexton, Beth-Anne Thye ... Fort Myers, FL
Sexton, Brenda A. ... Elkton, MD
Sexton, Brian P. ... New York, NY
Sexton, C. Anthony ... Tampa, FL
Sexton, C. Anthony, P.A. ... Tampa, FL
Sexton, Charles S. ... Sevierville, TN
Sexton, Charles S. ... Orange, TX
Sexton, Clifton ... Oneida, TN
Sexton, Clifton H. ... Huntsville, TN
Sexton, Cristie A. ... Fayetteville, NC
Sexton, D. David ... Knoxville, TN
Sexton, Daniel W. ... Jersey City, NJ
Sexton, David Bruce ... Gladstone, MO
Sexton, David J. ... St. Louis, MO
Sexton, David N. ... Bonita Springs, FL
Naples, FL
Sexton, Dorrance, Jr. ... Blue Hill, ME
Sexton, E. Shayne ... Jacksboro, TN
Sexton, Edward V., (P.C.) ... Phoenix, AZ
Sexton, Elizabeth Walter ... Wheaton, IL
Sexton, Eric C. ... Kansas City, MO
Sexton, Eugene L. ... Waseca, MN
Sexton & Fields, P.L.L.C. ... Fort Smith, AR
Sexton, Forest C. ... Pittsburgh, PA
Sexton, Francis X., Jr., (P.A.)
Coral Gables, FL
Sexton, Fred C., Jr. ... Shreveport, LA
Sexton, George C. ... Dover, TN
Sexton, Gerard J. ... Treasury Department, Office of the Comptroller of the Currency, GV
Sexton, Gladys L. ... Greeley, CO
Sexton, Indiya R. ... Philadelphia, PA
Sexton, J. Douglas ... Norcross, GA
Sexton, J. Scott ... Roanoke, VA
Sexton, J. Stan ... Salina, KS
Sexton, James F. ... San Diego, CA
Sexton, James J., III ... Far Rockaway, NY
Sexton, James, Jr. ... Silver Spring, MD
Sexton, James W. ... Boston, MA
Sexton, Jane Watson ... Fayetteville, AR
Sexton, Jay W. ... Haslett, MI
Sexton, Jeanne L. ... San Francisco, CA
Sexton, Jeffrey A. ... Louisville, KY
Sexton, Jeffrey B. ... Orlando, FL
Sexton, Joe R. ... Sevierville, TN
Sexton, Jonathan P. ... Conyers, GA
Sexton, Joseph Thye ... Fort Myers, FL
Sexton, Juliana C. ... Marietta, OH
Sexton, K. Edward, II ... Birmingham, AL
Sexton, Karen W. ... Mineola, NY
Sexton, Karla K. ... Bethpage, NY
Sexton, Kaye ... Orange, TX
Sexton, Kevin M. ... Albuquerque, NM
Sexton, L. Landis ... Montgomery, AL
Sexton Law Offices ... Columbus, OH
Sexton, Lee ... Jonesboro, GA
Sexton, Lee & Associates, P.C.
Jonesboro, GA
Sexton, Lloyd Y. ... Moss Point, MS
Sexton, Mark J. ... Minneapolis, MN
Sexton, Mary ... Portland, ME
Sexton, Mary Catherine ... Chicago, IL
Sexton, Micah D. ... Cushing, OK
Sexton, Michael B. ... Buffalo, NY
Sexton, Michael F. ... Chicago, IL
Sexton, Michael F. ... Boston, MA
Sexton, Michael J. ... Orange, CA
Sexton, Michael L. ... Overland Park, KS
Sexton, Michael V. ... Oroville, CA
Sexton, Michelle W. ... San Francisco, CA
Sexton, Nancy S. ... Carlsbad, CA
Sexton, Patricia A. ... Kansas City, MO
Sexton, Paul ... Tallahassee, FL
Sexton, Paul E., Jr. ... San Antonio, TX
Sexton, Peter S. ... Phoenix, AZ
Sexton, R. Gray ... Baton Rouge, LA
Sexton, Richard ... New York, NY
Sexton, Richard J. ... Mount Laurel, NJ
Philadelphia, PA
Sexton, Rick S. ... Decatur, GA
Sexton, Robert E. ... Columbus, OH
Sexton, Robert L. ... Bordentown, NJ
Sexton, Robert R. ... Birmingham, AL
Sexton, Roy D. ... Oneida, TN
Sexton, Sam, Jr. ... Fort Smith, AR
Sexton & Sexton ... Orange, TX
Sexton, Sheila M. ... Cleveland, OH
Sexton, Shelor, Latimer & Pryor
Kansas City, KS
Overland Park, KS
Sexton, Steven L. ... Reno, NV
Sexton, Terence P. ... West Hartford, CT
Sexton, Terrence J. ... Kansas City, MO
Sexton, Theodore L., Jr. ... Leavenworth, KS
Sexton, Thomas J. ... St. Paul, MN
Sexton, Thomas P. ... Columbus, OH
Sexton, Thomas W., III ... Chicago, IL
Sexton, William E., Jr. ... Columbia, MD
Sexton, William J. ... Los Angeles, CA
Sexton, William J., (Co., L.P.A.)
Cleveland, OH
Sextro, Gregory J. ... Denison, IA
Seybert, Janet Rose ... Aurora, CO
Seybert, Joanna ... Uniondale, NY
Seybert, John R. ... Garden City, NY
Seybold, David ... Addison, TX
Seybold, Edward P., Jr. ... New Orleans, LA
Seybold, Leo ... Bethesda, MD
Seybold, Thomas J. ... St. Petersburg, FL
Seybold, Thomas Woodward ... Baltimore, MD
Seybolt, Cameron R. ... Duluth, MN
Seybolt, Harry K. ... Washington, NJ
Seybolt, Harry K., A Professional Corporation
Washington, NJ
Seyburn, Bruce H. ... Southfield, MI
Seyburn & Hencken, P.C. ... Kalamazoo, MI
Seyburn, Kahn, Ginn, Bess, Deitch and Serlin, Professional Corporation
Detroit, MI
Southfield, MI
Seyburn, Lowell M. ... Kalamazoo, MI
Seyburn, Marc E. ... Southfield, MI
Seydel, J. Rutherford, II ... Atlanta, GA
Seydel, Robert E. ... Sinclairville, NY
Seydel, Rodney A., Jr. ... New Orleans, LA
Seyedin-Noor, Bahram ... Palo Alto, CA
Seyedin-Noor, Shahram ... Palo Alto, CA
Seyer, David V. ... Phoenix, AZ
Seyer, Kenneth J. ... Jefferson City, MO
Seyer, Mary K. ... Hudson, WI
Seyfang, Matthew G. ... Washington, DC
Seyfarth, Shaw, Fairweather & Geraldson
Los Angeles, CA
Sacramento, CA
San Francisco, CA
Washington, DC
Atlanta, GA
Chicago, IL
Boston, MA
New York, NY
Houston, TX
Seyfarth, Theodore H. ... Northbrook, IL
Seyfer, Gregory J. ... Cedar Rapids, IA
Seyfert, Franklin J. ... Media, PA
Seyfert, Valorie A. ... San Diego, CA
Seyferth, Francis G. ... Troy, MI
Seyferth, Francis G., & Associates, P.C.
Troy, MI
Seyferth, Horst R. ... Chicago, IL
Seyferth, Mary B. ... Department of Justice, Tax Division, GV
Seyferth, Patrick G. ... Bloomfield Hills, MI
Seyferth, Paul D. ... Kansas City, MO
Seyffer, Richard R. ... Phoenix, AZ
Seyfried, John P. ... Troy, MI
Seykora, Charles M. ... Minneapolis, MN
Seykora, James E. ... Billings, MT
Seyle, Michael R. ... San Diego, CA
Seyler, Axel P. ... New York, NY
Seyler, Julie B. ... New York, NY
Seyler, Mark P. ... New Orleans, LA
Seyler-James, Tamara ... Kansas City, MO
Seyman, John T. ... Sacramento, CA
Seymoe, Steven P. ... Tallahassee, FL
Seymon, Pamela S. ... New York, NY
Seymon-Hirsch, Barbara N.
Washington, DC
Seymore, Ann Elizabeth ... Sugar Land, TX
Seymore, Charles W. ... Sugar Land, TX
Seymore, Christopher ... Philadelphia, PA
Seymore & Harris, PLLC
Sugar Land, TX
Seymore, Malinda L. ... Fort Worth, TX
Seymour, Angie W. ... Stone Mountain, GA
Seymour, Anissa D. ... Los Angeles, CA
Seymour, Arthur G. ... Knoxville, TN
Seymour, Arthur G., Jr. ... Knoxville, TN
Seymour, Barbara L. ... Houston, TX
Seymour, Barbara M. ... Greenville, SC
Seymour, Barbara P. ... Salem, OR
Seymour, Barbara R. ... New York, NY
Seymour, Brian M. ... West Palm Beach, FL
Seymour, Carolyn K. ... Richfield, OH
Seymour, Christine M. ... Pittsburgh, PA
Seymour, Christine M. Simon ... Chardon, OH
Seymour, Christopher E. ... Fresno, CA
Seymour, Christopher H. ... New York, NY
Seymour, Clive ... Tulsa, OK
Seymour, Daniel A. ... White Plains, NY
Seymour, Daniel J. ... Detroit, MI
Seymour, Daniel J. ... Sun Prairie, WI
Seymour, David ... Studio City, CA
Seymour, Deana C. ... Jackson, TN
Seymour, Dennis O., Jr. ... San Diego, CA
Seymour, Donald B. ... Columbia, MD
Seymour, Donald C. ... Salem, OR
Seymour, Donald E. ... Pittsburgh, PA
Seymour, E. Daniel ... Wilsonville, OR
Seymour, Edw. J., Jr. ... Monroe, LA
Seymour, Ernest J. ... Norwalk, CA
Seymour, Eugene V. ... Omaha, NE
Seymour, Everett H., Jr. ... New York, NY
Seymour, Frederick J. ... Alhambra, CA
Seymour, Hubert E., Jr. ... Greensboro, NC
Seymour, J. Gordon ... Washington, DC
Seymour, James H. ... Palo Alto, CA
Seymour, Jeffrey S. ... Lake Oswego, OR
Seymour, Joel A. ... Appleton, WI
Seymour, John L. ... Houston, TX
Seymour, John L., III ... Minneapolis, MN
Seymour, Julie K. ... Chicago, IL
Seymour, Karen A. ... Overland Park, KS
Seymour, Karen Hoffman ... Denver, CO
Seymour, Karen Patton ... New York, NY
Seymour, Kremer, Nommensen, Morrissy & Koch ... Elkhorn, WI
Seymour, L. Scott ... Norfolk, VA
Seymour, Lauren ... Laguna Niguel, CA
Seymour, Linda C. ... Chicago, IL
Seymour, Margaret B. ... Florence, SC
Seymour, Mark O. ... Chatham, NJ
Seymour, Mary F. ... St. Paul, MN
Seymour, McNeil V., Jr. ... St. Paul, MN
Seymour, Melanie Shaw
Fort Walton Beach, FL
Metairie, LA
Seymour, Michael D. ... Pittsburgh, PA
Seymour, Michael J. ... Bethel Park, PA
Pittsburgh, PA
Seymour, Michael L. ... Tulsa, OK
Seymour, Milton A. ... Waterbury, CT
Seymour, Paul A., III ... Topeka, KS
Seymour, Philip A. ... Los Angeles, CA
Seymour, Philip H. ... Novi, MI
Royal Oak, MI
Seymour, R. Thomas ... Tulsa, OK
Seymour, Richard T. ... Washington, DC
Seymour, Richard W. ... Fort Pierce, FL
Seymour, Robert E. ... Ocala, FL
Seymour, Ross A. ... La Crosse, WI
Seymour, S. Jay ... Anchorage, AK
Seymour, Samuel H. ... Washington, DC
Seymour, Samuel W. ... New York, NY
Seymour & Scherr, P.L.L.C.
Washington, DC
Seymour, Scott J. ... Huntington Beach, CA
Seymour, Scott J. ... Madison, WI
Seymour & Seymour ... Chatham, NJ
Seymour & Seymour ... Sanford, NC
Seymour, Shelly A. ... Merced, CA
Seymour, Shirley Pittman ... Potomac, MD
Seymour, Stephanie K. ... Tulsa, OK
Seymour, Steven P. ... Effingham, IL
Seymour, Steven W. ... Portland, OR
Seymour, Teresa Weynne ... Englewood, CO
Seymour, Thomas H. ... Miami, FL
Seymour, Thomas H. ... Boston, MA
Seymour, Thomas J. ... Minneapolis, MN
Seymour, Trevlyan G. ... Austin, TX
Seymour, Tully H. ... Santa Ana, CA
Seymour, W. Schuyler ... Flint, MI
Seymour, Whitney North, Jr.
New York, NY
Seymour, William C. ... Austin, TX
Seymour, William F., IV ... Richmond, VA
Seymour, William L. ... Elkhorn, WI
Seymour, Woodrow W., Jr. ... Sanford, NC
Seymour-Harris, Barbara L. ... Houston, TX
Seymour III, Bartholomew A.
Bloomfield Hills, MI
Seyranian, Leon G. ... Oakland, CA
Seyring, Gerhard W. ... Mount Prospect, IL
Seys, Wade S. ... Grand Rapids, MI
Sezer, Lawrence K. ... Chicago, IL
Sezna, Edward W. ... Los Angeles, CA
Sezon, Marianne ... Jefferson, OH
Sfaelos, Emanuel G. ... Hauppauge, NY
Sfara, David L. ... Southbury, CT
Waterbury, CT
Sfarti, Julius ... North Miami Beach, FL
Sfasciotti, Robert F. ... Kenosha, WI
Sfeir, Javier Gonzalez ... San Diego, CA
Sfekas, C. James ... Ellicott City, MD
Sfekas, James S. ... Towson, MD
Sfekas, Lauren A. ... Greenbelt, MD
Sfekas, Stephen J. ... Baltimore, MD
Sferra, Anne Marie ... Columbus, OH
Sferra, Pasqual J. ... Seattle, WA
Sferra, Stephen J. ... Cleveland, OH
Sferrazza, Joseph ... Melville, NY
Sferrazza, Mary-Lynn ... Washington, DC
Sferrella, Nino A. ... Columbus, OH
Sferrino, Lori A ... Florham Park, NJ
Sfikas, Ellen M. ... Chicago, IL
Sfikas, Karambelas & Akaras, LLP
Washington, DC
Baltimore, MD
New York, NY
Sfikas, Perry ... Washington, DC
Baltimore, MD
Sfikas, Peter M. ... Chicago, IL
Sfiscko, Johanna M. ... Cleveland, OH
Sforza, Dina L. ... Morristown, NJ
New York, NY
Sforzini, Richard H., Jr. ... Montgomery, AL
Sfregola, Michael F. ... Los Angeles, CA
Sgambati, Anthony P., II ... Youngstown, OH
Sgambati, Stephanie L. ... New York, NY
Sgambettera, Matthew J. ... Boston, MA
Sganga, John B., Jr. ... Newport Beach, CA
Sgarlat, Michael J. ... Alexandria, VA
Sgarlat, Susan L. ... New York, NY
Sgarlata, Anthony B. ... Schenectady, NY
Sgarlata, Mark A. ... McLean, VA
Sgarlata, Philip J. ... Albany, NY
Sgarlato, Gina ... Staten Island, NY
Sgarlato, Richard J. ... Staten Island, NY
Sgarlato, Richard J., P.C. ... Staten Island, NY
Sgarlato, Robert A. ... Staten Island, NY
Sgarlato, Santo D. ... Brooklyn, NY
Sgarlato, Santo R., Jr. ... Brooklyn, NY
Sgarzi, Louis A. ... Canton, MA
Sgrignari, Lawrence C. ... Hamden, CT
Sgro, Anthony P. ... Las Vegas, NV
Sgro, Charles J.
Commodity Futures Trading Commission, Office of the General Counsel, GV
Sgro, Charles V. ... Ridgefield, NJ
Sgro, Gregory P. ... Springfield, IL
Sgro, Hanrahan & Blue, L.L.P.
Springfield, IL
Sgro & Hill ... Hammonton, NJ
Sgro, Jill A. ... Nashua, NH
Sgro, Michael A. ... Haddon Heights, NJ
Sgro, Peter R., Jr. ... Hagåtña, GU
Sgro, Vincent J. ... Hammonton, NJ
Sgroi, Fred L. ... Kansas City, MO
Sgroi, Robert J. ... Warwick, RI
Sgroi, Roy C. ... Birmingham, MI
Sgroi, Sandra L. ... Smithtown, NY
Sgrosso, Vincent L. ... Atlanta, GA
Sgueglia, Vincent A. ... Owego, NY
Sha, Leslie K. ... Kansas City, MO
Sha, Leslie K., P.C. ... Kansas City, MO
Shaaber, A. R. ... Jacksonville, FL
Sha'afi, Sheryl J. ... Farmington, CT
Shabaik, Nadia A. ... Los Angeles, CA
Shaban, Dan ... Westport, CT
New York, NY
Shaban, Ephraim W. ... Brooklyn, NY
Shaban, John T. ... New York, NY
Shaban, Tova G. ... Southfield, MI
Shabani, Michael M. ... Birmingham, AL
Shabani, Michael M., P.C.
Birmingham, AL
Shabanian, Victoria S. ... Los Angeles, CA
Shabason, Helen ... New York, NY
Shabasson, Daniel Scott ... New York, NY
Shabasson, Leonard ... Larchmont, NY
Shabat, Michael E. ... Chicago, IL
Shabaz, John C. ... Madison, WI
Shabaz, Pamela B. ... Chicago, IL
Shabbick, Barry C. ... Palmerton, PA
Shabecoff, Peter ... New York, NY
Shabel, Algeo & Shabel, A Professional Association ... Mount Laurel, NJ
Shabel, Daniel A. ... Bala Cynwyd, PA
Philadelphia, PA
Shabel, Kathryn M. Gilbertson
Bellmawr, NJ
Shabel, Norman ... Mount Laurel, NJ
Shabel, Scott Lee ... Los Angeles, CA
Shaber, Craig J. ... San Diego, CA
Shaber, Steven J. ... New York, NY
Shaber, Steven Mansfield ... Raleigh, NC
Shaberman, Marc P. ... West Bloomfield, MI
Shabino, Allen N. ... Bellevue, WA
Shablin, David V. ... Worcester, MA
Shabman, Stefanie Honig ... Brooklyn, NY
Shabo, Harold E. ... Los Angeles, CA
Shabowich, Ronald J. ... Peabody, MA
Shabsels, Charles ... New York, NY
Shabshelowitz, Andrew ... Fall River, MA
Shabsin, Anna A. ... Creve Coeur, MO
St. Louis, MO
Shabsin, Michael S. ... Clayton, MO
Shaby, John P. ... Culver City, CA
Shach, Marc E. ... Baltimore, MD
Shachar, Avishai ... New York, NY
Shachat, Gary M. ... North Miami Beach, FL
Shachat, Marc G. ... New Orleans, LA
Shachat, Martin P. ... Miami, FL
Shachat, Michael S. ... Seattle, WA
Shachok, Mary E. ... Salem, MA
Shachoy, Laura Ryan ... Dedham, MA
Shachoy, N. James, Jr. ... Boston, MA
Shachoy, Norman J. ... Boston, MA
Shachter, Alan S. ... Manassas, VA
Shachter, Ellen J. ... Cambridge, MA
Shachtman, Douglas A., & Associates
Wilmington, DE
Shachtman, Scott A. ... Kansas City, MO
Shack, Donald D. ... New York, NY
Shack, John G. ... Woburn, MA
Shack, Norman M. ... Methuen, MA
Shack, Peter K. ... Sacramento, CA
Shack, Richard M. ... Orange, CA
Shack & Siegel, P.C. ... New York, NY
Shack, Stephanie L. ... Baltimore, MD

Shack, Thomas G., Jr. .... **Washington, DC**
Shack, Thomas G., Jr., P.C., Law Offices of .... **Washington, DC**
Shack, William P. .... Methuen, MA
Shackelford, Alfred C., III
Charlottesville, VA
Shackelford, Allan D. .... Clarksdale, MS
Shackelford, Allan L. .... **Greensboro, NC**
Shackelford, C. Preston .... **Napa, CA**
Shackelford, Charles D. .... Dallas, TX
Shackelford, Charles M. .... San Diego, CA
Shackelford, Cynthia S. .... Cedarburg, WI
Shackelford, Donna M. .... Ironton, MO
Shackelford, Edward A. .... Springfield, VA
Shackelford, Gayle Newman .... Midland, TX
Shackelford, Honenberger, Thomas, Willis & Gregg, P.L.C. .... **Culpeper, VA**
Orange, VA
Shackelford, James B. .... **Fort Worth, TX**
Shackelford, Jan .... **Pensacola, FL**
Shackelford, Jennifer L. .... Potts Camp, MS
Shackelford, Jerry F. .... **Austin, TX**
Shackelford, John C. .... **Hazard, KY**
Shackelford, John C. .... **Dallas, TX**
Shackelford, John E. .... Asheville, NC
Shackelford, Jon E. .... **Southfield, MI**
Shackelford, Karl A. .... Austin, TX
Shackelford, Kelly J. .... Plano, TX
Shackelford, L. Michael .... Atlanta, GA
Shackelford, Larry W. .... **Atlanta, GA**
Shackelford, Les E., Jr. .... Dallas, TX
Shackelford, Margaret O'Connor
Pataskala, OH
Shackelford, Michael W. .... **Portland, OR**
Shackelford, Patricia A.
Corpus Christi, TX
Shackelford, Patricia Ann .... **Hartford, CT**
Shackelford, R. Scott .... **Kansas City, MO**
Shackelford, Randall W. .... **Lexington, MO**
Shackelford, Ray L. .... Houston, TX
Shackelford, Richard L. .... **Atlanta, GA**
Shackelford, Ricky L. .... **Los Angeles, CA**
Shackelford, Rosella M. .... Paris, TN
Shackelford, Tricia A. .... **Miami, FL**
Shackelford, Virginius R., III
Culpeper, VA
Orange, VA
Shackelford, Virginius R., Jr. .... **Orange, VA**
Shackelford, William S.
Federal Election Commission, Office of the General Counsel, GV
Shackle, H. Gene .... Canton, OH
Shacklee, C. Edward .... Arlington, VA
Shackleford, Dennis L. .... **El Dorado, AR**
Shackleford, Farrior, Stallings & Evans, Professional Association .... **Tampa, FL**
Shackleford, John M., Jr. .... El Dorado, AR
Shackleford, Phillips, Wineland & Ratcliff, P.A. .... **El Dorado, AR**
Shackleford, Richard
Department of Defense, Armed Services Board of Contract Appeals, GV
Shackleford, Thomas D. .... Mason, OH
Shackleton, Hazeltine and Bishop
Fairfield, NJ
Ship Bottom, NJ
Shackleton, Richard J. .... **Fairfield, NJ**
Ship Bottom, NJ
Shackleton, Sara .... **Houston, TX**
Shacklett, Curtis J. .... **Tulsa, OK**
Shacklette, Ross E. .... Bossier City, LA
Shackman, Beverly .... **Clark, NJ**
New York, NY
Shackman, Steven B. .... **New York, NY**
Shackter, Peter V. .... San Mateo, CA
Shacter, David M. .... West Los Angeles, CA
Shacter, Joseph B. .... Jacksonville, FL
Shacter, Kevin A. .... Hollywood, FL
Shacter, Michael H. .... **Washington, DC**
Shacter, Scott A. .... **Phoenix, AZ**
Shactman, Murray .... New York, NY
Shad, Charles Thomas .... **Jacksonville, FL**
Shad, Kerry A. .... **Raleigh, NC**
Shad, Leslie .... Atlanta, GA
Shadbegian, Karen M. .... Princeton, MA
Shadd, Audrey M.
Office Of Special Counsel, GV
Shadd, Deborah A. .... Cohasset, MA
Shadd, Robert W. .... **Providence, RI**
Shadden, John L. .... Hillsboro, OR
Shaddinger, Alan R. .... **Meadville, PA**
Shaddix, James W. .... **Houston, TX**
Shaddock, Carroll .... **Houston, TX**
Shaddock, George S. .... **Pascagoula, MS**
Shaddock, Joe E., & Associates
Wichita Falls, TX
Shaddock Law Firm .... **Pascagoula, MS**
Shaddock, Pamela A. .... **Greeley, CO**
Shaddock, Robert E. .... Austin, TX
Shaddock, Robert M. .... **Rochester, NY**
Shaddock, William C. .... Plano, TX
Shaddock, William E. .... **Lake Charles, LA**
Shaddox, Charles R. .... **San Antonio, TX**
Shaddox, Compere, Walraven & Good, P.C.
San Antonio, TX
Shaddox, Robert C. .... **Houston, TX**
Shadduck, E. Dean, Jr. .... Binghamton, NY
Shadduck, James E. .... Portland, OR
Shadduck, John H. .... Belvedere-Tiburon, CA
Shadduck, Robert N. .... Edina, MN
Shadduck Young & Brown, LLP
Annandale, MN
Buffalo, MN
Shade & Associates, P.A. .... Miami Beach, FL
Shade, Cory .... Coral Gables, FL
Shade, Cynthia S. .... United States Senate, Senatorial Assistants, GV

Shade, David C. .... Delaware, OH
Shade, Dean H. .... Portland, OR
Shade, James M. .... **Grand Rapids, MI**
Shade, Jane L. .... Santa Ana, CA
Shade, Joseph .... Fort Worth, TX
Shade, Kenny .... Burtonsville, MD
Shade, Leslie N., Jr. .... Miami Beach, FL
Shade, Matt .... **Atlanta, GA**
Shade, Michael R. .... Delaware, OH
Shade, Patricia .... Los Angeles, CA
Shade, Patrick L. .... Dayton, OH
Shade & Shade .... Delaware, OH
Shade, Sharon A. .... Miami Beach, FL
Shade, Thomas M. .... Decatur, IL
Shade, Wayne F. .... Carlisle, PA
Shade, William E. .... Greeley, CO
Shade, William H. .... Sacramento, CA
Shadeed, Linda Salim .... Grand Blanc, MI
Shadegg, John B. .... Phoenix, AZ
Shadek, John L. .... **Incline Village, NV**
Shadel, David F. .... Koror, TT
Shadel, Scott F. .... **Janesville, WI**
Shader, Gary E. .... Maitland, FL
Shader, Lance C. .... Brattleboro, VT
Shader, Lance C., P.C. .... Brattleboro, VT
Shadiack, Michael Anthony
Hackettstown, NJ
Morristown, NJ
Trenton, NJ
Shadid, Chas. A. .... Oklahoma City, OK
Shadid, Damon .... **Houston, TX**
Shadid, Danny K. .... Oklahoma City, OK
Shadid, Ellen Darlene .... Oklahoma City, OK
Shadid, James E. .... Peoria, IL
Shadid & Pipes .... Oklahoma City, OK
Shadid, Randel C. .... Edmond, OK
Shadid, Todd E. .... **Wichita, KS**
Shadis, Patricia V. .... Newcastle, ME
Shadis & Rosendo .... Newcastle, ME
Shadi-Saed, Sherli .... Uniondale, NY
Shadle, George H. .... Estherville, IA
Shadle, Paul W. .... **Chicago, IL**
Shadle, Ronald E. .... Oakbrook Terrace, IL
Shadle, Stephen P. .... **Yuma, AZ**
Shadle, Todd W. .... **Dallas, TX**
Shadley, Frederic X. .... **Cincinnati, OH**
Shadley, Kay L. .... New York, NY
Shadley, Sue A. .... **Indianapolis, IN**
Shadlock, Nadine Feiden .... **Albany, NY**
Shadmand, Sheila L. .... **Washington, DC**
Shadoan, George W. .... Washington, DC
Rockville, MD
Shadoan, Julie F. .... **Bowling Green, KY**
Shadoan and Michael, LLP
Washington, DC
Rockville, MD
Shadoan, William L. .... Wickliffe, KY
Shadoin, Robert E. .... **Ruston, LA**
Shadoin, Thomas Louis .... Topeka, KS
Shadowen, Cyril E. .... Louisville, KY
Shadowen, H. Leon, Jr. .... Richmond, VA
Shadowen, Steve D. .... **Harrisburg, PA**
Philadelphia, PA
Shadowens, Lamont W. .... Redwood City, CA
Shadowitz Associates, P.A.
Boca Raton, FL
Shadowitz, Beth I. .... **Boca Raton, FL**
Shadowitz, Mitchell L. .... **Boca Raton, FL**
New York, NY
Shadrawy, Bernard F. .... Boston, MA
Shadrawy, Bernard F., Jr. .... Boston, MA
Shadrick, Thomas S. .... Virginia Beach, VA
Shadrix, G. Gregory .... **Carrollton, GA**
Shadrix, G. Gregory, P.C. .... **Carrollton, GA**
Shadur, Ellen J. .... **Los Angeles, CA**
Shadur, Milton I. .... Chicago, IL
Shadur, Robert H. .... Chicago, IL
Shadwell, Ira M. .... Redding, CA
Shadwell, Ralph E., III .... San Diego, CA
Shadwell Keller, Julie A. .... Portsmouth, VA
Shadwick, Gerald .... Greeley, CO
Shadwick, Jay T. .... Kansas City, MO
Shadwick, Jeffrey A. .... Houston, TX
Shadyac, Richard C. .... Falls Church, VA
Gainesville, VA
Shadyac, Richard C., Jr. .... **Washington, DC**
Falls Church, VA
Shae, Douglas J. .... Wenatchee, WA
Shaeffer, Clinton E. .... Cedar Rapids, IA
Shaeffer, Douglas J. .... Seattle, WA
Shaeffer, Erika Solti .... **Burbank, CA**
Shaeffer, Fred J. .... **Norman, OK**
Shaeffer, George William, Jr. .... Irvine, CA
Shaeffer, J. Murry .... Cheyenne, WY
Shaeffer, Jane H. .... Tallahassee, FL
Shaeffer, John A. .... Flandreau, SD
Shaeffer, John J. .... **Los Angeles, CA**
Shaeffer, Laura A. .... **Norman, OK**
Shaeffer, Shaeffer & Kernal .... **Norman, OK**
Shaeffer, Walter E. .... Columbus, OH
Shaen, Michael M. .... Wildwood, NJ
Shaer, Karen B. .... New York, NY
Shaer, Robert H. .... **Boston, MA**
Shaev, David B. .... New York, NY
Shaevel & Krems .... Boston, MA
Shaevel, William H. .... Boston, MA
Shaevitz, Eric Gregg .... Jamaica, NY
Shaevitz, Jerald P. .... Los Altos, CA
Shaevitz, Mark Alan .... Jamaica, NY
Shaevitz, Oliver .... Jamaica, NY
Shaevitz & Shaevitz .... Jamaica, NY
Shaevsky, Mark .... **Detroit, MI**
Shaevsky, Thomas L. .... **Detroit, MI**
Shafer, Abe, IV .... **Weston, MO**
Shafer, Alexandra M. .... Phoenix, AZ
Shafer, Amy Pigg .... **Wheeling, WV**
Shafer, Andrew D. .... **Seattle, WA**

Shafer & Associates, P.A. .... Boca Raton, FL
River Edge, NJ
Shafer, B. Kay .... Glendale, CA
Shafer, B. Lyle .... Jackson, WY
Shafer & Bailey .... **Seattle, WA**
Shafer, Bernard W. .... Beverly Hills, CA
Shafer, Bradford J.
South San Francisco, CA
Shafer, Bradley K. .... **Wheeling, WV**
Shafer, Carson B. .... Atlanta, GA
Shafer, Charles B. .... Baltimore, MD
Shafer, Charles E. .... Cortland, NY
Tully, NY
Shafer, Charles L. .... Durango, CO
Shafer, Claudia Yvonne .... Santa Cruz, CA
Shafer, Creighton Preston .... **Orlando, FL**
Shafer, Cynthia A. .... **Cincinnati, OH**
Shafer, David A. .... Auburn, CA
Shafer, David M. .... **Detroit, MI**
Shafer, Davis, Ashley, O'Leary & Stoker, A Professional Corporation .... Midland, TX
Odessa, TX
Shafer, Dennis H. .... Ishpeming, MI
Shafer, Derek J. .... Topeka, KS
Shafer, Donna P. .... Falls Church, VA
Shafer, Edward F. .... Rochester, MN
Shafer, Edward M. .... Washington, DC
Shafer, Elizabeth McNalley .... Napa, CA
Shafer, Harry T. .... Long Beach, CA
Shafer, Howard S. .... **New York, NY**
Shafer, Hugh A. M., Jr. .... **McLean, VA**
Shafer, Jacqueline L. H. .... Langley, WA
Shafer, James E. .... **Louisville, KY**
Shafer, James E. .... **New York, NY**
Shafer, James M. .... **Indianapolis, IN**
Shafer, James W. .... **Seattle, WA**
Shafer, Jennifer .... New York, NY
Shafer, John L., III .... **Tulsa, OK**
Shafer, John W. .... Waukon, IA
Shafer, Kent E. .... **Detroit, MI**
Shafer, Lana L. .... Lansing, MI
Shafer, Larry F. .... Johnstown, OH
Shafer Law Office .... Williamsburg, IA
Shafer Law Office, L.C. .... **Platte City, MO**
Weston, MO
Shafer, Lewis R. .... Boca Raton, FL
River Edge, NJ
Shafer, Margaret E. (MaLiz)
Kansas City, MO
Shafer, Mary S. .... **Kansas City, MO**
Shafer, Michael D. .... Huntington Beach, CA
Shafer, Moen & Bryan, P.S. .... **Seattle, WA**
Shafer, Nelson E. .... Hudson, FL
Shafer, Paul D., Jr. .... **Meadville, PA**
Shafer, Phil J. .... Long Beach, CA
Shafer, Philip H. .... Ashland, OH
Shafer, Philip J. .... Towson, MD
Shafer, Philip M. .... Houston, TX
Shafer, Quint .... **Weston, MO**
Shafer, Randall J. .... Dallas, TX
Shafer, Raymond P. .... **Meadville, PA**
Shafer, Robert J. .... **Wilmington, DE**
Shafer, Robert L. .... New York, NY
Shafer, Robert L., Jr. .... Jacksonville, FL
Shafer, Robert M. .... Cortland, NY
Tully, NY
Shafer, Robert S., (P.A.) .... **Little Rock, AR**
Shafer, Robert T., Jr. .... Fort Myers, FL
Shafer, Roger S. .... Huntington Park, CA
Shafer & Shafer .... Waukon, IA
Shafer, Stephanie J. .... Denver, CO
Shafer, Stuart R., P.C. .... **Lansing, MI**
Shafer, Stuart Robert .... **Lansing, MI**
Shafer, Susan L. .... San Juan, PR
Shafer, Swick, Bailey, Irwin, Stack & Millin
Meadville, PA
Shafer, Theodore Charles .... Fort Pierce, FL
Shafer, Timothy A. .... Cranford, NJ
Shafer & Trotter, PLC .... **McLean, VA**
Shafer, Warren W. .... Alameda, CA
Shafer, William J. .... Waukon, IA
Shafer, William K. .... Williamsburg, IA
Shaff, Carl, II .... Los Angeles, CA
Shaff, David O. .... Clinton, IA
Shaff, Grace L. .... **Chicago, IL**
Shaff, Karen E. .... Des Moines, IA
Shaff, Louis A. .... Dallas, TX
Shaff, Martha L. .... **Davenport, IA**
Shaff, Michael E. .... **Irvine, CA**
Shaffar, Charles H. .... St. Ann, MO
Shaffer, Alan J. .... Los Angeles, CA
Shaffer, Allen .... Millersburg, PA
Shaffer, Andrew D. .... Waterford, MI
Shaffer, Andrew K. .... **Sunnyvale, CA**
Shaffer, Anne E. .... **Charleston, WV**
Shaffer & Associates, P.C. .... Fort Myers, FL
Shaffer, Barbara Ann .... **Blue Bell, PA**
Shaffer, Bonfiglio, Scerni & D'Elia, L.L.C.
Mount Laurel, NJ
Pleasantville, NJ
Philadelphia, PA
Shaffer, Brent C. .... **Wilmington, DE**
Shaffer, Brian W. .... **Philadelphia, PA**
Shaffer, Bruce L. .... **Sacramento, CA**
Shaffer, Bruce P., (P.C.) .... Boulder, CO
Shaffer, Butler D. .... Los Angeles, CA
Shaffer, Carmin K. .... Glendale, CA
Shaffer, Charles A. .... **Kingston, PA**
Shaffer, Charles Augustus .... Morgantown, WV
Shaffer, Charles E. .... Seneca Falls, NY
Shaffer, Charles M., Jr. .... **Atlanta, GA**
Shaffer, Charles Norman .... Greenbelt, MD
Shaffer, Charles T. .... **Butler, PA**
Shaffer, Chetuan L. .... San Francisco, CA
Shaffer, Clark R. .... Westminster, MD
Shaffer, Craig B. .... **Denver, CO**
Shaffer & Culbertson, L.L.P. .... **Austin, TX**
Shaffer, D. Kirk .... **Nashville, TN**

Shaffer, D. Scott .... **San Francisco, CA**
Shaffer, Daniel R. .... **Chicago, IL**
Shaffer, Darren G. .... **Irvine, CA**
Shaffer, David H. .... **Akron, OH**
Shaffer, David J. .... **Washington, DC**
Shaffer, David M. .... Los Angeles, CA
Shaffer, David S. .... **Washington, DC**
Shaffer, Denise Oakes .... Towson, MD
Shaffer, Donald .... New York, NY
Shaffer, Donald W. .... **Pittsburgh, PA**
Shaffer, E. Thomas .... **Macon, GA**
Shaffer, Earl E. .... Arlington, VA
Shaffer, Edward L. .... **Richmond, CA**
Shaffer, Edwin G. .... Wytheville, VA
Shaffer, Elizabeth Ann .... Salt Lake City, UT
Shaffer, Emmett C. .... Vienna, OH
Shaffer, Erin E. .... Washington, DC
Shaffer, F. Mike .... **Tacoma, WA**
Shaffer, Francis A. .... Silver Spring, MD
Shaffer, Franklin D. .... Corpus Christi, TX
Shaffer, Gary L. .... **Washington, DC**
Shaffer, Gary P. .... New York, NY
Shaffer, Gene .... Atlanta, GA
Shaffer, George A. .... Buffalo, MO
Shaffer, George A. .... Utica, NY
Shaffer, George D. .... Corpus Christi, TX
Shaffer, George E. .... San Antonio, TX
Shaffer, George W. .... Corpus Christi, TX
Shaffer, Gold & Rubaum, LLP
Los Angeles, CA
Shaffer, Gregory Jay .... **Baltimore, MD**
Shaffer, Gregory S. .... **New York, NY**
Shaffer, H. Elizabeth .... Richmond, VA
Shaffer, Hal Jonathan .... **Mount Laurel, NJ**
Shaffer, Harold .... Philadelphia, PA
Shaffer, Harold W., Jr. .... Richfield, OH
Shaffer, Harry G., III .... **Charleston, WV**
Shaffer, Harry G., Jr. .... **Madison, WV**
Shaffer, Henry R. .... Pittsburgh, PA
Shaffer, J. Michael .... **Kansas City, MO**
Shaffer, J. Nevin, Jr. .... **Austin, TX**
Shaffer, J. Scott .... Bloomington, IL
Shaffer, James A. .... St. Petersburg, FL
Shaffer, James H. .... Corpus Christi, TX
Shaffer, James W. .... **Kansas City, MO**
Shaffer, Jane E. .... **Chicago, IL**
Shaffer, Jason N. .... **Springfield, MO**
Shaffer, Jeffrey A. .... **Palm Beach, FL**
Shaffer, Jo A. .... San Francisco, CA
Shaffer, John C., Jr. .... **Menlo Park, CA**
Shaffer, John C., Jr., A Prof. Law Corp., Law Offices of .... **Menlo Park, CA**
Shaffer, John E. .... **Farmington, CT**
Shaffer, John H. .... **Hutchinson, KS**
Shaffer, John P. .... Pittsburgh, PA
Shaffer, John R. .... Steubenville, OH
Shaffer, John S. .... **Bryan, OH**
Shaffer, Jonathan D. .... **Vienna, VA**
Shaffer, Joseph C., Jr. .... Anderson, SC
Shaffer, Joseph F. .... Clarksburg, WV
Shaffer, K. Ann .... Waco, TX
Shaffer, K. John .... **Los Angeles, CA**
Shaffer, Kim A. .... Fairmont, MN
Shaffer, Kim M. .... **Rochester, NY**
Shaffer, Kristy C. .... Fort Myers, FL
Shaffer, Kyle Niki .... San Diego, CA
Shaffer Law Office .... Steubenville, OH
Shaffer, Layton, Hannam & Luna
Corpus Christi, TX
Shaffer, Lewis A. .... **Middlebury, CT**
Shaffer, Linda K. .... Pittsburgh, PA
Shaffer, Lloyd C. .... Syracuse, NY
Shaffer Lombardo Shurin, A Professional Corporation .... **Kansas City, MO**
Shaffer, Mark A. .... **Atlanta, GA**
Shaffer, Mark J. .... **Boston, MA**
Shaffer, Mark L. .... **Washington, DC**
Shaffer, Mark R. .... **Washington, DC**
Shaffer, Mark S.
Federal Energy Regulatory Commission, Office of the Commissioners, GV
Shaffer, Mark S. .... **Philadelphia, PA**
Shaffer, Mary M. .... **St. Louis, MO**
Shaffer, Matthew D. .... Houston, TX
Shaffer, Michael A. .... **Bryan, OH**
Shaffer, Michael D. .... **Philadelphia, PA**
Shaffer, Michael H. .... Redwood City, CA
Shaffer, Monica Wahl .... **Los Angeles, CA**
Shaffer, Neal H. .... Holliston, MA
Shaffer, Owen E. .... St. Paul, MN
Shaffer, Pamela J. .... Costa Mesa, CA
Shaffer, Patricia C. .... Lincoln, NE
Shaffer, Patricia I .... Duluth, MN
Shaffer, Peter H. .... Butler, PA
Shaffer, Philip .... Salina, KS
Shaffer, Phillip G. .... Denison, TX
Shaffer, Phillip G., P.C. .... Denison, TX
Shaffer, Pocrass & Gam .... Los Angeles, CA
Shaffer, Polly M. .... Philadelphia, PA
Shaffer, R. James .... Huntington Beach, CA
Shaffer, Randal C. .... **Dallas, TX**
Shaffer, Raymond & Dalton .... **Macon, GA**
Shaffer, Richard A. .... Woodland Hills, CA
Shaffer, Richard Allyn .... Westport, CT
Shaffer, Richard J., Jr. .... Lincolnton, NC
Shaffer, Richard S. .... Aurora, CO
Shaffer, Richard W. .... **Allentown, PA**
Shaffer, Richard W., Jr. .... **Allentown, PA**
Shaffer, Robert .... West Chester, PA
Shaffer, Robert G., II .... **Jacksonville, FL**
Shaffer, Robert H., Jr. .... **Los Angeles, CA**
Shaffer, Robert L. .... San Antonio, TX
Shaffer, Robert M. .... Frankfort, IN
Shaffer, Robert M.M. .... **Cincinnati, OH**
Shaffer, Robert T., III .... **Baltimore, MD**
Shaffer, Robert W., Jr. .... **Los Angeles, CA**
Shaffer, Roberta I. .... Washington, DC
Shaffer, Roger L. .... Boca Raton, FL

Shaffer, Roger L., Jr. ... Boca Raton, FL
Shaffer, Roger R., Jr. ... Hermitage, PA
Shaffer, Ronald J. ... Philadelphia, PA
Shaffer, Ronald L. ... Tulsa, OK
Shaffer, R. W. ... Ketchikan, AK
Shaffer, Scott A. ... New York, NY
Shaffer and Shaffer ... Charleston, WV
Madison, WV
Shaffer & Solomon, P.A. ... Greenbelt, MD
Shaffer, Stacy P. ... Westminster, MD
Shaffer, Stephen T. ... Philadelphia, PA
Shaffer, Steven A. ... San Francisco, CA
Shaffer, Steven D. ... Syracuse, NY
Shaffer, Theresa M. ... Baltimore, MD
Shaffer, Thomas G. ... Providence, RI
Shaffer, Thomas L. ... Notre Dame, IN
Shaffer, Thomas R. ... Coudersport, PA
Shaffer, Wayne A. ... Reno, NV
Shaffer, Wayne E. ... Bryan, OH
Shaffer, William A., Jr. ... Elmira, NY
Shaffer, William B., Jr. ... Cincinnati, OH
Shaffer, William K. ... Lawrenceburg, TN
Shaffer, William L. ... Palo Alto, CA
Shaffer, William R. ... Butler, PA
Shaffer, William Timothy ... Fort Myers, FL
Shaffer, Winfield T. ... Charleston, WV
Shafferman, David ... Millis, MA
Shafferman, Howard H. ... Washington, DC
Shafferman, Joel M. ... New York, NY
Shaffert, Kurt ... Department of Justice, Antitrust Division, GV
Shaffert, Robin L. ... McLean, VA
Shaffery, John ... Los Angeles, CA
Shaffir, Melvyn L. ... New York, NY
Shaffman, Scott E. ... Monterey, CA
Shaffner, Bruce G., P.A.
Fort Lauderdale, FL
Shaffner, David P. ... Atlanta, GA
Shaffner, David P., P.C. ... Atlanta, GA
Shaffner, Jerrold E. ... Plantation, FL
Shaffner, Paula D. ... Philadelphia, PA
Shaffner, Thomas D. ... Fryeburg, ME
Shaffner, William G. ... Pittsburgh, PA
Shafi, Susan Nancy ... San Diego, CA
Shafie, Behrouz ... Los Angeles, CA
Shafir, Anna ... Houston, TX
Shafir, Jeremiah A. ... Newton, MA
Shafir, Julia ... New York, NY
Shafir, Lois D. ... Oceanport, NJ
Shafir, Marc A. ... Oceanport, NJ
Shafiroff, Cynthia L. ... Los Angeles, CA
Shafiroff, Ira L. ... Los Angeles, CA
Shafis, Robert M. ... Chicago, IL
Shafit, Matthew E. ... New York, NY
Shafizadeh, Sherri S. ... Irvine, CA
Shafkowitz, David M. ... Perkasie, PA
Shafmaster, Sumner H.
North Miami Beach, FL
Shafner, Alan C. ... Denver, CO
Shafner, Jonathan L. ... Washington, DC
Shafner, Matthew ... Groton, CT
Shafner, Nathan J. ... Groton, CT
Shafner, Samuel M. ... Boston, MA
Shafnisky, Alene M. ... Chicago, IL
Shafor, Martha Jane ... Treasury Department, Internal Revenue Service, GV
Shafovaloff, Thomas E. ... Winter Park, FL
Shafran, Chaya R. ... New York, NY
Shafran, Howard E. ... New York, NY
Shafran, Irving ... New York, NY
Shafran, J. A. ... Los Angeles, CA
Shafran, Lynn A. ... New York, NY
Shafran, Milton Philip, (P.A.)
Fort Lauderdale, FL
Shafran & Mosley, P.C. ... New York, NY
Shafran, Nina ... Washington, DC
Shafran, Peter W. ... Danbury, CT
Stamford, CT
Hillsdale, NJ
Shafranski, James A. ... New Brunswick, NJ
Shafrin, Alan ... Milwaukee, WI
Shafritz, Megan J. ... New York, NY
Shafrock, Elizabeth ... Chino, CA
Shafron, Jason T. ... San Francisco, CA
Shafron, Mark H. ... Canoga Park, CA
Shafron, Shelly Jay ... Encino, CA
Shafron, Steven D. ... Cleveland, OH
Shafroth, Frank H. ... Denver, CO
Shafroth & Toll, P.C. ... Denver, CO
Shaft, Grant H. ... Grand Forks, ND
Shaft, Reis & Shaft, Ltd.
Grand Forks, ND
Shaftal, Max ... Chicago, IL
Shaftel, Cynthia ... Bedford, NY
Shaftel, David G. ... Anchorage, AK
Shaftel, David G., P.C., Law Offices of
Anchorage, AK
Shaftel, Eve ... Long Island City, NY
Shaftel, Hal S. ... New York, NY
Shafter, A. James ... Decatur, IL
Shafter, Allan D. ... Garden City, NY
Shafter, Bernard ... Garden City, NY
Shafter, Melissa ... Des Moines, IA
Shafter, Robert L. ... Stamford, CT
Shafter & Shafter ... Garden City, NY
Shafto & Ashbrook ... Monroe, LA
Shafto, Donald B. ... New York, NY
Shafto, Wesley S. ... Monroe, LA
Shafton, Anthony E. ... Los Angeles, CA
Shafton, Ben ... Vancouver, WA
Shafton, David G. ... Stevens Point, WI
Shafton, Edward ... Omaha, NE
Shafton, Judith Vera ... San Francisco, CA
Shafton, Kevin D. ... New York, NY
Shafton, Lester B. ... Los Angeles, CA
Shafton, Lori A. ... Beverly Hills, CA
Shafton, Robert M. ... Los Angeles, CA

Shafton-Kaplan, Judith V.
San Francisco, CA
Shagam, David ... Berkeley, CA
Shagam, Jerome I. ... Rockville Centre, NY
Shagan, Michael D. ... New York, NY
Shager, Merrie C.
Department of Agriculture, Board of Contract Appeals, GV
Shaghalian, Elizabeth A. ... New York, NY
Shaghzo, Armen ... Glendale, CA
Shaghzo, Jean M. Schanberger
San Francisco, CA
Shagin & Anstine LLC ... Harrisburg, PA
Shagin, Craig R. ... Harrisburg, PA
Shagin, Scott J. ... Fair Lawn, NJ
Shagley, Richard J. ... Terre Haute, IN
Shagory, Edward J. ... Boston, MA
Shagory and Shagory, P.C. ... Boston, MA
Shagoury, Paul B. ... Hyde Park, MA
Shagrin, Andrew Z. ... San Francisco, CA
Shagrin, Michael B. ... Cleveland, OH
Shagrin, Richard A. ... Seattle, WA
Shah, Afsheen Ashley ... East Meadow, NY
Shah, Alpita A. ... Chicago, IL
Shah, Ami P. ... Washington, DC
Shah, Amit B. ... St. Louis, MO
Shah, Angana R. ... Washington, DC
Shah, Anita V. ... San Jose, CA
Shah, Ankur D. ... Washington, DC
Shah, Asmi A. ... Santa Monica, CA
Shah, Bansari M. ... Chicago, IL
Shah, Barbara J. ... Bethel Park, PA
Shah, Barbara J., P.C. ... Bethel Park, PA
Shah, Chirag ... Washington, DC
Shah, Dayna C. ... General Accounting Office, Office of the General Counsel, GV
Shah, Devang ... Palo Alto, CA
Shah, Devang M. ... Rockville, MD
Shah, Dina K. ... Woodbridge, NJ
Shah, Dipawali ... Garden City, NY
Shah, Hiral H. ... New York, NY
Shah, Huma P. ... Chicago, IL
Shah, James C. ... Philadelphia, PA
Shah, Jay H. ... Harrisburg, PA
Philadelphia, PA
Shah, Jennifer A. ... Washington, DC
Shah, Kala ... Washington, DC
Shah, Kinnari P. ... San Francisco, CA
Shah & Kishore ... Rockville, MD
Shah Law Firm, The ... Harrisburg, PA
Philadelphia, PA
Shah, Manish S. ... San Francisco, CA
Shah, Marla B. ... Los Angeles, CA
Shah, Meha ... Washington, DC
Shah, Namita ... New York, NY
Shah, Namita Tripathi ... Hartford, CT
Shah, Nilay A. ... Los Angeles, CA
Shah, Nimish ... Cherry Hill, NJ
Shah, Niranjana I., (Ms.) ... Bronx, NY
Shah, Nisha ... Dallas, TX
Shah, Preeti G. ... Los Angeles, CA
Shah, Raj N. ... Chicago, IL
Shah, Rajat R. ... Washington, DC
Shah, Rajiv C. ... Bloomington, IL
Shah, Razi A. ... Sacramento, CA
Shah, Roopal ... Washington, DC
Shah, Sangeeta G. ... Southfield, MI
Shah, Sanjit S. ... New York, NY
Shah, Saurabh K. ... New York, NY
Shah, Seema R. ... Minneapolis, MN
Shah, Shefali A. ... Boston, MA
Shah, Sheila ... Richmond, CA
Shah, Shital A. ... Sandusky, OH
Shah, Sona R. ... New York, NY
Shah, Vimal K. ... Newark, NJ
Shahade, Loretta M. ... Pittsburgh, PA
Shahade, Samuel G. ... Johnstown, PA
Shahade, William G. ... Johnstown, PA
Shahady, Carl Joseph ... Pflugerville, TX
Shahady, John J. ... Fort Lauderdale, FL
Shahady, Thomas R. ... Fort Lauderdale, FL
Shahalayi, Chaye F. ... Los Angeles, CA
Shahan, Amy ... Dallas, TX
Shahan, Bridget ... Washington, DC
Shahan, E. Kathleen ... Department of Justice, Civil Division, GV
Shahan & Erwin ... Abilene, TX
Shahan, Gary H. ... Abilene, TX
Shahan, John A. ... Tarpon Springs, FL
Shahan, Michael R. ... Fayetteville, AR
Shahan, Steven C. ... Syracuse, NY
Shahan, Tully ... Brackettville, TX
Shahani, Ray K. ... San Francisco, CA
Shahar, Martine Safran ... Los Angeles, CA
Shahbazian, Steven L. ... Fresno, CA
Shahbazian, V. Blair ... Sacramento, CA
Shahdanian, John L., II ... Secaucus, NJ
Shaheed, David A. ... Indianapolis, IN
Shaheen, Anthony F. ... Utica, NY
Shaheen, Anthony J. ... Denver, CO
Shaheen, Arthur V. ... Richmond, VA
Virginia Beach, VA
Shaheen, Christopher T.
Minneapolis, MN
Shaheen, David T. ... Washington, DC
Shaheen & Farah ... Flint, MI
Shaheen, Frederick F. ... Washington, DC
Shaheen & Gordon, P.A. ... Concord, NH
Dover, NH
Shaheen, Jacobs & Ross, P.C. ... Detroit, MI
Shaheen, Kristen Teuchert
New Hartford, NY
Shaheen, L. Joseph, Jr. ... Tampa, FL
Shaheen, Matthew M. ... Cleveland, OH
Shaheen, Michael ... Edwardsville, IL
Shaheen, Michael E., Jr.
Treasury Department, Internal Revenue Service, GV

Shaheen, Michael J. ... St. Clairsville, OH
Shaheen, Nicholas L. ... Braintree, MA
Shaheen, Orr, Pearce, Griffin & Staat, P.C.
Chicago, IL
Shaheen, Philip J., Jr. ... Baton Rouge, LA
Shaheen, Randal M. ... Washington, DC
Shaheen, Raymond ... Chicago, IL
Shaheen & Shaheen, P.C. ... Richmond, VA
Virginia Beach, VA
Shaheen, V. David, Jr. ... Little Silver, NJ
Shaheen, Victor A. ... Richmond, VA
Virginia Beach, VA
Shaheen, William A., Jr. ... Flint, MI
Shaheen, William H. ... Concord, NH
Dover, NH
Shahi, Kaveh S. ... Rutland, VT
Shahian, Paul G. ... Andover, MA
Shahid, A. Peter, Jr. ... Charleston, SC
Shahid Law Office, LLC ... Charleston, SC
Shahid, Mary D. ... North Charleston, SC
Shahida, Stephen K. ... Washington, DC
Shahin, Robert S. ... Los Angeles, CA
Shahinfar, Darius ... Albany, NY
Shahinian, Armen ... Roseland, NJ
Shahinian, Dean V. ... United States Senate, Committee Legal Personnel, GV
Shahinian, George C. ... Los Alamitos, CA
Shahinian, Steven A. ... Roseland, NJ
Shah-Khan, S. Mujeeb ... Charlotte, NC
Shahlavi, Hooman ... Palo Alto, CA
Shahmoon, Eli R. ... New York, NY
Shahoian, Kenneth J. ... Petaluma, CA
Shahon, Leon J. ... Lakewood, CA
Shahood, George A. ... West Palm Beach, FL
Shahpar, Shahpar ... Phoenix, AZ
Shahri, Mitra T. ... Los Angeles, CA
Shahriari, K. Thomas ... Washington, DC
Shahvari, Mandana ... Philadelphia, PA
Shaia, Harry, Jr. ... Richmond, VA
Shaia, William H., Jr. ... Charlotte, NC
Shaievitz & Berowitz ... Bloomfield, NJ
Shaievitz, Sidney ... Bloomfield, NJ
Shaifer, Jerry A. ... Atlanta, GA
Shaiken & Associates, P.C. ... Hartford, CT
Shaiken, David M. S. ... Hartford, CT
Shaiken, Elliot B. ... Whitestone, NY
Shaiken, Mark A. ... Kansas City, MO
Shaikewitz, Richard P. ... Alton, IL
Shaikh, Anwar M. ... Staten Island, NY
Shaikh, Ayaz R. ... New York, NY
Shaikh-Bahai, Carrie A. ... New York, NY
Shaikun, Leon J. ... Louisville, KY
Shaikun, Michael G. ... Frankfort, KY
Louisville, KY
Shaikun, Philip ... Department of Justice, Civil Division, GV
Shailer, John L. ... Columbus, OH
Shailer, Philip S. ... Fort Lauderdale, FL
Shailer, Purdy & Jolly, P.A.
Fort Lauderdale, FL
Shailor, Nancy J. ... Modesto, CA
Shailor, William D. ... Farmington Hills, MI
Shaima, Michael Leo ... Temecula, CA
Shaiman & Associates, P.C.
Philadelphia, PA
Shaiman, Pamela ... Philadelphia, PA
Shaiman, Robert ... Denver, CO
Shaiman, S. Laurence ... Philadelphia, PA
Shaiman, Stephen A. ... Wayne, PA
Shain, Bernard L. ... Portland, OR
Shain, David L. ... Ventura, CA
Shain, H. Leland ... San Francisco, CA
Shain, Harold ... San Francisco, CA
Shain, Henry H. ... San Francisco, CA
Shain, Joel L. ... Bernardsville, NJ
Shain, Jonathan D. ... Horsham, PA
Shain, Melinda ... Portland, ME
Shain, Ray E. ... Williston Park, NY
Shain, Ray Elliot, P.C. ... Williston Park, NY
Shain, Rodney A., Jr. ... Sanford, ME
Shain, Schaffer & Rafanello, A Professional Corporation ... Bernardsville, NJ
Shain, Terry L. ... Woodland Hills, CA
Shainberg, Abe M. ... New York, NY
Shainberg, Andrew M. ... Newark, NJ
Shainberg, Charles C. ... Haddonfield, NJ
Shainberg, Raymond M. ... Memphis, TN
Shaine, Abigail A.
Federal Election Commission, Office of the General Counsel, GV
Shaine, Seth K. ... Cherry Hill, NJ
Shaines, Marsha Sue ... Washington, DC
Shaines & McEachern, Professional Association ... Portsmouth, NH
Shaines, Robert A. ... Portsmouth, NH
Shainess, Joseph J. ... Middletown, CT
Shainis, Aaron ... Washington, DC
Shainis & Peltzman, Chartered
Washington, DC
Shainman, Barry J. ... Middlebury, CT
Shainswit, Beatrice ... New York, NY
Shainswit, Seymour ... New York, NY
Shainwald, Sybil ... New York, NY
Shainwald, Sybil, A Prof. Corp., Law Offices of ... New York, NY
Shair, David K. A. ... Rockford, IL
Shair & Fishbon ... Boston, MA
Shaird, Willie B. ... Department of Labor, Office of the Solicitor, GV
Shajnfeld, Saul M. ... New York, NY
Shakabpa, W. Derek
Commodity Futures Trading Commission, Division of Enforcement, GV
Shakarchi, David ... Flushing, NY
Shakarchy, Jacob S. ... New York, NY
Shakarjian, John, Jr. ... Pontiac, MI
Shake, Ann O'Malley ... Louisville, KY
Shake, B. Keith ... Indianapolis, IN

Shake, James M. ... Louisville, KY
Shaked, Nitzhia B. ... Berkeley, CA
Shakely, Heidi Hamman ... Harrisburg, PA
Shakely, Robin Burke ... Sacramento, CA
Shakely, Ronald H. ... Evans City, PA
Shakely, William W. ... Harrisburg, PA
Shaker, Burton A. ... Andover, MA
Shaker, Christopher J. ... Niles, OH
Shaker, James M. ... Seattle, WA
Shaker, Joan Perkins ... Atlanta, GA
Shaker, Mitchell F. ... Warren, OH
Shaker, Robert I. ... Niles, OH
Shaker, Robert M.N. ... Norcross, GA
Shaker & Shaker ... Niles, OH
Shakes, David L. ... Colorado Springs, CO
Shakeshaft, Chernushin & Donohoe, P.C.
Colorado Springs, CO
Shakeshaft, Kenneth J.
Colorado Springs, CO
Shakeshaft, Thomas D. ... Chicago, IL
Shakespeare, Frank J. ... Du Bois, PA
Shakib, Kaivan M. ... New York, NY
Shakin, Alan C.
Consumer Product Safety Commission, Office of the General Counsel, GV
Shakin, Diane P. ... Los Angeles, CA
Shakin, Edward Harold ... Arlington, VA
Shakin, George ... Amherst, NH
Shaklan, Allen Y. ... New York, NY
Shaklee, Barbara J. ... Denver, CO
Shaklee, Richard J. ... Neptune, NJ
Shaklovitz, Robert D. ... Houston, TX
Shakman, Michael L. ... Chicago, IL
Shakman, Stephen A. ... St. Paul, MN
Shaknes, Alexander ... New York, NY
Shakoor, Adam A. ... Detroit, MI
Shakoor, Grubba & Miller, PLLC
Detroit, MI
Shakoori, Shaban ... Palo Alto, CA
Shakow, David Joseph ... Washington, DC
Shakow, John D. ... Washington, DC
Shakow, Peter J. ... Los Angeles, CA
Shakow, Susannah Wellford
Washington, DC
Shakula, Peter J. ... Chicago, IL
Shalaby, Mark A. ... Washington, DC
Shalala & Batal ... Rocky River, OH
Shalala, Edna C. ... Rocky River, OH
Shalant, Joseph L. ... Los Angeles, CA
Shalbrack, Michael Jon ... Rockford, IL
Shalek, Donna E. ... Valhalla, NY
Shalek, James H. ... White Plains, NY
Shalek, Jeffrey B. ... Miami, FL
Shalen, Barry R. ... Phoenix, AZ
Shalen, Stephen H. ... New York, NY
Shaler, Frank C. ... Birmingham, MI
Shaler, Patricia ... Scottsdale, AZ
Shalfi, Edward ... Brooklyn, NY
Shalgian, Robert E. ... Rockland, MA
Shalhoob, Margaret P. ... Bangor, ME
Shalhoob, Patricia A. ... Williamston, MI
Shalhoub, Donald G. ... Department of Labor, Office of the Solicitor, GV
Shalhoub, John J. ... Rutherford, NJ
Shalhoub, Michael D. ... New York, NY
Shalhoub, Paul V. ... New York, NY
Shalhoub, Robert M. W.
West Palm Beach, FL
Shalhoub, Robert M.W., P.A., Law Offices of
West Palm Beach, FL
Shalhoub, Susan C. ... Peace Corps, Office of the General Counsel, GV
Shalhoup, Julia B. ... Charleston, WV
Shalit, Brad D. ... Hackensack, NJ
Shalit, Melissa D. ... Sherman Oaks, CA
Shalit, Susan Mary ... San Francisco, CA
Shalita, Paul ... Trenton, NJ
Shalita, Paul ... Philadelphia, PA
Shaljian, Cammarata & O'Connor
Jersey City, NJ
Shaljian, Ronald H. ... Jersey City, NJ
Shalk, Colin M. ... Wilmington, DE
Shalkevich, Vladimir Mark
Los Angeles, CA
Shall, David C. ... Los Angeles, CA
Shallal, Jane ... Southfield, MI
Shallant, David E.
Department of Commerce, Patent and Trademark Office, GV
Shallbetter, Tami ... Spokane, WA
Shallcross, Doris D. ... Naples, FL
Shallcross, Gary Clayton ... Seaside, CA
Shallcross, Richard A. ... Tulsa, OK
Shalleck, James F.
Montgomery Village, MD
Shallenberger, Garvin F. ... Costa Mesa, CA
Shallenberger, Susan ... Chicago, IL
Shallenburger, Joe H. ... New York, NY
Shaller, David A. ... St. Louis, MO
Shaller, Elliot H. ... Washington, DC
Shaller, Frederick C. ... Pasadena, CA
Shaller, Kimberly W. ... Pasadena, CA
Shalley, James ... Kew Gardens, NY
Shallito, Vivian Teresa ... Covina, CA
Shallman, Mary E. ... New York, NY
Shallo, Scott D. ... Albany, NY
Shalloo, Denis ... San Francisco, CA
Shallow, Nancy E. ... Detroit, MI
Shalloway, C. Michael
West Palm Beach, FL
Shalloway, Edwin A. ... Alexandria, VA
Shalloway, G. Mark ... West Palm Beach, FL
Shalloway, Philip D. ... Fairfax, VA
Shalloway & Shalloway
West Palm Beach, FL
Shalloway, Stuart M. ... Small Business Administration, GV
Shally, Brian J. ... San Francisco, CA

Shally, Joanna .... New York, NY
Shalo, Abraham .... New York, NY
Shalof, Ann .... New York, NY
Shalom, Isaiah .... Cambridge, MA
Shalov, Barry D. .... New York, NY
Shalov, Lee S. .... New York, NY
Shalov Stone & Bonner .... New York, NY
Shalowitz, Howard A. .... St. Louis, MO
Shalowitz, Nancy L. .... Deerfield, IL
Shalowitz, Sidney .... Glencoe, IL
Shaltes, Craig R. .... Sacramento, CA
Shalton, Lonnie J. .... Kansas City, MO
Shaltz, David L. .... Lansing, MI
Shaltz, Jennifer J. .... Minneapolis, MN
Shaltz and Royal, P.C. .... Lansing, MI
Shalvoy, James A. .... Manhattan Beach, CA
Shalz, Ronald S. .... Colby, KS
Shama, Cynthia .... Akron, OH
Shama, Sharif S. .... Chicago, IL
Shamahs, Elizabeth Y. .... New York, NY
Shamaly, Chris M. .... Houston, TX
Shaman, Jeffrey M. .... Chicago, IL
Shaman, Wm. I. .... Dayton, OH
Shamansky, Robert N. .... Columbus, OH
Shamansky, Ronda S. .... Columbus, OH
Shamansky, Samuel H. .... Columbus, OH
Shamas, George J. .... Coral Gables, FL
Shamas, Jimmy E. .... Denver, CO
Shamas, Leonard A. .... Lowell, MA
Shamas, Mitchell E. .... Tulsa, OK
Shamas, Ralph D. .... Roswell, NM
Shamash, Charles .... Los Angeles, CA
Shambach, John L. .... Covington, IN
Shamban, Stephen E. .... Braintree, MA
Shambaugh, Cynthia .... Foster City, CA
Shambaugh, Kast, Beck & Williams, LLP
Fort Wayne, IN
Shambaugh, Stephen H. .... Fort Wayne, IN
Shambaugh, Thomas D. .... York, PA
Shambeau, Steven D. .... Waupaca, WI
Shamberg, James I. .... Grand Island, NE
Shamberg, Jeffrey S. .... Chicago, IL
Shamberg, John E. .... Kansas City, KS
Overland Park, KS
Kansas City, MO
Shamberg, Johnson & Bergman, Chartered
Kansas City, KS
Overland Park, KS
Kansas City, MO
Shamberg Marwell Hocherman Davis & Hollis, P.C. .... Mount Kisco, NY
White Plains, NY
Shamberg, R. Brock .... Anchorage, AK
Shamberg, Stephen C. .... Chicago, IL
Shamberg, Stuart R. .... Mount Kisco, NY
Shamberg, Wolf, McDermott & Depué
Grand Island, NE
Shamberger, David M. .... Boston, MA
Shamblin, Jason A. .... Birmingham, AL
Shamblin, John W. .... Phoenix, AZ
Shamblin, Renée E.Sandler .... Phoenix, AZ
Shamblin, Ronald B. .... Lapeer, MI
Shambon, Leonard M. .... Washington, DC
Shambour, Angela K. .... Pikeville, KY
Fargo, ND
Shamburek, Steven J. .... Anchorage, AK
Shamburger, John K. .... Fairfield Bay, AR
Shamek, Edward B. .... Goldendale, WA
Shamel, C. Richard, Jr. .... Boca Raton, FL
Shamel, C. Richard, Jr.
Deerfield Beach, FL
Shamel, C. Richard, Jr.
Fort Lauderdale, FL
Shamers, David S. .... Wilmington, DE
Shames, Alison B. .... San Francisco, CA
Shames & Byrum, P.C. .... Chesapeake, VA
Shames, Eric J. .... New York, NY
Shames, Harry .... New York, NY
Shames, Henry J. .... Santa Barbara, CA
Shames, Jack E. .... Red Bank, NJ
Shames, Jack E., P.A. .... Red Bank, NJ
Shames, Jerry .... Westport, CT
Shames, Mark I. .... St. Petersburg, FL
Shames, Mitchell H. .... Boston, MA
Shames, Steven F. .... Chesapeake, VA
Shamgochian, Edward G. .... Worcester, MA
Shami, Khaled .... Redwood City, CA
Shamieh and Awad-Rashmawi
Sacramento, CA
Shamieh, Elias Z. .... Sacramento, CA
Shamieh, Reem J. .... Los Angeles, CA
Shamieh, Sami I. .... Alamo, CA
Shamin, Rashid .... Palm Desert, CA
Shamir, Ruth .... Los Angeles, CA
Shamis, Edward A., Jr. .... Slidell, LA
Shamis, Edward A., Jr., A Professional Corporation .... Slidell, LA
Shamis, Max .... Long Beach, NY
Shamiyeh, A. Nick .... Walnut Creek, CA
Shamji, Simin Madatali .... San Francisco, CA
Shamlian, Harry T. .... Troy, NY
Shamo, M. John .... Detroit, MI
Shamon, George J. .... Auburn, NY
Shamon, Robt. E. .... Boston, MA
Shamon, Thomas J. .... Auburn, NY
Shamoon, Rona G. .... New York, NY
Shamos, Jeremy .... Denver, CO
Shamos, Michael I. .... Pittsburgh, PA
Shamouilian, Susan M. .... San Jose, CA
Shamoun, C. Gregory .... Dallas, TX
Shamp, Arduini & Hain .... Erie, PA
Shamp, Clinton A. .... Erie, PA
Shamp, Larry D. .... Naperville, IL
Shamp, Laura M. .... Atlanta, GA
Shampanier, Judith M. .... New York, NY
Shampo, G. Christopher .... Placerville, CA
Shampo, Jeffrey J. .... Madison, WI
Shampton, John Fredrick .... Fort Worth, TX

Shams, Howard .... New York, NY
Shams, Maurice .... Orlando, FL
Shams, Sidney H. .... Orlando, FL
Shamsai, Heather R. .... New York, NY
Shamsie, Sy S. .... Dallas, TX
Shamulka, George .... Endicott, NY
Shamulka, William E. .... Endicott, NY
Shamwell, Earl E., Jr.
National Labor Relations Board, Division of Administrative Law Judges, GV
Shamy, Edward P., Jr. .... North Brunswick, NJ
Shamy, George J., Jr. .... New Brunswick, NJ
Shamy, Jason E. .... New Brunswick, NJ
Shamy, John C. .... Somerset, NJ
Shamy, Shipers & Lonski, P.C.
New Brunswick, NJ
Shan, Xiaokui "Katie" .... Chicago, IL
Shanaberger, Jeffrey L. .... Princeton, NJ
Shanaberger, William G. .... Franklin, MI
Shanaberger & Zanolli, P.C. .... Franklin, MI
Shanabrook, Katherine R.
Department of Agriculture, Office of Inspector General, GV
Shanabrook, Michael D. .... New York, NY
Shanafelt, Randall V. .... St. Petersburg, FL
Shanafelt, Tab R. .... New York, NY
Shanagher, Denis F. .... San Francisco, CA
Shanahan, Angela .... Los Angeles, CA
Shanahan, Brian E. .... Philadelphia, PA
Shanahan, Brien W. .... Cleveland, OH
Shanahan, Bruce G. .... Los Angeles, CA
Shanahan, Clark A. .... Owosso, MI
Shanahan, Colleen A. .... Nashville, TN
Shanahan, Daniel E. .... Worcester, MA
Shanahan, David A. .... San Diego, CA
Shanahan, Donald E. .... Roseau, MN
Shanahan, Donald F. .... San Diego, CA
Shanahan, Donald G. .... South Pasadena, CA
Shanahan, Donald G., Jr.
South Pasadena, CA
Shanahan, Dumler, Swanson & Olsson, P.C.
Fort Collins, CO
Shanahan, Edmond F. .... Los Angeles, CA
Shanahan, George A. .... New York, NY
Shanahan, J. Kearney .... Washington, DC
Cleveland, OH
Shanahan, J. Robert .... San Marino, CA
Shanahan, James A. .... Chicago, IL
Indianapolis, IN
Shanahan, James P. .... Indianapolis, IN
Shanahan, James P. .... Livingston, NJ
Shanahan, James P. .... Syracuse, NY
Shanahan, James R., Jr. .... Washington, DC
Shanahan, Jas. A., Jr. .... Bedford, NH
Shanahan, John J., III .... Jersey City, NJ
Shanahan, John L. .... Hackensack, NJ
Shanahan, John P. .... Hebron, IN
Shanahan, Joseph F. .... New York, NY
Shanahan, Joseph P., Jr.
Manhattan Beach, CA
Shanahan, Joyce .... Chicago, IL
Shanahan, Karen F. .... Cleveland, OH
Shanahan, Kevin D. .... Lowell, MA
Shanahan, Kieran Joseph .... Greensboro, NC
Shanahan and Kremski, P.C. .... Owosso, MI
Shanahan, Laurence M. .... New York, NY
New York, NY
Shanahan, Laurence M., Law Office of
White Plains, NY
Shanahan, Lauri M. .... San Francisco, CA
Shanahan Law Firm, The
Washington, DC
Cleveland, OH
Shanahan, Linus H. .... Rochester, NH
Shanahan, Lori N. .... Chicago, IL
Shanahan, Margaret A. .... Chicago, IL
Shanahan, Mark J. .... Richmond, VA
Shanahan, Martin J., Jr. .... Joliet, IL
Shanahan, Maureen G. .... Los Angeles, CA
Shanahan, Maureen J. .... Pacific Palisades, CA
Shanahan, Michael H. .... Boston, MA
Shanahan, Michael S. .... Indianapolis, IN
Shanahan, Michelle M. .... Washington, DC
Shanahan, Patricia A. .... San Jose, CA
Shanahan, Paul F. .... Rochester, NY
Shanahan, Philip E. .... Anchorage, AK
Shanahan, Rebecca M. .... Indianapolis, IN
Shanahan, Richard A. .... Oklahoma City, OK
Shanahan, Richard P. .... Sacramento, CA
Shanahan, Robert J. .... Massapequa, NY
Shanahan, Robert J., Jr. .... Annandale, NJ
Shanahan, Sara J. .... Boston, MA
Shanahan & Shanahan .... South Pasadena, CA
Shanahan, Steven R. .... Fort Collins, CO
Shanahan, Thomas C. .... Athens, GA
Shanahan, Thomas C. .... Wilmette, IL
Shanahan, Thomas D. .... New York, NY
Shanahan, Thomas E. .... Calhoun, GA
Shanahan, Thomas F. .... Pittsburgh, PA
Shanahan, Thomas J. .... Chicago, IL
Shanahan, Thomas J. .... Buffalo, NY
Shanahan, Thomas M. .... Omaha, NE
Shanahan, T. L. .... Calhoun, GA
Shanahan, Ward A. .... Helena, MT
Shanahan, William E. .... Salem, MA
Shanahan, Wm. Patrick
Department of Commerce, Patent and Trademark Office, GV
Shanaman, Alan I. .... Birmingham, MI
Shanberg, Arnold N. .... Kansas City, MO
Shanberg, Edwin H. .... Chicago, IL
Shanberg, Mark H. .... Chicago, IL
Shanberg, Ross E. .... Irvine, CA
Shanberge, Jonathan P. .... Palo Alto, CA
Shanbhag, Manish .... Boston, MA
Shanbom, Jeffrey M. .... Ferndale, MI
Shanbour, Steve .... Oklahoma City, OK
Shanbron, Barry S. .... Plainview, NY

Shancer, Jeffrey M. .... Chicago, IL
Shand, David A. .... Ann Arbor, MI
Shand, J. Douglas .... Durango, CO
Shand, Newbold & Chapman, A Professional Corporation .... Durango, CO
Pagosa Springs, CO
Shandalow, Keith A. .... Palo Alto, CA
Shandell, Andrea T. .... Bethesda, MD
Shandell, Blitz, Blitz, Glass, Bookson & Kern, LLP .... New York, NY
Shandell, Hildy .... New York, NY
Shandell, Richard E. .... New York, NY
Shander, Barbara J. .... Philadelphia, PA
Shandler, Carole C. .... Encino, CA
Shandler, Chad M. .... Wilmington, DE
Shandler, Esther .... Culver City, CA
Shandler, Marc Adam .... Edison, NJ
Shandler, Phyllis Weinstein .... Haverstraw, NY
Shandles, Deborah A. .... Raleigh, NC
Shandles, H. Martin .... Northbrook, IL
Shandling, Fred I. .... Northbrook, IL
Shandling, Judith L. .... New York, NY
Shandloff, Ned M. .... Boca Raton, FL
Shandor, A. Kristin .... Salem, VA
Shandor, Lidia Boyduy .... Lake Forest, IL
Shandrick, Rebecca Lynn .... Denver, CO
Shands, Courtney, Jr. .... St. Louis, MO
Shands, Jack L. .... Forrest City, AR
Shands, James A. .... Birmingham, AL
Shands, Joan M. .... Upton, NY
Shands, Marian J. .... Gainesville, FL
Shands, Morgan P. .... Jackson, MS
Shands, Rodney E. .... New Albany, MS
Shands, Tina M. .... Austin, TX
Shands, Wm. Tyler .... Richmond, VA
Shandy, Donald K. .... Oklahoma City, OK
Shane, Alan R. .... Boca Raton, FL
Shane, Amy L. .... New York, NY
Shane, Arnold M. .... Palm Desert, CA
Shane, B. Jerome .... Plymouth Meeting, PA
Shane, Barbara Kanter .... Solon, OH
Shane, Barry .... Cleveland, OH
Shane, Charles F. .... Dayton, OH
Shane, Charles N., Jr. .... Dayton, OH
Shane, David L. .... Westlake Village, CA
Shane, David M. .... Mineola, NY
Shane, David N. .... Indianapolis, IN
Shane, David R. .... San Francisco, CA
Shane, Denise .... Sunnyside, NY
Shane & DiGiuseppe .... Westlake Village, CA
Shane, Ian .... New York, NY
Shane, J. Michael .... Olean, NY
Shane, Jeffrey A. .... Los Angeles, CA
Shane, Jeffrey A. .... Rockville, MD
Shane, Jeffrey N. .... Washington, DC
Shane, John R. .... Washington, DC
Shane, Joseph .... Los Angeles, CA
Shane, Mark S. .... Edison, NJ
Shane, Michael .... Miami, FL
Shane, Michael .... Cleveland, OH
Shane, Michael B. .... San Francisco, CA
Shane, Michael J. .... San Bernardino, CA
Shane, Michael J. .... El Paso, TX
Shane, Michael, P.A., Law Offices of
Fort Lauderdale, FL
Miami, FL
Shane and Paolillo, P.C. .... Newton, MA
Shane, Paul T. .... Newton, MA
Shane, Penny .... New York, NY
Shane, Peter M. .... Pittsburgh, PA
Shane, Raymond E. .... St. Louis, MO
Shane, Richard A. .... New York, NY
Shane, Richard J. .... Albuquerque, NM
Shane & Shane, L.P.A. .... Cleveland, OH
Shane, Stephen H. .... New York, NY
Shane, Steven C. .... Cincinnati, OH
Shane, Susan M. .... Cherry Hill, NJ
Shane, Suzanne V. .... Riverhead, NY
Shane & Taitz .... San Francisco, CA
Shane, Thomas R. .... Newton, MA
Shane, Tim A. .... Boca Raton, FL
Shane, Victor P. .... Chicago, IL
Shane, Virginia R. .... Winnemucca, NV
Shanebrook, Elaine A. .... West Bend, WI
Shanedling, Stanley V. .... Wayzata, MN
Shane-Held, Deborah .... Mountainside, NJ
Shanelec, Daniel J. .... Lyons, KS
Sterling, KS
Shaner, Constance H. .... Carlsbad, CA
Shaner, Daniel H. .... Fairfax, VA
Shaner, Daniel H., P.C. .... Fairfax, VA
Shaner, G. Neale .... Ft. Calhoun, NE
Shaner, James L. .... Tonka Bay, MN
Shaner, Jeffrey Ian .... Las Vegas, NV
Shaner, Jeffrey Ian, Ltd., A Professional Corporation .... Las Vegas, NV
Shaner & Lane, Law Office of .... Robinson, IL
Shaner, Leslie Ann .... Lynchburg, VA
Shaner, Mark K. .... Aurora, CO
Shaner, Mark L. .... Robinson, IL
Shaner, Roberta .... Philadelphia, PA
Shaner, Thomas Ray .... Vandergrift, PA
Shanes, Abraham .... Chicago, IL
Shanes, Jacqueline P. .... Newark, NJ
Shanes, Samuel .... Chicago, IL
Shanes, Scott A. .... Dallas, TX
Shanes & Shanes .... Chicago, IL
Shaney, Kevin R. .... Los Angeles, CA
Shaney, Mary Jo .... Kansas City, MO
Shaneyfelt, Donald L. .... Long Pine, NE
Shaneyfelt, Laura B. .... Wichita, KS
Shaneyfelt, Richard L. .... Port Townsend, WA
Shaneyfelt, William L. .... Jasper, IN
Shanfeld, Andrew B. .... St. Louis, MO
Shang, Jane K. .... Boston, MA
Shang, Wade Vincent .... Daly City, CA
Shang, Wendy Wan-Long .... Washington, DC
Shangler, Chas. .... Kansas City, MO

Shangler, Dean A. .... Chapel Hill, NC
Shangraw, Barbara A. .... Denver, CO
Shangraw, Michael D. .... Denver, CO
Shanholtz, Judy L. .... Clarksburg, WV
Shanholtzer, Steven T. .... Springfield, MO
Shanin, Donald B. .... Newark, NJ
Shanin, Jeffrey M. .... Lincolnwood, IL
Shanin, Steven R. .... Chicago, IL
Shanis, Jos. .... Philadelphia, PA
Shank, Aaron M. .... Springfield, OH
Shank, Allison .... Prospect Heights, IL
Shank, Anne .... Dayton, OH
Shank, C. Kenneth .... Woodbridge, NJ
Shank, Christopher K. .... Seattle, WA
Shank, Christopher S. .... Kansas City, MO
Shank, Craig E. .... Bellevue, WA
Shank, Daniel F. .... Houston, TX
Shank, Derek P. .... Glendale, AZ
Shank, Diane S. .... Cincinnati, OH
Shank, Edward L. .... Dayton, OH
Shank, Erin B. .... Waco, TX
Shank, Gary W. .... Floresville, TX
Shank, Jeffrey J. .... Houston, TX
Shank, Jeffrey S. .... Lancaster, PA
Shank, Jennifer Lea .... Kansas City, MO
Shank, Jerome B. .... Portland, OR
Shank, John L. .... Englewood, CO
Shank, John R., Jr. .... Kansas City, MO
Shank, Karen B. .... Crystal Lake, IL
Shank, Laue & Hamilton, P.C.
Kansas City, MO
Shank, Leanne M. .... Lexington, VA
Shank, Lisa M. .... Fairfax, VA
Shank, Margaret Little .... Humble, TX
Shank, Mark A. .... Dallas, TX
Shank, Robert D. .... Cincinnati, OH
Shank, Susan .... Houston, TX
Shank, Suzanne .... Overland Park, KS
Shank, Theresa L. .... Norcross, GA
Shank, Warren .... Des Moines, IA
Shank, Willard A. .... Sacramento, CA
Shank, William O. .... Chicago, IL
Shankel, Joan S. .... Fresno, CA
Shanken, Mandell K. .... Harrisburg, PA
Shanken, Mayor .... Phoenix, AZ
Shanker, Arthur L. .... Atlantic City, NJ
Shanker, Jay .... Los Angeles, CA
Shanker, Julius L. .... Beverly Hills, CA
Shanker, Lawrence H. .... Chicago, IL
Shanker, Michael L. .... New York, NY
Shanker, Morris G. .... Cleveland, OH
Shankin, Hilary G. .... Ventura, CA
Shank-Klein, Marina .... Miami, FL
Shank-Klein, Marina, P.A. .... Miami, FL
Shankland, Richard W. .... Kansas City, MO
Shankland, Robert L. .... Ann Arbor, MI
Shankle, Margaret E. .... Charlotte, NC
Shanklin, Carita T. .... San Francisco, CA
Shanklin, Charles E. .... Milford Center, OH
Shanklin, Cynthia K. .... Fort Worth, TX
Shanklin, Dennis L. .... Burbank, CA
Shanklin, Gregory D. .... Brooklyn, NY
New York, NY
Shanklin, Kenneth A. .... Wilmington, NC
Shanklin & McDaniel, L.L.P.
Wilmington, NC
Shanklin, Susan .... New York, NY
Shankman, Aaron .... Memphis, TN
Shankman, Abraham .... Syracuse, NY
Shankman, Alan D. .... Cleveland, OH
Shankman & Associates .... Lewiston, ME
Shankman, Bernard .... Washington, DC
Shankman, David S. .... Tampa, FL
Shankman, Jack L. .... Chicago, IL
Shankman, Leonard I. .... Bolton, CT
Shankman, Ned N. .... Los Angeles, CA
Shankman, Neil S. .... Lewiston, ME
Shankman, Stephen B. .... Memphis, TN
Shanks & Blackstock .... Knoxville, TN
Shanks, C. A. Dudley .... Jeffersonville, IN
Louisville, KY
Shanks, Donald L. .... Kansas City, MO
Shanks, Gary L. .... Woodland Hills, CA
Shanks, George M., Jr. .... Houston, TX
Shanks, George Warren .... Luray, VA
Shanks, George Warren, P.C. .... Luray, VA
Shanks, Gregory D. .... Knoxville, TN
Shanks & Herbert .... Washington, DC
Alexandria, VA
Shanks, Hershel .... Washington, DC
Shanks, Jas. P. .... Baird, TX
Shanks, Jason .... Fort Worth, TX
Shanks, Jo Anne .... Albuquerque, NM
Shanks, John A. .... Madison, MS
Shanks, John N., II .... Fishers, IN
Indianapolis, IN
Shanks, John T. .... Dayton, OH
Shanks, Jonathan Julius .... Surfside Beach, SC
Shanks, Krista Lyn .... Iowa City, IA
Shanks, Laurie .... Albany, NY
Shanks, Linda D. .... Denver, CO
Shanks, Margaret McCloskey
Board of Governors Of The Federal Reserve System, Office of the General Counsel, GV
Shanks, Mark R. .... Alexandria, VA
Shanks, Michael D. .... Hamilton, OH
Shanks, Patricia L. .... Los Angeles, CA
San Francisco, CA
Shanks, Philip T., III, Law Offices of
Cordova, TN
Shanks, Philip T., Jr. .... Decatur, AL
Shanks, Randall J. .... Council Bluffs, IA
Shanks, Richard C. .... Houston, TX
Shanks, Richard C., P.C. .... Houston, TX
Shanks, Rosalie .... San Diego, CA
Shanks, Ruthanne Brain .... Spring Valley, NY
Shanks, Siobhan .... Albany, NY

Shanks, Sylvia L.
General Accounting Office, Office of the General Counsel, GV
Shanks, Thomas A. ....Cleveland, OH
Shanks, Tritter & Associates, P.C.
Austin, TX
Dallas, TX
Fort Worth, TX
Houston, TX
Shanks, Wallace T. ....Brenham, TX
Shanks, William E., Jr. ....Birmingham, AL
Shankweiler, R. T. ....Fort Lauderdale, FL
Shanle, Maria M. ....Alameda, CA
Shanle, Marsha B. ....Santa Cruz, CA
Shanle, Tom ....San Jose, CA
Shanler, Dana Ellen ....New York, NY
Shanley, Anthony J. ....San Diego, CA
Shanley and Baker ....Washington, DC
Shanley, Barry E. ....Montrose, CA
Shanley, Brigid ....Mendham, NJ
Shanley, Charles J., Jr. ....New York, NY
Shanley, Daniel M. ....Los Angeles, CA
Shanley, Dion J. ....Grenada, MS
Jackson, MS
Oxford, MS
Shanley, Edward K. ....Attleboro, MA
Shanley, Gregory T. ....Olympic Valley, CA
Shanley, J. Michael ....Marshfield, MA
Shanley, James ....Boston, MA
Shanley, James A., Jr. ....Madison, CT
Shanley, James C. ....Chicago, IL
Shanley, Jean M. ....Teterboro, NJ
Shanley, John B. ....Pueblo, CO
Shanley, Judith A. ....Buffalo, NY
Shanley, Michael G. ....Indianapolis, IN
Shanley, Michael P., Jr. ....Albany, NY
Shanley, Mildred A. ....Brooklyn, NY
Shanley, P. Michael ....Oswego, NY
Shanley, Peter J. ....Wilmington, DE
Shanley, Sharon I. ....Honolulu, HI
Shanley, Susan Potter ....Montrose, CA
Shanley, Sweeney, Reilly & Allen, P.C.
Albany, NY
Shanley, Terence E. ....Troy, NY
Shanley, Thomas H. ....Denver, CO
Shanley, Thomas M. ....Greenwich, CT
Shanley, Timothy E. ....Newark, NJ
Shanley, Timothy J. ....Wheaton, IL
Shanley, Timothy W. ....Montpelier, VT
Shanley, William F. ....Yonkers, NY
Shanlian, Dennis J. ....Kent, WA
Shanman, James A. ....New York, NY
Shannahan, Joan C. ....Lincolnshire, IL
Shannahan, Regina E. ....New York, NY
Shannahan, William P. ....La Jolla, CA
Shanner, Robert B. ....San Diego, CA
Shanney-Saborsky, Regina T.
Los Angeles, CA
Shanni, Erik ....Woodbridge, NJ
Shannin, Nicholas A. ....Orlando, FL
Shannon, Arthur W. ....Bloomfield Hills, MI
Shannon, Belinda R.
Research Triangle Park, NC
Shannon, Bob E. ....Austin, TX
Shannon, Brendan Linehan
Wilmington, DE
Shannon, Brian D. ....Walnut Creek, CA
Shannon, Brian D. ....Lubbock, TX
Shannon, Brian G. ....Detroit, MI
Shannon, Careen B. ....New York, NY
Shannon, Carlton A., Jr. ....Charlotte, NC
Shannon, Charles V. ....Bethesda, MD
Shannon, Christopher A. ....Brookline, MA
Shannon, Claudine M. ....New York, NY
Shannon, Craig ....Missoula, MT
Shannon, Craig Criminal Defense Attorney
Missoula, MT
Shannon, Craig S. ....Des Moines, IA
Pella, IA
Shannon, Dale E. ....Fort Collins, CO
Shannon, Dana M. ....Itasca, IL
Shannon, Daniel E. ....Great Falls, MT
Shannon, David J. ....Minneapolis, MN
Shannon, David James ....Philadelphia, PA
Shannon, David L. ....New Smyrna Beach, FL
Shannon, David M. ....Santa Clara, CA
Shannon, David R. ....Chicago, IL
Shannon, David S. ....Portland, OR
Shannon, David Taylor ....Tucson, AZ
Shannon, Desiree T. ....Columbus, OH
Shannon, Edward H. ....Gainesville, GA
Shannon, Eugene W. ....Norfolk, VA
Shannon & Fleming, P.C. ....Phoenix, AZ
Shannon, Francis A., III ....Boston, MA
Shannon, Frank J., III ....Atlanta, GA
Shannon, Fred ....San Antonio, TX
Shannon, Gary P. ....Springfield, MA
Shannon, George A., Jr. ....Houston, TX
Shannon, Gerald P. ....Falls Church, VA
Shannon, Gladys ....Fort Worth, TX
Shannon, Gracey, Ratliff & Miller, L.L.P.
Euless, TX
Fort Worth, TX
Shannon, Gregory R. ....Reno, NV
Shannon, H. Linwood, III ....Evansville, IN
Shannon, J. Donald ....Somers, CT
Shannon, Jack H., Jr. ....New York, NY
Shannon, Jacquelyn M. ....Clearwater, FL
Shannon, James A. ....Albany, NY
Shannon, James C. ....Richmond, VA
Shannon, James D. ....Hazlehurst, MS
Shannon, James F. ....Cleveland, OH
Shannon, James J., Jr. ....Richmond, KY
Shannon, James P. ....Wayzata, MN
Shannon, James P. ....Old Bridge, NJ
Shannon, James P. ....Portland, OR
Shannon, James W. ....Hillsborough, CA
Shannon, James W., Jr. ....Washington, DC
Shannon, Janie A. ....San Antonio, TX
Shannon, Jean ....Malvern, PA
Shannon, Jeffrey C. ....Tampa, FL
Shannon, Jeremiah S. ....Chicago, IL
Shannon, Joe, Jr. ....Fort Worth, TX
Shannon, John B. ....Atlanta, GA
Shannon, John E., Jr. ....Stevens Point, WI
Shannon, John G. ....Racine, WI
Shannon, John H. ....Fairfield, CT
Shannon, John Hugh, P.A. ....Lakeland, FL
Shannon, John J. ....Bedminster, NJ
Shannon, John M. ....New Haven, CT
Shannon, John M. ....Skaneateles, NY
Shannon, John P., Jr. ....Washington, DC
Shannon, John Rex ....Meridian, MS
Shannon, John S. ....Norfolk, VA
Shannon, John T. ....Little Rock, AR
Shannon, Johnaaron ....Crofton, MD
Shannon & Johnson, P.C. ....Portland, OR
Shannon, Joseph J. ....Detroit, MI
Shannon, Joseph P. ....Chicago, IL
Naperville, IL
Shannon, Joseph Scott ....Wilmington, DE
Shannon, Joseph T., Jr. ....Quincy, MA
Shannon, Karla J. ....Sacramento, CA
Shannon, Kathleen E. ....New York, NY
Shannon, Kathleen Marie ....Denver, CO
Shannon, Kevin E. ....El Paso, TX
Shannon, Kevin R. ....Wilmington, DE
Shannon, Kevin R. ....Atlantic City, NJ
Shannon, Laura Delong ....Washington, DC
Shannon, Laurie J. ....Chicago, IL
Shannon, Lavinia Lewis ....Lakeland, FL
Shannon Law Associates ....Boston, MA
Shannon, Lee K. ....Portland, OR
Shannon, Lisa A. ....Phoenix, AZ
Shannon, Lori L. ....Chicago, IL
Shannon, Malcolm L., Jr. ....Denver, CO
Shannon, Marcy S. ....Hillsboro, OR
Shannon, Margaret ....Detroit, MI
Shannon, Margaret Barrett ....Houston, TX
Shannon, Martin, Finkelstein & Sayre, A Professional Corporation ....Houston, TX
Shannon, Mary E. ....Palo Alto, CA
Shannon, Mathew E. ....Phoenix, AZ
Shannon, Matthew A. ....Tarrytown, NY
Shannon, Matthew D.
Merit Systems Protection Board, Clerk of the Board, GV
Shannon, Maureen A. ....Pittsburgh, PA
Shannon, Michael G. ....Miami, FL
Shannon, Michael G. ....New York, NY
Shannon, Michael J. ....Greensboro, NC
Shannon, Michael K. ....Clayton, MO
Shannon, Michael N. ....Little Rock, AR
Shannon, Michael P. ....Cheshire, CT
Shannon, Michael R. ....Buffalo, NY
Shannon, Michael T. ....Columbus, OH
Shannon, Michael Timothy ....Pasadena, CA
Shannon, Michael T. M. ....Bethesda, MD
Shannon, Mitzi T. ....El Paso, TX
Shannon & Munn, PLLC ....Hazlehurst, MS
Shannon, Newell C. ....New York, NY
Shannon, Pat A. ....Kansas City, MO
Shannon, Patrick H. ....Washington, DC
Shannon, Patrick J. ....Murrysville, PA
Pittsburgh, PA
Shannon, Patrick J. ....Arlington, VA
Shannon, Patrick K. ....Sacramento, CA
Shannon, Patrick L. ....San Angelo, TX
Shannon, Patrick M. ....Sault Ste. Marie, MI
Shannon, Paul V. ....Worcester, MA
Shannon, P. B. ....San Angelo, TX
Shannon, Peter A. ....Old Forge, NY
Shannon, Peter M., Jr. ....Chicago, IL
Shannon, Philip T. ....New York, NY
Shannon, Porter, Johnson, Pfluger, Davis & Joynton, L.L.P. ....San Angelo, TX
Shannon, Preston C. ....Richmond, VA
Shannon, Raphael ....San Francisco, CA
Shannon, Raymond E. ....Cincinnati, OH
Shannon, Richard A. ....Brooklyn, NY
Shannon, Richard A. ....Austin, TX
Shannon, Robert H. ....Grand Blanc, MI
Shannon, Robert J. ....New York, NY
Shannon, Robert J. ....Stevens Point, WI
Shannon, Robert L., Jr. ....Atlanta, GA
Shannon, Robert M. ....Sacramento, CA
Shannon, Robert T. ....Chicago, IL
Shannon, Robert V. ....Chicago, IL
Shannon, Robert V. ....Newark, NJ
Shannon, Robert W. ....Vancouver, WA
Shannon, Rufus D. ....St. Louis, MO
Shannon, Scott ....Wilmington, DE
Shannon, Scott H. ....Portland, OR
Shannon, Sean James ....White Plains, NY
Shannon, Terence J. ....San Mateo, CA
Shannon, Thomas A. ....Alexandria, VA
Shannon, Thomas F. ....Washington, DC
Shannon, Thomas F. ....Syracuse, NY
Shannon, Thomas J. ....Chicago, IL
Mount Prospect, IL
Shannon, Thomas P. ....Milwaukee, WI
Shannon, Walter E. ....Port Huron, MI
Shannon, Walter J. ....Rochester, NY
Shannon, Wesley J. ....Atlanta, GA
Shannon, William E., Jr.
Palm Beach Gardens, FL
Shannon, William K. ....Rock Hill, SC
Shannon, William P. ....Austin, TX
Shannon, William T. ....Fairfax Station, VA
Shannon, William V., Jr. ....Roseville, CA
Shannon, Wm. Kevin ....Paducah, KY
Shannonhouse, James M. ....Charlotte, NC
Shannonhouse, Joseph G., IV
Oklahoma City, OK
Shannonhouse, Royal G., III
Annapolis, MD
Shanoff, Barry S. ....Washington, DC
Shanor, Stephen S. ....Carlsbad, NM
Shanor, Stuart D. ....Roswell, NM
Shanoski, Henry Ives ....Portland, ME
Shanoski, Paul ....Department of Commerce, Patent and Trademark Office, GV
Shanower, Jonathan B. ....Aurora, IL
Shansab, Yama A. ....McLean, VA
Shansby, Ronnald J.
General Services Administration, Public Buildings Service, GV
Shansky, Marjorie F. ....New Haven, CT
Shansky, Robert J. ....New York, NY
Shanstrom, Jack D. ....Billings, MT
Shantz, Arthur W., Jr. ....Columbus, OH
Shantz and Booker, Professional Corporation
Birmingham, MI
Detroit, MI
Shantz, Debra Mallonee ....Springfield, MO
Shantz, Frederick F. ....Liverpool, NY
Shantz, John F. ....Birmingham, MI
Shantz, Stephen H. ....Doylestown, PA
Shanus, Corey R. ....Purchase, NY
Shanus, Sarene Paula ....Mamaroneck, NY
Shanus, Stuart A. ....Los Angeles, CA
Shao, Mary Ann ....Ames, IA
Shao, Misara C. ....Los Angeles, CA
Shao, W. Ming ....Washington, DC
Shapack, Andrew I. ....New York, NY
Shapack, Claire K. ....Charlotte, NC
Shapack, Edward S. ....Charlotte, NC
Shapack, McCullough & Kanter, A Professional Corporation
Bloomfield Hills, MI
Shapack, Richard A. ....Naples, FL
Bloomfield Hills, MI
Shapack & Shapack, P.A. ....Charlotte, NC
Shapan, Harvey M. ....Dallas, TX
Shapard, Howard K. ....Washington, DC
Shapard, Edwin J. ....Oklahoma City, OK
Shapard, John E.
Federal Judicial Center, GV
Shapard & Shapard, Inc.
Oklahoma City, OK
Shapard, W. Allen ....Washington, DC
Shapazian, Larry H. ....Fresno, CA
Shape, John F. ....Grand Rapids, MI
Shape, Steven M. ....Northbrook, IL
Shape & Zuckerman ....Northbrook, IL
Shapera, Louis M. ....Northbrook, IL
Shapero, Arnold O. ....Southfield, MI
Shapero, Bertram M. ....West Palm Beach, FL
Shapero, Donald L. ....Santa Monica, CA
Shapero, Ephraim E. ....Syracuse, NY
Shapero, James I. ....Cleveland, OH
Shapero, Laurence A. ....Chicago, IL
Shapero, Lila ....Burlington, VT
Shapero, Martin M., (A Law Corporation)
Woodland Hills, CA
Shapero, McGinnis and Associates
Bedford Heights, OH
Cleveland, OH
Shapero, Michael I. ....Bedford Heights, OH
Cleveland, OH
Shapero, Neal E. ....Cleveland, OH
Shapero, Paul D., Law Offices of
Stamford, CT
Shapero & Shapero ....Woodland Hills, CA
Shapero, Steven J., (A Law Corporation)
Woodland Hills, CA
Shapero, Theodore A. ....Chicago, IL
Shapero, Walter ....Detroit, MI
Shapero, William L. ....Boca Raton, FL
Shapery, Sandor W. ....San Diego, CA
Shapey, Alan M. ....New York, NY
Shaphran, Wayne A. ....Sherman Oaks, CA
Shaphren, Paul H. ....Salt Lake City, UT
Shapin & Buchanan ....Tustin, CA
Shapin, Ruth D. ....Tustin, CA
Shapira, Albert C. ....Pittsburgh, PA
Shapira, Daniel H. ....Pittsburgh, PA
Shapira, Gary J. ....Erie, PA
Shapira, Hutzelman, Berlin & May
Erie, PA
Shapira, Jane A. ....Seattle, WA
Shapira, John S. ....Chicago, IL
Shapira, Ralph J. ....Los Angeles, CA
Shapira, Randy L. ....Erie, PA
Shapira, Saul F. ....Pittsburgh, PA
Shapira, Thomas B. ....Chicago, IL
Shapiro, A. Morton ....Cherry Hill, NJ
Shapiro, Abbe G. ....New York, NY
Shapiro, Abraham ....New York, NY
Shapiro Abrams Zedeck
Fort Lauderdale, FL
Plantation, FL
Shapiro, Adam J. ....New York, NY
Shapiro, Adam L. ....New York, NY
Shapiro, Adam M. ....Seattle, WA
Shapiro, Adam P. ....Brooklyn, NY
Shapiro & Adams, P.A. ....Plantation, FL
Shapiro, Alan ....New York, NY
Shapiro, Alan H. ....Boston, MA
Shapiro, Alan J. ....Cleveland, OH
Shapiro, Alan M. ....Department of Justice, Tax Division, GV
Shapiro, Alan N. ....New York, NY
Shapiro, Alayne Green ....Chestnut Hill, MA
Shapiro, Albert ....Brooklyn, NY
Shapiro, Albert ....Philadelphia, PA
Shapiro, Aleena R. ....New York, NY
Shapiro, Alexander ....New York, NY
Shapiro, Alexandra A.E. ....New York, NY
Shapiro, Alexis H. ....New York, NY
Shapiro, Alfred B. ....Baton Rouge, LA
Shapiro, Alison J. ....Washington, DC
Arlington, VA
Shapiro, Allan, & Associates, P.A.
Minneapolis, MN
Shapiro, Allan F. ....Minneapolis, MN
Shapiro, Allan M. ....Tarzana, CA
Shapiro, Alvin D., P.C. ....Aspen, CO
Overland Park, KS
Kansas City, MO
Shapiro, Amy ....Binghamton, NY
Shapiro, Amy L. ....Hackensack, NJ
Shapiro, Amy L. ....Milwaukee, WI
Shapiro, Andra L. ....New York, NY
Shapiro, Andrea ....New York, NY
Shapiro, Andrew E. ....Melville, NY
Shapiro, Andrew H. ....New York, NY
Shapiro, Andrew J. ....Department of Justice, Antitrust Division, GV
Shapiro, Andrew L. ....Encino, CA
Shapiro, Andrew L. ....Washington, DC
Shapiro, Andrew M. ....New York, NY
Shapiro, Anita D. ....New York, NY
Shapiro, Anita Rae ....Brea, CA
Shapiro, Ann E. L. ....Pittsburgh, PA
Shapiro, Anthony D. ....Seattle, WA
Shapiro, Arthur ....Middletown, NY
Shapiro, Arthur D. ....Narberth, PA
Shapiro & Associates ....Boston, MA
Dedham, MA
Shapiro & Associates ....New York, NY
Shapiro, Avner M. ....Department of Justice, Civil Rights Division, GV
Shapiro, Barbara K.
Federal Trade Commission, Bureau of Competition, GV
Shapiro, Barbara L. ....Albuquerque, NM
Shapiro, Barrie M. ....Lakewood, CO
Shapiro, Barry ....Phoenix, AZ
Shapiro, Barry H. ....Freehold, NJ
Shapiro, Barry R. ....Uniondale, NY
Shapiro, Barton
Department of Housing and Urban Development, Office of General Counsel, GV
Shapiro, Beilly, Rosenberg, Aronowitz, Levy & Fox, LLP ....New York, NY
Shapiro, Benjamin L. ....Boston, MA
Shapiro, Benjamin P. ....Chicago, IL
Shapiro, Bernard ....Los Angeles, CA
Shapiro, Bernard H. ....Rockford, IL
Shapiro, Bernard L. ....Stamford, CT
Shapiro, Bernard L. ....Philadelphia, PA
Shapiro, Bernard S. ....Miami, FL
Shapiro, Bernard S., (A Law Corp.)
Los Angeles, CA
Shapiro, Beth ....New York, NY
Shapiro, Beth J. ....Phoenix, AZ
Shapiro and Bettinger, LLP
Albuquerque, NM
Shapiro, Boris ....Philadelphia, PA
Shapiro, Bram ....Boston, MA
Shapiro, Brenda Bernstein ....Miami, FL
Shapiro, Brian ....Las Vegas, NV
Shapiro, Bruce H. ....Salt Lake City, UT
Shapiro, Bruce I. ....Las Vegas, NV
Shapiro, Bruce I., Ltd. ....Las Vegas, NV
Shapiro, Bruce L. ....Florham Park, NJ
Shapiro, Bruce S. ....Towson, MD
Shapiro, Buchman, Provine & Patton LLP
Walnut Creek, CA
Shapiro & Burson ....Fairfax, VA
Virginia Beach, VA
Shapiro, Burton J. ....Los Angeles, CA
Shapiro, C. Zadik ....San Francisco, CA
Shapiro, Carl B. ....San Anselmo, CA
Shapiro, Carl W. ....Santa Monica, CA
Shapiro, Carolyn ....Chicago, IL
Shapiro, Charles A. ....Bronx, NY
Shapiro, Charles D. ....New York, NY
Shapiro, Charlotte ....Kenosha, WI
Shapiro, Cheryl B. ....Mount Laurel, NJ
Shapiro, Cindy A. ....Manhattan Beach, CA
Shapiro, Claire L. ....Washington, DC
Shapiro, Clifford Harlan ....New York, NY
Shapiro, Clifford J. ....San Francisco, CA
Shapiro, Clifford J. ....Chicago, IL
Shapiro & Coleman ....North Massapequa, NY
Shapiro, Corey B. ....San Francisco, CA
Shapiro & Croland ....Hackensack, NJ
Shapiro & Daly ....Gardiner, ME
Shapiro, Daniel ....New York, NY
Shapiro, Daniel A. ....Miami, FL
Shapiro, Daniel A. ....Needham, MA
Shapiro, Daniel A. ....New York, NY
Shapiro, Daniel B. ....Boston, MA
Dedham, MA
Shapiro, Daniel C. ....Los Angeles, CA
Shapiro, Daniel C. ....Bolingbrook, IL
Shapiro, Daniel J. ....Baton Rouge, LA
Shapiro, Daniel J. ....St. Paul, MN
Shapiro, Daniel K. ....Los Angeles, CA
Shapiro, Daniel Lawrence ....Cleveland, OH
Shapiro, Daniel M. ....Los Angeles, CA
Shapiro, Daniel M. ....Mineola, NY
Shapiro, Daniel P. ....Chicago, IL
Shapiro, Daniel R. ....Hartford, CT
Shapiro, Daniel S. ....New York, NY
Shapiro, Daniel W. ....Albuquerque, NM
Shapiro, Daniel Z. ....Middletown, CT
Shapiro, Darwin ....Las Vegas, NV
Shapiro, Daryl M. ....Washington, DC
Shapiro, David ....Bronx, NY
Shapiro, David A. ....Chicago, IL
Shapiro, David A. ....Buffalo, NY
Shapiro, David B. ....Baltimore, MD
Shapiro, David B. ....Charleston, WV
Shapiro, David G. ....Philadelphia, PA
Shapiro, David H. ....Washington, DC
Shapiro, David H. ....New York, NY
Shapiro, David I. ....Washington, DC

Shapiro, David I. ....**New York, NY**
Shapiro, David J. ....Calabasas, CA
Shapiro, David J. ....**Seal Beach, CA**
Shapiro, David J. ....**Boston, MA**
Shapiro, David J. ....**New York, NY**
Shapiro, David L. ....**Chicago, IL**
Shapiro, David L. ....Cambridge, MA
Shapiro, David L. ....Austin, TX
Shapiro, David M. ....Bethesda, MD
Shapiro, David M. ....New York, NY
Shapiro, David M. ....**Richmond, VA**
Shapiro, David P. ....Washington, DC
Shapiro, David T. ....**Washington, DC**
Shapiro, David V. ....Jenkintown, PA
Shapiro, Dawn C. ....**New York, NY**
Shapiro, Deborah A. ....**New York, NY**
Shapiro, Deborah B. ....**New York, NY**
Shapiro, Deborah Dickson ....Middletown, CT
Shapiro, Deborah K. ....**White Plains, NY**
Shapiro, Debra ....Los Angeles, CA
Shapiro & Dector, P.A. ....**Boca Raton, FL**
Shapiro, Diane S. ....Rancho Cucamonga, CA
Shapiro, Dina L. ....**New York, NY**
Shapiro, D. J. ....St. Clair, MI
Shapiro, Donald A., (Ltd.) ....Chicago, IL
Shapiro, Dorothy L. ....Staten Island, NY
Shapiro, Douglas B. ....Ypsilanti, MI
Shapiro, E. Donald ....New York, NY
Shapiro, Edward A. ....**Boston, MA**
Shapiro, Edward D. ....**Chicago, IL**
Shapiro, Edward H. ....Nashville, TN
Shapiro, Edward I. ....New York, NY
Shapiro, Edward J. ....**Washington, DC**
Shapiro, Edward J. ....Mineola, NY
Shapiro, Edward M. ....**New York, NY**
Shapiro, Edwin ....Towson, MD
Shapiro, Edwin H. ....**Schaumburg, IL**
Shapiro, Edwin S. ....Briarcliff Manor, NY
Shapiro, Eileen F. ....New York, NY
Shapiro, Elizabeth J. ....Department of Justice, Civil Division, GV
Shapiro, Ellen Carol ....Brooklyn, NY
Shapiro, Ellen L. ....**New York, NY**
Shapiro, Ellen Louise ....Washington, DC
Shapiro, Ellen S. ....Department of Justice, Civil Division, GV
Shapiro, Emily F. ....St. Paul, MN
Shapiro, Eric L. ....New York, NY
Shapiro, Eugene A. ....Baltimore, MD
Shapiro, Evan ....**New York, NY**
Shapiro, Everett H. ....**Santa Rosa, CA**
Shapiro, Felicia ....New York, NY
Shapiro & Felty, P.L.L. ....Cleveland, OH
Shapiro, Floyd ....**Roseland, NJ**
Shapiro Forman & Allen LLP
New York, NY
Shapiro, Frances Alperin ....Philadelphia, PA
Shapiro, Frank H. ....**Boston, MA**
Shapiro, Fred D. ....**Cleveland, OH**
Shapiro, Fred D., Co., L.P.A.
Cleveland, OH
Shapiro, Fred L. ....Anna, IL
Shapiro, Fred L. ....White Plains, NY
Shapiro, Fred Richard ....**Santa Ana, CA**
Shapiro Fussell Wedge Smotherman Martin & Price, LLP ....**Atlanta, GA**
Shapiro, Gail B. ....**New York, NY**
Shapiro, Galvin, Shapiro, Piasta & Moran, A Professional Corporation
Santa Rosa, CA
Shapiro, Gary ....**Palo Alto, CA**
Shapiro, Gary A. ....Huntingdon Valley, PA
Shapiro, Gary E. ....Woodbury, NY
Shapiro, Gary E. ....Salt Lake City, UT
Shapiro, Gary J. ....**San Francisco, CA**
Shapiro, Gary J. ....Arlington, VA
Shapiro, Gary M. ....Irvine, CA
Shapiro, Gary S. ....East Brunswick, NJ
Shapiro, Gayle M. ....Skokie, IL
Shapiro, Gene J. ....Chicago, IL
Shapiro, Geoffrey Jerome ....**Cleveland, OH**
Shapiro, George H. ....Washington, DC
Shapiro, George J. ....**Reston, VA**
Shapiro, George J., P.C. ....**Reston, VA**
Shapiro, Gerald ....New York, NY
Shapiro, Gerald M. ....**Atlanta, GA**
Fairfax, VA
Shapiro, Gladys ....Gloucester, MA
Shapiro, Glenn A. ....Omaha, NE
Shapiro & Goodfriend ....Nanuet, NY
Shapiro, Gordon H. ....**Roanoke, VA**
Shapiro, Gordon M. ....**Dallas, TX**
Shapiro, Gregg D. ....**Boston, MA**
Shapiro, H. Adam ....Philadelphia, PA
Shapiro Haber & Urmy LLP ......**Boston, MA**
Shapiro, Hal S. ....**Washington, DC**
Shapiro, Harold A. ....Selden, NY
Shapiro, Harold B. ....Vineland, NJ
Shapiro, Harold D. ....**Chicago, IL**
Shapiro, Harold J. ....Gardiner, ME
Shapiro, Harold P. ....Washington, DC
Shapiro, Harriet C. ....New York, NY
Shapiro, Harriet S. ....Department of Justice, Office of the Solicitor General, GV
Shapiro, Harry ....New York, NY
Shapiro, Harry D. ....**Baltimore, MD**
Shapiro, Harry G. ....Cheyenne, WY
Shapiro, Harry S. ....Towson, MD
Shapiro, Harvey ....**New York, NY**
Shapiro, Harvey N. ....**Cherry Hill, NJ**
Philadelphia, PA
Shapiro, Harvey S. ....Cambridge, MA
Shapiro, Haskell ....Boston, MA
Shapiro, Helen D. ....**Chicago, IL**
Shapiro, Herbert L. ....Beach Haven, NJ
Shapiro, Hershel J. ....Denver, CO
Shapiro, Howard ....Chicago, IL
Shapiro, Howard ....**Albany, NY**
Shapiro, Howard ....Plano, TX
Shapiro, Howard A. ....**New York, NY**
Shapiro, Howard D. ....**Los Angeles, CA**
Shapiro, Howard E. ....**Washington, DC**
Shapiro, Howard M. ....**Washington, DC**
Shapiro, Howard, (P.C.) .....**New Orleans, LA**
Shapiro, Howard R. ....**Hackensack, NJ**
New York, NY
Shapiro, Hy ....**Miami, FL**
Shapiro, Hyman ....Bethesda, MD
Shapiro, Hyman R. ....Lake Worth, FL
Shapiro, Ilene E. ....**Chicago, IL**
Shapiro, Ira P. ....Princeton, NJ
Shapiro, Ira R. ....**North Miami Beach, FL**
Shapiro, Ira R., P.A.
North Miami Beach, FL
Shapiro, Ira S. ....**Washington, DC**
Shapiro, Irving ....Newton, MA
Shapiro, Irving S. ....**Wilmington, DE**
Shapiro, Isaac ....**New York, NY**
Shapiro, Isaac B. ....Chicago, IL
Shapiro, Isadore ....Newburgh, NY
Shapiro, Israel & Weiner, P.C.
Boston, MA
Shapiro, Ivan ....New York, NY
Shapiro, J. Ben ....**Atlanta, GA**
Shapiro, J. Jay ....Tarzana, CA
Shapiro, J. Jay ....Albany, NY
Shapiro, Jack E. ....Chicago, IL
Shapiro, Jack R. ....**New York, NY**
Shapiro, Jacob J. ....Lutherville, MD
Shapiro, Jacob M. ....Freeport, NY
Shapiro, Jacqueline E. ....Miami, FL
Shapiro, James A. ....**Stamford, CT**
Shapiro, James A. ....**Chicago, IL**
Shapiro, James B. ....**New York, NY**
Shapiro, James E. ....Milwaukee, WI
Shapiro, James J. ....Rochester, NY
Shapiro, Jamie E. ....New York, NY
Shapiro, Janet A. ....**Beverly Hills, CA**
Shapiro, Jason A. ....**Columbia, MD**
Shapiro, Jason A. ....**Ellicott City, MD**
Shapiro, Jason M. ....**Rockville, MD**
Shapiro, Jason Samuel ....West Babylon, NY
Shapiro, Jay B. ....**Miami, FL**
Shapiro, Jay L. ....**Phoenix, AZ**
Shapiro, Jay M. ....Chicago, IL
Shapiro, Jay M. ....Chestnut Hill, MA
Shapiro, Jeffrey B. ....**Miami, FL**
Shapiro, Jeffrey E. ....**Boston, MA**
Shapiro, Jeffrey G. ....Highland, NY
Shapiro, Jeffrey Ira ....Garden City, NY
Shapiro, Jeffrey J. ....New York, NY
Shapiro, Jeffrey K. ....**Washington, DC**
Shapiro, Jeffrey L. ....Union, NJ
Shapiro, Jeffrey M. ....**Woodbridge, NJ**
Shapiro, Jeffrey N. ....**Los Angeles, CA**
Shapiro, Jeffrey P. ....**Miami, FL**
Shapiro, Jeffrey Scott ....Hopewell, VA
Shapiro, Jennifer R. ....**Chicago, IL**
Shapiro, Jerold J. ....Chicago, IL
Shapiro, Jerome ....Bayonne, NJ
West Long Branch, NJ
Shapiro, Jerome C. ....**Kankakee, IL**
Shapiro, Jerome G. ....**New York, NY**
Shapiro, Jerrold M. ....Chicago, IL
Shapiro, Jerry ....Los Angeles, CA
Shapiro, Jerry I. ....Munster, IN
Shapiro, Jill A. ....Washington, DC
Shapiro, Joel ....Chicago, IL
Shapiro, Joel B. ....**Phoenix, AZ**
Shapiro, Joel C. ....**Philadelphia, PA**
Shapiro, Joel F. ....**Edison, NJ**
Shapiro, Joel G. ....**Chicago, IL**
Shapiro, Joel H. ....**Chicago, IL**
Shapiro, Joel M. ....Washington, DC
Shapiro, Joel S. ....Dayton, OH
Shapiro, John H. ....Miami, FL
Shapiro, John L. ....**San Juan, PR**
Shapiro, John T. ....**Chicago, IL**
Shapiro, Jonathan ....**Portland, ME**
Shapiro, Jonathan ....**Boston, MA**
Shapiro, Jonathan ....Alexandria, VA
McLean, VA
Shapiro, Jonathan A. ....**Boston, MA**
Shapiro, Jonathan G. ....**Palo Alto, CA**
Shapiro, Jonathan I. ....**New York, NY**
Shapiro, Jonathan, P.C. ....Alexandria, VA
Shapiro, Jonathan S. ....**New York, NY**
Shapiro, Jordan L. ....Malden, MA
Shapiro, Joseph C. ....New Canaan, CT
Shapiro, Joseph C. ....Margaretville, NY
Shapiro, Judah S. ....New York, NY
Shapiro, Judith A. ....**Washington, DC**
Shapiro, Judith Hope ....Chicago, IL
Shapiro, Judith Salkow ....**Los Angeles, CA**
Shapiro, Julie A. ....Los Angeles, CA
Shapiro, Julie Greenberg ....**Miami, FL**
Shapiro, Julius H. ....**Chicago, IL**
Palatine, IL
Shapiro, Karen L. ....Washington, DC
Shapiro, Keith J. ....**Chicago, IL**
Shapiro, Kendis & Associates Co., L.P.A.
Cleveland, OH
Shapiro, Kenneth A. ....**Atlanta, GA**
Shapiro, Kenneth J.
National Labor Relations Board, Office of the General Counsel, GV
Shapiro, Kenneth L. ....**Albany, NY**
Shapiro, Kenneth S. ....**Bala Cynwyd, PA**
Shapiro, Kenneth W.
Fort Lauderdale, FL
Shapiro, Kerry ....**San Francisco, CA**
Shapiro, Kimberly Ross ....**Coral Gables, FL**
Shapiro, Kristina Webb ....Baton Rouge, LA
Shapiro & Kurtin ....**Roanoke, VA**
Shapiro, Larry E. ....**Washington, DC**
Shapiro, Larry J. ....Tiburon, CA
Shapiro, Laura E. ....**Denver, CO**
Shapiro, Laura E., P.C., Law Office of
Denver, CO
Shapiro, Laura R. ....**New York, NY**
Shapiro, Lauren B. ....Orlando, FL
Shapiro, Laurence J. ....**Burbank, CA**
Shapiro, Laurence J. ....Morristown, NJ
Shapiro Law Firm ....**Tallahassee, FL**
Shapiro Law Firm, The .....**Beverly Hills, CA**
Los Angeles, CA
Shapiro, Lawrence G. ....New York, NY
Shapiro, Lawrence H.
Ocean Township, NJ
Shapiro, Lawrence M. ....**Minneapolis, MN**
Shapiro, Lawrence W. ....**New York, NY**
Shapiro, Lee J. ....Denver, CO
Shapiro, Lee J., P.C. ....Denver, CO
Shapiro, Lee S. ....La Mesa, CA
Shapiro, Leonard ....Huntington Woods, MI
Shapiro, Leonard A. ....McLean, VA
Shapiro, Leonard H. ....**Baltimore, MD**
Shapiro, Leonard H. ....**Owings Mills, MD**
Shapiro, Leonard H. ....**Towson, MD**
Shapiro, Leonard I. ....Cambridge, MA
Shapiro, Leonard N. ....**New York, NY**
Shapiro, Leonard P. ....**Nashua, NH**
Shapiro, Leonard P., P.A. ....**Nashua, NH**
Shapiro, Leonard & Robert, Law Offices of
New York, NY
Shapiro, Leslie H. ....**Boston, MA**
Shapiro, Lewis R. ....Chicago, IL
Shapiro & Liebman ....Chicago, IL
Shapiro, Lifschitz and Schram, P.C.
Washington, DC
Greenbelt, MD
Shapiro, Linda J. ....**Washington, DC**
Shapiro, Linda L. ....**St. Louis, MO**
Shapiro, Lisa A. ....**Cambridge, MA**
Shapiro, Lori Ann ....New York, NY
Shapiro, Lori J. ....**Atlanta, GA**
Shapiro, Louis Charles ....**Philadelphia, PA**
Shapiro & Lugo ....**San Juan, PR**
Shapiro, Lyle E. ....**Miami, FL**
Shapiro, Lynn A. ....Pasadena, CA
Shapiro, Lynn E. ....Washington, DC
Shapiro, M. David ....**Sarasota, FL**
Shapiro, Manson & Karbank ....**Aspen, CO**
Overland Park, KS
Kansas City, MO
Shapiro, Marc A. ....Treasury Department, Internal Revenue Service, GV
Shapiro, Marc H.
Research Triangle Park, NC
Shapiro, Marc L. ....Naples, FL
Shapiro, Marc S. ....Woodland Hills, CA
Shapiro, Marc S. ....**New York, NY**
Shapiro, Marilyn M. ....Kansas City, MO
Shapiro, Mark A. ....**New York, NY**
Shapiro, Mark A.J. ....**Miami, FL**
Shapiro, Mark D.
Administrative Office Of The United States Courts, GV
Shapiro, Mark D. ....**Voorhees, NJ**
Shapiro, Mark H., (P.C.) ....Southfield, MI
Shapiro, Mark J. ....**New York, NY**
Shapiro, Mark L. ....**Chicago, IL**
Shapiro, Mark R. ....**Boulder, CO**
Shapiro, Mark S. ....**Miami, FL**
Shapiro, Marshall D. ....Hull, MA
Shapiro, Marta Berl ....Brooklyn, NY
Shapiro, Martin ....**Miami Beach, FL**
Shapiro, Martin A. ....Ithaca, NY
Shapiro, Martin, Attorney At Law
Miami Beach, FL
Shapiro, Marvin A. ....Akron, OH
Shapiro, Marvin M. ....**New York, NY**
Shapiro, Marvin N. ....Los Angeles, CA
Shapiro, Marvin S., (P.C.)
Los Angeles, CA
Shapiro, Mary L. ....**San Francisco, CA**
Shapiro, Mathieu J. ....**Philadelphia, PA**
Shapiro, Matthew I. ....Cooper City, FL
Shapiro, Maxine R. ....**New York, NY**
Shapiro & Mayer ....Washington, DC
Shapiro & McKenzie ....Euless, TX
Shapiro, Melinda R. ....**Indianapolis, IN**
Shapiro, Melvin I. ....Cambridge, MA
Shapiro, Meryl ....**Brooklyn, NY**
Shapiro, Meryl J. ....Woodbridge, NJ
Shapiro, Michael ....Atlanta, GA
Shapiro, Michael ....Merrick, NY
Shapiro, Michael A. ....Deer Park, NY
Shapiro, Michael A., Law Offices of
Coconut Grove, FL
Cincinnati, OH
Shapiro, Michael B. ....**Boca Raton, FL**
Shapiro, Michael B. ....Atlanta, GA
Shapiro, Michael B. ....**Detroit, MI**
Shapiro, Michael D. ....New London, CT
Shapiro, Michael D., P.C. ....New London, CT
Shapiro, Michael F. ....Torrance, CA
Shapiro, Michael H. ....Los Angeles, CA
Shapiro, Michael J. ....**Chicago, IL**
Shapiro, Michael J. ....**New York, NY**
Shapiro, Michael J. ....**Cleveland, OH**
Shapiro, Michael L. ....Stratford, CT
Shapiro, Michael, (P.C.) ....**New York, NY**
Shapiro, Michael R. ....Beverly Hills, CA
Shapiro, Michael R. ....Newark, NJ
Shapiro, Michael R., P.C. ....Beverly Hills, CA
Shapiro, Michelle J. ....**New York, NY**
Shapiro & Miles ....La Jolla, CA
Santa Ana, CA
Walnut Creek, CA
Las Vegas, NV
Shapiro, Milton B. ....Nanuet, NY
Shapiro, Milton H. ....Chevy Chase, MD
Shapiro, Milton S. ....**New York, NY**
Shapiro, Minor H. ....Pittsburgh, PA
Shapiro, Mitchell C. ....**New York, NY**
Shapiro, Mitchell & Dupont LLP
Santa Monica, CA
Shapiro, Mitchell G. ....New York, NY
Shapiro, Mitchell J. ....Bethesda, MD
Shapiro, Mitchell S. ....**Los Angeles, CA**
Shapiro, Mitchell W. ....**Washington, DC**
Shapiro, Mona D. ....**Mount Kisco, NY**
Shapiro, Mortimer A. ....New York, NY
Shapiro, Morton ....Baltimore, MD
Shapiro, Morton A. ....New York, NY
Shapiro, Murray S. ....**Butler, PA**
Shapiro, Myra E. ....Jamaica, NY
Shapiro, Myron ....**Sun City, AZ**
Sun City West, AZ
Shapiro, Myron ....Fresno, CA
Shapiro, Myron ....**Miami, FL**
Shapiro, Nathan, (P.C.) ....New York, NY
Shapiro, Neal J. ....**Minneapolis, MN**
Shapiro, Neil K.
Executive Office Of The President, Office of Management and Budget, GV
Shapiro, Neil L. ....**San Francisco, CA**
Shapiro, Neil R. ....**New York, NY**
Shapiro, Nelson H. ....**Washington, DC**
Shapiro, Nina B. ....Lancaster, PA
Shapiro & Nordmeyer ....Edina, MN
Shapiro, Norma L. ....Philadelphia, PA
Shapiro, Norman ....**Middletown, NY**
Shapiro, Norman J. ....Los Angeles, CA
Shapiro, Norman M. ....Glen Ellyn, IL
Shapiro and Olander, A Professional Association ....**Washington, DC**
Baltimore, MD
Shapiro, Orie C. ....New York, NY
Shapiro, Pamela B. ....Foxboro, MA
Shapiro, Pat R.
Agency for International Development, Legal Advisers-Overseas, GV
Shapiro, Paul ....Frankfort, KY
Shapiro, Paul ....**Piscataway, NJ**
Shapiro, Paul A. ....**Tallahassee, FL**
Shapiro, Paul E. ....Boca Raton, FL
Shapiro, Paul G. ....Trenton, NJ
Shapiro, Paul I. ....**Teaneck, NJ**
Shapiro, Paul M. ....Storrs, CT
Shapiro, Paul S. ....Chicago, IL
Shapiro, Paul W. ....Corona Del Mar, CA
Shapiro, Paul Y. ....**Cleveland, OH**
Shapiro, Peter A. ....Orlando, FL
Shapiro, Peter E. ....**Garden City, NY**
Shapiro, Peter R. ....Mineola, NY
Shapiro, Peter T. ....**New York, NY**
Shapiro, Philip ....Cleveland, OH
Shapiro, Philip A. ....San Diego, CA
Shapiro, Philip J. ....Lake Success, NY
Shapiro, Philip S. ....Albany, NY
Shapiro, Phyllis ....St. Louis, MO
Shapiro, Price M. ....**Norfolk, VA**
Shapiro Professional Association
Minneapolis, MN
Shapiro, R. Peter ....Concord, NH
Shapiro, Rachel C. ....San Francisco, CA
Shapiro, Ralph ....Los Angeles, CA
Shapiro, Ralph ....Newburgh, NY
Shapiro, Ralph ....Columbus, OH
Shapiro, Ralph J. ....Beverly Hills, CA
Shapiro, Ralph L. ....Baltimore, MD
Shapiro, Rand E. ....Norfolk, VA
Shapiro, Randy L. ....**Washington, DC**
Shapiro, Raymond L. ....**Philadelphia, PA**
Shapiro, Regina F. ....Detroit, MI
Shapiro & Reid ....Kansas City, KS
Shapiro, Richard A. ....Scottsdale, AZ
Shapiro, Richard A. ....Sarasota, FL
Shapiro, Richard A. ....Chicago, IL
Shapiro, Richard A. ....Cherry Hill, NJ
Shapiro, Richard A. ....**New York, NY**
Shapiro, Richard A. ....White Plains, NY
Shapiro, Richard D. ....**Newark, NJ**
Shapiro, Richard Harry ....Chicago, IL
Shapiro, Richard I. ....New York, NY
Shapiro, Richard J. ....**Bridgeport, CT**
Shapiro, Richard J. ....Middletown, NY
Shapiro, Richard J. ....New York, NY
Shapiro, Richard M. ....**San Francisco, CA**
Shapiro, Richard M. ....Hamden, CT
Shapiro, Richard M. ....Bradenton, FL
Shapiro, Richard N. ....**Munster, IN**
Shapiro, Richard N. ....Philadelphia, PA
Shapiro, Richard N. ....Virginia Beach, VA
Shapiro, Richard P. ....Baltimore, MD
Shapiro, Richard P. ....**Parsippany, NJ**
Shapiro, Richard P., P.A. ....Baltimore, MD
Shapiro, Richard Scott ....Charleston, WV
Shapiro, Richard W. ....**Phoenix, AZ**
Shapiro, Rick J. ....**Columbus, OH**
Shapiro, Robert ....East Hampton, NY
Shapiro, Robert A. ....**Washington, DC**
Shapiro, Robert A. ....Department of Labor, Office of the Solicitor, GV
Shapiro, Robert A. ....Rochester, NY
Shapiro, Robert B. ....**Washington, DC**
New York, NY
Shapiro, Robert D. ....Miami, FL
Shapiro, Robert D. ....Boston, MA
Shapiro, Robert D. ....**Boston, MA**
Shapiro, Robert D. ....**Philadelphia, PA**
Shapiro, Robert D., P.A. ....Miami, FL
Shapiro, Robert E. ....**Chicago, IL**
Shapiro, Robert E. ....Westfield, NJ
Shapiro, Robert F. ....**Washington, DC**
Shapiro, Robert I. ....**Miami, FL**
Shapiro, Robert J. ....**Tampa, FL**
Shapiro, Robert J. ....**New York, NY**
Shapiro, Robert J. ....**Dallas, TX**
Shapiro, Robert L. ....**Los Angeles, CA**

Sharp, Henry, Cerniglia, Colvin & Weaver, L.L.C. ..... **Baton Rouge, LA**
Homer, LA
New Orleans, LA
Ruston, LA
Shreveport, LA
Sharp, Ira H. ..... Washington, DC
Sharp, J. Baxter, III ..... **Brinkley, AR**
Sharp, J. Daniel ..... **Los Angeles, CA**
San Francisco, CA
Sharp, J. Logan ..... **Memphis, TN**
Sharp, Jacqueline ..... Stamford, CT
Sharp, James B. ..... **Brinkley, AR**
Sharp, James B. ..... **Parsippany, NJ**
Sharp, James E. ..... **Washington, DC**
Sharp, James M. ..... Bowling Green, OH
Sharp, James Michael ..... Cleveland, TN
Sharp, James Patrick, Jr. ..... Houston, TX
Sharp, James R. ..... Springfield, MO
Sharp, Jan W. ..... Omaha, NE
Sharp, Jane E.
Department Of Veterans Affairs, Board of Veterans Appeals, GV
Sharp, Janice A. ..... Pasadena, CA
Sharp, Janice C. ..... **Conyers, GA**
Sharp, Jarmie, Dixon, Scholl & Bailey, P.A.
Albuquerque, NM
Sharp, Jas., Jr. ..... Monroe, LA
Sharp, Jeffery M. ..... University Park, PA
Sharp, Jeffrey ..... Glasgow, KY
Sharp, Jeffrey D. ..... Omaha, NE
Sharp, Jeffrey S. ..... **Chicago, IL**
Sharp, Jennifer ..... **St. Louis, MO**
Sharp, Joel H., Jr. ..... **Orlando, FL**
Sharp, Joel Randall ..... **Dallas, TX**
Sharp, John ..... Bloomfield Hills, MI
Sharp, John E. ..... San Rafael, CA
Sharp, John E. ..... Longview, TX
Sharp, John M. ..... Baton Rouge, LA
Sharp, John M. ..... Pine City, MN
Sharp, John M. ..... Hudson, OH
Sharp, John M. ..... Tulsa, OK
Sharp, John S. ..... Tulsa, OK
Sharp, John W. ..... **Traverse City, MI**
Sharp, John W. ..... Akron, OH
Sharp, Joseph A. ..... **Tulsa, OK**
Sharp, Joseph C. ..... **Atlanta, GA**
Sharp, Judith A. ..... Liberty, MO
Sharp, Karen Glasser ..... **Indianapolis, IN**
Sharp, Keith A. ..... **Los Angeles, CA**
Sharp, Kenneth W. ..... **Omaha, NE**
Sharp, Kent L. ..... La Jolla, CA
Sharp, Kevin Hunter ..... **Nashville, TN**
Sharp, Kevin J. ..... Modesto, CA
Sharp, Kim Howard ..... Danville, VA
Sharp, Kirsten ..... **Walnut Creek, CA**
Sharp, Kishásha Bruce ..... **Miami, FL**
Sharp, L. Diane ..... Niles, IL
Sharp, Lance D. ..... **Austin, TX**
Sharp, Larry D. ..... **Washington, DC**
Sharp, Larry G. ..... Flint, MI
Sharp, Laura Bellegie ..... **Austin, TX**
Sharp, Laurie Boston ..... **Birmingham, AL**
Sharp, Leslee R. ..... Raleigh, NC
Sharp, Lincoln V., Jr. ..... Boise, ID
Sharp, Lisa Johnson ..... **Birmingham, AL**
Sharp, Lucy P. N. ..... Jenkintown, PA
Sharp, Lynn S. ..... **Albuquerque, NM**
Sharp, Marcia L. ..... **Los Angeles, CA**
Sharp, Margaret B. ..... Los Angeles, CA
Sharp, Marjorie C. ..... Chicago, IL
Sharp, Mark E. ..... **Fairfax, VA**
Sharp, Marvin L. ..... Trenton, MO
Sharp, Mary Ann ..... Columbia, MD
Sharp, Mary Elizabeth ..... **Atlanta, GA**
Sharp, Mary Lee ..... San Francisco, CA
Sharp, Mary W. ..... Lexington, KY
Sharp, Matthew L. ..... **Reno, NV**
Sharp, Maureen Mahon ..... Montclair, NJ
Sharp, Maurice H. ..... Syracuse, NY
Sharp, McQueen, McKinley, Dreiling & Tate, P.A. ..... **Hugoton, KS**
Liberal, KS
Sublette, KS
Sharp, Melanie K. ..... **Wilmington, DE**
Sharp, Melvin ..... Dallas, TX
Sharp, Michael Daniel ..... **New York, NY**
Sharp, Michael J. ..... **New York, NY**
Sharp, Michael, Outten and Graham
Kitty Hawk, NC
Manteo, NC
Nags Head, NC
Sharp, Michael P. ..... **Dallas, TX**
Sharp, Michael R. ..... **Austin, TX**
Sharp, Mitchell E., Jr. ..... Durango, CO
Sharp, Nancy A. ..... **New York, NY**
Sharp, Noreen ..... Phoenix, AZ
Sharp, P. Trevor ..... Greensboro, NC
Sharp, Paul F., Jr. ..... Modesto, CA
Sharp, Peter ..... **New York, NY**
Sharp, Philip D. ..... San Diego, CA
Sharp, Phillip D. ..... **Houston, TX**
Sharp, R. Christopher ..... Racine, WI
Sharp, Ralph E., Jr. ..... Juneau, WI
Sharp, Rex A. ..... **Kansas City, MO**
Sharp, Richard M. ..... **Washington, DC**
Sharp, Richard T. ..... **New York, NY**
Sharp, Rick ..... Burlington, VT
Sharp & Ripley, PLLC ..... **Sevierville, TN**
Sharp, Robert B. ..... New Orleans, LA
Sharp, Robert D. ..... **Des Moines, IA**
Sharp, Robert Donald
Department of Justice, Criminal Division, GV
Sharp, Robert E. ..... Blue Springs, MO
Sharp, Robert E. ..... Racine, WI
Sharp, Robert F. ..... **Chicago, IL**
Sharp, Robert K. ..... **New York, NY**
Sharp, Robert K. ..... Nashville, TN
Sharp, Robert M. ..... **Jacksonville, FL**
Sharp, Robert W. ..... Northbrook, IL
Sharp, Robert W. ..... **Cleveland, OH**
Sharp, Robert W., Jr. ..... Ruston, LA
Sharp, Roberta J. ..... **San Antonio, TX**
Sharp, Robin Orosz ..... **Orlando, FL**
Sharp, Robt. L., Jr. ..... Houston, TX
Sharp, Robt. N. ..... El Sobrante, CA
Sharp, Rodney M. ..... **Belleville, IL**
St. Louis, MO
Sharp, Roger Jay ..... Vancouver, WA
Sharp, Roger T. ..... **Salt Lake City, UT**
Sharp, Ronald Case ..... **Bridgeport, CT**
New Haven, CT
Stamford, CT
Sharp, Ronald E. ..... **Sevierville, TN**
Sharp, Ronald L. ..... Dexter, MI
Sharp, Sallie Martin ..... Austin, TX
Sharp, Sam ..... Bryan, TX
Sharp, Sarah A. ..... Fresno, CA
Sharp, Sarah Helene ..... **Miami, FL**
Sharp, Scott W. ..... **Lubbock, TX**
Sharp & Sharp, P.A. ..... **Brinkley, AR**
Sharp, Shelly Y. ..... **Atlanta, GA**
Sharp & Smalling ..... San Antonio, TX
Sharp, Smith & Harrison, P.A.
Tampa, FL
Sharp, Stacey G. ..... Glendale, CA
Sharp, Stanley E. ..... Portland, OR
Sharp, Starkey ..... **Kitty Hawk, NC**
Sharp, Stefanie T. ..... **San Francisco, CA**
Sharp, Stephanie K. ..... Long Beach, CA
Sharp, Stephen D. ..... Chicago, IL
Sharp, Stephen R. ..... Kennett, MO
Sharp, Steven K. ..... Syracuse, NY
Sharp, Steven R. ..... **St. Louis, MO**
Sharp, Terence K. ..... Sacramento, CA
Sharp, Terrell Lee ..... **Benton, IL**
Mount Vernon, IL
Sharp, Terry, P.C., Law Office of
Benton, IL
Effingham, IL
Mount Vernon, IL
Sharp, Thomas E. ..... **Washington, DC**
Sharp, Thomas E., III ..... **Mobile, AL**
Sharp, Thomas R.
Steamboat Springs, CO
Sharp, Victoria Tkachenko ..... **Houston, TX**
Sharp, Wavie C. ..... San Antonio, TX
Sharp, Wendy C. ..... Los Angeles, CA
Sharp, William C. ..... Richmond, CA
Sharp, William L. ..... **Chicago, IL**
Sharp, William L. ..... Albany, NY
Sharp, William M., Sr. ..... **Tampa, FL**
Sharp, William P. ..... San Diego, CA
Sharp, William R. ..... Miami, OK
Sharp, William W. ..... Front Royal, VA
Sharp, Winifred Johnson
Daytona Beach, FL
Sharp, Wm. T. ..... Greenwood, IN
Sharpe, Alan A. ..... Los Angeles, CA
Sharpe, Albert P., III ..... **Cleveland, OH**
Sharpe, Ann M. ..... **Binghamton, NY**
Sharpe, B. Patrick ..... **Martinsville, VA**
Sharpe & Beavers ..... **Forrest City, AR**
Sharpe, Benny S. ..... **Rockingham, NC**
Sharpe, Beverly A. ..... Summit, NJ
Sharpe, Beverly P. ..... Knoxville, TN
Sharpe, Bradley T. ..... **Dallas, TX**
Sharpe & Buckner, PLLC
Rockingham, NC
Sharpe, Calvin W. ..... Cleveland, OH
Sharpe, Carol ..... Brooklyn, NY
Sharpe, Charles N., III ..... Dallas, TX
Sharpe, Christopher G. ..... Seattle, WA
Sharpe, Clifford C. ..... Mobile, AL
Sharpe, Craig M. ..... **Philadelphia, PA**
Sharpe, Curtis Randolph, Jr. ..... Hickory, NC
Sharpe, Daniel R. ..... **Buffalo, NY**
Sharpe, Darren ..... **McLean, VA**
Sharpe, David B. ..... **New Orleans, LA**
Sharpe, David C. ..... Jersey City, NJ
Sharpe, David J. ..... Washington, DC
Sharpe, David N. ..... **New York, NY**
Sharpe, David Ormond ..... Boston, MA
Sharpe, Donald E. ..... **Baltimore, MD**
Sharpe, Donna E. ..... **Memphis, TN**
Sharpe, Emily J. ..... Wilmette, IL
Sharpe, Ernest M. ..... **Grand Rapids, MI**
Sharpe, G. Calvin ..... **Oklahoma City, OK**
Sharpe, Gabler & Sharpe
Chambersburg, PA
Sharpe, Gardner, Jr. ..... Sarasota, FL
Sharpe, Gary L. ..... Syracuse, NY
Sharpe, Gary R. ..... Fond du Lac, WI
Sharpe, Glenn J. ..... Midwest City, OK
Sharpe, Graeme Ellis ..... Oakland, CA
Sharpe, Gwendolyn ..... Kansas City, KS
Sharpe, Harold ..... **Forrest City, AR**
Sharpe, J. McDowell ..... **Chambersburg, PA**
Sharpe, J. Shelby ..... **Fort Worth, TX**
Sharpe, Jean E. ..... Mount Kisco, NY
Sharpe, Jeremy C. ..... **Des Moines, IA**
Sharpe, Jimmy D. ..... Durham, NC
Sharpe, John H. ..... **Indianapolis, IN**
Sharpe, John McD., Jr.
Chambersburg, PA
Sharpe, John R. ..... Center Square, PA
Sharpe, Kieran ..... **Washington, DC**
Sharpe, Kirk H. ..... **Dallas, TX**
Sharpe & Krueger ..... **Kingsville, TX**
Sharpe, Leo F., Jr. ..... Portsmouth, VA
Sharpe, Leon E., P.A. ..... Miami, FL
Sharpe, Leon E., (P.A.) ..... Miami, FL
Sharpe, Linda J. L. ..... Sacramento, CA
Sharpe, Lisa A. ..... **Seattle, WA**
Sharpe, Margaret Land ..... Winston-Salem, NC
Sharpe, Mark E. ..... New York, NY
Sharpe, Mark S. ..... **Charleston, SC**
Sharpe, Melvin T., Jr. ..... Philadelphia, PA
Sharpe, Norah G. ..... San Francisco, CA
Sharpe & Oliver, L.L.P. ..... **Houston, TX**
Sharpe, Patrick M. ..... Mount Airy, NC
Sharpe, Philip E., Jr. ..... **Bellingham, WA**
Sharpe, Ralph E. ..... Treasury Department, Office of the Comptroller of the Currency, GV
Sharpe, Richard ..... **Culver City, CA**
Sharpe, Richard A. ..... **Cleveland, OH**
Sharpe, R. M., Jr. ..... **Houston, TX**
Sharpe, Robert C. ..... Springfield, IL
Sharpe, Robert E. ..... Cleveland, OH
Sharpe, Robert F., Jr. ..... Purchase, NY
Sharpe, Robert F., Jr. ..... Memphis, TN
Sharpe, Ronald E. ..... New York, NY
Sharpe, Ronald V. ..... **Syracuse, NY**
Sharpe, Ruth ..... Chestnut Hill, MA
Sharpe, Steven K. ..... **Cheyenne, WY**
Laramie, WY
Sharpe, Thomas E. ..... Columbus, OH
Sharpe, Thomas G. ..... **New York, NY**
Sharpe, Thomas G., Jr. ..... Brownsville, TX
Sharpe, Thomas M. ..... Fresno, CA
Sharpe & Tillman, A Professional Corporation ..... **Fort Worth, TX**
Sharpe, Timothy U. ..... **Baltimore, MD**
Sharpe, Tracy R., (P.A.)
West Palm Beach, FL
Sharpe, Valarie L. ..... **San Francisco, CA**
Sharpe, Valerie A. ..... San Francisco, CA
Sharpe, W. Smith, Jr. ..... **Minneapolis, MN**
Sharpe, William R. ..... Wheat Ridge, CO
Sharpe, William T. ..... Charlotte, NC
Sharpe, William T., P.A. ..... Charlotte, NC
Sharpe & Woo ..... Sacramento, CA
Sharpee, Michael J. ..... **Amarillo, TX**
Sharpelletti, Darrell J. ..... Riverhead, NY
Sharper, Ronald J. ..... Philadelphia, PA
Sharp-Gracia, Leeanne T.
Washington, DC
Sharphorn, Daniel H. ..... Ann Arbor, MI
Sharples, Carole Hansen ..... **Sacramento, CA**
Sharpless, Frederick K. ..... **Greensboro, NC**
Sharpless, Herbert H. ..... Lansing, MI
Sharpless, John Floyd ..... Tampa, FL
Sharpless, Lionel ..... Philadelphia, PA
Sharpless, Richard Kennedy
Chapel Hill, NC
Sharpless, Susan M. ..... Ontario, CA
Sharpless, William M. ..... **Jupiter, FL**
Sharpnack, Bigley, David & Rumple
Columbus, IN
Sharpnack, John T. ..... Indianapolis, IN
Sharps, Beverly ..... Ocean City, NJ
Sharps, Douglas R. ..... Louisville, KY
Sharpstein, Janice Burton ..... **Miami, FL**
Sharpstein, Richard A. ..... **Miami, FL**
Sharpstein & Sharpstein, P.A. ..... **Miami, FL**
Sharrar, Larry Logan ..... Houston, TX
Sharrard, Mark A. ..... Frankfort, KY
Sharrard, Richard F. ..... Edwardsville, IL
Sharratt, Bryan E. ..... Wheatland, WY
Sharratt, Helen P. ..... Anchorage, AK
Sharratt, James A. ..... San Diego, CA
Sharratt & Sharratt, P.C. ..... Wheatland, WY
Sharratt, Thomas W. ..... Medina, OH
Sharrer, Elizabeth A. ..... **Denver, CO**
Sharrett, W. Allan ..... **Emporia, VA**
Sharretts, Edward P., Jr. ..... Southampton, NY
Sharretts, Paley, Carter & Blauvelt, P.C.
Washington, DC
New York, NY
Sharretts, R. Carleton, Jr. ..... Fallston, MD
Sharrin, Andrea M. ..... Department of Justice, Civil Division, GV
Sharrit, Michael S. ..... **Jacksonville, FL**
Sharrock, Elizabeth R. ..... Oklahoma City, OK
Sharrock, James W. ..... **Oklahoma City, OK**
Sharrock, Kennedy Clare ..... Bucyrus, OH
Sharrock, Susan R. ..... Bristow, OK
Sharron, Stephanie ..... **Palo Alto, CA**
Sharrott, Douglas ..... **New York, NY**
Sharrow, David P. ..... **Boston, MA**
Sharrow, Joel David ..... **New York, NY**
Sharrow, Keith D. ..... Yuma, AZ
Sharrow, Regina M. ..... **Indianapolis, IN**
Sharrow, Ronald M. ..... Baltimore, MD
Sharrow, Ronald M., Chartered, Law Offices of
Baltimore, MD
Sharry, Janice V. ..... **Dallas, TX**
Shartel, James R. ..... Portland, OR
Shartin, Liane A. ..... Austin, TX
Shartin, Stacy D. ..... **Los Angeles, CA**
Sharton, Brenda Ruel ..... **Boston, MA**
Shartrand, Douglas A. ..... Latham, NY
Shartrand, Jo Ann ..... Latham, NY
Shartrand and Shartrand ..... Latham, NY
Sharts, John E., III ..... Springboro, OH
Shartsis, Arthur J. ..... **San Francisco, CA**
Shartsis, Friese & Ginsburg LLP
San Francisco, CA
Shartsis, Loretta Sue ..... Frazier Park, CA
Shartsis, Mary Jo ..... **San Francisco, CA**
Shartzer, Sandy ..... San Anselmo, CA
Sharum, Monica A. ..... Cheyenne, WY
Sharum, Stephen M. ..... **Fort Smith, AR**
Sharum, Timothy C. ..... **Fort Smith, AR**
Sharvelle, Sybil ..... Lafayette, IN
Sharvit, Eliav ..... **New York, NY**
Sharwell, George R. ..... Columbia, SC
Sharzer, Elizabeth Gale ..... Rossmoor, CA
Shasha, Gilbert ..... New London, CT
Shasha, Jennifer ..... **West Palm Beach, FL**
Shashaani, Ramona ..... La Jolla, CA
Shashank, Amit ..... **New York, NY**
Shashank, Svati Kania ..... **New York, NY**
Shashoua, Ezra ..... **Dallas, TX**
Shashy, Abraham N. M., Jr.
Washington, DC
Shashy, William A. ..... Montgomery, AL
Shasky, Brett M. ..... Fargo, ND
Shasteen & Crawford, P.C. ..... Lincoln, NE
Shasteen, H. E. Dan ..... Irvine, CA
Shasteen, Philip M. ..... **Clearwater, FL**
Tampa, FL
Shasteen, Rolf Edward ..... Lincoln, NE
Shastid, Jon B. ..... Modesto, CA
Shatan, Gregory S. ..... **New York, NY**
Shatford, Henry W. ..... Altadena, CA
Shatford & Shatford ..... Temple City, CA
Shatford, Walter T., II ..... Temple City, CA
Shatford, Walter T., III ..... Temple City, CA
Shatkin, Marc Steven ..... Buffalo, NY
Shatkin, Paul ..... Buffalo, NY
Shatkin and Shatkin ..... Buffalo, NY
Shatkin, Stephanie Thea ..... Brooklyn, NY
Shatley, Sanjo S. ..... **Miami, FL**
Shatsky, Howard Steven ..... Timonium, MD
Shattil, Emily Cameron ..... Lincoln, NE
Shatto, Dennis J. ..... **Harrisburg, PA**
Shattuck, Cathie A. ..... **Washington, DC**
Shattuck, Clarence E., Jr. ..... Chattanooga, TN
Shattuck, David N. ..... Lexington, KY
Shattuck & Elledge ..... Clinton, TN
Shattuck, Frank W. ..... Las Vegas, NV
Shattuck, Gary G. ..... Rutland, VT
Shattuck, George C. ..... **Syracuse, NY**
Shattuck, Jean ..... **San Francisco, CA**
Shattuck, Jeffery B. ..... **La Grange, GA**
Shattuck, Jerry H. ..... Clinton, TN
Shattuck, Joseph E. ..... Albuquerque, NM
Shattuck, Judson L., Jr. ..... Xenia, OH
Shattuck, Kelly T. ..... **Omaha, NE**
Shattuck, Lee V. ..... Stockton, CA
Shattuck, R. Cooper ..... **Tuscaloosa, AL**
Shattuck, Robert D., Jr. ..... **Birmingham, AL**
Shattuck, Robert V., Jr. ..... Galveston, TX
Shattuck, Sarah Bootes ..... Ashland, KS
Shattuck & Shattuck ..... Ashland, KS
Shattuck, Steven D. ..... **Baltimore, MD**
Shattuck, Steven R. ..... **Dallas, TX**
Shattuck, Tim R. ..... **Sioux Falls, SD**
Shattuck, William M. ..... **Phoenix, AZ**
Shattuck-Kaiser, Anne M. ..... Mentor, OH
Shatynski, Jennie L. ..... **New York, NY**
Shatz, Benjamin G. ..... **Los Angeles, CA**
Shatz, Chester ..... Natick, MA
Shatz, Eileen M. ..... Treasury Department, Internal Revenue Service, GV
Shatz, Harry ..... New York, NY
Shatz, Herbert A. ..... Tucson, AZ
Shatz, Howard ..... **New York, NY**
Shatz Meier Franzino & Scher, LLP
New York, NY
Shatz, Phillip ..... **Poughkeepsie, NY**
Shatz, Samuel J. ..... **Portland, ME**
Shatz, Sanford ..... **Calabasas, CA**
Shatz, Schwartz and Fentin, P.C.
Springfield, MA
Shatz, Stephen A. ..... **Springfield, MA**
Shatz, Steven F. ..... San Francisco, CA
Shatzen, Robert S. ..... Portland, OR
Shatzer, Alida Rife ..... Philadelphia, PA
Shatzer, Larry L., II ..... **Washington, DC**
Shatzer & Sheridan ..... Philadelphia, PA
Shatzer, William W. ..... Portland, OR
Shatzkin & Furman, L.L.P.
Great Neck, NY
Jericho, NY
Shatzkin, Gary E. ..... Boca Raton, FL
Shatzkin, Karen ..... **New York, NY**
Shatzkin, Morton L. ..... Encino, CA
Shatzkin, Peter J. ..... **Jericho, NY**
Shatzkin & Reiss ..... **New York, NY**
Shatzko, Robert ..... **Menlo Park, CA**
Shatzman and Associates, P.C.
Bingham Farms, MI
Shatzman, Jerald D. ..... **Bingham Farms, MI**
Shatzman, Kiki C.G. ..... Lincoln Park, MI
Shatzman, Pearl P. ..... St. Clair Shores, MI
Shaub, Ahmuty, Citrin & Spratt, LLP
Lake Success, NY
New York, NY
Shaub, David R. ..... **Los Angeles, CA**
Shaub, Eric Steven ..... New York, NY
Shaub, Henry Z. ..... **Lake Success, NY**
New York, NY
Shaub, Walter M., Jr.
Department Of Veterans Affairs, VA Regional Counsel Office, Washington, D.C., GV
Shaub & Williams ..... **Los Angeles, CA**
Shauck, Kimberly W. ..... Dallas, TX
Shaud, Russell C. ..... Jerome, ID
Shauf, Scott D. ..... **New York, NY**
Shaufer, Susan J. ..... Buckland, MA
Shaughnessey, Sheryl A. ..... **Southport, CT**
Shaughnessy, Brian C. ..... Manchester, NH
Shaughnessy, Brian P. ..... **Chicago, IL**
Wheaton, IL
Shaughnessy, Brian W. ..... **Washington, DC**
Shaughnessy, C. Patrick, Jr. ..... Scottsdale, AZ
Shaughnessy, Candace A. ..... Louisville, KY
Shaughnessy, Christopher J. ..... **Danville, KY**
Shaughnessy, Colleen T. ..... **Chicago, IL**
Shaughnessy, Daniel C. ..... Jacksonville, FL
Shaughnessy, Daniel C., Jr. ..... Herkimer, NY
Shaughnessy, David ..... Boston, MA
Shaughnessy, Dennis R. ..... **Wilmington, MA**
Shaughnessy, Edward P. ..... **Easton, PA**
Shaughnessy, E. F. ..... San Antonio, TX
Shaughnessy, Gregory R.
San Francisco, CA

Shaughnessy, James E. ....**Englewood, CO**
Shaughnessy, James M.
New Brunswick, NJ
New York, NY
Shaughnessy, James P. ....**Houston, TX**
Shaughnessy, James W. ....**Hartford, CT**
Shaughnessy, Joan M. ....Lexington, VA
Shaughnessy, John N. ....New Brunswick, NJ
Shaughnessy, John R., Jr. ....**Hartford, CT**
Shaughnessy, Joseph H. ....**Orlando, FL**
Shaughnessy, Kevin W. ....**Orlando, FL**
Shaughnessy Law Office
Grand Island, NE
St. Paul, NE
Shaughnessy, Mark W. ....**Boston, MA**
Shaughnessy, Mary A. ....Louisville, KY
Shaughnessy, Mary Katherine
Baltimore, MD
Shaughnessy, Maurice F. ....Boston, MA
Shaughnessy, Michael A., Jr. ....St. Louis, MO
Shaughnessy, Michael J. ....**St. Paul, NE**
Shaughnessy, Paul V. ....Waltham, MA
Shaughnessy, Robert J. ....**Washington, DC**
Shaughnessy, Robert J. ....Salt Lake City, UT
Shaughnessy, Robert J., Jr. ....Warren, NJ
Shaughnessy, Robert M. ....**San Diego, CA**
Shaughnessy, Ryan S. ....**St. Louis, MO**
Shaughnessy, Stephen W. ....Berkeley, CA
Shaughnessy, Sylvia Lewellyn
San Diego, CA
Shaughnessy, Thomas J. ....Greenwich, CT
Shaughnessy, Thomas M. ....Cleveland, OH
Shaughnessy, Todd M. .....**Salt Lake City, UT**
Shaughnessy, Volzer & Gagner, P.C.
Washington, DC
Shaughnessy, William D., Jr.
Baltimore, MD
Shaughnessy, William E. ....**Greenville, SC**
Shaughnessy, William H. ....Boston, MA
Shaughnessy, William M. ....Hartford, CT
Shaughnessy, Wm. P. ....Woburn, MA
Shaul, John P. ....Deerfield, IL
Shaul, Kathleen Evelyn ....**St. Louis, MO**
Shaul, Kimberly A. ....Brookfield, WI
Shaul, Roman Ashley ....**Tuscaloosa, AL**
Shaules, James ....Monterey, CA
Shaulis, Kathleen Krise ....Harrisburg, PA
Shaulis, Norman A. ....Somerset, PA
Shaull, James R. ....Charlotte, MI
Shaull & Shaull ....Charlotte, MI
Shaulson, Sam S. ....**New York, NY**
Shaulys, Gail S., Law Offices of
Glastonbury, CT
Shaunessy, Linda Ibach ....Austin, TX
Shaunessy, Michael A. ....**Austin, TX**
Shaunty, Leslie K. ....Houston, TX
Shaurette, James D. ....**Spokane, WA**
Shave, Betty-Ellen ....Department of Justice, Criminal Division, GV
Shave, Janice E. ....Seattle, WA
Shavel, Michael J. ....**Philadelphia, PA**
Shavell, Catherine ....**Boston, MA**
Shavell, Steven J. ....La Jolla, CA
Shavelson, Lynn Daly ....**New York, NY**
Shavelson, Sunny L. ....Absecon, NJ
Shaver, Alan M. ....**Stamford, CT**
New York, NY
Shaver, Barbara M. ....**Highland, IN**
Shaver, Benjamin M. ....Scottsbluff, NE
Shaver, Charles C., Jr. ....Houston, TX
Shaver, Charles E., Jr. ....**Huntsville, AL**
Shaver, Charles Rhett ....**Houston, TX**
Shaver, David B. ....Pickerington, OH
Shaver, David E. ....Lakewood, NJ
Shaver, Elizabeth A. ....Beachwood, OH
Shaver, Elizabeth Rott ....Grand Junction, CO
Shaver, Ernest Edward ....Phoenix, AZ
Shaver, Gary H. ....Longview, TX
Shaver, Harley W. ....Denver, CO
Shaver, Jeffery J. ....**Tyler, TX**
Shaver, J. L. (Jim), Jr. ....**Wynne, AR**
Shaver, John W. ....Albuquerque, NM
Shaver & Licht ....Denver, CO
Shaver, Mark A. ....**Tipp City, OH**
Shaver, Pamela B. ....Denver, CO
Shaver, Peter Vaughan ....Portland, OR
Shaver, Philip A. ....**Princeton, NJ**
Shaver, Rex A. ....Houston, TX
Shaver, Robert C. ....**Grand Rapids, MI**
Shaver, Robert E. ....Wichita, KS
Shaver, Robert L. ....**Boise, ID**
Shaver, Robert V., Jr. ....**Greensboro, NC**
Shaver, Scott W. ....**Denver, CO**
Shaver & Smith, P.A. ....**Wynne, AR**
Shaver, Steven R. ....Dallas, TX
Shaver, Suntag & Feuerstein ....Stockton, CA
Shaver, Susan L. ....Atlanta, GA
Shaver, Thomas R. ....Cincinnati, OH
Shaver, Thomas W. ....Woodland Hills, CA
Shaver, Wm. R. ....Lubbock, TX
Shaver, Yancey L. ....Marietta, GA
Shavers, Anna W. ....Lincoln, NE
Shavers, John J. ....Baltimore, MD
Shavers, Zoe A. ....Charleston, WV
Shavick, Robert M. ....Longboat Key, FL
Shavin, Eliot D. ....Dallas, TX
Shaviro, Daniel N.
Joint Committees And Commissions, GV
Shavitz, Elizabeth Stone
West Palm Beach, FL
Shavitz, Gregg I. ....**West Palm Beach, FL**
Shavitz, Ian A. ....**New York, NY**
Shavo, Christopher M. ....**Media, PA**
Shaw, A. Earl, Jr. ....East Greenwich, RI
Shaw, A. Reid ....Minneapolis, MN
Shaw, Abelina Madrid ....Honolulu, HI
Shaw, Adam M. ....**New York, NY**
Shaw, Adam R. ....**Albany, NY**
Shaw, Alan ....Pittsburgh, PA
Shaw, Alan Bradley ....Mesa, AZ
Shaw, Amanda Chapman ....Tully, NY
Shaw, Amber C. ....New Albany, IN
Shaw, Amy H. ....Lemon Grove, CA
Shaw, Andrew ....**Sarasota, FL**
Shaw, Andrew B. ....Philadelphia, PA
Shaw, Andrew H. ....**Chicago, IL**
Shaw, Andrew J. ....**New York, NY**
Shaw, Andrew M. ....Deer River, MN
Shaw, Andrew T. ....Randolph, NJ
Shaw, Angela D. ....**Orlando, FL**
Shaw, Ann ....Salisbury, MD
Shaw, Ann Lewise ....**McLean, VA**
Oakton, VA
Shaw, Anne M. ....Chicago, IL
Shaw, Anthony W. ....**Washington, DC**
Shaw, Arnold F. ....Washington, DC
Shaw, Arnold H. ....Lynbrook, NY
Shaw, Ashley L. ....**Washington, DC**
Shaw & Associates ....Dallas, TX
Shaw & Associates, A Professional Corporation
Houston, TX
Shaw, Barbara A. ....Raleigh, NC
Shaw, Barbara G. ....**Portland, ME**
Shaw, Barry N. ....**Ashland, OR**
Shaw, Benjamin M. ....Woodside, NY
Shaw, Bennie N., III ....Morristown, NJ
Shaw & Benson ....**San Antonio, TX**
Shaw, Betty M. ....St. Louis Park, MN
Shaw, Beverly T. ....**Tampa, FL**
Shaw, Bill M. ....Claremore, OK
Shaw, Brackley ....Washington, DC
Shaw, Bradford L. ....Fort Worth, TX
Shaw, Bransford, Veilleux & Roth, A Professional Corporation
Washington, DC
Shaw, Brian B. ....**Rochester, NY**
Shaw, Brian C. ....**Raleigh, NC**
Shaw, Brian F. ....Auburn, NY
Shaw, Brian L. ....**Chicago, IL**
Shaw, Bruce R. ....**Detroit, MI**
Shaw, Byron P. ....Kennewick, WA
Shaw, Carl D. ....**Houston, TX**
Shaw, Carol A. ....Long Beach, CA
Shaw, Carol W. ....Plano, TX
Shaw, Catherine A. ....**Portland, OR**
Shaw, Catherine L. ....**Milwaukee, WI**
Shaw, Charles ....Hackensack, NJ
Shaw, Charles A. ....St. Louis, MO
Shaw, Charles Anthony ....Prescott, AZ
Shaw, Charles C. ....**Rome, GA**
Shaw, Charles F., III ....Spring Lake, NJ
Shaw, Charles J. ....Waipahu, HI
Shaw, Charles M. ....Clayton, MO
Shaw, Cherry A. ....Tallahassee, FL
Shaw, Cheryl ....**Providence, RI**
Shaw, Cheryl A. ....Santa Barbara, CA
Shaw, Cheryl V. ....**Atlanta, GA**
Shaw, Chester ....Chestnut Ridge, NY
Shaw, Chih-Ming (Jimmy) ....Potomac, MD
Shaw, Christopher ....White Plains, NY
Shaw, Christopher D. ....Albuquerque, NM
Shaw, Christopher J. ....Cleveland, OH
Shaw, Christopher L. ....Layton, UT
Ogden, UT
Shaw, Clark L. ....Nashville, TN
Shaw, Colleen A. ....Hudson Falls, NY
Shaw & Currey ....Ithaca, NY
Shaw, Curtis G. ....Greenwood, SC
Shaw, Curtis S. ....**St. Louis, MO**
Shaw, Cuyler E., (A Law Corporation)
Honolulu, HI
Shaw, D. Jean ....Portland, OR
Shaw, Daniel F. ....**Pittsburgh, PA**
Shaw, Danny G. ....**New Orleans, LA**
Shaw, David A. ....New Haven, CT
Shaw, David A. ....**Seattle, WA**
Shaw, David B. ....**Pueblo, CO**
Shaw, David B. ....Pittsfield, IL
Shaw, David C. ....Hartford, CT
Shaw, David C. ....Owings Mills, MD
Shaw, David E. ....Madison, WI
Shaw, David L. ....**Chicago, IL**
Shaw, David L. ....**New York, NY**
Shaw, David M. ....Menlo Park, CA
Shaw, David M. ....**Palm Beach, FL**
Shaw, David M. ....**Evansville, IN**
Shaw, David M. ....Braintree, MA
Shaw, David P.
United States International Trade Commission, Office of Administrative Law Judges, GV
Shaw, David S. ....Highland, NY
Shaw, David Thomas ....Eutaw, AL
Shaw, Dayne ....Mc Keesport, PA
Shaw, Deborah A. ....New Castle, PA
Shaw, Deborah G. ....Los Angeles, CA
Shaw, Deborah L. ....**Portland, ME**
Shaw, Deborah Lewis ....**Elizabethtown, KY**
Shaw, Dennis H. ....**Louisville, KY**
Shaw, Dennis R.
Department of Defense, GV
Shaw, Detra P. ....**Miami, FL**
Shaw, Diana G. ....Santa Clarita, CA
Shaw, Diane K. ....Dallas, TX
Shaw, Dirk M. ....**Oklahoma City, OK**
Shaw, Don ....**Idabel, OK**
Shaw, Donald B. ....Pleasanton, CA
Shaw, Donald H. ....Davenport, IA
Shaw, Donald H., The Law Office of
New York, NY
Shaw, Donald J. ....Los Angeles, CA
Shaw, Donald R. ....Yakima, WA
Shaw, Donna M. ....**Chicago, IL**
Shaw, Dorian A. ....**New York, NY**
Shaw, Doris Kobrin ....Larchmont, NY
Shaw, Douglas A. ....Los Angeles, CA
Shaw, Douglas R. ....San Francisco, CA
Shaw, Douglas W. ....Columbus, OH
Shaw, E. Clay, Jr. ....Fort Lauderdale, FL
Shaw, Eden D. B. ....Jamaica, NY
Shaw, Edward ....Novi, MI
Shaw, Edward E. ....Spokane, WA
Shaw, Edward M., Law Offices of
New York, NY
Shaw, Edward R. ....Brainerd, MN
Shaw, Ekaterini P. ....Long Island City, NY
Shaw, Elizabeth ....Richmond, KY
Shaw, Elizabeth H. ....**Birmingham, AL**
Shaw, Elizabeth Kirksey ....Tuscaloosa, AL
Shaw, Elizabeth O. ....Davenport, IA
Shaw, Elliot S. ....West Palm Beach, FL
Shaw, Elliot S., P.A. ....West Palm Beach, FL
Shaw, Emily Marie ....Brooklyn, NY
Shaw, Eric C. ....**San Francisco, CA**
Shaw, Eric W. ....**New York, NY**
Shaw, Erin S. ....**Chicago, IL**
Shaw, Errol G. ....Bakersfield, CA
Shaw, Errol G., A P.C. ....Bakersfield, CA
Shaw, Ethan L. ....**Beaumont, TX**
Shaw, Eudora ....Concord, NH
Shaw, Eugene F. ....Starke, FL
Shaw, Eugene G. ....Memphis, TN
Shaw, Evans & Dallas LLC ....**Atlanta, GA**
Shaw, E. W. (Bill) ....**Enid, OK**
Pond Creek, OK
Shaw, Forrest G. ....Ann Arbor, MI
Shaw, Frank ....Houston, TX
Shaw, Frank C. ....**Washington, DC**
Shaw, Frank C. ....Binghamton, NY
Shaw, Frank E. ....Conway, AR
Shaw, Frank R. ....Fort Smith, AR
Shaw, Frank S., III ....**Tallahassee, FL**
Shaw, Frank W., Jr. ....San Francisco, CA
Shaw, Franklin G. ....**New Iberia, LA**
New Orleans, LA
Shaw, Frederic E., Jr ....United States Senate, Committee Legal Personnel, GV
Shaw, Frederick J. ....Bloomfield Hills, MI
Shaw, G. Jerry, Jr. ....**Washington, DC**
Shaw, G. Richard ....Chanute, KS
Shaw, G. William ....**Seattle, WA**
Shaw, Gareth D. ....Department of Commerce, Patent and Trademark Office, GV
Shaw, Garrin James, (Professional Corporation) ....**Los Angeles, CA**
Shaw, Gary L. ....Indianapolis, IN
Shaw, Gary Michael ....New York, NY
Shaw, Gene R. ....Cincinnati, OH
Shaw, George A., Jr. ....Atlanta, GA
Shaw, George C. ....Marysville, CA
Shaw, George F. ....Bay City, MI
Shaw, George T. ....**Boston, MA**
Shaw, George W. ....**Rochester, NY**
Shaw, Georgiana Elizabeth ....Weldon, CA
Shaw, Gerald B. ....Miami, FL
Shaw, Gerald E. ....Sanford, NC
Shaw, Gerald M. ....Corona Del Mar, CA
Shaw, Gerald M., A Professional Corporation
Corona Del Mar, CA
Shaw, Gloria E. ....San Jose, CA
Shaw, Gordon A. ....Milford, MA
Shaw, Gordon M. ....Washington, DC
Shaw, Gordon Peter ....Holyoke, MA
Shaw, Greer ....**Boston, MA**
Shaw, Gregory M. ....**New York, NY**
Shaw, Gregory R. ....**Boston, MA**
Shaw Group, The ....Novi, MI
Shaw Gussis Domanskis Fishman & Glantz
Chicago, IL
Shaw, Guy W. ....Abilene, TX
Shaw & Gwinn, P.C. ....Evansville, IN
Shaw, H. Lee, (P.C.) ....**Memphis, TN**
Shaw, H. Reid ....**New York, NY**
Shaw, Harold M. ....**Washington, DC**
Shaw, Harry O., III ....Mount Pleasant, SC
Shaw, Harry T. ....Port Henry, NY
Shaw, Helen Lessin ....Bethesda, MD
Shaw, Henry E., Jr. ....Delaware, OH
Shaw, Henry S. ....St. Louis, MO
Shaw, Hergenreter, Quarnstrom & Kocher, LLP
Topeka, KS
Shaw, Hewitt B., Jr. ....**Cleveland, OH**
Shaw, Horton R. ....Rye, NY
Shaw, Howard P. ....**Morristown, NJ**
Shaw, Ian D. ....**Cheyenne, WY**
Shaw, Ian G. ....New York, NY
Shaw, Irving C., Jr. ....Adrian, MI
Shaw, Irwin ....East Brunswick, NJ
Shaw, J. David ....Rutland, VT
Shaw, J. Gilbert ....Dallas, TX
Shaw, J. Kevin ....Houston, TX
Shaw, J. Michael ....**Fort Smith, AR**
Shaw, J. Stanley ....**Garden City, NY**
Shaw, Jack W., Jr. ....Orlando, FL
Shaw, James ....Simi Valley, CA
Shaw, James C. ....Oklahoma City, OK
Shaw, James Darryl ....Auburn, CA
Shaw, James E. ....Philadelphia, PA
Shaw, James H. ....Fort Worth, TX
Shaw, James I. ....Hilton Head Island, SC
Shaw, James K. ....**Chicago, IL**
Lincolnwood, IL
Shaw, James M. ....Hamburg, NY
Shaw, James M. ....San Antonio, TX
Shaw, James R. ....**Birmingham, AL**
Shaw, James T., III ....Dana Point, CA
Shaw, James T., The Law Offices of
Dana Point, CA
Shaw, James W., (P.A.) ....**Spartanburg, SC**
Shaw, Jana Beth ....Houston, TX
Shaw, Janee ....Boston, MA
Shaw, Janet P. ....Middlebury, VT
Shaw, Jason L. ....**Hudson, NY**
Poughkeepsie, NY
Shaw, Jean Craighead ....Homer, LA
Shaw, Jeff J. ....Valparaiso, IN
Shaw, Jeffrey ....New York, NY
Shaw, Jeffrey C. ....**Pueblo, CO**
Shaw, Jeffrey Craig ....Tallahassee, FL
Shaw, Jeffrey F. ....**St. Paul, MN**
Shaw, Jeffrey L. ....**Columbia, SC**
Shaw, Jeffrey Lee ....Lawton, OK
Shaw, Jeffrey T. ....**Chicago, IL**
Shaw, Jennifer ....**Seattle, WA**
Shaw, Jennifer Brown ....**Sacramento, CA**
Shaw, Jennifer S. ....**Coral Springs, FL**
Shaw, Jerome M. ....Southfield, MI
Shaw, Jim Franklin ....**Seattle, WA**
Shaw, Jo E. (Jed), Jr. ....Houston, TX
Shaw, John A. ....Bloomfield, CT
Shaw, John A. ....St. Louis, MO
Shaw, John C., Jr. ....Lisle, IL
Shaw, John D., Law Offices of ......Phoenix, AZ
Shaw, John E. ....Kosciusko, MS
Shaw, John E. ....Greensboro, NC
Shaw, John E. ....Everett, WA
Shaw, John F. ....Middletown, CT
Shaw, John G. ....**Fayetteville, NC**
Shaw, John K. ....**Anchorage, AK**
Shaw, John L. ....**Raleigh, NC**
Shaw, John L., Jr. ....Temple City, CA
Shaw, John M. ....Lafayette, LA
Shaw, John R. ....**Orange, CA**
Shaw, John R. ....**San Antonio, TX**
Shaw, John Robert ....Los Alamitos, CA
Shaw, John Spitaleri ....**Washington, DC**
Shaw, John T. ....Baltimore, MD
Shaw, John T. ....**St. Charles, MO**
Shaw, John W. ....**Los Angeles, CA**
Shaw, John W. ....**Wilmington, DE**
Shaw, John W. ....**Kansas City, MO**
Shaw, Jonathan M. ....**Seattle, WA**
Shaw, Joseph H., Jr. ....Hamburg, NY
Shaw, Joseph P. ....Phoenix, AZ
Shaw, Judy B. ....San Jose, CA
Shaw, Judy L. ....Oklahoma City, OK
Shaw, Julia ....Wilmington, DE
Shaw, Julie E. ....San Diego, CA
Shaw, Karen ....**Palo Alto, CA**
Shaw, Karen ....Mayfield Village, OH
Shaw, Katherine S. ....Burlington, MA
Shaw, Kathey I. ....Portland, OR
Shaw, Kayan ....Poughkeepsie, NY
Shaw, Keith G. ....Duluth, MN
Shaw, Kenneth N. ....Warren, OH
Shaw, Kenneth R. ....Brooklyn, NY
Shaw, Kevin A. ....**Chicago, IL**
Shaw, Kevin L. ....**Los Angeles, CA**
Shaw, Kim Donald ....Flint, MI
Shaw, Kimberly J. ....Columbia, MO
Shaw, Kirk C. ....**Mobile, AL**
Shaw, Kyle K. ....Dallas, TX
Shaw, L. Edward, Jr. ....**Hartford, CT**
Shaw, Larry D. ....Bethany, OK
Shaw, Laura J. ....**Cleveland, OH**
Shaw, Laura R. ....**New York, NY**
Shaw Law Firm ....**Fort Smith, AR**
Van Buren, AR
Shaw, Leander J., Jr. ....Tallahassee, FL
Shaw, Lee C. ....Chicago, IL
Shaw, Leland H., Jr. ....Port St. Lucie, FL
Shaw, Leo H. ....Oklahoma City, OK
Shaw, Leon ....Mineola, NY
Shaw, Leonard ....Novato, CA
Shaw, Leonora L. ....Chicago, IL
Shaw, Leslie J. ....**South Lake Tahoe, CA**
Stateline, NV
Shaw, Leslie Suzanne ....San Diego, CA
Shaw, Licitra, Bohner, Esernio & Schwartz, P.C. ....**Garden City, NY**
Mineola, NY
New York, NY
Shaw, Lin Jun ....**New York, NY**
Shaw, Linda ....**Rochester, NY**
Shaw, Lucien W. ....Santa Monica, CA
Shaw, M. Allan ....Naperville, IL
Shaw, M. Duane, Sr. ....Abilene, TX
Shaw, M. James ....Fort Lauderdale, FL
Shaw, Maddox, Graham, Monk & Boling, LLP ....**Carrollton, GA**
Cartersville, GA
Cedartown, GA
Dalton, GA
Rome, GA
Shaw, Malcolm L. ....Dallas, TX
Shaw, Mari M. ....**Philadelphia, PA**
Shaw, Marie Elizabeth ....Universal City, CA
Shaw, Marilyn ....Pullman, WA
Shaw, Marilyn Tebor ....**Washington, DC**
Shaw, Mark A. ....**Columbus, OH**
Shaw, Mark H. ....Santa Fe, NM
Shaw, Mark J. ....**Erie, PA**
Shaw, Mark R. ....**Dallas, TX**
Shaw, Marla Voss ....Dallas, TX
Shaw & Martin ....**Mount Vernon, IL**
Shaw, Martin ....New York, NY
Shaw, Marvin L. ....Willoughby, OH
Shaw, Mary Beth ....**Pittsburgh, PA**
Shaw, Matthew G. ....Geneva, IL
Shaw, Matthew G. ....New York, NY
Shaw, Matthew G., P.C. ....Geneva, IL
Shaw & McHolme ....Mc Keesport, PA
Shaw, Melanie M. ....Hyattsville, MD
Shaw, Melissa J. ....Westerville, OH
Shaw, Michael B. ....**Chicago, IL**
Shaw, Michael C. ....Aptos, CA
Shaw, Michael E. ....Seattle, WA
Shaw, Michael F. ....**Pierre, SD**
Shaw, Michael H. ....New York, NY
Shaw, Michael L.
Department Of Health And Human Services, GV

Shaw, Michael Patrick ..... Baltimore, MD
Shaw, Michael R. ..... Houston, TX
Shaw, Michael R. ..... St. George, UT
Shaw, Michael S. ..... Highland Park, IL
Shaw, Midori G. ..... Anchorage, AK
Shaw, Monica F. ..... Chicago, IL
Shaw & Morrison ..... Willoughby, OH
Shaw & Morrow, P.A. ..... Baltimore, MD
Towson, MD
Shaw, Nancy A. ..... San Marino, CA
Shaw, Nancy A. ..... Cleveland, OH
Shaw, Nancy Gierlich ..... Philadelphia, PA
Shaw, Nancy Russell ..... Charlotte, NC
Shaw, Nancy Russell, P.A. ..... Charlotte, NC
Shaw, Nelson V. ..... Texarkana, AR
Shaw, Nicholas J. ..... New York, NY
Shaw, Nina L. ..... Los Angeles, CA
Shaw, Norman ..... New York, NY
Shaw, Norman P. ..... Bar Harbor, ME
Shaw, Norman W., Jr. ..... Stockton, CA
Shaw, Nyanza ..... San Francisco, CA
Shaw, O'Brien & Crowley ..... Binghamton, NY
Shaw & O'Brien, LLP ..... San Diego, CA
Shaw, Pandora ..... Portland, ME
Shaw, Patricia ..... Lakeport, CA
Shaw, Patricia A. ..... New York, NY
Pittsburgh, PA
Shaw, Patrick ..... Dallas, TX
Shaw, Patrick D. ..... Springfield, IL
Shaw, Paul ..... Great Neck, NY
Shaw, Paul B., Jr. ..... Birmingham, AL
Shaw, Paul M. ..... Deer River, MN
Shaw, Paul W. ..... Boston, MA
Shaw, Paula M. ..... Walnut Creek, CA
Shaw, Peg ..... Washington, DC
Shaw, Pete ..... Connersville, IN
Shaw, Peter B. ..... West Long Branch, NJ
Shaw, Peter J. ..... Brooklyn, NY
Shaw, Peter L. ..... San Francisco, CA
Shaw, Peter L. ..... Philadelphia, PA
Shaw, Peter L., Law Offices of
Houston, TX
Shaw, Philip C. ..... Four Oaks, NC
Shaw, Philip M., Jr. ..... San Francisco, CA
Shaw & Pickle ..... Kosciusko, MS
Shaw Pittman ..... Washington, DC
New York, NY
McLean, VA
Shaw & Quigg, P.C. ..... Pueblo, CO
Shaw, R. Bruce ..... Columbia, SC
Shaw, R. Michael ..... Point Pleasant, WV
Shaw, Ralph W., (P.C.) ..... Denver, CO
Shaw, Randall Merritt ..... San Francisco, CA
Shaw, Randy D. ..... Lexington, KY
Shaw, Randy J. ..... Miami, FL
Shaw, Ray ..... Brooksville, FL
Shaw, Ray W. ..... Salem, OR
Shaw, Rebecca L. ..... St. Petersburg, FL
Shaw, Richard ..... West Grove, PA
Shaw, Richard A. ..... San Diego, CA
Shaw, Richard C. ..... Scottsdale, AZ
Shaw, Richard E. ..... Southfield, MI
Shaw, Richard F. ..... Pittsburgh, PA
Shaw, Richard H. ..... Hastings, MI
Shaw, Richard H. ..... Binghamton, NY
Shaw, Richard L.
Department Of Veterans Affairs,
Board of Veterans Appeals, GV
Shaw, Richard L. ..... Coral Gables, FL
Shaw, Richard L., II ..... Coral Gables, FL
Shaw, Richard M. ..... Philadelphia, PA
Shaw, Risa C. ..... Franklin Lakes, NJ
Shaw, Robert ..... Concord, NH
Shaw, Robert A. ..... New York, NY
Shaw, Robert B. ..... Winnfield, LA
Shaw, Robert B. ..... New York, NY
Shaw, Robert E. ..... Sacramento, CA
Shaw, Robert E. ..... Mount Vernon, IL
Shaw, Robert Edward ..... Washington, DC
Shaw, Robert G. ..... New York, NY
Shaw, Robert H. ..... Tuscaloosa, AL
Shaw, Robert H. ..... Platte City, MO
Shaw, Robert Hill, III ..... Charleston, SC
Shaw, Robert J. ..... Rockford, IL
Shaw, Robert J. ..... Grandville, MI
Shaw, Robert J. ..... Seattle, WA
Shaw, Robert L. ..... Phoenix, AZ
Shaw, Robert L. ..... Camarillo, CA
Shaw, Robert M. ..... Mount Olive, NJ
Shaw, Robert W. ..... White Plains, NY
Shaw, Roderick K., Jr. ..... Tampa, FL
Shaw, Rodrick L. ..... Lubbock, TX
Shaw, Ronald R. ..... Scotia, NY
Shaw, Ronald U. ..... Towson, MD
Shaw, Roxanne Klein ..... Houston, TX
Shaw, Roy W. ..... Temple City, CA
Shaw, Ruby L. ..... Missouri City, TX
Shaw, Russell C. ..... Cleveland, OH
Shaw, Russell C. ..... Houston, TX
Shaw, Ruth C. ..... Washington, DC
Shaw, Sabrina ..... Philadelphia, PA
Shaw, Samuel E. ..... Brookline, MA
Shaw, Samuel P. ..... Millerton, NY
Shaw, Sarah E. ..... Washington, DC
Shaw, Scott Morgan ..... Chattanooga, TN
Shaw, Sharon B. ..... Seattle, WA
Shaw & Shaw ..... Temple City, CA
Shaw & Shaw ..... Deer River, MN
Shaw & Shaw, P.C. ..... Hamburg, NY
Shaw, Sherri Kristine ..... Cedar Park, TX
Shaw, Sidney Wade ..... Cushing, OK
Shaw, Sonia ..... Ann Arbor, MI
Shaw Spangler, P.C. ..... Denver, CO
Shaw, Stacy Gamble ..... Los Angeles, CA
Shaw, Stanford E. ..... Orange, CA
Shaw, Stanford E. ..... Provo, UT
Shaw, Stanley S., Jr.
United States Tax Court, GV

Shaw & Stein ..... Point Pleasant, WV
Shaw, Stephanie A. ..... Boston, MA
Shaw, Stephanie L. ..... Washington, DC
Shaw, Stephen I.
Department of Housing and Urban
Development,
Office of General Counsel, GV
Shaw, Stephen K. ..... Cincinnati, OH
Shaw, Stephen M. ..... Del Mar, CA
Shaw, Stephen R. ..... Lima, OH
Shaw, Stephen W. ..... Birmingham, AL
Shaw, Steve F. ..... Nampa, ID
Shaw, Steven A. ..... Modesto, CA
Shaw, Steven A.
Department of the Air Force,
Office of the General Counsel, GV
Shaw, Steven G. ..... Mesquite, TX
Shaw, Steven J. ..... Huntsville, AL
Shaw, Steven M. ..... Long Beach, CA
Shaw, Steven R. ..... Syracuse, NY
Shaw, Steven W. ..... Castro Valley, CA
Shaw, Stuart F. ..... East Rockaway, NY
Shaw, Stuart Kent ..... Kansas City, MO
Shaw, Stuart R. ..... New York, NY
Shaw, Susan B. ..... Columbia, SC
Shaw, Susan Elizabeth ..... Washington, DC
Shaw, Susan King ..... New Haven, CT
Shaw, Susanne S. ..... Newport Beach, CA
Shaw, Terence L. ..... Reston, VA
Shaw, Terry L. ..... New Era, MI
Shaw, Theodore M. ..... New York, NY
Shaw, Theresa C. ..... Claremont, CA
Shaw, Thomas C. ..... Orlando, FL
Shaw, Thomas E. ..... Dallas, TX
Shaw, Thomas V. ..... Department of Commerce,
Patent and Trademark Office, GV
Shaw, Timothy F. ..... Lincoln, NE
Shaw, Timothy S. ..... Sarasota, FL
Shaw, Timothy W.
Fort Walton Beach, FL
Shaw, Toby D. ..... Evansville, IN
Shaw, Tracy ..... Nashville, TN
Shaw, Tyler A. ..... San Francisco, CA
Shaw, Van ..... Dallas, TX
Shaw, W. Irving ..... Emporia, KS
Shaw, W. Marshall, Jr. ..... Shreveport, LA
Shaw, Wallace N. ..... Freeport, TX
Shaw, Walter Gilmore ..... Phoenix, AZ
Shaw & Weitz ..... Los Alamitos, CA
Shaw & Wenzloff, P.C. ..... Bay City, MI
Shaw and Wilhoite ..... Connersville, IN
Shaw, William A. ..... Beverly Hills, CA
Shaw, William Alan ..... Sayre, PA
Shaw, William C. ..... Cocoa, FL
Shaw, William D. ..... Laguna Niguel, CA
Shaw, William G. ..... Brownwood, TX
Shaw, William G., Jr. ..... Dallas, TX
Shaw, William H., III ..... Gloucester, VA
Shaw, William H., Jr. ..... Kalamazoo, MI
Shaw, William Jac ..... Minden, NV
Shaw, William K., Jr. ..... Portsmouth, OH
Shaw, William R. ..... Ithaca, NY
Shaw, William W., Jr. ..... New Orleans, LA
Shaw, Wm. Tracey ..... Lynchburg, VA
Shaw, Y. Jessie ..... Alhambra, CA
Shawaf, Raad K. ..... Santa Monica, CA
Shawan, David Howald ..... Columbus, OH
Shaw-Bell, Nöelle L. ..... Richmond, VA
Shawcroft, David H. ..... Provo, UT
Shawcross, Raymond E. ..... Providence, RI
Shawde, John C. ..... Miami, FL
Shawe, Earle K. ..... Baltimore, MD
Shawe, Mark T. ..... Savannah, GA
Shawe & Rosenthal ..... Washington, DC
Baltimore, MD
Greenbelt, MD
Towson, MD
Shawe, Stephen D. ..... Baltimore, MD
Shaweker, Kenneth E. ..... Venice, FL
Shawger, G. Dawn ..... Dallas, TX
Shawhan, Peter B. ..... Albany, NY
Shawhat, Lois Gimpel ..... New York, NY
Shaw-Jackson, Jane ..... Clarksdale, MS
Shawler, Donald M. ..... Roswell, NM
Shawler, Omer T. ..... Marshall, IL
Shawler, Omer T., Law Offices ..... Marshall, IL
Shawley, Dianne ..... Department of Justice,
Environment and Natural Resources
Division, GV
Shaw-Lorello, Loretta ..... New York, NY
Shaw-Meadow, Robert K. ..... San Antonio, TX
Shaw-Milton, Alethea M. ..... McDonough, GA
Shawn, Erik L. ..... New York, NY
Shawn, Henri ..... Monticello, NY
Shawn, James L., III ..... Austin, TX
Shawn, Joel A. ..... San Francisco, CA
Shawn, Mann L.L.P. ..... Los Angeles, CA
Newport Beach, CA
San Diego, CA
San Francisco, CA
Washington, DC
Shawn, Stacey Lynn ..... Houston, TX
Shawn, William H. ..... Newport Beach, CA
Washington, DC
Shaw-pierson, Gail ..... Canton, MS
Shawver, Bruce A. ..... Davenport, IA
Shawver, Harry R., Jr. ..... Dallas, TX
Shawver, Harry R., Jr., P.C. ..... Dallas, TX
Shawver, Harry Reed, III ..... Dallas, TX
Shawver III, H. Reed, P.C. ..... Dallas, TX
Shawver, Judy A. ..... Davenport, IA
Shawver, Karl V., Jr. ..... Paola, KS
Shawver, N. Trip ..... Wichita, KS
Shawver, Robert A. ..... Westerly, RI
Shawver & Shawver ..... Davenport, IA
Shawver and Shawver ..... Paola, KS
Shawver, Thomas W. ..... Lenexa, KS
Shay, Albert W. ..... Washington, DC

Shay, Bernard Edward ..... Cincinnati, OH
Shay, Cynthia A. ..... Baltimore, MD
Shay, Dana R. ..... Fairmont, WV
Shay, David E. ..... Kansas City, MO
Shay, David G. ..... Melrose, MA
Shay, Dennis E. ..... Wichita, KS
Shay, Douglas E. ..... Wichita, KS
Shay, Edward F. ..... Philadelphia, PA
Shay, Edward N. ..... Orange, CT
Shay, Elaine ..... Brooklyn, NY
Shay, Elizabeth P. ..... Winnetka, IL
Shay, Frederick B.
Department of Commerce,
Patent and Trademark Office, GV
Shay, Garry S. ..... Pasadena, CA
Shay, John F., Jr. ..... Upper Marlboro, MD
Shay, John J., Jr. ..... White Plains, NY
Shay, Justin T. ..... Providence, RI
Shay, Kathleen M. ..... Philadelphia, PA
Shay, Keith ..... Chicago, IL
Shay, Kevin P. ..... San Antonio, TX
Shay, Lawrence F. ..... Media, PA
Philadelphia, PA
Shay, Lori A. ..... New York, NY
Shay, Madeline Lee Brunner ..... New York, NY
Shay, Mary C. ..... Washington, DC
Shay, Matthew R. ..... Columbus, OH
Shay, Michael E. ..... Wilton, CT
Shay, Michael E. ..... New York, NY
Shay, Michael P. ..... Bethlehem, PA
Shay, Michael W. ..... Cumberland, MD
Shay, Monique C. ..... Long Beach, CA
Shay, Patrick M. ..... Albuquerque, NM
Shay, Paul R. ..... Hoffman Estates, IL
Shay & Perbix ..... Decatur, IL
Shay, Richard H. ..... McLean, VA
Shay, Richard J. ..... Cortland, NY
Shay, Santee & Kelhart ..... Allentown, PA
Bethlehem, PA
Easton, PA
Stroudsburg, PA
Shay, Stephen E. ..... Boston, MA
Shay, Susan Knowles ..... Bloomington, IL
Shay, Timothy M. ..... Decatur, IL
Shay, W. Dixon, III ..... Washington, DC
Shay, W. Michael ..... Columbus, OH
Shay, Warren C. ..... Skowhegan, ME
Shay, William D., Jr. ..... Englewood, CO
Shay, William E. ..... Buzzards Bay, MA
Shay, William M. ..... Peoria, IL
Shaya, Robert A. ..... Farmington Hills, MI
Shayan, Roxana ..... Studio City, CA
Shaye, Marc K. ..... Washington, DC
Harbor Springs, MI
Shaye, Max M. ..... Southfield, MI
Shayer, Andrew A. ..... Purchase, NY
Shayer, W. Steven ..... Bakersfield, CA
Shayhorn, Harry C. ..... Philadelphia, PA
Shaykin, Steven M. ..... Schaumburg, IL
Shayler, George J. ..... Auburn, NY
Shayne, Adam M. ..... Washington, DC
Shayne, Dachs, Stanisci, Corker & Sauer
Garden City, NY
Mineola, NY
Shayne, David ..... Chicago, IL
Shayne & Greenwald Co., L.P.A.
Columbus, OH
Shayne, Lara ..... Chicago, IL
Shayne, Leslie Jay ..... Walhalla, SC
Shayne, Stanley H. ..... Columbus, OH
Shayne, William C. ..... New York, NY
Shayo, Allen B. ..... Phoenix, AZ
Shays, Henry C. ..... New York, NY
Shays & Murphy ..... New York, NY
Shays, Rona J. ..... New York, NY
Shays, Rothman & Heisler, L.L.P.
New York, NY
Shchuka, Karen L. ..... Wyomissing, PA
Shcolnek, Richard P. ..... Marina Del Rey, CA
Shdeed & Hartmann, Inc.
Oklahoma City, OK
Shdeed, William F., Jr. ..... Oklahoma City, OK
Shea, Adam K. ..... Santa Monica, CA
Shea, Alison K. ..... Phoenix, AZ
Shea, Allison ..... New York, NY
Shea, Ames B. ..... Hartford, CT
Shea, Andrew F. ..... Andover, MA
Shea, Andrew J. ..... Minneapolis, MN
Shea, Arthur J. ..... Memphis, TN
Shea & Associates ..... Batavia, OH
Cincinnati, OH
Lebanon, OH
Shea & Associates, P.A. ..... Tampa, FL
Shea, Barbara B.
Department Of Veterans Affairs,
Office of the General Counsel, GV
Shea, Barbara S. ..... Rowayton, CT
New York, NY
Shea, Barbara S., P.C. ..... Rowayton, CT
New York, NY
Shea, Barry F. ..... Danville, VA
Shea, Betty Jean ..... Los Angeles, CA
Shea, Beverly Ann ..... Winchester, KY
Shea, Brian C. ..... Chicago, IL
Shea, Bridget C.
Environmental Protection Agency,
Office of the General Counsel, GV
Shea & Carlyon, Ltd. ..... Las Vegas, NV
Shea, Carol L. ..... Burlington, VT
Shea, Catherine M.
Securities and Exchange Commission,
Division of Enforcement, GV
Shea, Charles A., III ..... Gearhart, OR
Shea, Charles A., III ..... Kingston, PA
Shea, Charles M. ..... Chicago, IL
Shea, Charles M., P.C. ..... Chicago, IL
Shea, Charles P. ..... San Francisco, CA
Shea, Charles T. ..... Burlington, VT

Shea, Clayton E. ..... Cincinnati, OH
Shea, Colleen N. ..... Raleigh, NC
Shea, Cornelius J. ..... Manchester, CT
Shea, Cynthia Ahlgren ..... East Hampton, NY
Shea, Daniel C. ..... Redwood City, CA
Shea, Daniel F. ..... Denver, CO
Shea, Daniel J. ..... Swansea, MA
Shea, Daniel L. ..... Rockville, MD
Shea, Daniel M. ..... Atlanta, GA
Shea, David B. ..... Ventura, CA
Shea, David J. ..... Houma, LA
Shea, David M. ..... Hartford, CT
Shea, Denise M. ..... Los Altos, CA
Shea, Dennis C. ..... Washington, DC
Shea, Dennis R. ..... Jenkintown, PA
Shea, Dente & Mosca, LLP ..... Kingston, PA
Shea, Diane S. ..... Washington, DC
Shea, Donald F. ..... Providence, RI
Shea, Donna M. ..... Department of State,
Office of the Legal Adviser, GV
Shea, D. P. ..... Boston, MA
Shea, Edith S. ..... Los Angeles, CA
Shea, Edmund L. ..... St. Petersburg, FL
Shea, Edward E. ..... New York, NY
Shea, Edward F. ..... Richland, WA
Shea, Edward F., III ..... Baltimore, MD
Shea, Edward F., Jr. ..... Baltimore, MD
Shea, Edward F., Jr. ..... Pasco, WA
Shea, Edward J. ..... Greenfield, MA
Shea, Edward M. ..... Worcester, MA
Shea, Edwin Timothy, III ..... Bakersfield, CA
Shea, Elaine F. ..... New York, NY
Shea, Elizabeth H. ..... Seattle, WA
Shea, Elizabeth M. ..... Chicago, IL
Shea, Emily G. ..... Worcester, MA
Shea, Emily J. ..... Charlotte, NC
Shea, Erin P. ..... New Orleans, LA
Shea, F. Scott ..... New York, NY
Shea, Felice K. ..... New York, NY
Shea, Francis Courtney ..... Manchester, CT
Shea, Francis J. ..... Jacksonville, FL
Shea, Francis J. ..... Chicopee, MA
Shea, Francis Jerome, P.A.
Jacksonville, FL
Shea, Francis X. ..... Ridgefield, CT
Shea, Frank J. ..... New Orleans, LA
Shea, Frank P., Jr. ..... Columbus, OH
Shea, Fredericka K. ..... Chicago, IL
Shea & Gardner ..... Washington, DC
Shea, Gary J. ..... Cedar Rapids, IA
Shea, George S. ..... Canton, MI
Shea, Gerald C. ..... Southport, CT
New York, NY
Shea, Gerald P. ..... Newburyport, MA
Shea, Gerald T. ..... San Luis Obispo, CA
Shea, Gerald W. ..... Springfield, IL
Shea, Glen C. ..... Gold River, CA
Shea, Gwyn "Wendy" R. ..... Memphis, TN
Shea, Heather E. ..... Woodstock, IL
Shea, Henry J. ..... Minneapolis, MN
Shea, Irina Sturam ..... New York, NY
Shea, Irl V., III ..... Dallas, TX
Shea, J. Michael ..... Tampa, FL
Shea, Jacqueline J. ..... Washington, DC
Shea, James A., Jr. ..... Atlanta, GA
Shea, James C. ..... East Montpelier, VT
Shea, James F. ..... Hartford, CT
Shea, James F., Jr. ..... Nappanee, IN
Shea, James J. ..... Fort Wayne, IN
Shea, James J. ..... Missoula, MT
Shea, James L. ..... Washington, DC
Baltimore, MD
Shea, James L. ..... Upper Darby, PA
Shea, James L., P.C. ..... Upper Darby, PA
Shea, James O'Connor ..... Branford, CT
Shea, James P. ..... Buffalo, NY
Shea, James P. ..... Yonkers, NY
Shea, James Patrick ..... Las Vegas, NV
Shea, James R., Jr. ..... Boston, MA
Shea, James T. ..... Alpharetta, GA
Shea, James T., IV ..... Knoxville, TN
Shea, James W. ..... North Branford, CT
Shea, James W. ..... New York, NY
Shea, Jane Hils ..... Cincinnati, OH
Shea, Janice Whelan ..... Hauppauge, NY
Shea, Jeanmarie B. ..... Hartford, CT
Shea, Jeffrey B. ..... San Francisco, CA
Shea, Jennifer L. ..... Minneapolis, MN
Shea, Jennifer L. ..... Ada, OH
Shea, Jeremy C. ..... Madison, WI
Shea, Jerome J., Jr. ..... Chula Vista, CA
Shea, Joanne Marshall ..... Palo Alto, CA
Shea, John A. ..... New Orleans, LA
Shea, John A. ..... Worcester, MA
Shea, John A. ..... Ann Arbor, MI
Shea, John A., A Prof. Law Corp.
New Orleans, LA
Shea, John C. ..... Berlin, CT
Shea, John C. ..... Richmond, VA
Shea, John D. ..... Philadelphia, PA
Shea, John D., P.C. ..... Midland, MI
Shea, John F. ..... Boston, MA
Shea, John F., III ..... East Hampton, NY
Riverhead, NY
Shea, John F., Jr. ..... Wantagh, NY
Shea, John G. ..... Bryn Mawr, PA
Shea, John J. ..... Montvale, NJ
Shea, John J., Jr. ..... Sarasota, FL
Shea, John L. ..... Albany, NY
Shea, John M. ..... Shrewsbury, MA
Shea, John M. ..... Columbus, OH
Shea, John P. ..... Manchester, NH
Shea, John P. ..... Philadelphia, PA
Shea, John R. ..... Lafayette, LA
Shea, John T. ..... Philadelphia, PA
Shea, Joseph A., Jr. ..... Newark, NJ
Shea, Joseph F. ..... Boston, MA
Shea, Joseph G. ..... Concord, MA

Shedlock, Andrew J., III ....Bethesda, MD
Shedlock, Jean ....New York, NY
Shedroff, Marcia I. ....Portsmouth, OH
Shedwill, Jamison K., Law Offices of
San Francisco, CA
Sheean, Cara A. ....San Francisco, CA
Sheean, Christopher T. ....Chicago, IL
Sheeber, Samantha ....New York, NY
Sheeckutz, William A., Jr.
East Meadow, NY
Sheed, Francis R. A. ....Washington, DC
Sheeder, Frank E., III ....Dallas, TX
Sheeder, Robert E. ....Dallas, TX
Sheedy, Amanda ....Morris, IL
Sheedy, Christopher M. ....Glendale, CA
Sheedy, Dennis M. ....Pittsburgh, PA
Sheedy, Eve Flegenheimer
Beverly Hills, CA
Sheedy, James W. ....Rock Hill, SC
Sheedy, John F. ....New York, NY
Sheedy, John J. ....New Haven, CT
Sheedy, John J., Jr. ....Dallas, TX
Sheedy, John V. ....Syracuse, NY
Sheedy, Kathleen A. ....Red Bank, NJ
Sheedy, Kathleen A. ....Kohler, WI
Sheedy, Michael C. ....Phoenix, AZ
Sheedy, Michael T. ....Milwaukee, WI
Sheedy, Nicholas Joseph ....Sacramento, CA
Sheedy, Patrick J. ....Haymarket, VA
Sheedy, Patrick T. ....Glendale, WI
Sheedy, Stacy H. ....Carmel, IN
Sheedy, Timothy G. ....Concord, NH
Sheedy-McGonagle, Catherine A.
Boston, MA
Sheeger, David Mitchell ....New York, NY
Sheeger, Floyd A. ....Freeport, NY
Sheeham, Mark T.
Department of Justice, GV
Sheehan, Adam D. ....Austin, TX
Sheehan, Alan H. ....Quincy, MA
Sheehan, Angela D. ....Annapolis, MD
Sheehan, Anthony L. ....Madison, WI
Sheehan, Anthony T. ....Department of Justice,
Tax Division, GV
Sheehan & Associates ....Newport, RI
Sheehan & Associates, P.L.C. ....Detroit, MI
Pontiac, MI
Rochester Hills, MI
Sheehan, Barbara A. ....New York, NY
Sheehan, Barnett, Hays, Dean & Pennington,
P.S.C. ....Danville, KY
Sheehan, Bartholomew A., III
New York, NY
Sheehan, Bartholomew A., Jr.
Summit, NJ
Sheehan, Bernard F. ....Old Saybrook, CT
Sheehan & Booser, LLP
Woodland Hills, CA
Sheehan, Brendan R. ....Melville, NY
Sheehan, C. Ann ....Wilmington, DE
Sheehan, C. Winston, Jr.
Montgomery, AL
Sheehan, Caitlin A. ....Winchester, MA
Sheehan, Carol A. ....Columbus, OH
Sheehan, Catherine F. ....Washington, DC
Sheehan, Cathy J. ....San Antonio, TX
Sheehan, Charles A. ....High Ridge, MO
Sheehan, Cherylann W. ....Dedham, MA
Sheehan, Christopher C. ....Rocky Hill, CT
Sheehan, Clifford J. ....Elizabeth, NJ
Sheehan, Colleen P. ....Chicago, IL
Sheehan, Constance Cae ....Hayward, CA
Sheehan & Couling, P.C. ....Grand Blanc, MI
Sheehan, Cynthia ....Indiana, PA
Sheehan, Cynthia E. ....Allston, MA
Sheehan, Daniel, & Associates, LLP
Dallas, TX
Sheehan, Daniel F.
Department of State, GV
Sheehan, Daniel F., Jr. ....St. Louis, MO
Sheehan, Daniel J. ....Dallas, TX
Sheehan, Daniel R. ....Burneyville, OK
Sheehan, Darlene M. ....Boston, MA
Sheehan, David J. ....Springfield, MA
Sheehan, David J. ....Newark, NJ
Sheehan, David M. ....Baltimore, MD
Sheehan, Denis K. ....Wheaton, IL
Sheehan, Dennis E. ....New York, NY
Sheehan, Dennis M. ....Pekin, IL
Sheehan, Dennis P. ....Binghamton, NY
Sheehan, Dennis P. ....West Chester, PA
Sheehan, Dennis W. ....Pekin, IL
Sheehan, D. J. ....Ashland, MA
Sheehan, Donald M. ....Pensacola, FL
Sheehan, E. Michael ....Fort Worth, TX
Sheehan, Earl C. ....Canton, OH
Sheehan, Edward D. ....Camden, NJ
Sheehan, Eileen Frances
Department of Justice, GV
Sheehan, Elizabeth A. ....Minneapolis, MN
Sheehan, Ellen B. ....West Chester, PA
Sheehan, Francis B. ....Montvale, NJ
Sheehan, Francis G. ....Braintree, MA
Sheehan, Francis M. ....New York, NY
Sheehan, Frederick J. ....Weymouth, MA
Sheehan, G. Dennis ....Fort Worth, TX
Sheehan, Gary R. ....Fairfax, VA
Sheehan, Gary R., Jr. ....Atlanta, GA
Sheehan, Gary R., Ltd. ....Fairfax, VA
Sheehan, George D., Jr. ....Philadelphia, PA
Sheehan, Gerald J. ....Bronx, NY
Sheehan, Gerald M. ....La Crosse, WI
Sheehan, Geralyn R. ....Atlanta, GA
Sheehan, Gregory D. ....Boston, MA
Sheehan, Gregory M., Jr. ....New Haven, MO
Sheehan and Grubb ....Beloit, WI
Sheehan, Heather K. ....Kingston, NY

Sheehan, Howard V., Jr.
Woodland Hills, CA
Sheehan, J. Christopher ....Boston, MA
Sheehan, J. Scott ....Houston, TX
Sheehan, J. Timothy ....Lake Placid, FL
Sebring, FL
Sheehan, James A. ....St. Petersburg, FL
Sheehan, James A., P.A. ....St. Petersburg, FL
Sheehan, James G. ....Philadelphia, PA
Sheehan, James G., Jr. ....Danville, KY
Sheehan, James J. ....Detroit, MI
Sheehan, James M. ....Lisle, IL
Sheehan, James M. ....Harrisburg, PA
Sheehan, James R. ....Bloomfield Hills, MI
Sheehan, Jane ....Augusta, ME
Sheehan, Jane Ennis ....Baltimore, MD
Sheehan, Janet A. ....Wheeling, WV
Sheehan, Jeffrey T. ....Rockville, MD
Sheehan, Jeffrey T., P.C. ....Rockville, MD
Sheehan, Jeremiah J. ....Carmel, NY
Sheehan, Jeremiah P. ....Roseland, NJ
Sheehan, Jeremiah P. ....New York, NY
Sheehan, Joanne Patricia ....Fairfield, CT
Sheehan, John A. ....Department of Justice,
Environment and Natural Resources
Division, GV
Sheehan, John B. ....Bentonville, AR
Sheehan, John D. ....Malvern, PA
Sheehan, John E. ....Beloit, WI
Sheehan, John F. ....Taunton, MA
Sheehan, John F. ....New York, NY
Sheehan, John F. ....Providence, RI
Sheehan, John J. ....Boston, MA
Dedham, MA
Sheehan, John J. ....Concord, MA
Sheehan, John J. ....Elmhurst, NY
Sheehan, John J. ....Point Lookout, NY
Sheehan, John J., Jr. ....Cleveland, OH
Sheehan, John K. ....St. Louis, MO
Sheehan, John L. ....Ruston, LA
Sheehan, John L. ....Central Islip, NY
Sheehan, John M. ....Wilmington, DE
Sheehan, John Q. ....Blauvelt, NY
Sheehan, John T., Jr. ....Newport, RI
Sheehan, Jon F. ....Boston, MA
Sheehan, Joseph F., Jr. ....Floral Park, NY
Sheehan, Joseph J. ....Los Angeles, CA
Sheehan, Joseph J. ....New York, NY
Sheehan, Joseph M. ....Burtonsville, MD
Sheehan, Joseph W. ....Fairbanks, AK
Sheehan, Joseph W. ....Mechanicville, NY
Sheehan, Judith Marie ....Essex, CT
Sheehan, Karen A. ....Boston, MA
Sheehan, Karen M. ....Roseland, NJ
Sheehan, Katherine A. ....Nashua, NH
Sheehan, Katherine C. ....Los Angeles, CA
Sheehan, Katherine M. ....Latham, NY
Sheehan, Kathleen A. ....Southfield, MI
Sheehan, Kathleen E. ....Springfield, MA
Sheehan, Kathleen K. ....Ellicott City, MD
Sheehan, Kathleen M. ....Louisville, KY
Sheehan, Kathleen M. ....Boston, MA
Sheehan, Kathleen Mary ....San Antonio, TX
Sheehan, Kathryn Mary ....Seattle, WA
Sheehan, Kathryn Olson ....Scarborough, ME
Sheehan, Kenneth E. ....New York, NY
Sheehan, Kenneth J. ....Washington, DC
Sheehan, Kenneth M. ....Jericho, NY
Sheehan, Kenneth R. ....Las Vegas, NV
Sheehan, Kevin D. ....Moorestown, NJ
Sheehan, Kevin J. ....
Department of Housing and Urban
Development, GV
Sheehan, Kevin M. ....Chicago, IL
Sheehan, Kevin P. ....New York, NY
Sheehan, Kimberly C. ....White Plains, NY
Sheehan Law Group Chtd., The
Bethesda, MD
Sheehan, Lawrence J. ....Los Angeles, CA
Sheehan, Lawrence J. ....Bronx, NY
Sheehan, Lawrence K. ....Omaha, NE
Sheehan, Leon E. ....La Crosse, WI
Sheehan, Linda M. ....San Francisco, CA
Sheehan, Lisa D. ....Baltimore, MD
Sheehan, Lisa M. ....Sandwich, MA
Sheehan, Lorraine M.
Lake Buena Vista, FL
Sheehan, Louis Joseph ....Harrisburg, PA
Sheehan & Lower ....Cary, IL
Chicago, IL
Sheehan, Margaret A. ....Washington, DC
Sheehan, Margaret M. ....Greenville, SC
Sheehan, Marguerite E. ....Edison, NJ
Sheehan, Mark ....Hartford, CT
Sheehan, Mark A. ....Philadelphia, PA
Sheehan, Martin P. ....Wheeling, WV
Sheehan, Mary Agnes ....Bethesda, MD
Sheehan, Mary M. ....Tulsa, OK
Sheehan, Maureen Walsh ....New York, NY
Sheehan, Michael B. ....Corpus Christi, TX
Sheehan, Michael B., P.C.
Corpus Christi, TX
Sheehan, Michael E. ....Reston, VA
Sheehan, Michael F. ....Scappoose, OR
Sheehan, Michael F. R. ....Commack, NY
Sheehan, Michael J. ....Chicago, IL
Sheehan, Michael J. ....Detroit, MI
Sheehan, Michael J. ....Concord, NH
Sheehan, Michael L. ....Portland, ME
Sheehan, Michael O. ....New Haven, CT
Sheehan, Michael T. ....New York, NY
Sheehan, Michael W. ....New London, CT
Sheehan, Michelle ....St. Louis, MO
Sheehan, Michelle J. ....Cleveland, OH
Sheehan, Miriam Vock ....Boston, MA
Sheehan, Myra A. ....Reno, NV
Sheehan, Nancy Drew ....Chicago, IL
Sheehan, Nancy J. ....Sacramento, CA

Sheehan, Nora Catherine ....New York, NY
Sheehan, Nora L. ....Washington, DC
Sheehan & Nugent, P.L.L.C.
Wheeling, WV
Sheehan, Pat ....Albuquerque, NM
Sheehan, Patricia A. ....Boston, MA
Sheehan, Patrick A. ....Biloxi, MS
Sheehan, Patrick J. ....New Berlin, IL
Springfield, IL
Sheehan, Patrick J. ....Las Vegas, NV
Sheehan, Patrick J. ....Concord, NH
Sheehan, Patrick J. ....New York, NY
Sheehan, Patrick K. ....San Antonio, TX
Sheehan Phinney Bass + Green, Professional
Association ....Concord, NH
Manchester, NH
Portsmouth, NH
Sheehan, Regina N. ....Covington, KY
Sheehan, Richard C. ....Norristown, PA
Sheehan, Richard G. ....Londonderry, NH
Sheehan, Richard H., Jr. ....Beverly Hills, CA
Sheehan, Richard J., Jr. ....Haverhill, MA
Sheehan, Richard J., (P.A.)
Minneapolis, MN
Sheehan, Robert C. ....New York, NY
Sheehan, Robert D. ....Rochester Hills, MI
Sheehan, Robert R. ....Chicago, IL
Sheehan, Robert W. ....New York, NY
Sheehan, Rosemary F. ....Dakota Dunes, SD
Sheehan, Rourke J. ....Bethesda, MD
Sheehan, Schiavoni, Mooradian and Jutras
Haverhill, MA
Sheehan, Sharon Buckley ....Aurora, IL
Sheehan and Sheehan, Lawyers, P.C.
New Berlin, IL
Springfield, IL
Sheehan, Sheehan & Stelzner, P.A.
Albuquerque, NM
Sheehan, Stafford ....Fall River, MA
Sheehan, Stanley S. ....Newcastle, WY
Sheehan, Stephen P. ....Providence, RI
Sheehan, Stephen R. ....Old Saybrook, CT
Sheehan, Sue Bak ....Washington, DC
Sheehan, Terrance P. ....Grand Blanc, MI
Sheehan, Terrence P. ....Dallas, TX
Sheehan, Thomas ....Levittown, NY
Sheehan, Thomas A. ....Kansas City, MO
Sheehan, Thomas A., III ....Tallahassee, FL
West Palm Beach, FL
Sheehan, Thomas C. ....New York, NY
Sheehan, Thomas F. ....Cleveland, OH
Sheehan, Thomas F. ....Keswick, VA
Sheehan, Thomas G. ....Jackson Heights, NY
Sheehan, Thomas M. ....New Canaan, CT
Sheehan, Thomas M. ....Cary, IL
Sheehan, Thomas P. ....North Andover, MA
Sheehan, Timothy ....New Britain, CT
Sheehan, Timothy J. ....New York, NY
Sheehan, Timothy J. ....Milwaukee, WI
Sheehan, Timothy M. ....Albuquerque, NM
Sheehan, Timothy P. ....Albany, NY
Sheehan, Timothy P. ....Rochester, NY
Sheehan, Tracy ....Tampa, FL
Sheehan, Vanessa M. ....Farmingdale, NY
Sheehan, Victoria Spann ....St. Louis, MO
Sheehan, Virginia Symmes ....Concord, NH
Sheehan, William B. ....New York, NY
Sheehan, William F. ....Washington, DC
Sheehan, William F. ....Silver Spring, MD
Sheehan, William F. ....Albany, NY
Sheehan, William F. ....Mechanicville, NY
Sheehan, William H. ....Dumas, TX
Sheehan, William H., III ....Peabody, MA
Sheehan, William J. ....Cocoa Beach, FL
Arlington, VA
Sheehan, William J. ....New Berlin, IL
Springfield, IL
Sheehan-Hemmingson, Jacqueline E.
New York, NY
Sheehe, Phillip J. ....Miami, FL
Ocala, FL
Sheehe & Vendittelli, P.A. ....Miami, FL
Sheehey, Christopher B. ....Charlotte, NC
Sheehey Furlong Rendall & Behm,
Professional Corporation ...Burlington, VT
Sheehey, Paul D. ....Burlington, VT
Sheehy, Christopher J. ....Garden City, NY
Sheehy, Dan R. ....Boulder, CO
Sheehy, Diane P. ....St. Paul, MN
Sheehy & Dillon ....Ansonia, CT
Sheehy, Donald J. ....Washington, DC
Sheehy, Douglas T. ....Menlo Park, CA
Sheehy, Edmund F., Jr. ....Helena, MT
Missoula, MT
Sheehy, Edward F. ....Orland Park, IL
Sheehy, Edward Maum ....Bridgeport, CT
Sheehy, Frances Diane
Coconut Creek, FL
Sheehy, Frances Diane
Fort Lauderdale, FL
Sheehy & Friedler ....Carle Place, NY
Sheehy, J. Robert ....Waco, TX
Sheehy, James E. ....Ansonia, CT
Sheehy, John C. ....Helena, MT
Sheehy, John F. ....Morro Bay, CA
Sheehy, John F., Jr. ....Waco, TX
Sheehy, John J. ....Jersey City, NJ
Sheehy, John J. ....Jersey City, NJ
Toms River, NJ
Sheehy, John L. ....Mequon, WI
Sheehy, John P. ....Minneapolis, MN
Sheehy, Joseph P. ....Toledo, OH
Sheehy, Karen Patruno ....Morristown, NJ
Sheehy, Kathleen ....New York, NY
Sheehy, Kathleen Dunn ....Minneapolis, MN
Sheehy, Kevin D. ....Los Angeles, CA
Sheehy, Kevin D. ....Santa Monica, CA
Sheehy, Kristine ....Boston, MA

Sheehy, Laura S. ....Redding, CA
Sheehy, Lovelace & Mayfield, P.C. A
Professional Corporation ....Temple, TX
Waco, TX
Sheehy, Lynn Abraham ....Detroit, MI
Sheehy, Marian ....Bellevue, WA
Sheehy, Martha ....Billings, MT
Sheehy, Maureen A. ....Emeryville, CA
Sheehy, Maureen E. ....Encino, CA
Sheehy, Michael K. ....Detroit, MI
Sheehy, Michael W. ....Coraopolis, PA
Sheehy, Neil K. ....Minneapolis, MN
Sheehy, Patrick J.
Department Of The Interior,
Bureau of Land Management, GV
Sheehy, Patrick R. ....Billings, MT
Sheehy, Paul R. ....Torrance, CA
Sheehy, R. Michael ....Bend, OR
Sheehy, Richard A. ....Houston, TX
Sheehy, Richard E. ....Scottsdale, AZ
Sheehy, Shawn K., Law Offices of
Boston, MA
Sheehy & Sheehy ....Jersey City, NJ
Toms River, NJ
Sheehy, Stephen M. ....Boston, MA
Sheehy, T. Kevin ....Wayne, NJ
Sheehy, Terrence C. ....Washington, DC
Sheehy, Thomas J. ....Big Sandy, MT
Sheehy, William ....Tyler, TX
Sheehy, William J. ....Livonia, MI
Sheehy, William Joseph ....Farmington, MI
Sheehy, William K. ....New York, NY
Sheehy, William M. ....West Paterson, NJ
Sheekey, Karen E. ....Philadelphia, PA
Sheeks, Charles Reed ....Indianapolis, IN
Sheeks, Ittenbach & Johnson
Indianapolis, IN
Sheeks, Joseph E. ....Petaluma, CA
Sheela, Barton C., III ....San Diego, CA
Sheeler, Charles F. ....Closter, NJ
Sheeler, Lisa A. ....New York, NY
Sheeley, Ann S. ....Middletown, RI
Sheeley, James M. ....Kansas City, KS
Sheeley, Michael J. ....Boise, ID
Sheeline, Paul C. ....Washington, DC
Sheely, Ben E. ....Gulfport, MS
Sheely, Harold E. ....Mechanicsburg, PA
Sheely, Michael A. ....Charlotte, NC
Sheely, Paul E. ....Kennewick, WA
Sheely, Sean C. ....New York, NY
Sheen, Christine E. ....Cary, IL
Sheen, Dennis M. ....Chicago, IL
Sheen, E. Jay ....Salt Lake City, UT
Sheen, Fulton J. ....Western Springs, IL
Sheen, Joseph F., Jr. ....Punta Gorda, FL
Sheen, Raymond H. ....San Francisco, CA
Sheen, Robert Sunghyuk ....Los Angeles, CA
Sheen, Terence M. ....Wheaton, IL
Sheen, Thomas J. ....St. Clair Shores, MI
Sheena, Rita Fishman ....Melville, NY
Sheeno, Ramsin ....Encino, CA
Sheer, Bonnie H. ....Newark, DE
Wilmington, DE
Sheer, H. Alain ....Federal Trade Commission,
Bureau of Consumer Protection, GV
Sheer, Leo R. ....New York, NY
Sheer, Norman ....White Plains, NY
Sheer, Richard M.
Department of Commerce,
Patent and Trademark Office, GV
Sheer, R. M. ....Acton, MA
Sheer, Seth A. ....Mamaroneck, NY
Sheeran, James R. ....Norfolk, VA
Sheeran, Kerri E. ....Boston, MA
Sheeran, Patrick E. ....Columbus, OH
Sheeran, Patrick J. ....Cortez, CO
Sheeran, Susan C. ....Madison, WI
Sheeran, Thomas M. ....Cincinnati, OH
Sheeran, Timothy J. ....Cleveland, OH
Sheerer, Benjamin B. ....Lorain, OH
Sheerer, R. James ....Cedar Falls, IA
Sheerin & Associates, LLC ....Denver, CO
Sheerin, Denise M. ....Binghamton, NY
Sheerin, Gary A. ....Carson City, NV
Sheerin, Howard H. ....Denver, CO
Sheerin, John G. ....Rolling Meadows, IL
Sheerin, John J. ....Glen Cove, NY
Sheerin, Patrick T. ....Boston, MA
Sheerin, Walsh & Keele ....Carson City, NV
Minden, NV
Sheers, Alexander M. ....New York, NY
Sheers, Nathan C. ....Washington, DC
Sheesley, James P., II ....New York, NY
Sheets, Chad ....Indianapolis, IN
Sheets, Charles P. ....Chicago, IL
Sheets, D. Mark ....Nashville, TN
Sheets, Elizabeth A. ....Palo Alto, CA
Sheets, Ernst & Diehl ....Lebanon, OH
Sheets, F. Stephen ....Evansville, IN
Sheets, Gary L. ....Phoenix, AZ
Sheets, Gary L. ....Hamilton, OH
Sheets, George A. ....Minneapolis, MN
Sheets, James B. ....Fort Worth, TX
Sheets, James E. ....Lebanon, OH
Sheets, Jennifer L. ....Pomeroy, OH
Sheets, Jody G. ....Amarillo, TX
Dallas, TX
Houston, TX
Sheets, Linda L. ....Galveston, TX
Sheets, Mark E. ....Gallipolis, OH
Sheets, Martin E., Jr. ....St. Louis, MO
Sheets, Paulann Hosler ....Groton, CT
Sheets, Philip A. ....Irvine, CA
Sheets, Ralph E. ....Fort Wayne, IN
Sheets, Robert N. ....Oklahoma City, OK
Sheets, Sandra C. ....Atlanta, GA
Sheets, Sandra Graham ....Lakeland, FL

Sheets, Scott K. ... **Charleston, WV**
Huntington, WV
Sheets, Stephan L. ... **Round Rock, TX**
Sheets, Thomas R. ... Las Vegas, NV
Sheets, Thomas Wade ... Decatur, IN
Sheets, Vickie R. ... St. Paul, MN
Sheets, Warren F. ... Gallipolis, OH
Sheetz, Darryl C. ... Washington, DC
Sheetz, Edward P. ... **Allentown, PA**
Sheetz, Jeffery H. ... **New York, NY**
Sheetz, Kenneth L. ... South Bend, IN
Sheetz, Martha G. ... Chicago, IL
Sheetz, Megan L. ... **New York, NY**
Sheetz, Michael N. ... **Boston, MA**
Sheetz, Richard D. ... **Troy, PA**
Sheetz, Roy A. ... **Alexandria, VA**
Sheetz, William D. ... Dallas, TX
Shef, Michael J. ... **Great Neck, NY**
New York, NY
Sheff, Andrew ... Indianapolis, IN
Sheff, Gary I. ... New York, NY
Sheff, Harold H. ... **Minneapolis, MN**
Sheff, Irving H. ... Boston, MA
Sheff, Kevin M. ... **Salt Lake City, UT**
Sheff, Neil J. ... **Los Angeles, CA**
Sheff, Ronald B. ... **Rockville, MD**
Sheffel, Jeffrey Phillip ... **Miami, FL**
Sheffer, Abner ... Great Neck, NY
Sheffer, Andrew R. ... **Marion, NC**
Sheffer, Brent A. ... **Columbus, OH**
Sheffer, Craig C. ... **Sacramento, CA**
Sheffer, Gregory M. ... **San Francisco, CA**
Sheffer • Hutchinson • Kinney
Evansville, IN
Bowling Green, KY
Frankfort, KY
Henderson, KY
Lexington, KY
Louisville, KY
Owensboro, KY
Paducah, KY
Sheffer, John A. ... **Owensboro, KY**
Sheffer, John B., II ... Williamsville, NY
Sheffer, Julianne P. ... Atlanta, GA
Sheffer, Karen E. ... **Columbus, OH**
Sheffer, Murphy & White ... Williamsville, NY
Sheffer, Ronald G. ... **Bowling Green, KY**
Frankfort, KY
Henderson, KY
Lexington, KY
Louisville, KY
Owensboro, KY
Paducah, KY
Shefferly, Jon B. ... Detroit, MI
Shefferly, Jon B., & Associates, P.C.
Detroit, MI
Shefferly, Phillip J. ... **West Bloomfield, MI**
Shefferly, Silverman & Morris, A Professional Corporation ... **Detroit, MI**
West Bloomfield, MI
Shefferman, Brian D. ... Rockville, MD
Shefferman, Scott A. ... Washington, DC
Sheffert, David G. ... Chicago, IL
Sheffey, David W. ... **New York, NY**
Sheffey, E. Summers ... Dade City, FL
Sheffey, Rita A. ... **Atlanta, GA**
Sheffey, Steven R. ... **Northbrook, IL**
Sheffey, Timothy D. ... Lebanon, PA
Sheffield, A. Daniel, Jr.
Colorado Springs, CO
Sheffield, Beth McDonald ... Marion, VA
Sheffield, Billy Joe ... Dothan, AL
Sheffield, Chaney M. ... **Los Angeles, CA**
Sheffield, Christopher E. ... Chambersburg, PA
Sheffield, David A. ... Alexandria, LA
Sheffield, Deborah Harrison
Columbia, SC
Sheffield, Donald L. ... Ashtabula, OH
Sheffield, Douglas M. ... Columbus, OH
Sheffield, Ellen E. ... Gambier, OH
Sheffield, Ernie M. ... Colquitt, GA
Sheffield, Frank E., P.A. ... Tallahassee, FL
Sheffield, Frank H., Jr. ... **New Bern, NC**
Sheffield, Haidee Oppie ... Pascagoula, MS
Sheffield & Harvey ... **Jamestown, RI**
Middletown, RI
Newport, RI
Portsmouth, RI
Sheffield, Homer G., Jr.
Santa Barbara, CA
Sheffield, Hope Reisman ... Wilmette, IL
Sheffield, J. Howard ... Jacksonville, FL
Sheffield, J. Howard, P.A. ... Jacksonville, FL
Sheffield, James Edward ... Richmond, VA
Sheffield, James R., III ... **Austin, TX**
Sheffield, Jeffrey T., (P.C.) ... **Chicago, IL**
Sheffield, Jim C. ... Huntsville, TX
Sheffield, Joel B. ... Sulphur Springs, TX
Sheffield, John W. ... **Birmingham, AL**
Sheffield, Joseph A. ... Graceville, FL
Sheffield, Keith Allen ... Birmingham, AL
Sheffield, Kim Lynette ... Fayetteville, PA
Sheffield, Lanny R. ... Jamestown, NY
Sheffield, Lawrence B., III ... Birmingham, AL
Sheffield, Lawrence B., Jr. ... Birmingham, AL
Sheffield, Linda Gray ... Bryan, TX
Sheffield, Lloyd S. ... El Paso, TX
Sheffield, Malvern J., Jr. ... Washington, DC
Sheffield, Mark S. ... Baltimore, MD
Sheffield, Mary W. ... Rolla, MO
Sheffield, Michael ... Amarillo, TX
Sheffield, Neal Y. R. ... San Antonio, TX
Sheffield, R. Wendell ... Birmingham, AL
Sheffield, Ricci S. ... Gambier, OH
Sheffield, Richard A. ... Reno, NV
Sheffield, Richard B. ... **Newport, RI**
Sheffield, Richard W. ... **Phoenix, AZ**
Provo, UT

Sheffield, Robert Michael ... **Atlanta, GA**
Sheffield, Ronald L. ... Little Rock, AR
Sheffield, Shari Leta ... Arlington, VA
Sheffield & Sheffield ... Gambier, OH
Sheffield, Sheffield and Sheffield, P.C.
Birmingham, AL
Sheffield, Sherwood H. ... Belton, TX
Sheffield, Tamara L. ... **Houston, TX**
Sheffield, Walter J., Attorney at Law, P.C.
Fredericksburg, VA
Sheffield, Walter Jervis
Fredericksburg, VA
Sheffield, Walter L., III ... Raleigh, NC
Sheffield, William C. ... **Princeton, NJ**
Sheffield, William P. ... Abingdon, VA
Sheffield, William R.
San Juan Capistrano, CA
Sheffield, Wm. T. ... Cincinnati, OH
Sheffler, Bruce G. ... **New York, NY**
Sheffler, Stephen K. ... Champaign, IL
Sheffler, Steven P. ... **Baldwin, NY**
Sheffy, A. Alan ... **Southington, CT**
Sheffy, Donald H. ... Bel Air, MD
Shefler, Deborah S. ... **San Francisco, CA**
Shefler, Jane Cantor ... Port Angeles, WA
Shefman, Benjamin ... New Braunfels, TX
Shefman, Randy Jay ... Denver, CO
Shefman, Stephen E. ... Southfield, MI
Shefren, Leonard W., (P.C.) ... Omaha, NE
Shefrin, Bradley N. ... **Denver, CO**
Shefrin, Deborah H. ... **Chicago, IL**
Shefsky & Froelich Ltd. ... **Chicago, IL**
Shefsky, Lloyd E. ... **Chicago, IL**
Sheft, Laurie Tribble ... **Boston, MA**
Sheft, Leonard A. ... **New York, NY**
Sheft, Mark A. ... **San Francisco, CA**
Sheft, Peter I. ... New York, NY
Sheftall, John McKay ... **Columbus, GA**
Sheftall, Scott D. ... **Miami, FL**
Sheftall & Torres, P.A. ... **Miami, FL**
Shefte, D. Frederick ... Springdale, AR
Shefte, Dalbert U. ... **Charlotte, NC**
Shefte, Pinckney & Sawyer, L.L.P
Charlotte, NC
Sheftel, Janice C. ... **Durango, CO**
Sheftel, Lynn A., Mr. ... Niles, OH
Sheftel, Stephen M. ... Wallingford, CT
Shefter, Bret A. ... Glendale, CA
Sheftman, Howard S. ... **Columbia, SC**
Shegerian, Carney R. ... Los Angeles, CA
Shegog-Whitlock, Hermia
Redondo Beach, CA
Shegon, Patrick M. ... **Montgomery, AL**
Shegos, Robert L. ... Davison, MI
Shegoski, Heidi G. ... **New York, NY**
Sheh, Lawrence J. ... Needham, MA
Shehab, Michael J. ... Detroit, MI
Shehabi, Soroush Ricard
Department of Justice,
Environment and Natural Resources
Division, GV
Shehadi, Paul V. ... **Philadelphia, PA**
Shehan, George A. ... Charlotte, NC
Shehan, J. Brooke, Jr. ... Annapolis, MD
Shehan, James C. ... New York, NY
Shehan, Mark T. ... **New York, NY**
Shehan, Suzanne M. ... **Omaha, NE**
Shehan, Thomas F., Jr. ... Belfast, ME
Shehan, Tomi J. ... Dallas, TX
Shehan, Wayne C. ... **St. Clair Shores, MI**
Shehane, Kristine Booker ... **Savannah, GA**
Shehee, Amy Carter ... Kevil, KY
Sheheen, Robert J. ... **Camden, SC**
Sheheen, Vincent Austin ... **Camden, SC**
Shehigian, Ruben B., Jr. ... Chicago, IL
Shei, Kashya K.H. ... **San Francisco, CA**
Sheidenberger, Michelle M. ... Sacramento, CA
Sheidlower, Arnold M. ... Great Neck, NY
Sheidlower, Donna F. ... New York, NY
Sheidlower, Eric S. ... **Carle Place, NY**
Sheidy, Charles W. ... Denver, PA
Sheiffer, David S. ... **New York, NY**
Sheih, Eugene ... **Minneapolis, MN**
Sheikerz, Mehdi Darius ... **Jacksonville, FL**
Sheikh, David J. ... **Chicago, IL**
Sheikh, Kashif Z. ... **New York, NY**
Sheikh, Kemal A. ... **New York, NY**
Sheil, David R. ... Houston, TX
Sheil, Denis R. ... Somers, NY
Sheil, Peter W. ... Los Angeles, CA
Sheil, Thomas Kevin ... Denver, CO
Sheil, Timothy E. ... **Washington, DC**
Sheil, William B., II ... Tulsa, OK
Sheil, William H. ... Maplewood, NJ
Sheild, Conway H., III
Newport News, VA
Sheils, Denis F. ... **Philadelphia, PA**
Sheils, J. Stephen ... **New York, NY**
Sheils, James B. ... **Springfield, MA**
Sheils, James H. ... Somers, NY
Sheils, Lawrence T. ... Boston, MA
Sheils, Max M., Jr. ... **Boise, ID**
Sheils, Paul C. ... La Grange, IL
Sheils, Paul T. ... Princeton, NJ
Sheils, Richard A., Jr. ... **Worcester, MA**
Sheils, Robert P., Jr., Law Offices of
Scranton, PA
Sheils, Robert P., Jr., Law Offices of
Wilkes-Barre, PA
Sheils, T. Craig ... **Richardson, TX**
Sheils, William J. ... **Portland, ME**
Sheils, Winnubst, Sanford & Bethune
Dallas, TX
Richardson, TX
Sheiman, Judith Ann ... Stamford, CT
Sheiman, Richard M. ... Trumbull, CT
Sheiman, Ronald L. ... **Westport, CT**
Sheiman, Stuart M. ... Bridgeport, CT

Shein, Benjamin P. ... Philadelphia, PA
Shein, David H. ... San Francisco, CA
Shein, James B. ... **Chicago, IL**
Shein, Jeffrey Steven ... Whitestone, NY
Shein, Joseph D. ... Philadelphia, PA
Shein, Joseph D., P.C. ... Philadelphia, PA
Shein, Marcia G., Law Offices of
Atlanta, GA
Shein & Shelton, L.L.C. ... **Washington, DC**
Rockville, MD
Shein, Todd A. ... **Rockville, MD**
Sheinbaum, James B. ... **Ghent, NY**
New York, NY
Sheinbaum, Jordan ... Pasadena, CA
Sheinbaum, Louis P. ... **New York, NY**
Sheinbein, Andrea ... Dallas, TX
Sheinbein, Robert A. ... Beverly Hills, CA
Sheinbein, Roger B. ... Beverly Hills, CA
Sheinbein, Roger B., A Professional Corporation ... Beverly Hills, CA
Sheinberg, George ... Brooklyn, NY
Sheinberg, Herbert G. ... **Pittsburgh, PA**
Sheinberg, Jill H. ... Park City, UT
Sheinberg, Lauren M. ... **San Antonio, TX**
Sheinberg, Lawrence P. ... New York, NY
Sheinberg, Michael Alan ... Brooklyn, NY
Sheinberg, Sidney J. ... Universal City, CA
Sheinberg, Wendy H. ... **Westbury, NY**
Sheindlin, Gerald ... Congers, NY
Sheinen, Kimberly C. ... **Philadelphia, PA**
Sheiner, Naomi F. ... New York, NY
Sheiness, Marc A. ... Houston, TX
Sheinfeld, Harry L. ... Department of Labor, Office of the Solicitor, GV
Sheinfeld, Ira S. ... **New York, NY**
Sheinfeld, Kari B. ... **Chicago, IL**
Sheinfeld, Maley & Kay, A Professional Corporation ... **Austin, TX**
Dallas, TX
Houston, TX
Sheinfeld, Meyer ... Oak Brook, IL
Sheinfeld, Myron M. ... **Houston, TX**
Sheinfeld, Stephen L. ... **New York, NY**
Sheinfeld, Steven ... Fort Lauderdale, FL
Sheinfeld, Steven, Law Offices of, P.A.
Fort Lauderdale, FL
Sheinfield, Frederick P. ... San Francisco, CA
Sheingold, Kathryn J. ... **Albany, NY**
Sheingold, T. Faye ... Mount Laurel, NJ
Sheinkman, Jacob ... New York, NY
Sheinkopf, Cheryl M. ... **Los Angeles, CA**
Sheinman, Jerome ... **Columbia, MD**
Sheinman, Martin M. ... Pittsburgh, PA
Sheinoff, Mitchel H. ... Media, PA
Philadelphia, PA
Sheintoch, Everett K. ... **Philadelphia, PA**
Sheinwald, Steven B. ... Garden City, NY
Sheinwold, Marcy D. ... **Melville, NY**
Sheiowitz, Gerald L. ... Bronx, NY
Sheivachman, Mark ... Pomona, NY
Sheive, Sarah W. ... **New York, NY**
Shek, Bernard C. ... **San Francisco, CA**
Shek, John R. ... **Boston, MA**
Shek, Peter S. ... Saginaw, MI
Sheka, John W. ... Mason City, IA
Shekarchian, Haleh ... Beverly Hills, CA
Shekarchian, Haleh, A Professional Corporation
Beverly Hills, CA
Shekell, Leslie Judson ... Paducah, KY
Shekell, Leslie Judson, PSC ... Paducah, KY
Shekerjian, Denise G. ... Charlotte, VT
Shekerko, J. James ... North Ridgeville, OH
Sheketoff & Homan ... **Boston, MA**
Sheketoff, Robert L. ... **Boston, MA**
Shekita, Melanie ... Raleigh, NC
Shekleton, Gerald T. ... **Chicago, IL**
Shekleton, James F. ... Pierre, SD
Shekletski, Gerald J. ... New Cumberland, PA
Shekou, Sally ... **San Francisco, CA**
Shekoyan, James E. ... **Fresno, CA**
Shelander, Mel W. ... Beaumont, TX
Shelar, Richard C. ... Leetonia, OH
Shelat, Bipin R. ... San Francisco, CA
Shelbourne, Peter Brandt ... Charleston, SC
Shelburne, Anne Howard, (MS.)
Owensboro, KY
Shelburne, Anne Pettus
Treasury Department,
Internal Revenue Service, GV
Shelburne, Jan P. ... New York, NY
Shelburne, Laura Lewis ... Palo Alto, CA
Shelburne, Lori B. ... **Lexington, KY**
Shelburne, Mark H. ... **Raleigh, NC**
Shelburne, Patrice ... **Washington, DC**
Shelburne, Ralph W. ... Houston, TX
Shelburne, Robert S. ... **Sacramento, CA**
Shelburne, Thomas D. ... Rogersville, TN
Shelburne, Timothy O. ... Owensboro, KY
Shelby & Associates, P.A. ... Goldsboro, NC
Shelby, Azelie Ziegler ... **Baton Rouge, LA**
Shelby, B. Kip ... Winterset, IA
Shelby, Barbara McCahon ... Buffalo, NY
Shelby & Bastian ... San Francisco, CA
Shelby & Cartee ... Birmingham, AL
Tuscaloosa, AL
Shelby, Chris L. ... Lebanon, IN
Shelby, David Alan ... Salisbury, NC
Shelby, David D. ... Birmingham, AL
Shelby, David J., II ... **Baton Rouge, LA**
Shelby & Edens, P.C. ... Lebanon, IN
Shelby, Eric J. ... **Los Angeles, CA**
Shelby, George J. ... San Francisco, CA
Shelby, Glenn T. ... Lakeland, FL
Shelby, Glenn T., P.A. ... Lakeland, FL
Shelby, Glenna Dudley ... Greenfield, IN
Shelby, James D. ... Cleveland, OH
Shelby, Jeffry A. ... **Kirkland, WA**
Shelby, Jerome ... **New York, NY**

Shelby, Joseph D. ... **Harrisburg, PA**
Shelby, Katherine L. ... **Indianapolis, IN**
Shelby, Laura S. ... **Houston, TX**
Shelby, Laura Wilson ... **Los Angeles, CA**
Shelby, Linda C. ... **Indianapolis, IN**
Shelby, Linda L. ... San Ramon, CA
Shelby, Mark Alan ... **Tulsa, OK**
Shelby, Paul R. ... Bowie, MD
Shelby, Richard C. ... Tuscaloosa, AL
Shelby, Robert J. ... **Salt Lake City, UT**
Shelby, Stuart ... Los Angeles, CA
Shelby, Thomas G. ... Downieville, CA
Shelden, Aaron E. ... **Encino, CA**
Shelden, Albert N. ... San Diego, CA
Shelden, Jamie R. ... **San Jose, CA**
Shelden, Jas. W. ... Rockford, IL
Shelden and Kulchin ... **Encino, CA**
Sheldon, A. Jerry ... **Jackson, MS**
Sheldon, Angela L. ... **Appleton, WI**
Sheldon, Ann P. ... Chicago, IL
Sheldon, Barbara L. ... Sacramento, CA
Sheldon, Betty Jo ... Los Angeles, CA
Sheldon, Bryan King ... **Los Angeles, CA**
Sheldon, Carl R. ... **New York, NY**
Sheldon, Charles D. ... Long Beach, CA
Sheldon, Charles T. ... **San Francisco, CA**
Sheldon, Christopher J. ... Indio, CA
Sheldon, Craig L. ... **New York, NY**
Sheldon, Dale W. ... Minnetonka, MN
Sheldon, Dale W., P.A. ... Minnetonka, MN
Sheldon, David C. ... **Ashtabula, OH**
Sheldon, David P. ... **Washington, DC**
Sheldon, Deborah S.C. ... **Seattle, WA**
Sheldon, Donald S. ... Bradford, MA
Sheldon, Donald W. ... Port Huron, MI
Sheldon, Elizabeth Torrant
Washington, DC
Sheldon, Ernest B. ... Pepperell, MA
Sheldon, Garrett ... Walsenburg, CO
Sheldon, Gary F. ... **Hartford, CT**
Sheldon, Geoffrey S. ... Santa Monica, CA
Sheldon, George H. ... Tallahassee, FL
Sheldon & Gordon, P.C. ... **Denver, CO**
Sheldon, Harvey M. ... **Chicago, IL**
Sheldon, Harvey M., Professional Corporation ... **Chicago, IL**
Sheldon, Henry E. ... Cincinnati, OH
Sheldon, James E. ... Chapel Hill, NC
Sheldon, James F. ... **Apple Valley, MN**
Sheldon, James P. ... Crofton, NE
Sheldon, James R., Jr. ... Buffalo, NY
Sheldon, James S. ... Des Plaines, IL
Sheldon, Janette Conaway ... Olathe, KS
Sheldon, Jeffrey G. ... **Pasadena, CA**
Upland, CA
Sheldon, Jeffrey L. ... Washington, DC
Sheldon, Jeffrey L. ... Washington, DC
Sheldon, Jeffrey Stuart ... Fountain Valley, CA
Sheldon, Jennifer B. ... Seattle, WA
Sheldon, John C. ... Bridgton, ME
Sheldon, John W. ... Baltimore, MD
Sheldon, Jonathan A. ... Boston, MA
Sheldon, Jordan & Dunham, L.L.P.
Beaumont, TX
Sheldon, Karin P. ... Washington, DC
Sheldon, Linda D. ... **Dallas, TX**
Sheldon, Lynette M. ... **Bloomfield Hills, MI**
Sheldon & Mak ... **Los Angeles, CA**
Newport Beach, CA
Pasadena, CA
Riverside, CA
San Bernardino, CA
Upland, CA
Sheldon & Mankin ... **Walnut Creek, CA**
Sheldon, Marcia D. ... Long Island City, NY
Sheldon, Marie A. ... **Honolulu, HI**
Sheldon, Marjorie E. ... **New York, NY**
Sheldon, Matthew R. ... **McLean, VA**
Sheldon, Michael A. ... **Denver, CO**
Sheldon, Michael R. ... Waterbury, CT
Sheldon, Patrick C. ... **Seattle, WA**
Sheldon, Paul A. ... **Chicago, IL**
Sheldon, Paul D. ... Sacramento, CA
Sheldon, Paul W. ... **San Antonio, TX**
Sheldon, Peter B. ... Groton, MA
Sheldon, Peter S. ... **Lansing, MI**
Sheldon, Richard B., Jr. (A Professional Corporation) ... **Los Angeles, CA**
Sheldon, Robert E. ... **Walnut Creek, CA**
Sheldon, Robert H. ... Houston, TX
Sheldon, Robert L. ... Roselle Park, NJ
Sheldon, Robert R. ... **Bridgeport, CT**
Sheldon, Robert S. ... Miami, FL
Pompano Beach, FL
Sheldon, Robin ... **Philadelphia, PA**
Sheldon, Robt. M. ... Alma, MI
Sheldon, Sam. H. ... Ottawa, KS
Sheldon, Sam S. ... **San Diego, CA**
Sheldon, Sarah McCauley ... Brookline, MA
Sheldon, Scot E. ... **Beaumont, TX**
Sheldon, Scott J. ... **Roseland, NJ**
Sheldon, Sherrie Lipsky
Universal City, CA
Sheldon, Steven D. ... Phoenix, AZ
Sheldon, Stuart A. ... **Washington, DC**
Sheldon & Sullivan ... Groton, MA
Sheldon, Suzanne ... **Boston, MA**
Sheldon, Timothy Q. ... Geneva, IL
Sheldon, Todd N. ... **Chicago, IL**
Sheldon, Toni A. ... Shelton, WA
Sheldon, Vern E. ... Fort Wayne, IN
Sheldon, Victoria Watt ... Olympia, WA
Sheldon, Wendy E. ... Washington, DC
Sheldon, Weston L. ... Delray Beach, FL
Sheldon, William D., III ... Pittsford, NY
Sheldon, William D., III, P.C. ... Pittsford, NY
Sheldon, Wilson S. ... **Florence, SC**
Sheldon, Wylie R. ... **San Francisco, CA**

Sheldrake, Warren Edward ....Irvington, NY
Sheldrick, Andrew W. ....New York, NY
Sheldrick, Emily A. ....Bellevue, WA
Shelesky, Raymond J. ....Fairfax, VA
Shelesny, Stephen G. ....Chicago, IL
Sheley, Raymond P. ....Atlanta, GA
Sheley, Russell G., Jr. ....Phoenix, AZ
Shelfer, Arthur J., Jr. ....Thomasville, GA
Shelfer, Charles L. ....Tallahassee, FL
Shelfer, David B. ....Sugar Land, TX
Shelfer, James O. ....Tallahassee, FL
Shelfer, William S., Jr. ....Decatur, GA
Shelger, James M. ....Houston, TX
Shelhamer, Amy ....Amarillo, TX
Shelhamer, Linda K. ....Billings, MT
Shelhorse, John ....St. Louis, MO
Sheligo, Beth C. ....Philadelphia, PA
Sheline, Miriam Hirsch ....Cincinnati, OH
Sheline, Robert C. ....Harlingen, TX
Shelist, Michael R. ....Chicago, IL
Shelist, Robert J. ....Chicago, IL
Shelkin, Scott P. ....Garden City, NY
Shelko, Loree J. ....Newark, NJ
Shelkofsky, Morris E., Jr. ....Tallahassee, FL
Shelkrot, Lisa B. ....Burlington, VT
Shell, Ann Katherine ....Burbank, CA
Shell, Bobbie T. ....Dallas, TX
Shell, Buford, Bufkin, Callicutt & Perry
Jackson, MS
Oxford, MS
Tupelo, MS
Shell, Carmack C. ....Clarksville, TN
Shell, Dale Coran ....Burnet, TX
Shell, David E. ....Ukiah, CA
Shell, Diane E. ....Orinda, CA
Shell, Donald J. ....Redmond, WA
Shell, Eddie G. ....Burnet, TX
Shell, Fleming, Davis & Menge, P.A.
Pensacola, FL
Shell, G. Richard ....Philadelphia, PA
Shell, J. Daniel ....Lewisburg, TN
Shell, Jay F. ....Little Rock, AR
Shell, Jerry B. ....Bradenton Beach, FL
Shell, Johnson, Andrews, Baskervill & Baskervill, P.C. ....Petersburg, VA
Shell, Kayla Paige ....Round Rock, TX
Shell, Kimberly Gould ....Albany, NY
Shell, Louis C. ....Petersburg, VA
Shell, Marilyn S. ....Fort Worth, TX
Shell, Phillip B. ....Murray, UT
Shell, Stephen B. ....Pensacola, FL
Shell, T. E. ....Stephenville, TX
Shell, Thurston A. ....Pensacola, FL
Shellabarger, John F. ....Santa Barbara, CA
Shellabarger, Mark S. ....Tampa, FL
Shellaberger, Donna J. ....Orleans, MA
Shellan, Ronald A., P.C. ....Portland, OR
Shelledy, Nancy L. ....Kansas City, MO
Shelledy, Patrick H. ....Spokane, WA
Shelledy, William R., Jr. ....Worland, WY
Shellenback, Stephanie B. ....Chicago, IL
Shellenbarger, Todd S. ....Valparaiso, IN
Shellenberg, Mary W. ....Chicago, IL
Shellenberger, David E. ....Boston, MA
Shellenberger, Grant C. ....Liberal, KS
Shellenberger, James A. ....Philadelphia, PA
Shellenberger, Scott D. ....Baltimore, MD
Shellenberger, Stephen W. ....Dallas, TX
Shellenberger, Thomas D. ....Newark, DE
Wilmington, DE
Sheller, Edgar L. ....Bronx, NY
Sheller, J. Garrett ....Salisbury, MD
Sheller, Jamie L. ....Philadelphia, PA
Sheller, John O. ....Louisville, KY
Sheller, John W., (A Professional Corporation) ....Santa Monica, CA
Sheller, Lee A. ....Baltimore, MD
Sheller, Ludwig & Badey, A Prof. Corp.
Marlton, NJ
Philadelphia, PA
Sheller, Patrick M. ....Rochester, NY
Sheller, Robert G. ....New York, NY
Sheller, Stephen A. ....Philadelphia, PA
Shelley, Anne-Marie ....New York, NY
Shelley, Anthony F. ....Washington, DC
Shelley & Bethea, P.L.C. ....Mesa, AZ
Shelley, Blackwell N. ....Richmond, VA
Shelley, Blackwell N., Jr. ....Richmond, VA
Shelley, Cherie ....Juneau, AK
Shelley, David N. ....Chicago, IL
Shelley, Deborah L. ....Houston, TX
Shelley, Diane Cardaci ....Morristown, NJ
Shelley, E. Eugene ....York, PA
Shelley, Elizabeth Pruett
Hilton Head Island, SC
Shelley, Geo. P. ....Austin, TX
Shelley, George S. ....Fort Lauderdale, FL
Shelley, Gerald L. ....Phoenix, AZ
Shelley, Gerald N. ....Costa Mesa, CA
Shelley, Gordon C. ....Reno, NV
Shelley & Graff, A Prof. Law Corp.
Pasadena, CA
Shelley, Heather O ....Wichita, KS
Shelley, Henry C., Jr.
Department of Defense, Office of the General Counsel, GV
Shelley, Herbert C. ....Washington, DC
Shelley, Heywood ....New York, NY
Shelley, Howard A., Jr. ....Cleveland, OH
Shelley, J. Barry ....Phoenix, AZ
Shelley, J. Gregory ....Indianapolis, IN
Shelley, J. LaMar ....Mesa, AZ
Shelley, James H. ....Hartsville, SC
Shelley, James R. ....Pensacola, FL
Shelley, Jerrold F. ....Yuma, AZ
Shelley, John A. ....Los Angeles, CA
Shelley, John E. ....Fresno, CA
Shelley, John F. ....Cleveland, OH
Shelley, Kathleen Q. ....Big Sandy, TX
Shelley, Kevin M. ....New York, NY
Shelley, Lewis E. ....Tallahassee, FL
Shelley, Linda Loomis ....Tallahassee, FL
Shelley, Mark E. ....Concord, NC
Shelley, Melvyn T. ....Phoenix, AZ
Shelley, Michael ....Tallahassee, FL
Shelley, Patrick D. ....Watsonville, CA
Shelley, Patrick M. ....Baltimore, MD
Shelley, Peter ....Boston, MA
Shelley, Peter Alan ....Boulder, CO
Shelley, Randall L., (A Professional Corporation) ....Sherman Oaks, CA
Shelley, Robert R. ....Pasadena, CA
Shelley, Scott C. ....New York, NY
Shelley, Staci Rhodes ....Mechanicsburg, PA
Shelley, Susanne M. ....Sacramento, CA
Shelley, Thomas McRoy, III
Columbia, SC
Shelley, W. Denis, (P.A.)
Daytona Beach, FL
Shelley, Wendy L. ....Lowell, MA
Shelley, William P. ....Philadelphia, PA
Shelley, W. P., Jr. ....Tallahassee, FL
Shelley-Hartle, Carolyn ....Sharon, PA
Shellhamer, Daniel N. ....Newark, NJ
Shellhorse, William Brent ....Fort Worth, TX
Shellhouse, Herbert D. ....Atlanta, GA
Shellist, Lore & Lazarz, P.C. ....Houston, TX
Shellist, Martin A. ....Houston, TX
Shellito, Christopher J.
Bedford Heights, OH
Shellman, Carolyn E. ....Austin, TX
Shellman, Dwight K., III, (P.C.)
Denver, CO
Shellman, Dwight K., Jr. ....Aspen, CO
Shellman, Jolene Lang ....Milwaukee, WI
Shellman & Ornitz, A Professional Corporation ....Aspen, CO
Shellow, Gilda B. ....Milwaukee, WI
Shellow, James M. ....Milwaukee, WI
Shellow, Jill R. ....Department of Justice, Tax Division, GV
Shellow, Shellow & Glynn, S.C.
Milwaukee, WI
Shellow-Lavine, Jill R. ....New York, NY
Shells, Lori L. ....Youngstown, OH
Shelly, Carl Hudson ....Pittsburgh, PA
Shelly, Carol A. ....Doylestown, PA
Shelly, Jeffrey S. ....Albany, NY
New York, NY
Shelly, Joseph D., III ....Chicago, IL
Shelly, Katherine M. ....Thompson, PA
Shelly, Lee W. ....Brielle, NJ
Shelly, Mitchell K. ....Mobile, AL
Shelly, Rita R. ....Saratoga, CA
Shelly, Stephen A. ....Quakertown, PA
Shelly, Thomas J., Jr. ....Philadelphia, PA
Shelly, Timothy S. ....Elkhart, IN
Shelmire, David H. ....Dallas, TX
Shelmon, Donald W. ....Rensselaer, IN
Shelnitz, Howard W. ....Waterbury, CT
Shelnitz, Mark A. ....Columbia, MD
Shelnut, Knowlton H., Jr. ....Lakeland, FL
Shelnut, Knowlton H., Jr., P.A.
Lakeland, FL
Shelnutt, Fred G. ....Marietta, GA
Shelnutt, J. Mark ....Columbus, GA
Shelnutt, John L. ....Atlanta, GA
Shelnutt, Mark D. ....Ocala, FL
Shelnutt, Stephen ....Arlington, VA
Shelomith, Zach B. ....Miami, FL
Shelor, Jesse S. ....Vinton, VA
Shelor, Karen L. ....Overland Park, KS
Shelor, Robert A., Jr. ....Spartanburg, SC
Shelor, Robert Michael ....Knoxville, TN
Shelowitz, Marc Allen ....Deerfield Beach, FL
Shelowitz & Mills, P.A.
Deerfield Beach, FL
Shelowitz, Paul A. ....Miami, FL
Shelquist, Robert K. ....Minneapolis, MN
Shelsby, Gilbert F., Jr. ....Newark, DE
Baltimore, MD
Shelson, James W. ....Jackson, MS
Shelson, Sandra M. ....Jackson, MS
Shelstad, Gary Duane ....Chula Vista, CA
Shelstad, Lori P. ....Chicago, IL
Shelters, Mary K. ....Calabasas, CA
Shelton, Adam J. ....West Hartford, CT
Shelton, Allen ....Hill City, KS
Shelton, Andrea Spencer ....Atlanta, GA
Shelton, Angel Fleetwood ....Indianapolis, IN
Shelton, Angela D. ....Baltimore, MD
Shelton, Arthur M., Jr. ....Oakland, CA
Shelton, Billy R. ....Lexington, KY
Pikeville, KY
Shelton, Billy W. ....Tupelo, MS
Shelton, Bob J. ....Dallas, TX
Shelton, Brandon M. ....Indianapolis, IN
Shelton, Brett ....Denver, CO
Shelton, Charles C. ....Baltimore, MD
Shelton, Charles E., II ....Los Angeles, CA
Shelton, Cheryl L. ....Orange, CA
Shelton, Christi A. ....Miami, FL
Shelton, Clarke & Phifer, L.L.P.
Pinehurst, NC
Southern Pines, NC
Shelton, Curtis A. ....Vancouver, WA
Shelton, Curtis R. ....Shreveport, LA
Shelton, Dana M. ....New Orleans, LA
Shelton, Daniel R. ....
Department of Agriculture, GV
Shelton, Danielle Marie ....Des Moines, IA
Shelton, David A. ....Chicago, IL
Shelton, David A. ....Indianapolis, IN
Shelton, David B. ....Orlando, FL
Shelton, David C. ....West Memphis, AR
Shelton, David C. ....Wilmington, DE
Shelton, David C. ....Memphis, TN
Shelton, David M. ....Seattle, WA
Shelton, Deborah K. ....Houston, TX
Shelton, Deborah M. ....Washington, DC
Shelton, Demetrius D. ....Berkeley, CA
Shelton, Dennis K. ....Seattle, WA
Shelton, Dominique R. ....Los Angeles, CA
Shelton, Donald E. ....Ann Arbor, MI
Shelton, Donald W., II ....Arlington, TX
Shelton, Dorothy Rees ....San Diego, CA
Shelton, Douglas J. ....Oklahoma City, OK
Shelton, Dowlen ....Houston, TX
Shelton, Edward S. ....Hartford, CT
Shelton, Elliot L. ....Los Angeles, CA
Shelton, Eric M. ....Buffalo, NY
Shelton, Fincourt B. C. ....Darby, PA
Shelton, Fred ....Othello, WA
Shelton, Frederick C., Jr. ....Dallas, TX
Shelton, Gary R. ....Arlington, TX
Shelton, George C., Jr. ....Indio, CA
Shelton, George L. ....Danbury, CT
Shelton, Gerald B., Jr. ....Rockford, IL
Shelton, Glen H., Jr. ....El Paso, TX
Shelton, Grace W. ....
Department of State, GV
Shelton, Gray W. ....Denton, TX
Shelton, Greg L. ....Decatur, AL
Shelton, Gregory D. ....New York, NY
Shelton, Gregory L. ....Tampa, FL
Shelton, Haskell ....Midland, MI
Shelton, Henry C., III ....Memphis, TN
Shelton, Horace P., Jr. ....Franklin, TN
Shelton, Hornor N. ....Houston, TX
Shelton, Howard W. ....Long Beach, CA
Shelton, J. Alison ....Thornton, CO
Shelton, J. Charles ....Tulsa, OK
Shelton, J. Keith ....Raymond, MS
Shelton, Jack ....Wichita, KS
Shelton, James F., Jr. ....Rockville, MD
Shelton, James R. ....Lafayette, LA
Shelton, James R. ....Houston, TX
Shelton, James T. ....Clarendon, TX
Shelton, Jeffery "Randy" ....Beaumont, TX
Shelton, Jeffrey L. ....Sacramento, CA
Shelton, Jerome H., Esq. ....Washington, DC
Shelton, Jerry C. ....Nashville, TN
Shelton, Jerry L. ....Beatrice, NE
Shelton, Jimmy D. ....Tupelo, MS
Shelton, Joe M. ....Sherman, TX
Shelton, John C. ....Atlanta, GA
Shelton, John R. ....Louisville, KY
Shelton, John R. ....Oklahoma City, OK
Shelton, John W. ....Palm Beach, FL
Shelton, Joseph P. ....Atlanta, GA
Shelton, Joseph Randall ....Morristown, TN
Shelton, Judith Treger ....Albany, NY
Buffalo, NY
Shelton, Julia B. ....Washington, DC
Shelton, Julie E. ....Lafayette, LA
Shelton, Julie Fretwell ....Roswell, GA
Shelton, Julie Page ....Chicago, IL
Shelton, Karen Wallach ....Atlanta, GA
Shelton, Kathryn Elizabeth
Alexandria, VA
Shelton, Kathryn R. ....Huntsville, AL
Shelton, Kathryne Ann ....Columbia, SC
Shelton, Kenneth ....Decatur, AL
Shelton, Kenneth N.
Research Triangle Park, NC
Shelton, Kenneth Wayne, Jr. ....Decatur, AL
Shelton, Kent A. ....Huron, SD
Shelton, Kevin C. ....Lake Ozark, MO
Shelton, Kristi A. ....Poway, CA
Shelton, Larry W. ....Norfolk, VA
Shelton Law Firm ....Chariton, IA
Shelton Law Firm ....Lake Ozark, MO
Shelton Law Firm ....Oklahoma City, OK
Shelton Law Office ....Columbia, SC
Shelton, Lawrence R. ....Kingston, NY
Shelton, Le Ann ....Bronx, NY
Shelton, Lee B. ....New York, NY
Shelton & Legendre ....Lafayette, LA
Shelton, Leslie ....Tulsa, OK
Shelton, Lisa Montgomery ....Austin, TX
Shelton, Lori Katrine ....Treasury Department, Internal Revenue Service, GV
Shelton, Mark ....Lutz, FL
Shelton, Mark, Professional Association
Lutz, FL
Shelton, Mark S. ....Washington, DC
Shelton, Martin R. ....Williamsburg, VA
Shelton, Max ....Memphis, TN
Shelton, Michael J. ....Rockville, MD
Shelton, Michael W. ....St. Louis, MO
Shelton, Michelle L. ....New York, NY
Shelton, Mimi Hastings ....Austin, TX
Shelton, Mykhanh P. ....Los Angeles, CA
Shelton, Nathaniel ....Littleton, CO
Shelton, Pamela Dowell ....Tulsa, OK
Shelton, Pat ....Houston, TX
Shelton, Paul D. ....Baltimore, MD
Shelton, Peter A. ....Washington, DC
Shelton, Peter K. ....Cleveland, OH
Shelton, Philip A. ....West Hartford, CT
Shelton, Phrasel L. ....Redwood City, CA
Shelton, R. Walton ....Austin, TX
Shelton, Ralph Conrad, II ....Santa Ana, CA
Shelton, Randolph E., Jr. ....Pinehurst, NC
Shelton, Raymond L. ....Louisville, KY
Shelton, Reuben A. ....St. Louis, MO
Shelton, Rhonda D. ....Oakland, CA
Shelton, Robert A. ....Baltimore, MD
Shelton, Robert C., Jr. ....Roseland, NJ
Shelton, Robert E. ....San Francisco, CA
Shelton, Rod ....Chula Vista, CA
Shelton, Ronene D. ....Oakton, VA
Shelton, Russell B. ....Dallas, TX
Shelton, Scott H. ....Cedar Mountain, NC
Shelton, Sheila S. ....Louisville, KY
Shelton, Shelly Harrell ....Winter Haven, FL
Shelton & Shelton ....Decatur, AL
Shelton & Shelton ....West Hartford, CT
Shelton, Stacy Glyn ....San Jose, CA
Shelton, Stephen R. ....Wichita Falls, TX
Shelton, Stephen R. ....Puyallup, WA
Shelton, Steven T. ....New York, NY
Shelton, Stuart E. ....Olympia, WA
Shelton, Stuart L. ....Department of Agriculture, Office of the General Counsel, GV
Shelton, Susan B. ....Oakbrook Terrace, IL
Shelton, Susan Leslie ....Tulsa, OK
Shelton, Talbot, Jr. ....Bonners Ferry, ID
Shelton, Tami J. ....Oklahoma City, OK
Shelton, Tammy F. ....De Kalb, IL
Shelton, Taryn V. ....New York, NY
Shelton, Thomas C. ....Atlanta, GA
Shelton, Thomas R. ....Lafayette, LA
Shelton, Timothy G. ....Chicago, IL
Shelton, Timothy Luke ....Tuscaloosa, AL
Shelton, Travis D. ....Lubbock, TX
Shelton, Travis D., P.C. ....Lubbock, TX
Shelton & Valadez, P.C. ....San Antonio, TX
Shelton, Valerie C. ....San Francisco, CA
Shelton, Vernon T. ....Glenwood Springs, CO
Shelton, Von H. ....Friendswood, TX
Shelton, W. Daniel ....Tucson, AZ
Shelton, Wade B. ....San Antonio, TX
Shelton, Walden E., Jr. ....San Antonio, TX
Shelton, Wayne C. ....Clarksville, TN
Shelton, William B. ....Dallas, TX
Shelton, William L. ....Chariton, IA
Shelton, William R. ....Cleveland, OH
Shelton, William R. ....Chesterfield, VA
Shelton-Dutcher, Mary Jo
Fountain Valley, CA
Sheltzer, Michael ....Visalia, CA
Sheluga, Lisa A. ....Bensalem, PA
Shelvy, Marjorie ....Los Angeles, CA
Shely, Donald E. ....Bloomfield Hills, MI
Shely, John B. ....Houston, TX
Shely, Lynda C. ....Washington, DC
Shely, Robert W. ....Phoenix, AZ
Shem, Mark W. ....San Jose, CA
Shema, Suzanne M. ....Tucson, AZ
Shema, Virginia K. ....Terre Haute, IN
Shemano, David B. ....Los Angeles, CA
Shemaria, Joseph, Law Offices of
Los Angeles, CA
Shemaria, Victoria R. ....Los Angeles, CA
Shemas, James F. ....Toledo, OH
Shemberg, Andrea R. ....Columbus, OH
Shemel, Sidney ....Flushing, NY
Shemeld, Gregory E. ....Franklinville, NY
Shemer, Daniel M. ....Baltimore, MD
Shemesh, Maximillian Tarkington
St. Paul, MN
Shemie, Lisa A. ....New York, NY
Shemin, Kenneth Robert ....Fayetteville, AR
Shemin Law Firm, A Professional Association ....Fayetteville, AR
Little Rock, AR
Shemin, Vicki L. ....Wellesley, MA
Shemke, Allan L. ....Santa Ana, CA
Shemke, Daniel R. ....Ann Arbor, MI
Shemke, Daniel R., P.C. ....Ann Arbor, MI
Shemler, Howard M. ....Fort Washington, MD
Shemo, Matthew M., Jr. ....Miami, FL
Shemonsky, Lisa G. ....San Diego, CA
Shemonsky, Natalie K. ....Silver Spring, MD
Shemrock, Bruce E. ....Fort Lauderdale, FL
Shems, Ronald A. ....Montpelier, VT
Shemtob, Lori Kessler ....Blue Bell, PA
Shemtob, Max D. ....Brooklyn, NY
Shemtob, Penny ....New York, NY
Shemwell, Cynthia W. ....Shreveport, LA
Shemwell, Robert H. ....Shreveport, LA
Shemwell, Robert H. "Lad", Jr.
Shreveport, LA
Shen, Bernard T. ....Seattle, WA
Shen, Ching-Lee ....New York, NY
Shen, Christine M. ....San Francisco, CA
Shen, Chunping ....Rosemead, CA
Shen, Edward Y. ....San Francisco, CA
Shen, Glenna ....Los Angeles, CA
Shen, I.C. Judy ....New York, NY
Shen, Leon Y. ....Montvale, NJ
Shen, Leonard H. ....Fairfield, CT
Shen, Martha A. ....Los Angeles, CA
Shen, Michael ....New York, NY
Shen, Michael M. ....Washington, DC
Shen, Nancy ....Minneapolis, MN
Shen, Simon ....San Francisco, CA
Shen, Y. Paige ....Long Beach, CA
Shen, Yu-Chi Paige ....Long Beach, CA
Shena, Sarah L. ....Visalia, CA
Shenai, Vasanth R. ....Cincinnati, OH
Shenas, George P. ....San Diego, CA
Shenas, George P., Inc. Law Offices of
San Diego, CA
Shenas, Peter, Law Offices of
San Diego, CA
Shenberg, Michael S. ....New York, NY
Shendalman, Elissa Jill ....New York, NY
Shendell, Gary R. ....West Palm Beach, FL
Shendell, Tamar Duffner
Lighthouse Point, FL
Shenefelt, Patricia F. ....Houston, TX
Shenefield, John H. ....Washington, DC
Shenekji, Raymond F. ....Wayne, NJ
Sheneman, Margaret ....San Francisco, CA
Shenfeld, Beth A. ....Los Angeles, CA
Shenfeld, Doreen W. ....Beverly Hills, CA
Shenfeld, Doreen Wener ....Sherman Oaks, CA
Shenfeld, Robert C. ....New York, NY
Shenfield, Christopher J.
New Orleans, LA

Sheppard, Joseph Dow, III **Springfield, MO**
Sheppard, Joseph L. .... Burleson, TX
Sheppard, Julie L. .... Tallahassee, FL
Sheppard, Kenneth A. .... Seattle, WA
Sheppard, Kenneth J. .... Idaho Falls, ID
Sheppard, Laura E. .... Boston, MA
Sheppard, Lawrence E. .... Olathe, KS
Sheppard, Lesli Lynn .... Vienna, VA
Sheppard, Linda J. .... Kansas City, MO
Sheppard, Lisa M. .... Winston-Salem, NC
Sheppard, M. Susan .... Philadelphia, PA
Sheppard, Mark B. .... Philadelphia, PA
Sheppard, Mark J. .... Cincinnati, OH
Sheppard, Mary Roberts .... Baltimore, MD
Sheppard, Michael A. .... Cuero, TX
Sheppard, Michael B. .... Washington, DC
Sheppard, Michael Gibbs .... Cincinnati, OH
Sheppard, Michael M. .... Richmond, VA
Sheppard, Michael R. .... Decatur, GA
Sheppard, Mullin, Richter & Hampton LLP **Costa Mesa, CA** **Los Angeles, CA** **San Diego, CA** **San Francisco, CA**
Sheppard, Nicholas J. .... Chappaqua, NY
Sheppard, Patricia M. B. .... Boston, MA
Sheppard, Paul T. .... Binghamton, NY
Sheppard, Phillip A. .... Cotuit, MA
Sheppard, Ralph H. .... New York, NY
Sheppard, Ray C. .... Akron, OH
Sheppard, Reed S. .... Albuquerque, NM
Sheppard, Richard C. .... Bay City, MI Saginaw, MI
Sheppard, Robert H. .... Troy, AL
Sheppard, Robert H. .... Charlotte, NC
Sheppard, Robert J. .... San Francisco, CA
Sheppard, Robert O. .... Syracuse, NY
Sheppard, Rodney J. .... Austin, TX
Sheppard, Stennett .... Enterprise, CA
Sheppard, Stephen R. .... Mobile, AL
Sheppard, Steven B. .... Woodbury, NY
Sheppard, Susan D. .... Austin, TX
Sheppard, Susan R. .... New York, NY
Sheppard, Sylvester G. .... Petersburg, VA
Sheppard, Thomas C., Jr. .... Fairmont, WV
Sheppard, Thomas R. .... Los Angeles, CA
Sheppard, Todd A. .... Manhattan, KS
Sheppard, Walter O. .... Fort Myers, FL
Sheppard, Warren J., Jr. **New Orleans, LA**
Sheppard, Weisberg & Miller San Francisco, CA
Sheppard, White & Thomas, P.A. **Jacksonville, FL**
Sheppard, William A., Jr. .... Evergreen, CO
Sheppard, William D. .... Springfield, MO
Sheppard, William J. .... Atlanta, GA
Sheppard, Wm. J. .... Jacksonville, FL
Sheppe, I. Jeremy .... Purchase, NY
Sheppe, Matthew H. .... New York, NY
Sheppeard, Cynthia J. .... Topeka, KS
Sheppeard, Laura K. Federal Energy Regulatory Commission, Office of the General Counsel, GV
Sheppeard, Sarah Y. .... Knoxville, TN
Sheppeard & Swanson, P.L.C. **Knoxville, TN**
Shepperd, Alfred L. .... San Antonio, TX
Shepperd, Anita L. .... Gainesville, FL
Shepperd, Chris .... Pella, IA
Shepperd, John R. .... Houston, TX
Shepps, Ben B. .... Mineola, NY
Shepps, Lawrence T. .... New York, NY
Shepro, Daniel .... Bridgeport, CT
Shepro, Justice W. .... Roscoe, IL
Shepro, Kenneth C. .... Chicago, IL
Shepro, Richard W. .... Chicago, IL
Sheps, Cynthia .... New York, NY
Sheps, Elaine Rudnick .... New York, NY
Sheps, Isaiah C. .... Suffern, NY
Sheps, Lewis .... Highland Park, NJ
Sheps, Mindy .... Los Angeles, CA
Sheps, Robert C. .... New York, NY
Sheps, Stephanie A. .... Boston, MA
Sheptak, Peter J. .... Palm Beach, FL
Sheptock, John J. .... Maplewood, NJ
Sheptow, Allen H. .... Kissimmee, FL
Shepura, Judy Bateman .... Birmingham, AL
Shequine, Elizabeth K. .... Poughkeepsie, NY
Sher, Adam H. .... New York, NY
Sher, Andrew .... Houston, TX
Sher, Audrey F. .... New York, NY
Sher, Barry G. .... New York, NY
Sher & Blackwell .... Washington, DC
Sher, Brian A. .... Chicago, IL
Sher, Byron D. .... Palo Alto, CA
Sher and Cummings .... Arlington, VA **Fairfax, VA**
Sher, Daphna R. .... Palo Alto, CA
Sher, David E. .... Arlington, VA
Sher, Denise L. .... Hempstead, NY
Sher, Diane Bernoff .... Philadelphia, PA
Sher, Donald J. .... St. Louis, MO
Sher, Elizabeth J. .... Morristown, NJ **New York, NY**
Sher Garner Cahill Richter Klein McAlister & Hilbert, L.L.C. .... New Orleans, LA
Sher, Harry D. .... Chicago, IL
Sher, Harry J. .... Philadelphia, PA
Sher, Howard S. .... Troy, MI
Sher, Jaimes .... Houston, TX
Sher, Jeffrey E. .... Houston, TX
Sher, Jeremy J. .... Washington, DC
Sher, Joel I. .... Baltimore, MD
Sher, Jonathon F. .... Los Angeles, CA
Sher, Karen B. .... New Orleans, LA
Sher, Kathleen J. .... Concord, NH
Sher, Lawrence J. .... Los Angeles, CA
Sher, Lawrence S. .... Washington, DC
Sher, Leopold Z., (P.C.) .... New Orleans, LA
Sher, Linda R. National Labor Relations Board, Office of the General Counsel, GV
Sher, Malcolm, Law Offices of **Walnut Creek, CA**
Sher, Marilyn .... Miami, FL
Sher, Merritt I. .... San Francisco, CA
Sher, Michael D. .... Chicago, IL
Sher, Michael L. .... New York, NY
Sher, Michael S. .... Boston, MA
Sher, Neal M. .... Washington, DC
Sher, Patricia R. .... Jacksonville, FL
Sher, Paul D. .... Washington, DC
Sher, Paul D. .... Jackson, MI
Sher, R. Joseph .... Department of Justice, Civil Division, GV
Sher, Richard J. .... St. Louis, MO
Sher, Richard P. .... St. Louis, MO
Sher, Robert B. .... Los Angeles, CA
Sher, Robert J. .... Chevy Chase, MD
Sher, Ronald A. .... White Plains, NY
Sher, Rosalie M. .... Burke, VA
Sher, Sidney .... Sacramento, CA
Sher, Stanley .... New York, NY
Sher, Stanley O. .... Washington, DC
Sher, Stephen N. .... Chicago, IL
Sher, Steven R. .... Philadelphia, PA
Sher, Susan S. .... Chicago, IL
Sher, Tara A. .... Washington, DC
Sher, Victor M. .... Sacramento, CA
Shera-Dal Cin, Deborah .... Plano, TX
Sheradsky, Saml., (P.A.) .... Coral Gables, FL
Sherak, Robin S. .... New York, NY
Sheran, Daniel J. .... Minneapolis, MN
Sheran, John M. .... Minneapolis, MN
Sheran, Robert J. .... Minneapolis, MN
Sheran, Thomas R. .... Minneapolis, MN
Sherar, Craig Z., (P.A.) .... Miami, FL
Sherard, D. N. .... Wheatland, WY
Sherard, James R. (Randy) .... Vicksburg, MS
Sherard, Marshall P., Jr. .... Anderson, SC
Sherard, Sherard and Johnson **Wheatland, WY**
Sherard, Stephen N. .... Wheatland, WY
Sheraw, Donald M. .... Albany, NY
Sheray, Sidney R. .... San Francisco, CA
Sherb, J. Michael .... New London, CT
Sherbakoff, Jeffry A. .... Sacramento, CA
Sherbakoff & Sherbakoff .... Sacramento, CA
Sherbanee, Anita Silvia .... Santa Ana, CA
Sherbell, Gary W. .... Brooklyn, NY
Sherbert, Adrienne E. .... Houston, TX
Sherbert, Bill .... Houston, TX
Sherbert & Campbell .... Houston, TX
Sherbert, Mark Thomas .... San Diego, CA
Sherbet, Eric M. .... New York, NY
Sherbill, Raymond J. .... Bethesda, MD
Sherbin, Aaron H. .... Farmington Hills, MI
Sherbin, David M. .... Southfield, MI
Sherbin, James L. .... Oakland, MD
Sherbin, Joshua A. .... Auburn Hills, MI
Sherbin, Linda S. .... Oakland, MD
Sherbondy, Dick E. .... Leawood, KS
Sherbow, David A. .... Baltimore, MD
Sherbow, Jeffrey S. .... Detroit, MI Troy, MI
Sherbow & Mitchell .... Detroit, MI Troy, MI
Sherbow, Theodore .... Baltimore, MD
Sherbrook, Harry J. .... Detroit, MI
Sherbrooke, Alan P. .... Seattle, WA
Sherbunt, Norbert J. .... Amsterdam, NY
Sherburn, Cynthia Jane .... Detroit, MI
Sherburne, Alan A. .... Tewksbury, MA
Sherburne, Amy E. .... San Francisco, CA
Sherburne, Eric J. .... Minneapolis, MN
Sherburne, James M. .... Minneapolis, MN
Sherburne, Jane C. .... Washington, DC
Sherburne Law Offices, P.A. **Minneapolis, MN**
Sherburne, Paul G. .... Milwaukee, WI
Sherburne, Powers & Needham, P.C. **Boston, MA**
Sherburne Beyer, Erin .... Lafayette, LA
Sherby, James W. .... St. Louis, MO
Sherby, Kathleen R. .... St. Louis, MO
Sherck, James R. .... Toledo, OH
Sherck, Timothy C. .... Chicago, IL
Sherdan, Carmelita Judith .... Rockville, MD
Sherden, Molly Haynes .... Boston, MA
Shere, Fazal A. .... Charleston, WV
Shere, Joel M. .... Ann Arbor, MI
Shere, Mark E. .... Indianapolis, IN
Shereda, Cynthia L. .... Fairfield, CT
Shereda, Joseph P. .... Chicago, IL
Shereff, Friedman, Hoffman & Goodman, LLP .... New York, NY
Shereff, Henry D. .... New York, NY
Sheren, Lesley .... Chicago, IL
Sherer, Barbara L. .... Edwardsville, IL
Sherer, Christopher A. .... Jasper, AL
Sherer, Donald B. .... Stamford, CT
Sherer, Dunham B. .... San Jose, CA
Sherer, Edward F. .... Baytown, TX
Sherer, Eric David .... San Antonio, TX
Sherer, Frank A., Jr. .... Middlebury, CT
Sherer, Joseph P. .... Melville, NY
Sherer, Leonard C. .... Pittsburgh, PA
Sherer, Mark C. .... Warsaw, IN
Sherer, Melinda S. .... Forest Hills, NY
Sherer, Robert J. .... Boston, MA
Sherer, Russell S. .... Roseville, MN
Sherer, Samuel A. .... Washington, DC
Sherer, Stephen T. .... Meridian, ID
Sherer, Trace J. .... Houston, TX
Sheres, Samuel .... Hallandale Beach, FL
Sheresky Aronson & Mayefsky, LLP **New York, NY**
Sheresky, Norman M. .... New York, NY
Sherfinski, John M. .... West Hartford, CT
Shergalis, Katharine .... New York, NY
Sherick, Jack .... Woodland Hills, CA
Sherick, Joseph H. .... Annandale, VA
Sherick Law Office .... Tucson, AZ
Sherick, Steven P. .... Tucson, AZ
Sherick, Tricia A. .... Detroit, MI
Sheridan, Adele A. .... Latham, NY
Sheridan, Allen L. .... New York, NY
Sheridan, Amy L. .... Washington, DC
Sheridan, Angelia J. .... Orlando, FL
Sheridan & Associates, P.C. .... Wheaton, IL
Sheridan, Barbara S. .... Asbury Park, NJ
Sheridan, Barrett C. .... Harrisburg, PA
Sheridan, Brian D. .... Ishpeming, MI
Sheridan, C. Michael .... Deerfield, MA
Sheridan & Carroll, LLP **Sacramento, CA**
Sheridan, Cathryn A. .... Cleveland, OH
Sheridan, Charlene M. .... Chicago, IL
Sheridan, Charles F., Jr. .... Concord, NH
Sheridan, Charles J. .... Olney, MD
Sheridan, Charles R. .... Arlington Heights, IL
Sheridan, Christine H. .... Philadelphia, PA
Sheridan, Christopher F. .... Ebensburg, PA
Sheridan, Daniel J. .... South Hadley, MA
Sheridan, Daniel J. .... Princeton, NJ
Sheridan, Daniel James .... Chicago, IL
Sheridan, Daniel M. .... Burnsville, MN
Sheridan, Daniel P. .... Prince Frederick, MD
Sheridan, David M. .... Farmington, CT
Sheridan, David R. .... Des Moines, IA
Sheridan, David R. .... Albany, NY
Sheridan, Debra M. .... Providence, RI
Sheridan, Desiree .... Bronx, NY
Sheridan, Desmond G. .... Greensboro, NC
Sheridan, Diane L. .... Allentown, PA
Sheridan, Drew S. .... Miami, FL
Sheridan, E. Gayle .... White Plains, NY
Sheridan, Edward A. .... Hamburg, NY
Sheridan, Edward P. .... Lansing, IL
Sheridan, Edwin A. .... Washington, DC **Fairfax, VA**
Sheridan, Eric James .... New York, NY
Sheridan, E. W. .... Long Beach, CA
Sheridan, Gabriel T. .... Seattle, WA
Sheridan, Gerald M., Jr. .... Wheaton, IL
Sheridan, H. Ford .... Helendale, CA
Sheridan, J. Brian .... Norfolk, VA
Sheridan, J. Michael .... Media, PA
Sheridan, Jack .... Morristown, NJ
Sheridan, Jack M. .... Rusk, TX
Sheridan, James A. .... Palo Alto, CA
Sheridan, James E. .... Adrian, MI
Sheridan, James M. .... Muskegon, MI
Sheridan, Jeffrey S Inver Grove Heights, MN
Sheridan, JoAl Cannon .... Jacksonville, TX
Sheridan, John D. .... Wormleysburg, PA
Sheridan, John J. .... Chicago, IL
Sheridan, John K., II .... Indianapolis, IN
Sheridan, John M. .... Southfield, MI
Sheridan, John P. .... Detroit, MI
Sheridan, John P. .... Troy, MI
Sheridan, John P. .... New York, NY
Sheridan, John P., Jr. .... Morristown, NJ **Trenton, NJ**
Sheridan, John R. .... Wilmington, DE
Sheridan, John T. .... Palo Alto, CA
Sheridan, Julia A. .... Portland, ME
Sheridan, Julie Mathy .... Albany, NY
Sheridan, Jullia A. .... Harrisburg, PA
Sheridan & Jump .... Columbus, OH
Sheridan, Kelly C. .... Schaumburg, IL
Sheridan, L. Kevin, Jr. .... New York, NY
Sheridan Law Offices, P.C. .... Allegan, MI
Sheridan, Lawrence K. .... Smithtown, NY
Sheridan, Loretta A. .... White Plains, NY
Sheridan, Mark F. .... Santa Fe, NM
Sheridan, Mark G. .... Chicago, IL
Sheridan, Mark T. .... Hillsborough, NC
Sheridan, Mary E. .... New York, NY
Sheridan, Megan Crowell .... Los Angeles, CA
Sheridan, Michael C. .... Santa Monica, CA
Sheridan, Michael J. .... Department of Justice, Immigration and Naturalization Service, GV
Sheridan, Michael J. .... Dearborn, MI
Sheridan, Michael J. .... Norristown, PA
Sheridan, Michael P. .... South Hadley, MA
Sheridan, Michael W. .... Brentwood, TN
Sheridan, Michele L. .... Washington, DC
Sheridan, Owen G. .... North East, PA
Sheridan, Pamela Anne .... Wilmette, IL
Sheridan, Patricia J. Department Of Veterans Affairs, Board of Contract Appeals, GV
Sheridan, Patricia Martin .... Wheaton, IL
Sheridan, Patrick E. .... Bozeman, MT
Sheridan, Paul A. .... Raleigh, NC
Sheridan, Paul F. .... Arlington, VA
Sheridan, Paul F., Jr. .... Washington, DC
Sheridan, Paul M., III .... Chicago, IL
Sheridan, Paul N. .... New York, NY
Sheridan, Peter C. .... Los Angeles, CA
Sheridan, Peter Edward .... Boston, MA
Sheridan, Peter F. .... Sweetwater, TX
Sheridan, Peter G. .... Trenton, NJ
Sheridan, Peter N. .... Atlanta, GA
Sheridan, Peter T. .... New York, NY
Sheridan, Philip F., Jr. .... Hackensack, NJ
Sheridan, Philip H., Jr. .... Columbus, OH
Sheridan, Philip H., (P.C.) .... Denver, CO
Sheridan, Philip J. .... Allegan, MI
Sheridan, R. Kelly .... Providence, RI
Sheridan, Richard J. .... San Francisco, CA
Sheridan, Richard M. .... Hartford, CT
Sheridan, Richard R. .... San Diego, CA
Sheridan, Robert .... Daly City, CA
Sheridan, Robert E. .... Tallahassee, FL
Sheridan, Robert E. .... Missoula, MT
Sheridan, Robert K. .... Woburn, MA
Sheridan, Robert P. .... Chicago, IL
Sheridan, Robin M. .... Pewaukee, WI
Sheridan Ross, P.C. .... Denver, CO
Sheridan, Sandra N. .... Vienna, VA
Sheridan, Scott E. .... Boston, MA **Providence, RI**
Sheridan & Sheridan .... South Hadley, MA
Sheridan, Shirley M. .... Southborough, MA
Sheridan, Stephanie A. **San Francisco, CA**
Sheridan, Stephen E. .... Allegan, MI
Sheridan, Steven J. .... Duluth, MN
Sheridan, Sue D. .... House of Representatives, Committee Legal Personnel, GV
Sheridan, Susan G. .... Columbus, OH
Sheridan, Susan J. .... Sacramento, CA
Sheridan, Suzanne M. Department of Education, Office of the General Counsel, GV
Sheridan, Thomas .... Philadelphia, PA
Sheridan, Thomas I., III .... New York, NY
Sheridan, Thomas I., Jr. .... New York, NY
Sheridan, Thomas J. .... Albany, NY
Sheridan, Thomas M. .... Portland, OR
Sheridan, Thomas P. .... Glastonbury, CT
Sheridan, Thomas W. .... Philadelphia, PA
Sheridan, Timothy F. .... Grand Rapids, MI **Troy, MI**
Sheridan, Timothy F. .... Forest Hills, NY
Sheridan, Todd A. .... Phoenix, AZ Sun City, AZ
Sheridan, Vickie A. .... New Smyrna Beach, FL
Sheridan, William A. .... Boston, MA
Sheridan, William C. .... Londonderry, NH
Sheridan, William C., P.A., Law Offices of **Londonderry, NH**
Sheridan, William G., Jr. .... Portland, OR
Sheridan, William J. .... Chicago, IL
Sheridan, William P. .... Leonia, NJ
Sheridan, William T. .... Baltimore, MD
Sheridan, Wilson E. .... Richmond, VA
Sheridan-Lucht, Gail A. .... Des Moines, IA
Sherif, Linda Y. .... San Francisco, CA
Sherif, Mahir Tewfik .... San Diego, CA
Sheriff, Dee Catherine .... Cincinnati, OH
Sheriff, James A. .... Milwaukee, WI
Sheriff, Mark J. .... Columbus, OH
Sheriff, Matthew P. .... Schaumburg, IL
Sheriff, Thomas M. .... Monrovia, CA
Sherin and Lodgen LLP .... Los Angeles, CA **Boston, MA**
Sherinian, Suzanne A. .... Sacramento, CA
Sherins, Dana M. .... New York, NY
Sherk, Arik A. .... Dayton, OH
Sherk, John K., III .... Kansas City, MO
Sherk, Jon Arthur .... Ada, MI
Sherk, Kenneth J. .... Phoenix, AZ
Sherk, Thomas Howard .... Birmingham, AL
Sherk, Wendell J. .... Florissant, MO
Sherk, William C. .... Dallas, TX
Sherl, Bernard .... New York, NY
Sherland, Barbara C. .... Seattle, WA
Sherland, Paul G. .... Charlottesville, VA
Sherley, Anne W. .... Baltimore, MD
Sherley, Frederick H. .... Washington, DC
Sherley, Robert Putman .... Washington, DC
Sherlin, Jacquelyn S. .... Fullerton, CA
Sherlin, M. Johanna .... Walnut Creek, CA
Sherline, Ann E. .... Washington, DC **Chicago, IL**
Sherling, Barber (Bob), Jr., P.C. .... Mobile, AL
Sherling, Barber (Bob), Jr. .... Mobile, AL
Sherlock, Daniel T. .... Chicago, IL
Sherlock, E. Todd .... Overland Park, KS
Sherlock, J. Richard .... Grand Rapids, MI
Sherlock, Jeffrey M. .... Helena, MT
Sherlock, Joel D., Jr. .... Austin, TX
Sherlock, John J. .... White Plains, NY
Sherlock, Kathleen A. .... Providence, RI
Sherlock, Lawrence W. .... Houston, TX
Sherlock, Margaret A. .... Rutherford, NJ
Sherlock, Mary E. .... Dover, DE
Sherlock & Nardi .... Kalispell, MT
Sherlock, Patrick D. .... Kalispell, MT
Sherlock, Patrick J. .... Chicago, IL
Sherlock, Paula F. .... Louisville, KY
Sherlock, Robert L. .... Irvine, CA
Sherlock, Ronald P. .... West Hartford, CT
Sherlock, Scott M. Environmental Protection Agency, Program Office Attorneys, GV
Sherlock, Sean Michael .... Irvine, CA
Sherlock, Victoria J. .... Houston, TX
Sherlock, Virginia Pitt .... Stuart, FL
Sherlock, William H. .... Eugene, OR
Shermak, Julie I. .... Washington, DC
Sherman, A. Haag .... Houston, TX
Sherman, A. Lawrence .... Lexington, KY
Sherman, Alan E. .... Newark, NJ **New York, NY**
Sherman, Alan E., Law Offices of Dallas, TX
Sherman, Albert .... River Vale, NJ
Sherman, Albert E. .... Midland, TX
Sherman & Allegretti .... Hammond, IN
Sherman, Allen .... Boca Raton, FL
Sherman, Andrew H. .... Newark, NJ **New York, NY**
Sherman, Andrew J. .... Washington, DC
Sherman, Andrew L. .... New York, NY
Sherman, Ann L. .... Portland, OR

Sherman, Anthony B. ... Chicago, IL
Sherman, Arnold B. ... Bethesda, MD
Sherman, Arthur ... Beverly Hills, CA
Sherman, Arthur ... Cambridge, MA
Sherman, Barry D. ... Hammond, IN
Sherman, Barry H. ... Oakbrook Terrace, IL
Sherman, Benson ... Bay Shore, NY
Sherman, Berton D.
Black River Falls, WI
Sparta, WI
Sherman & Bouknight, P.A.
Columbia, SC
Sherman, Brad J. ... Woodland Hills, CA
Sherman, Bradley A. ... Albany, NY
Sherman, Bradley A. ... Cleveland, OH
Sherman, Brendan J. ... Blue Bell, PA
Sherman, Brett D. ... New York, NY
Sherman, Bruce Eric ... Santa Monica, CA
Sherman, Bruce F., Jr. ... Honolulu, HI
Sherman, Bruce H. ... Franklinville, NJ
Sherman, Bruce P. ... Rockville, MD
Sherman, Bryn Hope ... Bethesda, MD
Sherman, Burton A. ... Northbrook, IL
Sherman, Burton S. ... New York, NY
Sherman, C. Leon ... Pittsburgh, PA
Sherman, C. Leon, & Associates, P.C.
Pittsburgh, PA
Sherman, Candyce Faith
West Bloomfield, MI
Sherman, Carol ... New York, NY
Sherman, Carol B. ... Los Angeles, CA
Sherman, Carol Weiss ... Stamford, CT
Sherman, Carole Runcie ... Calabasas, CA
Sherman, Carolyn J.
Securities and Exchange Commission,
Division of Corporation Finance, GV
Sherman, Cary Howard ... Washington, DC
Sherman & Castro ... Coral Gables, FL
Miami, FL
Sherman, Charles D. ... St. Johns, MI
Sherman, Charles I. ... Louisville, KY
Sherman, Charles W., Jr.
Washington, DC
Sherman, Charlotte A. ... Baltimore, MD
Sherman, Charna Eve ... Cleveland, OH
Sherman, Citron & Karasik, P.C.
New York, NY
Sherman, Claudine ... Rancho Santa Fe, CA
Sherman, Colin D. ... Metairie, LA
Sherman, Cori ... New York, NY
Sherman, Craig A. ... San Diego, CA
Sherman, Craig B. ... Fort Lauderdale, FL
Sherman, Craig E. ... Kirkland, WA
Sherman, Cynthia ... Cambridge, MA
Sherman, D. Terrell ... San Ramon, CA
Sherman, D. Warren, Jr. ... Lexington, MO
Sherman, Dana ... Tarzana, CA
Sherman, Daniel ... Bloomington, IN
Sherman, Daniel ... Norristown, PA
Sherman, Daniel H., IV ... Atlanta, GA
Sherman, Daniel J. ... Dallas, TX
Sherman, Daniel W. ... Chicago, IL
Sherman & Danielsen, Ltd. ... Plymouth, MN
Sherman, Darrell C. ... Phoenix, AZ
Sherman, Darryl H. ... Northbrook, IL
Sherman, Daryn Z. ... Department of State,
Foreign Service Officers (Overseas), GV
Sherman, David ... Rockville, MD
Sherman, David B. ... Philadelphia, PA
Sherman, David C. ... Westlake, OH
Sherman, David C., Co., L.P.A.
Westlake, OH
Sherman, David E. ... Union, NJ
Sherman, David G. ... West Palm Beach, FL
Sherman, David L. ... New York, NY
Sherman, David M. ... Denver, CO
Sherman, David R. ... Tucson, AZ
Sherman, David R., (Professional Law Corporation) ... Metairie, LA
Sherman, David S., III ... St. Louis, MO
Sherman, David W. ... Honolulu, HI
Sherman, Davis V. R. ... Baltimore, MD
Sherman, Debbie S. Harris ... Palm Desert, CA
Sherman, Deborah ... New York, NY
Sherman, Deming E. ... Providence, RI
Sherman, Dennis H. ... Cleveland, OH
Sherman, Diane B. ... New York, NY
Sherman, Diane C. ... New York, NY
Sherman, Don R. ... St. Louis, MO
Sherman, Douglas B. ... Hartford, CT
Sherman, Dunn, Cohen, Leifer & Yellig, P.C.
Washington, DC
Sherman, Earl I. ... Farmington Hills, MI
Sherman, Earl I., Associates, P.C.
Farmington Hills, MI
Sherman, Edw. L. ... Potomac, MD
Sherman, Edward F. ... New Orleans, LA
Sherman, Edward F., Jr. ... Los Angeles, CA
Sherman, Elinore ... San Jose, CA
Sherman, Elizabeth Jorgenson
Washington, DC
Sherman, Elliot M. ... Boston, MA
Sherman, Eric ... Los Angeles, CA
Sherman, Eric D. ... Newark, NJ
Sherman, Erwin A. ... Louisville, KY
Sherman, Eugene N. ... Los Angeles, CA
Sherman, Eugene T. ... Chicago, IL
Sherman, Francine T. ... Newton, MA
Sherman, Frank Howard ... Rochester, NY
Sherman, Frank R. ... Waltham, MA
Sherman, Fred Ross ... Glenview, IL
Sherman, Frederick "Rick" ... Deming, NM
Sherman, Fredrick E. ... New York, NY
Sherman & Fromme, P.C. ... Fairfax, VA
Sherman, Gary E. ... Fort Lauderdale, FL
Sherman, Gary E. ... Port Wing, WI
Sherman, Gary L. ... Providence, RI
Sherman, Gary S. ... Woodland Hills, CA
Sherman, George J. ... Hartford, CT
Sherman, Gerald H. ... Washington, DC
Sherman, Gerald J. ... Chicago, IL
Sherman, Gerald M. ... Minneapolis, MN
Sherman And Glenn, A Professional Corporation ... Woodland Hills, CA
Sherman, Glenn F. ... Marietta, GA
Sherman, Glenn F., & Associates, P.C.
Marietta, GA
Sherman, Glenn T. ... Los Angeles, CA
Sherman & Gordon, P.C. ... New York, NY
Sherman, H. Edward ... New Orleans, LA
Sherman, Harold ... Ridgefield, CT
Sherman, Harold A. ... Edison, NJ
Sherman, Harold J. ... West Palm Beach, FL
Sherman, Harris D. ... Denver, CO
Sherman, Harry ... New York, NY
Sherman, Harvey C. ... Los Angeles, CA
Sherman, Harvey W. ... Riverhead, NY
Sherman, Heather C. ... Minneapolis, MN
Sherman, Henry ... New York, NY
Sherman, Herbert I. ... Mountainside, NJ
Sherman, Herbert Scott ... East Brunswick, NJ
Sherman, Hope R. ... Cypress, CA
Sherman, Howard B. ... New York, NY
Sherman, Howard H. ... Bronx, NY
Sherman, Howard L. ... Chappaqua, NY
Sherman & Howard L.L.C.
Colorado Springs, CO
Denver, CO
Sherman, Ian M. ... Chicago, IL
Sherman, Ira ... Washington, DC
Rockville, MD
Sherman, Iris S.
Department Of Veterans Affairs,
Board of Veterans Appeals, GV
Sherman, Isaac ... New York, NY
Sherman, Ivan M. ... Bridgeton, NJ
Sherman, J. Daniel ... Cincinnati, OH
Sherman, Jack, Jr. ... Cincinnati, OH
Sherman, James B. ... Minneapolis, MN
Sherman, James D. ... Seattle, WA
Sherman, James E. ... St. Louis, MO
Sherman, James J. ... Tampa, FL
Sherman, James Marx ... Atlanta, GA
Sherman, James R. ... San Jose, CA
Sherman, James S. R. ... Roseland, NJ
Sherman, James W. ... Ellington, CT
Sherman, Janet Schmidt
Santa Monica, CA
Sherman, Janice L. ... Boston, MA
Sherman, Jay ... Encino, CA
Sherman, Jeffrey A. ... Denver, CO
Sherman, Jeffrey A. ... Atlanta, GA
Sherman, Jeffrey A. ... Bingham Farms, MI
Sherman, Jeffrey Adam ... Los Angeles, CA
Sherman, Jeffrey G. ... Chicago, IL
Sherman, Jeffrey M. ... Washington, DC
Sherman, Jeffrey M. ... St. Petersburg, FL
Sherman, Jeffrey M. ... Broomall, PA
Sherman, Jennifer ... Oak Brook, IL
Sherman, Jennifer L. ... Livonia, MI
Sherman, Jeremy P. ... Chicago, IL
Sherman, Jerold S. ... Burbank, CA
Sherman, Jerome B. ... New York, NY
Sherman, Jerome F. ... Lansing, MI
Sherman, Jerrold B., (P.C.) ... Southfield, MI
Sherman, Jo A. ... United States Senate,
Senatorial Assistants, GV
Sherman, Joan B. ... Somerset, NJ
Sherman, Joel B. ... Boston, MA
Sherman, John ... Ellsworth, KS
Sherman, John ... Woodbury, NY
Sherman, John B. ... New York, NY
Sherman, John E. ... Houston, TX
Sherman, John F., III ... Westborough, MA
Sherman, John Howland ... Crystal Lake, IL
Sherman, John L. ... Dickinson, ND
Sherman, John N., Jr. ... Chanute, KS
Sherman, John P. ... Manchester, NH
Sherman, John R. ... Boston, MA
Sherman, John S. ... Slingerlands, NY
Sherman, John W. ... Kenilworth, IL
Sherman, Jonathan ... Washington, DC
Sherman, Jonathan D. ... Chicago, IL
Sherman, Jonathan D.
Black River Falls, WI
Sparta, WI
Sherman, Jonathan L. ... New York, NY
Sherman, Jonathan M. ... Detroit, MI
Sherman, Joseph S. ... Secaucus, NJ
Sherman, Judith A. ... Ann Arbor, MI
Sherman, Jules J. ... San Clemente, CA
Sherman, Julie Locks ... Woodland Hills, CA
Sherman, Julius H. ... New York, NY
Sherman, Karen ... New York, NY
Sherman, Kathy Parden ... Mobile, AL
Sherman, Kay R. ... St. Louis, MO
Sherman, Kendra ... Columbus, OH
Sherman, Kenneth ... Salem, OR
Sherman, Kenneth, Jr. ... Salem, OR
Sherman, Kenneth L. ... Los Angeles, CA
Sherman, Kenneth P. ... Los Angeles, CA
Sherman, Kim Douglas ... Fort Lauderdale, FL
Sherman, Kirk B. ... San Antonio, TX
Sherman, Kirk D. ... Plymouth, MN
Sherman, Kristen W. ... Boston, MA
Providence, RI
Sherman, Kurt R. ... Syracuse, NY
Sherman, Kyle D. ... Atlanta, GA
Sherman & Lapidus, LLP ... San Diego, CA
Sherman, Larry H. ... Bingham Farms, MI
Sherman, Laura B. ... Washington, DC
Sherman, Laurence A. ... Chicago, IL
Sherman Law Offices ... Fort Lauderdale, FL
Sherman, Lawrence C. ... Cleveland, OH
Sherman, Lawrence E., Jr. ... Romney, WV
Sherman, Lawrence E., Jr., L.C.
Romney, WV
Sherman, Lawrence J. ... Washington, DC
Sherman, Lawrence M. ... San Diego, CA
Sherman, Lee A. ... Tustin, CA
Sherman, Lee S. ... Pennsauken, NJ
Sherman, Leigh Jennifer ... Saddle Brook, NJ
Sherman, Leonard W. ... Alexandria, VA
Sherman, Leslie E. ... San Francisco, CA
Sherman, Leslie J. ... New York, NY
Sherman, Leslie James ... Santa Monica, CA
Sherman, Lester I., (P.C.) ... Durango, CO
Sherman, Linda Bounds ... Jackson, MS
Sherman, Linda K. ... Boston, MA
Sherman, Linda L. ... Harrisonville, MO
Sherman, Lisa C. ... Spartanburg, SC
Sherman, Lisa F. ... Boston, MA
Sherman, Lisa G. ... Los Angeles, CA
Sherman, Lloyd A. ... New York, NY
Sherman, Lois Gilbert ... Sacramento, CA
Sherman, Loren D., II ... Encino, CA
Sherman, Lori S. ... New York, NY
Sherman, Lorraine R. ... St. Paul, MN
Sherman, Louis D. ... New York, NY
Sherman, Louis L., Jr. ... De Ridder, LA
Sherman, Lucile D. ... Tucson, AZ
Sherman, M. Andrew ... Pleasanton, CA
Sherman, M. Garth ... San Francisco, CA
Sherman, M. John ... Ithaca, NY
Sherman, Marc D. ... Lincolnwood, IL
Sherman, Margaret T., (Mrs.) ... Needles, CA
Sherman, Mark ... Tulsa, OK
Sherman, Mark Douglas ... Portland, OR
Sherman, Marne ... Columbia, SC
Sherman, Martin P. ... Palo Alto, CA
Sherman, Mary C. ... Minneapolis, MN
Sherman, Max ... Springfield, NJ
Sherman, Max E. ... Chicago, IL
Sherman, Max R. ... Austin, TX
Sherman, Meehan, Curtin & Ain, A Professional Corporation
Washington, DC
Sherman, Michael ... Stamford, CT
Sherman, Michael A. ... Los Angeles, CA
Sherman, Michael D. ... Washington, DC
Sherman, Michael D. ... Pittsburgh, PA
Sherman, Michael J. ... New York, NY
Sherman, Michael L. ... Chicago, IL
Sherman, Michael L. ... New York, NY
Sherman, Michael M. ... Philadelphia, PA
Sherman, Michael P. ... Minnetonka, MN
Sherman, Michael S. ... Stamford, CT
Sherman, Michael S. ... Chicago, IL
Sherman, Michael S. ... Kennett Square, PA
Sherman, Michael S., (P.C.)
Los Angeles, CA
Sherman, Michele C. ... Washington, DC
Sherman, Michelle ... Los Angeles, CA
Sherman, Milton ... New York, NY
Sherman, Milton N. ... Camarillo, CA
Sherman, Mitchell A. ... Boca Raton, FL
Sherman, Morris M. ... Minneapolis, MN
Sherman, Morris R. ... New York, NY
Sherman, Nancy M.
National Labor Relations Board,
Division of Administrative Law Judges, GV
Sherman, Natalie B. ... Baltimore, MD
Sherman, Nathanson & Miller, A Professional Corporation
Beverly Hills, CA
Los Angeles, CA
Sherman, Neil E. ... New York, NY
Sherman, Neil H. ... New York, NY
Sherman, Nina ... Toledo, OH
Sherman, Norman Eldredge ... Reading, MA
Sherman, Olsher & Sherman
Black River Falls, WI
Sparta, WI
Sherman, Patricia E. ... Troy, MI
Sherman, Paul ... Brooklyn, NY
Sherman, Paul E., Jr. ... Albany, NY
Sherman, Paul F. ... Springfield, MO
Sherman, Paul J. ... New York, NY
Sherman, Paul K.
Department of Commerce, GV
Sherman, Pauline ... New York, NY
Sherman, Peggy Brandenburg ... Atlanta, GA
Sherman, Peter ... Newark, OH
Sherman, Peter B. ... Washington, DC
Sherman, Peter Foster ... New York, NY
Sherman, Peter H. ... New York, NY
Sherman, Peter R. ... Washington, DC
Sherman, Philip ... Baltimore, MD
Sherman, Philip A. ... Clarksdale, MS
Sherman, Phyllis Z. ... Pennsauken, NJ
Sherman, Ralph ... Jericho, NY
New York, NY
Sherman, Ralph D. ... Hartford, CT
Sherman, Ralph D. ... West Hartford, CT
Sherman, Randall D. ... Hillsboro, MO
Sherman, Randall J. ... Newport Beach, CA
Sherman, Randolph S. ... New York, NY
Sherman, Ray W., Jr. ... Oakland, CA
Sherman, Richard ... Pasadena, CA
Sherman, Richard ... St. Louis, MO
Sherman, Richard A.
Fort Lauderdale, FL
Miami, FL
Sherman, Richard A. ... Providence, RI
Sherman, Richard A., P.A., Law Offices of
Fort Lauderdale, FL
Miami, FL
Sherman, Richard B. ... New York, NY
Sherman, Richard C. ... Springfield, NJ
Sherman, Richard C. ... Islip, NY
Sherman, Richard G. ... Los Angeles, CA
Sherman, Richard I. ... Berkeley, CA
Sherman, Richard Lloyd
Beverly Hills, CA
Sherman, Richard M., Jr.,(P.C.)
Newport Beach, CA
Sherman, Richard W. ... Germantown, MD
Sherman & Richichi ... Stamford, CT
Sherman, Rick D., Law Offices of
Phoenix, AZ
Sherman, Robert A. ... Boston, MA
Sherman, Robert A. ... Carthage, TX
Sherman, Robert J. ... Irvine, CA
Sherman Oaks, CA
Sherman, Robert J. ... Massapequa, NY
Sherman, Robert J. ... New York, NY
Sherman, Robert L. ... New York, NY
Sherman, Robert M. ... Irvine, CA
Sherman, Robert M. ... Fort Dodge, IA
Sherman, Robert N. ... Vista, CA
Sherman, Robert P. ... Boston, MA
Sherman, Robert P. ... Columbus, OH
Sherman, Robert R. ... Stockton, CA
Sherman, Robert S. ... Frankfort, KY
Sherman, Roger, (A Professional Corporation) ... Los Angeles, CA
Sherman, Roger B. ... Boston, MA
Sherman, Roger C. ... Washington, DC
Sherman, Roger L. ... Overland Park, KS
Sherman, Roger L., P.A. ... Overland Park, KS
Sherman, Roger M., P.A. ... Pensacola, FL
Sherman, Rosemary E. ... Brooklyn, NY
Sherman, Russell A. ... Elyria, OH
Sherman, Russell E. ... Fairfax, VA
Sherman, Ruthann ... Boston, MA
Sherman Salkow Petoyan & Weber, A Professional Corporation
Beverly Hills, CA
Los Angeles, CA
Sherman, Sam ... Brockton, MA
Sherman, Samenga, Federman, Donovan & Sambur, LLP ... Bay Shore, NY
Sherman, Sandra Brown ... Morristown, NJ
Sherman & Sandy ... Waterville, ME
Sherman, Sanford T. ... Irvine, CA
Sherman, Sara Lou ... Boston, MA
Sherman, Saul L. ... New York, NY
Sherman & Schachtman ... Chicago, IL
Sherman, Scott A. ... Austin, TX
Sherman, Scott D. ... Phoenix, AZ
Sherman, Scott G. ... Wilmington, NC
Sherman, Scott Kennedy ... Prairie Village, KS
Sherman, Scott L. ... Corpus Christi, TX
Sherman, Scott M. ... White Plains, NY
Sherman, Sean P. ... Washington, DC
Sherman, Seymour I. ... Chicago, IL
Sherman & Shalloway ... Alexandria, VA
Sherman, Sharon C.K. ... New York, NY
Sherman, Sharon Lynn ... Coronado, CA
Sherman, Sharon Lynn, A Professional Corporation ... Coronado, CA
Sherman & Sherman ... Los Angeles, CA
Santa Monica, CA
Sherman & Sherman ... Chicago, IL
Springfield, NJ
Sherman & Sherman, A Professional Corporation ... Los Angeles, CA
Sherman, Sherman, Murch & Johnnie, L.L.P. ... Salem, OR
Sherman & Sherman, P.C.
Bingham Farms, MI
Deming, NM
Sherman, Sherrill A. ... Englewood, CO
Sherman, Sidney ... Chicago, IL
Sherman, Sidney ... Bethesda, MD
Sherman, Sidney S. ... Northbrook, IL
Sherman, Silverstein, Kohl, Rose & Podolsky, A Professional Corporation
Camden, NJ
Cherry Hill, NJ
Lakewood, NJ
Pennsauken, NJ
Bala Cynwyd, PA
Sherman, Stacy L. ... Salisbury, MD
Sherman, Stephanie E.
Whitehouse Station, NJ
Sherman, Stephen A. ... Washington, DC
Sherman, Stephen A. ... Oklahoma City, OK
Sherman, Stephen A., & Associates
Oklahoma City, OK
Sherman, Stephen H. ... Washington, DC
Sherman, Stephen M. ... Indianapolis, IN
Sherman, Steve R. ... San Ramon, CA
Sherman, Steven E. ... San Francisco, CA
Sherman, Steven M. ... San Francisco, CA
Sherman, Steven M. ... Indianapolis, IN
Sherman, Steven M. ... St. Louis, MO
Sherman, Stuart A. ... Boca Raton, FL
Sherman, Stuart Lee ... Troy, MI
Sherman, Susan E. ... Bethesda, MD
Sherman, Susan H. ... Grand Rapids, MI
Sherman, Susan J. ... Department of Labor,
Office of the Solicitor, GV
Sherman, Susan M. ... Worcester, MA
Sherman, Suzanne ... West Caldwell, NJ
Sherman, Suzanne E., P.C.
West Caldwell, NJ
Sherman, Taff & Bangert, P.C.
Leawood, KS
Kansas City, MO
Sherman, Ted R. ... Pasadena, TX
Sherman, Teresa A. ... Spokane, WA
Sherman, Terry K. ... Columbus, OH
Sherman, Theodore S. ... Birmingham, MI
Sherman, Thomas D. ... Atlanta, GA
Sherman, Thomas G. ... Coral Gables, FL
Sherman, Thomas J. ... Cincinnati, OH
Sherman, Thomas L. ... Columbus, OH
Sherman, Thomas M., Jr. ... Pittsfield, MA
Sherman, Todd Brian ... Bronx, NY

Sherman, Troy Mayer ....Miami Beach, FL
Sherman, Valerie F. ....New York, NY
Sherman, Vicki Mae ....Jackson, MI
Sherman, Victor ....Santa Monica, CA
Sherman, Vilia G. ....Riverside, CA
Sherman, Vincent P. ....New York, NY
Sherman, W. Bradford ....Little Rock, AR
Sherman & Waldman, P.A.
Fort Lauderdale, FL
Sherman, William ....New York, NY
Sherman, William A., II ....Cincinnati, OH
Sherman, William B.
Fort Lauderdale, FL
Sherman, William B. ....Tamarac, FL
Sherman, William D. ....Palo Alto, CA
Sherman, William D. ....Cincinnati, OH
Sherman, William E. ....Department of Defense, Defense Commissary Agency, GV
Sherman, William E. ....Daytona Beach, FL
DeLand, FL
Sherman, William F. ....Little Rock, AR
Sherman, William M. ....Stamford, CT
Sherman, William R. ....Washington, DC
Sherman & Yaquinto, L.L.P. ....Dallas, TX
Shermer, Jonathan P., Jr. ....Russellville, AR
Shermet, Milton ....White Plains, NY
Shermeta, Chimko & Kilpatrick, P.C.
Ann Arbor, MI
Detroit, MI
Flint, MI
Grand Rapids, MI
Rochester Hills, MI
Shermeta, Douglass H. ....Detroit, MI
Rochester Hills, MI
Shermoen, Eugene C., Jr.
Minneapolis, MN
Shermoen, Jerome W.
International Falls, MN
Shermoen, Jerrod A. .....International Falls, MN
Shermoen, LeDuc & Jaksa, PLLP
International Falls, MN
Shermoen, Steven M., Law Office
International Falls, MN
Shern, Andrew T. ....St. Paul, MN
Shernoff, Bidart, Darras & Dillon
Claremont, CA
Los Angeles, CA
Palm Desert, CA
Pasadena, CA
Pomona, CA
Shernoff, Jeffrey L. ....New York, NY
Shernoff, William M., (P.C.)
Claremont, CA
Newport Beach, CA
Palm Desert, CA
Shernuk, Kurt J. ....Kansas City, KS
Sherod, Alec C. ....Denver, CO
Sheroke, Charles ....Coeur d'Alene, ID
Sheron, Christopher W. ....San Rafael, CA
Sheron, Marjorie F. ....Morristown, NJ
Sheronick, Mohammad H. ......Cedar Rapids, IA
Sherouse, Kenneth B., Jr. ....Miami, FL
Sherouse, Thomas M. ....Miami, FL
Sherow, Gary W. ....Ellenville, NY
Sherpy, Della L. Anderson ....Chicago, IL
Sherpy, R. Todd ....Columbia, SC
Sherr, Adam L. ....Seattle, WA
Sherr, Alan B. ....Boston, MA
Sherr, Anthony R. ....Blue Bell, PA
Sherr, Arthur ....New York, NY
Sherr, Bonnie S. ....Detroit, MI
Sherr, Brian J. ....Fort Lauderdale, FL
Sherr, Clifford M. ....Scottsdale, AZ
Sherr, Cynthia L. ....Hollywood, FL
Sherr, Cynthia L., P.A. ....Hollywood, FL
Sherr, Harry A. ....San Diego, CA
Sherr, Jonathan H. ....Loudon, TN
Sherr, Mitchell A. ....Fort Wayne, IN
Sherr, Morris M. ....Fresno, CA
Sherr, Norman A. ....Santa Barbara, CA
Sherr, Paul Berne ....Albany, NY
Sherr, Paul D. ....Birmingham, MI
Sherr, Paul D., P.C. ....Birmingham, MI
Sherr, Roger M. ....Farmington Hills, MI
Sherr, Ronald H. ....Philadelphia, PA
Sherr, Seymour Sy ....Sarasota, FL
Sherr, Steven N. ....San Francisco, CA
Sherr, Stuart D. ....Farmington Hills, MI
Sherr, William G. ....Allentown, PA
Sherraden, Mark ....Westwood, KS
Sherrard, Alexander C. ....Pittsburgh, PA
Sherrard, German & Kelly, P.C.
Pittsburgh, PA
Sherrard, James B. ....Elkton, MD
Sherrard, John Edgar ....Stuart, FL
Sherrard, John Edgar, P.A. ....Stuart, FL
Sherrard & McGonagle
Bainbridge Island, WA
Poulsbo, WA
Sherrard, Robert L. ....Millboro, VA
Sherrard & Roe, PLC ....Nashville, TN
Sherrard, Roger D. ....Poulsbo, WA
Sherrard, Thomas J., III ....Nashville, TN
Sherrard-Alvarez, Barbara L.
Rancho Cordova, CA
Sherr Duswalt, Geraldene ....New York, NY
Sherrell, George W., IV ....New York, NY
Sherrell, John B. ....Los Angeles, CA
Sherrell, Lynn M. ....Berkeley, CA
Sherrell, Robert E. ....Fitzgerald, GA
Sherren, James T. ....Ventura, CA
Sherrer, Charles W. ....Lafayette, CA
Sherrer, Gary C. ....Dothan, AL
Sherrer, John W., Jr. ....Vienna, GA
Sherrer, R. Benjamin ....Pryor, OK
Sherrer, Thomas J. ....Burlington, VT
Sherrer, Thomas J., A Professional Corporation
Burlington, VT

Sherrer, Wayman G. ....Oneonta, AL
Sherrerd, John J. F., Jr. ....Hood River, OR
Sherrets, Carl D. ....Dayton, OH
Sherrets, Hoffmann & Schiff, LLP
Centerville, OH
Dayton, OH
Kettering, OH
Oakwood, OH
Sherrets, James D. ....Omaha, NE
Sherrett, Maryhelen ....Portland, OR
Sherrick, Daniel W. ....Detroit, MI
Sherrick, James N. ....Villa Grove, IL
Sherrick, John A. ....Spokane, WA
Sherrick, John A., P.S. ....Spokane, WA
Sherrick, Richard D., II ....Los Angeles, CA
Sherriff, Andrew R. ....Westport, CT
Sherriff, Andrew R., Jr. ....Westport, CT
Sherriff, Angela S. ....Westport, CT
Sherriff, David J. ....Cleveland, OH
Sherriff & Sherriff ....Westport, CT
Sherriff, Susan R. ....Hayward, CA
Sherrill, Allen E. ....Miami, FL
Sherrill, Angela D. ....Miami, FL
Sherrill, Basil ....Clearwater, FL
Sherrill, Batts & Blizzard ....Athens, AL
Sherrill, Bruce ....Athens, AL
Sherrill, Carlyle ....Kannapolis, NC
Sherrill, Carlyle ....Salisbury, NC
Sherrill, Charles C., (P.A.) ....Pensacola, FL
Sherrill, Charles E., Jr. ....Kerrville, TX
Sherrill, Clifton W. ....Marco Island, FL
Sherrill, Crosnoe & Goff, A Professional Corporation ....Wichita Falls, TX
Sherrill, Everett C. ....Pilot Mountain, NC
Sherrill, George D., Jr. ....Duncan, OK
Sherrill, Gerald D. ....Phoenix, AZ
Sherrill, H. Virgil ....New York, NY
Sherrill, Henry F. ....Columbia, SC
Sherrill, Jackson H., III ....Savannah, GA
Sherrill, James E. ....Peachtree City, GA
Sherrill & Janes, PA ....Surfside Beach, SC
Sherrill, Jennifer D. ....Kansas City, MO
Sherrill, John A. ....Atlanta, GA
Sherrill, John C., III ....Mount Ulla, NC
Sherrill, John L. ....Surfside Beach, SC
Sherrill, John W. ....Wrightsville Beach, NC
Sherrill, Joseph N., Jr. ....Wichita Falls, TX
Sherrill, Kimberly A. ....Dearborn, MI
Sherrill, L. Stanford, Jr. ....Atlanta, GA
Sherrill, Linda S. ....Tucson, AZ
Sherrill, Mark David ....Charlottesville, VA
Sherrill, R. Kendall ....Tulsa, OK
Sherrill & Roof, L.L.P. ....Columbia, SC
Sherrill, Russell G., III ....Raleigh, NC
Sherrill, Susan J. ....Pleasanton, CA
Sherrill, Susan R. ....Atlanta, GA
Sherrill, W. Terry ....Charlotte, NC
Sherrill, William C., Jr. ....Tallahassee, FL
Sherrill, William N. ....Tucson, AZ
Sherrin, Jeffrey J. ....Albany, NY
Sherring, Neil K. ....Boston, MA
Sherrington, Paul A. ....New York, NY
Sherris, Theodore P. ....Garden City, NY
Sherritt, Craig Steven ....Fort Lauderdale, FL
Sherrod, Clarence ....Madison, WI
Sherrod, H. Floyd, Jr. ....Florence, AL
Sherrod, Henry F., III ....Sheffield, AL
Sherrod, Howell H., Jr. ....Johnson City, TN
Sherrod, J. Thomas ....Fremont, CA
Sherrod, J. Thomas, A Professional Corporation
Fremont, CA
Sherrod, John W. ....Douglasville, GA
Sherrod, Monte Lee ....El Paso, TX
Sherrod, Randall L. ....Canyon, TX
Sherrod, Stanley, Lincoln & Goldstein
Johnson City, TN
Sherrod, Susan M. ....Las Vegas, NV
Sherrod, Theodore R., Jr. ....Chicago, IL
Sherrod, Tonia ....New York, NY
Sherrod-Ali, Gilda ....Washington, DC
Sherron, Alvin B. ....Los Angeles, CA
Sherron, J. Kemp, III ....Raleigh, NC
Sherron, James E. ....Middletown, OH
Sherron, Steve P. ....Indianapolis, IN
Sherrow, Billy W. ....Lexington, KY
Sherrow, Dale E. ....Bellevue, WA
Sherrow, M. Michael ....New York, NY
Sherry, Alan G. ....Anchorage, AK
Sherry, Allan ....Woodsfield, OH
Sherry, Christine E. ....Menlo Park, CA
Sherry, Coleman & Holthouse, LLP
Newport Beach, CA
Sherry, Daniel I. ....Bowie, MD
Sherry, Daniel J. ....Newtown Square, PA
Sherry, Donna ....Boston, MA
Sherry, Edward N. ....West Palm Beach, FL
Sherry, Francis J. ....Philadelphia, PA
Wayne, PA
Sherry, Henry Allan ....Woodsfield, OH
Sherry, James M. ....Roslyn Heights, NY
Sherry, Jan Patrick ....Sacramento, CA
Sherry, Jeffrey S. ....Newport, KY
Sherry, John E. H. ....Ithaca, NY
New York, NY
Sherry, John Sebastian ....Pittsburgh, PA
Sherry, Jon David ....Brooklyn, NY
Sherry, Kathryn E. ....Woodsfield, OH
Sherry, Kevin L. ....Newport Beach, CA
Sherry, Leah ....Palo Alto, CA
Sherry, Leo C., Jr. ....Portland, OR
Sherry, Madeline M. ....Philadelphia, PA
Sherry, Mark J. ....Van Nuys, CA
Sherry, Mettery I., Jr. ....Metairie, LA
Sherry, Mettery I., Jr. ....New Orleans, LA
Sherry, Michael M. ....Woodstock, GA
Sherry & O'Neill ....New York, NY
Sherry, Paul J. ....Department of Energy, Office of the General Counsel, GV

Sherry, Peter J., Jr. ....Dearborn, MI
Sherry, Robert J. ....San Francisco, CA
Sherry, Robert Leo ....Milwaukee, WI
Sherry, Samuel M. ....Portland, ME
Sherry, Stephen F. ....Chicago, IL
Sherry, William T., Jr. ....Boston, MA
Shershin, Michael J., Jr. ....Atlanta, GA
Shertel, Michael Anthony Louis
Mays Landing, NJ
Sherter, Jeffrey H. ....Santa Monica, CA
Sherton, Corinne C. ....Salem, OR
Shertzer, Daniel H. ....Lancaster, PA
Shertzer, Daniel H., Jr. ....Lancaster, PA
Shertzer Law Offices ....Lancaster, PA
Shervheim, Lloyd O. ......Lake Havasu City, AZ
Sherwani, Fakhera Hina ....Suffern, NY
Sherwin, Benjamin E. ....New York, NY
Sherwin, Dennis J. ....Ontario, CA
Sherwin, Elaine C. ....Bradenton, FL
Sherwin, Elizabeth A. ....New York, NY
Sherwin, George R. ....Little Rock, AR
Sherwin, Gerald A. ....Stockton, CA
Sherwin & Gottlieb ....Fall River, MA
Sherwin, Gregory J. ....Los Angeles, CA
Sherwin, Howard ....New City, NY
Sherwin, Jay G. ....Ocala, FL
Sherwin, Jay S. ....Boston, MA
Sherwin, Jeffrey D. ....Middletown, NY
Sherwin, Jeffrey T. ....Northlake, IL
Sherwin, Joan M. ....Macomb, IL
Sherwin, Judith Schwartz ....Chicago, IL
Sherwin, Julia ....Oakland, CA
Sherwin, Louis H. ....Middletown, NY
Sherwin, Mark J. ....Elmwood Park, NJ
Sherwin, Michael R. ....Bridgeview, IL
Sherwin, Peter J. W. ....New York, NY
Sherwin, Philip N. ....Fort Myers, FL
Sherwin, Robert A. ....Chicago, IL
Sherwin, Robert A., Ltd. ....Chicago, IL
Sherwin, Scott D. ....Chicago, IL
Sherwin, Sidney ....Rego Park, NY
Sherwin, Theodore R. ....Chicago, IL
Sherwinter, Emily ....Atlanta, GA
Sherwinter McElroy Law Group, The
Atlanta, GA
Sherwood, Alan J. ....Oakland, CA
Sherwood, Alysoun J. ....White Plains, NY
Sherwood, Andrew R. ....Phoenix, AZ
Sherwood, Arthur L. ....Los Angeles, CA
Sherwood, Arthur M. ....Buffalo, NY
Sherwood, Arthur W. ....Baltimore, MD
Sherwood & Associates ....Woonsocket, RI
Sherwood, Charles A. ....New Haven, CT
Sherwood, Charles A., & Associates
New Haven, CT
Sherwood, Charles L. ....Tulsa, OK
Sherwood, Clare A. ....Bedford, NY
Sherwood, Daniel K. ....Wakefield, MA
Sherwood, Daniel K., P.C. ....Wakefield, MA
Sherwood, David ....Dallas, TX
Sherwood, David B. ....Boston, MA
Sherwood, David F. ....Glastonbury, CT
Sherwood, Devon F. ....Springfield, MO
Sherwood, Diane Elizabeth ....Wichita, KS
Sherwood, Don C., (P.C.)
Los Angeles, CA
Sherwood, Don H. ....Denver, CO
Sherwood, Donald S. ....Nyack, NY
Sherwood, Edwyn R. ....Bellevue, WA
Sherwood, Elizabeth P. ....Cincinnati, OH
Sherwood, Erin L. ....Akron, OH
Sherwood, Everett P. ....Stamford, CT
Sherwood, Frederick F. ....Helena, MT
Sherwood & Garlick, P.C. ....Norwalk, CT
Westport, CT
Sherwood, Geo. M. ....Timonium, MD
Sherwood, Gregory Don ....Austin, TX
Sherwood and Hardgrove
Los Angeles, CA
Sherwood & Harper ....Wichita, KS
Sherwood, Honecker & Bender
Springfield, MO
Sherwood, J. Carol, Jr. ....Valdosta, GA
Sherwood, Jack ....Glen Rock, NJ
Sherwood, James C. ....Fresno, CA
Sherwood, James C. ....New York, NY
Sherwood, Jason Tate ....Boston, MA
Sherwood, Jeffrey K. ....Washington, DC
Sherwood, John Charles ....Dallas, TX
Sherwood, John D. ....Wichita, KS
Sherwood, John F. ....Bellevue, WA
Sherwood, John F., Jr. ....Bellevue, WA
Sherwood, John K. ....Roseland, NJ
Sherwood, John M. ....San Francisco, CA
Sherwood, Julie M. ....Rochester, NY
Sherwood, Klein, Dudley & Abram, P.A.
Phoenix, AZ
Sherwood, Kurt N. ....Kalamazoo, MI
Sherwood, Laurie E. ....San Francisco, CA
Sherwood Law Offices ....Missoula, MT
Sherwood Law Offices ....Oxford, NE
Sherwood, Leo N. ....San Francisco, CA
Sherwood, Marc E. ....Chicago, IL
Sherwood, Margaret
North Miami Beach, FL
Sherwood, Mark C. ....Woodland Hills, CA
Sherwood, Marshall ....Panhandle, TX
Sherwood, Meryl P. ....New York, NY
Sherwood, Michael D. ....Vestal, NY
Sherwood, Michael J. ....Missoula, MT
Sherwood, Michael R. ....San Francisco, CA
Sherwood, Michelle A. ....Stamford, CT
Sherwood, Neil R. ....Buffalo, NY
Sherwood, Nicholas ....Bloomington, MN
Sherwood, Nicholas A. ......Department of State, Foreign Service Officers (Overseas), GV
Sherwood, O. Peter ....New York, NY
Sherwood, Pamela H. ....Indianapolis, IN

Sherwood & Pate, P.C. ....Erwin, TN
Johnson City, TN
Sherwood, Paul ....Stonington, ME
Sherwood, Paul J. ....Erwin, TN
Johnson City, TN
Sherwood, Peter A. ....Visalia, CA
Sherwood, Peter W. ....San Francisco, CA
Sherwood, Philip R. ....Woonsocket, RI
Sherwood, Ray D. ....Portland, OR
Sherwood, Rebecca J. ....Tulsa, OK
Sherwood, Richard E. ....Los Angeles, CA
Sherwood, Richard J. ....Albany, NY
Sherwood, Robert B., Jr. ....Washington, DC
Sherwood, Robt. B. ....Bellingham, WA
Sherwood, Rochelle N. ....Boston, MA
Sherwood, Roger ....Wichita, KS
Sherwood, Ruby B. ....New Rochelle, NY
Sherwood, Sam C., Jr. ....Kansas City, MO
Sherwood, Sandra Winslow ....Malden, MA
Sherwood, Scott ....Panhandle, TX
Sherwood, Scott D. ....Wildwood, NJ
Sherwood and Sherwood ....Stamford, CT
Sherwood and Sherwood ....Borger, TX
Panhandle, TX
Sherwood, Stanley C. ....Plantation, FL
Sherwood, Stanley G. ....New York, NY
Sherwood, Suzanne R. ....Baltimore, MD
Sherwood, Ted C. ....Tulsa, OK
Sherwood, Thomas G. ....Garden City, NY
Sherwood, Thomas Joel ....Ruskin, FL
Sherwood, Thomas M. ....San Francisco, CA
Sherwood, Toby ....San Francisco, CA
Sherwood, Todd K. ....Kenai, AK
Sherwood, W. Ben, (P.C.) ....Vestal, NY
Sherwood, William A. ....Houston, TX
Sherwood, William E. ....Sacramento, CA
Sherwood, William E. ....New City, NY
Sherwood, William F. ....Carbondale, IL
Sherwood, W. T., Jr. ....Arlington, VA
Sherwyn, Bernard A. ....Santa Barbara, CA
Sherwyn, David S. ....Ithaca, NY
Sherwyn, Donald S. ....Woodland Hills, CA
Sherwyn, Jack T. ....Los Angeles, CA
Sherzer, Harvey G. ....Washington, DC
Sherzer, Morton P. ....Decatur, GA
Sheshadri, Archana ....Cleveland, OH
Sheski, John ....Madison, WI
Shestack, Jerome J. ....Philadelphia, PA
Shestack, Julian ....New York, NY
Shestack & Shestack ....New York, NY
Shestack, Stuart G. ....New York, NY
Shestack & Young, LLP ....New York, NY
Shestakofsky, Stephen R. ....Boston, MA
Shestakov, Janet E. ....San Francisco, CA
Shestakova, Irina A. ....San Francisco, CA
Sheston, Stacey N. ....Sacramento, CA
Sheth, Gaurang Krishnavadan
San Francisco, CA
Sheth, Sameer Vijay ....Orlando, FL
Sheth, Shibani Y. ....Warren, OH
Shetka, Debra A. ....Palo Alto, CA
Shetlar, James R., Law Offices
Overland Park, KS
Shetler, Brian L. ....San Jose, CA
Shetler, Deena M.
Federal Communications Commission, Common Carrier Bureau, GV
Shetler & Spalding ....Alliance, OH
Shetler, Travis E. ....Tonopah, NV
Shetler, William B. ....Alliance, OH
Shetley, Donna Faye ....Spartanburg, SC
Shetley, Matthew R. ....Kennett, MO
Shetterly, Francine S. ....Salem, OR
Shetterly, Irick & Shetterly ....Dallas, OR
Shetterly, John A. ....Wellesley, MA
Shetterly, Kassie L. ....Denver, CO
Shetterly, Lane P. ....Dallas, OR
Shetterly, Michael M. ....Columbia, SC
Shetterly, Russell B. ....Columbia, SC
Shettle, Aubyn K., Jr. ....Dallas, TX
Shettle, Gregory R. ....West Hartford, CT
Shettle, Kenneth B. ....Middletown, CT
Shettle, Renee Wellford ....Gladwyne, PA
Shettle, W. E. ....Beaumont, TX
Shetty, Vaishali
Commodity Futures Trading Commission, Division of Enforcement, GV
Sheuerman, David ....San Jose, CA
Sheuerman, Martini and Tabari
San Jose, CA
Sheuerman, Philip
Department of the Air Force, Office of the General Counsel, GV
Shevach, Bernard ....Portland, OR
Shevade, Renu ....Paramus, NJ
Shevchuk, Donald E. ....New Britain, CT
Shevell, Jamie B ....Pleasantville, NY
Shevelson, J. Courtney ....Carmel, CA
Shevin, Arnold D. ....Miami, FL
Shevin, Eric D. ....Los Angeles, CA
Shevin, Harry A. ....West Palm Beach, FL
Shevin, Jerome H. ....Miami, FL
Shevin, Jerome H., Professional Association
Miami, FL
Shevin, Maurice L. ....Birmingham, AL
Shevin, Robert L. ....Miami, FL
Shevitz, David R., (P.C.) ....Chicago, IL
Shevitz, Richard E. ....Indianapolis, IN
Shevitz, Vivian ....Katonah, NY
Shevland, Laurence M. ....Havertown, PA
Shevlin, Brian C. ....Arlington, VA
Shevlin, Clay ....Irvine, CA
Shevlin, David A. ....New York, NY
Shevlin, Dennis W. ....Belleville, IL
Shevlin, Edmund P. ....St. Bonaventure, NY
Shevlin, George F., IV
House of Representatives, Congressional Assistants, GV

Shevlin, Glenn W. ....Scottsdale, AZ
Shevlin, Gregory L. ....Belleville, IL
Shevlin, John B., Jr. ....Boston, MA
Shevlin, John C. ....Palm Springs, CA
Shevlin, Linda Jenner ....Philadelphia, PA
Shevlin, Michael J. ....Arlington, VA
Shevlin, Patrick J. ....New York, NY
Shevlin & Smith ....Arlington, VA
Shevlin-Rizzo, Elisa ....New York, NY
Shevnock, Colleen M. ....Detroit, MI
Shevock, John P. ....Fort Lauderdale, FL
Shevock, John P., P.A. ....Fort Lauderdale, FL
Shevrin, Howard ....Roslyn, NY
Shevy, Patricia J. ....Albany, NY
Shew, D. Craig ....Ada, OK
Shew, Dianna Baker ....Nashville, TN
Shew, Elizabeth R. ....Lisbon Falls, ME
Shew, J. C. ....Middletown, OH
Shew & Lombardo, P.L.C. ....Phoenix, AZ
Shew, Michael J. ....Phoenix, AZ
Shew, Nancy M. ....Ada, OK
Shew, Sherman ....Brea, CA
Shewaga, Duane W. ....Campbell, CA
Shewan, Scott R. ....Clovis, CA
Sheward, Deborah L. ....Newark, NJ
New York, NY
Sheward, Richard S. ....Columbus, OH
Shewchuk, Jeffrey D. ....Minneapolis, MN
Shewchuk, Sonia A. ....Minneapolis, MN
Shewell, Alan D. ....Lompoc, CA
Shewmake, Baronian & McConnell
Richmond, VA
Shewmake, Charles W. ....Fort Worth, TX
Shewmake, Donna Griffith ......Richmond, VA
Shewmake, Floyd F., Jr. ....Kenosha, WI
Shewmake, Rex N., Jr. ....Prairie Village, KS
Shewmake, William H. ....Richmond, VA
Shewmaker, Carl W. ....Eureka, KS
Shewmaker, John B. ....St. Louis, MO
Shewmaker, John R. ....Irvine, CA
Shewmaker, Richard D. ....St. Louis, MO
Shewmaker, Stephen M. ....Danville, KY
Shewry, Steven M. ....San Diego, CA
Shey, Andrew M. ....New York, NY
Shey, Audrey ....Dix Hills, NY
Sheya, Kandace B. ....Phoenix, AZ
Sheybani, Kathryn M. ....Washington, DC
Sheybani, Mithra ....Los Angeles, CA
Sheyka, Joseph W. ....Chicago, IL
Sheyka, Robert F. ....New York, NY
Sheys, Kevin M. ....Washington, DC
Shi, J. Stephen ....Atlanta, GA
Shi, Jennie ....Philadelphia, PA
Shi, Lin ....New York, NY
Shi, Ting-Ting ....New York, NY
Shi, Tommy M. ....Montvale, NJ
Shia, Johnna M. ....Dayton, OH
Shia, Roxana Venecia ......Corpus Christi, TX
Shiah, Thomas H. ....Minneapolis, MN
Shiah, Thomas H., Ltd., Law Offices of
Minneapolis, MN
Shiao, Karen ....Los Angeles, CA
Shiaras, Michael P. ....Phoenix, AZ
Shiarella, Colleen Duffy ....Newark, NJ
Shiba, Wendy Christine ....Greenville, SC
Shibata, David ....Honolulu, HI
Shibata, Eileen Aiko ....Torrance, CA
Shibata, Naoyuki ....Los Angeles, CA
Shibata, Phyllis ....Pomona, CA
Shibayama, Scott T. ....Sacramento, CA
Shiber, Basil S. ....Menlo Park, CA
Shiber, William E. ....Baltimore, MD
Shibla, R. Stephen ....Harrisburg, PA
Shibley, Cathy M. ....Cleveland, OH
Shibley, Gregory J. ....North Palm Beach, FL
Shibley, Jeffery L. ....Tampa, FL
Shibley, Jeffery L., P.A., A Law Office of
Tampa, FL
Shibley, William H. ....Long Beach, CA
Shibley, William H. ....Los Angeles, CA
Newport Beach, CA
Shiboleth, Amnon ....New York, NY
Shiboleth, Yisraeli, Roberts & Zisman,
L.L.P. ....New York, NY
Shibuya, Patrick K. ....Los Angeles, CA
Shibuya, Toshifumi ....New York, NY
Shichman, Michael A. ....Great Neck, NY
Shichman, Robin E. Remis
Washington, DC
Shick, Alicia E. ....Miami, FL
Shick, Blair C. ....Cambridge, MA
Shick, Daniel S. ....Cincinnati, OH
Shick, Maureen Driscoll ....Chicago, IL
Shick, Mitchell K. ....Charleston, IL
Shick, Sondra Long ....Newton, MA
Shick, Susan F. ....Long Beach, CA
Shick & Tapella ....Charleston, IL
Shickich, Barbara Allan ....Seattle, WA
Shickich, Joseph E., Jr. ....Seattle, WA
Shickich, R. Michael ....Casper, WY
Shickler, Nancy Q. ....San Francisco, CA
Shideler, Blynn L. ....Pittsburgh, PA
Shideler, L. Grant ....Aurora, CO
Shideler, Shirley A. ....Indianapolis, IN
Shidler, Bradley Douglas ....Decorah, IA
Shidler, Constance L. ....Kansas City, MO
Shidler, Michael J. ....Denver, CO
Shidler, Michael J., & Associates, A
Professional Law Corporation ....Denver, CO
Shidlofsky, Lee H. ....Dallas, TX
Shidlovsky, Dan J. ....Pittsburgh, PA
Shie, Thomas E. ....Davenport, IA
Shieber, Benjamin M. ....Baton Rouge, LA
Shieber, William J. ....Washington, DC
Austin, TX
Shiebler, Christine R. ....Commack, NY
Shiebler, George L.
Whitehouse Station, NJ

Shieder, Daniel W., Jr. ....Dallas, TX
Shieh, Emily ....San Diego, CA
Shiekman, John L. ....Fort Lauderdale, FL
Shiekman, Laurence Z. ....Philadelphia, PA
Shiekman, Marjorie K. ....Philadelphia, PA
Shiekman, Philip M. ....Philadelphia, PA
Shiekman, Thomas D. ....Miami, FL
Shiel, Colleen Reppen ....Chicago, IL
Shiel, Daniel J. ....Kansas City, KS
Shiel, Michael C. ....Phoenix, AZ
Shiel, Samuel M. ....New York, NY
Shield, Axel A., II ....Paoli, PA
Shield, Ralph P. ....Manasquan, NJ
Shield, Robert H. ....Lexington, MA
Shield, Theodore P., P.L.C.
Long Beach, CA
Shield, William P., Jr. ....Detroit, MI
Shields, A. C., III ....Sarasota, FL
Shields, Alison R. ....New York, NY
Shields, Allison C. ....Melville, NY
Shields, Anne Y. ....New York, NY
Shields, Beth Kovacs ....Newport Beach, CA
Shields, Bradley W. ....Austin, TX
Shields, Britton & Fraser ....Dallas, TX
Shields, Buren R., III ....New Bern, NC
Shields, Carmel A. ....Brockton, MA
Shields, Carolyn J. ....Santa Monica, CA
Shields, Carrington ....Washington, DC
Shields, Charles A. ....Fairmont, WV
Shields, Charles Daniel ....Harrisburg, PA
Shields, Charles M. ....Galesburg, MI
Shields, Charles O. ....Dallas, TX
Shields, Christian D. ....Atlanta, GA
Shields, Christine P. ....Stamford, CT
Shields, Christopher ....Blue Bell, PA
Shields, Christopher J. ....Fort Myers, FL
Shields, Christopher M. ....Scranton, PA
Shields, Claude A. L. ....Pottsville, PA
Shields, Colleen D. ....Wilmington, DE
Shields, Cornelius C.
Department of Housing and Urban
Development, GV
Shields, Craig M. ....Glen Cove, NY
Shields, Dane ....Henderson, KY
Shields, David G. ....Maitland, FL
Shields, Day R. ....Stamford, CT
Shields, Deborah G. ....South Portland, ME
Shields, Debra A. ....New York, NY
Shields, Dennis J. ....Iowa City, IA
Shields, Dennis L. ....San Diego, CA
Shields, Dennis W. ....Tuscaloosa, AL
Shields, Donald J. ....Los Angeles, CA
Shields, Dwaine F. ....Sacramento, CA
Shields, Earle A. (Andy), III ....Austin, TX
Shields, Edward M. ....Colorado Springs, CO
Shields, Edward M., P.C.
Colorado Springs, CO
Shields, Eldon J. ....Overland Park, KS
Shields, Emerson H. ....St. John, KS
Shields, Frances R. ....Jackson, MS
Shields, Fred W., Jr. ....Charlottesville, VA
Shields, G. Thomas ....Greenville, MS
Shields, Geoffrey B. ....Chicago, IL
Shields, George T. ....Spokane, WA
Shields, Georgia E. ....Wheeling, IL
Shields, Ginger S. ....Greensboro, NC
Shields, Grady L. ....Raleigh, NC
Shields, Gregory W. ....Austin, TX
Shields & Gunter, P.C. ....Tuscaloosa, AL
Shields, H. Gordon, (P.C.) ....Phoenix, AZ
Shields, Heather J. ....Chicago, IL
Shields, Henry, Jr., (P.C.)
Los Angeles, CA
Shields, H. R. Hal ....Clovis, CA
Shields, J. Todd ....Houston, TX
Shields, Jack R. ....Batesville, IN
Shields, James A. ....Medina, OH
Shields, James Burr, II ....Phoenix, AZ
Shields, James C. ....Yorba Linda, CA
Shields, James D. ....Dallas, TX
Shields, James E. ....Gretna, LA
Shields, James F. ....Wallingford, CT
Shields, James J. ....Shrewsbury, MA
Shields, James M. ....Jamaica, NY
Shields, Jeffrey L. ....Salt Lake City, UT
Shields, Jeffrey W. (IBA) ....Irvine, CA
Shields, Jeffrey Weston
Salt Lake City, UT
Shields, Joann ....Salt Lake City, UT
Shields, John A. ....Rochester, NY
Shields, John B. ....New York, NY
Shields, John F. ....Santa Rosa, CA
Shields, John H. ....New York, NY
Shields, John H. ....San Antonio, TX
Shields, John Michael ....Riverhead, NY
Shields, John R. ....Everett, WA
Shields, Jon E. ....McLean, VA
Shields, Jordan B. ....Charlotte, NC
Shields, Joseph G. ....Syracuse, NY
Shields, Joseph L. ....Tallahassee, FL
Shields, Joseph M. ....Framingham, MA
Shields, Joseph R. ....West Chester, PA
Shields, Juli K. ....Mooresville, IN
Shields, Julia S. ....Department of Commerce,
Patent and Trademark Office, GV
Shields, Katheryn J. ....Kansas City, MO
Shields, Kathy E. M. ....Leesburg, VA
Shields, Kerry E. ....Gretna, LA
Shields, Kieran N. ....Portland, ME
Shields, Kimberly Cross ....Memphis, TN
Shields Law Office, P.A. ....St. John, KS
Shields Law Offices ....Irvine, CA
Shields, Les C. ....West Palm Beach, FL
Shields, Leslie ....Knoxville, TN
Shields, Lloyd N. ....New Orleans, LA
Shields, M. Lawrence, III ....West Mifflin, PA
Shields, Margaret G. ....Englewood, CO
Shields, Martin R. ....New Castle, IN

Shields, Mary C. ....Pinehurst, NC
Shields, Mary E. ....Chicago, IL
Shields, Merrill, (Ms.) ....Denver, CO
Shields, Michael A. ....Kalamazoo, MI
Shields, Michael C. ....Norristown, PA
Shields, Molly T. ....Minneapolis, MN
Shields Mott Lund L.L.P.
New Orleans, LA
Shields, N. Robert ....Woodburn, OR
Shields, Natalie Ann ....Towson, MD
Shields, Patricia P. ....Charlottesville, VA
Shields, Peter D. ....Washington, DC
Shields, R. Scott ....Houston, TX
Shields, Ralph B., III ....Vidalia, LA
Shields, Randal D. ....Columbia, SC
Shields, Regis A. ....New York, NY
Shields, Rhonda Michelle
Newport News, VA
Shields, Richard E. ....Mobile, AL
Shields, Richard F. ....Minneapolis, MN
Shields, Richard M. ....Clinton, MO
Shields, Richd. H. ....San Jose, CA
Shields, Robert ....San Diego, CA
Shields, Robert E. ....Atlanta, GA
Shields, Robert E. ....Philadelphia, PA
Shields, Robert J. ....Mineola, NY
Shields, Robert L., III ....Birmingham, AL
Shields, Robert L., Jr. ....Ellicott City, MD
Shields, Robert M. ....Bardonia, NY
Shields, Robert M., Jr. ....Hartford, CT
Shields, Robert S., Jr. ....New Bern, NC
Shields, Robert W. ....Boston, MA
Shields, Robyn ....Washington, DC
Shields & Rusk, P.C. ....Austin, TX
Shields, Russell M. ....Hiawatha, KS
Shields, Sarah M. ....San Francisco, CA
Shields, Scott W. ....Sturgis, KY
Shields, Sean ....New York, NY
Shields, Spencer C. ....Overland Park, KS
Shields, Stacy L. ....Philadelphia, PA
Shields, Stanley E. ....Oakland, CA
Shields, Stephen L. ....Memphis, TN
Shields, Stephen M. ....Columbus, OH
Shields, Susan B. ....Oklahoma City, OK
Shields, Susanna ....Dallas, TX
Shields, Sylvia J. ....Phoenix, AZ
Shields, Thomas C. ....Chicago, IL
Shields, Thomas E. ....Totowa, NJ
Shields, Thomas J. ....Davenport, IA
Shields, Thomas P. ....Vadnais Heights, MN
Shields, Timothy F. ....Irvine, CA
Shields, Toi ....Philadelphia, PA
Shields, V. Sue ....Indianapolis, IN
Shields, Wesley P. ....Houston, TX
Shields, Wilfred H., Jr. ....Annapolis, MD
Shields, William ....Boston, MA
Shields, William E. ....Sheridan, IN
Shields, William G., & Associates
Richmond, VA
Shields, William H. ....Fort Myers, FL
Shields, William H. ....Carrollton, TX
Shields, William M.
Department of Defense, GV
Shields, William M. ....Boston, MA
Shields, William M. ....Philadelphia, PA
Shields, William Scott ....Cincinnati, OH
Shields, William W., III ....Daphne, AL
Shields, Zachary T. ....Salt Lake City, UT
Shiell, Douglas J. ....Minneapolis, MN
Shiell, Lyall G., Jr. ....New Orleans, LA
Shiell, Warren R. ....Valley Cottage, NY
Shiells, Leon E. ....Menlo Park, CA
Shiells, Theodore F. ....Dallas, TX
Shiels, Alfred L. ....New York, NY
Shiels, Catherine M. ....Bridgewater, NJ
Shiels, Marnie R. ....Alexandria, VA
Shiels, Rosemary ....Chicago, IL
Shiels, Roy S. ....Dover, DE
Shiels, Thomas A. ....Dallas, TX
Shiely, Gerald L. ....San Antonio, TX
Shiely, James F., Jr. ....St. Paul, MN
Shiely, John S. ....Elm Grove, WI
Shiembob, Mark S. ....Richmond, VA
Shiener, Gale S. ....Farmington Hills, MI
Shientag, Florence P. ....New York, NY
Shienvold, Adam M. ....Harrisburg, PA
Shienvold, Michael Paul ....Hollywood, FL
Shier, Andrew ....Grand Rapids, MI
Shier, Carlton, IV ....Lexington, KY
Shier & Hanrahan ....Lexington, KY
Shier, Matthew J. ....San Francisco, CA
Shier, Robert C., Jr. ....Irvine, CA
Shier, Suzanne L. ....Chicago, IL
Shier, Tracy M. ....Seattle, WA
Shier, William T. ....Lexington, KY
Shierk, C. Kim ....Bloomfield Hills, MI
Shierling, Stephen P. ....Lockport, NY
Shiers, Barbara E. ....New York, NY
Shiers, Chrey, Cox & Caulkins
Port Orchard, WA
Shiers, Frank A. ....Port Orchard, WA
Shiever, Jerry L. ....Austin, TX
Shiff, Adam L. ....New York, NY
Shiff, Alan H. W. ....Bridgeport, CT
Shiff, Allison R. ....Phoenix, AZ
Shiff, Barbara S. ....Tustin, CA
Shiff, Harvey I. ....New York, NY
Shiff, J. Ronald ....Baltimore, MD
Shiff, Jonathan M. ....San Diego, CA
Shiff, Jonathan M., & Associates; Law Offices
of ....San Diego, CA
Shiff, Laurence ....New York, NY
Shiff, Philip Robert ....New Haven, CT
Shiff, Ralph M. ....Edison, NJ
Shiff and Schancupp ....New Haven, CT
Shiff, Sean Adam ....Minneapolis, MN
Shiff & Tisman ....New York, NY
Shiff, Wendy Lozinsky ....Baltimore, MD

Shiffer, David M. ....Bolingbrook, IL
Shiffermiller, Joy A. ....Lincoln, NE
Shiffermiller, Roger L. ....Omaha, NE
Shifflet, David E. ....Marion, OH
Shifflet, Kane & Konoske, LLP
Indian Wells, CA
Palm Springs, CA
Riverside, CA
San Bernardino, CA
San Diego, CA
Las Vegas, NV
Shifflet, William C. ....San Diego, CA
Shifflett, Leonard S. ....Chicago, IL
Shifflett, Walter Kyle ....Oklahoma City, OK
Shifflette, Larry D. ....Charleston, SC
Shiffman, Brad L. ....New York, NY
Shiffman, Gary ....Huntington Beach, CA
Shiffman, Howard G. ....Stamford, CT
Shiffman, Joyce ....New York, NY
Shiffman, Mark S. ....Pittsburgh, PA
Shiffman, Michael ....Plantation, FL
Shiffman, Michael A. (IBA)
San Francisco, CA
Shiffman, Paul ....Washington, DC
Falls Church, VA
Shiffman & Ricci, P.C. ....Washington, DC
Falls Church, VA
Shiffman, Sidney J. ....Utica, NY
Shiffman, Steven ....New York, NY
Shiffman, Theodore R. ....New York, NY
Shiffra, Robert ....Rocky River, OH
Shiffrin, Cynthia A. ....Oakland, CA
Shiffrin, Daniel ....Chicago, IL
Shiffrin, David E.
Federal Deposit Insurance Corporation, GV
Shiffrin, Steven H. ....Los Angeles, CA
Shifke, Howard J. ....Tampa, FL
Shifke, Howard J., P.A. ....Tampa, FL
Shifke, Patricia W. ....New York, NY
Shiflet, Hobart ....Ashtabula, OH
Shiflett, Sarah U. ....Gaffney, SC
Shiflett Rosen, Jennifer Elaine
Richmond, VA
Shifley, Charles W. ....Chicago, IL
Shifman, Arnold J. ....Royal Oak, MI
Shifman, Arnold R. ....Canton, OH
Shifman, Burton R. ....Southfield, MI
Shifman & Carlson, P.C. ....Southfield, MI
Shifman, Gail ....San Francisco, CA
Shifman, Howard L. ....Birmingham, MI
Shifman, Julie Cohen ....Cincinnati, OH
Shifman, Kenneth A. ....New York, NY
Shifman, Ronald J. ....Los Angeles, CA
Shifren, James A. ....New York, NY
Shifren, Nancy Z. ....New York, NY
Shifren, Ronald P. ....Hicksville, NY
Shifrin, Alan H. ....Schaumburg, IL
Shifrin, David A.(Dan) ....Tucson, AZ
Shifrin, Deanna S. ....Miami, FL
Shifrin, Debra S. ....Akron, OH
Shifrin, Edwin G. ....St. Louis, MO
Shifrin, Gerald B. ....Portland, OR
Shifrin, Jordan I. ....Buffalo Grove, IL
Shifrin, Margaret D. ....Austin, TX
Shifrin, Orrin S. ....Chicago, IL
Shifrin, Patsy White ....Towson, MD
Shifrin, Robin M. ....New York, NY
Shifris, Donald S. ....Northbrook, IL
Shifter, Barton D. ....Chula Vista, CA
Shigaki, Leslie E. ....New York, NY
Shigekane, Ronald M. ....Honolulu, HI
Shigekuni, Thomas N. ....Torrance, CA
Shigemoto, Thomas Y. ....Sacramento, CA
Shigemura, Donna L. ....Honolulu, HI
Shigemura, Gary Y. ....Honolulu, HI
Shigemura & Harakal, Attorneys At Law, A
Law Corporation ....Honolulu, HI
Shigemura, James Y. ....Honolulu, HI
Shigemura, Kristin S. ....Honolulu, HI
Shigetomi, Keith S. ....Honolulu, HI
Shigezawa, Yoshio ....Wailuku, HI
Shigley, Charles E. ....Seattle, WA
Shigley, Kenneth L. ....Atlanta, GA
Shigley Law Firm, L.L.C. ....Atlanta, GA
Shigo, Lynne ....Gainesville, FL
Shigo, Thomas S., Jr. ....Gainesville, FL
Shih, Alice L. ....New York, NY
Shih, Anna M. ....Bloomfield Hills, MI
Shih, Barbara W. ....Menlo Park, CA
Shih, Bernard Y. ....South Pasadena, CA
Shih, Bruce John ....Los Angeles, CA
Shih, Christine ....Flushing, NY
Shih, Christine ....Flushing, NY
Shih, Eric ....Los Angeles, CA
Shih, George C. ....New York, NY
Shih, Jennifer ....New York, NY
Shih, Linda P. ....San Francisco, CA
Shih, Michael M. ....New York, NY
Shih, Stephen T.
Equal Employment Opportunity
Commission,
Office of Federal Operations, GV
Shih, Theodore ....Denver, CO
Shih, Willard C. ....New York, NY
Shihab & Associates ....Columbus, OH
Shihab, Gus M. ....Columbus, OH
Shihab, Sam M. ....Columbus, OH
Shihadeh, Jameel M. ....Daly City, CA
Shikada, Holly T. ....Honolulu, HI
Shikany, Joseph F. ....Indianapolis, IN
Shiker, Brian L. ....Dallas, TX
Shikora, Hayes & Kaiser, LLP
Milwaukee, WI
Shikora, Jonathan E. ....Los Angeles, CA
Shikora, Ronald C. ....Milwaukee, WI
Shikuma, Craig K., (Atty. At Law, A Law
Corp.) ....Honolulu, HI
Shikuma, Michael H. ....Honolulu, HI

Shilberg, Nathan Mark ... San Diego, CA
Shildmyer, Kathleen M. ... Scottsdale, AZ
Shilensky, Michael D. ... Roslyn Heights, NY
Shilepsky, Nancy S. ... Boston, MA
Shiles, Carl Eugene, Jr. ... Chattanooga, TN
Shiles, Jerry E. ... Enid, OK
Shiles, Lawrence T. ... Tulsa, OK
Shiley, J. Bradford ... Portland, OR
Shiley, John G. ... Miami, FL
Shiling, Bloch and Hirsch, P.A.
Towson, MD
Shiling, Reuben ... Towson, MD
Shill, Cary S. ... Mays Landing, NJ
Shill, Otto S., III ... Mesa, AZ
Shill, Todd J. ... Harrisburg, PA
Shillaber, C. Russell ... Rochester, NH
Shilleh, Laila J. ... Lebanon, OH
Shillen, Dennis O. ... Woodstock, VT
Shillen, Gray & Powell, Professional Corporation ... Woodstock, VT
Shiller, Doris B. ... Westport, CT
Shiller, Jeffrey P. ... Baltimore, MD
Shiller, Mark A. ... Brookfield, WI
Mequon, WI
Shilliday, Daniel B. ... Houston, TX
Shilliday, Holly R. ... San Francisco, CA
Shilliday, Robert J., Jr. ... Atlanta, GA
Shilliday, Robert James, III
San Francisco, CA
Shillin, Beth I. ... New York, NY
Shilling, Alfred L. ... Richmond, VA
Shilling, Andrew T. ... Virginia Beach, VA
Shilling, C. William ... Harrisburg, PA
Shilling, Cameron G. ... Manchester, NH
Shilling, Kathryn L. ... Dallas, TX
Shilling, Leland Woodyard ... Purcell, OK
Shilling, Monica J. ... Los Angeles, CA
Shilling, Norman H ... Brooklyn, NY
Shilling, Patricia J. ... Ozark, MO
Shilling, Ralph F. ... St. Louis, MO
Shilling, Ralph F., Jr. ... Dallas, TX
Shilling, Sharon M. ... Easton, MD
Shilling & Shilling ... Richmond, VA
Shilling & Shilling, P.C. ... Ardmore, OK
Shilling, Susanne L. ... Richmond, VA
Shilling, Terry S. ... Elyria, OH
Shilling, Thomas K. ... Ardmore, OK
Shilling, William A., Jr. ... Carmel, NY
Shillinglaw, Thomas L. ... Corning, NY
Shillinglaw, William C., III ... Rock Hill, SC
Shillingstad, Hal A. ... Minneapolis, MN
Shillington, Beth C. ... Columbus, OH
Shillito, Beverly F. ... Dayton, OH
Shillito, Daniel G. ... Palm Springs, CA
Shillito & Giske, P.S. ... Tacoma, WA
Shillito, Noel P. ... Tacoma, WA
Shillman, David B. ... Cleveland, OH
Shillman, David S.
Securities and Exchange Commission, Division of Market Regulation, GV
Shillman, Jeffrey N. ... Southfield, MI
Shilobod, Dennis S. ... Greensburg, PA
Pittsburgh, PA
Shilobod, Leger & Ball, P.C.
Greensburg, PA
Pittsburgh, PA
Shiloh, Dekel ... New York, NY
Shiloh, Robert P. ... Pittsburgh, PA
Shils, Edward B. ... Philadelphia, PA
Shils, Jonathan R. ... Atlanta, GA
Shilson, Jason T. ... Chicago, IL
Shilt, Kristine D. ... Lee's Summit, MO
Shilton, David C. ... Department of Justice, Environment and Natural Resources Division, GV
Shilts, Gary L. ... Aurora, IL
Shilts, Nancy S. ... Southfield, MI
Shilts, Perry D. ... Fort Wayne, IN
Shilts, Richard D. ... Cranberry Township, PA
Shilub, Michael J. ... Los Angeles, CA
Shim, Alvin T. ... Honolulu, HI
Shim, Casey T. ... Los Angeles, CA
Shim, Daniel ... Atlanta, GA
Shim, Kie-Young ... Barrington, IL
Shim, Michael J. ... Philadelphia, PA
Shim, Paul J. ... New York, NY
Shim, Sung ... Berkeley, CA
Shim Tam Kirimitsu Chang ... Honolulu, HI
Shim, Youngtack ... Palo Alto, CA
Shim, Yumee Ann ... Philadelphia, PA
Shima, Douglas Todd ... Topeka, KS
Shima, Mary E. ... Seattle, WA
Shima, Patrick J. ... New York, NY
Shimabukuro, Bruce ... Mountain View, CA
Shimabukuro, Herbert K. ... Honolulu, HI
Shimabukuro, Peter T. ... Minneapolis, MN
Shimabukuro, Richard K. ... Ogden, UT
Shimabukuro, Ronald M.
Treasury Department, Office of the Comptroller of the Currency, GV
Shimada, Charlene Sachi
San Francisco, CA
Shimada, John H. ... Los Angeles, CA
Shimada, Yoshiki ... New York, NY
Shimahara, Bonnie K. ... Palo Alto, CA
Shimaji, Michael R. ... Glendale, CA
Shimalla, Amy Zylman ... Warren, NJ
Shimamoto, Peter ... New York, NY
Shimane, Robert ... San Jose, CA
Shimanek, R. Glade ... Springfield, OR
Shimanek, Robert F. ... Monticello, IA
Shimanek, Shimanek & Bowman
Monticello, IA
Shimanovsky, David L. ... Chicago, IL
Shimanowitz, Ronald ... Woodbridge, NJ
Shimasaki, Susan D. ... Los Angeles, CA
Shimato, Nao ... Los Angeles, CA
Shimazaki, Evelyn ... Mountain View, CA
Shimazaki, J. John ... Washington, DC
Shimazaki, Naoki ... Palo Alto, CA
Shimazaki, Tatsuji T. ... San Francisco, CA
Shimazu, Asako ... Honolulu, HI
Shimazu, Tad H. ... Seattle, WA
Shimazu, Wesley D. ... Honolulu, HI
Shimberg, Charles ... Haddonfield, NJ
Shimberg & Crohn ... Chicago, IL
Shimberg, James H. ... Tampa, FL
Shimberg, James H., Jr. ... Tampa, FL
Shimberg, Jessica K. ... Columbus, OH
Shimberg, Jonathan E. ... Chicago, IL
Shimberg, Robert A. ... Tampa, FL
Shimberg, Steven J. ... United States Senate, Committee Legal Personnel, GV
Shimeall, Kent M. ... Columbus, OH
Shimei, Barbara A. ... West Haven, CT
Shimek, Amy J. ... Anchorage, AK
Shimek, Andrew P. ... Minneapolis, MN
Shimek, Arthur A. ... Pensacola, FL
Shimek, Bruno A. ... Bryan, TX
Shimek, Daniel W. ... West Point, NY
Shimek, David ... Anchorage, AK
Shimek, Fara L. ... Detroit, MI
Shimek, Jerome J. ... Milwaukee, WI
Shimek, John J., III ... Erie, PA
Shimek, Mary E. ... Richardson, TX
Shimek, William G. ... Nashville, TN
Shimel, Ackerman, Theos & Spar
Charleston, SC
Shimel, Lisa K. ... Denver, CO
Shimelman, Arnold K. ... Hartford, CT
Shimer, Charles P. ... Richmond, VA
Shimer, Eric R. ... Bethlehem, PA
Shimer, G. Susan R. ... Armonk, NY
Shimer, Gloria K. ... Beverly Hills, CA
Shimer, Irving A. ... Beverly Hills, CA
Shimer, Katherine R. ... Williamsport, PA
Shimer, Leslie Ann ... Richmond, VA
Shimer, Zachary ... New York, NY
Shimizu, Edwin J. ... Honolulu, HI
Shimizu, Eileen ... Westmont, NJ
Philadelphia, PA
Shimizu, John B. ... Honolulu, HI
Shimizu, Kazuhiro ... Atlanta, GA
Shimizu, Wayne S. ... Lihue, HI
Shimkin, Barry E. ... New York, NY
Shimkin, Thomas K.E. ... Washington, DC
Shimko, Anna C. ... San Francisco, CA
Shimko, Timothy A. ... Cleveland, OH
Shimko, Timothy A., & Associates, A Legal Prof. Assn. ... Cleveland, OH
Shimkus, Alexander R. ... Peoria, IL
Shimkus, Charles J., Jr. ... Hartford, CT
Shimkus, Laura L. ... Summit, IL
Shimm, Melvin G. ... Durham, NC
Shimmel, Hill, Bishop & Gruender, P.C.
Phoenix, AZ
Shimmel, Joan C. ... Los Angeles, CA
Shimmel, Richard A ... Ventura, CA
Shimmel, Thomas R. ... Detroit, MI
Shimmin, Michael D. ... Boulder, CO
Shimoda, Nick Y. ... Montgomery, AL
Shimoda, Noriyuki ... San Francisco, CA
Shimoda, Walter T. ... Wailuku, HI
Shimoff, Irving ... Miami, FL
Shimoff, Paul M. ... Redlands, CA
Shimokaji, Michael A.
Newport Beach, CA
Shimola, Howard G. ... Cleveland, OH
Shimomoto, Paul B. ... Honolulu, HI
Shimomura, Ruby P. ... Glendale, CA
Shimon, Dani M. ... Minneapolis, MN
Shimon, Randal D. ... Las Vegas, NV
Shimonishi, Adrienne Y. ... Honolulu, HI
Shimotake, Jean E. ... New York, NY
Shimotake, Paul S. ... San Francisco, CA
Shimoura, James W. ... Troy, MI
Shimozono, Kenneth ... Honolulu, HI
Shimp, Karen J. ... Washington, DC
Shimp, William B. ... Columbus, OH
Shimpock, Kathy E. ... Tempe, AZ
Shimshak, Stephen J. ... New York, NY
Shimshidian, Ara A. ... New York, NY
Shimshidian, Laura ... New York, NY
Shin, Alexandra ... Los Angeles, CA
Shin, Alisa M. ... Philadelphia, PA
Shin, Brian Y. ... Los Angeles, CA
Shin, Chang-Shik ... San Francisco, CA
Shin, D.B. David ... New York, NY
Shin, Dennis K. ... Rowland Heights, CA
Shin, Doris Y. ... San Jose, CA
Shin, E. Peter ... Flushing, NY
Shin, Edward H. ... San Diego, CA
Shin, Grace J. ... Morristown, NJ
Shin, Grace U. ... South San Francisco, CA
Shin, Haeryung A. ... Boston, MA
Shin, Helen ... New York, NY
Shin, Ho Sik ... Department of Justice, Civil Division, GV
Shin, Irene M. ... San Francisco, CA
Shin, James ... Honolulu, HI
Shin, Ji Hye ... Los Angeles, CA
Shin, Jimmy M. ... Los Angeles, CA
Shin, John ... New York, NY
Shin, John H. ... New York, NY
Shin, Joong Sik ... Elkins Park, PA
Shin, Juliet Yoo ... New York, NY
Shin, Katherine Lee ... Los Angeles, CA
Shin, Kisu ... Santa Monica, CA
Shin, Michelle M. ... Honolulu, HI
Shin, Mya Saw ... Library of Congress, Law Library, GV
Shin, Sung H. ... Los Angeles, CA
Shin, Sung Mi ... Casselberry, FL
Shin, Susan C. ... New York, NY
Shin, Vivian S. ... Los Angeles, CA
Shin, Won ... Philadelphia, PA
Shin, Yoon J. ... New York, NY
Shinaberry & Meade, L.C. ... Charleston, WV
Shinaberry, Richard A. ... Toledo, OH
Shinaberry, Shannon L. ... Canton, OH
Shinaberry, Sterl F. ... Charleston, WV
Shinall, Greg ... Chicago, IL
Shinall, John M. ... Eatonton, GA
Shinall, Myrick Clements ... Atlanta, GA
Shinall, Nebl, Brown & Felt, LLC
Athens, GA
Atlanta, GA
Eatonton, GA
Columbia, SC
Shinall, R. Phillip, III ... Atlanta, GA
Shinaman, M. Aileen ... Rochester, NY
Shinaman, Todd R. ... Rochester, NY
Shinar, James R. ... Kalamazoo, MI
Shinas, Athanasios M. ... Albany, NY
Shinault, Jerome P. ... Mobile, AL
Shinaut, Richard K. ... El Paso, TX
Shinaver, Gary M. ... Fresno, CA
Shinay, Richard A. ... Portland, ME
Shinbaum, Abell, McLeod & Vann
Montgomery, AL
Shinbaum, Gail ... Houston, TX
Shinbaum, Kenneth ... Montgomery, AL
Shinbaum, Richard D. ... Montgomery, AL
Shinberg, Barry N. ... Denville, NJ
Shinberg, Ira H. ... Plaistow, NH
Shinbrot, Jeffrey S. ... Beverly Hills, CA
Shind, Laurence D. ... Boston, MA
Shindala, Carmen M. ... New Orleans, LA
Shindell, Anne B. ... Milwaukee, WI
Shindell, Ervin E. ... Chicago, IL
Shindell, James W., (P.A.) ... Miami, FL
Shindell Law Firm, LLC ... Milwaukee, WI
Shindell, Lawrence M. ... Milwaukee, WI
Shindell, Robert C. ... Boston, MA
Shindell, William I. ... Philadelphia, PA
Shinder, Earl W. ... Victorville, CA
Shinder, Jeffrey ... New York, NY
Shinder, Joseph J. ... Utica, NY
Shinder, Solomon ... Rochester, NY
Shinder, Suzan M. ... Waco, TX
Shinderman, Mark ... Los Angeles, CA
Shinderman, William ... Chatsworth, CA
Shindledecker, Tricia A. ... Santa Rosa, CA
Shindler, Donald A. ... Chicago, IL
Shindler, James V., Jr. ... Toledo, OH
Shindler, Martin L. ... New York, NY
Shindler, Neff, Holmes & Schlageter, L.L.P.
Toledo, OH
Shindler, Ronald D. ... Miami, FL
Shindler, Steven H. ... Des Moines, IA
Shindurling, Jon J. ... Idaho Falls, ID
Shine, Alfred J., Jr. ... Arcadia, CA
Shine, Allan M. ... Providence, RI
Shine, Cathleen ... New York, NY
Shine, Cathleen A. ... Harrisonville, MO
Shine, Christopher J. ... Salem, OR
Shine, Compton & Nelder, A P.C.
Downieville, CA
Grass Valley, CA
Nevada City, CA
Shine, D. Bruce ... Kingsport, TN
Shine, Daniel H. ... Dillon, SC
Shine, David N. ... New York, NY
Shine, Donald C. ... Chicago, IL
Shine, Donald P. ... Sun City, AZ
Shine, Edith S. ... Washington, DC
Shine, Edmund T. ... Kansas City, MO
Shine, Francis E., III ... Boca Raton, FL
Shine, Gerald J. ... Chicago, IL
Shine, Gerald P., Jr. ... Anderson, IN
Shine, James M. ... Juneau, AK
Shine, Joseph D. ... Columbia, SC
Shine, Judith G. ... St. Augustine, FL
Shine, Karin G. ... Sacramento, CA
Shine, Katherine ... Philadelphia, PA
Shine, Kenneth G. ... Duxbury, MA
Shine, Lawrence E. ... Fort Wayne, IN
Shine, Linda M. ... Jefferson City, MO
Shine & Mason Law Office
Kingsport, TN
Shine, Maureen T. ... Kansas City, MO
Shine, Patrick K. ... Spokane, WA
Shine, Patrick M. ... Chicago, IL
Shine, Philip J. ... Springfield, MA
Shine, Raymond E. ... Grass Valley, CA
Shine, Richard S. ... Bethesda, MD
Shine, Selwyn P. ... Brockton, MA
Shine, Shannon Oakes ... St. Louis, MO
Shine, Steven R. ... Fort Wayne, IN
Shine, Thomas E. ... Melbourne, FL
Shine, Thomas F. ... Melbourne, FL
Shine, Warren S. ... New York, NY
Shinehouse, B. R. ... Las Vegas, NV
Shinehouse & Duesing ... Las Vegas, NV
Shineman, David W, II ... Annapolis, MD
Shiner, Andrew ... Los Angeles, CA
Shiner, David B. ... Chicago, IL
Shiner, I. Randolph S. ... San Diego, CA
Shiner, James A. ... Tucson, AZ
Shiner, John R. ... Los Angeles, CA
Shiner, Keith T. ... Roanoke, VA
Shiner, Kenneth S. ... Oak Brook, IL
Shiner, Marc ... West Palm Beach, FL
Shiner, Michael A. ... Pittsburgh, PA
Shiner, Philip ... Los Angeles, CA
Shines, Gayle B. ... Chicago, IL
Shinevar, Peter O. ... New York, NY
Shiney, Fargo & Salcedo, A Law Corporation
Arcadia, CA
Sherman Oaks, CA
Shiney, Michael E. ... Arcadia, CA
Sherman Oaks, CA
Shiney, Richard D. ... Topeka, KS
Shingara, Valerie A. ... Milford, CT
Shing-Haw Teng, Shawn ... Covina, CA
Shingler, George P. ... Atlanta, GA
Shingler, Karen R. ... Burlington, VT
Shingler, Lois D. ... Savannah, GA
Shingler, Robert J. ... St. Petersburg, FL
Shingler, Ronald J. ... Antioch, CA
Shingler, William M., Sr. ... Donalsonville, GA
Shingles & Cappelli ... Blue Bell, PA
Norristown, PA
Philadelphia, PA
Plymouth Meeting, PA
Shingles, Stanley M. ... Blue Bell, PA
Shingleton, A. Bradley ... Washington, DC
Shingleton, Hoy G., Jr. ... Martinsburg, WV
Shingleton, Jeanne L. ... Atlanta, GA
Shingleton, Stephanie K. ... San Diego, CA
Shinglman, Gregory J. ... Chicago, IL
Shinholser, A. Edwin ... New Port Richey, FL
Shinholser, Olin W. ... Sebring, FL
Shining, Carolin Kay ... Novato, CA
Shinitzky, Edwin J. ... Chicago, IL
Shinjyu Global IP Counselors, LLP
Washington, DC
Shink, Susan Elise ... Grosse Pointe Farms, MI
Shinkarik, Michael ... Encino, CA
Shinkawa, Paul M. ... Austin, TX
Shinken, Leo ... Milwaukee, WI
Shinken, Milton ... Milwaukee, WI
Shinken & Shinken ... Milwaukee, WI
Shinkle, Daniel B. ... Lawrenceville, IL
Shinkle, David C. ... Des Moines, IA
Shinkle, Karen L. ... Covington, KY
Shinkle, Linda K. ... Auburn Hills, MI
Shinkle & Lynch ... Des Moines, IA
Shinkle, Noonan-Day & Hulse
Cedar Falls, IA
Shinkle, Norman D. ... Lansing, MI
Shinkle, Paul T. ... Cedar Falls, IA
Shinkle, Theodore L. ... Melbourne, FL
Shinkle, W. Michael ... Davenport, IA
Shinmoto, Lynn A. ... Los Angeles, CA
Shinmura, Yvonne R. ... Honolulu, HI
Shinn, Betty J. ... Pelham, AL
Shinn, Carl M. ... Lamar, CO
Shinn, Carmelita Reeder
Oklahoma City, OK
Shinn, Clinton W. ... Covington, LA
Shinn, Daniel W. ... Kansas City, MO
Shinn, David W. ... Kansas City, MO
Shinn, Ember Lee ... Oakland, CA
Shinn, James M. ... Huntington Beach, CA
Shinn, John P. ... Palo Alto, CA
Shinn, Maria L. ... Cleveland, OH
Shinn, Michael F. ... Yakima, WA
Shinn, Michael R. ... Portland, OR
Shinn, Paul B. ... Menlo Park, CA
Shinn, Paul B. ... Palo Alto, CA
Shinn, Phillip F. ... San Francisco, CA
Shinn, Robert George ... Manahawkin, NJ
Shinn, Robert William ... Richmond, VA
Shinn, Steerman & Shinn ... Lamar, CO
Shinn, Steven C. ... Solvang, CA
Shinn, Steven M. ... Honolulu, HI
Shinn, Steven M., A Law Corporation
Honolulu, HI
Shinn, Wendy S. ... Lamar, CO
Shinn, William E., Jr. ... Decatur, AL
Shinn, William W. ... Kansas City, MO
Shinnefield, Justin R. ... Cerritos, CA
Shinners & Cook, P.C. ... Saginaw, MI
Shinners, Craig E. ... Simi Valley, CA
Shinners, Gary W.
National Labor Relations Board, Office of the General Counsel, GV
Shinners, James J. ... Saginaw, MI
Shinners, John J. ... Saginaw, MI
Shinners, Richard E. ... St. Louis, MO
Shinnick, David M. ... Dallas, TX
Shinnick, Duane E. ... San Diego, CA
Shinnick, Edward K. ... San Francisco, CA
Shinnick, Josh M. ... Pleasanton, CA
Shinnick, Robert W. ... San Francisco, CA
Shinn-Jenkins, Terees M. ... Austin, TX
Shinnock, John B. "Jack" ... Columbus, OH
Shinoff, Daniel R. ... San Diego, CA
Shinofield, Richard E. ... Minneapolis, MN
Shinrod, Edward B. ... West Orange, NJ
Shinsato, Morris S. ... Lihue, HI
Shintani, Randal I. ... Honolulu, HI
Shintani, Scott K. ... Los Angeles, CA
Shintani, Terry T. ... Honolulu, HI
Shioda, Gene H. ... Los Angeles, CA
Shiok, Jessica L. ... Ellsworth, ME
Shiono, Masako C. ... New York, NY
Shiotani, Barney B. ... Los Angeles, CA
Shiotani & Inouye ... Los Angeles, CA
Shiotani, Kenneth S. ... Bath, NY
Shioya, Donna N. ... Sacramento, CA
Shipan, James V. ... Maple Heights, OH
Shiparski, Michael L. ... Grand Rapids, MI
Shipe, Andrew J.
Commodity Futures Trading Commission, Division of Enforcement, GV
Shipe, Cathy L. ... Orange, CA
Shipe, Edward A. ... Boca Raton, FL
Shipe, Edward A. ... Delray Beach, FL
Shipe, Kevin L. ... Fort Washington, PA
Shipe, S. Bradley ... Atlanta, GA
Shipers, William J. ... New Brunswick, NJ
Shipley, Andrew E. ... Arlington, VA
Shipley, Ann ... New York, NY
Shipley & Associates ... Fort Wayne, IN
Indianapolis, IN
Shipley & Associates, Ltd. ... Crystal Lake, IL
Shipley, Benjamin H., III ... Little Rock, AR
Shipley, Brison S. ... Boston, MA

Shipley, C. Frederick, IV
West Columbia, SC
Shipley, C. Gene ... Orlando, FL
Shipley, Charles W. ... Tulsa, OK
Shipley, Constance S. ... Naples, FL
Shipley, Curtis J. ... Charlotte, NC
Shipley, D. Michael ... Tacoma, WA
Shipley, Dale E. ... Warsaw, MO
Shipley, Danny S. ... Norfolk, VA
Shipley, David E. ... Columbia, SC
Shipley, David J. ... Princeton, NJ
Shipley, Donald K. ... Houston, TX
Shipley, Elizabeth M. ... Louisville, KY
Shipley, George T. ... Houston, TX
Shipley, Grant F. ... Fort Wayne, IN
Shipley, H. Anne ... Hollister, CA
Shipley & Horne, P.A. ... Largo, MD
Shipley, Howard N. ... Alexandria, VA
Shipley, James C. ... Ventura, CA
Shipley, James E. ... Wilmington, DE
Shipley, James R. ... Kingsport, TN
Shipley, Jeffrey C. ... Towson, MD
Shipley, Jennings & Champlin, P.C.
Oklahoma City, OK
Tulsa, OK
Shipley, Jerome V. ... Lake Placid, FL
Shipley, Jill N. ... Atlanta, GA
Shipley, John A. ... West Palm Beach, FL
Shipley, John C. ... Cherry Hill, NJ
Shipley, John C., Jr. ... Washington, DC
Shipley, Joseph E. ... Chicago, IL
Shipley, Lisa Hulen ... Chesterfield, VA
Shipley, Lori A. ... Phoenix, AZ
Shipley, Marietta M. ... Nashville, TN
Shipley, Mark T. ... Denver, CO
Shipley, Mary Lou ... Waxahachie, TX
Shipley, Michael S. ... Liberty, MO
Shipley, Nadia R. ... Concord, NH
Shipley, Parker L. ... Omaha, NE
Shipley, Richard H. ... San Diego, CA
Shipley, Richard J. ... Seattle, WA
Shipley, Robert A. ... Chicago, IL
Crystal Lake, IL
Waukegan, IL
Shipley, Robert L. ... Carlsbad, CA
Shipley, Robert L., A Professional Law Corporation ... Carlsbad, CA
Shipley, Robert M., II ... Springfield, OH
Shipley, Ronald A. ... Arlington, VA
Shipley, Russell W. ... Largo, MD
Shipley, Sally A. ... Tulsa, OK
Shipley, Stephanie A. ... Easton, MD
Shipley, Susan E. ... Knoxville, TN
Shipley, Susan J. ... Boston, MA
Shipley, William K. ... San Francisco, CA
Shipley, William L. ... Moncks Corner, SC
Shipley, William L., Jr. ... Fresno, CA
Shipley & Wilner, Ltd. ... Chicago, IL
Shipman, Alexander ... Los Angeles, CA
Shipman & Associates, L.L.P.
Wilmington, NC
Wrightsville Beach, NC
Shipman, B. Scott ... Athens, AL
Shipman, Bobette ... Elsberry, MO
Shipman, Charles W. (Chuck)
San Antonio, TX
Shipman, Christopher M. ... Easton, PA
Shipman, David C. ... Williamsport, PA
Shipman, David H. ... Idaho Falls, ID
Shipman, Dean J. ... Escanaba, MI
Shipman, Dianna L. ... Houston, TX
Shipman, Dixon & Livingston Co., L.P.A.
Dayton, OH
Sidney, OH
Troy, OH
West Milton, OH
Shipman, E. William S. ... Ann Arbor, MI
Detroit, MI
Grosse Pointe Farms, MI
Shipman, F. Lee ... Harrisburg, PA
Shipman, Gary A. ... Tallahassee, FL
Shipman, Gary K. ... Wilmington, NC
Shipman & Goodwin LLP ... Hartford, CT
Lakeville, CT
Stamford, CT
Shipman & Grifo, A Professional Corporation ... Easton, PA
Shipman, James D. ... Everett, WA
Shipman, James E. ... Cedar Rapids, IA
Shipman, James P. ... Denver, CO
Shipman, Jefferson J. ... Harrisburg, PA
Shipman, Jill Kelton ... Kansas City, MO
Shipman, Joan Eldridge ... New York, NY
Shipman, Lawrence S. ... Hartford, CT
Shipman, Lynn K. ... Philadelphia, PA
Shipman, Mark D. ... Salem, OR
Shipman, Mark S. ... Hartford, CT
Shipman, Matthew R. ... Indianapolis, IN
Shipman, Michael J. ... Dallas, TX
Shipman, Morgan E. ... Columbus, OH
Shipman, O. Douglas, III ... Memphis, TN
Shipman, Pamela L. ... Williamsport, PA
Shipman, Patricia ... Philadelphia, PA
Shipman, R. Perry ... Fowler, IN
Shipman, Richard E. ... Washington, DC
Shipman, Robert M. ... Huntsville, AL
Shipman, Ronald W. ... Easton, PA
Shipman, Sherry L. ... Fort Worth, TX
Shipman, Tanja K. ... Los Angeles, CA
Shipman, Walter J. ... San Francisco, CA
Shipman, Walter L. ... Lubbock, TX
Shipman, Warren W., III ... Fort Worth, TX
Shipman-Burns, Julie ... Lincoln, NE
Shipon, Marc B. ... Philadelphia, PA
Shipow, Mark S. ... Los Angeles, CA
Shipp, Brian E. ... Idabel, OK
Shipp, D. Shackelford ... Aspen, CO
Shipp, H. Tom ... Humble, TX
Shipp, Jeffrey C. ... Cincinnati, OH
Shipp, Joseph C., II ... Oakland, CA
Shipp, Marianne ... Irvine, CA
Shipp, Michael A. ... Newark, NJ
Shipp, Nathaniel W. ... Norwalk, CT
Shipp, Nathaniel W., LLC, Law Office of
Norwalk, CT
Shipp, Philip A. ... Kansas City, MO
Shipp, Rose Levada ... Louisville, KY
Shipp, Stephanie Teresa ... Houston, TX
Shipp, Thomas E., Jr. ... Cape Coral, FL
Shipp, Wallace E., Jr. ... Washington, DC
Shipp, Wayne E. ... Clearwater, FL
St. Petersburg, FL
Shipp, William M. ... Greenbelt, MD
La Plata, MD
Shippee, Patricia D. ... Princeton, NJ
Shippel, Lisa Glauber ... Roswell, GA
Shippen, Margaret S. ... Alpharetta, GA
Shipper, David W. ... New York, NY
Shipper, Jody L. ... San Francisco, CA
Shipper, Michael M. ... Mobile, AL
Shippey, Matthew P. ... Healdsburg, CA
Shippey, Sandra L. ... San Diego, CA
Shipps, Thomas H. ... Durango, CO
Shippy, Amelia Ellen ... Department of State, Foreign Service Officers (Overseas), GV
Shippy, Daren L. ... Tallahassee, FL
Shipsey, Gerald W. ... San Luis Obispo, CA
Shipsey & Seitz, Inc. ... San Luis Obispo, CA
Shipsey, Steven E. ... Salem, OR
Shipsey, Thomas E. ... Novato, CA
Shipstead, Patrick E. ... Costa Mesa, CA
Shiptoski, Richard C. ... Kingston, PA
Shipwash, Michael Scott ... Knoxville, TN
Shipway, Robert ... Oakland, CA
Shir, Guy M. ... West Palm Beach, FL
Shira, Donna L. ... New York, NY
Shira, William A., III ... Dayton, OH
Shiraishi, Ann S. ... San Jose, CA
Shiraishi, Clinton I. ... Lihue, HI
Shiraishi, Jolene J. ... Treasury Department, Internal Revenue Service, GV
Shiraishi & Murashige ... Lihue, HI
Shiraishi, Sherman T. ... Lihue, HI
Shiraki, Janna L. ... Honolulu, HI
Shirali, Asmita ... Cleveland, OH
Shiramizu, Curtis H. ... Lihue, HI
Shirar, Gerard ... Westford, MA
Shirazi, Ray I. ... New York, NY
Shircliff, David A. ... Indianapolis, IN
Shirdan, Lisette L. ... Philadelphia, PA
Shire, Bergstein & Galper ... Monessen, PA
Shire, Bernard S. ... Monessen, PA
Shire, Clark C. ... Chicago, IL
Shire, Donald S. ... Department of Labor, Office of the Solicitor, GV
Shire, Harold R. ... Beverly Hills, CA
Shire, Howard J. ... New York, NY
Shire, John D. ... Washington, DC
Shire, Lawrence ... New York, NY
Shire, Mark J. ... Monessen, PA
Shire, Miriam Lisa ... New York, NY
Shire, Richard K. ... Chicago, IL
Shire, Robert A. ... Newark, NJ
Shire, Sharon E. ... New York, NY
Shire & Shire ... Chicago, IL
Shirer, Albert D. ... Medina, OH
Shirer, Nelly Rocha ... Arlington, VA
Shirer, William L. ... Dallas, TX
Shires, Kevin T. ... Birmingham, AL
Shirey, Brian D. ... Georgetown, DE
Shirey, Daniel R. ... Evansville, IN
Shirey, Daniel R. ... Detroit, MI
Shirey, Stephen D. ... Denver, CO
Shirey, Van R. ... Columbus, OH
Shirey, Wayne A. ... Muncie, IN
Shirey, William ... Brooklyn, NY
Shiri, Robert R. ... Beverly Hills, CA
Shiriak, Ben David ... Woodbridge, NJ
Shirilla, Paul M. ... Detroit, MI
Shiring, Marie Jurbala ... Pittsburgh, PA
Shirinian, Ara H. ... San Francisco, CA
Las Vegas, NV
Shirinian & Roitman ... San Francisco, CA
Las Vegas, NV
Shirk, Adrienne E. ... Nutley, NJ
Shirk, Dennis H. ... Texarkana, TX
Shirk, J. Gary ... Naples, FL
Shirk, James A. ... Bloomington, IL
Shirk, Jennifer Conn ... Visalia, CA
Shirk, John O. ... Lancaster, PA
Shirk, Kenelm L., III ... Ephrata, PA
Shirk, Kenelm L., Jr. ... Ephrata, PA
Lancaster, PA
Lititz, PA
Shirk, Kenelm L., Law Offices ... Ephrata, PA
Shirk, Kevin G. ... Hillsdale, MI
Shirk, Reist, Wagenseller and Mecum
Ephrata, PA
Lancaster, PA
Lititz, PA
Quarryville, PA
Shirk, Roy D. ... Lancaster, PA
Shirk & Schrader ... Lakeview, OH
Shirk, Susan N. ... Atlantic City, NJ
Shirk, W. Bruce ... Washington, DC
Shirk, William E. ... Lakeview, OH
Shirk, William R. ... Morrison, IL
Mount Carroll, IL
Shirk, Work & Robinson, P.C.
Oklahoma City, OK
Shirkey, Jennifer E. ... Harrisonburg, VA
Shirkey, Linda Coleman ... Lansing, MI
Shirkey, Robert L. ... Kansas City, MO
Shirkey & Robertson ... Kansas City, MO
Shirlen, David A. ... Winston-Salem, NC
Shirley, A. Graham ... Raleigh, NC
Shirley, Alan ... Perry, IA
Shirley, Bonnie ... San Luis Obispo, CA
Shirley, C. Wilson ... Austin, TX
San Antonio, TX
Shirley, Candace H. ... Santa Rosa, CA
Shirley, Catherine T. ... Houston, TX
Shirley, Clarence H. ... Alpharetta, GA
Shirley, Clifford, Jr. ... Knoxville, TN
Shirley, Curtis E. ... Indianapolis, IN
Shirley, David S.V. ... Corvallis, OR
Shirley, Deborah L. ... Los Angeles, CA
Shirley, Donna Richardson
Birmingham, AL
Shirley, Evan R., Law Offices of
Honolulu, HI
Shirley, F. Douglas ... Watonga, OK
Shirley, Geoffrey G. ... Greeley, CO
Shirley, Heidi W. ... Los Angeles, CA
Shirley, J. Scott ... Columbia, SC
Shirley, Jacque L. ... Santa Monica, CA
Shirley, James Andrew "Drew"
Houston, TX
Shirley, James J. ... Springvale, ME
Shirley, James Q. ... Concord, NH
Manchester, NH
Shirley, James T., Jr. ... New York, NY
Shirley, John ... Scott City, KS
Shirley, John F. ... San Francisco, CA
Shirley, John N. ... Pearl, MS
Shirley, John O., & Associates
Baton Rouge, LA
Shirley, Jonathan W. ... Maitland, FL
Shirley, Julie S. ... Alpharetta, GA
Shirley, Kenneth D. ... Anaheim, CA
Shirley, Kevin ... New York, NY
Shirley, Kevin C. ... Punta Gorda, FL
Shirley, L. Merrill ... Elba, AL
Shirley, Lester W. ... Salinas, CA
Shirley, Lester W., A Professional Corporation
Salinas, CA
Shirley, Madeleine R. ... Miami, FL
Shirley, Mary Ann ... Eureka, KS
Shirley, Melissa M. ... Baton Rouge, LA
Shirley, Michael G. ... Austin, TX
Shirley, Michael G., A Professional Corporation ... Austin, TX
Shirley, Michael R. ... Edmond, OK
Shirley, Patti S. ... Kalamazoo, MI
Shirley, Powell & Finneseth ... Perry, IA
Shirley, R. Bryce ... Irvine, CA
Shirley, Raymond A., Jr. ... Knoxville, TN
Shirley, Ronald D. ... Colfax, WA
Shirley, Sarah J. ... Austin, TX
Shirley, Scott ... Tallahassee, FL
Shirley, Shannon Rochelle ... Tulsa, OK
Shirley & Shirley ... San Francisco, CA
Shirley, Stephen M. ... Pomona, CA
Shirley, Thomas E., (P.C.) ... Boston, MA
Shirley, Thomas Lloyd ... Indianapolis, IN
Shirley, Vikki R. ... Tallahassee, FL
Shirley, Wayne ... Albuquerque, NM
Shirley, William A. ... Westport, CT
Shirley, William A. ... St. Louis, MO
Shirley, William J. ... Mount Pleasant, MI
Shirley, William J., P.C. ... Mount Pleasant, MI
Shirley, Wilson S., Jr., (P.C.)
New Orleans, LA
Shiro, Burton G. ... Waterville, ME
Shiro, Louis J. ... Waterville, ME
Shiro & Shiro ... Waterville, ME
Shirodkar, Sanjay M.
Securities and Exchange Commission, Division of Corporation Finance, GV
Shiroff, Angelia M. ... Las Vegas, NV
Shiroff, Richard J. ... Easton, PA
Shiroishi, G. Kenneth ... Portland, OR
Shiroma, Geo. ... Honolulu, HI
Shiroma, Howard H. ... Hilo, HI
Shiroma-Bender, Paula ... Dallas, TX
Shirooni, Lucinda C. ... Covington, KY
Shirron, Phillip H. ... Sheridan, AR
Shirtcliff, Matthew B. ... Baker City, OR
Shirtz, Joseph F. ... New Brunswick, NJ
Shirvell, Maryann C. ... San Diego, CA
Shirwo, Darold M. ... Beverly Hills, CA
Shishem & Bailey ... Chicago, IL
Shishem, Edward M. ... Chicago, IL
Shishem, Karen L. ... Chicago, IL
Shishido, Glen E. ... Hawthorne, CA
Shishido, Nolan M. ... Portland, OR
Shishima, Gina N. ... Austin, TX
Shishko, Adrienne M. ... Boston, MA
Shishko, Steven M. ... Boston, MA
Shishkovsky, Katharine R.
Farmington Hills, MI
Shisler, Isaac Burkhart ... Telluride, CO
Shisler, Janna J. ... Indianapolis, IN
Shisler, R. Steven ... Media, PA
Philadelphia, PA
Shissias, Alexander ... Columbia, SC
Shissler, Marcia F. ... Haddonfield, NJ
Shiu, Kenneth K. ... Washington, DC
Shiu, Patricia A. ... San Francisco, CA
Shiv, Moina C. ... Los Angeles, CA
Shivakumar, Dhananjai ... New York, NY
Shive, Edward J. ... Oneida, NY
Shive, Robert E. ... Indianapolis, IN
Shivel, Charles E., Jr. ... Lexington, KY
Shively & Associates, P.C. ... Denver, CO
Yuma, CO
Shively, Carol J. ... Longmont, CO
Shively, Catherine E. ... Manchester, NH
Shively, Donald P. ... Angola, IN
Shively, George S. ... Newark, NJ
Shively, J. Mack ... Portland, OR
Shively, James E. ... Phoenix, AZ
Shively, James R. ... Birmingham, MI
Shively, Jeffrey A. ... Lakewood, OH
Shively, John D. ... Denver, CO
Shively, Judith A. ... Denver, CO
Yuma, CO
Shively, Kenneth O. ... Cape Coral, FL
Centerville, OH
Shively Law Offices, P.C. ... Casper, WY
Shively, Leslie C. ... Evansville, IN
Shively, Martin L. ... Redmond, WA
Shively, Orbie R. ... Baltimore, MD
Shively, Patricia G. ... Cincinnati, OH
Shively, Peter A. ... Madison, WI
Shively, Robert M. ... Casper, WY
Shively, Robert W. ... Lincoln, NE
Shively, Scotty McPheeters
Little Rock, AR
Shively, Sharon Brook ... Scottsdale, AZ
Shively, Strommen & Holst ... Longmont, CO
Shively, Tiffany Lee ... Denver, CO
Yuma, CO
Shiver, Christine Ann ... Brandon, FL
Shiver, David L. ... Sylvester, GA
Shiver, Donald L. ... Macon, GA
Shiver, Edwin C. ... Orinda, CA
Shiver, Frederick H. ... Dallas, TX
Shiver, Mai Sharif ... Chicago, IL
Shivers, Arthur C. ... St. Louis, MO
Shivers, Cassandra C. ... Los Angeles, CA
Shivers, David O. ... Chapel Hill, NC
Shivers, Donald M. ... Atlanta, GA
Shivers, Douglass B. ... Tallahassee, FL
Shivers, Gregg A. ... Cherry Hill, NJ
Shivers, Harriette H. ... Roanoke, VA
Shivers, Jerrald L. ... Jackson, MS
Shivers, Jesse E., Jr. ... Houston, TX
Shivers, Johnson & Wilson ... Atlanta, GA
Shivers, Marc T. ... Austin, TX
Shivers, Nancy Taylor ... San Antonio, TX
Shivers, Olin G. ... Tampa, FL
Shivers, Robert A. ... San Antonio, TX
Shivers, Shari Lynn ... Austin, TX
Shivers & Shivers ... San Antonio, TX
Shivers, Susan D. ... Geneva, IL
Shivers, Susan D., P.C., Law Office of
Geneva, IL
Shivers, Todd L. ... Chicago, IL
Shives, David E. ... Winston-Salem, NC
Shives, Martin L. ... San Diego, CA
Shives, Paula J. ... Orlando, FL
Lexington, KY
Shives, R. Craig ... Des Moines, IA
Shives, Robert A., Jr. ... San Ramon, CA
Shivietz, Michael T. ... Denville, NJ
Shiyou, Al ... Hattiesburg, MS
Shjeflo, Walter E., Jr. ... San Mateo, CA
Shklar, Mark A. ... St. Louis, MO
Shklar, Michael C. ... Newport, NH
Shklov, Mark T. ... Honolulu, HI
Shkolnick, Rodney ... Omaha, NE
Shkolnik, Barry J. ... Chicago, IL
Shkolnik, Hunter J. ... New York, NY
Shkolnik, Mark J. ... Chicago, IL
Shlachter, Robert A. ... Portland, OR
Shlackman, Mara ... Fort Lauderdale, FL
Shladovsky, David J. ... Los Angeles, CA
Shlaes, Carole ... Wichita, KS
Shlansky, David Jay ... Boston, MA
Shlanta, John A. ... New York, NY
Shlanta, Paul R. ... Lansing, MI
Shlaudeman, Katherine
San Francisco, CA
Shlay, Howard A. ... Lake Wales, FL
Shlemon, Paul R. ... Oak Ridge, TN
Shlens, Edmund N. ... Champaign, IL
Shlens, Steve H. ... Bakersfield, CA
Shlensky, William ... Cleveland, OH
Shlesinger, Arkwright & Garvey, LLP
Arlington, VA
Shlesinger, B. Edward, Jr. ... Arlington, VA
Shlesinger, Itzik ... Eugene, OR
Shlesinger, James E. ... Arlington, VA
Shlimbaum, C. Donald ... Islip, NY
Shlimbaum, Lark J. ... Islip, NY
Shlimbaum, Shlimbaum and Jablonski
Central Islip, NY
Islip, NY
Shlimovitz, Jack U. ... Milwaukee, WI
Shlonsky, Patricia A. ... Cleveland, OH
Shlufman, Daniel M. ... Garden City, NY
Shlufman, Martin A. ... Garden City, NY
Shluger, Kenneth L. ... Glastonbury, CT
Shluger, Robert J. ... Glastonbury, CT
Shmalo, Nathan J. ... New York, NY
Shmalo, Nathan S. ... Coral Gables, FL
Shmalo, Nathan S., P.A. ... Coral Gables, FL
Shmaruk, Alan J. ... New York, NY
Shmerelson, Samuel J. ... Camden, NJ
Shmerler, Laura R. ... Wilmington, DE
Cherry Hill, NJ
Philadelphia, PA
Shmerling, Gary T. ... Atlanta, GA
Shmidheiser, William E., III
Harrisonburg, VA
Shmidov, Juli ... Minneapolis, MN
Shmikler, Daniel A. ... Chicago, IL
Shmookler & Schwartz ... Allentown, PA
Shmookler, Stuart T. ... Allentown, PA
Shmukler, Joel M. ... Philadelphia, PA
Shmukler, Stanford ... Philadelphia, PA
Shmulewitz, Aaron ... New York, NY
Shnaider, Gennady ... San Diego, CA
Shnaider, Irving B. ... New Orleans, LA
Shneider, Gordon B. ... De Kalb, IL
Shneidman, Daniel L. ... Milwaukee, WI
Shneidman, Myers, Dowling & Blumenfield
Milwaukee, WI
Shnell, James H. ... Costa Mesa, CA
Shneyer, Paul A. ... New York, NY

Shneyer & Shen ....New York, NY
Shnider, Bruce J. ....Minneapolis, MN
Shnider, Ronald E. ....Sunrise, FL
Shniderman, Harry L. ....Washington, DC
Shniper, John ....Phoenixville, PA
Shoaf, Charles J. ....Wilmington, DE
Shoaf, Gerald D. ....Riverside, CA
Shoaf, Heather Marie ....Falls Church, VA
Shoaf, Larry D. ....Wichita, KS
Shoaf, Milton Bays, Jr. ....Salisbury, NC
Shoaf, N. B. Forrest ....Nashville, TN
Shoaf, Robert I. ....Anchorage, AK
Shoaff, Joseph A. ....Akron, OH
Shoaff, Thomas M. ....Fort Wayne, IN
Shoalmire, Kathryn Buckner ....Oxford, MS
Shoalmire, Lisa B. ....Texarkana, TX
Shoap, Joel W. ....Bowie, MD
Shoap, Richard Lee ....Shippensburg, PA
Shobe, Benj. F. ....Louisville, KY
Shobe, David C. ....Tampa, FL
Shobe, Georgia Anne ....Moncks Corner, SC
Shobe, William M., II ....Hendersonville, NC
Shoben, Elaine W. ....Champaign, IL
Shober, Bard L. ....Northfield, NJ
Shober, Cintra S. ....Arlington, MA
Shober, Joanna M. ....Fayetteville, NC
Shoberg, Jon C. ....San Diego, CA
Shochet, Stephen L. ....Boca Raton, FL
Shock, J. Randolph ....Fort Smith, AR
Shocket, Alan H ....Natick, MA
Shocket & Dockser ....Natick, MA
Shocket, Murray G. ....Natick, MA
Shockett, Steven L. ....Baltimore, MD
Shockett, William E. ....Miami, FL
Shockey, Charles R. ....Department of Justice, Environment and Natural Resources Division, GV
Shockey, David ....Syracuse, NY
Shockey, David D. ....Freeport, IL
Shockey, Gary L. ....Jackson, WY
Shockey, George R., Jr. ....New York, NY
Shockey, Helen A. ....Atlanta, GA
Shockey, John E. ....Washington, DC
Shockey, Larry Richard
San Francisco, CA
Shockey, Robert J. ....Nashville, TN
Shockey, Russell C. ....Roselle, IL
Shockey, William C. ....Baton Rouge, LA
Shockey & Ziober, A Professional Law Corporation ....Baton Rouge, LA
Shocklee, Erin R. ....St. Louis, MO
Shocklee, Rachelle M. ....Kansas City, MO
Shockley, A. Bonwill ....Virginia Beach, VA
Shockley, Brenda Yvonne, (P.C.)
Los Angeles, CA
Shockley, Brian D. ....Berlin, MD
Ocean City, MD
Shockley, Candice J. ....Bessemer, AL
Pelham, AL
Shockley, Carol ....Cleveland, OH
Shockley, Clay M. ....Mountain Home, ID
Shockley, Earl W. ....Lindale, TX
Shockley, Ernest V. ....Los Angeles, CA
Shockley, Everett P. ....Dublin, VA
Shockley, Gary C. ....Johnson City, TN
Nashville, TN
Shockley, James G. ....Victor, MT
Shockley, Kimberly Jo ....Clarksburg, WV
Shockley, Larry G. ....St. Louis, MO
Shockley, Meg S. ....Orange, CA
Shockley, Michael J. ....Irvine, CA
Shockley, Raymond C. ....Ocean City, MD
Shockley, Raymond H., Jr.
Cherry Hill, NJ
Short Hills, NJ
Philadelphia, PA
Shockley, Rob H. ....Boise, ID
Shockley, Rodney S. ....Marietta, GA
Shockley, Scott E. ....Muncie, IN
Shockley, Steven C. ....Indianapolis, IN
Shockley, William I. ....San Francisco, CA
Shockley, William T. ....Miami, FL
Shockling, Robt. J. ....Louisville, OH
Shockman & McKeegan, P.C.
Phoenix, AZ
Scottsdale, AZ
Shockman, Rosemary J. ....Scottsdale, AZ
Shockney, Dwight R. ....Dallas, TX
Shockro, Michael J. ....Los Angeles, CA
Shodeen, Anita L. ....Des Moines, IA
Shoeberg, Kevin K. ....Woodbury, MN
Shoeberg, Kevin K., P.A. ....Woodbury, MN
Shoebotham, Jonathan B. ....Houston, TX
Shoebotham, Katherine McIlroy
Houston, TX
Shoecraft, James W. ....Dallas, TX
Shoecraft, James W., P.C., Attorneys' Offices of ....Dallas, TX
Shoecraft, Robert D. ....San Diego, CA
Shoemake, Bransford ....Pawhuska, OK
Shoemake, David ....Collins, MS
Shoemake, Deborah J. ....Mobile, AL
Shoemake, Harold R. ....Houston, TX
Shoemake, James H. ....Houston, TX
Shoemake, Jim J. ....St. Louis, MO
Shoemake, Shockley T. ....Pawhuska, OK
Shoemaker, Alice ....Penn Yan, NY
Shoemaker, Bob ....Dallas, TX
Shoemaker, Bobby L. ....Bay Springs, MS
Shoemaker & Borbe ....Berlin, NJ
Shoemaker, Brian G. ....Springfield, MO
Shoemaker, Brian L. ....Albuquerque, NM
Shoemaker, C. Edwin ....Knoxville, TN
Shoemaker, Charles E., Jr. ....Allentown, PA
Shoemaker, Charles L. ....Edgewood, MD
Shoemaker, Charles O., Jr. ....Sunnyside, WA
Shoemaker, Charles R. ....Sacramento, CA
Shoemaker, Clifford J. ....Vienna, VA
Shoemaker, Connie ....New York, NY
Shoemaker, Curtis L. ....Spokane, WA
Shoemaker, D. Charles ....Hastings, NE
Shoemaker, Daniel A. R. ....Minneapolis, MN
Shoemaker, Douglas J. ....Houston, TX
Shoemaker, Douglas L. ....Columbus, OH
Shoemaker, Dwight L. ....Aledo, IL
Shoemaker, Edward G. ....Pittsburgh, PA
Shoemaker, Edward P. ....Dallas, TX
Shoemaker, Edwin J. ....Lockport, NY
Shoemaker, Faith Elaine ....Newnan, GA
Shoemaker, Frank A. ....Lansing, MI
Shoemaker, Fred J. ....Westerville, OH
Shoemaker, Fredric V. ....Boise, ID
Shoemaker, Geo. W. ....Spokane, WA
Shoemaker, George C., Jr. ....San Antonio, TX
Shoemaker, Gregory A. ....St. Louis, MO
Shoemaker, Gregory Mark ....New Bern, NC
Shoemaker, H. Lynn ....Kingsport, TN
Shoemaker, H. Reese, Jr. ....Frederick, MD
Shoemaker, Harry L., III ....Baton Rouge, LA
Shoemaker, Haven N., Jr., P.A.
Hampstead, MD
Shoemaker, Horman & Clapp, P.A.
Frederick, MD
Shoemaker & Horn ....Vienna, VA
Shoemaker, Irvin B. ....Berlin, NJ
Shoemaker, Jack ....Tallahassee, FL
Shoemaker, James Edward ....Binghamton, NY
Shoemaker, James G. ....New Port Richey, FL
Shoemaker, James H., Jr.
Newport News, VA
Shoemaker, James M., Jr. ....Greenville, SC
Shoemaker, James R. ....Frederick, MD
Shoemaker, James T. ....Wilkes-Barre, PA
Shoemaker, James W. ....Detroit Lakes, MN
Shoemaker, Jason Scott ....Frederick, MD
Shoemaker, Joan ....Pittsburgh, PA
Shoemaker, John B. (Ben) ......Cocoa Beach, FL
Shoemaker, John F. ....Omaha, NE
Shoemaker, John H. ....Akron, OH
Shoemaker, John Kyle ....Fort Myers, FL
Shoemaker, John L. ....Houston, TX
Shoemaker, John R. ....Minneapolis, MN
Shoemaker, John Robert ....Portland, OR
Shoemaker, John W. ....Columbus, OH
Shoemaker, Joseph J. ....Denver, CO
Shoemaker, Kathleen V. ....Fircrest, WA
Shoemaker, Kent A. ....Cincinnati, OH
Shoemaker, Kevin L. ....Columbus, OH
Shoemaker, Kimberly A. ....Norfolk, VA
Shoemaker, Lazarre, Daspit and Blackwell
Baton Rouge, LA
Shoemaker, Linda J. ....Boulder, CO
Shoemaker, Mark B. ....Cherry Hill, NJ
Shoemaker, Martha O., The Law Firm of
New York, NY
Shoemaker, Mary A. ....Cedar Rapids, IA
Shoemaker and Mattare, Ltd.
Arlington, VA
Shoemaker, Michele ....Stow, MA
Shoemaker, Monte R.
Altamonte Springs, FL
Shoemaker, Paul F. ....Minneapolis, MN
Shoemaker, Paul T. ....New York, NY
Shoemaker, Phillisa S. ....Denver, CO
Shoemaker, Raleigh A. ....Charlotte, NC
Shoemaker, Randall L.
Bloomfield Hills, MI
Shoemaker, Randle P. ....Jacksonville, FL
Shoemaker, Richard ....Birmingham, AL
Shoemaker, Robert B., Jr. ....Paoli, PA
Shoemaker, Robert C., Jr. ....Portland, OR
Shoemaker, Robert G. ....St. Petersburg, FL
Shoemaker, Robert G. ....Edmond, OK
Shoemaker, Robert W., III ....Concord, MA
Shoemaker, Ronald J. ....Arlington, VA
Shoemaker, Scot D. ....Vallejo, CA
Shoemaker & Shoemaker, P.L.C.
Minneapolis, MN
Shoemaker, Susan B. ....Edgerton, WI
Shoemaker, Tiffany ....Camden, NJ
Shoemaker, W. Joseph ....Denver, CO
Shoemaker, Wham, Krisor & Shoemaker
Denver, CO
Shoemaker & Witt ....Hastings, NE
Shoeman, Rosalie J. ....Morristown, NJ
Shoemate, Steven R. ....New York, NY
Shoen, Kimberly A. ....Somersworth, NH
Shoen, Lynn R. ....Las Vegas, NV
Shoen, Michael L. ....Paradise Valley, AZ
Shoenberg, Dana L. ....Department of Justice, Civil Rights Division, GV
Shoenberger, Allen E. ....Chicago, IL
Shoenberger, Elisabeth E. ....Chicago, IL
Shoenberger, Jon A. ....Palm Springs, CA
Shoener, Steven E. ....Dallas, TX
Shoener, Thomas J. ....New York, NY
Shoenfeld, Ingrid ....Mountain Lakes, NJ
Shoenfeld, Peter B. ....Santa Fe, NM
Shoenfeld, Peter B., P.A. ....Santa Fe, NM
Shoenfelt, Oscar L., III ....Baton Rouge, LA
Shoen-Morrison, Kimberly A.
Somersworth, NH
Shoenthal, Elliott A. ....Decatur, GA
Shoenthal, Lawrence E. ....Spring Valley, NY
Shoeps, Bernard S. ....Torrance, CA
Shoesmith, Mark G. ....Albuquerque, NM
Shoesmith, Thomas M. ....San Diego, CA
Shofar, Nick D. ....Cleveland, OH
Shoff, Mary Graham ....Rockville, MD
Shoff, Patricia A. ....Des Moines, IA
Shoffey, James ....Fort Smith, AR
Shoffner, Allen ....Shelbyville, TN
Shoffner, Freya Allen ....Boston, MA
Shoffner, Gary E. ....Santa Ana, CA
Shoffner, Jack Donald ....Chesterton, IN
Shoffner, Larry A. ....San Diego, CA
Shoffner, Lawrence R. ....Detroit, MI
Shoffner, Robert L., Jr. ....Greenville, NC
Shoffner, Robin D. ....Chicago, IL
Shofi, David M. ....Yorktown Heights, NY
Shofi, Hennen, Gramovot & Associates
Tampa, FL
Shofi, John D. ....Tampa, FL
Shofner, E. Elaine ....Atlanta, GA
Shofner, Elizabeth H. ....New York, NY
Shofner, Ginger Bobo ....Shelbyville, TN
Shofner, Jim D. ....Tulsa, OK
Shofner, John C. ....Shelbyville, TN
Shofner, William E. ....Nashville, TN
Shofstahl, Tyson B. ....New Orleans, LA
Shogan, Alexander J., Jr. ....Spokane, WA
Shogan, Jacqueline O. ....Pittsburgh, PA
Shogren, Gregory M. ....Yakima, WA
Shogren, Virginia ....San Diego, CA
Shohat, Edward R. ....Miami, FL
Shohat, Maria Beguiristain ....Miami, FL
Shohen, Wendi L. ....Philadelphia, PA
Shohet, Jeffrey M. ....San Diego, CA
Shoichet, Louis S. ....New York, NY
Shoiket, Igor ....Palo Alto, CA
Shoji, Aki Y. ....Palo Alto, CA
Shoker, Gursaran S.
West College Corner, IN
Shokohi, Nancy W. ....Los Angeles, CA
Shokrai, Maryam ....Newport Beach, CA
Sholar, John A. ....Alton, IL
Sholar, John P. ....Department of Justice, Civil Division, GV
Sholar, Terry M. ....Roanoke Rapids, NC
Shold, David M. ....Wickliffe, OH
Sholder, Iris E. ....Chicago, IL
Sholder, Joseph M. ....Santa Barbara, CA
Sholder, Stephen C. ....Williamsport, PA
Sholeen, Eden P. ....Houston, TX
Sholem, David B. ....Champaign, IL
Sholes, Andrew G. ....Warwick, RI
Sholes, Austin B. ....Wainscott, NY
Sholes, Bruce A. ....Scottsdale, AZ
Sholes, Bruce A., Law Offices of
Scottsdale, AZ
Sholes, David H. ....Warwick, RI
Sholes, Ronald J. ....New Orleans, LA
Sholes & Sholes ....Warwick, RI
Sholis, David R. ....San Diego, CA
Sholiton, Amy R. ....Newton, MA
Sholk, Steven H. ....Newark, NJ
Sholkoff, Jack S. ....Los Angeles, CA
Sholl, Barbara W. ....Northfield, IL
Sholl, Peter J. ....San Diego, CA
Sholl, Robert K. ....Milwaukee, WI
Shollenbarger, Kenneth E. ....Amarillo, TX
Shollenbarger, Ray H., Jr. ....Santa Fe, NM
Shollenberger, Allen R. ....Hamburg, PA
Wyomissing, PA
Shollenberger, Elizabeth A. ....Bronx, NY
Shollenberger & Januzzi, LLP
Harrisburg, PA
Shollenberger, Richard C., Jr. ....Chicago, IL
Shollenberger, Timothy A. ....Harrisburg, PA
Sholler, Lynne M. ....Breckenridge, CO
Sholley, Susan R. ....Los Angeles, CA
Sholly, John Thomas ....Knoxville, TN
Sholomson, Stephen L. ....Los Angeles, CA
Sholovitz, Arnold C. ....Simsbury, CT
Sholtis, Jonathan ....Mobile, AL
Sholts, Jill Johnson ....St. Paul, MN
Sholts, Thomas E. ....West Palm Beach, FL
Sholty, Anthony M. ....Juneau, AK
Sholtz, Michael C. ....Durham, NC
Sholz, Robert T. ....White Plains, NY
Shomade, Salmon A. ....Atlanta, GA
Shomaker, Mark W. ....College Station, TX
Shomaker, Thomas J. ....Omaha, NE
Shomali, Maha Elias ....Baltimore, MD
Shomber, Melissa A. ....Oklahoma City, OK
Shomberg, Robert ....New York, NY
Shomer, Evyn L. ....San Francisco, CA
Shomin, Kevin R. ....Milwaukee, WI
Shomloo, Naveed D. ....Portland, OR
Shomo, Casey D. ....North Palm Beach, FL
Shomo, R. Michael ....Denver, CO
Shomper, James D., Jr. ....Wilmington, DE
Shon, Debbie Leilani ....Los Angeles, CA
Shonafelt, Michael W. ....Irvine, CA
Shonder, Steven S. ....Chicago, IL
Shoneman, Charles H. ....Washington, DC
Shoneman, David T. ....Princeton, NJ
Shonfeld, Willard L. ....Melrose Park, IL
Shonfeld, Rachel H. ....Miami, FL
Shong, Jolene ....Rochester, MI
Shonk, Brian D. ....Lancaster, OH
Shonka, David C.
Federal Trade Commission, Office of the General Counsel, GV
Shonkwiler, Ayers & Rhoades
Monticello, IL
Shonkwiler, Daniel J. ....Washington, DC
Shonkwiler, James L., Jr. ....Lansing, MI
Shonkwiler, John F. ....Chicago, IL
Shonkwiler, John P. ....Monticello, IL
Shonkwiler, John W. ....Tigard, OR
Shonkwiler, Mark D.
Federal Election Commission, Office of the General Counsel, GV
Shonkwiler, Tatjana M. ....Washington, DC
Shonn, Daniel D., Jr. ....Buffalo, NY
Shontz, David B. ....New York, NY
Shontz, G. Brian ....Norwell, MA
Shontz, John M. ....Helena, MT
Shoob, Marvin H. ....Atlanta, GA
Shoob, Wendy L. ....Atlanta, GA
Shoobe and Bakarich, A Professional Corporation ....Paramus, NJ
Shoobe, Joanne ....Florham Park, NJ
Shoobe, Joel L. ....Paramus, NJ
Shoobridge Law Firm, P.C. ....Hobbs, NM
Shoobridge, William G. W. ....Hobbs, NM
Shoock & Jones, LLP ....Warwick, NY
Shoock, Paul S. ....Warwick, NY
Shook, Alex J. ....Morgantown, WV
Shook, Ann L. ....North Olmsted, OH
Shook, Chadwick Lester ....Jackson, MS
Shook, Charles A. ....Smiths Grove, KY
Shook, Charles D. ....Dayton, OH
Shook, Colleen M. ....Norfolk, VA
Shook, David C. ....Toledo, OH
Shook, David R. ....Lapeer, MI
Shook, Dennis N. ....Wagoner, OK
Shook, Donald J. ....Colorado Springs, CO
Shook, Douglas G. ....Phoenix, AZ
Shook, Gene E., Sr. ....North Olmsted, OH
Shook, Glenn D. ....San Antonio, TX
Shook, Hardy & Bacon L.L.P.
San Francisco, CA
Washington, DC
Miami, FL
Overland Park, KS
Kansas City, MO
Houston, TX
Shook, James A. ....Ocala, FL
Shook, James William
Federal Communications Commission, Mass Media Bureau, GV
Shook, Jeremy D. ....St. Louis, MO
Shook, Jimmy Nixon ....San Saba, TX
Shook, John B. ....Las Vegas, NV
Shook, John P. ....Los Angeles, CA
Shook, Joseph Stanley ....Coral Gables, FL
Shook, L. Arsinoe ....Philadelphia, PA
Shook, Langley R. ....Washington, DC
Shook, Lynn ....Greenville, SC
Shook, Lynn, P.C. ....Greenville, SC
Shook, Michael D. ....Torrance, CA
Shook, Neil E. ....Indianapolis, IN
Shook, Richard G. ....Sugar Land, TX
Shook, Robert C. ....Franklin, IN
Shook, Robert W. ....Crofton, MD
Shook & Shook ....North Olmsted, OH
Shook, Stephen H. ....Jacksonville, FL
Shook & Stone ....Las Vegas, NV
Shook, Susan M. ....Cincinnati, OH
Shook, William A. ....Washington, DC
Shookhoff, Andrew J. ....Nashville, TN
Shookman, Loyd A. ....Rancho Cordova, CA
Shoolman, Carl ....Rochester, NY
Shoolman, Ira M. ....Boston, MA
Shoolman Law Firm, P.C. ....Rochester, NY
Shooman, Alice H. ....Brooklyn, NY
Shooman, Harry M. ....Silver Spring, MD
Shoop, Corinne F. ....Southfield, MI
Shoop, Darcy A. ....Rockville, MD
Shoop, Deborah ....Farmington Hills, MI
Shoop, George J. ....Reading, PA
Shoop, John E. ....Concord, OH
Shoop, Lyn ....Columbia, MD
Shoop, Marcelle F. ....Magna, UT
Shoop, Melinda S. ....Harrisburg, PA
Shoop, Paul ....Malibu, CA
Shoop, Rex E. ....San Francisco, CA
Shoop, Robert H., Jr. ....Pittsburgh, PA
Shoop, Robert L. ....Colorado Springs, CO
Shooshan, Charles H., III ....West Hartford, CT
Shooster, Frank M. ....Margate, FL
Shooster, Frank Mallory, P.A. ....Margate, FL
Shoostine, Jeffrey H. ....Miami, FL
Shoot, Brian J. ....New York, NY
Shoot, Lawrence M. ....Miami, FL
Shopbell, Toshana ....Minneapolis, MN
Shope, John A. ....Boston, MA
Shope, Richard I. ....Greensboro, NC
Shope, Steven G. ....Knoxville, TN
Shope, Suzanne Seavello ....Atlanta, GA
Shope, Thomas D. ....Pittsburgh, PA
Shopf, Leslie A. ....Abilene, TX
Shopfner, David R. ....Washington, DC
Shopiro, Paula B. ....Lincolnshire, IL
Shopiro, Richard S. ....Chicago, IL
Shopkorn, Stanley B. ....New York, NY
Shopland, Linda F. ....Wilmington, DE
Shopneck, Craig H. ....Cleveland, OH
Shopneck, Patti A. ....Highlands Ranch, CO
Shopneck, Robert M. ....Denver, CO
Shopoff, Jeffrey W. ....San Francisco, CA
Shopteese, Debra ....Roxbury, MA
Shopulski, Donna K. ....Baltimore, MD
Shor, Alan Phillip ....Irving, TX
Shor, Frank, Law Offices of
Carrollton, TX
Shor, Jay Elliott ....Jenkintown, PA
Shor, Jeffrey A. ....New York, NY
Shor, Lester H. ....Denver, CO
Shor, Lloyd ....New York, NY
Shor, Martin ....Baltimore, MD
Shor, Michael L. ....Washington, DC
Shor, Michael T. ....Washington, DC
Shor, Nina ....Bethesda, MD
Shor, Robert Bartley ....Reading, MA
Shor, Stephen A. ....Kings Point, NY
Shorago, Alisa A. ....San Diego, CA
Shorall, John G., II ....Pittsburgh, PA
Shorall & Stevens, P.C. ....Flagstaff, AZ
Phoenix, AZ
Shorall, Thomas J., Jr. ....Phoenix, AZ
Shorb, John J. ....York, PA
Shorb, Randy R. ....Tulsa, OK
Shorb, Robert H. ....Chevy Chase, MD
Shorb, Shorb & Hast ....York, PA
Shorb, Thomas M. ....York, PA
Shorba, Jeffery ....Department of Justice, Bureau of Prisons, GV
Shore, Andrew ....Los Angeles, CA
Shore, Andrew D. ....Charlotte, NC

Shoup, Guy W. ... **San Jose, CA**
Shoup, Jennifer R. ... **Indianapolis, IN**
Shoup, Kim Elliott ... Angola, IN
Shoup, Mark Steven ... Victorville, CA
Shoup, Maryann Connolly ... Apple Valley, CA
Shoup, Steven V. ... Indianapolis, IN
Shoup, Tina L. ... **Burlington, VT**
Shoup, Wilson E. ... Angola, IN
Shoupe, Karen ... Powell, OH
Shoupe-Gorga, Sandra A.
Palm Springs, CA
Shourds, Charles W., Jr. ... Nashville, TN
Shouse, August E. ... **Houston, TX**
Shouse, Clint ... **Dallas, TX**
Shouse, David M. ... Louisville, KY
Shouse, E. E. ... Houston, TX
Shouse, Emily A. ... **Nashville, TN**
Shouse, Larry R. ... Kansas City, MO
Shouse, Neil ... Los Angeles, CA
Shouse & Raithel ... Kansas City, MO
Shouse, Weldon ... **Lexington, KY**
Shouse, William C. ... **Lexington, KY**
Shouse, William C. ... Louisville, KY
Shoush, Mark W. ... Scottsdale, AZ
Shousher, Mohamed ... Toledo, OH
Shouvlin, David P. ... **Columbus, OH**
Shovan, George O. ... New London, NH
Shovan, Michael J. ... Frankenmuth, MI
Saginaw, MI
Shovelin, Julia Manning ... Gastonia, NC
Shovers, Alan N. ... **Evansville, IN**
Shovers, Andrew C. ... **Atlanta, GA**
Shovers, Iman ... Atlanta, GA
Shovers, Norman ... Racine, WI
Shovlin, Bridget M. ... North Chicago, IL
Shovlin, Catherine Mary ... Tucson, AZ
Shovlin, George F. ... **Wilkes-Barre, PA**
Shovlin, Gerald Lee ... Mentor, OH
Shovlin, Hugh P. ... San Antonio, TX
Shovlin, Thomas A. ... Clementon, NJ
Showalter, Anne L. ... **Boston, MA**
Showalter, Barton Earl ... **Dallas, TX**
Showalter, David W., (P.C.) ... Bellaire, TX
Showalter, Donald E. ... **Harrisonburg, VA**
Showalter, Donald S.
Fort Lauderdale, FL
Showalter, Graham C. ... **Lewisburg, PA**
Showalter, J. Franklin, Jr. ... Bridgeport, WV
Showalter, J. Richard, II ... Topeka, KS
Showalter, Jeanette Baer ... Newport News, VA
Showalter, John A. ... **Kansas City, MO**
Showalter, John W. ... Department of Justice, Civil Division, GV
Showalter, Josiah T., Jr. ... Christiansburg, VA
Showalter, Judith A. ... Lutherville, MD
Showalter, Kent A., III ... **Orlando, FL**
Showalter, Paul M. ... Wyandotte, MI
Showalter, Robert D. ... **Denver, CO**
Showalter, Robert L. ... **Dayton, OH**
Showalter, Russell H., Jr. ... **Jacksonville, FL**
Showalter, Scott Irwin ... Goodland, KS
Showalter, Tamara E. ... **Lancaster, PA**
Showalter, Timothy A. ... Arkansas City, KS
Showalter, Welby C. ... Harrisonburg, VA
Showard, Sarah J. ... Tucson, AZ
Showell, Evan A. ... **Morristown, NJ**
Showen, Andrew V. ... Altamonte Springs, FL
Showen, James E. ... **Washington, DC**
Showen, Richard E.
Rancho Santa Fe, CA
Showen, Robert H. ... Walnut Creek, CA
Shower, Tyson M. ... **Sacramento, CA**
Showers, Barbara Wynne ... **Charleston, SC**
Showers, Bicknell J. ... Los Angeles, CA
Showers, Gregory K. ... **Clearwater, FL**
Showers, H. Robert, Jr. ... **McLean, VA**
Showers, Jack Paul ... Lafayette, LA
Showers, James A. ... **Hillsboro, TX**
Showers, Julie Hagen ... St. Paul, MN
Showers, Vina L. ... Oklahoma City, OK
Showfety, June E. ... **Concord, NC**
Showler, Scott ... **Redlands, CA**
Showley, Lon D. ... **San Diego, CA**
Showley & Thompson ... **San Diego, CA**
Showman, Wallace A. ... **New York, NY**
Shown, William G. ... San Antonio, TX
Shows, Cali & Burns ... **Baton Rouge, LA**
Shows, E. Wade ... **Baton Rouge, LA**
Shows, James W. ... Paso Robles, CA
Shows, John Howard ... **Jackson, MS**
Shows Law Firm, PLLC ... **Jackson, MS**
Shows, Marshall T., Jr. ... **Jackson, MS**
Shows, Scott A. ... Memphis, TN
Showstack, Louis ... New York, NY
Shoyer, Andrew W. ... **Washington, DC**
Shpall, Andrea ... **Denver, CO**
Shpall, Casey ... Denver, CO
Shpall, Mark H. ... Woodland Hills, CA
Shpeen, Alvin G. ... Trenton, NJ
Shpiece, Michael R. ... **Southfield, MI**
Shpigler, Debra R. ... Charleston, SC
Shpigler, Debra R., Co., LPA
Charleston, SC
Shpizner, Michael J. ... San Jose, CA
Shraberg, William L.
Department Of Health And Human Services, Social Security Administration, GV
Shrader, Cathleen M. ... **Fort Wayne, IN**
Shrader, Gerald R. ... Tulsa, OK
Shrader, Glenn C. ... **San Francisco, CA**
Shrader, Glenn J., Jr.
Oklahoma City, OK
Shrader, Heather A. ... Jefferson City, MO
Shrader, J. Carl ... Westbury, NY
Shrader, J. Thompson ... Amherst, VA
Shrader, Jeffrey G. ... **Amarillo, TX**
Shrader, John A. ... **Philadelphia, PA**
Shrader, Justin Hyde ... **Dallas, TX**
Shrader and Knapp, A Professional Corporation ... **Westport, CT**
Shrader, L. Douglas ... **Westport, CT**
Shrader, Natalie V. ... **East Chicago, IN**
Shrader, Patricia ... Los Angeles, CA
Shrader, Patricia Brown ... Sparks, MD
Shrader, Robert D., Jr. ... Richmond, VA
Shrader, William C. ... **Houston, TX**
Shrage, Harvey M. ... Springfield, MA
Shrager, David J. ... **Pittsburgh, PA**
Shrager, David S. ... **Philadelphia, PA**
Shrager, David S. ... Pittsburgh, PA
Shrager, Deborah E.
National Labor Relations Board, Office of the General Counsel, GV
Shrager, Ira B. ... Philadelphia, PA
Shrager, Isadore A. ... **Philadelphia, PA**
Shrager, James J. ... **Somerville, NJ**
Shrager, McDaid, Loftus, Flum & Spivey
Voorhees, NJ
Philadelphia, PA
Shragge, Mark B. ... San Francisco, CA
Shrago, Alvin H. ... New York, NY
Shraibati, Kimberly A. ... **Austin, TX**
Shraibati, Malek H. ... Los Angeles, CA
Shraiberg, Bradley Scott ... **Boca Raton, FL**
Shrair, David A. ... **Springfield, MA**
Shrair, Peter W. ... **Springfield, MA**
Shrake, Charles G. ... Roswell, GA
Shrake, Henry L., Jr. ... Houston, TX
Shrake, Marc J. ... **Minneapolis, MN**
Shrallow, Carrie L. ... **Providence, RI**
Shrallow, Dale Phillip ... Chicago, IL
Shrallow, Dane A. ... Mayfield Village, OH
Shralow, M. Melvin ... **Philadelphia, PA**
Shramenko, Andre ... **Secaucus, NJ**
Shramuk, Robert Alan ... Downers Grove, IL
Shrank, Brigette N. ... **Newark, NJ**
Shrank, Diane A. ... Centerville, MA
Shrank, Ian ... **New York, NY**
Shrauger & Dunn, P.C. ... Detroit, MI
Mount Clemens, MI
Shrauger, P. Robert ... Detroit, MI
Mount Clemens, MI
Shrayer, Alan C. ... Worcester, MA
Shreaves, Otto B., Jr. ... Richmond, VA
Shrecengost, R.L. ... Newport News, VA
Shreck, Morton M ... Suffern, NY
Shreckengost, Bryan K. ... **Pittsburgh, PA**
Shreder, Scott A. ... **San Antonio, TX**
Shreder, Steven P. ... Talihina, OK
Shreeves, Linda E. ... Los Angeles, CA
Shreeves, Sally ... **New York, NY**
Shreffler, Charles R. ... **Minneapolis, MN**
Shreffler Law Firm, P.A.
Minneapolis, MN
Shreffler, S. Gordon ... Oklahoma City, OK
Shreffler, William J. ... **Nashville, TN**
Shreiar, Barry R. ... Newport Beach, CA
Shreiber, Lisa S. ... **Buffalo, NY**
Shreibman, Stephanie Victoria
Philadelphia, PA
Shreiner, Grant P. ... Los Angeles, CA
Shreiner, J. Marlin ... Ephrata, PA
Lancaster, PA
Shrem, Marcia E. ... Mountainside, NJ
Shrenger, Erlinda G. ... Los Angeles, CA
Shrenger, Justin J., Law Offices of
Los Angeles, CA
Shrenkel, Jane P. ... Hempstead, NY
Shrensky, Jason A. ... **New York, NY**
Shrensky, Lewis F. ... Potomac, MD
Shreter, Stephanie ... Cherry Hill, NJ
Shreve, Dana S. ... Wilmington, DE
Shreve, David William ... **Altavista, VA**
Shreve, David William ... **Lynchburg, VA**
Rustburg, VA
Shreve, Dennis M. ... **Clarksburg, WV**
Shreve, Don F., Jr. ... **Las Vegas, NV**
Shreve, Julia K. ... **Charleston, WV**
Shreve, Marguerite R. ... **Bloomington, IN**
Shreve, Mark ... **Troy, MI**
Shreve, Mindy J. ... **Pittsburgh, PA**
Shreve, Nina ... **New York, NY**
Shreve, Patrick L. ... **Los Angeles, CA**
Shreve, Robert S. ... Greensburg, PA
Pittsburgh, PA
Shreve, Shannon C. ... Taunton, MA
Shreve, Steven T. ... **Pittsburgh, PA**
Shreve, William E., Jr. ... **Mobile, AL**
Shreve, William H. ... **Newport Beach, CA**
Shreves, Catherine E. ... Minneapolis, MN
Shreves, Frederick L., II ... **Fairfax, VA**
McLean, VA
Shreves, H. Bruce ... **New Orleans, LA**
Shreves, Helen C. ... Denver, CO
Shreves, John F. ... **New Orleans, LA**
Shreves, Keegan & Schudel, PLLC
Centreville, VA
Fairfax, VA
McLean, VA
Reston, VA
Shreves, Kenneth E. ... Union, NE
Shrewsberry, Lisa L. ... **Hawthorne, NY**
Shrewsbury, Dennis F. ... Plymouth, MI
Shrewsbury, Douglas R. ... St. Paul, MN
Shrewsbury, James F. ... St. Louis, MO
Shriberg, Glenn M. ... Boston, MA
Shribman, Jeffrey N. ... **Salem, MA**
Shride, Christopher S. ... **Belleville, IL**
Shrier, Hy S. ... Omaha, NE
Shrier, JoAnn ... Chicago, IL
Shrift, Emily ... **Washington, DC**
Shriftman, Elliott D. ... Manhasset, NY
Shriner, Cynthia T. ... Wilmington, NC
Shriner, Thomas L., Jr. ... **Milwaukee, WI**
Shrinsky, Jason L. ... **Washington, DC**
Shriro, Michelle E. ... **Dallas, TX**
Shriver, Alexander D. ... **Brattleboro, VT**
Shriver, Craig E. ... St. Paul, MN
Shriver, David G. ... McPherson, KS
Shriver, Donald L. ... Rockford, IL
Shriver, Donald P. ... Elgin, IL
Shriver, Ernest P. ... **Minneapolis, MN**
Shriver, Garner E. ... United States Senate, Committee Legal Personnel, GV
Shriver, Gary L. ... Apache Junction, AZ
Shriver, Gary L., P.C. ... Apache Junction, AZ
Shriver & Gordon, P.C. ... **Woodstock, GA**
Shriver, Jay M. ... **Mason City, IA**
Shriver, Mark Owings, IV
Woodstock, GA
Shriver, Molly M. ... Des Moines, IA
Shriver, Robert H., III ... Washington, DC
Shriver, Sargent ... **Washington, DC**
Shriver, Thomas H. ... Nashville, TN
Shroads, James L.
Amelia Island Plantation, FL
Jacksonville, FL
Shroba, Jane ... **Chicago, IL**
Shrock, Gregory J. ... **New York, NY**
Shrock, Rodney V. ... Kokomo, IN
Shrock, Steven J. ... **Millersburg, OH**
Shrode, W. Scott ... Evansville, IN
Shrode, Willard C. ... Evansville, IN
Shroder, Layne K. ... Bradenton, FL
Shroff, Anoop G. ... **Washington, DC**
Shroff, Kersi B. ... Library of Congress, Law Library, GV
Shroff, Ketki M. ... Rolling Meadows, IL
Shroff, Sabrina ... New York, NY
Shron, Bradley M. ... **Boston, MA**
Shron, Mitchell ... Hyde Park, NY
Shrontz, Craig H. ... **Bellevue, WA**
Shropshire, Charles A. ... Baton Rouge, LA
Shropshire, James K. ... Brentwood, TN
Shropshire, Jamie C., (Ms.) ... Lewiston, ID
Shropshire, Jerry ... Baton Rouge, LA
Shropshire, Karen Greer ... **Dallas, TX**
Shropshire, Sharon ... **Fort Worth, TX**
Shropshire & Shropshire ... Baton Rouge, LA
Shropshire, Steven L. ... **Portland, OR**
Shrosbree, Robert C. ... **Dearborn, MI**
Shrout, Howard L. ... Kansas City, MO
Shrout, Michael E. ... Owingsville, KY
Shroyer, David L. ... **Columbus, OH**
Shroyer, Donald R. ... Johnstown, PA
Shroyer, John W. ... **New York, NY**
Shroyer, Lee E. ... Mill Valley, CA
Shroyer, Lowell Allen ... Beech Grove, IN
Shroyer, Stephen H. ... Indianapolis, IN
Shroyer, Thomas J. ... **Minneapolis, MN**
Shroyer, William T. ... **Milwaukee, WI**
Shrull & Associates, A Professional Corporation
Fort Worth, TX
Shrull, Roland Lee ... Burlington, MA
Shrull, Roswald E. ... Fort Worth, TX
Shrum, Barry Neil ... **Nashville, TN**
Shrum, Kenneth W. ... Marble Hill, MO
Shrum, Wesley M. ... Merced, CA
Shrybman & Associates, P.C.
Silver Spring, MD
Shrybman, James A. ... Silver Spring, MD
Shryock, Charles M., III ... Seabrook, MD
Shryock, Dennis R. ... Fulton, MO
Shryock, E. Forrest, Jr. ... **Los Angeles, CA**
Shryock, John W. ... Willoughby, OH
Shryock, Kristine M. ... **Atlanta, GA**
Shryock, Richard W., Jr. ... Elkins, WV
Shtabsky, Janessa E. ... **Phoenix, AZ**
Shtasel, Laurence ... **Philadelphia, PA**
Shtasel, Sana F. ... Washington, DC
Shteamer, Michael B. ... **Kansas City, MO**
Shteamer, Richard M. ... Kansas City, MO
Shteir, Elliot ... Somerville, NJ
Shteir, Jon ... Somerville, NJ
Shteir-Dunn, Vicki J. ... Department of Labor, Office of the Solicitor, GV
Shtivelband, Inna ... Waltham, MA
Shtoyko, Julie A. ... Carmel, NY
Shu, Christina C. ... New York, NY
Shu, D'Andra Millsap ... **Houston, TX**
Shu, Glen ... **Houston, TX**
Shuai, Yee-Horn ... Pasadena, CA
Shuai, Yee-Jen ... Alhambra, CA
Shub, David ... **Greensboro, NC**
Shub, Jeffrey W. ... Salem, MA
Shub, Jonathan ... **Philadelphia, PA**
Shub, Lisa Horvath ... **San Antonio, TX**
Shub, Mark G. ... Boston, MA
Shub, Rachel Anne
Executive Office Of The President, Office of the U.S. Trade Representative, GV
Shub, Stefanie L. ... Stamford, CT
Shuba, John Kevin ... Salem, OR
Shuba, Timothy K. ... **Washington, DC**
Shubat, John G. ... **Indianapolis, IN**
Shubatt, Michael J. ... **Dubuque, IA**
Shubb, Carissa ... **San Francisco, CA**
Shubb, Glenn S. ... Encino, CA
Shubb, William B. ... Sacramento, CA
Shub-Condliffe & Condliffe, P.A.
Towson, MD
Shub-Condliffe, Judith ... Towson, MD
Shube, Eric S. ... **New York, NY**
Shube, Steven E. ... Irvine, CA
Shube, Susan E. ... **Anaheim, CA**
Shuben, Richard Warren, Law Office of
Canoga Park, CA
Shuben, Russell E. ... Westlake Village, CA
Shubert, Christian F. ... Lincoln, NE
Shubert, Donald J. ... **Hartford, CT**
Shubert, Jason A. ... Orlando, FL
Shubert, Lee Warner ... **Washington, DC**
Shubert, Norman A. ... **Chicago, IL**
Shubert, Ronald S. ... **Buffalo, NY**
Shubert, Susan A. ... Memphis, TN
Shubin, Andrew J. ... **State College, PA**
Shubin & Bass, P.A. ... **Miami, FL**
Shubin, Harry A. ... Miami Beach, FL
Shubin, Harry Benjamin ... **Arlington, VA**
Shubin, John K. ... **Miami, FL**
Shubin, Kimberly K. ... Longview, WA
Shubin, Susan Dishler ... Towson, MD
Shubinski, Carol A. ... **Hartford, CT**
Shubitowski, John K. ... Columbus, OH
Shubov, Dimitry ... New York, NY
Shubow, Lawrence D. ... **Boston, MA**
Shubow, Linda C. ... **St. Louis, MO**
Shubow, Morris S. ... Wellesley, MA
Shubrick, Adreme M. ... **New York, NY**
Shubrick, Edmund T. ... St. Petersburg, FL
Shucart, Martin E. ... Encino, CA
Shuchart, James (Jay) A. ... **Denver, CO**
Shuchat, Jeffrey L. ... **New York, NY**
Shuchman, James A. ... **Exeter, NH**
Shuchman & Krause-Elmslie, P.L.L.C.
Exeter, NH
Shuchman, Philip ... Newark, NJ
Shuck, Daniel B. ... **Sioux City, IA**
Shuck, Jeffrey A. ... **Peoria, IL**
Shuck, Jennifer A. ... Odenton, MD
Shuck, John D. ... New York, NY
Shuck, O. James ... Severna Park, MD
Shuck, Thomas E., (P.C.)
Los Angeles, CA
Shucker, Louis M. ... **Reading, PA**
Shuckra, L. Richard ... Peabody, MA
Shuckrow, Alan T. ... **Pittsburgh, PA**
Shucofsky, Joseph F. ... Cleveland, OH
Shucosky, Michael A. ... Wilkes-Barre, PA
Shuda, Scott A. ... Menlo Park, CA
Shudde, Athena ... San Diego, CA
Shudnow, Ronald A. ... Chicago, IL
Shudnow, Ronald A., LTD ... Chicago, IL
Shudofsky, Alisa D. ... **New York, NY**
Shudofsky, Sara ... New York, NY
Shudt, Edwyn L. ... **Troy, NY**
Shudtz, Peter J. ... **Richmond, VA**
Shue, Allison N. ... **Los Angeles, CA**
Shue, Charles Daniel, Jr. ... **Fort Smith, AR**
Shue, Robert B. ... McLean, VA
Shue, Tily ... San Francisco, CA
Shue, William A. ... Alexandria, VA
Shuebruk, Peter ... New York, NY
Shuetts, Howard P. ... Cincinnati, OH
Shuey, Benjamin P. ... Seattle, WA
Shuey, Carolyn A. ... **Bartlesville, OK**
Shuey, David F. ... Department of Justice, Environment and Natural Resources Division, GV
Shuey, David T. ... **Oakland, CA**
Shuey, Eugene E. ... West Palm Beach, FL
Shuey, Eugene E., P.A.
West Palm Beach, FL
Shuey, Gordon A. ... Orlando, FL
Shuey, James F. ... **New Orleans, LA**
Shuey, James F. ... Bairdford, PA
Shuey, John M. ... Shreveport, LA
Shuey, John M., Jr. ... Shreveport, LA
Shuey, Philip J., (P.C.) ... Englewood, CO
Shuey & Smith, L.L.C. ... Shreveport, LA
Shufelt, Gordon H.
Department Of Veterans Affairs, Board of Veterans Appeals, GV
Shufelt, Jennifer L. ... **Dallas, TX**
Shuff, Elizabeth C. ... Richmond, VA
Shuff, Geoffrey S. ... Camp Hill, PA
Shuff, George W., III ... Nashville, TN
Shuff, John D. ... **Costa Mesa, CA**
Shuff, Joseph A., III ... **Santa Ana, CA**
Shuff, Joseph A., III, A Prof. Law Corp., Law Offices of ... **Santa Ana, CA**
Shuff, Robert V. ... Springfield, IL
Shuff, Ronald F. ... Irving, TX
Shuff, Sheldon ... Department of Justice, Environment and Natural Resources Division, GV
Shuff, Steve C. ... Tiffin, OH
Shuffelton, David B., (Co., L.P.A.)
Fort Loramie, OH
Shuffett, James A. ... Lexington, KY
Shuffield, E. Wayne ... **San Antonio, TX**
Shuffield, Milton Gunn ... Beaumont, TX
Shuffield, W. Charles ... **Orlando, FL**
Shuffman, David K. ... New York, NY
Shuffstall, Dearald W. ... **Meadville, PA**
Shuford, A. Burton ... Charlotte, NC
Shuford & Associates ... **Dallas, TX**
Shuford, Best, Cagle, Brondyke, Wolcott & McClellan, P.A. ... **Asheville, NC**
Shuford, Caddell & Fraley ... **Salisbury, NC**
Shuford, Cornelia ... Indio, CA
Shuford, David G. ... **Richmond, VA**
Shuford, David W. ... **Dallas, TX**
Shuford, E. Graydon, Jr. ... Decatur, GA
Shuford, Forrest H., II ... Raleigh, NC
Shuford, Franklin L., Jr. ... Mobile, AL
Shuford, Harry A. ... Dallas, TX
Shuford, Hilary N. ... **Athens, GA**
Shuford, Hunter & Brown, P.A.
Charlotte, NC
Shuford, Jerry ... Indio, CA
Shuford, John F. ... **Asheville, NC**
Shuford, Mark C. ... **Richmond, VA**
Shuford, Meredith Amanda ... Lincolnton, NC
Shuford, Reginald T. ... Raleigh, NC
Shuford, Rubin & Gibney, P.C.
Richmond, VA
Shuford, Thomas M., Jr. ... Lincolnton, NC
Shuford, Wynn M. ... **Birmingham, AL**
Shufrin, Ronald C. ... Stoughton, MA
Shufro, Barbara R. ... **Palo Alto, CA**
Shufro, Gregory D. ... **New York, NY**

Shufro, Melissa ....Worcester, MA
Shufro, Norma Jean ....Southfield, MI
Shuftan, Robert L. ....Chicago, IL
Shuga, Gil ....Chandler, AZ
Shugar, Kamala Hollander ....Eugene, OR
Shugarman, Keith D. ....Washington, DC
Shugart, Amy E. ....San Diego, CA
Shugart, Gerry ....Atlanta, GA
Shugart, Jonathan L. ....Bakersfield, CA
Shuger, Marc S. ....Chicago, IL
Shughart, Dale F. ....Carlisle, PA
Shughart, Dale F., Jr. ....Carlisle, PA
Shughart, David S., III ....Phoenix, AZ
Shughart, Donald L. ....Kansas City, MO
Shughart, John A., Jr. ....Orlando, FL
Shughart Thomson & Kilroy, A Professional Corporation ....Denver, CO
Overland Park, KS
Kansas City, MO
Springfield, MO
Shugrue, Gerald E. ....Whitinsville, MA
Shugrue, John D. ....Chicago, IL
Shugrue & Pendergast ....Whitinsville, MA
Shugrue, Richard E. ....Omaha, NE
Shugrue-Schaffner, Catherine L. ......Omaha, NE
Shuh, Ann M. ....Tampa, FL
Shuh, Clarence J. ....San Jose, CA
Shuham, Martin J. ....Fort Lauderdale, FL
Shukan, David S. ....Los Angeles, CA
Shukas, Socrates N. ....Elmhurst, IL
Shukat Arrow Hafer & Weber L.L.P.
New York, NY
Shukat, Peter S. ....New York, NY
Shuken, Robert S. ....San Francisco, CA
Shuker, R. Scott ....Orlando, FL
Shukoff, Igor ....Rochester, NY
Shukovsky, Neil M. ....Philadelphia, PA
Shukur, Margaret A. ....Waltham, MA
Shula, Robert J. ....Indianapolis, IN
Shulan, Bruce C. ....New York, NY
Shulansky, Ralph M. ....Hartford, CT
Shulaw, Richard A. ....Owosso, MI
Shulaw, Richard A., P.C. ....Owosso, MI
Shulbank, Janet (Jenny) ......Philadelphia, PA
Shulby, Todd W. ....Fort Lauderdale, FL
Shuldberg, Kirt W. ....San Diego, CA
Shuldiner, Albert D. ....Washington, DC
Shuldiner, Alizon J. ....Evanston, IL
Shuldiner, Paul R., Law Offices of
Chicago, IL
Park Ridge, IL
Shuldiner, Paul R., Law Offices of
Park Ridge, IL
Shuldiner, Reed ....Washington, DC
Shulenberger, H. T. ....Miami, FL
Shulenberger, Susan J. ....Seattle, WA
Shuler, Alfred O. ....Apalachicola, FL
Shuler, Ann Adams ....Gainesville, GA
Shuler, Arthur K., Jr. ....Dallas, GA
Shuler, Crista Hogan ....Springfield, MO
Shuler, Franklin G., Jr. ....Columbia, SC
Shuler, Franklin M. ....Sumter, SC
Shuler, G. Phillip, III ....New Orleans, LA
Shuler, Gary R., Jr. ....Cincinnati, OH
Shuler, Gordon P. ....Columbus, OH
Shuler, Griffis Clark ....Taylorsville, NC
Winston-Salem, NC
Shuler, J. Gordon ....Apalachicola, FL
Shuler, Jack H. ....Naples, FL
Shuler, James L. ....Carlsbad, NM
Shuler, James M. ....Tampa, FL
Shuler, James O. ....Omaha, NE
Shuler, Jane Opitz ....Columbia, SC
Shuler, Jay A. ....Apalachicola, FL
Shuler, John F. ....Orangeburg, SC
Shuler, Karen M. ....Omaha, NE
Shuler, Kohath K. ....Mays Landing, NJ
Shuler, Matthew D. ....Cincinnati, OH
Shuler, M. D. ....Kingstree, SC
Shuler, Plank, Morgan & Brahm, A Legal Professional Association .....Columbus, OH
Shuler, Richard D. ....Lansing, MI
Shuler, Robert L. ....Yuba City, CA
Shuler, Samantha A. ....Columbus, OH
Shuler and Shuler ....Apalachicola, FL
Shuler, Stanton E., Jr. ....New Orleans, LA
Shuler, Stephanie D. ....New Orleans, LA
Shuler, Thomas S. ....Sardis, MS
Shulevitz, Deborah G. ....Newark, NJ
Shulevitz, Mel ....Portland, OR
Shuley, Keith A. ....Austin, TX
Shulick, William T. ....Blairsville, PA
Shulkin Hutton, Inc., P.S. ....Seattle, WA
Shulkin, Jerome ....Seattle, WA
Shulkin, Martin B. ....Boston, MA
Shulkin, Robert J. ....Los Angeles, CA
Shulkin, Steffen D. ....Santa Rosa, CA
Shulklapper, Gregg B. ....New York, NY
Shulklapper, Lester M. ....Albany, NY
Shull, Andrew D. ....Oxford, MS
Shull, Anthony B. ....Saugus, MA
Shull & Coyles ....Horseheads, NY
Shull, D. Carlton ....Sioux City, IA
Shull, Darren D. ....West Palm Beach, FL
Shull, Frederick H. ....Connersville, IN
Shull, J. Roger ....Stratford, CT
Shull, James M. ....Gate City, VA
Shull, Joe A. ....Washington, DC
Shull, John ....Springfield, IL
Shull, John R., Jr. ....Wausau, WI
Shull, Joseph W. ....Fort Wayne, IN
Shull, Kelley S. ....Columbia, SC
Shull, Lon H., III ....Mount Pleasant, SC
Shull, Luverne Eugene ....Gooding, ID
Shull, Mark E. ....Toledo, OH
Shull, Norris, Beeman & Schloss
Liberty, MO
Shull, Richard A. ....Wichita, KS
Shull, Robert A. ....Phoenix, AZ
Shull, Stephen ....Boston, MA
Shull, William E. ....Liberty, MO
Shull, William E. ....Houston, TX
Shullaw, Wayne A. ....Lafayette, LA
Shuller, Donald J. ....Cincinnati, OH
Shulman, Adley M. ....Hydesville, CA
Shulman, Alan D. ....Los Angeles, CA
Shulman, Alan L. ....New York, NY
Shulman, Allen L. ....Norcross, GA
Shulman, Alvin D. ....Chicago, IL
Shulman, Amy F. ....New York, NY
Shulman, Ann R. ....San Francisco, CA
Shulman, Arnold ....Decatur, GA
Shulman, Arnold G. ....Dearborn, MI
Shulman, Arthur E. ....Smithtown, NY
Shulman, Arthur Jay ....Livingston, NJ
Shulman, Barry M. ....Syracuse, NY
Shulman, Barry S. ....Lompoc, CA
Shulman, Bennett H. ....Chicago, IL
Shulman, Bernard H. ....Boca Raton, FL
Shulman, Beth ....Washington, DC
Shulman, Bruce N. ....Washington, DC
Shulman & Burns, P.C. ....Southfield, MI
Shulman, C. Daniel ....Syracuse, NY
Shulman, Carren B. ....New York, NY
Shulman, Charles C. ....New York, NY
Shulman, Christopher M. ....Tampa, FL
Shulman, Corinne S., (Mrs.) ......Hydesville, CA
Shulman, Curtin, Grundner, Regan & Snyder, P.C. ....Syracuse, NY
Shulman, Daniel R. ....Minneapolis, MN
Shulman, Daniel S. ....Highland Park, IL
Shulman, David A. ....Rochester, MN
Shulman, David B. ....Northampton, PA
Palmerton, PA
Shulman, David L. ....Minneapolis, MN
Shulman, Dean S. ....New York, NY
Shulman & Dobbs ....Commack, NY
Shulman, Donald L. ....Boston, MA
Shulman, Doreen F. ....Plainsboro, NJ
Shulman, E. Isaac ....New York, NY
Shulman, Edith I. ....Los Angeles, CA
Shulman, Edward Gary ....Paterson, NJ
Shulman, Frederic M. .....Woodcliff Lake, NJ
Shulman, Gary B., Ltd. ....Northbrook, IL
Shulman, George E. ....Deerfield Beach, FL
Shulman, Gerald S. ....Boston, MA
Shulman, Harold ....New York, NY
Shulman, Harry ....San Francisco, CA
Shulman, Harry ....Aspen, CO
Shulman, Howard ....Houston, TX
Shulman, Howard J. ....Bronx, NY
Shulman, Ilana M. ....New York, NY
Shulman, Irwin ....Stamford, CT
Shulman, Jacqueline L. ....Los Angeles, CA
Shulman, Jacqueline Z. ....Philadelphia, PA
Shulman, James D. ....Nashville, TN
Shulman, James H. ....Hartford, CT
Shulman, James (Ike) S. K. ....San Jose, CA
Shulman, Jason M. ....New York, NY
Shulman, Jay A. ....Baltimore, MD
Shulman, Jeffrey B. ....Dayton, OH
Shulman, Jerry L. ....Washington, DC
Shulman, Jessica A. ....Kansas City, MO
Shulman, John C. ....Minneapolis, MN
Shulman, Joseph ....Southfield, MI
Shulman, Joseph, P.C. ....Southfield, MI
Shulman, Judith A. ....Edmonds, WA
Shulman, Karen R. ....Santa Ana, CA
Shulman, Ken W. ....Boston, MA
Shulman, Larry R. ....Detroit, MI
Shulman, Laurence J. ....Secaucus, NJ
Shulman Law Offices ....San Jose, CA
Shulman, Lawrence A. ....Washington, DC
Greenbelt, MD
Rockville, MD
Shulman, Lawrence Bryant ....Detroit, MI
Shulman, Leonard B. ....Farmington Hills, MI
Shulman, Leonard M. ....Irvine, CA
Shulman, Lisa Ruth ....New York, NY
Shulman, Louis T. ....Dayton, OH
Shulman, Madelyn R. Spatt ....Mineola, NY
Shulman, Marc I. ....Southfield, MI
Shulman, Margaret A. R. ....Detroit, MI
Shulman, Martin ....Washington, DC
Shulman, Martin ....Jamaica, NY
Shulman, Max L. ....Brooklyn, NY
Shulman, Max R. ....New York, NY
Shulman & McBride ....Columbus, GA
Shulman, Michael Bradley
Washington, DC
Shulman, Michael C. ....Austin, TX
Shulman, Morton D. ....Averill Park, NY
Shulman, Murray ....West Springfield, MA
Shulman, Paul M. ....Syracuse, NY
Shulman, Regan A. ....New York, NY
Shulman, Richard M. ....Southfield, MI
Shulman, Robert ....Merrick, NY
Shulman, Robert A. ....New York, NY
Shulman, Robert H. ....Washington, DC
Shulman, Robert J. ....Quincy, CA
Shulman, Rogers, Gandal, Pordy & Ecker, P.A. ....Washington, DC
Greenbelt, MD
Rockville, MD
McLean, VA
Shulman, Ron E. ....Palo Alto, CA
Shulman, Ronald ....Andover, MA
Shulman, Roy A. ....Roseland, NJ
Shulman & Shabbick ....Allentown, PA
Northampton, PA
Palmerton, PA
Shulman, Sharon Sendyk
West Hempstead, NY
Shulman, Shulman & Siegel ....Encino, CA
Hydesville, CA
Shulman, Stephanie J. ....Santa Ana, CA
Shulman, Stephen C. ....New York, NY
Shulman, Stephen N. ....Washington, DC
Shulman, Steven ....Commack, NY
Shulman, Steven F. ....Las Vegas, NV
Shulman, Steven H. ....Boca Raton, FL
Shulman, Steven H., P.A. ....Boca Raton, FL
Shulman, Steven R. ....New York, NY
Shulman, Sydney ....Bayonne, NJ
Shulman, Teri L. ....Newburgh, NY
Shulman, Terrence D. ....Ann Arbor, MI
Shulman, Thomas E. ....Las Vegas, NV
Shulman, Walcott & Shulman, P.A.
Minneapolis, MN
Shulman & Wall ....Edgewater, NJ
Shulman, Warren S. ....Columbus, GA
Shulman, William S. ....Mobile, AL
Shulman, William Z. ....Edgewater, NJ
Shulmister, M. Ross ....Pompano Beach, FL
Shulock, Barry J. ....Chicago, IL
Shulock, David J. ....Concord, NH
Lebanon, NH
Shulruff, Joy Pava ....Chicago, IL
Shulruff, Lawrence ....Chicago, IL
Shulruff, Stuart P. ....Chicago, IL
Shulski, Debra A. ....Blue Bell, PA
Shulstad, Mariana R. ....Minneapolis, MN
Shulster, Stanley Anthony ....Ashland, OR
Shulter, Joseph W. ....San Antonio, TX
Shultes, Edwin M., III ....Sun City, CA
Shultie, David R. ....Denton, MD
Shultis, Gary D. ....Milwaukee, WI
Shultis, Russell A. ....Department of Labor, Office of the Solicitor, GV
Shultis, Timothy J. ....Hanover, PA
Shults, Albert J. ....Sacramento, CA
Shults, David A. ....Hornell, NY
Shults, David R. ....Erwin, TN
Shults, Douglas K. ....Erwin, TN
Shults, Eric ....Hornell, NY
Shults, Glen C., Law Offices of
Asheville, NC
Shults, Lois B. ....Erwin, TN
Shults, Pamela ....Wailuku, HI
Shults & Ray, LLP ....Little Rock, AR
Shults, Richard H. ....Pompano Beach, FL
Shults, Richard H., P.A.
Pompano Beach, FL
Shults, Robert ....Little Rock, AR
Shults, Robert A. ....Houston, TX
Shults, Roy L., (A Professional Corporation)
Los Angeles, CA
Shults and Shults ....Hornell, NY
Shults & Shults ....Erwin, TN
Shults, Steven T. ....Little Rock, AR
Shults, Theodore F.
Research Triangle Park, NC
Shults, Thomas D. ....Sarasota, FL
Shults, Victor S. ....Winston, OR
Shults, William O. ....Newport, TN
Shultz, Alan D. ....Wilmette, IL
Shultz & Associates, P.A. ....Dodge City, KS
Shultz, Benjamin M. ....Saginaw, MI
Shultz, Carl R. ....Harrisburg, PA
Shultz, Chad A. ....Atlanta, GA
Shultz, Charles A. ....Los Angeles, CA
Shultz, Craig ....Wichita, KS
Shultz, Dana Howard ....Oakland, CA
Shultz, Donald E. ....Dodge City, KS
Shultz, Donald R. ....Rapid City, SD
Shultz, Doralie J. ....Kew Gardens, NY
Shultz, Edward J. ....Knoxville, TN
Shultz, Erich M. ....Memphis, TN
Shultz, Eugene R. ....Reynoldsburg, OH
Shultz, Frederick W. ....Clayton, MO
Shultz, Gary L. ....Normal, IL
Shultz, Harold M. ....New York, NY
Shultz, Harold M., Jr. ....Laredo, TX
Shultz, Henry H. ....Newton, MA
Shultz, Jack L. ....Lincoln, NE
Shultz, Jack W. ....Dodge City, KS
Shultz, Jacqueline M. ....Dayton, OH
Shultz, James M. ....St. Paul, MN
Shultz, Jay C. ....Rapid City, SD
Shultz, J. G. ....Sioux Falls, SD
Shultz, John C. ....Phoenix, AZ
Shultz, John D. ....Los Angeles, CA
Shultz, John D. ....Dodge City, KS
Shultz, John F. ....Youngstown, OH
Shultz, John R. ....Mount Vernon, WA
Shultz, Joshuah S. ....Lauderhill, FL
Shultz, Joshuah S., P.A. ....Lauderhill, FL
Shultz, Lebert D. ....Kansas City, MO
Shultz, Mack H., Jr. ....Seattle, WA
Shultz, Michael M. ....Kansas City, KS
Shultz & Middlesworth, LLC ....Linwood, NJ
Shultz, Morris ....Bronxville, NY
Shultz, Robert H. ....Walnut, IL
Shultz, Robert H., Jr. ....Edwardsville, IL
Shultz & Rollins, Ltd. ....Phoenix, AZ
Tucson, AZ
Shultz, Silas H. ....Tucson, AZ
Shultz, Steven P. ....Saratoga Springs, NY
Shultz, Thomas M. ....Hanover, PA
Shultz, Timothy A. ....Topeka, KS
Shultz, William B. ....Amarillo, TX
Shultz, William D., Jr. ....Belleville, IL
Shultz, William W. ....Linwood, NJ
Shultz, W. O., II ....Austin, TX
Shumacker, Peter D. ....Santa Rosa Beach, FL
Shumacker, Ralph ....Chattanooga, TN
Shumacker & Thompson, P.C.
Chattanooga, TN
Shumadine, Anne Ballard ....Norfolk, VA
Shumadine, Conrad M. ....Norfolk, VA
Shumake, Darrel G. ....Columbus, KS
Shumake, David S. ....Oklahoma City, OK
Shumake, David Shawn ....Orange, VA
Shumake & Hilbert ....Oklahoma City, OK
Shumake, Jim David, (P.A.) ....Naples, FL
Shumaker, Albert L. ....Centre, AL
Shumaker, Bradley W. ....Houston, TX
Shumaker, Charles M., III
Los Angeles, CA
New York, NY
Shumaker, Chas. S. ....Weatherford, TX
Shumaker, Elisabeth A. ....Denver, CO
Shumaker, Gale C. ....Columbus, OH
Shumaker, Gordon W. ....St. Paul, MN
Shumaker, Gregory M. ....Washington, DC
Shumaker, Gregory S. ....Toledo, OH
Shumaker, H. Dennis ....Marietta, PA
Shumaker, J. Claire ....Olney, IL
Shumaker, James F. ....Athens, OH
Shumaker, Jody L. ....Avon Lake, OH
Shumaker, John G. ....Atlanta, GA
Shumaker, John G., P.C. ....Atlanta, GA
Shumaker, Loop & Kendrick, LLP
Tampa, FL
Charlotte, NC
Columbus, OH
Toledo, OH
Shumaker, M. James, (P.C.) ....Boston, MA
Shumaker, Mary Ann ....Birmingham, MI
Shumaker, Michael R. ....Washington, DC
Shumaker & Rice ....Centre, AL
Shumaker, Rick C. ....Texarkana, TX
Shumaker, Robert E. ....Madison, WI
Shumaker, Roger L. ....Cleveland, OH
Shumaker, Ronald L. ....Bakersfield, CA
Shumaker & Shumaker ....New Castle, PA
Shumaker Sragow & Steckbauer, LLP
Los Angeles, CA
Shumaker, Steven J. ....Minneapolis, MN
Shumaker, Theodore H. ....Milford, CT
Shumaker, Thomas A. ....Akron, OH
Shumaker, Thomas A. ....New Castle, PA
Shumaker, Thomas A. ....Pittsburgh, PA
Shumaker, Thomas C. ....Detroit, MI
Shumaker, Thomas E. ....Centreville, MI
Shumaker, Wilbur A. ....Gurnee, IL
Shumaker, William P. ....Yarmouth, ME
Shumaker Williams, A Professional Corporation ....Towson, MD
Harrisburg, PA
Lancaster, PA
Reading, PA
State College, PA
Shumaker-Holland, Judith B.
Highland Park, MI
Shuman, Abbie A. ....Southfield, MI
Shuman, Alice M. ....Monona, WI
Shuman, Ann K. ....Chicago, IL
Shuman Annand Bailey Wyant & Earles
Charleston, WV
Wheeling, WV
Shuman, Benjamin T. ....Orlando, FL
Shuman, Beth Liss ....Harrisburg, PA
Shuman, Bonnie Levy ....Malvern, PA
Shuman, Carl Harris ....Camp Hill, PA
Shuman, Christopher N. ....Atlanta, GA
Shuman, Clyde Alvin ....New York, NY
Shuman, D. Robert ....Sacramento, CA
Shuman, David L. ....Charleston, WV
Shuman, David E. ....La Jolla, CA
Shuman, Dean ....Dallas, TX
Shuman, Eric A. ....New Orleans, LA
Shuman, Erik P. ....Melbourne, FL
Orlando, FL
Shuman, Glenn A. ....Ocala, FL
Shuman, Harry M. ....Boston, MA
Shuman, Ira H. ....New York, NY
Shuman, Irving M. ....Buffalo, NY
Shuman, Jay Alan ....Yardley, PA
Shuman, Jerome ....Washington, DC
Shuman, John R.
Department of Commerce, GV
Shuman, John R., Jr. ....Palo Alto, CA
Shuman, Joseph D. ....Pittsburgh, PA
Shuman, Kip Brian ....Denver, CO
Shuman, Labron K. ....Narberth, PA
Shuman, Lisa Jane ....Treasury Department, Internal Revenue Service, GV
Shuman, Maria B. ....Boulder, CO
Shuman, Mark D. ....Melbourne, FL
Shuman, Mark P.
Securities and Exchange Commission, Division of Corporation Finance, GV
Shuman, Melvin R. ....Boston, MA
Shuman, Mona S. ....Atlanta, GA
Shuman, Morton J. ....Boston, MA
Shuman, Morton J. ....Framingham, MA
Shuman, P. Dennis ....Pensacola, FL
Shuman, Pamela G. ....Harrisburg, PA
Shuman, Randy M. ....Somerville, MA
Shuman, Robert A. ....Providence, RI
Shuman, Robert C. ....Lawrence, MA
Shuman, Robert D. ....New York, NY
Shuman, Robert Louis ....Morgantown, WV
Shuman, Robert R. ....Bloomfield Hills, MI
Shuman & Ross ....Providence, RI
Shuman, Scott M. ....Atlanta, GA
Shuman, Stanley J. ....Chicago, IL
Shuman, Stanley S. ....New York, NY
Shuman, Stephen K. ....Morgantown, WV
Shuman, Steven C. ....Los Angeles, CA
Shuman-Moore, Elizabeth ....Chicago, IL
Shumannfang, David G. ....Durham, NC
Shumar, Mark C. ....Modesto, CA
Shumar, Peter ....Traverse City, MI
Shumard, Jo A. ....Orlando, FL
Shumard, M. A., Jr. ....Boerne, TX
Shumard, Thomas J. ....Phoenix, AZ
Shumate, Alex ....Columbus, OH
Shumate, Amy M. ....Dothan, AL
Shumate & Bowling ....Knoxville, TN

Shumate, C. Keith ... North Royalton, OH
Shumate, Charles L. ... Reston, VA
Shumate, Cynthia L. ... Seattle, WA
Shumate, David R. ... Greenville, SC
Shumate & Dean, P.C. ... Henderson, TX
Shumate, Donna L. ... Sparta, NC
Shumate, Flaherty & Eubanks ... Berea, KY
Irvine, KY
Lexington, KY
Richmond, KY
Shumate, Gregory S. ... Covington, KY
Shumate, Jack D. ... Birmingham, MI
Shumate, James F., Jr. ... Meridian, MS
Shumate, Joe ... Henderson, TX
Shumate, Joe D. ... Pauls Valley, OK
Shumate, Keith ... Columbus, OH
Shumate, Kimberly Callery ... Columbus, OH
Shumate, Kimberly Winkenhofer
Elizabethtown, KY
Shumate, Kraftson & Sparrow, P.C.
Washington, DC
Fairfax, VA
Reston, VA
Shumate, Mark E. ... Albuquerque, NM
Shumate, Nicole Cober ... Washington, DC
Shumate, Rick F. ... Greensboro, NC
Shumate, Roger E. ... Casper, WY
Shumate, Thomas O. ... Nashville, TN
Shumate, Thomas W., IV ... Nashville, TN
Shumate, W. F., Jr., (P.C.) ... Knoxville, TN
Shumejda, Jeffrey S., Law Offices of
New York, NY
Shumejda, Jeffrey S., Law Offices of
Sleepy Hollow, NY
Shumener, Betty M. ... Los Angeles, CA
Shuminer, Alan J. ... Miami, FL
Shuminer, Alan J., P.A., Law Offices of
Miami, FL
Shumpert, Amy Patterson ... Aiken, SC
Shumpert, Floyd A. ... Terrell, TX
Shumpert, Gregory A. ... Terrell, TX
Shumpert, Krista Lenore ... Jackson, MS
Shumpert Law Offices ... Terrell, TX
Shumpert, Shanon ... Chicago, IL
Shumpert, Suzanne S. ... Terrell, TX
Shumsky, Anthony C. ... Traverse City, MI
Shumsky & Backman ... Portland, OR
Shumsky, Ellen B. ... Los Angeles, CA
Shumsky, George M. ... Portland, OR
Shumsky, Kenneth M. ... Atlantic City, NJ
Shumsky, Sabrina L. ... Westerville, OH
Shumway & Associates, LLC ... Ottawa, KS
Shumway, D. Rex, II ... Tempe, AZ
Shumway, Dale R. ... Mesa, AZ
Shumway, David L. ... Algona, IA
Shumway, Forrest N. ... San Diego, CA
Shumway, G. Charles, II ... Portland, ME
Shumway, G. Lynn ... Scottsdale, AZ
Shumway, Jeff A. ... Scottsdale, AZ
Shumway, Jeffrey L. ... Beverly Hills, CA
Shumway, John B.
Department of Housing and Urban
Development,
Office of General Counsel, GV
Shumway, Noel J. ... Santa Rosa, CA
Shumway, Robert B. ... Worcester, MA
Shumway, Roberta ... Houston, TX
Shumway, S. Brooks ... New York, NY
Shumway, Sharon J. ... Dallas, TX
Shumway & Spencer, LLC ... Fairfield, CT
Shumway, Susan ... Ottawa, KS
Shumway, Susan H. ... Fairfield, CT
Shumway, William C. ... Hendersonville, NC
Shumway, William Steven ... Rocklin, CA
Shunatona, Paul R. ... Dallas, TX
Shunk, John K. ... Denver, CO
Shunk, Michael W. ... Overland Park, KS
Shunk, Thomas H. ... Cleveland, OH
Shunnarah, Nader G. ... Louisville, KY
Shunnarah, Omar A. ... Birmingham, AL
Shunneson, Arnold W. ... Littleton, CO
Shuntich, Louis S. ... Newark, NJ
Shunway, Douglas M. ... Camarillo, CA
Shupack, Bernard M. ... Long Beach, CA
Shupack, Jeffrey S. ... New York, NY
Shupack, Paul M. ... New York, NY
Shupack, Richard A. ... Palo Alto, CA
Shupack, Robert A. ... Miami, FL
Shupack, Stephanie S. ... Livingston, NJ
Shupe, Caryl E. ... Iowa City, IA
Shupe, Cynthia L. ... Phoenix, AZ
Shupe, Deborah R.J. ... Columbia, SC
Shupe, Dwight A. ... Dallas, TX
Shupe and Finkelstein ... San Mateo, CA
Shupe, Gary L. ... Phoenix, AZ
Shupe, Harry G. ... Washington, DC
Shupe, J. Denny ... Philadelphia, PA
Shupe, James Barry ... Northglenn, CO
Shupe, John A. ... San Mateo, CA
Shupe, Larry L. ... Racine, WI
Shupe, Mark W. ... Bethesda, MD
Shupe, Matthew T. ... Burlington, IA
Shupe, Reagan & Wyne ... Santa Ana, CA
Shupe, R. Q., (A Professional Corporation)
Santa Ana, CA
Shupenus, Robert M. ... Decatur, IL
Shupert, Holly D. ... Rockville, MD
Shupik, Rudolph A. ... Bridgeport, CT
Shupik, Rudolph A., Jr. ... Chatham, VA
Shupik, Rudolph A., Jr. ... Danville, VA
Shuping & Morse ... Atlanta, GA
Shuping, S. Andrew, Jr. ... Atlanta, GA
Shupp, Diew M. ... San Antonio, TX
Shupp, Gary L. ... Colorado Springs, CO
Shuquem, Darrien O. ... Phoenix, AZ
Shur, Brett F. ... Atlanta, GA
Shur, Don ... Cologne, NJ
Shur, George M. ... De Kalb, IL
Shur, Henry ... Alexandria, VA
Shur, Irwin M. ... Milwaukee, WI
Shur, Joseph M. ... Rochester, NY
Shur, Luba ... Washington, DC
Shreveport, LA
Shur, Paul H. ... Princeton, NJ
Shurb, Sharon Marie ... San Antonio, TX
Shurberg, Jonathan S. ... Rockville, MD
Shurbet, N. Shannon ... Lima, OH
Shurdut, Jennifer H. ... New York, NY
Shure, Andrew F. ... Boston, MA
Providence, RI
Shure, Deane A. ... Greenbelt, MD
Rockville, MD
Rockville, MD
Tilghman, MD
Shure, H. William ... Bridgeport, CT
New Haven, CT
Shure, Leon R. ... Chicago, IL
Shure, Mark E. ... Chicago, IL
Shure, Marshall R. ... Baltimore, MD
Shure, Perez & O'Connor ... Greenbelt, MD
Rockville, MD
Swanton, MD
Takoma Park, MD
Tilghman, MD
Shure, Ralph George ... Rockville, MD
Shure, Richard D. ... Ellicott City, MD
Shure, Stanley H. ... Los Angeles, CA
Shureb, John M. ... Plymouth, MI
Shureen, D. Douglas ... Santa Rosa, CA
Shurell, Carolyn J. ... Cleveland, OH
Shuren, Allison Weber ... Washington, DC
Shuriah, Nerre ... Fort Lauderdale, FL
Shurin, Leland M. ... Kansas City, MO
Shurkin, Arnold G. ... Passaic, NJ
Shurkin & Fershing, A Professional Corporation
West Orange, NJ
Shurlds, Katherine ... Fayetteville, AR
Shurling, Judy ... Dallas, GA
Shurling, Judy, P.C. ... Dallas, GA
Shurlow, Nancy J. ... Pittsburgh, PA
Shurman, Gregory S. ... Atlanta, GA
Shurman, Steven W. ... Woodlyn, PA
Shurn, Anthony L. ... Treasury Department,
Office of Regulations and Rulings, GV
Shurn, Michael Anthony ... Winamac, IN
Shurn, Peter J., III ... Houston, TX
Shurn, Steven D. ... Houston, TX
Shurpin, Barbara T. ... Boca Raton, FL
Shurr, Barbara K. ... Chicago, IL
Shurr, Charles N., Jr. ... Reading, PA
Shurson-Repya, Debra J. ... St. Paul, MN
Shurte, Matthew R. ... Columbus, OH
Shurtleff, Donald O. ... Lincoln, NE
Shurtleff, Froeschner, Bunn & Aulgur
Columbia, MO
Shurtleff, John H. ... Chicago, IL
Shurtleff, Loramel P. ... Columbia, MO
Shurtleff, Mark W. ... Irvine, CA
Shurtleff, Russell Daniel ... Factoryville, PA
Shurtleff, W. Hunter ... Houston, TX
Shurtliff, M. Karl ... Boise, ID
Shurts, Patricia L. ... Eugene, OR
Shurts, William A. ... Lebanon, NJ
Shurtz, Alfred M. ... Fort Wayne, IN
Shurtz, David F. ... Fort Worth, TX
Shurtz, Michael ... Elko, NV
Shurtz, Nancy E. ... Eugene, OR
Shurtz, Richard F. ... Virginia Beach, VA
Shurtz, Richard J. ... Edmonds, WA
Shurtz, Robert W. ... Marietta, GA
Shurtz, Steven P. ... Chicago, IL
Shushan, Amber B. ... Atlanta, GA
Shushan, Jonathan M. ... New Orleans, LA
Shushan, Sally A. ... New Orleans, LA
Shushan, Sidney L., (P.C.)
New Orleans, LA
Shusky, Carl D. ... Nashville, TN
Shuss, Amy L. ... La Jolla, CA
Shuss, J. Logan ... Parsons, KS
Shust, Robert B. ... Pittsburgh, PA
Shusta, Timothy P. ... Tampa, FL
Shustak, Erwin J. ... San Diego, CA
New York, NY
Shustak Jalil & Heller, A Professional
Corporation ... San Diego, CA
New York, NY
Shusted, John P. ... Moorestown, NJ
Philadelphia, PA
Shusted, Thomas J. ... Westmont, NJ
Shusted, Thomas J., Jr. ... Westmont, NJ
Shuster, Andra J. ... Treasury Department,
Office of the Comptroller of the Currency,
GV
Shuster, Ariella L. ... New York, NY
Shuster, Carl H. ... Avon, CT
Shuster, David A. ... New York, NY
Shuster, David J. ... Baltimore, MD
Shuster, Elisabeth S. ... Harrisburg, PA
Shuster, Elwood H. ... Alliance, OH
Shuster, Frank B. ... Atlanta, GA
Shuster, Gary S. ... Los Angeles, CA
Shuster, George W. ... Cranston, RI
Shuster, Leroy P. ... Greenacres, WA
Shuster, Leroy P., P.S. ... Greenacres, WA
Shuster, Lynn A. ... Hubbard Woods, IL
Shuster, Marci ... New York, NY
Shuster, Melvin R. ... Philadelphia, PA
Shuster, Michael H. ... Atlanta, GA
Shuster, Michael J. ... San Francisco, CA
Shuster, Michael P. ... Cleveland, OH
Shuster, Michael S. ... New York, NY
Shuster, Morris M. ... Haverford, PA
Shuster, Myrna A. ... Toledo, OH
Shuster, Neil H. ... Trenton, NJ
Shuster, Richard H. ... Louisville, KY
Shuster, Richard M. ... Hastings, MI
Shuster, Rickel ... Wellesley, MA
Shuster, Robert A. ... Oyster Bay, NY
Shuster, Robert G. ... Gaithersburg, MD
Shuster, Robert L. ... Harrisburg, PA
Shuster, Rosen & Gallese, A Professional
Association ... Wellesley, MA
Shuster, Scott D. ... Boston, MA
Shuster, Thomas M. ... Woodville, OH
Shuster, Todd H. ... Boston, MA
Shusterman, Carl, Law Offices of
Los Angeles, CA
Shusterman, Murray H. ... Philadelphia, PA
Shusterman, Richard M. (IBA)
Philadelphia, PA
Shusterman, Robert J. ... Philadelphia, PA
Shusterman, Victoria ... Chicago, IL
Shustoff, Mark A. ... San Francisco, CA
Shuta, James M. ... St. Petersburg, FL
Shutack & Lavelle ... Lehighton, PA
Shutan, Peter H. ... Los Angeles, CA
Shutan, Robert H. ... Los Angeles, CA
Shute, Austin F. ... Kansas City, MO
Shute, Brian R. ... Anchorage, AK
Shute, Brian R., A Prof. Corp.
Anchorage, AK
Shute, David ... Chicago, IL
Shute, E. Clement, Jr. ... San Francisco, CA
Shute, Mihaly & Weinberger
San Francisco, CA
Shute, Richard M. ... Mercer Island, WA
Shute, Robert W. ... Holyoke, MA
Shuter, Bruce D. ... Philadelphia, PA
Shuter, Richard K. ... Los Angeles, CA
Shuteran, Sharon Elaine ... Telluride, CO
Shutes, Robert L. ... Edina, MN
Shutkin, John A. ... Norwalk, CT
New York, NY
Shutkin, William Andrew ... Boston, MA
Shutler, K. Eugene ... Las Vegas, NV
Shutler and Low ... Chantilly, VA
Shutler, Norman D., (P.C.) ... Chantilly, VA
Shutler, Sharon K.
Department of Commerce,
National Oceanic and Atmospheric
Administration, GV
Shutran, Richard ... New York, NY
Shutt, Judson H. ... Philadelphia, PA
Shutt, Nekki ... Columbia, SC
Shuttee, Anne ... Plano, TX
Shuttee, David A. ... Dallas, TX
Shutter, Deborah L. ... Fort Morgan, CO
Shutter, Jon D. ... Chicago, IL
Shutter, Steven G. ... Plantation, FL
Shutter, Walter D., Jr. ... Pittsburgh, PA
Shuttera, Robert J. ... Clearwater, FL
Shutterly, Michael T. ... Glen Allen, VA
Shutters, Peter G. ... Ocala, FL
Shutters, Peter G., P.A., Law Offices of
Ocala, FL
Shuttie, Edward A. ... Royal Oak, MI
Shuttlesworth, James S. ... Houston, TX
Shuttlesworth, Perry G., Jr.
Birmingham, AL
Shuttlesworth, Perry G., Jr., P.C.
Birmingham, AL
Shuttleworth & Ingersoll, P.C.
Cedar Rapids, IA
Dubuque, IA
Iowa City, IA
Waterloo, IA
Shuttleworth, James W., III ... Newburgh, NY
Shuttleworth, Keith J. ... Leawood, KS
Kansas City, MO
Shuttleworth, Kenneth R. ... Memphis, TN
Shuttleworth, Ruloff & Giordano, P.C.
Chesapeake, VA
Shuttleworth Ruloff & Giordano, P.C.
Newport News, VA
Virginia Beach, VA
Shuttleworth, Thomas B., II
Virginia Beach, VA
Shuttleworth, Thorpe ... New York, NY
Shuttleworth, William R.
Cedar Rapids, IA
Shuttleworth, Williams, Harper, Waring &
Derrick, P.L.L.C. ... Memphis, TN
Shutts, Anjela A. ... Des Moines, IA
Shutts & Bowen LLP
Fort Lauderdale, FL
Miami, FL
Orlando, FL
Tallahassee, FL
West Palm Beach, FL
Shutts, Eugene C. ... Joliet, IL
Shutts, Kenneth R., II ... Harrisburg, PA
Shutts, Robert D. ... Joliet, IL
Shutts, Shutts and Portlock ... Joliet, IL
Shutty, Angela J. ... Thousand Oaks, CA
Shutzer, Kenneth B. ... Lynn, MA
Shuvalov, Andrew ... Austin, TX
Shuwarger, Jeffrey ... Calabasas, CA
Shuzman, William I. ... Cleveland, OH
Shvartsman, Marina ... Encino, CA
Shvodian, Daniel T. ... Menlo Park, CA
Shwachman, Ben ... Covina, CA
Shwachman, Perry J. ... Chicago, IL
Shwarts, Robert S. ... Menlo Park, CA
Shwartz, Eve Ann ... Hamilton, NY
Shwartz, Mark L. ... New York, NY
Shwartz, Myron ... Columbus, OH
Shwartz, Patty ... Newark, NJ
Shwartz, Robert N. ... New York, NY
Shwayder, Donald P. ... Denver, CO
Shwed, Amy A. ... Scranton, PA
Shwedel, Marvin S. ... Bloomfield Hills, MI
Shweky, Barbara R. ... New York, NY
Shweky, Evan Y. ... Hartford, CT
Shwiff, Marvin G. ... Dallas, TX
Shwiff, Stephen M. ... Dallas, TX
Shwisberg, Eric B. ... San Diego, CA
Shy, David G. ... Fairview Heights, IL
Shy, DeWitt M., Jr. ... Memphis, TN
Shy, James C. ... Houston, TX
Shy, Jennifer A. ... Oakland, CA
Shyavitz, Abby P. ... Boston, MA
Shyavitz, Gerald L. ... Haverhill, MA
Shyavitz, Joel R. ... Lowell, MA
Shyavitz, John P. ... Haverhill, MA
Shyavitz and Shyavitz ... Haverhill, MA
Shyer, Bruce N., Jr. ... San Francisco, CA
Shyer, Herbert M. ... La Mirada, CA
Shyer, John D. ... New York, NY
Shyer, John H. ... Sacramento, CA
Shyer, Lisa ... Los Angeles, CA
Shyllon, Mohamed M. ... Raleigh, NC
Shyllon, Prince E. N. ... Raleigh, NC
Shyllon & Shyllon, P.A. ... Raleigh, NC
Shyloski, Jo Ann M. ... Norwich, CT
Shymanski, Henry J. ... Detroit, MI
Shymansky, Julia Marie ... Monroeville, PA
Shyn, Frank S. ... Beverly Hills, CA
Shyrock, Mickey ... Athens, TX
Shyrock, Mickey, P.C., Law Office of
Athens, TX
Shyshlak, Dean M. ... Portland, OR
Shyshlak, Dean M., P.C. ... Portland, OR
Shytle, B. Eric ... Columbia, SC
Shytles, R. Spencer ... Dallas, TX
Shytles, Robert W. ... Dallas, TX
Shyu, Lee (Limin), P.C.
Farmington Hills, MI
Shyu, Lee (Limin) ... Farmington Hills, MI
Sia, Jeffrey H. K. ... Honolulu, HI
Siaci, Djaouida ... Washington, DC
Siade, Troy S. ... St. Louis, MO
Siahatgar, Bijan R. ... Houston, TX
Siakotos, Ellen C. ... Carmel, IN
Siam, Hab M. ... Chicago, IL
Siam, Rana M. ... Austin, TX
Siamas, Harry A. ... Crawfordsville, IN
Siamas, John S. ... San Francisco, CA
Siamas, William N. ... San Jose, CA
Sian, Paul S. ... West Bloomfield, MI
Siana, Philip J. ... New Brunswick, NJ
Siana, Stephen V. ... Exton, PA
Siana and Vaughan, LLP ... Exton, PA
Philadelphia, PA
Sianni, Ralph N. ... Philadelphia, PA
Siano, Michele ... New York, NY
Siano, Vincent A. ... Elmwood Park, NJ
Siar, David E. ... Clearwater, FL
Sias, Michael E. ... Waupun, WI
Sias & Ranstrom, P.C. ... Chinook, MT
Sias, William C. ... Los Angeles, CA
Siavelis, Michael P. ... Chicago, IL
Sibal, Abner W. ... Alexandria, VA
Sibarium, Michael L. ... Washington, DC
Sibary, Scott ... Chico, CA
Sibay, Hala M. ... McLean, VA
Sibbernsen, E. Terry ... Omaha, NE
Sibbernsen, E. Terry, P.C. ... Omaha, NE
Sibbernsen, Richard D. ... Evanston, IL
Sibbett, Benjamin K. ... New York, NY
Sibbing, Henry ... Lake Geneva, WI
Sibbison, John H., III
Rolling Hills Estates, CA
Sibbison, John H., III, Professional Law
Corporation ... Rolling Hills Estates, CA
Sibbison, Wendy ... Greenfield, MA
Sibbitt, Jason Ty ... Indianapolis, IN
Sibble, Edward Matson, Jr., (P.C.)
Boston, MA
Sibbring, Donald A. ... Columbus, OH
Sibears, Daniel M. ... Washington, DC
Sibek, David P. ... Huntington, NY
Sibel, Steven J. ... Baltimore, MD
Sibell, Stanley J. ... Manhasset, NY
Siben, Andrew B. ... Bay Shore, NY
Siben & Ferber ... Hauppauge, NY
Siben, Gary L. ... Hauppauge, NY
Siben, Jacqueline ... Bay Shore, NY
Siben & Siben, LLP ... Bay Shore, NY
Central Islip, NY
Hauppauge, NY
Riverhead, NY
Siben, Sidney R. ... Bay Shore, NY
Siben, Stephen G. ... Bay Shore, NY
Siben, Walter ... Bay Shore, NY
Sibener, Paul S. ... Commack, NY
Siber, Victor ... New York, NY
Siberine, Raymond R. ... Roseland, NJ
Siberio, Ignacio ... Miami, FL
Siberon, Alfred ... Ponce, PR
Sibert, Charles F. ... Rochester, MI
Sibert, Charles M. ... Rochester, MI
Sibert & Sibert ... Rochester, MI
Sibert, Susan H. ... Cedar Rapids, IA
Sibert, Thomas J. ... Ebensburg, PA
Sibila, Jorge A. ... Miami, FL
Sibila, Regla M. ... Miami, FL
Sibilia, Robert ... Calabasas, CA
Sibilla, Guy A. ... Honolulu, HI
Sibilla & Wildman ... Honolulu, HI
Sibille, Christine M.
Securities and Exchange Commission,
Division of Market Regulation, GV
Sibiski, Kendel L. ... Annapolis, MD
Sibley, Daniel C. ... Dallas, TX
Sibley, David A. ... Corpus Christi, TX
Sibley, David M. ... Waco, TX
Sibley, Elizabeth K. ... Santa Monica, CA
Sibley, G. Waide ... Claremore, OK
Sibley, Gary D. ... Key West, FL
Sibley, Gary Warren ... Dallas, TX
Sibley, George R. ... Gloucester, MA
Sibley, Horace H. ... Atlanta, GA

Sibley, Jack N. ... **Atlanta, GA**
Sibley, James M. ... Atlanta, GA
Sibley, John A., III ... Atlanta, GA
Sibley, John J. ... Danbury, CT
Sibley, John W. ... Farmington Hills, MI
Sibley, Kathleen Quick ... **Beaumont, TX**
Sibley, Kenneth D. ... **Raleigh, NC**
Sibley, Kimberly Norris ... **Florence, AL**
Sibley, Mara J. ... **New York, NY**
Sibley, Margaret Hamlett ... Tulsa, OK
Sibley, Michele E. ... **Chicago, IL**
Sibley, Montgomery Blair ... **Miami, FL**
Sibley, Peter E. ... **San Francisco, CA**
Sibley, Phillip A. ... **Macon, GA**
Sibley, Quintus W. ... Milledgeville, GA
Sibley, Russell A. ... Rochester, NY
Sibley, Russell A., Jr. ... Tampa, FL
Sibley, Sam B., Jr. ... Augusta, GA
Sibley, Steven ... Montgomery, AL
Sibley, Steven Jude ... San Jose, CA
Sibley, Tarrant L. ... **Boston, MA**
Sibley, Thomas J. ... **Beaumont, TX**
Sibley, Thomas J., P.C. ... **Beaumont, TX**
Sibley & Voegtle, L.L.P. ... Dallas, TX
Sibley, W. Hugh ... Greensburg, LA
Sibner, Steven J. ... **Boca Raton, FL**
Sibold, James Scott ... Dunwoody, GA
Sibonga, Randi Maya ... Seattle, WA
Siboni, Michael C. ... **Ocala, FL**
Sibrava, John C. ... Chicago, IL
Sibrea, John E. ... Towson, MD
Sibrey, James W. ... Gainesville, FL
Sibum, Jennifer H. ... **Stroudsburg, PA**
Sica, Alfred F. ... New York, NY
Sica, Alfred F., P.C. ... New York, NY
Sica, Anthony ... **Roseland, NJ**
Sica, John ... Frederick, MD
Sica, Paul J. ... New Brunswick, NJ
Sica, Pauline E. ... Union City, NJ
Sica, Richard V. ... **Pittsburgh, PA**
Sica, Thomas A. ... **Albany, NY**
Sica, Vincent A. ... **Arcadia, FL**
Punta Gorda, FL
Sica, Vincent A., P.A. ... **Arcadia, FL**
Punta Gorda, FL
Sica, William J. ... New York, NY
Sicalides, Barbara T. ... **Philadelphia, PA**
Sicard, Kathleen A. ... Washington, DC
Sicard, Paula Marie ... Tampa, FL
Sicarelli, Darryl D., P.C. ... Metairie, LA
Sicari, Vincenzo A. ... Upper Saddle River, NJ
Siccardi, A. Joseph ... Golden, CO
Siceloff, Wendy E. ... Houston, TX
Sice-Sweger, Chantal M. ... Tucson, AZ
Sichel, Jonathan R. ... Los Angeles, CA
Sichel, Lucien J. ... Washington, DC
Sichel, Robert L. ... **Philadelphia, PA**
Sicheneder, Steven A. ... Forest Lake, MN
Sichenze, Andrew L. ... Brooklyn, NY
Sichenzia, Dominic J. ... Carle Place, NY
Sichenzia, Gregory ... **New York, NY**
Sichenzia, Ross & Friedman, LLP
New York, NY
Sicheri, Adolph P. ... Manahawkin, NJ
Sicherman, Marvin A. ... **Cleveland, OH**
Sichko, Francis C. ... Washington, PA
Sichko, Samuel C. ... **Boston, MA**
Sichko, William J., Jr. ... Overland Park, KS
Sichol, Brian A. ... **Suffern, NY**
Sichol, Douglas W. ... **Providence, RI**
Sichol & Hicks, P.C. ... **New City, NY**
Suffern, NY
Sichol, William R., Jr. ... **Suffern, NY**
Sichon, Dustin D. ... **Irvine, CA**
Sicilia, Anthony A. ... Carlsbad, CA
Sicilian, James ... **Hartford, CT**
Sicilian, John J. ... Miami, FL
Sicilian, Shirley Klenda ... Lawrence, KS
Siciliano, Alan R. ... **Lanham, MD**
Siciliano, Anthony ... **Youngstown, OH**
Siciliano, Anthony J. ... Springfield, MA
Siciliano, Anthony J., P.C., Law Offices of
Springfield, MA
Siciliano, Bradley A. ... Wayne, NJ
Siciliano, Carol Ann
Environmental Protection Agency,
Office of the General Counsel, GV
Siciliano, Dennis J. ... **Cleveland, OH**
Siciliano, Ellis, Dyer & Boccarosse
Fairfax, VA
Siciliano, Erin M. ... **Philadelphia, PA**
Siciliano, Gerard M. ... **Chattanooga, TN**
Siciliano, James M. ... Long Branch, NJ
Siciliano, Jill ... Los Angeles, CA
Siciliano, John A. ... **Vienna, VA**
Siciliano, John J. ... **Toledo, OH**
Siciliano, Joseph A. ... Stratford, CT
Siciliano, Joseph A. ... **Farmington Hills, MI**
Siciliano, Loretta ... **Los Angeles, CA**
Siciliano, Ralph A. ... **New York, NY**
Siciliano, Robert J. ... **Washington, DC**
Siciliano, Salvatore J. ... Voorhees, NJ
Siciliano, Stacey J. ... **Saddle Brook, NJ**
Siciliano, Stephen L.
Board of Governors Of The Federal Reserve
System,
Office of the General Counsel, GV
Siciliano, Thomas V. ... **Boca Raton, FL**
Siciliano, Thomas V., P.A.
Boca Raton, FL
Sick, Jonathan R. ... **Chicago, IL**
Sickal, James D. ... **Osage Beach, MO**
Sickal, James D. ... **Waynesville, MO**
Sickel, Avrom David ... Washington, DC
Sickel, Stephen V. ... Olathe, KS
Sickelco, Elizabeth A. ... Springfield, MA
Sickels, Charles W. ... **Reston, VA**
Sickels, Peter D. ... **Monroe, MI**
Sickels, Robert B. ... **Southfield, MI**
Sickels, Robert W. ... San Diego, CA
Sickenberger, Glenn E. ... **Philadelphia, PA**
Sickendick, Keith W. ... Kansas City, KS
Sickert, Dugal S. ... **North Chicago, IL**
Sicking, Albert G., Jr. ... Covington, OH
Sicking, Christoph Oliver ... **New York, NY**
Sicking, Richard A. ... **Coral Gables, FL**
Sicking, Richard A., P.A.
Coral Gables, FL
Miami, FL
Sickinger, Frank A. ... Basking Ridge, NJ
Sickinger, Gina ... **New York, NY**
Sickinger, Peter X. ... New York, NY
Sickinger, Robert J. ... **Bridgeport, CT**
Sickinger, William M. ... Ontario, CA
Temecula, CA
Sickinger, Wm. A. ... Metairie, LA
Sickle, David B. ... **Chicago, IL**
Sickle, Steven D. ... Woodland Hills, CA
Sickler, Christine Hayes ... San Diego, CA
Sickler, Jason A. ... Dallas, TX
Sickler, Jennifer S. ... **Houston, TX**
Sickler, Randall N. ... **Dickinson, ND**
Sickler, Sandra D. ... San Diego, CA
Sickles, Barry M. ... Coral Springs, FL
Sickles, Blaine T. ... Dublin, OH
Sickles, Kay E. ... **Philadelphia, PA**
Sickles, Louis, II ... **Philadelphia, PA**
Sickles, Mark H. ... **Austin, TX**
Sickles, Michael W. ... Troy, MI
Sickles, Robert E. ... Canton, OH
Sickles, W. Mark ... **Chicago, IL**
Wheaton, IL
Sickmen, Ronald M. ... Centereach, NY
Sicks, Philip E. ... Brooklyn, NY
Siclare, Clemente A. ... Staten Island, NY
Siclari, Victor R. ... Pittsburgh, PA
Sicner, John C. ... Atlanta, GA
Sico, Ann M. ... **Metairie, LA**
Sico, Craig M. ... **Corpus Christi, TX**
Sico, Jerome A. ... **Fort Myers, FL**
Sico, Thomas ... Columbus, OH
Sicola, Donna L. ... Bloomfield, NJ
Sicola, Michael A. ... **Livingston, NJ**
Sicola, Wendy H. ... Houston, TX
Sicoli, Robert D. ... Minneapolis, MN
Siconolfi, Rocco J. ... **New York, NY**
Sicora, Jerome J. ... St. Paul, MN
Sicula, Howard S. ... **Milwaukee, WI**
Sicula, Michelle ... Oakland, CA
Sicula, Paul E. ... Milwaukee, WI
Siculan, Nick ... Columbus, OH
Sicular, David R. ... **New York, NY**
Sicuro, Robert A. ... Columbus, OH
Sicuro, Thomas J. ... Ravenna, OH
Sicuso, Salvatore J. ... **Coral Gables, FL**
Siczewicz, Ann M. ... **Hartford, CT**
Sida, Arturo ... Orange, CA
Sidak, Donald C. ... Alexandria, LA
Sidak, Melinda Ledden ... Potomac, MD
Sidamon-Eristoff, Andrew ... New York, NY
Sidamon-Eristoff, Constantine
New York, NY
Sidamon-Eristoff, Simon ... Washington, DC
Sidari, Anthony P. ... Hazleton, PA
Sidaway, Katherine E. ... **Miami, FL**
Sidd, Diane ... Boston, MA
Sidd, Susan E. ... New York, NY
Siddall, Cynthia ... El Monte, CA
Siddall, David L. ... **Houston, TX**
Siddall, David R. ... **Washington, DC**
Siddall, James L. ... Naperville, IL
Siddall, Michael R. ... **Springfield, MA**
Siddall, Michael S. ... **Appleton, WI**
Sidd-Champion, Diane ... San Francisco, CA
Siddeek, John ... **Grand Junction, CO**
Siddens, Edward H. ... **Dayton, OH**
Siddens Law Office ... **Des Moines, IA**
Siddens, Robert N. ... **Des Moines, IA**
Siddiq, Nizam M. ... **New York, NY**
Siddiqi, Humma S. ... **Bloomfield Hills, MI**
Siddiqi, Numan J. ... **Newport Beach, CA**
Siddiqi, Salman Ahmad ... Richardson, TX
Siddique, Osama ... **New York, NY**
Siddiqui, Clark H. ... Acton, MA
Siddiqui, Faisal Bin ... Columbia, MD
Siddiqui, Maqsood H. ... Garden City, NY
Siddiqui, Muddassir Husain
Washington, DC
Siddiqui, Shahram M. ... **Philadelphia, PA**
Siddiqui, Waajid ... White Plains, NY
Siddons, Charles L. ... **Greenwich, CT**
Siddons, David W. ... Columbia, SC
Siddons, Pamela ... Danville, IN
Siddons, Scott V. ... **Dallas, TX**
Siddoway, Douglas J. ... **Spokane, WA**
Siddoway, Laurel H. ... **Spokane, WA**
Siddoway, R. Bryant ... **Houston, TX**
Sidebottom, W. Jeffrey ... **Lancaster, PA**
Sidel, Douglas J. ... Clayton, MO
Sidel, Kevin ... Kiowa, CO
Sidel, Mark ... New York, NY
Sidel, Paul R. ... Needham, MA
Sidel, Peter S. ... Barre, VT
Waitsfield, VT
Sidel & Pikulski ... Barre, VT
Waitsfield, VT
Sidel, Steven C. ... Bethesda, MD
Sidel, Susan P. ... New York, NY
Sidell, Arthur L., III ... Xenia, OH
Sidell, Barbara C. ... Newton, MA
Sidell, Gary M. ... Washington, DC
Sidell, John B. ... **San Diego, CA**
Sidell, Moss M. ... Boston, MA
Sidell, Robert B. ... **Las Vegas, NV**
Sidell, Scott D. ... Natick, MA
Sidelle, Ronald A. ... New York, NY
Sideman, Anat ... Los Angeles, CA
Sideman & Bancroft LLP
San Francisco, CA
Sideman, Joel ... Evanston, IL
Sideman, Mark J. ... San Antonio, TX
Sideman, Mark J., Inc. ... San Antonio, TX
Sideman, Michael S. ... San Diego, CA
Sideman, Richard J. ... **San Francisco, CA**
Sidener, Don H. ... College Park, GA
Sidener, Steven O. ... **San Francisco, CA**
Sider, Donald C. ... **Boca Raton, FL**
Sider, Donald C., & Assocaites, P.A.
Boca Raton, FL
Sider, Gail R. ... New York, NY
Sider, William E. ... **Detroit, MI**
Sideras, Leah D. ... **Portland, OR**
Sideras, Nancy ... Scappoose, OR
Sideris, James J. ... Pensacola, FL
Sideris, John J. ... Ashburn, VA
Sideris, Nicole J.
Department Of Veterans Affairs,
Office of the General Counsel, GV
Siderits, Matthew C. ... **Milwaukee, WI**
Siderius, Frank R. ... **Seattle, WA**
Siderius, Jeffrey A. ... **Chicago, IL**
Siderius, Linda L. ... **Denver, CO**
Siderius Lonergan ... **Seattle, WA**
Siderius, Michael E. ... **Seattle, WA**
Siderius, Raymond H. ... **Seattle, WA**
Siderius, Robert R., Jr. ... **Wenatchee, WA**
Siderman, Lori ... **Los Angeles, CA**
Siderman, Sergio Jose ... Los Angeles, CA
Siders, Barry L. ... Danville, CA
Siders, Wilbur L. ... Peru, IN
Sides, Clay R. ... Fallbrook, CA
Sides, Desmond ... **Poteau, OK**
Sides, Donald J. ... Decatur, AL
Sides, Jack D., Jr. ... **Dallas, TX**
Sides, Jimmie L. ... Jackson, CA
Sides, J. M. ... **Anniston, AL**
Sides, Oglesby, Held & Dick
Anniston, AL
Sides, R. Marie ... Harrison, MI
Sides, Terry A. ... **Montgomery, AL**
Sidikman, David S. ... Westbury, NY
Sidikman & Hoffmann ... Westbury, NY
Sidirourgos, John A. ... Coral Springs, FL
Sidkoff, Pincus & Green, P.C.
Philadelphia, PA
Sidle, A. Michael ... **Timonium, MD**
Sidle, Barton J. ... Towson, MD
Sidle, Daryl J. ... **Baltimore, MD**
Sidle, Kenneth I. ... **Los Angeles, CA**
Sidles, Sheila D. ... Centerville, IA
Sidley & Austin ... Los Angeles, CA
Washington, DC
Chicago, IL
New York, NY
Dallas, TX
Sidley & Bell LLP ... **Los Angeles, CA**
Sidley, Janna Beth ... Department of Justice,
Office of Justice Programs, GV
Sidley, Michael I. ... **Los Angeles, CA**
Sidley, Milton ... Los Angeles, CA
Sidley, Terrence A. ... Alexandria, VA
Sidlosca, Randall L. ... Miami, FL
Sidman, Andrew W. ... **New York, NY**
Sidman, Arnold B. ... **Atlanta, GA**
Sidman, Bernard ... Encino, CA
Sidman, Eric L. ... **Atlanta, GA**
Sidman, Helen Reeder ... Boston, MA
Sidman, James S. ... **Largo, FL**
Sidman, John R. ... Portland, OR
Sidman, Lawrence R. ... **Washington, DC**
Sidman, Mark H. ... **Washington, DC**
Sidman, Robert J. ... **Columbus, OH**
Sidman, Steven S. ... **Atlanta, GA**
Sidman, Thomas J. ... McLean, VA
Sidner, Mark C. ... Westerville, OH
Sidner, Svoboda, Schilke, Thomsen, Holtorf, Boggy & Nick ... **Fremont, NE**
Sidney, Arthur Dennis
Department of Commerce,
Office of the General Counsel, GV
Sidney, Ethel B. ... **New York, NY**
Sidney, Ross H. ... **Des Moines, IA**
Sidney, Sherwin ... Rego Park, NY
Sidney, Steven L. ... **Albertson, NY**
Sidney, Steven L., A Prof. Corp., The Law Firm of ... Woodbury, NY
Sido, Kevin R. ... **Chicago, IL**
Sido, Mary O'Neil ... Winnetka, IL
Sido, Nancy L. ... Clayton, MO
Sidor, David S. ... **Columbus, OH**
Sidor, Karl V. ... Roswell, GA
Sidorov, Jack D. ... Department of Justice,
Antitrust Division, GV
Sidorsky, Emily ... New York, NY
Sidorsky, Robert ... **New York, NY**
Sidoti, Christopher A. ... King Of Prussia, PA
Sidoti, Frank V. ... Rochester, NY
Sidoti, Joseph R. ... Rochester, NY
Sidoti, Mark S. ... **Newark, NJ**
Sidran, David R. ... **Walnut Creek, CA**
Sidran, Mark H. ... Seattle, WA
Sidrane, Steven Donald ... Brooklyn, NY
Sidweber, Robert W. ... Fort Lauderdale, FL
Sidweber, Robert W., P.A.
Fort Lauderdale, FL
Sidwell & Barrett ... Franklin, TN
Sidwell, Benj. C. ... Tampa, FL
Sidwell, James ... Albuquerque, NM
Sidwell, K. Thomas ... Franklin, TN
Sidwell, King E. ... **Sikeston, MO**
Sidwell Law Offices ... Kearney, NE
Sidwell, Robert C. ... Ashland, OH
Sidwell, Scott E. ... Kearney, NE
Sidwell, Susan V. ... **Nashville, TN**
Sieb, Douglas M. ... **Sarasota, FL**
Sieb, Douglas M., P.A. ... **Sarasota, FL**
Siebe, James E. ... Moscow, ID
Siebel, G. Edmund, Jr. ... Newport Beach, CA
Siebel, Matthew A. ... **Newark, NJ**
Siebel, Richard A., (P.C.) ... Chicago, IL
Siebel, Schofield & Varde ... Chicago, IL
Siebels, Leonard A. ... St. Louis, MO
Sieben, Grose, Von Holtum & Carey, Ltd.
Duluth, MN
Fairfax, MN
Lakeville, MN
Minneapolis, MN
St. Paul, MN
Sieben, Harry A., Jr. ... **Minneapolis, MN**
Sieben, John P. ... **Hastings, MN**
Sieben, Michael R. ... **Hastings, MN**
Sieben, Paul L. ... **Palo Alto, CA**
Sieben, Polk, LaVerdiere, Jones & Hawn, A Professional Association ... **Hastings, MN**
St. Paul, MN
Sieben, William R. ... **Minneapolis, MN**
Siebeneicher, S. Aaron ... **Alexandria, LA**
Siebenhaar, Michael K. ... **Chicago, IL**
Siebenmann, John F. ... Cedar Rapids, IA
Siebenschuh, Ellen ... **Cleveland, OH**
Sieber, Fred B. ... Redington Shores, FL
Sieber, Paul W. ... Hackensack, NJ
Siebers, Jack A. ... Grand Rapids, MI
Siebers, Jonathan J. ... **Grand Rapids, MI**
Siebers Mohney Associates, P.L.C.
Grand Rapids, MI
Siebers, Paulette L. ... **Madison, WI**
Siebers, Spencer ... **Salt Lake City, UT**
Siebers, Steven E. ... **Quincy, IL**
Siebers, William L. ... Chicago, IL
Sieberson, Stephen C. ... **Seattle, WA**
Siebert, Annette G. ... **Kansas City, MO**
Siebert, Caryn B. ... **Chicago, IL**
Siebert, Charles G. ... Ballwin, MO
Siebert, Dan E. ... **Louisville, KY**
Siebert, Edward W. ... Ballwin, MO
Siebert, Francis J. ... Scott City, MO
Siebert, J. Suzanne ... **San Francisco, CA**
Siebert, James C. ... Des Plaines, IL
Siebert, Jeanne M. ... **Pleasantville, NY**
Siebert & Johnson PLLC ... **Louisville, KY**
Siebert, Judson K. ... **Rye, NY**
White Plains, NY
Siebert, Kevin C. ... **Lincoln, NE**
Siebert, Kevin Christopher
San Diego, CA
Washington, DC
Siebert, Lawrence A. ... Stamford, CT
Siebert, Mark D. ... **Chicago, IL**
Siebert, Michael ... Eastland, TX
Siebert, Richard J. ... Chicago, IL
Siebert, Sherill ... **Detroit, MI**
Siebert, Steven G. ... **San Francisco, CA**
Siebert, Susan E. ... **Boston, MA**
Siebert, Thomas L. ... **Washington, DC**
Siebert, Werner ... Livonia, MI
Siebert, William A. ... Gladwin, MI
Siebert, William Newell ... Chicago, IL
Siebert, W.V. Bernie ... **Denver, CO**
Sieberth, John F., & Associates
Baton Rouge, LA
Siebigteroth, Sean M. ... **Grand Blanc, MI**
Siebman, Clyde M. ... **Plano, TX**
Sherman, TX
Siebman, Reynolds & Burg, LLP
McKinney, TX
Plano, TX
Sherman, TX
Siebold, Dennis J. ... Wilmington, DE
Siebold, Guy L. ... Alexandria, VA
Siebold & Hammelrath Co., L.P.A.
Cincinnati, OH
Siebold, Jack H. ... Lansing, MI
Siebrands, Doug ... **Thermopolis, WY**
Siebrecht, Stacie ... Boston, MA
Sieburg, Jeffrey J. ... Chicago, IL
Sieburth, Kathryn Lutomski
New York, NY
Sieck, A. Gerard ... **Deerfield, IL**
Sieck, Charles L. ... **Boca Raton, FL**
Sieck, John ... New York, NY
Sieck, Katherine ... **Newport Beach, CA**
Sieckmann, Gordon F. ... **St. Louis, MO**
Sieczkowski, Keith B. ... **Corpus Christi, TX**
Siedel, George J. ... Ann Arbor, MI
Sieder, Warren S. ... Calabasas, CA
Siedlarz, Joseph B., III ... **Media, PA**
Siedlecki, Andrew F. ... Waverly, NY
Siedlecki, Charles, & Associates, P.C.
Chicago, IL
Siedlecki, Charles T. ... Chicago, IL
Siedlecki, Dean A. ... Lutherville, MD
Siedlecki, Nancy T. ... Downers Grove, IL
Siedlecki, Robert, Jr. ... **Hartford, CT**
Siedlik, Mark S. ... Kansas City, MO
Siedman, Jack ... Bolinas, CA
Siedor, Greig R. ... Oak Brook, IL
Siedorf, Myron ... Los Angeles, CA
Siedow, Thomas A. ... Eau Claire, WI
Siedschlaw, Kurt D. ... Kearney, NE
Siedzikowski, Henry F. ... **Blue Bell, PA**
Harrisburg, PA
Reading, PA
Siefer, Daniel R. ... Detroit, MI
Siefer, Miriam L. ... Detroit, MI
Siefer, Patricia B. ... **Boston, MA**
Siefert, Jerry R. ... San Diego, CA
Siefert, John ... Milwaukee, WI
Siefert, Richard C. ... **Seattle, WA**
Siefert, Sharon A. ... **Los Angeles, CA**
Siefert, Steven W. ... San Diego, CA
Siefert-Sharp, Martha ... **Los Angeles, CA**

Sieff, Harmon .... **Santa Monica, CA**
Sieff, Harmon, A Law Corporation
Santa Monica, CA
Sieff, Laurie J. .... **Minneapolis, MN**
Sieff, Philip .... **Minneapolis, MN**
Siefferman, Floyd E., Jr.
Minneapolis, MN
Sieffert, Marion P. .... **Greenville, SC**
Siefken, Kevin H. .... **Albert Lea, MN**
Siefken, Mark H. .... **Austin, TX**
Siefkin, Robert M. .... Tucson, AZ
Siefkin, Susan D. .... Modesto, CA
Siefman, Jay N. .... **Farmington Hills, MI**
Sieg, Peter K. .... Gainesville, FL
Siegal, Arthur H. .... **Detroit, MI**
Siegal, Barry P. .... Chicago, IL
Siegal, Barry P., Ltd. .... Chicago, IL
Siegal, Bernice Daun .... Bellerose, NY
Siegal, Bradley G. .... **Birmingham, AL**
Siegal, Brian .... **Dallas, TX**
Siegal, Bruce Benjamin .... Atlanta, GA
Siegal, Byron J. .... Portsmouth, NH
Siegal, Charles D. .... **Los Angeles, CA**
Siegal, David M. .... Sarasota, FL
Albany, NY
Siegal, David M. .... New York, NY
Siegal, F. Don .... **Birmingham, AL**
Siegal, Floyd J. .... **Encino, CA**
Siegal, Helen L. .... **New York, NY**
Siegal, Howard D. .... Foxboro, MA
Siegal, Jacob J. .... Haverford, PA
Siegal, James G. .... New York, NY
Siegal, Joel D. .... **Englewood, NJ**
Newark, NJ
Siegal, Joel H., & Associates .... La Jolla, CA
San Francisco, CA
Siegal, Joel H., & Associates
Los Angeles, CA
San Diego, CA
Siegal, John .... **New York, NY**
Siegal, Jonathan .... **New York, NY**
Siegal Law Offices, LLC .... Sarasota, FL
Albany, NY
Siegal, Leonard J. .... Mountain View, CA
Siegal, Matthew W. .... **New York, NY**
Siegal, Richard A. .... Rolling Hills, CA
Siegal, Richard A. .... **New Haven, CT**
Stamford, CT
Siegal, Ronny Jo Greenwald
Englewood, NJ
Newark, NJ
Siegal, Susan L. .... Department of Justice, Criminal Division, GV
Siegal, Tod E.
Environmental Protection Agency, Office of the General Counsel, GV
Siegal, Warren B. .... Phoenix, AZ
Siegal, Yonina Z. .... **Hackensack, NJ**
New York, NY
Siegal, Zola .... Los Angeles, CA
Siegan, Bernard H. .... La Jolla, CA
Siegan, Jerold N. .... **Chicago, IL**
Siegan, Jerome A. .... **Chicago, IL**
Siegan, Kenneth R. .... Chicago, IL
Siegan, Renée S. .... **Detroit, MI**
St. Clair Shores, MI
Siegan, Robert J. .... Agoura Hills, CA
Siegan & Weisman, Ltd. .... Chicago, IL
Siegars, Jane C Koenitzer
Feeding Hills, MA
Siegars, Mark W. .... **Pittsfield, MA**
Siegeist, Susan M. .... **San Francisco, CA**
Siegel, Abe .... **New York, NY**
Siegel, Abraham .... Pacific Palisades, CA
Siegel, Adam B. .... New York, NY
Siegel, Adolph H. .... Lindenhurst, NY
Siegel, Alan .... **New York, NY**
Siegel, Alan B. .... Watchung, NJ
Siegel, Alan E. .... San Antonio, TX
Siegel, Alan H. .... **New York, NY**
Siegel, Alan M. .... New York, NY
Siegel, Albert .... Chicago, IL
Siegel, Alexander M. .... Fort Lauderdale, FL
Siegel, Alexandra L. .... **Dallas, TX**
Siegel, Alfred R. .... Bronx, NY
Siegel, Alison R. .... **Sacramento, CA**
Siegel, Allan M. .... **Washington, DC**
Falls Church, VA
Siegel, Allen G. .... **Washington, DC**
Siegel, Amy Beth .... Burlington, VT
Siegel, Andrew .... **New York, NY**
Siegel, Andrew .... Warwick, NY
Siegel, Andrew B. .... New York, NY
Siegel, Andrew J. .... Chicago, IL
Siegel, Andrew J. .... **Northampton, MA**
Siegel, Andrew J. .... Roseland, NJ
Siegel, Andrew J. .... **New York, NY**
Siegel, Andrew L. .... Fort Lauderdale, FL
Siegel, Andrew L. .... White Plains, NY
Siegel, Andrew L. .... **Dallas, TX**
Siegel, Andrew L., P.A. .... Fort Lauderdale, FL
Siegel, Andrew R. .... Jamestown, NY
Siegel, Andrew W. .... New York, NY
Siegel, Angela, The Law Office of
Garden City, NY
Siegel, Angela, The Law Office of
Mineola, NY
Siegel, Anita Joy .... **Morristown, NJ**
Siegel, Ann B. .... New York, NY
Siegel, Arleen L. .... **Memphis, TN**
Siegel, Arne .... Englewood, NJ
Siegel, Arnold G. .... **Chicago, IL**
Siegel, Arnon D. .... Washington, DC
Siegel, Arthur B. .... **Milford, PA**
Siegel, Arthur J. .... **Albany, NY**
Siegel, Arthur R. .... San Francisco, CA
Siegel, Barbara L. .... Cambridge, MA

Siegel, Barnett & Schutz, L.L.P.
Aberdeen, SD
Sioux Falls, SD
Siegel, Barris .... Beaver, PA
Siegel, Barry D. .... Boca Raton, FL
Siegel, Barry I. .... Parsippany, NJ
Siegel, Barry J. .... **Philadelphia, PA**
Siegel Bellovin & Karnas, P.C. .... Tucson, AZ
Siegel, Benjamin L. .... **Florham Park, NJ**
Siegel, Bernard F. .... **Miami, FL**
Siegel, Bernard L. .... **Philadelphia, PA**
Siegel, Bertram .... Teaneck, NJ
Siegel & Bonds .... **Charleston, SC**
Walterboro, SC
Siegel, Boris .... Encinitas, CA
Siegel, Bradd N. .... **Columbus, OH**
Siegel, Brain P. .... Baltimore, MD
Siegel, Brent G. .... **Gainesville, FL**
Siegel, Brent G., P.A. .... **Bronson, FL**
Gainesville, FL
Siegel, Brent M. .... Gurnee, IL
Siegel, Brian .... **Los Angeles, CA**
Siegel, Brian P. .... Department of Education, Office of the General Counsel, GV
Siegel, Brill, Greupner, Duffy & Foster, P.A.
Minneapolis, MN
Siegel, Bruce G. .... Birmingham, MI
Siegel, Byron E. .... San Francisco, CA
Southfield, MI
Siegel, Byron E., P.C. .... San Francisco, CA
Southfield, MI
Siegel, Carl E. .... **Boca Raton, FL**
Siegel, Carl M. .... Farmington Hills, MI
Siegel Carter & Dassow, LLP
Indianapolis, IN
Siegel, Cary M. .... New York, NY
Siegel, Catherine H. .... New Orleans, LA
Siegel, Chalif & Winn, P.C.
New York, NY
Siegel, Charles .... **New York, NY**
Siegel, Charles A. .... New Canaan, CT
Siegel, Charles H. .... Atlanta, GA
Siegel, Charles J. .... **Baltimore, MD**
Siegel, Charles John .... Bronx, NY
Siegel, Charles S., Law Offices of
Dallas, TX
Siegel, Cheryl .... **Parsippany, NJ**
Siegel, Christine H. .... Los Angeles, CA
Siegel, Christopher J .... **Cincinnati, OH**
Siegel, Clark B. .... **Los Angeles, CA**
Siegel, Claudine F. .... Westport, CT
Siegel, Cordell .... **St. Louis, MO**
Siegel, Dan .... Oakland, CA
Siegel, Dan K. .... **Menlo Park, CA**
Siegel, Daniel Isaiah .... Harrisburg, PA
Siegel, Daniel J. .... Marlton, NJ
Philadelphia, PA
Siegel, Daniel L. .... Sacramento, CA
Siegel, Daniel M. .... **Richmond, VA**
Siegel, Daniel R. .... Portola Valley, CA
Siegel, David .... **Los Angeles, CA**
Siegel, David A. .... **Columbus, GA**
Siegel, David A. .... Memphis, TN
Siegel, David Alan .... **Amherst, NY**
Buffalo, NY
Siegel, David B. .... **Washington, DC**
Siegel, David B. .... **Columbia, MD**
Siegel, David C., Law Offices of
San Diego, CA
Siegel, David D. .... Albany, NY
Siegel, David H. .... **Hartford, CT**
Siegel, David J. .... **Chicago, IL**
Siegel, David J. .... Patchogue, NY
Siegel, David L. .... St. Paul, MN
Siegel, David M. .... Allston, MA
Siegel, David M. .... Roslyn Harbor, NY
Siegel, David M. .... Nashville, TN
Siegel, David Marc .... Boston, MA
Siegel, David P. .... **Pittsburgh, PA**
Siegel, David T. .... Phoenix, AZ
Siegel, David W., (P.C.) .... **Atlanta, GA**
Siegel, Deanna L. .... Schenectady, NY
Siegel, Deborah E. .... Washington, DC
Siegel, Deborah E. .... Philadelphia, PA
Siegel, Deborah S. .... Marina Del Rey, CA
Siegel, Debra L. .... Kew Gardens, NY
Siegel, Dee Miller .... Encino, CA
Siegel, Donald H., P.C. .... **Boston, MA**
Siegel, Donald J. .... Boston, MA
Siegel, Donald R. .... Great Neck, NY
Siegel, Douglas H. .... **Grand Rapids, MI**
Siegel, Edmond B. .... Santa Monica, CA
Siegel, Edward .... Jacksonville, FL
Siegel, Edward F. .... Cleveland, OH
Siegel, Edward F., Co, L.P.A.
Cleveland, OH
Siegel, Edward M. .... New York, NY
Siegel, Edward R. .... **New York, NY**
Siegel, Edwin B. .... Woodland Hills, CA
Siegel, Elaine K. B. .... Chicago, IL
Siegel, Ellen Kersch .... **St. Louis, MO**
Siegel, Eric H. .... Flourtown, PA
Siegel, Eric L. .... Washington, DC
Siegel, Eric Stephen .... Laurel, MD
Siegel, Ethan D. .... **New York, NY**
Siegel, Eugene M. .... Hawaiian Gardens, CA
Siegel Fenchel & Peddy, P.C.
Garden City, NY
Mineola, NY
Siegel & Fotheringill L.L.C. .... Towson, MD
Siegel, Franklin .... New York, NY
Siegel, Franklin J. .... Miami, FL
Siegel, Franklin J., P.A. .... Miami, FL
Siegel, Fred .... Cleveland, OH
Siegel, Fred, Co., L.P.A. .... Cleveland, OH
Siegel, Frederic J. .... **New York, NY**
Siegel, G. Roger .... El Segundo, CA
Siegel, Gail .... **New York, NY**

Siegel, Gary .... Washington, DC
Rockville, MD
Siegel, Gary .... Coconut Creek, FL
Siegel, Gary M. .... **St. Louis, MO**
Siegel, Gary R. .... Miami, FL
Siegel, Gary R., P.A. .... Miami, FL
Siegel, George E. .... New York, NY
Siegel, Georgette J. .... Roseland, NJ
Siegel, Gerald D. .... Plainsboro, NJ
Siegel, Gerald M. .... Culver City, CA
Siegel, Gerald P. .... Silver Spring, MD
Siegel, Gerald W. .... United States Senate, Committee Legal Personnel, GV
Siegel, Gil Todd .... Beverly Hills, CA
Siegel, Gil Todd, A Professional Corporation
Beverly Hills, CA
Siegel, Gillian F. .... Chicago, IL
Siegel, Glenn E. .... **New York, NY**
Siegel, Glenn N. .... Port Charlotte, FL
Siegel, Greenfield, Hayes & Gross, P.L.C.
Detroit, MI
Southfield, MI
Siegel, Gregg B. .... Walnut Creek, CA
Siegel, Gregory B. .... Perrysburg, OH
Siegel, H. Warren .... Santa Ana, CA
Siegel, Harold A., Jr. .... Pottstown, PA
Siegel, Harold Aryai .... Greenbelt, MD
Siegel, Harold B.
Department Of Health And Human Services, Social Security Administration, GV
Siegel, Harold J. .... **Staten Island, NY**
Siegel, Harvey J. .... Baltimore, MD
Siegel, Herbert M. .... Buffalo, NY
Siegel, Hester, Saunders, Kahler & Manion
Rome, NY
Utica, NY
Waterville, NY
Siegel, Howard .... Teaneck, NJ
Siegel, Howard .... **New York, NY**
Siegel, Howard F. .... New York, NY
Siegel, Howard J. .... **Chicago, IL**
Siegel, Howard J. .... New York, NY
Siegel, Howard L. .... **Hartford, CT**
Siegel, Howard L. .... Rockville, MD
Siegel, Howard M. .... Kings Point, NY
Siegel, Hudson, Gee & Youngsma, LLP
Hastings, MI
Siegel & Hyatt, LLC .... Baltimore, MD
Siegel, Ira M., Law Offices of
Beverly Hills, CA
Siegel, Irvin .... Philadelphia, PA
Siegel, Irwin .... New York, NY
Siegel, Jack M. .... **Chicago, IL**
Siegel, Jack M. .... **New York, NY**
Siegel, James E. .... **New York, NY**
Siegel, James H. .... **San Diego, CA**
Siegel, James R.
Department Of Veterans Affairs, Board of Veterans Appeals, GV
Siegel, Jamie L. .... Tacoma, WA
Siegel, Jane L. .... **New York, NY**
Siegel, Jane M. .... Grand Rapids, MI
Siegel, Janet L. .... New York, NY
Siegel, Jay A. .... Los Angeles, CA
Siegel, Jay Alan .... New York, NY
Siegel, Jay M. .... Department of Justice, Civil Division, GV
Siegel, Jay M. .... Highland, NY
Siegel, Jay S. .... **Hartford, CT**
Siegel, Jeanne F. .... **New York, NY**
Siegel, Jeffrey A. .... **Albany, NY**
Siegel, Jeffrey A. .... Kew Gardens, NY
Siegel, Jeffrey M. .... **Hartford, CT**
Siegel, Jeffrey M. .... Lawrenceville, NJ
Siegel, Jeffrey N. .... **New York, NY**
Siegel, Jeffrey P. .... Los Angeles, CA
Siegel, Jeremy Scott .... San Antonio, TX
Siegel, Jerome A. .... New York, NY
Siegel, Jerome R. .... Tamarac, FL
Siegel, Jerrad S. .... New York, NY
Siegel, Jessica S. .... **Houston, TX**
Siegel, Jill Ann .... Bronx, NY
Siegel, Jodie M. .... **Miami, FL**
Siegel, Joel A. .... New York, NY
Siegel, Joel D. .... **Los Angeles, CA**
Siegel, Joel D. .... **Roseland, NJ**
Siegel, Joel E. .... **Chicago, IL**
Siegel, Joel H. .... Marietta, GA
Siegel, Joel S. .... **Chicago, IL**
Siegel, John J. .... Stamford, CT
Siegel, John M. .... Cleveland, OH
Siegel, Jonathan A. .... **Los Angeles, CA**
Siegel, Jonathan A. .... **New York, NY**
Siegel, Jonathan H. .... Oakland, CA
Siegel, Jonathan P. .... Monterey, CA
Siegel, Joseph A. .... New York, NY
Siegel, Joseph A. .... Toledo, OH
Siegel, Joseph W. .... Garden City, NY
Siegel, Joshua David .... Larchmont, NY
Siegel, Judith L. .... **New York, NY**
Siegel, Judith V. .... Durham, NC
Siegel, Julian L. .... Boston, MA
Siegel, Julie E. .... **New York, NY**
Siegel, Julie L. .... **St. Louis, MO**
Siegel, Julie T. .... Santa Barbara, CA
Siegel, Karen K.
Administrative Office Of The United States Courts, GV
Siegel, Karina .... **New York, NY**
Siegel, Kelleher, & Kahn .... Buffalo, NY
Siegel, Kenneth B. .... **Denver, CO**
Siegel, Kenneth E. .... **Alexandria, VA**
Siegel, Kenneth I. .... Brooklyn, NY
Siegel, Kenneth M. .... **Palo Alto, CA**
Siegel, Kenneth N. .... Elizabeth, NJ
Siegel, Kenneth S. .... Westport, CT
Siegel, Kenneth S. .... Tampa, FL
Siegel, Kenneth S., P.A. .... Tampa, FL

Siegel, Kent S. .... Farmington Hills, MI
Siegel, Kevin M. .... **Philadelphia, PA**
Siegel, Kirk G .... South Paris, ME
Siegel, Lalenya W. .... **New York, NY**
Siegel, Larry .... San Diego, CA
Siegel, Larry A. .... Buffalo Grove, IL
Siegel, Larry B. .... Walla Walla, WA
Siegel, Laura J. .... **New York, NY**
Siegel, Laurel H. .... **Boston, MA**
Siegel, Lauri Sussman .... Jenkintown, PA
Siegel, Lawrence R. .... **Virginia Beach, VA**
Siegel, Lee .... **New York, NY**
Siegel, Lee S. .... **Uniondale, NY**
Siegel, Leo B. .... San Ramon, CA
Siegel, Leonard .... **Beverly Hills, CA**
Siegel, Lesley Ann .... Pleasant Hill, CA
Siegel, Lewis W. .... **New York, NY**
Siegel & LeWitter .... Oakland, CA
Siegel, Linda Soreff .... Glencoe, IL
Siegel, Lipman, Dunay & Shepard, LLP
Boca Raton, FL
Siegel, Lisa B. .... **Boca Raton, FL**
Siegel, Lisa F. .... **New York, NY**
Siegel, Lisette .... Princeton, NJ
Siegel, Loren B. .... Oakbrook Terrace, IL
Siegel, Louis A. .... San Juan, PR
Siegel, Louis H., Law Offices of
Buffalo, NY
Siegel, Lowell R. .... Albany, NY
Siegel, Lynn .... **San Diego, CA**
Siegel, Lynn & Capitel, Ltd.
Bannockburn, IL
Siegel, Lynne F. .... Tigard, OR
Siegel, M. Drew .... Carrollton, TX
Siegel, Malinda S. .... Towson, MD
Siegel, Mara Jan .... Phoenix, AZ
Siegel, Marc J. .... **Chicago, IL**
Siegel, Marilyn C. .... Baltimore, MD
Siegel, Marilyn E. .... Alamo, CA
Siegel, Mark .... Phoenix, AZ
Siegel, Mark .... Knoxville, TN
Siegel, Mark I. .... Detroit, MI
Siegel, Mark Ira .... Sheridan, OR
Siegel, Mark Jordan .... Dallas, TX
Siegel, Mark S. .... San Diego, CA
Siegel, Marlena Lilian .... Philadelphia, PA
Siegel, Marshall E. .... Atlanta, GA
Siegel, Martha P. .... **San Francisco, CA**
Siegel, Martha S. .... Iowa City, IA
Siegel, Martin J. .... New York, NY
Siegel, Martin L. .... **Wilmington, DE**
Siegel, Martin S. .... **New York, NY**
Siegel, Martin W. .... Studio City, CA
Siegel, Marvin H. .... Miami, FL
Siegel, Marvin H. .... Boston, MA
Siegel, Marvin S. .... **Menlo Park, CA**
Siegel, Matthew J. .... **Philadelphia, PA**
Siegel, Max L. .... Indianapolis, IN
Siegel, Melvin .... Uniondale, NY
Siegel, Melvin N. .... Baltimore, MD
Siegel, Michael A. .... Seattle, WA
Siegel, Michael D. .... **St. Petersburg, FL**
Siegel, Michael E. .... Shaker Heights, OH
Siegel, Michael J. .... Naples, FL
Siegel, Michael L. .... **Chicago, IL**
Siegel, Michael S.
Department Of Veterans Affairs, Board of Veterans Appeals, GV
Siegel, Michael S. .... **New York, NY**
Siegel, Michael Simon .... Washington, PA
Siegel, Miles .... Boston, MA
Siegel, Moreno & Kramer .... San Diego, CA
Santa Ana, CA
Siegel, Morris J. .... Wantagh, NY
Siegel, Morton .... **Chicago, IL**
Siegel, Morton J. .... Hauppauge, NY
Siegel, Moses, Schoenstadt & Webster, P.C.
Chicago, IL
Siegel, Myron E. .... Bannockburn, IL
Siegel, Myron M. .... Kenmore, NY
Siegel, Nancy E. .... **Washington, DC**
Siegel, Nancy L. .... **Westmont, NJ**
Siegel, Nathan E. .... Baltimore, MD
Siegel, Ned L. .... Old Bridge, NJ
Siegel, Neil B. .... **Washington, DC**
Siegel, Neil F. .... **Pittsburgh, PA**
Siegel, Neil Y. .... **New York, NY**
Siegel & Nichols .... Long Beach, CA
Siegel, Norman E. .... **Kansas City, MO**
Siegel, Norman I. .... Rome, NY
Utica, NY
Siegel, O'Connor, Schiff & Zangari, P.C.
Hartford, CT
New Haven, CT
Siegel, P. Fred .... New Orleans, LA
Siegel, P. Joy .... Garrett Park, MD
Siegel, Paul .... Miami, FL
Siegel, Paul B. .... **Houston, TX**
Siegel, Paul J. .... **Woodbury, NY**
Siegel, Paul N. .... **Walterboro, SC**
Siegel, Peter M. .... Miami, FL
Siegel, Peter R. .... **Hollywood, FL**
Siegel, Philip H. .... Evansville, IN
Siegel, Philip J. .... **Atlanta, GA**
Siegel, Phyllis A. .... Los Angeles, CA
Siegel, Phyllis B. .... San Antonio, TX
Siegel, Phyllis Hochberg .... Los Angeles, CA
Siegel, Rhonda Z. .... **New York, NY**
Siegel, Richard .... **Minneapolis, MN**
Siegel, Richard A.
National Labor Relations Board, Office of the General Counsel, GV
Siegel, Richard A. .... Mineola, NY
Siegel, Richard D. .... **Washington, DC**
Siegel, Richard D. .... **Cincinnati, OH**
Siegel, Richard H. .... Denver, CO
Siegel, Richard H. .... **Atlanta, GA**
Siegel, Richard H. .... New York, NY

Siegel, Richard H. ... Cleveland, OH
Siegel, Richard H., Co., L.P.A. ... Cleveland, OH
Siegel, Richard M. ... New York, NY
Siegel, Richard S. ... Purchase, NY
Siegel, Rita G. ... Albuquerque, NM
Siegel, Rita G., A Professional Corporation ... Albuquerque, NM
Siegel, Robert ... Sun City West, AZ
Siegel, Robert A. ... Los Angeles, CA
Siegel, Robert Alan ... Jackson Heights, NY
Siegel, Robert G. ... Hartford, CT
Siegel, Robert H. ... East Hampton, NY
Siegel, Robert H. ... Cincinnati, OH
Siegel, Robert I. ... New Orleans, LA
Siegel, Robert I. ... Newark, NJ
Siegel, Robert J. ... Seattle, WA
Siegel, Robert K. ... Troy, MI
Siegel, Robert M. ... Miami, FL
Siegel, Robert P. ... Hawthorne, NY
Siegel, Robert P. ... New York, NY
Siegel, Robert W. ... Southfield, MI
Siegel, Roberta A. ... Portland, OR
Siegel, Robin J. ... Baltimore, MD
Siegel, Roger E. ... Brooklyn, NY
Siegel, Roger J. ... Farmington Hills, MI
Siegel, Ronald A. ... Washington, DC
Siegel, Ronald D. ... Tucson, AZ
Siegel, Ronald E. ... Chicago, IL
Siegel, Ronald H. ... West Orange, NJ
Siegel, Ronald L. ... Boca Raton, FL
Siegel, Ronald L., P.A. ... Boca Raton, FL
Siegel, Ronald O. ... Dallas, TX
Siegel, Ronald S. ... Birmingham, MI
Siegel, Ronald S., P.C. ... Birmingham, MI
Siegel, Ruth V. ... Albuquerque, NM
Siegel, Samuel ... Long Beach, CA
Siegel & Sanders, P.C. ... Portland, OR
Siegel, Sanford H. ... Albuquerque, NM
Siegel, Sanford J. ... East Northport, NY
Siegel, Sarah A. ... Chesterfield, MO
Siegel & Schiffman ... Garden City, NY
Siegel, Scott Howard ... Burbank, CA
Siegel, Seth M. ... New York, NY
Siegel Sevastianos, LLP ... St. Louis, MO
Siegel, Seymour E. ... Plainsboro, NJ
Siegel, Shana ... Lake Success, NY
Siegel, Shane C. ... Princeton, NJ
Siegel, Shari ... New York, NY
Siegel, Sharon ... Slingerlands, NY
Siegel, Sharon P. ... Worcester, MA
Siegel, Sharon R. ... Potomac, MD
Siegel, Sheldon M. ... San Francisco, CA
Siegel, Shelley ... West Orange, NJ
Siegel, Sherman H. ... Washington, PA
Siegel, Shirley Adelson ... New York, NY
Siegel & Siegel ... Farmington Hills, MI
Siegel & Siegel, P.C. ... Plainsboro, NJ
Siegel, Sindy Jill ... San Francisco, CA
Siegel, Sol ... Portland, OR
Siegel, Spencer Bryant ... Fort Lauderdale, FL
Siegel, Stacy LeBow ... Baltimore, MD
Towson, MD
Siegel, Stacy LeBow, L.L.C.
Baltimore, MD
Towson, MD
Siegel, Stanley ... New York, NY
Siegel, Stanley E., Jr. ... Minneapolis, MN
Siegel, Stanley H. ... Lewistown, PA
Siegel, Stanley L. ... New York, NY
Siegel, Stanley O. ... Key West, FL
Siegel, Stephan ... Freehold, NJ
Siegel, Stephan J. ... Forest Hills, NY
Siegel, Stephanie ... Washington, DC
Siegel, Stephen F. ... Lakeland, FL
Siegel, Stephen H. ... Miami, FL
Siegel, Stephen J. ... Chicago, IL
Siegel, Stephen S. ... Santa Cruz, CA
Siegel, Stephen S. ... Miami Lakes, FL
Siegel, Steve N. ... Cincinnati, OH
Siegel, Steven A. ... Dallas, TX
Siegel, Steven C. ... Boston, MA
Siegel, Steven E. ... Kew Gardens, NY
Siegel, Steven E., P.C. ... Kew Gardens, NY
Siegel, Steven F. ... New York, NY
Siegel, Steven M. ... San Diego, CA
Santa Ana, CA
Siegel, Steven M. ... Chicago, IL
Siegel, Steven Nathan ... Kew Gardens, NY
Siegel, Steven S. ... Denver, CO
Siegel, Steven S. ... Garden City, NY
Siegel & Sugar, P.A. ... Baltimore, MD
Owings Mills, MD
Siegel, Terri I. ... Los Angeles, CA
Siegel, Thomas L. ... Dallas, TX
Siegel, Timothy E. ... Portland, OR
Siegel, Todd H. ... New York, NY
Siegel, Todd M. ... Hillsboro, MO
Siegel, Tom M. ... Los Angeles, CA
Siegel, Tristan B.L. ... Washington, DC
Siegel, Trudy S. ... Fullerton, CA
Siegel, Valerie L. ... Greenbelt, MD
Siegel, Walter ... Melville, NY
Siegel, Warren Lewis ... Pleasant Hill, CA
Siegel, William C. ... River Ridge, LA
Siegel, William D. ... St. Paul, MN
Siegel, William D. ... Garden City, NY
Siegel, William L. ... Dallas, TX
Siegel, William M. ... Los Altos Hills, CA
Siegel, William W. ... New York, NY
Siegel, Yanai Zvi ... East Brunswick, NJ
Siegel, Zee ... Oakland, CA
Siegelaub, Steven M. ... Westport, CT
Siegelbaum, Heidi Ann ... Seattle, WA
Siegelbaum, Joseph R. ... Roseland, NJ
New York, NY
Siegel-Baum, Judith Ellen ... New York, NY
Siegelbaum, Sheri K. ... Secaucus, NJ
Siegelbaum, Stanley J. ... New York, NY
Siegell, Barbara C. ... Wilmington, DE
Siegelman, Burt A. ... Manhattan Beach, CA
Siegelman, Don ... Montgomery, AL
Siegelman, Harold L. ... Office of Personnel Management, GV
Siegelman, Jerry ... New York, NY
Siegelman, Rachael B. ... Atlanta, GA
Siegel, M.D., Julius ... Boston, MA
Siegeltuch, Andrew ... Westmont, NJ
Philadelphia, PA
Siegeltuch, Ronald A. ... New Orleans, LA
Siegeltuch, Ronald A., A Prof. Law Corp. ... New Orleans, LA
Siegendorf, Arden M. ... Tallahassee, FL
Siegenthaler, Craig P. ... Louisville, KY
Siegenthaler, John H. ... Mansfield, OH
Sieger, Charles E., Jr. ... Allentown, PA
Sieger, Christine M. ... Atlanta, GA
Sieger, Donald F. ... La Crosse, WI
Sieger, Edward D. ... Department of Labor, Office of the Solicitor, GV
Sieger, Hal E. ... Westbury, NY
Sieger, John A. ... Houston, TX
Sieger, John P. ... Chicago, IL
Sieger, Mary A. ... Jacksonville, FL
Sieger, Michelle L. ... Wheaton, IL
Sieger, Stuart M. ... Mineola, NY
Siegert, Edmund J. ... Chicago, IL
Siegert, Larry R. ... Plymouth, WI
Siegert, Laurel A. ... Amarillo, TX
Dallas, TX
Siegert, Michael T. ... Pittsburgh, PA
Siegert, Paul W. ... New York, NY
Siegert, William E. ... Stockton, CA
Siegesmund, Jean D. ... Cincinnati, OH
Siegesmund, John C., III ... Denver, CO
Siegesmund, Kristin A. ... Minneapolis, MN
Siegesmund, Rudolf O. ... Dallas, TX
Siegfeld, David E. ... Albany, NY
Siegfried, Arthur P. ... Red Bank, NJ
Siegfried, Daniel L. ... Cedar Rapids, IA
Siegfried, Elayne M. ... Norwalk, OH
Siegfried, Frederick M. ... St. Louis, MO
Siegfried, Heidi J. ... Oswego, NY
Siegfried, Jonathan D. ... New York, NY
Siegfried, Kurt S. ... Akron, OH
Siegfried, Mary F. ... San Francisco, CA
Siegfried, Mary K. ... Washington, DC
Siegfried, Paul D. ... New York, NY
Siegfried, Peter C. ... Purchase, NY
Siegfried, Rivera, Lerner De La Torre & Sobel, P.A. ... Coral Gables, FL
Fort Lauderdale, FL
Siegfried, Rivera, Lerner, De La Torre & Sobel, P.A. ... Miami, FL
Siegfried, Robert A. ... Albany, NY
Siegfried, Ruth L. ... Rockford, IL
Siegfried, Stephen D. ... Hampton Bays, NY
Siegfried, Stephen D., P.C. ... Hampton Bays, NY
Siegfried, Steven M. ... Miami, FL
Siegfried, Timothy J. ... Allentown, PA
Siegfried, Warren L. ... Pittsburgh, PA
Siegfried, Willis A. ... Pittsburgh, PA
Sieghardt, George A. ... Staten Island, NY
Sieglaff, Peter M. ... Boca Grande, FL
Siegle, Christopher P. ... Phoenix, AZ
Siegle, Eric W. ... New York, NY
Siegle, John G. ... Media, PA
Siegle, Liza Maurer ... Fort Lauderdale, FL
Siegle, Mary E. ... Fort Lauderdale, FL
Siegle & Sims P.C. ... New York, NY
Siegler, Adam ... Los Angeles, CA
Siegler, Douglas L. ... Washington, DC
Siegler, Edward J. ... Los Angeles, CA
Siegler, Ellen ... Washington, DC
Siegler, Ira S. ... Washington, DC
Siegler, John T. ... Washington, DC
Siegler, Lora C. ... Rochester, NY
Siegler, Richard ... New York, NY
Siegler, Steven ... Hackensack, NJ
Siegler, Sylvan ... Kansas City, MO
Siegler-Miller, Sara J. ... Portland, OR
Siegling, H. Carter ... Cayce, SC
Sieglitz, Frank E. ... Sacramento, CA
Siegman, Adam P. ... San Francisco, CA
Siegman, Hugh M. ... Santa Monica, CA
Siegman, Jerome ... Phoenix, AZ
Siegman, Robert M. ... Milwaukee, WI
Siegmund, Dirk W. ... Greensboro, NC
Siegmund, Frederick ... New York, NY
Siegmund, Joanne H. ... New York, NY
Siegmyer, Gerald S. ... Houston, TX
Siegner, A. Wes, Jr. ... Washington, DC
Siegner, Jodi ... Los Angeles, CA
Siegrist, Camden P. ... Charleston, WV
Siegrist, Christopher B. ... Houma, LA
Siegrist, Christopher B., A Law Corporation ... Houma, LA
Siegrist, David J. ... Britt, IA
Siegrist, Deborah A. ... Mount Holly, NJ
Siegrist, Edgar C. ... Clarksburg, WV
Siegrist, Harry E., III ... Austell, GA
Siegrist, Koller, Brightbill & Long ... Lebanon, PA
Siegrist, Robert E. ... Lebanon, PA
Siegrist, Stephen E. ... Haddonfield, NJ
Siegrist & White, PLLC ... Clarksburg, WV
Sieh, Frank O. ... Ventura, CA
Sieh, Gregory M. ... Cedar Rapids, IA
Sieh, Nancy M. ... Santa Barbara, CA
Sieh, Robert G. ... Seattle, WA
Siehl, David H. ... Federal Communications Commission, Wireless Telecommunications Bureau, GV
Siehl, Gregory L. ... San Jose, CA
Siehl, Jeffrey D. ... Cincinnati, OH
Siehl, Richard W. ... Columbus, OH
Siehndel, Ray D. ... Topeka, KS
Sieira-Alvarez, Esther M. ... New Brunswick, NJ
Sieja, Michael F. ... Phoenix, AZ
Sieke, Eric T. ... Los Angeles, CA
Sieke, Mark R., (P.C.) ... Los Angeles, CA
Sieker, Marie A. ... Madison, WI
Sieker & Matthews ... Madison, WI
Siekerka, Michele N. ... Trenton, NJ
Siekert, Friedrich A. P. ... Minneapolis, MN
Siekert, Linda M. ... Plano, TX
Siekman, Lane A. ... Rising Sun, IN
Siekman, Michael T. ... Washington, DC
Siekman, Thomas C. ... Houston, TX
Siel, Lon E. ... Concord, NH
Sielaff, Dale L. ... Peoria, IL
Sielaff, Jennifer L. ... Milwaukee, WI
Sielaty, Robert M. ... Arlington, VA
Sieleman, Jay ... Panama Canal Commission, Office of the General Counsel, GV
Sieler, Jean Ann S. ... Adrian, MI
Toledo, OH
Sieler, Lincoln D. ... Seattle, WA
Sieloff, James P. ... San Antonio, TX
Sieloff, Lori A. ... Taylor, MI
Sieloff, Paul ... Northport, NY
Sielski, Cynthia A. ... Little Valley, NY
Sielski, Philip R. ... Grand Haven, MI
Sieman, Barbara A. ... Libertyville, IL
Sieman, Harold ... Cleveland, OH
Sieman, Michael M. ... Libertyville, IL
Sieman, Nathan L. ... Warren, OH
Sieman & Sieman ... Libertyville, IL
Siemann, Catherine A. ... New York, NY
Siemann, Gregory J. ... Carroll, IA
Siembab, Peter ... Los Angeles, CA
Siembieda, Matthew J. ... Philadelphia, PA
Siemel, Sasha ... Albuquerque, NM
Siemen, Christopher W. ... Cleveland, OH
Siemens, James Burt ... Owego, NY
Siemens, John E., Jr. ... Ponte Vedra Beach, FL
Siemens, Kenneth E. ... St. Joseph, MO
Siemens, Mark A. ... New York, NY
Siemens, Reynold L. ... Los Angeles, CA
Siemens, Steven M. ... Los Angeles, CA
Siemer, Calvin ... Palo Alto, CA
Siemer, Deanne C. ... Saipan, TT
Siemer, Joseph E. ... St. Louis, MO
Siemer, Lawrence J. ... Jacksonville, FL
Siemer, Leighton & Love ... Columbus, OH
Siemer, Martin W. ... Effingham, IL
Siemer, Michael D. ... Houston, TX
Siemer, Q. Anthony ... Effingham, IL
Siemer, Richard C. ... Teutopolis, IL
Siemer, Robert E. ... Long Beach, CA
Siemer, Walter J. ... Columbus, OH
Siemering, Jack L. ... Bothell, WA
Siemers, John C. ... Anchorage, AK
Siemien, John M. ... Potomac, MD
Siemien, Mary P. ... Nuclear Regulatory Commission, Office of the General Counsel, GV
Siemietkowski, Missy Kelly ... Evans, GA
Charlottesville, VA
Sieminski, John ... Pittsburgh, PA
Sieminski, John D. ... Wilkes-Barre, PA
Sieminski, Marya V. ... Detroit, MI
Siemion, Huckabay, Bodary, Padilla, Morganti & Bowerman, P.C. ... Southfield, MI
Siemion, Piotr D. ... New York, NY
Siemion, Robert P. ... Southfield, MI
Siemon, Carol A. ... Lansing, MI
Siemon, Charles L. ... Boca Raton, FL
Chicago, IL
Siemon, Joyce M. ... Boca Raton, FL
Siemon, Larsen & Marsh ... Irvine, CA
Aspen, CO
Boca Raton, FL
Chicago, IL
Siems, Robert L. ... Baltimore, MD
Siems, Tierman T. ... Omaha, NE
Siena, John J. ... Hoffman Estates, IL
Siena, John R., Jr. ... Chicago, IL
Siener, Gary J. ... Los Angeles, CA
Siener, Gary J. ... Woodland Hills, CA
Siener, Ray ... Chattanooga, TN
Sieni, Francesca M. ... New York, NY
Sienicki, James J. ... Phoenix, AZ
Sienkiewicz, Jeffrey B. ... Kent, CT
New Milford, CT
Sienkiewicz & McKenna, P.C. ... Kent, CT
New Milford, CT
Sienkiewicz, Nancy ... Kent, CT
New Milford, CT
Sienko, David C. ... Dallas, TX
Sienko, Leonard E., Jr. ... Hancock, NY
Sienty, Meroslaw D. ... Beacon, NY
Siepker, Frank G. ... Chicago, IL
Siepman, Kenneth B. ... Indianapolis, IN
Siepmann, Paul K. ... Riverhead, NY
Siepmann, Willi H. ... San Francisco, CA
Sier, John M. ... Detroit, MI
Sieradzki, David L. ... Washington, DC
Sieradzki, David Seth ... Securities and Exchange Commission, Division of Market Regulation, GV
Sieradzki, James P. ... Clifton, NJ
Sieradzki, Maurice ... New York, NY
Sierawski, Stephen S. ... Mount Clemens, MI
Sierck, Alexander W. ... Washington, DC
Sierck, Carsten W. ... Cleveland Heights, OH
Sieren, John L. ... Fort Worth, TX
Siergiej, Bernard F. ... Ambler, PA
Siering, Michael ... Muscatine, IA
Sierk, Carroll H. ... Cleveland, OH
Sierka, Kevin J. ... Phoenix, AZ
Sierks, William R. ... St. Paul, MN
Sierleja, David A. ... Cleveland, OH
Sieron, Mark A. ... Orange Park, FL
Sierpina, Raymond J., Jr. ... Melrose, MA
Sierra, Alex R. ... Coral Gables, FL
Sierra, Alexander L. ... Tucson, AZ
Sierra, Charles H. ... San Antonio, TX
Sierra, David A. ... Orlando, FL
Sierra, David R. ... Las Vegas, NV
Sierra, Edward ... Beverly Hills, CA
Sierra, Elaine L. ... San Francisco, CA
Sierra, Gustafson & Sierra ... Tampa, FL
Sierra, John William ... Denver, CO
Sierra, Jorge Luis ... Colorado Springs, CO
Sierra, Jose R. ... Miami, FL
Sierra, Michael ... Tampa, FL
Sierra, Monica Lynn ... Tampa, FL
Sierra, Ralph J., Jr. ... San Juan, PR
Sierra, Richard Douglas ... Orlando, FL
Sierra, Timothy J. ... Tampa, FL
Sierra/Serapion ... San Juan, PR
Sierra-Enriquez, Gloria M. ... San Juan, PR
Sierra-Winn, Leticia ... Los Angeles, CA
Sierzega, Ronald P. ... Cherry Hill, NJ
Sies, Dennis Ellsworth ... Highland Heights, KY
Sies, Gary L. ... Columbus, OH
Sies, Jerry ... Los Angeles, CA
Siesco, Robert E. ... Phoenix, AZ
Siesel, Gerald F. ... Wapakoneta, OH
Siesel, Mark A. ... New York, NY
Siesel, Melissa ... Fort Lauderdale, FL
Siesennop, David A. ... Bloomington, MN
Siesennop, W. Wayne ... Milwaukee, WI
Siesko, David M. ... New York, NY
Siesky, James H. ... Naples, FL
Siesky, Pilon & Wood ... Naples, FL
Siess, Janie Hickok ... Stockton, CA
Siess, John T. ... La Fayette, GA
Siess, Kurt ... Houston, TX
Siesser, Steven C. ... Washington, DC
Siesser, Steven E. ... Roseland, NJ
Siev, Jordan W. ... New York, NY
Sieve, Brian D. ... Chicago, IL
Sieve, Carolyn E. ... Los Angeles, CA
Sieve, James E. ... Cincinnati, OH
Sieve, Philip L. ... Kansas City, KS
Sieveke, Donald W. ... Santa Ana, CA
Sieveke, Patricia A. ... Corona Del Mar, CA
Sieveking, Jill K. ... Concord, NH
Sieveking, Michelle L. ... St. Louis, MO
Sieven, Howard A. ... New York, NY
Sieven & Mammana ... New York, NY
Sieverding, Pauline A. ... Baltimore, MD
Sievers, Charles F. ... Manassas, VA
Sievers, Diane S. ... Springfield, MA
Sievers, Edward C., Jr. ... Paw Paw, MI
Sievers, Gretchen ... Chicago, IL
Sievers & Haigh ... Long Beach, CA
Sievers, Ian R. ... Seattle, WA
Sievers, James J., Jr. ... St. Louis, MO
Sievers, Jill M. ... Colleyville, TX
Sievers, Kathryn L. ... Monroe, WI
Sievers, Mark P. ... Irving, TX
Sievers, Ora L. ... Los Angeles, CA
Sievers, Patricia A. ... Little Rock, AR
Sievers, Paul J. ... Costa Mesa, CA
Sievers, Richard D. ... Lincoln, NE
Sievers, Ronald ... Long Beach, CA
Sievert, Janet L. ... Federal Communications Commission, Common Carrier Bureau, GV
Sievert, Richard D. ... Los Angeles, CA
Sievert, Ronald J. ... Beaumont, TX
Sievertson, Michael A. ... Schaumburg, IL
Sieving, Charles E. ... Washington, DC
Sieving, Michael M. ... Sacramento, CA
Sieving, Richard N. ... Sacramento, CA
Sievwright, Ralph B. ... Phoenix, AZ
Siew, Ambrose Chua Hai ... Deerfield, IL
Siewers, Daniel L. ... Vincennes, IN
Siewert, Donald J. ... New York, NY
Siewert, Patricia A. ... Raleigh, NC
Siewerth, Sarane Crowther ... Chicago, IL
Siex, Simone R. ... Atlanta, GA
Siferd, Richard E. ... Lima, OH
Siferd & Siferd ... Lima, OH
Siferd, Willis S. ... Lima, OH
Sifers, Charles L. ... Oklahoma City, OK
Sifers, Charles L., A Prof. Corp., Law Offices of ... Oklahoma City, OK
Sifers, Randall W. ... Washington, DC
Siff, Alan L. ... Akron, OH
Siff, Andrew P. ... New York, NY
Siff, Brian D. ... New York, NY
Siff, Daniel E. ... New York, NY
Siff, Ezra Y. ... Baltimore, MD
Siff, Lawrence M. ... Miami, FL
Siff, Marshall S. ... Chatsworth, CA
Siff, Michael D. ... Kew Gardens, NY
Siff, S. David ... Concord, NH
Siff, Scott ... Department of Justice, Environment and Natural Resources Division, GV
Siff, Steven E. ... Miami, FL
Sifferlen, Mark J. ... Indianapolis, IN
Sifferlen, Sandra Cha ... Indianapolis, IN
Sifferman, Mark S. ... Phoenix, AZ
Sifferman, Robert M. ... Bellevue, WA
Sifferman, Scott S. ... Mount Vernon, MO
Siffermann, Mary M. ... Washington, DC
Siffert, John Sand ... New York, NY
Sifford & Anderson, L.L.P. ... Dallas, TX
Sifford, Lewis R., (P.C.) ... Dallas, TX
Sifford, Lisa M. ... Baltimore, MD
Siffring, Robert R. ... Omaha, NE
Sifleet, Jean D. ... Boston, MA

Sifontes, Iris ... Denver, CO
Sifre, Adam L. ... New York, NY
Sifre, Antonio R. ... San Juan, PR
Sifre, David A. ... New York, NY
Sifre-Rodríguez, Jaime ... San Juan, PR
Sifrit, Robert C. ... Port Charlotte, FL
Sifton, Charles P. ... Brooklyn, NY
Sifuentes, Jesús ... Austin, TX
Sifuentes, John ... Austin, TX
Sifuentes, Loretta S. ... Beverly Hills, CA
Sigafoose, Jay W. ... Iowa City, IA
Sigal, Andrew C. ... Van Nuys, CA
Sigal, Gerald P. ... Reading, PA
Sigal, Howard ... Chicago, IL
Sigal, Laura Land ... New York, NY
Sigal, Marc ... Philadelphia, PA
Sigal, Michael S. ... Chicago, IL
Sigal, (Mike) Myer O., Jr. ... New York, NY
Sigal, Nathan A. ... West Hartford, CT
Sigal, Oren N. ... Newton, MA
Sigal, Randee E. ... New York, NY
Sigal, Richard L. ... New York, NY
Sigal, Roger H. ... Berkeley, CA
Sigal, Warren ... Albuquerque, NM
Sigalas, Cathy P. ... Herndon, VA
Sigale, David G. ... Chicago, IL
Sigale, Jordan A. ... Chicago, IL
Sigale, Keith A. ... Chicago, IL
Sigall, Beth T. ... Washington, DC
Sigall, Elana W. ... New York, NY
Sigall, Jule L. ... Washington, DC
Sigall, Leonard S. ... Reynoldsburg, OH
Sigall, Michael W. ... New York, NY
Sigalos, George L. ... Boca Raton, FL
Sigalow, Alan M. ... Jamaica, NY
Sigalow, David L. ... Orlando, FL
Sigalow, Steven E. ... Cleveland, OH
Sigars, L. Jana ... Miami, FL
Sigda, Eric B. ... New York, NY
Sigel & Albin ... Chicago, IL
Sigel, Allan A. ... Los Angeles, CA
Sigel, Allan A., P.C., Law Offices of
Los Angeles, CA
Sigel, Carin J. ... Washington, DC
Sigel, Edwin M. ... Dallas, TX
Sigel, Gabrielle ... Chicago, IL
Sigel, James L. ... Boston, MA
Sigel, John D. ... Boston, MA
Sigel, Jonathan R. ... Worcester, MA
Sigel, Marshall E. ... Boca Raton, FL
Sigel, Philip A. ... Coral Gables, FL
Sigel, Quentin (Doug) ... Austin, TX
Sigel, Ralph I. ... Worcester, MA
Sigel, Richard ... Manchester, NH
Sigel, Robt. H. ... Chicago, IL
Sigelbaum, Harvey C. ... New York, NY
Sigelko, Duane F. ... Chicago, IL
Sigelman, Daniel W. ... Atlanta, GA
Sigelman, Kenneth M., and Associates
Los Angeles, CA
Sigelman, Kenneth M., and Associates
San Diego, CA
Sigelman, Paul S. ... Beverly Hills, CA
Sigelman and Perlman ... Beverly Hills, CA
Sigelman, Sidney ... Staten Island, NY
Sigelmann, André ... New York, NY
Siger, Jeffrey M. ... New York, NY
Sigerman, Jon B., The Law Offices of
San Francisco, CA
Sigerman, Jon B., The Law Offices of
San Rafael, CA
Sigerson, Andrew C. ... Omaha, NE
Sigerson, David K. ... Ormond Beach, FL
Sigety, Charles E. ... New York, NY
Sigety, Elizabeth D. ... Doylestown, PA
Sigg, Eric W. ... Los Angeles, CA
Siggelakis, G. Theodore ... Hightstown, NJ
Siggelkow, Mary Beth ... Louisville, KY
Siggers, E. Gregory ... Clovis, CA
Siggins, Olga A. ... Magna, UT
Siggins, Peter J. ... San Francisco, CA
Siggins, Richard J. ... San Francisco, CA
Sighinolfi, Paul H. ... Bangor, ME
Sights, Gale E. ... Dunwoody, GA
Sigillito, Barbara M. ... New York, NY
Sigillito, Martin T. ... St. Louis, MO
Sigismondi, Anthony ... Hollywood, FL
Sigismonti, David L. ... Media, PA
Sigismonti, Thomas A. ... Jersey City, NJ
Sigl, Kelann Larguier ... New Orleans, LA
Sigl, Patrick B. ... Phoenix, AZ
Sigle, Trecia L. ... Denver, CO
Sigler, Ana Lourdes ... Miami, FL
Sigler, Arnold E. ... New York, NY
Sigler, Bob C. ... Torrington, WY
Sigler, Daniel C. ... Orange, CA
Sigler, Daniel J. ... Decatur, IN
Sigler, David Andrew ... United States Senate,
Senatorial Assistants, GV
Sigler, David L. ... Lake Charles, LA
Sigler, Edward A. ... Bloomfield Hills, MI
Sigler, J. Denmon ... Houston, TX
Sigler, James A. ... Granada Hills, CA
Sigler, James A. ... Paducah, KY
Sigler, Janice M. ... Richmond, VA
Sigler, John Charles ... Dover, DE
Sigler, Kimberly ... Newton, MA
Sigler, L. Lanning ... Albuquerque, NM
Sigler, M. Christopher ... Fairfax, VA
Sigler, Michael ... Charlotte, NC
Sigler, Michael D. ... McDonough, GA
Sigler, R. Bradley ... Jackson, TN
Sigler, Richard ... Burbank, CA
Sigler, Robert C. ... Omaha, NE
Sigler, Robert J. ... Corpus Christi, TX
Sigler, Robert M., Jr. ... Troy, MI
Sigler, Shirley Cherin ... New York, NY
Sigler & Smith Law Office ... Torrington, WY

Sigler, Sonya ... Mountain View, CA
Sigler, Stephen Thatcher ... San Diego, CA
Sigler, Todd E. ... Hermosa Beach, CA
Sigler, Victoria S. ... Miami, FL
Sigler, William E. ... Southfield, MI
Sigley, Randolph A. ... Colorado Springs, CO
Siglin, I. Steven, Jr. ... Costa Mesa, CA
Siglin, I. Steven, Jr., P.C. ... Costa Mesa, CA
Sigman, Adam Joshua ... Birmingham, AL
Sigman, Alfred H. ... Oakland, CA
Sigman, B. David ... Philadelphia, PA
Sigman, Barry S. ... Bingham Farms, MI
Sigman, David D. ... Houston, TX
Sigman, Gloria J. ... Columbus, OH
Sigman, Harry C. ... Los Angeles, CA
Sigman, Harry C., Professional Corporation
Los Angeles, CA
Sigman, Helen ... Chicago, IL
Sigman, Isiah ... Chatsworth, CA
Sigman, Janssen, Stack, Wenning & Wilson
Appleton, WI
Sigman, John M. ... Austin, TX
Sigman, Lance Bretton ... Newton, NC
Sigman, Larry A. ... Denver, CO
Sigman, Leigh A. ... Orlando, FL
Sigman, Lewis & Feinberg, P.C.
Oakland, CA
San Francisco, CA
San Jose, CA
Sigman, Lisa C. ... Orlando, FL
Sigman, Lisa K. ... San Francisco, CA
Sigman, Lloyd M. ... Arden, NC
Sigman, Louis E. ... Chicago, IL
Sigman, Michael ... Orlando, FL
Sigman, Michael, and Associates, Law
Offices of ... Orlando, FL
Sigman, Patricia R. ... Altamonte Springs, FL
Sigman, Phillip W. ... Altamonte Springs, FL
Sigman, Robert M. ... Appleton, WI
Sigman, Robert S. ... Altamonte Springs, FL
Sigman, Scott W. ... San Diego, CA
Sigman & Sigman, L.L.P. ... Austin, TX
Sigman & Sigman, P.A.
Altamonte Springs, FL
Sigman, Timothy E. ... Covington, KY
Athens, OH
Sigmier, Harry ... Cleveland, OH
Sigmon, C. Miller ... Raleigh, NC
Sigmon, Charles E., Jr. ... Middlesboro, KY
Sigmon, Clark, Mackie, Hutton & Hanvey,
P.A. ... Hickory, NC
Newton, NC
Sigmon, Darrell R. ... Denver, CO
Sigmon, Darrell R., P.C. ... Denver, CO
Sigmon, Gene ... Newton, NC
Sigmon, Jan Alison ... New York, NY
Sigmon, Mark S. ... Bethlehem, PA
Sigmon, Michael C. ... Cary, NC
Sigmon, P. Wayne ... Gastonia, NC
Sigmon & Sigmon ... Jersey City, NJ
Bethlehem, PA
Allentown, PA
Easton, PA
Sigmon, Sigmon and Isenhower
Newton, NC
Sigmon, Susanne M. ... Danville, VA
Sigmon, Teresa J. ... Memphis, TN
Sigmon, Teresa J., Law Office
Memphis, TN
Sigmon, William R. ... Hickory, NC
Sigmond, Bennett M. ... Denver, CO
Sigmond, Carol A. ... Woodbridge, NJ
Sigmond, Helen ... Alamosa, CO
Sigmond, Leif R., Jr. ... Chicago, IL
Sigmond, Richard B. ... Philadelphia, PA
Sigmund, Diane Weiss ... Philadelphia, PA
Sigmund, Eileen Barrett ... Phoenix, AZ
Sigmund, Jeffrey D. ... St. Louis, MO
Sigmund, Rebecca L. ... Atlanta, GA
Sigmund, Richard D., Law Offices of
Visalia, CA
Sigmund, Thomas J. ... Columbus, OH
Sigmund, Timothy T. ... St. Louis, MO
Signer, Gregory R. ... Knoxville, TN
Signet, Bradford R. ... Columbus, OH
Signet, Paul A. ... Springfield, VA
Signet, William D. ... Austin, TX
Signom, Robert E., II ... Dayton, OH
Signoracci, Diane M. ... Columbus, OH
Signorella, Terrence O'Riley ... Fort Myers, FL
Signorelli, Mark T. ... Duluth, MN
Signorelli, Nancy F. ... Bronx, NY
Signorelli, Richard E. ... New York, NY
Signorelli, Walter P. ... Yorktown Heights, NY
Signorello, Christopher J. ... Boston, MA
Signorello, Gina M. ... Cupertino, CA
Signori, Lawrence James
West Palm Beach, FL
Signorile, Vincent A. ... Jersey City, NJ
Signorille, Mary Ellen ... Washington, DC
Signs, Jennifer West ... Gulfport, MS
Sigoloff, Chas. S. ... St. Louis, MO
Sigoloff, J. E. ... St. Louis, MO
Sigoloff, Robert ... St. Louis, MO
Sigoloff & Sigoloff ... St. Louis, MO
Sigrist, Heather N.
Merit Systems Protection Board,
Office of Appeals Counsel, GV
Sigsbee, Cheryl Ann ... Washington, DC
Sigsbey, Eric E. ... Midland, TX
Siguenza, Peter C., Jr. ... Hagåtña, GU
Sigur, Nicholas Joseph ... Broussard, LA
Sigurdson, Kathleen A. ... Las Vegas, NV
Sigurski, Mark ... United States Senate,
Office of the Legislative Counsel, GV
Sigwarth, Paul J. ... Dubuque, IA
Sigworth, Craig L. ... Albany, NY
Sigworth, Heather A. ... Phoenix, AZ

Sigworth, Ronald Lee ... Washington, DC
Sihler, John C. ... Eugene, OR
Sihnhold, Robert H. ... St. Louis, MO
Siino, Ben P. ... White Plains, NY
Siino, Horace J. ... Brentwood, CA
Siino, Joseph K. ... San Francisco, CA
Siino, Salvatore G. ... New York, NY
Sikand, Renee C. ... Van Nuys, CA
Sikaras, James T. ... Belmont, NY
Sikelianos, Cynthia S. ... Albuquerque, NM
Sikellis, Robert N. ... Boston, MA
Siken, Jacob Leon ... Tucson, AZ
Sikes, April Allison ... Corsicana, TX
Sikes, Cheryl A. ... Macon, GA
Sikes, Douglas C. ... Beaumont, TX
Sikes, Ewing E., III ... Brownsville, TX
Sikes, Griffin ... Andalusia, AL
Sikes, Griffin, Jr. ... Montgomery, AL
Sikes, J. Robert ... Macon, GA
Sikes, John M., Jr. ... Atlanta, GA
Sikes, Larry E. ... St. Augustine, FL
Sikes, Laurence D., Jr. ... Houston, TX
Sikes, Lucinda A. ... Washington, DC
Sikes, Mark D., (P.C.) ... Lafayette, LA
Sikes, Martha B. ... Atlanta, GA
Sikes, Michael D. ... Miami, FL
Sikes, Randy ... Brownwood, TX
Sikes, Richard T. ... Chicago, IL
Sikes, Richard T., Jr. ... Chicago, IL
Sikes, Ronald W. ... Orlando, FL
Sikes, Stanley B. ... Selma, AL
Sikes, Vanice H., Jr. ... Savannah, GA
Sikes, Virginia P. ... Philadelphia, PA
Siket, Andrew G. ... Naples, FL
Sikich, Steve M. ... Lake Charles, LA
Sikirica, Jeffrey J. ... Gibsonia, PA
Sikka, Linda Sollish ... Williamsville, NY
Sikkel, Robert W. ... Holland, MI
Sikkel, William A., IV ... Grand Rapids, MI
Sikkelee, Louis W. ... Richmond, VA
Sikkema, Gary D. ... Toledo, OH
Sikkema, Jeffrey L ... Costa Mesa, CA
Sikkema, P. Dawn ... Department of Justice,
U. S. Parole Commission, GV
Sikkema, Sue A. ... Toledo, OH
Sikkenga, Scott R. ... Kalamazoo, MI
Sikkenga, William J. ... Ann Arbor, MI
Siklosi, David ... Athens, TN
Sikora, Frederick J. ... Warren, NJ
Sikora, Frederick J., P.A. ... Warren, NJ
Sikora, J. William ... Cleveland, OH
Sikora, John A. ... Milwaukee, WI
Sikora Law Firm, The, P.C. ... Piney Flats, TN
Sikora, Linda S. ... Bridgewater, NJ
Sikora, Maureen S. ... Orlando, FL
Sikora, Michael J., III ... Columbus, OH
Sikora, Mitchell J., Jr. ... Boston, MA
Sikora, Paul ... North Tonawanda, NY
Sikora, Paul E. ... New York, NY
Sikora, Peter ... Cleveland, OH
Sikora & Price, Incorporated ... Irvine, CA
Santa Ana, CA
Sikora, Ted R., II ... Denver, CO
Sikora, Tomasz J. ... Houston, TX
Sikora, Vincent A. ... Piney Flats, TN
Sikorski, Edmund J., Jr. ... Ann Arbor, MI
Sikorski, Edward H. ... San Diego, CA
Sikorski, Gerald E. ... Washington, DC
Sikorski, Henry E. ... Palo Alto, CA
Sikorski, John C. ... Springfield, MA
Sikorski, Joni Marie ... Orlando, FL
Sikorski, Laura Paglia ... Garden City, NY
Sikorski, Laurie J. ... Wheaton, IL
Sikorski, Robert J. ... Buffalo, NY
Sikorski, Robert S. ... New York, NY
Sikorsky, Igor I., Jr. ... Wethersfield, CT
Sikorsky, Joseph E. ... Belleville, PA
Lewistown, PA
Sikov, Irving ... Natrona Heights, PA
Sikov & Love, P.A. ... Pittsburgh, PA
Sikov, Seymour A. ... Pittsburgh, PA
Sikowitz, Joel ... Babylon, NY
Sikyta, Curtis A. ... Ord, NE
Spalding, NE
Sil, Chandani ... San Diego, CA
Siladie, Dawn K. ... Cherry Hill, NJ
Silagi, Robt. ... San Diego, CA
Silagy, Anne Piero ... Canton, OH
Silah, Anahid N. ... Los Angeles, CA
Silahian, Cary K. ... El Paso, TX
Silak, Cathy R. ... Boise, ID
Silak, Jane P. ... Houston, TX
Silak, John L. ... Houston, TX
Silak, Michele J. ... San Francisco, CA
Silakoski, Linda G. ... Jefferson, OH
Silane, Frank A. ... Los Angeles, CA
Silar, Scott L. ... Wilmington, DE
Philadelphia, PA
Silard, Stephen A. ... Washington, DC
Silas, Adrien L. ... Department of Justice,
Office of Legislative Affairs, GV
Silas, Lamont H. ... Washington, DC
Silas, Martina A., Law Offices of
Los Angeles, CA
Silbar, Lisa Welch ... Irvine, CA
Silbaugh, Timothy W. ... Butler, PA
Valencia, PA
Silber, Alan ... Weehawken, NJ
Silber, Albert J. ... Southfield, MI
Silber, Barry ... Columbia, MD
Silber, Barry L. ... Pensacola, FL
Silber, Barry L., P.A. ... Pensacola, FL
Silber, Benjamin A. ... Penns Grove, NJ
Silber, David ... Hartford, CT
Silber, David Barry ... Treasury Department,
Internal Revenue Service, GV
Silber, David J. E. ... Poughkeepsie, NY
Silber, Debra ... New York, NY

Silber, Douglas N. ... Baltimore, MD
Silber, Frank E. ... Raleigh, NC
Silber, Frederic S. ... New York, NY
Silber, Gary J. ... Walnut Creek, CA
Silber, Harry J. ... New York, NY
Silber, Harvey B. ... Freeport, NY
Silber, Jennifer ... Washington, DC
Silber, Jerome H. ... Department of Defense,
Defense Legal Services Agency, GV
Silber, Jerome S. ... Rye Brook, NY
Silber, Jonathan S. ... Washington, DC
Silber, Josh ... New York, NY
Silber, Lewis Maurice ... Wheaton, MD
Silber, Louis M. ... West Palm Beach, FL
Silber, Marian E. ... New York, NY
Silber, Mark R. ... Metuchen, NJ
Silber, Meyer Y. ... Los Angeles, CA
New York, NY
Silber, Nancy E. ... New York, NY
Silber, Nancy L. ... Philadelphia, PA
Silber, Norman I. ... New York, NY
Silber, Norman J. ... Miami, FL
Silber ★ Pearlman, P.C. ... Dallas, TX
Houston, TX
Lake Jackson, TX
Silber, Rachel N. ... Miami, FL
Silber, Reagan W. ... Dallas, TX
Silber, Richard F. ... Washington, DC
Silber, Richard J. ... Huntington Beach, CA
Silber, Richard J. ... Albany, NY
Silber, Ronald ... Elizabeth, NJ
Silber, Seth C. ... Washington, DC
Silber, Siegmar ... Clifton, NJ
Silber, Stacy Plotkin ... Greenbelt, MD
Silber, Susan ... Takoma Park, MD
Silber & Valente, P.A.
West Palm Beach, FL
Silberberg, Alan ... Littleton, MA
Silberberg, Amy M. ... Afton, MN
Silberberg, Charles T. ... Seal Beach, CA
Silberberg, David D. ... Memphis, TN
Silberberg, Fred ... Los Angeles, CA
Silberberg, Fred, P.C. ... Los Angeles, CA
Silberberg, Gary K. ... New York, NY
Silberberg, Henry J. ... Los Angeles, CA
New York, NY
Silberberg, Howard B. ... McLean, VA
Silberberg, Marc L. ... New York, NY
Silberberg, Marshall ... Irvine, CA
Silberberg, Michael ... Red Bank, NJ
Silberberg, Michael C. ... New York, NY
Silberberg, Nathan L. ... Pembroke Pines, FL
Silberberg, Paul ... New York, NY
Silberberg, Philip E. ... White Plains, NY
Silberberg, Rachelle G. ... Detroit, MI
Silberberg, Richard H. ... New York, NY
Silberberg, Steven A. ... Bedford, NH
Silberberg & Wasser ... McLean, VA
Silberberg, Wendy J. ... Department of Justice,
Criminal Division, GV
Silberblatt, Jay N. ... Pittsburgh, PA
Silberblatt, Mark I. ... New York, NY
Silberblatt, Neil W. ... White Plains, NY
Silberbusch, Barbara ... Beverly Hills, CA
Silberbusch, Susan Milek ... Dayton, OH
Silberfarb, Irving B. ... Brooklyn, NY
Silberfarb, Paul ... Opa Locka, FL
Silberfarb, Stephen R. ... Takoma Park, MD
Silberfein, Joey ... New York, NY
Silberfein, Stephen I. ... New York, NY
Silberfeld, Roman M. ... Los Angeles, CA
Silberfield, Laurieann ... Long Island City, NY
Silberg, David A. ... Los Angeles, CA
Silberg, Jay E., (P.C.) ... Washington, DC
Silberg, Martin I. ... Mineola, NY
Silberg, Ruth ... Rockville, MD
Silberg & Silberg ... Baltimore, MD
Silberg, Steven E. ... Baltimore, MD
Silbergeld, Alan Mark ... Washington, DC
Silbergeld, Arthur F. ... Los Angeles, CA
Silbergleid, Steven A. ... Argonne, IL
Silbergleit, Kenneth R. ... Mamaroneck, NY
Silbergleit, Stuart I. ... Albany, NY
Silberglied, Robert ... New York, NY
Silberglied, Russell C. ... Wilmington, DE
Silberglitt, Mark S. ... New York, NY
Silberhorn, Edward J. ... Reston, VA
Silbering, Robert H. ... New York, NY
Silberlicht, Irwin ... Plainview, NY
Silberling, Edwyn ... Huntington, NY
Silberling & Silberling ... Hauppauge, NY
Huntington, NY
Silberling, Stephen P. ... Hauppauge, NY
Huntington, NY
Silberman, Aaron P. ... San Francisco, CA
Silberman, Alan H. ... Chicago, IL
Silberman, Arnold London ... Pennsauken, NJ
Silberman, Arthur L. ... San Francisco, CA
Silberman, Charlotte ... Delray Beach, FL
Silberman & Cohn ... Irvine, CA
Silberman, Curt C. ... Florham Park, NJ
Silberman, Curt C., A Professional Corporation
Florham Park, NJ
Silberman, David
Federal Communications Commission,
Office of the General Counsel, GV
Silberman, David J. ... Roseland, NJ
New York, NY
Silberman, David J. ... Milwaukee, WI
Silberman, Deborah F.
Federal Housing Finance Board,
Office of General Counsel, GV
Silberman & DiFilippo, A Professional
Corporation ... Bala Cynwyd, PA
Silberman, Earl J. ... Columbus, OH
Silberman, Elana ... Brooklyn, NY
Silberman, Gary K. ... Jackson, MS
Silberman, Gil G. ... San Francisco, CA

Silberman, Gregory P. ....New York, NY
Silberman, Harvey A. ....Glendora, CA
Silberman, Herbert C. ....Atlantic Beach, NY
Silberman, Jay W. ....San Antonio, TX
Silberman, Jeffrey H. ....San Diego, CA
Silberman, Jeffrey L. ....Cherry Hill, NJ
Blue Bell, PA
Silberman, Jeffrey P. ....Santa Monica, CA
Silberman, Jeremy I. ....Roseland, NJ
Silberman, Jessica I. ....Los Angeles, CA
Silberman, John ....New York, NY
Silberman, John, Associates, PC
New York, NY
Silberman, Jon D.
Environmental Protection Agency, Office of Enforcement and Compliance Assurance, GV
Silberman, Judith Gail ....Annapolis, MD
Silberman, Laurence H. ....
United States Court Of Appeals District Of Columbia Circuit, GV
Silberman, Leonard J. ....Irvine, CA
Silberman, Marc N. ....Cleveland, OH
Silberman, Martin N. ....New York, NY
Silberman, Michael R. ....Birmingham, AL
Silberman, Michael S. ....Bala Cynwyd, PA
Silberman, Michael W. ....Philadelphia, PA
Silberman, Mickey ....Woodbury, NY
Silberman, Morris ....Clearwater, FL
Silberman, Morris, P.A. ....Clearwater, FL
Silberman, Morton B. ....White Plains, NY
Silberman, Patricia B. ....Finksburg, MD
Silberman, Paul ....Baltimore, MD
Silberman, Renee Birnberg ....Lincolnwood, IL
Silberman and Rhine, LLP ....New York, NY
Silberman, Richard D. ....Albany, CA
Silberman, Robert A. S. ....Boston, MA
Silberman, Robert H. ....Camp Springs, MD
Silberman, Robert H., P.A.
Camp Springs, MD
Silberman, Ronni Beth, (Ms.)
New York, NY
Silberman, Sidney J. ....New York, NY
Silberman, Stanley ....Solvang, CA
Silberman, Steven R. ....Towson, MD
Silberman, Todd H. ....San Antonio, TX
Silberman, Todd J. ....Portland, OR
Silberman, Wilbur G. ....Birmingham, AL
Silbermann, Barry D. ....Beverly Hills, CA
Silbermann, Gale ....Clearwater, FL
Silbermann, Jacqueline W. ....New York, NY
Silbermann, James M. ....Washington, DC
Silbermann, John G.
Small Business Administration, Office of the General Counsel, GV
Silbermann, Jonathan J. ....Staten Island, NY
Silbernagel, Brian C. ....Chicago, IL
Silberner, Jay M. ....Roseland, NJ
Silbersack, John W. ....Darien, CT
Silbersack, Mark L. ....Cincinnati, OH
Silberstein, Alan K. ....Philadelphia, PA
Silberstein, Andrew ....New York, NY
Silberstein, Arnold I. ....New York, NY
Silberstein & Associates ....Boston, MA
Silberstein, Awad & Miklos, P.C.
Garden City, NY
Silberstein, Beth N. ....New York, NY
Silberstein, Carol K. ....Teaneck, NJ
Silberstein, Daniel P. ....Short Hills, NJ
Silberstein, David M. ....Sarasota, FL
Silberstein, Dawn A. ....Piedmont, CA
Silberstein, Debra Rahmin ....Andover, MA
Silberstein, Eric B. ....White Plains, NY
Silberstein, Gail Fradin ....Boston, MA
Silberstein, James D. ....New York, NY
Silberstein, Janice ....New York, NY
Silberstein, Jerome D. ....Garden City, NY
Silberstein, Jo Ellen ....New York, NY
Silberstein, John ....New York, NY
Silberstein, Laurie S. ....New York, NY
Silberstein, Margery B. ....Washington, DC
Silberstein, Michael F. ....San Rafael, CA
Silberstein, Michael R. ....Freehold, NJ
New York, NY
Silberstein, Myra R. ....Hyattsville, MD
Silberstein, N. Ronald ....Chestnut Hill, MA
Silberstein, Pamela J. ....San Jose, CA
Silberstein, Pamela M. ....Arlington, VA
Silberstein, Peter J. ....Boston, MA
Silberstein, Rebecca F. ....New York, NY
Silberstein, Robert L. ....Peoria, IL
Silberstein, Ronald C. ....San Francisco, CA
Silberstein, Scott ....Stamford, CT
Silberstein, Sheryl K. ....Bloomfield Hills, MI
Silberstein, William M. ....Denver, CO
Silbert, Benjamin A. ....New York, NY
Silbert, Bernard L. ....Seattle, WA
Silbert, Bernard M. ....Los Angeles, CA
Silbert, Claudia E. ....New York, NY
Silbert, David J. ....San Francisco, CA
Silbert, Earl J. ....Washington, DC
Silbert & Garon ....Metairie, LA
New Orleans, LA
Silbert, Gerald ....New York, NY
Silbert, Harvey L. ....Los Angeles, CA
Silbert, Hiller & Sena, LLP
Upper Saddle River, NJ
New York, NY
Silbert, James D. ....New York, NY
Silbert, Jonathan E. ....New Haven, CT
Silbert, Julie Parelman ....New Orleans, LA
Silbert, Kenneth N. ....Orinda, CA
Silbert, Laurence ....Bellerose, NY
Silbert, Marc M. ....Philadelphia, PA
Silbert, Michael D. ....Camden, NJ
Philadelphia, PA
Silbert, Michael M. ....Chicago, IL
Silbert, Nancy S. ....New Orleans, LA

Silbert, Richard W. ....Norwalk, CT
Silbert, Ronald G. ....Chicago, IL
Silbert, Sarah A. ....Los Angeles, CA
Silbert, Scott E. ....New Orleans, LA
Silbert, Stephen D., (A Professional Corporation) ....Los Angeles, CA
Silberthau, Howard R. ....Waltham, MA
Silberthau, Paula R.
Federal Communications Commission, Office of the General Counsel, GV
Silberzweig, Lloyd T. ....San Jose, CA
Silberzweig, Robin T. ....New York, NY
Silbey, Victoria E. ....Wayne, PA
Silbey, William J. ....Madison, NJ
Silbiger, Arnold R. ....Baltimore, MD
Silbiger, Clifford B. ....Westminster, MD
Silbiger & Coleman ....Westminster, MD
Silbiger, David M. ....Baltimore, MD
Silbiger, Gary ....Los Angeles, CA
Silbiger & Honig ....Los Angeles, CA
Silbiger, Sara L. ....New York, NY
Silbiger, Thomas ....New York, NY
Silbowitz, Albert E. ....Atlantic Beach, NY
Silbowitz, Freda ....New York, NY
Silbowitz, Mitchell E. ....New York, NY
Silby, D. Wayne ....Washington, DC
Silc, Gary F. ....Ironwood, MI
Ashland, WI
Silcott, Daniel Lynn ....Chillicothe, OH
Silcott, Lori L. ....Columbus, OH
Silcox, Clark R. ....Washington, DC
Rosslyn, VA
Silcox, Teresa ....Salt Lake City, UT
Sildon & Evans Law Group, P.C.
Kansas City, MO
Sildon, Myron E. ....Kansas City, MO
Silecchia, Lucia Ann ....Washington, DC
Silecky Firm, The, A Professional Corporation ....Morristown, NJ
Silek, Joseph F., Jr. ....Front Royal, VA
Winchester, VA
Silen, Arthur R. ....Newton, MA
Silen, Harold ....Kentfield, CA
Silen, James S. ....Rush City, MN
Silen, Stephan R. ....San Francisco, CA
Silence, Joseph A. ....Phoenix, AZ
Sileneck, James P. ....New York, NY
Sileo, Anthony M. ....Newark, NJ
Sileo, Brett J. ....Houston, TX
Sileo, John D. ....New Orleans, LA
Sileo, Joseph S. ....Scranton, PA
Sileo, Michael A., Jr. ....Allen, TX
Sileo, Michael G., Jr. ....Garden City, NY
Siler, Arthur G. ....Boston, MA
Siler, Brent B. ....Washington, DC
Siler, Cheri L. ....Fayetteville, NC
Siler, Dale G. ....Logan, UT
Siler, David J. ....Mequon, WI
Siler, Duane Alan ....Washington, DC
Siler, E. Dennis ....Scottsdale, AZ
Siler, Edith E. ....Chicago, IL
Siler, Eugene E., Jr. ....London, KY
Siler, Harvey Alan ....Charleston, WV
Siler, J. Bernard ....Washington, DC
Siler, Jeffrey R. ....Garden City, NY
Siler, John P. ....Flint, MI
Siler, John W. ....Fort Pierce, FL
Siler, Joseph V. ....Garden Grove, CA
Siler Law Firm, The, P.C. ....Norcross, GA
Siler, Nancy Lucille ....Charlotte, NC
Siler, Patricia ....Garden City, NY
Siler, Robert F. ....Franklin, NC
Siler, Ronald L. ....Fort Worth, TX
Siler, Russell Oliver ....Harrisburg, PA
Siler, Timothy A. ....Norcross, GA
Siler, W. Thomas, Jr. ....Jackson, MS
Siler, William W. ....Memphis, TN
Siler-Nixon, Dawn ....Tampa, FL
Siles, Aladar F. ....Palatine, IL
Silets, Harvey M. ....Chicago, IL
Silets, Steven G. ....Chicago, IL
Siletti, Jennifer A ....New York, NY
Silfani, Daniel L. ....Bath, OH
Silfen, Andrew I. ....New York, NY
Silfen, Jill H. ....Los Angeles, CA
Silfen, Lori Lynn ....New York, NY
Silfen, Martin ....Atlanta, GA
Silfen, Martin E. ....Virginia Beach, VA
Silfen, Nina P. ....New York, NY
Silfen, Richard A. ....Philadelphia, PA
Silfen, Segal, Fryer & Shuster, P.C.
Atlanta, GA
Silfen, Stuart A. ....Chicago, IL
Silfen, Stuart, (P.C.) ....New York, NY
Silfen, Thomas E. ....Washington, DC
Silfin, Ira E. ....New York, NY
Silhan, Paul H. ....Ridge, NY
Silhasek, James ....Scottsdale, AZ
Silhavy, J. Mark ....East Hartford, CT
Silhavy, Jack C. ....Chicago, IL
Silhol, Michael L. ....Nashville, TN
Siliato, Anthony F. ....Newark, NJ
Siliciano, John A. ....Ithaca, NY
Silicon Valley Law Group, A Law Corporation ....San Jose, CA
Silien, Daniel A. ....Washington, DC
Silikovitz, Brian A. ....Boston, MA
Silikovitz, Harvey B. ....New York, NY
Silin, Steven D. ....Lewiston, ME
Siljeg, Charles E. ....Seattle, WA
Silk, Adler & Colvin, A Law Corporation
San Francisco, CA
Silk, Allen M. ....Princeton, NJ
Silk, Alyson R. ....Brooklyn, NY
Silk, Bunks & Suckle, P.C. ....New York, NY
Silk, Caroline T. ....New York, NY
Silk, David A. ....Boca Raton, FL
Silk, David M. ....New York, NY

Silk, David P. ....Portland, ME
Silk, David P.N. ....Cleveland, OH
Silk, Debra A. ....Boise, ID
Silk, Gerald H. ....New York, NY
Silk, James J. ....Washington, DC
Silk, James P., Jr. ....Toledo, OH
Silk, James P., Sr. ....Toledo, OH
Silk, John D. ....Chicago, IL
Silk, John K. ....Chicago, IL
Silk, John M. ....Seattle, WA
Silk, Joseph ....Glendale, CA
Silk, Jules ....Philadelphia, PA
Silk, Kenneth R. ....Encino, CA
Silk, Leonard D. ....Pittsburgh, PA
Silk, Mary Ellen ....Huntington, WV
Silk, Melvyn A. ....Sacramento, CA
Silk, Michael L. ....Los Angeles, CA
Silk, Nancy ....New York, NY
Silk, Norman B. ....Randolph, MA
Silk, Robert ....New York, NY
Silk, Robert H. ....New York, NY
Silk, Robin Kitzes ....New York, NY
Silk, Rosenberg & Abdo ....Randolph, MA
Silk, Sherrill M. ....Malibu, CA
Silk, Thomas ....San Francisco, CA
Silk, Thomas J. ....Cleveland, OH
Silk, Wm. A. ....Boulder, CO
Silke, David W. ....Seattle, WA
Silkenat, James R. ....New York, NY
Silkey, Alice L. ....St. Paul, MN
Silkey, John P. ....Tempe, AZ
Silkey, Robert F. ....Syracuse, NY
Silkiss, Emanuel ....Cliffside Park, NJ
Silko, Alan T. ....Pittsburgh, PA
Silkowitz, Andrea M. ....Newark, NJ
Silkowski, Stephen Edward ....Jacksonville, FL
Silks, Laurence B. ....Kansas City, MO
Silks, Louis A., Jr. ....Merriam, KS
Kansas City, MO
Silks, Louis A., Jr., P.C. ....Kansas City, MO
Silkwood, Larry R. ....Urbana, IL
Silkworth, Ronald A. ....Glen Burnie, MD
Silkworth, Ronald A., P.A.
Glen Burnie, MD
Silkworth, Stacy A. ....Murray Hill, NJ
Silky, Charles E. ....Muskegon, MI
Sill, Bryan W. ....Naperville, IL
Sill, Darlee E. ....Hollidaysburg, PA
Sill, David W. ....Drexel Hill, PA
Sill, Frederick O. ....Jackson, MI
Sill, Gerald M. ....Jefferson City, MO
Sill, Henry F. ....Scottsdale, AZ
Sill, James D., Jr. ....Shawnee, OK
Sill, Louis J., Jr. ....Kansas City, MO
Sill, Peter L. ....Tacoma, WA
Sill, Richard A. ....Montrose, CA
Sill, Sara ....New York, NY
Sill, Shannon B. ....Dallas, TX
Sill & Webster, Attorneys at Law, P.C.
Hollidaysburg, PA
Sill, William J. ....Washington, DC
Silla, David ....New York, NY
Silla, Julie D. ....Brooklyn, NY
Silla, Mark R. ....Fort Collins, CO
Sillars, Robert G. ....Clarence, NY
Sillas, Herman ....Los Angeles, CA
Sacramento, CA
Sillcocks, H. Jackson ....Chatham, MA
Silldorf, Burdman, Duignan & Eisenberg
Irvine, CA
San Diego, CA
Silldorf, Howard J., (A P.C.) ....San Diego, CA
Silleck, Joan Ritchie ....New York, NY
Siller, Gary J. ....Houston, TX
Siller, Gustavo, Jr. ....Chicago, IL
Siller, Konrad L. ....Ann Arbor, MI
Siller, Michael B. ....New York, NY
Siller, Scott H. ....Manhasset, NY
Siller, Sidney ....New York, NY
Siller, Stephen I. ....New York, NY
Siller Wilk LLP ....New York, NY
Sillerman, Michael T. ....New York, NY
Sillers, Cameron D. ....Langdon, ND
Sillery, James D. ....Athens, OH
Silletti, Nicholas C. ....New York, NY
Silletto, Gary L. ....Jeffersonville, IN
Silliker, Mark T. ....Harrisburg, PA
Silliker & Reinhold ....Harrisburg, PA
Silliman, Amy ....Portland, OR
Silliman, Craig L. ....Washington, DC
Silliman, Dean J. ....Pomona, CA
Silliman, Dena LaMoyne ....Norman, OK
Silliman, Dishman and Nickels
Danville, KY
Silliman, Henry H., III ....Wilmington, DE
Silliman, James O. ....Chicago, IL
Silliman, John E. ....Hartford, CT
Silliman, Keith G. ....Albany, NY
Silliman, Kenneth G. ....Cleveland, OH
Silliman, N. Reed ....Fort Wayne, IN
Silliman, Richard D. ....Universal City, CA
Silliman, Rich'd G. ....East Moline, IL
Silliman, Robert B. ....Marietta, GA
Silliman, Robert Todd ....Atlanta, GA
Silliman, Wendelin White ....Atlanta, GA
Sillin, Elizabeth H. ....Springfield, MA
Sillings, John S. ....Yonkers, NY
Sillins, Herbert J. ....Chicago, IL
Sillins, Wm. M. ....Columbus, OH
Sillis, John J. ....Sacramento, CA
Sillman, Gail D. ....Sudbury, MA
Sillmon, M. Rebecca ....Raleigh, NC
Sill-Rogers, Christine ....Kansas City, MO
Sills, Alan I. ....New York, NY
Sills, Alan J. ....University Heights, OH
Sills, Anne R. ....Boston, MA
Sills, Arthur M. ....West Bloomfield, MI

Sills Cummis Radin Tischman Epstein & Gross, A Professional Corporation
Atlantic City, NJ
Newark, NJ
New York, NY
Sills, Donna M. ....Columbia, MD
Sills, Edward M. ....New York, NY
Sills, Edward M. ....Austin, TX
Sills, Eric H. ....Albany, NY
Sills, G. Joseph, Jr. ....Baltimore, MD
Sills, Jason A. ....San Jose, CA
Sills, Jay Adam ....Riverside, CA
Sills, Jennifer E. ....Waterbury, CT
Sills, Joan H. ....Baltimore, MD
Sills, John D. ....Bloomfield Hills, MI
Traverse City, MI
Sills, John L. ....New York, NY
Sills, John W., III ....Staunton, VA
Sills, Jonathan Peter ....Baltimore, MD
Sills, Kenneth B. ....Daytona Beach, FL
Sills, Kenneth F. ....Baton Rouge, LA
Sills, Law, Essad, Fiedler & Charboneau, P.C.
Ann Arbor, MI
Bloomfield Hills, MI
Lansing, MI
Traverse City, MI
Sills, Milton ....Hayward, CA
Sills, Nancy M. ....Albany, NY
Sills, Nancy M. ....Glens Falls, NY
Sills, Nancy R. ....New York, NY
Sills, Randall L. ....West Palm Beach, FL
Sills, Richard P. ....Washington, DC
Sills, Robert ....San Francisco, CA
Sills, Robert L. ....Los Angeles, CA
Sills, Robert L. ....New York, NY
Sills, Steven D. ....Los Angeles, CA
Sillyman, Michael W. ....Phoenix, AZ
Silman, Ruth Hilary ....Cambridge, MA
Silna, Robin L. ....Sherman Oaks, CA
Silodor, Deborah A. ....Roseland, NJ
Silow, Gary ....Jenkintown, PA
Silow, Mark L. ....Philadelphia, PA
Silpe, Richard J. ....Philadelphia, PA
Silpe, Steven M. ....New York, NY
Sils, Anna K. ....New York, NY
Sils, Evan H. ....New York, NY
Silsbury, Lori M. ....Lansing, MI
Silsby, Herbert T., II ....Ellsworth, ME
Silsby, James A. ....Ellsworth, ME
Silsby, James A., Jr. ....Ellsworth, ME
Silsby, Liana C. ....Fort Lauderdale, FL
Silsby, Patricia Shields ....Olney, MD
Silsby, William J. ....Haddonfield, NJ
Silsby-Hardy, Carolyn A. ....Camden, ME
Silsdorf, Arthur R. ....New York, NY
Silten, Peter Ronald ....San Francisco, CA
Silton, Herbert ....Chicago, IL
Silton, Lawrence C. ....Appleton, WI
Silton, Leo J. ....Chestnut Hill, MA
Silton, Myles B. ....San Francisco, CA
Silton, Seifert, Carlson & Gamble, S.C.
Appleton, WI
Siluk, Richard S. ....Houston, TX
Silva, Alban P. ....Irvine, CA
Silva, Albert P. ....Tampa, FL
Silva, Alfredo L. ....Dallas, TX
Silva, Anthony D. ....San Francisco, CA
Silva, Anthony R. ....Coral Gables, FL
Silva, Antone L. ....Mattapoisett, MA
Silva, Antone R. ....Albany, NY
Silva, Antonio V. ....El Paso, TX
Silva, Antonio V., P.C. ....El Paso, TX
Silva & Associates, Ltd. ....Middletown, RI
Silva, Benjamin, Jr. ....Albuquerque, NM
Silva, Bernard R., Jr. ....Belmont, MA
Silva, Bernardo ....Los Angeles, CA
Silva, Bernardo M. ....San Francisco, CA
Silva, Betsy Rodriguez ....Tacoma, WA
Silva, Bradley A. ....Fresno, CA
Silva, Bruce E. ....Vista, CA
Silva, Carlos E. ....Miami, FL
Silva, Charles J., Jr. ....Menands, NY
Silva, Charles W. ....Provincetown, MA
Silva, Clasen & Raffalow ....Los Angeles, CA
Sherman Oaks, CA
Silva, Cristian P. ....Treasury Department, Internal Revenue Service, GV
Silva, Cristina R. ....Pittsburgh, PA
Silva, D. Elisabeth ....San Diego, CA
Silva, David A. ....Fresno, CA
Silva, David A. ....Lawrence, MA
Silva, David A. ....New York, NY
Silva, David R. ....Santa Fe, NM
Silva, Deborah M. ....Plymouth, MA
Silva, Diane L. ....Hayward, CA
Silva, Dirk E. ....Claremont, CA
Silva, Dirk E., P.C., Law Office of
Claremont, CA
Silva, Edward P. ....Franklin, TN
Silva, Elizabeth J. ....Denver, CO
Silva, Enrique ....Miami, FL
Silva, Eugene J. ....Houston, TX
Silva, F. Andrekita ....Seattle, WA
Silva, Fabio Roman ....Washington, DC
Silva, Fernando H ....Brooklyn, NY
Silva, Francis E., Jr. ....Hingham, MA
Silva, Francisco Tirado ....San Bernardino, CA
Silva, Frank S. ....San Diego, CA
Silva, Fred A. ....Modesto, CA
Oakdale, CA
Silva, Gail Linscott ....Clearwater, FL
Silva, Gregory A. ....Alameda, CA
Silva, Helen N. ....San Juan, PR
Silva, Humberto ....Weslaco, TX
Silva, James ....Indio, CA
Silva, James R. ....Olympia, WA
Silva, Joaquim F. ....Ludlow, MA
Silva, John M. ....Los Angeles, CA

Silva, Jon S. ... San Dimas, CA
Silva, Jorge E. ... Miami, FL
Silva, Jose A., Jr. ... El Paso, TX
Silva, José, Jr. ... Vineland, NJ
Silva, Jose Jr., Attorney at Law, P.C. Vineland, NJ
Silva, Joseph J. ... Bridgeport, CT
Silva, Juan L. ... Irvine, CA
Silva, Judy A. ... Concord, NH
Silva Lopez Graf Martinez & Alejo, S.C. San Diego, CA
Silva, Margarida M. ... Fall River, MA
Silva, Mario R. ... Rochester, NY
Silva, Mary Elise ... Vero Beach, FL
Silva, Michael B. ... Houston, TX
Silva, Michael F. ... New York, NY
Silva, Michele A. ... White Plains, NY
Silva, Miguel A. ... Miami, FL
Silva, Milton R. ... Fall River, MA
Silva, Paul ... Bristol, RI
Silva, Pete, Jr. ... Tulsa, OK
Silva, Phillip A. ... Fresno, CA
Silva, Regina ... San Diego, CA
Silva, Richard J., Jr. ... Fall River, MA
Silva, Rieder & Maestas, P.C. Albuquerque, NM
Silva, Riguer J. ... New Orleans, LA
Silva, Robert D. ... Hartford, CT
Silva, Robert M. ... Middletown, RI
Silva, Robin M. ... San Francisco, CA
Silva, Rolando A. ... San Juan, PR
Silva, Roy Z. ... Los Angeles, CA
Silva, Ruben R. ... San Antonio, TX
Silva & Silva ... Miami, FL
Silva & Simpson, L.L.P. ... Houston, TX
Silva, Theodore D. ... Seattle, WA
Silva, Theodore S., Jr. ... Washington, DC
Silva, Thomas J., Sr. ... San Jose, CA
Silva, Tiffany Doon ... San Francisco, CA
Silva, Timothy F. ... Boston, MA
Silva, Tracey A. ... Seattle, WA
Silva, William D. ... Washington, DC
Silva, Zoilo I. ... New York, NY
Silva Almeyda, Rafael E. ... San Juan, PR
Silva-Cofresí, José A. ... San Juan, PR
Silva-Cofresí, Maritza ... San Juan, PR
Silvaggio, Concetta A. ... Pittsburgh, PA
Silvaggio, Joseph D. ... Pittsburgh, PA
Silvain, Allison L. ... Baltimore, MD
Silvain, Peter B., Jr. ... Salisbury, MD
Silva-Martinez, Diane ... San Diego, CA
Silvano, Michael J. ... Cherry Hill, NJ
Silva-Ruiz, Pedro F. ... San Juan, PR
Silvas & Eaton ... Santa Ana, CA
Silvas, Manuel S. ... Phoenix, AZ
Silvas, Michael J. ... Santa Ana, CA
Silvas, Richard H. ... Corpus Christi, TX
Silva-Wiscovich, Guillermo J. San Juan, PR
Silveira, Garrett L. ... Highland, NY
Silveira, Lori Caron ... Providence, RI
Silveira, Maria De Fatima ... Reston, VA
Silveira, Marie Sovey ... Modesto, CA
Silveira, Mattos & Lewis ... Merced, CA
Silveira, Michael J. ... Modesto, CA
Silveira, Norbert R. ... San Jose, CA
Silveira, Ronald A., (A Professional Corporation) ... San Rafael, CA
Silveira, William, Jr. ... Visalia, CA
Silven, David C. ... Baker City, OR
Silven, Schmeits & Vaughan Baker City, OR
Silver, Aaron B. Z. ... Brooklyn, NY
Silver, Adam ... New York, NY
Silver and Ahern ... Boston, MA
Silver, Alan B. ... Hartford, CT
Silver, Alan B., LLC, Law Offices of Hartford, CT
Silver, Alan E., (P.C.) ... New Haven, CT
Silver, Alan I. ... Minneapolis, MN
Silver, Alan J. ... San Francisco, CA
Silver, Alan J. ... Elizabeth, NJ
Silver, Allan B. ... Troy, NY
Silver, Allan E. ... Great Neck, NY
Silver, Allen ... Belvidere, IL
Silver, Amelia W. ... New York, NY
Silver, Andrea Feldman ... Burbank, CA
Silver, Anne Gonte ... Bloomfield Hills, MI
Silver, Arnold B. ... Portland, OR
Silver & Arsht ... Ventura, CA
Westlake Village, CA
Silver & Associates, A Professional Corporation ... Southfield, MI
Silver, Barbara Oaks ... Bala Cynwyd, PA
Philadelphia, PA
Silver, Barry B. ... Newburgh, NY
Silver, Barry Lee ... Los Angeles, CA
Silver, Barry M. ... Boca Raton, FL
Silver, Barry M., P.A. ... Boca Raton, FL
Silver, Barry S., P.C. ... Northbrook, IL
Silver, Barry Stewart ... Northbrook, IL
Silver, Benj. J. ... Baltimore, MD
Silver, Bernard C. ... Tampa, FL
Silver, Bernard F. ... Miami, FL
Silver, Bernard F., P.A. ... Miami, FL
Silver, Beth G. ... Wilmington, DE
Silver, Beth L. (Balzer) ... Pittsburgh, PA
Silver, Beverly David ... Jericho, NY
Silver, Bobbi L., Law Offices of Stamford, CT
Silver, Brian R. ... Napa, CA
Silver & Brown, A Professional Corporation Fairfax, VA
Silver, Bruce F. ... Boca Raton, FL
Silver, Bruce F., P.A. ... Boca Raton, FL
Silver, Bryna S. ... Philadelphia, PA
Silver, Cara E. ... Santa Monica, CA
Silver, Carl C. ... Alpena, MI
Silver, Carol Ruth, Law Offices of San Francisco, CA
Silver, Cecilia A. P. ... Freehold, NJ
Silver, Charles S. ... Bloomfield, CT
Silver, Cherin ... Philadelphia, PA
Silver, Cole B. ... Voorhees, NJ
Silver, Cortland J., Jr. ... Tempe, AZ
Silver, Craig J. ... Irvine, CA
Silver, Craig L. ... Mount Airy, MD
Silver, Cynthia J. ... Ardmore, PA
Silver, Daniel ... Richboro, PA
Silver, Daniel A. ... New Britain, CT
Silver, Daniel A. ... Boston, MA
Silver, Daniel B. ... Washington, DC
Silver, Daniel H. ... Somerville, MA
Silver, Darren ... Los Angeles, CA
Silver, David ... Ventura, CA
Silver, David ... Washington, DC
Silver, David ... Roseland, NJ
Silver, David ... Greenville, NC
Silver, David C. ... Washington, DC
Silver, David F. ... Bennington, VT
Silver, David M. ... Langhorne, PA
Silver, David W. ... Northbrook, IL
Silver, David W. ... Lansing, MI
Silver & DeBoskey, A Professional Corporation ... Denver, CO
Silver, Debra L. ... New York, NY
Silver, Deirdre P. ... New York, NY
Silver, Dennis S. ... Sarasota, FL
Silver, Diane C. ... New Brunswick, NJ
Silver, Diane L. ... Phoenix, AZ
Silver & DiVergilis ... Pennsauken, NJ
Media, PA
Philadelphia, PA
Silver, Donald P. ... Los Angeles, CA
Silver, Donna ... Long Beach, CA
Silver, Dorothy ... Manchester, NH
Silver, Edgar P. ... Annapolis, MD
Baltimore, MD
Silver, Edmund P. ... Sarasota, FL
Silver, Edward ... New York, NY
Silver, Edward A. ... New York, NY
Silver, Edward F. ... Fair Lawn, NJ
Silver, Edward W. ... Bala Cynwyd, PA
Philadelphia, PA
Silver, Edwin ... Long Beach, CA
Silver, Elaine T. ... Stamford, CT
Silver, Elizabeth H. ... San Leandro, CA
Silver, Ellen A. ... Camp Springs, MD
Silver, Ellen Ann ... Woodbridge, NJ
Silver, Emanuel M. ... Los Angeles, CA
Silver, Eric C. ... Atlanta, GA
Silver, Eric C., P.C. ... Atlanta, GA
Silver, Evelyn B. ... New York, NY
Silver & Feldman ... Rochester, NY
Silver & Field, A Law Corporation
Los Angeles, CA
Silver, Franklin ... Oakland, CA
Silver & Freedman, A Professional Law Corporation ... Los Angeles, CA
Silver, Freedman & Taff, L.L.P. Washington, DC
Silver, Gabi Deborah ... Detroit, MI
Silver, Gail Cotton ... West Palm Beach, FL
Silver & Garvett, P.A. ... Miami, FL
Silver, Gary D. ... Monticello, NY
Silver, Gary S. ... Media, PA
Philadelphia, PA
Silver, Geoffrey S. ... Portland, OR
Silver, George E. ... Morristown, NY
Silver, Gerald D. ... New York, NY
Silver, Gerald J. ... Scarsdale, NY
Silver, Glenn H. ... Fairfax, VA
Silver, Golub & Teitell LLP
Bridgeport, CT
Danbury, CT
Fairfield, CT
Greenwich, CT
Hartford, CT
New Canaan, CT
Norwalk, CT
Stamford, CT
Silver, Gray, III ... Martinsburg, WV
Silver, Gray, Jr. ... Martinsburg, WV
Silver, Gregory K. ... Indianapolis, IN
Silver, Gregory S. ... Long Beach, CA
Silver, Harold ... Gainesville, FL
Silver, Harold, Law Offices of, P.A. Gainesville, FL
Silver, Harris R. ... Roseland, NJ
Silver, Harry R. ... Washington, DC
Silver, Hayden J., III ... Raleigh, NC
Silver, Henry ... Los Angeles, CA
Silver, Herbert B. ... Piedmont, SC
Silver, Herbert J. ... Somerset, NJ
New York, NY
Silver, Hilda M. ... Hollywood, FL
Silver, Holly A. ... Glendale, CA
Silver, Howard ... Southfield, MI
Silver, Howard D. ... Encino, CA
Silver, Howard D. ... Columbus, OH
Silver, Howard R. ... Bronx, NY
Silver, Howard S. ... Washington, DC
Silver, Ian ... New York, NY
Silver, Ira S. ... Miami, FL
Silver, Irene S. ... Scarsdale, NY
Silver, Irving ... Mobile, AL
Silver, Jack ... Santa Rosa, CA
Silver, James D. ... Miami, FL
Silver, James R. ... Aurora, OH
Silver, James W. ... San Francisco, CA
Silver, Jane C. ... Philadelphia, PA
Silver, Jane Hastings ... Richmond, IN
Silver, Janine ... New York, NY
Silver, Jason M. ... Beverly Hills, CA
Silver, Jay Kit ... Evanston, IL
Silver, Jay Sterling ... Miami, FL
Silver, Jed L. ... Atlanta, GA
Silver, Jeffrey ... New York, NY
Silver, Jeffrey A. ... Omaha, NE
Silver, Jeffrey A. ... Las Vegas, NV
Silver, Jeffrey I. ... Albany, NY
Silver, Jeffrey L. ... Columbia, SC
Silver, Jennifer ... New York, NY
Silver, Jerome ... Cleveland, OH
Silver, Jerome J. ... Hempstead, NY
Silver, Jessica D. ... Department of Justice, Civil Rights Division, GV
Silver, Joanna L. ... Brooklyn, NY
Silver, Joe L. ... Denver, CO
Silver, Joel Z. ... Washington, DC
Silver, John J. ... Denver, CO
Silver, John K. ... Santa Fe, NM
Silver, Jonathan ... Kew Gardens, NY
Silver, Jonathan D. ... Treasury Department, Internal Revenue Service, GV
Silver, Jonathan L. F. ... New York, NY
Silver, Jonathan M. ... New York, NY
Silver, Joseph G. ... Atlanta, GA
Silver, Joseph J. ... Columbus, OH
Silver, Joseph L. ... Newark, NJ
Silver, Joseph S. ... Tampa, FL
Silver, Karen E. ... Beverly Hills, CA
Silver, Katherine M. ... Houston, TX
Silver, Katz & Hurley ... San Jose, CA
Silver, Kenneth F. ... Southfield, MI
Silver, Kenneth P. ... Stony Point, NY
Silver, Kimberley Weber ... Raleigh, NC
Silver and Lake ... Morristown, NY
Silver, Larry D. ... Philadelphia, PA
Silver Law Firm, The, P.L.C. ... Phoenix, AZ
Silver, Lawrence ... Los Angeles, CA
Silver, Lawrence A. ... Brooklyn, NY
Silver, Lawrence B. ... San Francisco, CA
Silver, Lawrence S. ... Coral Gables, FL
Silver, Leda Soffran ... Santa Fe, NM
Silver, Lee I. ... Beverly Hills, CA
Silver, Lee T. ... Grand Rapids, MI
Silver, Leon B. ... Phoenix, AZ
Silver, Leonard R. ... Philadelphia, PA
Silver, Leslie Carter ... Washington, DC
Silver, Leslie E. ... Montville, NJ
Silver, Lori ... Carmel, CA
Silver, Lori ... Boston, MA
Silver, Lori A. ... East Brunswick, NJ
Silver, Louis D. ... San Jose, CA
Silver, Louis E., (P.C.) ... Houston, TX
Silver, Lynn B. ... Jenkintown, PA
Silver, Madeline ... Lawrence, NY
Silver, Marc A. ... Boston, MA
Silver, Marc F. ... Rockville, MD
Silver, Marc H. ... New York, NY
Silver, Marc S. ... Chicago, IL
Silver, Margaret B. ... Seattle, WA
Silver, Marjorie A. ... Huntington, NY
Silver, Mark S. ... San Bernardino, CA
Silver, Mark S. ... Harrisburg, PA
Silver, Marsha K. ... Austin, TX
Silver, Martin ... Hauppauge, NY
Silver, Martin ... Seattle, WA
Silver, Martin H. ... Dallas, TX
Silver, Marvin S., P.C. ... Worcester, MA
Silver, Mary Ellen F. ... Los Altos Hills, CA
Silver, Max R. ... Miami, FL
Silver, Melinda ... Santa Fe, NM
Silver, Melvin J. ... St. Paul, MN
Silver, Melvyn A. ... Elkhart, IN
Silver, Melvyn D. ... San Jose, CA
Silver, Meryl ... East Hartford, CT
Silver, Meyer ... Ardmore, PA
Silver, Michael E. ... Universal City, CA
Silver, Michael G. ... Philadelphia, PA
Silver, Michael G. ... Houston, TX
Silver, Michael J. ... Westlake Village, CA
Silver, Michael J. ... Augusta, KS
Silver, Michael J. ... Baltimore, MD
Silver, Michael J. ... St. Louis, MO
Silver, Michael N. ... Upper Darby, PA
Silver, Michael S. ... Detroit, MI
Silver, Milton L. ... Clayton, NJ
Silver, Mitchell ... Sanford, FL
Silver, Morris L. ... Rutland, VT
Silver, Morton F. ... New York, NY
Silver, Morton H. ... Homestead, FL
Silver, Murray M. ... Atlanta, GA
Silver & Nagler ... Seattle, WA
Silver, Nancy J. ... New York, NY
Silver, Nathan I. ... Bethesda, MD
Silver, Neil S. ... Denver, CO
Silver, Neil S. ... Southfield, MI
Silver Nuckolls, LLP ... Greenville, NC
Silver, Patricia M. ... Miami, FL
Silver, Paul ... Santa Rosa, CA
Silver, Paul ... Portland, OR
Silver, Paul A. ... Boston, MA
Providence, RI
Silver, Paul A. ... Olympia, WA
Silver, Paul F. ... St. Clair, MI
Silver, Paul G. ... Chicago, IL
Silver, Paul M. ... Wayne, PA
Silver, Paul M. ... Seattle, WA
Silver, Paula Kay ... Wellsburg, WV
Silver, Perry D. ... New York, NY
Silver, Perry S. ... Los Angeles, CA
Silver, Peter A. ... Indianapolis, IN
Silver, Peter M. ... Brookfield, WI
Silver, Philip M. ... Rochester, NY
Silver, Renée J. ... Woodbury, NY
Silver, Richard ... Bangor, ME
Silver, Richard ... Elizabeth, NJ
Silver, Richard A. ... Stamford, CT
Silver, Richard B. ... Santa Barbara, CA
Silver, Richard D. ... Worcester, MA
Silver, Richard H. ... New York, NY
Silver, Richard H. ... Philadelphia, PA
Silver, Richard M. ... Salinas, CA
Silver, Richard V. ... New York, NY
Silver, Robert ... Woodbridge, NJ
Silver, Robert B. ... Armonk, NY
Silver, Robert D. ... Ventura, CA
Silver, Robert D. ... Park Ridge, IL
Silver, Robert S. ... Philadelphia, PA
Silver, Robert Scott ... Los Angeles, CA
Silver, Roberta L. ... New York, NY
Silver, Robin ... Baltimore, MD
Silver, Roger A. ... Miami, FL
Silver, Ronald ... Coral Gables, FL
Silver, Ronald J. ... Worcester, MA
Silver, Roslyn O. ... Phoenix, AZ
Silver, Ross Z. ... New York, NY
Silver, Rugenia ... Washington, DC
Silver, S. Lance ... Philadelphia, PA
Silver, Sam I. ... Coral Gables, FL
Silver, Samuel M. ... Hollywood, FL
Silver, Samuel W. ... Philadelphia, PA
Silver, Sandra G. ... Pontiac, MI
Silver, Sanford ... Brooklyn, NY
Silver, Scott ... Los Angeles, CA
Silver, Scott A. ... Miami, FL
Silver, Scott H. ... Fort Lauderdale, FL
Silver, Scott L. ... New York, NY
Silver, Scott N. ... Linwood, NJ
Silver, Scott N., P.C. ... Linwood, NJ
Silver, Scott Z. ... Encino, CA
Silver, Sharon E. ... New York, NY
Silver, Sharon L. ... Commack, NY
Silver, Sheldon E. ... Brooklyn, NY
Silver, Sherry L. ... Florham Park, NJ
Silver, Shira A. ... New York, NY
Silver, Sidney J., (P.C.) ... Washington, DC
Silver & Silver ... Santa Rosa, CA
Silver & Silver ... Miami, FL
Silver & Silver ... Worcester, MA
Silver & Silver ... Scarsdale, NY
Silver & Silver ... Ardmore, PA
Philadelphia, PA
Silver & Silver, P.C. ... Washington, DC
Silver, Stacey Rubin ... Chicago, IL
Silver, Stanley ... San Fernando, CA
Silver, Stanley M., Jr. Altamonte Springs, FL
Silver, Stanley M., P.A. Altamonte Springs, FL
Silver, Stephen E. ... Phoenix, AZ
Silver, Stephen H. ... Santa Monica, CA
Silver, Stephen M. ... Lake Buena Vista, FL
Silver, Stephen N. ... Far Rockaway, NY
Silver, Steven A. ... Los Angeles, CA
Silver, Steven J. ... Phoenix, AZ
Silver, Steven R. ... Atlanta, GA
Silver, Steven W. ... Arlington, VA
Silver, Stuart R. ... Miami, FL
Silver, Sumner ... Worcester, MA
Silver, Susan ... Santa Monica, CA
Silver, Susan E. ... Northampton, MA
Silver, Susan M. ... Cincinnati, OH
Silver, Susan Remis ... Trenton, NJ
Silver, Tamra Lois ... Tarzana, CA
Silver & Taube ... San Jose, CA
Silver, Terry L. ... Mayfield Village, OH
Silver, Theodore A. ... New York, NY
Silver, Theodore J. ... Miami, FL
Silver, Theodore "Ted" Jack ... Miami, FL
Silver, Thomas A. ... Corpus Christi, TX
Silver & Tischler ... New York, NY
Silver, Tracy ... Los Angeles, CA
Silver, Voit & Thompson, P.C. ... Mobile, AL
Silver & Waldman, P.A. ... Miami, FL
Silver, Warren E. ... Chicago, IL
Silver, Warren M. ... Bangor, ME
Silver, Warren M., P.A. ... Bangor, ME
Silver, Wayne A., Law Offices of Palo Alto, CA
Silver, Wendy Bieber ... Philadelphia, PA
Silvera, Darryl J. ... Dallas, TX
Silvera, Hillel R. ... New York, NY
Silverang, Kevin J. ... Bryn Mawr, PA
Philadelphia, PA
Silverberg, Alan B. ... Chicago, IL
Silverberg, Alan H. ... Owings Mills, MD
Silverberg, Alice D. ... El Cajon, CA
Silverberg, Charles D., (A Professional Corporation) ... Los Angeles, CA
Silverberg, David J. ... Brooklyn, NY
Silverberg, David K. ... Buffalo, NY
Silverberg, Dean L. ... New York, NY
Silverberg, Donald M. ... Buffalo, NY
Silverberg, E. David ... Towson, MD
Silverberg, Edward L. ... Westlake Village, CA
Silverberg, Eric ... Xenia, OH
Silverberg, Fred Andrew Department of Commerce, Patent and Trademark Office, GV
Silverberg, Goldman and Bikoff, L.L.P. Washington, DC
Silverberg, Herbert M. ... Santa Fe, NM
Silverberg & Hunter, LLP ... Garden City, NY
Silverberg, James Lorin ... Washington, DC
Silverberg, Janet Lynn ... Chicago, IL
Silverberg, Jay L. ... New York, NY
Silverberg, Jeffrey D. ... Baltimore, MD
Silverberg, Jeroll R. ... New Canaan, CT
Silverberg, Jerome R. Fort Lauderdale, FL
Silverberg, Jos. H. ... Madison, WI
Silverberg, Kenneth H. ... Washington, DC
Silverberg, Kristen L. ... Washington, DC
Silverberg, Lawrence Eric ... New York, NY
Silverberg, Lee F. ... St. Paul, MN
Silverberg, LLoyd I. ... Pacific Palisades, CA
Silverberg, Margaret ... Washington, DC
Silverberg, Mary L. ... Pittsburgh, PA
Silverberg, Maxel (Bud) ... Dallas, TX

Silverberg, Michael ... New York, NY
Silverberg, Michael J. ... New York, NY
Silverberg, Paul K. ... Miami, FL
Silverberg, Philip C. ... New York, NY
Silverberg, Rachelle ... New York, NY
Silverberg, Randall J. ... Jacksonville, FL
Silverberg, Richard Joseph ... Philadelphia, PA
Silverberg, Robert ... Los Angeles, CA
Silverberg, Robert P. ... Washington, DC
Silverberg, Ronnie L. ... New York, NY
Silverberg, Sabrina E. ... New York, NY
Silverberg, Sanford M. ... Buffalo, NY
Silverberg, Sheldon ... New York, NY
Silverberg, Stephen C. ... Garden City, NY
Silverberg, Stephen C., P.C.
Garden City, NY
Silverberg, Stephen G. ... Glastonbury, CT
Silverberg, Stephen J. ... Garden City, NY
Silverberg, Steven J. ... Washington, DC
Silverberg, Steven M. ... White Plains, NY
Silverberg Stonehill & Goldsmith, P.C.
New York, NY
Silverberg, Todd L. ... Philadelphia, PA
Silverberg & Wade ... Washington, DC
Silverberg, Yood, Sellers, McGorry & Silverberg ... Buffalo, NY
Silverblatt, Alan Michael ... Philadelphia, PA
Silverblatt, Alan S. ... North Massapequa, NY
Silverblatt, Arthur F. ... Wilkes-Barre, PA
Silverblatt, Gene ... Killeen, TX
Silverblatt, Jonathan Edward
New York, NY
Silverblatt, Tiara B. ... Louisville, KY
Silverblatt, Todd ... Brooklyn, NY
Silverblatt & Townend ... Wilkes-Barre, PA
Silver-Boice, Nanci G. ... Bellaire, TX
Silverbush, Bradley S. ... New York, NY
Silverbush, Rhona ... New York, NY
Silverfine, Jeremy ... Boston, MA
Silverglade, Christine Cohan ... Deerfield, IL
Silverglate, Frances ... New York, NY
Silverglate & Good ... Boston, MA
Silverglate, Harvey A. ... Boston, MA
Silverglate, Katherine Clark ... Miami, FL
Silverglate, Samuel H. ... Miami, FL
Silverglate, Scot A. ... Miami Lakes, FL
Silverglate, Spencer H. ... Miami, FL
Silvergleid, Diane R. ... New York, NY
Silvergleid, Naomi ... Riverside, CA
Silverhart, Louis ... Pittsburgh, PA
Silveri, Jeffrey N. ... Ann Arbor, MI
Silveria, Kathryn Dowling ... Boston, MA
Silverii, Glenn L. ... Santa Ana, CA
Silverii, Glenn L., & Associates
Santa Ana, CA
Silverio & Hall ... Miami, FL
Naples, FL
Silverio, Mark V. ... Miami, FL
Naples, FL
Silverio, William R. ... Atlanta, GA
Silverlieb, Richard R. ... Livingston, NJ
Silverman, A. Jared ... West Orange, NJ
Silverman, Abby B. ... San Diego, CA
Silverman & Abramson ... Jenkintown, PA
Silverman, Adam ... Valley Stream, NY
Silverman, Adam ... Houston, TX
Silverman, Adam J. ... Miami, FL
Silverman, Adam M. ... Philadelphia, PA
Silverman, Adam P. ... Chicago, IL
Silverman, Alan ... Carle Place, NY
Silverman, Alan D. ... Philadelphia, PA
Silverman, Alan H. ... Washington, DC
Silverman, Alan H. ... Kalamazoo, MI
Silverman, Alan R. ... San Francisco, CA
Silverman, Albert A. ... Milwaukee, WI
Silverman, Albert S.
Palm Beach Gardens, FL
Silverman, Alex ... Tempe, AZ
Silverman, Alexei M. ... Washington, DC
Silverman, Allen H. ... Philadelphia, PA
Silverman, Allen P. ... Philadelphia, PA
Silverman, Alvin ... New York, NY
Silverman, Ami V. ... Los Angeles, CA
Silverman, Andrea L. ... Boston, MA
Silverman, Andrew ... Tucson, AZ
Silverman, Andrew ... Boston, MA
Silverman, Andrew D. ... Denver, CO
Silverman, Anna May ... Suffern, NY
Silverman, Arden B. ... Los Angeles, CA
Silverman, Arlene R. ... New York, NY
Silverman, Arnold B. ... Pittsburgh, PA
Silverman, Arthur ... Elkins Park, PA
Silverman, Arthur C. ... New York, NY
Silverman, Arthur H. ... Washington, DC
Silverman & Associates, L.L.C.
Bethesda, MD
Silverman & Associates, P.C. ... Vienna, VA
Silverman, B. Scott ... Los Angeles, CA
Silverman, Barbara Ann ... Miami, FL
Silverman, Barry G. ... Phoenix, AZ
Silverman, Barry J. ... Taylor, MI
Silverman, Barry P. ... New York, NY
Silverman, Benjamin ... Savannah, GA
Silverman, Bennet H. ... New York, NY
Silverman, Bennett L. ... Los Angeles, CA
Silverman, Bernard ... Liberty, NY
Silverman, Bernard S. ... Bay Shore, NY
Silverman, Bernard T. ... Larchmont, NY
Silverman, Bernice E. ... New York, NY
Silverman, Beth ... Cincinnati, OH
Silverman, Beverly W. ... Gainesville, FL
Silverman & Bluestein ... Jenkintown, PA
Silverman, Bradley Allan ... Miami, FL
Silverman, Brian C. ... Urbana, IL
Silverman, Brian C. ... Alliance, NE
Silverman, Bruce S. ... San Ramon, CA
Silverman, Caren R. ... Philadelphia, PA
Silverman, Carl D. ... Short Hills, NJ
Silverman, Carl L. ... Santa Clara, CA
Silverman, Carl S. ... Washington, DC
Silverman, Carol G. ... Skokie, IL
Silverman, Caryn M. ... New York, NY
Silverman, Cass & Singer, Ltd. ... Chicago, IL
Silverman, Charles J. ... Teterboro, NJ
Twinsburg, OH
Silverman, Charles M. ... Houston, TX
Silverman, Charles Z. ... Friday Harbor, WA
Silverman, Cheryl R. ... Coral Gables, FL
Silverman, Claudia ... Mammoth Lakes, CA
Silverman, Claudia Bravo
San Francisco, CA
Silverman, Clifford A. ... Chicago, IL
Homewood, IL
Silverman Collura Chernis & Balzano, P.C.
New York, NY
Silverman, Craig A. ... Denver, CO
Silverman, Craig Merrill ... Cambridge, MA
Silverman, Daena A. ... Livingston, NJ
Silverman, Daniel ... New York, NY
Silverman, Daniel S. ... La Jolla, CA
Silverman, David ... Englewood, CO
Silverman, David A. ... New Bedford, MA
Providence, RI
Silverman, David B. ... Washington, DC
Silverman, David B. ... Flushing, NY
Silverman, David C. ... Pennsauken, NJ
Silverman, David H. ... San Francisco, CA
Silverman, David J. ... Joliet, IL
Silverman, David John ... Northbrook, IL
Silverman, David L. ... Great Neck, NY
Silverman, David M. ... Washington, DC
Silverman, David W. ... New City, NY
Silverman, Deborah Ann ... Columbia, MD
Silverman, Debra Ann ... Great Neck, NY
Silverman & Decaria, Chartered
Carson City, NV
Gardnerville, NV
Incline Village, NV
Las Vegas, NV
Minden, NV
Reno, NV
Stateline, NV
Silverman, Dennis G. ... Baltimore, MD
Silverman, Diane Robson ... Richmond, VA
Silverman & DiLuccio ... Valley Stream, NY
Silverman, Donald H. ... Hauppauge, NY
Silverman, Donald J. ... Washington, DC
Silverman, Donald N. ... White Plains, NY
Silverman, Edward I. ... San Diego, CA
Silverman, Eldon E. ... Denver, CO
Silverman, Elissa F. ... Miami, FL
Silverman, Elizabeth A. ... Birmingham, MI
Silverman, Elizabeth A., P.C.
Birmingham, MI
Silverman, Elizabeth F. ... Cambridge, MA
Silverman, Elliot ... New York, NY
Silverman, Elsie Brown ... Amarillo, TX
Silverman, Eric F. ... New York, NY
Silverman, Eric G. ... New York, NY
Silverman, Eugene J. ... Baltimore, MD
Silverman, Factor and Godino
Burlington, MA
Silverman, Frances R. ... Coral Gables, FL
Silverman, Fred J. ... Willow Grove, PA
Silverman, Fred J., & Associates
Willow Grove, PA
Silverman Frimmer Bernheim & McDonnell, A Professional Corporation
Westmont, NJ
Philadelphia, PA
Silverman, Gary ... Beverly Hills, CA
Silverman, Gary ... Bethesda, MD
Silverman, Gary I. ... Silver Spring, MD
Silverman, Gary R. ... Chicago, IL
Silverman, Gary R. ... Reno, NV
Silverman, Geoffrey L.
West Bloomfield, MI
Silverman, George S. ... Burlington, MA
Silverman, Gerald ... Miami, FL
Silverman, Gerald ... Philadelphia, PA
Silverman, Harnes, Harnes, Prussin & Keller
New York, NY
Silverman, Harold C. ... North Easton, MA
Silverman, Harold I. ... Syracuse, NY
Silverman, Harry ... Perth Amboy, NJ
Silverman, Harvey A. ... Vienna, VA
Silverman, Henry H. ... Boston, MA
Silverman, Henry N. ... New Haven, CT
Silverman, Howard A. ... Detroit, MI
Silverman, Howard E. ... Chicago, IL
Silverman, Howard G. ... Philadelphia, PA
Silverman, Howard R. ... Deerfield, IL
Silverman, Howard S. ... Chicago, IL
Silverman, Ian Robert ... Philadelphia, PA
Silverman, Ina L. ... New Haven, CT
Silverman, Ira W. ... Dallas, TX
Silverman, Ira W., P.C. ... Dallas, TX
Silverman, Irene L. ... Los Angeles, CA
Silverman, Irving ... Newark, NJ
Silverman, Irwin B. ... Brooklyn, NY
Silverman, J. Daniel ... Wakefield, MA
Silverman, Jack H. ... Chicago, IL
Silverman, Jacob
Federal Energy Regulatory Commission, Office of the General Counsel, GV
Silverman, James D. ... Pittsburgh, PA
Silverman, James S. ... Omaha, NE
Silverman, Janet A. ... New York, NY
Silverman, Jared Richard
Washington, DC
Silverman, Jay B. ... White Plains, NY
Silverman, Jay M. ... Jackson, MI
Silverman, Jeffrey D. ... Northbrook, IL
Silverman, Jeffrey F. ... San Francisco, CA
Silverman, Jeffrey P. ... Towson, MD
Silverman, Jeffrey R. ... East Northport, NY
Silverman, Jennifer D. ... New York, NY
Silverman, Jeremy C. ... Atlanta, GA
Silverman, Jerry ... Long Beach, CA
Silverman, Jesse G., Jr. ... New York, NY
Silverman, Jill Tilton ... Troy, MI
Silverman, Joan C. ... New York, NY
Silverman, Joan P. ... Northport, NY
Silverman, Joan S. ... New York, NY
Silverman, Jody ... Burbank, CA
Silverman, Joel A. ... New York, NY
Silverman, Joel L. ... Atlanta, GA
Silverman, Jonathan ... Bethesda, MD
Silverman, Jonathan ... Sanford, NC
Silverman, Jonathan R. ... New York, NY
Silverman, Joseph E. ... New York, NY
Silverman, Joseph S. ... Brooklyn, NY
Silverman, Joshua B. ... Chicago, IL
Silverman, Joshua David ... Richmond, VA
Silverman, Julie A. ... Minneapolis, MN
St. Paul, MN
Silverman, Karen F. ... New York, NY
Silverman, Karen L. ... Los Angeles, CA
Silverman, Kay S. ... Scottsdale, AZ
Silverman, Kenneth M. ... New York, NY
Silverman, Kenneth P. ... Jericho, NY
Silverman & Krain ... Philadelphia, PA
Silverman & Kudisch, P.C. ... Boston, MA
Silverman, Kyle A.
North Palm Beach, FL
Silverman, Larry A. ... Pittsburgh, PA
Silverman, Larry J. ... New York, NY
Silverman, Laurence A. ... New York, NY
Silverman, Laurence A.
Yorktown Heights, NY
Silverman, Lawrence D. ... Miami, FL
Silverman, Lawrence H. ... New York, NY
Silverman, Lawrence M. ... Philadelphia, PA
Silverman, Lawrence S. ... Agoura Hills, CA
Silverman, Lenore A. ... Mill Valley, CA
Silverman, Leon, (P.C.) ... New York, NY
Silverman, Leon W. ... Philadelphia, PA
Silverman, Leonard ... New York, NY
Silverman, Leonard S. ... New York, NY
Silverman, Leonard Steven
New York, NY
Silverman, Leslie N. ... New York, NY
Silverman, Lewis H. ... White Plains, NY
Silverman, Lewis R. ... New York, NY
Silverman, Lisa G. ... Pittsburgh, PA
Silverman, Lloyd B. ... Boca Raton, FL
Silverman, Lora ... Los Angeles, CA
Silverman, Lorri A. ... Santa Ana, CA
Silverman, Louis A., P.C. ... Tempe, AZ
Silverman, Louis P. ... Altoona, PA
Silverman, Louis T. ... Philadelphia, PA
Silverman & Mailman ... Philadelphia, PA
Silverman, Marc A. ... Fort Lauderdale, FL
Silverman, Marc A. ... New York, NY
Silverman, Marc A. B. ... Clearwater, FL
Silverman, Marc A.B. ... Clearwater, FL
Silverman, Marc L. ... New York, NY
Silverman, Marc L. ... Bellevue, WA
Silverman, Marci J. ... Hartford, CT
Silverman, Maris W. ... Manhasset Hills, NY
Silverman, Marjorie A. ... New York, NY
Silverman, Mark ... San Francisco, CA
Silverman, Mark David ... Freeport, NY
Silverman, Mark J. ... Washington, DC
Silverman, Marlene K. ... Miami, FL
Silverman, Marshall M. ... Burbank, CA
Silverman, Martin ... Cleveland, OH
Silverman, Martin E. ... Lakewood, NJ
Silverman, Martin J. ... New York, NY
Silverman, Martin L. ... Chicago, IL
Silverman, Marvin ... Carmel, CA
Silverman, Marvin E. ... East Chicago, IN
Silverman, Matthew A. ... Scottsdale, AZ
Silverman, Meryl A. ...
Administrative Office Of The United States Courts, GV
Silverman, Michael ... Riverside, CA
Silverman, Michael ... Chicago, IL
Silverman, Michael ... Northfield, IL
Silverman, Michael ... Newark, NJ
Silverman, Michael D. ... New York, NY
Silverman, Michael E. ... Holmdel, NJ
Silverman, Michael E. ... Pittsburgh, PA
Silverman, Michael G. ... Los Angeles, CA
Silverman, Michael G. ... Los Angeles, CA
Silverman, Michael I. ... Wilmington, DE
Silverman, Michael J. ... Chicago, IL
Silverman, Milton ... Southfield, MI
Silverman, Milton A. ... New York, NY
Silverman, Milton J., Law Offices of
San Diego, CA
Silverman, Monroe ... Stamford, CT
Silverman, Moses ... New York, NY
Silverman, Nancy ... Washington, DC
Silverman, Nathan L. ... Toledo, OH
Silverman, Neal R. ... New York, NY
Silverman, Neill E. ... Bernardsville, NJ
Silverman, Noah H. ... New York, NY
Silverman, Noah J. ... Washington, DC
Silverman, Noel L. ... New York, NY
Silverman, Norma J. ... Mamaroneck, NY
Silverman, Norman H. ... Lansing, IL
Silverman, Norman R. ... Chicago, IL
Silverman & Olivas, P.C. ... Denver, CO
Silverman, Orion J. ... Lakewood, NJ
Silverman, Owen A. ... Tempe, AZ
Torrance, CA
Silverman, Owen A., Inc., A Professional Corporation ... Tempe, AZ
Torrance, CA
Silverman, Pamela B. ... New York, NY
Silverman, Pamela K. ... Charlotte, NC
Silverman, Paul H. ... New York, NY
Silverman, Penna, Pike & Gaige ... Dover, NH
Silverman Perlstein & Acampora, LLP
Jericho, NY
Silverman, Perry R. ... Columbus, OH
Silverman, Perry R., Co., L.P.A.
Columbus, OH
Silverman, Peter ... New York, NY
Silverman, Peter A. ... Chicago, IL
Silverman, Peter J. ... New York, NY
Silverman, Peter J. ... Houston, TX
Silverman, Peter R. ... Toledo, OH
Silverman, Philip C. ... Boston, MA
Silverman, Philip E. ... New York, NY
Silverman, Phillip B. ... Philadelphia, PA
Silverman, Phillip E. ... Anaheim, CA
Silverman, Phyllis N. ... Pittsburgh, PA
Silverman, Rachel S. ... Los Angeles, CA
Silverman, Ramon A. ... Savannah, GA
Silverman, Randi ... San Francisco, CA
Silverman, Randi J. ... Johnstown, PA
Silverman, Rhona A. ... New York, NY
Silverman, Richard B., (P.C.) ... Chicago, IL
Silverman, Richard H. ... Phoenix, AZ
Silverman, Richard S. ... Washington, DC
Silverman, Rick ... Los Angeles, CA
Silverman, Rick ... Tampa, FL
Silverman & Riley ... Denver, CO
Silverman, Robert ... Alamo, CA
Silverman, Robert ... Ambler, PA
Silverman, Robert ... Jenkintown, PA
Silverman, Robert A. ... Nutley, NJ
Silverman, Robert A. ... Philadelphia, PA
Silverman, Robert B. ... Lakewood, NJ
Silverman, Robert B. ... New York, NY
Silverman, Robert J. ... Boston, MA
Silverman, Robert J. ... Minneapolis, MN
Silverman, Robert M. ... Los Angeles, CA
Silverman, Robert M. ... Deerfield, IL
Silverman, Robert M. ... Haddonfield, NJ
Philadelphia, PA
Silverman, Robert M. ... Syracuse, NY
Silverman, Robert N. ... Salinas, CA
Silverman, Robert S. ... Detroit, MI
Silverman, Robin E. ... New York, NY
Silverman, Robyn B. ... New York, NY
Silverman, Rodbard & Smith, P.C.
Kalamazoo, MI
Silverman, Ronald H. ... Hempstead, NY
Silverman, Ronald H. ... King Of Prussia, PA
Silverman, Ronald I., (A Professional Corporation) ... Los Angeles, CA
Silverman, Ronald J. ... Hartford, CT
New York, NY
Silverman, Ronald J., (P.C.)
Beverly Hills, CA
Silverman, Ross O. ... Chicago, IL
Silverman & Rozier ... Lakewood, NJ
Silverman, Ruben D. ... Lakewood, NJ
Silverman, S Jonathan ... Chicago, IL
Silverman, Sam ... Lexington, MA
Silverman, Sam S. ... Grand Forks, ND
Silverman, Samuel ... Worcester, MA
Silverman, Samuel B. ... Amarillo, TX
Silverman, Samuel J. ... New York, NY
Silverman, Samuel K. ... Kalamazoo, MI
Silverman, Samuel L. ... Boston, MA
Silverman, Sara L. ... Lihue, HI
Silverman, Saul S. ... New York, NY
Silverman, Scott Aron ... Boston, MA
Silverman, Scott D. ... Bethesda, MD
Silverman, Scott J. ... Miami, FL
Silverman, Scott Jon ... Silver Spring, MD
Silverman, Scott R. ... Atlantic City, NJ
Silverman, Scott T. ... Tampa, FL
Silverman, Seymour ... Los Angeles, CA
Silverman, Sharon D. ... San Francisco, CA
Silverman, Sheldon ... Denver, CO
Silverman, Sherman A. ... Laguna Niguel, CA
Silverman, Sherman A., A Law Corp.
Laguna Niguel, CA
Silverman Shulman & Baker, P.C.
New York, NY
Silverman, Sidney B. ... New York, NY
Silverman & Silverman
San Francisco, CA
Silverman & Silverman ... Lakewood, NJ
Silverman & Silverman ... Amarillo, TX
Silverman, Sonia Savariego ... Miami, FL
Silverman, Stacey L. ... Miami, FL
Silverman, Stanley N. ... Montclair, NJ
Silverman, Stephen A., (P.L.C.)
Santa Monica, CA
Silverman, Stephen B. ... New York, NY
Silverman, Stephen E. ... Phoenix, AZ
Silverman, Stephen H. ... Jenkintown, PA
Silverman, Stephen M. ... Milwaukee, WI
Silverman, Stephen W. ... Springfield, MA
Silverman, Steve I. ... Miami, FL
Silverman, Steven ... Miami, FL
Silverman, Steven A. ... Eden Prairie, MN
Silverman, Steven B. ... Chicago, IL
Silverman, Steven B. ... Elkins Park, PA
Silverman, Steven B. ... Pittsburgh, PA
Silverman, Steven D.
Department of Justice, Tax Division, GV
Silverman, Steven D. ... Owings Mills, MD
Silverman, Steven D., P.A.
Owings Mills, MD
Silverman, Steven E.
Environmental Protection Agency, Office of the General Counsel, GV
Silverman, Steven E. ... Northbrook, IL
Silverman, Steven G. ... Detroit, MI
Silverman, Steven H. ... Los Angeles, CA
Silverman, Steven J. ... Fort Lauderdale, FL
Silverman, Steven M. ... New York, NY
Silverman, Steven, P.A. ... Miami, FL
Silverman, Stuart A. ... City of Industry, CA
Silverman, Stuart I. (IBA) ... **Washington, DC**

Silverman, Stuart J. .... Rockville Centre, NY
Silverman, Stuart M. West Palm Beach, FL
Silverman, Susan M. .... Frankfort, KY
Silverman, Susan M. .... Kew Gardens, NY
Silverman, Suzanne L. .... New York, NY
Silverman, Terry N. .... Gainesville, FL
Silverman, Terry N., Law Offices of Gainesville, FL
Silverman, Thomas D. Glenwood Springs, CO
Silverman, Thomas N. Palm Beach Gardens, FL
Silverman, Thomas N., P.A. Palm Beach Gardens, FL
Silverman, Timothy J. .... San Diego, CA
Silverman, Tracy E. .... Detroit, MI
Silverman, Warren E. .... Hollywood, FL
Silverman, William .... Washington, DC
Silverman, William M. .... New York, NY
Silverman, William S. .... Denver, CO
Silverman, Wm. L. .... Chicago, IL
Silvermintz, Mark M. .... Belleville, IL
Silvern, Mark C. .... Mountain View, CA
Silvernail, J. Preston .... Viera, FL
Silvernail, Susan J. .... Birmingham, AL
Silvernale, Grant Josiah, III .... Seattle, WA
Silvernale, Lawrence D. .... Seattle, WA
Silvernale, Marya Johanna .... Everett, WA
Silvernell, George R. .... Oneonta, NY
Silvers, Adam P. .... Mineola, NY
Silvers, Aimée Domínguez .... Los Angeles, CA
Silvers, Arnold J. .... Philadelphia, PA
Silvers, Bruce C. .... Hartford, CT
Silvers, Charles R. .... St. Petersburg, FL
Silvers, Clem H. .... El Dorado, KS
Silvers, Dean .... New York, NY
Silvers, Eileen S. .... New York, NY
Silvers, Eleanor Cohen .... El Cajon, CA
Silvers, Ellen Dee .... Aventura, FL
Silvers, G. Matthew .... Evanston, IL
Silvers, H. R., A Prof. Corp. Greeneville, TN
Silvers, Jane Fink .... Cincinnati, OH
Silvers, Jessica Perrin .... Los Angeles, CA
Silvers, Kyle A. .... Toledo, OH
Silvers, Laura R. .... New York, NY
Silvers, Laurie S. .... Boca Raton, FL
Silvers, Lorraine A. .... Los Angeles, CA
Silvers, Marcia J. .... Miami, FL
Silvers, Mark M., Jr. .... Savannah, GA
Silvers, Michael H. .... Los Angeles, CA
Silvers, Michael H., A Law Corporation Los Angeles, CA
Silvers, Morton L. .... San Francisco, CA
Silvers, Rachel A. .... San Francisco, CA
Silvers, Ruth .... Houston, TX
Silvers, Samuel M. .... New York, NY
Silvers, Simpson & Creasy, P.C. Savannah, GA
Silvers, Stephanie C. .... Los Angeles, CA
Silvers, Teri D. .... New York, NY
Silverschotz, Mark D. .... New York, NY
Silvershein, Daniel .... New York, NY
Silvershein, Daniel Michael .... New York, NY
Silvershein, Joel Michael Fort Lauderdale, FL
Silversher, Mark .... Telluride, CO
Silversmith, Jol A. .... Washington, DC
Silversmith, Lyle F. .... Brooklyn, NY
Silversmith, Mark .... New York, NY
Silversmith, Robert G. .... New York, NY
Silversmith, Sharon G. .... Albany, NY
Silverson, Jeffrey .... Brooklyn, NY
Silverson & Pareres .... New York, NY
Silverson, Robert M., Jr. .... New York, NY
Silverstein, Abraham .... Chicago, IL
Silverstein, Adam C. .... New York, NY
Silverstein, Adam G. .... Flourtown, PA
Silverstein, Alan .... North Palm Beach, FL
Silverstein, Alisa .... New York, NY
Silverstein, Allan Michael .... New York, NY
Silverstein, Allen .... Milwaukee, WI
Silverstein, Amy .... Boston, MA
Silverstein, Amy L. .... San Francisco, CA
Silverstein, Andrew .... New York, NY
Silverstein, Andrew B. .... Chevy Chase, MD
Silverstein, Anne K. .... St. Louis, MO
Silverstein, Arthur A. .... New York, NY
Silverstein, Audrey J. .... Philadelphia, PA
Silverstein, Barry .... Sarasota, FL
Silverstein, Barry D. .... Aventura, FL
Silverstein, Barry W. .... Brooklyn, NY
New York, NY
Silverstein, Bornstein & Thomas, S.C. Milwaukee, WI
Silverstein, Bruce L. .... Wilmington, DE
Silverstein, Burton .... Chicago, IL
Silverstein, Carl J. .... Monticello, NY
Silverstein, Carol K. .... Raleigh, NC
Silverstein, Charles .... Great Neck, NY
New York, NY
Silverstein & Cook, P.A. .... Raleigh, NC
Silverstein, Craig W. .... Washington, DC
Silverstein, Cynthia B. .... San Francisco, CA
Silverstein, Darryn L. North Miami Beach, FL
Silverstein, David .... Boston, MA
Silverstein, David A. .... Philadelphia, PA
Silverstein, David E. .... San Diego, CA
Silverstein, David L. .... Birmingham, AL
Silverstein, Deborah R. .... San Francisco, CA
Silverstein, Douglas N. Universal City, CA
Silverstein, Edward M. Federal Energy Regulatory Commission, Office of the Administrative Law Judges, GV
Silverstein, Elias .... Lanham, MD
Silverstein, Elliot S. .... Boston, MA
Silverstein, Evan .... Philadelphia, PA
Silverstein, Francine Nicole .... Atlanta, GA
Silverstein, Frank .... White Plains, NY
Silverstein, Fred Howard .... Ellicott City, MD
Silverstein, Gary T. .... New York, NY
Silverstein, Glen A. .... New York, NY
Silverstein, Gregg Alan .... Miami, FL
Silverstein, Harlan J. .... New York, NY
Silverstein, Harvey C. .... Albany, NY
Silverstein, Howard L. .... Miami, FL
Silverstein, Howard L., P.A. .... Miami, FL
Silverstein & Hurwitz, P.C. .... New York, NY
Silverstein, Ira .... Sunrise, FL
Silverstein, Ira B. .... Philadelphia, PA
Silverstein, Ira Isaac .... Chicago, IL
Silverstein, Irl R., (A Prof. Law Corp.) Gretna, LA
Silverstein, Jack Owen .... Brockton, MA
Silverstein, Jack S. .... Trenton, NJ
Silverstein, James I. .... San Francisco, CA
Silverstein, James J. .... Sherman Oaks, CA
Silverstein, James R. .... New Orleans, LA
Silverstein, Jay D. .... New York, NY
Silverstein, Jeffrey B. .... New York, NY
Silverstein, Jeffrey D. .... New York, NY
Silverstein, Jeffrey M., and Associates Dayton, OH
Silverstein, Jeffrey N. .... Burke, VA
Silverstein, Joel M. .... Roseland, NJ
Silverstein, John M. .... Raleigh, NC
Silverstein, Jonathan .... Boston, MA
Silverstein, Joseph B. .... Philadelphia, PA
Silverstein, Joshua M. .... Chicago, IL
Silverstein, Judi LaMountain New York, NY
Silverstein, Julius .... Chevy Chase, MD
Silverstein, Karen .... Ithaca, NY
Silverstein, Keith D. .... New York, NY
Silverstein, Keith D. .... New York, NY
Silverstein, Kenneth A. .... Hampton, NH
Silverstein Langer Newburgh & McElyea, LLP New York, NY
Silverstein, Larry .... New York, NY
Silverstein, Laurie Selber Wilmington, DE
Silverstein, Lawrence I. .... Boston, MA
Silverstein, Lawrence Mark .... Knoxville, TN
Silverstein, Lee .... Pennsauken, NJ
Silverstein, Leila Ellen .... Wallingford, CT
Silverstein, Leo .... New York, NY
Silverstein, Leo A. .... Chicago, IL
Silverstein, Leonard A. .... Atlanta, GA
Silverstein, Leonard L. .... Washington, DC
Silverstein, Lorne F. .... Baltimore, MD
Silverstein, Louis A. .... Ansonia, CT
Silverstein, M. Howard Department of Agriculture, Office of the General Counsel, GV
Silverstein, Marc .... Staten Island, NY
Silverstein, Marc Alan .... Cleveland, OH
Silverstein, Marc S. .... New York, NY
Silverstein, Margaret McAlister New Orleans, LA
Silverstein, Marita E. .... Southfield, MI
Silverstein, Mark .... Boston, MA
Silverstein, Mark C. .... New York, NY
Silverstein, Mark L. .... Newton, MA
Silverstein, Martin J., & Associates, L.L.C. Voorhees, NJ
Philadelphia, PA
Silverstein, Merle L. .... St. Louis, MO
Silverstein, Michael A. .... Providence, RI
Silverstein, Michael J. North Miami Beach, FL
Silverstein, Mitchell E. .... Miami, FL
Silverstein, Mitchell F. .... St. Louis, MO
Silverstein, Morris B. Federal Deposit Insurance Corporation, Professional Liability Section, GV
Silverstein and Mullens, P.L.L.C. Washington, DC
Silverstein, Murray B. .... St. Petersburg, FL
Silverstein, Nathan M. .... New Haven, CT
Silverstein, Nathan R. .... Newark, NJ
Silverstein & Osach, P.C. .... New Haven, CT
Silverstein, Owen Robert Bala Cynwyd, PA
Silverstein, Owen Robert Philadelphia, PA
Silverstein, P. Jason .... Santa Rosa, CA
Silverstein, Paul J. .... New York, NY
Silverstein, Paul N. .... New York, NY
Silverstein, Peter A. .... Great Neck, NY
Silverstein, Philip I. .... Brooklyn, NY
Silverstein, Ralph .... Brockton, MA
Silverstein, Randi S. .... Albany, NY
Silverstein, Richard .... Denver, CO
Silverstein, Richard Jay .... Palo Alto, CA
Silverstein, Richard P. .... New Haven, CT
Silverstein, Robert .... United States Senate, Committee Legal Personnel, GV
Silverstein, Robert .... Milwaukee, WI
Silverstein, Robert D. .... Santa Monica, CA
Silverstein, Robert M. .... Roseland, NJ
Silverstein, Robert P. .... Los Angeles, CA
Silverstein, Robert S. .... Parsippany, NJ
Silverstein, Sanford D. .... Flushing, NY
Silverstein, Scott E. .... Washington, DC
Silverstein, Scott G. .... Washington, DC
Silverstein, Sheryl Rubinstein La Jolla, CA
Silverstein, Stanley P. .... New York, NY
Silverstein, Steven .... Chicago, IL
Silverstein, Steven D. .... Tustin, CA
Silverstein, Steven M. .... Montvale, NJ
New City, NY
Silverstein, Stuart Y. .... Los Angeles, CA
Silverstein, Susan Ann .... Rochester, NY
Silverstein, Susan M. .... Silver Spring, MD
Silverstein, Thomas D. Securities and Exchange Commission, Division of Enforcement, GV
Silverstein, Victor C. .... Buffalo, NY
Silverstein, Walter C. .... New York, NY
Silverstein, Walter C., P.C. .... New York, NY
Silverstein-Wade, Judi L. .... San Jose, CA
Silversten, Ronald K. .... Warren, NJ
Silverstone, Adam H. .... New York, NY
Silverstone, Barbara R. .... Midland Park, NJ
Silverstone, David .... Hartford, CT
Silverstone & Koontz, P.C. .... Hartford, CT
Silverstone, Mark J. .... Austin, TX
Georgetown, TX
Silverstone, Paul H. .... New York, NY
Silverstone, Sophie .... Tucson, AZ
Silverstone, Stanley J. .... New York, NY
Silverstone & Stern .... Tucson, AZ
Silverstone, Susan M. .... New Hyde Park, NY
Silvert, Corinne G., Esq. .... Danbury, CT
Silvert, Donald J. .... Philadelphia, PA
Silvert, Leon .... Brooklyn, NY
Silver Taube, Ruth A. .... San Jose, CA
Silverthorn, Richard W. .... Milwaukee, WI
Silverthorn, Robert S., Jr. .... Louisville, KY
Silverthorn, Shane M. .... Tacoma, WA
Silverthorne, Katherine Andrea Washington, DC
Silverthorne, Willis C. .... San Francisco, CA
Silverton, Lawrence E. North Hollywood, CA
Silverton, Ronald R. .... Los Angeles, CA
Silvertooth, Lynn N. .... Sarasota, FL
Silvertrust, Raymond H. R. Highland Park, IL
Silvertrust & Silvertrust .... Highland Park, IL
Silver-Westrick, Avarelle .... Dana Point, CA
Silverwood, Harry E., Jr. .... Baltimore, MD
Silverwood, James R. Department of Justice, Criminal Division, GV
Silvester & Conroy .... Salt Lake City, UT
Silvester, Fred R. .... Salt Lake City, UT
Silvester, Kent William .... Sacramento, CA
Silvester, L. V., III .... Washington, DC
Silvester, Richard D. .... Concord, CA
Silvestri, Amy L. .... Columbus, OH
Silvestri, Arnold A. .... Chicago, IL
Silvestri, Christopher J. .... New York, NY
Silvestri, Frank A. .... New Orleans, LA
Silvestri, Frank J., Jr. .... Bridgeport, CT
Silvestri, Gary F. .... Toms River, NJ
Silvestri, George A., III .... Boston, MA
Silvestri, George J., Jr. .... Novato, CA
Silvestri, James P. C. .... Las Vegas, NV
Silvestri, Jeffrey A. .... Las Vegas, NV
Reno, NV
Silvestri, John H. .... Chicago, IL
Silvestri, John M. .... Chestertown, NY
Silvestri, John M. .... Pittsburgh, PA
Silvestri, Joseph M. .... New York, NY
Silvestri, Laurie A. .... Oakbrook Terrace, IL
Silvestri, Lawrence A. West Palm Beach, FL
Silvestri, Louis S. .... New York, NY
Silvestri, Lynette .... Staten Island, NY
Silvestri, Mary Anne .... Long Beach, CA
Silvestri & Massicot .... New Orleans, LA
Silvestri, Peter N. .... Chicago, IL
Silvestri, Philip S. .... Menlo Park, CA
Redwood City, CA
Silvestri, Stephen M. .... Baltimore, MD
Silvestri, Steven P. .... Redwood City, CA
Silvestrini, Jeffrey L. .... Salt Lake City, UT
Silvestro, Brian T. .... Southport, CT
Silvey, Charles D., Jr. .... Fairbanks, AK
Silvey, Donald K. .... Houston, TX
Silvey, Gregory G. .... Anchorage, AK
Silvey, Joseph F. .... Los Angeles, CA
Silvey, Michael R. .... Portland, OR
Silvey, Michael W. .... Fredericktown, MO
Silvey, Steve C. .... Chicago, IL
Silvi, Silvio M. .... Toms River, NJ
Silvia, Jane E. .... Springfield, MA
Silvia, Jeffrey A. .... Stockton, CA
Silvia, Jerald .... Fall River, MA
Silvia, Joseph H. .... Fall River, MA
Silvia, Judith A. .... Boston, MA
Silvia, Marilyn S. .... Princeton, NJ
Silvia, Paul D. .... Brockton, MA
Silvia, William P. .... Leominster, MA
Silvian, A. Lance .... East Chicago, IN
Silvian, David L. .... Boston, MA
Silvian, Sidney J. .... Columbus, OH
Silvis & Ambrose, P.C. .... Thomasville, GA
Silvis, Douglas K. .... Thomasville, GA
Silvis, James R. .... Greensburg, PA
Silvis, Jennifer K. .... Miami, FL
Silvis, Michael J. .... Eugene, OR
Silvius, Douglas D. .... Kansas City, MO
Silvus, David J. .... Clarksville, TN
Silvy, L. E. .... Brooklyn, NY
Silvyn, Jeffrey S. .... Tucson, AZ
Silvyn, Keri Lazarus .... Tucson, AZ
Silzer, Scot A. .... Winter Park, FL
Sim, Ashley S. H. .... Los Angeles, CA
Sim, J. Ronald .... Seattle, WA
Sim, Jennifer S. .... Menlo Park, CA
Sim, Michael P. .... Boca Raton, FL
Sim, Randolph B. .... Treasury Department, Office of the General Counsel, GV
Sim, Steven P. .... Los Angeles, CA
Sim, Victor H. .... Los Angeles, CA
Sima, Carlo .... Los Angeles, CA
Simafranca, Ryan D. .... Minneapolis, MN
Simafrance, Ryan .... Minneapolis, MN
Simakas, Alexander J. .... Pittsburgh, PA
Simakis, George K. .... Cleveland, OH
Simala, Jodi Ann .... Chicago, IL
Siman, Mark I. .... Trenton, NJ
Siman, Steven A. .... Troy, MI
Siman, Steven A., P.C. .... Troy, MI
Siman, Terry J. .... Spring House, PA
Simandl, Robert H. .... West Orange, NJ
Simandl, Robert J. .... Green Bay, WI
Madison, WI
Milwaukee, WI
Simandle, Jerome B. .... Camden, NJ
Simanek, Barbara A. .... Pittsburgh, PA
Simanek, Stephen A. .... Racine, WI
Simank, Deborah .... Corpus Christi, TX
Simank, Dow .... Oklahoma City, OK
Simank, Ronald A. .... Corpus Christi, TX
Simanski, John F., Jr. .... Baltimore, MD
Simanski, Joseph V. .... Plymouth, IN
Simantob, David .... Los Angeles, CA
Simantob, Lisa D. .... Los Angeles, CA
Simantov, A.Z. .... New York, NY
Simantov, Leora R. .... Towson, MD
Siman-Tov, Leslie A. .... Yorktown, VA
Simantz, Donald J. .... Aurora, IL
Simao, Salvador P. .... New York, NY
Simard, Joanne M. .... Hartford, CT
Simard, Kevin J. .... Boston, MA
Simard, Linda Sandstrom .... Boston, MA
Simard, Tana K. .... Denver, CO
Simard, Terri K. .... Minneapolis, MN
Simari, Paula V. .... Jamaica, NY
Simarski, Edward J. .... Milwaukee, WI
Simas, Alexander F. .... Santa Maria, CA
Simas, David M. .... Taunton, MA
Simas, Gina .... Los Angeles, CA
Simas, Juli L. .... Orlando, FL
Simas, Steven L. .... Sacramento, CA
Simasek, Robert G. .... Pittsburgh, PA
Simasko, James Matthew Mount Clemens, MI
Simasko, Leonard J. .... Mount Clemens, MI
Simasko, Patrick Michael Mount Clemens, MI
Simasko, Simasko & Simasko, P.C. Mount Clemens, MI
Simball, Barbara Joseph General Accounting Office, Office of the General Counsel, GV
Simberg, Bruce F. .... Hollywood, FL
Miami, FL
Simbol & Crossen .... Terre Haute, IN
Simbol, Nellie L. .... Terre Haute, IN
Simbole, Bernard J. .... Arlington, VA
Simbole, Bernard J., P.C. .... Arlington, VA
Simboli, Dorothy R. .... Boston, MA
Simbro, Robert P. .... Phoenix, AZ
Simburg, Ketter, Sheppard & Purdy, LLP Seattle, WA
Simburg, Melvyn Jay .... Seattle, WA
Simchak, Matthew S. .... Washington, DC
Simchak, Thomas G. .... Houston, TX
Simchowitz, Cyprienne .... Kansas City, MO
Simchuk, Carrie C. .... Seattle, WA
Simcic, Peter M., Jr .... Columbus, OH
Simcock, Stephen E. .... Frederick, MD
Simcoe, Daniel .... Grants Pass, OR
Simcoe, Edward F. .... Palos Hills, IL
Simcoe, Kathleen Woodruff .... Atlanta, GA
Simcoe, Steven W. .... Tulsa, OK
Simcox and Barclay .... Annapolis, MD
Simcox, Daniel W. .... Philadelphia, PA
Simcox, Edwin J. .... Indianapolis, IN
Simcox, Jeffrey H. .... Hatfield, PA
Simcox, John S. .... Annapolis, MD
Sime, Billy M. .... Salem, OR
Sime, Donald L. .... Waukegan, IL
Sime, Reba Howell .... Chattanooga, TN
Simecek, David J. .... Richfield, OH
Simei, Joseph A. .... Washington, DC
Simek, Ervin J. .... Barrington, IL
Simek, Patrick C. .... Lubbock, TX
Simels, Robert M. .... New York, NY
Simels, Robert M., P.C. .... New York, NY
Simen, Figura & Parker, P.L.C. .... Flint, MI
Simen, Sander H. .... Flint, MI
Simenauer, Jeffrey A. .... Phoenix, AZ
Simendinger, Donna L. .... Bellmore, NY
Simendinger, Mark .... Lebanon, OH
Simendinger, William E. South Burlington, VT
Simenon, Pierre N. .... Malibu, CA
Simenowitz, Steven H. .... Hauppauge, NY
Simens, Jay .... Garden City, NY
Simensen, Richard E. .... San Diego, CA
Simensky, Brenda T. .... New York, NY
Simensky, Glenn E. .... Brooklyn, NY
Simensky, Melvin .... New York, NY
Simenson, Caroline A. .... St. Louis Park, MN
Simenson, Kelly S. .... Chicago, IL
Simental, Luis Carlos .... San Diego, CA
Simeone, Annmarie .... Somerville, NJ
Simeone, Bruce .... Jefferson City, MO
Simeone, Donna Previti .... Boca Raton, FL
Simeone, Donna Previti, Attorney at Law Boca Raton, FL
Simeone, Frank T. .... Suffern, NY
Simeone, Gerard D. .... Fairfield, NJ
Simeone, John D. .... Walpole, MA
Simeone, Richard J. .... Fort Lauderdale, FL
Simeone, Richard J., Jr. .... West Orange, NJ
Simeone, Robert A. .... Colville, WA
Simeone, Salvatore A. .... Morristown, NJ
Simeone, Thomas J. .... Washington, DC
Simeone, Timothy J. .... Washington, DC
Simeonidis, Nicholas .... Greenwich, CT
Simeri, Joseph V. .... South Bend, IN
Simerlein, Steven J. .... San Diego, CA

Simerly, Janine S. .... San Francisco, CA
Simerman, Anne E. .... Fort Wayne, IN
Simerman, Marjorie .... Myrtle Beach, SC
Simerman, Marjorie, P.A. .... Myrtle Beach, SC
Simerson, Diane L. .... Minneapolis, MN
Simes, Alvin Leonard .... West Helena, AR
Simes, Jeffrey Alan .... Boston, MA
Simes, Joanne Schnurr .... Richmond, IL
Simes, Michael L. .... Phoenix, AZ
Simet, Anne Smith .... Buffalo, NY
Simeti, Thomas .... Stony Point, NY
Simhauser Law Office .... Springfield, IL
Simhauser, Louis E. .... Vero Beach, FL
Simhauser, Val C. .... Springfield, IL
Simhauser, Walter J. .... Springfield, IL
Simi, Roberta J. .... Santa Rosa, CA
Simiele, David L. .... Canton, OH
Salem, OH
Simiele, Thomas C. .... Westlake, OH
Simien, Clyde R. .... Lafayette, LA
Simien, Marshall J., Jr. .... New Orleans, LA
Simien & Miniex, A Prof. Law Corp.
Lafayette, LA
Simien, Reneé R. .... Cameron, LA
Lake Charles, LA
Simien, Tamara D. .... Baton Rouge, LA
Simile, Belinda H. .... Powell, OH
Simili, Lisa J. .... Derry, NH
Siminerio, Andrew C. .... Pittsburgh, PA
Siminerio, Anthony J. .... Medford, NY
Siminoff, Faren R. .... New York, NY
Siminoff, Ian W. .... Florham Park, NJ
New York, NY
Siminoff, Jeffrey M. .... Morristown, NJ
Siminoff, Julie B. .... New York, NY
Siminou, Stephen S. .... New York, NY
Siminovsky, Paul .... Brooklyn, NY
Simins, Richard M. .... Philadelphia, PA
Simins, Robert A. .... New York, NY
Siminski, Robert M. .... Troy, MI
Simio, Michael V. .... Morristown, NJ
Simison, David A. .... Annapolis, MD
Simke Chodos .... Los Angeles, CA
Simke, Stuart A. .... Los Angeles, CA
Simkin, Andrew T. .... Department of State,
Foreign Service Institute, GV
Simkin, Brian M. .... Department of Justice,
Civil Division, GV
Simkin, Carol F. .... New York, NY
Simkin, Deborah Morris .... Newton, MA
Simkin, Donald L. .... Richmond, IN
Simkin, Lawrence M. .... Richmond, IN
Simkin, Michael .... Chicago, IL
Simkin, Michael Jay .... Los Angeles, CA
Simkin, Morris N. .... New York, NY
Simkin, Samuel .... San Diego, CA
Simkin, Steven .... New York, NY
Simkins, Brenda H. .... Bloomington, IL
Simkins, Charles N. .... Northville, MI
Simkins, Christopher P. .... Washington, DC
Simkins, David K. .... St. Louis, MO
Simkins, Raymond G. .... San Jose, CA
Simkins, Rebecca G. .... Northville, MI
Simkins, Scott I. .... St. Petersburg, FL
Simkins, Scott I., P.A. .... St. Petersburg, FL
Simkins & Simkins, P.C. .... Detroit, MI
Northville, MI
Southfield, MI
Simkins, Steven C. .... Bloomington, IL
Simkins, Tara R. .... Augusta, GA
Aiken, SC
Simko, David J. .... Toledo, OH
Simko, James S. .... Denver, CO
Simko, John E. .... Sioux Falls, SD
Simko, John M. .... Crystal Lake, IL
Simko, John S. .... Boise, ID
Simko Law Firm, The, L.L.C.
Bridgeport, CT
Simko, Mark J. .... Middlesex, NJ
Simko, Patricia A. .... New York, NY
Simko, Stephen J., Jr.
Occupational Safety and Health Review Commission,
Administrative Law Judges, GV
Simko, V. Michael, Jr. .... Bridgeport, CT
Simko, Vincent M. .... Bridgeport, CT
Simkovic, Martin S. .... Miami, FL
Simkovitz, Wilbert .... Clawson, MI
Simkow, Michael P. .... Livonia, MI
Simkunas, Michael J. .... Oak Park, IL
Simkus, Michael P. .... Chicago, IL
Simler, Francis L. .... Cincinnati, OH
Simler, Michael W. .... Terre Haute, IN
Simlick, Linda C. T. .... Sacramento, CA
Simmang, Michael J. .... Giddings, TX
Simmang & Roesch, L.L.P. .... Giddings, TX
Simmelkjaer, Robert T. .... New York, NY
Simmelkjaer, Robert T., II .... New York, NY
Simmens, Adam F. .... Philadelphia, PA
Simmental, David A. .... El Paso, TX
Simmer, David R. .... Boston, MA
Simmer, Jared D. .... Pittsburgh, PA
Simmer, L. Keith .... Tyler, TX
Simmer, Robert W. .... Missouri City, TX
Simmer, Samuel S. .... Southfield, MI
Simmer, W. Scott .... Washington, DC
Simmerer, John M. .... Southfield, MI
Simmerman, Frank E., Jr.
Clarksburg, WV
Simmerman, George M., Jr. .... Pascagoula, MS
Simmerman, Sam O. .... Canton, OH
Salem, OH
Simmermon & Johnson, P.A.
Daytona Beach, FL
Orlando, FL
Simmermon, Robert W. .... Orlando, FL
Simmers, H. Edwin .... Bellingham, WA
Simmers, Walter W. .... Hartford, CT
Simmington, Glenn M. .... Flint, MI
Simmler, Robert W. .... Franklin, MA
Simmon, Paul C. .... Scottsdale, AZ
Simmon, Randall C., Law Office of
Temple, TX
Simmonds, Adolfo M. .... Palm Harbor, FL
Simmonds, Andrew R. .... New York, NY
Simmonds, Denise A. .... Washington, DC
Simmonds, James H. .... Arlington, VA
Simmonds, James M., III .... Del Rio, TX
Simmonds, Jean McCree .... Pittsburgh, PA
Simmonds, John E. .... Mankato, MN
Simmonds, John G. .... Whitehouse, NJ
Simmonds, Karen H. .... Seattle, WA
Simmonds, Michael R. .... San Francisco, CA
Simmonds, Nancy S. .... Auburn, NY
Simmonds, Rasheed A. .... Cincinnati, OH
Simmonds, Simmonds & Wright
Mankato, MN
Simmonds, Therese C. .... Mankato, MN
Simmonds-DiLoreto, Noelle .... Robinson, PA
Simmons, Abraham A. .... San Francisco, CA
Simmons, Alan R. .... Huntington, WV
Simmons, Alexander J., Jr. .... Atlanta, GA
Simmons, Amana Thompson .... McLean, VA
Simmons, Anderson M. .... Austin, TX
Simmons, Andrew T. .... San Diego, CA
Simmons, Anna Cunningham
Baton Rouge, LA
Simmons, Annie R. .... Atlanta, GA
Simmons, Barbara .... Fort Collins, CO
Simmons, Barbara J. .... Indianapolis, IN
Simmons, Barry E. .... Washington, DC
Simmons, Barry K. .... Sanford, FL
Simmons, Berkeley L. .... Elizabeth, WV
Simmons, Bobby D. .... Forest Park, GA
Simmons, Bonnie K. .... Westfield, IN
Simmons, Brent E. .... Lansing, MI
Simmons, Bret S. .... Bellingham, WA
Simmons, Brian E. .... Houston, TX
Simmons, Brian J. .... Rochester Hills, MI
Simmons, Brunson & Associates
Anniston, AL
Centre, AL
Fort Payne, AL
Gadsden, AL
Guntersville, AL
Oneonta, AL
Pell City, AL
Simmons, Bryan J. .... Hershey, PA
Simmons, Cameron B. .... Jeanerette, LA
Simmons, Charles .... New York, NY
Simmons, Charles A. .... New York, NY
Simmons, Charles B., Jr. .... Charlotte, NC
Simmons, Charles B., Jr. .... Greenville, SC
Simmons, Charles E. .... Topeka, KS
Simmons, Charles L., Jr. .... Baltimore, MD
Simmons, Charles O., Jr. .... Baton Rouge, LA
Simmons, Charles T. .... Washington, DC
Simmons, Charles W. .... Las Vegas, NV
Simmons, Christine R. .... Santa Ana, CA
Simmons, Christopher S.
Montgomery, AL
Simmons, Clarence G., Jr. .... Troy, NY
Simmons, Clarence, Jr. .... Gadsden, AL
Simmons, Clayton D. .... Sanford, FL
Simmons, Cleatous J. .... Orlando, FL
Simmons & Cleaver, LLP .... Canton, OH
Simmons & Clyne, P.A. .... Miami, FL
Port St. Lucie, FL
West Palm Beach, FL
Simmons, Consuella D. .... Houston, TX
Simmons, Craig .... Pasadena, CA
Simmons, Curtis W. .... Ann Arbor, MI
Simmons, D. Randy .... Juneau, AK
Simmons, Dale R. .... Indianapolis, IN
Simmons, Daniel K. .... Toms River, NJ
Simmons, Daniel R. .... Springfield, IL
Simmons, Darlene S. .... Orlando, FL
Simmons, David B. .... Kansas City, MO
Simmons, David C. .... Washington, DC
Alexandria, VA
Simmons, David E. .... Little Rock, AR
Simmons, David H. .... Orlando, FL
Simmons, David J. .... Canton, OH
Simmons, David L. .... Indianapolis, IN
Simmons, David N. .... Denver, CO
Simmons, David P. .... Olathe, KS
Simmons, Dawn G. .... Syracuse, NY
Simmons, Deanis L. .... Tazewell, VA
Simmons, Deborah Storey .... Dallas, TX
Simmons, Delores J. .... Birmingham, AL
Simmons, Denise .... Pittsburgh, PA
Simmons, Denise A. .... Montgomery, AL
Simmons, Dennis E. .... Las Vegas, NV
Simmons, Dennis E., Law Office of
San Francisco, CA
Simmons and Derr .... Winnfield, LA
Simmons, D'Lisa R. .... Houston, TX
Simmons, Donald C. .... Waterbury, CT
Simmons, Donald D. .... Perrysburg, OH
Simmons, Donald O. .... Gulfport, MS
Simmons, Doreen A. .... Syracuse, NY
Simmons, Douglas .... New York, NY
Simmons, Douglas J. .... Pittsburgh, PA
Simmons, Douglas K. .... Charlotte, NC
Simmons, Duncan M. .... Nevada City, CA
Simmons, Edward B. .... Tarboro, NC
Simmons, Edward W. .... Irvine, CA
Simmons, E. J. .... Portland, OR
Simmons, Ellen B. .... Boston, MA
Simmons, Erny G. .... Dallas, TX
Simmons, Esmeralda I. .... Brooklyn, NY
Simmons, Eugene A. .... Jackson, MS
Simmons, Evett L. .... Port St. Lucie, FL
Simmons, F. Chase .... Overland Park, KS
Simmons and Fields, P.A. .... Baltimore, MD
Simmons & Fleming .... Kokomo, IN
Simmons & Fletcher .... Houston, TX
Simmons, Forrest W. .... Portland, OR
Simmons, Frank C. .... Rancho Cordova, CA
Simmons, Franklin Bruce, III
Sharon Center, OH
Simmons, Frederick F. .... Spartanburg, SC
Simmons, Frederick L. .... Los Angeles, CA
Simmons, G. Lindsay .... Washington, DC
Simmons, Gary L. .... Altamonte Springs, FL
Simmons, Gary W. .... Elwood, IN
Simmons, Gayle Gladous .... Needham, MA
Simmons, George R. .... Cleveland, OH
Simmons, George W. F. .... Lopez, WA
Simmons, Gerald G. .... Columbus, OH
Simmons, Gerald W. .... Cincinnati, OH
Simmons, Geraldine C. .... Chicago, IL
Simmons, Gilmer T. .... Birmingham, AL
Simmons, Gordon B. .... Norristown, PA
Simmons, Gracella .... Baton Rouge, LA
Simmons, Gregory E. .... Sugar Land, TX
Simmons, Gregory K.
Charlotte Amalie, St. Thomas, VI
Simmons, Griffin & Lydon, L.L.P.
Columbia, SC
Simmons, Hal F., Professional Association
Albuquerque, NM
Simmons, Harry D. .... Shreveport, LA
Simmons, Harvey O., III .... Syracuse, NY
Simmons, Haven E. .... Ellicott City, MD
Simmons, Heather J.E. .... Detroit, MI
Simmons, Heber S., III .... Jackson, MS
Simmons, Heidi L. .... Nashville, TN
Simmons, Henry H. .... Jacksonville, FL
Simmons, Henry R., Jr. .... Chicago, IL
Simmons, Howard D. .... Atlanta, GA
Simmons, Howard D. .... New York, NY
Simmons, Howard D., P.C. .... Atlanta, GA
Simmons, Howard D., P.C. .... New York, NY
Simmons, Hunt, Simmons & Keehr
Olivia, MN
Simmons, Ian .... Washington, DC
Simmons, J. Earl, Jr. .... Philadelphia, PA
Simmons, J. Rawleigh .... White Stone, VA
Simmons, J. Scott .... Clearwater, FL
Simmons, J. Tayloe, Jr. .... Jackson, MS
Simmons, Jack H. .... Lewiston, ME
Simmons, Jack M., III .... Washington, DC
Simmons, Jack R. .... Miami, FL
Simmons, Jacolyn A. .... Washington, DC
Simmons, Jacqueline A. .... Indianapolis, IN
Simmons, James A. .... Prescott, AZ
Simmons, James Andrew .... Nashville, TN
Simmons, James C. .... Williamsville, NY
Simmons, James C. .... Williamsville, NY
Simmons, James C., Jr. .... Atlanta, GA
Simmons, James Charles .... Allentown, PA
Valley Forge, PA
Simmons, James E. .... Houston, TX
Simmons, James F. .... Detroit, MI
Simmons, James H. .... Sleepy Hollow, NY
Simmons, James L. .... Denver, CO
Simmons, James L. .... Houston, TX
Simmons, James R. .... Providence, RI
Simmons, Jan S. .... Chapel Hill, NC
Simmons, Jane Hummel .... Seattle, WA
Simmons, Jannace & Stagg, L.L.P.
East Meadow, NY
Simmons, Jay B. .... Bowling Green, KY
Simmons, Jay R. .... Sacramento, CA
Simmons, Jeffrey G. .... Atlanta, GA
Simmons, Jeffrey L. .... McArthur, OH
Simmons, Jeffrey L., and N. Robert Grillo
McArthur, OH
Simmons, Jeffrey R. .... Phoenix, AZ
Simmons, Joan P. .... Rosemont, IL
Simmons, Joanne Shipley .... Denton, TX
Simmons, Joe A. .... Findlay, OH
Simmons, John Anthony
North Hampton, NH
Simmons, John D. .... Granite City, IL
Simmons, John E. .... Boston, MA
Simmons, John F. .... Scottsbluff, NE
Simmons, John F. .... Dallas, TX
Simmons, John G. .... Idaho Falls, ID
Simmons, John H. .... Orlando, FL
Simmons, John P. .... Chicago, IL
Simmons, John R. .... Seattle, WA
Simmons, John R., Jr. .... Covington, LA
Simmons, John S. .... Columbia, SC
Simmons, John T., Jr. .... Missouri City, TX
Simmons, John W. .... Memphis, TN
Simmons, Jon T. .... Boise, ID
Simmons, Jonathan L. .... Los Angeles, CA
Simmons, Joseph G. .... Baton Rouge, LA
Simmons, Josephine S.
Federal Communications Commission,
Common Carrier Bureau, GV
Simmons, Joy A. .... Los Angeles, CA
Simmons, Joyce R. .... Houston, TX
Simmons, Judith W., (P.A.) .... Tampa, FL
Simmons, Julie K. .... Oklahoma City, OK
Simmons, Karen C. .... West Columbia, SC
Simmons, Karen D. .... Tallahassee, FL
Simmons, Kathie J. .... Bodega Bay, CA
Simmons, Kathleen D.
Newport Beach, CA
Simmons, Kathryn L. .... Lake Orion, MI
Simmons, Keith B. .... Nashville, TN
Simmons, Keith R. .... Shady Grove, PA
Simmons, Kenneth D. .... Cleveland, OH
Simmons, Kenneth J. .... Cambridge, MA
Simmons, Kenneth L. .... Clinton Township, MI
Simmons, Kenneth N. .... Shreveport, LA
Simmons, Kent A. .... Davenport, IA
Simmons, Kermit M. .... Winnfield, LA
Simmons, Kevin P. .... East Meadow, NY
Simmons, Lane R. .... Boise, ID
Simmons, Larry J., Jr. .... Beaumont, TX
Simmons, Larry Vernon .... Tulsa, OK
Simmons, Larry W. .... Springfield, TN
Simmons, Lauren J. .... New York, NY
Simmons Law Firm .... Memphis, TN
Simmons, Lawr. .... Ridgewood, NY
Simmons, L. D., II .... Charlotte, NC
Simmons, Leigh Beasley .... Birmingham, AL
Simmons, LeRoy A. .... Barstow, CA
Simmons, Lisa S. .... Chicago, IL
Simmons, Lonnie L. .... Pensacola, FL
Simmons, Lonnie L., P.A. .... Pensacola, FL
Simmons, Luann L. .... San Francisco, CA
Simmons, Luiz R. S. .... Silver Spring, MD
Simmons, Lyn M. .... Newport News, VA
Simmons, M. Ellen .... St. Louis, MO
Simmons, M. Reggie .... Franklinton, LA
Simmons, Madson & Snyder .... Las Vegas, NV
Simmons, Margaret P. .... Huntsville, AL
Simmons, Marshall .... Dallas, TX
Simmons, Martha .... Boston, MA
Simmons, Martin E. .... Nashville, TN
Simmons, Mary Davis .... Sacramento, CA
Simmons, Mary K. .... Gadsden, AL
Simmons, Maryellen .... Carrollton, GA
Simmons, Matthew O. .... Jonesboro, GA
Simmons, Mel J. .... Cincinnati, OH
Simmons, Melanie A. .... Washington, DC
Simmons, Michael A.
Small Business Administration,
Office of the General Counsel, GV
Simmons, Michael C. .... Woodbridge, NJ
New York, NY
Simmons, Michael D. .... Jackson, MS
Simmons, Michael E. .... Indianapolis, IN
Simmons, Michael R.
Department Of Veterans Affairs,
Office of the General Counsel, GV
Simmons, Michelle A. .... Angola, IN
Simmons, Milton L. .... Independence, OH
Simmons, Monica Michelle .... Memphis, TN
Simmons, M. T., Jr. .... Decatur, GA
Simmons, Nancy N. .... Denver, CO
Simmons, Nancy Rae .... Cedar Hill, MO
Simmons, Nathan D. .... Denver, CO
Simmons, Nelson, Jr. .... Decatur, AL
Simmons, Nicholas R. .... Los Angeles, CA
Simmons, Norbert A. .... New Orleans, LA
Simmons, Olsen, Ediger, Selzer, Ferguson & Carney, P.C. .... Alliance, NE
Bridgeport, NE
Scottsbluff, NE
Simmons, Pamela Robinson .... Durham, NC
Simmons, Patricia A. .... Oakland, CA
Simmons, Patrick H. .... Groesbeck, TX
Simmons, Paul A. .... Monongahela, PA
Simmons, Paul M. .... Salt Lake City, UT
Simmons, Paul S. .... Sacramento, CA
Simmons, Perrine, Albright & Ellwood, P.L.C. .... Cedar Rapids, IA
Simmons, Peter L. .... New York, NY
Simmons, Philip E. .... Tucson, AZ
Simmons, Philip S., Law Offices of
Encino, CA
Simmons Pitman Le Gros .... Jeanerette, LA
Simmons, Ralph A. .... Washington, DC
Simmons, Randy Clay .... Overland Park, KS
Simmons, Ray C. .... Fremont, NE
Simmons, Ray E. .... Wichita, KS
Simmons, Raymond H. .... Newport Beach, CA
Simmons, Raymond H. .... Salinas, CA
Simmons, Raymond H., Jr. .... Cambridge, MD
Simmons, Raymond J., Jr. .... Roseville, CA
Simmons, Rebecca .... San Antonio, TX
Simmons, Rebecca J. .... New York, NY
Simmons, Reginald D., & Associate, P.A.
Atlanta, GA
Augusta, GA
Aiken, SC
Simmons, Reginald Dale .... Atlanta, GA
Augusta, GA
Aiken, SC
Simmons, Richard J. .... Los Angeles, CA
Simmons, Richard S. .... Citrus Heights, CA
Simmons, Richard T., Jr.,(P.L.C.)
Metairie, LA
Simmons, Richard W. .... Charlotte, NC
Simmons, Richard W., II .... Sumter, SC
Simmons, Ritchie & Segal .... Los Angeles, CA
Simmons, Robert J. .... Clovis, CA
Simmons, Robert J. .... Detroit, MI
Simmons, Robert J. .... Fort Washington, PA
Simmons, Robert L. .... San Bernardino, CA
Simmons, Robert L. .... San Diego, CA
Simmons, Robert L. .... Atlanta, GA
Simmons, Robert L. .... Baltimore, MD
Simmons, Robert L. .... Cumberland, RI
Simmons, Robert L. .... Richardson, TX
Simmons, Robert M. .... Columbus, OH
Simmons, Robert S. .... Houston, TX
Simmons, Robert W. .... Charlotte, NC
Simmons, Roderick S. .... Seattle, WA
Simmons, Roderick W. .... Richmond, VA
Simmons, Roger C. .... Lauderhill, FL
Simmons, Roger C. .... Frederick, MD
Simmons, Ronnie M. .... Canoga Park, CA
Simmons, Ross G. .... San Diego, CA
Simmons, Roy G. .... Toms River, NJ
Simmons, Roy, III .... Mexia, TX
Simmons, Roy, Jr. .... Pearland, TX
Simmons, Russell E., Jr. .... Kingston, TN
Simmons, Rutledge A. .... Boston, MA
Simmons, Ryland P. .... Roanoke, VA
Simmons, S. Jnatel .... Philadelphia, PA
Simmons, Sam .... Florence, MS
Simmons, Sandra G. .... Hardinsburg, KY
Simmons, Sara .... Port St. Lucie, FL
Simmons, Sara A. .... San Francisco, CA
Simmons, Sarah R. .... Tucson, AZ

Simmons, Scott A. .... Richmond, VA
Simmons, Scott M. .... Russellville, AR
Simmons, Scott R. .... New Orleans, LA
Simmons, Sharón L. .... Jacksonville, FL
Simmons, Shayla Freeman
Department Of The Interior, Office of Legislation, GV
Simmons, Sherman H. .... Las Vegas, NV
Simmons, Sherwin P., (P.A.) .... Miami, FL
Simmons, Sheryl .... Houston, TX
Simmons, Sidney S., II .... Jacksonville, FL
Simmons & Simmons .... Atlanta, GA
Simmons & Simmons .... New York, NY
Simmons and Simmons .... Troy, NY
Simmons & Simmons .... Elizabeth, WV
Simmons & Simmons, P.C.
Birmingham, AL
Simmons & Simmons, P.C. .... Denver, CO
Simmons, Stacey J. .... Austin, TX
Simmons, Stephanie J. .... Chicago, IL
Simmons, Stephen J.
Fort Lauderdale, FL
Simmons, Stephen J. .... Cypress, TX
Simmons, Stephen J., P.A.
Fort Lauderdale, FL
Simmons, Steven C. .... Houston, TX
Simmons, Sue Haley .... Canton, MS
Jackson, MS
Simmons, Susan D. .... Elizabeth, WV
Simmons, Sylvia J. .... San Clemente, CA
Simmons, T. Austin .... Tampa, FL
Simmons, T. Clayton .... Shreveport, LA
Simmons, T. Dean .... Florham Park, NJ
Simmons, Tara .... St. Louis, MO
Simmons, Teri A. .... Atlanta, GA
Simmons, Terry .... Reno, NV
Simmons, Terry L. .... Dallas, TX
Simmons, Thomas E. .... Rapid City, SD
Simmons, Thomas J. .... Kokomo, IN
Simmons, Thomas J. .... Olivia, MN
Simmons, Timothy J. .... Colorado Springs, CO
Simmons, Ty Collin .... Dallas, TX
Simmons, Ungar, Helbush, Steinberg & Bright .... San Francisco, CA
Simmons, Valerie Pierre
Grand Rapids, MI
Simmons, Viall & Lee .... Seattle, WA
Simmons, Warren D. .... Olivia, MN
Simmons, Warren, Szczecko & McFee
Atlanta, GA
Decatur, GA
Simmons, Wayland A. .... Port Aransas, TX
Simmons, Wayne F. .... Andover, MA
Simmons, William .... San Diego, CA
Simmons, William B., Jr. .... Boston, MA
Simmons, William E. .... Oakland, CA
Simmons, William E. .... Clinton, MO
Simmons, William G. .... Rockville, MD
Simmons, William G. .... Seattle, WA
Simmons, William G., P.A. .... Rockville, MD
Simmons, William J., Jr. .... Corning, NY
Simmons, William J., Jr. .... Memphis, TN
Simmons, William M. .... Annapolis, MD
Simmons, William M. .... Boston, MA
Simmons, William R. .... New Braunfels, TX
Simmons, Wm. David .... Dallas, TX
Simmons, Young J. .... Ocala, FL
Simmons-Gill, Catherine .... Chicago, IL
Simms, Abby P.
National Labor Relations Board, Office of the General Counsel, GV
Simms, Alan H. .... Elizabeth, WV
Simms, Albert .... Taos, NM
Simms, Arthur E., Jr. .... Fayetteville, TN
Simms, Barry R. .... Oklahoma City, OK
Simms, Brian E. .... Newark, OH
Simms, Carolyn A. .... Washougal, WA
Simms, Charles C., III .... Bardstown, KY
Simms, Charles W. .... Ellicott City, MD
Simms, Christopher P. .... St. Louis, MO
Simms, Cicily .... Austin, TX
Simms, Cindy S. .... Brooklyn, NY
Simms, David L. .... Boston, MA
Simms, Debra G. .... Cleveland, OH
Simms, Dennis L. .... Anaheim, CA
Simms, Douglas G. .... Belleville, KS
Simms, Edward P. .... Cleveland, OH
Simms, Garfield B. .... Boston, MA
Simms, Gary L. .... San Francisco, CA
Simms, George E., III .... Brookeville, MD
Simms, Hamilton B. .... Springfield, KY
Simms, Harold F. .... Georgetown, KY
Simms, Howard Z. .... Macon, GA
Simms, J. Stephen .... Baltimore, MD
Frederick, MD
Simms, Jack L., Jr. .... Leesville, LA
Simms, Jeffrey, & Assoc., A P.C.
West Orange, NJ
Simms, John E., Jr. .... Baltimore, MD
Simms, John M. .... Lexington, KY
Simms, John M. .... Salem, VA
Simms, John Seth .... Clearwater, FL
Simms, Joseph S .... Cleveland, OH
Simms, Judith M. .... Sacramento, CA
Simms, Julie A. .... New York, NY
Simms, Keri Donald .... Birmingham, AL
Simms, Larry L. .... Washington, DC
Simms, Leah A. .... Miami, FL
Simms, Leroy H. .... Houston, TX
Simms, Linda Cunningham .... Thomson, GA
Simms, Marsha E. .... New York, NY
Simms, Marvin .... Great Neck, NY
Simms, Melanie F. .... Detroit, MI
Simms, Michael A. .... Cleveland, OH
Simms, N. Wayne, Jr. .... Montgomery, AL
Simms, Nathan F., III
Research Triangle Park, NC
Simms, Nicholas A. .... Houston, TX

Simms, Oliva .... Santa Barbara, CA
Simms, Patrice L.
Environmental Protection Agency, Office of the General Counsel, GV
Simms, Phillip J. .... Whitehouse, NJ
Simms, Quentin B. .... Altadena, CA
Simms, Rany L. .... Department of Commerce, Patent and Trademark Office, GV
Simms, Richard A. .... Sun Valley, ID
Santa Fe, NM
Simms, Richard E. .... Warwick, RI
Simms, Robert E. .... San Francisco, CA
Simms, Robert J. .... Tampa, FL
Simms, Roberta .... Forest Hills, NY
Simms, Robt. W. .... Fayetteville, TN
Simms, Sandra A. .... Honolulu, HI
Simms & Simms .... Fayetteville, TN
Simms & Stein, P.A. .... Sun Valley, ID
Santa Fe, NM
Simms, Stephen .... New York, NY
Simms, Stephen G. .... Matthews, NC
Simms, Stuart O. .... Towson, MD
Simms, Susan D. .... Hershey, PA
Simms, Susan L. .... Columbus, OH
Simms, Thomas W. .... Beavercreek, OH
Simms, William .... Brooklyn, NY
Simms, William A. .... Knoxville, TN
Simms, William E. .... Fayetteville, TN
Simnacher, Elroy D. .... Lubbock, TX
Simno, George R., III .... New Orleans, LA
Simoes, Fausto .... Newark, NJ
Simoes, James R. .... McLean, VA
Simoes, Kimberly P. .... Daytona Beach, FL
Simola, Ted O. .... Cheyenne, WY
Simoldoni, Charles J. .... Garfield, NJ
Simolike, Arlene .... Feasterville, PA
Philadelphia, PA
Simolunas, Alicia Anne .... Arlington, VA
Simon, A. Lysa .... Northridge, CA
Simon, Aaron H. .... Oakland, CA
Simon, Abbott .... New York, NY
Simon, Adam B. .... Waukegan, IL
Simon, Alan .... Burlingame, CA
Simon, Alan H. .... Van Nuys, CA
Simon, Alan H. .... Denver, CO
Simon, Alan M. .... Suffern, NY
Simon, Alan Richard .... Boca Raton, FL
Simon, Albert .... Los Angeles, CA
Simon, Alexander .... New York, NY
Simon, Alexander .... West Hempstead, NY
Simon, Alexander N. .... Richmond, VA
Simon, Alfred J., Jr. .... Louisville, KY
Simon, Alison Warren .... Miami, FL
Simon, Alvin A. .... Yonkers, NY
Simon, Amy Edelstein .... New York, NY
Simon, Andrea .... New York, NY
Simon, Angela C. .... Galena, IL
Dubuque, IA
Simon, Anne Gaiennie .... Opelousas, LA
Simon, Anne Lennan .... New Iberia, LA
Simon, Anne W. .... Department of State, Foreign Service Officers (Overseas), GV
Simon, Anthony G. .... St. Louis, MO
Simon, Anthony Luke .... Detroit, MI
Simon, Arnold L. .... Harrison, NJ
Simon, Arthur .... Rockville, MD
Simon, Arthur Gary .... Chicago, IL
Simon, Arthur J. .... Chicago, IL
Simon, Arthur M. .... Miami, FL
Simon & Associates .... Washington, DC
Simon, B. Daniel .... Columbia, MO
Simon, Barbara .... New York, NY
Simon, Barbara A. .... Housatonic, MA
Simon, Barry .... Philadelphia, PA
Simon, Barry E. .... Arlington Heights, IL
Simon, Barry E., P.C. .... Arlington Heights, IL
Simon, Barry J. .... Marina Del Rey, CA
Simon, Barry P. .... Forest Hills, NY
Simon, Barry S. .... Washington, DC
Simon, Basil T. .... Detroit, MI
Simon, Beau .... San Francisco, CA
Simon, Benjamin .... Deerfield Beach, FL
Simon & Berman .... Las Vegas, NV
Simon, Bert C. .... Jacksonville, FL
Simon, Bettina Solomon .... Dallas, TX
Simon, Betty A. .... Philadelphia, PA
Simon Borden, LLP .... Birmingham, AL
Simon, Bradford S. .... San Francisco, CA
Simon, Bradley D., Law Offices of
New York, NY
Simon, Bradley F. .... Chicago, IL
Simon, Brette S. .... Los Angeles, CA
Simon, Brian P. .... Los Angeles, CA
Simon, Bruce H. .... New York, NY
Simon, Bruce L. .... Burlingame, CA
Los Angeles, CA
Simon, Bruce S. .... Los Angeles, CA
Simon, Bruce S. .... New York, NY
Simon, Bruce W. .... Kansas City, MO
Simon, Carl E. .... San Francisco, CA
Simon, Carol B. .... San Diego, CA
Simon, Carol Bremer .... Hawthorne, CA
Manhattan Beach, CA
Simon, Carol Warren .... Rochester, NY
Simon, Carole .... New York, NY
Simon, Caroline K. .... New York, NY
Simon, Carrie A. .... Washington, DC
Simon, Cathy Ann .... Washington, DC
Simon, Charles F. .... Fairfax, VA
Simon, Charles L. .... Fort Lauderdale, FL
Simon, Charles S. .... Chicago, IL
Simon, Charles S., Ltd. .... Chicago, IL
Simon, Charles T. .... Rocky River, OH
Simon, Charles W., III .... Edmore, MI
Simon, Charles W., Jr. .... Stanton, MI
Simon, Christiana .... Woodbridge, NJ
Simon, Christopher .... Marietta, GA
Simon, Christopher P. .... Wilmington, DE

Simon, Claude A. C. .... New York, NY
Simon, Clinton S. .... Kansas City, KS
Simon, Craig F. .... Newburgh, NY
Simon, Craig F. .... Dallas, TX
Simon, Craig J. .... Phoenix, AZ
Simon, Craig S. .... Irvine, CA
Simon, Cynthia W. .... Washington, DC
Simon, Daniel A. .... Washington, DC
Simon, Daniel B., III .... Rockmart, GA
Simon, Daniel B., III, P.C. .... Rockmart, GA
Simon, Daniel I. .... Solvang, CA
Simon, Daniel K. .... Santa Barbara, CA
Simon, Daniel S. .... St. Paul, MN
Simon, Daniel S. .... Columbia, MO
Simon, Darcy L. .... Beverly Hills, CA
Simon, David .... New York, NY
Simon, David A. .... Bay Minette, AL
Simon, David A. .... House of Representatives, Congressional Assistants, GV
Simon, David D. .... New York, NY
Simon, David E. .... Hawthorne, CA
Manhattan Beach, CA
Simon, David F. .... Southfield, MI
Simon, David F. .... Blue Bell, PA
Simon, David Henry .... Los Angeles, CA
Simon, David L. .... Washington, DC
Simon, David M. .... Santa Clara, CA
Simon, David M. .... Chicago, IL
Simon, David O. .... New York, NY
Simon, David O. .... Cleveland, OH
Simon, David R. .... Newark, NJ
Simon, David R. .... Portland, OR
Simon, David Scott .... Chicago, IL
Simon, David W. .... San Bernardino, CA
Simon, David W. .... Milwaukee, WI
Simon, Deana L. .... Atlanta, GA
Simon, Debora Lynn .... Dallas, TX
Simon, Deborah H. .... Haddonfield, NJ
Philadelphia, PA
Simon, Declan Joseph .... Cleveland, OH
Simon & Demeter, P.A. .... Trenton, NJ
Simon, Dennis L. .... Neenah, WI
Simon, Diana J. .... Tucson, AZ
Simon, Diana P. .... Lafayette, LA
Simon, Diane P. .... Newport Beach, CA
Simon, Dolph B. H. .... Dallas, TX
Simon, Donald .... Clearwater, FL
Simon, Donald S. .... Oakland, CA
Simon & Dondero .... Miami, FL
Simon & Donohoe .... Ketchum, ID
Simon, Douglas E. .... Cherry Hill, NJ
Philadelphia, PA
Simon, Drabkin & Kamens .... New York, NY
Simon, E. Kelleher .... Covington, LA
Simon, Earl L. .... Chicago, IL
Simon, Earl L. .... Skokie, IL
Simon & Early, P.C. .... St. Louis, MO
Simon, Edgar, (A Professional Corporation)
Beverly Hills, CA
Simon, Edward .... Ketchum, ID
Simon, Edward E., Jr. .... Denver, CO
Simon, Edwin O. .... North Miami, FL
Simon, Eileen S. .... Purchase, NY
Simon, Ellen Beth .... Haddonfield, NJ
Simon, Ellen S. .... Cleveland, OH
Simon, Elliott M. .... Chicago, IL
Simon, Elmer P. .... Frankenmuth, MI
Simon, Elwood S. .... Birmingham, MI
Simon, Elwood S., & Associates, P.C.
Birmingham, MI
Simon, Emily .... Portland, OR
Simon & Enright, P.A. .... Morris Plains, NJ
Simon, Eric A. .... Coral Springs, FL
Simon, Eric A. P.A. .... Coral Springs, FL
Simon, Eric B. .... Santa Rosa, CA
Simon, Eric M. .... Cleveland, OH
Simon, Eric P. .... New York, NY
Simon, Ernest .... Pittsburgh, PA
Simon, Ernest D. .... Chicago, IL
Simon, Ernest G. .... Delray Beach, FL
Simon, Erwin S. .... Detroit, MI
Simon, Esther B. .... Tucson, AZ
Simon, Eugene C. .... Phoenix, AZ
Simon, Eugene M. .... North Miami, FL
Simon, Evelyn .... Dearborn, MI
Simon, Ezra .... White Plains, NY
Simon, Fakhoury, Tangalos & Frantz, PLC
Detroit, MI
Troy, MI
Simon, Fitzgerald, Cooke, Reed & Welch
Shreveport, LA
Simon, Francis M. .... Beaufort, SC
Simon, Frank R. .... Troy, MI
Simon, Fred R. .... Louisville, KY
Simon, Frederick A. .... North Brunswick, NJ
Simon, Frederick J. .... Worthington, OH
Simon, Frederick Jeffrey
East Brunswick, NJ
Simon, Gail R. .... Philadelphia, PA
Simon, Gary B. .... Milwaukee, WI
Simon, Gary J. .... New York, NY
Simon, Gary P. .... Miami, FL
Simon, Gary R. .... Burbank, CA
Simon, Gary Scott .... New York, NY
Simon, Gene M. .... Buffalo, NY
Simon, Geoffrey H. .... Denver, CO
Simon, George T. .... Chicago, IL
Simon, George T. .... Cleveland, OH
Simon, George V. .... Walnut Creek, CA
Simon, Gerald C. .... Detroit, MI
Simon, Geraldine .... Anchorage, AK
Simon, Gregg M. .... Chicago, IL
Simon, Gregory I. .... New York, NY
Simon, Gregory M. .... West Branch, MI
Simon, H. Leon .... Las Vegas, NV
Simon, H. Paul .... New Orleans, LA
Simon, H. Robert .... Hunt Valley, MD
Simon, Harlan M. .... Beachwood, OH

Simon, Harold .... Van Nuys, CA
Simon, Harold .... New York, NY
Simon, Harold S. .... Elizabeth, NJ
Simon, Harriet A.
Department Of Health And Human Services, Social Security Administration, GV
Simon, Harry L. .... Denver, CO
Simon, Harry L., P.C. .... Denver, CO
Simon, Harry W. .... Los Angeles, CA
Simon, Harvey .... Irving, TX
Simon, Helen L. .... Santa Ana, CA
Simon, Helene B. .... Bloomfield Hills, MI
Simon, Henry R. .... Millburn, NJ
New York, NY
White Plains, NY
Simon, Henry R. .... New York, NY
Scarsdale, NY
Simon, Henry W., Jr. .... Fort Worth, TX
Simon, Herbert A. .... Valley Stream, NY
Simon, Herman .... New York, NY
Simon Higgins & Moran, P.C.
Philadelphia, PA
Simon, Hinda B. .... Houston, TX
Simon, Howard A. .... San Francisco, CA
Simon, Howard L. .... Los Angeles, CA
Simon, Howard L. .... New York, NY
Simon, Howard M. .... Santa Barbara, CA
Simon, Hunter .... Los Angeles, CA
Simon, Ilan E. .... Newark, NJ
Simon, Ira H. .... East Setauket, NY
Simon, Irwin F .... New York, NY
Simon, J. Minos .... Lafayette, LA
Simon, J. Quentin .... Lafayette, LA
Simon, J. Stephen .... Scottsdale, AZ
Simon, Jacalyn Newman
West Bloomfield, MI
Simon, Jack H. .... Mesa, AZ
Simon, Jacob M. .... Los Angeles, CA
Simon, James E. .... Truckee, CA
Simon, James E. .... Lafayette, LA
Simon, James F. .... Stamford, CT
Simon, James F. .... Department of Justice, Environment and Natural Resources Division, GV
Simon, James F. .... New York, NY
Simon, James H. .... Boston, MA
Simon, James L. .... Longwood, FL
Simon, James L. .... Inverness, IL
Simon, James M. .... Los Angeles, CA
Simon, Jason T. .... Fort Lauderdale, FL
Simon, Jay .... Florham Park, NJ
Simon, Jay S. .... Dallas, TX
Simon, Jean-Marie .... Washington, DC
Simon, Jeanne Kramer .... Boca Raton, FL
Simon, Jeffrey B. .... Arlington, TX
Simon, Jeffrey J. .... Kansas City, MO
Simon, Jeffrey M. .... Skokie, IL
Simon, Jeffrey S. .... Long Beach, CA
Simon, Jeremy S. .... Washington, DC
Simon, Jerome B. .... Minneapolis, MN
Simon, Jerome C. .... St. Louis, MO
Simon, Jerry M. .... San Antonio, TX
Simon, Jessamyne M. .... Philadelphia, PA
Simon, Jo Anne .... Hempstead, NY
Simon, Jody .... Beverly Hills, CA
Simon, Joel K. .... New York, NY
Simon, Joel L. .... Baltimore, MD
Simon, Joel M. .... Encino, CA
Simon, Joel M. .... New York, NY
Simon, Joel N. .... Washington, DC
Simon, John A. .... Chicago, IL
Simon, John A. .... Cleveland, OH
Simon, John B. .... Chicago, IL
Simon, John F. .... Alexandria, LA
Simon, John F. .... New York, NY
Simon, John Franklin, Jr. .... Pensacola, FL
Simon, John G. .... North Little Rock, AR
St. Louis, MO
Simon, John J. .... St. Clair Shores, MI
Simon, John Jeffrey .... New Iberia, LA
Simon, John M. .... Boston, MA
Simon, John M. .... Roseland, NJ
Simon, John P. .... Chicago, IL
Simon, John R. .... Costa Mesa, CA
Simon, John Victor .... Lewiston, NY
Simon, Jonathan D. .... Washington, DC
Simon, Jonathan D. .... Cambridge, MA
Simon, Jonathan D. .... Houston, TX
Simon, Jordan O. .... Evanston, IL
Simon, Jorge A. .... Manchester, CT
Simon, Joseph A. .... Ann Arbor, MI
Simon, Joseph D. .... Garden City, NY
Simon, Joshua L. .... Frazer, PA
Simon, Joy R. .... New York, NY
Simon, Juan M. .... Redwood City, CA
Simon, Judith .... Las Vegas, NV
Simon, Judith .... Purchase, NY
Simon, Judith R. .... Woodland Hills, CA
Simon, Judy L. .... Kansas City, KS
Simon, Jules F. .... Los Angeles, CA
Simon, Julia A. .... Dallas, TX
Simon, Julie .... Washington, DC
Simon, Justin D. .... Washington, DC
Simon & Kane .... San Francisco, CA
Simon, Karla W. .... Washington, DC
Simon, Kathleen E. .... Covington, LA
Simon, Kell A. .... Birmingham, AL
Simon, Kenneth .... Mamaroneck, NY
Simon, Kenneth E. .... Detroit, MI
Simon, Kenneth J. .... Houston, TX
Simon, Kenneth M. .... Washington, DC
Simon, Kenneth O. .... Birmingham, AL
Simon, Kenneth W. .... Hartford, CT
Simon, Kevin Joseph .... Salt Lake City, UT
Simon, Kevin S. .... Chicago, IL
Simon, Kevin V. .... Cincinnati, OH
Simon, King D. .... Santa Rosa, CA
Simon, L. Linfield .... Lenox, MA

Simon, Lainie ... **Chicago, IL**
Simon, Larry J. ... Houston, TX
Simon, Lauren Beth ... Chicago, IL
Simon Law Firm, The ... **Cleveland, OH**
Simon Law Firm, The, P.C. ... Arlington, TX
Simon, Lawrence B. ... **New York, NY**
Simon, Lawrence M. ... New York, NY
Simon, Lawrence P., Jr. ... **Lafayette, LA**
Simon, Lawrence S. ... Piedmont, CA
Simon, Lennox J. ... Washington, DC
Simon, Leonard A. ... Boston, MA
Simon, Leonard B. ... **San Diego, CA**
Simon, Leonore M. ... Vancouver, WA
Simon, Leslie A. ... San Francisco, CA
Simon, Leslie A. ... Department of Justice, Civil Rights Division, GV
Simon, Leslie A. ... **New York, NY**
Simon, Leslie Norman ... Cross River, NY
Simon, Licata & Conklin ... Suffern, NY
Simon, Linda J. ... **Chicago, IL**
Simon, Lisa R. ... Department of the Army, Army Materiel Command, GV
Simon, Lisa T. ... Greenwich, CT
Simón, Lisette E. ... **Miami, FL**
Simon, Loretta A. ... **St. Louis, MO**
Simon, Lori E. ... Chicago, IL
Simon, Lori R. ... **Santa Ana, CA**
Simon, Louis, II (P.C.) ... **Lafayette, LA**
Simon & Lupo ... North Brunswick, NJ
Simon, Lyn Heywood, (Mrs.) ... Utica, NY
Simon, Mace Stephen ... Beverly Hills, CA
Simon, Marc G. ... **Tucson, AZ**
Simon, Marc L. ... **Las Vegas, NV**
Simon, Margaret Daniels ... Jeanerette, LA
Simon, Marguerite T. ... Hackensack, NJ
Simon, Maria ... Department of Justice, Civil Division, GV
Simon, Marilyn, & Associates
New York, NY
Simon, Mark ... Newark, NJ
Simon, Mark A. ... Denver, CO
Simon, Mark C. ... **Chicago, IL**
Simon, Mark S. ... Chicago, IL
Simon, Markus S. ... Southfield, MI
Simon, Marnie E. ... **Philadelphia, PA**
Simon, Martha J. ... San Francisco, CA
Simon, Martin ... Bethany, CT
Simon, Martin J. ... New York, NY
Simon, Martin R. ... Los Angeles, CA
Simon, Matthew D. ... **Tampa, FL**
Simon, Matthew D. ... New York, NY
Simon, Matthew J. ... New York, NY
Simon, McClosky & Scovell, Ltd.
Chicago, IL
Simon, McKinsey, Miller, Zommick, Sandor & Dundas, A Law Corporation
Irvine, CA
Long Beach, CA
Los Angeles, CA
Santa Ana, CA
Simon, Melvin A. ... **Hartford, CT**
Simon, Meyer ... Glenside, PA
Simon, Meyrowitz, Meyrowitz & Schlussel
New York, NY
Simon, Michael ... **Miami, FL**
Simon, Michael Arthur ... Stony Brook, NY
Simon, Michael B. ... Bay Shore, NY
Simon, Michael C. ... **Vancouver, WA**
Simon, Michael D. ... **West Palm Beach, FL**
Simon, Michael D. ... Pittsburgh, PA
Simon, Michael F. ... Newtown Square, PA
Simon, Michael G. ... **Weirton, WV**
Wheeling, WV
Simon, Michael H. ... **Portland, OR**
Simon, Michael J. ... Baton Rouge, LA
Simon, Michael J. ... **New York, NY**
Simon, Michael M. ... Islip, NY
Simon, Michael P. P. ... Florence, AZ
Simon, Michael S. ... **Los Angeles, CA**
Simon, Michael S. ... **Trenton, NJ**
Simon, Michael S. ... Buffalo, NY
Simon, Michael S. ... **New York, NY**
Simon, Michael W. ... **Boca Raton, FL**
Simon, Michelle J. ... **Garden City, NY**
Simon and Milner ... Valley Stream, NY
Simon, Mitchell J. ... Whitewater, WI
Simon, Mitchell M. ... Concord, NH
Simon, Morton J., Jr. ... **Philadelphia, PA**
Simon, Morton S. ... **Stamford, CT**
Simon, Morton S. ... Santa Fe, NM
Simon, Mrg ... Pierre, SD
Simon, Murray G. ... Newark, NJ
Simon, Nancy R. ... Cupertino, CA
Simon, Nannette ... **Burbank, CA**
Simon, Natalie A. ... Gloucester, MA
Simon, Nathan R. ... Cleveland Heights, OH
Simon, Nathanya Guritzky
Florham Park, NJ
Simon, Neil A. ... Washington, DC
Simon, Neil M. ... **Atlanta, GA**
Simon, Norman Christopher
New York, NY
Simon & Oppenheimer ... Santa Fe, NM
Simon, Otto E. ... Mobile, AL
Simon, Pamela H. ... **Statesville, NC**
Simon & Parashos ... San Diego, CA
Simon, Patrick O. ... Akron, OH
Simon, Paul J. ... St. Louis, MO
Simon, Paul, Jr. ... **St. Louis, MO**
Simon, Paul S. ... Tucson, AZ
Simon, Peragine, Smith & Redfearn, L.L.P.
New Orleans, LA
Simon, Peter L.D. ... **Santa Rosa, CA**
Simon, Peter N. ... Boulder, CO
Simon, Philip A. ... Santa Maria, CA
Simon, Philip H. ... Torrance, CA
Simon, Philip J. ... **Washington, DC**
Simon, Phyllis E. ... San Francisco, CA
Simon, Phyllis E. ... New City, NY
Simon, Priva H. ... Bronx, NY
Simon, R. Scott ... **Honolulu, HI**
Simon, Rachel L. ... **New York, NY**
Simon, Ramsey ... Mobile, AL
Simon, Ray ... Omaha, NE
Simon, Ray R. ... Omaha, NE
Simon, Raymond F. ... Chicago, IL
Simon, Raymond J. ... **New York, NY**
Simon & Rees ... Covington, LA
Simon, Richard ... Birmingham, AL
Simon, Richard ... Mesa, AZ
Simon, Richard ... Ventura, CA
Simon, Richard ... Northport, NY
Simon, Richard A. ... **Orlando, FL**
Simon, Richard A. ... Norristown, PA
Simon, Richard D. ... East Brunswick, NJ
Simon, Richard F. ... **New Brunswick, NJ**
Simon, Richard F., P.C.
New Brunswick, NJ
Simon, Richard G. ... San Bernardino, CA
Simon, Richard H. ... Boston, MA
Simon, Richard I. ... **West Orange, NJ**
Simon, Richard J. ... Indianapolis, IN
Simon, Richard K. ... **Los Angeles, CA**
Simon, Richard M. ... St. Louis, MO
Simon, Richard S. ... Forest Hills, NY
Simon, Richard U., Jr. ... **Fort Worth, TX**
Simon, Robert A. ... **Fort Worth, TX**
Simon, Robert B. ... Chicago, IL
Simon, Robert F. ... **Chicago, IL**
Simon, Robert F. ... **Maplewood, NJ**
Simon, Robert G. ... Pelham Manor, NY
Simon, Robert I. ... San Francisco, CA
Simon, Robert J. ... **Olean, NY**
Simon, Robert J. ... Houston, TX
Simon, Robert James ... Houston, TX
Simon, Robert L. ... **Orlando, FL**
Simon, Robert L. ... **New York, NY**
Simon, Robert M. ... Jersey City, NJ
Simon, Robert M. ... Morristown, NJ
Simon, Robert S. ... Los Angeles, CA
Simon, Robert S. ... Albuquerque, NM
Simon, Robert S. ... Oregon City, OR
Simon, Robin Barnett ... **Secaucus, NJ**
Simon, Robyn B. ... **Washington, DC**
Des Plaines, IL
Simon, Roger B. ... **Buffalo, NY**
Simon, Roger F. ... Austin, TX
Simon, Roger H., Jr. ... Evanston, IL
Simon, Roger L. ... Denver, CO
Simon, Roger N. ... **Washington, DC**
Simon, Ron ... **Houston, TX**
Simon, Ronald ... **Washington, DC**
Simon, Ronald E. ... Fairfield, NJ
Paterson, NJ
Simon, Ronald L., (P.A.) ... Minneapolis, MN
Simon, Ronald M. ... Miami, FL
Simon, Roy D., Jr. ... West Hempstead, NY
Simon, Russell C. ... Houston, TX
Simon, Ruth ... Malvern, PA
Simon, Ruth Ann ... West Bloomfield, MI
Simon, Ruth V. ... **Newark, NJ**
New York, NY
Simon, S. Gerald ... New Iberia, LA
Simon, Sabrina A. ... **Birmingham, AL**
Simon, Samuel H. ... **Columbus, OH**
Simon, Samuel J. ... Hollywood, FL
Simon, Samuel J. ... **Cincinnati, OH**
Simon, Samuel R. ... **Philadelphia, PA**
Simon, Sandra Wien ... Department of Justice, Civil Division, GV
Simon, Sanford ... Sun City, CA
Simon, Sara R. ... Parkersburg, WV
Simon, Sarver & Rosenberg, P.A.
East Orange, NJ
Fairfield, NJ
Paterson, NJ
Simon, Schindler & Sandberg, A Professional Association ... Miami, FL
Simon & Schmidt ... **Delray Beach, FL**
Simon, Scott ... Rancho Mirage, CA
Simon, Scott A. ... Boca Raton, FL
Simon, Scott A., P.A. ... Boca Raton, FL
Simon, Seymour F. ... **Chicago, IL**
Simon, Shaun Robin ... **Roseland, NJ**
Simon, Sheila Jeanne ... Murphysboro, IL
Simon, Sheldon M. ... Morris Plains, NJ
Simon, Shulamith ... **St. Louis, MO**
Simon, Sigalos & Spyredes, P.A.
Boca Raton, FL
Simon and Simon ... New Iberia, LA
Simon and Simon ... **Kansas City, MO**
Simon & Simon, Chartered Attorneys
Boca Raton, FL
Simon & Simon, Ltd. ... Hawthorne, CA
Manhattan Beach, CA
Simon & Simon, P.A. ... **Miami, FL**
Simon & Spitalli ... Chicago, IL
Simon, Stacy Deanne ... Dallas, TX
Simon, Stanley C. ... **Dallas, TX**
Simon, Stanley R. ... New York, NY
Simon, Stephanie D. ... **Chicago, IL**
Simon, Stephanie E. ... Southfield, MI
Simon, Stephen A. ... Washington, DC
Simon, Stephen A. ... **Covington, KY**
Simon, Stephen B., (A Prof. Corp.)
Sherman Oaks, CA
Simon, Stephen M. ... Minneapolis, MN
Simon, Steven B. ... Woodland Hills, CA
Simon, Steven Charles
West Palm Beach, FL
Simon, Steven E. ... Cincinnati, OH
Simon, Steven G. ... **Chicago, IL**
Simon, Steven J. ... Albany, NY
Simon, Steven P. ... Erie, PA
Simon, Steven R. ... **Miami, FL**
Simon, Steven W. ... **Miami, FL**
Simon, Stuart ... East Meadow, NY
Simon, Stuart A. ... **Beverly Hills, CA**
Simon, Stuart A. ... Richmond, VA
Simon, Stuart H. ... East Hanover, NJ
Simon, Stuart K. ... Seattle, WA
Simon, Sunny M. ... Cleveland, OH
Simon, Tamara M. ... **Chicago, IL**
Simon, Terri E. ... **New York, NY**
Simon, Terry H. ... Monroe, WA
Simon, Thelma B. ... Wilmette, IL
Simon, Thomas C. ... Mesa, AZ
Simon, Thomas C. ... **St. Louis, MO**
Simon, Thomas J. ... Ashtabula, OH
Simon, Thomas P. ... Elizabeth, NJ
Simon, Thomas P. ... **Burlington, VT**
Simon, Timothy Alan ... San Francisco, CA
Simon, Timothy J. ... Flint, MI
Pontiac, MI
Simon, Timothy J., P.C. ... Flint, MI
Simon, Todd F. ... East Lansing, MI
Simon, Turnbull & Martin, Chartered
Washington, DC
Alexandria, VA
Simon, Vickie I. ... **Philadelphia, PA**
Simon, Victor ... Great Neck, NY
Simon, Vivienne L. ... Newton, MA
Simon, W. Peter, Jr. ... Bethany, CT
Simon, Walter ... Silver Spring, MD
Simon, Warner & Doby, L.L.P.
Fort Worth, TX
Simon, Wayne ... Los Angeles, CA
Simon, William ... **Washington, DC**
Simon, William ... **White Plains, NY**
Simon, William A. ... **New York, NY**
Simon, William D. ... **Washington, DC**
Simon, William E., Jr. ... New York, NY
Simon, William G. ... Irvine, CA
Simon, William G. ... Ravenna, OH
Simon, William J. ... **Phoenix, AZ**
Simon, William J., The Law Offices of
Palm Springs, CA
Simon, William J., The Law Offices of
Riverside, CA
Simon, William J., The Law Offices of
San Bernardino, CA
Simon, William M. ... Savannah, GA
Simon, William P. ... Bethany, CT
Simon, William R., Jr. ... San Diego, CA
Simon, William S. ... Cleveland, OH
Simon, William Scott ... **Dublin, OH**
Simon, Wood & Crane ... Mobile, AL
Simon, Yvonne T. ... **Los Angeles, CA**
Simonaitis, Joseph E. ... Chicago, IL
Simoncelli, George B., Jr. ... Torrington, CT
Simoncic, Judy Lynn ... Melville, NY
Mineola, NY
Simoncini & Associates ... **San Jose, CA**
Simoncini, Carmela F. ... San Diego, CA
Simoncini, Kenneth D. ... **San Jose, CA**
Simoncini, Roland ... San Diego, CA
Simondi, Michael P. ... Newport Beach, CA
Simonds, Albert R., Jr. ... **Washington, DC**
Simonds, Barbara Yorra ... Fort Lauderdale, FL
Simonds, C. Victoria ... San Francisco, CA
Simonds, Dana Beernink ... **Santa Rosa, CA**
Simonds, David H. ... Bangor, ME
Simonds, David P. ... **New York, NY**
Simonds, Gordon ... San Francisco, CA
Simonds, Jerome H. ... **Washington, DC**
Simonds, John L. ... Belmont, MA
Simonds, Joshua L. ... **Burlington, VT**
Simonds, Marshall, (P.C.) ... **Boston, MA**
Simonds, Philip G. ... Maumee, OH
Simonds, Richard D., Jr. ... **New York, NY**
Simonds, Timothy R. ... **Chattanooga, TN**
Simonds, Vance C., Jr. ... **Irvine, CA**
Simonds, Victor John ... Austin, TX
Simonds, Walter S., Jr. ... Nacogdoches, TX
Simonds, Winslow, Willis & Abbott, A Professional Association ... **Boston, MA**
Simone, Brian J. ... Dedham, MA
Simone, Christopher F. ... **Great Neck, NY**
Simone, Dina L. ... San Jose, CA
Simone, Donald F. ... **New York, NY**
Simone, Francesco ... San Diego, CA
Simone, Francesco ... Lansing, MI
Simone, Frank C. ... Fort Lauderdale, FL
Simone, Frank J., Jr. ... **Fairfield, CT**
Simone, Gary H. ... Butler, PA
Cranberry Township, PA
Simone, Joseph R. ... **New York, NY**
Simone, Lisa ... **New York, NY**
Simone, Lisa Marie ... **Los Angeles, CA**
Simone, Martin ... **Los Angeles, CA**
Simone, Mathew W. ... La Mesa, CA
Simone, Roberts & Weiss, P.A.
Albuquerque, NM
Simone, Stephen J. ... Metairie, LA
Simone, Stephen M. ... **Albuquerque, NM**
Simone, Vincent N. ... Wildwood, NJ
Simoneau, Ann L. ... **Cambridge, MA**
Simoneaux, Diana V. ... Metairie, LA
Simoneaux, Earl W. ... New Orleans, LA
Simoneaux, F. Paul, III ... **New Orleans, LA**
Simoneaux, Frank P. ... **Baton Rouge, LA**
Simoneaux, Kelly C. ... **New Orleans, LA**
Simoneaux Ryan Carleton Rowe & Dunlap, L.L.C. ... **Baton Rouge, LA**
Simonek, Karen M. ... Bethesda, MD
Simonelli, David J. ... **Troy, MI**
Simonelli, Emilia A. ... **New York, NY**
Simonelli, Jerry ... Fairfax, VA
Simonelli, Joanne I. ... Lewiston, ME
Simonelli, Laurie Ebling ... **Troy, MI**
Simonelli, Lyssa M. ... **Las Vegas, NV**
Simonelli, Mark M. ... Willoughby, OH
Simonelli, Patrice L. ... **Boston, MA**
Simonelli, Patrick J. ... San Francisco, CA
Simonelli, Susan ... Boston, MA
Simones, Thomas C. ... New London, CT
Simonet, Edward W., III ... Stillwater, MN
Simonet, Edward W., Jr. ... Stillwater, MN
Simonet, J. Thos. ... St. Paul, MN
Simonet, Jose ... Miami Beach, FL
Simonet, Ross A. ... Merced, CA
Simonet, William F. ... Orlando, FL
Simonet, William F., P.A. ... Orlando, FL
Simonett, John E. ... **Minneapolis, MN**
Simonett, Paul J. ... **Mankato, MN**
Simonetta & Associates, P.A.
St. Petersburg, FL
Simonetta, Lisa A. ... **Des Moines, IA**
Simonetta, Russell S. ... St. Petersburg, FL
Simonette, Daniel R. ... New York, NY
Simonetti, Anthony G. ... Trenton, NJ
Simonetti, Bruce E. ... **New York, NY**
Simonetti, Carol G. ... Lorain, OH
Simonetti, David A. ... Charlotte, NC
Simonetti, David P. ... **New York, NY**
Simonetti, D. J. ... **Birmingham, AL**
Simonetti, John A. ... Cleveland, OH
Simonetti, John J. ... **Chicago, IL**
Simonetti, Katherine ... **Washington, DC**
Simonetti, Lisa M. ... **Los Angeles, CA**
Simonetti, Louis F., Jr. ... Mineola, NY
Simonetti, Michael ... Birmingham, AL
Simoni, Christopher ... Chicago, IL
Simoni, John B., Jr. ... **New York, NY**
Simoni, Peter P. ... Aliquippa, PA
Simoni, Stephen ... **New York, NY**
Simonian, Chas. G. ... San Leandro, CA
Simonian, Gary P. ... Los Angeles, CA
Simonian, Gregory C. ... **Menlo Park, CA**
Simonian, Gregory E. ... **Orange, CA**
Simonian, James K. ... Waukegan, IL
Simonian, Jeffrey D. ... Fresno, CA
Simonian, Kenneth C. ... Long Beach, CA
Simonian, Mark S. ... Los Angeles, CA
Simonian, Richard M. ... Worcester, MA
Simonian, Stephen M. ... Waukegan, IL
Simonini, David M. ... San Anselmo, CA
Simonini, Reno J. ... Madison, WI
Simonis, John F. ... **Costa Mesa, CA**
Simonis, Julian A. ... Los Angeles, CA
Simonis, Thomas A. ... **Milwaukee, WI**
Simonitis, William P. ... Mountainside, NJ
Simonitsch, Jean M. ... Kansas City, MO
Simonitsch, Judith M. ... Kansas City, MO
Simonoff, Anne R. ... Philadelphia, PA
Simonoff, Howard S. ... **Atlantic City, NJ**
Cherry Hill, NJ
Northfield, NJ
Simonoff, Rachael A. ... **Los Angeles, CA**
Simonpietri Monefeldt, Dennis A.
San Juan, PR
Simon-Pratt, Kimberly J. ... Uniontown, PA
Simons, Alan D. ... Norcross, GA
Simons, Alan M. ... **Atlanta, GA**
Simons, Albert, III ... **New York, NY**
Simons, Amy Jane, The Law Offices of
Denver, CO
Simons, Andrew J. ... Pueblo, CO
Simons, Andrew J. ... **Albuquerque, NM**
Simons, Andrew J. ... **Uniondale, NY**
Simons, Andrew J. ... Philadelphia, PA
Simons & Associates ... **Pittsfield, MA**
Simons, Barbara M. ... Washington, DC
Simons, Barry L. ... Miami, FL
Simons, Barry T. ... **Laguna Beach, CA**
Simons, Benton R. ... Rochester, NY
Simons, Bernard P. ... **Los Angeles, CA**
Simons, Broudy ... **Chicago, IL**
Simons, Charles E., III ... Aiken, SC
Simons, Charles T. ... **Oklahoma City, OK**
Simons, Chas. E., Jr. ... Aiken, SC
Simons, Christopher J. ... Salem, OR
Simons, Claude Ernest, Jr. ... **Raleigh, NC**
Simons, Claudia A.
Federal Trade Commission, Office of Congressional Relations, GV
Simons, Clay G., Jr. ... Boise, ID
Simons, Cuddy & Friedman, LLP
Santa Fe, NM
Simons, Daniel A. ... **Richmond, KY**
Simons, Daniel S. ... Fort Lauderdale, FL
Simons, David A. ... **Boston, MA**
Simons, David F. ... **Honolulu, HI**
Simons, David J. ... Hollywood, FL
Simons, Dennis S. ... Edna, TX
Simons, Diane G. ... **New York, NY**
Simons, Donald S. ... Los Angeles, CA
Simons, Douglas A. ... Chicago, IL
Simons, Edward A. ... Denver, CO
Simons, Elizabeth A. ... Roselle, IL
Simons, Ellen L. ... Chestnut Hill, MA
Simons, Emily ... New York, NY
Simons, Eugene R. ... Atlanta, GA
Simons, Frances E. ... Minneapolis, MN
Simons, Frank S., Jr. ... Colorado Springs, CO
Simons, Gary C. ... **Ocala, FL**
Simons, George L. ... Mobile, AL
Simons, Gerry G. ... Turners Falls, MA
Simons, Glenna L. ... Brazil, IN
Simons, Gordon E. ... Minneapolis, MN
Simons, Harold F. ... Hamilton, NY
Simons, J. Jay ... Fort Lauderdale, FL
Simons, J. Jay, P.A. ... Fort Lauderdale, FL
Simons, James F. ... Park Forest, IL
Simons, James M. ... Austin, TX
Simons, Jean E. ... Cold Spring, NY
Simons, Jean R. ... Fairfax, VA
Simons, Jerome A. ... Hollywood, FL
Simons, Jerome A., P.A. ... Hollywood, FL
Simons, Jerome J., Jr. ... **Minneapolis, MN**
Simons, John C. ... Chicago, IL
Simons, John C. ... **New York, NY**

Simons, John Charles
New Brunswick, NJ
Simons, Joseph J. .... **Washington, DC**
Simons, Katherine W. .... **Charleston, SC**
Simons, Keating L., III .... **Charleston, SC**
Simons & Keaveny .... **Charleston, SC**
Simons, Keith E. .... Hopkins, MN
Simons, Keith E., P.A. .... Hopkins, MN
Simons, Laird H., III .... **Palo Alto, CA**
Simons, Laura L. .... Clarkston, MI
Simons, Lawrence A. .... Nashville, TN
Simons, Lawrence B. .... Washington, DC
Simons, Lawrence D. .... **Woodland Hills, CA**
Simons, Lawrence J. .... Pueblo, CO
Simons, Leonard M. .... **Boston, MA**
Simons, Linnea Mitchell .... Denver, CO
Simons, Lowell J. .... Redding, CA
Simons & Marcus .... Boston, MA
Simons, Mark B. .... Martinez, CA
Simons, Mark G. .... **Reno, NV**
Simons, Michael .... **Houston, TX**
Simons, Michael H. .... Towson, MD
Simons, Michael J. .... Austin, TX
Simons, Michelle T. .... **Needham, MA**
Simons, Morton L. .... Washington, DC
Simons, Patricia K.
Department Of Veterans Affairs, Office of Employment Discrimination Complaints Adjudication, GV
Simons, Paul R. .... **Chicago, IL**
Simons, Philip Yale .... **New York, NY**
Simons, R. Eric .... Beaver, PA
Simons, Raymond B. .... River Forest, IL
Simons, Richard A. .... **Pittsfield, MA**
Simons, Richard D. .... **Rome, NY**
Simons, Rick .... Hayward, CA
Simons, Robert A. .... West Des Moines, IA
Simons, Robert A. .... **West Des Moines, IA**
Simons, Robert D. .... **Atlanta, GA**
Simons, Robert P. .... **Pittsburgh, PA**
Simons, Robert R., Jr. .... Camden, NJ
Simons, Ross Parker .... Pascagoula, MS
Simons, Sam J. .... Brazil, IN
Simons & Seeley, P.A. .... Fairfax, VA
Simons, Serena Gray .... **Washington, DC**
Simons, Sheldon M. .... Sarasota, FL
Simons & Simons .... Washington, DC
Simons & Simons .... Turners Falls, MA
Simons, Stephen L. .... **Battle Creek, MI**
Simons, Stevan Gregory .... Towson, MD
Simons, Steven A. .... Granada Hills, CA
Simons, Steven J. .... **Boston, MA**
Simons, Stuart M. .... Miami, FL
Simons, Susan Brunick .... **Sioux Falls, SD**
Simons, Thad W., Jr. .... St. Louis, MO
Simons, Thomas A., IV .... **Santa Fe, NM**
Simons, Thomas A., Jr. .... Cincinnati, OH
Simons, Thomas G. .... Turners Falls, MA
Simons, Thomas L. .... Orange, CA
Simons, Thomas Moss .... Lexington, VA
Simons, Thomas Moss, P.C. .... Lexington, VA
Simons, Valerie L. .... Department of Justice, Civil Rights Division, GV
Simons, William A. .... **New Haven, CT**
Simons, William P. .... Northfield, MN
Simons, William W. .... **Pittsfield, MA**
Simons • Wilson • Viola .... **Honolulu, HI**
Simons & Wiskin .... **New York, NY**
Simonsen, Carolyn M. .... Edgewater, MD
Simonsen, David R., Jr. .... Richmond, VA
Simonsen, Eric T. .... Indianapolis, IN
Simonsen, Gregory M.
Salt Lake City, UT
Simonsen, James H. .... New York, NY
Simonsen, Jan E. .... **Washington, DC**
Simonsen, Karen A. .... **Chicago, IL**
Simonsen, Lars P. .... **Windsor, NC**
Simonsen, Lisa L. .... Spokane, WA
Simonsen, Marilyn Y. .... **Phoenix, AZ**
Farmington Hills, MI
Simonsen & Mizel, L.L.P. .... **Phoenix, AZ**
Farmington Hills, MI
Simonsen, Richard D. .... Quimby, IA
Simonsen, Stephen A. .... Conroe, TX
Simonsen, Warren P. .... Treasury Department, Internal Revenue Service, GV
Simonsmeier, Larry M. .... Pullman, WA
Simon-Solomon, Bettina S. .... Dallas, TX
Simonson, Alexander .... Suffern, NY
Simonson, Archie E. .... Madison, WI
Simonson, Brian D. .... Hibbing, MN
Simonson & Cohen, P.C. .... **New York, NY**
Staten Island, NY
Simonson, David M. .... Department of Justice, Criminal Division, GV
Simonson, Edward B. .... Basalt, CO
Simonson, Eric .... **New York, NY**
Simonson, Eric J. .... **New Orleans, LA**
Simonson Hess & Leibowitz, P.C.
Jersey City, NJ
New York, NY
Simonson, James S. .... **Minneapolis, MN**
Simonson, Jared S. .... Fargo, ND
Simonson, John S. .... **Redwood City, CA**
Simonson, Jon A. .... **New Paltz, NY**
Simonson, Judith Kochmanski
Hastings, MI
Simonson, Karen J. .... Claremont, CA
Simonson, Kirstin H. .... Irvine, CA
Simonson, Larry W. .... Grand Rapids, MI
Simonson, Laurie K. .... **San Francisco, CA**
Simonson, Marsha E. .... Albuquerque, NM
Simonson, Mary Ellen .... **Phoenix, AZ**
Simonson, Michael .... Scottsdale, AZ
Simonson, Michael H. .... New York, NY
Simonson, Mikal .... Valley City, ND
Simonson, Nancy M. .... **Corpus Christi, TX**
Simonson, Neil W. .... Owatonna, MN
Simonson, Paul .... Jersey City, NJ
New York, NY
Simonson, Paul J. .... **Salt Lake City, UT**
Simonson, Richard A. .... Scottsdale, AZ
Simonson, Richard G. .... Glendale, CA
Simonson, Richard S. .... New London, CT
Simonson, Ronald A. .... Chisholm, MN
Simonson, Steven J. .... Minot, ND
Simonson, Terry A. .... Tulsa, OK
Simonson-Malott, Theresa .... Whiting, NJ
Simon-Spada, Susan M. .... **Parsippany, NJ**
Simontacchi, Steven A. .... **San Rafael, CA**
Simonton, David R. .... **Fresno, CA**
Simonton, Dennis E. .... Casey, IL
Simonton, Frank H., Jr. .... Houston, TX
Simonton, Gail .... Memphis, TN
Simonton, George L. .... **Cody, WY**
Simonton, James W. .... Parkersburg, WV
Simonton, Pamela A. .... **West Haven, CT**
Simonton, Richard A. .... Glendive, MT
Simonton and Simonton .... **Cody, WY**
Simonton, Stacey R. .... Akron, OH
Simonton, Stephen L. .... **Cody, WY**
Simonyi, Juli Z. .... Hackensack, NJ
Simor, Peter T. .... **New York, NY**
Simos, Paul E. .... **Los Angeles, CA**
Simos, Sandra Copenhaver .... **Charlotte, NC**
Simoson, William E. .... **New York, NY**
Simotas, Helen .... Houston, TX
Simotas, Lisa .... Department of Justice, Criminal Division, GV
Simoudis, Christina .... **Akron, OH**
Simovitch, Audra J. .... Charlestown, MA
Simowitz, Lee H. .... **Washington, DC**
Simowitz, Mark B. .... San Diego, CA
Simowitz, Scott E. .... **Fort Lauderdale, FL**
Simowski, Kevin G. .... Detroit, MI
Simpich, Frederick .... **Washington, DC**
Simpkins, Cheri Cole .... Kansas City, MO
Simpkins, Darryl W., Law Offices of
Belle Mead, NJ
Simpkins, Gilbert A. .... **White Plains, NY**
Simpkins, Glenda M. .... Lansing, MI
Simpkins, Karen L. .... Ypsilanti, MI
Simpkins, Kelly D. .... **Jackson, MS**
Simpkins, Kirk G. .... **Princess Anne, MD**
Simpkins, Lloyd L. .... Princess Anne, MD
Simpkins, Mark B. .... **Newport Beach, CA**
Simpkins, Michelle L. .... **Austin, TX**
Simpkins, Robert L. .... Fairview Heights, IL
Simpkins, Robert L. .... Evansville, IN
Simpkins, Scott D. .... **Cleveland, OH**
Simpkins & Simpkins, P.A. .... **Crisfield, MD**
Princess Anne, MD
Simpler, Gary L. .... **Baltimore, MD**
Simpler, M. Fredrick, Jr.
Montgomery, AL
Simplicio, Linda .... New York, NY
Simplot, Thomas M. .... Phoenix, AZ
Simpson, A. Bruce .... Lockport, LA
Simpson, A. Marie .... Minneapolis, MN
Simpson, Adam K. .... **San Diego, CA**
Simpson, Adele B. .... Ruidoso, NM
Simpson, Aherne & Garrity, Professional Corporation .... San Francisco, CA
San Mateo, CA
Simpson, Alan K. .... **Englewood, CO**
Cody, WY
Simpson, Alan M. .... **Phoenix, AZ**
Simpson, Alan M. .... **Fresno, CA**
Simpson, Alan M., P.C. .... **Phoenix, AZ**
Simpson, Albert D., III .... Houston, TX
Simpson, Albert L. .... Union, NJ
Simpson, Alexander G. .... **New York, NY**
Simpson, Allyson B. .... Glendale, CA
Simpson, Althea Lynn .... **Detroit, MI**
Simpson, Amy E. .... **Charlotte, NC**
Simpson, Ancel .... Kingfisher, OK
Simpson, Andrew C.
Christiansted, St. Croix, VI
Simpson, Andrew G. .... Alexandria, VA
Simpson, Andrew H. .... **Newport Beach, CA**
Simpson, Andrew J. .... Boulder, CO
Simpson, Anna L. .... Oakland, CA
Simpson, Arnold R. .... Covington, KY
Simpson, Arthur J., Jr. .... **Hackensack, NJ**
Simpson & Associates .... Philadelphia, PA
Simpson, Augustus A., Jr. .... Metairie, LA
Simpson Aycock, P.A. .... **Morganton, NC**
Simpson, B. Alan .... **Bowling Green, KY**
Simpson, Barry M. .... Pittsburgh, PA
Simpson, Beeton, Finegan & Jaworski, L.L.P.
Texas City, TX
Simpson, Benjamin R. .... **Wallace, ID**
Simpson, Bobby C. .... **Louisville, KY**
Simpson & Boyd, P.L.L.C.
Bridgeport, TX
Decatur, TX
Simpson, Bradford P. .... Columbia, SC
Simpson, Brian J. .... **San Bernardino, CA**
Simpson, Brian M. .... **Fort Wayne, IN**
Simpson, Bruce E. .... Kentwood, LA
Simpson, Bruce M. .... **Charlotte, NC**
Simpson, Bryan T. .... **Raleigh, NC**
Simpson, C. Allan .... Houston, TX
Simpson, C. Edward .... Los Angeles, CA
Simpson, C. Kristopher .... Washington, DC
Simpson, C. Michael .... Arlington, VA
Simpson, C. Robert, Jr. .... Norwalk, CA
Simpson, C. Taylor .... New Orleans, LA
Simpson, Cameron Denise
Fort Walton Beach, FL
Simpson, Carol Masden .... **Galesburg, IL**
Simpson, Carolyn L. .... New York, NY
Simpson, Carolyn R. .... Lawrence, KS
Simpson, Carter B. .... **Fairfax, VA**
Simpson, Cecil O., Jr.
Department of the Army, U.S. Army Legal Services Agency, GV
Simpson, Charles C., III .... **Bay Minette, AL**
Mobile, AL
Simpson, Charles E. .... **New York, NY**
Simpson, Charles Everett, Jr.
New Bern, NC
Simpson, Charles J. .... Indianapolis, IN
Simpson, Charles J. .... Vandalia, OH
Simpson, Charles J., Jr. .... **Washington, DC**
Simpson, Charles R., III .... Louisville, KY
Simpson, Cheryl A. .... **Charleston, WV**
Simpson, Christina M. .... Gettysburg, PA
Simpson, Christine B. .... Burlington, NC
Simpson, Christine V. .... Washington, DC
Simpson, Christopher .... Augusta, ME
Simpson, Christopher C. .... **Phoenix, AZ**
Simpson, Clason, Callahan & Giustina
Longmeadow, MA
Simpson, Clay B. .... **Palo Alto, CA**
Simpson, Cliff .... **Houston, TX**
Simpson, Colin C. E. .... Elk Grove Village, IL
Simpson, Colin M. .... **Englewood, CO**
Cody, WY
Simpson, Craig A. .... Oak Brook, IL
Simpson, Craig Evan .... **Pittsburgh, PA**
Simpson & Cross .... **Tifton, GA**
Simpson, Curtis C., III
Santa Barbara, CA
Simpson, Curtis, Law Offices
Santa Barbara, CA
Simpson & Cybak .... Chicago, IL
Simpson, D. Scott .... **Des Moines, IA**
Simpson, D. Timothy .... **Tyler, TX**
Simpson, D. William .... Salisbury, MD
Simpson, Dan R. .... **Morganton, NC**
Simpson, Daniel G. .... **New York, NY**
Simpson, Daniel P. .... Hackensack, NJ
Simpson, David A. .... San Francisco, CA
Simpson, David A.
Fort Walton Beach, FL
Simpson, David A. .... Charlotte, NC
Simpson, David B. .... Glendale, CA
Simpson, David B. .... **Hackensack, NJ**
New York, NY
Simpson, David B. .... Binghamton, NY
Simpson, David E. .... **Rock Hill, SC**
Simpson, David G. .... Winchester, VA
Simpson, David L. .... **Edwardsville, IL**
Simpson, David L., III .... Memphis, TN
Simpson, David L., IV .... Memphis, TN
Simpson, David M. .... Marietta, GA
Simpson, David T., Jr. .... **Charlotte, NC**
Simpson, David W. .... Chicago, IL
Simpson, David W. .... **Irving, TX**
Simpson, David W., Jr. .... Salisbury, MD
Simpson, Deborah .... Washington, DC
Simpson, Deborah L. .... Danville, IL
Simpson, Denise O. .... Daytona Beach, FL
Simpson, Dennis H. .... Marshall, MN
Wood Lake, MN
Simpson, Derek W. .... Huntsville, AL
Simpson, Diane W. .... **Lawrence, KS**
Simpson, Donald .... Vancouver, WA
Simpson, Donald C. .... Moorestown, NJ
Simpson, Donald C., P.C. .... Moorestown, NJ
Simpson, Donald R. .... **Hollywood, FL**
Simpson, Dong & Wingate, L.L.C.
Columbia, SC
Simpson, Douglas J. .... Milwaukee, WI
Simpson, Douglas K. .... **Los Angeles, CA**
Simpson, Douglas K. .... Hartford, CT
Simpson, Douglas P. .... Salt Lake City, UT
Simpson, Duncan A. .... **Dallas, TX**
Simpson, E. Budd .... **Juneau, AK**
Simpson, E. Philip A., Jr. .... Boston, MA
Simpson, E. A., Jr. .... **Atlanta, GA**
Simpson, Edward B., (A Professional Corporation) .... **Sacramento, CA**
San Francisco, CA
Squaw Valley, CA
Tahoe City, CA
Simpson, Edward F., Jr.
Ormond Beach, FL
Simpson, Edward L. .... **Portland, OR**
Simpson, Edwin T. .... Wheaton, IL
Simpson, Eleanor P. .... Webster Groves, MO
Simpson, Elizabeth .... Marianna, FL
Simpson, Elizabeth E. .... **Albuquerque, NM**
Simpson, Ellen Swartz .... Buffalo, NY
Simpson, Faust Y. .... Morganfield, KY
Simpson, Francis L. R. .... Peoria, IL
Simpson, Frank G., III .... **Louisville, KY**
Simpson, Frank L., Jr. .... Marietta, GA
Simpson, Fred A. .... **Houston, TX**
Simpson, Fred B. .... Huntsville, AL
Simpson, Fred, Jr. .... **Missoula, MT**
Simpson, Frederick B. .... **Albertson, NY**
Simpson, Frederick J. .... Jacksonville, FL
Simpson, G. Northrup, Jr. .... Chicago, IL
Simpson, Garrett W. .... Phoenix, AZ
Simpson, Gary D. .... Duluth, GA
Simpson, Gary Howard .... **Washington, DC**
Simpson, Gary Howard .... **Bethesda, MD**
Simpson, Gary Howard .... **Rockville, MD**
Simpson, Gary L. .... **Atlanta, GA**
Simpson, Georganna L., Law Offices of
Dallas, TX
Simpson, George A. .... Springfield, VA
Simpson, George Arthur .... Indianapolis, IN
Simpson, George B. .... Sturgis, KY
Simpson, George L., III .... Rocky Mount, NC
Simpson, Gerald .... Toms River, NJ
Simpson & Gigounas .... **Sacramento, CA**
San Francisco, CA
Squaw Valley, CA
Tahoe City, CA
Simpson, Glenn D. .... Washington, DC
Simpson, Glenn Edward .... White Plains, NY
Simpson, Gregory Todd .... Texas City, TX
Simpson, G.W. Skip, III, P.A.
New Smyrna Beach, FL
Simpson, Harold H. .... **Little Rock, AR**
Simpson, Helen L. .... Anchorage, AK
Simpson, Henderson & Carta
Fort Myers, FL
Simpson, Henry A. .... Atlanta, GA
Simpson, Henry E. .... **Birmingham, AL**
Simpson, Hugh A. .... Fort Worth, TX
Simpson, Hulen R. .... Southfield, MI
Simpson, Iain G. .... **Houston, TX**
Simpson, Ian C. .... **Troy, MI**
Simpson, J. Calvin .... San Francisco, CA
Simpson, J. Cedric .... Ann Arbor, MI
Simpson, J. Christopher .... **Atlanta, GA**
Simpson, J. Michael .... Fort Worth, TX
Simpson, J. Scott .... Jacksonville, FL
Simpson, Jack P. .... Jay, NY
Simpson, Jacqueline .... Cleveland, OH
Simpson, James A. .... Goshen, IN
Simpson, James A. .... **Birmingham, MI**
Simpson, James A. .... Morganton, NC
Simpson, James A., Jr. .... **Searcy, AR**
Simpson, James B. .... Berkeley, CA
Simpson, James C., Jr. .... **Gulfport, MS**
Simpson, James D. .... Washington, DC
Simpson, James E. .... **Birmingham, AL**
Simpson, James F. .... West Palm Beach, FL
Simpson, James F. .... Portland, OR
Simpson, James H. .... Lenoir City, TN
Simpson, James L., III .... Louisville, KY
Simpson, James M. .... **Memphis, TN**
Simpson, James M., Jr. .... **Little Rock, AR**
Simpson, James M., Jr. (P.A.)
Little Rock, AR
Simpson, James P. .... Texas City, TX
Simpson, James Pope .... Dallas, TX
Simpson, James R. .... Los Angeles, CA
Simpson, James Reid, II .... **Morganton, NC**
Simpson, Jan K. .... **Houston, TX**
Simpson, Jane L. .... College Park, MD
Simpson, Janella K. .... Orange, CA
Simpson, Janet M. .... **Kansas City, KS**
Simpson, Jay Dee .... Houston, TX
Simpson, Jay M. .... Dayton, OH
Simpson, Jean E. .... Tallahassee, FL
Simpson, Jeffrey K. .... **Wilmington, DE**
Simpson, Jeffrey R. .... **Yakima, WA**
Simpson, Jennifer L. .... **Seattle, WA**
Simpson, Jesse B. .... **Phoenix, AZ**
Simpson, Jody Lynn .... **Houston, TX**
Simpson, John .... Bowdon, GA
Simpson, John A. .... **San Diego, CA**
Simpson, John B., Jr. .... Forestville, MD
Simpson, John D. .... Marianna, FL
Simpson, John D. .... **Chicago, IL**
Arlington, VA
Simpson, John E. .... Savannah, GA
Simpson, John F. (Jack), Jr. .... Denver, CO
Simpson, John H. .... Chicago, IL
Simpson, John H. .... Massillon, OH
Simpson, John, III .... Lubbock, TX
Simpson, John K. .... Boise, ID
Simpson, John L. .... Oklahoma City, OK
Simpson, John M. .... **Washington, DC**
Simpson, John M. .... Kansas City, MO
Simpson, John M., P.C., P.A.
Kansas City, MO
Simpson, John P. .... Gaithersburg, MD
Simpson, John P. .... Emerald Isle, NC
Jacksonville, NC
Swansboro, NC
Simpson, John R. .... Springfield, IL
Simpson, John R. .... Everett, WA
Simpson, John R., Jr. .... **Winter Park, FL**
Simpson, John S. .... **Ridgeland, MS**
Simpson, John S. .... **Indiana, PA**
Simpson, John W. .... **Kansas City, MO**
Simpson, John W., Jr. PLLC
Bloomfield Hills, MI
Simpson, Johnny .... Columbia, SC
Simpson, Joseph A. .... **Fort Myers, FL**
Simpson, Joseph C. .... Memphis, TN
Simpson, Joseph H. .... Amite, LA
Simpson, Joseph S. .... **Toledo, OH**
Simpson, Julie
Environmental Protection Agency, Program Office Attorneys, GV
Simpson, Juliet M. .... **Chicago, IL**
Simpson, J. W., Jr. .... Conroe, TX
Simpson, K. Russell .... **Savannah, GA**
Simpson, Kablack & Bell .... **Indiana, PA**
Simpson, Karen .... Batavia, IL
Simpson, Kathryn Lease .... **Harrisburg, PA**
Simpson, Keith F. .... **Fresno, CA**
Simpson, Kendall C. .... Newport Beach, CA
Simpson, Kepler & Edwards, LC
Cody, WY
Simpson, Kerry Aileen .... **St. Louis, MO**
Simpson, Kimberly A. .... Orinda, CA
Simpson, Kimberly A. .... **Providence, RI**
Simpson, Kirsten L. .... Treasury Department, Internal Revenue Service, GV
Simpson, Kristy L. .... Wichita, KS
Simpson, Kristy L., P.A. .... Wichita, KS
Simpson, Kurt A. .... Jacksonville Beach, FL
Simpson, L. Kimbal .... Garland, TX
Simpson, Lane W. .... Lakeview, OR
Simpson, Larry D. .... **Tallahassee, FL**
Simpson, Lary C. .... Los Angeles, CA
Simpson, Laura K. .... Kansas City, MO
Simpson Law Offices .... **Louisville, KY**
Simpson Law Offices LLP .... **Atlanta, GA**
Simpson, Leah R. .... **Metairie, LA**
Simpson, Lee M. .... **Dallas, TX**

Simpson, Lester A., Jr. ... Salisbury, MD
Simpson, Linda A. ... New York, NY
Simpson, Linda W. ... Charlotte, NC
Simpson, Lisa T. ... New York, NY
Simpson, Lonnie L. ... Tampa, FL
Simpson, Lori A. ... Charleston, WV
Simpson, Lou Ann ... Des Moines, IA
Simpson, Lucia S. ... Detroit, MI
Simpson, Lucy Rain ... Window Rock, AZ
Simpson, Lyle L. ... Des Moines, IA
Simpson, Lyndon E. ... Fort Worth, TX
Simpson, M. Gregory ... Edina, MN
Simpson, Manliff M. ... Chicago, IL
Simpson, Marc D. ... Minneapolis, MN
Simpson, Margaret J. ... Chicago, IL
Simpson, Mark D. ... Philadelphia, PA
Simpson, Mark L. ... Little River, SC
Simpson, Mark R. ... Douglasville, GA
Simpson, Mark S. ... Hilton Head Island, SC
Simpson, Marla G. ... New York, NY
Simpson, Marva B. ... Atlanta, GA
Simpson, Marva D.
Securities and Exchange Commission, Office of the General Counsel, GV
Simpson, Mary K. ... San Jose, CA
Simpson, Mary K. ... Tallahassee, FL
Simpson, Matthew J. ... Stamford, CT
Simpson & McLaughlin ... Goshen, IN
Simpson, Meredith J. ... New York, NY
Simpson, Michael A. ... Bridgeport, TX
Decatur, TX
Simpson, Michael D. ... Washington, DC
Simpson, Michael Francis ... Knoxville, TN
Simpson, Michael H. ... Milwaukee, WI
Simpson, Michael J. ... Rapid City, SD
Simpson, Michael M. ... New Orleans, LA
Simpson, Michael N. ... Overland Park, KS
Simpson, Michael S. ... Denver, CO
Simpson, Michael S. ... Austin, TX
Simpson, Michael W. ... Moore, OK
Simpson, Murray S., Jr. ... Greenbelt, MD
Simpson, Nancy L. ... Sacramento, CA
Simpson, Nancy Stein ... Hackensack, NJ
New York, NY
Simpson, Natasha Denise ... Orange Park, FL
Simpson, Nathan B. ... Tampa, FL
Simpson, Nathaniel H. ... Southfield, MI
Simpson, Noah Henry, III ... Dallas, TX
Simpson, Noelle J. ... Department of the Army, Office, Chief of Engineers/Headquarters, U.S. Army Corps of Engineers, GV
Simpson, Norene L. ... Pueblo, CO
Simpson, Novice ... Houston, TX
Simpson, P. Edward ... Seattle, WA
Simpson, Patricia L. ... Farmington, NM
Simpson, Patrick J. ... Portland, OR
Simpson, Paul A. ... Fredericksburg, VA
Richmond, VA
Simpson, Paul F. ... Houston, TX
Simpson, Paul L. ... Selmer, TN
Simpson, Paul V. ... San Francisco, CA
Simpson, Pedro A. ... Mesa, AZ
Simpson, Peter F. ... Oak Brook, IL
Simpson, Phillip T. ... New York, NY
Simpson, Phillis Lu ... New York, NY
Simpson, Phyllis Alexander ... Antioch, TN
Simpson, Preston M. ... Sarasota, FL
Simpson, Ralph F. ... Tifton, GA
Simpson, Randall G. ... Anchorage, AK
Simpson, Randolph C. ... Los Angeles, CA
Simpson, Raymond ... La Grange, KY
Simpson, Raymond L.
Jacksonville Beach, FL
Simpson, Reagan W. ... Houston, TX
Simpson, Rebecca G. ... Peachtree City, GA
Simpson, Rebecca L. ... Cincinnati, OH
Simpson, Rebecca L. ... Longview, TX
Simpson, Rexford C. ... Torrance, CA
Simpson, Richard A. ... Washington, DC
Simpson, Richard B.
House of Representatives, Office of Law Revision Counsel, GV
Simpson, Richard C. ... Columbus, OH
Simpson, Richard D. ... Overland Park, KS
Simpson, Richard D., Jr. ... Irvine, CA
Simpson, Richard E.
Securities and Exchange Commission, Division of Enforcement, GV
Simpson, Richard S. ... Alexandria, VA
Simpson, Riley J. ... Gatesville, TX
Simpson, Robert A. ... Lakewood, CO
Simpson, Robert A. ... Eastlake, OH
Simpson, Robert E. ... Vienna, VA
Simpson, Robert E., Jr. ... Easton, PA
Simpson, Robert G. ... Redding, CA
Simpson, Robert G. ... Portland, OR
Simpson, Robert G. ... Houston, TX
Simpson, Robert J. ... Beverly Hills, CA
Simpson, Robert J. ... San Bernardino, CA
Simpson, Robert J. ... Owego, NY
Simpson, Robert L. ... Long Beach, CA
Simpson, Robert L. ... Fort Lauderdale, FL
Simpson, Robert L. ... Metairie, LA
Simpson, Robert L. ... Spokane, WA
Simpson, Robert Lee ... Virginia Beach, VA
Simpson, Robert M. ... Long Beach, CA
Simpson, Robert P. ... La Jolla, CA
Simpson, Robert P. ... Williamsville, NY
Simpson, Robert R. ... Hartford, CT
Simpson, Robert R. ... Knoxville, TN
Simpson, Robert V., Jr. ... Burlington, VT
Simpson, Robin D. ... Minneapolis, MN
Simpson, Roger A. ... Monticello, IL
Simpson, Roger M., Jr. ... Chicago, IL
Simpson, Roger N. ... San Antonio, TX
Simpson, Roger W. ... Los Angeles, CA
Simpson, Roland G. ... Los Angeles, CA
Simpson, Roland G., A Law Corporation
Los Angeles, CA
Simpson, Ronald V. ... Louisville, KY
Simpson, Ronald W. ... Corydon, IN
Simpson, Ross M. ... Bridgeport, TX
Decatur, TX
Simpson, Roy B., Jr. ... New York, NY
Simpson, Russell G., (P.C.) ... Boston, MA
Simpson, S. David ... Galesburg, IL
Simpson, Samuel L. ... Detroit, MI
Simpson, Samuel P., V ... Richmond, VA
Simpson, Samuel S. ... Stratford, CT
Simpson, Sara M. ... Monticello, AR
Simpson, Sarah Biety ... New York, NY
Simpson, Scott A. ... Wilmington, DE
Simpson, Scott E. ... Daytona Beach, FL
Ormond Beach, FL
Simpson, Scott L. ... Spokane, WA
Simpson, Sean D., Law Offices of
San Diego, CA
Simpson, Sean R. ... Los Angeles, CA
Simpson, Selden ... Amarillo, TX
Simpson, Shannon S. ... Huntsville, AL
Simpson, Shelley ... House of Representatives, Congressional Assistants, GV
Simpson, Shelley A. ... Montpelier, VT
Simpson, Shirley S. ... Phoenix, AZ
Simpson & Simpson
Fort Walton Beach, FL
Simpson & Simpson ... Morganfield, KY
Simpson, Simpson & Willisson
Huntsville, AL
Simpson, Skip, A Prof. Corp., Law Offices of
Dallas, TX
Simpson, Skip, Jr. ... Dallas, TX
Simpson, Sondra L. ... Austin, TX
Simpson, Stan Patrick ... Camden, NJ
Simpson, Stefanie Glasgow ... Dallas, TX
Simpson, Stephen C. ... Houston, TX
Simpson, Stephen K. ... Alexandria, VA
Simpson, Stephen W. ... Los Angeles, CA
Simpson, Stephen W. ... Philadelphia, PA
Simpson, Steven D. ... Raleigh, NC
Simpson, Steven D., P.A., Law Offices of
Raleigh, NC
Simpson, Steven P. ... Bluff, UT
Simpson, T. Justin ... Metairie, LA
Simpson, Terrence G. ... Narragansett, RI
Simpson Thacher & Bartlett
Palo Alto, CA
Universal City, CA
New York, NY
Columbus, OH
Simpson, Thomas ... Woodbury, NJ
Simpson, Thomas B., Jr. ... Lexington, KY
Simpson, Thomas C. ... Bloomfield Hills, MI
Simpson, Thomas E. ... Morganfield, KY
Simpson, Thomas L. ... Glendale, CA
Simpson, Thomas M. ... New York, NY
Simpson, Thomas R. ... Compton, CA
Simpson, Thomas R., Jr. ... La Plata, MD
Simpson, Thomas S. ... Racine, WI
Simpson & Thompson ... Corydon, IN
New Albany, IN
Simpson, Tillinghast, Sorensen & Lorensen
Juneau, AK
Simpson, Timothy J. ... Fairfield, NJ
Simpson, Travis H. ... Winston-Salem, NC
Simpson, Varya ... San Francisco, CA
Simpson, W. Kennedy ... Louisville, KY
Simpson, W. Roger ... Lancaster, PA
Simpson, W. Scott ... Department of Justice, Civil Division, GV
Simpson, Walter R. ... Kansas City, MO
Simpson, Warren L., Jr. ... Philadelphia, PA
Simpson, Wendell, Jr. ... Crestwood, KY
Simpson, William D. ... Shawnee, OK
Simpson, William F. ... Columbus, OH
Simpson, William F., Jr. ... Kinston, NC
Simpson, William H. ... York, PA
Simpson, William J. ... Costa Mesa, CA
Simpson, William John ... Rockford, IL
Simpson, William L. ... Englewood, CO
Cody, WY
Simpson, William P. ... Columbia, SC
Simpson, William Samuel ... Kalamazoo, MI
Simpson & Williams, P.A. ... Salisbury, MD
Simpson, Winifred D. ... Atlanta, GA
Simpson Woolley McConachie, L.L.P.
Dallas, TX
Simpson Zelenock, P.C. ... Birmingham, MI
Detroit, MI
Simpson-Brown, Susan ... Reading, PA
Simrill, Jack D. ... Hilton Head Island, SC
Simrill, T. Hugh, Jr. ... Rock Hill, SC
Simrin, Andy ... Salem, OR
Simrin, Stanley ... Bakersfield, CA
Simrin, Steven M. ... Oakland, CA
Simring, Jill Rona ... Fort Lauderdale, FL
Simring, Richard B. ... Miami, FL
Sims, A. Ward ... Charlottesville, VA
Sims, Aaron R. ... Woodward, OK
Sims, Alan D. ... Norcross, GA
Sims, Alan S. ... Cleveland, OH
Sims, Algie W., III ... St. Louis, MO
Sims, Allen ... Salt Lake City, UT
Sims, Alvin Jack ... Brockton, MA
Plymouth, MA
Sims, Andrew B ... New York, NY
Sims, Andrew D. ... Fort Worth, TX
Sims, Angela B. ... Chattanooga, TN
Sims, Ann Tilford ... Los Lunas, NM
Sims, Arthur D., II ... Orlando, FL
Sims, Arthur P. ... Baltimore, MD
Sims, August C. ... Pataskala, OH
Sims, Barbara L. ... Minneapolis, MN
Sims, Barbara M. ... Buffalo, NY
Sims, Barry A. ... North Little Rock, AR
Sims, Benham J., III ... Louisville, KY
Sims, Benjamin A. ... Ogden, UT
Sims & Boster ... Denver, CO
Sims, Brian Douglas ... New York, NY
Sims, Brian E. ... Oakland, CA
Sims, Bruce W. ... San Antonio, TX
Sims, Bryan A. ... Washington, DC
Sims, Bryan D. ... Las Vegas, NV
Sims, Byron J. ... Carlinville, IL
Sims, C. Garold ... Denver, CO
Sims, C. Randall ... Conway, AR
Sims, Carole P. ... Atlanta, GA
Sims, Carvel A. ... Baton Rouge, LA
Sims, Charles H., III ... Selma, AL
Sims, Charles M. ... Richmond, VA
Sims, Charles S. ... New York, NY
Sims, Christine ... Jacksonville, FL
Sims, Clyde ... Hubbard, TX
Sims, Darrell R. ... Metairie, LA
Sims, David A. ... Winter Springs, FL
Sims, David A. ... Elkins, WV
Sims, David A., P.C. ... Trenton, MI
Sims, David E. ... Detroit, MI
Sims, David J. ... Wheeling, WV
Sims, David L. ... Pine Bluff, AR
Sims, Dawn
Federal Communications Commission, Wireless Telecommunications Bureau, GV
Sims, Denise Tatum ... Hernando, MS
Sims, Dorothy Clay ... Gainesville, FL
Ocala, FL
Sims, Edgar H., Jr. (P.C.) ... Atlanta, GA
Sims, Edward S. ... Los Angeles, CA
Sims, Eileen J. ... Indianapolis, IN
Sims, Elise Epperson ... Bay St. Louis, MS
Sims, Eric, Jr. ... Brighton, CO
Sims, Ferman W. ... Crescent City, CA
Sims, Fleming & Spurlin, P.C. ... Tifton, GA
Sims, G. Brent ... Irvine, CA
Sims, G. Byron ... Houston, TX
Sims, G. Larry ... Daytona Beach, FL
Daytona Beach, FL
Maitland, FL
Sims, G. Reynolds ... Bloomfield Hills, MI
Sims, G. Reynolds, & Associates, P.C.
Bloomfield Hills, MI
Sims, Garland D. ... New York, NY
Sims, Genevieve C. ... Raleigh, NC
Sims, Geoffrey H. ... Fresno, CA
Sims, George N., Jr. ... Talladega, AL
Sims, Gerald A., Jr. ... Clayton, MO
Sims, Gerald N. ... San Diego, CA
Sims, Gerald N. ... Pass Christian, MS
Sims, Gerard C., Jr. ... Trenton, NJ
Sims, Glennis E. ... Dallas, TX
Sims, H. Blake ... Chattanooga, TN
Sims, H. Bryant ... West Palm Beach, FL
Sims, H. William, Jr. ... Longmont, CO
Sims and Hall ... Elkins, WV
Sims, Hannah E. ... Alameda, CA
Sims, Harriet J. ... St. Paul, MN
Sims, Henry R., Sr. ... Orangeburg, SC
Sims, H.J. ... San Diego, CA
Sims, Howard
Department of Housing and Urban Development, Washington, D. C. Office, GV
Sims, Hugo S., III ... Orangeburg, SC
Sims, Hugo S., Jr. ... Orangeburg, SC
Sims, Hunter W., Jr. ... Norfolk, VA
Sims, Iris K. ... Oak Park, IL
Sims, J. Scott ... Birmingham, AL
Sims, J. Scott ... Orlando, FL
Sims, Jack ... Hillsboro, TX
Sims, Jack B. ... San Antonio, TX
Sims, Jacqueline M.
Department Of Veterans Affairs, Office of the General Counsel, GV
Sims, James A., Jr. ... Oakland, CA
Sims, James L. ... San Francisco, CA
Sims, James R., III ... Washington, DC
Sims, Jason B. ... Cincinnati, OH
Sims, Jerry L. ... Atlanta, GA
Sims, Jodi Michelle ... Tuscaloosa, AL
Sims, Joe ... Washington, DC
Sims, John C. ... Lubbock, TX
Sims, John Cary ... Sacramento, CA
Sims, John D. ... Mount Olivet, KY
Sims, John E. ... Citrus Heights, CA
Sims, John I. ... Monaca, PA
Sims, John L. ... Hartselle, AL
Sims, John M. ... Albion, MI
Sims, John R. ... Neosho, MO
Sims, John R. ... Cincinnati, OH
Sims, John S., Jr. ... Tifton, GA
Sims, John W. ... New Orleans, LA
Sims, John W. ... Marshfield, MO
Sims, Johnson, Wood & Higdon
Neosho, MO
Sims, Jonathan D. ... New York, NY
Sims, Joseph A., Jr. ... Hammond, LA
Sims, Joseph Walker ... Hernando, MS
Sims, Joseph Walker ... Tunica, MS
Sims, Joy M. ... Nashville, TN
Sims, Kara Cline ... Boston, MA
Sims, Karen Ann ... Liberty, MO
Sims, Kathleen Healy ... Chester, NJ
Sims, Kathleen S. ... Seattle, WA
Sims, Kelly B. ... Winter Park, FL
Sims, Kelly B., P.A., Law Office of
Winter Park, FL
Sims, Kidd, Hubbert & Wilson
Lubbock, TX
Sims, L. David, (P.A.) ... Fort Myers, FL
Sims, L. Lee ... Dadeville, AL
Sims, Lana H., Jr. ... Columbia, SC
Sims, Larry U. ... Mobile, AL
Sims & Layton ... Alameda, CA
Monterey, CA
San Jose, CA
Santa Cruz, CA
Sims, Leon J. ... Doraville, GA
Sims, Liesche, Reagan, Wallace & Wallace, P.A. ... Coeur d'Alene, ID
Sims, Linda Fowler ... Detroit, MI
Sims & Lopez, P.A. ... Lawrenceville, GA
Sims, Luke E. ... Milwaukee, WI
Sims, M. Kent ... Wheeler, TX
Sims, M. Saylor ... Columbia, SC
Sims, Margaret Bowen ... Columbus, OH
Sims, Marguerita Brunson
Washington, DC
Sims, Mari Kristine ... Dallas, TX
Sims, Marilyn S. ... Houston, TX
Sims, Mark E. ... Cincinnati, OH
Sims, Mark Wesley ... Austin, TX
Sims, Marketa ... Pittsburgh, PA
Sims, Marney Collins ... Houston, TX
Sims, Martin L. ... Charlottesville, VA
Sims, Mary L. ... Philadelphia, PA
Sims, McCarty, Amat & Stakenborg, P.A.
Gainesville, FL
Jacksonville, FL
Ocala, FL
Sims & McCoid ... Wheeling, WV
Sims, Melanie E. ... Los Angeles, CA
Sims Moore Hill & Gannon, L.L.P.
Hillsboro, TX
Sims Moss Kline & Davis LLP
Atlanta, GA
New York, NY
Sims, Murray W., Jr. ... Flossmoor, IL
Sims, Nanette ... Birmingham, AL
Sims, Nathaniel ... Washington, DC
Sims, Nathaniel G. ... Mount Kisco, NY
Sims & Olsen ... Oakland, CA
Sims, Patricia L. Winfrey
Environmental Protection Agency, Office of Enforcement and Compliance Assurance, GV
Sims, Patrick H. ... Mobile, AL
Sims, Perry B. ... Sacramento, CA
Sims, Peter ... New York, NY
Sims, Phillip M. ... San Jose, CA
Sims, R. Stephen ... Savannah, GA
Sims, Ralph L. ... Anaheim, CA
Sims, Randall T. ... New York, NY
Sims, Randy D. ... Kansas City, MO
Sims, Rebecca L. ... Douglas, GA
Sims, Richard J. ... Cleveland, OH
Sims, Richard M., III ... Sacramento, CA
Sims, Richard P. ... Costa Mesa, CA
Sims, Ricky R. ... Teague, TX
Sims, Robert E. ... San Francisco, CA
Sims, Robert E. ... Louisville, KY
Sims, Robert L. ... Dallas, TX
Sims, Robert L., Jr. ... New York, NY
Sims, Robert P. ... San Antonio, TX
Sims, Roberta Willis ... Washington, DC
Sims, Roger W. ... Orlando, FL
Sims, Ronald L. ... Birmingham, AL
Sims, Ronald L. ... Orlando, FL
Sims, Ronald L., P.A. ... Orlando, FL
Sims, Ronald M. ... Hackettstown, NJ
Sims, Ronald S., Law Office of
Bakersfield, CA
Sims, Russell W. ... Walnut Creek, CA
Sims, S. Lamar ... Denver, CO
Sims, Savalle C. ... Washington, DC
Sims, Sheva M. ... Shreveport, LA
Sims, Shields ... Columbus, MS
Sims and Sims ... Louisville, KY
Sims and Sims ... Louisville, KY
Sims & Sims ... Columbus, MS
Sims & Sims, P.C. ... Brockton, MA
Plymouth, MA
Sims & Sprowl ... Costa Mesa, CA
Sims, Stacy L. ... Heidelberg, MS
Sims, Stephen M. ... Anchorage, AK
Sims, Stephen M. ... Fort Wayne, IN
Sims, Steven K. ... Oak Brook, IL
Sims, Steven M. ... Norman, OK
Sims, Steven O. ... Denver, CO
Sims, Steven R. ... Tyler, TX
Sims, Susan Snoot ... Bandera, TX
Sims, Terrance L. ... Phoenix, AZ
Sims, Thaddeus M. ... Dallas, TX
Sims, Theron L. ... Kansas City, MO
Sims, Thomas E. ... Kansas City, MO
Sims, Thomas J., (P.C.) ... Edinburg, TX
Sims, Thomas S. ... San Diego, CA
Sims, Tom ... New Augusta, MS
Sims, Tommy L. ... Lawton, OK
Sims, Trevin E. ... Santa Monica, CA
Sims, Van F. ... Paducah, KY
Sims, Victor Dwayne ... Cincinnati, OH
Sims, W. Scott ... Nashville, TN
Sims, Wallace A. ... Detroit, MI
Sims, Wayne R., (A Professional Corporation) ... Costa Mesa, CA
Sims, Wendell M. ... Charlotte, NC
Sims, William D., Jr. ... Dallas, TX
Sims, William F. ... Coeur d'Alene, ID
Sims, William H. ... Brockton, MA
Plymouth, MA
Sims, William J., III ... Phoenix, AZ
Sims, William M. ... Bakersfield, CA
Sims, William P. ... Hilton Head Island, SC
Sims, William R. ... Kershaw, SC
Sims, Wilson ... Nashville, TN
Sims, Wm. Dennis ... Louisville, KY
Sims, Yvonne C. M. ... Department of Labor, Employment Standards Administration, GV
Simsarian, Edward D. ... Whitinsville, MA
Worcester, MA

Simsarian, Kendall D. ....Fresno, CA
Simser, Thomas A., Jr. ....Orlando, FL
Simses, Richard M. ....Lake Charles, LA
New Orleans, LA
Houston, TX
Simses, Robert G. ....Palm Beach, FL
Vero Beach, FL
Simshauser, John V. ....Macomb, IL
Simshauser, Peter ....Los Angeles, CA
Simshaw, Calvin K. ....Vancouver, WA
Simson, Gary J. ....Ithaca, NY
Simson, Jean Birdsall ....New York, NY
Simson, John L. ....Washington, DC
Simson, Leon ....Portland, OR
Simson, Marguerite B. ....Honolulu, HI
Simstacolos, James G. ....Louisville, KY
Sims-Taylor, Lynne ....Syracuse, NY
Sims-Taylor, Lynne A. ....Palos Park, IL
Sims-West, James W. ....Bronx, NY
Simunic, Joan L. ....Louisville, KY
Simunic, Nancy H. ....Columbus, OH
Simuro, Valerie Theresa ....Brooklyn, NY
Simutis, Frank J. ....Watseka, IL
Simutis, Frank J., P.C., Law Offices of
Watseka, IL
Sinadinos, John G. ....Sacramento, CA
Sinadinos & Vryonis, R.L.L.P.
Sacramento, CA
Sinagra, Anthony C. ....Lakewood, OH
Sinagra, Frank J. ....Fort Lauderdale, FL
Sinai, David P. ....Reno, NV
Sinai, Robert W. ....Santa Rosa, CA
Sinai, Schroeder, Mooney, Boetsch & Bradley
Reno, NV
Sinai, Stuart ....Troy, MI
Sinaikin, Ronald A. ....Morristown, NJ
Sinaiko, Stephen M. ....New York, NY
Sinak, David L. ....Dallas, TX
Sinal, Paul A. ....Winston-Salem, NC
Sinanian, Shahe ....New York, NY
Sinanian, Zaven V. ....Los Angeles, CA
Sinapi Formisano & Coleman, Ltd.
Cranston, RI
Providence, RI
Sinapi, Richard A. ....Cranston, RI
Sinar, Scott A. ....Chicago, IL
Sinardi, Nick J. ....Tampa, FL
Sinars, Douglas M. ....Chicago, IL
Sinars, Theodore A. ....Chicago, IL
Sinas, Dramis, Brake, Boughton & McIntyre, P.C. ....Lansing, MI
Sinas, George T. ....Lansing, MI
Sinasohn, Gideon E. ....San Diego, CA
Sinasohn, John M. ....Encino, CA
Sinatra, Frank G. ....New York, NY
Sinatra, Geraldine A. ....Philadelphia, PA
Sinatra, John L., Jr. ....Cleveland, OH
Sinatra, Kathryn ....Rockville Centre, NY
Sinatra, Louis J. ....Philadelphia, PA
Sinatra, Michael P. ....Bloomfield, NJ
Sinatra, Steven ....New York, NY
Sinatro, Stephen J. ....Hartford, CT
Sinawski, Gary ....New York, NY
Sinay, Michael Paul ....Bethesda, MD
Sinay Phillips, Florence
San Francisco, CA
Sinback, Patricia H. ....Atlanta, GA
Sinback, Petrita Posada
West Valley City, UT
Sincerbeaux, Robert A. ....New York, NY
Sincerbeaux & Shrewsbury ....New York, NY
Sinchak & Bennett ....Wilton, CT
Sinchak, Karen K. ....Scottsdale, AZ
Sinchak, Karen K., P.C. ....Scottsdale, AZ
Sinchak, Thomas M. ....Wilton, CT
Sinclair, Alex M. ....Great Falls, VA
Sinclair, Andrea L. ....Cleveland, OH
Sinclair, Andrew T. ....Oakland, CA
Sinclair, Arthur W. ....Haymarket, VA
Sinclair, Barbara B. ....Chicago, IL
Sinclair, Brad A. ....Fargo, ND
Sinclair, Bradley H. ....St. Louis, MO
Sinclair, Bradley W. ....Melbourne, FL
Sinclair, Brian C. ....Irvine, CA
Sinclair, Bryan J. ....Washington, DC
Sinclair, Calder P. ....Atlanta, GA
Sinclair, Charles D. ....Des Moines, IA
Sinclair, Charles H. ....Miami, FL
Sinclair, Charles J. ....Paramus, NJ
Sinclair, Craig A. ....Redding, CA
Sinclair, Daniel Edward ....Pineland, FL
Sinclair, Daniel J. ....St. Louis, MO
Sinclair, Daniel J. ....Pittsburgh, PA
Sinclair, Daniel K. ....Gurnee, IL
Sinclair, Dawn R. ....Phoenix, AZ
Sinclair, Deborah Leah ....Delta, CO
Sinclair, Diane ....San Antonio, TX
Sinclair, Dionne G. ....New York, NY
Sinclair, Donald C., II ....Canonsburg, PA
Sinclair, E. David ....Vista, CA
Sinclair, F. Larry ....Roseville, CA
Sinclair & Ferg ....Chippewa Falls, WI
Sinclair, Gary M. ....Chicago, IL
Sinclair, Gerald A. ....Woodbury, NJ
Sinclair, Gerald A., P.C. ....Woodbury, NJ
Sinclair & Hill, A Law Corporation
Redding, CA
Sinclair, Howard V. ....Washington, DC
Sinclair, I.B., Law Offices ....Bellefonte, PA
Sinclair, I.B. ....Media, PA
State College, PA
Sinclair, J. Frederick ....Alexandria, VA
Sinclair, J. Frederick, P.C.
Alexandria, VA
Sinclair, J. Walter ....Twin Falls, ID
Sinclair, Jaclyn R. ....Seattle, WA
Sinclair, James A. ....West Des Moines, IA
Sinclair, James D. ....Detroit Lakes, MN
Sinclair, James S. ....Alton, IL
Sinclair, Jo-Anne ....Palo Alto, CA
Sinclair, John B. ....Towson, MD
Sinclair, John J. ....Olympia, WA
Sinclair, John J., P.S. ....Olympia, WA
Sinclair, John M. ....San Francisco, CA
Sinclair, John P. ....Wilmington, DE
Sinclair, Joseph T. ....The Woodlands, TX
Sinclair, Judith K. ....Dallas, TX
Sinclair, Kent D.B. ....Boston, MA
Sinclair, Kent, Jr. ....Charlottesville, VA
Sinclair, Larry P. ....Auburn, CA
Sinclair, Larry P. ....Roseville, CA
Sinclair, Larry P. ....Sacramento, CA
Sinclair, Larry R. ....Rusk, TX
Sinclair Law Firm, The ....Annapolis, MD
Bowie, MD
Millersville, MD
Sinclair, Linda J. ....San Diego, CA
Sinclair, Louis, Heath, Nussbaum & Zavertnik, P.A. ....Miami, FL
Sinclair, Marcie E. ....Chula Vista, CA
Sinclair, Mark A. ....Waterbury, VT
Sinclair, Martin H. ....Great Falls, MT
Sinclair, Mary G. ....Department of Labor, Office of Secretary, GV
Sinclair, Michael B.W. ....New York, NY
Sinclair, Michael V. ....Bozeman, MT
Sinclair, Murray M. ....Los Angeles, CA
Sinclair, Nancy Anderson
Great Falls, MT
Sinclair, Patricia Timko ....Los Angeles, CA
Sinclair, Paul A. ....Glen Allen, VA
Sinclair, Paul D. ....Kansas City, MO
Sinclair, Paul H. ....Indianapolis, IN
Sinclair, Paula Brown ....Twin Falls, ID
Sinclair, Phillip K. ....Spartanburg, SC
Sinclair, R. Allen ....Youngstown, OH
Sinclair, R. Allen & Assoc.
Youngstown, OH
Sinclair, R. Ronald ....Annapolis, MD
Bowie, MD
Millersville, MD
Sinclair, Randy W. ....Danville, VA
Sinclair, Randy W., P.C. ....Danville, VA
Sinclair, Richard C. ....Oakdale, CA
Sinclair, Rita Diane ....Long Beach, CA
Sinclair, Robert F. ....Roseville, CA
Sinclair, Robert J. ....Houston, TX
Sinclair, Roxanne Ellis ....Waterbury, CT
Sinclair, Sawyer, Thompson, Haynes & Cowing, P.C. ....Kansas City, KS
Kansas City, MO
Sinclair, Scott C. ....Shreveport, LA
Sinclair, Stacey J. ....Haddonfield, NJ
Sinclair, Susan A. ....Department of Justice, Criminal Division, GV
Sinclair, Talbot ....Port Charlotte, FL
Sinclair, Tana L. ....Arroyo Grande, CA
Sinclair, Timothy R. ....Bingham Farms, MI
Sinclair, V. Lee, Jr. ....Canton, OH
Sinclair, Vance L. ....Chippewa Falls, WI
Sinclair, Wayne A. ....Deerfield, IL
Sinclair, William B. ....Rockville, MD
Sinclair, William F. ....Wheeling, WV
Sinclair, Wilson & Bedore ....Auburn, CA
Roseville, CA
Sinclaire, Joel S. ....Baltimore, MD
Sinclaire, John, III ....North Charleston, SC
Sinclitico, Dennis J. ....Los Angeles, CA
Sinclitico, J. Anthony, III ....San Diego, CA
Sinco, Philip F. ....San Luis Obispo, CA
Sincoff, Arnon I. ....Beverly Hills, CA
Sincoff, Gregg M. ....Stamford, CT
Sincoff, Mark ....Pacific Grove, CA
Sincoff, Milton G. ....New York, NY
Sincoff, Richard J. ....Rockville, MD
Sincox, Allan R. ....Chicago, IL
Sindeband, Melissa M. ....Andover, MA
Sindel, Brian ....Roslyn Heights, NY
Sindel, Charles D. ....St. Louis, MO
Sindel, Richard H. ....St. Louis, MO
Sindel, Rosario Herrera ....El Segundo, CA
Sindel, Sandra Beth ....New York, NY
Sindel & Sindel, P.C. ....St. Louis, MO
Sindel, Wm. F. ....St. Louis, MO
Sindelar, Charles J. ....Glenview, IL
Sindelar, H. Richard, III
Department of State, Foreign Service Officers (Overseas), GV
Sindelar, H. Richard, III ....Houston, TX
Sindelar, Toni ....San Jose, CA
Sindell, David S. ....New York, NY
Seattle, WA
Sindell, Gail E. ....Cleveland, OH
Sindell, Jon S. ....San Francisco, CA
Sindell Law Offices, A Professional Corporation ....Los Angeles, CA
New York, NY
Seattle, WA
Sindell & Levy, Inc., P.S. ....Seattle, WA
Sindell, Lowe & Guidubaldi
Cleveland, OH
Sindell, Lowe & Guidubaldi
Cleveland, OH
Sindell, Richard I. ....Seattle, WA
Sindell, Steven A. ....Cleveland, OH
Sindell, Stuart L. ....New York, NY
Sindell, Young, Guidubaldi & Sucher, P.L.L.
Cleveland, OH
Sinden, Amy ....Seattle, WA
Sinden, Watson R. ....St. Petersburg, FL
Sinden, Watson R., P.A. ....St. Petersburg, FL
Sinder, Carl J. ....Champaign, IL
Sinder, Fredric L. ....Dayton, OH
Sinder, Janet L. ....Springfield, IL
Sinder, Jennifer Levin ....Indianapolis, IN
Sinder, Joan B. ....Willimantic, CT
Sinder, Ned F. ....Longboat Key, FL
Sinder, Scott ....Washington, DC
Sinder, Stuart J. ....New York, NY
Sinderbrand, Alvin ....New York, NY
Sinderbrand, Carl A. ....Madison, WI
Sinderbrand, David I. ....Atlantic City, NJ
Sinderbrand, Gregory M.
Los Angeles, CA
Sinderbrand, Paul J. ....Washington, DC
Sinderbrand, Steven A. ....Atlantic City, NJ
Sindermann, Robert P., Jr.
United States Postal Service, Law Department, GV
Sinders, John W., Jr. ....New Orleans, LA
Sindic Law Offices, S.C. ....Milwaukee, WI
Sindic, Richard R. ....Milwaukee, WI
Sindici, Gregg C. ....San Diego, CA
Sinding, Kate ....New York, NY
White Plains, NY
Sindle, Harvey B. ....New York, NY
Sindle, Roger A. ....Hendersonville, TN
Sindler, Mark A. ....Pittsburgh, PA
Sindler, Michael H. ....Washington, DC
Sindler, Steven M. ....Odenton, MD
Sindler, Trisha D. ....Miami, FL
Sindon, Betty B. ....Pearsall, TX
Sindon, James A. ....Pearsall, TX
Sindoni, John P. ....Syracuse, NY
Sindoni, Stephen A. ....Rancho Mirage, CA
Sindt, Conrad J. ....Battle Creek, MI
Sindt, Robert H. ....Washington, DC
Sindt, Russell J. ....Lakewood, CO
Sindyla, Robert J. ....Cleveland, OH
Sine, Albert ....Boca Raton, FL
Sine, Amy J. ....Oklahoma City, OK
Sine, Andrea R. ....La Plata, MD
Sine, David M. ....Long Beach, CA
Sine, Jeffrey A. ....New York, NY
Sine, Laurie ....Miami, FL
Sine, Wesley ....Salt Lake City, UT
Sineath, Lloyd E. ....Charleston, SC
Sinek, Jeffrey S. ....Los Angeles, CA
Sinek, Scott ....Santa Ana, CA
Sinel, Elliot Bruce ....New York, NY
Sinel, Frances Maria ....Denver, CO
Sinel, Norman M. ....Washington, DC
Sinell, Lyle B. ....San Francisco, CA
Sinelli, Mary Christine ....Baltimore, MD
Sinelli, Paul R. ....Redford, MI
Sinelnik, Alexander ....Berlin, NJ
Sinensky, Elisheva, (Mrs) ....Teaneck, NJ
Sinensky, Jeffrey ....New York, NY
Sinensky, Marc I. ....Boca Raton, FL
Siner, Bernard B. ....San Jose, CA
Siner, Charles P. ....Seattle, WA
Siner, Jonathan P. ....Chicago, IL
Siner, Steinbock, Hofmann & Pennypacker
San Jose, CA
Siner, Steven D. ....San Jose, CA
Siner, Suzanne ....Lafayette, LA
Sines, F. Alfred, Jr. ....Charleston, WV
Sines, James L. ....Cedar Rapids, IA
Sines, John B. ....Los Altos, CA
Sines, Travis L. ....Spokane, WA
Sinesi, Dominique V. ....Fairfax, VA
Sinesi, Don G. ....East Greenwich, RI
Sinetar, Raymond J. ....Los Angeles, CA
Sinex, Donald G. ....Houston, TX
Sinex, Jennifer J. ....San Diego, CA
Sinex, Thomas W. ....New Albany, IN
Sing, Lillian Kwok ....San Francisco, CA
Sing, Randall K. ....Honolulu, HI
Sing, Richard H. S. ....Honolulu, HI
Sing, William B. ....Houston, TX
Singal, Bruce A. ....Boston, MA
Singal, George Z. ....Bangor, ME
Singal, Laurence ....Oak Park, MI
Singarella, Paul N. ....Costa Mesa, CA
Singbush, Jack ....Ocala, FL
Singdahlsen, Jeffrey P.
Department of Justice, Office of Legal Counsel, GV
Singdahlsen, William E. ....Albuquerque, NM
Singe, Herbert R. ....Hillside, NJ
Singeltary, G. Richard ....Tavares, FL
Singer, A. Robert ....San Francisco, CA
Singer, Aaron J. ....West Covina, CA
Singer, Abraham ....Detroit, MI
Singer, Adam ....Newark, DE
Wilmington, DE
Singer, Alan ....Philadelphia, PA
Singer, Alan D. ....White Plains, NY
Singer, Alan M. ....Seattle, WA
Singer, Alexander T. ....Brooklyn, NY
Singer, Alfred L. ....Baltimore, MD
Singer, Alisa Margolis ....Chicago, IL
Singer, Allan W. ....Charlotte, NC
Singer, Allen M. ....San Francisco, CA
Singer, Alvin Ira ....Highland Park, IL
Singer, Andrew D. ....San Diego, CA
Singer, Andrew L. ....Vienna, VA
Singer, Andrew M. ....New York, NY
Singer, Andrew N. ....Middletown, OH
Singer, Andrew W. ....Washington, DC
Singer, Andrew W. ....New York, NY
Singer, Anne C. ....Camden, NJ
Singer, Anthony M. ....Wichita, KS
Singer, Arianne ....Albuquerque, NM
Singer, Arlene ....Toledo, OH
Singer, Arthur H. ....Las Vegas, NV
Singer & Associates, A Professional Corporation ....Washington, DC
Singer, Barbara Ann ....Miami Beach, FL
Singer, Barbara Conroy ....Brooklyn, NY
Singer, Barney
Small Business Administration, GV
Singer, Barry ....New York, NY
Singer, Bernard A. ....Hollywood, FL
Singer, Bernard A., P.A. ....Hollywood, FL
Singer, Bernard E. ....Harrison, NY
Singer, Bertram C. ....Tarzana, CA
Singer, Betsy Sundheim ....Tampa, FL
Singer, Bill T. ....New York, NY
Singer, Block & Matles ....Brooklyn, NY
Singer, Bonnie J. ....Washington, DC
Singer, Bonnie P. ....New York, NY
Singer & Boothe ....Winnsboro, LA
Singer, Brad C. ....Urbana, OH
Singer, Bradley C. ....Urbana, OH
Singer, Brent A. ....Bangor, ME
Singer, Brooke Erdos ....New York, NY
Singer, Brown & Barringer, Nevada LLC
Las Vegas, NV
Singer, Carla M. ....Santa Ana, CA
Singer, Carol B. ....Culver City, CA
Singer, Cass L. ....Hazel Park, MI
Singer, Cecile ....Chicago, IL
Singer, Charles A. ....Melville, NY
Singer, Charles W. ....Jensen Beach, FL
Singer, Clifford B. ....Waldwick, NJ
Singer, Craig D. ....Washington, DC
Singer & Crawford, A Professional Corporation
San Diego, CA
Singer, Cynthia L. ....Greenwich, CT
Singer, Dana S. ....Missoula, MT
Singer, Daniel E. ....St. Louis, MO
Singer, Daniel M. ....Washington, DC
Singer, Danielle S. ....Chicago, IL
Singer, David ....Stamford, CT
Singer, David A., Ltd. ....Crystal Bay, MN
Singer, David C. ....New York, NY
Singer, David E. ....Baltimore, MD
Singer, David Eli ....Bronx, NY
Singer, David H. ....New York, NY
Singer, David Harris ....Miami, FL
Singer, David Ira ....Elmsford, NY
Singer, David J. ....Newton, MA
Singer, David M. ....Greenwich, CT
Singer, David R. ....Los Angeles, CA
Singer, David W. ....Hollywood, FL
Singer, Deborah Ann ....Mineola, NY
Singer & Deutsch ....San Jose, CA
Singer, Donald F. ....Medford, MA
Singer, Donald H. ....Elmhurst, NY
Singer, Donald H., P.C. ....Elmhurst, NY
Singer, Donald L., Jr. ....Cortlandt Manor, NY
Singer, Donald Lee ....Peekskill, NY
Singer, Donald S. ....St. Louis, MO
Singer, Douglas E. ....Woodcliff Lake, NJ
Scarsdale, NY
Singer, Edward ....Bala Cynwyd, PA
Singer, Edward C ....Eugene, OR
Singer, Edward J. ....Los Angeles, CA
Singer, Edwin McMahon ....New York, NY
Singer, Elise E. ....Philadelphia, PA
Singer, Elizabeth A. ....Department of Justice, Civil Rights Division, GV
Singer, Elizabeth K. ....Northampton, MA
Singer, Ellen M. ....Eugene, OR
Singer, Eric H.
Consumer Product Safety Commission, Office of Compliance, GV
Singer, Eric L. ....Oakbrook Terrace, IL
Singer, Eric T. ....New York, NY
Singer, Erika K. ....Washington, DC
Singer, Eugene M. ....Harrison, NY
Singer, Ezra David ....Irving, TX
Singer, Farbman and White, P.A.
Hollywood, FL
Singer & Fedun ....Belle Mead, NJ
Singer, Fern H. ....Birmingham, AL
Singer, Frank ....Detroit, MI
Singer Frumento LLP ....New York, NY
White Plains, NY
Singer, Gail M. ....Chappaqua, NY
Singer, Gary J. ....Newport Beach, CA
Singer, Gary S. ....Fort Lauderdale, FL
Singer, George H. ....Minneapolis, MN
Singer, Gerald M. ....Palm Desert, CA
Singer, Gerald M. ....St. Louis Park, MN
Singer, Gerald M., P.A. ....St. Louis Park, MN
Singer, Gerald R. ....New York, NY
Singer, Gilbert ....Pompano Beach, FL
Singer, Gilbert M. ....Tampa, FL
Singer, Gino Josh ....New York, NY
Singer & Goger ....Newark, NJ
Singer, Goodman ....Tamarac, FL
Singer, Gregory F. ....Dayton, OH
Singer, Gregory Z. ....Addison, TX
Singer, Harold M. ....Treasury Department, Office of Regulations and Rulings, GV
Singer, Harry C. ....San Francisco, CA
Singer, Harry J. ....Edmond, OK
Singer, Henry A. ....New York, NY
Singer, Henry M. ....Chicago, IL
Singer, Herbert J. ....Chicago, IL
Singer, Hildtrude M. ....Long Island City, NY
Singer, Hope J. ....Burbank, CA
Singer, Howard A. ....Phoenix, AZ
Singer, Howard A. ....New York, NY
Singer, Howard M. ....New York, NY
Singer, Howard N. ....Phoenix, AZ
Singer, Irving ....Brooklyn, NY
Singer, Irving ....Hempstead, NY
Singer, Jack D. ....Cherry Hill, NJ
Singer, James A. ....St. Louis, MO
Singer, James E. ....Atlanta, GA
Singer, James I. ....St. Louis, MO
Singer, James M. ....Pittsburgh, PA
Singer, James S. ....Boston, MA
Singer, Jana B. ....Baltimore, MD
Singer, Janet C. ....Huntington, NY
Singer, Jani Kline ....Hallandale Beach, FL
Singer, Janice A. ....Atlanta, GA
Singer, Jeanne M. ....Gainesville, FL
Singer, Jeffrey ....Chicago, IL

Singer, Jeffrey ... New York, NY
Singer, Jeffrey B. ... Los Alamitos, CA
Singer, Jeffrey D. ... Roseland, NJ
Singer, Jeffrey Scott ... St. Louis, MO
Singer, Jeremy M. ... San Diego, CA
Singer, Jill D. ... Kansas City, MO
Singer, Joel ... Washington, DC
Singer, Joel R. ... Berkeley, CA
Singer, John A. ... Federal Trade Commission, Bureau of Consumer Protection, GV
Singer, John D. ... New York, NY
Singer, Jonas ... Bordentown, NJ
Mount Holly, NJ
Robbinsville, NJ
Singer, Jonathan E. ... Minneapolis, MN
Singer, Joseph H. ... Frankfort, IL
Singer, Joseph K. ... Plantation, FL
Singer, Joseph William ... Cambridge, MA
Singer, Judith ... New York, NY
Singer, Julian ... New York, NY
Singer, Julie L. ... Rochelle Park, NJ
Singer, Karen G. ... New York, NY
Singer, Karen M. ... Columbia, MD
Singer, Keith ... Miami, FL
Singer, Keith A. ... Tucson, AZ
Singer, Keith J. ... Lake Success, NY
Singer, Kent Lyman ... Denver, CO
Singer, Larry ... New York, NY
Singer, Larry A. ... Greensboro, NC
Singer, Larry D. ... Thiells, NY
Singer, Laura R. ... Washington, DC
Singer Law Offices, P.A. ... Overland Park, KS
Singer, Lawrence ... Philadelphia, PA
Singer, Lawrence A. ... Columbus, OH
Singer, Lawrence E. ... Chicago, IL
Singer, Lawrence H. ... New York, NY
Singer, Lea S. ... Manhasset, NY
Singer, Leah ... San Diego, CA
Singer, Leona R. ... Torrance, CA
Singer, Leonard ... Kansas City, MO
Singer, Leonard H. ... Washington, DC
Albany, NY
Singer, Leonard I. ... Lake Worth, FL
Singer, Leonard M. ... Boston, MA
Singer, Leonard S. ... Wayne, NJ
Singer, Leslie ... Department of Justice, Tax Division, GV
Singer, Lewis A. ... Hartford, CT
Singer, Linda C. ... Miami, FL
Singer, Linda C., P.A. ... Miami, FL
Singer, Linda R. ... Washington, DC
Singer, Lisa B. ... Birmingham, AL
Singer, Lisa D. ... Los Angeles, CA
Singer, Lisa R. ... Escondido, CA
Singer, Lloyd I ... New York, NY
Singer, Lon M. ... New York, NY
Singer, Loren A. ... Minneapolis, MN
Singer, Lori G. ... Newark, NJ
Singer, Louis H. ... New York, NY
Singer, Lucy A. ... St. Louis, MO
Singer, Lynne D. ... Minneapolis, MN
Singer, M. Neal ... Riverside, CA
Singer, Marc C. ... Newark, NJ
Singer, Maria A. ... Plantation, FL
Singer, Marian Staton ... New York, NY
Singer, Marilyn J. ... Cleveland, OH
Singer, Marion K. ... Greene, NY
Singer, Marjorie ... New York, NY
Singer, Mark D. ... Sarasota, FL
Singer, Mark E. ... Winnetka, IL
Singer, Mark E., P.C. ... Winnetka, IL
Singer, Mark Ellis ... Seal Beach, CA
Singer, Mark R. ... Overland Park, KS
Singer, Marsha Lynne ... Miami, FL
Singer, Martin D. ... Los Angeles, CA
Singer, Marvin I. ... Baltimore, MD
Singer, Max ... Medford, MA
Singer & McGirt, P.A. ... Charlotte, NC
Singer, Melanie Rabin ... Newport Beach, CA
Singer, Melvin J., (Co., L.P.A.) Pepper Pike, OH
Singer, Meredith L. ... Simsbury, CT
Singer, Michael ... Los Angeles, CA
Singer, Michael ... Harrison, NY
Singer, Michael D. ... Escondido, CA
Singer, Michael H. ... Las Vegas, NV
Singer, Michael H. ... New York, NY
Singer, Michael I. ... Vernon Hills, IL
Singer, Michael J. ... Department of Justice, Civil Division, GV
Singer, Michael K. ... Sterling, CO
Singer, Michael S. ... Los Angeles, CA
Singer, Michael S. ... West Palm Beach, FL
Singer, Michele I. ... New York, NY
Singer, Micki S. ... San Francisco, CA
Singer, Miriam Rogers ... St. Louis, MO
Singer, Mitchell F. ... Culver City, CA
Singer, Mitchell J. ... Falls Church, VA
Singer, Mitchell L. ... Matawan, NJ
Singer, Monroe S. ... New York, NY
Singer, Morris ... Long Beach, CA
Singer, Murray E. ... Forest Hills, NY
Singer, Myer R. ... Dennis Port, MA
Singer, N. Bruce ... Minneapolis, MN
Singer, Nancy ... Washington, DC
Singer, Nancy L. ... Washington, DC
Skillman, NJ
Singer, Naomi L. ... Morristown, NJ
Singer Netter Dowd & Berman New York, NY
Singer, Norman H., (P.C.) Washington, DC
Singer, Norman J. ... Tuscaloosa, AL
Singer, Norman J. ... Denver, CO
Singer, Norman P. ... Vienna, VA
Singer, Owen J. ... San Jose, CA
Singer, Pamela Egan ... Eugene, OR
Singer, Pasley, Holm, Timmons, Mathison & Curtis ... Ames, IA
Singer, Paul E. ... New York, NY
Singer, Paul H. ... Chicago, IL
Singer, Paul J. ... Akron, OH
Singer, Paul M. ... Pittsburgh, PA
Singer, Paula N. ... Newton, MA
Singer, Peter W. ... San Diego, CA
Singer, Philip ... New York, NY
Singer, Rachelle ... Irvine, CA
Singer, Ralph M., Jr. ... Hermosa Beach, CA
Singer, Randi Wolkenbreit ... New York, NY
Singer, Randy D. ... Norfolk, VA
Singer, Rebecca Anne ... Dallas, TX
Singer & Recht, Chartered ... Bethesda, MD
Singer, Renée R. Feldman ... New York, NY
Singer, Richard C. ... Melbourne, FL
Singer, Richard C. ... New York, NY
Singer, Richard C., P.A. ... Melbourne, FL
Singer, Richard G. ... Camden, NJ
Singer, Richard G. ... Raleigh, NC
Singer, Richard H., Jr. ... Morristown, NJ
Singer, Richard M. ... Washington, DC
Singer, Rick A. ... Hammond, LA
Singer, Rickie L. J. ... New York, NY
Singer, Rita ... Sacramento, CA
Singer, Robert ... Manchester, NH
Singer, Robert A. ... Greensboro, NC
Raleigh, NC
Singer, Robert E. ... Houston, TX
Singer, Robert I. ... Springfield, MA
Singer, Robert J. ... Farmington, MI
Singer, Robert J. ... Roseland, NJ
Singer, Robert M. ... Hamden, CT
Singer, Robert M., L.L.C., Law Offices of Hamden, CT
New Haven, CT
Singer, Robert N. ... Albuquerque, NM
Singer, Robert S. ... Miami, FL
Singer, Robert W. ... Mount Prospect, IL
Singer, Roger D. ... New York, NY
Singer, Roger M. ... Boston, MA
Singer, Ronald M. ... Kenosha, WI
Singer, Russell J. ... Richmond, VA
Singer, Samuel M. ... Silver Spring, MD
Singer, Samuel T. ... Winnsboro, LA
Singer, Sandra J. ... Boulder, CO
Singer, Saul J. ... Washington, DC
Singer, Scott ... New York, NY
Singer, Scott A. ... Mineola, NY
New York, NY
White Plains, NY
Singer, Scott N. ... New York, NY
Singer, Scott R. ... New York, NY
Singer, Scott W. ... San Francisco, CA
Singer, Scott W. ... Golden, CO
Singer, Seymour N. ... Coral Gables, FL
Singer, Sheila G. ... Sherman Oaks, CA
Singer, Sheldon ... Farmington Hills, MI
Singer, Sheldon F. ... Los Angeles, CA
Singer, Sheldon G. ... East Brunswick, NJ
Singer, Sheldon J. ... Bethesda, MD
Singer, Sheldon R. ... Overland Park, KS
Singer, Shelvin ... Skokie, IL
Singer, Sherry L. ... Valley Stream, NY
Singer, Sidney ... Houston, TX
Singer & Silvergleid, Inc. ... Riverside, CA
Singer & Singer ... Plantation, FL
Singer & Singer, A Professional Law Corporation ... Torrance, CA
Singer & Singer, Inc. ... Medford, MA
Singer & Singh ... Valley Stream, NY
Singer, Stanley ... New York, NY
Singer, Stephen ... New York, NY
Singer, Stephen J. ... Kew Gardens, NY
Singer, Stephen Sayre ... New York, NY
Singer, Steven B. ... New York, NY
Singer, Steven D. ... Boston, MA
Singer, Steven D. ... Enid, OK
Singer, Steven G. ... Cresskill, NJ
Singer, Steven M. ... Medford, MA
Singer, Steven T. ... Montclair, NJ
Singer, Stewart R. ... Philadelphia, PA
Singer, Stuart H. ... Miami, FL
Singer, Stuart L. ... Rock Hill, NY
Singer, Stuart R. ... Los Angeles, CA
Singer, Susan S. ... Newark, NJ
Singer, Sydnee R. ... Los Angeles, CA
Singer, T. Thomas ... Billings, MT
Singer, Terese J. ... Milwaukee, WI
Singer, Terry E. ... Washington, DC
Singer, Thomas C. ... Englewood, CO
Singer, Thomas D. ... Mc Connellsburg, PA
Singer, Thomas H. ... South Bend, IN
Singer, Thomas M. ... St. Louis, MO
Singer, Toby G. ... Washington, DC
Singer, Vernon D. ... St. Louis, MO
Singer, Warren J. ... New York, NY
Singer, William ... West Hartford, CT
Singer, William A. ... Ames, IA
Singer, William B. ... Cincinnati, OH
Singer, William S. ... Chicago, IL
Singer, William S. ... Belle Mead, NJ
Singer-Blumberg, Tara ... Niagara Falls, NY
Singer-Kaufman, Sue Ellen ... Detroit, MI
Singerman, Donna D. ... Solon, OH
Singerman, Egon P. ... Cleveland, OH
Singerman, Fredric S. ... Washington, DC
Singerman, Mark A. ... Annapolis, MD
Singerman, Marte V. ... Miami, FL
Singerman, Paul J. ... Cleveland, OH
Singerman, Paul Steven ... Miami, FL
Singewald, Christian J. ... Wilmington, DE
Singewald, Dean R. ... Madison, CT
New Haven, CT
Singewald, Dean R. ... Milford, CT
Singewald, Robert A. ... Wilton, CT
Singewald and Valkenburgh ... Wilton, CT
Singh, A. Paul ... Chicago, IL
Singh, Amarik K. ... Visalia, CA
Singh, Amit ... New York, NY
Singh, Amy K. ... Chicago, IL
Singh, Anita Lila ... Lakewood, CO
Singh, Gulwinder S. ... Irvine, CA
Singh, Gurpreet M. ... New York, NY
Singh, Harry M. ... Dallas, TX
Singh, Inderjeet K. ... Valley Stream, NY
Singh, Indie K. ... Valley Stream, NY
Singh, Iskah C. ... New York, NY
Singh, Jagpreet ... Washington, DC
Singh, Jaikaran ... San Diego, CA
Singh, Kanwal M. ... Modesto, CA
Singh, Kanwar M. ... Skokie, IL
Singh, Karan ... New York, NY
Singh, Krishna K. ... Amsterdam, NY
Singh, Kulvinder ... Marysville, CA
Singh, Laurie A. ... Fort Wayne, IN
Singh, Manisha ... Philadelphia, PA
Singh, Manny ... Fort Lauderdale, FL
Singh, Manpreet ... Treasury Department, Office of the Comptroller of the Currency, GV
Singh, Mia Makela ... Fort Lauderdale, FL
Singh, Mohinder ... Walnut Creek, CA
Singh, Neelam ... Chicago, IL
Singh, Padmini Environmental Protection Agency, Office of the General Counsel, GV
Singh, Premjit ... Chicago, IL
Singh, R. Nicholas ... Washington, DC
Singh, Rajinder ... Bethesda, MD
Singh, Ranjeev ... Washington, DC
Singh, Renu ... Arlington, VA
Singh, Sabita ... Boston, MA
Singh, Seema M. ... Princeton, NJ
Singh, Shane ... Sacramento, CA
Singh, Sharmila S ... Richmond Hill, NY
Singh, Shawn K. ... San Mateo, CA
Singh, Tanya ... New York, NY
Singh, Tina M. ... Palo Alto, CA
Singh, T.J. ... Newport Beach, CA
Singh, Vicki James ... Memphis, TN
Singha, Alexander Aman P. New York, NY
Singha, Chafica A. ... Tampa, FL
Singhal, Anuraag H. ... Fort Lauderdale, FL
Singhal, Dinesh ... Houston, TX
Singhal, Harish K. ... San Carlos, CA
Singhal, Raag ... Fort Lauderdale, FL
Singhal, Vani ... Chicago, IL
Singham, Shanker ... Miami, FL
Singhel, Timothy M. ... Mineola, NY
New York, NY
Singiser, Dana E. ... Washington, DC
Singiser, George W. ... Troy, NY
Single, Randall C. ... Los Angeles, CA
Single, Richard W., Sr. ... Sparks, MD
Single, Robert C. ... Bohemia, NY
Single, William, III ... Baltimore, MD
Single, William, IV ... Washington, DC
Singleman, Beverly J. ... Las Cruces, NM
Singler, Peter A. ... Sebastopol, CA
Singler, Peter A., Jr., Law Offices of Sebastopol, CA
Singler, Richard P. ... Chicago, IL
Singletary, Alvin D. ... Slidell, LA
Singletary, Britt R. ... Biloxi, MS
Jackson, MS
Singletary, C. Eston ... Lake Charles, LA
Singletary, Cary R. ... Tampa, FL
Singletary, Cary R., P.A. ... Tampa, FL
Singletary, Clarence E. ... Charleston, SC
Singletary, Cynthia A ... Elizabethtown, NC
Singletary, Daniel L. ... Jackson, MS
Singletary, E. McLeod ... Columbia, SC
Singletary, Fawn ... Ocala, FL
Singletary, Gary S. ... Cleveland, OH
Singletary, Howard E., Jr. ... Albemarle, NC
Singletary, J. Noland ... Baton Rouge, LA
Singletary, Kathleen H. ... Palos Park, IL
Singletary Law Firm, P.A. ... Tampa, FL
Singletary, M. Benjamin ... Tulsa, OK
Singletary, Molly D. ... Austin, TX
Singletary, Thomas H. ... Tampa, FL
Singletary & Thrash, P.A. ... Biloxi, MS
Jackson, MS
Singletary, Wayne M. ... Jacksonville, FL
Singletary, Wiggins Ellison, Jr. ... Atlanta, GA
Singletary, William E. ... Newark, NJ
Singletary, William H. ... Jackson, MS
Singleton, A. Louis ... Greenville, NC
Singleton, Alan R. ... Urbana, IL
Singleton, Amy C. ... Nashville, TN
Singleton, Ann E. ... Ellicott City, MD
Singleton & Associates ... Escondido, CA
San Diego, CA
Singleton, Bruce W. ... Somerset, KY
Singleton, Burleigh L. ... Atlanta, GA
Singleton & Burroughs, P.A. ... Conway, SC
Singleton, Charles R. ... Little Rock, AR
Singleton, Charles R., P.A. ... Little Rock, AR
Singleton & Cooksey, A Professional Corporation ... Houston, TX
Singleton, Crist, Austgen & Sears Hammond, IN
Munster, IN
Singleton, David G., Jr. ... Durham, NC
Singleton, David M. ... Mission Hills, CA
Singleton, David R. ... Tampa, FL
Singleton, Deborah W. Department Of Veterans Affairs, Board of Veterans Appeals, GV
Singleton, Debra Johnson ... Baltimore, MD
Singleton & Deeds ... Monterey, VA
Warm Springs, VA
Singleton, Diane A. ... Santa Rosa, CA
Singleton, Donald L. ... Carson, CA
Singleton, E. Dean ... Owensville, IN
Singleton, E. Lynn ... Greensburg, LA
Singleton, Eric C. ... Salt Lake City, UT
Singleton, Frank G. ... San Francisco, CA
Singleton, George W. ... Charleston, WV
Singleton, Gerald E. ... New York, NY
Singleton, Hamilton H. ... Camden, AR
Singleton & Herlihy ... Glens Falls, NY
Singleton, Howard H. ... Houston, TX
Singleton, Hutchens & Senter Fayetteville, NC
Singleton, James B. ... East Rutherford, NJ
Singleton, James K., Jr. ... Anchorage, AK
Singleton, Jeffrey L. ... Jonesboro, AR
Singleton, John A. ... Charleston, WV
Huntington, WV
Singleton, John A., PLLC ... Charleston, WV
Singleton, John B. ... St. Louis, MO
Singleton, John C. ... Monterey, VA
Warm Springs, VA
Singleton, John D. ... Oklahoma City, OK
Singleton, John M. ... Baltimore, MD
Singleton, John V., Jr. ... Houston, TX
Singleton, Joseph F. ... Conway, SC
Singleton, Judith S. ... Lutherville, MD
Singleton, Judy A. ... Dallas, TX
Singleton, Julie C. ... Indianapolis, IN
Singleton, Katherine W. ... Kingsport, TN
Singleton, Kenneth P. ... New York, NY
Singleton, Kristi ... Washington, DC
Singleton, Kristine R. ... El Segundo, CA
Singleton, Margaret M. ... Charleston, WV
Huntington, WV
Singleton, Marilyn M. ... San Francisco, CA
Singleton, Maureen R.M. ... Houston, TX
Singleton, Melinda ... Lee's Summit, MO
Singleton, Norman D. ... Tipton, IA
Singleton, Palmer C., Jr. ... Munster, IN
Singleton, Patience R. ... Washington, DC
Singleton, Philip A. ... Holyoke, MA
Singleton, R. Grant ... Myrtle Beach, SC
Singleton, Richard N., Jr. ... St. Louis, MO
Singleton, Richard V., II ... New York, NY
Singleton, Robert H. ... Houston, TX
Singleton, Robert H., Jr. ... Houston, TX
Singleton, Rudolph G., Jr. Fayetteville, NC
Singleton, Russell Neal ... Enid, OK
Singleton, Ruth ... New York, NY
Singleton, Sabrena K. ... Las Vegas, NV
Singleton, Sarah Michael ... Santa Fe, NM
Singleton, Shannon A. ... Atlanta, GA
Singleton, Sheila P. ... Pikeville, KY
Singleton & Singleton ... Mount Kisco, NY
White Plains, NY
Singleton & Singleton, P.A. Myrtle Beach, SC
Singleton, Stephanie L. ... Charlotte, NC
Singleton, Steven D. ... Tampa, FL
Singleton, Susan Cobb ... Greenville, SC
Singleton, Terry ... Escondido, CA
Singleton, Thomas J. ... Mount Kisco, NY
Singleton, W. James ... Shreveport, LA
Singleton, Whitney ... Mount Kisco, NY
Singleton-English, Tammy ... Pittsburgh, PA
Singley & Associates ... Cherry Hill, NJ
Philadelphia, PA
Singley & Beal, P.L.L.C. ... Washington, DC
Singley, Bernestine ... Duncanville, TX
Singley, Carl E. ... Philadelphia, PA
Singley, David J. ... Pittsburgh, PA
Singley, George J. ... Mount Laurel, NJ
Singley, J. Brent ... McLean, VA
Singley, Karan Y. ... Tuscaloosa, AL
Singley, Mark A. ... Washington, DC
Singley, Michael ... Austin, TX
Singley, Philip ... Columbia, MS
Singley, Robert S. ... San Francisco, CA
Singley, Timothy K. ... San Antonio, TX
Singley, Wendy G. ... San Francisco, CA
Singman, Bruce H. ... Pacific Palisades, CA
Singman, Ralph ... Tarzana, CA
Singman, Thomas M. ... Oakland, CA
Singmaster-Hernández, Helen Sacramento, CA
Singreen, Harry V. ... New Orleans, LA
Singreen, Shirley Basile ... New Orleans, LA
Singsank, Richard C. ... Burlington, IA
Singsen, Antone G., III ... Watertown, MA
Singsen, Michael P. ... San Francisco, CA
Sinha, Deborah Rosenberg ... New York, NY
Sinha, Hans P. ... New Orleans, LA
Sinha, Jessica ... Norwalk, CT
Sinha, Pankaj K. ... Washington, DC
Sinha, Ritu ... San Francisco, CA
Siniard, Brenda G. ... Chattanooga, TN
Siniard, McKinney & Braswell, P.C., The Law Firm of ... Athens, AL
Cullman, AL
Decatur, AL
Florence, AL
Guntersville, AL
Huntsville, AL
Moulton, AL
Russellville, AL
Scottsboro, AL
Tuscumbia, AL
Siniard, Tommy H. ... Huntsville, AL
Siniawer, Paul D. ... New York, NY
Siniawsky, Jeffrey S. ... Plantation, FL
Siniawsky, Jeffrey S., P.A. ... Plantation, FL
Sinick, Edward S. ... New York, NY
Sinick, Marshall Sanford Washington, DC
Sinicki, Mary Kay ... Las Vegas, NV
Sinicki, Michael S. ... Binghamton, NY

Sinicropi, Patricia Louise .... Department of Energy, GV
Sinift, Bruce E. .... Berkeley, CA
Sin-I Ma, Sandy .... Raleigh, NC
Sininger, William R. .... Muskegon, MI
Sinins, Susan T. .... Newark, NJ
Siniscalchi, Aniello Frank .... Springfield, MA
Siniscalco, Gary R. .... San Francisco, CA
Sinisi, Stephen P. .... Paramus, NJ
Sinisi, Van Dam & Sproviero .... Paramus, NJ
Sink, Ann Marie .... Chicago, IL
Sink, Caroline Wannamaker .... Charlotte, NC
Sink, Charles M. .... San Francisco, CA
Sink, Deborah A. .... Charleston, WV
Sink, George .... Charleston, SC
Sink, George, Accident & Injury Law Offices of, P.A. .... Charleston, SC
Sink, Henry H., Jr. .... Raleigh, NC
Sink, Irvin R. .... Lexington, NC
Sink, John M. .... Santa Barbara, CA
Sink, Kevin L. .... Raleigh, NC
Sink, L. Wallace .... Hampton, VA
Sink, Powers, Sink & Potter, L.L.P.
Cary, NC
Raleigh, NC
Sink, Robert C. .... Charlotte, NC
Sink, Thomas Reed .... Cloverdale, CA
Santa Rosa, CA
Sink, William Fenton, Law Offices of .... Honolulu, HI
Sinkel, Ginny .... Boston, MA
Sinkeldam, Gary P. .... San Diego, CA
Sinkeldam, Gary P., Law Office of .... Las Vegas, NV
Sinkewicz, Joseph F., Jr. .... Buffalo, NY
Sinkfield, Richard H. .... Atlanta, GA
Sinkfield, Richard H., III .... Washington, DC
Sinkfield, Rita D. .... New York, NY
Sinkhorn, Mark W. .... Westerville, OH
Sinkiewicz, Mark Steven .... Beckley, WV
Sinkin, Judy G. .... Washington, DC
Sinkin, Lanny Alan .... Hilo, HI
Sinkins, Todd A. .... Vienna, VA
Sinkkanen, Dreama D. .... Clarksburg, WV
Sinkler & Boyd, P.A. .... Charleston, SC
Columbia, SC
Greenville, SC
Sinkler, G. Dana .... Charleston, SC
Sinko, Glenn S. .... Pittsburgh, PA
Sinko, Michael D. .... Haddonfield, NJ
Sinkoff, Steven B. .... Southfield, MI
Sinkov, Michael .... Los Angeles, CA
Sinkovics, Jeffrey K. .... Peru, IN
Sinks, Thomas W. .... Greensboro, NC
Sinkula, Deborah K. .... Cincinnati, OH
Sinkway, Steven E. .... Pittsburgh, PA
Sinkwitts, Scott Joseph .... Birmingham, MI
Sinn, Andrew J. .... Hoopeston, IL
Sinn, David R. .... Peoria, IL
Sinn, Deanna Newlon .... Akron, OH
Sinn, Fitzsimmons, Cantoli, West & Pardes, P.A. .... Point Pleasant Beach, NJ
Sinn, G. Albert .... Worland, WY
Sinn, Jack F. .... Point Pleasant Beach, NJ
Sinn, Laura .... Boston, MA
Sinn, Leroy G. .... Washington, DC
Sinn, Patricia L. .... Library of Congress, Copyright Office, GV
Sinn, Rebecca H. .... Southfield, MI
Sinn, Valerie W. .... Cincinnati, OH
Sinn, William G. .... Birmingham, MI
Sinn-Bailey, Holly Ann .... Kenton, OH
Sinner, Angela K. .... Phoenix, AZ
Sinnette, Charles S. .... Ashland, KY
Sinnette, Kevin P. .... Ashland, KY
Sinniger, Jean-Luc .... New York, NY
Sinniger, Karin B. .... Chicago, IL
Sinning, Gordon R., II .... Rancho Santa Fe, CA
Sinnis, Stellio .... Boston, MA
Sinnitt, C. Joseph .... Tacoma, WA
Sinnitt, Lisa .... Tacoma, WA
Sinnitt, Paul .... Tacoma, WA
Sinnitt & Sinnitt, Inc., P.S. .... Tacoma, WA
Sinno, Sheila M. .... Columbus, OH
Sinnott, Bradley K. .... Columbus, OH
Sinnott, Christine E. .... Marina, CA
Sinnott, Christopher J. .... Erie, PA
Sinnott, Dito, Moura & Puebla
Los Angeles, CA
San Francisco, CA
Sinnott, Edmund W. .... Chicago, IL
Sinnott, Eleanor Coe .... Boston, MA
Sinnott, James A. .... Pleasant Hill, CA
Sinnott, James H. .... Atlanta, GA
Sinnott, Jessica M. .... Fairfax, VA
Sinnott, John P. .... New York, NY
Sinnott, John W. .... New Orleans, LA
Sinnott, Laura J. .... Newark, NJ
Sinnott, Nuckols & Logan, P.C.
Midlothian, VA
Richmond, VA
Sinnott, Randolph P. .... Los Angeles, CA
Sinnott, Raymond J., III .... Midlothian, VA
Sinnott, Richard J. .... Boston, MA
Sinnott, Richard J. .... Albany, NY
Sinnott, Stephen P. .... Chicago, IL
Sinnott, Timothy S. .... Indianapolis, IN
Sinnott, William F. .... Boston, MA
Sinnreich & Francisco .... Macon, GA
Sinnreich, Jonathan .... Hauppauge, NY
New York, NY
Sinnreich, Naomi B. .... New York, NY
Sinnreich Wasserman & Grubin, LLP
Hauppauge, NY
New York, NY
Sinnreich, William .... Plainview, NY
Sinodis, John G. .... Phoenix, AZ
Sinoff, Barry S. .... Jacksonville, FL
Sinoff, Barry S., P.A., Law Office of .... Jacksonville, FL
Sinofsky, Darren E. .... Pittsfield, MA
Sinofsky, Linda B. .... West Paterson, NJ
Sinon, Frank A. .... Harrisburg, PA
Sinon, Gina M. .... Pleasantville, NY
Sinon, John W. .... Williston Park, NY
Sinon, John W., P.C. .... Williston Park, NY
Sinopole, Roberta C. .... Towson, MD
Sinopoli, Debra L. .... Akron, OH
Sinopoli & Sinopoli, Co., L.P.A. .... Akron, OH
Sinopoli, Vito F. .... Akron, OH
Sinor, Andrew J. .... Birmingham, AL
Sinor, Andrew J., Jr. .... Birmingham, AL
Sinor, Howard E., Jr. .... New Orleans, LA
Sinor, Keith .... Grand Island, NE
Sinor Law Off. .... Grand Island, NE
Sinor, Lindsay Lankford .... Birmingham, AL
Sinor, Morris L. .... Durham, NC
Sinoway, Ronald M. .... Miranda, CA
Sinoway, Stephen L. .... Annandale, NJ
Sinowitz, Betty E. .... Washington, DC
Sinowski, Thomas C. .... Atlanta, GA
Sinquefield, R. Steven .... Madison, MS
Sinreich & Associates .... New York, NY
Sinreich, Ellen .... New York, NY
Sinrich, Diane W. .... Watertown, MA
Sinrich, Gary A. .... Hinesville, GA
Sinrich, Norman .... New York, NY
Sinrich, Scott S. .... Worcester, MA
Sinrod, Donald E. .... Rockville, MD
Sinrod, Eric J. .... San Francisco, CA
Sinrod, Lisa D. .... Alexandria, VA
Sinrod & Tash .... Washington, DC
Sins, Stacy C. .... Atlanta, GA
Sinsel, Charles A., III .... Martinsburg, WV
Sinser, Sabrina .... Los Angeles, CA
Sinsheimer, Alan J. .... New York, NY
Sinsheimer and Meltzer, Inc., P.S. .... Seattle, WA
Sinsheimer, Richard .... Los Angeles, CA
Sinsheimer, Robert S. .... Boston, MA
Boston, MA
Sinsheimer, Schiebelhut & Baggett, A Professional Corporation
Paso Robles, CA
San Luis Obispo, CA
Santa Maria, CA
Sinsheimer, Stuart J. .... Seattle, WA
Sinsheimer, W. John .... Seattle, WA
Sinsheimer, Warren A., III .... San Luis Obispo, CA
Sinsheimer, Warren J. .... New York, NY
Sinski, Douglas C. .... Syosset, NY
Sinsky, Ellwood A. .... Owings Mills, MD
Sinsley, Barbara A. .... Tampa, FL
Sinsley, Jay I. .... Tampa, FL
Sinson, Junie L., (Mr.) .... Chicago, IL
Sintek, W. Richard .... Sacramento, CA
Sinton, Richard J. .... Basking Ridge, NJ
Sinton, Scott J. .... Deerfield, IL
Sinton, Stephen J. .... Shandon, CA
Sinton, Thomas P. .... Frederick, MD
Sinturel, Catherine .... New York, NY
Sintz, Campbell, Duke & Taylor .... Mobile, AL
Sintzenich, Henry D. .... Springfield, IL
Sinuk, John C. .... New Brunswick, NJ
Sinunu, James N. .... San Francisco, CA
Sinunu, Karyn K. .... San Jose, CA
Sinykin, Daniel .... Madison, WI
Sinykin, H. Robert .... Los Angeles, CA
Sinz, John A. .... Nacogdoches, TX
Sinzinger, Richard A. .... Dallas, TX
Siok, Jan M. .... Boston, MA
Siokos, James C. .... Columbia, SC
Sioli, Frank J., Jr. .... Miami, FL
Sion, Jeffrey S. .... New York, NY
Sion, L. Gilles .... New York, NY
Sion, Steven M. .... Los Angeles, CA
Sioris, Gregory A. .... New York, NY
Sioris & Molumby .... New York, NY
Sioss, Robert J. .... La Jolla, CA
Siotka, Anne M. .... Bedminster, NJ
Sioukas, Chris J. .... Sacramento, CA
Sipan, Richard C. .... Las Vegas, NV
Sipari, Orazio (Ross) .... Chicago, IL
Sipchen, James J., Jr. .... Chicago, IL
Sipe, Billy K., Jr. .... Kingman, AZ
Sipe & Chapman .... Sandusky, OH
Sipe, Charles Y. .... Charlottesville, VA
Sipe, Christopher J. .... Wilmington, DE
Sipe, Connie J. .... Anchorage, AK
Sipe, David L. .... Sandusky, OH
Sipe, Dean A., Law Offices of .... Tucson, AZ
Sipe, Dennis L. .... Marietta, OH
Sipe, Donald J. .... Augusta, ME
Sipe, Donald L. .... Prophetstown, IL
Sipe, Frederic C. .... Indianapolis, IN
Sipe, Ilene G. .... Tucson, AZ
Sipe, James R. .... Harrisonburg, VA
Sipe, Michael P. .... San Diego, CA
Sipe, Nicholas P. .... Columbia, SC
Sipe, Pankow, Han, Rumely & Hehner, A Professional Association .... Indianapolis, IN
Sipe, Samuel M., Jr. .... Washington, DC
Sipe, Stephanie R. .... Harrisonburg, VA
Sipe, W. Henry, III .... Rock Hill, SC
Siper, Brian M. .... New York, NY
Siper, Robert M. .... New York, NY
Sipes, Christopher N. .... Washington, DC
Sipes, Darren Austin .... Brandenburg, KY
Sipes, Janni S. .... San Diego, CA
Sipes Law Firm, P.C. .... El Paso, TX
Sipes, Marilyn .... Beverly Hills, CA
Sipes, Marlene T. .... Columbia, SC
Sipes, Michael K. .... Sacramento, CA
Sipes, Ralph E. .... Anderson, IN
Sipes, Rodney W. .... Edinburg, TX
Sipes, Samuel S. .... El Paso, TX
Sipes, W. Russell .... Indianapolis, IN
Sipes-Early, Kimberly A. .... Chicago, IL
Sipherd, Ronald K. .... Oakland, CA
Sipich, Kathleen L. .... Sauk Rapids, MN
Sipio, William J. .... New York, NY
Sipiora, David E. .... Denver, CO
Sipkins, Peter W. .... Minneapolis, MN
Sipkins, Robert C. .... Minnetonka, MN
Sipkins, Thomas M. .... Minneapolis, MN
Siple, Kathleen K. .... San Jose, CA
Siple, Randolph E. .... Ventura, CA
Siple, Susan D. .... Ventura, CA
Siplin, Gary A. .... Miami, FL
Orlando, FL
Siplin, Gary A., P.A., & Associates
Miami, FL
Orlando, FL
Siporin, Sandra .... Culver City, CA
Siporin, Sheldon .... Brooklyn, NY
Siporin, Steven .... West Bloomfield, MI
Sipos, Andrew L., Jr. .... Miami, FL
Sipos, Andrew L., Jr., P.A. .... Miami, FL
Sipos, John J. .... Albany, NY
Sipos, John M. .... Seneca Falls, NY
Sipos, Michael J. .... Santa Monica, CA
Sipos, Richard A. .... Oakland, CA
Sipos, Ronald A. .... Grand Island, NY
Sipos, Susan A. .... Syosset, NY
Sipos, Thomas M. .... Santa Monica, CA
Sipos, Victor A. .... Phoenix, AZ
Sipp, John Peter .... Staten Island, NY
Sipp, Nancy Newton .... New York, NY
Sippel, Eric M. .... San Francisco, CA
Sippel, John W., Jr. .... Baltimore, MD
Sippel, Kenneth J. .... Mount Calvary, WI
Sippel, Mark A. .... Scottsdale, AZ
Sippel, Mark A., P.C. .... Scottsdale, AZ
Sippel, Richard L. .... Federal Communications Commission, Office of Administrative Law Judges, GV
Sippel, Rodney W. .... St. Louis, MO
Sippel, Sharon M. .... Oklahoma City, OK
Sippel, Thomas .... Macon, GA
Sippel, Thomas J. .... Rockville, MD
Sippel, William C. .... Chicago, IL
Sippel, William L. .... Minneapolis, MN
Sippell, Kraig .... Grand Blanc, MI
Sipper, Mark A. .... Gibsonia, PA
Sipper, Robert J. .... New City, NY
Sipperly, Carol L. .... New York, NY
Sipperly, David P. .... East Setauket, NY
Sipperly, David W. .... North Andover, MA
Sipperly, Peter C. .... Saratoga Springs, NY
Sipple, David F. .... Savannah, GA
Sipple, Hansen, Emerson & Schumacher
Clarkson, NE
Columbus, NE
Sipple, James D. .... Clifton, NJ
Sipple, John M., Jr. .... Washington, DC
Sipple, Mark M. .... Columbus, NE
Sipple, Martin B. .... Tallahassee, FL
Sipples, Kyle C. .... St. Johnsbury, VT
Sipples, Peter M. .... Clinton, CT
Sipprell, David E. .... High Point, NC
Sipprell, Ralph C. .... Portland, OR
Sipprelle, Keith A. .... Los Angeles, CA
Siprelle, Ann M. .... Sacramento, CA
Sipress, Mannie .... Brooklyn, NY
Sipser, I. Philip .... New York, NY
Sipser, Margaret Ann .... New York, NY
Sipser, William Joseph .... New York, NY
Siqueiros, John A. .... Los Angeles, CA
Siqueland, Herman S. .... Bellevue, WA
Sir, Brian T. .... Chicago, IL
Sir, Martin S. .... Nashville, TN
Sira, Stephen N. .... Justice, IL
Sirabian, John .... Fresno, CA
Siraco, Alan .... Oakland, CA
Siraco, Michael Joseph .... Tewksbury, MA
Siracusa, Frank M. .... Chicago, IL
Siracusa, J M .... Miami, FL
Siracusa, John G. .... Williamsville, NY
Siracusa, John M. .... Miami, FL
Siracusa, Joseph .... Syracuse, NY
Siracusa, Lawrence Stephen .... San Francisco, CA
Siracusa, Mary C. .... Atlantic City, NJ
Siracusa, Richard A. .... Washington, DC
New York, NY
Siracusa, Thomas G. .... Chicago, IL
Siracusano, Louis V. .... East Rockaway, NY
Siracuse, Andrew V. .... Rochester, NY
Siracuse, George J. .... New York, NY
Siracuse, Philip L. .... Los Angeles, CA
Siragusa, Charles W. .... Chicago, IL
Siragusa, Edward A. .... Garden City, NY
Siragusa, Michael A. .... St. Augustine, FL
Sirak, Jane A. .... West Palm Beach, FL
Sirak, Norman L. .... Massillon, OH
Siratovich, Thomas A. .... Denver, CO
Sirbu, Gary M. .... Oakland, CA
Sircar, Ketaki .... Merrillville, IN
Sircher, Denise M. .... Chicago, IL
Sircus, Gary M. .... Chicago, IL
Sircus, Mindy Crandus .... Chicago, IL
Sireci, Thomas J., Jr. .... Key West, FL
Sireci, Vincent A. .... New York, NY
Sirefman, Josef P. .... Glen Head, NY
Sirera, David P. .... Covington, LA
Sirera, Julie Lynn .... New Orleans, LA
Sirera, Virginia E. .... Metairie, LA
Sires, Bruce D. .... Los Angeles, CA
Sires, Carlos M. .... Miami, FL
Sires, N. Gruber, Jr. .... Seneca, SC
Sires, Ronald L. .... Glendale, CA
Sirgado, Jo Anne E. .... New York, NY
Sirgado, Michael A. .... New York, NY
Sirgo, Elizabeth Smyth .... Metairie, LA
Sirh, Michael Helbert Peter .... House of Representatives, Congressional Assistants, GV
Sirhal, Charles M. .... Bloomfield Hills, MI
Sirhal, Charles M., P.C. .... Bloomfield Hills, MI
Sirhall, Lawrence George, Jr. .... Boise, ID
Siri, Katherine D. .... Santa Rosa, CA
Siriani, Richard .... Southfield, MI
Siriani, Richard J., P.C. .... Southfield, MI
Sirianni, Stephen J. .... Seattle, WA
Sirianni & Youtz .... Seattle, WA
Sirianno, Marlene Toni .... Jamestown, NY
Siriano, Anthony F. .... Bronx, NY
Siriano, DePalma & Bernstein .... Bronx, NY
Sirias, Deborah F. .... Beverly Hills, CA
Sirica, Micheal R. .... Watertown, CT
Sirich, Scott H. .... Detroit, MI
Sirico, John A. .... Stamford, CT
Sirico, John P., II .... Parsippany, NJ
Sirignano, David A. .... Securities and Exchange Commission, Division of Corporation Finance, GV
Sirignano, George A., Jr. .... White Plains, NY
Sirignano, Michael A. .... Uniondale, NY
Sirignano, Michael Fuller .... Cross River, NY
Sirignano, P. Raymond .... White Plains, NY
Sirignano, Paul D. .... New York, NY
White Plains, NY
Sirilla, George M. .... Washington, DC
Siringas, Athina T. .... Detroit, MI
Siris, Michael J. .... New York, NY
New York, NY
Siris, Stuart .... Garden City, NY
Siritzky, Brian .... Washington, DC
Sirk, Denise L. .... Miami, FL
Sirk, Timothy M. .... Keyser, WV
Sirkin, Alan L. .... Cincinnati, OH
Sirkin, Arthur L. .... Palm Coast, FL
Sirkin, David Andrew .... San Francisco, CA
Sirkin, Debra J. .... Orlando, FL
Sirkin, Edward A. .... Miami, FL
Sirkin, Evan R. .... Woodland Hills, CA
Sirkin, H. Louis .... Cincinnati, OH
Sirkin, Jean Justyn .... Denver, CO
Sirkin, Joel H. .... Boston, MA
Sirkin, Joshua A. .... Miami, FL
Sirkin and McClymonds, P.A. .... Miami, FL
Sirkin, Michael S. .... New York, NY
Sirkin, Mina .... Woodland Hills, CA
Sirkin, Pamela .... North Hollywood, CA
Sirkin Pinales Mezibov & Schwartz
Burlington, KY
Covington, KY
Cincinnati, OH
Sirkin, Stephen R. .... Lyons, NY
Sirkin, Stuart A. .... Pension Benefit Guaranty Corporation, Other Lawyers in Staff or Executive Positions, GV
Sirkis, Arthur K. .... Hackettstown, NJ
Sirkis, Judith E. .... Phoenix, AZ
Sirko, Samuel D. .... Houston, TX
Sirlin, Alan R. .... Valley Stream, NY
Sirlin, Daniel .... Old Westbury, NY
Sirlin Gallogly & Lesser, P.C.
Cherry Hill, NJ
Philadelphia, PA
Sirlin, H. Scott .... Los Angeles, CA
San Francisco, CA
Sirlin, Jon C. .... Cherry Hill, NJ
Philadelphia, PA
Sirlin, Keith .... Pontiac, MI
Sirlin, Keith, & Associates, P.C. .... Pontiac, MI
Sirlin, Kenneth .... Melville, NY
New York, NY
Sirlin, Kenneth, P.C. .... Melville, NY
New York, NY
Sirlin, Reuben .... Mamaroneck, NY
Sirlin, Roger H., & Associates .... Mamaroneck, NY
Sirman, John N. .... Austin, TX
Sirmans, David E. .... Memphis, TN
Sirmans, G. Allan .... Homestead, FL
Sirmans, L. Paul .... Atlanta, GA
Sirmans, Matthew A. .... Pensacola, FL
Sirmans, Robert H. .... Washington, DC
Sirmon, Cynthia Brannon .... Birmingham, AL
Sirmon, Pamela Cook .... Amarillo, TX
Sirmons, Ben H., Jr. .... Greensboro, NC
Sirmons, Don T. .... Panama City, FL
Sirna, A. Ronald, Jr., (P.C.) .... Flint, MI
Sirna, Salvatore T. .... Long Beach, CA
Siro, Rik N. .... Kansas City, MO
Sirodoeva, Olga N. .... New York, NY
Sirois, David R. .... Hamden, CT
Sirois & Maser, P.C. .... Hamden, CT
Sirois, Saml. F. .... Bloomington, IN
Sirok, James S. .... Honolulu, HI
Siroka, Martin I. .... New York, NY
Sironi, Sylvia L. .... Washington, DC
Sirop, Kevin M. .... St. Louis, MO
Siros, Steven M. .... Chicago, IL
Siroskey, Nicholas E. .... Dearborn, MI
Sirota, Anne F. .... Syracuse, NY
Sirota, Barry W. .... Fair Lawn, NJ
Sirota, Beverly S. .... Maplewood, NJ
Sirota, Dorine C. .... Wall Township, NJ
Sirota, Frances S. .... White Plains, NY
Sirota, Fredric J. .... Morristown, NJ
Sirota, Gary L. .... Encinitas, CA
Sirota, George G. .... Miami, FL

Sirota, Howard B. ... New York, NY
Sirota, Ian M. ... Westmont, NJ
Sirota, Jonathan E. ... Maplewood, NJ
Sirota, Louis ... New York, NY
Sirota, Mark A. ... Pleasantville, NY
Sirota, Michael D. ... Hackensack, NJ
Sirota, Michael L. ... Chicago, IL
Sirota, Neil P. ... New York, NY
Sirota, Rachell Roffé ... New York, NY
Sirota, Rima ... Washington, DC
Sirota, Robert S. ... Passaic, NJ
Sirota, Samuel J. ... Maplewood, NJ
Sirota and Sirota ... Maplewood, NJ
Sirota & Sirota, LLP ... New York, NY
Sirota, Wilbert H. ... Baltimore, MD
Sirote & Permutt, P.C. ... Birmingham, AL
Huntsville, AL
Mobile, AL
Montgomery, AL
Sirote, Susan Lynn ... Bronx, NY
Sirotic, Steven ... New York, NY
Sirotkin, Lynn Loeb ... Kew Gardens, NY
Sirotkin, Michael D. ... Montpelier, VT
Sirotkin & Necrason ... Montpelier, VT
Sirotkin, Sherri G. ... Columbia, MD
Sirott, Herbert N. ... Chicago, IL
Sirott, Jack ... Bristol, PA
Sirott & Reimel ... Bristol, PA
Sirower, Brian ... Phoenix, AZ
Sirowitz, Herbert ... Pittsburgh, PA
Sirr, Francis A. ... Boulder, CO
Sirridge, Patrick M. ... San Francisco, CA
Sirtori, Michael J. ... Portland, OR
Sirugo, David A. ... La Porte, IN
Sirulnik, Eric S. ... Washington, DC
Sirus, Richard A. ... Chicago, IL
Sirutis, Donna M. ... Boston, MA
Sirvaitis, Algis ... Cleveland, OH
Mentor, OH
Sirvattha, Camille N. ... Honolulu, HI
Sirvén, José E. ... Miami, FL
Sirven, Silvia M. ... Newark, NJ
Siry, Lawrence J. ... Chatham, NY
Sisak, Janine E. ... New York, NY
Sisak, Mary J. ... Washington, DC
Sisam, Edwin L. ... Minneapolis, MN
Sisca, Eileen R. ... Pittsburgh, PA
Sisca, Francis J. ... Port Chester, NY
Sisca, Joseph S. ... Pittsburgh, PA
Sisco, Dale R. ... Tampa, FL
Sisco, Donna A. ... Woodbridge, NJ
Sisco, James G. ... St. Augustine, FL
Sisco, Kenneth ... New Brunswick, NJ
Sisco, Kenneth D. ... Long Beach, CA
Sisco, Lynn ... Aberdeen, SD
Sisco, Lynn ... Aberdeen, SD
Sise, Paul M. ... Tampa, FL
Sise, Daniel M. ... Belleville, IL
Sise, Joseph M. ... Bronx, NY
Sise, Richard E. ... Amsterdam, NY
Sise, Robert J. ... Amsterdam, NY
Sise, Robin Lynch ... Albany, NY
Sise, Sarah Roe ... St. Louis, MO
Sise & Sise ... Amsterdam, NY
Sise, Thomas E. ... Amsterdam, NY
Sisemoore, Jeffrey B. ... Kingston, NH
Sisemoore, Nancy V. ... Manchester, NH
Sisemoore Professional Association
Kingston, NH
Sisemore, Patricia ... San Francisco, CA
Sisemore, William L. ... Klamath Falls, OR
Sisinni, Andrew J. ... Erie, PA
Sisitsky, Adam L. ... Boston, MA
Sisitsky, Alan D. ... Springfield, MA
Sisitsky, Lawrence R. ... Springfield, MA
Sisitsky, Mark K. ... Washington, DC
Sisk, Bart N. ... Memphis, TN
Sisk, Charles L. ... Boulder, CO
Sisk, Curtis B. ... Fresno, CA
Sisk, Daniel A. ... Albuquerque, NM
Sisk, Darrel B. ... St. Louis, MO
Sisk, Denise Renee ... Boston, MA
Sisk, Edward J. ... New York, NY
Sisk, Eugene B. ... Universal City, TX
Sisk, Fred E. ... La Junta, CO
Sisk, Gregory C. ... Des Moines, IA
Sisk, Harry T., Jr. ... Chestertown, MD
Sisk, J. Jackson ... St. Louis, MO
Sisk, J. Timothy ... Conroe, TX
Sisk, J. Timothy, P.C. ... Conroe, TX
Sisk, K. Dennis ... Richmond, VA
Sisk, Marcus W., Jr. ... Washington, DC
Sisk, Mark D. ... Wilmington, DE
Sisk, P. Douglas ... Philadelphia, PA
Sisk, Raymond W. ... Boston, MA
Sisk, Robert J. ... New York, NY
Sisk & Van Voorhis ... Universal City, TX
Sisk, Wallace T., Jr ... Katy, TX
Siska, Jean M. ... Las Vegas, NV
Siske, Roger C. ... Chicago, IL
Siskel, Howard B. ... Los Angeles, CA
Siskel, Sharyn ... Van Nuys, CA
Siskin, Cheryl E. ... Wilmington, DE
Siskin, Jerrold A. ... Hartford, CT
New York, NY
Siskin, Mark J. ... Tucker, GA
Siskin, Marshall I. ... Santa Monica, CA
Siskin, Michael A. ... New York, NY
Siskin, Robin H. ... Brooklyn, NY
Siskin, Susie F. ... Atlanta, GA
Siskind, Arthur M. ... New York, NY
Siskind, David A. ... Mansfield, MA
Siskind, Donald H. ... New York, NY
Siskind, Donald J. ... New York, NY
Siskind, Eliot ... Glen Burnie, MD
Siskind, Grady, Rosen & Hoover, P.A.
Baltimore, MD
Siskind, Gregory Howard ... Nashville, TN
Siskind, Harris C. ... Miami, FL
Siskind, Ira L. ... Los Angeles, CA
Siskind, Jay S. ... Houston, TX
Siskind, Jeffrey M. ... Baltimore, MD
Siskind, Keith R. ... Glen Burnie, MD
Siskind, Lawrence A. ... Los Angeles, CA
Siskind, Lawrence J. ... San Francisco, CA
Siskind, Lawrence M. ... Brockton, MA
Siskind, Lawrence M., Law Offices Of
Brockton, MA
Siskind, Marcy A. ... Armonk, NY
Siskind, Marvin S. ... Troy, MI
Siskind, Neal ... Brockton, MA
Siskind, Neil S. ... New York, NY
Siskind, Paul M. ... Wellesley, MA
Siskind, Ralph W. ... Philadelphia, PA
Siskind, Sarah E. ... Madison, WI
Siskind Susser Haas & Chang ... Memphis, TN
Nashville, TN
Siskind, William L. ... Baltimore, MD
Siskind, Wm. ... New York, NY
Sisko, Robert E. ... Lancaster, PA
Siskovic, Carole N. ... Cleveland, OH
Sisler, David G. ... Dallas, TX
Sisler, Eric Lee ... Lexington, VA
Sisler, Matthew J. ... Missoula, MT
Sisler, William E. ... Freeport, IL
Sisley, G. William ... Stamford, CT
Sisley, Jeffrey A. ... Port Washington, WI
Sislin, Paul ... Bingham Farms, MI
Sislin, Paul, P.C. ... Bingham Farms, MI
Sislo, Andrew ... Philadelphia, PA
Sislowski, David ... Bellevue, WA
Sisman, Hyman ... Los Angeles, CA
Sisneros, Darlene ... Denver, CO
Sisneros, Patrick D. ... Santa Rosa, CA
Sisneros, Roger L. ... San Francisco, CA
Sisodia, Teesta ... Bradenton, FL
Sisolak, Andrew M. ... Salinas, CA
Sisolak, James G. ... Brookfield, WI
Sisolak & Labros ... Brookfield, WI
Sison, Benjamin C., Jr. ... Hagåtña, GU
Siss, Alfred A., Jr. ... Midland Park, NJ
Siss, Darryl W. ... Midland Park, NJ
Siss, Gregory A. ... Evergreen Park, IL
Sissel, Gary L. ... Moline, IL
Sissel, Kenneth M. ... Atlanta, GA
Sisselman, Barry A. ... Van Nuys, CA
Sisselman, David I. ... Miami, FL
Sisselman, Kerry Pauline ... Indianapolis, IN
Sisselman, Martin L. ... Roseland, NJ
Sisselman, S. Michele ... Watertown, MA
Sisselman & Schwartz, LLP ... Roseland, NJ
Sisserson, James A. ... Maitland, FL
Sisskind, David W. ... New York, NY
Sisskind, Harvey A. ... Encino, CA
Sissman, Ben G. ... Memphis, TN
Sissman, Brooke ... St. Louis, MO
Sissman, Elissa M. ... Treasury Department,
Internal Revenue Service, GV
Sissman, Jack J. ... Albany, NY
Sissman, Mark ... Columbia, MD
Sissman, Peter L. ... Arlington, VA
Sissman, Richard M. ... McLean, VA
Sisson, Atkins & Becker ... Middletown, OH
Sisson, B. David ... Norman, OK
Sisson, B. David ... Oklahoma City, OK
Sisson, Bernard M. ... Triangle, VA
Sisson, David J. ... Milwaukee, WI
Sisson, Edward H. ... Washington, DC
Sisson, F. Glen ... Memphis, TN
Sisson, Frank E., III ... New Canaan, CT
Stamford, CT
Sisson, Frank E., III, Law Offices of
New Canaan, CT
Sisson, Jill ... Crown Point, IN
Gary, IN
Sisson, Jill ... Valparaiso, IN
Sisson, Jill B. W. ... Golden, CO
Sisson, Joyce Winston ... Norfolk, VA
Sisson, Julie C. ... Novi, MI
Sisson & Knutson ... Anchorage, AK
Sisson, Louis F., III ... Fort Myers, FL
Sisson, Louis F., III, P.A. ... Fort Myers, FL
Sisson, Norman L. ... Baton Rouge, LA
Sisson, Pamela J. ... Lansing, MI
Sisson, Paul T., Sr. ... Adelphi, MD
Sisson, Rod R. ... Anchorage, AK
Sisson, Roger G. ... Nashville, TN
Sisson, Sheldon M. ... Las Vegas, NV
Sisson, Stephanie M. ... New Orleans, LA
Sisson, Thomas E. ... San Antonio, TX
Sisson, Thomas E. (Pete) ... Germantown, TN
Sisson, Timothy M. ... Farmington Hills, MI
Sisson, Vincent A. ... Middletown, OH
Sisson, William H. ... Mobile, AL
Sissons, Christopher J. ... Billerica, MA
Sistare & Associates ... Fort Lauderdale, FL
Sistare, Janet P. ... Hartford, CT
Sistare, Susan P. ... Fort Lauderdale, FL
Sistek, Johanna F. ... San Francisco, CA
Sistevaris, George ... Fort Wayne, IN
Sisti, John G. ... New Paltz, NY
Sisti, Thomas R. ... United States Senate,
Committee Legal Personnel, GV
Sisto, James E. P. ... Columbus, OH
Sisto, James J. ... Pittsfield, MA
Sistos, Roberta R. ... Los Angeles, CA
Sistrunk & Associates ... Atlanta, GA
Decatur, GA
Jonesboro, GA
Marietta, GA
Sistrunk, George W., III ... Charlotte, NC
Sistrunk, Hezekiah, Jr. ... Atlanta, GA
Sistrunk, Karen R. ... Washington, DC
Sistrunk, Laurie ... Jacksonville, FL
Sistrunk, Michael R. ... Metairie, LA
Sistrunk, Ralph E. ... Jacksonville, FL
Sisul, J. Jerome ... Chicago, IL
Sisul, Thomas J. ... Downers Grove, IL
Sisun, Mark A. ... Denver, CO
Sit, Po Y. ... New York, NY
Sitar, Douglas J. ... Roseland, NJ
Sitar, Duane D. ... Atlanta, GA
Sitar, Laura K. ... Santa Ana, CA
Sitarchuk, Eric W. ... Philadelphia, PA
Sitarski, Lynne A. ... Philadelphia, PA
Sitarz, John W. ... Hartford, CT
Sitchler, Patricia Flora ... San Antonio, TX
Sitchman, Barton ... Washington, DC
Sitcoff, Jeremy A. ... Denver, CO
Sitcov, Michael ... Department of Justice,
Civil Division, GV
Sitcov, Steven ... Seattle, WA
Siteman, Karen B. ... Beverly Hills, CA
Sites, Edward E. ... Madras, OR
Sites, Edward J. ... Yardley, PA
Sites, James P. ... Billings, MT
Sites, Richard L. ... Columbus, OH
Sites, Thomas C. ... Los Angeles, CA
Sitgreaves, James Y. ... South Padre Island, TX
Sither, John Wright ... Department of Justice,
Environment and Natural Resources
Division, GV
Sitiriche-Torres, Angel L. ... Caguas, PR
Sitkin, James M. ... San Francisco, CA
Sitkin, Jonathan K. ... Bellingham, WA
Sitkin, Lisa M. ... San Francisco, CA
Sitkin, Peter E. ... Emeryville, CA
Sitko, Anthony G. ... Chicago, IL
Sitko, Edward S. ... Bowie, MD
Sitko, Margaret K. ... Pittsburgh, PA
Sitko, Mary F. ... Chicago, IL
Sitko, Richard L. ... Cleveland, OH
Sitkoff, Donna L. ... Gainesville, FL
Sitkoff, Samuel ... Roslyn, NY
Sitkoff, Samuel, P.C. ... Roslyn, NY
Sitkoff, Stephen David ... Los Angeles, CA
Sitkowski, Matthew J. ... Miami, FL
Sitkowski, Robert J. ... Hartford, CT
Sitler, Martin H. ... Jacksonville, NC
Sitley, Stephen Langdon
Hoffman Estates, IL
Sitlinger, Curt ... Louisville, KY
Sitlinger, Lee E. ... Louisville, KY
Sitlinger, McGlincy, Steiner, Theiler & Karem ... Louisville, KY
Sitman, Jacob M. ... Newark, NJ
Sitner, Amy M. ... Detroit, MI
Farmington Hills, MI
Sitner, Scott D. ... Bingham Farms, MI
Sitner, Scott D., P.C. ... Bingham Farms, MI
Sitnick, Irving ... New York, NY
Sitnick, Joseph ... Washington, DC
Sitnick, Stanley A. ... Portland, OR
Sitomer, Alvin L. ... New York, NY
Sitomer, David J. ... Washington, DC
Sitoski, Robert M. ... Philadelphia, PA
Sitoski, Robert M., P.C. ... Philadelphia, PA
Sitrick, David H. ... Skokie, IL
Sitrick, James B. ... New York, NY
Sitrin, Harris ... Albany, NY
Sitrin, Sherman ... New York, NY
Sitte, Klaus D. ... Missoula, MT
Sittenauer, Teresa L. ... Topeka, KS
Sittenfeld, Linda R. ... Naples, FL
Sitter, Douglas R. ... Durango, CO
Sitter, Douglas R., LLC ... Durango, CO
Sitter, J. Gerard ... Itasca, IL
Sitter, James P., (Chtd.) ... Las Vegas, NV
Sitter, Lester D. ... Littleton, CO
Sitterding, Martha Ann ... Westminster, MD
Sitterley, Kermit C. ... Lancaster, OH
Sitterley and Vandervoort ... Lancaster, OH
Sitterley, William J. ... Lancaster, OH
Sitterly, Elizabeth ... Fond du Lac, WI
Sitterly, Rebecca ... Albuquerque, NM
Sitterson, Curtis H. ... Miami, FL
Sittig, Debra S. ... Sioux Falls, SD
Sittig, Marshall P. ... Van Nuys, CA
Sittler, Douglas E. ... Moberly, MO
Sittler, Lester A. ... Fly Creek, NY
Sittler, Ronald K. ... Los Angeles, CA
Sitton, C. McLaurin ... Atlanta, GA
Conyers, GA
Sitton, Claude McLaurin ... Conyers, GA
Sitton, Claude S. ... Morganton, NC
Sitton, Clinton Whetstone, Law Offices of
Atlanta, GA
Sitton, Janie Allison ... Department of Justice,
Civil Rights Division, GV
Sitton, Jaye ... Morganton, NC
Sitton, Juleigh ... Valdese, NC
Sitton, Larry B. ... Greensboro, NC
Sitton, Ron B. ... New York, NY
Sitton, Sam C. ... Oklahoma City, OK
Sitton, William L., Jr. ... Charlotte, NC
Sittu, John David ... Phoenix, AZ
Sitver, Morton ... Phoenix, AZ
Sitz, David N. ... Northbrook, IL
Sitz, Donald H. ... Davenport, IA
Sitz, Thomas E. ... Denver, CO
Sitzer, Harvey Allan ... Los Angeles, CA
Sitzer, Matthew O. ... Chicago, IL
Sitzer, Michael F. ... Costa Mesa, CA
Sitzer, Nina Momtazee ... Chicago, IL
Sitzer, William ... St. Louis, MO
Sitzes, Madeline D. ... Houston, TX
Sitzes, Steven L. ... Providence, RI
Sitzler, William E. ... Mount Holly, NJ
Sitzman, Karen D. ... Omaha, NE
Sitzman, Michael A. ... San Francisco, CA
Sitzman, R. Richard ... Norman, OK
Sitzmann, Christopher G. ... Appleton, WI
Sitzmann, Dean J. ... Lincoln, NE
Sitzmann, Thomas G. ... Boston, MA
Siu, Chi-Yim ... New York, NY
Siu, Joanne L. ... Palo Alto, CA
Siu, Woon-Wah ... Chicago, IL
Siudak, Lynn Anne ... Mineola, NY
Siudara, Leonard A. ... Bloomfield Hills, MI
Siurek, Mark ... Houston, TX
Siuta, Patricia Ann ... Minneapolis, MN
Siuzdak, Robert M. ... Naugatuck, CT
Sivananthan, Prithviraj S. ... Phoenix, AZ
Sivanich, Lisa Hancy ... Milwaukee, WI
Sivaslian & Lawrence ... Torrington, CT
Sivaslian, Peter K. ... Torrington, CT
Sive, David ... New York, NY
White Plains, NY
Sive, Lesley Ann ... Los Angeles, CA
Sive, Paget & Riesel, P.C. ... New York, NY
White Plains, NY
Sively, Susan Kirkpatrick ... Jamaica, NY
Siver & Associates, P.L.L.C. ... Lansing, MI
Siver, James Anthony ... Lansing, MI
Siver, Keith D. ... Nassau, NY
Siverd, Robert J. ... Highland Heights, KY
Siverhus, Hope Hunter ... Fox Point, WI
Siverling, A. Ross ... Ashland, OH
Sivert, John Michael ... Minneapolis, MN
Sivertsen, David R. ... Houston, TX
Sivertsen, Jeffrey T. ... Salt Lake City, UT
Sivertsen, John B. ... Atlanta, GA
Sivertsen, John W., Jr. ... Juneau, AK
Sivertsen, Sharon Powers
Federal Deposit Insurance Corporation,
Liquidation Branch, GV
Sivertson, Alf E. ... St. Paul, MN
Sivertson and Barrette, A Professional Association ... St. Paul, MN
Sivertson, Wayne A. ... Minneapolis, MN
Sivesind, Erik J. ... Walnut Creek, CA
Sivesind, James A. ... Costa Mesa, CA
Los Angeles, CA
Sivic, Sybil Yvette ... Inverness, FL
Ocala, FL
Sivick, Robert J. ... Omaha, NE
Siviglia, Peter ... New York, NY
Sivilli, Rachel ... Fort Lauderdale, FL
Sivils, Daniel B. ... Springfield, MO
Sivils, James L., Jr. ... Springfield, MO
Sivils, James L., Jr., P.C. ... Springfield, MO
Sivin, Philip M. ... New York, NY
Sivinski, Greg A. ... Dallas, TX
Sivinski, John A. ... Cleveland, OH
Sivitz, David R. ... Freeport, NY
Sivolella, John J. ... New York, NY
Sivon, James C. ... Washington, DC
Sivright, David H., Jr. ... Clinton, IA
Sivyer, Neal A. ... Tampa, FL
Siwak, Ellen Levy ... St. Louis, MO
Siwak, Todd B. ... Bourbon, MO
Siwek, Donna M. ... Buffalo, NY
Siwek, James J. ... Worth, IL
Siwek, Laurie A. ... Chicago, IL
Siwek, Reuben M. ... Scarsdale, NY
Siwica, Richard P. ... Orlando, FL
Siwierka, Michael J. ... Houston, TX
Siwik, Christine J. ... Chicago, IL
Siwik, Lori L. ... Akron, OH
Siwik, Mark R. ... Richfield, OH
Six, Catherine M. ... Baltimore, MD
Six, Charles Edward ...
Administrative Office Of The United States
Courts, GV
Six, Elizabeth Brand ... Kansas City, MO
Six, Fred N. ... Topeka, KS
Six, Marjeta Duzevic ... San Diego, CA
Six, Steve N. ... Overland Park, KS
Sixbey, Daniel W. ... Arlington, VA
McLean, VA
Sixbey, Friedman, Leedom & Ferguson, P.C.
Washington, DC
Arlington, VA
Fairfax, VA
McLean, VA
Sixel, Nancy J. ... River Falls, WI
Sixta, Don J. ... Baltimore, MD
Harrisburg, PA
Sixta, John A., Jr. ... Corpus Christi, TX
Sixta, John A., Jr., P.C. ... Corpus Christi, TX
Siy, Lucio Steven ... Wauwatosa, WI
Size, Richard J. ... Van Nuys, CA
Sizeland-Ross, Lisa A. ... Ogdensburg, NY
Sizemore, Burns & Gillmore, P.A.
Newton, KS
Sizemore, Carl E. ... San Diego, CA
Sizemore, Charles E., Jr. ... Norfolk, VA
Sizemore, Charles E., Jr., P.C. ... Norfolk, VA
Sizemore, Dale H., Jr. ... Lenexa, KS
Sizemore, Hadley ... McPherson, KS
Sizemore, J. Paul ... Birmingham, AL
Sizemore, James E. ... Winston-Salem, NC
Sizemore, James M., Jr. ... Montgomery, AL
Sizemore, Kenneth A. ... London, KY
Sizemore, Lamar W., Jr. ... Atlanta, GA
Macon, GA
Sizemore, Laura M. ... New York, NY
Sizemore, Lawrence E. ... Oklahoma City, OK
Sizemore, Lawrence E., Inc., P.C.
Oklahoma City, OK
Sizemore, Mary H. ... Tallassee, AL
Sizemore, Michael S. ... Newton, KS
Sizemore, Nada K. Morin ... New Haven, CT
Sizemore, Patrick A. ... Santa Rosa, CA
Sizemore, Polly D. ... Greensboro, NC
Sizemore, Russell F. ... Charlotte, NC
Sizemore, Russell S. ... Elizabethtown, KY
Sizemore, Stephen G. ... Raleigh, NC
Sizemore, Steven Weir ... Asheville, NC
Sizemore, Tanya D. ... Riverside, CA
Sizemore, Thomas E. ... Detroit, MI

Sizemore, Victor K. ... **Placitas, NM**
Santa Teresa, NM
Sizemore, Victor K. ... Santa Teresa, NM
Sizemore, W. James, Jr. ... **Albany, GA**
Sizemore, William E. ... **Tampa, FL**
Sizensky, Jill M. ... New Haven, CT
Sizer, Henry S. ... Washington, DC
Sizer, Judith R. ... Waltham, MA
Sizer, Theresé M. ... West Bend, WI
Sizoo, Joseph A. ... Pinehurst, NC
Sizoo, Wesley ... **Walnut Creek, CA**
Sjaarda, Donald S. ... Fountain Valley, CA
Sjaarda, Donald S., A Prof. Corp.
Fountain Valley, CA
Sjaastad, Gerald D. ... Elbert, CO
Sjoberg, John Matthew ... **Austin, TX**
Sjoberg, Kathi ... Farmington, UT
Sjoberg, Mark A. ... **Warwick, RI**
Sjoberg, Roy A. ... Woodbury, MN
Sjoberg & Tebelius, P.A. ... Woodbury, MN
Sjoberg & Votta Law Offices
Providence, RI
Warwick, RI
Sjoberg, William C. ... **Washington, DC**
Sjoblom, J. Andrew ... **Los Angeles, CA**
Sjoblom, Thomas V.
Securities and Exchange Commission,
Division of Enforcement, GV
Sjodin, Keith E. ... Waconia, MN
Sjogreen, Martha L. ... **New York, NY**
Sjögren, Dee Anne ... **St. Louis, MO**
Sjogren, Michael P. ... New York, NY
Sjogren, Robert E. ... **Costa Mesa, CA**
Sjogren, Robert T. ... Lemon Grove, CA
Sjogren, Thomas F. ... Duluth, MN
Sjogren, Torbjorn B. ... **St. Louis, MO**
Sjogren, Wade R. ... Bridgeton, NJ
Sjoholm, Jack F. ... **Minneapolis, MN**
Sjoholm, John J. ... Schaumburg, IL
Sjoholm, William E. ... **Minneapolis, MN**
Sjoholm-Sierchio, Kristi Anne
Los Angeles, CA
Sjolander, Amy L. ... **Los Angeles, CA**
Sjoquist, Mary M. ... **Washington, DC**
Sjoquist, Paul L. ... Minneapolis, MN
Sjostrand, Donalyn C. ... Eureka, CA
Sjostrand, George W. ... San Bernardino, CA
Sjostrom, Craig D. ... Arlington, WA
Sjostrom, Donald R. ... Wayzata, MN
Sjostrom, Elizabeth ... Mount Vernon, WA
Sjostrom, Jay A. ... Edina, MN
Sjostrom, Jonathan ... **Tallahassee, FL**
Sjostrom, Kevin J. ... **Milwaukee, WI**
Sjostrom & Lofthus ... Wayzata, MN
Sjostrom, Susan D. ... Deerfield, IL
Sjostrom, William K., Jr.
Minneapolis, MN
Sjovall, John M. ... **Waco, TX**
Sjovall, John P. ... Danbury, CT
Sjue, Garth H. ... Williston, ND
Sjulin, Carl J. ... **Lincoln, NE**
Skaalerud, Erik ... Central Islip, NY
Skaar, Arthur L., Jr. ... Belle Mead, NJ
Skaar, Barbara J. ... Lowell, MA
Skaar, Harvey E. ... Minneapolis, MN
Skaar, James D. ... **Geneva, IL**
Skaar, Kris K. ... Marietta, GA
Skaar & McCullough ... Minneapolis, MN
Skaar, Randall T. ... **Minneapolis, MN**
Skaats, Donna Richer ... Norwich, CT
Skabelund, Gregory N. ... Logan, UT
Skabronski, Jill C. ... Twin Falls, ID
Skacevic, Stephen M. ... Los Angeles, CA
Skadden, Arps, Slate, Meagher & Flom (Illinois) ... **Chicago, IL**
Skadden, Arps, Slate, Meagher & Flom LLP
Los Angeles, CA
Palo Alto, CA
San Francisco, CA
Wilmington, DE
Washington, DC
Boston, MA
Newark, NJ
New York, NY
Houston, TX
Skadden, Michael J. ... Houston, TX
Skadow, Ronald R. ... Tryon, NC
Skaer, Arthur W., Jr. ... **Wichita, KS**
Skaer, Susan J. ... **Mountain View, CA**
Skaf, Alfred J. ... Boca Raton, FL
Skafar, Janet M. ... **Palo Alto, CA**
Skaff, Bridgette B. ... **Ann Arbor, MI**
Skaff, Didi M. ... New York, NY
Skaff, Kristen E. ... **Detroit, MI**
Skaff, Stephanie P. ... **San Francisco, CA**
Skaff, Victor S., III ... **Roanoke, VA**
Skafidas, Arthur B. ... Tampa, FL
Skager, Philip R. ... High Point, NC
Skaggs, Amy R. ... **Chicago, IL**
Skaggs, Barbara W. ... Acton, MA
Skaggs, Betina D. ... Marietta, GA
Skaggs, Clayton C. ... **Wichita, KS**
Skaggs, Darcy A. ... Big Bear Lake, CA
Skaggs, David E. ... **Denver, CO**
Washington, DC
Skaggs, Diana L. ... Louisville, KY
Skaggs, Elizabeth Wells ... **Washington, DC**
Skaggs, Ernest ... Fayetteville, WV
Skaggs, Gail E. ... Denver, CO
Skaggs & Garza, L.L.P. ... **McAllen, TX**
Skaggs, Jack C., Jr. ... Brownsville, TX
Skaggs, Jamy Mitchell ... **Tyler, TX**
Skaggs, John A., II ... Bentonville, AR
Skaggs, John B. ... **McAllen, TX**
Skaggs, John H. ... **Charleston, WV**
Skaggs, Linda S. ... **Kansas City, MO**
Skaggs, Mark D. ... Peoria, IL
Skaggs, Marylynn E. ... **Greensboro, NC**
Skaggs, Robert C., Jr. ... Toledo, OH
Skaggs, Robert H. ... Billings, MT
Skaggs, Roy B., II ... Mesa, AZ
Skaggs, Sanford M. ... **Walnut Creek, CA**
Skaggs, Shirley ... **Charleston, WV**
Skaggs, Vicki M. ... **McAllen, TX**
Skaggs, William C. ... **Knoxville, TN**
Skaggs, William Kerry ... **Las Vegas, NV**
Skaggs, Wyatt R. ... Laramie, WY
Skahan, Gerald Daniel ... Memphis, TN
Skahill, Theresa M. ... Bradenton, FL
Skahn, Steven L. ... **Grand Rapids, MI**
Skain, James R. ... Jefferson City, MO
Skaine, Theresa M. ... **Saratoga Springs, NY**
Skaist, Howard A. ... **Hillsboro, OR**
Skaist, Lisa K. ... **Los Angeles, CA**
Skaist, Mark L. ... **Newport Beach, CA**
Skakel, Deborah A. ... **New York, NY**
Skakles, Greg J. ... Anaconda, MT
Skakun, John M. ... Canton, OH
Skakun, Mark J., III ... **Akron, OH**
Skala, Brian Oliver ... Americus, GA
Skala, Jason E. ... **Santa Barbara, CA**
Skala, Mary Frances ... **Duluth, MN**
Skala, Michael J., Jr., Law Office of
Sacramento, CA
Skala, Murray L. ... **New York, NY**
Skala, Roland L. ... Yakima, WA
Skala, Whitney M. ... **San Diego, CA**
Skalaban, Peter J., Jr. ... **Washington, DC**
Skalak, John P. ... **Las Vegas, NV**
Skalak, William H. ... Portland, OR
Skalangya, Nancy S. ... Bethlehem, PA
Skalbania, Alexander J. ... Seattle, WA
Skalbania, Richard H. ... **Seattle, WA**
Skalberg, Randall K. ... Sartell, MN
Skale, Andrew ... **Washington, DC**
Skale, Stephen H. ... Philadelphia, PA
Skaleris, Athena ... **Madison, WI**
Skalet, Steven A. ... Washington, DC
Skaletsky and Mannis, P.C. ... Chicago, IL
Skaletsky, Scott ... Chicago, IL
Skaletzky, Harry ... Sacramento, CA
Skalitzky, William G. ... **Chicago, IL**
Skalka, David J. ... **Omaha, NE**
Skalka, Douglas S. ... **New Haven, CT**
Southport, CT
Skalka, Michael B. ... New York, NY
Skall, David W. ... **Cleveland, OH**
Skall, Gregg P. ... **Washington, DC**
Skalland, Lyle B. ... Charlotte, MI
Skaller, David Matthew ... **New York, NY**
Skallerud, William R. ... **Minneapolis, MN**
Skalley, Marion Fagan ... Baton Rouge, LA
Skalmoski, Thomas L. ... **Milwaukee, WI**
Skalmowski, Armin A.
Huntington Beach, CA
Skalniak, Joseph W. ... Pittsburgh, PA
Skalnik, Brinton ... Skiatook, OK
Skalski, Joseph C. ... Clearwater, FL
Skalsky, Wade J. ... **Phoenix, AZ**
Skambis, Christopher C. ... **Orlando, FL**
Skambis, Kathleen L. Maloney
Orlando, FL
Skanchy, Randall N. ... **Salt Lake City, UT**
Skancke, Nancy J. ... **Washington, DC**
Skandalakis, Peter J. ... La Grange, GA
Skandalis, George ... **Syracuse, NY**
Skane, Elizabeth Ann ... San Diego, CA
Skane, Thomas J. ... **Irvine, CA**
Skantz, Donald W. ... Oswego, NY
Skapars & Morin ... **Boston, MA**
Skapars, Z. John ... **Boston, MA**
Skapik, Geralyn L. ... **Riverside, CA**
Skar, Robert E. ... Thermopolis, WY
Skarakis, Gus E. ... Sacramento, CA
Skarbek, James ... Philadelphia, PA
Skarbek, William Joseph, Jr ... Fort Myers, FL
Skarbnik, Jack A. ... Boynton Beach, FL
Skarbnik, John H. ... **Roseland, NJ**
Skarbnik-Kirmser, Michelle ... Princeton, NJ
Skarda, James Jay ... Chicago, IL
Skarda, Jeffrey J. ... Houston, TX
Skarda, Lynell G. ... **Clovis, NM**
Skarda, Michael W. ... **Dallas, TX**
Skardon, James T. ... Phoenix, AZ
Skare, Robert M. ... **Minneapolis, MN**
Skare, Samuel E.
General Services Administration,
Office of Regional Counsel, GV
Skare, Thomas M. ... **Cloquet, MN**
Skarecky, Dennis J. ... **Phoenix, AZ**
Skarecky & Holder, A Professional Association ... **Phoenix, AZ**
Skarky, Earl A. ... **Oklahoma City, OK**
Skarlatos, Bryan C. ... **New York, NY**
Skarlatos, Nicholas J. ... Murray Hill, NJ
Skarlatos and Zonarich ... Harrisburg, PA
Steelton, PA
Skarmeas, Arthur P. ... Boston, MA
Skaro, Ann A. ... Corpus Christi, TX
Skaro, Ann A., P.C. ... Corpus Christi, TX
Skarpetowski, Carol ... Flemington, NJ
Skarr, Ronald J. ... Western Springs, IL
Skarren, William E. ... Jericho, NY
Skarsgard, Gordon L. ... Albuquerque, NM
Skarstad, Dennis W. ... **Portland, OR**
Skarvan, Dennis C. ... Peoria, IL
Skarvelis, Michele K. ... Charlottesville, VA
Skarzynski, James A. ... **New York, NY**
Skatell, Christopher P. ... Youngwood, PA
Skates, Jeffrey ... **Leesburg, FL**
Skates, John R. ... Canton, GA
Skatoff, Jeffrey Howard ... **Washington, DC**
Skatvold, Paul O. ... Hawley, MN
Moorhead, MN
Skau, Anne C. ... Ridgewood, NJ
Skau, Creighton C. ... Carson City, NV
Skaug, Bruce D. ... Nampa, ID
Skavdahl, Duane R. ... Cincinnati, OH
Skavdahl, John H. ... Harrison, NE
Skavdahl, Scott W. ... **Casper, WY**
Skavdahl & Wickersham ... Harrison, NE
Skavina, Joseph A. ... Cohoes, NY
Skavina, Paul E. ... Rome, NY
Skawin, Michael A. ... **Arlington, TX**
Skawski, John J. ... Chicago, IL
Skay, Jacqueline M. ... **Escondido, CA**
Vista, CA
Skay, Michael C. ... New York, NY
Skeans, David W. ... Cleveland, OH
Skeary, Michael J. ... Boston, MA
Skeath, John E. ... San Jose, CA
Skebba, Jamie B. ... **Glendale, CA**
Skedd, Lloyd J. ... Helena, MT
Skedelsky, Marvin D. ... Whitestone, NY
Skedsvold, Kevin O. ... **Atlanta, GA**
Skeel, Henke, Evenson & Roberts
Seattle, WA
Skeel, Peter B. ... **Pittsburgh, PA**
Skeele, Joan Williams ... La Conner, WA
Skeels, Jennifer Fouts ... Park Ridge, IL
Skeels, Paul L. ... Santa Paula, CA
Skeels, Robert A. ... Jacksonville Beach, FL
Skeen, Carla ... Santa Fe, NM
Skeen, Cynthia V.R. ... **Denver, CO**
Skeen, David G. ... Port Hadlock, WA
Skeen, David S. ... South Charleston, WV
Skeen, David W. ... **Baltimore, MD**
Skeen, Donna D. ... Dallas, TX
Skeen, H. Keith ... Huntington, WV
Skeen, Harold C. ... Richmond, VA
Skeen, James D. ... **Baltimore, MD**
Skeen, James E. ... **Charlottesville, VA**
Skeen, Jannece-Marie ... Pocatello, ID
Skeen & Johnson ... **Charlottesville, VA**
Skeen, Joseph Ike ... Washington, DC
Skeen, Kennad L. ... Ripley, WV
Skeen, Larry L. ... Ripley, WV
Skeen, Marc L. ... **Irving, TX**
Skeen, Marnie S. ... **San Diego, CA**
Skeen, Matthew D. ... **Denver, CO**
Skeen, Melissa Gay ... Fort Myers, FL
Skeen, Michael W. ... Augusta, GA
Skeen, Randall L. ... Salt Lake City, UT
Skeen, Rayma ... Boulder, CO
Skeen, Richard C. ... **Salt Lake City, UT**
Skeen, Robert G. ... Baltimore, MD
Skeen, Robert H., Jr. ... **Charleston, WV**
Skeen, Samuel P. ... Pittsburgh, PA
Skeen, Shelly Lynn ... Dallas, TX
Skeen and Skeen ... Ripley, WV
Skeen & Skeen, P.C. ... **Denver, CO**
Skeen, Spencer C. ... **San Diego, CA**
Skeen, William A. ... **Baltimore, MD**
Skeens, David M. ... **Kansas City, MO**
Skeens, Deborah DePaul ... Charleston, WV
Skeens, Edward John, (P.A.) ... Suitland, MD
Skeens, Edwin L. ... **Columbus, OH**
Skeens, James Norman ... Glendale, AZ
Skeens, Troy W., Jr. ... Cincinnati, OH
Skeens, William A. ... Overland Park, KS
Skeer, David ... Naples, FL
Skeer, W. Thom ... Ridgecrest, CA
Skees, Hugh O. ... Florence, KY
Skees, Tony D. ... **Philadelphia, PA**
Pittsburgh, PA
Skees, William L., Jr. ... **Louisville, KY**
Skees-Helly, Sally ... Pittsford, VT
Skeeter, Carolene Y. ... New York, NY
Skeeters, Bennett & Wilson ... **Radcliff, KY**
Skeeters, Donald E. ... **Radcliff, KY**
Skeffington, Donald J., Jr.
Bloomington, MN
Skeffington, James J. ... **Providence, RI**
Skeffington, James J., Jr ... **Boston, MA**
Skeffington, John F. ... **Chicago, IL**
Skeffington, Keyna Pidcock
Minneapolis, MN
Skeffington, Thomas J. ... Newark, NJ
New York, NY
Skefos, Catherine H. ... Memphis, TN
Skefos, Harry J. ... **Memphis, TN**
Skehan, Philip J. ... **Rochester, NY**
Skehan, Thomas H. ... Okemos, MI
Skehan, William M. ... New York, NY
Skehen, Kelley L. ... Albuquerque, NM
Skeins, Harry, Jr. ... Fredericksburg, TX
Skeith, Paul ... Austin, TX
Skeith, Robert P. ... **Tulsa, OK**
Skekloff, Daniel J. ... **Fort Wayne, IN**
Skekloff, Scot T. ... **Fort Wayne, IN**
Skelding, Jack M., Jr. ... **Tallahassee, FL**
Skelding, Labasky & Daws, A Professional Association ... **Tallahassee, FL**
Skelding, Susan E. ... Commerce, CA
Skellenger Bender, A Professional Service Corporation ... **Seattle, WA**
Skellenger, David ... **Seattle, WA**
Skelley, Dana M. ... Kansas City, KS
Skelley, Joseph T. ... Fort Lee, NJ
Skelley, Matthew D. ... Fort Lee, NJ
Skelley, Patrick J., II ... **Roanoke, VA**
Skelley Rottner P.C. ... **Hartford, CT**
West Hartford, CT
Skelley, Susan C. ... **Boston, MA**
Skellie, Sheila K. ... Largo, FL
Skelly / Deininger ... Atlanta, GA
Skelly, Christopher M. ... Phoenix, AZ
Skelly, Edward J. ... Sherman Oaks, CA
Skelly, Elizabeth Joy Reza ... Boston, MA
Skelly, Garrett ... Tustin, CA
Skelly, George J. ... **Boston, MA**
Skelly, James M. ... New York, NY
Skelly, James T. ... Metairie, LA
Skelly, Joseph G. ... **Harrisburg, PA**
Skelly, Kenneth B. ... **New York, NY**
Skelly, Kerry A. Walsh ... Louisville, KY
Skelly, Laurence J. ... Scarsdale, NY
Skelly, Muriel R ... Reno, NV
Skelly, Noreen P. ... Sacramento, CA
Skelly, Paul C. ... **Washington, DC**
Skelly, Richard M. ... Atlanta, GA
Skelly, Sheehan & Peevers ... Reno, NV
Skelly, Thomas M. ... Dearborn, MI
Skelly, Timothy O. ... **Wood Dale, IL**
Skelnik, Josette M. ... Elgin, IL
Skelnik, Mary E. ... **Dallas, TX**
Skelos, Dean G. ... **Mineola, NY**
Skelton, Arch M. ... Dallas, TX
Skelton, Arch M., P.C. ... Dallas, TX
Skelton, Barnet B., Jr. ... Houston, TX
Skelton, Barnet B., Jr., P.C. ... Houston, TX
Skelton, Beverly B., (Ms.) ... Dallas, TX
Skelton, Bryan L. ... **Edwardsville, IL**
Skelton & Cooley ... Missoula, MT
Skelton, David ... San Diego, CA
Skelton, Deborah M. ... **Cedar Rapids, IA**
Skelton, H. Gray, Jr. ... Marietta, GA
Skelton, Harold N. ... **Auburn, ME**
Skelton, Henry T. ... Athens, TX
Skelton, Ike, Jr. ... Lexington, MO
Skelton, J. Hampton ... **Austin, TX**
Skelton, J. Russell ... **Phoenix, AZ**
Skelton, James R. ... **Coshocton, OH**
Skelton, James R. ... North Royalton, OH
Skelton, James W., Jr. ... Houston, TX
Skelton, Jan ... Treasury Department,
Internal Revenue Service, GV
Skelton, Jane E. ... **Bangor, ME**
Skelton, Jefferson P.W. ... **Jackson, MS**
Skelton, Jeffrey J. ... Indianapolis, IN
Skelton, Jim ... Abilene, TX
Skelton, John ... **Redwood City, CA**
Skelton, John H. ... Seattle, WA
Skelton, John L., Jr. ... Marietta, GA
Skelton, John R. ... **Boston, MA**
Skelton, Joseph R. ... **Coshocton, OH**
Skelton, Joseph S. ... Hartwell, GA
Skelton, Kathryn E. ... **Chicago, IL**
Skelton, L. Wayne ... Houston, TX
Skelton, Larry Charles ... Corinth, MS
Skelton, Mark A. ... **Rogersville, TN**
Skelton, Marvin L. ... Houston, TX
Skelton, Mary H. ... Birmingham, AL
Skelton, Meghan S. ... Department of Justice,
Tax Division, GV
Skelton, Michael A. ... **Tampa, FL**
Skelton, Pamela ... **Denver, CO**
Skelton, Pamela J. ... Memphis, TN
Skelton, Patricia Cowan ... **Indianapolis, IN**
Skelton, Patrick W. ... **Tampa, FL**
Skelton, Pelton & Pelton ... Abilene, TX
Skelton, R. Duane ... **Sacramento, CA**
Skelton, Ralph T., Jr.
Saint Simons Island, GA
Skelton, Richard D. ... Oak Park, IL
Skelton, Richard S. ... Dayton, OH
Skelton, Robert A. ... **Coshocton, OH**
Skelton, Robert M. ... Glen Burnie, MD
Skelton, Robert R. ... Missoula, MT
Skelton, Robert W. ... Sparks, MD
Skelton, Roy C. ... Clearwater, FL
Skelton, Scott C. ... **Lufkin, TX**
Skelton, Stephen R. ... Mount Vernon, WA
Skelton and Steuber, P.A. ... Russellville, AR
Skelton, Steven M. ... Eugene, OR
Skelton, Taintor & Abbott, A Professional Corporation ... **Auburn, ME**
Lewiston, ME
Skelton, Thomas M. ... **White Plains, NY**
Skelton, Timothy L. ... **Los Angeles, CA**
Skelton & Tims ... Mount Vernon, WA
Skelton, Walter L. ... Little Rock, AR
Skelton, William B., II ... **Auburn, ME**
Skelton, William Douglas ... Russellville, AR
Skelton, William H. ... **Knoxville, TN**
Skelton, William K. ... **Auburn, ME**
Skelton, Willis and Bennett
St. Petersburg, FL
Skelton, Woody & Arnold ... **Austin, TX**
Skemp, Anthony J. ... **Milwaukee, WI**
Skemp, Daniel C. ... La Crosse, WI
Skemp, Daniel C., Jr. ... La Crosse, WI
Skemp, Douglas W. ... Dallas, TX
Skemp, Elizabeth ... Dallas, TX
Skemp, Joseph J., Jr. ... **La Crosse, WI**
Skemp, Kim John ... **Platteville, WI**
Skemp, Robert C. ... **La Crosse, WI**
Skemp, Robert H. ... Salinas, CA
Skemp & Skemp ... Dallas, TX
Skemp, Theodore J. ... La Crosse, WI
Skemp, William G. ... **La Crosse, WI**
Skemp, William, Law Firm, S.C.
La Crosse, WI
Skemp, William P. ... **La Crosse, WI**
Skenandore, Francis R. ... Oneida, WI
Skender, Marilyn L. ... **Reno, NV**
Skene, Annette R. ... Mobile, AL
Skene, G. Neil, Jr. ... Washington, DC
Skene, George N. ... Macon, GA
Skene, Mary L. ... Metter, GA
Skene, Robert D. ... **Edison, NJ**
New York, NY
Skennion & Associates ... Dallas, TX
Skennion, Michael G. ... Dallas, TX
Skenyon, John M. ... **Boston, MA**
Skepnek & Maddox, P.A. ... **Lawrence, KS**
Skepnek, William J. ... **Lawrence, KS**
Skeppstrom, Joan Craun ... Norfolk, VA
Skerik, Dale O. ... Huntington Beach, CA
Skerjanec, Carol DeHaven ... Vale, OR
Skerpon, Joseph M. ... **Washington, DC**
Skerpon, Lynn Loughlin ... Bowie, MD

Skerrett, Cassandra D. ..... Brevard, NC
Skerritt, Daniel H. ..... Portland, OR
Skerritt, Tina L. ..... Leominster, MA
Skerry, Ann M. ..... Cleveland, OH
Skerry, David P. ..... Medford, MA
Skerry, Ethan A. ..... New York, NY
Skerry, Jeffrey J. ..... Boston, MA
Skerry, Jon T. ..... Salem, MA
Skerry, Joseph H., III ..... Boston, MA
Skerry, Richard A., Jr. ..... Boston, MA
Skestos, George A. ..... Columbus, OH
Sketch, Michael M. ..... Covington, KY
Skewes, Klosterbuer & Vajgrt ..... Luverne, MN
Skewes, Mort B. ..... Luverne, MN
Skewes, Thomas T. ..... Fort Madison, IA
Skewes, William A., II ..... Denver, CO
Skewes, William F. ..... Denver, CO
Skewes, William F. ..... Evergreen, CO
Skey, Christopher N. ..... Chicago, IL
Skey, Dumont & Matejek, A Professional Corporation ..... Princeton, NJ
Skey, W. S. Gerald ..... Princeton, NJ
Skiba, Carol ..... Albuquerque, NM
Skiba, David J. ..... North Eastham, MA
Skiba, Gary V. ..... Erie, PA
Skiba, Steven E. ..... Detroit, MI
Skibbe, Sheryl L. ..... Los Angeles, CA
Skibell, Arthur ..... Dallas, TX
Skibell, Carl A. ..... Dallas, TX
Skibiel, Mark A. ..... Morrow, GA
Skibine, George T.
Department Of The Interior, Bureau of Indian Affairs, GV
Skibinski, J. Michael ..... Stoughton, WI
Skibinski, Kenneth P.
Ocean Township, NJ
Skibinsky, Clifford G.
Commodity Futures Trading Commission, Division of Enforcement, GV
Skibitsky, Gregory S., Jr. ..... Scranton, PA
Skidan, Irene ..... New York, NY
Skidd, Thomas P., Jr. ..... Stamford, CT
Skidelsky, Allon D. ..... Deerfield, IL
Skidgel, David L. ..... Kansas City, MO
Skidmore, Alan J. ..... Long Beach, CA
Skidmore & Alderson, P.A.
Cumberland, MD
Skidmore, Alfred J. ..... Hicksville, NY
Skidmore, Archie W. ..... Akron, OH
Skidmore & Associates Co., L.P.A.
Akron, OH
Skidmore, Bradley C. ..... Atlanta, GA
Skidmore, Brian K. ..... Akron, OH
Skidmore, Cathy Ann ..... Coraopolis, PA
Skidmore, Charles E. ..... Lexington, KY
Skidmore, Charles G. ..... Cincinnati, OH
Skidmore, Claudia M. ..... Medina, OH
Skidmore, David A., Jr. ..... Cincinnati, OH
Skidmore, David L. ..... Grand Rapids, MI
Skidmore, Eric E. ..... Akron, OH
Skidmore, H. Gregory ..... Cumberland, MD
Skidmore, Henry L. ..... Bellevue, WA
Skidmore, Henry L., P.S. ..... Bellevue, WA
Skidmore, Jonathan B. ..... Dallas, TX
Skidmore, L. Randolph ..... Napa, CA
St. Helena, CA
Skidmore, L. Thomas ..... Medina, OH
Skidmore, Lawrence E. ..... Auburn, CA
Skidmore, Lawrence J. ..... Kansas City, MO
Skidmore, Lee Thomas ..... Medina, OH
Skidmore, Mark A. ..... Phoenix, AZ
Skidmore, Nancy A. ..... Secaucus, NJ
Skidmore, Paul E. ..... Tuscaloosa, AL
Skidmore, Robert D. ..... Colville, WA
Skidmore, Robert G. ..... Sulphur Springs, TX
Skidmore, Ruth Ann ..... Grand Rapids, MI
Skidmore, Scott K. ..... Reidsville, NC
Skidmore, Susan E. ..... Monroe, LA
Skidmore, Thomas A. ..... Akron, OH
Skidmore, Thomas D. ..... Bushnell, FL
Skidmore, Wallace E., Jr. ..... Seattle, WA
Skidmore, William V. .....
Department of Commerce, GV
Skiena, Alan N. ..... New York, NY
Skier, Andrew Mark ..... Montgomery, AL
Skier, Barbara J. ..... Acton, CA
Skierski, Douglas D. ..... Dallas, TX
Skievaski, Janice K.
Fort Walton Beach, FL
Panama City, FL
Pensacola, FL
Skievaski, Kim Anthony ..... Pensacola, FL
Skiff, Kenneth ..... Phoenix, AZ
Skiff, Peter K. ..... Alexandria, VA
Skiff, William B., II ..... Burlington, VT
Skiffington, Anna M. ..... Chicago, IL
Skiffington, Lawrence S.
Manitou Springs, CO
Skifstad, Jason E. ..... Silverdale, WA
Skigen, Gloria M. ..... New York, NY
Skigen, Patricia S. ..... New York, NY
Skigen, Robert H. ..... Smithtown, NY
Skigen, Wayne D. ..... San Francisco, CA
Skigin, Cheryl A. ..... Orange, CA
Skiko, Peter G. ..... Chicago, IL
Skiko, Tracy L. ..... Los Angeles, CA
Skikos, Gregory T. ..... San Francisco, CA
Skikos, Ida Samawi ..... Redwood City, CA
Skikos, Steven J. ..... Newport Beach, CA
San Francisco, CA
Skiles, Elizabeth H. ..... Laramie, WY
Skiles, James H. ..... Washington, DC
Skiles, Jay L. ..... Salem, OR
Skiles, Jonathan M. ..... Fresno, CA
Skiles, Mason F. ..... Laramie, WY
Skiles, Nicholas E. ..... Wilmington, DE
Skiles, Richard R. ..... Indianapolis, IN
Skiles, Shelley E. ..... Atlanta, GA
Skiles, Terri ..... West Palm Beach, FL
Skiljan, David R. ..... Cincinnati, OH
Skiljan, Jeff M., (P.C.) ..... Carlsbad, CA
Skilken, Lynne ..... Cincinnati, OH
Skilken, Melissa S. ..... Chicago, IL
Skilken, Ralph A., Jr. ..... Dayton, OH
Skilken & Replogle, LLP ..... Dayton, OH
Skilken, Thomas E. ..... Dayton, OH
Skillen, Lesley Ann ..... New York, NY
Skillen, Richard, Jr. ..... Cleveland, OH
Skillen, Sandra B. ..... Macon, GA
Skillern, Beth ..... Portland, OR
Skillern, Christopher L. ..... Dallas, TX
Skillern, Frank F. ..... Lubbock, TX
Skillern, Frederick B. ..... Denver, CO
Skillicorn, Thomas H. ..... Watsonville, CA
Skillin, Bruce K. ..... Waltham, MA
Skillin, Robert A. ..... Santa Monica, CA
Skilling, Elizabeth E. S. ..... Richmond, VA
Skilling, James C. ..... Richmond, VA
Skilling, Mark C. ..... Oakland, CA
Skilling, Raymond I. ..... Chicago, IL
Skillings-Goff, Janice E. ..... Salem, MA
Skillington, G. Lee ..... Washington, DC
Skillman, A. Dix ..... Belle Mead, NJ
Skillman, B. Scott ..... New Orleans, LA
Skillman, B. Scott, PLC ..... New Orleans, LA
Skillman, Deborah L. ..... Bel Air, MD
Skillman, Gregory E. ..... Eugene, OR
Skillman, Henry H. ..... Philadelphia, PA
Skillman, Richard W. ..... Washington, DC
Skillman, Stephen ..... Trenton, NJ
Skillman, William B. ..... Baton Rouge, LA
Skilton, Anne M. ..... Lansing, MI
Skilton, Christine Bishop ..... Nashua, IA
Skilton, David H. ..... Nashua, IA
Skilton, John S. ..... Madison, WI
Skilton, Robert H., III ..... Southfield, MI
Skilton, Thomas E. ..... Washington, DC
Skinazi, Heather R. ..... Los Angeles, CA
Skindell, Michael J. ..... Cleveland, OH
Skinder, Richard D. ..... Newark, NJ
Skindrud, Michael E. ..... Madison, WI
Skingle, Denise L ..... Columbus, OH
Skingle, Ronald A. ..... Cleveland, OH
Skinker, Donald R. ..... Fredericksburg, VA
Skinker, Michael T. ..... Department of Energy, Office of the General Counsel, GV
Skinner, Alice J. ..... Montgomery, AL
Skinner, Allison O. ..... Birmingham, AL
Skinner, Asa Allen ..... Leesville, LA
Skinner & Associates ..... Greenville, SC
Skinner, Beth Osborne ..... Lebanon, VA
Skinner, Blake Knowles ..... Denver, CO
Skinner, Brent D. ..... Menomonie, WI
Skinner, Brian J. ..... Elkins, WV
Skinner, Carol Nolan ..... Baldwin, WI
New Richmond, WI
Skinner, Chad A. ..... Palo Alto, CA
Skinner, Charles M. ..... Lutsen, MN
Skinner, Christon ..... Oak Harbor, WA
Skinner, Christopher L. ..... Chevy Chase, MD
Skinner, Christopher S. ..... Salem, MA
Skinner, Claire E. ..... Elkhart, IN
Skinner, Daniel E. ..... Mission Viejo, CA
Skinner, Dara ..... Gulfport, MS
Skinner, Darren C. ..... Washington, DC
Skinner, David C. ..... Birmingham, AL
Skinner, David C., L.L.C. ..... Birmingham, AL
Skinner, David L. ..... Albuquerque, NM
Skinner, David L., Jr. ..... San Francisco, CA
Skinner, David L., P.C. ..... Albuquerque, NM
Skinner, David R. ..... Bay City, MI
Skinner, David Rupert ..... Boise, ID
Skinner, David V. ..... El Toro, CA
Skinner, David W. ..... San Leandro, CA
San Leandro, CA
Skinner, Desiree Taber ..... New Brunswick, NJ
Skinner, Donald D. ..... Seattle, WA
Skinner, Ed ..... Altoona, IA
Skinner, Elizabeth Anne ..... Minneapolis, MN
Skinner, Elton A. ..... San Antonio, TX
Skinner Fawcett ..... Boise, ID
Skinner, Gardner W., Jr. ..... Boise, ID
Skinner, George S. ..... Arlington, VA
Skinner, Gina Williamson ..... Salem, OR
Skinner, Gregory A. ..... Ankeny, IA
Skinner, Gregory M. ..... Belleville, IL
Skinner, Gregory S. ..... Incline Village, NV
Skinner, Gwen Denoux ..... Birmingham, AL
Skinner, Gwynne L. ..... Seattle, WA
Skinner, H. Craig ..... Denver, CO
Skinner, H. Edward ..... Little Rock, AR
Skinner, Halcyon E. ..... Jacksonville, FL
Skinner, Halcyon G. ..... Hartsdale, NY
Skinner, Howard W. ..... Jacksonville, FL
Skinner, Ira, Jr. ..... Des Moines, IA
Skinner, J. Wesley ..... Atlanta, GA
Skinner, Jack ..... Greenwood, AR
Skinner, Jeffery R. ..... Flint, MI
Skinner, Jeffrey A. ..... San Francisco, CA
Skinner, Jeffrey E. ..... Hernando, MS
Skinner, Jeffrey T. ..... Raleigh, NC
Skinner, Jerome L. ..... Cincinnati, OH
Skinner, Jill Dian ..... Carlsbad, CA
Skinner, Jim ..... Galesburg, IL
Skinner, Joel D., Jr. ..... Hudson, WI
Skinner, Joel R. ..... Chicago, IL
Skinner, John C. ..... Boston, MA
Skinner, John C., Jr. ..... Charles Town, WV
Skinner, John G. ..... Atlanta, GA
Skinner, John H. ..... Jacksonville, FL
Skinner, John J., Jr. ..... New York, NY
Skinner, John M. ..... Williamston, NC
Skinner, John W. ..... Lafayette, CA
Skinner, Jonathan P. ..... Boston, MA
Skinner, Joseph F. ..... Florham Park, NJ
Skinner, Joseph H. ..... Grand Junction, CO
Skinner, J. T. ..... Batesville, AR
Skinner, Kathleen A. ..... Oakland, CA
Skinner, Kathy Mace ..... Nevada, IA
Skinner & Kees ..... Leesville, LA
Skinner, L. Michael ..... Cedar Rapids, IA
Skinner, Laura L. ..... Durham, NC
Skinner, Laurence E. ..... Washington, DC
Skinner Law Firm, P.A. ..... Greenwood, AR
Skinner Law Offices, P.C. ..... Altoona, IA
Skinner, Leary G. ..... Liberty, MO
Skinner, Lemoine, III ..... San Francisco, CA
Skinner, Leslie E ..... Santa Clara, CA
Skinner, Linda Scott ..... Mission, KS
Skinner, Louvin Hitt ..... New Orleans, LA
Skinner, Madonna M. R. ..... Brainard, NE
Skinner, Margaret Manzon ..... Waltham, MA
Skinner, Marie C. ..... Mendota Heights, MN
Skinner, Mary Jacobs ..... Chicago, IL
Skinner, Mary Just ..... Montpelier, VT
Skinner, Mary T. ..... Durham, NC
Skinner, Matthew L. ..... Rapid City, SD
Skinner, Matthew R. ..... Fairfield, OH
Skinner, Melissa L. ..... Windsor, NC
Skinner, Michael A. ..... San Francisco, CA
Skinner, Michael D. ..... Lafayette, LA
Skinner, Michael F. ..... Lansing, MI
Skinner, Michael L. ..... Grand Prairie, TX
Skinner, Mikell Grafton ..... Louisville, KY
Skinner, Peter G. ..... New York, NY
Skinner, Philip G. ..... Atlanta, GA
Skinner, R. Bradley ..... Altoona, IA
Skinner, Randy A. ..... Greenville, SC
Skinner, Renée ..... Dallas, TX
Skinner, Richard A. ..... Boise, ID
Skinner, Richd. H. ..... Houston, TX
Skinner, Robert A. ..... Boston, MA
Skinner, Robert A. ..... Dayton, OH
Skinner, Robert A. ..... Toledo, OH
Skinner, Robert J. ..... Chicago, IL
Skinner, Robert J. ..... New Orleans, LA
Skinner, Robert L. ..... Santa Barbara, CA
Skinner, Robert N., Jr. ..... Nashville, TN
Skinner, Robert R. ..... Charles Town, WV
Inwood, WV
Skinner, Roger C. ..... Wichita, KS
Skinner, Samuel K. ..... Washington, DC
Chicago, IL
Skinner, Sandra L. ..... Springfield, MO
Skinner, Schofield & Higley, S.C.
Menomonie, WI
Skinner, Scott M. ..... Montpelier, VT
Skinner, Shannon J. ..... Seattle, WA
Skinner, Sonia L. ..... Boston, MA
Skinner, Stanford J. ..... Birmingham, AL
Skinner, Stanley T. ..... San Francisco, CA
Skinner, Stephanie D. ..... New Orleans, LA
Skinner, Stephen C. ..... Oakland, CA
Skinner, Stephen D. ..... Dallas, TX
Skinner, Stephen D., & Associates, P.C.
Dallas, TX
Skinner, Stephen G. ..... Seattle, WA
Skinner, Sutton, Watson & Rounds
Tahoe City, CA
Incline Village, NV
Las Vegas, NV
Reno, NV
Skinner, T. Julian, Jr. ..... Birmingham, AL
Skinner, Tammy Spivack ..... Atlanta, GA
Skinner, Thomas J., IV ..... Birmingham, AL
Skinner, Tracey E. ..... Baltimore, MD
Skinner, Troy A. ..... Altoona, IA
Skinner, Walter I. ..... Colorado Springs, CO
Skinner, Wildeboer & Ogden, L.L.P.
Bay City, MI
Skinner, William A. ..... Akron, OH
Skinner, William F. C., Jr. ..... Decatur, GA
Skinner, William J. ..... Rockville, MD
Skinner, William L. ..... Decatur, GA
Skinner, William P. ..... Washington, DC
Skinner, William P., Jr. ..... Raleigh, NC
Skinner, William S. ..... Cherry Hill, NJ
Skinner, William T, IV ..... Littleton, NC
Skinner, Wilson F., Jr. ..... Williamsburg, VA
Skinner-Lewis, Frances J. ..... Chicago, IL
Skinner-Pfarr, Ann M. ..... Indianapolis, IN
Skipp, Jonathan W. ..... Miami, FL
Skipp, Stefan R. ..... Chestertown, MD
Skipper, Chester L. ..... St. Petersburg, FL
Skipper, Christopher Alton
Surfside Beach, SC
Skipper & Day ..... St. Petersburg, FL
Tampa, FL
Skipper, Frank P., Jr. ..... Dallas, TX
Skipper, Gigi Garber ..... Lakeland, FL
Skipper, H. Curtis ..... New Port Richey, FL
Spring Hill, FL
Skipper, H. Curtis, P.A., Law Offices of
New Port Richey, FL
Spring Hill, FL
Skipper, Herman L. ..... Dededo, GU
Skipper, J. Ronald ..... Longboat Key, FL
Sarasota, FL
Skipper, James M., Jr. ..... Americus, GA
Skipper, Jesse L. ..... St. Petersburg, FL
Skipper, Kathryn Nutt ..... Department of State, Office of the Legal Adviser, GV
Skipper, Kathy Long ..... Birmingham, AL
Skipper, Leigh M ..... Philadelphia, PA
Skipper, Linda M. ..... Stuart, FL
Skipper, M. Ann ..... Birmingham, AL
Skipper, Mark J. ..... Fort Lauderdale, FL
Skipper, Nathan R., Jr. ..... New Bern, NC
Skipper, Ronald G. ..... San Bernardino, CA
Skipper, Sallie D. ..... New Port Richey, FL
Skipper, Stephen L. ..... Orlando, FL
Skipper, Walter J. ..... Milwaukee, WI
Skipper-Dotta, Rhonda ..... Galt, CA
Skipton, John A. ..... Pinehurst, NC
Skipton, Stephen R. ..... Kolonia, TT
Skipwith, Donald L. ..... Houston, TX
Skipworth, Robert A. ..... El Paso, TX
Skipworth, Robert T. ..... Rochester, NY
Skipworth, Timothy K. ..... Dallas, TX
Skir, Eugene D. ..... Mineola, NY
Skirbunt, James R. ..... Cleveland, OH
Skirbunt, Sharon A. ..... Cleveland, OH
Skirbunt & Skirbunt, Co., L.P.A.
Akron, OH
Chardon, OH
Cleveland, OH
Painesville, OH
Skirnick, Maria A. ..... New York, NY
Philadelphia, PA
Skirnick, Robert A. ..... New York, NY
Philadelphia, PA
Skirtich, Paul E. ..... Pittsburgh, PA
Skirvin & Larimer ..... Cincinnati, OH
Skirvin, Steven R. ..... Salt Lake City, UT
Skitol, Robert A. ..... Washington, DC
Skittone, John R. ..... Chicago, IL
Skiver, Robert E. ..... Raleigh, NC
Skiver, Stephen A. ..... Toledo, OH
Skivington, Dale E. ..... Rochester, NY
Skivington, Peter K. ..... Geneseo, NY
Scottsville, NY
Skjeie, David F. ..... Los Angeles, CA
Skjeie, Iver E. ..... Sacramento, CA
Skjelset, Douglas G. ..... Missoula, MT
Skjerven, Morrill, MacPherson, Franklin & Friel LLP ..... Cupertino, CA
Fremont, CA
Milpitas, CA
Mountain View, CA
Newport Beach, CA
Palo Alto, CA
San Francisco, CA
San Jose, CA
Santa Clara, CA
Sunnyvale, CA
Austin, TX
Skjerven, Paul W. ..... Los Gatos, CA
Skjerven, Richard H. ..... Austin, TX
Skjerven, Wendy C. ..... Minneapolis, MN
Skjervold, Kristafer E. ..... Shorewood, MN
Skjervold Law Office ..... Shorewood, MN
Skjervold, Paul A. ..... Shorewood, MN
Skjold, Benjamin R. ..... Chicago, IL
Skladal, George W. ..... Anchorage, AK
Skladany, Barney J., Jr. ..... Washington, DC
Skladany, Linda Arey ..... Washington, DC
Skladany, Terri ..... Phoenix, AZ
Sklaire, David ..... Hollywood, FL
Sklamba, Stephen G. ..... Metairie, LA
Sklamba & Thomas, A Professional Law Corporation ..... Metairie, LA
Sklamberg, Marvin S. ..... New York, NY
Sklan, Mark L. ..... Costa Mesa, CA
Sklansky, David A. ..... Los Angeles, CA
Sklansky, Joseph J. ..... Boston, MA
Sklansky, Paul E. ..... Fairfax, VA
Sklansky, Ronald L. ..... Madison, WI
Sklar, Adam B. ..... Boca Raton, FL
Sklar, Adam J. ..... Hackensack, NJ
Sklar, Alan C. ..... Las Vegas, NV
Sklar, Albert L. ..... Baltimore, MD
Sklar, Amy ..... Commack, NY
Sklar, Andrew ..... Cherry Hill, NJ
Sklar, Arnold ..... Los Angeles, CA
Sklar, Arthur E. ..... Atlantic City, NJ
Sklar, Barry N. ..... Jenkintown, PA
Sklar, Bradley J. ..... Birmingham, AL
Sklar, Brandon N. ..... New York, NY
Sklar, Cary P.
Office Of Special Counsel, GV
Sklar, Catherine A. ..... Asheville, NC
Sklar, Charles B. ..... Baton Rouge, LA
Sklar, Claudia M. ..... Hartford, CT
Sklar, Craig A. ..... New York, NY
Sklar, Daniel M. ..... Los Angeles, CA
Sklar, Daniel M., A Professional Law Corporation ..... Los Angeles, CA
Sklar, Daniel R. ..... Wharton, TX
Sklar, Daniel W., (P.C.) ..... Manchester, NH
Sklar, David A. ..... Seattle, WA
Sklar, David J. ..... Manchester, MI
Sklar, Debbie-Ann R. ..... Manchester, NH
Sklar, Edward J. ..... San Francisco, CA
Sklar, Gary Martin ..... Beverly Hills, CA
Sklar, Gerald W. ..... Richmond, VA
Sklar, Glenn ..... New York, NY
Sklar, Harris J. ..... Philadelphia, PA
Sklar, Henry R. ..... Philadelphia, PA
Sklar, Howard Mark ..... Bronx, NY
Sklar, James E. ..... Birmingham, MI
Sklar, Jeffrey A. ..... Los Angeles, CA
Sklar, Jerald H. ..... Memphis, TN
Sklar, Jerry ..... New York, NY
Sklar, Joel ..... Boston, MA
Sklar, Joel B. ..... Memphis, TN
Sklar, John ..... Detroit, MI
Sklar, Jordan ..... New York, NY
Sklar, Judith B. ..... San Jose, CA
Sklar, Kenneth M. ..... New York, NY
Sklar, Kwasnik & Sklar ..... Cherry Hill, NJ
Sklar, Lawrence E. ..... Shelton, CT
Sklar, Lawrence F. ..... Bingham Farms, MI
Sklar, Leon ..... Staten Island, NY
Sklar, Leonard M. ..... Los Angeles, CA
Sklar, Lori J. ..... West New York, NJ
Sklar, Marshall A. ..... New York, NY
Sklar, Martin D. ..... New York, NY
Sklar, Marvin P. ..... Baltimore, MD
Sklar, Michael D. ..... Atlantic City, NJ
Sklar, Michael L. ..... Chicago, IL
Sklar, Mitchell C. ..... Cherry Hill, NJ
Sklar, Morton H. ..... Washington, DC

Sklar, Neal Ian ... Fort Lauderdale, FL
Sklar, Paul R. ... New York, NY
Sklar, Ronald J. ... San Francisco, CA
Sklar, Ronald S. ... Jenkintown, PA
Sklar, Ruben ... Miami, FL
Sklar, S. Jay ... Philadelphia, PA
Sklar, Scott David ... Hicksville, NY
Sklar, Scott W. ... Palm Springs, CA
Sklar, Stanley L. ... New York, NY
Sklar, Stanley P. ... Chicago, IL
Sklar, Steven A. ... Millburn, NJ
Sklar, Steven H. ... Chicago, IL
Sklar, Steven I. ... New York, NY
Sklar, Steven V. ... Baltimore, MD
Sklar, Stuart A. ... Farmington Hills, MI
Sklar, Stuart M. ... Philadelphia, PA
Sklar, Teri H. ... San Francisco, CA
Sklar, Warren A. ... Cleveland, OH
Sklar Warren Conway Williams & Rosenfeld LLP ... Las Vegas, NV
Sklar, Wilford N. ... Riverside, CA
Sklar, William P. ... West Palm Beach, FL
Sklaren, Cary Stewart ... New York, NY
Sklaren, Linda Genero ... New York, NY
Sklarew, Christina
General Accounting Office,
Office of the General Counsel, GV
Sklarew, Peter ... Department of Justice,
Tax Division, GV
Sklarin, Ila Siegel ... San Francisco, CA
Sklarin, Richard S. ... White Plains, NY
Sklaroff, Jeffrey B. ... New York, NY
Sklaroff, Michael ... Philadelphia, PA
Sklaroff, Murray ... Jericho, NY
Sklaroff, Neil ... Philadelphia, PA
Sklarosky, Joseph F. ... Wilkes-Barre, PA
Sklarsky, Alan H. ... Cherry Hill, NJ
Northfield, NJ
Sklarsky, Charles B. ... Chicago, IL
Sklarz, Mark G. ... New Haven, CT
Sklaver, Alfred ... Yorktown Heights, NY
Sklaver, Gary P. ... New Haven, CT
Sklaver, Harvey M. ... Yorktown Heights, NY
Sklaver, Laura M. ... New Haven, CT
Sklaver, Randy Gail ... New City, NY
Sklaw, Laurence ... Livingston, NJ
Sklencar, Brad L. ... San Antonio, TX
Sklenicka, Jane E. ... Glencoe, MN
Skliar, Michael H. ... New York, NY
Sklodowski & Franklin ... Chicago, IL
Sklodowski, Robert L. ... Chicago, IL
Sklorman, Sheryl L. ... Tampa, FL
Skloss, Ronald G. ... Austin, TX
Sklover, Alan L. ... New York, NY
Sklover, Beverly Jacks Schwarz
Washington, DC
Sklover, Himmel & Bernstein, LLP
New York, NY
Sklover, Jacob ... Penfield, NY
Sklover, Lawrence ... New York, NY
Sklover, Lori ... New York, NY
Sklover, Philip B.
Equal Employment Opportunity
Commission,
Office of the General Counsel, GV
Sklute, Jessica ... New York, NY
Skluth, Nancy ... New York, NY
Skobin, Alan Jon ... North Hills, CA
Skoblow, David V. ... New York, NY
Skocelas, Nancy G. ... Kalamazoo, MI
Skoch & Churchmack ... Cleveland, OH
Skoch, Edwin A., II ... Portland, OR
Skoch, Gerald ... Cleveland, OH
Skochdopole, James A. ... Dallas, TX
Skochdopole, Robert A. ... Omaha, NE
Skocypec, Ronald J. ... Los Angeles, CA
Skoczulek, Robert W. ... Boston, MA
Skoda, Edward F. ... Gloversville, NY
Skoda, Regina Whelan ... Marshall, TX
Skodol, C. Harold ... Pittsburgh, PA
Skoff, Abraham Y. ... Hackensack, NJ
New York, NY
Skofstad, Philip G. ... Gresham, OR
Skog, Carl ... Grosse Pointe, MI
Skog, Paul R. ... Evanston, WY
Skogen, Sandra L. ... Irving, TX
Skogen, Tony R. ... Los Angeles, CA
Skogg, Kenneth K. ... Denver, CO
Skogland, John E., Jr. ... San Antonio, TX
Skoglind, David M. ... Milwaukee, WI
Skoglund, Jeffrey M. ... Belleville, IL
Skoglund, Lawrence J. ... Minneapolis, MN
Skoglund, Patti J. ... St. Paul, MN
Skoglund, Raymond Francis ... Boston, MA
Skoglund, Rodney Lee ... Akron, OH
Skoglund, Ruth ... Allentown, PA
Skogstrom, George W., Jr. ... Braintree, MA
Skogstrom, James W. ... Springfield, OH
Skojec, Laura Gail ... Wappingers Falls, NY
Skojec, Michael W. ... Baltimore, MD
Skojec, Sheila A.
Department of Transportation,
Federal Aviation Administration, GV
Skok, Franz J. ... Westfield, NJ
New York, NY
Skok, Fred V. ... Painesville, OH
Skok, Lawrence Joseph
Gaithersburg, MD
Skok, Paul Joseph, Law Offices of
Denver, CO
Skok, Phillip P. ... Chewelah, WA
Skok, Stuart Muntzing ... Gaithersburg, MD
Skok, W. Thomas ... Costa Mesa, CA
Skokan, Dean ... Fremont, NE
Wahoo, NE
Skokos, Bequette & Billingsley, P.A.
Little Rock, AR
Skokos, Peter Z. ... Sarasota, FL

Skokos, Theodore C. ... Little Rock, AR
Skokos, Theodore C., Jr. ... Little Rock, AR
Skokoski, Frank J., Jr. ... Hazleton, PA
Skokus, George S. ... Ocean Grove, NJ
Skol, Armand G. ... Modesto, CA
Skola, Arthur H. ... San Diego, CA
Skola, Thomas J. ... Miami, FL
Skola, Winton & Larson ... San Diego, CA
Skole, Michelle ... Bensalem, PA
Skoler, Abbott & Presser, P.C.
Enfield, CT
Greenfield, MA
Northampton, MA
Pittsfield, MA
Springfield, MA
Westfield, MA
Worcester, MA
Skoler, Daniel L. ... Falls Church, VA
Skoler, Elizabeth F. ... New York, NY
Skoler, George A. ... New York, NY
Skolfield, John T., Jr. ... Winter Park, FL
Skolfield, Sheldon D. ... Portland, ME
Skoll, Gabrielle J. ... Harrisburg, PA
Skoller, Charles E. ... New York, NY
Skoller, Fran M. ... New York, NY
Skoller, Lori ... Westfield, NJ
Skoller, Richard M. ... New York, NY
Skoller, Ronald A. ... Tulsa, OK
Houston, TX
Skoller, Stephen H. ... Morristown, NJ
Skolnick, Andrew W. ... Fairfield, CT
Skolnick & Associates, P.A.
Minneapolis, MN
Skolnick, Barry G. ... Plainsboro, NJ
Skolnick, Barry S. ... Norcross, GA
Skolnick, David J. ... New Haven, CT
Skolnick, David W. ... Woodbridge, CT
Skolnick, Gerald ... New York, NY
Skolnick, Harvey M. ... Port Chester, NY
Skolnick & Hochberg, P.C. ... New York, NY
Skolnick, Holly R. ... Miami, FL
Skolnick, Howard Gerald ... Spring, TX
Skolnick, Jay M. ... Youngstown, OH
Skolnick, Jennifer ... Los Angeles, CA
Skolnick, Julie F. Rosenbaum
National Labor Relations Board,
Office of Board Members, GV
Skolnick, Kenneth A. ... Evanston, IL
Skolnick, Kerry B. ... Philadelphia, PA
Skolnick, Leslie ... New York, NY
Skolnick, Malcolm H. ... Houston, TX
Skolnick, Mark ... New York, NY
Skolnick, Michael F. ... Salt Lake City, UT
Skolnick, Richard B. ... Beverly Hills, CA
Beverly Hills, CA
Skolnick, Ross A. ... Longview, TX
Skolnick, S. Harold ... Miami, FL
Skolnick, Scott E. ... Feeding Hills, MA
Skolnick, Steven E. ... St. Paul, MN
Skolnick, Steven M. ... Roseland, NJ
Skolnick, William R. ... Minneapolis, MN
Skolnicki, Mark
Department of Transportation,
U. S. Coast Guard, GV
Skolnik, Bruce L. ... Tucson, AZ
Skolnik, Deborah R. ... New York, NY
Skolnik, Edward L. ... White Plains, NY
Skolnik, Fred S. ... East Meadow, NY
Skolnik, Gayle L. ... Indianapolis, IN
Skolnik, Kathleen L. ... Orleans, MA
Skolnik, Kenneth L. ... Chicago, IL
Skolnik, McIntyre & Tate Esquires, Ltd.
Providence, RI
Skolnik, Miriam ... New York, NY
Skolnik, Peter L. ... Roseland, NJ
Skolnik, Richard A. ... Providence, RI
Skolnik, Robert M. ... Maywood, NJ
Skolnik, Ronald B. ... Parlin, NJ
Skolnik, Steven D. ... New York, NY
Skoloff, Gary N. ... Livingston, NJ
Morristown, NJ
Skoloff & Wolfe ... Paterson, NJ
Elizabeth, NJ
Livingston, NJ
Morristown, NJ
Newark, NJ
Skolos, Mark C. ... Black River Falls, WI
Skolrood, Mark R. ... Roanoke, VA
Skolrood, Robert K. ... Roanoke, VA
Skomal, Bernard George ... San Diego, CA
Skomal, Daniel J ... St. Louis, MO
Skomba, David Arthur ... Baltimore, MD
Skomorowsky, Peter ... New York, NY
Skomp, John K. ... Phoenix, AZ
Skomski, Charles ... Monessen, PA
Skon, Linda D. ... Phoenix, AZ
Skonberg, John M. ... San Francisco, CA
Skonberg, Kurt ... New York, NY
Skonce, Ralph T., Jr. ... Cleveland, OH
Skone, Edward R. ... Bellevue, WA
Skoney, Lesa Hartley ... Nashville, TN
Skoney, Michael J. ... Buffalo, NY
Skonieczny, Conrad J. ... Waukegan, IL
Skonieczny, Stephen W. ... New York, NY
Skoning, Gerald D. ... Chicago, IL
Skonnord, Eric ... Minneapolis, MN
Skontos, George J. ... Chicago, IL
Skoog, Mark T. ... Minneapolis, MN
Skoog, Norma ... Cincinnati, OH
Skoog, Ralph E. ... Topeka, KS
Skoog, Ralph E., P.A. ... Topeka, KS
Skoog, Richard O. ... Ottawa, KS
Skoog, Richard O., P.A. ... Ottawa, KS
Skoog, Roger J. ... Washington, NJ
Skoog, William A., Jr. ... San Diego, CA
Skootsky, Seth M. ... San Francisco, CA
Skop, Charles ... New York, NY
Skopetz, Alexander ... Spring Hill, FL

Skopetz, Alexander, P.A. ... Spring Hill, FL
Skopic, Kyle Elizabeth ... Fairfax, VA
Skopil, Otto R., Jr. ... Portland, OR
Skopp, Andrew E. ... Chicago, IL
Skopp, Arnold ... Brooklyn, NY
Skopp, Fredric M. ... Miami, FL
Skoppek, Juergen O. ... Lansing, MI
Skor, Anita M. ... Mineola, NY
Skor, Douglas L. ... St. Paul, MN
Skor, Gerald L. ... Dallas, TX
Skora, Eugene J. ... Alexandria, VA
Skora, Mary Elizabeth ... Richmond, VA
Skora, Susan S. ... Grand Rapids, MI
Skorczeski, Thomas L. ... St. Paul, MN
Skord, Jennifer L. ... Durham, NC
Skordahl, Kristi L. ... Minneapolis, MN
Skordal, Lynn M. ... Seattle, WA
Skordas, Gregory G. ... Salt Lake City, UT
Skorecki, Adam S. ... Atlanta, GA
Skorepa, Thomas A. ... Rock Island, IL
Skoretz, Lenita ... San Bernardino, CA
Skorheim, James M. ... Laguna Hills, CA
Skorheim Law Office ... Great Falls, MT
Skorheim, Randall O. ... Great Falls, MT
Skoric, Bryan Alan ... Cheyenne, WY
Skorich, Dan ... DeWitt, MI
Skorich, Elaine L. ... St. Clairsville, OH
Skorin, Yurii ... Chicago, IL
Skorina, Christopher ... Columbus, OH
Skorko, John E. ... Derry, NH
Skornia Law Firm, The ... Palo Alto, CA
San Francisco, CA
San Jose, CA
Skornia, Thomas A. ... San Jose, CA
Skornicka, Carol ... Madison, WI
Skoro, Linda ... Department of Commerce,
Patent and Trademark Office, GV
Skoro, Peter ... Annandale, VA
Skoronski, Stephen M. ... Chicago, IL
Skorubskas, Rima L. ... Chicago, IL
Skorupa, Frank J. ... Columbus, NE
Skorupa, Robert John ... Boston, MA
Skorupka, Michael W. ... Indianapolis, IN
Skorzewski, Cynthia A. ... West Haven, CT
Skotnicki, Michael C. ... Birmingham, AL
Skotynsky, Walter J. ... Toledo, OH
Skoufalos, Llorca & Ziccardi, LLP
New York, NY
Skoufalos, Peter ... New York, NY
Skoufalos, Stephan ... Stamford, CT
New York, NY
Skoufatos, Nikitas ... Youngstown, OH
Skoumal, Steve M. ... Chapel Hill, NC
Skouras, George ... Astoria, NY
Skousen, John E. ... Mesa, AZ
Skousen, John K. ... Newport Beach, CA
Skousen, Judy ... Morro Bay, CA
Skousen, Kenneth E. ... San Bernardino, CA
Skousen, Michael J. ... Mesa, AZ
Skousen, Richard E. ... Mesa, AZ
Skousen, Robert J. ... Torrance, CA
Skousen & Skousen, A Law Corporation
San Bernardino, CA
Skousen, Skousen, Gulbrandsen & Patience, P.C. ... Apache Junction, AZ
Mesa, AZ
Phoenix, AZ
Skousen, Steven C. ... Scottsdale, AZ
Skousen, William J. ... Mesa, AZ
Skoutelas, John S. ... Fairless Hills, PA
Skouteris, George E. ... Memphis, TN
Skouteris, George E., Jr. ... Memphis, TN
Skouteris Law Firm ... Memphis, TN
Skouteris, Michael C. ... Memphis, TN
Skov, Peter T. ... New Orleans, LA
Skov, Steven L. ... Dallas, TX
Skove, Thomas M. ... Akron, OH
Cleveland, OH
Skover, David M. ... Tacoma, WA
Skovgaard, Barry C. ... New York, NY
Skovgaard, Robert A. ... Stamford, CT
Skovholt, Nancy J. ... San Diego, CA
Skovron, Jeffrey L. ... Boulder, CO
Skovron, Jeffrey L., P.C. ... Boulder, CO
Skovron, Stephen E. ... Philadelphia, PA
Skovronski, Annette Nicki
San Francisco, CA
Skow, Ardell W. ... Baldwin, WI
Skow, Charles A. ... Chico, CA
Skow, Cynthia A.
Department Of Veterans Affairs,
Board of Veterans Appeals, GV
Skow, J. Wesley ... San Francisco, CA
Skow, James D. ... Sacramento, CA
Skow, Jon B. ... Racine, WI
Skow, William J. ... Toledo, OH
Skowron, David R. ... Chicago, IL
Skowronek, Andrew Dieter
Washington, DC
Skowronek, John C. ... Minot, ND
Skowronek, Kenneth J. ... Flemington, NJ
Skowronski, Eugene A. ... Derby, CT
Skowronski, John P. ... Palo Alto, CA
Skowronski, Joseph P., Jr. ... Danville, IL
Skowronski & Skowronski ... Derby, CT
Skowronski, Theodore E. ... Derby, CT
Skowronski, Thomas E. ... Fort Wayne, IN
Skoy, Robert I. ... Freeport, NY
Skoy, Robert I., P.C. ... Freeport, NY
Skoyles, Karen ... Detroit Lakes, MN
Skozen, Joseph L. ... Merrillville, IN
Skozen, Joseph M. ... Merrillville, IN
Skrabak, Carol Kelly ... McLean, VA
Skrabec, David J. ... Chardon, OH
Skrainka, Stephen W. ... St. Louis, MO
Skrak, Ellen T. ... Albuquerque, NM
Skramstad, Robert C. ... Detroit, MI
Skrandel, Jerome F. ... North Palm Beach, FL

Skrandel, John Joseph Robert
North Palm Beach, FL
Skrapits, Frank M. ... Northampton, PA
Skrapits, Juliana ... Allentown, PA
Skrasek, Ada Marie ... Fort Worth, TX
Skrede, Stephanie M. ... Florham Park, NJ
Skreen, Janet L. ... Port Orchard, WA
Skrel, Vicki Heltman ... Chicago, IL
Skrenes, Ronald T. ... Stevens Point, WI
Skrentny, Stanley T. ... Highland, IN
Skretny, William M. ... Buffalo, NY
Skrha, Joseph Raymond, Law Offices of
Kenai, AK
Skrhak, John M., Jr. ... Dallas, TX
Skrief, Charles W. ... St. Paul, MN
Skrien, Michael Allen ... Kennett, MO
Skrine, Bruce E. ... Boston, MA
Skrip, Daniel G. ... Boston, MA
Skripek, Jean E. ... San Diego, CA
Skripek, Joseph P. ... Fairfield, NJ
Skripko, Robert W., Jr. ... Santa Ana, CA
Skripol, Paul G. ... Unionville, CT
Skrivan, Kent A. ... Naples, FL
Skrivanek, Joseph J., III ... Caldwell, TX
Skrivanek, Robert A., Jr. ... Boston, MA
Skrivanek, Stephen G. ... Des Moines, IA
Skrivanie, Oliver T. ... Two Rivers, WI
Skroback, Andrew Evans ... New York, NY
Skrobarcek, James A. ... Corpus Christi, TX
Skrobot, David A. ... Columbus, OH
Skrobot, Pope, Levy & Fisher, LLP
Columbus, OH
Westerville, OH
Skrocki, Anthony M. ... Sacramento, CA
Skrocki, John M. ... Philadelphia, PA
Skrod, Walter F. ... Paramus, NJ
Skrodzki, Richard J. ... Summit, IL
Skropits, Amy E. ... Bucyrus, OH
Skrupa, Rosemary M. ... Omaha, NE
Skryd, David A. ... North Riverside, IL
Skryd, Joseph G. ... Wheaton, IL
Skryd, Paul J. ... North Riverside, IL
Skrypak, John K. ... New York, NY
Skrypak, Karl T. ... Pittsburgh, PA
Skrzat, Stephen M. ... Montgomeryville, PA
Skrzyniarz, William J., Law Offices of
Beverly Hills, CA
Skrzynski, Carl E. ... Birmingham, MI
Skrzynski, John M. ... Pontiac, MI
Skrzypczak, Julie A. ... Tulsa, OK
Skrzypczak, Robert C. ... Weehawken, NJ
Skrzypek, Josef W. ... Springfield, MA
Skube, John C. ... La Mesa, CA
Skubecz, Ronald H. ... Harrisburg, PA
Skubel, Marimichael O.
Federal Trade Commission,
Bureau of Competition, GV
Skubel, Stephen C. ... Department of Energy,
Office of the General Counsel, GV
Skubik, Daniel Walter ... Riverside, CA
Skubik, Jacqueline M. ... Islandia, NY
Skubis, Stanley J. ... Clifton Park, NY
Skubisz, Gregory R. ... Calumet City, IL
Skubisz, Gregory R. ... Joliet, IL
Skubitz, Dan J. ... Wichita, KS
Skubitz, John M. ... Le Sueur, MN
Skucas, Alexas D. ... New York, NY
Skucas, Ruta Kalvaitis
Federal Energy Regulatory Commission,
Office of the Administrative Law Judges, GV
Skudlarek, Joseph J. ... Omaha, NE
Skudlarek, Stephen J. (Jack), Jr.
Milford, CT
Skudstad, Michael S. ... Crescent City, CA
Skufca, Christopher J. ... Cincinnati, OH
Skufca, Ronald A. ... Charlotte, NC
Skula, Emil R. ... New Brunswick, NJ
Skulina, Michael S. ... Findlay, OH
Skulina, Thomas R. ... Cleveland, OH
Skulina, Thomas R. ... Westlake, OH
Skullerud, Jerry ... San Diego, CA
Skulley, Brooke E. ... Worcester, MA
Skulnik, Steven ... New York, NY
Skulski, Brooke ... New York, NY
Skulsky, Sabina L. ... Los Angeles, CA
Skultety, Alice H. ... Lincoln, NE
Skumanich, Nonna ... Durham, NC
Skupa, William S. ... Las Vegas, NV
Skupa, William S., Esq., P.C.
Las Vegas, NV
Skupien, Geraldine S. ... Pittsburgh, PA
Skupin, Charles G. ... Detroit, MI
Skupniewitz, Joseph W. ... Madison, WI
Skupnik, George J., Jr. ... St. Louis, MO
Skupp, Alan R. ... New York, NY
Skuras, G. Deno ... Clinton Township, MI
Skuret, Daniel D. ... Ansonia, CT
Skuris, Stephen J. ... San Diego, CA
Skurka, Larry ... Boca Raton, FL
Skurka, Mark ... Corpus Christi, TX
Skurman, Paul S. ... New York, NY
Skurnick, Benjamin D. ... New York, NY
Skurnik, Linda ... East Meadow, NY
Skuros, George J. ... Chicago, IL
Skuster, William D. ... Des Plaines, IL
Skutnik, Bolesh J. ... East Longmeadow, MA
Skutnik, Carol M. ... Cleveland, OH
Skvarla, John E., III ... Hillsborough, NC
Skvir, Natalea ... Needham, MA
Skvirsky, Leonard R. ... Springfield, MA
Skwarcan, Shelly M. ... Indianapolis, IN
Skwarek & Associates ... Oakbrook Terrace, IL
Skwarek, Wayne M. ... Oakbrook Terrace, IL
Skwierawski, Audrey ... Washington, DC
Skwierawski, Michael J. ... Milwaukee, WI
Skwierawski, Paul J. ... Arlington, VA
Skwiertz, Albert A., Jr. ... New York, NY
Sky, Mary G. ... Oakland, CA

Sky, Theodore ...Department of Education, Office of the General Counsel, GV
Skydel, Elliot ...Lake Success, NY
Skydell, Norman B. ...New York, NY
Skye, John J. ...Tampa, FL
Skye, William C. ...Bridgeton, NJ
Skyer, David C. ...San Diego, CA
Skyer, Regina Pagirsky ...Forest Hills, NY
Skyers, Eroll V. ...Bridgeport, CT
Skyers, Sharon A. ...Bridgeport, CT
Skyers & Skyers, P.C. ...Bridgeport, CT
Skyler, Nelson D. ...Houston, TX
Skyles, Ada ...Chicago, IL
Skypakewych, Roman A. ...Warren, MI
Skypala, Danielle J. ...Cherry Hill, NJ
Skypala, Edward A. ...Pottstown, PA
Skypeck, Don D. ...Phoenix, AZ
Skytte, Eric J. ...Minneapolis, MN
Slaatten, Marilyn J. ...Hawthorne, NY
Slabach, Frederick G. ...Costa Mesa, CA
Slabach, Marjorie A. ...Santa Rosa, CA
Slabach, Stephen H., Law Offices of San Mateo, CA
Slabaugh, Julie ...Ely, NV
Slabaugh, Susan K. ...Akron, OH
Slabaugh, William F. ...Akron, OH
Slabey, Vernon A. ...Wooster, OH
Slabouz, Timothy James ...Columbia, SC
Slaby, Andrew F. ...Brookfield, WI
Slaby, David M. ...Nevada, MO
Slaby, David W. ...Menlo Park, CA
Slaby, Deda, Marshall, Reinhard & Fuhr LLP ...Park Falls, WI
Phillips, WI
Slaby, James J., Jr. ...Los Angeles, CA
Slaby, John W. ...Phillips, WI
Slaby, Lynn C. ...Akron, OH
Slaby, Richard A. ...Augusta, GA
Slaby, Robert P. ...Crofton, MD
Slachetka, Joseph J. ...Franklinville, NJ
Slachter, David ...Miami Lakes, FL
Slack, Chad M. ...Santa Barbara, CA
Slack, Chandra K. ...Concord, CA
Slack, Charlotte T. ...Pecos, TX
Slack, Charmaine L. ...Atlanta, GA
Slack, Cynthia A. ...Fairlawn, OH
Slack, Dan M. ...Champaign, IL
Slack & Davis, L.L.P. ...Austin, TX
Slack, Edmund J. ...Madison, WI
Slack, Eric W. ...Toledo, OH
Slack, Harry A., Jr. ...Coquille, OR
Slack, James P. ...Santa Ana, CA
Slack, Jeffrey Scott ...St. Paul, MN
Slack, John D. ...Arlington, TX
Slack, John M., III ...Charleston, WV
Slack, K. Thomas ...Phoenix, AZ
Slack, Kenneth M. ...Bellaire, TX
Slack, Kenneth R. ...Madison, WI
Slack, Mark A. ...Naples, FL
Slack, Mark R. ...Salem, OH
Slack, Michael L. ...Austin, TX
Slack, Michelle R. ...Department of Justice, Civil Division, GV
Slack, Richard W. ...New York, NY
Slack, Robert L. ...Fairmont, WV
Slack, Slack and Stone ...Coquille, OR
Slack, Sue Barrett ...Miami, FL
Slack, Terri Tribble ...Oak Ridge, TN
Slack, Thomas H. ...Overland Park, KS
Slack, Thomas H. ...Kansas City, MO
Slack, Todd R. ...New Orleans, LA
Slack, William E., Jr. ...Philadelphia, PA
Slack, William P. ...La Fayette, GA
Slack, William P., P.C. ...La Fayette, GA
Slacter, David A. ...Bethesda, MD
Sladczyk, George, Jr. ...Beaumont, TX
Slade, Andrea Y. ...Los Angeles, CA
Slade, Arthur R. ...St. Petersburg, FL
Slade & Associates, P.C. ...New York, NY
Slade, Charles Kenneth, Jr. ...Fairhope, AL
Slade, Charles M., Jr. ...Rich Square, NC
Slade, Charles R., Jr. ...Columbia, MD
Slade, Christy Gherlein ...Washington, DC
Slade, David ...Middleton, MA
Slade, David R. (IBA) ...New York, NY
Slade, Douglas D. ...Rome, GA
Slade, Edwin W. ...Doylestown, PA
Slade, Elizabeth Ohman ...New York, NY
Slade, Elliott K., Jr. ...Dennis, MA
Slade, Eugene E. ...Deerfield, IL
Slade, George B. ...Austin, TX
Slade, George H. ...Greenville, MS
Slade, George K., Jr. ...Vineland, NJ
Slade, Georgiana J. ...New York, NY
Slade, Gordon W., Jr. ...San Antonio, TX
Slade, H. Geoffrey, Sr. ...Fayetteville, GA
Slade, Herbert T. ...Camillus, NY
Slade, Ira L. ...New York, NY
Slade, Jeffrey C. ...New York, NY
Slade, Jodi Beth ...Great Neck, NY
Slade, John F., III ...Leonardtown, MD
Slade, Ken Russell ...Wakefield, RI
Slade, Kenneth H. ...Washington, DC
Boston, MA
Slade, L. Keith ...Houston, TX
Slade, Lynn H. ...Albuquerque, NM
Slade, Melvin S. ...New York, NY
Slade, Michael G. ...Minneapolis, MN
Slade, Paul H. ...Bolton, MA
Slade, Robert E. ...Beverly Hills, CA
Slade, Sam Mitchell, Jr. ...Spartanburg, SC
Slade, Shelley R. ...Department of Justice, Civil Division, GV
Slade, Sondra K. ...Berwyn, PA
Slade, Thomas B., III ...Jacksonville, FL
Slade, Thomas E. ...Rockville Centre, NY
Slade, William E. ...Washington, DC
Sladek, Bradley ...Grand Rapids, MI
Sladek, Dennis J. ...Colorado Springs, CO
Sladek, John R. ...Iowa City, IA
Sladek, Maureen ...Armonk, NY
Sladek, William L. ...Dallas, TX
Slader, David L. ...Portland, OR
Sladic, Allyson Martin ...Richmond, VA
Sladic, David F. ...Houston, TX
Sladic, Nicholas G. ...Richmond, VA
Sladkin, Colleen Lin ...Washington, DC
Sladkus, Harvey I. ...New York, NY
Sladkus, Jeffrey B. ...Atlanta, GA
Sladkus, Steven D. ...River Edge, NJ
New York, NY
Sladnick, Clifford M. ...Chicago, IL
Sladoje, Douglas ...Westerville, OH
Sladoje, Mark, Jr. ...Columbus, OH
Sladon, Ronald B. ...Winchester, KY
Slaff, Sara ...Baltimore, MD
Slaff, Susan M. ...Newark, NJ
Slafsky, John L. ...Palo Alto, CA
Slaga, Julie E. ...Houston, TX
Slaga, Sandra J. ...Rockford, IL
Slagel, Allan T. ...Chicago, IL
Slagel, Steven L. ...Bartlesville, OK
Slager, Jennifer L. ...Stamford, CT
Slager, Lynne E. ...Jackson, MI
Slager, Paul A. ...Stamford, CT
Slager, Susan E. ...Sacramento, CA
Slagg, H. Keith ...Rome, GA
Slagg, Stanley D. ...Kansas City, MO
Slaggie, E. Leo
Nuclear Regulatory Commission, Office of the General Counsel, GV
Slagh, Jonathan W. ...Cassopolis, MI
Slaght, William W. ...Clearwater, FL
Slagle, Barry C. ...Milwaukee, WI
Slagle, Bernard & Gorman, A Professional Corporation ...Kansas City, MO
Slagle, Beth Ann ...Pittsburgh, PA
Slagle, David W. ...Salt Lake City, UT
Slagle & Gist
Hot Springs National Park, AR
Slagle, Jack A. ...Muncie, IN
Slagle, James William ...Marion, OH
Slagle, Jefferson B. ...Norcross, GA
Slagle, Jeffrey J. ...Falls City, NE
Slagle, Jim ...Marion, OH
Slagle, John H. ...Kansas City, MO
Slagle, John W. ...Dayton, OH
Slagle, Kendra Sexton ...Alabaster, AL
Slagle, L. Orin, Jr. ...Tallahassee, FL
Slagle, Larry V. ...Massillon, OH
Slagle, L. B. ...Santa Anna, TX
Slagle, Mark D. ...Johnson City, TN
Slagle, Michael A. ...Terre Haute, IN
Slagle Morgan & Ellsworth, LLP
Seattle, WA
Slagle, R. C., III ...Sherman, TX
Slagle & Rhodes
Hot Springs National Park, AR
Slagle, Richard J. ...Greenwich, CT
Slagle, Richard L.
Hot Springs National Park, AR
Slagle, Richard M. ...Seattle, WA
Slagle, Stephany Rush
Hot Springs National Park, AR
Slagle, Susan ...Jacksonville, FL
Slagle, Susan, P.A. ...Jacksonville, FL
Slagle, Thomas D. ...Norway, MI
Slagle, Thomas J. ...Juneau, AK
Slagle, Thomas J. ...Knoxville, TN
Slagter, John P. ...Cleveland, OH
Slahor, Stephenie ...Palm Springs, CA
Slaiby, Samuel E. ...Torrington, CT
Slaight, Joanne D. ...Washington, DC
Slaikeu, Diane W. ...Austin, TX
Slaiman, Gary D. ...Washington, DC
Slain, John J. ...New York, NY
Slajchert, Michael C. ...Chicago, IL
Slak, Frank V., Jr. ...Spokane, WA
Slak, Milan D. ...Nashville, TN
Slakas, Kevin D. ...New York, NY
Slakey, Monica M. ...San Francisco, CA
Slakter, Jeffrey D. ...Dallas, TX
Slama, Jo Lynn ...Oklahoma City, OK
Slama, Joseph J. (IBA)
Fort Lauderdale, FL
Slama, Mark A. ...New Brunswick, NJ
New York, NY
Slama, Richard C., Jr. ...Media, PA
Slama, Robert J. ...Jacksonville, FL
Slama, Robert J., P.A. ...Jacksonville, FL
Slamar, Charles, Jr. ...Chicago, IL
Slamar, Paul T. ...Chicago, IL
Slameka, Robert E. ...Detroit, MI
Slamkowski, William T. ...Denver, CO
Slamowitz, Mitchell G. ...Syosset, NY
Slamowitz, Todd R. ...Washington, DC
Slanda, Scott R. ...Orlando, FL
Slane, Charles D. ...Minneapolis, MN
Slane, Charles J. ...Harrisburg, PA
Slane, Cindy R. ...Hamden, CT
Slane, Harold ...Sedona, AZ
Slane, John F., Jr. ...Greenwich, CT
Slanec, Darra Ososki ...Detroit, MI
Slanec, Darra Ososki ...Mount Clemens, MI
Slaney, Mary Jo M. ...McLean, VA
Slaney, Michael A. ...Dallas, TX
Slaney, Paul H. ...New York, NY
Slaney, Richard E. ...Richmond, VA
Slania, Michael A. ...Tucson, AZ
Slanina, Charles ...Wilmington, DE
Slaninger, Frank P. ...Denver, CO
Slank, Eileen J. ...Ann Arbor, MI
Slank, Noreen L. ...Southfield, MI
Slankard, Kenton G. ...Springfield, MO
Slanker, Barbara Olsen ...Champaign, IL
Slanover, Russell C. ...New York, NY
Slansky, David L. ...Portland, OR
Slansky, Douglas A. ...Naperville, IL
Slap, Albert J. ...Plymouth Meeting, PA
Slap, Leonard Q. ...Boston, MA
Slape, Dale V. ...Wichita, KS
Slape, Erin C. ...Los Angeles, CA
Slape & Howard, Chtd. ...Wichita, KS
Slape, Phillip Bradley ...Wichita, KS
Slappey, E. Scott ...Atlanta, GA
Slappey & Sadd ...Atlanta, GA
Slasinski-Griem, Carolyn ...Detroit, MI
Slason, Lawrence G. ...Bellows Falls, VT
Slasor, Susan ...Flagstaff, AZ
Slass, Larry H. ...Philadelphia, PA
Slatas, Reed A. ...Hartford, CT
Slate, Cook & Waters ...Decatur, AL
Slate, Daniel H. ...Los Angeles, CA
Slate, David L. ...Palo Alto, CA
Slate, H. L. (Buddy) ...Little Rock, AR
Slate, Ilene R. ...Chicago, IL
Slate, Irvin C., Jr. ...Granite City, IL
Slate, James R. ...Richmond, VA
Slate, Jerold S. ...Poughkeepsie, NY
Slate, Joseph E., Jr. ...Cary, NC
Slate and Leoni, A Professional Corporation
Long Beach, CA
Los Angeles, CA
Van Nuys, CA
Slate, Mary Beth ...Montgomery, AL
Slate, Pamela Beard ...Birmingham, AL
Slate, Peter J. ...Chicago, IL
Slate, Ralph E. ...Decatur, AL
Slate, Rex W. ...Birmingham, AL
Slate, Rudolph W. ...Tupelo, MS
Slate, Scott Alan ...Decatur, AL
Slate, William ...Markesan, WI
Slate, William B. ...New Haven, CT
Slate-Cook, Cynthia R. ...Decatur, AL
Slaten, Clifton E. ...Montgomery, AL
Slaten, D. Reed ...Anchorage, AK
Slater, Adam M. ...Livingston, NJ
Slater, Albert H., III ...Greensburg, PA
Slater, Alice J. ...New York, NY
Slater, Allen R. ...Kansas City, MO
Slater, Alvin J. ...Boston, MA
Slater, Amy E. ...Philadelphia, PA
Slater, Andrew R. ...West Palm Beach, FL
Slater, Angela D. ...Newark, NJ
Slater, Anne C. ...Belvedere-Tiburon, CA
Slater & Associates, P.C. ...Gilbert, AZ
Slater, Barbara B. ...Providence, RI
Slater, Benjamin R., III ...New Orleans, LA
Slater, Benjamin R., Jr. ...New Orleans, LA
Slater, Bill J. ...Pana, IL
Slater, Brent R. ...Bangor, ME
Slater, Brian V. ...New York, NY
Slater, Bruce H. ...Mineola, NY
Slater, Calvin A. ...Pasadena, CA
Slater, Carole S., The Law Office of
New York, NY
Slater, Charles E. ...Tallahassee, FL
Slater, Chris D. ...Muskegon, MI
Slater, Claude K. ...Jacksonville, FL
Slater and Cole, P.C. ...New York, NY
Slater, Craig A. ...Buffalo, NY
Slater, Dan ...Costa Mesa, CA
Slater, Daniel B. ...Canon City, CO
Slater, Darin ...Mt. Pleasant, IA
Slater, David B. ...Needham, MA
Slater, David M. ...New York, NY
Slater, David P. ...New York, NY
Slater, David W. ...Pana, IL
Slater, Deborah R. ...Hartford, CT
Slater, Debra ...San Francisco, CA
Slater, Debra A. ...Milwaukee, WI
Slater, Doris Hale ...Pleasanton, CA
Slater, Ferdinand A. ...Hancock, ME
Slater, Gary E. ...San Diego, CA
Slater, Gary M. ...Los Angeles, CA
Slater, Gary R. W. ...Federal Way, WA
Slater, Gerald R. ...Mendota Heights, MN
Slater, Herbert J. ...Boca Raton, FL
Slater, Howard L. ...Hartford, CT
Slater, Ilene J. ...New York, NY
Slater, J. Timothy ...Bellingham, WA
Slater, James E. ...Sarasota, FL
Slater, James E., (P.A.) ...Orlando, FL
Slater, James Lawrence ...Palm Harbor, FL
Slater, James M. ...Santa Barbara, CA
Slater, James S. ...North Bergen, NJ
Slater, James W. ...Akron, OH
Slater, Jeffery S. ...Scottsdale, AZ
Slater, Jeffrey G. ...Orlando, FL
Slater, Jeffrey M. ...Woodland Hills, CA
Slater, Jerry ...New York, NY
Slater, Jerry W. ...Wausau, WI
Slater, John, III ...Chicago, IL
Slater, John J., III ...Boston, MA
Slater, John M. ...Tulsa, OK
Slater, John R. ...Cleveland, OH
North Canton, OH
Slater, John T. ...Bellingham, WA
Slater, John W., Jr. ...Memphis, TN
Slater, Joseph E. ...Washington, DC
Slater, Joseph M., Law Office of
Melville, NY
Slater, Kenneth R., Jr. ...New Britain, CT
Slater, Kent ...Macomb, IL
Slater, King and Gross ...Atlanta, GA
Slater Law Firm, A Professional Corporation
New Orleans, LA
Slater, Lawrence B. ...Gilbert, AZ
Slater, Lawrence M. ...Salem, MA
Slater, Lee ...Oklahoma City, OK
Slater, Leslie E. ...Powell, OH
Slater, Lindsay Jay ...Medford, OR
Slater, Lourdes M. ...New York, NY
Slater, Mandel E. ...Randolph, MA
Slater, Marc B. ...Marlton, NJ
Slater, Marcus B., Jr. ...Washington, DC
Slater, Mark K. ...San Francisco, CA
Slater, Martin R. ...Los Angeles, CA
Slater, Matthew D. ...Washington, DC
Slater, Michael P. ...Fresno, CA
Slater, Michael W. ...Lakewood, OH
Slater, Mildred Fletcher ...Middleburg, VA
Slater, Mildred Fletcher ...Upperville, VA
Slater, Nanci ...Brooklyn, NY
Slater, Nanci M. ...Brooklyn, NY
Slater, Pamela B. ...Telluride, CO
Slater, Patricia Kennedy ...Indianapolis, IN
Slater, Paul D. ...Woodland Hills, CA
Slater, Paul E. ...Chicago, IL
Slater, Paul F. ...New York, NY
Slater, Peggy H. ...Chicago, IL
Slater, Peter M. ...Cleveland, OH
Slater, Peter O. ...Sacramento, CA
Slater, Phyllis ...Tallahassee, FL
Slater, R. Winston ...Algonquin, IL
Slater, Ralph D. ...Santa Monica, CA
Slater, Ralph E. ...Wilton, CT
Slater, Randy Scott ...Atlanta, GA
Slater, Richard C. ...Cheyenne, WY
Slater, Richard N. ...New York, NY
Slater, Richard V. ...Jamestown, NY
Slater, R. J. ...St. Louis, MO
Slater, Robert C. ...Schaumburg, IL
Slater, Robert I. ...Los Angeles, CA
Slater, Robert L. ...New York, NY
Slater, Rochelle Price ...Chicago, IL
Slater, Ronald L. ...Erie, PA
Slater, Scott S. ...San Diego, CA
Santa Barbara, CA
Slater & Sgarlato, P.C. ...Brooklyn, NY
Staten Island, NY
Slater & Shub, P.A. ...Salem, MA
Slater & Slater ...Bellingham, WA
Slater, Stacey B. ...New York, NY
Slater, Stacey C. ...Portland, OR
Slater, Stephen H. ...New City, NY
Slater, Steven H. ...Dallas, TX
Slater, Terry D. ...Grand Junction, CO
Slater, Thomas F. ...Jacksonville, FL
Slater, Thomas G. ...Frederick, MD
Slater, Thomas G., Jr. ...Richmond, VA
Slater, Thomas P. ...Des Moines, IA
Slater, Thomas S. ...Des Moines, IA
Slater, Timothy T. ...Madison, NJ
Slater, Valerie A. ...Washington, DC
Slater, Vanderpool & Breakstone
Melville, NY
Slater, Whedon ...Longboat Key, FL
Slater, William A. ...Stamford, CT
Slater & Young, P.A. ...Palm Harbor, FL
Slater & Zeien, L.L.P. ...Washington, DC
Slater & Zurz ...Akron, OH
Slater-Jansen, Susan B. ...New York, NY
Slatery, Herbert H., III ...Knoxville, TN
Slates, John William, III ...Dallas, TX
Slates, Michael D. ...Rockford, IL
Slates, Roger ...Huntington Beach, CA
Slates, Ronald P. ...Los Angeles, CA
Slates, Ronald P., P.C. ...Los Angeles, CA
Slates, Sue Ann ...Department of Justice, Executive Office for United States Trustees, GV
Slatin, Carol M. ...San Francisco, CA
Slatinshek, Frank M. ...Alexandria, VA
Slatkin, Avrin ...Tenafly, NJ
Slatkin, Jason E. ...Coral Springs, FL
Slatkin, Murray ...Stevenson, MD
Slatkin, Russell S. ...Southfield, MI
Slatkin, Sander Jay ...Denver, CO
Slatkin, Sheldon Theodore
Coral Springs, FL
Slatkin & Slatkin, Chartered
Coral Springs, FL
Fort Lauderdale, FL
Slatkin, Stephanie C. ...Chicago, IL
Slatkin, Stewart ...Southfield, MI
Slatkin, Walter ...Denver, CO
Slatkow, Steve A. ...Pacific Grove, CA
Slatky, Glenn J. ...Kewaunee, WI
Slatky, Wolske & Mehn ...Kewaunee, WI
Slatoff, Robert Todd ...Fort Lauderdale, FL
Slaton, Curtis F. ...Dayton, OH
Slaton, D. David ...Little Rock, AR
Slaton, Harrison A. ...Maplewood, NJ
Slaton, J. Paul ...Lexington, KY
Slaton, James E. ...Augusta, GA
Slaton, Jeffrey B. ...Sacramento, CA
Slaton, Juliette Robinson ...Los Angeles, CA
Slaton, Lewis R. ...Atlanta, GA
Slaton, Loretta N. ...Chatsworth, CA
Slaton, Melanie V. ...Los Angeles, CA
Slaton, Melissa J. ...Vero Beach, FL
Slaton, Nicole E. Dale ...Sacramento, CA
Slaton, Randolph R. ...Honolulu, HI
Slaton, Sandra Lynn ...Phoenix, AZ
Slaton, Susan Y. ...Boca Raton, FL
Slatt, Abner P. ...New York, NY
Slatt & Lane ...New York, NY
Slatten, James E., III ...Lafayette, LA
Slatten, Robert E. ...San Diego, CA
Slatten, S. Christopher ...Shreveport, LA
Slattengren, Linn A. ...Center City, MN
Slatter, Jason B. ...Salt Lake City, UT
Slatter, Lindsay Kohut ...Santa Cruz, CA
Slattery, Alan D. ...Lincoln, NE
Slattery, Brian J. ...Short Hills, NJ
Slattery, Christine Kentopp ...Chicago, IL
Slattery, Daniel B. ...Denver, CO
Slattery, Daniel J. ...Chicago, IL
Slattery, Daniel J. ...South Bend, IN
Slattery, Daniel J., Jr. ...Department of Labor, Office of Secretary, GV

Slattery, Dennis D. ....Pasadena, CA
Slattery, E. Michael, III ....Plattsmouth, NE
Slattery, Eve ....Boston, MA
Slattery, Francis J. ....Oshkosh, WI
Slattery, Frank P. ....Santa Clara, CA
Slattery, Gerald F., Jr. ....New Orleans, LA
Slattery, Geraldine S. ....Atlanta, GA
Slattery & Hausman, Ltd. ....Waukesha, WI
Slattery, Helen M. ....Tequesta, FL
Slattery, James J., Jr. ....Cincinnati, OH
Slattery, James L. ....Largo, FL
Slattery, James M. ....Falls Church, VA
Slattery, James P. ....Brooklyn, NY
Slattery, Jeanette N. ....Treasury Department, Bureau of Alcohol, Tobacco and Firearms, GV
Slattery, Jeffrey D. ....Kansas City, MO
Slattery & Jespersen, A Professional Corporation ....Short Hills, NJ
Slattery, Jill S. ....Verona, NJ
Slattery, Jim ....Washington, DC
Slattery, John ....Elk Point, SD
Slattery, John B., Jr. ....Springhill, LA
Slattery, Kerrin Brennan ....Chicago, IL
Slattery, Lawrence J. ....New York, NY
Slattery, Lisa J. ....Mentor, OH
Slattery, Lisa J., Co., L.P.A. ....Mentor, OH
Slattery, Mary Ann ....Kansas City, KS
Slattery, Mary F. ....Department of Defense, Defense Legal Services Agency, GV
Slattery, Mary H. ....Brookfield, WI
Slattery, Michael K. ....Costa Mesa, CA
Slattery, Michael Robert ....Baltimore, MD
Slattery, R. Timothy ....Wilmington, DE
Slattery & Rawson, P.C.
Overland Park, KS
Kansas City, MO
Slattery, Raymond J., III ....Westlake, OH
Slattery, Richard G. ....Washington, DC
Slattery, Robert A. ....Waukesha, WI
Slattery, Robert K. ....Freeport, IL
Slattery, Robert M. ....Walnut Creek, CA
Slattery, Robert V., Jr. ....Los Angeles, CA
Slattery, Scott E. ....Milwaukee, WI
Slattery, Shannon E. ....Phoenix, AZ
Slattery, Thomas K. ....Washington, DC
Slattery, Timothy J. ....Manhasset, NY
Slattery, William C. ....Short Hills, NJ
Slattery, William H. ....New York, NY
Slattery, William P. ....Santa Fe, NM
Slatton, Christina M. ....Los Angeles, CA
Slattum, Kevin J. ....Los Angeles, CA
Slatus, Robert E. ....New York, NY
Slatz, Daniel J. ....New York, NY
Slaugh, Leslie W. ....Provo, UT
Slaughter, Alan L. ....Payson, AZ
Slaughter, Alexander H. ....Richmond, VA
Slaughter, Alicia A. ....Frisco, TX
Slaughter, Anne-Marie ....Cambridge, MA
Slaughter, Beverly Jo ....New York, NY
Slaughter, Christopher L.
Charleston, WV
Slaughter, D. French, III
Charlottesville, VA
Slaughter, Daniel K. ....San Francisco, CA
Slaughter, David B. ....Orlando, FL
Slaughter, David B., Law Offices of
Orlando, FL
Slaughter, David W. ....Salt Lake City, UT
Slaughter, Donald B. ....Des Moines, WA
Slaughter, Donald E. ....Corona Del Mar, CA
Slaughter, Donald O. ....Omaha, NE
Slaughter, Edward, Jr. ....Princeton, NJ
Slaughter, Edward M. ....Arkadelphia, AR
Slaughter, Edward R., Jr.
Charlottesville, VA
Slaughter, Frank L. ....Bristol, TN
Slaughter, Frank L., Jr. ....Bristol, TN
Slaughter, Fred L. ....Santa Monica, CA
Slaughter, Gail E. ....Morristown, NJ
Slaughter, H. Craig ....Charleston, WV
Slaughter, Harold M. ....Dallas, TX
Slaughter, Harrison T., Jr. ....Orlando, FL
Slaughter, J. Melanie ....Gainesville, FL
Slaughter, James B. ....Washington, DC
Slaughter, James C. ....Houston, TX
Slaughter, James H. ....Greensboro, NC
Slaughter, Jeffrey R. ....Indianapolis, IN
Slaughter, Jennifer C. ....Charlottesville, VA
Slaughter, John E., Jr. ....Clearwater, FL
Slaughter, John Edward, III
Charlottesville, VA
Slaughter, Katherine E. ....Charlottesville, VA
Slaughter, Kenneth S. ....Washington, DC
Slaughter, Kevin E. ....Chicago, IL
Slaughter, Kristi A. ....Houston, TX
Slaughter, L. Charles ....Amarillo, TX
Slaughter, L. Walter ....Falls Church, VA
Slaughter, Leigh ....
Department of Energy, GV
Slaughter, Logan A. ....Houston, TX
Slaughter, M. Brian ....Birmingham, AL
Slaughter, M. Bryan ....Charlottesville, VA
Richmond, VA
Slaughter, Malcolm E. ....Anaheim, CA
Slaughter, Marjorie P. ....Birmingham, AL
Slaughter, Mark E. ....Virginia Beach, VA
Slaughter, Marshall G. ....Lake Alfred, FL
Slaughter and May ....New York, NY
Slaughter, Melanie Ann ....New York, NY
Slaughter, Michael G. ....East Lansing, MI
Slaughter, Milton Lawrenc ....Brooklyn, NY
Slaughter, Molly E. ....Rapid City, SD
Slaughter, Nathaniel G., III ....Atlanta, GA
Slaughter, Nicole B. ....Wilmington, NC
Slaughter, Percy C. ....Palos Heights, IL
Slaughter, Peter D. ....Santa Barbara, CA
Slaughter, R. James ....San Francisco, CA
Slaughter, Raymond T. ....Denver, CO
Slaughter, Robert C., III ....Wilmington, NC
Slaughter, Robert L. ....Albemarle, NC
Slaughter, Robert L., III ....Los Angeles, CA
Slaughter, Robert L., Jr. ....San Diego, CA
Slaughter, Robert Z. ....Troy, MI
Slaughter, Ruth N. ....Washington, DC
Slaughter & Slaughter ....Corona Del Mar, CA
Slaughter & Slaughter ....Bristol, TN
Slaughter, Thomas ....Knoxville, TN
Slaughter, Thomas L. ....Des Moines, IA
Slaughter, Thos. A., Jr. ....Atlanta, GA
Slaughter, Todd E. ....Redding, CA
Slaughter, Vernon L. ....Atlanta, GA
Slaughter & Virgin, P.C. ....Atlanta, GA
Slaughter, W. James ....Corona Del Mar, CA
Slaughter, Wayne B., Jr. ....Boise, ID
Slaughter, Wayne B., Jr. ....Houston, TX
Slaughter, William A. ....Philadelphia, PA
Slaughter, William H., III ....Metairie, LA
Slaughter, William L. ....Columbus, GA
Slaughter, William M. ....Birmingham, AL
Slaughter, William M. ....Ventura, CA
Slaughter, William N. ....Athens, GA
Slaughter, Wm. V. ....Richmond, VA
Slaughter-Bormann, Ovette
Los Angeles, CA
Slauson, Gale W. ....Victorville, CA
Slauson, John G. ....Cincinnati, OH
Slaven, James J. ....Brea, CA
Slaven, Matthew A. ....St. Paul, MN
Slaven, Robert Michael ....Louisville, KY
Slaven, Terrence M. ....Phoenix, AZ
Slavens, Bob J. ....Davenport, IA
Slavens, James E. ....Bettendorf, IA
Slavens, James K. ....Fillmore, UT
Slavens, Joe B. ....Davenport, IA
Slavens, John M. ....Dayton, OH
Slavens, John S. ....Fort Myers Beach, FL
Slavens, Julie M. ....Indianapolis, IN
Slavens, Kathleen M. ....Youngstown, OH
Slavens, Kenneth A. ....St. Louis, MO
Slavens, Mark T. ....Livonia, MI
Slavens, Mark T., P.C. ....Canton, MI
Livonia, MI
Plymouth, MI
Slavet, Arnold L. ....Boston, MA
Slavet, Beth S.
Merit Systems Protection Board, Board Members, GV
Slavet, Jeffrey ....New City, NY
Slavet & Lefkowitz ....New City, NY
Slavett, Lawrence D. ....Woodland Hills, CA
Slavicek, Brett L ....Phoenix, AZ
Slavich, John ....Dallas, TX
Slavick, Betty S. ....Milwaukee, WI
Slavick, Garrick R. ....Brick, NJ
Slavick, Scott J. ....Chicago, IL
Slavik, Donald H. ....Milwaukee, WI
Slavik, James W. ....Chadron, NE
Slavik, Leigh Flesher ....Cupertino, CA
Slavin, Barton L. ....New York, NY
Slavin, Bruce M. ....San Francisco, CA
Slavin, Catherine B. ....Philadelphia, PA
Slavin, Cheryl A. ....Brooklyn, NY
Slavin, David A. ....New York, NY
Slavin, Denise Noonan ....Miami, FL
Slavin, Donald F. ....Denver, CO
Slavin, Donald F., A Professional Corporation
Denver, CO
Slavin, Edward A., Jr. ....Houston, TX
Slavin, Edward J. ....Woodmere, NY
Slavin, Eric W. ....Tucson, AZ
Slavin, Francis J. ....Phoenix, AZ
Slavin, Francis J., P.C. ....Phoenix, AZ
Slavin, Franklin P., Jr. ....Wytheville, VA
Slavin, Glenn C. ....Woodbridge, NJ
Slavin, Howard A. ....Los Angeles, CA
Slavin, Howard I. ....Larchmont, NY
Slavin, Howard L. ....Denver, CO
Slavin, James D., III ....Cheshire, CT
Slavin, James S., Jr. ....Shrewsbury, MA
Slavin, Jane R. ....New York, NY
Slavin, Janet D. ....New York, NY
Slavin, Jeffrey F. ....Cleveland, OH
Slavin, Joan E. ....Chicago, IL
Slavin, John C. ....Kirksville, MO
Slavin, Joseph ....New York, NY
Slavin, Ken K. ....El Paso, TX
Slavin, L. Susan ....Jericho, NY
Slavin, Laurie R. ....North Miami Beach, FL
Slavin, Leslie Crane ....Boston, MA
Slavin, Lorraine ....Greenwich, CT
Slavin, Louis J. ....Tucson, AZ
Slavin, Mark B. ....North Miami Beach, FL
Slavin, Mark F. ....Chicago, IL
Slavin, Maureen T. ....Robbinsville, NJ
Slavin, Michael A. ....Miami, FL
West Palm Beach, FL
Slavin, Milton A. ....Salmon, ID
Slavin, Patricia ....New York, NY
Slavin, Richard ....Bridgeport, CT
Westport, CT
Slavin, Richard C. ....Worthington, OH
Slavin, Robert E. ....Westlake Village, CA
Slavin, Sherman R. ....Watertown, CT
Slavin, Stauffacher & Scott, LLC
Watertown, CT
Slavin, Stephen M. ....Chicago, IL
Slavin, Timothy J. ....Morrison, IL
Slavina, Marina ....San Francisco, CA
Slavin-Coslel, Judith A. ....Irvine, CA
Slavis, Harry, (Ltd.) ....Chicago, IL
Slavis, Peter D. ....Fort Lauderdale, FL
Slavish, Timothy M. ....Pittsburgh, PA
Slavit & Gill, P.C. ....Washington, DC
Slavit, Howard G. ....Washington, DC
Slavit, Ira S. ....New York, NY
Slavit, Leonard S. ....New York, NY
Slavitt, Ben J. ....Newark, NJ
Slavitt, Connery & Vardamis
Norwalk, CT
Slavitt, David W. ....Beverly Hills, CA
Slavitt, Earl B., (P.C.) ....Los Angeles, CA
Slavitt, Evan ....Boston, MA
Slavitt, Fish & Cowen, P.A. ....Newark, NJ
Slavitt, Howard A. ....San Francisco, CA
Slavitt, John E. ....Newark, NJ
Slavitt, Joshua R. ....Philadelphia, PA
Slavitt, Richard L. ....West Orange, NJ
Slavitt, Robert A. ....Norwalk, CT
Slavkin, David S. ....St. Louis, MO
Slavkin, Robert E. ....Harrisburg, PA
Slavkin, Wendy L. ....Los Angeles, CA
Slavney, John D. ....Deerfield, IL
Slavney, Morris ....Madison, WI
Slaw, Steven L. ....Chicago, IL
Slaw, Terry D. ....Schaumburg, IL
Slawe, Louis E. ....Philadelphia, PA
Slawik, Harold J. ....Redwood City, CA
Slawinski, Steven J. ....Milwaukee, WI
Slawinski-Bracconeri, Toni ....Pomona, NY
Slawkowski, David J. ....Chicago, IL
Slawotsky, Joel ....New York, NY
Slawsby, Stuart W. ....Hingham, MA
Slawsky, David P. ....Concord, NH
Slawsky, Norman J. ....Atlanta, GA
Slawsky, Toby D. ....Philadelphia, PA
Slawson, Byron Bart ....Birmingham, AL
Slawson, Byron Bart, P.C. ....Birmingham, AL
Slawson, Christina Anne ....Los Angeles, CA
Slawson Cunningham Whalen & Stewart, P.L. ....Palm Beach Gardens, FL
Slawson, D. Scott ....Newport Beach, CA
Slawson, Donna B. ....Durham, NC
Slawson, Guenton C., Jr.
New Orleans, LA
Slawson, Karen V. ....Provo, UT
Slawson, Kurt T. ....Washington, DC
Slawson, MaryGray ....Grand Rapids, MI
Slawson, Richard W., (P.A.)
Palm Beach Gardens, FL
Slawson, Thomas M. ....Arlington, VA
Slawson, W. David ....Los Angeles, CA
Slawta, Kathleen N. ....Bethesda, MD
Slawter, William F. ....Asheville, NC
Slay, Craig L. ....Brandon, MS
Slay, Francis G. ....St. Louis, MO
Slay, Joann G. ....Quincy, FL
Slay, Kelly S. ....Fort Lauderdale, FL
Slayback, Paul C. ....Costa Mesa, CA
Slaybaugh, Debra L. ....Fresno, CA
Slaybod, Sheldon M. ....Toledo, OH
Slayden, Amy A. ....Huntsville, AL
Slayden, Bruce W., II ....Houston, TX
Slayden, Daniel P. ....Joliet, IL
Slayden, Nancy Staff ....Tallahassee, FL
Slayden, Rhonda K. ....Little Rock, AR
Slaydon, Kathleen Amelia ....Houston, TX
Slaydon, Kathleen Amelia, P.C.
Houston, TX
Slaydon, Roger J. ....Winston-Salem, NC
Slayen, Gary ....
Treasury Department, GV
Slaymaker, Laura Lyon ....Lancaster, PA
Slaymaker and Nelson, P.A. ....Homosassa, FL
Inverness, FL
Slaymaker, Samuel C. ....Lancaster, PA
Slaymaker, Thomas E. ....Homosassa, FL
Inverness, FL
Slayne, Kevin F. ....Boston, MA
Slayne, Leigh Earls ....Boston, MA
Slayton, Bain and Clary ....Lawrenceville, VA
Slayton, Don L. ....Woodland Hills, CA
Slayton, Donald R. ....Eugene, OR
Slayton, Douglas S. ....Peoria, IL
Slayton, Fran Cannon ....Lynchburg, VA
Slayton, Franklin M. ....South Boston, VA
Slayton, Jack L. ....Austin, TX
Slayton, James A. ....Oklahoma City, OK
Slayton, James A., P.C. ....Oklahoma City, OK
Slayton, Jeffery M. ....Seattle, WA
Slayton, John H. ....Arlington, VA
Slayton, Julie ....Los Angeles, CA
Slayton, Katherine A. ....Costa Mesa, CA
Slayton, Linwood R., Jr. ....Atlanta, GA
Slayton, Marshall M. ....Charlottesville, VA
Slayton, Olan A. ....Columbus, GA
Slayton, R. Duane ....Elgin, IL
Slayton, Roderic H. ....Orange, VA
Slayton, Roderic H., P.C. ....Orange, VA
Slayton, Russell O., Jr. ....Lawrenceville, VA
Slayton, Scott H. ....Union, NJ
Slayton, Thomas F. ....Toledo, OH
Slayton, Wendy L. Rhyne ....Topeka, KS
Slazinski, Stanley H. ....Detroit, MI
Slazinski, Stephen E. ....Detroit, MI
Slead, Roger W. ....Kansas City, MO
Slear, Wendy L. ....Philadelphia, PA
Slease, Clyde H., III ....Washington, DC
Pittsburgh, PA
Slease, Clyde Harold ....Midlothian, VA
Sleasman, Daniel M. ....Albany, NY
Sleater, Keith L. ....Aurora, CO
Sleater, Mary C. ....Kirkwood, MO
Sleater, Nancy C. ....Kirkwood, MO
Sleater, Regina L. ....Kirkwood, MO
Sleater, Sharon G. ....Kirkwood, MO
Sleater, Susan M. ....Department of Justice, Civil Division, GV
Sleater, W. W. ....Kirkwood, MO
Slebir, John L. ....San Francisco, CA
Slechta, Donald B. ....Hays, KS
Slechter, Mat A. ....Louisville, KY
Sledd, Charles M. ....Chatsworth, CA
Sledd, Herbert D. ....Lexington, KY
Sleder, Ted N. ....Atlanta, GA
Sledge, Brian L. ....Austin, TX
Sledge, Carla Williams ....Boulder, CO
Sledge, David L. ....Memphis, TN
Sledge, Edward C. ....Baltimore, MD
Sledge, Edward S., III ....Mobile, AL
Sledge, Frank D. ....Denver, CO
Sledge, Henry E., Jr. ....Knoxville, TN
Sledge, James J. ....Tuscaloosa, AL
Sledge, James S. ....Anniston, AL
Sledge, Jimmy Ried, Jr. ....Houston, TX
Sledge, Kristi L. ....Raleigh, NC
Sledge, Lawrence D. ....Baton Rouge, LA
Sledge, Margaret M. ....New Orleans, LA
Sledge, Michael D. ....New Orleans, LA
Sledge, Roland E. ....Houston, TX
Sledge, Roland L. ....Valley, AL
Sledge, Scott H. ....Hammond, LA
Sledge, T. Mark ....Jackson, MS
Sledge, William R. ....Memphis, TN
Sledjeski, Thomas C. ....Melville, NY
Sledz, Henry W., Jr. ....Chicago, IL
Sledzik, Chester S. ....New Britain, CT
Sledzik & McGuire ....New Britain, CT
Sledzik, Peter P. ....Jacksonville, FL
Sledzik, Steven T. ....New York, NY
Sledziona, Frank W. ....Hamden, CT
Slee, Andrew J. ....Montrose, CO
Slee, Debora A. ....St. Paul, MN
Slee, Dennis ....Northridge, CA
Slee, Malcolm C. ....Washington, DC
Slee, Richard Alan ....Columbus, OH
Sleek, Diane Elizabeth ....Augusta, ME
Sleeman, William Craig ....Troy, MI
Sleeper, Bradley J. ....Boise, ID
Sleeper, Carolyn Reinhard ....Marlton, NJ
Sleeper, Donald N., Jr. ....Burlington, MA
Sleeper, Eric W. ....Newark, NJ
New York, NY
Sleeper, F. Bruce ....Portland, ME
Sleeper, Gary C. ....Anchorage, AK
Sleeper, Gary W. ....Oklahoma City, OK
Sleeper, Mason C. ....New York, NY
Sleeper & Sleeper ....Burlington, MA
Sleet, Daniel H. ....Tampa, FL
Sleet, Gregory M. ....Wilmington, DE
Sleeth, Boyd C. ....Oakland, CA
Sleeth, Jack M., Jr. ....San Diego, CA
Sleeth, Joseph C., Jr. ....Houston, TX
Sleeth, Larry K. ....Baton Rouge, LA
Sleeth, Tim E. ....Jacksonville, FL
Sleeth, Walter J. ....San Francisco, CA
Sleggs, Todd W. ....Cleveland, OH
Sleggs, Todd W., & Associates
Cleveland, OH
Slehofer, Richard D. ....Westlake Village, CA
Sleigh, David C. ....St. Johnsbury, VT
Sleight, David J. ....Buffalo, NY
Sleight, Roger W. ....San Francisco, CA
Sleight, Scott R. ....Seattle, WA
Sleight, Theresa F. ....St. Louis, MO
Sleight, Virginia M. ....Lake George, NY
Sleik, Thomas S. ....La Crosse, WI
Sleiman, Peter D. ....Jacksonville, FL
Slein, John J. ....Milwaukee, WI
Sleisenger, Thomas P. ....Los Angeles, CA
Slemboski, James E. ....St. George, UT
Slemmer, Carl W., Jr. ....Moorestown, NJ
Slemons, Dale Edward ....Martinsburg, WV
Slen, Rolf O. ....Albert Lea, MN
Slenker, Neil A. ....York, PA
Slenkovich, Keith ....Palo Alto, CA
Slenn, Bradley ....Cherry Hill, NJ
Philadelphia, PA
Slentz, Robert J. ....Castle Rock, CO
Slenzak, Laura M. ....Auburn Hills, MI
Slep, Keith A. ....Belfast, NY
Wellsville, NY
Slepchuk, Peter P., Jr. ....Springfield, MA
Slepetis, Laura ....Brookville, NY
Slepian, Alan W. ....Bethesda, MD
Slepian, Charles G. ....New York, NY
Slepian, David Craig ....Fairfield, CT
Slepian, Jack I. ....Bayside, NY
Slepian, Ronald P. ....Mobile, AL
Slepian, Steven D. ....Phoenix, AZ
Slepicka, Frank B. ....Chicago, IL
Slepicka, Nancy L. ....Greenbelt, MD
La Plata, MD
Slepin, Harrison & Feuer ....Boca Raton, FL
Slepin, Matthew M. ....Tallahassee, FL
Slepin & Slepin ....Tallahassee, FL
Slepin, Stephen Marc ....Boca Raton, FL
Tallahassee, FL
Slepkow, Martin P. ....East Providence, RI
Slepkow, Matthew D. ....East Providence, RI
Slepkow, Milton S. ....East Providence, RI
Sleppy, David A. ....Cornelia, GA
Slesnick & Casey ....Miami, FL
Slesnick, David J. ....Pittsburgh, PA
Slesnick, Donald D., II ....Miami, FL
Sless, Jacob B. ....Philadelphia, PA
Sless, Kathryn Suzanne ....Linwood, NJ
Sletta, Stephen J. ....Colorado Springs, CO
Slette, Gary D. ....Twin Falls, ID
Sletteland, George B. ....Mequon, WI
Sletten, Douglas D. ....Garrison, ND
Sletten, Steven Eugene (IBA)
Los Angeles, CA
Sletto, Mark A. ....Eagan, MN
Sletvold, Jennifer Riddle ....Philadelphia, PA
Sletvold, Robert Einar ....Easton, PA
Sleuwen Guerrero, Markus ....Chicago, IL
Sleva, William G. ....Bedford, IN
Sleven, Paul J. ....New York, NY
Slevin, Barry S. ....Washington, DC
Slevin, Cindy ....Denver, CO
Slevin, Edward D. ....Philadelphia, PA

Slevin, Gerald T. ... New York, NY
Slevin & Hart, P.C. ... Washington, DC
Slevin, John A. ... Peoria, IL
Slevin, Maribeth ... Mineola, NY
Slevin, Mary Elizabeth ... Albany, NY
Slevin, Michael J. ... Denville, NJ
Slevin, Patrick J. ... Washington, DC
Slevin, Robert P. ... New York, NY
Slevin, Sheila
Securities and Exchange Commission, Division of Market Regulation, GV
Slewett, Franklyn R. ... Plainview, NY
Slewett, Nathan ... Miami, FL
Slewett, Robert D.
North Miami Beach, FL
Slewett, Robert D., P.A. ... Aventura, FL
Fort Lauderdale, FL
Miami, FL
North Miami Beach, FL
Slewitzke, Ronald T. ... Chicago, IL
Sley, Benjamin B. ... Cleveland, OH
Slez, Anthony F., Jr. ... Westport, CT
Slez, Margaret J. ... Westport, CT
Slezak, David G. ... Mayfield Heights, OH
Slezak, Deborah A. ... Niskayuna, NY
Slezak, Edward M. ... New York, NY
Slezak, John A. ... Oxnard, CA
Slezak, Marilyn K. ... Olathe, KS
Slezak, Rebecca A. ... Albany, NY
Slezak, Richard E. ... Salem, OR
Slezak, Thomas R., Jr. ... Las Vegas, NV
Slezak, Walter T. ... Chicago, IL
Slicer, Charles W., III ... Dayton, OH
Slicer, Charles W., Jr. ... Dayton, OH
Slicer, K. Penny R. ... Kansas City, MO
Slicer, Paul A. ... Point Lookout, MO
Slicer, William R. ... Charleston, WV
Slichter, Donald A. ... Palo Alto, CA
Slicker, Frederick K. ... Tulsa, OK
Slicker, William D. ... St. Petersburg, FL
Slicker, William D., P.A. ... St. Petersburg, FL
Slider, Linda C. ... Walnut Creek, CA
Slife, Courtney A. ... Albert Lea, MN
Slife, E. V., Jr. ... Hawarden, IA
Slifer, Karl R. ... San Ramon, CA
Slifer, Russell D. ... Minneapolis, MN
Slifkin, Anne R. ... Raleigh, NC
Slifkin & Axe ... Philadelphia, PA
Slifkin, Clara L. ... Los Angeles, CA
Slifkin, Daniel ... New York, NY
Slifkin, Debra L. ... Philadelphia, PA
Slifkin, Irving ... Stamford, CT
Slifkin, Morrie ... New City, NY
Slifkin, Morton A. ... Philadelphia, PA
Slifkin, Neal L. ... Rochester, NY
Slifko, John Robert ... Reading, PA
Slifko, Sharon G. ... Phoenix, AZ
Slifman, Marilyn Sandra ... Costa Mesa, CA
Sligar, Benjamin R. ... Tacoma, WA
Sligar, James S. ... New York, NY
Sliger, Herbert J., Jr. ... Phoenix, AZ
Sligh, Jesse J. ... Philadelphia, PA
Sligh, John A., Jr. ... Atlanta, GA
Slights, Ellen W. ... Wilmington, DE
Slights, Joseph R., III ... Wilmington, DE
Slijepcevich, Daniel ... San Francisco, CA
Slike, John E. ... Camp Hill, PA
Slim, Jules P. ... Irving, TX
Slimak, Darryl R. ... State College, PA
Sliman, Richard W. ... Gulfport, MS
Slimbaugh, Kimberly A. ... Syracuse, NY
Slimm, Jamie A. ... Haddonfield, NJ
Slimm, John L. ... Cherry Hill, NJ
Slimmer, Kenneth H. ... Garden Grove, CA
Slimp, Fredrick A., II ... Sacramento, CA
Slimp, John R. ... San Antonio, TX
Slimp, Kenneth H. ... Winters, TX
Sliney, Thomas E., (P.A.) ... Boca Raton, FL
Slinger, Diane ... Farmington Hills, MI
Slingerland, E. Gilman, Jr. ... Maplewood, NJ
Slingerland, Edward G. ... Maplewood, NJ
Slingerland, J. Jeffery ... Milton, FL
Slingerland, Jack C. ... Sycamore, IL
Slingerland, John H. ... Chelmsford, MA
Slingerland and Slingerland ... Maplewood, NJ
Slingland, Bernstein & van Hartogh
Pompton Lakes, NJ
Slingland, George W. ... Hawthorne, NJ
Slingluff, Charles H. ... Ijamsville, MD
Slininger, Arthur P. ... Canby, OR
Slinkard, Howard L. ... Rogers, AR
Slinkard Law Firm, A Professional Association
Rogers, AR
Slinkard, Mary Vassallo ... Philadelphia, PA
Slinkard, Robert W. ... Kiowa, KS
Medicine Lodge, KS
Slinkard, Theodore L. ... Fresno, CA
Slinkman, F. Kendall
West Palm Beach, FL
Slinkman, Richard K.
West Palm Beach, FL
Slinkman & Slinkman, P.A.
West Palm Beach, FL
Slinn, Peter L. ... Seattle, WA
Slinskey, Jenifer C. ... Pittsburgh, PA
Slipakoff, Barbra ... Fort Lauderdale, FL
Slipian, Sally I. ... Clayton, MO
Slipock, Arthur H. ... Granada Hills, CA
Slipock, Samantha ... Los Angeles, CA
Slipow, Larry B. ... Virginia Beach, VA
Slipow, Robusto & Kellam, P.C.
Virginia Beach, VA
Slipp, Elena ... Weehawken, NJ
Slipp, Ellen ... New York, NY
Slipp, Jonathan M. ... Newport Beach, CA
Slipp, Peter T. ... Methuen, MA
Slipski, Cheryl L. ... Philadelphia, PA
Slipski, Ronald E. ... Youngstown, OH
Sliskovich, Joseph V. ... Los Angeles, CA
Slisz, Mary L. ... Buffalo, NY
Slisz, Richard C. ... Buffalo, NY
Sliter, Charles F. ... Bellevue, OH
Slitt, Aaron P. ... Hartford, CT
Slitt & Gerace ... Hartford, CT
Slitt, Wayne L. ... Hartford, CT
Sliva, Amy Logan ... Pensacola, FL
Slive & Slive ... Cleveland, OH
Slive, Steven H. ... Cleveland, OH
Slivinska, Diana ... Oakmont, PA
Slivinski, Dennis L. ... Ventura, CA
Slivinski, Robert H. ... Selinsgrove, PA
Slivka, Andrew P. ... Garfield Heights, OH
Slivka, Donell A. ... Sacramento, CA
Slivka, John M. ... Cleveland, OH
Slivka, Richard P. ... Denver, CO
Slivka Robinson Waters & O'Dorisio, A Professional Corporation ... Denver, CO
Slivka, William ... New York, NY
Slivka, William J. ... Arlington, VA
Slivkin, Richard H. ... Los Angeles, CA
Slivon, Fred P., Jr. ... Princeton, NJ
Sliwa, Cynthia A. ... Torrance, CA
Sliwa, Daniel J. ... Dearborn, MI
Sliwa & Lane ... Buffalo, NY
Sliwa, Stanley J. ... Buffalo, NY
Sliwa, Susanne M. ... Las Vegas, NV
Sliwinski, Bronislaw ... Chalfont, PA
Sliwinski, Mary Anne ... Chicago, IL
Sliwinski, Teddy ... Cleveland, OH
Sliwka, Justine M. ... Northville, MI
Sliz, Jeffrey R. ... Lawrenceville, GA
Slizeski, Richard M. ... San Francisco, CA
Slizewski, Edward J. ... Los Angeles, CA
Slizewski, Emil ... Newton, MA
Sloame, Stuart C. ... Washington, DC
Sloan, Aaron P. ... Toledo, OH
Sloan, Allan Poe, III ... Charleston, SC
Sloan, Allen ... Window Rock, AZ
Sloan, Amy E. ... Washington, DC
Sloan, Andrea ... Beaverton, OR
Sloan, Andrea J. ... McLean, VA
Sloan, Andrea L. ... Austin, TX
Sloan, Arthur M. ... Dallas, TX
Sloan and Associates ... Chicago, IL
Sloan and Associates, Inc. ... Chicago, IL
Sloan & Associates, P.C. ... Washington, DC
Sloan, Barbara A. ... Boca Raton, FL
Sloan, Barbara A. ... New York, NY
Sloan, Barbara L.
Equal Employment Opportunity Commission, Office of the General Counsel, GV
Sloan, Bart ... Dallas, TX
Sloan, Betty H. ... Tulsa, OK
Sloan, Betty Sue M. ... Columbia, SC
Sloan Bobrick & Oldfield, Inc. P.S.
Tacoma, WA
Sloan, Breece W. ... Walnut Creek, CA
Sloan, Bryan ... New York, NY
Sloan, Carl R. ... New York, NY
Sloan, Carol J. ... Mehoopany, PA
Sloan, Carolyn Brock ... Overland Park, KS
Sloan, Carolyn Dunnum ... Downey, CA
Sloan, Catherine R. ... Washington, DC
Sloan, Charles W. ... Vienna, VA
Sloan, Chas. H. ... Richmond, MO
Sloan, Cheryl Leigh Thornton ... Charlotte, NC
Sloan, Christine O. ... Columbia, SC
Sloan, Christopher H.K. ... Boston, MA
Sloan, Clark J. ... Tucson, AZ
Sloan, Clifford M. ... Washington, DC
Sloan, Colleen A. ... Buffalo, NY
Sloan, Cynthia M.
Department of Commerce, Patent and Trademark Office, GV
Sloan, Cyrus T., III ... Marion, SC
Sloan, D. Clay ... Walnut Ridge, AR
Sloan, David B. ... Covington, KY
Sloan, David E. ... Salt Lake City, UT
Sloan, David M. ... Redwood City, CA
Sloan, David M. ... Houston, TX
Sloan, David N. ... Flushing, NY
Sloan, David Scott ... Boston, MA
Sloan, David W. ... New York, NY
Sloan, David W. ... Cleveland, OH
Sloan, Donna Crosby ... Atlanta, GA
Sloan, Douglas T. ... Fresno, CA
Sloan, D. R., Jr. ... Duluth, GA
Sloan, E. Ned ... Washington, DC
Sloan, Edith ... Washington, DC
Sloan, Edward S. ... Kansas City, MO
Sloan & Eland ... Hoxie, KS
Sloan, Eldon ... Topeka, KS
Sloan, Elizabeth Ann ... Reading, PA
Sloan, Eric B. ... Washington, DC
Sloan, Eva L., (Mrs.) ... Milledgeville, GA
Sloan, F. Blaine ... Fort Garland, CO
Sloan, F. Linton, Jr. ... Tampa, FL
Sloan & Feldman ... Haddonfield, NJ
Berwyn, PA
Philadelphia, PA
Sloan, Frances V. ... Brooklyn, NY
Sloan, Frank ... Covington, LA
Sloan, G. Rogers ... Vicksburg, MS
Sloan, Gary L. ... Olathe, KS
Sloan, Gerald T. ... Lake Orion, MI
Sloan, Gordon ... Salem, OR
Sloan, Graham F. ... Little Rock, AR
Sloan, Greg P. ... Columbia, SC
Sloan, Gregory Brandon ... Modesto, CA
Sloan, Harry E. ... Los Angeles, CA
Sloan, Harvey F. ... Pittsburgh, PA
Sloan, Jack C. ... Denver, CO
Sloan, Jacqueline H. ... Los Angeles, CA
Sloan, James B. ... Lake Forest, IL
Sloan, James C. ... Buffalo, NY
Sloan, James D. ... Denver, CO
Sloan, James D. ... LaBelle, FL
Sloan, James D., Jr. ... Anniston, AL
Sloan, James E. ... Houston, TX
Sloan, James F. ... Fallon, NV
Sloan, James L. ... Little Rock, AR
Sloan, James M., III ... Providence, RI
Sloan, James R. ... Austin, TX
Sloan, James W. ... Topeka, KS
Sloan, Janet M. ... Harrisburg, PA
Sloan, Jeffrey ... San Francisco, CA
Sloan, Jeffrey S. ... San Francisco, CA
Sloan, Jeremy S. ... New York, NY
Sloan, Jerry ... Akron, OH
Sloan, Jerry S. ... Chattanooga, TN
Sloan, J. F. (Jim), III ... Walnut Ridge, AR
Sloan, John B. ... Lufkin, TX
Sloan, John D., Jr. ... Longview, TX
Sloan, John Donovan, Jr. ... Dallas, TX
Sloan, John E. ... Lake Orion, MI
Sloan, John F. ... Peoria, IL
Sloan, John J., Jr. ... Livonia, MI
Sloan, John P. ... Anchorage, AK
Sloan, John R. ... Ridgway, CO
Sloan, John Reeves ... New Bern, NC
Wilmington, NC
Sloan, John W. ... Baltimore, MD
Sloan, Judy Beckner ... Los Angeles, CA
Sloan, Karin ... Syracuse, NY
Sloan, Karl F. ... Olympia, WA
Sloan, Kathleen L. ... Olathe, KS
Sloan, Kenneth W. ... Dallas, TX
Sloan Law Firm ... Walnut Ridge, AR
Sloan, Leonard A. ... Washington, DC
Sloan, Leslie J. ... New York, NY
Sloan, Linda Rekas ... Providence, RI
Sloan, Lisa M. ... Philadelphia, PA
Sloan, Listrom, Eisenbarth, Sloan & Glassman, L.L.C. ... Overland Park, KS
Topeka, KS
Sloan, Lynn D. ... Fort Pierce, FL
Sloan, Maceo K. ... Durham, NC
Sloan, Malcolm Todd ... Phoenix, AZ
Sloan, Margaret A. ... Menlo Park, CA
Sloan, Marilyn ... Harrison, NY
Sloan, Marilyn D. ... Seattle, WA
Sloan, Mark M. ... Dallas, TX
Sloan, Martin C. ... McKees Rocks, PA
Sloan, Mary Ann ... Atlanta, GA
Sloan, Mary Ellen ... Salt Lake City, UT
Sloan, Mary Margaret ... Arlington, VA
Sloan, Matthew E. ... Los Angeles, CA
Sloan, Matthew H. ... Phoenix, AZ
Sloan, Mel ... Chicago, IL
Sloan, Michael ... McKinney, TX
Sloan, Michael A. ... Austin, TX
Sloan, Michael C. ... Washington, DC
Sloan, Michael J. ... Atlanta, GA
Sloan, Michael L. ... Pasadena, CA
Sloan, Mike H. ... Las Vegas, NV
Sloan, Millard J. ... Olympia, WA
Sloan, Nanci Oliver ... Atlanta, GA
Sloan, Nathan B. ... Harrison, NY
Sloan, Norman D. ... Los Angeles, CA
Sloan, Norman L. ... Winston-Salem, NC
Sloan, Pamela M. ... New York, NY
Sloan, Paul G. ... San Rafael, CA
Sloan, Peter B. ... Kansas City, MO
Sloan, Peter M. ... Los Angeles, CA
Sloan, Philip M., Jr. ... Westerly, RI
Sloan, Philip R. ... Tacoma, WA
Sloan, Phillip E. ... New York, NY
Sloan, Price A. ... Kansas City, MO
Sloan & Price, P.C. ... Longview, TX
Sloan, R. Brannon, Jr. ... Little Rock, AR
Sloan, R. John, Jr. ... Omak, WA
Sloan, R. Stedman, Jr. ... Columbia, SC
Sloan, Ralph W. ... Atlanta, GA
Sloan, Ray C. ... Hoxie, KS
Sloan, Rebecca ... Orlando, FL
Sloan, Richard D. ... Ho-Ho-Kus, NJ
Sloan, Richard S. ... Washington, DC
Sloan, Robert A. ... Haddonfield, NJ
Berwyn, PA
Philadelphia, PA
Sloan, Robert D. ... Plainville, CT
Sloan, Robert E. ... Houston, TX
Sloan, Robert F. ... Bayonne, NJ
Sloan, Robert G. ... Albuquerque, NM
Sloan, Robert, III ... Baltimore, MD
Sloan, Robert L. ... Newark, NJ
Sloan, Robert V., (P.C.) ... Washington, DC
Sloan, Rubens & Peeples
West Memphis, AR
Sloan, Sam Ross, III ... Houston, TX
Sloan, Shadow ... Houston, TX
Sloan, Sharon Nader ... Los Angeles, CA
Sloan, Sheldon H. ... Los Angeles, CA
Sloan, Stephen R. ... Albany, NY
Sloan, Stephen R. ... Salt Lake City, UT
Sloan, Stevan E. ... New York, NY
Sloan, Steven J. ... Plainsboro, NJ
Sloan, Steven T. ... Athens, OH
Sloan, Steven W. ... Dallas, TX
Sloan, Stuart ... Orlando, FL
Sloan & Swedish ... Vienna, VA
Sloan, T. Dwight ... Birmingham, AL
Sloan, Thomas H., Jr. ... San Francisco, CA
Sloan, Timothy Ann ... Bay City, TX
Sloan, Timothy C.
Department of Commerce, National Telecommunications & Information Administration, GV
Sloan, Timothy J. ... Panama City, FL
Sloan, Todd M., Law Offices of
Los Angeles, CA
Sloan, Todd M., Law Offices of
Malibu, CA
Sloan, Vickie Lynn ... Department of Justice, Justice Management Division, GV
Sloan, Victor T. ... Uxbridge, MA
Sloan, Virginia A. ... Tyler, TX
Sloan, Walter F. ... Dallas, TX
Sloan, William E. ... Lexington, KY
Sloan, William M. ... San Francisco, CA
Sloan, William M. ... Grants Pass, OR
Sloan, William T. ... Oxford, MS
Sloan-Altieri, Anibelle ... San Juan, PR
Sloane, Abigail ... New York, NY
Sloane, Adam C. ... Washington, DC
Sloane, Carol Herman ... Vero Beach, FL
Sloane, Charles B. ... Philadelphia, PA
Sloane, Craig ... New York, NY
Sloane, Craig A. ... New York, NY
Sloane, Daniel A. ... Denver, CO
Sloane, David A. ... Hauppauge, NY
Sloane, Dianne Herland ... Woodbury, NJ
Sloane, Douglas A. ... Reno, NV
Sloane, Emily A. ... Evanston, IL
Sloane, Gloria F. Kaplan ... Merrick, NY
Sloane, Howard G. ... New York, NY
Sloane, Ira P., Law Offices of
Smithtown, NY
Sloane, Jason C. ... Beverly Hills, CA
Sloane, Jay R. ... Cary, NC
Sloane, Jeffrey G. ... Las Vegas, NV
Sloane, Jennifer L. ... Orlando, FL
Sloane, Jonathan C. ... St. Louis, MO
Sloane, Karen L. ... Palm Beach, FL
Sloane, L. Ted. ... Davenport, IA
Sloane, Leonard A. ... Media, PA
West Chester, PA
Sloane, Madeleine E. ... San Francisco, CA
Sloane, Marc Kerry ... Baltimore, MD
Sloane, Margaret A. ... Chapel Hill, NC
Sloane, Marilyn ... Harrison, NY
Sloane, Martin A. ... New York, NY
Sloane, Maureen R., P.C. ... Portland, OR
Sloane, Nancy F. ... Spokane, WA
Sloane, Owen J. ... Los Angeles, CA
Sloane, Peter D. ... Seal Beach, CA
Sloane, Peter S. ... New York, NY
Sloane, Raffaele & Schuster, P.C. ... Media, PA
Sloane, Raymond T. ... Garden City, NY
Sloane, Richard ... Philadelphia, PA
Sloane, Robert D. ... Plantation, FL
Sloane, Stephen Marc ... Los Angeles, CA
Sloane, Susan K. ... Boston, MA
Sloane and Walsh, LLP ... Boston, MA
Sloane, Wendi E. ... Chicago, IL
Sloane, William H. ... New York, NY
Sloane, William I. ... Dedham, MA
Sloane, William Martin ... Carlisle, PA
Sloan-Menninger, Kimberly K.
Santa Ana, CA
Sloas, Steven A. ... Memphis, TN
Sloat, Bonnie Kerwin ... Moline, IL
Sloat, Gerald C. ... Boulder, CO
Sloat, Gerald C., P.C. ... Boulder, CO
Sloat, Karen Joanne ... Glenwood Springs, CO
Sloat, Loren R. ... Nappanee, IN
Wakarusa, IN
Sloat, Robert E. ... Chicago, IL
Sloat, Robert W. ... Pasadena, CA
Sloate, Alan R. ... Larchmont, NY
Sloate, Pamela M. ... Old Greenwich, CT
Slobasky, Michael R. ... Washington, DC
Slobey, Jay R. ... Nashville, TN
Slobig, Robert J. ... Chicago, IL
Slobin, Cary A. ... Dallas, TX
Slobin, Gary ... New York, NY
Slobin, Lester H. ... Houston, TX
Slobin, Sanford J. ... Houston, TX
Slobod, Elaine Z. ... Goshen, NY
Slobod, Jack D. ... Tarrytown, NY
Sloboda, Joseph D. ... Bronx, NY
Slobodian, Markian R., Law Offices of
Harrisburg, PA
Slobodien, Andrew M. ... Chicago, IL
Slobodien, David J. ... Murray Hill, NJ
Slobodien, Myron L. ... Los Angeles, CA
Slobodin, Alan M. ... Washington, DC
Slobodin, Jack L. ... Menlo Park, CA
Slobodkin, Sidney A. ... Franklin, MA
Wellesley, MA
Sloca, Steven L. ... Los Angeles, CA
Slocomb, Paul D. ... Chicago, IL
Slocomb, Paul T. ... St. Louis, MO
Slocombe, Jeffrey A. ... Edwardsburg, MI
Slocombe, Walter B.
Department of Defense, GV
Slocum, A. Terry ... Santa Cruz, CA
Slocum & Boddie, P.C. ... Springfield, VA
Slocum, Carol Ann ... Cherry Hill, NJ
Slocum, Charles W. ... Wellton, AZ
Slocum, David K. ... Mount Sterling, IL
Slocum, Gail L. ... San Francisco, CA
Slocum, Garth J. ... Kinderhook, NY
Slocum, George Q. ... Ossining, NY
Slocum, J. Michael ... Springfield, VA
Slocum, Joyce D. ... Richardson, TX
Slocum, Lee R. ... Cincinnati, OH
Slocum, Lisa M. ... Newark, NJ
Slocum, Mary Ellen Goman ... Columbia, SC
Slocum, Priscilla F. ... Los Angeles, CA
Slocum, Richard C. ... Aurora, IL
Slocum, Robert B. ... Chicago, IL
Slocum, Robert R. ... Mobridge, SD
Slocum, Ronald James ... Owego, NY
Slocum, Shaun M. ... Cheshire, CT
Slocum, Shaun M., LLC, Law Offices of
Cheshire, CT
New Haven, CT
Slocum, Theodore T. N. ... Long Beach, CA
Slocumb, Howard B. ... Homerville, GA
Slocumb, L. Kathryn ... Winston-Salem, NC

Slocumb, Robert S. ... Macon, GA
Slocumb, Thomas ... Oakland, CA
Slocumb, William H. ... Bakersfield, CA
Sloderbeck, Vonda L. ... San Jose, CA
Slodki, Alan H. ... Chicago, IL
Slodov, Michael D. ... Cleveland, OH
Sloey, James H. ... San Pedro, CA
Slogar, John Michael ... Houston, TX
Slogoff, Reed J. ... Cherry Hill, NJ
Philadelphia, PA
Slom, Samuel J. ... Miami, FL
Slom, Wm. ... Philadelphia, PA
Sloma, Anthony P. ... Toledo, OH
Slomak, Michael J. ... Cleveland, OH
Sloman, E. Michael ... Boston, MA
Sloman, Gary ... Brooklyn, NY
Sloman, Jay E. ... Atlanta, GA
Sloman, Jeffrey H. ... Fort Lauderdale, FL
Sloman, Judith F. ... Atlanta, GA
Sloman, Marvin S. ... Dallas, TX
Sloman, Robert A. ... Bloomfield Hills, MI
Slomann, Jeffrey Robert ... Santa Ana, CA
Slomanson, William R. ... San Diego, CA
Slome, Ernest ... San Diego, CA
Slome, Thomas R. ... Garden City, NY
New York, NY
Slome, Troy H. ... Los Angeles, CA
Slomiak, Scott A. ... Redwood City, CA
Slomin, Michael S. ... Morristown, NJ
Slominski, Jaleh K. ... Lynchburg, VA
Slominski, James M. ... Los Angeles, CA
Slominski, Michael J. ... Gladstone, OR
Slomka, Howard P. ... Atlanta, GA
Slomka, Irwin M. ... New York, NY
Slomon, Joel A. ... Rockville Centre, NY
Slomovic, Ephraim ... New York, NY
Slomovitz, Murray C. ... Southfield, MI
Slomovitz-Glaser, Penny S. ... Holtsville, NY
Slomowitz, Alan ... Washington, DC
Slomowitz, Diane ... Milwaukee, WI
Slomowitz, Scott M. ... Philadelphia, PA
Slomski, Raymond J. ... Phoenix, AZ
Slomski, Raymond J., P.C., Law Offices of
Phoenix, AZ
Slomski, Robert ... Thompson Falls, MT
Slomsky, W. David ... Pittsburgh, PA
Slomsky, Joel Harvey ... Philadelphia, PA
Slon, Sandra G. ... Los Angeles, CA
Slonaker, Jerry P. ... Richmond, VA
Slonaker, Norman D. ... New York, NY
Slonaker, Robert A. ... Phoenix, AZ
Slonaker, Ronald W. ... Ocala, FL
Slonaker, Ronald W., & Associates, P.A.
Ocala, FL
Slonaker, Stanley M. ... Phoenix, AZ
Slonaker, William M., Sr. ... Dayton, OH
Slone, Benton & Long PSC
Lexington, KY
Slone, Charles R. ... Richmond, TX
Slone, Daniel K. ... Richmond, VA
Slone, David N. ... Palo Alto, CA
Slone, Fred A. ... Atlanta, GA
Slone, Frederick T. ... Anchorage, AK
Slone, Gordon R. ... Frankfort, KY
Slone, James E. ... Grundy, VA
Slone, James J. ... Campbell, CA
Slone, James M. ... Kansas City, MO
Slone, Jennifer L. ... Orlando, FL
Slone, Jerry Wayne ... Hindman, KY
Slone, Michael C. ... Lexington, KY
Slone, Michelle ... Lexington, KY
Slone, Ondine C. ... New York, NY
Slone, Randolph C. ... Slidell, LA
Slone, Randy G. ... Hindman, KY
Slone, Richard A. ... New Hyde Park, NY
Slone, Robert H. ... Greensburg, PA
Slone, Ronnie Merel ... Prestonsburg, KY
Slone, Tara L. ... Detroit, MI
Slonecker, Michael L. ... Orlando, FL
Sloneker, J. Michael ... Baltimore, MD
Slone-Stiven, Ruth A. ... Dayton, OH
Sloniewsky, Andrew J. ... Washington, DC
Sloniewsky, Roman
Department of Commerce,
Office of the General Counsel, GV
Slonim, Arthur H. ... St. Louis, MO
Slonim, Bert L. ... New York, NY
Slonim, Donn P. ... Bridgewater, NJ
Slonim, Hope E. ... Department of Commerce,
Patent and Trademark Office, GV
Slonim, Howard R. ... New York, NY
Slonim, Howard R., P.C. ... New York, NY
Slonim, Jeffrey I. ... New York, NY
Slonim, Marc D. ... Seattle, WA
Slonim, Michael L. ... New York, NY
Slonim, Nancy Cowger ... Chicago, IL
Slonim, Scott ... Rolling Meadows, IL
Sloop, Everett E. ... Oklahoma City, OK
Sloop, John R. ... Sanford, FL
Slootmaker, Leonard W. ... Richmond, CA
Slootsky, Steven E. ... Fort Lauderdale, FL
Sloper, Val D. ... Salem, OR
Slorby, Robert J. ... Minot, ND
Slorby, Tom P. ... Minot, ND
Slosberg, Howard S. ... Fort Lauderdale, FL
Slosberg, Jared A. ... Los Altos, CA
Slosberg, Laurie ... New York, NY
Slosberg, Lee R. ... Owings Mills, MD
Slosberg, Myles J. ... Boston, MA
Slosberg, Richard B. ... Portland, ME
Slosberg, Saml. H. ... Gardiner, ME
Slosberg, William J. ... Washington, DC
Slosbergas & Fernandez, L.L.P. ... Miami, FL
Slosbergas, Nelson ... Miami, FL
Slosky, Brent T. ... Denver, CO
Slosky, Robert S. ... Denver, CO
Sloss, Andrew G. ... St. Clair Shores, MI
Sloss, David A. ... New York, NY
Sloss, David L. ... Palo Alto, CA
Sloss, John ... New York, NY
Sloss, Katherine ... Newark, NJ
Sloss, Larry N., Jr. ... Lawrenceville, IL
Sloss Law Office, P.C. ... New York, NY
Sloss, Peter B. ... New Orleans, LA
Sloss, Peter F. ... San Francisco, CA
Sloss, Robert H. ... Mountain View, CA
Sloss, Robert James ... La Crescenta, CA
Slossberg, David A. ... Milford, CT
Slossberg, Lynn T. ... Boca Raton, FL
Slosser, Hudgins & Struse, P.L.C., Law
Offices of ... Tucson, AZ
Slosser, Paul D. ... Tucson, AZ
Slota, Deanna L. ... Bryn Mawr, PA
Slota, Robert E. ... Bryn Mawr, PA
Slota, Robert E., A Prof. Corp., Law Offices
of ... Bryn Mawr, PA
Philadelphia, PA
Slota, Robert E., Jr. ... Bryn Mawr, PA
Slota, Thomas J. ... Chicago, IL
Slotchiver, Daniel S. ... Charleston, SC
Slotchiver, Irvin J. ... Charleston, SC
Slotchiver & Slotchiver, L.L.P.
Charleston, SC
Hollywood, SC
Mount Pleasant, SC
Slotchiver, Stacey L. ... Charleston, SC
Slotchiver, Stephen M. ... Charleston, SC
Slote, Adam G. ... San Francisco, CA
Slote, Charles D. ... Stockton, CA
Slote, Lawrence C. ... Denver, CO
Slote, Lawrence C., P.C. ... Denver, CO
Slotegraaf, Eric P. ... Milwaukee, WI
Sloter, Eric P. ... Louisville, KY
Slother, T. Gregory ... Tampa, FL
Slothower, Jeffrey D. ... Ellensburg, WA
Slothower, Jim N. ... Bend, OR
Slotkin, David P. ... Washington, DC
Slotkin, F. Robert, Jr. ... Atlanta, GA
Slotkin, Jacquelyn H. ... San Diego, CA
Slotkin, Mark ... New York, NY
Slotkin, Mark I. ... Cherry Hill, NJ
Philadelphia, PA
Slotkin, Matthew B. ... Raleigh, NC
Slotkin, Richard M. ... Teaneck, NJ
Slotkin, Robert J. ... Fort Lauderdale, FL
Slotkin, Samantha D. ... Los Angeles, CA
Slotkin, Seth D. ... New York, NY
Slotky, Solomon ... Chicago, IL
Slotnick, Barry I. ... New York, NY
Slotnick, Barry Ivan, (P.C.)
New York, NY
Slotnick, Carl S. ... New York, NY
Slotnick, Fay D. ... Alexandria, VA
Slotnick, George H. ... Ventura, CA
Slotnick, Kenneth J. ... New York, NY
Slotnick, Lawrence M. ... Boston, MA
Slotnick, Marc J. ... Charleston, WV
Slotnick, Marcia Katz ... Columbus, OH
Slotnick, Melvin M. ... North Syracuse, NY
Slotnick, Michael C. ... Coral Gables, FL
Slotnick, Philip ... Boston, MA
Slotnick & Schwartz ... Williamstown, NJ
Slotnick, Shapiro & Crocker, L.L.P.
New York, NY
Slotnick, Stephen C. ... Juneau, AK
Slotnick, Steven J. ... New York, NY
Slotnick, Steven M. ... Williamstown, NJ
Slotnick, Stuart Philip ... Brooklyn, NY
Slotnik, Gerald ... Brooklyn, NY
Slotnik, Joanne C. ... Salt Lake City, UT
Slotnik, Sol V. ... New York, NY
Sloto, James R. ... Miami, FL
Slotoroff, Joseph G. ... Margate City, NJ
Slotsema, Daniel J. ... Grand Rapids, MI
Slott, Arnold H., (P.A.) ... Jacksonville, FL
Slott & Barker ... Jacksonville, FL
Slott, Barry R. ... Asbury Park, NJ
Slott, Robert W. ... New York, NY
Slottee, Richard A. ... Portland, OR
Slotten, Douglas L.
Federal Communications Commission,
Common Carrier Bureau, GV
Slotter, William A. ... Allentown, PA
Slotznick, Benjamin ... Mount Gretna, PA
Slotznick, Michael ... West Chester, PA
Slough, Bob D. ... Cortez, CO
Slough, Connealy, Irwin & Madden
Kansas City, MO
Slough, David C. ... Columbia, SC
Slough, Fred L. ... Kansas City, MO
Slough, J. Helen ... Cleveland, OH
Slough, John E. ... Charlottesville, VA
Slough, Marsha G. ... Riverside, CA
Sloup, George P. ... Edwards, CA
Slous, Joan ... Department of Justice,
Immigration and Naturalization Service, GV
Slous, Laurence ... Upper Montclair, NJ
Slovacek, Joseph O. ... Houston, TX
Slovak, Baron & Empey, LLP
Palm Springs, CA
Slovak, J. David ... Great Falls, MT
Slovak, Patricia Costello ... Chicago, IL
Slovak, Susan ... New York, NY
Slovak, Thomas S. ... Palm Springs, CA
Slovek, Robert M. ... Omaha, NE
Sloven, Linda J. ... San Francisco, CA
Slovenko, Ralph ... New Orleans, LA
Slovensky, David E. ... Atlanta, GA
Slovensky, Heather Kern ... Atlanta, GA
Slovensky, John C. ... North Canton, OH
Slovensky, Lawrence A. ... Atlanta, GA
Slover, Frank ... Atlanta, GA
Slover, George, Jr. ... Dallas, TX
Slover, George P. ... Department of Justice,
Antitrust Division, GV
Slover, Jack G., Jr. ... Atlanta, GA
Slover, John A., Jr. ... Moline, IL
Slover & Loftus ... Washington, DC
Slover, Roland M. ... Jackson, MS
Slover, Sarah ... New York, NY
Slover, William A. ... Princeton, NJ
Slover, William L. ... Washington, DC
Sloves, Evan Barry ... New York, NY
Slovick, Edward, (Ltd.) ... Chicago, IL
Slovin, Gary M. ... Honolulu, HI
Slovin, Judith ... Boston, MA
Slovin, Nathan ... Livingston, NJ
Slovin, Randy T. ... Cincinnati, OH
Slovin, Richard A. ... Chicago, IL
Slovin, Scott M. ... Cincinnati, OH
Slovin, Sherri Goren ... Cincinnati, OH
Slovin, Sherri Goren, Co., L.P.A.
Cincinnati, OH
Slovinsky, Claudia ... New York, NY
Slovinsky, Gustavo B. ... Chula Vista, CA
Slovinsky, Mary P. ... Chula Vista, CA
Slovinsky and Slovinsky ... Chula Vista, CA
Slovis, Harvey J. ... Bronx, NY
Slovis, Michael R. ... Chicago, IL
Slovis, Norbert J. ... Knoxville, TN
Sloviter, Dolores K. ... Philadelphia, PA
Slovut, Brian J. ... Minneapolis, MN
Slowe, Arthur P. ... Boston, MA
Slowe, Linda M. ... Westford, MA
Slowe, Nancy A. ... Woodbridge, NJ
Slowe, Richard E., Jr. ... North Attleboro, MA
Slowen, W. Thomas ... Clayton, GA
Slowey, William B. ... Detroit, MI
Slowiaczek, John S. ... Omaha, NE
Slowiak, J. Marcus ... Annapolis, MD
Slowiak, J. Marcus, P.A. ... Annapolis, MD
Slowik, Donald C. ... Columbus, OH
Slowik, Henry M. ... Redding, CA
Slowik, Marcia Resnick
Charlotte Amalie, St. Thomas, VI
Slowinski Atkins ... New York, NY
Newark, NJ
Slowinski, Joseph L. ... Fort Lauderdale, FL
Slowinski, Matthew S. ... Newark, NJ
New York, NY
Slowinski, Richard L. ... Washington, DC
Sloyer, Michael N. ... New York, NY
Sluck, John ... St. Paul, MN
Slucter, David L. ... San Bernardino, CA
Sluder, Donald P. ... Jacksonville, FL
Sluga, Gena LoPresto ... Phoenix, AZ
Slugg, Mary Ellen ... Falls Church, VA
Slugg, Ramsay H. ... Fort Worth, TX
Sluggett, Jeffrey V.H. ... Grand Rapids, MI
Sluggett, Jerome V. ... Grand Rapids, MI
Sluis, Paul M. ... Oakland, CA
Sluis, Ralph E. ... Old Saybrook, CT
Sluiter, Jack R. ... Wyoming, MI
Slukich, Richard R. ... Covington, KY
Slungaard, Rolv ... Baldwin, WI
Slunt, Joseph B.
Federal Maritime Commission,
Bureau of Enforcement, GV
Slusarchuk, Cheryl L. ... Chicago, IL
Slusarczuk, Marko M. G. ... Ann Arbor, MI
Slusarz, G. Vincent ... Newbury, OH
Slusher, Aimee C. ... Round Rock, TX
Slusher, Boone ... McAllen, TX
Slusher, Harry R. ... Seattle, WA
Slusher, Jeffrey L. ... Santa Clara, CA
Slusher, Jeremy E. ... Tampa, FL
Slusher, Lee B. ... Arvada, CO
Slusher, Rodney B. ... Florence, AL
Slusher, Stephen A. ... Albuquerque, NM
Slusher, Terry A. ... Orlando, FL
Slusher, Vincent P. ... Dallas, TX
Slusky, Howard J. ... Southfield, MI
Slusky, Jerry M. ... Omaha, NE
Slusky, Ronald D. ... Murray Hill, NJ
Sluss, Andrew Ray ... Detroit, MI
Sluss, Michael J. ... Pittsburgh, PA
Sluss, Stephen Craig ... Charleston, WV
Slusser, Amber L. ... Southfield, MI
Slusser, Andrea B. ... Newport News, VA
Slusser, Christopher B. ... Hazleton, PA
Slusser & Frost, LLP ... Houston, TX
Slusser, Jennifer Jernigan
Wilmington, NC
Slusser, Kenneth A. ... Farmington Hills, MI
Slusser, Scott T. ... Wilmington, NC
Slusser, William C. ... Houston, TX
Slute, Amy D. ... Hackensack, NJ
Slutes, Sakrison, Grant, Hill & Rubin, P.C.
Tucson, AZ
Slutes, Tom ... Tucson, AZ
Slutkin, Andrew G. ... Baltimore, MD
Slutkin & Rubin, LLP ... Baltimore, MD
Slutsker, David A. ... Miami Beach, FL
Slutsky, Allen R. ... Chicago, IL
Slutsky, Bradley A. ... Atlanta, GA
Slutsky, David A. ... Ellenville, NY
Slutsky, David S. ... Brockton, MA
Slutsky, Donald B. ... Philadelphia, PA
Slutsky, June Clayton ... Cincinnati, OH
Slutsky, Kenneth J. ... Roseland, NJ
Slutsky, Michael A. ... Brockton, MA
Slutsky, Michael H. ... Chicago, IL
Slutsky, Norman L. ... Cincinnati, OH
Slutsky & Slutsky ... Brockton, MA
Slutsky & Slutsky Co., L.P.A.
Cincinnati, OH
Slutter, Regis E. ... Alexandria, VA
Slutz, Leonard D. ... Cincinnati, OH
Slutzky, Irving ... Niles, IL
Slutzky, Jay A. ... Niles, IL
Slutzky, Jerrold E. ... Tampa, FL
Slutzky, Richard O. ... New York, NY
Slutzky, Rodney C. ... Chicago, IL
Slutzky, Stanley K. ... Atlanta, GA
Slutzky, Steven J. ... New York, NY
Slutzky, Wolfe and Bailey, LLP
Atlanta, GA
Marietta, GA
Smyrna, GA
Sluyter, Crystal D. ... San Clemente, CA
Sluyter & Schuster ... San Clemente, CA
Sluzar & Black ... Endwell, NY
Sluzar, Joseph J. ... Endwell, NY
Sluzas, Alex R. ... Philadelphia, PA
Sly, John T. ... Albany, NY
Sly, Peter W. ... Oakland, CA
Sly, Richard A. ... Portland, OR
Sly, Thomas S. ... Decatur, IL
Slye & Burrows ... Watertown, NY
Slye, John S. ... Tallahassee, FL
Slye, Kathryn A. ... Miami, FL
Slye, Robert J. ... Watertown, NY
Slye, Ronald C. ... New Haven, CT
Slye, Terry L. ... St. Paul, MN
Slye, William R. ... White Plains, NY
Slykas, Scott P. ... Chicago, IL
Chicago, IL
Slyker, Steven ... Ventura, CA
Slykhouse, George J. ... Grand Rapids, MI
Slyman, Dennis J. ... Greensburg, PA
Slyman, Jeffrey D. ... Dayton, OH
Slyn, Alan T., Law Office ... Louisville, KY
Slyngstad, Charles E. ... Los Angeles, CA
Slywynsky, V. Mark ... Detroit, MI
Slyz, George ... New York, NY
Smaage, Beth C. ... Sacramento, CA
Smaby, Jonathan E. ... Dallas, TX
Smachetti, Emily M. ... Nashville, TN
Smades, Ira P. ... Ambler, PA
Smading, Daniel E. ... Wichita, KS
Smading, Daniel G. ... Marietta, GA
Smaga, Dennis V. ... Sherman Oaks, CA
Smagac, Sandra ... Las Vegas, NV
Smagala, Gerald J. ... Alexandria, VA
Smagowski, Yarek M. ... Fairfax, VA
Smagula, John W. ... New York, NY
Smaha, John L., (A Professional Law
Corporation) ... San Diego, CA
Smaha, Katherine M. ... Gainesville, FL
Smaha, Leslie E. ... Marshalltown, IA
Smaha, Swysgood & Daley ... San Diego, CA
Smail, David W. ... Washington, DC
Smail, Harry F., Jr. ... Greensburg, PA
Smail, Laurence M. ... Newport News, VA
Smail, Thomas E., Jr. ... Sacramento, CA
Smaistrla, Charles J. ... Austin, TX
Smalbach, Peter A. ... San Francisco, CA
Smalbein, Paul W., Jr. ... Daytona Beach, FL
Smaldone, Paul J. ... Buffalo, NY
Smaldone, Paul J. ... Wantagh, NY
Smalec, Mark S. ... White Plains, NY
Smales, Sandra L. ... Boston, MA
Smalheer, Bruce C. ... Chardon, OH
Smalkin, Frederic N. ... Baltimore, MD
Smalkin, Valerie Leonhart ... Monkton, MD
Small, A. Ann Kelsay ... Henderson, NV
Small, A. Thomas ... Raleigh, NC
Small, A. G. ... San Rafael, CA
Small, Amy Rosenberg ... Riverwoods, IL
Small, Andrew B. ... New York, NY
Small, Andrew C. ... Chicago, IL
Small, Andrew D. ... Chicago, IL
Small, Andrew M. ... Minneapolis, MN
Small, Angela R. ... Los Angeles, CA
Small, Anthony M. ... Syracuse, NY
Small, Arthur Atwell, II ... Stockton, CA
Small, Arthur M. ... Indianapolis, IN
Small, Audra J. ... Rockville, MD
Small, Barry L. ... Philadelphia, PA
Small, Benjamin F. ... Rockford, IL
Small, Bobby J. ... Indianapolis, IN
Small, Bradley S. ... Santa Monica, CA
Small, Bradley W. ... Nashville, IL
Small, C. Neal ... Memphis, TN
Small, Carolyn L. ... San Francisco, CA
Small, Charles E. ... Fresno, CA
Small, Charles E. ... San Francisco, CA
Small, Charles F. ... Newburyport, MA
Small, Charles H. ... New York, NY
Small, Christopher James
Winston-Salem, NC
Small, Clarence M., Jr. ... Birmingham, AL
Small, Clay G. ... Plano, TX
Small, Clyde ... Red Bluff, CA
Small, Craig & Werkenthin, A Professional
Corporation ... Austin, TX
San Angelo, TX
San Antonio, TX
Small, Daniel A. ... Washington, DC
Small, Daniel I. ... Boston, MA
Small, Daniel P., (P.C.) ... Richmond, VA
Small, Daniel W. ... Nashville, TN
Small, David ... New York, NY
Small, David A. ... Dallas, TX
Small, David L. ... Houston, TX
Small, David M. ... Tacoma, WA
Small, Dean D. ... Chicago, IL
Small, Doreen G. ... New York, NY
Small, Douglas D. ... South Bend, IN
Small, Edward ... Cleveland, OH
Small, Edward C. ... Austin, TX
Small, Edwin W. ... Knoxville, TN
Small, Elizabeth ... New York, NY
Small, Elizabeth R. ... Franklin, MA
Small, Elizabeth S. ... Providence, RI
Small, Eugene L. ... New York, NY
Small, F. McCauley, Jr. ... San Jose, CA
Small, Frank A. ... Palo Alto, CA
Small, Frederick ... Boston, MA
Small, G. Elvin, III ... Elizabeth City, NC
Small, George E. ... Bellingham, WA
Small, Gillian, G.M. ... Oakland, CA

Smiedt, Donna J. ....Dallas, TX
Smierciak, Robert M. ....Chicago, IL
Smietanka, Allan J. ....Chicago, IL
Smietanka, John A. ....Grand Rapids, MI
Smietanka, Paul A. ....Helena, MT
Smietanka, Raymond V. ....Stevensville, MI
Smietanski, Alan F. ....Kankakee, IL
Smietanski, Debra K., (P.A.) ....Tampa, FL
Smiga, David L. ....Pittsburgh, PA
Smigel, Anderson & Sacks
Harrisburg, PA
Smigel, LeRoy ....Harrisburg, PA
Smigel, Scott B. ....Montecito, CA
Smigelski, Brian R. ....Milwaukee, WI
Smigelski, William S. ....Alpena, MI
Smigelskis, Marianne R. ....Chicago, IL
Smigiel, Chester W. ....Chicago, IL
Smigiel, Joseph S., Jr. ....Grand Rapids, MI
Smigielski, Mary A. ....Chicago, IL
Smigielski, Paul J. ....Rochester Hills, MI
Smigliani, Paul W. ....San Diego, CA
Smigliani, Suzanne Lovelace
San Diego, CA
Smigosky, Kristina Gilbertson ....Towson, MD
Smigulec, Michael ....Clinton Township, MI
Smikle, Richard A. ....Indianapolis, IN
Smilack, Stanley ....Washington, DC
Smilan, Laurie B. ....Palo Alto, CA
Smiland & Khachigian ....Los Angeles, CA
San Clemente, CA
Smiland, William M. ....Los Angeles, CA
Smilanick, Diane ....University Heights, OH
Smilay, Steven L. ....Los Angeles, CA
Smiler, Scott M. ....New York, NY
Smiles, Barbara J. ....Naperville, IL
Smiles, Jennifer L. ....Morristown, NJ
Smiles, Joan E. ....Los Angeles, CA
Smiles, Robert G., Jr. ....Martinsburg, WV
Smiles, Terri-Lynne B. ....Columbus, OH
Smiley, Ann M. ....Middleton, WI
Smiley, Brian N. ....Atlanta, GA
Smiley, Bruce M. ....Los Angeles, CA
Smiley, Carl T. ....Palos Verdes Estates, CA
Smiley, Charles A., Jr. ....Dayton, OH
Smiley, Charles, & Associates ....Dayton, OH
Smiley, Charles W. ....Kansas City, MO
Smiley, Clare B., Jr. ....Uniontown, AL
Smiley, Cynthia C. ....Austin, TX
Smiley, David W. ....Bend, OR
Smiley, Donald B. ....Scottsdale, AZ
Smiley, Donald V., Jr. ....Los Angeles, CA
Smiley, Eileen M. ....Washington, DC
Smiley, Evan D. ....Costa Mesa, CA
Smiley, Gary A. ....Lincolnwood, IL
Smiley, George S., Jr. ....Buena Park, CA
Smiley, Guy I. ....New York, NY
Smiley, Harold U., Jr. ....Wyoming, MI
Smiley & Holst ....Wyoming, MI
Smiley, James Ian ....Baltimore, MD
Smiley, Janine M. ....Madison, WI
Smiley, Joan E. ....Department of Justice, Civil Division, GV
Smiley, John C. ....Denver, CO
Smiley, John R. ....Ventura, CA
Smiley, John T. ....Carrollton, OH
Smiley, Kathleen L. ....Gulfport, MS
Smiley, Laurie A. ....Seattle, WA
Smiley Law Office ....Portage, WI
Smiley, Mark C. ....Detroit, MI
Smiley, Martha E. ....Austin, TX
Smiley, Martin ....New York, NY
Smiley, Michael S. ....Hartford, CT
Smiley, Michael S. ....Amarillo, TX
Smiley, Prentis, Jr. ....Yorktown, VA
Smiley, Raymond E. ....Muskegon, MI
Smiley, Rhonda ....Kansas City, MO
Smiley, Robert N. ....Utica, MI
Smiley, Robert R., III ....Elk, CA
Charleston, SC
Smiley, Robert R., P.C. ....Elk, CA
Charleston, SC
Smiley, Robert W. ....Pittsburgh, PA
Smiley, Robert W., Jr. ....Logandale, NV
Smiley, Russell M.
Palm Beach Gardens, FL
Smiley, Schwartz & Captain ....New York, NY
Smiley, Scott William ....Tallahassee, FL
Smiley, Stafford ....Washington, DC
Smiley, Stanley R. ....Torrance, CA
Smiley, Thomas G. ....St. Petersburg, FL
Smiley, Tiare Bowe ....Raleigh, NC
Smiley, William A. ....Portage, WI
Smiley, W. M., Jr. ....St. Petersburg, FL
Smilgin, John F ....New York, NY
Smilie, Carolyn J. ....Alexandria, LA
Smilie, Dal ....Helena, MT
Smilie, Scott W. ....Chicago, IL
Smiling, A. Mark ....Tulsa, OK
Smiljanich, Terry A. ....St. Petersburg, FL
Tampa, FL
Smilk, David M. ....Broomall, PA
Smilley-Weiner, Debra A. ....Bethesda, MD
Smillie, Deborah A. ....Los Angeles, CA
Smillie, Douglas J. ....Allentown, PA
Smillie, John A. ....Marlborough, MA
Smillie, Keith O. ....Ann Arbor, MI
Smillie-Scavelli, Patricia ....Staten Island, NY
Smilow, Edward L. ....Newport Beach, CA
Smilow, Lynn V. ....Orange, CA
Smilow, Mark D. ....New York, NY
Smilowitz, Alan ....West Hempstead, NY
Smink, Bryce William ....Virginia Beach, VA
Smink, Linda ....Metuchen, NJ
Smink Thomas & Assocs., P.C.
Virginia Beach, VA
Smink, Tiffany West ....Denver, CO
Smirch, James McCord ....Idaho Falls, ID
Smircina, Blair E. ....Norfolk, VA
Smircina, John E. ....Alexandria, VA
Smirl, Richard W. ....Long Beach, CA
Smirlock, Daniel ....Clifton Park, NY
Smirman, Preston H. ....Troy, MI
Smirni, Allan D. ....Sunnyvale, CA
Smirnoff, Andrew P. ....San Francisco, CA
Smirnoff, Irving ....Derby, CT
Smirnoff, Tracy Wilson ....Cleveland, OH
Smirti, Stephen J., Jr. (P.C.)
Uniondale, NY
Smirz, James W. ....Lexington, KY
Smirz & Toliver, P.L.C. ....Lexington, KY
Smisek, Jeffery A. ....Houston, TX
Smissaert, John H. ....Tiburon, CA
Smissman, Clarine F., (Mrs.) ....Orlando, FL
Smit, Bernardus J. ....Piedmont, CA
Waldport, OR
Smit, Hans ....New York, NY
Smit, Keith R. ....Sturgis, SD
Smit, Leonard J. ....St. Joseph, MI
Smit, Peter A. ....Grand Rapids, MI
Smit, Rebecca A. ....Georgetown, TX
Smit, Robert H. ....New York, NY
Smit, Steven D. ....Austin, TX
Smitas, Daniel J. ....Albany, NY
Smitas, David A. ....Beverly Hills, CA
Smitch, Marjorie ....Olympia, WA
Smitelli, Janet Heller ....Mineola, NY
Smith / Cotton ....Holly Springs, MS
Tupelo, MS
Smith, A. Frank, III ....Houston, TX
Smith, A. Frank, Jr. ....Houston, TX
Smith, A. Jeffrey ....Dallas, TX
Smith, A. Meilus ....Barre, MA
Smith, A. Randall ....Redwood City, CA
Smith, A. Russell ....Jacksonville, FL
Smith, A. Russell ....Akron, OH
Smith, A. Russell ....Akron, OH
Smith, A. Thomas, III
Oakbrook Terrace, IL
Smith, A. Zachary, III ....Charlotte, NC
Smith, A. B., Jr. ....Grand Rapids, MI
Smith, Abbe ....Washington, DC
Smith Abbot, L.L.P. ....New York, NY
Smith, Adam Clayton ....San Francisco, CA
Smith, Adam L. ....Atlanta, GA
Smith, Adam M. ....Newark, NJ
Smith, Adam M. ....King Of Prussia, PA
Smith, Adam W. ....Fairfax, VA
Smith, Adrian C. ....Chicago, IL
Smith, Adrian C. ....Pittsburgh, PA
Smith, Adrienne Goebel ....Macon, GA
Smith, Adrienne Sullivan ....Bronxville, NY
Smith, Aimee La Buy ....Laurel, MD
Smith, Aker, Grossman & Hollinger LLP
Norristown, PA
Smith, Alan B. ....Brunswick, GA
Smith, Alan C. ....Seattle, WA
Smith, Alan D. ....Boston, MA
Smith, Alan D.
Charlotte Amalie, St. Thomas, VI
Smith, Alan D. ....Seattle, WA
Smith, Alan E. ....Stockton, CA
Smith, Alan I. ....Jersey City, NJ
Smith, Alan J. ....Watsonville, CA
Smith, Alan L. ....Salt Lake City, UT
Smith, Alan Lee ....Jackson, MS
Smith, Alan Lee ....Jackson, MS
Smith, Alan M. ....Flint, MI
Smith, Alan P. ....Rydal, PA
Smith, Alan R. ....Grand Rapids, MI
Smith, Alan T. ....Fayetteville, NC
Smith, Albert A. ....Saginaw, MI
Smith, Albert B., III ....Cleveland, MS
Smith, Albert C. ....Palo Alto, CA
Smith, Albert V. ....Spartanburg, SC
Smith, Albert W. ....Park Ridge, IL
Smith, Alden H., Jr. ....Nashville, TN
Smith, Alex F., Jr. ....Shreveport, LA
Smith, Alexander G. ....Jacksonville, FL
Smith, Alexander M. ....Oneonta, AL
Smith, Alexander P. ....Norfolk, VA
Smith, Alexander P., and Associates, P.C.
Norfolk, VA
Smith, Alexander W. ....Atlanta, GA
Smith, Alexandra ....Dallas, TX
Smith, Alexandra K. ....Seattle, WA
Smith, Alexis M. ....Knoxville, TN
Smith, Alfred C. ....Denver, CO
Smith, Alfred E. ....Los Angeles, CA
Smith, Alfred E. ....New York, NY
Smith, Alfred E., Jr. ....New Haven, CT
Smith, Alfred E., Jr. ....Chattanooga, TN
Smith, Alfred F., Jr. ....Birmingham, AL
Smith, Alfred G., II ....Miami, FL
Smith, Alfred J., Jr. ....Stamford, CT
Smith, Alfred L., Jr. ....Richmond, VA
Smith, Alfred L., Jr. ....Richmond, VA
Smith, Alisa L. ....Nashville, TN
Smith, Alison B. ....Memphis, TN
Smith, Alison L. ....Houston, TX
Smith, Alison T. ....Pittsburgh, PA
Smith, Alistair J. H. ....Kalamazoo, MI
Smith, Allan C. ....Vacaville, CA
Smith, Allan F. ....Ann Arbor, MI
Smith, Allan F. ....San Antonio, TX
Smith, Allan R. ....Jonesboro, GA
Smith, Allan R., P.C. ....Jonesboro, GA
Smith, Allan W. ....Richmond, VA
Smith, Allan W., P.C. ....Richmond, VA
Smith, Allen C. ....Stoughton, MA
Smith, Allen C. ....Charlotte, NC
Smith, Allen D. ....Fayetteville, NC
Smith, Allen D. ....Steelton, PA
Smith, Allen D. ....Columbia, SC
Smith, Allen H. ....York, PA
Smith, Allen, Jr. ....Helena, MT
Smith, Allen L., III ....New Orleans, LA
Smith, Allen L., Jr. ....Lake Charles, LA
Smith, Allen M. ....Riverhead, NY
Smith, Allen, Mendenhall, Delaney & Associate
Alton, IL
Smith, Allen R. ....Winter Haven, FL
Smith, Allen R. ....Albuquerque, NM
Smith, Allen R., P.A. ....Winter Haven, FL
Smith, Allen W. ....Glastonbury, CT
Smith Alling Lane, P.S. ....Tacoma, WA
Smith, Allison B. ....Hammond, IN
Smith, Allison E. ....Albany, OR
Smith, Allison K. ....Rancho Cordova, CA
Smith, Allison M.
Department of Transportation, Federal Highway Administration, GV
Smith, Allison P. ....Birmingham, AL
Smith, Alton J. ....Irvine, CA
Smith, Alton J., A Professional Corporation
Irvine, CA
Smith, Alton L. ....Austin, TX
Smith, Alva C., Jr. ....Baton Rouge, LA
Smith, Alva E. ....Dallas, TX
Smith, Alvah O. ....Atlanta, GA
Smith, Alvin W., Jr. ....San Jose, CA
Smith, Alwin A. ....Sulphur Springs, TX
Smith, Alys Choi ....Chicago, IL
Smith, Alys Portman ....Morristown, NJ
Smith, Amber L. ....Oklahoma City, OK
Smith, Amos ....St. Louis, MO
Smith, Amy A. ....Westby, WI
Smith, Amy B. ....Washington, DC
Smith, Amy Bryson ....Nashville, TN
Smith, Amy D. ....Madisonville, TX
Smith, Amy E. ....Chicago, IL
Smith, Amy Elizabeth ....Atlanta, GA
Smith, Amy K. ....Winston-Salem, NC
Smith, Amy L., (P.A.)
West Palm Beach, FL
Smith, Amy Lynne ....Lake Placid, NY
Smith, Amy M. ....Sulphur Springs, TX
Smith, Amy M. ....Clarksburg, WV
Smith, Anastasia Watson ....College Park, MD
Smith, Ande A. ....Portland, ME
Smith, Anderson, Baker & Long ....York, PA
Smith, Anderson, Blount, Dorsett, Mitchell & Jernigan, L.L.P. ....Raleigh, NC
Research Triangle Park, NC
Smith, Andrea Kitzis ....Morristown, NJ
Smith, Andrea L. ....Denver, CO
Smith, Andrea L. ....Cincinnati, OH
Smith, Andrea L. ....Philadelphia, PA
Smith, Andrea Teves ....Lakeland, FL
Lake Wales, FL
Winter Haven, FL
Smith, Andrew A. ....Northport, AL
Smith, Andrew A. ....Department of Justice, Environment and Natural Resources Division, GV
Smith, Andrew C. ....Columbus, OH
Smith, Andrew D. ....Honolulu, HI
Smith, Andrew G. ....St. Louis, MO
Smith, Andrew H. ....New York, NY
Smith, Andrew J. ....Sacramento, CA
Smith, Andrew J. ....Portland, OR
Smith, Andrew L. ....Mobile, AL
Smith, Andrew L. ....Carrollton, TX
Smith, Andrew M. ....Birmingham, AL
Smith, Andrew M.
Securities and Exchange Commission, GV
Smith, Andrew M. ....Boca Raton, FL
Smith, Andrew M. ....Cherry Hill, NJ
Smith, Andrew M. ....New York, NY
Smith, Andrew M., Jr. ....Freehold, NJ
Smith, Andrew Mason ....Alexandria, LA
Smith, Andrew O. ....Columbus, OH
Smith, Andrew P. ....La Quinta, CA
Smith, Andrew P. ....Rhinelander, WI
Smith, Andrew T. ....Rockford, IL
Smith, Andrew T. ....Dayton, OH
Smith, Andrew Trevor ....Frankfort, KY
Smith, Andrew V. ....Fallbrook, CA
Smith, Andrew V. ....San Francisco, CA
Smith, Andrews, Rogers & Brady
Tampa, FL
Smith, Andrine K. ....San Francisco, CA
Smith, Angela M. ....Indianapolis, IN
Smith, Angela R. ....Elkhart, IN
Smith, Angela Todd
National Labor Relations Board, Office of the General Counsel, GV
Smith, Angela Townsend ....Olathe, KS
Smith, Angelia D. ....Columbia, SC
Smith, Anita J. ....Dallas, TX
Smith, Anita Tucker ....New York, NY
Smith, Ann Bailey ....Louisville, KY
Smith, Ann K. ....Cerritos, CA
Smith, Ann Kane ....Los Angeles, CA
Smith, Ann Kowal ....Cleveland, OH
Smith, Ann Kristine ....Sullivan, IN
Smith, Ann Krueger ....Jacksonville, FL
Smith, Ann L. ....Independence, KS
Smith, Ann L. ....Wausau, WI
Smith, Ann Lonergan ....Pasadena, CA
Smith, Ann M. ....Chicago, IL
Smith, Ann Marie ....San Diego, CA
Smith, Ann Ustad ....Madison, WI
Smith, Anna T.
Department of Defense, GV
Smith, Annalyn G. ....San Antonio, TX
Smith, Anne Brouwers ....Sun Prairie, WI
Smith, Anne D. ....Washington, DC
Smith, Anne Ferris ....McLean, VA
Smith, Anne K. ....Indianapolis, IN
Smith, Anne Martin ....Paducah, KY
Smith, Anne N. ....Newark, NJ
Smith, Anne Orsi ....Des Arc, AR
Smith, Anne Orsi ....Little Rock, AR
Smith, Anneli R. ....Salt Lake City, UT
Smith, Annette ....Marietta, GA
Smith, Anthony ....Department of Commerce, Patent and Trademark Office, GV
Silver Spring, MD
Smith, Anthony E. ....Kansas City, MO
Smith, Anthony L. ....Austin, TX
Smith, Antonia G. ....Laguna Hills, CA
Smith, April ....Oneonta, NY
Smith, April E. ....Dallas, TX
Smith, Archer D., III ....Atlanta, GA
Smith, Archie L. ....Asheboro, NC
Smith, Archie L., III ....Durham, NC
Smith, Archie L., Jr. ....Asheboro, NC
Smith, Ariel M.
Charlotte Amalie, St. Thomas, VI
Smith, Arlene G. ....Bloomfield Hills, MI
Smith, Armin H., Jr. ....Tampa, FL
Smith & Armstrong ....Louisville, KY
Smith, Arnold ....Wilmington, NC
Smith, Arnold & Gyben, LLP ....Irvine, CA
Smith, Arnold M. ....Hawthorne, NJ
Smith, Aron L. ....Pearl River, NY
Smith, Arthur ....Beverly Hills, CA
Smith, Arthur A., Jr. ....Boston, MA
Smith, Arthur B., Jr. ....Chicago, IL
Smith, Arthur D. ....Moscow, ID
Smith, Arthur D. ....Edgartown, MA
Smith, Arthur E. ....Roanoke, VA
Smith, Arthur G. ....Lynchburg, VA
Smith, Arthur H. ....Toledo, OH
Smith, Arthur J. ....New York, NY
Smith, Arthur J. ....Pittsburgh, PA
Smith, Arthur J., P.C. ....Pittsburgh, PA
Smith, Arthur K., III ....Dallas, TX
Smith, Arthur L. ....St. Louis, MO
Smith, Arthur L., III ....Columbus, GA
Smith, Arthur R., Jr. ....Grand Junction, CO
Smith, Arthur Thad ....Denver, CO
Smith & Ashburn, P.A.
Fort Lauderdale, FL
Jacksonville, FL
Miami, FL
Orlando, FL
Pensacola, FL
Tallahassee, FL
Tampa, FL
Smith, Ashley Ann ....Houston, TX
Smith, Athena Platis ....Hinsdale, IL
Smith, Aubry ....New York, NY
Smith, Audra ....Augusta, ME
Smith, Audrey A. ....San Francisco, CA
Smith, Audrey Anne ....Burlingame, CA
Smith, Autherine B. ....Philadelphia, PA
Smith, Avery ....Pensacola, FL
Smith, B. Anne ....Atlanta, GA
Smith, B. Dixie ....Houston, TX
Smith, B. Jack ....Tulsa, OK
Smith, B. Rush, III ....Columbia, SC
Smith, B. Ward ....Dearborn, MI
Smith, Bachman S., III ....Charleston, SC
Smith, Baker A. ....Marietta, GA
Smith Bakke Hovland & Oppegard
Moorhead, MN
Bismarck, ND
Fargo, ND
Smith, Ballard & Logan, P.A.
Tallahassee, FL
Smith, Banks M. ....San Antonio, TX
Smith, Banks T. ....Dothan, AL
Smith, Barbara ....Dallas, TX
Smith, Barbara C.
Securities and Exchange Commission, Division of Corporation Finance, GV
Smith, Barbara F. ....Albany, NY
Smith, Barbara Hawley ....Nashville, TN
Smith, Barbara J. ....Cleveland, OH
Smith, Barbara Jensen ....Concord, NH
Smith, Barbara Jo ....Salem, OR
Smith, Barbara L. ....Wilkes-Barre, PA
Smith, Barbara Lee ....Washington, DC
Smith, Barbara Lee ....Chicago, IL
Smith, Barbara O'Neil ....Cambridge, MA
Smith, Barbara P. ....Brooklyn, NY
Smith, Barbara Quinn ....Sandusky, OH
Smith, Barbara R. ....Berkeley, CA
Smith, Barbara Rudolph ....Miami, FL
Smith, Barbara W. ....Rockford, IL
Smith, Barlow ....Austin, TX
Smith, Barney M., Jr. ....Macomb, IL
Smith, Barry A. ....Los Angeles, CA
Smith, Barry F.
Department Of Health And Human Services, GV
Smith, Barry L. ....Jackson, OH
Smith, Barry Lee ....Warren, PA
Smith, Barry Lynn ....Tulsa, OK
Smith, Barry M. ....New York, NY
Smith, Barry Paul ....El Segundo, CA
Smith, Barry R. ....Braintree, MA
Smith, Barry R. ....Framingham, MA
Smith, Barry R. ....Kalamazoo, MI
Smith, Barry V. ....Rome, GA
Smith, Bart A. ....River Grove, IL
Smith, Bartlett B. ....Milford, MI
Smith, Bartlett, Heeke, Carpenter, Lewis & Thompson ....Jeffersonville, IN
Louisville, KY
Smith, Barton A. ....Milpitas, CA
Smith, Barton S. ....Fort Worth, TX
Smith, Bassett, Purcell & Koenig
Atlanta, GA
Smith, Bea Ann ....Austin, TX
Smith, Beatrice M. ....Beaumont, TX
Smith, Beeks & Hodges ....Twin Falls, ID
Smith, Belinda A. ....Houston, TX
Smith & Bemenderfer ....Indianapolis, IN
Smith, Ben Barrett ....Batesville, MS
Smith, Ben W. ....McAllen, TX

Smith, Benjamin .... **Pittsfield, MA**
Smith, Benjamin Franklin, Jr. .... Marietta, GA
Smith, Benjamin J. .... **Minneapolis, MN**
Smith, Benjamin, Jr. .... Waycross, GA
Smith, Benjamin M., III .... **Fairfax, VA**
Smith, Benjamin M., Jr.
Fredericksburg, VA
Smith, Bennett E. .... Jackson, MS
Smith, Bentley & Hartnett
Redwood City, CA
Smith, Berkeley Ashton .... St. Helens, OR
Smith, Berl A. .... **Jonesboro, AR**
Smith, Berl S. .... **Jonesboro, AR**
Smith, Bernadette M. .... Atlanta, GA
Smith, Bernadette T. .... **Philadelphia, PA**
Smith, Bernard A. .... Cleveland, OH
Smith, Bernard J. .... Buffalo, NY
Smith, Bernard J. .... **Cleveland, OH**
Smith, Bernard K. .... McMinnville, TN
Smith, Bernard L. .... **Washington, DC**
Smith, Bernard L. .... The Dalles, OR
Smith, Bernard Patrick .... Marblehead, MA
Smith, Bernard S. .... Lafayette, LA
Smith & Bertelsen .... Washington, DC
Smith, Beth Ann .... Waynesboro, GA
Smith, Beth Ann .... North Lima, OH
Smith, Betty .... Salem, OR
Smith, Betty Jean R. .... Nahunta, GA
Smith, Beverly A. .... **Mineola, NY**
Riverhead, NY
Smith, Beverly H. .... **Tallahassee, FL**
Smith, Beverly J. .... **Oakland, CA**
Smith, Beverly K. .... **Tulsa, OK**
Smith, Beverly McQueary .... Huntington, NY
Smith, Bill Lee .... Cumberland, MD
Smith, Bill T., Jr. .... **Boca Raton, FL**
Smith, Bill T., Jr., P.A. .... **Boca Raton, FL**
Smith, Billy, Jr. .... **Las Vegas, NV**
Smith, Billy R. .... Atlanta, GA
Smith, Billy R. .... Houston, TX
Smith, Billy R., P.C. .... Houston, TX
Smith, Bing .... Ventura, CA
Smith, B. J. .... Mesquite, TX
Smith, Blake J. .... **Macon, GA**
Smith, Blane A. .... **Rancho Cordova, CA**
Smith, Blucher .... Edinburg, TX
Smith, Bob A. .... Oklahoma City, OK
Smith, Bobby Dean .... Anchorage, AK
Smith, Bonner, Law Offices of
Lubbock, TX
Smith, Bonnie Bridgers .... **Jackson, MS**
Smith, Bonnie M. .... Los Angeles, CA
Smith, Boston W. .... Oklahoma City, OK
Smith, Bovill, Fisher, Meyer & Borchard, P.C. .... **Bay City, MI**
Flint, MI
Frankenmuth, MI
Midland, MI
Saginaw, MI
Smith, Brad .... Tulsa, OK
Smith, Brad C. .... Ogden, UT
Smith, Brad E. .... **Coeur d'Alene, ID**
Spokane, WA
Smith, Brad H. .... **Cincinnati, OH**
Smith, Bradford C. .... New York, NY
Smith, Bradford J. .... **Boston, MA**
Smith, Bradford James .... Baltimore, MD
Smith, Bradford S. .... Atlantic City, NJ
Smith, Bradley .... San Jose, CA
Smith, Bradley A. .... Corpus Christi, TX
Smith, Bradley C. .... Dayton, OH
Smith, Bradley E. .... Latrobe, PA
Smith, Bradley Guy .... **Lakeland, FL**
Smith, Bradley J .... Fremont, OH
Smith, Bradley L. .... **Ann Arbor, MI**
Smith, Bradley P. .... **New York, NY**
Smith, Bradley S. .... Cleveland, OH
Smith, Bradley W .... Argonne, IL
Smith, Bradley W. .... **Jackson, MS**
Smith, Bradley Y. .... **New York, NY**
Smith, Bradshaw .... Van Buren, MO
Smith, Brandenburg, Starkweather & Knochelmann .... Cincinnati, OH
Smith, Brandon D. .... San Francisco, CA
Smith & Bratcher, P.C. .... **Waco, TX**
Smith, Brenda C. .... Oxnard, CA
Simi Valley, CA
Smith, Brenda J. .... Louisville, KY
Smith, Brenda J. .... Canandaigua, NY
Smith, Brenda Joyce .... Lewisburg, WV
Smith, Brenda K. .... San Marcos, TX
Smith, Brenda V. .... Washington, DC
Smith, Brendan P. .... Providence, RI
Smith, Brendan P., A Professional Corporation
Providence, RI
Smith, Brent P. .... **La Crosse, WI**
Smith, Brent W. .... **Los Angeles, CA**
Smith, Bret A. .... **Muskogee, OK**
Smith, Brett A. .... **Dallas, TX**
Smith, Brett Warren .... Spokane, WA
Smith, Brian A. .... **New York, NY**
Smith, Brian A. E. .... **San Francisco, CA**
Smith, Brian B. .... **Birmingham, MI**
Smith, Brian C. .... Minneapolis, MN
Smith, Brian C. .... Hamilton, MT
Smith, Brian C. .... **Chattanooga, TN**
Smith, Brian D. .... **San Francisco, CA**
Smith, Brian D. .... Denver, CO
Smith, Brian D. .... **Hartford, CT**
Smith, Brian D. .... Miami Beach, FL
Smith, Brian D. .... **Marietta, GA**
Smith, Brian D. .... Joliet, IL
Smith, Brian D. .... **Shreveport, LA**
Smith, Brian D. .... Belvidere, NJ
Smith, Brian D., P.C. .... Denver, CO
Smith, Brian Douglas .... Arnold, MO
Smith, Brian E. .... **Yuma, AZ**
Smith, Brian E. .... Department of Justice, Federal Bureau of Investigation, GV
Smith, Brian E., The, Law Firm
Phoenix, AZ
Tucson, AZ
Yuma, AZ
Smith, Brian Edward .... Gilbert, AZ
Smith, Brian Edward, P.C. .... Gilbert, AZ
Smith, Brian F. .... **New York, NY**
Smith, Brian G. .... Chester, PA
Smith, Brian H. .... **Elkins Park, PA**
Smith, Brian J. .... **North Chicago, IL**
Smith, Brian J. .... **Missoula, MT**
Smith, Brian J. .... Albany, NY
Smith, Brian Jonathan .... Jacksonville, FL
Smith, Brian K. .... Evansville, IN
Smith, Brian L. .... **Waterbury, CT**
Smith, Brian L. .... Shawnee, KS
Smith, Brian L. .... Gallatin, TN
Smith, Brian Lester .... Des Moines, IA
Smith, Brian M. .... **Detroit, MI**
Smith, Brian M. .... Troy, MI
Smith, Brian R. .... **Hartford, CT**
Smith, Brian S. .... Department of Justice, Civil Division, GV
Smith, Brian T. .... **Dallas, TX**
Smith, Brian W. .... **Bridgeport, CT**
Smith, Brian W. .... **Washington, DC**
Smith, Brian W. .... West Palm Beach, FL
Smith, Brian W. .... Lewis, IN
Smith, Brian W., P.A. .... West Palm Beach, FL
Smith, Brice L. .... Portland, OR
Smith, Brigid M. .... Stamford, CT
Smith & Brink, P.C. .... **Boston, MA**
Lynnfield, MA
Quincy, MA
Springfield, MA
Smith, Briscoe R. .... **New York, NY**
Smith, Brock .... **Decatur, TX**
Smith, Brook McCray .... **Ann Arbor, MI**
Smith, Brook McCray, P.C.
Ann Arbor, MI
Smith, Brooke E. .... Houston, TX
Smith & Brooker, P.C. .... **Bay City, MI**
Saginaw, MI
Smith, Brooks M. .... **Richmond, VA**
Smith, Brooks R. .... **Atlanta, GA**
Smith Bros. Law Office .... Grand Ledge, MI
Smith, Brown B. .... **San Diego, CA**
Smith, Bruce .... Bronx, NY
Smith, Bruce A. .... Vincennes, IN
Smith, Bruce A. .... Washington, IN
Smith, Bruce A. .... **Lincoln, NE**
Smith, Bruce A. .... **Syracuse, NY**
Smith, Bruce A. .... **Longview, TX**
Smith, Bruce B. .... Magee, MS
Smith, Bruce C. .... **Scottsdale, AZ**
Smith, Bruce C. .... San Diego, CA
Smith, Bruce C. .... **Atlanta, GA**
Smith, Bruce D. .... Medford, OR
Smith, Bruce E. .... **Indianapolis, IN**
Smith, Bruce E. .... **Nicholasville, KY**
Smith, Bruce E. .... **Alliance, OH**
Smith, Bruce E. .... **Eugene, OR**
Smith, Bruce F. .... **Boston, MA**
Smith, Bruce G. .... **Denver, CO**
Smith, Bruce I. .... **Grand Island, NE**
Smith, Bruce J. .... Vero Beach, FL
Smith, Bruce L. .... **Toledo, OH**
Smith, Bruce L. .... Titusville, PA
Smith, Bruce M. .... Gainesville, FL
Smith, Bruce M. .... Wilmette, IL
Smith, Bruce M. .... Plymouth Meeting, PA
Smith, Bruce M. .... Dakota Dunes, SD
Smith, Bruce Macon .... **Memphis, TN**
Smith, Bruce P. .... **Washington, DC**
Smith, Bruce R. .... **Lexington, KY**
Smith, Bruce T. .... West Des Moines, IA
Smith, Bruce W. .... **Portland, ME**
Smith, Bryan D. .... **Idaho Falls, ID**
Smith, Bryan F. (Buck), Jr. .... **Dallas, TX**
Smith, Bryan J. .... **Pittsburgh, PA**
Smith, Bryan L. .... Tulsa, OK
Smith, Bryan W. .... **Topeka, KS**
Smith, Bryant K. .... Peachtree City, GA
Smith, Bryant M. .... Austin, TX
Smith, Bundy, Bybee & Barnett, P.C.
Charleston, SC
Mount Pleasant, SC
Smith, Burdette C. .... Longboat Key, FL
Smith, Burke E. .... Kenton, OH
Smith, Burke Q. .... New York, NY
Smith, Burnett & Larson, L.L.C.
Larned, KS
Smith, Burry, Herman & Miller, P.C.
Decatur, IN
Smith, Burton C., Jr. .... Waynesville, NC
Smith, Buss & Jacobs, LLP
New York, NY
Yonkers, NY
Smith, Byron O. .... Indian Wells, CA
Smith, C. Ander .... **Denver, CO**
Smith, C. Bradley .... Cody, WY
Smith, C. Byron, Jr. .... North Little Rock, AR
Smith, C. Christopher .... Lumberton, NC
Smith, C. Christopher, P.A. .... Lumberton, NC
Smith, C. Emanuel .... Tupelo, MS
Smith, C. Giles, Jr. .... **Kalamazoo, MI**
Smith, C. Holt, III .... **Jacksonville, FL**
Smith, C. Jerome .... **Hammond, IN**
Smith, C. Joseph .... San Francisco, CA
Smith, C. Lamont .... Denver, CO
Smith, C. Lynwood, Jr. .... Huntsville, AL
Smith, C Matthew A. .... **Jacksonville, IL**
Smith, C. McFerrin, III .... DeLand, FL
Smith, C. Michael .... San Jose, CA
Smith, C. Paul .... **Frederick, MD**
Smith, C. Paul .... **Rockville, MD**
Smith, C. Ron .... **Atlanta, GA**
Smith, C. Roscoe .... Indianapolis, IN
Smith, C. Ross, III .... Sandusky, OH
Smith, C. Vandiver .... Charlotte, NC
Smith, C. Wayne .... Homer, LA
Smith, C. Wesley .... Aiken, SC
Smith, C. William .... **Washington, DC**
Smith, Calvin E. .... Wernersville, PA
Smith, Cameron M., Jr. .... **Irvine, CA**
Smith Campbell & Paduano
New York, NY
Smith, Candace J. .... **Covington, KY**
Smith, Candace L. .... Houston, TX
Smith, Candace N. .... **Atlanta, GA**
Smith, Candice C. .... Houston, TX
Smith & Cannon .... **Lewiston, ID**
Smith, Carey E. .... Austin, TX
Smith, Carey H. .... **Worcester, MA**
Smith, Carey W. .... **Washington, DC**
Smith, Carissa M. .... **Palo Alto, CA**
Smith, Carl E. .... Boston, MA
Smith, Carl E. .... Ava, MO
Smith, Carl F. .... Lakewood, CO
Smith, Carl H., Jr. .... **Bay City, MI**
Smith, Carl J., Jr. .... Washington, PA
Smith, Carl M. .... Washington, DC
Smith, Carl Michael .... **Oklahoma City, OK**
Smith, Carla J. .... Minneapolis, MN
Smith, Carlos C. .... **Chattanooga, TN**
Smith & Carlson .... Reading, PA
Smith & Carlson, P.C. .... **Austin, TX**
Georgetown, TX
Killeen, TX
Round Rock, TX
Temple, TX
Waco, TX
Smith, Carlton B. .... Madison, NJ
Smith, Carlton S., Jr. .... **Boston, MA**
Smith, Carmen D. .... Atlanta, GA
Smith, Carmen L. .... **Seattle, WA**
Smith, Carol A. .... Auburn Hills, MI
Smith, Carol A. .... Olympia, WA
Smith, Carol Ann .... **Birmingham, AL**
Smith, Carol B. .... Kingsport, TN
Smith, Carol E. .... Purchase, NY
Smith, Carol Elizabeth .... Baltimore, MD
Smith, Carol Jean .... Montgomery, AL
Smith, Carol L. .... Palo Alto, CA
Smith, Carol L. .... New Lenox, IL
Smith, Carol Lisa .... **Albuquerque, NM**
Smith, Carol Lisa .... Santa Fe, NM
Smith, Carol Z. .... **Kansas City, MO**
Smith, Carole .... Chicago, IL
Smith, Caroline A. .... **Boston, MA**
Smith, Caroline G. .... **Oakland, CA**
Smith, Caroline LaCour .... Panama City, FL
Smith, Caroline Wahle .... Ocala, FL
Smith, Carolyn E. .... **Denver, CO**
Smith, Carolyn E.
Joint Committees And Commissions, GV
Smith, Carolyn F. .... **Irvine, CA**
Smith, Carolyn L. .... Dodgeville, WI
Smith, Carolyn M. .... Centreville, VA
Smith, Carolyn S. .... Ponca City, OK
Smith, Carolyn Tucker .... Charleston, WV
Smith, Carolynne .... Los Angeles, CA
Smith & Carr, P.C. .... **Houston, TX**
Smith, Carrie L. .... **Walnut Creek, CA**
Smith, Carrie L. .... **Buffalo, NY**
Smith, Carroad, Levy, Arpino & Finkel, LLP
Commack, NY
Smith, Carroll D. .... San Anselmo, CA
Smith, Carroll E. .... Fredericksburg, VA
Smith, Carroll J. .... Rowland Heights, CA
Smith, Carson .... Amarillo, TX
Smith, Carthel L., Jr. .... Lexington, TN
Smith, Cary C. .... Rochester, NY
Smith, Cary F. .... Anniston, AL
Smith, Cary S. .... Fremont, CA
Smith, Caryl Greenberg .... **Atlanta, GA**
Smith & Cashion, PLC .... **Nashville, TN**
Smith, Casper, Smith & Alexander, L.L.P.
Asheboro, NC
Smith, Cassidy, Platt, Harris & Radabaugh, P.A.
Lakeland, FL
Smith, Catharine Marie .... Albertville, AL
Smith, Catherine Bukowski .... **Houston, TX**
Smith, Catherine J. .... **Somerset, NJ**
Smith, Catherine Roseman .... Ho-Ho-Kus, NJ
Smith, Catherine S.
Environmental Protection Agency, Office of Enforcement and Compliance Assurance, GV
Smith, Catherine W. .... **Edinburg, TX**
Smith, Catherine Wright .... **Seattle, WA**
Smith, Cathleen Robson .... **Atlanta, GA**
Smith, Cathleen W. .... **Rochester, NY**
Smith, Cathy E. .... **Portland, OR**
Smith, Cathy L. .... Houston, TX
Smith, Cecelia C. .... Tallahassee, FL
Smith, Cecial C. .... Lake Oswego, OR
Smith, Cecil D. .... Memphis, TN
Smith, Cecil L. .... **Dallas, TX**
Smith, Ced L. .... Chardon, OH
Smith, Celeste A. .... **New York, NY**
Smith, Chadbourn H. .... **Bar Harbor, ME**
Smith, Chadwick .... Tulsa, OK
Smith, Chadwick H. .... **Helena, MT**
Smith, Chapman L., Jr. .... **Miami, FL**
Smith, Charlene .... Topeka, KS
Smith, Charles A. .... Helena, MT
Smith, Charles A. .... Williamsburg, VA
Smith, Charles B. .... South San Francisco, CA
Smith, Charles B. .... Park Ridge, IL
Smith, Charles B. .... **New York, NY**
Smith, Charles B. .... Philadelphia, PA
Smith, Charles B. .... Columbia, SC
Smith, Charles C., Jr. .... Cameron, TX
Smith, Charles D. .... **Columbus, OH**
Smith, Charles D., IV .... Washington, DC
Smith, Charles Derek .... Annandale, VA
Smith, Charles Duvall .... Upper Marlboro, MD
Smith, Charles E. .... Fort Smith, AR
Smith, Charles E. .... Vero Beach, FL
Smith, Charles E. .... Meridian, MS
Smith, Charles E. .... Arlington, TX
Smith, Charles E. .... Baytown, TX
Smith, Charles E. .... Seattle, WA
Smith, Charles F. .... Dardanelle, AR
Smith, Charles F. .... **Chicago, IL**
Smith, Charles F., Jr. .... **Jim Thorpe, PA**
Smith, Charles F., Jr. .... Wausau, WI
Smith, Charles Frederick .... Washington, DC
Smith, Charles G. .... **Los Angeles, CA**
Smith, Charles H. .... Long Beach, CA
Smith, Charles H. .... **Dallas, TX**
Smith, Charles H., III .... **Roanoke, VA**
Smith, Charles H., Jr. .... Abingdon, VA
Smith, Charles Henry .... Alexandria, VA
Smith, Charles J. .... **Redwood City, CA**
Smith, Charles J. .... Columbus, OH
Smith, Charles James .... Corpus Christi, TX
Smith, Charles K. .... Petersburg, IL
Smith, Charles K. .... Hartsville, TN
Smith, Charles L. .... **Council Bluffs, IA**
Smith, Charles L. .... **San Antonio, TX**
Smith, Charles L., III .... Missouri Valley, IA
Smith, Charles L., Jr. .... Pasadena, CA
Smith, Charles M. .... Sepulveda, CA
Smith, Charles M. .... **Northbrook, IL**
Smith, Charles M. .... Kearny, NJ
Smith, Charles M. .... Bensalem, PA
Smith, Charles Marshall .... Tucson, AZ
Smith, Charles R. .... Tucson, AZ
Smith, Charles R. .... Washington, DC
Smith, Charles R. .... Cumming, GA
Smith, Charles R. .... Bluefield, WV
Smith, Charles R., Jr. .... **Huntsville, AL**
Smith, Charles R., Jr. .... **Pittsburgh, PA**
Smith, Charles R., P.C. .... Tucson, AZ
Smith, Charles S. .... **Monroe, LA**
Smith, Charles S. .... Easton, PA
Smith, Charles T. .... Overland Park, KS
Smith, Charles T. .... **Portland, OR**
Smith, Charles T. .... **Georgetown, SC**
Smith, Charles T., II .... Washington, DC
Smith, Charles W. .... **Melbourne, FL**
Smith, Charles W. .... Waukegan, IL
Smith, Charles W. .... Norristown, PA
Smith, Charles W. .... **Keyser, WV**
Smith, Charles W., Jr. .... Gainesville, GA
Smith, Charles W., Jr. .... **Saco, ME**
Smith, Charles Z. .... Olympia, WA
Smith, Charley L. .... Bellville, TX
Smith, Charlotte A. .... Tulsa, OK
Smith, Charlotte Louisa .... Newark, NJ
Smith, Charlotte Mitchell .... **Chicago, IL**
Smith, Charlton S. .... **Portland, ME**
Smith, Chas. C. .... New York, NY
Smith, Chas. C., Jr. .... Cameron, TX
Smith, Cheryl A. .... Fayetteville, GA
Smith, Cheryl D. .... Hurst, TX
Smith, Cheryl I. .... **Springfield, MA**
Smith, Cheryl K. .... Dallas, TX
Smith, Cheryl Rivera .... Dallas, TX
Smith, Cheryl Watson .... **Roanoke, VA**
Smith, Chester & Ann Smith .... Pasadena, CA
Smith, Chester B. .... Coudersport, PA
Smith, Chester H. .... United States Senate, Committee Legal Personnel, GV
Smith, Chester L. .... Virginia Beach, VA
Smith, Chester Leo .... Pasadena, CA
Smith, Chester R. .... Palm Springs, CA
Smith, Chesterfield .... Washington, DC
Miami, FL
Smith, Chris M. .... **New York, NY**
Smith and Christensen, L.L.P.
Charlotte, NC
Smith, Christian F. .... **Jacksonville, FL**
Smith, Christina A. .... **Minneapolis, MN**
Smith, Christina J. .... **Los Angeles, CA**
Smith, Christina L. .... Charleston, WV
Smith, Christina Monroe .... Arlington, VA
Smith, Christina N. .... **Cleveland, OH**
Smith, Christine Boersma .... Orinda, CA
Smith, Christine E. .... Chicago, IL
Smith, Christine H. .... **Cupertino, CA**
Smith, Christine J. .... **New York, NY**
Smith, Christine M. .... Miami, FL
Smith, Christine M. .... Omaha, NE
Smith, Christine M. .... New York, NY
Smith, Christine Ranieri .... River Edge, NJ
Smith, Christopher .... Santa Cruz, CA
Smith, Christopher .... Westlake Village, CA
Smith, Christopher .... **Washington, DC**
Smith, Christopher .... Taylor, MI
Smith, Christopher A. .... **Florence, AL**
Smith, Christopher A. .... **Indianapolis, IN**
Smith, Christopher A. .... Clarksville, TN
Smith, Christopher B. .... Milford, MI
Smith, Christopher E. .... East Lansing, MI
Smith, Christopher F. .... **New York, NY**
Smith, Christopher G. .... **Raleigh, NC**
Smith, Christopher H. .... Jacksonville, FL
Smith, Christopher J. .... Tucson, AZ
Smith, Christopher J. .... **Bridgeport, CT**
Smith, Christopher J. .... **Tampa, FL**
Smith, Christopher J. .... **Tavares, FL**
Smith, Christopher J.
Bloomfield Hills, MI
Smith, Christopher J. .... Charlottesville, VA
Smith, Christopher L.
Fort Lauderdale, FL
Smith, Christopher L. .... Cheyenne, WY
Smith, Christopher M. .... **San Diego, CA**
Smith, Christopher M. .... Cut Off, LA

Smith, Christopher M. .... St. Louis, MO
Smith, Christopher N. .... Macon, GA
Smith, Christopher R. .... Boston, MA
Smith, Christopher R. .... Kansas City, MO
Smith, Christopher, A Prof. Law Corp.
Santa Cruz, CA
Smith, Christopher E., P.C. .... Taylor, MI
Smith, Christopher S. .... Beaumont, TX
Smith, Christopher Sax .... Charleston, WV
Smith, Christopher T. .... Greenfield, IN
Smith, Christy .... Ankeny, IA
Smith, Cinda K. .... Bethesda, MD
Smith, Cindy .... Seattle, WA
Smith, Cindy T. .... Des Moines, IA
Smith, C. J. Keller .... Detroit, MI
Smith, Clara E. .... Pensacola, FL
Smith, Clare K. .... Toledo, OH
Smith, Clarence A. .... Washington, DC
Smith, Clark .... Raleigh, NC
Smith Clark Delesie Bierley Mueller & Kadyk .... Tampa, FL
Smith, Clark & Holzapfel .... Columbus, OH
Smith & Clark, Law Offices of
Grand Prairie, TX
Smith, Clark R. .... Boston, MA
Smith, Clark W. .... West Palm Beach, FL
Smith, Claude D., Jr. .... Macon, GA
Smith, Claude, Jr. .... Jacksonville, FL
Smith, Claude S., III .... Charleston, WV
Smith, Claudia A. .... New York, NY
Smith, Claudius C. .... Madison, TN
Smith, Clay M. .... Los Angeles, CA
Smith, Clay R. .... Helena, MT
Smith, Clayton G. .... Houston, TX
Smith, Clayton L. .... Houston, TX
Smith, Clifford B. .... Prairie Village, KS
Smith, Clifford Edward, Jr. .... St. Paul, MN
Smith, Clifford H. .... Ketchikan, AK
Smith, Clifford H., A Prof. Corp., Law Offices of .... Ketchikan, AK
Smith, Clifton S., Jr. .... Los Angeles, CA
Smith, Clint W. .... Mesa, AZ
Smith, Clint W., P.C. .... Mesa, AZ
Phoenix, AZ
Smith, Clinton B. .... Mount Kisco, NY
Smith, Clinton G., Jr. .... Harrisburg, PA
Smith, Clinton L. .... San Diego, CA
Smith, Clinton W. .... Williamsport, PA
Smith, Clinton W. .... Charleston, WV
Smith, Clyde A. .... Montgomery, AL
Smith, Clyde A., Jr. .... Beckley, WV
Smith & Co .... Seattle, WA
Smith, Coby D. .... Fort Worth, TX
Smith and Cockett .... Mountain City, TN
Smith, Cody W., Jr. .... Charleston, SC
Smith, Colby A. .... Washington, DC
Smith, Colette G. .... New York, NY
Smith, Colette Mulrenan .... Philadelphia, PA
Smith, Colin .... Chicago, IL
Smith, Colin J. .... McLean, VA
Smith, Colin L. .... Roscommon, MI
Smith, Colleen Duffy .... San Jose, CA
Smith & Collins, L.L.P. .... Dallas, TX
Smith & Colner .... Columbus, OH
Smith, Colten Wade .... Austin, TX
Smith and Condeni, Co., L.P.A.
Cleveland, OH
Smith, Constance D. .... Denver, CO
Smith, Constance F. .... Baltimore, MD
Smith, Conway W., III
Newport News, VA
Smith, Corey J. .... Department of Justice, Tax Division, GV
Smith, Corinne E. .... Washington, DC
Smith, Cornelius C., Jr. .... Princeton, NJ
Smith, Cortez .... Los Angeles, CA
Smith, Cory W. .... Austin, TX
Smith, Court D. .... Dallas, TX
Smith, Courtlandt L. .... Charleston, WV
Smith, Courtney Alexa .... Springdale, AR
Smith, Courtney Craig, Jr. .... Philadelphia, PA
Smith & Coury .... Woodsfield, OH
Smith, Cox & Associates .... Charleston, SC
Smith, Craig .... Los Angeles, CA
Smith, Craig .... Austin, TX
Smith, Craig .... Seattle, WA
Smith, Craig A. .... Los Angeles, CA
Smith, Craig A. .... Santa Maria, CA
Smith, Craig A. .... Venice, CA
Smith, Craig A. .... Buzzards Bay, MA
Smith, Craig A. .... St. Louis, MO
Smith, Craig A. .... Columbus, OH
Smith, Craig A. .... Eugene, OR
Smith, Craig A. .... Salem, OR
Smith, Craig A. .... Newtown, PA
Smith, Craig Alden .... Springfield, MO
Smith, Craig B. .... Wilmington, DE
Smith, Craig Cordell .... Bismarck, ND
Smith, Craig D. .... Worcester, MA
Smith, Craig D. .... Jackson, MS
Smith, Craig E. .... Baltimore, MD
Smith, Craig E. .... Gettysburg, SD
Onida, SD
Smith, Craig G. .... Milwaukee, WI
Smith, Craig H. .... White Stone, VA
Smith, Craig Hamilton
Fort Lauderdale, FL
Smith, Craig J. .... Easton, PA
Smith, Craig L. .... Yakima, WA
Smith, Craig Lindsay .... New York, NY
Smith, Craig M. .... Deerfield, IL
Smith, Craig R. .... Boston, MA
Smith, Craig S. .... Corpus Christi, TX
Smith, Craig S. .... Corpus Christi, TX
Smith, Craig T. .... Westwood, KS
Smith, Craig T. .... Boston, MA
Smith, Craig W. .... Los Angeles, CA

Smith Crane Robinson & Parker LLP
Los Angeles, CA
Torrance, CA
Smith, C. R. E. .... Oakland, CA
Smith & Crebessa .... Brandenburg, KY
Smith, Crystal Y. .... St. Louis, MO
Smith, Cullen .... Waco, TX
Smith, Currie & Hancock LLP
Atlanta, GA
Smith, Curtis D. .... Minneapolis, MN
Smith, Curtis L. .... Oklahoma City, OK
Smith, Curtis Reed .... Idaho Falls, ID
Smith, Curtis V. .... Littleton, CO
Smith, Cynthia A. .... New York, NY
Smith, Cynthia B. .... Atlanta, GA
Smith, Cynthia Borgfeld .... Georgetown, TX
Smith, Cynthia Buehrer .... Perrysburg, OH
Smith, Cynthia C. .... Boston, MA
Smith, Cynthia "C. C."
Oklahoma City, OK
Smith, Cynthia Dodd .... San Antonio, TX
Smith, Cynthia E. .... Roswell, GA
Smith, Cynthia E. .... Milwaukee, WI
Smith, Cynthia G. .... Department of State, Foreign Service Officers (Overseas), GV
Smith, Cynthia Gail .... Somers, NY
Smith, Cynthia K. .... Missoula, MT
Smith, Cynthia L. .... Stamford, CT
Smith, Cynthia L. .... Portland, OR
Smith, Cynthia M. .... Edina, MN
Smith, Cynthia M. .... St. Louis, MO
Smith, Cynthia Phillips .... Lafayette, IN
Smith, Cyril Elliot .... New York, NY
Smith, Cyril V. .... Baltimore, MD
Smith, D. Andrew C. .... New York, NY
Smith, D. Beecher, II .... Memphis, TN
Smith, D. Berkeley .... Waterloo, IA
Smith, D. Briggs, Jr. .... Batesville, MS
Smith, D. Brooks .... Johnstown, PA
Smith, D. Christopher .... Minneapolis, MN
Smith, D. Clark, Jr. .... Lexington, NC
Smith, D. Culver, III
West Palm Beach, FL
Smith, D. Gordon .... Portland, OR
Smith, D. Jack, Jr. .... Memphis, TN
Smith, D. Jacques .... Washington, DC
Smith, D. Jesse .... Tucson, AZ
Smith, D. Joe .... Durham, NC
Smith, D. Neil .... Daingerfield, TX
Smith, D. Robert .... Greenville, TX
Smith, D. Scott .... Cartersville, GA
Smith, D. Shannon .... Cincinnati, OH
Smith, D. St. J. .... Corpus Christi, TX
Smith, D. Todd .... Dallas, TX
Smith, D. Zackary .... Visalia, CA
Smith, D. Zane .... Ventura, CA
Smith, DaCosta, Jr. .... Weston, WV
Smith, Dale .... Fruitland, ID
Smith, Dale .... Jefferson City, MO
Smith, Dale B. .... Sloan, IA
Smith, Dale D. .... New Orleans, LA
Smith, Dale L. .... Adrian, MI
Smith, Dale L. .... Hermiston, OR
Smith, Dale L. .... Richmond, VA
Smith, Dale L., P.C. .... Adrian, MI
Smith, Dale P. .... Toccoa, GA
Smith, Damian M. .... St. Louis, MO
Smith, Damon Quinn .... Florence, AL
Smith, Dan C., III .... Houston, TX
Smith, Dana .... Brownwood, TX
Smith, Dana K. .... St. Paul, MN
Smith, Dana M. .... Riverside, CA
Smith & Danamraj, A Professional Corporation .... Dallas, TX
Smith, Danelle J. .... Las Vegas, NM
Smith, Dani D. .... Dallas, TX
Smith, Daniel A. .... Jacksonville, FL
Smith, Daniel A. .... New Orleans, LA
Smith, Daniel A. .... Lyons, NE
Omaha, NE
Smith, Daniel B. .... Princeton, AL
Smith, Daniel B., Attorney at Law, P.C.
Princeton, AL
Smith, Daniel C. .... Washington, DC
Smith, Daniel C. .... Washington, DC
Smith, Daniel C.
Department of Transportation, Federal Railroad Administration, GV
Smith, Daniel C. .... Tacoma, WA
Smith, Daniel E. .... Cerritos, CA
Smith, Daniel E. .... Washington, DC
Smith, Daniel E. .... Greensboro, NC
Smith, Daniel F. .... Jefferson City, MO
Smith, Daniel G. .... Hanover, NH
Smith, Daniel Hoyt .... Seattle, WA
Smith, Daniel J. .... San Jose, CA
Smith, Daniel J. .... Washington, DC
Smith, Daniel J. .... Fort Worth, TX
Smith, Daniel J. .... Grand Prairie, TX
Smith, Daniel Jon .... Minneapolis, MN
Smith, Daniel L. .... Overland Park, KS
Smith, Daniel L. .... Savannah, TN
Smith, Daniel L., Jr. .... North Palm Beach, FL
Smith, Daniel P. .... Nashville, TN
Smith, Daniel R. .... Austin, TX
Smith, Daniel S. .... Berryville, AR
Smith, Daniel S. M. .... Englewood, CO
Smith, Daniel T. .... Denver, CO
Smith, Daniel T. .... Chestertown, NY
Smith, Daniel Thomas .... Akron, NY
Smith, Daniel U. .... Kentfield, CA
Smith, Daniel V. .... Bloomfield Hills, MI
Smith, Daniel W. .... Carmichael, CA
Smith, Daniel W. .... Chicago, IL
Smith, Daniel W. .... Des Moines, IA
Smith, Daniel W. .... Puyallup, WA
Smith, Danielle A. .... Northville, MI

Smith, Danielle M. ....
United States Tax Court, GV
Smith, Danielle M. .... Lafayette, LA
Smith, Danielle V. .... Denver, CO
Smith, Dannette L. .... Minneapolis, MN
Smith, Danny L. .... Boaz, AL
Smith, Danny R. .... Spartanburg, SC
Smith, Daria Ann .... Elizabeth, NJ
Smith, Darin D. .... Cedar Rapids, IA
Smith, Darin P. .... Boston, MA
Smith, Darlene Payne .... Houston, TX
Smith, Darrel D. .... Las Vegas, NV
Smith, Darrell C. .... Tampa, FL
Smith, Darrell Duane .... San Marcos, CA
Smith, Darrell F. .... Globe, AZ
Smith, Darrell Frank .... San Antonio, TX
Smith, Darrell L. .... Olathe, KS
Smith, Darrell W. .... Dallas, TX
Smith, Darryl A. .... Santa Clara, CA
Smith & Darst, LLP .... Walnut Creek, CA
Smith, Daryl L. .... Covina, CA
Smith and Davenport .... Manassas, VA
Smith, David .... Springfield, OH
Smith, David .... Philadelphia, PA
Smith, David .... Greensboro, VT
Smith, David A. .... Little Rock, AR
Smith, David A. .... Irvine, CA
Smith, David A. .... Atlanta, GA
Smith, David A. .... Oregon, IL
Smith, David A. .... Bedford, IN
Smith, David A. .... Columbus, MS
Smith, David A. .... St. Louis, MO
Smith, David A. .... Garden City, NY
Smith, David Atmar, (P.C.) .... Victoria, TX
Smith, David B. .... Lexington, NE
Smith, David B. .... Westfield, NJ
Smith, David B. .... Buffalo, NY
Charlotte Amalie, St. Thomas, VI
Smith, David B. .... Greensboro, NC
Smith, David B. .... Philadelphia, PA
Smith, David B. .... Alexandria, VA
Smith, David B. .... Milwaukee, WI
Smith, David Burnell .... Scottsdale, AZ
Smith, David C. .... Mesa, AZ
Smith, David C. .... Irvine, CA
Westlake Village, CA
Smith, David C. .... Santa Monica, CA
Smith, David C. .... West Hartford, CT
Smith, David C. .... Wilmington, DE
Smith, David C. .... Augusta, GA
Aiken, SC
Smith, David C. .... Winston-Salem, NC
Smith, David C. .... McSherrystown, PA
Smith, David C. .... Bluefield, WV
Smith, David C., Jr. .... Washington, DC
Smith, David Carlson .... Santa Fe, NM
Smith, David Carlson, P.C. .... Santa Fe, NM
Smith, David D. .... Norman, OK
Smith, David D. .... Spokane, WA
Smith, David E. .... Benton, AR
Smith, David E. .... Sacramento, CA
Smith, David E. .... Kailua-Kona, HI
Smith, David E. .... Knoxville, TN
Smith, David E. .... Richmond, VA
Smith, David Earl .... Phoenix, AZ
Smith, David E.B. .... Chicago, IL
Smith, David F. .... Washington, DC
Smith, David F. .... Rockford, IL
Smith, David F. .... Baltimore, MD
Smith, David F. .... Buffalo, NY
Smith, David Fayette .... Russell Springs, KY
Smith, David F. B. .... Washington, DC
Smith, David G. .... Pensacola, FL
Smith, David G. .... New York, NY
Smith, David H. .... Little Rock, AR
Smith, David H. .... San Ramon, CA
Smith, David H. .... Midland, TX
Smith, David H. .... Seattle, WA
Smith, David Henry .... Henderson, NV
Smith, David I. .... Burlington, NC
Smith, David J. .... San Diego, CA
Smith, David J. .... Decatur, IL
Smith, David J. .... Cedar Rapids, IA
Smith, David J. .... Bel Air, MD
Smith, David J. .... Newton, MA
Smith, David J. .... Salt Lake City, UT
Smith, David J. .... Kirkland, WA
Smith, David J., P.S. .... Kirkland, WA
Smith, David James .... Miami, FL
Smith, David K. .... Cleveland, OH
Smith, David K. .... Salt Lake City, UT
Smith, David Kelly .... Calhoun, GA
Smith, David L. .... Denver, CO
Smith, David L. .... Denver, CO
Smith, David L. .... Tampa, FL
Smith, David L. .... Atlanta, GA
Smith, David L. .... Macon, GA
Smith, David L. .... Decatur, IL
Smith, David L. .... Charlotte, MI
Smith, David L. .... China, MI
Smith, David L. .... Grand Rapids, MI
Smith, David L. .... Branson, MO
Smith, David L. .... St. Louis, MO
Smith, David L. .... New York, NY
Smith, David L. .... North Canton, OH
Smith, David L. .... Ashland, OR
Smith, David L. .... Breinigsville, PA
Smith, David L. .... Austin, TX
Smith, David L. .... Corpus Christi, TX
Smith, David L., (P.C.)
Farmington Hills, MI
Smith, David L., P.C., Law Office of
Corpus Christi, TX
Smith, David Langolf .... Tipton, IN
Smith, David Laurence .... Carrollton, GA
Smith, David Leon, III .... Birmingham, AL
Smith, David M. .... Birmingham, AL
Smith, David M. .... Washington, DC

Smith, David M.
Federal Labor Relations Authority, Office of the Solicitor, GV
Smith, David M. .... Chicago, IL
Smith, David M. .... Springfield, IL
Smith, David M. .... Houston, TX
Smith, David M. .... Wausau, WI
Smith, David N. .... Cambridge, MA
Smith, David N. .... Austin, TX
Smith, David O. .... Riverside, CA
Smith, David O. .... Corbin, KY
Smith, David P. .... Durango, CO
Smith, David P. .... Portland, OR
Smith, David P., (A Prof. Law Corp.)
Alexandria, LA
Smith, David Patterson, Jr. .... Austin, TX
Smith, David R.
Department Of Health And Human Services, Office of the General Counsel, GV
Smith, David R. .... Miami, FL
Smith, David R. .... Savannah, GA
Smith, David R. .... Hyattsville, MD
Smith, David R. .... Kansas City, MO
Smith, David R. .... Albany, NY
Smith, David Randolph, & Associates
Nashville, TN
Smith, David Russell .... Atlanta, GA
Smith, David S. .... Beverly Hills, CA
Smith, David S. .... New York, NY
Smith, David S. .... New York, NY
Smith, David S. .... New York, NY
Smith, David S. .... New York, NY
Smith, David S. .... Allentown, PA
Smith, David S. .... Pittsburgh, PA
Smith, David S. .... McLean, VA
Smith, David Shane .... Richmond, VA
Smith, David Symington .... Winter Haven, FL
Smith, David T. .... Gainesville, FL
Smith, David V. .... Memphis, TN
Smith, David V. .... Arlington, TX
Smith, David W. .... Richmond, KY
Smith, David W. .... Kansas City, MO
Smith, David W. .... New York, NY
Smith, David W., III .... Gastonia, NC
Smith, David William .... Montgomery, AL
Smith, David William .... Philadelphia, PA
Smith, David Y. .... Woodland Hills, CA
Smith, David Z. .... Chicago, IL
Smith & Davis .... Portland, OR
Smith, Dawn .... Atlanta, GA
Smith, D. C. .... Vero Beach, FL
Smith, Dean Arthur .... Portland, OR
Smith, Dean E. .... Akron, OH
Smith, Dean H. .... Tulsa, OK
Smith, Dean J. .... Los Angeles, CA
Smith, Dean J. .... Kansas City, KS
Smith, Dean O. .... Wichita, KS
Smith, Dean P. .... Buffalo, NY
Smith, DeAnn Foran .... Troy, MI
Smith, Deanna Dean .... Houston, TX
Smith Debnam Narron Wyche Story & Myers, L.L.P. .... Raleigh, NC
Smith & DeBonis .... Highland, IN
La Porte, IN
Smith, Deborah A. .... Kansas City, MO
Smith, Deborah A. .... Brooklyn, NY
Smith, Deborah Alley .... Birmingham, AL
Smith, Deborah Ann .... Austin, TX
Smith, Deborah Jo .... Bentonville, AR
Smith, Deborah Kathleen .... Portland, OR
Smith, Deborah Kaye Whiddon
Andalusia, AL
Smith, Deborah L. .... San Francisco, CA
Smith, Deborah L. .... Whitehall, PA
Smith, Deborah Lee .... Chicago, IL
Smith, Deborah M. .... Department of Justice, Environment and Natural Resources Division, GV
Smith, Deborah M. .... Madison, WI
Smith, Deborah S. .... Helena, MT
Smith, Debra A. .... Oakland, CA
Smith, Debra A. .... Riverside, CA
Smith, Debra A. .... Pottsville, PA
Smith, Debra K. .... Chicago, IL
Smith, Debra K. .... Jasper, IN
Smith, Debra Kaye .... Jasper, IN
Smith, Debra L. .... Denver, CO
Smith, Debra L. .... Watertown, MA
Smith, Debra R. .... Denver, CO
Smith, Debra R. .... New York, NY
Smith DeFeo .... Dallas, TX
Smith, DeHaven L. .... Baltimore, MD
Smith, Deirdre Karen .... Boulder, CO
Smith, Deirdre M. .... Portland, ME
Smith, Deirdre O'Meara .... St. Louis, MO
Smith, Delaine R. .... Memphis, TN
Smith, Delavan .... Wassaic, NY
Smith, Delbert D. .... Washington, DC
Smith, Delisa Anderson .... Lawton, OK
Smith, Dell W. .... Soda Springs, ID
Smith, Delman W. .... Los Gatos, CA
Smith, Delores I. .... Santa Monica, CA
Smith Demahy and Drake .... Miami, FL
Smith, DeMaurice Fitzgerald
Washington, DC
Smith, Demian .... Denver, CO
Smith, Denice .... Houston, TX
Smith, Denise A. .... Media, PA
Smith, Denise Lynn .... Ravenna, OH
Smith, Denise M. .... West Bloomfield, MI
Smith, Denise M. .... Cincinnati, OH
Smith, Denise Mendez .... Tallahassee, FL
Smith, Dennis .... Seattle, WA
Smith, Dennis A. .... Arapaho, OK
Smith, Dennis C. .... Houston, TX
Smith, Dennis D. .... Beverly Hills, CA
Smith, Dennis Dustin
Fort Lauderdale, FL

Smith, Dennis J. ... Roseland, NJ
Smith, Dennis J. ... Fairfax, VA
Smith, Dennis L. ... St. Paul, MN
Smith, Dennis L. ... Kerrville, TX
Smith, Dennis N. ... Ballwin, MO
Smith, Dennis O. ... Hutchinson, KS
Smith, Dennis O., Chartered
Hutchinson, KS
Smith, Dennis Paul ... Richmond, VA
Smith, Dennis R. ... Boston, MA
Smith, Dennis T. ... Hackensack, NJ
Smith, Dennis W. ... Canton, MO
Smith, Dennis Wm. ... San Jose, CA
Smith, Derek B. ... Oklahoma City, OK
Smith, Derek C. ... Washington, DC
Smith, Derek C. ... Chicago, IL
Smith, Derek E. ... Los Angeles, CA
Smith, Derek L. ... Richmond, VA
Smith, Derick R. ... Katy, TX
Smith, Derrick C. ... Nashville, TN
Smith, Derrick H. ... Lake City, FL
Smith, Deverich, Ellison & Harraka, A Professional Corporation ... Irvine, CA
Smith, Devin ... Itasca, IL
Boston, MA
Smith, DeWayne ... Troy, OH
Smith, Dewey ... Carrollton, GA
Smith, Dewey J., Jr. ... Monroe, LA
Smith, Diana L. ... Los Angeles, CA
Smith, Diana Lynn ... Northville, MI
Smith, Diane A. ... Anchorage, AK
Smith, Diane B. ... Albany, NY
Smith, Diane Green ... Chicago, IL
Smith, Diane K. ... Somerville, NJ
Smith, Diane M. ... Lansing, MI
Smith, Diane M. ... Arlington, VA
Smith, Diane R. ... Irvine, CA
Smith, Diane Stern ... Northbrook, IL
Smith, Diane V. ... Tacoma, WA
Smith, Diane Vaksdal ... Englewood, CO
Smith, Diane Y. ... Tomball, TX
Smith, Diann L. ... Washington, DC
Smith, Dianne ... Research Triangle Park, NC
Smith, Dianne Baquet ... Los Angeles, CA
Smith, Dianne J. ... Chevy Chase, MD
Smith, Dianne L. ... Tulsa, OK
Smith, Dickey, Smith, Hasty & Dempster, P.A.
Fayetteville, NC
Smith & Diment, A Professional Corporation
Carrollton, GA
Smith, DJ ... Cedar Rapids, IA
Smith, D. Lamar, P.A. ... Jacksonville, FL
Smith, Dock G., Jr. ... Robbins, NC
Smith, Dolores Silva
Board of Governors Of The Federal Reserve System,
Division of Consumer and Community Affairs, GV
Smith, Dolores V. Mason ... New Orleans, LA
Smith, Dominic L. ... Philadelphia, PA
Smith, Don A. ... Fort Smith, AR
Smith, Don C. ... Minneapolis, MN
Smith, Don C., Jr. ... Colorado Springs, CO
Smith, Don G. ... Gun Barrel City, TX
Smith, Don H. ... Atlanta, GA
Smith, Don L. ... Lawton, OK
Smith, Don L. ... Nashville, TN
Smith, Donald A. ... Tampa, FL
Smith, Donald A. ... Niles, IL
Smith, Donald A. ... Birmingham, MI
Smith, Donald A. ... Gulfport, MS
Smith, Donald A., Jr. ... Woodbury, NJ
Smith, Donald A. W. ... Rochester, NY
Smith, Donald B. ... Tuscaloosa, AL
Smith, Donald B. ... De Bary, FL
Smith, Donald B., Jr. ... Defiance, OH
Smith, Donald B., Sr. ... Lansdale, PA
Smith, Donald C. ... Dodge City, KS
Smith, Donald C., Jr. ... Denver, CO
Smith, Donald D. ... Marietta, GA
Smith, Donald D. ... Minneapolis, MN
Smith, Donald E. ... Palm Desert, CA
Smith, Donald E. ... Sarasota, FL
Smith, Donald F. ... Snyder, NY
Smith, Donald F., Jr. ... Reading, PA
Smith, Donald G. ... Santa Barbara, CA
Smith, Donald H. ... Phoenix, AZ
Smith, Donald H. ... Pine Bluff, AR
Smith, Donald H. ... Washington, DC
Smith, Donald H. ... Louisville, KY
Smith, Donald H. ... Pittsburgh, PA
Smith, Donald J. ... La Grange, KY
Smith, Donald J. ... Oklahoma City, OK
Smith, Donald K. ... Sterling, CO
Smith, Donald L. ... Los Gatos, CA
Smith, Donald L. ... Jacksonville, FL
Smith, Donald L. ... Alton, IL
Smith, Donald L. ... Ames, IA
Smith, Donald L. ... New York, NY
Smith, Donald L. ... Raleigh, NC
Smith, Donald L., A Prof. Corp.
Los Gatos, CA
Smith, Donald L., Jr. ... Columbus, OH
Smith, Donald Lamar, Jr.
Jacksonville, FL
Smith, Donald M. ... Westminster, MD
Smith, Donald O. ... Boston, MA
Smith, Donald P. ... Chicago, IL
Smith, Donald P. ... Short Hills, NJ
Smith, Donald P., Jr. ... Buffalo Creek, CO
Smith, Donald R. ... Bridgeport, CT
Smith, Donald R. ... North Palm Beach, FL
Smith, Donald R. ... Lafayette, IN
Smith, Donald R. ... Northville, MI
Smith, Donald R. ... Dallas, TX
Smith, Donald R., A Prof. Corp., Law Office of
Dallas, TX
Smith, Donald S. ... Tempe, AZ
Smith, Donald S. ... Washington, DC
Smith, Donald S. ... Indianapolis, IN
Smith, Donald S. ... Olathe, KS
Smith, Donald S. ... Tulsa, OK
Smith, Donald T. ... Fort Worth, TX
Smith, Donald T., P.C. ... Fort Worth, TX
Smith, Donald W. ... Solana Beach, CA
Smith, Donald W. ... Washington, DC
Smith, Donald W. ... Columbia, MO
Smith, Donald W. ... Yonkers, NY
Smith, Donald W. ... Madison, WI
Smith, Donna Aronoff ... St. Louis, MO
Smith, Donna Dyer ... Memphis, TN
Smith, Donna H. ... Boston, MA
Smith, Donna L. ... Grove, OK
Vinita, OK
Smith, Donna M. ... Parkersburg, WV
Smith, Donnie E. ... Edmond, OK
Smith & Doran, A Professional Corporation
Morristown, NJ
Smith, Doreen ... Collegeville, PA
Smith, Doris A. ... Philadelphia, PA
Smith, Dorothy M. ... Birmingham, MI
Smith, Douglas A. ... Atlanta, GA
Smith, Douglas C. ... Riverside, CA
Smith, Douglas C. ... Honolulu, HI
Smith, Douglas C. ... Bay City, MI
Smith, Douglas C. ... El Paso, TX
Smith, Douglas D. ... Los Angeles, CA
Smith, Douglas D. ... San Francisco, CA
Smith, Douglas Dean ... Portland, OR
Smith, Douglas E. ... Gainesville, GA
Smith, Douglas E. ... Seattle, WA
Smith, Douglas G. ... Livonia, MI
Smith, Douglas G. ... Pittsburgh, PA
Smith, Douglas G., Jr. ... Atlanta, GA
Smith, Douglas H. ... Lake Alfred, FL
Smith, Douglas H. ... Providence, RI
Smith, Douglas K. ... Tacoma, WA
Smith, Douglas K., P.S., Law Offices of
Tacoma, WA
Smith, Douglas L. ... Sacramento, CA
Smith, Douglas L. ... Panama City, FL
Smith, Douglas L. ... Sheridan, MT
Smith, Douglas M. ... Walnut Creek, CA
Smith, Douglas M. ... Augusta, ME
Dover-Foxcroft, ME
Smith, Douglas M. ... Bellefontaine, OH
Smith, Douglas M. ... Newport News, VA
Smith, Douglas N. ... Napa, CA
Smith, Douglas O., Jr. ... Fort Smith, AR
Smith, Douglas P. ... Irvine, CA
Smith, Douglas R. ... Bethesda, MD
Smith, Douglas S. ... Santa Ana, CA
Smith, Douglas W. ... Atlanta, GA
Smith, Douglas W. ... Chicago, IL
Smith, Douglas Willets
Federal Energy Regulatory Commission,
Office of the General Counsel, GV
Smith & Dowdy ... Northport, AL
Smith & Downey, A Professional Association
Washington, DC
Baltimore, MD
Hauppauge, NY
Smith, D. R. ... Ocala, FL
Smith & Drake ... McGehee, AR
Smith, Duane P. ... Pinetop, AZ
Smith, Duane W. ... Beatrice, NE
Smith, Dudley B. ... Brookings, OR
Smith & Duggan LLP ... Boston, MA
Smith, Duncan C. ... Beaverton, OR
Smith, Duncan C., III ... Washington, DC
Smith, Durward A. ... Lincoln, NE
Smith, Dustan T. ... Iselin, NJ
New York, NY
Smith, Dwayne E. ... Kansas City, MO
Smith, Dwight C., III ... Washington, DC
Smith, Dwight D. ... San Francisco, CA
Smith, Dwight E. ... Chappell, NE
Smith, Dwight L. ... Tulsa, OK
Smith, Dwyer and Bliss, P.C.
Keene Valley, NY
Lake Placid, NY
Smith, Dylan D. ... New York, NY
Smith, E. Alfred ... Voorhees, NJ
Philadelphia, PA
Smith, E. Bruce ... Lexington, NE
Smith, E. Byron ... Barnesville, GA
Smith, E. Gary ... Santa Ana, CA
Smith, E. Hardy ... Tucson, AZ
Smith, E. Kendrick ... Atlanta, GA
Smith, E. Lee ... New York, NY
Smith, E. O'Malley ... Danbury, CT
Smith, E. Randall ... Houston, TX
Smith, E. Randall, P.C. ... Houston, TX
Smith, E. Scott ... Atlanta, GA
Smith, E. Steeves ... Mitchell, SD
Smith, E. Tyler ... Greenville, SC
Smith, E. Watson ... Mobile, AL
Smith, E. Wayne ... Liberty, MS
Smith, E. Wray ... Montgomery, AL
Smith, Earl Q. ... St. Louis, MO
Smith, Earl W. ... Austin, TX
Smith, Ed T. ... Bonham, TX
Smith, Eddie D. ... Winston-Salem, NC
Smith, Eddy R. ... Knoxville, TN
Smith, Edgar C., III ... Mission Viejo, CA
Smith, Edgar J., Jr. ... Greenwich, CT
Smith, Edgar L. ... Lewisburg, WV
Smith, Edgar Q. ... Houston, TX
Smith, Edmond B., Jr. ... Pittsburgh, PA
Smith, Edmund C. ... Salem, MA
Smith, Edw. L. ... Niagara Falls, NY
Smith, Edw. N., Jr. ... Marshall, TX
Smith, Edw. W. ... Edmond, OK
Smith, Edw. W. ... Hilton Head Island, SC
Smith, Edward ... Longmont, CO
Smith, Edward A. ... Roseville, CA
Smith, Edward A. ... Sacramento, CA
Smith, Edward A. ... Stamford, CT
Smith, Edward A. ... Kansas City, MO
Smith, Edward C. ... New York, NY
Smith, Edward C. ... Philadelphia, PA
Smith, Edward D. ... Long Beach, CA
Smith, Edward D. ... Atlanta, GA
Smith, Edward D. ... Kankakee, IL
Smith, Edward Egan ... San Francisco, CA
Smith, Edward F. ... West Campton, NH
Smith, Edward F. ... Youngstown, OH
Smith, Edward F., III ... Boca Raton, FL
Smith, Edward G. ... Easton, PA
Smith, Edward G. ... Spartanburg, SC
Smith, Edward H. ... Burbank, CA
Smith, Edward H., Jr. ... Bristol, CT
Smith, Edward J. ... Chicago, IL
Smith, Edward J. ... Deerfield, IL
Smith, Edward J. ... Louisville, KY
Smith, Edward J. ... Bangor, ME
Smith, Edward J. ... Boston, MA
Smith, Edward J., III ... Syracuse, NY
Smith, Edward J., Jr. ... Washington, DC
Smith, Edward L. ... Kansas City, MO
Smith, Edward L. ... New York, NY
Smith, Edward L., III ... Buffalo, NY
Smith, Edward L., Jr. ... Park Hills, KY
Smith, Edward L.D. ... Mobile, AL
Smith, Edward M. ... Grand Rapids, MI
Smith, Edward M. ... Dayton, OH
Smith, Edward M. ... Dallas, TX
Smith, Edward N. ... Fort Wayne, IN
Smith, Edward P. ... Darien, CT
Smith, Edward P. ... Greenfield, MA
Smith, Edward P. ... New York, NY
Smith, Edward R. ... Lubbock, TX
Smith, Edward S. ...
United States Court Of Appeals For The
Federal Circuit, GV
Smith, Edward T. ... Norcross, GA
Smith, Edward T. ... New York, NY
Smith, Edward T. ... Akron, OH
Smith, Edward T. ... Pittsburgh, PA
Smith, Edward V., III ... Dallas, TX
Smith, Edwin A., III ... Baton Rouge, LA
Smith, Edwin A., Jr. ... Baton Rouge, LA
Smith, Edwin D., V ... Kansas City, MO
Smith, Edwin Dudley ... Overland Park, KS
Smith, Edwin E. ... Boston, MA
Smith, Edwin H. ... Kansas City, MO
Smith, Edwin L. ... New York, NY
Smith, Edwin M. ... Austin, TX
Smith, Edwin M., Jr. ... Los Angeles, CA
Smith, Edwin P. ... Philadelphia, PA
Smith, Edwin P., & Associates, P.C.
Philadelphia, PA
Smith, Edwin R. ... Fort Myers Beach, FL
Evansville, IN
Smith, Edwin R. ... Ottawa, KS
Smith, Edwin R. ... Bar Harbor, ME
Smith, Edwin W. ... Erie, PA
Smith, Edwina C. ... Kansas City, MO
Smith, Eileen Kuklis ... Albany, NY
Smith, Elaine ... Philadelphia, PA
Smith, Elaine D. ... Newberg, OR
Smith, Elaine M. ... Los Angeles, CA
Smith, Elbert G. ... Springfield, OH
Smith, Elbridge W. ... Honolulu, HI
Smith, Eleanor Cattron ... Ferndale, MI
Smith, Eleanor H. ... Washington, DC
Smith, Eleanor W. ... Middlebury, VT
Smith, Elinor P. ... Tampa, FL
Smith, Eliot F. ... Wilson, NC
Smith, Elisa W. ... San Francisco, CA
Smith, Elizabeth ... New York, NY
Smith, Elizabeth A. ... San Diego, CA
Smith, Elizabeth A. ... Indianapolis, IN
Smith, Elizabeth A. ... New York, NY
Smith, Elizabeth C. ... Tucson, AZ
Smith, Elizabeth C. ... San Francisco, CA
Smith, Elizabeth Casteel ... Memphis, TN
Smith, Elizabeth Childers ... McLean, VA
Smith, Elizabeth D. ... Washington, DC
Smith, Elizabeth G. ... Seattle, WA
Smith, Elizabeth H. ... Mendham, NJ
Smith, Elizabeth J. ... Greenville, SC
Smith, Elizabeth J. ... Brentwood, TN
Smith, Elizabeth J. ... Eau Claire, WI
Smith, Elizabeth L. ... Denver, CO
Smith, Elizabeth M. ... Hartford, CT
Smith, Elizabeth P. ... White Plains, NY
Smith, Elizabeth Page ... New York, NY
Smith, Elizabeth Shaw ... Santa Ana, CA
Smith, Elizabeth T. ... Columbus, OH
Smith, Elizabeth-Ann Neufeld
Bismarck, ND
Smith, Ellen C. ... Waukegan, IL
Smith, Ellen M. ... New York, NY
Smith, Ellen Resnick ... Washington, DC
Smith, Ellen S. ... Atlanta, GA
Smith, Ellen Schrader ... Fort Worth, TX
Smith, Ellen W. ... Hackensack, NJ
Smith, Ellen W. ... New York, NY
Smith, Elliot F. ... San Francisco, CA
Smith Elliott Smith & Garmey, P.A.
Saco, ME
Sanford, ME
Smith, Ellis C. ... La Grange, GA
Smith, Ellis P. ... Quincy, FL
Smith, Ellison D., IV ... Charleston, SC
Smith, Elting H. ... Old Lyme, CT
Smith, Elting H., Jr. ... Scarborough, ME
Smith, Elva E. ... Columbus, OH
Smith, Elvera Wollitz ... Oakland, CA
Smith, Elvin E., III ... Dallas, TX
Smith, Elwayne E. ... Downey, CA
Smith, Elwayne E., Inc. ... Downey, CA
Smith & Ely, LLP ... Birmingham, AL
Smith & Ely, P.A. ... Rutherford, NJ
Smith, Elzy J. ... Clarksdale, MS
Smith, Emery W. ... Cleveland, OH
Smith, Emily A. ... San Francisco, CA
Smith, Emily K. ... Phoenix, AZ
Smith, Emlee Hilliard ... Chicago, IL
Smith, Emory C. ...
Department of the Navy, GV
Smith, Endicott ... Boston, MA
Smith, Eric A. ... Boston, MA
Smith, Eric A. ... Portland, OR
Smith, Eric B. ... Hugoton, KS
Smith, Eric B. ... Norristown, PA
Smith, Eric C. ... Pasadena, CA
Smith, Eric D. ... Southfield, MI
Smith, Eric H. ... Washington, DC
Smith, Eric J. ... Farmington Hills, MI
Smith, Eric K. ... Atlanta, GA
Smith, Eric L. ... Newport Beach, CA
Smith, Eric M. ... Pittsburgh, PA
Smith, Eric P. ... New Haven, CT
Smith, Eric P. ... State College, PA
Smith, Eric S. ... Saipan, TT
Smith, Eric T. ... Pittsburgh, PA
Smith, Eric W. ... Irvine, CA
Smith, Eric W. ... Kansas City, MO
Smith, Eric W. ... Totowa, NJ
Smith, Erica L. ... Toledo, OH
Smith, Erick C. ... Cleveland, OH
Smith, Erika B. ... San Francisco, CA
Smith, Erin E. ... New York, NY
Smith, Erin M. ... Greenwood Village, CO
Smith, Ernest W. ... Jeffersonville, IN
Smith, Ernest W. ... Henryetta, OK
Smith, Eskridge E., Jr. ... Baton Rouge, LA
Bossier City, LA
Smith, Esme C. ... San Francisco, CA
Smith, Esta M. ... New York, NY
Smith, Esther Belenker
Department of Commerce,
Patent and Trademark Office, GV
Smith, Ethan W. ... Huntingdon, PA
Smith, Eubanks, Smith & Tumlin, P.C.
Marietta, GA
Smith, Eugene ... East Hanover, NJ
Smith, Eugene A. ... Raleigh, NC
Smith, Eugene H. ... Palo Alto, CA
Smith, Eugene H. (Chip) ... Naples, FL
Smith, Eugene L. ... Liberal, KS
Smith, Eugene L. ... Dearborn, MI
Smith, Eugene L. ... Houston, TX
Smith, Eugene M. ... Chicago, IL
Smith, Eugene R. ... Masury, OH
North Lima, OH
Smith, Eugene T. ... Washington, DC
Smith, Eulyse M. ... Memphis, TN
Smith, Eunice E. ... San Antonio, TX
Smith, Evan ... Portland, ME
Smith, Evan Jason ... Cherry Hill, NJ
Allentown, PA
Bala Cynwyd, PA
Philadelphia, PA
Smith, Evan L. ... Pomona, CA
Smith, Evan R. ... Tysons Corner, VA
Smith, Evan Thomas ... Chicago, IL
Smith, Evanden Cade ... San Francisco, CA
Smith & Evans ... Louisville, KY
Smith, Evelyn S. ... Cumming, GA
Smith, Everet F. ... Indianapolis, IN
Smith, Everett Algernon
Fort Lauderdale, FL
Smith, Everett I. ... Hackensack, NJ
Smith, Everett, Jr.
Securities and Exchange Commission,
Division of Corporation Finance, GV
Smith, Everett L. J., Jr. ... Denver, CO
Smith, Ewing, Jr. ... Murfreesboro, TN
Smith, F. Glenn, III ... Dallas, TX
Smith, F. Kelly ... Denver, CO
Smith, F. LaGard ... Malibu, CA
Smith, F. Richards, III ... Provo, UT
Smith & Falcone, A Professional Corporation ... Lynchburg, VA
Smith, Farrell D. ... Corpus Christi, TX
Smith, Farrell M. ... Corpus Christi, TX
Smith, Farrell Matthew
Albuquerque, NM
Smith, Favor R. ... Lake Placid, NY
Smith, Feddeler, Smith & Miles, P.A.
Lakeland, FL
Smith, Felicia Claire ... Miami, FL
Smith, Felicia Zeltman ... Bristol, PA
Smith, Felix E. ... Ontario, CA
Smith & Fels, P.C. ... Springfield, MO
Smith, Felton W. ... Birmingham, AL
Smith & Feola, P.C. ... Phoenix, AZ
Smith, Fern L. ... Oklahoma City, OK
Smith, Fern M. ... San Francisco, CA
Smith, Ferr ... Canton, MS
Smith, Finkelstein, Lundberg, Isler and Yakaboski, LLP ... Riverhead, NY
Smith Fisher ... Richfield, MN
Smith & Fleming ... Atlanta, GA
Smith, Fletcher N., III ... Chicago, IL
Smith, Fletcher Nathaniel, Jr. ... Greenville, SC
Smith, Floyd L., III ... Bayfield, CO
Smith, Floyd V. ... Anchorage, AK
Smith, Floyd W., Jr. ... Racine, WI
Smith & Forbes ... Plainfield, NJ
Smith, Ford R. ... Sacramento, CA
Smith, Forest ... Elizabethtown, KY
Smith, Forrest ... Dallas, TX
Smith, Forrest B. ... Glendale, CA
Smith, Forrest M. ... St. Louis, MO
Smith, Forrest M., III ... San Antonio, TX
Smith, Forrest S. ... Santa Fe, NM
Smith, Frances K. ... Hockessin, DE
Smith, Frances L. ... Trenton, NJ

Smith, Frances M. ....Houston, TX
Smith, Francis Audley, Jr. ....New Roads, LA
Smith, Francis E. ....Northridge, CA
Smith, Francis I. ....Portland, OR
Smith, Francis J., Jr. ....Albany, NY
Smith, Francis L. ....Roeland Park, KS
Smith, Francis M. ....Sioux Falls, SD
Smith, Francis P. ....Phoenix, AZ
Smith, Francis S. ....Washington, DC
Smith, Francis William ....Worcester, MA
Smith, Francis W. K. ....Cambridge, MA
Smith, Frank ....Washington, DC
Smith, Frank A. ....Pittsfield, MA
Smith, Frank A., III ....Boston, MA
Smith, Frank A., III & Associates, P.C. Boston, MA
Smith, Frank D., Jr. ....Cartersville, GA
Smith, Frank F., Jr. ....Houston, TX
Smith, Frank G. ....Ogden, UT
Smith, Frank G., III ....Atlanta, GA
Smith, Frank H., Jr. ....Los Angeles, CA
Smith, Frank J. ....Bellerose, NY
Smith, Frank J., III ....Chicago, IL
Smith, Frank K. ....Ocean City, NJ
Smith, Frank Murray ....Des Moines, IA
Smith, Frank R. ....Los Angeles, CA
Smith, Frank S. ....Plain City, OH
Smith, Frank Tupper, Jr. ....Dallas, TX
Smith, Frank Tupper, Jr. & Associates, P.C. Dallas, TX
Smith, Frank V., III ....Kansas City, MO
Smith, Frank W., Jr. ....Seattle, WA
Smith, Frankie Fields ....Mobile, AL
Smith, Franklin D. ....Elkin, NC
Smith, Franklin Jennings, Jr. Columbia, SC
Smith, Franklin L. ....Seattle, WA
Smith, Franklin N. ....Salt Lake City, UT
Smith, Fred A., III ....Chicago, IL
Smith, Fred C. ....Cincinnati, OH
Smith, Fred C., Jr. ....Lawton, OK
Smith, Fred Chris ....Santa Fe, NM
Smith, Fred D., Jr. ....Martinsville, VA
Stuart, VA
Smith, Fred J. ....Williamsville, NY
Smith, Fred J., Jr. ....Raleigh, NC
Smith, Fred N. ....Towanda, PA
Smith, Frederic L., Jr. ....Birmingham, AL
Smith, Frederic M. ....Pasadena, CA
Smith, Frederick Bradford ....Southfield, MI
Smith, Frederick C., Jr. ....Camp Hill, PA
Smith, Frederick D. ....Gainesville, FL
Smith, Frederick D. ....Seattle, WA
Smith, Frederick D., Jr. ....Quincy, MA
Smith, Frederick E. ....Los Angeles, CA
Smith, Frederick E. ....Doylestown, PA
Smith, Frederick E., Jr. ....Norristown, PA
Smith, Frederick J. ....Milwaukee, WI
Smith, Frederick James West Bloomfield, MI
Smith, Frederick P. ....Puyallup, WA
Smith, Frederick R. ....Pittsburg, KS
Smith, Frederick T. ....Atlanta, GA
Smith, Frederick T. ....Newark, NJ
Smith, Frederick W. ....Oakdale, CA
Smith, Fredk. D. ....San Francisco, CA
Smith, Fredric A. ....Southfield, MI
Smith, Fredric L. ....Columbus, OH
Smith, Fredricka G. ....Miami, FL
Smith, Freed, Heald & Chock, P.C. Portland, OR
Smith Freed, Heald & Chock, P.C. Vancouver, WA
Smith, Freling H. ....Albany, NY
Smith & Friedman ....Philadelphia, PA
Smith & Fuller, P.A. ....Tampa, FL
Smith, Fulton M., III ....San Francisco, CA
Smith, Furman, Jr. ....Atlanta, GA
Smith, G. Bert, Jr., Law Firm of Andrews, TX
Smith, G. Boone, III ....Macon, GA
Smith, G. Brian ....Milwaukee, WI
Smith, G. Clifton ....San Bernardino, CA
Smith, G. Daryl ....Greensburg, IN
Smith, G. David ....Dallas, TX
Smith, G. Elaine ....Treasury Department, Bureau of Alcohol, Tobacco and Firearms, GV
Smith, G. Emmett ....Glens Falls, NY
Smith, G. Guy ....Media, PA
Smith, G. Hampton, III ....Birmingham, AL
Smith, G. Kenneth ....Swiftwater, PA
Smith, G. Lee, Jr. ....Carrollton, GA
Smith, G. Lynn ....Dallas, TX
Smith, G. Mark ....Lafayette, IN
Smith, G. Michael ....Atlanta, GA
Smith, G. Michael ....Myrtle Beach, SC
Smith, G. Murrell, Jr. ....Sumter, SC
Smith, G. Nelson, III ....Pleasanton, CA
Smith, G. Pearson, Jr. ....Indianapolis, IN
Smith, G. Rand ....Columbus, OH
Smith, G. Rand, Co., L.P.A., Law Offices of Columbus, OH
Smith, G. Sid ....Office of Government Ethics, Office of General Counsel and Legal Policy, GV
Smith, G. Thomas ....Pensacola, FL
Smith, G. Thomas ....Clarksburg, WV
Smith, G. Wellington ....Austin, TX
Smith, G. Wellington, P.C. ....Austin, TX
Smith, G. William ....St. Paul, MN
Smith, G. Wynn, Jr. ....Walnut Creek, CA
Smith, Gad ....Kansas City, MO
Smith, Gail R. ....Mount Vernon, WA
Smith, Gaillen R. ....Los Angeles, CA
Smith, Gaines W. ....Charleston, SC
Smith, Gale F. ....Cheyenne, OK
Smith & Gamblin ....Lexington, NC

Smith, Gambrell & Russell, LLP Washington, DC
Atlanta, GA
Smith, Gamson, Diamond & Olney Portland, OR
Smith, Gare A. ....United States Senate, Senatorial Assistants, GV
Smith, Garrett K. ....New York, NY
Smith, Garrett M. ....Charlottesville, VA
Smith, Garth V. ....Santa Cruz, CA
Smith, Gary A. ....Mesa, AZ
Smith, Gary A. ....Antioch, CA
Smith, Gary Arlen ....Philadelphia, PA
Smith, Gary C. ....Birmingham, AL
Smith, Gary E. ....Connersville, IN
Smith, Gary E. ....Mount Olive, NJ
Smith, Gary E. ....Rochester, NY
Smith, Gary E. ....Dallas, TX
Smith, Gary E. ....Beloit, WI
Smith, Gary F. ....Hauppauge, NY
Smith, Gary H. ....Chicago, IL
Smith, Gary H. ....Alexandria, VA
Smith, Gary H., III ....Aiken, SC
Smith, Gary H., P.C., Law Offices of Chicago, IL
Smith, Gary J. ....Washington, DC
Smith, Gary K. ....Memphis, TN
Smith, Gary L. ....Newark, DE
Smith, Gary L. ....Wilmington, DE
Smith, Gary L. ....Springfield, IL
Smith, Gary L. ....Kansas City, MO
Smith, Gary L. ....Lebanon, MO
Smith, Gary L. ....Wauseon, OH
Smith, Gary L. ....Pittsburgh, PA
Smith, Gary M. ....Hoffman Estates, IL
Smith, Gary M. ....St. Louis, MO
Smith, Gary M. ....Akron, OH
Smith, Gary Mitchel ....New York, NY
Smith, Gary N. ....West Sacramento, CA
Smith, Gary R. ....Atlanta, GA
Smith, Gary S. ....Pinson, AL
Smith, Gary V. ....Miami, FL
Smith, Gary W. ....Atlanta, GA
Smith, Gary W. ....Boston, MA
Smith, Gary W. ....Charlotte, NC
Smith, Gary W. ....Woodsfield, OH
Smith, Gary William ....Sedalia, MO
Smith, Gavin H. ....Houston, TX
Smith, Gayle R. ....Philadelphia, PA
Smith, Gaylord G. ....Kansas City, MO
Smith, Gendler, Shiell, Sheff & Ford, P.A. Minneapolis, MN
Smith, Gene A. ....Alvin, TX
Smith, Gene C. ....Springfield, MO
Smith, Gene Collison ....Raleigh, NC
Smith, Gene E. ....Del Mar, CA
Smith, Gene F. ....Galveston, TX
Smith, Gene M., (Ms.) Department of State, GV
Smith, Gene R. ....New Orleans, LA
Smith, Genese Dopson ....Kentfield, CA
Smith, Geo. C. ....Miami, FL
Smith, Geo. R. ....Xenia, OH
Smith, Geoff G. ....Traverse City, MI
Smith, Geoffrey A. ....Fairfax, VA
Smith, Geoffrey D. ....Tallahassee, FL
Smith, Geoffrey D. ....White Plains, NY
Smith, Geoffrey L. ....Livonia, MI
Smith, Geoffrey Maxwell ....Charleston, SC
Smith, Geoffrey S. ....Philadelphia, PA
Smith, George A. ....Universal City, CA
Smith, George A. ....Englewood, CO
Smith, George A. ....New York, NY
Smith, George A., II ....Huntsville, AL
Smith, George A., Jr. ....Tallahassee, FL
Smith, George A., Jr. ....Spring House, PA
Smith, George Anthony ....Atlanta, GA
Smith, George B. ....Georgetown, DE
Smith, George B. ....Atlanta, GA
Smith, George B. ....Albany, NY
Smith, George B., III ....Portland, ME
Smith, George C. ....Washington, DC
Smith, George C. ....Columbus, OH
Smith, George D. ....Lexington, KY
Smith, George E. ....Hartford, WI
Smith, George Earl ....Montgomery, AL
Smith, George E. R. ....Southbury, CT
Smith, George F. ....Fenton, MO
Smith, George H. ....Santa Cruz, CA
Smith, George L. ....Greenwich, CT
Smith, George L. ....Bellevue, WA
Smith, George L., Jr. ....Hampton, VA
Smith, George L., Jr., Ltd. ....Hampton, VA
Smith, George M. ....Charleston, WV
Smith, George P., II ....Washington, DC
Smith, George T. ....Marietta, GA
Smith, George W. ....Muskogee, OK
Smith, Gerald A. ....Baltimore, MD
Smith, Gerald A. ....Seattle, WA
Smith, Gerald A., Jr. ....Nashville, TN
Smith, Gerald C. ....Oakland, CA
Smith, Gerald Floyd ....Greenwood, IN
Smith, Gerald J. ....El Paso, TX
Smith, Gerald K. ....Phoenix, AZ
Smith, Gerald K. ....San Ramon, CA
Smith, Gerald L. ....Columbus, OH
Smith, Gerald M. ....St. Louis, MO
Smith, Gerald M. ....New York, NY
Smith, Gerald M. ....Avon Lake, OH
Smith, Gerald M., Jr. ....Norwich, CT
Smith, Gerald S. ....Harrisburg, PA
Smith, Gerald W., (P.C.) ....Pekin, IL
Smith, Geraldine A. ....Parsippany, NJ
Smith, Gerard F., Law Office of Denville, NJ
Smith, Gerard X. M. ....Cherry Hill, NJ
Philadelphia, PA
Smith, Geri M. ....Cleveland, OH

Smith & Giacometti ....Westmont, NJ
Philadelphia, PA
Smith, Gibson, Jr. ....York, PA
Smith, Gibson L., Jr. ....Charlotte, NC
Smith, Gilbert A. ....Bradenton, FL
Smith, Gilbert A. ....Palm Harbor, FL
Smith, Gilbert A., Jr. ....Bradenton, FL
Smith, Gilbert D., P.C. ....Arlington, TX
Smith, Gilbert Davis ....Arlington, TX
Smith, Gilbert F. ....Pomona, CA
Smith, Gilbert L., Jr. ....Chagrin Falls, OH
Smith, Gilliam and Williams ....Buford, GA
Clarkesville, GA
Cleveland, GA
Dahlonega, GA
Dawsonville, GA
Gainesville, GA
Smith & Gilstrap ....Marshall, TX
Smith, Gina G. ....Tallahassee, FL
Smith, Gina Marie ....Riverdale, MD
Smith & Glauser ....Salt Lake City, UT
Smith, Glee S., Jr. ....Larned, KS
Lawrence, KS
Smith, Glen A. ....Los Angeles, CA
Smith, Glen A. ....Belle Mead, NJ
Smith, Glen E. ....Miami, FL
Smith, Glen E. ....Baton Rouge, LA
Smith, Glen M. ....Santa Rosa, CA
Smith, Glen O., Jr. ....Cleveland, OH
Smith, Glen P. ....Atlanta, GA
Smith, Glenn A. ....Palo Alto, CA
San Francisco, CA
Smith, Glenn C. ....United States Senate, Committee Legal Personnel, GV
Smith, Glenn D. ....Los Angeles, CA
Smith, Glenn D. ....Uniondale, NY
Smith, Glenn E. ....Fort Worth, TX
Smith, Glenn E. ....Cheyenne, WY
Smith, Glenn J. ....Wayne, NJ
Smith, Glenn L. ....Des Moines, IA
Smith, Glenn N. ....Fort Lauderdale, FL
Smith, Glenn R. ....Keene, NH
Smith, Glenn W. ....Marquette, MI
Smith, Goldstein, Magram & Berenato, A Professional Corporation ...Burlington, NJ
Smith, Gomer, Jr. ....Oklahoma City, OK
Smith, Gordon A. ....Atlanta, GA
Smith, Gordon B. ....Savannah, GA
Smith, Gordon C. ....Denver, CO
Smith, Gordon D. ....Gig Harbor, WA
Smith, Gordon H. ....Chicago, IL
Smith, Gordon H. ....Manchester, ME
Smith, Gordon H., Jr. ....Milwaukee, WI
Smith, Gordon J. ....Washington, DC
Smith, Gordon K. ....Lake Kiowa, TX
Smith, Gordon L. ....West St. Paul, MN
Smith, Gordon L. ....Greenwood, MS
Smith, Gordon R. ....Indianapolis, IN
Smith, Gordon S. ....Southfield, MI
Smith, Gordon W. ....Nashville, TN
Smith, Grady F. ....Chamblee, GA
Smith, Graham N. ....Lafayette, LA
Smith, Graham W. ....Orchard Park, NY
Smith & Granberg ....San Francisco, CA
Smith, Grant B. ....Atlanta, GA
Smith, Grant J. ....Fort Lauderdale, FL
Smith, Grant W. ....Nashville, TN
Smith, Granville B. ....Twin Falls, ID
Smith, Greenleaf & Brooks ....Liberal, KS
Smith, Greer M. ....San Francisco, CA
Smith, Greg K. ....Denver, CO
Smith, Greg L. ....Winston-Salem, NC
Smith, Gregg D. ....New York, NY
Smith, Gregg L. ....Birmingham, AL
Smith, Gregg R. ....Spokane, WA
Smith, Greggory M. ....Holdenville, OK
Smith, Gregory ....Camden, NJ
Smith, Gregory A. ....Denver, CO
Smith, Gregory A. ....Washington, DC
Smith, Gregory A. ....Washington, DC
Smith, Gregory A. ....Washington, IN
Smith, Gregory A. ....Salem, OR
Smith, Gregory A. ....Spokane, WA
Smith, Gregory A., R.N., P.C. ....Salem, OR
Smith, Gregory B. Federal Deposit Insurance Corporation, GV
Smith, Gregory B. ....Muncie, IN
Smith, Gregory C. ....Palo Alto, CA
Smith, Gregory C. ....Denver, CO
Smith, Gregory C. ....Metairie, LA
Smith, Gregory D. ....Pensacola, FL
Smith, Gregory D. ....Clarksville, TN
Smith, Gregory D. ....Nashville, TN
Smith, Gregory D. ....Tyler, TX
Smith, Gregory D., P.A. ....Pensacola, FL
Smith, Gregory Dean ....Washington, DC
Smith, Gregory E. ......Department of the Army, Office of the General Counsel, GV
Smith, Gregory E. ....Detroit, MI
Smith, Gregory E. ....Las Vegas, NV
Smith, Gregory F. ....Oak Brook, IL
Smith, Gregory G. ....Birmingham, AL
Smith, Gregory G. ....Fort Smith, AR
Smith, Gregory G. ....Chicago, IL
Smith, Gregory G. ....Great Falls, MT
Smith, Gregory H. ....Concord, NH
Smith, Gregory J. ....Fresno, CA
Smith, Gregory J. ....Denver, CO
Smith, Gregory J. ....Chicago, IL
Smith, Gregory J. ....Springfield, MO
Smith, Gregory K. ....Washington, DC
Smith, Gregory K. ....Clinton, NJ
Smith, Gregory L. ....San Francisco, CA
Smith, Gregory L. ....Oak Park, IL
Smith, Gregory L. ....Louisville, KY
Smith, Gregory M. ....Laguna Beach, CA
Smith, Gregory M. ....Chicago, IL
Smith, Gregory N. ....Redmond, WA

Smith, Gregory P. ....Bushnell, FL
Orlando, FL
Tavares, FL
Smith, Gregory R. ....Los Angeles, CA
Smith, Gregory R. ....Portland, ME
Smith, Gregory R. ....St. Louis, MO
Smith, Gregory S. ....Atlanta, GA
Smith, Gregory S. ....New York, NY
Smith, Gregory Scott ....Fremont, CA
Smith, Gregory Scott ....Atlanta, GA
Smith, Gregory V. ....Monticello, MN
Smith, Gregory V. ....Madison, WI
Smith, Gregory V., & Associates Monticello, MN
Smith, Gregory W. ....Denver, CO
Smith, Gregory W. ....Augusta, GA
Smith, Gregory W. ....Grand Ledge, MI
Smith, Gregory W. ....Madison Heights, VA
Smith, Gregry Scott ....Paw Paw, MI
Smith, Gretchen N. ....Phoenix, AZ
Smith, Gretchen Wegmann ....Houston, TX
Smith, Griffin ....Little Rock, AR
Smith, Griffin, Jr. ....Little Rock, AR
Smith, Grigg, Shea & Klinker, A Professional Corporation ....Cherokee, IA
Orange City, IA
Primghar, IA
Sibley, IA
Sutherland, IA
Smith, Grimsley, Bauman, Pinkerton, Petermann & Wells
De Funiak Springs, FL
Destin, FL
Fort Walton Beach, FL
Smith & Guenther, P.C. ....Great Falls, MT
Missoula, MT
Smith, Guy C. ....Washington, DC
Smith, Guy Porter ....Los Angeles, CA
Smith, Guy W. ....New Orleans, LA
Smith, G. W. King ....Anderson, SC
Smith, Gwendolyn Chisholm Baltimore, MD
Smith, Gwynn Kelly ....Gallatin, TN
Smith, H. Arthur, Jr. ....Pennington, NJ
Smith, H. Bradley ....Frankfort, KY
Smith, H. Brooks ....Locust Valley, NY
Smith, H. Charles ....Rancho Cucamonga, CA
Smith, H. Daniel ....Omaha, NE
Smith, H. David, Jr. ....Baton Rouge, LA
Smith, H. Davidson, III ....El Paso, TX
Smith, H. Guy ....Dallas, TX
Smith, H. Guy, Jr. (P.A.) ....Lakeland, FL
Smith, H. Jill ....Las Vegas, NV
Smith, H. Lawrence ....Grand Rapids, MI
Smith, H. Mayo ....Little Rock, AR
Smith, H. Parker
Cape May Court House, NJ
Smith, H. Presley ....Jesup, GA
Smith, H. Richard ....Des Moines, IA
Smith, H. Russell ....Detroit, MI
Smith, H. Scott ....Washington, DC
Smith, H. Selwyn ....Manassas, VA
Smith, H. Stratton, III ....Tampa, FL
Smith, H. Stratton, III, P.A. ....Tampa, FL
Smith, H. Suzanne ....Atlanta, GA
Smith, H. T., P.A. ....Miami, FL
Smith, H. Terrence ....Toledo, OH
Smith, H. Vance ....Tampa, FL
Smith, H. William, III ....Stamford, CT
Smith, Hal M. ....Baltimore, MD
Smith & Hale ....Centerville, OH
Columbus, OH
Delaware, OH
Dublin, OH
Lancaster, OH
Marysville, OH
New Albany, OH
Newark, OH
Smith & Hallinger ....Lancaster, PA
York, PA
Smith and Hamm, P.A. ....Lake Alfred, FL
Winter Haven, FL
Smith, Hancock & Zollinger ....Rexburg, ID
Smith & Hanna ....Salt Lake City, UT
Smith, Hannah & Parker, P.C. Valdosta, GA
Smith, Hansell L. ....Marietta, GA
Smith & Hansen ....Omaha, NE
Smith, Hardy B. ....Mobile, AL
Smith, Harland L. ....Milford, MA
Smith, Harley M. ....St. Louis, MO
Smith, Harmon T., Jr. ....Gainesville, GA
Smith, Harold ....Chevy Chase, MD
Smith, Harold C., Jr. ....Rockville, MD
Smith, Harold D., P.A., Law Offices Fort Lauderdale, FL
Smith, Harold F., Jr. ....Memphis, TN
Smith, Harold G. ....Woodbridge, NJ
Smith, Harold H. ....Concord, NC
Smith, Harold (Hal) ......Fort Lauderdale, FL
Smith, Harold P. (Peter) ....Oakland, CA
Smith, Harold R. ....La Grange, KY
Smith, Harold S., II ....Indianapolis, IN
Smith & Harper ....Helena, MT
Smith & Harrington ....Eastman, GA
Smith, Harris & Goyette, P.L.C. ....Flint, MI
Smith & Harris, LLP ....Mount Kisco, NY
Smith, Harrison C. ....Washington, DC
Sterling, VA
Smith, Harrison E. ....Nashua, NH
Smith, Harrison, Law Offices of Redding, CA
Shasta, CA
Smith, Harrison W., Jr. ....Columbus, OH
Smith, Harry A., III ....Elkins, WV
Smith, Harry B. ....Miami, FL
Smith, Harry B. ....Guaynabo, PR
Smith, Harry C. ....Bay Minette, AL

Smith, Harry E. ..... Moscow, PA
Smith, Harry F. ..... Fairfield, CT
Smith, Harry J. ..... Mountain City, TN
Smith, Harry J., Jr. ..... River Grove, IL
Smith, Harry L. ..... Marietta, OH
Smith, Harry R., Jr. ..... Glenn Dale, MD
Smith, Harvey ..... Roseland, NJ
Smith, Harvey R. ..... Dallas, TX
Smith, Harvey Y. ..... Department of Justice, United States Marshals Service, GV
Smith and Haskell, L.L.P.
Spartanburg, SC
Smith & Hassler ..... Houston, TX
Smith Haughey Rice & Roegge, P.C.
East Lansing, MI
Grand Rapids, MI
Lansing, MI
Traverse City, MI
Smith, Hawkins, Hollingsworth & Reeves, LLP ..... Macon, GA
Smith, Hayden, Jr. ..... Newark, NJ
Smith, Heather Bussing ..... Windsor, CA
Smith, Heather C. ..... Atlanta, GA
Smith, Heidi E. ..... Sacramento, CA
Smith, Heidi L. ..... Manhattan Beach, CA
Smith, Helane H. ..... New Rochelle, NY
Smith, Heldt & McKeone ..... Lexington, NE
Smith, Helen Bunt ..... Pasadena, CA
Smith, Helen C. ..... Memphis, TN
Smith, Helen C. Theo ..... Birmingham, AL
Smith, Helen T. ..... Portland, OR
Smith & Helman ..... Louisville, KY
Smith Helms Mulliss & Moore, L.L.P.
Atlanta, GA
Charlotte, NC
Greensboro, NC
Raleigh, NC
Research Triangle Park, NC
Wilmington, NC
Winston-Salem, NC
Smith, Heman B. ..... Sacramento, CA
Smith & Hemingway ..... Spokane, WA
Smith, Hemmesch & Burke ..... Chicago, IL
Smith, Henry A., III ..... Baltimore, MD
Smith, Henry B., Jr. ..... Monroe, NC
Smith, Henry C. ..... Goldsboro, NC
Smith, Henry E. ..... Chicago, IL
Smith, Henry Grady ..... Warner Robins, GA
Smith, Henry L., Jr. ..... Louisville, KY
Smith, Henry O., III ..... New York, NY
Smith, Henry R. ..... Augusta, GA
Smith, Henry R., P.C. ..... Augusta, GA
Smith, Henry T. ..... Roswell, GA
Smith, Herbert D. ..... Alva, OK
Smith, Herbert F., Jr. ..... Orland Park, IL
Smith, Herbert G., II ..... Washington, DC
Smith, Herbert J., Jr. ..... Bowling Green, KY
Smith, Herbert Richard Harrison
Redding, CA
Shasta, CA
Smith, Herbert S. ..... Los Angeles, CA
Smith, Herman Edward ..... Barnwell, SC
Smith, Herman F. (Bud) ..... Klamath Falls, OR
Smith, Herman J., Jr. ..... Boston, MA
Smith, Herman T. ..... Los Angeles, CA
Smith & Hiatt, P.A. ..... Fort Lauderdale, FL
Smith, Hilda Trapp, & Associates
Florence, AL
Smith, Hillary B. ..... Farmingdale, NY
Smith, Hillary B. ..... New York, NY
Smith Himmelmann, Attorneys at Law, A Law Corporation ..... Honolulu, HI
Smith & Hinton ..... Richmond, VA
Smith & Hirsch ..... Nashville, TN
Smith Hirsch & Brody ..... Southfield, MI
Smith, Hoke, III ..... Fort Walton Beach, FL
Smith, Hollie A. ..... Memphis, TN
Nashville, TN
Smith, Holly H. ..... Washington, DC
Smith, Holly L. ..... Springdale, AR
Smith, Holly N. ..... Medford, OR
Smith & Holmes, P.C. ..... Raleigh, NC
Smith, Homer A. ..... Oklahoma City, OK
Smith, Hood, Perkins, Loucks, Stout & Orfinger ..... Daytona Beach, FL
Smith & Hooper, Texas Trial Lawyers
Houston, TX
Smith & Hopen, P.A. ..... Clearwater, FL
Smith, Horace A. ..... Columbia, SC
Smith, Horace C. ..... Spartanburg, SC
Smith, Horace, Jr. ..... Daytona Beach, FL
Smith, Horace L., Jr. ..... Chattanooga, TN
Smith, Horton ..... Seattle, WA
Smith, Horton, P.S. Inc. ..... Seattle, WA
Smith, Houston D., III ..... Atlanta, GA
Smith, Houston Madison ..... Terrell, TX
Smith, Houston M., Law Offices of, P.C.
Terrell, TX
Smith, Howard A. ..... New York, NY
Smith, Howard & Ajax, LLP ..... Atlanta, GA
Smith, Howard B. ..... Birmingham, MI
Smith, Howard B. ..... Uniontown, PA
Smith, Howard E. ..... Bronxville, NY
Smith, Howard E., Jr. ..... Geneva, IL
Smith, Howard J. ..... Los Angeles, CA
Smith, Howard J. ..... St. Louis, MO
Smith, Howard J., Jr. ..... Houston, TX
Smith, Howard M. ..... Needham, MA
Smith, Howard N. ..... Jackson, MS
Smith, Howard P. ..... Hampton, VA
Smith, Howard W. ..... Trenton, NJ
Smith, Howard W., Jr. ..... Alexandria, VA
Smith, H. T. ..... Miami, FL
Smith, Huckaby & Graves, P.A.
Huntsville, AL
Smith, Hudson, Hammond & Alston, P.C.
Manassas, VA
Smith, Hugh E. ..... St. Petersburg, FL
Smith, Hugh E., Jr. ..... Dunwoody, GA
Smith, Hugh M. ..... Glen Rose, TX
Smith, Hugh N. ..... Tampa, FL
Smith, Hugh R. H. ..... Chevy Chase, MD
Smith, Hugh V., Jr. ..... Montgomery, AL
Smith, Hugh V., Jr., A Professional Corporation ..... Auburn, AL
Montgomery, AL
Smith, Hugh W. ..... Leesburg, AL
Smith Hulsey & Busey ..... Jacksonville, FL
Smith, Hurley D. ..... Dearborn, MI
Smith, I. Henry, Jr. ..... Shreveport, LA
Smith, Ian D. ..... Santa Barbara, CA
Smith, Ian R. ..... Cincinnati, OH
Smith, Ilam E. ..... Louisville, KY
Smith, Ilana ..... Los Angeles, CA
Smith, Ingrid A. ..... San Francisco, CA
Smith, Irvin D. ..... Eugene, OR
Smith, Irvin S. ..... New Orleans, LA
Smith, Irving D., Jr. ..... Seattle, WA
Smith, Isaac Keahi ..... Honolulu, HI
Smith, Isiah C. ..... West Palm Beach, FL
Smith, Israel ..... Tyler, TX
Smith, Issac N., Jr. ..... Charleston, WV
Smith, Ivan C. ..... Columbus, OH
Smith, Ivan D. ..... New York, NY
Smith, Ivan H. ..... North Little Rock, AR
Smith, Ivan L. ..... Akron, OH
Smith, Ivan W. ..... Ijamsville, MD
Smith, Ivy A., Jr. ..... New Orleans, LA
Smith, J. Adrian ..... Gulfport, MS
Smith, J. Alan ..... Lima, OH
Smith, J. Allen ..... Newark, NJ
Smith, J. Allen ..... Dallas, TX
Smith, J. Alvernon, Jr. ..... Richmond, VA
Smith, J. Anthony ..... Ontario, CA
Smith, J. Anthony ..... Washington, DC
Smith, J. Arthur, III ..... Baton Rouge, LA
Smith, J. Barry ..... San Luis Obispo, CA
Smith, J. Bond, Jr. ..... New York, NY
Smith, J. Bradley ..... Jefferson, GA
Smith, J. Breck ..... Wilmington, DE
Smith, J. Brett ..... Sherman, TX
Smith, J. Brian ..... Albuquerque, NM
Smith, J. Bruce ..... Bellingham, WA
Smith, J. Burleson ..... San Antonio, TX
Smith, J. Charles, III ..... Mount Airy, MD
Smith, J. Clay, Jr. ..... Washington, DC
Smith, J. Clinton, Jr. ..... Buford, GA
Smith, J. Craig ..... Salt Lake City, UT
Smith, J. Curtis ..... Dunlap, TN
Smith, J. David ..... Menlo Park, CA
Smith, J. David ..... Clayton, GA
Smith, J. David ..... Baton Rouge, LA
Smith, J. David ..... Williamsport, PA
Smith, J. David, Jr. ..... Lexington, KY
Smith, J. Dimmitt ..... Seattle, WA
Smith, J. Donally ..... Atlanta, GA
Smith, J Douglas
Hot Springs National Park, AR
Smith, J. Douglas ..... Riverview, MI
Smith, J. Earl ..... Dothan, AL
Smith, J. Edward ..... Morristown, NJ
Smith, J. Edwin ..... Houston, TX
Smith, J. Emory, Jr. ..... Columbia, SC
Smith, J. Harmon, III ..... Wynne, AR
Smith, J. Holder, Jr. ..... Valdosta, GA
Smith, J. Hulbert ..... Fort Worth, TX
Smith, J. Keith ..... Louisville, KY
Smith, J. Kellum, Jr. ..... New York, NY
Smith, J. Layne ..... Tallahassee, FL
Smith, J. Linwood ..... Baltimore, MD
Smith, J. MacAlpine ..... Bellefontaine, OH
Smith, J. Mark ..... Denver, CO
Smith, J. Martin ..... Olympia, WA
Smith, J. Maxwell ..... Phenix City, AL
Smith, J. Michael ..... West Palm Beach, FL
Smith, J. Michael ..... Winfield, KS
Smith, J. Michael ..... Grand Rapids, MI
Smith, J. Michael ..... Salem, OR
Smith, J. Michael ..... Texarkana, TX
Smith, J. Michael ..... Purcellville, VA
Smith, J. Mitchell ..... Beaumont, TX
Smith, J. Myron ..... Prattville, AL
Smith, J. Nevin ..... Carrollton, GA
Smith, J. Patrick ..... La Porte, IN
Smith, J. Paul ..... Bloomfield Hills, MI
Smith, J. Philip ..... Memphis, TN
Smith, J. Randolph ..... Monroe, LA
Smith, J. Randolph ..... Richmond, VA
Smith, J. Randolph, Jr. ..... Martinsville, VA
Smith, J. Richard ..... Naples, FL
Smith, J. Richard ..... Stow, MA
Smith, J. Richard ..... Kansas City, MO
Smith, J. Robert ..... Colquitt, GA
Smith, J. Robert ..... Seattle, WA
Smith, J. Ron ..... Lakeland, FL
Smith, J. Russel ..... Silver Spring, MD
Smith, J. Ryan ..... New York, NY
Smith, J. Scott ..... Sacramento, CA
Smith, J. Shaffer ..... Beverly Hills, CA
Smith, J. Stanley ..... Dublin, GA
Smith, J. Stephen ..... Covington, KY
Smith, J. Stewart ..... Harrison, NY
Smith, J. Stuart ..... Orlando, FL
Smith, J. Theodore ..... Columbus, OH
Smith, J. Timothy ..... Birmingham, AL
Smith, J. Timothy ..... Fayetteville, AR
Smith, J. Timothy, P.C. ..... Birmingham, AL
Smith, J. Travis ..... Cody, WY
Smith, J. Troy, Jr. ..... Greenville, NC
New Bern, NC
Smith, J. Wellford ..... Virginia Beach, VA
Smith, Jack ..... Albuquerque, NM
Smith, Jack B. ..... Department of Defense, Defense Legal Services Agency, GV
Smith, Jack B. ..... Decatur, GA
Smith, Jack D.
Federal Deposit Insurance Corporation, Litigation Branch, GV
Smith, Jack F. ..... Englewood, CO
Smith, Jack K. ..... Dallas, TX
Smith, Jack L. ..... Denver, CO
Smith, Jack L. ..... Miami, OK
Smith, Jack L., P.C. ..... Miami, OK
Smith, Jack M. ..... Marietta, GA
Smith, Jack O. ..... Ellsworth, ME
Smith, Jack R. ..... Granada Hills, CA
Smith, Jack W. ..... Dothan, AL
Smith & Jackson ..... Lebanon, MO
Smith, Jackson B., Jr. ..... Houston, TX
Smith, Jackson C.
Department Of Health And Human Services, Social Security Administration, GV
Smith, Jackson L. ..... Colorado Springs, CO
Smith, Jacob D. ..... Indianapolis, IN
Smith, Jacob J. ..... Eureka, CA
Smith, Jacob L. ..... Lynden, WA
Smith, Jacob W. ..... Rockland, MA
Smith, Jacqueline ..... Houston, TX
Smith, Jacquelyn D. ..... Birmingham, AL
Smith, Jak M. ..... Tupelo, MS
Smith & Jakubowski ..... Abington, PA
Philadelphia, PA
Smith, James A. ..... Menlo Park, CA
Smith, James A. ..... Fort Lauderdale, FL
Smith, James A. ..... Chicago, IL
Smith, James A. ..... Chicago, IL
Smith, James A. ..... New Orleans, LA
Smith, James A. ..... Boston, MA
Smith, James A. ..... Detroit, MI
Smith, James A. ..... Falcon Heights, MN
Smith, James A. ..... Cleveland, OH
Smith, James A., Jr. ..... Seattle, WA
Smith, James Allan ..... Atlanta, GA
Smith, James A.N. ..... San Francisco, CA
Smith, James Andrew ..... Greenville, SC
Smith, James B. ..... Chicago, IL
Smith, James B. ..... Biddeford, ME
Smith, James B. ..... Galena Park, TX
Smith, James B., Jr. ..... San Antonio, TX
Smith, James Bayard ..... Metuchen, NJ
Smith, James C. ..... Carson City, NV
Smith, James C. ..... Charlotte, NC
Smith, James C., Jr. ..... Yorktown, VA
Smith, James Clark ..... Middletown, OH
Smith, James Cloudis ..... Tallahassee, FL
Smith, James D. ..... Phoenix, AZ
Smith, James D. ..... Wilmington, NC
Smith, James D. ..... Austin, TX
Smith, James D. ..... Houston, TX
Smith, James D., Law Offices of
Tuscaloosa, AL
Smith, James Dale ..... Mobile, AL
Smith, James David (J.D.) ..... Harlan, KY
Smith, James David, Jr. ..... Florence, SC
Smith, James E. ..... Fairhope, AL
Smith, James E. ..... San Luis Obispo, CA
Smith, James E. ..... Washington, DC
Smith, James E. ..... Chicago, IL
Smith, James E. ..... Augusta, ME
Smith, James E. ..... Boston, MA
Smith, James E. ..... Las Vegas, NV
Smith, James E. ..... Houston, TX
Smith, James E., II ..... Keyser, WV
Smith, James E. (Jay) ..... Los Angeles, CA
Smith, James E., Jr. ..... Little Rock, AR
Smith, James E., Jr. ..... Kenner, LA
Metairie, LA
New Orleans, LA
Slidell, LA
Smith, James E., Jr. ..... Carthage, MS
Smith, James E., Jr. ..... Columbia, SC
Smith, James E., Jr., P.A. ..... Columbia, SC
Smith, James E., Ltd. ..... Las Vegas, NV
Smith, James E., P.C. ..... Fairhope, AL
Smith, James F. ..... Davis, CA
Smith, James F. ..... Atlanta, GA
Smith, James F. ..... Chicago, IL
Smith, James F. ..... Charles City, IA
Smith, James F. ..... Omaha, NE
Smith, James G. ..... Monroe, LA
Smith, James G. ..... Flint, MI
Smith, James G. ..... New York, NY
Smith, James G. F. ..... Chicago, IL
Smith, James H. ..... Long Beach, CA
Smith, James H. ..... Santa Barbara, CA
Smith, James H. ..... Tampa, FL
Smith, James H. ..... Thomasville, GA
Smith, James H. ..... Shawneetown, IL
Smith, James H. ..... Indianapolis, IN
Smith, James H. ..... Falmouth, MA
Smith, James H. ..... Eatontown, NJ
Smith, James H. ..... Yorktown, VA
Smith, James H. (Buck) ..... Lexington, TX
Smith, James H., III ..... Cincinnati, OH
Smith, James H., P.C. ..... Shawneetown, IL
Smith, James H., P.C. ..... Falmouth, MA
Smith, James J. ..... Tampa, FL
Smith, James J. ..... Garnett, KS
Smith, James K. ..... San Diego, CA
Smith, James K., Jr. ..... Newark, NJ
Smith, James L. ..... Orange, CA
Smith, James L. ..... Pekin, IL
Smith, James L. ..... Dallas, TX
Smith, James L., III ..... Atlanta, GA
Smith, James Lonnie ..... Picayune, MS
Smith, James M. ..... Phoenix, AZ
Smith, James M. ..... Palo Alto, CA
Smith, James M. ..... Baltimore, MD
Smith, James M. ..... Lexington, MA
Smith, James M. ..... Springfield, MA
Smith, James M. ..... Detroit, MI
Smith, James M. ..... St. Louis, MO
Smith, James M. ..... Newark, NJ
Smith, James M. ..... Cleveland, OH
Smith, James M. ..... Reading, PA
Smith, James M. ..... Decaturville, TN
Smith, James M. ..... Memphis, TN
Smith, James McCauley ..... Montgomery, AL
Smith, James Michael ..... Birmingham, AL
Smith, James Michael ..... McGehee, AR
Smith, James N. ..... McGehee, AR
Smith, James N. ..... Decaturville, TN
Smith, James O. ..... Washington, DC
Smith, James P. ..... Huntsville, AL
Smith, James P. ..... Atlanta, GA
Macon, GA
Smith, James P., III ..... New York, NY
Smith, James Patrick ..... Houston, TX
Smith, James Patrick, P.C. ..... Houston, TX
Smith, James Peeler ..... Raleigh, NC
Smith, James Q. ..... Wichita Falls, TX
Smith, James R. ..... Middlebury, CT
Smith, James R. ..... Tampa, FL
Smith, James R. ..... Chicago, IL
Smith, James R. ..... Louisville, KY
Smith, James R. ..... Durand, MI
Smith, James R. ..... Sister Bay, WI
Sturgeon Bay, WI
Smith, James R., II ..... Mt. Gilead, OH
Smith, James R., Jr. ..... Valdosta, GA
Smith, James Randolph ..... Nashville, TN
Smith, James, Rowlett & Cohen, L.L.P.
Greensboro, NC
Smith, James S. ..... Oak Park, IL
Smith, James S. ..... Portsmouth, OH
Smith, James S., III ..... Waukegan, IL
Smith, James S., Jr. ..... Rockwood, TN
Smith, James Stephen ..... Covington, KY
Smith, James Stuart ..... Portland, OR
Smith, James T. ..... Philadelphia, PA
Smith, James T., Jr. ..... Towson, MD
Smith, James U., III ..... Louisville, KY
Smith, James W. ..... Little Rock, AR
Smith, James W. ..... Daytona Beach, FL
Smith, James W. ..... Athens, GA
Smith, James W. ..... Hinesville, GA
Smith, James W. ..... Muncie, IN
Smith, James W. ..... Kalamazoo, MI
Smith, James W. ..... Syracuse, NY
Smith, James W. ..... Troy, NY
Smith, James W. ..... Stigler, OK
Smith, James W., Jr. ..... Pacoima, CA
Smith, James W., Jr. ..... Houston, TX
Smith, James W., Jr. ..... Pearsall, TX
Smith, James Walker ..... New York, NY
Smith, James Wilson ..... Phoenix, AZ
Smith, Jamie S. ..... Chicago, IL
Smith, Jan M. ..... Savannah, GA
Smith, Jana E. ..... Metairie, LA
Smith, Jana Jawan ..... Huntsville, AL
Smith, Jane Creekmore ..... Birmingham, AL
Smith, Jane D. ..... Englewood, CO
Smith, Jane Krueger ..... Marinette, WI
Smith, Jane Oliver ..... Manassas, VA
Smith, Jane Simkin ..... Millbrook, NY
Smith, Jane Snoddy ..... St. Louis, MO
Smith, Jane T. ..... Fresno, CA
Smith, Janene M. ..... Washington, DC
Smith, Janet D. ..... Hightstown, NJ
Smith, Janet Gerald ..... Nutley, NJ
Smith, Janet H. ..... Cleveland, OH
Smith, Janet Hugie ..... Salt Lake City, UT
Smith, Janet Jo ..... Denver, CO
Smith, Janet K. ..... Chicago, IL
Smith, Janet L. ..... Tallahassee, FL
Smith, Janet L. ..... Seattle, WA
Smith, Janet M. ..... Boston, MA
Smith, Janice E. ..... Las Vegas, NV
Smith, Janice K. ..... New York, NY
Smith, Janice M. ..... Oklahoma City, OK
Smith, Janice M. ..... Pittsburgh, PA
Smith, Janice N. ..... Atlanta, GA
Smith, Janie F. ..... Centralia, IL
Smith, Janine ..... Culver City, CA
Smith, Janis C. ..... Alexandria, VA
Smith, Janis M. ..... Parkesburg, PA
Smith, Janna Eaton ..... Atlanta, GA
Smith, Jared O. ..... Safford, AZ
Smith, Jared R. ..... Novato, CA
Smith, Jas. B. ..... El Cerrito, CA
Smith, Jas. M. ..... Dracut, MA
Smith, Jason D. ..... Washington, DC
Smith, Jason R. ..... Madison, WI
Smith, Jason Randal ..... Key West, FL
Smith, Jason W. ..... Longview, TX
Smith, Jay A. ..... Latham, NY
Smith, Jay B. ..... Winchester, MA
Smith, Jay C. ..... Bakersfield, CA
Smith, Jay D. ..... Santa Barbara, CA
Smith, Jay E. ..... Los Angeles, CA
Smith, Jay Earl ..... Las Vegas, NV
Smith, Jay H. ..... Eugene, OR
Smith, Jay L. ..... Palos Park, IL
Smith, Jay L. ..... Jefferson City, MO
Smith, Jay T. ..... Washington, DC
Smith, J. B. ..... Hammond, IN
South Bend, IN
Smith, J. B. ..... Portland, OR
Smith, J. D. ..... Atlanta, GA
Smith, J.D. ..... Seattle, WA
Smith, J. D., (P.A.) ..... Pensacola, FL
Smith, Jean Delaney ..... New York, NY
Smith, Jeanette E. ..... Miami, FL
Smith, Jeanette E., & Associates, P.A.
Miami, FL
Smith, Jeanette Louise ..... Sacramento, CA
Smith, Jeanette M. ..... Omaha, NE
Smith, Jeanne ..... Atlanta, GA
Smith, Jeanne A. ..... Corvallis, OR
Smith, Jeannette C. ..... Johnson City, TN
Smith, Jeannine M. ..... Washington, DC

Smith, Jeff D. ... Huntsville, AL
Smith, Jeff Forrest ... Dallas, TX
Smith, Jefferson S. ... San Diego, CA
Smith, Jefferson V., Jr. ... Greenville, SC
Greer, SC
Smith, Jeffery E. ... Columbus, OH
Smith, Jeffrey ... Long Beach, CA
Smith, Jeffrey ... Department of Commerce, Patent and Trademark Office, GV
Smith, Jeffrey A. ... Santa Ana, CA
Smith, Jeffrey A. ... Oskaloosa, IA
Smith, Jeffrey A. ... New York, NY
Smith, Jeffrey A. ... Towanda, PA
Smith, Jeffrey A. ... Trenton, TN
Smith, Jeffrey B. ... Phoenix, AZ
Smith, Jeffrey B. ... Brea, CA
Ontario, CA
Palm Desert, CA
Pasadena, CA
Smith, Jeffrey B. ... Fort Lauderdale, FL
Smith, Jeffrey B. ... Baltimore, MD
Smith, Jeffrey B., Law Offices of
Long Beach, CA
Smith, Jeffrey C. ... Washington, DC
Smith, Jeffrey C. ... Columbus, MS
Smith, Jeffrey C. ... Poteau, OK
Smith, Jeffrey C. ... Memphis, TN
Smith, Jeffrey Carl ... Tuscaloosa, AL
Smith, Jeffrey Carlin ... Austin, TX
Smith, Jeffrey D. ... Riverside, CA
Smith, Jeffrey D. ... Kalamazoo, MI
Smith, Jeffrey D. ... Teaneck, NJ
Smith, Jeffrey D. ... Northport, NY
Smith, Jeffrey E. ... Columbus, OH
Smith, Jeffrey E. ... Philadelphia, PA
Smith, Jeffrey F. ... Harrisburg, PA
Smith, Jeffrey G. ... New York, NY
Smith, Jeffrey H. ... Washington, DC
Smith, Jeffrey H. ... Lake Buena Vista, FL
Smith, Jeffrey H. ... Valparaiso, IN
Smith, Jeffrey K. ... New Orleans, LA
Smith, Jeffrey L. ... Denver, CO
Smith, Jeffrey L. ... New Orleans, LA
Smith, Jeffrey L. ... Greensboro, NC
Smith, Jeffrey M. ... Los Angeles, CA
Smith, Jeffrey M. ... Atlanta, GA
Smith, Jeffrey M. ... Chicago, IL
Smith, Jeffrey M. ... Boston, MA
Smith, Jeffrey M. ... St. Paul, MN
Smith, Jeffrey M. ... Ironton, OH
Smith, Jeffrey Norman ... Chicago, IL
Smith, Jeffrey P. ... Los Angeles, CA
Smith, Jeffrey P. ... Fort Wayne, IN
Smith, Jeffrey Paul ... Skokie, IL
Smith, Jeffrey Q. ... New York, NY
Smith, Jeffrey R. ... Delphi, IN
Smith, Jeffrey S. ... Sunnyvale, CA
Smith, Jeffrey S. ... Priest River, ID
Smith, Jeffrey S. ... Danville, VA
Smith, Jeffrey S., & Associates ... Easton, PA
Smith, Jeffrey T. ... Washington, DC
Smith, Jeffrey T. ... Perrysburg, OH
Smith, Jeffrey T., (P.C.) ... Brandon, VT
Smith, Jeffrey W. ... Montgomery, AL
Smith, Jeffry W. ... Madison, WI
Smith & Jenkins, P.C. ... Atlanta, GA
Marietta, GA
Smith, Jennifer ... Los Angeles, CA
Smith, Jennifer ... Siler City, NC
Smith, Jennifer ... Texas City, TX
Smith, Jennifer A. ... Washington, DC
Smith, Jennifer A. ... Reno, NV
Smith, Jennifer C. ... Washington, DC
Smith, Jennifer C. ... Austin, TX
Smith, Jennifer D. ... Southfield, MI
Smith, Jennifer E. Gale ... Syracuse, NY
Smith, Jennifer G. ... New York, NY
Smith, Jennifer Grant ... Madison, WI
Smith, Jennifer J. ... Falls Church, VA
Smith, Jennifer L. ... Lafayette, LA
Smith, Jennifer L. ... St. Joseph, MI
Smith, Jennifer M. ... Washington, DC
Smith, Jennifer M. ... West Des Moines, IA
Smith, Jennifer M. ... Montclair, NJ
Smith, Jennifer R. ... Birmingham, AL
Smith, Jennifer R. ... Princeton, NJ
New York, NY
Smith, Jennings T. ... Irving, TX
Smith, Jenny Lynn ... Birmingham, AL
Smith, Jenny Namanworth
Cincinnati, OH
Smith & Jensen ... Chesterfield, VA
Glen Allen, VA
Richmond, VA
Smith, Jeraldine B. ... Freeport, TX
Smith, Jere C. ... Marietta, GA
Smith, Jere K. ... Santa Fe, NM
Smith, Jeriel C. ... Los Angeles, CA
Smith, Jerome B. ... Encino, CA
Smith, Jerome D. ... Montgomery, AL
Smith, Jerome M. ... Grand Rapids, MI
Smith, Jerome R. ... Reading, PA
Smith, Jerry ... Department of Commerce, Patent and Trademark Office, GV
Smith, Jerry ... Hereford, TX
Smith, Jerry A., P.C. ... Colorado Springs, CO
Smith, Jerry A., (P.C.)
Colorado Springs, CO
Smith, Jerry B. ... Du Quoin, IL
Smith, Jerry E. ... Houston, TX
Smith, Jerry J. ... Fountain Valley, CA
Smith, Jerry L. ... Flagstaff, AZ
Smith, Jerry L. ... New York, NY
Smith, Jerry L. ... Tulsa, OK
Smith, Jerry M. ... Winston-Salem, NC
Smith, Jerry M. ... Torrington, WY
Smith, Jerry N. ... Amarillo, TX
Smith, Jerry, P.C. ... Hereford, TX

Smith, Jerry V. ... Lewiston, ID
Smith, Jerry V. ... Dickson, TN
Smith, Jess H. ... Torrington, CT
Smith, Jess M., III ... Dayton, OH
Smith, Jessica ... Raleigh, NC
Smith, Jessica Cullen ... Los Angeles, CA
Smith, Jessie L. ... Harrisburg, PA
Smith, Jill A. ... Cleveland, OH
Smith, Jill C. ... Watertown, MA
Smith, Jill D. ... Bethesda, MD
Smith, Jill Galbreath ... Overland Park, KS
Smith, Jill Janine ... Albuquerque, NM
Smith, Jill K. ... Mount Clemens, MI
Smith, Jill L. ... Los Angeles, CA
Smith, Jim D. ... Yuma, AZ
Smith, Jimmy C. ... Union City, TN
Smith, J. L. ... San Augustine, TX
Smith, Joan E. ... San Francisco, CA
Smith, Joan E. ... Augusta, GA
Smith, Joanalys B. ... Austin, TX
Smith, Joanna Carey ... Chapel Hill, NC
Smith, Joanne C. ... Boston, MA
Smith, Joanne M. ... St. Paul, MN
Smith, Joanne Tawny ... Fort Lauderdale, FL
Smith, Joe E. ... Des Moines, IA
Smith, Joel A. ... Baltimore, MD
Smith, Joel D. ... Lancaster, PA
York, PA
Smith, Joel E. ... Rochester, NY
Smith, Joel E. ... Seattle, WA
Smith, Joel H. ... Columbia, SC
Smith, Joel McCabe ... Los Angeles, CA
Smith, Joel P., Jr. ... Eufaula, AL
Smith, Joel R. ... Jamestown, KY
Smith, Joel S. ... San Diego, CA
Smith, Johanna ... Boston, MA
Smith & John ... Shreveport, LA
Smith, John ... New York, NY
Smith, John A. ... Willow Springs, IL
Smith, John A. ... San Antonio, TX
Smith, John A., III ... Jersey City, NJ
Smith, John A., III ... Corpus Christi, TX
Smith, John Andrew ... Charleston, WV
Smith, John Anthony ... New York, NY
Smith, John B. ... Fort Lauderdale, FL
Smith, John Brem ... Charlotte, NC
Smith, John C. ... Boca Raton, FL
Smith, John C. ... Annapolis, MD
Smith, John C. ... St. Paul, MN
Smith, John C. (Bud), Jr., A Professional Corporation ... San Francisco, CA
Smith, John C. (Bud), Jr.
San Francisco, CA
Smith, John C. (Jack) ... Bellevue, WA
Smith, John C., Jr. ... Media, PA
Philadelphia, PA
Smith, John Cash ... Beaumont, TX
Orange, TX
Smith, John C. B., Jr. ... Columbia, SC
Smith, John Charles Thompson ... Auburn, IN
Smith, John Churchman ... Media, PA
West Chester, PA
Smith, John Churchman, & Associates, P.C.
Cherry Hill, NJ
Media, PA
Philadelphia, PA
West Chester, PA
Smith, John Coventry, Jr. ... Arlington, VA
Smith, John D. ... Department of Commerce, Patent and Trademark Office, GV
Smith, John D. ... Columbia, MO
Smith, John D. ... Franklin, OH
Springboro, OH
Smith, John Da Grosa ... Philadelphia, PA
Smith, John E.
Department of Justice, GV
Smith, John E. ... Missoula, MT
Smith, John E. ... New York, NY
Smith, John E. ... New York, NY
Philadelphia, PA
Smith, John E. ... Falls Church, VA
Smith, John E., II ... Houston, TX
Smith, John E., III ... Fitzgerald, GA
Smith, John F. ... Louisville, KY
Smith, John F., III ... Philadelphia, PA
Smith, John F. "Sandy" ... Atlanta, GA
Smith, John Frederick ... San Diego, CA
Smith, John G. ... Washington, DC
Smith, John G. ... Chicago, IL
Smith, John G. ... Crofton, MD
Smith, John Garland ... Tallassee, AL
Smith, John Gordon ... Middletown, NY
Smith, John H. ... Gainesville, GA
Smith, John H. ... Keokuk, IA
Smith, John H ... Baton Rouge, LA
Smith, John H. ... Pittsburgh, PA
Smith, John H., III ... Brea, CA
Smith, John Hamilton ... Charleston, SC
Smith, John J. ... Birmingham, AL
Smith, John J., Jr. ... Trenton, NJ
Smith, John Joseph ... Washington, DC
Smith, John Joseph ... Okemos, MI
Smith, John Joseph, Jr. ... Birmingham, AL
Smith, John Joseph, Jr., P.C.
Birmingham, AL
Smith, John K. ... Hayward, CA
Smith, John L. ... Louisville, KY
Smith, John Lawrence ... Tempe, AZ
Smith, John L. B. ... Fresno, CA
Smith, John Leslie ... Spartanburg, SC
Smith, John Lynn ... Oakland, CA
Smith, John M. ... Department of the Air Force, Office of the Judge Advocate General, GV
Smith, John M. ... Charlotte, NC
Smith, John M. ... New Philadelphia, OH
Smith, John M. ... Elizabethtown, PA
Lancaster, PA
Smith, John M. ... Pittsburgh, PA

Smith, John M. ... Barnwell, SC
Smith, John M. ... Longview, TX
Smith, John MacDonald ... Petaluma, CA
Smith, John Martin ... Auburn, IN
Smith, John R. ... Memphis, TN
Smith, John R. ... Center, TX
Smith, John R., Jr. ... Jacksonville, FL
Smith, John Richard ... Washington, DC
Smith, John Roger ... DeLand, FL
Smith, John Russell, Jr.
West Palm Beach, FL
Smith, John S. ... San Diego, CA
Smith, John S. ... Tampa, FL
Smith, John S. ... Lebanon, KY
Smith, John Stuart ... Washington, DC
Rochester, NY
Smith, John Thomas, II ... Washington, DC
Smith, John V., II ... Chicago, IL
Smith, John W. ... Boca Raton, FL
Smith, John W. ... Macon, GA
Smith, John W. ... Wilmington, NC
Smith, John W. ... Odessa, TX
Smith, John W., III ... Denver, CO
Smith, John Ward ... Maitland, FL
Smith, John Wesley ... Walnut Creek, CA
Smith & Johnson, Attorneys, P.C.
Bellaire, MI
Beulah, MI
Cadillac, MI
Kalkaska, MI
Lansing, MI
Traverse City, MI
Smith, Jon Michael ... Austin, TX
Smith, Jon Michael, The Law Offices of
Austin, TX
Smith, Jon R. ... Yuma, AZ
Smith, Jon W. ... Memphis, TN
Smith, Jonathan B. ... Kalispell, MT
Smith, Jonathan C. ... Milwaukee, WI
Smith, Jonathan D. ... New Port Richey, FL
Spring Hill, FL
Smith, Jonathan D. ... Baltimore, MD
Smith, Jonathan M. ... Washington, DC
Smith, Jonathan P. ... Norfolk, MA
Smith, Jonathan R. ... Dallas, TX
Smith, Jonathan Scott ... Columbia, MD
Ellicott City, MD
Smith, Jonathan W. ... Columbia, SC
Smith, Jones & Fawer, L.L.P.
Covington, LA
New Orleans, LA
Smith, Joni D. ... Kings Mountain, NC
Smith, Jordan H. ... Detroit, MI
Smith, Jordan P. ... Salmon, ID
Smith, Joscelyn E. ... Jamaica, NY
Smith, Jose ... North Miami Beach, FL
Smith, Joseph A. ... New York, NY
Smith, Joseph A. ... New York, NY
Smith, Joseph A., Jr. ... Rocky Mount, NC
Smith, Joseph C. ... New York, NY
Smith, Joseph C., Jr. ... Denver, CO
Smith, Joseph Conrad ... Southfield, MI
Smith, Joseph Conrad, and Associates, P.C.
Detroit, MI
Southfield, MI
Smith, Joseph E. ... Birmingham, AL
Smith, Joseph E. ... Oakland, CA
Smith, Joseph E. ... Bronson, FL
Smith, Joseph E. ... Ocala, FL
Smith, Joseph F. ... Dallas, TX
Smith, Joseph F., III ... Denver, CO
Smith, Joseph F., Jr. ... Fort Lauderdale, FL
Smith, Joseph H. ... Foster City, CA
Smith, Joseph, LTD. ... Hampton, VA
Newport News, VA
Smith, Joseph Michael ... Abington, PA
Philadelphia, PA
Smith, Joseph P. ... Anaheim, CA
Smith, Joseph P. ... Philadelphia, PA
Smith, Joseph S. ... Indianapolis, IN
Smith, Joseph S. ... Boston, MA
Smith, Joseph W. ... Fort Lauderdale, FL
Smith, Joshua L. ... Chicago, IL
Smith, Joy ... La Canada Flintridge, CA
Smith, Joyce ... Spokane, WA
Smith, Joyce Y. ... San Francisco, CA
Smith, J. P. ... Toledo, OH
Smith, J. R. ... Richmond, VA
Smith, Judith A. ... Ontario, CA
Smith, Judith A. ... Denver, CO
Smith, Judith K. ... Los Angeles, CA
Smith, Judith L. ... Buffalo Grove, IL
Smith, Judith M. ... Sarasota, FL
Smith, Juereta P. ... San Antonio, TX
Smith, Jules L. ... Rochester, NY
Smith, Julia E. ... Tallahassee, FL
Smith, Julia E. ... Norfolk, VA
Smith, Julia F. ... Clarksville, TN
Smith, Julian B., Jr. ... Metter, GA
Smith, Julian C., Jr. ... Carson City, NV
Smith, Julian J. ... Gainesville, TX
Smith, Julie A. ... Los Angeles, CA
Smith, Julie A. ... Columbus, OH
Smith, Julie C. ... Moorestown, NJ
Smith, Julie Eason ... Daytona Beach, FL
Smith, Julie F. ... Los Angeles, CA
Smith, Julie L. ... North Haven, CT
Smith, Juliette ... New York, NY
Smith, Julious P., Jr. ... Detroit, MI
Richmond, VA
Smith, Julius C. ... Minneapolis, MN
Smith, Julius C., III ... Greensboro, NC
Smith, June A. ... New Bedford, MA
Smith, Justin ... Department of Justice, Environment and Natural Resources Division, GV
Smith, Justin Bayly ... Orlando, FL
Smith, Justin C. ... San Francisco, CA

Smith, Justin Luke ... Troy, MI
Smith, Justin M. ... Medford, OR
Smith, Justine D. ... Annapolis, MD
Smith, Jyll A. ... Department of Commerce, Patent and Trademark Office, GV
Smith, K. Clay ... Indianapolis, IN
Smith and Kagawa ... Danville, IL
Smith, Kaighn, Jr. ... Portland, ME
Smith & Kane, P.A. ... Bel Air, MD
Smith, Kaori Horikawa ... Belleville, IL
St. Louis, MO
Smith, Kara Ann ... San Francisco, CA
Smith, Karalee H. ... Boston, MA
Smith, Karen ... Berkeley, CA
Smith, Karen ... San Francisco, CA
Smith, Karen A. ... Englewood, CO
Smith, Karen A. ... New York, NY
Smith, Karen D. ... Columbus, OH
Smith, Karen D. ... Houston, TX
Smith, Karen J. ... New York, NY
Smith, Karen L. ... Englewood, CO
Smith, Karen L. ... Hagerstown, MD
Smith, Karen L. ... Plano, TX
Smith, Karen M. ... Orlando, FL
Smith, Karen M., P.A. ... Cocoa, FL
Fort Pierce, FL
Gainesville, FL
Lakeland, FL
Melbourne, FL
Ocala, FL
Orlando, FL
Rockledge, FL
Sanford, FL
Tampa, FL
Titusville, FL
Winter Park, FL
Smith, Karen M. (Sutton)
Chattanooga, TN
Smith, Karen MacRae
Securities and Exchange Commission, Office of Equal Employment Opportunity, GV
Smith, Karen P. ... Chicago, IL
Smith, Karen R. ... Los Angeles, CA
Smith, Karen R. ... Tampa, FL
Smith, Karen R. ... Merrill, WI
Smith, Karen S. ... San Francisco, CA
Smith, Karen S. ... Bronx, NY
Smith, Kari A. ... Houston, TX
Smith, Karl Harold ... Las Vegas, NV
Smith, Karyn R. ... San Francisco, CA
Smith, Kate DeVries ... Minneapolis, MN
Smith, Katharine E. ... New York, NY
Smith, Katherine A. ... Jackson, MS
Smith, Katherine C. Hart ... Akron, OH
Smith, Katherine M. ... Edwardsville, IL
Smith, Katherine Mary ... Grand Rapids, MI
Smith, Kathleen A. ... Titusville, FL
Smith, Kathleen A. ... Brockton, MA
Smith, Kathleen A. ... Philadelphia, PA
Smith, Kathleen Conley
Department of Justice, Office of Attorney Personnel Management, GV
Smith, Kathleen DeSales Gast
Baltimore, MD
Smith, Kathleen Duffy ... Wilmington, DE
Smith, Kathleen E. ... Ocean City, MD
Smith, Kathleen F. ... Buffalo, NY
Smith, Kathleen G. ... Beverly Hills, CA
Smith, Kathleen Goodpasture
Columbia, SC
Smith, Kathleen Janetatos ... Oxnard, CA
Smith, Kathleen K. ... Chicago, IL
Smith, Kathleen M.
Department of the Air Force, Office of the General Counsel, GV
Smith, Kathleen Salome ... El Paso, TX
Smith, Kathryn Eden "Kate"
Santa Barbara, CA
Smith, Kathryn Hackney ... Brunswick, GA
Smith, Kathryn Harner ... New Haven, CT
Smith, Kathryn K. ... Minneapolis, MN
Smith, Kathy A. ... San Diego, CA
Smith, Kathy Kaplan ... Delray Beach, FL
Smith, Kathy Rae ... Frankfort, IN
Smith, Katuria E. ... Seattle, WA
Smith, Katzenstein & Furlow LLP
Wilmington, DE
Smith Kaufman LLP ... Los Angeles, CA
Smith & Kaye ... South Euclid, OH
Smith, Kayla D. ... Dallas, TX
Smith, Keefe & Moraghan ... Torrington, CT
Smith, Keith A. ... Charlotte, NC
Smith, Keith E. ... Princeton, NJ
Philadelphia, PA
Smith, Keith J. ... Washington, DC
Smith, Keith P. ... Phoenix, AZ
Smith, Keith T. ... Northfield, NJ
Smith, Keith W. ... Atlanta, GA
Smith, Keller, Miner & O'Shea
Buffalo, NY
Smith, Kelli Burris ... Beaumont, TX
Smith, Kelli M. ... Naperville, IL
Smith, Kelly Kalandyk ... Boston, MA
Smith, Kelly M. ... Allentown, PA
Smith, Kelly T. ... Sacramento, CA
Smith, Kelly W. ... Menlo Park, CA
Smith, Kelly W. ... Menlo Park, CA
Smith, Kelly W. ... Atlanta, GA
Smith, Kelsey J. ... Fort Collins, CO
Smith, Kembra L. ... Atlanta, GA
Smith, Ken J. ... Newton, IA
Smith, Ken McFarlane ... Arlington, VA
Smith, Ken McFarlane, P.C.
Arlington, VA
Smith, Ken W. ... Hazlehurst, GA

Smith, M. Robert F. .... Portland, OR
Smith, M. Shane .... Salt Lake City, UT
Smith, M. Stephen .... Miami, FL
Smith, M. Steve .... Houston, TX
Smith, M. Tyler .... Gainesville, GA
Smith, M. Van .... Mountain View, CA
Smith, M. A., A P.L.C. .... Arcadia, CA
Smith & Mabley, PLC .... Farmington Hills, MI
Smith, Mac, Law Office of
Weatherford, TX
Smith, MacDonald .... Sioux City, IA
Smith, Mack Arthur .... Florence, SC
Smith, Mackinnon, Greeley, Bowdoin, Edwards, Brownlee & Marks, P.A.
Orlando, FL
Smith, Macklyn A. .... Lawrenceville, GA
Smith, Maggie L. .... Indianapolis, IN
Smith, Majcher & Mudge, L.L.P.
Austin, TX
Smith, Malcolm A. .... San Francisco, CA
Smith, Malcolm B.E. .... Northampton, MA
Smith, Malcolm George .... Inglewood, CA
Smith, Malcolm P. .... Atlanta, GA
Smith, Malcolm R., (P.A.) .... Stuttgart, AR
Smith, Malcom C. .... Austin, TX
Smith, Malcom D., Jr. .... Tulsa, OK
Smith, Maley & Douglas .... Indianapolis, IN
Smith, Mara Shapiro .... Chicago, IL
Smith, Marc .... Encino, CA
Smith, Marc A. .... Department of Justice, Environment and Natural Resources Division, GV
Smith, Marc D. .... Toledo, OH
Smith, Marc J. .... Rockville, MD
Smith, Marcel .... Lexington, KY
Smith, Marcene J. .... De Smet, SD
Smith, Marci L. .... Los Angeles, CA
Smith, Marcia A. .... Corbin, KY
Smith, Marcia B. .... Waterbury, CT
Smith, Marcia B. .... Albany, NY
Smith, Marcus A. J. .... New Orleans, LA
Smith, Marcus E., Jr. .... Dallas, TX
Smith, Marcus H. .... Washington, DC
Smith, Marcus Lynn .... Greenville, SC
Smith, Marcy Lynn .... Wetumpka, AL
Smith, Mareta J. .... Kansas City, MO
Smith, Margaret A. .... Los Gatos, CA
Smith, Margaret A.
Securities and Exchange Commission, Division of Market Regulation, GV
Smith, Margaret Ann .... Alexandria, VA
Smith, Margaret B. .... Dallas, TX
Smith, Margaret Coburn .... Portland, ME
Smith, Margaret H. .... Bakersfield, CA
Smith, Margaret I. .... Denver, CO
Smith, Margaret M. .... Seattle, WA
Smith, Margaret R. .... New York, NY
Smith, Margery Weir .... Boise, ID
Smith, Marguerite A. .... Riverhead, NY
Smith, Maria A. .... Cleveland, OH
Smith, Marianne C. .... Moscow, PA
Scranton, PA
Smith, Marianne Demetral
Department of Labor, Office of the Solicitor, GV
Smith, Marianne DuVal .... Hartford, CT
Smith, Marilyn Koch .... St. Louis, MO
Smith, Marilyn M. .... Pasadena, CA
Smith, Marilyn Ray .... Cambridge, MA
Smith, Marilyn S. .... Seattle, WA
Smith, Marion, II .... Atlanta, GA
Smith, Marjorie A. .... Norfolk, VA
Smith, Marjorie J. .... Poughkeepsie, NY
Smith, Marjorie L. .... Stony Brook, NY
Smith, Marjorie M. .... Tappan, NY
Smith, Marjorie O. .... South Orange, NJ
Smith, Mark .... Flint, MI
Smith, Mark .... Elmira, NY
Smith, Mark .... Philadelphia, PA
Smith, Mark .... Pierre, SD
Smith, Mark A. .... El Segundo, CA
Smith, Mark A. .... Lake Forest, CA
Smith, Mark A. .... Washington, DC
Smith, Mark A. .... Itasca, IL
Smith, Mark A. .... Indianapolis, IN
Smith, Mark A. .... St. Louis, MO
Smith, Mark A. .... Omaha, NE
Smith, Mark A. .... Albuquerque, NM
Smith, Mark A. .... Mount Kisco, NY
Smith, Mark A. .... Cleveland, OH
Smith, Mark A. .... Columbia, SC
Smith, Mark A., III .... Atlanta, GA
Smith, Mark A., III, P.C. .... Atlanta, GA
Smith, Mark A., Jr. .... Toledo, OH
Smith, Mark Andrew .... Houston, TX
Smith, Mark B. .... Cincinnati, OH
Smith, Mark B. .... Vienna, VA
Smith, Mark B., Co., L.P.A. .... Cincinnati, OH
Smith, Mark C. .... New York, NY
Smith, Mark D. .... Rancho Cordova, CA
Smith, Mark D. .... Boston, MA
Smith, Mark D. .... Monroe, MI
Smith, Mark D. .... Dallas, TX
Smith, Mark Damon .... Quincy, IL
Smith, Mark Daniel .... Charlottesville, VA
Smith, Mark E. .... Washington, DC
Smith, Mark E. .... Savannah, GA
Smith, Mark E. .... Dallas, TX
Smith, Mark E. .... Madison, WI
Smith, Mark F. .... Cincinnati, OH
Smith, Mark H. .... Riverside, CA
Smith, Mark H. .... Lake Wales, FL
Smith, Mark H. .... Louisville, KY
Smith, Mark J. .... Gardena, CA
Smith, Mark J. .... Chicago, IL
Smith, Mark J. .... Davenport, IA
Smith, Mark J. .... Philadelphia, PA
Smith, Mark Joseph .... West Palm Beach, FL
Smith, Mark K. .... Princeton, NJ
Smith, Mark L. .... Carthage, MO
Smith, Mark L. .... North Smithfield, RI
Smith, Mark Lee .... Pensacola, FL
Smith, Mark Lee, P.A.
Fort Walton Beach, FL
Milton, FL
Pensacola, FL
Smith, Mark M. .... San Francisco, CA
Smith, Mark P. .... Cape Coral, FL
Smith, Mark Paul .... Fort Wayne, IN
Smith, Mark R. .... San Ramon, CA
Smith, Mark R. .... Indianapolis, IN
Smith, Mark R. .... Grand Rapids, MI
Smith, Mark R. .... Oxford, MS
Smith, Mark R. .... Lawton, OK
Smith, Mark S. .... Long Beach, CA
Smith, Mark S. .... Treasury Department, Internal Revenue Service, GV
Smith, Mark S. .... Skokie, IL
Smith, Mark S. .... Bellefonte, PA
Smith, Mark S. .... Lubbock, TX
Smith, Mark S. .... Virginia Beach, VA
Smith, Mark Stanton .... San Antonio, TX
Smith, Mark T. .... Boston, MA
Smith, Mark T. .... Lincoln, NE
Smith, Mark T. .... Gallatin, TN
Smith, Mark T. .... Dallas, TX
Smith, Mark W. .... Department of Education, Office of the General Counsel, GV
Smith, Mark W. .... Metairie, LA
Smith, Mark W. .... New York, NY
Smith, Mark W. .... New York, NY
Smith, Mark W. .... Towanda, PA
Smith, Mark W. .... Chattanooga, TN
Smith, Mark W. .... Austin, TX
Smith, Mark W. .... Milwaukee, WI
Smith, Marla A. .... Los Angeles, CA
Smith, Marlena .... Birmingham, AL
Smith, Marlene A. .... Chicago, IL
Smith, Marlin D. .... Barrow, AK
Smith, Marlin R. .... Plano, TX
Smith, Marlyn F., (Mr.) .... Norristown, PA
Smith, Marschall I. .... Northbrook, IL
Smith, Marschall I. .... Northbrook, IL
Smith, Marsh .... Southern Pines, NC
Smith, Marsha D. .... Oxford, MD
Smith, Marsha H. .... Boise, ID
Smith, Marshall E., III .... Fairfield, AL
Smith, Marshall H. .... Alton, IL
Smith, Marshall H. .... Lexington, MS
Smith, Marshall H., Jr. .... Memphis, TN
Smith & Marshall, Law Office of
Hammond, IN
Smith, Marshall, Weaver and Vergon
Cleveland, OH
Smith, Martha Carolyn
Federal Maritime Commission, Bureau of Enforcement, GV
Smith, Martha L. .... Londonderry, NH
Smith, Martha Riegel .... Harrisburg, PA
Smith Martin .... Kenner, LA
Metairie, LA
New Orleans, LA
Slidell, LA
Smith & Martin .... Wichita Falls, TX
Smith, Martin A. .... Chicago, IL
Smith, Martin A., Jr. .... Slidell, LA
Smith, Martin E. .... Binghamton, NY
Smith, Martin F. .... Seattle, WA
Smith, Martin F., Jr. .... Hampton, NH
Smith, Martin J. .... Los Angeles, CA
Smith, Martin J. .... Eastpointe, MI
Smith, Martin L. .... Torrance, CA
Smith, Martin L. .... Seattle, WA
Smith, Martin R., Jr. .... Charleston, WV
Smith, Martin T. .... Poplarville, MS
Smith, Marty .... Ocala, FL
Smith, Marvin H. .... Federalsburg, MD
Smith, Marvin J. .... Great Falls, MT
Smith, Marvin L. .... Miami, OK
Smith, Marvin M. .... Idaho Falls, ID
Smith, Marvin Neil, Jr. .... Greeneville, TN
Smith, Marvin R. .... Pontiac, MI
Smith, Marvin S., Jr. .... Dallas, TX
Smith, Mary A. .... Corinth, MS
Smith, Mary Anne .... Chicago, IL
Smith, Mary Anne .... Norway, ME
Smith, Mary Anne .... Milwaukee, WI
Smith, Mary Augusta .... New York, NY
Smith, Mary Beth .... Concord, NC
Smith, Mary C. .... Lansing, MI
Smith, Mary C. .... Toledo, OH
Smith, Mary Claffey .... Vidalia, GA
Smith, Mary E. .... Columbus, OH
Smith, Mary E. .... Toledo, OH
Smith, Mary H. .... Albuquerque, NM
Smith, Mary H. .... White Plains, NY
Smith, Mary J. .... Rexburg, ID
Smith, Mary John .... Charlottesville, VA
Smith, Mary Kay .... Columbus, OH
Smith, Mary Keib .... Syracuse, NY
Smith, Mary L.
Executive Office Of The President, Office of Policy Development, GV
Smith, Mary Leslie .... Miami, FL
Smith, Mary Lou .... Washington, DC
Smith, Mary Mann .... Ridgefield, CT
Smith, Mary Martha .... Savannah, TN
Smith, Mary T.
Environmental Protection Agency, Program Office Attorneys, GV
Smith, Mary T. Schmitt
Bloomfield Hills, MI
Smith, Mary-Louise, (Mrs.) .... Rocklin, CA
Smith, Mastin G. .... Nashville, TN
Smith, Mathew G. .... Chicago, IL
Smith, Matthew A. .... Los Angeles, CA
Smith, Matthew A. .... New York, NY
Smith, Matthew B. .... Peoria, IL
Smith, Matthew J. .... Tucson, AZ
Smith, Matthew J. .... Sacramento, CA
Smith, Matthew J. .... Paramus, NJ
Smith, Matthew J. .... Albany, NY
Smith, Matthew Jon .... Cincinnati, OH
Smith, Matthew P. .... Seattle, WA
Smith, Matthew S.
Department of Commerce, Patent and Trademark Office, GV
Smith, Matthew S. .... Orlando, FL
Smith, Matthew T. .... Greenville, OH
Smith, Matthew Tolbert .... Troy, MI
Smith, Matthew W. .... Eden, NC
Smith, Matthew W. .... Kingsport, TN
Smith, Maura E. Caffrey .... Lawrence, MA
Smith, Maura T. .... Kissimmee, FL
Smith, Maureen .... New York, NY
Smith, Maureen D. .... Concord, NH
Smith, Maureen O'Hara .... Millbrae, CA
Smith, Maureen R. .... Chicago, IL
Smith & Maurer .... Las Vegas, NV
Smith, Maurice B. .... Sacramento, CA
Smith, Maurras, Cohen, Redd & Horan, PLC .... Fort Smith, AR
Smith, Maury D. .... Montgomery, AL
Smith, Max J., Jr. .... Hershey, PA
Smith, Max M. .... Frankfort, KY
Smith, Max W. .... Liberty, MO
Smith, Maxine S. .... Lake Havasu City, AZ
Smith, Maxwell P. .... Fort Wayne, IN
Smith & Mazak Co., L.P.A. .... Akron, OH
Smith Mazure Director Wilkins Young Yagerman & Tarallo, P.C. .... Bronx, NY
Brooklyn, NY
Jamaica, NY
Mineola, NY
New Rochelle, NY
New York, NY
Peekskill, NY
Staten Island, NY
White Plains, NY
Yonkers, NY
Smith & McArty .... Jackson, MS
Smith, McCabe and Costello .... Bend, OR
Smith McCullough, P.C. .... Denver, CO
Smith, McDaniel & Donahue
Pleasanton, CA
Smith, McDowell & Ginn
Sulphur Springs, TX
Smith & McElwain .... Sioux City, IA
Smith & McMaster, P.C. .... Newtown, PA
Smith, McNeill .... Greensboro, NC
Smith, Megan A. .... San Jose, CA
Smith, Megan G. .... Olympic Valley, CA
Smith, Mel .... Houston, TX
Smith, Melanie .... New York, NY
Smith, Melanie Karsh .... Baltimore, MD
Smith, Meleta G. .... Dallas, TX
Smith, Melinda A. .... Sherman Oaks, CA
Smith, Melinda Watts .... Fort Worth, TX
Smith, Melissa .... Marshall, TX
Smith, Melissa A. .... Lancaster, TX
Smith, Melissa E. .... Lowell, AR
Smith, Melissa J. .... Indianapolis, IN
Smith, Melissa M. .... Washington, DC
Smith, Melissa Uelk .... Madison, WI
Smith, Melton V. .... Houston, TX
Smith, Melven E. .... Ogden, UT
Smith, Mequio, Koning, VanWagoner & Beck, P.C. .... Kalamazoo, MI
Portage, MI
Smith, Meredyth A. .... Baltimore, MD
Smith, Merideth H. .... Rochester, NY
Smith, Merlin J. .... San Diego, CA
Smith, Merrill E. .... Washington, DC
Smith, Merrill & Peffer, A Professional Corporation .... San Ramon, CA
Smith, Merton V., II
Department Of Health And Human Services, GV
Smith & Metalitz, L.L.P. .... Washington, DC
Smith, Mettie M. .... Annapolis, MD
Smith, Michael A. .... Arcadia, CA
Smith, Michael A. .... San Bernardino, CA
Smith, Michael A. .... Denver, CO
Smith, Michael A. .... Dunnellon, FL
Smith, Michael A. .... Chicago, IL
Smith, Michael A. .... Eldora, IA
Smith, Michael A. .... Papillion, NE
Smith, Michael A. .... Columbus, OH
Smith, Michael A. .... Arlington, TX
Smith, Michael A. .... Madison, WI
Smith, Michael B. .... Mobile, AL
Smith, Michael B. .... Tucson, AZ
Smith, Michael B. .... Woodland Hills, CA
Smith, Michael B. .... Houston, TX
Smith, Michael B. .... Tacoma, WA
Smith, Michael C. .... Torrance, CA
Smith, Michael C. .... La Grange, GA
Smith, Michael C. .... New Orleans, LA
Smith, Michael C. .... Hattiesburg, MS
Smith, Michael C. .... Santa Fe, NM
Smith, Michael C. .... Dallas, TX
Smith, Michael C. .... Marshall, TX
Smith, Michael D. .... Tuscaloosa, AL
Smith, Michael D. .... Claremont, CA
Smith, Michael D. .... Washington, DC
Smith, Michael D. .... Pensacola, FL
Smith, Michael D. .... Columbus, GA
Smith, Michael D. .... Chicago, IL
Smith, Michael D. .... Mount Clemens, MI
Smith, Michael D. .... Columbus, OH
Smith, Michael D. .... San Antonio, TX
Smith, Michael D. .... Milwaukee, WI
Smith, Michael Dallas .... Fort Wayne, IN
Smith, Michael E. .... Fresno, CA
Smith, Michael E. .... New York, NY
Smith, Michael E. .... Cleveland, OH
Smith, Michael E. .... Oklahoma City, OK
Smith, Michael E. .... Oklahoma City, OK
Smith, Michael F. .... Fountain Valley, CA
Smith, Michael F. .... Detroit, MI
Smith, Michael F. .... Tulsa, OK
Smith, Michael F. .... Ambler, PA
Smith, Michael F. .... Houston, TX
Smith, Michael G. .... Little Rock, AR
Smith, Michael G. .... Berkeley, CA
Smith, Michael G. .... Wailuku, HI
Smith, Michael G. .... Overland Park, KS
Smith, Michael G. .... Ada, OK
Smith, Michael G. .... Amarillo, TX
Smith, Michael George .... Salem, OR
Smith, Michael H. .... Denver, CO
Smith, Michael H. .... Des Moines, IA
Smith, Michael H. .... Waterville, ME
Smith, Michael H. .... North Chelmsford, MA
Smith, Michael H. .... New York, NY
Smith, Michael H. .... New York, NY
Smith, Michael H. .... Houston, TX
Smith, Michael J. .... San Diego, CA
Smith, Michael J. .... Ventura, CA
Smith, Michael J. .... Walnut Creek, CA
Smith, Michael J. .... Hartford, CT
Boston, MA
Providence, RI
Smith, Michael J. .... Miami, FL
Smith, Michael J. .... Doraville, GA
Smith, Michael J. .... Chicago, IL
Smith, Michael J. .... Rockford, IL
Smith, Michael J. .... Flint, MI
Smith, Michael J. .... Minneapolis, MN
Smith, Michael J. .... St. Louis, MO
Smith, Michael J. .... Turnersville, NJ
Philadelphia, PA
Smith, Michael J. .... Albany, NY
Smith, Michael J. .... New York, NY
Smith, Michael J. .... Philadelphia, PA
Smith, Michael J. .... Philadelphia, PA
Smith, Michael J. .... Seneca, SC
Smith, Michael J. .... Edmonds, WA
Smith, Michael J., and Associates
Sterling Heights, MI
Smith, Michael J., Jr. .... Pelham Manor, NY
Smith, Michael Jay .... Indianapolis, IN
Wabash, IN
Smith, Michael Jens F. .... Fresno, CA
Smith, Michael John .... St. Louis, MO
Smith, Michael Joseph .... Houston, TX
Smith, Michael K. .... Nashville, TN
Smith, Michael L. .... Santa Barbara, CA
Smith, Michael L. .... Tampa, FL
Smith, Michael L. .... Sioux City, IA
Smith, Michael L. .... Traverse City, MI
Smith, Michael L. .... St. Louis, MO
Smith, Michael L. .... Beachwood, OH
Smith, Michael L., (Co., L.P.A.) .... Sidney, OH
Smith, Michael Lee .... Treasury Department, Office of Regulations and Rulings, GV
Smith, Michael M. .... Atlanta, GA
Smith, Michael M. .... Macon, GA
Smith, Michael M. .... Midvale, UT
Smith, Michael P. .... San Jose, CA
Smith, Michael P. .... Baton Rouge, LA
Smith, Michael P. .... Baltimore, MD
Smith, Michael P. .... Mayville, NY
Smith, Michael P. .... Silver Creek, NY
Smith, Michael Paul .... Towson, MD
Smith, Michael R. .... Anchorage, AK
Smith, Michael R. .... Berkeley, CA
Smith, Michael R. .... Denver, CO
Smith, Michael R. .... Washington, DC
Smith, Michael R. .... Atlanta, GA
Smith, Michael R. .... Indianapolis, IN
Smith, Michael R. .... Hillsdale, MI
Smith, Michael R. .... Milwaukee, WI
Smith, Michael Robert .... Midlothian, VA
Smith, Michael S. .... Santa Clara, CA
Smith, Michael S. .... Perry, FL
Smith, Michael S. .... West Palm Beach, FL
Smith, Michael S. .... West Palm Beach, FL
Smith, Michael S. .... Chicago, IL
Smith, Michael S. .... New York, NY
Smith, Michael S. .... Philadelphia, PA
Smith, Michael Steven .... New York, NY
Smith, Michael T. .... Los Angeles, CA
Smith, Michael T. .... Lawrenceville, GA
Smith, Michael T. .... Anderson, SC
Smith, Michael Todd .... Columbia, SC
Smith, Michael V. .... Gordon, NE
Rushville, NE
Smith, Michael W. .... New York, NY
Smith, Michael W. .... Pittsburgh, PA
Smith, Michael W. .... Richmond, VA
Smith, Michael W. .... Bellevue, WA
Smith, Michael W. .... Lodi, WI
Smith, Michele A.
Department of Defense, GV
Smith, Michele A. .... Buffalo, NY
Smith, Michele A. .... Sandusky, OH
Smith, Michele E. .... Chicago, IL
Smith, Michele G. .... Greensboro, NC
Smith, Michele L. .... Rockville, MD
Smith, Michele L. .... Ashland, WI
Smith, Michele Y. .... Beaumont, TX
Smith, Michelle B. .... Covington, GA
Smith, Michelle D. .... Washington, DC
Smith, Michelle D. .... Pittsburgh, PA
Smith, Michelle J. .... Kalamazoo, MI
Smith, Michelle L. .... Dallas, TX
Smith, Michelle L. .... Elkhorn, WI
Smith, Michelle Mindy Gross
Minneapolis, MN
Smith, Mickey W. .... Pueblo, CO
Smith, Miguel A. .... San Diego, CA

Smith, Mike ... Columbus, GA
Smith, Mike ... Mc Comb, MS
Smith and Milam, P.C. ... Lexington, TN
Smith, Milan D., Jr. ... Torrance, CA
Smith & Miller, LLP ... Santa Rosa, CA
Smith & Miller, P.C. ... Richmond, VA
Smith, Milo W. ... Henderson, NV
Smith, Milton A. ... Chevy Chase, MD
Smith, Milton A. ... Spartanburg, SC
Smith, Milton B. ... St. Paul, MN
Smith, Milton C. ... Dallas, TX
Smith, Milton C. ... Seattle, WA
Smith, Milton L. "Skip", III Colorado Springs, CO
Smith, Milton R., Jr. ... Towson, MD
Smith, Milton W., Jr. ... Scottsville, KY
Smith, Miriam A. ... San Francisco, CA
Smith, Mitchell B. ... Boca Raton, FL
Smith, Mitchell C. ... Atlantic City, NJ
Smith, Mitchell J. ... Florissant, MO
Smith, M L ... Bowie, MD
Smith, Molly K. ... Portland, OR
Smith, Mona ... Bellevue, WA
Smith, Monica A. ... Portland, OR
Smith, Monica M. ... Oregon City, OR
Smith, Monte G. ... Cincinnati, OH
Smith, Montgomery L. ... Houston, TX
Smith, Montgomery "Monte" W. St. Louis, MO
Smith & Moore ... Dallas, TX
Smith & Moreno, P.A. ... Columbia, SC
Smith, Morgan ... Denver, CO
Smith, Morgan C. ... San Francisco, CA
Smith, Morton A., (P.C.) White Plains, NY
Smith, M. P., & Assocs., P.C. Fort Wayne, IN
Smith, M. Steve, & Associates Houston, TX
Smith Mullin ... West Orange, NJ
Montclair, NJ
Smith & Mullis ... Valdosta, GA
Smith, Munson ... Victoria, TX
Smith, Murdaugh, Little & Bonham, L.L.P. Houston, TX
Smith, Murdo T. ... Hartford, CT
Smith & Murdock, P.C. ... Indianapolis, IN
Smith, Murl E. ... Houston, TX
Smith & Murphy ... North Augusta, SC
Smith, Murphy & Schoepperle Buffalo, NY
Smith, Murphy and Taliaferro, A Professional Corporation ... Warsaw, VA
Smith, Musgrove & McCord Batesville, MS
Smith, Myron C. ... Fairfax, VA
Smith, N. Gregory ... Baton Rouge, LA
Smith, N. Kent ... Indianapolis, IN
Smith, N. Lindsey ... Cleveland, OH
Smith, N. Randy ... Pocatello, ID
Smith, N. Richard ... San Francisco, CA
Smith, N. A. ... Crockett, TX
Smith, Nana G. H. ... Lincoln, NE
Smith, Nanci A. ... Rutland, VT
Smith, Nancy A. F. ... Cleveland, OH
Smith, Nancy B. ... Denver, CO
Smith, Nancy C. ... Los Angeles, CA
Smith, Nancy C. ... Washington, DC
Smith, Nancy E. ... San Francisco, CA
Smith, Nancy E. ... Rochester, NY
Smith, Nancy Erika ... Montclair, NJ
Smith, Nancy F. ... Charlotte, NC
Smith, Nancy Graham ... Marlton, NJ
Smith, Nancy Janet ... Farmington, MI
Smith, Nancy Leser ... Cincinnati, OH
Smith, Nancy M. ... Worcester, MA
Smith, Nancy Myers ... North Hollywood, CA
Smith, Nancy Spencer ... Boston, MA
Smith, Nancy Y. ... Kissimmee, FL
Smith, Naomi Behar ... Fort Lauderdale, FL
Smith, Nathan B. ... Charlottesville, VA
Smith, Nathan H. ... Portland, ME
Smith, Nathan H. ... Richmond, VA
Smith, Nathan John ... Ledgewood, NJ
Smith, Nathan S. ... Sausalito, CA
Smith, Nathaniel B. ... New York, NY
Smith, Nathaniel Byron ... Hollidaysburg, PA
Smith, Nathaniel C. ... Chapel Hill, NC
Smith, Neal E. ... Des Moines, IA
Smith, Neal & Karam, P.C. San Antonio, TX
Smith, Neal T. ... Tyler, TX
Smith, Neil A. ... San Francisco, CA
Smith, Neil B. ... Hamilton, OH
Smith, Neil B. ... Salt Lake City, UT
Smith, Neil J. ... Paramus, NJ
Smith, Nelson ... El Paso, TX
Smith, Nelson & Clement ... Friendswood, TX
Smith & NeSmith ... Oneonta, AL
Smith, Neville ... Manchester, KY
Smith, Neville, Law Firm of Manchester, KY
Smith, Newell D. ... Seattle, WA
Smith, Newman Jackson ... Charleston, SC
Smith, Nicholas ... Plymouth, MI
Smith, Nichole ... Burbank, CA
Smith, Nick ... Duluth, MN
Smith, Nicole Montagnet ... Shreveport, LA
Smith, Nina Nelson ... Columbia, SC
Smith, Nina Q. ... Miami, FL
Smith, Noah M. ... McLean, VA
Smith, Noel I. ... Chicago, IL
Smith, Noland W. ... Murphy, NC
Smith, Norbert J. ... Greensburg, PA
Smith, Norbert P. ... Mankato, MN
Smith, Norborne G., Jr. ... Goldsboro, NC
Smith, Norman ... Griffin, GA
Smith, Norman A. ... Charlotte, NC
Smith, Norman A., P.A. ... Charlotte, NC
Smith, Norman B. Office of Government Ethics, Office of General Counsel and Legal Policy, GV
Smith, Norman B. ... North Miami, FL
Smith, Norman B. ... Greensboro, NC
Smith, Norman C. ... Burlington, VT
Smith, Norman D. ... Lakewood, NJ
Smith, Norman E. ... Littleton, CO
Smith, Norman Estes ... Dunwoody, GA
Smith, Norman Estes, P.C. ... Dunwoody, GA
Smith, Norman F. ... Vista, CA
Smith, Norman J. ... Kissimmee, FL
Smith, Norman L. ... San Diego, CA
Smith, Norman L. ... Baltimore, MD
Smith, Norman Lee ... Atlanta, GA
Smith, Norman M. ... Stuttgart, AR
Smith, Norman P. ... Sidney, OH
Smith, Norman R. ... Hudson, OH
Smith, Norman T. ... Columbus, OH
Smith, Norman W. ... Dallas, TX
Smith, Normand F., III ... Boston, MA
Smith and Nowlin ... Ventura, CA
Smith, Numa L., Jr. ... Washington, DC
Smith, Nyle B. ... Portland, OR
Smith, O. Douglas ... North Augusta, SC
Smith, O. Whitman ... Burlington, VT
Smith, O'Hare & Mesenbrink Silverdale, WA
Smith & Oldmixon, P.L.L.C. Poplarville, MS
Smith, Oliver A. ... New York, NY
Smith, Oliver A., III ... Knoxville, TN
Smith, Olivia Constance ... Montclair, NJ
Smith, Olivia L. Hudson ... Denver, CO
Smith, Olivia Lee ... Marylhurst, OR
Smith, Ollie D. ... Birmingham, AL
Smith, Ormond N. ... Staten Island, NY
Smith, Orren R. ... Chipley, FL
Smith, Ortrie D. ... Kansas City, MO
Smith, Oscar B., Jr. ... Webster, WI
Smith, Oscar D., Jr. ... Columbus, GA
Smith, Oscar M. ... Rome, GA
Smith, Otis ... Phoenix, AZ
Smith, Owen C. ... Rye Brook, NY
Smith, Owen T. ... Syosset, NY
Smith, P. David ... Ouray, CO
Smith, P. Douglas ... Birmingham, AL
Smith, P. Glen ... Kansas City, MO
Smith, P. McCoy ... New York, NY
Smith, P. Nelson, Jr. ... Columbus, MS
Smith, Pachter, McWhorter & D'Ambrosio, P.L.C. ... Washington, DC
Fairfax, VA
Vienna, VA
Smith, Page Thomas ... Wilson, NC
Smith, Paige A. ... Atlanta, GA
Smith, Palmer ... Seattle, WA
Smith, Pamela A. ... Boston, MA
Smith, Pamela G. ... Chicago, IL
Smith, Pamela G. ... Boston, MA
Smith, Pamela I. ... St. Petersburg, FL
Smith, Pamela I., P.A. ... St. Petersburg, FL
Smith, Pamela J. ... Department of Justice, Office of Legislative Affairs, GV
Smith, Pamela J. ... Portland, ME
Smith, Pamela J. ... Newton, MA
Smith, Pamela Joy ... Orlando, FL
Smith, Pamela L. Federal Communications Commission, Office of the General Counsel, GV
Smith, Pamela S. ... Plano, TX
Smith & Paris, P.C. ... Anniston, AL
Smith Parker ... Minneapolis, MN
Smith, Parker B. ... Ponte Vedra Beach, FL
Smith, Parker B., P.A. ... Jacksonville, FL
Ponte Vedra Beach, FL
Smith, Parker H. Cape May Court House, NJ
Smith Partnership, The, P.C. ... St. Louis, MO
Smith, Patricia ... Tulsa, OK
Smith, Patricia A. ... Cherry Hill, NJ
Smith, Patricia A. ... New York, NY
Smith, Patricia A. ... Columbus, OH
Smith, Patricia A. ... Alexandria, VA
Smith, Patricia A. ... Gig Harbor, WA
Smith, Patricia Ann ... Livonia, MI
Smith, Patricia Clifton ... Tulsa, OK
Smith, Patricia J. ... Minneapolis, MN
Smith, Patricia K. ... Erie, PA
Smith, Patricia L. ... Birmingham, MI
Smith, Patricia M. ... Bronxville, NY
Smith, Patricia M. ... Philadelphia, PA
Smith, Patricia McCoy ... Walnut Creek, CA
Smith, Patricia R. ... Baker, LA
Smith, Patrick C. ... Monterey, CA
Smith, Patrick C. ... Pittsburg, KS
Smith, Patrick C. ... Baltimore, MD
Smith, Patrick Charles ... Campbell, CA
Smith, Patrick D. ... Des Moines, IA
Smith, Patrick F. ... Columbus, OH
Smith, Patrick J. ... Washington, DC
Smith, Patrick J. ... Chicago, IL
Smith, Patrick J. ... Downers Grove, IL
Smith, Patrick J. ... Rockville, MD
Smith, Patrick J. ... Columbus, OH
Smith, Patrick J. ... Dallas, TX
Smith, Patrick K. ... Dayton, OH
Smith, Patrick L. ... Missoula, MT
Smith, Patrick M. ... San Diego, CA
Smith, Patrick N. ... Los Angeles, CA
Smith, Patrick R. ... Tampa, FL
Smith, Patrick S. ... Los Angeles, CA
Smith, Patrick T. ... Overland Park, KS
Smith, Patrick T. ... Louisville, KY
Smith, Patrick T. ... Mitchell, SD
Smith, Patti L. ... Allentown, PA
Smith, Paul ... Port Washington, WI
Smith, Paul A. ... Bisbee, AZ
Smith, Paul A. ... Chicago, IL
Smith, Paul A., Sr. ... Baltimore, MD
Smith, Paul B. ... Boulder, MT
Smith, Paul B. ... Santa Fe, NM
Smith, Paul B. ... Wewoka, OK
Smith, Paul C. ... San Rafael, CA
Smith, Paul C. ... Monroeville, PA
Smith, Paul D. ... Houston, TX
Smith, Paul E. ... Boulder, CO
Smith, Paul E. ... Wilkes-Barre, PA
Smith, Paul E. ... Bellevue, WA
Smith, Paul English ... Huntington, WV
Smith, Paul F. ... Pasadena, CA
Smith, Paul G. ... Birmingham, AL
Smith, Paul G. ... Sacramento, CA
Smith, Paul G. ... Carmel, IN
Smith, Paul H. ... Boardman, OH
Smith, Paul H. ... San Antonio, TX
Smith, Paul K. ... Los Angeles, CA
Smith, Paul L. ... Horseshoe Bay, TX
Smith, Paul L., and Associates, P.C. Horseshoe Bay, TX
Smith, Paul M. ... Irvine, CA
Smith, Paul M. ... Moosup, CT
Putnam, CT
Smith, Paul M. ... Washington, DC
Smith, Paul M. ... Atlanta, GA
Smith, Paul M. ... Omaha, NE
Smith, Paul M., Jr. ... Chicago, IL
Smith, Paul Overton ... San Ramon, CA
Smith, Paul R. ... Sacramento, CA
Smith, Paul R. ... Minneapolis, MN
Smith, Paul R. ... Albuquerque, NM
Smith, Paul S. ... Department of Transportation, Office of the General Counsel, GV
Smith, Paul S., III ... Seattle, WA
Smith, Paul T. ... San Francisco, CA
Smith, Paul V. ... Honolulu, HI
Smith, Paul Vernon ... Perry, FL
Smith, Paul W. ... Vista, CA
Smith, Paul W. ... Houston, TX
Smith, Paul Wilson ... Houston, TX
Smith, Paula A. ... Worcester, MA
Smith, Paula B. ... Atlanta, GA
Smith, Paula E. ... Dallas, TX
Smith, Paula Ferguson ... Atlanta, GA
Smith, Paula J. ... Denver, CO
Smith, Paula K. ... Atlanta, GA
Smith, Paula K. ... Salt Lake City, UT
Smith, Paula S. ... New York, NY
Smith, Paula Y. ... Austin, TX
Smith, Payton ... Seattle, WA
Smith, Pearl Crosby ... Cocoa, FL
Smith, Pedersen and Smith Orchard Park, NY
Smith, Peirce B. ... Attleboro, MA
Smith & Peltzer, A Professional Corporation San Marcos, CA
Smith & Pendry ... Xenia, OH
Smith, Perry J. ... Gonzales, LA
Smith, Perry M. ... Worcester, MA
Smith & Perry, P.A. ... Bainbridge, GA
Smith, Perry S., Jr. ... Waukegan, IL
Smith, Pete A. ... Covington, KY
Smith, Peter ... Jacksonville, FL
Smith, Peter A. ... Kentfield, CA
Smith, Peter A. ... St. Louis, MO
Smith, Peter A. ... Statesville, NC
Smith, Peter A. ... McMurray, PA
Smith, Peter B. ... Boca Raton, FL
Smith, Peter B. ... Richmond, VA
Smith, Peter B., P.A. ... Boca Raton, FL
Smith, Peter E. ... Wampsville, NY
Smith, Peter F. ... Clearfield, PA
Smith, Peter G. ... New York, NY
Smith, Peter G. ... Dallas, TX
Smith, Peter H. ... Modesto, CA
Smith, Peter H. ... San Andreas, CA
Smith, Peter H. ... Atlanta, GA
Smith, Peter J. ... Roseland, NJ
Smith, Peter J. ... Grants Pass, OR
Smith, Peter J. ... Jenkintown, PA
Smith, Peter Julian ... Carson City, NV
Smith, Peter K. ... Quitman, MS
Smith, Peter K. ... Gloversville, NY
Smith, Peter K., Ltd. ... Quitman, MS
Smith, Peter L. ... San Francisco, CA
Smith, Peter L. ... New York, NY
Smith, Peter, Law Offices ... Niles, MI
Smith, Peter N. ... Orlando, FL
Smith, Peter S. ... Los Angeles, CA
Smith, Peter S. ... Concord, NH
Smith, Peter Thomas ... Sycamore, IL
Smith, Peter W. ... Niles, MI
Smith, Peter W. ... Littleton, NH
Smith, Peter W. ... Morristown, NJ
Smith, Peter W. ... New York, NY
Smith, Peter W., IV ... Norfolk, VA
Smith Peterson Law Firm Council Bluffs, IA
Omaha, NE
Smith, Peyton N. ... Austin, TX
Smith, Pheobe S. ... Houston, TX
Smith, Philip ... New York, NY
Smith, Philip ... Portland, OR
Smith, Philip B., Jr. ... Paris, TX
Smith, Philip C. ... Canton, GA
Smith, Philip C. ... Salisbury, MD
Smith, Philip C. ... Westfield, MA
Smith, Philip E. ... Irvine, CA
Smith, Philip E. ... Stamford, CT
Smith, Philip E. ... Greensboro, NC
Smith, Philip G. ... Pocahontas, AR
Smith, Philip G. ... Louisiana, MO
Smith, Philip G., P.A. ... Pocahontas, AR
Smith, Philip H. ... Talladega, AL
Smith, Philip Hawley ... Tucson, AZ
Smith, Philip H. W. ... Fort Lee, NJ
Smith, Philip J. ... Atlanta, GA
Smith, Philip J. ... Boston, MA
Smith, Philip J. ... East Lansing, MI
Smith, Philip J. ... New York, NY
Smith, Philip J. ... New York, NY
Smith, Philip J. ... Asheville, NC
Smith, Philip K. ... Memphis, TN
Smith, Philip M. ... New York, NY
Smith, Philip N. ... Lake Buena Vista, FL
Smith, Philip N., Jr. ... New York, NY
Smith, Philip R. ... Westfield, MA
West Springfield, MA
Smith, Philip S. ... Cincinnati, OH
Smith, Philip Wesley ... Gaithersburg, MD
Smith, Philippa J. ... New York, NY
Smith, Phillip E. ... Irvine, CA
Smith, Phillip F., Jr. ... Denver, CO
Smith, Phillip H. ... Minneapolis, MN
Smith, Phillip J. ... Cincinnati, OH
Smith, Phillip K. ... Tulsa, OK
Smith, Phillip K., Jr. ... Palm Desert, CA
Smith, Phillip M. (Matt) Grand Junction, CO
Smith, Phillip N., Jr. ... Dallas, TX
Smith, Phillip R. ... Lafayette, IN
Smith, Phillip R. ... Martinsville, IN
Smith, Phillip R., P.C. ... Martinsville, IN
Smith, Phillip S. ... Leesburg, FL
Smith, Phillip S. ... Kansas City, MO
Smith, Phillip S., P.C. ... Kansas City, MO
Smith, Phillip W. ... Hoopa, CA
Smith, Phillip W. ... Leitchfield, KY
Smith, Phillip W., P.S.C. ... Leitchfield, KY
Smith, Phillips, Mitchell, Scott & Rutherford Batesville, MS
Hernando, MS
Smith & Powers ... Charlevoix, MI
Petoskey, MI
Smith, Prentice L. G., Jr. ... Baker, LA
Smith, Preston W. ... Rome, GA
Smith, Price & Wright ... Rome, GA
Smith, Priscilla J. ... New York, NY
Smith, Putnam C. ... Cumming, GA
Smith, Putnam Clark, P.C. Cumming, GA
Smith, Quentin H., Prof. Corp. San Jose, CA
Smith, R. Clarke ... Rutland, VT
Smith, R. Craig ... Philadelphia, PA
Smith, R. Curtis, II ... Hattiesburg, MS
Smith, R. Daniel, Jr. ... Plano, TX
Smith, R. Dillon ... Chicago, IL
Smith, R. Eric ... Salt Lake City, UT
Smith, R. Evan ... Washington, DC
Smith, R. Gail ... Nashville, TN
Smith, R. Gaylord ... San Diego, CA
Smith, R. Gordon ... Richmond, VA
Smith, R. Jeffrey ... Hartford, CT
Smith, R. Lee ... Jacksonville, FL
Smith, R. Lee, P.A. ... Jacksonville, FL
Smith, R. Louis ... Canton, OH
Smith, R. Lynn ... San Francisco, CA
Smith, R. Michael ... Baltimore, MD
Smith, R. Michael ... Columbus, OH
Smith, R. Milton ... Northridge, CA
Smith, R. Patrick ... Palo Alto, CA
Smith, R. Pete ... Overland Park, KS
Kansas City, MO
Smith, R. Rucker ... Americus, GA
Smith, R. Scott ... Denver, CO
Smith, R. Scott ... Kansas City, MO
Smith, R. Shearn ... Houston, TX
Smith, R. Theodore ... Decatur, GA
Smith, R. Todd ... Dayton, OH
Smith, R. Troy ... Dallas, TX
Smith, R. Wayne ... Ruston, LA
Smith, R. William ... Pasadena, CA
Smith, Rachel E. ... Washington, DC
Smith, Rachel E. ... Lincoln, NE
Smith, Rachel J. ... Cheyenne, WY
Smith, Rachel L. ... McLean, VA
Smith, Radford W. ... Clearwater, FL
Smith, Rainey ... Ada, MI
Smith, Ralph A. ... Charles City, IA
Smith, Ralph Allen ... Norman, OK
Smith, Ralph C. ... Fresno, CA
Smith, Ralph C. ... Dearborn, MI
Smith, Ralph C. ... Fairfax, VA
Smith, Ralph C., Jr. ... Bainbridge, GA
Smith, Ralph E. ... New Orleans, LA
Smith, Ralph E. ... Butler, MO
Smith, Ralph E., PLC ... New Orleans, LA
Smith, Ralph Edwin ... Southfield, MI
Smith, Ralph G. ... Columbus, OH
Smith, Ralph H., II ... Birmingham, AL
Smith, Ralph H., III ... Pittsburgh, PA
Smith, Ralph H., Jr. ... Bend, OR
Smith, Ralph J. ... Walnut Creek, CA
Smith, Ralph J. ... Boston, MA
Smith, Ralph K., Jr. ... New York, NY
Smith, Ralph R. ... Oklahoma City, OK
Smith, Ralph R. ... Olympia, WA
Smith, Ralph R., 3rd ... Cherry Hill, NJ
Smith, Ralph T. ... Bemidji, MN
Smith, Ralph W., Jr. ... Albany, NY
Smith, Ramona F. ... Denver, CO
Smith, Randall ... Chicago, IL
Smith, Randall ... St. Paul, MN
Smith, Randall A. ... Irvine, CA
Smith, Randall A., (P.C.) New Orleans, LA
Smith, Randall B. ... Melville, NY
Smith, Randall B., P.C. ... Melville, NY
Smith, Randall C. ... Maitland, FL
Smith, Randall D. ... Indianapolis, IN
Smith, Randall D. ... Chesapeake, VA

Smith, Randall E. ... Saco, ME
Smith, Randall L. ... Houston, TX
Smith, Randall M. ... San Francisco, CA
Smith, Randall M. ... Farmington Hills, MI
Smith, Randall P. ... Saginaw, MI
Smith, Randall R. ... Atlanta, GA
Smith, Randall T. ... Lincoln, NE
Smith, Randolph C. ... Philadelphia, PA
Smith, Randolph L. ... Boston, MA
Providence, RI
Smith, Randy H. ... Traverse City, MI
Smith, Randy J. ... La Crosse, WI
Smith, Randy L., Law Offices of
Springfield, MO
Smith, Ranscht, Connors, Mutino, Nordell & Sirignano, P.C. ... Stamford, CT
New York, NY
White Plains, NY
Smith, Ransome M. ... Fresno, CA
Smith, Ray E. ... Boise, ID
Smith, Ray G. ... Iowa Park, TX
Smith, Ray S., III ... Atlanta, GA
Smith, Ray S., Jr.
Hot Springs National Park, AR
Smith, Raymond C. ... Fayetteville, AR
Smith, Raymond C., P.A. ... Fayetteville, AR
Smith, Raymond D. ... Dallas, TX
Smith, Raymond F. ... Yaphank, NY
Smith, Raymond G. ... Louisville, KY
Smith, Raymond H., Jr. ... Marietta, OH
Smith, Raymond J. ... Chicago, IL
Smith, Raymond L., Jr. ... Louisville, KY
Smith, Raymond S. ... Oak Forest, IL
Smith, Reba Sloan ... Lillington, NC
Smith, Rebecca A. ... Philadelphia, PA
Smith, Rebecca Beach ... Norfolk, VA
Smith, Rebecca C. ... McLean, VA
Smith, Rebecca J. ... Los Angeles, CA
Smith, Rebecca K. ... New York, NY
Smith, Rebecca L. ... Muscatine, IA
Smith, Rebecca Lynn ... Encino, CA
Smith, Rebecca R. ... San Diego, CA
Smith, Rees R. ... Marietta, GA
Smith, Regan James Reno ... Berlin, MD
Ocean City, MD
Smith, Regina Holzhausen ... Franklin, IN
Smith, Reginald B., Jr. ... Sherman, TX
Smith, Reginald H., Jr. ... Cambridge, MA
Smith, Reginald K. ... Kannapolis, NC
Smith, Reginald Ross ... Houston, TX
Smith, Reginald W. ... Tuscaloosa, AL
Smith, Reid B. ... Los Angeles, CA
Smith, Reid B. ... Columbia, SC
Smith, Reid E., Jr. ... Ormond Beach, FL
Smith, Renato L. ... Chicago, IL
Smith, Rendel W. ... St. Petersburg, FL
Smith, Renee M. ... Wampsville, NY
Smith, Rensselaer J., IV ... Irvine, CA
Smith, Rex D. ... Atlanta, GA
Smith, Rex Q. ... Portland, OR
Smith, Richard A. ... Eureka, CA
Smith, Richard A. ... Irvine, CA
Smith, Richard A. ... New Fairfield, CT
Smith, Richard A. ... Cheboygan, MI
Smith, Richard A. ... Greenwood, MS
Smith, Richard A. ... Chattanooga, TN
Smith, Richard A. ... Irving, TX
Smith, Richard A. ... Alexandria, VA
Smith, Richard A. ... Yakima, WA
Smith, Richard A., P.C. ... Cheboygan, MI
Smith, Richard B. ... Milford, CT
Smith, Richard B.
Federal Trade Commission, Bureau of Competition, GV
Smith, Richard B. ... Park Forest, IL
Smith, Richard B. ... Boston, MA
Smith, Richard B. ... New York, NY
Smith, Richard B. ... Richmond, VA
Smith, Richard C. ... Phoenix, AZ
Smith, Richard C. ... Scottsdale, AZ
Smith, Richard C. ... Los Angeles, CA
Smith, Richard C. ... Oklahoma City, OK
Smith, Richard C. ... Horsham, PA
Smith, Richard C. ... Philadelphia, PA
Smith, Richard C. ... Edinburg, TX
Smith, Richard C. ... Yakima, WA
Smith, Richard C., & Associates, A Professional Corporation ... Edinburg, TX
Smith, Richard Caldwell ... Miami, FL
Smith, Richard Carlton ... Cupertino, CA
San Francisco, CA
San Jose, CA
San Rafael, CA
Santa Rosa, CA
Walnut Creek, CA
Smith, Richard Carlton, A Professional Corporation ... Cupertino, CA
San Francisco, CA
San Jose, CA
San Rafael, CA
Santa Rosa, CA
Walnut Creek, CA
Smith, Richard D. ... Los Angeles, CA
Smith, Richard D.
Federal Communications Commission, Common Carrier Bureau, GV
Smith, Richard D. ... Topeka, KS
Smith, Richard D. ... Gaithersburg, MD
Smith, Richard D. ... Warren, NJ
Smith, Richard E. ... Birmingham, AL
Smith, Richard E. ... Long Beach, CA
Smith, Richard E.
Department Of Veterans Affairs, Board of Veterans Appeals, GV
Smith, Richard E. ... Chicago, IL
Smith, Richard E. ... Topeka, KS
Smith, Richard E. ... Arlington, MA
Smith, Richard E. ... Longview, TX
Smith, Richard E. ... Richmond, VA
Smith, Richard E., Jr. ... Vicksburg, MS
Smith, Richard E. T. ... Wahpeton, ND
Smith, Richard F. ... Boston, MA
Smith, Richard F. ... Vienna, VA
Smith, Richard F., Jr. ... Cleveland, OH
Smith, Richard G. ... Boise, ID
Smith, Richard G. ... Keene, NH
Smith, Richard G. ... Chagrin Falls, OH
Smith, Richard H. ... Bella Vista, AR
Smith, Richard H. ... Washington, DC
Smith, Richard H. ... Tallahassee, FL
Smith, Richard J. ... Huntsville, AL
Smith, Richard J. ... Waukegan, IL
Smith, Richard J. ... Boston, MA
Smith, Richard J. ... Rochester, MN
Smith, Richard J. ... Gulfport, MS
Smith, Richard J. ... Albuquerque, NM
Smith, Richard J. ... Austin, TX
Smith, Richard J. ... Milwaukee, WI
Smith, Richard J., Jr. ... Branford, CT
Smith, Richard J., Jr., P.C. ... Branford, CT
Smith, Richard Joyce ... Greenwich, CT
Smith, Richard K. ... Burley, ID
Smith, Richard K. ... Savanna, IL
Smith, Richard K. ... Nashville, TN
Smith, Richard K., Jr. ... Los Angeles, CA
Smith, Richard L. ... Little Rock, AR
Smith, Richard L. ... Sarasota, FL
Smith, Richard L. ... Hawarden, IA
Smith, Richard L. ... Albany, NY
Smith, Richard L. ... Rochester, NY
Smith, Richard L., Jr. ... Dallas, TX
Smith, Richard M. ... Tallahassee, FL
Smith, Richard M. ... Mound City, KS
Smith, Richard M. ... Pittsburgh, PA
Smith, Richard M., Jr. ... Phoenix, AZ
Smith, Richard McCallister ... Nashville, TN
Smith, Richard N. ... Connersville, IN
Smith, Richard O. ... Columbus, GA
Smith, Richard P. ... West Hartford, CT
Smith, Richard P. ... Detroit, MI
Smith, Richard P. ... Syracuse, NY
Smith, Richard S. ... Rutland, VT
Smith, Richard S., Jr. ... Little Rock, AR
Smith, Richard S., Jr. ... Hartford, CT
Smith, Richard T. ... Pasadena, CA
Smith, Richard T. ... Atlanta, GA
Marietta, GA
Smith, Richard T. ... Beatrice, NE
Smith, Richard T. ... Westmont, NJ
Smith, Richard V. ... San Francisco, CA
Smith, Richard W. ... San Bernardino, CA
Smith, Richard W. ... West Sacramento, CA
Smith, Richard W. ... Washington, DC
Smith, Richard W. ... Orlando, FL
Smith, Richard W. ... Portland, ME
Smith, Richard W. ... Lincoln, NE
Smith, Richard W. ... Staunton, VA
Smith, Rick ... Silverdale, WA
Smith, Rick E. ... Highland Park, IL
Smith, Rickert & Smith ... River Grove, IL
Smith, Ricky B. ... Lamesa, TX
Smith, R.K., Jr. ... Harrisburg, PA
Smith, R. O. ... Erwin, TN
Smith, Robb L. ... Naples, FL
Smith, Robert ... Elm Grove, WI
Smith, Robert A. ... East Hampton, CT
Smith, Robert A. ... Washington, DC
Smith, Robert A. ... Kaneohe, HI
Smith, Robert A. ... Indianapolis, IN
Smith, Robert A. ... St. Louis, MO
Smith, Robert A. ... Morristown, NJ
Smith, Robert A. ... Troy, NY
Smith, Robert A., A Law Corporation
Kaneohe, HI
Smith, Robert A., Jr.
Fort Lauderdale, FL
Smith, Robert B. ... Atlanta, GA
Smith, Robert B. ... Jesup, GA
Smith, Robert B. ... Boston, MA
Smith, Robert B. ... New York, NY
Smith, Robert B. ... Oklahoma City, OK
Smith, Robert B. ... Portland, OR
Smith, Robert B. ... Pittsburgh, PA
Smith, Robert B. ... Dallas, TX
Smith, Robert B., III ... Richmond, VA
Smith, Robert B., III, P.C. ... Richmond, VA
Smith, Robert B., Jr. ... Lexington, NC
Smith, Robert Bailey, IV ... Richmond, VA
Smith, Robert Barr ... Norman, OK
Smith, Robert Borthwick ... Los Angeles, CA
Smith, Robert Brandon ... Denver, CO
Smith, Robert Burton ... Lansing, MI
Smith, Robert C. ... Glendale, CA
Los Angeles, CA
Smith, Robert C.
General Services Administration, Office of the General Counsel, GV
Smith, Robert C. ... New Orleans, LA
Smith, Robert C. ... Columbia, MO
Smith, Robert C. ... Billings, MT
Smith, Robert C. ... New York, NY
Smith, Robert C., Jr. ... Elmhurst, IL
Smith, Robert C., Jr. ... Oklahoma City, OK
Smith, Robert D. ... Centerville, MA
Smith, Robert D. ... Manchester, NH
Smith, Robert D., III ... Little Rock, AR
Smith, Robert Dane ... Highlands Ranch, CO
Smith, Robert E. ... Palm Springs, CA
Smith, Robert E. ... Lansing, MI
Smith, Robert E. ... New York, NY
Smith, Robert E. ... Raleigh, NC
Smith, Robert E. ... Philadelphia, PA
Smith, Robert E. ... Block Island, RI
Smith, Robert E. ... Bellevue, WA
Smith, Robert F. ... Florence, AL
Smith, Robert F. ... Northbrook, IL
Smith, Robert F. ... Louisville, KY
Smith, Robert F. ... Dennis Port, MA
Smith, Robert F. ... Babylon, NY
Smith, Robert F. ... Columbus, OH
Smith, Robert G. ... New York, NY
Smith, Robert G. ... Stoneville, NC
Smith, Robert G., (P.C.) ... Baltimore, MD
Smith, Robert H. ... Mobile, AL
Smith, Robert H. ... Miami, FL
Smith, Robert H. ... Chicago, IL
Smith, Robert H. ... Newton, MA
Smith, Robert H. ... Chapel Hill, NC
Smith, Robert H. ... Columbus, OH
Smith, Robert H. ... Amarillo, TX
Smith, Robert H. ... Irving, TX
Smith, Robert H., Jr. ... Hartford, CT
Smith, Robert I. ... Waldorf, MD
Smith, Robert J. ... Larkspur, CA
Smith, Robert J. ... Mountain View, CA
Smith, Robert J. ... Sepulveda, CA
Smith, Robert J. ... Washington, DC
Smith, Robert J.
Department Of Health And Human Services, Social Security Administration, GV
Smith, Robert J. ... Baltimore, MD
Smith, Robert J. ... Binghamton, NY
Smith, Robert J. ... New York, NY
Smith, Robert J. ... Syracuse, NY
Smith, Robert J. ... Raleigh, NC
Smith, Robert J. ... Richmond, VA
Smith, Robert J. ... Charleston, WV
Smith, Robert J. ... Madison, WI
Smith, Robert J., Jr. ... Chicago, IL
Smith, Robert James ... Marietta, OH
Smith, Robert K. ... Santa Barbara, CA
Smith, Robert L. ... Huntington Beach, CA
Smith, Robert L. ... Kailua-Kona, HI
Smith, Robert L. ... Rockford, IL
Smith, Robert L. ... Wichita, KS
Smith, Robert L. ... St. Paul, MN
Smith, Robert L. ... Poplar Bluff, MO
Smith, Robert L. ... Brewster, NY
Smith, Robert L. ... Zanesville, OH
Smith, Robert L. ... Tulsa, OK
Smith, Robert L. ... Nashville, TN
Smith, Robert L., A Law Corporation
Kailua-Kona, HI
Smith, Robert L., P.C. ... Tulsa, OK
Smith, Robert Leach ... Fort Lauderdale, FL
Smith, Robert Lee ... Amarillo, TX
Smith, Robert Lee ... The Woodlands, TX
Smith, Robert Lee, P.C.
The Woodlands, TX
Smith, Robert Lewis ... Chicago, IL
Smith, Robert M. ... McGehee, AR
Smith, Robert M. ... Los Angeles, CA
Smith, Robert M. ... Chicago, IL
Smith, Robert M. ... Minneapolis, MN
Smith, Robert M. ... Philadelphia, PA
Smith, Robert M. ... San Antonio, TX
Smith, Robert M., Jr. ... Jacksonville, FL
Smith, Robert M., Law Offices of
San Francisco, CA
Smith, Robert McD. ... Birmingham, AL
Smith, Robert McLanahan, III ... Norfolk, VA
Smith, Robert Merritt ... Fort Collins, CO
Smith, Robert N. ... Washington, DC
Smith, Robert O. ... Grand Rapids, MI
Smith, Robert P. ... Tallahassee, FL
Smith, Robert P. ... New York, NY
Smith, Robert P. ... Monroe, WI
Smith, Robert Perry ... Littleton, CO
Smith, Robert R. ... Washington, DC
Annapolis, MD
Owings Mills, MD
Smith, Robert R. ... Atlanta, GA
Smith, Robert R. ... Pella, IA
Smith, Robert R., Jr. ... Dallas, TX
Smith, Robert Ray ... Austin, TX
Smith, Robert S. ... Hartford, CT
Smith, Robert S. ... New York, NY
Smith, Robert Sellers ... Huntsville, AL
Smith, Robert Steen ... Tulsa, OK
Smith, Robert T. ... Detroit, MI
Smith, Robert T. ... Salt Lake City, UT
Smith, Robert Thornton ... New York, NY
Smith, Robert V. ... Austin, TX
Smith, Robert W. ... Denver, CO
Smith, Robert W. ... Middlebury, CT
Smith, Robert W. ... Orlando, FL
Smith, Robert W. ... Atlanta, GA
Smith, Robert W. ... Elgin, IL
Smith, Robert W. ... Portland, ME
Smith, Robert W. ... Neligh, NE
Smith, Robert W. ... Newark, NJ
Smith, Robert W. ... Providence, RI
Smith, Robert W., Jr. ... Baltimore, MD
Smith, Robert Wood ... Kalamazoo, MI
Smith, Robert Z., Jr. ... Columbia, MD
Smith, Roberta H. ... New York, NY
Smith, Robin Christine ... Brooklyn, NY
Smith, Robin D. ... Department of Justice, Civil Division, GV
Smith, Robin J. ... Danbury, CT
Smith, Robin L. ... Hartford, CT
Smith, Robin M. ... Los Angeles, CA
Smith, Robin R. ... Baltimore, MD
Smith, Robin Simpson ... Salyersville, KY
Smith, Robin Whitlock ... Chicago, IL
Smith, Robt. H. ... Oklahoma City, OK
Smith, Robt. L. ... Springfield, NE
Smith, Robyn E. ... Nashville, TN
Smith, Rod G. ... Tulsa, OK
Smith, Rodger D. ... Wilmington, DE
Smith, Rodger F., Jr. ... Westport, CT
Smith, Rodger L. ... Luray, VA
Smith, Rodney L. ... Denver, CO
Smith, Rodney L. ... Charleston, IL
Smith, Rodney R. ... Homer, NE
Smith, Rodney W. ... Gainesville, FL
Smith, Rodney W. ... Neligh, NE
Smith, Roger A. ... Folsom, CA
Smith, Roger A. ... Sacramento, CA
Smith, Roger A. ... Troy, MI
Smith, Roger D. ... Scottsdale, AZ
Smith, Roger H. ... Brookville, IN
Smith, Roger I. ... Albuquerque, NM
Smith, Roger K. ... Los Angeles, CA
Smith, Roger K ... Nashville, TN
Smith, Roger L. ... Barrington, IL
Smith, Roger Louis ... Glen Burnie, MD
Smith, Roger S. ... New York, NY
Smith, Roger S. ... Pottstown, PA
Smith, Roger T. ... Asheville, NC
Smith, Roger W. ... Raleigh, NC
Smith, Roger W., III ... Corning, NY
Smith, Roger W., Jr. ... Raleigh, NC
Smith, Rolfes & Skavdahl Co., L.P.A.
Cincinnati, OH
Smith, Rolland F. ... Lake Placid, FL
Smith, Ron ... Steamboat Springs, CO
Smith, Ronald A. ... Yardley, PA
Smith, Ronald B. ... Stuart, FL
Smith, Ronald C. ... Chicago, IL
Smith, Ronald C. ... Indianapolis, IN
Smith, Ronald D. ... Dover, DE
Smith, Ronald D. ... Topeka, KS
Smith, Ronald D. ... Shreveport, LA
Smith, Ronald E. ... Clearwater, FL
Smith, Ronald E. ... Atlanta, GA
Smith, Ronald E. ... Fairfax, VA
Smith, Ronald G. ... Cincinnati, OH
Smith, Ronald H. ... Washington, DC
Smith, Ronald K. ... Muncie, IN
Smith, Ronald L. ... Los Angeles, CA
Smith, Ronald Lee ... Columbus, OH
Smith, Ronald P. ... Knoxville, TN
Smith, Ronald Patrick ... St. Paul, MN
Smith, Ronald R. ... Bellevue, OH
Smith, Ronald R. ... Madison, WI
Smith, Ronald S. ... Beverly Hills, CA
Smith, Ronald S. ... Springfield, MA
Smith, Ronald S. ... Bloomfield Hills, MI
Smith, Ronald S., A Law Corporation
Beverly Hills, CA
Smith, Ronald V. ... Trenton, NJ
Smith, Ronnie L. ... Easley, SC
Smith, Rory Dean ... Chicago, IL
Smith, Rose, Finley, Harp & Price, A Professional Corporation ... Eldorado, TX
San Angelo, TX
Smith, Rose Z. ... Rockland, MA
Smith, Rosemary Claire
Federal Election Commission, Office of the General Counsel, GV
Smith, Ross Menefee ... Houston, TX
Smith, Ross W. ... Summit, NJ
Smith, Roy ... West Paterson, NJ
Smith, Roy ... New York, NY
Smith, Roy A., Jr. ... Jackson, MS
Smith, Roy E. ... Las Vegas, NV
Smith, Roy L. ... Pawcatuck, CT
Smith, Roy L., Jr. ... Phenix City, AL
Smith, Roy McBee ... Spartanburg, SC
Smith, Roy P. ... Department of Labor, Office of Secretary, GV
Smith, Roy W. ... Houston, TX
Smith, Royce E.
Department Of Veterans Affairs, Office of the General Counsel, GV
Smith, Rozalind ... Oak Ridge, TN
Smith, Rozalind T. ... Anniston, AL
Smith, Ruben A. ... Irvine, CA
Los Angeles, CA
Smith & Ruch ... Burbank, CA
Smith, Rudolph K. ... Brooklyn, NY
Smith, Rufus R., Jr. & Associates
Dothan, AL
Smith, Rupert Jasen ... Fort Pierce, FL
Smith, Rush S., Jr. ... Atlanta, GA
Smith, Rusha C. ... Birmingham, AL
Smith, Russell A. ... Grand Ledge, MI
Smith, Russell A. ... Montauk, NY
New York, NY
Smith, Russell A. ... Peekskill, NY
Smith, Russell A. ... Waco, TX
Smith, Russell & Associates ... Dallas, TX
Smith, Russell B. ... Dallas, TX
Smith, Russell C. ... Raeford, NC
Smith, Russell D. ... Kansas City, MO
Smith, Russell F., III ... Department of Justice, Environment and Natural Resources Division, GV
Smith, Russell J. ... San Francisco, CA
Smith, Russell K. ... Palo Alto, CA
Smith, Russell L. ... Washington, DC
Smith, Russell L. ... Waco, TX
Smith, Russell M. ... White Plains, NY
Smith, Russell R. ... Houston, TX
Nacogdoches, TX
Smith, Russell W. ... Toccoa, GA
Smith, Rutherford, P.A. ... Summerville, SC
Smith, Rutherford P. C. ... Summerville, SC
Smith, Ryan A. ... Scottsdale, AZ
Smith, Ryan M. ... Charlotte, NC
Smith, S. Amelia ... Washington, DC
Smith, S. Berne ... Camp Hill, PA
Smith, S. Cheri ... Baton Rouge, LA
Smith, S. Christie, IV (A Professional Corporation) ... Leesville, LA
Smith, S. Craig ... Paris, IL
Smith, S. Craig ... Dallas, TX
Smith, S. David ... Houston, TX
Smith, S. David, Jr., (P.C.) ... Rome, GA
Smith, S. Dawn ... Palo Alto, CA
Smith, S. Frank, Jr. ... Bowling Green, KY

Smith, S. Hayes ... New York, NY
Smith, S. Henslee, Law Offices of ... Tustin, CA
Smith, S. Kent ... Southern Pines, NC
Smith, S. Kinnie, Jr. ... New York, NY
Smith, S. Lloyd ... Alexandria, VA
Smith, S. Price, Jr. ... Wichita Falls, TX
Smith, S. Russell, Jr. ... Louisville, KY
Smith, S. Sonjia ... Charlottesville, VA
Smith, Sabbatini & McLeary, PLLC ... Memphis, TN
Smith, Salem C. ... Charleston, WV
Smith, Salesia, V., P.A. ... West Palm Beach, FL
Smith, Salesia Vanette ... West Palm Beach, FL
Smith, Sally A. ... Rochester, NY
Smith, Sally Ann ... Rockford, IL
Smith, Sally Womack ... Mocksville, NC
Smith, Sam G., Jr. ... Knoxville, TN
Smith, Sam J. ... Sunnyvale, CA
Smith, Sam J. ... Tampa, FL
Smith, Samuel ... El Paso, TX
Smith, Sandell Lee ... Research Triangle Park, NC
Smith, Sandra ... Los Angeles, CA
Smith, Sandra A. ... Boston, MA
Smith, Sandra G. ... Gainesville, FL
Smith, Sandra Helen ... Warwick, RI
Smith, Sandra J. ... Los Angeles, CA
Smith, Sandra L. ... Department Of Veterans Affairs, Board of Veterans Appeals, GV
Smith, Sandra McDermott ... Syracuse, NY
Smith, Sanford K. ... Rock Springs, WY
Smith, Sara A. ... Walnut Creek, CA
Smith, Sara L. ... Miami, FL
Smith & Sarafiny ... Hartford, WI
Smith, Sarah Curran ... Pottsville, PA
Smith, Sarah D. ... Albuquerque, NM
Smith, Sarah Day ... Tulsa, OK
Smith, Sarah E. ... Charleston, WV
Smith, Sasha A. ... New York, NY
Smith, Sauer & DeMaria ... Pensacola, FL
Smith & Schaffer, P.C. ... Denver, CO
Smith, Schneider, Stiles, Hudson, Serangeli, Mallaney & Shindler, P.C. ... Des Moines, IA
Smith, Schoder & Roddenberry, P.A. ... Daytona Beach, FL
Smith, Schroeder & O'Connell ... Atlanta, GA
Decatur, GA
Smith & Schultz, LLP ... Eastpointe, MI
Smith, Schuyler S. ... Jacksonville, FL
Smith, Scott ... Dallas, TX
Smith, Scott A. ... Santa Ana, CA
Smith, Scott A. ... Boston, MA
Smith, Scott A. ... Minneapolis, MN
Smith, Scott A. ... St. Louis, MO
Smith, Scott A. ... Westerville, OH
Smith, Scott A. ... Seattle, WA
Smith, Scott Alan ... Great Neck, NY
Smith, Scott B. ... Birmingham, AL
Smith, Scott Bryant ... West Palm Beach, FL
Smith, Scott C. ... San Diego, CA
Smith, Scott C. ... San Francisco, CA
Smith, Scott C. ... Atlanta, GA
Smith, Scott C. ... Canandaigua, NY
Smith, Scott C. ... Cleveland, OH
Smith, Scott C. ... New Holland, PA
Smith, Scott D. ... Atlanta, GA
Smith, Scott D. ... Gulfport, MS
Smith, Scott E. ... Fayetteville, AR
Smith, Scott E., Co., L.P.A. ... Columbus, OH
Smith, Scott Elliot ... Columbus, OH
Smith, Scott F. ... Sterling Heights, MI
Smith, Scott F. ... New York, NY
Smith, Scott F. ... Akron, OH
Smith, Scott G. ... West River, MD
Smith, Scott G. ... Grand Rapids, MI
Smith, Scott H. ... Rochester, NY
Smith, Scott J. ... Chicago, IL
Smith, Scott L. ... Las Vegas, NV
Smith, Scott M. ... San Bernardino, CA
Smith, Scott M. ... Rome, GA
Smith, Scott M. ... Cambridge, IL
Smith, Scott M. ... Rochester, NY
Smith, Scott O. ... Los Angeles, CA
Smith, Scott R. ... New York, NY
Smith, Scott R. ... Spokane, WA
Smith, Scott T. ... Menlo Park, CA
Smith, Scott V. ... San Francisco, CA
Smith, Scott W. ... Grand Marais, MN
Smith, Scott W. ... Cheyenne, WY
Smith & Seagle ... Dothan, AL
Smith, Sean Kevin ... Falls Church, VA
Smith, Sean O., (P.C.) ... Bismarck, ND
Smith, Sean R. ... Atlanta, GA
Smith, Sean R.H. ... Carrollton, OH
Smith, Seana Holly ... New York, NY
Smith, Segel & Sowalsky ... Boston, MA
Smith & Sellers ... Murfreesboro, TN
Smith, Selma L.D. ... Mobile, AL
Smith, Seslee S. ... Savannah, GA
Smith, Seymour A. ... Hackensack, NJ
Smith, S. F. Raymond ... Pineville, WV
Smith, Shannon D. ... Los Angeles, CA
Oklahoma City, OK
Smith & Shapiro ... New York, NY
Smith, Shapleigh, Jr. ... Burlington, VT
Smith, Sharon D. ... New Orleans, LA
Smith, Sharon D. ... Baltimore, MD
Smith, Sharon E. ... Atlanta, GA
Smith, Sharon J. ... Austin, TX
Smith, Sharon L. ... National Aeronautics And Space Administration, GV
Smith, Sharon Leigh ... Raleigh, NC
Smith, Sharon M. Ruppe ... Fayetteville, NC
Smith, Sharon R. ... Bend, OR
Smith, Sharon R. ... Dallas, TX
Smith, Sharyn Lynn ... Tallahassee, FL
Smith & Shaw ... West Long Branch, NJ
Smith, Shawn Allyson ... Mineola, NY
Smith, Shawn D. ... Key West, FL
Smith, Shawn E. ... Columbus, OH
Smith, Shawn Patrick ... Bloomfield Hills, MI
Smith, Shay, Farmer & Wetta, L.L.C. ... Wichita, KS
Smith, Shayne D. ... Conway, AR
Smith, Sheila A. ... Reno, NV
Smith, Sheila M. ... Fresno, CA
Smith, Sheldon A. ... Bismarck, ND
Smith, Sheldon H. ... Denver, CO
Smith, Sheldon M. ... Edgewater, NJ
Smith, Shelley Ilene ... Los Angeles, CA
Smith, Shelley R. ... Chicago, IL
Smith, Shellie Freeman ... Phoenix, AZ
Smith, Shelly R. ... Sandusky, MI
Smith, Shelton L. ... Walnut Creek, CA
Smith, Shelton, P.C. ... Houston, TX
Smith, Sherman N., III ... Vero Beach, FL
Smith, Sherman W. ... Los Angeles, CA
Smith, Sherman W., III ... Deerfield Beach, FL
Smith, Sherri L. ... Poway, CA
Smith, Sherri R. ... Kansas City, KS
Smith, Sherrilynn S. ... Hampden, ME
Smith, Sherry H. ... Berkeley, CA
Smith, Sherry L. ... Oklahoma City, OK
Smith, Sherwood H., Jr. ... Raleigh, NC
Smith, Sheryl Kramer ... Louisville, KY
Smith, Shew, Scrivner & Corbin, P.C. ... Tishomingo, OK
Smith, Shew, Scrivner, Corbin & Watts
Oklahoma City, OK
Ada, OK
Smith, Shirley A. ... Reno, NV
Smith, Shirley J. ... Canfield, OH
Smith, Shirley R. ... Nashville, TN
Smith, Sidney ... Baltimore, MD
Smith, Sidney E. ... Coeur d'Alene, ID
Smith, Sidney E. ... Pontiac, IL
Smith, Sidney E. ... Raleigh, NC
Smith, Sidney O., III ... Los Angeles, CA
Smith, Sidney O., Jr. ... Atlanta, GA
Smith, Sidney R. ... Washington, DC
Smith, Sidney W., Jr. ... Bloomfield Hills, MI
Smith, Silbar, Parker & Woffinden, LLP ... Irvine, CA
Smith, Simeon C., III ... Leesville, LA
Smith, Skottowe W., Jr. ... Charlotte, NC
Smith, Sky E. ... Miami, FL
Smith, Slade E. ... San Francisco, CA
Smith Smart, PLLC ... Seattle, WA
Tacoma, WA
Smith and Smith ... Mobile, AL
Smith & Smith ... Stuttgart, AR
Smith & Smith ... Beverly Hills, CA
Los Angeles, CA
Smith & Smith ... Fort Lauderdale, FL
Smith & Smith ... Vero Beach, FL
Smith & Smith ... Corbin, KY
Smith and Smith ... Louisville, KY
Smith & Smith ... Milford, MI
Smith & Smith ... Carthage, MS
Smith and Smith ... Wilmington, NC
Smith & Smith ... Avon Lake, OH
Smith & Smith ... Perrysburg, OH
Smith & Smith ... Henryetta, OK
Smith & Smith ... Oklahoma City, OK
Smith & Smith ... Tulsa, OK
Smith & Smith ... Easton, PA
Smith & Smith ... Memphis, TN
Smith & Smith ... Savannah, TN
Smith & Smith ... Dallas, TX
Smith & Smith ... Gig Harbor, WA
Smith and Smith, A Law Corporation ... Baker, LA
Smith & Smith, A Prof. Corp. ... Rockland, MA
Smith, Smith & Harter, LLP ... Santa Ana, CA
Smith, Smith Law Offices, P.A. ... Albuquerque, NM
Smith & Smith, LLP ... Cullman, AL
Smith, Smith & Montgomery ... Bellefontaine, OH
Smith and Smith, P.A. ... Jacksonville, FL
Smith, Smith & Parker, P.A. ... Lake City, FL
Mayo, FL
Perry, FL
Smith & Smith, P.C. ... Phenix City, AL
Smith & Smith, P.C. ... Portland, OR
Smith & Smith, P.C. ... Sherman, TX
Smith, Smith & Smith ... Baton Rouge, LA
Smith, Smith & Smith, L.L.P. ... Dallas, TX
Smith, Somerville & Case, L.L.C. ... Baltimore, MD
Smith, Sovik, Kendrick & Sugnet, P.C. ... Syracuse, NY
Smith, Spencer ... Austin, TX
Smith, Spencer A. ... Tucson, AZ
Smith, Speranza, Pusateri, Fitzgerald, Foltz, May and Farrugia ... Lockport, NY
Smith, Spires & Peddy, P.C. ... Birmingham, AL
Smith, Spurgeon E. ... Los Angeles, CA
Smith, Stacey D. ... Eugene, OR
Smith, Stacey Kekich ... Seattle, WA
Smith, Stacey L. ... Levittown, PA
Smith, Stacey R. ... Chickasha, OK
Smith, Stacie K. ... Phoenix, AZ
Smith, Stacy ... Philadelphia, PA
Smith, Stacy A. ... Viroqua, WI
Smith, Stacy Britton ... Orlando, FL
Smith, Stacy L. ... Oklahoma City, OK
Smith, Stafford L. ... Seattle, WA
Smith, Stan D. ... Little Rock, AR
Smith, Stanford J., Jr. ... Wichita, KS
Smith, Stanford S. ... Cleveland, OH
Smith, Stanley A. ... Harrisburg, PA
Smith, Stanley D. ... Del Mar, CA
Smith, Stanley E. ... Abilene, TX
Smith, Stanley G. ... Plainfield, NJ
Smith, Stanley H. ... Indianapolis, IN
Smith, Stanley H., Jr. ... Atlanta, GA
Smith, Stanley K. ... Alabaster, AL
Smith, Stanley L., Jr. ... Stockton, CA
Smith, Stanley Q. ... Jackson, MS
Smith, Stanley R. ... Florence, AL
Smith, Stanley R. ... San Diego, CA
Smith, Stanley R. ... American Fork, UT
Smith, Stanley S. ... Grove City, OH
Smith, Stanley Valladares ... New York, NY
Smith, Stanley W. ... San Francisco, CA
Smith, Stanton K., Jr. ... Jackson, MI
Smith & Stark ... Santa Monica, CA
Smith, Stefan Prentiss ... Houston, TX
Smith, Steibel, Alexander & Saskor, P.C. ... New York, NY
Smith, Stephanie A. ... Austin, TX
Smith, Stephanie E. ... San Francisco, CA
Smith, Stephanie M. ... Newport Beach, CA
San Diego, CA
Smith, Stephanie M. ... St. Petersburg, FL
Smith, Stephanie M. ... Prairie Village, KS
Las Vegas, NV
Smith, Stephanie M., Chartered ... Prairie Village, KS
Smith, Stephen ... Longview, TX
Smith, Stephen A. ... Lake City, FL
Perry, FL
Smith, Stephen A. ... Houston, TX
Smith, Stephen A. ... Seattle, WA
Smith, Stephen A., P.A. ... Lake City, FL
Smith, Stephen Blaine ... Dallas, TX
Smith, Stephen C. ... Barbourville, KY
Smith, Stephen C. ... Bangor, ME
Smith, Stephen C. ... Pittsburgh, PA
Smith, Stephen C. ... Seattle, WA
Smith, Stephen Chadwick ... Lock Haven, PA
Smith, Stephen D. ... United States Court Of Appeals For The Armed Forces, GV
Smith, Stephen D. ... Indianapolis, IN
Smith, Stephen D. ... St. Louis, MO
Smith, Stephen D. ... St. Louis, MO
Smith, Stephen E. ... Irvine, CA
Smith, Stephen E. ... Littleton, CO
Smith, Stephen E. ... Louisville, KY
Smith, Stephen E. ... Minneapolis, MN
Smith, Stephen E. ... Houston, TX
Smith, Stephen E., Jr. ... Paducah, KY
Smith, Stephen Edward ... Chicago, IL
Smith, Stephen F. ... Washington, DC
Smith, Stephen F. ... Priest River, ID
Sandpoint, ID
Smith, Stephen G., Jr. ... Memphis, TN
Smith, Stephen H. ... Huntington Beach, CA
Smith, Stephen H. ... Los Angeles, CA
Smith, Stephen J. ... Clinton, IL
Smith, Stephen J. ... Owatonna, MN
Smith, Stephen J. ... St. Louis, MO
Smith, Stephen J. ... Columbus, OH
Smith, Stephen J. ... Kent, OH
Smith, Stephen J. ... Philadelphia, PA
Smith, Stephen J. ... Houston, TX
Smith, Stephen J. ... Racine, WI
Smith, Stephen J., Jr. ... Norristown, PA
Smith, Stephen K. ... Flagstaff, AZ
Smith, Stephen Kendall ... Indianapolis, IN
Smith, Stephen L. ... San Diego, CA
Smith, Stephen L. ... Minneapolis, MN
Smith, Stephen L. ... Charlotte, NC
Smith, Stephen L. ... New Bremen, OH
Smith, Stephen Lee ... Indianapolis, IN
Smith, Stephen M. ... Long Beach, CA
Smith, Stephen M. ... Hampton, VA
Smith, Stephen Michael ... Nashville, TN
Smith, Stephen N. ... Hillsboro, TX
Smith, Stephen O. ... St. Louis, MO
Smith, Stephen P., III ... Jacksonville, FL
Smith, Stephen P., Jr. ... Jacksonville, FL
Smith, Stephen Page ... Department of Energy, Office of the General Counsel, GV
Smith, Stephen R. ... Phoenix, AZ
Smith, Stephen R. ... Phoenix, AZ
Smith, Stephen R. ... Washington, DC
Smith, Stephen R. ... Melbourne, FL
Smith, Stephen R. ... Lisle, IL
Smith, Stephen R. ... New York, NY
Smith, Stephen R. ... Hendersonville, NC
Smith, Stephen R., P.C. ... Phoenix, AZ
Smith, Stephen Ray, P.C. ... Houston, TX
Smith, Stephen S. ... Los Angeles, CA
Smith, Stephen S. ... Upper Darby, PA
Smith, Stephen T. ... Worthington, MA
Smith, Stephen T. ... Raleigh, NC
Smith, Stephen T. ... Houston, TX
Smith, Stephen W. ... Washington, DC
Smith, Stephen W. ... Henryetta, OK
Smith, Stephen William ... Houston, TX
Smith, Sterling H. ... Washington, DC
Smith, Stern & Friedman, P.C. ... Dallas, TX
Smith, Steve ... Bryan, TX
Smith, Steve D. ... Wenatchee, WA
Smith, Steven A. ... Modesto, CA
Smith, Steven A. ... Minneapolis, MN
Smith, Steven A. ... New York, NY
Smith, Steven A. ... Utica, NY
Smith, Steven A. ... Houston, TX
Smith, Steven Allen ... Portland, OR
Smith, Steven Allen, P.C. ... Portland, OR
Smith, Steven B. ... Colorado Springs, CO
Smith, Steven B. ... Salt Lake City, UT
Smith, Steven Blakely ... Greenville, SC
Smith, Steven C. ... Cullman, AL
Smith, Steven C. ... Santa Ana, CA
Smith, Steven C. ... Anderson, IN
Smith, Steven C. ... Richfield, MN
Smith, Steven C. ... Scottsbluff, NE
Smith, Steven Charles ... Portland, OR
Smith, Steven D. ... Anchorage, AK
Smith, Steven D. ... Phoenix, AZ
Smith, Steven D. ... Fresno, CA
Smith, Steven D. ... Columbus, GA
Smith, Steven D., P.C. ... Anchorage, AK
Smith, Steven Daniel ... Norwalk, CT
Smith, Steven E. ... Sherman Oaks, CA
Smith, Steven E., (A Professional Corporation) ... Los Angeles, CA
Smith, Steven G., Law Office of ... Mesa, AZ
Smith, Steven H. ... Hollywood, FL
Smith, Steven H. ... Jackson, MS
Smith, Steven H. ... Portland, OR
Smith, Steven I. ... Los Angeles, CA
Smith, Steven J. ... Fresno, CA
Smith, Steven J. ... Fort Collins, CO
Smith, Steven L. ... San Francisco, CA
Smith, Steven L. ... Atlanta, GA
Smith, Steven L. ... Cincinnati, OH
Smith, Steven L. ... Philadelphia, PA
Smith, Steven Lee ... Columbus, OH
Smith, Steven M. ... Boston, MA
Smith, Steven M. ... Dallas, TX
Smith, Steven M. ... Fort Worth, TX
Smith, Steven M. ... Houston, TX
Smith, Steven P. ... Wichita, KS
Smith, Steven Paul ... Atlanta, GA
Smith, Steven R. ... Los Angeles, CA
Smith, Steven R. ... San Diego, CA
Smith, Steven R. ... Chicago, IL
Smith, Steven R. ... Riverdale, MD
Smith, Steven R. ... Great Neck, NY
Smith, Steven R. ... Cincinnati, OH
Smith, Steven R. ... Toledo, OH
Smith, Steven R. ... Chamberlain, SD
Smith, Steven R. ... Collierville, TN
Smith, Steven R. ... Dallas, TX
Smith, Steven S. ... Littleton, CO
Smith, Steven S. ... Oklahoma City, OK
Smith, Steven Selwyn ... Manassas, VA
Smith, Steven Taylor ... Great Barrington, MA
Pittsfield, MA
Smith, Steven W. ... Atlanta, GA
Smith, Steven W. ... Baltimore, MD
Smith, Steven W. ... Philadelphia, PA
Smith, Steven W. ... Olympia, WA
Smith, Steven Ware ... Dallas, TX
Smith, Stewart G. ... Detroit, MI
Smith, Stewart K. ... Houston, TX
Smith, Stewart R. ... San Marino, CA
Smith, Stewart R. ... East Wenatchee, WA
Smith, Stoddard ... Brunswick, ME
Smith, Stoddard L., P.A. ... Brunswick, ME
Smith & Stone ... Amarillo, TX
Smith, Storrs, Wilson & McConnell, P.C. ... Amarillo, TX
Smith, Stourton Scott ... Cleveland, OH
Smith, Stratton, Wise, Heher & Brennan ... Princeton, NJ
Smith & Strauss ... De Kalb, IL
Sycamore, IL
Smith & Strege, Ltd. ... Wahpeton, ND
Smith, Stuart ... Chicago, IL
Smith, Stuart ... Waco, TX
Smith, Stuart A. ... Santa Ana, CA
Smith, Stuart A. ... New York, NY
Smith, Stuart C. ... Daingerfield, TX
Smith, Stuart D. ... New York, NY
Smith, Stuart E. ... Huntsville, AL
Smith, Stuart H. ... New Orleans, LA
Smith, Stuart I. ... Alexandria, VA
Smith, Stuart R. ... Washington, DC
Smith, Stuart S. ... Media, PA
Smith, SueLyn ... Washington, DC
Smith, Sumner H. ... Lynn, MA
Smith, Sumner N. ... Charlotte, NC
Smith & Supraski, P.A. ... North Miami Beach, FL
Smith, Susan A. ... Washington, DC
Smith, Susan B. ... Newtown, PA
Smith, Susan D. ... Chicago, IL
Smith, Susan E. M. ... Wilmette, IL
Smith, Susan Ferraro ... Cleveland, OH
Smith, Susan Gunnells ... Mobile, AL
Smith, Susan Hunter ... Austin, TX
Smith, Susan J. ... Harrisburg, PA
Smith, Susan Jane ... Detroit, MI
Smith, Susan Jean ... Doylestown, PA
Smith, Susan K. ... Phoenix, AZ
Smith, Susan K. ... Avon, CT
Hartford, CT
Smith, Susan K. ... Minneapolis, MN
Smith, Susan L. ... Menlo Park, CA
Smith, Susan L. ... Department of Justice, Criminal Division, GV
Smith, Susan L. ... Atlanta, GA
Smith, Susan L. ... Wichita, KS
Smith, Susan L. ... Salem, OR
Smith, Susan M. ... Great Barrington, MA
Smith, Susan M. ... New York, NY
Smith, Susan McGuire ... Huntsville, AL
Smith, Susan Moloney ... Richmond, VA
Smith, Susan T. ... Downers Grove, IL
Smith, Susan W. ... San Jose, CA
Smith, Susanna B. ... Anniston, AL
Smith, Susanne S. ... St. Paul, MN

Smith & Susson, A Prof. Corp.
Santa Ana, CA
Smith, Suzanne A. .... Los Angeles, CA
Smith, Suzanne Constance .... Bozeman, MT
Smith, Suzanne E. K. .... Brooklin, ME
Smith, Suzanne L. .... New York, NY
Smith, Suzanne S. .... York, PA
Smith, Suzeanne E. .... Salem, MA
Smith, Suzelle M. .... Los Angeles, CA
Smith, Suzette Marie .... New Orleans, LA
Smith, Sydney Albert .... Elba, AL
Smith, Sydney P. .... Miami, FL
Smith, Sydney R. .... New York, NY
Smith, Sydney S., (Mrs.) .... Phenix City, AL
Smith, Sylvia A. .... Santa Monica, CA
Smith, Sylvia J. .... Tulsa, OK
Smith, T. Andrew .... Nashville, TN
Smith, T. Bruce .... Fresno, CA
Smith, T. Byron .... Raleigh, NC
Smith, T. Edward .... Beverly Hills, CA
Smith, T. Fitzgerald .... Walnut, CA
Smith, T. Kenan .... Knoxville, TN
Smith, T. Mark .... Los Angeles, CA
Smith, T. Michael .... Naples, FL
Smith, T. Murray .... Dallas, TX
Smith, T. Rhett .... Pensacola, FL
Smith, T. Scott .... Sherman, TX
Smith, Tad R. .... El Paso, TX
Smith, Taffiny Louise .... Montgomery, AL
Smith, Taliaferro, Purvis & Boothe
Jonesville, LA
Smith, Tamara .... Columbus, OH
Smith, Tamara A. .... El Cajon, CA
Smith, Tamara J. .... Boston, MA
Smith, Tammeryn M. .... Baton Rouge, LA
Smith, Tammy A. .... Passaic, NJ
Smith, Tammy C. .... Philadelphia, MS
Smith, Tamra L. (Tami) .... Shelbyville, TN
Smith, Tana Fredrick .... Muskogee, OK
Smith, Tangela D. .... New York, NY
Smith, Tardiff & Hayes, A Law Corporation
San Luis Obispo, CA
Smith, Taylor B. .... Columbus, MS
Corinth, MS
Tupelo, MS
Smith, Taylor & Johnson .... Clinton, IL
Smith, Ted A. .... Scottsdale, AZ
Smith, Ted A.V. .... Santa Rosa, CA
Smith, Ted D. .... Denver, CO
Smith, Ted E. .... Manhattan, KS
Smith, Ted, Jr. .... Killeen, TX
Smith, Ted L. .... Batesville, MS
Smith, Tefft W. .... Washington, DC
Chicago, IL
Smith, Templeton .... Pittsburgh, PA
Smith, Templeton, Jr. .... Pittsburgh, PA
Smith, Teresa K. Murray .... Blountville, TN
Smith, Teri Hayes .... Gadsden, AL
Smith, Terral R. .... Austin, TX
Smith, Terrance L. .... Highland, IN
La Porte, IN
Smith, Terrell W. .... Salt Lake City, UT
Smith, Terrence .... Florham Park, NJ
New York, NY
Philadelphia, PA
Smith, Terrence A. .... Fort Lauderdale, FL
Smith, Terry .... New York, NY
Smith, Terry C. .... Blue Springs, MO
Smith, Terry D. .... Buffalo, NY
Smith, Terry H.
Department Of Veterans Affairs,
Board of Veterans Appeals, GV
Smith, Terry J. .... Chicago, IL
Smith, Terry J. .... Grand Ledge, MI
Smith, Terry L. .... Long Beach, CA
Smith, Terry L. .... Columbia City, IN
Smith, Terry L. .... Monticello, IN
Smith, Terry L. & Associates, P.C.
Columbia City, IN
Smith, Terry P. .... Houston, TX
Smith, Theadore M. .... San Diego, CA
Smith, Theodore B., III .... Harrisburg, PA
Smith, Theodore F., Jr. .... Indianapolis, IN
Smith, Theodore H. .... Pleasantville, NJ
Smith, Theodore J., III .... Los Angeles, CA
Smith, Theodore K. .... Washington, DC
Smith, Theodore M. .... Denver, CO
Smith, Theodore R. .... Suwanee, GA
Smith, Theodore S. .... Florham Park, NJ
Smith & Thiel, Law Offices .... Missoula, MT
Smith & This, Co., L.P.A.
New Bremen, OH
Smith, Thomas .... Lansing, MI
Smith, Thomas A. .... Cameron Park, CA
Smith, Thomas A. .... Tampa, FL
Smith, Thomas A. .... Chicago, IL
Smith, Thomas A. .... Birmingham, MI
Smith, Thomas A., Jr. .... Cullman, AL
Smith, Thomas B. .... Washington, DC
Smith, Thomas B. .... Orlando, FL
Smith, Thomas B. .... St. Petersburg, FL
Smith, Thomas Bailey .... Pickens, SC
Smith, Thomas C. .... Washington, DC
Smith, Thomas C. .... Chicago, IL
Indianapolis, IN
Smith, Thomas C. .... Covington, KY
Smith, Thomas C. .... Dallas, TX
Smith, Thomas D. .... Perrysburg, OH
Smith, Thomas D. .... Philadelphia, PA
Smith, Thomas Dixon .... Albany, NY
Smith, Thomas E. .... Chicago, IL
Smith, Thomas E. .... Billings, MT
Smith, Thomas E. .... Chattanooga, TN
Smith, Thomas E., III .... Atlanta, GA
Smith, Thomas E., Jr. .... Columbia, SC
Pamplico, SC
Smith, Thomas F. .... Harrison, ME
Smith, Thomas Fenton .... Aspen, CO
Smith, Thomas G. .... Hartford, CT
Smith, Thomas G. .... Zebulon, GA
Smith, Thomas G. .... Westland, MI
Smith, Thomas G. .... Atlantic City, NJ
Pleasantville, NJ
Smith, Thomas G. .... Rochester, NY
Smith, Thomas G. .... Syracuse, NY
Smith, Thomas G. .... Pittsburgh, PA
Smith, Thomas G. .... Arlington, VA
Smith, Thomas Gordon .... Culpeper, VA
Smith, Thomas H. .... Kansas City, MO
Smith, Thomas J.
Commodity Futures Trading Commission,
Division of Trading and Markets, GV
Smith, Thomas J. .... Belleville, IL
St. Louis, MO
Smith, Thomas J. .... New Orleans, LA
Houston, TX
Smith, Thomas J. .... New York, NY
Smith, Thomas J. .... Elyria, OH
Smith, Thomas J. .... Pittsburgh, PA
Smith, Thomas J. .... Memphis, TN
Smith, Thomas J. .... San Antonio, TX
Smith, Thomas J., III .... Richmond, KY
Smith, Thomas J., III
West Long Branch, NJ
Smith, Thomas J., Jr. .... West Long Branch, NJ
Smith, Thomas Jason .... Houston, TX
Smith, Thomas L. .... Highland, IN
Smith, Thomas L., Jr. .... Atlanta, GA
Smith, Thomas L., (P.A.) .... Boise, ID
Smith, Thomas M. .... Prestonsburg, KY
Smith, Thomas M. .... Dallas, TX
Smith, Thomas M. .... Spokane, WA
Smith, Thomas McGinn .... Redwood City, CA
Smith, Thomas O., P.C. .... Bismarck, ND
Smith, Thomas P. .... Chicago, IL
Smith, Thomas P. .... Upper Marlboro, MD
Smith, Thomas P. .... Lawrence, MA
Smith, Thomas P., Jr. .... Alexandria, VA
Smith, Thomas Peter, Jr. .... Washington, DC
Smith, Thomas R. .... Danville, IL
Smith, Thomas R. .... Princeton, NJ
Smith, Thomas R. .... Buffalo, NY
Smith, Thomas R. .... Syracuse, NY
Smith, Thomas R. .... Cincinnati, OH
Smith, Thomas R. .... Nashville, TN
Smith, Thomas R., Jr. .... New York, NY
Smith, Thomas Raymond .... Casper, WY
Smith, Thomas Royall .... Boston, MA
Smith, Thomas S. .... Dothan, AL
Smith, Thomas S. .... Denver, CO
Smith, Thomas S. .... Spokane, WA
Smith, Thomas S. .... Laramie, WY
Smith, Thomas S., Jr. .... Trenton, NJ
Smith, Thomas T. .... Bemidji, MN
Smith, Thomas T. .... Austin, TX
Smith, Thomas Verner .... Jackson, TN
Smith, Thomas W. .... New York, NY
Yonkers, NY
Smith, Thomas W. .... New York, NY
Smith, Thomas W. .... Greensburg, PA
Smith, Thomas W. .... Falls Church, VA
Smith, Thomas W., III .... San Marcos, CA
Smith, Thomas W., III .... Manassas, VA
Smith, Thompson & Shaw, P.A.
Tallahassee, FL
Smith, Thorn M. .... Rock Island, IL
Smith, Tiffanie R. .... Ellicott City, MD
Smith, Tim W. .... Memphis, TN
Smith, Timothy A. .... Phoenix, AZ
Smith, Timothy A. .... Orlando, FL
Smith, Timothy A. .... Brooklyn, NY
Smith, Timothy A. .... Camden, NY
Smith, Timothy A. .... Cincinnati, OH
Smith, Timothy B. .... Lawrenceville, GA
Smith, Timothy B. .... Dallas, TX
Smith, Timothy Bryan .... San Antonio, TX
Smith, Timothy C. .... San Francisco, CA
Smith, Timothy D. .... Kent, OH
Smith, Timothy Daly .... Portland, OR
Smith, Timothy Dean .... Greensboro, NC
Smith, Timothy E. .... House of Representatives,
Congressional Assistants, GV
Smith, Timothy F. .... New York, NY
Smith, Timothy J. .... St. Louis, MO
Smith, Timothy L. .... San Francisco, CA
Smith, Timothy M. .... Sacramento, CA
Smith, Timothy M. .... Boston, MA
Smith, Timothy O. .... Danville, IL
Smith, Timothy P. .... San Rafael, CA
Smith, Timothy P. .... Detroit, MI
Smith, Timothy P. .... Manchester, NH
Smith, Timothy P. .... Morristown, NJ
Smith, Timothy Paul .... Traverse City, MI
Smith, Timothy R. .... Princeton, NJ
Smith, Timothy R. .... Keene Valley, NY
Lake Placid, NY
Smith, Timothy R. .... Pittsburgh, PA
Smith, Timothy Ross .... Fort Smith, AR
Smith, Timothy T. .... Lanham, MD
Smith, Timothy T. .... Avon Lake, OH
Smith, Timothy V., (P.C.) .... New York, NY
Smith, Timothy W. .... Chicago, IL
Smith, Timothy W., P.A. .... Kenansville, NC
Smith, Timothy Wayne .... Kenansville, NC
Smith, Tina A. .... Kansas City, MO
Smith, Tito S. .... Palatka, FL
Smith, T.J. .... Louisville, KY
Smith, Todd A. .... Chicago, IL
Smith, Todd A. .... Lansing, MI
Smith, Todd A. .... Bedford, TX
Smith, Todd & Farrell, P.C. .... Indianapolis, IN
Smith, Todd G. .... Madison, WI
Smith, Todd L. .... Fort Lauderdale, FL
Smith, Todd, Law Firm, The .... Bedford, TX
Grapevine, TX
Smith, Todd M. .... Cleveland, OH
Smith, Todd Michael .... Bakersfield, CA
Smith, Todd Stewart .... Syracuse, NY
Smith & Tollefson .... Owatonna, MN
Smith, Tom C. .... Virginia Beach, VA
Smith, Tom D. .... Washington, DC
Smith, Tom K. .... McRae, GA
Smith, Tommy E. .... Heber Springs, AR
Smith, Tommy L. .... Austin, TX
Houston, TX
Smith and Toner .... Doylestown, PA
Smith, Tonya L. .... Capistrano Beach, CA
Smith, Tonya M. .... Newark, NJ
Smith, Toxey H., Jr. .... Biloxi, MS
Smith, Toxey Hall .... Los Angeles, CA
Smith and Tozian, P.A. .... Tampa, FL
Smith, Tracie Grove .... Savannah, GA
Smith, Tracy A. Heinzman
Washington, DC
Smith, Tracy Annette .... Newport, KY
Smith, Tracy Jackson .... Knoxville, TN
Smith, Tracy M. .... St. Paul, MN
Smith, Tracy S. .... San Francisco, CA
Smith, Traver Clinton, Jr. .... Boston, MA
Smith, Travis Calvin .... Oklahoma City, OK
Smith, Trevor A. .... Louisville, KY
Smith, Trey .... Dallas, TX
Smith, Tricia .... Belvidere, IL
Smith, Tricia A. .... Del Mar, CA
Smith, Tricia B. .... McDonough, GA
Smith, Trina B. .... Charleston, WV
Smith, Trisha L. .... New York, NY
Smith, Tristine Grimes .... South Portland, ME
Smith, Troy A. .... Department of the Army,
U.S. Army Legal Services Agency, GV
Smith, Troy B. .... Los Angeles, CA
Smith, Troy K. .... Jacksonville, FL
St. Augustine, FL
Smith, Troy V. .... Tyler, TX
Smith, Truett .... Elberton, GA
Smith, Truman H. .... Fayetteville, AR
Smith, Trystan B. .... Salt Lake City, UT
Smith, Turner P. .... New York, NY
Smith, Turner T., Jr. .... Washington, DC
Smith, Turner Taliaferro .... Manassas, VA
Smith, Tyce S., Sr. .... Waynesville, MO
Smith, Tye H. .... Oklahoma City, OK
Smith, Tyler D. .... Boise, ID
Smith, Tyler J. .... Pittsburgh, PA
Smith, Tyson D., Jr .... Monroe, GA
Smith & Uloth, P.C. .... Dallas, TX
Smith, Ulrich W. .... Las Vegas, NV
Smith, Underwood & Perkins, A Professional
Corporation .... Dallas, TX
Smith & Ure .... Santa Ana, CA
Smith, V. James .... Los Angeles, CA
Smith, V. Roland .... Draper, UT
Smith, Valerie A. .... Los Angeles, CA
Smith, Valerie A. .... Santa Ana, CA
Smith, Valerie J. .... Baltimore, MD
Smith, Valerie L. .... San Francisco, CA
San Jose, CA
Smith, Valerie Michelle .... Kankakee, IL
Smith, Valjean R., (Mr.) .... Springfield, IL
Smith, Van .... Chevy Chase, MD
Smith, Van P. .... Muncie, IN
Smith & Van Bibber .... Charleston, WV
Smith, Vance A. .... Louisville, KY
Smith, Vanessa L. .... Chicago, IL
Smith, Vann .... Little Rock, AR
Smith, Vardaman Kimball (Vick), III
Hattiesburg, MS
Smith & Ventura .... Los Gatos, CA
Smith, Verena .... Cincinnati, OH
Smith, Vernon Alan .... Niwot, CO
Smith, Vernon F. .... San Rafael, CA
Smith, Vernon K. .... Boise, ID
Smith, Vernon L. .... Waco, TX
Smith, Veronica Anzalone .... Grove City, PA
Smith, Vicki Haynes .... Longview, TX
Smith, Vicki L. .... Portland, OR
Smith, Victor .... Lake Alfred, FL
Smith, Victor H. .... Washington, DC
Smith, Victor Harlan .... Walker, MN
Smith, Victor J. .... Houston, TX
Smith, Victoria .... Chicago, IL
Smith, Victoria Bolling .... Oxford, MS
Smith, Victoria F. .... New York, NY
Smith, Victoria L. .... Kansas City, MO
Smith, Victoria L. .... New York, NY
Smith, Victoria Lynn .... Toledo, OH
Smith, Vincent M. .... New York, NY
Smith, Virgil M. .... Gadsden, AL
Smith, Virginia C. .... Department of Labor,
Pension and Welfare Benefits, GV
Smith, Virginia D. .... Hudson, NY
Smith, Virginia S. .... Salt Lake City, UT
Smith, Virginia Stanton .... Pittsfield, MA
Williamstown, MA
Smith, V. M. Manning .... Beaufort, SC
Smith, W. Alan, Jr. .... Lynchburg, VA
Smith, W. Bailey .... Newport Beach, CA
Smith, W. Britton, Jr. .... Charlotte, NC
Smith, W. Bryan .... Brentwood, TN
Smith, W. Craig .... Augusta, GA
Smith, W. Creighton .... Houston, TX
Smith, W. Crit .... Tallahassee, FL
Smith, W. David, Jr. .... Hooksett, NH
Smith, W. Douglas .... Jacksonville, FL
Saint Marys, GA
Smith, W. Everett .... Columbia, SC
Smith, W. Graham, Jr. .... Williamson, WV
Smith, W. Gregory .... Birmingham, AL
Smith, W. Holt .... Madisonville, TN
Smith, W. Hutchins, III .... Chattanooga, TN
Smith, W. Kelly .... Orlando, FL
Smith, W. Kevin .... Louisville, KY
Smith, W. Lance, III .... Savannah, GA
Smith, W. Lawrence .... Tampa, FL
Smith, W. Lewis, Jr. .... Charlotte, NC
Smith, W. Lindsay .... Greenville, SC
Smith, W. Mark .... Washington, DC
Smith, W. Osmond, III .... Yanceyville, NC
Smith, W. Patrick .... Nashville, TN
Smith, W. Randolph .... West Keansburg, NJ
Smith, W. Reed .... New Orleans, LA
Smith, W. Richard, Jr. .... Hartford, CT
Smith, W. Richard, Jr. .... Atlanta, GA
Smith, W. Ritchie, Jr. .... Fayetteville, NC
Smith, W. Stanford .... Rockville, MD
Smith, W. Stephen .... Washington, DC
Smith, W. Steve .... Houston, TX
Smith, W. Terry, Jr. .... Memphis, TN
Smith, W. Thomas .... Boston, MA
Smith, W. Truett .... San Angelo, TX
Smith, W. Wheeler .... Birmingham, AL
Smith & Wade .... Indianapolis, IN
Smith, Wade C. .... Dallas, TX
Smith, Wade M. .... Raleigh, NC
Smith, Wade V. .... Austin, TX
Smith, Wade W., Jr. .... Youngstown, OH
Smith, Walker Bledsoe, Ms.
Department of Justice,
Environment and Natural Resources
Division, GV
Smith, Walker Gordon .... Sausalito, CA
Smith, Wallace B. .... Virginia Beach, VA
Smith, Wallace E. .... Walnut Creek, CA
Smith, Wallace J. .... Sacramento, CA
Smith, Wallace M. .... Austin, TX
Smith, Walsh & Brisbin .... San Francisco, CA
Smith, Walsh, Clarke & Gregoire
Great Falls, MT
Smith, Walstein, Jr. .... Waco, TX
Smith, Walter .... Macon, GA
Smith, Walter A. .... Atlanta, GA
Smith, Walter A. .... Bala Cynwyd, PA
Smith, Walter A., III .... Bethesda, MD
Smith, Walter A., Jr. .... Washington, DC
Smith, Walter B. .... Panama City, FL
Smith, Walter E. .... Santa Ana, CA
Smith, Walter E. .... St. Petersburg, FL
Smith, Walter F.
Department of Justice, GV
Smith, Walter H. .... Owensboro, KY
Smith, Walter H. .... Columbia, SC
Smith, Walter J. .... Houston, TX
Smith, Walter J., Jr. .... Washington, DC
Baltimore, MD
Smith, Walter J., (P.A.)
Fort Walton Beach, FL
Smith, Walter K. .... Lawrence, MA
Smith, Walter L. .... Baton Rouge, LA
Smith, Walter L., Jr. .... Baton Rouge, LA
Smith, Walter Landry .... Baton Rouge, LA
Smith, Walter M. .... Wilmington, NC
Smith, Walter R. .... Dartmouth, MA
New Bedford, MA
Smith, Walter S., Jr. .... Waco, TX
Smith, Walter W. .... Pulaski, NY
Smith, Walton N. .... Atlanta, GA
Smith, Ward .... Philadelphia, PA
Smith, Ward G. .... Mayfield Heights, OH
Smith & Warren .... Oklahoma City, OK
Smith, Warren E. .... Plainfield, NJ
Smith, Warren G. .... Canton, OH
Smith, Warren H. .... Dallas, TX
Smith, Warren J. .... Columbus, OH
Smith, Warren M. .... Nashville, TN
Smith Waters Hughes, Ltd. .... Peoria, IL
Smith, Wayman F., III .... St. Louis, MO
Smith, Wayne A. .... Phoenix, AZ
Smith, Wayne A. .... Troy, MI
Smith, Wayne D. .... New York, NY
Smith, Wayne E. .... Boston, MA
Smith, Wayne E. .... Kansas City, MO
Smith, Wayne H. .... Heflin, AL
Smith, Wayne LaRue .... Key West, FL
Smith, Wayne M. .... Los Angeles, CA
Smith, Wayne N. .... Richmond, VA
Smith, Wayne O. .... St. Petersburg, FL
Smith, Wayne O. .... Paxton, IL
Smith, Wayne O., P.A. .... St. Petersburg, FL
Smith, Wayne P. .... Schenectady, NY
Smith, Wayne R. .... New York, NY
Smith, Wayne Richard .... Petoskey, MI
Smith, Wayne S. .... Dallas, TX
Smith, Wayne V. R. .... Walnut Creek, CA
Smith, Wayne W. .... Irvine, CA
Los Angeles, CA
Smith, Webb .... Carbondale, IL
Smith, Webb A. .... Lansing, MI
Smith, Wedon T. .... Jonesville, LA
Smith, Welch & Brittain .... Atlanta, GA
McDonough, GA
Stockbridge, GA
Smith, Wendall H. .... Atlanta, GA
Smith, Wendell A. .... Woodbridge, NJ
Smith, Wendell A. .... Austin, TX
Smith, Wendell K. .... Grandview, MO
Smith, Wendy B. .... Pittsburgh, PA
Smith, Wendy E. D. .... Pittsburgh, PA
Smith, Wendy H. .... Roseland, NJ
Smith, Wendy J. .... Fort Lauderdale, FL
Smith, Wendy W. .... San Francisco, CA
San Jose, CA
Smith, Wesley B. .... Rutherford, NJ
Smith, Wesley F. .... Topeka, KS
Smith, Wesley J. .... Los Angeles, CA
Smith, Wesley M. .... Kansas City, KS
Smith & West .... Springfield, OH
Smith, Weston F. .... Bradenton, FL
Smith, W. G. .... Wilmington, NC
Smith, Wheeler .... Minneapolis, MN
Smith, White, Sharma & Halpern, A
Professional Association .... Atlanta, GA
Smith, Whitfield C. .... Decatur, GA

Smith, Whitney ...... Beverly, MA
Smith, Whitney ...... New York, NY
Smith, Whitney ...... Seattle, WA
Smith, Wilbur C., III ...... Fort Myers, FL
Smith, Wilbur, Law Firm ...... Fort Myers, FL
Smith, Wilburn, III ...... Laguna Niguel, CA
Smith, Wilfred J., Jr. ...... Wilmington, DE
Smith, William A. ...... Solvang, CA
Smith, William A. ...... Dallas, TX
Smith, William A. ...... Hampton, VA
Smith, William A., Jr. ...... Batavia, NY
Smith, William A., Jr. ...... Cary, NC
Smith, William Arthur, II
Washington, DC
Smith, William B. ...... San Francisco, CA
Smith, William B. ...... Ventura, CA
Smith, William B. ...... Tampa, FL
Smith, William B. ...... Clinton, IL
Smith, William B. ...... Midland, TX
Smith, William B. ...... Virginia Beach, VA
Smith, William B., III ...... St. Louis, MO
Smith, William B., P.A. ...... Tampa, FL
Smith, William B. B. ...... Atlanta, GA
Smith, William Bradford, Jr.
Greenwich, CT
Smith, William Bruce ...... Bartow, FL
Smith, William C. ...... Washington, DC
Smith, William C. ...... Portland, ME
Smith, William C. ...... Philadelphia, PA
Smith, William C. ...... North, SC
Smith, William C., III ...... Atlanta, GA
Smith, William C., III ...... Jackson, MS
Smith, William C., Jr. ...... Prairieville, LA
Smith, William C., Jr. ...... Jackson, MS
Smith, William C., Jr. ...... Raleigh, NC
Smith, William Clancy ...... Pittsburgh, PA
Smith, William D. ...... New York, NY
Smith, William D. ...... Rochester, NY
Smith, William D. ...... Mt. Vernon, OH
Smith, William D. ...... Spearman, TX
Smith, William Darr ...... Atlanta, GA
Smith, William Dean ...... San Diego, CA
Smith, William Douglas ...... Spartanburg, SC
Smith, William E. ...... San Francisco, CA
Smith, William E. ...... Washington, DC
Smith, William E. ...... Americus, GA
Smith, William E. ...... Springfield, MA
Smith, William E. ...... Evart, MI
Smith, William E. ...... Lockport, NY
Smith, William E. ...... Providence, RI
Smith, William E. ...... Denton, TX
Smith, William E., III ...... Clarksville, IN
Smith, William E., Jr ...... Florence, AL
Smith, William E., Jr. ...... Los Angeles, CA
Smith, William F. ...... Department of Commerce,
Patent and Trademark Office, GV
Smith, William F. ...... Miami, FL
Smith, William F. ...... Chicago, IL
Smith, William F. ...... Pearl River, NY
Smith, William F. ...... Tulsa, OK
Smith, William F., II ...... Birmingham, AL
Smith, William F., Jr. ...... Russellville, AR
Smith, William F., P.C. ...... Chicago, IL
Smith, William Frank ...... Wichita Falls, TX
Smith, William G. ...... Los Angeles, CA
Smith, William G. ...... Garland, TX
Smith, William George
Rancho Palos Verdes, CA
Smith, William H. ...... Cleveland, OH
Smith, William H. ...... Harrisburg, PA
Smith, William H. ...... Danville, VA
Smith, William H. ...... Clarksburg, WV
Smith, William H., III ...... Mendenhall, MS
Smith, William H., III ...... Philadelphia, PA
Smith, William H., Jr. ...... Des Moines, IA
Smith, William H., Jr. ...... Sandusky, OH
Smith, William H., Jr., (P.C.) ...... Tucker, GA
Smith, William J. ...... Little Rock, AR
Smith, William J. ...... Fresno, CA
Smith, William J. ...... Santa Rosa, CA
Smith, William J. ...... Columbus, GA
Smith, William J. ...... Van Buren, ME
Smith, William J. ...... Westmont, NJ
Smith, William J. ...... New York, NY
Smith, William J. ...... Pittsburgh, PA
Smith, William J. ...... Newberry, SC
Smith, William J. ...... Corsicana, TX
Smith, William J. ...... Houston, TX
Smith, William J. ...... Wenatchee, WA
Smith, William Jarrel, Jr. ...... Falls Church, VA
Smith, William Joseph H. ...... Washington, DC
Smith, William K. ...... Mission Viejo, CA
Smith, William K. ...... Cleveland, OH
Smith, William L. ...... Arnold, CA
Smith, William L. ...... Yazoo City, MS
Smith, William L., II ...... Columbia, SC
Smith, William L., Jr. ...... Denver, CO
Smith, William L., Jr. ...... Chicago, IL
Smith, William M. ...... Palo Alto, CA
Smith, William M. ...... New York, NY
Smith, William Marion ...... Natchez, MS
Smith, William McBee ...... Spartanburg, SC
Smith, William N. ...... Atlanta, GA
Smith, William O. ...... Greensburg, IN
Smith, William P. ...... Chicago, IL
Smith, William P. ...... Boston, MA
Quincy, MA
Smith, William P. ...... Pittsburgh, PA
Smith, William P. ...... Quitaque, TX
Smith, William P., III ...... Atlanta, GA
Smith, William P., Jr. ...... Rochester, NY
Smith, William R. ...... Fort Myers, FL
Smith, William R. ...... Wichita, KS
Smith, William R. ...... Marquette, MI
Smith, William R., P.A. ...... Fort Myers, FL
Smith, William S. ...... Des Moines, IA
Smith, William S. ...... Waterloo, IA
Smith, William S. ...... Shrewsbury, MA
Smith, William S. ...... Pittsburgh, PA
Smith, William S., III ...... Burlington, VT
Smith, William T. ...... Franklin Lakes, NJ
Smith, William T., III ...... Salisbury, MD
Smith, William T., III ...... Kansas City, MO
Smith, William T., III, P.A. ...... Salisbury, MD
Smith, William Thomas ...... Albany, GA
Smith, William U. ...... Clearfield, PA
Smith, William W. ...... Birmingham, AL
Smith, William W. ...... Booneville, MS
Smith, William W. ...... Goldsboro, NC
Smith, William W. ...... Charleston, WV
Smith & Williams ...... Las Vegas, NV
Smith, Willie, Jr. ...... Gulfport, MS
Smith, Willie T., Jr. ...... Greenville, SC
Smith, Willis B., Jr. ...... Texarkana, AR
Smith, Wilson, (P.A.) ...... Miami, FL
Smith, Wilson R. ...... Dublin, GA
Vidalia, GA
Smith, Wilton J.
Department of Transportation,
Federal Aviation Administration, GV
Smith, Winston G. ...... Houston, TX
Smith, Winston R. ...... Amarillo, TX
Smith, Winthrop S., Jr. ...... Milford, CT
Smith, Winton C., Jr. ...... Memphis, TN
Smith, Wm. B. ...... Chicago, IL
Smith, Wm. Benjamin ...... Charlotte, NC
Smith, Wm. Michael ...... Yuma, AZ
Smith, Wm. Michael ...... Miamisburg, OH
Smith, Wm. Randolph ...... Washington, DC
Smith, Wm. Randolph ...... Houston, TX
Smith, Wm. Reece, Jr. ...... Tampa, FL
Smith, Wm. Ronald ...... Fairbanks, AK
Smith, Wm. Scott ...... Houston, TX
Smith, Wm. Tousley ...... Cleveland, OH
Smith, W. N. Harrell, IV ...... Washington, DC
Smith, Woodrow Davis ...... San Diego, CA
Smith, Woody D. ...... Coffeyville, KS
Smith, W. P. Colin, Jr. ...... Boston, MA
Smith, Wrede H., Jr. ...... Madison, WI
Smith, Wright W. ...... Rome, GA
Smith, Wyman G., III ...... Fairfield, CA
Napa, CA
Smith, Yaphet L. ...... Palo Alto, CA
Smith, Young M., Jr. ...... Hickory, NC
Smith, Yvonne Soucie ...... Sun City Center, FL
Smith, Z. Hershel ...... Providence, RI
Smith, Zachary ...... Walnut Creek, CA
Smith, Zachary M. ...... Sacramento, CA
Smith, Zane D. ...... Chicago, IL
Smith & Zuccarini, P.S. ...... Bellevue, WA
Seattle, WA
Smith-Adam, Louisa ...... North Palm Beach, FL
Smitham, Craig H. ...... Dallas, TX
Smithart, Andrew J., III ...... Tuscaloosa, AL
Smithart, Elizabeth C. ...... Union Springs, AL
Smith-Ashford, Monica L ...... Nashville, TN
Smithberg, Ellen ...... New York, NY
Smithberg, Nicholas ...... New York, NY
Smithburn, J. Eric ...... Notre Dame, IN
Smith-Burris, Stephanie ...... Del Rio, TX
Smith-Daniel, Paula D. ...... Greensboro, NC
Smithdeal, Elizabeth C. ...... Greenwood, SC
Smithdeal, Joseph C. ...... Greenwood, SC
Smith-Delach, Kathleen ...... Washington, PA
Smithee, John ...... Amarillo, TX
Smithee, Robert W. ...... Lubbock, TX
Smither, J. Michael ...... Louisville, KY
Smither, John H. ...... Houston, TX
Smither, John J., (P.C.) ...... Houston, TX
Smither, Margaret H. ...... Mechanicsville, VA
Smither, Martin, Henderson & Blazek, P.C.
Huntsville, TX
Smitherman, Barry T. ...... Houston, TX
Smitherman, Carole C. ...... Birmingham, AL
Smitherman, Christopher J. ...... Bryan, TX
Smitherman, David B. ...... Clearwater, FL
Smitherman, Dianne ...... Birmingham, AL
Smitherman, E. Thomas, Jr.
Hot Springs National Park, AR
Smitherman, Geralyn G. ...... Washington, DC
Smitherman, L. Don ...... Oklahoma City, OK
Smitherman Law Firm, The, L.C.
Bossier City, LA
Shreveport, LA
Smitherman, Robert J. ...... Danville, VA
Smitherman, Shannon ...... Dallas, TX
Smitherman, Tanya Tyer ...... Dallas, TX
Smitherman, William C. ...... Tucson, AZ
Smitherman, William T. ...... Providence, RI
Smithern, Michelle A. ...... Akron, OH
Smithers, Barbara B. ...... Orlando, FL
Smithers, Barbara L. ...... Purchase, NY
Smithers, Brett ...... Ojai, CA
Smithers, Edward W. ...... San Jose, CA
Smithers, Eric Robert ...... Syracuse, NY
Smithers, F. Sydney, IV ...... Pittsfield, MA
Smithers & Jemela ...... New Braunfels, TX
Smithers Law Firm ...... San Jose, CA
Smithers, Michael B. ...... New Braunfels, TX
Smithers, Paul E. ...... San Diego, CA
Smithers, Roy O. ...... Austin, TX
Smithers, William S., Jr. ...... Richmond, VA
Smithey, Phyllis N.
United States International Trade
Commission,
Office of the General Counsel, GV
Smithey, Stephanie Alden
Indianapolis, IN
Smith-George, Deborah W.
Newport News, VA
Richmond, VA
Smith-George, Jonathan A.
Newport News, VA
Richmond, VA
Smith-Haszto, Kathleen A. ...... Chicago, IL
Smith-Hess, Iris ...... Los Angeles, CA
Smith-Hill & Bedell ...... Portland, OR
Smith-Hill, John ...... Portland, OR
Smith-Hill, Norma P. ...... Hempstead, NY
Smith-Hoffman, S. Jean ...... Brooklyn, NY
Smithies, Ronald H. ...... New York, NY
Smith Katz, Marni A. ...... Bridgeport, CT
Smith-Lalla, Lori ...... Miami, FL
Smith-Lee, Emily E. ...... Boston, MA
Smith Lee, Jennifer ...... Lafayette, LA
Smithline, Frederick E. ...... New York, NY
Smithline, Todd P. ...... Mountain View, CA
Smithline-Shirley, Janet ...... Milledgeville, GA
Saint Simons Island, GA
Smithline-Shirley, Janet, & Associates, P.C.
Milledgeville, GA
Saint Simons Island, GA
Smith-Malfatti, Jena ...... New Orleans, LA
SmithMidford, Robert A. ...... Richmond, VA
Smithmier, Dennis W. ...... Lawson, MO
Smithmier, Dennis W., P.C. ...... Lawson, MO
Smith-Miller, Judith Kristie ...... Jackson, MS
Vicksburg, MS
Smith-Mines, Lita ...... Commack, NY
Smith-Monahan, Richard W. ...... Cincinnati, OH
Smith-Pittman, Mabel H. ...... Chesapeake, VA
Smith-Rodrigue, L. Dawn
Baton Rouge, LA
Smith-Ross, Susan ...... Chicago, IL
Smith-Secret, Tijiuana R. ...... Omaha, NE
Smithson, Al ...... San Diego, CA
Smithson, Amy B. ...... Cincinnati, OH
Smithson, Andrew J. ...... Trenton, NJ
Smithson, Carol M.L. ...... Los Angeles, CA
Smithson, David E. ...... Madison, WI
Smithson, David M. ...... Los Angeles, CA
Smithson, Grant ...... Charlotte, NC
Smithson, Harry F. ...... Columbia, SC
Smithson, James L. ...... Boston, MA
Smithson, Jennifer A. ...... Universal City, CA
Smithson & Kardaras ...... San Diego, CA
Smithson, Lowell L. ...... Kansas City, MO
Smithson, Stephen W. ...... Morristown, NJ
Smithson, Thomas L. ...... Escanaba, MI
Smithson, William Charles ...... Topeka, KS
Smithson-Corl, Laura ...... Rochester, NH
Smith T, John W. ...... Birmingham, AL
Smith T, Mandi ...... Birmingham, AL
Smith-Tintor, Sarah Ann ...... Sandusky, OH
Smithton, W. Shane ...... Woodward, OK
Smith-Vaniz, W. Larry ...... Canton, MS
Jackson, MS
Smith-Ward, Kimberly A. ...... Baltimore, MD
Smith-Weiss, Brenda C. ...... Nashua, NH
Smithweiss, Erik D. ...... New York, NY
Smith-Weiss, Shepard & Durmer, P.C.
Nashua, NH
Smithwick & Belendiuk, P.C.
Washington, DC
Smithwick, Gary S. ...... Washington, DC
Smithwick, George T. ...... Danville, CA
Smith Williamson, Beverly
Tuscaloosa, AL
Smith-Woertz, Ardith R. ...... Topeka, KS
Smith-Yancey, Lindsay K. ...... Charleston, SC
Smith-Yancy, Lindsay K.
North Charleston, SC
Smithyman, Lee M. ...... Overland Park, KS
Smithyman & Zakoura, Chartered
Overland Park, KS
Smitke, Raymond ...... Port Charlotte, FL
Smitko & Gary, Law Offices of
Houma, LA
Smitko, Jerri G. ...... Houma, LA
Smits, Andrew A. ...... Newport Beach, CA
Smits, Annmarie P. ...... New York, NY
Smits, Anthony J. ...... Hartford, CT
Smits, Connie ...... Berlin, WI
Smits, G. William ...... Council Bluffs, IA
Smits, Kelly J. ...... Nashville, TN
Smits, Patricia Garity ...... Morristown, NJ
Smits, Pete A. ...... Austin, TX
Smits, Robert K. ...... New York, NY
Smits, Steven P. ...... Oshkosh, WI
Smits, Stuart L., & Assoc., A Prof. Law
Corp. ...... Sacramento, CA
Smits, Stuart Lansing ...... Sacramento, CA
Smitson, Patricia Mann ...... Cincinnati, OH
Smitten, John A. ...... Clearwater, FL
Smitter, Henry R. ...... Grand Rapids, MI
Smittkamp, James C. ...... Boulder, CO
Smittkamp, Walters & Farus, LLC
Boulder, CO
Smizik, Frank I. ...... Boston, MA
Smoak, Evan L. ...... New York, NY
Smoak, Gerald C. ...... Beaufort, SC
Smoak, Gerald C., Jr. ...... Walterboro, SC
Smoak, I. A., III ...... Walterboro, SC
Smoak, I. A., Jr. ...... Walterboro, SC
Smoak, Lewis Tyson ...... Washington, DC
Greenville, SC
Smoak, Marion H. ...... McLean, VA
Smoak, Pamela J. ...... Panama City, FL
Smoak, Richard ...... Panama City, FL
Smoak, Robert A., Jr. ...... Aiken, SC
Smock, C. Diane ...... Greenville, SC
Smock, Erica L. ...... Oregon City, OR
Smock and Etling ...... Terre Haute, IN
Smock, Henry C.
Charlotte Amalie, St. Thomas, VI
Smock, James F. ...... Sarasota, FL
Smock, Jon D. ...... Sacramento, CA
Smock, Julia Z. ...... Phoenix, AZ
Smock Law Offices, A Professional
Corporation
Charlotte Amalie, St. Thomas, VI
Smock, Morgan R. ...... San Francisco, CA
Smock, S. Bradford ...... Frankfort, KY
Smock, Thomas A. ...... Pittsburgh, PA
Smock, Thomas F. ...... Las Vegas, NV
Smock, Timothy R. ...... Phoenix, AZ
Smock and Weinberger ...... Phoenix, AZ
Smock, William, G. ...... Terre Haute, IN
Smodish, Michael P. ...... Boynton Beach, FL
Smodish, Susan D. ...... New York, NY
Smoger & Associates, P.C. ...... Oakland, CA
Dallas, TX
Smoger, Gerson H. ...... Oakland, CA
Smoger, Ilene J. ...... Dallas, TX
Smoger, Michael S. ...... La Mesa, CA
Smoger, Steven W. ...... Margate City, NJ
Smoke, Daniel W. ...... San Bernardino, CA
Smoke, G. Arthur, Jr. ...... Fresno, CA
Smoke, Gary S. ...... Jersey City, NJ
New York, NY
Smoke, Richard E. ...... Grand Rapids, MI
Smokelin, Jennifer A. ...... Pittsburgh, PA
Smoker, Constance M. ...... Lancaster, PA
Smoker, Jennafer M. ...... Washington, DC
Smoker, Marion R. ...... Phoenix, AZ
Smoker, Michael D. ...... Lancaster, PA
Smoker, Thomas R., & Associates
Waukegan, IL
Smokler, David N. ...... Huntington Woods, MI
Smokler, Henry S. ...... New York, NY
Smokler, Sandra K. ...... Burbank, CA
Smokler, Sanford ...... New York, NY
Smokowicz, Jan A. ...... Milwaukee, WI
Smola, Barnet ...... New Bedford, MA
Smola, Peter ...... New Bedford, MA
Smolak, Jan M. ...... Auburn, NY
Smolak, John T. ...... Boston, MA
Smolak, Mark E. ...... Portland, OR
Smolar, Curtis E. ...... San Francisco, CA
Smolar, Jessica Lieber ...... Pittsburgh, PA
Smolar, Kenneth ...... Pittsburgh, PA
Smolarek, Daniel Lawrence
Cheektowaga, NY
Smolarek, Mary Alice ...... Baltimore, MD
Smolarz, Roy B. ...... New York, NY
Smolek, Gary W. ...... St. Augustine, FL
Smolek, Jeffrey A. ...... Troy, MI
Smolek, Kristin Stiles ...... Troy, MI
Smolen, Donald E. ...... Tulsa, OK
Smolen, Gary F. ...... Omaha, NE
Smolen, Herbert ...... Philadelphia, PA
Smolen, Jack ...... Great Neck, NY
Smolen, James J. ...... Missouri City, TX
Smolen, Jason D. ...... Vienna, VA
Smolen, Lee M. ...... Chicago, IL
Smolen & Plevy P.C. ...... Washington, DC
Fairfax, VA
Vienna, VA
Smolen, Rebecca Rosenberger
Philadelphia, PA
Smolen, Robert M. ...... Mount Laurel, NJ
Smolen, Robin Beth
Federal Communications Commission,
Common Carrier Bureau, GV
Smolen, Stuart D. ...... Washington, DC
Smolen, Theodore F. ...... Waltham, MA
Smolen, Wendy Miller ...... Charlotte, NC
Smolens, Jack ...... Tarzana, CA
Smolens, Mark F. ...... Chicago, IL
Smolens, Robert M. ...... New York, NY
Smolenski, J. Robert ...... Grand Rapids, MI
Smolenski, Michael R. ...... Grand Rapids, MI
Smolenski, Raymond M. ...... Westbury, NY
Smolenski, Robert J. ...... Honolulu, HI
Smolenski, Sara J. ...... Grand Rapids, MI
Smolenski & Wooddell ...... Honolulu, HI
Smoler, Barry M.
Federal Energy Regulatory Commission,
Office of the General Counsel, GV
Smoler, Bruce J. ...... Miami, FL
Smoler, Robert J. ...... Chicago, IL
Smoler, Tedia K. ...... Waukesha, WI
Smoler, William ...... Madison, WI
Smolev, Richard G. ...... Chicago, IL
Smolev, Steven P. ...... Miami, FL
Smolev, Terence E. ...... Melville, NY
Mineola, NY
Smolevitz, Mindy K. ...... Woodbury, NY
Smoley, Lewis M. ...... Secaucus, NJ
Smoley, Robert A. ...... Miami, FL
Smoley, William A. ...... St. Cloud, MN
Smoliar, Burton B. ...... Kansas City, MO
Smolich, Andrew J. ...... Sacramento, CA
Smolik, Mark A. ...... Cleveland, OH
Smolin, David M. ...... Birmingham, AL
Smolin, Gerard, Jr. ...... San Diego, CA
Smolin, Michele ...... Cleveland, OH
Smolin, Stan ...... Long Beach, CA
Smolin, Vessela ...... Carlsbad, CA
Smolinski, Robert P. ...... Syracuse, NY
Smolinski, Thomas A. ...... Pittsburgh, PA
Smolinski, William A. ...... Syracuse, NY
Smolinsky, Joseph H. ...... New York, NY
Smolinsky, Paul D. ...... Bethesda, MD
Smolinsky, Sidney J. ...... Philadelphia, PA
Smolizza, Christian M. ...... New York, NY
Smoljanovich, Pamela ...... Weirton, WV
Smolk, Edward C. ...... Tallmadge, OH
Smolka, Christopher J. ...... Buffalo, NY
Smolka, Edward R. ...... New York, NY
Smolka, Eugene J. ...... Buffalo, NY
Smolka, Peter H. ...... Alexandria, VA
Smolker, David ...... Tampa, FL
Smolker, Jennifer Ann ...... El Segundo, CA
Smolker, Theodore I. ...... Madison, WI
Smolkin, Stanley A. ...... Long Beach, CA
Smolla, Rodney A. ...... Williamsburg, VA
Smollar, Paul R. ...... Washington, DC
Smollen, Jonathan A.
Federal Trade Commission,
Bureau of Consumer Protection, GV
Smollen, Lindasue ...... Boulder, CO

Smollens, Guralnick & Frazer
New York, NY
Smollens, Steven W. ... New York, NY
Smoller, Gerald J. ... Buffalo Grove, IL
Smoller, Jodi M. ... Northbrook, IL
Smoller, Jonathan L. ... Los Angeles, CA
Smoller, Kenneth J. ... Boston, MA
Smoller, Robert A. ... Chicago, IL
Smollett, C. Jean ... Lakewood, CO
Smollins, John F., Jr. ... Providence, RI
Smolnik, Danny M. ... Hartford, CT
Smolover, Deborah S. ... Department of Justice, Office of the Deputy Attorney General, GV
Smolow & Landis ... Trevose, PA
Smolow, Mitchell A. ... Hazleton, PA
Smolow, Ronald J. ... Trevose, PA
Smolowitz, Barry M. ... Kings Park, NY
Smolowitz, Sindee M. ... Laguna Beach, CA
Smolski, Robert J. ... Philadelphia, PA
Smolskis, Joseph V. ... Waterbury, CT
Smook, Naomi ... New York, NY
Smooke, Brian G. ... Atlanta, GA
Smooke, Michael G. ... Los Angeles, CA
Smookler, David A. ... Newton, MA
Smookler, Lynn M. ... Poughkeepsie, NY
Smoot, Alan L. ... Rapid City, SD
Smoot & Associates, P.C. ... Boston, MA
Smoot, Beth Y. ... Raleigh, NC
Smoot, C. Timothy ... Los Angeles, CA
Smoot, C. Timothy ... Torrance, CA
Smoot, Carolyn Bailey ... Marion, IL
Smoot, David E. ... Salt Lake City, UT
Smoot, Douglas A. ... Charleston, WV
Smoot, E. Brayton ... Washington, IN
Smoot, J. Tom, III ... Fort Myers, FL
Smoot, J. Tom, III, P.A. ... Fort Myers, FL
Smoot, James R. ... Valparaiso, IN
Smoot, John D. K. ... McLean, VA
Smoot, John E. ... Willits, CA
Smoot Law Office ... Rapid City, SD
Smoot, Oliver R., Jr. ... Washington, DC
Smoot, Paul J. ... San Mateo, CA
Smoot, Peter C. ... Los Angeles, CA
Smoot & Pitts ... Beaufort, SC
Hilton Head Island, SC
Smoot, Roland N. ... Los Angeles, CA
Smoot, Shelby W., (P.A.) ... Kingsport, TN
Smoot, Steven F. ... Boston, MA
Smoot, Steven M. ... Houston, TX
Smoot, Tom, Jr. ... Fort Myers, FL
Smoot, W. Davis ... Lancaster, PA
Smoot, Warren K. ... Phoenix, AZ
Smoot, William M.
Hilton Head Island, SC
Smoots, Carol A. ... Washington, DC
Smoots, Michael A., Jr.
Overland Park, KS
Smoots, Patricia K. ... Chicago, IL
Smoragiewicz, Edward R. ... Hartford, CT
Smorodsky, Myroslaw ... Rutherford, NJ
Smorodsky & Stawnychy, P.A.
Rutherford, NJ
Smoron, Michael J. ... Crystal Lake, IL
Smorto, Arnold D. ... Ebensburg, PA
Smorto, Persio, Webb & McGill
Ebensburg, PA
Johnstown, PA
Smotherman, Ira J., Jr. ... Atlanta, GA
Smotherman, Keena L. ... Austin, TX
Smotherman, Richard ... Guthrie, OK
Smothers, David A. ... Oakhurst, CA
Smothers, Paul J. ... Birmingham, MI
Smothers, Thomas W. ... High Point, NC
Smotkin, Howard S. ... St. Louis, MO
Smotrich, Thomas W. ... Tarzana, CA
Smouse, Dennis B. ... Omaha, NE
Smouse, Gregory R. ... Baltimore, MD
Towson, MD
Smouse, H. Russell ... Baltimore, MD
Towson, MD
Smouse, Randall Forsyth ... Baltimore, MD
Smouse, Scott ... Seattle, WA
Smout, Cheryl L. ... Department of Justice, Environment and Natural Resources Division, GV
Smoyer, Amy R. ... Kittanning, PA
Smoyer, Ann L. ... Helena, MT
Smoyer, Divonne ... Washington, DC
Smoyer, Stanley C. ... Princeton, NJ
Smrek, Carol A. ... New Hyde Park, NY
Smriga, John C. ... Bridgeport, CT
Smrtka, George M. ... Troy, MI
Smrtka, George M., P.C. ... Troy, MI
Smuck, John C. ... Washington, DC
Smucker, Conrad J. ... Washington, DC
Smucker, Donald W. ... Sarasota, FL
Smucker, Donald W., P.A. ... Sarasota, FL
Smucker, John E., II ... Lancaster, PA
Smucker, Steven R. ... Portland, OR
Smuckler, Elizabeth L. ... Los Angeles, CA
Smuckler, Gary S. ... Washington, DC
Smuda, Cynthia ... St. Louis, MO
Smuda, Marie Elayne ... Chicago, IL
Smukler, Ilisa J. ... Philadelphia, PA
Smukler, Joseph ... Philadelphia, PA
Smukler, K. Bennett ... Visalia, CA
Smukler, Larry M. ... Concord, NH
Smukler, Lisa Meltser ... Philadelphia, PA
Smukler, Richard C. ... Plymouth Meeting, PA
Smukler, Victor E. ... New York, NY
Smul, Spencer G. ... New York, NY
Smulian, Andrew M. ... Miami, FL
Smulkowski, Ziemowit T. ... Chicago, IL
Smull, Ronald E. ... Columbia, MO
Smullian, Ronald M.
Department of Transportation, Surface Transportation Board, GV
Smullin, Alix ... Swampscott, MA

Smullin, Wm. David ... Mountain View, CA
Smulow, Daniel I. ... Salem, MA
Smulow, Judith L. ... New York, NY
Smulowitz, William J. ... Kingston, PA
Smulyan, Yale H. ... San Francisco, CA
Smurl, Paul F. ... New York, NY
Smurr, Peter H. ... Carmichael, CA
Smurthwaite, Richard ... Eugene, OR
Smurthwaite, Richard G. ... Salt Lake City, UT
Smurzynski, Kenneth C. ... Washington, DC
Smurzynski, Thomas V. ... Boston, MA
Smutek, Richard B. ... Warren, MI
Smutny, Abby Cohen ... Washington, DC
Smutny, David F. ... Department of Justice, Antitrust Division, GV
Smyer, Connie L. ... Gilbert, AZ
Smyer, Joel P. ... Fort Worth, TX
Smyer, Marc Adam ... San Francisco, CA
Smyers, Robyn Minter ... New York, NY
Smyk, Bruce C. ... Binghamton, NY
Smyk, Smyk & Fahrenz, LLP
Binghamton, NY
Smyk, Stephen ... Binghamton, NY
Smyk, Stephen D. ... Binghamton, NY
Smykowski, Robert Allen ... Poway, CA
Smyle, Sue Ellen ... Costa Mesa, CA
Smyler, Denise J ... Philadelphia, PA
Smyler, Henry I. ... Miami, FL
Smyley, Kevin T. ... New York, NY
Smylie, Robert & Associates
Los Angeles, CA
Smylie, Robert E. ... Boise, ID
Smylie, Robert O. ... Los Angeles, CA
Smylie, Russell ... San Pedro, CA
Smylie, Sallie G. ... Chicago, IL
Smylie, Scott A. ... San Diego, CA
Smylie, Van Dusen & Magliozzi
San Diego, CA
Smyly, R. Carlton ... Birmingham, AL
Smyly, Terry R. ... Montgomery, AL
Smyre, Charles O. ... Denison, TX
Smyrl & Giddens ... Pasadena, TX
Smyrl, Peter J. ... Media, PA
Smyrl, R. Michael ... Pasadena, TX
Smyrniotis, George P. ... Chicago, IL
Smyrnos, George J., Jr. ... Yuba City, CA
Smyrski, Martha M. ... Montpelier, VT
Smyrski, Steven W. ... Los Angeles, CA
Smyser, Charles A. (Skip) ... Boise, ID
Parma, ID
Smyser, Craig ... Houston, TX
Smyser, Howard D. ... Burley, ID
Smyser, J. Andrew ... Harrisburg, PA
Smyser, James O. ... Department of Defense, Office of the General Counsel, GV
Smyser, Jay M. ... Chicago, IL
Smyser Kaplan & Veselka, L.L.P.
Houston, TX
Smyser, Kathryn Vanderbeck ... Houston, TX
Smyser, Susan Diane ... Azusa, CA
Smyth, Bernard B. ... Wilmington, NC
Smyth, Bruce T. ... Los Angeles, CA
Smyth, Damian B. ... San Francisco, CA
Smyth, Daniel J. ... Mount Holly, NJ
Smyth, Daniel T., Jr. ... Oak Brook, IL
Smyth, Daniel T., Jr., Ltd. ... Oak Brook, IL
Smyth, Deborah W. ... Gaithersburg, MD
Smyth & Devereux, P.C. ... Irvine, CA
Smyth, Donald A. ... Houston, TX
Smyth, Duncan ... Ann Arbor, MI
Smyth & Dunn ... La Crosse, WI
Smyth, Edmund J.M. ... Huntington, NY
Smyth, George H. ... Houston, TX
Smyth, Gerard A. ... Hartford, CT
Smyth, J. Douglas ... Amarillo, TX
Smyth, James E., II ... Las Vegas, NV
Smyth, Jeffrey A. ... Seattle, WA
Smyth, Jeffrey A., P.S. ... Seattle, WA
Smyth, Jerome E. ... Green Bay, WI
Smyth, Joan Stevens ... Sherman Oaks, CA
Smyth, John A., III ... Birmingham, AL
Smyth, John E. ... Stamford, CT
Smyth, John M. ... Downers Grove, IL
Smyth, John R. ... Cheyenne, WY
Smyth, Joseph ... Newark, NJ
Smyth, Joseph P. ... Fairfax, VA
Smyth, Justice D., III ... Tuscaloosa, AL
Smyth, Karen Ann ... Troy, MI
Smyth, Kristin M. ... Midvale, UT
Smyth & Lack ... Huntington, NY
Melville, NY
Smyth, Lisa ... Boston, MA
Smyth, Lorraine Kay ... Irvine, CA
Santa Ana, CA
Smyth, Maria M. ... Trenton, NJ
Smyth, Mark T. ... Luverne, AL
Smyth, Michael T. ... San Diego, CA
Smyth, Nigel S. ... Fairfax, VA
Smyth, Patrick H. ... Chicago, IL
Smyth, Paul B. ... Department Of The Interior, Office of the Solicitor, GV
Smyth, Raoul ... Irvine, CA
Smyth, Robert M. ... Cincinnati, OH
Smyth, Robert P. ... La Crosse, WI
Smyth, Robert V., II ... Nashville, TN
Smyth, Robert W., Jr. ... Chicago, IL
Smyth, Ross J. ... Charlotte, NC
Smyth, Sallee S. ... Houston, TX
Smyth, Sarah W. ... Olympia, WA
Smyth, Scott J. ... Austin, TX
Smyth and Smyth ... Fairfax, VA
Smyth, Stephen G. ... Phoenix, AZ
Smyth, Sue Cady ... Waukesha, WI
Smyth, Theodore B. ... Raleigh, NC
Smyth, Theresa A. ... Buffalo, NY
Smyth, Thomas A. ... Babylon, NY
Smyth, Todd R. ... Department of Labor, Office of Secretary, GV

Smyth, Todd W. ... Charleston, SC
Smyth, Vincent A. ... Huntington, NY
Smyth, William J. ... Kennebunk, ME
Smyth, W. O., Jr. ... Austin, TX
Smythe, Andrew C. ... Spokane, WA
Smythe, David M. ... Nashville, TN
Smythe, David R. ... Lynchburg, VA
Smythe, Ellen D. ... Arlington, VA
Smythe, Hebe R. ... Phoenix, AZ
Smythe, Henry B. ... Charleston, SC
Smythe, Henry B., Jr. ... Charleston, SC
Smythe, Julien R. ... Houston, TX
Smythe, Laura C. ... Appleton, WI
Smythe & Lee ... Waukegan, IL
Smythe, Lisa ... Boston, MA
Smythe, Lucy M. ... Perry, MI
Smythe, Marianne K. ... Washington, DC
Smythe, Marie T. ... Cleveland, OH
Smythe, Peter Christian ... Dallas, TX
Smythe, Robert M. ... Auburn, WA
Smythe & Smythe ... Auburn, WA
Smythe, Stacey L. ... Auburn, WA
Smythe, Susan M. ... Charleston, SC
Smythe, Terry J. ... Waukegan, IL
Smythe, Therese Trouche ... Charleston, SC
Smythers, Michael R. ... Norfolk, VA
Smyth-Mendoza, Shannon K.
Redwood City, CA
Smyth Rush, Mary-Ann ... London, KY
Smyton, James W. ... Buffalo, NY
Snabes, Mauraleen A. ... Charlevoix, MI
Snable, Anthony D. ... Birmingham, AL
Snaden, Sandra L. ... Simsbury, CT
Snader, Robert M. ... Los Angeles, CA
Snadon, Daryl N. ... Dallas, TX
Snaid, Leon J. ... San Diego, CA
Snaider, Andrés ... Houston, TX
Snaider, Benson A. ... New Haven, CT
Snaider, Benson A., P.C. ... New Haven, CT
Snair, William ... Royal Palm Beach, FL
Snaith, Phillip Harvey ... Fort Lauderdale, FL
Snakard, Charles R. ... Dallas, TX
Snakard, Stephen A. ... Chicago, IL
Skokie, IL
Snape, William J., III ... Washington, DC
Snapka, Kathryn ... Corpus Christi, TX
Snapp, Bryan A. ... Allentown, PA
Snapp, Cassandra A. ... West Palm Beach, FL
Snapp, David H. ... Dodge City, KS
Snapp, Donald R. ... Newton, KS
Snapp, Erik W. A. ... Chicago, IL
Snapp, Harvey J. ... Newton, KS
Snapp, Howard E. ... St. Clair Shores, MI
Snapp, Jeffrey C. ... Bellefontaine, OH
Snapp, Jon C. ... Washington, KS
Snapp, Kent ... Kansas City, MO
Snapp, Maribeth D. ... Oklahoma City, OK
Snapp, Mary E. ... Redmond, WA
Snapp, Randall J. ... Tulsa, OK
Snapp, Sandra ... Department of Commerce, Patent and Trademark Office, GV
Snapp, Sandra S. ... Greenville, SC
Snapp, Thomas A. ... Knoxville, TN
Snapp, Tina L. ... Department of Commerce, Patent and Trademark Office, GV
Snapp, William A. ... Houston, TX
Snapp, William D. ... Atlanta, GA
Snapp Danberg, Barbara ... Wilmington, DE
Snapper, Michael A. ... Grand Rapids, MI
Snare, Jonathan L. ... San Antonio, TX
Snare, Susan J. ... Dallas, TX
Snarr, Brian B. ... New York, NY
Snarr, George G., Jr. ... Winchester, VA
Snarr, Steven W. ... Salt Lake City, UT
Snarski, Eugene M. ... Waukegan, IL
Snarskis, John E. ... Portland, OR
Snarskis, Ruta S. ... Galveston, TX
Snashall, James G. ... New York, NY
Snashall, Robert C. ... Portland, OR
Snashall, Robert C., Jr. ... Department of Labor, Office of the Solicitor, GV
Snashall, Robert R., III ... Syracuse, NY
Snauffer, Mark W. ... Fresno, CA
Snavely, Brent A. ... Bloomfield Hills, MI
Snavely, Brent A., P.C.
Bloomfield Hills, MI
Detroit, MI
Snavely, David A. ... Holland, OH
Snavely, Donald V. ... Missoula, MT
Snavely, Ed ... Houston, TX
Snavely, Gordon A. ... Bloomfield Hills, MI
Bloomfield Hills, MI
Snavely, Gordon A., P.C.
Bloomfield Hills, MI
Snavely, Henry U. ... Orlando, FL
Snavely, Jeffrey D. ... Toledo, OH
Snavely, Joel M. ... Erie, PA
Snavely Law Firm ... Missoula, MT
Snavely, Luther M., III ... Las Vegas, NV
Snavely, Michael E. ... Columbus, OH
Snavely, Scott A. ... Tallahassee, FL
Snavely, Stephen K. ... Defiance, OH
Snavely, Stephen K., Co., L.P.A.
Defiance, OH
Napoleon, OH
Snavley, J. Trent ... Sidney, OH
Snead, Caren J. ... Deerfield Beach, FL
Snead, Charles D., Jr. ... Coeur d'Alene, ID
Snead, Charles G. ... King George, VA
Snead, Cozette ... Springfield, OH
Snead, George P. ... Fredericksburg, VA
Snead, Harry L., Jr. ... Richmond, VA
Snead, J. Lee ... Garden City, NY
Snead, James E. ... Santa Fe, NM
Snead, Janice L. ... Riverhead, NY
Snead, Jeffrey W. ... Dayton, OH
Snead, John A. ... Colonial Heights, VA
Snead, Kathleen Marie ... Denver, CO

Snead, Margaret Allison ... Mount Pleasant, SC
Snead, Margaret E. ... Bethesda, MD
Snead, Maxwell A., Jr. ... Denver, CO
Snead, Paul ... Roswell, NM
Snead & Promis ... Denver, CO
Snead, Rayner V. ... Washington, VA
Snead, Rayner V., Jr. ... Lynchburg, VA
Snead, Samuel A. ... Asheville, NC
Snead, Stephen H. ... Springfield, MO
Snead, W. David ... Washington, DC
Snead, Warren L. ... Greeneville, TN
Snead, William B., Jr. ... Roanoke, VA
Snead, William E., Law Office of
Albuquerque, NM
Snead, William G. ... Fairfax, VA
Snead, William O. P., III ... Fairfax, VA
Sneath, Henry M. ... Pittsburgh, PA
Sneath, Stan ... Conshohocken, PA
Sneath, Wm. Stanley ... Conshohocken, PA
Sneathen, Carl L. ... Doraville, GA
Sneathern, Charles D. ... Torrance, CA
Sneathern, Kenneth Andrew
East Prairie, MO
Sneberger, Nora E. ... Charlotte, NC
Sneckenberg, W. J., & Associates
Chicago, IL
Sneckenberg, William J. ... Chicago, IL
Sned, Pruitt, D'Angio & Tucker, P.A.
West Palm Beach, FL
Sned, William H., Jr.
West Palm Beach, FL
Snedaker, Robert H., III ... Columbus, OH
Sneddon, Emily ... Little Rock, AR
Sneddon, Thomas W., Jr. ... Santa Barbara, CA
Snedegar, Suzanne M. ... Bethesda, MD
Snedeker, Donnie E. ... Basking Ridge, NJ
Snedeker, James D. ... Hackensack, NJ
Snedeker, Larry H. ... Nashville, TN
Snedeker, Steven J. ... Brookfield, WI
Snedeker, William P. ... Highland Park, NJ
Sneden, Curtis S. ... Topeka, KS
Snediker, David E. ... Stamford, CT
Snee, Bryant G. ... Department of Justice, Civil Division, GV
Snee, Charles E., III ... Rochester, NY
Snee, Joseph F., Jr. ... Bel Air, MD
Snee, Tina L. ... Falls Church, VA
Sneed, Albert L., Jr. ... Asheville, NC
Sneed, Brenda D. ... Northbrook, IL
Sneed, Carl D. ... Herrin, IL
Sneed, Chelsea A. ... Los Angeles, CA
Sneed, Claude J., Jr. ... Bradenton, FL
Sneed, Dewitt T., Jr. ... Chattanooga, TN
Sneed, Earl R. ... Lubbock, TX
Sneed, George E. ... Oklahoma City, OK
Sneed, Horace Geoffrey
Treasury Department, Office of the Comptroller of the Currency, GV
Sneed, Hugh B. ... Jackson, MS
Sneed, James H. ... Washington, DC
Sneed, James L. ... Tulsa, OK
Sneed, Jason M. ... Overland Park, KS
Sneed, Jeffrey J. ... Atlantic Beach, FL
Sneed, Jerome E. ... Austin, TX
Sneed, Joe ... Austin, TX
Sneed, John P. ... Jackson, MS
Sneed, Joseph T. ... San Francisco, CA
Sneed, Julie K. ... Austin, TX
Sneed, Julie S. ... Tampa, FL
Sneed Lang, P.C. ... Tulsa, OK
Sneed, Letta F. ... Washington, DC
Sneed, Lucian Lamar ... Cumming, GA
Sneed, Maree F. ... Washington, DC
Sneed, Mary L. ... Orlando, FL
Sneed, Paul A. ... Finleyville, PA
Sneed, Rankin ... Huntsville, AL
Sneed, Richard D., Jr. ... Fort Pierce, FL
Sneed, Richard D., Jr., P.A.
Fort Pierce, FL
Sneed, Robert C. ... Austin, TX
Sneed, Robert W. ... Jackson, MS
Sneed, Ronald E. ... Black Mountain, NC
Sneed, Spencer C. ... Anchorage, AK
Sneed, Thomas Nelson ... Madisonville, KY
Sneed, Tracy L. ... Calabasas, CA
Sneed, Vine & Perry, a Prof. Corp.
Georgetown, TX
Austin, TX
Sneed, William C., Jr. ... Sacramento, CA
Sneed, William L. ... Pontotoc, MS
Sneed, William M. ... Chicago, IL
Sneed, William W. ... Topeka, KS
Sneed, Woodrow B.
Department Of The Interior, Bureau of Indian Affairs, GV
Sneeden, David G. ... Wilmington, NC
Sneeringer, Eugene M. ... Albany, NY
Ballston Spa, NY
Troy, NY
Sneeringer, Eugene M., Jr. ... Albany, NY
Ballston Spa, NY
Troy, NY
Sneeringer, Eugene M., Jr.
Saratoga Springs, NY
Sneeringer, Robert J. ... Albany, NY
Ballston Spa, NY
Sneeringer, Stephen G. ... St. Louis, MO
Sneeringer, Thomas M. ... Washington, DC
Sneff, Wendy Robin
Federal Deposit Insurance Corporation, Resolutions Section, GV
Sneider, Carol S. ... Boston, MA
Sneider, Glenn J. ... North Bay Village, FL
Sneider, James R. ... Northfield, IL
Sneider & Joyce, Law Offices of
Northfield, IL

Snow, Marcus L., Jr., P.A., Law Offices of ... Lakeland, FL
Orlando, FL
Tampa, FL
Snow, Mark H. ... Libertyville, IL
Snow, Mark P. ... Portland, ME
Snow, Martin B. ... Chicago, IL
Snow, Mary C. ... Denver, CO
Snow, Mary C ... Tampa, FL
Snow, Mary L. ... San Antonio, TX
Snow, Michael L. ... Minneapolis, MN
Snow, Nancy J. ... Portland, OR
Snow, Norman S. ... Fort Wayne, IN
Snow, Nuffer, Engstrom, Drake, Wade & Smart, A Professional Corporation ... St. George, UT
Salt Lake City, UT
Snow, P. Thomas ... Richmond, IN
Snow, Paul V. ... New Smyrna Beach, FL
Snow, Peter G. ... Burley, ID
Snow, Phil, Jr. ... Houston, TX
Snow, Phyllis F. ... Detroit, MI
Snow, R. Brian ... Nashua, NH
Snow, Ralph C., Jr. ... Savannah, GA
Snow, Ralph M., Jr. ... Athens, GA
Snow, Randall G. ... Department of the Air Force, Office of the Judge Advocate General, GV
Snow, Randolph L. ... Canton, OH
Snow, Randy L. ... Murfreesboro, TN
Snow, Raymond A. ... Somerville, MA
Snow, Raymond M. ... Fremont, CA
Snow, Raymond P., Jr. ... Sylvania, OH
Snow, Rebecca ... Washington, DC
Snow, Richard A. ... Atlanta, GA
Snow, Richard A. ... Chicago, IL
Snow, Robert Bruce ... Brooksville, FL
Snow, Robert Bruce, P.A. ... Brooksville, FL
Snow, Robert F. ... Department Of The Interior, Office of the Solicitor, GV
Snow, Robert H. ... Chicago, IL
Snow, Rod W. ... Denver, CO
Snow, Rodney G. ... Salt Lake City, UT
Snow, Roman J. ... Grand Rapids, MI
Snow, Ronald J. ... Denver, CO
Snow, Ronald L. ... Concord, NH
Snow & Sauerteig ... Fort Wayne, IN
Snow & Skager ... High Point, NC
Snow & Snow ... Los Angeles, CA
Snow & Snow ... Provincetown, MA
Snow & Snow ... Astoria, OR
Snow & Snow, Ltd. ... Chicago, IL
Snow, Stanley Howard ... Calverton, MD
Snow, Stephen E. ... Tuscaloosa, AL
Snow, Stephen L. ... Santa Clarita, CA
Snow, Steven E. ... Providence, RI
Snow, Steven E. ... St. George, UT
Snow, Steven T. ... Boston, MA
Snow, Stuart W. ... Florence, SC
Snow, Susan ... Bridgeview, IL
Snow, Susan Chester ... Signal Mountain, TN
Snow, Terri Murrell ... Hoover, AL
Snow, Terry L. ... Davenport, WA
Spokane, WA
Snow, Terry N. ... Cumberland Center, ME
Snow, Terry N., P.A. ... Cumberland Center, ME
Snow, Thomas A. ... Tampa, FL
Snow, Thomas G. ... Department of Justice, Criminal Division, GV
Snow, Tom M. ... Dallas, TX
Terrell, TX
Snow, Tower C., Jr. ... San Francisco, CA
Snow, V. Lowry ... St. George, UT
Snow, Vernon L. ... Provo, UT
Snow, Vicki L. ... Atlanta, GA
Snow, W. Prentice ... Newark, OH
Snow, Wayne B. ... Oklahoma City, OK
Snow & Whitworth ... Angleton, TX
Houston, TX
Snow, Windell G. ... Wichita, KS
Snow, Windell G., P.A. ... Wichita, KS
Snow, Zachary ... New York, NY
Snowden, Alison Welles ... McLean, VA
Snowden, Andrea Dylan ... Lincoln, NE
Snowden, Arthur H., II ... Anchorage, AK
Snowden, Barry H. ... Houston, TX
Snowden, Bradley C. ... Martinsburg, WV
Snowden, C. Franklin, III ... Montgomery, AL
Snowden, Esther Ann ... Sequim, WA
Snowden, Greg ... Meridian, MS
Snowden, Howard L. ... Quincy, IL
La Grange, MO
Snowden, J. Bayard, III ... Memphis, TN
Snowden, J. Raymond ... Columbus, OH
Snowden, James A. ... Lincoln, NE
Snowden, James H. ... Quincy, IL
La Grange, MO
Snowden, John R. ... Lincoln, NE
Snowden, Kelly J. ... San Francisco, CA
Snowden, L. R. ... Detroit, MI
Snowden, Margaret M. ... Burlingame, CA
Snowden, Mike ... Fort Lauderdale, FL
Snowden, Pamela E. ... Los Angeles, CA
Snowden, Peter A. ... Westlake Village, CA
Snowden, Phillip H. ... Kansas City, MO
Snowden, Randolph F. ... Napa, CA
Snowden & Snowden ... Quincy, IL
La Grange, MO
Snowden, Susan R. Stuckey ... Martinsburg, WV
Snowden, W. Scott ... Napa, CA
Snowden, William G. ... Forrest City, AR
Snowdon, Andrew L. ... Securities and Exchange Commission, Division of Enforcement, GV
Snowdon, H. Taft, Jr. ... Federal Communications Commission, Mass Media Bureau, GV
Snowdon, John A., Jr. ... Pompton Plains, NJ
Snowdon, Marlee Adams ... Houston, TX
Snowdon, Richard W., III ... Washington, DC
Snowdy, J. Sterling ... La Place, LA
Snowe, Alan M. ... Hicksville, NY
Snowfield, John ... St. Paul, MN
Snowiss, Alvin L. ... Lock Haven, PA
Snowiss, Steinberg & Faulkner, LLP ... Lock Haven, PA
Snowman, M. Stanley ... Millinocket, ME
Snowman, Stacy ... San Francisco, CA
Snoxell, James E. ... Minneapolis, MN
Snuffer, Denver C., Jr. ... Sandy, UT
Snuggs, Charles C. ... Lubbock, TX
Snuggs, M. Ann ... Washington, DC
Snuggs, Wayne M. ... Jackson, MS
Snukals, Arnold B. ... Richmond, VA
Snukals, Beverly W. ... Richmond, VA
Snure, Clark B. ... Des Moines, WA
Snure, Michael J. ... Winter Park, FL
Snurkowski, Carolyn M. ... Tallahassee, FL
Snyder, A. Margaret S. ... Pittsburgh, PA
Snyder, Adam G. ... Bellevue, WA
Snyder, Alan C. ... Laguna Hills, CA
Snyder, Alan M. ... New York, NY
Snyder, Alexander L.W. ... New York, NY
Snyder, Alge & Welch ... Ada, OH
Findlay, OH
Snyder, Allen C. ... San Diego, CA
Snyder, Allen R. ... Washington, DC
Snyder, Allison A. ... New York, NY
Snyder, Allison J. ... Houston, TX
Snyder, Amy ... Washington, DC
Snyder, Amy H. ... Davenport, IA
Dallas, TX
Snyder, Amy Miller ... Greenville, SC
Snyder, Andrea ... Philadelphia, PA
Snyder, Andrea W. ... Portland, OR
Snyder, Andrew C. ... Englewood, CO
Snyder, Andrew W. ... Scottsbluff, NE
Snyder, Ann E. ... Kingwood, WV
Snyder, Ann L. ... Akron, OH
Snyder, Arthur ... Edina, MN
Snyder, Arthur I. ... Miami, FL
Snyder, Arthur K. ... Los Angeles, CA
Snyder, Arthur R. ... Dallas, TX
Snyder Associates ... Cleveland, OH
Snyder & Associates, P.A. ... Wilmington, DE
Snyder, Barry C. ... Greensboro, NC
Snyder, Barry Clifford ... Santa Barbara, CA
Snyder, Barry M. ... North Miami Beach, FL
Snyder, Barry M., P.A. ... North Miami Beach, FL
Snyder, Bayard J. ... Wilmington, DE
Snyder, B. B., Jr. ... Santa Cruz, CA
Snyder, Benjamin N. ... Charleston, WV
Snyder, Bernard ... Fairfield, CT
Snyder, Bernard A. ... La Grange, IL
Snyder, Bertram E. ... Boston, MA
Snyder, Beryl L. ... Elmwood Park, NJ
Snyder, Bradley A. ... Encino, CA
Snyder, Bradley L. ... Columbus, OH
Snyder, Brent C. ... Seattle, WA
Snyder, Brock R. ... Topeka, KS
Snyder, Bruce D. ... Glendale, CA
Snyder, Bruce H. ... Roseland, NJ
Snyder, Bruce R. ... Fort Wayne, IN
Snyder, Bryan R., (A Professional Corporation) ... Costa Mesa, CA
Los Angeles, CA
San Diego, CA
Snyder, Burt L. ... Honolulu, HI
Snyder, Burt L., A Law Corporation ... Honolulu, HI
Snyder, Burton H. ... Hershey, PA
Snyder, Carroll E. ... Danville, IL
Snyder, Cathi Cozen ... Philadelphia, PA
Snyder, Chad A. ... Minneapolis, MN
Snyder, Charles A., (P.C.) ... New Orleans, LA
Snyder, Charles C. ... Oak Brook, IL
Snyder, Charles Edward ... Bethany, OK
Snyder, Charles L., Jr. ... Steubenville, OH
Snyder, Charles R. ... Bellingham, WA
Snyder, Charles V., Jr. ... Denver, PA
Lancaster, PA
Snyder, Charles W. ... Savannah, GA
Snyder, Charles W. ... Madison, WI
Snyder, Christie L. ... Seattle, WA
Snyder, Christina A. ... Los Angeles, CA
Snyder, Christopher John ... Cincinnati, OH
Snyder, Clark L. ... Indianapolis, IN
Snyder, Clarke, Fouts & Associates ... Waukegan, IL
Snyder, Clement H., Jr. ... Preston, MN
Snyder, Clifford Eugene, Jr. ... Frederick, MD
Snyder, Constance A. ... Toledo, OH
Snyder, Cornelius & Hunter ... Pleasant Hill, CA
Snyder, Craig J.J. ... New York, NY
Snyder, Craig M. ... Provo, UT
Snyder, Craig R. ... Addison, NY
Snyder, D. James ... Oldsmar, FL
Snyder, D. Joseph ... New Bern, NC
Snyder, Daniel ... Portland, OR
Snyder, Daniel C. ... Washington, DC
Snyder, Daniel F. ... Park Falls, WI
Snyder, Daniel G. ... Lehighton, PA
Snyder, Daniel M. ... Ada, OH
Findlay, OH
Snyder, Darin W. ... San Francisco, CA
Snyder, David A. ... Voorhees, NJ
Snyder, David B. ... Dillingham, AK
Snyder, David B. ... Cincinnati, OH
Snyder, David B. ... Philadelphia, PA
Snyder, David F. ... Washington, DC
Snyder, David K. ... Stillwater, MN
Snyder, David L. ... Morris, CT
Snyder, David L. ... Baltimore, MD
Snyder, David L. ... Buffalo, NY
Snyder, David L. ... New York, NY
White Plains, NY
Snyder, David M. ... Tampa, FL
Snyder, David M. ... Clinton, NJ
Snyder, David M., P.A., Mediation & Law Offices of ... Tampa, FL
Snyder, David R. ... San Diego, CA
Snyder, David S. ... Washington, DC
Snyder, David S. ... Southfield, MI
Snyder, David V. ... Cleveland, OH
Snyder, David W. ... Pittsburgh, PA
Snyder, Dean E. ... Northfield, IL
Snyder, Debbie C. ... St. Louis, MO
Snyder, Deborah J. ... Los Angeles, CA
Snyder, Deborah K. ... New Haven, CT
Snyder, Debra S. ... Philadelphia, PA
Snyder, Dominique ... Los Angeles, CA
Snyder, Donald E. ... Henrietta, NY
Snyder, Donald E., Jr. ... Lowville, NY
Snyder, Donald J. ... New Hartford, NY
West Winfield, NY
Snyder, Donald J., Jr. ... Latrobe, PA
Philadelphia, PA
Snyder, Donald W. ... Slatington, PA
Snyder, Donn L. ... Harrisburg, PA
Snyder, Donna J. ... Ann Arbor, MI
Snyder, Donna L. ... Dallas, TX
Snyder, Donovan C. ... Salt Lake City, UT
Snyder, Dorothy M. ... Penn Valley, CA
Snyder, Douglas B. ... Rockville, MD
Snyder, Douglas J. ... Miami, FL
Snyder, Douglas J. ... Fairfax, VA
Snyder, Douglas P. ... Los Angeles, CA
Snyder, E. Kenneth ... Seattle, WA
Snyder, Edgar M. ... Pittsburgh, PA
Snyder, Edward A. ... Chicago, IL
Snyder, Edward A. ... Chattanooga, TN
Snyder, Edward C. ... McAllen, TX
Snyder, Edward J. ... Department of Justice, Tax Division, GV
Snyder, Edward J. ... West Seneca, NY
Snyder, Edward L. ... Holland, OH
Snyder, Edward M., Jr. ... Dallas, TX
Snyder, Edward S. ... Roseland, NJ
Snyder, Edwin L. ... Brookville, PA
Snyder, Edwin M. ... Dallas, TX
Snyder & Ek, S.C. ... Oconomowoc, WI
Snyder, Elisabeth M. ... Boston, MA
Snyder, Ellen K. ... Annandale, VA
Snyder, Emanuel Philip ... McLean, VA
Snyder, Emmor F. ... Girard, OH
Snyder, Eric J. ... Westbury, NY
Snyder, Eric J., (P.C.) ... St. Louis, MO
Snyder, Ervin D. ... Wiscasset, ME
Snyder, Eufrona A. ... Irvine, CA
Snyder, Eugene I. ... Des Plaines, IL
Snyder, Evan Harrison ... Philadelphia, PA
Snyder, Frances E. ... Washington, DC
Snyder, Frank V. ... Greenwich, CT
Snyder, Franklin Bliss ... Evanston, IL
Snyder, Frederick E. ... Cambridge, MA
Snyder, Frederick R., Jr. ... Miami, FL
Snyder, Fredrick R. ... Reading, PA
Snyder, G. Joseph ... Cameron Park, CA
Snyder, Gail R. ... Boston, MA
Snyder, Gary A. ... Dayton, OH
Snyder, Gary E. ... Atlanta, GA
Snyder, Gary J. ... Burlington, IA
Snyder, Gary P. ... Walnut Creek, CA
Snyder, Gary P. ... Olive Branch, MS
Snyder, Gay H. ... Brooklyn, NY
Snyder, Gayle L. ... Cuyahoga Falls, OH
Snyder, Geoffrey W. ... Jackson, MI
Snyder, George B. ... New York, NY
Snyder, George E. ... Bloomfield Hills, MI
Detroit, MI
Snyder, George E., Jr. ... Hagerstown, MD
Snyder, George L., Jr. ... Buffalo, NY
Snyder, George M. ... Orange, CA
Snyder, George T. ... Pittsburgh, PA
Snyder, George W. K., Jr. ... Atlanta, GA
Snyder, Gerald C., Jr. ... Waukegan, IL
Snyder, Gerard J. ... Dolgeville, NY
Snyder, Giles D. H. ... Charleston, WV
Snyder, Gina R. ... Atlanta, GA
Snyder, Glen W. ... Elkins Park, PA
Snyder, Glenn ... Arlington, VA
Snyder, Glenn Q. ... San Francisco, CA
Snyder, Gordon B. ... Raymond, NH
Snyder, Gregory C. ... Environmental Protection Agency, Office of Enforcement and Compliance Assurance, GV
Snyder, Gregory M. ... Manchester, PA
Snyder, Gregory T. ... Crystal Lake, IL
Snyder, Guy E. ... Chicago, IL
Snyder, H. Ralph, Jr. ... Thousand Oaks, CA
Snyder, Hancock & Ashworth, A Professional Corporation ... South Pasadena, CA
Snyder, Harold W. ... Marina Del Rey, CA
Snyder, Harris W. ... Crawford, NE
Snyder, Harry D. ... Saratoga Springs, NY
Snyder, Harry G. ... Waukesha, WI
Snyder, Harry M. ... San Francisco, CA
Snyder, Harry M., Jr. ... Arlington, VA
Snyder & Hassig ... New Martinsville, WV
Snyder, Helene M. ... Chicago, IL
Snyder, Henry K. ... Greenwich, CT
Snyder, Herbert C., Jr. ... Fort Wayne, IN
Snyder, Herman ... Boston, MA
Providence, RI
Snyder, Hilarie E. ... Baltimore, MD
Snyder, Hillary L. ... Portland, OR
Snyder, H. L. ... Charleston, WV
Snyder, Howard A. ... Encino, CA
Snyder, Howard J. ... New York, NY
Snyder, Howard M. ... Phoenix, AZ
Snyder, Howard R. ... Hauppauge, NY
Snyder, Howard T. ... Jacksonville, FL
Snyder, Irvin J. ... Camden, NJ
Snyder, J. Dudley ... New Braunfels, TX
Snyder, J. Jared ... Albany, NY
Snyder, J. Kevin ... Los Angeles, CA
Snyder, Jack H. ... Moreno Valley, CA
Orange, CA
Snyder, Jack R. ... Indianapolis, IN
Snyder, Jacob N. ... Philadelphia, PA
Snyder, James A. ... Kansas City, MO
Snyder, James A. ... Murray Hill, NJ
Snyder, James B. ... St. Louis, MO
Snyder, James C. ... Indianapolis, IN
Snyder, James C., Jr. ... Atlanta, GA
Snyder, James D. ... Clifton Forge, VA
Snyder, James Eugene, Jr. ... Lexington, NC
Snyder, James G. ... Saratoga Springs, NY
Snyder, James H., Jr. ... Maryville, TN
Snyder, James L. ... Chagrin Falls, OH
Snyder, James M. ... Chicago, IL
Snyder, James M. ... Reading, PA
Snyder, James N. ... Lawrence, KS
Snyder, James R. ... Cedar Rapids, IA
Snyder, James R. ... Charleston, WV
Snyder, James T. ... Syracuse, NY
Snyder, James W. ... Appleton, WI
Snyder, Jason ... New York, NY
Snyder, Jean Maclean ... Chicago, IL
Snyder, Jeffrey A. ... Palo Alto, CA
Snyder, Jeffrey D. ... Dayton, OH
Snyder, Jeffrey D. ... Philadelphia, PA
Snyder, Jeffrey F. ... Neenah, WI
Snyder, Jeffrey L. ... Washington, DC
Snyder, Jeffrey L. ... Troy, MI
Snyder, Jeffrey M. ... Bethesda, MD
Snyder, Jennifer A. ... New York, NY
Snyder, Jennifer C. ... Boston, MA
Snyder, Jennifer R. ... New York, NY
Snyder, Jerome F. ... Las Vegas, NV
Snyder, Jerry A. ... Allentown, PA
Snyder, Jerry L. ... Lincoln, NE
Snyder, Jerry M ... Reno, NV
Snyder, Jerry N. ... Denver, CO
Snyder, Jill Aranson ... Chicago, IL
Snyder, Jill R. ... Rockville, MD
Snyder, Jill R. ... Bethlehem, PA
Snyder, Jim C. ... Seattle, WA
Snyder, Joan P. ... Portland, OR
Snyder, Joe L. ... Shelton, WA
Snyder, John A. ... Decatur, GA
Snyder, John A. ... State College, PA
Snyder, John A., II ... New York, NY
Snyder, John B. ... Winnetka, IL
Snyder, John C. ... Berwyn, PA
Snyder, John D. ... West Chester, PA
Snyder, John G. ... Boston, MA
Snyder, John H. ... Rutherfordton, NC
Snyder, John J. ... Atlanta, GA
Snyder, John, Jr. ... Norwalk, CT
Snyder, John L. ... Chicago, IL
Snyder, John L. ... Kansas City, MO
Snyder, John M. ... Washington, DC
Snyder, John O. ... Milford, DE
Snyder, John R. ... Boston, MA
Snyder, John S. ... Pullman, WA
Snyder, Jon H. ... Charleston, WV
Snyder, Joseph M. ... Syracuse, NY
Snyder, Joseph P. L. ... Atlanta, GA
Snyder, Joseph R. ... Pasadena, CA
San Francisco, CA
Snyder, Joy Irving ... Kansas City, MO
Snyder, Judy Danelle ... Portland, OR
Snyder, Julie E. ... Philadelphia, PA
Snyder & Jumper ... Wiscasset, ME
Snyder, Kathryn M. ... Rochester, MN
Snyder, Kathy L. ... Morgantown, WV
Snyder, Kay R. ... St. Cloud, MN
Snyder, Keith D. ... Brookeville, MD
Snyder, Keith S. ... Asheville, NC
Snyder, Kenneth F. ... Cincinnati, OH
Cleveland, OH
Snyder, Kent G. ... Irvine, CA
Snyder, Kent V. ... Portland, OR
Snyder, Kevin J. ... Saratoga Springs, NY
Snyder, Kiley, Toohey & Corbett, LLP ... Saratoga Springs, NY
Snyder, King C. ... Tempe, AZ
Snyder, Klaus O. ... Sumner, WA
Snyder, Klaus O., P.S. ... Sumner, WA
Snyder, Kristin A. ... San Jose, CA
Snyder, L. Miles ... Sacramento, CA
Snyder, Larry H. ... Columbus, OH
Snyder, Larry R. ... Dayton, OH
Snyder, Laurence R. ... Cleveland, OH
Snyder, Laurie A. ... Arlington, VA
Snyder, Lawrence A. ... Los Angeles, CA
Snyder, Lawrence G. ... Southfield, MI
Snyder, Leah Meshelle ... Fort Myers, FL
Snyder, Lee Ann ... Encino, CA
Snyder, Lee H. ... Philadelphia, PA
Snyder, Lee M. ... Baltimore, MD
Snyder, Leonard A. ... Rochester, NY
Snyder, Leonard R. ... College Park, MD
Snyder, LeRoy, Jr. ... Fresno, CA
Snyder, Leslie B., Jr. ... Lafayette, CA
Snyder, Leslie C. ... New York, NY
Snyder, Leslie I. ... Coral Gables, FL
Miami, FL

Soberman & Rosenberg .... Edgewater, NJ
Lake Success, NY
Soberman, Stuart L. .... Fairfax, VA
Sobers, Sharon .... Cincinnati, OH
Sobetzer, John G. .... Plymouth, NH
Sobhan, Zafar .... **New York, NY**
Sobhani, Koorosh .... Bethesda, MD
Sobie, Merril .... White Plains, NY
Sobie, Rebecca J. .... **San Bernardino, CA**
Sobien, Wayne J. .... Winter Springs, FL
Sobieraj, Jacob L. .... Detroit, MI
Sobieraj, James R. .... **Chicago, IL**
Sobieraj, Ronald E. .... New London, CT
Sobieski, James L. .... Los Angeles, CA
Sobieski, John .... **Los Angeles, CA**
Sobieski, John L., Jr. .... Knoxville, TN
Sobieski, Messer & Associates
Knoxville, TN
Sobieski, Ralph P. .... Berea, OH
Sobieski, Wanda G. .... **Knoxville, TN**
Sobiloff, Elfriede F. .... Millbrae, CA
Sobiloff, Stephen .... Topeka, KS
Sobin, Carole .... **New York, NY**
Sobin, Clifford B. .... Gaithersburg, MD
Sobin, Louise .... Roslyn Heights, NY
Sobin, Sturgis M. .... **Washington, DC**
Sobkiewicz, Erik .... **Pittsburgh, PA**
Sobkoviak, Amie M. .... Plainfield, IL
Sobkowski, Gregory A. .... **Merrillville, IN**
Portage, IN
Sobkowski, Mary H. .... Portland, OR
Soble, Elaine K. .... Highland Park, IL
Soble, H. David .... Alexandria, VA
Soble International Law PLLC
Washington, DC
Soble, James B. .... **Tampa, FL**
Soble, Jeffrey A. .... **Chicago, IL**
Soble, Kenneth H. .... Chestnut Hill, MA
Soble, Marc S. .... **Mission Viejo, CA**
Soble, Mark R. .... Sacramento, CA
Soble, Marlena J. .... Waltham, MA
Soble, Peter M. .... Rock Island, IL
Soble, Richard A. .... Detroit, MI
Soble, Richard S. .... **Detroit, MI**
Soble, Stephen M. .... Washington, DC
Soble, Stephen M. .... San Antonio, TX
Soble, VanDam & Berenson
Chestnut Hill, MA
Soblick, Martin D. .... San Diego, CA
Sobnosky, Edward N. .... Youngstown, OH
Sobo, Aryn J. .... **New York, NY**
Sobo, Gary M. .... Middletown, NY
Sobo & Levine .... Fort Lauderdale, FL
Sobo, Theodore P. .... Fort Lauderdale, FL
Sobocinski, Edward Z. .... **Hockessin, DE**
Sobocinski, Eric J. .... **Durham, NC**
Sobocinski, Joseph S. .... New York, NY
Sobocinski, Michelle A. .... **Milwaukee, WI**
Sobocinski, Nancy L. .... Orange, CT
Sobocinski, Sandra M. .... Milwaukee, WI
Soboda, Robert J. .... Cumberland, RI
Soboeiro, John Anibal ...... Treasury Department, Office of the Comptroller of the Currency, GV
Sobol, Alan J. .... **Hartford, CT**
Sobol, Brian L. .... **Minneapolis, MN**
Sobol, Ellis J. .... Denver, CO
Sobol, Ephraim .... Paramus, NJ
New York, NY
Sobol, Gerald L. .... **New York, NY**
Sobol, I Harry .... Washington, DC
Sobol, Joanna .... **Los Angeles, CA**
Sobol, Lawrence R. .... **St. Louis, MO**
Sobol, Marjorie R.S. .... Eugene, OR
Sobol, Martin J. .... **Philadelphia, PA**
Sobol, Michael R. .... Eugene, OR
Sobol, Michael W. .... **San Francisco, CA**
Sobol, Neal H. .... Glendale, CA
Sobol, Neil L. .... **Dallas, TX**
Sobol, Paul R. .... Lombard, IL
Sobol, Peter B. .... New York, NY
Sobol, Richard B. .... Slidell, LA
Sobol, Robert N. .... **Philadelphia, PA**
Sobol, Thomas M. .... **Boston, MA**
Sobol, Yael Wohlberg .... Paramus, NJ
New York, NY
Sobolewski, Ann M. .... **Boston, MA**
Sobolewski, James M. .... **Sacramento, CA**
Sobolewski, John J. .... New York, NY
Sobolik, Blake S. .... **Hallock, MN**
Sobolik, Dennis M. .... **Hallock, MN**
Sobon, Wayne P. .... **Palo Alto, CA**
Soborski, Barbara K. .... Boston, MA
Sobota, David T. .... **Kirkland, WA**
Sobota, Henry F. .... **Syracuse, NY**
Sobota, John R. .... Wilkes-Barre, PA
Sobota, Raymond J. .... Wilkes-Barre, PA
Sobota, Stephen M. .... Madison, WI
Sobota, Thomas J. .... **Madison, WI**
Sobotik, John J. .... Madison, WI
Sobotka, Andrew L. .... Department of Justice, Tax Division, GV
Sobotka, David S. .... Reading, PA
Sobotka, Frank J. .... Cicero, IL
Sobotka, Victor D. .... Towson, MD
Sobotka, Virginia A. .... Dearborn, MI
Sobral, Germaine Wright .... Falls Church, VA
Sobral, Russell J. .... New Bedford, MA
Sobran, Thomas P. .... Hingham, MA
Sobran, Thomas P., P.C. .... Hingham, MA
Sobrino, Maria E. .... **Sunnyvale, CA**
Sobrino, Oswald P. .... Shaker Heights, OH
Sobul, David A. .... **San Francisco, CA**
Soby, Dayton E. .... **Minneapolis, MN**
Socarides, Richard C.
Executive Office Of The President, GV
Socarras, Michael P. .... **Kansas City, MO**
Socci, Donato .... Flushing, NY
Socci, Nicholas F. .... New City, NY
Socci, Robert A. .... **Houston, TX**
Soccio, E. Michael .... Riverside, CA
Socey, Rudolph A., Jr. .... **Trenton, NJ**
Socha, Alexa A. .... Long Beach, CA
Socha, Charles Q. .... **Denver, CO**
Socha, Daniel P. .... Chicago, IL
Socha, Francis M. .... Harrisburg, PA
Socha, George J., Jr. .... **Minneapolis, MN**
Socha, Jack A. .... Las Vegas, NV
Socha, Kenneth M. .... Washington, DC
Socha, Mark M. .... Simsbury, CT
Socha, Mary Antoinette
West Springfield, MA
Socha, Michael M. .... **Pittsburgh, PA**
Socha, Robert F. .... Linden, NJ
Socha, Stephen E. .... Fresno, CA
Sochacki, Christopher J. .... **Hartford, CT**
Sochacki, John B. .... Atlantis, FL
Sochaczewski, Morris .... Baltimore, MD
Sochanchak, Paul A. .... **Cherry Hill, NJ**
Sochats, Laverne L. .... Pittsburgh, PA
Socher, Cori L. .... Allenhurst, NJ
Sochia, David .... **Dallas, TX**
Sochin, Lori A. .... **Miami, FL**
Sochocki, Timothy D. .... **Ann Arbor, MI**
Sochor, Robert A. .... Florham Park, NJ
Sochynsky, Yaroslav .... **San Francisco, CA**
Socias, Manuel .... Orlando, FL
Socie, David G. .... **Washington, DC**
Sock, Arnold Forrest .... Los Angeles, CA
Sockbeson, Henry J. .... Ledyard, CT
Sockel, Christian P. .... **Reading, PA**
Sockett, Lisa R.
Federal Communications Commission, Office of Plans and Policy, GV
Sockett, Maureen Ann .... **New York, NY**
Sockett, Mitchell C. .... **Honolulu, HI**
Socknat, John D. .... **Washington, DC**
Sockol & Associates, P.A. .... **Clearwater, FL**
St. Petersburg, FL
Tampa, FL
Sockol, David J. .... **St. Petersburg, FL**
Sockol, Marc A. .... **Palo Alto, CA**
Sockowitz, Ira Mitchell
Department of Commerce, Office of the General Counsel, GV
Sockrider, Bolin, Anglin & Batte, A Professional Law Corporation
Bossier City, LA
Shreveport, LA
Sockrider, H. F., Jr. .... **Shreveport, LA**
Socks, Harold L. "Buddy"
San Antonio, TX
Sockwell, Christopher V.
Lawrenceburg, TN
Sockwell, W. Stephen, Jr.
Federal Trade Commission, Bureau of Competition, GV
Socol, Donna Kaner .... **Chicago, IL**
Socol, Randy .... **San Diego, CA**
Socolof, Joan E. .... Franklin Lakes, NJ
Socoloff, Irwin H.
National Labor Relations Board, Division of Administrative Law Judges, GV
Socoloff, Jane Ballenger
National Labor Relations Board, Office of Board Members, GV
Socolofsky, John H. .... Salem, OR
Socolov, Albert H. .... New York, NY
Socolow, Ari B. .... Atlanta, GA
Socolow, Ari B., P.C. .... Atlanta, GA
Socolow, Brian R. .... **New York, NY**
Socolow, John M. .... **New York, NY**
Socransky, Lisa E. .... Los Angeles, CA
Sod, Paul M. .... Woodmere, NY
Soda, Jennifer L. .... Philadelphia, PA
Soda, Rodney Lee, Law Offices of
Palm Desert, CA
Sodaro, Anselm .... Baltimore, MD
Sodaro, Jennifer Prager .... Oak Brook, IL
Sodaro, Kenneth J. .... Buffalo, NY
Sodd, Glenn A. .... **Corsicana, TX**
Dallas, TX
Soddy, Susan J .... Logan, OH
Sodeman, William A., Jr. .... Toledo, OH
Soden, Bruce G. .... **Syracuse, NY**
Soden, Denis F. .... Richmond, VA
Soden, Glenn W. .... Columbus, OH
Soden, Julie Morris .... San Diego, CA
Soden, Mark A. .... Corona Del Mar, CA
Soden, Mary Ann .... Long Beach, CA
Soden, Richard A. .... **Boston, MA**
Soden, Steven D. .... **Kansas City, MO**
Soder, Robert F. .... Madisonville, KY
Soderbeck, Pamela M. .... **Santa Monica, CA**
Soderberg, Ann Gottberg .... **Wichita, KS**
Soderberg, Darlene D. .... **Rockford, IL**
Soderberg, Elizabeth A. .... **Minneapolis, MN**
Soderberg, Geraldine M. .... **Campbell, CA**
Soderberg, Gregory V. .... **Atlanta, GA**
Soderberg, Harold J. .... Minneapolis, MN
Soderberg, James E. .... **Escanaba, MI**
Soderberg, Janet M. .... **Chicago, IL**
Soderberg, Jeffrey W. .... **Media, PA**
Soderberg, Jerome M. .... Mound, MN
Soderberg, John V. .... **Uniondale, NY**
Soderberg, Jon A. .... Washington, DC
Soderberg & Pittman .... Mound, MN
Soderberg, Roger K. .... Boston, MA
Soderberg, Scott H. .... Minneapolis, MN
Soderberg, Suzanne C. .... Florham Park, NJ
Soderberg, Thomas A. .... **Atlanta, GA**
Soderblom, Peter J. .... Allentown, PA
Soderbloom, Marc R. .... **Baraboo, WI**
Soderborg, Ray L. .... Sandy, UT
Soderborg, Robert B., Jr. .... Santa Barbara, CA
Sodergren, Arnold P. .... Simi Valley, CA
Sodergren, Daniel G. .... San Jose, CA
Sodergren, Harold G. .... San Francisco, CA
Sodergren, Thomas L. .... Jefferson City, MO
Soderholm, R. Erik .... Honolulu, HI
Soderholm, Robert G. .... Boston, MA
Soderland, David M. .... **Seattle, WA**
Soderland, Douglas R. .... **Seattle, WA**
Soderland Waechter, PLLC .... **Seattle, WA**
Soderling, Gail S. .... Warren, MI
Soderlund, David A. .... North Charleston, SC
Soderman, Anthony R. .... Minneapolis, MN
Soderman, Kenneth J. .... Darien, CT
Soderman, Paul J. .... West Orange, NJ
Soderna, Andrew P. .... **Chicago, IL**
Soderquist, Kirk A. .... **Bellevue, WA**
Soderquist, Larry D. .... **Nashville, TN**
Soderquist, Philip R. .... **San Francisco, CA**
Soderstedt, Jeffrey P. .... Lancaster, PA
Soderstrom, Edward H., II .... Chicago, IL
Soderstrom, Reed .... **Minot, ND**
Soderstrom, Robert S. .... **Chicago, IL**
Soderstrom, William R. .... **Milwaukee, WI**
Soderstrum, Brenton D. .... **Des Moines, IA**
Sodikoff, Robert N. .... **Chicago, IL**
Sodini, Gregg S. .... **Hackensack, NJ**
Sodini, Orlando R. .... **Pittsburgh, PA**
Sodini, Ronald P. .... Chicago, IL
Sodipe, Olukayode A. .... Burr Ridge, IL
Sodko, Jeffrey D. .... Atlanta, GA
Sodolak, Brian G. .... Sealy, TX
Sodolak, Michael E. .... Sealy, TX
Sodomsky, Allan L. .... Reading, PA
Sodonis, Arunas A .... Long Beach, CA
Sodono, Anthony, III .... Hackensack, NJ
Sodoro, Daly & Sodoro, P.C.
Council Bluffs, IA
Lincoln, NE
Omaha, NE
Papillion, NE
Sodoro, Emil F. .... **Omaha, NE**
Sodoro, John R. .... **Omaha, NE**
Sodos, Boris .... Menomonee Falls, WI
Sodos, Erving .... **San Francisco, CA**
Sodos & Kafkas, S.C. .... Milwaukee, WI
Sodos, Nadja S. .... **Washington, DC**
Sodos, Saul R. .... Mount Prospect, IL
Sodos, Sidney .... Milwaukee, WI
Sodowick, George Y. .... **Roseland, NJ**
Sodowsky, Elden R. .... Fairfax, VA
Soe, Garson C. .... San Ramon, CA
Soebbing, Ralph K. .... St. Louis, MO
Soebke, Bernard M. .... **Garden City, NY**
Soechting, Charles E. .... San Marcos, TX
Soeder, Arnold H. .... Buffalo, NY
Soeder, Lisa P. .... **Hartford, CT**
New York, NY
Soefje, Timothy B. .... **San Antonio, TX**
Soefker, Curt R. .... **Memphis, TN**
Soegeng, Jemy .... **Washington, DC**
Soehl, Harold J. .... St. Petersburg, FL
Soehle, Tracy Morse .... **Boston, MA**
Soehlig, Deborah Jo .... Chicago, IL
Soeiro, David V. .... New York, NY
Soeka, Eva M. .... Milwaukee, WI
Soelberg, Glenn B. .... Laguna Beach, CA
Soelberg, Scott L. .... **Salt Lake City, UT**
Soelling, Christopher J. .... **Seattle, WA**
Soelter, Wilfrid W. H. .... Upland, CA
Soenksen, Paul .... **Honolulu, HI**
Soennichsen, Eric W. .... Ballston Spa, NY
Soens, Roger J., Sr. .... Avalon, NJ
Soet, H. David .... Grand Rapids, MI
Soeten, Jan, Jr. .... Cleveland, OH
Sofaer, Abraham D. .... Palo Alto, CA
Sofaer, David A. .... **San Francisco, CA**
Sofelkanik, Victor R. .... West Los Angeles, CA
Sofen, Ronald S. .... **Los Angeles, CA**
Sofer, Avner D. .... **Parker, AZ**
Sofer, Joseph .... New York, NY
Soffa & Devitt .... Whitewater, WI
Soffa, JoAnna R. .... **Washington, DC**
Soffa, Sam J. .... Whitewater, WI
Soffar, Charles E. .... Houston, TX
Soffar, William D. .... Bellaire, TX
Soffen, Marvin C. .... **New York, NY**
Soffen, Stephen A. .... **Washington, DC**
Soffer, Adam M. .... **Minneapolis, MN**
Soffer, Benjamin E. .... **Santa Monica, CA**
Soffer, Howard H. .... Bensalem, PA
Soffer, Jennifer Anne .... Austin, TX
Soffer, Jonathan H. .... Mill Valley, CA
Soffer, Joseph .... New York, NY
Soffer, Lewis J. .... **Menlo Park, CA**
Soffer, Mary Beth (Ponte) .... **St. Louis, MO**
Soffer, Rachel E. .... **Minneapolis, MN**
Soffer, Robert J.
Federal Deposit Insurance Corporation, GV
Soffer, Sanford .... Albany, NY
Soffer, Steven I. .... Houston, TX
Soffer, Victor K. .... New York, NY
Sofferin, Lisa T. .... **Buffalo, NY**
Soffey, Douglas M. .... Garden City, NY
Soffian & Allen .... Haddonfield, NJ
Soffian, Gregory S. .... **Cherry Hill, NJ**
Soffian, Warren L. .... Haddonfield, NJ
Philadelphia, PA
Soffientini, Raymond J. .... **New York, NY**
Soffientini, Robert .... New York, NY
Soffietti, Johnson, Teegen, Phillips & Ortiz, Ltd. .... Fox Lake, IL
Soffin, Michael L. .... **Richmond, VA**
Soffin, Nicole E. .... **New York, NY**
Sofge, David P. .... **Miami, FL**
Sofia, Frank .... New York, NY
Sofield, Richard C.
Department of the Air Force, Office of the General Counsel, GV
Sofio, Margaret A. .... **Englewood, CO**
Sofocleous, Frank .... **Greenbelt, MD**
Sofocleous, Michael .... **Reston, VA**
Soforenko & Associates, P.C. .... Chicopee, MA
Soforenko, Joel .... Chicopee, MA
Soforenko, Marjorie S. .... Springfield, MA
Soforo, Federico .... El Paso, TX
Sofos, Evdokia .... New York, NY
Sofranko, George Bernard, Jr. .... Canfield, OH
Sofris, Michael N. .... Santa Monica, CA
Softcheck, Daniel J. .... **Joliet, IL**
Softcheck, John E. .... Batavia, IL
Softness, David R. .... **Miami, FL**
Softness, Michele B. .... Hackensack, NJ
Sogard, David B. .... Grand Forks, ND
Sogard, Patrick Oliver .... **Williston, ND**
Sogg, Nancy Walsh .... Cleveland, OH
Sogg, Wilton S. .... **Cleveland, OH**
Sogge, Eric .... **Portland, OR**
Sogge, Ronald R. .... St. Clair Shores, MI
Sogi, Francis Y. .... **New York, NY**
Sogi, J. James .... Kailua-Kona, HI
Soglin, Paul R. .... Madison, WI
Sogn, Jon C. .... **Sioux Falls, SD**
Sognier, John W. .... **Atlanta, GA**
Savannah, GA
Sogocio, Rico M. .... **Miami, FL**
Sogol, Joel L. .... **Tuscaloosa, AL**
Sogomonian, Aram M. .... Moreno Valley, CA
Soh, Kenneth S. .... **Houston, TX**
Soh, Suzanna J. L. .... New York, NY
Soha & Lang, P.S. .... **Seattle, WA**
Soha, Steven .... **Seattle, WA**
Sohagi, Margaret Moore .... **Los Angeles, CA**
Sohaili, Hushmand .... **Los Angeles, CA**
Sohaili, Masood .... **Los Angeles, CA**
Sohan, James P. .... Louisville, KY
Sohan, Patrick J. .... **Louisville, KY**
Sohcot and Jacks .... East Haven, CT
Sohigian, Michael R. .... Los Angeles, CA
Sohigian, Ronald M. .... Los Angeles, CA
Sohinki, Stephen M.
Department of Energy, GV
Sohl, Charles E. .... Hartford, CT
Sohl, John H. .... **Wahoo, NE**
Sohlgren, Eric C. .... **Irvine, CA**
Sohm, Keith E. .... Salt Lake City, UT
Sohm, Norbert H. .... Albany, KY
Sohmer, Alec G. .... Brockton, MA
Sohmer, Olivia .... New York, NY
Sohmer, Stephen M. .... **New York, NY**
Sohn, Alan E., Law Offices of .... **Chicago, IL**
Sohn, Andrew W. .... **Chicago, IL**
Sohn, Chang M. .... New York, NY
Sohn, Craig W. .... **Naples, FL**
Sohn, Daryl F. .... **St. Louis, MO**
Sohn, David .... Lawrence, NY
Sohn, David M. .... **Washington, DC**
Sohn, Garry D. .... **Freeport, NY**
Sohn, Gerald .... Jacksonville, FL
Sohn, Gigi B. .... Washington, DC
Sohn, Herbert .... Chicago, IL
Sohn, Howard Allan .... **Tavernier, FL**
Sohn, Howard, P.A. .... **Tavernier, FL**
Sohn, Ivy E. .... Wellesley, MA
Sohn, Jeremy .... **Wheeling, WV**
Sohn, John J. .... New York, NY
Sohn, Joshua S. .... **New York, NY**
Sohn, Michael N. .... **Washington, DC**
Sohn, Nancy .... Chicago, IL
Sohn, Richard Chongsoo .... **Kirkland, WA**
Sohn, Rina Leigh .... Tulsa, OK
Sohn, Robert D. .... San Antonio, TX
Sohn, William S. .... Hinsdale, IL
Sohn, Youngjin .... **New York, NY**
Sohnen, Barbara C. .... Denver, CO
Sohnen, Harvey .... Walnut Creek, CA
Sohngen, S. William, Jr. .... Bay Pines, FL
Sohnlein, Julie A. .... **Palm Springs, CA**
San Bernardino, CA
Sohns, Gregory E. .... **New York, NY**
Sohns, Robert C., Jr. .... Houston, TX
Sohon, Julian A., Jr. .... Fairfield, CT
Sohon, Michael C. .... Bridgeport, CT
Sohonage, Kirk Steven .... **Uniontown, PA**
Sohr, David J. .... Davenport, IA
Soibelman, Adam J. .... **Encino, CA**
Soicher, Lawrence G. .... New York, NY
Soiefer, Alan J. .... **New York, NY**
Soiefer, Hilary M. .... Scarsdale, NY
Soifer, Aviam .... West Hartford, CT
Soifer, Carl .... Philadelphia, PA
Soifer, Howard J. .... **Lansing, MI**
Soifer, Jan .... **Austin, TX**
Soifer, Jonathan P. .... **St. Louis, MO**
Soifer, Lawrence M. .... Albuquerque, NM
Soifer, Mark .... **Atlantic City, NJ**
Soifer, Michael D. .... Coconut Creek, FL
Soifer, Robert .... Oviedo, FL
Soiferman, Milton D. .... Philadelphia, PA
Soignet, Donald M. .... Metairie, LA
Soignet, Joseph S. .... Thibodaux, LA
Soignier, D. Brian .... Durango, CO
Soika, Helmut E. .... New York, NY
Soika, John J. .... Davis, CA
Soileau, Charles E. .... **Rayne, LA**
Soileau, Curtis L. .... Beaumont, TX
Soileau, Donald .... Mamou, LA
Soileau, Isaac H., Jr. .... **New Orleans, LA**
Soileau, John L. .... **Cocoa, FL**
Soileau Law Offices .... Mamou, LA
Soileau, Nicholas .... Mamou, LA
Soileau, Rudie R., Jr. .... Lake Charles, LA
Soileau, Steven E. .... **Shreveport, LA**
Soileau, W. Glenn .... Breaux Bridge, LA
Soilis, Fred C. .... Pittsburgh, PA
Soini, Wayne .... Boston, MA
Soiret, Jacques E. .... **Los Angeles, CA**
Soisson, Amy M. .... **Boston, MA**

Solloway, Cozata ....Stamford, CT
Solloway, Robert G. ....Indianapolis, IN
Sollows, William E. ....Dallas, TX
Solls, Joseph J. ....Peoria, IL
Solls, Mark A. ....Nashville, TN
Solman & Hunter, P.A. ....Caribou, ME
Solman, Richard D. ....Caribou, ME
Solman, Richard N. ....Caribou, ME
Solmen, Daniel J. ....Salem, OH
Solmi, Vicki R. ....Culver City, CA
Solmonson, Garry W. ....San Jose, CA
Solmonson, Sheldon C. ....Merced, CA
Solmonson, Steven J. ....New York, NY
Solmor, Deborah G. ....Chicago, IL
Solmor, Fran ....Irvine, CA
Solmor-Mordini, Jane ....Chicago, IL
Solms, Charles, III ....Bedford, NH
Solms, Charles, III, P.A. ....Bedford, NH
Solms & Price, P.A. ....Miami, FL
Solms, William O., Jr. ....Miami, FL
Solmson, William S. ....Memphis, TN
Solmssen, Arthur R. G. ....Philadelphia, PA
Solmssen, Arthur R.G., Jr.
Philadelphia, PA
Solmssen, Peter Y. ....Pittsfield, MA
Solner, Michael C. ....Van Nuys, CA
Solner, Robert J. ....Sylvan Lake, MI
Solnick, Jay L. ....Philadelphia, PA
Solnick, Nancy Neff ....Plymouth Meeting, PA
Solnick, Paul B. ....Plymouth Meeting, PA
Solnick & Solnick, LLC
Plymouth Meeting, PA
Solnik, Bernard A. ....Washington, DC
Solnit, Ben A. ....New Haven, CT
Solny, Sanford ....New York, NY
Solo, David H. ....Irvine, CA
Solo, Gail D., (A Professional Corporation)
Los Angeles, CA
Solo, Ian Noel ....Inglewood, CA
Solo, Julia A. ....New York, NY
Solo, Richard D. ....Longboat Key, FL
Solochek, Albert ....Milwaukee, WI
Solochek, Marc R. ....Huntington, WV
Solock, Mark W. ....Chicago, IL
Solod, Arnold S. ....Boston, MA
Solodar, Lenora Hoffer ....Richmond, VA
Solodar, Michael W. ....Richmond, VA
Solodar & Solodar ....Richmond, VA
Solodar, Todd E. ....Allentown, PA
Solodky, Barry A. ....Lancaster, PA
Solodky, Howard N. ....Washington, DC
Solof, Wendy M. ....Cherry Hill, NJ
Soloff, Alison F. ....Philadelphia, PA
Soloff, Donald M. ....Philadelphia, PA
Soloff, Donald M., P.C. ....Philadelphia, PA
Soloff, Harold A. ....Norwich, CT
Soloff, Michael E. ....Los Angeles, CA
Soloff, Peter J. ....Philadelphia, PA
Soloff, Randi J. ....Massapequa Park, NY
Soloff, Sharon B. ....New York, NY
Soloff, Stacey F. ....Miami, FL
Soloman, Carol L. ....Nashville, TN
Soloman, Howard M. ....Philadelphia, PA
Solome-Rodriguez, Joan V. ....New York, NY
Solomey, Joseph
Department of Transportation,
Federal Highway Administration, GV
Solomiany, Alex ....Miami, FL
Solomiany, Alex, P.A. ....Miami, FL
Solomiany, Marvin L. ....Atlanta, GA
Solomich, Thomas R. ....Pittsburgh, PA
Solomine, Anthony M. ....New Haven, CT
Solomita, Michael V. ....New York, NY
Solomito, John H. ....New Bedford, MA
Solomon, A. Bernard ....Charleston, SC
Solomon, Abner ....Miami, FL
Solomon, Alan M. ....Meriden, CT
Solomon, Alex Lee ....Morgantown, WV
Solomon, Alfred B. ....Chicago, IL
Solomon, Alice J. ....Holmdel, NJ
Solomon, Alison Roberts ....Atlanta, GA
Solomon, Allan B., (P.A.) ....Boca Raton, FL
Solomon, Amy Fisch ....Los Angeles, CA
Solomon, Andrew ....Indianapolis, IN
Solomon, Andrew A. ....Pottsville, PA
Solomon, Andrew D. ....New York, NY
Solomon, Andrew H. ....West Nyack, NY
Solomon, Andrew M. ....Cranbury, NJ
Solomon, Andrew P. ....New York, NY
Solomon, Arthur M. ....Chicago, IL
Solomon, Aurel ....Canton, OH
Solomon, Ava ....Jamaica, NY
Solomon, Barbara A. ....New York, NY
Solomon, Barbara Davis ....Washington, DC
Solomon, Barry ....Oak Brook, IL
Solomon, Barry A. ....Summit, NJ
Solomon & Behrendt ....Chicago, IL
Solomon & Benedict, P.A. ....Tampa, FL
Solomon, Benjamin B. ....Philadelphia, PA
Solomon, Benna Ruth ....Chicago, IL
Solomon, Berschler, Warren, Schatz & Flood,
P.C. ....Norristown, PA
Solomon, Beth J. ....Riverwoods, IL
Solomon, Brian D. ....Orlando, FL
Solomon, Budman, Stricker & Schwartz,
L.L.P. ....Charleston, SC
Solomon, Burt Allen ....South Orange, NJ
New York, NY
Solomon, Carl L. ....Columbia, SC
Solomon, Cecil L. ....Houston, TX
Solomon, Charles E., Jr. ....La Grange, GA
Solomon, Charles M. ....Dallas, TX
Solomon, Charles S. ....Santa Fe, NM
Solomon, Charles Thomas ....Cheyenne, WY
Solomon, Cheryl A. ....Washington, DC
Solomon, Clifford M. ....New York, NY
Solomon, Craig H. ....Hackensack, NJ
New York, NY
Solomon, Cristina Portela ....Houston, TX
Solomon, Cynthia Anne ....Charleston, SC
Solomon, Dale S. ....New York, NY
Solomon, Damaris M. ....Passaic, NJ
Solomon, Daniel ....
Department of Labor, GV
Solomon, Daniel ....Boston, MA
Solomon, Daniel H. ....Morristown, NJ
Solomon, Davia ....North Hollywood, CA
Solomon, David ....Helena, AR
Solomon, David A. ....Englewood, CO
Solomon, David B. ....Chicago, IL
Solomon, David H.
Federal Communications Commission,
Office of the General Counsel, GV
Solomon, David R. ....Baltimore, MD
Solomon, Deborah S. ....Boston, MA
Solomon, Dennis M. ....West Palm Beach, FL
Solomon, Dianne L. ....Boston, MA
Solomon, Don J. ....Hatboro, PA
Solomon, Donald M. ....Boston, MA
Solomon, Dori Beth ....Dulles, VA
Solomon, Dori Staller ....Fort Lauderdale, FL
Solomon, Douglas H. ....Cleveland, OH
Solomon, Douglas P. ....San Francisco, CA
Solomon, Douglas Paul
Fort Lauderdale, FL
Miami, FL
Solomon, Earl S., Jr. ....Greenville, MS
Solomon, Edward, Jr. ....Ebensburg, PA
Solomon, Edward Robert ....
Department of Justice, GV
Solomon, Edward S. ....Huntington, NY
Solomon, Elaine D. ....Philadelphia, PA
Solomon, Elise S. ....New York, NY
Solomon, Ellen ....New York, NY
Solomon, Ellen H. ....Palo Alto, CA
Solomon, Elliot N. ....New London, CT
Solomon, Eric ....Novato, CA
Solomon, Eric L. ....New York, NY
Solomon, Eric R. ....Huntington Valley, PA
Solomon, Eskel Haymes ....Los Angeles, CA
Solomon, Francine R. ....Wilmington, DE
Solomon, Francine R., P.A. ......Wilmington, DE
Solomon, Frank E. ....San Francisco, CA
Solomon, Franklin P. ....Cherry Hill, NJ
Solomon, G. Michael ....Stillwater, OK
Solomon, Gary ....Jenkintown, PA
Solomon, Gary B. ....Sharon, PA
Solomon, Gary Bruce ....Dallas, TX
Solomon, Gary S. ....Jamaica, NY
Solomon, Gene ....Fort Myers, FL
Solomon, George J. ....New York, NY
Solomon, Gerald ....Greenbelt, MD
Solomon, Gerald I. ....San Diego, CA
Solomon, Gerald L. ....Boston, MA
Solomon, Gerald R. ....Uniontown, PA
Solomon, Gilbert S. ....Pittsburgh, PA
Solomon, Glenn D. ....Owings Mills, MD
Solomon, Glenn E. ....Los Angeles, CA
Solomon, Gloria B. ....Washington, DC
Solomon, Grace Ferraro ....Hollywood, FL
Solomon, Greta E. ....Bridgeport, CT
Westport, CT
Solomon, Grindle, Silverman & Spinella
San Diego, CA
Solomon, H. Mark ....Melrose Park, PA
Solomon, Harold ....Miami, FL
Solomon, Harold ....Rockville Centre, NY
Solomon, Harold L. ....Albany, NY
Solomon, Harold N. ....Chicago, IL
Solomon, Harris K. ....Fort Lauderdale, FL
Solomon, Harry M. ....Miami, FL
Solomon, Harry M., P.A. ....Miami, FL
Solomon, Harvey E. ....Denver, CO
Solomon, Henry A. ....Arlington, VA
Solomon, Herbert J. ....San Diego, CA
Solomon, Herbert W. ....Mineola, NY
Solomon, Herbie L. ....Albany, GA
Solomon, Howard ....New York, NY
Solomon, Howard B. ....New York, NY
Solomon, J. Howard ....Teaneck, NJ
Solomon, Jack ....Pompano Beach, FL
Solomon, Jack ....Verona, NJ
Solomon, Jack E. ....Pittsburgh, PA
Solomon, Jack, Jr. ....Chicago, IL
Solomon, Jack L. ....New York, NY
Solomon, James R., Jr. ....Montgomery, AL
Solomon, Jane S. ....New York, NY
Solomon, Jason Scott ....Newark, NJ
Solomon, Jay B. ....New York, NY
Solomon, Jay I. ....Atlanta, GA
Solomon, Jay M. ....Elmsford, NY
Solomon, Jeanne R. ....New York, NY
Solomon, Jed E. ....San Francisco, CA
Solomon, Jeffrey D. ....Pittsburgh, PA
Solomon, Jeffrey, Law Office of
Cooper City, FL
Hollywood, FL
Solomon, Jeffrey, Law Office of
Fort Lauderdale, FL
Solomon, Jerome S. ....New York, NY
Solomon, Jerri L. ....Los Angeles, CA
Solomon, Jerry M. ....Rochester, NY
Solomon, Joan G. ....Chicago, IL
Solomon, Joel C. ....Lincolnwood, IL
Solomon, Joel S. ....Cherry Hill, NJ
Philadelphia, PA
Solomon, John ....Washington, PA
Solomon, John C. ....Beverly, MA
Solomon, John F., Jr. ....Norristown, PA
Solomon, John W. ....Akron, OH
Solomon, Jonathan ....New Castle, PA
Solomon, Jordan S. ....Roseland, NJ
Solomon, Joseph ....New York, NY
Solomon, Joseph A. ....Montrose, CO
Solomon, Judith E. ....La Jolla, CA
Solomon, Julie N. ....New York, NY
Solomon, Julius E. ....Highwood, IL
Solomon, Karen O. ....Treasury Department,
Office of the Comptroller of the Currency,
GV
Solomon, Kay S. ....Los Angeles, CA
Solomon, Keith H. ....Douglas, GA
Solomon, Kenneth ....St. Louis, MO
Solomon, Kenneth O. ....Laguna Beach, CA
Solomon, Kenneth O. ....Laguna Beach, CA
Solomon, Kenneth S. ....Lake Oswego, OR
Solomon, Kim Keenan ....Washington, DC
Solomon, Krupnikoff, Wyskiel & Gerber, P.C.
Meriden, CT
Solomon, Lafe E.
National Labor Relations Board,
Office of Board Members, GV
Solomon, Lanny M. ....Cleveland, OH
Solomon, Larry E. ....Tampa, FL
Solomon, Larry S. ....Washington, DC
Solomon, Larry T. ....Kingman, KS
Solomon, Laurel E. ....Durham, NC
Solomon, Lauren ....New York, NY
Solomon, Lawrence ....Philadelphia, PA
Solomon, Lawrence O. ....Morganton, NC
Solomon, Lee E. ....Mountain View, CA
Solomon, Leonard V. ....Chicago, IL
Solomon, Lesley ....Modesto, CA
Solomon, Lewis D. ....Kansas City, MO
Solomon, Lewis J. ....Garden City, NY
Solomon, Leymon ....Houston, TX
Solomon, Lisa ....New York, NY
Solomon, Lisa M. ....Boston, MA
Solomon, Lois ....Wilmette, IL
Solomon, Lois R. ....Northbrook, IL
Solomon, Lori J. ....New York, NY
Solomon, Louis E. ....Bronx, NY
Solomon, Louis M. ....Treasury Department,
Internal Revenue Service, GV
Solomon, Louis M. ....New York, NY
Solomon, Louis M. ....New York, NY
Solomon, M. Dean ....Houston, TX
Solomon, Marc ....Pocasset, MA
Solomon, Marilyn Ann ....Winchester, VA
Solomon, Marion B. ....Hackensack, NJ
Solomon, Mark ....San Diego, CA
Solomon, Mark A. ....Las Vegas, NV
Solomon, Mark A. ....Princeton, NJ
Solomon, Mark B. ....Los Angeles, CA
Solomon, Mark B. ....Lexington, MA
Solomon, Mark E. ....Winter Park, FL
Solomon, Mark J. ....Redwood City, CA
Solomon, Mark J. ....Ithaca, NY
Solomon, Mark R. ....Bloomfield Hills, MI
Detroit, MI
Solomon, Mark S. ....Fort Lauderdale, FL
Solomon, Mark S. ....Dallas, TX
Solomon, Martin J. ....Phoenix, AZ
Solomon, Martin M. ....Deerfield Beach, FL
Solomon, Martin M. ....Brooklyn, NY
Solomon, Martin P. ....New York, NY
Solomon, Marvin ....Tampa, FL
Solomon, Marvin M. ....Washington, DC
Solomon, Marvin, P.A. ....Tampa, FL
Solomon, Melissa J. ....Boston, MA
Solomon, Melvin R. ....Hackensack, NJ
Solomon, Melvyn J. ....New York, NY
Solomon, Melvyn J., P.C. ....New York, NY
Solomon, Michael ....Freeport, NY
Solomon, Michael A. ....New York, NY
Solomon, Michael B. ....North Miami, FL
Solomon, Michael B. ....Melville, NY
Solomon, Michael B., P.A.
North Miami, FL
Solomon, Michael D. ....Levittown, NY
Solomon, Michael D. ....New York, NY
Solomon, Michael D. ....New York, NY
Solomon, Michael F. ....Washington, DC
Solomon, Michael I. ....Brooklyn, NY
Solomon, Michael L. ....Cleveland, OH
Solomon, Michael L. ....Camp Hill, PA
Solomon, Michael R. ....San Francisco, CA
Solomon, Michael T. ....West Sacramento, CA
Solomon, Milton D. ....New York, NY
White Plains, NY
Solomon, Mindy Fletcher
Fort Lauderdale, FL
Solomon, Mitchell J. ....New York, NY
Solomon & Mitchell, PLLC ....Durham, NC
Solomon, Morris J. ....Harrisburg, PA
Solomon & Moskowitz, P.C.
New York, NY
Solomon, Nadine H. ....New York, NY
Solomon, Nancy M. ....Los Angeles, CA
Solomon, Natalie C. ....New York, NY
Solomon, Neal S. ....Princeton, NJ
Solomon, Neil B. ....Chicago, IL
Solomon, Norman E. ....Nashville, TN
Solomon, Norman E. & Associates
Nashville, TN
Solomon, Ori ....New York, NY
Solomon, Owen S. ....Santa Monica, CA
Solomon, Patrick J. ....Rochester, NY
Solomon, Paul D. ....Vernon, NJ
Solomon, Paul D. ....Lawrence, NY
Solomon, Paul D. ....Austin, TX
Solomon, Paul R. ....New Haven, CT
Solomon Pearl Blum & Quinn LLP
Denver, CO
New York, NY
Charlotte Amalie, St. Thomas, VI
Solomon, Peter M. ....Londonderry, NH
Solomon, Phillip E. ....Long Beach, CA
Solomon, Phyllis C. ....New York, NY
Solomon, Phyllis T. ....San Francisco, CA
Solomon, R. Adrian ....Rochester, NY
Solomon, R. Jeremy ....Tallahassee, FL
Solomon & Ramer ....Vernon, NJ
Solomon, Randall J. ....Bloomfield Hills, MI
Solomon, Randall L. ....Cleveland, OH
Solomon, Rayman L. ....Chicago, IL
Solomon, Raymond ....Irvington, NY
Solomon, Relihan & Blake, P.C.
Phoenix, AZ
Solomon, Richard A. ....San Diego, CA
Solomon, Richard A. ....Santa Ana, CA
Solomon, Richard A. ....Washington, DC
Solomon, Richard A. ....Orlando, FL
Solomon, Richard A. ....Lawrence, NY
Solomon, Richard A. ....Houston, TX
Solomon, Richard B. ....New York, NY
Solomon, Richard B. ....New York, NY
Solomon, Richard C. ....Los Angeles, CA
Solomon, Richard E. ....Towson, MD
Solomon, Richard G. ....Hyattsville, MD
Solomon, Richard P. ....Los Angeles, CA
Solomon, Richard R. ....Aurora, IL
Solomon, Rick R. ....Seattle, WA
Solomon, Robert A. ....Denver, CO
New York, NY
Solomon, Robert A. ....New Haven, CT
Solomon, Robert A. ....Dallas, TX
Solomon, Robert H. ....Livingston, NJ
Solomon, Robert H. ....Long Beach, NY
Solomon, Robert J. ....Duluth, GA
Solomon, Robert N. ....New York, NY
Solomon, Robert S. ....Chicago, IL
Solomon, Robert S. ....Livingston, NJ
Solomon, Robert S. ....Morristown, NJ
Solomon, Robert W. ....Henderson, NV
Solomon, Robin M. ....Washington, DC
Solomon & Robinson ....Washington, DC
Solomon, Rodney ....Boston, MA
Solomon, Ronald E. ....Fort Lauderdale, FL
Solomon, Ronald E., P.A., The Law Offices
of ....**Fort Lauderdale, FL**
Solomon, Ronni D. ....Miami, FL
Solomon, Ross ....New Windsor, NY
Solomon, Russell A., & Associates
Metairie, LA
Solomon, Russell A., P.L.C. ....Metairie, LA
Solomon, Saul ....Nashville, TN
Solomon, Saul Jay ....Norristown, PA
Solomon, Scott ....Coral Gables, FL
Solomon, Scott A. ....Los Angeles, CA
Solomon, Scott E. ....New York, NY
Solomon, S.E. Anne ....Coeur d'Alene, ID
Solomon, Selig ....Baltimore, MD
Solomon, Shana M. ....Denver, CO
Solomon, Sharon M. ....San Francisco, CA
Solomon, Sharon R. ....New York, NY
Solomon, Shelia ....Bloomfield Hills, MI
Solomon, Sherman & Gabay
Philadelphia, PA
Solomon, Sherri A. ....Yarmouth, ME
Solomon, Sidney N. ....Lake Success, NY
Solomon, Sirak ....Washington, DC
Solomon & Solomon ....Greenville, MS
Solomon and Solomon, P.C. ....Albany, NY
Solomon, Stanford R. ....Tampa, FL
Solomon, Stanley A. ....Stamford, CT
Solomon, Stanley G. ....New York, NY
Solomon, Stanley H. ....New York, NY
Solomon, Stanley J., (P.A.)
Daytona Beach, FL
Solomon, Stefanie C. ....Montrose, CO
Solomon, Stephanie D. ....Walnut Hill, FL
Solomon, Stephanie L. ....New York, NY
Solomon, Stephen B. ....Minneapolis, MN
Solomon, Stephen D. ....Washington, DC
Solomon, Stephen E. ....Beverly Hills, CA
Solomon, Stephen E. ....Los Angeles, CA
Solomon, Stephen G. ....Oklahoma City, OK
Solomon, Stephen L. ....New York, NY
Solomon, Stephen L. ....New York, NY
Solomon, Stephen R. ....Dayton, OH
Solomon, Stephen Warren
Playa Del Rey, CA
Solomon, Steven ....Los Angeles, CA
Solomon, Steven ....Moorestown, NJ
Solomon, Steven ....New York, NY
White Plains, NY
Solomon, Steven A. ....Department of State,
Office of the Legal Adviser, GV
Solomon, Steven A. ....Manchester, NH
Solomon, Steven B. ....Burlingame, CA
Solomon, Steven E. ....Myrtle Beach, SC
Solomon, Steven G. ....Evanston, IL
Solomon, Steven J. ....Miami, FL
Solomon, Steven Y. ....Rochester, NY
Solomon, Sudi A., (Ms.) ....Trenton, NJ
Solomon, Susan L. ....New York, NY
Solomon, Susan M. ....Chicago, IL
Solomon, Susan R. F. ....Los Banos, CA
Palo Alto, CA
Solomon, Suzanne ....San Francisco, CA
Solomon, Suzanne A. ....New York, NY
Solomon, Teddy ....Alma, GA
Solomon, Terri M. ....Morristown, NJ
New York, NY
Solomon, Thomas J. ....Pittsford, NY
Solomon, T. J., II ....Gastonia, NC
Solomon, Toby ....Livingston, NJ
Solomon, Todd A. ....Chicago, IL
Solomon, Valerie N. ....Albany, NY
Solomon, Vernard G. ....Marshall, TX
Solomon, Vivian Raits ....Portland, OR
Solomon, W. Howard ....Jacksonville, FL
Solomon, Walter L. ....New York, NY
Solomon Ward Seidenwurm & Smith, LLP
Imperial, CA
La Jolla, CA
San Diego, CA
Solomon and Weinberg LLP
Hackensack, NJ
New York, NY
Solomon, William B., Jr. ....Detroit, MI

Solomon, William G. ... Houston, TX
Solomon, William G., IV ... Macon, GA
Solomon, William H. ... Stoneham, MA
Solomon, William I. ... Arlington, VA
Solomon, Zauderer, Ellenhorn, Frischer & Sharp ... New York, NY
Solomonian, Patrick ... Irvine, CA
Solomons, A. G., Jr. ... Estill, SC
Solomons, Burt R. ... Carrollton, TX
Solomons, Ella K. ... New York, NY
Solomons, Mark E. ... Washington, DC
Solomonson, Minnie F. South Padre Island, TX
Solomont, Charles L. ... Boston, MA
Solomont, Meyer ... Lowell, MA
Solomson, Stephen H. ... Hartford, CT
Solon, Arthur M. ... Albuquerque, NM
Solon, Cheryl ... Brighton, CO
Solon, James D. ... Chicago, IL
Solon, John J. ... Dallas, TX
Solon, Miriam B. ... New York, NY
Solon, Patrick F. ... Chicago, IL
Solon, Paul ... San Francisco, CA
Solondz, Irvin L. ... Newark, NJ
Solop, Christopher ... Jackson, MS
Solorio, Esequiel ... Modesto, CA
Solorio, Paula J. ... San Francisco, CA
Solorzano, Edward F. ... Montebello, CA
Soloshatz, David A. ... New York, NY
Soloski, Warren J., (P.C.) ... Los Angeles, CA
Solot, Alan R. ... Tucson, AZ
Solot, Ray M. ... Denver, CO
Solotar, Gavin D. ... New York, NY
Solotaroff, Jason L. ... New York, NY
Solotke, James S. ... Chicago, IL
Solotke, Manuel ... Chicago, IL
Solotke, Sylvia G. ... Chicago, IL
Solotkin, Nancy A. ... San Francisco, CA
Solotoff, Eric S. ... Short Hills, NJ
Solotoff, Lawrence ... Great Neck, NY
Solotorovsky, Julian ... Chicago, IL
Solotoy, Percy ... Santa Monica, CA
Solov, Laurence Gregory ... Los Angeles, CA
Solov, Lessing C. ... Los Angeles, CA
Solov, Mark D. ... Miami, FL
Solov, Tanya ... Chicago, IL
Solovan, John M., II ... St. Clairsville, OH
Solovay, Edlin & Eiseman ... New York, NY
Solovay, Michael B. ... New York, NY
Solovay, Norman ... New York, NY
Solovay, Wendy P. ... Rochester, NY
Solove & Blair ... Lancaster, PA
Solove, Deborah A. ... Albuquerque, NM
Solove, Deborah A. ... Columbus, OH
Solove, Larry M. ... Columbus, OH
Solove, M'liss K. ... Columbus, OH
Solove, Richard S. ... Lancaster, PA
Solove, Robert A. ... Miami, FL
Solove, Ronald L. ... Columbus, OH
Solove & Solove, Professional Association Miami, FL
Solove, Tracye K. ... Miami, FL
Soloveitzik, Charles S. ... Westerly, RI
Soloveitzik, Harold B. ... Westerly, RI
Solovy, Jerold S. ... Chicago, IL
Solovy, Joel J. ... Chicago, IL
Solovy, Jonathan S. ... Seattle, WA
Solovy, Mark A. ... Chicago, IL
Solovy, Susan M. ... Evanston, IL
Solow, Alan P. ... Chicago, IL
Solow, Andrew K. ... New York, NY
Solow, Joel ... Newark, NJ
Solow, Joseph A. ... Hauppauge, NY
Solow, Linda J. ... Richmond, CA
Solow, Michael B. ... Chicago, IL
Solow, Sheldon L. ... Chicago, IL
Solow, Shelley M. ... Huntsville, TX
Solow, Steven P. ... Department of Justice, Environment and Natural Resources Division, GV
Solowan, Richard Allen ... Woodbury, NY
Soloway, Belle ... Dedham, MA
Soloway, Brett D. ... Northbrook, IL
Soloway, Carolyn Frazier ... Atlanta, GA
Soloway, Daniel M. ... Pensacola, FL
Soloway, Daniel M., P.A. ... Pensacola, FL
Soloway, David H. ... Morristown, NJ
Soloway, David N. ... Atlanta, GA
Soloway, Herman J. ... New York, NY
Soloway, Howard B. ... Los Angeles, CA
Soloway, Irving J. ... West Orange, NJ
Soloway, Jay N. ... New York, NY
Soloway, Jennifer S. ... Sacramento, CA
Soloway, Joy M. ... Houston, TX
Soloway, Julie L. ... Chicago, IL
Soloway, Louis ... East Meadow, NY
Soloway, Marilyn L. ... Galveston, TX
Soloway, Norman P. ... Tucson, AZ
Manchester, NH
Soloway, Robert A. ... New York, NY
Soloway, Scott M. ... Bedford, MA
Soloway, Steven A. ... Beverly Hills, CA
Soloway, Todd ... New York, NY
Soloway, Dawn Reddy ... Boston, MA
Solowey, Eric ... Boston, MA
Solowiej, Sandra M. Federal Labor Relations Authority, Authority Member Staff, GV
Solowkowski, Jason ... Newark, NJ
Solowsky, Adam D. ... New York, NY
Solowsky, Jay ... Miami, FL
Soloy, William J. ... Sterling Heights, MI
Solsberry, L. Bernell ... Sonoita, AZ
Solsberry, R. Frazier ... Charlottesville, VA
Solsky, Stuart T. ... New York, NY
Solsrud, Gregory A. ... Minneapolis, MN
Solstad, Elizabeth A. ... Sacramento, CA
Solstad, Mark T. ... Minneapolis, MN

Solt, Christine G. ... Boston, MA
Solt, Frederick W. ... Princeton, NJ
Solt, John R. K. ... Allentown, PA
Solt, Lloyd E. ... Fort Myers, FL
Solt, Lloyd E., P.A. ... Fort Myers, FL
Solt, Robert L., III ... Toledo, OH
Soltan, Charles C. ... Augusta, ME
Soltan, Star S. ... San Diego, CA
Soltan, Suzanne M. ... Chicago, IL
Soltani, Ali ... Beverly Hills, CA
Soltani, Tony F. ... Epsom, NH
Soltau, Hans H., (Co., L.P.A.) Centerville, OH
Solter, Donald Duane ... Wichita, KS
Solter, George D. ... Towson, MD
Solter, Lee P. ... Mission, KS
Solter, Myron W. ... Poolesville, MD
Soltermann, Jeffrey L. ... Jacksonville, IL
Soltero, Carlos R. ... Austin, TX
Soltero, David F. ... Millburn, NJ
Soltero, Nona M. ... Portland, OR
Soltesz, Jas. ... Lincoln Park, MI
Soltesz, Susan C. ... Iselin, NJ
Soltis, Ann M. ... Washington, DC
Soltis, August R. ... Pompton Plains, NJ
Soltis, Cassandra A. ... Washington, DC
Soltis, Christine Fitzgerald Salt Lake City, UT
Soltis, Debra ... Washington, DC
Soltis, Frank J. ... Trenton, NJ
Soltis, James L. ... Lansing, MI
Soltis, Keith J. ... Detroit, MI
Soltis, Martha Beach ... Farmington Hills, MI
Soltis, Michael J. ... Stamford, CT
Soltis, Robert A. ... Kalamazoo, MI
Soltis, Robert Alan ... San Diego, CA
Soltis, Robert R. ... Parma, OH
Soltis, Stephen J. ... Los Angeles, CA
Soltis, Stephen R. ... Lexington, SC
Soltis, Steve M. ... Columbus, OH
Soltman, Neil M. ... Los Angeles, CA
Soltman, Nelson A. ... Chicago, IL
Soltman, Ronald P. ... Nashville, TN
Soltman, Steven B. ... Westlake Village, CA
Solton, Mikhail Y. ... New York, NY
Solton, Robert T. ... Downey, CA
Solton Rosen & Balakhovsky LLP New York, NY
Soltow, Christopher R. ... Thousand Oaks, CA
Soltys, Darlene M. ... Washington, DC
Soltys, John J. ... Seattle, WA
Soltysinski, Henry M., Jr. ... Chicago, IL
Soltysinski, Henry M., Jr., Ltd. ... Chicago, IL
Soltz, David A. ... Philadelphia, PA
Soltz, Edwin M. ... Overland Park, KS
Soltz, Evan David ... Kansas City, MO
Soltz, Judith E. ... Philadelphia, PA
Soltz, Maurice B. ... Kansas City, MO
Soltz & Shankland, A P.C. ... Kansas City, MO
Solum, Conrad R., Jr. ... Los Angeles, CA
Solum, Gregory R. ... Edina, MN
Solum & Hopper ... Chicago Heights, IL
Solum, Richard B. ... Minneapolis, MN
Solum, Wallace G. ... Chicago Heights, IL
Solum-Middleton, Lorraine A. Pacific Palisades, CA
Solverson, Christy W. ... Carbondale, IL
Solverud, Erik O. ... St. Louis, MO
Solveson, George H. ... Milwaukee, WI
Solvibile, Nicole C. ... Springfield, NJ
Solvibile, William R. ... Philadelphia, PA
Solvin, Francis J. ... Hillsborough, CA
Solymos, Peter D. ... Shrewsbury, PA
York, PA
Solymosy, Roger K. ... New York, NY
Solze, Norman P. ... Fremont, OH
Soma, John T. ... Denver, CO
Soma, Marie A. ... Waterford, MI
Somach, Richard Brent ... Allentown, PA
Somach, Stuart L. ... Sacramento, CA
Somach, Susan Deborah ... Washington, DC
Somach & Wester ... Allentown, PA
Bethlehem, PA
Somaia, Sunil R. ... Apple Valley, CA
Soman, James W. ... Fennimore, WI
Soman, Peter A. ... Santa Clarita, CA
Soman, William David ... Coral Gables, FL
Sombathy, Julie Ann ... Panama City, FL
Panama City Beach, FL
Sombathy, Robert S. ... Panama City, FL
Somberg, Judith E. ... Cambridge, MA
Somberg, Norman ... Miami, FL
Somberg, Norman, P.A. ... Miami, FL
Somberg, Reed B. ... Miami, FL
Som de Cerff, Johanna L. Treasury Department, GV
Somelofske, Martin J. ... Fairfax Station, VA
Somer, Abraham ... Los Angeles, CA
Somer, Harold ... East Meadow, NY
Somer, Herbert I. ... Hempstead, NY
Somer, Jason M. ... New York, NY
Somer, Robert M. ... Fairfax, VA
Somer, Stanley J. ... Commack, NY
Somer, Stuart ... Los Angeles, CA
Somer, Thomas J. ... Olympia Fields, IL
Somera, Peter J., Jr. ... Fort Lauderdale, FL
Somerlot, Douglas K. ... Chicago, IL
Somers, A. Jeffrey ... Meriden, CT
Somers, Allan C. ... Springfield, IL
Somers, Andrew L., Jr. ... Madison, WI
Somers, Angela J. ... New York, NY
Somers & Associates ... Upland, CA
Somers, Barbara B. ... Tampa, FL
Somers, Brent R. ... Kirkland, WA
Somers, Christine D. ... Butte, MT
Somers, Christopher A. ... Fairfax, VA
Somers, Clayton D. ... Raleigh, NC
Somers, Clifford L. ... Tampa, FL

Somers, Constance R. ... San Antonio, TX
Somers, Dale L. ... Topeka, KS
Somers, Daniel E. ... Morristown, NY
Somers, Douglas E. ... Tacoma, WA
Somers, Eric S. ... San Francisco, CA
Somers, Fred L., Jr. ... Atlanta, GA
Somers, Fred L., Jr., P.C. ... Atlanta, GA
Somers, George B., Jr. ... Long Branch, NJ
Somers, George W. ... Indianapolis, IN
Somers, H. Peter ... Philadelphia, PA
Somers, Harold M. ... Los Angeles, CA
Somers, Heather M. ... Chicago, IL
Somers, Holly J. ... Lake Oswego, OR
Somers, James V. ... Hartford, CT
Somers, Jeffrey D. ... Meriden, CT
Somers, Jeffrey P. ... Waltham, MA
Somers, Jerome H., (P.C.) ... Boston, MA
Somers, Jocelyn B. ... Portland, OR
Somers, John ... Minneapolis, MN
Somers, John C. ... Flushing, NY
Somers, John O. ... Minneapolis, MN
Somers, John S. ... Bakersfield, CA
Somers, Karen M. ... Virginia Beach, VA
Somers, Kathryn M. ... Chicago, IL
Somers, Kirk L. ... Toledo, OH
Somers, Kristina E. ... Milwaukee, WI
Somers, Lawrence B. ... Winston-Salem, NC
Somers, Margery Nan ... Los Angeles, CA
Somers, Marilyn R. ... Southfield, MI
Somers, Mark C. ... Rochester, NY
Somers, Mark W. ... Dearborn, MI
Somers, Michael E. ... Long Beach, CA
Somers, Nancy ... Malvern, PA
Somers, Nancy M. ... Las Vegas, NV
Somers, Pamela ... Los Angeles, CA
Somers, Paul ... Amesbury, MA
Somers, Paul C. ... Cambridge, MA
Somers, Paul P. ... Worthington, OH
Somers, Peter A. ... Westfield, NJ
Somers, Robb and Robb ... Newton, KS
Somers, Robert B. ... Richardson, TX
Somers, Robert Bruce Federal Communications Commission, Mass Media Bureau, GV
Somers, Robert Vance ... Salisbury, NC
Somers, Ronald M. ... The Dalles, OR
Somers, Susan B. ... Albany, NY
Somers, Susan Linda ... Miami, FL
Somers, Thomas H. ... Portland, ME
Burlington, VT
Somers, Thomas W. ... Upland, CA
Somers, Torry R. ... Las Vegas, NV
Somers, Vali M. ... Seattle, WA
Somers, Vesna Tereza ... Seattle, WA
Somerset, E. Patricia ... Bronx, NY
Somerset, John S. ... Birmingham, AL
Somerset, Margaret E. ... Rochester, NY
Somersille, Valerie G. ... Albany, NY
Somerstein, Barry E. Fort Lauderdale, FL
Somerstein, Bruce ... New York, NY
Somerstein, Bruce & Associates, P.C. New York, NY
Somerstein, Evin L. ... Atlanta, GA
Somerstein, Jonathan J. Lake Success, NY
Somerstein, Mark K. Fort Lauderdale, FL
Somerstein, Mark R. ... New York, NY
Somerstein & Pike ... Brooklyn, NY
Somerstein, Stephen A. ... Brooklyn, NY
Somervell, Katherine S. ... Portland, OR
Somervill, Cynthia B. ... Highlands Ranch, CO
Somerville, Andera Hurt ... Birmingham, AL
Somerville, Andrea G. ... Sun City, AZ
Somerville, Atwell W. ... Orange, VA
Somerville, Deborah A. ... New York, NY
Somerville, Don E. ... Capistrano Beach, CA
Somerville, Frank Walker ... Orange, VA
Somerville, George A. ... Richmond, VA
Somerville, George R., III ... Austin, TX
Somerville, John ... Chicago, IL
Somerville, John H. ... Baltimore, MD
Somerville, John Q. ... Birmingham, AL
Somerville, Kathlene J. ... San Diego, CA
Somerville, Kurt F. ... Boston, MA
Somerville, Lawrence W. ... Arcadia, CA
Somerville, Lee A. ... Bingham Farms, MI
Somerville, Linda S. ... Pittsburgh, PA
Somerville, Mark S. ... Alexandria, VA
Woodbridge, VA
Somerville, Martha H. ... Baltimore, MD
Somerville, Ormond ... Birmingham, AL
Somerville, Richard A. ... Neshanic Station, NJ
Somerville, Scott W. ... Purcellville, VA
Somerville, Sellers & Wilkinson, Ltd. Orange, VA
Somerville, William G., III Birmingham, AL
Somerville, Wm. J. D., III ... Lutherville, MD
Somerville-Hawes, Susan C. M. Baltimore, MD
Somerwitz, Herbert S. ... New York, NY
Somes, Charles J. ... Irving, TX
Somes, Janet C. ... Rochester, NY
Somheil, Eric D. ... Brazil, IN
Somit, Jed ... Oakland, CA
Somlo, Steven G. ... Albany, NY
Somma, Charles A., Jr. ... Richmond, VA
Somma, Donna ... New York, NY
Somma, Michael S., Jr. ... Brooklyn, NY
Somma, Peter J., Jr. ... Stamford, CT
Somma, Ralph A. ... Farmingdale, NY
Somma, Robert ... Boston, MA
Sommar, James C. ... Lansdale, PA
Sommar, Kevin J. ... Lansdale, PA
Sommar, Tracy & Sommar ... Lansdale, PA
Sommars & Bertsch, L.L.C. ... St. Louis, MO

Sommars, Donna M. ... St. Louis, MO
Sommaruga, Mark J. ... Hartford, CT
Sommella, Pasquale ... White Plains, NY
Sommer, Amelia M. ... Lockport, NY
Sommer, Amy Karig ... Glen Rock, NJ
Sommer, Andrew J. ... San Francisco, CA
Sommer, Andrew L. (IBA) ... New York, NY
Sommer & Associates, P.C. ... Washington, DC
Sommer & Barnard, Attorneys at Law, PC Indianapolis, IN
Sommer and Bear ... Beverly Hills, CA
Encino, CA
Sommer, Bradley E. ... Mineola, NY
Sommer, Cheryl Pick ... Santa Fe, NM
Sommer, Christiane ("Tiane") L. Atlanta, GA
Sommer, Christopher ... New York, NY
Sommer, Clifford G. ... New York, NY
Sommer, D. Kevin ... Loves Park, IL
Sommer, Dean S. ... Albany, NY
Sommer, Deborah A. ... Miami, FL
Sommer, Edmund T., Jr. Department of Transportation, Maritime Administration, GV
Sommer, Edward V. ... Chicago, IL
Sommer, Elizabeth M. ... New York, NY
Sommer, Eric M. ... Santa Fe, NM
Sommer, Evelyn M. ... New York, NY
Sommer, Fox, Udall, Othmer & Hardwick, P.A. ... Santa Fe, NM
Sommer, Fred S. ... Rockville, MD
Sommer, Gary A. ... Houston, TX
Sommer, Gary M. ... Syracuse, NY
Sommer, Gary O. ... Toledo, OH
Sommer, George A. ... Scottsbluff, NE
Sommer, George W. ... Fernandina Beach, FL
Sommer, Gerald I. ... Washington, DC
Sommer, Glenn S. ... Miami, FL
Sommer, Glenn S., P.A. ... Miami, FL
Sommer, Harrison W. ... Woodland Hills, CA
Sommer, Harvey D. ... West Palm Beach, FL
Sommer, Hyman Cal ... Old Bethpage, NY
Sommer, Irving Occupational Safety and Health Review Commission, Administrative Law Judges, GV
Sommer, James A. ... Fredonia, NY
Sommer, James K. ... Indianapolis, IN
Sommer, Janet ... Palo Alto, CA
Sommer, Jason J. ... Sacramento, CA
Sommer, Jeffrey R. ... West Chester, PA
Sommer, Jennifer L. ... Walnut Creek, CA
Sommer, Joanne D. ... Doylestown, PA
Sommer, John R. ... Los Angeles, CA
Sommer, John R. ... Louisville, KY
Sommer, Jonathan E. ... Houston, TX
Sommer, Joseph A. ... Santa Fe, NM
Sommer, Joseph C. ... Columbus, OH
Sommer, Joseph D. ... Cambridge, MA
Sommer, Joseph H. ... New York, NY
Sommer, Joseph J. ... North Canton, OH
Sommer, Joseph M. ... New York, NY
Sommer, Joseph P. ... St. Louis, MO
Sommer, Joseph P., & Associates, P.C. St. Louis, MO
Sommer, Karl H. ... Santa Fe, NM
Sommer, Karl W., Jr. ... Martins Ferry, OH
Sommer, Keith A. ... Martins Ferry, OH
St. Clairsville, OH
Sommer, Kenneth A. ... New York, NY
Sommer, Kurt A. ... Santa Fe, NM
Sommer, Leonard ... New York, NY
Sommer, Liberati & Hoffman Co., L.P.A. Martins Ferry, OH
St. Clairsville, OH
Sommer, Lyndon P. ... Belleville, IL
St. Louis, MO
Sommer, Mark F. ... Frankfort, KY
Louisville, KY
Sommer, Mary E. ... Stamford, CT
Sommer, Melanie S. ... Boston, MA
Sommer, Michael C. ... Arlington, VA
Sommer, Michael L. ... Maplewood, NJ
Sommer, Michael S. ... New York, NY
Sommer, Mitchel ... Long Beach, NY
Sommer, Murray I. ... New York, NY
Sommer, N. Theodore ... Binghamton, NY
Sommer, Nancy L. ... New York, NY
Sommer, Olk, Schroeder & Payant Antigo, WI
Rhinelander, WI
Sommer, Patricia ... Edmond, OK
Sommer, Patricia ... Waunakee, WI
Sommer, Paul R. ... Beverly Hills, CA
Encino, CA
Sommer, Paul S. ... New York, NY
Sommer, Peter J. ... Baltimore, MD
Sommer, Peter K. ... Buffalo, NY
Sommer, Richard E. ... Rhinelander, WI
Sommer, Richard F. ... Milpitas, CA
Sommer, Richard H. ... New York, NY
Sommer, Richard H. ... San Antonio, TX
Sommer, Rick J. ... Cincinnati, OH
Sommer, Robert B. ... Pittsburgh, PA
Sommer, Robert G. ... Ocala, FL
Sommer, Roger A. ... Morton, IL
Sommer, Ronald W. ... Tucson, AZ
Sommer, Rudolph ... New York, NY
Sommer, Scott A. ... Walnut Creek, CA
Sommer, Seymour D. ... Beverly Hills, CA
Sommer & Steele, L.L.C. ... Baltimore, MD
Sommer, Stephanie ... Washington, DC
Sommer, Susan L. ... New York, NY
Sommer, Thomas W. ... Loveland, CO
Sommer, William D. ... San Diego, CA
Sommer, William E. ... San Diego, CA
Sommer, William F., Jr. ... North Branch, NJ
Sommerdyke, John M. ... Grand Rapids, MI

Sommerer, Carl J., II ....Minneapolis, MN
Sommerer & Schultz ....Minneapolis, MN
Sommerfeld, Amanda C. ......Los Angeles, CA
Sommerfeld, David W. ....Birmingham, MI
Grosse Pointe Farms, MI
Sommerfeld, Donald D. ....Billings, MT
Sommerfeld, George ....Scarsdale, NY
Sommerfeld, Gretchen ....Cambridge, MA
Sommerfeld, Joan E. ....Denver, CO
Sommerfeld, Lawrence ....Atlanta, GA
Sommerfeld, Michael John ....Ann Arbor, MI
Sommerfeld, Nicholas U. ....Boston, MA
Sommerfelt, Gary J. ....Dallas, TX
Sommerfield, Robert D. ....New York, NY
Sommerhalter, Stephen W.
San Francisco, CA
Sommerhauser, Peter M. ....Milwaukee, WI
Sommerman, Andrew B. ....Dallas, TX
Sommerman, Andrew B., P.C. ....Dallas, TX
Sommermeyer, Brett W. ....Portland, OR
Sommermeyer, Mayo ....Fort Collins, CO
Sommerness, William D. ....Duluth, MN
Sommero, Grace M. ....New York, NY
Sommers, Amy L. ....Seattle, WA
Sommers, Andrew ....New York, NY
Sommers, Andrew Clark ....Albany, NY
Sommers, Ashton L. ....Baton Rouge, LA
Sommers, Bernard J. ....Newburgh, NY
Sommers, Bruce W. ....Brooklyn, NY
Sommers, Cindy M. ....Chesterfield, VA
Sommers, Conrad H. ....Dallas, TX
Sommers, Daniel S. ....Washington, DC
Sommers, David G. ....New York, NY
Sommers, David S. ....Houston, TX
Sommers, Diane L. ....Freehold, NJ
Sommers, Donald H. ....Albany, NY
Sommers, Elizabeth Boone ....Albany, NY
Sommers, Emily E.
Federal Deposit Insurance Corporation,
Professional Liability Section, GV
Sommers, Frank F., IV, Law Offices of
San Francisco, CA
Sommers, George ....Hoboken, NJ
New York, NY
Sommers, Harold S. ....New York, NY
Sommers, Howard M. ....New York, NY
Sommers, Howard N. ....Los Angeles, CA
Sommers, Hubert R. ....Encino, CA
Sommers, James R. ....Waukesha, WI
Sommers, Janis M. ....Bloomington, IL
Sommers, Jennifer Clarke ....Boston, MA
Sommers, John Gerard ....Woodbury, NY
Sommers, John M. ....Northfield, NJ
Sommers, John Marcus ....Wichita, KS
Sommers, Karen Nicholson ......San Diego, CA
Sommers, Lawrence A. ....Detroit, MI
Sommers, Lawrence Edmund ....Chicago, IL
Sommers, Louise ....New York, NY
Sommers, Louise, Law Offices of
New York, NY
Sommers, Mara Beth ....Miami, FL
Sommers, Margaret L. ....Rosemead, CA
Sommers, Margaret L. ....Cody, WY
Sommers, Mark S. ....Washington, DC
Sommers, Mary K. ....North Chicago, IL
Sommers, Norman S. ....Southfield, MI
Sommers, Oscar L. "Jack"
The Woodlands, TX
Sommers, Richard A. ....Aberdeen, SD
Sommers, Richard D. ....Los Angeles, CA
Sommers, Robert L. ....San Francisco, CA
Sommers, Robert L. ....Dallas, TX
Sommers, Robert M. ....Springfield, MO
Sommers, Ronald J. ....Houston, TX
Sommers, Sally M. ....Englewood, CO
Sommers, Samuel A., Jr. ....Selma, AL
Sommers, Sandra Becher ....Cleveland, OH
Sommers, Sandra J. ....Indianapolis, IN
Sommers, Schwartz, Silver & Schwartz, P.C.
Detroit, MI
Southfield, MI
Sommers, Scott R. ....Houston, TX
Sommers, Scott R., P.C. ....Houston, TX
Sommers & Sommers ....Encino, CA
Sommers & Sommers, LLP ....Albany, NY
Sommers, Stephen P. ....Pasadena, CA
Sommers, Stephen V. ....San Antonio, TX
Sommers, Steven E. ....San Diego, CA
Sommers, Steven L. ....Fort Lauderdale, FL
Sommers, Steven M. ....Denver, CO
Sommers, Susan Jill ....Westbury, NY
Sommers, Susan V. ....Atlanta, GA
Sommers, Thomas S. ....Milwaukee, WI
Sommers, Wendi E. ....Encino, CA
Sommers, William J., Jr.
New Orleans, LA
Sommers, William W. ....San Antonio, TX
Sommerstein, Gary ....Los Angeles, CA
Sommerstein, John Fitzgerald ....Boston, MA
Sommerstein, Robert B. ....Buffalo, NY
Sommerville, Albert L., Jr.
Webster Springs, WV
Sommerville, Frank ....Houston, TX
Sommerville, John J. ....Minneapolis, MN
Sommerville, Michael F. ....Boston, MA
Sommerville, Molly ....Denver, CO
Sommerville, Robert C., (P.A.) ....Miami, FL
West Palm Beach, FL
Sommervold, Arlo D. ....Sioux Falls, SD
Sommervold, Peter W. ....Sioux Falls, SD
Sommese, Dennis A. ....Sacramento, CA
Sommese, Dennis A.
South Lake Tahoe, CA
Sommi, Michael J. ....New York, NY
Sommo, Charles, III ....Boston, MA
Sommovilla, Randall J. ....Philadelphia, PA
Somogye, Tammy M. ....Overland Park, KS
Somogyi, Edward Lloyd ....Shell Beach, CA
Somogyi, Elaine ....El Dorado Hills, CA
Somogyi, Lloyd E. ....San Luis Obispo, CA
Somoza, James L. ....New York, NY
Somoza, John H. ....New York, NY
Somoza, Michael F. ....New Orleans, LA
Somoza-Colombani, Guillermo A.
San Juan, PR
Somple, Neysa M. ....Brecksville, OH
Somppi, William A. ....San Jose, CA
Somps, Michael P. ....Carson City, NV
Somrak, David J. ....Cleveland, OH
Somsen, Henry N., Jr. ....New Ulm, MN
Somsen, Jon H. ....Orlando, FL
Somsen, Schade & Franta, PLC
Mankato, MN
New Ulm, MN
Somson, Barbara C. ....Washington, DC
Somvichian, Whitty ....San Francisco, CA
Somyak, John, & Associates ....Houston, TX
Son, Anthony H. ....Beverly Hills, CA
Son, David Won-Ihl ....Louisville, KY
Son, James R. ....Evansville, IN
Son, Landon F. ....Tucson, AZ
Son, Rosa E. ....New York, NY
Sona, Steven P. ....Woodbridge, NJ
Sonageri, Donna Yurow ....Hackensack, NJ
Sonageri & Fallon ....Hackensack, NJ
Garden City, NY
Sonageri, James L. ....Hackensack, NJ
Garden City, NY
Sonberg, Richard T. ......Hilton Head Island, SC
Sonberg, Steven ....Fort Lauderdale, FL
Miami, FL
Sonda, James D. ....Chicago, IL
Sondag, Patrick A. ....Council Bluffs, IA
Sondag, Robert H. ....Minneapolis, MN
Sondag, Thomas W. ....Portland, OR
Sondag, Victor H. ....Waterloo, IL
Sondak, Robert M. ....Miami, FL
Sondak, Robyn ....Hartford, CT
Sondalle, Daniel D. ....Princeton, WI
Sonday, Henry F., Jr. ....Kansas City, KS
Sonde, Theodore ....Washington, DC
Sondee, Racine & Doren, P.L.C.
Traverse City, MI
Sondee, Ronald W. ....Traverse City, MI
Sondej, Denise ....Chicago, IL
Sondej, Thad F. ....Liverpool, NY
Sondel, Robert ....Tonawanda, NY
Sonder, Tami Suzanne ....Fresno, CA
Sonderby, Christopher P. ......San Francisco, CA
Sonderby, Peter R. ....Chicago, IL
Peoria, IL
Sonderby, Peter R., P.C. ....Chicago, IL
Sonderby, Stephen ....Chicago, IL
Sonderby, Susan Pierson ....Chicago, IL
Sonderegger, Diane C. ....Omaha, NE
Sonderen, John W. ....Portland, OR
Sondergaard, Lisa A. ....Madera, CA
Sondergaard, Steven J. ....Defiance, OH
Sondericker, William F. ....New York, NY
Sonderlick, Marlene G. ....Pelham Manor, NY
Sonderling, Roy J. ....Miami Beach, FL
Sonderman, Andrew J. ....Columbus, OH
Sonderman, Carl G. ....Kennewick, WA
Sonders, Mark R. ....Albany, NY
Sonders, Ricki Valerie
Oklahoma City, OK
Sondes, Brian ....Metairie, LA
Sondgerath, Van L. ....Covington, KY
Sondgeroth, Kenneth L.
Bullhead City, AZ
Sondheim, Harry B. ....Los Angeles, CA
Sondheimer, David ......Colorado Springs, CO
Sondheimer, David ....Denver, CO
Pueblo, CO
Sondheimer, Joshua N. ....San Francisco, CA
Sondhi, Jay ....Long Beach, CA
Sondik, Kenneth I. ....Medina, OH
Sondler, Bruce I. ....Providence, RI
Sondler Salvadore & Associates
Providence, RI
Sondock, Ruby Kless ....Houston, TX
Sondrall, Steven A. ....Brooklyn Park, MN
Sondreal, Lynn A. ....Milwaukee, WI
Sondreal, Mark S. ....Moorhead, MN
Sone, Jeffrey M. ....Dallas, TX
Sone, Maurice A. ....Chicago, IL
Soneff, George M. ....Santa Monica, CA
Sonenberg, Steven R. ....Southfield, MI
Sonenblick, Jerry ....Tucson, AZ
Sonenklare, Richard H. ....Plainview, NY
Sonenshein, David A. ....Philadelphia, PA
Sonenshein, Joel A. ....Garberville, CA
Sonenshine, Allyson W. ....Los Angeles, CA
San Francisco, CA
Sonenshine, Daniel A. ....Costa Mesa, CA
Sonenshine, H. Marshall ....New York, NY
Sonenstein, David M. ....Las Vegas, NV
Sonenthal & Overall, PC
Washington, DC
Sonenthal, Robert B. ....Washington, DC
Sonentz-Papazian, Vicken ....Washington, DC
Soneral, Christine Mason ....Lansing, MI
Sones, Kathy D. ....Purvis, MS
Sones, Marla D. ....Lafayette Hill, PA
Sones, Randall D. ....Hanover, MD
Sonesen, Loren ....Miami, FL
Sonet, Emile H., III ....King Of Prussia, PA
Sonet, Jerrold M. ....New York, NY
Sonet, Richard ....New York, NY
Sonfield, Brian Joseph ....Washington, DC
Sonfield, Robert L., Jr. ....Houston, TX
Sonfield & Sonfield, A Prtnship incl. Prof.
Corps. ....Los Angeles, CA
Fairfax, VA
Song, Alfred H. ....Sacramento, CA
Song, Chulho P. ....San Diego, CA
Song, David S. ....New York, NY
Song, Elenne ....New York, NY
Song, Jane I. ....Boston, MA
Song, John S. K. ....Aurora, CO
Song, Joon W. ....Los Angeles, CA
Song, Kristina M. ....New York, NY
Song, Lawrence J. ....Los Angeles, CA
Song, Margaret U. ....San Francisco, CA
Song, Marsha Farris ....Huntersville, NC
Song, Moses K. ....Dallas, TX
Song, Natasha J. ....Los Angeles, CA
Song Oswald & Mondress, PLLC
Seattle, WA
Song, Peter ....New York, NY
Song, Philip D. ....Charlotte, NC
Song, Sandra ....New York, NY
Song, Seungtaik ....Palo Alto, CA
Song, Simone Y. ....New York, NY
Song, Soo C. ....Department of Justice,
Office of Tribal Justice, GV
Song, Tailim ....Arlington, TX
Song, Wayne ....Los Angeles, CA
Song, Wayne H. ....Los Angeles, CA
Song, William ....Philadelphia, PA
Song, William H. ....Seattle, WA
Song, Woosuk (Brent) ....Los Angeles, CA
Songer, Donald J. ....Bellflower, CA
Songer, Hugo C. ....Jasper, IN
Songer, Michael J. ....Washington, DC
Songer, Richard E. ....San Diego, CA
Songer, Vester ....Hugo, OK
Songer, Vickie Y. ....Bakersfield, CA
Songer, William H. ....San Diego, CA
Songstad, L. Allan, Jr. ....Irvine, CA
Songstad, Randall & Ulich ....Irvine, CA
Songstad, Randy N. ....Memphis, TN
Songstad, Steven Booth ....Wailuku, HI
Songy, Edward A. ....Plaquemine, LA
Songy, Lisa A. ....Dallas, TX
Songy, Randall C. ....Lafayette, LA
Sonheim, Helm, Less & Williams, L.L.P.
Arvada, CO
Westminster, CO
Sonheim, Robert H. ....Arvada, CO
Soni, Anjili ....Chicago, IL
Soni, Leena ....Chicago, IL
Soni, Pragna ....Washington, DC
Soni, Sushma ....Department of Justice,
Civil Division, GV
Sonia, Gailyc ....Stoughton, MA
Sonies, Jared M. ....Herndon, VA
Soniker, Hilton ....New York, NY
Sonju, Scott D. ....Vancouver, WA
Sonju, Vincent E. ....Crookston, MN
Sonkin, Andrea Laurel ....Chicago, IL
Sonkin, Fromson, Kess & Koberna Co., L.P.A.
Cleveland, OH
Sonkin, Irving A. ....Seattle, WA
Sonkin & Klein ....Seattle, WA
Sonkin, Leo ....Lake Worth, FL
Sonkin, Loren M. ....Cleveland, OH
Sonkin, Michael A. ....White Plains, NY
Sonkin, Mitchell I. ....New York, NY
Sonkin, Richard ....New York, NY
Sonkin, Rick D. ....Cleveland, OH
Sonkin, Shale S. ....Cleveland, OH
Sonkin, Steven Lee ....New York, NY
Sonn, Adam S. ....Somerville, NJ
Sonn & Associates, P.A.
Fort Lauderdale, FL
Miami, FL
Sonn, David E. ....Greene, NY
Sonn, David E. ....Wenatchee, WA
Sonn, Jeffrey R. ....Fort Lauderdale, FL
Sonn, Marilyn D.
Federal Communications Commission,
Office of the General Counsel, GV
Sonn, Paul K. ....New York, NY
Sonnabend, Caryl J. ....Sparta, NJ
Sonnabend, Cynthia K. ....Hackensack, NJ
Sonnabend, Peter J. ....Boston, MA
Sonne, Carl W. ....San Diego, CA
Sonne, Frances G. ....Allentown, PA
Sonne, Frances G., P.C. ....Allentown, PA
Sonne, J. Robert ....Salt Lake City, UT
Sonne, James A. ....Richmond, VA
Sonne, Scott W. ....San Diego, CA
Sonne, Stephen ....New York, NY
Sonneborn, Barbara W.
West Palm Beach, FL
Sonneborn, H. Andrew ....Indianapolis, IN
Sonneborn, Herbert M., Jr. ....Wheeling, WV
Sonneborn, James L. ....Syracuse, NY
Sonneborn Law Offices ....Syracuse, NY
Sonneborn, Marcy ....New York, NY
Sonneborn, Marcy ....White Plains, NY
Sonneborn Rutter Cooney Klingensmith &
Eyler, P.A. ....West Palm Beach, FL
Sonneborn, Thomas F. ....Springfield, IL
Sonnefeldt, Jerome M. ....Chicago, IL
Sonnega, Steven P. ....Martinsville, IN
Sonnemaker, Harry H., Jr. ....Peoria, IL
Sonnemaker & Sonnemaker, P.C. ....Peoria, IL
Sonneman, Joseph A. ....Juneau, AK
Sonneman, Karin L. ....Winona, MN
Sonneman Law Office ....Winona, MN
Sonnen, Craig A. ....Columbus, OH
Sonnenberg, Amy J. ....Houston, TX
Sonnenberg & Anderson ....Chicago, IL
Sonnenberg, Andrea L. ....Los Angeles, CA
Sonnenberg, Eric H. ....Honolulu, HI
Sonnenberg, Glenn A. ....Los Angeles, CA
Sonnenberg, Jay T. ....Houston, TX
Sonnenberg, Katharine L. ....Bethesda, MD
Sonnenberg, Lin ....Nespelem, WA
Sonnenberg, Raymond J. ....Harrisonville, MO
Sonnenberg, Scott A. ....Beverly Hills, CA
Sonnenberg, Stephen P. ....Los Angeles, CA
Sonnenberg, Steven P. ....Chicago, IL
Sonnenberg, Susan C. ....Kansas City, MO
Sonnenberg, William C.
Department of Education, GV
Sonnenblick, Gerald N. ....Freehold, NJ
Sonnenblick, Judith M. ....Philadelphia, PA
Sonnenblick, Parker & Selvers, A
Professional Corporation ....Freehold, NJ
Sonnenblick, Scott Ian ....New York, NY
Sonnenborn, Donald E. ....New York, NY
Sonnenborn, Monroe R. ....New York, NY
Sonnenburg, William K. ....Sheboygan, WI
Sonnenburg & Zelpe ....Sheboygan, WI
Sonnenfeld, Fred I. ....New York, NY
Sonnenfeld, Jennifer L. ....Tampa, FL
Sonnenfeld, Kenneth H. ....New York, NY
Sonnenfeld, Marc J. ....Philadelphia, PA
Sonnenfeld & Richman ....New York, NY
Sonnenfeldt, Neil ....New Hyde Park, NY
Sonnenklar, Alan H. ....New York, NY
Sonnenklar, Beth S. ....Los Angeles, CA
Sonnenklar, Mark J. ....Los Angeles, CA
Sonnenreich, David N. ....Salt Lake City, UT
Sonnenreich, Michael R. ....Washington, DC
Sonnenreich & Roccograndi
Washington, DC
Sonnenschein, Adam ....Boston, MA
Sonnenschein, Edward, Jr.
Los Angeles, CA
Sonnenschein, Eric A. ....Brooklyn, NY
Sonnenschein, Irving ....New York, NY
Sonnenschein, J. Dorian
Newport Beach, CA
Sonnenschein, Michael D. ....Oviedo, FL
Sonnenschein Nath & Rosenthal
Los Angeles, CA
San Francisco, CA
Washington, DC
Chicago, IL
Kansas City, MO
St. Louis, MO
New York, NY
Sonnenschein Sherman & Deutsch
New York, NY
Sonnenthal, Peter Y. ....Denver, CO
Sonner, Andrew L. ....Rockville, MD
Sonner, David A. ....Los Angeles, CA
Sonnesyn, David N. ....Longmont, CO
Sonnesyn Law Firm, The ....Longmont, CO
Sonnesyn, Rolf E. ....Minneapolis, MN
Sonnett, Anthony E. ....Los Angeles, CA
Sonnett, Neal R. ....Miami, FL
Sonnett, Neal R., P.A. ....Miami, FL
Sonnhalter, Aaron ....Los Angeles, CA
Sonnhalter, Joy B. ....Cleveland, OH
Sonnich, Richard L. ....Kansas City, MO
Sonnie, Marilyn W. ....New York, NY
Sonnier, Blaise M. ....Lafayette, LA
Sonnier, Brent G. ....Lafayette, LA
Sonnier, Charles R., (Law Corporation)
Abbeville, LA
Sonnier, G. Robert ....Austin, TX
Sonnier, Gerard J. ....Houston, TX
Sonnier, Margret L. ....Houston, TX
Sonnier, Scott J. ....New Orleans, LA
Sonnier & Trahan ....Abbeville, LA
Sonnino, Edward A. ....New York, NY
Sonntag, Jennine T. ....Milwaukee, WI
Sonntag, Jolana Faye ....Brainerd, MN
Sonntag, Richard A. ....Scottsdale, AZ
Sonntag, Richard A. ....Jersey City, NJ
Sonntag, Thomas M. ....Sidney, NE
Sonntag, W. Scott ....Greenbelt, MD
Sonoda, Midori ....New York, NY
Sonom, Ronald G. ....Miami, FL
Sonosky, Chambers, Sachse & Endreson
Washington, DC
Sonosky, Chambers, Sachse, Miller &
Munson ....Anchorage, AK
Juneau, AK
Sonosky, Jerome N. ....Washington, DC
Sons, Kathy M. ....Joliet, IL
Sonsini, Larry W. ....Palo Alto, CA
Sonsini, Matthew W. ....Palo Alto, CA
Sonsino, Isaas D. ....New York, NY
Sonson, Alex M. ....Waipahu, HI
Sonstein, Paul W. ....Voorhees, NJ
Sonstein, Paul W., P.C. ....Voorhees, NJ
Sonstroem, Jed P. ....Columbia, SC
Sontag, Christine M. ....Santa Barbara, CA
Sontag, James L. ....Nowata, OK
Sontag, Jocelyn A. ....New York, NY
Sontag, Leo ....Boston, MA
Sontag, Michael D. ....Nashville, TN
Sontag, Scott M. ....New York, NY
Sontag, Stephanie ....San Diego, CA
Sontchi, Christopher S. ....Wilmington, DE
Sontich, Joseph P., Jr. ....Youngstown, OH
Sontich, Joseph P., Sr. ....Youngstown, OH
Sontz, Herbert O. ....New York, NY
Sonu, Andrew Chanho ....Washington, DC
Sonzogni, Louis A., Jr. ....Allentown, PA
Sonzogni, Stephanie ....Roseland, NJ
Soo, Kenneth A. ....Raleigh, NC
Soobert, Allan M. ....Alexandria, VA
Soobzokov, Aslan ....Paterson, NJ
Soobzokov, Kazbek ....Santa Ana, CA
Soocher, Stan ....New York, NY
Sood, Surendra J., M.D. ....Modesto, CA
Soodek, Caroline S. ....Chicago, IL
Soodik, Lynn ....Los Angeles, CA
Soodik, Michael J. ....Pasadena, CA
Soofer, Ramin ....Los Angeles, CA
Soofian, David A. ....Atlanta, GA
Sooho, Sharyn T. ....Newton, MA
Soo Hoo, Bentley M. ....Los Angeles, CA
Soohoo, Cynthia ....New York, NY
Soo Hoo, George N. ....Rockville, MD

SooHoo, Kwok M. ....New York, NY
SooHoo, Linda ....New York, NY
Soo Hoo, Mona C. ....Los Angeles, CA
Soohoo, Nancy ....Lexington, MA
Soo Hoo, William F. ....Sacramento, CA
Sook, Prescott C. ....Albany, NY
Sook, Prescott C., Law Firm of ....Albany, NY
Sookram, Carolyn M. ....Tampa, FL
Soom, Daniel S. ....Canfield, OH
Soomekh, Karen A. ....Los Angeles, CA
Soong, Arthur J. ....New York, NY
Soong, Dana L. ....San Francisco, CA
Soong, Danny C. ....Orange, CA
Soong, James W. ....Palo Alto, CA
Soong, May H. ....Chicago, IL
Soong, Melvin K. ....Honolulu, HI
Soong, Michael K. ....Lihue, HI
Soong, Zosan S. ....Rochester, NY
Soons, Jeffrey P. ....Charlottesville, VA
Soons & Soons ....Englewood, NJ
New York, NY
Soons, William R. ....Englewood, NJ
New York, NY
Sooper, Martin ....San Francisco, CA
Soopper, Samuel
Federal Energy Regulatory Commission, Office of the General Counsel, GV
Soos, Charles J. ....Princeton, NJ
Soos, Charles J., P.C. ....Princeton, NJ
Soos, Robert W. ....Staten Island, NY
Soos, Wm. G. ....Cleveland, OH
Soosaipillai, Miruni ....Redwood City, CA
Soosman, Barry F. ....Los Angeles, CA
Sooter, Lacie L. ....Dallas, TX
Sooter, Ricky L. ....Alexandria, LA
Sooter & Savoie, L.L.P. ....Alexandria, LA
Sooter, Victor H. ....Alexandria, LA
Sootes, Lisa Schafroth ....Dallas, TX
Sooudi, Shiva A. ....New York, NY
Sooy, C. Darrell ....San Francisco, CA
Sooy, Charles D. ....San Francisco, CA
Sooy, Jennifer E. ....Springboro, OH
Sooy, Kathleen Taylor ....Richmond, VA
Sooy, Richard R. ....San Diego, CA
Las Vegas, NV
Sopchick, Michael K. ....Washington, DC
Sopel, George C. ....Boston, MA
Soper, Allen B., Jr. ....Slater, MO
Soper, David B. ....Houston, TX
Soper, Dawn J. ....Salt Lake City, UT
Soper, Dent & Logan, P.A. ....Tupelo, MS
Soper, James C., (Inc.) ....Oakland, CA
Soper, James J. ....Miami, FL
Soper, James R. ....Salt Lake City, UT
Soper, Jeanne M. ....Washington, DC
Soper, Jerry A. ....Davenport, IA
Soper, Katharine B. ....Ann Arbor, MI
Soper, Kevin M. ....Towson, MD
Soper, Michael G. ....Tupelo, MS
Soper, Nancy E. ....Mineola, NY
Soper, Paul F. ....Nashville, TN
Soper, Philip ....Ann Arbor, MI
Soper, Robert G. ....Los Angeles, CA
Soper, Rochael M. ....New York, NY
Soper, Stanley E. ....Park City, UT
Soper, Virginia J. ....Grand Rapids, MI
Sopher, Edward D. ....New York, NY
Sopher, Jeanne Welch ....Pittsburgh, PA
Sopher, Jerry S. ....Baltimore, MD
Sopher, John P. ....Oklahoma City, OK
Sopher, Meridith F. ....New York, NY
Sopher, Valerie Esther ....El Cerrito, CA
Sophie, Kenneth J., Jr. ....Chicago, IL
Sophir, Jayme L.
National Labor Relations Board, Office of the General Counsel, GV
Sophir, Mark D., (P.C.) ....Belleville, IL
St. Louis, MO
Sophir, Stephen P. ....Port Washington, NY
Sophocles, Mark T. ....Philadelphia, PA
Sophocles, Michael S., (P.C.) ....Boston, MA
Sophos, Constantine ....West Orange, NJ
Sophrin, Gail ....Rutland, VT
Sophy, Daniel M. ....Phoenix, AZ
Sophy, Michael M. ....Phoenix, AZ
Sophy and Sophy ....Phoenix, AZ
Sopinski, Timothy E. ....Lincoln, NE
Sopinsky, Brian I. ....Philadelphia, PA
Sopkin, Gregory E. ....Denver, CO
Sopkin, Rebecca Rains ....Denver, CO
Sopko, James ....Stuart, FL
Sopko, Jeffrey J. ....Cleveland, OH
Sopko, John S. ....Parsippany, NJ
Sopko, Nussbaum & Inabnit
South Bend, IN
Sopko, Thomas C. ....South Bend, IN
Soponis, Gaylin G. ....Gainesville, FL
Sopp, John A. ....Arlington, VA
Sopp, Richard D. ....Folsom, CA
Sopp, Teresa J. ....Jacksonville, FL
Sopp, William V. ....Boston, MA
Sopper Oliva & Associates, P.C.
San Antonio, TX
Sopranik, Victoria J. ....Lexington, KY
Soprano, Juliane ....Falmouth, MA
Sopt, John F. ....Birmingham, MI
Sopuch, John A., III ....Chicago, IL
Sopuch Nouhan Higgins & Arnett, L.L.P.
Chicago, IL
Dallas, TX
Sopwith, Laurie J. ....Sacramento, CA
Sor, Yvonne S. ....Chicago, IL
Sora, Cynthia D. ....Trenton, NJ
Soraci, Robert J. ....Gainesville, FL
Soraghan, Joseph R. ....St. Louis, MO
Soraghan, Patricia Cahill ....New Bern, NC
Soraghan, Thomas C. ....Belleville, IL
St. Louis, MO
Sorak, Nancy B. ....Memphis, TN
Soran, James J., III ....Denver, CO
Soran, Robert P. ....Redwood City, CA
Soranno, Carl J. ....Roseland, NJ
Soranno, Linda J. ....Minneapolis, MN
Soranno, Richard S. ....Manchester, CT
Soranno, Richard T. ....New Boston, MI
Sorantino, Sandra A. ....Tuckahoe, NJ
Sorapure, Cornelius E., Jr. ....Morristown, NJ
Sorbello, John R. ....Crown Point, IN
Sorbello, John R., P.C. ....Crown Point, IN
Sorbello, Joseph C. ....Riverside, CA
Sorber, Linda E. ....Odessa, TX
Sorbo, John ....La Mesa, CA
Sorce, C. Becket ....New York, NY
Sorce, David S. ....Fairport, NY
Sorce, Joseph P. ....Chicago, IL
Sorce, Robert J. ....Phoenix, AZ
Sorcher, Alan E. ....Washington, DC
Sorci, Michael R. ....Kalamazoo, MI
Sorcinelli, William J. ....Spokane, WA
Sordahl, Fredrick H., Jr. ....Pryor, OK
Sordello, Richard J., Jr. ....Modesto, CA
Sordello, Suzanne C. ....San Jose, CA
Sorden, Dale L. ....Milwaukee, WI
Sordi, John R. ....Albertson, NY
Sordi, Michael C. ....Glen Cove, NY
Sordi, Nicholas A. ....Glen Cove, NY
Sordi, Nicholas A., Jr. ....Glen Cove, NY
Sordi and Sordi, LLP ....Glen Cove, NY
Mineola, NY
Sordyl, Eugene E. ....Flint, MI
Sordyl, Kimberly A. ....Lansing, MI
Soref, Randye B. ....Los Angeles, CA
Soreff, Paul ....Seattle, WA
Sorejian, Samuel S. ....Encino, CA
Sorell, Louis S. ....New York, NY
Sorell, Peter B. ....Uniondale, NY
Sorelle, Alicia Carrington ....Elk City, OK
SoRelle, A. W., III ....Amarillo, TX
So Relle, Sara ....Abilene, TX
Sorem, Barbara L. ....Los Angeles, CA
Sorem, Gentra Abbey ....Tulsa, OK
Sorem & Pastore, Lawyers ....San Diego, CA
Sorem, Richard L. ....San Diego, CA
Soren, Marshall ....Chicago, IL
Sorensen, Allen B. ....Provo, UT
Sorensen, Andrew D. ....St. Paul, MN
Sorensen, Andrew K. ....Anchorage, AK
Sorensen, Andrew W. ....Madison, WI
Sorensen, Anita M. ....Madison, WI
Sorensen, Annette F. ....Salt Lake City, UT
Sorensen, Arthur H. ....Atlantic Highlands, NJ
Sorensen, Bonnie S. ....Palo Alto, CA
Sorensen, Candace Lynn ....Grand Rapids, MI
Sorensen, Carlie B. ....Washington, DC
Sorensen, Carlotta H. ....Salem, OR
Sorensen, Carolyn J. ....St. Paul, MN
Sorensen, David A. ....Indianapolis, IN
Sorensen, David F. ....Philadelphia, PA
Sorensen, David W. ....Las Vegas, NV
Sorensen, Dawn ....Minneapolis, MN
Sorensen, Dean C. ....Boise, ID
Sorensen, Donald J. ....Minneapolis, MN
Sorensen, Donna J. ....Cedar Rapids, IA
Sorensen, Douglas A. ....Dallas, TX
Sorensen, Douglas J. ....Novato, CA
Sorensen, Evan B. ....Los Angeles, CA
Sorensen, Gary R. ....Williston, ND
Sorensen, George C. ....Springfield, IL
Sorensen, Glen V. ....Salem, OR
Sorensen, Harvey R. ....Wichita, KS
Sorensen, Heidi A. ....Washington, DC
Sorensen, Henry T., II ....Tampa, FL
Sorensen, Howard D.
Department of Education, Office of the General Counsel, GV
Sorensen, Ingrid ....Boston, MA
Sorensen, Ingrid R. ....Bridgeton, NJ
Sorensen, J. Douglas ....Norfolk, VA
Sorensen, James A. ....Chicago, IL
Sorensen, John K. ....Scottsbluff, NE
Sorensen, John M. ....Lafayette, IN
Sorensen, John R. ....San Diego, CA
Sorensen, Judi G. ....Salt Lake City, UT
Sorensen, Karen L. ....Rockford, IL
Sorensen, Karen S. ....Kentfield, CA
Sorensen, Kenneth J.
Bloomfield Hills, MI
Sorensen, Kerry L. ....Tustin, CA
Sorensen, Kristen H. ....New York, NY
Sorensen, Kurt ....Lincoln, CA
Sorensen, Laura P. ....Chicago, IL
Sorensen, Laury P. ....Westwood, MA
Sorensen, Lawrence T.
Santa Barbara, CA
Sorensen, Linda ....San Francisco, CA
Sorensen, Mahlon L. ....Casper, WY
Sorensen, Marien ....Sacramento, CA
Sorensen, Melvin N. ....Seattle, WA
Sorensen, Michael R. ....Seattle, WA
Sorensen, Murray Jim ....Blackfoot, ID
Sorensen, Myron L. ....Salt Lake City, UT
Sorensen, Nancy L. ....Seattle, WA
Sorensen, Neil ....San Rafael, CA
Sorensen, Nick H. ....Houston, TX
Sorensen, Otto E. ....San Diego, CA
Sorensen, Paul T. ....Grand Rapids, MI
Sorensen, Peter W. ....Phoenix, AZ
Sorensen, Philip J. ....Ashland, WI
Sorensen, Robert H. ....Chicago, IL
Sorensen, Robert J. ....Minneapolis, MN
Sorensen, Robin G. ....Granby, CT
Sorensen, Ruth ....Alturas, CA
Sorensen, Sharp ....Chicago, IL
Sorensen, Stephen ....Los Angeles, CA
Sorensen, Stephen F. ....Juneau, AK
Sorensen, Stephen J. ....Fairfax, VA
Sorensen, Theodore C. ....New York, NY
Sorensen, W. Stephen ....Melbourne, FL
Sorensen, Wendi A. ....Phoenix, AZ
Sorensen, William B., Jr. ....Wichita, KS
Sorensen & Zimmerman, A Professional Corporation ....Scottsbluff, NE
Sorensen-Jolink, Scott ....Portland, OR
Sorensen-Jolink, Trubo, Williams, McIlheny & Williams ....Portland, OR
Sorenson, A. Bridget ....Los Angeles, CA
Sorenson, Alfred R. ....Phoenix, AZ
Sorenson, Amy F. ....San Francisco, CA
Sorenson, Arne M. ....Washington, DC
Sorenson, Brett B. ....Oklahoma City, OK
Sorenson, C. Peter ....Eugene, OR
Sorenson, Charles A. ....Jacksonville, FL
Sorenson, Charles W., Jr. ....Boston, MA
Sorenson, Christopher J.
Minneapolis, MN
Sorenson, Cole Dean ....Phoenix, AZ
Sorenson, D. James ....Albuquerque, NM
Sorenson, Daniel D. ....Costa Mesa, CA
Rancho Cucamonga, CA
Sorenson, David G. ....Newton, IA
Sorenson, David G., P.C. ....Newton, IA
Sorenson, David W. ....Logan, UT
Sorenson, Derek L. ....Phoenix, AZ
Sorenson, Eric C. ....New York, NY
Sorenson, Eric J., Jr. ....Lynchburg, VA
Sorenson, Gail ....Albany, NY
Sorenson, Gayle A. ....Idaho Falls, ID
Sorenson, George ....Mesa, AZ
Sorenson, George R. ....Phoenix, AZ
Sorenson & Hach ....Dallas, TX
Sorenson, James E. ....Tallahassee, FL
Sorenson, Jeffrey G. ....Peoria, IL
Sorenson, Joe C. ....Palo Alto, CA
Sorenson, Johnny J. ....Phoenix, AZ
Sorenson, Karl E. ....San Diego, CA
Sorenson, Keith C. ....Redwood City, CA
Sorenson, Kenneth M. ....Honolulu, HI
Sorenson, Kristine M. ....Chicago, IL
Sorenson, Maura B.
West Palm Beach, FL
Sorenson, Michael P. ....Miami, FL
Sorenson, Michele A. ....Virginia Beach, VA
Sorenson, Moore, Evens, Marshall & Rocco
Phoenix, AZ
Sorenson, Morris J. ....Santa Rosa, CA
Sorenson, Owen L. ....St. Paul, MN
Sorenson, Paul R. ....Fort Worth, TX
Sorenson, R. Paul ....Las Vegas, NV
Sorenson, Randall C. ....Kingsland, GA
Sorenson, Richard G. ....Los Angeles, CA
Sorenson, Rick G. ....Fort Worth, TX
Sorenson, Robert E. ....Hortonville, WI
Sorenson, S. Brent ....Tulsa, OK
Sorenson, S. Charles, Jr. ....Minneapolis, MN
Sorenson, Sigurd Ansgar ....New York, NY
Sorenson, Stephen J. ....Salt Lake City, UT
Sorenson, Steve L. ....Las Vegas, NV
Sorenson, Steven R. ....Ripon, WI
Sorenson, Stuart L. ....Minneapolis, MN
Sorenson, Timothy W. ....Dallas, TX
Soressi, James A. ....Great Neck, NY
Sorett, Henry P. ....Boston, MA
Sorey, Charles E. II ....Vicksburg, MS
Sorey, Gloria Jean ....Omaha, NE
Sorey, Lynn Hughes ....Raleigh, MS
Sorg, Gerard R. ....St. Marys, PA
Sorg, Gregory M. ....Littleton, NH
Sorg, H. Peter, Jr. ....Seattle, WA
Sorg, Steven V. ....Somerset, KY
Sorge, Christine M. ....Washington, DC
Sorge, Gary W. ....Lawrenceburg, IN
Sorge, Gina M. ....Livingston, NJ
Sorge, Robert H. ....Hammond, IN
Sorge, Robert J. ....Brooklyn, NY
Sorgen, David L. ....New York, NY
Sorgen, Lawrence S. ....Hiawassee, GA
Sorgen, Michael S., Law Offices of
San Francisco, CA
Sorgenfrei, Robert L. ....Santa Maria, CA
Sorgente, Natalia T. ....New York, NY
Sorgi, David E. ....Boston, MA
Sorgi, Leonard S. ....New York, NY
Sorgi, Louis V., Jr. ....Raynham, MA
Sorgi & Mellencamp, LLP ....Milwaukee, WI
Sorgi, Michael L. ....Milwaukee, WI
Sorgi, Peter ....Boston, MA
Sorgie, Lee B. ....Pompano Beach, FL
Sorgini, Richard C. ....Lake Worth, FL
Sorgini, Robert C. ....Lake Worth, FL
Sorgini & Sorgini, P.A. ....Lake Worth, FL
Soria, Dora I. ....Houston, TX
Soria, G. Craig ....Sarasota, FL
Soria, William O. ....Salinas, CA
Sorial, George A. ....Morristown, NJ
Soriano & Associates ....Portland, OR
Soriano, Brian E. ....San Francisco, CA
Soriano, Daniel C., Jr. ....Somerville, NJ
Soriano, Elizabeth S. ....Ridgewood, NJ
Soriano, Enrico C. ....Washington, DC
Soriano, Geoffrey D. ....Somerville, NJ
Soriano, Gregory B. ....Portland, OR
Soriano, Henkel, Salerno, Biehl & Matthews, A Professional Corporation ....Roseland, NJ
Soriano, Jack J. ....Roseland, NJ
Soriano, Jerry L. ....Bremerton, WA
Soriano, Jocelyn M. ....San Francisco, CA
Soriano, John D. ....Franklin Lakes, NJ
Soriano, Joseph M. ....South Orange, NJ
Soriano, Laurie L. ....Los Angeles, CA
Soriano, Lawrence E. ....Bremerton, WA
Soriano, Mark Russell ....Los Angeles, CA
Soriano, Max D. ....Seattle, WA
Soriano, Milton H. ....Seattle, WA
Soriano, Nicholas M. ....White Plains, NY
Soriano, Robert A. ....Tampa, FL
Soriano & Soriano ....Somerville, NJ
Soriano & Soriano ....Bremerton, WA
Soriano, William J. ....Roseland, NJ
Soriano-Vesagas, Maria Rita
Beverly Hills, CA
Sorice, Mark L. ....Greensburg, PA
Soricelli, Gary P. ....Massapequa, NY
Sorich, John M. ....Irvine, CA
Los Angeles, CA
Sorich, Samuel ....Sacramento, CA
Sorid, Robyn ....New York, NY
Soriero, Donald J. ....Middletown, NJ
Sori-Marin, Mariano L. ....Chicago, IL
Sorin, David J. ....Princeton, NJ
New York, NY
Sorin, Francis ....Jersey City, NJ
Sorin, Marc ....Memphis, TN
Sorin, Marvin ....Cleveland, OH
Sorin, Mindy Okeon ....Memphis, TN
Sorin, Richard E. ....Memphis, TN
Sorin, Robert J. ....New York, NY
Sorini, Marc E. ....Washington, DC
Sorini, Sandra L. ....Ann Arbor, MI
Soris, Johanna ....Boston, MA
Sorise, Domnick J. ....Clinton, MI
Sorkin, Bernard R. ....New York, NY
Sorkin, David E. ....Chicago, IL
Sorkin, David J. ....New York, NY
Sorkin, Ira L. ....New York, NY
Sorkin, Jerome D. ....Washington, DC
Sorkin, Joan Ross ....Scarsdale, NY
Sorkin, John E. ....New York, NY
Sorkin, John R. ....Hollywood, FL
Sorkin, John R., P.A. ....Hollywood, FL
Sorkin, Laurence T. ....New York, NY
Sorkin, Linda Watkins
Department of Transportation, Federal Transit Administration, GV
Sorkin, Paul D. ....Boston, MA
Sorkin, Risa G. ....Boston, MA
Sorkin, Robin Siegel ....Hollywood, FL
Sorkin, Saul ....Great Neck, NY
Sorkin, Scott J. ....Richmond, VA
Sorkin, Stuart H., P.C. ....Washington, DC
Sorkow, Alan ....Glendale, CA
Sorkow, Harvey R. ....Hackensack, NJ
Sorkowitz, Alan J. ....New York, NY
Sorlie, John D. ....Bend, OR
Sorlie, Oscar J., Jr. ....Fergus Falls, MN
Sorlien, Jerry L. ....Moses Lake, WA
Sorlien, Richard C. ....Philadelphia, PA
Sorling, Northrup, Hanna, Cullen and Cochran, Ltd. ....Springfield, IL
Sorman, Cynthia M. ....Escondido, CA
Sorman, Richard J. ....Chicago, IL
Sormani, Leo L. ....Bronx, NY
Sormani, Nannette ....Houston, TX
Sornberger, George R. ....Somerset, KY
Sornson, Robert O. ....Detroit, MI
Sorocco, Douglas J. ....Oklahoma City, OK
Sorochinsky, Michael I.
Santa Monica, CA
Sorochty, Matthew Peter ....Wichita, KS
Soroeta Alzaga, Jose M. ....San Juan, PR
Sorohan, Diedra L. ....Atlanta, GA
Sorohan, Lawrence J., II
New Orleans, LA
Soroka, Anthony ....Baltimore, MD
Soroka, David M. ....Department of Commerce, Patent and Trademark Office, GV
Soroka, Mark S. ....New York, NY
Soroka, Michael H. ....Garden City, NY
Soroka, Walter ....Chicago, IL
Sorokin, Cheryl A. ....San Francisco, CA
Sorokin, Ethel Silver ....Hartford, CT
Sorokin, Gross & Hyde, P.C.
Hartford, CT
Rocky Hill, CT
Simsbury, CT
Sorokin, Jack E. ....Fullerton, CA
Sorokin, Leo T. ....Boston, MA
Sorokin, Peter S. ....Hartford, CT
Sorokin, Sharon L. ....Philadelphia, PA
Soroko, John J. ....Philadelphia, PA
Soroko, Richard S. ....San Francisco, CA
Sorokoff, Caroline ....New York, NY
Sorokoff, David H. ....New York, NY
Sorokoty, Walter G. ....Naples, FL
Sorokowski, Andrew ....Cambridge, MA
Soroky, William A. ....Woodland Hills, CA
Sorola, Diane ....Lafayette, LA
Sorola, Diane A., A Professional Law Corporation ....Lafayette, LA
Sorolis, Maria N. ....Tampa, FL
Sorondo, Alicia Otazo ....Miami, FL
Soronen, Laurence J. ....Albany, NY
Soronen, Vera L. ....Houston, TX
Soronen, William P., Jr. ....Albany, NY
Soroosh, Fariba R. ....Saratoga, CA
Sorosky, Sheldon M. ....Chicago, IL
Sorota, Alan M. ....Miami, FL
Sorota, Joseph J., Jr. ....Clearwater, FL
Sorota, Joseph J., Jr., P.A. ....Clearwater, FL
Sorota, Pamela B. ....Columbia, MD
Sorota, Pamela B., P.A. ....Columbia, MD
Sorota, Samuel S. ....North Miami Beach, FL
Soroy, H. Michael ....Los Angeles, CA
Sorrell, Ann ....Newark, NJ
Sorrell, Anderson, Lehrman, Maixner & Ridulfo, L.L.P. ....Corpus Christi, TX
Sorrell, Clyde H., Jr. ....Washington, DC
Rockville, MD
Sorrell, Elisa T. ....Union, NJ
Sorrell, Jack M. ....Pearsall, TX
Sorrell, Jay R. ....Pearsall, TX
Sorrell, John B. ....Washington, DC
Sorrell, Karen M. ....Newton, NJ

Sorrell, Keith D. ......Poplar Bluff, MO
Sorrell, Larry D. ......Castle Rock, CO
Sorrell, Lisa Winston ......Dallas, TX
Sorrell, Margaret Jackson ......Sumter, SC
Sorrell, Mark K. ......Southaven, MS
Sorrell, Michael ......Dallas, TX
Sorrell, Paul N. ......Los Angeles, CA
Sorrell, Randall Vernon ......Greenfield, IN
Sorrell and Sindon ......Pearsall, TX
Sorrell, Todd M. ......Los Angeles, CA
Sorrell, W. Drew ......New York, NY
Sorrell, Whitney Lynn ......Phoenix, AZ
Sorrell, William E. ......St. Louis, MO
Sorrell, William H. ......Montpelier, VT
Sorrells, Adam ......Chico, CA
Sorrells, A. T. ......Atlanta, GA
Sorrells, Elizabeth Ann
Department of Transportation, Federal Railroad Administration, GV
Sorrells, Linda Gale ......Austin, TX
Sorrells, Marvin W. ......Monroe, GA
Sorrells, Reginald L. ......Montgomery, AL
Sorrells, Teddy P. ......New Orleans, LA
Sorrells, W. Bradley ......Charleston, WV
Sorrells, W. Bradley, LC ......Charleston, WV
Sorrels, Barry ......Dallas, TX
Sorrels, James S. ......Edmonds, WA
Sorrels, Randall Owen ......Houston, TX
Sorrels, Stephen Matthew ......Buffalo, NY
Sorrels, W. Scott ......Atlanta, GA
Sorren, William P. ......Miami, FL
Sorrenti, David P. ......Brockton, MA
Sorrenti & Delano, P.A. ......Brockton, MA
Sorrentino, Anthony J. ......Omaha, NE
Sorrentino, Anthony V. ......Las Vegas, NV
Sorrentino, Charlene H. ......Miami, FL
Sorrentino, Eileen Z. ......Springfield, MA
Sorrentino, Frank L. ......Woodbury, NJ
Sorrentino, James S. ......Lancaster, PA
Sorrentino, Jeanine Marie ......Phoenix, AZ
Sorrentino, Joan ......Chatham, NJ
Sorrentino, Joanne ......Flanders, NJ
Sorrentino, John M. ......Maywood, IL
Sorrentino, John R. ......New York, NY
Sorrentino, Joseph M. ......Princeton, NJ
Sorrentino, Joseph N. ......Los Angeles, CA
Sorrentino, Joseph R. ......New York, NY
Sorrentino, Joseph V. ......Bronx, NY
Sorrentino, Mark Anthony ......Baltimore, MD
Sorrentino, Matthew R. ......Allentown, PA
Sorrentino, P. A. ......Chicago, IL
Sorrentino, Paul F. ......San Diego, CA
Sorrentino, Susan C. ......Mukwonago, WI
Sorrentino, Vincent J. ......Buffalo, NY
Sorrick, Floyd D., Jr. ......Washington, KS
Sorrow, Christopher P. ......Atlanta, GA
Sorrow, Susan ......Athens, GA
Sorsaia, Mark A. ......Hurricane, WV
Sorscher, Laura B. ......Bensalem, PA
Sorte, M. James ......Wolf Point, MT
Sorteberg, Kenneth K. ......Columbia, MD
Sortedahl, Kenneth N., II ......Spring Valley, WI
Sortino, Anthony M. ......Rochester, NY
Sortino, Anthony T. ......Tomball, TX
Sortland Law Office ......Minneapolis, MN
Sortland, Paul A. ......Minneapolis, MN
Sortor, Carolyn ......Dallas, TX
Sortor, Katherine M. ......Stamford, CT
Sortor, Shirley M. ......Milwaukee, WI
Sortor, William H. ......San Francisco, CA
Sorum, Mary G. ......Detroit Lakes, MN
Sorvaag, Jim L. ......Overland Park, KS
Sorvari, Karen C. ......Buies Creek, NC
Sorvino, Heidi Jan ......Morristown, NJ
Sorvino, Kerry L. ......Chicago, IL
Sos, Emil F., Jr. ......Chesterland, OH
Sos, Renata M. ......San Francisco, CA
Sosa, Carlos E. ......Encino, CA
Sosa, Edward M. ......El Paso, TX
Sosa, Gloria ......New York, NY
Sosa, Heileen ......Miami, FL
Sosa, Joaquin A. ......Van Nuys, CA
Sosa, José A. ......Brooklyn, NY
Sosa, Jose D. ......West Palm Beach, FL
Sosa, Jose M. ......West Palm Beach, FL
Sosa, Lisa M. ......Hartford, CT
Sosa Lloréns, Cruz Neris & Associates
San Juan, PR
Sosa, Meryl Camin ......Northbrook, IL
Sosa, Pablo A. ......New York, NY
Sosa, R. Thomas ......Los Angeles, CA
Sosa, Steven C. ......Santa Monica, CA
Sosalla, Robert E. ......Cedar Rapids, IA
Sosa-Lloréns, José A. ......San Juan, PR
Sosa-Lloréns, José Alberto ......San Juan, PR
Sosa-Padró, Carlos R. ......San Juan, PR
Sosbe, Patricia McGaughey
Crawfordsville, IN
Sosby, Teresa Gail ......Miami, FL
Soschin, Alan B. ......Washington, DC
Soscia, Anthony M., Jr. ......New York, NY
Soscia, Elizabeth D. ......Washington, DC
Sosebee, Carl R.
Agency for International Development, Office of the General Counsel, GV
Sosebee, Hugh D. ......Forsyth, GA
Sosebee, Hugh D., Jr. ......Forsyth, GA
Sosebee, Robyn Ice ......Atlanta, GA
Sosenko, Eric J. ......Ann Arbor, MI
Sosensky, Steven C. ......New Haven, CT
Soshnick, Andrew Z. ......Indianapolis, IN
Soshnick, Harold F. ......Great Neck, NY
Soshnick, Michael L. ......Mineola, NY
Sosich, Anthony G. ......San Diego, CA
Sosin, David B. ......Palos Heights, IL
Sosin, Jeremy S. ......New York, NY
Sosin & Lawler, Ltd. ......Palos Heights, IL
Sosin, Martin, (Inc.) ......Santa Monica, CA
Sosin, Michael A. ......Southfield, MI
Sosin, Ralph ......Bingham Farms, MI
Sosin, Robert M. ......Bingham Farms, MI
Sosin, Theodore M. ......Indianapolis, IN
Sosinski, David A. ......Kansas City, MO
Sosinsky, Bernard ......Plainview, NY
Sosinsky, Frederick L. ......New York, NY
Sosinsky, Joel I. ......New York, NY
Sosis, Richard A. ......New Rochelle, NY
Soska, Christine Vernard ......New Albany, OH
Soske, Joshua L., Jr. ......San Francisco, CA
Soskin, Marvin S. ......Atlanta, GA
Soskin, Richard N. ......Eden Prairie, MN
Soskin, Rollin J. ......Skokie, IL
Soskin, Ronald M. ......Indianapolis, IN
Soskin, Stephen P. ......Los Angeles, CA
Soskin, William H., Law Offices of
Monterey, CA
Soskis, Joque H. ......Jacksonville, FL
Soskis, Mosetta S. ......Jacksonville, FL
Sosland, Daniel L. ......Rockland, ME
Sosland, Karl Z. ......Hackensack, NJ
Sosland, Martin A. ......Dallas, TX
Sosler, Evan R. ......New York, NY
Sosler, Karen E. ......Albany, NY
Soslow, Joanne R. ......Philadelphia, PA
Soslowsky, James A. ......Mesa, AZ
Sosman, Martha B. ......Boston, MA
Sosna, Donna Marie ......Brooklyn, NY
Sosna, Jeremy D. ......Minneapolis, MN
Sosna, Michael B. ......Henderson, NC
Sosnaud, Jeffrey ......Portland, ME
Sosnay, William ......Madison, WI
Sosne, David A. ......St. Louis, MO
Sosne, Elinor D.
Securities and Exchange Commission, Division of Enforcement, GV
Sosne, Jeffrey J. ......Lenox, MA
Sosne, Pamela G. ......Washington, DC
Sosnick, Barbara E. ......Washington, DC
Sosnick, Charles J. ......New York, NY
Sosnick, Ernest ......Beverly Hills, CA
Sosnick, Fredric ......New York, NY
Sosnick, Randall D. ......Redwood City, CA
Sosnik, Howard L. ......Fort Lee, NJ
Garden City, NY
New York, NY
Sosnik, Matthew A. ......New York, NY
Sosnik, Tracey G. ......New York, NY
Sosnkowski, Alexandra E. ......The Dalles, OR
Sosnoff, Nora ......Augusta, ME
Sosnoff, Sandra S. ......New Haven, CT
Sosnoski, Kenneth ......Norwalk, CT
Sosnosky, Kristen P. ......Boston, MA
Sosnov, Amy W. ......West Atlantic City, NJ
Norristown, PA
Sosnov, Leonard N. ......Philadelphia, PA
Sosnov, Steven R. ......Norristown, PA
Sosnow & Freed ......New York, NY
Sosnow, Kelly J. ......Los Angeles, CA
Sosnow, Sherman F. ......New York, NY
Sosnowicz, Michael T. ......Philadelphia, PA
Sosnowitz, Linda J. ......New York, NY
Sosnowski, Blaze H. ......Boonton, NJ
Sosnowski, Leonard S. ......Madison, WI
Sosnowski, Michael A. ......Hollidaysburg, PA
Sosnowski, Michael S. ......Monterey, CA
Sosnowski, Paul T.
National Credit Union Administration, Office of General Counsel, GV
Soso, Daniel P. ......Chicago, IL
Sosothikul, Janette H. ......Pasadena, CA
Soss, Harvey Preston ......Brooklyn, NY
Soss, Marc J. ......Sarasota, FL
Sossaman, Dennis J. ......Memphis, TN
Sossaman, William L. ......Memphis, TN
Sossen, Lee D. ......New York, NY
Sossen, R. Robert, Jr. ......Utica, NY
Sossi, Frank Thomas ......Akron, OH
Sossi, Mark ......Brownsville, TX
Sosslau, Allan ......Greenbelt, MD
Sosslau, Allan, P.A. ......Greenbelt, MD
Sossner, Edward M. ......Albany, NY
Sosso, Anna Maria ......Pittsburgh, PA
Sosso, Anthony R., Jr ......Pittsburgh, PA
Sosso, Michael P. ......Pittsburgh, PA
Sossomon, Creighton W. ......Highlands, NC
Sossong, Anna Marie ......Harrisburg, PA
Sossong, Michael A. ......Ebensburg, PA
Sostaric, Jennifer ......Oak Brook, IL
Sostarich, Mark E. ......Milwaukee, WI
Sostchin, David M., Law Offices of
Hialeah, FL
Sostchin, Guillermo ......Miami, FL
Sostek, Bruce S. ......Dallas, TX
Sostek, Joan Sprince ......Dallas, TX
Sostman, Ellen L. ......Rocky Hill, CT
Sostoi, Martin W. ......Montpelier, OH
Sostowski, Lorraine ......Washington, DC
Sostre Law Office, The ......Boulder, CO
Sostre, Shirley ......Boulder, CO
Sostre-Oquendo, Shirley ......Boulder, CO
Sostrin, Ellen M. ......Chicago, IL
Sostrin, Jennifer Lynn ......Los Angeles, CA
Sotak, Joseph E. ......South Euclid, OH
Sotak, Mark W. ......Westerville, OH
Sotak, Paul ......Scranton, PA
Sotak, Ronald Michael ......Ames, IA
Sotel, Phillip K. ......Pasadena, CA
Sotelo, Martha Leary ......McLean, VA
Sotelo, Thomas Paul ......Fairfax, VA
Soter, Gary S. ......Tarzana, CA
Soter, Mary K. C. ......Dayton, OH
Soter, Nicholas G. ......San Francisco, CA
Soter, R. Paul, Jr. ......San Francisco, CA
Soter, William J. ......Columbus, OH
Sotera, Mary C. ......Cleveland, OH
Soth, William R., (P.A.) ......Minneapolis, MN
Sotherland, Paul L. ......Birmingham, AL
Sothmann, James G. ......Davenport, IA
Sothoron, Richard H., Jr.
Upper Marlboro, MD
Sotier, Raymond O. ......St. Louis, MO
Sotile, Vincent J., Jr. ......Donaldsonville, LA
Sotir & Goldman ......Jamestown, NY
Sotir, Lisa M. ......McLean, VA
Sotir, Richard L., Jr. ......Jamestown, NY
Sotirakis, John A. ......Astoria, NY
Sotiras, Sylvia A. ......Chicago, IL
Sotirhos, Maria E. ......Seattle, WA
Sotiriou, Evan R. ......St. Louis, MO
Sotiriou, Setiri S. ......Long Island City, NY
Sotiroff & Abramczyk, P.C.
Bingham Farms, MI
Detroit, MI
Sotiroff, Keith A. ......Bingham Farms, MI
Sotiroff, Philip ......Bingham Farms, MI
Sotis, Mary J. ......New York, NY
Sotland, Jeffrey ......Harrisburg, PA
Sotland, Jeffrey C. ......Philadelphia, PA
Soto, Alejandro ......El Paso, TX
Soto, Alfonso, III ......El Paso, TX
Soto, Andrew K.
Federal Energy Regulatory Commission, Office of the General Counsel, GV
Soto, Angela Downey
Fort Lauderdale, FL
Soto, Anthony J. ......Coral Gables, FL
Soto, Antonio J., III ......Miami, FL
Soto, Benjamin M. ......Rockville, MD
Soto, Carlos E. Carrasquillo ......San Juan, PR
Soto, Carlos R. ......Houston, TX
Soto, Catalina ......Chicago, IL
Soto, Christopher D. ......Phoenix, AZ
Soto, Denise S. ......Santa Fe, NM
Soto, Dionisio Tinsay ......San Francisco, CA
Soto, Domingo ......Mobile, AL
Soto, Edward ......Miami, FL
Soto, Franklin ......Paterson, NJ
Soto, Gloria E. ......Atlantic City, NJ
Soto, Henrietta ......Boston, MA
Soto, James A. ......Nogales, AZ
Soto, James E. ......Houston, TX
Soto, Javier Alberto ......Miami, FL
Soto, Joseph R. ......Houston, TX
Soto, Juan B. ......San Juan, PR
Soto, Julia A. M. ......Tucson, AZ
Soto Law Group, The, P.A.
Fort Lauderdale, FL
Soto, Louis D. ......Menlo Park, CA
Soto, Marcia ......Miami, FL
Soto, Marcia, P.A. ......Miami, FL
Soto, Maria L. ......Miami, FL
Soto, Martin & Coogan, P.C. ......Nogales, AZ
Soto, Michael ......Columbus, OH
Soto, Michele ......Newark, NJ
Soto, Milenia I. ......Houston, TX
Soto, Oscar E. ......Fort Lauderdale, FL
Soto, Philip L. ......Huntington Park, CA
Soto, Ricardo ......San Diego, CA
Soto, Roberta Macias ......Los Angeles, CA
Soto, Sara ......Miami, FL
Soto, Sharon Carlstedt ......New York, NY
Soto, Sylvia ......Thousand Oaks, CA
Soto Hestres, Catalino ......Canovanas, PR
Sotolongo, Ariel L. ......Los Angeles, CA
Sotolongo, Wendy C. ......Durham, NC
Soto-Maldonado, Evette ......New York, NY
Sotomayor, Felix ......New York, NY
Sotomayor, Jess E. ......Glendale, CA
Sotomayor, Rande Sherman
Los Angeles, CA
Sotomayor, Sonia ......New York, NY
Sotomayor, Victor ......San Francisco, CA
Sotomayor Santos, Rene F. ......Ponce, PR
Soto-Miranda, Ricardo E. ......San Juan, PR
Sotoodeh & Associates ......Santa Ana, CA
Sotoodeh, Babak ......Los Angeles, CA
Santa Ana, CA
Sotoodeh, Pamela G. ......Houston, TX
Sotorrio, Rene A. ......Coral Gables, FL
Sotorrio, Rene A., P.A., Law Offices of
Coral Gables, FL
Miami, FL
Sotos, David Joseph ......Cincinnati, OH
Sotos, George J. ......Wheaton, IL
Sotos, James G. ......Itasca, IL
Sotos, Lisa Ann ......Columbus, OH
Sotos, Peter G. ......New York, NY
Sotos, Sarah Hansen ......Des Plaines, IL
Sotos, Victor H. ......Montecito, CA
Sotsky, Lester ......Washington, DC
Sotsky, Marvin M. ......Louisville, KY
Sott, Herbert ......Detroit, MI
Sotta & Crane ......Joplin, MO
Sotta, Donald E. ......Joplin, MO
Sottilare, Santo J. ......Vero Beach, FL
Sottile, Anthony, III ......Indiana, PA
Sottile, Bruce J. ......Van Nuys, CA
Sottile & Hopkins, L.L.P
Mount Pleasant, SC
Sottile, James, IV ......Washington, DC
Sottile, Kenneth R. ......Spangler, PA
Sottile, Nicholas C. ......Mount Pleasant, SC
Sottile, Robert J. ......New York, NY
Sottile, Thomas V. ......Bala Cynwyd, PA
Sottile, Timothy B. ......Westlake Village, CA
Sotto, Lisa J. ......New York, NY
Sottosanti, Carl ......Malvern, PA
Sottosanti, Deborah A. ......Reading, PA
Sottosanti, Martha H. ......San Diego, CA
Souaid, Robert G. ......Miami Beach, FL
Soublet, Brian G. ......San Francisco, CA
Soublet, Bruce A. ......Berkeley, CA
Soublet, Erika E. ......Portland, OR
Soubly, Diane M. ......Detroit, MI
Souchek and Kimble ......Seward, NE
Souchon, Harry V. ......New Orleans, LA
Soucie, Buchman, Grover & Bolt, Ltd.
Anoka, MN
Soucie, Fred M. ......Anoka, MN
Soucie, Jerry L. ......Lincoln, NE
Soucie, Michele Polito ......Cleveland, OH
Soucie, Paul M. ......Westlake, OH
Soucy, David J. ......Fort Kent, ME
Soucy, John A. ......Cumberland Foreside, ME
Soucy, Robert L., Jr. ......Coral Springs, FL
Soud, A. C., Jr. ......Jacksonville, FL
Soud, Adrian G. ......Jacksonville, FL
Soud, Jeffrey D. ......Jacksonville, FL
Soud, Kelly L. ......Tampa, FL
Soud, Linda M. ......Jacksonville, FL
Soudah, Randa G. ......New York, NY
Souder, Andrew M. ......Philadelphia, PA
Souder, Angelia R. ......Atlanta, GA
Souder, Billye G. ......Roanoke, TX
Souder, Elvin R. ......Souderton, PA
Souder, Rosenberger, Bricker, Buschman & Maza ......Souderton, PA
Souder, Susan ......Baltimore, MD
Souder, W. Granger, Jr. ......Bowling Green, OH
Souder-Fox, Susan ......Philadelphia, PA
Souders, Bradley D. ......Tampa, FL
Souders, Bradley D., P.A. ......Brandon, FL
Clearwater, FL
Tampa, FL
Souders, David M. ......Department of Justice, Civil Division, GV
Souders, Donald E., Jr. ......Phillipsburg, NJ
Souders, J. Scott ......Newport Beach, CA
Souders, Jean F. ......St. Louis, MO
Souders, Kenneth M. ......Toledo, OH
Souders & Levine ......Olivette, MO
Souders, Ronald L. ......Horsham, PA
Souders, Terry P. ......Garden Grove, CA
Soudry, Roslyn ......Los Angeles, CA
Souers, Loren E., Jr. ......Canton, OH
Souers, P. Eric ......Oak Brook, IL
Souffrant, Emmanuella ......New York, NY
Souffront, Carlos A. ......Miami, FL
Souffront, Carlos O. ......San Juan, PR
Souffront, Luis Oscar ......Washington, DC
Souhlas, Ernest N. ......Covington, LA
Souhrada, Nannette (Nicki)
San Diego, CA
Souk, Fred S. ......Washington, DC
Souk, James E. ......Urbana, IL
Soukas, William C. ......New York, NY
Soukenik, Anthony J. ......St. Louis, MO
Soukenik, John P., Jr. ......Washington, DC
Soukup, Christopher E. ......Pepper Pike, OH
Soukup, David W. ......Seattle, WA
Soukup, Earle ......Placentia, CA
Soukup, Gerald W. ......Baltimore, MD
Soukup, Jeffrey Edward ......Wantagh, NY
Soukup, John F. ......Los Angeles, CA
Soukup, Lynn A., (P.C.) ......Washington, DC
Soukup & Schiff, LLP ......Los Angeles, CA
Soukup, William W. ......Anaheim, CA
Soulanille, Nicole D.
Export-Import Bank of The United States, Office of the General Counsel, GV
Soule, Andrew N. ......Dallas, TX
Soule, Augustus W., Jr. ......Boston, MA
Soule, Charles M. ......Brookfield, WI
Soule, David B. ......Wiscasset, ME
Soule, David B., Jr. ......Wiscasset, ME
Soule, Edward B. ......Topeka, KS
Soule, Elizabeth Ann ......Framingham, MA
Soule, Gary T. ......St. Louis, MO
Soule, George W. ......Minneapolis, MN
Soule, Gregory D. ......Minneapolis, MN
Soule, Hardyn B. ......Tacoma, WA
Soule, Jennifer K. ......Chicago, IL
Soule, Joel V. ......Grand Rapids, MI
Soule, John G. ......Austin, TX
Soulé, Kent E. ......San Francisco, CA
Soule, Kevin M. ......Chicago, IL
Soule, Leah M. ......Albany, NY
Soule, Leslie, Kidder, Sayward & Loughman, P.L.L.C. ......Laconia, NH
Salem, NH
Soulé, Margo C. ......Kansas City, MO
Soule, Mark L. ......Anoka, MN
Soule, Matthew D. ......Los Angeles, CA
Soule, Michael S. ......Philadelphia, PA
Soule, Robert G. ......Boston, MA
Soule, Samuel A. ......Rock Springs, WY
Soule, Scott A. ......New Orleans, LA
Soule, Soule & Logan ......Wiscasset, ME
Soule, Stephen J. ......Burlington, VT
Soule, Steven E. ......Los Angeles, CA
Soule, Steven W. ......Tulsa, OK
Soule, Theodore W. ......Pensacola, FL
Soule, Theodore W., P.A. ......Pensacola, FL
Souleles, Thomas S. ......Chicago, IL
Soulema, Solomon ......Los Angeles, CA
Soulen, Allison Rutland ......Washington, DC
Soules, Luther H., III ......San Antonio, TX
Soules & Wallace, Attorneys at Law, A Prof. Corp. ......Austin, TX
San Antonio, TX
Soules, William ......Minnetonka, MN
Soulier, Ruth Elizabeth ......Fairfax, VA
Soulios, Steven A. ......New York, NY
Souliotis, George ......Hartford, CT
Soulis, David P. ......Cartersville, GA
Soullier, John E. ......Harper Woods, MI
Soulliere, Dacia ......Pocatello, ID
Soulsby, Peter W. ......Hartford, CT
Soult, John G. ......Clearfield, PA
Soult, Launcelot E., Jr. ......Clearfield, PA
Soumas, Gregory C. ......Boston, MA
Soumilas, Nevan ......Cherry Hill, NJ

Soumoff, Cynthia ... Foster City, CA
Soundararajan, Srinivasan ... Washington, DC
Soupios, Val A. ... New York, NY
Sourant, James D. ... Friday Harbor, WA
Souras, Louis G. ... Los Angeles, CA
Sourbeer, Emory R. ... Atlanta, GA
Sourial, Wynn Heather ... Los Angeles, CA
Souris, Christopher Nicholas ... Boston, MA
Souris, J. G. ... Vernon, TX
Souris, Theodore ... Chicago, IL
Souris, Theodore G. ... Lakewood, OH
Sourlis, Virginia K. ... Red Bank, NJ
Sours, John D. ... Atlanta, GA
Sours, Matthew J. ... Atlanta, GA
Sourwine, Julien G. ... Reno, NV
Sous, Ramon S. ... Seymour, CT
Sousa, Angela M. ... Los Angeles, CA
Sousa, Anthony G. ... San Francisco, CA
Sousa, Anthony J. ... Los Angeles, CA
Sousa, Barbara Anne ... Boston, MA
Sousa, Barbara C. ... Los Angeles, CA
Sousa, Bettie Kelley ... Raleigh, NC
Sousa, Bruce B. ... Gustine, CA
Sousa, Danielle A. ... Mansfield, MA
Sousa, David P. ... Raleigh, NC
Sousa, Edward M. ... San Jose, CA
Sousa, Edward Ramos ... New York, NY
Sousa, G. Gary ... Bayside, NY
Sousa, George E. ... Somerville, MA
Sousa, Gerald W. ... South Easton, MA
Sousa, Henry J., Jr. ... Norton, MA
Sousa, John L. ... United States Senate, Committee Legal Personnel, GV
Sousa, Louis A. ... Providence, RI
Sousa, Michael ... Albuquerque, NM
Sousa, Ricardo Manuel ... Boston, MA
Sousa, Sheila Cabral ... Warwick, RI
Sousa, Stephanie A. ... Brockton, MA
Sousa, Stephen J. ... Springfield, MA
Sousa, Vicki J. ... Tulsa, OK
Sousie, Lawrence A. ... New York, NY
Souss, Jorge ... San Juan, PR
Souss, Jorge E. ... San Juan, PR
Soussan, Gerard J. ... Beverly Hills, CA
Soussan, Susan S. ... Houston, TX
Soussloff, Andrew D. ... New York, NY
Soutar, Douglas L. ... Greenwich, CT
Soutendijk, Dirk R. ... Wayne, NJ
Souter, David H. ... Supreme Court Of The United States, GV
Souter, Don V. ... Grand Rapids, MI
Souter, Kimberly Hays ... Tulsa, OK
Souter, M. Alan ... Bristow, OK
Souter, Milton M. ... Anchorage, AK
Souter, Patrick D. ... Dallas, TX
Souter, Sydney S. ... Princeton, NJ
Souter and Voliva ... Princeton, NJ
South, Alan E. ... Kansas City, MO
South, Arthur R. ... Lawton, OK
South & Associates, P.C. ... Kansas City, MO
South, B. Claire ... Indianapolis, IN
South, Brett K. ... Reno, NV
South, Daryl M. ... Murfreesboro, TN
South, Dual Scott ... Orlando, FL
South, Galen R. ... Chicago, IL
South, George B., III ... New York, NY
South, J. Todd ... Winter Park, FL
South, Jackey W. ... Lake Charles, LA
South, Jayne L. ... New York, NY
South, Jerry G. ... Sausalito, CA
South, Leslie Elaine ... Flossmoor, IL
South, Mark O. ... Blountsville, AL
South, Melinda H. ... Richmond, VA
South, Myrna Lynn ... Idaho Falls, ID
South, Pamela D. ... Lawrenceville, GA
South, Rhysa Griffith ... Richmond, VA
South, Richard W. ... Austin, TX
South, Steven D. ... Arlington, VA
South, William H. ... Fort Myers, FL
Southall, David M. ... Columbia, MD
Southall, Kenneth ... Atlanta, GA
Southall, Orian C. ... Placentia, CA
Southall, Richard J. ... Kansas City, MO
Southall, Samantha L. ... New York, NY
Philadelphia, PA
Southall, Valentine W., Jr. ... Amelia, VA
Southam, Lynn Wm. ... Aurora, CO
Southard, Bret J. ... Williamsport, PA
Southard, C. Dennis, IV ... Washington, DC
Southard, Calvin B. ... Atlanta, GA
Southard, Charles Gary ... Wichita Falls, TX
Southard, Cristin A. ... Lexington, KY
Southard, Elizabeth S. ... Tallahassee, FL
Southard, Jeffrey C. ... Richmond, VA
Southard, Jeffrey S. ... Kansas City, MO
Southard, John B., Jr. ... Middletown, KY
Southard, Leo A. ... Dickson City, PA
Southard, Melville, Jr. ... New York, NY
Southard, Perry N. ... Lexington, KY
Southard, Robert W. ... Ann Arbor, MI
Southard, Sean W. ... Los Angeles, CA
Southard, Stephen R. ... Cape Girardeau, MO
Southard, Stephen S. ... Lockport, NY
Southard, Terence J. ... Cincinnati, OH
Southard, Warren R. ... Wichita, KS
Southard, William G. ... Boston, MA
Southard, William H. ... Greeley, CO
Southcombe, R. Michael ... Boise, ID
Southcotte, David Geoffrey, Sr. ... Fitchburg, MA
Souther, Albert E. ... Dover, NH
Souther, Eugene P. ... New York, NY
Souther, G. Stuart ... Woodbridge, NJ
Souther, John B. ... Portland, OR
Souther, R. Michael ... Brunswick, GA
Souther, R. Michael, P.C. ... Brunswick, GA
Souther, Thomas McCarthy ... New York, NY
Southerland, Carolyn Brostad ... Houston, TX
Southerland, Edward M. ... Tucker, GA
Southerland, Harold P. ... Tallahassee, FL
Southerland, Harry Lamont ... Durham, NC
Southerland, Henry deLeon, Jr. ... Birmingham, AL
Southerland, J. Michael ... Plymouth, MI
Southerland, James Alfred ... Atlanta, GA
Houston, TX
Southerland, James D. ... Benton, LA
Southerland, Leslie J. ... Tulsa, OK
Southerland, Mary N. ... Chattanooga, TN
Southern & Allen ... Little Rock, AR
Southern, Brent E. ... Jackson, MS
Southern, Byron S. ... Little Rock, AR
Southern, Charles B., Jr. ... Caruthersville, MO
Southern, Charles W. ... Knoxville, TN
Southern, Donn A. ... Memphis, TN
Southern, E. Reid, P.C. ... Mesa, AZ
Southern, Frederick W., Jr. ... Midwest City, OK
Southern, J. Todd ... El Paso, TX
Southern, James G. ... Marietta, GA
Southern, Jana Lane ... Memphis, TN
Southern, Kathleen Pepi ... Raleigh, NC
Southern, Noceeba Donnetta ... Detroit, MI
Southern, Richard ... Jefferson City, MO
Southern, Richard Allen ... New York, NY
Southern, Robert A. ... Chicago, IL
Southern, Robert A. ... Gurnee, IL
Southern, Robert E. ... Great Bend, KS
Southern, Samuel O. ... Raleigh, NC
Southern, Tawnya L. ... Los Angeles, CA
Southers, Eleanor K. ... Los Angeles, CA
Southers, Frank R. ... San Antonio, TX
Southers, Philip L. ... Department of Agriculture, Office of the General Counsel, GV
Southerst, Mark E. ... Dallas, TX
Southey, Byron M. ... Bishop, CA
Southgate, Adrienne G. ... Providence, RI
Southgate, James C. ... Albany, NY
Southgate, Richard W. ... Boston, MA
Southmayd, Andrew K. ... Georgetown, DE
Southon, Edward H. ... Seattle, WA
Southon, Taryn S. ... New Orleans, LA
Southward, Rock A. ... San Francisco, CA
Southward, Wayne E. ... Dayton, OH
Southwell, Alexander H. ... New York, NY
Southwell, Brian C. ... United States Senate, Committee Legal Personnel, GV
Southwell, E. Lee, III ... Atlanta, GA
Southwell, Gilbert L., III ... Milwaukee, WI
Southwell & O'Rourke, P.S. ... Spokane, WA
Southwell & Thompson ... Portland, OR
Southwell, Todd R. ... Chicago, IL
Southwell, Wm. G. ... Portland, OR
Southwick, A. Thomas ... Newark, NJ
Southwick, Benjamin ... Richland Center, WI
Southwick, Holly S. ... Bellevue, WA
Southwick, James D. ... Minneapolis, MN
Southwick, James T. ... Houston, TX
Southwick, Jeffrey P. ... Oklahoma City, OK
Southwick, Jerlyn S. ... Indianapolis, IN
Southwick, Julia B. ... Raleigh, NC
Southwick, Michael J. ... Westport, CT
Southwick, Richard R. ... Syracuse, NY
Southwick, Solace Kirkland ... Houston, TX
Southwick, Stephen W. ... Cedar Rapids, IA
Southwood, John D. ... Jacksonville, FL
Southworth, Ann ... Cleveland, OH
Southworth, Augustus R., III ... Waterbury, CT
Southworth, George A. ... Pocatello, ID
Southworth, Glenn D. ... Cleveland, OH
Southworth, Gregory J. ... Seattle, WA
Southworth, Hamilton, III ... San Diego, CA
Southworth, James E. ... Philadelphia, PA
Southworth, John F., Jr. ... Hixson, TN
Southworth, Karl ... Janesville, WI
Southworth, Kenneth A., III ... Edgartown, MA
Southworth, Laurel J. ... New York, NY
Southworth, Louis S., II ... Charleston, WV
Southworth, Michele ... Swarthmore, PA
Southworth, Mike ... Springfield, IL
Southworth, Peter Keller ... Sacramento, CA
Southworth, Robert, III ... Richland, WA
Southworth, William W. ... Boston, MA
Souto, Edward P. ... Goshen, NY
Souto, Silvia C. ... Elmsford, NY
Soutter, Nicholas B. ... Cohasset, MA
Soutter, Thomas D. ... Providence, RI
Soutullo, Catherine J. ... Gretna, LA
Soutullo, Scott Wayne ... Birmingham, AL
Mobile, AL
Souvall, Harry H. ... Salt Lake City, UT
Souvé, Todd W. ... Dayton, OH
Souvenir, Carole L. ... Portland, OR
Souveroff, Michael W. ... Buena Park, CA
Souweidane, Edward E. ... Mount Clemens, MI
Souweine, Jonathan Z. ... Northampton, MA
Souza, Brett J. ... Irvine, CA
Souza, Christian T. ... Dallas, TX
Souza, Christian T. & Sandra Reynolds ... Dallas, TX
Souza, Emma Burns ... Tracy, CA
Souza, James P. ... San Diego, CA
Souza, Jennifer L. ... Cleveland, OH
Souza, Joanne E. ... Fall River, MA
Souza, John C. ... Pocatello, ID
Souza, John M. ... Fall River, MA
Souza, Joseph C. ... Louisville, KY
Souza, Karen E. ... New Haven, CT
Souza, Kevin A. ... Honolulu, HI
Souza, Leo D. ... Kaneohe, HI
Souza, Matthew F. ... Columbus, IN
Souza, Randall L. ... Providence, RI
Souza, Ronald J. ... San Francisco, CA
Souza, Wayne G. ... Norfolk, VA
Souza, William F. ... North Miami, FL
Souza, William Joseph ... Beverly Hills, CA
Souza-Rasile, Lea Ann ... Miami, FL
Souzon, Jane C. ... Environmental Protection Agency, Office of the General Counsel, GV
Sova, Christopher J. ... Washington, DC
Sova, Donna J. ... Secaucus, NJ
Sova, Gregory ... Toledo, OH
Sova, Laura L. ... Chicago, IL
Sova, Rosemary ... Columbus, OH
Sovak, Christopher J. ... New York, NY
Sovel, Charles ... Philadelphia, PA
Soven, Abby ... Los Angeles, CA
Soven, Alan R. ... Miami, FL
Soven, Andrew J. ... Philadelphia, PA
Soven, Joshua H. ... Department of Justice, Antitrust Division, GV
Soven & Wax ... Miami, FL
Sovereign, Diane ... San Francisco, CA
Sovereign, Jerry A. ... San Bernardino, CA
Sovereign, K. L. ... Lake Elmo, MN
Sovereign, Stacey L. ... Department of Justice, Office of Professional Responsibility, GV
Soverinsky, Randall J. ... Farmington Hills, MI
Sovern, Grant ... Boston, MA
Sovern, Jane M. ... New York, NY
Sovern, Jeff ... Jamaica, NY
Sovern, Michael I. ... New York, NY
Sovern, Steve ... Cedar Rapids, IA
Sovick & Wolpert ... Charleston, WV
Sovie, Donald E. ... Irvine, CA
Sovie, Susan A. ... Watertown, NY
Soviero, Anthony C. ... Delray Beach, FL
Soviero, D. J. ... San Francisco, CA
Soviero, Joseph F., Jr. ... Garden City, NY
Sovik, Laurence F. ... Syracuse, NY
Sovine, Brett D. ... Charlotte, NC
Sovis, Michael V. ... Hastings, MN
Sovocool, Daniel R. ... San Francisco, CA
Sovocool, Roger B. ... Ithaca, NY
Sovronsky, Ruth ... Commack, NY
Sowa, Edward P., Jr. ... Providence, RI
Sowa, Elizabeth S. ... Knoxville, TN
Sowa, Ferdinand B. ... New Bedford, MA
Sowa, Glenn M. ... Geneva, IL
Lisle, IL
Sowa, Nancy Kent ... Philadelphia, PA
Sowa, Paul ... Trabuco Canyon, CA
Sowa, Paul F. ... Los Angeles, CA
Sowa, Robert Reed ... Sutton, WV
Sowa, Sharon ... Valparaiso, IN
Sowa, Walter J., Jr. ... Everett, WA
Sowada, Felix J. ... Gillette, WY
Sowah, Francis N. ... New York, NY
Sowah, Margaret O. ... New York, NY
Sowald, Beatrice K. ... Columbus, OH
Sowald, Heather G. ... Columbus, OH
Sowald, Sowald & Clouse ... Columbus, OH
Sowalsky, Jerome S. ... Vienna, VA
Sowalsky, Joel M. ... Boston, MA
Sowande & Associates, P.C. ... Brooklyn, NY
Sowande, Beverly Folasade ... Brooklyn, NY
Sowar, Gerard D. ... Dayton, OH
Soward, Larry R. ... Austin, TX
Sowards, John A. ... Columbia, SC
Sowards, John S., Jr. ... Lexington, KY
Madisonville, KY
Sowards, Ray W. ... Milpitas, CA
Sowash, Carson & Ferrier ... Athens, OH
Sowash, Jonathan ... Athens, OH
Sowden, Christopher J. ... Hartford, CT
Sowder, James L. ... Dallas, TX
Sowder, John G. ... Providence Forge, VA
Sowder, Madison ... Lubbock, TX
Sowder, Michael D. ... Atlanta, GA
Sowder, William C. ... Lubbock, TX
Sowders, A. Glenn, Jr. ... Kansas City, MO
Sowders, Henry C., III ... Edmond, OK
Sowders, Maria Benecki ... Tyler, TX
Sowders, Steven A. ... Los Angeles, CA
Sowell, Alan M. ... Nashville, TN
Sowell, Charles L. ... Houston, TX
Sowell, Ernest E. ... Houston, TX
Sowell, Gregory C. ... Tifton, GA
Sowell, J. Ralph, Jr. ... Jackson, MS
Sowell, James B. ... Treasury Department, Departmental Offices, GV
Sowell, James W. ... Dickson, TN
Sowell, Jason B., Jr. ... Dallas, TX
Sowell, Jim W. ... Quanah, TX
Sowell, Joseph A., III ... Nashville, TN
Sowell, Kenneth E. ... Simpsonville, SC
Sowell, Leamon R., Jr. ... Detroit, MI
Sowell, Malcolm ... Sonoma, CA
Sowell, Matthew W. ... Jacksonville, FL
Sowell, Matthew W., P.A. ... Jacksonville, FL
Sowell, Myzell ... Detroit, MI
Sowell, Paul ... New York, NY
Sowell, Robert E. ... Bellflower, CA
Sowell & Sandifer, P.C. ... Tifton, GA
Sowell, Stephanie E. ... New York, NY
Sowell, Stephen L. ... Mobile, AL
Sowell, Susan L. ... Charlotte, NC
Sowell, Thornwell F. ... Columbia, SC
Sowell Todd Laffitte Beard & Watson, L.L.C. ... Columbia, SC
Sower, Phyllis A. ... Frankfort, KY
Sowerbutts, David J. ... Bristol, PA
Sowerby, David N. ... Fort Pierce, FL
Sowerby, James B. ... Chicago, IL
Sowerby, Richard G., Jr. ... Raleigh, NC
Sowerby, Vincent D. ... Brunswick, GA
Sowers, Christopher K. ... Brooklyn, NY
Sowers, D. Eric ... St. Louis, MO
Sowers, Donald G. ... Encino, CA
Long Beach, CA
Los Angeles, CA
Newport Beach, CA
Ontario, CA
Orange, CA
Oxnard, CA
Pasadena, CA
Torrance, CA
Universal City, CA
West Covina, CA
Sowers, Edward E. ... Indianapolis, IN
Sowers, George M. ... Richmond, IN
Sowers, James J. ... San Francisco, CA
Sowers, Jayson W. ... Seattle, WA
Sowers, Leonard N. ... Florence, AZ
Sowers, Michele R. ... Dallas, TX
Sowers, Roy G., III ... Burgaw, NC
Sowers, Thomas E. ... Atlanta, GA
Sowers, Walter P., II ... Harrisonburg, VA
Sowerwine, Orvis ... New York, NY
Sowg, Tailim ... Dallas, TX
Sowinski, Edward A., Jr. ... Youngstown, OH
Sowinski, Karen C. ... Woodinville, WA
Sowinski, William A., Jr. ... St. Paul, MN
Sowinski-Fix, Patricia ... Waukegan, IL
Sowle, Allen M. ... Irving, TX
Sowle, Allen M., Jr. ... San Francisco, CA
Sowle, Donald N. ... Mount Pleasant, MI
Sowle, Leslie A. ... Los Angeles, CA
Sowle, Mary E. ... Chicago, IL
Sowle, Stephen D. ... Chicago, IL
Sowles, J. Kenneth ... Burlington, VT
Sowles, Marcia K. ... Department of Justice, Civil Division, GV
Sownie, Peter ... Scottsdale, AZ
Sowsy, Craig F. ... Newton, MA
Sowyrda, Mary Ellen ... Quincy, MA
Sowyrda, Michael W. ... Worcester, MA
Sox, James A. ... New Hope, PA
Sox, Jonathan W. ... Reston, VA
Sox, Richard N., Jr. ... Tallahassee, FL
Sox, Thomas E. ... Ambler, PA
Soy, Rosa H. ... Montclair, NJ
Soya, Stanley R. ... Washington, DC
Soyars, John Thomas ... Hopkinsville, KY
Soyars-Berman, Julia A. ... Washington, DC
Soybel, Arthur ... New York, NY
Soycher, Mark D. ... Bloomfield, CT
Soycher & Winslow, LLC ... Bloomfield, CT
Soyka, David L. ... Newton, MA
Soypher, Howard B. ... Baltimore, MD
Soyster, Margaret Blair ... New York, NY
Soyster, Matthew D. ... St. Petersburg, FL
Soza, Alfredo A. ... Odessa, TX
Soza, Jeffrey C. ... Los Angeles, CA
Soza, Robert L., Jr. ... San Antonio, TX
Sozan, Michael L. ... Department of Justice, Executive Office for Immigration Review, GV
Sozansky, Michael W., Jr. ... Flemington, NJ
Sozio, Alan ... Los Angeles, CA
Sozio Law Offices ... Springfield, VT
Sozio, Maria L. ... Springfield, VT
Sozio, Stephen G. ... Cleveland, OH
Spaanstra, James R. ... Denver, CO
Spacapan, Edward, Jr. ... Chicago, IL
Spacapan, Lise T. ... Chicago, IL
Spaccasi, Lawrence M. F. ... Washington, DC
Space, Richard T. ... Newport Beach, CA
Space, Socrates J. ... New Philadelphia, OH
Space & Space ... New Philadelphia, OH
Space, Theodore M. ... Hartford, CT
Space, Zachary T. ... New Philadelphia, OH
Spacek, Edward G. ... New York, NY
Spacek, Eric A. ... Washington, DC
Fairfax, VA
Spacek, John F. ... Cudahy, WI
Spach, Madison S., Jr. ... Newport Beach, CA
Spack, Barbara S. ... San Francisco, CA
Spack, Harry ... Roswell, GA
Spackey, Thomas Melvin ... Brighton, MI
Spackman & Co., A Limited Liability Company ... Dallas, TX
Spackman, David G. ... Boston, MA
Spackman, Hugh S. ... Santa Barbara, CA
Spackman, Paul ... Los Angeles, CA
Spackman, Thomas James, Jr. ... Dallas, TX
Spackman, Thomas M. ... Boston, MA
Spacone, Andrew Carl ... Providence, RI
Spada, Anthony J. ... Grosse Pointe, MI
Spada, Ardam & Ershowsky, P.C. ... Smithtown, NY
Spada, Arthur L. ... Hartford, CT
Spada, Charles T. ... New York, NY
Spada, D. Joseph ... Montebello, CA
Spada, David M. ... Oak Brook, IL
Spada, David P. ... Brookline, MA
Spada, Deborah D. ... Barrington, IL
Spada, Eugene R. ... Albany, NY
Spada, Francis Xavier ... Leonia, NJ
Spada, Frank M., Sr. ... Olivebridge, NY
Spada, Frank P., Jr. ... Blue Bell, PA
Spada, Gerald F. ... Newark, NJ
Spada, Justine Lisa ... Albany, NY
Spada, Lawrence J. ... Smithtown, NY
Spada, Leonard Louis ... Boston, MA
Spada, Robert W. ... Detroit, MI
Spada, Teresa D. ... Washington, DC
Spadaccini, Dino ... Trenton, NJ
Spadaccini, Louis A. ... Newington, CT

Spadaccini, Maria P. ... New York, NY
Spadaccini, Michael ... San Francisco, CA
Spadacene, Joseph C. ... Pittsburgh, PA
Spadafor, Christine J. ... Boston, MA
Spadafora, John E. ... Buffalo, NY
Spadafora, Jo-Una ... New York, NY
Spadafora, Luigi ... New York, NY
Spadafora, Mario A. ... Dearborn Heights, MI
Spadafore, Emil M., Jr. ... Meadville, PA
Spadafore, Neville K. ... San Jose, CA
Spadafore, Scott William ... Monongahela, PA
Spadaro, Donald R. ... Fort Lauderdale, FL
Spadaro, James J., Jr. ... Philadelphia, PA
Spadaro, John S. ... Wilmington, DE
Spadaro, Stephanie J. ... New York, NY
Spade, Dana R. ... Aurora, CO
Spade, Eric F. ... Cleveland, OH
Spade, Gina M. ... Washington, DC
Spade, Holland B. ... Frankfort, KY
Spade, James F. ... Harrisburg, PA
Spade, John A. ... Hagåtña, GU
Spader, David J. ... Harrisburg, PA
Spader, Dean J. ... Vermillion, SD
Spader, Robert J. ... Silverdale, WA
Spades, Michael W., Jr. ... Little Rock, AR
Spadlin, G.D. ... San Luis Obispo, CA
Spado, James A. ... Charlotte, NC
Spadone, Donald ... Hamilton, MT
Spadone, Melina ... New York, NY
Spadoni, Charles B. ... Hartford, CT
Spadoni, Christopher T. ... Bethlehem, PA
Spadoni, Eileen ... Irvine, CA
Spadoni, Gino, Jr. ... Eureka, CA
Spadoni, Peter A. ... Wenatchee, WA
Spadora, John C. ... Union City, NJ
Spadorcia, Jon F. ... Indianapolis, IN
Spadoro, George A., Jr. ... Woodbridge, NJ
New York, NY
Spadoro & Hilson ... New Brunswick, NJ
Woodbridge, NJ
New York, NY
Spadoro, Mark A. ... Chicago, IL
Spadoro, Nicholas J. ... Edison, NJ
Spadt, Jonathan Henry ... Valley Forge, PA
Spady, James R. ... Seattle, WA
Spaeder, Roger C. ... Washington, DC
Spaeder-Younkin, Joan C.
Lake Forest, CA
Spaeth, Anton P. ... Houston, TX
Spaeth, Belinda ... St. Louis, MO
Spaeth, Bernard L. "Jerry", Jr.
Des Moines, IA
Spaeth, Bret A. ... Findlay, OH
Spaeth, C. Grant ... Palo Alto, CA
Spaeth, Earl C. ... Washington, DC
Kalamazoo, MI
Spaeth, Edmund B., Jr. ... Philadelphia, PA
Spaeth, Edward J. ... Cincinnati, OH
Spaeth, Frederick A. ... Simsbury, CT
Spaeth, Gary L. ... Helena, MT
Spaeth, George A. ... San Francisco, CA
Spaeth, Harry M., Jr. ... Philadelphia, PA
Spaeth, Jonathan S. ... Washington, DC
Spaeth, Joseph L. ... San Rafael, CA
Spaeth, Juliana M. ... Atlanta, GA
Spaeth, Karl Henry ... Conshohocken, PA
Spaeth, Keith M. ... Fairfield, OH
Spaeth, Kevin B. ... Cape Girardeau, MO
Spaeth, Kevin B. ... Grand Forks, ND
Spaeth, Mark ... Watonga, OK
Spaeth & McGrath ... San Francisco, CA
Spaeth, Melvin ... Washington, DC
Spaeth, Nicholas J. ... Palo Alto, CA
Spaeth, Paul H. ... Dayton, OH
Spaeth, Paul H., Co., L.P.A. ... Dayton, OH
Spaeth, Peter A. ... Boston, MA
Spaeth, Peter H. ... Red Bank, NJ
Spaeth, Rosemary W. ... Newton, MA
Spaeth, Sidney J. ... Fargo, ND
Spaeth, Steven M.
Federal Communications Commission,
Common Carrier Bureau, GV
Spaeth, Susan M. ... Palo Alto, CA
Spaeth, Terrence R. ... Eau Claire, WI
Spaeth, Thelen, Van Voorhis & Jasmer
Grand Forks, ND
Spaeth, Wayne E. ... Smithtown, NY
Spaetti, Charles A. ... Evansville, IN
Spafford & Associates ... Salt Lake City, UT
Spafford, Donald L., Jr. ... Honolulu, HI
Spafford, Earl S. ... Salt Lake City, UT
Spafford, Gay, Ferro & Ivy ... Dallas, TX
Spafford, Michael L. ... Washington, DC
Spagat, David ... Oak Park, IL
Spagat, Martin, (P.C.) ... Chicago, IL
Spagat, Robert ... San Francisco, CA
Spagna, Rocco J. ... Chicago, IL
Spagna, Susan L. ... New York, NY
Spagnardi, Joseph M.
Research Triangle Park, NC
Spagnola, Gary S. ... Bridgewater, NJ
Spagnola, Mary M. ... Fort Pierce, FL
Spagnola, Samuel S. ... Concord, NC
Spagnola, Susan Sturges ... New York, NY
Spagnoletti, Robert James ... Washington, DC
Spagnoli, Charles C. ... Syracuse, NY
Spagnoli, Christine D. ... Santa Monica, CA
Spagnoli, Deborah Ann ... Bakersfield, CA
Spagnoli, Joseph W. ... Cranford, NJ
Spagnoli, Michael D. ... Hartford, CT
Spagnoli, Paul D., Jr. ... New York, NY
Spagnolo, Leonard F. ... Pittsburgh, PA
Spagnuolo, Carl J. ... Boca Raton, FL
Spagnuolo, Mario L. ... Bedford, NY
Spagnuolo, Vincent P. ... East Lansing, MI
Spahn, Elizabeth K. ... West Hartford, CT
Spahn, G. Daniel ... Steubenville, OH
Spahn, Gary J. ... Richmond, VA

Spahn, Gay Ann ... Appleton, WI
Spahn, George C. ... Rockville Centre, NY
Spahn, Harvis, Greenberg & Broida
Columbia, MD
Spahn, Jeff C., Jr. ... Wichita, KS
Spahn, John C. ... Los Angeles, CA
Spahn, Kenneth E. ... Boca Raton, FL
Spahn, Merrill M., Jr ... Lancaster, PA
Spahn, Michael J. ... New York, NY
Spahn, Philip C. ... Merrillville, IN
Spahn, Philip F., Jr. ... Rochester, NY
Spahn, Ronald L. ... Columbia, MD
Spahn, Stephanie C. ... Washington, DC
Spahn, Susan J. ... Omaha, NE
Spahn, Thomas E. ... Richmond, VA
Spahn, Thomas J. ... Westchester, IL
Spahn, Thomas J. & Associates, P.C.
Westchester, IL
Spahr, Boyd L., Jr. ... Blue Bell, PA
Spahr, Chesterfield A. ... San Francisco, CA
Spahr, Ellen L. ... Chicago, IL
Spahr, Jon R. ... Newark, OH
Spahr, Karl E. ... Cleburne, TX
Spahr, Kenneth G., Jr. ... Akron, OH
Spahr, Laurence Charles ... Hollis, NY
Spahr, M. Jeffry ... Norwalk, CT
Spahr, Michael G. ... Marietta, OH
Spahr, Natalie J. ... Houston, TX
Spahr, Robert A. ... Peru, IN
Spahr, Steven O. ... Harrisburg, PA
Spaht, Carlos G. ... Baton Rouge, LA
Spaht, Katherine S. ... Baton Rouge, LA
Spaht, Paul H. ... Baton Rouge, LA
Spaid, Brian M. ... Franklin, PA
Spaid, Noel W. ... Del Mar, CA
Spain, Amy E. ... Memphis, TN
Spain, Anthony P. ... New York, NY
Spain, Astrid R. ... San Diego, CA
Spain, C. Compton ... Mahopac, NY
Spain, Charles A., Jr. ... Houston, TX
Spain, Charles H., Jr. ... Cleveland, OH
Spain, Darius J. ... Bridgeport, CT
Spain, David A. ... Orlando, FL
Spain, Debra Deames ... Montgomery, AL
Spain, Edward O. ... Troy, NY
Spain, Fully R. ... Warren, OH
Spain, Gary J. ... Visalia, CA
Spain & Gillon, L.L.C. ... Birmingham, AL
Spain, H. Daniel ... Houston, TX
Spain & Hastings ... Houston, TX
Spain, Jack H., Jr. ... Richmond, VA
Spain, James E. ... Poplar Bluff, MO
Spain, Jerry J. ... San Francisco, CA
Spain, John A. ... Cincinnati, OH
Spain, John F. ... Bethel, CT
Spain, Judith W. ... Richmond, KY
Spain, Kenneth W. ... Kansas City, MO
Spain, Margaret E. ... Forney, TX
Spain, Mary R. ... Richmond, VA
Spain, Melvyn N. ... New York, NY
Spain, Merrell and Miller, L.L.P.
Poplar Bluff, MO
Spain, Michael C. ... West Palm Beach, FL
Spain, Michael Louis ... San Antonio, TX
Spain, Nancy M. ... Chicago, IL
Spain, Norman N. ... Ardsley, NY
Spain, Paul L. ... Adamsville, AL
Spain, Ralph ... Gainesville, GA
Spain, Richard C. ... Chicago, IL
Schaumburg, IL
Northborough, MA
Spain, Samuel P. ... Poplar Bluff, MO
Spain, Spain & Varnet, P.C. ... Chicago, IL
Homewood, IL
Schaumburg, IL
Northborough, MA
Spain, Thomas B. ... Madisonville, KY
Spain, Thomas D. ... Troy, NY
Spain, Thomas J. ... Salisbury, MD
Spain, William C. ... Oakland, CA
Spain, William D., Jr. ... Mahopac, NY
Spain, William E. ... Richmond, VA
Spainhour, Brian W. ... Atlanta, GA
Spainhour, C. Timothy ... Conway, AR
Spainhour, Carla G., (P.A.)
Little Rock, AR
Spainhour, Carole ... Blowing Rock, NC
Spainhour, Elise Givhan ... Louisville, KY
Shepherdsville, KY
Spainhour, John E., Jr. ... Louisville, KY
Shepherdsville, KY
Spainhour, Sterling A. ... Columbia, SC
Spainhour, T. Howard ... Norfolk, VA
Spainhour, William Erwin ... Concord, NC
Spainhoward, Rebecca A. ... Columbus, OH
Spaite, Paul W. ... Cincinnati, OH
Spaite, Paul W., Co., L.P.A. ... Cincinnati, OH
Spaits, Kim L. ... Bloomington, IL
Spajer, Allen M. ... Gary, IN
Spajic, Robert ... Portland, OR
Spak, Bernard R. ... Chicago, IL
Spak, David G. ... Chicago, IL
Spak, David G. ... Northfield, IL
Spak, Donald F. ... Chicago, IL
Spak, Gregory J. ... Washington, DC
Spak, Lorin M. ... Barrington, IL
Spak, Marsha C. ... Chicago, IL
Spak, Michael I. ... Chicago, IL
Spak, Nancy H. ... San Antonio, TX
Spak, Theodore ... Chicago, IL
Spak, Walter J. ... Washington, DC
Spake, Todd W. ... Fort Worth, TX
Spaka, Gerald A. ... Moreno Valley, CA
Spalatin, Mario S. ... Wauwatosa, WI
Spalding, Albert D., Jr. ... Detroit, MI
Spalding, Andrew F. ... Houston, TX
Spalding, Arthur C. ... Grand Rapids, MI
Spalding, Benedict J. ... Kansas City, MO

Spalding, Bethany P. ... Fairbanks, AK
Spalding, Catherine H. ... Louisville, KY
Spalding, Catherine W. ... Randolph, MA
Spalding, Charles G. ... Brunswick, GA
Spalding, D. Andrew ... South Bend, IN
Spalding, David B. ... Alliance, OH
Spalding, Drew ... Government Printing Office,
Office of General Counsel, GV
Spalding, Francis O. ... San Francisco, CA
Spalding, Henry C., III ... Richmond, VA
Spalding, Hughes, Jr. ... Atlanta, GA
Spalding, James H. ... Nashville, TN
Spalding, Jeffery S. ... Grand Rapids, MI
Spalding, John E. ... Houston, TX
Spalding, John L. ... Covington, KY
Spalding, John Phinizy ... Atlanta, GA
Spalding, Joseph C. ... Louisville, KY
Spalding, Judy M. ... Dallas, TX
Spalding, Karin I. ... Rochelle Park, NJ
Spalding, Kirsten S. ... San Francisco, CA
Spalding, Larry H. ... Sarasota, FL
Spalding, Laura H. ... Houston, TX
Spalding, Lester Helm ... Lebanon, KY
Spalding, Maria S. ... Hartford, CT
New Haven, CT
Spalding, Mark J. ... Del Mar, CA
Spalding, Michael ... San Francisco, CA
Spalding, Michael F. ... Louisville, KY
Spalding, Philip F. ... San Francisco, CA
Spalding, Rita C. ... Brunswick, GA
Spalding, Robert K. ... Chesterfield, MO
Spalding, Robert M. ... Chicago, IL
Spalding, Roger S. ... Philadelphia, PA
Spalding, Rosemary G. ... Indianapolis, IN
Spalding, Samuel Todd ... Lebanon, KY
Spalding, Sloan T. ... Columbus, OH
Spalding, Staci F. ... Houston, TX
Spalding, Steven L. ... Lexington, KY
Spalding, Thad D. ... San Antonio, TX
Spalding, Thomas L.
Rancho Cucamonga, CA
Spalding, Thomas L., Law Offices of
Rancho Cucamonga, CA
Spalding & Ujczo Co., L.P.A. ... Westlake, OH
Spalding, Wallace H., III ... Louisville, KY
Spalding, Wallace H., Jr. ... Louisville, KY
Spalding, Walter T., Jr. ... Westlake, OH
Spalding, Warren S. ... Philadelphia, PA
Spalding, William R. ... Atlanta, GA
Spalding, William W. ... Lancaster, PA
Lebanon, PA
Philadelphia, PA
Reading, PA
Spalitta, Salvadore V. ... New Orleans, LA
Spalj, Gregory T. ... Minneapolis, MN
Spall, Cynthia C. ... West Palm Beach, FL
Spall, Gerald R. ... Vineland, NJ
Spall, Hugh M., Jr. ... Ellensburg, WA
Spall, James A. ... Helena, MT
Spall, John F. ... Hawley, PA
Spall and Magnotta ... Hawley, PA
Spall, Thomas L. ... North Palm Beach, FL
Spalla, A. J. Jim ... Tallahassee, FL
Dayton, OH
Spalla, Andrea L. ... New York, NY
Spalla, Joseph R. ... Avon, CT
Spalla, Salvatore J. ... Dayton, OH
Spalla & Spalla ... Dayton, OH
Spallas, Gregory L. ... Fresno, CA
San Francisco, CA
San Luis Obispo, CA
Spallas, Nichlas P. ... Tucson, AZ
Spalletta, Sandra L. ... Washington, DC
Spallina, Fred V. ... Porterville, CA
Spallina & Krase ... Porterville, CA
Spallina, Randi Perry ... Los Angeles, CA
Spallina, William F. ... Newton, MA
Spallino, James, Jr. ... Cleveland, OH
Spallo, August V. ... Kansas City, MO
Spallo, Joseph P. ... Kansas City, MO
Spallo & Spallo ... Kansas City, MO
Spallone, James F. ... New London, CT
Spalo, William M. ... Chicago, IL
Spaloss, Henry F. ... Nashua, NH
Spaloss & Rosson ... Nashua, NH
Spalsbury, Clark S., Jr. ... Estes Park, CO
Spalten, David E. ... Atlanta, GA
Spalter, David H. ... Miami, FL
Spalter, Pamela ... Davie, FL
Spalter, Robyn Jeana ... New Orleans, LA
Spalter, Ruth Ann ... Everett, WA
Spalter, Samuel A. ... Brooklyn, NY
Spaltro, James P. ... Orange, CA
Spalty, Edward R. ... Olathe, KS
Kansas City, MO
Spalvins, K. Karl ... Knoxville, TN
Spaly, Gregory A. ... Ann Arbor, MI
Spamer, Jeffrey J. ... Phoenix, AZ
Spampinato, William J. ... Hudson, NY
Span, Gerald ... Atlantic City, NJ
Newark, NJ
New York, NY
Span, Miriam N. ... Elizabeth, NJ
Span, Patrick J. ... Minnetonka, MN
Span, Robert S. ... Los Angeles, CA
Spanagel, George W. ... Parma Heights, OH
Spanagel, Kenneth R. ... Parma, OH
Spanakos, John M. ... Brooklyn, NY
Spanakos, Michel ... New York, NY
Spanakos & Spanakos ... Brooklyn, NY
Spanakos, William M. ... Brooklyn, NY
Spanbauer, Wendy L. ... Charlotte, NC
Spanbock, Jonathan H. ... New York, NY
Spanbock, Maurice S. ... New York, NY
Spander, Deborah L. ... Los Angeles, CA
Spandorf, Leo ... Uniondale, NY
Spandorf, Rochelle Buchsbaum
Los Angeles, CA

Spaneas, Catherine A. ... Clifton Park, NY
Spanel, Claudette M. ... Dayton, OH
Spaner, Ann A. ... Charleston, WV
Spang, Brian Edward ... Chicago, IL
Spang, Christopher Alfred ... Reading, PA
Spang, David F. ... Reading, PA
Spang, Donald F. ... Reading, PA
Spang, Kenneth O., III ... Blue Bell, PA
Spang, Lynn ... San Francisco, CA
Spangelo, James W. ... Havre, MT
Spangelo, Waldo N. ... Havre, MT
Spangenberg, Caroline W. ... Atlanta, GA
Spangenberg, David P. ... Marinette, WI
Spangenberg, Eric Karl ... Portola Valley, CA
Spangenberg, Erich Lawson
Los Angeles, CA
Spangenberg, James A.
General Accounting Office,
Office of the General Counsel, GV
Spangenberg, Jennifer ... Layton, UT
Spangenberg, Shibley & Liber LLP
Cleveland, OH
Spangenberg, William Charles ... Wheeling, IL
Spangler, Andrew M. ... Chicago, IL
Spangler, Craig D. ... Berea, OH
Spangler, Daniel R. ... Casper, WY
Spangler, David B. ... Greensboro, NC
Spangler, David B., P.A. ... Greensboro, NC
Spangler, David C. ... Washington, DC
Spangler, Donald M. ... Tallahassee, FL
Spangler, E. Douglas, Jr. ... Sarasota, FL
Spangler, E. Douglas, P.A. ... Sarasota, FL
Spangler, Ellen P. ... Denver, CO
Spangler, Frederick S. ... York, PA
Spangler, Garland S. ... Pearisburg, VA
Spangler, Garland S., P.C. ... Pearisburg, VA
Spangler, Gary G. ... Knoxville, TN
Spangler, Georlen K. ... Henderson, NV
Spangler, J. Christopher ... Sedalia, MO
Spangler, J. Robert, II ... Woodland, CA
Spangler, James C. ... Chicago, IL
Spangler, James Robert ... San Diego, CA
Spangler, Jeffrey T. ... Philadelphia, PA
Spangler, Jennings & Dougherty, P.C.
Crown Point, IN
Gary, IN
Hammond, IN
Merrillville, IN
Valparaiso, IN
Spangler, Jerry Lee ... Somerset, PA
Spangler, John H. ... West Chester, PA
Spangler, John I., III ... Atlanta, GA
Spangler, John M. ... Frankfort, KY
Spangler, John T. ... Missoula, MT
Spangler, Kathleen A. ... Baltimore, MD
Spangler, Kathleen Bone ... Houston, TX
Spangler, Kenneth L. ... New York, NY
Spangler, Kent S. ... Evanston, WY
Spangler, Kirk L. ... Salem, OR
Spangler, Laura S. ... Dallas, TX
Spangler, Lore K. ... Los Angeles, CA
Spangler, Lynne Sindoni ... Berwyn, PA
Spangler, M. Todd ... Fresno, CA
Spangler, Mark S. ... Wakefield, RI
Spangler, Matthew M. ... Rio Rancho, NM
Spangler, Melissa D. ... Columbus, OH
Spangler, Michael W. ... Bryan, OH
Montpelier, OH
Spangler, Nancy A. ... Washington, DC
Reston, VA
Spangler, Richard L., Jr. ... Lincoln, NE
Spangler, Robert W. ... Belton, MO
Harrisonville, MO
Spangler, Ronald T. ... Merrillville, IN
Spangler, Shannon L. ... San Francisco, CA
Spangler, Stan L. ... Denver, CO
Spangler, Theodore V., Jr. ... Boise, ID
Spangler, Viiu ... Los Angeles, CA
Spangler, Walter L. ... Posen, IL
Spangler-Weiss, Jane R. ... Paoli, PA
Spaniac, Katharine L. ... San Bernardino, CA
Spanich, Jason John ... Tahlequah, OK
Spaniel, Edward Francis, Jr.
Philadelphia, PA
Spanier, A. Orli ... New York, NY
Spanier, Alan F. ... Oakland, CA
Spanier, David B. ... New York, NY
Spanier, Irving L. ... Great Neck, NY
Spanier, Judith L. ... New York, NY
Spanier, Kristen L. ... Los Angeles, CA
Spanier, Maury L. ... Purchase, NY
Spaniol, Joseph F., Jr. ... Bethesda, MD
Spaniola, Anthony M.
Bloomfield Hills, MI
Spaniola, Paul R. ... Ludington, MI
Spaniola, William P. ... Muskegon, MI
Spaniolo, James D. ... Miami, FL
Spaniolo, M. R. ... Lansing, MI
Spanjers, Craig M. ... Winter Haven, FL
Spann, Anthony J. ... Dunkirk, NY
Spann, Anthony J., P.C. ... Dunkirk, NY
Spann, Bob J. ... Corpus Christi, TX
Spann, Calvin D. ... Los Angeles, CA
Spann, Charles C. ... Albuquerque, NM
Spann, Charles E. ... Richardson, TX
Spann, Charles W. ... Las Vegas, NV
Reno, NV
Spann, Girardeau A. ... Washington, DC
Spann, James J., Jr. ... Dunkirk, NY
Spann, John Arthur, III ... Nashville, TN
Spann, Kathryn C. ... New York, NY
Spann, Kenneth L. ... Gunnison, CO
Spann, Kimbra R. ... Nashville, TN
Spann, Latimer & Hollowwa
Albuquerque, NM
Spann, Richard E. ... Lancaster, CA
Spann, Richard H. ... Columbus, MS
Spann, Robert F. ... Nashville, TN

Spann, Stephen P. ....Nashville, TN
Spann, Terrance A. ....Department of the Army, U.S. Army Legal Services Agency, GV
Spannaus, Warren R. ....Minneapolis, MN
Spanne, David L. ....El Cerrito, CA
Spanner, Bruce A. ....Richland, WA
Spanner, Robert A. ....Menlo Park, CA
Spanner, Robert A., A Prof. Corp., Law Offices of ....Menlo Park, CA
Spanninger, Beth Anne ....Philadelphia, PA
Spano, Brian J. ....Denver, CO
Spano, Ellen ....Basking Ridge, NJ
Spano, Frank T. ....New York, NY
Spano, Joseph A. ....Port Jervis, NY
Spano, Karen M. ....Chatham, NJ
Spano, Michael ....Auburn, NY
Spano, Michele M. ....New York, NY
Spano, Robert A. ....Redding, CA
Spano, Rosemary C. ....New York, NY
Spano, Sal A. ....Garden City, NY
Spano, Salvatore ....Wantagh, NY
Spano, Salvatore R. ....San Jose, CA
Spano, Stephen ....Saugus, MA
Spano, V. Ross ....Jacksonville, FL
Tampa, FL
Spano-Harting, Lisa M. ....Painesville, OH
Spanopoulos, Lynda Wray ....Memphis, TN
Spanos & Black ....Walnut Creek, CA
Spanos, Charles V. ....Claremont, NH
Spanos, Christopher J. ....Peoria, IL
Spanos, Evanthia ....Oakland, CA
Spanos, George C. ....Sacramento, CA
Spanos, George D. ....Petoskey, MI
Spanos, George G. ....Stockton, CA
Spanos, George V. ....Walnut Creek, CA
Spanos, Harry V. ....Newport, NH
Spanos, James C. ....Peabody, MA
Spanos, Katherine A. ....Sacramento, CA
Spanos, Olympia Critikou ....Houston, TX
Spanos, Paul G. ....Cleveland, OH
Columbus, OH
Spanos, Peter R. ....Atlanta, GA
Spanos, Theodore G. ....Los Angeles, CA
Spanoulis, Constantine A.
Virginia Beach, VA
Spansel, Mark J. ....New Orleans, LA
Spanton, Conway L. ....Geneseo, IL
Spanton, Donald M. ....Melville, NY
New York, NY
Spanton & Parsoff, LLP ....Melville, NY
Mineola, NY
New York, NY
Riverhead, NY
Spanyer, H. Beckham ....Louisville, KY
Spar, A. Albert ....Los Angeles, CA
Spar, Harold S. ....Daly City, CA
Spar, Harvey M. ....Charleston, SC
Spar, Julie L. ....New York, NY
Spar, Michael R. ....West Orange, NJ
Spar, Rebecca K. ....Hackensack, NJ
Spar, Robert A. ....Baltimore, MD
Spar, Robert J. ....Department of Commerce, Patent and Trademark Office, GV
Sparacino, Anthony J., Jr. ....Beckley, WV
Sparacino, Jack R. ....Belle Vernon, PA
Sparacino, John J. ....Houston, TX
Sparacino, Michael W. ....East Meadow, NY
Sparacio & Allen ....Chicago, IL
Sparacio, Robert D. ....Bloomingdale, IL
Sparacio, Steven J. ....Chicago, IL
Sparaco, Christine A. ....Stamford, CT
Sparaco, Richard ....Cherry Hill, NJ
Sparaco, Robert J. ....Garden City, NY
Sparaco, Susan A. ....Auburn, ME
Sparagna, Diana Biafora ....Reseda, CA
Sparagna, Francis A., Jr. ....Reseda, CA
Sparagna, Giovanna T. ....Washington, DC
Sparagna, Sparagna, Ferrone & Ferrone
Bakersfield, CA
Los Angeles, CA
Reseda, CA
Sparagna, Stephanie A. ....Los Angeles, CA
Sparago, Lorraine H. ....Garden City, NY
Sparano, Kim E. ....Montclair, NJ
Sparber, Byron L. ....Miami, FL
Sparber, Ferguson, Ponder & Ryan, A Professional Law Corporation
San Diego, CA
Sparber, Frank A.
Federal Energy Regulatory Commission, Office of the General Counsel, GV
Sparber, Kim A. ....Corona, NY
Sparber, Neil G. ....New York, NY
Sparber, Norman H. ....New York, NY
Sparber, Richard E. ....San Diego, CA
Sparber, Roy M. ....New York, NY
Sparby, Delray L. ....Thief River Falls, MN
Spare, Amy L. ....Houston, TX
Spare, Philip H. ....Mechanicsburg, PA
Spare, Richard N. ....Pottstown, PA
Sparer, Alan B. ....West Islip, NY
Sparer, Alan W. ....San Francisco, CA
Sparer, Robert A. ....New York, NY
Sparer, William J. ....Chicago, IL
Sparger, Kevin W. ....Jonesboro, GA
Sparger, Steven L. ....Savannah, GA
Spargo, Alan D. ....Old Saybrook, CT
Spargo, Michael N. ....Lorton, VA
Spargo, Thomas J. ....East Berne, NY
Spargo, Wendy R. ....Bangor, ME
Spargur, Jon L., Jr. ....Winston-Salem, NC
Spark, Andrew Bennett ....Sarasota, FL
Spark, Jeffrey ....Nashville, TN
Spark, Matthew J. ....Palo Alto, CA
Sparkes, James E. ....Syracuse, NY
Sparkes, Phillip M. ....Albany, NY
Sparklin, Rex D. ....Seminole, FL
Sparkman, Allen ....Denver, CO
Sparkman, Ann ....San Francisco, CA
Sparkman & Associates, P.C. ....Denver, CO
Sparkman, Catherine A. G. ....Denver, CO
Sparkman & Davison, L.L.P.
Wichita Falls, TX
Sparkman, Jackie B. ....Philadelphia, PA
Sparkman, James D. ....Rockford, IL
Sparkman, James T. ....Fort Lauderdale, FL
Miami, FL
Sparkman, Janet P. ....Nashville, TN
Sparkman, John C. ....New York, NY
Sparkman, Jon B. ....Manchester, NH
Sparkman, Joseph B. ....Portland, OR
Sparkman, Joseph M., Jr. ....Southaven, MS
Sparkman, Lynn O. ....Sparta, TN
Sparkman, Michael E. ....Hartselle, AL
Sparkman and Quinn, P.A. ....Naples, FL
Sparkman, Richard D. ....Naples, FL
Sparkman, Richard D. ....Angier, NC
Sparkman, Richard D., & Associates, P.A.
Angier, NC
Sparkman, Robb & Mason
Fort Lauderdale, FL
Miami, FL
Sparkman, Roy T. ....Wichita Falls, TX
Sparkman, Steven L. ....Tampa, FL
Sparkman, Susan K. ....Denver, CO
Sparks, A. Gilchrist, III ....Wilmington, DE
Sparks, Andrew W. ....Portland, ME
Sparks, Anne Charette ....Raleigh, NC
Sparks, Anne L. ....Houston, TX
Sparks, Arthur L. ....Wichita, KS
Sparks, Bertel M. ....Durham, NC
Sparks, Beth Meiers
Colorado Springs, CO
Sparks, Billy S. ....Overland Park, KS
Sparks, Bonnie S. ....St. Louis, MO
Sparks, Braden W. ....Dallas, TX
Sparks, Braden W., P.C. ....Dallas, TX
Sparks, Brian C. ....Tampa, FL
Sparks, C. Michael ....Williamson, WV
Sparks, Charles H. ....Portland, OR
Sparks, Charles L. (Larry) ....Birmingham, AL
Sparks, Craig L. ....Vail, CO
Sparks, Daniel D. ....Birmingham, AL
Sparks, Daniel R. ....Louisa, KY
Sparks, Danielle R. ....Columbus, OH
Sparks, David ....Paducah, KY
Sparks, David R. ....Tupelo, MS
Sparks, David T. ....Bowling Green, KY
Sparks, David W. ....Irvine, CA
Sparks, Deidre Lynn ....Palo Alto, CA
Sparks, Derek H. ....Dallas, TX
Sparks, Douglas C. ....Sacramento, CA
Sparks, Elizabeth A. ....Cedar Rapids, IA
Sparks, Eric S. ....Scottsdale, AZ
Tucson, AZ
Sparks, Eric Slocum, P.C. ....Scottsdale, AZ
Tucson, AZ
Sparks, Galen M. ....Dallas, TX
Sparks, George O., Jr. ....New Windsor, MD
Sparks, Gil ....Wenatchee, WA
Sparks, Grant C. ....Georgetown, TX
Sparks, Harold S., III ....Fort Worth, TX
Sparks, Herbert B. ....Edmonton, KY
Sparks, Herbert B., Jr. ....Birmingham, AL
Sparks, Herschel E., Jr. ....Miami, FL
Sparks, J. Steven ....Phoenix, AZ
Sparks, J. Timothy ....Charlotte, NC
Sparks, Jack N. ....Florham Park, NJ
Sparks, Jacqueline R. ....Palo Alto, CA
Sparks, James D., Jr. ....Monroe, LA
Sparks, James J. ....San Carlos, CA
Sparks, James, Jr. ....Beaumont, TX
Sparks, Jeffrey C. ....Redondo Beach, CA
Sparks, Jeffrey C. ....Orlando, FL
Sparks, Jeffrey C., P.A. ....Orlando, FL
Sparks, Jeffrey W. ....Prescott, AZ
Sparks, Jennifer A. ....Phoenix, AZ
Sparks, Jerry D. ....Chicago, IL
Sparks, Jerry G. ....McMinnville, OR
Sparks, Jerry R. ....Beverly Hills, CA
Sparks, Jesse F., Jr. ....Orlando, FL
Sparks, Joe P. ....Scottsdale, AZ
Sparks, John A. ....Grove City, PA
Sparks, John Hunt ....Oklahoma City, OK
Sparks, John R. ....Grand Rapids, MI
Sparks, John R., Jr. ....Lancaster, PA
Philadelphia, PA
Reading, PA
Sparks, John T. ....Atlanta, GA
Sparks, Jonathan W. ....Greenwich, CT
Sparks, Karen ....Seattle, WA
Sparks, Karen A. ....Walnut Creek, CA
Sparks, Karol K. ....Indianapolis, IN
Sparks, Keith A. ....Bardstown, KY
Sparks, Keith F. ....Loomis, CA
Sparks, Kenneth ....Colorado Springs, CO
Sparks, Kenneth C. ....Kalamazoo, MI
Sparks, Kenneth F. ....Chicago, IL
Sparks, Kenneth R. ....Springfield, VA
Sparks, Kenneth W. ....Weimar, TX
Sparks, Kyra L. ....Selma, AL
Sparks, Lee ....Woodward, OK
Sparks, Lee Ann ....Atlanta, GA
Sparks, Leonard, III ....Houston, TX
Sparks, Linda ....Brunswick, ME
Sparks, Lonnie F. ....Spokane, WA
Sparks, Lyle Wayne ....Chicago, IL
Sparks, Lynne W. ....Marietta, GA
Sparks, M. Randolph ....Charlotte, NC
Sparks, Marcia L. ....Prospect, KY
Sparks, Margaret R. ....New York, NY
Sparks, Michael T. ....Sacramento, CA
Sparks, Nancy S. ....Memphis, TN
Sparks, Nelson T. ....Louisa, KY
Sparks, Norma Doctor ....Honolulu, HI
Sparks, O. C. "Rusty" ....Little Rock, AR
Sparks, Oswald Claude ....Little Rock, AR
Sparks, Randy C., Jr. ....Virginia Beach, VA
Sparks, Reuben K., III
Colorado Springs, CO
Sparks, Rex V. ....Norfolk, VA
Sparks, Ricky E. ....Frankfort, KY
Sparks, Robert A. ....Fairbanks, AK
Sparks, Robert H. ....Detroit, MI
Sparks, Robert K. ....Las Vegas, NV
Sparks, Robert M. ....Atlanta, GA
Sparks, Robert R. ....Covington, KY
Sparks, Robert R., Jr. ....McLean, VA
Sparks, Robert W. ....New York, NY
Sparks, Robin A. ....Hempstead, NY
Sparks, Robin V. ....Birmingham, AL
Sparks, Sam ....Austin, TX
Sparks, Sam D. ....San Angelo, TX
Sparks, Scott R. ....Ellensburg, WA
Sparks, Serena L. ....Riverdale, GA
Sparks, Seth L. ....Albuquerque, NM
Santa Fe, NM
Sparks, Sheila L. ....Reston, VA
Sparks, Stephen L. ....Jackson, MS
Sparks, Stephen S. ....Kansas City, MO
Sparks, Steven R. ....Media, PA
Sparks, Steward A., III ....Cumming, GA
Sparks, Susan E. ....Madison, IN
Sparks, Susan E. ....Angleton, TX
Sparks, Susan L. ....San Diego, CA
Sparks, Tehan & Ryley, P.C. ....Phoenix, AZ
Scottsdale, AZ
Sparks, Thomas D. ....Bakersfield, CA
Sparks, Thomas E. ....Fordyce, AR
Sparks, Thomas E., Jr.
San Francisco, CA
Sparks, Thomas L. ....Okemos, MI
Sparks, Thomas R. ....Raleigh, NC
Sparks, Timothy J. ....Palo Alto, CA
Sparks, Ty M. ....Canadian, TX
Sparks, W. Donald ....Media, PA
Sparks, W. Donald, II ....Wilmington, DE
Sparks, W. E. "Bill" ....Tulsa, OK
Sparks, William B. ....Woodbury, NJ
Sparks, William D. ....Cedartown, GA
Sparks, William Earl ....Tulsa, OK
Sparks, William F. ....Rome, GA
Sparks, William J. A. ....Columbia, MD
Sparks, William K. ....Louisville, KY
Sparks, William R. ....Canton, OH
Sparks, Willis B., III ....Macon, GA
Sparks Willson Borges Brandt & Johnson, P.C. ....Colorado Springs, CO
Sparks, Wood T. ....Monroe, LA
Sparler, Kenneth J. ....York, PA
Sparler, Sylvia A. ....West Palm Beach, FL
Sparlin, Derry Dean, Jr. ....Washington, DC
Sparlin, Ronald G. ....Joplin, MO
Sparling, Betty Ann ....Melville, NY
Sparling, Cynthia L. ....Oklahoma City, OK
Sparling, Densford and Reynolds, P.A.
Lexington Park, MD
Sparling, Gary A. ....Seattle, WA
Sparling, George R. ....Lexington Park, MD
Sparling, John E. ....New York, NY
Sparling, Joy L. ....Chicago, IL
Sparling, Randy J. ....Minneapolis, MN
Sparling, Richard P. ....Washington, DC
Sparling, Tobin Andrews ....Houston, TX
Sparno, Thomas A. ....Roseland, NJ
Sparr, Daniel B. ....Denver, CO
Sparr, David K. ....Oshkosh, WI
Sparr, David K., S.C., Associates
Oshkosh, WI
Sparr, Faith M. ....Kansas City, MO
Sparr, Jennifer Hernden ....San Antonio, TX
Sparr, Stephen G. ....Denver, CO
Sparrenberger, William H. ....Indianapolis, IN
Sparrough, Ann R. ....Upper Marlboro, MD
Sparrow, Amy C. ....Palo Alto, CA
Sparrow, Calvin N. ....Carmel, IN
Sparrow, David J. ....Bloomfield Hills, MI
Sparrow, Donald G. ....Greensboro, NC
Sparrow, George N., Jr. ....Fayetteville, GA
Sparrow, George N., Jr., P.C.
Fayetteville, GA
Sparrow, Herbert G., III ....Detroit, MI
Sparrow, J. Callen ....Birmingham, AL
Sparrow, J. Raymond, Jr. ....Reston, VA
Sparrow, James B. ....Danville, KY
Sparrow, Jason B. ....Greensboro, NC
Sparrow, John P. ....Oakland, CA
Sparrow, Keithley B. ....Toledo, OH
Sparrow, Laurie Joy ....Bronx, NY
Sparrow & Lavette, P.C.
Birmingham, AL
Sparrow, Marvin ....Boston, MA
Sparrow, Marvin R. ....Raleigh, NC
Sparrow, Mary Ireland
Department of Commerce, Patent and Trademark Office, GV
Sparrow, Miriam Lane ....New York, NY
Sparrow, Nancy J. ....Louisville, KY
Sparrow, Richard S. ....Sarasota, FL
Sparrow, Robert E. ....Kew Gardens, NY
Sparrow, Ruth S. ....Philadelphia, PA
Sparrow, Sarah F. ....Greensboro, NC
Sparrow, Sidney G. ....Kew Gardens, NY
Sparrow, Sophie M. ....Claremont, NH
Sparrow, Sparrow, Singer & Schreiber
Kew Gardens, NY
Sparrow, W. Clayton, Jr. ....Atlanta, GA
Sparrow, Warren ....Winston-Salem, NC
Sparschu, Mark S. ....Dearborn, MI
Spartichino, George W. ....Cambridge, MA
Spartin, Debbie Beecher, (P.C.)
Washington, DC
Spartis, Gary L. ....Columbus, OH
Spartz, Donald H. ....Le Center, MN
Spartz, Laura L. ....Eagan, MN
Sparwath, Stephen H. ....Marietta, GA
Spasser, Leslie F. ....Atlanta, GA
Spat, Meryl A. ....Waterbury, CT
Spata, Frank F. ....Houston, TX
Spata, Michael C. ....Visalia, CA
Spatafora, Samuel J.
Grosse Pointe Shores, MI
Spatafore, John A. ....San Luis Obispo, CA
Spatafore, Marcus A. ....Pittsburgh, PA
Spatari, Richard J. ....Liverpool, NY
Spataro, Carl L., Jr. ....Reston, VA
Spataro, Christopher J. ....Elkhart, IN
Spataro, John C. ....New York, NY
Spataro, John F. ....Meadville, PA
Spataro, Michael ....New York, NY
Spataro, Peter F. ....St. Louis, MO
Spataro, Stephen A. ....Santa Monica, CA
Spatcher, George I., Jr. ....Attleboro, MA
Spater, Alexander M. ....Columbus, OH
Spater, Benjamin F. ....San Francisco, CA
Spater, Gittes, Schulte & Kolman
Columbus, OH
Spates, Dennis P. ....New York, NY
Spath, Gregg A. ....Warren, NJ
Spath, John M. ....Grosse Pointe, MI
Troy, MI
Spath, Linda C. ....San Francisco, CA
Spath, M. Kristin ....Manchester, NH
Spath, Thomas E. ....New York, NY
Spath, Walter F., III ....San Francisco, CA
Spathis, George J. ....Chicago, IL
Spatola, Jo-Anne B. ....Elizabeth, NJ
Spatoliatore, Lucian V. ....New York, NY
Spatorico, Derrick A. ....Rochester, NY
Spatt, Arthur D. ....Uniondale, NY
Spatt, David M. ....Saunderstown, RI
Spatt, Robert E. ....New York, NY
Spatuzza, John G. ....Chicago, IL
Spatuzza and Spatuzza ....Chicago, IL
Spatz, Alan B. ....Los Angeles, CA
Spatz, Bilha ....Jamaica, NY
Spatz, Carl A. ....Miami, FL
Spatz, Hilary Ann ....Pittsburgh, PA
Spatz, Joanne ....Elmhurst, IL
Spatz, Laura E. ....San Antonio, TX
Spatz, Mark M. ....Fort Lauderdale, FL
Spatz, Robert L. ....Annandale, VA
Spatz, Russell A. ....Miami, FL
Spatz, William J. ....New York, NY
Spatz, William V. ....Treasury Department, Internal Revenue Service, GV
Spatzek, James F., Jr. ....Chicago, IL
Spatzer, Samuel M. ....Miami, FL
Spaude, Stuart J. ....Appleton, WI
Spaugh, Robert G. ....Winston-Salem, NC
Spaulding, Alayne L. ....Everett, WA
Spaulding, Alyson E. ....Buffalo, NY
Spaulding, Anthony A. ....Santa Monica, CA
Spaulding, Arthur O., Jr. ....Irvine, CA
Spaulding, Bernard L. ....Logan, WV
Spaulding, Brian L. ....Springdale, AR
Spaulding, Cathryn ....Wellesley, MA
Spaulding, Christopher D. ....Des Moines, IA
Spaulding, Donald O. ....Roseville, CA
Spaulding, Douglas K. ....Washington, DC
Spaulding, Earl L. ....Sacramento, CA
Spaulding, Gregory G. ....Santa Rosa, CA
Spaulding, Harold G. C. ....Santa Rosa, CA
Spaulding, Jill ....Fresno, CA
Spaulding, Karla R. ....Orlando, FL
Spaulding, Kenneth B. ....Durham, NC
Spaulding, Larry D. ....Des Moines, IA
Spaulding, Lawrence O., Jr. ....Orleans, MA
Spaulding, Linda D. ....Oakland, CA
Spaulding, Linda Rae, (P.A.)
Fort Lauderdale, FL
Spaulding, Lynette V. ....White Plains, NY
Spaulding, Matthew F. ....Culver City, CA
Spaulding McCullough & Tansil LLP
Santa Rosa, CA
Spaulding, O. Connor ....Hurricane, WV
Spaulding, Paul L. ....Richmond, VA
Spaulding, Paul P., III ....San Francisco, CA
Spaulding, Ralph D. ....Albany, NY
Spaulding, Randal I. ....Roundup, MT
Spaulding, Robert Frank ....Olympia, WA
Spaulding, Robert M. ....Buffalo, NY
Spaulding, Roger H. ....San Diego, CA
Spaulding, Sally Anne ....St. Louis Park, MN
Spaulding, Sandra R. ....San Jose, CA
Spaulding, Scott W. ....Chicago, IL
Spaulding, Stephanie G. ....Pittsburgh, PA
Spaulding, Steven S. ....San Francisco, CA
Spaulding, Suzanne E. ....United States Senate, Senatorial Assistants, GV
Spaulding, Thomas B. ....Sacramento, CA
Spaulding, Thomas F. ....Portland, OR
Spaulding, Thomas F., P.C. ....Portland, OR
Spaulding-Ruddell, Janet A. ....Hartford, CT
Spaull, Elaine M. ....Rochester, NY
Spaunhorst, Bradley V. ....St. Louis, MO
Spaustat, James H. ....Hermosa Beach, CA
Spaw, David E. ....Cleveland, OH
Spaw, Peter S. ....Phoenix, AZ
Spawn, Coy U., Jr. ....Houston, TX
Spayd, Robert V. ....Dayton, OH
Spayde, Barbara Faye ....Long Beach, MS
Spayde, White & Anderson ....Oskaloosa, IA
Spayne, Timothy C. ....Norwich, CT
Spayth, Guy R., Jr. ....Wheaton, IL
Spaziani, Charles H. ....Easton, PA
Spaziano, Gini P. ....Providence, RI
Spaziano, Jennifer L. ....Los Angeles, CA
Spaziano, Virginia ....Providence, RI
Speagle, Tina K. ....Lansing, MI
Speake, Harold L. ....Moulton, AL
Speake, Scott L. ....New Orleans, LA

Speaker, Alexandre ... New York, NY
Speaker, David K. ... Rocky River, OH
Speaker, Homer A. ... Shepherdstown, WV
Speaker Law Firm, P.C. ... Atlanta, GA
Speaker, Mark D. ... Princeton, NJ
New York, NY
Speaker, Peter J. ... Bethlehem, PA
Harrisburg, PA
Speaker, Sharyl Poulson ... Scottsdale, AZ
Speaker, Susan J. ... Tulsa, OK
Speaker, Theodore A. ... Atlanta, GA
Speakman, Claudia J. ... Columbus, OH
Speakman, Michael S. ... Auburn, AL
Speakman, Riethmuller, Svidro & Allison
Washington, PA
Speakman, Valerie B. ... Memphis, TN
Speakman, William E., Jr. ... Washington, PA
Speaks, Christopher G. ... Clanton, AL
Speaks, Francis W., Jr. ... Clanton, AL
Speaks, Francis Wm. ... Clanton, AL
Speaks, John C. ... New York, NY
Speaks, Peter ... Harrisburg, PA
Speaks, William M., Jr. ... Winston-Salem, NC
Speal, Gerald K. ... Babylon, NY
Speal, Sherry Lee ... Babylon, NY
Speal and Speal ... Babylon, NY
Spear, Alan L.
Federal Deposit Insurance Corporation, Liquidation Branch, GV
Spear, Alison D. ... Los Angeles, CA
Spear, Amy Reidbord ... Pittsburgh, PA
Spear, Barry W. ... Norfolk, VA
Spear & Blackburn, P.S.C. ... Vanceburg, KY
Spear, Bradley H. ... Van Nuys, CA
Spear, Bruce A. ... San Diego, CA
Spear, C. Scott ... Philadelphia, PA
Spear, Charles S. ... Oakland, CA
Spear, Curt G., Jr. ... Newport News, VA
Spear, David ... Pine City, MN
Spear, David B. ... Pittsburgh, PA
Spear, Donald A. ... Brunswick, ME
Spear, E. Eugene ... Bridgeport, CT
Spear, Earle T. ... Boston, MA
Spear, Garry R. ... Boca Raton, FL
Spear, Gary Randall ... Mobile, AL
Spear, George E., II ... Swanton, VT
Spear, H. Dyke N., Jr. ... Hartford, CT
Spear, Harvey M. ... New York, NY
Spear, Howard ... Randolph, NJ
Spear, J. Bartley, Jr. ... Cameron, MO
Spear, James A. ... Deerfield, IL
Spear, Jeffrey C. ... Portland, OR
Spear, Jeffrey W. ... Pittsburgh, PA
Spear, John Barlow ... Durango, CO
Spear, John D., Law Offices of
Bonita Springs, FL
Spear, Jonathan L. ... McLean, VA
Spear, Julia C. ... Metairie, LA
Spear, Karen C. ... Tucson, AZ
Spear, Kathleen Kelly ... Northfield, IL
Spear, Laura M. ... Philadelphia, PA
Spear, Leonard ... Philadelphia, PA
Spear, Lloyd E. ... Vanceburg, KY
Spear, Louis L. ... Chicago, IL
Spear, Mark E. ... Mobile, AL
Spear, Martin J. ... Los Angeles, CA
Spear, Mercer P. ... Panama City, FL
Spear, Noel M. ... Roseland, NJ
Spear, Rand ... Philadelphia, PA
Spear, Richd. J. ... Oakland, CA
Spear, Robin L. ... New York, NY
Spear, Rosanne F. ... Philadelphia, PA
Spear, Ruth ... Richmond, CA
Spear, Samuel L. ... Philadelphia, PA
Spear, Sandra L. ... Arlington, VA
Spear, Scott A. ... Washington, DC
Spear, Scott T. ... Providence, RI
Spear, Shane R. ... Midland, TX
Spear, Steven C. ... Whitewater, WI
Spear & Swanson ... Pine City, MN
Spear, Timothy ... Kansas City, MO
Houston, TX
Spear, Tracie D. ... Washington, DC
Spear, Vanessa M. ... San Francisco, CA
Spear, Wilderman, Borish, Endy, Spear and Runckel ... Haddonfield, NJ
Philadelphia, PA
Spear, William E. ... Juneau, AK
Speare, Allen C., Law Office of
San Jose, CA
Speare and Hughey ... Media, PA
Speare, Richard ... San Diego, CA
Speare, Robert N. ... Media, PA
Speare, William J. ... Billings, MT
Speare, William J. ... Billings, MT
Spearing, Mary C. ... Washington, DC
Spearing, Michael I. ... Huntsville, AL
Spearing, Neil M. ... Ambler, PA
Spearing, Scott S. ... Boston, MA
Spearman, Glen A. ... San Diego, CA
Spearman, Huey W. ... Waycross, GA
Spearman, Lori Anne ... Grapevine, TX
Spearman, Patricia H. ... Durham, NC
Spearman, Richard L. ... Fort Smith, AR
Spearman, Robert W. ... Raleigh, NC
Spearman, Theodore F.
Bainbridge Island, WA
Spearman, Theodore, P.C.
Bainbridge Island, WA
Spears, Alan L. ... Allegany, NY
Spears & Associates Co., L.P.A.
Ironton, OH
Spears, Barnes, Baker, Wainio, & Whaley, L.L.P. ... Durham, NC
Spears, Berry D. ... Austin, TX
Spears, Bonnie R. ... Thomasville, GA
Spears, Brian ... Atlanta, GA
Spears, Carleton B. ... San Antonio, TX
Spears, Carlson, Lindsey & Anderson
Cable, WI
Hayward, WI
Washburn, WI
Spears, Charles M. ... Bowie, MD
Spears, Charles Steven ... La Jolla, CA
Spears, Christopher C. ... Peoria, IL
Spears, Claudos G. ... St. Petersburg, FL
Spears, D. Michael ... Clearwater, FL
Spears, David ... New York, NY
Spears, David E. ... Portsmouth, OH
Spears, David R. ... Ironton, OH
Spears, Dennis W. ... North Kansas City, MO
Spears, Diane C. ... Memphis, TN
Spears, Diane W. ... Boston, MA
Spears, Donald M. ... Malvern, AR
Spears, Douglas C. ... Orlando, FL
Spears, Duncan T. ... Atlanta, GA
Spears, Frank H. ... Portland, OR
Spears, Franklin Scott, Jr. ... Austin, TX
Spears, Gilda F. ... Tucker, GA
Spears, Grady M. ... Lafayette, LA
Spears, Gregory P. ... Dayton, OH
Spears, Harold C. ... Charlotte, NC
Spears, Harold D. ... Ironton, OH
Spears, Hugh D. ... Dallas, TX
Spears, Iric Vonn ... Clearwater, FL
Spears, James B., Jr. ... Charlotte, NC
Spears, James C., Jr. ... Spartanburg, SC
Spears, James Herbert ... Lincoln, NE
Spears, James M. ... Washington, DC
Spears, Jeffry S. ... Rockford, IL
Spears, Jim D. ... Fort Smith, AR
Spears, John F., Jr. ... Des Plaines, IL
Spears, John W., Jr. ... Atlanta, GA
Spears, Kenneth L. ... Oklahoma City, OK
Spears, Kenneth L., P.C.
Oklahoma City, OK
Spears, Kenneth R. ... Lake Charles, LA
Spears, L. Gene, Jr. ... Houston, TX
Spears, Larry L. ... Monmouth, IL
Spears, Larry M. ... Oklahoma City, OK
Spears Law Firm, The
Oklahoma City, OK
Spears Law Offices ... Malvern, AR
Spears, Lawrence D. ... Bismarck, ND
Spears, Marshall T., Jr. ... Durham, NC
Spears, Marvin E. ... Tulsa, OK
Spears, Melvin S. ... Beverly Hills, CA
Spears, Michael E. ... Spartanburg, SC
Spears, Michael E., P.A. ... Spartanburg, SC
Spears, Mitchell A. ... Montevallo, AL
Spears, Moore, Rebman & Williams
Chattanooga, TN
Spears, Natalie J. ... Chicago, IL
Spears, Rachel Epps ... Atlanta, GA
Spears, Ray E.
Environmental Protection Agency, Office of Enforcement and Compliance Assurance, GV
Spears, Richard A. ... Lafayette, LA
Spears, Richard A. ... New Iberia, LA
Spears, Richard W. ... Lexington, KY
Spears, Rita L. ... Tempe, AZ
Spears, Robert A. ... Midland, TX
Spears, Robert E., Jr. ... Atlanta, GA
Spears, Robert F. ... Austin, TX
Spears, Robert L. ... Watertown, SD
Spears, Robert M. ... Cable, WI
Washburn, WI
Spears, Robert W. ... Lake City, CO
Spears, Ronald A. ... Phoenix, AZ
Spears, Ronald D. ... Taylorville, IL
Spears, Ronald S ... Medina, OH
Spears, Sally ... San Antonio, TX
Spears, Scott D. ... Meridian, ID
Spears, Sonja M. ... New Orleans, LA
Shreveport, LA
Spears & Spears ... New Orleans, LA
Shreveport, LA
Spears & Spears ... Ironton, OH
Portsmouth, OH
Spears, Stephen D. ... Downers Grove, IL
Spears, Steven G. ... Houston, TX
Spears, Sylvia L. ... San Francisco, CA
Spears, Ted D. ... Locust Grove, GA
Spears, Terrence M. ... Dixon, IL
Spears, Timothy Paul ... Cincinnati, OH
Spears, William D. ... Onida, SD
Spear-Smith, Garrett ... Omaha, NE
Spears-Petersen, Carolyn H.
San Antonio, TX
Speary, William A., Jr. ... Chicago, IL
Speas, Caron E. ... Welaka, FL
Speas, Denise L.
Securities and Exchange Commission, Office of Compliance Inspections and Examinations, GV
Speas, Edwin M., Jr. ... Raleigh, NC
Spease, Laura R. ... Oakland, CA
Speca, John M. ... Kansas City, MO
Specchio, Lisa Anna ... Glendale, CA
Specchio, Michael R. ... Reno, NV
Specchio, Richard K.
South Lake Tahoe, CA
Spece, Roy G., Jr. ... Tucson, AZ
Spechalske, Jon M. ... Mobile, AL
Spechalske, Richard A. ... Cleveland, OH
Spechler, Arthur I. ... Voorhees, NJ
Spechler, Jay S. ... Fort Lauderdale, FL
Specht, Alan I. ... New York, NY
Specht, Darla Scranton ... Lamar, CO
Specht, Frank Evans ... Atlanta, GA
Specht, Frederick L. ... Chicago, IL
Specht, Linda B. ... San Antonio, TX
Specht, Lisa ... Los Angeles, CA
Specht, Lisa A. ... Orlando, FL
Specht, Michael B. ... Nyack, NY
Specht, Randolph Stephen
Oklahoma City, OK
Specht, Robert J. ... Trafford, PA
Specht, Scott A. ... Atlanta, GA
Specht, U. H. (Woody) ... Dallas, TX
Specht, Yvonne S. ... Dallas, TX
Specia, Arden Anne ... San Antonio, TX
Specia, Ashley C. ... San Antonio, TX
Specia, John J., Jr. ... San Antonio, TX
Special, Teresa Ann ... Victoria, TX
Speciale, Charles J. ... Fairfax, VA
Speciale, George H. ... Salt Lake City, UT
Speciale, John D. ... Woodland Hills, CA
Specian, Patricia A. ... Cleveland, OH
Specie, Karen K. ... Gainesville, FL
Speciner, David P. ... New York, NY
Speciner, Mark J. ... New York, NY
Speck & Aanestad, A Professional Corporation ... Ketchum, ID
Speck, Aaron T., Law Office of ... Taylor, MI
Speck, Adrian D. ... Dallas, TX
Speck, Alisa Berne ... Houston, TX
Speck, Christian A. ... Marysville, CA
Speck, Connie L. ... Eugene, OR
Speck, David W. ... Harrisburg, PA
Speck, F. Allen ... Kansas City, MO
Speck, Fred ... Chicago, IL
Speck, James F. ... Kansas City, MO
Speck, James F., P.C. ... Kansas City, MO
Speck, James P. ... Ketchum, ID
Speck, Laura J. ... Houston, TX
Speck, Mark James ... San Diego, CA
Speck, Michael R. ... Woodbridge, NJ
Speck, Nancy L. ... Towson, MD
Speck, Paul J. ... Bend, OR
Speck, Paula K. ... Department of Justice, Tax Division, GV
Speck Philbin Attorneys, A Professional Corporation ... Oklahoma City, OK
Speck, Randall L. ... Washington, DC
Speck, Sue Vansau ... Houston, TX
Speck, Wayne F. ... San Antonio, TX
Speck, Wm. H. ... Bethesda, MD
Specker, Ellen C. ... Department of Justice, Tax Division, GV
Specker, Robert G. ... Menlo Park, CA
Speckhals, Trent B. ... Atlanta, GA
Speckhard, Donald K. ... Greensboro, NC
Speckhard, Joel T. ... Valparaiso, IN
Speckhard, Rebecca A. ... Milwaukee, WI
Speckhard, Stanley E. ... Greensboro, NC
Speckman, Ann Willard ... Seattle, WA
Speckman, David L., Law Offices of
San Diego, CA
Speckman & Hoback ... Louisville, KY
Speckman, Thomas W.
Hoffman Estates, IL
Speckman, Thomas W. ... Louisville, KY
Speckmann, James E. ... St. Paul, MN
Specks, Ernest E. ... Dallas, TX
Specks, Gary L. ... Chicago, IL
Specks & Goldberg ... Chicago, IL
Specks, Granvil I. ... Chicago, IL
Specktor, Bruce A. ... St. Paul, MN
Specter, Arlen ... Philadelphia, PA
Specter, Donald H. ... San Quentin, CA
Specter, Elaine ... Erie, PA
Pittsburgh, PA
Specter, Howard A. ... Erie, PA
Pittsburgh, PA
Specter, Jill Ossenfort ... Irvine, CA
Specter Law Offices, P.C. ... Erie, PA
Specter, Marianna E. ... Pittsburgh, PA
Specter, Richard B. ... Irvine, CA
Specter, Ronald C. ... San Francisco, CA
Specter, Shanin ... Philadelphia, PA
Specter Specter Evans & Manogue, P.C.
Pittsburgh, PA
Specthrie, Jared ... New York, NY
Specthrie, Mark ... Middletown, NY
Spector, Abraham ... Silver Spring, MD
Spector, Abraham ... Brooklyn, NY
Woodmere, NY
Spector, Alan J. ... Lincolnshire, IL
Spector, Alan M. ... Department of Defense, Armed Services Board of Contract Appeals, GV
Spector, Albert B., Jr. ... Scottsdale, AZ
Spector, Amy ... Boston, MA
Spector, Andrew R. ... Miami, FL
Spector, Ann F. ... Chittenango, NY
Spector, Arthur J. ... Bay City, MI
Spector, Barbara ... Campbell, CA
Spector, Barry S. ... Washington, DC
Spector, Barry W. ... Denver, CO
Spector, Bennett A. ... Beverly Hills, CA
Spector, Bertha A. ... Baltimore, MD
Spector, Brian A. ... St. Louis, MO
Spector, Brian D. ... Florham Park, NJ
Spector, Brian F. ... Miami, FL
Spector, Brian N. ... Phoenix, AZ
Spector, Bruce R. ... Baltimore, MD
Spector, Carl J. ... St. Louis, MO
Spector, Carl S. ... New York, NY
Spector, Claire G. ... Brooklyn, NY
Spector & Cohen, LLP ... Santa Ana, CA
Spector, Craig D. ... Hackensack, NJ
Spector, Daniel I. ... Sacramento, CA
Spector, David ... Brooklyn, NY
Spector, David I. ... West Palm Beach, FL
Spector, David M. ... Los Altos Hills, CA
Spector, David M. ... Chicago, IL
Spector, David N. ... Columbus, OH
Spector, Donald M. ... New York, NY
Spector, Douglas M. ... Great Neck, NY
Spector, Douglas M. ... Great Neck, NY
Spector, Edward M. ... Cedar Rapids, IA
Spector, Edward S. ... Buffalo, NY
Spector & Ehrenworth, P.C.
Florham Park, NJ
Spector, Elliot B. ... West Hartford, CT
Spector, Eric S. ... Arlington, VA
Spector, Erica S. ... New York, NY
Spector, Eugene A. ... Philadelphia, PA
Spector & Feldman, LLP ... New York, NY
Spector, Frank W. ... Timonium, MD
Spector, Gabriel E. ... West Long Branch, NJ
Spector Gadon & Rosen, P.C.
Moorestown, NJ
Philadelphia, PA
Spector, Gary Ford ... Tucson, AZ
Spector, Gary M. ... Cleveland, OH
Spector, George L. ... New York, NY
Spector, Herman ... Baltimore, MD
Spector, J. Paul ... Beverly Hills, CA
Spector, J. Steven ... Kearny, NJ
Spector, James M. ... New York, NY
Spector, Jeffrey A. ... Washington, DC
Spector, Jeffrey A. ... Washington, DC
Spector, Jeremy A. ... Philadelphia, PA
Spector, Jeremy D. ... Washington, DC
Spector, Jesse ... Lauderhill, FL
Spector, Joel A. ... Orlando, FL
Spector, Joel J. ... New York, NY
Spector, John A. ... Windham, CT
Spector, John P. ... Milwaukee, WI
Spector, Joseph R. ... Largo, FL
Spector, Julie A. ... Seattle, WA
Spector, Kenneth L. ... Chicago, IL
Spector, Larry H. ... Philadelphia, PA
Spector, Laura A. ... Manchester, NH
Spector Law Firm ... Campbell, CA
Spector Law Offices, P.C. ... Scottsdale, AZ
Spector, Lawrence A. ... New York, NY
Spector, Lawrence H. ... Skokie, IL
Spector, Leonard C. ... Brooklyn, NY
Spector, Leonard S. ... United States Senate, Committee Legal Personnel, GV
Spector, Louis ... Falls Church, VA
Spector, Marc T. ... Hollywood, FL
Spector, Mark A. ... Washington, DC
Spector, Marshal P. ... Aloha, OR
Spector, Martin W. ... Philadelphia, PA
Spector, Michael G. ... Santa Ana, CA
Spector, Michael J. ... Milwaukee, WI
Spector, Michael S. ... Department of Justice, Antitrust Division, GV
Spector, Michelle B. ... New York, NY
Spector, Mindy J. ... New York, NY
Spector, Morgan ... Lancaster, CA
Spector, Nancy A. ... San Diego, CA
Spector, Neal S. ... Garden City, NY
Spector, Neil C. ... Tampa, FL
Spector, Norman C. ... Boston, MA
Hingham, MA
Spector, Paul R. ... Philadelphia, PA
Spector, Philip H. ... New York, NY
Spector, Phillip L. ... Washington, DC
New York, NY
Spector, Rachel ... Minneapolis, MN
Spector, Richard S. ... Chicago, IL
Spector, Richard S., Ltd. ... Chicago, IL
Spector, Robert G. ... Norman, OK
Spector, Robert L. ... Fort Lauderdale, FL
Spector, Robert L., A Professional Association
Fort Lauderdale, FL
Spector, Robert M. ... Minneapolis, MN
Spector, Robert S. ... Cleveland, OH
Spector, Ronald L. ... San Francisco, CA
Spector, Rose ... Austin, TX
Spector & Roseman, A Professional Corporation ... San Diego, CA
Philadelphia, PA
Spector, Ross A. ... San Francisco, CA
Spector, Scott P. ... Palo Alto, CA
Spector, Seymour ... Lido Beach, NY
Spector, Sharman ... San Francisco, CA
Spector, Solomon R. ... Santa Cruz, CA
Spector, Solomon R. ... Skokie, IL
Spector, Stanley S. ... Ocean Township, NJ
Spector, Stephen L. ... Santa Monica, CA
Spector, Stephen L. ... Tallahassee, FL
Spector, Steven Barry ... Takoma Park, MD
Spector, Steven David ... Glenview, IL
Spector, Steven M. ... Los Angeles, CA
Spector, Steven R., (P.A.) ... Englewood, NJ
Spector, Steven W. ... Los Angeles, CA
Spector, Susan A. ... New York, NY
Spector, Sweeney & Wolfe, L.L.C.
St. Louis, MO
Spector, Sydney M. ... White Plains, NY
Spector, Tappa & Nathan ... Rock Island, IL
Spector, Wayne H. ... White Plains, NY
Spector, Wendy R. ... Eureka, CA
Spector, William D. ... Los Angeles, CA
Spector, Yale R. ... Timonium, MD
Spedale, Charles E. ... Baton Rouge, LA
Spedale, Gerald M. ... Houston, TX
Spedale, Iris R. ... Vienna, VA
Spedale, Rhodes J., Jr. ... New Orleans, LA
Spee, David R. ... Paia, HI
Speece, Janet L. ... Cleveland, OH
Speece, Joseph M., Jr. ... Muncie, IN
Speece, Robert L. ... Willoughby Hills, OH
Speece, Steven E. ... Wayne, PA
Speed, Bryant G., II ... Atlanta, GA
Speed, Carolyn W. ... Fort Smith, AR
Speed, Chester A. ... Louisville, KY
Speed, Christopher K.
West Palm Beach, FL
Speed, Clifton Thomas ... Greensburg, LA
Speed, Elena V. ... San Francisco, CA
Speed, Fred M., Jr. ... Dublin, OH
Speed, Gary N. ... Little Rock, AR
Speed, Jackson ... San Antonio, TX
Speed, James T. ... Meridian, MS

Speed, Lea Hall ... **Memphis, TN**
Speed, Leslie B. ... **Baltimore, MD**
Speed, Linda Shearer ... **Louisville, KY**
Speed, Mark D. ... **New York, NY**
Speed, Marvin B., (P.A.) ... Meridian, MS
Speed, Phyllis A. ... **Fort Worth, TX**
Speed, Robert E. ... Houston, TX
Speed, Robert E., P.C. ... Houston, TX
Speed & Rogers, P.A. ... **Little Rock, AR**
Speed, Wallace ... **Atlanta, GA**
Speed, William G., IV ... Rocky Hill, CT
Speed, William W. ... **Dallas, TX**
Speed-Bost, Regina Y. ... **Washington, DC**
Speedlin, Phylis J. ... **San Antonio, TX**
Speedy, George W. ... Camden, SC
Speedy, Kim A. ... Flint, MI
Speedy, Timothy D. ... **Morristown, NJ**
Speegle, C. Max ... Edmond, OK
Speegle, Christopher F. ... Cambridge, MA
Speegle, Jerome E. ... **Mobile, AL**
Speegle, Mike W. ... Oklahoma City, OK
Speelman, Eleanor L. ... Columbus, OH
Speelman, Joseph F. ... **Houston, TX**
Speelmon, April A. ... **Mesa, AZ**
Speer, Alfred A., II ... St. Louis, MO
Speer, Alfred A., II, P.C. ... St. Louis, MO
Speer, Alfred W. ... Baton Rouge, LA
Speer, Amie B. ... Denver, CO
Speer & Associates ... Wheaton, IL
Speer, Brenda L. ... Colorado Springs, CO
Speer, Brownlow M. ... Boston, MA
Speer, Charles F. ... **Olathe, KS**
Kansas City, MO
Speer, Dana S. ... **Houston, TX**
Speer, David M. ... **Clarion, PA**
Speer, Denise L. ... Baltimore, MD
Speer, Doris L. ... New York, NY
Speer, Earlene Y. ... Altamont, TN
Speer, Edward I. ... New York, NY
Speer, G. Andrew ... Sanford, FL
Speer, G. William ... **Atlanta, GA**
Speer, Gary D. ... Torrance, CA
Speer, Grace Elizabeth ... Brownsville, TN
Speer, Harold Glenn, Jr. ... Memphis, TN
Speer, Holliday & Veatch ... **Olathe, KS**
Speer, Howard E. ... **Eugene, OR**
Speer, Hoyt, Jones, Poppe & Wolf Lawyers, P.C. ... **Eugene, OR**
Speer, James G. ... **Phoenix, AZ**
Speer, James M., Jr. ... **El Paso, TX**
Speer, James W. ... Richmond, VA
Speer, Jeffery F. ... **Lafayette, LA**
Speer, John B. ... Albuquerque, NM
Speer, John C. ... **Memphis, TN**
Speer, John P. ... Little Falls, NY
Speer, Kevin P. ... **Indianapolis, IN**
Speer, Kymberly E. ... San Francisco, CA
Speer, Larry D. ... **Oklahoma City, OK**
Speer, Lloyd L. ... Wheaton, IL
Speer, Marshall and Associates, P.C.
St. Louis, MO
Speer, Michael R. ... **Livingston, NJ**
Speer, Neal E. ... Albuquerque, NM
Speer, Pamela K. ... West Palm Beach, FL
Speer, R. Tanswell ... Dallas, TX
Speer, Rebecca A. ... San Francisco, CA
Speer, Richard A. ... **Chicago, IL**
Speer, Richard L. ... Toledo, OH
Speer, Roy M. ... New Port Richey, FL
Speer, Steven E. ... Tucker, GA
Speer, Susan C. ... **Atlanta, GA**
Speer, Thomas A. ... **Sanford, FL**
Speer, Thomas A., P.A. ... **Sanford, FL**
Speer, W. Morgan ... **Palm Beach, FL**
Speer, W. Morgan, P.A. ... **Palm Beach, FL**
Speer, Wilson E., (P.A.) ... **Olathe, KS**
Speers, Cathy ... **Nashville, TN**
Speers, Jay S. ... **Albany, NY**
Speers, JoAnne ... Sacramento, CA
Speers, Lisa N. ... Great Falls, VA
Speers, Robert L. ... **Aurora, IL**
Speers, Thomas J. ... **Norristown, PA**
Speers, Thomas J. ... **Plymouth Meeting, PA**
Speers, William C. ... Colorado Springs, CO
Speerschneider, Timm P. ... **Madison, WI**
Speert, Berryl A. ... **Baltimore, MD**
Spees, Frank W., Jr. ... Incline Village, NV
Spees, Judith A. ... Incline Village, NV
Spees, Sherry D. ... Los Angeles, CA
Spees & Spees ... Incline Village, NV
Spees, Stanley K. ... Paducah, KY
Speese, E. L. Clark ... **Augusta, GA**
Martinez, GA
Speeter, Johnson, Hautman & Hamilton
Minneapolis, MN
Speeter, Lea DeSouza ... Minneapolis, MN
Speeter, Richard H. ... Minneapolis, MN
Speeter, Robert L. ... Minneapolis, MN
Speeter, Robert M. ... Minneapolis, MN
Speetjens, Amy L. ... Treasury Department,
Internal Revenue Service, GV
Speetjens, Cynthia H. ... **Jackson, MS**
Spegal, Karen L. ... Newport, KY
Spegar, Lawrence A.J. ... Blakely, PA
Spegele, Janet C. ... Hartford, CT
Spegman, Gerard A. ... Portsmouth, NH
Spehar, Danielle M. ... **Detroit, MI**
Spehr, Richard A. ... **New York, NY**
Speice, Donald E. ... Hollidaysburg, PA
Speich, Jeffery H. ... **Santa Barbara, CA**
Speicher, Howard P. ... **Boston, MA**
Speicher, John A. ... Fishers, IN
Speicher, John J. ... **Fleetwood, PA**
Reading, PA
Speicher, Stephen ... Lincoln, NE
Speicher, W. Glenn, Jr. ... Columbia, MD
Speicher, Wm. S. ... Indianapolis, IN
Speichinger, Susan L. ... Shelbyville, IN
Speid, Marian H. ... Hackensack, NJ
Speidel, C. Edward ... **Bridgewater, NJ**
Speidel, Donald L. ... **Baltimore, MD**
Speidel, Edward J. ... Boston, MA
Speidel, Elizabeth J. ... Greenville, SC
Speidel, Elizabeth West ... **Chicago, IL**
Speidel, Harry W. ... **Reading, PA**
Speidel Law Firm ... **Wenatchee, WA**
Speidel, Mary M. ... **Victoria, TX**
Speidel, Richard E. ... Chicago, IL
Speidel, Richard Henry ... **Washington, DC**
Speidel, Russell J. ... **Wenatchee, WA**
Speidel, T. Michael ... **Minneapolis, MN**
Speier, Gary J., Jr. ... **Minneapolis, MN**
Speier, John E. ... St. Paul, MN
Speier, Leonard M. ... New York, NY
Speigel, Howard A. ... Winter Park, FL
Speight, H. Max ... **Dresden, TN**
Martin, TN
Speight, John B. "Jack" ... **Cheyenne, WY**
Speight, Jonnie L. ... **Roanoke, VA**
Speight, Kent W. ... **Red Wing, MN**
Speight, Mark C. ... General Accounting Office,
Office of the General Counsel, GV
Speight, Monica Foust ... Greensboro, NC
Speight, Watson and Brewer
Greenville, NC
Speights, Daniel A. ... **Hampton, SC**
Speights, Grace E. ... **Washington, DC**
Speights, Jason B. ... **San Antonio, TX**
Speights, Nathaniel H. ... Washington, DC
Speights & Runyan ... **Hampton, SC**
Speikers, David G. ... Seattle, WA
Speilburg, G. David ... St. Clair, MI
Speiller, William M. ... Camden, NJ
Speir, Bonnie D. ... Fircrest, WA
Speir, Chas. A. ... Birmingham, AL
Speir, Clifton E. ... Houston, TX
Speir, George B. ... **Walnut Creek, CA**
Speir, Tiffany L. ... Fircrest, WA
Speir, Wyeth Holt, III ... **Montgomery, AL**
Speirs, C. Kevin ... **Salt Lake City, UT**
Speirs, Joanne C. ... Denver, CO
Speirs, R. Dean ... Denver, CO
Speirs, Richard A. ... **New York, NY**
Speirs, Verne H. ... Montgomery, AL
Speirs, William C. ... South Laguna, CA
Speiser, Arlene ... Santa Ana, CA
Speiser, Bella S. ... Newton, MA
Speiser, E. Pat ... Springfield, MO
Speiser, I. Bruce ... **Los Angeles, CA**
Speiser, James ... Yonkers, NY
Speiser, Jeffrey ... **Roseland, NJ**
Speiser, Karen Marie ... **St. Louis, MO**
Speiser Krause, A Professional Corporation
Irvine, CA
Miami, FL
Dallas, TX
Arlington, VA
Speiser Krause Nolan & Granito, A Professional Corporation ... **New York, NY**
Speiser, Laurence A. ... **Las Vegas, NV**
Speiser, Laurence A., Ltd. ... **Las Vegas, NV**
Speiser, Mark A. ... Fort Lauderdale, FL
Speiser, Mark A. ... **New York, NY**
Speiser, Stephen E. ... Hoboken, NJ
Speiser, Steven ... New York, NY
Speiser, Stuart M. ... **Irvine, CA**
New York, NY
Arlington, VA
Speisman, Albert ... Highland Park, IL
Speisman, Albert, & Associates, P.C.
Highland Park, IL
Speiss, Thomas J. ... **Laguna Beach, CA**
Speizer, Jeanne J. ... Boston, MA
Speizer, Nancy Rosenblum ... Pasadena, CA
Spekman, Hyman S. ... New York, NY
Spekter, Michael L. ... Washington, DC
Speleotis, Charles J. ... **Boston, MA**
Spelfogel, Douglas E. ... **Garden City, NY**
Spelfogel, Evan J. ... **New York, NY**
Spelfogel, Scott D. ... **Boston, MA**
Spelhaug, Lisa ... **Chicago, IL**
Spelhaug, Robert B. ... **Rochester, MN**
Spelich, John W. ... Dearborn, MI
Spelios, George P. ... Flushing, NY
Spelios, Louis C. ... **Atlanta, GA**
Spelke, Norman L. ... Elko, NV
Spelke, Robert A. ... Department of Justice,
Drug Enforcement Administration, GV
Spelke, Sherwood R. ... Stamford, CT
Spell, Carrol L., Jr. ... Lafayette, LA
Spell, Carrol L., Sr. ... Rayne, LA
Spell, Carrol L., Sr., Ltd. ... Rayne, LA
Spell, Cynthia L. ... **Baltimore, MD**
Spell, Karen R. ... Cooper City, FL
Spell, L. Penn, Jr. ... **Atlanta, GA**
Spell, Robert L. ... **Jackson, MS**
Spell, Scott E. ... **Los Angeles, CA**
Spell, Suzanne Thomas ... Atlanta, GA
Spell, William E. ... Clinton, MS
Spella, James A. ... West Bend, WI
Spellacy, Bourke G. ... **Hartford, CT**
Spellacy, John A. ... Grand Rapids, MN
Spellacy, John F. ... Fort Lauderdale, FL
Spellacy, Kevin A. ... **St. Cloud, MN**
Spellacy, Leo M. ... Cleveland, OH
Spellacy, Leo M., Jr. ... **Cleveland, OH**
Spellacy, Patrick Shawn
Fort Lauderdale, FL
Spellacy, Patrick Shawn, P.A.
Fort Lauderdale, FL
Spellacy, Suzanne M. ... **Minneapolis, MN**
St. Paul, MN
Spellane, Joanne B. ... **New York, NY**
Spellane, Philip G. ... **Rochester, NY**
Spellane, Thomas P. ... **Greenwich, CT**
New York, NY
Spellberg, Geoffrey ... San Francisco, CA
Spellberg, Norman ... Walnut Creek, CA
Spellbring, William B., Jr.
Upper Marlboro, MD
Speller, Dennis J. ... Williamsville, NY
Speller, Dennis J., P.C. ... Williamsville, NY
Speller, Glenn J. ... East Amherst, NY
Speller, Jennifer G. ... **Syracuse, NY**
Spellerberg, Thomas R. ... Tiffin, OH
Spellings, Margaret Burns ... **Dallas, TX**
Spellings, Robert D. ... Austin, TX
Spelliscy, M.J. ... **New York, NY**
Spellman, Ann C. ... **Des Moines, IA**
Spellman, Arthur N. ... Ballston Spa, NY
Spellman, Barbara A. ... Charlottesville, VA
Spellman, Blondell K. ... Atlantic City, NJ
Spellman, Daniel J. ... Des Moines, IA
Perry, IA
Spellman, David C. ... **Seattle, WA**
Spellman, David J., III ... Davie, FL
Spellman, Dean M. ... Walnut Creek, CA
Spellman, Debra A. ... **Buffalo, NY**
Spellman, Ellen B. ... **Los Angeles, CA**
San Diego, CA
Spellman, James E. ... Ilion, NY
Spellman, James L. ... Des Moines, IA
Spellman, James P. ... Santa Ana, CA
Spellman, John D. ... **Seattle, WA**
Spellman, John M. ... Garden City, NY
Spellman, Julie T. ... **New York, NY**
Spellman, Kevin M. ... Smithtown, NY
Spellman, Lawrence E. ... **Concord, NH**
Spellman, Mark A.
Small Business Administration,
Office of the General Counsel, GV
Spellman, Mark E. ... Des Moines, IA
Perry, IA
Spellman, Mark Howard ... Gaithersburg, MD
Spellman, Martin E. ... Des Moines, IA
Perry, IA
Spellman, Mary B. ... Des Moines, IA
Spellman, Michael J. ... Madison, CT
Spellman, Patrick J. ... Des Moines, IA
Perry, IA
Spellman, Paul R. ... **Dallas, TX**
Spellman, Richard A. ... Omaha, NE
Spellman, Spellman, Spellman, Spellman,
Kealhofer & Spellman ... Des Moines, IA
Perry, IA
Spellman, Steven J. ... **Denver, CO**
Spellman, Thomas J., III ... New York, NY
Spellman, Thomas J., Jr. ... Smithtown, NY
Spellman, Thomas L. ... Des Moines, IA
Perry, IA
Spellman, Victoria ... Suffield, CT
Spellman & Walsh, LLP ... Garden City, NY
Spellmeyer, Don Robert ... New York, NY
Spellmire, George W., Jr. ... **Chicago, IL**
Spellmire, Robert J. ... Santa Monica, CA
Spells, Ned L., Jr. ... **Pittsburgh, PA**
Spells, Thelma C. ... Pittsburgh, PA
Spellun, Arnold ... **New York, NY**
Spelman, Harold J. ... West Chicago, IL
Spelman, James C. ... Rockford, IL
Spelman, James Walter ... Boulder, CO
Spelman, John H. ... **St. Joseph, MI**
Spelman, Katherine C.
San Francisco, CA
Spelman, Kimberly Dunn ... **Baltimore, MD**
Spelman, Laurence A. ... **New York, NY**
Spelman, Mark G. ... Orchard Park, NY
Spelman, Mary Ann G.
Yorktown Heights, NY
Spelman, Peter ... **Beverly Hills, CA**
Spelman, Randolph W. ... Northport, NY
Spelman & Sauer, P.C. ... **St. Joseph, MI**
Spelman & Spelman ... Yorktown Heights, NY
Spelman, Stephen E. ... Springfield, MA
Spelman, Thomas L. ... Terre Haute, IN
Spelman, William M. ... **New York, NY**
Spelman, William V. ... Yorktown Heights, NY
Spelts, Richard J. ... Littleton, CO
Speltz, Louis J. ... **Minneapolis, MN**
Spelzini, Denise F. ... Sacramento, CA
Spenard, Albert W. ... Madisonville, KY
Spenard, David A. ... **Washington, DC**
Spenard, David E. ... Frankfort, KY
Spence, A. Hartie ... Lake Charles, LA
Spence, Adam ... **McLean, VA**
Spence, Amanda ... **Raleigh, NC**
Spence, Amy E. ... **San Francisco, CA**
Spence, Andrew J. ... **Fairfax, VA**
Spence, Arthur G. ... Beverly Hills, CA
Spence, Bob ... Brady, TX
Spence, Bruce A. ... **Tulsa, OK**
Spence, C. David ... Los Altos, CA
Spence, C. Norman ... **Albany, GA**
Spence, Charles C. ... **Idaho Falls, ID**
Spence, Charles W. ... Greenville, SC
Spence, Christopher A. ... Buffalo, NY
Spence, Christopher A., P.C. ... Buffalo, NY
Spence, Craig H. ... **San Antonio, TX**
Spence, Custer, Saylor, Wolfe & Rose
Ebensburg, PA
Hollidaysburg, PA
Indiana, PA
Johnstown, PA
Somerset, PA
Spence, Danie I. ... Santa Ana, CA
Spence, Darcie Ellen ... Manchester, NH
Spence, David A. ... Clinton, IL
Spence, David B. ... Austin, TX
Spence, David L. ... Winston-Salem, NC
Spence, David P. ... **Alexandria, LA**
Spence, David R. ... **Seattle, WA**
Spence, David W. ... Treasury Department,
Office of Regulations and Rulings, GV
Spence, Debra L. ... **Overland Park, KS**
Spence, Donald H., Jr. ... Washington, DC
Burtonsville, MD
Spence, E. Berton ... **Birmingham, AL**
Spence, Edward B. ... Lansing, MI
Spence, Edward J. ... Library of Congress,
Congressional Research Service, GV
Spence, Edward J., III ... Pittsfield, MA
Spence, Edward P. ... Clarksville, TN
Spence, Eric Richard ... **Raleigh, NC**
Spence, Fay F. ... Norfolk, VA
Spence, Fred R., Jr. ... Houston, TX
Spence, G. Bruce ... Ukiah, CA
Spence, Gene P. ... Omaha, NE
Spence, Gerry L., P.C. ... **Jackson, WY**
Spence, H. Aleta M. ... Atlanta, GA
Spence, Hal ... New Smyrna Beach, FL
Spence, Harrison M. ... Appleton, WI
Spence, Helen J. ... Christiansburg, VA
Spence, Herman, III ... **Charlotte, NC**
Spence, Howard T. ... Lansing, MI
Spence, J. Michael ... Augusta, GA
Spence, J. Michael, P.C. ... Augusta, GA
Spence, James E., Jr. ... Atlanta, GA
Spence, James O. ... Lexington, SC
Spence, J. B. ... Miami, FL
Orlando, FL
Spence, John C., III ... Los Angeles, CA
Spence, Joseph M. ... McLean, VA
Spence, Joseph W. ... **Fort Worth, TX**
Spence, Julian C. ... Norcross, GA
Spence, Kenneth F., III ... **St. Paul, MN**
Spence, Kent W. ... **Jackson, WY**
Spence, Kohler, Christie & Pulver, P.A.
Baltimore, MD
Towson, MD
Spence, Kristi Cotton ... **San Mateo, CA**
Spence, Lee H. ... **Washington, DC**
Spence, Leon ... Livonia, MI
Spence, Linda C. ... Cherry Hill, NJ
Spence, Lori A. ... **Plainfield, IN**
Spence, Lou R. ... Houston, TX
Spence, Mark A. ... **New Port Richey, FL**
Spence, Mark A., P.A.
New Port Richey, FL
Spence, Mark C. ... Kansas City, MO
Spence, Martha W. ... Portland, OR
Spence, Michael W. ... **Salt Lake City, UT**
Spence, Moriarity & Schuster, LLC
Salt Lake City, UT
Jackson, WY
Spence, O. Wayne ... **Columbus, GA**
Spence & Paschall ... Hearne, TX
Spence, Paul W. ... **Baltimore, MD**
Spence, Philip A. ... **Houma, LA**
Spence, R. Noel ... Clear Spring, MD
Spence, Randall ... **Minneapolis, MN**
Woodbury, MN
Spence, Ricke & Thurmer, P.A.
St. Paul, MN
Spence, Robert A. ... Smithfield, NC
Spence, Robert A., Jr. ... **Smithfield, NC**
Spence, Robert B. ... Geneva, IL
Spence, Robert J. ... East Meadow, NY
Spence, Robert M. ... Troy, MI
Spence, Ronald G. ... Denver, CO
Spence, Royce A. ... Falls Church, VA
Spence, Russell, Jr. ... **Minneapolis, MN**
Spence, Russell M. ... Woodbury, MN
Spence, Scarlett H. ... **Philadelphia, PA**
Spence & Spence, P.A. ... **Smithfield, NC**
Spence, Stanley P. ... Alexandria, VA
Spence, Stephen E. ... Detroit, MI
Spence, Stephen W. ... **Wilmington, DE**
Spence, Steven A. ... Indianapolis, IN
Spence, Susan F. ... Springfield, MO
Spence, Susan L. ... **Baltimore, MD**
Spence, Susan L. ... Trenton, NJ
Spence, Terry ... Dearborn Heights, MI
Spence, Thomas K. ... Concord, NC
Spence, Thomas W. ... **St. Paul, MN**
Spence, V. Bryant ... Hearne, TX
Spence, Virgil C. ... Marietta, GA
Spence, Virgil C., P.C. ... Marietta, GA
Spence, W. Mark ... Nags Head, NC
Spence, W. Ross ... **Houston, TX**
Spence, William A. ... Tampa, FL
Spence, William A. ... **Chicago, IL**
Spence, William E. ... Alpharetta, GA
Spence, William M. ... Chandler, AZ
Spence, William M., P.C. ... Chandler, AZ
Spence, Wm. C. ... Houston, TX
Spencer, Aaron G.B. ... **Raleigh, NC**
Spencer, Alfred, III ... Gaithersburg, MD
Spencer, Andrea M. ... **Metairie, LA**
Spencer, Ann Morelli ... Bloomington, MN
Spencer, Anna L. ... Birmingham, AL
Spencer, Anne ... Owatonna, MN
Spencer, Anthony G. ... **Richmond, VA**
Spencer, Archibald ... **Minneapolis, MN**
Spencer, Arnold A. ... **Dallas, TX**
Spencer & Associates, P.C. ... **Houston, TX**
Spencer, Barbara A. ... Pasadena, CA
Spencer, Barbara C. ... San Francisco, CA
Spencer, Bevin ... **Albany, NY**
Spencer, Bonnie-Easterly ... **Houston, TX**
Spencer, Boyd ... Norristown, PA
Spencer, Brad W. ... **Washington, DC**
Spencer, Brett Marshall ... West Union, OH
Spencer, Bruce M. ... **Helena, MT**
Spencer, Bryan S. ... Austin, TX
Spencer, C. Gerald ... Quitman, GA
Spencer, C. Thomas ... Spencer, IN
Spencer, Calvin S., Jr. ... **Charlottesville, VA**
Spencer, Carlton Wentworth ... Boston, MA
Spencer, Cary W. ... Malibu, CA
Spencer, Chad B. ... **Athens, MI**
Spencer, Chad B. ... **Battle Creek, MI**

Spencer, Chandra Gehri ..... Pasadena, CA
Santa Ana, CA
Spencer, Charles E., Jr. ..... Sacramento, CA
Spencer, Charles G. ..... Aiken, SC
Spencer, Charles L. ..... Baton Rouge, LA
Spencer, Charles S. ..... College Park, MD
Spencer, Charles W. ..... Wheaton, IL
Spencer, Charles W. ..... Dallas, TX
Spencer, Christopher C. ..... Richmond, VA
Spencer, Christopher S. ..... Madison, WI
Spencer, Clarinda S. ..... Portland, OR
Spencer, Claybourne C. ..... Ocala, FL
Spencer, Cliff E. ..... Portland, OR
Spencer, Clifford M., Jr. ..... Birmingham, AL
Spencer, Clifton C. ..... Dallas, TX
Spencer, Corwin C. ..... Oakley, KS
Spencer, Cox & Warren ..... Fort Worth, TX
Spencer, Craig A. ..... Philadelphia, PA
Spencer, Craig D. ..... Towson, MD
Spencer, Craig S. ..... Oakland, CA
Spencer, Crystal Collins ..... Pensacola, FL
Spencer, Cynthia A. ..... Garland, TX
Spencer, Cynthia L. ..... Sunnyvale, CA
Spencer, Daniel K. ..... White Plains, NY
Spencer, Daniel M. ..... Bend, OR
Spencer, Dave C. ..... Longview, WA
Spencer, David ..... St. Louis, MO
Spencer, David B. ..... New Orleans, LA
Spencer, David D. ..... Seattle, WA
Spencer, David E. ..... New York, NY
Spencer, David H. ..... New York, NY
Spencer, David J. ..... Minneapolis, MN
Spencer, David J. ..... Austin, TX
Spencer, David M. ..... Wiscasset, ME
Spencer, Dean R. ..... Lisle, IL
Spencer, Deborah J. ..... Tulsa, OK
Spencer, Delia A. ..... Dallas, TX
Spencer, Diane B. ..... Wilton Manors, FL
Spencer, Donald H. ..... Madison, AL
Spencer, Douglas C. ..... Oakley, KS
Spencer, Douglas Charles ..... La Habra, CA
Spencer, Douglas F. ..... Hillsboro, OR
Spencer, Douglas R. ..... Eugene, OR
Spencer, Earl W. ..... Houston, TX
Spencer, Edward H. ..... Scarsdale, NY
Spencer, Edward J., III ..... Syracuse, NY
Spencer, Elaine L. ..... Seattle, WA
Spencer, Eldon J., Jr. ..... St. Paul, MN
Spencer, Ellen G. ..... Ellicott City, MD
Spencer, Elmer ..... West Union, OH
Spencer, Emily B. ..... Denver, CO
Spencer, Eric A. ..... Sherman Oaks, CA
Spencer, Eric Roland ..... Roanoke, VA
Spencer, Eric Roland, P.C. ..... Bedford, VA
Fincastle, VA
Roanoke, VA
Rocky Mount, VA
Spencer, Ernest O., III ..... Jackson, MS
Spencer, Eugene P., II ..... Dothan, AL
Spencer Fane Britt & Browne LLP
Kansas City, KS
Overland Park, KS
Kansas City, MO
Spencer & Filson, P.C. ..... Lexington, VA
Spencer, Frank ..... San Diego, CA
Spencer & Frank ..... Washington, DC
Spencer, Frank ..... Jackson, MS
Spencer, Franklin T. ..... Little Rock, AR
Spencer, Franklin T., P.A.
Little Rock, AR
Spencer, Frederick S. "Rick"
Mountain Home, AR
Spencer, Fredrick R. ..... Anderson, IN
Spencer, Garold L. ..... Oklahoma City, OK
Spencer, Gary L. ..... Morrison, IL
Spencer, Gary S. ..... Dallas, TX
Spencer, Gary V. ..... Irvine, CA
Spencer, Geoffrey H. ..... San Bernardino, CA
Santa Ana, CA
Spencer, George C. ..... Portland, OR
Spencer, George H. ..... Washington, DC
Spencer, George H. ..... San Antonio, TX
Spencer, George H., Jr. ..... San Antonio, TX
Spencer, Gilbert G., Jr. ..... Great Neck, NY
Spencer, Gleason, Hebe & Rague
Wellsboro, PA
Spencer, Glenn L. ..... Greenville, SC
Spencer, Gordon J. ..... Merced, CA
Spencer, Graham & Holderman
Washington, DC
Spencer, Gregory Scott
San Francisco, CA
Spencer, Harold E. ..... Chicago, IL
Spencer, Harry G. ..... Tigard, OR
Spencer & Honey ..... Richmond, VA
Spencer, Howard W. ..... Broken Bow, NE
Spencer, I. G., Jr. ..... Louisville, KY
Spencer, J. Fred, Jr. ..... Jackson, MS
Spencer, J. Greg ..... Salt Lake City, UT
Spencer, J. Jeffers ..... Houston, TX
Spencer, J. Michael
Christiansted, St. Croix, VI
Spencer, J. Stuart ..... Cedarville, MI
Spencer, James A. ..... San Diego, CA
Spencer, James A. ..... Middleburgh, NY
Spencer, James C. ..... Indianapolis, IN
Spencer, James C., Jr. ..... Graham, NC
Spencer, James Corwin ..... Wichita, KS
Spencer, James G. ..... Milan, MO
Spencer, James L. ..... Ventura, CA
Spencer, James L. ..... Madison, MS
Spencer, James L. ..... Seattle, WA
Spencer, James P. ..... St. Paul, MN
Spencer, James T. ..... Carson City, NV
Spencer, James V., III ..... Birmingham, AL
El Dorado, AR
Spencer, Jane E. ..... Grangeville, ID
Spencer, Janet M. ..... Jamaica, NY
Spencer, Jeffrey A. ..... Buffalo, NY
Spencer, Jeffrey A. ..... Richmond, VA
Spencer, Jeffrey W. ..... Cortland, NY
Spencer, Jesse Neal ..... Portland, OR
Spencer, J. H. ..... Erin, TN
Spencer, Jill Wilemon ..... San Francisco, CA
Spencer, Jody L. ..... Chattanooga, TN
Spencer, John C. ..... Pensacola, FL
Spencer, John G. ..... Livonia, MI
Spencer, John M.
Federal Communications Commission,
Wireless Telecommunications Bureau, GV
Spencer, John M. ..... Briarcliff Manor, NY
Spencer, John M. ..... New Carlisle, OH
Spencer, John Marvin ..... St. Joseph, MO
Spencer, John S. ..... Sausalito, CA
Spencer, John W. ..... Brookline, MA
Spencer, John Wesley, Jr. ..... Elkton, MD
Spencer, John Wesley, Jr., P.A. ..... Elkton, MD
Spencer, Jon William ..... Kirksville, MO
Spencer, Jonathan R. ..... Vienna, VA
Spencer, Joseph A. ..... Sacramento, CA
Spencer, Joseph F. ..... Bronxville, NY
Spencer, Karen H. ..... Jackson, MS
Spencer, Karen L. ..... Getzville, NY
Spencer, Karen Lambart
Colorado Springs, CO
Spencer, Karen M. ..... Muskegon, MI
Spencer, Karen Y. ..... Palo Alto, CA
Spencer, Kathelen V. ..... Columbus, GA
Spencer, Katherine S. ..... Jackson, WY
Spencer, Kelly R. ..... Lowell, MA
Spencer, Kenneth F. ..... Los Angeles, CA
Spencer, Kerry Jane ..... Southfield, MI
Spencer, Kerwin L. ..... Wellington, KS
Spencer, Kevin ..... Miami, FL
Spencer, Kevin J. ..... New York, NY
Spencer and Klein, Professional Association
Miami, FL
Spencer, Larry ..... Jackson, MS
Spencer Law Firm ..... Lancaster, PA
Spencer Law Firm ..... Chesterfield, SC
Pageland, SC
Spencer, Lee B., Jr. ..... New York, NY
Spencer, Leland H. ..... Honolulu, HI
Spencer, Leslie Y. ..... Cleveland, OH
Spencer, Lewis D. ..... Chicago, IL
Spencer, Lloyd ..... McCordsville, IN
Spencer, Lloyd H., III ..... Washington, DC
Spencer, Lorna A. ..... Phoenix, AZ
Spencer, Lorraine Hess ..... Atlanta, GA
Spencer, Lowell E. ..... Paintsville, KY
Spencer, Lydia D. ..... Los Angeles, CA
Spencer, Lynne Delanty ..... Philadelphia, PA
Spencer, M. Randall ..... Fort Wayne, IN
Spencer, Marc I. ..... West Palm Beach, FL
Spencer, Margaret Gilliam
Englewood, CO
Spencer, Margaret Poles ..... Richmond, VA
Spencer, Margaret S. ..... Washington, DC
Spencer, Marguerite L. ..... St. Paul, MN
Spencer, Mariann Twist ..... Schaumburg, IL
Spencer, Marilynn Mika ..... San Diego, CA
Spencer, Mark D. ..... Oklahoma City, OK
Spencer, Mark G. ..... San Diego, CA
Spencer, Mark J. ..... Newport Beach, CA
Spencer, Mary Anne ..... Bradenton, FL
Spencer, Mary E. ..... Columbia, SC
Spencer, Matthew J. ..... Manteo, NC
Spencer, Matthew S. ..... Harrison, NY
Spencer, Mayme F. ..... Chicago, IL
Spencer, Melvin J. ..... Oklahoma City, OK
Spencer, Merritt ..... Tomball, TX
Spencer, Merritt N. ..... Austin, TX
Spencer, Michael B. ..... Los Angeles, CA
Spencer, Michael C. ..... New York, NY
Spencer, Michael G. ..... Aberdeen, WA
Spencer, Michael H. ..... Charleston, WV
Spencer, Michael J. ..... Bloomington, IN
Spencer, Michael L. ..... Memphis, TN
Spencer, Michelle D. ..... Santa Cruz, CA
Spencer, Natalie A. ..... Scottsdale, AZ
Spencer, Nathan ..... Brownsville, TN
Spencer, Pamela McAfee
Warner Robins, GA
Spencer, Patricia V. ..... Santa Ynez, CA
Spencer, Patrick Cook Hanalei, II
Colorado Springs, CO
Spencer, Patti S. ..... Lancaster, PA
Spencer, Paul A. ..... Seattle, WA
Spencer, Phelps, Dunbar & Marks
New Orleans, LA
Spencer, Philip P. ..... New Orleans, LA
Spencer, Polly Jackson ..... San Antonio, TX
Spencer & Pridavka, P.C. ..... Dallas, TX
Spencer, R. Keith ..... Fort Worth, TX
Spencer, R. Kevin ..... Dallas, TX
Spencer, Ralph W. ..... New Kensington, PA
Spencer, Reid M. ..... Norfolk, VA
Spencer, Reuben ..... New York, NY
Spencer, Richard A. ..... Portland, ME
Spencer, Richard A. ..... Springfield, OH
Spencer, Richard C., Law Offices of
Los Angeles, CA
Spencer, Richard E.
Agency for International Development,
Other Offices of A.I.D., GV
Spencer, Richard H. ..... Kansas City, MO
Spencer, Richard H., Jr. ..... Portland, ME
Spencer, Richard L. ..... Houston, TX
Spencer, Richard L., P.C. ..... Houston, TX
Spencer, Richard R., Jr.
Florham Park, NJ
Spencer, Richard W. ..... Santa Ana, CA
Spencer, Robert B., Jr. ..... Dillwyn, VA
Spencer, Robert E. ..... Dickson, TN
Spencer, Robert F. ..... Westfield, NJ
Spencer, Robert F., Jr. ..... New Orleans, LA
Spencer, Robert J. ..... Amherst, MA
Spencer, Robert L. ..... Washington, DC
Spencer, Robert N. ..... Denver, CO
Spencer, Robert N., IV ..... Palmetto, FL
Spencer, Robert W. ..... Tarrytown, NY
Spencer, Robert W., Jr. ..... Akron, OH
Spencer, Robin M. ..... Chicago, IL
Spencer, Robin R. ..... Minneapolis, MN
Spencer, Roger K. ..... Phoenix, AZ
Spencer, Ronald D. ..... New York, NY
Spencer, Russell ..... Watertown, NY
Spencer, Sandra L. ..... Denver, CO
Cheyenne, WY
Spencer, Sarah Carmack
Oklahoma City, OK
Spencer, Scott B. ..... Libby, MT
Spencer, Scott & Dwyer, P.C. ..... Joplin, MO
Spencer, Scott E. ..... Toledo, OH
Spencer, Scott H. ..... Lancaster, PA
Spencer, Shaun B. ..... Boston, MA
Spencer, Sherna Gay ..... Lauderhill, FL
Spencer & Spencer ..... Birmingham, AL
El Dorado, AR
Spencer & Spencer, Professional Association
Rock Hill, SC
Spencer, Stephen C. ..... Napa, CA
Spencer, Stephen W. ..... Des Moines, IA
Spencer, Stephen W. ..... Amarillo, TX
Spencer, Steven A. ..... Murray Hill, NJ
Spencer, Steven D. ..... Philadelphia, PA
Spencer, Steven E. ..... Los Angeles, CA
Spencer, Steven J. ..... New York, NY
Spencer & Stewart ..... Madison, MS
Spencer & Stone ..... Boston, MA
Spencer, Susan L. ..... Atlanta, GA
Spencer, Terry Reed ..... Salt Lake City, UT
Spencer, Thomas C. ..... Lexington, VA
Spencer, Thomas E. ..... Fort Myers, FL
Spencer, Thomas G. ..... Philadelphia, PA
Spencer, Thomas P. ..... Atlanta, GA
Spencer, Thomas R., Jr. ..... Miami, FL
Spencer, Timothy R. ..... Richmond, VA
Spencer, Trevor L. ..... Santa Barbara, CA
Spencer & Tyra ..... Hamilton, AL
Jackson, MS
Spencer, Victor A. ..... Salt Lake City, UT
Spencer, W. Chaplin, Jr. ..... Rock Hill, SC
Spencer, W. Thomas ..... Miami, FL
Spencer, Warren J. ..... Fort Worth, TX
Spencer, Warwick F.M. ..... Memphis, TN
Spencer, Wayne D. ..... Waipahu, HI
Spencer, Wayne R. ..... Newport News, VA
Spencer, William A. ..... St. Louis, MO
Spencer, William C. ..... Fairfield, CT
Spencer, William C. ..... Columbus, MS
Jackson, MS
Tupelo, MS
Memphis, TN
Spencer, William C. ..... Rock Hill, SC
Spencer, William Collins, Jr. ..... Tupelo, MS
Spencer, William D. ..... Smithville, TN
Spencer, William Gregory ..... Washington, DC
Spencer, William O., Jr. ..... Chesterfield, SC
Pageland, SC
Spencer, William P. ..... New Smyrna Beach, FL
Spencer, William S. ..... Hollywood, FL
Spencer, William W. ..... Columbus, OH
Spencer, William W. ..... Seattle, WA
Spencer, Wm. L. ..... Youngstown, OH
Spencer-Ayres, Cynthia ..... Sacramento, CA
Spencer-Benard, Sabrina E. ..... Tampa, FL
Spenceri, Pasquale D. ..... Omaha, NE
Spencer-James, Angela ..... New York, NY
Spender, Robb & Black, A Professional Corporation ..... Flint, MI
Spender, Steven F. ..... Flint, MI
Spendlove, Gretta C. ..... Salt Lake City, UT
Spendlove, Larry V. ..... Salt Lake City, UT
Spengler, Carolyn White ..... Fort Wayne, IN
Spengler, Daniel G. ..... Bath, PA
Spengler, E. Gordon ..... Irvine, CA
Spengler, Kurt M. ..... Orlando, FL
Spengler, Larri Irene ..... Juneau, AK
Spengler, Mark P. ..... Granite City, IL
Spengler, Mark P., P.C. ..... Granite City, IL
Spengler Nathanson P.L.L. ..... Toledo, OH
Spengler, Patricia Wise ..... Bowling Green, OH
Spengler, Robert Dale ..... Bound Brook, NJ
Spengler, Silas ..... New York, NY
Spengler, Teo ..... San Francisco, CA
Spenn, Theodore R. ..... Danforth, IL
Watseka, IL
Speno, M. Jeffrey ..... Mill Valley, CA
Speno, Sarah R. ..... New York, NY
Spensieri, Bernard M. ..... Jersey City, NJ
Spensley, James W. ..... Denver, CO
Spensley, W. Robert ..... Clovis, CA
Spenzer, Sherry Newman ..... Elyria, OH
Sper, Jane ..... Richmond, VA
Sper, T. Dwight ..... Las Vegas, NV
Spera, Christopher P. ..... McLean, VA
Spera, George T., Jr. ..... New York, NY
Spera, Johnna S. ..... Arlington, VA
Spera, Stephen P. ..... Lombard, IL
Spera, Thomas M. ..... Boston, MA
Sperandeo & Donegan ..... New Haven, CT
Sperandeo, Richard ..... Hartsdale, NY
Sperandeo, Richard P. ..... New Haven, CT
Sperandio, Kenneth J., Jr.
San Francisco, CA
Sperando, Maria P. ..... Stuart, FL
Speranza, Anthony ..... Ridgewood, NJ
Speranza, Bates and De Pree ..... Chicago, IL
Lake Forest, IL
Speranza, Carmen V. ..... Chicago, IL
Lake Forest, IL
Speranza, Christine Hough ..... Lake Forest, IL
Speranza, Jack D. ..... Easton, MA
Speranza, John F. ..... Rochester, NY
Speranza, Paul S., Jr. ..... Rochester, NY
Speranza, Peter A. ..... Lake Forest, IL
Speranza, Stephanie L. ..... Detroit, MI
Speranza, Stephen V. ..... Lake Forest, IL
Speranza, Thomas H. ..... Philadelphia, PA
Speranza, William J. ..... Stamford, CT
Speranzella, Charles J., Jr. ..... Lakeland, FL
Speranzini, David ..... Milford, CT
Sperazza, Eugene D. ..... Wilkes-Barre, PA
Sperbeck, Jean A. ..... Gainesville, FL
Sperbeck, Richard S. ..... Virginia Beach, VA
Sperber, Anthony J. ..... San Francisco, CA
Sperber, David S. ..... Encino, CA
Sperber, Denenberg and Barany, P.C.
New York, NY
Sperber, Jack R. ..... Denver, CO
Sperber, Jerome M. ..... Hartford, CT
Sperber, Jonathan E. ..... Juneau, AK
Sperber, Joseph J. ..... New York, NY
Sperber, Joseph J., IV ..... New York, NY
Sperber, Lawrence J. ..... Encino, CA
Sperber, Leonard R. ..... Mineola, NY
Sperber, Mark D. ..... Elizabeth, NJ
Sperber, Nancy B. ..... Los Angeles, CA
Sperber, Steven B. ..... New York, NY
Sperber, Susan Strebel ..... Denver, CO
Sperber, Thomas S. ..... Cincinnati, OH
Sperber, Timothy P. ..... Diamond Springs, CA
Sperduto, Kim Hoyt ..... Washington, DC
Sperduto Law Firm, The, P.L.C.
Washington, DC
Spere, Jeffrey R. ..... Portland, OR
Spere, Kathryn McFerron ..... Portland, OR
Speregen, Adam B. ..... Brooklyn, NY
Sperendi, Michael F. ..... Garden City, NY
Spergel, Barry A. ..... Washington, DC
Spergel, Jonathan H. ..... Bala Cynwyd, PA
Sperka, Shlomo ..... Detroit, MI
Sperka, Stacy J. ..... New York, NY
Sperkacz, Zorian ..... Miami, FL
Sperl, Kenneth J. ..... Columbus, OH
Sperla, John T. ..... Grand Rapids, MI
Sperlak, Deborah A. ..... Denver, CO
Sperlein, Dennis Gill ..... San Francisco, CA
Sperline, Evan E. ..... Ephrata, WA
Sperline, Jeffrey T. ..... Kennewick, WA
Sperling, Adam L. ..... Youngstown, OH
Sperling, Allan G. ..... New York, NY
Sperling, Andrew N. ..... New York, NY
Sperling, Barbara W. ..... Bronx, NY
Sperling, Bruce S. ..... Chicago, IL
Sperling, Craig A. ..... Washington, DC
Sperling, David ..... Huntington, NY
Sperling, David M. ..... Huntington, NY
Sperling, Dean P. ..... Santa Ana, CA
Sperling, Donald N. ..... Rockville, MD
Falls Church, VA
Sperling & Framm ..... Baltimore, MD
Sperling, Frederick J. ..... Chicago, IL
Sperling, Gary H. ..... New York, NY
Sperling, George E., Jr. ..... Santa Monica, CA
Sperling, Gerri L. ..... Pittsburgh, PA
Sperling, Harvey J. ..... Brooklyn, NY
Sperling, Henry ..... Bronx, NY
Sperling, Jac K. ..... Denver, CO
Sperling, James D. ..... Boston, MA
Sperling, Jeffrey C. ..... Chicago, IL
Sperling, Joanne G. ..... New York, NY
Sperling, Jonathan D. ..... Baltimore, MD
Sperling, Jonathan M. ..... New York, NY
Sperling, Joy Harmon ..... Morristown, NJ
Sperling, Lawrence I.
Environmental Protection Agency,
Office of Enforcement and Compliance
Assurance, GV
Sperling, Lawrence W. ..... Ann Arbor, MI
Ypsilanti, MI
Sperling, Lee Todd ..... Springfield, MA
Sperling, Leonard J. ..... Baltimore, MD
Sperling, Mack ..... Greensboro, NC
Sperling, Michael S. ..... Milwaukee, WI
Sperling, Mortimer ..... New York, NY
Sperling, Peter E. ..... New Orleans, LA
Sperling, Priscilla C. ..... Glencoe, IL
Sperling, Robert B. ..... Wilmington, DE
Sperling, Robert Y., (P.C.) ..... Chicago, IL
Sperling, Robt. J. ..... Lynbrook, NY
Sperling, Samuel ..... Baltimore, MD
Sperling, Sharon T. ..... Gainesville, FL
Sperling, Sheldon J. ..... Muskogee, OK
Sperling & Slater, A Professional Corporation ..... Chicago, IL
Sperling, Steven D. ..... Orange, CA
Sperling, Veronica A. ..... Boulder, CO
Sperling, Victor ..... Youngstown, OH
Sperling, Warren F. ..... Haddon Heights, NJ
Philadelphia, PA
Spern, William L. ..... Woodhaven, MI
Spero, A. J. ..... Falls Church, VA
Spero, Brian J. ..... Providence, RI
Spero, C. Michael ..... New York, NY
Spero, Gary M. ..... Santa Ana, CA
Spero & Jorgenson, P.C. ..... Cambridge, MA
Spero, Keith E. ..... Cleveland, OH
Spero, Mackey A. ..... Milwaukee, WI
Spero, Michael A. ..... Princeton, NJ
Spero, Morton B. ..... Petersburg, VA
Spero, Nancy E. ..... Los Angeles, CA
Spero, Norman R. ..... Huntington, WV
Spero, Peter ..... Santa Monica, CA
Spero, Peter, Professional Corporation
Los Angeles, CA
Santa Monica, CA
Spero & Rosenfield Co., L.P.A.
Cleveland, OH
Spero, Scott A. ..... Cleveland, OH
Spero, Stanley J. ..... Cambridge, MA

Speroff, R. Scott ... Cleveland, OH
Speronis, Lee Peter ... West Babylon, NY
Speros, J. William ... Cleveland, OH
Speros, James A. ... Phoenix, AZ
Speros, James M. ... Marion, OH
Speros, Michael C. ... Memphis, TN
Sperow, Elisabeth Heather
Department of Justice, Civil Division, GV
Sperow, Janice L. ... San Diego, CA
Sperrazza, Daniel J. ... Buffalo, NY
Sperrazza, Sara Sheldon ... Lockport, NY
Sperring, Randall J. ... San Francisco, CA
Sperring, Richard F. ... Miami, FL
Sperry, Alexander M. ... San Jose, CA
Sperry & Bowman ... South Haven, MI
Sperry, Bruce J. ... Plant City, FL
Sperry, David G. ... Independence, MO
Sperry, Derral K. ... Houston, TX
Sperry, Edward L. ... Denver, CO
Sperry & Feland ... Mandan, ND
Sperry, Floyd L., Jr. ... Warsaw, MO
Sperry, Gerald A. ... Stockton, CA
Sperry, Harvey L. ... New York, NY
Sperry, J. Glenn ... South Haven, MI
Sperry, James H. ... Worland, WY
Sperry, Joseph H. ... Houston, TX
Sperry, Julia L. ... Portland, OR
Sperry, Leavenworth P., Jr. ... Middlebury, CT
Sperry, Leonard M., Jr.
Belvedere-Tiburon, CA
Sperry, Margaret ... Springfield, MA
Sperry, Mark L., III ... Burlington, VT
Sperry, Martin J. ... Fort Lauderdale, FL
Sperry, Matthew C.
United States Tax Court, GV
Sperry, Richard D. ... Roxbury, CT
Sperry, Robert M. ... Woodland Hills, CA
Sperry, S. Jess ... Baton Rouge, LA
Sperry, Samuel A. ... San Francisco, CA
Sperry, Shannon ... Seattle, WA
Sperry, Shapiro & Kashi, P.A.
Fort Lauderdale, FL
Sperry, Stephen C. ... Litchfield, MN
Sperry, Weinberg & Cohen ... New York, NY
Sperry Young & Stoecklein
San Diego, CA
Sperry, Zoda & Kane ... Princeton, NJ
Trenton, NJ
Sperstad, Kari J. ... Chicago, IL
Spertus, James W. ... Santa Ana, CA
Spertus, Tammy C. ... Santa Ana, CA
Spery, Robert M. ... Salisbury, MD
Sperzel, Edward J. ... Smithtown, NY
Speser, Philip ... Washington, DC
Spesia, Ayers & Ardaugh ... Joliet, IL
Spesia, Christian G. ... Joliet, IL
Spesia, Douglas F. ... Joliet, IL
Spesia, John M. ... Joliet, IL
Spessard, Robert W., Jr. ... Floyd, VA
Spessert, Robert D. ... Tucson, AZ
Spetalnick, Jon P. ... Atlanta, GA
Speth & Blackmon ... Marion, SC
Speth, Charles T. ... Marion, SC
Speth, Charles T., II ... Columbia, SC
Speth, King & Riedmiller ... Wichita, KS
Speth, Maria Crimi ... Phoenix, AZ
Speth, Sally Wiggins ... Columbia, SC
Speth, Steven L. ... Wichita, KS
Spetnagel, Thomas M. ... Chillicothe, OH
Spetrino, Michael J. ... Akron, OH
Spett, Eric J. ... Dallas, TX
Spett, Peter M. ... New York, NY
Spetter, Ruth M. ... Portland, OR
Spetter, Victoria C. ... Brooklyn, NY
Spevacek, Charles E. ... Minneapolis, MN
Spevack, Arnold D. ... Washington, DC
Spevack, Barry A. ... Chicago, IL
Spevack, Robert G. ... New York, NY
Spevak, Albert ... Santa Monica, CA
Spevak, Bradley D. ... Houston, TX
Spevak, Eric S. ... Cherry Hill, NJ
Spevak, Marcus ... Brooklyn, NY
Spevak, Stacey C. ... New York, NY
Spewak, David S. ... St. Louis, MO
Spewak, Steven B. ... St. Louis, MO
Speyer, Bennett H. ... Toledo, OH
Speyer, Britt S. ... Washington, DC
Speyer, David Blair ... Pasadena, CA
Speyer, Debra G. ... Philadelphia, PA
Speyer, James F. ... Los Angeles, CA
Speyer, John M. ... Melville, NY
New York, NY
Speyer, Jos. L. ... Kansas City, MO
Speyer, Kenneth J. ... New Britain, CT
Speyer, Lawrence S. ... Chicago, IL
Speyer, Paul Harold ... Willoughby, OH
Speyer & Perlberg ... Melville, NY
New York, NY
Speyer, Pieter D. ... La Jolla, CA
Speyer, Thomas J. ... Buffalo, NY
Spezia, Nancy J. ... Ann Arbor, MI
Spezia, Roy A. ... Austin, TX
Speziale, Marcia Jean ... Hamden, CT
Speziale, Paul ... Lodi, NJ
Middle Village, NY
Speziale, Thomas A. ... Woodbury, NY
Speziali, Albert ... New London, CT
Speziali, David A. ... Voorhees, NJ
Speziali, Greenwald, Kueny & Hawkins, P.C.
Voorhees, NJ
Sphar, Michelle A. ... Pittsburgh, PA
Sphar, Steven R. ... Sacramento, CA
Spheeris, Andrew M. ... Milwaukee, WI
Sphikas, C. George ... Honolulu, HI
Spialter, David C. ... Columbus, OH
Spialter, Howard D. ... Union, NJ
Spicer, Annetta L. ... Heppner, OR
Spicer, Anthony J. ... El Monte, CA
Spicer, Barbara Ann ... Timonium, MD
Spicer, Bruce R. ... Harrisburg, PA
Spicer, Carol Vadimsky ... Somerville, NJ
Spicer, Cathy A. ... Seattle, WA
Spicer, Charles L. ... Rochester Hills, MI
Spicer, Chas. B., Jr. ... Palestine, TX
Spicer, Dan E. ... Denver, CO
Spicer, David T. ... Seattle, WA
Spicer, David W. ... North Palm Beach, FL
Spicer, Debra A. ... Detroit, MI
Spicer, Don L., Jr. ... Colorado Springs, CO
Spicer, Donna M. ... Riverhead, NY
Spicer, Flynn & Rudstrom ... Oxford, MS
Chattanooga, TN
Knoxville, TN
Memphis, TN
Nashville, TN
Spicer, G. Stephen ... Fort Smith, AR
Spicer, Glen M. ... Albany, NY
Spicer, Gregory J. ... Macon, GA
Spicer, Hiram H. ... Arlington, VA
Spicer, Ibn D. ... Washington, DC
Spicer, Jerry A. ... Dayton, OH
Spicer, Joe D. ... Memphis, TN
Nashville, TN
Spicer, John D ... Hurst, TX
Spicer, Kenneth J. ... Westerville, OH
Spicer, M. John ... Gold Beach, OR
Spicer, Malcolm F., Jr. ... Towson, MD
Spicer, Mary Ann ... Calabasas, CA
Spicer, Mary F. ... Akron, OH
Spicer, Michael F. ... Princeton, NJ
Spicer, M. John, P.C. ... Gold Beach, OR
Spicer, Nicholas Goodenough ... Berkley, MI
Spicer, Oscar F. ... Gettysburg, PA
Spicer, Patrick P. ... Bel Air, MD
Spicer, Phillip R., Jr. ... San Antonio, TX
Spicer, Richard E. ... Nashville, TN
Spicer, Richard G. ... Hastings, MN
Spicer, Robert E., Jr. ... Richmond, VA
Spicer, S. Gary ... Grosse Pointe, MI
Spicer, Thomas G. ... South Miami, FL
Spicer, Valerie Ann ... Memphis, TN
Spicer, Willard F. ... Akron, OH
Spickard, Douglas V. ... Glendale, CA
Spickard & Leibson ... Louisville, KY
Spickard, Mack T. ... Brighton, MI
Spickard, Susan P., (P.S.C.) ... Louisville, KY
Spickard, Todd S. ... Dallas, TX
Spickelmier, Keith D. ... Houston, TX
Spickerman, James W. ... Eugene, OR
Spickler, Beth E. ... New York, NY
Spickler, Daniel L. ... Lewiston, ID
Spickler, David C.
Department Of Veterans Affairs,
Board of Veterans Appeals, GV
Spickler, Lisa S. ... Richmond, VA
Spicola, A. G., Jr. ... Tampa, FL
Spicola, Brigid Mahoney ... Minnetonka, MN
Spicola, G. C., Jr. ... Tampa, FL
Spicola, Guy W. ... Tampa, FL
Spicola, Joseph G., Jr. ... Tampa, FL
Spicola & Larkin, P.A. ... Tampa, FL
Spicuzza, Richard P. ... Park Ridge, IL
Spidel, Douglas A. ... Toledo, OH
Spidel, George J. ... Dayton, OH
Spidi, John J. ... Washington, DC
Spidi, Mary Alice Donner
Federal Deposit Insurance Corporation,
Liquidation Branch, GV
Spiece, Mary Ellen ... Tucson, AZ
Spiecens, Camil P. ... New York, NY
Spiecker, Frank F. ... Grand Junction, CO
Spiecker, Hanlon & Gormley, L.L.P.
Grand Junction, CO
Spieczny, Nancy J. ... San Diego, CA
Spieczny, Thomas A. ... El Paso, TX
Spiegel, Adam G. ... Los Angeles, CA
Spiegel, Albert A. ... Los Angeles, CA
Spiegel, Andrew ... Boulder, CO
Spiegel, Andrew, P.C. ... Boulder, CO
Spiegel, Andrew R. ... Haddon Heights, NJ
Bala Cynwyd, PA
Spiegel, Andrew R., A Professional Corporation
Haddon Heights, NJ
Bala Cynwyd, PA
Spiegel, Arthur ... Miami, FL
Spiegel & Associates ... San Francisco, CA
Spiegel & Associates LLC ... Goshen, NY
Spiegel & Associates, LLC ... New York, NY
Spiegel, Audrey A. ... New York, NY
Spiegel, Barry R. ... Philadelphia, PA
Spiegel, Bennett L. ... Los Angeles, CA
Spiegel, Beth Ellen ... North Miami, FL
Spiegel Brown & Fichera ... Fishkill, NY
Poughkeepsie, NY
Spiegel, Carol Bouman ... Tampa, FL
Spiegel, Charles ... San Francisco, CA
Spiegel, Charles H. ... Bronx, NY
Spiegel, Charles J. G., Jr. ... Bronx, NY
Spiegel, Charles S. ... Lexington, KY
Spiegel, Craig R. ... Los Angeles, CA
Spiegel, Daniel J. ... Minneapolis, MN
Spiegel, Daniel L. ... Washington, DC
Spiegel, David J. ... West Hartford, CT
Spiegel, David M. ... Portland, OR
Spiegel, David R.
Federal Trade Commission,
Bureau of Consumer Protection, GV
Spiegel & DeMars ... Chicago, IL
Spiegel, Donald H. ... Chattanooga, TN
Spiegel, Edward H. ... Bayside, NY
Spiegel, Evan N. ... Los Angeles, CA
Spiegel, Greg Christopher ... Los Angeles, CA
Spiegel, H. Jay ... Arlington, VA
Spiegel, Harry ... Los Angeles, CA
Spiegel, Harvey R. ... Atlanta, GA
Spiegel, Henri I. ... Miami Beach, FL
Spiegel, Howard J. ... Miami, FL
Spiegel, Irving L. ... Metuchen, NJ
Spiegel, James A., S.C. ... Madison, WI
Spiegel, James A., S.C. ... Madison, WI
Spiegel, Jay H. ... Pittsburgh, PA
Spiegel, Jayson L. ... Department of the Army,
Office of the Assistant Secretary of the Army
(Manpower & Reserve Affairs), GV
Spiegel, Jeffrey ... Tuxedo, NY
Spiegel, Jerrold B. ... New York, NY
Spiegel, Jody L. ... Los Angeles, CA
Spiegel, Joelle Hillory ... Chicago, IL
Spiegel, John ... Washington, DC
Spiegel, John J. ... Miami, FL
Spiegel, John J., P.A. ... Miami, FL
Spiegel, John L. ... Bucyrus, OH
Spiegel, John L. ... Pittsburgh, PA
Spiegel, John W. ... Los Angeles, CA
Spiegel, Joseph H. ... Southfield, MI
Spiegel, Joseph H., P.C., Law Offices of
Southfield, MI
Spiegel, Joseph L. ... Poughkeepsie, NY
Spiegel, Lance S. ... Beverly Hills, CA
Spiegel, Laurence H. ... Lake Oswego, OR
Spiegel, Lawrence J. ... Coral Gables, FL
Spiegel, Lawrence S. ... New York, NY
Spiegel Liao & Kagay ... San Francisco, CA
Spiegel, Linda F. ... Hackensack, NJ
Spiegel, Linda F. ... Hackensack, NJ
Spiegel, Lisa ... San Francisco, CA
Spiegel, Mark A. ... Los Angeles, CA
Spiegel, Mark L. ... Chicago, IL
Spiegel, Martin F. ... Springfield, MO
Spiegel, Martin Ted ... Chicago, IL
Spiegel, Mary Ann ... Westmont, IL
Spiegel, Mathias Lloyd ... New York, NY
Spiegel & McDiarmid ... Washington, DC
Spiegel, Merrill S. ... Washington, DC
Spiegel, Michael ... Los Angeles, CA
Spiegel, Michael H. ... New York, NY
Spiegel, Michael I. ... San Francisco, CA
Spiegel, Michael L. ... New York, NY
Spiegel, Musawwir ... Sacramento, CA
Spiegel, Nancy Ann ... Albany, NY
Spiegel, Ori D. ... Hartford, CT
Spiegel, Paul A. ... San Francisco, CA
Spiegel, Richard A. ... Honokaa, HI
Spiegel, Robert I., (P.C.) ... Chicago, IL
Spiegel, Robert M. ... Cincinnati, OH
Spiegel, Ronald L. ... Los Angeles, CA
Spiegel, S. Arthur ... Cincinnati, OH
Spiegel, Scott D. ... Louisville, KY
Spiegel, Simone A. ... Deerfield Beach, FL
Spiegel, Stephen Jay ... Los Angeles, CA
Spiegel, Steven
Environmental Protection Agency,
Office of Enforcement and Compliance
Assurance, GV
Spiegel, Steven J. ... Goshen, NY
Spiegel, Steven M. ... Metairie, LA
Spiegel, Stuart ... Chicago, IL
Spiegel, Susan C. ... Maryland Heights, MO
Spiegel, Ted W. ... Sellersburg, IN
Louisville, KY
Spiegel, Vitabile & Ychelson
Los Angeles, CA
Spiegel, Walter C. ... Boston, MA
Spiegel, Walter E. ... Dayton, OH
Spiegel, Yasmin C. ... Davis, CA
Spiegelberg, Frank D. ... Tulsa, OK
Spiegelberger, William R. ... New York, NY
Spiegelman, Anne R. ... Department of Justice,
Antitrust Division, GV
Spiegelman & Edwards ... Los Angeles, CA
Spiegelman, Guy G. ... Miami, FL
Spiegelman, Jack ... Los Angeles, CA
Spiegelman, Kenneth S. ... Miami, FL
Spiegelman, Leland C. ... San Francisco, CA
Spiegelman, Max ... Miami, FL
Spiegelman, Richard D. ... Harrisburg, PA
Philadelphia, PA
Spiegelman, Robert A. ... New York, NY
Spiegelman, Robert I. ... Miami, FL
Spiegelman & Spiegelman ... Miami, FL
Spiegelman, Steve J. ... Los Angeles, CA
Spiegle, William E., III ... Ocean City, NJ
Spiegleman, Donald E. ... Denver, CO
Spiegleman, Julie L. ... Denver, CO
Spiegler, Bruce A. ... Weehawken, NJ
Spiegler, Howard N. ... New York, NY
Spiegler, Joseph A. ... Chicago, IL
Spiegler, Lee R. ... Denver, CO
Spiegler, Mark A. ... San Diego, CA
Spiegler, Nina G. ... Bronx, NY
Spiegler, Stanley M. ... New York, NY
Spiehler, Andrew C., Jr. ... New Orleans, LA
Spiek, Thuy-Anh T. ... Phoenix, AZ
Spiekerman, Charles H. ... Pontiac, MI
Spiekerman, Michael ... Huntington Beach, CA
Spiekerman, Nancy ... Atlanta, GA
Spiekermann, Gloria W. ... Westport, CT
Spiel, Timothy R. ... Denver, CO
Spielbauer, Thomas J. ... San Jose, CA
Spielberg, Anne ... Washington, DC
Spielberg, David C. ... San Francisco, CA
Spielberg, Joshua M. ... Cherry Hill, NJ
Northfield, NJ
Spielberg, Lawrence Bruce ... New York, NY
Spielberg, Leonard I. ... White Plains, NY
Spielberg, Marc A. ... Barnegat Light, NJ
Spielberg, Matthew M. ... Castro Valley, CA
Spielberg, Regina M. ... Paramus, NJ
Spielberg, Susan Barbara ... Richmond, VA
Spielberger, Andrew J. ... Los Angeles, CA
Spielberger, Diana ... Los Angeles, CA
Spielberger, Joan E. ... Fairfax, VA
Spielberger, John R. ... Bel Air, MD
Spielberger, Ronald J. ... Darien, CT
Spieler, Albert ... Boca Raton, FL
Spieler & Associates, P.A. ... Miami, FL
Spieler, Gregg ... Miami, FL
Spieler, Laurie A. ... Tampa, FL
Spieler, Stanley H. ... Miami, FL
Spieler, William M. ... St. Louis, MO
Spielfogel, Daniel J. ... Westlake Village, CA
Spielfogel, Keith ... Chicago, IL
Spielfogel, Kenneth ... New York, NY
Spieller, Kent A. ... Beverly Hills, CA
Spieller, L. Christian ... San Jose, CA
Spielman, Alan L. ... Philadelphia, PA
Spielman, Alan L., Ltd. ... Philadelphia, PA
Spielman, Andrew L. ... Denver, CO
Spielman, Cynthia A. ... Santa Rosa, CA
Spielman, David J. ... Burlington, VT
Spielman, Earl S. ... Houston, TX
Spielman, Edgar E., Jr. ... Baton Rouge, LA
Spielman, Elena ... Albuquerque, NM
Spielman, Ephraim ... Atlanta, GA
Spielman, I. Bradford ... Brooklyn, NY
Spielman, John Christian ... Kennett, MO
Spielman, John M. ... New Haven, CT
Spielman, John R. ... Amherst, VA
Spielman, Joseph M., III ... De Land, IL
Spielman & Kassimir, P.C. ... New York, NY
Spielman, M. Roy ... Newport Beach, CA
Spielman, Mark J. ... Southfield, MI
Spielman, Michael A.
United States Tax Court, GV
Spielman, Robert ... Bloomsburg, PA
Wilkes-Barre, PA
Spielman, Robert A. ... New York, NY
Spielman, Robert M. ... New York, NY
Spielman, Ronald M. ... Monroe, WI
Spielman, Stefan A. ... San Francisco, CA
Spielman, Stephen A. ... Jenkintown, PA
Spielman, Stuart ... Treasury Department,
Internal Revenue Service, GV
Spielman, Sumner J. ... Van Nuys, CA
Spielmann, Daniel J. ... Green Bay, WI
Spielvogel, Janet L. ... The Woodlands, TX
Spielvogel, Leonard ... Merritt Island, FL
Spielvogel, Paul David ... The Woodlands, TX
Spier, Alan R. ... Hartford, CT
Spier, Howard A. ... Miami, FL
Spier, Ian P. ... White Plains, NY
Spier, Peter C. ... Chicago, IL
Spier, Randi ... New York, NY
Spier, Richard G. ... Portland, OR
Spier, Robert E. ... Macomb Township, MI
Spierer, Howard ... Liberty Corner, NJ
Spierer, Robert J. ... Santa Clarita, CA
Spierer, Steven F. ... Redondo Beach, CA
Spierer, Woodward, Corbalis & Goldberg
Englewood, CO
Redondo Beach, CA
Spiering, James F. ... Monterey, CA
Spiering, Kevin J. ... Cincinnati, OH
Spiering, Kristi J. ... San Francisco, CA
Spiering, M. Susan ... Corpus Christi, TX
Spiering, Swartz & Kennedy
Monterey, CA
Spiers, Jeffrey E. ... Houston, TX
Spiers, John B., Jr. ... Radford, VA
Spiers, Lynn H. ... Houston, TX
Spiers, Sherry A. ... Tallahassee, FL
Spiers, William A ... Portland, OR
Spiert, Ken ... Columbus, OH
Spies, Charles R. ... Washington, DC
Spies, Frank S. ... Grand Rapids, MI
Spies, Greg T. ... Kansas City, MO
Spies, Harlan R. ... Dover, OH
Spies, Janet R. ... Denver, CO
Spies, Kimberley S. ... Kansas City, MO
Spies, L. Tyler ... Louisville, KY
Spies, Leon F. ... Iowa City, IA
Spies, Nancy J.
Occupational Safety and Health Review
Commission,
Administrative Law Judges, GV
Spies, P. L. ... Austin, TX
Spies, Powers & Robinson, P.C.
Denver, CO
Spies, Richard E. ... Lynchburg, VA
Spies, Richard T. ... Austin, TX
Spies, Robert ... Los Angeles, CA
Spies, Roland ... Bloomington, IL
Spies, Thomas J. ... Roseland, NJ
Spies, William A. ... Longmont, CO
Spiesman, Audrey ... Crystal Lake, IL
Spiesman, Thomas ... Morristown, NJ
New York, NY
Spiess, Barbara J. ... Ann Arbor, MI
Spiess, Charles J. ... New York, NY
Spiess, Erik K. ... Sacramento, CA
Spiess, F. Harry, Jr. ... Wayne, PA
Spiess, G. Peter ... Phoenix, AZ
Spiess, Gary A. ... Boston, MA
Spiess, James ... Riverhead, NY
Spiess, Marcia Wane ... Detroit, MI
Spiess, Robert C. ... Pompton Plains, NJ
Spiess & Short, P.C. ... Phoenix, AZ
Spiess, Susan E. ... Silver Spring, MD
Spiessbach, Peter M. ... Denver, CO
Spieth, Bell, McCurdy & Newell Co., L.P.A.
Cleveland, OH
Spieth, Cynthia M. ... Charleston, SC
Spievack, Edwin B. ... Bethesda, MD
Spievack, Jay B. ... New York, NY
Spievack, Linda J. ... Marietta, GA
Spievak, James R., (P.C.) ... San Diego, CA
Spiewak, Alan E. ... New York, NY
Spiewak, Gary R. ... East Brunswick, NJ
Spiezio, Julie ... Washington, DC
Spiezio, Nicholas J. ... Washington, DC
Spigai, Tracey Ann ... Prince Frederick, MD

Spigarelli, Fred ..... **Pittsburg, KS**
Branson, MO
Spigarelli, Kala Ann ..... **Pittsburg, KS**
Spigarelli, McLane & Short ..... **Girard, KS**
Pittsburg, KS
Branson, MO
Spigel, Jeffrey S. ..... **Washington, DC**
Spigel, Jonathan Mark ..... **Dallas, TX**
Spigel-Link, Amy Lynn ..... Fort Lauderdale, FL
Spigelmyer, Terri K. ..... Homer, AK
Spigle, David B. ..... Fincastle, VA
Spigle, John E. ..... South Bend, IN
Spigle, Kenneth Ira ..... **Newton, MA**
Spigle & Roe ..... Fincastle, VA
Spigler, Manuel A. ..... Trevose, PA
Spigner, Martin A. ..... Cranbury, NJ
Spigner, Reedy Macque ..... Plano, TX
Spignesi, John J. ..... Woburn, MA
Spika, Nicholas C. ..... St. Paul, MN
Spike, Allen S. ..... Elyria, OH
Spike & Meckler ..... Elyria, OH
Spike, Neil H. ..... Elyria, OH
Spiker, Douglas E. ..... **Columbus, OH**
Spiker, Michael I. ..... **Charleston, WV**
Ripley, WV
Spiker, William E. ..... Cadiz, OH
Spiker, William J. ..... Alliance, OH
Spikes, A. Trent ..... Dodge City, KS
Spikes & Gleason ..... Dodge City, KS
Spikes, Harry T. ..... Washington, DC
Spikes, Jesse J. ..... **Atlanta, GA**
Spikes, Larry B. ..... **Wichita, KS**
Spikes, Martha A. ..... **Irvine, CA**
Spikes, M. R. ..... San Antonio, TX
Spilde, Lori E. ..... Rapid City, SD
Spile & Siegal, LLP ..... **Encino, CA**
Los Angeles, CA
Spile, Steven D. ..... **Encino, CA**
Spilger, Michael ..... El Cajon, CA
Spilger, Ursula I. ..... **Houston, TX**
Spilhaus, Karl ..... Boston, MA
Spiliakos, John S. ..... Lincoln, MA
Spiliopoulos, Elaine M. ..... Ottawa, IL
Spiliotes, Lauren Talner
Chevy Chase, MD
Spiliotes, Nicholas J. ..... **Washington, DC**
Spilka, Adam R. ..... New York, NY
Spilka, Cheryl M. ..... Old Bridge, NJ
Spilka, Jane ..... Boston, MA
Spilka, Karen E. ..... Ashland, MA
Spilka, Mathew J. ..... Woodland Hills, CA
Spilka, Max D. ..... Las Vegas, NV
Spilker, Brenda S. ..... **Lincoln, NE**
Spilker, H. Larry ..... Idaho Falls, ID
Spilker, Lawrence J. ..... New Cumberland, PA
Spilker, Lester W. ..... Clayton, MO
Spilker, Marcy J. ..... Lewiston, ID
Spilker, Roy F. ..... Indianapolis, IN
Spilkin, Andrew Z. ..... **Detroit, MI**
Spilkin, Larry J. ..... Southfield, MI
Spilkin, Shapiro & Feeney, P.C.
Southfield, MI
Spilko, Howard T. ..... **New York, NY**
Spilky, Robert M. ..... Garden City, NY
Spilky & Spilky ..... Garden City, NY
Spill, Joy B. ..... **Miami, FL**
Spillan, Lawrence Michael ..... Washington, DC
Spillane, Ann M. ..... Chicago, IL
Spillane, Brian D. ..... Purchase, NY
Spillane, Dennis K. ..... Bronx, NY
Spillane, Eugene P. ..... Parsippany, NJ
Spillane, Frank H. ..... Easton, MA
Spillane, Garrett H., Jr. ..... Foxboro, MA
Spillane, Jay M. ..... **Los Angeles, CA**
Spillane, John J. ..... **Dallas, TX**
Spillane, John K. ..... Los Angeles, CA
Spillane, John M. ..... **Denver, CO**
Spillane, John W. ..... Worcester, MA
Spillane, Joseph R. ..... South Bend, IN
Spillane, Lester W. ..... Napa, CA
Spillane, Mary H. ..... **Seattle, WA**
Spillane, Michael Robert ..... Milford, MA
Spillane, Philip F. ..... **New Milford, CT**
Spillane, Rita-Jane ..... Sacramento, CA
Spillane, Suzanne V. ..... **Los Angeles, CA**
Spillane, Thomas B., Jr.
Bloomfield Hills, MI
Spillane, Todd L. ..... San Diego, CA
Hartford, CT
Spillane, William ..... Columbia, SC
Spillard, Robert R. ..... Port Huron, MI
Spiller, Amy Beth ..... Cincinnati, OH
Spiller, Brad J. ..... Philadelphia, PA
Spiller, Carlton T. ..... **Woodbridge, NJ**
Spiller, David ..... Jacksboro, TX
Spiller, Dudley P. ..... **Denver, CO**
Spiller, James M. ..... Jacksboro, TX
Spiller, John E. ..... **Immokalee, FL**
Spiller, John K. ..... **Houston, TX**
Spiller, Keith P. ..... **Cincinnati, OH**
Spiller • McProud ..... **Nevada City, CA**
Spiller, Mildred Vallerini ..... Trenton, NJ
Spiller, Nathaniel I. ..... Department of Labor, Office of the Solicitor, GV
Spiller, Peter N. ..... **Phoenix, AZ**
Spiller, Robert M., Jr. ..... Rockville, MD
Spiller & Spiller ..... Jacksboro, TX
Spiller, Steven T. ..... **Nevada City, CA**
Spillers, Charles L. ..... Atlanta, GA
Spillers, G. C., Jr. ..... Tulsa, OK
Spillers, George L. ..... Wheeling, WV
Spillers, Paul D. ..... **Monroe, LA**
Spillias, Kenneth G.
West Palm Beach, FL
Spillias, William A. ..... Boca Raton, FL
Spillis, Peter K. ..... **Miami, FL**
Spillman, C. Fairley ..... **Washington, DC**
Spillman, Don Lewis, Jr. ..... Corning, NY

Spillman, Janice L. ..... Nashville, TN
Spillman, John H. ..... **Atlanta, GA**
Spillman, Joseph B., Jr. ..... Baltimore, MD
Spillman, Ray A. ..... Durham, NC
Spillman, Thomas A. ..... **Atlanta, GA**
Spillman, Tracey Ford ..... **Dallas, TX**
Spillman, William P., Jr. ..... Wellington, TX
Spillner, Elizabeth V. ..... **Fresno, CA**
Spillner, Justus C. ..... **Fresno, CA**
Spilman, Amy ..... Southfield, MI
Spilman, Joseph L., III ..... **Metairie, LA**
Spilman, Joseph L., Jr. ..... Bethesda, MD
Spilman, Maia T. ..... New York, NY
Spilman Thomas & Battle, PLLC
Charleston, WV
Martinsburg, WV
Morgantown, WV
Parkersburg, WV
Weirton, WV
Spilman, Wade F. ..... **Austin, TX**
Spilotro, John V. ..... **Las Vegas, NV**
Spilotro & Kulla, Chartered
Las Vegas, NV
Spils, Carol A. ..... United States Senate, Senatorial Assistants, GV
Spilsbury, George C. ..... **Phoenix, AZ**
Spilsbury, John L. ..... Pittsburgh, PA
Spilsbury, Sue ..... New Orleans, LA
Spilseth, Donald M. ..... Willmar, MN
Spina, Anthony ..... Columbus, OH
Spina, Anthony F. ..... **Chicago, IL**
Spina, Dean A. ..... **Cedar Rapids, IA**
Spina, Dolores Marie ..... **Philadelphia, PA**
Spina, E. Lynn Murphy ..... Galloway, OH
Spina, F. Christopher ..... Pittsburgh, PA
Spina, Felicia ..... **Chicago, IL**
Spina, Francis A. ..... **Chicago, IL**
Spina, Francis X. ..... Pittsfield, MA
Spina, Frank M., II ..... Philadelphia, PA
Spina, Frank S. ..... Anaheim, CA
Spina, James B. ..... Homewood, IL
Spina, John D. ..... **Chicago, IL**
Spina, John P. ..... Pittsburgh, PA
Spina, John Paul ..... Pittsburgh, PA
Spina, Kenneth P. ..... **Chicago, IL**
Spina, McGuire & Okal, A Professional Corporation ..... **Chicago, IL**
Spina, Michael J. ..... Plainsboro, NJ
Spina, Naomi A. ..... **Los Angeles, CA**
Spina, Nicholas M. ..... Melrose Park, IL
Spina, Nicholas M. & Associates, P.C.
Melrose Park, IL
Spina, Patrick J. ..... Elmwood Park, NJ
Spina, Paul J. ..... Louisville, KY
Spina, Paul J., III ..... **Birmingham, AL**
Spina & Spina ..... Pittsburgh, PA
Spina, Stephen M. ..... **Washington, DC**
Spina, Teresa ..... Woodbury, NY
Spina, Thomas J. ..... Birmingham, AL
Spina, Thomas, Jr. ..... Albany, NY
Spinac, Mitchell H. ..... Kingston, NY
Spina-Hampton, Lauren ..... Weddington, NC
Spinak & Gray ..... **New York, NY**
Spinak, Jane Marcia ..... New York, NY
Spinak, Michael D. ..... Chicago, IL
Spinak, Robert ..... **New York, NY**
Spinale, Camille ..... **Philadelphia, PA**
Spinale, John S. ..... South Easton, MA
Spinale, John T. ..... South Easton, MA
Spinale, Joseph M. ..... **Melrose, MA**
Spinale, Rebecca R. ..... Miami, FL
Spinar, Thomas L. ..... Crete, NE
Spinardi, Karen R. ..... **Merced, CA**
Spinasanta, Roxane ..... Cicero, IL
Spinato, Michael E. ..... Ridgewood, NJ
Spindel, Bernard B. ..... Warwick, NY
Spindel, Frederic T. ..... **Washington, DC**
Spindel, Marla P. ..... **Washington, DC**
Spindel, Norman W. ..... **Roseland, NJ**
Spindel, Peter ..... Miami, FL
Spindel, Sally ..... Bay Harbor Islands, FL
Spindel, Steven H. ..... Los Angeles, CA
Spindell, Cyndi A. ..... Berkeley, CA
Spindell, Frederic A. ..... Studio City, CA
Spindell, Robert F. ..... Kenilworth, IL
Spindelman, Norman M. ..... **Rochester, NY**
Spinden, Paul M. ..... Kansas City, MO
Spindler, Bruce K. ..... **San Antonio, TX**
Spindler, Ellen M. ..... **New York, NY**
Spindler, George E. ..... San Leandro, CA
Spindler, George S. ..... Chicago, IL
Spindler, James F., Jr. ..... Crystal River, FL
Spindler, James F., Jr., P.A.
Crystal River, FL
Spindler, James W. ..... Lincoln, MA
Spindler, Jeffrey S. ..... **New York, NY**
Spindler, John F. ..... **Stamford, CT**
Spindler, John M. ..... Manitowoc, WI
Spindler, Judith A. ..... Omaha, NE
Spindler, Judith A., P.C. ..... Omaha, NE
Spindler, Kenneth J. ..... San Diego, CA
Spindler, Laurie A. ..... **Wichita, KS**
Dallas, TX
Spindler, Stephen ..... Albion, IN
Spine, Mary Lou ..... Coraopolis, PA
Spinella, A. Paul ..... **Hartford, CT**
Spinella, David M. ..... Providence, RI
Spinella, Edward F. ..... **Hartford, CT**
Spinella, Frank P., Jr. ..... **Concord, NH**
Spinella, Jack T. ..... Montclair, NJ
Spinella & Jaffe, P.C. ..... **Hartford, CT**
New Haven, CT
New London, CT
Stamford, CT
Spinella, Joseph A. ..... Clifton, NJ
Spinella, Nicholas A. ..... Richmond, VA
Spinella, Owings & Shaia, A Professional Corporation ..... Richmond, VA

Spinella, Stephen M. ..... San Diego, CA
Spinelli, Benjamin L., Jr. ..... Florham Park, NJ
Spinelli, Catherine ..... Elk Grove, CA
Spinelli, Charles J. ..... Staten Island, NY
Spinelli, Domenic D. ..... **Sacramento, CA**
Spinelli, Frederick A. ..... New York, NY
Spinelli, Giovanni E. ..... **New York, NY**
Spinelli, Nicholas J. ..... **Roseland, NJ**
Spinelli, Pamela A. ..... Rochelle Park, NJ
Spinelli, Peter Joseph ..... **Rochester, NY**
Spinelli, Robert N. ..... **Philadelphia, PA**
Spinelli, Stephen A. ..... Brooklyn, NY
Spinelli, Thomas, Sr. ..... **Garden City, NY**
Spinelli, William M. ..... Scottsdale, AZ
Spinelli-Noseda, Carlos J. ..... **New York, NY**
Spinello, John F., Jr ..... Trenton, NJ
Spinello, Richard B. ..... Rio Rancho, NM
Spinello, Sean J. ..... Roseland, NJ
Spineti, Daniel C. ..... **Hartford, CT**
Spinetta, Peter L. ..... Martinez, CA
Spingarn, Jerome H. ..... Washington, DC
Spingarn, Mitchell H. ..... Paterson, NJ
Spingarn & Sachs ..... Union City, NJ
Spingler, Frank J., Jr. ..... Washington, DC
Spingola, Peter M. ..... **Chicago, IL**
Spini, David S. ..... **Watsonville, CA**
Spiniello, Alan P. ..... Hackensack, NJ
Spining, W. Carl ..... **Nashville, TN**
Spink & Butler ..... **Boise, ID**
Spink, Carole A. ..... **Chicago, IL**
Spink, Edith J. ..... St. Louis, MO
Spink, James W. ..... **Burlington, VT**
Spink, John C. ..... Middleboro, MA
Spink, Michael T. ..... **Boise, ID**
Spink, Myra Jane A. ..... Painesville, OH
Spink, Prudence C. ..... Medina, OH
Spink, Rodger L. ..... Plantation, FL
Spink, Roland B. ..... Painesville, OH
Spinka, Dorothy W., (Mrs.) ..... Chicago, IL
Spinks, Adrian B. ..... Detroit, MI
Spinks, Anna Smith ..... Austin, TX
Spinks, Brent J. ..... Tyler, TX
Spinks, Gerald W. ..... San Diego, CA
Spinks, Hugh F. ..... **Little Rock, AR**
Spinks, James D. ..... De Kalb, MS
Spinks, James E. ..... Virginia Beach, VA
Spinks, Lee A. ..... **Charlotte, NC**
Spinks, Lynwood L. ..... Los Angeles, CA
Spinks, Susan G. ..... College Station, TX
Spinnato, John M. ..... **New York, NY**
Spinnato, Joseph E. ..... Brooklyn, NY
Spinnell, Andrew J. ..... **New York, NY**
Spinnelli, Victor ..... **East Meadow, NY**
Spinner, Beth P. ..... New York, NY
Spinner, Dittman, Federspiel & Dowling
Delray Beach, FL
West Palm Beach, FL
Spinner, Grant F. ..... Fernandina Beach, FL
Spinner, Gregory P. ..... **Los Angeles, CA**
Spinner, Ileane ..... Brooklyn, NY
Spinner, James A. ..... **Pocatello, ID**
Spinner, Jeffrey Arlen ..... Riverhead, NY
Spinner, Jerome ..... Deer Park, NY
Spinner, Joseph J. ..... Washington, DC
Spinner, Lisa C. ..... Malibu, CA
Spinner, Marina A. ..... **New York, NY**
Spinney, Richard B. ..... Stamford, NY
Spino, Gianpiero ..... **Boston, MA**
Spinogatti, Richard L. ..... **New York, NY**
Spinola, Cynthia A. ..... Pittsfield, MA
Spinrad, Alan M. ..... **Portland, OR**
Spinrad, Frederick L. ..... Los Angeles, CA
Spinrad, John Clay ..... **Atlanta, GA**
Spinrad, Max ..... **West Orange, NJ**
Spinrad, Ruben ..... Indianapolis, IN
Spinthourakis, Frances ..... **Miami, FL**
Spinuzzi, John A. ..... Denton, TX
Spiotta, Hollye P. ..... Collierville, TN
Spiotto, James E. ..... **Chicago, IL**
Spira, Beadle & McGarrell, P.A.
Melbourne, FL
Palm Bay, FL
Spira, David J. ..... **Chicago, IL**
Spira, Herbert L. ..... United States Senate, Committee Legal Personnel, GV
Spira, Immanuel I. ..... Los Angeles, CA
Spira, Jack B. ..... **Palm Bay, FL**
Spira, James M. ..... **Melrose Park, IL**
Spira, Kirsten E. ..... **Madison, WI**
Spira, Kirsten Hicks ..... **Santa Monica, CA**
Spira, Leslie G. ..... Schaumburg, IL
Spira, Maurice H. ..... Oak Park, IL
Spira, Michelle Stein ..... **Cleveland, OH**
Spira, Robert A. ..... Riverside, CA
Spira, Robert M. ..... **Cleveland, OH**
Spira, Samuel R. ..... **Los Angeles, CA**
Spira, Susan G. ..... Los Angeles, CA
Spirakis, David J. ..... New York, NY
Spirakis, George N. ..... Myrtle Beach, SC
Spirakis, Haar and Rhodes, L.L.P.
Myrtle Beach, SC
Spirakis, James G. ..... Ventura, CA
Spirduso, Craig D. ..... Austin, TX
Spire, Alvin ..... Woodland Hills, CA
Spire, Garry A. ..... Los Angeles, CA
Spirer, Alan R. ..... **Westport, CT**
Spirer & Cott ..... **Westport, CT**
Spirer & Goldberg, P.C. ..... **Washington, DC**
Rockville, MD
Spirer, Julian H. ..... **Washington, DC**
Rockville, MD
Spirer, Laren E. ..... **New York, NY**
Spires, Edward J. ..... Rochester, NY
Spires, Joseph Edward ..... **Augusta, GA**
Spires, Mark H., Jr. ..... Jamaica, NY
Spires, Robin T. ..... Shreveport, LA
Spires, Thomas S. ..... **Birmingham, AL**

Spirgel, Larry M.
Securities and Exchange Commission, Division of Corporation Finance, GV
Spirgel, Peter R. ..... **Cherry Hill, NJ**
Philadelphia, PA
Spirgen, Dennis R. ..... **Cleveland, OH**
Spiridakis, John N. ..... Long Island City, NY
Spiridigliozzi, Michelle L. ..... **Boston, MA**
Spirito, John, Jr. ..... Providence, RI
Spirito, Joseph P., Jr. ..... **Torrance, CA**
Spirito, Kim Thurman ..... Burbank, CA
Spirito, Lavinia Theodoli ..... Lexington, KY
Spirito, Maryellen C. ..... **Columbus, OH**
Spiritos, Celia G. ..... **McLean, VA**
Spiritos, Samuel M. ..... **Rockville, MD**
McLean, VA
Spirko, Richard A. ..... Richardson, TX
Spirn, Arthur L. ..... Hempstead, NY
Spirn, Daniel A. ..... **St. Louis, MO**
Spirn, Jonathan M. ..... Boston, MA
Spirn, Joshua Ian ..... Cambridge, MA
Spirn, Lawrence F. ..... Woodbury, NY
Spirn, Michelle J. ..... **St. Louis, MO**
Spirn, Ronald A. ..... **Westbury, NY**
Spirn, Stuart D. ..... **Williamsburg, VA**
Spirn, Tarley, Robinson and Tarley, P.L.L.C.
Williamsburg, VA
Spiro, Adina T. ..... **New York, NY**
Spiro, Alan M. ..... **Boston, MA**
Spiro, Alexander C. S. ..... New York, NY
Spiro, Alfred E. ..... Fort Lee, NJ
Spiro, Daniel A. ..... Department of Justice, Civil Division, GV
Spiro, David K. ..... **Richmond, VA**
Spiro, Edward M. ..... **New York, NY**
Spiro, Ellen L. ..... Simsbury, CT
Spiro, Ira ..... **Beverly Hills, CA**
Spiro, James M. ..... Sylva, NC
Spiro, James M., P.A. ..... Sylva, NC
Spiro, Jessica L. ..... Birmingham, MI
Spiro & Markosky ..... Danbury, CT
Spiro, Miriam Rena ..... New York, NY
Spiro, Peter J. ..... Hempstead, NY
Spiro, Randy ..... Beverly Hills, CA
Spiro, Robert B. ..... Raleigh, NC
Spiro, Susan F. ..... Lawrenceville, NJ
Spiro, Vanessa G. ..... New York, NY
Spiro, Walter M.B. ..... **Albany, NY**
Spiro, William B. ..... Chicago, IL
Spiroff, Harlan J. ..... **Oakbrook Terrace, IL**
Spiroff, Kero ..... St. Louis, MO
Spiroff, Thomas W.
Dearborn Heights, MI
Spiropoulos, Andrew C. ..... Oklahoma City, OK
Spiropoulos, Carmen K. ..... **Chicago, IL**
Spiropoulos, Ellen K. ..... **Oklahoma City, OK**
Spiros, Andrew G. ..... Katonah, NY
Spiros, James ..... Danville, IL
Hoopeston, IL
Spiros, Michael J. ..... Lambertville, MI
Spirou, Evelyn ..... Walnut Creek, CA
Spirra, Richard R. ..... **San Diego, CA**
Spirt, Andrew R. ..... Philadelphia, PA
Spirt, H. David ..... Blue Bell, PA
Spirt, Jay B. ..... **Towson, MD**
Spiry, A. William ..... **Britton, SD**
Spiry & Frohling, LLP ..... **Britton, SD**
Spisak, Harry W. ..... Homestead, FL
Spisak, Leslie J. ..... Cleveland, OH
Spisak, Michael J. ..... **Toledo, OH**
Spisak, Susanne M. ..... **Indianapolis, IN**
Spisek, Milan P. ..... **Mineola, NY**
New York, NY
White Plains, NY
Spishock, Robin A. ..... Stroudsburg, PA
Spitaels, Randy J. ..... Nappanee, IN
Spital, Jeanne Katz ..... **Miami, FL**
Spitale, Leonardo ..... Miami, FL
Spitale, Leonardo, Jr. ..... Miami, FL
Spitalli, Joseph A. ..... Chicago, IL
Spitalney, Leslie S. ..... **Washington, DC**
Spitalnick, David A. ..... Northfield, NJ
Spitalnick, Robert E. ..... Great Neck, NY
Spitalnik, Alyson M. ..... **Chicago, IL**
Philadelphia, PA
Spitalnik, Mark ..... Denver, CO
Spitalnik, Richard ..... **San Francisco, CA**
Spithogiannis, Michael J. ..... **Fairfield, NJ**
Carle Place, NY
Spitko, David M. ..... Allentown, PA
Spitko, E. Gary ..... Indianapolis, IN
Spitkovsky, Robert, Jr. ..... **Chicago, IL**
Spitler, Calvin D. ..... Lebanon, PA
Spitler, Charles L. ..... New Madrid, MO
Spitler, Corey E. ..... Wooster, OH
Spitler, Daniel M., Jr. ..... Pelham, AL
Spitler, Daniel T. ..... **Bowling Green, OH**
Spitler, Harley J. ..... San Francisco, CA
Spitler, Kevin W. ..... Kenmore, NY
Spitler and Kilgore ..... Lebanon, PA
Spitler, Kristina Keech ..... **Manassas, VA**
Spitler, Mark ..... **Buffalo, NY**
Spitler, Robert E. ..... **Bowling Green, OH**
Spitler, Steven L. ..... **Bowling Green, OH**
Spitler, Steven M. ..... Toledo, OH
Spitler, Vogtsberger & Huffman, LLP
Bowling Green, OH
Findlay, OH
Rossford, OH
Toledo, OH
Spitler, Wendy L. ..... Orlando, FL
Spitler & Williams-Young, Co, L.P.A.
Toledo, OH
Spitofsky, David B. ..... Norristown, PA
Spitser, James L. ..... Los Angeles, CA
Spitters, Laurence L., Jr. ..... **San Jose, CA**
Spitters, Louis ..... **San Jose, CA**

Spittler, John J., Jr. .... Boca Raton, FL
Miami, FL
Spittler, John W. .... Gold River, CA
Spittler, Richard L. .... Norfolk, NE
Spittler, Russell W. .... Irvine, CA
Spitulnik, Charles A. .... Washington, DC
Spitz, Alan .... Chicago, IL
Spitz, Alice .... New York, NY
Spitz, Andrew L. .... Poughkeepsie, NY
Spitz, Arnold .... New York, NY
Spitz, Brian D. .... Cleveland, OH
Spitz, Charles W. .... Philadelphia, PA
Spitz, Chas. H. .... Tallahassee, FL
Spitz, David M. .... Northbrook, IL
Spitz, Edward A. .... Anderson, SC
Spitz, Gary Franklin .... Floral Park, NY
Spitz, Gary M. .... East Meadow, NY
Spitz, Gregory G. .... Cincinnati, OH
Spitz, Hugo M. .... Charleston, SC
Spitz, J. George .... Poughkeepsie, NY
Spitz, James A., Jr. .... Rochester, NY
Spitz, James C. .... West Palm Beach, FL
Spitz, James E. .... Cleveland, OH
Spitz, Jane Murvin .... Olney, IL
Spitz, Jeffrey .... Los Angeles, CA
Spitz, Jennifer M. .... Longmont, CO
Spitz, Joel H. .... Chicago, IL
Spitz, Jonathan J. .... Atlanta, GA
Spitz, Kevin .... Marshfield, MA
Spitz, Leslie Nancy .... Brooklyn, NY
Spitz, Marcy B. .... Southfield, MI
Spitz, Mark A. .... Cincinnati, OH
Spitz, Marsha M. .... Chicago, IL
Spitz, Michael B. .... Attleboro, MA
Spitz, Neil H. .... New York, NY
Spitz, Oscar .... Corpus Christi, TX
Spitz, Rachel D. .... Wellesley, MA
Spitz, Robert J. .... Ontario, CA
Spitz, Sherman M. .... Irvine, CA
Spitz, Stephen A. .... San Francisco, CA
Spitz, Stephen J. .... Chicago, IL
Spitz, Stephen L. .... Washington, DC
Spitz, Steven S. .... Los Angeles, CA
Spitz, Terry L. .... Salinas, CA
Spitza, Kenneth J. .... Warren, MI
Spitza, Winnie McConnell .... Fraser, MI
Spitzbard, Kenneth S. .... West Haven, CT
Spitzberg, Irving J., Jr. .... Fairfax, VA
Spitzberg, Marian .... Dallas, TX
Spitze, Cherie A. .... Sonora, CA
Spitzen, Jay M. .... Palo Alto, CA
Spitzer, Addis, Susman & Krull
Chicago, IL
Spitzer, Adelbert L. .... Boston, MA
Spitzer, Alvin L. .... New City, NY
Spitzer, Anne L. .... Gainesville, FL
Spitzer, Arthur B. .... Washington, DC
Spitzer, Barry H. .... Sacramento, CA
Spitzer, Bruce C. .... Chicago, IL
Spitzer, Charles A. .... Jackson, TN
Spitzer, Charles E. .... Grafton, OH
Spitzer, Christopher & Arvanites
Danvers, MA
Spitzer, Daniel A. .... Buffalo, NY
Spitzer, Daniel B. .... Encino, CA
Spitzer, Daniel G. .... Durango, CO
Spitzer, David C. .... New York, NY
Spitzer, David D. .... Reno, NV
Spitzer, Eddie
Hot Springs National Park, AR
Spitzer & Feldman, P.C. .... New York, NY
Spitzer, Franklin H. .... Philadelphia, PA
Spitzer, Gary S. .... Los Angeles, CA
Spitzer, Glenn L. .... Sacramento, CA
Spitzer, Gregory E. .... Chicago, IL
Spitzer, Herbert A., Jr. .... Marion, IN
Spitzer, Hugh D. .... Seattle, WA
Spitzer, Jamie Morris .... Orange, CA
Spitzer, Jean .... Pacific Palisades, CA
Spitzer, John B. .... Toledo, OH
Spitzer, John B. .... Philadelphia, PA
Spitzer, John B., Jr. .... Boulder, CO
Spitzer, Joseph S. .... Azle, TX
Spitzer, Karl G. .... Danvers, MA
Spitzer, Lyman F. .... Toledo, OH
Spitzer, M. James .... New York, NY
Spitzer, M. James, Jr. .... New York, NY
Spitzer, Marc L. .... Phoenix, AZ
Spitzer, Mark A. .... Los Angeles, CA
Spitzer, Mark E. .... Marion, IN
Spitzer, Matthew L. .... Los Angeles, CA
Spitzer, Michael E. .... Hohenwald, TN
Spitzer, Richard C. .... Rockville, MD
Spitzer, Richard C., P.C. .... Rockville, MD
Spitzer, Robert B. .... Seattle, WA
Spitzer, Robert C. .... Harrisburg, PA
Spitzer, Robert Damon
Incline Village, NV
Spitzer, Robert G. .... Riverside, CA
Spitzer, Scott L. .... Totowa, NJ
Spitzer, Stephen A. .... Woodbridge, NJ
Spitzer, Stephen M. .... Tyler, TX
Spitzer, Steven .... Torrance, CA
Spitzer & Struc .... Incline Village, NV
Spitzer, Stuart T. .... Freeport, NY
Spitzer, Susan Michelle .... Los Angeles, CA
Spitzer, Thomas .... Warren, MI
Spitzer, Thomas N. .... Portland, OR
Spitzer, Toby E. .... Basking Ridge, NJ
Spitzer, Todd A. .... Santa Ana, CA
Spitzer, Vlad G. .... Stamford, CT
Spitzer, Wilbur J. .... Deerfield Beach, FL
Spitzer, Yael .... Roslyn Heights, NY
Spitzfaden, Harold John .... New York, NY
Spitzfaden, Robert S. .... Juneau, AK
Spitzig, John R. .... Rolling Meadows, IL
Spitzig, William L. .... San Francisco, CA
Spitzli, Donald H., Jr. .... Virginia Beach, VA
Spitzmiller, Frank M. .... Vero Beach, FL
Spitzmiller, John C. .... Buffalo, NY
Spitzmueller, Lawrence J. .... Cincinnati, OH
Spitznagel, David R. .... Key Largo, FL
Spitzzeri, Alfred A. .... Wheaton, IL
Spitzzeri, Joseph F. .... Chicago, IL
Spiva, Bruce .... Washington, DC
Spiva, Howard E. .... Savannah, GA
Spiva, Howard E., P.C. .... Savannah, GA
Spiva, J. Walter .... Orlando, FL
Spiva, Joseph L. .... Fairfield, CA
Spiva, Joseph L. .... Woodland, CA
Spiva, Wayne E. .... Douglasville, GA
Spivack, Aaron .... Chicago, IL
Spivack, Amy J. .... Fort Lauderdale, FL
Spivack, Andrew L. .... Chicago, IL
Northbrook, IL
Spivack, Byron H. .... New York, NY
Spivack, Deborah E. .... Wilmington, DE
Spivack, Dennis R. .... Wilmington, DE
Spivack, Edith I. .... New York, NY
Spivack, Edmund S. .... Rockville, MD
Spivack, Gary I. .... Philadelphia, PA
Spivack, Gerald W. .... Cherry Hill, NJ
Philadelphia, PA
Spivack, Gordon B. .... New York, NY
Spivack, Joel R., Law Office of
Cherry Hill, NJ
Spivack, Leo J. .... Miami, FL
Spivack, Lisa M. .... New York, NY
Spivack, Louis M. .... Tucson, AZ
Spivack, Mona Sedky
Federal Trade Commission,
Bureau of Consumer Protection, GV
Spivack, Peter S. .... Washington, DC
Spivack, Richard Cary .... Forest Hills, NY
Spivack, Scott K. .... Orlando, FL
Spivack, Shelley R. .... Flint, MI
Spivack, Stephen R. .... Washington, DC
Spivack, Thomas M. .... Glendale, CA
Spivack, Trina L. .... Fair Oaks, CA
Spivak, Barbara L. .... New York, NY
Spivak, Burton .... New York, NY
Spivak, David B. .... New York, NY
Spivak, Jennifer L. .... Annapolis, MD
Spivak, Joel .... Great Neck, NY
Spivak, Joel A. .... Los Angeles, CA
Spivak, Jonah H. .... Pittsburgh, PA
Spivak, Karl L. .... Philadelphia, PA
Spivak, Kevin R. .... Washington, DC
Spivak, Leonard A. .... New York, NY
Spivak, Lipton, Watanabe, Spivak & Moss LLP .... New York, NY
Spivak, Marc E. .... Chicago, IL
Spivak, Marjorie Giller .... Washington, DC
Spivak, Mark B. .... Cherry Hill, NJ
Spivak, Mark R. .... Washington, DC
Spivak, Marvin J. .... Arlington, VA
Spivak & Meiselas .... Great Neck, NY
Spivak, Milton .... Brooklyn, NY
Spivak, Paul H. .... Denver, CO
Spivak, Richd. W. .... Philadelphia, PA
Spivak, Sharon B. .... San Diego, CA
Spivak, Steven B. .... New York, NY
Spivak, Susan I. .... Venice, CA
Spivak, William B., Jr. .... Los Angeles, CA
Spivey & Ainsworth, P.C. .... Austin, TX
Houston, TX
Spivey, Andrew C. .... Waycross, GA
Spivey, Angela M. .... Oxford, MS
Spivey, Anita V. .... Denville, NJ
Spivey, Barry F. .... Sarasota, FL
Spivey, Broadus A. .... Austin, TX
Spivey, Carlton & Edenfield, P.C.
Swainsboro, GA
Spivey, Corey J. .... Los Angeles, CA
Spivey, Cynthia G. .... Winston-Salem, NC
Spivey, David C. .... Franklin, NC
Highlands, NC
Spivey, Dawn Michelle .... Miami, FL
Spivey, Donna R. .... Chicago, IL
Spivey, Gary D. .... Colorado Springs, CO
Spivey, Gorden W. .... Elizabeth City, NC
Spivey, Gregory Glen .... Corpus Christi, TX
Spivey, Gwendolyn L. .... Tallahassee, FL
Spivey, H. Michael .... Mauldin, SC
Spivey, I. William, II .... Orlando, FL
Spivey, James K. .... San Antonio, TX
Spivey, Jerry L. .... Wilmington, NC
Spivey, John Neal .... Tallahassee, FL
Spivey, John William, III .... Little Rock, AR
Spivey, Joseph M., III .... Richmond, VA
Spivey, Karen Drabik .... Westminster, MD
Spivey, Karen L. .... Beaumont, TX
Spivey, Karen T. .... Milledgeville, GA
Spivey, Kathryn Joyce
Providence Forge, VA
Spivey, LaDonna B. .... Ozark, AL
Spivey, Lloyd G., Jr. .... Canton, MS
Spivey, Louise Wilkinson .... Lakeland, FL
Spivey, Marvin M., Jr. .... Raleigh, NC
Spivey, Michael J.
Export-Import Bank of The United States,
Office of the General Counsel, GV
Spivey, Michael O. .... Washington, DC
Spivey, Patricia R. .... Cape Canaveral, FL
Spivey, Philip B. .... Milledgeville, GA
Spivey, Philip B., P.C. .... Milledgeville, GA
Spivey, Rex J. .... Irving, TX
Spivey, Richard A. .... Kingsport, TN
Spivey, Richard C. .... Macon, GA
Spivey, Robin V. .... Powder Springs, GA
Spivey, Ronald E. .... Winston-Salem, NC
Spivey, Scott W. .... Macon, GA
Spivey, Stacey D. .... Oklahoma City, OK
Spivey, Stephen D. .... Ocala, FL
Spivey, Thomas W. .... Victorville, CA
Spivey, Tricia A. .... Fort Myers, FL
Spivey, W. Edgar .... Norfolk, VA
Spivey, W. Michael .... Rocky Mount, NC
Spivey, Wayne R. .... Philadelphia, PA
Spivok, Jordan M. .... Bethesda, MD
Spiwak, Andrew D. .... Chicago, IL
Spiwak & Iezza .... Westlake Village, CA
Spiwak, Lisa E. .... Westlake Village, CA
Spix, Krupp & Reece, P.C. .... Atlanta, GA
Spix, Mark Van .... Atlanta, GA
Spizer, Bruce, A Professional Law Corporation .... New Orleans, LA
Spizer, David "Bruce" .... New Orleans, LA
Spizer, Gregory Steven .... Philadelphia, PA
Spizer, Howard M. .... Scranton, PA
Tunkhannock, PA
Spizer, S. W. .... Los Angeles, CA
Spizler, Bruce C. .... Baltimore, MD
Spizz, Alex .... New York, NY
Spizz & Cooper .... Mineola, NY
Spizz, Harvey W. .... Mineola, NY
Spizz, Sheldon N. .... Manalapan, NJ
Spizziri, John A., Sr. (P.C.) .... Wyckoff, NJ
Spizziri, Sandra S. .... Wyckoff, NJ
Spizzirri, Paul M. .... Chicago, IL
Spizzirri, Richard D. .... New York, NY
Spizzirri, William E. .... Chicago, IL
Spizzirro, Louis M. .... Yonkers, NY
Spizzo, James A. .... Chicago, IL
Spjut, Robert J. .... San Francisco, CA
Splain, Jeanne T. .... Lakewood, OH
Splain, John F. .... Cincinnati, OH
Splain, Julianne .... Simsbury, CT
Splain, Thomas Matthew .... Rochester, NY
Splaine, Neal F. .... Boston, MA
Splan, Myrna Good .... Newport News, VA
Splane, Stephanie I. .... San Francisco, CA
Splawn, Charles R. .... Winston-Salem, NC
Splawn, Homer B. .... Yakima, WA
Splawn and Simpson, P.C. .... Lubbock, TX
Spletzer, Ann Lisa .... Stamford, CT
Spletzer, Christine A. .... New York, NY
Splinter, Robert G. .... Lomita, CA
Splitek, Lynn J. .... Madison, WI
Splitt, David A. .... Washington, DC
Splitt, Ronald G. .... La Moure, ND
Splivalo, Michael Norman .... Fresno, CA
Splude, Michelle A. .... Chicago, IL
Spodak, Sharon T. .... New York, NY
Spodarek, Janice Gail .... Grand Ledge, MI
Spodek & Barrett .... New York, NY
Spodek, Ellen M. .... New York, NY
Spodek, Jules L. .... Brooklyn, NY
Spodek, Lance Roger .... New York, NY
Spodek, Lance Roger, P.C. .... New York, NY
Spoden, James E. .... Erie, PA
Spoden, M. Clark .... Nashville, TN
Spodnick, Jonathan E. .... Trumbull, CT
Spoede, David L.
Department of Defense, GV
Spoehr, Milton .... Berlin, WI
Spoeneman, Steven E. .... St. Louis, MO
Spoeri, John W. .... Chicago, IL
Spoeri, Robert F., Jr. .... Los Angeles, CA
Spoerk, Jeffrey K. .... Milwaukee, WI
Spofford, Chris A. .... Houston, TX
Spofford, David J. .... Boca Raton, FL
Spofford, Geoffrey E. .... Worcester, MA
Spofford, George E., IV .... Tampa, FL
Spofford, Juliana E. .... Worcester, MA
Spognardi, Mark A. .... Chicago, IL
Spohler, Norman G. .... Toledo, OH
Spohn, Clifford C. .... Marion, OH
Spohn, James F. .... Madison, WI
Spohn, Kurt W. .... Honolulu, HI
Spohn, Monica L. .... Hamilton, OH
Spohn, Monica L. .... Oxford, OH
Spohn, Richard B. .... San Francisco, CA
Spohn, Robert D. .... Saxonburg, PA
Spohn & Robertson .... Napa, CA
Spohn, Rosemary Ann .... Gibbsboro, NJ
Spohn, Verner J., Jr. .... Tucson, AZ
Spohn, Vincent M. .... Napa, CA
Spohrer, George A. .... Kingston, PA
Spohrer, Jonathan A. .... Kingston, PA
Spohrer, Jonathan A. .... Wilkes-Barre, PA
Spohrer, Robert F. .... Jacksonville, FL
Spohrer, Wilner, Maxwell & Matthews, P.A.
Jacksonville, FL
Spoja, James E. .... Denver, CO
Spoja, William A., Jr. .... Lewistown, MT
Spokane Lawyer, P.S. .... Spokane, WA
Spoke, Nicholas M. .... Cleveland, OH
Spokes Foley, P.L.C. .... Burlington, VT
Spokes, Jennifer J. .... Washington, DC
Spokes, Richard A. .... Burlington, VT
Spokes, Susan E. .... Portland, ME
Spokoiny, Larry S. .... Mercer Island, WA
Spokojny, Anthony S. .... Southfield, MI
Spokony, David .... Bronx, NY
Spolan, Harmon .... Philadelphia, PA
Spolan, Michael L. .... El Cerrito, CA
Spolar, Stephen B. .... Pittsburgh, PA
Spole, Kenneth M. .... Syosset, NY
Spolin, Scott J., (P.L.C.)
Santa Monica, CA
Spolin, Silverman & Cohen LLP
Los Angeles, CA
Santa Monica, CA
Spoll, Lisbeth R. .... Wethersfield, CT
Spollen, John F. .... Greenlawn, NY
Spollen, John W. .... New York, NY
Spollen, Thomas P. .... Staten Island, NY
Spolter, David .... San Diego, CA
Spolter, Jerry .... San Francisco, CA
Spolter, Loring N. .... Fort Lauderdale, FL
Spolter, McDonald & Mannion, A Professional Corporation
San Francisco, CA
Spoltman, Stephen J. .... Fort Wayne, IN
Spoltore, Leslie .... Wilmington, DE
Spolyar, Geoffrey J. .... Los Angeles, CA
Spolzino, Robert A. .... White Plains, NY
Spomer, Dorothy W. .... Cairo, IL
Spomer, Stephen L. .... Cairo, IL
Spomer, Waldemar C. .... Cairo, IL
Spon, Ronald D. .... Mansfield, OH
Sponaugle, George I., II .... Franklin, WV
Sponaugle, Kevin C. .... Franklin, WV
Sponaugle, Mary Mongiovi .... Lancaster, PA
Sponaugle, S. Woodrow .... Rye Beach, NH
Sponaugle & Sponaugle .... Franklin, WV
Sponaugle, Thomas B. .... York, PA
Sponberg, Ronald T. .... Houston, TX
Sponcler, Maurice M., Jr. .... Dalton, GA
Sponder, Emanuel .... Hollywood, FL
Sponder, Jeffrey M. .... Parsippany, NJ
Sponer, Dennis M. .... Las Vegas, NV
Spong, Alison E. .... Palo Alto, CA
Spong, Ernest M., III .... Winnsboro, SC
Spong, J. Kershaw .... Columbia, SC
Spong, Keith A. .... Elgin, IL
Spong, Lawrence E. .... Detroit, MI
Spong, Richard C. .... Joplin, MO
Sponheim, Rolf A. .... Minnetonka, MN
Sponholtz, Elizabeth A. .... Knoxville, TN
Sponsel, Thane Tyler, Jr. .... Houston, TX
Sponseller, Alan W. .... Akron, OH
Sponseller, Daniel J. .... Pittsburgh, PA
Sponseller, James M. .... Paulding, OH
Sponseller, John N. .... Canton, OH
Sponseller, Nancy L., Law Offices of
Columbus, OH
Sponseller, Nancy L., Law Offices of
Dublin, OH
Sponseller, Richard W. .... Alexandria, VA
Sponseller, Steven R. .... Sunnyvale, CA
Sponseller, Timothy S. .... Chambersburg, PA
Sponsler, George C., III .... Bethesda, MD
Sponsler, Margret A. G.
Half Moon Bay, CA
Sponsler, Thomas .... Portland, OR
Sponsler, Thomas H. .... San Francisco, CA
Sponsler, Warren K. .... Tampa, FL
Sponzilli, Edward G. .... Somerville, NJ
Sponzilli, Gina T. .... Walnut Creek, CA
Sponzo, Marilyn A. .... Springfield, MA
Sponzo, Maurice J. .... Hartford, CT
Sponzo, Richard T. .... Hartford, CT
Spoo, Gregory M. .... Rochester, MN
Spoo, James .... Reno, NV
Spool, James .... Charleston, SC
Spoon, Dan L. .... Missoula, MT
Spoon, Elliot A. .... Detroit, MI
Spoon, S. Alec .... Montgomery, AL
Spoonemore, Jerry W. .... Seattle, WA
Spoonemore, Richard E. .... Seattle, WA
Spooner & Burnett .... New York, NY
Spooner, Charles W. .... Kansas City, MO
Spooner, Eric P. .... Washington, DC
Spooner, Jack B. .... St. Louis, MO
Spooner, John B. .... New York, NY
Spooner, Leonard J. (Skip) .... Greenville, SC
Spooner, Mark J. .... Los Angeles, CA
Spooner, Much & Ammann, P.C.
Salem, OR
Spooner, Nancy Killien .... Washington, DC
Spooner, Ralph C. .... Salem, OR
Spooner, Richard F. .... Rochester, NY
Spooner, Sandra P. .... Department of Justice,
Civil Division, GV
Spooner, Sarah W.
Federal Labor Relations Authority,
Authority Member Staff, GV
Spooner, Scott D. .... Springfield, IL
Spooner, Scott Kelley .... Lawrenceville, GA
Spooner & Spooner, P.C.
Kansas City, MO
Spooner, Stanley C. .... Arlington, VA
Spooner, William .... Paynesville, MN
Spooner, William Charles
Kansas City, MO
Spooner, William J. .... Grand Rapids, MN
Spooner, Wright, Farrell & Ryan
Springfield, MA
Spoonhour, James M. .... Orlando, FL
Spoont, Maxwell B. .... Ithaca, NY
Spoor, Carol DeNardo .... Seattle, WA
Spoor, David C. .... San Antonio, TX
Spoor, Julia L. .... Indianapolis, IN
Spoor, Laura S. Schulte .... Los Angeles, CA
Spoor, Richard D. .... Fort Mitchell, KY
Spore, Jerry P. .... Jackson, TN
Spore, Judson P., Jr. .... Perrysburg, OH
Spore, Richard R., III .... Memphis, TN
Sporer Law Firm, P.C.
West Des Moines, IA
Sporer, Theodore F. .... West Des Moines, IA
Sporkin, Andrew B.
Securities and Exchange Commission,
Division of Enforcement, GV
Sporkin, Stanley
United States District Court For The District
Of Columbia, GV
Sporleder, Dale E. .... Indianapolis, IN
Sporleder, James G. .... South Barrington, IL
Sporn, Arthur D. .... New York, NY
Sporn, Benjamin .... Lawrence, NY
Sporn, Benjamin T. .... New York, NY
Sporn, Charles M. .... Brooklyn, NY
Sporn, Judith B. .... Westport, CT
Sporn, Lee S. .... New York, NY
Sporn, Paul E. .... Norwell, MA
Sporn, Richard A. .... New York, NY
Yorktown Heights, NY
Sporn, Robert .... New York, NY
Sporn, Saml. P. .... New York, NY

Sporn, Samuel P. ... **New York, NY**
Sporrer, Daniel J. ... Pittsburgh, PA
Spors, Karen E. ... Delavan, WI
Sport, Thomas E. ... **Luverne, AL**
Sposaro, Anthony J. ... Chester, NJ
Sposato, Janis Ann ... Department of Justice, Justice Management Division, GV
Sposato, Michael Gabriel ... **San Diego, CA**
Sposeep, Michael L. ... Wabash, IN
Sposeto, Dominic J. ... Sonoma, CA
Spositi, Julie L. ... **Voorhees, NJ**
Sposito, James A. ... Scranton, PA
Sposto, Ernest A. ... **Wilkes-Barre, PA**
Spota, Thomas J. ... Hauppauge, NY
Spotila, Jennifer M. ... Philadelphia, PA
Spoto, Douglas A. ... Jamestown, NY
Spoto, Keith P. ... Lakeland, FL
Spoto, Mark D. ... **Reston, VA**
Spoto & Slater ... Jamestown, NY
Spotswood, J. Brooke ... Hayes, VA
Spotswood, Richard D. ... San Francisco, CA
Spotswood, Robert K. ... **Birmingham, AL**
Spotswood, William S., Jr. ... Springfield, VA
Spott, Curtis M. ... Exeter, CA
Spott, Erika A. ... King Of Prussia, PA
Spott, Patrick M. ... **Duluth, MN**
Spottiswood, David J. ... **Sacramento, CA**
Spotts, David A. ... Washington, DC
Spotts, David M. ... **Ashtabula, OH**
Spotts, David M. ... **Cleveland, OH**
Spotts, Meade A. ... **Richmond, VA**
Spotts, Michael K. ... Stuart, FL
Spotts, Richard C. ... Chicago, IL
Spotts, Smith, Fain & Buis, P.C.
Chesterfield, VA
Henrico, VA
Richmond, VA
Spotts-Cantwell, Gail ... **Kansas City, MO**
Spottswood, John M., Jr. ... **Key West, FL**
Spottswood, Robert A. ... **Key West, FL**
Spottswood, Spottswood & Spottswood
Key West, FL
Spottswood, William B. ... **Key West, FL**
Spotwood, Barbara R. Blade ... Gary, IN
Spotz, Richard T., Jr. ... **Cleveland, OH**
Spracker, Marilyn S. ... Chicago, IL
Spracker, Stanley M. ... **Washington, DC**
Sprader, Bobbie S. ... **Columbus, OH**
Sprader, Paul L. ... **Nashville, TN**
Spradley, J. Mark ... **Little Rock, AR**
Spradley & Riesmeyer, A Professional Corporation ... **Kansas City, MO**
Spradley, Ronald C. ... **Kansas City, MO**
Spradley, Scott W. ... **Orlando, FL**
Spradley, Susan Tassell ... **Orlando, FL**
Spradley & Tassell ... Orlando, FL
Spradley, Webb ... Dallas, TX
Spradley, William J., III ... **Jacksonville, FL**
Spradlin, Daniel K. ... **Orange, CA**
Spradlin, David A. ... Houston, TX
Spradlin, David L. ... Hyattsville, MD
Spradlin, J. Elizabeth ... **Asheville, NC**
Spradlin, J. Elizabeth ... **Henderson, NC**
Madison, NC
Spradlin, James R. ... Houston, TX
Spradlin, Katherine J. ... Mansfield, TX
Spradlin, Phaedra ... Lexington, KY
Spradlin, Phyllis ... Austin, TX
Spradlin, Shane M. ... **Washington, DC**
Spradlin, Simon ... Poteau, OK
Spradlin, Thomas Richard ... Los Angeles, CA
Spradlin-Dahn, Linda Theresa
Severna Park, MD
Spradling, Albert M., III
Cape Girardeau, MO
Spradling, Alpern, Friot & Gum, L.L.P.
Elk City, OK
Oklahoma City, OK
Spradling, A. M., Jr.
Cape Girardeau, MO
Spradling, Cameron M. ... Irving, TX
Spradling, Charles G., Jr. ... Anniston, AL
Spradling, Gary J. ... **San Diego, CA**
Spradling, James R. ... Carthage, MO
Spradling, John T. ... Oklahoma City, OK
Spradling, Kevin K. ... **St. Louis, MO**
Spradling, Mark R. ... **Houston, TX**
Spradling, Marshall C. ... Charleston, WV
Spradling & Query ... Charleston, WV
Spradling & Spradling
Cape Girardeau, MO
Spradling, T. Scott ... **Oklahoma City, OK**
Spradling Wyman, L.L.C. ... Carthage, MO
Spraetz, D. Lynn ... **Cincinnati, OH**
Sprafkin, David C. ... New York, NY
Sprafkin, Samuel M. ... New York, NY
Spragens, David W. ... **Nashville, TN**
Spragens, Janet R. ... Washington, DC
Spragens, Jeffrey G. ... Washington, DC
Spragens, Robert M. ... Lebanon, KY
Spragens, Robert M., Jr. ... Lebanon, KY
Spragens, Smith & Higdon, P.S.C.
Lebanon, KY
Spragg, Heather A. ... **Los Angeles, CA**
Spragg, Robert J. ... **New York, NY**
Spragins, Alan W. ... Wenatchee, WA
Spragins, Barnett, Cobb & Butler, PLC
Jackson, TN
Spragins, H. Scot ... **Grenada, MS**
Jackson, MS
New Albany, MS
Oxford, MS
Sprague, Alice G. ... San Francisco, CA
Sprague, Allen E. ... Fremont, CA
Sprague, Anne V. ... Roanoke, VA
Sprague & Associates, P.A. ... **New York, NY**
Sprague, Bernard ... Red Cloud, NE
Sprague, C. Christopher ... Newark, NJ
Sprague, Charles Edward ... Cleveland, OH
Sprague, Charles W. ... **Brookfield, WI**
Sprague, Clarence E. ... Santa Ana, CA
Sprague, Clarence E. ... Dunedin, FL
Sprague, Dale M. ... McPherson, KS
Sprague, Dawn ... Boston, MA
Sprague, Dianne M. ... Clarksville, TX
Sprague, Donald L. ... Flourtown, PA
Sprague, E. Sue ... **Washington, DC**
Sprague, Edward L. ... St. Louis, MO
Sprague, Eugene M. ... **Denver, CO**
Sprague, Florence ... Maplewood, MN
Sprague, Frederick O. ... Cadillac, MI
Sprague, G. Keith ... San Bernardino, CA
Sprague, Gary D. ... **Palo Alto, CA**
Sprague, George R. ... Cambridge, MA
Sprague, Gretchen L. ... Brooklyn, NY
Sprague, Holly ... Pleasant Hill, CA
Sprague, Hugh A. ... Jefferson City, MO
Sprague, James R. ... Columbus, OH
Sprague & Jeske, P.A. ... Tampa, FL
Sprague, Jill Andrews ... **Palo Alto, CA**
Sprague, John R., III ... Riverhead, NY
Sprague, John Reno ... Belleville, IL
Sprague, John Reno, Jr. ... Belleville, IL
Sprague, Jonathan B. ... **Philadelphia, PA**
Sprague, Jonathan W. ... Caribou, ME
Sprague, Judith A. ... **Philadelphia, PA**
Sprague, Karen A. ... Long Grove, IL
Sprague, Katherine E. ... St. Paul, MN
Sprague, Kendra Colton ... Chehalis, WA
Sprague, Lauren D. ... Savannah, GA
Sprague, Leah Whitney ... Boston, MA
Sprague & Lewis, Ltd. ... Lancaster, PA
Sprague, Madelon ... **Cleveland, OH**
Sprague, Marcia C.
Department of Education, Office of the General Counsel, GV
Sprague, Mary Gabrielle ... **Washington, DC**
Sprague, Michael J. ... Hackensack, NJ
Sprague, Michael L. ... Bakersfield, CA
Sprague, Michael T. ... Houston, TX
Sprague, Michelle Annjanette ... Brighton, CO
Sprague, Neil E. ... **Kansas City, MO**
Sprague, Patrick F. ... Tampa, FL
Sprague, Paul K. ... Warwick, RI
Sprague, Peter ... Jamaica, NY
Sprague, Peter R. ... Belmont, NY
Sprague, Richard A. ... Haddonfield, NJ
Lancaster, PA
Media, PA
Philadelphia, PA
Sprague, Richard S. ... Bellevue, WA
Sprague, Richard W. ... Pasadena, CA
Sprague, Robert ... San Francisco, CA
Sprague, Robert C. ... Bloomfield Hills, MI
Sprague, Robert F. ... **Findlay, OH**
Sprague, Robert J. ... Belleville, IL
Sprague, Robert W. ... **St. Paul, MN**
Sprague, Ron A. ... **San Antonio, TX**
Sprague, Sandra B. ... Belchertown, MA
Sprague, Sharon A. ... Washington, DC
Sprague & Sprague ... Belleville, IL
Sprague & Sprague ... Haddonfield, NJ
Media, PA
Philadelphia, PA
Sprague, Stephen J. E. ... **Albuquerque, NM**
Sprague, Thomas A. ... Haddonfield, NJ
Lancaster, PA
Media, PA
Philadelphia, PA
Sprague, Thomas C. ... La Grange, IL
Sprague, Victoria Elisabeth
New York, NY
Sprague, W. Douglas ... **San Francisco, CA**
Chicago, IL
Sprague, Wayne Elliot ... Tallahassee, FL
Sprague, Wesley T. ... **Houston, TX**
Sprague, William R. ... Denver, CO
Sprague, William T. ... Phoenix, AZ
Sprague, William W. ... St. Johnsbury, VT
Sprague-Embree, Susan E. ... Spokane, WA
Spraguer, Patricia A. ... **New York, NY**
Spraic, Mark A. ... **Pasadena, CA**
Spraic, Mark A., A Law Corporation
Los Angeles, CA
Pasadena, CA
Sprain, Robert H., Jr. ... **Birmingham, AL**
Sprain, Theresa M. ... **Winston-Salem, NC**
Spraitzar, Curtis L. ... Birmingham, AL
Spraitzar, Stephen S. ... **San Francisco, CA**
Spraker, Gary A. ... **Anchorage, AK**
Spraker, I. Burton ... **Orlando, FL**
Spraker, Lynne W. ... **Stuart, FL**
Spraker & Prinz ... **Stuart, FL**
Spraley, Thomas E. ... Gainesville, GA
Sprang, Kermit N. ... **Irvine, CA**
Spranger, Deborah Landan ... **Berwyn, PA**
Spranger, Susan G. ... Washington, DC
Spransy, Joseph W. ... Birmingham, AL
Spraragen, Joseph M. ... **New York, NY**
Spratley, Dawn S. ... **Birmingham, MI**
Spratley, Derek L. ... **Knoxville, TN**
Spratley, Margaret Kinney
Salt Lake City, UT
Spratley, Richard K. ... Murray, UT
Spratley, William A. ... Columbus, OH
Spratlin, Arthur Dennis, Jr. ... **Jackson, MS**
Spratling, Benjamin B., III
Birmingham, AL
Spratling, Gary R. ... San Francisco, CA
Spratling, Ronald N., Jr. ... Salt Lake City, UT
Spratt, Adrian ... New York, NY
Spratt, Craig T. ... Pembroke, MA
Spratt, David H. ... **Washington, DC**
Spratt, Donald R. ... Baltimore, MD
Spratt, Gwendolyn D. ... **Atlanta, GA**
Spratt, Jacqueline L. ... Department of Justice, Civil Rights Division, GV
Spratt, James Dean, Jr. ... **Atlanta, GA**
Spratt, James T. ... Los Angeles, CA
Spratt, John M., Jr. ... York, SC
Spratt, Joseph M. ... **Conway, PA**
Spratt, Michael D. ... Tacoma, WA
Spratt, Patricia S. ... **Chicago, IL**
Spratt, Robert Gilroy, III ... **Charlotte, NC**
Spratt, William G. ... **Lake Success, NY**
Spratt, William J., Jr. ... **Miami, FL**
Sprau, Julie L. ... Chanhassen, MN
Sprauer, Constance D. ... **Boston, MA**
Spraul, Daniel G. ... Cincinnati, OH
Spraul, Holly Doan ... Cincinnati, OH
Spraul, Stephen G. ... Cincinnati, OH
Spraul, Susan M ... **St. Louis, MO**
Spraul, Veith & Doan ... Cincinnati, OH
Spray & Associates, PLLC ... Union Lake, MI
Spray, Gould & Bowers, A Professional Corporation ... **Los Angeles, CA**
Tustin, CA
Ventura, CA
Spray, J. L. ... Adams, NE
Lincoln, NE
Spray, Judd R. ... Marquette, MI
Spray, Kathryn R.S. ... Union Lake, MI
Spray, Vann Allan ... **Gadsden, AL**
Sprayberry, Brad A. ... Columbus, OH
Sprayberry, James B. ... Auburn, AL
Sprayregen, James H. M. ... **Chicago, IL**
Sprayregen, Joel J. ... **Chicago, IL**
Spreadbury, Andrew W. ... Washington, DC
Spreadbury, Véronique A. ... Washington, DC
Sprecace, David A. ... **Denver, CO**
Sprecace, David A., P.C. ... **Denver, CO**
Sprecher, A. Grant ... Philadelphia, PA
Sprecher, Averum J. ... Middletown, CT
Sprecher, Christina I. ... **New Orleans, LA**
Sprecher, Christina M. ... **Cincinnati, OH**
Sprecher, Jeffrey K. ... Reading, PA
Sprecher, Kevin S. ... **Cincinnati, OH**
Sprecher, Max J. ... **Los Angeles, CA**
Sprecher, Stephanie Irene ... Casper, WY
Sprechman & Associates, P.A.
Fort Lauderdale, FL
Miami, FL
Sprechman, Jordan A. ... New York, NY
Sprechman, Steven B. ... **Miami, FL**
Spreen, Harold J. ... New York, NY
Spreen, Robert H. ... Loma Linda, CA
Sprehn, Boyd L. ... San Francisco, CA
Spreitzer, John R. ... Farmington Hills, MI
Spreitzer, Michelle Deneau ... **Southfield, MI**
Spreng, Kevin S. ... **Minneapolis, MN**
Spreng, Michael R. ... **Cleveland, OH**
Sprengel, Jennifer Winter ... **Chicago, IL**
Sprengelmeyer, Victor V. ... East Dubuque, IL
Sprenger, Heleen A. ... **New York, NY**
Sprenger & Lang, P.L.L.C.
Washington, DC
Minneapolis, MN
Sprenger, Michael T. ... **Cleveland, OH**
Sprenger, Paul C. ... **Washington, DC**
Sprengnether, Michael T. ... **Chicago, IL**
Wheaton, IL
Sprenkle, Jason B. ... **Charlotte, NC**
Sprenkle, Stephanie Jean
Philadelphia, PA
Sprenkle, Stephen D. ... Salinas, CA
Sprentall, David A. ... **Phoenix, AZ**
Spretnak, Robert P. ... **Las Vegas, NV**
Spreyer, Abigail Kay ... **Chicago, IL**
Spreyer, Marbeth M. ... **Arlington, VA**
Sprick, Gary G. ... Fayette, MO
Sprick, Robert F. ... Orlando, FL
Spridgeon, Timothy M. ... Tampa, FL
Sprie, Ingo W., Jr. ... **New York, NY**
Spriegel, David D. ... Buffalo, NY
Sprigg, Roger ... Tustin, CA
Spriggs, Edward J., Jr.
Agency for International Development, Other Offices of A.I.D., GV
Spriggs, Everett L. ... **Riverside, CA**
Spriggs, Heather A. ... **Irvine, CA**
Spriggs & Hollingsworth ... **Washington, DC**
Spriggs, James O. ... Kensington, MD
Spriggs, James P. ... **Antwerp, OH**
Spriggs, James P. ... **Paulding, OH**
Spriggs, Jennifer Dover
Department of Justice, Tax Division, GV
Spriggs, Karyl Terese ... Washington, DC
Spriggs, Kent ... Tallahassee, FL
Spriggs, Richard T. ... Denver, CO
Spriggs, Ronald T. ... Amarillo, TX
Spriggs, Scott B. ... **Riverside, CA**
Spriggs, Stacey A. ... Hernando, MS
Spriggs, William J. ... **Washington, DC**
Sprigman, Charles J., Jr. ... Woodbury, NJ
Sprik, Dale, & Associates, P.C.
Grand Rapids, MI
Sprik, Dale R. ... **Grand Rapids, MI**
Spring, Andrew L. ... Greenwich, CT
Spring, Arthur Carl ... Johnstown, NY
Spring, Arthur J. ... **White Plains, NY**
Spring, David M. ... Brooklyn, NY
Spring, Douglas J. ... Hollywood, FL
Spring, Frank L. ... Albuquerque, NM
Spring, Gary W. ... **Akron, OH**
Spring, Gilbert M. ... Lufkin, TX
Spring, Heather ... **Washington, DC**
Spring, Herbert A., Jr. ... Cleveland, OH
Spring, J. Paul ... San Diego, CA
Spring, James J., III ... **Houston, TX**
Spring, Jolie C. ... **Lexington, MA**
Spring, Julia C. ... New York, NY
Spring, Laura L. ... **Syracuse, NY**
Spring, Linda E. ... **Waukegan, IL**
Spring, M. Edward ... **Bellevue, WA**
Spring, Margaret F. ... Washington, DC
Spring, Mark S. ... **Irvine, CA**
Sacramento, CA
Spring, Milissa R. ... **Vienna, VA**
Spring and Raghavan, LLP ... Albany, NY
Spring, Raymond L. ... Topeka, KS
Spring, Robert E. ... **New York, NY**
Spring, Ronnie H. ... **Morristown, NJ**
Spring, S. Stephen, II ... Covington, LA
Spring, Stanley A. ... **Pensacola, FL**
Spring, Stephen R. ... Albany, NY
Spring, Stuart S. ... West Linn, OR
Spring, Thomas C. ... San Francisco, CA
Spring, Truman E., Jr. ... **Dallas, TX**
Spring, William L. ... **Cleveland, OH**
Springate, Betty A. ... Lawrenceburg, KY
Springate, James O. ... Versailles, KY
Springate, Jerry L. ... Lawrenceburg, KY
Springberg, Laurence B. ... **Las Vegas, NV**
Springborg, Raymond ... Holmdel, NJ
Springborg, Geo. R. ... St. Paul, MN
Springborn, Harvey E. ... Maumee, OH
Springborn, John K. ... St. Louis, MO
Springel, Adam H. ... **Irvine, CA**
Springel, Barry L. ... **Cleveland, OH**
Springel & Fink, L.L.P. ... **Irvine, CA**
Springer, Allen D. ... Brooklyn, NY
Springer, Amy Mandel ... **Denver, CO**
Springer, Ann L. ... Department of Justice, Civil Division, GV
Springer, Barbara S. ... **Denver, CO**
Springer, Barry A. ... Mount Prospect, IL
Springer, Barry A., P.C. ... Mount Prospect, IL
Springer, Barton J. ... **Chicago, IL**
Springer, Bettye S. ... **Fort Worth, TX**
Springer, Boyd J. ... **Chicago, IL**
Springer, Bradford W. ... **Chicago, IL**
Springer, Burt ... Houston, TX
Springer, Bush & Perry, A Professional Corporation ... **Coraopolis, PA**
Pittsburgh, PA
Springer, Byron E. ... **Lawrence, KS**
Springer, Casey & Dienstag, P.C.
Barrington, IL
Chicago, IL
Springer, Charles E. ... Carson City, NV
Springer, Christine A. ... Redford, MI
Springer, Claudia Z. ... **Philadelphia, PA**
Springer, Clement F. ... Lake Bluff, IL
Springer, Clement F., Jr. ... **Chicago, IL**
Springer, Curtis H. ... Montgomery, AL
Springer, Cynthia K. ... **Indianapolis, IN**
Springer, Dale V. ... Lansing, MI
Springer, David E. ... **Washington, DC**
Springer, David E. ... **Chicago, IL**
Springer, David S. ... Florham Park, NJ
Springer, Denise B. ... **Pittsburgh, PA**
Springer, Edward L. ... **Pittsburgh, PA**
Springer, Edward M. ... **Barrington, IL**
Chicago, IL
Springer, Edwin E. ... San Antonio, TX
Springer, Eric C. ... **Pittsburgh, PA**
Springer, Eric W. ... **Pittsburgh, PA**
Springer, Felix J. ... **Hartford, CT**
Stamford, CT
Springer, Frank David ... Mocksville, NC
Springer, Frederick J. ... **Tallahassee, FL**
Springer, George C., Jr. ... New Britain, CT
Springer, Gerald C. ... Newport Beach, CA
Springer and Haseltine ... Springfield, MO
Springer, Howard ... Jersey City, NJ
Springer, J. Jeffrey ... **Denton, TX**
Springer, James E. ... Fort Wayne, IN
Springer, James E., P.C. ... Fort Wayne, IN
Springer, James M., Jr. ... Stillwater, OK
Springer, James P. ... Department of Justice, Tax Division, GV
Springer, James vanR. ... **Washington, DC**
Springer, James W. ... **Peoria, IL**
Springer, Jeffrey A. ... **Denver, CO**
Springer, Jeffrey B. ... Rockville, MD
Springer, Jeffrey Z. B. ... **Los Angeles, CA**
Springer, John L. ... **Aurora, CO**
Springer, John W. ... **Charlotte, NC**
Springer, Jonathan L. ... Windsor, VT
Springer, Jonathan L., P.C., Law Office of
Windsor, VT
Springer, Jonathan S. ... **Portsmouth, NH**
Springer, Joseph G. ... **Minneapolis, MN**
Springer, Judy McIntire ... **Philadelphia, PA**
Springer, Julia A. ... Washington, DC
Springer, Julie A. ... **Austin, TX**
Springer, Karen A. ... **Fort Wayne, IN**
Springer, Ken R. ... Newark, NJ
Springer, Kimberly N. ... **St. Louis, MO**
Springer, Kristi M. ... **Los Angeles, CA**
Springer, Lawrence J. ... New Orleans, LA
Springer, Lawrence R. ... **Youngstown, OH**
Springer, Lewis E., Jr. ... St. Johnsbury, VT
Springer, Lyle & Watt L.L.P. ... **Denton, TX**
Springer, M. Rebecca ... Fort Lauderdale, FL
Springer, Marc ... Brookline, MA
Springer, Marilee J. ... **Indianapolis, IN**
Springer, Mario D. ... **New York, NY**
Springer, Mark T. ... Fort Lauderdale, FL
Springer, Matt Lawrence ... **Herndon, VA**
Springer, Mel ... Laguna Hills, CA
Springer, Michael B. ... Reno, NV
Springer, Michael Craig ... Baytown, TX
Springer, Nathaniel E., Jr. ... New York, NY
Springer, Norman H. ... Las Vegas, NV
Springer, Norman L., Jr. ... Council Bluffs, IA
Springer, Norman & Workman
Longview, WA
Springer, Olga M. ... Chicago, IL
Springer, Pamela Davis ... Los Angeles, CA
Springer, Patrick M. ... Kalispell, MT

Springer, Paul D. ....Los Angeles, CA
Springer, Peter E. ....Santa Fe, NM
Springer, Randel S. ....Winston-Salem, NC
Springer, Richard S. ....Portland, OR
Springer, Richard W. ....Palm Springs, FL
Springer, Robert E. ....Sullivan, IN
Springer, Robert H. ....Palm Springs, FL
Springer, Robert P. ....Sunapee, NH
Springer, Robert T. ....St. Louis, MO
Springer, Roger W. ....Los Angeles, CA
Springer, Rosemary J. ....San Francisco, CA
Springer, Ross E. ....Indianapolis, IN
Springer, Sarah P. ....Meridian, MS
Springer, Stanley G. ....Pomona, CA
Springer & Steinberg, A Professional Corporation ....Denver, CO
Springer, Stephen D. ....Plano, TX
Springer, Stephen G. ....Houston, TX
Springer, Stephen J. ....Philadelphia, PA
Springer, Steven A. ....Dallas, TX
Springer, Steven E. ....Indianapolis, IN
Springer, Stewart G. ....Birmingham, AL
Springer, Thomas E. ....Addison, IL
Springer, Tracy ....New York, NY
Springer, W. Bruce ....St. Louis, MO
Springer, Wallace N., Jr. ....Springfield, MO
Springer, William G. ....Bellevue, WA
Springer, William L. ....Marshalltown, IA
Springfield, Craig R. ....Washington, DC
Springfield, James F. ....Cordova, TN
Springfield, Mark A. ....Raleigh, NC
Springfield, (Ms.) Freddie M.W. ....Elyria, OH
Springfield, Stephen F. ....Birmingham, AL
Springfield, William R. ....Mesquite, TX
Springford, Cathy A. ....Auburn, CA
Springgate, Jack R. ....Houston, TX
Springgate, John P. ....Reno, NV
Springgate, Margaret M. ....Reno, NV
Springgay, Peggy L. ....San Jose, CA
Springhetti, David A. ....Houston, TX
Springman, Mary Adele ....Cleveland, OH
Springman, Ronald W., Jr. ....Cincinnati, OH
Springmann, Franz F. ....Orlando, FL
Springmann, Kurt E. ....San Diego, CA
Springmann, Theresa Lazar ....Merrillville, IN
Springmeyer, Don ....San Diego, CA
Springmeyer, Jon K. ....Carson City, NV
Springob, Tarn M. ....Houston, TX
Springs, Clare H. ....San Francisco, CA
Springs, Darryl M. ....Houston, TX
Springs, E. Shane ....Arkadelphia, AR
Springs, Eli Baxter, IV ....Charlotte, NC
Springs, Michael A.
Research Triangle Park, NC
Springs, Sandra J. ....Oakland, CA
Springs, Suzanne ....Palo Alto, CA
Springstead & Bostic, P.C. ....Fremont, MI
Hart, MI
Springstead, Douglas A. ....Hart, MI
Springstead, Harold N. ....Hackensack, NJ
Springstead, John W. ....Brooksville, FL
Springstead, Julie A. ....Hart, MI
Springstead, Robert D. ....Fremont, MI
Hart, MI
Springsteen, George S. ....Washington, DC
Springut, Milton ....New York, NY
Springwater, Jane ....San Francisco, CA
Sprink, Jeffrey L. ....San Antonio, TX
Sprink, Jeffrey L., P.C. ....San Antonio, TX
Sprinkel & Burau, LLC
Incline Village, NV
Reno, NV
Sprinkel, George A., IV ....Orlando, FL
Sprinkel, Stephen S. ....Incline Village, NV
Reno, NV
Sprinkel, Wilbur H. ....Reno, NV
Sprinkle, Coffield and Stackhouse
High Point, NC
Sprinkle, David J. ....Seattle, WA
Sprinkle, Douglas W. ....Birmingham, MI
Sprinkle, J. Wayne ....Portsmouth, VA
Sprinkle, Jack W. ....Mobile, AL
Sprinkle, Leslie A. ....San Francisco, CA
Sprinkle, Philip M., II
West Palm Beach, FL
Sprinkle, Richard P. ....Kansas City, MO
Sprinkle, S. Charles ....Libby, MT
Sprinkle, Sharon H. ....Rocky Mount, NC
Sprinkle, Steven R. ....Austin, TX
Sprinkle, Vincent G. ....Fort Worth, TX
Sprinkles, Catherine C. ....San Jose, CA
Sprinkles, Leonard B. ....Saratoga, CA
Sprinkles, Randolph S. ....San Jose, CA
Sprinz, Maurice F. ....Sarasota, FL
Sprio, Arete ....Albany, NY
Spritz, Gary M. ....Beverly Hills, CA
Spritz, Gary R. ....Wilmington, DE
Spritz, Keith B. ....Appleton, WI
Spritz, Nancy S. ....Baltimore, MD
Spritz, Norton ....New York, NY
Spritzer, Henry M. ....New Brunswick, NJ
Spritzer, Lois ....St. Louis, MO
Spritzer, Marlene Alpern ....Durham, NC
Spritzer, Martin A. ....Pittsboro, NC
Spritzer, Ralph S. ....Tempe, AZ
Spritzer, Ronald M. ....Department of Justice, Environment and Natural Resources Division, GV
Spritzer, Rose C. ....New Brunswick, NJ
Sprizzo, John E. ....New York, NY
Sproat, Barbara J. ....Menlo Park, CA
Sproat, CarolynH. ....Baltimore, MD
Sproat, Christine ....Poughkeepsie, NY
Sproat, John W. ....Columbus, OH
Sproat, Ronald G. ....Oakland, CA
Sproat, S. Mark ....Chicago, IL
Sproat, Vicki L. ....Fort Myers, FL
Sprock, Charles M., Jr. ....Syracuse, NY
Sprock, Martin C. ....Des Moines, IA
Sprock, Richard J. ....New York, NY
Sprofera, Salvatore W. ....Boston, MA
Sproger, Charles E. ....Chicago, IL
Sprogis, Carolyn E. ....Oakland, CA
Sprole, Frank A. ....Darien, CT
Sprole, John ....Des Moines, IA
Sprole, Jonathan K. ....Stamford, CT
Sprole, Karen E. ....Dallas, TX
Sprole, Robert R. ....Ithaca, NY
Sproles, D. Leon ....Rome, GA
Sproles, Donald R. ....Knoxville, TN
Sproles, Gregory W. ....Summersville, WV
Sprong, David J. ....Roseland, NJ
Sprong, Douglas R. ....East St. Louis, IL
Spronz, Steven C. ....Los Angeles, CA
Sprott and Clarkson ....Winnsboro, SC
Sprott, James D. ....Harrison, AR
Sprott, Joel Randal ....Houston, TX
Sprott, Kingswood, Jr. ....Lakeland, FL
Sprott, Oliver W., Jr. ....Houston, TX
Sprotzer, Ira B. ....Jamesburg, NJ
Sproul, Alan H., II ....New York, NY
Sproul, Catherine E. ....Sacramento, CA
Sproul, Christopher ....San Francisco, CA
Sproul, Curtis Cutter ....Sacramento, CA
Sproul, Don E. ....Houston, TX
Sproul, Gayle C. ....Philadelphia, PA
Sproul, Gene C. ....Orangevale, CA
Sproul, Harvey L. ....Lenoir City, TN
Sproul & Hinton ....Lenoir City, TN
Loudon, TN
Sproul, J. Martin ....San Rafael, CA
Sproul, Margaret ....Pemaquid, ME
Sproul, Peter M. ....Walnut Creek, CA
Sproul, Stanley E. ....Augusta, ME
Sproule, Clare M. ....New York, NY
Sproule, Dianne M. ....Chicago, IL
Sproule, Michael H. ....New York, NY
Sproule, R. Gordon, Jr. ....Birmingham, AL
Sproule, Randy ....Madison, WI
Sproule, Robert C. ....New York, NY
Sproule, Robert H. ....Seattle, WA
Sproule, Tracy ....Birmingham, AL
Sproule, William P. ....Pleasant Grove, AL
Sproull, Frederick A.R. ....Aspinwall, PA
Sproull, J. Ruth ....Tempe, AZ
Sproull, James E., Jr. ....Ocala, FL
Sproull, John F., Jr. ....Palatka, FL
Sproull, Steven H. ....Austin, TX
Sprouls, John R. ....New York, NY
Sprouls, Joseph W. ....Hartford, CT
Sprouls, Patrick B. ....Chatham, NJ
Sprouls, R. Tracy ....Artesia, NM
Roswell, NM
Sprouls, Robert F. ....New York, NY
Sprouls, Walter A. ....Essex Fells, NJ
Sprouse, Curtis Steven ....Knoxville, TN
Sprouse, Daniel T. ....Pauls Valley, OK
Sprouse, Dennis M. ....Sallisaw, OK
Sprouse, E. Blaine ....Nashville, TN
Sprouse & Ferguson ....Charleston, WV
Sprouse, Harlow L. ....Amarillo, TX
Sprouse, J. Edward ....Columbus, GA
Sprouse, James M. ....Charleston, WV
Sprouse, Keith W. ....Marysville, KS
Sprouse, Kenneth M. ....Northridge, CA
Sprouse, Marvin E., III ....Dallas, TX
Sprouse, Mary L. ....Las Vegas, NV
Sprouse, R. Scott ....Seneca, SC
Sprouse, Smith & Rowley, P.C. A Professional Corporation ....Amarillo, TX
Sprouse, Tucker & Ford, P.C.
Columbus, GA
Sprouse Cauble, Lisa Lee ....Austin, TX
Sproviero, Frank V. ....Hackensack, NJ
Sproviero, Scott G. ....Paramus, NJ
Sprow, Betsy Hawman ....Reading, PA
Sprow, Howard T. ....Albany, NY
Sprowl, Charles R. ....Chicago, IL
Sprowl, David A. ....Costa Mesa, CA
Sprowl, James A. ....Washington, DC
Chicago, IL
Sprowl, Milton L. ....Dayton, OH
Sprowls, Jeffrey P. ....McLean, VA
Sprowls, Jeffrey P., P.C. ....McLean, VA
Sprowls, John R. ....Pauls Valley, OK
Sprowls, Paul Alan ....Tallahassee, FL
Spruance, H. Douglas, III ....Spokane, WA
Spruance, William H. ....Oroville, CA
Spruce, Susan ....Houston, TX
Spruce, Tracey E. ....Boston, MA
Spruce, William ....Fort Lauderdale, FL
Spruch, Seymour ....Staten Island, NY
Spruell, Alyce Manley ....Eutaw, AL
Fayette, AL
Spruell, Alyce Manley ....Tuscaloosa, AL
Spruell, Billy L. ....Atlanta, GA
Spruell, Raymond L., Jr. ....Fort Smith, AR
Spruell Taylor & Associates, P.C.
Atlanta, GA
Spruiell, Franklin H., Jr. (P.C.)
Shreveport, LA
Spruiell, J. Patrick ....Canton, TX
Spruiell, Michael L. ....Tyler, TX
Spruill, E. Carol ....Durham, NC
Spruill, Frank P., Jr. ....Rocky Mount, NC
Spruill, James A., III ....Cheraw, SC
Spruill, Joseph E., III ....Richmond, VA
Spruill, Joseph E., Jr. ....Tappahannock, VA
Spruill, Kerry L. ....Marksville, LA
Spruill, Richard L. ....Jackson, MS
Spruill, W. Duvall ....Columbia, SC
Spruill, W. Murray, Jr. ....Raleigh, NC
Spruit, Richard M. ....Grand Rapids, MI
Sprung, Arnold ....Tarrytown, NY
Sprung, Harvey ....Hyde Park, NY
Sprung, Jeffrey T. ....Seattle, WA
Sprung, John B. ....New York, NY
Sprung, Kramer, Schaefer & Briscoe
Tarrytown, NY
Sprung, Marshall S. ....Los Angeles, CA
Sprung, Peter C. ....New York, NY
Sprung, Sarah ....New York, NY
Sprunger, Barton T. ....Indianapolis, IN
Sprunger, Noble ....Placerville, CA
Sprunger, Powell L. ....San Jose, CA
Sprunger, Richard L. ....Los Angeles, CA
Sprunger, Rick L. ....Berne, IN
Sprunger, Sue A. ....Raleigh, NC
Sprunk, Bethany Anne ....Wyandotte, MI
Sprunk, Thomas R. ....Sandusky, OH
Sprunt, Hugh H., Jr. ....Richardson, TX
Spry, Donald F., II ....Bangor, PA
Stroudsburg, PA
Spry, W. Dennie ....Winston-Salem, NC
Spry, William D., Jr. ....Winston-Salem, NC
Spuches, Gregory James
North Syracuse, NY
Spuches, John P. ....New York, NY
Spudeas, Christina L. ....Fort Lauderdale, FL
Spudis, Barbara C. ....Chicago, IL
Spuehler, Donald R. ....Los Angeles, CA
Spuhler, Earl R. ....Flint, MI
Spuhler, Kent R. ....Jacksonville, FL
Spula & Spula ....Niagara Falls, NY
Spula, Wm. B. ....Niagara Falls, NY
Spulak, Thomas J. ....Washington, DC
Spuller, Susan E. ....Seattle, WA
Spunaugle, Vaughn E. ....El Sobrante, CA
Spund, Mark E. ....New York, NY
Spung, Bartley Stiers ....Montgomery, AL
Spungen, Sharon S. ....Grand Rapids, MI
Spungin, Lawrence D. ....Universal City, CA
Spungin, Scott A. ....Santa Monica, CA
Spunt, Jerome B. ....Providence, RI
Spurgeon, Edward D. ....Salt Lake City, UT
Spurgeon, Jani Lynn ....Plattsburgh, NY
Spurgeon, John M. ....Denver, CO
Spurgeon, Larry D. ....Wichita, KS
Spurgeon, Michael W. ....Anderson, IN
Spurgeon, Paul E., Jr. ....Mt. Vernon, OH
Spurgeon, Roberta Kaye ....Cleveland, OH
Spurgeon, Sandra ....Paintsville, KY
Spurgeon, Sybil Louise
Virginia Beach, VA
Spurgeon, Thomas K. ....San Antonio, TX
Spurgers, Michael Ray ....Wichita Falls, TX
Spurgin, Gerald ....Tampa, FL
Spurgin & Jaramillo, P.A. ....Tampa, FL
Spurgin, John H., II ....Kingwood, TX
Spurgin, M. Evelyn ....Annapolis, MD
Spurgin, Stephen ....Fort Stockton, TX
Spurgis, John T. ....Jackson, MI
Spuria, David A. ....Dallas, TX
Spurlark, Susan ....Oakland, CA
Spurlin, John C. ....Tifton, GA
Spurlin, Margaret H. ....Washington, DC
Spurlin, Robert E. ....Frankfort, KY
Spurlin, Tamela J. ....Danville, KY
Spurling, Clarence H. ....Gardiner, ME
Spurling, David E. ....Boise, ID
Spurling, Dennis F. ....Houston, TX
Spurling, Dennis M. ....Haverhill, MA
Spurling, Dennis M., P.C. ....Haverhill, MA
Spurling, James Casey ....Sacramento, CA
Spurling Law Offices ....Gardiner, ME
Spurling, Mark ....Rockville, CT
Spurlock, Ben L., Jr. ....Indianapolis, IN
Spurlock, Burl W. ....Prestonsburg, KY
Spurlock, Charles T. ....Boston, MA
Spurlock, David W. ....Birmingham, AL
Spurlock, Donna S. ....Chattanooga, TN
Spurlock, James E. ....Huntington, WV
Spurlock, Jeffrey M. ....Irvine, CA
Spurlock, Joe C., II ....Dallas, TX
Spurlock, Michael ....Columbus, OH
Spurlock, Michael ....El Paso, TX
Spurlock, Odile F. ....Chattanooga, TN
Spurlock, Robert J. ....Phoenix, AZ
Spurlock, Ronda Yvette ....Franklin, TN
Spurlock, Sears, Pry, Griebling & McBride
Bucyrus, OH
Spurlock, Stacey B. ....Santa Ana, CA
Spurlock, Susan Hicks ....Boston, MA
Spurney, Frank G., Jr. ....Belleville, KS
Spurney & Spurney ....Belleville, KS
Spurr, Christin Popp ....Newport, KY
Spurr, James E. ....Kalamazoo, MI
Spurr, Jon Charles ....Terre Haute, IN
Spurr, Sophie L. ....Blue Hill, ME
Spurr, William R. ....Seattle, WA
Spurrier, Clinton L. ....Lenox, IA
Mt. Ayr, IA
Spurrier, Donald N. ....Huntsville, AL
Spurrier, Mark G. ....Finksburg, MD
Spurrier, Rice, Wood & Hall ....Decatur, AL
Huntsville, AL
Spurrier, Stanley, III ....Wichita, KS
Spurzem, Peter R. ....Hollister, CA
Spustek, Maria S. ....San Jose, CA
Sputz, Alan W. ....New York, NY
Spyhalski, Paul R. ....Austin, MN
Spyke, Nancy Perkins ....Pittsburgh, PA
Spyker, Marvin Lloyd ....Frisco, CO
Spykman, Erik D. ....Lafayette, IN
Spyksma, Sarah V. J. ....Los Angeles, CA
Spyra, Dennis J. ....Pittsburgh, PA
Spyratos, E. Angelo ....Downers Grove, IL
Spyratos, Ethel ....Chicago, IL
Spyredes, Anastasios Tom
Boca Raton, FL
Spyres, Theodore G. ....Milwaukee, WI
Spyridon, Gregg L. ....Covington, LA
Metairie, LA
Spyridon, Koch, Wallace & Palermo, L.L.C.
Covington, LA
Metairie, LA
New Orleans, LA
Spyroboulos, Dionysios S. ....Forest Hills, NY
Spyropoulos, George E. ....Washington, DC
Spyropoulos, Katerina ....Melville, NY
Spyropoulos, Michael ....Peekskill, NY
Spyropoulos, Soula J. ....Park Ridge, IL
Spyros, Nicholas L., Jr. ....Palo Alto, CA
Spytek, Eryk J. ....Chicago, IL
Squadron, Anne Strickland ....Bronx, NY
Squadron, Ellenoff, Plesent & Sheinfeld, LLP ....Los Angeles, CA
New York, NY
Squadron, Howard M. ....New York, NY
Squadron, Richard J. ....Newark, DE
Squarcy and Associates ....Sea Girt, NJ
Squarcy, Charlotte Van Horne ....Sea Girt, NJ
Squarrell, Marcus L. ....Denver, CO
Squatrito, Dominic J. ....Hartford, CT
Squeglia, Elisabeth A. ....Columbus, OH
Squeo, Eugene P. ....Jersey City, NJ
New York, NY
Squeo, Robin L ....Worthington, OH
Squeri, Doris Ann ....Foster City, CA
Squeri, James D. ....San Francisco, CA
Squeri, Stephen J. ....Cleveland, OH
Squeri, Thomas H. ....Watsonville, CA
Squibb, George S., Jr. ....Jamestown, RI
Squibb, John D. ....Houston, TX
Squibb, Wallace S. ....Springfield, MO
Squier, James D. ....Houston, TX
Squier, Moira J. ....Cincinnati, OH
Squier, Robert M., Jr. ....Indianapolis, IN
Squiers, Deborah K. ....New York, NY
Squiers, Jay D. ....Newark, NJ
Squiers, Mary P. ....Needham, MA
Squiers and Policinski ....Cassopolis, MI
Squiers, Robert J., Jr. ....Detroit, MI
Squillace, Mark S. ....Laramie, WY
Squillace, Michael L. ....Columbus, OH
Squillace, Scott E. ....San Francisco, CA
Squillacote, George F. ....Milwaukee, WI
Squillante, Bruce J. ....Ada, MI
Squillante, David G. ....Toledo, OH
Squillante, Robert N. ....West Paterson, NJ
Squillaro, Thomas S. ....San Diego, CA
Squire, Andrew ....New York, NY
Squire, Bruce M. ....Mesa, AZ
Squire, Daniel H. ....Washington, DC
Squire, Geri Landau ....Hackensack, NJ
Squire, Harris G. ....Tulsa, OK
Squire, Jane E. ....San Francisco, CA
Squire, Jeffrey H. ....New York, NY
Squire, Jeffrey P. ....St. Marys, OH
Squire, Kelly Lyn ....Milwaukee, WI
Squire, Madelyn Carol ....Washington, DC
Squire, Orin L. ....Orofino, ID
Squire, Paul D. ....New York, NY
Squire, Percy ....Columbus, OH
Squire, Richard M. ....Philadelphia, PA
Squire, Ryan C. ....Los Angeles, CA
Squire, Sanders & Dempsey L.L.P.
Phoenix, AZ
Washington, DC
Jacksonville, FL
Miami, FL
New York, NY
Cleveland, OH
Columbus, OH
Houston, TX
Squire, Sidney ....New York, NY
Squire, Steven F. ....Fort Lauderdale, FL
Squire, Steven F., Chartered
Fort Lauderdale, FL
Squire, Tamara A. ....Columbus, OH
Squire, Thomas S. ....Syracuse, NY
Squire, Walter C. ....New York, NY
Squire, William ....Roseland, NJ
Squires, Barry P. ....Carnegie, OK
Squires, Charles J. ....Joliet, IL
Squires & Cordrey ....New York, NY
Squires, Cynthia ....Glide, OR
Squires, Donald B. ....Fremont, CA
Squires, Donald M. ....Treasury Department, Internal Revenue Service, GV
Squires, Douglas W. ....Visalia, CA
Squires, Elizabeth K.
White Sulphur Springs, WV
Squires, George L. ....Department of Justice, Tax Division, GV
Squires, Herbert E. ....Philadelphia, PA
Squires, James Austin ....Norfolk, VA
Squires, James Drew ....Arlington, VA
Squires, Janna L. ....Philadelphia, PA
Squires, Jay T. ....Minneapolis, MN
Squires, Jeffrey E. ....Bath, NY
Squires, Jeffrey L. ....Washington, DC
Squires, Jeffrey L., P.C. ....Alexandria, VA
Squires, Jodi ....Punta Gorda, FL
Squires, John A. ....Morristown, NJ
Squires, John B. ....Las Vegas, NV
Squires, John D. ....Dayton, OH
Squires, John F. ....Mission Viejo, CA
Squires, John H. ....Chicago, IL
Squires, John L., III ....Richmond, VA
Squires, Julaan ....Conway, SC
Squires, Kate L. ....Dallas, TX
Squires, Katherine L. ....Dallas, TX
Squires, Kendall M. ....San Diego, CA
Squires, Kenneth C. ....Houston, TX
Squires, Lawrence S. ....San Francisco, CA
Squires, Lawton W. ....New York, NY
Squires & Lopez ....Portland, OR
Squires, Malcolm H., Jr.
Department of the Army, U.S. Army Court of Criminal Appeals, GV

Squires, Mark E. ....**Philadelphia, PA**
Squires, Richard A. ....**Carle Place, NY**
Squires, Rod S. ....**Waco, TX**
Squires, Rodger D. ....**Minneapolis, MN**
Squires, T. Grey ....**Orlando, FL**
Squires, Thomas B. ....Akron, OH
Squires, Vernon P. ....**Cedar Rapids, IA**
Squires, Vernon T. ....Downers Grove, IL
Squires, Wendy Jo ....Portland, OR
Squires, William ....Los Angeles, CA
Squires, William J., III ....Exton, PA
Squires, William R., III ....**Seattle, WA**
Squires-Lee, Debra A. ....**Boston, MA**
Squirrell, David J. ....**White Plains, NY**
Squitero, John R. ....**Miami, FL**
Squitieri, Generoso ....Paramus, NJ
Squitieri, Janet ....New York, NY
Squitieri, Lee ....**New York, NY**
Squitieri, S. Paul ....Bronx, NY
Squitiero, Geoffrey L. ....**Bridgeport, CT**
Squyres, B. Newal ....**Boise, ID**
Squyres, Mary M. ....**Chicago, IL**
Squyres, Roland E. ....Houston, TX
Srader, Sabra J. ....**Lubbock, TX**
Sraga, Alan T. ....**Chicago, IL**
Chicago Heights, IL
Srager, Leslie ....**New York, NY**
Sragow, Daniel E. ....Princeton, NJ
Sragow, Darry A. ....**Los Angeles, CA**
New York, NY
Sragow, William J. ....Cherry Hill, NJ
Srail, Donald J. ....Galloway, OH
Sralla, Tim G. ....**Fort Worth, TX**
Sramek, Gerald J. ....Palos Heights, IL
Srebnick, Howard M. ....**Miami, FL**
Srebnick, Michael G. ....Miami, FL
Srebnick, Scott A. ....**Miami, FL**
Srebro, Anne M. ....Dallas, TX
Sredni, Lilian ....North Miami Beach, FL
Sreenan & Cain, P.C. ....**Rockford, IL**
Sreenan, Charene E. ....Miami, FL
Sreenan, Gregory P. ....**Miami, FL**
Sreenan, Gregory P., P.A., Law Offices of
Miami, FL
Sreenan, Michael J. ....Chicago, IL
Srejovic, Nina K. ....**San Francisco, CA**
Sremack, William M. ....Akron, OH
Srere, Mark A. ....**Washington, DC**
Sreter, Albert J. ....Lexington, MA
Srholez, Joseph T., III ....Sussex, NJ
Sriberg, Robert M. ....Newton, MA
Sribnick, Howard L. ....
Department of Justice, GV
Sridharan, Priya ....**Los Angeles, CA**
Sridharan, Savitha ....**San Francisco, CA**
Srikantiah, Jayashri ....**San Francisco, CA**
Srinivasan, Gautam
Environmental Protection Agency, Office of the General Counsel, GV
Srinivasan, Gregg D. ....**New York, NY**
Srinivasan, Latha M. ....**Cleveland, OH**
Sriram, Kaushik P. ....Houston, TX
SRIS, P.C. ....**Fairfax, VA**
Manassas, VA
Sriskandarajah, Atchuthan "Sris"
Manassas, VA
Srivastava, Alok K. ....**Kansas City, MO**
Srochi, Julie J. ....**Atlanta, GA**
Sroczynski, Michael E. ....Boston, MA
Srodes, Paul G. ....Arlington Heights, IL
Srodulski, Marc L. ....Chicago, IL
Sroges, Richard W. ....New Orleans, LA
Srogota, Holly ....**Moorestown, NJ**
Philadelphia, PA
Sroka, Daniel M. ....**Greensboro, NC**
Raleigh, NC
Sroka, Frank J. ....**Chicago, IL**
Sroka, Frederick W. ....Danville, CA
Sroka, Jennifer Dole ....Buffalo, NY
Sroka, Louis S. ....Garden City, NY
Sroka, Marianne Dennstedt ....Lakewood, OH
Sroka, Scott L. ....**Buffalo, NY**
Sroloff, Sheldon ....Beverly Hills, CA
Srolovic, Lemuel M. ....**New York, NY**
White Plains, NY
Sroufe, Delmar L., (P.C.) ....**Houston, TX**
Srouji, Afif S. ....Brentwood, TN
Srour, Danielle R. ....**Washington, DC**
Srour, Deborah R. ....**New York, NY**
Srsen, Nicholas J., Jr. ....Salinas, CA
Srsic, Daniel W. ....**Columbus, OH**
Srstka, Cynthia Lacey ....Sioux Falls, SD
Srstka, Donald Nicholas ....Sioux Falls, SD
Srstka, William J., Jr. ....Sioux Falls, SD
Srstka, William J., Sr. ....Sioux Falls, SD
Sruba, Anne L. ....Newport Beach, CA
Srulovitz, Jeffrey ....**Chicago, IL**
Srulowitz, Marvin ....New York, NY
Srulowitz, Sander ....New York, NY
Srygley, Paul D. ....**Tallahassee, FL**
Ssekandi, Francis M. ....New York, NY
Ssutu, Louis ....Santa Monica, CA
Ssutu, Louis, A Prof. Corp.
Santa Monica, CA
Staab, Andrew E. ....St. Paul, MN
Staab, Diane D. ....**Purchase, NY**
Staab, Diane M. ....Lincoln, NE
Staab, Donald C. ....Hays, KS
Staab, Edward W., III ....Fort Lauderdale, FL
Staab, Gary G. ....New York, NY
Staab, Lawrence J.
Department of Commerce, Patent and Trademark Office, GV
Staab, Louise Betcher ....**Denver, CO**
Staab, Martin R. ....Louisville, CO
Staab, Michael J. ....**Chicago, IL**
Staab, William C. ....Monroe, LA
Staack, Anselm C. ....Juneau, AK
Staack, James A. ....Clearwater, FL
Staack & Klemm, P.A. ....Clearwater, FL
Staack, Thomas L. ....**Waterloo, IA**
Staadeker, David ....Cincinnati, OH
Staaden, Constance A. ....Racine, WI
Staaf, Monica S. ....**Norwell, MA**
Staak, Joseph C. ....**Atlanta, GA**
Staal, Robert J. ....San Francisco, CA
Staar, William A. ....Milford, CT
Staas, Carl K. ....Jacksonville, FL
Staas & Halsey LLP ....**Washington, DC**
Staas, H. J. ....**Washington, DC**
Staas, Laurie ....Chicago, IL
Staas, William E., III ....**Mount Laurel, NJ**
Philadelphia, PA
Staat, Lawrence G. ....**Chicago, IL**
Staats, David ....**Wilmington, DE**
Staats, David, P.A., Law Office of
Wilmington, DE
Staats, Harwood H. ....Cudahy, WI
Staats, Keith W. ....Springfield, IL
Staats, Larry E. ....Columbus, OH
Staats, Marilyn Kay ....Oklahoma City, OK
Staats, Richard H. ....Cudahy, WI
Staats, Robert B. ....Panama City, FL
Staats & Staats ....Cudahy, WI
Staats & White ....Panama City, FL
Stabbe, Mitchell H. ....**Washington, DC**
Stabell, Edward R., III ....**Savannah, GA**
Staben, Kopsick & McCollum, P.C.
Waukegan, IL
Staber, David F. ....**Dallas, TX**
Stabile, Arthur J. ....Tustin, CA
Stabile, Diane ....Mount Pleasant, SC
Stabile, Gary D. ....Manhattan Beach, CA
Stabile, Jana S. ....**San Jose, CA**
Stabile, Joanne ....Mount Vernon, NY
Stabile, Maria Treglia ......Treasury Department, Internal Revenue Service, GV
Stabile, Mark R. ....**Pittsburgh, PA**
Stabile, Mary K. ....Andover, NJ
Stabile, Michael R., Jr. ....**Pittsburgh, PA**
Stabile, Paul A. ....Pasadena, CA
Stabile, Steven L. ....Woodbridge, NJ
Stabile, Thomas P. ....Orange, CA
Stabile, Victor P. ....**Harrisburg, PA**
Philadelphia, PA
Stabinski, Luis ....Miami, FL
Stabinski, Richard E. ....**Philadelphia, PA**
Stabinsky, Allon ....**Menlo Park, CA**
Stabinsky, Harvey, M.D. ....Armonk, NY
Stabler, Eric A. ....**New York, NY**
Stabler, James B. ....Phoenix, AZ
Stabler, James M. ....Dallas, TX
Stabler, Jed A. ....West Palm Beach, FL
Stabler, Jeffrey C. ....Lawton, OK
Stabler, L. Vastine, Jr. ....**Birmingham, AL**
Stabler, Pamela Hays ....**Houston, TX**
Stabler, Steven Barry ....Santa Monica, CA
Stabler, W. Laird, III ....**Wilmington, DE**
Stabler, W. Laird, Jr. ....**Wilmington, DE**
Stabler, Wendie Cohen ....**Wilmington, DE**
Stables, William L., Jr. ....Harrisonburg, VA
Stablie, Maria T. ....New York, NY
Stabnick, Courtney C. ....**Burlington, MA**
Stabnick, Richard T. ....**Glastonbury, CT**
Stabrawa, David J. ....Chicago, IL
Stacchini, Michael J. ....**New York, NY**
Stacell, Mark Alan ....Austin, TX
Stacer, Jefferson L. ....San Diego, CA
Stacer, Richard K. ....San Diego, CA
Stacey, Brett D. ....**Milwaukee, WI**
Stacey, Brian J. ....Plymouth, MI
Stacey, Calvin J. ....**Billings, MT**
Stacey, Christ S. ....Naperville, IL
Stacey, Cindy S. ....Conyers, GA
Stacey, Cindy S., P.C. ....Conyers, GA
Stacey, Daniel T. ....Columbia, SC
Stacey, David R. ....Palatine, IL
Stacey, Donald R. ....Bedford, NH
Stacey, Eve A. Piemonte ....Boston, MA
Stacey, Francyne ....**Ann Arbor, MI**
Stacey, George K. ....**Memphis, TN**
Stacey, Hutson, Stacey & Powers, A Legal Professional Association
Columbiana, OH
Stacey, Jas. A. ....Sandusky, OH
Stacey, Joseph S. ....Tacoma, WA
Stacey, Kathleen Z. ....Glen Allen, VA
Stacey, Kelly M. ....Charleston, IL
Stacey, Kelly M. ....Akron, OH
Stacey, Kim T. ....Fort Wayne, IN
Stacey, Lawrence W. ....**Columbiana, OH**
Stacey, Lawrence W., II ....**Columbiana, OH**
Stacey, Leslie Sullivan ....Dayton, OH
Stacey, Marsha K. ....Sioux Falls, SD
Stacey, Michael L. ....Detroit, MI
Stacey, Paul H. ....Wheaton, IL
Stacey, Reid ....Topeka, KS
Stacey, Rex D. ....Hastings, MN
Stacey, Richard Wayne ....Honolulu, HI
Stacey, Robert E., Jr. ....Portland, OR
Stacey, Sherman L. ....**Woodland Hills, CA**
Stacey & Walen ....**Billings, MT**
Stacey, William E., Jr.
Fort Lauderdale, FL
Stach, Christine M. ....**Fort Wayne, IN**
Stach, David Joseph ....**Anderson, IN**
Fort Wayne, IN
Marion, IN
Stach, Dennis ....Riverside, CA
Stach, Marc Allan ....Irving, TX
Stach, Mark A. ....Dublin, OH
Stach, Sharon Marie ....Chicago, IL
Stach, Victoria F. ....**Chicago, IL**
Stache, Dale ....Beaverton, OR
Stachel, Kenneth J. ....Pittsburgh, PA
Stachel, Robert D., Jr. ....Sierra Vista, AZ
Stachenfeld, Avi J. ....Oakland, CA
Stachenfeld, Bruce M. ....**New York, NY**
Stachiw, Mark A. ....**Dallas, TX**
Stachler, John H. ....**Dayton, OH**
Stachler, Robert G. ....**Cincinnati, OH**
Stachler, Thomas L. ....**Cincinnati, OH**
Stachnik, Raymond E. ....**Chicago, IL**
Stachowiak, Christopher S. ....**Phoenix, AZ**
Stachowiak, Keith R. ....**Mequon, WI**
Milwaukee, WI
Racine, WI
Stachowiak, Robert W. ....Akron, OH
Stachowski, Karen H. ....Nashville, TN
Stachowski, Michael J. ....Buffalo, NY
Stachowski, Michael J., P.C. ....Buffalo, NY
Stachtiaris, Chris Alexander .....Canonsburg, PA
Stachtiaris, Theodore J. ....**New York, NY**
Stachura, James M. ....Howell, MI
Stachura, Joseph T. ....Riverwoods, IL
Stachyra, Frank E. ....Chicago, IL
Stachyra & Penn ....Chicago, IL
Stack, Allen M. ....Honolulu, HI
Stack, Alvin A. ....**Milwaukee, WI**
Stack, Andrea Carol ....New York, NY
Stack, Ann Marie ....**Savannah, GA**
Stack, Bonnie L. ....Berkeley, CA
Stack, Brian J. ....**Miami, FL**
Stack, Brian J. ....Covington, KY
Stack, C. Stephen, Jr. ....**Jackson, MS**
Stack, Charles D. ....Cleveland, OH
Stack, Charles M. ....Cleveland, OH
Stack, Charles R., (P.A.) ....Melbourne, FL
Miami, FL
Stack, Christopher J. ....Warren, RI
Stack, Daniel ....Suffern, NY
Stack, Daniel J. ....Highland, IL
Stack, David R. ....**New York, NY**
Stack, Donald D. J. ....Atlanta, GA
Stack, Douglas L. ....North Platte, NE
Stack, Felice R. ....Philadelphia, PA
Stack Fernandez Anderson Harris & Wallace, P.A. ....**Fort Lauderdale, FL**
Miami, FL
Stack & Filpi, Chartered ....**Chicago, IL**
Stack, Francis J. ....Sylvania, OH
Stack, George ....Houston, TX
Stack, Gerald A. ....Cheyenne, WY
Stack, Gerald F. ....**Syracuse, NY**
Stack, Heather ....**New York, NY**
Stack, Ilene W. ....**New York, NY**
Stack, James F. ....Chicago, IL
Stack, Jane M. ....New York, NY
Stack, John R. ....Mount Vernon, NY
Stack, John Timothy ....Columbia, SC
Stack, John W. ....Chicago, IL
Stack, Joseph M. ....Hoboken, NJ
Stack, Kevin J. ....**Glendale, CA**
Stack, Laura Barton ....**Washington, DC**
Stack, Lawrence R. ....Chicago, IL
Stack, Louis J. ....**Meadville, PA**
Stack, Melissa K. ....**Los Angeles, CA**
Stack, Melvin D. ....**Daytona Beach, FL**
Stack, Michael A. ....**Cheboygan, MI**
Stack, Michael D. ....Oklahoma City, OK
Stack, Michael J., III ....Philadelphia, PA
Stack, Michael J., Jr. ....Philadelphia, PA
Stack, Michael R.
Agency for International Development, Other Offices of A.I.D., GV
Stack, Paul F. ....**Chicago, IL**
Stack, Richard A. ....Barstow, CA
Stack, Richard A., Jr. ....**Appleton, WI**
Stack, Richard L. ....**Los Angeles, CA**
Stack, Richard L. ....Glen Burnie, MD
Stack, Robert B. ....**Washington, DC**
Stack, Robert J. ....Richardson, TX
Stack, Robert T. ....**New York, NY**
Stack & Rogers ....**Atlanta, GA**
Stack, Rosemary ....Syracuse, NY
Stack, Shari S. ....**Houston, TX**
Stack, Sharon R. ....Cheboygan, MI
Stack & Stack, P.C. ....Philadelphia, PA
Stack, Stephen A., Jr. ....**Philadelphia, PA**
Stack, Susan Barr ....Daytona Beach, FL
Stack, Thomas F., Jr. ....Norwood, MA
Stack, Thos. F. ....San Mateo, CA
Stack, W. E., Jr. ....Midland, TX
Stack, William J. ....**Houston, TX**
Stack, William J., Jr. ....**Atlanta, GA**
Stack, William S. ....Encino, CA
Stackable, Frederick L. ....Lansing, MI
Stackel, Dean ....**Los Angeles, CA**
Stacker, Edwin J. ....**Fort Lauderdale, FL**
Stacker, Howard G. ....**Minneapolis, MN**
Stacker, Patrick C. ....**Long Beach, CA**
Stacker, Patrick C. ....**Los Angeles, CA**
Stackhouse, Dale E. ....**Indianapolis, IN**
Stackhouse, Harry B. ....**Pensacola, FL**
Stackhouse, John E. H. ....New York, NY
Stackhouse, Lee F. ....High Point, NC
Stackhouse, Martin E. ....Hartford, CT
Stackhouse, Neil ....**Atlantic City, NJ**
Pleasantville, NJ
Stackhouse, Peter K. ....**Arlington, VA**
Stackhouse, R. Clinton, Jr. ....**Norfolk, VA**
Stackhouse, Robert C. ....**Norfolk, VA**
Stackhouse, Smith & Nexsen ....**Norfolk, VA**
Portsmouth, VA
Virginia Beach, VA
Stackhouse, Susan G. ....Fairfield, CA
Stackler, Barbara W. ....Chicago, IL
Stackler and Holstein, Law Offices of
Chicago, IL
Stackler, Ronald E. ....Lake Villa, IL
Stackman, Garrett L. ....**Madison, NJ**
Stacknik, Wesley R., (P.A.) ....Seminole, FL
Stackpole, Carol A. ....Manchester, NH
Stackpole, David B. ....**Stowe, VT**
Stackpole & French ....**Stowe, VT**
Stackpole, Harrison C. ....**Troy, MI**
Stackpole, John E. ....New York, NY
Stackpole, Kerin E. ....**Burlington, VT**
Stackpole, William ....Lawrenceville, NJ
Stackpoole, William R. ....Detroit, MI
Stacks, Leslie R. ....**Charlotte, NC**
Stacom, Beau Claire ....**Los Angeles, CA**
Stacy, Burton E., Jr. ....**Fayetteville, AR**
Stacy, Charles A. ....**Bluefield, VA**
Stacy, Charles B. ....**Charleston, WV**
Stacy, Chris A. ....Houston, TX
Stacy, Chris A., & Associates, P.C.
Houston, TX
Stacy, Daniel W., Jr. ....**Georgetown, SC**
Stacy, David H. ....**Denver, CO**
Stacy, Elizabeth M. ....**Dallas, TX**
Stacy, Frances H. ....Houston, TX
Stacy, G. Palmer, III ....Raleigh, NC
Stacy, George W. ....Bainbridge, GA
Stacy, Gilbert L. ....Savannah, GA
Stacy & Griffith ....Beckley, WV
Stacy, Holly Ring ....Gainesville, FL
Stacy, Horace E., Jr. ....**Lumberton, NC**
Stacy, James D., II ....Beckley, WV
Stacy, Mark A. ....Boston, MA
Stacy, Michael D. ....**Dallas, TX**
Stacy, Neera Rellan ....**New York, NY**
Stacy, Peter L. ....**Pasadena, CA**
Stacy, Pierce P., III ....Bryan, TX
Stacy, Robert C., II ....**McLean, VA**
Stacy, Robert F., Jr. ....**Oxford, MS**
Stacy, Roy L. ....**Dallas, TX**
Stacy, Sanders & McAlpine, LLP
Atlanta, GA
Stacy, Stephanie F. ....**Lincoln, NE**
Stacy, Stroud P. ....**Atlanta, GA**
Stacy, Tatum R. ....Jackson, MS
Stacy, Theodore L. ....Valparaiso, IN
Stacy, Thomas G. ....Lawrence, KS
Stade, Nancy K. ....Rockville, MD
Stadeker, Marcia Bull ....**Birmingham, AL**
Stadel, Renee A. ....Providence, RI
Stadelman, Gary R. ....Pittsburgh, PA
Stadelman, H. James ....**Orlando, FL**
Stadelman, H. Rudy C., (P.C.)
Cottonwood, AZ
Stadelman, Richard J. ....Shawano, WI
Stadfeld, L. Seth ....**Boston, MA**
Stadfeld, Max S. ....**Baltimore, MD**
Stadheim & Grear ....**Chicago, IL**
Stadheim, Rolf O. ....**Chicago, IL**
Stadiem, William H. ....Santa Monica, CA
Stading & Assocs., A Prof. Corp.
El Paso, TX
Stading, Donald R. ....**Lincoln, NE**
Stading, Ronald J. ....El Paso, TX
Stadler, Brian M. ....**New York, NY**
Stadler, Frances M. ....**Washington, DC**
Stadler & Harris, P.A.
New Smyrna Beach, FL
Titusville, FL
Stadler, Harry ....Woodbridge, NJ
Stadler, James A. ....Denver, CO
Stadler, James R. ....**Grand Rapids, MI**
Stadler, Jeffrey L. ....**Uniondale, NY**
Stadler, John B. ....Milwaukee, WI
Stadler, John S. ....Boston, MA
Stadler, Katherine ....**Madison, WI**
Stadler, Lewis B. ....Pawling, NY
Stadler, Linda L. ....**New Orleans, LA**
Stadler, Lynda R. ....**New York, NY**
Stadler, Mark ....**Pittsburgh, PA**
Stadler, Michael M. ....**Freehold, NJ**
Stadler, Richard E. ....**Titusville, FL**
Stadler, Ronald S. ....Brookfield, WI
Stadler, Sara K. ....**Atlanta, GA**
Stadler, Sara R. ....**New Haven, CT**
Stadler & Schott, S.C. ....Brookfield, WI
Stadnicar, Joseph W. ....Beavercreek, OH
Stadnicki, Alfred A. ....**Washington, DC**
Stadnik, Thomas J.R. (IBA) ....**New York, NY**
Stadter, Gregory E. ....Vancouver, WA
Stadter, Taunia Davis ....Little Rock, AR
Stadtlander, Lindsay L. ....**Las Vegas, NV**
Stadtmauer, Allan W. ....Boston, MA
Stadtmauer, Arnold L. ....**Clifton, NJ**
Stadtmauer Bailkin, LLP ....**New York, NY**
Stadtmauer, Catherine S. ....New York, NY
Stadtmauer, David I. ....**New York, NY**
Stadtmauer, Gary D. ....**Florham Park, NJ**
Stadtmauer, Marc A. ....**New York, NY**
Stadtmauer, Richard Paul ....Florham Park, NJ
Stadtmauer, Seymour M. ....Morristown, NJ
Stadtmauer, Steven ....**Clifton, NJ**
Stadtmauer, Steven A. ....**Millburn, NJ**
New York, NY
Stadtmauer, Susan Burton ....Bryn Mawr, PA
Stadtmauer, Warren K. ....Clifton, NJ
Stadtmueller, J. P. ....Milwaukee, WI
Stadtmueller, Ronald E. ....San Diego, CA
Stadulis, Lawrence P. ....**Washington, DC**
Stadum, Steven D. ....Portland, OR
Staebler, Charles A., Jr. ....Louisville, KY
Staebler, Clifford R ....Jackson Heights, NY
Staebler, Jonathan ....**Cumberland, MD**
Staebler, Michael B. ....**Washington, DC**
Detroit, MI
Staed, Robert E., Jr. ....St. Louis, MO
Staed, Thomas W. ....Daytona Beach, FL
Staedtler, Richard P. ....Madison, WI
Staeheli, Gregory G. ....Spokane, WA
Staeheli, Richard A. ....Spokane, WA
Staehely, Al, Jr. ....Houston, TX
Staehle, Richard W. ....Akron, OH
Staehle, Sandra J. ....Philadelphia, PA
Staehle, William E. ....East Hanover, NJ
Staehr, Lawrence R. ....New York, NY

Staelin, Earl H. ... Austin, TX
Staenberg, Marc R. ... Los Angeles, CA
Staerk, James W. ... Roslyn, PA
Staes, Andrew T. ... Chicago, IL
Staes, Michelle Saunders ... Orlando, FL
Staes, Steven M. ... Atlanta, GA
Staev, Julius ... Dallas, TX
Stafanini, Thomas F. ... Rochester, NY
Staff, Andrew W. ... Quincy, IL
Staff, Hubert G. ... Quincy, IL
Staff, Karen L. ... New York, NY
Staff, Kenneth C. ... Jenkintown, PA
Staff, Marcia J. ... Denton, TX
Staff, Richard J. ... Madison, WI
Staff, Richard W. ... Houston, TX
Staff & Staff ... Quincy, IL
Staffa, Joseph ... New York, NY
Staffa, Kimberly A. ... St. Petersburg, FL
Staffa, Thomas F. ... New York, NY
Staffanson, Kristin J. ... Chicago, IL
Staffaroni, Robert J. ... New York, NY
Staffel, Timothy J. ... Santa Maria, CA
Staffelbach, Dennis ... Tupelo, MS
Staffier, David William ... Somerville, MA
Staffier, John R. ... Washington, DC
Staffieri, Nicholas J. ... Philadelphia, PA
Staffieri, Victor A. ... Louisville, KY
Staffin, Alvin M. ... Plymouth Meeting, PA
Staffin, Bruce E. ... Richardson, TX
Staffin, Elliot B.
Securities and Exchange Commission, Division of Corporation Finance, GV
Stafford, Albert H., II ... Edna, TX
Stafford, Allan M. ... Garland, TX
Stafford & Allison ... Woodville, TX
Stafford, Blakeney ... Palo Alto, CA
Stafford, Bobby B. ... Alexandria, VA
Stafford, Brenda Eady ... Florham Park, NJ
Stafford, Carl F. ... Detroit, MI
Stafford, Catherine B. ... Minneapolis, MN
Stafford, C. E. ... Battle Creek, MI
Stafford, Charles E., Jr. ... Indio, CA
Stafford, Charles F., Jr. ... Olympia, WA
Stafford, Curtis K., Jr. ... Baton Rouge, LA
Stafford, David ... Raton, NM
Stafford, David B. ... New York, NY
Stafford, Dawn ... San Bernardino, CA
Stafford, Derek J. ... San Francisco, CA
Stafford, Diane R. ... Kansas City, MO
Stafford, E. Kay, Jr. ... Dublin, GA
Vidalia, GA
Stafford, E. Michael ... Lansing, MI
Stafford, Elaine K. ... Lakewood, CO
Stafford, Elizabeth A. ... Detroit, MI
Stafford, Forney B. ... LaBelle, FL
Stafford, Frederick E. ... Paramus, NJ
Stafford Frey Cooper, Professional Corporation ... Seattle, WA
Stafford, G. William ... Washington, DC
Stafford, G. Woody ... Colonial Heights, VA
Stafford, Gail A ... Jacksonville, FL
Stafford, George Clinton ... Oakland, CA
San Francisco, CA
Stafford, George L. ... Slater, MO
Stafford, Gordon O., Jr. ... San Antonio, TX
Stafford, Gregory W. ... Pittsboro, NC
Stafford, Grove, Jr. ... Alexandria, LA
Stafford, H. Craig ... Atlanta, GA
Stafford & Hall, L.L.P. ... Santa Ana, CA
Stafford, Harry R., Jr. ... Hartville, MO
Stafford, Harry W. ... Woodville, TX
Stafford, Harte Peary ... Bethesda, MD
Stafford, J. Steven ... Dyersburg, TN
Stafford, James L. ... Washington, DC
Stafford, James T., (P.C.) ... Houston, TX
Stafford, Jane L. ... Kansas City, MO
Stafford, Jane R. ... Richmond, VA
Stafford, Janet Maire ... University Park, PA
Stafford, Jeffrey J. ... Carmel, IN
Stafford, Jerry T. ... Peoria, IL
Stafford, Joanne ... Detroit, MI
Stafford, Joel D. ... Oklahoma City, OK
Stafford, John E. ... Charlestown, MA
Stafford, John G., Jr. ... Dallas, TX
Stafford, John H. ... Department of Justice, Federal Bureau of Investigation, GV
Stafford, John J., (P.C.) ... Inverness, IL
Stafford, John M. ... Denver, CO
Stafford, John P., Jr. ... Chestertown, MD
Stafford, John T., Jr. ... Lakewood, CO
Stafford, Joseph G., & Associates
Cleveland, OH
Stafford, Josephine Howard ... Tampa, FL
Stafford, Karen Leikkanen
Charlottesville, VA
Stafford, Kathi Jean ... Los Angeles, CA
Stafford, Kathleen L. ... Houston, TX
Stafford, L. Scott ... Little Rock, AR
Stafford Law Offices ... Boynton Beach, FL
Garden City, NY
Stafford Law Offices ... Hampton Bays, NY
Stafford, Leonard L. ... Fort Lauderdale, FL
Stafford, Leslie M. ... Dallas, TX
Stafford, Lynn R. ... Portland, OR
Stafford, Margaret ... Madison, WI
Stafford, Mark A. ... Winston-Salem, NC
Stafford, Mark C. ... Burnsville, MN
Stafford, Mary F. ... Chicago, IL
Stafford, Mary J. ... Baltimore, MD
Stafford, Mary J. ... Dayton, OH
Stafford, Michael A. ... Liberty, TX
Stafford, Michael E. ... Lake George, NY
Stafford, Michael J. ... Marlton, NJ
Stafford, Michael N. ... Glendale, CA
Stafford, Michael N. ... Los Angeles, CA
Stafford, Michael P. ... Boynton Beach, FL
Garden City, NY
Stafford, Michele R. ... San Mateo, CA
Stafford & Neal, S.C. ... Madison, WI
Stafford, Nicole W. ... Austin, TX
Stafford, O'Connor & Adsit ... Weedsport, NY
Stafford, Pamela ... Randolph, VT
Stafford, Philip O. ... New York, NY
Stafford, Randall A. ... Houston, TX
Stafford, Raymond K. ... New York, NY
Stafford, Regis W., Jr. ... Pittsburgh, PA
Stafford, Richard D. ... Norfolk, NE
Stafford, Richard H. ... Chippewa Falls, WI
Stafford, Robert A. ... Claremont, CA
Stafford, Robert E. ... Hampton Bays, NY
Stafford, Robert G. ... Columbus, OH
Stafford, Robert L. ... Houston, TX
Stafford, Robert P. ... Portland, OR
Stafford, Robt. T. ... Rutland, VT
Stafford, Rodney J. ... San Jose, CA
Stafford, Ronald B. ... Plattsburgh, NY
Stafford Rosenbaum LLP ... Madison, WI
Sun Prairie, WI
Stafford, Roxane ... Santa Ana, CA
Stafford, Ryan K. ... Exeter, NH
Stafford, Sarah A. ... Halstead, KS
Stafford, Sean Reagan ... Santa Ana, CA
Stafford, Shane L. ... Lake Worth, FL
Stafford, Shannon ... Seattle, WA
Stafford, Shawn D. ... Atlanta, GA
Stafford, Shawn D., P.C. ... Atlanta, GA
Stafford & Stafford, L.L.C. ... Lakewood, CO
Stafford, Stephanie J. ... Dallas, TX
Stafford, Stewart & Potter
Alexandria, LA
Colfax, LA
Jena, LA
Leesville, LA
Marksville, LA
Natchitoches, LA
Oberlin, LA
Ville Platte, LA
Stafford, Stormie ... Miami, FL
Stafford, Thomas ... Holmdel, NJ
Stafford, Thomas O. M., Jr. ... Alexandria, LA
Stafford, Thomas R. ... Xenia, OH
Stafford, Timothy A. ... New York, NY
Stafford, Timothy J. ... Santa Ana, CA
Stafford, Tracy E. ... Wilton Manors, FL
Stafford, Tracy E. ... Chesapeake, VA
Stafford, Trombley, Owens & Curtin, P.C.
Plattsburgh, NY
Stafford, Troy J. ... Charlotte, NC
Stafford, Vincent A. ... Cleveland, OH
Stafford, Walter V. ... Los Angeles, CA
Stafford, Warren S. ... Springfield, MO
Stafford, William H., Jr. ... Tallahassee, FL
Stafford, William J. ... San Francisco, CA
Stafford, William John ... Hollywood, FL
Stafford, William P., II ... Bluefield, WV
Stafford, William V. ... Irvine, CA
Stafira, John P. ... Tulsa, OK
Stafko, Ralph E. ... Department of Agriculture, Food Safety and Inspection Service, GV
Stafman, Edward S. ... Tallahassee, FL
Stafne, Albert J., Jr. ... Bettendorf, IA
Stafne, Lewis, Jasper, Alexander & Preacher, an Assn. of Sole Practitioners ... Bettendorf, IA
Stafne, Philip D. ... Fargo, ND
Stafsholt, Jon ... Glenwood, MN
Stafslien, Joan B. ... San Diego, CA
Stafstrom, John F., Jr. ... Bridgeport, CT
Hartford, CT
Stamford, CT
Stag, Michael G. ... New Orleans, LA
Stage, David A. ... Omaha, NE
Stage, Douglas R. ... Warwick, NY
Stage, Edma C. ... Van Nuys, CA
Stage, Gail Marie ... Miami, FL
Stage, Gary L. ... Indianapolis, IN
Lexington, KY
Stage, Jon K. ... Fort Lauderdale, FL
Stage, Rebecca E. ... Warwick, NY
Stage & Stage ... Warwick, NY
Stageberg, Mark N. ... Minnetonka, MN
Stageberg, Roger V. ... Minneapolis, MN
Stageman, Daniel B. ... Colorado Springs, CO
Stageman, Richard F. ... Des Moines, IA
Stagen, Frank P. ... Seattle, WA
Stager, Danielle M. ... Falls Church, VA
Stagg, Bonnie R. ... San Diego, CA
Stagg, C. Lawrence ... Tampa, FL
Stagg, Dard F. ... Huntington, NY
Stagg, David J. ... New York, NY
Stagg, Howard J., IV ... Sacramento, CA
Stagg, Howard J., IV, A Prof. Corp.
Sacramento, CA
Stagg, Lawrence A. ... Ringgold, GA
Stagg, M. Kimberly ... Nashville, TN
Stagg, Michael K. ... Nashville, TN
Stagg, Nancy ... New York, NY
Stagg, Nancy L. ... San Diego, CA
Stagg, R. Paulette ... Terre Haute, IN
Stagg, Regina A. ... Los Angeles, CA
Stagg, Richard B. ... Phoenix, AZ
Stagg, Robert E., Jr. ... Atlanta, GA
Stagg, Thomas E. ... East Meadow, NY
Stagg, Tom ... Shreveport, LA
Stagg, William L. ... Charlotte, NC
Stagg, William W. ... Lafayette, LA
Staggard, Richard A.
Jacksonville Beach, FL
Staggers, Allen C., Jr. ... Marshall, TX
Staggers, Daniel C. ... Keyser, WV
Staggers, Harley O., Jr. ... Keyser, WV
Staggers, Melissa L. ... Pittsburgh, PA
Staggers & Staggers ... Keyser, WV
Staggs, Daniel T. ... Redwood City, CA
Staggs, David R. ... San Diego, CA
Staggs, Dawn Lei ... Tulsa, OK
Staggs, Frank M., Jr. ... Houston, TX
Staggs, H. Bradley ... Tampa, FL
Staggs, Nancy C. ... Madera, CA
Staggs, Russell K. ... Hollywood, CA
Stagliano, David A. ... New York, NY
Stagliano & DeWeese, P.A. ... Wildwood, NJ
Stagliano, Gregory G. ... Media, PA
Stagliano, Gregory G., P.C. ... Media, PA
Stagliano, Paul T. ... Atlanta, GA
Stagliano, Ronald J. ... Wildwood, NJ
Stagman, David J. ... Chicago, IL
Stagnaro, Eugene J., Jr. ... Cincinnati, OH
Stagnaro, Gene A. ... Batavia, OH
Stagnaro, Jeffrey G. ... Cincinnati, OH
Stagnaro-Green, Doreen ... Oradell, NJ
Stagnato, Gerard Wm. ... Freehold, NJ
Stagner, Brian S. ... Fort Worth, TX
Stagner & Corley ... Bonham, TX
Sherman, TX
Stagner, Cynthia L. ... Sherman, TX
Stagner, David M. ... Sherman, TX
Stagner, Deborah R. ... Sanford, NC
Stagner, Morris D. ... Clovis, NM
Stagner, Robert D. ... Orange, CA
Stagnitto, Salvatore L. ... San Jose, CA
Stagno, Anthony ... Schaumburg, IL
Stagnolia, Carla Hounshel
Indianapolis, IN
Stagnone, Lauren A. ... Boston, MA
Staha, Scott T. ... Corpus Christi, TX
Staha, Vada L. ... Corpus Christi, TX
Stahancyk, Gearing & Rackner, P.C.
Astoria, OR
Bend, OR
Portland, OR
Stahancyk, Jody L. ... Portland, OR
Stahel, Harry C. ... New Orleans, LA
Staheli, M. Reed ... Milwaukee, WI
Stahl, Alan G. ... Houston, TX
Stahl, Alberta P. ... Beverly Hills, CA
Stahl, Allison ... West Palm Beach, FL
Stahl, Allison C. ... New York, NY
Stahl, Bennett L. ... San Antonio, TX
Stahl & Brashler ... Chicago, IL
Stahl, Brent G. ... Austin, TX
Stahl, Carl ... White Plains, NY
Stahl, Charles E., III ... Detroit, MI
Stahl, Charles S., Jr. ... Wheaton, IL
Stahl, Cheryl Blume ... Tuscaloosa, AL
Stahl, Craig L. ... Houston, TX
Stahl, David M. ... Chicago, IL
Stahl & DeLaurentis ... Mount Laurel, NJ
Philadelphia, PA
Stahl, Dennis J. ... Irvine, CA
Stahl, Dirck H. ... Evansville, IN
Stahl, Douglas ... New York, NY
Stahl, E. Thos. W. ... Baltimore, MD
Stahl, Eliza D. ... New York, NY
Stahl, Eric ... Dallas, TX
Stahl, Eric A. ... Junction City, KS
Stahl, Eric M. ... Seattle, WA
Stahl, Frank B., Jr. ... Houston, TX
Stahl, G. E. ... Amarillo, TX
Stahl, Gerald ... New York, NY
Stahl, Gerald R., Law Offices of
Grand Rapids, MI
Stahl, Harry S. ... Irvine, CA
Stahl & Horblit, LLC ... Summit, NJ
New York, NY
Stahl, Hortense ... Beverly Hills, CA
Stahl, Howard H. ... Washington, DC
Stahl, Irving M. ... Southfield, MI
Stahl, J. David ... Seattle, WA
Stahl, James E. ... San Francisco, CA
Stahl, James E. ... North Brunswick, NJ
Stahl, James E. ... New York, NY
Stahl, Jane M. ... Chattanooga, TN
Stahl, Jeffrey J. ... Chicago, IL
Stahl, John C. ... San Antonio, TX
Stahl, John Matthew ... Arlington, VA
Stahl, John T. ... Fremont, OH
Stahl, John W. ... Tuscaloosa, AL
Stahl, Joseph B. ... New Orleans, LA
Stahl, K. Paul ... Helena, MT
Stahl, Kenneth L. ... East Rutherford, NJ
Stahl, Lawrence A. ... Washington, DC
Stahl, Leopold ... New Orleans, LA
Stahl, Linda R. ... Dallas, TX
Stahl, Louis A. ... Phoenix, AZ
Stahl, Madonna ... Troy, NY
Stahl, Maria D. ... Boston, MA
Stahl, Martens & Bernal, L.L.P.
Austin, TX
Stahl, Michael J. ... New York, NY
Stahl, Michael R. ... Anchorage, AK
Stahl, Noel F. ... Nashville, TN
Stahl, Norbert ... Palo Alto, CA
Stahl, Norman H. ... Concord, NH
Stahl, Pamela M. ... Charlottesville, VA
Stahl, Paul Steven ... Fairfax, VA
Stahl, Philip C. ... Chicago, IL
Stahl, Richard J., Law Offices of
Fairfax, VA
Stahl, Robert G. ... Birmingham, MI
Stahl, Robert G. ... Summit, NJ
Stahl, Robert Miles, IV ... Towson, MD
Stahl, Robt. J., Jr. ... San Diego, CA
Stahl, Roger Matthew ... Rochester, MN
Stahl, Ronald M. ... Aberdeen, MD
Stahl, Roy H. ... Bryn Mawr, PA
Stahl, Samuel T. ... Detroit, MI
Stahl, Saul J. ... New York, NY
Stahl, Scott B. ... Dallas, TX
Stahl, Sherri M. ... Chevy Chase, MD
Stahl, Sidney ... Dallas, TX
Stahl & Stahl, P.C. ... Tuscaloosa, AL
Stahl, Stanley P. ... Mount Laurel, NJ
Philadelphia, PA
Stahl, Susan L. ... Philadelphia, PA
Stahl, Thomas H., (P.C.)
Kansas City, MO
Stahl, Thomas L. ... Albuquerque, NM
Stahl, Thomas W. ... Tallahassee, FL
Stahl, Tycho H. E. ... Boston, MA
Stahl, William F. ... Junction City, KS
Stahl, William N. ... New York, NY
Stahl, William P. ... New York, NY
Stahl, William T. ... Iuka, MS
Stahl & Zelmanovitz ... New York, NY
Stahla, Edward A. ... Sitka, AK
Stahl-Don, Karen ... Riverdale, NY
Stahle, Diane M. ... Des Moines, IA
Stahle, Phillip J. ... Saginaw, MI
Stahle, Robert J. ... Sioux City, IA
Stahlecker, Gerald F., III ... Philadelphia, PA
Stahler, Alan ... Lawrence, NY
Stahler, Cathy A. ... Cupertino, CA
Stahler, Elliot J. ... Beverly Hills, CA
Stahler, Harold ... Boston, MA
Stahley, Edward L. ... Merritt Island, FL
Stahley, Edward L., P.A. ... Merritt Island, FL
Stahlfeld, Susan K. ... Seattle, WA
Stahlheber, Robt. H. ... Webster Groves, MO
Stahlhut, Eric H.J. ... Fort Wayne, IN
Stahlhuth, John H. ... St. Louis, MO
Stahlhuth, Richard J. ... St. Louis, MO
Stahlhuth, William R. ... Eureka, MO
St. Louis, MO
Washington, MO
Stahlin, Jeremy A. ... Boston, MA
Stahlman, Christine ... Hillsboro, MO
Stahlman, Jill Elaine ... Marietta, GA
Stahlman, Kimberly J. ... Washington, DC
Stahlschmidt, Robert H. ... Sarasota, FL
Stahly, J. Mark ... Helena, MT
Stahman, Myrna A. I. ... Boise, ID
Stahman, Robert W. ... Boise, ID
Stahmann, Benjamin C. ... Provo, UT
Stahmer, H. Charles ... Bozeman, MT
Stahnke, Jay M. ... Mesa, AZ
Stahnke, Jerry L. ... Mesa, AZ
Stahnke & Stahnke ... Mesa, AZ
Stahnke, Tad ... New York, NY
Stahr, Don B. ... Wichita, KS
Stahr, John R. ... Costa Mesa, CA
Stahr, John T. ... Department of Justice, Environment and Natural Resources Division, GV
Stahr, Scott M. ... Chicago, IL
Stahr, Thomas E. ... Chicago, IL
Stahr, Thomas J. ... Bath, NY
Stahzhuth & Rudder, L.C. ... Eureka, MO
St. Louis, MO
Washington, MO
Staib, A.M. Nancee ... Cleveland, OH
Staib, Catherine C. ... Frankfort, KY
Staib, Mark E. ... Cleveland, OH
Staiger, Carl F. ... Philadelphia, PA
Staiger, Charles W. ... St. Clair, MI
Staiger, Frank O. ... Port Huron, MI
Staiger, Maria A. ... Seattle, WA
Staiger, Warren A. ... San Francisco, CA
Staight, Lisa, Law Office of ... Irvine, CA
Staihar, Steven J. ... Kennewick, WA
Staikos, John P. ... Stamford, CT
Stailey, Robert V. ... Englewood, CO
Staiman, Ari ... New York, NY
Staiman, Richard P. ... Williamsport, PA
Stainback, Frank ... Owensboro, KY
Stainback, Paul J. ... Henderson, NC
Stainback & Satterwhite ... Henderson, NC
Stainbrook, Charmaine ... Santa Rosa, CA
Stainbrook, Craig M. ... Santa Rosa, CA
Staine, Mary E. ... Houston, TX
Staine, Ross ... Houston, TX
Staine, Ross, Jr. ... Houston, TX
Stainer, Kenneth L. ... Tulsa, OK
Stainer, Randolph P. ... Tulsa, OK
Staines, Anthony J. ... Covington, LA
Metairie, LA
Staines, Brian B. ... Wethersfield, CT
Staines & Eppling, A Professional Law Corporation ... Covington, LA
Metairie, LA
New Orleans, LA
Staines, Joseph J. ... Los Angeles, CA
Stains, Scott ... Dallas, TX
Stainthorp, John L. ... Chicago, IL
Stainton, Jeffrey L. ... Cincinnati, OH
Stainton, William W. ... Lancaster, PA
Stair, Carol J. ... San Francisco, CA
Stair, Jeffrey C. ... Tucker, GA
Stair, John R. ... Knoxville, TN
Stair, Kent T., (P.C.) ... Atlanta, GA
Stair, L. Caesar, III ... Knoxville, TN
Stair, Richard ... Lenoir City, TN
Stair, Richard, Jr. ... Knoxville, TN
Stairs Dillenbeck Finley & Merle
New York, NY
Stairs, Elizabeth A. ... New York, NY
Stairs, Stanley T., (P.C.) ... New York, NY
Staisey, Leonard C. ... Pittsburgh, PA
Staiti, Peter F. ... Fairhaven, MA
Staitman, Jack M. ... Encino, CA
Staitman Snyder Tannenbaum & Dorenfeld, LLP ... Encino, CA
Los Angeles, CA
Stajduhar, Michael W. ... Charleston, WV
Stake, Charles D.
Department of Defense, GV
Stake, Daniel P. ... Oklahoma City, OK
Stake, Michael F. ... Woodward, OK
Stake, Robert B., III ... Arroyo Grande, CA
Stake, Sylvia L. G. ... Hagåtña, GU
Stakelum, Piercy J., IV ... Naples, FL
Stakelum, P.J., III, (Professional Corporation) ... Metairie, LA

Stakely, Charles A. .... **Montgomery, AL**
Stakely, Frank J. .... **Montgomery, AL**
Stakem, Paul J. .... Cumberland, MD
Stakem, Richard J., Jr. .... Ponce Inlet, FL
Stakem, Ronald E. .... **Oklahoma City, OK**
Stakeman, Kurt C. .... **Winston-Salem, NC**
Stakenborg, Elizabeth .... Gainesville, FL
Ocala, FL
Staker & Associates, Tax & Estate Plann. Attys., P.C. .... Camarillo, CA
Staker, Frederick G., III .... Huntington, WV
Staker, John R. .... Yorktown Heights, NY
Staker, Kevin G. .... Camarillo, CA
Staker, Lance R. .... **Chicago, IL**
Staker, Robert J. .... Huntington, WV
Staker, Steven L. .... Santa Ana, CA
Stalbaum, Michael B. .... Norristown, PA
Stalbrink, Richard R., Jr. .... Michigan City, IN
Stalcup & Atkerson, LLP .... **Dallas, TX**
Stalcup, Brett B. .... **Dallas, TX**
Stalcup, Joe A. .... Dallas, TX
Stalcup, Randy S. .... Wichita, KS
Stalcup, Wayne L. .... Brownsburg, IN
Stalder, Diane Desfor .... **Newport Beach, CA**
Stalder, Jeffery B. .... **Denver, CO**
Stalder, Joseph E. .... Redondo Beach, CA
Staley, Alicia .... Sumter, SC
Staley, Allan R. .... **Newport News, VA**
Staley, Ann K. .... Valparaiso, IN
Staley, Brian Edward .... **Houston, TX**
Staley, Charles R. .... **Chicago, IL**
Staley, Darsee R. .... Portland, OR
Staley, Debra Sue .... New York, NY
Staley, Edmund J. .... Hartford, CT
Staley, Harry A. .... Bakersfield, CA
Staley, Harry L. .... Purchase, NY
Staley, Howard .... Fairbanks, AK
Staley, Jack E. .... Dayton, OH
Staley, James A. .... Milford, OH
Staley, James R. .... **Houston, TX**
Staley, Jane E. .... Dayton, OH
Staley, Jeffrey J. .... Cincinnati, OH
Staley, Jobson & Wetherell, A Professional Corporation .... **Pleasanton, CA**
Staley, Joe H., Jr. .... Dallas, TX
Staley, John F. .... **Pleasanton, CA**
Staley, John L. .... San Diego, CA
Staley, Kay S. .... Houston, TX
Staley, Lynn .... St. Louis, MO
Staley, Mary E. .... Marietta, GA
Staley, Mary Tuck .... **Washington, DC**
Staley, Matt C. .... Lima, OH
Staley, Michael B. .... Ocala, FL
Staley, Nicole .... **Harrisburg, PA**
Staley, Patricia L. .... **Jackson, MI**
Staley, Paul D. .... **San Diego, CA**
Staley, Regis E., Jr. .... Garden City, NY
Staley, Robert B. .... Monroe, LA
Staley, Robert H. .... **San Francisco, CA**
Staley, Robert W., Jr. .... Salem, OR
Staley, Roger H. .... Fort Lauderdale, FL
Staley, Thomas B. .... **Little Rock, AR**
Staley, Thomas J. .... New Haven, CT
Staley, Thomas L. .... **Dallas, TX**
Staley, Timothy W. .... **Washington, DC**
Staley, William C. .... **Woodland Hills, CA**
Staley, William J. .... **Pittsburgh, PA**
Staley-Burley, Gina C. .... Lima, OH
Stalf, Dale A. .... **Cincinnati, OH**
Stalford, Mark P. .... Freehold, NJ
Stalford, Terry J. .... **Dallas, TX**
Stalfort, John A. .... **Baltimore, MD**
Stalions, Stuart M. .... Evansville, IN
Stalions, William C. .... Fort Lauderdale, FL
Stalk, Robyn F. .... **Los Angeles, CA**
Oxnard, CA
Stalker, Clark M. .... Chicago, IL
Stalker, David K. .... Godfrey, IL
Stalker, Peter, II .... Detroit, MI
Stalker, Robert A., Jr. .... Seattle, WA
Stalker, Robert D. .... Flint, MI
Stalker, Scott M. .... **Batesville, AR**
Stalker, Timothy W. .... Amherst, NH
Stall, Astor & Goldstein .... **Los Angeles, CA**
Stall, David A. .... Costa Mesa, CA
Stall, David T. .... Virginia, MN
Stall, Eric W. .... **Claremore, OK**
Tulsa, OK
Stall, Herman .... Schenectady, NY
Stall, Mark G. .... Covington, KY
Stall, R. Niven .... Indianapolis, IN
Stall, Richard J., Jr. .... **Los Angeles, CA**
Stall, Robert J., Jr. .... San Diego, CA
Stall, Todd S. .... LaGrangeville, NY
Poughkeepsie, NY
Stalland, K. Peter .... Stillwater, MN
Stalland, Luther M. .... Bloomington, MN
Stallard, Carl E. .... Orlando, FL
Stallard, David R. .... Park City, UT
Stallard, David S. .... **Cincinnati, OH**
Stallard, Diana Renee .... Tulsa, OK
Stallard, Jean Markham .... New Orleans, LA
Stallard, Kenneth G. .... **Washington, DC**
Arlington, VA
Stallard, Kent V. .... **Kansas City, MO**
Stallard, Russell R. .... Virginia Beach, VA
Stallard, Terri R. .... **Lexington, KY**
Stallard, Thomas W. .... Woodland, CA
Stallard, W. Patrick .... **Louisville, KY**
Stallard, Wayne M. .... Onaga, KS
Stallard, William B. .... **Abingdon, VA**
Stallbaumer, Sharon A. .... **Leawood, KS**
Stallcup, Stephen W. .... **Birmingham, AL**
Stallcup, Timothy P. .... Phoenix, AZ
Staller, Alan C. .... **Atlantic City, NJ**
Staller, Cary F. .... Hauppauge, NY
Staller, Jonah M. .... Denver, CO
Stalling, Joe E. .... Dallas, TX
Stallings, Brenda N. .... Little Rock, AR
Stallings, C. G. .... Fort Wayne, IN
Stallings, Clyde .... Durant, OK
Stallings, Clyde, Inc. .... Durant, OK
Stallings, David D. .... Downey, CA
Stallings, Dinah Marriage .... Austin, TX
Fort Worth, TX
Houston, TX
Stallings, Don L. .... Austin, TX
Fort Worth, TX
Houston, TX
Stallings, Freeman .... Dallas, TX
Stallings, G. Thorne, Jr. .... Blanchard, OK
Stallings, Hamilton & Fox, P.C.
Lebanon, TN
Stallings, J. Gilbert .... **New York, NY**
Stallings, J. Vance .... **Newport News, VA**
Stallings, James R., Jr. .... Lebanon, TN
Stallings, Jeanette Ann .... **Carrollton, TX**
Stallings, Jerry L. .... Calhoun City, MS
Stallings, John C. .... **Prescott, AZ**
Stallings, John R. .... **Wichita, KS**
Stallings, Joseph H. .... **New Bern, NC**
Raleigh, NC
Stallings, Kimberly M. .... **Washington, DC**
Stallings, Kurt .... Fort Worth, TX
Stallings, Lisa R. .... Department of the Navy, Office of the Judge Advocate General, GV
Stallings, Mark A. .... **Norfolk, VA**
Stallings, Martin F. .... Hartly, DE
Stallings, Moody E. .... Virginia Beach, VA
Stallings, Moody E., Jr. .... Virginia Beach, VA
Stallings, Noel Joan .... Pecos, NM
Stallings, Norman .... **Tampa, FL**
Stallings, Norman, Jr. .... Tampa, FL
Stallings, Paul E. .... **Houston, TX**
Stallings, Paul W. .... Oyster Bay Cove, NY
Stallings & Richardson, P.C.
Virginia Beach, VA
Stallings, Robert George .... Louisville, KY
Stallings, Robert S. .... Atlanta, GA
Stallings, Ronald D. .... **Atlanta, GA**
Stallings, Samuel James .... Louisville, KY
Stallings & Stallings .... Louisville, KY
Stallings, Stephen A. .... **Westport, CT**
New York, NY
Stallings, Stephen A.
Department of the Navy, Office of the Judge Advocate General, GV
Stallings, Stephen S. .... **Miami, FL**
Stallings, Stewart C. .... Memphis, TN
Stallings, Susan Camille
Oklahoma City, OK
Stallings, Thomas J. .... **Richmond, VA**
Stallings, William H. .... Department of Justice, Antitrust Division, GV
Stallings, William S. .... Washington, DC
Stallion, Mark E. .... **St. Louis, MO**
Stallknecht, Leslie Ruth .... Woodbridge, VA
Stallknecht, Ruth L. .... Sacramento, CA
Stallman, Edwin .... Elizabeth, NJ
Stallman, Karen L. .... Benton, IL
Stallman, Michael A. .... **San Francisco, CA**
Stallman, Michael D. .... New York, NY
Stallone, Albert A. .... Reading, PA
Stallone, Dianna R. .... Northampton, MA
Stallone, James A. .... Reading, PA
Stallone, James A., P.C. .... Reading, PA
Stallone, Joseph A. .... Melville, NY
Stallone, Joseph A. .... **Corpus Christi, TX**
Stallone, Patricia M. .... New York, NY
Stallones, Kyle D. .... **Houston, TX**
Stallones, Troy M. .... Tomball, TX
Stalls, Frederick D. .... Fort Pierce, FL
Stallsmith, William P., Jr.
Virginia Beach, VA
Stallsworth, Bruce A. .... Oklahoma City, OK
Stallter, David R. .... **Oak Brook, IL**
Stallwood, Robert K. .... Indianapolis, IN
Stallworth, Deirdre L. .... Philadelphia, PA
Stallworth, Stanley B. .... **Chicago, IL**
Stallworth, William L. .... Dayton, OH
Stalmack, John M. .... **Chicago, IL**
Stalmack, Joseph .... **Chicago, IL**
Hammond, IN
Stalmack, Joseph, & Associates, P.C.
Chicago, IL
Crown Point, IN
Hammond, IN
Valparaiso, IN
Stalnaker, Becker, Buresh, Gleason & Farnham, P.C. .... **Omaha, NE**
Stalnaker, Edw. B. .... **Augusta, GA**
Stalnaker, Faith K. .... Heathrow, FL
Stalnaker, Howard W. .... St. Albans, VT
Stalnaker, J. Anderson .... **Norfolk, VA**
Stalnaker, Lance K. .... Tampa, FL
Stalnaker, Phil A. .... Pikeville, KY
Stalnaker & Smith, P.A. .... Heathrow, FL
Stalnaker, Thomas D. .... **Omaha, NE**
Stalnaker, Timothy L. .... St. Louis, MO
Stalnaker, Wallace F., Jr. (P.A.)
Heathrow, FL
Stalnaker, William J. .... **Portland, OR**
Staloch, Heidi L. .... **Minneapolis, MN**
Stalonas, Michael D. .... New York, NY
Stalowicz, Roger J. .... Richmond, VA
Stalter, J. Brian .... **New York, NY**
Stalter & Kennedy, LLP .... **Boston, MA**
Stalter, Lisle A. .... Waukegan, IL
Stalter, Oliver W., (P.C.) .... **Boston, MA**
Stalter, William R. .... **Kansas City, MO**
Stalteri, Lisa Hayhurst .... **Burlingame, CA**
Stalzer, Barbara B., (P.C.) .... **Atlanta, GA**
Stalzer, Louis F. .... Phoenix, AZ
Stalzer, Patricia J. .... Phoenix, AZ
Stalzer, Thomas J. .... **Atlanta, GA**
Stam, Bradley D. .... Seattle, WA
Stam, Fordham & Danchi, P.A. .... **Apex, NC**
Stam, Heidi
Securities and Exchange Commission, Division of Investment Management, GV
Stam, Jacqueline I. .... **Richland, WA**
Stam, Paul .... **Apex, NC**
Stam, Paul N. .... **Irvine, CA**
Stam, Yvonne K. .... **Fort Wayne, IN**
Staman, Barbara W. .... **San Francisco, CA**
Staman, Sara M. .... Philadelphia, PA
Stamas, Arthur .... Chicago, IL
Stamas, George P. .... **Washington, DC**
Baltimore, MD
Stamas, Theodore A. .... Carle Place, NY
Stamas, Theodore S. .... New York, NY
Stamat, Paul N. .... Indian Head Park, IL
Stamatakos, Alyssa .... **Hammond, IN**
Stamatakos, Philip S. .... **Chicago, IL**
Stamatakos, Theodore C. .... **Chicago, IL**
Stamataky, Evans J. .... New York, NY
Stamatelos, Dan .... West Des Moines, IA
Stamatelos & Kenyon, P.C.
West Des Moines, IA
Stamatis, John N. .... Lorain, OH
Stamatis, Peter S. .... Chicago, IL
Stamatis, Peter S., Law Offices of, P.C.
Chicago, IL
Stamato, Anthony G. .... **Chicago, IL**
Stamato, Juliana .... **Los Angeles, CA**
Stamato, Philomena M. .... Binghamton, NY
Stambaugh, Curtis N. .... **Harrisburg, PA**
Stambaugh, Gerald M. .... **Mason City, IA**
Stambaugh, Gregory E. .... **Manassas, VA**
Stambaugh, Reginald G.
West Palm Beach, FL
Stambaugh, Reginald G., P.A.
West Palm Beach, FL
Stambaugh, Robert J. .... **Winter Haven, FL**
Stambaugh, Steven D. .... York, PA
Stambaugh, Susan M. .... New York, NY
Stambaugh, William C. .... Richmond, KY
Stambler, Arthur .... Wickford, RI
Stambler, Errol H. .... **Beverly Hills, CA**
Stambler, Errol H. .... **Los Angeles, CA**
Stambler, Olga .... **Chicago, IL**
Stambler-Wolfe, Terry .... **Los Angeles, CA**
Stambler-Wolfe, Terry
Redondo Beach, CA
Stambor, Howard .... **Seattle, WA**
Stamboulidis, George A. .... Garden City, NY
Stambul, Richard A. .... Los Angeles, CA
Stambulis, John C., (Ltd.) .... Hickory Hills, IL
Stamell, Erik .... **Detroit, MI**
Stamell, Jared .... **New York, NY**
Stamell & Schager, LLP .... **New York, NY**
Stamelman, Andrew J. .... **Morristown, NJ**
Stamelman, Laurence C. .... Freehold, NJ
Stamen, Randall S. .... Riverside, CA
Stamen, Robert A. .... **Miami, FL**
Stamer, Cynthia M. .... **Dallas, TX**
Stamer, Howard .... New York, NY
Stamer, Michael S. .... **New York, NY**
Stamets, Connie S. .... **Dallas, TX**
Stamets, Eric C. .... Department of the Army, Office of the Judge Advocate General, GV
Stamets Law Office .... Red Oak, IA
Stamets, Russell A. .... **Chicago, IL**
Stamets, Thomas E. .... Red Oak, IA
Stamey, David E, Jr .... **Winter Haven, FL**
Stamey, Ernest N. .... Lake Worth, FL
Spruce Pine, NC
Stamey, Frank R. .... **Abilene, TX**
Stamey, Joseph B. .... **Natchitoches, LA**
Stamey Law Firm, A Professional Law Corporation .... **Leesville, LA**
Natchitoches, LA
Stamey, Susanne E. .... **Los Angeles, CA**
Stamilio, Nancy N. .... Slidell, LA
Stamires, Natalie D. .... **Orange, CA**
Stamler, Jeffrey S. .... New York, NY
Stamler, Joseph H. .... Stony Creek, CT
Stamler, Patricia A. .... **Southfield, MI**
Stamler, Shelly B. .... Miami, FL
Stamm, Alan .... Los Angeles, CA
Stamm, Arthur .... Conroe, TX
Stamm, Blake D. .... Honolulu, HI
Stamm, Charles H., III .... **New York, NY**
Stamm, Charles H., IV .... **Baltimore, MD**
Stamm, Douglas A. .... Beaverton, OR
Stamm, Earl T. .... Harrisburg, PA
Stamm, Edward N. .... Miami, FL
Stamm, Fred .... Markesan, WI
Stamm, Garry R. .... **Indianapolis, IN**
Stamm, Gregory .... Buffalo, NY
Stamm, Henry N. .... Floral Park, NY
Stamm, Jan H. .... **Wauseon, OH**
Stamm, Janice Lorraine .... Tahoe City, CA
Stamm, Janis .... Mc Kean, PA
Stamm, Leonard R. .... **Greenbelt, MD**
Stamm, Mary Anne .... Springfield, MA
Stamm, Michael J .... Hollywood, MD
Stamm, Michael W. .... **New York, NY**
Stamm, Nancy J. .... **San Francisco, CA**
Stamm, Paul Christian, Jr.
Kilmarnock, VA
Stamm, Philip M. .... New York, NY
Stamm, R. David .... Hartford, CT
Stamm, Richard A. .... Middleboro, MA
Stamm, Richard I. .... **Chicago, IL**
Stamm, Ronald W. .... Los Angeles, CA
Stamm, Susan M. .... **Englewood, CO**
Stamm, Todd .... Olympia, WA
Stamm, Vikki S. .... Kearney, NE
Stamm, Warren Jay .... Coral Gables, FL
Stamm & Wilsnack .... Markesan, WI
Stamman, James E. .... East Lansing, MI
Stammberger, Gayle L.
Westlake Village, CA
Stammel, Matthew R. .... **Dallas, TX**
Stammel, Nicole Woods .... **Fort Worth, TX**
Stammel, Thomas S. .... **Philadelphia, PA**
Stammer, McKnight, Barnum & Bailey
Fresno, CA
Stammer, William .... Westport, CT
Stammich, Kurt C. .... Chicago, IL
Stamnes, Paul A. .... **Portland, OR**
Stamos, Christopher W. .... **Boston, MA**
Stamos, Constantine .... **Hackensack, NJ**
Stamos, Deborah Elsasser .... New York, NY
Stamos, Gregory .... Long Beach, CA
Los Angeles, CA
Stamos, James A. .... Chicago, IL
Stamos, James A., Ltd. .... Chicago, IL
Stamos, James J. .... **Chicago, IL**
Stamos, John J. .... **Chicago, IL**
Stamos, Nikos A. .... Glendale, CA
Stamos, Theophani K. .... Arlington, VA
Stamos & Trucco .... **Chicago, IL**
Stamos-Salotto, Theoni .... **Purchase, NY**
Stamoulas, Maria A. .... Washington, DC
Stamoulis, Paul A. .... Hazlet, NJ
Stamoulis, Stamatios .... **New York, NY**
Stamp, Andrew H. .... **Portland, OR**
Stamp, Charles, Jr. .... Roswell, GA
Stamp, David W. .... **Waterloo, IA**
Stamp, Duane M. .... **Dallas, TX**
Stamp, Frederick P., Jr. .... Wheeling, WV
Stamp, Kimberly R. .... **Houston, TX**
Stamp, Leon F., Jr. .... **Mobile, AL**
Stamp, Linda L.
Federal Deposit Insurance Corporation, Corporate Affairs Section, GV
Stamp, Lloyd V. .... Long Beach, CA
Stamp, Martin F., Jr. .... **Orlando, FL**
Stamp, Matthew E. .... Columbus, OH
Stamp, Michael W., Law Offices of
Monterey, CA
Stamp, Neal R. .... Ithaca, NY
Stamp, Vincent B. .... **Cincinnati, OH**
Stamp, Zack .... Springfield, IL
Stampelos, Charles A. .... **Tallahassee, FL**
Stampen, Kristine M. .... **Madison, WI**
Stamper, Adam T. .... **Medford, OR**
Stamper, Conni L. .... Spokane, WA
Stamper, Debra K. .... Louisville, KY
Stamper, Gary L. .... **Columbia, MO**
Stamper, Geoffrey .... Wichita, KS
Stamper, Gerald G. .... **Tulsa, OK**
Stamper, Hadley & Reasor .... **Antlers, OK**
Atoka, OK
Stamper, J. Harlan .... **Kansas City, MO**
Stamper, James N. .... Denver, CO
Stamper, James W. .... **Tulsa, OK**
Stamper, Janelle G. .... Albuquerque, NM
Stamper, Jeffrey D. .... Louisville, KY
Stamper, Joe .... **Antlers, OK**
Stamper, John W. .... **Los Angeles, CA**
Stamper, Kevin C. .... Seattle, WA
Stamper, Kevin T. .... Wichita, KS
Stamper, Linda A. .... Boston, MA
Stamper, Mark C. .... **New Castle, IN**
Stamper, Maxwell H., Jr. .... Dayton, OH
Stamper, Peggy Jo .... **Crown Point, IN**
Stamper, R. Marc .... **Fresno, CA**
Stamper, Randall L. .... Coeur d'Alene, ID
Seattle, WA
Spokane, WA
Stamper, Rubens, Stocker & Smith, P.S.
Coeur d'Alene, ID
Seattle, WA
Spokane, WA
Stamper, Thomas E. .... Clarksville, TN
Stampfel, J. Raymond
Middleburg Heights, OH
Stampfer, Noam .... Portland, OR
Stampfl, Robert J. .... Miami Lakes, FL
Stampley, David A. .... **New York, NY**
Stampley, Gilbert E. .... New Orleans, LA
Stampley, Herbert G. .... Jackson, MS
Stampolis & Kobrow .... Sugar Grove, IL
Stampolis, Marjorie Friedl .... Sugar Grove, IL
Stampone & D'Angelo, P.C. .... Jenkintown, PA
Stampone, Joseph P. .... Jenkintown, PA
Stampone, Vincenzo .... **Secaucus, NJ**
Stampp, Maureen M. .... **New York, NY**
Stamps, Amanda .... **Dallas, TX**
Stamps, Dana A. .... Vandalia, OH
Stamps, Randall H. .... Hendersonville, TN
Stamps, Regina T. .... **Atlanta, GA**
Stamps, Robert B. .... Birmingham, AL
Stamps, Robert F.
Department of the Air Force, Office of the General Counsel, GV
Stamps, Robert J. .... Metairie, LA
Stamps, Spurgeon Martin D., III
Tampa, FL
Stamps, Susan D. .... **Concord, MA**
Stamps, Thomas Paty, Law Office of
Atlanta, GA
Stamps, Tina Whitehead .... **Dothan, AL**
Stamps-Henderson, Sumari .... Denver, CO
Stampur, William J. .... New York, NY
Stamy, Karin L. .... **Norfolk, VA**
Stanage, Jody K. .... Ruston, LA
Stanaitis, Georgia A. .... **Philadelphia, PA**
Stanaland, Elizabeth M. .... **Greensboro, NC**
Stanaland, Terence B. .... **Greensboro, NC**
Stanard, Chandler Kite .... Mobile, AL
Stanard, James J. .... Cleveland, OH
Stanard, Margaret Kazdin .... Cleveland, OH
Stanard, Mark A. .... Denver, CO
Stanard & Mark, P.C. .... Mobile, AL
Stanard, Roger L. .... **Tarzana, CA**
Stanat, Erika N.D. .... **Rochester, NY**
Stanaway, Gina M. .... **Minneapolis, MN**
Stanback, A. Leon, Jr. .... Durham, NC

Stanback, Willard A. ....Philadelphia, PA
Stanberry, Thomas E. ....Minneapolis, MN
Stanberry, William B., Jr. ....Houston, TX
Stanbury Fishelman Wisner & Adsit
Los Angeles, CA
Stanbury, George R. ....Los Angeles, CA
Stanbury, Jerome ....Lanham, MD
Stancati, Joseph A. ....Toledo, OH
Stancati, Ross F. ....Kalamazoo, MI
Stancati & Zausner ....Kalamazoo, MI
Stancato, Vincent J. ....Staten Island, NY
Stanceu, James T. ....Akron, OH
Stanceu, Timothy Charles
Washington, DC
Stanchak, David G. ....McKinney, TX
Stanchak, Kathleen Ivan ....Clifton, NJ
Stanchfield, Michael A. ....Minneapolis, MN
Stanchina, Christopher J. ....Cherry Hill, NJ
Stancik, Donald B. ....Richland, WA
Stancik & Goodchild, A Professional Association ....Derry, NH
Stancik, Joseph V. ....Derry, NH
Stancil, Hale Ralph ....Bushnell, FL
Stancil, James E. ....Baltimore, MD
Stancil, James W. ....Mount Holly, NC
Stancil, Lisa Joi ....Baltimore, MD
Stancil, Paul J. ....Houston, TX
Stancil & Rhines ....Baltimore, MD
Stancil, Richard H. ....Hiawassee, GA
Stancil, Shannon d'Layne ....Tampa, FL
Stancill, Christine E. ....South Pasadena, CA
Stancill, Susan A. ....Chapel Hill, NC
Stancioff, Lissette S. ....Miami, FL
Stanclift, Tucker C. ....Glens Falls, NY
Stanco, Michael J. ....Northport, NY
Stanculescu, Dana ....San Francisco, CA
Stanczak, David L. ....Bloomington, IL
Stanczak, Frank ....Birmingham, MI
Stanczak, Frederick M. ....Syracuse, NY
Stanczak, Michael P. ....Waukegan, IL
Stanczak, Stephen P. ....Palm Desert, CA
Stanczak, William R. ....Waukegan, IL
Stanczyk, Benjamin C. ....Detroit, MI
Stanczyk, Boleslaus I. ....Ann Arbor, MI
Stanczyk, Matthew J. ....Detroit, MI
Stanczyk, Suzanne C. ....Detroit, MI
Stand, Darren B. ....Dallas, TX
Standa, Mark P. ....Chicago, IL
Standage, Douglas H. ....Mesa, AZ
Standage, Rodney H. ....Albany, NY
Standal, Thomas P. ....Kalamazoo, MI
Standard, James R. ....Monmouth, IL
Standard, James W., Jr. ....Atlanta, GA
Standard, Kenneth G. ....New York, NY
Standard, Matthew L.
Oklahoma City, OK
Standard, Michael B. ....New York, NY
Standard, Michael W. ....Vail, CO
Standard Weisberg, P.C. ....New York, NY
Standefer, Malinda Clawson
Lubbock, TX
Standefer, Mark C. ....Chicago, IL
Standefer, Paul ....Austin, TX
Standefer, Peggy J. ....San Diego, CA
Standefer, Richard B.
Department Of Veterans Affairs, Board of Veterans Appeals, GV
Standeffer, Brislane & Griffith
Anderson, SC
Seneca, SC
Standeffer, J. David ....Anderson, SC
Standel, David Greg ....Brooklyn, NY
Standel, Richard R., Jr. ....Richardson, TX
Standen, Daniel J. ....New York, NY
Standen, Jeffrey A. ....Salem, OR
Standen, Julian O. ....San Francisco, CA
Standen, Kara A. ....Miami, FL
Standen, Mark E. ....Portland, ME
Stander, Irvin ....Philadelphia, PA
Stander, James A. ....Littleton, CO
Stander, John J. ....San Francisco, CA
Stander, Roena Mae ....Homewood, IL
Stander, Stephen F. ....New York, NY
Stander, Thomas A. ....Rochester, NY
Standerfer, Gregory P. ....Dallas, TX
Standifer, Daniel S. ....Covina, CA
Standifer, John J., Jr. ....Tucson, AZ
Standifer, Rick ....Paris, TX
Standiferd, Cary L. ....Topeka, KS
Standiford, Steven A. ....New York, NY
Standing, J. Howard ....Tarzana, CA
Standing Bear, Geoffrey M.
Pawhuska, OK
Standish, Angela R. ....St. Louis, MO
Standish, Arthur M. ....Charleston, WV
Standish and Birmingham ....Los Angeles, CA
Standish, Daniel J. ....Washington, DC
Standish, Gail J. ....Los Angeles, CA
Standish, Linda S. ....Cleveland, OH
Standish, Michael Robert ....Decatur, GA
Standish, Myles E. ....Greensboro, NC
Standish, Patricia ....Pacific Grove, CA
Standish, Peter D. ....New York, NY
Standish, Samantha L. ....Santa Barbara, CA
Standish, Susan Manning ....New York, NY
Standish, Thomas ....Las Vegas, NV
Standish, William J. ....Los Angeles, CA
Standish, William L. ....Pittsburgh, PA
Standke, Greene & Greenstein, Ltd.
Minnetonka, MN
Standke, Robert A. ....Minnetonka, MN
Standlee, Christopher G. ....Wichita, KS
Standlee, Michael C. ....Palo Alto, CA
Standlee, Robert G. ....Houston, TX
Standlee, Russell P. ....Chicago, IL
Standler, Ronald B. ....Andover, MA
Concord, NH
Standley, Barry L. ....Evansville, IN
Standley & Gilcrest ....Columbus, OH
Dublin, OH
Zanesville, OH
Standley, J. Stewart ....Littleton, CO
Standley, Jeffrey S. ....Dublin, OH
Standley, John J. ....Coronado, CA
Standley, Joseph W. ....Ocala, FL
Standley, Joseph W., P.A. ....Ocala, FL
Standley, Larry W. ....Houston, TX
Standley, Mason S. ....San Antonio, TX
Standley, Thomas R. ....Findlay, OH
Standly, J. Kirk ....Dallas, TX
Standridge, David A. ....Albuquerque, NM
Standridge, Denise C. ....Sacramento, CA
Standridge, James O. ....Tuscaloosa, AL
Standridge, Richard E. ....Kansas City, MO
Stane, Beverly W. ....Pasadena, CA
Stanec, Kathryn M. ....Medina, OH
Stanecker, Charles A. ....Phoenix, AZ
Stanek, Bernard W., Jr. ....Pittsburgh, PA
Stanek & Boyle ....San Jose, CA
Stanek, Carl J. ....Cleveland, OH
Stanek, Debra J. ....Chicago, IL
Stanek, Eileen G. ....Atlanta, GA
Stanek, Frank J. ....Morgantown, WV
Stanek, Frederick D. ....Seymour, CT
Stanek, Herbert S. ....San Jose, CA
Stanek, Marthe C. ....San Francisco, CA
Stanek, Martin J. ....Pittsburgh, PA
Stanek, Matthew E. ....San Jose, CA
Stanek, Robert S. ....Southington, CT
Stanek & Smith ....Lyons, NE
Omaha, NE
Stanek, Veronica M. ....Troy, MI
Stanek, William C. ....Lyons, NE
Omaha, NE
Stanek, William J. ....Orange, CA
Stanewich, Robert B. ....Phoenix, AZ
Stanfa, Anne Casey ....St. Charles, IL
Stanfa, Michael A. ....Kankakee, IL
Stanfa, Thomas J. ....Geneva, IL
Stanfield, Cyril C., III ....Los Angeles, CA
Stanfield, Diane C. ....Los Angeles, CA
Stanfield, E. Neil ....Oklahoma City, OK
Stanfield, Gary D. ....Vienna, VA
Stanfield, Gregory M. ....Pleasant Hill, CA
Stanfield, Hall & Poole, P.L.L.C.
Jackson, MS
Stanfield, Henry L. ....Boca Raton, FL
Stanfield, James A. ....Atlanta, GA
Stanfield, James Caleb ....Paris, IL
Stanfield, James F. ....Tallahassee, FL
Stanfield, Janet L. ....Redlands, CA
Stanfield, Jeffrey L. ....Denver, CO
Washington, DC
Stanfield, John ....East Point, GA
Stanfield, John E. ....Laramie, WY
Stanfield, Jon M. ....Fort Sill, OK
Stanfield, Paul W. ....Austin, TX
Stanfield, Percy S. ....Jackson, MS
Stanfield, Phillip H. ....Phoenix, AZ
Stanfield, Richard L. ....Richardson, TX
Stanfield, Robert B. ....Sherman, TX
Stanfield, Sally F. ....Randallstown, MD
Stanfield, Sandra Valerie ....Canoga Park, CA
Stanfield, Tommy G. ....Lubbock, TX
Stanfield & Wightman, P.A. ....Phoenix, AZ
Stanfield, William A. ....Casa Grande, AZ
Stanfill, Alan ....Glendora, CA
Stanfill, Frankie K. ....Lexington, TN
Stanfill, Stan B. ....Anchorage, AK
Stanfill, Wm. Bruce ....Houston, TX
Stanford, Andrew A. ....Bowling Green, KY
Stanford, Barbara J. ....Cleveland, OH
Stanford & Bohannon, P.A. ....Marietta, GA
Stanford, Brad C. ....Portland, OR
Stanford, Bruce F. ....Anchorage, AK
Stanford, Bruce H. ....Boston, MA
Stanford, C. Glenn, (P.C.) ....Atlanta, GA
Stanford, Charles ....New York, NY
Stanford, C. L. ....Canton, TX
Stanford, Clifford S. ....Atlanta, GA
Stanford, D. Reardon ....Alexandria, LA
Stanford, Dan L. ....San Diego, CA
Stanford, Dawan P. ....Palo Alto, CA
Stanford, Donald G. ....Dallas, TX
Stanford, Donald M., Jr. ....Chapel Hill, NC
Stanford, Douglas G. ....Jacksonville, FL
Stanford, Dwight E. ....Rancho Santa Fe, CA
Stanford, E. Ray, Jr. ....Atlanta, GA
Stanford, Elliot E. ....Pacific Palisades, CA
Stanford, E. R., Jr. ....Silver Spring, MD
Stanford, Eric A. ....Pomona, CA
Stanford, Ernest H., Jr. ....Marietta, GA
Stanford, Fagan & Giolito ....Atlanta, GA
Stanford, Gary R. ....Austin, TX
Stanford, Glenn J. ....San Francisco, CA
Stanford, Jacqueline A. ....New York, NY
Stanford, James C. ....Chapel Hill, NC
Stanford, John H., Jr. ....Atlanta, GA
Stanford, John Paul ....Dallas, TX
Stanford, John W. ....Virginia Beach, VA
Stanford, Karen M. ....Miami, FL
Stanford, K. C. ....Tucson, AZ
Stanford, Kenyann Brown ....Raleigh, NC
Stanford Law Firm ....Houston, TX
Stanford Law Offices, S.C.
Milwaukee, WI
Stanford, Lee E. ....Kansas City, MO
Stanford, Lee R., Jr. ....Topeka, KS
Stanford, Leland A. ....Mays Landing, NJ
Stanford, M. Denise ....Raleigh, NC
Stanford, Marvin R. ....New Albany, MS
Oxford, MS
Stanford, Mary Bassett ....Concord, MA
Stanford, Morgan C. ....Atlanta, GA
Stanford, Natalie Diann ....Oklahoma City, OK
Stanford, Patricia Martin ....Jacksonville, FL
Stanford, Patricia Martin, P.A.
Jacksonville, FL
Stanford, Paul ....Los Angeles, CA
Stanford, Peter A. ....Milwaukee, WI
Stanford, Randolph L. ....Raleigh, NC
Stanford, Richard A. ....Houston, TX
Stanford, Richard L. ....Dallas, TX
Stanford, Richard W., Jr. ....Santa Ana, CA
Stanford, Robert J. ....Washington, DC
Stanford, Rochelle ....San Diego, CA
Stanford, Roger C. ....New Bedford, MA
Stanford & Schall ....New Bedford, MA
Stanford, Sherman ....Opelousas, LA
Stanford, Stanley L. ....Cincinnati, OH
Stanford, Stephen J. ....Toledo, OH
Stanford, Susanne J. ....San Diego, CA
Stanford, Teresa G. ....Lakewood, OH
Stanford, Terry S. ....Dallas, TX
Stanford, Theodore D. ....Annandale, VA
Stanford, Thomas James
West Palm Beach, FL
Stanford, Timothy U. ....Dallas, TX
Stanford, Tina G. ....Columbus, GA
Stanford, Vactor H. ....Dallas, TX
Stanford & Walls ....Dallas, TX
Stanford, Wendy E. ....Los Angeles, CA
Stanford, William L., Jr. ....Durham, NC
Stang, David P., P.C. ....Washington, DC
Stang, Donald J. ....Oakland, CA
Stang, Harry R. ....Santa Monica, CA
Stang, Heather L. ....New York, NY
Stang, James I. ....Los Angeles, CA
Stang, John E. ....Wichita, KS
Stang, John J. ....La Crosse, KS
Stang, Lynn Anton ....Denver, CO
Stang, Mark A. ....Chicago, IL
Stang, Michael H. ....Overland Park, KS
Stang, Richard E. ....Warwick, RI
Stang, Ronald B. ....Overland Park, KS
Stang, Thomas A. ....Seattle, WA
Stang, William L. ....Pittsburgh, PA
Stanga, Alonzo T., III ....Metairie, LA
Stanga & Mustian, P.L.C. ....Metairie, LA
Stanganelli, Joseph L. ....Boston, MA
Stange, Dean T. ....Madison, WI
Stange, Gerald D. ....Athens, WI
Stange, Richard T. ....Greensboro, NC
Stange, Robert W. ....Towson, MD
Stange, Wiseman & Hanson ....Towson, MD
Stangel, John W. ....Manitowoc, WI
Stangel, Maria E. ....Naperville, IL
Stangeland, L. Alan ....Tulsa, OK
Stangel-Plowe, Dana ....New York, NY
Stangenes, Ina ....San Jose, CA
Stanger, Abraham M. ....New York, NY
Stanger, Bernard E. ....New City, NY
Stanger, Bruce H. ....Hartford, CT
Stanger, Daniel J. ....Alexandria, VA
Stanger, Douglas S. ....Atlantic City, NJ
Cherry Hill, NJ
Northfield, NJ
Stanger, George H., Jr. ....Bridgeton, NJ
Stanger, Jeffrey D. ....Teaneck, NJ
New York, NY
Stanger, Kim C. ....Boise, ID
Stanger, Lawrence N. ....New York, NY
Stanger, Leo ....Red Bank, NJ
Stanger, Lisa ....New York, NY
Stanger, Marlene Z. ....Newport Beach, CA
Stanger, Neva L. ....Pittsburgh, PA
Stanger, Nicole D. ....Cleveland, OH
Stanger, Philip C. ....Worthington, OH
Stanger, Philip F. ....Sacramento, CA
Stanger, Ronald R. ....Orem, UT
Stangl, Terri L. ....Saginaw, MI
Stangland, Elaine
Export-Import Bank of The United States, Office of the General Counsel, GV
Stangle, Gregory L. ....Chicago, IL
Stangler, Edelman & Binder
Carle Place, NY
Stangler, Harold J. ....Carle Place, NY
Stanglin, Deborah A. ....Yorktown Heights, NY
Stanhagen, William H. ....Alexandria, VA
Stanham, Nicholas ....Miami, FL
Stanhaus, James S. ....Chicago, IL
Stanhope, William H. ....Atlanta, GA
Stanich, Albert M. ....Milwaukee, WI
Stanich, Janis K. ....Seattle, WA
Stanich, Robert A. ....St. Paul, MN
Stanich, Tanya M. ....New York, NY
Stanichak, Joseph M. ....Aliquippa, PA
Stanicki, Robert R ....Clark, NJ
Staniec, Denise Y. ....Chicago, IL
Staniec, Marjan P. ....Chicago, IL
Stanier, Julie V. ....Pittsburgh, PA
Stanifer, David H. ....Tazewell, TN
Stanifer & Stanifer ....Tazewell, TN
Stanifer, Wm. R. ....Tazewell, TN
Staniford, Geoffrey T. ....San Francisco, CA
Staniford-Chen, Lynnette D. ....Eureka, CA
Stanimirovic, Violet ....North Miami, FL
Stanis, John B. ....Chicago, IL
Stanisci, Thomas W. ....Mineola, NY
Stanish, John R. ....Hammond, IN
Stanish, Margaret M. ....Las Vegas, NV
Stanish, Tanya J. ....Chicago, IL
Stanisha, Therese J. ....Chicago, IL
Stanisil, Eileen M. Collet ....Cleveland, OH
Stanislaus, Tara Allen ....Sherman, TX
Stanislaw Ashbaugh, LLP ....Seattle, WA
Stanislaw, James ....San Francisco, CA
Stanislaw, R. Miles ....Seattle, WA
Stanislaw, William C. ....Pittsburgh, PA
Stanislawczyk, Marc A. ....Washington, DC
Stanislawski, Gary S. ....Milwaukee, WI
Stanislawski, Howard J. ....Washington, DC
Staniszewski, John M. ....St. Clair Shores, MI
Stanitz, Christopher ....Warren, OH
Stank, Kenneth E. ....Indianapolis, IN
Stankee, Glen A. ....Fort Lauderdale, FL
Stankevich, George C. ....Shelter Island, NY
Stankevich, George C., P.C.
Shelter Island, NY
Stankevich, Mark ....Los Angeles, CA
Stankewich, Paul J. ....New Haven, CT
Stankewicz, Steven M. ....Kalamazoo, MI
Stankiewicz, Anthony K. ....Boston, MA
Stankiewicz, Kevin G. ....East Lansing, MI
Stanko, Edward R. ....Algonac, MI
Stanko, Elaine Pennington ....Lancaster, PA
Reading, PA
Stanko, Gary G. ....Anniston, AL
Stanko, Glenn A. ....Champaign, IL
Stanko, Kevin M. ....Troy, MI
Stanko, Paul D. ....Crown Point, IN
Stanko, Richard A. ....Media, PA
Stankoski, Daniel Robert, Jr. ....Fairhope, AL
Stankoski, J. Clark ....Fairhope, AL
Stankovich, David P. ....Greenville, PA
Stankow, David G. ....Mesa, AZ
Stankowski, James A. ....Los Angeles, CA
Stankowski, Thaddeus ....Milwaukee, WI
Stanley, Alison M. ....Detroit, MI
Lansing, MI
Stanley, Amy L. Schaner ....Washington, DC
Baltimore, MD
Stanley, Andrea Eveler ....York, PA
Stanley, Anne E. ....Bronxville, NY
Stanley, Anthony J. ....Los Angeles, CA
Stanley, Anya ....Los Angeles, CA
Stanley, Ashley C. ....Atlanta, GA
Stanley, Avery L. ....Vanceburg, KY
Stanley, Barbara Ellis ....Houston, TX
Stanley, Barbara McC. ....Baltimore, MD
Stanley, Baroody, O'Toole ....Baltimore, MD
Stanley and Bertram, P.S.C.
Vanceburg, KY
Stanley & Bratcher ....McMinnville, TN
Stanley, Brian J. ....Oklahoma City, OK
Stanley, Brian K. ....Phoenix, AZ
Stanley, Bruce E. ....Pittsburgh, PA
Stanley, Bruce M., Sr. ....Fort Myers, FL
Stanley, Bryan J. ....Tampa, FL
Stanley, Burton J. ....Sacramento, CA
Stanley, Byron B. ....Corning, IA
Stanley, C. Franklin, Jr. ....Tabor City, NC
Stanley, C. Haydon ....Louisville, KY
Stanley, C. Paul, III ....Wytheville, VA
Stanley, Carol MacMillan
Delray Beach, FL
Stanley, C. B. ....Houston, TX
Stanley, Christopher ....Georgetown, TX
Stanley, Christophe L. ....New York, NY
Stanley, Chrystal D. ....Lexington, KY
Stanley, Craig M. ....Detroit, MI
Stanley, Daniel C., Jr. ....Castleton, VA
Stanley, Daniel J. ....Tustin, CA
Stanley, Daniel L. ....Detroit, MI
Lansing, MI
Stanley, Davey L. ....Ocean Isle Beach, NC
Stanley, David ....Kansas City, MO
Stanley, David E. ....Los Angeles, CA
Stanley, David E. ....Baton Rouge, LA
Stanley, David E., A PLC ....Baton Rouge, LA
Stanley, David H. ....Menlo Park, CA
Stanley, David L. ....Carmi, IL
Stanley, David M. ....Davenport, IA
Muscatine, IA
Stanley, David W. ....Washington, DC
Stanley, Deborah C. ....Richmond, VA
Stanley, Deborah F. ....Oswego, NY
Stanley, Debra Owen ....Concord, NH
Stanley, Deirdre ....Irving, TX
Stanley, Dewey Brian ....Bel Air, MD
Stanley, Diane D. ....Fairfax, VA
Stanley, Donald E. ....Cleveland, GA
Stanley, Donald L. ....Greensboro, NC
Stanley, Donald W., Jr. ....Tampa, FL
Stanley, Douglas J. ....St. Louis, MO
Stanley, Douglas L. ....Wichita, KS
Stanley, E. Blaine ....Philadelphia, PA
Stanley, E. Glynn, Jr. ....Fairfield, CA
Stanley, E. Paul ....Daytona Beach, FL
Stanley, Earl R ....Washington, DC
Stanley, Edith F. ....Louisville, KY
Stanley, Edmund C. ....Los Angeles, CA
Stanley, Edward D. ....Columbus, OH
Stanley, Edwin ....Solana Beach, CA
Stanley, Elizabeth M. ....Washington, DC
Stanley, Eugene S. ....San Antonio, TX
Stanley, Fenton ....Malvern, AR
Stanley & Flanagan, L.L.C.
New Orleans, LA
Stanley, Forrest F. ....Cleveland, OH
Stanley, Frank C., Jr. ....Chicago, IL
Stanley, Frank E. ....Grand Rapids, MI
Stanley, Frank J., III ....Bridgewater, NJ
Stanley, Frank, P.C. ....Grand Rapids, MI
Stanley, Frederic, Jr. ....Altamonte Springs, FL
Stanley, G. Steve ....DeLand, FL
Stanley, Gary L. ....Washington, DC
Stanley, Gay Parker ....Goldsboro, NC
Stanley, Gene A., Jr. ....Knoxville, TN
Stanley, George H. ....Syracuse, NE
Stanley, Gyneth S. ....Clearwater, FL
Stanley, H. Ronald ....Columbia, SC
Stanley, Harold M. ....Los Angeles, CA
Stanley, Harry M. ....Santa Maria, CA
Stanley, Heather J.C. ....Bakersfield, CA
Stanley, Hugh M., Jr. ....Cleveland, OH
Stanley, J. Alfred, Jr. ....Orlando, FL
Stanley, J. Keith ....Beaumont, TX
Stanley, J. Lee, III ....Stone Mountain, GA
Stanley, J. Snowden, Jr., ...Baltimore, MD
Stanley, Jack S. ....Pauma Valley, CA

Stanley, James A., Jr. ... Jacksonville, FL
Stanley, James Charles, II
Birmingham, AL
Stanley, James F. ... Overland Park, KS
Stanley, James F., III ... Golden, CO
Stanley, James G. ... Costa Mesa, CA
Stanley, James K. ... San Diego, CA
Stanley, James Miller, Jr. ... Greenville, NC
Stanley, James R. ... Chicago, IL
Stanley, James T. ... Anchorage, AK
Stanley, Janelle ... Scottsdale, AZ
Stanley, Jann ... San Francisco, CA
Stanley, Jean A. ... Johnson City, TN
Stanley, Joan C. ... Boston, MA
Stanley, John C., Jr. ... Great Falls, MT
Stanley, John D. ... Carmi, IL
Stanley, John D. ... Allentown, PA
Stanley, John F. ... Marco Island, FL
Naples, FL
Stanley, John Neil ... Tustin, CA
Stanley, John P. ... Washington, DC
Stanley, John V. ... San Marcos, CA
Stanley, Joseph A. ... Taylor, MI
Stanley, Joseph P. ... Syracuse, NY
Stanley, Joseph W. ... Washington, DC
Stanley, Julie Anne ... Richmond, VA
Stanley, Julie Muse ... Hingham, MA
Stanley, Justin A. ... Chicago, IL
Stanley, Karin L. ... Ocean Isle Beach, NC
Stanley, Karlyn D. (IBA) ... **Washington, DC**
Stanley, Kathryn V. ... Montgomery, AL
Stanley, Keith E. ... Treasury Department, Internal Revenue Service, GV
Stanley, Kelly N. ... Muncie, IN
Stanley, Kimberly S. ... La Jolla, CA
Stanley, K. L. ... Peru, IN
Stanley, Kris-Ann ... Lancaster, OH
Stanley, Kristal S. Otto ... Chicago, IL
Stanley, L. Jerome ... Baton Rouge, LA
Stanley, Lande & Hunter, A Professional Corporation ... Moline, IL
Rock Island, IL
Davenport, IA
Muscatine, IA
Wilton, IA
Stanley, Larry B. ... McMinnville, TN
Stanley, Larry B., Jr. ... McMinnville, TN
Stanley, Laurel S. ... Oakland, CA
Stanley Law Office ... Carmi, IL
Stanley, Lawrence E. ... Trenton, NJ
Stanley, Linda J. ... Austin, TX
Stanley, Lisa DeAnn ... New York, NY
Stanley, L. Jerome, P.C. ... Baton Rouge, LA
Stanley, Lowell A. ... Norfolk, VA
Stanley, Lu Ann ... Dayton, OH
Stanley, Mandel & Iola, P.C. ... Dallas, TX
Stanley, Marc R. ... Dallas, TX
Stanley, Mark ... Lancaster, PA
Stanley, Mark R. ... Carmi, IL
Stanley, Mark S. ... Tulsa, OK
Stanley, Mary ... Cleveland, OH
Stanley, Mary Booth Miller ... Indianapolis, IN
Stanley, Matthew W. ... Tacoma, WA
Stanley, Merton ... Kokomo, IN
Stanley, Meta K. ... Grants Pass, OR
Stanley, Michael A. ... Baltimore, MD
Stanley, Michael J. ... Oswego, NY
Stanley, Michael J. ... Houston, TX
Stanley, Michael P. ... Austin, TX
Stanley, Mitchell A. ... Cleveland, OH
Stanley, Nancy E. ... Washington, DC
Stanley, Neil A. ... Washington, DC
Stanley, Nita K. ... Ridgeway, VA
Stanley, Norma ... Orlando, FL
Winter Park, FL
Stanley, Patricia A. ... Coeur d'Alene, ID
Stanley, Patricia Sue ... Canton, NC
Stanley, Peter T. ... Billings, MT
Stanley, Philip E. ... Tampa, FL
Stanley, Powers & Matyola ... Bridgewater, NJ
Stanley, Raiford, Jr. ... Decatur, GA
Stanley & Rhodes, L.L.P. ... Greenville, NC
Stanley, Richard B. ... Encino, CA
Stanley, Richard B. ... Baltimore, MD
Stanley, Richard C. ... New Orleans, LA
Stanley, Richard E., Jr. ... Chicago, IL
Stanley, Richard L. ... Beaufort, NC
Emerald Isle, NC
Stanley, Richard L. ... Houston, TX
Stanley, Richard M. ... Naples, FL
Stanley, Richard R. ... North Quincy, MA
Stanley, Robert E. ... Atlanta, GA
Stanley, Robert Kirk ... Indianapolis, IN
Stanley, Robert L. ... Santa Fe, NM
Stanley, Robert W. ... Atlanta, GA
Stanley, Roberta G. ... Fort Lauderdale, FL
Stanley, Ronald D. ... Columbia, IL
Stanley, Ronald R. ... Medina, OH
Stanley, S. Alan ... Miami, FL
Stanley, Sabrina A. ... San Jose, CA
Stanley & Schadt, P.C., Law Offices of
Anchorage, AK
Stanley, Scott A. ... Drexel Hill, PA
Stanley, Sherry A. ... Miami, FL
Stanley, Stacy Charles ... Texarkana, TX
Stanley, Stacy L. ... Myrtle Beach, SC
Stanley & Stanley ... Ocean Isle Beach, NC
Stanley, Stanley & Fisher ... Cleveland, OH
Stanley, Stephanie ... San Luis Obispo, CA
Stanley, Stephen C. ... Mount Prospect, IL
Stanley, Steven M. ... Bakersfield, CA
Stanley, Susan C. ... San Diego, CA
New York, NY
Stanley, Susan D. ... Bridgeport, CT
Stanley, Tamar C. ... Washington, DC
Stanley, Teresa A. ... Folsom, CA
Stanley, Thomas A. ... Tarzana, CA
Stanley, Thomas C. ... Myrtle Beach, SC

Stanley, Thomas E. ... Everett, WA
Stanley, Thomas G. ... Grand Rapids, MI
Stanley, Thomas M. ... Houston, TX
Stanley, Timothy D. ... Albuquerque, NM
Stanley, V. Earl, Jr. ... Lawrenceville, VA
Stanley, Valerie J. ... Rockville, MD
Stanley, W. Lloyd, Jr. ... Chattanooga, TN
Stanley, William D. ... Bartlesville, OK
Stanley, William J. ... Jonesboro, AR
Stanley, William M., Jr. ... Fairfax, VA
Stanley, William P. ... Yreka, CA
Stanley, William P. ... South Bend, IN
Stanley Wines Law Firm, The, P.A.
Winter Haven, FL
Stanmar, Reginald S. ... La Salle, IL
Stanmeyer, William A. ... Great Falls, VA
Stann, Frederick R. ... Gastonia, NC
Stannard, Constance P. ... Coralville, IA
Stannard, Frederick F. ... Scottsdale, AZ
Stannard, Gregory F. ... Culver City, CA
Stannard, Paula M. ... Chicago, IL
Stanner, Daniel L. ... Chicago, IL
Stanner, James W. ... Oceanside, CA
Stanners, Edward J., Jr.
Farmington Hills, MI
Stanny, Brian T. ... Pittsburgh, PA
Stano, Michael ... Stillwater, OK
Stano, Paul J. ... Cleveland, OH
Stano, Phillip E. ... Washington, DC
Stano, Robert E. ... Vincennes, IN
Stano, Susan L. ... North Royalton, OH
Stanoch, John M. ... Minneapolis, MN
Stanonis, Frank Lee ... Tampa, FL
Stanos, Steve P. ... Youngstown, OH
Stanosheck, Melissa A. ... Omaha, NE
Stanosz, David J. ... Milwaukee, WI
Stanowski, John W. ... Saline, MI
Stansberry, Don C., III ... Huntsville, TN
Stansberry, Don C., Jr. ... Washington, DC
Stansberry, Lloyd D. ... Alvin, TX
Stansberry, Lloyd D., P.C. ... Alvin, TX
Stansberry, Tony W. ... Knoxville, TN
Stansberry, Schoenberger & Scheck
Upper Sandusky, OH
Stansbury, Carlton D. ... Milwaukee, WI
Stansbury, Claude B. ... Washington, DC
Stansbury, Daniel W. ... Dallas, TX
Stansbury, Edward P. ... Beckley, WV
Stansbury, Graham P. ... St. Petersburg, FL
Stansbury, Harry C. ... New Orleans, LA
Stansbury, J. Nathan ... Lafayette, LA
Stansbury, J. Robert ... London, KY
Stansbury, John P. ... Benton Harbor, MI
Stansbury, Karen A. ... Wilton, CT
Stansbury, Kim P. ... Morgan City, LA
Stansbury, Kim P., A Prof. Law Corp.
Morgan City, LA
Stansbury, Michael E. ... Seattle, WA
Stansbury, Olin M., Jr. ... El Dorado, KS
Stansbury, Philip R. ... Washington, DC
Stansbury, R. Douglas ... Cedarburg, WI
Stansbury, Richard T. ... Annapolis, MD
Baltimore, MD
Stansbury, Richard T., A Professional Association ... Annapolis, MD
Baltimore, MD
Stansbury, Roger A. ... Albuquerque, NM
Stansbury, Ronald C. ... Cleveland, OH
Stansbury, Thomas A. ... Chicago, IL
Stansbury, Thomas O. ... Richmond, TX
Stansbury, Todd M. ... Washington, DC
Stansbury, Travis A. ... Beverly Hills, CA
Stansbury, Zoellers & Hudson ... London, KY
Stansel, Lynn A. ... New York, NY
Stansel, Mary E. ... United States Senate, Senatorial Assistants, GV
Stansel, Teresa L. ... Cincinnati, OH
Stansel, Teresa L. ... Cincinnati, OH
Stansell, Jane E. ... Chico, CA
Stansell, Joe B. ... Seattle, WA
Stansell, Leland E., Jr. ... Miami, FL
Stansell, Leland E., Jr., P.A. ... Miami, FL
Stansell, Maxine R. ... Seattle, WA
Stansell, O. B. "Bud", Jr. ... Tampa, FL
Stansell, Quintin G. ... San Antonio, TX
Stansell, Robert F. ... San Diego, CA
Stansell, Robert F., A Professional Law Corporation ... San Diego, CA
Stansell, Theodore L. ... Monmouth, IL
Stansell, Whitman & Baber
Galesburg, IL
Monmouth, IL
Oquawka, IL
Stansell-Gamm, Martha J.
Department of Justice, Criminal Division, GV
Stansell-Gamm, Richard T.
Department of Labor, Office of Secretary, GV
Stansen, Brent F. ... St. Louis, MO
Stansen, Paul ... Calabasas, CA
Stansfield, Jared W. ... Boston, MA
Stansfield, Julie E. ... Chicago, IL
Stansfield Law Firm, P.S. ... Quincy, WA
Stansfield, Mark E. ... Quincy, WA
Stansfield, Robert H., Law Offices
Covington, GA
Stansfield, Robert J. ... Salt Lake City, UT
Stansfield, Thomas F. ... Westminster, MD
Stansfield, Wayne C. ... Philadelphia, PA
Stanshine, Gerald S. ... Philadelphia, PA
Stanshine, Martin ... Philadelphia, PA
Stanshine & Sigal, P.C. ... Philadelphia, PA
Stansky, Joan M. ... New Castle, DE
Stansky, Joseph ... Huntington, NY
Stansky, Mildred ... New York, NY
Stant, Frederick T., III
Virginia Beach, VA

Stant, Frederick T., Jr. ... Virginia Beach, VA
Stant, John Tyler ... Norfolk, VA
Stanton, Aaron H. ... Chicago, IL
Stanton, A. J., III ... Orlando, FL
Stanton, A. J., Jr. ... Orlando, FL
Stanton, Alexis J. ... Phoenix, AZ
Stanton, Allan J. ... Phoenix, AZ
Stanton, Andrew Y.
Department of Agriculture, Office of the General Counsel, GV
Stanton, Ann Marie ... Tempe, AZ
Stanton, Antcliff & Briggs, P.C.
El Paso, TX
Stanton & Associates, A Professional Corporation ... Washington, DC
Stanton, Boston H. ... Denver, CO
Stanton, Bruce E. ... San Jose, CA
Stanton, Bruce E. ... New York, NY
Stanton, Charles P. ... New York, NY
Stanton, Cheryl A. ... Minneapolis, MN
Stanton, Cheryl M. ... Washington, DC
Stanton, Christopher R.M. ... Seattle, WA
Stanton, Christopher T. ... St. Paul, MN
Stanton, Clark ... San Francisco, CA
Stanton, Clay, Tom, Chapman & Crumpton, Attorneys at Law, A Law Corporation
Honolulu, HI
Stanton, Colin ... Newark, NJ
Stanton, Courtney Wilder ... Jacksonville, FL
Stanton, Cynthia J. ... Summersville, WV
Stanton, Daniel T. ... Chicago, IL
Stanton, David A.
United States Postal Service, Law Department, GV
Stanton, David B. ... Bakersfield, CA
Stanton, David D. ... St. Louis, MO
Stanton, David M. ... Elko, NV
Stanton, David N. ... Pinckneyville, IL
Stanton, David R. ... Portland, OR
Stanton, David W. ... Cincinnati, OH
Stanton, David W. ... Columbia, SC
Stanton & Davis ... Marshfield, MA
Stanton, Diane E. ... Orlando, FL
Stanton, Diane R. ... San Francisco, CA
Stanton, Donald F. ... Paradise, CA
Stanton, Donald J. ... Newton, MA
Stanton, E. Scott ... Summersville, WV
Stanton, Edward ... Morristown, NJ
Stanton, Elizabeth M. ... Columbus, OH
Stanton, Emmett C. ... Palo Alto, CA
Stanton, Erin E. ... Radnor, PA
Stanton, Frances J. ... Oklahoma City, OK
Stanton, Fred R. ... Miami, FL
Stanton, G. Patrick, Jr. ... Fairmont, WV
Stanton, G. Russell, Jr. ... Memphis, TN
Stanton, Gary G. ... Chicago, IL
Stanton & Gasdick, P.A. ... Orlando, FL
Stanton, Gelene M. ... Chicago, IL
Stanton, George P., III ... Fairmont, WV
Stanton, Gideon T., III ... New Orleans, LA
Stanton, Glenn A. ... Visalia, CA
Stanton, Gregory E. ... Palo Alto, CA
Stanton, Gregory H.
Department of State, GV
Stanton, Gregory J. ... Phoenix, AZ
Stanton, Harold G. ... Hardin, MT
Stanton, Harold J. ... Encino, CA
Stanton, Henry J. ... Yorktown Heights, NY
Stanton, Hugh W., Jr. ... Cordova, TN
Stanton, Hughes, Diana, Salsberg, Cerra & Mariani, P.C. ... Morristown, NJ
Newark, NJ
Stanton, J. Alex, IV ... Hartsville, SC
Stanton, Jacqueline A. M. ... Forest Hills, NY
Stanton, James A. ... Honolulu, HI
Stanton, James D., The Law Offices of
Dallas, TX
Stanton, James L. ... Omaha, NE
Stanton, James Patrick, Jr. ... Palm Harbor, FL
Stanton, James V. ... Washington, DC
Stanton, Janice E. ... Kansas City, MO
Stanton, Jeanne F. ... Cincinnati, OH
Stanton, Jeffrey D. ... Logansport, IN
Stanton, Jennifer Tope ... Norfolk, VA
Stanton, Jill ... San Francisco, CA
Stanton, Jimmie R. ... Houston, TX
Stanton, John ... Oceanside, CA
Stanton, John E., Jr ... Buffalo, NY
Stanton, John F. ... Meriden, CT
Stanton, John F. ... Washington, DC
Stanton, John G. ... Mountain View, CA
Stanton, John J. ... Los Angeles, CA
Stanton, John Maloney ... Washington, DC
Stanton, John P. ... Newark, DE
Stanton, John R. ... Chicago, IL
Stanton, John R., Jr. ... Long Beach, CA
Stanton, John S. ... Washington, DC
Stanton & Jones ... Hartsville, SC
Stanton, Joseph ... Boston, MA
Stanton, Joseph B. ... Orlando, FL
Stanton, Joseph P. ... Jenkintown, PA
Stanton, Julia A. ... Long Beach, CA
Stanton, Julie ... Brooklyn, NY
Stanton, Karen M. ... Chicago, IL
Stanton, Kathryn L. ... Oaks, PA
Stanton, Kathryn M. ... Los Angeles, CA
Stanton, Kay & Watson, LLP
Sacramento, CA
San Francisco, CA
Stanton, Kevin J. ... Purchase, NY
Stanton, L. Vance ... Dallas, TX
Stanton & Lang ... Lynnfield, MA
Stanton, Laura K. ... Los Angeles, CA
Stanton, Laurence A. ... Loveland, CO
Stanton Law Corporation ... Encino, CA
Los Angeles, CA
Stanton Law Offices, P.A. ... Columbia, SC
Stanton, Lisa E. ... Newport Beach, CA

Stanton, Lois Ann ... Beaumont, TX
Stanton, Loren K., (Mr.) ... Ketchikan, AK
Stanton, Louis L. ... New York, NY
Stanton, M. Baron ... Columbia, SC
Stanton, Margaret M ... Brooklyn, NY
Stanton, Marian L. ... Encino, CA
Stanton, Marie A. ... Green Bay, WI
Stanton, Marie A., S.C., Law Offices of
Green Bay, WI
Stanton, Mariela R. ... Kew Gardens, NY
Stanton, Marion J. ... San Francisco, CA
Stanton, Mark A. ... Cleveland, OH
Stanton, Mark J. ... Trenton, NJ
Stanton, Mark Kevin ... New York, NY
Stanton, Mark L. ... Piscataway, NJ
Stanton, Marta I. ... Agoura Hills, CA
Stanton, Melanie ... Traverse City, MI
Stanton, Michael F. ... Chicago, IL
Stanton, Michael J. ... Somerville, NJ
Stanton, Michael K. ... New York, NY
Stanton, Michael K., Jr. ... Stamford, CT
Stanton, Michael P. ... Ocean City, NJ
Stanton, Michael R. ... San Diego, CA
Stanton, Mitchel T. ... Woodland Hills, CA
Stanton, Nancy C. ... Fall River, MA
Stanton, Patricia ... Chicago, IL
Stanton, Patricia M. ... Dallas, TX
Stanton, Patrick M. ... Morristown, NJ
Stanton, Patrick T. ... Chicago, IL
Stanton, Paul I. ... Los Angeles, CA
Stanton, Paul R. ... Miami, FL
Stanton, Peter D. ... Framingham, MA
Stanton, Peter James ... San Antonio, TX
Stanton, Philip H. ... Spokane, WA
Stanton, R. Thomas ... New York, NY
Cleveland, OH
Stanton, R. B. ... Pasadena, TX
Stanton • Redlingshafer, L.L.C.
Kansas City, MO
Stanton, Reginald ... Morristown, NJ
Stanton, Richard J. ... Boston, MA
Stanton, Richard K. ... Miami, FL
Stanton, Richard M. ... Chicago, IL
Stanton, Richard M. ... Lynnfield, MA
Stanton, Richard P. ... Washington, DC
Stanton, Richard W. ... Lakewood, CO
Stanton, Robert D. ... Big Rapids, MI
Stanton, Robert D., P.C. ... Big Rapids, MI
Stanton, Robert E. ... White Salmon, WA
Stanton, Robert J. ... Newark, NY
Stanton, Robert J. ... Tulsa, OK
Stanton, Robert L. ... Chicago, IL
Stanton, Robert M. ... Pittsburgh, PA
Stanton, Robert Q. ... Dallas, TX
Stanton, Robert R. ... Fayetteville, NC
Stanton, Robin Curtis ... Columbia, SC
Stanton, Robyn B.
South San Francisco, CA
Stanton, Roger C. ... West Palm Beach, FL
Stanton, Roger D. ... Prairie Village, KS
Kansas City, MO
Stanton, Roger L. ... Los Angeles, CA
Stanton, Ross H., Jr. ... St. Petersburg, FL
Stanton, Scott M. ... San Diego, CA
Stanton, Sherri C. ... Schaumburg, IL
Stanton, Shirley J. ... Fairmont, WV
Stanton and Stanton ... Fairmont, WV
Stanton, Stephen G. ... Napa, CA
Stanton, Stephen G. ... Drexel Hill, PA
Stanton, Steven T. ... Edwardsville, IL
Stanton & Stieh, P.A. ... Piscataway, NJ
Stanton, Stuart R. ... Buffalo Grove, IL
Stanton, Susan A. ... Houston, TX
Stanton, T. Harrison ... Jackson, MI
Stanton, Tara A. ... Washington, DC
Stanton, Teresa C. ... Miami, FL
Stanton, Thomas ... Dallas, TX
Stanton, Thomas E. ... San Francisco, CA
Stanton, Thomas E. ... El Paso, TX
Stanton, Thomas G. ... Seattle, WA
Stanton, Thomas J. ... Washington, DC
Stanton, Thomas L., Jr. ... Boston, MA
Stanton, Thomas L., Jr. ... Houston, TX
Stanton, Thomas M. ... Bakersfield, CA
Stanton, Thomas M. ... Neenah, WI
Stanton, Thomas R. ... Washington, DC
Stanton, Thomas W. ... Rapid City, SD
Stanton, Timothy J. ... Chicago, IL
Stanton, Timothy J., Jr. ... Milton, MA
Stanton, Timothy S. ... Ocala, FL
Stanton, Vernon, Jr. ... Philadelphia, PA
Stanton, Victoria M. ... Albany, NY
Stanton, W. Clark ... San Francisco, CA
Stanton, Walter J., III ... Miami, FL
Stanton, Warren M. ... San Pedro, CA
Stanton, Wayne S. ... New York, NY
Stanton, Wendell ... Billings, MT
Stanton, William B. ... Denver, CO
Stanton, William E. ... Marshfield, MA
Stanton, William E. ... Millbrook, NY
Stanfordville, NY
Stanton, William E. ... Poughkeepsie, NY
Stanton, William J. ... Warwick, RI
Stanton, Wynn G. ... Dallas, TX
Stanton Kelly, Lenore J. ... McLean, VA
Stanton-Rossi, Patricia ... New Port Richey, FL
Stanula, Edward F. ... South Holland, IL
Stanush, David P. ... San Antonio, TX
Stanway, J. Clark ... Fort Lauderdale, FL
Stanway, Roger G. ... Hollywood, FL
Stanway, S. Gregg ... Hotchkiss, CO
Stanwicks, David M. ... Worcester, MA
Stanwood, James Tanner ... Chico, CA
Stanwood & Price ... Palo Alto, CA
Stanwood, Thomas R. ... Palo Alto, CA
Stanwyck, Michele Ann
San Luis Obispo, CA
Stanwyck, Peter M. ... Oakland, CA

Stanwyck, Steven J. ....Los Angeles, CA
Stanyar, Carole M. ....Detroit, MI
Stanyer, Brent T. ....Spokane, WA
Stanzel, John C. ....Manchester, NH
Stanziale, Benjamin A. ....West Orange, NJ
Stanziale & Campanile ....West Orange, NJ
Stanziale, Carla Alix ....Montclair, NJ
Stanziale & Carpentier, LLP .....Mineola, NY
Stanziale, Charles A., Jr. ....Montclair, NJ
Trenton, NJ
Stanziale, David C. ....Newark, NJ
Stanziale, Gina M. ....Rahway, NJ
Stanziale, Henry ....Mineola, NY
Stanziani, Janis Marie ....Saugus, MA
Stanziani, Robert A. ....Lynnfield, MA
Stanziano, Mark J. ....Somerset, KY
Stanziola, Carmen R. ....Reading, PA
Stanziola, Claudio M. ....Scotch Plains, NJ
Stanziola, James A. ....Overland Park, KS
Stanzione, Alphonse A., Jr. ....Toms River, NJ
Stanzione, John J. ....Downingtown, PA
Reading, PA
West Chester, PA
Stanzione, Joseph ....Catskill, NY
Stanzione, Karen J. ....Philadelphia, PA
Stanzione, Ralph F. ....New Brunswick, NJ
Stanzione, Richard D. ....Toms River, NJ
Stanzione, Sharon L. ....Merrillville, IN
Stanzione, Stanzione & Martone, P.A.
Toms River, NJ
Stanzler, Alan L. ....Boston, MA
Stanzler Funderburk & Castellon LLP
Los Angeles, CA
San Francisco, CA
Stanzler, Jordan ....Los Angeles, CA
San Francisco, CA
Stanzler, Milton ....Providence, RI
Stanzler, Paul E. ....Boston, MA
Stapans, Edwin A. ....Providence, RI
Stapel, Julie K. ....Washington, DC
Stapel, Robert Owen ....Denver, CO
Stapell, Raymond J. ....Hamburg, NY
Stapen, Adam P. ....Denver, CO
Stapert, Bart ....New Orleans, LA
Staph, Jack A. ....Twinsburg, OH
Stapke & Harris, LLP ....Los Angeles, CA
Stapke, Mark R. ....Los Angeles, CA
Staple, Elliot P. ....New York, NY
Staple, Gregory C. ....Washington, DC
Staple, Irwin ....New Rochelle, NY
Staple, Nanci Klein ....Jersey City, NJ
Staple, Peter D. ....Palo Alto, CA
Staplefield, Veronica C. ....Greenwich, CT
Stapler, Alfred ....Philadelphia, PA
Stapler, Evan Lee ....Bremen, GA
Stapler, Richard N., Jr.
Salt Lake City, UT
Staples, Ariadne ....New York, NY
Staples, Barry ....Marietta, GA
Staples, Barry M. ....Carrollton, GA
Staples, Barry, P.C. ....Marietta, GA
Staples, Bernard C. ....Ellsworth, ME
Staples, Charles T. ....Columbus, GA
Staples, Craig A. ....Vancouver, WA
Staples, Craig L. ....Concord, NH
Staples, D. Christian, III ....Louisville, KY
Staples, Debra G. ....Philadelphia, PA
Staples, Donald P. ....Richmond, VA
Staples, Edwin H., II ....Annapolis, MD
Staples, F. Dudley, Jr. ....Ijamsville, MD
Staples, Fred R. ....Richland, WA
Staples, Gail T. ....Huntington, WV
Staples, George A., Jr. ....Fort Worth, TX
Staples, Gregory W. ....Los Angeles, CA
Staples, J. Edward ....Cornelia, GA
Staples, J. Peter ....Portland, OR
Staples, James G. ....Chicago, IL
Staples, Jeffrey M. ....Houston, TX
Staples, John N., III ....San Francisco, CA
Staples, Kevin G. ....Vancouver, WA
Staples, Lang & Associates ....Pensacola, FL
Staples, Leonard J. ....Ashburnham, MA
Staples, Lorraine Carol ....Morristown, NJ
Staples, Lyle N. ....Westminster, MD
Staples, Michele A. ....Irvine, CA
Staples, Randy ....Dallas, TX
Staples, Richard F. ....Providence, RI
Staples, Richard N. ....Kansas City, MO
Staples, Scott D. ....Glens Falls, NY
Staples, Shirley ....New York, NY
Staples, Thomas C. ....Pensacola, FL
Staples, Waller Redd, III ....Richmond, VA
Staples, William H. ....Walnut Creek, CA
Stapleton, Alfred B. ....Providence, RI
Stapleton, Anne B. ....Latham, NY
Stapleton, Benjamin F. ....New York, NY
Stapleton, Brian T. ....New York, NY
Stapleton, Carol M. ....Washington, DC
Stapleton, Carolyn L. ....Honolulu, HI
Stapleton, Caron L. ....San Francisco, CA
Stapleton, Charles M. ....Baltimore, MD
Stapleton, Clyde L. ....Lexington, KY
Stapleton & Colden ....Drexel Hill, PA
Stapleton, David R. ....Jamestown, NY
Stapleton, Denise Terry ....Morristown, TN
Stapleton, E. Dunn ....Albany, GA
Stapleton, E. Martin ....St. Paul, MN
Stapleton, Gerard V. ....Hempstead, NY
Stapleton, James A. ....Los Altos, CA
Stapleton, James A. ....Reading, PA
Stapleton, James F. ....Stamford, CT
Stapleton, James J.
Department Of Health And Human Services,
Social Security Administration, GV
Stapleton, James J. ....Newark, NJ
Stapleton, Jerry L. ....Harlingen, TX
Stapleton, John F. ....St. Louis, MO
Stapleton, John O. ....Fort Lauderdale, FL
Stapleton, John W., Jr. ....Kansas City, MO
Stapleton, John Warren ....Huntington, WV
Stapleton, Jonathan C. ....New York, NY
Stapleton, Joseph P. ....Sevierville, TN
Stapleton, Joseph T. ....Cherry Hill, NJ
Philadelphia, PA
Stapleton, Keith E. ....Cedar Rapids, IA
Stapleton, Kevin ....Covina, CA
Stapleton, Laura ....Dallas, TX
Stapleton, Laura Lee ....Austin, TX
Stapleton Law Offices, L.C.
Huntington, WV
Stapleton, Lillian F ....Holyoke, MA
Stapleton, Margaret ....Chicago, IL
Stapleton, Mark A. ....Hartford, CT
Stapleton, Mark S. ....Rogersville, TN
Stapleton, Marlin G. ....Tustin, CA
Stapleton, Marlin G., Jr. ....Tustin, CA
Stapleton, Michael J. ....Lafayette, IN
Stapleton, Michael P. ....Dedham, MA
Stapleton & Nisenson ....Newark, NJ
Stapleton, Nolan & Hynes ....St. Paul, MN
Stapleton, Patrick J., III ....Philadelphia, PA
Stapleton, Rachel A. ....Milwaukee, WI
Stapleton, Ranah L. ....Montgomery, AL
Stapleton, Richard B. ....Lansing, MI
Stapleton, Richard D. ....Meriden, CT
Stapleton, Robert J. ....Mineola, NY
Stapleton, Scott G. ....Huntington, WV
Stapleton & Stapleton ....Covina, CA
Stapleton & Stapleton, A Professional Association ....Tustin, CA
Stapleton, Stephanie D. ....Chicago, IL
Stapleton, Stephen C. ....Dallas, TX
Stapleton, Steven F. ....Grand Rapids, MI
Stapleton, Steven M. ....Chico, CA
Oroville, CA
Stapleton, Susan L. ....Palo Alto, CA
Stapleton, Susannah M. ....Wethersfield, CT
Stapleton, T. David ....Auburn, NY
Stapleton, Theodore N., II ....Atlanta, GA
Stapleton, Theodore N., P.C. ....Atlanta, GA
Stapleton, Thomas J., Jr. ....Drexel Hill, PA
Stapleton, Thomas L. ....New York, NY
Stapleton, Thomas M. ....Elmont, NY
Stapleton, Ulys J. ....Grants Pass, OR
Stapleton, Victoria Prusas ....Covina, CA
Stapleton, Walter K. ....Wilmington, DE
Stapleton, Warren J. ....Phoenix, AZ
Stapleton, Whittington, Curtis & Boswell
Brownsville, TX
Harlingen, TX
Stapleton, William B. ....Georgetown, OH
Stapleton, William F. ....Holyoke, MA
Stapleton, William H., Jr.
Department of Justice,
Criminal Division, GV
Stapleton, William J. ....Ann Arbor, MI
Stapleton, William J. ....Lansing, MI
Stapleton, William J., P.C. ....Lansing, MI
Stapleton, William M. ....Kansas City, MO
Stapleton, William. T. ....Chaska, MN
Stapleton, William W. ....Filer City, MI
Stapley, R. Lind ....Seattle, WA
Stapor, Marcella A. ....New York, NY
Stapp, Dan F. ....New Orleans, LA
Stapp, Fred T., Jr. ....Jacksonville, FL
Stapp, Gary L., Law Office of, The
Fairbanks, AK
Stapp, Gerald L. ....Denver, CO
Stapp, Gregory A. ....Pottsville, PA
Stapp, James A. ....New Orleans, LA
Stapp, John W., IV ....Nashville, TN
Stapp, K. Scott ....Demopolis, AL
Stapp & Martin, P.A. ....Jacksonville, FL
Stapp, Melanie K. ....New York, NY
Stapp, Randee Layne ....Denver, CO
Stapp, Steven J. ....Clinton, IL
Stapp, William E. ....Houston, TX
Stapper, Erik J. ....New York, NY
Stapper & Van Doren ....New York, NY
Star, Bailee Rebecca ....Jamaica Plain, MA
Star, Bernard ....Cliffside Park, NJ
Star, B. J. ....Indian Rocks Beach, FL
Star, Carlene ....Las Vegas, NV
Star, Gregg ....New York, NY
Star, James A. ....Chicago, IL
Star, Leon P. ....Chicago, IL
Star, Linda ....Los Angeles, CA
Star, Robert M. ....Chicago, IL
Star, Robert R. ....Encino, CA
Star, Ronald H. ....San Francisco, CA
Star, Sara Crown ....Chicago, IL
Star, Scott A. ....San Diego, CA
Star, Steven E. ....Mineola, NY
New York, NY
Stara, Nancy J. ....Lincoln, NE
Starace, Arlene T. ....Fairfax, VA
Starace, Vincent D. ....Mineola, NY
Staran, John D. ....Bloomfield Hills, MI
Starbird, Alisa T. ....Houston, TX
Starbird, Jeffrey W. ....Minneapolis, MN
Starbird, Russell B. ....Houston, TX
Starbird, Russell B., P.C. ....Houston, TX
Starbird, Zackary ....Boise, ID
Starble, Jonathan M. ....Hartford, CT
Starbranch, Harry N. ....Augusta, ME
Starbranch, Harry N., Jr.
Portsmouth, NH
Starbranch, Linda J. ....Dover, NH
Starbuck, C. Gerald ....Denver, CO
Starbuck, Charles E. ....Kalamazoo, MI
Starbuck, Dane C. ....Winchester, IN
Starbuck, David L. ....Denver, CO
Starbuck, Dustin Michael ....Richmond, VA
Starbuck, John ....Berkeley, CA
Starbuck, John D. ....Chattanooga, TN
Starcevic, Joseph F. ....Fairfield, IA
Starcevich, Lisa Marie ....Chicago, IL
Starcevich, M. Jean ....San Jose, CA
Starcher, Ann R. ....Charleston, WV
Starcher, Charles Cecil ....Corpus Christi, TX
Starcher, Douglas E., (P.A.) ....Orlando, FL
Starcher, Larry V. ....Charleston, WV
Starcher, Mollianne ....Morgantown, WV
Starchman, Donald J. ....Mariposa, CA
Starck, Andrew P. ....Arlington Heights, IL
Starck, Christopher C. ....Waukegan, IL
Starck, Douglas H. ....Milwaukee, WI
Starck, Thomas W. ....Chicago, IL
Starck, Walter J. ....Chicago, IL
Starcke, John L. ....Seguin, TX
Starczewski, Lisa M. ....Philadelphia, PA
Starczewski, Marja ....Seattle, WA
Starczewski, Michael T. ....Philadelphia, PA
Starek, Roscoe B., III ....Washington, DC
Starer, Ann R. ....Scarsdale, NY
Starer, Brian D. ....New York, NY
Stares, Diana ....Pittsburgh, PA
Starfield, David W. ....Fort Washington, PA
Starfield, Lawrence E. ....Dallas, TX
Starfield & Payne, P.C.
Fort Washington, PA
Philadelphia, PA
Stargardter, GailAnn Y. ....Seattle, WA
Stargatt, Bruce M. ....Wilmington, DE
Stargel, John K. ....Mulberry, FL
Stargel, Joseph H., Jr. ....Gainesville, GA
Stargel, Rogena ....Cincinnati, OH
Stargell, Leslie Spiegel ....Rustburg, VA
Stargiotti, Joseph A. ....White Plains, NY
Starich, Frederic R. ....Reno, NV
Staricha, Lance ....St. Paul, MN
Stariha, James R. ....Muskegon, MI
Starin, Mary Kay Wheeler, (P.C.) ....Butte, MT
Starin, Robert D. ....Seattle, WA
Staring, Christopher P. ....Phoenix, AZ
Tucson, AZ
Staring, Diana H. ....Berkeley, CA
Staring, Graydon S. ....San Francisco, CA
Staring, Merlin H. ....Bowie, MD
Staring, Merlin H., and Ralphine R. Staring
Bowie, MD
Staring, Ralphine R. ....Bowie, MD
Starinieri, Nicholas J. ....Philadelphia, PA
Staris, Ina ....Boston, MA
Starishevsky, Edward ....Bronx, NY
Stark, Aida O.
Department Of Health And Human Services,
Office of the General Counsel, GV
Stark, Alan M. ....West Orange, NJ
Stark, Albert M. ....Princeton, NJ
Stark, Alice W. ....Dover, DE
Stark, Allana F. ....New York, NY
Stark, Amel ....Princeton, NJ
Stark, Amron, Liner & Narotsky, LLP
New York, NY
Stark, Andrew W. ....Columbus, OH
Stark, Andria ....Oklahoma City, OK
Stark, Andria, P.C. ....Oklahoma City, OK
Stark, Arthur B. ....Miami, FL
Stark, Barbara ....Newark, NJ
Stark, Barbara Kahn ....New Haven, CT
Stark, Blooma ....Chicago, IL
Stark, Brian A ....Bronx, NY
Stark, Brian J. ....Milwaukee, WI
Stark, Carol A. ....Schaumburg, IL
Stark, Charles A.
Department Of Health And Human Services,
Social Security Administration, GV
Stark, Charles B., Jr. (P.C.)
San Francisco, CA
Stark, Charles D. ....Santa Rosa, CA
Stark, Charles G. ....Houston, TX
Stark, Charles H. ....Altamonte Springs, FL
Stark, Charles H. ....Manistique, MI
Stark, Charles S. ....Department of Justice,
Antitrust Division, GV
Stark, Christopher J. ....Springfield, MO
Stark, Cliff A. ....Tulsa, OK
Stark & Crooks ....Mayfield, KY
Stark, Crumley & Jacobs ....Fort Dodge, IA
Stark, Daniel ....Basking Ridge, NJ
Stark, Daniel C. ....Department of Justice,
Criminal Division, GV
Stark, David Evan ....Garden City, NY
Stark, David M. ....Buffalo, NY
Stark, David M. ....New York, NY
Stark, David W. ....Denver, CO
Stark, Dean A. ....St. Louis, MO
Stark, Deborah L. C. ....Los Angeles, CA
Stark, Deborah Rose ....Princeton, NJ
Stark, Debra Pogrund ....Chicago, IL
Stark, Dennis H. ....Terre Haute, IN
Stark, Dennis M. ....Columbus, IN
Stark, Derek W. ....Calabasas, CA
Stark, Dewey W., Jr. ....Dallas, TX
Stark, Don F. ....Memphis, TN
Stark, Donald D. ....Houston, TX
Stark, Donald R. ....Portland, OR
Stark Doninger & Smith ....Indianapolis, IN
Stark, Douglas T. ....Harrisonburg, VA
Stark, Edward C. ....Santa Monica, CA
Stark, Elwood V., Jr. ....Bel Air, MD
Havre de Grace, MD
Stark, Eric R. ....Medford, OR
Stark, F. John, III ....Minneapolis, MN
Stark, Gary ....Cairo, IL
Stark, Gary R. ....Portland, OR
Stark, George M., P.A. ....Tampa, FL
Stark, George Miles ....Tampa, FL
Stark, Gerald V. ....Scottsdale, AZ
Stark and Gordon ....Royal Oak, MI
Stark, Gregg J. ....Indianapolis, IN
Stark, Gregory S. ....Maitland, FL
Stark, H. Allan ....Crystal Lake, IL
St. Charles, IL
Stark and Hammack, P.C. ....Medford, OR
Stark, Harry S. ....Traverse City, MI
Stark, Harvey G. ....Van Nuys, CA
Stark, Henry L. ....Houston, TX
Stark, Homer M. ....Lawrenceville, GA
Stark, Howard A. ....Rochester, NY
Stark, Isabel Brawer ....Hackensack, NJ
Stark, J. Norman ....Cleveland, OH
Stark, J. Robert ....Scottsdale, AZ
Stark, Jack T. ....Fort Worth, TX
Stark, James E., Jr. ....Grand Rapids, MI
Stark, James H. ....New York, NY
Stark, James M. ....Fort Lauderdale, FL
Stark, Jarmila ....Chicago, IL
Stark, Jay ....Hackensack, NJ
New York, NY
Stark, Jeffrey ....New York, NY
Stark, Jeffrey G. ....Mineola, NY
Stark, Jeffrey M. ....Plano, TX
Stark, Jeffrey P. ....Anchorage, AK
Stark, Jeffrey P. ....Oakland, CA
Stark, Jeffrey R. ....Torrance, CA
Stark, Jerome D. ....Orange, CA
Stark, Jerome D., P.C. ....Orange, CA
Stark, Joanne Trifilo ....Phoenix, AZ
Las Vegas, NV
Stark, John B. ....Hermitage, TN
Stark, John C. ....Indianapolis, IN
Stark, John N. ....Austin, TX
Stark, John R.
Securities and Exchange Commission,
Division of Enforcement, GV
Stark, John T. ....Omaha, NE
Stark, Jon R. ....Palo Alto, CA
Stark, Jonathan E. ....Princeton, NJ
Stark, Jonathan L. ....Cleveland, OH
Stark, Joseph L. ....Los Angeles, CA
Stark, Julie ....New York, NY
Stark, Justin W. ....Billings, MT
Stark, Kathy A. ....Miami, FL
Stark and Keenan ....Havre de Grace, MD
Stark & Keenan, A Professional Association
Bel Air, MD
Stark, Kelly S. ....Memphis, TN
Stark, Kenneth B. ....Cleveland, OH
Stark & Knoll Co., L.P.A. ....Akron, OH
Stark, LaVar E. ....Ogden, UT
Stark, Lawrence J. ....Chicago, IL
Stark, Lee E. ....Los Angeles, CA
Stark, Leland Alan ....Santa Monica, CA
Stark, Leland Alan, A Law Corporation
Santa Monica, CA
Stark, Leo P. ....Columbus, OH
Stark, Leonard L. ....New York, NY
Stark, Leonard P. ....Wilmington, DE
Stark, Linda A. ....New York, NY
Stark, Lisa J. ....Department of Justice,
Civil Rights Division, GV
Stark, Lisa K. ....Eau Claire, WI
Stark & Little ....Baltimore, MD
Stark, Lorraine A. ....Thornton, CO
Stark, Margo D. ....Boston, MA
Stark, Martha E. ....Brooklyn, NY
Stark, Maurie E. ....Fort Dodge, IA
Stark, Mei-lan E. W. ....Burbank, CA
Stark, Michael ....New Brunswick, NJ
Stark, Michael J. ....Juneau, AK
Stark, Michael L. ....Akron, OH
Stark, Michael P. ....Phoenix, AZ
Stark, Michele P. ....Denver, CO
Stark, Nadine R. ....Sayreville, NJ
Stark, Nathan J. ....Washington, DC
Stark, Norman A. ....Erie, PA
Stark, Norman H. ....Erie, PA
Stark, Patrick J. ....Long Beach, CA
Stark, Patrick V. ....Dallas, TX
Stark, Paul ....Indianapolis, IN
Stark, Paul G. ....Westminster, CA
Stark, Penny R. ....Carle Place, NY
Stark, Peter R. ....Milford, CT
Stark, R. Keith ....Boca Raton, FL
Troy, MI
Stark, R. Stephen ....Prairieville, LA
Stark, Rachel L. ....Princeton, NJ
Stark, Randall R. ....Chicago, IL
Stark, Rasak & Clarke ....Los Angeles, CA
Torrance, CA
Stark, Reagan & Finnerty, P.C.
Boca Raton, FL
Detroit, MI
Traverse City, MI
Troy, MI
Stark, Richard A. ....Medford, OR
Stark, Richard C. ....Washington, DC
Stark, Richard E. ....Atlanta, GA
Stark, Richard J. ....New York, NY
Stark, Richard L. ....Buffalo, NY
Stark, Richard S. ....Gainesville, TX
Stark, Robert J. ....New York, NY
Stark, Robert N. ....Sacramento, CA
Stark, Robert R., Jr. ....Denver, CO
Stark, Rodney L. ....Phoenix, AZ
Stark, Rodney L. ....Manchester, NH
Stark, Rodney L., P.A., Law Office of
Manchester, NH
Stark, Roger D. ....Washington, DC
Stark, Ronald J. ....Houston, TX
Stark, Sally H. ....Portland, OR
Stark, Sanford W. ....Washington, DC
Stark, Sharon M. ....Washington, DC
Stark, Sheila ....Washington, DC
Stark, Sheila Christine ....Washington, DC
Stark, Sheldon J. ....Royal Oak, MI

Stark & Stark, A Professional Corporation Lawrenceville, NJ
Princeton, NJ
Trenton, NJ
Stark, Stephen H. ... New York, NY
Stark, Stephen J. ... Jefferson City, MO
Stark, Stephen J. ... Chattanooga, TN
Stark, Stephen K. ... Kuna, ID
Stark, Stephen L. ... Oklahoma City, OK
Stark, Stephen M. ... Wichita, KS
Stark, Stephen S. ... Santa Barbara, CA
Stark, Steven David ... Belmont, MA
Stark, Steven E. ... Miami, FL
Stark, Steven W. ... Athens, TX
Stark, Susan A. ... Newark, NJ
Stark, Susan E. ... Redwood City, CA
Stark, Tami Scarola ... New York, NY
Stark, Theresa A. ... Treasury Department, Departmental Offices, GV
Stark, Thomas A. ... Bend, OR
Stark, Thomas H., Law Offices of Durham, NC
Stark, Thomas H., Law Offices of Research Triangle Park, NC
Stark, Thomas, III ... Amelia, VA
Stark, Thomas, IV ... Glen Allen, VA
Stark, Thomas M. ... Las Vegas, NV
Stark, Thomas M. ... Riverhead, NY
Stark, Thomas M., Chtd. ... Las Vegas, NV
Stark, Timothy C. ... Mayfield, KY
Stark, Tina L. ... New York, NY
Stark, Todd Evan ... Los Angeles, CA
Stark, Vincent J. ... Chicago, IL
Stark, Vivien I. ... New York, NY
Stark, Wallace C. ... Woods Hole, MA
Stark, Wells, Rahl, Field & Schwartz Walnut Creek, CA
Stark, Wells, Rahl, Schwartz & Schieffer Oakland, CA
Stark, Wendy E. ... Cleveland, OH
Stark, William A. ... Houma, LA
Stark, William D. ... Salem, OR
Stark, William D., III ... Fort Pierce, FL
Stark, William Dean ... Starkville, MS
Stark, William K. ... Sacramento, CA
Starke, Diane D. ... Tallahassee, FL
Starke, Glenn O. ... Milwaukee, WI
Starke, Harold E., Jr. ... Richmond, VA
Starke, Henry C. ... Oklahoma City, OK
Starke, Jane Sutter ... Washington, DC
Starke, Jane Wells ... Los Alamos, NM
Starke, Karen L. ... Richmond, VA
Starke, Leonardo Da Vinci ... Miami, FL
Starke, R. Penfield ... Washington, DC
Starke, Richard C. L. ... Treasury Department, Internal Revenue Service, GV
Starke, Sheldon Philip ... Cleveland, OH
Starke, Wallace M. ... Richmond, VA
Starke, Walter M. ... Birmingham, AL
Starkel, W. Dennis ... Missoula, MT
Starken, R. Timothy ... Ottumwa, IA
Starker, Alan ... Philadelphia, PA
Starker, Jeffrey D. ... Orlando, FL
Starkes, Dale J. ... Winamac, IN
Starkes, F. Xavier ... Columbia, SC
Starkes Law Offices ... Winamac, IN
Starkey, Brad S. ... Bucyrus, OH
Starkey, Charles E. ... Brick, NJ
Toms River, NJ
Starkey, Charles P. ... Portland, OR
Starkey, Chris K. ... Fort Wayne, IN
Starkey, Cynthia D. ... Chandler, AZ
Livermore, CA
Starkey, David H. ... Columbus, OH
Starkey, David J. ... Lockport, NY
Starkey, Douglas E. ... Indianapolis, IN
Starkey, E. Patrick ... Roanoke, VA
Starkey, Earle J. ... New York, NY
Starkey, Elizabeth B. ... New York, NY
Starkey, Erin A. ... Dayton, OH
Starkey & Gatz ... Colby, KS
Starkey, H. David ... Colby, KS
Starkey, Hugh V. A. ... Boston, MA
Starkey, J. Shane ... Dayton, OH
Starkey, James G. ... Brooklyn, NY
Starkey, Jeffrey N. ... Mesquite, NV
St. George, UT
Starkey, John M. ... Bethel, AK
Starkey, Joseph E., Jr. ... Pittsburgh, PA
Starkey, Kelly, Blaney & White ... Brick, NJ
Manasquan, NJ
Toms River, NJ
Starkey, Kenneth S., Jr. ... Kansas City, MO
Starkey, Laurence E. ... Jefferson, OH
Starkey, Lawrence V., P.C. ... Atlanta, GA
Starkey, Leland D. ... Anaheim, CA
Starkey, Martha T. ... Indianapolis, IN
Starkey, Melissa N. ... Minneapolis, MN
Starkey, Patricia A. ... Stratford, CT
Starkey, Paul M. ... Sacramento, CA
Starkey, Peter B. ... New York, NY
Starkey, Richard ... Parkersburg, WV
Starkey, Richard B. ... Waldorf, MD
Starkey, Richard C. ... Indianapolis, IN
Starkey, Robert L. ... Beverly Hills, CA
Starkey, Ronald K. ... Akron, OH
Starkey, Sharon E. ... Baton Rouge, LA
Starkey, Sheila T. ... Washington, DC
Starkey & Stoll, Ltd. ... Bucyrus, OH
Starkey, Thomas L. ... Upper Marlboro, MD
Starkman, Gary L. ... Chicago, IL
Starkman, Jay ... Miami, FL
Starkman, Mark R. ... Miami, FL
Starkman, Mark T. ... Poughkeepsie, NY
Starkman, Milton I. ... Fort Lauderdale, FL
Starkman, Morris ... Cherry Hill, NJ
Starkman, Paul E. ... Chicago, IL
Starkman, Robert D. ... Southfield, MI
Starkman, Roxana M. ... Miami, FL
Starkoff, Alan G. ... Columbus, OH
Starkoff, Harvey H. ... Boca Raton, FL
Starkoff, Jack Richard ... Cleveland, OH
Starkopf, Lawrence S. ... Chicago, IL
Starkovich, Lynn M. ... Minneapolis, MN
Starks, Anthony Charles ... San Diego, CA
Starks, Benjamin E., Sr. ... Chicago, IL
Starks, Cammy C. ... Los Angeles, CA
Starks, Daniel J. ... Minnetonka, MN
Starks, Dennis J. Department of Transportation, Surface Transportation Board, GV
Starks, H. Powell ... Louisville, KY
Starks, Homer C. ... Naples, FL
Starks, Isaac J. ... Matteson, IL
Starks, Joe E., (P.C.) ... Dallas, TX
Starks, Leslie J., Mr. ... Chicago, IL
Starks, Michael D. ... Orlando, FL
Starks, Samuel J. ... Stamford, CT
Starkweather, David A. ... Lafayette, IN
Starkweather, Frederic H., Jr. Gold Beach, OR
Starkweather, Harold C. ... Miami, FL
Starkweather, John P. ... Chicago, IL
Starkweather, Michael W. ... Cincinnati, OH
Sandy, UT
Starkweather, Rodney J. ... Albuquerque, NM
Starkweather, Sarah M. ... New York, NY
Starkweather, Van A. ... Manchester, CT
Starkweather, William H. Salt Lake City, UT
Starleaf, David C. ... Burbank, CA
Starler, Michael H. ... Malibu, CA
Starler, Michael H., Law Corporation Malibu, CA
Starley, Sandra ... Moab, UT
Starlin, Keith J. ... Albany, NY
Starlin, T. W. ... Columbus, GA
Starling, Arleen A. ... Middleburg, FL
Starling, Bruce C. ... Orlando, FL
Starling, C. Gordon, Jr. ... New Orleans, LA
Starling, Donald A. ... Douglas, GA
Starling, F. Steven ... Marietta, GA
Starling, H. Ray, Jr. ... Kailua, HI
Starling, John M. ... Titusville, FL
Starling, Kenneth G. ... Washington, DC
Starling, L. Q. ... Los Angeles, CA
Starling, Luther D., Jr ... Smithfield, NC
Starling, M. Jefferson, III Birmingham, AL
Starling, Richard E., Jr. ... Pineville, LA
Starling, Richard S. ... Charlotte, NC
Starling, Shelby L., Jr. ... Anniston, AL
Starling, Thomas I. ... Jackson, MS
Starmann, Allison Wisk ... Chicago, IL
Starn, Jonathan P. ... Findlay, OH
Starn, Larry M. ... Sacramento, CA
Starn, Peter ... Honolulu, HI
Starn, Peter, A Law Corporation, Law Offices of ... Honolulu, HI
Starner, Patricia Moran ... Philadelphia, PA
Starnes & Atchison LLP ... Birmingham, AL
Mobile, AL
Starnes & Becker ... Emeryville, CA
Starnes, Bill ... Huntsville, AL
Starnes, Curtis R. ... Overland Park, KS
Starnes, D. Edward, III ... Huntsville, AL
Starnes, David W. ... Beaumont, TX
Starnes, DeAngelo Environmental Protection Agency, Office of the General Counsel, GV
Starnes, Dorothy L. ... Nashville, TN
Starnes, Gary W. ... Chattanooga, TN
Starnes, Gregory S. ... Sioux Falls, SD
Starnes, Hugh E. ... Fort Myers, FL
Starnes, James E. ... Savannah, GA
Starnes, James E., P.C., Law Offices of Savannah, GA
Starnes, James H. ... Birmingham, AL
Starnes, James Wright ... Springfield, MO
Starnes, Jeffrey M. ... Conyers, GA
Starnes, Joel D., Jr. ... Midland, TX
Starnes, Mac A. ... Midland, TX
Starnes, Marjorie ... Fort Myers, FL
Starnes, Marjorie, P.A. ... Cape Coral, FL
Fort Myers, FL
Starnes, O. E. ... Asheville, NC
Starnes, Richard A. ... Jefferson City, MO
Starnes, Robert C. ... Memphis, TN
Starnes, Steven D. ... Monroe, NC
Starnes, Tanya ... Emeryville, CA
Starnes, Thomas E. ... Washington, DC
Starnes, Thomas M. ... Morganton, NC
Starnes, W. Brian ... Knoxville, TN
Starnes, W. Stancil ... Birmingham, AL
Starnes & Wilkes ... Guntersville, AL
Starnes, William B., II ... Edwardsville, IL
Starns, Brian Michael ... Hood River, OR
Starns, Byron E., Jr. ... St. Paul, MN
Starns, Douglas E. ... Walnut Creek, CA
Starns, Larry D. ... Minneapolis, MN
Starobin, A. Fred ... Washington, DC
Starobin, Aaron ... Milwaukee, WI
Starobin, Amy L. ... Stamford, CT
Starobin & Associates ... Milwaukee, WI
Staron, Sonja ... Dallas, TX
Staropoli, C. Curtis ... Wilmington, DE
Philadelphia, PA
Staropoli, Catherine M. ... Larchmont, NY
Staropoli, Joseph J., Jr. ... White Plains, NY
Staropoli, Michael W. ... Portland, OR
Staros, Barbara J. ... Tallahassee, FL
Staroschuck, Bernadette M. Philadelphia, PA
Pittsburgh, PA
Starosciak, Matthew W. ... Detroit, MI
Starr, Alexander P. Federal Communications Commission, Common Carrier Bureau, GV
Starr, Allan ... New York, NY
Starr, Allan H. ... Philadelphia, PA
Starr, Amelia T. R. ... New York, NY
Starr, Arthur D. ... Baltimore, MD
Starr Austen Tribbett & Myers Logansport, IN
Starr, Bart, Jr. ... Birmingham, AL
Starr, Bernard H. ... Pittsfield, MA
Starr, Bert ... Dallas, TX
Starr, Bert ... Plano, TX
Starr, Bruno A. ... Chicago, IL
Starr, Carol L. ... Pittsburgh, PA
Starr, Carolyn M. ... Hamden, CT
Starr, C. M., II ... Bakersfield, CA
Starr, Craig A. ... Eugene, OR
Starr, Cynthia ... Quincy, CA
Starr, Daniel B. ... Fort Wayne, IN
Starr, Daniel M. ... Chicago, IL
Starr & Daniell, P.C. ... Chattanooga, TN
Starr, David A. ... Washington, DC
Starr, David S. ... Dallas, TX
Starr, Dawn E. ... Washington, DC
Starr, Debra Hope ... Los Angeles, CA
Starr, Dominic A. ... Myrtle Beach, SC
Starr, Donald F. ... Des Moines, IA
Starr, Edward H., Jr. ... Richmond, VA
Starr, Emily S. ... Fitchburg, MA
Worcester, MA
Starr, Enid M. ... Boston, MA
Starr, Ephraim ... Albuquerque, NM
Starr, Eric C. ... San Francisco, CA
Starr, F. Albert ... Block Island, RI
Cranston, RI
Starr • Finley LLP ... San Francisco, CA
Starr, Gary S. ... Hartford, CT
Starr, Gayle Phillips ... San Francisco, CA
Starr, Gern, Davison & Rubin, A Professional Corporation ... Roseland, NJ
New York, NY
Starr, Gregory S. ... Fort Lauderdale, FL
Starr, Gregory S., P.A. Fort Lauderdale, FL
Starr, H. David ... Washington, DC
Starr, H. James ... Lansing, MI
Starr, Harold P. ... Philadelphia, PA
Starr, Helen P. ... Washington, DC
Starr, Helmut M. ... St. Louis, MO
Starr, Henry Phillip ... Nevada City, CA
Starr, Ian M. ... Boston, MA
Starr, Ira M. ... Roseland, NJ
Starr, Irving ... Arlington, VA
Starr, Isidore ... Scottsdale, AZ
Starr, Ivar M. ... Miami Beach, FL
Starr, J. Michael ... Eugene, OR
Starr, J. William ... Gretna, LA
Starr, James D. ... Duluth, MN
Starr, James R. ... Concord, NH
Starr, Jay M. ... Bryn Mawr, PA
Starr, Jay M., Attorney-at-Law, P.C. Bryn Mawr, PA
Starr, Jeffrey ... Melville, NY
Starr, Jennifer Charwat ... Tenafly, NJ
Starr, Jim ... Crested Butte, CO
Starr, John A. ... Memphis, TN
Starr, John B., Jr. ... New York, NY
Starr, John M. ... Concord, CA
Starr, John W. ... Aspen, CO
Starr, Jon D. ... Tulsa, OK
Starr, Joseph A. ... Birmingham, MI
Starr, Judith R. Securities and Exchange Commission, Division of Enforcement, GV
Starr, Judson W. ... Washington, DC
Baltimore, MD
Towson, MD
Starr, Keith W. ... Tyler, TX
Starr, Kelly A. ... Chicago, IL
Starr, Kenneth I. ... Port Washington, NY
Starr, Kenneth R. ... Chattanooga, TN
Starr, Kenneth W. ... Washington, DC
New York, NY
Starr, Kent Wade ... Dallas, TX
Fort Worth, TX
Starr, Kerry Doherty ... Pittsburgh, PA
Starr, Kim Dale ... Fort Collins, CO
Starr, Larry W. ... Texarkana, TX
Starr, Laurence M. ... Boston, MA
Starr, Laurie F. ... Cleveland, OH
Starr, Laurie F., Co., L.P.A. ... Cleveland, OH
Starr, Leonard E., III ... Sandston, VA
Starr, Leonard E., III, P.C. ... Sandston, VA
Starr, Leonard W. ... El Paso, TX
Starr, Linda C. ... Santa Clara, CA
Starr, Lynn Acker ... San Francisco, CA
Starr, Madonna Kissel ... Treasury Department, Office of the Comptroller of the Currency, GV
Starr, Malcolm W. ... Providence, RI
Starr, Mark D. ... Lincoln, NE
Starr, Mark I. ... Carmel, CA
Starr, Mark M. ... Hibbing, MN
Starr, Mark T. ... Blue Bell, PA
Starr, Marlon F. ... Atlanta, GA
Starr, Martin ... Miami, FL
Starr, Marvin B. ... Walnut Creek, CA
Starr, Michael ... New York, NY
Starr, Michael E. ... Tyler, TX
Starr, Michael J. ... Boston, MA
Starr, Michael S. ... Matawan, NJ
Starr, Milton E. ... Memphis, TN
Starr, Nichole ... Atlanta, GA
Starr, Nina ... Pleasant Hill, CA
Starr, Paul Byron ... Houston, TX
Starr, Paul J. ... Stoughton, MA
Starr, Philip ... Beverly Hills, CA
Starr, Philip J. ... Inglewood, CA
Starr, Randolph W. ... Loveland, CO
Starr, Randolph W., P.C. ... Loveland, CO
Starr, Richard M. ... New York, NY
Starr, Robert ... Old Westbury, NY
Starr, Robert H. ... Trussville, AL
Starr, Robert S., (P.C.) ... New York, NY
Starr & Rowells ... Chicago, IL
Starr, Samuel M. ... Boston, MA
Starr, Samuel P. ... Washington, DC
Starr, Scott L. ... Logansport, IN
Starr, Sherman H., Jr. ... Boston, MA
Starr, Sheryl C. ... Boston, MA
Starr, Stephen Z. ... New York, NY
Starr, Steven B. ... Edina, MN
Starr, Steven J. ... Dallas, TX
Starr, Stuart, Chartered, Law Offices of Fort Lauderdale, FL
Starr, Stuart J. ... Fort Lauderdale, FL
Starr, Susan K. ... Bronx, NY
Starr, Susan L. P. Equal Employment Opportunity Commission, Office of the General Counsel, GV
Starr, Susanne E. ... Minneapolis, MN
Starr, Theodore L. ... Hiawatha, KS
Starr, Thomas A. ... Boyd, WI
Starr, Todd M. ... Cortez, CO
Starr, Vildan ... New York, NY
Starr & Vinson, P.C. ... Eugene, OR
Starr, Wade ... Dallas, TX
Starr, Warren D. ... Port Washington, NY
Starr, Wendy B. ... Port Washington, NY
Starr, Wendy J. ... London, OH
Starr, William D. ... Boston, MA
Starr, William Joseph ... Manchester, NH
Starr, Zachary Alan ... New York, NY
Starre, Gary A. ... Los Angeles, CA
Starrels, Andrew J. ... Los Angeles, CA
Starrett, Carl H., II ... La Mesa, CA
Starrett, Clyde F. ... McCook, NE
Starrett, Frederick K. ... Overland Park, KS
Starrett, Harry L. ... West Orange, NJ
Starrett, Jay R. ... Milwaukee, WI
Starrett, Judith A. ... Charlotte, NC
Starrett, Jung-Ock ... Cambridge, MA
Starrett, Keith ... Mc Comb, MS
Starrett, Kevin L. ... Cleveland, OH
Starrett & Klinghoffer, A Professional Corporation ... West Orange, NJ
Starrett, Laura L. ... Jacksonville, FL
Starrett, Loyd M. ... Boston, MA
Starrett, Lucinda ... Los Angeles, CA
Starrett, Randall M., II ... Middleburg, VA
Starrett, Richard T. ... Jackson, MS
Starrett, Sarah J. ... Washington, DC
Starrett, Tracey Bogen ... Sarasota, FL
Starrett, William C., II ... Newport Beach, CA
Starritt, Joseph W., III ... San Francisco, CA
Starritt, Sam D. ... Grand Junction, CO
Starritt-Burnett, Cari ... Killeen, TX
Starrs, Arthur F., Jr. ... Plano, TX
Starrs, Charles G. ... Germantown, MD
Starrs, Elizabeth A. ... Denver, CO
Starrs, Erika Jongejan ... Seattle, WA
Starrs, Thomas J. ... Vashon, WA
Starry & Associates, P.C. ... Houston, TX
Starry, Stuart J. ... Houston, TX
Starshak, James L. ... Honolulu, HI
Starsia, Victor ... White Plains, NY
Starsick, Joseph J., Jr. ... Charleston, WV
Starsky, Jeffrey M. ... Sacramento, CA
Starsky & Kirk, L.L.P. ... Sacramento, CA
Starson, Peter P., Jr. ... Los Angeles, CA
Start, Richard F. ... Pittsburgh, PA
Startsman, Daniel B., Jr. ... Cincinnati, OH
Startup, Thomas A. ... New York, NY
Startzel, Todd R. ... Spokane, WA
Startzman, Jeffrey P. ... Dayton, OH
Startzman, Thos. L. ... Columbus, OH
Staruch, W. Scott ... Lemoyne, PA
Staruck, James E. ... Chicago, IL
Starwood, Janet W. ... Wyncote, PA
Starzak, Jocelyn Ann ... Washington, DC
Starzel, Robert F. ... San Francisco, CA
Starzyk, Michael A. ... Houston, TX
Starzynski, James S. ... Albuquerque, NM
Stasa, Mark J. ... Detroit, MI
Stasa, Renata M. ... San Antonio, TX
Stasack, Stephen A. ... Troy, NY
Staschak, Michael C. ... Pittsburgh, PA
Stascia, Lawrence R. ... Chicago, IL
Stasel, Stanley R. ... Minneapolis, MN
Staser, John S. ... Evansville, IN
Stasevich, Nicholas J. ... Detroit, MI
Stash, Robert G. ... Pittsburgh, PA
Stashevsky, Yury ... Chatsworth, CA
Stashik, Anthony G. ... Anaheim, CA
Stashio, Joseph ... Salisbury, MA
Stashower, Arthur L. ... Los Angeles, CA
Stasiak, Tiffanie D. ... Englewood, CO
Stasiewicz, Suzanne ... Columbus, OH
Stasio, Andrew F., Jr. ... Fort Worth, TX
Stasio, Renee L. ... New York, NY
Stasio & Stasio, P.C. ... Fort Worth, TX
Stasio, Stephen M. ... Fort Worth, TX
Stasior, Laura H. ... New York, NY
Stasiowski, John F. ... Boston, MA
Stasiuk, George P. ... New York, NY
Stasiuk, Walter P. ... New York, NY
Stasiulis, Paul S. ... Memphis, TN
Stasiulis, Stanley P. ... Effingham, IL
Staskal, Douglas F. ... Des Moines, IA
Stasko, Nanette L. ... Somers, NY
Stasko, Paul A. ... Farmingdale, NY
Staskunas, Anthony J. ... Milwaukee, WI
Staskus, Kim David ... San Jose, CA
Staskus, Michael J. ... San Jose, CA

Staskus, Phillip A. .... Houston, TX
Stasney, Jo Allison .... Dallas, TX
Stasney, John J., III .... Dallas, TX
Stasnopolis, Dee H. .... Bakersfield, CA
Stasny, C. David .... Bryan, TX
Stasny, Ronald P. .... Beeville, TX
Staso, E. Blythe, Jr. .... De Kalb, IL
Stassen, John H., (P.C.) .... Chicago, IL
Stassen, William Harold .... Philadelphia, PA
Stassi, John A., II .... New Orleans, LA
Stassi, Michelle .... Columbus, OH
Stassi, Robert G. .... Metairie, LA
Stassi, Robert S. .... New Orleans, LA
Stassin, Larry D. .... Hammond, IN
Stassinopoulos, Nancy .... San Diego, CA
Stassinos, Gail .... Carmichael, CA
Stasson, Shelley A. .... West Bloomfield, MI
Stassun, Peter G. .... Fort Lauderdale, FL
Philadelphia, PA
Stastney, Hoyt R. .... Milwaukee, WI
Stastney, Shad L. .... New York, NY
Stastny, Stephen .... Department of Defense,
Defense Legal Services Agency, GV
Stastny, Steven M. .... Birmingham, AL
Stasz, Peter J. .... Westfield, MA
Staszewski, Glen .... Department of Justice,
Civil Division, GV
Staszewsky, Victor .... Minneapolis, MN
Staszower, Steven .... Beverly Hills, CA
Statchen, Robert R. .... Stamford, CT
State, David J. .... Buffalo, NY
State, Douglas R. .... Kearney, NE
State, John F. .... Cleveland, OH
State, Yeagley & George .... Kearney, NE
Stateman, Keith E. .... New York, NY
Staten, Earl P. .... Salt Lake City, UT
Staten, Jacqueline .... Garden Grove, CA
Staten, Kevin J. .... Little Rock, AR
Staten, Marjorie .... Southfield, MI
Staten, Richard N. .... Orlando, FL
Staten-Hayes, Kimberly A. .... Anchorage, AK
Stater Law Office .... Canton, MS
Stater, Lisa Anne .... Atlanta, GA
Stater, Stacey L. .... St. Louis, MO
Stater, Stanley F., III .... Canton, MS
Stater, William J. .... Eugene, OR
States, Dale L. .... Phoenix, AZ
States, John P. .... Bloomington, IL
Statesman, Kirsten Aminta
Leonardtown, MD
Stateson, Joseph Y. .... San Antonio, TX
Statfeld, George N. .... New York, NY
Statfeld, George N., P.C. .... New York, NY
Statfield, Cary N. .... Indianapolis, IN
Stathacos & Bellas .... Buffalo, NY
Stathacos, Dean C. .... Buffalo, NY
Stathakis, John J. .... Anderson, SC
Stathakis, Regan Pendleton .... Greenville, SC
Statham, H. Wayne .... Galesburg, IL
Statham, James W. .... Detroit, MI
Statham & McCray .... Evansville, IN
Statham, Scott .... Houston, TX
Statham, William E. .... Evansville, IN
Stathas, Charles J. .... Madison, WI
Stathas, James A. .... Los Angeles, CA
Stathas, Lynn M. .... Madison, WI
Stathatos, Gerasimia .... Lake Success, NY
Stathis, Anna M. .... New York, NY
Stathis, Lucinda Meekins .... Bradenton, FL
Stathis, William T. .... New York, NY
Stathopoulos, Angela .... Tampa, FL
Stathopoulos, Harry J. .... Charlotte, NC
Stathopoulos, James W. .... Sandwich, MA
Stathopulos, Andrew .... Englewood, CO
Stathopulos and Associates, P.C.
Englewood, CO
Stathos, Amy A. .... Los Angeles, CA
Stathos, Michael .... River Forest, IL
Stathos, Sam G. .... Columbia, SC
Stathos, Tony J., (A P.C.) .... Sacramento, CA
Statile, Dominick C. .... Glastonbury, CT
Statile, Richard P. .... Raleigh, NC
Statile, William J., (A Prof. Law Corp.)
Escondido, CA
Statkus, Carol .... Cheyenne, WY
Statkus, Jerry .... Germantown, WI
Statland & Buckley, P.C. .... Washington, DC
Statland, Donald A. .... Chicago, IL
Statland, Edward M. .... Washington, DC
Statland, Jay L. .... Chicago, IL
Statland, Sherryl Gayle .... Rockville, MD
Statler, John A. .... Harrisburg, PA
Statler, John C. .... Lamar, CO
Statler, Peter L. .... Cape Girardeau, MO
Statler, Teresa A. .... Portland, OR
Statman, Alan J. .... Washington, DC
Statman, Alan J. .... Cincinnati, OH
Statman, Eric D. .... New York, NY
Statman, Harris & Bardach, LLC
Cincinnati, OH
Dayton, OH
Statman, Russell K. .... New York, NY
Statom, Lila .... Nashville, TN
Staton, A. Lee, III .... Santa Ana, CA
Staton, Arthur, Jr. .... Kalamazoo, MI
Staton, Georgia A. .... Phoenix, AZ
Staton, Gwyn E. .... Seattle, WA
Staton, Jack W. .... Imperial, CA
Staton, James C. .... Dayton, OH
Staton, James S. .... Raleigh, NC
Staton, John C., Jr. .... Atlanta, GA
Staton, John S. .... Charlotte, NC
Staton, Jon T. .... Waurika, OK
Staton, Katherine A. .... New York, NY
Staton, Katherine A. .... Dallas, TX
Staton, Kerry D. .... Washington, DC
Baltimore, MD
Staton, Lee .... Santa Ana, CA
Staton, Louise G. .... Mullens, WV
Staton, Mack S. .... Santa Barbara, CA
Staton, Perkinson, Doster, Post, Silverman & Adcock, P.A. .... Sanford, NC
Staton, Raymond J. .... Los Angeles, CA
Staton, Robert E. .... Columbia, SC
Staton, Robert H. .... Indianapolis, IN
Staton, Robert V. .... Washington, DC
Staton, Shawna Y. .... Raleigh, NC
Staton, W. Richard .... Mullens, WV
Staton, Wayne C. .... Oxford, OH
Staton, Wayne, Co., L.P.A. .... Oxford, OH
Staton, William Wayne .... Sanford, NC
Statsinger, Steven M. .... New York, NY
Statsky, William P. .... San Francisco, CA
Statt, Daniel A. .... Seattle, WA
Statter, Humphrey .... New York, NY
Statton, Christopher J. .... Midland, TX
Statton, Edward C. .... Buford, GA
Statum, Fred C., III .... Nashville, TN
Statum, Lauren A. .... Federalsburg, MD
Statuta, Mildred Reynolds .... Worcester, MA
Statute, Louis F. .... Cherry Hill, NJ
Statz, Brian Andrew .... Indianapolis, IN
Statz, James I. .... Madison, WI
Statz, Susan C. .... Shoreview, MN
Statza, Gerald R. .... Chicago, IL
Statzer, Darrell E., Jr. .... Decatur, IL
Statzer, Darrell E., Jr. .... Sullivan, IL
Statzer, Joni Elizabeth .... Cincinnati, OH
Staub, Craig G. .... Los Angeles, CA
Staub, D. Joshua .... Encino, CA
Staub, David K. .... Chicago, IL
Staub, Jerry K., Law Office of .... Glendale, CA
Staub, Keith M. .... Los Angeles, CA
Staub, Michael K. .... Spokane, WA
Staub, Murray .... Mountainside, NJ
Staub, Perry R., Jr. .... New Orleans, LA
Staub, Rex B. .... Des Moines, IA
Staub, Richard S. .... Carson City, NV
Staub, Sandra J. .... Springfield, MA
Staub, Stacey S. .... Cleveland, OH
Staub, Thomas F. .... Columbus, OH
Staubach, Stephanie M. .... Dallas, TX
Stauber, Aaron D. .... Lawrence, NY
Stauber, Alan W. .... Englishtown, NJ
Stauber, Alvin .... Tallahassee, FL
Stauber, Donald J. .... New York, NY
Stauber, Lawrence B., Jr. .... Duluth, MN
Stauber & Lien .... Duluth, MN
Stauber, Mark J. .... Winfield, IL
Stauber, Patrick D. .... Searcy, AR
Stauber, Ronald J. .... Los Angeles, CA
Stauber, Sherwin .... Miami Beach, FL
Stauber, Thaddeus J. .... Chicago, IL
Staubes, Christopher B., III
Charleston, SC
Staubes, Christopher B., Jr.
Charleston, SC
Staubes, Tanya Gunter .... Mount Pleasant, SC
Staubitz, Arthur F. .... Deerfield, IL
Staubitz, Sheldon H. .... Schaumburg, IL
Staubus, Barry P. .... Johnson City, TN
Staubus, Bradley K. .... Chicago, IL
Staubus, Martin A. .... Napa, CA
Staubus, P. Keith .... Dallas, TX
Stauch, Arabo, Dickow and Ward, P.C.
Farmington Hills, MI
Stauch, Barbara J. .... Denver, CO
Stauch, George J., Jr. .... Lapeer, MI
Stauch, Konrad .... Farmington Hills, MI
Stauch & Shook, PLC .... Flint, MI
Lapeer, MI
Stauch, Thomas R. .... Dallas, TX
Staud, Aloysius J. .... Philadelphia, PA
Staudacher, Regina Marie .... Detroit, MI
Staudenmaier, Beth A. Buchanan
Dayton, OH
Staudenmaier, Craig J. .... Harrisburg, PA
Staudenmaier, Heidi McNeil .... Phoenix, AZ
Staudenmaier, L. William .... Phoenix, AZ
Staudenmaier, L. William .... Milwaukee, WI
Staudenmaier, Mary L. .... Marinette, WI
Stauder, Cindy .... O'Fallon, IL
Stauder, Lloyd P. .... Trumbull, CT
Stauder, Michael H. .... North Palm Beach, FL
Pahokee, FL
Staudinger, Deborah Kim
Washington, DC
Staudinger, Henry J., (P.C.) .... Tucson, AZ
Staudt, Daniel J. .... Orlando, FL
Staudt, E. Roman, III .... Canton, OH
Staudt, James .... White Plains, NY
Staudt, Jon L. .... Des Moines, IA
Staudt, Michael A. .... Sidney, OH
Staudt, Ronald W. .... Chicago, IL
Staudt, Susan Bernau .... Cedar Falls, IA
Staudt-Killea, Sandra L. .... New York, NY
Staudtuhar, Tara Lynn .... Fremont, CA
Stauff, Deidra L. .... Santa Monica, CA
Stauffacher, Charles D. .... Watertown, CT
Stauffacher, Dean W. .... Cedar Rapids, IA
Stauffacher, Jill D. .... Austin, TX
Stauffacher, Michael F. .... Huntsville, TX
Stauffacher, Raymond H., Jr. .... Houston, TX
Stauffacher, Walter A. .... Yakima, WA
Stauffenger, Leonard W. .... Akron, OH
Stauffer, Betsy G. .... Seattle, WA
Stauffer, Edward C. .... Fort Wayne, IN
Stauffer, Eric P. .... Portland, ME
Stauffer, Gerald M. .... Newport Beach, CA
Stauffer, J. Kent .... Colorado Springs, CO
Stauffer, J. Robt. .... Mechanicsburg, PA
Stauffer, James S. .... Claremore, OK
Stauffer, Jeanne E. .... Tucson, AZ
Stauffer, Jerry .... Memphis, TN
Stauffer, John H. .... Canal Winchester, OH
Stauffer, John H., Jr. .... Topeka, KS
Stauffer, Kent T. .... New York, NY
Stauffer, Mannix, Rommel, Decker & Dulany, L.L.C. .... Alexandria, VA
Fairfax, VA
McLean, VA
Stauffer, Mark R. .... Orlando, FL
Stauffer, Melvyn J. .... Sandusky, OH
Stauffer, Monica L. .... Morenci, AZ
Stauffer, Neal E. .... Tulsa, OK
Stauffer, Robert F. .... Vienna, VA
Stauffer, Robert L. .... Pottstown, PA
Stauffer, Robert R. .... Chicago, IL
Stauffer, Ronald E. .... Washington, DC
Stauffer, Scott .... Macomb, IL
Stauffer, Scott W. .... Aurora, CO
Stauffer, Susan A. .... Washougal, WA
Stauffer, Susan P. .... Cleveland, OH
Stauffer, Suzan L. .... San Jose, CA
Stauffer, Terry A. .... Fort Wayne, IN
Stauffer, Timothy D. .... Columbus, OH
Stauffer, Ward D. .... Kansas City, KS
Stauffer, William L., Jr. .... McLean, VA
Staugaard, William L. .... Mount Clemens, MI
Staulcup, James M., Jr. .... Lisle, IL
Staum, Tim A. .... Minneapolis, MN
Staunton, Kevin P. .... Minneapolis, MN
Staunton, Thomas M. .... Chicago, IL
Staurset, Sverre O. .... Tacoma, WA
Stausboll, Anne .... Sacramento, CA
Stauss, Edward F., III .... Baton Rouge, LA
Stauss, Edward F., Jr. .... New Orleans, LA
Stauss, Eileen M. .... Seattle, WA
Stauss, Karl .... Vista, CA
Stautberg, Jon M. .... Houston, TX
Stautberg, Julia A. .... Cincinnati, OH
Stautberg, Lee M. .... Cincinnati, OH
Stautberg, Peter J. .... Cincinnati, OH
Stauts, Helen C. .... Nevada City, CA
Stautz, Jane Ann Siggelkow
Indianapolis, IN
Stautz, Jeffrey M. .... Indianapolis, IN
Stava, Jeffrey A. .... Irvine, CA
Stave, Gregg M. .... Chapel Hill, NC
Stave, Howard D. .... Forest Hills, NY
Stave, P.C. .... Omaha, NE
Stave, Ronald H. .... Omaha, NE
Stavely, John F. .... Boulder, CO
Stavely, Richard W. .... Wichita, KS
Staver, Allen W. .... Denver, CO
Staver & Associates .... Orlando, FL
Staver, Mathew D. .... Orlando, FL
Staver, Peter J. .... Taylor, MI
Stavert, John L. .... San Francisco, CA
Stavile, Patrice D. .... New York, NY
Stavin, Richard A., and Associates
Encino, CA
Stavin, Richard A., and Associates
Los Angeles, CA
Stavinoha, James E. .... Richmond, TX
Stavinoha, Werner J. .... Weimar, TX
Stavins, Frederick C., Jr. .... Champaign, IL
Stavins, Ralph L. .... Glenview, IL
Stavins, Richard Lee .... Chicago, IL
Stavis & Kornfeld, L.L.P. .... New York, NY
Stavis, Paul F. .... Albany, NY
Stavis, Roger L. .... New York, NY
Stavish, Matthew Wade .... Bethesda, MD
Arlington, VA
Leesburg, VA
Stavish, Sabrina Crowley .... Denver, CO
Stavish, Theodore J., Jr. .... Denver, CO
Stavisky, Arthur .... Great Barrington, MA
Stavisky, Elizabeth Z. .... Lafayette Hill, PA
Stavisky, Jeffrey .... Baltimore, MD
Stavitsky, Bruce J. .... Upper Saddle River, NJ
Stavlas, Catherine McCallie
Washington, DC
Greenbelt, MD
Stavlas, Nicholas G. .... Baltimore, MD
Stavnezer, Jessica R. .... Merced, CA
Stavnicky, Michael R. .... Cleveland, OH
Stavola, Joseph M. .... Greensboro, NC
Stavole, C. Anthony .... Cleveland, OH
Stavole & Miller .... Cleveland, OH
Stavole, William J. .... Cleveland, OH
Stavrakis, Catherine M. .... Washington, DC
Stavrakis, Steve .... Tampa, FL
Stavrides, Stephen .... St. James, NY
Stavrides, Thalia Marie .... Hauppauge, NY
Stavrinakis, Leonidas Emanuel
Charleston, SC
Stavropoulos, George .... Brooklyn, NY
Stavropoulos, George T. .... Boston, MA
Stavropoulos, Peter J. .... Chicago, IL
Stavropoulos, Sandra M. .... Chicago, IL
Stavropoulos, Thomas C. .... Chicago, IL
Stavros, Andrew W. .... Salt Lake City, UT
Stavros, Catherine D. .... Fort Mitchell, KY
Stavros, Charles W. .... Boston, MA
Stavros, George P. .... Ashland, KY
Stavros, James P. .... Ashland, KY
Stavros, Joan A. .... Warren, NJ
New York, NY
Stavros, Marilyn E. .... Portland, ME
Stavros, Peter J. .... Louisville, KY
Stavsky, Averim .... New York, NY
Stawasz, Michael .... Boston, MA
Stawiarski, Lawrence V. .... Brighton, MI
Stawiarski, Leo C., Jr. .... Englewood, CO
Houston, TX
Stawicki, Charlene Ann M. .... Topsfield, MA
Stawicki, Jean M. .... Colchester, CT
Stawicki, John L. .... Colchester, CT
Stawicki and Stawicki .... Colchester, CT
Stawnychy, Petro R. .... Rutherford, NJ
Stawski, Amy A. .... Bloomfield Hills, MI
Stawski, Christopher J. .... Milwaukee, WI
Stay, Ronald J. .... Atlanta, GA
Stayart, Gregory Alan .... Lindenhurst, IL
Stayer, Mark A. .... Portland, OR
Stayin, Randolph J. .... Washington, DC
Stayman, Robert F. .... Evansville, IN
Stayn, Susan .... Boston, MA
Stayton, Angelina M. .... Tampa, FL
Kansas City, MO
Stayton, Brian F. .... Tampa, FL
Overland Park, KS
Stayton, Herbert J., Jr. .... Maple Shade, NJ
Stayton, James K. .... Louisville, KY
Stayton, John W., Jr. .... Austin, TX
Stayton, Thomas G. .... Indianapolis, IN
Stazer, Alan K. .... Los Angeles, CA
Stazzone, Victor Philip .... Aurora, CO
Stea, Bernard F. .... Portland, OR
Stea, Daniel E. .... Oakland, CA
Stead, Ben .... Des Moines, IA
Stead, Calvin R. .... Bakersfield, CA
Stead & Company, P.C. .... Grand Rapids, MI
Stead, Douglas P. .... Columbus, OH
Stead, Edward B. .... Dallas, TX
Stead, Gerald H. .... Tampa, FL
Stead, Gerald H., P.A. .... Tampa, FL
Stead & Heath, P.C. .... Oklahoma City, OK
Stead, Mark A. .... Lynn, MA
Stead, Robert E. .... St. Louis, MO
Stead, Robert R. .... Grand Rapids, MI
Stead, Robin .... Oklahoma City, OK
Stead, Susan Teigland .... Columbus, OH
Steadham, John M. .... Gainesville, FL
Steadman, Bernard W. .... Salem, CT
Steadman, Charles W. .... Washington, DC
Steadman, Clayton D. .... Augusta, GA
Steadman, Frank M., Jr. .... Summit, NJ
Steadman, Gary L. .... Taylors, SC
Steadman, Hollis S. .... Lake Bluff, IL
Steadman, James R. .... Girard, PA
Steadman, John W., (P.A.)
Fort Lauderdale, FL
Steadman, Joseph D. .... Mobile, AL
Steadman, Judith D. .... Littleton, CO
Steadman, Juliette M. .... Palo Alto, CA
Steadman, Kathy A. .... Phoenix, AZ
Steadman, Kyle J. .... Wichita, KS
Steadman, Lewis T. .... Chicago, IL
Arlington, VA
Steadman, Lewis T., Jr. .... Chicago, IL
Steadman, Linda Bridgers .... Mobile, AL
Steadman, Marquita B. .... Rockville, MD
Steadman, Paul R. .... Chicago, IL
Steadman, R. Webb .... Hartford, CT
Steadman, Robert A. .... Traverse City, MI
Steadman, Robert L. .... Raynham, MA
Steadman, Sarah D., (Mrs.) .... Kailua-Kona, HI
Steadman, Susan K. .... Hattiesburg, MS
Steadman, Todd C.
White River Junction, VT
Steadman-Martin, Nancy .... Red Bank, NJ
Steadry, Gretchen E. .... Minneapolis, MN
Steady, Scott I. .... Tampa, FL
Steaffens, M. Ava .... Costa Mesa, CA
Steagall, Barry M. .... St. Petersburg, FL
Steagall, Fred R. .... Ozark, AL
Steagall, Henry B., II .... Ozark, AL
Steagall, Henry B., III .... Ozark, AL
Steagall, Henry B., III, Law Offices of
Daleville, AL
Ozark, AL
Steagall, Richard L. .... Peoria, IL
Steager, Dale W. .... Charleston, WV
Steak, Charles A. .... Gold Beach, OR
Steakley, Edward D. .... Houston, TX
Steakley, Mark E. .... Houston, TX
Steakley, Roderic G. .... Huntsville, AL
Steakley & Wetsel .... Abilene, TX
Colorado City, TX
Snyder, TX
Sweetwater, TX
Steakley, Zollie C. .... Sweetwater, TX
Stealey, James Irvin .... Parkersburg, WV
Stealey, Patricia A. .... Cleveland, OH
Steamer, Julie B. .... New York, NY
Steans, Phillip M. .... Menomonie, WI
Steanson, Norman G., Jr.
North Kansas City, MO
Stear, Melissa D. .... Washington, DC
Stearman, James A. .... Fullerton, CA
Stearman, Jeffrey D. .... Placentia, CA
Stearn, Douglas W. .... Department of Justice,
Civil Division, GV
Stearn, Martin E. .... Encino, CA
Stearn, Mitchell A. .... Washington, DC
Stearn, Robert Alan .... Chicago, IL
Stearn, Robert J., Jr. .... Wilmington, DE
Stearn, Todd J. .... Farmington Hills, MI
Stearney, Ronald A., (Ltd.) .... Chicago, IL
Stearns, Alan B. .... Hallowell, ME
Stearns, Andrew V. .... San Jose, CA
Stearns, Barry T. .... Boston, MA
Stearns, Beth R. .... Parsippany, NJ
Stearns, Brett C. .... San Francisco, CA
Stearns, Christopher .... San Diego, CA
Stearns & Clemons .... Los Angeles, CA
Stearns, Craig E. .... New York, NY
Stearns, David B. .... Boca Raton, FL
Stearns, David G. .... Sarasota, FL
Stearns, Douglas H. .... Portland, OR
Stearns, Eugene E. .... Miami, FL
Stearns, F. Cole .... Dallas, TX
Stearns, Frank W. .... Fairfax, VA
Stearns, Franklin F., Jr. .... Portland, ME
Stearns, Franklin G. .... Boston, MA
Stearns, Frederick A. .... Washington, DC
Stearns, Fredric W. .... Atlanta, GA
Forsyth, GA
Stearns, Geoffrey B. .... Santa Barbara, CA
Stearns, George F., Jr. .... Bethesda, MD

Stearns, George K. ... Stowe, VT
Stearns, Gross, Moore & Rusch, A Prof. Corp. Whittier, CA
Stearns, Harward A. ... Whittier, CA
Stearns, James C. ... Washington, DC
Stearns, James R. ... Dunedin, FL
Stearns, James R. ... Walled Lake, MI
Stearns, Janet R. ... Boston, MA
Stearns, Jeffrey C. ... Fallbrook, CA
Stearns, Jeffrey T. ... Brewton, AL
Stearns, Jennifer D. ... Miami, FL
Stearns, Joan E.T. ... San Antonio, TX
Stearns, Jodie L. ... Bowling Green, OH
Stearns, John F. ... San Diego, CA
Stearns, Jon D. ... Chagrin Falls, OH
Stearns, Joseph T. ... Newark, NJ
New York, NY
Stearns, Karen Beth ... Atlanta, GA
Stearns, Katherine G. ... Chicago, IL
Stearns, Krista S. ... Anchorage, AK
Stearns, Laurie ... Redwood City, CA
Stearns, Mary ... Los Angeles, CA
Stearns, Mary A. ... Marietta, GA
Stearns, Maxwell L. ... Arlington, VA
Stearns, Michael ... Houston, TX
Stearns, Michael E. ... Fort Lauderdale, FL
Stearns, Nancy ... New York, NY
Stearns, Nicole R. ... Richland, WA
Stearns, Parks H. ... Dallas, TX
Stearns, Patricia H. ... Los Altos, CA
Stearns, Richard C. ... Treasury Department, Office of Thrift Supervision, GV
Stearns, Richard D. ... Columbus, OH
Stearns, Richard G. ... Boston, MA
Stearns, Richard M. ... Kinston, NC
Stearns, Robert L. ... Saginaw, MI
Stearns, Robert S. ... Mission Hills, CA
Stearns, Roger S. ... Cleveland, OH
Stearns, Rollin A. ... East Holden, ME
Stearns, Ryan E. ... Torrance, CA
Stearns, Sam B. ... Jacksonville, FL
Stearns, Sherman C. ... McGregor, TX
Stearns, Susan A. ... Evergreen, CO
Stearns, Timothy H. ... Mount Shasta, CA
Stearns Weaver Miller Weissler Alhadeff & Sitterson, P.A. ... Fort Lauderdale, FL
Miami, FL
Tampa, FL
Stearns, William A. ... Batavia, OH
Stears, George T. ... Chicago, IL
Stears, Marie B. ... Boulder, CO
Steates, Alison L. ... New Hartford, NY
Steates, F. Paul ... New Hartford, NY
Steates, Francis C. ... New Hartford, NY
Steates Remmell Steates & Dziekan New Hartford, NY
Stebbings, Robert Y. ... New York, NY
Stebbins, Bradley, Wood & Harvey, Professional Association ... Hanover, NH
Lebanon, NH
Norwich, VT
Stebbins, Carol G. ... Mt. Vernon, OH
Stebbins, Charles C., III ... Augusta, GA
Stebbins, Charles C., Jr. ... Darien, GA
Stebbins & Coffey ... North Bend, OR
Stebbins, Dana Brewington
Washington, DC
Annapolis, MD
Stebbins, Douglas B. ... New York, NY
Stebbins, Edward C. ... New Canaan, CT
Stebbins, Enid R. ... Philadelphia, PA
Stebbins, Gail Duffie ... Augusta, GA
Stebbins, James C. ... Charleston, WV
Huntington, WV
Stebbins, John Storrs ... Hanover, NH
Norwich, VT
Stebbins, Michael B. ... Plymouth, MI
Stebbins, Michael J. ... Pensacola, FL
Stebbins, Michael R. ... North Bend, OR
Stebbins, Michael W. ... Palo Alto, CA
Stebbins, Raymond ... Weymouth, MA
Stebbins, Robert A. ... Eustis, FL
Stebbins, Robert B. ... New York, NY
Stebbins, Rowland, III ... Corning, NY
Stebbins & Stebbins ... Eustis, FL
Stebbins, Thomas R. ... Toledo, OH
Stebbins, William J. ... Oxford, MI
Stebel, Bernard ... New York, NY
Woodbury, NY
Stebel & Paseltiner, P.C. ... Woodbury, NY
Stebelton, Aranda & Snider, A Legal Professional Association ... Columbus, OH
Lancaster, OH
Stebelton, Gerald L. ... Lancaster, OH
Stebelton, Richard A. ... Youngstown, OH
Stebenne, David L. ... Columbus, OH
Stebenne, Marisa ... Severna Park, MD
Stebens, Glen A. ... Santa Ana, CA
Stebens, Robert E. ... Worthington, OH
Steber, Alan Barnes ... Houston, TX
Steber, Jill S. ... Plymouth Meeting, PA
Steber, Michael T. ... Milwaukee, WI
Stebick, Michael R. ... Buffalo, NY
Stebing, David G. ... Anchorage, AK
Stebleton, Roger V. ... El Cajon, CA
Stebner, Kenneth E. ... Rawlins, WY
Stec, Daria M. ... Department of Education, Office of the General Counsel, GV
Stec, Gary L. ... Grand Rapids, MI
Troy, MI
Stec, Jeffrey L. ... Cincinnati, OH
Stec, John M. ... Glenview, IL
Stec, Marc R. ... Alexandria, VA
Stec, Sean C. ... Chicago, IL
Stec, Stan B. ... Chicago, IL
Steccato, Carl L. ... New York, NY
Stecco, John T. ... Grand Rapids, MI
Stecco, Larry J., (P.C.) ... Flint, MI

Stecewycz, Joseph ... Boston, MA
Stechel, Howard J., P.C. ... Los Angeles, CA
Stechel, Howard J., P.C. ... Los Angeles, CA
Stechel, Ira B. ... New York, NY
Stecher, Beth A. ... Boston, MA
Stecher, Bridget ... West Caldwell, NJ
Stecher, David J. ... Boise, ID
Stecher, Esta Eiger ... New York, NY
Stecher Jaglom & Prutzman, LLP
New York, NY
Stecher, Jamie B.W. ... New York, NY
Stecher, Jill R. ... Sacramento, CA
Stecher, Joe W. ... Fremont, NE
Stecher, Leonard ... New York, NY
Stecher, Michael J. ... San Francisco, CA
Stecher, Stacy K. ... San Francisco, CA
Stecher, Steven A. ... Bixby, OK
Tulsa, OK
Stecher, William T. ... Silver Spring, MD
Stechert, Robert B. ... Basking Ridge, NJ
Stechler, Gail ... Teaneck, NJ
Stechman, Scott D. ... Uniondale, NY
Stechmann, John Henry
Redwood Falls, MN
Stechow, David R. ... Birmingham, MI
Stechschulte, George ... Mount Clemens, MI
Stechschulte, Mark ... McLean, VA
Stecich, Marianne ... Tarrytown, NY
Stecina, Susan Q. ... Phoenix, AZ
Steck, David L. ... West Chester, PA
Steck, Emil, Jr. ... Pasadena, CA
Steck, Frederick E. ... Memphis, TN
Steck, Garrett David ... Anderson, SC
Steck, Hans W. ... Indianapolis, IN
Steck, Henry E. ... Fort Worth, TX
Steck, James M. ... Upland, CA
Steck, Janine M. ... Lebanon, IN
Steck, Phillip G. ... Albany, NY
Steckbauer, William W. ... Los Angeles, CA
New York, NY
Steckbeck, Mark D. ... Indianapolis, IN
Steckel, Edward I. ... Chambersburg, PA
Steckel, Martin H. ... Atlanta, GA
Steckel, Randy E. ... Seattle, WA
Steckel, Raymond F. ... New York, NY
Steckel, Simon T. ... Miami, FL
Steckel & Stopp ... Schnecksville, PA
Slatington, PA
Steckel, Susan J. ... Burlington, VT
Montpelier, VT
Steckel, Susan J., P.C. ... Montpelier, VT
Steckel, William A. ... Slatington, PA
Steckelberg, Cheryl Whitten ... Lincoln, NE
Steckelis, Michael J. ... Madison, WI
Steckelman, Peter ... Los Angeles, CA
Stecker, Carl R. ... Salem, OR
Stecker, Donald P. ... San Antonio, TX
Stecker, James C. ... Columbus, NE
Stecker, Pavel K. ... Buffalo, NY
Stecker, Richard C. ... Bloomfield Hills, MI
Steckiel, Richard E. ... Providence, RI
Steckiw, Andrew E. ... Philadelphia, PA
Stecklair, Francis X. ... Morrisville, PA
Stecklein, Alan J. ... Kansas City, KS
Stecklein, C. Brett ... Dallas, TX
Steckler, Bruce W. ... Dallas, TX
Steckler, David E. ... Great Neck, NY
Steckler, David T. ... Fredericksburg, VA
Steckler, Gary R. ... St. Landry, LA
Steckler, Gutman, Morrissey & Murray
New York, NY
Steckler, Henry I. ... Fairfield, CT
Steckler, Judith J. ... Norwalk, CT
Steckler & Ryan ... Indianapolis, IN
Steckler, Sanford R. ... Biloxi, MS
Steckler, Sharon ... St. Louis, MO
Steckler, Todd C. ... New York, NY
Steckler, W. Rudolph ... Indianapolis, IN
Steckling, John W. ... Clarkston, MI
Steckling, Kimberly S. ... San Diego, CA
Steckloff, I. Mark ... Detroit, MI
Stecklow, David S. ... Hollywood, FL
Steckman, Lawrence A. ... New York, NY
Steckman, Lois ... Cold Spring Harbor, NY
Steckmest, Lawrence D. ... Los Angeles, CA
Steckowych, Kerry P. ... Goffstown, NH
Steckroth, Donald H. ... Newark, NJ
Steco, Janice V. (Benante) ... Media, PA
Stecopoulos, Nicholas ... New York, NY
Stecz, Eric J. ... Warren, OH
Steddom, Mary B. ... Ocala, FL
Steddom, Mary B., P.A. ... Ocala, FL
Stedeford, Walter R. ... Jacksonville, FL
Stedelin, Mark W. ... Centralia, IL
Stedem, Deanne R. ... Kansas City, MO
Stedem, Edwin J., Jr. ... Dearborn, MI
Stedfast, Jeffrey M. ... Norfolk, VA
Stedge, Tanya M. ... New York, NY
Stedham, Brenda S. ... Anniston, AL
Stedina, Aloysius P. ... White Plains, NY
Steding, Sue F. ... Indio, CA
Stedman, Alfred B. ... Granada Hills, CA
Stedman, Barbara Epstein ... Wellesley, MA
Stedman, Carling H. ... Miami, FL
Stedman, Charles N. ... Burlington, NC
Stedman, Fershee & Fershee, L.L.P.
Petoskey, MI
Stedman, Hugh J. ... Atlanta, GA
Stedman, J. Russell ... San Francisco, CA
Stedman, Lynn G., III ... Petoskey, MI
Stedman, Randy M. ... Portland, OR
Stedman, Richard R. ... Columbus, OH
Stedman, Robert S. ... Victorville, CA
Stedman, Robert W., (P.C.)
Newport Beach, CA
Stedman, Sharon Lee ... Orlando, FL
Stedman, Sharon Lee, P.A. ... Orlando, FL
Stedman, Stuart West ... Houston, TX

Stedronsky, George R. ... Winter Park, FL
Stedronsky, H. James ... Farmington, CT
Stedry, Marie F. ... Atlanta, GA
Stedtfeld, Todd ... St. Paul, MN
Steeb, Earl F. ... St. Joseph, MO
Steeb, Merrill M. ... St. Joseph, MO
Steece, Thomas J. ... Oklahoma City, OK
Steed, C. Val ... Las Vegas, NV
Steed, Christian A. ... Houston, TX
Steed & Collins ... Orlando, FL
Steed, D'Angela Proctor ... Pittsburgh, PA
Steed, David L. ... Nashville, TN
Steed, David W. ... Wichita, KS
Steed, Derek B. ... Burlington, NC
Steed, Donald Russell ... Sacramento, CA
Steed, Emily R. ... Boston, MA
Steed, F. Wade ... Birmingham, AL
Steed, Gene E. ... Perryton, TX
Steed, Hudell McCelvey ... Sugar Land, TX
Steed, James A. ... Washington, DC
Steed, James M. ... Austin, TX
Steed, Jerry T. ... San Antonio, TX
Steed, Joel J. ... Dallas, TX
Steed, Joel J., A Prof. Corp., Law Offices of
Clarksville, TX
Dallas, TX
Steed, Julia Ann ... Metairie, LA
Steed, Michael R. ... North Hollywood, CA
Steed, Richard N. ... Austin, TX
Steed, Robert L. ... Atlanta, GA
Steed, Thomas W., III ... Rocky Mount, NC
Steed, Wilton E. ... Pine Bluff, AR
Steedle, Roger C. ... Absecon, NJ
Atlantic City, NJ
Deptford, NJ
Steedle, Roger C., P.A., Law Offices of
Woodbury, NJ
Absecon, NJ
Atlantic City, NJ
Deptford, NJ
Steedman, Richard B. ... Evansville, IN
Steedman, Robert ... Anaheim, CA
Steedman, Wayne D. ... Baltimore, MD
Steefel, David S. ... Denver, CO
Steefel, Edward R. ... San Francisco, CA
Steefel, Levitt & Weiss, A Professional Corporation ... San Francisco, CA
Stamford, CT
Steeg, Glenn D. ... Kalamazoo, MI
Steeg, Howard R. ... Bristol, CT
Steeg, Moise S., Jr. ... New Orleans, LA
Steeg Newton Connelly & Emmons, P.C.
Kalamazoo, MI
Steeg and O'Connor, L.L.C.
New Orleans, LA
Steeg, Robert M. ... New Orleans, LA
Steege, Brandi R. ... Newport Beach, CA
Steege, Catherine L. ... Chicago, IL
Steege, Donald T. ... Bella Vista, AR
Steege, Peter O. ... Beaver, PA
Steegmann, Edward P. ... Indianapolis, IN
Steeh, George C., III ... Mount Clemens, MI
Steel, Adrian L., Jr. ... Washington, DC
Steel, Angela M. ... San Francisco, CA
Steel, Barry C. ... Towson, MD
Steel, Bellman, Ritz & Clark, P.C.
New York, NY
Steel, Brian E. ... Atlanta, GA
Steel, Charles L., IV ... Raleigh, NC
Research Triangle Park, NC
Steel, Christopher C. ... Indianapolis, IN
Steel, Cynthia D. ... Las Vegas, NV
Steel, Debra Dunn ... Costa Mesa, CA
Steel, Donald B. ... Lakewood, NJ
Red Bank, NJ
Whiting, NJ
Steel, Elizabeth Kate ... Westborough, MA
Steel, Emily R. ... New York, NY
Steel, Florence Dubrow ... Burlington, NJ
Haddonfield, NJ
Steel, Frank E., Jr. ... Akron, OH
Steel, Gary L. ... New Braunfels, TX
Steel, George E. ... Nashville, AR
Steel, George E., Jr. ... Nashville, AR
Steel, George W. ... Flint, MI
Troy, MI
Steel Hector & Davis LLP ... Key West, FL
Miami, FL
Naples, FL
Tallahassee, FL
West Palm Beach, FL
Steel, James F. ... Gulfport, MS
Jackson, MS
Steel, Jim Bob ... Nashville, AR
Steel, John D. ... Atlanta, GA
Steel, John H., Law Offices of
Telluride, CO
Steel, John M. ... Seattle, WA
Steel, Kathy D. ... San Francisco, CA
Steel, Kenneth C., III ... Jacksonville, FL
Steel, Laura Nachowitz ... Washington, DC
Steel, Lewis M. ... New York, NY
Steel, Mary A. ... San Jose, CA
Steel, Michael J. ... San Francisco, CA
Steel, Philip G. ... Haddonfield, NJ
Steel, Richard D. ... Philadelphia, PA
Pittsburgh, PA
Steel, Robert W. ... Yuba City, CA
Steel, Rudnick & Ruben ... Philadelphia, PA
Pittsburgh, PA
Steel, Sally L. ... Lynchburg, VA
Steel, Sari J. ... Los Angeles, CA
Steel, Shawn ... Beverly Hills, CA
Steel, Simon A. ... New York, NY
Steel, Spencer M. ... Southfield, MI
Steel & Steel ... Nashville, AR
Steel & Steel ... Haddonfield, NJ
Steel, Tere Richardson ... Biloxi, MS

Steel, Terrence J. ... Akron, OH
Cleveland, OH
Steel, William L. ... Irvine, CA
Steele, Alan ... Middletown, CT
Steele, Albert N., Jr. ... Valparaiso, IN
Steele, Alexandria M. ... Dennis, MA
Steele, Alison M. ... St. Petersburg, FL
Steele, Allan L. ... Ventura, CA
Steele, Amanda K. ... Traverse City, MI
Steele, Anne E. ... San Bruno, CA
Steele, Anthony J. ... Clearwater, FL
Steele, Anthony R. ... Knoxville, TN
Steele, Arnold O. ... Bend, OR
Steele, Athornia, (Mr.) ... Columbus, OH
Steele, Bennett ... Yonkers, NY
Steele, Beth A. ... Norwich, CT
Steele, Betty K. ... Providence, RI
Steele, Brad D. ... Muncie, IN
Steele, Bradley T. ... Longview, TX
Steele, Brent E. ... Bedford, IN
Steele, Brice, IV ... Brighton, CO
Steele, Bruce J. ... Los Angeles, CA
Steele, Byron W. ... Bedford, IN
Steele, C. Carlyle ... Greenville, SC
Steele, C. Thomas, Jr. ... Burlington, NC
Steele, Carol B. ... Ada, MI
Steele, Carolyn S. ... Boise, ID
Steele, Cathy ... St. Louis, MO
Steele, Cathy, P.C., The Law Office of
St. Louis, MO
Steele, C. F. ... Houston, TX
Steele, Charles D. ... Van Wert, OH
Steele, Charles J. ... Washington, DC
Steele, Charles N. ... Washington, DC
Steele, Charles R. ... Clarksburg, WV
Steele, Cheryl D. ... Charlotte, NC
Steele, Christine Carey ... Cincinnati, OH
Steele, Clayton C. ... New York, NY
Steele, Clifford J. ... Atlanta, GA
Steele, Clifford J., A Prof. Corp., Law Offices of ... Atlanta, GA
Steele, Clifford R. ... Miami, FL
Steele, Craig A. ... Los Angeles, CA
Steele, Cynthia L.K. ... Toledo, OH
Steele, D. David ... San Francisco, CA
Steele, Dana E. ... Denver, CO
Steele, Daniel G. ... Department of Justice, Environment and Natural Resources Division, GV
Steele, Daniel P. ... Detroit, MI
Steele, Darren ... Stuart, FL
Steele, Dathard V. ... Columbus, OH
Steele, David F. ... Monroeville, AL
Steele, David H. ... Jackson, KY
Steele, David R. ... Covington, KY
Steele, Dawn C. ... Palo Alto, CA
Steele, Deborah Brewer ... Charlotte, NC
Steele, Deborah Pitcher ... Washington, DC
Steele, Deborah Williams ... Baltimore, MD
Steele, Denise A. ... Detroit, MI
Steele, Diena A. ... New York, NY
Steele, Donald B. ... Kansas City, MO
Steele, Donald H. ... Salt Lake City, UT
Steele, Donald W. ... Beverly Hills, CA
Steele, Donnalee R. ... San Francisco, CA
Steele, Douglas L. ... Washington, DC
Steele, Dwight C. ... Walnut Creek, CA
Steele, E. Boyd ... Grand Junction, CO
Steele, Eden C. ... Denver, CO
Steele, Elizabeth M. ... Englewood, CO
Steele, Eric D. ... Milwaukee, WI
Steele, Ethan ... Tucson, AZ
Steele, Eugene H. ... Fort Lauderdale, FL
Steele, Eugenia L. ... Los Angeles, CA
Steele, Floyd W. ... Flint, MI
Saginaw, MI
Steele, Fred W. ... Brighton, CO
Steele, Gary T. ... Pine Brook, NJ
Steele, George L. ... Culver City, CA
Steele, Glenn H. (Pete), Jr. ... Beaumont, TX
Steele, Gregory W. ... North Chicago, IL
Steele, H. John ... Washington, DC
Steele & Hanson, P.A.
Fort Lauderdale, FL
Miami, FL
Steele, Harriet M. W. ... Germantown, OH
Steele, Heidi J. ... Chicago, IL
Steele, Howard L., Jr. ... Houston, TX
Steele, J. Brian ... Merrillville, IN
Steele, J. Kent ... Idyllwild, CA
Steele, J. Rodman, Jr.
West Palm Beach, FL
Steele, Jackson N. ... Charlotte, NC
Steele, Jacqueline B. ... Plainview, NY
Steele, James P. ... Washington, DC
Steele, James T., Jr. ... Harrisburg, PA
Steele, James W. ... St. Louis, MO
Steele, James W. ... Conroe, TX
Steele, Janet L. ... McLean, VA
Steele, Jared Bentley Seneca
Pension Benefit Guaranty Corporation, Office of the General Counsel, GV
Steele, Jay Frederick ... Atlanta, GA
Steele, Jeffrey ... Sacramento, CA
Steele, Jeffrey A. ... Detroit, MI
Steele, Jeffrey P. ... Waltham, MA
Steele, Jerry ... Phoenix, AZ
Steele, Jill Humphreys ... Hastings, MI
Steele, Johan A. ... New York, NY
Steele, John C. ... Los Angeles, CA
Steele, John C. ... Denver, CO
Steele, John D. ... St. Louis, MO
Steele, John D., Jr. ... Buffalo, NY
Steele, John Donald ... Northumberland, PA
Steele, John E. ... Jacksonville, FL
Steele, John J. ... Palo Alto, CA
Steele, John M., (P.A.) ... Minneapolis, MN
Steele, John R. ... Plankinton, SD

Steele, John W. ... Fredericksburg, VA
Richmond, VA
Steele, John W., III ... Columbia, MD
Steele, John-Henry M. ... New Haven, CT
Steele, Joseph B. ... Erie, PA
Steele, Joseph W., V ... Los Angeles, CA
Steele, K. David ... Atlanta, GA
Steele, Karen A. ... Salem, OR
Steele, Karen J. ... Springfield, IL
Steele, Karen L. ... Altoona, PA
Steele, Katherine M. ... Seattle, WA
Steele, Kathie F. ... Oregon City, OR
Steele, Kelly Dean ... Iowa City, IA
Steele, Kendall D. ... Phoenix, AZ
Steele, Kevin E. ... Merrillville, IN
Steele, Kim D. ... Wichita, KS
Steele, Kimberly M. ... Tulsa, OK
Steele, Krista Dianne ... Houston, TX
Steele, Kurt D. ... Winnetka, IL
Steele, Kyle Christophen ... Dallas, TX
Steele, L. Denise ... Irving, TX
Steele, L. Marika ... Lafayette, LA
Houston, TX
Steele, Larry A. ... Vernal, UT
Steele, Larry J. ... Walnut Ridge, AR
Steele, Larry J. ... Decatur, GA
Steele, Lawrence B., III ... Georgetown, DE
Steele, Lawrence B., III, Professional Association ... Georgetown, DE
Steele, Lawrence J. ... Seattle, WA
Steele, Lewis F. ... Albany, NY
Steele, Linda Hopkins ... Olathe, CO
Steele, Lisa ... Dallas, TX
Steele, Lisa J. ... Bolton, MA
Steele, Lisa L. ... Pittsburgh, PA
Steele, Louise A. ... Sun Valley, CA
Steele, M. Kathleen ... Tuscaloosa, AL
Steele, Margaret L. ... Westerly, RI
Steele, Martha L. ... Richmond, VA
Steele, Mary E. ... Seattle, WA
Steele, Mary Jo H. ... Chicago, IL
Steele, Merilyn M. ... Irvine, CA
Steele, Michael H. ... Kosciusko, MS
Steele, Michael L. ... Foothill Ranch, CA
Steele, Michael W. ... Honolulu, HI
Steele, Molly ... Dallas, TX
Steele, Myron T. ... Dover, DE
Steele, Nevett, Jr. ... Towson, MD
Steele, Nevett, Jr., P.A. ... Towson, MD
Steele, Ney B. ... Chesterfield, SC
Steele & Page, P.C. ... Conroe, TX
Steele, Parker Blair ... Birmingham, AL
Steele, Patricia D.
Christiansted, St. Croix, VI
Steele, Patricia M. ... Washington, DC
Steele, Patrick J., The Law Offices of
Bakersfield, CA
Steele, Patrick K. ... Houston, TX
Steele, Patrick M. ... Tacoma, WA
Steele, Paul M. ... Los Gatos, CA
Steele, Perry L. ... Tulsa, OK
Steele, Philip L. ... Hartford, CT
Steele, R. Lawrence ... Merrillville, IN
Portage, IN
Steele, R. Michael ... Leawood, KS
Steele, R. Philip ... Alpha, IL
Steele, Ralph W., II ... Bozeman, MT
Steele, Randall P. ... Glen Carbon, IL
Steele, Reed F. ... Irving, TX
Steele, Rhonda V. ... Birmingham, AL
Steele, Richard A. ... Austin, TX
Steele, Richard G. ... Palo Alto, CA
Steele, Richard G. ... Cape Girardeau, MO
Steele, Richard M. ... Charleston, SC
Steele, Richard P. ... Houston, TX
Steele, Robert B. ... La Salle, IL
Steele, Robert D. ... New York, NY
Steele, Robert E., Jr. ... Macon, GA
Steele, Robert G. ... Clarksburg, WV
Steele, Robert J., Jr ... Cleveland, OH
Steele, Robert M. ... San Diego, CA
Steele, Robert M. ... Washington, DC
Nashville, TN
Steele, Robert P. ... Madison, WI
Steele, Roberta L. ... Oakland, CA
Steele, Robin ... South San Francisco, CA
Steele, Rodney J. ... Brookings, SD
Steele, Rodney R. ... Montgomery, AL
Steele, Roger G. ... Grand Island, NE
Steele, Russell E. ... Kirksville, MO
Steele & Sales, P.S. ... Seattle, WA
Steele, Sally A. ... Tunkhannock, PA
Steele, Sandra C. ... Boston, MA
Steele, Sarah O. ... Wichita, KS
Steele, Schuyler G. ... Newport, ME
Steele, Scott L. ... Brownwood, TX
Steele, Scott N. ... Portland, OR
Steele, Shari ... Washington, DC
Steele, Silcox & Browning, P.C.
Washington, DC
Steele, Spencer ... Lake Success, NY
Steele, Steele, McSoley & McSoley
Bedford, IN
Steele & Steele, P.C. ... Plankinton, SD
Steele, Stephen C. ... Marietta, GA
Steele, Steven J. ... Seattle, WA
Steele, Susan N. ... Plankinton, SD
Steele, Sydney L ... Indianapolis, IN
Steele, Thomas D. ... Nashville, TN
Steele, Thomas G., The Law Offices of
Clarksburg, WV
Steele, Thomas H. ... San Francisco, CA
Denver, CO
Steele, Thomas L. ... Wichita, KS
Steele, Thomas L. ... Columbus, OH
Steele, Thomas P. ... Northbrook, IL
Steele, Thomas T. ... Tampa, FL
Steele, Thomas Wardlaw ... Nashville, TN

Steele, Todd B. ... Brownwood, TX
Steele, Todd P. ... Refugio, TX
Steele, Tracy L. ... Washington, DC
Steele, Ulmschneider & Eberhard
Fort Wayne, IN
LaGrange, IN
Steele, Vickie R. ... Columbia, SC
Steele, W. Trent ... Palm Beach Gardens, FL
Steele, Walter ... Indianapolis, IN
Steele, Walter A. ... Denver, CO
Steele, Walter W., Jr. ... Dallas, TX
Steele, Wayne E. ... Crawfordsville, IN
Steele, Wendy A. ... Frederick, MD
Steele, William B., III ... Austin, TX
Steele, William H. ... Mobile, AL
Steele, William J. ... Columbus, OH
Steele, William Pressley, Jr. ... Anderson, SC
Steele, William S., Jr. ... Danbury, CT
Steele, William Steven ... Bryan, TX
Steele-Donner, Amy ... Miami, FL
Steeler, Jonathan H. ... Denver, CO
Steelhammer, Daniel C. ... Bend, OR
Steelhammer & Miller, A Professional Corporation ... Houston, TX
Steelhammer, Neva ... Houston, TX
Steelhammer, Robert H. ... Houston, TX
Steelman, Barry A. ... Chattanooga, TN
Steelman, Barry L. ... Baltimore, MD
Steelman, Barry L., P.A. ... Baltimore, MD
Towson, MD
Steelman, David C. ... North Andover, MA
Steelman, David L. ... Rolla, MO
Steelman, Dorman L. ... Salem, MO
Steelman, Frank ... Bryan, TX
Steelman & Gaunt ... Rolla, MO
Steelman, Henry ... Los Angeles, CA
Steelman, J. Robert ... Haymarket, VA
Steelman, Joe W. ... Houston, TX
Steelman, Kathryn Everett
Hot Sulphur Springs, CO
Steelman, Ken E. ... Irvine, CA
Steelman, Michael G. ... Bushnell, IL
Steelman, Robert C. ... Anchorage, AK
Steelman, Robert E. ... Greenville, SC
Steelman, Robert W. ... Grand Rapids, MI
Steelman, Ronald ... Laguna Niguel, CA
Steelman, Samuel C., Jr. ... College Park, MD
Steelman, Susan B. ... Birmingham, AL
Steelman, Thomas W., Jr. ... Blue Springs, MO
Steelmon, Edward C. ... Columbus, GA
Steely, Clay Martindale ... Houston, TX
Steely, E. Newton, Jr. ... Greenbelt, MD
Steely, Ellen C. ... Duncan, OK
Steely, Janice L. ... Baltimore, MD
Steely, Lisa Elizabeth ... Jacksonville, FL
Steely, Melody L. ... Circleville, OH
Steely, Rachel Powitzky ... Houston, TX
Steely, Robert L. ... Cleveland, OH
Steen, B. Gail ... Norfolk, NE
Steen, Barbara J. ... New York, NY
Steen, Bruce M. ... Charlotte, NC
Steen, Carl R. ... Irvine, CA
Steen, Charles H. ... Dallas, TX
Steen, Charles M. ... New Orleans, LA
Steen, Daniel K. ... Washington, DC
Steen, Daniel V. ... Akron, OH
Steen, David Jay, Jr. ... Tulsa, OK
Steen, David W. ... Tampa, FL
Steen, Deborah Ann ... Santa Cruz, CA
Steen, Edward A. ... Saddle Brook, NJ
Steen, Ellen B. ... Washington, DC
Steen, Frances P. ... Hartford, CT
Steen, Geraldine C. ... Minnetonka, MN
Steen, Irene C. ... Richmond, KY
Steen, Jason A. ... Anchorage, AK
Steen, Jeffrey C. ... Chicago, IL
Steen, Jeffrey S. ... Uniondale, NY
Steen, John T., Jr. ... San Antonio, TX
Steen, Jon R. ... Boardman, OH
Steen, Jonathan O. ... Jackson, TN
Steen, Julia S. ... Boston, MA
Steen, Larry D. ... Elkhorn, WI
Steen, Leslie W. ... Little Rock, AR
Steen, Lias J. ... Houston, TX
Steen, Lisa Marie ... Hermosa Beach, CA
Steen, Marilyn D. ... Pacifica, CA
Steen & McShane, L.L.C.
New Orleans, LA
Steen, Nancy E. ... Hattiesburg, MS
Steen, P. Russell ... Mount Olive, AL
Steen, Pamela L. ... Patchogue, NY
Steen, Paul E. ... Tempe, AZ
Steen Reynolds & Dalehite, LLP
Jackson, MS
Steen, Richard H. ... Willingboro, NJ
Steen, Ronald G., Jr. ... Huntsville, AL
Steen, Samuel ... Miami, FL
Steen, Samuel G., Jr. ... Catonsville, MD
Steen, Samuel, P.A. ... Miami, FL
Steen, Sharon L. ... Arlington, VA
Steen, Stephen M., Jr. ... Odessa, TX
Steen, Tempe B. ... Bethany Beach, DE
Steen, William T. ... New Orleans, LA
Steenbergh, James C. ... Catskill, NY
Steenbergh, Robert M. ... New York, NY
Steenblik, Gerrit M. ... Phoenix, AZ
Steenblik, Roelof Scott ... Salt Lake City, UT
Steenburg, Earl D., Law Offices of
Ballston Spa, NY
Steenburg, Edward D. ... Ogallala, NE
Steenburg, Thomas N. ... Hartford, CT
Steen-Dente, Ellen M. ... Peabody, MA
Steenhoek, Preston J. ... Phoenix, AZ
Steenken, F. Lewis ... Fayetteville, AR
Steenkolk, Tony J. ... Boise, ID
Steenlage, Keith E. ... Westmont, NJ
Steenland, Brad P. ... Hasbrouck Heights, NJ
Steenland, Catherine B. ... Roseville, MI

Steenland, Deborah S. ... Boston, MA
Steenland, Douglas M. ... St. Paul, MN
Steenland, Peter R., Jr.
Department of Justice, Civil Division, GV
Steen Melville, Margaret ... Boston, MA
Steeno, David L. ... Big Rapids, MI
Steeno, Michael P. ... St. Louis, MO
Steenrod & Darling, P.C. ... Denver, CO
Steenrod, Ralston W. ... Louisville, KY
Steenrod, Robert L., Jr. ... Denver, CO
Steensland, Greg W. ... Council Bluffs, IA
Steenson, Anita Flannigan ... Milford, CT
Steenson, Brian A. ... Portland, OR
Steenson, Brian A., P.C. ... Portland, OR
Steenson, Charles Thomas ... Lincoln, NE
Steenson, Daniel V. ... Boise, ID
Steenson, Mary E. ... Minneapolis, MN
Steenson and Schumann ... Portland, OR
Steenson, Todd D. ... Chicago, IL
Steenson, Tom ... Portland, OR
Steep, Mary Ann ... Mequon, WI
Steer, Dulaney G. "Dee" ... Fort Worth, TX
Steer, John R. ... United States Senate, Senatorial Assistants, GV
Steer, Marc H. ... Deerfield, IL
Steer, Reginald D. ... San Francisco, CA
Steer, Richard L. ... New York, NY
Steer, Susan R. ... San Francisco, CA
Steere, Allen C. ... Fort Wayne, IN
Steere, Bradley L. ... Glocester, RI
Steere, Douglas N. ... Bedford, NH
Steere, J. Douglas
United States Court Of Appeals For The Federal Circuit, GV
Steere, Jennifer K. ... Columbus, OH
Steere, Kimberly Sue ... Portage, IN
Steere, Martin E. ... Los Angeles, CA
Steere, Paul W. ... Seattle, WA
Steere, Peter K. ... Seattle, WA
Steere, Robert D. ... Springfield, IL
Steerman, Amy F. ... Collingswood, NJ
Philadelphia, PA
Philadelphia, PA
Steerman, David J. ... Philadelphia, PA
Steerman, Donald L. ... Lamar, CO
Steerman & Felixon, P.C. ... Philadelphia, PA
Steerman, William ... Philadelphia, PA
Steers, George W. ... Seattle, WA
Steers, Lester L. B. ... Lebanon, OR
Steers, Newton I., Jr. ... Bethesda, MD
Steers, R. Lee, Jr. ... Franklin, KY
Steers & Steers, P.S.C. ... Franklin, KY
Steers Sullivan, Professional Corporation
Indianapolis, IN
Noblesville, IN
Steese, Charles W. ... Denver, CO
Steese, Steven M. ... Los Angeles, CA
Steeve, Rolf G., Jr. ... Vista, CA
Steevens, Mark James ... Newport Beach, CA
Steever, Harry S. ... Concord, NH
Steever, Scott Loren ... Santa Rosa, CA
Steeves, Frank L. ... Milwaukee, WI
Steeves & Graff ... Standish, ME
Steeves, Linda M. ... Plymouth, MA
Steeves, Michael B. ... Clearwater, FL
Steeves, Michael B., P.A. ... Clearwater, FL
Steeves, Myron E. ... Newport Beach, CA
Steeves, Richard G. ... Standish, ME
Steeves, Robert F.
Department Of Health And Human Services, Food & Drug Administration, GV
Steeves, Robert J., Jr. ... Boston, MA
Stefan, Gregory D. ... Virginia Beach, VA
Stefan, Karl L. ... Reading, PA
Stefan, Marc A. ... Washington, DC
Stefan, Pamela ... Vassar, MI
Stefan, Robt. N. ... San Ramon, CA
Stefan, Victor F. ... San Jose, CA
Stefanacci, Mark E. ... Ho-Ho-Kus, NJ
Stefancin, Jocelyn ... Wooster, OH
Stefancin, Robert M. ... Akron, OH
Stefaneas, Telly ... Chicago, IL
Stefanelli, Frank D. ... Roseland, NJ
Stefanelli, Richard F. ... Gaithersburg, MD
Stefanelli, Thomas M. ... Palm Springs, CA
Stefani, Brady G. ... Troy, MI
Stefani, Catherine M. ... Walnut Creek, CA
Stefani, Daniel R. ... Chicago, IL
Stefani, John N. ... Albany, NY
Stefani, Kristopher S. ... Brockton, MA
Stefani, Laura A. ... Washington, DC
Stefani, Linda B. ... Chicago, IL
Stefani, Michael L. ... Troy, MI
Stefani, Randall H. ... Des Moines, IA
Stefani, Raymond R. ... Cedar Rapids, IA
Stefani, Raymond R., II
Cedar Rapids, IA
Stefani, Richard A. ... Cedar Rapids, IA
Stefani, Robert J., Jr. ... New Orleans, LA
Stefani, Robert L. ... Bloomfield Hills, MI
Stefani, Ronald L. ... San Jose, CA
Stefaniak, Alan L. ... Park Ridge, IL
Stefaniak, David A. ... Medina, NY
Stefaniak, James D. ... Columbus, OH
Stefaniak, Thomas P., Jr. ... Crown Point, IN
Stefanic, Michael P., II ... Boise, ID
Stefanich, Carol A. ... Ocean Township, NJ
Stefanich, Matthew W. ... Joliet, IL
Stefanich, Matthew W., Jr. ... Chicago, IL
Stefanich, McGarry, Wols, Okrei & Braun, Ltd.
Joliet, IL
Stefanick, Jennifer L. ... Newark, NJ
Stefanik, Debra L. ... Peoria, IL
Stefanik, Dennis J. ... Oakdale, PA
Stefanik, Thomas J., Jr. ... Cleveland, OH
Stefanini, John A. ... Framingham, MA
Stefanis, Maria S. ... Norfolk, VA
Stefaniuk, Daniel M. ... Chattanooga, TN

Stefanki, John E. ... Sacramento, CA
Stefanki, John E., A Professional Corporation
Sacramento, CA
Stefankiewicz, David A. ... Wildwood, NJ
Stefanko, Michael J. ... Massillon, OH
Stefanko, Robert J. ... Pittsburgh, PA
Stefano, Joseph M. ... New York, NY
Stefano, Marc A. ... Fresno, CA
Stefano, Vincent, Jr. ... Burbank, CA
Stefanon, Anthony ... Harrisburg, PA
Stefanon, Robert M. ... Herminie, PA
Stefanos, Chris L. ... Downers Grove, IL
Stefanoudakis, Lori S. ... Denver, CO
Stefanoudakis, Michael Nikolaos
Denver, CO
Stefanovski, Laura Popoff ... Erie, PA
Stefanowicz, Elizabeth W. ... Washington, DC
Stefanowicz, John F. ... Wyomissing, PA
Stefanowicz, Lydia C. ... Florham Park, NJ
Stefans, Arthur ... Chicago, IL
Stefans, Donald J. ... Chicago, IL
Stefans, Laurance A. ... Chicago, IL
Stefans & Stefans ... Chicago, IL
Stefanski, Brett A. ... Crowley, LA
Stefanski, D. Kim ... Canton, OH
Cleveland, OH
Youngstown, OH
Stefanski, Donald S. ... Buffalo, NY
Stefanski, J. Michael ... Crowley, LA
Stefanski, Scott A. ... Crowley, LA
Stefanski, Stephen A. ... Crowley, LA
Stefanski, Thomas J. ... Los Angeles, CA
Stefanson, Plambeck & Foss
Moorhead, MN
Stefanson, Randolph E. ... Moorhead, MN
Stefany, David J. ... Tampa, FL
Steff, Alfred L., Jr. ... Beaver, PA
Steffan & Associates ... Washington, DC
Fairfax, VA
Steffan, Edwin F. ... Alden, NY
Steffan, Frederick V. ... Everett, WA
Steffan, Genevieve R. ... Clarence, NY
Steffan, John D. ... Washington, DC
Fairfax, VA
Steffan, Joseph C. ... Hartford, CT
Steffan, Kim K. ... Hillsborough, NC
Steffan, Michael N. ... Devils Lake, ND
Steffan, Richard D. ... Auburn, CA
Steffan, Thomas A. ... Alden, NY
Steffan, Thomas W. ... Buffalo, NY
Steffanetta, Gary Lee ... Farmingdale, NY
Steffas, Irene Arfaras ... Roswell, GA
Steffe, Eric K. ... Washington, DC
Steffe, Juliette M. ... Chicago, IL
Steffe, Shirley A. ... Des Moines, IA
Steffee, Laura J. ... Columbus, OH
Steffel, James J. ... Battle Creek, MI
Steffel, Jeffrey J. ... East Lansing, MI
Steffel, Robert A. ... Madison, WI
Steffel, Sherry ... Madison, WI
Steffel and Steffel ... Battle Creek, MI
Steffel, Vern J., Jr. ... Battle Creek, MI
Steffen, Bernard E. ... Minneapolis, MN
Steffen, Catherine ... Virginia Beach, VA
Steffen, Daniel P. ... Osceola, WI
Steffen, David T. ... San Francisco, CA
Steffen, Donald K. ... San Francisco, CA
Steffen, E. Andrew ... Indianapolis, IN
Steffen, Eugene A. ... Manassas, VA
Steffen, F. John, Jr. ... Elgin, IL
Steffen, Frederick J. ... Elgin, IL
Steffen, Gary E. ... Dallas, TX
Steffen, James C. ... Minneapolis, MN
Steffen, James R. ... Minneapolis, MN
Steffen, Jeffrey C. ... Portland, OR
Steffen, John K. ... Minneapolis, MN
Steffen, John R. ... Frankfort, KY
Steffen, John T. ... Las Vegas, NV
Steffen, Joseph J., Jr. ... Blacksburg, VA
Steffen, Kelly & Steffen ... Elgin, IL
Steffen, Leo J., Jr. ... Des Moines, IA
Steffen, Mala B. ... Nazareth, PA
Steffen, Mark R. ... Kankakee, IL
Steffen, Marvin E. ... Norfolk, VA
Steffen, Michael H. ... Sacramento, CA
Steffen, Phillip J. ... Department of the Army, Office, Chief of Engineers/Headquarters, U.S. Army Corps of Engineers, GV
Steffen, Phillip T., Jr. ... Davenport, IA
Steffen, Richard A. ... Des Moines, IA
Steffen, Sally A. ... Philadelphia, PA
Steffen, Scott T. ... Modesto, CA
Steffen, Suzanne M. ... Philadelphia, PA
Steffen, Thomas L. ... Las Vegas, NV
Steffen, Victoria A.
Cape May Court House, NJ
Steffen, Wallace R. ... Cleveland, OH
Steffen, Zona ... Los Angeles, CA
Steffenhagen, John J. ... Minneapolis, MN
Steffenhagen, Timothy J. ... Minneapolis, MN
Steffens, Betty J. ... Tallahassee, FL
Steffens, John L. ... Libertyville, IL
Steffens, John S. ... West Des Moines, IA
Steffens, Karen M. ... Charlotte, NC
Steffens, Paul A. ... Charlotte, NC
Steffens, Richard J. ... Menasha, WI
Steffens, Roger S. ... Trenton, NJ
Steffens, Ronald W. ... Waukesha, WI
Steffens, Thomas L. ... Edina, MN
Steffens, William Vern ... Broken Bow, NE
Steffensen, Brian W., P.C.
Salt Lake City, UT
Steffensen, D. David, Jr. ... Irvine, CA
Steffensen, David W., P.C.
Salt Lake City, UT
Steffensen, Herman & Doggett, LLC
Boston, MA
Steffensen, Jon E. ... Boston, MA

Steffensen • Law • Office
Salt Lake City, UT
Steffensen, Mark A. ... New York, NY
Steffens-Guzmán, Carlos A. ... San Juan, PR
Steffenson, Dane L. ... Atlanta, GA
Steffenson, Douglas S. ... Chicago, IL
Steffenson, Mark V. ... Minneapolis, MN
Steffenson, Paul C. ... Minneapolis, MN
Steffes, James C. ... Creston, IA
Steffes, Kenyon & Nielsen, P.C. ... Creston, IA
Steffes, Larry R. ... Washington, DC
Steffes & Macmurdo ... Baton Rouge, LA
Monroe, LA
Steffes, Paul R. ... Cleveland, OH
Steffes, Richard W. ... Beaver Dam, WI
Steffes, William E. ... Baton Rouge, LA
Steffey, Charles E. ... Minneapolis, MN
Steffey, Fred H. ... Jacksonville, FL
Steffey, Fred H., Professional Association
Jacksonville, FL
Steffey, Matthew S. ... Jackson, MS
Steffey, Susan Latham ... Jackson, MS
Steffin, William C., (A Professional Corporation) ... Los Angeles, CA
Steffish, George John, III ... Butler, PA
Steffl, Flood & Gerlach, P.C. ... Troy, MI
Steffl, James C. ... Troy, MI
Stefflre, Greg P. ... Long Beach, CA
Stefflre, Greg P., A Law Corporation
Long Beach, CA
Stefflre, James P. ... Reno, NV
Stefflre, Karen ... New York, NY
Steffy, Edwin T., Jr. ... Baltimore, MD
Steffy, Paul M. ... Los Angeles, CA
Steffy, Willis ... Canton, OH
Stefin, Roger H. ... Fort Lauderdale, FL
Stefko, Daniel P. ... Pittsburgh, PA
Stefl, Scott Richard ... Mentor, OH
Steflik, Joseph J., Jr. ... Binghamton, NY
Stefonek, Karen Marie ... Oakland, CA
Stefonowicz, Michel W. ... Crosby, ND
Steg, Betsy M. ... Clearwater, FL
Stegall, Charles T. ... Phoenix, AZ
Stegall, Dale L. ... Brentwood, TN
Stegall, Daniel Richard ... Chesapeake, VA
Stegall, Daniel Richard, A Professional Law Corporation ... Chesapeake, VA
Stegall, Donald L. ... Fort Worth, TX
Stegall, James Ron ... Chattanooga, TN
Stegall, Jo H., III ... Rome, GA
Stegall, Laurie R. ... Greensboro, NC
Stegall, Lisa A. ... Dallas, TX
Stegall, Martha Bost ... Columbus, MS
Tupelo, MS
Stegall, Nancy J. ... Fresno, CA
Stegall, Randall C. ... Fort Worth, TX
Stegall, Ray A. ... Knoxville, TN
Stegall, Whitney ... Murfreesboro, TN
Stegall, William A., Jr. ... Salt Lake City, UT
Stege & Associates Co., L.P.A.
Cleveland, OH
Stege, Charles E. ... Villa Park, IL
Stege, Edward Richard ... Cleveland, OH
Stege, George R., III ... Bainbridge Island, WA
Seattle, WA
Stege, Kurt M. ... Madison, WI
Stege, Scott H. ... Majuro, TT
Stege, William L. ... Pompano Beach, FL
Stegeland, Garry J. ... Weehawken, NJ
Stegelmann, Bodie J. ... Goshen, IN
Stegeman, Christian B. ... Cincinnati, OH
Stegeman, Russell S. ... Gretna, LA
Stegeman, Toni I. ... St. Louis, MO
Stegemann, Patricia B. ... Chittenango, NY
Stegemann, Traci J. ... Washington, DC
Stegemoeller, Andrew B. ... Albany, NY
Stegemoeller, Sarah Mueller ... Chicago, IL
Stegemoller, Sharon E. ... Danville, IN
Stegen, Monti J. ... San Francisco, CA
Steger, Betsy S. ... Mayville, NY
Steger, Brian M. ... Houston, TX
Steger, Catherine B. ... Reston, VA
Steger, Christopher H. ... Chattanooga, TN
Steger, Evan E. ... Indianapolis, IN
Steger, Hugh L. ... Dallas, TX
Steger, Jeffrey I. ... Department of Justice, Antitrust Division, GV
Steger, Karen O'Brien ... Stuart, FL
Steger, Mark J. ... Chicago, IL
Steger, Mary Lynn ... Clinton, IA
Steger, Merlin A. ... Des Moines, IA
Steger, Michael A. ... Pittsburgh, PA
Steger, Michael D. ... Santa Monica, CA
Steger, S. Martijn ... Columbus, OH
Steger, Sam T. ... Stuart, FL
Steger & Steger, P.A. ... Stuart, FL
Steger, Steven G. ... Chicago, IL
Steger, Susan S. J. ... Macon, GA
Steger, Susan Z. ... San Francisco, CA
Steger, William K. ... Bloomington, IN
Steger, William M. ... Tyler, TX
Steggall, Walter J., Jr. ... Cedar Rapids, IA
Steggerda, Todd R. ... Philadelphia, PA
Stegich, Deborah A. ... New York, NY
Stegich, Stephen R., III ... New York, NY
Stegina, Gary W. ... East Haven, CT
Stegink, Lisa A. ... Chicago, IL
Steglich, David M. ... Minneapolis, MN
Stegmaier, David D. ... Honolulu, HI
Stegmaier, Jennifer S. ... Chicago, IL
Stegmaier, Patricia Gray
West Des Moines, IA
Stegman, Brian W. ... Mount Olive, NJ
Stegman & Caragozian ... Los Angeles, CA
Stegman, Catherine ... Lincoln, NE
Stegman, Clement A., Jr. ... Chicago, IL
Stegman, Daphne M. ... Beverly Hills, CA
Stegman, David R ... San Diego, CA
Stegman, Edwin B. ... Los Angeles, CA
Stegman, James R. ... Bingham Farms, MI
Stegman, James R., P.C.
Bingham Farms, MI
Stegman, Laurie Michelle
Washington, DC
Stegman, Mark J. ... Belleville, IL
Stegman, Michael J. ... Cincinnati, OH
Stegman, Michael J., Co., LPA
Cincinnati, OH
Stegman, Richard W. ... Los Angeles, CA
Stegmayer, John E. ... Saugerties, NY
Stegmeier, Eleanor A. ... Costa Mesa, CA
Stegmeyer, Charles F. ... Belleville, IL
Stegmeyer, Charles H., Jr. ... Belleville, IL
Stegmeyer & Stegmeyer ... Belleville, IL
Stegner, Dennis E. ... Springfield, OH
Stegner, Jean N. ... Zionsville, IN
Stegner, John R. ... Moscow, ID
Stegner, Michael E. ... Camden, SC
Stegossi, Laura E. ... Philadelphia, PA
Stehl, Richard L. ... New York, NY
Stehle, William L. ... Columbus, OH
Stehle, William L., Co., L.P.A.
Columbus, OH
Stehlik, Anna L. ... Hastings, NE
Stehlik, Frederick D. ... Omaha, NE
Stehlik, Galen E. ... Grand Island, NE
Stehlik, Jerry N. ... Seattle, WA
Stehlik, L. Joe ... Pawnee City, NE
Stehlik, Noreene C. ... Department of Justice, Tax Division, GV
Stehling, M. Scott ... Kerrville, TX
Stehmer, Karl H. ...
National Aeronautics And Space Administration, GV
Stehno, Richard G. ... Lapeer, MI
Stehr, Ayn W. ... Baton Rouge, LA
Stehr, Donald L. ... Grosse Pointe, MI
Stehr, Judith I. ... Los Angeles, CA
Stehura, Janelle K. ... Indianapolis, IN
Stehura, Paul ... Columbus, OH
Steib, Charles H. ... St. Louis, MO
Steib, Curt F. ... San Angelo, TX
Steib, Michael B. ... Middletown, NJ
Steib, Michael B., P.A. ... Middletown, NJ
Steib, Raymond S., Jr. ... Gretna, LA
Steib, Sylvia Taylor ... Reserve, LA
Steiber, Richard I. ... Bridgeport, CT
Steiber & Schopick ... Bridgeport, CT
Steiber, Stanley J. ... Reno, NV
Steich, Thomas J. ... Rockville, MD
Steichen, Mark J. ... Madison, WI
Steichen, Mary J. ... Dallas, TX
Steichen, Randall R. ... Seattle, WA
Steichen, Thomas E. ... Tulsa, OK
Steichen, Thomas F. ... Minneapolis, MN
Steiden, Eric A. ... Cincinnati, OH
Steider & Jakob, P.C. ... Albuquerque, NM
Steider, Timothy D. ... Albuquerque, NM
Steidl, Daniel H. ... Bronxville, NY
Steidl, Kenneth ... Pittsburgh, PA
Steidl & Steinberg ... Pittsburgh, PA
Steidl, Thomas F. ... Madison, WI
Steidle, Lucy M. ... St. Louis, MO
Steidle, William A., Jr. ... Pittsburgh, PA
Steidley, J. Dwayne ... Claremore, OK
Steidley, Jeffrey W. ... Houston, TX
Steidley, Julie A. ... Midland, TX
Steidley ★ Kim Law Firms, The
Houston, TX
Steidley & Neal ... McAlester, OK
Steidley, W. G. "Gil", Jr. ... McAlester, OK
Steidlmayer, Leo ... Colusa, CA
Steidlmayer, Mark G. ... Yuba City, CA
Steidtmann, Charles E. ... San Francisco, CA
Steier, Alan E. ... Santa Rosa, CA
Steier, Donald H. ... Los Angeles, CA
Steier, Douglas B. ... Fort Myers, FL
Steier, Guy R. ... Beloit, KS
Steier, Larry J. ... Omaha, NE
Steier, Mark S. ... West Hartford, CT
Steiert, James T. ... Lakewood, CO
Steiert, Jan N. ... Denver, CO
Steiert, Robert M. ... Littleton, CO
Steif, Paul ... Flushing, NY
Steifman, Daniel A. ... Brooklyn, NY
Steig, A. Bret ... Westfield, NJ
Steig, Thomas A. ... Long Beach, CA
Steigelfest, Jack G. ... Hartford, CT
Steigenberger, Maria N. ... Dallas, TX
Steiger, Andrew R. ... Wayne, NJ
Steiger, Daniel N. ... Cleveland, OH
Steiger, David A. ... Chicago, IL
Steiger, David J. ... Sandusky, OH
Steiger, Frederick M. ... St. Louis, MO
Steiger, Gene L., (Ltd.) ... Flagstaff, AZ
Steiger, James G. ... Norfolk, VA
Steiger, Joan C. ... Springfield, MA
Steiger, John W. ... Portland, OR
Steiger, Jon ... Manasquan, NJ
Steiger, Jon Robert ... Bloomfield Hills, MI
Steiger, Jonathan Miller
Federal Trade Commission, Office of the General Counsel, GV
Steiger, Joseph R. ... Chicago, IL
Steiger, Mirit D. ... New York, NY
Steiger, Norman A. ... Rockville Centre, NY
Steiger, Robert C. ... Philadelphia, PA
Steiger, Robert D. ... San Antonio, TX
Steiger, Sheldon G. ... Cleveland, OH
Steiger, Steiger & Meyers ... Mercersburg, PA
Steiger, Susan J. ... New York, NY
Steiger, Thomas B. ... Mercersburg, PA
Steiger, Thomas B., Jr. ... Mercersburg, PA
Steiger, Walt A. ... Los Angeles, CA
Steiger, William S. ... Philadelphia, PA
Steiger, Zev ... Highland Park, IL
Steigerwald, David P.
Colorado Springs, CO
Steigerwald, James H. ... Philadelphia, PA
Steigerwald, Jean M. ... Dayton, OH
Steigerwald, Michelle L.
San Francisco, CA
Steigerwald, Robert S. ... Chicago, IL
Steigerwald, Steven A. ... Garden City, NY
Steigerwalt, Debra A. ... Los Angeles, CA
Steigerwalt, Wardell F. ... New Tripoli, PA
Steiglehner, Thomas J. ... Arkville, NY
Steigleman, Walter A.
Fort Walton Beach, FL
Pensacola, FL
Steigleman, Walter A., P.A.
Fort Walton Beach, FL
Pensacola, FL
Steigler, Lowell E. ... Miami, FL
Steiglitz, Eric B. ... New York, NY
Steigman, Elizabeth C. ... New York, NY
Steigman, Ernest R. ... New York, NY
Steigman, Jennifer E. ... Aventura, FL
Boca Raton, FL
Fort Lauderdale, FL
West Palm Beach, FL
Steigman, Meredith L. ... New York, NY
Steigman, Richard M. ... New York, NY
Steigman, William F. ... Brooklyn, NY
Steigmann, Michael A. ... Chicago, IL
Steigmann, Robert J. ... Urbana, IL
Steigmeyer, Paul S. ... Fort Wayne, IN
Steigner, Carolyn Butler ... Lexington, SC
Steiker, Andrew R. ... Granada Hills, CA
Steiker, Carol S. ... Cambridge, MA
Steiker, James G., & Associates
Philadelphia, PA
Steil, George K., Jr. ... Janesville, WI
Steil, George K., Sr. ... Janesville, WI
Steil, John R. ... Janesville, WI
Steil, Paul W. ... St. Cloud, MN
Steilberg, Peter, III ... Seattle, WA
Steilen, James R. ... Minneapolis, MN
Steiling, Kevin ... Boston, MA
Steiman, Henry M. ... Los Angeles, CA
Steiman, Michael ... Philadelphia, PA
Steiman, Susan H.
Federal Communications Commission, Office of the General Counsel, GV
Steimel, James L. ... Waukesha, WI
Steimel, Joe B. ... Wichita Falls, TX
Steimel Law Office ... Millersburg, OH
Steimel, Lyndon B. ... Phoenix, AZ
Steimel, Norman C., III ... St. Charles, MO
Steimel, Samuel M. ... Millersburg, OH
Steimel, Walter E. ... Washington, DC
Steimel, Walter E. ... Fort Worth, TX
Steimer, Elizabeth A. ... New Kensington, PA
Steimer, Natacha D. ... Washington, DC
Steimer, William M. ... Charlotte, NC
Steimle, Andrew J. ... Manitowoc, WI
Stein, A. William ... Ross, CA
Stein, Aaron J. ... Atlanta, GA
Stein, Aaron Lee ... Gaithersburg, MD
Stein, Abbe Pomerance ... New York, NY
Stein, Adam ... Chapel Hill, NC
Stein, Adam I. ... New York, NY
Stein, Adam J. ... New York, NY
Stein, Adrienne ... Santa Cruz, CA
Stein, Aimee D. ... Miami, FL
Stein, Alan Curtis ... Manhasset, NY
Stein, Alan J. ... New York, NY
Stein, Alan L. ... Tucson, AZ
Stein, Alan L. ... Denver, CO
Stein, Alan L. ... Orangeburg, NY
Stein, Alan M. ... Williston Park, NY
Stein, Alec C. ... Los Angeles, CA
Stein, Alexander E. ... Philadelphia, PA
Stein, Alison J. ... Los Angeles, CA
Stein, Allan J. ... Washington, DC
Stein, Allan M. ... Miami, FL
Stein, Allan R. ... Camden, NJ
Stein, Allison Zousmer ... Chicago, IL
Stein, Alvin M. ... New York, NY
Stein, Amy ... Lauderhill, FL
Stein, Amy L. ... Encino, CA
Stein, Andrew D. ... Woodland Hills, CA
Stein, Andrew L. ... New York, NY
Stein, Andrew M. ... Bellflower, CA
Stein, Anthony Asher ... Kansas City, MO
Stein, Arland T. ... Pittsburgh, PA
Stein, Arnold B. ... Chicago, IL
Stein, Arnold M. ... Morristown, NJ
Stein, Arnold P. ... Maitland, FL
Stein, Arthur ... Pittsfield, MA
Stein, Arthur ... Forked River, NJ
Stein, Arthur, & Associates, Law Offices
Forked River, NJ
Toms River, NJ
Stein, Aryeh E. ... Baltimore, MD
Stein, Barbara E. ... Mamaroneck, NY
Stein, Barbara F. ... Los Angeles, CA
Stein, Barbara Flum ... Collingdale, PA
Stein, Barry A. ... Miami, FL
Stein, Barry A. ... Philadelphia, PA
Stein, Barry G. ... Washington, DC
Stein, Barry J. ... Atlanta, GA
Stein & Battalia ... Larchmont, NY
Stein, Benjamin ... Forest Hills, NY
Stein, Bennett L. ... Newport News, VA
Stein, Bernard Dane ... Miami, FL
Stein, Bernard S., S.C. ... Milwaukee, WI
Stein, Bernice B. ... Roseland, NJ
Stein, Bliablias, McGuire, Pantages & Gigl, LLP ... Livingston, NJ
Stein, Bobbie ... San Francisco, CA
Stein, Bonnie S. ... Morrisville, PA
Stein, Bradley H. ... Miami, FL
Stein, Brett B. ... Memphis, TN
Stein, Brian D. ... Oakland, CA
Stein, Bruce ... Kalamazoo, MI
Stein, Burton ... Plymouth Meeting, PA
Stein, Burton K. ... West Conshohocken, PA
Stein, Carey M. ... Chicago, IL
Stein, Carl M. ... Sacramento, CA
Stein, Carolyn Johnson ... San Francisco, CA
Stein, Carolyn Stafford ... Boston, MA
Stein, Carrie A. ... Bloomington, IN
Stein & Casciola ... San Luis Obispo, CA
Stein, Cathy McNeil ... Chicago, IL
Stein, Charles D. ... Chicago, IL
Stein, Charles F., III ... Towson, MD
Stein & Cherney, Ltd. ... Chicago, IL
Stein, Cheryl D. ... Washington, DC
Stein, Cheryl L. ... Buffalo, NY
Stein, Chris ... Columbus, TX
Stein, Cliff M. ... Voorhees, NJ
Stein, Clifford A. ... Amarillo, TX
Stein, Clifford H. ... New York, NY
Stein & Cohen ... Philadelphia, PA
Stein, Craig ... New York, NY
Stein, Craig D. ... Fort Lauderdale, FL
Stein, Craig Edward ... Miami Beach, FL
Stein, Craig Edward, P.A. ... Miami, FL
Miami Beach, FL
Stein, Craig J. ... Los Angeles, CA
Stein, Cynthia Weiss ... Norristown, PA
Stein, Daniel J. ... Greensboro, NC
Stein, Daniel N. ... San Francisco, CA
Stein, David ... New York, NY
Stein, David ... Philadelphia, PA
Stein, David A. ... Oakland, CA
Stein, David A. ... Washington, DC
Stein, David A. ... New York, NY
Stein, David A. ... New York, NY
Stein, David D. ... San Francisco, CA
Stein, David D. ... Milwaukee, WI
Stein, David H. ... Newark, NJ
Stein, David J. ... New City, NY
Stein, David J., Sr. ... Milford, IA
Stein, David John, Jr. ... Milford, IA
Stein, David K., & Associates
Columbus, OH
Stein, David L. ... New York, NY
Stein, David M. ... Irvine, CA
Stein, David M. ... Chicago, IL
Stein, David S. ... Stamford, CT
Stein, Deborah M. ... Des Moines, IA
Stein, Debra B. ... Detroit, MI
Stein, Dennis L. ... New City, NY
New York, NY
Stein, Deon R. ... Sacramento, CA
Stein, Diana E. ... Washington, DC
Stein, Dinah S. ... Miami, FL
Stein, Donald J. ... Cherry Hill, NJ
Stein, Donald M. ... Canton, OH
Stein, Donald S. ... Washington, DC
Stein, Douglas E. ... Sacramento, CA
Stein, Douglas H. ... Miami, FL
Stein, Douglas W. ... Albany, NY
Utica, NY
Stein, E. William ... Portland, OR
Stein, Edward A. ... Clifton, NJ
Stein, Edward I. ... Northbrook, IL
Stein, Edward J. ... New York, NY
Stein, Edward K. ... Covington, VA
Stein, Edward M. ... Satellite Beach, FL
Stein, Edward R. ... Ann Arbor, MI
Stein, Edward S. ... Norfolk, VA
Stein, Edward T., Law Offices of
Chicago, IL
Stein, Edwin R. ... Rockville Centre, NY
Stein, Eileen M. ... Shady Side, MD
Stein, Elaine F. ... New York, NY
Stein, Elaine M. ... Freehold, NJ
Stein, Eleanor ... Albany, NY
Stein, Eleanor B. ... Kokomo, IN
Stein, Elias H. ... Philadelphia, PA
Stein, Elizabeth ... Department of Justice, Civil Division, GV
Stein, Elizabeth Ruf ... Miami, FL
Stein, Ellen Dennis ... Baltimore, MD
Stein, Elliott V. ... New York, NY
Stein, Ellyn J. ... Los Angeles, CA
Stein, Eric ... Boise, ID
Stein, Eric ... Ann Arbor, MI
Stein, Eric L. ... Dallas, TX
Stein, Ernest D. ... Livingston, NJ
Stein, Ernest R. ... Akron, OH
Stein, Estelle B. ... Brooklyn, NY
Stein, Ethan D. ... Florham Park, NJ
Stein, Eugene H. ... Minneapolis, MN
Stein, Eugene P. ... New York, NY
Stein, F. Robert ... New York, NY
Stein & Flugge, LLP ... Los Angeles, CA
Stein, Ford, Schaaf & Towzey, L.L.P.
Clearwater, FL
St. Petersburg, FL
Tampa, FL
Stein, Frederick M. ... Philadelphia, PA
Stein, Frederick W. ... Oak Brook, IL
Stein, Frederick W. ... Wheaton, IL
Stein, G. Barker, Jr. ... Montrose, AL
Stein, Gail E. ... Nashville, NC
Stein, Gary A. ... Washington, DC
Rockville, MD
Stein, Gary E. ... Columbus, OH
Stein, Gary L. ... Pottstown, PA
Stein, Gary M. ... Miami, FL
Stein, Gary S. ... Hackensack, NJ
Stein, Gayle Baumgarten
Philadelphia, PA
Stein, Geoffrey E. ... New York, NY
Stein, George N. ... New York, NY
Stein, Gerald A. ... New York, NY
Stein, Gerald A. ... Philadelphia, PA
Stein, Gerald A., P.C. ... Philadelphia, PA

Steinbach, Frank, III
West Des Moines, IA
Steinbach, Harold I. .... **Hackensack, NJ**
New York, NY
Steinbach, John W. .... Cicero, NY
Steinbach, Karen .... **Princeton, NJ**
Steinbach, Leonard J .... Springfield, NJ
Steinbach, Mark H., (P.C.) .... Washington, DC
Steinbach, R. Scott .... Dallas, TX
Steinbach, Robert M. .... Maynard, MA
Steinbach, Roch .... Forest Grove, OR
Steinbach, Ronald D. .... Irvine, CA
Steinbach, Sheldon E. .... Washington, DC
Steinbach & Steinbach, A Professional
Corporation .... Dallas, TX
Steinbach, Steven A. .... **Washington, DC**
Steinback, Jeffrey B. .... Chicago, IL
Steinback, Steven C. .... **Chicago, IL**
Steinbart, Neal W. .... **Indianapolis, IN**
Steinbarth, Gregg J. .... Rockville, MD
Steinbarth, Len .... San Diego, CA
Steinbauer, Charles P. .... **Brainerd, MN**
Steinbaum, Robert S. .... Newark, NJ
Steinbeck, Carl E. .... Dallas, TX
Steinbeck, Mark .... **Fort Myers, FL**
Steinberg, Abby L. .... Fort Lauderdale, FL
Steinberg, Abby L., P.A.
Fort Lauderdale, FL
Steinberg, Abram .... Monsey, NY
Steinberg, Alan .... Allentown, PA
Steinberg, Alan J. .... **St. Louis, MO**
Steinberg, Alan J. .... **Pittsburgh, PA**
Steinberg, Alan M. .... **Santa Rosa, CA**
Steinberg, Alex .... **Manhattan Beach, CA**
New York, NY
Steinberg, Allan R. .... Chicago, IL
Steinberg, Allen T. .... Lincolnshire, IL
Steinberg, Anastasia L. .... Scotts Valley, CA
Steinberg, Andrew B. .... Dallas, TX
Steinberg, Andrew D. .... Los Angeles, CA
Steinberg, Andrew E. .... Houston, TX
Steinberg, Andrew J. ...... Department of Justice, Immigration and Naturalization Service, GV
Steinberg, Andrew J. .... Springfield, MA
Steinberg, Anita .... Santa Monica, CA
Steinberg, Ann R. .... Chevy Chase, MD
Steinberg, Arthur .... **New York, NY**
Steinberg, Arthur H. .... New York, NY
Steinberg, Arthur I.
Federal Communications Commission, Office of Administrative Law Judges, GV
Steinberg, Arthur J. .... **New York, NY**
Steinberg, Arvin L. .... Fort Lauderdale, FL
Steinberg, Avery .... Yonkers, NY
Steinberg, Barbara A. .... Skokie, IL
Steinberg Barness Foster & Foley LLP
Los Angeles, CA
Manhattan Beach, CA
New York, NY
Steinberg, Barry P. .... **Washington, DC**
Steinberg, Beatrice D. .... Forest Hills, NY
Steinberg, Benjamin B. .... Minneapolis, MN
Steinberg, Bennet .... **New York, NY**
Steinberg, Bert William .... Great Neck, NY
Steinberg, Beth R. .... Williamsville, NY
Steinberg, Bettye .... New York, NY
Steinberg, Beverlee G. .... Houston, TX
Steinberg, Beverly G. .... **New York, NY**
Steinberg, Brad Lee, Law Offices of
New York, NY
Steinberg, Bradley D. .... **Chicago, IL**
Steinberg, Brenda S. .... **Framingham, MA**
Steinberg, Bruce M. .... Brooklyn, NY
Steinberg, Burtker & Grossman, Ltd.
Chicago, IL
Steinberg, Carol J. .... New York, NY
Steinberg, Carol R. .... Boston, MA
Steinberg & Cavaliere, LLP ...... **Stamford, CT**
New York, NY
White Plains, NY
Steinberg, Charles E. .... Stuart, FL
Steinberg, Charles E., P.A. .... Stuart, FL
Steinberg, Charles J. .... Los Angeles, CA
Steinberg, Charles L. .... Orlando, FL
Steinberg, Charles M. .... Chicago, IL
Steinberg, Charles R. .... **Cocoa, FL**
Steinberg, Christine H. .... East Rutherford, NJ
Steinberg, Cori B. .... **Los Angeles, CA**
Steinberg, Daniel L. .... **Salem, OR**
Steinberg, Daniel M. .... **Sacramento, CA**
Steinberg, Daniel S. .... **New York, NY**
Steinberg, Darin J. .... **Philadelphia, PA**
Steinberg, Darrell S. .... **Sacramento, CA**
Steinberg, David A., (A Professional Corporation) .... **Los Angeles, CA**
Steinberg, David I., & Associates
Clinton, MD
Glen Burnie, MD
Silver Spring, MD
Steinberg, David L. .... **Bloomfield Hills, MI**
Steinberg, David L. .... Poughkeepsie, NY
Steinberg, David S. .... Basking Ridge, NJ
Steinberg, Debra Brown .... **New York, NY**
Steinberg, Donald R. .... **Boston, MA**
Steinberg, Douglas A. .... **Alexandria, VA**
Steinberg, Edward B. .... Baltimore, MD
Steinberg, Edwin A. .... Miami, FL
Steinberg, Elliot G. .... San Francisco, CA
Steinberg, Ellis .... Los Angeles, CA
Steinberg, Ellsworth H. .... Baltimore, MD
Steinberg & Emery .... Santa Rosa, CA
Steinberg, Emily .... New York, NY
Steinberg, Eric .... **New York, NY**
Steinberg, Ethan S. .... San Francisco, CA
Steinberg, Evan L. .... Hackensack, NJ
Steinberg, Faith S. .... Marlton, NJ
Steinberg, Frances S. .... Chicago, IL

Steinberg, Franklyn C., III
Somerville, NJ
Steinberg, Franklyn C., III, P.C.
Newark, NJ
Somerville, NJ
Steinberg, Frederic .... Beverly Hills, CA
Steinberg, Frederick W. .... **Pittsburgh, PA**
Steinberg, Gabriel N. .... Atlanta, GA
Steinberg, Gary Philip .... Rochester, NY
Steinberg, Gary R. .... Newport Beach, CA
Steinberg, Gary R. .... **Garden City, NY**
Steinberg, Gerald L. .... Cleveland, OH
Steinberg, Geraldine .... San Jose, CA
Steinberg & Girsh, P.C. .... Philadelphia, PA
Steinberg, H. Arthur .... Los Angeles, CA
Steinberg, H. Michael .... Denver, CO
Steinberg, Harold D. .... **New York, NY**
Steinberg, Harold M. .... Holland, OH
Steinberg, Harold S. .... **New York, NY**
Steinberg, Harriette M. .... Westbury, NY
Steinberg, Harriette M., P.C. .... Westbury, NY
Steinberg, Harris I. .... **San Diego, CA**
Steinberg, Harry .... **New York, NY**
Steinberg, Harvey A. .... **Denver, CO**
Steinberg, Harvey B. .... **Rockville, MD**
Rockville, MD
Steinberg, Harvey L. .... **Midland, MI**
Steinberg, Herbert .... Beverly Hills, CA
Steinberg, Herbert Noel .... Kew Gardens, NY
Steinberg, Herman S. .... **New York, NY**
Steinberg, Herman W. .... Paterson, NJ
Steinberg, Hillary C. .... **Philadelphia, PA**
Steinberg, Howard E. .... **New York, NY**
Steinberg, Howard J. .... **Los Angeles, CA**
Steinberg, Howard M. .... Guttenberg, NJ
New York, NY
Steinberg, Howard M. .... Ridgewood, NJ
Steinberg, Irving G. .... Chicago, IL
Steinberg, Isaiah .... Camden, NJ
Steinberg, Jack .... Seattle, WA
Steinberg, James A. .... Poughkeepsie, NY
Steinberg, James B. .... United States Senate, Committee Legal Personnel, GV
Steinberg, James D. .... **Atlanta, GA**
Steinberg, James J. .... Eureka, CA
Steinberg, Jay A. .... **Chicago, IL**
Steinberg, Jay D. .... New York, NY
Steinberg, Jeffrey .... Santa Rosa, CA
Steinberg, Jeffrey .... Boca Raton, FL
Steinberg, Jeffrey G. .... Stamford, CT
White Plains, NY
Steinberg, Jeffrey M. .... **Springfield, NJ**
Steinberg, Jeffrey M. .... New York, NY
Steinberg, Jeffrey S.
Federal Communications Commission, Wireless Telecommunications Bureau, GV
Steinberg, Jerald R. .... Louisville, KY
Steinberg, Jill E. .... Philadelphia, PA
Steinberg, Jill M. .... **Memphis, TN**
Steinberg, Jim J. .... Rancho Bernardo, CA
San Diego, CA
Steinberg, Jody .... Woodland Hills, CA
Steinberg, Joel .... **Fairfax, VA**
Steinberg, Joel, & Associates, P.C.
Washington, DC
Alexandria, VA
Fairfax, VA
Manassas, VA
Woodbridge, VA
Steinberg, Joel M. .... New York, NY
Steinberg, John .... Berkeley, CA
Steinberg, John D. .... **Laguna Beach, CA**
Steinberg, John D. .... Wisconsin Rapids, WI
Steinberg, Jonathan G. .... Minneapolis, MN
Steinberg, Jonathan H. .... **Los Angeles, CA**
Steinberg, Jonathan R.
United States Court Of Veterans Appeals, GV
Steinberg, Jonathan R. .... New York, NY
Steinberg, Joseph L. .... Hartford, CT
Steinberg, Joseph LeVow .... **Roseland, NJ**
Steinberg, Kalman .... **Los Angeles, CA**
Steinberg, Kenneth J. .... Durham, NC
Steinberg, Kenneth M. .... Pittsburgh, PA
Steinberg, Kevin B. .... Philadelphia, PA
Steinberg, Kimberly A. .... **Farmington, CT**
Steinberg, Kip Evan .... **San Francisco, CA**
Steinberg & Lamb .... Chicago, IL
Steinberg, Laura .... **Boston, MA**
Steinberg Law Firm, P.C. .... Houston, TX
Steinberg, Law Offices, S.C. .... Brookfield, WI
Steinberg, Lawrence B.
Fort Lauderdale, FL
Steinberg, Lawrence B., (P.C.)
Beverly Hills, CA
Steinberg, Lawrence E. .... Dallas, TX
Steinberg, Lawrence W. .... Santa Monica, CA
Steinberg, Lee Anne .... **Los Angeles, CA**
Steinberg, Leigh W. .... Newport Beach, CA
Steinberg, Lennard B. .... **Philadelphia, PA**
Steinberg, Leon I. .... Minneapolis, MN
Steinberg, Leonard A. .... **Anchorage, AK**
Steinberg, Leonard N. .... Forest Park, GA
Steinberg, Les A. .... **St. Louis, MO**
Steinberg, Lewis G. .... **Lock Haven, PA**
Steinberg, Lewis R. .... **New York, NY**
Steinberg & Linn, P.A. .... Fort Myers, FL
Naples, FL
Port Charlotte, FL
Steinberg, Lisa Huwer .... Cincinnati, OH
Steinberg, Louis .... Baltimore, MD
Steinberg, Lynn .... Great Neck, NY
Steinberg, Mal .... Fort Lauderdale, FL
Steinberg, Marc I. .... Dallas, TX
Steinberg, Marc Robert .... **Lansdale, PA**
Steinberg, Marcia Jean .... Sacramento, CA
Steinberg, Marjorie R. .... Staten Island, NY
Steinberg, Marjorie S. .... **Los Angeles, CA**

Steinberg, Mark .... Hartford, CT
Steinberg, Mark .... Gainesville, FL
Steinberg, Mark A. .... Fort Myers, FL
Naples, FL
Port Charlotte, FL
Steinberg, Mark A. .... Asbury Park, NJ
Steinberg, Mark R. .... **Los Angeles, CA**
Steinberg, Mark S. .... Miami, FL
Steinberg & Marks, P.A. .... Clark, NJ
Steinberg, Marty .... **Miami, FL**
Steinberg, Matthew B.
Bowling Green, KY
Steinberg, Matthew S. .... **Los Angeles, CA**
Steinberg, Maurice .... Augusta, GA
Steinberg, Maynerd I. .... **Chicago, IL**
Steinberg, Melissa .... New York, NY
Steinberg, Melvin A. .... **Baltimore, MD**
Steinberg, Meredith P. .... **Milwaukee, WI**
Steinberg, Merrick D. .... **Fort Lee, NJ**
Steinberg, Merrill E. .... **San Francisco, CA**
Steinberg, Michael .... Tampa, FL
Steinberg, Michael .... Glencoe, IL
Steinberg, Michael .... Rochester, NY
Steinberg, Michael A. .... **Wilmington, DE**
Steinberg, Michael G. .... **New York, NY**
Steinberg, Michael H. .... **Los Angeles, CA**
Steinberg, Michael H. .... **Pittsburgh, PA**
Steinberg, Michael L. .... New York, NY
Steinberg, Michael M. .... San Diego, CA
Steinberg, Michael R. .... New York, NY
Steinberg, Michael W. .... **Washington, DC**
Steinberg, Michelle N. .... Burlington, VT
Steinberg, Mindy .... North Woodmere, NY
Steinberg & Moorad .... Newport Beach, CA
Steinberg, Morton M. .... **Chicago, IL**
Steinberg, Murray .... Bronx, NY
Steinberg, Nisan A. .... **Los Angeles, CA**
Steinberg, Norman .... Floral Park, NY
Steinberg, Nutter & Brent
Los Angeles, CA
Santa Monica, CA
Woodland Hills, CA
Steinberg, O'Connor & Burns, P.L.L.C.
Detroit, MI
Steinberg, Paul B. .... **Miami Beach, FL**
Steinberg, Paul G. .... Incline Village, NV
Steinberg, Paul H., (P.C.) .... Southfield, MI
Steinberg, Paul I. .... **New York, NY**
Steinberg, Peter J. .... Dover, MA
Steinberg, Peter M. .... Santa Monica, CA
Steinberg, Peter M., A Law Corp.
Santa Monica, CA
Steinberg, Peter T. .... **Santa Monica, CA**
Steinberg, Philip .... Cape Coral, FL
Steinberg, Philip A. .... **Bala Cynwyd, PA**
Steinberg, Polacek & Goodman
Chicago, IL
Steinberg, Quentin .... Seattle, WA
Steinberg, R. Philip .... **Philadelphia, PA**
Steinberg, Ralph .... Tampa, FL
Steinberg, Ralph J. .... Santa Cruz, CA
Steinberg & Raskin, P.C. .... **New York, NY**
Steinberg, Richard A. .... Skokie, IL
Steinberg, Richard A. .... **New York, NY**
Steinberg, Richard A. .... **Alexandria, VA**
Steinberg, Richard H. .... Newton, MA
Steinberg, Richard H. .... **West Orange, NJ**
Steinberg, Richard J. .... Brookfield, WI
Steinberg, Richard L. .... **Miami Beach, FL**
Steinberg, Richard L. .... **Detroit, MI**
Steinberg, Richard L. .... Chester, PA
Steinberg, Richard S. .... St. Joseph, MO
Steinberg, Rick Aaron .... **Philadelphia, PA**
Steinberg, Robert .... Los Angeles, CA
Steinberg, Robert .... **Los Angeles, CA**
Steinberg, Robert A. .... **Los Angeles, CA**
Steinberg, Robert A. .... **Cincinnati, OH**
Steinberg, Robert B. .... Los Angeles, CA
Steinberg, Robert B. .... Kew Gardens, NY
Steinberg, Robert D. .... Philadelphia, PA
Steinberg, Robert E. .... Fairfield, IA
Steinberg, Robert E. .... New York, NY
Steinberg, Robert G. .... East Islip, NY
Steinberg, Robert H. .... **Los Angeles, CA**
Steinberg, Robert H. .... Middleburg, PA
Steinberg, Robert J. .... Catonsville, MD
Steinberg, Robert K. .... Los Angeles, CA
Steinberg, Robert K. .... Farmington, MI
Steinberg, Robert Lee .... Allentown, PA
Steinberg, Robert S. .... South Miami, FL
Steinberg, Robert S. .... **Boston, MA**
Steinberg, Ronald A. .... Farmington Hills, MI
Steinberg, Ronald F .... Miami, FL
Steinberg, Ruth C. .... New York, NY
Steinberg, S. Keven .... **Santa Monica, CA**
Steinberg, Sally L. .... Princeton, NJ
Steinberg, Sara Jane .... **New York, NY**
Steinberg, Saul J. .... Camden, NJ
Philadelphia, PA
Steinberg, Scott A., Law Offices of
New York, NY
Steinberg, Seth J. .... Foster City, CA
Steinberg, Seymour .... New York, NY
Steinberg, Seymour P. .... Berkeley, CA
Steinberg & Shapiro .... Southfield, MI
Steinberg, Shari L. .... **New York, NY**
Steinberg, Sharon L. .... New York, NY
Steinberg, Sidney R. .... **Philadelphia, PA**
Steinberg, Spitz, Goldberg, Pearlman, Holmes & White, L.L.P. .... **Charleston, SC**
Goose Creek, SC
Mount Pleasant, SC
North Charleston, SC
Steinberg, Stacy K. .... **Anchorage, AK**
Steinberg, Stanley R. .... Newport Beach, CA
Steinberg & Steinberg .... Santa Monica, CA
Steinberg & Steinberg, L.L.C.
St. Louis, MO

Steinberg & Steinberg, Ltd. .... Chicago, IL
Steinberg, Steinberg & White, P.C.
Augusta, GA
Steinberg, Stephen .... Clark, NJ
Steinberg, Stephen C. .... Brockton, MA
Steinberg, Stephen H. .... Augusta, GA
Steinberg, Stephen P. .... Acton, MA
Steinberg, Stephen R. .... Bridgehampton, NY
Steinberg, Steven P. .... **Baltimore, MD**
Steinberg, Stuart M. .... Woodland Hills, CA
Steinberg, Stuart M. .... Garden City, NY
Steinberg, Stuart T. .... **Philadelphia, PA**
Steinberg, Susan Renee .... Baltimore, MD
Steinberg, Sylvan J. .... **New Orleans, LA**
Steinberg, Ted L. .... Beverly Hills, CA
Steinberg, Todd I. .... **Greenbelt, MD**
Rockville, MD
Steinberg, Tracey Loren .... New York, NY
Steinberg, William H. .... Endicott, NY
Steinberg & Yaffe, P.A. .... **Miami, FL**
Miami Beach, FL
Steinberger, Chaim T. .... New York, NY
Steinberger, David P. .... **Washington, DC**
Steinberger, Emanuel .... Garden City, NY
Steinberger, Erica H. .... **New York, NY**
Steinberger & Feldherr .... Garden City, NY
Steinberger, Frank J. .... Schuyler, NE
Steinberger, Gary J. .... Fort Worth, TX
Steinberger, J. Scott .... **Albuquerque, NM**
Steinberger, Jeffrey W. .... Beverly Hills, CA
Steinberger, Jeffrey W., A P.C.
Beverly Hills, CA
Steinberger, John C. .... **Washington, DC**
Steinberger, John C. .... **El Paso, TX**
Steinberger, John S., Jr. .... Kenmare, ND
Steinberger, Joseph .... Rockland, ME
Steinberger, Karl R. .... **Pascagoula, MS**
Steinberger, Mark N. .... **Jenkintown, PA**
Steinberger, Mitchell J. .... **Costa Mesa, CA**
Steinberger, Richard L. .... St. Helena, CA
Steinberger, Rita A. .... Westport, CT
Steinberger, Robert J. .... San Diego, CA
Steinbock, Elmer Lincoln .... Concord, CA
Steinbock, Mark A. .... Beachwood, OH
Steinbock, Miriam .... **Oakland, CA**
Steinbock, Natalie B. .... Albany, NY
Steinbock, Phillip M. .... San Jose, CA
Steinbock-Sinclair, Robert .... Oak Brook, IL
Steinborn, Stanley D. .... Lansing, MI
Steinborn, Steven B. .... **Washington, DC**
Steinbrecher, Alan K. .... **Los Angeles, CA**
Steinbrecher, Bradley K. .... **Washington, DC**
Steinbrecher, Michael J. .... San Francisco, CA
Steinbrecher & Ross LLP .... New York, NY
Steinbrecher, Stephen .... New York, NY
Steinbrecher, William P. .... **Chicago, IL**
Steinbrenner, Carl A. .... **Rochester, NY**
Steinbrenner, Carl J. .... Sweet Valley, PA
Steinbrenner, Gerald W. .... **Missoula, MT**
Steinbrinck, Richard J. .... Green Bay, WI
Steinbrink, Stuart H. .... New York, NY
Steinbrink, William H. .... Shaker Heights, OH
Steinbronn, Richard E. .... **Fort Wayne, IN**
Steinbruegge, Robert W. .... Rome, GA
Steinbrunner, Christina .... Ashland, KY
Steinbugler, Kathryn .... **West Point, PA**
Steinburg, Carwile, Herzik & Prieto
Houston, TX
Steinburg, Rodney V. .... **Houston, TX**
Steincamp, Charles C. .... **Wichita, KS**
Steincolor, Deborah .... New York, NY
Steincross, G. Warren .... Minneapolis, MN
Steindam, Michael L. .... New York, NY
Steindel, Sarah H. .... Glen Ridge, NJ
Steindl, Ethel J. .... New York, NY
Steindler, Curt S. .... Los Angeles, CA
Steindler, Howard A. .... **Cleveland, OH**
Steindler, Thomas P. .... **Washington, DC**
Steindorf, Michael C. .... **Dallas, TX**
Steindorf, Robert H. .... **White Plains, NY**
Steine, M. Harry .... Augusta, GA
Steine, Robert Owen .... Aurora, CO
Steinebrey, Rebecca .... Denver, CO
Steinebrey, Rebecca, P.C. .... Denver, CO
Steineckert, R. Gene .... **San Diego, CA**
Steineckert & Shotwell, A Professional Corporation .... **San Diego, CA**
Steinemann, George C. .... **Sandusky, OH**
Steiner, Alan .... Peekskill, NY
Steiner, Alan E. .... **Albany, NY**
Steiner, Alfred .... **Dallas, TX**
Steiner, Alison .... Hattiesburg, MS
Steiner, Andrew D. .... **Anchorage, AK**
Steiner, Ann Buntin .... **Nashville, TN**
Steiner, Ann Mendelson .... Pittsburgh, PA
Steiner, Arthur J. .... **Washington, DC**
Steiner, Ashley M. .... **Atlanta, GA**
Steiner, Barbara S. .... **Chicago, IL**
Steiner, Barry J. .... Sacramento, CA
Steiner, Barry N. .... **New York, NY**
Steiner, Beat U. .... **Denver, CO**
Steiner, Benjamin D. .... **Chicago, IL**
Steiner, Beth Sears .... San Francisco, CA
Steiner & Blotnik .... Buffalo, NY
Steiner, Bradford A. .... **Seattle, WA**
Steiner, Bradford E. .... Boston, MA
Steiner, Brian R. .... **Philadelphia, PA**
Steiner, Bruce D. .... **Hackensack, NJ**
New York, NY
Steiner, C. Michael .... Washington, IN
Steiner, Carl L. .... Chicago, IL
Steiner, Carolyn L. .... Shaker Heights, OH
Steiner, Catherine A. .... **Los Angeles, CA**
Steiner, Catherine Whitehurst
Baltimore, MD
Steiner, Chris E. .... Toledo, OH
Steiner, Christian M. .... **New York, NY**
Steiner, Christine .... Los Angeles, CA

Steiner, Clarence ... Coconut Grove, FL
Steiner, Clarence H. ... Pittsburgh, PA
Steiner, Crum & Baker ... Montgomery, AL
Steiner, Cynthia Holder ... Dallas, TX
Steiner, Daniel ... Boston, MA
Steiner, Darling, Hutchinson & Wilson LLP
Denver, CO
Steiner, David A. ... New York, NY
Steiner, David A. ... Redmond, WA
Steiner, David L. ... Indianapolis, IN
Steiner, David M. ... Springfield, NJ
Steiner, David M. ... New York, NY
Steiner, David P. ... New Orleans, LA
Steiner, David Paul ... Los Angeles, CA
Steiner, David R. ... Fort Wayne, IN
Steiner, Deborah L. ... Chicago, IL
Steiner, D. G. ... Tacoma, WA
Steiner, Diane B. ... New York, NY
Steiner, Donald C. ... Rochester, MN
Steiner, Dwight E. ... Omaha, NE
Steiner & Ebeling, LL.P ... White Plains, NY
Steiner, Edward E. ... Cincinnati, OH
Steiner, Edward J. ... Kittanning, PA
Steiner, Erwin H. ... Eau Claire, WI
Steiner, Fern M. ... San Diego, CA
Steiner, Frank ... Nashville, TN
Steiner, Frank G. ... Department of Agriculture, Agricultural Research Service, GV
Steiner, Frederick K., Jr. ... Phoenix, AZ
Steiner, Gaar W. ... Milwaukee, WI
Steiner, Geoffrey B. ... Tampa, FL
Steiner, Geoffrey B., & Associates, P.A.
Tampa, FL
Steiner, Harriet A. ... Sacramento, CA
Steiner, Henry H. ... New York, NY
Steiner, Henry J. ... Cambridge, MA
Steiner, Henry J. ... Myerstown, PA
Steiner, Irene A. ... New York, NY
Steiner, Jack J. ... Kittanning, PA
Steiner, Jack W., Jr. ... Louisville, KY
Steiner, Jacob ... New York, NY
Steiner, James D. ... Minneapolis, MN
Steiner, Jeanne ... Phoenix, AZ
Steiner, Jeffrey B. ... New York, NY
Steiner, Jeffrey E., (P.C.) ... Los Angeles, CA
Steiner, Jeffrey S. ... Boca Raton, FL
Steiner, Jeremy S. ... Hopkins, MN
Steiner, Jerome M., Jr. ... San Francisco, CA
Steiner, Jerry H. ... Pleasantville, NJ
Steiner, Joel D. ... Seaford, NY
Steiner, Joel H. ... Chicago, IL
Steiner, John L. ... Anchorage, AK
Steiner, John M. ... Boston, MA
Steiner, John M. ... Erie, PA
Steiner, John S. ... St. Louis, MO
Steiner, Jonathan B. ... Los Angeles, CA
Steiner, Jonathan H. ... Honolulu, HI
Steiner, Jonathan L. ... San Francisco, CA
Steiner, Judith A. ... Akron, OH
Steiner, Julian ... New York, NY
Steiner, Julie E. ... New York, NY
Steiner, Julius M. ... Philadelphia, PA
Steiner, K. James, Jr. ... Honolulu, HI
Steiner, Katherine R. ... White Plains, NY
Steiner, Keith J. ... Honolulu, HI
Steiner, Keith J., A Law Corporation
Honolulu, HI
Steiner, Kenneth K. ... Jackson, MS
Steiner, LaDonna L. ... West Haven, CT
Steiner, Laurie G. ... Cleveland, OH
Steiner, Lawrence R., (P.A.)
Altamonte Springs, FL
Steiner, Lee N. ... New York, NY
Steiner, Leonard ... Beverly Hills, CA
New York, NY
Steiner, LeRoy M. ... St. Louis, MO
Steiner & Libo, Professional Corporation
Beverly Hills, CA
Steiner, Linda J. ... Cheyenne, WY
Steiner, Margaret L. ... Phoenix, AZ
Steiner, Maria L. ... New York, NY
Steiner, Mark A. ... San Francisco, CA
Steiner, Mark E. ... Georgetown, DE
Milford, DE
Milford, DE
Steiner, Mark H. ... Fort Wayne, IN
Steiner, Mark R. ... Dallas, TX
Steiner, Martin B. ... Sacramento, CA
Steiner, Matt ... Los Angeles, CA
Steiner, Matthew J. ... Palo Alto, CA
Steiner, Merrill R. ... Philadelphia, PA
Steiner, Michael F ... San Francisco, CA
Steiner, Michael J. ... San Francisco, CA
Steiner, Michael S. ... Delray Beach, FL
Steiner, Neil A. ... New York, NY
Steiner, Neil S. ... Beverly Hills, CA
Steiner Norris PLLC ... Seattle, WA
Steiner, Patricia J. ... Basking Ridge, NJ
Steiner, Paul J., Law Offices of
San Francisco, CA
Steiner, Paul L. ... Miami, FL
Steiner, Paula Ryan ... Georgetown, DE
Steiner, Peter Jack ... San Jose, CA
Steiner, Peter N. ... Corpus Christi, TX
Steiner, R. James ... Concord, NH
Steiner, Rebel R., Jr. ... Los Angeles, CA
Steiner, Renae D. ... Minneapolis, MN
Steiner, Richard A. ... Phoenix, AZ
Steiner, Richard G. ... Gretna, LA
Steiner, Richard G., A P.C. ... Gretna, LA
Steiner, Richard J. ... Buffalo, NY
Steiner, Richard N. ... Chicago, IL
Steiner, Robert C. ... Salt Lake City, UT
Steiner, Robert G. ... San Diego, CA
Steiner, Robert I. ... New York, NY
Steiner, Roberta ... Milwaukee, WI
Steiner, Roger W. ... Kansas City, MO
Steiner, Russell A. ... Newark, OH

Steiner & Saffer, A Professional Law Corporation ... Los Angeles, CA
Steiner, Samuel J. ... Seattle, WA
Steiner, Sandoe & Cooper ... Myerstown, PA
Steiner, Sanford L. ... Kalamazoo, MI
Steiner, Sarah Kramer ... New York, NY
Steiner & Schoenfeld ... Milwaukee, WI
Steiner, Scott J. ... Grand Rapids, MI
Steiner, Scott J. ... White Plains, NY
Steiner, Segal, Muller & Donan
Philadelphia, PA
Reading, PA
Steiner, Sidney B. ... New Orleans, LA
Steiner, Stacey L. ... Charleroi, PA
Steiner and Steiner ... Kittanning, PA
Steiner & Steiner ... Nashville, TN
Steiner, Stephen D. ... Millbrae, CA
Steiner & Stern Co., L.P.A. ... Cleveland, OH
Steiner, Susan C. ... Portland, ME
Steiner, Thomas D. ... New York, NY
Steiner, Tracey B. ... Arlington, VA
Steiner, Valerie ... Hackensack, NJ
Steiner, Wilfred A., Jr. ... Detroit, MI
Steiner, Wilfred Eric
Farmington Hills, MI
Steiner, William F. ... Cleveland, OH
Steiner, William L. ... Pittsburgh, PA
Steinert, Eric M. ... Los Angeles, CA
Steinert, N. Steven ... Charleston, SC
Steinert, Raymond L. ... Anaheim, CA
Steinert, Robert M. ... North Massapequa, NY
Steinerts, Vanessa T. ... Tamarac, FL
Steines, Ann Munson ... Cincinnati, OH
Steines, Charles M. ... Cleveland, OH
Steines, John P., Jr. ... New York, NY
Steines, Stanley B. ... Morrison, IL
Steinfeld, Adam ... New York, NY
Steinfeld, Bart R. ... New York, NY
Steinfeld, Betsy C. ... Wheeling, WV
Steinfeld Boldt Wagner & Weiner
Louisville, KY
Steinfeld, Bruce R. ... Atlanta, GA
Steinfeld, Craig L. ... Morristown, NJ
Steinfeld, Dede S. ... San Francisco, CA
Steinfeld, Eugene M. ... Margate, FL
Steinfeld, James F. ... Louisville, KY
Steinfeld, Jeffrey B. ... Hackensack, NJ
Steinfeld, Joel B. ... Ventura, CA
Steinfeld, Joseph L., Jr. ... Washington, DC
Steinfeld, Mallary ... Morristown, NJ
Steinfeld, Melissa A. ... San Antonio, TX
Steinfeld, Philip A. ... Newark, NJ
Steinfeld, Reid L. ... Calabasas, CA
Steinfeld, Samuel ... Louisville, KY
Steinfeld, Shayna M. ... Atlanta, GA
Steinfeld, Susan Frances ... Los Angeles, CA
Steinfeldt, Oren J. ... Hopkins, MN
Stein-Ferguson, Karen L.
Indianapolis, IN
Stein-Fernandez, Nora L.
King Of Prussia, PA
Steinfield, Arlene Switzer ... Dallas, TX
Steinfield, Joseph D. ... Boston, MA
Steinfink, Barry ... White Plains, NY
Steinfink, Jamie ... New York, NY
Steingard, Richard M. ... Los Angeles, CA
Steingard, Sharon L. ... Philadelphia, PA
Steingard, Steven M. ... Philadelphia, PA
Steingart, Bonnie Kayatta ... New York, NY
Steingart, Danl. G. ... New York, NY
Steingart, David J. ... Minneapolis, MN
Steingart, Jack M. ... Garden City, NY
Steingarten, Jeffrey L. ... New York, NY
Steingass, Bruce D. ... Pandora, OH
Steingass, Jonathan M. ... Medina, OH
Steingass, Susan R. ... Madison, WI
Steinger, Charles S. (IBA) ... Des Moines, IA
Steingisser, I. Robert ... Long Beach, CA
Steinglass, Henry J. ... New York, NY
Steingold, Andy B. ... Tampa, FL
Steingold, David S. ... Detroit, MI
Steingold, David S., P.C. ... Detroit, MI
Steingold, Eugene ... Chicago, IL
Steingold, Fred S. ... Ann Arbor, MI
Steingold, Jeffrey M. ... Virginia Beach, VA
Steingold, Laura R. ... Huntington Beach, CA
Steingold, Neal R. ... Providence, RI
Steingold, Ron ... Bellevue, WA
Steingold, Shrader & Angelidis
Richmond, VA
Steingold, Stuart G. ... Washington, DC
Steingraber, Peter C. ... Providence, RI
Steingraber, Stuart G. ... Santa Ana, CA
Steingut, Robert ... New York, NY
Steingut, Theodore S. ... New York, NY
Steinhafel, Michael W. ... Elm Grove, WI
Steinhagen, Daniel J. ... Edina, MN
Steinhagen, Renée ... Newark, NJ
Steinhagen, Rita Clare ... North Branch, MN
Steinhardt, Ann B. ... New Orleans, LA
Steinhardt, Barbara J. ... Sacramento, CA
Steinhardt, Doris E. ... New York, NY
Steinhardt, Douglas J. ... Belvidere, NJ
Steinhardt, Frederick D. ... Southfield, MI
Steinhardt, Jeffrey D. ... Redmond, WA
Steinhardt, Joyce S. ... Englewood, CO
Steinhardt, Louis H. ... Stoughton, MA
Steinhardt, Marsha L. ... Brooklyn, NY
Steinhardt, Michael D. ... Glen Burnie, MD
Steinhardt, Paul C. ... San Diego, CA
Steinhardt, Ralph G., III ... Washington, DC
Steinhardt, Raphael ... Miami Beach, FL
Steinhardt, Steven B. ... Albany, NY
Steinhart, Amy E. ... Evansville, IN
Steinhart, Ashley ... Roseland, NJ
Steinhart, Barry N. ... New York, NY
Steinhart & Falconer, LLP
San Francisco, CA

Steinhart, Jason G. ... Princeton, NJ
Steinhart, Lance J.M. ... Duluth, GA
Steinhart, Mitchell I. ... Rochelle Park, NJ
Steinhart, Steven Y. ... Lake Success, NY
Steinhart, Terran T. ... Los Angeles, CA
Steinhauer, Arthur J. ... New York, NY
Steinhauer, Esther H. ... New York, NY
Steinhauer, Gillian ... Boston, MA
Steinhauer, John S. ... Akron, OH
Steinhauer, Joshua R. ... San Francisco, CA
Steinhauer, Lorie E. ... Southfield, MI
Steinhauer, Paul R. ... San Francisco, CA
Steinhauer, R.E. ... Berkeley, CA
Steinhaus, Brian T. ... Menomonee Falls, WI
Steinhaus, Christopher James
Tallahassee, FL
Steinhaus, Robert D ... Buffalo, NY
Steinhaus, William P. ... Atlanta, GA
Steinhause, Darryl ... San Diego, CA
Steinhauser, Bennie F., Jr. ... San Antonio, TX
Steinhauser, Jeff R. ... Houston, TX
Steinhauser, Lore C. ... Stamford, CT
Steinhauser, Michael R. ... Flatonia, TX
Steinhauser, Rebecca J. ... Defiance, OH
Steinheider, John F. ... Nebraska City, NE
Steinheimer, Cassel & Polley, Law Offices of
Reno, NV
Steinheimer, Connie J. ... Reno, NV
Steinheimer, M. Max ... Sonora, CA
Stockton, CA
Reno, NV
Steinheimer, Michael G. ... Temple, TX
Steinheimer, Riggio, Haydel & Mordaunt, A Professional Law Corporation
Sonora, CA
Stockton, CA
Steinheimer, Robert ... Rockville, MD
Steinheimer, Vickie L. ... San Francisco, CA
Steinher, Jan Hatcher ... Cincinnati, OH
Steinhilber, August W., III ... Fairfax, VA
Steinhilber, August William
Columbia, MD
Steinhilber, Jack D. ... Oshkosh, WI
Steinhilber, Robert E. ... Virginia Beach, VA
Steinhilber, Robert V. ... Plantation, FL
Steinhilber, Steven D. ... Kansas City, MO
Steinhilber, Swanson, Mares, Marone & McDermott ... Oshkosh, WI
Steinhilper, Frank A. ... Gainesville, GA
Steinhoff, Aaron M. ... Las Vegas, NV
Steinhoff, David F. ... Denver, CO
Steinhoff, Gean A. ... Imperial Beach, CA
Steinhoff, Rainer E. ... Columbus, OH
Steinhoff, Scott A. ... Birmingham, MI
Steinhoff, Steven J. ... Eagle, WI
Steinholz, Bari Allison ... New York, NY
Steinhorn, Allan W. ... Washington, DC
Greenbelt, MD
Steinhorn, Irwin H. ... Oklahoma City, OK
Steinhour, Jan Adele
Colorado Springs, CO
Denver, CO
Steinhour, Paul E. ... Springfield, IL
Steinhouse, Carl L. ... Cleveland, OH
Steinig, Michael A. ... Washington, DC
Steiniger, Michael G. ... Encino, CA
Steininger, Daniel J. ... Milwaukee, WI
Steininger, Donald B. ... Fort Wayne, IN
Steininger, Michael G. ...
Small Business Administration, GV
Steininger, Ronald ... San Jose, CA
Steinitz, Jeffrey M. ... Forest Hills, NY
Steinitz, Jeffrey M. ... New York, NY
Steinkamp, John G. ... Fayetteville, AR
Steinkamp, John L. ... Fort Wayne, IN
Steinkamp, Robert T. ... Overland Park, KS
Steinke, Andr é ... Bronx, NY
Steinke, Kurt A. ... Troy, MI
Steinke, Mark ... Steamboat Springs, CO
Steinke, Marvin R. ... Belleville, IL
Steinke, Maureen Maher ... Tempe, AZ
Steinke, Paul F. ... Chicago, IL
Steinke, Robert R. ... Columbus, NE
Steinke, Suzanne M. ... Los Angeles, CA
Steinke, Ted ... Dallas, TX
Steinke, Terri L. ... Flagstaff, AZ
Steinke, Thomas F. ... San Diego, CA
Steinken, Richard P. ... Chicago, IL
Steinkirchner, Frank B. ... Wichita, KS
Steinkoenig, Kristine M. L. ... Baltimore, MD
Steinkraus, Paul D. ... Dearborn, MI
Steinkraus, Walter J. ... Minnetonka, MN
Steinkrauss, Joseph C., Law Office of
Boston, MA
Steinkrauss, Joseph C., Law Office of
Lexington, MA
Steinkruger, Niesje J. ... Fairbanks, AK
Steinlage, Michael J. ... St. Paul, MN
Steinlage, Paul N. ... Wausau, WI
Steinle, Alfred A. ... Jourdanton, TX
Steinle, Eric M. ... Oakland, CA
Steinle, Jack P. ... Mount Vernon, MO
Steinle, Janice A., & Associates, P.C.
Littleton, CO
Steinle, Janice Ann ... Littleton, CO
Steinle, Jeffrey J. ... Minneapolis, MN
Steinle, Leon F. ... Jourdanton, TX
Steinle, Michael J. ... Milwaukee, WI
Steinle, Renee Mueller ... Minneapolis, MN
Steinle, Roland J., Jr. ... Milwaukee, WI
Steinle, S. Eric ... Hutchinson, KS
Steinle, W. Timothy ... Milwaukee, WI
Steinley, Martin H. ... San Diego, CA
Steinman, Charles D. ... Rochester, NY
Steinman Cooper Wiscarson
Portland, OR
Steinman, David R. ... Washington, DC
Steinman, Dennis ... Portland, OR

Steinman, Donald I. ... Jamaica, NY
Steinman, Edward H. ... Santa Clara, CA
Steinman, Emily Yerman ... New York, NY
Steinman, Gregory D. ... Albuquerque, NM
Steinman, Harvey B. ... Columbia, MD
Steinman, Howard A. ... Hartford, CT
Steinman, Jack ... New York, NY
Steinman, Jay A. ... Miami, FL
Steinman, Jay R. ... Irvine, CA
Steinman, Jeffrey Q. ... Encino, CA
Steinman, Joan E. ... Chicago, IL
Steinman, Joel ... Morrisville, PA
Steinman, Kathryn G. ... New York, NY
Steinman, Leonard D. ... New York, NY
Steinman, Lester D. ... White Plains, NY
Steinman, Lewis ... New York, NY
Steinman, Martha N. ... New York, NY
Steinman, Melissa Landau
Washington, DC
Steinman, Morton H. ... Glendale, CA
Steinman, Ness & Robinson, The Law Offices of ... Riverside, CA
San Diego, CA
Santa Ana, CA
Steinman, Paul D. ... Pittsburgh, PA
Steinman, Peter E. ... Glendale, CA
Steinman, Peter L. ... Los Angeles, CA
Steinman, Ralph ... New York, NY
Steinman, Randy Eder ... New York, NY
Steinman, Robert ... New York, NY
Steinman, Robert C. ... St. Johns, MI
Steinman, Steven J. ... New York, NY
Steinman, Susan G. ... Princeton, NJ
Steinman, Walter Z. ... Wyncote, PA
Steinman, William B. Fenning
Washington, DC
Steinmanis, Karl S. ... Cincinnati, OH
Steinmann, Bert ... The Woodlands, TX
Steinmann, David P. ... New York, NY
Steinmann, Edwin H., Jr.
Jefferson City, MO
Steinmann, Eric J. ... Wrightwood, CA
Steinmann, Frederick ... Baltimore, MD
Steinmann, Frederick M. ... St. Charles, MO
Steinmann, Joan M. ... Los Angeles, CA
Steinmann, Michael A. ... Fair Oaks, CA
Steinmark, Frank Joseph ... Seattle, WA
Steinmayer, Janet L. ... Stamford, CT
Stein-McCarthy, Nancy
West Palm Beach, FL
Stein-McCarthy, Nancy I. ... Montclair, NJ
Steinmeier, William D., P.C.
Jefferson City, MO
Steinmeier, William Dann
Jefferson City, MO
Steinmetz, Alan H. ... Clearwater, FL
Steinmetz, Alan M. ... Woodmere, NY
Steinmetz, Alan M., L.L.C. ... Woodmere, NY
Steinmetz, Alfred G. ... Whippany, NJ
Steinmetz, Ann ... Albuquerque, NM
Steinmetz, Arthur P. ... Cleveland, OH
Steinmetz, Calvin ... Washington, DC
Steinmetz, Charles E. ... Des Moines, IA
Steinmetz, Christian G. ... Milwaukee, WI
Steinmetz, Christian J., III ... Savannah, GA
Steinmetz, Daniel F., Jr. ... Pennsauken, NJ
Steinmetz, David S. ... White Plains, NY
Steinmetz, Debra ... New York, NY
Steinmetz, Deetta H. ... Indianapolis, IN
Steinmetz, Donald W. ... Madison, WI
Steinmetz, Douglas R. ... Stamford, CT
Steinmetz, Fred H. ... Los Angeles, CA
Steinmetz, Harry J. ... Indianapolis, IN
Steinmetz, Herbert C., Jr. ... Aurora, IL
Steinmetz, John W. ... Boston, MA
Steinmetz, Kim D. ... Phoenix, AZ
Steinmetz, Martin R. ... Tulsa, OK
Steinmetz, Matthew E. ... Chicago, IL
Steinmetz, Richard B., Jr. ... Greenwich, CT
Steinmetz, Richard C., Jr. ... Milwaukee, WI
Steinmetz, Robert D. ... Tucson, AZ
Steinmetz, Robert Francis ... Cleveland, OH
Steinmetz, Robert L. ... Louisville, KY
Steinmetz, Roberta F. ... Tulsa, OK
Steinmetz, Sheri P. ... West Hartford, CT
Steinmetz, Steven ... Hartford, CT
Steinmetz, Steven B. ... Greenwich, CT
Steinmetz, Thomas A. ... Horsham, PA
Steinmetz, Weinberg & Moats
Washington, DC
Steinmetz, William H. ... Palo Alto, CA
Steinmetz, William R. ... Milwaukee, WI
Steinmeyer, Amanda Graham
Hampton, SC
Steinmeyer, Anthony J.
Department of Justice, Civil Division, GV
Steinmeyer, Burnell E., Jr. ... North Platte, NE
Steinmeyer, Edwin Andrew
Tallahassee, FL
Steinmeyer, F. E., III ... Tallahassee, FL
Steinmeyer, Heather C. ... Chicago, IL
Steinmeyer, Judy I. ... Thousand Oaks, CA
Steinmeyer, Julie Rome ... Tallahassee, FL
Steinmeyer, Leslie P. ... St. Louis, MO
Steinmeyer, Patricia E. ... La Grange, IL
Steinmeyer, Peter A. ... Chicago, IL
Steinmeyer, Randall Henry ... St. Paul, MN
Steinmeyer, Robert J. ... Fullerton, CA
Steinmeyer, William B. ... Thousand Oaks, CA
Steinmeyer, William B., Inc.
Thousand Oaks, CA
Steinnafel-Lappe, Ellen ... New Berlin, WI
Steinour, Carol A. ... Harrisburg, PA
Steinowitz, Bruce L. ... White Plains, NY
Steinsapir, Laurence D. ... Los Angeles, CA
Steinschriber, Frank ... Encino, CA
Steinshouer, Darrel G. ... Wichita, KS
Steinsnyder, Jeffrey N. ... Bradenton, FL

Steinthal, James .... **New York, NY**
Steinthal, Kenneth L. .... **New York, NY**
Steinthal, Susan J. .... **New York, NY**
Steinvarzel, Ronald E. .... **Morristown, NJ**
Steinvoort, Sandra L. .... Salt Lake City, UT
Steinwall, Susan D. .... **Minneapolis, MN**
Steinway, Barry A. .... Birmingham, MI
Steinway, Daniel M. .... **Washington, DC**
Steinwedel, Louis Wm. .... Baltimore, MD
Steinwurtzel, Richard A. .... **Washington, DC**
New York, NY
Steinwurtzel, Robert N. .... **Washington, DC**
Steirer, Mark W. .... **Dallas, TX**
Steiskal, A. Robert .... Youngstown, OH
Steitz, James K. .... St. Louis, MO
Stejkowski, David G. .... **Chicago, IL**
Stejskal, Jerry L. .... Omaha, NE
Stek, Stanley J. .... **Grand Rapids, MI**
Steketee, John P. .... Grand Rapids, MI
Steketee, John Powers .... Chicago, IL
Steketee, Peter W. .... Grand Rapids, MI
Stekler, Beth A. .... **Washington, DC**
Stekloff, Neil B. .... **Stamford, CT**
Steklov-Hahn, Einat .... New York, NY
Stelacone, Jay A. .... **Washington, DC**
Stelben, Brian T. .... Fairfield, CT
Stelboum, Barry S. .... **New York, NY**
Stelck, Jane E. .... **Washington, DC**
Steldt, Frank A. .... Noblesville, IN
Stelea, Barbara J. .... North Canton, OH
Steles, Nickolas J. .... **Tuscumbia, AL**
Stelk, Roger William .... Arlington Heights, IL
Stell, C. Robert .... **Oklahoma City, OK**
Stell, John E., Jr. .... **Winder, GA**
Stell, Jos. .... La Canada Flintridge, CA
Stell, Michael D. .... **El Paso, TX**
Stella, Annette N. Castro .... San Francisco, CA
Stella, C. Craig .... **Fort Lauderdale, FL**
Stella, C. Craig, P.A., Law Offices of
Fort Lauderdale, FL
Stella, Frances B. .... Harrison, NY
Stella, George E. .... Westbury, NY
Stella, Joseph M. .... **New York, NY**
Stella, Joseph N. .... **Chicago, IL**
Stella, Lucy M. .... Fort Worth, TX
Stella, Michael .... Harrison, NY
Stella, Michael T., Jr. .... Lawrence, MA
Stella, Paul J. .... Ridgefield, CT
Stella, Ronald M. .... **Grand Rapids, MI**
Stella, Walter M. .... **San Francisco, CA**
Stellabotte, John C. .... **New York, NY**
Stellato, Donald E. .... Chicago, IL
Stellato, Frederick J. .... **Philadelphia, PA**
Stellato, John M. .... New Bedford, MA
Stellato, Louis E. .... Cleveland, OH
Stellato, Patrick M. .... Albany, NY
Stellato & Schwartz, Ltd. .... Chicago, IL
Stellberger, Lowell C. .... Livonia, MI
Stelle, John P. .... Brazil, IN
Stelle, Roger T. .... **Schaumburg, IL**
Steller, Brian G. .... **Roseland, NJ**
Steller, Bridget Rahilly .... Poughkeepsie, NY
Steller, James R. .... Columbus, OH
Steller, Robert A. .... **Los Angeles, CA**
San Diego, CA
Stelley, Arthur F. .... Waco, TX
Stelley, John C. .... Boston, MA
Stellick, Robert C., Jr. .... Madison, WI
Stelling, Andrea Mote .... Columbus, OH
Stelling, Leon L. .... Cole Camp, MO
Stelling, Otto C., Jr. .... San Francisco, CA
Stellings, Brande M. .... **New York, NY**
Stellings, David S. .... **New York, NY**
Stellingwerf, Frank .... Detroit, MI
Stellitano, Patrick .... **Austin, TX**
Stelljes, Charles F. .... **Danbury, CT**
Stelljes, Roger J. .... Minneapolis, MN
Stellmach, William T. .... New York, NY
Stellman, Leslie R. .... **Baltimore, MD**
Stellman, William J. .... Pinehurst, NC
Stellmann, Elizabeth P.S.
Hunt Valley, MD
Stellmon, John M. .... Lewiston, ID
Stello, Jamie C. .... Punxsutawney, PA
Stello, Joseph R. .... Brooklyn, NY
Stellpflug, C. David .... **De Pere, WI**
Stellpflug, Janet Scheel .... **Minneapolis, MN**
Stellpflug, Janssen, Nell & Hammer, S.C.
De Pere, WI
Green Bay, WI
Stellpflug, Luke R. .... Anoka, MN
Stellute, Joseph J. .... Hampton, VA
Stellwagen, Robert H., Jr. .... **Pasadena, CA**
Stelly, Alex J., Jr. .... **Beaumont, TX**
Stelly, Anton J. .... **Richmond, VA**
Stelly, Herbert J., Sr. .... Gulfport, MS
Stelly, J. Kevin .... **Lafayette, LA**
Stelly, Lisa C. .... Phoenix, AZ
Stelly, Nora M. .... **Lafayette, LA**
Stelly, Paxton K. .... **Metairie, LA**
Stelly, W. Chad .... **Metairie, LA**
Stelmach, Mark R. .... New Orleans, LA
Stelmach, Steven, Jr. .... Troy, MI
Stelman, Jeffrey L. .... **Salem, MA**
Stelman, Michael N. .... **Salem, MA**
Stelnicki, Phillip J. .... Chicago, IL
Stelogeannis, George A., (P.A.) .... Ocala, FL
Stelogeannis & Tucker .... Ocala, FL
Stelt, James R. .... Williamston, MI
Steltemeier, R. William, Jr. .... **Nashville, TN**
Steltemeier & Westbrook .... **Nashville, TN**
Steltenkamp, Gerald Lawrence
Cleveland, OH
Steltenpohl, Garth F. .... Powell Butte, OR
Steltenpohl, Robert H. .... Cincinnati, OH
Stelter, Daniel C. .... **Dayton, OH**
Stelter, Katherine L. .... Seattle, WA
Stelter, Mark A. .... Conroe, TX
Stelter, N. Richard .... Chicago Heights, IL
Stelter, Susan L. .... Manhattan Beach, CA
Stelts, Anne Elizabeth .... **Rock Hill, SC**
Steltzlen, Janelle H. .... Tulsa, OK
Stelwagon, William M. .... **New York, NY**
Stelzenmuller, C. V. .... **Birmingham, AL**
Stelzer, Edward A. .... **New York, NY**
Stelzer, Gregory L. .... **Chicago, IL**
Stelzer, J. T. .... **Bryan, OH**
Stelzer, Kerry Lynn .... Boston, MA
Stelzer, Lance R., (P.A.) .... Miami, FL
Stelzer, Michael F. .... St. Louis, MO
Stelzer, Peter J. .... Dorchester, MA
Stelzig, Tim .... **Washington, DC**
Stelzner, Luis G. .... **Albuquerque, NM**
Stem, Christi C. .... **Smithfield, NC**
Stem, Frederick R. .... Milford, NJ
Stem, Robert .... Marlin, TX
Stem & Stem .... Milford, NJ
Stember, John .... **Erie, PA**
Greensburg, PA
Stember, John .... **Pittsburgh, PA**
Stember, Lesa K. .... **Fort Lauderdale, FL**
Stember, Mark L. .... **Des Moines, IA**
Stemberger & Associates, P.C.
Newnan, GA
Peachtree City, GA
Stemberger, Edward J. .... **Washington, DC**
Stemberger, John, A Prof. Assoc., Law Offices of .... **Kissimmee, FL**
Orlando, FL
Sanford, FL
Stemberger, John T. .... **Orlando, FL**
Stemberger, Tony R. .... **St. Paul, MN**
Stemberger, William J., Jr. .... **Newnan, GA**
Stember-Ottensmeier, Darla D.
Oskaloosa, KS
Stembler, William J. .... Atlanta, GA
Stemen, Robin M. .... **San Diego, CA**
Stemen, Sue Ellen .... Indianapolis, IN
Stemerick, David M. .... Indianapolis, IN
Stemerman, Steven L. .... Las Vegas, NV
Stemke, Russell S. .... Mount Pleasant, SC
Stemle, Angela D. .... **Indianapolis, IN**
Stemler, Alison M. .... **Louisville, KY**
Stemler, Edward E. .... Everett, WA
Stemler, Janet Simmons .... **Long Beach, CA**
Stemler, Patty Merkamp
Department of Justice, Criminal Division, GV
Stemler, Robert J. .... **Long Beach, CA**
Stemm, Mark S. .... **Columbus, OH**
Stemmans, W. Michael .... Baton Rouge, LA
Stemmer, Donald R. .... Pennsauken, NJ
Stemmer, Linda S. H. .... Union City, IN
Stemmler, Beth Ann .... **Morristown, NJ**
Stemmler, David F. .... **Pittsburgh, PA**
Wheeling, WV
Stemmler, Frederick J. .... **Irvine, CA**
Stemmler, James A. .... St. Louis, MO
Stemmler, John A. .... **Memphis, TN**
Stemmons, Randee S. .... Mount Vernon, MO
Stemmons, Robert .... Mount Vernon, MO
Stemmons, Stemmons & Cowherd
Mount Vernon, MO
Stempel, Alan R. .... **Ridgefield, CT**
Stempel, Andrea H. .... **New York, NY**
Stempel Bennett Claman & Hochberg, P.C.
New York, NY
Stempel, Dyanne L. .... Universal City, CA
Stempel, Ivy B. .... **New York, NY**
Stempel, James A. .... **Chicago, IL**
Stempel, James I. .... New York, NY
Stempel, Jeffrey W. .... Tallahassee, FL
Stempel, Joan V. .... Boston, MA
Stempel, Karen Ostrow .... Washington, DC
Stempel, Lee A. .... New York, NY
Stempel, Oscar S. .... Los Angeles, CA
Stempel, Richard C. .... New York, NY
Stempel, Samuel B. .... **Chicago, IL**
Stempel, Scott A. .... **Washington, DC**
Stempel, Vincent F. .... Garden City, NY
Stempel, William D. .... New Haven, CT
Stempien, Catherine S. .... Liberty Corner, NJ
Stempien, Gregory J. .... Livonia, MI
Stempien, Gregory J., P.C. .... Livonia, MI
Stempien, James Henry .... Columbus, OH
Stempien, Jeanne .... Detroit, MI
Stempien, Marvin R. .... **Southfield, MI**
Stempien, Ronald J. .... Meriden, CT
Stempkovski, Richard C., Jr.
Minneapolis, MN
Stempler, Andrew P. .... Boston, MA
Stempler, David S., (P.C.) .... Washington, DC
Stempler, Howard E. .... Worcester, MA
Stempler, Jack L. .... Alexandria, VA
Stempler, Judith F. .... **New York, NY**
Stempler, Larry A. .... **Florham Park, NJ**
Stempler, Marilyn D. (IBA) .... **Boston, MA**
Stempler, Mark N. .... Department of Defense, Armed Services Board of Contract Appeals, GV
Stempler, Michael .... Silver Spring, MD
Stempler, Randall I. .... New York, NY
Stempler, Randi K. .... New York, NY
Stempler, Robert .... **Los Angeles, CA**
Stempler, Robert .... **Palm Desert, CA**
Stempler, Stanley .... **New York, NY**
Stemplewicz, John T.
Department of Justice, Civil Division, GV
Stempson, David W. .... Lincoln, NE
Stemwedel, Charles G. .... Palatine, IL
Stemwedel, John A. .... Hopewell Junction, NY
Sten, John A. .... Boston, MA
Stenard Sabitt, Karen M. .... Eugene, OR
Stenback, Sara Lynn .... **Bloomfield Hills, MI**
Stenberg, Dean E. .... San Jose, CA
Stenberg, Donald B. .... Lincoln, NE
Stenberg, F. Joe .... San Antonio, TX
Stenberg, Neal E. .... **Lincoln, NE**
Stenberg, Richard A. .... **New York, NY**
Stenberg, Sunseri, Roe & Pickard
San Jose, CA
Stencel, Debra N. .... **Washington, DC**
Stenchever, Marc R. .... Seattle, WA
Sten-Clanton, Albert E. .... Dorchester, MA
Stendahl, Pamela J. .... **Portland, OR**
Stendardi, Gloria .... Las Vegas, NV
Stender, Albert N. .... Cranford, NJ
Stender, Christopher .... El Centro, CA
Stender, F. Frederick .... Madison, WI
Stender & Hernandez .... Cranford, NJ
Stender, Marjorie A. .... **San Diego, CA**
Stender, Mark K. .... **San Diego, CA**
Stender, Marvin .... **San Francisco, CA**
Stender, Steven A. .... **Chicago, IL**
Stendig, Barry S. .... New York, NY
Stene, George R. .... San Diego, CA
Stene, Jean S. .... Chula Vista, CA
Steneck, Joanne B. .... Augusta, ME
Stenehjem, Leland M., Jr. .... Fargo, ND
Stenehjem, Mark L. .... **Williston, ND**
Stenehjem, Wayne K. .... Grand Forks, ND
Stenersen, Doris R. .... Fremont, CA
Stenerson, Todd M. .... **Washington, DC**
Stenfeldt, Lillian G. .... **Palo Alto, CA**
Stengel, Bridget Ann .... Rock Island, IL
Stengel, Bruce V. .... Newport, IN
Stengel, Elizabeth B. .... **Memphis, TN**
Stengel, George J. (Dick) .... San Antonio, TX
Stengel, James L. .... **New York, NY**
Stengel, John P. .... Lancaster, PA
Stengel, Karen M. .... **Washington, DC**
Stengel, L. Edward, Jr. .... Sheboygan, WI
Stengel, Lawrence E. .... Lancaster, PA
Stengel, Lawrence F. .... Lancaster, PA
Stengel, Lisa C. .... Sheboygan, WI
Stengel, Michael J. .... **Memphis, TN**
Stengel, Michael J., P.C. .... **Memphis, TN**
Stengel, Robert F. .... Rocky Hill, CT
Stengel, Robert M. .... Doylestown, PA
Wilkes-Barre, PA
Stengel, Robert M., P.C. .... Doylestown, PA
Stengel, Scott A. .... **Washington, DC**
Stengel, Stuart S. .... Great Neck, NY
Stengel, William R., Jr. .... Rock Island, IL
Stenger, Daniel F. .... **Washington, DC**
Stenger & Finnerty .... **Buffalo, NY**
Stenger, Frank W. .... Washington, DC
Stenger, George W. .... St. Paul, MN
Stenger, Georgianna Ringler .... Johnstown, PA
Stenger, James A. .... **Washington, DC**
Stenger, Jenny Lynn Hebert
Washington, DC
Stenger, John H. .... Lansing, MI
Stenger, John H. .... **Buffalo, NY**
Stenger, John J. .... **Dallas, TX**
Stenger, Julie .... **St. Louis, MO**
Stenger, Kenneth M. .... Poughkeepsie, NY
Wappingers Falls, NY
Stenger, Mark G. .... Cincinnati, OH
Stenger, Mitchell M. .... **Buffalo, NY**
Stenger, Phillip S. .... **Grand Rapids, MI**
Stenger, Ralph T. .... Belleville, IL
Stenger, Robert G. .... Hartland, WI
Stenger, Robert L. .... Louisville, KY
Stenger, Ronald K. .... Springfield, MO
Stenger, Stacey A. .... Springfield, MO
Stenger & Stenger, P.C.
Grand Rapids, MI
Holland, MI
Stenger, Steven V. .... **St. Louis, MO**
Stenger, Susan E. .... **Boston, MA**
Stenger, Suzanne K. .... **Grand Rapids, MI**
Stengle, Dan R. .... **Tallahassee, FL**
Stenglein, Dulce M. .... **Houston, TX**
Stenglein, Mike .... **Houston, TX**
Stengren, Ralph L. .... **Washington, DC**
Stenholm, Chris W. .... **Fort Worth, TX**
Stenhouse, D. Scott .... **Atlanta, GA**
Stenhouse, Wallace J., Jr. .... Chicago, IL
Stenicka, Charles E., III .... Brookfield, WI
Steninger Balkenbush & Free, LLC
Denver, CO
Steninger, John A. .... Denver, CO
Stenken, Joseph F. .... Cincinnati, OH
Stenlake, Rodney L. .... New York, NY
Stenlake, Ronald P. .... Allen, TX
Stenlake, Ronald W. .... Los Angeles, CA
Stenlund, Paula M. .... **Dubuque, IA**
Stenman, Eric G. .... San Diego, CA
Stenmark, Lizbeth J. .... Louisville, CO
Stenmoe, Gregory J. .... **Minneapolis, MN**
Stenn, Edgar H. .... Oak Brook, IL
Stennes, Matthew L. .... **Washington, DC**
Stennes, Matthew Lorris .... Washington, DC
Stennes, Stephen L. .... **Montevideo, MN**
Stennes, Todd M. .... **Chicago, IL**
Stennett, Carolyn P. .... **Syracuse, NY**
Stennett, Donald L. .... **Charleston, WV**
Stennett, Jack C. .... Torrance, CA
Stennett, John L. .... San Diego, CA
Stennett, John P. .... San Diego, CA
Stennett & Stennett .... San Diego, CA
Stennett, Steven D. .... **Indianapolis, IN**
Stennett, Wilkinson & Peden, A Professional Association .... Jackson, MS
Stennett, William C. .... Tupelo, MS
Stennett-Yancey, Paula N. .... Meridian, MS
Stennis, Gail .... Amarillo, TX
Stennis, Hardy R. .... Macon, MS
Stennis, John Hampton .... **Jackson, MS**
Stensaas, Scott .... Flint, MI
Stenshoel, Eric .... **New York, NY**
Stensland, Craig W. .... Peoria, IL
Stensland, Dean A. .... **Missoula, MT**
Stenson, Daniel A. .... **San Francisco, CA**
Stenson, Gary L. .... St. Paul, MN
Stenson, Joseph James .... Detroit, MI
Stenson, Michael P. .... Sacramento, CA
Stenson, Robert E. .... Los Angeles, CA
Stenson, Suzanne H. .... **Dallas, TX**
Stenson, Thomas G. .... New York, NY
Stenstedt, Anders E. .... **San Francisco, CA**
Stenstrom, Dennis G. .... San Diego, CA
Stenstrom, Douglas .... **Sanford, FL**
Stenstrom, McIntosh, Colbert, Whigham & Simmons, P.A. .... **Sanford, FL**
Stenstrom, Robert B. .... Bethesda, MD
Stent, Ernest R. .... **Sun City, AZ**
Stenton, Kimberly S. .... Los Angeles, CA
Stenton, W. John .... **Marquette, MI**
Stentz, Jon W. .... **Bethesda, MD**
Stenuf, Theodore W. .... Minoa, NY
Stenz, Robert D. .... Woodbury, NY
Stenzel, Dennis E. .... **Portland, OR**
Stenzel, Douglas L. .... Ventura, CA
Stenzel, Gary R., P.S. .... Spokane, WA
Stenzel, Paulette L. .... East Lansing, MI
Stenzel & Price .... Spokane, WA
Stenzel, Robert D. .... Queens Village, NY
Stenzel, Robt. J. .... Minnetonka, MN
Steorts, Sharon .... Charleston, WV
Stepakoff, Mark H. .... Worcester, MA
Stepakoff, Michael .... Tampa, FL
Stepakoff, Sherri Federbush .... **Boston, MA**
Stepan, Chad J. .... **Minneapolis, MN**
Stepan, Linda L. .... Cleveland, OH
Stepan, M. Jean .... St. Paul, MN
Stepan, Paul H. .... Chicago, IL
Stepanchenko, Vadim D.
Redwood City, CA
Stepanek, Michael J., Jr. .... South Bend, IN
Stepanek, Walter .... Cleveland, OH
Stepanek, William J. .... Cleveland, OH
Stepanenko, George .... San Jose, CA
Stepaniak, Kurt E. .... South Bend, IN
Stepaniak, Mark J. .... **Cincinnati, OH**
Stepanian, Leo M. .... Butler, PA
Stepanian, Leo M., II .... Butler, PA
Stepanian, Michael .... San Francisco, CA
Stepanian & Muscatello .... Butler, PA
Stepanian, Steven A., II .... Pittsburgh, PA
Stepanic, Mary J. .... Columbus, OH
Stepanich, Thomas P. .... Waukegan, IL
Stepanicich, Gregory W.
San Francisco, CA
Stepanishen, William .... Canton, MA
Stepanovic, Ronald A. .... **Cleveland, OH**
Stepanovich, Donald .... Highland, IN
Stepanovich, John G. .... **Virginia Beach, VA**
Stepans, Edward R. .... **San Francisco, CA**
Stepanski, Lisa A. .... **Costa Mesa, CA**
Stepanski, Marcelyn A.
Farmington Hills, MI
Stepanuk, Kevin D. .... Cherry Hill, NJ
Stepek, Daniel T. .... Mount Clemens, MI
Stepek, Mark W. .... Mount Clemens, MI
Stephan, Albert J., Jr. .... St. Louis, MO
Stephan, Carl E. .... Albany, NY
Stephan, Charles Michael .... **Cincinnati, OH**
Stephan, Cheryl B. .... La Porte, IN
Stephan, Daniel D. .... Fort Lauderdale, FL
Stephan, David A. .... **Dallas, TX**
Stephan, E. Douglas .... **Lexington, KY**
Stephan, Edmund A., III .... Chicago, IL
Stephan, Edwin C. .... Sturgeon Bay, WI
Stephan, Este J. .... **Pittsburgh, PA**
Stephan, George J. .... **Los Angeles, CA**
Stephan, George P. .... Hartford, CT
Stephan, Gregory D. .... **San Diego, CA**
Stephan, John S. .... San Francisco, CA
Stephan, Katharina R. .... Haddonfield, NJ
Stephan, Kenneth C. .... Lincoln, NE
Stephan, Kvanvig, Stone & Trainor
Boise, ID
Sun Valley, ID
Twin Falls, ID
Stephan Law Office .... Valley City, ND
Stephan, Lisa M. .... **Garden City, NY**
Stephan, Michael E. .... Minnetonka, MN
Stephan, Oringher, Richman & Theodora, P.C. .... **Costa Mesa, CA**
Los Angeles, CA
Stephan, Paul Edmond .... San Francisco, CA
Stephan, Peter D. .... Xenia, OH
Stephan, Phyllis Marie .... New York, NY
Stephan, Rayna A. .... Costa Mesa, CA
Stephan, Reinhard G. .... Winter Park, FL
Stephan, Richard A. .... Valley City, ND
Stephan, Robert D. .... **Denver, CO**
Stephan, Robert J. .... Grand Rapids, MI
Stephan, Robert J., Jr. .... Phoenix, AZ
Stephan, Robert, Jr., P.C. .... Phoenix, AZ
Stephan, Robert M. .... **Stamford, CT**
Stephan, Robert T. .... Wichita, KS
Stephan, Robert W. .... **Twin Falls, ID**
Stephan, Robin C. .... **New York, NY**
Stephan, Scott W. .... **Pittsburgh, PA**
Stephan, Steven Patrick
Overland Park, KS
Stephan, Summer Sabraw .... San Diego, CA
Stephan, Susan Hayes .... **Minneapolis, MN**
Stephan, Ted Marc .... Melbourne, FL
Stephan, Thomas L. .... Altamonte Springs, FL
Stephan, Thomas L., P.A.
Altamonte Springs, FL
Stephan, Wayne P. .... Dayton, OH
Stephanakis, George A. .... New York, NY
Stephani, Otto C., Jr. .... Wheaton, IL
Stephan-Nolan, Donna M. .... **Bedminster, NJ**
Stephanoff, Susan M. .... **Cleveland, OH**
Stephanos, Ann M. .... Washington, DC
Stephanou, Stephen J. .... Sherman Oaks, CA

Stephenson, Jay C. ..... Marietta, GA
Stephenson, Jeffrey G. ..... St. Paul, MN
Stephenson, John C. ..... Centerville, MA
Stephenson, John D., Jr. ..... Great Falls, MT
Stephenson, John E., Jr. ..... Atlanta, GA
Stephenson, John M. ..... Albany, GA
Stephenson, John M., Jr. ..... Dallas, TX
Stephenson, John W. ..... Palatka, FL
Stephenson, Joy ..... Burbank, CA
Stephenson, Kathleen A. ..... Philadelphia, PA
Stephenson, Kathryn A. ..... Nashville, TN
Stephenson, Kent R. ..... Houston, TX
Stephenson, Kevin L. ..... San Diego, CA
Las Vegas, NV
Stephenson, Larry A. ..... Fuquay-Varina, NC
Stephenson, Larry C. ..... Kennewick, WA
Stephenson, Lawrence D. ..... Edina, MN
Stephenson, Leland D. ..... Fresno, CA
Stephenson, Lisa ..... New York, NY
Stephenson, Lucius H. ..... Monterey, VA
Stephenson, Lynne A. ..... San Jose, CA
Stephenson, M. Michael ..... Shelbyville, IN
Stephenson, Mack ..... Springfield, IL
Stephenson, Mandi D. Fort Lauderdale, FL
Stephenson, Marcia A. ..... Baltimore, MD
Stephenson, Margaret Laurel ..... Dallas, TX
Stephenson, Maria I. O'Byrne New Orleans, LA
Stephenson, Maria V. ..... Bellmore, NY
Stephenson, Marilee ..... Portsmouth, OH
Stephenson, Mark C. ..... Philadelphia, PA
Stephenson, Mark D. ..... Minneapolis, MN
Stephenson, Mark E. ..... Lorain, OH
Stephenson, Mark G. ..... Rochester, MN
Stephenson, Marsha L. ..... Las Vegas, NV
Stephenson, Martha King ..... Fayetteville, GA
Stephenson, Martha S. ..... Little Rock, AR
Stephenson, Mason W. ..... Atlanta, GA
Stephenson, Mathew ..... San Francisco, CA
Stephenson, Matthews & Chávarri, LLC New Orleans, LA
Stephenson & McKay, L.L.P. Victoria, TX
Stephenson, Michael M. ..... San Pedro, CA
Stephenson, Michelle M. ..... Troy, MI
Stephenson, Nancy G. ..... Seattle, WA
Stephenson, Nancy S. ..... Albany, GA
Stephenson, Natalie C. ..... Charlotte, NC
Stephenson, Nicole M. ..... Hamilton, OH
Stephenson, Patricia Federal Trade Commission, Offices of Commissioners, GV
Stephenson, Patrick C. ..... Omaha, NE
Stephenson, Paul H., III ..... Jackson, MS
Stephenson, Phillip E. ..... Marion, IN
Stephenson, Phyllis Pattillo Corpus Christi, TX
Houston, TX
Stephenson, Polly Clarke ..... Hillsborough, CA
Stephenson, R. Jack ..... Seattle, WA
Stephenson, R. Lee ..... Richmond, VA
Stephenson, Ralph W., Jr. ..... Baton Rouge, LA
Stephenson, Rebecca ..... Marietta, GA
Stephenson, Rebecca B. ..... Lexington, KY
Stephenson, Rebecca K. ..... Birmingham, AL
Stephenson, Richard C. ..... Lexington, KY
Stephenson, Richard C. ..... Cary, NC
Stephenson, Richard G. San Francisco, CA
Stephenson, Richard I. ..... Wichita, KS
Stephenson, Richard L. New Philadelphia, OH
Stephenson, Richard S. ..... Ripley, WV
Stephenson, Robert B. ..... Albuquerque, NM
Stephenson, Robert H. ..... Cook, MN
Virginia, MN
Stephenson, Robert J., IV ..... Greenville, SC
Stephenson, Robert M. ..... Chicago, IL
Stephenson, Robert R. ..... Pittsburgh, PA
Stephenson, Robert R., II New Philadelphia, OH
Stephenson, Robert S. ..... Buffalo, NY
Stephenson, Robert T. ..... New York, NY
Stephenson, Robert Timothy Washington, DC
Stephenson, Ronald G. ..... Portland, OR
Stephenson, Ronald L. ..... St. Petersburg, FL
Stephenson, Roscoe B., III ..... Covington, VA
Stephenson, Roscoe B., Jr. ..... Covington, VA
Stephenson, Ross C. ..... Fort Worth, TX
Stephenson, Roy E. ..... Santa Fe, NM
Stephenson, Sam L. ..... Greenville, SC
Stephenson, Scott D. ..... Chicago, IL
Stephenson, Scott E. ..... Wichita Falls, TX
Stephenson, Shanda M. ..... Costa Mesa, CA
Stephenson, Sheryl N. ..... Baltimore, MD
Stephenson & Stephenson Los Angeles, CA
San Pedro, CA
Stephenson, Stephenson & Carrothers Dover, OH
New Philadelphia, OH
Stephenson & Sutcliffe ..... Rochester, MN
Stephenson, Tenley ..... Boston, MA
Stephenson, Thomas L. ..... Greenville, SC
Stephenson, Tom R. ..... Oklahoma City, OK
Watonga, OK
Stephenson, Travis C. ..... Boulder, CO
Stephenson, W. Michael ..... Anchorage, AK
Stephenson, W. Monroe ..... New Orleans, LA
Stephenson, W. Turner, III Roanoke Rapids, NC
Stephenson & Webber ..... Oklahoma City, OK
Watonga, OK
Stephenson, William K., Jr. ..... Columbia, SC
Stephenson, William Vincent Bowling Green, OH
Stephenson, Worley, Garratt, Schwartz, Garfield & Prairie ..... San Diego, CA
Stephenson-Kuhn, Leigh D. ..... Portland, OR
Stepherson, Angela M. ..... Austin, TX
Stephson, Amy J. ..... Seattle, WA
Stepien, Scott Andrew ..... Niagara Falls, NY
Stepka, Michael S. ..... Traverse City, MI
Stepke, Kenneth E. ..... Danville, IL
Stepkin, Charles ..... San Francisco, CA
Stepler, Howard R., Jr. ..... Frederick, MD
Stepler, Mary Ann ..... Frederick, MD
Stepler, Sharon J. Strange Lawrenceville, GA
Stepleton, Bonnie M. ..... Albuquerque, NM
Stepleton, James V. ..... St. Louis, MO
Stepleton, Kimberly S. ..... Toledo, OH
Stepner, Donald L. ..... Covington, KY
Stepner, Jeffrey A. ..... Covington, KY
Stepnicka, Craig D. ..... Oak Brook, IL
Stepno, Norman H. ..... Alexandria, VA
Stepnowski, Edward L. ..... Oak Park, IL
Stepnowski, Francis E. ..... Chicago, IL
Steponovich & Associates, A Professional Law Corporation ..... Irvine, CA
Steponovich, Michael J., Jr. ..... Irvine, CA
Steponovich, Stephen A. Huntington Beach, CA
Stepovich, Sonia Mireya-Iriarte San Diego, CA
Stepp & Beauchamp LLP Newport Beach, CA
Stepp, Christopher Samuel Hendersonville, NC
Stepp, David R. ..... Los Angeles, CA
Washington, DC
Stepp, Donna B. ..... Monroe, NC
Stepp, Elizabeth ..... New York, NY
Stepp, Groce & Associates Hendersonville, NC
Stepp, Jad J. ..... Houston, TX
Stepp, James W. ..... Houston, TX
Stepp, Jerry L. ..... Atlanta, GA
Stepp, John Edd, Jr. ..... Los Angeles, CA
Stepp, Kenneth S. ..... Inverness, FL
Stepp, Kenneth S., P.A., P.S.C. Inverness, FL
Stepp, LaChelle D. ..... Indianapolis, IN
Stepp, Leigh A. ..... Sacramento, CA
Stepp, Robert E. ..... Columbia, SC
Stepp & Sullivan, P.C. ..... Galveston, TX
Houston, TX
Stepp, Tali R. Department of Labor, GV
Stepp, Thomas E., Jr. Newport Beach, CA
Stepp, W. Harley, Jr. ..... Hendersonville, NC
Steppacher, William C. ..... Scranton, PA
Stepper, Michael ..... New York, NY
Stepper, Steven Mark ..... New York, NY
Steppick, Daniel C. ..... Fort Worth, TX
Steproe, Nancy A. ..... New York, NY
Steps, B. Jill ..... Fairfield, CT
Stepter, Charles R., Jr. ..... Orlando, FL
Stepto, Rebecca L. ..... Charleston, WV
Steptoe, E. Jason National Aeronautics And Space Administration, Office of the General Counsel, GV
Steptoe, James D. ..... Martinsburg, WV
Steptoe & Johnson ..... Charleston, WV
Clarksburg, WV
Fairmont, WV
Martinsburg, WV
Morgantown, WV
Parkersburg, WV
Wheeling, WV
Steptoe & Johnson LLP ..... Phoenix, AZ
Los Angeles, CA
Washington, DC
Steptoe, Mary Lou ..... Washington, DC
Steptoe, Philip P., III ..... Chicago, IL
Steptoe, Robert M. ..... Martinsburg, WV
Steptoe, Robert M., Jr. ..... Clarksburg, WV
Steptoe, Thomas W., Jr. ..... Charles Town, WV
Ster, Brian T. ..... Indianapolis, IN
Sterba, Anne M. ..... Washington, DC
Sterba, Jeanne A. ..... Claremont, CA
Sterba, M. John, Jr. ..... New York, NY
Sterba, Melanie M. ..... Schererville, IN
Sterba, Richard A. ..... Washington, DC
Sterba-Boatwright, Sandra Corpus Christi, TX
Sterbach, Charles R. ..... Phoenix, AZ
Sterbakov, Jill E. ..... Philadelphia, PA
Sterbcow, Paul M. ..... New Orleans, LA
Sterben, Colleen F. ..... Buffalo, NY
Sterbenz, Christopher A. ..... Vienna, VA
Sterbenz, Jolanta ..... Washington, DC
Sterbenz, Stanley R. ..... South Miami, FL
Sterbick, Abel & Sterbick ..... Tacoma, WA
Sterbick, John A. ..... Tacoma, WA
Sterbick, Michael J. ..... Tacoma, WA
Sterbick, Peter L. ..... Tacoma, WA
Sterbick-Nelson, Lou Anne ..... Bisbee, AZ
Sterbin, Johanna E. ..... New York, NY
Sterbinsky, Stephen R. ..... Gardner, MA
Sterchi, Charles F., III ..... Knoxville, TN
Sterchi, Karen L. ..... Los Angeles, CA
Sterchi, Thomas N. ..... Kansas City, MO
Stercho, Olena ..... Jenkintown, PA
Stercho, Yuriy P. ..... King Of Prussia, PA
Stere, Gary S. ..... Atlantic Beach, FL
Steren, E. John ..... Washington, DC
Steren, Marc N. ..... Rockville, MD
Steren, Paula T. ..... West Chester, PA
Sterenberg, Solomon Martin Lanham, MD
Sterenbuch, Martin ..... Bethesda, MD
Sterenfeld, Alan J. ..... Westbury, NY
Sterenfeld, Herbert W. ..... New York, NY
Steres, Mark ..... Los Angeles, CA
Stergas, David W. ..... Norwalk, CT
Sterger, Kass ..... San Diego, CA
Stergio, Anthony G. ..... Houston, TX
Stergio, Gerald P. ..... Hartford, CT
Stergios, J. Fred ..... Massillon, OH
Stergios & Kurtzman Co., L.P.A. Massillon, OH
Stergios, Paul J. ..... Massillon, OH
Stergios, Pericles G. ..... Massillon, OH
Stergios, Peter D. ..... New York, NY
Stergos, Mary K. ..... St. Louis, MO
Sterinbach, Howard B. ..... New York, NY
Steringer, C. Robert ..... Portland, OR
Sterio, James F. ..... Wakefield, MA
Sterk, Calvin J. ..... Lansing, MI
Sterk, Gwendolyn J. ..... Summit, IL
Sterk, Stewart E ..... New York, NY
Sterkel, Alice V. ..... St. Louis, MO
Sterkel, Deborah A. ..... Chickasha, OK
Oklahoma City, OK
Sterkel, Timothy R. ..... Cleveland, OH
Sterken, Thomas A. ..... Seattle, WA
Sterlacci, Michael J. ..... Jersey City, NJ
Sterlacci, Michael V. ..... Palm Beach, FL
New York, NY
Sterle, Frank ..... Paradise, CA
Sterle, Joseph A. ..... Texarkana, TX
Sterling, Abigail-Mary ..... New York, NY
Sterling, Alan DeNeve ..... Costa Mesa, CA
Sterling, Alinor C. ..... New Haven, CT
Sterling, Barry H. ..... Sebastopol, CA
Sterling, Beau ..... Las Vegas, NV
Sterling, Brian R. ..... New York, NY
Sterling & Clack ..... San Francisco, CA
Sterling, Craig ..... San Francisco, CA
Sterling, Craig A. ..... San Francisco, CA
Sterling, David Brent ..... Fayetteville, AR
Sterling, David D. ..... Houston, TX
Sterling, David F. ..... Chicago, IL
Sterling, David W. ..... Hope, AR
Sterling, Davis Watson ..... Encinitas, CA
Sterling, Debra G. ..... Baltimore, MD
Sterling, Dee M. ..... Norfolk, VA
Sterling, Donald R. ..... Roy, UT
Sterling, Donald T. ..... Beverly Hills, CA
Sterling, Edward E. ..... Kansas City, MO
Sterling, Elizabeth R. B. ..... Austin, TX
Sterling & Fausett ..... Fayetteville, AR
Sterling, Felix S. ..... Palo Alto, CA
Sterling, Frances W. ..... Riverside, CA
Sterling, Gabriel Stephen, III Washington, DC
Sterling, Graham L., III ..... Los Angeles, CA
Sterling, Harry J. ..... Fairview Heights, IL
Sterling, Harry J., P.C. ..... Fairview Heights, IL
Sterling, Harry M. ..... Denver, CO
Sterling, Herbert P. ..... Tampa, FL
Sterling, Hillard M. ..... Chicago, IL
Sterling, Ian W. ..... New York, NY
Sterling, J. Robert ..... Pontiac, MI
Sterling, Janis Ann ..... Prescott, AZ
Sterling, John E. ..... Monument, CO
Sterling, John F. ..... Dallas, TX
Sterling, John K. ..... Dallas, TX
Sterling, John L. ..... Cleveland, OH
Sterling, John W., Jr. ..... Walnut Creek, CA
Sterling, Judith Lee ..... Honolulu, HI
Sterling, Julius H. ..... San Antonio, TX
Sterling, Kevin A. ..... Chicago, IL
Sterling, Laurence G. ..... Sebastopol, CA
Sterling, Lea Ann ..... Columbus, OH
Sterling, Leon P. ..... Denver, CO
Sterling, Lisa D. ..... Newport Beach, CA
Sterling, M. John ..... Pittsburgh, PA
Sterling, Marcia Kemp ..... San Rafael, CA
Sterling, Mark A. ..... Miami, FL
Sterling, Michael E. ..... Issaquah, WA
Sterling, Michael L. ..... Norfolk, VA
Sterling, Michelle ..... New York, NY
Sterling, Nathaniel ..... Palo Alto, CA
Sterling, Patricia M. ..... Uniondale, NY
Sterling, Paul Gary ..... San Francisco, CA
Sterling, Peter J. ..... Bloomfield, CT
Sterling, Rand E. ..... Houston, TX
Sterling, Randall C. ..... Escondido, CA
Sterling, Raymond J. ..... Troy, MI
Sterling, Richard J. ..... Tyngsborough, MA
Sterling, Richard T. ..... Midland, MI
Sterling, Richard W. ..... Belleville, IL
Sterling, Robert V. ..... Maumee, OH
Sterling & Schilling, P.C. ..... Pontiac, MI
Sterling, Scott A. ..... Anchorage, AK
Sterling, Scott Andrew ..... Washington, DC
Sterling, Scott E. ..... Arlington, VA
Sterling, Scott L. ..... Orlando, FL
Sterling, Scott L., Law Offices of Orlando, FL
Sterling, Stacy B. ..... Los Angeles, CA
Sterling, Suzanne K. ..... Miami, FL
Sterling, Terry N. ..... San Angelo, TX
Sterling, Terry S. ..... Santa Rosa, CA
Sterling, Thomas C. ..... Hagåtña, GU
Sterling, Thomas D. ..... Chicago, IL
Sterling, Thomas E. ..... State College, PA
Sterling, Thomas W. W., III ..... Pittsburgh, PA
Sterling, Timothy F. ..... Tulsa, OK
Sterling & Tucker ..... Honolulu, HI
Sterling, W. Dawson ..... Houston, TX
Sterling, Wayne L. ..... Bogalusa, LA
Sterling, William C., Jr. ..... New York, NY
Sterling, William E., Jr. ..... Austin, TX
Sterling, William F. ..... Milwaukee, WI
Sterling, William Fisher Westfield Center, OH
Sterling, William N. ..... Los Angeles, CA
Sterling, William W. ..... Sausalito, CA
Sterling, Yvonne ..... Bonita, CA
Sterlinski, Donald J. ..... Tony, WI
Sterman, Gary M. ..... Buffalo, NY
Sterman, Karina Bess ..... Los Angeles, CA
Sterman, Lynn R. ..... Wilmette, IL
Sterman, Milton ..... Arlington, VA
Stermasi, Julie ..... Treasury Department, Office of Regulations and Rulings, GV
Stermer, Daniel J. ..... Fort Lauderdale, FL
Stermer, G. Scott ..... Mount Morris, MI
Stermer, J. Richard ..... Montevideo, MN
Stermer, Robert A. ..... Ocala, FL
Stermitz, Mark L. ..... Missoula, MT
Stermock, Michael C. ..... Lancaster, PA
Stern, Abraham J. ..... Chicago, IL
Stern, Adina T. ..... Irvine, CA
Stern, Aimee Morgan ..... Wheeling, WV
Stern, Akiba ..... New York, NY
Stern, Alan J. ..... Garden City, NY
Stern, Alan J., P.C. ..... Garden City, NY
Stern, Alan N. ..... Denver, CO
Stern, Allan M. ..... Mineola, NY
Stern, Alvin L. ..... New York, NY
Stern, Amy R. ..... Lansdale, PA
Stern, Ana Marie ..... Los Angeles, CA
Stern & Anderson, P.A. ..... Minneapolis, MN
Stern, Andrew J. ..... Philadelphia, PA
Stern, Andrew L. ..... Morristown, NJ
Stern, Andrew M. ..... New York, NY
Stern, Andrew R. ..... Boston, MA
Stern, Andrew W. ..... New York, NY
Stern, Ann Barnett ..... Houston, TX
Stern, Anne E. ..... Denver, CO
Stern, Arthur J. ..... Beachwood, OH
Stern, Arthur L., III ..... Tallahassee, FL
Stern, Arthur O. ..... Boston, MA
Stern, Arthur R. ..... New York, NY
Stern, Asher ..... Deerfield, IL
Stern, Audrey S. ..... Parsippany, NJ
Stern, Avidan J. ..... Chicago, IL
Stern, Barbara L. ..... Lincolnshire, IL
Stern, Barry J. ..... Springfield, MA
Stern, Becky J. ..... Dallas, TX
Stern, Benjamin S. ..... Milwaukee, WI
Stern, Bennett M. ..... Livingston, NJ
Stern Berenbroick, L.L.C. ..... Paramus, NJ
Stern, Bernard ..... Phoenix, AZ
Stern, Bradford M. ..... Cherry Hill, NJ
Stern, Brian P. ..... Livingston, NJ
New York, NY
Stern, Brian S. ..... Richmond, CA
Stern, Brian S. ..... Arlington, VA
Stern, Brian Todd ..... Dover, NH
Stern, Brian Todd, P.A. ..... Dover, NH
Stern, Bruce ..... New York, NY
Stern, Bruce E. ..... Trumbull, CT
Stern, Bruce H. ..... Princeton, NJ
Stern, Bruce M. ..... Newburgh, NY
Stern, Carey E. ..... Brighton, MA
Stern, Carl L. Department of Justice, GV
Stern, Carla F. ..... Atlanta, GA
Stern, Carla M. ..... Department of Justice, Antitrust Division, GV
Stern, Carol C. ..... Newark, NJ
Stern, Carol Meyer ..... White Plains, NY
Stern, Carole ..... Washington, DC
Stern, Charles A. ..... Chicago, IL
Stern, Charles D. ..... Sunland, CA
Stern, Charles E. ..... Madison, WI
Stern, Charles L., Jr. ..... New Orleans, LA
Stern, Charles M. ..... Los Angeles, CA
Stern, Chester J. ..... Denver, CO
Stern, Claude M. ..... Palo Alto, CA
Stern, Claudia J. ..... New York, NY
Stern, Clifford J. ..... New York, NY
Stern, Colin D. ..... Bensalem, PA
Stern, Craig ..... New York, NY
Stern, Craig A. ..... United States Senate, Committee Legal Personnel, GV
Stern, Craig J. ..... San Rafael, CA
Stern, Dale A. ..... Sacramento, CA
Stern, Dana E. ..... Washington, DC
Stern, Daniel R. ..... San Antonio, TX
Stern, Daniel W. ..... Harrisburg, PA
Stern, David ..... Washington, DC
Stern, David ..... Arlington, VA
Stern, David A. ..... Florham Park, NJ
Stern, David A. ..... Tonawanda, NY
Stern, David B. ..... Los Angeles, CA
Stern, David E. ..... Philadelphia, PA
Stern, David H. ..... Los Angeles, CA
Stern, David J. ..... New York, NY
Stern, David Lyle ..... Brooklyn, NY
Stern, David M. ..... Santa Monica, CA
Stern, David M. ..... Salem, MA
Stern, David M. ..... New York, NY
White Plains, NY
Stern, David N. ..... Atlanta, GA
Stern, David S. ..... De Kalb, IL
Stern, David S. ..... Rochester, NY
Stern, Dawn P. ..... Philadelphia, PA
Stern, Dean ..... Los Angeles, CA
Stern, Debbi R. ..... Palo Alto, CA
Boston, MA
Stern, Deborah ..... Washington, DC
Stern, Denise L. ..... Portland, OR
Stern, Diehl, Cornish & Jensen Albert City, IA
Storm Lake, IA
Stern, Donald ..... La Canada Flintridge, CA
Stern, Donald A. ..... New York, NY
Stern, Donald J. ..... Los Angeles, CA
Stern, Donald K. ..... Boston, MA
Stern, Donald L. ..... Omaha, NE
Stern, Doris L. ..... Playa Del Rey, CA
Stern, Douglas N. ..... Philadelphia, PA

Stern, Douglas R. ... Milwaukee, WI
Stern, Douglas W. ... Los Angeles, CA
Stern, Dubrow & Marcus, A Professional Corporation ... Maplewood, NJ
Morristown, NJ
Newark, NJ
Stern, Duke Nordlinger ... St. Petersburg, FL
Stern, E. Louis ... Sarasota, FL
Stern & Edlin, P.C. ... Atlanta, GA
Stern, Edward ... San Francisco, CA
Stern, Edward A. ... Conshohocken, PA
Stern, Edward M. ... Newton, MA
Stern, Edward W. ... Denver, CO
Stern, Elizabeth Espin ... Washington, DC
Stern and Elkind ... Denver, CO
Stern, Ellen J. ... Trenton, NJ
Stern, Elliot M. ... Fort Lauderdale, FL
Stern, Elliott ... Rochester, NY
Stern, Ellis R. ... Beverly Hills, CA
Stern, Emily ... New York, NY
Stern, Eric A. ... Washington, DC
Stern, Eric L. ... Philadelphia, PA
Stern, Erika Aronson ... New York, NY
Stern, Ernest ... Columbus, OH
Stern, Ernest M. ... Washington, DC
Stern, Eugene ... Woodmere, NY
Stern, Eugene B. ... Los Angeles, CA
Stern, Fay Taub ... Woodmere, NY
Stern, Felecia L. ... New York, NY
Stern, Frances R. ... Boise, ID
Stern, Frank ... New York, NY
Stern, Frederick C. ... New York, NY
Stern, Fredric W. ... Los Angeles, CA
Stern, Fredrick H. ... Encino, CA
Stern, Fredrick Paul ... Bohemia, NY
Stern, Gail M. ... Baltimore, MD
Stern, Gail S. ... Hamden, CT
Stern, Gary B. ... Chicago, IL
Stern, Gary E. ... Hackensack, NJ
Stern, Gary J. ... Chicago, IL
Stern, Gary M. ... Los Angeles, CA
Stern, Gary M. ... Steubenville, OH
Stern, Gary N. ... Los Angeles, CA
Palm Springs, CA
Stern, Geoffrey ... Columbus, OH
Stern, George ... Northridge, CA
Stern, George S. ... Atlanta, GA
Stern, Gerald ... New York, NY
Stern, Gerald D. ... Palo Alto, CA
Stern, Gerald M. ... Washington, DC
Stern, Gidon D. ... New York, NY
Stern, Glenn E. ... Monrovia, CA
Stern, Glenn R. ... Lakewood, NJ
Stern & Goldberg ... Beverly Hills, CA
Los Angeles, CA
Stern & Gonzalez ... Livingston, NJ
New York, NY
Stern & Greenberg ... Newark, NJ
Roseland, NJ
Stern, Gregory ... Blue Bell, PA
Stern, Gregory E. ... Houston, TX
Stern, Gregory K. ... Chicago, IL
Stern, Gregory K., P.C. ... Chicago, IL
Stern, H. Peter ... Mountainville, NY
Stern, Hal T. ... Rockville, MD
Stern, Hamilton ... Northbrook, IL
Stern, Harold ... Huntington Woods, MI
Stern, Harold S. ... Cleveland, OH
Stern, Harry L. ... Brooklyn, NY
Stern, Harry M. ... Kensington, MD
Stern, Harvey L. ... Lawrenceville, NJ
Stern, Helen F. ... Los Angeles, CA
Stern & Hellman, Ltd. ... Chicago, IL
Stern, Henry H., Jr. ... St. Louis, MO
Stern, Henry J. ... New York, NY
Stern, Herbert A. ... Iselin, NJ
Stern, Herbert G. ... Columbus, OH
Stern, Herbert J. ... Roseland, NJ
Stern, Herbert L., III ... Denver, CO
Stern, Herbert L., Jr. ... Chicago, IL
Stern, Herman ... Montebello, CA
Stern, Hildy S. ... Sacramento, CA
Stern, Hillary A. ... Department of Justice, Civil Division, GV
Stern, Holly C. ... Newark, NJ
Stern, Horace ... Philadelphia, PA
Stern, Horace A. ... Philadelphia, PA
Stern, Howard ... Paramus, NJ
Stern, Howard J. ... New York, NY
Stern, Howard J. ... Houston, TX
Stern, Howard L., The Law Office of
Camp Springs, MD
Stern, Howard M. ... Garden City, NY
Stern, Howard S. ... Cleveland, OH
Stern, Ilene B. ... White Plains, NY
Stern, Irving C. ... Houston, TX
Stern, J. Leonard ... Santa Monica, CA
Stern, Jack ... Staten Island, NY
Stern, Jack G. ... New York, NY
Stern, Jack M. ... Englewood, CO
Stern, Jacqueline M. ... San Diego, CA
Stern, Jacqueline O. ... New York, NY
Stern, James A. ... Steubenville, OH
Stern, James F. ... Longboat Key, FL
Stern, James F. ... Milwaukee, WI
Stern, James L.
Department of Transportation, Board of Contract Appeals, GV
Stern, James M. ... San Diego, CA
Stern, James M. ... Denver, CO
Stern, James M. ... Belleville, IL
Stern, James Russell ... Chicago, IL
Stern, Jamie E. ... New York, NY
Stern, Janet S. ... Fort Lee, NJ
Stern, Janice Livesay ... Albion, MI
Stern, Jason A. ... New York, NY
Stern, Jeffrey ... New York, NY
Stern, Jeffrey A. ... Brookline, MA
Stern, Jeffrey A. ... Cleveland, OH
Stern, Jeffrey B. ... Washington, DC
Stern, Jeffrey M. ... Houston, TX
Stern, Jeffrey Ross ... New York, NY
Stern, Jeffrey S. ... Los Angeles, CA
Stern, Jeffrey S. ... Boston, MA
Stern, Jennifer ... Las Vegas, NV
Reno, NV
Stern, Jennifer K. ... Englewood, CO
Stern, Jerome H. ... Hallandale Beach, FL
Stern, Jerome H. ... Chicago, IL
Stern, Jerrold S. ... Sanibel, FL
Stern, Jerry R. ... Encino, CA
Stern, Jill Abeshouse ... Washington, DC
Stern, Jill T. ... Pittsburg, CA
Stern, Joan N. ... Philadelphia, PA
Stern, Joanne B. ... Costa Mesa, CA
Stern, Joel S. ... New York, NY
Stern, John C. ... Chicago, IL
Stern, John H. ... Indianapolis, IN
Stern, John J. ... Paramus, NJ
Stern, John M., Jr. ... Anchorage, AK
Stern, John N. ... Winnetka, IL
Stern, Jonathan A. ... New York, NY
Stern, Jonathan L. ... Washington, DC
Stern, Jonathan M. ... Washington, DC
Stern, Jordan ... New York, NY
Stern, Jos. ... Farmingdale, NY
Stern, Joseph ... Fort Collins, CO
Stern, Joseph A. ... New York, NY
Stern, Joyce Reuben ... Rockville, MD
Stern, Judith R.S. ... Boston, MA
Stern, Judith Susan ... New York, NY
Stern, Julian N. ... Palo Alto, CA
Stern, Julie Rose ... Pittsburgh, PA
Stern, Julius ... New York, NY
Stern, Karen L. ... Worcester, MA
Stern, Karl S. ... Houston, TX
Stern Keiser Panken & Wohl, LLP
New York, NY
White Plains, NY
Stern, Kenneth D. ... Boca Raton, FL
Stern, Kenneth D. ... Merrick, NY
Stern, Kenneth D., P.A. ... Boca Raton, FL
Stern, Kenneth H. ... Denver, CO
Stern, Kenneth J. ... Huntington, NY
Stern, Kenneth S. ... New York, NY
Stern, Kevin E. ... Washington, DC
Stern & Klepfer, L.L.P. ... Asheboro, NC
Burlington, NC
Greensboro, NC
High Point, NC
Winston-Salem, NC
Stern, Kresslein & Thornton, P.A.
Frederick, MD
Stern, Larry E. ... Minneapolis, MN
Stern, Laurence C. ... Glen Rock, NJ
Stern, Laurence Michael ... Rye, NY
Stern, Laurence R. ... New York, NY
Stern, Lavinthal Norgaard & Kapnick
Englewood, NJ
Hackensack, NJ
Livingston, NJ
Newark, NJ
Stern, Lawrence F. ... Los Angeles, CA
Stern, Lawrence I. ... Los Angeles, CA
Stern, Lawrence M. ... New York, NY
Stern, Lawrence Mark ... New York, NY
Stern, Lawrence P. ... Englewood Cliffs, NJ
Stern, Lawrence S. ... Bethesda, MD
Stern, Leo G. ... Minneapolis, MN
Stern, Leonard A., II ... Dallas, TX
Stern, Leslie F. ... Long Island City, NY
Stern, Leslie R. ... Boston, MA
Stern, Levy & Pellegrino, LLP
New York, NY
Stern, Lewis A., (P.C.) ... New York, NY
Stern, Lilian S. ... Tarrytown, NY
Stern, Linda C. ... San Bernardino, CA
Stern, Lisa ... Los Angeles, CA
Stern, Lisa A. ... Baltimore, MD
Stern, Lisa D. ... Royersford, PA
Stern, Lisa E. ... Newark, NJ
Stern, Lisa M. ... New York, NY
Stern, Lowell R. ... Washington, DC
Stern, Lynne ... Washington, DC
Stern, Lynne Rothschild ... Metairie, LA
Stern, Marc ... New York, NY
Stern, Marc D. ... New York, NY
Stern, Marc I. ... Los Angeles, CA
Stern, Marc J. ... Inwood, NY
Stern, Marc M. ... Los Angeles, CA
Stern, Marc O. ... San Diego, CA
Stern, Marc S. ... Seattle, WA
Stern, Margaret B. ... Portland, OR
Stern, Margo BeVier ... Washington, DC
Stern, Mark ... Westport, CT
Stern, Mark ... Department of Justice, Civil Division, GV
Stern, Mark A. ... Detroit, MI
Stern, Mark D. ... Somerville, MA
Stern, Mark D. ... Goshen, NY
Stern, Mark E. ... Wyandotte, MI
Stern, Mark O. ... Springfield, IL
Stern, Mark S. ... Milwaukee, WI
Stern, Marsha ... New York, NY
Stern, Marshall M. ... Huntington Station, NY
Stern, Martin A. ... New Orleans, LA
Stern, Martin D. ... Coral Gables, FL
Stern, Martin L. ... Washington, DC
Stern, Martin L. ... Chicago, IL
Stern, Marvin A. ... Sacramento, CA
Stern, Marvin A. ... Boston, MA
Stern, Marvin R. ... Washington, DC
Stern, Mary Mannion ... Albuquerque, NM
Stern, Matthew D. ... Austin, TX
Stern, Maurice M. ... Tucson, AZ
Stern, Max D. ... Boston, MA
Stern, Maximilian H. ... San Francisco, CA
Stern, Maxwell & Associates, L.L.C.
Chicago, IL
Stern, Michael ... Palo Alto, CA
Stern, Michael ... House of Representatives, Congressional Assistants, GV
Stern, Michael A. ... Minneapolis, MN
Stern, Michael A. ... New York, NY
Stern, Michael B. ... St. Louis, MO
Stern, Michael C. ... Montrose, CO
Stern, Michael D. ... Taneytown, MD
Stern, Michael E. ... New York, NY
Stern, Michael E. ... New York, NY
Stern, Michael G. ... New York, NY
Stern, Michael Jay ... Los Angeles, CA
Royal Oak, MI
Stern, Michael L. ... Los Angeles, CA
Stern, Michael P. ... Vienna, VA
Stern, Michael R. ... Old Saybrook, CT
Stern, Michael R. ... Queensbury, NY
Stern, Michael R. ... Vienna, VA
Stern, Michael S. ... Long Island City, NY
Stern, Michael Z. ... Austin, TX
Stern, Michel P. ... Bellevue, WA
Stern, Michelle L. ... Encino, CA
Stern, Michelle W. ... Denver, CO
Stern, Milton R. ... Brooklyn, NY
Stern, Milton R. ... Painesville, OH
Stern, Mindy H. ... New York, NY
Stern, Mitchell A. ... Cleveland, OH
Stern, Mitchell B. ... New York, NY
Stern & Montana ... New York, NY
Stern, Morris ... Maplewood, NJ
Stern, Morris M. ... Los Angeles, CA
Stern, Nancy Ann ... New York, NY
Stern, Nat ... Tallahassee, FL
Stern, Nathan ... Mineola, NY
Stern, Nathan ... Steubenville, OH
Stern, Neal A. ... New York, NY
Stern, Neil P. ... Chicago, IL
Stern, Nelson M. ... New York, NY
Stern, Neubauer, Greenwald & Pauly, A Professional Corporation
Santa Monica, CA
Stern & Newton, A Professional Corporation
Granby, CO
Stern, Norman L. ... Sherman Oaks, CA
Stern, Norman W. ... Southfield, MI
Stern, Norman W., P.C. ... Southfield, MI
Stern, Patrick ... Indianapolis, IN
Stern, Paul G. ... Los Angeles, CA
Stern, Peter C. ... Cardiff-By-The-Sea, CA
Stern, Peter J. ... Walnut Creek, CA
Stern, Peter M. ... Springfield, MA
Stern, Peter M. ... New York, NY
Stern, Peter R. ... New York, NY
Stern, Peter S. ... Livingston, NJ
Stern, Peter S., Law Office of
Palo Alto, CA
Stern, Philip D. ... Millburn, NJ
Stern, Philip Edward ... Newark, NJ
Stern, Philip H. ... New York, NY
Stern, Philip J. ... Minneapolis, MN
Stern, Philip W. ... Houston, TX
Stern, Phillip L. ... Chicago, IL
Stern, Rachelle ... New York, NY
Stern, Ralph D. ... Hayward, CA
Stern & Ramthun ... Milwaukee, WI
Stern, Rebecca J. ... Chattanooga, TN
Stern, Rebecca Rae ... Los Angeles, CA
Stern, Rhonda Liebman ... Chicago, IL
Stern, Richard ... New York, NY
Stern, Richard A. ... Norristown, PA
Stern, Richard B. ... Conshohocken, PA
Stern, Richard F. ... Jenkintown, PA
Stern, Richard H. ... Washington, DC
Stern, Richard L. ... Huntington, NY
Stern, Richard L. ... New York, NY
Stern, Richard M. ... San Diego, CA
Stern, Richard N. ... Guttenberg, NJ
Stern, Richard S. ... Washington, DC
Rockville, MD
Stern, Richard Winant ... New York, NY
Stern & Rindner ... Goshen, NY
Stern, Robert A. ... Gainesville, FL
Stern, Robert A. ... Gaithersburg, MD
Stern, Robert A. ... Hackensack, NJ
Stern, Robert A. ... New York, NY
Stern, Robert A. ... New York, NY
Stern, Robert A., P.A. ... Gainesville, FL
Stern, Robert C. ... New Orleans, LA
Stern, Robert E. ... York, PA
Stern, Robert G. ... Tampa, FL
Stern, Robert H.
Department of Justice, GV
Stern, Robert J. ... Maynard, MA
Stern, Robert J. ... Philadelphia, PA
Stern, Robert L. ... Chicago, IL
Stern, Robert M. ... Los Angeles, CA
Stern, Robert S. ... Los Angeles, CA
Stern, Robert T. ... Mineola, NY
Stern, Robert W. ... West Bloomfield, MI
Stern, Robert W. ... Cleveland, OH
Stern, Robin ... Brattleboro, VT
Stern, Robyn C. ... New York, NY
Stern, Roger C. ... Los Angeles, CA
Stern, Roger D. ... Palo Alto, CA
Stern, Roger D. ... New York, NY
Stern, Ronald A. ... Washington, DC
Stern, Ronald H. ... Cincinnati, OH
Stern, Ronald J. ... Department of Commerce, Patent and Trademark Office, GV
Stern, Ronald M. ... Southfield, MI
Stern, Ronald S. ... Granby, CO
Stern, Ronald William ... Alexandria, VA
Stern & Rotheiser ... Chicago, IL
Stern, Russell H. ... East Meadow, NY
Stern, Ryan M. ... Denver, CO
Stern, Samuel A. ... Washington, DC
Stern, Samuel A. ... New York, NY
Stern, Samuel L. ... Minneapolis, MN
Stern, Sandra B. ... Encino, CA
Stern, Sandra Kohler ... Mequon, WI
Stern, Sandra R. ... San Francisco, CA
Stern, Sandra Schnitzer ... New York, NY
Stern & Schrage ... Westport, CT
Stern, Scott L. ... New York, NY
Stern, Seymour ... Miami, FL
Stern, Seymour B. ... Frederick, MD
Stern, Shapiro, Weissberg & Garin
Boston, MA
Stern, Sharon H. ... New York, NY
Stern, Shirley ... New Hyde Park, NY
Stern, Slate J. ... Santa Fe, NM
Stern, Sonya Z. ... Ann Arbor, MI
Stern, Stacey Jo ... Dallas, TX
Stern, Stanley ... Hackensack, NJ
Stern, Stephen ... Chicago, IL
Stern, Stephen B. ... Baltimore, MD
Stern, Stephen J. ... Los Angeles, CA
Stern, Stephen M. ... Steubenville, OH
Stern, Stephen R., (P.C.) ... New York, NY
Stern and Stercho ... Jenkintown, PA
Stern & Stern ... Omaha, NE
Stern & Stern, P.C. ... Merrick, NY
Stern, Stern & Stern Co., L.P.A.
Steubenville, OH
Stern, Steven B. ... Chicago, IL
Stern, Steven D. ... Cordova, TN
Stern, Steven E. ... Chicago, IL
Stern, Steven H. ... Islandia, NY
Stern, Steven L. ... Newport Beach, CA
Stern, Steven T. ... Philadelphia, PA
Stern, Stewart J. ... Philadelphia, PA
Stern, Stuart M. ... New Milford, NJ
Stern, Susan H. ... Boca Raton, FL
Stern, Susan Rubin ... Short Hills, NJ
Stern, Theodore N. ... Dulles, VA
Stern, Thomas H. ... Chicago, IL
Stern, Thomas M. ... Denver, CO
Stern, Thomas M. ... Chapel Hill, NC
Stern, Todd D. ...
Executive Office Of The President, GV
Stern, Todd E. ... Woburn, MA
Stern, Todd M. ... Beverly Hills, CA
Stern, Todd R. ... Tampa, FL
Stern, Todd R., & Associates, P.A.
Tampa, FL
Stern, T. S., Jr. ... Greenville, SC
Stern, W. Rod ... Irvine, CA
Stern, Walter E., III ... Albuquerque, NM
Stern, Walter W., III ... Union Grove, WI
Stern, Warren R. ... New York, NY
Stern, William B. ... Hollywood, FL
Stern, William C. ... New York, NY
Stern, William E. ... Boston, MA
Stern, William L. ... San Francisco, CA
Stern, William M. ... Orlando, FL
Stern, William S.
Securities and Exchange Commission, Office of the General Counsel, GV
Stern, William S. ... Southfield, MI
Stern, Wolf H. ... Newport Beach, CA
Stern, Wynne B., Jr. ... New York, NY
Stern, Zachary D. ... New York, NY
Sternad, Trudy K.
Department Of Veterans Affairs, Board of Veterans Appeals, GV
Sternagel, Chris A. ... Longview, WA
Sternal, Guy J. ... Tacoma, WA
Sternal, Lee N. ... Pueblo, CO
Sternal, Lee N., P.C. ... Pueblo, CO
Sternat, Christian M. ... Houston, TX
Sternat, Edward D. ... Flushing, NY
Sternau, Thomas R. ... New York, NY
Sternbach, David G. ... New York, NY
Sternbach, Mitchell ... Rockville Centre, NY
Sternbach, Robert A., Law Office of
New York, NY
Sternback, Cary Richard ... Marlboro, NJ
Sternbane, Leonard ... Shrewsbury, MA
Sternbaum, Marc J. ... Miami, FL
Sternberg, Adam ... Greenvale, NY
Sternberg, Alan J. ... Walnut Creek, CA
Sternberg, Alan L. ... Denver, CO
Sternberg, Alan L. ... Bloomington, IL
Sternberg, Arthur B. ... Chicago, IL
Sternberg, Bernard ... Lauderhill, FL
Sternberg, Christopher J. ... Louisville, KY
Sternberg, Craig S. ... Seattle, WA
Sternberg, Daniel S. ... New York, NY
Sternberg, David E. ... Philadelphia, PA
Sternberg, David Evan ... New York, NY
Sternberg, David J. ... Mentor, OH
Sternberg, David M. ... Walnut Creek, CA
Sternberg, Donna Udin ... Philadelphia, PA
Sternberg & Eagle ... Phoenix, AZ
Sternberg, Elden R. ... St. Louis, MO
Sternberg, Erik M. ... New York, NY
Sternberg, Fred ... Wantagh, NY
Sternberg, Frederick J. ... Graham, NC
Sternberg, Frederick J., P.A. ... Graham, NC
Sternberg, Gerald C. ... Madison, WI
Sternberg, Harvey J. ... Bryn Mawr, PA
Sternberg, Henry ... New York, NY
Sternberg, Jamie J. ... San Diego, CA
Sternberg, Jeffrey S. ... Birmingham, MI
Sternberg, Jennifer S. ... Southfield, MI
Sternberg, Jeremy M. ... Boston, MA
Sternberg, John D. ... Denver, CO
Sternberg, Jonathan ... New York, NY
Sternberg, Jordana R. ... Atlanta, GA
Sternberg, Joseph S. ... Philadelphia, PA
Sternberg, Joseph V. ... New York, NY
Sternberg, Kenneth S. ... New York, NY

Sternberg, L. Louis., (Mr.)
Spring Valley, NY
Sternberg, Laurie J. ....New York, NY
Sternberg, Linda J. ....Boston, MA
Sternberg, Mark A. ....Chicago, IL
Sternberg, Melvin ....Phoenix, AZ
Sternberg, Michael J. ....Feasterville, PA
Sternberg, Newman, & Associates
Akron, OH
Sternberg, Paul J. ....Binghamton, NY
Sternberg, Phillip L.
Farmington Hills, MI
Sternberg, Richard ....Akron, OH
Sternberg, Richard S. ....Washington, DC
Potomac, MD
Sternberg, Richard W. ....St. Louis, MO
Sternberg, Robert A. ....Buffalo Grove, IL
Sternberg, Rolf M. ....Hoosick Falls, NY
Bennington, VT
Sternberg, Ronald E. ....New York, NY
Sternberg, Ronald S. ....Morristown, NJ
Sternberg, Sandor W. ....Cleveland, OH
Sternberg, Scott J. ....St. Petersburg, FL
Sternberg, Sheldon H. ....Phoenix, AZ
Sternberg, Sheryl ....Chicago, IL
Sternberg & Singer, Ltd. ....Phoenix, AZ
Sternberg, Stacey ....Los Angeles, CA
Sternberg, Susan R. ....Brooklyn, NY
Sternberg, Terence M. ....Woodland Hills, CA
Sternberg, Theresa M. ....Boston, MA
Sternberg Thomson Okrent & Scher
Seattle, WA
Sternberg, Valerie K. ....Chicago, IL
Sternberg & Zeid Co., L.P.A.
Chardon, OH
Cleveland, OH
Mentor, OH
Painesville, OH
Sternberger, Eric ....San Rafael, CA
Sternberger, Marc L. ....Pittsburgh, PA
Stern-Bird, Margaret ....Washington, DC
Stern-Brown, Vicki L. ....Atlanta, GA
Sterne, Colleen K. ....Santa Barbara, CA
Sterne, John H., Jr. ....Washington, DC
Sterne, Kessler, Goldstein & Fox P.L.L.C.
Washington, DC
Sterne, Robert Greene ....Washington, DC
Sternenberg, Kathleen A. ....Manchester, NH
Sterner, Anders R. ....Brooklyn, NY
Sterner, Christopher B. ....Albany, NY
Sterner, Dan G. ....Indianapolis, IN
Sterner, Edwin B. ....Seattle, WA
Sterner, John P. ....Salisbury, MD
Sterner, Karen L. ....Baltimore, MD
Sterner, M. Joseph ....Atlanta, GA
Sterner, Robert R. ....Fulton, MO
Sterner, Susan T. ....Monterey, CA
Sterner, Victor L. ....Flushing, NY
Sternfeld, David I. ....Oakland, CA
Sternfeld, William M. ....Los Angeles, CA
Sternfels, Felix J. ....Napoleonville, LA
Sternfels, Lewis B. ....Los Angeles, CA
Sternfels, Robert B. ....Stockton, CA
Sternfels, Urvan Ruiz ....Washington, DC
Sternfield, Scott F. ....Wheeling, IL
Sternhagen, William G. ....Helena, MT
Sternheim, Bobbi C. ....New York, NY
Sternheimer, Joann ....Hackensack, NJ
Sternick, Michael A. ....Paterson, NJ
Sternick, Michael J. ....Denver, CO
Sternicki, Donna L. ....Las Vegas, NV
Sternik, James E. ....Chicago, IL
Sternin, Bernard ....Rockville Centre, NY
Sternin, Erica L. ....New York, NY
Sternke, Myrl B. ....Hannibal, MO
Sternklar, Cindy ....New York, NY
Sternklar, Jeffrey D. ....Boston, MA
Sternklar, Theodore ....New York, NY
Sternlicht, David G. ....New York, NY
Sternlicht, David N. ....New York, NY
Sternlicht, Jennifer ....New York, NY
Sternlicht, Leo ....Riverhead, NY
Sternlicht, Mark A. ....Fayetteville, NC
Sternlicht, Melissa R. ....Cleveland, OH
Sternlicht, Norman ....Brooklyn, NY
Sternlicht, Steven A. ....East Islip, NY
Sternlieb, Charlotte R. ....Palm Desert, CA
Sternlieb, David F. ....New York, NY
Sternlieb & Dowd, L.L.C.
Hackensack, NJ
Sternlieb, Edward I. ....Miami, FL
Sternlieb, Joanne R. ....New York, NY
Sternlieb, Lynne R. ....Deerfield, IL
Sternlieb, Michael ....Hackensack, NJ
Sternlight, Jean R. ....Tallahassee, FL
Sternlof, Karl-Erik ....Norwich, CT
Sternman, Joel W. ....New York, NY
Sternoff, Joshua H. ....New York, NY
Sterns, Floyd A. ....Lincoln, NE
Sterns, Gerald C. ....Oakland, CA
Sterns, James E. ....New City, NY
Sterns, Joel H. ....Trenton, NJ
Sterns, Patricia Margaret ....Phoenix, AZ
Sterns, Randy K. ....Tampa, FL
Sterns, Richard S. ....Skowhegan, ME
Sterns and Tennen ....Phoenix, AZ
Sterns & Walker, Law Offices of
Oakland, CA
Sterns & Weinroth, A Professional
Corporation ....Atlantic City, NJ
Trenton, NJ
Sterns, William S., III ....New York, NY
Sternschuss, David G. ....New Rochelle, NY
Sternstein, Alan B. ....Rockville, MD
Sternstein, Allan J. ....Chicago, IL
Sternstein, Bruce L. ....Miami, FL
Sternstein, Marilyn E. ....Deptford, NJ
Sternstein, Philip S. ....Boston, MA

Sternthal, Robert ....New York, NY
Sterrett, Grace ....Albany, NY
Sterrett, James R. ....Chicago, IL
Sterrett, Joel A. ....Tempe, AZ
Sterrett, Michael L. ....Pleasant Hill, CA
Sterrett, Robert W., Jr. ....Atlanta, GA
Sterrett, Samuel B. ....Washington, DC
Sterrett, Samuel B., Jr. ....Washington, DC
Sterrett, Tate K. ....Charlotte, NC
Sterrett, Wm. W. ....Slater, MO
Sterrette, Dawana Merritt
Washington, DC
Sterritt, Christopher J. ....
United States Court Of Appeals For The
Armed Forces, GV
Sterritt, James R. ....Shreveport, LA
Sterritt, Thos. J. ....Nashville, TN
Sterrn, Richard C. ....Bethesda, MD
Sterthous, Michael G. ....Albany, NY
Stertz, H. William, Jr. ....Saginaw, MI
Tawas City, MI
Stertz, Kurt N. ....St. Cloud, MN
Stertz, Weaver & Cline, P.C. .....Saginaw, MI
Tawas City, MI
Stertzer, Annette L. ....Washington, DC
Sterud, Shari L. ....Albuquerque, NM
Sterup, Robert L. ....Billings, MT
Sterzer, Brian N. ....Long Beach, CA
Stesch, David K. ....Baltimore, MD
Stesiak, Jeffrey J. ....South Bend, IN
Stesis, Louis G. ....Media, PA
Stesney, Linda A. ....New York, NY
Stetch, Jack ....Brooklyn, NY
Stetfelt, Chester C., Jr. ....Metairie, LA
Stetfelt, Chester, Jr., APLC ....Metairie, LA
Stethem, James H. ....Cincinnati, OH
Stetina Brunda Garred & Brucker, A
Professional Corporation
Laguna Hills, CA
Stetina, Kit M., (Mr.) ....Laguna Hills, CA
Stetler, Alan K. ....Rochester, NY
Stetler, Bradley S. ....Burlington, VT
Stetler, C. Joseph ....Washington, DC
Stetler, David J. ....Chicago, IL
Stetler, David W. ....San Leandro, CA
Stetler & Duffy, Ltd. ....Chicago, IL
Stetler & Gribbin ....York, PA
Stetler, Mark M. ....Dallas, TX
Stetler, Ronald L. ....Naples, FL
Stetler, Ronald N. ....Boston, MA
Stets & Hardisty ....Waynesburg, PA
Stets, John A. ....Waynesburg, PA
Stets, Robert D. ....Harrisburg, PA
Stetson, Alan R. ....Overland Park, KS
Stetson, Anne ....Boston, MA
Stetson, Barrett W. ....Dallas, TX
Stetson, Catherine Baker
Albuquerque, NM
Stetson, Catherine E. ....Washington, DC
Stetson, Christine L. ....Dallas, TX
Stetson, David J. ....Versailles, KY
Stetson, David P. ....Pittsfield, VT
Stetson, Donavon K. ....Lisbon, ND
Stetson, Everett C. ....Chicago, IL
Stetson, Genevieve C. ....Machias, ME
Stetson, James Lee ....Chicago, IL
Stetson, James W. ....Boston, MA
Stetson, John C. ....Westbury, NY
Stetson, John Edwin ....Camden, ME
Stetson, Karen L. ....Miami Beach, FL
Stetson Law Offices, P.C.
Albuquerque, NM
Stetson, Michael R. ....San Pedro, CA
Stetson, Richard ....Scottsdale, AZ
Stetson, Robert C. ....Portola Valley, CA
Stetson, Robert G. ....Falmouth, MA
Stetson, Roger T. ....Des Moines, IA
Stetson, Rufus E., Jr. ....Augusta, ME
Stetson, Tracy Elizabeth .....Laguna Niguel, CA
Stetter, Debra L. ....Chicago, IL
Stetter, Roger A. ....New Orleans, LA
Stettin, Eric L. ....Fort Lauderdale, FL
Stettin, Herbert ....Miami, FL
Stettin, Herbert, P.A. ....Miami, FL
Stettin, Jacob J. ....El Segundo, CA
Stettine, Richard A. ....Islip, NY
Stettler, David M. ....Sherman Oaks, CA
Stettner, Barbara Ann
Securities and Exchange Commission,
Office of International Affairs, GV
Stettner, Derek C. ....Milwaukee, WI
Stettner, Eisenberg & Morris ....Glendora, CA
Stettner, Kenneth R. ....Denver, CO
Stettner, Miller and Cohn, P.C.
Colorado Springs, CO
Denver, CO
Stettner, Pamela P. ....Glendora, CA
Stetz, Carl E. ....New York, NY
Stetzer, Claudene Losey
Fort Lauderdale, FL
Stetzer, William T. ....Dodge City, KS
Stetzler, Kip A. ....Kansas City, MO
Stetzner, Leah Manning ....Decatur, IL
Steuart, Charles R. ....Treasury Department,
Office of Regulations and Rulings, GV
Steuart, George C. ....Washington, DC
Steuart, Timothy G. ....Inglewood, CA
Steuber, David E. ....San Jose, CA
Steuber, David W. ....Los Angeles, CA
Steuber, Kristin Clark ....Russellville, AR
Steubing, Mary M. ....Billerica, MA
Steubing, R. Bruce ....Sacramento, CA
Steuch, Michael N. ....Los Angeles, CA
Steude, William L. ....Ann Arbor, MI
Steuer, Arlene B. ....Cleveland, OH
Steuer, David S. ....Palo Alto, CA
Steuer, Eliot ....New York, NY

Steuer, Escovar & Berk Co., L.P.A.
Cleveland, OH
Hudson, OH
Solon, OH
Westlake, OH
Steuer, Katherine B.
Environmental Protection Agency,
Office of Enforcement and Compliance
Assurance, GV
Steuer, Michael A. ....Santa Barbara, CA
Steuer, Michael J. ....Eau Claire, WI
Steuer, Richard B. ....Cleveland, OH
Steuer, Richard M. ....New York, NY
Steuer, Shelley ....Northampton, MA
Steuer-Miller, Ellyn ....New York, NY
Steuerwald, Gregory E. ....Danville, IN
Steuerwald, Harold A. ....Bellport, NY
Steuerwald, John K. ....Media, PA
Steuk, William C. ....Sandusky, OH
Steuk, Wm. R.S. ....Sandusky, OH
Steury, Ellen Hochstedler
Washington, DC
Steury, Wesley N. ....Fort Wayne, IN
Stevanovic, Dragic D. ....Buffalo, NY
Stevason, John C. ....Portland, OR
Steve, Nadja Choroszylow ......Plymouth, MA
Steve, Paul A. ....Loudonville, NY
Steveken, Susan T. ....Hastings, MN
Stevelman, Paul D. ....Greenwich, CT
Steven, Eric M. ....Spokane, WA
Steven, Eric M., P.S. ....Spokane, WA
Steven, Lee A. ....Washington, DC
Steven, Michael T. ....Andover, ME
Steven, Murielle J. ....New York, NY
Stevener, Arthur B., Jr. ....El Reno, OK
Stevenot, James W. ....Indianapolis, IN
Stevens, Albert J. ....Garden City, NY
Stevens, Albert M. ....Presque Isle, ME
Stevens, Allen L. ....New Canaan, CT
Stevens, Alton C. ....Waterville, ME
Stevens, Amy W. ....Nashville, TN
Stevens, Anastasia S. ....Albuquerque, NM
Stevens, Andrea K. R. ....Jeffersonville, IN
Stevens, Ann Benedetto ....Washington, DC
Stevens, Ann D. ....Roseland, NJ
Stevens, Ann H.
Federal Communications Commission,
Common Carrier Bureau, GV
Stevens, Anne K. ....Kennesaw, GA
Stevens, Anne K. ....Cleveland, OH
Stevens, Anthony J. ....Bartow, FL
Stevens, Arthur J. ....New York, NY
Greensboro, NC
Stevens, Arthur W., III ....Brookings, OR
Medford, OR
Stevens & Associates ....Atlanta, GA
Norcross, GA
Stevens, Bagley & Stevens
Fayetteville, TN
Stevens, Baldo & Freeman, L.L.P.
Lake Charles, LA
Beaumont, TX
Houston, TX
Stevens, Barbara ....Columbus, IN
Stevens, Barry W. ......Department of Education,
Office of the General Counsel, GV
Stevens, Ben D. ....Houston, TX
Stevens, Betsy Macmillan
Springfield, MA
Stevens, Betty L. ....Syracuse, NY
Stevens, Blaine C. ....Ozark, AL
Stevens, Bradford L. ....St. Louis, MO
Stevens, Bradley J. ....Phoenix, AZ
Stevens & Brand, L.L.P. ....Lawrence, KS
Stevens, Brian E. ....Brooklyn Center, MN
Stevens, Brian K. ....Woodstock, IL
Stevens, Brian K., Law Office of
Richmond, VA
Stevens, Brian M. ....Vacaville, CA
Stevens, Bruce M. ....El Toro, CA
Stevens, Bryan ....Quincy, MA
Stevens, Buddy ....Angleton, TX
Stevens, Burton L. ....Woodbury, CT
Stevens, C. Daniel ....Richmond, VA
Stevens, C. Eric ....Nashville, TN
Stevens, C. Joseph ....Hamlin, WV
Stevens, Carl J. ....Virginia Beach, VA
Stevens, Carl R. ....Agoura Hills, CA
Irvine, CA
Stevens, Carol Ann ....New Brunswick, NJ
New York, NY
Stevens, Carol D. ....Windham, NY
Stevens, Carole K. ....Dallas, TX
Stevens, Carolyn B. ....New York, NY
Stevens, Carroll & Carveth ....Milford, CT
New Haven, CT
Stevens, Carroll D. ....New Haven, CT
Stevens, Carter J. ....Waterloo, IA
Stevens, Casey W. ....Atlanta, GA
Stevens, Catherine A. ....Columbia, MD
Stevens, Catherine B. ....Atlanta, GA
Stevens, Catherine M. ....Lexington, KY
Stevens, Charles E. ....Blue Ridge, GA
Stevens, Charles J. ....Sacramento, CA
Stevens, Charles J., Jr. ....Cranford, NJ
Stevens, Charles P. ....Milwaukee, WI
Stevens, Charles T. ....Phoenix, AZ
Stevens, Cheryl A. ....Oakland, CA
Stevens, Christine E. ....Newport Beach, CA
Stevens, Christopher M. ....Los Angeles, CA
Stevens, Christopher W. ....Roanoke, VA
Stevens, Clark V. ....St. Clair Shores, MI
Stevens, Clark V., Professional Corporation
St. Clair Shores, MI
Stevens, Clay M. ....Louisville, KY
Stevens, Clay R. ....Irvine, CA
Stevens, Clifford E., Jr. ....Washington, DC
Stevens, Clifford W. ....Stockton, CA

Stevens, Connie J. ....Lancaster, PA
Stevens, Constance F. ....Fremont, CA
Stevens, Correale F. ....Hazleton, PA
Stevens, Craig C. ....San Mateo, CA
Stevens, Craig R. ....Tarzana, CA
Stevens, Craig R. ....Fort Myers, FL
Stevens, Craig S. ....Oak Brook, IL
Stevens, Cristian Matthew ......Kansas City, MO
Stevens, Curt ....New York, NY
Stevens, Curtis L. ....Minneapolis, MN
Stevens, Cynthia Bushnell ....Chicago, IL
Stevens, Daniel D. ....Granada Hills, CA
Stevens, Daniel J. ....Augusta, ME
Stevens, Darrell W. ....Chico, CA
Stevens, David ....Mattoon, IL
Stevens, David A. ....San Diego, CA
Stevens, David A. ....Inkster, MI
Stevens, David A. ....Afton, VA
Stevens, David B. ....Seattle, WA
Stevens, David E. ....Raynham, MA
Stevens, David John ....Littleton, CO
Stevens, David O. ....Houston, TX
Stevens, David P. ....Montgomery, AL
Stevens, David R. ....Palo Alto, CA
Stevens, David S. ....Highland, IN
Stevens, Davis, Miller & Mosher, L.L.P.
Washington, DC
Baltimore, MD
Alexandria, VA
Tysons Corner, VA
Stevens, Dawn E. ....San Antonio, TX
Stevens, Dawn M. ....Fredericksburg, VA
Stevens, Deborah C. ....Knoxville, TN
Stevens, Dennis R. ....New Iberia, LA
Stevens, Dinah
Administrative Office Of The United States
Courts, GV
Stevens, Don C., II ....Phoenix, AZ
Stevens, Donald E. ....Thousand Oaks, CA
Stevens, Donald E. ....Branford, CT
Stevens, Donald E., A Professional Law
Corporation ....Thousand Oaks, CA
Stevens, Donald F. ....Secaucus, NJ
Stevens, Donald M. ....Alexandria, KY
Stevens, Donald T. ....Lawton, OK
Stevens, Donna ....Oak Ridge, TN
Stevens, Douglas M. ....Costa Mesa, CA
Stevens, Douglas M. ....St. Paul, MN
Stevens, Douglas M. ....Parsippany, NJ
Stevens, Douglas R. ....Washington, DC
Stevens, Douglas R. ....Chicago, IL
Stevens, Drummond & Gifford
Walnut Creek, CA
Stevens, E. Dan ....Alva, FL
Stevens, E. Seward ....Litchfield, CT
Stevens, Edith M. ....Boulder, CO
Stevens, Edward ....Ventura, CA
Stevens, Edward Hamilton, III
Shreveport, LA
Stevens, Edward Henry ....Tuscaloosa, AL
Stevens, Edward S. ....Kansas City, MO
Stevens, Edwards & Hallock, P.C.
Gillette, WY
Stevens, Elizabeth G. ....Orlando, FL
Stevens, Ellen B. ....Warren, MI
Stevens, Elwood C., Jr. ....Morgan City, LA
Stevens, Engels, Bishop & Sprague
Presque Isle, ME
Stevens, Eric P. ....Raleigh, NC
Stevens, Essie F. ....Silver Spring, MD
Stevens, Eugene ....Cleveland, OH
Stevens, Eva B. ....Chicago, IL
Stevens, E. W. Dann ....Buffalo, NY
Eden, NY
Stevens, Felicia ....Harrison, NY
Stevens, Francis E. ....Gillette, WY
Stevens, Frank C. ....Chicago, IL
Stevens, Frank M. ....Walnut Creek, CA
Stevens, Fred A. ....Cleveland, OH
Stevens, Frederick H. ....Evergreen, AL
Stevens, Frederick W. ....Secaucus, NJ
Stevens, G. Rawson ....Shenandoah, IA
Stevens, G. Sefton ....Charlotte, NC
Stevens, Gail E. ....Fort Lauderdale, FL
Stevens, Garrett B.
Department of Agriculture,
Office of the General Counsel, GV
Stevens, Gary D. ....Laguna Niguel, CA
Stevens, Gary G. ....Washington, DC
Stevens, Gene C. ....Phoenix, AZ
Stevens, Gene F. ....Dallas, TX
Stevens, George A ....Lexington, MA
Stevens, George F. ....Albuquerque, NM
Stevens, George L., Jr. ....Birmingham, AL
Stevens, George N. ....Arlington, VA
Stevens, George R. ....Medford, OR
Stevens, Gerald M. ....Bethesda, MD
Stevens, Gerald M. ....Flint, MI
Owosso, MI
Stevens, Gerard King ....Baltimore, MD
Stevens, Gina M. ....Library of Congress,
Congressional Research Service, GV
Stevens, Glenn E. ....Beverly Hills, CA
Stevens, Glenn H. ....Longmont, CO
Stevens, Gordon D. ....Houston, TX
Stevens, Graydon G. ....Portland, ME
Stevens, Gregg D. ....Department of Justice,
Tax Division, GV
Dallas, TX
Stevens, Gregory B. ....Department of Justice,
Criminal Division, GV
Stevens, Gregory L. ....Spokane, WA
Stevens, Gregory W. ....Salt Lake City, UT
Stevens, H. Jay ....Orlando, FL
Stevens, Harold Burr ....Stowe, VT
Stevens, Harold, (P.A.) ....Fort Myers, FL
Stevens, Harold S. ....West Palm Beach, FL
Stevens, Harold W. ....Everett, MA

Stevens, Harrell L. .... Dallas, TX
Stevens, Harris, Guernsey & Connolly, P.C.
East Lyme, CT
New London, CT
Niantic, CT
Stevens & Hayes .... Coldwater, MI
Stevens, Helen M. E. .... Fort Myers, FL
Stevens, Henry L., III .... Kenansville, NC
Stevens, Henry S. .... Phoenix, AZ
Stevens, Herbert F. .... Washington, DC
Stevens, Hjordis C. .... Napa, CA
Stevens, Holly B. .... Atlanta, GA
Stevens, Howard L. .... New York, NY
Stevens, Howard S. .... Baltimore, MD
Stevens, Howard S. .... Allentown, PA
Stevens, Hugh .... Raleigh, NC
Stevens, J. Benjamin .... Spartanburg, SC
Stevens, J. Grant .... Beaumont, TX
Stevens, J. Joshua, Jr. .... West Point, MS
Stevens, J. Randell .... Dallas, TX
Stevens, James A. .... Richmond, TX
Stevens, James C. .... San Diego, CA
Stevens, James C. .... Bossier City, LA
Stevens, James C., Jr. .... Chicago, IL
Stevens, James D. .... Elkhart, IN
Stevens, James D. .... Troy, MI
Stevens, James D. .... Oklahoma City, OK
Stevens, James E. .... San Francisco, CA
Stevens, James E. .... Rockford, IL
Stevens, James E. .... Kuttawa, KY
Stevens, James G., Jr. .... Syracuse, NY
Stevens, James H. .... Plymouth Meeting, PA
Stevens, James L., Jr. .... Woodland, CA
Stevens, James M. .... Tarpon Springs, FL
Stevens, James P. .... Jacksonville, FL
Stevens, James P., Jr. .... Loris, SC
Stevens, James R., Jr. .... Houston, TX
Stevens, James Randall .... Westwood, NJ
Stevens, James W. .... Philadelphia, PA
Stevens, James W. .... Angleton, TX
Stevens, Jan .... Sacramento, CA
Stevens, Jane G. .... New York, NY
Stevens, Jane Greengold .... Brooklyn, NY
Stevens, Janet E. .... Suamico, WI
Stevens, Jason D. .... Charleston, WV
Stevens, Jason S. .... New York, NY
Stevens, Jeanine L. .... Chicago, IL
Stevens, Jeffrey Dean .... Salt Lake City, UT
Stevens, Jeffrey N. .... Boston, MA
Stevens, Jennifer J. .... Auburn, WA
Stevens, Jennifer L. .... Washington, DC
Stevens, Jeron L. .... Spring, TX
Stevens, Joan Gress .... Chicago, IL
Stevens, Joanne Ellen .... Mineola, NY
Stevens, Joanne Ellen, P.C. .... Mineola, NY
Stevens, Joe D. .... Hattiesburg, MS
Stevens, Joe M., Jr. .... Houston, TX
Stevens, John A. .... Troy, MI
Stevens, John A. .... Ithaca, NY
Stevens, John B., Jr. .... Beaumont, TX
Stevens, John C. .... Muscatine, IA
Stevens, John C., III .... Newburyport, MA
Stevens, John H. .... Westport, CT
Stevens, John H. .... Boston, MA
Stevens, John H. .... Jackson, MS
Stevens, John M. .... St. Petersburg, FL
Stevens, John M. .... Jackson, MS
Stevens, John M. .... Norristown, PA
Stevens, John M., Jr. .... Boston, MA
Stevens, John N., Law Offices
Bloomington, IL
Stevens, John P. .... Novato, CA
Stevens, John P. ....
Supreme Court Of The United States, GV
Stevens, John R. .... Bakersfield, CA
Stevens, John R. .... Fredericksburg, VA
Stevens, John S. .... Stillwater, OK
Stevens, John Shorter .... Asheville, NC
Stevens, John Spencer .... Chicago, IL
Stevens, John V., Jr. .... Riverside, CA
Stevens, John W. .... Grand Rapids, MI
Stevens, John W. .... Cedarburg, WI
Stevens, John W., III
Fort Lauderdale, FL
Stevens & Johnson .... Allentown, PA
Stevens, Jonathan C. .... Orange, CA
Stevens, Jonathan H. .... Burlington, VT
Stevens, Joseph .... New Brunswick, NJ
Stevens, Joseph J. .... Chicago, IL
Stevens, Joseph P. .... Brooklyn, NY
Stevens, Joyce E. .... Arlington, TX
Stevens, Joyce E. .... Fort Worth, TX
Stevens, Joyce P. .... Morehead, KY
Stevens, Judith Anne .... New York, NY
Stevens, Julian B., Jr. .... Annapolis, MD
Stevens, Julie A. .... Portland, OR
Stevens, Karen .... Milwaukee, WI
Stevens, Karen L. .... Department of Justice, Civil Rights Division, GV
Stevens, Karen L. .... Harrisburg, PA
Stevens, Karen Pedersen .... Sacramento, CA
Stevens, Karen Pedersen, A Professional Corporation .... Sacramento, CA
Stevens, Karen S .... Denver, CO
Stevens, Katherine G. .... Orlando, FL
Stevens, Keith H. .... San Francisco, CA
Stevens, Kelly H. .... Los Angeles, CA
Stevens, Kenneth G. .... Fort Lauderdale, FL
Stevens, Kenneth M. .... Wichita, KS
Stevens, Kenneth M., P.A. .... Wichita, KS
Stevens, Kent R. .... Washington, DC
Stevens, Kent W. .... Phoenix, AZ
Stevens, Kerry B. .... New York, NY
Stevens, Kevin A. .... Suffern, NY
Stevens, Kimberly C.
North Wilkesboro, NC

Stevens & Kramer, A Professional Corporation .... Agoura Hills, CA
Irvine, CA
Stevens, Kristin Binder .... Chicago, IL
Stevens, L. Austin .... Smithfield, NC
Stevens, L. Bruce, Jr. .... Dayton, OH
Stevens, Lance L. .... Jackson, MS
Stevens, Lauren C.
Research Triangle Park, NC
Stevens, Lauren L. .... Palo Alto, CA
Stevens, Laurence B. .... Phoenix, AZ
Stevens, Laurence E. .... Albany, NY
Stevens Law Firm, P.C. .... Loris, SC
Myrtle Beach, SC
Stevens Law Office .... Stowe, VT
Stevens Law Office .... Cedarburg, WI
Stevens, Lawrence E. .... Salt Lake City, UT
Stevens, Lawrence T. .... Redwood City, CA
Stevens, Lawrence W. .... Stockton, CA
Stevens, Lawrence W. .... Olympia, WA
Stevens, Lee A. .... Detroit, MI
Stevens & Lee, A Professional Corporation
Wilmington, DE
Cherry Hill, NJ
Harrisburg, PA
Lancaster, PA
Lehigh Valley, PA
Philadelphia, PA
Reading, PA
Scranton, PA
Wayne, PA
Wilkes-Barre, PA
Stevens and Leibow, P.C. .... Phoenix, AZ
Stevens, Leo J. .... Grand Rapids, MI
Stevens, LeRoy E. .... Chicago, IL
Stevens, Les H. .... Boca Raton, FL
Stevens, Lewis T. .... Decatur, TX
Stevens, Liesel Brand .... San Francisco, CA
Stevens, Lillian M. .... Los Angeles, CA
Stevens, Linda A. .... El Paso, TX
Stevens, Linda K. .... Chicago, IL
Stevens, Littman & Biddison, LLC
Boulder, CO
Vail, CO
Stevens, Lyle E. .... Paso Robles, CA
Stevens, Lynn Gatlin .... Conway, SC
Stevens, M. Carol .... Palo Alto, CA
Stevens, M. Richard .... Kotzebue, AK
Stevens & Mack .... Cleveland, OH
Stevens, Marcia Elissa .... Huntsville, AL
Stevens, Margo L. .... Treasury Department, Internal Revenue Service, GV
Stevens, Marijean Raffetto .... Trenton, NJ
Stevens, Marilyn R. .... Quincy, MA
Stevens, Mark .... Newport Beach, CA
Stevens, Mark .... Chicago, IL
Stevens, Mark .... San Antonio, TX
Stevens, Mark A. .... Willingboro, NJ
Philadelphia, PA
Stevens, Mark B. .... Twentynine Palms, CA
Stevens, Mark Curtis .... New York, NY
Stevens, Mark D. .... Meadville, PA
Stevens, Mark E.
Environmental Protection Agency, Office of Congressional and Legislative Affairs, GV
Stevens, Mark J. .... Los Angeles, CA
Stevens, Mark J. .... Orange, CA
Stevens, Mark L. .... Haverhill, MA
Stevens, Mark S. .... New Brunswick, NJ
Stevens, Mark W. .... Galveston, TX
Stevens, Marshall M. .... Elgin, IL
Stevens, Mary C. .... Tempe, AZ
Stevens, Mary E. .... Kuttawa, KY
Stevens, Mary E. G. .... Washington, DC
Stevens, Mary Harding .... Washington, DC
Stevens, Mary Lamberton .... Parkland, PA
Stevens, Mary M. .... Madison, WI
Stevens, Mary Margaret Zerse .... Papillion, NE
Stevens, Matthew A. .... Washington, DC
Stevens, McGhee, Morgan, Lennon, O'Quinn & Toll .... Wilmington, NC
Stevens, Melissa Ann .... Frankfort, KY
Stevens, Michael .... Texarkana, TX
Stevens, Michael C. .... Dedham, MA
Stevens, Michael D. .... Los Angeles, CA
Stevens, Michael D. .... Clarksdale, MS
Stevens, Michael D. .... Yankton, SD
Stevens, Michael D. .... Wimberley, TX
Stevens, Michael G. .... Ventura, CA
Stevens, Michael J. .... Toledo, OH
Stevens, Michael L. .... Washington, DC
Stevens, Michael L. .... Atlanta, GA
Stevens, Michael L. .... Louisville, KY
Stevens, Michael N. .... New York, NY
Stevens & Minter .... Secaucus, NJ
Stevens, Mitchell A. .... Concord, CA
Stevens, Mitchell D. .... Dallas, TX
Stevens, Mitchell F. .... St. Louis, MO
Stevens, Morris L. .... Pittsburg, KS
Stevens, Nance F .... Poplarville, MS
Stevens, Nathaniel .... Boston, MA
Stevens, Neal R. .... New York, NY
Stevens, Nicholas .... Roseland, NJ
Stevens, Norman E. .... Los Angeles, CA
Stevens, Norman E., Professional Corporation
Los Angeles, CA
Stevens, Norman Lawrence, III
Houston, TX
Stevens & O'Connell LLP
Sacramento, CA
Stevens, Olu A. .... Louisville, KY
Stevens, Paige R. .... Niantic, CT
Stevens, Pamela J. .... San Francisco, CA
Stevens, Pamela Sawyer .... Wellesley, MA
Stevens & Parker, P.A. .... Spartanburg, SC
Stevens, Pascha R. Moller
Santa Cruz, CA

Stevens, Patricia A. .... Paso Robles, CA
Stevens, Patricia M. .... Bangor, ME
Stevens, Patrick Kenneth .... Madison, WI
Stevens, Paul C. .... Morley, MI
Stevens, Paul E. .... Youngstown, OH
Stevens, Paul E., (Co., L.P.A.)
Youngstown, OH
Stevens, Paul H. .... Lafayette, CO
Stevens, Paul L. .... Doylestown, PA
Stevens, Paul Schott .... Washington, DC
Stevens, Pauline M. .... Los Angeles, CA
Stevens, Peter H. .... Norwalk, CA
Stevens, Peter L. .... Chicago, IL
Stevens, Peter M. .... Lake Charles, LA
Stevens, Peter N. .... Plainsboro, NJ
New York, NY
Stevens, Phillip M. .... Lansing, MI
Stevens, Phineas .... Jackson, MS
Stevens, Preston V. .... Odessa, TX
Stevens, R. Whitney, Jr. .... Fayetteville, TN
Stevens, Ralph A. .... Mesa, AZ
Stevens, Ralph H. .... Prestonsburg, KY
Stevens, Ralph P. .... Coldwater, MI
Stevens, Randolph J. .... Portland, OR
Stevens & Rau, A Professional Corporation
Angleton, TX
Stevens, Ray .... West Columbia, TX
Stevens, Ray N. .... Columbia, SC
Stevens, Raymond Lyn .... Beaumont, TX
Stevens, Rebecca L. .... Cary, NC
Stevens, Rhea C. .... Richmond, TX
Stevens, Richard A. .... Chicago, IL
Stevens, Richard A. .... Annapolis, MD
Stevens, Richard B. .... Berkeley, CA
Stevens, Richard C. .... Dayton, OH
Stevens, Richard D. .... Norman, OK
Stevens, Richard F. .... Allentown, PA
Stevens, Richard G. .... Battle Creek, MI
Stevens, Richard H. .... Springfield, MO
Stevens, Richard J. .... Chicago, IL
Stevens, Richard J. .... Fargo, ND
Stevens, Richard James .... Chicago, IL
Stevens, Richard K., Jr.
Plymouth Meeting, PA
Stevens, Richard L. .... Davenport, IA
Stevens, Richard L. .... Boston, MA
Stevens, Richard L. .... Geneva, OH
Stevens, Richard O. .... San Francisco, CA
Stevens, Richard W. .... Washington, DC
Stevens, Richard W. .... Jenkintown, PA
Stevens, Richard W. .... Philadelphia, PA
Stevens, Richard Y. .... Raleigh, NC
Stevens, Rita J. .... Wichita Falls, TX
Stevens, Robert C. .... Atlanta, GA
Stevens, Robert E. .... Portland, ME
Stevens, Robert E. .... Rochester, NY
Stevens, Robert E. .... Bluffton, SC
Hilton Head Island, SC
Hilton Head Island, SC
Stevens, Robert G. .... Covington, KY
Stevens, Robert H., Jr. .... Cary, NC
Stevens, Robert L. .... Thomson, GA
Stevens, Robert L. .... Hubbard, OH
Stevens, Robert L. .... Salt Lake City, UT
Stevens, Robert S. .... Los Angeles, CA
Stevens, Robert W. .... Radcliff, KY
Stevens, Robt. J. .... Los Angeles, CA
Stevens, Rodney J. .... Columbia, MO
Stevens, Roger E., (P.C.) .... Boulder, CO
Stevens, Roger R. .... New Rochelle, NY
Stevens, Roland R. .... Modesto, CA
Stevens, Ronald A. .... Santa Fe, NM
Stevens, Ronald C. .... Santa Barbara, CA
Stevens, Ronald F. .... Niantic, CT
Stevens, Ronald S. .... Atlanta, GA
Norcross, GA
Stevens, Ronald W. .... Washington, DC
Stevens, Ronald W. .... Bronson, FL
Stevens, Rosslyn Coldwell
Los Angeles, CA
Stevens, Rowland S., II .... Phoenix, AZ
Stevens, Roy A. .... Bridgewater, NJ
Stevens, Russell L. .... Fallbrook, CA
Stevens, Ryan E. .... Corpus Christi, TX
Stevens, S. Marie .... Lawrenceburg, KY
Stevens, Sallie Jacobs .... Louisville, KY
Stevens, Sam R. .... Cleveland, OH
Stevens, Samuel S. .... Palo Alto, CA
Stevens, Samuel S. .... Santa Cruz, CA
Stevens, Sandra L. .... Los Angeles, CA
Stevens, Sandra Tvarian .... Washington, DC
Stevens, Sarah .... Washington, DC
Stevens, Sarah S. .... Mount Airy, NC
Stevens, Scott E. .... Minneapolis, MN
Stevens, Scott E. .... Longview, TX
Stevens, Scott J. .... Indianapolis, IN
Stevens, Scott K. .... Belton, TX
Stevens, Scott M. .... Cumming, GA
Stevens, Scudder G. .... Kennett Square, PA
Stevens, Scudder G., A Professional Association .... Kennett Square, PA
Stevens, Shannon K. .... Chicago, IL
Stevens, Sharon Cox .... Keizer, OR
Stevens, Shawn K. .... Milwaukee, WI
Stevens, Sheila Boothby .... Madison, WI
Stevens, Sheldon D., P.A.
Merritt Island, FL
Stevens, Stanley M. .... Chicago, IL
Stevens, Stephanie L. .... San Antonio, TX
Stevens, Steven B. .... Los Angeles, CA
Stevens & Stevens .... San Francisco, CA
Stevens & Stevens .... Kuttawa, KY
Stevens, Summer .... Los Angeles, CA
Stevens, Susan Fisher .... Billings, MT
Stevens, Suzanne M. .... Glendale, CA
Stevens, Sylvia E. .... Lake Oswego, OR
Stevens, Tamatha A. .... Indianapolis, IN
Stevens, Theodore F. .... Anchorage, AK

Stevens, Thomas A. .... Wilmington, DE
Stevens, Thomas C. .... Cleveland, OH
Stevens, Thomas E. .... San Francisco, CA
Stevens, Thomas J. .... Durham, NC
Stevens, Thomas J., Jr. .... Trevose, PA
Stevens, Thomas J., P.A. .... Durham, NC
Stevens, Thomas L. .... Evanston, IL
Stevens, Thomas P. .... Trevose, PA
Stevens, Thomas R. .... San Antonio, TX
Stevens, Thomas Robert .... Mineola, NY
Stevens, Timothy J. .... San Mateo, CA
Stevens, Timothy J. .... Buffalo, NY
Stevens, Timothy S. .... Midland, MI
Stevens, Timothy T. .... Allentown, PA
Stevens, Todd F. .... San Diego, CA
Stevens, Travis, Fortin & Lukenbill
Plymouth, IN
Stevens, W. Jack .... Hamlin, WV
Stevens, Wade C. .... Fort Wayne, IN
Stevens, Wallace L. .... Truckee, CA
Stevens, Walter E. .... Miami, FL
Stevens, Walter S. .... Rochester, NY
Stevens & Ward, P.A. .... Jackson, MS
Stevens & Weiss, P.C. .... San Antonio, TX
Stevens, William F. .... Atlanta, GA
Stevens, William Henry, Jr. .... Boston, MA
Stevens, William J. .... Crown Point, IN
Stevens, William K. .... Naples, FL
Stevens, William L. .... Waterbury, CT
Stevens, William L. .... Danville, KY
Stevens, William M. .... Chicago, IL
Stevens, William R. .... Rome, NY
Stevens, William R., Jr. .... Tucson, AZ
Stevens, William S. .... Philadelphia, PA
Stevens, Wilmer B. .... Naples, FL
Stevens, Winfred A. .... Bangor, ME
Stevens, Wyatt Shorter .... Asheville, NC
Stevens-Black, Lisa .... Los Angeles, CA
Stevenson, Adlai E. .... Chicago, IL
Stevenson, Alec B., III .... Dallas, TX
Stevenson, Allan J. .... Washington, DC
Stevenson & Ammons, L.C. .... Houston, TX
Stevenson, Amy M. Fulmer
Columbus, OH
Stevenson, Andrew L. .... Redding, CA
Stevenson, Andrew R. .... White Plains, NY
Stevenson, Ann L. .... Fort Worth, TX
Stevenson, Arthur L. .... Boston, MA
Stevenson & Associates .... Atlanta, GA
Stevenson, Ben M. .... Montgomery, TX
Stevenson, Benjamin D. .... Boston, MA
Stevenson, Blake D. .... Sacramento, CA
Stevenson, Brent M. .... Salt Lake City, UT
Stevenson, Britt .... Louisville, KY
Stevenson, Bruce E. .... Melbourne, FL
Stevenson, C. Scott .... Providence, RI
Stevenson, Charles C. .... Brockton, MA
Stevenson, Charles M. "Tex"
Covington, LA
Stevenson, Christine M. .... Roseland, NJ
Stevenson, Clinton R. .... Los Angeles, CA
Stevenson, Daniel G. .... Riverside, CA
Stevenson, Daniel J. .... Oxnard, CA
Stevenson, Daniel L. .... Patchogue, NY
Stevenson, David E. .... Chicago, IL
Stevenson, David E. .... Rockville, MD
Stevenson, David G. .... Houston, TX
Stevenson, David R. .... Houston, TX
Stevenson, David S. .... Louisville, KY
Stevenson, Deborah L. .... Atlanta, GA
Stevenson, Donald M. "Steve"
Stockton, CA
Stevenson, Donald W. .... Painted Post, NY
Stevenson, Douglas Bruce .... New York, NY
Stevenson, Douglas E. .... Ludington, MI
Stevenson, Edward B. .... Roseland, NJ
Stevenson, Edward E. .... Denver, CO
Stevenson and Emerson .... Memphis, TN
Stevenson, Eric .... Washington, DC
Stevenson, Eric D. .... Pensacola, FL
Stevenson, Ernest B. .... Chagrin Falls, OH
Stevenson, Evelyn M. .... Pablo, MT
Stevenson, F. David .... Albany, OR
Stevenson, Frank E. .... Noblesville, IN
Stevenson, Frank E., II .... Dallas, TX
Stevenson, Franklin W. .... West Hartford, CT
Stevenson, Gary E. .... Farmington, MO
Stevenson, George N. .... Lansing, MI
Stevenson, George W. .... Memphis, TN
Stevenson, George W., III .... Cherry Hill, NJ
Stevenson, Gordon M., Jr. .... Boston, MA
Stevenson, H. James .... Fort Lauderdale, FL
Stevenson, H. Thomas .... Ogden, UT
Stevenson, Henderson & Garrett, PLLC
Houston, TX
Stevenson, Henry E. .... New York, NY
Stevenson, Hotz, DiPonio & Bullock, L.L.P.
Southfield, MI
Stevenson, Howard L. .... Indianapolis, IN
Stevenson, Hugh G.
Federal Trade Commission, Bureau of Consumer Protection, GV
Stevenson, Hugh O. .... Washington, DC
Stevenson, Ian R. .... Chicago, IL
Stevenson, Ivan K., Law Offices of
Rolling Hills Estates, CA
Stevenson, Ivan K., Law Offices of
Santa Ana, CA
Stevenson, J. Donald, Jr. .... Dallas, TX
Stevenson, J. John .... Watertown, CT
Port Washington, NY
Stevenson, Jack C. .... Santa Barbara, CA
Stevenson, James D. .... Dallas, TX
Stevenson, James F. .... Sidney, OH
Stevenson, James L. .... Phoenix, AZ
Stevenson, James L. .... Walnut Creek, CA
Stevenson, James P. .... Joliet, IL
Stevenson, James W., Jr. .... Chicago, IL

Stevenson, Jay K. .... Dallas, TX
Stevenson, Jeffrey W. .... Chicago, IL
Stevenson, Jerome E. .... Palm Springs, CA
Stevenson, Jill M. .... Des Moines, IA
Stevenson, Joanne Turner .... Centralia, IL
Stevenson, Joel B. .... Asheville, NC
Stevenson, John A. .... Centralia, IL
Stevenson, John C. .... Livonia, MI
Stevenson, John F. .... Hartford, CT
Stevenson, John G., Jr. .... Quincy, IL
Stevenson, John Hart .... Houston, TX
Stevenson, John M. .... New York, NY
Stevenson, John W. .... Owensboro, KY
Stevenson, John W., Jr. .... Houston, TX
Stevenson, Jon C. .... Colorado Springs, CO
Stevenson, Joseph L. .... Troy, MI
Stevenson, Judith M. .... Columbus, OH
Stevenson, Julie Vick .... Naperville, IL
Stevenson, Justin J., III .... New York, NY
Stevenson, Karen .... San Jose, CA
Stevenson, Karen L. .... Los Angeles, CA
Stevenson, Kathleen .... Syracuse, NY
Stevenson, Kelly Sanders .... Memphis, TN
Stevenson Keppelman Associates Ann Arbor, MI
Stevenson, Kevin D. .... Bowie, MD
Stevenson, Krista A. .... Sacramento, CA
Stevenson, L. John, Jr. .... Seattle, WA
Stevenson, Lacey .... Basking Ridge, NJ
Stevenson, LaMarr .... Arlington, TX
Stevenson, Laura E. .... Atlanta, GA
Stevenson, Laurel .... Kansas City, MO Springfield, MO
Stevenson, Lawrence P. .... Tallahassee, FL
Stevenson, Lee Ann .... New York, NY
Stevenson, Leo J. .... Kalamazoo, MI
Stevenson, Lisa J. .... Washington, DC
Stevenson, Mack B. .... Marietta, GA
Stevenson, Malcolm G. .... Washington, DC
Stevenson, Marcus .... Houston, TX
Stevenson, Margaret .... Edison, NJ
Stevenson, Marisa Fera .... Pittsburgh, PA
Stevenson, Mark A. .... Sioux Falls, SD
Stevenson, Martha Roth .... Manchester, VT
Stevenson, Michael A. .... Southfield, MI
Stevenson, Michael D. .... San Francisco, CA
Stevenson, Michael D. .... Las Vegas, NV
Stevenson, Michael E. .... Olympia, WA
Stevenson, Michael J. Securities and Exchange Commission, Division of Enforcement, GV
Stevenson, Michele A. .... Collegeville, PA
Stevenson, Nancy Federal Communications Commission, Cable Services Bureau, GV
Stevenson, Neil .... New York, NY
Stevenson, Nicholas .... Chicago, IL
Stevenson, Norman W. .... Charleston, SC
Stevenson, Paul D. .... New York, NY
Stevenson, Paul E. .... Las Vegas, NV
Stevenson, Paul H. .... Detroit, MI
Stevenson, Philip D. .... Boston, MA
Stevenson, R. Scott .... Atlanta, GA
Stevenson, Raymond .... Stoneham, MA
Stevenson, Raymond H. Prospect Heights, IL
Stevenson, R. C. .... Sweeny, TX
Stevenson, Richard M. .... Sacramento, CA
Stevenson, Richard W. .... Harrisburg, PA
Stevenson, R. J. (Randy) .... Omaha, NE
Stevenson, Robert A. .... New York, NY
Stevenson, Robert B. .... Ann Arbor, MI
Stevenson, Robert H. .... Pittsburgh, PA
Stevenson, Robert H. .... Seattle, WA
Stevenson, Robert W. La Canada Flintridge, CA
Stevenson, Roger J. .... Akron, OH
Stevenson, Roseann C. .... Los Angeles, CA
Stevenson, Roslyn L. .... Hollywood, FL
Stevenson, Russell B., Jr. .... Reston, VA
Stevenson, S. Lee, Jr. .... Rochester, NY
Stevenson, Scot A. .... Barberton, OH
Stevenson, Scot B. .... Los Angeles, CA
Stevenson, Scott M. .... Charlotte, NC
Stevenson, Scott W. .... Charlotte, NC
Stevenson, Shanon R. .... Atlanta, GA
Stevenson & Smith .... Ogden, UT
Stevenson, Stanford L., III Wilmington, DE
Stevenson, Steven L. .... Savannah, MO
Stevenson, Susan C. .... San Diego, CA
Stevenson, Susan Crowley .... Houston, TX
Stevenson, Tamara Smith .... Simi Valley, CA
Stevenson, Tami Edith .... Plantation, FL
Stevenson, Tasha Williams .... Dallas, TX
Stevenson, Terry B. .... Burbank, CA
Stevenson, Theodore, III .... Dallas, TX
Stevenson, Theresa Osterman San Diego, CA
Stevenson, Thomas L. .... Pittsburgh, PA
Stevenson, Timothy E. .... Cambridge, MA
Stevenson, Todd L. .... Dubuque, IA
Stevenson, Virginia Leggett Washington, DC Charlotte, NC
Stevenson, W. Malcolm .... New Orleans, LA
Stevenson, W. Scott .... Atlanta, GA
Stevenson, William B. .... Aurora, CO
Stevenson, William B. .... Beltsville, MD
Stevenson, William H., Jr. .... Sumter, SC
Stevenson, William J. .... East Rutherford, NJ
Stevenson, William W. Canal Winchester, OH
Stevenson, Wm. J. .... Chicago, IL
Stevenson, Young W. .... Montgomery, AL
Stevenson, Yvonne M. .... Edmonds, WA
Stevenson & Zabowski .... Collegeville, PA

Stevenson-Lawrence, Kimberly A. Cleveland, OH
Stever, Arthur C., III .... Watertown, NY
Stever, Donald W., Jr. .... New York, NY
Stever, Tara C. .... New York, NY
Steverango, Laird P. .... San Francisco, CA
Steverman, Benjamin W., Jr. .... Hartford, CT
Stevers, Stephen L. .... Las Cruces, NM
Steverson, L. Neil .... Richmond, VA
Steverson, Mark L. .... New York, NY
Steverson, Randall K. .... Honolulu, HI
Steverson-Wright, Janet W. .... Portland, OR
Steves, David A. .... Sarasota, FL
Steves, Edward M. .... New York, NY
Steves, Marshall T., Jr. .... San Antonio, TX
Steves, Sterling W. .... Fort Worth, TX
Stevick, Sayre E. .... Palo Alto, CA
Stevinson, Douglas A. .... New Brunswick, NJ New York, NY
Stevinson, Stanley R. .... Morristown, NJ
Stevning-Roe, Ann E. .... Marshfield, WI
Stevralia, James H. .... New York, NY
Steward, Bob G. .... Carrollton, TX
Steward, Brian C. .... San Antonio, TX
Steward, Carleen M. .... Princeton, NJ
Steward, Christopher Wayne .... San Diego, CA
Steward, David G. .... Riverside, CA
Steward, David S. .... Des Moines, IA
Steward, Evelyne R. .... Los Angeles, CA
Steward, H. Dean .... Santa Ana, CA
Steward, Harry D. .... Carlsbad, CA
Steward, James B. .... Ishpeming, MI
Steward, Jennifer A. .... Miami, FL
Steward, John .... Boston, MA
Steward, Kimberly S. Hot Springs National Park, AR
Steward, Lawrence A. .... Indianapolis, IN
Steward, Lorna L. .... Eureka, CA
Steward, Matthew A. .... Salt Lake City, UT
Steward, Merrill F. .... Stamford, CT
Steward, Mimi (Mildred) .... Silver Spring, MD
Steward, Pierre L. .... Orlando, FL
Steward, Priscilla .... New York, NY
Steward & Sheridan, P.L.C. .... Ishpeming, MI
Stewart, A. Amy .... Atlanta, GA
Stewart, A. DeLoach .... Florence, AL
Stewart, A. Obie .... Palm Beach, FL West Palm Beach, FL
Stewart, Alan D. .... Tampa, FL
Stewart, Alan M. .... Columbia, SC
Stewart, Alan R. .... Charlotte, NC
Stewart, Alan R. .... Salt Lake City, UT
Stewart, Albert, Jr. .... Springfield, OH
Stewart, Alberta .... New York, NY
Stewart, Alison L. .... San Francisco, CA
Stewart, Allan F. .... St. Louis, MO
Stewart, Allen M. .... Dallas, TX
Stewart, Allen W. .... Broomall, PA
Stewart, Alton K., Jr. .... Conroe, TX
Stewart, Amy .... Atlanta, GA
Stewart, Amy A. .... Atlanta, GA
Stewart, Amy L. .... Indianapolis, IN
Stewart, Amy Lee .... Little Rock, AR
Stewart, Amy M. .... Louisville, KY
Stewart, Amy Watson .... Birmingham, AL
Stewart, Andrew M. .... Redlands, CA
Stewart, Andrew R. .... Washington, DC
Stewart, Andrew R.A. .... Dallas, TX
Stewart, Andrew T. .... Enfield, NH
Stewart, Andy .... Jackson, MS
Stewart, Angel Duggan .... Canton, NY
Stewart, Angela M. .... Portland, OR
Stewart, Ann H. .... Columbus, IN
Stewart, Ann K. .... Dallas, TX
Stewart, Anneke Joan .... Long Beach, CA
Stewart, Annette .... Dallas, TX
Stewart, Annette Y. .... White Plains, NY
Stewart, Anthony J. .... New Orleans, LA
Stewart, Anthony L. .... Washington, DC
Stewart, Ardis L. .... Olympia Fields, IL
Stewart, Arnie L. .... Boston, MA
Stewart, Arthur A. .... Dallas, TX
Stewart, Arthur J. .... Warren, PA
Stewart, Ashton L. .... Baton Rouge, LA
Stewart & Associates, A Professional Law Association .... Wilmington, DE Las Vegas, NV
Stewart, Austin E., II .... San Francisco, CA
Stewart, Barbara G. H. .... Concord, NH
Stewart, Barbara L. .... Greensboro, NC
Stewart, Barney, III .... Charlotte, NC
Stewart, Bernard F. .... Ann Arbor, MI
Stewart, Beryl W. .... Wayne, OH
Stewart, Betsy Ann T. .... Independence, MO
Stewart, Beverly A. .... Tulsa, OK
Stewart, Bingham M. .... Baton Rouge, LA
Stewart & Black .... Madison, TN
Stewart, Blair W., Jr. .... Palo Alto, CA
Stewart, Bonnie D. .... Hartford, CT
Stewart & Bourque, P.C. .... Phoenix, AZ
Stewart, Boyd .... Del City, OK
Stewart, B. R. .... Edinburg, TX
Stewart, Brenda J. .... Montvale, NJ
Stewart, Brenda M. .... Treasury Department, Internal Revenue Service, GV
Stewart, Brent P. .... Rock Hill, SC
Stewart, Brian K. .... Pasadena, CA
Stewart, Brian P. .... Santa Ana, CA
Stewart, Brian S. .... Malone, NY
Stewart, Bruce D. .... Harrisburg, IL
Stewart, Bruce F. .... Sacramento, CA
Stewart, Bruce J. .... Nashville, TN
Stewart, Bruce L. .... Wichita, KS
Stewart, Bryan K. .... Tipp City, OH
Stewart, Burks & Carroll .... Picayune, MS
Stewart & Byrom .... Milton, FL
Stewart, Byron A., Jr. .... Independence, MO
Stewart, Byron G. .... Independence, MO

Stewart, C. Evan .... New York, NY
Stewart, C. Jean .... Denver, CO
Stewart, C. Van Leuven .... Baltimore, MD
Stewart, Cameron A. .... Los Angeles, CA
Stewart, Carl E. .... Midland, TX
Stewart, Carl J., Jr. .... Gastonia, NC
Stewart, Carl M. "Hap" .... Jacksonville, FL
Stewart, Carol Ann .... Salt Lake City, UT
Stewart, Carol H. .... Birmingham, AL
Stewart, Carole Lynn .... Houston, TX
Stewart, Carolyn House .... Tampa, FL
Stewart, Caron H. .... Dunn, NC
Stewart, Carter M. .... San Francisco, CA
Stewart, Catharine H. .... Indianapolis, IN
Stewart, Catherine .... Philadelphia, PA
Stewart, Catherine A. .... Bridgeport, CT
Stewart, Catherine M. .... Tucson, AZ
Stewart, Charles A. .... Oakbrook Terrace, IL
Stewart, Charles A., III .... Montgomery, AL
Stewart, Charles Addison, III Roseland, NJ New York, NY
Stewart, Charles B., Jr. .... Beverly Hills, CA
Stewart, Charles Brent .... Columbia, MO
Stewart, Charles C. .... Bedford, OH
Stewart, Charles C., Jr. .... Donalsonville, GA
Stewart, Charles D. .... Birmingham, AL
Stewart, Charles E., III .... Pawling, NY
Stewart, Charles E., Jr. .... New York, NY
Stewart, Charles G. .... Paonia, CO
Stewart, Charles G. .... Oakley, KS
Stewart, Charles I. .... Dallas, TX
Stewart, Charles L., Jr. .... Glencoe, IL
Stewart, Charles Richard .... Greenville, SC
Stewart, Charles T. .... Delray Beach, FL
Stewart, Charles V. .... Washington, DC
Stewart, Charles W., IV .... Bartlesville, OK
Stewart, Chas. W., Jr. .... Fayetteville, AR
Stewart, Chris .... Skaneateles, NY
Stewart, Christian D. .... Kansas City, MO Amarillo, TX
Stewart, Christophe G. .... Louisville, KY
Stewart, Clarence E. .... Pittsburgh, PA
Stewart, Claudia .... Naples, FL
Stewart, Coke Morgan .... Washington, DC
Stewart, Cook, Constance, Stewart & Minton, L.L.C. .... Independence, MO
Stewart, Corey A. .... Washington, DC
Stewart, Craig A. .... New York, NY
Stewart, Craig E. .... San Francisco, CA
Stewart, Craig E. .... Denver, CO
Stewart, Craig E. .... Boston, MA
Stewart, Craig Herschel .... Knoxville, TN
Stewart, Craig M. .... Columbus, OH
Stewart, Cresey D. .... Seattle, WA
Stewart, Curtis C. .... Chapin, SC
Stewart, Cynthia A. .... Jackson, MS
Stewart, Cynthia K. .... Austin, TX
Stewart, Cynthia L. .... Louisville, KY
Stewart, Cynthia L. .... Columbia, MD
Stewart, Cynthia Vuille .... Department of State, Office of the Legal Adviser, GV
Stewart, D. Jay .... Claxton, GA
Stewart, D. Wayne .... Englewood, CO
Stewart, Damien G. .... Washington, DC
Stewart, Dana E. .... Los Angeles, CA
Stewart, Daniel A. .... Fort Smith, AR
Stewart, Daniel C. .... Bloomington, IN
Stewart, Daniel C. .... Dallas, TX
Stewart, Daniel J. .... Minneapolis, MN
Stewart, Daniel J. .... Albany, NY
Stewart, Daniel MacLaren .... Red Bank, NJ New York, NY
Stewart, Daniel P. .... San Jose, CA
Stewart, Daniel W. .... Reno, NV
Stewart, Daniel W., Ltd., A Professional Corporation .... Reno, NV
Stewart, Darnley Dickinson New York, NY
Stewart, Darrell G. .... San Antonio, TX
Stewart, Darrell G., PLLC, Law Office of San Antonio, TX
Stewart, David A. .... Fort Wayne, IN
Stewart, David A. .... Portland, OR
Stewart, David A., Jr. .... Pascagoula, MS
Stewart, David C. .... Anchorage, AK
Stewart, David C. .... Lynn, IN
Stewart, David C. .... Seattle, WA
Stewart, David J. .... Atlanta, GA
Stewart, David K. .... Los Angeles, CA
Stewart, David L. .... Washington, DC
Stewart, David M. .... Flint, MI
Stewart, David M. .... New York, NY
Stewart, David M. .... San Antonio, TX
Stewart, David O. .... Washington, DC
Stewart, David P. .... Department of State, Office of the Legal Adviser, GV
Stewart, David P. .... St. Paul, MN
Stewart, David R. .... Madison, NC
Stewart, David R. .... New York, NY
Stewart, David W. .... Indianapolis, IN
Stewart, David W. .... Gulfport, MS
Stewart, David Wayne .... Carmel, IN
Stewart, Dawn C. .... Washington, DC
Stewart, Dean .... Somerset, KY
Stewart, Deborah A. .... Naples, FL
Stewart and De Chant Co., L.P.A. Cleveland, OH
Stewart, Deirdre O'Brien .... Chester, NJ
Stewart, Delano S. .... Tampa, FL
Stewart, Dennis .... San Diego, CA
Stewart, Dennis G. .... Rayville, LA
Stewart, Dennis L. .... Fort Lauderdale, FL
Stewart, D. Jay, P.C. .... Claxton, GA
Stewart, Don F. .... Memphis, TN
Stewart, Don R. .... Arlington, TX
Stewart, Donald A. .... Sarasota, FL
Stewart, Donald C. .... Lynn, MA

Stewart, Donald J. .... Mobile, AL
Stewart, Donald W. .... Anniston, AL
Stewart, Donald W. .... Gadsden, AL
Stewart, Donald W. .... Oakland, CA
Stewart, Doris A. .... Houston, TX
Stewart, Douglas E., (P.C.) .... Houston, TX
Stewart, Douglas W. San Juan Capistrano, CA
Stewart Due Doyle & Pugh, LLP Indianapolis, IN
Stewart, Duncan J. .... New York, NY
Stewart, Duncan W. .... Houston, TX
Stewart, Dwayne Royce .... Willows, CA
Stewart, E. Roger .... Cleveland, OH
Stewart, Edward C. .... Denver, CO
Stewart, Edward S. .... North Creek, NY
Stewart, Edward W. .... Waukesha, WI
Stewart, Edward W., Jr. .... Manchester, NH
Stewart and Edwards .... Winchester, TN
Stewart & Elder, A Professional Corporation Oklahoma City, OK
Stewart, Elizabeth A. .... Washington, DC
Stewart, Elizabeth J. .... Phoenix, AZ
Stewart, Elizabeth J. .... New Haven, CT
Stewart, Ellen E. .... Denver, CO
Stewart, Ellen Gusikoff .... San Diego, CA Philadelphia, PA
Stewart, Ellen P. .... Dallas, TX
Stewart, Emilie F. .... Austin, TX
Stewart, Emma F. .... Irving, TX
Stewart, Ernest W. .... Madison, MS
Stewart, Estes & Donnell .... Nashville, TN
Stewart, Eugene A. .... Brookville, IN
Stewart, Eugene David .... Eagle Pass, TX
Stewart, Evans & Hafner, P.A. Vero Beach, FL
Stewart, Fernande Welsh .... Torrance, CA
Stewart Firm, The, P.C. .... Mobile, AL
Stewart, Floyd D. .... Clayton, MO
Stewart, Forrest R. .... Giddings, TX
Stewart, Foster A., Jr .... Portland, ME
Stewart, Frank H. .... Cincinnati, OH
Stewart, Frank S. .... Tampa, FL
Stewart, Fred C. .... Franklin, VA
Stewart, Fred L. .... Colville, WA
Stewart, Frederick B. .... Franklin, VA
Stewart, Frederick N. .... Leavenworth, KS
Stewart, G. Cope, III .... Washington, DC
Stewart, G. Michael .... Dallas, TX
Stewart, G. Russell .... New London, CT
Stewart, G. Todd .... Houston, TX
Stewart, Gail Grant .... Bellevue, WA
Stewart, Gail S. .... Albuquerque, NM
Stewart, Gail Woodson .... Houston, TX
Stewart, Gale B., (Ms.) .... Little Rock, AR
Stewart, Garry D. .... Pasadena, CA
Stewart, Gary .... Allegan, MI
Stewart, Gary A. .... Bloomfield Hills, MI
Stewart, Gary D. .... Des Moines, IA
Stewart, Gary N. .... Warwick, RI
Stewart, Garylle B. .... Fargo, ND
Stewart, Gayle Richard .... Rock Springs, WY
Stewart, Gaylord L. .... San Diego, CA
Stewart, Geoffrey S. .... Washington, DC
Stewart, Geoffrey S. .... New York, NY
Stewart, George A. .... Concord, NH
Stewart, George C. .... Ann Arbor, MI
Stewart, George Daniel .... Milton, FL
Stewart, George J. .... Pittsburgh, PA
Stewart, George L., II .... Pittsburgh, PA
Stewart, George N. .... Pittsburgh, PA
Stewart, George Scott, III .... Philadelphia, PA
Stewart, Gerald A. .... Metairie, LA
Stewart, Gerald H. .... Tarzana, CA
Stewart, Geraldine H. .... Fairbanks, AK
Stewart, Glenn .... Corsicana, TX
Stewart, Gordon M. .... Palo Alto, CA
Stewart, Gordon W. .... Wilmington, DE Las Vegas, NV
Stewart, Green & McGowan .... Carmel, CA
Stewart, Gregory A. .... Houston, TX
Stewart, Gregory J. .... Buffalo, NY
Stewart, Gregory K. .... Little Rock, AR
Stewart, Gregory K. .... Carmi, IL
Stewart, Gregory M. .... Norton, VA
Stewart, Gregory T. .... Tallahassee, FL
Stewart, Gwyneth G. .... Cincinnati, OH
Stewart, H. Malcolm, III .... Goshen, NY
Stewart, Hallie E. .... Concord, CA
Stewart, Harold L. .... Presque Isle, ME
Stewart, Harold L., II .... Presque Isle, ME
Stewart, Harold W. .... Alhambra, CA
Stewart & Harris .... Pasadena, CA
Stewart, Harry A. .... Orlando, FL
Stewart, Harry A., Jr. .... Phoenix, AZ
Stewart, Harry A., Jr., P.C. .... Phoenix, AZ
Stewart, Hazel L. .... Yonkers, NY
Stewart, Heather J. .... Washington, DC
Stewart, Heidi Rai .... Pittsburgh, PA
Stewart, Helen H., Law Office of Concord, MA
Stewart, Helen M. .... San Marino, CA
Stewart, Helene R. .... Reston, VA
Stewart, Henry S. .... Rochester, NY
Stewart, Herman I., Jr. .... De Ridder, LA
Stewart, Howard P. .... Department of Justice, Environment and Natural Resources Division, GV
Stewart, Hugh W. .... Tucson, AZ
Stewart Humpherys Burchett Sandelman & Molin .... Chico, CA
Stewart, I. Daniel, Jr. .... Salt Lake City, UT
Stewart & Irwin, Professional Corporation Indianapolis, IN
Stewart, J. Benton, II .... Tampa, FL
Stewart, J. Darin .... Winter Park, FL
Stewart, J. Douglas .... Gainesville, GA
Stewart, J. Frank .... Los Angeles, CA

Stewart, J. Frank .... Angola, IN
Coldwater, MI
Stewart, J. Hamilton, III ..... Washington, DC
Charleston, SC
Greenville, SC
Nashville, TN
Stewart, J. Mark .... Winchester, TN
Stewart, J. Milton .... Baytown, TX
Stewart, J. Sebastian .... Minneapolis, MN
Stewart, J. Steven .... Macon, GA
Stewart, J. Williams .... Minneapolis, MN
Stewart, Jack C. .... Hillsboro, MO
Stewart, Jack L. .... Columbus, OH
Stewart, Jack L. .... Keizer, OR
Stewart, Jack N. .... Salina, KS
Stewart, Jack W., Jr. .... Asheville, NC
Stewart, Jacqueline M .... Catonsville, MD
Stewart, Jacqueline W. .... Palo Alto, CA
Stewart, James .... Roseland, NJ
Stewart, James A. .... Madison, WI
Stewart, James B. .... Bridgeport, CT
Southport, CT
Stewart, James C. .... Washington, DC
Stewart, James C. .... Washington, DC
Stewart, James C. .... Rochester, NY
Stewart, James C., Jr. .... Naples, FL
Stewart, James D. .... Minneapolis, MN
Stewart, James D. .... San Antonio, TX
Stewart, James D., and Associates, Inc.
San Antonio, TX
Stewart, James E. .... Shreveport, LA
Stewart, James E. .... Ann Arbor, MI
Stewart, James G. .... Portland, OR
Stewart, James H. .... Iron Mountain, MI
Duluth, MN
Stewart, James H. .... Fargo, ND
Stewart, James H., Jr. .... Harrisburg, PA
Stewart, James J. .... Los Angeles, CA
Stewart, James K. .... Washington, DC
Stewart, James M. .... Temecula, CA
Stewart, James M. .... Singer Island, FL
Stewart, James M. .... Montesano, WA
Stewart, James M. "Mac" .... Dallas, TX
Stewart, James R. .... Los Angeles, CA
Stewart, James R., Jr. ...... West Palm Beach, FL
Stewart, James T. .... Springfield, VA
Stewart, James V. .... St. Petersburg, FL
Stewart, James W. .... San Jose, CA
Stewart, James W. .... Salt Lake City, UT
Stewart, James Y. .... Birmingham, MI
Stewart, Jami L., Ms. .... Oklahoma City, OK
Stewart, Jan C. .... Washington, DC
Stewart, Jan L. .... Olney, MD
Stewart, Jan L., P.A. .... Olney, MD
Stewart, Jane B. .... New York, NY
Stewart, Jane Lauren Buel .... Drain, OR
Eugene, OR
Stewart, Janet Blair .... Columbus, OH
Stewart, Janet E. .... Omaha, NE
Stewart, Janet Elizabeth ..... Oklahoma City, OK
Stewart, Janet Marie .... Oklahoma City, OK
Stewart, Janice M. .... Portland, OR
Stewart, Jay B. .... Austin, TX
Stewart, Jay T. .... Phoenix, AZ
Stewart, Jeanne Fennell .... Westport, CT
Stewart, Jeff .... Winchester, TN
Stewart, Jefferson D. .... New Orleans, LA
Jackson, MS
Stewart, Jeffrey B. .... Atlanta, GA
Stewart, Jeffrey J. .... Fort Washington, MD
Stewart, Jeffrey L. .... Dallas, TX
Stewart, Jeffrey T. .... Southfield, MI
Stewart, Jeffrey W. .... New York, NY
Stewart, Jelahn
Pension Benefit Guaranty Corporation,
Office of the General Counsel, GV
Stewart, Jennifer .... San Francisco, CA
Stewart, Jennifer .... Houston, TX
Stewart, Jerry A. .... Grand Prairie, TX
Stewart, Jerry W. .... Benton, AR
Stewart, Jimmy .... San Angelo, TX
Stewart, Joan .... Tallahassee, FL
Stewart, Joanne I .... Costa Mesa, CA
Stewart, Joel .... Fort Lauderdale, FL
Stewart, John .... New York, NY
Stewart, John .... Norristown, PA
Stewart, John A. .... Woodbridge, CT
Stewart, John A. .... Dallas, TX
Stewart, John A., Jr. .... New Orleans, LA
Stewart, John B. .... Sarasota, FL
Stewart, John B. .... Springfield, MA
Stewart, John B. .... San Antonio, TX
Stewart, John C. .... Denver, CO
Stewart, John C. .... Plymouth, MI
Stewart, John C. .... Toledo, OH
Stewart, John C. .... Fort Worth, TX
Stewart, John C. .... Seattle, WA
Stewart, John C., Jr. .... Myrtle Beach, SC
Stewart, John D. .... Winter Park, FL
Stewart, John D. .... Philadelphia, PA
Stewart, John E. .... Cherry Hill, NJ
Stewart, John F. .... Covina, CA
Stewart, John F. .... Fort Myers, FL
Stewart, John Frith .... Crestwood, KY
Louisville, KY
Stewart, John H. .... Buena Park, CA
Stewart, John H. .... St. Petersburg, FL
Stewart, John I., Jr. .... Washington, DC
Stewart, John J., Jr. .... Mineola, NY
Riverhead, NY
Stewart, John (Jack) P. .... Mansfield, OH
Stewart, John (Jack) P. .... Mansfield, OH
Stewart, John K. .... San Francisco, CA
Stewart, John L. .... Murphysboro, IL
Stewart, John L. .... Indianapolis, IN
Stewart, John Mitchell .... Vero Beach, FL
Stewart, John R. .... La Junta, CO
Stewart, John R. (Jack) .... Kenilworth, NJ
Stewart, John R., Jr. .... Fayetteville, GA
Stewart, John S. .... New York, NY
Stewart, John Spencer .... Portland, OR
Stewart, John T. .... Chapel Hill, NC
Stewart, John W. .... Louisville, KY
Stewart, John W. .... Lincoln, NE
Stewart, Jomo K. .... San Jose, CA
Stewart, Jon A. .... Louisville, KY
Stewart, Jonathan C. .... Nashville, TN
Stewart, Jonathan M. .... Arcadia, LA
Stewart, Jose A. .... Dallas, TX
Stewart, Joseph .... Penacook, NH
Stewart, Joseph A. .... Chicago, IL
Stewart, Joseph D. .... Naples, FL
Stewart, Joseph G. .... Birmingham, AL
Stewart, Joseph G. .... St. Louis, MO
Stewart, Joseph G., Jr. .... Montgomery, AL
Stewart, Joseph W. .... Arlington, TX
Stewart, Joyce E. .... Moorefield, WV
Stewart, Joyner & Jordan-Holmes, P.A.
Jacksonville, FL
Tampa, FL
Stewart, Judith A. .... Chicago, IL
Stewart, Judith A. .... Indianapolis, IN
Stewart, Judith G. .... Chapel Hill, NC
Stewart, Julia Smeds .... Birmingham, AL
Stewart, Justin C. .... Salt Lake City, UT
Stewart, Karen A. .... Sacramento, CA
Stewart, Karen L. .... Louisville, KY
Stewart, Karl A. .... Greenwich, CT
Stewart, Katherine Bell .... Dallas, TX
Stewart, Katherine Mahan .... Spooner, WI
Stewart & Keevil, L.L.C. .... Columbia, MO
Jefferson City, MO
Stewart, Kendra Tamara .... New York, NY
Stewart, Kenneth B. .... Raleigh, NC
Stewart, Kenneth B. .... Oregon City, OR
Stewart, Kenneth E. .... Oakbrook Terrace, IL
Stewart, Kenneth L. .... Dallas, TX
Stewart, Kenneth P. .... Wichita, KS
Stewart, Kenneth S. .... Rosemead, CA
Stewart, Kent O. .... Indianapolis, IN
Stewart, Keslie .... San Francisco, CA
Stewart, Kevin D. .... Spokane, WA
Stewart & Keyes .... Fort Myers, FL
Stewart, Kim A. .... Mission Viejo, CA
Stewart, Kirk .... Cleveland, OH
Stewart, Kirsten B. .... Denver, CO
Minneapolis, MN
Stewart, Kristen Larkin .... Pittsburgh, PA
Stewart, Kristin D. .... St. Cloud, MN
Stewart, L. Jack .... Picayune, MS
Stewart, Lance L. .... Jackson, MS
Stewart, Larry A. .... Alexandria, LA
Stewart, Larry D. .... Encino, CA
Stewart, Larry E. .... Cumming, GA
Stewart, Larry M. .... Stuart, FL
Stewart, Larry M., P.A. .... Stuart, FL
Stewart, Larry S. .... Miami, FL
Stewart, Laura E. .... Los Angeles, CA
Stewart, Laura J. .... Cambridge, MA
Stewart, Lauri Beth .... Bloomfield Hills, MI
Stewart Law Group, The, P.C.
Birmingham, AL
Stewart Law Office, P.C. .... Norton, VA
Stewart, Lawrence C., Jr. .... Winter Haven, FL
Stewart, Lawrence E. .... Cleveland, OH
Stewart, Leasa M. .... Oklahoma City, OK
Stewart, Lee H. .... Birmingham, AL
Stewart, Leonard L. .... Pittsburgh, PA
Stewart, Leonard W. .... Brooklyn, NY
Stewart, Leslie E., (Ms) .... Harrisonville, MO
Stewart, Leslie M. .... Houston, TX
Stewart, Lester H. .... Everett, WA
Stewart, L. F. .... Winchester, TN
Stewart, Linda Susan .... Pittsburgh, PA
Stewart, Lindsay D. .... Beaverton, OR
Stewart, Lindsay, III .... Cynthiana, KY
Stewart, Lois J. .... Santa Monica, CA
Stewart, Lorrie S. .... Los Angeles, CA
Stewart, Lucinda A.
Department of Education,
Office of the General Counsel, GV
Stewart, Lyle B. .... Denver, CO
Stewart, Lyndy Chang .... San Francisco, CA
Stewart, Lynn C. .... Atlanta, GA
Stewart, Lynn Kellene .... Baltimore, MD
Stewart, Lynne F. .... New York, NY
Stewart, Lynne F., Law Office of
New York, NY
Stewart, Lynne S. .... Pittsburgh, PA
Stewart, M. Deane .... Louisville, KY
Stewart, M. Eliza .... Albuquerque, NM
Stewart, Malcolm H. .... Fresno, CA
Stewart, Malcolm L. .... Department of Justice,
Office of the Solicitor General, GV
Stewart, Malcolm N. .... Fairfield, PA
Stewart & Mann, P.C. .... Edinburg, TX
Stewart, Marcia Kaye .... Smithfield, NC
Stewart, Margaret Ann .... Jackson, MS
Stewart, Margaret G. .... Chicago, IL
Stewart, Marguerite H. .... McMinnville, TN
Stewart, Maria Morris .... Austin, TX
Stewart, Marikay .... DeLand, FL
Stewart, Marilyn J. .... Alamo, CA
Stewart, Mark C. .... Toledo, OH
Stewart, Mark M. .... Los Angeles, CA
Stewart, Mark R., III .... Cheyenne, WY
Stewart, Mark R.B. .... New York, NY
Stewart, Mark S. .... Philadelphia, PA
Stewart, Mark S. .... Fort Worth, TX
Stewart, Mark Scott .... Harrisburg, PA
Stewart, Martin .... New York, NY
Stewart, Martin A. .... Dallas, TX
Stewart, Martin A., P.C., Law Offices of
Dallas, TX
Stewart, Marvin L., Jr. .... Birmingham, AL
Stewart, Mary A. .... Clovis, CA
Stewart, Mary Ann .... Covington, KY
Stewart, Mary Elizabeth .... Concord, NC
Stewart, Mary M. .... Orlando, FL
Stewart, Mary M. .... St. Louis, MO
Stewart, Matthew J. .... Owosso, MI
Stewart, Maurice L. .... St. Louis, MO
Stewart, Max B. .... Carthage, IL
Stewart, McCormick, McArdle & Sorice
Greensburg, PA
Stewart, Melanie McCaa .... Memphis, TN
Stewart, Melinda C.H. .... Vacaville, CA
Stewart, Melinda J. .... San Jose, CA
Stewart, Melissa Anne .... Lexington, KY
Stewart, Melissa K. .... Lawrenceville, GA
Stewart, Melissa Ruman .... Dallas, TX
Stewart, Melody J. .... Cleveland, OH
Stewart, Melvin & Frost, LLP
Gainesville, GA
Stewart, Michael .... New York, NY
Stewart, Michael A., Sr. .... Cullman, AL
Stewart, Michael B. .... Bloomfield Hills, MI
Stewart, Michael C. .... Oklahoma City, OK
Stewart, Michael D. .... Costa Mesa, CA
Stewart, Michael D. .... Greeley, CO
Stewart, Michael D. .... Fort Lauderdale, FL
Stewart, Michael D., P.A.
Fort Lauderdale, FL
Stewart, Michael G. .... Nashville, TN
Stewart, Michael J. .... Newport Beach, CA
Stewart, Michael J.
Department of Agriculture,
Office of the Judicial Officer, GV
Stewart, Michael J. .... Greensburg, PA
Stewart, Michael Kevin .... Atlanta, GA
Stewart, Michael L. .... New Orleans, LA
Stewart, Michael M. .... Oklahoma City, OK
Stewart, Michael P. .... Los Angeles, CA
Stewart, Michael R. .... Grinnell, IA
Stewart, Michael R. .... Minneapolis, MN
Stewart, Michael T. .... Maplewood, NJ
New York, NY
Stewart, Mildred L. .... Bronx, NY
Stewart, Milton D. .... Phoenix, AZ
Stewart, Milton R. .... Portland, OR
Stewart, Monte N. .... Provo, UT
Stewart, Monte Neil .... Las Vegas, NV
Stewart, Morton B. .... Richmond, VA
Stewart, Myles C. .... Tucson, AZ
Stewart, N. John, Jr.
New Port Richey, FL
Stewart, N. John, Jr., P.A.
New Port Richey, FL
Stewart, N. Johnson, Jr.
New Port Richey, FL
Stewart, N. Scott .... Renton, WA
Stewart, N. Simone .... Washington, DC
Stewart, Nancy .... Morristown, NJ
Stewart, Nancy Black .... Tallahassee, FL
Stewart, Nancy Davis .... Pittsburgh, PA
Stewart, Nathan B. .... Hillsboro, MO
Stewart, Ned A., Jr. .... Texarkana, AR
Stewart & Neilson .... Philadelphia, PA
Stewart, Nelson R. .... Annapolis, MD
Stewart, Norman R. .... Buffalo, NY
Stewart Occhipinti & Makow, LLP
Roseland, NJ
New York, NY
Stewart, Pamela .... Ruston, LA
Stewart, Pamela S. .... Houston, TX
Stewart, Patricia .... Annandale, VA
Stewart, Patricia D. .... Norwell, MA
Stewart, Patricia Jerome .... Phoenix, AZ
Stewart, Patricia W. Cobb .... Scottsboro, AL
Stewart, Patrick .... Apple Valley, MN
Stewart, Patrick J. .... Washington, DC
Baltimore, MD
Stewart, Patrick Lester .... Chantilly, VA
Stewart, Paul A. .... Newport Beach, CA
Stewart, Paul A. .... San Francisco, CA
Stewart, Paul P. .... Port Washington, NY
Stewart, Paul W. .... Memphis, TN
Stewart, Paula M. .... Columbia, SC
Stewart, Perry P. .... Washington, DC
Stewart, Peter A., III .... Jackson, MS
Stewart, Peter B. .... Indianapolis, IN
Stewart, Peter G. .... Roseland, NJ
Stewart, Peyton, Crawford, Crawford & Stutt
Racine, WI
Stewart, Philip O. .... Middletown, VA
Stewart, Philip W. .... San Antonio, TX
Stewart, Phillip L. .... Carmel, IN
Stewart, Plant & Blumenthal, LLC
Baltimore, MD
Stewart, Potter, Jr. .... Brattleboro, VT
Stewart, Potter, Jr., Law Offices, P.C.
Brattleboro, VT
Stewart, R. Scott .... Langdon, ND
Stewart, Ramsey R. .... San Diego, CA
Stewart, Randall L. .... Vancouver, WA
Stewart, Raymond C. .... Falls Church, VA
Stewart, Raymond J. .... Washington, DC
Stewart, Reda J. .... Leesburg, FL
Stewart, Renee LeVay .... Nashville, TN
Stewart, R.F. (Ben), III .... Birmingham, AL
Stewart, Richard A. .... Moreno Valley, CA
Stewart, Richard B. .... New York, NY
Stewart, Richard C. .... Roseland, NJ
Stewart, Richard C., II .... Stamford, CT
Stewart, Richard C., Law Offices of
New Canaan, CT
Stewart, Richard C. H. .... Jamaica Plain, MA
Stewart, Richard E. .... Chapel Hill, NC
Stewart, Richard F. .... Burbank, CA
Stewart, Richard F., A Professional Corporation
Burbank, CA
Stewart, Richard G., Jr. .... Irving, TX
Stewart, Richard M. .... Simi Valley, CA
Stewart, Richard M. .... St. Louis, MO
Stewart, Richard M. .... Akron, OH
Stewart, Richard N. P. .... Cincinnati, OH
Stewart, Richard W. .... Absecon, NJ
Stewart, Richard W. .... Lemoyne, PA
Stewart, Rickee S. .... Los Angeles, CA
Stewart, Robb .... Dallas, TX
Stewart, Robb & Associates, P.C.
Dallas, TX
Stewart, Robb P. .... Dallas, TX
Stewart, Robert A. .... Moorestown, NJ
Stewart, Robert A. .... New York, NY
Stewart, Robert A. .... Seattle, WA
Stewart, Robert B. .... Birmingham, AL
Stewart, Robert B. .... Anchorage, AK
Stewart, Robert B. .... Tulsa, OK
Stewart, Robert B., III .... Huntingdon, PA
Stewart, Robert C. .... Naperville, IL
Stewart, Robert D. .... Boston, MA
Stewart, Robert D. .... Seattle, WA
Stewart, Robert D., Jr. .... Oklahoma City, OK
Stewart, Robert E. .... Danville, IN
Stewart, Robert E. .... Pittsburgh, PA
Stewart, Robert Forrest, Jr.
Wilmington, DE
Philadelphia, PA
Stewart, Robert G. .... Gloucester, MA
Stewart, Robert G., P.C. .... Gloucester, MA
Stewart, Robert H. .... West Des Moines, IA
Stewart, Robert J. .... York, PA
Stewart, Robert J., III .... Syracuse, NY
Stewart, Robert K., Jr. .... Anchorage, AK
Stewart, Robert L., Jr. .... Phoenix, AZ
Stewart, Robert L., Jr. .... Richmond, VA
Stewart, Robert M. .... Houston, TX
Stewart, Robert P. .... Shallotte, NC
Stewart, Robert P., III .... Houston, TX
Stewart, Robert R. .... Englewood, CO
Stewart, Robert S. .... Glens Falls, NY
Stewart, Robert T. .... Austin, TX
Stewart, Robert W. .... Corte Madera, CA
Stewart, Robert W. .... Miami, FL
Stewart, Robert W. .... St. Louis, MO
Stewart, Robert W. .... Athens, OH
Stewart, Robert W. .... Norfolk, VA
Stewart, Robert W., Jr., A Law Corporation
Palm Desert, CA
Stewart, Robert W., P.A. .... Miami, FL
Stewart, Robin Leslie .... Sacramento, CA
San Francisco, CA
Stewart, Roderick N. .... Delta, CO
Stewart, Rodney D. .... Oklahoma City, OK
Stewart & Roelandt .... Crestwood, KY
Stewart, Roger T. .... Irvine, CA
Stewart, Roger W. .... Austin, TX
Stewart, Roland M. .... Chicago, IL
Stewart, Roma Jones .... Chicago, IL
Stewart, Ronald B. .... Corbin, KY
Stewart, Ronald E. .... Chico, CA
Stewart, Ronald S. .... Castro Valley, CA
Stewart, Ronni P. .... Marina Del Rey, CA
Stewart, Rose D. .... Atlanta, GA
Stewart, Rosemary .... Washington, DC
Stewart, Roy D. .... Racine, WI
Stewart, Roy J.
Federal Communications Commission,
Mass Media Bureau, GV
Stewart, Russell J. .... Park Ridge, IL
Stewart, Russell O. .... Denver, CO
Stewart, Russell R. .... Panama City, FL
Stewart, S. Grant .... Willow Street, PA
Stewart, S. Kent .... Birmingham, AL
Stewart, S. Porter, II .... Florence, SC
Stewart, Sabrina E. .... Fort Worth, TX
Stewart, Sandra C. .... Los Angeles, CA
Stewart, Sandra J .... Montgomery, AL
Stewart, Sandra L. .... Las Vegas, NV
Stewart, Sandra Lynne .... Fort Stockton, TX
Stewart, Sara B. .... Red Bank, NJ
Stewart, Sarah Hicks .... Mobile, AL
Stewart, Sarah J. .... New York, NY
Stewart, Sarah L.
Federal Mine Safety and Health Review
Commission,
Office of the General Counsel, GV
Stewart, Scott E. .... Washington, DC
Stewart, Scott E. .... Cleveland, OH
Stewart, Scott E. .... San Antonio, TX
Stewart, Scott F. .... Rainbow City, AL
Stewart, Scott M. .... Chicago, IL
Stewart, Scott Michael .... Winston-Salem, NC
Stewart, Sean C. .... Denver, CO
Stewart, Shailah T. .... Boston, MA
Stewart, Shameka L. .... Escondido, CA
Stewart, Shane R. .... Concord, NH
Stewart, Shannon .... Indianapolis, IN
Stewart, Sheila .... Houston, TX
Stewart, Shortridge & Coates, P.C.
Denver, CO
Englewood, CO
Stewart & Smith .... Anniston, AL
Stewart & Smith .... Lexington, NE
Stewart Sokol & Gray, LLC
Portland, OR
Stewart & Steele, P.C. .... Oregon City, OR
Stewart, Stephanie J. .... Tampa, FL
Stewart, Stephen C. .... Garden Grove, CA
Stewart, Stephen D. .... Springfield, MO
Stewart, Stephen P. .... Raleigh, NC
Stewart, Stephen W. .... San Angelo, TX
Stewart, Steve .... Houston, TX
Stewart, Steven D. .... Jeffersonville, IN
Stewart, Steven H. .... Salt Lake City, UT
Stewart, Steven Jay .... Chicago, IL
Stewart, Steven Wayne .... Washington, DC
Stewart and Stewart .... Washington, DC
Stewart and Stewart .... Carmel, IN
Stewart & Stewart .... Arcadia, LA
Stewart & Stewart .... Conroe, TX

Stewart & Stewart ... Houston, TX
Stewart & Stewart ... Franklin, VA
Stewart & Stewart Law Offices, Inc., P.S., A Prof. Serv. Corp. ... Montesano, WA
Stewart, Stewart & O'Neil ... Walnut Creek, CA
Stewart & Stewart, P.A. ... Dunn, NC
Stewart, Sue Stern ... Rochester, NY
Stewart, Susan C. ... Newbury Park, CA
Benton Harbor, MI
Stewart, Susan E. ... Seattle, WA
Stewart, Susan K. ... San Diego, CA
Stewart, Susan P. ... Steubenville, OH
Stewart, Susan R. ... Elkin, NC
Stewart, Suzan M. ... Des Moines, IA
Stewart, Sylvia D. ... Paso Robles, CA
Stewart, T. Chris ... Minneapolis, MN
Stewart, Tab Timothy ... New York, NY
Stewart, Tamara C. ... Los Angeles, CA
Stewart, Tammy M. ... Metairie, LA
Stewart, Tarun M. ... New York, NY
Stewart, Terence P. ... Washington, DC
Stewart, Theodore M. ... Atlanta, GA
Stewart, Therese M. ... San Francisco, CA
Stewart, Thomas A. ... Los Angeles, CA
Stèwart, Thomas A. ... Boca Raton, FL
Stewart, Thomas B. ... Juneau, AK
Stewart, Thomas C. ... Lafayette, LA
Stewart, Thomas C. ... Morgantown, WV
Stewart, Thomas E. ... Madison, TN
Stewart, Thomas F. ... Sacramento, CA
Stewart, Thomas F. ... Silver City, NM
Stewart, Thomas H. ... Covington, KY
Stewart, Thomas L. ... Birmingham, AL
Stewart, Thomas L. (Larry) ... Nashville, TN
Stewart, Thomas Lee ... St. Louis, MO
Stewart, Thomas M. ... Highlands Ranch, CO
Stewart, Thomas M. ... Oak Park, IL
Stewart, Thomas N., III ... Walnut Creek, CA
Stewart, Thomas N., Jr. ... Walnut Creek, CA
Stewart, Thomas S. ... Kansas City, MO
Stewart, Thomas S. ... Kearney, NE
Stewart, Thomas Scott ... Edwardsville, IL
Stewart, Thomas W. ... Chicago, IL
Stewart Tilghman Fox & Bianchi, P.A. ... Miami, FL
Stewart, Timothy A. ... Hagåtña, GU
Stewart, Timothy L. ... Milwaukee, WI
Stewart, Timothy T. ... Jefferson City, MO
Stewart, Todd A. ... Charlotte, NC
Stewart, Todd S. ... Harrisburg, PA
Stewart, Todd S., (P.A.) ... Palm Beach Gardens, FL
Stewart, Tom B., Jr. ... Jacksonville, FL
Stewart, Tonya ... Albuquerque, NM
Stewart, Tracy L. ... Redondo Beach, CA
Stewart, Tracy Lynn ... Dearborn, MI
Stewart, Valentina ... Lahaina, HI
Stewart, Valerie L. ... Dublin, CA
Stewart, Vaughan O. ... Lake Jackson, TX
Stewart, Vaughn M., II ... Anniston, AL
Stewart, Vernon Kirkland ... Dunn, NC
Stewart, Victor E. ... New York, NY
Stewart, Victoria A. ... Los Angeles, CA
Stewart, Virginia K. ... Panama City, FL
Stewart, W. Jackson ... Casper, WY
Stewart, W. Kelly ... Dallas, TX
Stewart, W. Layton ... St. Louis, MO
Stewart, W. Paul ... Dallas, TX
Stewart, W. Woodrow ... Gainesville, GA
Stewart, Wallace D. ... Sarasota, FL
Stewart, Walter A. ... Springfield, MA
Stewart, Walter A. ... Philadelphia, PA
Stewart, Walter A., Jr. ... New Canaan, CT
Stewart, Walter R. ... Madison, WI
Stewart, Wayne ... Clinton Township, MI
Stewart, Wilkinson & Wilson ... Memphis, TN
Stewart, William A. ... Chicago, IL
Stewart, William Benton ... Birmingham, AL
Stewart, William C., Jr. ... San Diego, CA
Stewart, William D., (A P.C.) ... Glendale, CA
Stewart, William E. ... Annawan, IL
Kewanee, IL
Stewart, William E. ... Lathrup Village, MI
Stewart, William F. ... Los Angeles, CA
Stewart, William F. ... Shelbyville, KY
Stewart, William F. ... Philadelphia, PA
Stewart, William G. ... Wilson, NC
Stewart, William Gerald ... Charlotte, NC
Stewart, William Grant ... Wasilla, AK
Stewart, William J. ... Santa Barbara, CA
Stewart, William J. ... Vero Beach, FL
Stewart, William J. ... Montesano, WA
Stewart, William K., Jr. ... Blue Bell, PA
Stewart, William Kirk ... Carmel, CA
Stewart, William L. ... Fort Myers, FL
Stewart, William L. ... Gulfport, MS
Stewart, William M. ... Roslyn Heights, NY
Stewart, William R. ... East St. Louis, IL
Stewart, William R. ... Cleveland, OH
Stewart, William Ray ... Topeka, KS
Stewart, William S. ... Chapel Hill, NC
Stewart, William T. ... Portland, ME
Stewart, William W. ... Washington, DC
Stewart, William W., Jr. ... Raleigh, NC
Stewart, Winburn E. ... Macon, GA
Stewart, Wm. H. ... Saucier, MS
Stewart, Wm. J., III ... Dallas, TX
Stewart, Wm. L. ... Aptos, CA
Stewart, Wm. R. ... Topeka, KS
Stewart, Wm. W. ... Birmingham, AL
Stewart, Wood & Branca ... Norristown, PA
Stewart, Zlimen & Jungers ... Minneapolis, MN
Stewart-Johnson, Lynne ... Cleveland, OH
Stewart-Magee, Candace Burnes ... Odenville, AL
Stewart-Murray, Karen L. ... Southfield, MI
Stewart-Roberts, Diane M. ... La Grande, OR
Stewman, G. Kevin ... Mineola, NY
Steyaert, Lynn L. ... Lakewood, CO
Steyer, Allan ... San Francisco, CA
Steyer, Hume R. ... New York, NY
Steyer Lowenthal Boodrookas & Walker LLP ... San Francisco, CA
Steyer, Murray ... White Plains, NY
Steyer, Richard Alan ... Washington, DC
Steyer & Sirota ... White Plains, NY
Steyermark, Paul R. ... Wilmington, DE
Steyn, William R. ... Annandale, VA
Sthay, Gerald P. ... Naperville, IL
Stiansen, Stanley G. ... New York, NY
Stibbe Simont Monahan Duhot ... New York, NY
New York, NY
Stibbs & Burbach, P.C. ... Houston, TX
The Woodlands, TX
Stibbs, John H. "Jack", Jr. ... The Woodlands, TX
Stibel & Toulan, LLP ... Boston, MA
Stibel, William A. ... Boston, MA
Stiberth, Thomas J. ... Elgin, IL
Stibich, Michael L. ... Johnstown, PA
Stibolt, Dori K. ... West Palm Beach, FL
Stibolt, Victor D. ... Portland, OR
Stice, John F. ... Sacramento, CA
Stice, Michael D. ... Kingsport, TN
Stice, Steven Lee ... Norman, OK
Stich, Angell, Kreidler, Brownson & Ballou, P.A. ... Minneapolis, MN
Stich, Carl J., Jr. ... Cincinnati, OH
Stich, David P. ... Denver, CO
New York, NY
Stich, Frank J., Jr. ... New Orleans, LA
Stich, George N., Jr. ... Slidell, LA
Stich, Janet I. ... Akron, OH
Stich, Lori J. ... Grand Rapids, MI
Stich, Mary Brennan ... San Antonio, TX
Stich, Robert T. ... Minneapolis, MN
Sticha, James J. ... Minneapolis, MN
Stichel, H. Mark ... Baltimore, MD
Stichel, Henry W., Jr. ... Baltimore, MD
Sticher, Clifford A. ... Jonesboro, GA
Stichinsky, Jeffrey S. ... Brooklyn, NY
Stichler, Paul J. ... Orange City, FL
Stichman Hoke Fels ... Vancouver, WA
Stichman, John R. ... Vancouver, WA
Stichnoth, Frederick ... Riverdale, MD
Stichter, Don M. ... Tampa, FL
Stichter, John A. ... Essex, CT
New York, NY
Stichter, Kevin P. ... Charlotte, NC
Stichter, Philip W. ... Columbus, OH
Stichter, Riedel, Blain & Prosser, P.A. ... Tampa, FL
Stichter, Scott A. ... Tampa, FL
Stick, John J. ... New Orleans, LA
Stick, Michael A. ... Chicago, IL
Stick, Michael J. ... Boston, MA
Stick, Susan L. ... Menlo Park, CA
Sticka, Ronald R. ... Eugene, OR
Sticka, Ronald R., P.C. ... Eugene, OR
Stickan, Christian H. ... Cleveland, OH
Stickel, Brandt R. ... Santa Cruz, CA
Stickel, Frahn & Lloyd ... Chatham, NJ
Stickel, Frederick G., III ... Cedar Grove, NJ
Stickel, George A. ... New Brunswick, NJ
Stickel, Koenig & Sullivan ... Cedar Grove, NJ
Stickel, Matthew J. ... Oconomowoc, WI
Stickel, Thomas A. ... New York, NY
Stickel, Thomas Lee ... East Palestine, OH
Darlington, PA
Stickell, Gary R. ... Mesa, AZ
Stickells, Austin T. ... Boston, MA
Stickelman, Timothy G. ... New York, NY
Stickel-Martinez, Melody ... Pembroke Pines, FL
Stickevers, John J. ... Boston, MA
Stickgold, Marc ... San Francisco, CA
Stickle, Jeffrey Robert ... Washington, DC
Sticklen, Charles J., Jr. ... Joplin, MO
Sticklen, Kathryn A. ... Boise, ID
Sticklen Law Firm, The ... Joplin, MO
Stickler, Daniel L. ... Charleston, WV
Stickler, David F. ... La Crosse, WI
Stickler, K. Bruce ... Chicago, IL
Stickler & Nelson ... Chicago, IL
Stickler, Paul ... Oak Park, IL
Stickler, Rachael A. ... Charleston, WV
Stickler, Robert H. ... Steamboat Springs, CO
Stickler, Steven C. ... New York, NY
Stickler, Timothy N. ... Newport Beach, CA
Stickler, Tom J. ... Alvin, TX
Stickles, J. Kate ... Wilmington, DE
Philadelphia, PA
Stickles, James S., Jr. ... Chicago, IL
Stickles, Kennedy & Van Steenburgh ... New York, NY
Stickles, Milton J., Jr. ... Washington, DC
Stickles, Robert J. ... Newark, NJ
Stickley, Dillina Wimer ... Harrisonburg, VA
Stickley, Robert S. ... Philadelphia, PA
Stickley, Walter J., Jr. ... West Chester, PA
Sticklor, Donald ... Brooklyn, NY
Sticklor, Marilyn L. ... Boston, MA
Stickman, David R. ... Omaha, NE
Stickman, Jon R. ... Washington, DC
Stickney, Bernard ... Bethesda, MD
Stickney, Brian ... Marietta, GA
Stickney, David R. ... San Francisco, CA
Stickney, Elisabeth S. ... Boston, MA
Stickney, Frank G. ... Elk Point, SD
Stickney & Groe ... Elk Point, SD
Stickney, Herbert H. ... Bonsall, CA
Stickney, John M. ... Cleveland, OH
Stickney, Lawrence E. ... Los Angeles, CA
Stickney, Robin B. ... Indianapolis, IN
Stickney, R. W. ... Tampa, FL
Stickney, Scott M. ... Seattle, WA
Stickney, Thomas M. ... Cleveland, OH
Stickney, Timothy P. ... Key Biscayne, FL
Stickrath, Thomas J. ... Columbus, OH
Stidham & Associates, P.S.C. ... Lexington, KY
Stidham, Chuck R. ... Cincinnati, OH
Stidham & Crow ... Paragould, AR
Stidham, Daniel Troy ... Paragould, AR
Stidham, Erik F. ... Boise, ID
Stidham, G. Steven ... Tulsa, OK
Stidham, Garnie Cliff ... Lexington, KY
Stidham, Gregory R. ... Checotah, OK
Stidham, Jonathan ... Bartow, FL
Stidham, Lisa A. ... Buffalo, NY
Stidham, Lynn C. ... Lexington, KY
Stidham, Michael A. ... Jackson, KY
Stidham & Stidham, P.A. ... Bartow, FL
Stidham, Tamara A. ... Montgomery, AL
Stidham, Wofford Hampton ... Bartow, FL
Stidolph, Robert A. ... Forest Hills, NY
Stie, John S. ... Sacramento, CA
Stieb, Jeffrey D. ... Albany, GA
Stiebel, Christina Hall ... Long Beach, NY
Stiebel, Mark A. ... Cincinnati, OH
Stiebel, Michael S. ... Hartford, CT
Stieber Campbell, P.C. ... Dallas, TX
Stieber, David G. ... Dallas, TX
Stieber, Kathryn A. ... Chicago, IL
Stieber, Michael H. ... Livingston, NJ
Stieber, Thomas M. ... Minneapolis, MN
Stieber & Veloric ... Livingston, NJ
Stief, Barbara ... San Diego, CA
Stief, Christopher P. ... Paoli, PA
Stief, Gerard J. ... Washington, DC
Stief, James E. ... Cleveland, OH
Stief, Michael J., III ... Pittsburgh, PA
Stief, Michael J., Jr. ... Newtown, PA
Stief, Waite, Gross, Sagoskin & Gilman ... Newtown, PA
Stiefel, Aaron ... New York, NY
Stiefel, Abigail L. ... Teaneck, NJ
New York, NY
Stiefel, Carol G. ... Miami, FL
Stiefel, Charles W. ... Coral Gables, FL
Stiefel & Cohen ... New York, NY
Stiefel, Edward P. ... Catskill, NY
Stiefel, Fred ... Victor, IA
Stiefel, George ... New York, NY
Stiefel, Holly June ... Wilmington, DE
Stiefel, Jack G. ... Buffalo, NY
Stiefel, Jan M. ... Northampton, MA
Stiefel, Jay Robert ... Philadelphia, PA
Stiefel, Jeanne M. ... Lawrenceville, NJ
Marlton, NJ
Stiefel, John C. ... Chicago, IL
Stiefel, John R., Jr. ... Jacksonville, FL
Stiefel, Linda Shields ... Louisville, OH
Stiefel, Maurice B. ... New York, NY
Stiefel, Reid A. ... Elk Grove Village, IL
Stiefel & Winans ... Catskill, NY
Stiefer, Sands Littlefield ... Austin, TX
Stieff, J. Preston ... Salt Lake City, UT
Stiefler, Kurt ... Newport Beach, CA
Stieg, Edward C. ... Los Angeles, CA
Stieg, Harold E. ... Detroit, MI
Stieg, Sharon B. ... Winter Park, FL
Stiegel, Lori A. ... Washington, DC
Stiegel, Michael A. ... Chicago, IL
Stiegelmeier, Kurt G. ... Denver, CO
Stieger, Danielle O. ... McLean, VA
Stiegler, Alan L. ... St. Louis Park, MN
Stiegler, Anthony M. ... San Diego, CA
Stiegler, Kerianne M. ... Metairie, LA
Stiegler, Mayo H. ... La Jolla, CA
Stieglitz, A. Blackwell ... Miami, FL
Stieglitz, Albert N. ... Boston, MA
Stieglitz, Val H., III ... Columbia, SC
Stiehl, Donald W. ... Piscataway, NJ
Stiehl, John T. ... Milford, PA
Stiehl, Frederick F. ... Environmental Protection Agency, Office of Enforcement and Compliance Assurance, GV
Stiehl, Harley ... Belleville, IL
Stiehl, James P. ... Belleville, IL
Stiehl, Paul W. ... Hillsdale, NJ
Stiehl, William D. ... East St. Louis, IL
Stiehl, William D., Jr. ... Belleville, IL
Stiehm Law Office ... Alexandria, VA
Stiehm, Patrick H. ... Alexandria, VA
Stiehm, Peter J. ... Minneapolis, MN
Stiehm, Ralph G. ... Alexandria, VA
Stiel, David H., III ... Franklin, LA
Stiel, Mary M. ... Pontiac, MI
Stiele, Douglas F. ... Minneapolis, MN
Stieler, Scott R., III ... Summit, NJ
Stien, Andrew J. ... Fort Lauderdale, FL
Stien, Barry G. ... Washington, DC
Stien, Braunstein & Associates, P.C. ... Washington, DC
Stieneker, Stephen L. ... Denver, CO
Stiennon, David R. J. ... Madison, WI
Stiennon, Patrick J. G. ... Madison, WI
Stientjes, Harlan C. ... Olympia, WA
Stientjes, Michael J. ... Park Ridge, IL
Stiepan, James L. ... Newport Beach, CA
Stiepel, Henry R. ... Costa Mesa, CA
Stieper, Nelson B. ... Troy, MI
Stier, Aaron R. ... Elizabeth, NJ
Stier, Anderson & Malone ... Washington, DC
Skillman, NJ
Stier, Brian E. ... Fort Wayne, IN
Stier, Bruce N. ... Fort Wayne, IN
Stier, Byron G. ... New York, NY
Stier, Carl ... Bloomfield, NJ
Stier, Charles H., Jr. ... Beavercreek, OH
Stier, Christian J. ... Ashland, MA
Stier, Daniel D. ... Madison, WI
Stier, Edwin H. ... Skillman, NJ
Stier, Jeff A. ... New York, NY
Stier, Jude Lawrence ... Liberty, NY
Stier, Mark ... Department of Justice, Tax Division, GV
Stier, Max ... Washington, DC
Stier, Mitchell J. ... East Rutherford, NJ
Stier, Robert H., Jr. ... Portland, ME
Stier, Robert I. ... Seattle, WA
Stier, Serena D. ... Iowa City, IA
Stierberger, Edward A. ... Union, MO
Stierer, Richd. T. ... West Palm Beach, FL
Stierhoff, John R. ... Annapolis, MD
Stierholz, Kristina L. C. ... Minneapolis, MN
Stierle, David S. ... Simpsonville, KY
Stierle, James E. ... Louisville, KY
Stierman, Charles F. ... Milwaukee, WI
Stierman, Matthew V. ... Council Bluffs, IA
Stierwald, Louis, Jr. ... New Orleans, LA
Stierwalt, Brian K. ... St. Louis, MO
Stierwalt, Thomas L. ... Fremont, OH
Stiesmeyer, Vera Ann ... Phoenix, AZ
Stievater, Willard J. ... Boston, MA
Stifel, Orville E., II ... Cleveland, OH
Stifelman, Frank L. ... Roseland, NJ
Stiff, Eric J. ... Sacramento, CA
Stiff, Glenn G. ... Roswell, NM
Stiff, John S. ... Albuquerque, NM
Stiff, L. Graves, III ... Birmingham, AL
Stiff, Michael R. ... Denver, CO
Stiff, Michael R. ... Joliet, IL
Stiffarm, Denise L. ... Seattle, WA
Stifelman, Gary S. ... Los Angeles, CA
Stiffle, Dean A. ... New York, NY
Stiffler, George W. ... Washington, DC
Stiffler, Harry A., Jr. ... Washington, PA
Stiffler, J. Eric ... Fort Myers, FL
Stiffler, Lori D. ... Houston, TX
Stiffler, Mark S. ... San Diego, CA
Stifler, William C. ... Baltimore, MD
Stiftel, Albert J. ... Wilmington, DE
Stifter, John J., IV ... Woodland Hills, CA
Stigall, Humphrey, Lucas, Henry, Stigall & Dollar, L.C. ... Kansas City, MO
Stigall, James F. ... Kansas City, MO
Stigall, Jeff ... Kansas City, MO
Stigall, R. Stephen ... Philadelphia, PA
Stigall, Scott O. ... Tampa, FL
Stigall, Zane A. ... Houston, TX
Stiger, Colleen M. ... Boca Raton, FL
Stiger, R. Barry ... Roseland, NJ
Stiger, Timothy Allen ... Chickasha, OK
Stigger, Cara Wells ... Louisville, KY
Stigger, G. Bruce ... Louisville, KY
Stigger, George E. ... Henderson, KY
Stigger, Robert E. ... Chicago, IL
Stigi, John P., III ... Palo Alto, CA
Stigler, David M. ... Windsor, CT
Stigler, George L. ... Waterloo, IA
Stigler, Margaret M. ... Columbus, OH
Stigler, Samuel J., III ... Washington, DC
Stigliani-O'Keefe, Linda A. ... New York, NY
Stiglitz, Bruce M., (A P.C.) ... Los Angeles, CA
Stiglitz, Jan, (Mr.) ... San Diego, CA
Stiglitz, Matthew R. ... La Plata, MD
Stiglmeier, Gary F. ... Albany, NY
Stikeleather, Michael H. ... Indianapolis, IN
Stikelether, Graham W., Jr. ... Vero Beach, FL
Stikeman Elliott ... New York, NY
Stikker, Barbara Cohen ... San Francisco, CA
Stikker, Judy ... Billings, MT
Stikker, Thomas J. ... San Francisco, CA
Stile, Christina M. ... Mount Kisco, NY
Stile, David ... Akron, OH
Stile, Walter L., III ... Chico, CA
Stiles, Andrea Rowse ... Richmond, VA
Stiles, Brian Lee ... Sedro Woolley, WA
Stiles, Brock David ... Sedro Woolley, WA
Stiles Byrum & Horne, L.L.P. ... Charlotte, NC
Stiles, David J. ... Salisbury Mills, NY
Stiles, David M., Jr. ... Beaumont, TX
Stiles, David (Trey) M., III ... Houston, TX
Stiles, David V. ... Bakersfield, CA
Stiles, Deborah F. ... New York, NY
Stiles, Debra J. ... Maplewood, MN
Stiles, Douglas W. ... Waukegan, IL
Stiles, Edi S. ... Los Angeles, CA
Stiles, Everett D. ... Little Rock, AR
Stiles, Harold J. ... Newark, NY
Stiles, Henry A., III ... Fort Lauderdale, FL
Stiles, Henry E., II ... Spokane, WA
Stiles, Jane E. ... Boston, MA
Stiles, Jeff ... Stanton, KY
Stiles, John K. ... Louisville, KY
Stiles, John O. ... Merrillville, IN
Stiles, Joseph G. ... Houston, TX
Stiles, Kenneth R. ... Pittsburgh, PA
Stiles, Kevin P. ... Providence, RI
Stiles, Kirk P. ... Augusta, GA
Stiles, Leon N., Jr. ... Chicago, IL
Stiles, Leonard K. ... Bremerton, WA
Stiles, Mark D. ... Norfolk, VA

Stippich, Barbara J. ... Milwaukee, WI
Stippich, Matthew J. ... Milwaukee, WI
Stippich, Tanya M. ... Chicago, IL
Stippler, A. David ... Indianapolis, IN
Stirba, Anne M. ... Salt Lake City, UT
Stirba & Hathaway, A Professional Corporation ... Salt Lake City, UT
Stirba, Peter ... Salt Lake City, UT
Stires, Hannah A. ... Federal Trade Commission, Bureau of Consumer Protection, GV
Stires, Sally ... Weston, CT
Stirewalt, Thomas E., Jr. ... Metairie, LA
Stiriti, August M. ... Watertown, MA
Stiritz, Anna Gabrielle Sanford ... Russellville, AR
Stirling, Amy L. ... Royal Oak, MI
Stirling, Ann M. ... Charleston, SC
Stirling, Bryan P. ... Columbia, SC
Stirling, Clark T. ... Santa Barbara, CA
Stirling, Deborah Jane ... United States Senate, Committee Legal Personnel, GV
Stirling, E. Tillman ... Washington, DC
Stirling, Helen L. ... Albuquerque, NM
Stirling, Helen L., P.C. ... Albuquerque, NM
Stirling, Howard J. ... Buffalo, NY
Stirling, James W. ... Atlanta, GA
Stirling & Kleintop ... Honolulu, HI
Stirling, Lawrence W. ... San Diego, CA
Stirling, Linda Bradley ... Securities and Exchange Commission, Office of the General Counsel, GV
Stirling, M. David ... Sacramento, CA
Stirling, Mark J. ... Metairie, LA
Stirling & O'Connell, P.A. ... Charleston, SC
Stirling, Patricia ... Albany, NY
Stirling, Robert B. ... Martinez, CA
Stirling, Scot C. ... Phoenix, AZ
Stirling, Scott T. ... Toledo, OH
Stirling, Thomas L., Jr. ... Honolulu, HI
Stirman, Charles E. ... Fort Collins, CO
Stirman, Donald S. ... The Woodlands, TX
Stirman & Kennedy, P.C. ... The Woodlands, TX
Stirn, Craig ... Fort Collins, CO
Stirone, E. Marco ... Morristown, NJ
Stirparo, Steven J. ... Wilmington, DE
Stirrat, Pamela R. ... Wellesley, MA
Stirsman, David Asher ... Indianapolis, IN
Stirton, Charles P. ... Tucson, AZ
Stirtz, Jerry C. ... Minden, NE
Stis, Diane L. ... Indianapolis, IN
Stiska, John C. ... San Diego, CA
Stiskin, Howard L. ... San Francisco, CA
Stiskin, Ronald Elliot ... Monsey, NY
Stiso, Pat V. ... New Rochelle, NY
Stiss, Betsy Sherwin ... Coral Gables, FL
Stiss, Carey A. ... Miami, FL
Stiss, Sol B. ... Miami, FL
Stitch, Ronald K. ... Thousand Oaks, CA / Ventura, CA
Stitch, Ronald K. ... Westlake Village, CA
Stitcher, Felecia F. ... Scottsdale, AZ
Stiteler, David W. ... Salem, OR
Stiteler, Laurie S. ... Hondo, TX
Stites, Anthony M. ... Fort Wayne, IN
Stites, Catherine M. ... Los Angeles, CA
Stites, Gregory B. ... Kansas City, MO
Stites & Harbison ... Washington, DC / **Atlanta, GA** / **Jeffersonville, IN** / **Frankfort, KY** / **Hyden, KY** / **Lexington, KY** / **Louisville, KY**
Stites, Hill, Wilson & Knopp ... Manhattan, KS
Stites, Hopkins & Fair ... Kansas City, MO
Stites, J. Walker, III ... Louisville, KY
Stites, James W., Jr. ... Louisville, KY
Stites, Jef T. ... Tulsa, OK
Stites, Jeffrey ... Minneapolis, MN
Stites, John F. ... Manhattan, KS
Stites, John H., III ... Louisville, KY
Stites, Mark A. ... Kansas City, MO
Stites, McElwain & Fowler ... Louisville, KY
Stites, O. R., Jr. ... Overland Park, KS
Stites, Richard E. ... Bloomington, IL
Stites, Robert B. ... Woodbury, NJ
Stites, Robert T. ... Fort Worth, TX
Stites, Robert T., A Prof. Corp., Law Offices of ... Fort Worth, TX
Stites, Ronald J., (P.C.) ... Kansas City, MO
Stites, Thomas E. ... Oakes, ND
Stites, William D. ... Seattle, WA
Stith, Chris E. ... Detroit, MI
Stith, Clark D. ... Rock Springs, WY
Stith, David V. ... Plano, TX
Stith, F. Blackwell ... New Bern, NC
Stith, Garland Lee, Jr. ... Fairfax, VA
Stith, James L. ... Park City, UT
Stith, John S. ... Cincinnati, OH
Stith, Kimberly Gee ... Houston, TX
Stith, Laura D. ... Kansas City, MO
Stith, Michael R. ... Sharon Center, OH
Stith, Nancy Chiles ... Charleston, SC
Stith, Paul D. ... Lexington, KY
Stith, Pier M. ... Houston, TX
Stith, R. Bruce, III ... Lexington, KY
Stith, R. Bruce, III, P.S.C. ... Lexington, KY
Stith, Richard T., III ... Valparaiso, IN
Stith, Robin S. ... Columbus, OH
Stith & Stith, P.A. ... New Bern, NC
Stith & Stith, P.C. ... Plano, TX
Stith, Virginia R. ... Suitland, MD
Stith, W. Curtis, Jr. ... Baltimore, MD
Stith, William ... Plano, TX
Stitham, Kevin L. ... Dover-Foxcroft, ME
Stitle, Stephen A. ... Indianapolis, IN
Stits, Dana Joseph ... Santa Ana, CA
Stitser, Robert D. ... Reno, NV
Stitt, Antoinette M. ... Pensacola, FL
Stitt, Charles H. ... Kansas City, MO
Stitt, Charles L. ... Kansas City, MO
Stitt, David T. ... Fairfax, VA
Stitt, Donald K. ... Madison, WI / Milwaukee, WI
Stitt, James R. ... Westminster, CO
Stitt, James R., P.C. ... Westminster, CO
Stitt, John W. ... York, PA
Stitt, Klein & Daday ... Arlington Heights, IL
Stitt, LeMoine D., Jr. ... Arlington Heights, IL
Stitt, Nikki ... Chicago, IL
Stitt, Raoul C. ... Kansas City, MO
Stitt, Rebecca L. ... Torrance, CA
Stitt, Richard P. ... Kansas City, MO
Stitt, Sarah J. ... Ann Arbor, MI / Toledo, OH
Stitt, Stephen D. ... Springdale, AR
Stitt and Stitt ... York, PA
Stitt, Susan B. ... Springfield, IL
Stitt, Susan K. ... Hermosa Beach, CA
Stitt, Thomas P., Sr. ... Easton, PA
Stitt, Todd Harrison ... Los Angeles, CA
Stittleburg, Philip C. ... La Farge, WI
Stitz, Leonard W. ... San Dimas, CA
Stitzel, D. Howard, III ... Plant City, FL
Stitzel Law Group, The ... Plant City, FL / Tampa, FL
Stitzel, Page & Fletcher, P.C. ... Burlington, VT
Stitzel, Steven F. ... Burlington, VT
Stitzel, Veronica Prostko ... Plant City, FL
Stitzenberg, Donald E. ... Iselin, NJ
Stitzer, H. Todd ... Stamford, CT
Stitzer, Laurie Faber ... Kirksville, MO
Stivale, Lee A. ... Springfield, PA
Stivarius, John C., Jr. ... Atlanta, GA
Stiven, James F. ... San Diego, CA
Stiven, Janet A. ... Chicago, IL
Stivender, James C. ... Gadsden, AL
Stiver, Charles E., Jr. ... Miami, FL
Stiver, Vernon ... Loveland, OH
Stivers, B. Robert ... London, KY
Stivers, Elizabeth Williams ... Portland, ME
Stivers, Franklin A. ... London, KY
Stivers, Gregory N. ... Bowling Green, KY
Stivers, Mark Emmons ... Stephenson, VA
Stivers, Neal S. ... South Sioux City, NE
Stivers, Paul W. ... Atlanta, GA
Stivers, Robert M., Jr. ... Oak Ridge, TN
Stivers & Stivers ... London, KY
Stiverson, Keith Ann ... Austin, TX
Stix, Margaret P. ... New York, NY
Stix, Sally A. ... Madison, WI
Stix, Wayne P. ... White Plains, NY
St-Laurent, Claude ... Greenville, SC
StLouis, Barbara ... Fresno, CA
Stluka, Ben W. ... Houston, TX
Stoa, Gordon R. ... Spokane, WA
Stoakley, Yvor E. ... Glen Ellyn, IL
Stobaugh, David F. ... Seattle, WA
Stobaugh, Jennifer C. ... Dallas, TX
Stobaugh, Kevin C. ... Napa, CA
Stobb, David G. ... Southfield, MI
Stobbs, Gregory A. ... Troy, MI
Stobbs, Jane L. ... Aurora, CO
Stobbs, John Dale ... Alton, IL
Stobbs, R. Russell ... Weston, WV
Stobbs and Sinclair, Ltd. Law Offices ... Alton, IL
Stobbs, Stephen A. ... Alton, IL
Stober, Fillis W. ... Hartford, CT
Stober, James ... Cincinnati, OH
Stober, John M. ... Vernon, CT
Stober, Mary R. ... Sacramento, CA
Stober, Ralph K. ... Canoga Park, CA
Stober, Wilson S. ... Indianapolis, IN
Stoberski, Holly S. ... Las Vegas, NV
Stoberski, Michael E. ... Las Vegas, NV
Stobierski, John J. ... Greenfield, MA
Stobierski, Pamela H. ... Greenfield, MA
Stobierski & Stobierski ... Greenfield, MA
Stobs, Donald W., Jr. ... Miami Shores, FL
Stobs & Fitzgerald ... Miami Shores, FL
Stocco, Joseph M. ... Minneapolis, MN
Stochholm, Eric H. ... Chatham, NJ
Stochl, Richard D. ... Charles City, IA / Cresco, IA / New Hampton, IA
Stock, Alan J. ... Pittsburgh, PA
Stock, Alice ... New York, NY
Stock, Alice B. ... New York, NY
Stock, Angharad Grimes ... Pittsburgh, PA
Stock, Aric L. ... Dallas, TX
Stock, Arthur ... Philadelphia, PA
Stock, Carol M. ... Seattle, WA
Stock, Charles Alan ... Crookston, MN
Stock, Christopher W. ... Port Washington, WI
Stock, Cindy Lee ... Las Vegas, NV
Stock, Cletus H. ... Roanoke, VA
Stock, Daniel M. ... Dearborn, MI
Stock, Darrell K. ... Lincoln, NE
Stock, David J. ... San Jose, CA
Stock, Donald A. ... Hagåtña, GU
Stock, E. Kendall ... Leesburg, VA
Stock, Edward ... Philadelphia, PA
Stock, Edwin L. ... Reading, PA
Stock, Elise M. ... Philadelphia, PA
Stock, Gail Cromer ... Dallas, TX
Stock, Garry A. ... San Diego, CA
Stock, Heidi J. ... Falls Church, VA
Stock, Ian J. ... Palo Alto, CA
Stock, Jack ... Westport, CT
Stock, James H., Jr. ... Memphis, TN
Stock, Jamie Alicia ... Tulsa, OK
Stock, Janine C. ... Fullerton, CA
Stock, John F. ... Columbus, OH
Stock, John P., III ... Wheaton, IL
Stock, Jonathan K. ... Columbus, OH
Stock, Kevin L. ... Seattle, WA
Stock, Lauri J. ... San Diego, CA
Stock and Leader, A Professional Corporation ... Brogue, PA / Glen Rock, PA / Hallam, PA / Shrewsbury, PA / Stewartstown, PA / **York, PA**
Stock, Leon O. ... Miami, FL
Stock, Linda M. ... Los Angeles, CA
Stock, Margaret D. ... Anchorage, AK
Stock, Michael T., Sr. ... Glendale, CA
Stock & Moeller, L.L.C. ... Anchorage, AK
Stock, Nancy Wieben ... Santa Ana, CA
Stock, Otto F., Jr. ... Dayton, OH
Stock & Patterson ... Butler, PA
Stock, Paul H. ... Raleigh, NC
Stock, Philip W. ... Stroudsburg, PA
Stock, Robert J. ... Los Angeles, CA
Stock, Robert J. ... Butler, PA
Stock, Roy H. ... Albany, NY
Stock, Ruth A. ... Mobile, AL
Stock, Sheldon K. ... St. Louis, MO
Stock, Sherman E. ... Hales Corners, WI
Stock, Stuart C. ... Washington, DC
Stock, Susan Hilary ... Tulsa, OK
Stock, Thomas A. ... Federal Mine Safety and Health Review Commission, Office of the Commissioners, GV
Stock, Thomas J. ... Mineola, NY
Stock, Timothy F. ... Arlington, VA
Stock, Timothy J. ... Sacramento, CA
Stock, Timothy R. ... Pittsburgh, PA
Stock, Wallace L. ... Cheyenne, WY
Stock, William A. ... Philadelphia, PA
Stockalper, Patrick E. ... Manhattan Beach, CA
Stockard, Bruce A. ... Dallas, TX
Stockard, James A. ... Dallas, TX
Stockard, James A., Jr. ... Dallas, TX
Stockberger, James L. ... St. Louis, MO
Stockbridge, Allen ... Park City, UT
Stockbridge, Edward T. ... Houston, TX
Stockbridge, M. Virginia ... Houston, TX
Stockburger, Bruce C. ... Roanoke, VA
Stockburger, Jean D. ... Little Rock, AR
Stockburger, Susan Zlomke ... Warwick, NY
Stockdale, Bruce R. ... Washington, DC
Stockdale, Carolyn M. ... Newark, NJ
Stockdale, Charles B. ... Albany, NY
Stockdale, Daniel L. ... Des Moines, IA
Stockdale, David C. ... Cincinnati, OH
Stockdale, Donald K., Jr. ... Federal Communications Commission, Common Carrier Bureau, GV
Stockdale, Earl H., Jr. ... Department of the Army, Office of the General Counsel, GV
Stockdale, Helen Sarett ... Sacramento, CA
Stockdale & Hodges ... Woodland Hills, CA
Stockdale, J. Paul ... Ogden, UT
Stockdale, John E. ... Woodland Hills, CA
Stockdale, Lee L. ... Department of the Army, U.S. Army Legal Services Agency, GV
Stockdale, Mark G. ... Seattle, WA
Stockdale, Ned A. ... Estherville, IA
Stockdale, Scott J. ... Torrance, CA
Stockdale, Susan L. ... Denver, CO / Kansas City, MO
Stockdale, Susan R. ... Des Moines, IA
Stockdale, William G. ... Omaha, NE
Stockdon, Wallace B. ... Richmond, VA
Stockel, Eric G. ... Los Angeles, CA
Stockel, John H. ... Perth Amboy, NJ
Stockel & Press ... New York, NY
Stockel, Robert H. ... New York, NY
Stockel, Susan R. ... Los Angeles, CA
Stockell, Catherine H. ... New York, NY
Stockell, Duncan C. ... Walterboro, SC
Stockell, Henry C., Jr. ... Brunswick, ME
Stockell, Mercer L. ... New York, NY
Stockenberg, Richard A. ... St. Louis, MO
Stocker, Allan H. ... Bartlesville, OK
Stocker, Barbara Larkin ... Santa Ana, CA
Stocker, Cathy Lee ... Enid, OK
Stocker, C. W., III ... Fort Worth, TX
Stocker, David E. ... Cincinnati, OH
Stocker, Eva Marie ... Department of Labor, Office of the Solicitor, GV
Stocker, Frederick J. ... San Diego, CA
Stocker, Jay F. ... Irvine, CA
Stocker, Jeffrey Donald ... Jenkintown, PA
Stocker, Jennifer Jo ... Kansas City, MO
Stocker, Joel L. ... Miami, FL
Stocker, John J. ... Chicago, IL
Stocker, John M., Jr. ... Newport Beach, CA
Stocker, John R. ... Costa Mesa, CA
Stocker, Kevin T. ... Kenmore, NY
Stocker, Lynne G. ... San Francisco, CA
Stocker, Michael A. ... Houston, TX
Stocker, Robert W., II ... Detroit, MI / Lansing, MI
Stocker, Steven E. ... North Canton, OH
Stocker, Steven R. ... Spokane, WA
Stocker, Thomas H. ... Lakewood, CO
Stocker, Thomas H., P.C. ... Lakewood, CO
Stocker, William ... San Juan Capistrano, CA
Stockett, Don L. ... Sacramento, CA
Stockett, Peter M., Jr. ... United States Senate, Committee Legal Personnel, GV
Stockey, William E. ... Pittsburgh, PA
Stockfield, Howard F. ... New York, NY
Stockford, Daniel C. ... Lewiston, ME
Stockham, Connie Ray ... Birmingham, AL
Stockham, Richard J., III ... Birmingham, AL
Stockham, Ronald L. ... Morrisville, PA
Stockham, Ronald L., P.C. ... Morrisville, PA
Stockham & Stockham, P.C. ... Birmingham, AL
Stockham, Susan L. ... Sarasota, FL
Stockham, Susan L., P.A., Law Offices of ... Sarasota, FL
Stockhamer, Neil ... Garden City, NY
Stockhausen, Deborah L. ... Ballwin, MO
Stockholm, Gene ... West Columbia, SC
Stockholm, Jeffrey E. ... Albany, NY
Stockholm, Kristin M. ... San Diego, CA
Stocking & Crotteau ... Lamoine, ME
Stocking, Don ... Conroe, TX
Stocking, Don ... Conroe, TX
Stocking, Frederick B. ... Lamoine, ME
Stocking, James L. ... Milwaukee, WI
Stocking, John A. ... Milwaukee, WI
Stocking, Kathryn A. ... Durham, NC
Stocking, Kathryn E. ... Yuma, AZ
Stocking, R. Michael ... Seattle, WA
Stocking, Richard R. ... Port Orchard, WA
Stockland, Thomas D. ... Fayetteville, AR
Stockland & Trantham, P.A. ... Fayetteville, AR
Stockler, Lawrence J. ... Southfield, MI
Stockler, Lawrence J., & Associates, Law Offices of, P.C. ... Southfield, MI
Stockler, Paul D. ... Anchorage, AK
Stockley, Dale L. ... Sandwich, IL
Stockley, Darleen J. ... Chicago, IL
Stockley, Griffin J. ... Little Rock, AR
Stockley, Jeffery E. ... Santa Monica, CA
Stockli, John P., Jr. ... Albany, NY
Stockli, Patricia Betz ... Albany, NY
Stocklin & Simpson Co., A Legal Professional Association ... Dayton, OH
Stocklin, Valerie ... Dayton, OH
Stockman, Becky Bowen ... Bismarck, ND
Stockman & Bedsole ... Mobile, AL
Stockman, Brien D. ... Charlotte, NC
Stockman, Cori Gayle ... Los Angeles, CA
Stockman, Diane O. ... Minneapolis, MN
Stockman, Eric J. ... New Haven, CT
Stockman, Gene W. ... Alexandria, VA
Stockman, Gerald R. ... Lawrenceville, NJ
Stockman, Gerald R., P.C. ... Lawrenceville, NJ
Stockman, Harry M. ... St. Louis, MO
Stockman, Jacque G. ... Fargo, ND
Stockman, Jeanne W. ... Washington, DC
Stockman, John F. ... Minneapolis, MN
Stockman, Lewis ... New York, NY
Stockman, Louis A. ... Duluth, MN
Stockman, Mark William ... Bismarck, ND
Stockman, Michael I. ... Valencia, CA
Stockman, Paul K. ... Pittsburgh, PA
Stockman, Samuel L. ... Mobile, AL
Stockman Wallach Lentz & Gamell, LLP ... New York, NY
Stockman, William E. ... Fort Myers, FL
Stockmann, Peter H. ... Jamesville, NY
Stockmar, Ted P. ... Denver, CO
Stockmaster, Ann Marie ... Cleveland, OH
Stockmeyer, E. William ... Portland, ME
Stockmeyer, Norman Otto, Jr. ... Lansing, MI
Stock-Patterson, Lynn M. ... Butler, PA
Stockrahm, Daniel M. ... Detroit, MI
Stocks, Bruce D. ... Denver, CO
Stocks and Fentin, LLP ... San Diego, CA
Stocks, Janis K. ... San Diego, CA
Stocks, Jerrold H. ... Decatur, IL
Stocks, John F. ... West Springfield, MA
Stocks, John J. ... Springfield, MA
Stocks, John S. ... Auburn, WA
Stocks, Lubie M. ... Winterville, NC
Stocks, Peter Joseph ... Brighton, MA
Stocks, Susan M. Camp ... Federal Trade Commission, Bureau of Consumer Protection, GV
Stocks, William L. ... Greensboro, NC
Stocks, William M. ... Waldo, AR
Stockschlaeder, McDonald & Sules, P.C. ... New York, NY
Stockschlaeder, Paul F. ... New York, NY
Stocksdale, Alan H. ... Baltimore, MD
Stocksdale, Jarrell & Cvach ... Baltimore, MD
Stocksdale, Robert L. ... Baltimore, MD
Stockslager, Matthew J. ... Akron, OH
Stockstill, Byron Jake ... Picayune, MS
Stockstill, Corinne ... San Francisco, CA
Stockstill, Doris K. ... San Antonio, TX
Stockstill, Lowell E. ... Springfield, OH
Stockstill, Marshall J. ... Lafayette, LA
Stockstill, P. A. ... Houston, TX
Stockstill, Robert W., Jr. ... Los Angeles, CA
Stockstill, Susan R. ... Santa Fe, NM
Stockton, A. L. Waldo ... Jacksonville, FL
Stockton, Alice C. ... Trenton, NJ
Stockton, Barker & Mead ... Albany, NY
Stockton, Ben B., Jr. ... Morganfield, KY
Stockton, Bette Kane ... San Francisco, CA
Stockton, Carolyn Christine ... Phoenix, AZ
Stockton, Christopher R. ... Moorestown, NJ
Stockton, Cleveland J. ... Modesto, CA
Stockton, Darla K. ... Dallas, TX
Stockton, David A. ... Atlanta, GA
Stockton, David S. ... Munford, TN
Stockton, Eugene L. ... Kewanee, IL
Stockton, Gilchrist B., Jr. ... Atlantic Beach, FL
Stockton & Hing, P.A. ... Phoenix, AZ / Scottsdale, AZ
Stockton, James A. ... Lake Buena Vista, FL

Stokes, Nanci G. ... Secaucus, NJ
Stokes, Ogden ... Nashville, TN
Stokes, Pamela P. ... Corpus Christi, TX
Stokes, Paul R. ... Morehead, KY
Stokes, Ralph E. ... Wakefield, RI
Stokes, Ray E. ... Baltimore, MD
Stokes, Richard F. ... Georgetown, DE
Stokes, Richard M.
Egg Harbor Township, NJ
Stokes, Robert C. ... Houston, TX
Stokes, Robert C., III ... Tampa, FL
Stokes, Robert D. ... Austin, TX
Stokes, Robert G. ... Lakeland, FL
Stokes, Robert J. ... Dallas, TX
Stokes, Robert J., Jr. ... Houston, TX
Stokes, Robert, Jr. ... Kirkland, WA
Stokes, Robert M. ... Warren, NJ
Stokes, Robert N. ... Columbia, MD
Stokes, Sarah M. ... Tallahassee, FL
Stokes, Scott Andrew ... Madison, WI
Stokes, Sean A. ... Washington, DC
Stokes, Sharon Douglas ... Atlanta, GA
Stokes, Sherwood L. ... Haines City, FL
Stokes, Steeves, Rowe & Hamer
Arcata, CA
Eureka, CA
Stokes, Stephen W. ... Alpharetta, GA
Stokes, Susan E. ... Minneapolis, MN
Stokes, Tammy McClendon
Birmingham, AL
Stokes, Ted A. ... Bagdad, FL
Stokes, Terry ... Oklahoma City, OK
Stokes, Theodore H. ... Carson City, NV
Stokes, Theophilus O., III ... Greensboro, NC
Stokes, Thomas D., III ... Richmond, VA
Stokes & Thompson ... Charleston, SC
Stokes & Throckmorton ... Long Branch, NJ
Stokes, Tia M. ... Pittsburgh, PA
Stokes, Timms & Bell, P.L.C. ... Norfolk, VA
Virginia Beach, VA
Stokes, Timothy M. ... Charlotte, NC
Stokes, Tracey J. ... Chicago, IL
Stokes, W. Douglas ... Hopewell, VA
Stokes, W. Lee ... Bozeman, MT
Stokes, Wanda M. ... Southfield, MI
Stokes, William B. ... Salina, KS
Stokes, William D. ... Washington, DC
Stokes, William R. ... Augusta, ME
Stokes, William R., II ... Wellsboro, PA
Stokes, William R., Jr. ... Brewton, AL
Stokes, William S. ... Des Moines, IA
Stokes & Winter ... Carson City, NV
Stokes, Wm. ... Plymouth, MI
Stokes, Wm. Roy ... Brewton, AL
Stokesbury, Janet C. ... Hartford, CT
Stokesbury, William C. ... Farmington, CT
Stokes Carver, Cynthia L.- ... Bartlesville, OK
Stokey, Richard J. ... Irvine, CA
Washington, DC
Stokfisz, Steven T. ... Dearborn, MI
Stokinger, Carol A. ... New York, NY
Stokinger, Mary A. ... New York, NY
Stokke, Allan H. ... Santa Ana, CA
Stokke, Diane R. ... Seattle, WA
Stokke, John P. ... New York, NY
Stokke, Leslie E. ... Cedar Rapids, IA
Stokke & Riddet, A Professional Corporation
Santa Ana, CA
Stokley, Eileen Currie ... Trenton, NJ
Stokley, Janette E. ... Oakland, CA
Stokley, Jennifer M.
Colorado Springs, CO
Stokley, Jimmie D. ... Kennett, MO
Stokley, Linda A. ... Houston, TX
Stokols, Gwen Patricia ... Bethesda, MD
Stokols, Niki Frank ... Westlake Village, CA
Stokstad, Peter J. ... Missoula, MT
Stokwitz, Stephen S. ... Harrisburg, PA
Stolar, Allen D. ... Boca Raton, FL
Stolar, Bernadine J. ... Los Angeles, CA
Stolar, Brian M. ... Short Hills, NJ
Stolar, Brian S. ... Mineola, NY
Stolar, David M. ... Bay Harbor Islands, FL
Stolar, Donna ... Chicago, IL
Stolar, Henry S. ... Fenton, MO
Stolar, Kathleen S. ... White Plains, NY
Stolar, Leah L. ... Houston, TX
Stolar, Leonard U. ... Miami Beach, FL
Stolar, Margaret M. ... Mandeville, LA
Columbus, OH
Stolar, Martin R. ... New York, NY
Stolar, Martina M. ... San Diego, CA
Stolar, Merle L. ... Tucson, AZ
Stolar Partnership, The ... Belleville, IL
St. Louis, MO
Stolar, Steven R. ... Beverly Hills, CA
Stolarick, Ruth Ann ... Memphis, TN
Stolarik, Debbra ... New York, NY
Stolarik, Robert J. ... Fort Myers, FL
Stolarski, Deborah L ... Sealy, TX
Stolarski, Edward J. ... Philadelphia, PA
Stolarski, Michael ... Chicago, IL
Stolarsky, Lon D. ... Cleveland, OH
Stolarsky, Marc L. ... Cleveland, OH
Stolarun, Edward L.
Department of the Army,
Army Materiel Command, GV
Stolarz, John B. ... Baltimore, MD
Stolba, Lou E. ... Orlando, FL
Stolba, Norman E. ... Palos Verdes Estates, CA
Stolbach, Diane ... Springfield, NJ
Stolbach, Gary ... Dallas, TX
Stolbach, Michael S. ... Gaithersburg, MD
Stolbach, Richard K. ... Monsey, NY
Stolbach, Richard M. ... Washington, DC
Stolbach, Scott B. ... Springfield, NJ
Stolberg, Donald H ... Detroit, MI
Stolberg, Lawrence R. ... Arlington Heights, IL
Stolberg & Pence ... Fort Lauderdale, FL
Stolberg, Vicki L. ... Tampa, FL
Stolberg, William H. ... Fort Lauderdale, FL
Stolbun, Bernard S. ... Houston, TX
Stolbun, Sam L. ... Sugar Land, TX
Stoldt, Derek Michael ... New York, NY
Stoldt, Horan and Kowal, A Professional Corporation ... Hackensack, NJ
Stoldt, Sydney V., Jr. ... Hackensack, NJ
Stolebarger, Robert L. ... Salt Lake City, UT
Stolee, Anne M. ... Washington, DC
Stolee, Mary E. ... Minneapolis, MN
Stolen, Lyder J., Jr. ... Greenwood Village, CO
Stoler, Alan G. ... Omaha, NE
Stoler, Eugene L. ... New York, NY
Stoler, Jeffrey M. ... Boston, MA
Stoler, Jonathan ... New York, NY
Stoler, Louis M. ... Houston, TX
Stoler, Mark ... Columbia, MD
Stoler, Robert M. ... Tampa, FL
Stoleson, Mark A. ... Dallas, TX
Stolfa, David G. ... Englewood, CO
Stolfa, Margaret R. ... Boston, MA
Stolfi, John M. ... Hauppauge, NY
Stolgitis, Colleen W. ... Westerly, RI
Stolgitis, William C. ... Arlington, VA
Stolhandske, Matt ... San Antonio, TX
Stolhandske, Tom ... San Antonio, TX
Stolhandske, William F. ... San Antonio, TX
Stoliar, Neil M. ... Newport Beach, CA
Stoliker, Jack Mark ... New Orleans, LA
Stoline, Dean F. ... Gaithersburg, MD
Stolk, Robin L. ... Springfield, MA
Stolker, Leah R. ... Philadelphia, PA
Stolker, Richard S. ... Rockville, MD
Stolker, Richard S., P.A. ... Rockville, MD
Stolkin, Ronald J. ... Phoenix, AZ
Tucson, AZ
Stolkowski, Elizabeth ... Pittsburgh, PA
Stoll, Albert G., Jr. ... San Francisco, CA
Stoll, Amy E. ... Tampa, FL
Stoll, C. Patrick ... Rancho Cordova, CA
Stoll, Carl B., Sr. ... Chicago, IL
Stoll, Charles W. ... Glendale, CA
Stoll, Charley M. ... Camarillo, CA
Stoll, Charley M., A Professional Corporation
Camarillo, CA
Stoll, Christopher F. ... San Francisco, CA
Stoll, Christopher J. ... Highland Park, IL
Stoll, David J. ... New York, NY
Stoll, David L. ... Phoenix, AZ
Stoll, Edward J., Jr. ... Cleveland, OH
Stoll, Geoffrey L. ... Bucyrus, OH
Stoll, George C. ... San Francisco, CA
Stoll, Gerhard ... San Francisco, CA
Stoll, Ian T. ... New York, NY
Stoll, J. Robert ... Chicago, IL
Stoll, James W. ... Boston, MA
Stoll, Jeffrey R. ... Fort Lauderdale, FL
Stoll, Joseph J. ... Philadelphia, PA
Stoll, Judith A. ... New York, NY
Stoll, Kara Farnandez ... Washington, DC
Stoll, Keenon & Park, LLP
Frankfort, KY
Henderson, KY
Lexington, KY
Louisville, KY
Stoll, Kimberly Kramer ... Boston, MA
Stoll, Kimberly Kvistad ... Milwaukee, WI
Stoll, Mark T. ... Hillsboro, MO
Stoll, Martin A. ... New York, NY
Stoll, Mary L. ... Seattle, WA
Stoll, Michael L. ... Madison, WI
Stoll, Miskin, Hoffman & Badie
New York, NY
Stoll, Myron S. ... Cleveland, OH
Stoll, N. Robert ... Portland, OR
Stoll, Neal R. ... New York, NY
Stoll, Nussbaum & Polakov, A Professional Corporation ... Los Angeles, CA
Stoll, R. Ryan ... Chicago, IL
Stoll, Randy R. ... York, NE
Stoll, Richard G. ... Washington, DC
Stoll, Richard M. ... Tustin, CA
Stoll, Richard M. ... New York, NY
Stoll, Robert J., Jr. ... Los Angeles, CA
Stoll, Robert L. ... Department of Commerce,
Patent and Trademark Office, GV
Stoll, Robert S. ... New York, NY
Stoll, Ronald M. ... Phoenix, AZ
Stoll, Samuel J. ... New York, NY
Stoll, Sheryl Clark ... Pittsburgh, PA
Stoll, Stanley K. ... Salt Lake City, UT
Stoll, Steven M. ... Fort Lauderdale, FL
Stoll Stoll Berne Lokting & Shlachter, P.C.
Portland, OR
Stoll, Thomas G. ... Kansas City, MO
Stoll, V. Edwin ... Kansas City, MO
Stoll, William F., Jr. ... Columbus, OH
Stoll, Wm. J. ... Springfield, OH
Stollar, Kim I. ... Boston, MA
Stoll-DeBell, Kirstin L. ... Denver, CO
Stolle, Dennis P. ... Indianapolis, IN
Stolle, Edward R. ... Virginia Beach, VA
Stolle, Russell R. ... Austin, TX
Stolle, Scott A. ... San Antonio, TX
Stolle, Susan Kulp ... Prairie Village, KS
Stollenwerck, Allyson Serxner
Department of Justice,
Office of the Deputy Attorney General, GV
Stollenwerck, Henry ... Dallas, TX
Stollenwerck, Moore & Silverberg, P.C.
Dallas, TX
Stollenwerck, Sam S. ... Dallas, TX
Stollenwerck, Tom J. ... Dallas, TX
Stoller, Barbara W. ... Morristown, NJ
Stoller, Bernard M. ... Dallas, TX
Stoller, Bert L. ... Silver Spring, MD
Stoller, Daniel E. ... New York, NY
Stoller, Danny D. ... Elkhorn, NE
Stoller, David A. ... New Bern, NC
Stoller, David T. ... Matawan, NJ
Stoller, Debra G. ... Boston, MA
Stoller, Drew A. ... Viera, FL
Stoller, Fritz M. ... New Orleans, LA
Stoller, Harry ... Cincinnati, OH
Stoller, Helen B. ... Mount Kisco, NY
Stoller, Herbert ... New York, NY
Stoller, Irving ... Los Angeles, CA
Stoller, James J. ... El Paso, IL
Stoller, John R. ... Bloomfield Hills, MI
Stoller, Kenneth A. ... Hollywood, FL
Stoller, Larry A. ... Spirit Lake, IA
Stoller, Lawrence B. ... New York, NY
Stoller, Lee J. ... New York, NY
Stoller, Leon L. ... Miami, FL
Stoller, Linda A. ... Wellesley, MA
Stoller, Max ... New York, NY
Stoller, Max A. ... Lowell, MA
Stoller, Michael A. ... New York, NY
Stoller, Paul L. ... Phoenix, AZ
Stoller, Philip D. ... New York, NY
Stoller, Robert C. ... Arlington Heights, IL
Stoller, Robert E. ... Anchorage, AK
Stoller, Stewart D. ... Oak Brook, IL
Stoller, Todd Benjamin ... Dallas, TX
Stoller, Warren E. ... New York, NY
Stoller & Wingert ... Spirit Lake, IA
Stolley, Scott P. ... Dallas, TX
Stolliker, Brian J. ... Ramona, CA
Stollings, Harley E. ... Summersville, WV
Stollman, Bernard ... Kingston, NY
Stollman, Bernard H. ... Troy, MI
Stollman, Beth T. ... West Bloomfield, MI
Stollman, Marc D. ... Boca Raton, FL
Stolls, Michele ... New York, NY
Stolmack, Amanda H. ... Fresno, CA
Stolman, Anne Loevy ... Chicago, IL
Stolman, Marc D. ... Belvedere-Tiburon, CA
Stolman, Theodore B. ... Los Angeles, CA
Stolmeier, Patrick J. ... San Antonio, TX
Stoloff, Alfred H. ... Portland, OR
Stoloff, Joel M. ... Philadelphia, PA
Stoloff, Jonathan D.
Board of Governors Of The Federal Reserve System,
Office of the General Counsel, GV
Stoloff, Neil H. ... Washington, DC
Stoloff, Peter F. ... Portland, OR
Stoloff, Peter F., P.C. ... Portland, OR
Stoloff, Richard A. ... Monticello, NY
Stoloff, Robert H. ... Trenton, NJ
Stoloff, Scott ... West Palm Beach, FL
Stoloff, Sheva ... Huntingdon Valley, PA
Stoloff, Sonia S. ... New Haven, CT
Stolove, Evan S. ... Washington, DC
Stolow, David M. ... New York, NY
Stolowitz, Joel P. ... Hauppauge, NY
Stolowitz, Micah D. ... Portland, OR
Stolp, Loren P. ... East Hartford, CT
Stolp, Robert W. ... Ithaca, NY
Stolpe, Charles T. ... San Francisco, CA
Stolper, Antonia E. ... New York, NY
Stolper, Daniel W. ... Madison, WI
Stolper, Max A. ... Washington, DC
Stolper, Michael ... New York, NY
Stolper, Rita M. ... Cincinnati, OH
Stolper, Steven L. ... Milwaukee, WI
Stolper, Warren H. ... Madison, WI
Stolper & Wilcox ... Madison, WI
Stolpestad, James A. ... St. Paul, MN
Stolpman • Krissman • Elber • Mandel & Katzman LLP ... Long Beach, CA
Los Angeles, CA
Stolpman, Mark S. ... Fergus Falls, MN
Stolpman, Preethi G. ... Beaverton, OR
Stolpman, Thomas G. ... Long Beach, CA
Los Angeles, CA
Stolson, Jack A. ... Venice, FL
Stolt, Marsha ... Minneapolis, MN
Stolt, Robert J. ... Augusta, ME
Stolte, Keith M. ... Chicago, IL
Stolte, Sharon L. ... Overland Park, KS
Stoltenberg, Clyde D. ... Lawrence, KS
Stoltenberg, Eric C. ... Harrisburg, PA
Stoltenberg, Herbert W. ... Cedar Crest, NM
Stolting, Steven J. ... Tallahassee, FL
Stoltman, Thomas P. ... Minneapolis, MN
Stoltz, Elizabeth S. ... Woodland, CA
Stoltz, Gerald D. ... Washington, DC
Stoltz, Henry C., Jr. ... Columbia, MO
Stoltz, John R. ... Columbus, WI
Stoltz, Kathryne A. ... Los Angeles, CA
Stoltz, Melvin I. ... Milford, CT
Stoltz, Michael R. ... Midland, TX
Stoltz, Randy M. ... Boca Raton, FL
Stoltz, Richard A. ... Dallas, TX
Stoltz, Richard B., Jr. ... Chicago, IL
Stoltz, Seth S. ... Dodgeville, WI
Stoltz, Stephen P. ... Lexington, KY
Stoltz, Steven ... San Francisco, CA
Stoltz, Terry L. ... New York, NY
Stoltze, Bruce H. ... Des Moines, IA
Stoltzfus, J. Robert ... Philadelphia, PA
Stoltzfus, James A. ... Wilmington, DE
Stoltzfus, John B. ... Minneapolis, MN
Stoltzfus, Lorraine C. ... Madison, WI
Stoltzmann, William A. ... Minneapolis, MN
Stoltzner, Thomas J. ... North Port, FL
Stolworthy, Kevin R. ... Las Vegas, NV
Stolz, Charles J. ... Benkelman, NE
Ogallala, NE
Stolz, Daniel M. ... Millburn, NJ
Stolz, Irwin W., Jr. ... Atlanta, GA
Stolz, John S. ... Hackettstown, NJ
Morristown, NJ
Trenton, NJ
Stolz, Joseph E., Jr. ... Gaithersburg, MD
Stolz, Katherine M. ... Phoenix, AZ
Stolz, Paul C. ... Chicago, IL
Stolz, Preble ... Berkeley, CA
Stolz, Robert M. ... Brooklyn, NY
Stolz, Samuel S. ... New York, NY
Stolz, Whit F. ... Alpharetta, GA
Stolzar, Michael I. ... New York, NY
Stolzar, Peter H. ... New York, NY
Stolzberg, Karen Gale ... Portland, OR
Stolzberg, Maxwell ... New York, NY
Stolzberg, Michael M. ... Pasadena, CA
Stolzberg, Robert A. ... Boston, MA
Stolze, David M. ... St. Louis, MO
Stolze, Steven J. ... North Little Rock, AR
St. Louis, MO
Stolzenberg, Gelles & Zilber, P.A.
Miami, FL
Stolzenberg, Howard B. ... White Plains, NY
Stolzenberg, Joseph ... New York, NY
Stolzenberg, Keith H. ... Miami, FL
Stolzenberg, Marc ... New York, NY
Stolzer, Bradley ... Manchester, NH
Stolzer, Daniel R. ... Cleveland, OH
Stolzer, Ernest R. ... Mineola, NY
New York, NY
Stolzer, Paul E. ... Murray Hill, NJ
Stolzer, Renate A. ... Chicago, IL
Stolzer, Susan C. ... New York, NY
Stolzman, Alison A. ... New York, NY
Stolzman, Barry A. ... Irvine, CA
Stolzman, Robert I. ... Providence, RI
Stolzy, Lisa ... Riverside, CA
San Bernardino, CA
Stoma, Meredith Kaplan ... Livingston, NJ
Stombaugh, Christopher D.
Platteville, WI
Stombaugh, Ronald D. ... Monmouth, IL
Stomberg, Nannette ... Fresno, CA
Stomberg, Stephanie R. ... Chicago, IL
Stombler, Miriam L. ... San Francisco, CA
Stomel, Alan J. ... Los Angeles, CA
Stomel, Elliot S. ... Westmont, NJ
Stomel, Terry B. ... Bridgeton, NJ
Cherry Hill, NJ
Stomma, Peter C. ... Racine, WI
Stommel, R. Robert ... Indianapolis, IN
Stommel, Robert J. ... Naples, FL
Stommes, Julia L. (Jill) ... Dallas, TX
Stompoly, John G. ... Tucson, AZ
Stompoly, Stroud, Glicksman & Erickson, P.C. ... Tucson, AZ
Stompor, John Frank ... New York, NY
Stomski, Laura J. ... Department of Labor,
Office of the Solicitor, GV
Stonage, Charles L. ... Pittsburgh, PA
Stonaker, Janice B. ... Princeton, NJ
Stonaker, Joseph L. ... Princeton, NJ
Stonberg, Michael L. ... New York, NY
Stonberg, Naomi R. ... Wellesley, MA
Stonbraker, Jon ... Denver, CO
Stone, Aaron T. ... Inver Grove Heights, MN
Stone, Adam ... Pascagoula, MS
Stone, Adele I. ... Hollywood, FL
Stone, Adrienne ... Seattle, WA
Stone, A. J., Jr. ... Hampton, VA
Stone, Alan ... Houston, TX
Stone, Alan G. ... Lewiston, ME
Stone, Alan J. ... Wilmington, DE
Stone, Alan J. ... Pittsburgh, PA
Stone, Alan R. ... Boston, MA
Stone, Albert L., Jr. ... Danielsville, GA
Stone, Alec G. ... Brandenburg, KY
Stone, Alfred E. ... Fountain Valley, CA
Stone, Allan B. ... New York, NY
Stone, Allen E. ... Vestal, NY
Stone, Allyson Anne ... Rockport, ME
Stone, Amy M. ... Groton, CT
Stone, Andrena L. ... Anchorage, AK
Stone, Andrew C. ... Westminster, MD
Stone, Andrew D. ... Denver, CO
Stone, Andrew D. ... Miami, FL
Stone, Andrew D. ... Pelham, NY
Stone, Andrew G. ... Marblehead, MA
Stone, Andrew H. ... Salt Lake City, UT
Stone, Andrew M. ... Pittsburgh, PA
Stone, Andrew P. ... New York, NY
Stone, Anne F. ... New York, NY
Stone, Antoinette R. ... Philadelphia, PA
Stone, April Bennett ... Boulder, CO
Stone, Arnold J. ... Santa Monica, CA
Stone, Arnold M. ... Emerald Isle, NC
Stone, Art ... Forney, TX
Stone, Arthur C., Jr. ... Raleigh, NC
Stone and Associates, A Professional Corporation ... Denver, CO
Stone & Associates, P.C. ... Williamsburg, VA
Stone, Audrey ... Brooklyn, NY
Stone, Barry J. ... West Palm Beach, FL
Stone & Baxter, LLP ... Macon, GA
Warner Robins, GA
Stone, Ben H. ... Gulfport, MS
Jackson, MS
Stone, Benjamin A. ... Atlanta, GA
Stone, Benjamin J. ... New York, NY
Stone, Biber & O'Toole, P.C. ... Troy, MI
Stone, Blair C. ... Seattle, WA
Stone, Bonita L. ... Chicago, IL
Stone, Bonnie M. ... Bronx, NY
Stone, Bradford ... St. Petersburg, FL
Stone, Bret A. ... Santa Barbara, CA
Stone, Brian J. ... Sacramento, CA
Stone, Brian M. ... New Haven, CT
Stone, Bruce ... Miami, FL
Stone, Bruce Braxton ... Montgomery, AL

Stone, Bruce C. .... Minneapolis, MN
Stone, Bruce M. .... Saline, MI
Stone, Bruce W. .... Fairfield, NJ
Stone, Burgess W. .... Atlanta, GA
Stone, Burton W. .... Garden City, NY
Stone, Byron T. .... San Antonio, TX
Stone, C. Randall .... Williamsburg, VA
Stone, Calvin R. .... Venice, FL
Stone & Campbell .... Cassopolis, MI
Niles, MI
Stone, Candice .... Atlanta, GA
Stone, Carol Thomas .... Washington, DC
Fairfax, VA
Stone, Catherine A. .... Los Angeles, CA
Stone, Cathleen Douglas .... Boston, MA
Stone, Charles D. .... Chicago, IL
Stone, Charles F. .... Chicago, IL
Stone, Charles H. .... New Cumberland, PA
Stone, Charles H. .... Walla Walla, WA
Stone, Charles M. .... Martinsville, VA
Stone, Charles V. .... Modesto, CA
Stone, Charles W. .... Fort Pierce, FL
Stone, Christina E. .... Watertown, NY
Stone, Christina M. .... La Habra, CA
Stone, Christopher B. .... Washington, DC
Stone, Christopher D. .... Los Angeles, CA
Stone, Christopher L. .... Palo Alto, CA
Stone, Christopher R. .... East Hartford, CT
Stone, Christopher R. .... Boston, MA
Stone, Clarence L., Jr. .... Detroit, MI
Stone, Clark S. .... San Jose, CA
Stone, Claudia .... Los Angeles, CA
Stone, Claudia E. .... Pompton Plains, NJ
Stone, Clifton .... New York, NY
Stone, Colette F. .... Walnut Creek, CA
Stone, Connie J. .... Atlanta, GA
Stone, Craig A. .... Harrisburg, PA
Stone, Craig R. .... Sunrise, FL
Stone, D. Barry .... Amarillo, TX
Stone, D. Stephen, Jr. .... Alliance, OH
Stone, Dale B. .... Birmingham, AL
Stone, Dale J. .... Jacksonville, FL
Stone, Dana R. .... San Francisco, CA
Stone, Daniel .... Providence, RI
Stone, Daniel B. .... Washington, DC
Stone, D'Ann Rouse .... St. Petersburg, FL
Stone, David .... Miami, FL
Stone, David .... New York, NY
Stone, David .... Houston, TX
Stone, David C. .... Hartford, CT
Stone, David C. .... Troy, MI
Stone, David E. .... North Miami, FL
Stone, David E. .... Northbrook, IL
Stone, David E. .... Alexandria, LA
Stone, David G. .... Algonquin, IL
Stone, David Hean .... New Cumberland, PA
Stone, David J. .... Houston, TX
Stone, David L. .... San Francisco, CA
Stone, David L., (P.C.) .... New Orleans, LA
Stone, David N. .... McHenry, IL
Stone, David P. .... Northbrook, IL
Stone, David P. .... New York, NY
Stone, David P. .... Dallas, TX
Stone, David, P.A. .... Miami, FL
Stone, David S. .... Chicago, IL
Stone, David S. .... Ramsey, NJ
Stone, David T. .... Vernon, CT
Stone, David W., IV .... Anderson, IN
Stone, David Z. .... Fort Lauderdale, FL
Stone, Dean A. .... Macomb, IL
Stone, Deanna P. .... Rocky Mount, VA
Stone, Deborah L. .... Alpharetta, GA
Stone, Deborah R. .... Palm Desert, CA
San Diego, CA
Stone, Debra C. .... New York, NY
Stone, Debra F. .... New York, NY
Stone, Debra L. .... Trenton, NJ
Stone, Dennis J. .... Jacksonville, FL
Stone, Derek C. .... Wilsonville, OR
Stone, Diana L. .... Madison, WI
Stone, Dolginer & Wenzel, A Law Corporation .... Los Angeles, CA
Stone, Donald E. .... Miami, FL
Stone, Donald G. .... Spokane, WA
Stone, Donald L. .... Encino, CA
Stone, Donald P. .... Kalamazoo, MI
Stone, Donald P. .... Niles, MI
Stone, Donald R. .... Washington, DC
Stone, Dorothy C. .... Denver, CO
Elizabeth, CO
Stone, Douglas S. .... Kansas City, MO
Stone & Doyle .... Los Angeles, CA
Pasadena, CA
Stone, Dwight C. .... Forest Hill, MD
Stone, Dwight W., II .... Baltimore, MD
Stone, E. Harrison .... Towson, MD
Stone, E. Randolph .... Greenville, SC
Stone, Earl .... Chicago, IL
Stone, Edmund C., Jr. .... Princeton, WV
Stone, Edward A. .... Louisville, KY
Stone, Edward C. .... Marietta, GA
Stone, Edward H. .... Irvine, CA
Stone, Edward H. .... Chicago, IL
Stone, Edward H., P.C. .... Irvine, CA
Stone, Edward J. .... Geneseo, IL
Stone, Edward J. .... Annapolis, MD
Baltimore, MD
Stone, Edward S. .... New York, NY
Stone, Edwin C. .... Radford, VA
Stone, Elhanan C. .... New York, NY
Stone, Elizabeth A. .... Los Angeles, CA
Stone, Elizabeth C. .... Atlanta, GA
Stone, Ellen C. .... Brownsville, TX
Stone, Ellen D. .... Lexington, MA
Stone, Elliot W. .... New York, NY
Stone, Emmy Harper .... Parker, CO
Stone, Eric Alan .... New York, NY

Stone, Eric L.
Consumer Product Safety Commission, Office of Compliance, GV
Stone, Erin Eileen .... Alexandria, VA
Stone, Erin S. .... Atlanta, GA
Stone, Errol L. .... Chicago, IL
Stone, Errol M. .... Austin, TX
Stone, Evan D. .... New York, NY
Stone, Evan Mead .... San Diego, CA
Stone, F. L. Peter .... Dover, DE
Stone, F. R. Josh .... Norcross, GA
Stone, Frank B. .... New York, NY
Stone, Frank C. .... Atlanta, GA
Stone, Franklin H. .... New York, NY
Stone, Fred M. .... New York, NY
Stone, Frederick H. .... Springfield, IL
Stone, Gail F. .... New York, NY
Stone, Garrett A. .... Washington, DC
Stone, Gary L. .... Pasadena, CA
Stone, Gary P. .... Chicago, IL
Stone, Gary S. .... Jamaica, NY
Stone, Geoffrey F. .... Topsfield, MA
Stone, Geoffrey M. .... Boston, MA
Stone, Geoffrey R. .... Chicago, IL
Stone, George E. .... Newark, OH
Stone, George S., Jr. .... New York, NY
Stone & Gerken, P.A. .... Eustis, FL
Stone, Glenna L. .... Atlanta, GA
Stone, Gordon P., III .... Stamford, CT
Stone, Granade & Crosby, P.C.
Bay Minette, AL
Daphne, AL
Foley, AL
Stone, Gregory E. .... Encino, CA
Stone, Gregory M. .... Baltimore, MD
Stone, Gregory P. .... Los Angeles, CA
Stone & Griffin .... St. Petersburg, FL
Stone, H. Ernest .... South Hamilton, MA
Stone, Harlan S. .... Pittsburgh, PA
Stone, Harold A. .... San Francisco, CA
Stone, Harold B. .... Knoxville, TN
Stone, Harrison & Turk, P.C.
Radford, VA
Stone, Harry L. .... Rockville, MD
Stone, Harvey M. .... New York, NY
Stone & Hayes .... Columbus, MS
Stone, Heather M. .... Boston, MA
Stone, Helen L. .... Miami, FL
Stone, Helen R. .... Boulder, CO
Stone, Henry .... New York, NY
Stone, Henry S. .... Culver City, CA
Stone, Henry S., A Professional Corporation
Culver City, CA
Stone, Herbert .... Huntington, NY
Stone, Higgs & Drexler .... Memphis, TN
Stone, Hilary Manson .... Santa Barbara, CA
Stone & Hiles, LLP .... Beverly Hills, CA
Los Angeles, CA
Stone & Hinds, P.C. .... Knoxville, TN
Stone, Hoffman .... Rochester, NY
Stone, Hoke .... Lambert, MS
Stone, Horace E. .... Detroit, MI
Stone, Howard A. .... Miami, FL
Stone, Howard L. .... Santa Monica, CA
Stone, Howard L. .... Chicago, IL
Stone, Howard R. .... Golden, CO
Stone, Hubert L. .... Corpus Christi, TX
Stone, Hugh W. .... Blairsville, GA
Stone, Huntley .... Boulder, CO
Bridgeport, CT
Stone, Huntley J. .... Easton, CT
Stone, Ira M. .... Exeter, NH
Stone, Irving E., Jr. .... Clive, IA
Stone, J. Carson, III .... Nashville, TN
Stone, J. Ed .... Siler City, NC
Stone, J. Homer, Jr. .... Memphis, TN
Stone, J. Jacques .... New York, NY
Stone, J. Lawton .... San Antonio, TX
Stone, J. Lawton, Law Offices of, P.C.
San Antonio, TX
Stone, Jack A., Law Offices of
Evansville, IN
Stone, Jack Dell, Jr. .... Dallas, TX
Stone, Jack R. .... Lewistown, MT
Stone, Jacob .... Boston, MA
Stone, Jacquelyn E. .... Richmond, VA
Stone, James A. .... Reno, NV
Stone, James B. .... Romulus, MI
Stone, James C., III .... Louisville, KY
Stone, James D. .... Newport Beach, CA
Stone, James D. .... Towson, MD
Stone, James D. .... Macatawa, MI
Stone, James E., Jr. .... Orange, CA
Stone, James J. .... Honolulu, HI
Stone, James K. .... Santa Ana, CA
Stone, James L. .... Denver, CO
Stone, James M. .... Durham, NC
Stone, James M. .... Cleveland, OH
Stone, James Mauliola Keaka, Jr.
Honolulu, HI
Stone, James R. .... Washington, DC
Stone, James W. .... Hagerstown, MD
Stone, Jan E. .... Chicago, IL
Stone, Jane Lipscomb .... Austin, TX
Stone, Janice .... Santa Monica, CA
Stone, Jay L. .... Salt Lake City, UT
Stone, Jay W. .... Grand Rapids, MI
Stone, Jean .... Waipahu, HI
Stone, Jean A. .... Nashville, TN
Stone, Jean Vernon .... Dayton, OH
Stone, Jeanette K. .... Killeen, TX
Stone, Jed .... Chicago, IL
Stone, Jed, Ltd., The Law Offices of
Chicago, IL
Stone, Jeffrey A. .... Pensacola, FL
Stone, Jeffrey B. .... New York, NY
Stone, Jeffrey D. .... Des Moines, IA
Stone, Jeffrey E. .... Chicago, IL

Stone, Jeffrey M. .... Marlton, NJ
Stone, Jeffrey P. .... Rochester, NY
Stone, Jeffrey S. .... Sacramento, CA
Stone, Jeffrey W. .... Buffalo, NY
Stone, Jennifer Drew .... Montclair, NJ
Trenton, NJ
Stone, Jennifer K. .... Thermopolis, WY
Stone, Jennifer L. .... Los Angeles, CA
Stone, Jennifer L. .... Albuquerque, NM
Stone, Jeri .... Austin, TX
Stone, Jerome A. .... Stuart, FL
Stone, Jerry H. .... Bloomington, IL
Stone, Jerry L. .... Oklahoma City, OK
Stone, Jesse C. .... Augusta, GA
Statesboro, GA
Swainsboro, GA
Stone Jessup, P.C. .... Tulsa, OK
Stone, Jill Haavig .... Tacoma, WA
Stone, Joel A. .... Chicago, IL
Stone, John A. .... South Orange, NJ
Stone, John B. .... San Francisco, CA
Stone, John D. .... Norcross, GA
Stone, John E. .... Memphis, TN
Stone, John F. .... Minneapolis, MN
Stone, John G. .... Syracuse, NY
Stone, John H. .... Chula Vista, CA
Stone, John H. .... West Des Moines, IA
Stone, John K. P., III .... Boston, MA
Stone, John L., III .... Greensburg, LA
Stone, John M. .... Charlottesville, VA
Stone, John S. .... Portland, OR
Stone, John W. .... Topeka, KS
Stone, John W., III .... Nashville, TN
Stone, Jonathan B. .... Los Angeles, CA
Stone, Jonathan R. .... Washington, DC
Stone, Jos. M. .... Chevy Chase, MD
Stone, Joseph D., Jr. .... Waco, TX
Stone, Joseph L., (P.C.) .... New York, NY
Stone, Joseph L. .... Chicago, IL
Stone, Joseph R. .... Philadelphia, PA
Stone, Judith Ellen .... Merrick, NY
Stone, Judy Roché .... Lincoln, NE
Stone, Juliet L. .... Los Angeles, CA
Stone, J. V. .... Dayton, OH
Stone, Kaplan & Chapman, P.C.
Macon, GA
Warner Robins, GA
Stone, Karen M. .... Lansdale, PA
Stone, Karine C. M. .... New York, NY
Stone, Katherine E., (P.C.) .... Ventura, CA
Stone, Katherine Grunwald .... Burbank, CA
Stone, Katherine Van Wezel .... Ithaca, NY
Stone, Kathleen C. .... Boston, MA
Stone, Kathleen S. .... Houston, TX
Stone, Kathryn .... Department of the Army, Office of the Judge Advocate General, GV
Stone, Kaye Ellis .... Huntsville, TX
Stone, Keith J. .... San Diego, CA
Stone, Kenneth C. .... Dallas, TX
Stone, Kenneth C., Jr. .... Oklahoma City, OK
Stone, Kenneth D. .... Sandpoint, ID
Stone, Kenneth H. .... San Diego, CA
Stone, Kenneth R. .... Sacramento, CA
Stone, Kenneth W. .... Greensboro, NC
Stone, Kerwin B. .... Beaumont, TX
Stone, Kice H., Jr. .... Macon, GA
Stone, Kimberly A. .... Worcester, MA
Stone, Kimberly J. .... Chicago, IL
Stone, Kirk L. .... Greenville, SC
Stone, Kirsten Schneberger .... Mason, OH
Stone, Kristine De Serpa .... San Francisco, CA
Stone LaFaver & Shekletski
New Cumberland, PA
Stone, Laird B. .... Twin Falls, ID
Stone, Laura Elena .... Chevy Chase, MD
Stone, Laura S. .... Los Angeles, CA
Stone, Laurie M. .... Los Angeles, CA
Stone Law Office .... Brandenburg, KY
Stone, Lawrence D. .... Denver, CO
Stone, Lawrence H. .... Los Angeles, CA
Stone, Lawrence M., (P.C.)
Los Angeles, CA
Stone, Lawrence S. .... Brooklyn, NY
Stone, Lea Ann P. .... Washington, DC
Stone, Lee Dan, III .... Tazewell, TN
Stone, Leon C. .... Princeton, IN
Stone, Leonard .... Teaneck, NJ
Stone, Leonard H. .... Las Vegas, NV
Stone, Lester .... Chicago, IL
Stone, Lewis Bart .... New York, NY
Stone, Lewis Bart .... New York, NY
Stone, Lewis W. .... Eustis, FL
Mount Dora, FL
Stone, Leyton & Gershman, A Professional Corporation .... St. Louis, MO
Stone, Linda May, (Mrs.) .... Los Angeles, CA
Stone, Linda Sanders .... Metairie, LA
Stone, Lisa .... Los Angeles, CA
Stone, Lisa A. .... Indianapolis, IN
Stone, Lisa M. .... Seattle, WA
Stone, Lois A. .... Los Angeles, CA
Stone, Loren R. .... Skokie, IL
Stone, Lorrie Lee .... Honolulu, HI
Stone, Louis .... New Bedford, MA
Stone, Lowrey S. .... Blakely, GA
Stone, Lynn Korman .... Westport, CT
Stone, M. Blake, L.P.A., Inc. .... Wooster, OH
Stone Mandia, L.L.C. .... Neptune, NJ
Stone, Marc D. .... Kansas City, MO
Stone, Marc D. .... Cleveland, OH
Stone, Marc H. .... Dallas, TX
Stone, Marc J., (P.A.) .... Miami, FL
Stone, Marcia .... Los Angeles, CA
Stone, Margaret A. .... Mobile, AL
Stone, Margaret E. .... Radford, VA
Stone, Margaret R. .... Grover Beach, CA
Santa Maria, CA
Stone, Mark .... New York, NY

Stone, Mark D. .... Miami, FL
Stone, Mark Edward .... Dayton, OH
Stone, Mark H. .... Bridgewater, MA
Stone, Mark J. .... Washington, DC
Rockville, MD
Vienna, VA
Stone, Mark P. .... Stamford, CT
Stone, Marrie K. .... Irvine, CA
Stone, Martha .... Hartford, CT
Stone, Martha Kaufman .... Cleveland, OH
Stone, Martin .... Lake Placid, NY
Stone, Martin .... Cleveland, OH
Stone, Martin E. .... Coquille, OR
Stone, Marty M. .... Chattanooga, TN
Stone, Mary Jeanne .... Fall River, MA
Stone, Matthew P. .... Atlanta, GA
Stone, Maurice L. .... Hackensack, NJ
Stone, McGuire & Benjamin .... Chicago, IL
Northbrook, IL
Stone, Melanie Stephens .... Atlanta, GA
Stone, Melissa M. .... Boston, MA
Stone, Meredith Barg .... Windsor, CT
Stone, Merrill B. .... Parsippany, NJ
New York, NY
Stone, Michael .... Bristol, NH
Stone, Michael A. .... Chicago, IL
Stone, Michael A. .... Birmingham, MI
Stone, Michael B. .... Seal Beach, CA
Stone, Michael F. .... South Yarmouth, MA
Stone, Michael H. .... Roswell, NM
Stone, Michael H. .... New York, NY
Stone, Michael J. .... Boston, MA
Stone, Michael John .... New Brunswick, NJ
Stone, Michael K. .... Stamford, CT
Stone, Michael L. .... Wilmette, IL
Stone, Michael N. .... Lake Oswego, OR
Stone, Michael P., Law Office of
Pasadena, CA
Riverside, CA
Stone, Michael R. .... Modesto, CA
Stone, Michael S. .... New York, NY
Stone, Michael T. .... San Francisco, CA
Stone, Michael T. .... Seattle, WA
Stone, Michel L. .... Panama City, FL
Stone, Michele .... New York, NY
Stone, Michelle E. .... Vestal, NY
Stone, Miriam E. .... St. Paul, MN
Stone, Mitchell A. .... Jacksonville, FL
Stone, Mitchell A., & Associates, P.A.
Jacksonville, FL
Stone & Moore, Chartered .... Chicago, IL
Wheaton, IL
Merrillville, IN
Stone, Morris .... Huntington Beach, CA
Stone, Morton L. .... Cleveland, OH
Stone, Murray .... St. Louis, MO
Stone, N. Susan .... Houston, TX
Stone, Nancy A. .... Juno Beach, FL
Stone, Nancy B. .... Washington, DC
Stone, Nancy J. .... Amarillo, TX
Stone, Nancy Komer .... Cincinnati, OH
Stone, Nancy Robin .... New York, NY
Stone, Natalie Pages .... Los Angeles, CA
Stone, Nathan L. .... Denver, CO
Stone, Neil H .... San Antonio, TX
Stone, Nina C. .... Corpus Christi, TX
Stone, Nina E. .... New York, NY
Stone, Norborne C., Jr. .... Bay Minette, AL
Daphne, AL
Foley, AL
Stone, Norina K. S. .... Harrisburg, PA
Stone, Norman .... Novato, CA
Stone, Norman R., III .... Baltimore, MD
Stone, Norman R., Jr. .... Baltimore, MD
Stone, Ollie E. .... Tinley Park, IL
Stone, Otis D.
Hot Springs National Park, AR
Stone & Palmgren .... Geneseo, IL
Stone, Pamella A. .... Santa Ana, CA
Stone, Parker J. .... Syracuse, NY
Stone, Patricia A. .... Beaumont, TX
Stone, Patricia Jo, (P.C.) .... Denver, CO
Stone, Patti .... New York, NY
Stone, Patton, Kierce & Freeman
Bessemer, AL
Stone, Paul .... Sullivan, IL
Stone, Paul B. .... Austin, TX
Stone, Paul D. .... Pleasantville, NY
Stone, Paul L. .... Sullivan, IL
Stone, Paul Russo .... San Antonio, TX
Stone, Paula G. .... Southfield, MI
Stone, Paula L. .... Norristown, PA
Stone, Peter G. .... San Jose, CA
Stone, Peter J. .... Milwaukee, WI
Stone, Peter M. .... Costa Mesa, CA
Stone, Peter Robert .... Sacramento, CA
Stone, Peter T. .... Honolulu, HI
Stone, Philip M. .... Worcester, MA
Stone, Philip M., Jr. .... Minneapolis, MN
Stone, Phillip C. .... Bridgewater, VA
Stone, Phillip C., Jr. .... Harrisonburg, VA
Stone, Phillip J. .... Clear Lake, IA
Stone, Phillip M. .... Reno, NV
Stone, Pigman, Walther, Wittmann & Hutchinson, L.L.P. .... New Orleans, LA
Stone, Pogrund & Korey .... Chicago, IL
Stone •Pregliasco •Haynes •Buba, L.L.P.
Louisville, KY
Stone, Price .... Dallas, TX
Stone, R. Bryan .... Corpus Christi, TX
Stone, R. Kenny .... Statesboro, GA
Stone, R. Kenny, P.C. .... Statesboro, GA
Stone, R. Thomas .... Birmingham, AL
Stone, R. Timothy .... Los Angeles, CA
Stone, Rafael A. .... Los Angeles, CA
Stone, Ralph E. .... San Francisco, CA
Stone, Ralph K. .... Boston, MA
Stone, Ralph M. .... New York, NY

Stone, Randall I. ... **Southfield, MI**
Stone, Randall M. ... Department of Justice, Environment and Natural Resources Division, GV
Stone, Randolph C. ... **Burley, ID**
Stone, Raybun F., Jr. ... Ocala, FL
Stone, Raymond E., Jr. ... East Hartford, CT
Stone, Rebecca Batdorf ... Shillington, PA
Stone, Rebecca Carter ... **Atlanta, GA**
Stone & Reid ... South Yarmouth, MA
Stone, Rena C. ... **Newport Beach, CA**
Stone, Rena Denton ... **Los Angeles, CA**
Stone, Renee ... Department Of The Interior, Office of the Solicitor, GV
Stone, Richard A. ... **Beverly Hills, CA**
Stone, Richard A. ... Geneseo, IL
Stone, Richard A. ... Springfield, IL
Stone, Richard B. ... Montgomery, AL
Stone, Richard B. ... Department of State, GV
Stone, Richard B. ... Chicago, IL
Stone, Richard B. ... **Neptune, NJ**
Stone, Richard B. ... New York, NY
Stone, Richard B. ... Black Mountain, NC
Stone, Richard B. ... Corpus Christi, TX
Stone, Richard C. ... Hayward, CA
Stone, Richard D. ... Russell, KY
Stone, Richard D. ... Waurika, OK
Stone, Richard H. ... **New York, NY**
Stone, Richard J. ... **Miami, FL**
Stone, Richard J. ... **Portland, OR**
Stone, Richard L. ... **Los Angeles, CA**
Stone, Richard L. ... **New York, NY**
Stone, Richard L. ... Jacksonville, TX
Stone, Richard M. ... **Cincinnati, OH**
Stone, Richard R. ... Department of Justice, Civil Division, GV
Stone, Richard S. ... Campbell, CA
Stone, Richard W. ... Wentworth, NC
Stone, Richard W., II ... **New York, NY**
Stone & Richardson, Professional Corporation ... **Detroit, MI**
Stone, Robert ... **New York, NY**
Stone, Robert A. ... **New York, NY**
Stone, Robert B. ... Hagerstown, MD
Stone, Robert B. ... Morgantown, WV
Stone, Robert C. ... Lexington, KY
Stone, Robert C. ... **Grand Rapids, MI**
Stone, Robert D. ... **Anchorage, AK**
Stone, Robert D. ... Chicago, IL
Stone, Robert D. ... Delmar, NY
Stone, Robert E. ... Miami, FL
Stone, Robert E. ... Vero Beach, FL
Stone, Robert F. ... Hilton Head Island, SC
Stone, Robert H. ... Dallas, TX
Stone, Robert J. ... Marion, IA
Stone, Robert J., Jr. ... San Francisco, CA
Stone, Robert L. ... Chicago, IL
Stone, Robert L. ... **Piscataway, NJ**
Stone, Robert L. ... Cincinnati, OH
Stone, Robert L., and Associates, P.C. ... Chicago, IL
Stone, Robert M. ... **Long Beach, CA**
Stone, Robert M. ... **Los Angeles, CA**
Stone, Robert M. ... New York, NY
Stone, Robert M. ... Medford, OR
Stone, Robert N. ... **Los Angeles, CA**
Stone, Robert N. ... **Stamford, CT**
Stone, Robert N. ... **Minneapolis, MN**
Stone, Robert R. ... Santa Barbara, CA
Stone, Robert S. ... White Plains, NY
Stone, Robert S. ... Cleveland, OH
Stone, Robert S. ... **Knoxville, TN**
Stone, Robert W. ... Duarte, CA
Stone, Robert W. ... **Palo Alto, CA**
Stone, Robert W. ... **Boulder, CO**
Stone, Robin F. ... Los Angeles, CA
Stone, Robin L. ... Orchard Park, NY
Stone, Robt. S. ... Portland, OR
Stone, Rodney G. ... Napa, CA
Stone, Rodney J. ... **Los Angeles, CA**
Stone, Roger A. ... Memphis, TN
Stone, Roger E. ... Buffalo, NY
Stone, Roger W. ... **Cedar Rapids, IA**
Stone, Ronald A. ... Woodbridge, CT
Stone, Ronald E. ... Sacramento, CA
Stone, Ronald J. ... **Springfield, IL**
Stone, Ronald J. ... New York, NY
Stone, Ronald L. ... Wichita, KS
Stone, Ronald L. ... Nashville, TN
Stone, Ronald M. ... **Los Angeles, CA**
Stone, Ronald M. ... Ashland, MA
Stone, Ronald W. ... **McMinnville, OR**
Stone, Ronit M. ... **Los Angeles, CA**
Stone & Rosenblatt, A Law Corporation ... **Encino, CA**
Stone, Roy C. ... Escondido, CA
Stone, Russell B. ... Lorain, OH
Stone, Russell D. ... Wilmington, NC
Stone, S. Craig, II ... **Las Vegas, NV**
Stone, S. Robert, III ... Boca Raton, FL
Stone, S. Scott ... **Orlando, FL**
Stone, Sam L. ... Fortuna, CA
Stone, Sam V., Jr. ... **Austin, TX**
Stone, Samuel B., (A Professional Corporation) ... **Irvine, CA**
Stone, Samuel C. ... **Tulsa, OK**
Stone, Samuel Spencer ... Cincinnati, OH
Alexandria, VA
Morgantown, WV
Stone, Sandra E. ... **San Francisco, CA**
Stone, Sara M. Benchoff ... Nacogdoches, TX
Stone, Sarah A. ... **Washington, DC**
Stone, Saul ... **New Orleans, LA**
Stone, Scot ... Federal Communications Commission, Wireless Telecommunications Bureau, GV
Stone, Scot A. ... **Dayton, OH**
Stone, Scott ... Lynbrook, NY
Stone, Scott A. ... **Overland Park, KS**
Stone, Scott H. ... **New York, NY**
Stone, Scott N. ... **Washington, DC**
Stone, Scott S. ... **Evansville, IN**
Stone, Scott W. ... **Duncan, OK**
Stone & Semento, P.A. ... Mount Dora, FL
Stone, Seymour ... Sarasota, FL
Stone, Shalom D. ... **Roseland, NJ**
Stone, Shari ... Fort Lauderdale, FL
Stone, Sharon A. ... **Chico, CA**
Oroville, CA
Stone, Sharon R. ... Tucson, AZ
Stone, Sheehy, Rosen & Byrne ... Boulder, CO
Stone, Sheldon ... Teaneck, NJ
Stone, Sherwin J. ... **Chicago, IL**
Stone, Sidney L. ... **St. Louis, MO**
Stone, Sigrid C. ... **Washington, DC**
Stone, Stacey M. ... **Winston-Salem, NC**
Stone, Stanley E. ... Seattle, WA
Stone, Stanley H. ... Encino, CA
Stone, Stephen J. ... Atlanta, GA
Stone, Stephen J. ... **Lubbock, TX**
Stone, Stephen M. ... Orlando, FL
Stone, Stephen Scott ... Orlando, FL
Stone, Stephen W. ... **Marion, IL**
Stone, Steven ... Fort Washington, PA
Stone, Steven David ... Alexandria, VA
Stone, Steven David, P.C. ... Alexandria, VA
Stone, Steven E. ... **Los Angeles, CA**
Stone, Steven F. ... Palo Alto, CA
Stone, Steven H. ... Encino, CA
Stone, Steven J. ... Ventura, CA
Stone, Steven J. ... **Washington, DC**
Stone, Steven M. ... **Chicago, IL**
Stone, Steven M. ... **St. Louis, MO**
Stone, Steven W. ... **Washington, DC**
Stone, Stewart G. ... Sanford, FL
Stone, Stewart, Jr. ... **San Jose, CA**
Stone & Stone ... Encino, CA
Stone & Stone ... Teaneck, NJ
Stone & Stone ... Vestal, NY
Stone & Stone ... Dayton, OH
Stone & Stone ... **Pittsburgh, PA**
Stone & Stone ... Corpus Christi, TX
Stone, Stone & Creem ... **Boston, MA**
Stone & Stone, Law Offices of ... Corpus Christi, TX
Stone & Stone, P.C. ... Jacksonville, TX
Stone, Susan ... **San Antonio, TX**
Stone, Susan A. ... **Chicago, IL**
Stone, Susan J. ... New York, NY
Stone, Susan W. ... La Jolla, CA
Stone & Sutton, P.A. ... **Panama City, FL**
Stone, Suzanne L. ... New York, NY
Stone, Thatcher A. ... **New York, NY**
Stone, Theodore M. ... **Minneapolis, MN**
Stone, Thomas A. ... Columbus, OH
Stone, Thomas B., Jr., Law Offices of ... Annapolis, MD
Rockville, MD
Stone, Thomas E. ... Madison, FL
Stone, Thomas F. ... Santa Barbara, CA
Stone, Thomas K. ... Louisville, KY
Stone, Thomas P. ... **Houston, TX**
Stone, Thomas S. ... **Little Rock, AR**
Stone, Timothy M. ... Anchorage, AK
Stone, Todd I. ... **Fort Lauderdale, FL**
Stone, Todd R. ... Chula Vista, CA
Stone, Trudy Burns ... **Honolulu, HI**
Stone, Truman A. ... Portland, OR
Stone, V. Rafael ... **Seattle, WA**
Stone, Van C. ... Topeka, KS
Stone, Victor D. L. ... Department of Justice, Criminal Division, GV
Stone, Victor J. ... Urbana, IL
Stone, Waldo F. ... **Tacoma, WA**
Stone, Walter B. ... San Jose, CA
Stone, Walter L. ... **Washington, DC**
Stone, Walter R. ... **Baltimore, MD**
Stone, Walter R. ... **Providence, RI**
Stone, Ward D. (Jerry), Jr. ... **Morgantown, WV**
Stone, Ward, Jr. ... **Macon, GA**
Stone, Wayne Ronald ... Tacoma, WA
Stone, Wilford H. ... **Cedar Rapids, IA**
Stone, Willard E. ... Walnut Creek, CA
Stone, Willard Gregory ... Walnut Creek, CA
Stone, William A. ... Fresno, CA
Stone, William A. ... Everett, WA
Stone, William C. ... Louisville, KY
Stone, William C. ... **Portland, OR**
Stone, William C., (P.C.) ... **Boston, MA**
Stone, William E., III ... **Dallas, TX**
Stone, William E., III ... Houston, TX
Stone, William F. ... **Destin, FL**
Stone, William F. ... **Fort Walton Beach, FL**
Stone, William F., Jr. ... Martinsville, VA
Stone, William G. ... **Chicago, IL**
Stone, William H. ... Tavares, FL
Stone, William H. ... Columbus, IN
Stone, William J. ... Department of Labor, Office of the Solicitor, GV
Stone, William S. ... Cape Coral, FL
Stone, William S. ... Blakely, GA
Stone, William S., P.C. ... Blakely, GA
Stone, William T. ... **Jacksonville, FL**
Stone, William T. ... Williamsburg, VA
Stone, Wilton E., Jr. ... **Valdosta, GA**
Stone & Wood ... Santa Monica, CA
Stone, Worthy, Reynolds & Joyce, A Professional Corporation ... **Martinsville, VA**
Stonebarger, D. Gregory ... Silver Lake, KS
Stoneberg, Paul E. ... **Marshall, MN**
Stonebraker, Deborah K. ... Glencoe, IL
Stonebraker, John D. ... **Davenport, IA**
Stonebraker, Kelly L. ... **Chicago, IL**
Stonebreaker, Karen W. ... **San Francisco, CA**
Stonebrook, Martha Smith ... Salt Lake City, UT
Stoneburner, Christina A. ... **Hackensack, NJ**
Stoneburner, Gresham R. ... **Jacksonville, FL**
Stoneburner, Lewis T. ... **Richmond, VA**
Stoneburner, Robert D. ... Paynesville, MN
Stoneburner, Terri ... New Ulm, MN
Stoneburner, William D. ... Belton, TX
Stonecipher, Cunningham, Beard & Schmitt, P.C. ... **Pittsburgh, PA**
Stonecipher, Hugh Brett ... **Lexington, KY**
Stonecipher, Mark K. ... **Oklahoma City, OK**
Stonecipher, Reilly L. ... Austin, TX
Stonecipher, Sheryl C. ... Columbus, OH
Stonecipher, Timothy R. ... **London, OH**
Stonecipher, Tom W. ... **Bozeman, MT**
Stone-Creem, Cynthia ... **Boston, MA**
Stonecypher, William W. ... Brandon, MS
Stonefield, Samuel ... Springfield, MA
Stone-Haas, Sandra ... New York, NY
Stoneham, John M. ... Beaumont, TX
Stone-Harrington, Kathleen ... Springfield, MA
Stonehill, David H. ... Merrick, NY
Stonehill, David N. ... Cincinnati, OH
Stonehill, David N., Co., L.P.A. ... Cincinnati, OH
Stonehill, David S. ... New York, NY
Stonehill, Eric ... **Rochester, NY**
Stonehill, Jeffrey Adam ... New York, NY
Stonehill, Jeremy ... **Chicago, IL**
Stonehill, Robert ... **New York, NY**
Stonehill, Roberta L. ... Forked River, NJ
Stonehocker, J. Scott ... Tulsa, OK
Stonehouse, James A. ... Alameda, CA
Stonehouse & Silva ... Alameda, CA
Stone-Jeraj, Laura Ruth ... **Honolulu, HI**
Stoneking, Gary ... **Minneapolis, MN**
Stonelake, Benjamin G., Jr. ... **Cherry Hill, NJ**
Philadelphia, PA
Stoneman, Chandler & Miller LLP ... **Boston, MA**
Stoneman, Christopher G. ... Woodstock, VT
Stoneman, James P., II ... Claremont, CA
Stoneman, Kathleen Ann Allmon ... Carrollton, OH
Stoneman Law Offices, Ltd. ... Phoenix, AZ
Stoneman, Mark L. ... **St. Louis, MO**
Stoneman, Martin ... **Birmingham, MI**
Stoneman, Martin L. ... Phoenix, AZ
Stoneman, S. Sidney ... Boston, MA
Stoneman, Susan K. ... **Richmond, VA**
Stoneman, Tracy Pride ... **Colorado Springs, CO**
Stoneman, Tracy Pride, P.C. ... **Colorado Springs, CO**
Stoneman, Ward Chalmers ... Oakland, CA
Stonemetz, Claude A. ... Atlantic Beach, FL
Stoner, Allen R. ... **Decatur, AL**
Stoner & Associates, P.C. ... Rochester, NY
Stoner, Barbara Carol ... Oklahoma City, OK
Stoner, Barbara Fox ... Costa Mesa, CA
Stoner, Bowers & Gray, P.A. ... **Lexington, NC**
Stoner, Bruce H., Jr. ... Department of Commerce, Patent and Trademark Office, GV
Stoner, C. Timothy ... Philadelphia, PA
Stoner, Charles A. ... Houston, TX
Stoner, Charles E. ... **Westminster, MD**
Stoner, Clifford E. ... Rockford, IL
Stoner, Craig Alan ... **Denver, CO**
Stoner, Daniel Justus ... Oklahoma City, OK
Stoner, Douglas E. ... **Schenectady, NY**
Stoner, Edward N., II ... **Pittsburgh, PA**
Stoner, Gordon G. ... Federal Deposit Insurance Corporation, Liquidation Branch, GV
Stoner, Gregory W. ... Orlando, FL
Stoner, J. David ... Bala Cynwyd, PA
Stoner, James R. ... Washington, DC
Stoner, Jeffrey Lynn ... Lemoyne, PA
Stoner, Jeffrey R. ... **Philadelphia, PA**
Stoner, Jennifer L. ... **Jacksonville, FL**
Stoner, Joel B. ... Bowling Green, KY
Stoner, John A. ... Charlottesville, VA
Stoner, John E. ... **Irvine, CA**
Stoner, John, Jr. ... Palo Alto, CA
Stoner, Katherine ... Bethesda, MD
Stoner, Katherine E. ... Pacific Grove, CA
Stoner, Kimberly K. ... San Antonio, TX
Stoner, Linda ... Bellefontaine, OH
Stoner, Lisa K. ... Jenison, MI
Stoner, Mark D. ... Indianapolis, IN
Stoner, Max T. ... Rochester, NY
Stoner, Michael A. ... Atlanta, GA
Stoner, Michael B. ... **Dayton, OH**
Stoner, Nancy K. ... Environmental Protection Agency, Program Office Attorneys, GV
Stoner, Norman A., (A Prof. Corp.) ... San Jose, CA
Stoner, Paul G., Jr. ... **Lexington, NC**
Stoner, Preston & Boswell, Chartered ... **Westminster, MD**
Stoner, Ralph V., Jr. ... Indianapolis, IN
Stoner, Ray C. ... **Pittsburgh, PA**
Stoner, Richard B. ... Columbus, IN
Stoner, Richard D. ... **Orlando, FL**
Stoner, Robert P. ... **Valparaiso, IN**
Stoner, Ronald L. ... Wilmington, DE
Stoner, Sandra W. ... Harrisburg, PA
Stoner, Scott D. ... **Lansing, MI**
Stoner, Scott W ... Princeton, NJ
Stoner, Tamara A. ... **Bethesda, MD**
Frederick, MD
Stoner, W. Scott ... **Princeton, NJ**
Stoner, Wayne L. ... **Boston, MA**
Stoner, Welsh and Schmidt ... Pacific Grove, CA
Stoner, William E. ... **Los Angeles, CA**
Stoner, William E. ... Springfield, MO
Stoner-Barone, Denise ... Batavia, OH
Stonerock, Bobbie J. ... Columbus, OH
Stonerock, Jeffrey A. ... **Washington, DC**
Stones, Adele V. ... **Key West, FL**
Stones & Cardenas ... **Key West, FL**
Stonesifer and Kelley ... **Gettysburg, PA**
Hanover, PA
Stonestreet, Daphne K. ... **De Bary, FL**
Stonestreet, F. David ... Providence, RI
Stonestreet, Hardeman L. ... Salt Lake City, UT
Stonestreet, Janice Perry ... Gig Harbor, WA
Stonestreet, Marianne K. ... Charleston, WV
Stonestreet, Wayne S. ... **Bluefield, WV**
Stone-Turesky, Gayle ... **Boston, MA**
Stoney, Carl J., Jr. ... **San Francisco, CA**
Stoney & Gouldon ... Charleston, SC
Stoney, Randell C., Jr. ... **Charleston, SC**
Stoney, Richard S. W. ... Charleston, SC
Stoney, Robert J. ... **Fairfax, VA**
Stoney and Stoney ... Linville Falls, NC
Stoney, Thomas P., II ... Linville Falls, NC
Stong, Elizabeth S. ... **New York, NY**
Stong, Roger A. ... **Oklahoma City, OK**
Stonger, R. Rex ... Kansas City, KS
Stonich, John A. ... San Jose, CA
Santa Cruz, CA
Stonick, Anthony J. ... Miami Beach, FL
Stonitsch, John R. ... Lexington, KY
Stonner, Dean F. ... **Newton, IA**
Stonner, John P. ... Canton, NY
Stonner, Kent E. ... Tuscola, IL
Stoodley, Dale G. ... Philadelphia, PA
Stoodt, Douglas A. ... San Diego, CA
Stoody, Amy Menkes ... **Newport Beach, CA**
Stoody, Amy Menkes, P.C. ... **Newport Beach, CA**
Stoody, John H. ... Environmental Protection Agency, Program Office Attorneys, GV
Stookal, Marc B. ... Chicago, IL
Stookey, Duane S. ... Olympia, WA
Stookey, John A. ... **Phoenix, AZ**
Stookey, Sarah L. ... Vancouver, WA
Stooksberry, John ... **McKinney, TX**
Stooksberry, M. Scott ... **Arlington, TX**
Stool, Anna E. ... **Houston, TX**
Stool, Matthew ... Philadelphia, PA
Stool, Max ... Del Rio, TX
Stoolman, Jeffrey S. ... Trenton, NJ
Stoopack, Helayne Oberman ... **New York, NY**
Stoopler, Eric ... Philadelphia, PA
Stoops, Barbara L. ... Detroit, MI
Stoops, Charles C., Jr. ... Pittsburgh, PA
Stoops, Daniel J. ... **Flagstaff, AZ**
Stoops, Elden E., Jr. ... North Manchester, IN
Stoops, Fred E., Sr. ... Tulsa, OK
Stoops & Kloberdanz, PLC ... Phoenix, AZ
Stoops, Richard D. ... **Albuquerque, NM**
Stoops, Susan E. ... **Richmond, VA**
Stoops, Thomas A. ... Phoenix, AZ
Stoorman, Karen ... Detroit, MI
Stoorman, Samuel J. ... Denver, CO
Stoos, William Kevin ... **Sioux City, IA**
Stoot, Denise H.M.C. ... **New York, NY**
Stoothoff, Judith ... Columbus, OH
Stootsberry, Kristie D. ... Department of Housing and Urban Development, GV
Stopa, John R. ... Columbus, OH
Stopa, Mark T. ... Foxboro, MA
Stopar, Jeffrey M. ... Warren, OH
Stopczynski, Kenneth M. ... Iron Mountain, MI
Stopeck, Howard L. ... Atlanta, GA
Stopek, Alan J. ... New York, NY
Stopek, Seth ... Miami, FL
Stopek, Seth, P.A. ... Miami, FL
Stoper, Richard L., Jr. ... **Cleveland, OH**
Stopford, Jeffrey M. ... Media, PA
Stophel, Glenn C. ... **Chattanooga, TN**
Stophel, John C. ... **Chattanooga, TN**
Stopher, Edward H. ... **Louisville, KY**
Stopher, Joseph E. ... **Louisville, KY**
Stopher, Robert E. ... **Louisville, KY**
Stopka, Albert J., III ... Lynn Haven, FL
Stopka, Albert J., III, P.A. ... Lynn Haven, FL
Stopka, Richard W. ... Huntley, IL
Stopnik, Scott H. ... New York, NY
Stopol, Larry N. ... **New York, NY**
Stopol, Leonora M. ... Woodland Hills, CA
Stopp, Charles W. ... Slatington, PA
Stopp, Margaret T. ... Pensacola, FL
Stoppello, Frank W., Law Offices of ... Boise, ID
Stoppello, James H. ... San Rafael, CA
Stoppello, Kathryn J. ... Morristown, NJ
Stoppels, C. Mark ... **Grand Rapids, MI**
Stopperan, Allan W. ... **Kansas City, MO**
Stopperan, Robert A. ... **Kansas City, MO**
Stopperich, Mark C. ... Washington, PA
Stoppert, Gale I. ... New York, NY
Stopsky, David C. ... Plainview, NY
Stopyra, Thomas P. ... Auburn, NY
Storaasli, Elizabeth A. ... **Duluth, MN**
Storace, A. Thomas ... Albany, NY
Storaker, Ronald J. ... Sheboygan, WI
Storar, Andrew C. ... **Dayton, OH**
Storaska, Joey A. ... **Sunbury, PA**

Stout, James D. .... **Bridgeport, IL**
Robinson, IL
Stout, James M. .... San Antonio, TX
Stout, James R. .... Orange, CA
Stout, James Ray .... Yukon, OK
Stout, Jas. J. .... Wauwatosa, WI
Stout, Jason J. .... **Atlanta, GA**
Stout, Jay H. .... Encinitas, CA
Stout, Joan M. .... **New York, NY**
Stout, Jodie W. .... Delhi, LA
Stout, John D. .... **Bloomfield Hills, MI**
Stout, John E.
Charlotte Amalie, St. Thomas, VI
Stout, John H. .... **Minneapolis, MN**
Stout, John H. .... Norman, OK
Stout, John J. .... **Charlotte, NC**
Stout, Juanita Kidd .... Philadelphia, PA
Stout, Kathleen M. .... Santa Barbara, CA
Stout, Kimberly A. .... **Denver, CO**
Stout, Kimberly W. .... Birmingham, MI
Stout, Koehler .... Butte, MT
Stout, Koehler, P.C. .... Butte, MT
Stout, L. Bruce .... **Atlanta, GA**
Stout, Larry R. .... **Daytona Beach, FL**
Stout, Laura P. .... **Washington, DC**
Stout Law Office .... **Marion, KY**
Paducah, KY
Stout, Lina Lee S. .... Durham, NC
Stout, Lowell .... **Hobbs, NM**
Stout, Lu Ann .... **Oklahoma City, OK**
Stout, Lynn A. .... Washington, DC
Stout, M. Jan .... **Kansas City, MO**
Stout, M. Kathleen .... Olympia, WA
Stout, Marilyn Harmon .... **Greensboro, NC**
Stout, Mark .... **Hobbs, NM**
Stout, Mark D. .... **Houston, TX**
Stout, Mark W. .... Fort Worth, TX
Stout, Michael A. .... **Salt Lake City, UT**
Stout, Michael L. .... Albuquerque, NM
Roswell, NM
Stout, Michael Ward .... **New York, NY**
Stout, Mikel L. .... **Wichita, KS**
Stout, Neal C. .... St. Louis, MO
Stout, Otis W. .... Clio, MI
Stout, Otis W., P.C. .... Clio, MI
Stout, Patricia A. .... Anaheim, CA
Stout, Patricia R. .... Atlanta, GA
Stout, R. Mark .... Oklahoma City, OK
Stout, Randall C. .... Chattanooga, TN
Stout, Randolph W. .... **Denton, TX**
Stout, Ray Franklin .... Ada, OK
Stout, Reed A. .... **Los Angeles, CA**
Stout, Richard Alan .... Portland, OR
Stout, Richard E. .... Edmond, OK
Stout, Richard H. .... **Nashville, TN**
Stout, Richard M. .... Weldon Spring, MO
Stout, Richard S. .... Brea, CA
Stout, Rick M. .... St. Charles, MO
Stout, Robert A. .... **Eugene, OR**
Stout, Robert E. .... Waterford, MI
Stout, Robert L., Jr. .... **Chicago, IL**
Stout, Roderick P. .... **Mobile, AL**
Stout, Ronald C. .... San Diego, CA
Stout, Rose H. .... **Raleigh, NC**
Stout & Rossler .... **Mobile, AL**
Stout, Stephanie L. .... Orange, CA
Stout, Stephen N. .... Richmond, VA
Stout & Stout .... **Hobbs, NM**
Stout, Susan L. .... Roseville, CA
Stout, Susan Lando .... Cheswick, PA
Stout & Thomas .... **New York, NY**
Stout, Thomas A., Jr. .... Washington, DC
Stout, Thomas C. .... Fremont, OH
Stout, Thomas W. .... Louisville, KY
Stout, Uxa, Buyan & Mullins, LLP
Irvine, CA
Stout, W. Lee .... **Ponca City, OK**
Stout, W. Ronald .... **Pittsburgh, PA**
Stout, Walter W., III .... Richmond, VA
Stout, Weldon W. .... **Muskogee, OK**
Stout, William A. .... **Houston, TX**
Stout, William A., Jr. .... Cincinnati, OH
Stout, William C. .... Pensacola, FL
Stout and Winterbottom .... Albuquerque, NM
Roswell, NM
Stoutenburg, Daniela P. .... **Los Angeles, CA**
Stoutenburg, Mark W. .... **New York, NY**
Stoutimore, John R. .... Fort Worth, TX
Stoutland, Julie A. .... **Minneapolis, MN**
Stoutner, Jeffrey B., (P.C.) .... Clinton, IA
Stout-Tabackman, Leslie A.
Washington, DC
Stoutz, Edwin A., Jr. .... New Orleans, LA
Stouwie, Kevin W. .... San Antonio, TX
Stouwie, Valerie Barth .... Laredo, TX
Stovall, Amianna .... **New York, NY**
Stovall, Bill, II .... Dallas, TX
Stovall, Blanche Vivian .... Houston, TX
Stovall, Brenda J. .... Department of Labor,
Office of the Solicitor, GV
Stovall, Carla J. .... Topeka, KS
Stovall, Christopher R. .... Atlanta, GA
Stovall, Cynthia M. .... Boulder, CO
Stovall, Cynthia M. .... **Denver, CO**
Stovall, Eric A. .... **Reno, NV**
Stovall, Eric A., Ltd. .... **Reno, NV**
Stovall, Everett S. .... Lake Jackson, TX
Stovall, Fred S. .... **Dallas, TX**
Stovall, Gerald L. .... **Louisville, KY**
Stovall Goodman Wallace, P.C. .... **Avon, CO**
Vail, CO
Stovall, Harry J. .... Culver City, CA
Stovall, Howard L. .... **Chicago, IL**
Stovall, J. Hunter .... Southern Pines, NC
Stovall, J. Philip .... Des Moines, IA
Stovall, James E. .... **Metairie, LA**
Stovall, James F., III .... Tucker, GA
Stovall, James K. .... **Chicago, IL**
Stovall, James M. .... Scarborough, ME
Stovall, James T., III .... Washington, DC
Stovall, James Wm. .... **Avon, CO**
Stovall, Jerry L., Jr. .... **Baton Rouge, LA**
Stovall, John F. .... Bakersfield, CA
Stovall, John W. .... **Stockton, CA**
Stovall, Joyce M. .... **San Bernardino, CA**
Stovall, Julia E. .... Brentwood, TN
Stovall, Kimberly A. .... Dallas, TX
Stovall, Kimberly A., & Associates, P.C.
Dallas, TX
Stovall, Lois H. Grace .... Chevy Chase, MD
Stovall, Marcy Tench .... **Bridgeport, CT**
Stovall, Michael C., Jr. .... Tulsa, OK
Stovall, Murray P., III .... Birmingham, AL
Stovall, Nicole Elise .... **Melville, NY**
Stovall, Richard Franklin, Jr. .... Houston, TX
Stovall, Richard K. .... **Columbus, OH**
Stovall & Somyak .... Houston, TX
Stovall, Thomas J., Jr. .... Seabrook, TX
Stovall, W. Thomas, II
Upper Marlboro, MD
Stovall Gilbert, Helen .... **Austin, TX**
Stovash, Robert J. .... **Orlando, FL**
Stovell, L. Bryce
Securities and Exchange Commission,
Office of Filings and Information Services,
GV
Stover, Alan B. .... Bethesda, MD
Stover, Alfred B. .... St. Joseph, MO
Stover, Allison A. .... **North Charleston, SC**
Stover, Andrew D. .... **Chicago, IL**
Stover, Bernard H. .... Traverse City, MI
Stover, Charles M. .... Birmingham, AL
Stover, Cromer & Bennett .... King, NC
Stover, David C. .... **Kansas City, MO**
Stover, David E. .... **Harrisburg, PA**
Stover, David F. .... Arlington, VA
Stover, D. C. .... Sebring, FL
Stover, DeAnn C. .... Lincoln, NE
Stover, Donald R. .... **Denver, CO**
Stover, Earl B. .... Beaumont, TX
Stover, Elizabeth .... Phoenix, AZ
Stover, Fallany O. .... **Birmingham, AL**
Stover, Frederick M. .... Montgomery, TX
Stover, Gaynor K. .... Tucson, AZ
Stover, Glenn A. .... **San Francisco, CA**
Stover, Gregg E. .... **Kalamazoo, MI**
Stover, Harney B., Jr. .... Milwaukee, WI
Stover, Hayes C. .... **Pittsburgh, PA**
Stover, Jack M. .... **Harrisburg, PA**
Stover, James .... **Dayton, OH**
Stover, James .... Philadelphia, PA
Stover, Jay Elton .... **Rainbow City, AL**
Stover, Jeffrey W. .... **Bellefonte, PA**
Stover, John D. .... **Lufkin, TX**
Stover, John O., Jr. .... **Allentown, PA**
Stover, John O., Jr. .... **Emmaus, PA**
Stover, John R. .... **Chicago, IL**
Stover, Jon R.
Federal Communications Commission,
Common Carrier Bureau, GV
Stover, Joseph G. .... Dallas, TX
Stover, Kim R. .... Tulsa, OK
Stover, Laura M. .... Scottsdale, AZ
Stover, Lora Lee .... Spokane, WA
Stover, Martha E. .... Tustin, CA
Stover, Michael A. .... Department of Justice,
U. S. Parole Commission, GV
Stover, Michael A. .... **Baltimore, MD**
Stover, Michal F. .... Denver, CO
Stover, Phillip G. .... **Denver, CO**
Stover, Richard E. .... King, NC
Stover, Robert F. .... McPherson, KS
Stover, S. Philip .... Quinter, KS
Stover, Scott W. .... **Austin, TX**
Stover & Sherbin .... Oakland, MD
Stover, Shirley A. .... **Dallas, TX**
Stover, Sid S. .... Jasper, TX
Stover, Stephan W. .... Columbus, OH
Stover, Suzanne .... General Accounting Office,
Office of the General Counsel, GV
Stover, Thomas C., Jr. .... Marblehead, MA
Stover, Thomas E. .... Washington, NJ
Stover, Thomas L. .... **Longmont, CO**
Stover, Timothy J. .... Twin Falls, ID
Stover, W. Dwight .... Oakland, MD
Stover, Wayne .... Alexandria, VA
Stover, William Wesley, Jr. .... Jackson, MS
Stoverink, David F. .... Carthage, IL
Stover-Springer, Deborah A.
Pension Benefit Guaranty Corporation,
Office of Inspector General, GV
Stoviak, John F. .... **Berwyn, PA**
Philadelphia, PA
Stovic, Ralph F. .... Green Bay, WI
Stovitz, Chuck H. .... Venice, CA
Stovitz, James E. .... Glendale, CA
Stovitz, Laura K. .... Los Angeles, CA
Stovitz, Ronald W. .... San Francisco, CA
Stovsky, Carol G. .... **Dublin, OH**
Stovsky, Michael D. .... **Cleveland, OH**
Stovsky, Richard P. .... Cleveland, OH
Stow, Elizabeth Glenn .... Atlanta, GA
Stow, Frederic S., III .... Tucson, AZ
Stow, Virginia D. .... Fort Lauderdale, FL
Stowater, Todd A. .... Algona, IA
Stowe, Carl H. .... Greenville, IL
Stowe, Charles K. .... Greenville, IL
Stowe, Charles R.B. .... Huntsville, TX
Stowe, Daniel E. .... **Spokane, WA**
Stowe, David L. .... Traverse City, MI
Stowe, Edward M. .... Danville, VA
Richmond, VA
Roanoke, VA
Virginia Beach, VA
Stowe, Erick D. .... **Denver, CO**
Stowe, Hugh A. .... **Houston, TX**
Stowe, John R. .... Los Angeles, CA
Stowe, John V. .... Minneapolis, MN
Stowe Law Firm, The, P.C. .... Danville, VA
Richmond, VA
Roanoke, VA
Virginia Beach, VA
Stowe, Randolph D. .... Norfolk, VA
Stowe, Richard E. .... Spencerport, NY
Stowe, Robert J. .... Franklin, MI
Stowe, S. Christopher, Jr. .... Warwick, RI
Stowe, Susan E. .... Washington, DC
Stowe, Susan Ramirez .... El Paso, TX
Stowe, Terrance W. .... Irvine, CA
Stowe, Thomas P., Jr. .... Wetumpka, AL
Stowe, Walter B., Jr. .... New York, NY
Stowe, William S. .... Boston, MA
Stowell, Alan M. .... Washington, DC
Stowell, Anton & Kraemer, P.A.
Destin, FL
Tallahassee, FL
Stowell, Brian Jensen .... **Bakersfield, CA**
Stowell, Brian L. .... **Aspen, CO**
Stowell, Cindy .... Bellaire, TX
Stowell, Doris D. .... Phillipsburg, KS
Stowell, Douglas L. .... **Destin, FL**
Tallahassee, FL
Stowell, Frederick C. .... Naperville, IL
Stowell & Friedman .... **Chicago, IL**
Stowell, Gary F., Sr. .... Haddon Heights, NJ
Stowell, Jon K. .... Indianapolis, IN
Stowell, Kruml & Geweke, P.C. .... **Ord, NE**
Stowell, Marilyn J. .... Fairbanks, AK
Stowell, Mary .... **Chicago, IL**
Stowell, Rand N., Jr. .... Weld, ME
Stowell, Randy L. .... **St. Petersburg, FL**
Stowell, Richard P. .... **Chicago, IL**
Stowell, Robert D. .... **Ord, NE**
Stowell, Robyn Nordin .... **Phoenix, AZ**
Stowell, Shawn R. .... **Roseland, NJ**
Stowell & Stowell, Chartered
Phillipsburg, KS
Stowell, Walter H., III .... **Boston, MA**
Stowell, William R. .... Quincy, IL
Stowell, Wm. H. .... Phillipsburg, KS
Stowers, Arthur B., Jr. .... Knoxville, TN
Stowers, Craig F. .... **Anchorage, AK**
Stowers, Dean A. .... **Des Moines, IA**
Stowers, Fred G. .... **Atlanta, GA**
Stowers, Gerard R. .... **Charleston, WV**
Stowers, Gregory A. .... Indianapolis, IN
Stowers, Harry E., Jr. .... Santa Fe, NM
Stowers, Hayes, Clark & Roane
Atlanta, GA
Stowers, John C. .... Austin, TX
Stowers, Joyce .... Albuquerque, NM
Stowers, Linda J. .... Winston-Salem, NC
Stowers, Margaret E. .... **New York, NY**
Stowers, Mark E. .... Atlanta, GA
Stowers, Michael R. .... **Des Moines, IA**
Stowers, Phillip M. .... Charleston, WV
Stowers, Ronald Gene .... Tallahassee, FL
Stowers, Russell B. .... **Tucson, AZ**
Stowers, Scott B. .... Indianapolis, IN
Stowers, Zoe A. .... Racine, WI
Stowick, Paul C. .... Chicago, IL
Stowick, Paul J. .... Chicago, IL
Stowick & Stowick .... Chicago, IL
Stowman, David L. .... Detroit Lakes, MN
Stowman, Jeffrey D. .... **Ottawa, KS**
Stoxen, John M. .... **St. Paul, MN**
Stoy, Lisa C. .... **Troy, MI**
Stoy, Michael S. .... Boise, ID
Stoyanoff, David J. .... **Richmond, VA**
Stoychoff, Paul M. .... Troy, MI
Stoyko, William N. .... **Richmond, VA**
Straatsma, B. Derek .... **Los Angeles, CA**
Straatsma, Thomas E., Jr. .... Lansing, MI
Strabala, Joseph L. .... **San Francisco, CA**
San Francisco, CA
Strabone, Conrad J. .... Rego Park, NY
Strabuk, Janissa A. .... **Seattle, WA**
Stracci, Paul G. .... **Merrillville, IN**
Stracco, Christopher John
Morristown, NJ
Stracener, Carol E. .... Baton Rouge, LA
Stracener, Douglas N. .... Baton Rouge, LA
Stracener, Nealon .... Baton Rouge, LA
Stracener, Stacey Perkins .... **Jackson, MS**
Stracener, Stracener & Stracener
Baton Rouge, LA
Stracener, W. Eric .... **Jackson, MS**
Stracener, Warren C. .... El Dorado Hills, CA
Straceski, Laura M. .... East Hartford, CT
Strachan, Camille J. .... **New Orleans, LA**
Strachan, Gordon C. .... **Park City, UT**
Strachan, Green, Miller & Olender
Cleveland, OH
Strachan, Harry L., III .... St. Louis, MO
Strachan, Jane A. .... New York, NY
Strachan, John R. .... Anchorage, AK
Strachan, Kristine .... **Park City, UT**
Strachan, Michael K. .... Houston, TX
Strachan, Nell B. .... **Baltimore, MD**
Strachan & Strachan, P.C. .... **Park City, UT**
Strachan, Stuart R. .... Los Angeles, CA
Strachan, Thomas C., III .... Chicago, IL
Strachan, William M. .... **Santa Monica, CA**
Strachan, William R. .... Cleveland, OH
Strache, Vivian Clara .... **Washington, DC**
Stracher, Cameron A. .... **Washington, DC**
Stracher, Leslie .... Fort Lauderdale, FL
Stracher, Richard L. .... Lake Success, NY
Strachman, David J. .... Providence, RI
Strachman, Philip .... Silver Spring, MD
Straci, Ronald A. .... New York, NY
Strack, Andrea L. .... **Springfield, NJ**
Strack, Gael B. .... San Diego, CA
Strack, Nii, Sphikas & Jung .... Honolulu, HI
Strack, Robert R. .... Jericho, NY
Strack, Scott T. .... Honolulu, HI
Strack, Thomas C. .... Waterloo, IA
Stracka, Daniel .... Bridgeport, CT
Strackbein, Howard E. .... Aransas Pass, TX
Stracker, Elaine C. .... **Cupertino, CA**
Stracks, Robert J. .... Chicago, IL
Strada, Henry Clayton .... **Yonkers, NY**
Strada, William E., Jr. .... Stamford, CT
Stradar, Elizabeth A. .... **Newburgh, NY**
Stradar, George F., Jr. .... **Newburgh, NY**
Strader, Ann W. .... **Pittsburgh, PA**
Strader, Charles J. .... Portland, OR
Strader, Clancy .... Mentor, OH
Strader, Donald W. .... Miami, FL
Strader, J. Kelly .... Los Angeles, CA
Strader, James D. .... **Pittsburgh, PA**
Wheeling, WV
Strader, Kent David .... Chicago, IL
Strader, Richard H. .... Charlotte, NC
Strader, Timothy L. .... Corona Del Mar, CA
Strader, Timothy R. .... **Portland, OR**
Stradinger, J. Michael .... Prairie Village, KS
Stradley, David A. .... Los Angeles, CA
Stradley, Fred S. .... **Dallas, TX**
Stradley, J. David .... Raleigh, NC
Stradley, J. Lindsay, Jr. .... **Atlanta, GA**
Stradley, Mark E. .... **Dallas, TX**
Stradley, Noranne .... Salem, NJ
Stradley, Ronon, Stevens & Young, LLP
Wilmington, DE
Washington, DC
Cherry Hill, NJ
Malvern, PA
Philadelphia, PA
Stradley, Stephanie Greer .... **Houston, TX**
Stradley, William J. .... **Austin, TX**
Houston, TX
Stradley, Wilson .... Philadelphia, PA
Stradley & Wright .... **Dallas, TX**
Stradling, Barbara J. .... Rockville, MD
Stradling, Fritz R. .... **Newport Beach, CA**
Stradling, Sandra A. .... **Newport Beach, CA**
Stradling Yocca Carlson & Rauth, A Professional Corporation
Newport Beach, CA
San Francisco, CA
Stradtman, G. Leighton .... **Atlanta, GA**
Strady, Barbara L. .... **Middletown, OH**
Straeb, Chas H. .... Colorado Springs, CO
Straetmans, Mark E. .... **Detroit, MI**
Straface, David J. .... Morgantown, WV
Straface, Mark William .... Westminster, CO
Strafaci, Frank T. .... Brooklyn, NY
Strafaci, Irene Frances .... Brooklyn, NY
Strafaci, M. John .... New London, CT
Straff, Donna E. .... Pleasanton, CA
Straffi, Daniel E. .... Toms River, NJ
Straggas, Catherine S. .... **Philadelphia, PA**
Straggas, George D. .... Newport Beach, CA
Strahan, Christopher C., Law Office of
West Orange, NJ
Strahan, Frank H. .... DeLand, FL
Strahan, Jeffery V. .... **El Paso, TX**
Strahan, John .... Topeka, KS
Strahan, Kenneth H. .... Humble, TX
Strahan, Lyle E. .... Madison, WI
Strahan, Marie P. .... Baltimore, MD
Strahan, Martin M. .... **Denton, TX**
Strahan, Richard D. .... Houston, TX
Strahan, Thomas W. .... Minneapolis, MN
Straher, Michael P. .... **Philadelphia, PA**
Strahl, Dan L. .... Greenfield, IN
Strahl, Murray S. .... Clarksville, IN
Strahley, Charles O. .... **New York, NY**
Strahlstrom, L. Elizabeth .... **Irvine, CA**
Strahn, Eric L. B. .... Reading, PA
Strahorn, Derrick A. .... Dayton, OH
Strahota, Robert D.
Securities and Exchange Commission,
Office of International Affairs, GV
Straight, Catherine Ashley .... Sacramento, CA
Straight, Earl K., Jr. .... Austin, TX
Straight, Matthew B. .... **Bellevue, WA**
Straight, Samuel C. .... **Salt Lake City, UT**
Straile, David W. .... Gaithersburg, MD
Strain, Alan R. .... **Memphis, TN**
Strain, Charles E. .... Cincinnati, OH
Strain, Charles M. .... **Uniondale, NY**
Strain, Dale M. .... **Grand Rapids, MI**
Strain, Daniel T., Jr. .... **Dalton, GA**
Strain, David .... **San Francisco, CA**
Strain, David B. .... Austin, TX
Strain, Denise O'Brien .... New York, NY
Strain, Dennis, Mayhall & Bates, L.L.P.
Baton Rouge, LA
Lafayette, LA
New Orleans, LA
Strain, Dennis W. .... Harrisburg, PA
Strain, Edward E., III .... **Cornelia, GA**
Strain, Geo. L. .... Beulah, CO
Strain, Howard G. .... **Cleveland, OH**
Strain, James A. .... **Indianapolis, IN**
Strain, James R., Jr. .... **Covington, LA**
Strain, James R., Jr. .... **Slidell, LA**
Strain, Jana K. .... Indianapolis, IN
Strain, John A. .... **Long Beach, CA**
Strain, John F. .... Richmond, IN
Strain, John M. .... **Rome, GA**
Strain, Joseph F., Jr. .... Philadelphia, PA
Strain, Lisa L. .... Rochester, NY
Strain, Mark .... **Austin, TX**
Strain, Marla Carrie .... Sacramento, CA
Strain, Michael W. .... **Sturgis, SD**
Strain, Murphy & Vander Wal, P.C.
Grand Rapids, MI
Strain, Paul F., (P.C.) .... **Baltimore, MD**
Strain, Robert T. .... Clearwater, FL

Strain & Rosenberger, A Law Corporation
Long Beach, CA
Los Angeles, CA
Strain, S. Mark .... San Bernardino, CA
Strain, Steven H. .... Jasper, TN
Strain, Wesley B., (P.L.L.C.) .... Midland, TX
Strain, William S. .... Baton Rouge, LA
Lafayette, LA
Strair, Randee Lynn .... Philadelphia, PA
Strait, Anthony J. .... Kansas City, MO
Strait, Brian A. .... Rochester, NY
Strait, David R. .... Watertown, SD
Strait, Denise L. .... New York, NY
Strait, Gerald E. .... Elyria, OH
Strait, John A. .... Tacoma, WA
Strait, Karl M. .... Richmond, VA
Strait Law Firm .... Dardanelle, AR
Strait, Loraine H. .... Miramar, FL
Strait, Michael Paul .... Colorado Springs, CO
Strait, Paul S. .... New York, NY
Strait, Scott D. .... Council Bluffs, IA
Strait, W. David .... Louisville, KY
Strait, William C. .... Brooklyn Park, MN
Strait, William D. .... Dardanelle, AR
Strait, William H. .... New Orleans, LA
Strait, William J. .... Lincoln, NE
Straite, David A. .... New York, NY
Straith, Donald B. .... Warren, MI
Straith, Joan C. .... Atlanta, GA
Straith-Miller, Edward A.
Indianapolis, IN
Straka, Angeline C. .... New York, NY
Straka, Donald J. .... Rantoul, IL
Straka, John A., III .... Pittsburgh, PA
Straka, Joseph A. .... Laguna Niguel, CA
Straka, Joseph J. .... Cleveland, OH
Straka, Patrick J. .... Omaha, NE
Straka, Thomas J. .... Dubuque, IA
Strakeljahn, Thomas H. .... Lancaster, WI
Stralen, John T. .... Sacramento, CA
Straley, Jack C. .... Fenton, MI
Straley, Mark K. .... Tampa, FL
Straley, Stephen J. .... Hollywood, FL
Straley, Stephen J., P.A. .... Hollywood, FL
Stralka, Daniel C. .... Chicago, IL
Stralka, Gregory T. .... Cleveland, OH
Stralka, Kenneth R. .... Garfield Heights, OH
Stralka, Paul .... Chicago, IL
Stralka, William F. .... Agoura Hills, CA
Stram, Thomas W. .... Grosse Pointe Park, MI
Strama, Brenda T. .... Houston, TX
Strama, Keith .... Austin, TX
Strambi, Robert Christopher
Sacramento, CA
Stramel, Todd R. .... Hays, KS
Stramer, Hyman I. .... Brooklyn, NY
Stramiello, Grace A. .... West Orange, NJ
Stramiello, Michael, Jr. .... Naples, FL
Stramondo, Lesa M. .... Lexington, MA
Stramondo, Salvatore F. .... Boston, MA
Stramondo, Salvatore F. .... Lexington, MA
Strampe, Frederick J. .... Milwaukee, WI
Stranahan, Duane, Jr. .... Naples, FL
Stranahan, James A., III .... Mercer, PA
Stranahan, James A., IV .... Mercer, PA
Stranahan, John Q. .... Mercer, PA
Stranahan, Robert F., III .... Raleigh, NC
Stranahan, Stranahan & Cline
Mercer, PA
Stranburg, Brooke A. .... New York, NY
Stranburg, Marshall C. .... Tulsa, OK
Stranburg, Nell Fickie .... Tallahassee, FL
Strance, Elizabeth A. .... Kailua-Kona, HI
Strance & Nakoa .... Kailua-Kona, HI
Stranch, James G., III .... Nashville, TN
Stranch, Jane Branstetter .... Nashville, TN
Strand, Anna Marie .... Springfield, NJ
Strand, Arnelle M. .... New Port Richey, FL
Strand, Arnelle M., P.A.
New Port Richey, FL
Strand, David E. .... Somerset, NJ
Strand, David L. .... Decorah, IA
Strand, David N. .... San Francisco, CA
Strand, David R. .... New York, NY
Strand, Edna B. .... Camarillo, CA
Strand, Edwin .... Colorado Springs, CO
Strand, Helen E. .... Los Angeles, CA
Strand, Howard E. .... Lamoni, IA
Strand, Ivan .... Boise, ID
Strand, Jennifer J. .... Lincoln, NE
Strand, Joan H. .... Washington, DC
Strand, Jynine A. .... Menomonee Falls, WI
Strand, Leof T. .... Albuquerque, NM
Strand, Leof T., Attorney at Law, P.C.
Albuquerque, NM
Strand, Leonard T. .... Cedar Rapids, IA
Strand, Lisa R. .... Buffalo, NY
Strand, Margaret N. .... Washington, DC
Strand, Marguerite S. .... San Diego, CA
Strand, Mary .... Tyler, TX
Strand, Mary E. .... Minneapolis, MN
Strand, Meadows & Webb
Colorado Springs, CO
Strand, Peter E. .... Houston, TX
Strand, Peter J. .... Chicago, IL
Strand, Robert E. .... Honolulu, HI
Strand, Roger G. .... Phoenix, AZ
Strand, Scott R. .... Minneapolis, MN
Strand & Seaborn .... San Francisco, CA
Strand, Sheldon A. .... Middletown, OH
Strand, Sherri Cranmore .... St. Louis, MO
Strand, Stratton C. .... Raleigh, NC
Strandberg, Brita Dagmar
Washington, DC
Strandberg, Douglas F.
Friday Harbor, WA
Strandberg, Rebecca Newman
Bethesda, MD
Strandberg, Thomas A. .... Milwaukee, WI
Strandburg, Katherine J. .... Chicago, IL
Strande, Jeffrey J. .... Wausau, WI
Strandell, Valerie N. .... Reno, NV
Strandemo, Guy T. .... Walker, MN
Strandemo, Neut L.
Inver Grove Heights, MN
Strandemo & Sheridan, P.A.
Inver Grove Heights, MN
Strandemo Jahner, Jacqueline A.
Bismarck, ND
Strandholm, Karen S. .... Southgate, MI
Strandlie, Julie M. .... Arlington, VA
Strandlie, Julie M., P.C. .... Arlington, VA
Strandlund, Roger L. .... Moline, IL
Strandmo, Dana D. .... Maple Grove, MN
Strandmo, Mark R. .... San Antonio, TX
Strandness, Paul A. .... Minneapolis, MN
Strandt, Billie Jean .... Milwaukee, WI
Strandtman, Lisa K. .... Honolulu, HI
Strandwitz, Rebecca M. .... Austin, TX
Strang, Albert W. .... San Diego, CA
Strang, Allen L. .... Auburn Hills, MI
Strang, Amy E. .... Mineola, NY
Strang, Arthur I. .... Marblehead, MA
Strang, Carter E. .... Cleveland, OH
Strang, Dean A. .... Milwaukee, WI
Strang, Eileen .... Chicago, IL
Strang, Ewing Bradley Connell
Chattanooga, TN
Strang, Fletcher, Carriger, Walker, Hodge & Smith, PLLC .... Chattanooga, TN
Strang, Joseph K. .... Mineola, NY
Strang, Kirk D. .... Madison, WI
Strang, Philip R. .... Chattanooga, TN
Strang, Robert M. .... Cherry Hill, NJ
Strange, Alexander T., II .... Gladwin, MI
Strange, Bill D. .... Grove, OK
Strange, Brian R. .... Los Angeles, CA
Strange, D. Clark, Jr. .... Jackson, MS
Strange, Elizabeth A. .... Department of Justice, Civil Division, GV
Strange, Farrell & Johnson, P.C.
Sioux Falls, SD
Strange, Frances Ellen Hewitt
Shreveport, LA
Strange, George J. .... Dallas, TX
Strange, Gerald .... Chicago, IL
Strange, Hal M. .... Georgetown, SC
Strange & Hoey .... Los Angeles, CA
San Diego, CA
Strange, Jeffrey .... Wilmette, IL
Strange, Jeffrey, & Associates .... Wilmette, IL
Strange, Jennifer L. .... Vienna, VA
Strange, John Naumann .... Annapolis, MD
Strange, Luther G. .... Arlington, TX
Strange, Luther J., III .... Birmingham, AL
Huntsville, AL
Washington, DC
Strange, Margaret J. .... Hartford, CT
Strange, Mark W. .... Knoxville, TN
Strange, Mary Lou .... Houston, TX
Strange, Owen W. .... Los Angeles, CA
Strange, Randall S. .... Boca Raton, FL
Strange, Rickey G. .... Midland, TX
Strange, Robert F. .... Los Angeles, CA
Strange, Roosevelt, Jr. .... Allston, MA
Strange, Ross E. .... Greensboro, NC
Strange, Sammie P., Jr. .... Roland, AR
Strange, Sidney B. .... Sioux Falls, SD
Strange, Stephan L. .... Dallas, TX
Strange, Steven B. .... Dallas, TX
Strange, Steven L. .... Los Angeles, CA
Strange, Steven W. .... Fort Worth, TX
Strange, Steven W. .... Mansfield, TX
Southlake, TX
Strange, William B., III .... Dallas, TX
Strange, William P. .... Lawrenceville, IL
Strange-Boston, Lauren G. .... Knoxville, TN
Strangeways, Erik .... Jamaica, NY
Strangfeld, William C. .... Cincinnati, OH
Strangis, Ralph .... Minneapolis, MN
Strang-Kutay, April L. .... Harrisburg, PA
Strangman, Ida M. .... Fullerton, CA
Strangman, John F. .... Stockton, CA
Stranick, Robert F. .... Media, PA
Straniere, Philip S. .... Staten Island, NY
Straniere, Robert A. .... New York, NY
Strankman, Felicia C. .... Oakland, CA
Strankman, Gary E. .... San Francisco, CA
Stranko, Denise F. .... Atlanta, GA
Stranko, Timothy P. .... Morgantown, WV
Strann, Daniel R. .... Garland, TX
Stranne, Steven K. .... Washington, DC
Stranquist, Robyn L. .... Ferguson, MO
Stransky, George E., Jr. .... Camden, NJ
Stransky, Joseph C. .... Dunellen, NJ
Strapp, Christopher E. .... Hartford, CT
Strapp, Francis J. .... Lawrenceville, NJ
Strapp, Francis J., Jr. .... Trenton, NJ
Strapp, Myrna Linett .... Los Angeles, CA
Strapp, Paul E. .... Cranbury, NJ
Strapp, Robert M. .... Urbana, OH
Strapp, W. Joseph .... Los Angeles, CA
Stras, Marcela B. .... Washington, DC
Strasavich, Michael David .... Mobile, AL
Strasbaugh, Wayne R. .... Philadelphia, PA
Strasberg, Lindsey M. .... Beverly Hills, CA
Strasburg, Mary .... Seattle, WA
Strasburg, Mary, P.S. .... Seattle, WA
Strasburg, Sari Ann .... Manchester, NH
Strasburger, John B. .... Houston, TX
Strasburger, John H. .... Seattle, WA
Strasburger, Pamela S. .... Houston, TX
Strasburger & Price, L.L.P. .... Austin, TX
Corpus Christi, TX
Dallas, TX
Houston, TX
San Antonio, TX
Strasburger, Thomas R.
Colorado Springs, CO
Straser, Richard A.
Department of Commerce, Patent and Trademark Office, GV
Strasfeld, Stuart A. .... Youngstown, OH
Strasheim, Frederick R. .... Omaha, NE
Strasheim, Jerrold L. .... Omaha, NE
Strashun, Brenda P. .... Union, NJ
Strashun, Jeffrey M. .... Union, NJ
Straske, Paul A. .... Tampa, FL
Straske, Stephen B., II .... Tampa, FL
Strasner, Stuart B. .... Oklahoma City, OK
Strasnick, Robert M. .... Salem, MA
Strass, Bernard M. .... Phoenix, AZ
Strassberg, Bradley M.
Salt Lake City, UT
Strassberg, Evan S. .... Salt Lake City, UT
Strassberg, Jonathan E. .... Hamilton, NJ
Strassberg, Louis .... New York, NY
Strassberg, Maura Irene .... Des Moines, IA
Strassberg, Milton .... New York, NY
Strassberg, Richard M. .... New York, NY
Strassberg, Robert .... New York, NY
Strassberg, Stanley .... Los Angeles, CA
Strassberg & Strassberg, P.C.
New York, NY
Strassberg, Todd .... New York, NY
Strassburg, Peter J. .... Norwalk, CT
Strassburg, Bernard .... Silver Spring, MD
Strassburg, Roger W., Jr. .... Phoenix, AZ
Strassburger, David Alan .... Pittsburgh, PA
Strassburger, Edwin J. .... Pittsburgh, PA
Strassburger, Eugene B., III .... Pittsburgh, PA
Strassburger McKenna Gutnick & Potter, A Professional Corporation
Greensburg, PA
Pittsburgh, PA
Strassburger, Philip C. .... New York, NY
Strassburger, Raymond L.
United States Senate, Committee Legal Personnel, GV
Strassel, Joseph R. .... Santa Monica, CA
Strasser, Alan D. .... Washington, DC
Strasser, Albert E. .... Cincinnati, OH
Strasser, Andrew M. .... Chicago, IL
Strasser & Associates, A Professional Corporation .... Hackensack, NJ
Newark, NJ
Nutley, NJ
Paramus, NJ
Strasser, Bernard H. .... Ormond Beach, FL
Strasser, Christine G. .... Detroit, MI
Strasser, Dale L. .... Freeman, SD
Marion, SD
Strasser, Dale L., P.C. .... Freeman, SD
Marion, SD
Strasser, David J. .... Pittsburgh, PA
Strasser, Dennis M. .... Seattle, WA
Strasser, Elmer .... Norwood, OH
Strasser, Gayle Mortola .... Dallas, TX
Strasser, George L. .... Fresno, CA
Strasser, Gregory J. .... Schofield, WI
Strasser, JoAnn M. .... Cincinnati, OH
Strasser, Joel David .... San Bernardino, CA
Strasser, Jos. L. .... West Des Moines, IA
Strasser, Kristofer K. .... Atlanta, GA
Greenville, SC
Strasser, Kurt A. .... Hartford, CT
Strasser, Michael .... Garland, TX
Strasser, Peter G. .... New Orleans, LA
Strasser, Peter J. .... Batavia, OH
Strasser, Resetar & DeLuna .... Garland, TX
Strasser, Richard C.
Securities and Exchange Commission, Division of Market Regulation, GV
Strasser, Robert H. .... Dayton, OH
Strasser, Robert J. .... Portland, OR
Strasser, Steven Z. .... Bellevue, WA
Strasser, Thomas F. .... Columbus, OH
Strasser, Virginia
Federal Energy Regulatory Commission, Office of the General Counsel, GV
Strasser, William .... Newark, NJ
Strasser, William I. .... Paramus, NJ
Strasser & Yde, S.C. .... Schofield, WI
Strassfeld, Anne F. .... Cleveland, OH
Strassfeld, Gail S. .... Newton, MA
Strassfield, Richard J. .... White Plains, NY
Strassfield, Robert N. .... Cleveland, OH
Strasshofer, Roland H., Jr.
Chagrin Falls, OH
Strassler, Heidi W. .... Department of Labor, Office of the Solicitor, GV
Strassler, Marc A. .... Carteret, NJ
Strassman, Carol D. .... Cleveland, OH
Strassman, Harvey .... Los Angeles, CA
Strassman, Richard A. .... New York, NY
Strassman, Sandra E. .... Naperville, IL
Strassmann, Franz J. .... Belmont, MA
Strassner, Anne L. .... New York, NY
Strassner, Dianne Lawson .... St. Louis, MO
Strassner, Meryl Lynn .... New York, NY
Strassner, Peter S. .... St. Louis, MO
Strassner, Sandra D. .... Los Angeles, CA
Strasz, Thomas E. .... Mount Clemens, MI
Straszheim, Janelle Sherfy
Washington, DC
Stratakis, Christ .... New York, NY
Stratakis, John C. .... New York, NY
Stratakos, Marion D. .... Charlotte, NC
Stratas, Nicholas A., IV .... Raleigh, NC
Stratas & Weathers .... Raleigh, NC
Strate, George J. .... Wheat Ridge, CO
Strategic Law Partners .... Los Angeles, CA
Strategos, Gena C. .... El Segundo, CA
Stratemeier, Edward H. .... Kansas City, MO
Stratemeyer, Daniel S. .... Louisville, KY
Paducah, KY
Strater, David .... York, ME
Strater, Donald B. .... Des Moines, IA
Strater, Nicholas S. .... York, ME
Strater & Strater, P.A. .... York, ME
Stratford, Carol .... Palo Alto, CA
Stratford, Dale E. .... Ogden, UT
Stratford, Haines D. .... Layton, UT
Stratford, Holly H. .... Bedford, MA
Stratford, Richard J.K.
Department of State, GV
Stratford, Stephen .... Jacksonville, FL
Stratford, Stephen, P.A., Law Offices of
Jacksonville, FL
Stratford, Tracy K. .... Cleveland, OH
Stratford-Jones, Kathleen A.
La Crescenta, CA
Strath, Wm. R. .... Wakefield, MA
Strathearn, Bruce D. .... Menomonee Falls, WI
Strathern, Arthur D. .... Department of Justice, Immigration and Naturalization Service, GV
Strathman, Chad W. .... Minneapolis, MN
Strathman, Charles O., Jr. .... El Segundo, CA
Strathman, Joshua A. O. .... New York, NY
Stratigakos, Helen .... Tampa, FL
Stratigos, Peter A. .... Oak Brook, IL
Stratis, Michael D. .... Brooklyn, NY
Stratis, Michael S. .... Hinsdale, IL
Stratman, Gregg J. .... Omaha, NE
Stratman, J. Terry .... Chicago, IL
Stratman, Jeffrey E. .... Aurora, IN
Stratman, John W. .... Cleveland, OH
Stratman, Scott C. .... Walnut Creek, CA
Stratman, Scott M. .... Evansville, IN
Stratman, Steven F. .... Omaha, NE
Stratman, Victoria Dagy .... Pasadena, CA
Stratmann, David A. .... St. Louis, MO
Stratmann, Gayle G. .... St. Louis, MO
Stratmeyer, Hubert .... Bellevue, WA
Stratmoen, Sally O.
Department of Agriculture, Food Safety and Inspection Service, GV
Stratmore, Robert D. .... Alamo, CA
Stratos, Joseph, Jr. .... Philadelphia, PA
Stratos, Kimarie R. .... Coral Gables, FL
Strattan, Sara E. .... Canton, OH
Strattard, Scott C. .... Saginaw, MI
Strattner, Mark William
Library of Congress, Law Library, GV
Strattner, Timothy J. .... Milwaukee, WI
Stratton, Alisa L. .... New York, NY
Stratton, Amy E. .... Quincy, MA
Stratton Ballew .... Seattle, WA
Yakima, WA
Stratton, Barbara H. .... Wilmington, DE
Stratton, Barbara J. .... Tacoma, WA
Stratton, Beth Maxwell .... Fresno, CA
Stratton, Brent D. .... Chicago, IL
Stratton, Bruce .... Springfield, IL
Stratton, C. Bruce .... Liberty, TX
Stratton, C. Jairus, III .... Seattle, WA
Stratton, C. Mark .... Austin, TX
Stratton, C. William .... Lawton, OK
Stratton, Carlin H. .... New York, NY
Stratton, Carole A. .... Annapolis, MD
Stratton & Cavin, P.A. .... Albuquerque, NM
Stratton, Charles E. .... Pittsburgh, PA
Stratton, Charles S., (P.A.)
Tallahassee, FL
Stratton, Constance N. .... Newport, NH
Stratton, Cynthia Day .... Houston, TX
Stratton, Daniel P. .... Pikeville, KY
Stratton, David B. .... Wilmington, DE
Stratton, David B. .... Washington, DC
Baltimore, MD
Rockville, MD
Stratton, David C. .... Pikeville, KY
Stratton, David S. .... Clinton, OK
Stratton, Douglas J. .... Norfolk, NE
Stratton, Douglas L. .... Denver, CO
Stratton, Eugene Y. .... Burnet, TX
Stratton, Evelyn J. .... Columbus, OH
Stratton, G. Robinson, III .... Edmond, OK
Stratton, Gardner N. .... Boston, MA
Stratton, Gibby M. .... Seattle, WA
Stratton, H. Duane .... Oklahoma City, OK
Stratton, Harold D., Jr.
Albuquerque, NM
Stratton Hogg & Maddox, P.S.C.
Pikeville, KY
Whitesburg, KY
Stratton, James H., Jr. .... Ebensburg, PA
Stratton, Jane L. .... Emeryville, CA
Stratton, John R., Inc. .... Austin, TX
Stratton, Judy D. .... New York, NY
Stratton, Karen E. .... Portland, OR
Stratton, Karyn D. .... Maywood, IL
Stratton, Kathleen M. .... Washington, DC
Stratton, Kathleen W. .... Vero Beach, FL
Stratton, Kayla A. J. .... Sioux City, IA
Stratton, Kenneth B. .... Palo Alto, CA
Stratton, Larry .... Encino, CA
Stratton, Laura K. .... Frankfort, KY
Stratton, Lisa C. .... Minneapolis, MN
Stratton, Louise B. .... Tucson, AZ
Stratton, Maria E. .... Los Angeles, CA
Stratton, Marvin D. .... Petersburg, IN
Stratton, Maureen M. .... Chicago, IL
Stratton, Michael A. .... Bridgeport, CT
Stratton & Monaco .... Oxford, NY
Stratton, Monty E. .... Bartlesville, OK
Stratton, Peter C. .... De Witt, NY
Stratton, Phil .... Conway, AR
Stratton & Ptak, P.C. .... Norfolk, NE
Stratton, Rex B. .... Seattle, WA
Stratton, Richard D. .... Birmingham, AL
Stratton, Richard J. .... San Francisco, CA

Stratton, Richard V. ... Lake Oswego, OR
Stratton, Robert H. ... Hermitage, TN
Stratton, Robert W. ... Baton Rouge, LA
Stratton, Sandra K. ... Fulton, MO
Stratton, Sara Ravenhill ... Topeka, KS
Stratton, Sheryl ... Arlington, VA
Stratton, Stephen L. ... Oklahoma City, OK
Stratton, Stone, Kopec & Sturm
Springfield, IL
Stratton, Susan L. ... Stamford, CT
Stratton, Tami L. West ... Overland Park, KS
Stratton, Terry T. ... Palm Desert, CA
Stratton, Thomas C. ... Seattle, WA
Stratton, W. Thomas, Jr. ... Topeka, KS
Stratton, Walter L. ... New York, NY
Stratton, Wayne T. ... Topeka, KS
Stratvert, Bruce N. ... Department of Justice, Civil Division, GV
Stratvert, William K. ... Albuquerque, NM
Straub, Betse C. ... Long Beach, CA
Straub, Bruce G. ... Tulsa, OK
Straub, Chester J. ... New York, NY
Straub, Christopher C. ... Lancaster, PA
Straub, Christopher L. ... Tucson, AZ
Straub, Donald A. ... Harwood Heights, IL
Straub, E. Frederick, Jr. ... Paducah, KY
Straub, F. Scott ... Shreveport, LA
Straub, Hugh Ramsay ... New Orleans, LA
Straub, J. Kurt ... Philadelphia, PA
Straub, James M. ... St. Joseph, MI
Straub, John C. ... Maumee, OH
Straub, John L. ... Toledo, OH
Straub, Joseph J. ... Algona, IA
Straub, Marcia F. ... Peoria, IL
Straub, Michael J. ... Bethel, VT
Straub, Nancy Elizabeth ... New York, NY
Straub, Peggy E. ... Milwaukee, WI
Straub, Peter T. ... Alexandria, VA
Straub, Phillip B. ... Chicago, IL
Straub, R. Richard ... St. Louis, MO
Straub, Raymond R., III ... Phoenixville, PA
Straub, Robert ... Decatur, AL
Straub, Robert A. ... Troy, MI
Straub, Roberta J. ... San Bernardino, CA
Straub, Seaman & Allen, P.C.
Grand Rapids, MI
Grandville, MI
St. Joseph, MI
Straub, Stephanie E. ... Cleveland, OH
Straub, William E. ... Orchard Park, NY
Straube, Diana Marie ... Buffalo, NY
Straube, Michele ... Salt Lake City, UT
Straubel, Michael S. ... Valparaiso, IN
Strauber, Donald I ... New York, NY
Strauch, Arnold Bruce ... Charleston, SC
Strauch, C. Randolph ... Bucyrus, OH
Strauch, George J. ... Flushing, NY
Strauch, Jack M. ... Winston-Salem, NC
Strauch, John L. ... Cleveland, OH
Strauch & Kiernan ... Flushing, NY
Strauch, Morris L. ... Memphis, TN
Strauch, Robert G. ... Sacramento, CA
Strauch, Thomas N. ... Detroit, MI
Strauch, Timothy B. ... Great Falls, MT
Strauchler, Adam E. ... Richmond, VA
Strauchler, Paul D. ... Roseland, NJ
Straud, Michael A. ... Aurora, CO
Straugh, Deanna K. ... Beverly Hills, CA
Straughan, Ben D. ... Seattle, WA
Straughan, Charles N. ... Naples, FL
Straughan, Laurel B. ... McRae, GA
Straughan, Mark W. ... McRae, GA
Straughan & Straughan ... McRae, GA
Straughan, William T. ... McRae, GA
Straughn, Carol J. ... Los Angeles, CA
Straughn, Jack ... Winter Haven, FL
Straughn, Loren E. ... Richmond, CA
Straughn, Richard E. ... Winter Haven, FL
Straughn, Robert O. ... Minneapolis, MN
Straughn, Straughn & Turner, P.A.
Winter Haven, FL
Straughn, Valerie A. ... New York, NY
Straus, Alan G. ... New York, NY
Straus, Alan J. ... New York, NY
Straus, Alan J., P.C. ... New York, NY
Straus, Arnold M., Jr. ... Pembroke Pines, FL
Straus, Brandon B. ... Treasury Department, Office of the General Counsel, GV
Straus, Charles B., III ... Worcester, MA
Straus, Daniel E. ... Englewood, NJ
Straus, David R. ... Washington, DC
Straus, Douglas C. ... Richmond, CA
Straus, Elisabeth S. ... Hudson, NY
Poughkeepsie, NY
Straus, Eric M. ... Detroit, MI
Straus, Geri Sue ... Boca Raton, FL
Straus, Jack B., Jr. ... Dallas, TX
Straus, Jay Bradley ... New York, NY
Straus, Jeffrey A. ... Scarsdale, NY
Straus, Jerry C. ... Washington, DC
Straus, Jill-Ellyn ... Brighton, CO
Straus, Joel K. ... San Bruno, CA
Straus, Joseph J. ... Seattle, WA
Straus, Karen ... Chicago, IL
Straus, Karl H. ... Asheville, NC
Straus, Lee ... Burbank, CA
Straus, Lee M. ... Department of Justice, Civil Division, GV
Straus, Leonard H. ... Los Angeles, CA
Straus, Michael ... New York, NY
Straus, Oscar S., III ... Brooklyn, NY
Straus, Paul Allan ... New York, NY
Straus, R. James ... Louisville, KY
Straus, Robert H. ... Bronx, NY
Straus, Robert H. ... Brooklyn, NY
Straus, Robert H. ... Newbury, OH
Straus, Stephen D. ... Hawthorne, NY

Straus, Susan K.
Securities and Exchange Commission, Office of the General Counsel, GV
Straus, Thomas J. ... Dayton, OH
Straus, Thomas R. ... Steubenville, OH
Straus, Timothy A. ... Altamonte Springs, FL
Straus, V. Michael ... Washington, DC
Straus, V. Michael, P.C. ... Washington, DC
Straus, William M. ... New Bedford, MA
Strausbaugh, Daniel J. ... Kansas City, MO
Strausbaugh, Dean ... Columbus, OH
Strausbaugh, Jeffrey A. ... Defiance, OH
Strausberg, Gary I. ... Baltimore, MD
Strause, Edgar A. ... Columbus, OH
Strause, Howard F. ... Great Falls, MT
Strause, Michelle
Hot Springs National Park, AR
Strause, Randall S. ... Louisville, KY
Strauser, Robert W. ... Austin, TX
Strausfeld, Laura ... New York, NY
Strausman, Jack E. ... Washington, DC
Strausner, Rachelle L. ... Atlanta, GA
Strauss, Abby F. ... New York, NY
Strauss, Alan H. ... Modesto, CA
Strauss, Alan Michael ... New York, NY
Strauss, Alfred C. ... Allentown, PA
Strauss, Andrew A. ... Asheville, NC
Strauss, Andrew L. ... Wilmington, DE
Strauss, Angelique P. ... Fanwood, NJ
Strauss, Anthony L. ... Minneapolis, MN
Strauss, Anthony R. ... Ventura, CA
Strauss, April M. ... San Francisco, CA
Strauss, Arthur M. ... New York, NY
Strauss & Asher ... San Diego, CA
Strauss, Asher & Zeitlin, P.C.
San Diego, CA
Strauss, Ashley Dianne ... Santa Fe, NM
Strauss and Associates, A Professional Law Corporation ... New Orleans, LA
Strauss & Associates, P.A. ... Asheville, NC
Strauss, Audrey ... New York, NY
Strauss, Barbara J. ... Goshen, NY
Strauss, Barry M. ... New York, NY
Strauss, Benjamin ... Wilmington, DE
Strauss, Benjamin ... Philadelphia, PA
Strauss, Benton C. ... Deerfield, IL
Strauss, Bernard ... Jamaica, NY
Strauss, Bernard I. ... New Rochelle, NY
Strauss, Berney L. ... New Orleans, LA
Strauss, Betsy ... Napa, CA
Strauss, Brian L. ... Philadelphia, PA
Strauss, Bruce E. ... Mission, KS
Kansas City, MO
Strauss, Carl ... Freeport, NY
Strauss, Catherine B. ... Philadelphia, PA
Strauss, Charles Louis ... Houston, TX
Strauss, Cynthia Fein ... Seattle, WA
Strauss, Dale K. ... Midland, TX
Strauss, David A. ... Chicago, IL
Strauss, David A. ... New Orleans, LA
Strauss, David Adam ... Garden City, NY
Strauss, David E. ... Bayside, NY
Strauss, David J. ... San Diego, CA
Strauss, David J. ... Cleveland, OH
Strauss, David L. ... Lisle, IL
Strauss, Deborah C. ... Los Angeles, CA
Strauss, Debra M. ... Southport, CT
Strauss, Derek M. ... Boulder, CO
Strauss, Diana L. ... San Diego, CA
Strauss, Donna E. ... Nyack, NY
Strauss, Douglas A. ... New Haven, CT
Strauss, Edward K. ... Pittsburgh, PA
Strauss, Elise I. ... Lake Success, NY
Strauss, Ellen L. F. ... Weston, CT
Strauss, Elyse G. ... Woodmere, NY
Strauss, Emanuel D. ... Herndon, VA
Strauss, Eric J. ... Lawrence, KS
Strauss, Eric R. ... Allentown, PA
Bethlehem, PA
Jim Thorpe, PA
Strauss, Eric W. ... Berkeley, CA
Strauss, Factor & Lopes ... Providence, RI
Strauss, Forrest ... White Plains, NY
Strauss, Francine Rachelle ... Washington, DC
Strauss, Gary D. ... Farmington Hills, MI
Strauss, Gary J. ... New York, NY
Strauss, Gary J. ... Seattle, WA
Strauss, Gerald L. ...
Department of Justice, GV
Strauss, Gordon C. ... Princeton, NJ
Strauss, Gordon M. ... Cincinnati, OH
Strauss, Gus J. ... Hallettsville, TX
Strauss, Harvey F. ... Norristown, PA
Strauss, Hazel C. F. ... Jamaica, NY
Strauss, Henry J. ... Wimberley, TX
Strauss, Homer Charles, Jr.
San Antonio, TX
Strauss, Howard T. ... Los Angeles, CA
Strauss, Isabelle R. ... West Orange, NJ
Strauss, James M. ... Iselin, NJ
New York, NY
Strauss, James S. ... New York, NY
Strauss, Jane ... Minneapolis, MN
Strauss, Jay F. ... New York, NY
Strauss, Jay Richard ... Lafayette, CA
Strauss, Jeffrey E. ... Monterey Park, CA
Strauss, Jeffrey E. ... Springfield, NJ
Strauss, Jeffrey M. ... Chicago, IL
Strauss, Jeffrey T. ... New York, NY
Strauss, Jerome M. ... Naples, FL
Strauss, Jerry ... Minneapolis, MN
Strauss, Jesse H. ... Newark, NJ
Strauss, Jo Ann ... Minneapolis, MN
Strauss, Joanne H. ... Austin, TX
Strauss, Joe E. ... Flemington, NJ
Strauss, Joel B. ... New York, NY
Strauss, John L. ... Macon, GA
Strauss, John T. ... Covington, GA

Strauss, Jon ... Atlanta, GA
Strauss, Jonathan ... Chicago, IL
Strauss, Jonathan A. ... Minneapolis, MN
Strauss, Joseph E. ... New York, NY
Strauss, Julie ... San Diego, CA
Strauss, Julie Alexa ... Vienna, VA
Strauss, Karen G. ... Brooklyn, NY
Strauss, Karen O. ... Irvine, CA
Strauss, Kit J. ... Austin, TX
Strauss, Lawrence J. ... Akron, NY
Strauss, Leigh R. ... Los Angeles, CA
Strauss, Leo, Jr. ... New York, NY
Strauss, Lori Olitsky ... Philadelphia, PA
Strauss & Malk ... Chicago, IL
Deerfield, IL
Strauss, Marc J. ... Sycamore, IL
Strauss, Marcelle Suzanne ... Irvine, CA
Santa Ana, CA
Strauss, Marci L. ... Fort Lauderdale, FL
Strauss, Marilyn B. ... Miami, FL
Strauss, Mark A. ... New York, NY
Strauss, Mark F. ... Somerville, NJ
Strauss, Mark G. ... New York, NY
Strauss, Mary M. ... San Antonio, TX
Strauss, Maureen B. ... San Diego, CA
Strauss, Michael J. ... Washington, DC
Strauss, Michael R. ... Clifton, NJ
New York, NY
Strauss, Michael R. ... Port Jefferson, NY
Strauss, Michael S. ... Deerfield, IL
Strauss, Michael S. ... Boston, MA
Strauss, Mindy F. ... Plainview, NY
Strauss, Neal J. ... Department of Energy, Office of the General Counsel, GV
Strauss, Neibauer, Anderson & Ramirez, A Professional Corporation ... Modesto, CA
Strauss Nickerson LLP ... Lafayette, CA
San Francisco, CA
Walnut Creek, CA
Strauss, Olin B. ... Jourdanton, TX
Strauss, Pamela S. ... Washington, DC
Strauss, Patrick O. ... Dallas, TX
Strauss, Paul L. ... Chicago, IL
Strauss, Peter A. ... New York, NY
Strauss, Peter J. ... New York, NY
Strauss, Peter James ... Chicago, IL
Strauss, Peter L. ... New York, NY
Strauss, Philip L. ... San Francisco, CA
Strauss, Philip Reed ... New York, NY
Strauss, Randall Edward ... Modesto, CA
Strauss, Randolph H. ... Fort Lauderdale, FL
Strauss, Randolph H., P.A.
Fort Lauderdale, FL
Strauss, Ray ... North Miami Beach, FL
Strauss, Richard E. ... New York, NY
Strauss, Richard E. L. ... San Diego, CA
Strauss, Richard M. ... Brooklyn, NY
Strauss, Richard S. ... Denver, CO
Strauss, Robert A. ... St. Louis, MO
Strauss, Robert D. ... Atlanta, GA
Strauss, Robert E. ... Los Angeles, CA
Strauss, Robert F. ... Minneapolis, MN
Strauss, Robert J. ... State College, PA
Strauss, Robert S. ... Washington, DC
Dallas, TX
Strauss, Robert W. ... Dallas, TX
Strauss, Ronald I. ... Miami, FL
Strauss, Rosalyn Kohen ... Atlanta, GA
Strauss, Ruth Ann ... San Francisco, CA
Strauss, Sara H. ... New York, NY
Strauss, Schomber & Williams, P.A.
Miami, FL
Strauss, Scott H. ... Washington, DC
Strauss, Scott J. ... Garden City, NY
Strauss, Scott Michael ... Little Rock, AR
Strauss, Sheryl ... Minnetonka, MN
Strauss, Sidney F. ... New York, NY
Strauss, Stanley P. ... Newark, NJ
Strauss, Stanley R. ... Washington, DC
Strauss, Stephen D. ... Cincinnati, OH
Strauss, Stephen Gerard ... St. Louis, MO
Strauss, Stephen J. ... Los Angeles, CA
Strauss, Stephen J. ... Sherman Oaks, CA
Strauss, Stephen N. ... Selden, NY
Strauss, Steven B. ... Houston, TX
Strauss, Steven D. ... Hilo, HI
Strauss, Steven D. ... Toledo, OH
Strauss, Steven M. ... San Diego, CA
Strauss, Suanne Smith ... Philadelphia, PA
Strauss, Susan Lee ... Bronx, NY
Strauss & Tauriello ... Flemington, NJ
Strauss, Thomas J. ... New York, NY
Strauss & Troy, A Legal Professional Association ... Covington, KY
Cincinnati, OH
Strauss • Uritz, A Professional Corporation
Ventura, CA
Strauss, Victor C., Jr. ... St. Louis, MO
Strauss & Walker, P.C. ... Covington, GA
Strauss, Walter ... New York, NY
Strauss, William L. ... Washington, DC
Strauss, William V. ... Cincinnati, OH
Straussman, Richard ... New York, NY
Strausz, William L. ... Los Angeles, CA
Strautman, Carolyn M.
Glenwood Springs, CO
Strautmanis, Michael A.
Agency for International Development, Office of the General Counsel, GV
Strauts, Maureen Calabrese
Oakbrook Terrace, IL
Strautz, Elizabeth M. ... Columbus, OH
Stravalle-Schmidt, Ann R. ... Hartford, CT
Stravers, Randall C. ... Oskaloosa, IA
Stravino, Allison Fields ... Buffalo, NY
Stravinskas, Lisa ... Elk Grove Village, IL
Stravitz, Eric N. ... Baltimore, MD
Straw, Andrew U. ... Fredericksburg, VA

Straw, Ann L. ... Burr Ridge, IL
Straw, Bill ... North Hollywood, CA
Straw, Charles A. ... Washington, DC
Straw, George M. ... Denver, CO
Straw, Gerald K. ... Troy, MI
Straw & Gough ... Los Angeles, CA
Straw, James T. ... San Ramon, CA
Straw, Lawrence J., Jr. ... Los Angeles, CA
Straw, Ralph L., Jr. ... Jersey City, NJ
Straw-Boone, Melanie Lee ... Louisville, KY
Strawbrich, Robert C. ... Austin, TX
Strawbridge, Allen J., Jr. ... Dresden, TN
Strawbridge, Caroline J. ... Tuscaloosa, AL
Strawbridge, David A. ... New York, NY
Strawbridge, Douglas A. ... Minnetonka, MN
Strawbridge, Jill E. ... New York, NY
Strawbridge, Richard Wm ... Chicago, IL
Strawbridge, Ronald H. ... Fayette, AL
Strawbridge, Ronald H. ... Vernon, AL
Strawbridge, Steven J. ... Indianapolis, IN
Strawbridge & Strawbridge ... Dresden, TN
Strawderman, Dennis L. ... Eureka, MO
Strawgate, Susan L. ... Briarcliff Manor, NY
Strawinski, James S. ... Atlanta, GA
Strawinski, Paul V. ... River Vale, NJ
Strawley, Faith ... Cherry Hill, NJ
Philadelphia, PA
Strawman, Erica L. ... Cincinnati, OH
Strawn, Allison L. ... Houston, TX
Strawn, Bradley E. ... Atlanta, GA
Strawn, Christopher C. ... San Antonio, TX
Strawn, David U. ... Maitland, FL
Strawn, David V. ... Charlotte, NC
Strawn, David V., P.C. ... Charlotte, NC
Strawn, Elizabeth L. ... Delray Beach, FL
Strawn, Evan A. ... Bloomington, IL
Strawn, James R. ... Canton, OH
Strawn, James R. ... Houston, TX
Strawn, Joel T. ... Delray Beach, FL
Strawn, John R., Jr. ... Houston, TX
Strawn, Julie M. ... Sterling Heights, MI
Strawn, Julie M., P.C. ... Sterling Heights, MI
Strawn, Louis F. ... Atlanta, GA
Dallas, TX
Strawn, Marvin I. ... Milwaukee, WI
Strawn, Monaghan & Cohen, P.A.
Delray Beach, FL
Fort Lauderdale, FL
Strawn, Ralph K., Jr. ... Gadsden, AL
Strawn, Roy W. ... Edwardsville, IL
Strawn, S. Mark ... Houston, TX
Strawn, Sue ... Houston, TX
Strawn, Thomas H., Jr. ... Dyersburg, TN
Strawn, Valery Paige Clark
Mount Vernon, IL
Strawser, Amy B. ... Charlotte, NC
Strax, Lisa ... Beechhurst, NY
Strayer, Ann L. ... San Francisco, CA
Strayer, Douglas C. ... Lexington, KY
Strayer, Hilary ... Iowa City, IA
Strayer, Jay B. ... Oak Brook, IL
Strayer, Joy D. ... Glendale, CA
Strayer, Kerry David ... Springfield, MA
Strayer Law Office ... Iowa City, IA
Strayer, R. Thomas ... Johnstown, PA
Strayer, Stephen B. ... Liberty, MO
Strayer, Susan L. ... Columbus, OH
Strayhan, Dennis C. ... Los Angeles, CA
Strayhan, Harvey L., Jr. ... Metairie, LA
Strayhorn, Cherry Jan ... Miami, FL
Strayhorn, Donald R. ... Chicago, IL
Strayhorn, E. Bruce ... Fort Myers, FL
Strayhorn, Earl E. ... Chicago, IL
Strayhorn, Eugene H.
Department Of Health And Human Services, Social Security Administration, GV
Strayhorn, Guy R. ... Fort Myers, FL
Strayhorn, Ralph N., Jr.
Winston-Salem, NC
Strayhorn & Strayhorn ... Fort Myers, FL
Strayhorne, Robert J. ... Annandale, VA
Strazinsky, David F. ... Greensburg, PA
Strazulo, Dennis D. ... Sacramento, CA
San Francisco, CA
Strazza, William ... Chatham, NJ
Strazzante, Salvatore R. ... Des Plaines, IL
Strazzella, James ... Philadelphia, PA
Strazzeri, Francis A. ... Rochester, NY
Strazzulla, John J. ... Quincy, MA
Strazzullo, John F., (P.A.) ... Pennsauken, NJ
Stream, Charles A. ... Oskaloosa, IA
Stream, Kenneth B. ... Riverside, CA
Stream & Stream, Inc. ... Riverside, CA
Stream, Theodore K. ... Riverside, CA
Streams, Mark ... Los Angeles, CA
Strear, Michelle ... Los Angeles, CA
Streater, Harold S. ... Winona, MN
Streater, Lisa M. ... Tampa, FL
Streater, Michael H. ... St. Paul, MN
Streater & Murphy, P.A. ... Winona, MN
Streb, John R. ... Kenmore, NY
Streb, Joseph S. ... Columbus, OH
Streb, Joseph S., Co., L.P.A.
Columbus, OH
Streb, Patrick B. ... Oakland, CA
Streb, Porter & Meyer, P.C. ... Geneseo, NY
Streb, Roger G. ... Geneseo, NY
Strebe, Galen G. ... Madison, WI
Strebel, Milton J. ... Kenmore, NY
Strebel, Sandra J. ... Washington, DC
Streber, Danielle M. ... Chicago, IL
Streble, Susan A. ... Riverside, CA
Streblow, Sara L. ... Gillett, WI
Streby, John ... Flint, MI
Streck, David L. ... Chicago, IL
Streck, Eric T. ... New York, NY
Streck, Frederick L., III ... Fort Worth, TX
Streck, Steven M. ... Madison, WI

Strecker & Associates, P.C. ... Tulsa, OK
Strecker, David E. ... Tulsa, OK
Strecker, Gerard R.
Department of Commerce, Patent and Trademark Office, GV
Strecker, Marc S. ... Newport Beach, CA
Strecker, Richard E. ... Akron, OH
Streckert, Binder & Streckert ... Chicago, IL
Streckert, Herbert P. ... Chicago, IL
Streckert, Kenneth E. ... Chicago, IL
Streckfus, George M. ... Louisville, KY
Stred, Kristin H. ... Seattle, WA
Stredler, Jeffrey L. ... Norfolk, VA
Streed, Craig K. ... Laguna Hills, CA
Streed, Danielle L. ... Kalamazoo, MI
Streed, Mark D. ... Minneapolis, MN
Streed, Stephen Gilbert ... Brainerd, MN
Streefland, Elizabeth Marie ... Burnsville, MN
Streefland, Russell L. ... Burnsville, MN
Streeky-Genet, Heidi ... Evanston, IL
Streelman, Bryan P. ... Golden, CO
Streen, Steven J. ... Kansas City, MO
Streen, Steven J., P.C. ... Kansas City, MO
Streep, Stephen ... Charlottesville, VA
Streeper, Richard D. ... San Diego, CA
Streepey, Jefferson K. ... Louisville, KY
Streepy, Jack B. ... Cleveland, OH
Streepy, Robert S. ... Kansas City, KS
Street, Benjamin A. ... Grundy, VA
Street, C. Daniel ... Monroe, LA
Street, Cassius E., Jr. ... Lansing, MI
Street, Craig A. ... Springfield, MO
Street, D. Randolph ... Monroe, LA
Street, Daniel A. ... Sacramento, CA
Street, Daniel W. ... Dallas, TX
Street, David A. ... Grundy, VA
Street, David E. ... Department of Justice, Environment and Natural Resources Division, GV
Street, David G. ... Springfield, MA
Street, David P. ... Washington, DC
Street, Dyanna Oian ... Minneapolis, MN
Street, Erica C. ... Minneapolis, MN
Street, F. Lawrence ... Atlanta, GA
Street, G. Leroy ... Dallas, TX
Street, George D., (P.C.) ... Dallas, TX
Street, Gerald I. H. ... Dover, DE
Street, Grua, Maire & Young, P.L.C.
Lansing, MI
Street, H. A. ... Grundy, VA
Street, Harold M. ... Muskegon, MI
Street, J. Stephen ... Honolulu, HI
Street, James B. ... Seattle, WA
Street, James H. ... Grundy, VA
Street, James J. ... St. Paul, MN
Street, James R. ... Aurora, IL
Street, James Timothy ... Franklin, TN
Street, James W. ... Cardiff-By-The-Sea, CA
Street, James W., A Prof. Corp., Law Offices of
Cardiff-By-The-Sea, CA
Street, Jeffrey R. ... Portland, OR
Kirkland, WA
Street, John ... Tulsa, OK
Street, John B. ... Chillicothe, OH
Street, John G. ... Oklahoma City, OK
Street, John G. ... Fort Worth, TX
Street, John S., Jr. ... Chillicothe, OH
Street, Joseph G. ... San Antonio, TX
Street, Kevin J. ... Savannah, GA
Street, Kimbrough ... Seattle, WA
Street, Lairold M. ... Department of Commerce, Office of the General Counsel, GV
Street, Malcolm B., Jr. ... Anniston, AL
Street, Malorie Melrose ... San Jose, CA
Street, Mary Nagle ... Boulder, CO
Street, Mathew H. ... Washington, DC
Street, N. D. ... Grundy, VA
Street, Nicholas ... Gastonia, NC
Street, Paul S. ... Boise, ID
Street, Phillip H. ... Atlanta, GA
Street, R. John ... Chicago, IL
Street, Richard L. ... Waterbury, CT
Street, Robert D. ... Corvallis, OR
Street, Roger Reid, Jr. ... Franklin, TN
Street, Stacy L., (Mr.) ... Elizabethton, TN
Street & Street, Law Offices of ... Monroe, LA
Street, Street, Street, Scott & Bowman
Grundy, VA
Street, Thomas A. ... Rockford, IL
Street, W. David ... Annapolis, MD
Street, W. Scott, III ... Richmond, VA
Street, William Michael ... Monroe, LA
Streete, Stephen R. ... Lake Charles, LA
Streeter, Arthur L., II ... Lexington, MA
Streeter, Barry W. ... West Columbia, SC
Streeter, Harrison ... Champaign, IL
Streeter, Henry S. ... Boston, MA
Streeter, Jack ... Reno, NV
Streeter, James K. ... Billings, MT
Streeter, John W. ... Los Angeles, CA
Streeter, Jon B. ... San Francisco, CA
Streeter, Jonathan R. ... Washington, DC
Streeter, Kim ... St. Petersburg, FL
Streeter, Lauri Croce ... San Diego, CA
Streeter, Linda L. ... Pasadena, CA
Streeter, Lucille Anderson ... Washington, DC
Streeter, Patricia A. ... Chicago, IL
Detroit, MI
Streeter, Richard E. ... Cleveland, OH
Streeter, Richard H. ... Washington, DC
Streeter, Ruth C. ... Albuquerque, NM
Streeter, Tom ... San Diego, CA
Streeter, William J. ... Newton, IA
Streeter, William P. ... Pekin, IL
Streetman, James P., III ... Jackson, MS
Streetman & Meeks ... Crossett, AR
Hamburg, AR
Streetman, Thomas S. ... Crossett, AR

Streeto, James B. ... Middletown, CT
Streets, Edward W. ... Oakland, CA
Streets, Harold M. ... Greenville, KY
Streets, Jeffrey L. ... Houston, TX
Streets, Jill M. ... Encino, CA
Streets, Lori E. ... Charleston, WV
Streets, William C. ... Fairfax, VA
Streett, Alex G. ... Russellville, AR
Streett, Diane Clarke ... Wilmington, DE
Streett, Emily W. ... Washington, DC
Streett, Julian D. ... Little Rock, AR
Streett Law Firm ... Dardanelle, AR
Russellville, AR
Streett, Sharon Carden ... Little Rock, AR
Streett, Timothy Ryan ... Bel Air, MD
Streff, Denise A. ... Chicago, IL
Streff, Tim B. ... Omaha, NE
Streff, William A., Jr. ... Chicago, IL
Strefling, Marklan M. ... Minneapolis, MN
Strefling, Neil A. ... Troy, MI
Strege, Fred ... Wahpeton, ND
Streger, Steven S. ... Irvine, CA
Strehl, Donald M. ... Mount Clemens, MI
Strehle, Andrew P. ... Boston, MA
Strehle, Phillip A. ... Waterford, MI
Strehli, Charles L. ... Austin, TX
Strehlow, Debra G. ... Minneapolis, MN
Strehlow, Nancy A. ... San Antonio, TX
Strehlow, Wm. Monty ... Casselton, ND
Streib, Kelley T.D. ... Evans City, PA
Streib, S. Michael ... Pittsburgh, PA
Streib, Victor L. ... Ada, OH
Streiber, Les J., III ... Boerne, TX
Streibich, Bruce W., Law Offices of
Charlotte Amalie, St. Thomas, VI
Streibich, Wayne ... Moorestown, NJ
Philadelphia, PA
Streich, Arnold J. ... Chicago, IL
Streich, David M. ... Ainsworth, NE
Streich, Elton F., Jr. ... Menomonee Falls, WI
Streich, Eric ... New York, NY
Streich, Eric, P.C. ... New York, NY
Streich, Judith A. ... Fargo, ND
Streich Lang, A Professional Association
Phoenix, AZ
Tucson, AZ
Streich, Sharon A. ... Aurora, CO
Streicher, David C. ... Portland, OR
Streicher, Deborah J. ... Oakland, CA
Streicher, James C.
Grosse Pointe Farms, MI
Streicher, James F. ... Cleveland, OH
Streicher, Michelle L. ... Troy, MI
Streicher, Paul D. ... Chicago, IL
Streicher, Richard P. ... New York, NY
Streicher, Sharon A. ... Secaucus, NJ
Streichler, Stuart A. ... Key Biscayne, FL
Streichman, Samuel I. ... Payson, AZ
Streicker, Gail ... Portland, OR
Streicker, James R. ... Chicago, IL
Streicker, John Harrison ... New York, NY
Streicker, Richard Daniel ... Burbank, CA
Streifender, Thomas R. ... Milwaukee, WI
Streifer, Jonathan ... San Francisco, CA
Streifer, Robert N. ... San Francisco, CA
Streiff, Charles J. ... Pittsburgh, PA
Streiff, Stephen R. ... Houston, TX
Streiker, S. Dean ... Leawood, KS
Streiker, Stephen D. ... Leawood, KS
Streim, Eliot R. ... Hartford, CT
Streim, Lorin R. ... Brattleboro, VT
Streimer, Laura Ann ... North Hollywood, CA
Streinz, James Ray ... Portland, OR
Streisand, Adam F. ... Los Angeles, CA
Streisfeld, Harrison A. ... Briarcliff Manor, NY
Streisfeld, Jeffrey D. ... Lake Success, NY
Streisfeld, Jonathan M.
Fort Lauderdale, FL
Streisfeld, Karen M. ... Hackensack, NJ
Streisfeld, Seymour S. ... Lake Success, NY
Streisinger, Cory ... Portland, OR
Streit, David R. ... Houston, TX
Streit, Edward F., Jr. ... Aurora, IL
Streit, Elizabeth M. ... Chicago, IL
Streit, Gary J. ... Cedar Rapids, IA
Streit, James D. ... Fort Wayne, IN
Streit, Kenneth M. ... Madison, WI
Streit, Martin S. ... Fort Lee, NJ
Streit, Michael D. ... Wichita, KS
Streit, Michael J. ... Des Moines, IA
Streit, Peterson, Hall & Keeney, L.L.P.
Houston, TX
Streit, Richard J. ... Chicago, IL
Streit, Ruth A. ... St. Louis, MO
Streit, Susan A. ... Santa Ana, CA
Streit, Thomas E. ... West Palm Beach, FL
Streit, Thomas J. ... Aurora, IL
Streiter, Michael C. ... Austin, TX
Streitfeld, Jeffrey E. ... Fort Lauderdale, FL
Streit-Kefalas, Beverly K. ... Milford, CT
Streitwieser, Jary V. ... Tampa, FL
Streitz, Mary J. ... Minneapolis, MN
Streitz, R. Jeanne ... San Francisco, CA
Streitz, Robert J. ... Minneapolis, MN
Streitz, Thomas A. ... Minneapolis, MN
Streitz, Wayne C. ... Pitman, NJ
Strekall, Stephen J. ... Billings, MT
Strelau, Nancy A. ... Denver, CO
Strelec, Frank ... Sarasota, FL
Strelecky, Robert A. ... Lisle, IL
Strelitz, Robert ... Boston, MA
Strelitz, Steven L. ... San Diego, CA
Strelitz, Susan J. ... El Paso, TX
Strelkoff, Joseph J. ... Madison, NJ
Strella, Joseph W., Jr. ... Walnut Creek, CA
Strella, Paul V. ... Washington, DC

Strellis, Faulbaum, Walsh & Field, Chartered ... Belleville, IL
Waterloo, IL
Strellis, Gregg E. ... Chicago, IL
Strellis, Jack A. ... Waterloo, IL
Strellis, Spencer W. ... Oakland, CA
Strelou, Karen Lee ... Columbus, OH
Strelov, Jerome J. ... New York, NY
Strelow, E. R. ... Riverside, CA
Strelow, William R. ... Southfield, MI
Streltzer, Adam Lee ... Encino, CA
Strelzik, Alan ... Newton, NJ
Strelzik, Stella M. ... Bridgewater, NJ
Stremba, Lee W. ... New York, NY
Stremel, A. Mark ... Manhattan, KS
Stremel, Gregory ... Neosho, MO
Stremlau, William M. ... Essex, CT
Stremler, Darrell J. ... Northbrook, IL
Stremming, Troy Alan ... Kansas City, MO
Strempel, Sandra A. ... Burlington, VT
Strench, Bibb Lamar ... Washington, DC
Strench, William G. ... Louisville, KY
Streng, Frank W. ... White Plains, NY
Streng, Fred L. ... Merchantville, NJ
Streng, Walter L. ... Brooklyn, NY
Streng, William P. ... Houston, TX
Strenge, Kraig T. ... Lafayette, LA
Strenger, Laurence N. ... Los Angeles, CA
New York, NY
Strenger, Lester ... Dallas, TX
Strenger, Sanford ... Uniondale, NY
Strenger, Saul W. ... Newburgh, NY
Strength, Brian P. ... Montgomery, AL
Strength, C. Mark ... Birmingham, AL
Strening, William R. ... Plainfield, IL
Strenio, Andrew J., Jr. ... Washington, DC
Strenio, Gerald J. ... Santa Barbara, CA
Strenk, Charles A. ... Morristown, NJ
Strenk, Michael J. ... Commack, NY
Strenkowski, Edward A. ... Houston, TX
Strenski, James P. ... Indianapolis, IN
Strenski, Robert F. ... Denver, CO
Strent, Amy B. ... Washington, DC
Strent, Robert A. ... New York, NY
Strentz, Stacey N. ... Stafford, VA
Strepey, Steven Burton ... Louisville, KY
Streppa, Alfred L. ... Rochester, NY
Streppa, Domenic L. ... Fairport, NY
Stretch, Brian Joseph ... San Rafael, CA
Stretch, Charlotte K. ... Chicago, IL
Stretch, Christopher E. ... Cupertino, CA
Stretch, Joseph P. ... San Francisco, CA
Stretch, Mary Ann ... Palo Alto, CA
Stretch, Maureen ... Natick, MA
Stretcher, Daniel E. ... Oakdale, LA
Stretcher, Keith ... Midland, TX
Stretton, John G. ... Hartford, CT
Stretton, Samuel C. ... Philadelphia, PA
West Chester, PA
Stretz, Matthew J. ... Kansas City, MO
Streubel, David A. ... Albuquerque, NM
Streuli, Konrad ... Saunderstown, RI
Streusand, Sabrina L. ... Austin, TX
Streva, Joseph R., Jr. ... Lafayette, LA
Strevell, Robert S. ... Houston, TX
Strever & Hansen ... Cedar Falls, IA
Strever, Harold B. (Duke), Jr.
Cedar Falls, IA
Strever, Kevin K. ... Newport, OR
Streyffeler, Kurt A. ... Fort Myers, FL
Streyffeler, Kurt A., P.A. ... Fort Myers, FL
Streza, Nicholas ... Avon Lake, OH
Streza, Ralph ... Cleveland, OH
Streza, Richard E., (A Professional Corporation) ... Irvine, CA
Streznewski, Alexandra J. ... Albany, NY
Striano-Bates, Lisa R. ... Belleville, IL
Strianse, Peter J. ... Nashville, TN
Striar, Eliot G. ... Columbia, MD
Striar, James G. ... Bronx, NY
Striar, Michael P. ... Hollywood, FL
Stribling, F. Kent ... Jackson, MS
Stribling, G. Carroll, Jr. ... St. Louis, MO
Stribling, James M. ... Madison, MS
Stribling, Jay V. ... El Paso, TX
Stribling, Jess H. ... Washington, DC
Stribling Law Firm, The, Ltd.
Albuquerque, NM
Stribling, Tom ... Austin, TX
Stribling, Wade H. ... Atlanta, GA
Strich, Gabrielle L. ... Cranbury, NJ
Doylestown, PA
Strichartz, Ina Lee ... Department of Justice, Civil Division, GV
Strichartz, James L. ... Seattle, WA
Strichartz, Jeffrey H. ... Farmington Hills, MI
Strick, Christine M. ... Cincinnati, OH
Strick, Gerald J. ... Phoenix, AZ
Strick, Kenneth ... Boca Raton, FL
Strick, Nancy L. ... Washington, DC
Strick, Susan P. ... Los Angeles, CA
Stricker, Cathey A. ... Los Angeles, CA
Stricker, Cynthia D. ... Minneapolis, MN
Stricker, Dana ... Valhalla, NY
Stricker, George, Jr. ... Cincinnati, OH
Stricker, Jack W. ... Newport Beach, CA
Stricker, James J. ... New York, NY
Stricker, Michael A. ... Charleston, SC
Stricker, Ralph T. ... Jonesboro, AR
Stricker, Robert P. ... San Diego, CA
Stricker, Thomas L., Jr. ... New Berlin, WI
Strickland, Anne R. ... Birmingham, AL
Strickland, Annette W. ... Kinston, NC
Strickland, Arthur P., Law Office of
Fincastle, VA
Strickland, Arthur P., Law Office of
Roanoke, VA
Strickland, Brent C. ... Baltimore, MD

Strickland, C. David ... Covington, GA
Strickland, C. Deen ... Folkston, GA
Waycross, GA
Strickland, C. Thomas ... Jacksonville, FL
Strickland, C. Thomas, P.A.
Jacksonville, FL
Strickland, C. Wesley
San Juan Capistrano, CA
Strickland, Carter H. ... Syracuse, NY
Strickland, Charles D. ... Covington, GA
Strickland, Charles D. ... Lavonia, GA
Strickland, Charles W. ... Shreveport, LA
Strickland & Chesnutt ... Winder, GA
Strickland, Christopher S. ... Atlanta, GA
Strickland, Cindy Hansel ... Phoenix, AZ
Strickland, D. Michael ... Greenville, NC
Strickland & Dailey, P.C.
San Antonio, TX
Strickland, Darlene ... Chicago, IL
Strickland, David A. ... Seattle, WA
Strickland, David L. ... Washington, DC
Strickland, Dean W. ... Tulsa, OK
Strickland, Delphene ... Tallahassee, FL
Strickland, Dennis J., Sr. ... Waycross, GA
Strickland, Diane M. ... Roanoke, VA
Strickland, Donald B. ... Goldsboro, NC
Strickland, Donald E. ... Albany, GA
Strickland, Donald R. ... Raleigh, NC
Strickland, Donald W. ... Hartford, CT
Strickland, Donald W. ... Chattanooga, TN
Strickland, E. Ansel, Jr. ... Birmingham, AL
Strickland, Edith A. ... Belton, TX
Strickland, Edwin A. ... Birmingham, AL
Strickland, Elroy ... Alcoa Center, PA
Strickland, Frank B. ... Atlanta, GA
Strickland, Fred P., Jr. ... Louisville, MS
Strickland, Frederick D. ... Wilmington, DE
Strickland & Garmon ... Waycross, GA
Strickland, Gary ... Hartford, CT
Strickland, Gray M. ... Tulsa, OK
Strickland, H. Allen ... San Antonio, TX
Strickland, H. Jerome ... Macon, GA
Strickland Haapala Altura Harnett Maguire & Thompson LLP ... Oakland, CA
Strickland, Henry C., III ... Birmingham, AL
Strickland, Howard J., Jr. ... Macon, GA
Strickland, Hugh A. ... Carrollton, IL
Strickland, J. Allison ... New York, NY
Strickland, J. Tim ... Bartow, FL
Strickland, J. William ... Richmond, VA
Strickland, Jack V., Jr. ... Fort Worth, TX
Strickland, James B. ... Spotsylvania, VA
Strickland, James R. ... Jacksonville, NC
Strickland, James R. ... Eugene, OR
Strickland, James S., Jr. ... Memphis, TN
Strickland, Jane ... Boston, MA
Strickland, Janet A. ... New York, NY
Strickland, Janet M. ... Daytona Beach, FL
Strickland, Jas. T. ... Mobile, AL
Strickland, Jerome R. ... Denver, CO
Strickland, John E. ... Philadelphia, PA
Strickland, John M. ... Sarasota, FL
Strickland, John S. ... Austin, TX
Strickland, Joseph M. ... Columbia, SC
Strickland, Joseph Whitsitt ... Birmingham, AL
Strickland, Joshua G. ... Nashville, TN
Strickland, Joy ... Farm Credit Administration, Regulatory Enforcement Division, GV
Strickland, Julia B. ... Los Angeles, CA
Strickland, Julia Beecher
Falls Church, VA
Strickland, J. W. ... Spartanburg, SC
Strickland, Katherine (Kate)
St. Johnsbury, VT
Strickland and Keels, P.A. ... Chester, SC
Strickland, Kelly W. ... Dallas, TX
Strickland Law Firm, The ... Tulsa, OK
Strickland, LeRoy N. ... Rochester, NY
Strickland, Lucy D. ... Murfreesboro, TN
Strickland, M. Suzy ... Houston, TX
Strickland, Marcia Will ... Santa Barbara, CA
Strickland, Marion O. ... Vidalia, GA
Strickland, Mark B. ... Gulfport, MS
Strickland, Mark Edward
Washington, DC
Strickland, Matthew T. ... Macon, GA
Strickland, Maurice R. ... Newark, NJ
Strickland, Michael G. ... Montgomery, AL
Strickland, Michael G., P.C.
Montgomery, AL
Strickland, Michael W. ... Fayetteville, NC
Strickland, Michele L. ... New Haven, CT
Strickland & Molhem, P.A. ... Tampa, FL
Strickland, Monica Lee ... Midland, TX
Strickland, N. Kathleen
San Francisco, CA
Strickland, N. Wes ... Tallahassee, FL
Strickland, Nancy Easley ... Fort Worth, TX
Strickland, Patricia C. ... Fairfield, CA
Strickland, Paul A. ... Shreveport, LA
Strickland, Phil D. ... Dallas, TX
Strickland, R. Michael ... Raleigh, NC
Strickland, Rebekah G. ... Atlanta, GA
Strickland, Richard A. ... Tampa, FL
Strickland, Richard F. ... El Centro, CA
Strickland, Richard K. ... Brunswick, GA
Strickland, Robert L. ... San Antonio, TX
Strickland, Robert Thomas ... Columbia, SC
Strickland, Roderick D. ... Detroit, MI
Strickland, Rodney G., Jr. ... Palo Alto, CA
Strickland, Roy B. ... Gulfport, MS
Strickland, Scott L. ... San Jose, CA
Strickland, Sidney L., Jr. ... Washington, DC
Strickland, Stan ... Orlando, FL
Strickland, Stephen A. ... Birmingham, AL
Strickland, Steven A. ... Tampa, FL
Strickland, Steven K. ... Little Rock, AR

Strickland & Strickland, LLP
Covington, GA
Strickland & Strickland, P.C. ......**Tucson, AZ**
Strickland, Sylvan W. ....Tallahassee, FL
Strickland, T. Whitney, Jr. ....Tallahassee, FL
Strickland, Thomas E. ....Goldsboro, NC
Strickland, Thomas M. ....Athens, GA
Strickland, Timothy W. ....**Houston, TX**
Strickland, Tracy ....**Pasadena, CA**
Santa Ana, CA
Strickland, W. Michael ....Winder, GA
Strickland, William D. ....Decatur, GA
Strickland, William Daryl
Los Angeles, CA
Strickland, William E. ....**Tucson, AZ**
Strickland, William E., Jr. ....**Tucson, AZ**
Strickland, William E., Jr. ......Peterborough, NH
Strickland, William J. ....**Richmond, VA**
Strickland, William L. ....Washington, DC
Strickland, William M. ....Cornelia, GA
Strickland, William R. ....**Oakland, CA**
Strickland, Wilton L.
Fort Lauderdale, FL
Strickland, Wilton L., P.A.
Fort Lauderdale, FL
Strickland, Zoe C.
United States Postal Service,
Law Department, GV
Stricklen, Charles W. ....Anaheim, CA
Strickler, Charles S., Jr. ....Philadelphia, PA
Strickler, David R. ....**Somerville, NJ**
Strickler, David W. ....San Antonio, TX
Strickler, Elmer D. ....Summersville, WV
Strickler, Eric S. ....**Wichita, KS**
Strickler, George E., Jr.
Bowling Green, KY
Strickler, George M., Jr. (A Professional
Corporation) ....New Orleans, LA
Strickler, J. Glenwood ....Roanoke, VA
Strickler, Jeffrey P. ....Portland, OR
Strickler, Jo Harriet ....New Orleans, LA
Strickler, Lee A. ....Fort Gratiot, MI
Strickler, Matthew M. ....**Philadelphia, PA**
Strickler, Meg ....**Decatur, GA**
Strickler, Mitchell L. ....Washington, DC
Strickler, Randal L. ....Milan, OH
Strickler, Randal L., Co., L.P.A. ....Milan, OH
Strickler, Robert M. ....**York, PA**
Strickler, Scott H.
Occupational Safety and Health Review
Commission,
Office of the General Counsel, GV
Strickler, Scott Michael ....**Bethesda, MD**
Strickler, Stephen A. ....Virginia Beach, VA
Strickler, Susan A. ....New York, NY
Strickler, Thomas F. ....Mishawaka, IN
Stricklett, Robert A. ....Greensburg, PA
Stricklin & Associates ....Houston, TX
Stricklin, C. Vance, Jr.
West Columbia, SC
Stricklin, Clifford ....Plano, TX
Stricklin, Donald F. ....Encino, CA
Stricklin, Donald R. ....Houston, TX
Stricklin, Elizabeth King ....Blythewood, SC
Stricklin, G. Gail ....Oklahoma City, OK
Stricklin, Jessica A. ....Decatur, IL
Stricklin, Lance L. ....Houston, TX
Stricklin, Lee A., Jr. ....Jackson, MS
Stricklin, Nancy ....Coeur d'Alene, ID
Stricklin, Samuel M. ....**Dallas, TX**
Stricklin, Steven M. ....**Houston, TX**
Stricklin, Timothy W. ....Coeur d'Alene, ID
Stricklin, William A. ....Honolulu, HI
Stricklin, William A., A Law Corporation
Honolulu, HI
Stricklin, William J. ....Franklin, TN
Strickling, Douglas K. ....Boise, ID
Strickling, Lawrence E.
Federal Communications Commission,
Common Carrier Bureau, GV
Strickman, Carol ....Oakland, CA
Strickon, Harvey A. ....**New York, NY**
Strickroot, John C. ....**Miami, FL**
Strickroot, John C., Jr. ....Miami, FL
Strickroth, Michael J. ....**Santa Ana, CA**
Stricks, Richard B. ....La Place, LA
Strickstein, Herbert J. ....Los Angeles, CA
Strid, Lawrence A. ....Laguna Hills, CA
Stride, Craddock & Stride ....**Chicago, IL**
Stride, Herbert F. ....**Chicago, IL**
Stride, Herbert L. ....**Chicago, IL**
Stride, John A. ....Fort Worth, TX
Stride, Jon P. ....**Portland, OR**
Stride, Megan M. ....**Boston, MA**
Stride-Saran, Deborah A. ....**Chicago, IL**
Strididron, Iver A.
Charlotte Amalie, St. Thomas, VI
Stridsberg, Roger C. ....Cincinnati, OH
Striebeck, Lewis E., Jr. ....**Belleville, IL**
St. Louis, MO
Striebeck, William R. ....Greenville, MS
Striebeck, William R., P.A. ....Greenville, MS
Striebel, Charlotte ....Minneapolis, MN
Strieber, Leslie J., III ....Boerne, TX
Strieber, Richard A. ....San Antonio, TX
Strief, Robt. E. ....Dallas, TX
Striefsky, Linda A. ....**Cleveland, OH**
Striegel, Bernard M., Jr. ....Akron, OH
Striegel, June A. ....Jefferson City, MO
Striegel, Louis E. ....Stigler, OK
Striegel, Lynda Joy ....Oaks, PA
Striemer, Katherine A. ....Sacramento, CA
Strier, Todd J. ....New York, NY
Strifert, William K. ....Minneapolis, MN
Striffler, Edgar P. ....Mc Keesport, PA
Striffler, Eugene, Jr. ....**Mount Olive, NJ**
Striffler, Stephanie L. ....Salem, OR
Strifling, Jan S. ....**Columbia, SC**
Strifling, Jan S., P.A. ....**Columbia, SC**
Strigel, Melanie J. ....Little Rock, AR
Strigenz, Mandy L. ....**Omaha, NE**
Strigenz, Thomas P., Law Offices of
Omaha, NE
Striggles, Theodore W. ....**New York, NY**
Striggow, Kathleen W. ....Toledo, OH
Strike, Barry W. ....**San Francisco, CA**
Strike, Jane F. ....Stuart, FL
Striker, Chad D. ....**Minneapolis, MN**
Striker, Robert L. ....**Minneapolis, MN**
Striker, Steven R. ....**San Diego, CA**
Strikis, Silvija A. ....**Washington, DC**
Strikol, Stella ....Chicago, IL
Strikowsky, Bruce M. ....**Millburn, NJ**
New York, NY
Striler, Robert L. ....**St. Louis, MO**
Striley, Lawrence W. ....Hinton, WV
Strimaitis, Andrew K. ....**Chicago, IL**
Strimaitis, Jonas V. ....Simsbury, CT
Strimaitis, Jura L. ....Swampscott, MA
Strimaitis, Romualdas ....San Jose, CA
Strimbeck, Lee A. ....Littleton, NH
Strimbeck & Morrison, P.L.L.C.
Littleton, NH
Strimbu, Victor, Jr. ....**Cleveland, OH**
Strimel, J. Jay ....**Dallas, TX**
Strimel, Mary N. ....**Washington, DC**
Strimling, Wendy S. ....San Francisco, CA
Strimple, Erin McNiece ....**Laredo, TX**
San Antonio, TX
Strimple, Shelly D. ....Richmond, TX
Strindberg, Erik ....**Salt Lake City, UT**
Strinden, Jon E. ....Fargo, ND
Strine, Alice W. ....Media, PA
String, Kevin L. ....Cleveland, OH
Stringari, Arthur M. ....Detroit, MI
Stringari, Fritz & Ahearn, P.C. ....Detroit, MI
Stringer, Ann L. ....Petoskey, MI
Stringer, Anthony R. ....Lakewood, OH
North Ridgeville, OH
Stringer, Arthur Henry ....Miami Beach, FL
Stringer, Benjamin A. ....**Springfield, MO**
Stringer, Charles M. ....Seattle, WA
Stringer, Daniel P. ....Lakewood, OH
North Ridgeville, OH
Stringer, David N. ....Chicago, IL
Stringer, Douglas (IBA) ....Portland, OR
Stringer, Elizabeth A. ....Washington, DC
Stringer, H. Patrick, Jr. ....**Towson, MD**
Stringer, J. Byron ....Baton Rouge, LA
Stringer, Jeffrey L. ....Kansas City, MO
Stringer, Jennifer Schooley ....**Richmond, VA**
Stringer, John D. ....Washington, DC
Stringer, John E. ....San Francisco, CA
Stringer, Kenneth N. ....Dallas, TX
Stringer, Larry J. ....**Bloomfield Hills, MI**
Stringer, L. E. ....**Oklahoma City, OK**
Stringer, Mark K. ....Provo, UT
Stringer, Martha M. ....**Sacramento, CA**
Stringer, Montgomery & Montgomery
Talladega, AL
Stringer, N. Martin ....**Oklahoma City, OK**
Stringer, Nanette Schulze ....**Palo Alto, CA**
Stringer, Patrick F. ....Charleston, SC
Stringer, Quentin ....Jackson, MS
Stringer, Richard E. ....Sebastian, FL
Stringer, Robert B. ....**San Francisco, CA**
Stringer, Robert H., Jr. ....Marietta, GA
Stringer & Rohleder, Ltd. ....**St. Paul, MN**
Stringer, Ronald E. ....**New York, NY**
Stringer, Ruth Sensenbrenner
San Bernardino, CA
Stringer & Stringer ....Lakewood, OH
North Ridgeville, OH
Stringer, Tamara J. ....**Charlotte, NC**
Stringer, Thomas E., Sr. ....Tampa, FL
Stringer, Thomas L. ....Dexter, MI
Stringer, Thomas M. ....Fergus Falls, MN
Stringer, Warren, Jr. ....Mequon, WI
Stringfellow & Associates, A Law
Corporation ....**Los Angeles, CA**
Stringfellow, Blair B., III ....Jacksonville, FL
Stringfellow, David J. ....Houston, TX
Stringfellow, Dean M. ....Glendale, CA
Stringfellow, Forrest W. ....**Jackson, MS**
Stringfellow, Henry R. ....**Decatur, GA**
Stringfellow, James S. ....**New York, NY**
Stringfellow, Victoria A. ....**Jackson, MS**
Stringfellow, Walter A. ....**Los Angeles, CA**
Stringfellow, William R. ....Little Rock, AR
Stringfield Law Office ....**Elko, NV**
Stringfield, Thomas L. ....**Elko, NV**
Stringham, Barton L. ....Washington, DC
Stringham, Daniel ....Newark, NJ
Stringham, Don A. ....Salt Lake City, UT
Stringham & Hillman ....Tulare, CA
Stringham, Jack F., II ....**Nashville, TN**
Stringham, John C. ....**Salt Lake City, UT**
Stringham, Kelly J. ....**Boston, MA**
Stringham, Robert P. ....Tulare, CA
Stringham, Ward R. ....Tulare, CA
Stringini, Robert F. ....Addison, IL
Strip, A. C. ....Columbus, OH
Strip, Fargo, Schulman & Hoppers Co., A
Legal Professional Association
Columbus, OH
Stripinis, Jean S. ....Brockton, MA
Striplin, Geo. P. ....Inola, OK
Stripling, Craig ....Nacogdoches, TX
Stripling, Dana K. ....Bastrop, TX
Stripling, David C. ....Newnan, GA
Stripling, George M. ....Birmingham, AL
Stripling, James C. ....Newnan, GA
Stripling, James L. ....**Fort Worth, TX**
Stripling, Louis F. ....Atlanta, GA
Stripling, McMichael & Stripling, P.A.
Gainesville, FL
Lake City, FL
Ocala, FL
Stripling, Morgan M. ....Nacogdoches, TX
Stripling, Philip ....San Mateo, CA
Stripling, Robert A. ....**Dallas, TX**
Stripling, Robert O., Jr. ....**Gainesville, FL**
Stripling, Rorie, Pedersen & Floyd, L.L.P.
Nacogdoches, TX
Stripling, Sylvia A. K. ....**Gainesville, FL**
Stripling, Wesley C., IV ....Fort Worth, TX
Stripling, William B., Jr. ....Vicksburg, MS
Stripp, George E. ....Ypsilanti, MI
Stripp, Stephen A. ....Trenton, NJ
Stripto, Vincent L. ....**Red Bank, NJ**
Strisar, Mary Lou ....Marquette, MI
Strite, David Scott ....**Louisville, KY**
Strite & Schildt, A Professional Association
Hagerstown, MD
Stritehoff, John C., Jr. ....Belvidere, NJ
Stritmatter Kessler Whelan Withey
Hoquiam, WA
Seattle, WA
Stritmatter, Paul L. ....**Hoquiam, WA**
Strittmatter, A. N. ....Monticello, IA
Strittmatter, Jacqueline B. ....Clinton, CT
Strittmatter, Jeffrey Thomas
Pittsburgh, PA
Strittmatter, Nicholas L. ....Monticello, IA
Stritzel, Stacey L. ....**Rochester, NY**
Stritzke, Jerry Dale ....Tulsa, OK
Strizak, Ira R. ....Chicago, IL
Strizever, William J. ....New York, NY
Strizic, A. Michael ....Denver, CO
Strnad, Martin F. ....Albany, NY
Strnad, Robt. G. ....Naperville, IL
Strnad, Sonya ....Collingswood, NJ
Strnal, James A. ....Chicago, IL
Strnisha, Herman J. ....Rocky River, OH
Stroad, Charles S. ....Detroit, MI
Stroba, Richard D. ....Allegan, MI
Kalamazoo, MI
Strobaugh, Terence P. ....Philadelphia, PA
Strobel, Ben E. ....Solon, OH
Strobel, Carol S. ....**Westmont, NJ**
Strobel, Charles E. ....Rochester, NY
Strobel, Christopher S. ....Overland Park, KS
Strobel, Elizabeth B. ....Greeley, CO
Strobel, Eric J. ....**Baltimore, MD**
Strobel, G. Robyn ....Arlington, TX
Strobel, Gil M. ....**Washington, DC**
Strobel & Hanna ....Pawleys Island, SC
Strobel & Hanson, P.A. ....**Red Wing, MN**
Strobel, Jack C. ....**Red Wing, MN**
Strobel, John A. ....**Chicago, IL**
Strobel, Joseph A. ....Wheaton, IL
Strobel, Ken W. ....**Dodge City, KS**
Strobel, Kevin L. ....Greeley, CO
Strobel, Lloyd J. ....San Mateo, CA
Strobel, Lynne J. ....**Arlington, VA**
Strobel, Martin J. ....**Toledo, OH**
Strobel, Mary H. ....Santa Monica, CA
Strobel, Pamela B. ....Chicago, IL
Strobel, Richard C. ....Cinnaminson, NJ
Strobel, Richard H. ....Treasury Department,
Departmental Offices, GV
Strobel, Richard W. ....Pawleys Island, SC
Strobel, Robert O. ....Brookside, NJ
Strobel, Russ M. ....**Chicago, IL**
Stroben, Laila ....**Burbank, CA**
Strober, Alan E. ....Kearny, NJ
Strober, Eric S. ....**New York, NY**
Strober, Frederick D. ....**Philadelphia, PA**
Strober, Lynne ....**West Orange, NJ**
Stroberg, Roland H. ....**Gainesville, GA**
Strobert, Andrew F. ....**New York, NY**
Strobl, Annie K. ....**Chicago, IL**
Strobl, Carla Ippolito ....**Atlanta, GA**
Strobl Cunningham Caretti & Sharp, P.C.
Bloomfield Hills, MI
Strobl, Edward J., Jr. ....Polk City, IA
Strobl, Gregory F. ....Houston, TX
Strobl, Thomas J. ....Bloomfield Hills, MI
Stroble, Joseph C. ....West Sayville, NY
Stroble, Joseph J. ....**Jackson, MS**
Stroble, Kelvin M. ......Department of the Navy,
Office of the Judge Advocate General, GV
Stroble, Larry J. ....**Indianapolis, IN**
Strobos, Eben H. ....**New York, NY**
Strobos, Jur ....**Washington, DC**
Strobos, Katharine ....**New York, NY**
Strobridge, Mary Ann ....Boulder, CO
Strobridge, Maurice E. ....Newark, NY
Strochak, Adam P. ....**Washington, DC**
Strochak, Kimberley S. ....**New York, NY**
Strochlic, Jerry J. ....**New York, NY**
Strock, Barton S. ....Hollywood, FL
Strock, Christine R. ....Texas City, TX
Strock, Jon F. ....Gladstone, OR
Strock, Marcus H. ....**New York, NY**
Strock, William C. ....**Dallas, TX**
Strode, Janelle D. ....**North Chicago, IL**
Strode, Joseph A. ....**Pine Bluff, AR**
Strode, Roger D., Jr. ....**Milwaukee, WI**
Strode, William C. ....**Sarasota, FL**
Strodel & Cass ....Syracuse, NY
Strodel, Joseph D. ....Syracuse, NY
Strodel, Richard H. ....Arlington, VA
Strodel, Robert C. ....**Peoria, IL**
Strodel, Robert C., Ltd. ....**Galesburg, IL**
Pekin, IL
Peoria, IL
Stroder, Allen R. ....Odessa, TX
Strods, Jonis J. ....Skaneateles, NY
Strodthoff, Kristine M. ....**Milwaukee, WI**
Strodtman, Thomas D. ....**Indianapolis, IN**
Stroebel, Andrew W. ....Olton, TX
Stroebel, Christopher J. ....**Chicago, IL**
Stroebel, Edward ....**Wapakoneta, OH**
Stroebel, George W., Jr. ....Schenectady, NY
Stroebel, John S. ....Philadelphia, PA
Stroebel & Johnson, P.L.L.C.
Charleston, WV
Lewisburg, WV
Stroebel, Kristi L. ....Metairie, LA
Stroebel, Meyer & Jaffke, P.C.
Frankenmuth, MI
Saginaw, MI
Stroebel, Paul M. ....Charleston, WV
Stroebel, Robert J. ....Frankenmuth, MI
Saginaw, MI
Stroedecke, Warren S. ....Carlstadt, NJ
Stroeher, Mark H. ....Fredericksburg, TX
Stroehmann, Kristen G. ....**Kansas City, MO**
Stroemer, Christine L. ....**St. Paul, MN**
Stroetz, Edward W., Jr. ....**Atlanta, GA**
Stroffe, James D. ....**Irvine, CA**
Strogatz, Ian A. L. ....**Philadelphia, PA**
Stroger, John H., Jr. ....Chicago, IL
Strogoff, Stanford L. ....Worcester, MA
Stroh, Alice V. ....**St. Louis, MO**
Stroh, Andrea R. ....**Katy, TX**
Stroh, Christine Elizabeth
Washington, DC
Stroh, David L. ....Dayton, OH
Stroh, David W. ....Fairfax, VA
Stroh, Duane C. ....Glendale, CA
Stroh, Gary E. ....Cleveland, OH
Stroh, Herbert A. ....Glendale, CA
Stroh, Jack ....Jackson, MS
Stroh, Jacqueline M. ....**San Antonio, TX**
Stroh, John A. ....**Columbus, IN**
Stroh, John H. ....Findlay, OH
Stroh, John J., Jr. ....**Erie, PA**
Stroh, Kyle J. ....**Columbus, OH**
Stroh, Lynda M. ....Buffalo, NY
Stroh, Michael E. ....Milwaukee, WI
Stroh, Robert M. ....**Philadelphia, PA**
Stroh, Saml. Y. ....Pittsburgh, PA
Stroh, Steven E. ....Lisle, IL
Stroh, Thomas M. ....Cleveland, OH
Stroh, Timothy J. ....Chicago, IL
Stroh, William C. ....**Houston, TX**
Strohauer, Gary N. ....**Clearwater, FL**
Strohbehn, Edward L., Jr.
San Francisco, CA
Strohbehn, Michael D. ....**Kansas City, MO**
Strohecker, Albert J., III ....Rohnert Park, CA
Strohl, Paul E. ....**Houston, TX**
Strohl, Tammy ....**Naples, FL**
Strohl, Tammy, P.A. ....**Naples, FL**
Strohl, Thomas M. ....Davis, CA
Strohm, Bruce C. ....Chicago, IL
Strohm, Douglas S. ....**Wheaton, IL**
Strohm, Lawrence G., Jr. ....**Media, PA**
Strohm, Leslie Chambers ....**St. Louis, MO**
Strohm, Peter R. ....**Lakewood, NJ**
Strohm, Richard L. ....**Phoenix, AZ**
Strohm, Ronald A. ....Chicago, IL
Strohm, Scott B. ....**Kansas City, MO**
Strohman, John M. ....Pierre, SD
Strohman, Joseph L., Jr. ....**Ventura, CA**
Strohmenger, Thomas C. ....**Hartford, CT**
Hartford, CT
Strohmeyer, Fritz ....**Stamford, CT**
Strohmeyer, Nancy Helen ....New York, NY
Strohmeyer, Robert W. ....**Port Angeles, WA**
Strohmeyer, Robert W., Jr.
Indianapolis, IN
Strohmeyer, Todd S. ....**Mobile, AL**
Strohmeyer, William ....**Denver, CO**
Strohsahl, Edward E. ....Saugerties, NY
Strohschein, Alan J. ....Columbus, WI
Strohschein, Linda M. ....**Chicago, IL**
Strohschein, Stephen P. ....**Baton Rouge, LA**
Strohson, Malcolm P. ....Phoenix, AZ
Stroia & Associates, P.C. ....Southgate, MI
Stroia, Audrey C. ....Southgate, MI
Stroia, Eugene J. ....Southgate, MI
Stroik, Lawrence M. ....Fort Worth, TX
Stroik, Patricia Borchert ....West Bend, WI
Stroik, William L. ....**Appleton, WI**
Stroili, Peter A. ....**New York, NY**
Strojny, Andrew M. ....Department of Justice,
Civil Rights Division, GV
Strojny, Duane A. ....Lansing, MI
Strojny & Rollo ....Taunton, MA
Strojny, Suzanne R.
Department Of Health And Human Services,
Office of the General Counsel, GV
Strojny, Thaddeus ....Taunton, MA
Strok, Lisa Bynum ....Orange, CA
Strok, Philip E. ....**Costa Mesa, CA**
Stroka, Albert A. ....Blue Island, IL
Stroker, R. James ....Orlando, FL
Stroker, Richard Porter ....Columbia, SC
Strokes, C. Blaine ....Denver, CO
Strokoff & Cowden, P.C. ....**Harrisburg, PA**
Strokoff, Elliot A. ....**Harrisburg, PA**
Strokoff, Sandra L.
House of Representatives,
Office of Legislative Counsel, GV
Strole, Donald G. ....Lawrence, KS
Stroll, Denise P. ....Somerville, MA
Stroll, Theodore J. ....San Francisco, CA
Strolle, David P., Jr. ....San Antonio, TX
Strolle, Stephanie T. ....**San Antonio, TX**
Strollo, Lauren M. ....**Short Hills, NJ**
Strollo, Richard, Jr. ....**New York, NY**
Strom, Andrew L. ....San Francisco, CA
Strom, Barry ....Ithaca, NY
Strom, Betty Carolyn ....York, SC
Strom, Bruce D. ....Elgin, IL
Strom, Cassie A. ....St. Louis, MO
Strom, Cindy M. ....**Cerritos, CA**

Strom, Cordia A. .... Washington, DC
Strom, David G. .... Chicago, IL
Strom, Dennis .... New York, NY
Strom, Elana E. .... Arlington, VA
Strom, Eric .... Chicago, IL
Strom, Harold L. .... Moraga, CA
Strom, J.P., Jr. .... Columbia, SC
Strom, Karen .... Garden City, NY
Strom, Kathy Silberthau .... Washington, DC
Strom, Larry J. .... Greenbelt, MD
Strom, Lise K. .... Washington, DC
Strom, Louis J. .... San Juan Capistrano, CA
Strom, Lyle E. .... Omaha, NE
Strom, Lynn M. .... Bakersfield, CA
Strom, Mark N. .... Beverly Hills, CA
Strom, Michael A. .... Chicago, IL
Strom, Michael R. .... Hastings, MN
Strom, Milton G. .... New York, NY
Strom, Milton L. .... Atlantic Beach, NY
Strom, Neal B. .... Chicago, IL
Strom, Neva D. .... New York, NY
Strom, Paul L. .... Escanaba, MI
Strom, Peter W. .... Escanaba, MI
Strom, Repay & McCutchan .... Elgin, IL
Strom, Richard .... Richardson, TX
Strom, Robb Michael .... Los Angeles, CA
Strom, Robt. C. .... Craigmont, ID
Strom, Sewell, Larson & Popp .... Belvidere, IL
Strom, Stephen E. .... Cape Girardeau, MO
Strom, Steven R. .... Hartford, CT
Strom, Susan R. .... Cleveland, OH
Strom, Tim A. .... Duluth, MN
Strom, Tracy O. .... Fort Walton Beach, FL
Strom & Young, L.L.P. .... Columbia, SC
Stroman, Cynthia A.M. .... Washington, DC
Stroman, Jacob Paul, IV .... Norfolk, VA
Stroman, Nancy Lynne .... Troy, MI
Stroman, Ralph P. .... Conway, SC
Stroman, Watts B. .... Pawleys Island, SC
Stroman, William J. .... Del Rio, TX
Stromberg, Amy V. .... Buffalo, NY
Stromberg, Anne C. .... San Mateo, CA
Stromberg, Bentley G. .... Lewiston, ID
Stromberg, Burle U. .... Portsmouth, VA
Stromberg, Clifford D. .... Washington, DC
Stromberg, David S. .... Walnut Creek, CA
Stromberg, G. Thomas, Jr.
Los Angeles, CA
Stromberg, Ingrid S. .... Arlington, TX
Stromberg, Jackson C. .... San Francisco, CA
Stromberg, Jeffrey T. .... Davis, CA
Yuba City, CA
Stromberg Law Firm .... Walnut Creek, CA
Stromberg, M. Gage, III .... Spokane, WA
Stromberg, Mark .... Dallas, TX
Stromberg, Marsan Kay .... St. Louis, MO
Stromberg, Michael S. .... Mineola, NY
Stromberg, Richard C.
San Francisco, CA
Stromberg, Robert E. .... Washington, DC
Stromberg, Robert H. .... Erwin, TN
Stromberg, Ross E. .... Los Angeles, CA
Stromberg, Spencer A.W. .... Spokane, WA
Stromberg & Stromberg, PLLC
Spokane, WA
Stromberg, Trygve L. .... Walnut Creek, CA
Stromberg, Wallis S. .... Denver, CO
Stromberger, John C. .... San Antonio, TX
Strombom, Karen L. .... Tacoma, WA
Strombotne, Mark L. .... San Jose, CA
Strome, Philip .... Salem, MA
Strome, William F. .... Pittsburgh, PA
Stromer, Duane L. .... Osage Beach, MO
Stromfeld, Lary .... New York, NY
Stromgren, David A. .... Duluth, MN
Stroming, Gilbert J., II .... Chester, NJ
Stromire, Bistline, Miniclier & Griffith
Cocoa, FL
Stromire, Leon .... Cocoa, FL
Stromme, Gary L. .... Oakland, CA
Stromme, Roy B. .... Minneapolis, MN
Strommen, Gregory G. .... Rapid City, SD
Strommen, James M. .... Minneapolis, MN
Strommen, Roselyn T. .... Longmont, CO
Strommer, Geoffrey D. .... Portland, OR
Strommer, Susan P. .... Winston-Salem, NC
Stromsem, William R. .... Bethesda, MD
Stromseth, Jane E. .... Washington, DC
Stromsheim & Associates
San Francisco, CA
Stromsheim, Reidun .... San Francisco, CA
Stromsness, Chris M. .... Weed, CA
Stromsta, Jon K. .... Rosemont, IL
Stromswold, Hugh C. .... Spokane, WA
Stromswold, Todd M. .... Mankato, MN
Stronach, George T., III .... Wilson, NC
Stronberg, Michael D. .... Whitefish, MT
Stronczer, Michelle P. .... Cleveland, OH
Strone, Michael J. .... Stamford, CT
Strong, Alison .... Newark, NJ
Strong, Andrea J. .... New York, NY
Strong, Andrew Lovell .... Houston, TX
Strong, Angela J. .... Washington, DC
Strong, Angelique J. .... Troy, MI
Strong, Ann L. .... Philadelphia, PA
Strong, Ann P. H. .... Malvern, PA
Strong, Arthur M.
Federal Trade Commission,
Bureau of Competition, GV
Strong, Arthur R. .... Rushville, IL
Strong, Blakeman & Schrock, Ltd.
Pontiac, IL
Strong, Bret L. .... The Woodlands, TX
Strong, Brian D. .... Mesa, AZ
Strong, Brian P. .... York, PA
Strong, Carter .... Washington, DC
Strong, Catherine E. .... Green Bay, WI
Strong, Charles P., Jr. .... Hagerstown, MD
Strong, Christina Woodward .... Princeton, NJ
Strong, Clive J. .... Boise, ID
Strong, Craig S. .... Detroit, MI
Strong, Cynthia G. .... Atlanta, GA
Strong, David B. .... New York, NY
Strong, David B. .... Burlington, WA
Strong, David L. .... Redwood City, CA
Strong, David R. .... Fort Lauderdale, FL
Strong, Dewitt J. .... Eagle River, WI
Strong, Don S. .... Oklahoma City, OK
Strong, Edward B. .... Birmingham, AL
Strong, Edward J. .... Culver City, CA
Strong, Eileen B. .... Treasury Department,
Internal Revenue Service, GV
Strong, Eric M. .... Riverside, CA
Strong, Frank H. .... Maryville, MO
Strong, Frank H., Jr. .... Maryville, MO
Strong, Frank R. .... Washington, DC
Strong, Frank R. .... Burlington, NC
Strong, Franklin Wallace, Jr. .... Columbia, SC
Strong, Fred Clegg .... New Orleans, LA
Strong, Frederic E. .... Issaquah, WA
Strong, Gayle Lynn .... Denver, CO
Strong, George B. .... Houston, TX
Strong, George G., Jr. .... Los Angeles, CA
Strong, George V., III .... Berwyn, PA
Strong, Glen F. .... Salt Lake City, UT
Strong, Glen W. .... Oak Grove, LA
Strong, H. Whitfield, Jr. .... Auburn, AL
Birmingham, AL
Montgomery, AL
Strong & Hanni, A Professional Corporation
Salt Lake City, UT
Strong, Harlan B. .... Minneapolis, MN
Strong, Harry P., Jr. .... St. Paul, MN
Strong & Heyburn .... Houston, TX
Strong, Hope, III, (P.A.) .... Winter Park, FL
Strong, Howard .... Reseda, CA
Strong, Jack B. .... Austin, TX
Strong, James B. .... Olympia, WA
Strong, James M., VI .... Harrisburg, PA
Strong, James R. .... St. Louis, MO
Strong, James W. .... Thomaston, ME
Strong, Jay V., Jr. .... Towson, MD
Strong, John F. .... Seattle, WA
Strong, John M. .... New York, NY
Strong, John VR., Jr. .... New Brunswick, NJ
Strong, John VR., Jr. .... Plainsboro, NJ
Somerville, NJ
Strong, John W. .... Tucson, AZ
Strong, Jonathan
Department of Housing and Urban
Development,
Office of General Counsel, GV
Strong, Jonathan .... Boston, MA
Strong, Jonnie .... New York, NY
Strong, Joseph T. .... Clarion, PA
Strong, Judith M. .... Kansas City, MO
Strong, Julianna K. .... Riverside, CA
Strong, Kathleen Diane
San Juan Capistrano, CA
Strong, Kenneth F. .... Novato, CA
Strong, Kenneth L. .... Pontiac, IL
Strong, Kenneth W. .... Baltimore, MD
Strong, Kenneth W., P.A. .... Baltimore, MD
Strong, Kimberly R. .... McLean, VA
Strong, Klasing & Williamson, P.C.
Birmingham, AL
Strong & Konat, P.S. .... Seattle, WA
Strong, Laurie M. .... Grand Rapids, MI
Strong Law Firm, The .... Chesapeake, VA
Strong Law Firm, The, A Professional Corporation .... Springfield, MO
Strong, Lisa Cooper .... Paducah, KY
Strong, M. Sheppard .... Austin, TX
Strong, Maria S. .... Washington, DC
Strong, Mark J. .... Baltimore, MD
Strong, Michael D. .... Kansas City, MO
Strong, Michael L. .... Berwyn, PA
Strong, Michael R. .... Chesapeake, VA
Strong & Morales .... San Juan Capistrano, CA
Strong, Nancy Kramer .... Houston, TX
Strong, Patricia L. .... Minneapolis, MN
Strong, Patricia M. .... Hartford, CT
Strong, Patrick V. .... Houston, TX
Strong, Peter A. .... Nyack, NY
Strong, Peter H. .... Los Angeles, CA
Strong, Philip L. .... Cranbury, NJ
Strong, Pipkin, Nelson, Bissell & Ledyard, L.L.P. .... Beaumont, TX
Houston, TX
Strong and Pugh, P.A. .... Phoenix, AZ
Strong, R. Blair .... Spokane, WA
Strong, R. Keith .... Great Falls, MT
Strong, Rachel Lisa .... Washington, DC
Strong, Randall B. .... Baytown, TX
Strong, Richard A. .... Los Angeles, CA
Strong, Richard C. .... Fresno, CA
Strong, Richard R. .... Akron, OH
Strong, Richard W. .... Green Bay, WI
Strong, Richard Wm .... Yucaipa, CA
Strong, Robert A. .... Nashville, TN
Strong, Robert A. W. .... Birmingham, MI
Strong, Robert C. .... San Diego, CA
Strong, Robert C. .... Edmonds, WA
Strong, Robert H., Jr. .... Chestertown, MD
Strong, Robert L. .... Westwood, MA
Strong, Rodney C. .... Chattanooga, TN
Strong, Serena A. .... Houston, TX
Strong, Sidney J. .... Seattle, WA
Strong, St. Clair G., Jr. .... Thousand Oaks, CA
Strong, Stephen K. .... Seattle, WA
Strong, Steve A. .... Bryan, TX
Strong, Steven C. .... Salt Lake City, UT
Strong, Steven Mark .... Dallas, TX
Strong, Stevens & Hamilton, P.C.
Plymouth Meeting, PA
Strong & Strong .... Green Bay, WI
Strong & Strong, A Professional Corporation
Maryville, MO
Strong, Thomas .... Springfield, MO
Strong, Thomas H. .... Baltimore, MD
Strong, Thomas J. .... Greenwich, CT
Strong, Timothy B. .... Jacksonville, FL
Strong, Timothy M. .... Pittsburgh, PA
Strong, Tony .... Juneau, AK
Strong, Tully, Tully & Crouch, Ltd.
Minneapolis, MN
Strong, Walker, Doepfner & Royse, P.C.
Dallas, TX
Strong, Walter G., Jr. .... Sulphur, LA
Strong, William K. .... Phoenix, AZ
Strong, William R. .... Clarion, PA
Strong, William S. .... Boston, MA
Strong, W. O., III .... Houston, TX
Stronge, David G. .... Pismo Beach, CA
Strongin, Debbie .... New York, NY
Strongin, Howard F. .... New York, NY
Strongin, Jeffrey M. .... Palm Springs, CA
Strongin, Landey .... New York, NY
Strongin, Michael .... Corona Del Mar, CA
Strongin, Norema K. .... Rowland Heights, CA
Strongin, Robert H. .... New York, NY
Strongin, Seymour .... Washington, DC
Strongin, Stuart J. .... Chicago, IL
Strongosky, Christopher M.
Las Vegas, NV
Strongwater & Cherniak .... Atlanta, GA
Strongwater, Jay L. .... Atlanta, GA
Strons, William J. .... Chicago, IL
Stronski, James K. .... New York, NY
Stronski, Neil P. .... New York, NY
Stroo, James C. .... Irving, TX
Strooband, Michael .... Eugene, OR
Stroock, Margaret M. .... Denver, CO
Stroock & Stroock & Lavan LLP
Los Angeles, CA
Washington, DC
Miami, FL
Boston, MA
New York, NY
Strootman, Gary William .... Cambridge, MN
Strop, William H. .... Miami, FL
Strop, William H. .... St. Joseph, MO
Strop, William H., P.C. .... St. Joseph, MO
Strope, Boyd W. .... O'Neill, NE
Strope, Cindy Goddard .... Princeton, WV
Strope, Krotter & Gotschall, P.C.
O'Neill, NE
Strophy, Richard A. .... Olympia, WA
Stropkai, James L. .... Lansing, MI
Strople, Christopher W. .... Newport Beach, CA
Strople, Raymond H. .... Portsmouth, VA
Strople, Sharon Thompson .... Santa Ana, CA
Stropp, Robert H., Jr. .... Washington, DC
Stropus, Ruta K. .... De Kalb, IL
Strosberg, Gail E. .... New Haven, CT
Stroschein, Charles M. .... Lewiston, ID
Strosnider, R. Barry .... Westmont, NJ
Stross, Howard C. .... Palm Harbor, FL
Stross Law Firm, A Professional Association
Palm Harbor, FL
Strossen, Nadine .... New York, NY
Stroster, Michael E. .... Grand Rapids, MI
Strote, Joel R. .... Woodland Hills, CA
Strote, Ronald P. .... Bloomfield Hills, MI
Strother, Ann M. .... Universal City, TX
Strother, Bart L. .... Kansas City, MO
Strother, Channing D., Jr.
Washington, DC
Strother, Don D. .... Memphis, TN
Strother, E. French .... San Antonio, TX
Strother Firm, The, P.A.
Mountain Home, AR
Strother, George B. .... Madison, WI
Strother, Harvey Q. .... Marietta, GA
Strother, Jack G. .... Seattle, WA
Strother, James M. .... Des Moines, IA
Strother, James O. .... Springdale, AR
Strother, Jeffrey A. .... Boise, ID
Strother, Jodi L. .... Mountain Home, AR
Strother, John F. .... Bridgeport, CT
Strother, John R. (Jack), III
Savannah, GA
Strother, John R., Jr. .... Atlanta, GA
Strother, Judith Cook .... Mountain Home, AR
Strother, Justin .... Houston, TX
Strother, Lane H. .... Mountain Home, AR
Strother, Macon D. .... Houston, TX
Strother, Mary B. .... Boston, MA
Strother, Philip Carter .... Richmond, VA
Strother, Ralph T. .... Waco, TX
Strother, Robert S. .... Lexington, KY
Strother, Robin D. .... Farmington, NM
Strother, Saml. L. .... St. Petersburg, FL
Strother & Stafford, P.S.C. .... Lexington, KY
Strother, T. McCullough .... Dallas, TX
Strother, Thomas W. .... Pompton Plains, NJ
Strother, Todd A. .... Chicago, IL
Strothers, Dwayne B. .... Norfolk, VA
Strothman, Doreen A. .... Hyattsville, MD
Upper Marlboro, MD
Strothman, Eleanor Shawfield
Chappaqua, NY
Strothman, John H. .... Minneapolis, MN
Strothman, Lloyd F., Jr.
Pompano Beach, FL
Strothman, Sara A. .... Minneapolis, MN
Strothmann, Wayne P. .... Clinton, MO
Strotkamp, Audie L. .... Newton, KS
Peabody, KS
Strotman, Andrew D. .... Lincoln, NE
Omaha, NE
Strott, George G., Jr. .... Seaford, DE
Salisbury, MD
Strott, George G., Jr., P.A. .... Seaford, DE
Salisbury, MD
Strott, Lynn W. .... Baltimore, MD
Strott, Peter H. .... Atlanta, GA
Strotz, Bruce H. .... Albuquerque, NM
Strotz, Caroline M. .... San Francisco, CA
Strotz, Peter A. .... Oakland, CA
Stroube, H. Rey, III, (P.C.) .... Houston, TX
Stroube, Mary K. .... Woodland, CA
Stroud, A. Neil ....
Department of the Navy, GV
Stroud, Alan L. .... Dallas, TX
Stroud, A. M., III .... Shreveport, LA
Stroud, Andrew W. .... Sacramento, CA
Stroud, Barbara L. .... Austin, TX
Stroud, Barron L., Jr. .... Baltimore, MD
Stroud, Belynda Reine .... Memphis, TN
Stroud, Carter .... Oakland, CA
Stroud, Cynthia K. .... Florham Park, NJ
Stroud, David G. .... Wexford, PA
Stroud, Delia .... Philadelphia, PA
Stroud, Donald R. .... Madison, WI
Stroud, Donald R., Jr. .... Greenville, NC
Stroud, Donna S. .... Zebulon, NC
Stroud, Geraldine G. .... Washington, DC
Stroud, Greer H., (Mrs.) .... Orange, CA
Stroud, Gretchen R. .... Palo Alto, CA
Stroud, H. Toney .... Charleston, WV
Stroud, Howard M. .... Hattiesburg, MS
Stroud, J. Keith .... Winston-Salem, NC
Stroud, J. Stanley .... Haverford, PA
Stroud, James A. .... Dallas, TX
Stroud, James C. .... Philadelphia, PA
Stroud, James L. .... Tucson, AZ
Stroud, John F., III .... Texarkana, TX
Stroud, John F., Jr. .... Little Rock, AR
Stroud, John V. .... Sacramento, CA
Stroud, Joseph E., Jr. .... Jacksonville, NC
Swansboro, NC
Stroud, Joseph O., Jr. .... Jacksonville, FL
Stroud, Keith M. .... Charlotte, NC
Stroud, Kenneth M. .... Indianapolis, IN
Stroud, M. Allyn .... Shreveport, LA
Stroud, Nancy E. .... Boca Raton, FL
Stroud, Philip A. .... Mobile, AL
Stroud, Ramey .... Lyons, OR
Stroud, Ramey R., P.C. .... Lyons, OR
Stroud, Rhathelia .... Decatur, GA
Stroud, Robert D. .... Batesville, AR
Stroud, Robert E. .... Charlottesville, VA
Stroud, Robert R. .... Madison, WI
Stroud, Robert R., Sr. .... Cincinnati, OH
Stroud, Roy W. .... Universal City, TX
Stroud, Seward Ritchey .... Madison, WI
Stroud, Stephen D. .... Sioux City, IA
Stroud, Steven R. .... Rocky Mount, NC
Stroud, Stuart L. .... Kinston, NC
Stroud, Ted W. .... East Lansing, MI
Stroud, Thomas E. .... Boca Raton, FL
Stroud, W. Randall .... Raleigh, NC
Stroud, William M. .... Chicago, IL
Stroud, William R., Jr. .... Raleigh, NC
Stroud, Willink & Howard, LLC
Madison, WI
Stroud, Zahava Aroesty .... Los Angeles, CA
Strouf, Yvonne J. .... Phoenix, AZ
Strough, Dale A. .... Watseka, IL
Strougo, Robert I. .... New York, NY
Stroumbakis, Nicholas C. .... Wilkes-Barre, PA
Stroumbakis, Toula .... New York, NY
Stroumtsos, C. John .... New Brunswick, NJ
Stroup & Bakerink .... Tracy, CA
Stroup, Carol A. .... Irvine, CA
Stroup, Catherine Anne .... Columbus, OH
Stroup, Danny M. .... Longview, TX
Stroup & de Goede .... Fresno, CA
Stroup, Erhart & Wurster, P.C.
Petoskey, MI
Stroup, Gordon E. .... Bedford, PA
Stroup, James L. .... Tracy, CA
Stroup, James W. .... Fort Lauderdale, FL
Stroup, James W., P.A.
Fort Lauderdale, FL
Miami, FL
Stroup, Janis I. .... Baltimore, MD
Stroup, John F. .... Lawrenceburg, IN
Stroup & Jones, L.L.P. .... Longview, TX
Stroup, Kenneth E., Jr. .... Morristown, NJ
Stroup, Kevin K. .... Marshall, MN
Stroup, Kim H. .... Macon, GA
Stroup, Marsha R. .... Denver, CO
Stroup, Nathaniel W. .... Petoskey, MI
Stroup, R. Keith .... Washington, DC
Stroup, Richard Lee .... Washington, DC
Stroup, Robert C. .... Fort Worth, TX
Stroup, Robert H. .... New York, NY
Stroup, Robert L., II .... Fargo, ND
Stroup, Robert L., III .... Fargo, ND
Stroup, Robert W. .... Fresno, CA
Stroup, Robin .... Schuylerville, NY
Stroup, Robin Fry .... White River, SD
Stroup, Roger K. .... Portland, OR
Stroup, Stanley S. .... Minneapolis, MN
Stroup, Stephen G. .... Philadelphia, PA
Stroup & Stroup .... Bedford, PA
Stroup, Thomas A. .... Washington, DC
Stroup, Walter M. .... Saratoga Springs, NY
Stroupe, John C., Jr. .... Hickory, NC
Stroupe, Joyce A. .... Baltimore, MD
Stroupe, Kerri J. .... Pensacola, FL
Stroupe, Odes L., Jr. .... Raleigh, NC
Stroupe, Ross .... Columbia, MO
Stroupe, Ross, P.C. .... Columbia, MO
Strouse, Benjamin S. .... New York, NY
Strouse, Daniel S. .... Tempe, AZ
Strouse, David James .... Los Angeles, CA
Strouse, Harry D. .... Chicago, IL
Strouse, Harry E. .... Ashland, PA

Strouse, Jeffrey B. ... Tampa, FL
Strouse, Jeffrey B., P.A. ... Tampa, FL
Strouse, Jonathan E. ... Chicago, IL
Strouse, Keith J. ... Ashland, PA
Strouse, Melvin J. ... Roanoke, VA
Strouse, Nancy J. ... Topeka, KS
Strouse, Richard L. ... Philadelphia, PA
Strouse, Richard S. ... Atlanta, GA
Strouse, Strouse & Snyder ... Ashland, PA
Strouss, Carleton O. ... Harrisburg, PA
Strouss, Cynthia M. ... Seattle, WA
Strouss, David C. ... Boston, MA
Strouss, Jill M. ... Harrisburg, PA
Strout, Arthur E. ... Rockland, ME
Strout, Cynthia L. ... Anchorage, AK
Strout, Dana F. ... Camden, ME
Strout, Dana F., P.C. ... Camden, ME
Strout, David ... Seattle, WA
Strout, Douglas M. ... Jacksonville, NC
Strout, Linda J. ... Seattle, WA
Strout, Monte W. ... Tahlequah, OK
Strout & Payson, P.A. ... Rockland, ME
Strouts, Scott J. ... Minneapolis, MN
Strovel, Marcus G. ... Baltimore, MD
Strowbridge, Patricia L. ... Orlando, FL
Strowd, Richard E.
Research Triangle Park, NC
Stroyd, Arthur H. ... Pittsburgh, PA
Strozdas, Jerome M. ... Springfield, OH
Strozier, Hardy M., III
Santa Barbara, CA
Strozyk-Ciervo, Helen ... Willingboro, NJ
Strozza, Nicholas ... Reno, NV
Strub, Michael H., Jr. ... Los Angeles, CA
Strubbe, John L. ... Cincinnati, OH
Strubbe, Joseph A. ... Chicago, IL
Strubbe, Mary Rose ... Chicago, IL
Strubbe, Thomas F. ... Chicago, IL
Strubbe, Thomas R. ... Olathe, KS
Strubbe, William B. ... Cincinnati, OH
Strubeck, Louis R., Jr. ... Dallas, TX
Struben, Christopher F. ... Kearny, NJ
Strubhar, Burton E. ... Pensacola, FL
Strubhar, Reta M. Chaney
Oklahoma City, OK
Strubhar, Richard D. ... Yukon, OK
Strubhar, Rustin J. ... Oklahoma City, OK
Strubin, Raymond G. ... Oakland, MD
Strubinger, Gerald F., Jr ... Palmerton, PA
Struble, Alan R. ... Dallas, TX
Struble, Charles A. ... Phoenix, AZ
Struble, Eric D. ... Gainesville, FL
Struble, George P. ... Riverdale, NJ
Struble, James D. ... Dallas, TX
Struble, Kenneth R. ... Battle Creek, MI
Struble, Michelle L. ... Buffalo, NY
Struble, R. Bryan, Jr. ... Atlanta, GA
Struble, Robert B. ... Toccoa, GA
Struble, Robert B. ... Oklahoma City, OK
Struble, Robert P. ... Pittsburgh, PA
Struble, Roger D. ... Salina, KS
Struble, Siri ... Battle Creek, MI
Struble, Wayne D. ... Minneapolis, MN
Struby, Carl W. ... Kansas City, MO
Struc, Vera Anne ... Incline Village, NV
Struck, Carolyn P. ... Modesto, CA
Struck, Daniel J. ... Chicago, IL
Struck, Daniel P. ... Phoenix, AZ
Struck, James D. ... Modesto, CA
Struck, Jeane ... San Francisco, CA
Struck, Jody ... Oakland, CA
Struck, Kenneth H. ... Cherry Hill, NJ
Struck, MaryAnn K. ... North Hollywood, CA
Struck, Patricia D. ... Madison, WI
Struckhoff, Eugene C., III ... Lebanon, NH
Struckmann, Donald K. ... Roseville, CA
Struckmann, J. Casey ... Front Royal, VA
Struckmann & White, P.C. ... Front Royal, VA
Struckmeyer and Wilson ... Phoenix, AZ
Strudell, Richard L. ... St. Louis, MO
Strudler, Conrad J. ... Fanwood, NJ
Strudler, Randi L. ... New York, NY
Strudwick, Lewis C. ... Baltimore, MD
Strueber, Thomas J. ... Atlanta, GA
Struebing, Steven R. ... Junction City, KS
Manhattan, KS
Strueh, Karen Ruse ... Bloomfield, IN
Linton, IN
Struell, Fabienne D. ... Los Angeles, CA
Strufe, Frederick E. ... Dwight, IL
Struffolino, Stephen C. ... Methuen, MA
Strug, Jeffrey N. ... Los Angeles, CA
Strug, Lowell A. ... New York, NY
Strug, Paul D. ... Houston, TX
Strugalski, Greg ... Cleveland, OH
Strugats, Robert ... Shelter Island, NY
Strugatz, Charles R. ... Jericho, NY
Strugatz, Donna L. ... New York, NY
Strugatz, Michael David ... Iselin, NJ
Short Hills, NJ
Struger, Marlene S. ... Cleveland, OH
Struhar, Melanie ... Chicago, IL
Struhl, Morton E. ... Alhambra, CA
Torrance, CA
Struhl, Morton E. ... Van Nuys, CA
Struhs, J. Pasco ... New York, NY
Struif, L. James ... Alton, IL
Struif Law Office, The ... Alton, IL
Struif, Scott ... Alton, IL
Struk, Randolph T. ... Pittsburgh, PA
Struke, Theodore O. ... Pittsburgh, PA
Strukelj, Mark S. ... Sugar Land, TX
Strull, James R. ... New York, NY
Strulowitz, Eric A. ... Roseland, NJ
Strulowitz, Herbert M. ... Randolph, NJ
Strulowitz, Michael J. ... Nutley, NJ
Strulowitz & Spear ... Randolph, NJ
Strulson, Richard D. ... Los Angeles, CA

Strum, Irving F. ... Linden, NJ
Strum, Irwin M. ... Brooklyn, NY
Strum, James C. ... Wilmington, DE
Strum, Jay G. ... New York, NY
Strum, Jessica ... Huntington Beach, CA
Strum, Jonathan M. ... Treasury Department,
Internal Revenue Service, GV
Strum, Michelle F. ... Woodbury, NY
Strum, Mollie ... New York, NY
Strum, Neal H. ... Baltimore, MD
Strum, Neil D. ... Studio City, CA
Strum, Stephen M. ... Belleville, IL
St. Louis, MO
Strumillo, Donald R. ... Burr Ridge, IL
Strumor, Arlene S. ... Santa Fe, NM
Strumor, Robert M. ... Albuquerque, NM
Santa Fe, NM
Strumpf, Burton D. ... New York, NY
Strumpf, Lance Steven ... Redondo Beach, CA
Strumpf, Linda ... New Canaan, CT
Strumpf, Susan Feinberg ... Northridge, CA
Strumpfler, Robert L.
North Massapequa, NY
Strumski, Joseph F., Jr. ... Raynham, MA
Yarmouth Port, MA
Strumwasser, David A. ... White Plains, NY
Strumwasser, Michael J. ... Santa Monica, CA
Strumwasser, Robert A. ... Randolph, MA
Strumwasser & Woocher ... Santa Monica, CA
Strunck, Thomas F. ... Washington, DC
Strunin, Robert J. ... Miami, FL
Strunk, AlbertL. ... Warren, NJ
Strunk, Bonnie ... Syracuse, NY
Strunk, Christopher D. ... Philadelphia, PA
Plymouth Meeting, PA
Strunk, Debra P. ... Gilroy, CA
Strunk, Donald J. ... Pittsburgh, PA
Strunk, Geoffrey Mark ... Cherry Hill, NJ
Strunk, June O. ... Belvedere-Tiburon, CA
Strunk, Lucas D. ... Glastonbury, CT
Strunk, Mary A. ... Chicago, IL
Strunk, Nica B. ... Riverhead, NY
Strunk, Rebecca A. ... Florence, KY
Strunk, Rosemary ... Scottsdale, AZ
Strunk, Sarah A. ... Englewood, CO
Strunk, T. Russell, Jr. ... Fort Wayne, IN
Strunk, Tiffany S. ... Pascagoula, MS
Strunk, Tommy L. ... Indianapolis, IN
Strunk, Wayne E. ... Cleveland, OH
Strunsky, Cheryl B. ... Everett, MA
Strup, David P. ... Findlay, OH
Toledo, OH
Strupp, Cory N. ... New York, NY
Strupp, David J. ... New York, NY
Strupp, Robert J. ... Vienna, VA
Strupp, Werner ... Washington, DC
Struse, Robert M. ... Tucson, AZ
Strusinski & Associates ... St. Paul, MN
Strusinski, Donna L. ... St. Paul, MN
Struss, David H. ... New York, NY
Struss, Violet ... Minneapolis, MN
Strusz, Mary Jo ... Chicago, IL
Struthers, Alex, Jr. ... Los Angeles, CA
Struthers, Caroline J. ... Wilmington, NC
Struthers, David R. ... Denver, CO
Struthers, James A. ... Minneapolis, MN
Struthers, James F. ... Palo Alto, CA
Struthers, Margo S. ... Minneapolis, MN
Struthers, Melvin, Jr. ... Cedar Rapids, IA
Struthers, Richard E. ... Minneapolis, MN
Struthers, Terry John ... Boulder, CO
Struthers, William ... Livermore, CA
Strutin, Mitchell S. ... Philadelphia, PA
Strutt, Barry R. ... White Plains, NY
Strutt, Charles F. ... Des Moines, IA
Strutt, David S. ... Des Moines, IA
Strutt, Holly M. ... Stamford, CT
Strutz, William A. ... Bismarck, ND
Struve, Andrew H. ... Anaheim, CA
Struve, Donald William ... San Antonio, TX
Struve, Guy Miller ... New York, NY
Struve, John G. ... Pendleton, OR
Struve, Kevin B. ... Des Moines, IA
Struve, Larry D. ... Carson City, NV
Struve, Robin L. ... Chicago, IL
Struwin, Jack M. ... St. Joseph, MI
Struxness, Gregory E. ... Portland, OR
Struyk, Robert J. ... Minneapolis, MN
Struyk, William C. ... New York, NY
Struzzi, Peter H. ... Westport, CT
Struzzieri, Michele S. ... Treasury Department,
Office of Regulations and Rulings, GV
Strye, John A. ... Chicago, IL
Strye, Steven L. ... Milwaukee, WI
Stryjnik, Iowna ... New York, NY
Stryker, Amy L. ... Houston, TX
Stryker, Cathleen M. ... San Antonio, TX
Stryker, David A. ... Pennington, NJ
Stryker, David M. ... New York, NY
Stryker, Dennis J. ... San Diego, CA
Stryker, Duensing, Casner & Dollison
Christiansted, St. Croix, VI
Cruz Bay, St. John, VI
Charlotte Amalie, St. Thomas, VI
Stryker, Eric K. ... Las Vegas, NV
Stryker, Gary L. ... Oakland, CA
Stryker, Hird ... Omaha, NE
Stryker, John W., (P.C.)
Charlotte Amalie, St. Thomas, VI
Stryker, Joseph M. ... Carthage, NC
Stryker, Kevin A. ... Wheeling, WV
Stryker, Nina B. ... Philadelphia, PA
Stryker, Russell F. ... Augusta, ME
Stryker, Steven C. ... Houston, TX
Stryker, Susan ... Trenton, NJ
Stryker, Susan L. ... Omaha, NE
Stryker, Tams & Dill LLP ... Newark, NJ
New York, NY

Stryker, Wendy ... New York, NY
Stryker, William Flint ... Reno, NV
Strzalka, Eugene B. ... Shelby Township, MI
Strzalka, Philip R. ... Chicago, IL
Strzelecki, Stanley A., Jr. ... Palos Heights, IL
Strzesynski, Michelle A. ... Toledo, OH
Strzetelski, George T. ... Burlington, MA
Strzyinski, Kathy J. ... Toledo, OH
Strzyz, Karen M. ... Department of Commerce,
Patent and Trademark Office, GV
Stuaan, Mark D. ... Indianapolis, IN
Stuaan, Mark D. ... Indianapolis, IN
Stuard, John M. ... Warren, OH
Stuard, Rhett M. ... Indianapolis, IN
Stuardi, A. Edwin, III ... Mobile, AL
Stuart, Albert D. ... Marathon, FL
Stuart, Alexander F. ... San Jose, CA
Stuart, Alice M. ... New York, NY
Stuart, Anne ... Boston, MA
Stuart, Anthony C. ... Roseland, NJ
Stuart, Antony ... Los Angeles, CA
Stuart, B. Jordan ... Fort Lauderdale, FL
Stuart, Barbara G. ... Minneapolis, MN
Stuart, Beverly A. ... Pasadena, CA
Stuart, Biolchini, Turner & Givray
Tulsa, OK
Stuart & Branigin ... Indianapolis, IN
Stuart & Branigin ... Lafayette, IN
Stuart, Brian J. ... Sioux Falls, SD
Stuart & Broz ... Bowling Green, KY
Stuart, Bruce C. ... Newport Beach, CA
Stuart, Bruce H. ... Albany, NY
Stuart, Bruce S. ... San Jose, CA
Stuart, Carmon J. ... Greensboro, NC
Stuart, Carolyn Tobiason ... San Jose, CA
Stuart, Catherine R. ... Raleigh, NC
Stuart, Charles E. ... Parker, CO
Stuart, Charles F., Jr. ... McLean, VA
Stuart, Charles M., Jr. ... Greenville, SC
Stuart, Cheryl G. ... Tallahassee, FL
Stuart, Christopher J. ... Chicago, IL
Stuart, Claude LeRoy, III ... Houston, TX
Stuart, Clinton Ryan ... Baton Rouge, LA
Stuart & Clover ... Shawnee, OK
Stuart, Colbern C. ... San Diego, CA
Stuart, D. Scott ... Grand Rapids, MI
Stuart, Dale A., & Associates ... Waterford, MI
Stuart, Dan D. ... Colorado Springs, CO
Stuart, Dana Catheen ... Liberal, KS
Stuart, Daniel E. ... Overland Park, KS
Stuart, Daniel K., Law Offices of
Beverly Hills, CA
Stuart, David A. ... Alcester, SD
Stuart, David A. ... Clinton, TN
Stuart, David C. W. ... Versailles, KY
Stuart, David L. ... Charleston, WV
Stuart, David W. ... Los Angeles, CA
Stuart, Debra J. ... Miami, FL
Stuart, Diana I. ... Portland, OR
Stuart, Diana P. ... Plano, TX
Stuart, Don W. ... North Miami Beach, FL
Stuart, Donald B. ... Nashville, TN
Stuart, Donald D. ... Seattle, WA
Stuart, Donald L. ... Austin, TX
Stuart, Donald R. ... Indianapolis, IN
Stuart, Douglas A. ... King Of Prussia, PA
Stuart, Douglas G. ... Wagoner, OK
Stuart, Douglas L. ... Santa Monica, CA
Stuart, Douglas S. ... Albuquerque, NM
Stuart, Duncan A. ... Midland, MI
Stuart, E. Page ... Shepherdsville, KY
Stuart, Edward C. ... Elkhart, IN
Stuart, Elizabeth D. ... New York, NY
Stuart, Elizabeth G. ... Rockland, ME
Stuart, Enid Nagler ... New York, NY
Stuart, Eugene N., III ... San Francisco, CA
Stuart, Flora Templeton ... Bowling Green, KY
Stuart, Frederick A. ... Broadview, IL
Stuart, Frieda & Hammond, P.C.
Duncan, OK
Stuart, Garfield D. ... Columbia, SC
Stuart, Gary L. ... Phoenix, AZ
Stuart, George Rogers Clark ... Abingdon, VA
Stuart, Gerry & Schlimgen, LLP
Sioux Falls, SD
Stuart, Glen R. ... Philadelphia, PA
Stuart, Hardwick, Jr. ... Columbia, SC
Stuart, Harold C. ... Tulsa, OK
Stuart, Harold E. ... Stamford, CT
Stuart, Harvey ... New York, NY
Stuart, Henry L. ... Carlisle, PA
Stuart, Holly L. ... Sacramento, CA
Stuart, Jacqueline B. ... New York, NY
Stuart, James ... Upper Marlboro, MD
Stuart, James D. ... Los Angeles, CA
Stuart, James L. ... Raleigh, NC
Stuart, James L., Jr. ... Pittsburgh, PA
Stuart, James M. ... Bakersfield, CA
Stuart, James Michael ... Carlisle, AR
Stuart, James R. ... Aitkin, MN
Stuart, James R., III ... Washington, DC
Stuart, James T. ... Shawnee, OK
Stuart, James W. ... Troy, MI
Stuart, Janet M. ... Lakeland, FL
Stuart, Jennifer L. ... Wellesley, MA
Stuart, Joan B. ... Haverford, PA
Stuart, John B. ... Tulsa, OK
Stuart, John D. ... Atlanta, GA
Stuart, John H. ... Dallas, TX
Stuart, John M. ... Duncan, OK
Stuart, John W. ... Portland, OR
Stuart, Joseph S. ... Irvine, CA
Stuart, Joseph W. ... Arlington, VA
Stuart, Kenneth J. ... New York, NY
Stuart, Kenneth K. ... Englewood, CO
Stuart, Kim N. ... Phoenix, AZ
Stuart, Lane R. ... San Luis Obispo, CA
Stuart, Larry D. ... Pawhuska, OK

Stuart, Laurence E. ... Houston, TX
Stuart Law Firm, A Professional
Corporation ... Los Angeles, CA
Stuart Law Firm, PLLC ... Raleigh, NC
Stuart Law Offices, P.C. ... Marshall, MI
Stuart, Lawrence G. ... Niagara Falls, NY
Stuart, Lochlan T. ... St. Paul, MN
Stuart, Louis J. ... Pueblo, CO
Stuart, Louise J. ... Newport Beach, CA
Stuart, Marc F. ... Trenton, NJ
Stuart, Marcia L. ... Washington, DC
Stuart, Margaret Mary ... Eugene, OR
Stuart, Mark Andrew ... Niskayuna, NY
Stuart, Mark F. ... Marshall, MI
Stuart, Martha Phillips ... Washington, DC
Stuart, Martin A. ... Golden, CO
Stuart, Mary B. ... Santa Rosa, CA
Stuart, Mary Hurley ... Denver, CO
Stuart, Mary Morgan ... La Crescenta, CA
Stuart, Mary Zimick ... Granby, MA
Stuart, Maurice E. ... Waco, TX
Stuart, Mia Lidde ... Morristown, NJ
Stuart, Michael C. ... New York, NY
Stuart, Michael D. ... Houston, TX
Stuart, Nancy ... Richmond, CA
Stuart, Nancy D. ... Montgomery, AL
Stuart, Naomi L. ... Overland Park, KS
Stuart, Natalie Talmage ... Bowling Green, KY
Stuart, Pamela B. ... Washington, DC
Garden City, NY
Stuart, Peter F. ... Groton, CT
Stuart, R. Wallace
United States Information Agency,
Office of the General Counsel, GV
Stuart, Richard H. ... Montrose, VA
Stuart, Richard J. ... Long Island City, NY
Stuart, Richard P. ... Avon Lake, OH
Stuart, Rissa A. ... Hanford, CA
Stuart, Robert ... Washington, DC
Stuart, Robert A., Jr. ... Springfield, IL
Stuart, Robert D., Jr. ... Lake Forest, IL
Stuart, Robert L. ... Kansas City, KS
Dallas, TX
Stuart, Robert R. ... Wichita Falls, TX
Stuart, Robin R. ... Houston, TX
Stuart, Roger E. ... New York, NY
Stuart, Rose Driver ... Prosperity, SC
Stuart, Ross T. ... Knoxville, TN
Stuart, Rupert A. ... Fayetteville, AR
Stuart, Sarah Eaton ... New York, NY
Stuart, Scot D. ... Okanogan, WA
Stuart, Scott Y. ... Uniondale, NY
Stuart, Sharon D. ... Sacramento, CA
Stuart, Sharon Donaldson
Birmingham, AL
Stuart, Stephen A. ... Sacramento, CA
Stuart, Stephen K. ... Tampa, FL
Stuart, Steven J. Duca ... Larkspur, CA
Stuart & Strickland, P.A. ... Tampa, FL
Stuart, Susan D. ... Smithtown, NY
Stuart, Susan S. ... Marietta, GA
Stuart, Tinley, Peters, Thorn, Hughes, Faust & Madsen ... Council Bluffs, IA
Omaha, NE
Stuart, Tod L. ... Phoenix, AZ
Stuart & Van Riper ... Clinton, TN
Stuart, Vernon ... Albany, NY
Stuart & Walker, P.A.
Fort Lauderdale, FL
Stuart, Walter B., IV ... Houston, TX
Stuart, William C. ... Des Moines, IA
Stuart, William H., III ... Chico, CA
Stuart, William R., III ... Newark, NJ
Stuart, William T. ... Milwaukee, WI
Stuart, William W. ... Chicago, IL
Stub, Jacob A. O., III ... Berkeley, CA
Stubbee, Kirk A. ... Chicago, IL
Stubbeman, David G. ... Abilene, TX
Stubbeman, McRae, Sealy, Laughlin & Browder, Inc. ... Midland, TX
Odessa, TX
Stubbeman, Robert F. ... Bandera, TX
Stubberud, Laura E. Wunsch
Las Vegas, NV
Las Vegas, NV
Stubbins, Brent A. ... Zanesville, OH
Stubbins, James B. ... Zanesville, OH
Stubbins, Mark W. ... Zanesville, OH
Stubblebine, Kevin J. ... Pittsburgh, PA
Stubblebine, Scott D. ... Sandusky, OH
Stubblefield, Andrea S. ... Independence, MO
Stubblefield, Carol B. ... New York, NY
Stubblefield, Carol D. ... Chicago, IL
Stubblefield, D. Lyman ... Amarillo, TX
Stubblefield, David S. ... Dallas, TX
Stubblefield, Dennis A. ... Los Angeles, CA
Stubblefield, J. Stephen ... Jackson, MS
Stubblefield, James W. ... San Diego, CA
Stubblefield, Jo Anne P. ... Atlanta, GA
Stubblefield, Julie H. ... Asheboro, NC
Stubblefield, Mallette & Harvey, P.A.
Jackson, MS
Stubblefield, Merry Peterson
Albuquerque, NM
Stubblefield, Michael E. ... Fort Smith, AR
Stubblefield, Michael E., P.A.
Fort Smith, AR
Stubblefield, Patricia L. ... Tulsa, OK
Stubblefield, Robert D. ... Woodland Hills, CA
Stubblefield, Robert J. ... Tulsa, OK
Stubblefield, Ronald J. ... Tulsa, OK
Stubblefield, Ross E. ... Blue Springs, MO
Stubbs, A. Thomas ... Atlanta, GA
Stubbs, A. Thomas ... Decatur, GA
Stubbs, Albert W. ... Columbus, GA
Stubbs, Alice Carson ... Raleigh, NC
Stubbs, Allston J. ... Durham, NC
Stubbs, Barry ... San Mateo, CA

Stubbs, Brian P. .... **San Mateo, CA**
Stubbs, Bruce L. .... Wichita, KS
Stubbs, Byron L. .... Salt Lake City, UT
Stubbs, C. David .... Anniston, AL
Stubbs, Carol D. .... Phoenix, AZ
Stubbs, Charles W. .... Oklahoma City, OK
Stubbs, Clifford K. .... **Lenexa, KS**
Stubbs, Cole, Breedlove, Prentis & Biggs
Durham, NC
Stubbs, Diane J. .... Department of Energy, Office of the General Counsel, GV
Stubbs, Donald G. .... Kansas City, MO
Stubbs, Donald H. .... **Columbia, SC**
Stubbs, Genevieve G. .... College Station, TX
Stubbs, George L., Jr. .... Shelbyville, IN
Stubbs, Gregory E. .... **Walnut Creek, CA**
Stubbs, H. Frank .... Tacoma, WA
Stubbs, H. Frank, Inc., P.S. .... Tacoma, WA
Stubbs, John R. .... Manhattan Beach, CA
Stubbs, Joseph E. .... **Washington, DC**
Stubbs, Kara Trouslot .... **Kansas City, MO**
Stubbs & Leone, A Professional Corporation
Walnut Creek, CA
Stubbs, Luisa Livia Belluomini
Birmingham, AL
Stubbs, M. Francis .... Reidsville, GA
Stubbs, Matthew E. .... **Cincinnati, OH**
Stubbs & Meltzer .... Shelbyville, IN
Stubbs, Michael D. .... Joliet, IL
Stubbs & Perdue, P.A. .... **New Bern, NC**
Raleigh, NC
Stubbs, Peter J. .... Sacramento, CA
Stubbs, Ralph E. .... Long Branch, NJ
Stubbs, Richard A. .... Denver, CO
Stubbs, Richard L. .... **Boise, ID**
Stubbs, Richard U., Jr. .... **Springfield, MA**
Worcester, MA
Stubbs, Robert C. .... Tucson, AZ
Stubbs, Robert D. .... Smithfield, NC
Stubbs, Robert S., II .... Canton, GA
Stubbs, Robert S., III .... **Cumming, GA**
Stubbs, S. Markey .... **Columbia, SC**
Stubbs, Sally E. .... Houston, TX
Stubbs, Samuel E. .... **Houston, TX**
Stubbs & Schubart, P.C. .... Tucson, AZ
Stubbs, Sidney A. .... **West Palm Beach, FL**
Stubbs & Stubbs .... **San Mateo, CA**
Stubbs, Thomas H., Jr. .... Hamilton, OH
Stubbs, Todd A. .... Great Falls, MT
Stubbs, Trawick H., Jr. .... **New Bern, NC**
Raleigh, NC
Stubbs, Tyra H. .... **Boise, ID**
Stubbs, V. Joseph .... **Los Angeles, CA**
Stubbs, W. Terrell .... Mendenhall, MS
Stubbs, Walter H. .... Gallatin, TN
Stubbs, William, Firm .... **Lafayette, LA**
Stubbs, William P., Jr. .... **Lafayette, LA**
Stubenberg & Durrett .... **Honolulu, HI**
Stubenberg, James A. .... **Honolulu, HI**
Stubenberg, Melissa K. .... **Wilmington, DE**
Stubenvoll, Eric D. .... **Chicago, IL**
Stuber, Charles W. .... **Dallas, TX**
Stuber, Charles W., Jr. .... Falls Church, VA
Stuber, Holly Nylander .... St. Louis, MO
Stuber, James A. .... West Palm Beach, FL
Stuber, James R. .... Chicago, IL
Stuber, John D. .... Columbus, OH
Stuber, John P. .... La Crosse, WI
Stuber, Larry W. .... **Corvallis, OR**
Stuber, Martin D. .... Denver, CO
Stuber, Paul Drew .... Boulder, CO
Stuber, Thomas K. .... Baltimore, MD
Stubington, Julie K. .... **Los Angeles, CA**
Stubington, Mark J. .... **Burbank, CA**
Stubins, J. David .... **Atlanta, GA**
Stubits, William C. .... **Moorestown, NJ**
Philadelphia, PA
Stublarec, Stephen .... **San Francisco, CA**
Stubler, Mark K. .... Jefferson City, MO
Stubley, M. Stephen .... Charleston, SC
Stubley, Mark M. .... **Greenville, SC**
Stubner, James W., Jr. .... **Seattle, WA**
Stubson, Susan Chapin .... **Casper, WY**
Stubson, Timothy M. .... **Casper, WY**
Stubstad, David J. .... **Omaha, NE**
Stuchel, Beth E. .... **Hoffman Estates, IL**
Stuchin, Miles M. .... New York, NY
Stuchiner, A. Martin .... New York, NY
Stuchiner, Jerry Wolf .... Calexico, CA
Stuchiner, Milton M. .... Brooklyn, NY
Stuchiner, Steven M. .... New York, NY
Stuchiner, Theresa B. .... Fort Lee, NJ
Stuck, Gregory A. .... Northumberland, PA
Sunbury, PA
Stuck, Haven L. .... **Rapid City, SD**
Stuck, T. Lynn .... Lockhart, TX
Stuckal, Elizabeth .... Fairfield, CT
Stuckel, David W. .... Peoria, IL
Stuckenschmidt, Dean L. .... Fresno, CA
Stuckenschneider, Ted .... Birmingham, AL
Stuckenschneider, Ted, P.C.
Birmingham, AL
Stucker, Bruce A. .... **Orlando, FL**
Stucker, Michael W. .... **Garland, TX**
Stucker, Robert E. .... Miami, FL
Stucker, Robert J. .... **Chicago, IL**
Stucker, Susan V. .... **Altamonte Springs, FL**
Stuckert, Robbin J. .... Sycamore, IL
Stuckert and Yates .... **Newtown, PA**
Stuckey, Aaron K. .... **Portland, OR**
Stuckey, Brent .... **Vincennes, IN**
Stuckey, David W. .... **Toledo, OH**
Stuckey, Donald J. .... **Auburn, IN**
Stuckey, E. Stephanie .... Athens, GA
Stuckey, Fata & Segars .... Bishopville, SC
Stuckey, Felix .... Oakland, CA
Stuckey, James A. .... **New Orleans, LA**
Stuckey, James A. .... **Charleston, SC**

Stuckey, James G., III .... Marietta, GA
Stuckey, James M. .... Stuart, FL
Stuckey, Jason Ashton .... **Birmingham, AL**
Stuckey, Jay C., Jr. .... Phoenix, AZ
Stuckey, Jeffery V. .... **Lansing, MI**
Stuckey, Jim O., II .... Columbia, SC
Stuckey, John M. .... **Lafayette, IN**
Stuckey, John M., Jr. .... **Atlanta, GA**
Stuckey, Karen M. .... **San Diego, CA**
Stuckey, Katherine P. .... Greenwood, MS
Stuckey, Kent D. .... Columbus, OH
Stuckey, Kurt A. .... Wauseon, OH
Stuckey Law Offices, LLC
Charleston, SC
Stuckey, Lisa F. .... **Atlanta, GA**
Stuckey, Mark A. .... **Sandusky, OH**
Stuckey, Mark L. .... **Atlanta, GA**
Stuckey & McRae .... Phoenix, AZ
Stuckey, Michael K. .... St. Petersburg, FL
Stuckey & Price .... Oakland, CA
Stuckey, Richard N. .... **Denver, CO**
Stuckey, Richard N., P.C. .... **Denver, CO**
Stuckey, Shannon Smith .... **Columbia, SC**
Stuckey and Stuckey .... Greenwood, MS
Stuckey, Ward B. .... Platte City, MO
Stuckey, W. S., Jr. .... Greenwood, MS
Stucki & Associates, A Prof. Limited Liability Company .... **Dallas, TX**
Irving, TX
Stucki, David E. .... Canton, OH
Stucki, Hans U. .... Chicago, IL
Stucki, Jay R. .... **Irving, TX**
Stucki, Marvin R. .... Idaho Falls, ID
Stucki, Paul D. .... Laguna Hills, CA
Stuckler, Patti .... **New York, NY**
Stuckmeyer, Lester C., Jr. .... Fayetteville, AR
Stucko, James K. .... **Chicago, IL**
Stucko, James K., Jr. .... **Columbus, OH**
Stuckwisch, William J. .... **Washington, DC**
Stucky, Alan .... **Waco, TX**
Stucky, Dale M. .... **Wichita, KS**
Stucky, Gregory J. .... **Wichita, KS**
Stucky, Jean S. .... Department of Energy, Office of the General Counsel, GV
Stucky, Natalie J. .... **Indianapolis, IN**
Stucky, Nicholas G. .... Sacramento, CA
Stucky, Scott W. .... United States Senate, Committee Legal Personnel, GV
Stucky, Thomas L. .... Fort Wayne, IN
Stucky, Timothy E. .... Fort Wayne, IN
Stuczynski, David J. .... Seattle, WA
Stuczynski, James J. .... **Erie, PA**
Studach, Guy A. .... Springfield, IL
Studarus, John Eldon .... Sacramento, CA
Studdard, Don .... **El Paso, TX**
Studdard, Gregory N. .... Atlanta, GA
Studdard, John D. .... Friendswood, TX
Studdard, Joseph N. .... **Columbus, MS**
Studdard & Melby, A Professional Corporation .... **El Paso, TX**
Van Horn, TX
Studdert-Kennedy, Theodore J.
Waitsfield, VT
Studebaker, Donald R. .... **McLean, VA**
Studebaker, Jack F., A Professional Corporation
San Diego, CA
Studebaker, Jennifer M. .... Jackson, MS
Studebaker, John T. .... Sacramento, CA
Studebaker, Johnna L. .... Santa Fe, NM
Studebaker, Kent E. .... Gladstone, OR
Studebaker, Lauren D. .... Issaquah, WA
Studemeyer, J. Gregory .... Columbia, SC
Studen, Greg E. .... Mentor, OH
Studen, Laura R. .... Wellesley, MA
Studenberg, Philip W. .... Klamath Falls, OR
Studenmund, John D. .... **Columbus, OH**
Studenny, J. Richard .... **Tulsa, OK**
Studenny, J. Richard, P.C. .... **Tulsa, OK**
Studensky, James E. .... Waco, TX
Student, Marjorie M. .... Naples, FL
Student, Michael J. .... **New York, NY**
Studeny, John Michael .... **Pittsburgh, PA**
Studer, Donald E. .... Monroe, LA
Studer, Elizabeth W. .... Norcross, GA
Studer, Eugene A. .... Seattle, WA
Studer, Jacqueline L. .... **Boulder, CO**
Studer, James, Law Offices of
Simi Valley, CA
Studer, Jerome C., Jr. .... **Chicago, IL**
Studer, John A. .... Sopchoppy, FL
Studer, Judith A. W. .... **Casper, WY**
Studer, Larry P. .... Orlando, FL
Studer, Martin R. .... Bozeman, MT
Studer, Raymond J. .... Columbus, OH
Studer, Stanley S. .... San Antonio, TX
Studer, Stephen A. .... **Mishawaka, IN**
Studer, Stephen W. .... **Milford, CT**
Studer, William P. .... **Minneapolis, MN**
Studholme & Cooke .... Boulder, CO
Studholme, John A. .... Boulder, CO
Studin, Robert A. .... Birmingham, AL
Studinski, Jason T. .... Madison, WI
Studley, Andrea L. .... **Boston, MA**
Studley, David W. .... **San Francisco, CA**
Studley, Donald C. .... Cleveland, GA
Studley, Janet R. .... **Washington, DC**
Studley, John E. .... Middleboro, MA
Studley, John H. .... Hingham, MA
Studley, Michael H. .... **Boston, MA**
Studley, Mitchell J. .... Brooklyn, NY
Studlien, Susan E. T. .... Boston, MA
Studly, Paul A. .... Cleveland, OH
Studner, Jon M. .... Upper Marlboro, MD
Studnicha, Cynthia H. .... Youngstown, OH
Studnicka, James R. .... **Chicago, IL**
Studnicki, Adam A. .... **Phoenix, AZ**
Studnicky, Lawrence J., III
New York, NY

Studstill, Daniel L. .... Nashville, GA
Studstill, Kenneth A. .... **Titusville, FL**
Studstill, Kenneth A., P.A. .... **Titusville, FL**
Studstrup, S. Kirk .... Augusta, ME
Studt, Donald A. .... Birmingham, MI
Studt, Robert R. .... **Madison, WI**
Studtmann, Earl I. .... Portage, IN
Studwell, James R. .... **Tucson, AZ**
Studwell, Spencer L. .... New York, NY
Studwell, Thomas W. .... **New York, NY**
Studybaker, Steven L. .... Fort Myers, FL
Studzinski, Christine S. .... Philadelphia, PA
Studzinski, Edward A. .... Dolton, IL
Studzinski, Edward P. .... Chicago, IL
Studzinski, William, Jr. .... **Boston, MA**
Stueben, Christian P. .... Fort Lee, NJ
Stueber, Frederick G. .... Cleveland, OH
Stueber, Jennifer L. .... **Cleveland, OH**
Stueber, Thomas J. .... **Minneapolis, MN**
Stuebing, Bradley F. .... Houston, TX
Stuebing, John D. .... **Boston, MA**
Stueckemann, Cathy S. .... Orange Park, FL
Stueckemann, Walter F. .... Jetmore, KS
Stuedeman, Amy Lynn .... **Birmingham, AL**
Stuehringer, James W. .... **Tucson, AZ**
Stuehrk, Christine M.
Whitehouse Station, NJ
Stuehrmann, Raymond L.
Thousand Oaks, CA
Stuehrmann, Raymond L. .... **Ventura, CA**
Westlake Village, CA
Stuelpnagel, John B. .... Denver, CO
Stuemke, Jay E. .... **Dallas, TX**
Stuen, Thomas E. .... **Bellingham, WA**
Stuenkel, Mark E. .... **Southfield, MI**
Stuenzi, Daniel Paul .... Woodstock, IL
Stuenzi, Daniel, P.C. .... Woodstock, IL
Stuermer, Michael P. .... **Buffalo, NY**
Stueve, Patrick J. .... **Kansas City, MO**
Stuever, Fred Ray .... Miami, FL
Stuff, Ronald R. .... **Charlotte, NC**
Stufflebeam, Dwain H. .... Blackfoot, ID
Stufflebeam, Scott .... Blackfoot, ID
Stufft, David F. .... Kalispell, MT
Stufko, Stephen W., Jr. .... Wayne, NJ
Stugelmeyer, Brenda J. .... **Milwaukee, WI**
Stuhan, Richard G. .... **Cleveland, OH**
Stuhl, Dari B. .... Ann Arbor, MI
Stuhl, George Z. .... Fayetteville, NC
Stuhl, Joseph M. .... **Dallas, TX**
Stuhl, Seth A. .... **New York, NY**
Stuhlbarg, Richard L. .... **Torrance, CA**
Stuhlbarg, Steven F. .... **Cincinnati, OH**
Stuhldreher, Augustus F. .... Akron, OH
Stuhldreher, Elizabeth A. .... Atlanta, GA
Stuhldreher, George W. .... **Cleveland, OH**
Stuhldreher, John M. .... Arlington, VA
Stuhldreher, Justin M. .... Houston, TX
Stuhler & Borchers, L.L.P.
St. Charles, MO
Stuhler, Eric O. .... **St. Charles, MO**
Stuhler, Gregory E. .... Norcross, GA
Stuhley, Jon R. .... Newport Beach, CA
Stuhlsatz, Douglas Charles .... Wichita, KS
Stuhltrager, Gary W. .... Deptford, NJ
Stuhr, Charles .... **San Francisco, CA**
Stuhr, Cortvl, Miller & Ashley
San Francisco, CA
Stuhr & Drell .... Joliet, IL
Stuhr, Fredk. .... Asheville, NC
Stuhr, George M. .... Joliet, IL
Stuhr, Richard W. .... Columbus, OH
Stuhr, Sarah H. .... **Oklahoma City, OK**
Stukane, Thomas J. .... **Kenilworth, NJ**
Stukel, John D. .... San Francisco, CA
Stukel, Virginia S. .... Boise, ID
Stukenberg, Michael W.
Corpus Christi, TX
Stukenborg, Charlene L.H. .... **Dayton, OH**
Stukes, Thomas S. .... **Greensboro, NC**
Stukey, Linda S., & Associates
Dayton, OH
Stula, Ken .... Athens, GA
Stulac, Francine M. .... **Milwaukee, WI**
Stulb, Joseph G., Jr. .... Schertz, TX
Stulbach, Marlene .... **New York, NY**
Stulberg, Barry A. .... **Redmond, WA**
Stulberg, Dorothy B. .... Oak Ridge, TN
Stulberg, Edward Barry .... Farmington, MI
Stulberg, Elaine Grand
Farmington Hills, MI
Stulberg, Jeffrey D. .... Atascadero, CA
Stulberg, Leslie A. .... Chicago, IL
Stulberg, Robert .... **Los Angeles, CA**
Stulberg, Robert B. .... **New York, NY**
Stulce, Arnold A., Jr. .... **Chattanooga, TN**
Stulce & Yantis .... **Chattanooga, TN**
Stulgies-Clauss, Andrea .... **Chicago, IL**
Stulgin, Paul R. .... Tucson, AZ
Stuligross, Joseph P. .... **Pittsburgh, PA**
Stull, Cathy A. .... Lansing, MI
Stull, Christopher J. .... Wheaton, IL
Stull, Corey L. .... **Lincoln, NE**
Stull, Gordon B. .... Pratt, KS
Stull, Jeanette .... **Lincoln, NE**
Stull, John M. .... **Wilmington, DE**
Stull, Malcolm H. .... Patchogue, NY
Stull, Malcolm H., P.C. .... Patchogue, NY
Stull, Melissa K. .... Rochester, NY
Stull, R. Jeffrey .... Tampa, FL
Stull, Tracy L. .... Miamisburg, OH
Stull, William M. .... Sacramento, CA
Stuller, Erwin L. .... Los Angeles, CA
Stuller, Sandra M. .... Aspen, CO
Stuller, Virginia M. .... New Berlin, WI
Stuller, W. Stuart .... **Boulder, CO**
Stulmaker, Mark L. .... **Buffalo, NY**
Stulman, Martha .... **Los Angeles, CA**

Stulting, Janet S. .... **Hartford, CT**
Stults & Balber, P.C. .... **New York, NY**
Stults, Fred M., Jr. .... **Gary, IN**
Stults, Frederick M., III .... **Gary, IN**
Stults, Harold L., Jr. .... **New York, NY**
Stults, Robert M. .... Roseburg, OR
Stults, Rosalyn .... Salem, MA
Stults & Stults .... **Gary, IN**
Stultz, Billie Ann
Department of Transportation, Federal Railroad Administration, GV
Stultz, Cheryl A. .... **Washington, DC**
Stultz, Elliot A. .... **New York, NY**
Stultz, J. Hoyte, III .... Eden, NC
Stultz, J. Hoyte, Jr. .... Eden, NC
Stultz, Jennifer L. .... **Wichita, KS**
Stultz, Michael L. .... Norfolk, VA
Stultz, Norman F. .... Plymouth, MA
Stultz, Paul R. .... Omaha, NE
Stultz, Ralph W. .... LaGrangeville, NY
Stultz, Robert L. .... Weston, WV
Stum, Douglas M. .... **Austin, TX**
Stumacher, Mark D. .... Staten Island, NY
Stuman, Gregory J. .... San Diego, CA
Stumbaugh, Paul D. .... Mangum, OK
Stumberg, H. K. .... St. Charles, MO
Stumberg, Nancy H. .... **Eagle Pass, TX**
San Antonio, TX
Stumberg, Robert K. .... Washington, DC
Stumbo, Barber & Moak, P.S.C.
Hazard, KY
Prestonsburg, KY
Stumbo, Gregory D. .... Hazard, KY
Prestonsburg, KY
Stumbo, Hanson & Hendricks .... Topeka, KS
Stumbo, Janet L. .... Prestonsburg, KY
Stumbo, John E. .... Topeka, KS
Stumbo, Walter G. .... Topeka, KS
Stumbos, David E. .... **Concord, CA**
Stumler, Rebecca J. .... Columbus, OH
Stumm, Richard L. .... **Atlanta, GA**
Stumme Law Office .... Denver, IA
Stumme, Lawrence A., Jr. .... Denver, IA
Stumo, Mary E. .... **Minneapolis, MN**
Stump, Barbara A. .... Lansing, MI
Stump, Barbara Orsburn .... York, PA
Stump, Christopher A. .... **Lancaster, PA**
Stump, Christopher Keith .... Ketchikan, AK
Stump, Crystal S. .... Charleston, WV
Stump, Daniel C. .... **Pompano Beach, FL**
Stump, Gary D. .... Des Moines, IA
Stump, Gary L. .... Orlando, FL
Stump, Harry H., II .... Pittsburgh, PA
Stump, Jeffrey W. .... **Atlanta, GA**
Stump, Joanne Roman .... Treasury Department, Office of Regulations and Rulings, GV
Stump, John C. .... **Charleston, WV**
Stump, John R. .... **Orlando, FL**
Stump, John R. .... Lansing, MI
Stump, John S. .... **McLean, VA**
Stump, Jonathan A. .... **Peoria, IL**
Stump, Joshua P. .... **Eugene, OR**
Stump, J. W. .... San Diego, CA
Stump, Kenneth A. .... **Cleveland, OH**
Stump, Kimberly M. .... Xenia, OH
Stump, Lisa O. .... **St. Louis, MO**
Stump, Mark A. .... **Oakland, CA**
Stump, Mark W. .... **Riverside, CA**
Stump, Michael J. .... **Bakersfield, CA**
Stump, Perry F., Jr. .... **La Porte, IN**
Stump, Randall C. .... Georgetown, TX
Stump, Randall L. .... **Dayton, OH**
Stump, Storey & Callahan, P.A.
Orlando, FL
Stump & Stump .... Ketchikan, AK
Stump, T. Douglas .... **Oklahoma City, OK**
Stump, Tom .... Nashville, TN
Stump, W. Clark .... Ketchikan, AK
Stumpe, Karen M. .... **Peoria, IL**
Stumpf, Alan E. .... Columbia, IL
Stumpf, Andrea E. .... **Bethesda, MD**
Stumpf, Bruce G. .... Albuquerque, NM
Stumpf Craddock Massey & Pulman, A Professional Corporation .... **Beaumont, TX**
Houston, TX
San Antonio, TX
Stumpf, David B. .... Bloomington, IL
Stumpf, Dugas, LeBlanc, Papale & Ripp
Donaldsonville, LA
Gretna, LA
Stumpf, Elizabeth S. .... **St. Louis, MO**
Stumpf, Felix F. .... Reno, NV
Stumpf, Frederick W. .... **Houston, TX**
Stumpf, Harry C. .... Gretna, LA
Stumpf, J. Eugene .... York, PA
Stumpf, James J. .... Omaha, NE
Stumpf, Joan A. .... **New York, NY**
Stumpf, Juliet P. .... Department of Justice, Civil Rights Division, GV
Stumpf, Kathryn J. .... Pitman, NJ
Stumpf, Larry A. .... **Miami, FL**
Stumpf, Marguerite N. .... Freeport, NY
Stumpf, Mark H. .... **Washington, DC**
Stumpf, Maura C., Attorney at Law
Arlington, MA
Stumpf, Richard H. .... New York, NY
Stumpf, Robert J., Jr. .... **San Francisco, CA**
Stumpf, Samuel E., Jr. .... **Nashville, TN**
Stumpf, Thomas J. .... **Georgetown, DE**
Stumpf, Vickers & Sandy, P.A.
Fenwick Island, DE
Georgetown, DE
Rehoboth Beach, DE
Seaford, DE
Stumpf, Walter L., Jr. .... **Houston, TX**
Stumpff, Andrew W. .... **New York, NY**
Stumpff & Guggenmos .... Broken Bow, NE
Stumpff, Steven O. .... Broken Bow, NE

Stumpff, Timothy E. .... Washington, DC
Stumphauzer, Kenneth S. .... Amherst, OH
Stumpp & Bond, LLP .... New York, NY
Stumpp, Edward A. .... Glendale, CA
Stumpp, Gary D. .... New York, NY
Stumreiter, Harold R. .... Madison, WI
Stumreiter, John J. .... Los Angeles, CA
Stundtner, Elizabeth A. .... Rochester, NY
Stunich, Andrew J. .... Eureka, CA
Stunson, Jeffrey F. .... Elizabethtown, IL
Stuntebeck, Clinton A. .... Philadelphia, PA
Stuntz, Jean A. .... Denton, TX
Stuntz, Linda Gillespie .... Washington, DC
Stunz, Fonda, Nichols, Kiyuna, Horton & Flinders, LLP .... Nyssa, OR
Ontario, OR
Stunz, Gene .... Nyssa, OR
Stup, Carolyn K. .... Washington, DC
Stup, Robert E., Jr. .... Washington, DC
Stupak, Bart T. .... Menominee, MI
Stupak & Bergman, P.C. .... Escanaba, MI
Menominee, MI
Stupak, David M. .... Battle Creek, MI
Stupak, Frank A., Jr. .... Escanaba, MI
Menominee, MI
Stupar, Branko .... Washington, DC
Stupar, James R. .... Monterey, CA
Stupar, Michael P. .... Milwaukee, WI
Stupar, Schuster & Cooper, S.C.
Milwaukee, WI
Stuparich, John N. .... Tampa, FL
Stuparich, Nancy Ann M. .... Pensacola, FL
Stupel, Eric .... Miami Beach, FL
Stupica, Terri L. .... Mayfield Heights, OH
Stupka, Renee A. .... Defiance, OH
Stuppi, Craig .... Los Angeles, CA
Stuppi, Sarah M. .... Los Angeles, CA
Stuppi, Stuart Craig .... San Francisco, CA
Stupsker, Charles A. .... Toledo, OH
Stupski, Betsy L. .... Tallahassee, FL
Stupski, Q. Tod .... Tallahassee, FL
Sturbaum, Karl R. .... Indianapolis, IN
Sturc, John H. .... Washington, DC
Sturchio, Rebecca G. .... North Wales, PA
Sturcken, Charles G. .... New York, NY
Sturcken, Kyle R. .... New York, NY
Sturdevant, Calvin E. .... Baltimore, MD
Sturdevant, Charles F., Jr. .... San Diego, CA
Sturdevant, Dan C. D. .... Kansas City, MO
Sturdevant, Howard T. .... Prairie Village, KS
Sturdevant, James A. .... Bellingham, WA
Sturdevant, James C. .... San Francisco, CA
Sturdevant Law Firm, The, A Professional Corporation .... San Francisco, CA
Sturdevant, Michael G. .... Minot, ND
Sturdevant, Patricia .... San Francisco, CA
Sturdevant, Sonia M. .... Duluth, MN
Sturdivant, Deverita C.
Charlotte Amalie, St. Thomas, VI
Sturdivant, E. Jane .... Memphis, TN
Sturdivant, Harold A. .... Griffin, GA
Sturdivant, J. Walker .... Greenville, MS
Sturdivant, James M. .... Tulsa, OK
Sturdivant, James R. .... Birmingham, AL
Sturdivant, Jocelyn M. .... Washington, DC
Sturdivant, Mark L. .... Reno, NV
Sturdivant, Wayne P. .... Amarillo, TX
Sturdy, Charles H. .... Boston, MA
Sturdy, Raymond O., Jr. .... Detroit, MI
Sturdy, Thomas C. .... Salt Lake City, UT
Sturek, Stephen E., Jr. .... Macon, GA
Sturge, Karl E. .... Miami, FL
Sturgell, Robert A. .... Washington, DC
Sturgeon, A. Holmes, III .... Woodville, MS
Sturgeon, A. Thomas, Jr. .... Louisville, KY
Sturgeon, Al, Law Offices of
Sioux City, IA
Sturgeon, Allyson K. .... Louisville, KY
Sturgeon, Alonzo H. .... Woodville, MS
Sturgeon, Ben L. .... Dallas, TX
Sturgeon & Boyd .... Ferriday, LA
Sturgeon, E. Allen .... Mission Viejo, CA
Sturgeon, Gregory W. .... Atlanta, GA
Sturgeon, James M., Jr. .... Charleston, WV
Sturgeon, Jim R. .... St. Charles, IL
Sturgeon, John .... Ferriday, LA
Sturgeon, John A. .... Los Angeles, CA
Sturgeon, Keller, Phillips, Gee & O'Leary, A Professional Corporation
San Francisco, CA
Sturgeon, Paul Richard .... Belleville, IL
Sturgeon, Peter J. .... Pittsfield, MA
Sturgeon, Ritchie J. .... Milwaukee, WI
Sturgeon, Robert C. .... Lawrence, KS
Sturgeon, Robert T. .... Los Angeles, CA
Sturgeon & Sturgeon .... Woodville, MS
Sturgeon, Suzanne .... Bloomington, IN
Sturgeon, Thomas E., III .... St. Louis, MO
Sturgeon, William B. .... San Francisco, CA
Sturgeon-Garcia, David
San Francisco, CA
Sturges, C. Boyd, III .... Louisburg, NC
Sturges, Clyde W. .... Glendale, CA
Sturges, Conrad B., Jr. .... Louisburg, NC
Sturges, David R. .... Glenwood Springs, CO
Sturges, David R., P.C.
Glenwood Springs, CO
Sturges, David W. .... New Ulm, MN
Sturges, Ernest W., Jr. .... Punta Gorda, FL
Sturges, Francis W. .... Charlotte, NC
Sturges, Houston & Johanson, P.C.
Albuquerque, NM
Sturges, Jennifer L. .... Laguna Beach, CA
Sturges, Joe A. .... Albuquerque, NM
Sturges Law Offices .... Le Mars, IA
Sturges, Leatha J. .... New York, NY
Sturges & Mathes .... Southbury, CT
Woodbury, CT
Sturges, Peter W. .... San Francisco, CA
Sturges, Philip .... San Francisco, CA
Sturges, Philip P. .... New York, NY
Sturges, Robert A. .... Aurora, OH
Sturges, Robert B. .... Miami, FL
Sturges, Robert S. .... San Jose, CA
Sturges, Scott F. .... Columbus, OH
Columbus, OH
Sturges, Sharon A. .... Anchorage, AK
Sturges, Sheldon Love .... Monroe, NC
Sturges, William H. .... Charlotte, NC
Sturges, William S. .... Le Mars, IA
Sturges, William W. .... Charlotte, NC
Sturgess, David E. .... Hartford, CT
Sturgess, Robert H. .... Jacksonville, FL
Sturgill, Ann D. .... Lexington, KY
Sturgill, Barkley J. .... Prestonsburg, KY
Sturgill, Barkley J., Jr. .... Prestonsburg, KY
Sturgill, Don S. .... Lexington, KY
Sturgill, Donna L. .... Sacramento, CA
Sturgill, Ellen Easom .... Prestonsburg, KY
Sturgill & Hunt .... Prestonsburg, KY
Sturgill, Jack R., Jr. .... Baltimore, MD
Sturgill, Jeffery A. .... Wise, VA
Sturgill & Kennedy .... Wise, VA
Sturgill, Russell I. .... Perrysburg, OH
Sturgill, Stephen J. .... Boise, ID
Sturgill, Thomas C. .... Lexington, KY
Sturgill, Timothy A. .... Frankfort, KY
Sturgill, Turner, Barker & Moloney, PLLC
Lexington, KY
Sturgill, William J., & Associates
Norton, VA
Sturgis, Ann C.McNutt .... Park City, UT
Sturgis, Carroll W., Jr. .... McAllen, TX
Sturgis, J. Graham, Jr. .... Charleston, SC
Sturgis, James K. .... West Palm Beach, FL
Sturgis, Kathy A. .... Fort Myers, FL
Sturgis, K.D. .... Raleigh, NC
Sturgis, Ness, Brunsell & Assaf, A Prof. Corp.
Emeryville, CA
Sturgis, Radford .... Fort Myers, FL
Sturgis, Sherree L. .... Camp Hill, PA
Sturgul, Paul A. .... Ironwood, MI
Ashland, WI
Sturgul, Paul A. .... Hurley, WI
Sturgul, Paul A. .... Minocqua, WI
Sturiale, Glory .... San Francisco, CA
Sturim, Allan .... Kew Gardens, NY
Sturim and Nizin .... Kew Gardens, NY
Sturing, Mark A. .... Detroit, MI
Farmington Hills, MI
Sturino, Denean K. .... Chicago, IL
Sturino, Michael J. .... Bellwood, IL
Sturkey, O. Lee .... McCormick, SC
Sturla, Jan C. .... Santa Ana, CA
Sturley, Michael F. .... Austin, TX
Sturm, Ann Black .... Frankfort, KY
Sturm, Arlen R. .... Kelso, WA
Sturm, Barry .... Chicago, IL
Sturm, C. Robert .... San Francisco, CA
Sturm, Charles A. .... Austin, TX
Sturm, Charles W. .... Brookfield, WI
Sturm, Daniel E. .... San Rafael, CA
Sturm, David C. .... New York, NY
Sturm, David G. .... Manchester, NH
Sturm, Edward W., IV .... Santa Ana, CA
Sturm, Glenn W. .... Atlanta, GA
Sturm, Gregory W. .... Vincennes, IN
Sturm, Howard S. .... Louisville, KY
Sturm, Igor .... Haddonfield, NJ
Sturm, Ira A. .... New York, NY
Sturm, Irving F. .... Clark, NJ
Sturm, James R. .... Madison, WI
Sturm, Jeffrey S. .... Merrillville, IN
Sturm, John F. .... Washington, DC
Sturm, Joy E. .... Washington, DC
Sturm, Kevin W. .... Spartanburg, SC
Sturm, L. Roland .... Columbia, MD
Sturm, Martin R. .... Detroit, MI
Sturm, Michael .... Wheeling, WV
Sturm, Michael L. .... Washington, DC
Sturm, Michael O. .... Des Moines, IA
Omaha, NE
Sturm, Nancy L. .... Milwaukee, WI
Sturm, Paletti & Wilson .... Louisville, KY
Sturm, Patrick R. .... San Mateo, CA
Sturm, Paul R. .... Fort Wayne, IN
Sturm, Paul W. .... New York, NY
Sturm, Raymond L. .... Austin, TX
Sturm, Rex L. .... Rockville, MD
Sturm, Sharon Louise .... Washington, DC
Sturm, Smith & Parmenter, Law Offices of
Vincennes, IN
Sturm & Sturm .... Frankfort, KY
Sturm, Susan P. .... Philadelphia, PA
Sturm, Teresa L. .... Idaho Falls, ID
Sturm, Timothy L. .... Orlando, FL
Sturm, Victor A. .... Pearland, TX
Sturm, Warren A. .... Minneapolis, MN
Sturm, William C. .... Milwaukee, WI
Sturm, William H., Jr. .... Myerstown, PA
Sturm, William P. .... Frankfort, KY
Sturman, Brian J., Jr. .... Alpharetta, GA
Sturman, David .... Encino, CA
Sturman, Deborah M. .... New York, NY
Sturman, Gloria J. .... Las Vegas, NV
Sturman, Herbert D. .... Los Angeles, CA
Sturman, Martin L., (A Professional Corporation) .... Los Angeles, CA
Sturman, Milton .... Irving, TX
Sturman, Randy Linda .... San Diego, CA
Sturman, Stephen G. .... Bronx, NY
Sturman, Susan M. .... Washington, DC
Sturman, William L., Jr. .... Stamford, CT
Sturmanis, John M. .... Champaign, IL
Sturmer, Debra Steel .... San Francisco, CA
Sturms, David A. .... Chicago, IL
Sturn, Gregory L. .... Warrington, PA
Sturner, Andrew S. .... New York, NY
Sturns, Louis E. .... Arlington, TX
Sturr, Geoffrey M.T. .... Phoenix, AZ
Sturrock, Deborah A. .... Los Angeles, CA
Sturrup, Robert M. .... Fort Lauderdale, FL
Sturrup, Robert M., P.A.
Fort Lauderdale, FL
Stursberg, C. Walter, Jr. .... New York, NY
Stursberg & Veith .... New York, NY
Sturtevant, Albert D. .... Washington, DC
Sturtevant, Brereton .... Alexandria, VA
Sturtevant, Charles L. .... Chicago, IL
Sturtevant, Craig M. .... Irving, TX
Sturtevant, Elwood R. .... Louisville, KY
Sturtevant, Jill M. .... Los Angeles, CA
Sturtevant, Kimberlee J. .... Burlington, VT
Sturtevant, Richard D. .... Tempe, AZ
Sturtevant, Richard H. .... Charlottesville, VA
Sturtevant, Thomas C., Jr. .... Augusta, ME
Sturtevant, Tracy (Uran)
Thousand Oaks, CA
Sturtevant, Wayne A. .... Noblesville, IN
Sturtz, Alec L. .... Saginaw, MI
Sturtz, Anne M. .... Columbus, OH
Sturtz, Barry A. .... Spring Valley, NY
Sturtz, Craig A. .... Columbus, OH
Sturtz, Cristin C. .... Columbus, OH
Sturtz, Donna Preston .... Baltimore, MD
Sturtz, Gregory S. .... Lakewood, CO
Sturtz, Laurence E. .... Columbus, OH
Sturtz, Matthew S. .... Baltimore, MD
Sturtz, Maxwell A. .... Roslyn Heights, NY
Sturtz, Philip R. .... Saginaw, MI
Sturtz, Robert D. .... Albert Lea, MN
Sturtz, Ronald M. .... Roseland, NJ
Sturtz & Sturtz, P.C. .... Saginaw, MI
Sturtz, William R. .... Albert Lea, MN
Sturwold, Dawn .... Bellingham, WA
Sturz, Janet M. .... Williston Park, NY
Sturz, Robert .... New York, NY
Sturzenegger, Kim K. .... Lincoln, NE
Sturzenegger, Lisa H. .... Los Angeles, CA
Stus, Erin Flannery .... Houston, TX
Stusek, Thomas J. .... Billings, MT
Red Lodge, MT
Stusiak, J. Michael .... Sacramento, CA
Stuska, Russell A. .... Golden, CO
Stusse, Michael B. .... West Yarmouth, MA
Stussy, Susan Agnes .... Kansas City, KS
Stutchfield, E. Martin .... Providence, RI
Stute, David J. .... Madison, WI
Stute, William F., Jr. .... Minneapolis, MN
Stutes, Keith A. .... Lafayette, LA
Stutes, Ronald D. .... Austin, TX
Stutes, Russell J., Jr. .... Lake Charles, LA
Stutesman, Paul, Law Office of
Kalamazoo, MI
Stuteville, Walter M. .... Kirkland, WA
Stuth, Harry P. .... Dallas, TX
Stuth, Harry P., Jr. .... Dallas, TX
Stutheit, Andrea B. .... Littleton, CO
Stutheit, Brian K. .... Denver, CO
Stutin, Cathy M. .... Fort Lauderdale, FL
Stutin, Corey R. .... Winter Springs, FL
Stutland, Gary .... Chicago, IL
Stutler, Bernard G. .... Knoxville, IL
Stutler, Larry E. .... Lamar, CO
Stutler, Timothy C. .... San Diego, CA
Stutman, Alan I. .... Brooklyn, NY
Stutman, David J. .... Philadelphia, PA
Stutman, Edward A. .... Department of Justice, Criminal Division, GV
Stutman, Jack .... Los Angeles, CA
Stutman, Joni D. .... Reston, VA
Stutman, Louis L. .... New York, NY
Stutman, Michael D. .... New York, NY
Stutman, Michael J. .... Philadelphia, PA
Stutman, Richard L. .... Philadelphia, PA
Stutman, Robert A. .... Cranbury, NJ
Robbinsville, NJ
Fort Washington, PA
Stutman, Robert A., P.C., Law Offices Of
Cranbury, NJ
Fort Washington, PA
Stutman, Robin M. .... Department of Justice, Civil Rights Division, GV
Stutman, Roni .... West Haven, CT
Stutman, Steven W. .... New York, NY
Stutman, Treister & Glatt, Professional Corporation .... Los Angeles, CA
Stutman, William J. .... New York, NY
Stuto, Peter F. .... Albany, NY
Stutsman, Bruce E. .... Jacksonville, FL
Stutsman, Cynthia Halse
Lake Oswego, OR
Stutsman, David B. .... Belleville, IL
Stutsman, David T. .... Elkhart, IN
Stutsman, Dennis Michael .... Morehead, KY
Stutsman, Judith A. .... Fresno, CA
Stutsman and Mulvaney .... Elkhart, IN
Goshen, IN
Mishawaka, IN
South Bend, IN
Valparaiso, IN
Warsaw, IN
Stutsman, Peter Joseph .... Lubbock, TX
Stutsman & Thames, P.A.
Jacksonville, FL
St. Augustine, FL
Stutt, John Barry .... Racine, WI
Stuttard, Gavin .... San Diego, CA
Stutte, Charles L. .... Fayetteville, AR
Stuttler, Elissa M. .... Franklin, PA
Stuttman, Joel .... New York, NY
Stuttman, Karen L. .... New York, NY
Stutts, Charles L. .... Tampa, FL
Stutts, Elizabeth Butterworth
Richmond, VA
Stutts, Eugene P. .... Birmingham, AL
Stutts, James H. .... Sweetwater, TN
Stutts, Joe Ross .... Houston, TX
Stutts, Phillip G. .... Birmingham, AL
Stutts, Shane T. .... High Point, NC
Stutts, William F., Jr. .... Austin, TX
Stutz, Barbara J. .... Toledo, OH
Stutz, Benjamin R. .... Lake Oswego, OR
Stutz, Daniel R. .... Beverly Hills, CA
Stutz, Eric F. .... Black River Falls, WI
Stutz, Gallagher, Artiano, Shinoff & Holtz, A Professional Corporation .... Imperial, CA
Irvine, CA
Los Angeles, CA
Orange, CA
San Diego, CA
Temecula, CA
Stutz, Joanne B. .... Lenexa, KS
Stutz, Jonah L. .... Birmingham, MI
Stutz, Lara R. .... Detroit, MI
Stutz & Lister .... Black River Falls, WI
Stutz, Lynn C. .... San Jose, CA
Stutz, Miller, & Urtz, LLC .... Denver, CO
Vail, CO
Stutz, Paul F. .... Toledo, OH
Stutz, R. Gregory .... Denver, CO
Vail, CO
Stutz, Robert B. .... Chicago, IL
Stutz, Sidney A. .... San Diego, CA
Stutz, Thomas B. .... Sherman Oaks, CA
Stutz, Thomas B., A Professional Corporation
Sherman Oaks, CA
Stutz, Thomas J. .... Dallas, TX
Stutz, Toba Beth .... Pound Ridge, NY
Stutzman, Andrew K. .... Philadelphia, PA
Stutzman & Bromberg, A Professional Corporation .... Dallas, TX
Stutzman, David E. .... New York, NY
Stutzman, Drew K. .... Savannah, GA
Stutzman, Kellie Lynn .... Detroit, MI
Stutzman, Mark E. .... El Cajon, CA
Stutzman, Morris .... Wooster, OH
Stutzman, Myron D. .... Dallas, TX
Stutzman, Sherri Lee .... Manhattan, KS
Stutzman, Stacey L. .... Libertyville, IL
Stutzman, Thomas Chase .... San Jose, CA
Stutzman, Thomas Chase, A Professional Corporation .... San Jose, CA
Stutzman, Weldon B. .... Boise, ID
Stuurmans, Jan .... Minneapolis, MN
Stuurmans, Jan, P.A. .... Minneapolis, MN
Stuursma, Ann M. .... Grand Rapids, MI
Stuver & George, P.C. .... Rifle, CO
Stuver, John Jeffrey .... Mexia, TX
Stuver, Thomas W. .... Rifle, CO
Stuyvesant & Benton .... Carlisle, IA
Stuyvesant, Robert L. .... Carlisle, IA
Stuzane, Michael B. .... Ventura, CA
Stuzin, Albert .... Garden City, NY
Stuzin, Charles B. .... Coral Gables, FL
Stuzin, Daniel M. .... Miami, FL
Stuzin, Laura A. .... Orlando, FL
Stuzin, Marcy G. .... New York, NY
Stuzin, Nancy S. .... New York, NY
Stuzin, Randolph A. .... New York, NY
Stuzin & Stuzin .... Garden City, NY
Stuzin, Theodore D. .... Garden City, NY
Stwora-Hail, Stephen G. .... Sacramento, CA
Styduhar, Robert J. .... Columbus, OH
Styer, Craig A. .... Exton, PA
Styer, David L. .... Milwaukee, WI
Styer, Paul A. .... Benicia, CA
Styer, Ryan D. .... North Canton, OH
Styers, Jeffrey Scott .... San Diego, CA
Styers, M. Gray, Jr. .... Raleigh, NC
Styers, Mitchell Glenn .... Raleigh, NC
Styers, Randall G. .... New York, NY
Styers, Robt. L. .... Winston-Salem, NC
Styka, Edward J. .... Villa Park, IL
Styka, Ronald J. .... Lansing, MI
Styka, Sandra K. .... Buffalo, NY
Stykes, Donna McCabe .... Island Park, NY
Style, Robert P. .... Bala Cynwyd, PA
Philadelphia, PA
Styler, Donald P. .... Milwaukee, WI
Styler, Kostich, LeBell, Dobroski & McGuire
Milwaukee, WI
Styles, Angela Barbee .... Washington, DC
Styles, David T. .... San Francisco, CA
Styles, Edward D. .... Milwaukee, WI
Styles, Jack B. .... Raleigh, NC
Styles, Kathleen M.
Department of Commerce, Office of the General Counsel, GV
Styles, Keith R. .... Washington, DC
Styles, Kenneth R. .... Walnut Creek, CA
Styles, Lisa Campagna .... Pittsburgh, PA
Styles, Mark .... Albuquerque, NM
Styles, Mark G. .... Mequon, WI
Styles, Michael J. .... Fort Lauderdale, FL
Styles, Paul L., Jr. .... Atlanta, GA
Styles, Paula J. .... Brooklyn, NY
Styles & Pumpian .... Milwaukee, WI
Styles, W. Brooks .... North Charleston, SC
Styles, W. M. .... Black Mountain, NC
Styles-Anderson, Sharon D.
Washington, DC
Styliades, George N. .... Cherry Hill, NJ
Styliades & Mamas .... Cherry Hill, NJ
Stylianou, Harry .... Englewood Cliffs, NJ
Stylianou, Katie .... Clifton, NJ
Stylianou, Katie, P.C. .... Clifton, NJ
Stylianou, Steve G. .... Dearborn, MI
Stylianou, Theresa .... New York, NY
Styn & Garland, A Professional Corporation
San Diego, CA

Sugarman, Carl M. .... Miami, FL
Sugarman, David B. .... Norman, OK
Sugarman, David W. .... Worcester, MA
Sugarman, Elizabeth .... Houston, TX
Sugarman, Gary S. .... Baldwin, NY
Sugarman, Irving C. .... San Francisco, CA
Sugarman, Irwin J. .... New York, NY
Sugarman, Jeal .... Hackensack, NJ
Sugarman, Jill .... West Orange, NJ
Sugarman, Julian J. .... Kenmore, NY
Sugarman, Kenneth D. .... New York, NY
Sugarman, Kenneth J. .... Austin, TX
Sugarman, Lawrence J. .... Boston, MA
Sugarman, Mark Jon .... New York, NY
Sugarman, Marvin H. .... New York, NY
Sugarman, Myron G. .... San Francisco, CA
Sugarman, Neil .... Boston, MA
Sugarman, Paul R. .... Boston, MA
Sugarman, Paul W. .... San Francisco, CA
Sugarman, Renan I. .... Chicago, IL
Sugarman, Richard L. .... Potomac, MD
Sugarman, Risa Sue .... Bronx, NY
Sugarman, Robert G. .... New York, NY
Sugarman, Robert J. .... Washington, DC
Doylestown, PA
Philadelphia, PA
Sugarman, Robert S. .... Chicago, IL
Sugarman, Roger P. .... Columbus, OH
Sugarman, Rogers, Barshak & Cohen, P.C.
Boston, MA
Sugarman, Ronald S. .... Beverly Hills, CA
Sugarman, Scott A. .... San Francisco, CA
Sugarman, Shari Lee .... Melville, NY
Sugarman, Stephen D. .... Berkeley, CA
Sugarman, Steven L., & Associates
Cherry Hill, NJ
Berwyn, PA
Sugarman, Steven R. .... Kenmore, NY
Sugarman, Stuart .... Portland, OR
Sugarman and Sugarman, P.C.
Boston, MA
Sugarman, Wallace, Manheim & Schoenwald
Auburn, NY
Buffalo, NY
Syracuse, NY
Sugarmann, Richard A. .... New Haven, CT
Sugarmann, Steven A .... New Haven, CT
Sugarmann and Sugarmann .... New Haven, CT
Sugarmon, R. B., Jr. .... Memphis, TN
Sugarmon, Tarik B. .... Memphis, TN
Sugars, Steven L. .... Pasadena, CA
Sugawara, Joyce, Ms. .... Los Angeles, CA
Sugayan, Catalina J. .... Chicago, IL
Sugayan, Norbert W., Jr. .... Seattle, WA
Sugden, Henry H., III .... Crystal Lake, IL
Sugden, John H. .... Ventura, CA
Sugden, Mariah L. .... Ely, NV
Sugden, Samuel M., (P.C.) .... New York, NY
Sugerman, David F. .... Portland, OR
Sugerman, David L. .... New York, NY
Sugerman, Donald F. .... Bloomfield Hills, MI
Sugerman, Irving B. .... Akron, OH
Sugerman, Jeremy .... San Francisco, CA
Sugerman, Leonard .... West Chester, PA
Sugerman, Martin A.
University Heights, OH
Sugg, Bryant L. .... Newport News, VA
Sugg, Edgar H., Jr. .... Memphis, TN
Sugg, Irvin D. .... South Boston, VA
Sugg, James R. .... New Bern, NC
Sugg, Kevin G. .... Exton, PA
Sugg, Randolph Palmer, (P.C.)
Raleigh, NC
Sugg, Reed W. .... Belleville, IL
St. Louis, MO
Sugg, Richard H., Jr. .... Englewood, CO
Sugg, Robert P., Sr. .... Jackson, MS
Suggett, Wayne R. .... Albuquerque, NM
Suggs, Alvin .... Houston, TX
Suggs, B. Scott .... Florence, SC
Suggs, David L. .... Newport Beach, CA
Minneapolis, MN
Suggs, Fred W., Jr. .... Birmingham, AL
Greenville, SC
Suggs, George O. .... St. Louis, MO
Suggs, James M., Jr. .... Irving, TX
Suggs & Kelly, Lawyers, P.A.
Columbia, SC
Florence, SC
Myrtle Beach, SC
Suggs, Ken .... Columbia, SC
Suggs, Michele S. .... Chicago, IL
New York, NY
Suggs, Neal M. .... Seattle, WA
Suggs, Robert E. .... Baltimore, MD
Suggs, Robert V. .... Greensboro, NC
Suggs, Robert V., P.A. .... Greensboro, NC
Suggs, Spradling & Associates, P.C.
Irving, TX
Sughroue, Patrick R. .... Grand Rapids, MI
Sughroue, Patrick R., P.C.
Grand Rapids, MI
Sughrua Law Firm .... Seattle, WA
Sughrua, Thomas P. .... Seattle, WA
Sughrue, Dennis M. .... New York, NY
Sughrue, John .... Clearfield, PA
Sughrue, Mion, Zinn, Macpeak & Seas, PLLC .... Menlo Park, CA
Washington, DC
Sughrue, O. Stevens, Jr. .... Boston, MA
Sughrue, Richard C., (P.C.)
Washington, DC
Sugierski, Chester S., Jr. .... Lansing, MI
Sugihara, Glenn P. .... San Jose, CA
Sugimoto, Douglas K. .... Los Angeles, CA
Sugimoto, Gregory C. .... Honolulu, HI
Sugimura, Audrey M. .... Washington, DC
Sugimura, Yuriko J. .... Honolulu, HI

Sugin, Linda .... New York, NY
Sugino, Mark M. .... New York, NY
Sugino, Philip M. .... Torrance, CA
Sugisaka, Keiko L. .... Minneapolis, MN
Sugita, Erin N. .... Honolulu, HI
Sugita, Kenneth Y., (Atty. At Law, A Law Corp.) .... Honolulu, HI
Sugiyama, Dylan .... New York, NY
Sugiyama, George Y. .... Washington, DC
Sugiyama, Jennifer Paul .... Berkeley, CA
Sugiyama, John H. .... San Francisco, CA
Suglia, Peter D. .... New York, NY
Suglia, Robert P. .... Providence, RI
Suglia, William F. .... Miller Place, NY
Suglis, Michael T. .... Carson City, NV
Sugnet, William E. .... Syracuse, NY
Sugrue, Daniel .... Forest Hills, NY
Sugrue, Diane E. .... East Hanover, NJ
Sugrue, Marcia C. .... Philadelphia, PA
Sugrue, Mary J. .... Bloomfield, NJ
Sugrue, Stephen R. .... New York, NY
Suh, Ann Sungmie .... Washington, DC
Suh, Cathlin .... Los Angeles, CA
Suh, Christine H. .... Los Angeles, CA
Suh, Eda U. .... Honolulu, HI
Suh, Haekyoung .... Somerville, NJ
Suh, Howard S. .... New York, NY
Suh, Ja H. .... Westlake Village, CA
Suh, Ja K. .... Tampa, FL
Suh, Joseph E. .... New York, NY
Suh, Katherine Tong-Shin
Washington, DC
Suh, Kenneth .... New York, NY
Suh, Kevin M. K. .... Ventura, CA
Suh, Min S. .... Cherry Hill, NJ
Philadelphia, PA
Suh, Patricia M. .... New York, NY
Suh, Su K. .... Portland, OR
Suh, Sung-Hee .... New York, NY
Suh, Susanna Mary .... New York, NY
Suh, Y. John .... New York, NY
Suh, Young J. .... Redwood City, CA
Suh, Yun Won .... Los Angeles, CA
Suhadolnik, William L. .... Waukegan, IL
Suhar, Andrew W. .... Youngstown, OH
Suhar, Roger T., Jr. .... Chicago, IL
Suhayda-Vogt, Martha A. .... Matawan, NJ
Suher, Jeffrey L. .... Pittsburgh, PA
Suher, Kathleen Kenney .... Rochester, NY
Suher, Mark L. .... Rochester, NY
Suher, Sidney .... Rochester, NY
Suher Katchmar, Suzanne V. .... Denver, CO
Suhl, David .... Lexington, MA
Suhler, Frederick S., Jr. .... Rochester, MN
Suhr, Charles M. .... Harrisburg, PA
Suhr, David M. .... Denver, CO
Suhr, Frank B. .... New Braunfels, TX
Suhr, Frederick C. .... Madison, WI
Suhr, J. Nicholas .... Newark, NJ
New York, NY
Suhr, John Nicholas, Jr. .... Charlotte, NC
Suhr, Lloyd C. .... Bismarck, ND
Suhr, Nicole O'Neal .... Springfield, MO
Suhr, Paul A. .... Raleigh, NC
Suhr, Paul H. .... Danbury, CT
Suhr, Peter C. .... Redwood City, CA
Suhr, Tong S. .... Los Angeles, CA
Suhr, Tong S., P.C. .... Los Angeles, CA
Suhrada, Melanie K. .... New York, NY
Suhre, John F.
Equal Employment Opportunity Commission,
Office of the General Counsel, GV
Suhre, Karen K. .... Dallas, TX
Suhre, Walter A., Jr. .... St. Louis, MO
Suhrheinrich, Richard J. .... Detroit, MI
Lansing, MI
Suhy, Michael W. .... Mount Clemens, MI
Suib, Margaret K. .... Norwalk, CT
Suica, Donald M. .... Treasury Department,
Internal Revenue Service, GV
Suich, David P. .... Dayton, OH
Suich, Jennifer L. .... Minneapolis, MN
Suich, Joseph .... Syracuse, NY
Suing, Dean F. .... Omaha, NE
Suing, Marina M. .... Portland, OR
Suino, Nicklaus .... Grand Blanc, MI
Suire, Raymond A. .... San Antonio, TX
Suisman, Charles .... New London, CT
Suisman, Marjorie .... Boston, MA
Suisman, S. Joel .... New London, CT
Suisman, Shapiro, Wool, Brennan, Gray & Greenberg, P.C. .... Groton, CT
New London, CT
Norwich, CT
Suissa, Harry A. .... Silver Spring, MD
Suissa, Harry A., P.C. .... Silver Spring, MD
Suissa, Nadine Z. .... Hollywood, FL
Suit, Edward K. .... Cleveland, OH
Suit, Jesse M., III .... Norfolk, VA
Suit, Marvin W. .... Flemingsburg, KY
Suit, McCartney & Price .... Flemingsburg, KY
Suite, Dominique T. .... Fort Lauderdale, FL
Suiter & Associates P.C. .... Omaha, NE
Suiter, James R. .... Bedford, TX
Suiter, Sean Patrick .... Omaha, NE
Suiters, Larry T. .... Arlington, VA
Suits, Adam Matthew G .... Orleans, MA
Suits, Douglas J. .... San Diego, CA
Suits, Jennifer K. .... St. Charles, MO
Suitter Axland, A Professional Law Corporation .... Salt Lake City, UT
Suitter, Francis H. .... Salt Lake City, UT
Suizzo, Anthony G. .... Wilmette, IL
Sujack, Gregory P. .... Chicago, IL
Sujat, Frederick J., Jr. .... Baltimore, MD
Suk, Charles James .... Rochester, MN
Suk Law Firm .... Rochester, MN

Suk, Robert G. .... Rochester, MN
Suk, Robert G., Law Offices, P.A.
Rochester, MN
Suk, Steve C. .... Washington, DC
Sukalo, Charles .... Clinton, MD
Sukatos, George J. .... Providence, RI
Sukel, Steven P. .... Freehold, NJ
Sukenic, Howard D. .... Phoenix, AZ
Sukenik, Dana H. .... Chicago, IL
Sukenik, Martin C. .... New York, NY
Sukert, David A. .... Simsbury, CT
Sukhadwala, Muniz P. .... Washington, DC
Sukhdeo, Devand A. .... Miami, FL
Sukhia, Kenneth W. .... Tallahassee, FL
Sukhman, Michael Yuri .... New York, NY
Sukin Law Group, A Professional Corporation
New York, NY
Sukin, Michael F. .... New York, NY
Nashville, TN
Sukin Rush Law Group .... Nashville, TN
Sukkar, James .... Troy, MI
Sukkar, Mazen M. .... Hollywood, FL
Sukkar, Mazen M., P.A. .... Hollywood, FL
Sukloff, Donald M. .... Binghamton, NY
Sukloff & Schanz .... Binghamton, NY
Suko, Lonny R. .... Yakima, WA
Suko, Todd A. .... Washington, DC
Sukol, Dena .... Philadelphia, PA
Sukol, Judith A. .... Department of Energy,
Office of the General Counsel, GV
Sukol, Robert M. .... House of Representatives,
Office of Law Revision Counsel, GV
Sukoneck, Ira D. .... Livingston, NJ
Sukonik, Patricia .... King Of Prussia, PA
Sukovich, Diana C. .... Newark, NJ
Sukovich, Robert A. .... Cranford, NJ
Sukrau, Janis .... Irvine, CA
Sukup & Grimm, P.C. .... Grand Rapids, MI
Sukup, Joseph .... Grand Rapids, MI
Sukys, Gregory L. .... Department of Justice,
Environment and Natural Resources
Division, GV
Sukys, Paul A. .... Mansfield, OH
Sulaiman, Fatima .... Washington, DC
Sulaiman, Nada S. .... Washington, DC
Sulak, Timothy M. .... Austin, TX
Sulami, Susan S. .... Bethesda, MD
Sulau, W. Charles .... Cincinnati, OH
Sulau, William C. .... Cincinnati, OH
Sulcove, Jan G. .... Chambersburg, PA
Suldan, Joel I. .... Baltimore, MD
Sulds, Jonathan L. .... New York, NY
Sulé, Aparna P. .... New York, NY
Sulek, Joseph L. .... St. Clair Shores, MI
Suleman, Fatai Aderemi .... Laurel, MD
Sulen, Andrew, Jr. .... South Bend, IN
Sulenski, Jeffrey M. .... San Jose, CA
Sulentic, Alison McMorran .... Pittsburgh, PA
Sulentic, James M. .... Omaha, NE
Sulentic, Stephen A. .... Mesa, AZ
Islamorada, FL
Sulentor, William J. .... Long Beach, CA
Sules, Richard T. .... New York, NY
Sules, Roy S. .... Pollock Pines, CA
Suleski, Steven R. .... Madison, WI
Sulesky, Edward F. .... Concord, MA
Suleta, Sharon .... Philadelphia, PA
Sulewski, Christine A. .... Lafayette, IN
Sulewski, James A. .... Toledo, OH
Sulfaro, Carl A. .... Brooklyn, NY
Sulfaro, Susan K. .... Brighton, MI
Sulger, Francis X. .... New York, NY
Sulham, Priscilla L. .... Seattle, WA
Sulhoff, James D. .... Avoca, IA
Sulhoff, Paul H. .... Hiwasse, AR
Sulik, John J. .... Jacksonville, FL
Sulik, Joseph G. .... Kew Gardens, NY
Sulik, William P. .... Washington, DC
Sulimowicz, Sharon M. .... Ithaca, NY
Sulin, Thomas M. .... Glen Burnie, MD
Sulin, Victor A. .... Severn, MD
Sulit-Peralejo, Apple .... Cherry Hill, NJ
Sulkes, Carol F. .... Rolling Meadows, IL
Sulkin, Robert M. .... Seattle, WA
Sulkosky, Douglas D. .... Tacoma, WA
Sulkowski, Cheryl .... Auburn Hills, MI
Sulla, Jennifer .... Los Angeles, CA
Sullan, Curt T. .... Denver, CO
Sullan, Scott F. .... Denver, CO
Sullen, Evelyn L. .... Detroit, MI
Sullenbarger, Daniel J. .... Houston, TX
Sullenberger, Douglas R. .... Atlanta, GA
Sullenberger, Lloyd C. .... Orange, VA
Sullenberger, Mary Love .... Atlanta, GA
Sullens, Jack W. .... Santa Ana, CA
Sullinger, Murvyl M. .... Pittsburg, KS
Sullinger, Tami L. .... Pittsburg, KS
Sullins, Adam J. .... Los Angeles, CA
Sullins, Fred .... Houston, TX
Sullins, Johnston, Rohrbach & Magers
Houston, TX
Sullins, Paul .... Bella Vista, AR
Sullins, Stephanie A. .... Dallas, TX
Sullins, Stephen Lee .... Oklahoma City, OK
Sullins, Thomas Neal .... Tacoma, WA
Sullins, Tony .... Boise, ID
Sullins, W. Thomas, II .... Casper, WY
Sullivan, A. Michael .... Clayton, MO
Sullivan, A. Michael, Jr. .... Washington, DC
Sullivan, Admire & Sullivan, Professional Association .... Coral Gables, FL
Sullivan, Alan L. .... Salt Lake City, UT
Sullivan, Alan R. .... Flint, MI
Troy, MI
Sullivan, Albert W. .... Boston, MA
Sullivan, Aleita A. .... Mendenhall, MS
Sullivan, Alexa A. .... San Francisco, CA
Sullivan, Alice D. .... San Diego, CA

Sullivan, Alicia L. .... Rowayton, CT
Sullivan, Allan J. .... Miami, FL
Sullivan, Allen F. .... New York, NY
Sullivan, Amy C. .... Jacksonville, FL
Sullivan, Andrea J. .... Woodbridge, NJ
Sullivan, Andrea M. .... Richmond, VA
Sullivan, Angela J. .... Cranston, RI
Sullivan, Angie .... Oklahoma City, OK
Sullivan, Anita M. .... Houston, TX
Sullivan, Ann K. .... Norfolk, VA
Sullivan, Ann M. .... Santa Barbara, CA
Sullivan, Anne E. .... Arlington, VA
Sullivan, Anne H.
Securities and Exchange Commission,
Office of the General Counsel, GV
Sullivan, Anne M. .... North Andover, MA
Sullivan, Anneil H. .... Miami, FL
Sullivan, Annie L. .... Chapel Hill, NC
Sullivan, Anthony C. .... Indianapolis, IN
Sullivan, Arthur C., Jr. .... Lowell, MA
Sullivan, Arthur E. .... Scarborough, NY
Sullivan, Arthur J. .... Indianapolis, IN
Sullivan, Arthur J., Jr. .... Montclair, NJ
Sullivan, Arthur V. .... Walpole, MA
Sullivan, Arthur V., Jr. .... Encinitas, CA
Sullivan & Associates .... Los Osos, CA
San Luis Obispo, CA
Sullivan Ave & Holston .... Dallas, TX
Sullivan, Bailey and Bailey, A Professional Association .... Pompano Beach, FL
Sullivan, Barbara A. .... Somerset, KY
Sullivan, Barbara J. .... Chicago, IL
Sullivan, Barbara J. .... Wilmington, NC
Sullivan, Barrie G., II .... Denver, CO
Sullivan, Barry .... Los Angeles, CA
Sullivan, Barry .... Honolulu, HI
Sullivan, Barry .... Lexington, VA
Sullivan, Barry A. .... Anoka, MN
Sullivan, Bart C. .... Belleville, IL
St. Louis, MO
Sullivan, Bat P., Jr. .... New Orleans, LA
Sullivan, Bernadette L. .... Boston, MA
Sullivan, Beth Ann Levine .... Punta Gorda, FL
Sullivan, Beverly C. .... Greeneville, TN
Sullivan, Bob .... Laurel, MS
Sullivan, Bob L. .... Mabank, TX
Sullivan, Bonnie A. .... Washington, DC
Sullivan & Boyd .... Jacksonville, FL
Sullivan, Bradley W. .... Sutter Creek, CA
Sullivan, Brenda E. W. .... Mattapan, MA
Sullivan, Brendan V., Jr. .... Washington, DC
Sullivan & Bress, P.C. .... Boston, MA
Sullivan, Brian .... Bloomfield Hills, MI
Sullivan, Brian A. .... Wilmington, DE
Sullivan, Brian D. .... Atlanta, GA
Sullivan, Brian D. .... Parsippany, NJ
New York, NY
Sullivan, Brian D. .... Cleveland, OH
Sullivan, Brian E. .... Wichita, KS
Sullivan, Brian G. .... Bowling Green, KY
Sullivan, Brian J. .... Fall River, MA
Sullivan, Brian J. .... Burlington, VT
Sullivan, Brian James .... Detroit, MI
Sullivan, Brian L. .... Reno, NV
Sullivan, Brian L. .... New York, NY
Sullivan, Brian M. .... Portland, OR
Sullivan, Brian P. .... Princeton, NJ
Sullivan, Brian P. .... Blue Bell, PA
Sullivan, Brian R. .... Chelmsford, MA
Sullivan, Brian R. .... Southfield, MI
Sullivan, Brian R., (P.C.) .... Austin, TX
Sullivan, Brian S. .... Cincinnati, OH
Sullivan, Brian T. .... Chicago, IL
Sullivan, Bridget A. .... Minneapolis, MN
Sullivan, Bridget K. .... Denver, CO
Sullivan, Brogan T. .... Kansas City, MO
Sullivan, Bruce Miles .... Stony Brook, NY
Sullivan, Bruce R. .... Albany, NY
Sullivan Brummond & Denk
St. Louis, MO
Sullivan, C. David .... Libertyville, IL
Sullivan, C. Randolph .... Richmond, VA
Sullivan, C. Timothy, Jr. .... Greenville, SC
Sullivan, C. Wilson .... Wilton, NH
Sullivan, Caleb W. .... Santa Ana, CA
Sullivan, Carol S. .... Lawton, OK
Sullivan, Carolyn .... New York, NY
Sullivan, Carolyn A. .... Milwaukee, WI
Sullivan, Carolyn B. .... Boston, MA
Sullivan, Carolyn G. .... Boston, MA
Sullivan, Carroll .... Mobile, AL
Sullivan, Catherine D. .... Washington, DC
Sullivan, Catherine E. .... Cambridge, MA
Sullivan, Catherine M. .... Grand Rapids, MI
Sullivan, Catherine M. .... Syracuse, NY
Sullivan, Catherine Patrick .... Haverhill, MA
Sullivan, Chad J. .... Evansville, IN
Sullivan, Charles A. .... Vero Beach, FL
Sullivan, Charles A. .... Newark, NJ
Sullivan, Charles A., Jr. .... Vero Beach, FL
Sullivan, Charles B. .... Wilton, NH
Sullivan, Charles B., Jr. .... Arlington, VA
Sullivan, Charles E., Jr. .... Houston, TX
Sullivan, Charles F. .... Telluride, CO
Sullivan, Charles F. .... Jamesport, NY
Sullivan, Charles J. .... Bellmore, NY
Sullivan, Charles J. .... Syracuse, NY
Sullivan, Charles J. .... Wayland, NY
Sullivan, Charles J. .... Houston, TX
Sullivan, Charles Joseph, Jr.
College Park, MD
Sullivan, Charles L. .... Kalamazoo, MI
Sullivan, Charles R. .... San Francisco, CA
Sullivan, Charles S. .... New York, NY
Sullivan, Charles W. .... Oceanside, CA
Sullivan, Charles W. .... Albuquerque, NM
Sullivan, Charles W., Jr. .... Boston, MA

Sullivan, John J. ... Cincinnati, OH
Sullivan, John J. ... Seattle, WA
Sullivan, John Joseph ... Phoenix, AZ
Sullivan, John Joseph ... New York, NY
Sullivan, John K. ... Cleveland, OH
Sullivan, John L. ... Boise, ID
Sullivan, John L. ... Chicago, IL
Sullivan, John L. ... Portland, ME
Sullivan, John L. ... Boston, MA
Sullivan, John L. ... Oakdale, MN
Sullivan, John L. ... St. Louis, MO
Sullivan, John L. ... Santa Fe, NM
Sullivan, John L. ... Corpus Christi, TX
Sullivan, John L., III ... McLean, VA
Sullivan, John L., Jr. ... Naples, FL
Sullivan, John L., Jr. ... Charlotte, NC
Sullivan, John M. ... Burlingame, CA
Sullivan, John M. ... San Jose, CA
Sullivan, John M. ... St. Paul, MN
Sullivan, John M. ... Las Vegas, NV
Sullivan, John M. ... Concord, NH
Sullivan, John M. ... Southampton, NY
Sullivan, John Martin, Jr. Santa Barbara, CA
Sullivan, John P. ... Chicago, IL
Sullivan, John P. ... Naperville, IL
Sullivan, John P. ... Winnetka, IL
Sullivan, John P. ... Boston, MA
Sullivan, John P. ... St. Louis, MO
Sullivan, John P. ... West Orange, NJ
Sullivan, John P. ... Whitesboro, NY
Sullivan, John P., D.D.S., LTD, Law Office of Naperville, IL
Sullivan, John P., Jr. ... Irving, TX
Sullivan, John Patrick ... Fairfax, VA
Sullivan, John Paul ... Boston, MA
Sullivan, John R. ... Midlothian, IL
Sullivan, John R. ... Salisbury, MD
Sullivan, John R. ... Concrete, WA
Sullivan, John T. ... Boulder, CO
Sullivan, John T. Federal Mine Safety and Health Review Commission, Office of the General Counsel, GV
Sullivan, John T. ... Chicago, IL
Sullivan, John T. ... New York, NY
Sullivan, John T., Jr. ... Oswego, NY
Sullivan, John T., Jr. ... Rochester, NY
Sullivan, John V. ... House of Representatives, Office of Parliamentarian, GV
Sullivan, John W. ... New York, NY
Sullivan, John W., Jr. ... Chattanooga, TN
Sullivan, John-David ... Fort Collins, CO
Sullivan, Jon P. ... Des Moines, IA
Sullivan, Jonathan K. ... Poteau, OK
Sullivan, Joseph A. ... Chicago, IL
Sullivan, Joseph A. ... Bloomfield, IN
Sullivan, Joseph A. ... Detroit, MI
Sullivan, Joseph A. ... Philadelphia, PA
Sullivan, Joseph B. ... Detroit, MI
Sullivan, Joseph C. ... Morristown, NJ
Sullivan, Joseph C., Jr. ... Mobile, AL
Sullivan, Joseph C., Jr. ... Boston, MA
Sullivan, Joseph D. ... Washington, DC
Sullivan, Joseph D. ... Randolph, NJ
Sullivan, Joseph D. ... Cleveland, OH
Sullivan, Joseph E. ... San Diego, CA
Sullivan, Joseph F. ... Salinas, CA
Sullivan, Joseph F. ... York, ME
Sullivan, Joseph F. ... New York, NY
Sullivan, Joseph F., Jr. ... Boston, MA
Sullivan, Joseph G. ... Omaha, NE
Sullivan, Joseph J., III ... New York, NY
Sullivan, Joseph M. ... Great Falls, MT
Sullivan, Joseph M. ... Fairfax, VA
Sullivan, Joseph M. ... Seattle, WA
Sullivan, Joseph M., Jr. ... Dallas, TX
Sullivan, Joseph M., P.C., The Law Offices of Fairfax, VA
Sullivan, Joseph P. ... Salisbury, MD
Sullivan, Joseph P. ... Boston, MA
Sullivan, Joseph P. ... Hingham, MA
Sullivan, Joseph P. ... New York, NY
Sullivan, Joseph P. ... New York, NY
Sullivan, Joseph P. ... Philadelphia, PA
Sullivan, Joseph P., Jr. ... Hingham, MA
Sullivan, Joseph P., P.A. ... Salisbury, MD
Sullivan, Joseph R. ... Mobile, AL
Sullivan, Joseph R. ... Dallas, TX
Sullivan, Joseph T. ... Newton, MA
Sullivan, Joseph X. ... Cambridge, MA
Sullivan, Jude M. ... Chicago, IL
Sullivan, Judith J. ... Morristown, NJ
Sullivan, Julia E. ... Washington, DC
Sullivan, Julia Ryan ... Cleveland, OH
Sullivan, Julie A. ... Kalamazoo, MI
Sullivan, Julie M. ... New York, NY
Sullivan, Justin M. ... Hartford, CT
Sullivan, K. Michael ... Lewisburg, PA
Sullivan, Kandy K. ... Rancho Cucamonga, CA
Sullivan, Karen ... Wilmington, DE
Sullivan, Karen E. C. ... Round Rock, TX
Sullivan, Karen M. ... Fort Lauderdale, FL
Sullivan, Katherine McG. ... Hartford, CT
New York, NY
Sullivan, Kathleen A. ... Atlanta, GA
Sullivan, Kathleen A. ... Boston, MA
Sullivan, Kathleen A. ... Syracuse, NY
Sullivan, Kathleen C. ... Brockton, MA
Sullivan, Kathleen F. ... Washington, DC
Sullivan, Kathleen F. ... Baltimore, MD
Sullivan, Kathleen M. ... Palo Alto, CA
Sullivan, Kathleen M. ... Washington, DC
Sullivan, Kathleen M. ... New York, NY
Sullivan, Kathleen N. ... Manchester, NH
Sullivan, Keely J. ... Boston, MA
Sullivan, Keith F. ... Glendale, CA
Sullivan, Keleigh René ... Collins, MS
Sullivan, Kelli Lister ... Columbia, SC
Sullivan, Kelly C. ... Fairview Heights, IL
Sullivan, Kenneth A. ... Winchester, IN
Sullivan, Kenneth E., Jr. ... Sacramento, CA
Sullivan, Kenneth L. ... Fall River, MA
Sullivan, Kenneth Michael ... Chicago, IL
Sullivan, Kenneth R. ... San Francisco, CA
Sullivan, Kenneth T. ... Englewood, CO
Sullivan, Kenneth W. ... Chicago, IL
Sullivan, Kent ... Kansas City, MO
Sullivan, Kent C. ... Houston, TX
Sullivan, Kent P. ... Duncan, OK
Sullivan, Kerry D. ... Dallas, TX
Sullivan, Kerry L. ... Denver, CO
Sullivan, Kerry S. ... New York, NY
Sullivan, Kevin A. ... St. Louis, MO
Sullivan, Kevin A. ... Dallas, TX
Sullivan, Kevin B. ... Corvallis, OR
Sullivan, Kevin C. ... Hartford, CT
Sullivan, Kevin F. ... Peoria, IL
Sullivan, Kevin F. ... Meredith, NH
Sullivan, Kevin F., P.A. ... Meredith, NH
Sullivan, Kevin Gerard ... Fairfax, VA
Sullivan, Kevin J. ... Juneau, AK
Sullivan, Kevin J. ... Boston, MA
Sullivan, Kevin J. ... Braintree, MA
Sullivan, Kevin J. ... North Andover, MA
Sullivan, Kevin J. ... Springfield, MA
Sullivan, Kevin J. ... Buffalo, NY
Hamburg, NY
Sullivan, Kevin J. ... New York, NY
Sullivan, Kevin J., P.C., Law Offices of Braintree, MA
Sullivan, Kevin M. ... San Francisco, CA
Sullivan, Kevin M. ... Cleveland, OH
Sullivan, Kevin M. ... Fairfax, VA
Sullivan, Kevin P. ... Escondido, CA
Sullivan, Kevin P. ... Ogden, UT
Sullivan, Kevin P. ... Seattle, WA
Sullivan, Kevin R. ... Washington, DC
Sullivan, Kevin S. ... Chelmsford, MA
Sullivan, Kevin T. ... Idaho Falls, ID
Ketchum, ID
Sullivan, Kevin T. ... Northbrook, IL
Sullivan, Kevin W. ... Webster, MA
Sullivan, Kiernan James ... White Plains, NY
Sullivan & Kight, Attorney at Law, L.L.C. Forsyth, GA
Sullivan, Kimberly ... Charlotte, NC
Sullivan, Kirby ... Moore Haven, FL
Sullivan, Kirk N. (IBA) ... **Glendale, CA**
Sullivan, Kriste Kissner ... Houston, TX
Sullivan, Kristin Rodgers ... Providence, RI
Sullivan, L. Paul ... Rockville, CT
Sullivan & Largey ... Boston, MA
Quincy, MA
Sullivan, Larry A. ... Vale, OR
Sullivan, Larry D. ... New Castle, DE
Sullivan, Larry D., P.A. ... New Castle, DE
Sullivan, Laura ... Cleveland, OH
Sullivan, Laura M. Federal Trade Commission, Bureau of Consumer Protection, GV
Sullivan, Laura P. ... Bloomington, IL
Sullivan, Laura Z. ... Mount Clemens, MI
Sullivan, Lauraine D. ... Washington, DC
Sullivan Law Corporation Los Angeles, CA
Sullivan Law Firm ... Ithaca, NY
Sullivan Law Firm, P.C. ... Columbia, SC
Sullivan Law Group ... Phoenix, AZ
Sullivan Law Office ... Lawton, OK
Sullivan Law Offices, P.C. ... Cheyenne, WY
Sullivan, Lawrence A. ... Los Angeles, CA
Sullivan, Lawrence C. ... Burlington, MA
Sullivan, Lawrence M. ... Wilmington, DE
Sullivan, Lawrence M. Department Of Veterans Affairs, Board of Veterans Appeals, GV
Sullivan, Lawrence P. ... Fargo, ND
Sullivan, Lawrence R. ... Gaithersburg, MD
Sullivan & Leavitt, P.C., Law Offices of Novi, MI
Sullivan, Leo ... San Diego, CA
Sullivan, Leo J. ... North Kingstown, RI
Sullivan, Leo J., III ... Waukegan, IL
Sullivan, Leslie D. ... Greenville, SC
Sullivan & Leyden, P.C. ... Wayland, NY
Sullivan, Lianne C. ... Cambridge, MA
Sullivan, Linda B. ... Lexington, KY
Sullivan, Linda J. ... Santa Monica, CA
Sullivan, Linda J. ... New London, CT
Sullivan, Linda L. ... Utica, NY
Sullivan, Lisa A. ... Cincinnati, OH
Sullivan, Lisa M. ... Chicago, IL
Sullivan, Lisa M. ... Lansing, MI
Sullivan, Lisa Petricone ... San Francisco, CA
Sullivan, Lori ... Garden City, NY
Sullivan, Lori B. ... Louisville, KY
Sullivan, Louis B. (Dee), III ... Houston, TX
Sullivan, Louis G., II ... Anderson, SC
Sullivan, Lovell Wayne ... Jenks, OK
Sullivan & Lynch, P.C. ... Boston, MA
Sullivan, Lynn A. ... Chicago, IL
Sullivan, M. Sean ... Nashville, TN
Sullivan, M. Todd ... Raleigh, NC
Sullivan, M. Virginia ... New York, NY
Sullivan, Malcolm K. ... Forsyth, GA
Sullivan & Maniscalco ... West Orange, NJ
Sullivan, Marcia W., (P.C.) ... Chicago, IL
Sullivan, Margaret ... Ridgewood, NJ
Sullivan, Margaret C. ... Scituate, MA
Sullivan, Margaret E. ... New Haven, CT
Sullivan, Margaret H. ... San Diego, CA
Sullivan, Margaret M. ... Laconia, NH
Sullivan, Margaret Pedrick San Antonio, TX
Sullivan, Marian E. Department of the Air Force, Office of the General Counsel, GV
Sullivan, Marita C. ... Chicago, IL
Sullivan, Mark A. ... Spring Lake, NJ
Sullivan, Mark A., Jr. ... Freehold, NJ
Sullivan, Mark D. ... Denver, CO
Sullivan, Mark D. ... Chelmsford, MA
Sullivan, Mark D. ... New York, NY
Sullivan, Mark D., III ... Greenville, SC
Sullivan, Mark E. ... Raleigh, NC
Sullivan, Mark E. ... Cleveland, OH
Sullivan, Mark E., P.A., Law Offices of Raleigh, NC
Sullivan, Mark F. ... Thousand Oaks, CA
Sullivan, Mark J. ... Indio, CA
Sullivan, Mark J. ... Palm Springs, CA
Sullivan, Mark J. ... Dubuque, IA
Sullivan, Mark J. ... Falls Church, VA
Sullivan, Mark K. ... Indianapolis, IN
Sullivan, Mark L. ... Boston, MA
Sullivan, Mark P. ... Butte, MT
Sullivan, Mark R. ... Princeton, NJ
Sullivan, Mark R. ... Pittsburgh, PA
Sullivan, Mark S. ... New York, NY
Sullivan, Mark Tod ... Salida, CA
Sullivan, Mark W. ... Fort Worth, TX
Sullivan, Mark X. ... Indianapolis, IN
Sullivan & Marshall ... Green Village, NJ
New York, NY
Sullivan, Marshall A. ... Omaha, NE
Sullivan & Marston, P.A. ... Wilmington, DE
Sullivan, Martha ... San Francisco, CA
Sullivan, Martha J. ... Nacogdoches, TX
Sullivan, Martha S. ... Cleveland, OH
Sullivan, Martin F., Jr. ... Louisville, KY
Sullivan, Martin J. ... Newark, NJ
Sullivan, Martin P. ... Washington, DC
Sullivan, Mary Ann ... Oak Park, IL
Sullivan, Mary Anne ... Department of Energy, Office of the General Counsel, GV
Sullivan, Mary Beth Securities and Exchange Commission, Office of the Inspector General, GV
Sullivan, Mary Colligan ... Trenton, NJ
Sullivan, Mary E. ... Los Angeles, CA
Sullivan, Mary E. ... Wayland, NY
Sullivan, Mary G. ... Belleville, IL
St. Louis, MO
Sullivan, Mary G. ... Boston, MA
Sullivan, Mary Kate ... San Francisco, CA
Sullivan, Mary M. ... Lakeside, CA
Sullivan, Mary M. ... New York, NY
Sullivan, Mary M. ... Olean, NY
Sullivan, Mary Morrissey ... Boston, MA
Sullivan, Mary P. ... Walnut Creek, CA
Sullivan, Mary Secor ... Boston, MA
Sullivan, Mary Susan ... Los Angeles, CA
Sullivan, Mary W. ... Cincinnati, OH
Sullivan, Maryellen C. ... Floral Park, NY
Sullivan, Mason D. ... Oak Park, IL
Sullivan & Matheson ... South Natick, MA
Sullivan, Matthew ... Branford, CT
Sullivan, Matthew J. ... Austin, TX
Sullivan, Matthew P. ... Walnut Creek, CA
Sullivan, Matthew S. ... Kinston, NC
Sullivan, Maura D. ... Boston, MA
Sullivan, Maura J. ... Boston, MA
Sullivan, Maureen ... Shepherdsville, KY
Sullivan, Maureen ... Derry, NH
Sullivan, Maureen ... New York, NY
Sullivan, Maureen W. ... Buffalo, NY
Sullivan, Maurice H., Jr. ... Brighton, MA
Sullivan, Maurice H., Jr., P.C. ... Brighton, MA
Sullivan, Maurice Henry, III ... Boston, MA
Sullivan, Maurice J. ... Reno, NV
Sullivan, McBride, Hess & Youngblood, P.C. Albany, NY
Sullivan & McDermott ... Boston, MA
Sullivan, McDonald, Bramley & Brody, A Professional Corporation ... La Jolla, CA
San Diego, CA
Sullivan, Meghan Boldvay ... Springfield, MA
Sullivan & Metcalf ... Oswego, NY
Sullivan, Michael ... San Diego, CA
Sullivan, Michael ... Ashland, OH
Sullivan, Michael A. ... Atlanta, GA
Sullivan, Michael A. ... Boston, MA
Sullivan, Michael A. ... Cleveland, OH
Sullivan, Michael B. ... St. Louis, MO
Sullivan, Michael Brice ... Englewood, CO
Sullivan, Michael C. ... San Diego, CA
Sullivan, Michael D. ... Washington, DC
Sullivan, Michael D. ... Rolling Meadows, IL
Sullivan, Michael D. ... Jackson, MS
Sullivan, Michael D. ... Cedar Grove, NJ
Sullivan, Michael Deuel ... Washington, DC
Sullivan, Michael E. ... Roswell, GA
Sullivan, Michael E. ... Hastings, NE
Sullivan, Michael E. ... Reno, NV
Sullivan, Michael E. ... Trenton, NJ
Sullivan, Michael F. ... Alamo, CA
Sullivan, Michael F. ... Evergreen Park, IL
Sullivan, Michael F. ... Concord, NH
Sullivan, Michael F. ... Columbus, OH
Sullivan, Michael F., A Prof. Corp. Alamo, CA
Sullivan, Michael G. ... Washington, DC
Sullivan, Michael G. ... Lafayette, LA
Sullivan, Michael G. ... Columbia, SC
Sullivan, Michael G., P.C. ... Columbia, SC
Sullivan, Michael J. ... San Francisco, CA
Sullivan, Michael J. ... Orlando, FL
Sullivan, Michael J. ... Woodstock, IL
Sullivan, Michael J. ... Scituate, MA
Sullivan, Michael J. ... Detroit, MI
Sullivan, Michael J. ... Southfield, MI
Sullivan, Michael J. ... Morristown, NJ
Sullivan, Michael J. ... Fredonia, NY
Sullivan, Michael J. ... Corpus Christi, TX
Sullivan, Michael J. ... Casper, WY
Sullivan, Michael K. ... Cherry Hill, NJ
Sullivan, Michael L. ... Chicago, IL
Sullivan, Michael L. ... Omaha, NE
Sullivan, Michael M. ... Huntsville, AL
Sullivan, Michael M. ... Boston, MA
Sullivan, Michael M. ... Natick, MA
Sullivan, Michael M. ... Minneapolis, MN
Sullivan, Michael P. ... Jacksonville, FL
Sullivan, Michael P. ... Miami, FL
Sullivan, Michael P. ... Chicago, IL
Sullivan, Michael P. ... Louisville, KY
Sullivan, Michael P. ... Cambridge, MA
Sullivan, Michael P. ... Minneapolis, MN
Sullivan, Michael P. ... Duncan, OK
Sullivan, Michael P., Jr. ... Minneapolis, MN
Sullivan, Michael R. ... Los Angeles, CA
Sullivan, Michael R. ... Oakland, CA
Sullivan, Michael R. ... Sewanee, TN
Sullivan, Michael T. ... Chicago, IL
Sullivan, Michael T. ... Boston, MA
Providence, RI
Sullivan, Michael T. ... Kings Park, NY
Sullivan, Michael T. ... New York, NY
Sullivan, Michael T. ... New York, NY
Sullivan, Michael T., Jr. ... Buffalo, NY
Sullivan, Michelle ... Chicago, IL
Sullivan, Michelle C. ... San Diego, CA
Sullivan, Mike ... Poteau, OK
Sullivan, Mikki Rosemary ... San Diego, CA
Sullivan, Mitchell ... Corona Del Mar, CA
Sullivan, Monica T. ... Chicago, IL
Sullivan, Mortimer A., Jr. ... Orchard Park, NY
Sullivan, Mountjoy, Stainback & Miller, P.S.C. ... Henderson, KY
Owensboro, KY
Sullivan, N. Colleen ... Dallas, TX
Sullivan, Nancy ... New York, NY
Sullivan, Nancy A. ... Minneapolis, MN
Sullivan, Neal C. ... Boston, MA
Sullivan, Neal E. ... Washington, DC
Sullivan, Neil P. ... Walnut Creek, CA
Sullivan, Nora B. ... Buffalo, NY
Sullivan, Norman C. ... Stockton, CA
Sullivan, Norman C., Jr. New Orleans, LA
Sullivan & Oliverio ... Batavia, NY
Buffalo, NY
Jamestown, NY
Niagara Falls, NY
Sullivan, Orville W. ... Brawley, CA
Sullivan, Owen Michael ... Allentown, PA
Sullivan, Pamela J. ... New York, NY
Sullivan, Pamela S. ... Anchorage, AK
Sullivan Papain Block McGrath & Cannavo P.C. ... Hackensack, NJ
Mineola, NY
New York, NY
Sullivan, Patrice Harris ... New Orleans, LA
Sullivan, Patricia ... Pendleton, OR
Sullivan, Patricia A. ... New York, NY
Sullivan, Patricia A. ... Vale, OR
Sullivan, Patricia A. ... Providence, RI
Sullivan, Patricia A. ... Warwick, RI
Sullivan, Patricia Ann ... Boston, MA
Sullivan, Patricia C. ... Bridgeport, CT
Westport, CT
Sullivan, Patricia J. ... Royal Oak, MI
Sullivan, Patricia L. ... San Diego, CA
Sullivan, Patrick A. ... Spokane, WA
Sullivan, Patrick D. ... Indianapolis, IN
Sullivan, Patrick D. ... Duncan, OK
Sullivan, Patrick D. ... Houston, TX
Sullivan, Patrick E. ... Clay Center, NE
Sullivan, Patrick G. ... Andover, MA
Sullivan, Patrick H. ... New York, NY
Sullivan, Patrick J. ... Oakland, CA
Sullivan, Patrick J. ... Oceanside, CA
Sullivan, Patrick J. ... Chicago, IL
Sullivan, Patrick J. ... Chicago, IL
Sullivan, Patrick J. ... Chicago, IL
Sullivan, Patrick J. ... Boston, MA
Sullivan, Patrick J. ... Minneapolis, MN
Sullivan, Patrick J. ... Papillion, NE
Sullivan, Patrick J. ... Jericho, NY
Sullivan, Patrick J. ... Austin, TX
Sullivan, Patrick Joseph ... Rockford, IL
Grand Rapids, MI
Sullivan, Patrick Lewis ... Bel Air, MD
Sullivan, Patrick M. ... Butte, MT
Sullivan, Patrick N. ... Lawton, OK
Sullivan, Patrick W. ... Albuquerque, NM
Sullivan & Patten, P.A. ... Wolfeboro, NH
Sullivan, Paul C. ... Washington, DC
Sullivan, Paul C. ... Cumberland, MD
Sullivan, Paul D. ... Punta Gorda, FL
Sullivan, Paul D. ... Duncan, OK
Sullivan, Paul E. ... Lexington, KY
Sullivan, Paul E. ... Irving, TX
Sullivan, Paul F. ... Los Angeles, CA
Sullivan, Paul F. ... Silver Spring, MD
Sullivan, Paul G. ... Pittsburgh, PA
Sullivan, Paul J. ... Scituate, MA
Sullivan, Paul J. ... Weymouth, MA
Sullivan, Paul J. ... Grand Rapids, MI
Sullivan, Paul K., Jr. ... Guilford, CT
Sullivan, Paul M., Jr. West Palm Beach, FL
Sullivan, Paul M., Jr., P.A. West Palm Beach, FL
Sullivan, Paul N. ... Nashville, TN
Sullivan, Paul O. ... Clearwater, FL
Poughkeepsie, NY
Sullivan, Paul T. ... Plantation, FL
Sullivan, Paul T. ... Boston, MA
Sullivan, Paul T. ... St. Louis, MO

Sullivan, Paul T. ... Montclair, NJ
Sullivan, Paul V. ... Providence, RI
Sullivan, Paula M. ... Vacaville, CA
Sullivan, Peggy ... Blacksburg, VA
Sullivan, Peggy J. ... West Monroe, LA
Sullivan, Peter (IBA) ... **Los Angeles, CA**
Sullivan, Peter ... Garden City, NY
Sullivan, Peter ... New York, NY
Sullivan, Peter A. ... New York, NY
Sullivan, Peter B. ... Buffalo, NY
Sullivan, Peter D. ... Chicago, IL
Sullivan, Peter M. ... United States Senate, Committee Legal Personnel, GV
Sullivan, Peter M. ... Boston, MA
Sullivan, Peter R. ... New York, NY
Sullivan, Peter W. Agency for International Development, Legal Advisers-Overseas, GV
Sullivan, Philip J. ... San Diego, CA
Sullivan, R. Alexander ... Rock Hill, SC
Sullivan, R. Michael ... Owensboro, KY
Sullivan, Ralph A. ... Belmont, CA
Sullivan, Ralph C. ... Boston, MA
Sullivan, Ralph G. ... Elizabeth, NJ
Sullivan, Ralph H. Environmental Protection Agency, Program Office Attorneys, GV
Sullivan, Ray T., Jr. ... Riverside, CA
Sullivan, Raymond ... Dallas, TX
Sullivan, Raymond F., Jr. Washington, DC
Sullivan, Raymond J. ... Tampa, FL
Sullivan, Raymond L. ... San Francisco, CA
Sullivan, Rebecca Kathleen San Francisco, CA
Sullivan, Reis, Sanchy & Logan, LLC Torrington, CT
Sullivan, Rhonda Kaye ... Dallas, TX
Sullivan, Richard A. ... Hingham, MA
Manchester, NH
Sullivan, Richard B. ... Rochester, NY
Sullivan, Richard C., Jr. Falls Church, VA
Sullivan, Richard D. ... Lapeer, MI
Sullivan, Richard D., Law Offices of Houston, TX
Sullivan, Richard F. ... Worcester, MA
Sullivan, Richard G. ... Birmingham, AL
Sullivan, Richard J. ... Decatur, IN
Sullivan, Richard J. ... Hauppauge, NY
Sullivan, Richard J. ... New York, NY
Sullivan, Richard J. ... Toledo, OH
Sullivan, Richard K. ... Milford, MA
Sullivan, Richard K., Jr. ... Springfield, MA
Sullivan, Richard L. C. ... Columbia, SC
Myrtle Beach, SC
Sullivan, Richard M. ... Louisville, KY
Sullivan, Richard P. ... Biddeford, ME
Sullivan, Richard P. ... Williamsville, NY
Sullivan, Richard P. ... Westerly, RI
Sullivan, Richard Patrick, Jr. Anchorage, AK
Sullivan, Richard T. ... Buffalo, NY
Sullivan, Richard T., Jr. ... Boston, MA
Sullivan Rivero & Moscowitz, P.A. Miami, FL
Sullivan & Rizzo ... Belmont, CA
Sullivan, Robert B. ... Kansas City, MO
Sullivan, Robert C. ... Dallas, TX
Sullivan, Robert C. ... Arlington, VA
Sullivan, Robert C., Jr. ... New York, NY
Sullivan, Robert D. ... Milwaukee, WI
Sullivan, Robert E. ... Edwards, CA
Sullivan, Robert E. ... San Francisco, CA
Sullivan, Robert E. Department Of Veterans Affairs, Board of Veterans Appeals, GV
Sullivan, Robert E. ... Boston, MA
Sullivan, Robert E. ... Framingham, MA
Sullivan, Robert E. ... Grand Haven, MI
Sullivan, Robert E. ... Southfield, MI
Sullivan, Robert E. ... Wahoo, NE
Sullivan, Robert E., Jr. ... Southfield, MI
Sullivan, Robert F. ... Louisville, KY
Sullivan, Robert F. ... Hamilton, NY
Sullivan, Robert F. ... New Berlin, WI
Sullivan, Robert G. ... Mineola, NY
New York, NY
Sullivan, Robert G. ... Providence, RI
Sullivan, Robert J. ... Danville, CA
Westport, CT
Sullivan, Robert J. ... Sacramento, CA
Sullivan, Robert J. ... Torrington, CT
Sullivan, Robert J. ... Missoula, MT
Sullivan, Robert J. ... New York, NY
Sullivan, Robert J. ... New York, NY
Sullivan, Robert J. ... Portland, OR
Sullivan, Robert, Jr. ... Lebanon, PA
Sullivan, Robert K. ... Chicago, IL
Sullivan, Robert L. ... Washington, DC
Sullivan, Robert L. ... Bloomington, IL
Sullivan, Robert L. ... Nashville, TN
Sullivan, Robert L., Jr. ... Fresno, CA
Sullivan, Robert, Law Offices of Danville, CA
Westport, CT
Sullivan, Robert M. ... Hastings, NE
Sullivan, Robert M. ... New York, NY
Sullivan, Robert N. ... Berkeley Heights, NJ
Sullivan, Robert P. ... Fairfield, CT
Sullivan, Robert P. ... Chelmsford, MA
Sullivan, Robert P. ... Portsmouth, NH
Sullivan, Robert R. ... Fairfax, VA
Sullivan, Robert T. ... Midland, TX
Sullivan, Robert W. ... Aurora, CO
Sullivan, Robert W. ... Hartford, CT
Sullivan, Robert W. ... Vinita, OK
Sullivan, Robert W. ... Fort Mill, SC
Sullivan, Roberta J. ... Kansas City, MO
Sullivan, Robin S. ... Santa Paula, CA
Sullivan, Robt. ... Boston, MA
Sullivan, Robt. ... Watertown, MA
Sullivan, Robt. E. ... Missoula, MT
Sullivan, Robt. L. ... Lindale, TX
Sullivan, Roger ... Santa Cruz, CA
Sullivan, Roger C. ... Dallas, TX
Sullivan, Roger F. ... Fall River, MA
Sullivan, Roger H. ... McLean, VA
Sullivan, Roger J. ... Towson, MD
Sullivan, Roger L. ... Fargo, ND
Sullivan, Roger M. ... Kalispell, MT
Sullivan, Roger M., (A Professional Corporation) ... Los Angeles, CA
Sullivan, Roger M., Law Offices of Branford, CT
Sullivan, Ronald F. ... San Francisco, CA
Sullivan, Ronald M. ... Danbury, CT
Sullivan, Ronald M. ... Owensboro, KY
Sullivan, Ronald N. ... Boston, MA
Sullivan, Ronald S., Jr. ... Washington, DC
Sullivan, Rose Ann C. Colorado Springs, CO
Sullivan, Roseanne ... Columbus, OH
Sullivan, Rosemary A. ... Langhorne, PA
Newtown, PA
Sullivan, Rosemary E. ... Houston, TX
Sullivan, Roy M., Jr. ... Stone Mountain, GA
Sullivan, Rozanne Franke ... Glen Ridge, NJ
Sullivan, Russell W. ... Washington, DC
Sullivan, Ruth D. ... San Francisco, CA
Sullivan, Ruth S., & Associate Dadeville, AL
Sullivan, Sally A. ... Boulder, CO
Sullivan, Sally L. ... Issaquah, WA
Sullivan, Samuel H. ... Griffin, GA
Sullivan, Samuel L., Jr. ... Jasper, AL
Sullivan, Sarah Toevs ... Kansas City, MO
Sullivan, Schoen, Campane & Connon, L.L.C. Hartford, CT
Sullivan, Scot A. ... Ballwin, MO
Sullivan, Scott C. ... Rockford, IL
Sullivan, Scott E. ... Dallas, TX
Sullivan, Scott J. ... Liberty, MO
Sullivan, Scott L. ... New York, NY
Sullivan, Scott P. ... Duncan, OK
Sullivan, Scott Randall Oklahoma City, OK
Sullivan, Sean M. ... Chicago, IL
Sullivan, Sean M. ... Chicago, IL
Sullivan, Sean M. ... Chicago, IL
Sullivan, Sean P. ... Las Vegas, NV
Sullivan, Sean P. ... Lawton, OK
Sullivan, Sean R. ... Pittsburgh, PA
Sullivan, Sean Thomas ... Northampton, MA
Sullivan, Selby W. ... Orlando, FL
Sullivan, Shannon A. ... Chicago, IL
Sullivan, Shannon S. ... Wheaton, IL
Sullivan, Shaun S. ... New Haven, CT
Sullivan, Shauna J. ... Atlanta, GA
Sullivan, Shaunna L. ... Los Osos, CA
San Luis Obispo, CA
Sullivan, Shawn J. ... Concord, NH
Sullivan, Shawn M. ... Evansville, IN
Sullivan, Shawn M. ... Providence, RI
Sullivan, Shawn Neill ... Jackson, MS
Sullivan, Shawn P. ... Altoona, PA
Sullivan, Sheila M. ... Madison, WI
Sullivan, Sherri Berkbigler ... St. Louis, MO
Sullivan, Sherwood M. ... Menlo Park, CA
Sullivan, Sheryl S. ... Oklahoma City, OK
Sullivan, Sheryl S., P.C. Oklahoma City, OK
Sullivan & Smith ... Norwich, NY
Sullivan, Smith, Hauser & Noonan, Ltd. Waukegan, IL
Sullivan, Sorgi and Dimmock ... Boston, MA
Sullivan, Stacey A. ... Los Angeles, CA
Sullivan, Stacey Hayden ... Salt Lake City, UT
Sullivan & Steinbarth ... San Diego, CA
Sullivan, Stephanie M. ... Morristown, NJ
Sullivan, Stephen ... Batavia, IL
Sullivan, Stephen C. ... Sun City Center, FL
Tampa, FL
Sullivan, Stephen G. ... Palo Alto, CA
Sullivan, Stephen J. ... Denver, CO
Sullivan, Stephen M. ... New Orleans, LA
Sullivan, Stephen P. ... Washington, DC
Sullivan, Stephen T. ... Phoenix, AZ
Sullivan, Stephen W. ... Vancouver, WA
Sullivan, Steven ... Minneapolis, MN
Sullivan, Steven M. ... Baltimore, MD
Sullivan, Steven R. ... St. Louis, MO
Sullivan, Stolier & Daigle, A Professional Law Corporation ... New Orleans, LA
Sullivan, Stuart C. ... Tulsa, OK
Sullivan, Stuart C., III ... Spotsylvania, VA
Sullivan, Sue Ann ... Boston, MA
Sullivan & Sullivan ... Santa Paula, CA
Sullivan & Sullivan ... Waterbury, CT
Sullivan & Sullivan ... Overland Park, KS
Phillipsburg, KS
Sullivan and Sullivan ... Bel Air, MD
Sullivan & Sullivan ... Framingham, MA
Sullivan & Sullivan ... Hingham, MA
Sullivan & Sullivan ... Webster, MA
Sullivan and Sullivan ... Jackson, MS
Sullivan & Sullivan ... Laurel, MS
Sullivan & Sullivan ... Cincinnati, OH
Sullivan & Sullivan ... North Kingstown, RI
Sullivan & Sullivan, A Professional Corporation ... Langhorne, PA
Newtown, PA
Sullivan & Sullivan, LLP
Chelmsford, MA
Sullivan & Sullivan, Ltd. ... Cleveland, OH
Sullivan, Sullivan & Nahigian, LLP Boston, MA
Sullivan & Sullivan, P.A. A Professional Corporation ... Montclair, NJ
Sullivan and Sullivan, P.C. ... Denver, CO
Sullivan & Sullivan, P.C. ... Norwell, MA
Sullivan & Sullivan, PLC ... Henderson, KY
Sullivan, Sullivan & Snelling Harrisburg, PA
Lebanon, PA
Sullivan, Sullivan & Thacker Vero Beach, FL
Sullivan, Susan E. ... Easton, MA
Sullivan, Susan Kipps ... Arlington, VA
Sullivan, Susan Koehler ... Los Angeles, CA
Sullivan, Susan M. ... New York, NY
Sullivan, Susan M. ... Columbus, OH
Sullivan, Susan R. Environmental Protection Agency, Office of Enforcement and Compliance Assurance, GV
Sullivan, Susan R. ... Brownsville, TX
McAllen, TX
Sullivan, Susanne K. ... Houston, TX
Sullivan, Suzanne M. ... Lincoln, RI
Sullivan & Tabaracci, A Professional Corporation ... Missoula, MT
Sullivan Taylor, P.C. ... Wheaton, IL
Sullivan, Ted ... Lakewood, CA
Sullivan, Ted E. ... Minneapolis, MN
Sullivan, Terence A. ... Rockville, CT
Sullivan, Terence M. ... New York, NY
Sullivan, Terrance C. ... Atlanta, GA
Columbus, GA
Sullivan & Terranova ... Portland, OR
Sullivan, Terrence D. ... Raleigh, NC
Sullivan, Terrence P. ... Cleveland, OH
Sullivan, Terry ... Rolling Meadows, IL
Sullivan, Terry Anne ... Corvallis, OR
Sullivan, Terry K. ... Baltimore, MD
Sullivan, Terry L. ... Washington, DC
Sullivan, Terry M. ... Danville, AR
Sullivan, Theodore M. ... Washington, DC
Sullivan, Theresa M. ... Burbank, CA
Sullivan, Thomas ... Kansas City, MO
Sullivan, Thomas ... Brownsville, TX
Sullivan, Thomas B. ... Palos Heights, IL
Sullivan, Thomas C. ... Hartford, CT
Sullivan, Thomas C. ... Jacksonville, FL
Sullivan, Thomas C. ... Philadelphia, PA
Sullivan, Thomas E. ... Downers Grove, IL
Sullivan, Thomas F. ... Chicago, IL
Sullivan, Thomas F. ... Melrose, MA
Sullivan, Thomas F. ... Wellesley, MA
Sullivan, Thomas F. ... New York, NY
Sullivan, Thomas F., Jr. ... Worcester, MA
Sullivan, Thomas H. ... Overland Park, KS
Phillipsburg, KS
Sullivan, Thomas H. ... Boston, MA
Sullivan, Thomas H. ... New York, NY
Sullivan, Thomas J. ... Fort Lauderdale, FL
Sullivan, Thomas J. ... Worcester, MA
Sullivan, Thomas J. ... Jackson, MI
Sullivan, Thomas J. ... Lansing, MI
Sullivan, Thomas J. ... Elmira, NY
Sullivan, Thomas J. ... New York, NY
Sullivan, Thomas J., Professional Corporation Jackson, MI
Sullivan, Thomas J. M., Sr. ... Naperville, IL
Sullivan, Thomas M. ... Littleton, CO
Sullivan, Thomas M. Environmental Protection Agency, Office of Congressional and Legislative Affairs, GV
Sullivan, Thomas M. ... Boston, MA
Sullivan, Thomas M. ... New Bedford, MA
Sullivan, Thomas M. ... Detroit, MI
Sullivan, Thomas M., Jr. ... Denver, CO
Sullivan, Thomas N. ... Hartford, CT
Sullivan, Thomas P. ... Plano, TX
Sullivan, Thomas P., (Ltd.) ... Chicago, IL
Sullivan, Thomas P., (P.C.) ... Alameda, CA
Sullivan, Thomas Q. ... Alexandria, VA
Sullivan, Thomas R. ... Mankato, MN
Sullivan, Thomas R. ... Staten Island, NY
Sullivan, Thomas V. ... White Plains, NY
Sullivan, Thomas W. ... Tucson, AZ
Sullivan & Thoreson ... Seattle, WA
Sullivan, Timon V. ... Tampa, FL
Sullivan, Timothy ... Los Angeles, CA
San Francisco, CA
Sullivan, Timothy ... Washington, DC
Sullivan, Timothy A. ... Minneapolis, MN
Sullivan, Timothy A. Fort Washington, PA
Sullivan, Timothy C. ... Cincinnati, OH
Sullivan, Timothy D. ... North Andover, MA
Sullivan, Timothy E. ... Galesburg, IL
Sullivan, Timothy F. ... Chicago, IL
Sullivan, Timothy F. ... Media, PA
Sullivan, Timothy F., Jr. ... Portage, IN
Sullivan, Timothy G. ... Pittsburgh, PA
Sullivan, Timothy G., Jr. ... San Mateo, CA
Sullivan, Timothy J. ... San Diego, CA
Sullivan, Timothy J. ... Detroit, MI
Sullivan, Timothy J. ... Wolfeboro, NH
Sullivan, Timothy J. ... Hackensack, NJ
Sullivan, Timothy J. ... Philadelphia, PA
Sullivan, Timothy J. ... Williamsburg, VA
Sullivan, Timothy J., Jr. ... Pittsfield, MA
Sullivan, Timothy J., P.A. ... Wolfeboro, NH
Sullivan, Timothy Jay ... Denver, CO
Sullivan, Timothy L. ... Needham, MA
Sullivan, Timothy M. ... Chicago, IL
Sullivan, Timothy M. ... New York, NY
Sullivan, Timothy M. ... Cleveland, OH
Sullivan, Timothy M. ... Altoona, PA
Sullivan, Timothy P. ... Santa Ana, CA
Sullivan, Timothy P. ... New York, NY
Sullivan, Timothy P. ... Raleigh, NC
Sullivan, Timothy P. ... Seattle, WA
Sullivan, Timothy R. ... Fresno, CA
Sullivan, Timothy T. J. ... Lowell, MA
Sullivan, Timothy W. ... Indianapolis, IN
Sullivan, Timothy W. ... Garden City, NY
Sullivan, Timothy W., P.C. ... Garden City, NY
Sullivan, T. J. ... Washington, DC
Sullivan, Todd P. ... Miami, FL
Sullivan, Tom ... Houston, TX
Sullivan, Tonya L. ... Houston, TX
Sullivan, Tracey F. ... New York, NY
Sullivan & Tumlinson ... Alexandria, VA
Sullivan, Ulric R. ... New York, NY
Sullivan, Victor J., Jr. ... Pittsburgh, PA
Sullivan & Villios ... New York, NY
Sullivan, Vincent E. ... San Diego, CA
Sullivan, Virginia M. ... Florham Park, NJ
Sullivan, Virginia Vance ... Los Angeles, CA
Sullivan, W. Howard ... Norwich, NY
Sullivan, W. Patrick ... Milwaukee, WI
Sullivan, Walter B. ... Norwell, MA
Sullivan, Walter F. ... Framingham, MA
Sullivan, Walter J. ... Philadelphia, PA
Sullivan, Walter J., Jr. ... Boston, MA
Sullivan, Walter L. ... Norwell, MA
Sullivan, Ward, Bone, Tyler & Asher, P.C.
San Francisco, CA
Deerfield Beach, FL
Detroit, MI
Grand Rapids, MI
Southfield, MI
Traverse City, MI
Sullivan & Ward, P.C. ... Des Moines, IA
Sullivan, Warren ... San Francisco, CA
Sullivan, Warren G. ... St. Louis, MO
Sullivan, Weinstein & McQuay Boston, MA
Sullivan, Wendall ... Cincinnati, OH
Sullivan Wertz McDade & Wallace, A Professional Corporation ... San Diego, CA
Sullivan, Willard A. ... Charleston, WV
Sullivan, William ... Riverside, CA
San Diego, CA
Sullivan, William A. ... Westlake Village, CA
Sullivan, William Allen ... New York, NY
Sullivan, William B. ... Oak Park, IL
Sullivan, William B. ... Laurel, MS
Sullivan, William B. ... Winston-Salem, NC
Sullivan, William C. ... Lincoln, AL
Sullivan, William C. ... Wellesley, MA
Sullivan, William C., Jr. ... Springfield, NJ
Sullivan, William D. ... Wilmington, DE
Sullivan, William Daniel ... Washington, DC
Sullivan, William F. ... San Diego, CA
Sullivan, William F. ... Peabody, MA
Sullivan, William F. ... Quincy, MA
Sullivan, William F., IV ... Miami, FL
Sullivan, William F., Jr. ... Boston, MA
Sullivan, William F., Jr. ... Philadelphia, PA
Sullivan, William F., (P.A.) Lighthouse Point, FL
Sullivan, William G. ... Corona, CA
Sullivan, William G. ... Chicago, IL
Sullivan, William G. ... Chanhassen, MN
Sullivan, William H. ... Riverside, CA
Sullivan, William H. ... East Falmouth, MA
Sullivan, William H. ... Oklahoma City, OK
Sullivan, William J., A Professional Corporation Albuquerque, NM
Sullivan, William J., III ... Birmingham, AL
Sullivan, William J., Jr. ... Birmingham, AL
Sullivan, William L. ... Henderson, KY
Sullivan, William M. ... Ronkonkoma, NY
Sullivan, William P. ... Phoenix, AZ
Sullivan, William P. Securities and Exchange Commission, Division of Enforcement, GV
Sullivan, William P., III ... Atlanta, GA
Sullivan, William P., Jr. ... Ithaca, NY
Sullivan, William R. ... Wakefield, MA
Sullivan, William R. ... Mill Creek, WA
Sullivan, William R., Jr. ... Chicago, IL
Sullivan, William T. ... Potomac, MD
Sullivan, William T. ... Bellmore, NY
Sullivan, William T. ... San Antonio, TX
Sullivan, William W., (P.C.) ... Danbury, CT
Sullivan, Willis E., III ... Boise, ID
Sullivan, Winnifred F. ... Lexington, VA
Sullivan & Worcester LLP Washington, DC
Boston, MA
New York, NY
Sullivan, Workman & Dee Los Angeles, CA
Sullivan, Z. Kent ... Missoula, MT
Sullivan, Zane K. ... Missoula, MT
Sullivan-Bisceglia, Susan M. New York, NY
Sullivan Brown, Deborah ... North Liberty, IN
Sullivan-Flock, Kerry ... Black River Falls, WI
Sullivan-Ford, Diane ... Rockville, MD
Sullivan-Friedberg, Mary E. Livingston, NJ
Sullivan-Kight, Karen T. ... Forsyth, GA
Sullivan-Summers, Beth ... Mooresville, IN
Sullivan Sutton, Erin A. ... St. Paul, MN
Sullivant, Elle ... Kansas City, MO
Sullivant, J. Milton ... Lawrence, KS
Sullivant, Larry B. ... Gainesville, TX
Sullivant, Sullivant & Meurer, L.L.P. Gainesville, TX
Sullivant, W. Benton (Ben) Gainesville, TX
Sullivant, William B. ... Gainesville, TX
Sullivan-Walsh, Morgan T. ... Purchase, NY
Sullivent, Thomas J., Jr. ... Tulsa, OK
Sulloway, Alvah W. ... Kittery Point, ME

Sulloway & Hollis, P.L.L.C. ......Concord, NH
Sullwold, Jane Cosgriff ......Oakland, CA
Sully, Cynthia Sue ......Las Vegas, NV
Sully, Ira B. ......Columbus, OH
Sully, Paige L. ......Richland, WA
Sully, Sarah E. ......New York, NY
Sully, W. Leslie, Jr. (Chartered) Las Vegas, NV
Sulman, Frances J. ......Los Angeles, CA
Sulman, Jeffrey M. ......New York, NY
Sulman, Stuart M. ......Seattle, WA
Sulmasy, Glenn M. ......New London, CT
Sulmeyer, Irving ......Los Angeles, CA
Sulmeyer, Kupetz, Baumann & Rothman, A Professional Corporation Los Angeles, CA
Sulmonetti, Alfred T. ......Portland, OR
Sulner, Andrew ......New York, NY
Sulock, S. Mark ......Haddon Heights, NJ
Suls, Robert Andrew ......Towson, MD
Sulser, Adrian P. ......St. Louis, MO
Sulser, Carol A. ......Roanoke, VA
Sulser, Floyd M., Jr. ......Jackson, MS
Sulsky, Leonard ......Hopewell Junction, NY
Sult, James B. ......Prescott, AZ
Sult, Nathan J. ......Honolulu, HI
Sultan & Associates, Ltd. ......Skokie, IL
Sultan, Berin ......Boston, MA
Sultan, Bruce I. ......Santa Monica, CA
Sultan, Frederick W., IV ......Austin, TX
Sultan, Gregg ......Beverly Hills, CA
Sultan, Gregory ......Skokie, IL
Sultan, James L. ......Boston, MA
Sultan, Jeffrey E., (P.C.) ......Los Angeles, CA
Sultan, Jennifer ......New York, NY
Sultan, Larry A. ......Skokie, IL
Sultan, Lila S. ......Department of Justice, Office of Justice Programs, GV
Sultan, Manal Commodity Futures Trading Commission, Division of Enforcement, GV
Sultan, Melody R. ......New York, NY
Sultan, Olivier ......New York, NY
Sultan, Peter L. ......Washington, DC
Sultan, Shaheda Federal Energy Regulatory Commission, Office of the General Counsel, GV
Sultan, Stephen G. ......New York, NY
Sultanik, Jeffrey T. ......Lansdale, PA
Sultanik, Samuel ......New York, NY
Sultemeier, William H., IV ......Houston, TX
Sulton, Anne T. ......Englewood, CO
Sulton, Gloria R. ......Department of Energy, Office of the General Counsel, GV
Sultzbach, Kelly E. ......Cincinnati, OH
Sulzbach, Christi Rocovich Santa Barbara, CA
Sulzbach, Denise C. ......Bel Air, MD
Sulzbach, J. Michael ......New Haven, CT
Sulzbach, Pamela ......San Diego, CA
Sulzbacher, Lawrence ......Chicago Heights, IL
Sulzberg, Ann H. Securities and Exchange Commission, Division of Enforcement, GV
Sulzberg, Jill ......Chicago, IL
Sulzberger, Carl L. ......Newark, NJ
Sulzberger, Eric W. ......Miami Beach, FL
Sulzberger, Eugene W. ......Miami Beach, FL
Sulzberger, Jennifer Lee ......New York, NY
Sulzberger & Sulzberger, Law Offices of Miami Beach, FL
Sulzby, William D., Jr. ......Cullman, AL
Sulzenfuss, Alan L. ......Salida, CO
Sulzer, Deborah M. ......Metairie, LA
Sulzer, Dorene ......San Diego, CA
Sulzer, James M. ......Chicago, IL
Sulzer, Joseph ......Chillicothe, OH
Sulzer, Kenneth D. ......Los Angeles, CA
Sulzer, Richard P. ......Metairie, LA New Orleans, LA
Sulzer & Shopiro, Ltd. ......Chicago, IL
Sulzer, Stephen L. ......Washington, DC
Sulzer, Victor L. ......Aurora, CO
Sulzer, William E. ......Bronxville, NY
Sulzner & Associates ......San Diego, CA
Sulzner, Bruce E. ......San Diego, CA
Sulzynsky, Wolodymyr R. Department of State, Office of the Legal Adviser, GV
Sum, Juliann J. ......Berkeley, CA
Sum, Michael E. ......Lafayette, IN
Sum, Sylvia ......Salem, OR
Sum, Vincent ......New York, NY
Suma, Margaret A. ......Detroit, MI
Sumalpong, Joanne S. ......Santa Barbara, CA Ventura, CA
Suman, Daniel O. ......Miami, FL
Suman, Edward W. ......San Bruno, CA
Suman, Margaret K. ......Seattle, WA
Sumarriva, Marco R. ......Emeryville, CA San Francisco, CA
Sumber, Edward I. ......Carmel, NY White Plains, NY
Sumber, Edward I., P.C. ......Carmel, NY
Sumberg, Alan ......Des Plaines, IL
Sumberg, Craig L. ......New York, NY
Sumberg, John C., (P.A.) ......Miami, FL
Sumberg, Paul P. ......Skowhegan, ME
Sumberg, Simon ......Norwalk, CT
Sumblin, Anne Stone ......Birmingham, AL
Sume, Kayser O. ......Los Angeles, CA
Sumell, Mary Jean ......Charlotte, NC
Sumerfield, V. P., Jr. ......Bedminster, NJ
Sumerfield, William H. ......Hood River, OR
Sumerford, Rees M. ......Brunswick, GA
Sumey, Benita J. ......Uniontown, PA
Sumi, John W. ......Wichita, KS
Sumi, Maryann ......Madison, WI
Sumich, Darren D. ......Belle Chasse, LA
Sumida, Clyde E. ......Honolulu, HI
Sumida, Floye N., (Ms.) ......Seattle, WA
Sumida, Osami ......New York, NY
Sumida, Steven E. ......Anchorage, AK
Sumihiro, Gary K. ......Ada, MI
Suminski, John H. ......Morristown, NJ
Suminski, Richard J. ......Harrisburg, PA
Sumits, Andrea P. ......San Francisco, CA
Sumlin, Lynn Murrell ......Atlanta, GA
Sumliner, Bernard B. ......New York, NY
Summa, Dale P. ......Angleton, TX
Summa, Joseph B. ......Waterbury, CT
Summa, Philip ......Charlotte, NC
Summa, Robert T. ......St. Louis, MO
Summa & Ryan, P.C. ......Hartford, CT New Haven, CT Waterbury, CT
Summar, Robt. W. ......Chattanooga, TN
Summars, Paul G. ......Oklahoma City, OK
Summe, Fred H. ......Covington, KY
Summe, Kimberly Anne ......New York, NY
Summe, Kurt Andrew ......Cincinnati, OH
Summe, Peter J. ......Fort Wright, KY
Summer, Barry H. ......Galveston, TX
Summer, Barry N. Securities and Exchange Commission, Division of Corporation Finance, GV
Summer, Bernard ......North Bellmore, NY
Summer, C. Scott J. ......Providence, RI
Summer, Chandelle Turner ......Gainesville, GA
Summer, D. Scott ......Nampa, ID
Summer, Daniel A. ......Gainesville, GA
Summer, David B., Jr. ......Columbia, SC
Summer, Donald L. ......Buffalo, NY
Summer, E. Janice ......Austin, TX
Summer, Ellen Stern ......New York, NY
Summer, Fern ......New York, NY
Summer, Fred A. ......Columbus, OH
Summer, Joel S. ......Kirkland, WA
Summer, Mark B. ......Glendale, CA
Summer, Martha Leeann ......Panama City, FL
Summer, Martin M. ......Detroit, MI
Summer, Robert S. ......Bronx, NY
Summer, Sol G. ......New York, NY
Summerall & Bailey, P.A. ......Aiken, SC Edgefield, SC
Summerall, Charles P., IV ......Charleston, SC
Summerall, Henry, Jr. ......Aiken, SC
Summerfield, Craig A. ......Chicago, IL
Summerfield, Cynthia B. ......Skokie, IL
Summerfield, David B. ......Gate City, VA
Summerfield, E. Pete ......Owings Mills, MD
Summerfield, George C., Jr. ......Chicago, IL
Summerfield, Herbert G., Jr. ......Pittsburgh, PA
Summerfield, J. Zane ......Fayetteville, WV
Summerfield, John A. ......Park Ridge, IL
Summerfield, Phillip R. ......San Antonio, TX
Summerfield & Summerfield ......Park Ridge, IL
Summerfield, Walter I., Jr. Bala Cynwyd, PA
Summerfield, Willen, Silverberg & Limsky, P.A. ......Owings Mills, MD
Summerford, Alice Tatum ......Tuscaloosa, AL
Summerford, Curtis K., Jr. ......Florence, SC
Summerford, E. Clark ......Tuscaloosa, AL
Summerford, Gerald N. ......Fort Worth, TX
Summerford, Joe A. ......Fayetteville, AR
Summerford, Lee Alton ......Savannah, GA
Summerford, R. Eric ......Decatur, AL
Summerford & Stoner ......Decatur, AL
Summerford, T. Kenneth ......Florence, SC
Summerford & Zelinski ......Fayetteville, AR
Summergrad, Eric Securities and Exchange Commission, Office of the General Counsel, GV
Summerhays, Diana L. ......Los Angeles, CA
Summerhays, Joanne ......Austin, TX
Summerhays, Lawrence L. Salt Lake City, UT
Summerhays, Lowell V. ......Salt Lake City, UT
Summerhays, Robert Rees ......Dallas, TX
Summerhill, Michael J. ......Cleveland, OH
Summerill & Hull, A Professional Corporation Toms River, NJ Whiting, NJ
Summerill, Joseph J., III ......Toms River, NJ Whiting, NJ
Summerlin, Anne Valley ......Decatur, GA
Summerlin, Connor & Cline Winter Haven, FL
Summerlin, Daniel C. ......Roanoke, VA
Summerlin, Glenn R. ......Stevensville, MD
Summerlin, James W. ......Claremore, OK
Summerlin, Karen Holbrook ......Tifton, GA
Summerlin, Roy C. ......Winter Haven, FL
Summerlin, Suzanne Fannon Tallahassee, FL
Summerlin, V. Gene ......Lincoln, NE
Summerour, J. Michael ......Riverside, CA
Summerour, Ronald W. ......San Mateo, CA
Summers, A. Hugh ......Palestine, TX
Summers, A. Kent ......Carmichael, CA
Summers, Alan ......San Francisco, CA
Summers, Alicia Lehnes ......Alexandria, VA
Summers, Allan D. ......Franklin Square, NY
Summers, Amy Joy ......Studio City, CA
Summers & Anderson ......Charlottesville, VA
Summers, André D. ......Franklin, MA
Summers, Angela Lee ......Louisville, KY
Summers, Ann H. ......Sylvania, OH
Summers, Anne E. ......Bismarck, ND
Summers, Anthony M. ......San Diego, CA
Summers, Anthony W., III ......Oak Brook, IL
Summers, Brad T. ......Portland, OR
Summers, Brent G. ......Portland, OR
Summers, Brett F. ......New York, NY
Summers, C. James ......Charlottesville, VA
Summers, Carla A. ......Deerfield, IL
Summers, Carole A. ......Tucson, AZ
Summers, Cathleen H. ......The Woodlands, TX
Summers, Cecil C. ......Winston-Salem, NC
Summers, Charnelle H., Jr. ......Key Largo, FL
Summers, Clark H., Jr. ......Santa Rosa, CA
Summers, Clinton D. ......Poplar Bluff, MO
Summers, Clive W. ......Stuart, FL
Summers, Clyde W. ......Philadelphia, PA
Summers, Compton, Wells and Hamburg, Professional Corporation ......St. Louis, MO
Summers, Craig S. ......Newport Beach, CA
Summers, Craig W. ......Princeton, NJ
Summers, Cynthia Porter ......Cincinnati, OH
Summers, Dan R. ......Seattle, WA
Summers, David B. ......Cape Girardeau, MO
Summers, David E. ......Thorntown, IN
Summers, David G. ......Kansas City, MO
Summers, David M. ......Englewood, CO
Summers, Deborah ......Houston, TX
Summers, Debra S. ......Palo Alto, CA
Summers, Dennis W. ......Madison, TN
Summers, Diana S.Brodman Downers Grove, IL
Summers, Diane S. ......Bristol, CT
Summers, Donald C. ......Webster, NY
Summers, E. Elizabeth ......Oakland, CA
Summers, Edward L. ......Knoxville, TN
Summers, Edwin C. ......Northridge, CA
Summers, Erica L. ......Washington, DC
Summers, Ernest, III ......Chicago, IL
Summers, Frank L., Jr. ......Staunton, VA
Summers, Frank W., II ......Abbeville, LA
Summers, Frederick C., III ......Dallas, TX
Summers, Frederick C., III, P.C. Dallas, TX
Summers, Gary L. ......Tavares, FL
Summers, Glen E. ......Denver, CO Chicago, IL
Summers, Glenn ......Omaha, NE
Summers, Grant E. ......Shreveport, LA
Summers, H. Meade, Jr. ......St. Louis, MO
Summers, H. Scott ......Kahoka, MO
Summers, Hardy ......Oklahoma City, OK
Summers, Harry Jacobs Federal Election Commission, Office of the General Counsel, GV
Summers, Holten D. ......Urbana, IL
Summers, J. Vernon ......Frederick, MD
Summers, James B. ......Memphis, TN
Summers, James M. ......San Antonio, TX
Summers, James W. ......Rusk, TX
Summers, Jane ......New York, NY
Summers, Janis L. United States International Trade Commission, Office of Tariff Affairs & Trade Agreements, GV
Summers, Jeffrey A. ......Van Wert, OH
Summers, Jerry H. ......Chattanooga, TN
Summers, Jillora Herdman ......Lebanon, OH
Summers, John S. ......Philadelphia, PA
Summers & Johnson ......Kansas City, KS Kansas City, MO
Summers, Jon R. ......Portland, OR
Summers, Jon S. ......Los Angeles, CA
Summers, Jonathan B. ......Albany, NY
Summers, Jonathan W. ......Harrisville, WV
Summers, Julia Clare ......Oklahoma City, OK
Summers, Julian S. ......Palm Desert, CA
Summers, Kelli Barr ......Goodlettsville, TN
Summers, Kenneth Kelly Grand Junction, CO
Summers, Kevin N. ......Southfield, MI
Summers, Kim S. ......Kansas City, MO
Summers, Lawrence L. ......Chicago, IL
Summers, Layman Allen ......Carbondale, IL
Summers, Lewis P., III ......Arlington, VA
Summers, Linda Delacourt Cleveland, OH
Summers, Linden D., III ......Oneonta, NY
Summers, Lisa D. ......Painesville, OH
Summers, Lloyd R. ......Portland, OR
Summers, Lorraine A. ......Cleveland, OH
Summers, Lorraine L. ......New Orleans, LA
Summers, L. T. Archer Department of Agriculture, GV
Summers, Lynn M. ......Miami, FL
Summers, Marc T. ......New Orleans, LA
Summers, Mark A. ......Middletown, OH
Summers, Maureen A. ......San Diego, CA
Summers, McDonnell, Walsh & Skeel Pittsburgh, PA
Summers, Melody J. ......San Francisco, CA
Summers, Michael G. ......Marquette, MI
Summers, Nancy Ann ......South Barrington, IL
Summers, Nancy E.F. ......Potomac, MD
Summers, Patricia L. ......Fort Worth, TX
Summers, Patrick C. ......Minneapolis, MN
Summers, Paul D., Jr. ......Charlottesville, VA
Summers, Paul G. ......Somerville, TN
Summers, Paul R. ......Somerville, TN
Summers, Paul W. ......Torrington, CT
Summers, Paul W. ......Bismarck, ND
Summers & Pence, A Professional Corporation Marquette, MI
Summers, Philip A. ......Gibson City, IL
Summers, Phillip C. ......Houston, TX
Summers, Preston M. ......Abbeville, LA
Summers, Pritchett and Blaich, P.C. Poplar Bluff, MO
Summers, R. Scott ......Lexington, KY
Summers, R. Scott ......Morgantown, WV
Summers, Reed N. ......Rochester, NY
Summers, Reed Noble ......Rochester, NY
Summers, Renee ......Fort Worth, TX
Summers, Richard E. ......Elkhart, IN
Summers, Richard W. ......Atlanta, GA
Summers, Robert ......Austin, TX
Summers, Robert B. ......Austin, TX
Summers, Robert C. ......Pasadena, CA
Summers, Robert F. ......St. Louis, MO
Summers, Robert H., Jr. ......Chicago, IL
Summers, Robert I. ......New York, NY
Summers, Robert P. ......Stuart, FL
Summers, Robert S. ......Ithaca, NY
Summers, Robert S. ......Ithaca, NY
Summers, Roger C. ......Fort Wayne, IN
Summers, Ronald James ......Rochester, NY
Summers, Ronald L. ......Del Mar, CA
Summers, Ross J. ......Fort Washington, MD
Summers, Scott K. ......Chicago, IL Oak Park, IL
Summers, Scott L. ......Charleston, WV
Summers, Sean B. ......Kansas City, MO
Summers, Sean E. ......Fayetteville, NC
Summers & Shives, A P.C. ......San Diego, CA
Summers, Sidney N. ......Atlanta, GA
Summers, Stephen J. ......Pittsburgh, PA
Summers, Steven C. ......Philadelphia, PA
Summers, Steven P. ......Portland, OR
Summers, Steven R. ......Stayton, OR
Summers, Stuart G. ......Cincinnati, OH
Summers, Sue Ellen ......Birmingham, AL
Summers & Summers ......Gibson City, IL
Summers, Sunshine A. ......La Mirada, CA
Summers, Sylvester, Jr. ......Cleveland, OH
Summers, Terrance M. ......Kansas City, MO
Summers, Thomas Carey ......Baltimore, MD Towson, MD
Summers, Thomas J. ......Euless, TX
Summers, Thomas R. ......St. Joseph, MO
Summers, Timothy J. ......San Francisco, CA
Summers & Vargas Co., L.P.A. Beachwood, OH
Summers Vargas & Resnick Co., L.P.A. Cleveland, OH
Summers, W. Dennis ......Atlanta, GA
Summers, William L. ......Coral Gables, FL
Summers, William L. ......Cleveland, OH
Summers & Wyatt, P.C. ......Chattanooga, TN Cleveland, TN
Summersett, Katrina Renee ......Troy, MI
Summersgill, Michael J. ......Boston, MA
Summerson, Carl H. ......Harrisburg, PA
Summerville, Clyde W. ......Seattle, WA
Summerville, Eric A. ......Jersey City, NJ
Summerville, Jay A. ......St. Louis, MO
Summerville, Jessiephine W. ......Detroit, MI
Summerville, Karen J. ......Seattle, WA
Summerville, Mark Hart ......Boston, MA
Summerville, Patricia L. Hot Springs National Park, AR
Summerville, Radding & Campbell Jersey City, NJ
Summerville, Rebecca L. ......Missoula, MT
Summerville, Sarah Falkner Department of Defense, GV
Summerville, Thomas D. ......Philadelphia, PA
Summerwill, Suzanne ......Iowa City, IA
Summey, Jamal Montez ......Murfreesboro, NC
Summey, Lemuel M. ......Los Altos, CA
Summey, Robert G. ......Forest City, NC
Summey, Sidney C., Jr. ......Birmingham, AL
Summit Law Group, PLLC ......Seattle, WA
Summit, Natasha M. ......Anchorage, AK
Summit, Paul E. ......Boston, MA
Summit, Steven C. ......South Glastonbury, CT
Summit, Stuart A. ......New York, NY
Summitt, Marilyn K. ......Fort Lauderdale, FL
Summitt, Marilyn K., P.A. Fort Lauderdale, FL
Summitt, Paul C. ......Falls Church, VA
Summitt, Robert M. ......Chattanooga, TN
Summons, Sarah F. ......Stamford, CT
Summonte, Joseph F., Jr. ......Sarasota, FL
Summy, Greg E. ......Norfolk, VA
Summy, Paul "Scott" ......Dallas, TX
Sumnar, Edmund J. O. ......Orlando, FL
Sumner, A. Welles ......Roseland, NJ
Sumner, Amy A. ......Denver, CO
Sumner & Anderson ......Beaufort, SC
Sumner, Ann E. ......Greenville, SC
Sumner & Auser ......Fulton, NY
Sumner, Bobby G. ......Charlotte, NC
Sumner, Bret A. ......Washington, DC
Sumner, Brian E. ......Hallowell, ME
Sumner, Bruce W. ......Orange, CA
Sumner, D. Jay ......Washington, DC
Sumner, Daniel R. ......Warwick, RI
Sumner, Daniel Y. ......Jacksonville, FL
Sumner, David W. ......Blue Bell, PA
Sumner, David W. ......Philadelphia, PA
Sumner, Elizabeth Neisler ......Gastonia, NC
Sumner, Ellen McGee ......Boston, MA
Sumner, Fred I. ......Fulton, NY
Sumner, H. Randolph ......Gastonia, NC
Sumner, Hugh L. ......Berwick, PA
Sumner, Ivan Todd ......Tallahassee, FL
Sumner, J. Clinton, Jr. ......Rome, GA
Sumner, James C. ......Winona, MS
Sumner, James L., Jr. ......Montgomery, AL
Sumner, Jas. D., Jr. ......Los Angeles, CA
Sumner, Jessie J., (Miss) ......Sheldon, IL
Sumner, John H. ......Columbus, OH
Sumner, John M. ......Winona, MS
Sumner, John P. ......Minneapolis, MN
Sumner, Kathleen G. ......Greensboro, NC
Sumner, Kenneth H. ......San Francisco, CA
Sumner, L. Cartan, Jr. ......St. Louis, MO
Sumner, Lawrence C. ......St. Louis, MO
Sumner, Leah Fallin ......Newnan, GA
Sumner, Leann A. ......San Diego, CA
Sumner, Lisa P. ......Roanoke, VA
Sumner & Mann, P.A. ......Dade City, FL
Sumner, Matthew A. ......West Paterson, NJ

Sumner, Michael E. .... **Newnan, GA**
Sumner, Michael E., P.C. .... **Newnan, GA**
Sumner, Molly P. .... Salt Lake City, UT
Sumner, Neil .... Islip, NY
Sumner, Patricia A. .... Department of Justice, Office of the Inspector General, GV
Sumner, Paul F. .... Madras, OR
Sumner & Peters .... Rochester Hills, MI
Warren, MI
Sumner, Phyllis B. .... Chicago, IL
Sumner, Quentin T. .... Rocky Mount, NC
Sumner & Riexinger, L.L.C. .... Atlanta, GA
Sumner, Robert B. .... Douglas, GA
Sumner, Robert D. .... Dade City, FL
Sumner, Robert D. .... Atlanta, GA
Sumner, Robert T. .... **Gastonia, NC**
Sumner, Robert W. .... **Raleigh, NC**
Sumner, Ron R. .... Rochester Hills, MI
Warren, MI
Sumner, Sandra S. .... Goose Creek, SC
Sumner, Sara E. .... Chicago, IL
Sumner & Schick .... Dallas, TX
Sumner, Scott .... **Rapid City, SD**
Sumner, Scott H. Z. .... **Walnut Creek, CA**
Sumner, Scott J. .... Rochester Hills, MI
Sumner, Steve .... Dallas, TX
Sumner, Steve W. .... Greenville, SC
Sumner, Susan Hurt .... **Valdosta, GA**
Sumner, Thomas R. .... Chicago, IL
Sumner, Tracy J., P.A. .... Tallahassee, FL
Sumner, Tracy Jeanne .... Tallahassee, FL
Sumner, Walter E. .... Atlanta, GA
Sumners & Carter .... **New Albany, MS**
Sumners, George & Dortch, P.C.
Trenton, NJ
Sumners, John S. .... **Minneapolis, MN**
Sumners, Lester F. .... **New Albany, MS**
Sumners, Martin C. .... Trenton, NJ
Sumners, Minor C., Jr. .... Jackson, MS
Sumners, Peter L. .... Washington, DC
Sumners, Thomas W., Jr. .... Trenton, NJ
Sumnick, Steven L. .... **Walnut Creek, CA**
Sumnik, George A. .... **Detroit, MI**
Sumoski, Diane M. .... **Dallas, TX**
Sump, David H. .... **Norfolk, VA**
Sumpter, Alfred V. .... Del Rio, TX
Sumpter, Chester L. .... **Cleveland, OH**
Sumpter, Dennis R. .... Sulphur, LA
Sumpter, Gail M. .... Agoura Hills, CA
Sumpter, James F. .... Richmond, VA
Sumpter, Jeffrey L. .... Woodland Hills, CA
Sumpter, Marilee .... Sacramento, CA
Sumpter, Rodney E. .... **Reno, NV**
Sumpter, Scott S. .... **Topeka, KS**
Sumpter, W. David, III .... Murphy, NC
Sumption, Nancy .... Department of Defense, Defense Legal Services Agency, GV
Sumrall, H. Cassedy, Jr.
Delray Beach, FL
Sumrall, H. Cassedy, Jr., Professional Association .... **Delray Beach, FL**
Sumrall, Katherine R. .... **Raleigh, NC**
Sumrall, Kathryn H. .... **Birmingham, AL**
Sumrall & Marshall .... Jackson, MS
Sumrall, O. Malcolm, Jr. .... Mobile, AL
Sumrall, Roger S. .... **Atlanta, GA**
Sumrall, William W. .... **Laurel, MS**
Sumrall, Wm. Andy .... Jackson, MS
Sumrell, Raymond E. .... **New Bern, NC**
Sumrell, Sugg, Carmichael, Hicks & Hart, P.A. .... **New Bern, NC**
Sumrow, Galen Ray .... Rockwall, TX
Sumrow, Matthew A. .... **Woodland Hills, CA**
Sumrow, Shad E. .... **Dallas, TX**
Sumrow-Pirch, Charlotte Dale
Fountain Valley, CA
Sumsion, Richard G. .... Salt Lake City, UT
Sumsion, Steven R. .... Springville, UT
Sumski, Bill J. .... Los Angeles, CA
Sumsky, Michael A. .... Mineola, NY
Sumter, Geraldine .... **Charlotte, NC**
Sumulong, Lorraine .... Beverly Hills, CA
Sumwalt, Vernon Edward .... Rock Hill, SC
Sumwalt, Vernon R. .... **Columbia, SC**
Florence, SC
Sun, Able M. .... New York, NY
Sun, Alexander F. .... Monterey Park, CA
Sun, Alexander K. .... Miami, FL
Sun, Andy Y. .... Ellicott City, MD
Sun, Bonnie .... Los Angeles, CA
Sun, Brian A. .... **Santa Monica, CA**
Sun, Caroline M. .... Jamaica, NY
Sun, Catherine .... **New York, NY**
Sun, Gerald T. .... New York, NY
Sun, Gregory R. .... Chicago, IL
Sun & Ho .... **Tustin, CA**
Sun, Hong .... **Los Angeles, CA**
Sun, Hsiang-ning (Sean) .... Philadelphia, PA
Sun, Irene C. .... **Los Angeles, CA**
Sun, Jeffrey C. .... New York, NY
Sun, Jennifer Y. .... **Miami, FL**
Sun, Joan F. .... Tacoma, WA
Sun, John L. .... Los Angeles, CA
Sun, Joyce J. .... **New York, NY**
Sun, Lazarus N. .... **Los Angeles, CA**
Sun, Lisa S.Y. .... New York, NY
Sun, Michael Tse-Wen .... Beverly Hills, CA
Sun, Patricia V.
Department of Transportation, Federal Railroad Administration, GV
Sun, Paul K., Jr. .... **Raleigh, NC**
Sun, Raymond .... **Tustin, CA**
Sun, Steven T. .... Woodland Hills, CA
Sun, T. Eric .... **San Francisco, CA**
Sun, Thomas .... Brooklyn, NY
Sun, Y. Ping .... **New York, NY**
Suna, Aron L. .... New York, NY
Suna, Steven A. .... **Atlanta, GA**
Sunada, Claire Midori .... Aiea, HI
Sunada, Craig S.
Rolling Hills Estates, CA
Sunberg, Cindy R. .... Kansas City, MO
Sunberg, Kenneth M. .... **Caldwell, NJ**
Sunberg, Randall B. .... **Princeton, NJ**
Sunbury, Gerald T. .... Columbus, OH
Sunby, David E. .... **Wausau, WI**
Sund, Gary L. .... Sequim, WA
Sundack, Tracie A. .... **White Plains, NY**
Sundack, Tracie A., L.L.C. .... **New York, NY**
White Plains, NY
Sundahl, John Alan .... **Cheyenne, WY**
Sundahl, Powers, Kapp & Martin, L.L.C.
Cheyenne, WY
Sundall, Herb C. .... **Kennebec, SD**
Sundall, Linda S. .... Champlin, MN
Sundar, Era F. .... Miami, FL
Sundar, Ram .... **New York, NY**
Sundara, Ravi .... **St. Louis, MO**
Sundaram, Kannan .... New York, NY
Sundaravej, Pimkaeo .... **New York, NY**
Sunday, Andrea Ellen .... Boston, MA
Sunday, Constance B. .... Houston, TX
Sunday, Dawn S. .... Mechanicsburg, PA
Sunday, Edward C. .... **The Woodlands, TX**
Sunday, Jeffery H. .... Wilkes-Barre, PA
Sunday, Jeffrey A. .... Orlando, FL
Sunday, Kay L. .... **San Diego, CA**
Sunday, Mark R. .... San Diego, CA
Sunday, Steven E. .... Upper Marlboro, MD
Sunday, William L. .... Mechanicsburg, PA
Sunday, William L. and Dawn S. Sunday
Mechanicsburg, PA
Sundback, Mark F. .... **Washington, DC**
Sundberg, Alan C. .... Tallahassee, FL
Sundberg, E. Kent .... Provo, UT
Sundberg, Eugene C., Jr. .... **Erie, PA**
Sundberg, Gary M. .... Phoenix, AZ
Sundberg, Jan L. .... Seattle, WA
Sundberg, Kathleen A. .... Richmond, VA
Sundberg, Kris J. .... Mercer Island, WA
Sundberg, Kurt L. .... **Erie, PA**
Sundberg, Margaret A. .... **Seattle, WA**
Sundberg & Mousel .... Phoenix, AZ
Sundberg, Paul A. .... **Chicago, IL**
Sundberg, Robert C., II .... Atlanta, GA
Sundberg, Susan L.
Small Business Administration, Office of the General Counsel, GV
Sundbery, Sidney C. .... **Houma, LA**
Sundburg, Alan Dean .... **Washington, DC**
Sundby, Gunnar A. .... Atchison, KS
Sundby, Herbert C. .... Portland, OR
Sundby, Scott Edwin .... San Francisco, CA
Sunde, Einar .... Palo Alto, CA
Sunde, Linda Neff .... **Carmel, CA**
Sunde, Olson, Kircher and Zender, P.L.C.
Madelia, MN
St. James, MN
Sunde, Richard W. .... Mounds View, MN
Sunde, Steven R. .... St. James, MN
Sundeen, Marcia H. .... **Washington, DC**
Sundeen, Matthew E. .... Denver, CO
Sundeen, Neal S. .... **Phoenix, AZ**
Sundeen, Neal S., P.C. .... **Peoria, AZ**
Phoenix, AZ
Sundeen, Randall J., Law Office of
Simi Valley, CA
Sundeen, Ross L. .... **Watford City, ND**
Sundeen, Ruben .... Oakland, CA
Sundel, Arnold H. .... Brooklyn, NY
Sundel, Michael B. .... Alexandria, VA
Sundelin, Peter A. .... West Barnstable, MA
Sundell, Daniel R. .... **Minneapolis, MN**
Sundell, Lanny S. .... Santa Cruz, CA
Sundell, Robert E. .... Maryville, MO
Sundell, Stephen D. .... **Rochester, NY**
Sundelson, David .... Berkeley, CA
Sunden, Gary .... New York, NY
Sunderdick, Vincent J. .... Arlington, VA
Sunderland, Allison M.
Santa Monica, CA
Sunderland, Beverly F. .... Northampton, MA
Sunderland, Charles M. .... Tampa, FL
Sunderland, Craig G. .... Burbank, CA
Sunderland, David G. .... Vandalia, OH
Sunderland & Diaz .... Buford, GA
Sunderland, Don D. .... **Amarillo, TX**
Sunderland, Gerard P. .... **Baltimore, MD**
Sunderland, James P. .... Overland Park, KS
Sunderland, Jeremy H. .... **Burbank, CA**
Sunderland, John T. .... **Columbus, OH**
Sunderland, Kaye E. .... Salem, OR
Sunderland, Louis B. .... **Milford, IL**
Watseka, IL
Sunderland, Louise A. .... Chicago, IL
Sunderland, Magali V. .... **Honolulu, HI**
Sunderland & Moore .... Vandalia, OH
Sunderland, Murphy, Spenn, Johnson and Luebchow .... Cissna Park, IL
Danforth, IL
Milford, IL
Watseka, IL
Sunderland, Philip G. .... Washington, DC
Sunderland, Richard H. .... Chattanooga, TN
Sunderland, Rodney S. .... Rice Lake, WI
Sunderland, Sandra J. .... Glastonbury, CT
Sunderland, Sean A. .... Redmond, WA
Sunderland, T. Stanley .... Buford, GA
Sunderman, David P. .... Delaware, OH
Sunderman, John D. .... Deshler, OH
Sunderman, Lisa M. .... Fort Worth, TX
Sunderman, Robert E. .... Cincinnati, OH
Sunderman, William A. .... **Charleston, IL**
Sundermann, Deborah R.
Corpus Christi, TX
Sundermann, J. Howard, Jr. .... Cincinnati, OH
Sundermeier, Christopher J.
Palo Alto, CA
Sundermeyer, Michael S. .... **Washington, DC**
Sundermier, Karen A. .... **San Francisco, CA**
Sundermier, Paul J. .... Salem, OR
Sundet & Associates .... La Crosse, WI
Sundet, R. Samuel .... Oshkosh, WI
Sundet, Ray A. .... La Crosse, WI
Sundgaard, Stephen R. .... Dallas, TX
Sundheim, Brian C. .... **Chicago, IL**
Sundheim, Frederick G. .... Stuart, FL
Sundheim, Frederick G., Jr. .... **Stuart, FL**
Sundheim, George M. .... Chicago, IL
Oak Brook, IL
Sundheim, George M., III .... **Palo Alto, CA**
Sundheim, Joanne K. .... Wilmington, DE
Sundheim, Nancy Straus .... **Blue Bell, PA**
Sundheim, Robert B. .... **Cleveland, OH**
Sundheim, Stephen J. .... **Philadelphia, PA**
Sundheim, Steven R. .... White Plains, NY
Sundheimer, Marlene .... Cleveland, OH
Sundholm, Charles A. .... Los Altos, CA
Sundick, Gary N.
Securities and Exchange Commission, Division of Enforcement, GV
Sundie, Rufus C. .... Miami, FL
Sundin, David Stephen .... California, KY
Sundling, Roger R. .... **Grand Forks, ND**
Sundlof, Kenneth C., Jr. .... **Phoenix, AZ**
Sundly, Matthew J. .... **Santa Ana, CA**
Sundmaker, Earl F., III .... **New Orleans, LA**
Sundmaker, Thomas P. .... Stroudsburg, PA
Sundock, Jon Michael .... Nashville, TN
Sundook, Steven B. .... **Fort Myers, FL**
Sundquist, Deborah K. .... Eagan, MN
Sundquist, Elizabeth Larson .... Edina, MN
Sundquist, Jack .... Gillette, WY
Sundquist, John .... Crystal Falls, MI
Sundquist, Raymond H. .... Seattle, WA
Sundquist, Richard A. .... **Detroit, MI**
Sundquist, Thomas E. .... Rocklin, CA
Sundram, Clarence J. .... Albany, NY
Sundstedt, Frank E., Jr. .... Los Angeles, CA
Sundstedt, Michael J. .... Newport Beach, CA
Sundstrand, Warren D. .... Paw Paw, MI
Sundstrom, Judith W. S. .... El Sobrante, CA
Sundstrom, William E., (P.A.)
Tallahassee, FL
Sundt, Ann N. .... Rockville, MD
Sundt, John H. .... **Phoenix, AZ**
Sundvall, Sheila A. .... **Chicago, IL**
Sundvold, Stephen J. .... Fountain Valley, CA
Sundwall, Catherine H. .... Silver Spring, MD
Sunenblick, Reben, Benjamin & March
Portland, ME
Sunenblick, Stephen .... Portland, ME
Suneson, Michael J. .... Fall River, MA
Sung, Audrey L. .... **San Francisco, CA**
Sung, Chan Woo .... **New York, NY**
Sung & Co., P.C. .... New York, NY
Sung, Donald D. .... New York, NY
Sung, Helen E. .... **San Francisco, CA**
Sung, Hyen-ae Jane .... **San Francisco, CA**
Sung, Jacqueline H. .... **San Francisco, CA**
Sung, John C.E. .... **Maitland, FL**
Sung, Ki Jun .... **Washington, DC**
Sung, Lawrence M. .... Washington, DC
Sung, Linda Ya-Ning .... **Palo Alto, CA**
Sung, Raymond T. .... **Los Angeles, CA**
Sung, Sharon O. .... **San Francisco, CA**
Sung, Tak K. .... Fairfax, VA
Sung, Thomas C. C. .... New York, NY
Sung, Vera .... New York, NY
Sung, Wu-fung .... Houston, TX
Sungaila, Mary-Christine (M.C.)
Los Angeles, CA
Sung Kepner, Kristina .... **Columbus, OH**
Suni, Ellen Y. .... Kansas City, MO
Suniga, Gail E. .... **Palo Alto, CA**
Suniville, Gerald H. .... **Salt Lake City, UT**
Sunkel, Margaret L. .... **New Orleans, LA**
Sunkel, Morris A. .... **Valparaiso, IN**
Sunkel, William M. .... **New York, NY**
Sunkin, David I. .... Beverly Hills, CA
Sunkin, Neil M. .... **Los Angeles, CA**
Sunkin, Roberta J. .... Chandler, AZ
Sunleaf, Robert S. .... Naperville, IL
Sunleaf, Roger W. .... Montezuma, IA
Sunne, Celia T. .... Atlanta, GA
Sunne, Kenneth A. .... **Clearwater, FL**
Sunne & Locke, P.A. .... **Clearwater, FL**
Sunnen, John W. .... San Diego, CA
Sunner, John A. .... Longwood, FL
Sunner, Kimberly Noworyta .... **Orlando, FL**
Sunner, Richard G. .... Longwood, FL
Sunness, Eric A. .... **Fort Collins, CO**
Sunseri, J. Douglas .... **Metairie, LA**
Sunseri, James M. .... Huntington Beach, CA
Sunseri, James V. .... San Jose, CA
Sunseri, Salvatore J. .... San Jose, CA
Sunshine, Amy .... **New York, NY**
Sunshine, Andrew B. .... San Clemente, CA
Sunshine, Atkins, Minassian & Tafuri, P.A.
River Edge, NJ
Sunshine, Barbara K. .... Plantation, FL
Sunshine, David M. .... **Burlington, VT**
Richmond, VT
Sunshine, Donald M. .... **New York, NY**
Sunshine, Ilene Robinson .... **Boston, MA**
Sunshine, Jeffrey A. .... Lake Success, NY
Sunshine, Jeffrey A., P.C. .... Lake Success, NY
Sunshine, Joel M. .... **Garden City, NY**
Sunshine, Mark .... Pelham, NY
Sunshine, Marvin H. .... River Edge, NJ
Sunshine, Paul D. .... Dover, DE
Sunshine, Paul H. .... **Palo Alto, CA**
Sunshine, Randall J. .... **Santa Monica, CA**
Sunshine, Richard I. .... East Hampton, NY
Sunshine, Robert S. .... **New York, NY**
Sunshine, Slott & Sunshine, P.C.
New York, NY
Sunshine, Steven C. .... **Washington, DC**
Sunshine, Steven H. .... **Irvine, CA**
Sunstein, Bruce D. .... **Boston, MA**
Sunstein, Cass R. .... Chicago, IL
Suntag, Dana A. .... Stockton, CA
Suntharam, Khannan .... **Houston, TX**
Suntum, Joseph P. .... **Rockville, MD**
Sunu, H. Wesley .... **Chicago, IL**
Sunukjian, Nancy M. .... Cohoes, NY
Sunukjian, Peter D. .... **Irvine, CA**
Sunwoo, Albert .... **Hawthorne, NY**
Suo, Sidney J. .... **Washington, MI**
Suo, Sidney J., P.C. .... **Washington, MI**
Suojanen, Wayne W. (Bill) .... **Irvine, CA**
Suomala, Robert L. .... **Los Angeles, CA**
Suozzi, Joseph A. .... **Mineola, NY**
Suozzi, Joseph M. .... Glen Cove, NY
Suozzi, Michael A. .... Pleasantville, NY
Suozzi, Paul J. .... **Buffalo, NY**
Suozzi, Thomas R. .... Glen Cove, NY
Suozzo, James C. .... **Westwood, NJ**
Suozzo, Joseph F. .... Trenton, NJ
Suozzo, Marie D. .... Morristown, NJ
Suozzo, Ralph .... **Manchester, NH**
Sup, Bryan R. .... **Chicago, IL**
Supan, Donald A. .... Santa Clara, CA
Supan, Gregory P. .... **Dallas, TX**
Supance & Howard .... **Tiffin, OH**
Supance, James D. .... **Tiffin, OH**
Supancic, Ronald Melin, Law Offices of
Woodland Hills, CA
Supancich, Michael Jack .... **Portland, OR**
Supanich, Dennis M. .... **Los Angeles, CA**
Supcoe, Donald C. .... Charleston, WV
Supcoff, Marc H. .... **New York, NY**
Super, David A. .... **Washington, DC**
Super, David A. .... Washington, DC
Super, Reed W. .... San Francisco, CA
Superfine, Richard J. .... **Chicago, IL**
Superfon, Laurie S. .... Phoenix, AZ
Superko, Colleen .... **Boston, MA**
Supernaw, Kathleen R. .... Tulsa, OK
Superville, Maurice C., Jr. .... Paris, TX
Supica, James W., Jr. .... Lenexa, KS
Supik, Frank J. .... **Washington, DC**
Supina, Gerald J. .... Ionia, MI
Supinger, Jeffrey L. .... **Spokane, WA**
Supinka, Michael J. .... Indiana, PA
Supinka & Supinka .... Indiana, PA
Supinka, Vivian F. .... Indiana, PA
Supino, Anthony M., Law Offices
West Orange, NJ
New York, NY
Supino, David J. .... New York, NY
Supinski, Henry W. .... Wilmington, DE
Supinski, Lyssa S. .... **St. Cloud, MN**
Supko, Mark M. .... **Washington, DC**
Suplee, Dennis R. .... **Philadelphia, PA**
Suplee, Katherine A. .... Union, NJ
Supler, Robin L. .... Fort Lauderdale, FL
Supman, Jack .... Lancaster, OH
Supnick, Richard B. .... Cherry Hill, NJ
Supnick, Samuel L. .... Camden, NJ
Supnik, Michael L. .... Delray Beach, FL
Supnik, Paul D. .... **Beverly Hills, CA**
Supnik, Paul D. .... **Los Angeles, CA**
Supon, Arthur G. .... Hicksville, NY
Supovitz, Ruth H. .... Albany, NY
Supowit, Jeffrey A. .... **Bingham Farms, MI**
Supowit, Stuart E. .... Valencia, CA
Supowitz, Paul A. .... Pittsburgh, PA
Supp, Joseph J. .... New York, NY
Supp, Lawrence J. .... **Hackettstown, NJ**
Suppa, Elizabeth A. .... Philadelphia, PA
Suppa, Jerry Michael .... **San Diego, CA**
Suppa, Ronald A. .... Westlake Village, CA
Suppa, Suzanne M. .... **Boston, MA**
Suppa, Trucchi & Lee, A Professional Corporation .... **San Diego, CA**
Supperstein, Scott M. .... Portland, OR
Supple, Brenda Kay .... **Miami, FL**
Supple, Charles M. .... Austin, TX
Fort Worth, TX
Houston, TX
Supple, Christopher J. .... Boston, MA
Supple, Gregory D. .... Beacon, NY
Wappingers Falls, NY
Supple, James B. .... **Franklin, LA**
Supple, John L. .... **San Francisco, CA**
Supple, John L. .... Beacon, NY
Supple, John Richard, Jr. .... Brooklyn, NY
Supple, Paul B. .... Beacon, NY
Supple, Paul C. .... Tustin, CA
Supplee, Edw. A. .... Baltimore, MD
Supplee, Henry A. .... Frederick, MD
Supplee, Robert S. .... **West Chester, PA**
Supplee, Robert S., P.C. .... **Media, PA**
West Chester, PA
Supran, Bryan A. .... **Boston, MA**
Supran, George P. .... **West Palm Beach, FL**
Supranowitz, Brian M. .... Brooklyn, NY
Supraski, Louis A.
North Miami Beach, FL
Suprenant, Leon J., Jr. .... Ventura, CA
Suprenuk, Christian P. .... **Philadelphia, PA**
Suprunowicz, Michael R.
Schenectady, NY
Supton, Paul D. .... Oakland, CA
Sur, Elizabeth Farrelly .... **Philadelphia, PA**
Sur, Richard Christopher
Minneapolis, MN
Sur, Wilma .... **Honolulu, HI**
Sura, Theodore J. .... Inkster, MI
Surabian, Vincent G. .... Treasury Department, Internal Revenue Service, GV

Surace, Cathy S. ... Landover, MD
Surace-Smith, Kathryn ... Redmond, WA
Suraci, F. Skip ... Tulsa, OK
Suraci, Joseph A. ... Kew Gardens, NY
Suraj, Gita C. ... San Francisco, CA
Sural, Jeffrey R. ... Eaton Rapids, MI
Surampudi, Rakesh ... Atlanta, GA
Suran, Frederick A. ... Milwaukee, WI
Suran & Suran ... Milwaukee, WI
Surane, James W. ... Charlotte, NC
Surasky, Bernard A. ... Naples, FL
Surasky, Charles W. ... Atlanta, GA
Surasky, Stephen K. ... Langley, SC
Suravitz, Louis ... Scranton, PA
Surbaugh, Linda A. ... Denver, CO
Surbeck, Catherine Tanaka
Philadelphia, PA
Surbeck, David A. ... Philadelphia, PA
Surbeck, John F., Jr. ... Fort Wayne, IN
Surber, Charles M., Jr. ... Charleston, WV
Surber, Jennifer C. ... Dallas, TX
Surber, Joel Patrick ... Dallas, TX
Surber, Julie J. ... San Bernardino, CA
Surber, Nell D. ... Cincinnati, OH
Surbey, D. Ronald ... Fort Lauderdale, FL
Surchin, Alan D. ... New York, NY
Surdacki, M. Eleanor ... Bayonne, NJ
Surdell, Steven M. ... Chicago, IL
Surdy, Joseph F. ... Newark, NJ
Surdyk, Leonard S. ... Chicago, IL
Surdyk, Robert J. ... Dayton, OH
Surdyk, Thomas M. ... Libertyville, IL
Surdykowski, Andrew J. ... Atlanta, GA
Sure, Kathryn A. ... San Jose, CA
Sureck, Philip ... Oklahoma City, OK
Sureff, J. Seymour ... Baltimore, MD
Surena, Andre M. ... Department of State, Office of the Legal Adviser, GV
Surenian, Jeffrey R. ... Toms River, NJ
Surett, Corey H. ... Boston, MA
Surette, J. Edward, III ... Wakefield, MA
Surette, Paul E. ... North Easton, MA
Surette, Robert J. ... Clearwater, FL
Surface, J. Frank ... Jacksonville, FL
Surface, Katheryn E. ... Richmond, VA
Surfus, Gerald C. ... Sarasota, FL
Surfus & Prosch ... Sarasota, FL
Surgalla, John B. ... Buffalo, NY
Surgalla, Kathleen E. ... Rochester, NY
Surgalla, Michael J., Jr.
Department of Justice, Criminal Division, GV
Surgan, Andrew ... Rego Park, NY
Surgener, Brian W. ... Lansing, MI
Surgent, George F. ... Mahwah, NJ
Surgent, Jay V. ... Wayne, NJ
Surgent, Thomas J. ... Dallas, TX
Surgeon, Donald L. ... Bethel, AK
Surges, Edward N. ... Chicago, IL
Surges, Nicole B. ... Minneapolis, MN
Surgis, Valentine ... Jackson, MS
Surgner, W. Hildebrandt, Jr.
Richmond, VA
Surguine, Arthur G., Jr. ... Fort Wayne, IN
Surguine, Michael E. ... Kansas City, MO
Surh, Helen H. ... San Francisco, CA
Suri, Mark K. ... Chicago, IL
Suri, Neerja ... Albany, NY
Albany, NY
Suri, Sharan Kaur ... Washington, DC
Suri, Vivek S. ... New York, NY
Suria, Ellen Q. ... Philadelphia, PA
Suria, Fred G., Jr. ... Chicago, IL
Suria, John R. ... Philadelphia, PA
Suriano, Costantino P. ... New York, NY
Suriano, Donald J. ... Chicago, IL
Suriano, Rosaria A. ... Newark, NJ
Suriano, William P. ... Riverside, IL
Surick, Stuart ... Trenton, NJ
Surie, Irving ... Chicago, IL
Suriel, Nicomedes E. ... Phoenix, AZ
Surillo Gutiérrez, Adela ... San Juan, PR
Surillo-Peña, Hilda M. ... San Juan, PR
Surillo-Pumarada & Dahdah Ramirez
Mayaguez, PR
Surillo-Pumarada, Juan M.
Mayaguez, PR
Surin, Elizabeth C. ... Philadelphia, PA
Surin, William T. ... Ottawa, IL
Surinak, Lawrence R. ... Joliet, IL
Suringa, Dirk J ... Washington, DC
Surinsky, Allen H. ... St. Louis, MO
Surkamp, Richard E., Jr. ... Blue Ash, OH
Surkin, Dean L. ... New York, NY
Surkin, Elliot M. ... Boston, MA
Surkin, Ronald H. ... Media, PA
Surla, Gia F. ... Houston, TX
Surlas, Jeffrey R., (P.A.) ... Miami, FL
Surles, Catherine ... Durham, NC
Surles, John C. ... Charlotte, NC
Surles, Martha W. ... Charlotte, NC
Surles, Oliver S. ... Tarboro, NC
Surles, Robert Edward ... Summerville, GA
Surles, Robert H. ... Wilmington, DE
Surles, Susan N. ... Charlotte, NC
Surlin, Matthew Tobias ... Los Angeles, CA
Surloff, Ellen L. ... Pittsburgh, PA
Surloff, Howard B. ... New York, NY
Surloff, Samuel M. ... Los Angeles, CA
Surma, Carl J. ... Hastings, MI
Surma, Carol J. ... Farmington Hills, MI
Surma, John Daniel ... Brookfield, WI
Surmaitis, George P. ... Charleston, WV
Surman, Christine M. ... Philadelphia, PA
Surman, Gregory A. ... Brick, NJ
Whiting, NJ
Surman, Gregory L. ... Los Angeles, CA
Surman, John K. ... Springfield, IL

Surnamer, Franklin J. ... Allentown, PA
Surovell, Jackson, Colten & Dugan, P.C.
Alexandria, VA
Arlington, VA
Fairfax, VA
Leesburg, VA
Manassas, VA
Surovell, Robert J. ... Fairfax, VA
Surovell, Scott Anthony ... Fairfax, VA
Surovik, Bob J. ... Abilene, TX
Surowiec, John T. ... Highland, IN
Surowiec, William J. ... Miami, FL
Surowka, Michael G. ... Binghamton, NY
Surpin, Mayersohn and Edelstone
Los Angeles, CA
Surpin, Shelley H. ... Los Angeles, CA
Surpless, Donn C. ... Durham, NH
Surplice & Gould ... Green Bay, WI
Surprenant, David E. ... Worcester, MA
Surprenant, Dennis R. ... Boston, MA
Surprenant, Dominic ... Los Angeles, CA
Surprenant, Katherine A. ... New York, NY
New York, NY
Surprenant, Mark C. ... New Orleans, LA
Houston, TX
Surprenant, Monica Tufano
New Orleans, LA
Surprenant, Robert L. ... New Bedford, MA
Surprenant, Therese L. ... Austin, TX
Surpris, Daphnee ... New York, NY
Surprise, Cynthia J. ... Boston, MA
Surprise, James W. ... Memphis, TN
Surr, John V. ... Bethesda, MD
Surrano, Charles J., III ... Phoenix, AZ
Surrano & Massey, P.C. ... Kingman, AZ
Phoenix, AZ
Yuma, AZ
Surratt, David G. ... Dallas, TX
Surratt, Donean S. ... Beaumont, TX
Surratt, J. Phillip ... Ann Arbor, MI
Surratt, John R. ... Winston-Salem, NC
Surratt, John R., P.A.
Winston-Salem, NC
Surratt, Kathy A. ... St. Louis, MO
Surratt-McIntosh, Donna L. ... Sanford, FL
Surrell, Veronica ... Tulsa, OK
Surrena, Marlene Martin ... Philadelphia, PA
Surrency, Robert E. ... Watkinsville, GA
Surrency, Ronald D. ... Gainesville, FL
Surrett, Carl J. ... Augusta, GA
Surrett & Coleman, P.A. ... Appling, GA
Augusta, GA
Surrette, Robert A. ... Chicago, IL
Surrick, R. Barclay ... Media, PA
Surridge, Afton & Franzel
Bloomfield Hills, MI
Surridge, Robert C., III ... Kansas City, MO
Surridge, Sally B. ... Kansas City, MO
Surrisi, Cynthia M. ... Honolulu, HI
Surso, Kathryn A. ... Chicago, IL
Surtees, Suzanne P. ... Los Angeles, CA
Surtida, Hilda C. ... Santa Ana, CA
Surtz, Daniel T. ... Florham Park, NJ
Survant, Bradley J. ... Atlanta, GA
Macon, GA
Survis, Lorraine Kooby ... Teterboro, NJ
Suryadevara, Omkarmurthy K.
San Jose, CA
Suryanarayan, Rajaram ... Providence, RI
Suryanarayan, Sankar ... Washington, DC
Sus, Geo. M. ... Chicago, IL
Susa, James M. ... Phoenix, AZ
Susac, Karen L. Komlos ... Portland, OR
Susag, James M. ... Minneapolis, MN
Susak, Frank J. ... Portland, OR
Susak, Gary J. ... Portland, OR
Susak & Powell, P.C. ... Portland, OR
Susalla, Malinda L. ... West Lafayette, IN
Midland, TX
Susan, Bogdan A. ... Columbia, MO
Susan, Douglas ... New Brunswick, NJ
Susaneck, Fredrick R.
West Palm Beach, FL
Susanin, Helene McGuinn
Newtown Square, PA
Susanin, Roger D. ... King Of Prussia, PA
Susano, Charles D., Jr. ... Knoxville, TN
Susany, John P. ... Akron, OH
Susca, McClung & Paul, P.C.
San Antonio, TX
Susca, Nancy E. ... Mineola, NY
Susca, Peter N. ... San Antonio, TX
Susca-Sabino, Mary Jane
Queens Village, NY
Susco & Associates Co., L.P.A.
Centerville, OH
Susco, Michael E. ... Centerville, OH
Suse, Philip F. ... Chicago, IL
Susee, Edward J. ... Richfield, MN
Susee, James J. ... Salem, OR
Susee, Jan H. ... Richfield, MN
Susee & Lee, Ltd. ... Richfield, MN
Susemihl, McDermott, Miller & Cowan, P.C.
Colorado Springs, CO
Susemihl, Peter M. ... Colorado Springs, CO
Susen, John W. ... Windsor, CT
Susens, Stephanie ... New York, NY
Sushak, Frank R. ... Minneapolis, MN
Sushchyk, Paul M. ... Worcester, MA
Sushelsky, Jay E. ... St. Louis, MO
Sushelsky, Maxine ... Boston, MA
Sushon, William J. ... New York, NY
Susi, Andrew P. ... McLean, VA
Susi, Dan W. ... Erie, PA
Susi, Doreen M. ... Phoenix, AZ
Susi, Mark E. ... Gardiner, ME
Susi, Mart Sven ... Thousand Oaks, CA
Susi, Peter ... Santa Barbara, CA

Susi, Samuel ... Boca Raton, FL
Susi, Ted ... Skowhegan, ME
Susich, J. Thomas ... Carson City, NV
Susie, Daniel F., (P.C.) ... Dallas, TX
Susina, Mark S. ... Chicago, IL
Susk, Robert A. ... San Francisco, CA
Suskauer Law Firm, The, P.A.
West Palm Beach, FL
Suskauer, Michelle R. ... West Palm Beach, FL
Suskauer, Scott ... West Palm Beach, FL
Suski, David A. ... Washington, DC
Suski, Gregory D. ... San Francisco, CA
Suski, Gregory D. ... San Rafael, CA
Suski, Jeanne M. ... Kenmore, NY
Suskin, E. Kenneth ... Libertyville, IL
Suskin, Howard S. ... Chicago, IL
Suskin, James S. ... Montpelier, VT
Suskin, Steven P. ... Phoenix, AZ
Suskin, Stuart F. ... North Miami Beach, FL
Suskind, Barbara ... Walnut Creek, CA
Suskind, I. Russell ... Newark, OH
Susko, A. Richard ... New York, NY
Susko, Andrew F. ... Philadelphia, PA
Susko, John C. ... Pensacola, FL
Susko, Paul John ... Erie, PA
Susko, Robert N. ... Atlanta, GA
Susko, Robert N., P.C. ... Atlanta, GA
Suslak, George R. ... Lynnfield, MA
Suslak, John W. ... Lynn, MA
Suslensky, Alexander ... New York, NY
Susler, David G. ... Schaumburg, IL
Susler, Janis M. ... Chicago, IL
Susler, Marshall A. ... Decatur, IL
Suslow, Lawrence ... Armonk, NY
Susman, Alan H. ... Phoenix, AZ
Susman, Allen E. ... Beverly Hills, CA
Susman, Arthur T. ... Chicago, IL
Susman & Associates ... Chicago, IL
Susman, Barbara A. ... Chicago, IL
Susman, Benjamin L. ... Monarch Beach, CA
Susman, Bernard ... St. Louis, MO
Susman, Dana M. ... New York, NY
Susman, Duffy & Segaloff, P.C.
New Haven, CT
Susman, Frank ... St. Louis, MO
Susman Godfrey L.L.P. ... Los Angeles, CA
Dallas, TX
Houston, TX
Seattle, WA
Susman, Harry P. ... Houston, TX
Susman, Howard E. ... San Diego, CA
Susman, Matthew C. ... New Haven, CT
Susman, Michael ... New Haven, CT
Susman, Michael B. ... Chicago, IL
Susman, Morton L. ... Houston, TX
Susman, Richard L. ... Colorado Springs, CO
Denver, CO
Pueblo, CO
Susman, Robert M. ... St. Louis, MO
Susman, Schermer, Rimmel & Shifrin, L.L.C. ... St. Louis, MO
Susman, Stephen D., (P.C.) ... Dallas, TX
Houston, TX
Susman, Susan D. ... Brooklyn, NY
Susman, Thomas M. ... Washington, DC
Susman, Warren I. ... Mineola, NY
Susman & Watkins ... Chicago, IL
Susmarski, Hain & Logue ... Erie, PA
Susmarski, Ronald J. ... Erie, PA
Susnar & Geesey ... West Palm Beach, FL
Susnar, Lisa M. ... West Palm Beach, FL
Susnick, Ruth L. ... New York, NY
Susnow, Arthur ... Brooklyn, NY
Susnow, Mark ... San Rafael, CA
Susnow, Robert L. ... Los Angeles, CA
Susoeff, Steve ... San Francisco, CA
Susolik, Edward ... Santa Ana, CA
Suson, Anita Bolton ... Houston, TX
Suson, David V. ... Houston, TX
Susong, Andrew Kirk ... Greensboro, NC
Susong, Walter L. ... Conyers, GA
Suss, Asher C. ... New York, NY
Suss, Donald B. ... Frazer, PA
Suss, Paul E. ... Aventura, FL
Suss, Ronald S. ... Edison, NJ
Suss, Stuart B. ... West Chester, PA
Sussan, Leslie A.
Department Of Health And Human Services, GV
Sussan, Theodore A. ... Spotswood, NJ
Susse, Sandra ... Springfield, MA
Susseles, Maxine Judi ... New York, NY
Sussely-House, Laura ... San Diego, CA
Susser, Allen ... Saddle Brook, NJ
Susser, Andrew ... New York, NY
Susser, Bennet ... Newark, NJ
New York, NY
Susser, Danielle F. ... Detroit, MI
Susser, Elliot I. ... Lake Success, NY
Susser, Gary E. ... Boynton Beach, FL
Susser, Howard J. ... Boston, MA
Susser, Leslie ... New York, NY
Susser, Lynn S. ... Memphis, TN
Susser, Peter A. ... Washington, DC
Susser, Philip J. ... San Francisco, CA
Susser, Steven ... Southfield, MI
Sussillo, Joseph M. ... Brooklyn, NY
Sussin, Robert D. ... Los Angeles, CA
Sussin, Robert D., A Professional Corporation
Los Angeles, CA
Sussis, Mitchell Cole ... Murray Hill, NJ
Susskind, Amanda F. ... Los Angeles, CA
Susskind, Judith A. ... Southfield, MI
Susskind, M. Stanley ... Bayonne, NJ
Susskind, Stuart R. ... Cincinnati, OH
Susskind & Susskind ... Bayonne, NJ
Sussman, Alan L. ... Clifton, NJ
Sussman, Alexander R. ... New York, NY

Sussman, Alexandra K. ... Albany, NY
Sussman, Allen Z. ... Los Angeles, CA
Sussman and Altwarg ... Bloomfield, NJ
Sussman, Amy R. ... Mineola, NY
Sussman, Andrea L. ... Boston, MA
Sussman, Andrew D. ... Pittsburgh, PA
Sussman, Andrew J. ... San Diego, CA
Sussman, Andrew M. ... Santa Ana, CA
Sussman, Ann L. ... Denver, CO
Sussman, Arthur M. ... Chicago, IL
Sussman, Bernard J. ... Washington, DC
Sussman, Carl B. ... Chicago, IL
Sussman, Daniel L. ... Jericho, NY
Syosset, NY
Sussman, David A. ... Roseland, NJ
Sussman, David H. ... San Jose, CA
Sussman, David S. ... East Orange, NJ
Sussman, David W. ... New York, NY
Sussman, Dean E. ... Los Angeles, CA
Sussman, Dov ... Fort Myers, FL
Sussman, Edie ... Santa Rosa, CA
Sussman, Edna Rubin ... Scarsdale, NY
Sussman, Edward C. ... Washington, DC
Sussman, Edward I. ... Boca Raton, FL
Sussman, Elliott ... New York, NY
Sussman, Eric J. ... Garden City, NY
Sussman, Eric L. ... Hartford, CT
Sussman, Ericka A. ... Washington, DC
Sussman, Everett G. ... Stamford, CT
Sussman, F. Richard ... New York, NY
Sussman, Frederick C. ... Annapolis, MD
Sussman, Gary Y. ... Portland, OR
Sussman, Gilbert L. ... Silver Spring, MD
Sussman, H. Steven ... Miami, FL
Sussman, Harold ... Liberty, NY
Sussman, Harold ... Mineola, NY
Sussman, Harvey A. ... Plainsboro, NJ
Sussman, Herbert T. ... Jacksonville, FL
Sussman, Howard S. ... New York, NY
Sussman, Ilene ... New York, NY
Sussman, Ilene M. ... Brooklyn, NY
Sussman, Ira E. ... Oakbrook Terrace, IL
Sussman, J. Bruce ... New Britain, CT
Sussman, Jacqueline M. ... New York, NY
Sussman, Janet R. ... New York, NY
Sussman, Jason R. ... Cleveland, OH
Sussman, Jeffrey B. ... Chicago, IL
Sussman, Jeffrey H. ... Beverly Hills, CA
Sussman, Jerome ... Brooklyn, NY
Sussman, Jerome J. ... Los Angeles, CA
Sussman, Jerry
Department of State, GV
Sussman, Jessica ... New York, NY
Sussman, Jill H. ... Bayside, NY
Sussman, Joel W. ... Clifton, NJ
Sussman, Karen L. ... College Park, MD
Sussman, Kathryn Gilson
Farmington Hills, MI
Sussman, Lawrence R., Law Offices of
San Francisco, CA
Sussman, Lee R. ... Cherry Hill, NJ
Philadelphia, PA
Sussman, Leo ... Great Neck, NY
Sussman, Leonard, (P.A.) ... Miami, FL
Sussman, Lewis K. ... Burlington, VT
Sussman, Marc ... Portland, OR
Sussman, Marc A. ... Sacramento, CA
Sussman, Marc J. ... Flint, MI
Sussman, Marianne L. ... White Plains, NY
Sussman, Mark L. ... Woodbury, NY
Sussman, Mark R. ... Hartford, CT
Sussman, Mark S. ... North Miami Beach, FL
Sussman, Marsha R. ... Miami Beach, FL
Sussman, Martin S. ... Jericho, NY
Sussman, Marvin ... New York, NY
Sussman, Marvin S. ... New York, NY
Sussman, Michael H. ... Baltimore, MD
Sussman, Michael S. ... Goshen, NY
Sussman, Mitchell E. ... New York, NY
Sussman, Mitchell R. ... Palm Springs, CA
Sussman, Monica Hilton ... Washington, DC
Sussman, Nancy E. ... Burbank, CA
Sussman, Nancy Rubin ... Hartford, CT
Sussman, Neil ... Seattle, WA
Sussman, Neil A. ... New York, NY
Sussman, Oscar ... Chapel Hill, NC
Sussman, Paul J. ... Chicago, IL
Sussman, Ralph B. ... East Orange, NJ
Sussman, Raymond S. ... Hartsdale, NY
Sussman, Reed ... Boston, MA
Sussman, Richard ... Nyack, NY
Sussman, Richard L. ... New York, NY
Sussman, Richd. C. ... Camarillo, CA
Sussman, Robert C. ... Westport, CT
Sussman, Robert J. ... Bloomfield, NJ
Sussman, Robert J. ... New York, NY
Sussman, Robert J. ... Houston, TX
Sussman, Robert L.
Department of Labor, GV
Sussman, Robert M. ... Washington, DC
Sussman, Robert M., (P.A.) ... Palm City, FL
Sussman, Ronald L. ... Dallas, TX
Sussman, Ronald R. ... New York, NY
Sussman, Ross A. ... Minneapolis, MN
Sussman, Samuel ... Salem, OR
Sussman, Samuel J. ... Brooklyn, NY
Sussman, Selig & Ross ... Chicago, IL
Sussman Shank Wapnick Caplan & Stiles, LLP ... Portland, OR
Sussman Sollis Ebin Tweedy & Wood, LLP
New York, NY
Sussman, Stacy J. ... New York, NY
Sussman, Stephen ... Red Bank, NJ
New York, NY
Sussman, Steven A. ... Marlborough, MA
Sussman, William C. ... Miami, FL
Sussman, William C., P.A. ... Miami, FL
Sussman, William I. ... New York, NY

Sutton, Laura K. ... Manchester, MI
Sutton Law Firm ... Myrtle Beach, SC
Sutton Law Group, The ... San Jose, CA
Sutton, Lawrence T. ... Campbell, CA
Sutton, Leland D. ... Jacksonville, TX
Sutton, Leonard v. B. ... Denver, CO
Sutton, Linda I. ... Chillicothe, OH
Sutton, Linda L. ... Lansing, MI
Sutton, Lisa L. ... Olympia, WA
Sutton, Lois Michelle ... Oklahoma City, OK
Sutton, Loren A. ... Tinian, TT
Sutton, M. Dean ... San Jose, CA
Sutton Mandell & Sutton ... New York, NY
Sutton, Mark H. ... Bloomfield Hills, MI
Sutton, Mark L. ... Los Angeles, CA
Sutton, Mary Ann ... Missoula, MT
Sutton, Matthew ... Medford, OR
Sutton, Maximillian C. ... Columbus, OH
Sutton, McCurdy & Stone, P.A.
Baltimore, MD
Sutton & Melonakis, P.A. ... Denver, CO
Littleton, CO
Sutton, Michael F. ... Orlando, FL
Sutton, Michael O. ... Dallas, TX
Sutton, Michael R. ... Baldwin, NY
Sutton, Michael S. ... Mission Viejo, CA
Sutton, Michael T. ... Florence, KY
Sutton, Micheal W. ... Niwot, CO
Sutton, Michelle R. ... Washington, DC
Sutton & Montoto, P.A., Professional
Association ... Miami, FL
Sutton, Morris ... New York, NY
Sutton and Murphy ... Mission Viejo, CA
Sutton, Nancy E. ... San Angelo, TX
Sutton, Nathan M. ... Overland Park, KS
Sutton, Neal S. ... Houston, TX
Sutton, Neil W. ... Bridgeport, CT
Sutton, Nicholas J., Jr. ... San Francisco, CA
Sutton, Oliver C., II ... New York, NY
Sutton, Pamela Dru ... Panama City, FL
Sutton, Paul E. ... Shawnee, OK
Sutton, Paul J. ... New York, NY
Sutton, Peggy A. ... Morgan Hill, CA
Sutton, Percy E. ... New York, NY
Sutton, Peter A. ... Chicago, IL
Sutton, Peter H. ... Boston, MA
Sutton, Ralph J. ... New York, NY
Sutton, Randall ... Port Orchard, WA
Sutton, Randall P. ... Salem, OR
Sutton, Randy J. ... New Orleans, LA
Sutton, Ray Sandy ... Kansas City, MO
Sutton, Raymond L., Jr. ... Denver, CO
Sutton, Raymond M. ... Sherman Oaks, CA
Sutton, Richard C. ... Tallapoosa, GA
Sutton, Richard C. ... Honolulu, HI
Sutton, Richard C., Jr. ... Honolulu, HI
Sutton, Richard C., P.C. ... Tallapoosa, GA
Sutton, Richard D. ... Toms River, NJ
Sutton, Richard L. ... Wilmington, DE
Sutton, Richard S. ... Dayton, OH
Sutton, Robert A. ... Baltimore, MD
Sutton, Robert Alan ... Philadelphia, PA
Sutton, Robert M., Jr. ... Myrtle Beach, SC
Sutton, Robert W. ... Burbank, CA
Sutton, Roger B. ... Greensboro, NC
Sutton, Roger L. ... Charles City, IA
Sutton, Ronald A. ... Lockport, NY
Sutton, Ronald L. ... Junction, TX
Sutton, Ronald R. ... Williamston, MI
Sutton, Ronnie N. ... Pembroke, NC
Sutton, Roy W., III ... Dallas, TX
Sutton, S. Brett ... Fresno, CA
Sutton, S. Guy ... Greenwich, CT
Sutton, S. Robert ... Washington, DC
Sutton, Samuel J. ... Phoenix, AZ
Sutton, Shane Henty ... New York, NY
Sutton, Shane Henty, P.C., Law Office of
New York, NY
Sutton, Shawn M. ... Bay City, MI
Sutton, Sherry N. ... Columbia, SC
Sutton, Stanford H. ... Greenwich, CT
Sutton, Stephen B. ... Kansas City, MO
Sutton, Stephen C. ... Cleveland, OH
Sutton, Stephen F. ... Vernon, CT
Sutton, Stephen W. ... Braintree, MA
Sutton, Steven R. ... New York, NY
Sutton, Stewart Andrew
Gaithersburg, MD
Sutton, Stewart Andrew
Germantown, MD
Sutton, Susan E. ... Wilmington, NC
Sutton, Susan L. ... San Jose, CA
Sutton, Susan M. ... Detroit, MI
Sutton & Sutton ... Shreveport, LA
Sutton, Tara D. ... Minneapolis, MN
Sutton, Terry J. ... Watertown, SD
Sutton, Thomas D. ... Langhorne, PA
Sutton, Thomas David ... Charleston, SC
Sutton, Thomas H. ... Carmi, IL
Sutton & Troge's Law Office
Charles City, IA
Sutton, W. Brad ... Salina, KS
Sutton, Wesley D. ... Columbia, SC
Sutton, William B., Jr. ... Clinton, NC
Sutton, William D. ... Pittsburgh, PA
Sutton, William D. ... The Woodlands, TX
Sutton, William F. ... Philadelphia, PA
Sutton, William F., Jr. ... Nashville, TN
Sutton, William H., (P.A.) ... Little Rock, AR
Sutton, William L., Jr. ... Atlanta, GA
Sutton, William M. ... Houston, TX
Sutton, William R., P.A. ... Baltimore, MD
Sutton, William S. ... Atlanta, GA
Sutton, Zella M. Smith ... Harrisburg, PA
Sutton, Zook F. ... Piedmont, CA
Sutton-Glasby, Gloria M. ... San Diego, CA
Suttora, David J. ... Carriere, MS

Sutula, John D. ... Cleveland, OH
Sutula, John J. ... Cleveland, OH
Sutula, Kathleen A. ... Cleveland, OH
Sutz, Debbie J. ... Marina Del Rey, CA
Suuberg, Ina I.V. ... Barrington, RI
Suuberg, Margaret Reardon
Worcester, MA
Suuck, Juergen O. ... Los Angeles, CA
Suvari, Elizabeth C. ... Department of State,
Foreign Service Officers (Overseas), GV
Suve, Heather A. ... Kansas City, MO
Suver, Jami K. ... Ashland, KY
Suver, Katie A. ... Albany, OR
Suwanto, Fabiola M. ... San Mateo, CA
Suwczinsky, Liza Danielle ... San Diego, CA
Suwinski, Craig S. ... Lakeland, FL
Suyat, Emily R. ... Denver, CO
Suyat, Frank William ... Denver, CO
Suyat, Reginald J. ... Menlo Park, CA
Suyat, Stanley D. ... Honolulu, HI
Suydam, John J. ... New York, NY
Suyemoto, Joe K. ... Nashua, NH
Suyenaga, Dawn ... Honolulu, HI
Suzan, Kenneth D. ... New York, NY
Suzenski, Robert ... Phoenix, AZ
Suzenski, Robert, P.C. ... Phoenix, AZ
Suzich, George H. ... Signal Mountain, TN
Suzukawa, Steven C. ... Compton, CA
Suzuki, Anri ... Washington, DC
Suzuki, Carol M. ... Staten Island, NY
Suzuki, Carole S. ... Los Angeles, CA
Suzuki, Darren M. ... Honolulu, HI
Suzuki, David A. ... San Francisco, CA
Suzuki, David Y. ... Honolulu, HI
Suzuki, Elton K. ... Honolulu, HI
Suzuki & Goo, A Law Corp. ... Honolulu, HI
Suzuki, Hidefumi ... New York, NY
Suzuki, Iori ... New York, NY
Suzuki, Jennifer Wong ... San Francisco, CA
Suzuki, Joan K. ... Palo Alto, CA
Suzuki, Junji ... San Francisco, CA
Suzuki, Kaoruhiko ... Los Angeles, CA
Suzuki, Lola Li ... Honolulu, HI
Suzuki, Norman H. ... Honolulu, HI
Suzuki, Paul T. ... Los Angeles, CA
Suzuki, Peter M. ... Parsippany, NJ
Suzuki, Russell A. ... Wahiawa, HI
Suzuki, Shari ... Treasury Department,
Office of Regulations and Rulings, GV
Suzuki, Shauna L. ... Stamford, CT
Suzuki, Takehiko ... Los Angeles, CA
Suzumoto, Mark Ken ... Los Angeles, CA
Suzzan, Steven I. ... New York, NY
Svab, Stephen
Federal Communications Commission,
Mass Media Bureau, GV
Svagzdys, John J. ... Brockton, MA
Svalina Law Firm, P.A. ... Beaufort, SC
Hilton Head Island, SC
Svalina, Nicholas B. ... Deerfield, IL
Svalina, Samuel L., P.A. ... Beaufort, SC
Svalina, Samuel S. ... Beaufort, SC
Svalstad, Neal C. ... Los Angeles, CA
Svalstad, Ronald L. ... Spring Valley, CA
Svalya, Phillip G. ... Cupertino, CA
Svalya, Phillip G., Inc. ... Cupertino, CA
Svanascini, Kathy ... Palos Heights, IL
Svanascini, Michael ... Chicago, IL
Svanda, Todd A. ... Lansing, MI
Svaren, David A. ... Burlington, WA
Svarre, Andrew C. ... New York, NY
Svarstad, Claudia J. ... Aurora, CO
Svartz, Steven H.
Federal Labor Relations Authority,
Office of the General Counsel, GV
Svarvari, Stanley A. ... Eau Claire, WI
Svat, Laura A. ... Washington, DC
Svat, Mark S. ... Cleveland, OH
Svatek, Amy L. ... Washington, DC
Svaty, Ron ... Ellsworth, KS
Svaty, Sherman & Hoffman, L.L.C.
Ellsworth, KS
Svec, David M. ... Berwyn, IL
Svec, Milton A., Associates ... Berwyn, IL
Sveeggen, G. E. ... Minneapolis, MN
Sveen, Jeffrey T. ... Aberdeen, SD
Svehla, Ray L. ... York, NE
Svei, Dore ... Seattle, WA
Sveikauskas, Maria L. ... Boston, MA
Svejda, Mark D. ... Scottsdale, AZ
Svejda, Mark D., P.C. ... Scottsdale, AZ
Svendsen, John T. ... Sturgis, MI
Svendsen, Kara L. ... Philadelphia, PA
Svendsen, Sean E. ... Alameda, CA
Svendsen, Sharon L. ... Boulder, CO
Svendson, Troye A. ... Baton Rouge, LA
Svenson, A. Christine ... Chicago, IL
Svenson, Charles O. ... New York, NY
Svenson, Ernest E. ... New Orleans, LA
Svenson, Judith M. ... Barrington, IL
Svenson, Vesta ... Detroit, MI
Svensson, H. Torbjorn ... Minneapolis, MN
Svensson, Kelli Anne ... Omaha, NE
Svensson, Leonard R. ... Costa Mesa, CA
Sverchek, Joseph P. ... New York, NY
Sverdlik, Irving ... Granite Springs, NY
Sverdrup & Barnes ... Libby, MT
Sverdrup, Lawrence H. ... Libby, MT
Sveska, Kim J. ... Detroit, MI
Svet, Don J. ... Albuquerque, NM
Svetanics, Milton F., Jr. ... St. Louis, MO
Svetanoff, Gerald N. ... Gary, IN
Svetanoff, Richard E. ... Michigan City, IN
Svetcov, Sanford ... San Francisco, CA
Svete, Jacqueline A. ... Chardon, OH
Svete, Joseph T. ... Chardon, OH
Svete, McGee & Carrabine, Co., L.P.A.
Chardon, OH

Svetlic, Michael J. ... Kansas City, MO
Svetlic & Wieland ... Kansas City, MO
Svetlov, Marina ... Roseland, NJ
Svets, Robert J. ... Greenville, SC
Svetz, Holly Emrick ... Washington, DC
Svidro, Daniel F. ... Washington, PA
Svihla, Randall S. ... Arlington, VA
Svikis, Andis ... Kalamazoo, MI
Svilar, Daniel P. ... Riverton, WY
Svingen, Athens, Russell & Hagstrom, PLLP
Fergus Falls, MN
Svingen, R. Kristian ... Fergus Falls, MN
Svirsko, Alex L., Jr. ... Ebensburg, PA
Svirsko, Dawn L. ... Johnstown, PA
Svirsky, Gary ... New York, NY
Svirsky, Peter S. ... Point Reyes Station, CA
Svisco, Rosa S. ... East Amherst, NY
Svitak, Linda S. ... Minneapolis, MN
Svitenko, Paul L. ... San Francisco, CA
Svoboda, Brian G. ... Washington, DC
Svoboda, Charles D. "Chick"
St. Petersburg, FL
Svoboda, Charles R. ... Kansas City, MO
Svoboda & Chebatoris ... Weeping Water, NE
Svoboda, Craig Gordon
South San Francisco, CA
Svoboda, Eric C. ... Wichita, KS
Svoboda, Frank B. ... Ogallala, NE
Svoboda, Frank J., Jr. ... Dayton, OH
Svoboda, George E. ... Fremont, NE
Svoboda, Gerald L. ... Minneapolis, MN
Svoboda, J. Steven ... Boston, MA
Svoboda, Janet S. ... Kansas City, MO
Svoboda, Jeffrey J. ... Birmingham, MI
Svoboda, John A. ... Omaha, NE
Svoboda, John L. ... Eugene, OR
Svoboda, Joseph E. ... Springfield, IL
Svoboda, Joseph V. ... Little Rock, AR
Svoboda and Mitts, P.C. ... Kansas City, MO
Svoboda, Nancy A. ... Omaha, NE
Svoboda, Paul A. ... Chicago, IL
Svoboda, Ronald D. ... Weeping Water, NE
Svobodny, Richard A. ... Juneau, AK
Svogun, Thomas V. ... Newport, RI
Svonavec, Patrick P. ... Somerset, PA
Svonkin & Gedge, P.C.
West Hartford, CT
Svonkin, Mark J. ... West Hartford, CT
Svoren, Nina M. ... Toccoa, GA
Swabowski, Thomas J. ... Chicago, IL
Swaby, Christopher Andrew
Washington, DC
Swacina, Paul ... Corpus Christi, TX
Swack, James C., Jr. ... Hermitage, TN
Swacker, Frank W. ... St. Petersburg, FL
Swade, Leonard ... Springfield, MA
Swaden Law Offices ... Edina, MN
Swaden, Martin L. ... Edina, MN
Swadey, Robert J. ... Cleveland, OH
Swados, Robert O. ... Buffalo, NY
Swaebe, Geoffrey, Jr. ... New York, NY
Swafford, C. Matt ... Kansas City, MO
Swafford, Cheri K. ... Oklahoma City, OK
Swafford, Claude G. ... Jasper, TN
Swafford, Clinton H. ... Winchester, TN
Swafford, C. P., Sr. ... Dayton, TN
Swafford, David R. ... Pikeville, TN
Swafford, Gregory ... New Orleans, LA
Swafford, Harold ... Carson City, NV
Swafford, Harold L. ... Columbia, SC
Swafford, Herbert T. ... Phoenix, AZ
Swafford, Howard G. ... Jasper, TN
Swafford, Howard Graham, Jr. ... Jasper, TN
Swafford, Jack D. ... Caldwell, ID
Swafford, Jack T. ... Pasadena, CA
Swafford, Lori L. ... Torrance, CA
Swafford, Lynne D. ... Dayton, TN
Swafford, Michael R. ... St. Louis, MO
Swafford, Paul A. ... Jasper, TN
Swafford, Peters, Priest & Colvin
Winchester, TN
Swafford, Roberta A. ... Wethersfield, CT
Swafford, Russell Anne ... Dunlap, TN
Swafford, Susan M. ... Alexandria, VA
Swafford & Swafford ... Dayton, TN
Jasper, TN
Swafford & Swafford ... Pikeville, TN
Swafford, Tara L. ... Nashville, TN
Swafford, Theresa Ann ... Chattanooga, TN
Swafford, Thomas A. ... Nashville, TN
Swagart, Harry A., III ... Columbia, SC
Swagart & Walker, P.A. ... Columbia, SC
Swager, Douglas E. ... San Francisco, CA
Swagert, Dean R., Jr. ... New York, NY
Swagerty, Evelynne LaMarris ... Franklin, MA
Swagler, Richard C., Jr. ... Washington, DC
Swaidan, Karl I. ... Pasadena, CA
Swailes, Harold J. ... Belle Plaine, IA
Swails, J. Edward ... Washington, DC
Swaim, C. Hall ... Boston, MA
Swaim, C. Thomas ... Boston, MA
Swaim, Donald E. ... Albuquerque, NM
Swaim, Frederick W., Jr. ... New Orleans, LA
Swaim, G. Don, (P.C.) ... Irving, TX
Swaim, George T. ... Kankakee, IL
Swaim, J. David, Jr. ... Dallas, TX
Swaim, J. Scott ... Kankakee, IL
Swaim, James A. ... Troy, MI
Swaim, James E. ... Dayton, OH
Swaim, Jeffrey E. ... Worcester, MA
Swaim, Jill D. ... Boston, MA
Swaim, Kristie J. ... Kirksville, MO
Swaim, M. Mort ... Foley, AL
Northport, AL
Swaim, Mark A. ... Houston, TX
Swaim, Michael E. ... Salem, OR
Swaim, Michael E., P.C., Law Offices of
Salem, OR

Swaim, M. Mort, P.C. ... Foley, AL
Northport, AL
Swaim, Phillip B. ... Westport, CT
Swaim, R. Kurt ... Bloomfield, IA
Swaim, Robyn Renee ... Rolla, MO
Swaim & Schrandt, P.C.
Albuquerque, NM
Swaim, Stephen ... Columbus, OH
Swaim & Swaim, Ltd. ... Kankakee, IL
Swaim, Thomas P. ... Raleigh, NC
Swaim, William G. ... Austin, TX
Swain, Albert Craig ... Huntsville, AL
Swain, Andrew D. ... Philadelphia, PA
Swain, Barbara G. ... Baltimore, MD
Swain, Brennan C. ... Los Angeles, CA
Swain, Carl B. ... Sacramento, CA
Swain, Clifford H. ... Philadelphia, PA
Swain, David E. ... Tempe, AZ
Swain, Dennis M. ... Manistee, MI
Swain & Dipolito LLP ... Long Beach, CA
Los Angeles, CA
Swain, E. Curtis ... Wilmington, DE
Swain, Earl G. ... Montrose, MI
Swain, Eugene K. ... Hartford, CT
Swain, Francis E. ... Siler City, NC
Swain, Frank S. ... Washington, DC
Swain, Frank T., Jr. ... Westfield, NJ
Swain, Gregory J. ... Arnold, MD
Swain, Hartshorn & Scott ... Peoria, IL
Swain, Henry G. ... Grand Rapids, MI
Swain, Jennifer Fox ... Birmingham, AL
Swain, John E. ... Houston, TX
Swain, John E., Jr. ... Louisville, KY
Swain, Jonathan T. ... Milwaukee, WI
Swain, Kenneth A. ... Monroe, NC
Swain, Kevin W. ... Topeka, KS
Swain, Kimberly Carol ... Oakland, CA
Swain, Kinney M. ... Greenville, MS
Swain, L. Kevin ... Boise, ID
Swain, Lawrence A. ... Overland Park, KS
Kansas City, MO
Swain, Margaret E., Law Offices of
Baltimore, MD
Swain, Maureen Redlin ... Cleveland, OH
Swain, Meta V. ... Jackson, MS
Swain, Michael L. ... Long Beach, CA
Swain, Paul E., III ... Tulsa, OK
Swain, Paul W., Jr. ... Bloomington, IN
Swain, Philip C. ... Boston, MA
Swain, Ray F. ... Siler City, NC
Swain, Rhonda F. ... Lincoln, MA
Swain, Richard A. ... Mentor, OH
Swain, Robert E. ... Rockford, IL
Swain, Robert L. ... San Diego, CA
Swain, Robert W. ... Department of Labor,
Office of the Solicitor, GV
Swain, Robert W., Jr. ... Appleton, WI
Swain, Scott A. ... Las Vegas, NV
Reno, NV
Swain, Stanley W. ... Bala Cynwyd, PA
Swain, Stephen C. ... Virginia Beach, VA
Swain, Stephen Louis ... Walnut Creek, CA
Swain, Steven J. ... Washington, DC
Swain, Stevenson & Moore, A Professional
Association ... Asheville, NC
Swain, Susan B. ... San Jose, CA
Swain & Swain ... Greenville, MS
Swain, Theodore M. ... Chicago, IL
Swain, Tim ... Peoria, IL
Swain, Timothy A. ... Butler, PA
Swain, Timothy W. ... Peoria, IL
Swain, Walter B., Jr. ... Greenville, MS
Swain, William L. ... Cleveland, OH
Swain, William R. ... Jacksonville, FL
Swain, William R., & Associates
Jacksonville, FL
Swain, William R., Jr. ... Cordova, TN
Swain, William S., (P.A.) ... Russellville, AR
Swainbank, John A. ... St. Johnsbury, VT
Swainbank, Morrissette & Neylon
St. Johnsbury, VT
Swaine, Harris, Sheehan & McClure, P.A.
Lake Placid, FL
Sebring, FL
Swaine, J. Michael ... Lake Placid, FL
Sebring, FL
Swaine, James E. ... New Haven, CT
Swaine, Richard S. ... St. Cloud, FL
Swainson, William A. ... Cheyenne, WY
Swainston, Colin C. ... Irvine, CA
Swainston, George W. ... Reno, NV
Swainston, Howard D. ... Los Angeles, CA
Swainston, Kurt C. ... Los Angeles, CA
Swainston, Paul C. ... Spokane, WA
Swajanen, Derek G. ... Marquette, MI
Swajian, Dawn M. ... Palm Desert, CA
Swajian, Gregory A. ... Palm Desert, CA
Swajian & Swajian ... Palm Desert, CA
Swales, William B. ... Augusta, ME
Swalina, Douglas W. ... Houston, TX
Swallen, Elizabeth P. ... Westport, CT
Swaller, Katherine Cogswell ... St. Louis, MO
Swallow, Bradley J. ... Baltimore, MD
Swallow, John E. ... Draper, UT
Swallow, Joseph P. ... Alpena, MI
Swallow, Julia ... Midland, TX
Swallow, Lyle S. ... San Francisco, CA
Swallow, Michael T. ... Mission, SD
Swallow, Sarah S. ... Kalamazoo, MI
Swallows, Beverly B. ... Corpus Christi, TX
Swalm, John M., III ... Naples, FL
Swalm & Murrell, P.A. ... Naples, FL
Swalsky, Stephen J. ... Albany, NY
Swalve, Peggy A. ... Las Vegas, NV
Swalwell, Chauncey M. ... Los Angeles, CA
Swam, Elwood E. ... Hampstead, MD
Swaminathan, Gopal ... Washington, DC
Swan, Alan C. ... Coral Gables, FL

Swan, Alan H. ... Tifton, GA
Swan, Alfred J. ... Forest Hills, NY
Swan, Allen G. ... Haverhill, MA
Swan, Anthony A. ... Montclair, NJ
Swan, Arthur R. ... Rochester, MN
Swan, Barbara J. ... Madison, WI
Swan, Barry R. ... San Bernardino, CA
Swan, Betsey Boardman ... Albany, NY
Swan, Carol Lynn ... Annapolis, MD
Swan, Carpenter, Wallis & McKenzie
Hemet, CA
Sun City, CA
Temecula, CA
Swan, Cynthia J. ... Minneapolis, MN
Swan, D. Richard, (P.C.) ... Hemet, CA
Sun City, CA
Swan, Dana J. ... Clarksdale, MS
Swan, Daniel B. ... Hingham, MA
Swan, David I. ... Pittsburgh, PA
Swan, David P. ... Medfield, MA
Swan, David S. ... Atlanta, GA
Swan, Deborah Dallas ... Dallas, TX
Swan, Donald M., Jr. ... Bethlehem, PA
Swan, Edw. P. ... Coral Gables, FL
Swan, Edward Patrick "Pat", Jr.
San Diego, CA
Swan, Edward T. ... Chicago, IL
Swan, Eric J. ... Philadelphia, PA
Swan, George S. ... Greensboro, NC
Swan, H. Titus ... Holdrege, NE
Swan, Henry M. ... Providence, RI
Swan, Hugo, Jr. ... Little Rock, AR
Swan, Ive A.
Charlotte Amalie, St. Thomas, VI
Swan, Jeffrey A. ... Glenview, IL
Swan, John T. ... San Diego, CA
Swan, Joseph B., Jr. ... Phoenix, AZ
Swan, Joseph G. ... Los Angeles, CA
Swan, Kathleen J. ... Chicago, IL
Swan, Kevin D. ... Seattle, WA
Swan, Mark S. ... Salt Lake City, UT
Swan, Michael J. ... Vero Beach, FL
Swan, Michael K., (P.C.) ... Houston, TX
Swan, Michael R. ... Dallas, TX
Swan, Pamela Pelekis ... Montgomery, AL
Swan, Patty G. ... Hartford, CT
Swan, Peter G. ... Highland Park, IL
Swan, Peter N. ... Eugene, OR
Swan, Richard H.
United States Information Agency, Office of the General Counsel, GV
Swan, Richard R. ... Denver, CO
Swan, Robert C. ... Phoenix, AZ
Swan, Robert E. ... Oakton, VA
Swan, Robert F., Jr. ... Miami, FL
Swan, Robert G. ... Phoenix, AZ
Swan, Sheila Tobie ... Warwick, RI
Swan, Sheldon B. ... Oklahoma City, OK
Swan, Steven J. ... Keokuk, IA
Swan, Theodore H., Jr. ... Abington, PA
Swan, Thomas H. ... Sausalito, CA
Swan, Thomas T. ... Pittsburgh, PA
Swan, Thornley K. ... Kaysville, UT
Swan, Timothy M. ... Merrillville, IN
Swan, Turner ... Los Angeles, CA
Swan, W. Briscoe ... Houston, TX
Swan, W. Bryant, Jr. ... Thomson, GA
Swan, Wayne D. ... Salt Lake City, UT
Swan, William H. ... Phoenix, AZ
Swan, William H., III ... Norfolk, VA
Swan, William L. ... Albany, GA
Swan, Winifred Lynn ... Natick, MA
Swan, Wm. H. ... East Quogue, NY
Swanberg, Chrisman L. ... Sacramento, CA
Swanberg, Gorham E. ... Great Falls, MT
Swanberg, Robt. F. ... Helena, MT
Swandal, Bonnie ... Livingston, MT
Swandal, Douglass & Gilbert, P.C.
Livingston, MT
Swandal, William Nels ... Livingston, MT
Swandby, Lawrence L. ... St. Paul, MN
Swander, George J. ... Brewster, NY
Swander, Richard C. ... Elk Grove Village, IL
Swander, Steven H. ... Fort Worth, TX
Swaneck, Anthony J. ... Columbus, OH
Swanekamp, Charles C. ... Buffalo, NY
Swanenburg, Michael S. ... Towson, MD
Swaner, Jack D. ... Black Butte Ranch, OR
Swaney, Allyson ... Patuxent River, MD
Swaney, Charles D. ... Springfield, OH
Swaney, Dennis ... Cincinnati, OH
Swaney, James O., Jr. ... Independence, MO
Swaney, Jeffrey R. ... St. Louis, MO
Swaney, Richard G. ... Holland, MI
Swaney & Thomas ... Holland, MI
Swaney, Thomas E. ... Chicago, IL
Swanger, Alfred L. ... Marina Del Rey, CA
Swanger, Derry W. ... Austin, TX
Swanger, Harry F. ... St. Louis, MO
Swanger, James P. ... Vancouver, WA
Swanger, James R. ... Des Moines, IA
Swanger, Peter A. E. ... New York, NY
Swanger, Russel S., Jr. ... Camp Hill, PA
Swanhart, Lani-Kai ... Yakima, WA
Swanholt, Erik K. ... San Diego, CA
Swanick, Christa L.
Fort Walton Beach, FL
Swanick, David R., III ... Niceville, FL
Swanick, Linda Thompson ... Tampa, FL
Swanicke, Paul T. ... Bridgewater, NJ
Swanicke, Paul T. ... Martinsville, NJ
Swanigan, Vivienne A. ... Los Angeles, CA
Swaniger, Peri H. ... Oxford, CT
Swaninger, C. Robert ... Dayton, OH
Swanis, Eric W. ... Las Vegas, NV
Swank & Assoc. Co., L.P.A. ... Newark, OH
Swank, Audrey Benson ... Tampa, FL
Swank, Ben R., Jr. ... Kansas City, MO
Swank, Ben R., Sr. ... Lee's Summit, MO
Swank, Clayton J. ... Covington, LA
Swank, Damon R.
Rancho Palos Verdes, CA
Swank, David ... Norman, OK
Swank, David M. ... Denver, CO
Swank, Deborah R. ... Kansas City, MO
Swank, Debra L. ... Lansdale, PA
Swank, Donald L. ... Woodhaven, MI
Swank, Elizabeth K. ... Laguna Hills, CA
Swank, J. Gerard ... Newark, OH
Swank, James W., Jr. ... Oklahoma City, OK
Swank, Kimberly A. ... Greenville, NC
Swank, Pamela A. ... Richardson, TX
Swank, Robert W. ... Monroe, WI
Swank, William A. ... Houston, TX
Swank, William K. ... Los Angeles, CA
Swank, William L., II ... Atlanta, GA
Swankin, David A. ... Washington, DC
Swankin & Turner ... Washington, DC
Swanko, Edward H. ... Lake City, FL
Swann, Bill ... Knoxville, TN
Swann, Clair L. ... San Jose, CA
Swann, Cynthia G. ... Washington, DC
Swann, Deborah ... Treasury Department, Internal Revenue Service, GV
Swann, Elizabeth ... St. Charles, MO
Swann, Erin E. ... Greenville, SC
Swann, Eugene M. ... Orinda, CA
Swann, Gerald C., Jr. ... Montgomery, AL
Swann, Hadley & Alvarez, P.A.
Orlando, FL
Winter Park, FL
Swann, Henry T., III ... St. Augustine, FL
Swann, James P., Jr. ... Atlanta, GA
Swann, Jerre B. ... Atlanta, GA
Swann, Jerre B., Jr. ... Atlanta, GA
Swann, John A. ... Atlanta, GA
Swann, K. Michael ... Winter Park, FL
Swann, Michael A. ... Lexington, NC
Swann, Michael A., P.A. ... Lexington, NC
Swann, Peter B. ... Phoenix, AZ
Swann, Philip D. ... Burton, MI
Swann, Richard H. M. ... Miami, FL
Swann, Richard R. ... Winter Park, FL
Swann, Samuel L. ... Springfield, TN
Swann, Sharron Lawson ... Austin, TX
Swann, Stephen L. ... Arlington, VA
Swann, Thomas D. ... Waco, TX
Swann, Tommy J. ... Lubbock, TX
Swann, Tracy d. ... Burbank, CA
Swann, W. A. ... Pensacola, FL
Swann, William J., Jr. ... Gulfport, MS
Swanner, Charles B. ... Houston, TX
Swanner, David A. ... Myrtle Beach, SC
Swanner, John W. L. ... Baton Rouge, LA
Swanner, William J., III ... Virginia Beach, VA
Swansen, Samuel T. ... Blue Bell, PA
Swansen, Samuel T., P.C. ... Blue Bell, PA
Swansiger, Erin R. ... Washington, DC
Swansinger, John ... Cleveland, OH
Swanson, A. J. ... Sioux Falls, SD
Swanson, Alan H. ... Chicago, IL
Swanson, Alfred M., Jr. ... Chicago, IL
Swanson, Allison C. ... St. Paul, MN
Swanson, Amy K. ... Parkersburg, IA
Swanson, Angela Althoff
West Des Moines, IA
Swanson, Anne V. ... Wheaton, IL
Swanson, Arthur C. ... Dallas, TX
Swanson, Arthur D. ... Renton, WA
Swanson, Arthur R. ... Rockford, IL
Swanson, Arvid J. ... Sioux Falls, SD
Swanson, Barbara J. ... Gurnee, IL
Swanson, Barry J. ... Englewood, CO
Swanson, Barry K. ... Topeka, KS
Swanson, Betty Jane ... Miami, FL
Swanson, Bevevino and Millin, P.C.
Tionesta, PA
Warren, PA
Swanson, Boad S. ... Superior, WI
Swanson, Bonnie M. ... Yakima, WA
Swanson, Bradley D. ... Pine River, MN
Swanson & Bratschun, L.L.C.
Denver, CO
Englewood, CO
Swanson, Brent A. ... Green Bay, WI
Swanson, Brett J. ... Salt Lake City, UT
Swanson, Brian R. ... Menlo Park, CA
Swanson & Brown, Ltd. ... Palos Heights, IL
Swanson, Bruce E. ... Red Oak, IA
Swanson, Burt E. ... St. Paul, MN
Swanson & Campbell ... Fort Wayne, IN
Swanson, Carl L., Jr. ... Richardson, TX
Swanson, Carl M. ... Tampa, FL
Swanson, Carl M. ... Portland, OR
Swanson, Carl W. ... North Brunswick, NJ
Swanson, Carol B. ... St. Paul, MN
Swanson, Carolann Austin
Fort Myers, FL
Swanson, Chad A. ... Waterloo, IA
Swanson, Charles ... Racine, WI
Swanson, Charles A. ... Cleveland, OH
Swanson, Charles W. ... Knoxville, TN
Swanson & Cherry, LLP ... Atlanta, GA
Swanson, Christopher M. ... Houston, TX
Swanson, Clara P. ... Newport News, VA
Swanson, Conrad ... Plant City, FL
Swanson, Conrad T. ... Fort Collins, CO
Swanson & Cowan, LLP ... Morristown, TN
Swanson, Craig D. ... San Diego, CA
Swanson, Curtis C. ... Madison, WI
Swanson, Cynthia Stump ... Gainesville, FL
Swanson, D. Keith ... Salem, OR
Swanson, Dale T. ... Durham, NH
Swanson, Daniel ... Arlington Heights, IL
Swanson, Daniel D. ... Southfield, MI
Swanson, Daniel G. (IBA) **... Los Angeles, CA**
Swanson, Daniel K. ... Austin, MN
Swanson, Daniel T. ... Columbus, OH
Swanson, David A. ... St. Joseph, MI
Swanson, David A. ... Lenoir, NC
Swanson, David C. ... Milwaukee, WI
Swanson, David Hodges, Jr. ... Columbus, OH
Swanson, David L. ... Corvallis, OR
Swanson, David L. ... Austin, TX
Swanson, David L. ... Dallas, TX
Swanson, David M. ... Charleston, SC
Swanson, David P. ... Minneapolis, MN
Swanson, David W. ... New York, NY
Swanson, David W. ... Tionesta, PA
Warren, PA
Swanson, Dennis V. ... Oakland, CA
Swanson & Dettmann ... Crystal Falls, MI
Escanaba, MI
Hancock, MI
Iron Mountain, MI
Marquette, MI
Menominee, MI
Sault Ste. Marie, MI
Swanson, Diane S. ... St. Louis, MO
Swanson, Donald A., Jr. ... Dallas, TX
Swanson, Donald C., Jr. ... Fort Wayne, IN
Swanson, Donald L. ... Omaha, NE
Swanson, Douglas A. ... Portland, OR
Swanson, Douglas E. ... Waukesha, WI
Swanson, Duane T. ... Sun City, AZ
Swanson, Edrei G. ... Washington, DC
Swanson, Edward N. ... Pilot Mountain, NC
Swanson, Edward T. ... Los Angeles, CA
Swanson, Edward W. ... San Francisco, CA
Swanson, Edward W. ... Ballston Lake, NY
Swanson, Eleanor Knoll ... Omaha, NE
Swanson, Elizabeth D. ... Des Moines, IA
Swanson, Elizabeth L., Law Office of
Los Angeles, CA
Swanson, Eric ... Yakima, WA
Swanson, Eric J.
Securities and Exchange Commission, Office of Compliance Inspections and Examinations, GV
Swanson, Eric T. ... Kansas City, MO
Swanson, Erik C. ... West Palm Beach, FL
Swanson, Gary L. ... Montrose, CO
Swanson, Gary M. ... Minneapolis, MN
Swanson, Geoffrey S. ... Titusville, FL
Swanson, George E. ... Atlanta, GA
Swanson, Gerald D. ... Tulsa, OK
Swanson and Gieser, A Professional Corporation ... San Diego, CA
Santa Ana, CA
Swanson, Gordon D. ... Sturgis, SD
Swanson, H. Paul ... San Diego, CA
Swanson, Harry B. ... Reno, NV
Swanson, Hedwig C. ... Encino, CA
Swanson, Helene Emilie
San Francisco, CA
Swanson, Hilbert D. ... Apache Junction, AZ
Swanson, Hollace S. W. ... New York, NY
Swanson, Howard D. ... Grand Forks, ND
Swanson, J. Gregory ... Liberal, KS
Swanson, J. Toger ... Omaha, NE
Swanson, Jack O. ... Bellingham, WA
Swanson, Jack W. ... Ouray, CO
Swanson, James A. ... Oak Brook, IL
Swanson, James R. ... New Orleans, LA
Swanson, James R. ... Salem, VA
Swanson, James W. ... Merced, CA
Swanson, Jane E. ... Pittsburgh, PA
Swanson, Jane K. ... The Woodlands, TX
Swanson, Jay L. ... Minneapolis, MN
Swanson, Jay W. ... New York, NY
Swanson, Jeffery J. ... Redding, CA
Swanson, Jeffrey R. ... Parsippany, NJ
Swanson, Jeffrey W. ... Tulsa, OK
Swanson, Joanne Geha ... Detroit, MI
Swanson, Joel E. ... Carroll, IA
Swanson, John C. ... Burlington, VT
Swanson, John C. ... Seattle, WA
Swanson, John E. ... Des Moines, IA
Swanson, John W. ... Denver, CO
Swanson, Jon K. ... Des Moines, IA
Swanson, Jonathan A. ... Honolulu, HI
Swanson, Judith Ann ... Columbus, OH
Swanson, Judith Lynn ... Portland, OR
Swanson, Julia S. ... Santa Barbara, CA
Swanson, Julie A. ... Chicago, IL
Swanson, June F. ... Pittsburgh, PA
Swanson, Kara W. ... Boston, MA
Swanson, Karen W. ... Bronxville, NY
Swanson, Kari M. ... Tampa, FL
Swanson, Karin H. ... Riverdale, NJ
Swanson, Keith E. ... Marquette, MI
Swanson, Kelly H. ... Las Vegas, NV
Swanson, Keri N. ... Minneapolis, MN
Swanson, Kim L. ... Columbus, OH
Swanson, Kyle B. ... Winnemucca, NV
Swanson, L. Alan ... Redding, CA
Swanson & Lange ... Burlington, VT
Swanson, Laurence ... Aurora, IL
Swanson Law Firm ... Red Oak, IA
Villisca, IA
Swanson Law Offices, Chtd. ... Las Vegas, NV
Swanson, Leigh J. ... Bensenville, IL
Swanson, Lenard C. ... Chicago, IL
Wheaton, IL
Swanson, Les, Jr. ... Portland, OR
Swanson, Linda Alden ... Sausalito, CA
Swanson, Linda J. ... Denver, CO
Swanson, Lisa ... New York, NY
Swanson, Lisa Robinson ... Oakland, CA
Swanson & Loberg ... Ellsworth, WI
Swanson, Lucia D. ... New York, NY
Swanson & Lyons, P.C. ... Detroit, MI
Taylor, MI
Swanson, M. Anne ... Washington, DC
Swanson, M. Susan ... Toledo, OH
Swanson, Maren L. ... Northfield, MN
Swanson, Mark ... Miami, FL
Swanson, Mark A. ... Seattle, WA
Swanson, Mark D. ... Red Oak, IA
Swanson, Mark J. ... Mount Clemens, MI
Swanson, Mark R. ... Atlanta, GA
Swanson, Mark W. ... Sacramento, CA
Swanson, Marla Lynn ... Piedra, CA
Swanson, Martin & Bell ... Chicago, IL
Geneva, IL
Kankakee, IL
Rockford, IL
Waukegan, IL
Wheaton, IL
Woodstock, IL
Swanson, Mary A. S. ... Riverside, CA
Swanson, Mary Ellen Rosen ... Chicago, IL
Swanson, Maynard F., Jr. ... Dade City, FL
Swanson & McNamara, LLP
San Francisco, CA
Swanson & McVay ... Omaha, NE
Swanson, Melodie C. ... Las Vegas, NV
Swanson, Melodie C., A Professional Law Corporation ... Las Vegas, NV
Swanson, Michael F. ... Denver, CO
Swanson, Michael G. ... Roseville, MN
Swanson, Michael J. ... Issaquah, WA
Swanson, Michael Shane
Minneapolis, MN
Swanson Midgley, LLC ... Kansas City, MO
Overland Park, KS
Swanson, Nancy H. ... Poughkeepsie, NY
Swanson, Ostlie & Associates, P.A.
Crookston, MN
Swanson, Otto F. ... Marina Del Rey, CA
Swanson, Palmer J. ... Sacramento, CA
Swanson, Patricia L. ... Yorba Linda, CA
Swanson, Paul D. ... Los Angeles, CA
Swanson, Paul D. ... Seattle, WA
Swanson, Paul G. ... Oshkosh, WI
Swanson, Paul R. ... Detroit, MI
Taylor, MI
Swanson, Peter C. ... Chicago, IL
Swanson, R. Alan, Law Offices of
Olympia, WA
Swanson, R. Gregory ... Omaha, NE
Swanson, R. Joel ... Houston, TX
Swanson, R. John ... Red Oak, IA
Villisca, IA
Swanson, Ralph J. ... Danville, IL
Swanson, Ralph J., III ... San Jose, CA
Swanson, Randy E. ... Naples, FL
Swanson, Raymond C., (P.S.) ... Seattle, WA
Swanson, Rebecca Beata ... Columbus, OH
Swanson, Rhonda ... Pine City, MN
Swanson, Richard D. ... Auburn Hills, MI
Swanson, Richard G. ... Minneapolis, MN
Swanson, Richard J. ... Indianapolis, IN
Swanson, Richard M. ... Conifer, CO
Swanson, Richard N. ... Morristown, TN
Swanson, Richard P. ... New York, NY
Swanson, Richard S. ... Seattle, WA
Swanson, Richard W. ... Grand Marais, MN
Swanson, Richard W. ... Marysville, WA
Swanson, Robert ... Denver, CO
Swanson, Robert B.
Department Of Veterans Affairs, Board of Veterans Appeals, GV
Swanson, Robert D. ... Sacramento, CA
Swanson, Robert E. ... Ridgewood, NJ
Swanson, Robert G. ... New York, NY
Swanson, Robert K. ... Redding, CA
Swanson, Robert K. ... Denver, CO
Swanson, Robert L. ... Racine, WI
Swanson, Robert P. ... Milan, IL
Swanson, Robert S. ... Clear Lake, IA
Swanson, Robert S., P.C. ... Clear Lake, IA
Swanson, Robert W. ... Austin, TX
Swanson, Ronald H. ... Minneapolis, MN
Swanson, Ronald V. ... Milton, FL
Swanson, Sandra Fisher ... Lakewood, NY
Swanson, Scott O. ... Pendroy, MT
Swanson, Scott W. ... St. Paul, MN
Swanson, Shane E. ... Mount Pleasant, SC
Swanson, Sharon Munson
Westlake Village, CA
Swanson, Shawna M. ... Palo Alto, CA
Swanson, Sheila Hegy ... Chicago, IL
Swanson, Shelley N. ... Spokane, WA
Swanson & Sperling, P.A. ... Gainesville, FL
Swanson, Steffi A. ... Bellevue, NE
Swanson, Stephen C. ... New York, NY
Swanson, Stephen T. ... Los Angeles, CA
Swanson, Stephen W. ... New York, NY
Swanson, Steven F. ... Marina Del Rey, CA
Swanson, Steven J. ... Balsam Lake, WI
Swanson, Steven P. ... Burlington, IA
Swanson, Sue A. ... South Barrington, IL
Swanson, Susan J. ... St. Paul, MN
Swanson, Susan R. ... Portland, OR
Swanson, Susan S. ... Rockwall, TX
Swanson, Suzanne K. ... Oklahoma City, OK
Swanson and Swanson ... Marina Del Rey, CA
Swanson, Terrence E. ... Des Moines, IA
Swanson, Therese M. ... Olympia, WA
Swanson, Thomas A. ... Novato, CA
Swanson, Thomas A. ... Houghton Lake, MI
Swanson, Thomas & Coon ... Portland, OR
Swanson, Todd E. ... Los Angeles, CA
Swanson, Trent A. ... Sioux Falls, SD
Swanson, Troy Christopher
Baltimore, MD
Swanson, Vernon A. ... Hiwasse, AR
Swanson, Victoria C.
Colorado Springs, CO
Denver, CO
Swanson, W. Howard ... Gurnee, IL

Swanson, Wallace M. ... Dallas, TX
Swanson, Walter ... San Jose, CA
Swanson, Warren L. ... Palos Heights, IL
Swanson, Wayne H. ... Crookston, MN
Swanson, William F., Jr. ... Pittsburgh, PA
Swanson, William G. ... Brooklyn Park, MN
Swanson, William R. ... Wellesley, MA
Swanson-Bowers, Rebecca L.
West Hartford, CT
Swanson-Hull, Camie J. ... Indianapolis, IN
Swanson-Mace, Kristin ... Orlando, FL
Swanson-Murray, Heather ... Grand Island, NE
Swanston, Charles ... Salinas, CA
Swanston, Frederick T., Jr.
New York, NY
Swanston, Samara F. ... Lindenhurst, NY
Swanstrom, Deborah A. ... Washington, DC
Swanstrom, Don L. ... Sandpoint, ID
Swanstrom, H. William ... Houston, TX
Swanstrom, Michelle Hoyt ... Huxley, IA
Swanstrom, Roger ... Boise, ID
Swantek, Susan Shannon ... Ann Arbor, MI
Swantko, Stephen ... Havertown, PA
Swantkowski, Jeffery R. ... Houston, TX
Swanton, Robert T., Jr. ... Waco, TX
Swanton, Sandra L. ... Cincinnati, OH
Swanton, Sheryl S. ... Waco, TX
Swanton, Thomas P. ... Boston, MA
Swanton, Wm. F. ... Casper, WY
Swanum, Vernon D. ... Duluth, MN
Swanwick, Rebecca Ann ... Lenexa, KS
Swanwick, W. Miguel ... Lafayette, LA
Swanz, Donald J. ... Franklinville, NY
Swanz, Gretchen H. ... Boston, MA
Swanz, Sarah P. ... Washington, DC
Swapp, J. Craig ... Salt Lake City, UT
Swapp, Russell B. ... Boston, MA
Swarb, Richard R. ... Fort Worth, TX
Swarbrick, John B., Jr. ... Indianapolis, IN
Swarbrick, Richard C., (P.A.)
Piscataway, NJ
Sward, Ellen ... Sacramento, CA
Sward, Gillian A. ... Redwood City, CA
Sward, James R. ... East Hartford, CT
Sward, Janice E. ... Sacramento, CA
Sward, Robert E. ... Indianapolis, IN
Sward, Ruth ... Santa Monica, CA
Sward, Stephen E. ... Chicago, IL
Swardenski, Jay G. ... Chicago, IL
Swark, Robt. N. ... Sioux Falls, SD
Swarner & Fitzgerald ... Riverside, CA
Swarns, Christina Allison ... Philadelphia, PA
Swarny, Pamela Streb ... Bolivar, OH
Swarr, Frank J. ... Baton Rouge, LA
Swarsensky, Gerald D. ... St. Paul, MN
Swart, Chester A. ... Bellflower, CA
Swart, Douglas J. ... Hauppauge, NY
Swart, Gregory W. ... Columbus, OH
Swart, Howard Michael ... Chicago, IL
Waukegan, IL
Swart, James A. ... Charleston, WV
Swart, Jeffrey J. ... Atlanta, GA
Swart, John P. (Jack) ... Jacksonville, NC
Swart, Michael ... Orchard Park, NY
Swart, Randal A. ... Tucson, AZ
Swart, Robert H. ... Washington, DC
Swart, William E. ... Dallas, TX
Swarth, George S. ... Palo Alto, CA
Swarthout, Andrew M. ... Santa Fe, NM
Swarthout, Kenneth L., Jr.
Ocean Springs, MS
Swarthout, Mark Wellington
Bloomfield Hills, MI
Swarthout, Russell L. ... Detroit, MI
Swartley, Christopher B. ... Missoula, MT
Swartley, Richard E. ... Jacksonville, FL
Swartling, David D. ... Seattle, WA
Swartling, Richard K. ... Venice, FL
Swartout, Steven H. ... Canandaigua, NY
Rochester, NY
Swarts, James L. ... Clayton, MO
Swarts, John L., III ... Fort Scott, KS
Swarts, Kem W. ... Breckenridge, CO
Swarts, Kem W., P.C. ... Breckenridge, CO
Swarts, Russell E., Jr. ... Oklahoma City, OK
Swarts, William B., III ... Westport, CT
Swartsel, Vernon ... Orlando, FL
Swartz, Berman ... Los Angeles, CA
Swartwood, Charles B. ... Elmira, NY
Swartwood, Charles B., III ... Worcester, MA
Swartwood, Gregory D. ... Orlando, FL
Swartwood, Thomas M. ... New York, NY
Swartwout, Ann M. ... Beverly Hills, MI
Swartwout, Charles J. ... Belleville, IL
St. Louis, MO
Swartwout, Kristen ... Brattleboro, VT
Swartwout, Willis B., III ... Hartland, WI
Swartz, Alan J. ... Sharon, MA
Swartz, Alan L. ... Providence, RI
Swartz, Albert F. ... Warren, OH
Swartz, Andrew H. ... Monterey, CA
Swartz, Andrew L. ... Albany, NY
Swartz, Barbara ... New York, NY
Swartz, Bridget O. ... Phoenix, AZ
Swartz, Bruce C. ... Washington, DC
Swartz, Campbell & Detweiler
Wilmington, DE
Mount Laurel, NJ
Allentown, PA
Harrisburg, PA
Media, PA
Philadelphia, PA
Scranton, PA
West Chester, PA
Swartz, Carl ... Santa Ana, CA
Swartz, Charles A. ... Irvine, CA
Swartz, Charles I. ... Warren, OH
Swartz, Charles R. ... Richmond, VA

Swartz, Christopher A. ... Saginaw, MI
Swartz, Clifford S. ... Des Moines, IA
Swartz, Conrad M. ... Worcester, MA
Swartz, Craig A. ... Trevose, PA
Swartz, D'Arcy T. ... Long Beach, CA
Swartz, David Adam ... Los Angeles, CA
Swartz, David J. ... Haverhill, MA
Swartz, David S. ... Ann Arbor, MI
Swartz, David W. ... Reading, PA
Swartz, D. E. ... Worcester, MA
Swartz, Dean E. ... Washington, DC
Swartz, Debra C. ... Philadelphia, PA
Swartz, Deiadra Dissen ... Parker, CO
Swartz, Donald K. ... Steubenville, OH
Swartz, Donna F. ... Agoura Hills, CA
Swartz, Douglas W. ... Denver, CO
Swartz, Edward M. ... Boston, MA
Swartz, Eric S. ... Henry, IL
Swartz, Franklin A. ... Norfolk, VA
Swartz, Fredric A. ... Boston, MA
Swartz, Fredrick L. ... Beatrice, NE
Lincoln, NE
Swartz, George T. ... Fort Myers, FL
Swartz, Gerald Neal, Law Offices, The
New York, NY
Swartz, Gordon E. ... Jersey City, NJ
Swartz, Heather Fisher ... Steubenville, OH
Swartz, Heidi L. ... Palo Alto, CA
Swartz, Howard H. ... Louisville, KY
Swartz, J. Robert ... Shaker Heights, OH
Swartz, Jacob ... Los Angeles, CA
Swartz, James A. ... Boston, MA
Swartz, James F., III ... Allentown, PA
Swartz, James F., Jr. ... New York, NY
Swartz, James L. ... Tulsa, OK
Swartz, Jean V. ... Springfield, VA
Swartz, Jeffrey A. ... Norfolk, VA
Swartz, Jeffrey D. ... Miami, FL
Swartz, Jeffrey L. ... Waukon, IA
Swartz, Joan E. ... Boston, MA
Swartz, Joan M. ... St. Louis, MO
Swartz, John F. ... Phoenix, AZ
Swartz, John J. ... Saginaw, MI
Swartz, John J., Jr. ... Saginaw, MI
Swartz, John L. ... Springfield, IL
Swartz, Joseph A. ... Boston, MA
Swartz, Joseph B. ... Cleveland, OH
Swartz, Joshua ... Los Angeles, CA
Swartz, Judy L. ... Ionia, MI
Swartz, Justin M. ... Chicago, IL
Swartz, Karl R. ... Wichita, KS
Swartz, Kenneth A. ... Morton Grove, IL
Swartz, Kenneth A., Ltd. ... Morton Grove, IL
Swartz, Kenneth M. ... Miami, FL
Swartz, Kim H. ... Los Angeles, CA
Swartz, Kristina B. ... Miami, FL
Swartz, Larry A. ... Albany, NY
Swartz, Laura Lynn ... Baltimore, MD
Swartz, Lawrence B., (P.C.) ... Denver, CO
Swartz, Lawrence D. ... Wenham, MA
Swartz, Lee C. ... Harrisburg, PA
Swartz, Linda K. ... Stockton, CA
Swartz, Linda Z. ... New York, NY
Swartz, Lloyd C. ... Topeka, KS
Swartz, Louis ... Los Angeles, CA
Swartz, Margaret Warren ... Richmond, VA
Swartz, Marjorie C. ... Sacramento, CA
Swartz, Mark A. ... Abingdon, VA
Charleston, WV
Swartz, Mark D. ... Philadelphia, PA
Swartz, Mark L. ... Amesbury, MA
Swartz, Mark R. ... Sacramento, CA
Swartz, Martha S. ... Philadelphia, PA
Swartz, Mary I. ... New York, NY
Swartz, Mary J. ... Charleston, WV
Swartz, Matthew B. ... San Diego, CA
Swartz, Melinda A. ... Milwaukee, WI
Swartz, Melvin Jay ... Scottsdale, AZ
Swartz, Merrill C. ... Marshalltown, IA
Swartz, Michael ... Los Angeles, CA
Swartz, Michael E. ... New York, NY
Swartz, Michael R. ... Pittsburgh, PA
Swartz, Michael S. ... San Mateo, CA
Swartz, Michael S. ... Somerville, MA
Swartz, Morris B. ... Syracuse, NY
Swartz, Neal James ... Department of Justice,
Office of Justice Programs, GV
Swartz, Paul B. ... Wichita, KS
Swartz, Peter H. ... Syracuse, NY
Swartz & Reed ... Washington, DC
Swartz, Richard A., Jr. ... Slidell, LA
Swartz, Richard Steven ... Philadelphia, PA
Swartz, Richard W. ... Los Angeles, CA
Swartz, Robert A. ... Los Angeles, CA
Swartz, Robert J. ... New York, NY
Swartz, Robert N. ... Grand Rapids, MI
Swartz, Ronald J. ... Great Neck, NY
Swartz, Russell C. ... Rosemead, CA
Swartz, Russell J. ... Redding, CA
Swartz, Saul David ... Rochester, NY
Swartz, Scott D. ... Orem, UT
Swartz, Scott E. ... Cleveland, OH
Swartz, Stephen M. ... Omaha, NE
Swartz, Stephen W. ... Bethesda, MD
Swartz, Steven ... Great Neck, NY
Swartz & Stump ... Abingdon, VA
Swartz & Stump, L.C. ... Charleston, WV
Swartz & Swartz ... Los Angeles, CA
Swartz & Swartz ... Boston, MA
Swartz & Swartz ... Great Neck, NY
Swartz, Terry R. ... West Palm Beach, FL
Swartz, Thomas Byrne ... San Francisco, CA
Swartz, Thomas F. ... Brooklyn, NY
Swartz, Todd Barry ... Boston, MA
Swartz, Warren G. ... Savannah, GA
Swartz & Wilson ... Saginaw, MI
Swartzbaugh, E. David ... Kansas City, MO

Swartzbaugh, Jeffrey H.
Department of Housing and Urban Development,
Office of General Counsel, GV
Swartzbaugh, Marc L. ... Cleveland, OH
Swartzberg & Duggan, S.C. ... Milwaukee, WI
Swartzberg, Pamela Muller ... Charlotte, NC
Swartzberg, Sandy ... Milwaukee, WI
Swartzendruber, Michael A. ... Dallas, TX
Swartzfager, Helen E. ... Laurel, MS
Swartzfager, Jon A. ... Laurel, MS
Swartzfager, Paul G. ... Laurel, MS
Swartzfager, Paul G., Jr. ... Laurel, MS
Swartzfager, Polly S. ... Denver, CO
Chicago, IL
Swartzfager & Swartzfager ... Laurel, MS
Swartzkopf, Walter K., Jr. ... Altoona, PA
Swartzle, Brock A. ... Ann Arbor, MI
Swartzman, Daniel ... Chicago, IL
Swartzmeyer, Sarah E. ... Chicago, IL
Swary, Mark F. ... Cleveland, OH
Swarz, Raymond F. ... Portsmouth, RI
Swasey, Charlton J. ... Plaistow, NH
Swasey, Jo Ann F. ... Santa Clara, CA
Swatek, Martha ... Geneva, IL
Swatek, Richard L. ... St. Louis, MO
Swatek, Susan Sanders ... Tulsa, OK
Swatek, Timothy P. ... Lake Geneva, WI
Swatek, William E. ... Pelham, AL
Swatez, Harold H., A Prof. Corp.
El Toro, CA
Swathwood, Jason Michael ... Indianapolis, IN
Swatkoski, John G. ... Wilkes-Barre, PA
Swatsler, Todd Shawn ... Columbus, OH
Swatt, Patricia Lynn ... Culver City, CA
Swaty, Charles R. ... Mabelvale, AR
Swaty, Joseph W. ... Sheridan, AR
Swauger, Melissa A. ... Camp Hill, PA
Swauger, Terry A. ... Warren, OH
Swaun, John W. ... Miami, FL
Swavely, Gary R., Jr. ... Reading, PA
Swavely, Melinda C. ... Hagåtña, GU
Sway, Michael Andrew ... Cincinnati, OH
Swaya, Matthew E. ... Seattle, WA
Swaye, Stacey L. ... Miami, FL
Swayne, G. Barrett, Jr. ... Arcadia, CA
Swayne, Gary J. ... Paris, TN
Swayne, John A. ... Orofino, ID
Swayne Law Firm, The ... Paris, TN
Swayne, Robert F. ... Paris, TN
Swayne, S. David ... Moscow, ID
Swayze, Charles J., Jr. ... Greenwood, MS
Swayze, David S. ... Dover, DE
Wilmington, DE
Swayze, John M. ... Washington, DC
Swayze, Julie Fleming ... Jackson, MS
Swayze, Mary A. ... Miami, FL
Swayze, Thomas A., Jr. ... Tacoma, WA
Swayze, W. Stephen ... Dallas, TX
Swayze, Walter H., III ... Philadelphia, PA
Swe, Sana ... Los Angeles, CA
Sweaney, Robert E. ... Richmond, VA
Sweany, Garett G. ... Department of State,
Foreign Service Officers (Overseas), GV
Swearengen, Anita Elizabeth ... St. Louis, MO
Swearengen, James C. ... Jefferson City, MO
Swearengen, James E. ... Memphis, TN
Swearengen, Michael K. ... Cleveland, OH
Swearengen, Monte L. ... Austin, TX
Swearer, Dell Marie Shanahan
Hutchinson, KS
Swearer, John B. ... Hutchinson, KS
Swearer, William B. ... Hutchinson, KS
Swearingen, Arlen C. ... Eugene, OR
Swearingen, Brad M. ... North Aurora, IL
Swearingen, Bradley W. ... Washington, IL
Swearingen, E. S. "Worth", Jr. ... Aiken, SC
Swearingen, Floyd G. ... Metairie, LA
Swearingen, Gary D. ... Seattle, WA
Swearingen, Glenda F. ... Marianna, FL
Swearingen, James D. ... Pensacola, FL
Swearingen, Kenneth R., Jr.
St. Petersburg, FL
Swearingen, Mark J. ... St. Louis, MO
Swearingen, Patrick H., Jr.
San Antonio, TX
Swearingen, Robert A. ... Bryan, TX
Swearingen, Sidney H. ... San Antonio, TX
Swearingen, Thomas J. ... Little Rock, AR
Swearingen, Thomas J. ... Port Arthur, TX
Swearingen, Walter E. ... New York, NY
Swearinger, Bill ... Los Angeles, CA
Swearinger, Eddy R. ... Salem, OR
Swearinger, Ronald E. ... Los Angeles, CA
Sweasy, William W. ... Green Bay, WI
Sweat, Andrew D. ... Jackson, MS
Sweat, Daniel W. ... Shelby, NC
Sweat, David L. ... Daytona Beach, FL
Sweat, David R. ... Athens, GA
Sweat, David R. ... Arlington, TX
Sweat, Donald A. ... Albany, GA
Sweat, Forrest W., Jr. ... Waycross, GA
Sweat, Gary L. ... Canonsburg, PA
Sweat & Giese, P.A. ... Athens, GA
Sweat, J. Wade ... Jackson, MS
Sweat, Justin Wade ... Tupelo, MS
Sweat & Passarello ... Canonsburg, PA
Sweat, Richard W. ... San Diego, CA
Sweat, Scott H. ... Heber City, UT
Sweat, Steven M. ... Encino, CA
Sweat, Thomas L., Jr. ... Corinth, MS
Sweat, William A., Jr. ... Lakeland, FL
Sweat, William A., Jr., P.A. ... Lakeland, FL
Sweatt, A. Morris ... Columbia, MS
Sweatt, Donald L. ... Graham, TX
Sweatt, Donald L., P.C. ... Graham, TX
Sweatt, Jason M. ... Rochester, NY
Sweatt, Millard E., Jr. ... Dallas, TX

Sweatt, Robert C., Jr. ... Kingsland, GA
Sweazea, Kevin R. ... Los Lunas, NM
Swecker, Mary Beth B. ... Greensboro, NC
Swecker, Robert S. ... Alexandria, VA
Sweda, Edward L., Jr. ... Boston, MA
Sweda, Kip M. ... Cleveland, OH
Swedback, Julie K. ... St. Paul, MN
Swedberg, Amy J. ... Minneapolis, MN
Swedberg, Byron L. ... Bellingham, WA
Swedberg, Jon L. ... Monterey, CA
Swedberg, Richard L. ... Chicago, IL
Swedelson, David C. ... Los Angeles, CA
Swedelson & Gottlieb ... Los Angeles, CA
Sweder, Kenneth A. ... Boston, MA
Sweder & Ross LLP ... Boston, MA
Sweders, Peter A. P., Sr. ... Naperville, IL
Swedish, Charles J. ... Vienna, VA
Swedlaw, Henry J. ... Baton Rouge, LA
Swedlow, Butler, Levine, Lewis & Dye Co., L.P.A. ... Columbus, OH
Swedlow, Gerald H. ... Columbus, OH
Swedlow, Leif ... Oklahoma City, OK
Swedlow, Stephen A. ... Chicago, IL
Swedlund, Paul S. ... Rapid City, SD
Swedmark, Gayle Smith ... Tallahassee, FL
Swedo, Jeffrey A. ... Irvine, CA
Swee, Jean A. ... Bloomington, IL
Sweebe, Richard D. ... Cleveland, OH
Columbus, OH
Sweeda, Ronald P. ... Wilkes-Barre, PA
Sweedler, Charles C. ... Cherry Hill, NJ
Philadelphia, PA
Sweedler, Ian K. ... San Francisco, CA
Sweedler, Michael J. ... New York, NY
Sweek, Walter H. ... Portland, OR
Sween & Beres, P.C. ... Eldora, IA
Sween, Birger M. ... Hackensack, NJ
Sween, Harlan G. ... Minneapolis, MN
Sween, Jim R. ... Eldora, IA
Sween, Paul V. ... Austin, MN
Sween & Salazar, Ltd. ... Minneapolis, MN
Sweeney, Adam Daniel ... Los Angeles, CA
Sweeney, Allyn L. ... Boise, ID
Sweeney, Ann C. ... New York, NY
Sweeney, Anna Shubik ... Chester, CT
Sweeney, Anthony E. ... Port Chester, NY
Sweeney, Asher W. ... Columbus, OH
Sweeney, Barbara J. ... Springfield, MA
Sweeney, Barry M. ... White Plains, NY
Sweeney, Bernadette ... Rockville, MD
Sweeney, Bernard L. ... Falls Church, VA
Sweeney, Bonny E. ... San Diego, CA
Sweeney, Borer & Ostrow, Professional Association ... St. Paul, MN
Sweeney, Brenda ... Taylorville, IL
Sweeney, Brendan ... Philadelphia, PA
Sweeney, Brian E. ... Sacramento, CA
Sweeney, Brian Francis ... Gaithersburg, MD
Sweeney & Calabrese ... White Plains, NY
Sweeney, Carol Ann ... Norristown, PA
Sweeney, Carol Meehan ... Philadelphia, PA
Sweeney, Charles A. ... Mendham, NJ
Sweeney, Charles A., Jr. ... South Bend, IN
Sweeney, Charles V. ... Madison, WI
Sweeney, Charles W., III ... Philadelphia, PA
Sweeney, Charlotte N. ... Denver, CO
Sweeney, Cheryl R. ... Monroe, MI
Sweeney, Christine Mullen ... Austin, TX
Sweeney, Christopher W. ... Fairfield, CA
Sweeney, Clayton A. ... Pittsburgh, PA
Sweeney, Clayton A., Jr. ... Philadelphia, PA
Sweeney, Clayton T. ... Birmingham, AL
Sweeney, Cohn, Stahl & Vaccaro
New York, NY
Scarsdale, NY
White Plains, NY
Sweeney, Colleen C. ... Fairfax, VA
Sweeney, Constance M. ... Springfield, MA
Sweeney, Craig C. ... Irving, TX
Sweeney, Craig V. ... Metairie, LA
Sweeney, D. Patrick ... Springfield, MO
Sweeney, Dabagia, Thorne, Janes & Pagos, L.L.P. ... La Porte, IN
Michigan City, IN
Sweeney, Daniel ... Philadelphia, PA
Sweeney, Daniel B. ... Philadelphia, PA
Sweeney, Daniel B. ... Lynchburg, VA
Sweeney, Daniel C. ... Manassas, VA
Sweeney, Daniel J. ... Burbank, CA
Sweeney, Daniel J. ... Washington, DC
Sweeney, Daniel J., Law Offices of
Pleasantville, NY
Sweeney, Daniel L. ... Orlando, FL
Sweeney, Daniel R. ... Butte, MT
Sweeney, David B. ... Seattle, WA
Sweeney, David F., Jr. ... Warwick, RI
Sweeney, David J. ... Portland, OR
Sweeney, David M. ... Mayfield Heights, OH
Sweeney, Deidre A. ... New York, NY
Sweeney, Dennis J. ... Spokane, WA
Sweeney, Dianne L. ... San Jose, CA
Sweeney, Don ... Santa Barbara, CA
Sweeney, Donald B., Jr. ... Birmingham, AL
Sweeney, Donald J. P. ... Philadelphia, PA
Sweeney, Donald W. ... New York, NY
Sweeney, Edward ... Monett, MO
Sweeney, Edward C. ... Downingtown, PA
Reading, PA
West Chester, PA
Sweeney, Edward J. ... Brooklyn, NY
Sweeney, Edward J., Jr.
West Yarmouth, MA
Sweeney, Edward S. ... Salt Lake City, UT
Sweeney, Edward V. ... Monett, MO
Sweeney, Eileen C. ... Towson, MD
Sweeney, Ellen ... Braintree, MA
Sweeney, Ellen M. ... Norristown, PA
Sweeney, Emilia L. ... Seattle, WA

Swegle, Thomas W. ....Department of Justice, Environment and Natural Resources Division, GV
Swegles, Frederick F. ....Port Huron, MI
Swegles, William H. ....Los Angeles, CA
Swegman, George E. ....Washington, DC
Sweig, Allan G. ....Chicago, IL
Sweig, Howard B. ....Denver, CO
Sweigard, Edward C. ....Chicago, IL
Sweigart, David V. ....Boston, MA
Sweigart, Krista Anne ....Washington, DC
Sweigart, Raymond L. ....Washington, DC
Sweigert, David C. ....Monterey, CA
Sweigert, Philip K. ....Seattle, WA
Sweitzer, A. Lawrence ....Madison, WI
Sweitzer, Brett G. ....Philadelphia, PA
Sweitzer, Cristine Kepple ....Oakland, MD
Sweitzer, David E. ....Pittsburgh, PA
Sweitzer, George T., Jr. ....Harrisonville, MO
Sweitzer, Harvey C. ....Salt Lake City, UT
Sweitzer, Kathleen A. ....Chicago, IL
Swelbar, Gaylord W. ....Duluth, MN
Swem, Lisa L. ....Lansing, MI
Swenarton, Jeffrey D. ....Kalamazoo, MI
Swendiman, Alan R. ....Washington, DC Baltimore, MD Rockville, MD
Swendiman, Kathleen S. Library of Congress, Congressional Research Service, GV
Swendseid, John O. ....Las Vegas, NV Reno, NV
Swendseid & Stern ....Las Vegas, NV Reno, NV
Swendson, William A. ....Oconomowoc, WI
Swendson/Menting Law Ltd. Oconomowoc, WI
Sweney, Michael E. ....St. Louis, MO
Sweney, Richard Wayne Coeur d'Alene, ID
Sweney, Robert L. ....St. Louis, MO
Swennen, Jean-Pierre ....Irvine, CA
Swennes, Ellen F. ....Washington, DC
Swennumson, Glenn R. West Des Moines, IA
Swenor, Rita L. ....San Francisco, CA
Swensen, Anne ....Salt Lake City, UT
Swensen & Gray ....Portland, OR
Swensen, James G., Jr. Salt Lake City, UT
Swensen, Jan C. ....Pittsburgh, PA
Swensen, Kathryn Ann ....New York, NY
Swensen, Keith R. ....Portland, OR
Swensen, Neal C. ....Tustin, CA
Swensen Perer & Kontos ....Pittsburgh, PA
Swensen Perer & McCandless ....Erie, PA
Swensen, Richard D. ....Warren, MI
Swensen, Timothy G. ....Kansas City, MO
Swensen, Tyler Q. ....Phoenix, AZ
Swenson, Bradley J. ....Minneapolis, MN
Swenson, Bruce A. ....Derby, KS
Swenson, Bruce E. ....Havre, MT
Swenson, C. David ....Washington, DC
Swenson, Carl A. ....St. Paul, MN
Swenson, Carol C. ....Palo Alto, CA
Swenson, Carol L. ....Tulsa, OK
Swenson, Chad W. ....Sioux Falls, SD
Swenson, Chester D. ....Albert Lea, MN
Swenson, Christopher C. ....St. Louis, MO
Swenson, Connie ....Gresham, OR
Swenson, Craig C. ....Hackensack, NJ
Swenson, Dan R. ....Denver, CO
Swenson, Darel F. ....Plymouth, MN
Swenson, David D. ....Concordia, KS
Swenson, David G. ....Waco, TX
Swenson, David P. ....Washington, DC
Swenson, Deborah C. ....Minneapolis, MN
Swenson, Douglas G. ....Pine City, MN
Swenson, Elizabeth von Fischer University Heights, OH
Swenson, Eric D. ....San Diego, CA
Swenson, Eric D. ....Oyster Bay, NY
Swenson, Eric, Jr. ....Spur, TX
Swenson, Eric P. ....Salt Lake City, UT
Swenson, Erik G. ....Minneapolis, MN
Swenson, Frederick L. ....Boulder, CO
Swenson, Garrett W., Jr. ....Hauppauge, NY
Swenson, Gary A. ....Basking Ridge, NJ
Swenson, George W., Jr. ....Washington, DC
Swenson, Geralyn T. ....Buffalo, NY
Swenson, Glen W. ....Buffalo, MN
Swenson, Gregory S. ....Woodbury, MN
Swenson, Guy A., Jr. ....Concord, NH
Swenson, Hal N. ....Salt Lake City, UT
Swenson, Harold H. ....Phoenix, AZ
Swenson, Houston L. ....Indianapolis, IN
Swenson, H. W. ....Madison, MN
Swenson, Ingrid L. ....Portland, OR
Swenson, Irving G. ....Chicago, IL
Swenson, James E., Jr. ....Sacramento, CA
Swenson, James S. ....Northridge, CA
Swenson, James S. ....Kansas City, MO
Swenson, John Forbes ....Glencoe, IL
Swenson, John J. ....Los Angeles, CA
Swenson, John R. ....Columbia, MO
Swenson, Joseph D. ....Boulder, CO
Swenson, Karen B. ....Columbus, OH
Swenson, Kathryn Ashbaugh ....Atlanta, GA
Swenson, Kenneth L. ....Sacramento, CA
Swenson, Kenneth W. ....Universal City, CA
Swenson, Kevin D. ....Salt Lake City, UT
Swenson, Kurt M. ....Manchester, NH
Swenson Law Office ....Albert Lea, MN
Swenson, Lawrence S. ....Penngrove, CA
Swenson Lervick Syverson Anderson Trosvig & Jacobson, P.A. ....Alexandria, MN
Swenson, Lily Fu ....Washington, DC
Swenson, Louise ....Sunriver, OR
Swenson, Marianne ....Boston, MA
Swenson, Mart W. ....Eau Claire, WI
Swenson, Matthew Ray ....Pittsburgh, PA
Swenson & Nelson ....Dawson, MN Madison, MN
Swenson, Paul E. ....Danbury, CT
Swenson, Paul N. ....Burnsville, MN
Swenson, Peter G. ....Chicago, IL
Swenson, R. A. ....San Antonio, TX
Swenson, Raymond Takashi Salt Lake City, UT
Swenson, Rebecca E. ....Washington, DC
Swenson, Rebecca P. ....Troy, IL
Swenson, Richard C. ....Glenwood, IA
Swenson, Richard L. ....Omaha, NE
Swenson, Robert C. ....Alexandria, MN
Swenson, Robert H. ....Moorhead, MN Fargo, ND
Swenson, Robt. W. ....Salt Lake City, UT
Swenson, Roger L. ....Madison, MN
Swenson, Sandra ....Philadelphia, PA
Swenson, Scott ....Denver, CO
Swenson, Severt, Jr. ....Gooding, ID
Swenson, Stanley F. ....Houston, TX
Swenson, Stephen James ....Hampton, IA
Swenson, Thomas ....Boulder, CO
Swenson, Vernon, Retter, Uri, Brewer & Long Concordia, KS
Swenson, Victoria J. ....Pasadena, TX
Swenson & Whitacre, P.C. ....Glenwood, IA
Swenson, William P. ....Houston, TX
Swent, F. Rae ....Alexandria, LA
Swent, William B. ....Greenville, SC
Swenty, Peter W. ....Cincinnati, OH
Swepston, Donald S. ....Columbus, OH
Swerbilow, Howard M. Merritt Island, FL
Swerdlin & Hassid ....New York, NY
Swerdlin, Joyce S. ....New York, NY
Swerdlin, Mark J. ....Baltimore, MD
Swerdloff, Arthur ....New York, NY
Swerdloff, Arthur J. ....Costa Mesa, CA
Swerdloff, David A. ....Stamford, CT
Swerdloff, Ileen P. ....West Hartford, CT
Swerdloff, Mark H. ....West Hartford, CT
Swerdloff, Nicolas ....Miami, FL
Swerdloff, Scott J. ....New York, NY
Swerdloff & Swerdloff ....West Hartford, CT
Swerdlove, Arthur P. ....Wichita Falls, TX
Swerdlove, Nathan B. ....Chicago, IL
Swerdlow, Alan E. ....Oakland, CA
Swerdlow, David F. ....Princeton, NJ
Swerdlow, Edith L. ....Beverly Hills, CA
Swerdlow Florence Sanchez & Rathbun, A Law Corporation ....Beverly Hills, CA Los Angeles, CA
Swerdlow, Harry B. ....Beverly Hills, CA
Swerdlow, Janet I. ....Beverly Hills, CA
Swerdlow, John D. ....Ann Arbor, MI
Swerdlow, Jonathan A. ....Beverly Hills, CA
Swerdlow, Marc ....Chicago, IL
Swerdlow, Marleen Roosth ....Beaumont, TX
Swerdlow, Richard ....Hollywood, FL
Swerdlow, Robert M. ....Los Angeles, CA
Swerdlow, Seymour ....Beverly Hills, CA
Swerdzewski, Joseph Federal Labor Relations Authority, Office of the General Counsel, GV
Sweren, Marci E. ....New York, NY
Sweren, Melvin R. ....Baltimore, MD
Swergold, Henry G. ....New York, NY
Swergold, Jon L. ....Jacksonville, FL
Swergold, Nathaniel M. ....Cedarhurst, NY
Swerin, Leon M. ....Madison, WI
Swerk, Robert W. ....Seattle, WA
Swerling, Jack B. ....Columbia, SC
Swernofsky, Steven A. ....Los Altos, CA
Swers, Andrew T. ....Washington, DC
Swersky, Alfred D. ....Alexandria, VA
Swertfeger, L. Jack, Jr. ....Atlanta, GA
Swetcky, Beverly A. ....Springfield, MA
Swete, Donald R. ....Camillus, NY
Sweterlitsch, Martha J. ....Columbus, OH
Swetland, Donald J. ....Kirtland, OH
Swetman, Glenn L. M. ....New Orleans, LA
Swetnam, Daniel R. ....Columbus, OH
Swetnam, Douglas S. ....Indianapolis, IN
Swetnam and Houff ....Luray, VA
Swetnam, Tony E. ....Kansas City, MO
Swetnick, Robert N. ....New York, NY
Swetow, Carol ....Boston, MA
Swets, David W. ....Grand Rapids, MI
Swets, Joel B. ....Boston, MA
Swets, Roger A. ....Grand Rapids, MI
Swetschinski, Galia ....San Francisco, CA
Swett, Ann Hastings ....Bethesda, MD
Swett, Brian I. ....Chicago, IL
Swett, Daniel R. ....Chicago, IL
Swett, Eric R. ....San Francisco, CA
Swett, Frank P., Jr. ....Pago Pago, TT
Swett, Gwendolynne Dell ....Media, PA
Swett, H. Andrew ....Fort Myers, FL
Swett, Jay T. ....Ivy, VA
Swett, Jeremy F. ....Lexington, MA
Swett, John E. ....Rochester, NY
Swett, Kathleen Claire ....Waukegan, IL
Swett, Leonard W. ....South Bristol, ME
Swett, Matthew J. ....Philadelphia, PA Wayne, PA
Swett, Trevor W., III ....Washington, DC
Swett, Valerie ....Boston, MA
Swetz, Alan G. ....East Orange, NJ Fairfield, NJ Paterson, NJ
Swetz, James A. ....Stroudsburg, PA
Sweyd, Bruce ....Laguna Hills, CA
Swezey, C. Lawrence ....Palo Alto, CA
Swezey, John W. ....Martinsville, VA
Swezey, Kenneth Neal ....New York, NY
Swhear, John C. ....Indianapolis, IN
Swhier, Claudia V. ....Indianapolis, IN
Swhier, Robert D., Jr. ....Indianapolis, IN
Swiader, Michael C. ....Washington, DC
Swiatek, Glenn M. ....Fort Walton Beach, FL
Swiatek, Jeffrey F. ....Buffalo, NY
Swiatek, Maria S. ....Palo Alto, CA
Swiatek, Mark J. Department Of Veterans Affairs, Board of Veterans Appeals, GV
Swiatek, Michael G. ....Chicago, IL
Swiatek, Thomas Marshall Los Angeles, CA
Swiatek, Virginia McDaniel Downingtown, PA
Swiatek, W. Jay ....Johnston, RI
Swiatkiewicz, Stephen J. ....New York, NY
Swiatocha, John ....East Hartford, CT
Swibel, Howard J. ....Chicago, IL
Swibel, Lawrence B. ....Chicago, IL
Swibel, Steven W. ....Chicago, IL
Swicegood, Teri Hays ....Conway, AR
Swicegood, Thomas E. ....Louisville, KY
Swichar, Edward I. ....Philadelphia, PA
Swichar, Jonathan L. ....Philadelphia, PA
Swichkow, Morton C. ....Richardson, TX
Swick, Bernhard R. ....Grosse Ile, MI
Swick, Charles J. ....Meadville, PA
Swick, Daniel A. ....Roseland, NJ
Swick, Gerard A. ....Chicago, IL
Swick, James E. ....Lakewood, CA
Swick, James R. ....Phillipsburg, NJ
Swick, Jeffrey D. ....Columbus, OH
Swick, John C. ....Meadville, PA
Swick, Kevin L. ....Cincinnati, OH
Swick, Larry E. ....Elwood, IN
Swick Law Office ....Phillipsburg, NJ
Swick, Loren ....Lakewood, CO
Swick, Mary Leiter ....Omaha, NE
Swick, Michael F. ....Duluth, GA
Swick, Richard L. ....Washington, DC Bowie, MD
Swick, Robert A. ....Washington, DC
Swick & Shapiro, P.C. ....Washington, DC
Swick, Susan M. ....Phoenix, AZ
Swickard, Christopher D. ....Topeka, KS
Swickard, Jack Neil ....Newport Beach, CA
Swickle, Ilene J. ....Fort Lauderdale, FL
Swickle, Marc K. ....Fort Lauderdale, FL
Swickle, Robert E. ....Detroit, MI
Swid, Scott A. ....Stratford, WI **Wausau, WI**
Swide, Fred A. ....Benicia, CA
Swider, David L. ....Indianapolis, IN
Swider, Robert A. ....Portland, OR
Swiderski, Alex M. ....Anchorage, AK
Swiderski, James S. ....Milwaukee, WI
Swiderski, Joseph D. ....Margate, FL
Swiderski, Pamela A. ....Bremen, IN
Swiderski, Robert S. North Massapequa, NY
Swidler, Arthur E. ....Trenton, NJ
Swidler, Barry ....Brooklyn, NY
Swidler Berlin Shereff Friedman, LLP Washington, DC New York, NY
Swidler, Ira J. ....Chicago, IL
Swidler, Joseph C. ....Washington, DC
Swidler, Louis ....Lincolnwood, IL
Swidler, Mary T. ....Albany, NY
Swidler, Michael J. ....New York, NY
Swidler, Robert N. ....Troy, NY
Swidler, Simon ....New York, NY
Swidler, Steven A., (P.C.) ....New York, NY
Swieca, John J. Treasury Department, GV
Swiech, Robert A. ....Chicago, IL
Swiedler, Alan M. ....New York, NY
Swiedler, Ernest ....New Rochelle, NY
Swien, Kathleen Ann ....Chicago, IL
Swienton, Cynthia K. ....Farmington, CT
Swier, Scott P. ....Lenox, IA
Swier, Scott R. ....Watertown, SD
Swierczynski, Diane ....Cambridge, MA
Swierenga, Donald J. ....Grand Rapids, MI
Swiers, Thomas C. ....Fairfax, VA
Swierzbinski, Annette I. ....New York, NY
Swierzbinski, Paul S. ....Dover, DE
Swierzewski, Ann M. ....Springfield, MA
Swierzewski, Jon S. ....Minneapolis, MN
Swierzewski, Matthew A. King Of Prussia, PA
Swiess, John J. ....Westmont, IL
Swietlik, John M. ....Milwaukee, WI
Swietlik, John M., Jr. ....Milwaukee, WI
Swietlik, Walter J. ....Port Washington, WI
Swift, A. Earl ....Houston, TX
Swift, Achia Y. ....San Francisco, CA
Swift, Amy U. ....Kirkland, WA
Swift and Associates ....Dallas, TX
Swift, Benjamin A. ....Chicago, IL
Swift, Bert L. ....Joshua Tree, CA
Swift, Betsy A. ....Columbus, OH
Swift, Brian T. ....Beaumont, TX
Swift, Byron ....Washington, DC
Swift, Carolyn J.A. ....Washington, DC
Swift, Catherine M. ....Helena, MT
Swift, Charlotte G. ....Spring Valley, NY
Swift, Charmayne S. ....Anaheim, CA
Swift, Cheryl Goldstein ....Decatur, GA
Swift, Christopher J. ....Cleveland, OH
Swift, Clifford D. ....Camp Hill, PA
Swift, Clinton P. ....Denver, CO
Swift, Currie, McGhee & Hiers Atlanta, GA
Swift, Daniel H. ....Manchester, IA
Swift, Daniel L. ....Boston, MA
Swift, David ....Hudson, OH
Swift, David A. ....Decatur, GA
Swift, David A. ....Columbus, OH
Swift, Dean A. ....North Canton, OH
Swift, Dennis ....Fort Worth, TX
Swift, Donald L., III ....Atlanta, GA
Swift, Donn A. ....New Haven, CT
Swift, Douglas M., Jr. ....Winchester, VA
Swift, Douglas M., Jr., P.C. Winchester, VA
Swift, Ed ....Houston, TX
Swift, Edward P. ....Gaithersburg, MD
Swift, Ernest ....Palestine, TX
Swift & Finlayson ....Fort Wayne, IN
Swift, Francis L. ....Boston, MA
Swift, Frank M. ....Atlanta, GA
Swift, Freeman B. ....Eden Prairie, MN
Swift, G. Lee ....San Marcos, TX
Swift, George H., III ....Stuart, FL
Swift, Gretchen L. ....Eddyville, KY
Swift, Grover ....Fort Worth, TX
Swift, Grover, Jr. ....Fort Worth, TX
Swift, H. Melvin, Jr. ....Pasadena, CA
Swift, Harry R. ....York, PA
Swift, Henry J. ....Osceola, AR
Swift, Herbert ....Newberg, OR
Swift, Hollis G. ....Springfield, IL
Swift, Jack H. ....Chula Vista, CA
Swift, Jack H. ....San Diego, CA
Swift, James G. ....Birmingham, AL
Swift, James P. ....Riverwoods, IL
Swift, James P., III ....Atlantic City, NJ
Swift, James W. ....Middlebury, VT
Swift, Jan Whitehead ....Lafayette, LA
Swift, Jane Wilcox ....Atlanta, GA
Swift, Jerry R. ....Troy, MI
Swift, Joel H. ....De Kalb, IL
Swift, John B., III ....Newburgh, NY
Swift, John G. ....Lafayette, LA
Swift, John H. ....Columbus, GA
Swift, John L. ....Des Moines, IA
Swift, John Q. ....Manchester, IA
Swift, Joseph R. ....St. Louis, MO
Swift, Joshua E. ....Department of Justice, Environment and Natural Resources Division, GV
Swift, Judith A. ....Dallas, TX
Swift, Kathleen H. ....Wyckoff, NJ
Swift, Kelley P. ....New York, NY
Swift, Ken ....St. Paul, MN
Swift Law Office, P.C. ....Arlington, VA
Swift, Lawrence David ....New York, NY
Swift, Malcolm S. ....El Segundo, CA
Swift, Marie C. ....Boston, MA
Swift, Marvin S., Jr. ....Phoenix, AZ
Swift, MaryAnn Farrell ....Philadelphia, PA
Swift, Mathews D. ....Columbus, GA
Swift, Michael A. ....Indianapolis, IN
Swift, Minear & Hansen ....Des Moines, IA
Swift, Nancy L. ....New York, NY
Swift, Pattie P. ....San Luis, CO
Swift, Peter J. ....Washington, DC
Swift, Phelps H., Jr. ....Jackson, WY
Swift, Popuch & Sinclair ....Chicago, IL
Swift, R. E. ....Palestine, TX
Swift, Richard E., Jr. ....Palestine, TX
Swift, Richard F. ....Washington, DC
Swift, Robert A. ....Philadelphia, PA
Swift, Robert E. ....Newberg, OR
Swift, Robert J. ....Houston, TX
Swift, Robert J., Jr. ....Jefferson City, MO
Swift, Sally C. ....New York, NY
Swift, Samuel R. ....San Jose, CA
Swift, Saundra G. ....Tallahassee, FL
Swift, Sharon A. ....Buffalo, NY
Swift, Spears & Harper, L.L.P. Lake Charles, LA
Swift, Stephen A. ....Cedar Rapids, IA
Swift, Stephen Christopher ....Arlington, VA
Swift, Stephen H. ....Colorado Springs, CO
Swift, Stephen J. United States Tax Court, GV
Swift, Susan Freya ....Fair Oaks, CA
Swift, Susan R. ....Los Angeles, CA
Swift and Swift ....Manchester, IA
Swift & Swift ....Newberg, OR Palestine, TX
Swift, Theodore W. ....Lansing, MI
Swift, Thomas A. ....Warren, OH
Swift, Thomas F. ....New York, NY
Swift, Thomas L. ....Brunswick, GA
Swift, Thomas N., II ....Mesa, AZ
Swift, Thomas Nye ....Chicago, IL
Swift, Timothy J. ....Santa Ana, CA
Swift & VanBuskirk ....Decatur, GA
Swift, Whitney L. ....Austin, TX
Swift, William B. ....Lake Charles, LA
Swift, William C. G., Jr. ....New Haven, CT New York, NY
Swift, William D. ....Fort Wayne, IN Indianapolis, IN
Swift, William J. ....Providence, RI
Swift, William N. ....Amarillo, TX
Swift, William P. ....Barnstable, MA
Swift, Yolanda V. Small Business Administration, Office of the General Counsel, GV
Swig, Esta S. ....Sausalito, CA
Swig, Steven L. ....San Francisco, CA
Swigart, Charles B. ....Huntingdon, PA
Swigart, James A. ....Auburn, WA
Swigart, Jefferey F. ....Frazer, PA
Swigart, Jennifer ....Huntingdon, PA
Swigart, John J., Jr. ....Newport Beach, CA
Swigart & Suss ....Frazer, PA
Swigart, William R. ....Wauseon, OH
Swiger, Brian R. ....Charleston, WV
Swiger, Cynthia G. ....Chicago, IL

Swiger, Elinor P. ... Chicago, IL
Swiger, Ernest C. ... Clarksburg, WV
Swiger, James E. ... Fairfax, VA
Swiger, Karen Patricia ... Bronx, NY
Swiger, Kelley, Harragan & Schott ... New York, NY
Swiger, Michael A. ... **Washington, DC**
Swigert, Brett L. ... **Eustis, FL** / Summerfield, FL
Swigert, Brett L., P.A. ... **Eustis, FL**
Swigert, Daniel Lee ... Plano, TX
Swigert, J. Mack ... **Cincinnati, OH**
Swigert, Stephen B. ... South Windsor, CT
Swigert, Thomas P. ... **Minneapolis, MN**
Swigert, William T. ... Ocala, FL
Swiggart & Agin, LLC ... **Boston, MA**
Swiggart, Carolyn C. ... Darien, CT
Swiggart, James M. ... Nashville, TN
Swiggart, William F. ... **Boston, MA**
Swiggett, R. Horace, Jr. ... Graham, NC
Swihart, Beverly H. ... Argos, IN
Swihart, David E. ... **Goshen, IN**
Swihart, Fred J. ... Lincoln, NE
Swihart, R. Dale ... St. Louis, MO
Swihart, Steven T. ... Denver, CO
Swihart, Thomas A. ... Fort Wayne, IN
Swihart, Thomas D. ... Fort Wayne, IN
Swill, Douglas B. ... **Chicago, IL**
Swill, Lisa Z. ... River Edge, NJ
Swiller, Jennifer F. ... **Hermosa Beach, CA**
Swillinger, Alison Looney ... Salt Lake City, UT
Swillinger, Jeffrey A. ... **Dayton, OH**
Swillinger, Steven R., (Co., L.P.A.) ... Cincinnati, OH
Swim, Debra A. ... Tallahassee, FL
Swim, Jessica L. ... Louisville, KY
Swim, Keith D., Jr. ... Bryan, TX
Swim, Michael A. ... Treasury Department, Internal Revenue Service, GV
Swim, Richard O. ... Virginia Beach, VA
Swimelar, Mark W. ... Syracuse, NY
Swimley, Barbara L. ... Oklahoma City, OK
Swimmer, Adolph H. ... Lilburn, GA
Swimmer, David L. ... Miami, FL
Swimmer, David L., P.A. ... Miami, FL
Swimmer, David R. ... St. Louis, MO
Swimmer, Gerald E. ... **Woodcliff Lake, NJ**
Swimmer, John S. ... Black River Falls, WI
Swimmer, Margaret A. ... **Tulsa, OK**
Swimmer, Michael A. ... **New York, NY**
Swimmer, Ross O. ... **Tulsa, OK**
Swimmer, Sylvia ... Clifton, NJ
Swimmer & Weber, P.A. ... Clifton, NJ
Swinburn, Charles ... **Washington, DC**
Swinburnson, Kurt D. ... Lihue, HI
Swindell, B. Jay ... **Glennville, GA**
Swindell, Benny E. ... Russellville, AR
Swindell, Edgar M. ... Department Of Health And Human Services, Office of the General Counsel, GV
Swindell, Gary W. ... **Charlotte, NC**
Swindell, Jerome A. ... **Washington, DC**
Swindell, Lewis H., IV ... Greenville, NC
Swindell, Michael S. ... **Greenville, SC**
Swindell, Patrick A. ... **Amarillo, TX**
Swindell, Scott W. ... **Vancouver, WA**
Swindell, Virginia Mixon ... Houston, TX
Swindells, Charles ... Portland, OR
Swindells, Pamela A. ... **Long Beach, CA**
Swindle, Grady L. ... Stephenville, TX
Swindle, Grady L., P.C., Law Offices of ... Stephenville, TX
Swindle, Hugh Tristram ... Birmingham, AL
Swindle, James H., Jr. ... **Little Rock, AR**
Swindle, Mack Ed ... **Fort Worth, TX**
Swindle, Michael B. ... Kissimmee, FL / **Kissimmee, FL** / **Orlando, FL**
Swindle and Nunnery ... Doniphan, MO
Swindle, R. Vance ... Birmingham, AL
Swindle, Shane R. ... **Phoenix, AZ**
Swindle, Stephen D. ... **Salt Lake City, UT**
Swindle, Thomas D. ... Doniphan, MO
Swindle & Tiffany ... **Kissimmee, FL** / **Orlando, FL** / **Sanford, FL**
Swindle, William R. ... **Tampa, FL**
Swindlehurst, Joseph T. ... **Livingston, MT**
Swindlehurst, Rodney Leon ... Palmdale, CA
Swindler, Geoffrey D. ... **Spokane, WA**
Swindler, James C. ... **Las Vegas, NV**
Swindler, Jo Anne ... Securities and Exchange Commission, Office of International Affairs, GV
Swindler, John R. ... Washington, DC
Swindler, Michael L. ... **Harrisburg, PA**
Swindler, Wm. F. ... Norfolk, VA
Swindling, Linda Byars ... **Carrollton, TX**
Swindoll, James F., Law Offices of ... **Little Rock, AR**
Swindoll, Robert E. ... Jackson, MS
Swinehart, Howard E. ... Troy, OH
Swinehart, James R. ... **Chicago, IL**
Swinehart, Richard E. ... Seneca Falls, NY
Swinehart and Sherr ... Fort Wayne, IN
Swinehart, Thomas H. ... Boise, ID
Swinehart, William R. ... **Sunbury, PA**
Swiney, D. Michael ... **Knoxville, TN**
Swiney, Mark D. ... Tulsa, OK
Swinford, C. William, Jr. ... Lexington, KY
Swinford, Jack E. ... Talladega, AL
Swinford, John ... **Cynthiana, KY**
Swinford, John W., Jr. ... Oklahoma City, OK
Swinford, Leslie B., Jr. ... Columbus, OH
Swinford & Sims, P.S.C. ... **Cynthiana, KY**
Swing, Anne Y. ... Tampa, FL
Swing, Bradford ... **Miami, FL**
Swing, Bridget Davis ... **Savannah, GA**
Swing, Christopher F. ... **Akron, OH**
Swing, John Temple ... New York, NY
Swing, Ross G. ... Los Angeles, CA
Swingen, Amy L. ... Vancouver, WA
Swingen, Eldred M. ... **Madison, WI**
Swinger, W. Lynn ... **Sidney, OH**
Swingle, Gary L. ... **Denver, CO**
Swingle, Loren C. ... White Plains, NY
Swingle, Sharon ... **Washington, DC**
Swingle, Susan A. ... **Chicago, IL**
Swingler, Lana R. ... Carmel, IN
Swingley, James ... **San Diego, CA**
Swingruber, Jill P. ... Delmar, NY
Swink, Don G. ... Portland, OR
Swink, Gilbert R., Jr. ... Norfolk, VA
Swink, Jack W. ... La Canada Flintridge, CA
Swink, Swink & Swink ... Miami, FL
Swink, William J., Jr. ... Miami, FL
Swinnen, James E. ... **New Orleans, LA**
Swinney, D. Kirk ... Austin, TX
Swinney, Richard B. ... Chatsworth, CA
Swinson, Curtis R. ... **Dallas, TX**
Swinson, Gwynn T. ... Raleigh, NC
Swinson, Scott A. ... Phoenix, AZ
Swinson, Sidney K. ... **Tulsa, OK**
Swinson, Thomas E. ... Del Rio, TX
Swinson, Wendi M. ... **Louisville, KY**
Swint, Dan David ... Houston, TX
Swint, Thomas W. ... Grants Pass, OR
Swint-Levin, Diane T. ... Bel Air, MD
Swinton, Barbara Green ... Oklahoma City, OK
Swinton, Daniel S. ... Clark, NJ
Swinton, David M. ... **Des Moines, IA**
Swinton, Duane M. ... **Spokane, WA**
Swinton, Jeffrey C., (P.C.) ... **Salt Lake City, UT**
Swinton, Lisa G.T. ... Lincoln, NE
Swinton, Paul S. ... **West Des Moines, IA**
Swinton, Richard B. ... Coronado, CA
Swinton, Stephen P. ... **San Diego, CA**
Swintosky, Kimberly Quarles ... **Raleigh, NC**
Swirbalus, Mark E. ... **Boston, MA**
Swire, James B. ... **New York, NY**
Swire, Lawrence J. ... **White Plains, NY**
Swire, Marvin S. W. ... Portland, OR
Swiren, Alfred M. ... Coral Gables, FL
Swiren, L. Bruce ... Orlando, FL
Swirles, Frank M. ... Rancho Santa Fe, CA
Swirnoff, Michael A. ... Portland, OR
Swirnow, Stephen G. ... New York, NY
Swirski, Alan J.J. ... Department of Justice, Tax Division, GV
Swirsky, Barry S. ... Media, PA
Swirsky, Gerald R. ... **Hartford, CT**
Swirsky, Joan Ohlbaum ... **Philadelphia, PA**
Swirsky, Keith G. ... **Washington, DC**
Swirsky, Sherry A. ... **Philadelphia, PA**
Swirsky, Steven M. ... **New York, NY**
Swischer, Nicholas L. ... Nevada, MO
Swisher, Anthony W. ... **Washington, DC**
Swisher, Arthur Kyle ... Edmond, OK
Swisher, Barbara A. ... Rochester, MN
Swisher, Carol M. ... **Oak Brook, IL**
Swisher & Cohrt, P.L.C. ... **Waterloo, IA**
Swisher, Crady ... Sewickley, PA
Swisher, Deanna ... **Lansing, MI**
Swisher, Donald P. ... Seattle, WA
Swisher, George W. ... Oskaloosa, KS
Swisher, Gerald J. ... Findlay, OH
Swisher, Jack G. ... Houston, TX
Swisher, James L. ... Greensboro, NC
Swisher, James T., Sr. ... Baltimore, MD
Swisher, John E. ... St. Petersburg, FL
Swisher, John E., P.A. ... St. Petersburg, FL
Swisher, John W. ... Charleston, WV
Swisher, Karen N. ... Midlothian, VA
Swisher, Kathryn M., Law Office of ... Memphis, TN
Swisher, Kirsten A. ... Linwood, NJ
Swisher, Laura Anne ... Laurel, MD
Swisher, Michael P. ... Lee's Summit, MO
Swisher, Michael P., P.C. ... Lee's Summit, MO
Swisher, Peter N. ... Richmond, VA
Swisher, Richd. F. ... Oakland, CA
Swisher, Robert G. ... Richland, WA
Swisher, Robert L. ... **Lexington, KY**
Swisher, Samuel D. ... Chicago, IL
Swisher, Scott A. ... Oakland, CA
Swisher, Stephen P. ... Charleston, WV / Dunbar, WV
Swisher, Thomas D. ... Dowagiac, MI
Swisher, Thomas K. ... Ellicott City, MD
Swisher, Thomas R. ... Columbus, OH
Swisher, William A. ... Towson, MD
Swiss, Daniel R. ... **Albuquerque, NM**
Swiss, David M. ... Kansas City, MO
Swiss, Gerald F. ... **Redwood City, CA**
Swiss, Marsha E. ... **Washington, DC**
Swiss, Sally A. ... Chicago, IL
Swiss, Susan M. ... Schaumburg, IL
Swiss, Thomas C. ... **Baltimore, MD**
Swisstack, Kenneth M. ... **New York, NY**
Swistak, Janet ... Farmington Hills, MI
Swistak, Jennifer M. ... Pittsburgh, PA
Swit, Michael A. ... **Washington, DC**
Switala, Gilbert B., Jr. ... **Dayton, OH**
Switalski, David B. ... **Tallahassee, FL**
Switalski, Mark S. ... Roseville, MI
Switalski, Michael M. ... Dousman, WI
Switalski, William J. ... Tampa, FL
Switkay, H. Coleman ... **Philadelphia, PA**
Switkay, Henry M. ... Washington, DC
Switkay, Howard W. ... Philadelphia, PA
Switkes, Robert L. ... Miami Beach, FL
Switko, Shari J. ... Hamden, CT
Switnicki, George ... Brooklyn, NY
Switz, Wrightson J. ... Overland Park, KS
Switzer, Angela Spears ... **Houston, TX**
Switzer, Ann Elizabeth ... **Rockford, IL**
Switzer, Barbara H. ... **Crystal Lake, IL**
Switzer, Bobby C. ... Odessa, TX
Switzer, Boyd V. ... Richmond, VA
Switzer, Bradley N. ... Montrose, CO
Switzer, Bruce D. ... Crossett, AR
Switzer, David B. ... Hot Springs National Park, AR
Switzer, Donald H. ... **Cleveland, OH**
Switzer, Donald K. ... Rogers, AR
Switzer, Erwin O., III ... St. Louis, MO
Switzer, Frederick M. ... St. Louis, MO
Switzer, Frederick M., III ... **St. Louis, MO**
Switzer, H. Duane ... **Cleveland, OH**
Switzer, James E. ... Clinton, MO
Switzer, Jeffrey John ... **Memphis, TN**
Switzer, Jerry L., Jr. ... **Chicago, IL**
Switzer, Jill ... Los Angeles, CA
Switzer, Joan E. ... Princeton, NJ
Switzer, Joseph P. ... **Chicago, IL**
Switzer, Justin V. ... **Houston, TX**
Switzer, Kenneth M. ... **Nashville, TN**
Switzer Law Office ... Crossett, AR
Switzer, Michael A. ... **Minneapolis, MN**
Switzer, Michael H. ... New York, NY
Switzer, Peter S. ... **Rockford, IL**
Switzer, Ralph V. ... Fort Collins, CO
Switzer, Regina Ann ... Oklahoma City, OK
Switzer, Richard L. ... Frazer, PA
Switzer, Robert E. ... Jacksonville, NC
Switzer, Robert G. ... Irvine, CA
Switzer, Robert J. ... Santa Monica, CA
Switzer, Robert L. ... **Oak Brook, IL**
Switzer, Robert O. ... San Antonio, TX
Switzer, Stephen W. ... **Lexington, KY**
Switzer, Thomas E. ... **Columbus, OH**
Switzer, William L., Jr. ... Omaha, NE
Swobe, C. Coe ... Reno, NV
Swoboda, Craig F. ... Omaha, NE
Swoboda, John H. ... St. Louis, MO
Swofford, C. Gaston ... Clyde, TX
Swofford, Michael J. ... **Seattle, WA**
Swofford, Robert ... **Houston, TX**
Swofford, Stephen R. ... **Chicago, IL**
Swogger, Amy Margaret ... Traverse City, MI
Swogger, Karen J. F. ... Eureka Springs, AR
Swogger, Michael J. ... **Traverse City, MI**
Swogger, Phillip S. ... Salem, OR
Swoish, Marc C. ... Bingham Farms, MI
Swokowski, Jay G. ... Anoka, MN
Swomley, Joanna R. ... **New York, NY**
Swomley, John G. ... **New York, NY**
Swonger, Ronald L. ... Hillsboro, OH
Swonke, Gerard J. ... **Houston, TX**
Swope, Andrew L. ... **Harrisburg, PA**
Swope & Brown, P.A. ... **Charleston, SC**
Swope, Cardillo, P.A. ... **Clearwater, FL** / **Plant City, FL** / **Tampa, FL**
Swope, Dale M. ... **Tampa, FL**
Swope, David A. ... Ossining, NY
Swope, Denise Grainger ... Charleston, SC
Swope, Derek C. ... **Princeton, WV**
Swope, Douglas H. ... San Diego, CA
Swope, Gregory D. ... Canton, OH
Swope, Harold W. ... Harrisburg, PA
Swope, Jay A. ... Denver, CO
Swope, Jeffrey ... **Boston, MA**
Swope, John F. ... Manchester, NH
Swope, Joseph Albert, Jr. ... St. Louis, MO
Swope, Karin Bornstein ... **Seattle, WA**
Swope, Kristy ... **Reynoldsburg, OH**
Swope, Leslie Ann ... **Tampa, FL**
Swope, M. Charles ... Minneapolis, MN
Swope, Michael J. ... **Philadelphia, PA**
Swope, R. Hain ... **Newark, NJ**
Swope, Richard F. ... **Reynoldsburg, OH**
Swope, Richard M. ... Virginia Beach, VA
Swope, Scott P. ... **Clearwater, FL**
Swope and Swope ... **Columbus, OH** / **Reynoldsburg, OH**
Swope, Thomas A. ... **Middletown, OH**
Swope, Thomas A., Jr. ... Ebensburg, PA
Swope, V. Raymond, III ... Redwood City, CA
Swope, W. Barry ... Miami Shores, FL
Swope, William E. ... **Washington, DC**
Swope, William K. ... **Charleston, SC**
Swope, William L. ... Findlay, OH
Swope, William M. ... **Honolulu, HI**
Swope, William R. ... Birmingham, AL
Swor & Gatto ... St. Paul, MN
Swor, Michael ... St. Paul, MN
Swor, Stacy W. ... Mill Valley, CA
Swor, William W. ... Detroit, MI
Sword, Carl H., Jr. ... **New York, NY**
Sword, Dean W., Jr. ... Portsmouth, VA
Sword, Floyd, Moody, Bohannon, Eaves, Fernandez, Olds & Murphy ... **Richmond, KY**
Sword, John D. ... **Richmond, KY**
Sword, Larry F. ... Somerset, KY
Sword, Michael Dean ... **New York, NY**
Swords, Daniel J. ... Springfield, MA
Swords, Denis C. ... **Lafayette, LA**
Swords, Margaret D. ... **Lafayette, LA**
Swords, Mark C. ... **Chicago, IL**
Swords, Mary C. ... East Longmeadow, MA
Swords, Patricia A. ... Rockville, CT
Swords, Peter ... New York, NY
Swortwood, Robert B. ... **Riverside, CA**
Swotes, Alan J. ... Philadelphia, PA
Swoyer, James F., Jr. ... Oskaloosa, KS
Swoyer, Martha Ann ... Oskaloosa, KS
Swoyer, Shelley ... Jefferson City, MO
Swoyer & Simms ... Belleville, KS
Swoyer and Swoyer ... Oskaloosa, KS
Swydan, Miriam A. ... **Washington, DC**
Swyer, David H. ... Albany, NY
Swyer, Leonard P. ... Montpelier, VT
Swyer-Novak, Jill ... Blue Bell, PA
Swyers, Christopher C. ... **Wichita, KS**
Swyers, Curtis A. ... San Antonio, TX
Swyers, Matthew H. ... **Falls Church, VA**
Swyers, Walter J., Jr. ... Louisville, KY
Swygert, H. Patrick ... Philadelphia, PA
Swygert, Michael I. ... St. Petersburg, FL
Swygert-Smith, Regina ... Upperville, VA
Swymer, George S., Jr. ... Milford, MA
Swynford, Agnew, III ... Falls Church, VA
Swyrydenko, Nicholas ... Akron, OH
Swysen, Catherine J. ... **Santa Barbara, CA**
Swysgood, Robert M. ... San Diego, CA
Swytak, Stephen C. ... Santa Ana, CA
Syat, Scott M. ... Quincy, MA
Syatt, Andrea H. ... Sudbury, MA
Sybert, Cornelius F., Jr. ... Ellicott City, MD
Sybert, Curtis J. ... Groveport, OH
Sybesma, Benjamin C. ... West Sacramento, CA
Sybesma, Edward D., Jr. (P.C.) ... **Costa Mesa, CA**
Syc, Allan R. ... Long Grove, IL
Syck, Rebekah R. ... **Duluth, MN**
Sydney, Herbert P. ... New York, NY
Sydney, Kristen Jean ... Columbus, OH
Sydney, Robert F. ... Newton, MA
Sydney, Ronny Metz ... Brookline, MA
Sydney, Seif & Amster ... New York, NY
Sydnor, Debra A. R. ... **Atlanta, GA**
Sydnor, Edgar Starke ... **Birmingham, AL**
Sydnor, J. Allen, Jr. ... **Birmingham, AL**
Sydnor, Marda W. ... **Birmingham, AL**
Sydnor, Thomas D., II ... **Washington, DC**
Sydnor, William W. ... **Altamonte Springs, FL**
Sydor, Harry N. ... Pittsburgh, PA
Sydow, Kelli McDonald ... Houston, TX
Sydow, Michael D. ... **Houston, TX**
Sydow, Teresa P. ... Marysville, CA
Syed, Khader M. ... New York, NY
Syed, Simin H. ... New York, NY
Sye-Payne, Vivian A. ... Philadelphia, PA
Syer, Elizabeth V. ... **Richmond, VA**
Syfan, R. David ... **Gainesville, GA**
Syfan, T. Treadwell ... **Gainesville, GA**
Syfert, Scott D. ... **Charlotte, NC**
Syfrett, Clayton Raymond ... Panama City, FL
Syfrett, Raymond L. ... Panama City, FL
Sygenda, Susan ... Philadelphia, PA
Syger, Elizabeth S. ... **Alameda, CA**
Sygman, Forrest ... Coral Gables, FL
Sygulla, Richard J. ... Sheldon, IL
Syke & Associates ... Denver, CO
Syke, Cameron J. ... Denver, CO
Syken, Kenneth ... Philadelphia, PA
Syken, Susan Wilding ... White Plains, NY
Sykes, A. Randolph ... **Sevierville, TN**
Sykes, Aisha J. ... **Richmond, VA**
Sykes, Alan L. ... Rice Lake, WI
Sykes, Alan O. ... Chicago, IL
Sykes, Andrew G. ... Mount Lebanon, PA
Sykes, Angela D. ... Department of Commerce, Patent and Trademark Office, GV
Sykes, Bernard G. ... Norwood, MA
Sykes, Brian L. ... **Norfolk, VA**
Sykes, Bryan William ... **Tampa, FL**
Sykes, C. Scott, Jr. ... Irving, TX
Sykes, Carnes, Bourdon & Ahern, P.C. ... **Chesapeake, VA** / **Norfolk, VA** / **Virginia Beach, VA**
Sykes, Charles E. ... **Houston, TX**
Sykes, Charmaine N. ... **New Orleans, LA**
Sykes, Christine E. ... Washington, DC
Sykes and Cole ... **Barnstable, MA** / **Chatham, MA** / **Hyannis, MA**
Sykes, Curtis L. ... New York, NY
Sykes, Dan W. ... **Fort Worth, TX**
Sykes, Dana B. ... Richmond, VA
Sykes, Daniel E. ... **Baltimore, MD**
Sykes, David F. ... Santa Ana, CA
Sykes, David K. ... New Bedford, MA
Sykes, David T. ... **Philadelphia, PA**
Sykes, Diane Schwerm ... Milwaukee, WI
Sykes, Dorothy J. ... Orange, CA
Sykes, Douglas A. ... Englewood, CO
Sykes, Douglas G. ... Oakland, CA
Sykes, Eileen C. ... **New Orleans, LA**
Sykes, G. Paris, Jr. ... **Atlanta, GA**
Sykes, Gordon L. ... **Raynham, MA**
Sykes, Howard R., Jr. ... **Virginia Beach, VA**
Sykes, J. Kenneth ... Norwood, MA
Sykes, James B., III ... Ridgeland, MS
Sykes, James E. ... Chicago, IL
Sykes, Jeff R. ... **Boise, ID**
Sykes, Jeffrey A. ... **Oakland, CA**
Sykes, John M., III ... **New York, NY**
Sykes, Judith K. ... Baltimore, MD
Sykes, Judith L. ... New York, NY
Sykes, Kerry Riordan ... San Francisco, CA
Sykes, Kevin L. ... **Columbus, OH**
Sykes, Larry A. ... **Lexington, KY**
Sykes Law Office ... Rice Lake, WI
Sykes, Lawrence R. ... Yonkers, NY
Sykes, Lynn ... **Atlanta, GA**
Sykes, Maurice L. ... **Buffalo, NY**
Sykes, Melvin Francis ... Solomons, MD
Sykes, Melvin J. ... **Baltimore, MD**
Sykes, Nathan A. ... **Portland, OR**
Sykes, Paul ... **Birmingham, AL**
Sykes, Phillip R. ... **Clarksville, TN**
Sykes, Phillip S. ... **Jackson, MS**

Sykes, Raymond M., Jr. ....Nashville, NC
Sykes, Richard T. ....Van Nuys, CA
Sykes, Robert B. ....Salt Lake City, UT
Sykes, Robert B., & Associates, P.C. Salt Lake City, UT
Sykes, Robert G. ....Minneapolis, MN
Sykes, Robert J. ....Irvine, CA
Sykes, Robert R. ....Midland, TX
Sykes, Robert S., Jr. ....Ionia, MI
Sykes, Roland E. ....Langhorne, PA
Sykes, Ronald G. ....Washington, DC
Sykes, Susan E. ....Greenville, SC
Sykes & Sykes ....Norwood, MA
Sykes, Teresa Rahm ....Dallas, TX
Sykes, Thomas D. ....Washington, DC
Sykes, Tracy Allan ....Boston, MA
Sykes, W. Steve ....Tallahassee, FL
Sykes, William G. ....Virginia Beach, VA
Sykes, William I., Jr. ....Gainesville, GA
Sykes, William R. ....Kalamazoo, MI
Sykes & Wynn, PLLC ....Sevierville, TN
Sykora, J. Anthony ....Sandusky, MI
Sykora, James J. ....Oklahoma City, OK
Sykora, Jennifer L. ....Chicago, IL
Sykora, Lora C. ....Brookfield, WI
Sykora, Robert W. ....Minneapolis, MN
Sykora, Wilfred F. National Labor Relations Board, Office of the General Counsel, GV
Sykstus, Ronald C. ....Huntsville, AL
Sykulski, George H. ....Encino, CA
Syler, William L. ....Cape Girardeau, MO
Syll, William H., Jr. ....New Orleans, LA
Sylla, John R. ....Kentfield, CA
Sylling, Ronald O. ....Denver, CO
Sylva, David R. ....Campbell, CA
Sylva, David R., A Prof. Corp., Law Offices of Campbell, CA
Sylva, Julia ....Los Angeles, CA
Sylva, Julianne C. ....San Jose, CA
Sylva, Kenneth J. ....Sacramento, CA
Sylva, Nancy Burke ....Campbell, CA
Sylva, Shirley J., Law Offices of East Harwich, MA
Sylvain, Robert S. ....Las Vegas, NV
Sylvan, Robert T. ....Jamaica, NY
Sylvan, W. Coleman ....Dallas, TX
Sylvanus, John J. ....York, PA
Sylver, Peter T. ....New York, NY
Sylvester, Alan F. ....Burlington, VT
Sylvester, Amy E. ....Burlington, VT
Sylvester, Anne L. ....Honolulu, HI
Sylvester, Anne M. ....New Port Richey, FL
Sylvester, Anthony J. ....Morristown, NJ
Sylvester, April Louise ....Newport Beach, CA
Sylvester, Barbara Jo ....Tacoma, WA
Sylvester, Bradley P. ....Wichita, KS
Sylvester, Brett S. ....Washington, DC
Sylvester, Cheryl A. Department Of The Interior, Office of the Solicitor, GV
Sylvester, Christine J. ....Charlotte, NC
Sylvester, Cortney G. ....Minneapolis, MN
Sylvester, Craig L. ....Hartford, CT
Sylvester, D. Beau ....Alexandria, LA
Sylvester, David ....Washington, DC
Sylvester, David J. ....Burlington, VT
Sylvester, Donald W. ....Sioux City, IA
Sylvester, Esther R. ....Philadelphia, PA
Sylvester, Eugene P. ....Clifton, NJ
Sylvester, James A. ....Morristown, NJ
Sylvester, James A., Jr. ....Zephyrhills, FL
Sylvester, James V. ....Austin, TX
Sylvester, Jeffrey R. ....Las Vegas, NV
Sylvester, John J. ....Boston, MA
Sylvester, John M. ....Pittsburgh, PA
Sylvester, John T. ....Baltimore, MD
Sylvester, John T. ....Mount Morris, NY
Sylvester, Jon H. ....San Francisco, CA
Sylvester, Joseph H. ....Derby, CT
Sylvester, Kathryn R. ....Hartford, CT
Sylvester, Kenneth J. ....Atlantic City, NJ
Sylvester, Lala Brittain ....Natchitoches, LA
Sylvester, Laura Norton ....Alexandria, LA
Sylvester Law Office, P.C. ....Tucson, AZ
Sylvester, Lee ....Los Angeles, CA
Sylvester & Maley, Inc. ....Burlington, VT
Sylvester, Mary Alice ....Denver, CO
Sylvester & Oppenheim ....Los Angeles, CA Woodland Hills, CA
Sylvester, Patricia L. ....Providence, RI
Sylvester & Polednak ....Las Vegas, NV
Sylvester, Robert E. ....Bethesda, MD
Sylvester, Robt. S. ....Chatham, MA
Sylvester, Russell L. ....Natchitoches, LA
Sylvester, Sandra R. ....Manassas, VA
Sylvester, Stephen F. Department Of Veterans Affairs, Board of Veterans Appeals, GV
Sylvester, Steven E. ....Boston, MA
Sylvester, Thomas P. ....Tucson, AZ
Sylvester, Thomas R. ....Honolulu, HI
Sylvester, Timothy F. ....Los Angeles, CA
Sylvester, Torrey A. ....Houlton, ME
Sylvester, Warren G. ....Wheaton, IL
Sylvester, William R. ....Birmingham, AL
Sylvestri, Paul D. ....Rochester, NY
Sylvia, Jane L. ....Wheaton, IL
Sylvia, John F. ....Boston, MA
Sylvia, Lisa Marie ....Washington, DC
Sylvia, Mark G. ....Providence, RI
Sylvia, Robert F. ....Boston, MA Providence, RI
Sylvia, Russell J. ....Boston, MA
Sylvor & Richman, LLP ....New York, NY
Sylvor, Robert ....New York, NY
Sylwester, Timothy A. ....Salem, OR
Sylwestrzak, Theodore B. ....Detroit, MI

Sym, John A. ....Boston, MA
Symanski, Charles W. Department Of Veterans Affairs, Board of Veterans Appeals, GV
Symanski, George A., Jr. ....Fairfax, VA
Symanski, Stan ....Tulsa, OK
Symansky, Joan F. ....Washington, DC
Symansky, Richard D. ....Latham, NY
Symchych, Janice M. ....Minneapolis, MN
Symczak, Paul E. ....Washington, DC
Syme, James J., Jr. ....Glendale, AZ
Syme, Michael H. ....Pittsburgh, PA
Symes, Clint A. ....San Angelo, TX
Symes, David P. R. ....Portland, OR
Symes, Deborah M. ....Fresno, CA
Symes, Gavin A. ....Boston, MA
Symington, James W. ....Washington, DC
Symington, John C. ....Sugar Land, TX
Symington, Stuart, Jr. ....St. Louis, MO
Symkowick, Joseph R. ....Sacramento, CA
Symm, Ron A. ....Bakersfield, CA
Symmes, Charles W. ....Indianapolis, IN
Symmes, Voyles, Zahn, Paul & Hogan Indianapolis, IN
Symmes, William D. ....Spokane, WA
Symmes, William M. ....Spokane, WA
Symmonds, Charles G. ....Dallas, TX
Symmonds, Robert N. ....Emporia, KS
Symmonds, Rodney H. ....Emporia, KS
Symmonds & Symmonds ....Emporia, KS
Symon, Colette C. ....Darien, CT
Symon, D. Russell ....San Francisco, CA
Symon, James ....Chapel Hill, NC
Symon, Robert J. ....Washington, DC
Symon, William M., Jr. ....Kansas City, MO
Symonds, Daniel C. ....Detroit, MI
Symonds, Elizabeth Federal Mine Safety and Health Review Commission, Office of the Commissioners, GV
Symonds, Elsa Ornelas ....San Antonio, TX
Symonds, Gary L. ....Saugus, CA
Symonds, Jay P. ....Worcester, MA
Symonds, Margaret B. ....Houston, TX
Symonds, R. John ....Wisconsin Rapids, WI
Symonds, Robert H. ....Laurel, MD
Symonds, Robert L., Jr. ....Wilmington, DE
Symonds, Sheryl Anne ....Edmonds, WA
Symonds, William J. ....Seattle, WA
Symonovicz, Philippe, (P.A.) Fort Lauderdale, FL
Symons, Andrew L. ....Bellevue, WA
Symons, David G. ....Los Angeles, CA
Symons, Dorothy B. ....New York, NY
Symons, Edward L., Jr. ....Pittsburgh, PA
Symons, Howard J. ....Washington, DC
Symons, Jeri Marie ....Red Bluff, CA
Symons, Karlin S. ....Minneapolis, MN
Symons, Leonard B. ....West Babylon, NY
Symons, Maggie J. ....Seattle, WA
Symons, Mary L. ....San Francisco, CA
Symons, Melanie Ann ....Helena, MT
Symons, Nancy F. ....San Jose, CA
Symons, Noel H. ....Washington, DC
Symons, Ralph W. ....Miami, FL
Symons, Ralph W., P.C. ....Miami, FL
Symons, Richard R. ....Grand Rapids, MI
Symons, Robin Taylor ....Miami, FL
Symons, Ryerson ....New York, NY
Symons, S. Adam ....Harrisburg, PA
Sympson, Richard E. ....Houston, TX
Symula-Nahikian, Lisa ....Pontiac, MI
Synakowski, Daniel G. ....Wellsville, NY
Synan, Tracy ....Jefferson City, MO
Synar, Alan E. ....Edmond, OK
Synchef, James S. ....Chicago, IL
Synchef, Richard M. ....San Rafael, CA
Synek, Henry T. ....Chicago, IL
Synek, Michael J. ....Kearney, NE
Synenberg & Marein ....Cleveland, OH
Synenberg, Roger M. ....Cleveland, OH
Synhorst, John V. ....Des Moines, IA
Synmoie, Patrick L. ....New York, NY
Synnes, Mark A. ....House of Representatives, Office of Legislative Counsel, GV
Synnestvedt, John T. ....Philadelphia, PA
Synnestvedt & Lechner LLP Philadelphia, PA
Synnestvedt, Yorvar Evan ....Kempton, PA
Synnott, Aidan ....New York, NY
Synnott, Andrew J. ....Boston, MA
Synnott, Linda ....Oak Ridge, TN
Synodi, Christine S. ....Hartford, CT
Synon, Imogene Mary ....Key West, FL
Synovec, Debra K. ....Minneapolis, MN
Sype, John E. ....Rockford, IL
Sypek, Arthur R., Jr. ....Trenton, NJ
Sypek, Maria Marinari ....Trenton, NJ
Sypek, Richard A. ....Springfield, MA
Sypher, Richard B. ....New York, NY
Syphers, Janet ....Campbell, CA
Sypniewski, Edward G. ....Grand Rapids, MI
Sypniewski, Michael A. ....Rochester, NY
Sypolt, Cynthia ....Spokane, WA
Syprett, Jim D. ....Sarasota, FL
Syprett, Meshad, Resnick, Lieb, Dumbaugh, Jones & Krotec, P.A. ....Sarasota, FL
Sypula McIntosh ....Sarasota, FL
Sypula, Philip J. ....Sarasota, FL
Sypulski, Jamie G. ....Chicago, IL
Syra, Kimberly A. ....Albuquerque, NM
Syracopoulos, Nicholas C. ....Akron, OH
Syracuse, Marion J. ....Maplewood, NJ
Syracuse, Russell D. ....Chicago, IL
Syracuse, Vetus J. ....Cleveland, OH
Syracuse, Vincent J. ....New York, NY
Syrbick, Angela M. ....Boston, MA
Syrdal, Daniel D. ....Seattle, WA

Syre, Mia Thelde ....Seattle, WA
Syrek, Gregory T. ....Clifton, NJ
Syrek, Walter ....New York, NY
Syren, Lester K. ....Anchorage, AK
Syrett, Spencer Andrew ....Columbia, SC
Syria, Ronald D. ....Kirkland, WA
Syring, Erin E. ....Wichita, KS
Syring, Paul F. ....Toledo, OH
Syring and Syring ....Toledo, OH
Syring, William J. ....Toledo, OH
Syring-Petrocchi, Tina A. Minneapolis, MN
Syrios, Jeffrey L. ....Wichita, KS
Syrios, M. William ....Wichita, KS
Syrnick, Mark S. ....Melbourne, FL
Syrnyk, Irene M. ....Stamford, CT
Syroney, David J. ....Cleveland, OH
Syrop, Nancy H. ....Marietta, GA
Syrowik, David R. ....Southfield, MI
Syrowik, Paul R. ....San Diego, CA
Syrup, Christopher D. ....St. Louis, MO
Syrvalin, Kristine C. ....Cleveland, OH
Syska, Krysia J. ....Boston, MA
Syska, Mark R. ....Evanston, IL
Sysko, Dennis J. ....Glen Burnie, MD
Sysol, Brad H. ....Kalamazoo, MI
Sysol, Theodore M. ....Garden City, NY
Syta, Thomas J. ....Los Angeles, CA
Syth, Kathryn S. ....Billings, MT
Sytsma, Fredric A. ....Grand Rapids, MI
Sytsma, John H. ....Seeley Lake, MT
Sytsma, John H., P.A. ....Seeley Lake, MT
Syverson, Bradley ....Minneapolis, MN
Syverson, Gary I. ....Alexandria, MN
Syverson, Todd W. ....Huntley, IL Marengo, IL Wonder Lake, IL
Syverson, William R. ....St. Cloud, MN
Syvertson, D. G. ....Clark, SD
Syvertson & Neill ....Clark, SD
Syverud, Eric C. ....Cedar Rapids, IA
Sywilok, John W. ....Hackensack, NJ Paterson, NJ
Syx, Deborah A. ....Detroit, MI
Syz, Anthony E. ....New York, NY
Syz, Jing-Kai ....New York, NY
Szabad, George M. ....New York, NY
Szabadi, Peter ....Los Angeles, CA
Szabados, Lester M. ....Youngstown, OH
Szabados, Rudy J. ....Corpus Christi, TX
Szabat, Ronald P. ....Washington, DC
Szablewicz & Bundick, P.C. ....Accomac, VA
Szablewicz, James J. ....Accomac, VA
Szabo and Angus, PLLC ....McLean, VA
Szabo, Cindy L. ....Morristown, NJ
Szabo, David S. ....Boston, MA
Szabo, Douglas B. ....Fort Myers, FL
Szabo, Elizabeth ....New York, NY
Szabo, Elizabeth M. ....New York, NY
Szabo, Gabriel S., Jr. ....Cleveland, OH
Szabo, Helen E. ....Flemington, NJ
Szabo, Howard K., Law Offices of Los Angeles, CA
Szabo, Jeffrey S. ....Amherst, OH
Szabo, Joella M. ....Pittsburgh, PA
Szabo, John L. Nuclear Regulatory Commission, Office of the General Counsel, GV
Szabo, John Z. ....Cleveland, OH
Szabo, Joseph A. ....Milwaukee, WI
Szabo, Laura J. V. ....Washington, DC
Szabo, Lawrence J. ....Sherman Oaks, CA
Szabo, Monika V. ....New York, NY
Szabo, Paul E. ....Cleveland, OH
Szabo, Paul S., Jr. ....Jamaica, NY
Szabo, Peter J. ....Benicia, CA
Szabo, Raoul E. ....East Patchogue, NY
Szabo, Raoul E., P.C. ....East Patchogue, NY
Szabo, Robert G. ....Washington, DC
Szabo, Spencer & Mulally, A Professional Corporation ....Sherman Oaks, CA
Szabo, Stephen J., III ....Tampa, FL
Szabo, Susan R. ....Los Angeles, CA
Szabo, Timothy T. ....Woodbridge, VA
Szabo, Valerie ....McLean, VA
Szabo, Zelnick & Erickson, P.C. Woodbridge, VA
Szadkowski, M. A. ....Clarksburg, NJ
Szafarowicz, Diane L. ....Boston, MA
Szaferman, Barry D. ....Lawrenceville, NJ
Szaferman, Lakind, Blumstein, Watter & Blader, P.C. ....Lawrenceville, NJ New Brunswick, NJ Princeton, NJ Trenton, NJ
Szaflarski, Mark ....Chicago, IL
Szafran, Elizabeth D. ....Wake Forest, NC
Szafran, James L. ....Plymouth, MI
Szafranic, Lisa M. ....Chattanooga, TN
Szafranski, Jill M. ....Pittsburgh, PA
Szaj, Christine M. ....Dallas, TX
Szajna, John J. ....Chambersburg, PA
Szak, Dona ....Houston, TX
Szakats, Patricia A. ....Newark, NJ
Szala, Scott J. ....Chicago, IL
Szalkowski, Charles ....Houston, TX
Szallar, Gregory A. ....Pittsburgh, PA
Szaller, James F. ....Cleveland, OH
Szambelan, Michelle Dimond ....Spokane, WA
Szander, Dinah L. ....San Francisco, CA
Szanto, Ivan G. ....Wilmington, DE
Szanto, Melissa J. ....Houston, TX
Szanyi, Kevin A. ....Buffalo, NY
Szapary, Christophe ....New Orleans, LA
Szapiro, Miriam ....Takoma Park, MD
Szarek, Milton L. ....Coventry, RI
Szarka, Agnes Peresztegi ....New York, NY
Szarka, Louis K. ....White Plains, NY

Szarke, Steven B. ....Buffalo, MN
Szarkowicz, Edward A., Jr. Rolling Meadows, IL
Szarmack, Stephen M. ....Chicago, IL
Szaro, Stanley J. ....New York, NY
Szary, George J. ....Albany, NY
Szasz, Kata ....New York, NY
Szasz, Paul C. ....Germantown, NY
Szathmary, Bela, (Mr.) ....Sanibel, FL
Szathmary, Robert ....Roanoke, VA
Szatkowski, Thomas S. ....Parsippany, NJ
Szatrowski, Robert P. ....New York, NY
Szautner, Christian A. ....Philadelphia, PA
Szczebak, Richard A. ....Boston, MA
Szczeblewski, Gary J. ....Sesser, IL
Szczecin, David F ....Chicago, IL
Szczecina, Eugene L., Jr. ....New York, NY
Szczecko, Joseph ....Decatur, GA
Szczepaniak, Amy J. ....Albuquerque, NM
Szczepaniak, Richard J. ....Toledo, OH
Szczepaniak, William E. ....Seal Beach, CA
Szczepanik, Carol Ann ....Cleveland, OH
Szczepanowski, Lidia D. ....Smithtown, NY
Szczepanski, Deborah L. ....Merrillville, IN
Szczepanski, Edward W. ....Houston, TX
Szczepanski, Kevin D. ....Buffalo, NY
Szczepanski, Peter G. ....Los Alamitos, CA
Szczepanski, Slawomir (Steve) Z. Chicago, IL
Szczepkowski, Edward J. Los Angeles, CA
Szczesniak (Sez-nee-ak), Andrew W. White Plains, NY
Szczesny, Brett ....Westport, CT
Szczesny, J. Charles ....Ellicott City, MD
Szczesny, Loren D. ....Pottstown, PA
Szczesny, Michael A. ....Lansing, MI
Szczesny, Ronald W. ....Madison Heights, MI
Szczesny, Vasiliki P. ....Baltimore, MD Beltsville, MD
Szczubelek, John F. ....Lansing, MI
Szczucinski, Susan D. ....Kansas City, MO
Szczupakiewicz, Ted ....Waukesha, WI
Szczygiel, Anthony H. ....Buffalo, NY
Szczytko, Michael P. ....Grand Rapids, MI
Sze, Helen W. Y. ....San Francisco, CA
Sze, Hoyt Y. ....San Francisco, CA
Sze, Stanley ....Palo Alto, CA
Szecsy, Alek P. ....Poughkeepsie, NY
Szegda & Gerbing ....New York, NY
Szegda, Michael A. ....New York, NY
Szegedy-Maszak, Peter B. Washington, DC
Szego, Stephen Donald Oliver ....Chicago, IL
Szejner, Ronald ....Chicago, IL
Szekely, Charles S. ....Denver, CO
Szekely, Michael ....Elyria, OH
Szeker, Julie Konneker ....Charlotte, NC
Szekeres, Gabor L. ....Irvine, CA
Szekeres, John C. L. ....Brooklyn, NY
Szekunda, Raymond T. ....Commerce, CA
Szela, Laura ....Newton, MA
Szeligo, Vincent P. ....Pittsburgh, PA
Szemiot, Richard J. ....Union, NJ
Szemraj, Roger Raymond House of Representatives, Congressional Assistants, GV
Szenberg, Avi I. ....New York, NY
Szender, James R. ....Anchorage, AK
Szendrey, Keith A. ....Linwood, NJ
Szendrey Ramos, María Teresa San Juan, PR
Szenicer, Harry L. ....Syosset, NY
Szep, Edward F. ....West Orange, NJ
Szep, Ronald J. ....Miami, FL
Szepesi, Judith A. ....Sunnyvale, CA
Szeptycki, Leon F. ....Arlington, VA
Szerejko, James J. ....Hartford, CT
Szeremeta, Stephen P. ....McLean, VA
Szerlag, David J. ....Providence, RI
Szerlip, Nathan H. ....Nyack, NY
Szerlip, William A. ....Morristown, NJ
Szesny, Henry C. ....Chicago, IL
Szeto, Anna ....Worcester, MA
Szeto, Edwin Y. ....Washington, DC
Szeto, Jennie ....Houston, TX
Szeto, Paul Pak-Leung ....New York, NY
Szeto, Yim M. ....Houston, TX
Szewczak, David A. ....Philadelphia, PA
Szewczuk, John C. ....New York, NY
Szewczyk, Edward J. ....Belleville, IL
Szewczyk, John R. ....Bakersfield, CA
Szewczyk, Phrances L. ....Middletown, CT
Szewczyk, Robyn R. Davis ....Granby, MA
Szigetvari, Paul O. ....Rolling Meadows, IL
Szilagyi, Catherine A. ....Washington, DC
Szilagyi, Flora ....Washington, DC
Szilagyi, Frank J. ....Hartford, CT
Szilagyi, Gregg E. ....Chicago, IL
Szilagyi, Richard A. ....Columbus, OH
Szilagyi, Robert C. ....La Porte, IN
Szilagyi, Sherry ....Elkridge, MD
Szilvas, Alexander J. ....Cleveland, OH
Szimonisz, Louise M. ....Buffalo, NY
Szipl, Joerg-Uwe ....Arlington, VA
Szkaradek, Michael W. ....Santa Ana, CA
Szklany, Stanley J. ....North Dartmouth, MA
Szkolnik, Fred Milton ....Los Angeles, CA
Szlachetka, Stanley A. ....Springfield, MA
Szlenker, Charles J. ....Arlington, VA
Szlichta, Christopher D. ....Stillwater, OK
Szlichta & Ramsey ....Stillwater, OK
Szlinis, William J. ....Romulus, MI
Szlosek, Richard W. ....Northampton, MA
Szmagala, Taras G., Jr. ....Painesville, OH
Szmuszkovicz, Kathryn E. Washington, DC
Szmyt, Pamela J. ....Springfield, MA

Tackett, Stephen L. .... Hazard, KY
Tackett, Steven J. .... Austin, TX
Tackett, Victor E. .... Louisville, KY
Tackett, Victor Edward, Jr. .... Louisville, KY
Tackett, Virginia .... Little Rock, AR
Tackett-Hunt, Cristy .... Chicago, IL
Tackitt, Mark B. .... Seattle, WA
Tackitt, Sylvan W. .... Bloomington, IN
Tackman, Alan R. .... Glenwood, NM
Tackney, Stephen B. .... Washington, DC
Tackowiak, Bruce J. .... Los Angeles, CA
Tacoma, Kenneth Lee .... Cadillac, MI
Tacon, Avelin P., III .... Olympia, WA
Tacopina, Joseph .... Hackensack, NJ
New York, NY
Tacticos, George .... Purchase, NY
Tacy, Susan A. .... Van Nuys, CA
Tada, Hajime .... San Francisco, CA
Tadajweski, Ann E. .... New York, NY
Tadano, Joseph T. .... Phoenix, AZ
Tadayon, Afshin .... Las Vegas, NV
Tadda, Erik M. .... Baton Rouge, LA
Taddei, Kathleen Caldwell .... Providence, RI
Taddeo, Anthony B., Jr. .... Baltimore, MD
Taddeo, Frank A., Jr. .... New York, NY
Taddeo, Frank J. .... Fort Lauderdale, FL
Taddeo, Joseph A., Jr. .... Rochester, NY
Taddeo, Joseph A., Sr. .... Rochester, NY
Taddeo, Joseph H. .... Cleveland, OH
Taddeo, Karen M. .... Syracuse, NY
Taddeucci, Deborah J. .... Irvine, CA
Taddonio, Gregory L. .... Canton, OH
Taddonio & Heed, P.C. .... Mineola, NY
Taddonio, Michael F. .... Rochester, NY
Taddonio, Robert S. .... Mineola, NY
Taddune, Paul J. .... Aspen, CO
Taddune, Paul J., P.C. .... Aspen, CO
Snowmass Village, CO
Tadduni, Charles A. .... Trenton, NJ
Tade, Jeanmarie Brock .... Houston, TX
Tade, Jeffrey L. .... Salinas, CA
Taden, Michael L. .... Chicago, IL
Tader, Mark W. .... Wheaton, IL
Tadje, James B. .... Ogden, UT
Tadla, James A. .... Poland, OH
Tadla, James, LLC .... Poland, OH
Tadler, Ariana J. .... New York, NY
Tadler, Robert J. .... Roslyn Heights, NY
Tadlock, C. Craig .... Dallas, TX
Tadlock, Kimberly L. .... Little Rock, AR
Tadlock, Lyn Davaly .... Hayward, CA
Tadlock, Terry G. .... San Francisco, CA
Tadlock, Warren L. .... Charlotte, NC
Tadlock, Zackary G. .... Atlanta, GA
Tadmor, Rachel C. .... Worcester, MA
Tadolini, Antoinette M. .... Long Beach, CA
Tadros, Daniel A. .... New Orleans, LA
Tadros, David S., (P.A.)
West Palm Beach, FL
Tadros, Niveen .... Los Angeles, CA
Tadrowski, Daniel G. .... Vero Beach, FL
Tady, Brandon K. .... Los Angeles, CA
Tady, George R. .... Seattle, WA
Tadych, Jason T. .... Chicago, IL
Tadych, Michael J. .... Raleigh, NC
Taebel, Scott W. .... Columbus, OH
Taecker, Tami J. .... Newport Beach, CA
Taekman, Jennifer .... Lafayette, CA
Taenzer, Friedman, Ettenson & Stockton, P.C.
Moorestown, NJ
Taenzer, Uri Hugo .... Moorestown, NJ
Taetle, Andrea W. .... New York, NY
Tafapolsky, Alan .... San Francisco, CA
Tafara, Ethiopis .... Washington, DC
Tafarella, Santi, Jr. .... Lancaster, CA
Tafaro & Flynn, P.A. .... Basking Ridge, NJ
Elizabeth, NJ
Morristown, NJ
Newark, NJ
New Providence, NJ
Tafaro, Lynda Albano .... New Orleans, LA
Tafaro, Stephen J. .... New Providence, NJ
Tafe, Edward J. .... San Francisco, CA
Tafe, Elizabeth M.
National Labor Relations Board,
Office of Board Members, GV
Tafe, H. Lawrence, III .... Boston, MA
Tafe, Joseph J. .... Department of Justice,
Criminal Division, GV
Tafel, Rosann D. .... Louisville, KY
Tafelski, Michael D. .... Kennett Square, PA
Tafelski, Paul J. .... Detroit, MI
Taff, Angus Broward, Jr. .... Tallahassee, FL
Taff, Barry P., (P.C.) .... Washington, DC
Taff, E. Wayne .... Kansas City, MO
Taff, Frank D. .... Topeka, KS
Taff & Hayes .... Tallahassee, FL
Taff, James C. .... Boston, MA
Taff, Robert H. .... Toms River, NJ
Taff, T. Michael .... North Miami Beach, FL
Taffae, Alfred M. .... New York, NY
Taffae, Seth J. .... New York, NY
Taffany, David J. .... Troy, NY
Taffe, Christopher V. .... Rochester, NY
Taffe, Elizabeth Deutsch .... Rochester, NY
Taffe, Paula M. .... Chicago, IL
New York, NY
Taffel, Shelley Iris .... Boston, MA
Taffera, Louis R. .... White Plains, NY
Taffet, Allan N. .... New York, NY
Taffet, Gary A. .... Newark, NJ
Taffet, Linda R. .... Framingham, MA
Taffet, Richard S. .... New York, NY
Taffet, Steven, Law Offices of
Boulder, CO
Taffet, Steven, Law Offices of .... Denver, CO
Taffet, William B. .... Boca Raton, FL
Taffora, Raymond P. .... Madison, WI

Taff-Rice, Anita C. .... San Francisco, CA
Taffuri, Rosina .... Brooklyn, NY
Taflan, Deborah L. .... Durham, NC
Taflan, James M. .... Helena, MT
Tafoya, Alaurice M. .... Denver, CO
Tafoya, Fernando .... San Francisco, CA
Tafoya, Kathleen M. .... Denver, CO
Tafoya, Michael G. .... Phoenix, AZ
Tafoya, Robert N. .... Los Angeles, CA
Tafoya, Robert S. .... Bakersfield, CA
Tafreshi, Sepi N. .... Concord, CA
Tafro, Alexander J. .... Roseland, NJ
Tafro, Angela V. .... Morristown, NJ
Tafro, Joseph, Jr. .... West Caldwell, NJ
Tafro, Leonard J. .... Fairfield, NJ
Taft, Alexander T., Jr. .... Goshen, KY
Taft, Barbara I.
Federal Deposit Insurance Corporation,
Resolutions Section, GV
Taft, Claudia L. .... New York, NY
Taft, Diana G. .... Simsbury, CT
Taft, Dudley S. .... Cincinnati, OH
Taft, Franklin R. .... Vallejo, CA
Taft, Frederick I. .... Cleveland, OH
Taft, Geoffrey .... Albany, CA
Taft, George .... Department of State,
Office of the Legal Adviser, GV
Taft, George .... Kansas City, MO
Taft, Homer S. .... Rocky River, OH
Taft, James L., Jr. .... Cranston, RI
Taft, Jeffrey P. .... Washington, DC
Taft, John A. .... St. Paul, MN
Taft, Jonathan D. .... Chicago, IL
Taft, Judith .... New York, NY
Taft, Kathleen M. .... Spokane, WA
Taft, Kingsley L. .... Boston, MA
Taft, Lee .... Cambridge, MA
Dallas, TX
Taft, Leroy B. .... Los Angeles, CA
Taft, Leroy B., A Professional Law Corporation
Los Angeles, CA
Taft, Lynne A. .... Flint, MI
Taft, Mackin, Grovdahl, Henault & Hancock,,
P.S. .... Spokane, WA
Taft, Martin S. .... New York, NY
Taft & McSally .... Cranston, RI
Providence, RI
Taft, Nathaniel B. .... White Plains, NY
Taft, Peter R., (A Professional Corporation)
Los Angeles, CA
Taft, Peter S. .... Albany, NY
Taft, R. Guy .... Cincinnati, OH
Taft, Richard G. .... Oklahoma City, OK
Taft, Robert .... Peterborough, NH
Taft, Robert A., II .... Columbus, OH
Taft, Robert W. .... New York, NY
Taft, Roger H. .... Erie, PA
Taft, Ronald S. .... New York, NY
Taft, Ronald S., P.C. .... New York, NY
Taft, Russell Parker .... Vallejo, CA
Taft Securities Litigation, P.C.
San Francisco, CA
Taft, Seth C. .... Cleveland, OH
Taft, Sheldon A. .... Columbus, OH
Taft, Stettinius & Hollister LLP
Covington, KY
Cincinnati, OH
Cleveland, OH
Columbus, OH
Taft, Taft & Haigler .... Greenville, NC
Taft, Thomas F. .... Greenville, NC
Taft, Tony R. .... Houston, TX
Taft, William H., IV .... Washington, DC
Taft, William L. .... Monroe, MI
Taft, William W. .... Cleveland, OH
Taft-Carter, Sarah .... Cranston, RI
Tafuri, Anthony A. .... Lindenhurst, NY
Tafuri, David M. .... Washington, DC
Tafuri, Robert J. .... River Edge, NJ
Tafuri, Sandra .... New York, NY
Tag & Associates, P.C. .... Washington, DC
Tag, Howard M. .... Washington, DC
Taga, Glenn N. .... Glenwood Springs, CO
Honolulu, HI
Tagaropulos, I. M., P.C. .... Houston, TX
Tagaropulos, I. M. .... Houston, TX
Tagart, David D. .... Lincoln, ME
Tagatac, Paul S. .... Waterbury, CT
Tagawa, Barry K. .... San Francisco, CA
Tagawa, Barry K., A Prof. Corp., The Law
Office of .... San Francisco, CA
Tager, Cheryl B. .... New York, NY
Tager, Clifford L. .... Danbury, CT
Tager, Evan M. .... Washington, DC
Tager, Jeff S. .... Bloomfield, CT
Tager, Richard N. .... Bethesda, MD
Tagerman, Neil A. .... Newton, MA
Tagg, Howard .... Tyler, TX
Tagg, Paul F. .... Dallas, TX
Taggart, Allen P. .... Boulder, CO
Taggart, Barbara J. .... Washington, DC
Taggart, Brent C. .... Columbus, OH
Taggart, Carolyn A. .... Cincinnati, OH
Taggart, Clare Kelly .... Gaithersburg, MD
Taggart, Cox, Hays, Zacour & Lanham, A
Legal Professional Association
Wooster, OH
Taggart, David R. .... Shreveport, LA
Taggart, Deborah S. .... Los Angeles, CA
Taggart, Douglas A. .... Ogden, UT
Taggart, Eugene G. .... New Orleans, LA
Taggart, Frank, III .... Longview, TX
Taggart, Georgana .... Cincinnati, OH
Taggart, Gregory H. .... Cody, WY
Taggart & Hawkins, A Professional
Corporation .... San Francisco, CA
Taggart, J. William .... Akron, OH
Taggart, James R. .... San Francisco, CA

Taggart, James W. .... Wooster, OH
Taggart, Jeanette H. .... San Jose, CA
Taggart, Jennifer McCabe
Cambridge, MA
Taggart, Jennifer T. .... Los Angeles, CA
Taggart, John C. .... Raleigh, NC
Taggart, John K., III .... Charlottesville, VA
Taggart, John Yeatman .... New York, NY
Taggart, Karen .... Anoka, MN
Taggart, Keith .... Boston, MA
Taggart, Leigh C. .... Ithaca, NY
Taggart, Max S., II .... Ontario, OR
Taggart, Morton, Ogden, Staub, Rougelot,
Brocato & O'Brien, L.L.C.
New Orleans, LA
Taggart, Patrick J. .... Baraboo, WI
Taggart, Patrick J. .... Reedsburg, WI
Sauk City, WI
Wonewoc, WI
Taggart, R. Andrew .... Jackson, MS
Taggart, Richard C. .... Salt Lake City, UT
Taggart, Robert D. .... San Francisco, CA
Taggart, Robert L. .... Indianapolis, IN
Taggart, Sonia E. .... Carson City, NV
Taggart & Taggart .... Ontario, OR
Taggart, Tara S. .... Columbia, SC
Taggart, Thomas M. .... Columbus, OH
Taggart, Thomas P. .... Adrian, MI
Taggart, Thomas R. .... Savannah, GA
Taggart, Thomas Terrell, Jr.
Locust Grove, VA
Taggart, Ward S. .... Trenton, NJ
Taggart, William .... Erie, PA
Taggart, William E., Jr.
San Francisco, CA
Tagge, Fredk. A. .... Littleton, CO
Tagge, Stephen A. .... Springfield, IL
Taggersell, Vilean .... Kittery, ME
Taggi, Christopher A. .... Newport News, VA
Taghioff, David M. .... Beverly Hills, CA
Tagle, Hilda .... Brownsville, TX
Tagler, George J. .... Chicago, IL
Tagli, Hugo, Jr. .... Chicago, IL
Taglia, Anthony R. .... Chicago, IL
Taglia, Daniel Paul .... Chicago, IL
Taglia, Fette, Dumke, Passaro & Kahne, P.C.
St. Joseph, MI
Taglia, John J. .... Austin, TX
Taglia, Paul A. .... St. Joseph, MI
Taglia, Peter R. .... New York, NY
Tagliaferri, Alfred J. .... Norristown, PA
Tagliaferri, Daniel D. .... San Francisco, CA
Tagliaferri, Michael .... Thousand Oaks, CA
Tagliaferri, Ronald .... Cranston, RI
Tagliaferro, Victor J. .... Somerville, MA
Tagliagambe, Anthony F. .... New York, NY
Taglianetti, Libro G., Jr. .... Philadelphia, PA
Tagliareni, Joan E. .... Boston, MA
Tagliarini, Thomas C. .... Oakland, CA
Tagliavia, Margaret D. .... Carrollton, TX
Tagliavini, Carlo A. .... Westfield, MA
Taglieri, James W. .... Washington, DC
Taglieri, Michael Christopher
New York, NY
Taglioli, Quintes D. .... Allentown, PA
Tagrin, Marnold .... Boston, MA
Tagtmeier, Brian J. .... Houston, TX
Tagtow, Patrick K. .... Houston, TX
Taguchi, Taren .... Honolulu, HI
Tague, Brian P., (P.A.) .... Miami, FL
West Palm Beach, FL
Tague, Charles J., Jr. .... Bryn Mawr, PA
Tague, Cynthia Vanden Heuvel
Bronxville, NY
Tague, John F., III .... Bronxville, NY
Tague, Michael J. .... Champaign, IL
Tague, P. Arthur .... Denver, CO
Tague, P. Arthur, P.C. .... Denver, CO
Tague, Rick W. .... Bloomington, MN
Tague, Robert G. .... New Lexington, OH
Tague, Roland .... Oklahoma City, OK
Tague, Suzanne M., (P.C.)
Costa Mesa, CA
Tague & Vanden Heuvel, LLP
Bronxville, NY
Tahajian, Gerald Lee .... Fresno, CA
Tahan, Kathryn Case .... St. Louis, MO
Tahan, Theodore M. .... St. Louis, MO
Tahan, Theodore M., Jr. .... St. Louis, MO
Tahbaz, Christopher K. .... New York, NY
Tahbaz, Leah .... New York, NY
Taheny, John J., Jr. .... San Francisco, CA
Taheny, Kevin A. .... San Mateo, CA
Taheri, Amy M. .... Casper, WY
Taheri, Marshall M. .... Houston, TX
Taheri, Michael S. .... Buffalo, NY
Taheripour-Sedaghat, M. Michelle
Sherman Oaks, CA
Tahernia, Susan .... McLean, VA
Tahmassebi, Stefan B. .... Fairfax, VA
Tahmin, Despina M. .... Washington, DC
Tahnk-Johnson, Raymond L. .... Eagan, MN
Tahsuda, Jacqueline Sandoval
Cazenovia, NY
Tahsuda, John .... Cazenovia, NY
Taht, Ronald L. .... Ocean City, NJ
Taht, Stanton & McCrosson, A Professional
Corporation .... Ocean City, NJ
Tahvonen, Randy L. .... St. Johns, MI
Tahyar, Margaret .... New York, NY
Tai, Chang Hsien .... North Hollywood, CA
Tai, Cynthia Toshiye .... Kealakekua, HI
Tai, Ernest .... San Francisco, CA
Tai, Henry M. .... Honolulu, HI
Tai, Linda W. .... Los Angeles, CA
Tai, Luther .... New York, NY
Tai, Mae .... San Francisco, CA
Tai, Ta Van .... Cambridge, MA

Tai, Tiffany W. .... Pasadena, CA
Taiani, Gennaro V. .... Queens Village, NY
Taibi, Anthony D. .... Raleigh, NC
Taibl, Steven M. .... Boston, MA
Taibl, William E. .... Milwaukee, WI
Taibleson, Michael W. .... Milwaukee, WI
Taich, Harry H. .... Cleveland, OH
Taich, Timothy F. .... Livermore, CA
Taicher, Michael A. .... South Easton, MA
Taichert, Robert D. .... Albuquerque, NM
Taichman, Laura R. .... New York, NY
Taichman-Robins, Susan N.
Bala Cynwyd, PA
Taieb, Steven N. .... Mount Laurel, NJ
Taigman, Michelle Epstein .... Detroit, MI
Taigman, Robert .... Lake Hiawatha, NJ
Taigue, Richard J. .... New York, NY
Tailer, Peter L. .... Hanover, NH
Taillefer, Joseph M., Jr. .... Sacramento, CA
Taillefer, Laurence A. .... West Springfield, MA
Tailleur, Joan P. .... West Coxsackie, NY
Taillon, Karen L. .... Newport Beach, CA
Taima, June A. .... Philadelphia, PA
Taiman, Edward C., Jr. .... Hartford, CT
Taine, Charles R. .... Miami, FL
Tainiter, Nancy L. .... Southampton, NY
Taintor, Christopher C. .... Portland, ME
Taintor, F. Andrews .... Naples, FL
Taintor, F. Andrews, P.A. .... Naples, FL
Taintor, Frederick G. .... Auburn, ME
Taintor, Jane S. .... Scarborough, ME
Taintor, Patrick C. .... Chattanooga, TN
Taira, Darryl M. .... Honolulu, HI
Taira, Eric M. .... Torrance, CA
Taira, Muriel M. .... Honolulu, HI
Taisey, Robert D. .... New York, NY
Taishoff, Howard A. .... Great Neck, NY
Taishoff, Lewis C. .... New York, NY
Taishoff, Robert P. .... Skaneateles, NY
Tait, Albert Lewis, Jr.
Oklahoma City, OK
Tait, Amy C. .... Columbus, OH
Tait & Associates .... Oregon City, OR
Tait, Christina .... Cleveland, OH
Tait, Christopher .... Yakima, WA
Tait, Colin C. .... Hartford, CT
Tait, Dana .... Dallas, TX
Tait, Donna R. .... Tacoma, WA
Tait, Edward T. .... Washington, DC
Tait, Eric J. .... Oregon City, OR
Tait, J. Minor, Jr. .... Memphis, TN
Tait, James C. .... Oregon City, OR
Tait, Jeffrey A. .... Binghamton, NY
Tait, John Reid .... Lewiston, ID
Tait, John T. .... Columbus, OH
Tait, Monica E. .... Los Angeles, CA
Tait, Robert E. .... Columbus, OH
Tait, Thomas J. .... St. Paul, MN
Tait, William J., Jr. .... Tallahassee, FL
Tait, William, Jr. .... Quincy, MA
Tait, William R., Jr. .... Mays Landing, NJ
Taitano, Carlos L. .... Hagåtña, GU
Taitano, Carlos Lujan, P.C. .... Hagåtña, GU
Taite, George T. .... Jersey City, NJ
Taite, Ralph .... Dallas, TX
Taitelman, Donald S. .... Milwaukee, WI
Taitelman, Michael A. .... Los Angeles, CA
Taitsman, Julie K. .... Cambridge, MA
Taitt, Edwin .... New York, NY
Taitz, Ariel B. .... New York, NY
Taitz, Emanuel .... Los Angeles, CA
Taitz, Robert J. .... San Francisco, CA
Taitz, Steven C. .... Patchogue, NY
Tajfel, Doran .... Lakewood, NJ
Tajiri, Taku .... New York, NY
Tak, Thomas A. .... Boston, MA
Takabuki, Glen S. .... Honolulu, HI
Takabuki, Matsuo .... Honolulu, HI
Takac, Michael G. .... Tallahassee, FL
Takach, Karen .... New York, NY
Takacs, Alison M. .... Cambridge, MA
Takács, Cynthia M. .... Beverly Hills, CA
Takács, Cynthia M., Law Offices of, P.C.
Beverly Hills, CA
Takacs, Gary J. .... St. Petersburg, FL
Tampa, FL
Takacs, Heni .... St. Louis, MO
Takacs, James D. .... Boston, MA
Takacs, Kenneth S., Jr. .... Tampa, FL
Takacs, Stephen J. .... Columbus, OH
Takacs, William E. .... Toledo, OH
Takaesu, Toshimitsu .... Seattle, WA
Takafuji, June H. .... New York, NY
Takahashi, Ben K. .... Los Angeles, CA
Takahashi, Bradley D. .... Short Hills, NJ
Takahashi, Brian .... Torrance, CA
Takahashi, Herbert R. .... Honolulu, HI
Takahashi, Irene .... San Francisco, CA
Takahashi, Ken .... Denver, CO
Takahashi, Kenichi .... Honolulu, HI
Takahashi, Kyoko .... New York, NY
Takahashi, Lane Y. .... Honolulu, HI
Takahashi, Linda B. .... Sherman Oaks, CA
Takahashi, Mark M. .... Phoenix, AZ
Takahashi, Masui & Vasconcellos
Honolulu, HI
Takahashi, Sakae .... Honolulu, HI
Takahashi, Steven Shigeru .... Seattle, WA
Takahashi, Takeshi .... New York, NY
Takahata, Sandra Y. .... Honolulu, HI
Takaichi, Drew C. .... San Jose, CA
Takakjian, Debra .... New York, NY
Takakjian, Paul .... Encino, CA
Long Beach, CA
Los Angeles, CA
Ontario, CA
Orange, CA
Oxnard, CA

Takakjian, Sowers & Sitkoff LLP
Alhambra, CA
Beverly Hills, CA
Burbank, CA
Downey, CA
Encino, CA
Englewood, CA
Fullerton, CA
Glendale, CA
Hollywood, CA
Laguna Niguel, CA
Long Beach, CA
Los Angeles, CA
Malibu, CA
Newhall, CA
Newport Beach, CA
Norwalk, CA
Ontario, CA
Orange, CA
Oxnard, CA
Pasadena, CA
Pomona, CA
Rancho Cucamonga, CA
Riverside, CA
San Bernardino, CA
Santa Ana, CA
Santa Monica, CA
Torrance, CA
Universal City, CA
Van Nuys, CA
Ventura, CA
West Covina, CA
Westminster, CA
Whittier, CA
Takamatsu, Robert T., (Atty. At Law, A Law Corp.) ... Honolulu, HI
Takamine, Dwight ... Hilo, HI
Takamine, Kathleen Yoko ... San Antonio, TX
Takamiya, Cori Ann C. ... Honolulu, HI
Takano, Jessica May ... San Francisco, CA
Takano, Jojiro ... San Francisco, CA
Takara, Edward ... Shreveport, LA
Takaro, Martha ... Portland, OR
Takarsh, Toni Harvey ... Charleston, WV
Takas, Marianne ... Silver Spring, MD
Takas, Stephen P., Jr. ... San Antonio, TX
Takase, Cathy L. ... Honolulu, HI
Takase, Gerald Allan ... Hilo, HI
Takash, Terry ... Chicago, IL
Takash, Timothy E. ... Chicago, IL
Takasugi, Douglas J. ... Wenatchee, WA
Takasugi, Jon R. ... Los Angeles, CA
Takasugi, Robert M. ... Los Angeles, CA
Takasugi, Russell H. ... Simi Valley, CA
Takasumi, Laura L. ... Portland, OR
Takata, Keith A. ... San Francisco, CA
Takata, Kevin K. ... Honolulu, HI
Takata, Timothy D. ... Los Angeles, CA
Takatsuka, Andy Hiroshi
Los Angeles, CA
Takayama, Ken H. ... Honolulu, HI
Takayama, Linda Chu ... Honolulu, HI
Takayanagi, Yuichiro ... Schaumburg, IL
Takayesu, Ben G. ... Kula, HI
Takeda, Keith T. ... New York, NY
Takefman, Joyce ... Chicago, IL
Takehara, Greg R. ... Garden City, NY
Takehara, Ronald M., Law Offices of
Los Angeles, CA
Takehara, Ronald M., Law Offices of
Santa Monica, CA
Takei, Jonathan H. ... Palo Alto, CA
Takei, Taketsugu ... San Jose, CA
Takemiya, Fred ... Oakland, CA
Takemoto, James H. ... Baton Rouge, LA
Taken, Mark A. ... Plano, TX
Taken, Michael E. ... Milwaukee, WI
Taken, Philip E. ... Dallas, TX
Taken, Theresa A. ... San Francisco, CA
Takenaka, Toshiko ... Seattle, WA
Takenouchi, Tom ... Pasadena, CA
Takesh, Fahi ... Los Angeles, CA
Taketa, Allyson S. ... Los Angeles, CA
Taketa, Anthony J. ... Los Angeles, CA
Taketa, Donn S. ... Westlake Village, CA
Taketa, Marilyn N. ... Palo Alto, CA
Taketa, Raymond M. ... Oakland, CA
Takeuchi, Derrick K. ... Los Angeles, CA
Takeuchi, Kevin K. ... Costa Mesa, CA
Takeuchi, Lisa M. M. ... Houston, TX
Takeuchi, Robert H. ... Los Angeles, CA
Takeuchi, Robert S. ... Bellevue, WA
Takeuchi, Stephen R. ... Jacksonville, FL
Takeuchi, Yukiko ... New York, NY
Takeyama, Roy Y. ... Honolulu, HI
Takeyama & Sullivan ... Honolulu, HI
Takeyasu, Carrie L. ... Oakland, CA
Takiff, Herman J. ... Elizabeth, NJ
Takiff, Raymond J. ... Boca Raton, FL
Takiff, Sanford ... Highland Park, IL
Takitani, Anthony P. ... Wailuku, HI
Takla, Danielle A. ... Indianapolis, IN
Taknint, Rachel L. ... Milwaukee, WI
Takoudes, Lisa C. ... New York, NY
Taksar, Jodi Zucker ... Beverly Hills, CA
Taksar, Mary L.
Federal Election Commission,
Office of the General Counsel, GV
Taksin, Aaron ... Glenview, IL
Taku, Yoichiro ... Palo Alto, CA
Takumi, Larry T. ... Honolulu, HI
Takura, Tamotsu ... Seattle, WA
Takushi, Funaki, Wong & Stone, Attorneys At Law, A Law Corporation
Honolulu, HI
Takushi, Roy E. ... Honolulu, HI
Takvorian, S. Theodore ... Hackensack, NJ
Tal, Tomer ... Palo Alto, CA

Talab, F. (Patrick) H. ... Southfield, MI
Talabach, Frederick G. ... Walpole, MA
Talaber, Stephen John ... Bronx, NY
Taladay, John M. ... Washington, DC
Taladay, Matthew B. ... Du Bois, PA
Talafous, Joseph J. ... Jersey City, NJ
Talaga, Bruce J. ... Chicago, IL
Talaga, James C. ... Carpinteria, CA
Talaganis, Dean S. ... Mentor, OH
Talaie, Mohammad Ali ... Los Angeles, CA
Talamante, David M. ... Phoenix, AZ
Talamante, Ryan J. ... Phoenix, AZ
Talamantes, Mark ... San Francisco, CA
Talamantez, Paul, Jr. ... San Antonio, TX
Talamo, Albert V. ... Garden City, NY
Talamo & Volesko, P.C. ... Garden City, NY
Talan, Randall G. ... Chicago, IL
Talan, Steven R. ... Garden City Park, NY
Talanker, Alyssa L. ... Albany, NY
Talansky, Gerald L. ... Atlanta, GA
Talarchyk, Tina M. ... West Palm Beach, FL
Talarick, Julia C. ... Roseland, NJ
Talarico, Anthony G. ... Lyndhurst, NJ
Talarico & Associates, P.C. ... Troy, MI
Talarico, George R. ... Morristown, NJ
Talarico, Guy F. ... New York, NY
Talarico, Joseph D. ... Pittsburgh, PA
Talarico, Joseph M. ... Chicago, IL
Talarico, Mary C. ... Chicago, IL
Talarico, Michael J. ... Duluth, MN
Talarico, Pasquale J. ... Voorhees, NJ
Talarico, Paula Marie ... Troy, MI
Talarico, Robert N. ... Danbury, CT
Talarico, Samuel J., Jr. ... Fort Wayne, IN
Talarico, Thomas S. ... Erie, PA
Talarides, Christine K. ... Palo Alto, CA
Talaska Law Firm, The, PLLC
Houston, TX
Talaska, Robert J. ... Houston, TX
Talasnik, Murray A. ... Mays Landing, NJ
Talavera, Gary Joseph ... Torrance, CA
Talavera, Henry ... Dallas, TX
Talavera, Jessamine Rose ... Parkersburg, WV
Talay, John ... New York, NY
Talbert, Alison W. ... Gainesville, FL
Talbert, Angelia C. ... Washington, DC
Talbert & Associates, P.C. ... Alton, IL
St. Louis, MO
Talbert, Bernard M. ... Chicago, IL
Talbert, Bonford R. ... Tiffin, OH
Talbert, Cecily T. ... San Francisco, CA
Talbert, Denise J. ... Kansas City, MO
Talbert, Eugene ... Tyler, TX
Talbert, Hugh M. ... Alton, IL
St. Louis, MO
Talbert, J. Andrew
Fort Walton Beach, FL
Panama City, FL
Pensacola, FL
Talbert, Jeffrey T. ... Virginia Beach, VA
Talbert & McDaniel ... Weslaco, TX
Talbert, Michael R., Sr. ... Richmond, VA
Talbert, Patricia M. ... Roseland, NJ
Talbert, Paul M. ... New York, NY
Talbert, Phillip A. ... Department of Justice,
Office of Professional Responsibility, GV
Talbert, Pierre C., Jr. ... Chicago, IL
Talbert, Richard C. ... Cleveland, OH
Elyria, OH
Talbert, Richard D. ... College Station, TX
Talbert, Richard D., P.C.
College Station, TX
Talbert, Richard S. ... Weslaco, TX
Talbert, Robert S. ... La Habra, CA
Talbert, Robin J. ... Washington, DC
Talbert, Ronald J. ... Andrews, SC
Talbert, Tamra ... Huntington Beach, CA
Talbert, W. David, II ... Jacksonville, FL
Talbert, Wanda McGuire ... Yanceyville, NC
Talbert, William D. ... Cedarburg, WI
Talbert Sifford, Evangeline ... Atlanta, GA
Talbot, A. David ... Anchorage, AK
Talbot, Alan M. ... Walnut Creek, CA
Talbot, Anne ... Washington, DC
Talbot, Annie ... Providence, RI
Talbot, Aubert D. ... Gonzales, LA
Talbot, Brent A. ... New Orleans, LA
Talbot, C. Scott ... Reston, VA
Talbot, Carmouche & Marcello, A Prof. Law Corp. ... Gonzales, LA
Talbot, Cary L. ... New York, NY
Talbot, Daniel J. ... Oklahoma City, OK
Talbot & Ducker ... Dayton, OH
Talbot, Earl A. ... Chicago, IL
Talbot, Edmond E., III ... Blair, NE
Talbot, Elizabeth Hessman
United States Court Of Veterans Appeals, GV
Talbot, Etta A. ... Costa Mesa, CA
Talbot, Fabené W. ... Houston, TX
Talbot, Frank M., II ... Bartow, FL
Talbot, Fred A. ... Richmond, VA
Talbot, Geoffrey ... North Miami, FL
Talbot, George E., Jr. ... Portsmouth, VA
Talbot, Gerald J. ... Metairie, LA
Talbot, Gerard J. ... New York, NY
Talbot, Gregory R. ... Washington, DC
Talbot, Heidi Primack ... Sacramento, CA
Talbot, J. Michael ... Skowhegan, ME
Talbot, J. Michael ... Onancock, VA
Talbot, J. Thomas ... Newport Beach, CA
Talbot, James S. ... Bakersfield, CA
Talbot, James S. ... New York, NY
Talbot, James W. ... Seattle, WA
Talbot, Jill S. ... Washington, DC
Talbot, John J. ... Chicago, IL
Talbot, John P. (Jack) ... Pine Bluff, AR
Talbot, Jonathan E. ... Westlake Village, CA

Talbot, Joseph H., III ... Nashville, TN
Talbot, Kathryn S. ... New Orleans, LA
Talbot, Kent L. ... Fort Worth, TX
Talbot, Kevin Howard ... Woodstock, IL
Talbot, Leslie D. ... Sarasota, FL
Talbot, Linda M. ... Houston, TX
Talbot, Lori B. ... Dallas, TX
Talbot, Mark M. ... Edinburg, TX
Talbot, Marshall E. ... Overland Park, KS
Talbot, Maurice P., Jr. ... Washington, DC
Talbot, Michael E. ... Las Vegas, NV
Talbot, Michael J. ... Detroit, MI
Talbot, Morgan ... McAllen, TX
Talbot, Nathan A. ... Boise, ID
Talbot, Pamela ... Boston, MA
Talbot, Patrick M. ... Miami, FL
Talbot, Paul W. ... Fort Worth, TX
Talbot, Peter ... Media, PA
Talbot, Ralph W., Jr. ... Miami, FL
Talbot, Richard J. ... Weymouth, MA
Talbot, Richard J. ... Keene, NH
Talbot, Richard R. ... Cheshire, CT
Talbot, Robert E. ... San Francisco, CA
Talbot, Robert J. ... Seattle, WA
Talbot, Steven D. ... Moses Lake, WA
Talbot, Steven D., P.S. ... Moses Lake, WA
Talbot & Talbot, P.A. ... Machias, ME
Talbot, Thomas B., Jr. ... Dayton, OH
Talbot, Thomas W. ... Macon, GA
Talbot, Timothy K. ... Sacramento, CA
Talbot, Tina M. ... Santa Ana, CA
Talbot, William B. ... Machias, ME
Talbot, William B., Jr. ... Machias, ME
Talbot, William T. ... Nevada, IA
Talbot & Wong, A Professional Corporation
McAllen, TX
Talbott, Alan J. ... San Diego, CA
Talbott, Alex F. ... Louisville, KY
Talbott & Alsop ... Burlington, VT
Talbott, Ben J., Jr. ... Louisville, KY
Talbott, Chad D. ... Louisville, KY
Talbott, D. Casey ... Toledo, OH
Talbott, Dennis M. ... San Francisco, CA
Talbott, Edwin M., Jr. ... Timonium, MD
Talbott, Frank E. ... Burlington, VT
Talbott, Frank, III ... Danville, VA
Talbott and Gallagher, A Professional Corporation ... McLean, VA
Talbott, Graham W. ... San Bernardino, CA
Talbott, Harold B. ... Columbus, OH
Talbott, Harold G. ... Holiday, FL
Talbott, James N. ... Malibu, CA
Talbott, Jeremiah J.
Fort Walton Beach, FL
Panama City, FL
Pensacola, FL
Talbott, Jerry D. ... Yakima, WA
Talbott, Joanne M. ... Paducah, KY
Talbott, John C. ... Louisville, KY
Talbott, John C. ... McLean, VA
Talbott, John S., III ... Lexington, KY
Talbott, Kirk L. ... Washington, DC
Talbott, M. Lizabeth ... New Orleans, LA
Talbott, Marvin S. ... Winner, SD
Talbott, Mary Kathleen ... Wynne, AR
Talbott, Patricia A. ... Chehalis, WA
Talbott, Richard E. ... Portland, OR
Talbott, Richard H., Jr. ... Elkins, WV
Talbott, Sandra Gail ... Sacramento, CA
Talbott, Simpson, Gibson & Davis, P.S.
Yakima, WA
Talbott, William W. ... Webster Springs, WV
Talbott-Schehl, Kathy J. ... St. Louis, MO
Talboy, Frank L. ... Boise, ID
Talboy, Robert W. ... Boise, ID
Talburt, Aubrey L. ... Miami, FL
Talbutt, Glenda M. ... Boise, ID
Talcott, Anne M. ... Portland, OR
Talcott, Brian R ... Portland, OR
Talcott, Darrel A. ... West Salem, WI
Talcott, Frederick L. ... Berkeley, CA
Talcott, James K. ... Greensboro, NC
Talcott, James R. ... Houston, TX
Talcott, Joel D. ... Redwood City, CA
Talcott, Jonathan H. ... Washington, DC
Talcott, Kelly D. ... New York, NY
Talcott, Kent P. ... Ann Arbor, MI
Talcott, Lightfoot, Vandevelde Sadowsky, Medvene & Levine ... Los Angeles, CA
Talcott, Marilyn S. ... Berkeley, CA
Talcott, Patricia L. ... Cherry Hill, NJ
Blue Bell, PA
Talcott, Robert M. ... Los Angeles, CA
Talcott, Steven J. ... Laguna Hills, CA
Talcott, Thomas J. ... Cleveland, OH
Talcott, Vern H. ... Boca Raton, FL
Talcott, William T., Jr. ... Worcester, MA
Talcott, Worthington H., Jr.
Rockville, MD
Talda, Richard A. ... Dayton, OH
Taldone, Nicholas J. ... Clearwater, FL
Talebi, Denise ... Delaware, OH
Taleff, Mark A. ... Albany, OR
Taleff, Ward E. ... Great Falls, MT
Talegaonkar, Neil S. ... Richmond, VA
Taleisnik, Martin ... Fresno, CA
Talel, Eva Coben ... New York, NY
Talen, Bruce L. ... St. Louis, MO
Talen, Edward J. ... Grand Rapids, MI
Talenfeld, Deborah Berlin ... Miami, FL
Talenfeld, Elliot C. ... Phoenix, AZ
Talenfeld, Howard M.
Fort Lauderdale, FL
Talens, James M. ... Washington, DC
Talent, Brenda Lyons ... Chesterfield, MO
Talent, James M. ... Chesterfield, MO
Talent, Milton O. ... St. Louis, MO
Talenti, Samuel D. ... Pittsburgh, PA

Taler, Elliott ... St. Paul, MN
Talerico, Eugene M., Jr ... Scranton, PA
Talerico, James A. ... Atlanta, GA
Talerman, Jason R. ... Walpole, MA
Talero, Ximena ... Washington, DC
Talesnick, Alan L. ... Denver, CO
Talesnick, Richard S. ... New York, NY
Talesnick, Stanley ... Indianapolis, IN
Talesnick, Stephen A. ... Los Angeles, CA
Talesnik, Sonja ... New York, NY
Talev, Peter N. ... Liverpool, NY
Talevi, Jacqueline F. Ward ... Roanoke, VA
Talevi, Steven J. ... Roanoke, VA
Talia, Melanie A. ... New Orleans, LA
Talia, Peter M. ... Patterson, CA
Taliaferro, Bruce O. ... Tulsa, OK
Taliaferro, Dan W. ... Montgomery, AL
Taliaferro, Diale Duane, II ... Dearborn, MI
Taliaferro, Don H. ... Griffin, GA
Taliaferro, George W., Jr. ... Cincinnati, OH
Taliaferro, Harry T., III ... Warsaw, VA
Taliaferro, Harry T., Jr. ... Richmond, VA
Taliaferro, Henry A. ... Jonesville, LA
Taliaferro, Henry B., Jr.
Oklahoma City, OK
Taliaferro, Lewis E.
La Canada Flintridge, CA
Taliaferro, Lilton R., Jr. ... Philadelphia, PA
Taliaferro, Mark, Jr. ... Birmingham, AL
Taliaferro, Mehling, Shirooni & Carran
Covington, KY
Cincinnati, OH
Taliaferro, Monroe ... Kansas City, MO
Taliaferro, Peter W. ... Baltimore, MD
Taliaferro, Philip, III ... Covington, KY
Taliaferro, R. Henry ... Birmingham, AL
Taliaferro, Richard S. ... Rossville, GA
Taliaferro, Russell G. ... Escondido, CA
Taliaferro, R. Y. ... El Dorado, KS
Taliaferro, Stephen ... Cassville, MO
Taliaferro, T. Cass
General Services Administration,
Office of Regional Counsel, GV
Taliaferro, Tracy Lee ... Petersburg, VA
Taliaferro, Viola J. ... Bloomington, IN
Taliaferro, Weldon S. ... Cartwright, OK
Amarillo, TX
Taliaferro, William Craig ... Austin, TX
San Antonio, TX
Taliaferro, William L., Jr. ... Norfolk, VA
Taliana, Lawrence O. ... Edwardsville, IL
Talianoff, Rubin & Rubin ... Miami, FL
Talieh, Koorosh ... Washington, DC
Talierco, John B. ... Downingtown, PA
Talierco, John B., Jr. ... Downingtown, PA
Talierco & Talierco ... Downingtown, PA
Talieri, Peter ... Boston, MA
Talifer, Henry ... Los Angeles, CA
Talikka, Ischie, Talikka & Wilson, Co., L.P.A.
Painesville, OH
Talikka, Kirsti S. ... Painesville, OH
Talikka, Leo J. ... Painesville, OH
Talisman, Amy B. ... Fort Lauderdale, FL
Talisman, Charles E. ... Washington, DC
Talisman, Harold L. ... Washington, DC
Talisman, Jonathan ... Treasury Department,
Departmental Offices, GV
Talisman, Patrice A. ... Miami, FL
Taliuaga, Alan J. ... Staten Island, NY
Talivaga, Alan J. ... Marlboro, NJ
Talkin, Richard B. ... Columbia, MD
Talkin, Richard B., P.A. ... Columbia, MD
Talkington, Alan ... San Francisco, CA
Talkington, Fred M. ... Dallas, TX
Talkington, Robert V. ... Iola, KS
Talkington, Scott R. ... Montgomery, AL
Talkington, Timothy ... Boulder, CO
Talkington, Victoria W. ... San Rafael, CA
Talkovsky, Steven H. ... Washington, DC
Talkow, Andrew M. ... Hillside, NJ
Talkow, Michael S. ... Hillside, NJ
Tall, Christopher Taliferro ... Cleveland, OH
Tall, Clifford H. ... Myrtle Beach, SC
Tall, Clifford H., P.A. ... Myrtle Beach, SC
Tall, David M. ... Bellevue, WA
Tall, Laura A. ... San Bernardino, CA
Tall, Sheri Lynne ... Walnut Creek, CA
Tallach, Timothy M. ... Memphis, TN
Tallackson, Christine J. ... Ancram, NY
Tallackson, Jeffrey S. ... New York, NY
Tallaksen, James J. ... Hartford, CT
Tallaksen, Laura Kennedy ... Atlanta, GA
Tallakson, Alfred T. ... Poughkeepsie, NY
Tallan, Martin B. ... New York, NY
Tallan, Mitchell M. ... Columbus, OH
Tallant, David, Jr. ... Chicago, IL
Tallant, Ellen A. ... Oklahoma City, OK
Tallant, Frederick C., Jr. ... Atlanta, GA
Tallant, James W. ... Downers Grove, IL
Tallant, James W., & Associates, Ltd.
Downers Grove, IL
Tallant Law Offices ... Atlanta, GA
Tallant, Mack D. ... Robbinsville, NC
Tallant, Ralph E., Jr. ... Chattanooga, TN
Tallarico, Lorraine M. ... Garden City, NY
Tallarigo, Matthew ... Cincinnati, OH
Tallas, Annmarie L. ... Houston, TX
Tallberg, James N. ... Hartford, CT
Talle, Herman L. ... Minneapolis, MN
Talle, Kenneth R. ... Hopkins, MN
Tallen, Steven M. ... Minneapolis, MN
Tallent, Charles J. ... Canajoharie, NY
Tallent, Jack M., II ... Knoxville, TN
Tallent, Jennifer Leigh ... Madisonville, TN
Tallent, Stephen E. ... Washington, DC
Taller, Martin ... Anaheim, CA

Taller, Martin, A Prof. Law Corp. **Anaheim, CA**
Los Angeles, CA
Taller, Y. David ....Forest Hills, NY
Tallerico, Catherine A. ....**Denver, CO**
Tallerico, Thomas J. ....**Detroit, MI**
Tallett, John H. ....Indian Wells, CA
Talley, Andrew A. ....Orange, CA
Talley, Anthony, Hughes & Knight, L.L.C. **Bogalusa, LA**
Mandeville, LA
Talley, Audrey C. ....**Philadelphia, PA**
Talley, Barry W. ....Del City, OK
Talley, Caroline S. ....**Atlanta, GA**
Talley, Carolyn D. ....Treasury Department, Financial Management Service, GV
Talley, Cecil W. ....**Shreveport, LA**
Talley, Charles R. ....**New Orleans, LA**
Talley, Claude E. ....Tulsa, OK
Talley, Cristina L ....Anaheim, CA
Talley, Crystal D. ....**Boston, MA**
Talley, Damon R. ....**Hodgenville, KY**
Talley, Damon R., P.S.C. ....**Frankfort, KY**
Hodgenville, KY
Talley & Darden, P.C. ....Dallas, GA
Marietta, GA
Talley, David Allen ....Suisun, CA
Talley, David W., Jr. ....Magnolia, AR
Talley, David W., Jr., P.A. ....Magnolia, AR
Talley, Debra ....Hondo, TX
Talley, Douglas L. ....Akron, OH
Talley, Edward Garner, Jr. ....**Richmond, VA**
Talley, George T. ....**Valdosta, GA**
Talley, Gerald W.
Board of Governors Of The Federal Reserve System, Division of Information Resources Management, GV
Talley, Gregory T. ....**Valdosta, GA**
Talley, James B. ....Marietta, GA
Talley, James B., Jr. ....**Dallas, GA**
Talley, James E. ....Bogalusa, LA
Talley, James M., Jr. ....**Charlotte, NC**
Talley, James Michael ....**Orlando, FL**
Talley, James W. ....Escondido, CA
Talley, Jeffrey B. ....Dallas, GA
Talley, Jennifer Leigh ....Dallas, TX
Talley, Jill H. ....**Los Angeles, CA**
Talley, John D. ....Longview, TX
Talley, John S. ....Downers Grove, IL
Talley, Kimberly M. ....**Los Angeles, CA**
Talley, Lisa F. ....**San Francisco, CA**
Talley, Lynn P. ....Knoxville, TN
Talley, Martha J. ....**Washington, DC**
Talley, Michael D. ....**Joplin, MO**
Talley, Michael F. ....Greenville, SC
Talley, Monroe R. ....Houston, TX
Talley, Ouida Dawn ....Orange Park, FL
Talley, Pamala W. ....San Angelo, TX
Talley, Patrick A., (P.C.)
New Orleans, LA
Talley, Paul Richard ....Dandridge, TN
Talley, & Perrine ....Norman, OK
Talley, Randall C. ....Rockford, IL
Talley, Richard B. ....Norman, OK
Talley, Rita Douglas ....Oklahoma City, OK
Talley, Robert A. ....**Memphis, TN**
Talley, Robert E. ....**Conyers, GA**
Talley, Robert M. ....**Wayne, PA**
Talley, Robin G., Mr. ....Oklahoma City, OK
Shawnee, OK
Talley, Ron D. ....**Atlanta, GA**
Talley & Sharp, P.C. ....**Conyers, GA**
Talley, Steven K. ....**Denver, CO**
Talley, Stuart C. ....**Long Beach, CA**
Talley, Susan Gayle, (P.C.)
New Orleans, LA
Talley & Talley ....Hobart, OK
Talley, Thomas N. ....**New York, NY**
Talley, Thomas W. ....Hobart, OK
Talley, Walter A., Jr. ....San Bernardino, CA
Talley, Walter R. ....Bradenton, FL
Talley, William A., Jr. ....Palmyra, VA
Talley, William, Jr. ....Cambridge, MA
Talley, William W. ....Hobart, OK
Talley-Morris, Neva B. ....Little Rock, AR
Tallia, Glenn E. ....Department of Commerce, National Oceanic and Atmospheric Administration, GV
Tallian, Karen R. ....Munster, IN
Tallichet, J. H., Jr. ....Houston, TX
Tallichet, Julian C., Jr. ....Bandera, TX
Tallis, Andrew Charles ....Brooklyn, NY
Tallis, Mitchell B. ....Brooklyn, NY
Tallmadge, Jennifer ....**Charlotte, NC**
Tallmadge, Mark M. ....**Florham Park, NJ**
Tallmadge, Philip J. ....**Brookfield, WI**
Tallmadge, Therese Noonan ....Madison, NJ
Tallmadge, Thomas F., Jr. ....**Atlanta, GA**
Tallmadge, Wallace, Hahn, Smith & Walsh, P.C. ....Denver, CO
Tallman, C. Darren ....Parkersburg, WV
Tallman, Christa B. ....Lansing, MI
Tallman, Evangeline V. ....Worcester, MA
Tallman, Garth T. ....Citrus Heights, CA
Tallman, Howard R. ....**Denver, CO**
Tallman, Hudders & Sorrentino, P.C.
Allentown, PA
Bethlehem, PA
Tallman, James T. ....**Pittsburgh, PA**
Tallman, John B., III ....Madison, WI
Tallman, John D. ....Grand Rapids, MI
Tallman, John E. ....Mount Prospect, IL
Tallman, John W. ....Chattanooga, TN
Tallman, Karen A. ....El Segundo, CA
Tallman, Lori A. ....**Davison, MI**
Tallman, Lori A., PLC ....**Davison, MI**
Flint, MI

Tallman, Richard C. ....**Seattle, WA**
Tallman, Richard J. ....**Santa Clara, CA**
Tallman, Robert G. ....**Allentown, PA**
Tallman, Robert W. ....Santa Clara, CA
Tallman & Severin, LLP ....**Seattle, WA**
Tallon, Daniel J. ....Placitas, NM
Tallon, Deborah L. ....Santa Ana, CA
Tallon, James P. ....**New York, NY**
Tallon, Michael J. ....Scottsville, NY
Tallon, Michael J., P.C. ....Scottsville, NY
Tallon, Patrick A. ....Hinsdale, IL
Tallow, Samuel ....Delray Beach, FL
Tallroth, Laura S. ....**Chicago, IL**
Talluto Cursain, Gina ....**New Orleans, LA**
Tally, B. J., Jr. ....**Bay City, MI**
Tally, John B., Jr. ....**Birmingham, AL**
Tally, John C. ....**Fayetteville, NC**
Tally, John R. ....Columbia, SC
Tally, Linda Suzanne ....Carrollton, KY
Tally, Lou ....Mount Dora, FL
Tally, Mary Ann ....**Fayetteville, NC**
Tally, Robert ....Winston-Salem, NC
Tally, Robert, A Professional Corporation
Winston-Salem, NC
Tally and Tally ....Scottsboro, AL
Tally & Tally ....**Fayetteville, NC**
Tally, Webster C. ....**Bay City, MI**
Tally, William G. ....Scarsdale, NY
Tally, William Kevin ....Bay Springs, MS
Tally, William W. ....Scottsboro, AL
Tallyn, William L. ....Clearlake, CA
Talmadge, Fred Philip ....Sierra Vista, AZ
Talmadge, Herman E. ....Hampton, GA
Talmadge, Jeffrey D. ....**Austin, TX**
Talmadge, John E. ....**Atlanta, GA**
Talmadge, Joseph D., Jr. ....**Dothan, AL**
Talmadge, Keith R. ....**San Diego, CA**
Talmadge, Philip A. ....Olympia, WA
Talmadge, Richard E. ....New York, NY
Talmadge, Scott D. ....**New York, NY**
Talmadge, Sherrie R. ....Boston, MA
Talmadge, Stephen P., (P.C.) ....Tucson, AZ
Talmadge, W. Wells ....**Portland, OR**
Talmadge, William C. ....**Washington, DC**
Talmage, Charles A. E. ....**Elkhart, IN**
Talmage, Constance C. ....Englewood, CO
Talmage, Deborah M. ....Santa Barbara, CA
Talmage, Heidi L. ....Hamlin, WV
Talmage Law Offices, P.C. ....**Elkhart, IN**
Talmage, William H. ....Dayton, OH
Talman, David A. ....Worcester, MA
Talmas, Bernard W. ....Los Angeles, CA
Talmo, Ronald R. ....Santa Ana, CA
Talmor, Orly Shery ....Glendale, CA
Talmud, Howard J. ....New York, NY
Talner, Nancy L. ....Seattle, WA
Talney, Ronald G. ....Salem, OR
Talon, Bernard D. ....Farmington Hills, MI
Talon, Lawrence Stuart ....Detroit, MI
Talon, Marianne G. ....Detroit, MI
Talpalatsky, Semion ....Newport Beach, CA
Talpers, Merrill R. ....**Kansas City, MO**
Talpins, Stephen K. ....Hollywood, FL
Talpis, Matthew B. ....**Dallas, TX**
Talpos & Arnold, P.C. ....Troy, MI
Talpos, John C. ....Troy, MI
Talsky, John E. ....Greenfield, WI
Talsky, Lori E. ....**Southfield, MI**
Talsma, Marc A. ....Grand Rapids, MI
Talsness, Eric N. ....St. Paul, MN
Talson, Steven M. ....Department of Justice, Civil Division, GV
Talt, Alan R. ....**Pasadena, CA**
Talt, Stephen S. ....**Pasadena, CA**
Taltavull, W. Warren, III ....**Washington, DC**
Talton, Andrew Lee, Jr. ....Inglewood, CA
Talton, David H. ....**Pasadena, CA**
Talton, Helmut F. ....Texarkana, TX
Talton, Hugh C., Jr. ....Beaufort, NC
Talton, Hugh C., Jr., P.A. ....Beaufort, NC
Talton, Jerry O. ....Front Royal, VA
Talton, Robert E. ....Pasadena, TX
Talty, Dennis P. ....Philadelphia, PA
Talty, Dennis P., P.C. ....Philadelphia, PA
Talty, Edward ....Bronx, NY
Talty, Francis J. ....Cleveland, OH
Talty, Francis T. ....Lowell, MA
Talty, Karen M. ....**Chicago, IL**
Talty, Kathleen A. ....**Baltimore, MD**
Talty, Patricia A. Sullivan ....Lowell, MA
Talty, Patrick E. ....Cleveland, OH
Talty and Talty, P.C. ....Lowell, MA
Talus, Gregory S. ....**Canon City, CO**
Talvacchia, John A. ....Mount Laurel, NJ
Talvacchia, John L. ....**Boston, MA**
Talvacchia, Nicholas F. ....**Atlantic City, NJ**
Talwalkar, Nandu A. ....Costa Mesa, CA
Talwani, Indira ....**San Francisco, CA**
Talwani, Rajeev M. ....**Los Angeles, CA**
Talwar, Anjali ....**San Francisco, CA**
Talwar, Rinku ....Jacksonville, FL
Tam, Christine ....**Los Angeles, CA**
Tam, James K. ....**Honolulu, HI**
Tam, Jane Kwok Ping ....**Washington, DC**
Tam, John E. ....Wailuku, HI
Tam, Maria W. ....Monterey Park, CA
Tam, O'Connor, Henderson, Taira & Yamauchi, Attorneys At Law, A Law Corporation ....**Honolulu, HI**
Tam, Raymond J. ....Honolulu, HI
Tam, Virginia M. ....**New York, NY**
Tam, William M. ....**Honolulu, HI**
Tama, Cheryl R. ....**Chicago, IL**
Tama, Debra ....**New York, NY**
Tama, Noreen ....**Fairfax, VA**
Tamaddon, Ray ....Beverly Hills, CA
Tamagini & Bloomenthal, P.C.
Waltham, MA

Tamagini, James E. ....Waltham, MA
Tamagini, James E., Jr. ....**Boston, MA**
Tamagni, Lisa Jordan
Executive Office Of The President, GV
Tamaki, Blaine L. ....Yakima, WA
Tamaki, Donald K. ....**San Francisco, CA**
Tamanaha, Susan E. ....Honolulu, HI
Tamanini, David F. ....Harrisburg, PA
Tamanini, Jan Matthew ....Harrisburg, PA
Tamaoki, Sunny ....Costa Mesa, CA
Tamarazzo, Dominick ....**Coral Gables, FL**
Tamarelli, Alan W. ....**Pittsburgh, PA**
Tamargo, Amy M. ....**Tampa, FL**
Tamargo, Eduardo ....**San Juan, PR**
Tamargo, Mauricio J.
House of Representatives, Congressional Assistants, GV
Tamargo, Ted R. ....**Tampa, FL**
Tamarin, Bruce Michael ....New York, NY
Tamarin, Harold W. ....New York, NY
Tamarin, Jeffrey M. ....**New York, NY**
Tamarin, Lloyd B. ....Staten Island, NY
Tamarkin, Ivan L. ....Cincinnati, OH
Tamaro, Therese Wynne ....Walnut Creek, CA
Tamaroff, Chad J. ....Aventura, FL
Tamaroff, Paul K. ....Atlanta, GA
Tamas, Adam I. ....Rancho Cordova, CA
Tamas, Alice J. ....Miami, FL
Tamasco, Anthony M. ....Denville, NJ
Tamases, Peter J. ....San Francisco, CA
Tamashasky, Anne L. ....Hamilton, OH
Tamashiro, Gail M. ....**Honolulu, HI**
Tamasik, Catherine E. ....**Teaneck, NJ**
Tamasy, Joe ....Cypress, TX
Tamayne, Donna T. ....**Hackensack, NJ**
Tamayo, Anita Margaret ....**Miami, FL**
Tamayo, Jeannette P. ....Chicago, IL
Tamayo, John Marc ....**Bartow, FL**
Tamayo, Josefina Maria ....Tampa, FL
Tamayo, Stephen C. ....Fairfield, CA
Tamayo, William R. ....San Francisco, CA
Tamayo, Yvonne A. ....Orlando, FL
Tambaro, Joseph L. ....**New York, NY**
Tambascia, John J., Jr. ....Cherry Hill, NJ
Tambasco, Annette M. ....**Albany, NY**
Tambasco, Catherine A. ....Toms River, NJ
Tambasco, Daniel J. ....Woodbury, NY
Tambe, Jayant W. ....**New York, NY**
Tamblyn, George O. ....Mercer Island, WA
Tamblyn, Mark J. ....**San Francisco, CA**
Tamblyn, Sue Stepp ....Mercer Island, WA
Tamblyn & Tamblyn, P.C.
Mercer Island, WA
Tambone, Patricia L. ....Concord, MA
Tambor, Matthew H. ....Los Angeles, CA
Tamborelli, John V. ....**Los Angeles, CA**
Tamborello, Gus G. ....**Houston, TX**
Tamborlane, Rebecca L. ....Mountainside, NJ
Tamborlane, Theodosia A. ....Mountainside, NJ
Tambornino, John L. ....Minneapolis, MN
Tamborra, Sabino P. ....Norwich, CT
Tamborski, Peter E. ....**Cincinnati, OH**
Tamburelli, Thomas J. ....**Pennsauken, NJ**
Tamburelli, Thomas T. ....Pennsauken, NJ
Tamburello Hanlon & Waggener
San Francisco, CA
Tamburello, Leonardo ....**Morristown, NJ**
Tamburello, Philip V. ....Baltimore, MD
Tamburello, Tony ....**San Francisco, CA**
Tamburine, Sidney E. ....San Diego, CA
Tamburine, Susan A. ....San Diego, CA
Tamburini, Michael M. ....**Kansas City, MO**
Tamburino, Gerard C. ....Verona, NJ
Tamburo, Anthony M. ....New Orleans, LA
Tamburo, Esther G. ....**Washington, DC**
Tamburo, Nina H. ....Naperville, IL
Tamburo, Salvatore P. ....**Washington, DC**
Tamburo, Valerie ....**Princeton, NJ**
Tamburo, Vincent A. ....South Bend, IN
Tamburri, Mark L. ....**Pittsburgh, PA**
Tamburri & Tamburri ....Livingston, NJ
Tamburri, William J., Jr. ....Livingston, NJ
Tamburrino, Ron M. ....Cleveland, OH
Tamburrino, Salvatore M. ....Philadelphia, PA
Tamburro, David A. ....Deerfield Beach, FL
Tamburro, James V. ....Towaco, NJ
Tambussi, William M. ....**Camden, NJ**
Westmont, NJ
Tamchin, Stephen M. ....Walnut Creek, CA
Tameling & Associates, P.C. ....Oak Brook, IL
Tameling, Connie M. ....**Chicago, IL**
Tameling, Eva W. ....Oak Brook, IL
Tameling, Gretta A. ....Wheaton, IL
Tamen, Frank H. ....Miami, FL
Tamen, Jack ....New York, NY
Tamer, Fred J. ....Mount Clemens, MI
Tamer, Steven ....Encino, CA
Tames, Pamela C. ....New York, NY
Tamez, Lydia G. ....**Redmond, WA**
Tami, Molly T. ....Cincinnati, OH
Tamietti, Robert L., Law Offices of
Truckee, CA
Tamillow, Terry N. ....Wood Dale, IL
Tamin, Alex O. ....**Los Angeles, CA**
Taminosian, Stephen J. ....Fort Myers, FL
Tamir, Denise M. ....Miami, FL
Tamis, Donald H. ....Seymour, CT
Tamisiea, David A. ....Dallas, TX
Tamisiea, John P. ....**Chicago, IL**
Tamiya, Sharon L. ....**Irvine, CA**
Westlake Village, CA
Tamke, James K. ....South Bend, IN
Tamkin, Alvin C. ....**Newton, MA**
Tamkin, Daniel S. ....**New York, NY**
Tamkin, Gregory S. ....**Denver, CO**
Tamkin & Hochberg, LLP ....**Newton, MA**
Tamkin, Jill S. ....Miami, FL
Tamkin, Jonathan D. ....**Newton, MA**

Tamkin, Michelle S. ....Van Nuys, CA
Tamkin, Priscilla M. ....Los Angeles, CA
Tamkin, Samuel J. ....Chicago, IL
Tamlyn, Thomas T., Jr. ....**New York, NY**
Tamm, Bradley R. ....Honolulu, HI
Tamm, James E. ....**Bloomfield Hills, MI**
Tamm, John R. ....Daytona Beach, FL
Tamm, Linda Ratnik ....Boston, MA
Tamm, Meinhard, Jr. ....Houston, TX
Tamm, R. Eugene ....Daytona Beach, FL
Tamm, Rudra, (Mr.) ....Byram, CT
Tamm & Tamm ....Daytona Beach, FL
Tammadge, Kathleen Donovan
Washington, DC
Arlington, VA
Tamman, David M. ....**Los Angeles, CA**
Tammany, D. Timothy ....Philadelphia, PA
Tammaro, Bradford L. ....Columbus, OH
Tammaro, Deborah S. ....Lakewood, OH
Tammaro, Domenick J. ....**New York, NY**
Tammaro, Katherine E. ....**Chicago, IL**
Tammaro, Michael S.
West Palm Beach, FL
Tammelleo, A. David, & Associates
Providence, RI
Tammelleo, David A. ....Providence, RI
Tammelleo, Katherine ....Providence, RI
Tammen, Arnold W. ....Muskegon, MI
Tammi, Bruce A. ....Milwaukee, WI
Tammi, Nancy D. ....Fairfield, NJ
Tammik, Maria D. ....Millbrook, NY
Tamminga, Roland R. ....Gilford, NH
Tamoney, Thomas H. ....West Hartford, CT
Tamoney, Thomas H., Jr. ....Purchase, NY
Tamony, Michael K. ....San Francisco, CA
Tamor, Jovita P. ....**San Jose, CA**
Tamor, Richard A. ....Oakland, CA
Tamoria, Leonor ....Honolulu, HI
Tamoshunas, Algy ....**Tarrytown, NY**
Tamplain, Kenneth F., Jr.
New Orleans, LA
Tamplin, Emory E., Jr. ....Bradenton, FL
Tampling, Andrew W., Jr. ....Prattville, AL
Tampone, Anita P. ....Ardsley, NY
Tamposi, James N., Jr. ....Bedford, NH
Tamposi, Peter N. ....**Manchester, NH**
Tamraz, Joel F., Law Offices of
Los Angeles, CA
Tamres, Herbert J. ....Oyster Bay, NY
Tamsberg, M. Catherine ....Raleigh, NC
Tamsen & Associates ....Melville, NY
Newburgh, NY
Tamsen, David B. ....Allen Park, MI
Tamsen, Peter ....Melville, NY
Newburgh, NY
New York, NY
Tamsen, Timothy C. ....**Goshen, NY**
Tamsen, Timothy C. ....**New Windsor, NY**
Tamsett, Clifton M., Jr. ....Albany, NY
Tamsky, Melanie B. ....**St. Louis, MO**
Tamuleviz, Charles A. ....**Providence, RI**
Tamulewicz, Ellyn B. ....**Cleveland, OH**
Tamulewicz, Jan ....**New York, NY**
Tamulonis, Frank L., Jr. ....**Pottsville, PA**
Tamulonis, Peter G. ....**Indianapolis, IN**
Tamulski, James J. ....**San Francisco, CA**
Tamura, Harry T. ....Honolulu, HI
Tamura, Jan M. ....**Honolulu, HI**
Tamura, Kaoru ....Los Angeles, CA
Tamura, Ronald S. ....**Los Angeles, CA**
Tamura, Susan ....**San Francisco, CA**
Tamura, Susan J. ....Oakland, CA
Tamzarian, Armen ....**Los Angeles, CA**
Newport Beach, CA
Tamzarian, Vaughn V. ....Manchester, NH
Tan, Alwin S. M. ....Pasadena, CA
Tan, Anne E. W. ....Phillipsburg, NJ
Tan, Carina M. ....**San Jose, CA**
Tan, Carol B. ....Washington, DC
Tan, Cedric C.Y. ....**Memphis, TN**
Tan, Colleen A. ....**New York, NY**
Tan, David S. ....**San Francisco, CA**
Tan, Eda Su Ling ....San Francisco, CA
Tan, Francesca ....**Morgantown, WV**
Tan, Herbert J. ....East Orange, NJ
Tan, Jon T. ....New York, NY
Tan, Lawrence ....Rowland Heights, CA
Tan, Madeleine M. L. ....**New York, NY**
Tan, Margaret Anaya ....Sacramento, CA
Tan, Michael W. ....Baltimore, MD
Tan, Mox ....**Chicago, IL**
Tan, Pei-San ....**New York, NY**
Tan, Pheng Theng ....**Washington, DC**
Tan, Robert Lew ....Los Angeles, CA
Tan, Robert N. ....**Santa Ana, CA**
Tan & Sakiyama ....Los Angeles, CA
Tan, Sharon M. ....Decatur, GA
Tan, Stephen J. ....**Seattle, WA**
Tan, Steven W. ....Cleveland, OH
Tan, S. Y. ....Honolulu, HI
Tan, Teresa ....Phoenix, AZ
Tan, Victor ....Albany, CA
Tan, William ....Tarrytown, NY
Tan, William L. ....Los Angeles, CA
Tana, Chinin ....**San Francisco, CA**
Tana, Kathleen M. ....**Philadelphia, PA**
Tanabe, Charles Y. ....Denver, CO
Tanabe, Craig A. ....**Hackensack, NJ**
Tanabe, David C. ....Honolulu, HI
Tanabe, Grant S. ....**Honolulu, HI**
Tanabe, Robin J. ....Fremont, CA
Tanacea, Kendra L. ....San Francisco, CA
Tanaka, Aida Saracevic ....**Chicago, IL**
Tanaka, Cary T. ....**Honolulu, HI**
Tanaka, Clayton S. ....Sacramento, CA
Tanaka, David F. ....Deerfield, IL
Tanaka, Diana ....New York, NY
Tanaka, Dwight T. ....Honolulu, HI

Tanner, James Roddy (Rod)
Fort Worth, TX
Tanner, James Roscoe
New Smyrna Beach, FL
Tanner, Jeanne Marian ... Washington, DC
Tanner, Jeremy K. ... Greenville, NC
Tanner, Jill A. ... Portland, OR
Tanner, Jill Harris ... Indianapolis, IN
Tanner, John C. ... Atlanta, GA
Tanner, John E. ... Winchester, IN
Tanner, John J. ... Tulsa, OK
Tanner, John Joseph ... Indianapolis, IN
Tanner, John K. ... Department of Justice,
Civil Rights Division, GV
Tanner, John M. ... Denver, CO
Tanner, John R. ... Hollywood, FL
Tanner, John S. ... Union City, TN
Tanner, John W. ... Daytona Beach, FL
Tanner, John W., III ... Dearborn, MI
Tanner, John W., P.A. ... Daytona Beach, FL
Tanner, Kathleen Gormley ... St. Louis, MO
Tanner Law Firm, P.A.
Daytona Beach, FL
Lakeland, FL
New Smyrna Beach, FL
Tanner, LeAnn M. ... Fuquay-Varina, NC
Tanner, Leonard R., Jr.
Lookout Mountain, GA
Tanner, Lester J. ... New York, NY
Tanner, Lynn S. ... New York, NY
Tanner, Malcolm L. ... Birmingham, AL
Tanner, Marc S. ... Boise, ID
Tanner, Mark ... Orangeville, UT
Tanner, Mark R. ... San Jose, CA
Tanner, Mark W. ... Philadelphia, PA
Tanner, Martha B. ... San Antonio, TX
Tanner, Martin S. ... Salt Lake City, UT
Tanner, Mary C. ... Buffalo, NY
Tanner, Mathewson & Hansgen
London, OH
Mechanicsburg, OH
Tanner, Matthew D. ... Chicago, IL
Tanner, Michael ... Miami, FL
Tanner, Michael A. ... Atlanta, GA
Tanner, Michael D. ... Dallas, TX
Tanner, Michael D. ... San Antonio, TX
Tanner, Michael G. ... Jacksonville, FL
Tanner, Millicent A. ... Louisville, KY
Tanner, Morris A., Jr. ... Duncanville, TX
Tanner, Mulkey & Gordon, P.C.
Newport News, VA
Yorktown, VA
Tanner, Neil Boyden ... Philadelphia, PA
Tanner, Patrick L. ... Salt Lake City, UT
Tanner, Paula V. ... Sacramento, CA
Tanner, Peggy H. ... Springfield, IL
Tanner, Perry A., Jr. ... Livingston, TX
Tanner, Philip G. ... Columbus, OH
Tanner Propp, LLP ... New York, NY
Tanner, R. Marshall ... Costa Mesa, CA
Tanner, Rashelle C. ... Seattle, WA
Tanner, Rebecca Greer ... Miami, FL
Tanner, Regina M. ... Visalia, CA
Tanner, Richard A. ... Upper Montclair, NJ
Tanner, Robert B. ... Ironton, OH
Tanner, Robert C. ... Tuscaloosa, AL
Tanner, Robert E., Jr. ... Jacksonville, FL
Tanner, Robert E., Jr. ... Columbus, OH
Tanner, Robert G. ... Atlanta, GA
Tanner, Robert L. ... San Jose, CA
Tanner, Robert S. ... Washington, DC
Tanner, Rod, & Associates, P.C.
Fort Worth, TX
Tanner & Rogel, P.A. ... Fuquay-Varina, NC
Tanner, Russell G. ... Escondido, CA
Tanner, Scott A. ... Franklin, IN
Tanner, Sharon Howard ... Jacksonville, FL
Tanner, Sharon L. ... Caldwell, OH
Tanner, Shelby L., Jr. ... Birmingham, AL
Tanner, Stephen A. ... Parsippany, NJ
Tanner, Stephen E. ... Woodstock, GA
Tanner, Sterling M. ... Las Vegas, NV
Tanner, Steven M. ... New York, NY
Tanner & Tanner ... Birmingham, AL
Tanner & Tanner ... Winchester, IN
Tanner & Tanner ... Barnegat, NJ
Tanner & Tanner ... Salt Lake City, UT
Tanner, Thomas W. ... Covington, LA
Tanner, Timothy N. ... New York, NY
Tanner, Troy F. ... Washington, DC
Tanner, W. Rhett ... Atlanta, GA
Tanner, William G. ... Lawrenceville, GA
Tanner, William P., III ... Irvine, CA
Tannery, Dick W. ... Lawton, OK
Tannesen, James T. ... Seattle, WA
Tanney, Catherine J.
Occupational Safety and Health Review
Commission,
Office of the General Counsel, GV
Tanney, Eno, Tanney, Griffith & Ingram,
P.A. ... Clearwater, FL
Tanney, William Drew ... Clearwater, FL
Tanney, William J. ... Clearwater, FL
Tannian, John F. ... Orlando, FL
Tannich, Betsy R. ... Warrenton, VA
Tannler, Michael J. ... Lawrenceville, NJ
Tannon, Elizabeth M. ... Louisville, KY
Tannon, Jay Middleton ... Louisville, KY
Tannous, Marlo B. ... Columbus, OH
Tannous, Robert J. ... Columbus, OH
Tannucilli, Alex J. ... Kearny, NJ
Tano, Lilliana ... Los Angeles, CA
Tano, Mervyn L. ... Denver, CO
Tanona, Mary A. ... Worcester, MA
Tanoos, Anthony A. ... Terre Haute, IN
Tanoue, Donna A. ... Honolulu, HI
Tanoue, Michael N. ... Honolulu, HI
Tanoue, Tami A. ... Denver, CO

Tanoury, John L. ... Columbus, OH
Tanoury, Mark P. ... Menlo Park, CA
Tanoury, William A. ... Detroit, MI
Tanous, E. Najla ... Houston, TX
Tanous, James J. ... Buffalo, NY
Tanous, Wakine G. ... East Millinocket, ME
Tanowitz, Ellen Rappaport
Framingham, MA
Tanquilut, Eric J. ... Chicago, IL
Tans, Gordon J ... Anchorage, AK
Tan-Sanchez, Charisma T. ... Urbana, IL
Tanselle, John W. ... Indianapolis, IN
Tansey, Andrew L. ... New York, NY
Tansey, Bernard J. ... Whitestone, NY
Tansey, Charles M., Jr. ... Farmington, NM
Tansey, Estelle R. ... Auburn, CA
Tansey, Fanning, Haggerty, Kelly, Convery
and Tracy ... Woodbridge, NJ
Staten Island, NY
Tansey, Francis X., Jr. ... Marshfield, MA
Tansey, J. Brian ... Riverdale, MD
Tansey, James G. ... Chicago, IL
Tansey, James J. ... Washington, DC
Tansey, James J. ... Richmond, VA
Tansey, John T. ... Washington, DC
Annapolis, MD
Tansey, Mary Stewart ... Springfield, MO
Tansey, Robert J., Jr. ... Minneapolis, MN
Tansey, Roger K., Jr. ... Irwindale, CA
Tansey, Thomas F. ... Woodbridge, NJ
Tansey, Thomas J., II ... Fort Lauderdale, FL
Tansil, Abner J. ... Grand Blanc, MI
Tansil, Jan Gabrielson ... Santa Rosa, CA
Tansil, Mark ... Santa Rosa, CA
Tansill, David A. ... Atlanta, GA
Tansill, Frederick J. ... McLean, VA
Tansill, Frederick J., & Associates, LLC
Washington, DC
McLean, VA
Tansill, Frederick R. ... Washington, DC
Tansill, Joseph E. ... Oshkosh, WI
Tansimore, Jeffrey D.
National Labor Relations Board,
Office of Board Members, GV
Tanski, James M. ... Hartford, CT
Tanski, Joseph C. ... Boston, MA
Tanski, Ronald J. ... Buffalo, NY
Tanski, Sharon Wirkus ... Monroeville, PA
Tanski, Thadeus A. ... Clifton, NJ
Tansley, Michael G. ... Waterbury, CT
Tant, Clarence P. ... Fairfax, VA
Tantari, Mark R. ... Toledo, OH
Tante, T. Edward, IV ... Columbus, GA
Tantillo, Mary E. ... Milpitas, CA
Tantillo, R. Michael ... Canandaigua, NY
Tantillo, Steven J. ... Chicago, IL
Tantleff, Cohen and Tantleff ... Brooklyn, NY
Tantleff, Edward Daniel ... Brooklyn, NY
Tantleff, Ivan L. ... Brooklyn, NY
Tanton, Joyce R. ... Corona Del Mar, CA
Tantra, Dina A. ... Columbus, OH
Tantum & Hamrick ... Knightdale, NC
Tantum, John E. ... Knightdale, NC
Tanur, Rachel D. ... New York, NY
Tanzer, David A. ... Vail, CO
Tanzer, David A., & Associates, P.C.
Vail, CO
Tanzer, Jacob B. ... Portland, OR
Tanzer, Jeffrey M. ... Los Angeles, CA
Tanzer, Lois B. ... Hartford, CT
Tanzer, Matthew O. ... Cleveland, OH
Tanzer, Richard ... Los Angeles, CA
Tanzer, Solomon ... Flushing, NY
Tanzer, Steven D. ... New York, NY
Tanzer, Tobi ... Minneapolis, MN
Tanzey, Carla Wood ... Mexico, MO
Tanzi, C. William ... Greenwich, CT
New York, NY
Tanzi, Lisa J. ... Redmond, WA
Tanzie, Annisha M. ... Dallas, TX
Tanzillo, Andrew R. ... Hammond, IN
Tanzillo, Barbara E. ... Palo Alto, CA
Tanzillo, Paul A. ... Chicago, IL
Tanzine, John M., III ... Columbus, GA
Tanzler, Hans G., III ... Jacksonville, FL
Tanzler, Hans G., Jr. ... Jacksonville, FL
Tanzman, Edward A. ... Argonne, IL
Tanzman, Mitchell A. ... New York, NY
Tanzman, Roy H. ... Woodbridge, NJ
Tanzy, Jerry ... El Paso, TX
Tao, Cathy H. ... Los Angeles, CA
Tao, Elizabeth J. Yalin ... New York, NY
Tao, Ellen S. ... Washington, DC
New York, NY
Tao, Eric V. ... San Francisco, CA
Tao, James F. ... Rochester, NY
Tao, Joan C. ... San Francisco, CA
Tao, Josephine J. ... Washington, DC
Tao, Leonard Michael ... Department of Energy,
Office of Hearings and Appeals, GV
Tao, Louis L.S. ... Washington, DC
Tao, Terry T. ... Cerritos, CA
Tao, Theresa V. ... Palo Alto, CA
Tao, X. Ben ... Honolulu, HI
Taomae, Patrick Y. ... Honolulu, HI
Taomae & Tamanaha, A Law Corporation
Honolulu, HI
Taoras, Bronius K. ... Cleveland, OH
Taormina, Anthony S. ... Metairie, LA
Taormina, Robert A. ... Ada, MI
Taormino, Frank J. ... Brooklyn, NY
Taosaka, Ross N. ... Honolulu, HI
Tapanes, Mario A. ... Los Angeles, CA
Tapanes, Mario U. ... Los Angeles, CA
Taparauskas, Paul ... Houston, TX
Tape, Linda W. ... St. Louis, MO
Tapella, Carlena L. ... Sacramento, CA
Tapella, William R. ... Charleston, IL

Tapfar, Gregory R. ... White Plains, NY
Tapfer, Kimberly E. ... Denver, CO
Taphorn, Joseph B. ... Poughkeepsie, NY
Tapia, Arthur A. ... San Jose, CA
Tapia & Aviles ... San Juan, PR
Tapia, John Albert ... Elmhurst, NY
Tapia, Lorenzo E. ... Albuquerque, NM
Tapia, Raul R. ... Washington, DC
Tapia, Rebecca A. ... Downey, CA
Tapia, Rosalia Burgueño ... San Jose, CA
Tapia, Sergio C., II ... Los Angeles, CA
Tapia, Steven P. ... Redmond, WA
Tapia, Thomas E. ... Las Vegas, NM
Tapia-Flores, Angel L. ... San Juan, PR
Tapia-Ruano, Carlina ... Chicago, IL
Tapie, Rebecca A. ... New York, NY
Tapley, D. Duston, Jr. ... Vidalia, GA
Tapley, Kate ... Washington, DC
Taplin, A. Russell ... San Francisco, CA
Taplin, Arlene C. ... Marysville, WA
Taplin, Dennis M. ... Carmichael, CA
Taplin, Edgar L., Jr. ... Fairfax, VA
Taplin, Irvin, Jr. ... Sacramento, CA
Taplin, Jay A. ... Fort Lauderdale, FL
Taplin, Lisa M. ... Everett, WA
Taplin, Martin W. ... Bay Harbor Islands, FL
Taplin, Norman E. ... West Palm Beach, FL
Taplits, Steven ... Franklin Lakes, NJ
Taplitz, Richard D. ... San Francisco, CA
Tapocsi-Lohmeyer, Jo Anne ... Valparaiso, IN
Tapogna, Anthony M. ... Hartford, CT
Tapp, Barry M.
Department Of Veterans Affairs,
Office of the General Counsel, GV
Tapp, George Michael ... Oklahoma City, OK
Tapp, John Sky
Hot Springs National Park, AR
Tapp, John W. ... Seattle, WA
Tapp, Michael G. ... Houston, TX
Tapp, Richard Lee, Jr. ... Charleston, SC
Tapp, Richard N. ... Greenville, SC
Tapp, Richard N., P.A. ... Greenville, SC
Tapp, Tylar ... Hot Springs National Park, AR
Tappa, James L. ... Rock Island, IL
Tappa, Robert Francis ... Rock Island, IL
Tappa, Tonya S. ... Rock Island, IL
Tappan, Charles S. ... Cincinnati, OH
Tappana, Gary W. ... St. Louis, MO
Tappe, Lee A. ... Platte, SD
Tappel, Catherine A. ... Portland, OR
Tappendorf, Julie A. ... Chicago, IL
Tapper, Jack W. ... Las Vegas, NV
Tapper, Joseph M. ... Bloomfield, CT
Tapper, Joyce Katz ... Baltimore, MD
Tapper, Mark L. ... Springfield, VT
Tapper, Patricia E. ... Houston, TX
Tapper, Steven M. ... Gainesville, GA
Tapper, Una R. ... New York, NY
Tapper-Catrillo, Barbara ... Jersey City, NJ
Tappin, C. William ... Pasadena, CA
Taps, Marc E. ... Tallahassee, FL
Taps, Richard T. ... Columbus, OH
Tapscott, Andrew J. ... Richmond, VA
Tapscott, Barbara M. ... Des Moines, IA
Tapscott, Leo J. ... Des Moines, IA
Tapscott, Michael D. ... Tupelo, MS
Tapscott, Robert W., Jr. ... Birmingham, AL
Tapscott, William Ken, Jr. ... Dallas, TX
Tapson, Stephen A. ... Placerville, CA
Taqi, Syeda ... Detroit, MI
Tara, Annee ... Auburn, ME
Tara, Christopher J. ... Rolling Hills, CA
Tara, John S. ... Brockton, MA
Tarab, Margaret Burke ... Garden City, NY
Taraba, Gary W. ... Dallas, TX
Tarabicos, Larry J. ... Wilmington, DE
Tarabicos, Stephanie M. ... Wilmington, DE
Tarabour, Albert ... Jensen Beach, FL
Tarabour, Sheila W. ... West Orange, NJ
Tarachas, Achilles J. ... Saginaw, MI
Taracido, M. D. ... New York, NY
Taracks, Barry K. ... Clearwater, FL
New Port Richey, FL
Tampa, FL
Taradash, Alan R. ... Albuquerque, NM
Taradash & Bentley ... McHenry, IL
Taradash, Christine R. ... Phoenix, AZ
Taradash, John William ... Phoenix, AZ
Taradash, Mary K. ... McHenry, IL
Taradash, Randall M. ... McHenry, IL
Taraday, Jeffrey ... Seattle, WA
Taragin, Arnold C. ... Baltimore, MD
Tarajano, Jose R., Jr. ... Long Island City, NY
Tarallo, Mark J. ... Boston, MA
Tarallo, Michelle ... De Kalb, IL
Tarallo, Nicholas ... New York, NY
Tarallo, Phillip S. ... Schaumburg, IL
Taran, Jesse ... New York, NY
Taran, Larissa Omelchenko
United States Postal Service,
Law Department, GV
Tarangioli, Edward G., Jr. ... Plano, TX
Tarango, Marcos M. ... Los Angeles, CA
Tarango, Ruben ... San Diego, CA
Tarantelli, Louis E. ... Elmira, NY
Tarantine, Richard R. ... Pittsburgh, PA
Tarantino, Andrew G., Jr. ... Coram, NY
Tarantino, Arthur E. ... Washington, DC
Tarantino, Carmen P. ... Buffalo, NY
Tarantino, Dennis J. ... Glens Falls, NY
Tarantino, John A. ... Boston, MA
Providence, RI
Tarantino, Joseph Burke ... Washington, DC
Tarantino, L. Gerald ... Boston, MA
Tarantino, Lynda M. ... Buffalo, NY
Tarantino, Mark P. ... Columbus, NJ
Tarantino, Richard P. ... Glens Falls, NY
Tarantino, Rosemary ... Springfield, MA

Tarantino, Salvatore ... San Diego, CA
Tarantino, Thomas E. ... New York, NY
Tarantino, Thomas J. ... Cleveland, OH
Tarantino, Walter R. ... Carson City, NV
Taranto, Frank S. ... San Jose, CA
Taranto, Jacob, III ... Metairie, LA
Taranto, Jenean M. ... Slingerlands, NY
Taranto, Joseph A. ... Metairie, LA
Taranto, Leon B. ... Washington, DC
Taranto, Norah C. ... Chalmette, LA
Taranto, Richard G. ... Washington, DC
Taranto, Thomas J. ... Wakefield, MA
Taranto, Thomas M. ... Jamaica, NY
Taranto, Vincent P. ... Glen Cove, NY
Tarantola, Leslie E. ... Camp Springs, MD
Tarantowicz, Laurie A. ... Washington, DC
Tarara, Alfonso P. ... St. Paul, MN
Taras, Bert ... Brooklyn, NY
Taras, Mitchell ... New York, NY
Taraschi, Carl L. ... Burlington, NJ
Taraschi, Mitchell W. ... Roseland, NJ
Tarasczuk, Christina ... Duluth, MN
Tarasevich, Deborah A. ... Washington, DC
Tarasevich, Matthew ... Portland, ME
Tarasi, Elizabeth M. ... Pittsburgh, PA
Tarasi Law Firm, The, P.C.
Pittsburgh, PA
Tarasi, Louis M., Jr. ... Pittsburgh, PA
Taraska, Joseph Martin ... Orlando, FL
Taraska, Sharon L. ... Stamford, CT
Taraskus, Edward A. ... Philadelphia, PA
Tarasuk, George J. ... Hamtramck, MI
Tarasuk, Steven ... New York, NY
Taratuta, Stephen M. ... Detroit, MI
Taravella, Christopher A. ... Southfield, MI
Tarawally, Sorie S. ... Jackson, MS
Tarazi, Carla V. ... San Francisco, CA
Tarbe, Susan ... Miami, FL
Tarbell, Eaton W., III ... Concord, NH
Tarbell, Eaton W., Jr. ... Concord, NH
Tarbell Professional Association
Concord, NH
Tarbell, Robt. E. ... Woodland Hills, CA
Tarbert, David J. ... Gainesville, FL
Tarbert, David J. ... Zanesville, OH
Tarbert, Molly L. ... Zanesville, OH
Tarbert, Todd R. ... Bellevue, WA
Tarbet, David W. ... Boston, MA
Tarbet, Karen E. ... Oakland Park, FL
Tarbet, Kenneth H. ... Seattle, WA
Tarbet, Michael J. ... Santa Monica, CA
Tarbox, Charles C. ... Gettysburg, PA
Tarbox, Eric J. ... Columbus, OH
Tarbox, Frank K. ... Philadelphia, PA
Tarbox, Jonathan A. ... Coral Springs, FL
Tarbox, Max R. ... Lubbock, TX
Tarbox, Max R., & Associates ... Lubbock, TX
Tarbox, Robert V. ... Edina, MN
Tarbox, Scott M. ... Denver, CO
Tarbox, Thomas R. ... Minneapolis, MN
Tarbox, Thomas T. ... Des Moines, IA
Tarbuck, Joseph Q. ... Pensacola, FL
Tarbutton, Benjamin R. ... Atlanta, GA
Tarbutton, Roger L. ... Olathe, KS
Tarby, Joseph R., III ... Woburn, MA
Tarby, Richard M. ... Washington, DC
Tarchala, William F. ... Stockton, CA
Tarcher, Abraham J. ... Lake Worth, FL
Tarcher, Herbert P. ... Bronx, NY
Tarchi, Elizabeth Aguilar ... San Francisco, CA
Tarchinski, Theresa A. ... Akron, OH
Tarcza & Gelderman, L.L.C.
New Orleans, LA
Tarcza, Robert E. ... New Orleans, LA
Tardera, John E. ... New York, NY
Tardie, Kenneth A. ... Mount Clemens, MI
Tardif, David E. ... Concord, NH
Tardif, Michael E. ... Olympia, WA
Tardif, Paul R. ... West Yarmouth, MA
Tardif, Robert E., Jr. ... Fort Myers, FL
Tardif, Robt. G. ... Miami, FL
Tardif, Shapiro and Cassidy ... Concord, NH
Tardiff, David C., Law Offices of
Beverly Hills, CA
Tardiff, John G. ... Winthrop, MA
Tardiff, Kristine S. ... Department of Justice,
Environment and Natural Resources
Division, GV
Tardiff, Mary Ann ... Santa Barbara, CA
Tardiff, Neil S. ... San Luis Obispo, CA
Tardiff, Richard M. ... Boston, MA
Tardiff, Robert F., Jr. ... San Bernardino, CA
Tardio, James ... Greenville, KY
Tarduno, Mary E. ... Los Angeles, CA
Tardy, Ann ... Palo Alto, CA
Tardy, Cassandra L. ... Toledo, OH
Tardy, Joshua A. ... Newport, ME
Tardy, Sabrina ... Washington, DC
Tardy, Thomas W., III ... Jackson, MS
Tarella, James A. ... North Brunswick, NJ
Tarella & Liftman ... North Brunswick, NJ
Taren, Jeffrey L. ... Chicago, IL
Tarenzi, Carla F. ... Forest Hills, NY
Tareshawty, Brian J. ... Youngstown, OH
Targ, David ... New York, NY
Targ, Elyse K. ... Miami, FL
Targ, Robert I. ... Miami, FL
Targan, Amy ... West Orange, NJ
Targan, Anthony A. ... Southfield, MI
Targan, Donald G. ... Atlantic City, NJ
Targan, Donald G., & Associates, A Prof.
Corp. ... Atlantic City, NJ
Targan, Holli Hart ... Detroit, MI
Targan, Ronald G. ... West Orange, NJ
Targan, Royal G., (P.C.) ... Dearborn, MI
Targer, Lloyd R. ... New York, NY
Targia, Anthony B. ... Buffalo, NY
Targia, Joseph ... Christiansted, St. Croix, VI

Tasoff, Diane E. ....Encino, CA
Tasoff, Richard J. ....Encino, CA
Tasoff, Ron Jeffrey ....Encino, CA
Tasoff and Tasoff ....Encino, CA
Los Angeles, CA
Tasolides, John N. ....Jericho, NY
Tass, Morris H. ....Cuyahoga Falls, OH
Tassan, Bruce A. ....Washington, DC
Tassan, Louis S. ....Garden City, NY
Tassan, Luisa A. ....Sudbury, MA
Tassano, Al ....Stockton, CA
Tassche, Edmund R. ....Gaithersburg, MD
Tasse, James L. ....Lakewood, OH
Tasse, Jeffrey L. ....Cleveland, OH
Tassel, Neil S. ....Boston, MA
Tassell, David C. ....Orlando, FL
Tassell-Getman, Terri L. ....Des Moines, IA
Tassi, Arthur J. ....Cleveland, OH
Tassi, Denise Jakabcin ....Alexandria, VA
Tassi, Elaine ....Chardon, OH
Tassi, Julie A. ....Washington, DC
Tassie, Deborah S. ....Toledo, OH
Tassie, H. Clifford ....Port Angeles, WA
Tassie, James G. ....Elyria, OH
Tassie, Peter N. ....Dearborn, MI
Tassillo, John M., Jr. ....Roseland, NJ
Tassin, James ....Tuscumbia, AL
Tassin, Kristin Kittrell ....Houston, TX
Tassin, Terry J., Jr. ....Portland, OR
Tassinari, Robert ....Springfield, MA
Tassinari, Robert P., Jr.
Yorktown Heights, NY
Tassinari, Vincent P. ....Los Angeles, CA
Tasso, Jon P. ....Tampa, FL
Tasso, Peter G., Jr. ....Albuquerque, NM
Tassone, Augustine C. ....Grass Valley, CA
Tassone, Bruno J. ....Chicago, IL
Tassone, Caterina P. ....Chicago, IL
Tassone & Eler ....Jacksonville, FL
Tassone, Eric C. ....Tampa, FL
Tassone, Frank J., Jr. ....Jacksonville, FL
Tassone, Joseph V. ....Dayton, OH
Tassone, Karen R. ....Beverly Hills, CA
Tassone, Marc J. ....Boston, MA
Tassone, Marlene C. ....Los Angeles, CA
Tassoni, Frank A. ....Attleboro, MA
Tasy, Stephen P. ....Warren, NJ
Tata, Elaine R. ....Holyoke, MA
Tata, Robert M. ....Norfolk, VA
Tata, Vijay S. ....New York, NY
Tataje, Sandra ....Hackensack, NJ
Tatalovich, Milan ....Girard, OH
Tatar, Howard J. ....Chicago, IL
Tatar, Jerome A. ....Oak Brook, IL
Tatar, Lauren D. W. ....Chicago, IL
Tatar, Leonard B. ....Houston, TX
Tatara, Irene ....Golf, IL
Tatarian, Brian I. ....Fresno, CA
Tatarian, Kenneth H. ....Boston, MA
Tatarsky, David M. ....Greenwood, SC
Tatarsky, Kathleen Ozak ....Canton, OH
Tataru, Terry, Co., L.P.A. ....Columbus, OH
Tataru, Terry L. ....Columbus, OH
Tataryn, Andrew M. ....Minneapolis, MN
Tatayon, Sheila M. ....Rancho Cordova, CA
Tate, Alan D. ....Los Angeles, CA
Tate, Alan R. ....Providence, RI
Wakefield, RI
Taté& Associates ....Atlanta, GA
Tate & Associates ....Richmond, TX
Tate, Atwood B. ....Glen Burnie, MD
Tate, Bernadette A. ....Omaha, NE
Tate, Beth B. ....Charlotte, NC
Tate, Bomba & Shelton, PLLC
Cedar Mountain, NC
Tate & Bywater, Ltd. ....Washington, DC
La Plata, MD
Alexandria, VA
Sterling, VA
Vienna, VA
Woodbridge, VA
Tate, C. Richard, Jr. ....High Point, NC
Tate, Carol L. ....St. Louis, MO
Tate, Caryn I. ....Tucson, AZ
Tate, Charles M. ....Greensboro, NC
Tate, Cheryl J. ....Cleveland, OH
Tate, Christopher F. ....Washington, DC
Tate, Claire Lavender ....Sherman, TX
Tate, D. Lynn ....Amarillo, TX
Tate, David A. ....Loudonville, NY
Tate, David K. ....Winston-Salem, NC
Tate, David L. ....Wichita Falls, TX
Tate, David W. ....Palo Alto, CA
Tate, Davie, Jr. ....Clarion, PA
Tate, Deborah Miller ....Providence, RI
Tate, Deborah T. ....Nashville, TN
Tate, Donald J. ....Mamou, LA
Tate, Donald J., Jr. ....Hoosick Falls, NY
Tate, Douglas A. ....Kokomo, IN
Tate, E. Murray, Jr. ....Hickory, NC
Tate, Earl S. ....Longview, TX
Tate and Edwards, P.L.L.P.
Statesville, NC
Tate, Edwin A., II ....Atlanta, GA
Tate & Elias ....Providence, RI
Wakefield, RI
Tate, Elizabeth D. ....Merrillville, IN
Tate, Emory A. ....Chicago, IL
Tate, Eric A. ....Palo Alto, CA
Taté, Ernest N. ....Atlanta, GA
Tate, Erton Frank ....Wichita Falls, TX
Tate, Farrell D.
National Labor Relations Board, Office of the General Counsel, GV
Tate, Frederick G. ....New York, NY
Tate, George J. ....Abbeville, LA
Tate, Gowan & Wilson, P.L.L.C.
Wichita Falls, TX

Tate, Granville, Jr. ....Jackson, MS
Tate, H. Richard, Jr. ....Knoxville, TN
Tate, H. Simmons, Jr. ....Columbia, SC
Tate, Hardy H. ....Sheridan, WY
Tate, Harry G. ....Durango, CO
Tate, Harry G., P.C. ....Durango, CO
Tate, Iris A. ....New Orleans, LA
Tate, J. David ....Bellaire, TX
Tate, J. Martin ....Salt Lake City, UT
Tate, James R. ....Vienna, VA
Tate, James S., Jr. ....Nashville, TN
Tate, James T., Jr. ....Department of Defense, Defense Legal Services Agency, GV
Tate, James W., II ....Henderson, KY
Tate, Jeanne LaRue ....San Jose, CA
Tate, Jeanne Trudeau ....Tampa, FL
Tate, Jeffrey E. ....Oklahoma City, OK
Tate, Joanna Davis ....Dallas, TX
Tate, John E. ....Omaha, NE
Tate, John E. ....New Bremen, OH
Tate, John E., Jr. ....Cedar Mountain, NC
Tate, John H., II ....San Antonio, TX
Tate, John H., Jr. ....Marion, VA
Tate, John L. ....Louisville, KY
Tate, John R. ....Los Angeles, CA
Tate, Jonathan O. ....Ronkonkoma, NY
Tate, Jonathan O., P.C. ....Ronkonkoma, NY
Tate, Joseph A. ....Philadelphia, PA
Tate, Joseph S. ....Marion, VA
Tate, June B. ....Chicago, IL
Tate, Karen J. ....Houston, TX
Tate, Karen L. ....Adrian, MI
Tate, Kathryn Willcox ....
Department of Labor, GV
Tate, Kearney ....Eunice, LA
Tate, Kimberly Cash ....Madison, WI
Tate, Kirk W. ....Austin, TX
Tate, Larry E. ....Boonville, MO
Tate, Larry I. ....Raleigh, NC
Tate, Laura K. ....Pittsburgh, PA
Tate, Lauren E. ....San Francisco, CA
Tate, Lavern, (Mr.) ....Florence, AL
Tate Law Firm, The ....Bristol, TN
Kingsport, TN
Abingdon, VA
Bristol, VA
Gate City, VA
Grundy, VA
Tate, Law Firm, The ....Lebanon, VA
Tate Law Firm, The ....Marion, VA
Wise, VA
Tate, Lazarini & Beall, PLC
Memphis, TN
Tate, Ltd., A Prof. Law Corp. ....Eunice, LA
Tate, Lucy Lynch ....Charlotte, NC
Tate, Maj-Le R. ....Los Angeles, CA
Tate, Mark A. ....Savannah, GA
Tate, Mark T., Jr. ....Tampa, FL
Tate, Mary Lynn ....Abingdon, VA
Tate, Matthew Bernard ....Philadelphia, PA
Tate, Maurice "Marty", III
The Woodlands, TX
Tate, Michael E. ....Schenectady, NY
Tate, Milton Y., Jr. ....Brenham, TX
Tate, Monice Tate ....Memphis, TN
Tate, Monroe D., II ....Picayune, MS
Tate, Patricia E. ....Atlanta, GA
Tate, Patrick H. ....Fort Payne, AL
Tate, Patrick H., P.A. ....Fort Payne, AL
Tate, Penfield W., III ....Denver, CO
Tate, R. Tim ....Houston, TX
Tate, Ragan S. ....Dallas, TX
Tate, Ralph B. ....Birmingham, AL
Tate, Ralph R. ....Salt Lake City, UT
Tate, Raymond A., Jr. ....Anderson, SC
Tate, Regina Williams ....Quincy, MA
Tate, Ricardo L. ....Chicago, IL
Tate, Richard G. ....San Antonio, TX
Tate, Richard L. ....Richmond, TX
Tate, Robert E. ....Mineola, NY
Tate, Robert G. ....Birmingham, AL
Tate, Robert J. ....Pittsburgh, PA
Tate, Robert T., Jr. ....Wilton, CT
Tate, Robert W. ....Seattle, WA
Tate, Rodger L. ....Washington, DC
Tate, Ronald G., Jr. ....Greenville, SC
Tate, S. Lester, III ....Cartersville, GA
Tate, S. Shepherd ....Memphis, TN
Tate, Samuel McDowell ....Morganton, NC
Tate, Sarah E. ....Treasury Department, Internal Revenue Service, GV
Tate, Sarah Lindsay ....Raleigh, NC
Tate, Sharon L. ....Los Angeles, CA
Tate, Shepherd D. ....Memphis, TN
Tate, Sonja R. ....Augusta, GA
Tate, Stanley D. ....Seattle, WA
Tate, Stanley L. ....Carrollton, GA
Tate, Stephen ....Westport, CT
Tate, Steven G. ....Statesville, NC
Tate, Stuart L. ....Ponca City, OK
Tate, Susan P. ....Athens, GA
Tate, T. Scott ....San Francisco, CA
Tate, Tamara Powell ....Irvine, CA
Tate & Tate ....Houston, TX
Tate & Tate, P.C. ....Denver, CO
Tate, Thomas B. ....South St. Paul, MN
Tate, Thomas H. ....Los Angeles, CA
Tate, Thomas J. ....Indianapolis, IN
Tate, Thomas T. ....Lawrenceville, GA
Tate, Tom ....Proctor, OK
Tate, Walter E. ....Fort Worth, TX
Tate, Wayne P. ....San Juan Capistrano, CA
Tate, Wayne R. ....Hugoton, KS
Tate, William B., II ....Irvine, CA
Tate, William D. ....Grapevine, TX
Tate, William H. ....Nashville, TN

Tate, Young, Morphis, Bach and Taylor, L.L.P. ....Hickory, NC
Newton, NC
Tateishi & Associates ....Honolulu, HI
Wailuku, HI
Tateishi, Michael K. ....Wailuku, HI
Tatel, Barry M. ....Roanoke, VA
Tatel, David S.
United States Court Of Appeals District Of Columbia Circuit, GV
Tatelbaum, Charles M. ....Naples, FL
Tatelbaum, Hyman P. ....Miami Beach, FL
Tatelbaum, Mark F. ....Washington, DC
Tatelman, Karen ....Denver, CO
Tatelman, Susan D. ....Revere, MA
Tatem, David G. ....Houston, TX
Tatem, James A., III ....Houston, TX
Tatem, James A., Jr. ....Houston, TX
Tatem, James H. ....Fredericksburg, VA
Tatem, Stephen B., Jr. ....El Paso, TX
Tatem, Valarie Ann ....Detroit, MI
Tate-Mathis, Jacqueline D. ....Austin, TX
Taten, Bruce M. ....Houston, TX
Taten, Michael E. ....Dallas, TX
Tateoka, Reid ....Salt Lake City, UT
Tateosian, John ....Hampstead, NH
Tater, Steve W. ....Bedford Heights, OH
Cleveland, OH
Taterka, Bruce D. ....Morristown, NJ
Taterka, Steven Andrew
Kingston Springs, TN
Tateronis, Arthur A. ....Auburn, MA
Tateronis, Craig M. ....Boston, MA
Tatevosian, Karine ....Los Angeles, CA
Tatevossian, Armond A. ....Orange, CA
Tatford, Archie C., Jr. ....New Orleans, LA
Tatge, David B. ....Washington, DC
Tatgenhorst & Bruestle ....Cincinnati, OH
Tatgenhorst, Robert ....Cincinnati, OH
Tatham, Charles H. ....Birmingham, MI
Tatham, Michael F. ....Fresno, CA
Tatham, Robert B., (P.C.) ....Eastpointe, MI
Tatham, Thos. L. ....Miami, FL
Tatich Downing & Shirley ....Maitland, FL
Tatich, Philip ....Maitland, FL
Tatigian, Harry C. ....Livonia, MI
Tatikian, Katherine ....Los Angeles, CA
Tatken, Morton J. ....Detroit, MI
Tatkenhorst, Mark Andrew ....Dallas, TX
Tatkin, David A. ....Phoenix, AZ
Tatkin, Lowell W. ....Los Angeles, CA
Tatlock, John H. ....Denver, CO
Tatlock, William ....New York, NY
Tatlow, Gary A. ....Moberly, MO
Tatlow & Gump ....Moberly, MO
Tatlow, Michael Q. ....New Brunswick, NJ
Tatlow, Paul V. ....Philadelphia, PA
Tatlow, Phillip A. ....St. Louis, MO
Tatlow, Rebecca J. ....Springfield, MO
Tatman, Molly Jennifer ....New York, NY
Tatnall, Susan B. ....Batavia, IL
Tato, Joseph A. ....Newark, NJ
Tatoian, Phillip E., Jr. ....Willow Grove, PA
Tatoian, Richard M. ....Enfield, CT
Tatol, Julie G. ....Miami, FL
Tatom, Kyle D. ....Abilene, TX
Tatom, Marx F., II ....Huntsville, AL
Tatone, Kathy A. ....Minneapolis, MN
Tatone, Paul M. ....Bloomington, MN
Tatone, Paul M., P.A. ....Bloomington, MN
Tatonetti, Stephen M. ....Cherry Hill, NJ
Tatooles, Dean J. ....Chicago, IL
Tatooles, Foley, Kluever & Gibson
Chicago, IL
Tatooles, James P. ....Wheeling, IL
Tatooles, John J. ....Chicago, IL
Tator, Malcolm R. ....Ventura, CA
Tatro Coffino Zeavin Bloomgarden LLP
Los Angeles, CA
San Francisco, CA
Tatro, René P. ....Los Angeles, CA
San Francisco, CA
Tatro, Susan M. ....Albany, NY
Tatro, Timothy J. ....San Diego, CA
Tatro, Todd R. ....Clovis, CA
Tatsuda, Charles ....Minneapolis, MN
Tatsugi & Associates ....Los Angeles, CA
Tatsugi, Kenji ....Los Angeles, CA
Tatsuguchi, Emmeline S. ....San Francisco, CA
Tatsui, Kiyoko ....Los Angeles, CA
Tattan, William C. ....Worcester, MA
Tattenbaum, Ian ....New York, NY
Tatter, Sarah Jane ....River Forest, IL
Tattersall, Hargreaves V., III ....Las Vegas, NV
Tattersall, J. C. Wm. ....Elyria, OH
Tatterson, Jeffrey D. ....Russell, KY
Tattoni, Julie Riley ....Princeton, NJ
Tatulli, Anthony ....Short Hills, NJ
Tatum, Alan C. ....Houston, TX
Tatum, Allyn C. ....Little Rock, AR
Tatum, Anthony P. ....Atlanta, GA
Tatum, Brian Steed ....Atlanta, GA
Tatum, C. Albert, III ....Dallas, TX
Tatum, Charles B. "Barry" ....Lebanon, TN
Tatum, Charles C., Jr. ....Jasper, AL
Tatum, Charles C. Jr., P.C. ....Jasper, AL
Tatum, Christine Petersen ....Boca Raton, FL
Tatum, Connie D. ....Wichita, KS
Tatum, Daniel L. ....Fort Worth, TX
Tatum, Danny W. ....Ruston, LA
Tatum, David M. ....Dallas, TX
Tatum, Edwin B. ....Clovis, NM
Tatum, Elizabeth Gray ....Atlanta, GA
Tatum, Erika Perrone ....Montgomery, AL
Tatum, F. Lloyd ....Henderson, TN
Tatum, Frank D., Jr. ....San Francisco, CA
Tatum, Franklin M., III ....Los Angeles, CA
Richmond, VA

Tatum, Fred M., Jr. ....Galveston, TX
Tatum, H. Eugene, III ....Durham, NC
Tatum, I. Dyke ....Nashville, TN
Tatum, J. Thomas, II ....Danville, AR
Tatum, James M., Jr. ....Durham, NC
Tatum, James T., Jr. ....Huntsville, AL
Tatum, J. C., III ....Fayetteville, TX
Tatum, Jeffery Anne ....Menlo Park, CA
Tatum, John G. ....Dallas, TX
Tatum, John H. ....Lufkin, TX
Tatum, John L. ....West Bloomfield, MI
Tatum, John L., P.C. ....West Bloomfield, MI
Tatum, John M. ....Atlanta, GA
Savannah, GA
Tatum, John M., III ....Beaufort, SC
Tatum, John S. ....Aurora, CO
Tatum, John T. ....Danville, AR
Tatum & Jones ....Nashville, TN
Tatum, Kenny ....Milwaukee, WI
Tatum, Kenyatta L. ....Chicago, IL
Tatum, L. Kay ....Washington, DC
Tatum, Lloyd R. ....Henderson, TN
Tatum, Luan ....Lufkin, TX
Tatum, Lynn Mullady ....Henderson, TN
Tatum, Mark C. ....Kansas City, MO
Tatum, Mary Ellen ....Salinas, CA
Tatum & McDowell ....Clovis, NM
Tatum, Patrick M. ....Jackson, MS
Tatum, Paul E., Jr. ....Nacogdoches, TX
Tatum, Rife and Tatum ....Danville, AR
Tatum, Stephen L. ....Fort Worth, TX
Tatum, Stephen Mark ....Shreveport, LA
Tatum, Tatum & Weinman ....Henderson, TN
Tatum, Thomas R. ....Fort Lauderdale, FL
Tatum, Tom ....Whitehouse, TX
Tatum, Vickie C. ....Austin, TX
Tatum, William Blanton ....Huntsville, AL
Tatusko, Wayne G. ....McLean, VA
Taub, Adam G. ....Southfield, MI
Taub, Amy Rosenthal ....Hartsdale, NY
Taub, Andrew L. ....Huntington, NY
Taub, Arnold T. ....New York, NY
Taub, Barry ....New York, NY
Taub, Bruce F. ....Memphis, TN
Taub, Cynthia L. ....Washington, DC
Taub, Daniel S. ....New York, NY
Taub, David L. ....New York, NY
Taub, David M. ....Los Angeles, CA
Taub, Deborah M. ....Roseland, NJ
Taub, Dena R. ....Boca Raton, FL
Taub, Edward L. ....Portland, OR
Taub, Eli I. ....Schenectady, NY
Taub, Eli I., P.C., Law Firm of
Schenectady, NY
Taub, Elliot H. ....New York, NY
Taub, Elston A. ....Union, NJ
Taub, Glenn M. ....Naples, FL
Taub, Herman ....New York, NY
Putnam Valley, NY
Taub, Iven R. ....Harrison, NY
Taub, Iven R. ....New York, NY
Taub, Jeffrey D. ....New York, NY
Taub, Jennifer Lynn ....Lexington, MA
Taub, Jennifer S. ....Stamford, CT
Taub, Joelle B. ....New York, NY
Taub, Jonathan ....Washington, DC
Taub, Kathy S. ....Chicago, IL
Taub, Kenneth M. ....Brooklyn, NY
Taub, Lawrence N. ....Largo, MD
Taub, Lawrence S., (P.C.) ....Santa Fe, NM
Taub, Linda Marsha ....Woodbury, NY
Taub, Loren R. ....New York, NY
Taub, Malcolm S. ....New York, NY
Taub & Marder ....New York, NY
Taub, Melissa M. ....Stamford, CT
Taub, Melvin S. ....Fairfield, NJ
Taub, Michael J. ....New York, NY
Taub, Michael L. ....White Plains, NY
Taub, Michele Elise ....New York, NY
Taub, Nadine H. ....Newark, NJ
Taub, Peter S. ....New York, NY
Taub, Philip B. ....Manchester, NH
Taub, Randi E. ....Garden City, NY
Taub, Randy Ford ....Richardson, TX
Taub, Richard F. ....Boca Raton, FL
Taub, Richard S. ....Scottsdale, AZ
Taub, Robert, & Associates ....Tacoma, WA
Taub, Robert B. ....Tacoma, WA
Taub, Robin B. ....Washington, DC
Bethesda, MD
Taub, Samuel ....Boynton Beach, FL
Taub, Shmuel D. ....Brooklyn, NY
Taub, Shmuel D., P.C. ....Brooklyn, NY
Taub, Simon ....Beverly Hills, CA
Taub, Stephen R. ....Garden City, NY
Taub, Steven C. ....New York, NY
Taub, Steven P. ....Washington, DC
Taub, Steven P. ....Waukegan, IL
Taub and Taub ....Fairfield, NJ
Taub & Taub, P.A. ....Boca Raton, FL
Taub, Theodore C., (P.A.) ....Tampa, FL
Taub, Zisl H. ....Chicago, IL
Taub Corrigan, Katherine T.
Newport Beach, CA
Taube, Donald H. ....Marion, OH
Taube, Donna G. ....Bronx, NY
Taube, Eric J. ....Austin, TX
Taube, Gerald ....Portsmouth, NH
Taube, Gregory M. ....Atlanta, GA
Taube, Jack, (P.C.) ....Syosset, NY
Taube, Kenneth P. ....Chicago, IL
Taube, Lawrence U. ....West Palm Beach, FL
Taube, Richard S. ....Memphis, TN
Taube, Robt. J. ....Lansing, MI
Taube, Seth T. ....Newark, NJ
Taubenblatt, Joel D.
Federal Communications Commission, Wireless Telecommunications Bureau, GV

Taubenblatt, Leonard ... New York, NY
Taubenblatt & Mopper ... New York, NY
Taubeneck, T. D. ... Mount Laurel, NJ
Taubenfeld, David R. N. ... Dallas, TX
Taubenfeld, Elaine M. ... Los Angeles, CA
Taubenfeld, Harry S. ... Cedarhurst, NY
Taubenfeld, Howard J. ... Dallas, TX
Taubenfeld, Marc W. ... Dallas, TX
Taubenhaus, Barbara A. ... Boston, MA
Taubenhaus, David A. ... Houston, TX
Tauber, Aaron E. ... New York, NY
Tauber, Adele S. ... New York, NY
Tauber, Arnold J. ... Brooklyn, NY
Tauber, Ayelet Vita ... White Plains, NY
Tauber, Charles ... Freeport, NY
Tauber, Frederic J. ... Park Ridge, NJ
Tauber, Joel D. ... Southfield, MI
Tauber, Joseph ... Baltimore, MD
Tauber, Joseph N. ... Stamford, CT
Tauber, Mark J. ... Washington, DC
Tauber, Marshall S. ... Bloomfield Hills, MI
Tauber, Michael G. ... Boston, MA
Providence, RI
Tauber, Paul J. ... San Francisco, CA
Tauber, Raymond R. ... Culver City, CA
Tauber, Rhett L. ... Merrillville, IN
Tauber, Robin A. ... New York, NY
Tauber, Thomas S. ... Des Moines, IA
Tauber, Wm. A. ... Bronx, NY
Tauber, Yale D. ... New York, NY
Taubert, Nicholas D. ... Chicago, IL
Taubin, Michael J. ... Garden City, NY
Taubin, Robin L. ... New York, NY
Taub-Joyce, Felice ... St. Louis, MO
Taublieb, Edward J. ... Buffalo, NY
Taubman, Bruce D. ... Cleveland, OH
Taubman, Daniel M. ... Denver, CO
Taubman, Elliot ... Block Island, RI
Taubman, Fredric P. ... Miami, FL
Taubman, Glenn M. ... Springfield, VA
Taubman, Joseph ... New York, NY
Taubman Law Offices, Ltd. ... Block Island, RI
Taubman, Lon S. ... Phoenix, AZ
Taubman, Lon S., P.C. ... Phoenix, AZ
Taubman, Louis ... New York, NY
Taubman, Nadis & Gorosh, P.C.
Southfield, MI
Taubman, Philip E. ... New York, NY
Taubman, Richard M. ... Southfield, MI
Taubman, Simpson, Young & Sulentor
Long Beach, CA
Los Angeles, CA
Newport Beach, CA
Taucher, Peter A. ... Troy, MI
Tauchert, Patricia A. ... Palatine, IL
Tauder, Milton C. ... Verona, NJ
Taue, Patricia I. ... Los Angeles, CA
Taufen, Mary Anne Glennon ... Media, PA
Taufer, Paul A. ... Philadelphia, PA
Tauger, Debra J. ... Los Angeles, CA
Tauger, Martin J. ... Englewood, CO
Tauger, Michael J. ... Englewood, CO
Tauger, Paul Nathan ... Costa Mesa, CA
Tauke, A. W. (Tony) ... Council Bluffs, IA
Tauke, Dale B. ... Chicago, IL
Tauke, Thomas J. ... Dubuque, IA
Taul, Thomas M., III ... Mobile, AL
Taulane, John B., III ... Jenkintown, PA
Taulane, John B., Jr. ... Jenkintown, PA
Taulbee, Dan R. ... Statesboro, GA
Taulbee, Edward O., IV ... Lafayette, LA
Taulbee & Escott, L.L.C. ... Lafayette, LA
Taulbee, George M. ... Charlotte, NC
Taum, R. Malia ... Honolulu, HI
Tauman, Charles S. ... Portland, OR
Tauman, Daniel S. ... Lake Worth, FL
Highland Park, IL
Tauman, Leonard K. ... Auburn, CA
Tauman, Nancy S. ... Oregon City, OR
Taunt, Charles J. ... Birmingham, MI
Taunt, Charles J., & Associates, P.L.L.C.
Birmingham, MI
Taunton, Dana G. ... Montgomery, AL
Taunton, James L. ... Macon, GA
Taunton, Keith R. ... Houston, TX
Taurek, Michael T. ... Orange, CA
Tauriello, Joseph C. ... Secaucus, NJ
Tauriello, Joseph John ... Elma, NY
Tauriello, William G. ... Flemington, NJ
Taurino, T.A. ... Los Angeles, CA
Taurinskas, P. James ... South St. Paul, MN
Taurinskas, P. James, P.A.
South St. Paul, MN
Taurman, John D. ... Washington, DC
Taurman, Kenneth R., Jr. ... New Albany, IN
Taurman, Lois J. ... Louisville, KY
Tauro, G. Joseph ... Swampscott, MA
Tauro, Joseph L. ... Boston, MA
Taus, Barry S. ... New York, NY
Taus, David M. ... Scotch Plains, NJ
Taus, Douglas ... New York, NY
Taus, James P. ... Salem, OH
Taus, Marla Wolfe ... Hackensack, NJ
New York, NY
Taus, Michael ... Pacific Palisades, CA
Taus, Robert L. ... San Antonio, TX
Tausch, Louise E. ... Texarkana, TX
Tausch, Michael C. ... Vancouver, WA
Tausche, Charles A. ... Chicago, IL
Tauscheck, Aloys L. ... Sheboygan, WI
Tauscher, Brian M. ... Washington, DC
Tauscher, Michael J. ... Troy, MI
Tauscher, Michael J., P.C. ... Detroit, MI
Troy, MI
Tausend, Fredric C. ... Seattle, WA
Tausk, Gene P. ... Houston, TX
Tauskey, Thomas F. ... Denver, CO
Tausner, Eric R. ... Minneapolis, MN
Taussig, Andrew R. ... New York, NY
Taussig, David C. ... Denver, CO
Taussig, Elaine M. ... Chicago, IL
Taussig, Eric A. ... Rye Brook, NY
Taussig, Gabriel ... New York, NY
Taussig, Greggory Paul ... Sarasota, FL
Taussig, John E. ... Glendale, CA
Taussig, John G., III ... Boulder, CO
Taussig, John G., Jr. ... Boulder, CO
Taussig, Peter E. ... Berkeley, CA
Taussig, Stuart K. ... Chicago, IL
Taussig & Taussig ... Boulder, CO
Taussig, William C. ... Boston, MA
Taute, Don W. ... Lincoln, NE
Tautkus, Rita E. ... San Francisco, CA
Tautvydas, Daiva K. ... Seattle, WA
Tauzer, Stephen M. ... Bakersfield, CA
Tauzin, Kevin P. ... Lafayette, LA
Tauzin, Kevin P., A Professional Law Corporation ... Lafayette, LA
Tavakoli, Shahram ... Los Angeles, CA
Tavakoli, Shiva ... San Francisco, CA
Tavana, John P. ... Washington, IL
Tavani, Lisa Hibner ... Atlantic City, NJ
Tavano, Joseph T. ... San Diego, CA
Tavano, Louis J. ... Las Vegas, NV
Tavano, Louis J., Jr. ... Bridgeport, CT
Tavares, Abilio, Jr. ... Los Angeles, CA
Tavares, Christine E. ... Tacoma, WA
Tavares, Lisa Ann ... Treasury Department, Internal Revenue Service, GV
Tavares, Raymond A. ... Tampa, FL
Tavares, Stephen A. ... Tampa, FL
Tavarez, Jose J. ... El Paso, TX
Taveira, August C. ... South Dartmouth, MA
Tavel, Andrew G. ... New York, NY
Tavel, Corey A. ... New York, NY
Tavel, Eric T. ... Lake Success, NY
Tavel, Jeffrey P. ... Central Islip, NY
Tavel, R. J. ... Indianapolis, IN
Tavel, Sherry D. ... Deer Park, TX
Tavel, Sherry D., P.C. ... Deer Park, TX
Tavel & Thea ... New York, NY
Tavella, David F. ... New York, NY
Tavelli, McDermott & Seldin ... Ithaca, NY
Tavelli, Paul N. ... Ithaca, NY
Tavenner, John S. ... Laredo, TX
Tavenner, Lisa A. ... Brunswick, ME
Tavenner, Lynn Lewis ... Richmond, VA
Tavenner, R. Gaines ... Richmond, VA
Tavenner, Thomas W. ... Boothbay Harbor, ME
Tavenner, Thomas W., Jr. ... Boston, MA
Tavera, Alfredo M. ... San Antonio, TX
Tavera, Leonard M ... Los Angeles, CA
Taveras, Angel ... Providence, RI
Taverni, Linda Troy ... Albany, NY
Tavernier, Ernest M. ... Orange, CA
Tavernier, Gregory J. ... Stillwater, MN
Tavernini, Marie McKenney ... Alexandria, VA
Taves, Barbara L. ... Las Vegas, NV
Taves, Harry J. ... Wadena, MN
Taves, J. Patrick ... Fairfax, VA
Taves, John D. ... Upland, CA
Tavetian, Gary E. ... Los Angeles, CA
Tavi, Andrew J. ... Detroit, MI
Tavill, Gregory J. ... Rancho Cucamonga, CA
Taviss, Michael L. ... Menlo Park, CA
Tavitas, Adam ... Merrillville, IN
Tavitas, Anthony F. ... Merrillville, IN
Tavitas, Elizabeth Thoman ... Crown Point, IN
Tavitian, Katherine R. ... Deerfield, IL
Tavlian, Philip E. ... Fresno, CA
Tavlin, John ... Lincoln, NE
Tavlin, Michael J. ... Lincoln, NE
Tavolacci, Carl E. ... Brooklyn, NY
Tavolaro, Karen B. ... Tucson, AZ
Tavolier, David R. ... Cleveland, OH
Tavolieri, Scott A. ... Jacksonville, FL
Tavormina, John W. ... Houston, TX
Tavoularis, Leonidas M.
Mount Clemens, MI
Tavoularis, Sperry ... Santa Ana, CA
Tavrides, Matthew A. ... Orlando, FL
Tavrides, Matthew A., P.A. ... Orlando, FL
Tavss, Fletcher, Maiden & King, P.C.
Norfolk, VA
Portsmouth, VA
Virginia Beach, VA
Tavss, John E. ... New York, NY
Tavss, Mona Binder ... Potomac, MD
Tavss, Richard J. ... Norfolk, VA
Tavtigian, Kirk ... Boston, MA
Tavzel, Erik R. ... New York, NY
Taw, Harold ... Seattle, WA
Tawa, Christopher E. ... Newton, MA
Tawa, John E., Jr. ... Irvine, CA
Tawares, Lisa A.
Treasury Department, GV
Tawasha, Carolyn J. ... San Francisco, CA
Taweel, A. Tony ... Detroit, MI
Taweel, David S. ... Fairfax, VA
Tawil, Nadir N. ... Fairfax, VA
Tawil, Nadir N., P.C. ... Fairfax, VA
Tawil, Ralph D. ... West Long Branch, NJ
Tawney, Kenneth E. ... Charleston, WV
Tawshunsky, Alan N. ... Treasury Department, Internal Revenue Service, GV
Tawwater, Larry A. ... Oklahoma City, OK
Tax, Estate & Business Law N.A. LLC
Albuquerque, NM
Taxay, Marc P. ... Palo Alto, CA
Taxay, Michael D. ... Department of Justice, Civil Division, GV
Taxay, William R. ... Pittsburgh, PA
Taxerman, Alan R. ... New York, NY
Taxin, David R. ... New York, NY
Taxin, Sharon Kay ... New York, NY
Taxis, Alfred L., Jr. ... Norristown, PA
Taxman, Eugene ... Kansas City, MO
Taxman, Glenn D. ... Chicago, IL
Taxman, Marc A. ... Chicago, IL
Taxman, Phillip ... Chicago, IL
Taxman, Phillip, Ltd. ... Chicago, IL
Taxy, Mark Alan ... Oakland, CA
Taxy, Neil E. ... San Francisco, CA
Tay, Bernard J. ... Lawrence, MA
Tay, Mark H. ... Lawrence, MA
Tay & Tay ... Lawrence, MA
Tayback, Christopher ... Los Angeles, CA
Tayback, Clare Phillips ... Los Angeles, CA
Tayback, M. Gordon ... Baltimore, MD
Tayer, Donald S. ... San Francisco, CA
Tayler, C. William ... Washington, DC
Tayler, William C. ... San Diego, CA
Taylerson, Robert S. ... Metairie, LA
Taylerson, Robert S., A Prof. Law Corp.
Metairie, LA
Tayloe, Benjamin O., Jr. ... Washington, DC
Tayloe, Gordon B., Jr. ... Norfolk, VA
Tayloe, Laura C. ... Washington, DC
Tayloe, Ryal W. ... New Bern, NC
Wilmington, NC
Taylor, A. Alexander, II ... Chattanooga, TN
Taylor, A. Blenn, Jr. ... Brunswick, GA
Taylor, A. Jeffry ... Rutland, VT
Taylor, A. Lavar ... Santa Ana, CA
Taylor, Abbi S. ... Decatur, GA
Taylor, Adam D. ... Bedford, MA
Taylor, Adam R. ... Los Angeles, CA
Taylor, Adams, Lowe & Hutchinson, A Professional Corporation
Salt Lake City, UT
Taylor, Al ... Houston, TX
Taylor, Alan ... Camden, NJ
Taylor, Alan B. ... Orlando, FL
Taylor, Albert J., Jr. ... Portsmouth, VA
Taylor, Albert Q., Jr. ... Greenville, SC
Taylor, Alexander C. ... Hartford, CT
Taylor, Alexander M. ... Knoxville, TN
Taylor, Alexis P. ... Chicago, IL
Taylor, Alice B. ... Needham, MA
Taylor, Alicia D. ... Irvine, CA
Taylor, Alicia E. ... Santa Monica, CA
Taylor, Alison ... Harrisburg, PA
Taylor, Alison J. ... Buffalo, NY
Taylor, Allan B. ... Hartford, CT
Taylor, Allan E. ... Boston, MA
Taylor, Allan J. ... Delray Beach, FL
Taylor, Allen M. ... Milwaukee, WI
Taylor, Alvin E. ... Bloomfield, CT
Taylor, Alvin E. ... Portsmouth, NH
Taylor, Alvin N. ... New Orleans, LA
Taylor, Amalia L. ... Los Angeles, CA
Taylor, AmySue ... Columbus, OH
Taylor, AmySue, Co., L.P.A. ... Columbus, OH
Taylor, Andrea L. ... Kansas City, MO
Taylor, Andrea L. ... Milwaukee, WI
Taylor, Andrew A. ... Saint Marys, GA
Taylor, Andrew D., Jr. & Associates
Charlotte, NC
Taylor, Andrew E. ... Alexandria, VA
Taylor, Andrew E., Jr. ... Boston, MA
Taylor, Andrew M. (Andy) ... Austin, TX
Taylor, Andrew P. ... Newark, DE
Taylor, Angela R. ... Sumter, SC
Taylor, Ann Caroline ... Chicago, IL
Taylor, Ann E. ... Mobile, AL
Taylor, Ann S. ... Austin, TX
Taylor, Anna Diggs ... Detroit, MI
Taylor, Anne ... Cambridge, MA
Taylor, Anne ... Columbus, OH
Taylor, Anne T. ... McLean, VA
Taylor, Anson W. H., Jr. ... Philadelphia, PA
Taylor, Arles A., Jr. ... Durham, NC
Taylor, Arnold S. ... Covington, KY
Taylor, Arthur G. ... New York, NY
Taylor, Arthur H. ... Miami, FL
Taylor, Arthur Haymore ... Kearney, NE
Taylor & Associates ... Dayton, OH
Taylor & Associates, P.C. ... Fort Wayne, IN
Taylor, Barbara A. ... New York, NY
Taylor, Barbara E. ... Los Angeles, CA
Taylor, Barbara G. ... Annapolis, MD
Taylor, Barbara J. ... Yorba Linda, CA
Taylor, Barbara J. ... Pearisburg, VA
Taylor, Barbara M. ... Northfield, VT
Taylor, Barbara T. ... Cocoa Beach, FL
Taylor, Barney D. ... Oklahoma City, OK
Taylor, Barry E. ... Palo Alto, CA
Taylor, Barry M. ... Huntington, WV
Taylor, Barry R. ... Virginia Beach, VA
Taylor, Barry W. ... Jupiter, FL
Taylor, Basil H. ... San Antonio, TX
Taylor, Bauer & Densford ... Bloomington, IN
Taylor, Bayard ... Dover, AR
Taylor, Ben D. ... Dallas, TX
Taylor, Ben F. ... Glendale, CA
Taylor, Benji Forbes ... Raleigh, NC
Taylor, Bernard ... Atlanta, GA
Taylor, Bert P. ... Birmingham, AL
Taylor, Bessie M. ... Gary, IN
Taylor, Beth McCahill ... Houston, TX
Taylor, Betty Lou ... Lebanon, TN
Taylor, Bobby R. ... Austin, TX
Taylor, Boyd F. ... London, KY
Taylor, Brad ... Houston, TX
Taylor, Bradley ... Wellsboro, PA
Taylor, Bradley G. ... Bellevue, WA
Taylor, Bradley J. ... Atlanta, GA
Taylor, Bradley S. ... Denver, CO
Taylor, Bradley T. ... Long Beach, CA
Taylor, Brandes Ovenia ... Washington, DC
Taylor, Brenda S. ... Tampa, FL
Taylor, Brent D. ... Indianapolis, IN
Taylor, Brent H. ... New York, NY
Taylor, Bret E. ... Peoria, IL
Taylor, Brewster B. ... Alexandria, VA
Taylor, Brian J. ... Philadelphia, PA
Taylor, Brian K. ... Alameda, CA
Taylor, Brian L. ... Great Falls, MT
Taylor, Brian L. ... New York, NY
Taylor, Brian P. ... Neosho, MO
Taylor, Brian P. ... New York, NY
Taylor, Brian S. ... North Chicago, IL
Taylor, Brian Zachary ... New Bern, NC
Taylor, Bridgette M. ... Los Angeles, CA
Taylor, Brinson & DeLoatch ... Tarboro, NC
Taylor, Brion, Buker & Greene
Fort Lauderdale, FL
Miami, FL
Taylor, Bruce A. ... Fairfax, VA
Taylor, Bruce A., Jr. ... Atlanta, GA
Taylor, Bruce E. ... Neosho, MO
Taylor, Bruce L. ... Englewood, CO
Taylor, Bruce P. ... St. Petersburg, FL
Taylor, Burrage, Foster, Mallett & Downs
Claremore, OK
Taylor, Butterfield, Riseman, Clark, Howell and Churchill, P.C. ... Lapeer, MI
Taylor, Byron F. ... Chicago, IL
Taylor, C. Bruce ... Traverse City, MI
Taylor, C. Christina ... Lexington, MA
Taylor, C. Eugene ... Canton, IL
Taylor, C. Gordon ... San Jose, CA
Taylor, C. Reeves ... Keyser, WV
Taylor, Calvin D. ... Pascagoula, MS
Taylor, Capp P. ... Tampa, FL
Taylor, Cara M. ... Universal City, CA
Taylor, Carey ... Columbia, SC
Taylor, Carl D., Jr. ... Alexandria, VA
Taylor, Carl E. ... Hartford, CT
Taylor, Carl L. ... Springfield, VA
Taylor, Carla B. ... Orlando, FL
Taylor & Carls, P.A. ... Daytona Beach, FL
Orlando, FL
Taylor, Caroline E. ... Atlanta, GA
Taylor, Carolyn ... San Diego, CA
Taylor, Carolyn A. ... Houston, TX
Taylor, Carolyn E. ... New York, NY
Taylor, Carolyn L. ... Nashville, TN
Taylor, Carrie T. ... Salt Lake City, UT
Taylor, Carroll S. ... Honolulu, HI
Taylor, Carson ... Burbank, CA
Taylor, Carson N. ... Modesto, CA
Taylor, Cary C. ... Kingsport, TN
Taylor, Catharin R. ... Cincinnati, OH
Taylor, Catherine A. ... Minneapolis, MN
Taylor, Catherine C. ... Tulsa, OK
Taylor, Catherine Derrick ... Columbia, SC
Taylor, Catherine H. ... Hawthorne, NY
Taylor, Cathryn M. ... Los Angeles, CA
Taylor & Cawthorne, Ltd. ... Tucson, AZ
Taylor, Celeste J. ... Minneapolis, MN
St. Paul, MN
Taylor, Cerese Crawford ... Tampa, FL
Taylor, Chaney Wes ... Batesville, AR
Taylor, Charles A. ... Lexington, KY
Taylor, Charles A. ... Clifton Park, NY
Taylor, Charles A., III ... Washington, DC
Taylor, Charles B. ... Chicago, IL
Taylor, Charles D. ... Harrisburg, IL
Taylor, Charles E. ... Atlanta, GA
Taylor, Charles E. ... Alexandria, VA
Taylor, Charles E. ... McLean, VA
Taylor, Charles E., III ... St. Louis, MO
Taylor, Charles E., P.C. ... McLean, VA
Taylor, Charles G., III ... Knoxville, TN
Taylor, Charles H. ... San Francisco, CA
Taylor, Charles H. ... Winston-Salem, NC
Taylor, Charles M. ... Philadelphia, PA
Taylor, Charles O. ... Metairie, LA
Taylor, Charles Phillip ... Warner Robins, GA
Taylor, Charles R. ... Valencia, CA
Taylor, Charles R. ... Detroit, MI
Taylor, Charles Trudrung ... Fresno, CA
Taylor, Cheri M. ... Washington, DC
Taylor, Cheri Price ... Silver Spring, MD
Taylor, Chestopher L. ... Los Angeles, CA
Taylor, Chris G. ... San Angelo, TX
Taylor, Christa D. ... Denver, CO
Taylor, Christian C. ... Chicago, IL
Taylor, Christina Fulks ... Orlando, FL
Taylor, Christine ... Gallatin, TN
Taylor, Christine L. ... Madison, WI
Taylor, Christine M.
United States Postal Service, Law Department, GV
Taylor, Christopher C. ... Sacramento, CA
Taylor, Christopher C. ... San Diego, CA
Taylor, Christopher H. ... Austin, TX
Taylor, Christopher M. ... Denver, CO
Taylor, Christopher M. ... Boston, MA
Taylor, Christopher O. ... Philadelphia, PA
Taylor & Cire ... Galveston, TX
Houston, TX
Taylor, Clarence B. ... Las Vegas, NV
Taylor, Clarence W. ... Wilmington, DE
Taylor, Clark K. ... Lindon, UT
Salt Lake City, UT
Taylor, Clark W. ... Baton Rouge, LA
Taylor, Claudia M. ... New York, NY
Taylor, Clifford W. ... Lansing, MI
Taylor, Clyde M., Jr. ... Tallahassee, FL
Taylor, Connie W. ... Lewiston, ID
Taylor, Cooper E., Jr. ... Atlanta, GA
Taylor, Corey E. ... Irvine, CA
Taylor, Corey J. ... Kansas City, MO
Taylor & Correa, P.C. ... San Antonio, TX
Taylor, Covington & Smith, P.A.
Jackson, MS
Taylor, Craig D. ... Department of Commerce, Patent and Trademark Office, GV
Taylor, Craig F. ... Minneapolis, MN
Taylor, Craig G. ... Boise, ID

Taylor, Curtis G. ....Grand Junction, CO
Taylor, Curtis Stanley ....Mansfield, OH
Taylor, Cynthia J. Z. ....Davenport, IA
Taylor, D. Brooke ....Charlotte, NC
Taylor, D. Clay, P.A. ....Minneapolis, MN
Taylor, D. Mitchell ....Fresno, CA
Taylor, Damian C. ....Miami, FL
Taylor, Damian C. ....Pensacola, FL
Taylor, Dan N. ....Provo, UT
Taylor, Dana M. ....Louisville, KY
Taylor, Dana R. ....Portland, OR
Taylor, Dane E. ....Cumberland, MD
Taylor, Daniel A. ....Boston, MA
Taylor, Daniel A., Jr. ....Houston, TX
Taylor, Daniel E. ....Fort Lauderdale, FL
Taylor, Daniel G. ....Atlanta, GA
Taylor, Daniel H. ....Baton Rouge, LA
Taylor, Daniel J. ....Jackson, TN
Taylor, Daniel K. ....Lancaster, PA
Taylor, Daniel L. ....Crawfordsville, IN
Taylor, Daniel L. ....Hawthorne, NY
Taylor, Daniel Loyd ....Memphis, TN
Taylor, Daniel M., Jr. ....Pittsburgh, PA
Taylor, Daniel P. ....Weirton, WV
Taylor, Daniel R. ....Penn Yan, NY
Taylor, Daniel R., Jr. ....Winston-Salem, NC
Taylor, Daniel T., III ....Louisville, KY
Taylor, Danyelle M. ....New Orleans, LA
Taylor, Darlene D. ....Houston, TX
Taylor, Darrell W. ....Houston, TX
Taylor, Daryl S. ....Arlington, VA
Taylor, David ....De Kalb, IL
Taylor, David A. ....Danville, KY
Taylor, David A. ....Jefferson City, MO
Taylor, David B. ....Euclid, OH
Taylor, David C., Jr. ....Fayetteville, NC
Taylor, David E. ....Columbia, SC
Taylor, David F. ....Santa Monica, CA
Seattle, WA
Taylor, David F. ....Houston, TX
Taylor, David G. ....Lewisburg, TN
Taylor, David Glenn ....Charleston, SC
Taylor, David H. ....Dallas, TX
Taylor, David J. ....Washington, DC
Taylor, David K. ....Oneonta, NY
Taylor, David K. ....Nashville, TN
Taylor, David L. ....Indianapolis, IN
Taylor, David L. ....Cambridge, MA
Sterling, MA
Taylor, David L. ....Joplin, MO
Webb City, MO
Taylor, David L., Jr. ....Florham Park, NJ
Taylor, David M. ....Wilmington, DE
Taylor, David M. ....Dallas, TX
Taylor, David R. ....Albany, NY
Taylor, David R., III ....Toledo, OH
Taylor, David S. ....Clarksville, AR
Taylor, David S. ....Washington, DC
Taylor, Dawson ....Lake Worth, FL
Taylor, Dawson ....Seattle, WA
Taylor, Day & Currie
Fernandina Beach, FL
Jacksonville, FL
Taylor, Deborah Essig ....Dallas, TX
Taylor, Debra F. ....Charlotte, NC
Taylor, DeeAnn M. ....Irvine, CA
Taylor, Denker & Boguski
Mount Laurel, NJ
Taylor, Dennis J. ....Ridgefield Park, NJ
Taylor, Dennis K. ....Traverse City, MI
Taylor, Dennis R. ....Topeka, KS
Taylor, Derek ....Morehead City, NC
Taylor, Des M. ....Austin, TX
Taylor, Diana M. Shera ....St. Helens, OR
Taylor, Diana R. ....Eugene, OR
Taylor, Diane F. ....Los Angeles, CA
Taylor, Diane Hess ....Everett, WA
Taylor, Don ....Liberty, TX
Taylor, Don A. ....Fayetteville, AR
Taylor, Don F. ....Chicago, IL
Taylor, Don Peter William ....Olympia, WA
Taylor, Donald A. ....New York, NY
Taylor, Donald C. ....Newark, DE
Wilmington, DE
Taylor, Donald E. ....Woodbridge, NJ
Taylor, Donald H. ....Houston, TX
Taylor, Donald R. ....Austin, TX
Taylor, Donald R. ....Williamsburg, VA
Taylor, Donald T. ....Kansas City, KS
Taylor, Donald W. ....Houston, TX
Taylor, Donald Wayne, Jr. ....Hazard, KY
Prestonsburg, KY
Taylor, Donna Farrell ....Neligh, NE
Taylor, Donna M. ....Atlantic City, NJ
Taylor, Donnie R. ....Ahoskie, NC
Taylor, Douglas B. ....Louisville, KY
Taylor, Douglas B. ....New Middletown, OH
Taylor, Douglas C. ....Cincinnati, OH
Taylor, Douglas E. ....Sevierville, TN
Taylor, Douglas John ....Minneapolis, MN
Taylor, Douglas L. ....Bartlesville, OK
Taylor, Douglas R. ....Gardena, CA
Taylor, Douglas W. ....Saginaw, MI
Taylor, Douglas W. ....Mattydale, NY
Taylor, Douglas W., P.C. ....Saginaw, MI
Taylor, Duane, Barton & Gilman, LLP
Boston, MA
Providence, RI
Taylor, Dudley W. ....Knoxville, TN
Taylor, Duncan H., Jr. ....Irvine, CA
Taylor & Dunham, L.L.P. ....Austin, TX
Taylor, Durryl D. ....Marshall, NC
Taylor, Durward M. ....Washington, DC
Taylor, Dwight ....Collinsville, IL
Taylor, Dyer Justice ....Weems, VA
Taylor, E. Allen, Jr. ....Fort Worth, TX
Taylor, E. Dwight ....Aurora, CO
Taylor, E. Hugh ....San Francisco, CA
Taylor, E. Hunter ....Mount Holly, NJ
Taylor, E. Jane ....Akron, OH
Taylor, Earl ....Milwaukee, WI
Taylor, Earl B. ....Opelousas, LA
Taylor, Earle R., III ....Atlanta, GA
Taylor, Edgar, III ....Lebanon, TN
Taylor, Edgar P. ....San Jose, CA
Taylor, Edward A. ....New York, NY
Taylor, Edward C. ....Jackson, MS
Taylor, Edward D. ....Los Angeles, CA
Taylor, Edward M. ....Smithtown, NY
Taylor, Edward M., Jr. ....Dayton, OH
Taylor, Edward R ....San Francisco, CA
Taylor, Edward W. ....Richmond, VA
Taylor, Edward W. ....Kent, WA
Taylor, Edwin E. ....Baltimore, MD
Taylor, Edwin H. ....Sunnyvale, CA
Denver, CO
Taylor & Egusquiza, P.A. ....Miami, FL
Taylor, Eileen McDermott ....Charlotte, NC
Taylor, Eleanor F. ....Chelsea, MA
Taylor, Elenor Rita ....Los Angeles, CA
Taylor, Elissa ....Dallas, TX
Taylor, Elizabeth A. ....Boston, MA
Taylor, Elizabeth B. ....Milwaukee, WI
Taylor, Elizabeth G. ....Washington, DC
Taylor, Elizabeth Grooms ....Akron, OH
Taylor, Elizabeth Joan ....Detroit, MI
Taylor, Elizabeth L. ....Minneapolis, MN
Taylor, Elizabeth M. ....New York, NY
Taylor, Elizabeth Newlin
Albuquerque, NM
Taylor, Elliott N. ....Salt Lake City, UT
Taylor, Ellisa A. ....Toledo, OH
Taylor, Ellisa A. ....Worthington, OH
Taylor, Eloise ....Port Richey, FL
Taylor, Emilia J. A. ....New York, NY
Taylor, Emily J. ....Tampa, FL
Taylor, Eric ....St. Louis, MO
Taylor, Eric C. ....Los Angeles, CA
Taylor, Eric J. ....Tallahassee, FL
Taylor, Eric Jon ....Atlanta, GA
Taylor, Eric K. ....Las Vegas, NV
Reno, NV
Taylor, Eric P. ....New York, NY
Taylor, Ernest G., Jr. ....Jackson, MS
Taylor, Ernest G., Jr., PLLC ....Jackson, MS
Taylor, Errol B. ....New York, NY
Taylor, Errol D. ....St. Joseph, MO
Taylor, Eugene P. ....Calabasas, CA
Taylor, Evan ....Owensboro, KY
Taylor, Evelyn ....Hamilton, OH
Taylor, F. Chet ....Minneapolis, MN
Taylor, F. Lawrence, Jr. ....Spokane, WA
Taylor, F. Michael ....Augusta, GA
Aiken, SC
Taylor & Faust, A Professional Corporation
San Francisco, CA
Taylor, Faye ....San Rafael, CA
Taylor, Fayette G. ....San Francisco, CA
Taylor, Feilmeyer & Wendl P.L.C.
Guthrie Center, IA
Taylor, Finley L. ....Costa Mesa, CA
Taylor, Fitch J. ....Madison, WI
Taylor, Floyd W. ....Oklahoma City, OK
Taylor, Frances O. ....Baltimore, MD
Taylor, Francis Alvin ....Washington, DC
Taylor, Francis M. ....West Caldwell, NJ
Taylor, Frank A. ....Orlando, FL
Taylor, Frank A. ....Minneapolis, MN
Taylor, Frank G. ....Mobile, AL
Taylor, Frank W., Jr. ....Kansas City, MO
Taylor, Fred H. ....Fort Wayne, IN
Taylor, Frederick J. ....Portage, MI
Taylor, Frederick K. ....San Diego, CA
Taylor, Frederick R. ....Arlington, VA
Taylor, G. Anthony ....St. Louis, MO
Taylor, G. Branch ....Chevy Chase, MD
Taylor, G. Kent ....Twin Falls, ID
Taylor, G. Kimbrough, Jr. ....Atlanta, GA
Taylor, G. Randall ....Simpsonville, SC
Taylor, G. Randall, P.A. ....Simpsonville, SC
Taylor, Gabrielle L.A. ....Tallahassee, FL
Taylor, Gail W. ....Los Angeles, CA
Taylor, Ganson & Perrin, L.L.P.
Beverly, MA
Boston, MA
Taylor, Gary A. ....Austin, TX
Taylor, Gary G. ....Indianapolis, IN
Taylor, Gary G. ....Onawa, IA
Taylor, Gary L. ....Santa Ana, CA
Taylor, Gary L. ....Wheaton, IL
Taylor, Gary R. ....Toledo, OH
Taylor, Gauntt & Guess ....Temple, TX
Taylor, Gene S. ....Tallahassee, FL
Taylor, Geo. M. ....Glen Burnie, MD
Taylor, Geoffrey L. ....Westlake Village, CA
Taylor, Geoffrey Michael ....Washington, DC
Taylor, Geoffrey N. ....Pittsburgh, PA
Taylor, Georganne Brown ....Prestonsburg, KY
Taylor, George F., Jr. ....Miami, FL
Taylor, George F., Jr., P.A. ....Miami, FL
Taylor, George G. ....Redwood City, CA
Taylor, George LeCroy ....El Dorado, AR
Taylor, George M., III ....Birmingham, AL
Taylor, George O., Jr.
Department Of Health And Human Services,
Social Security Administration, GV
Taylor, George R. ....Redwood City, CA
Taylor, Gerald B., Jr. ....Birmingham, AL
Taylor, Gerald H. ....Canastota, NY
Taylor, Gerald L. ....Midwest City, OK
Taylor, Gerald M. ....Tampa, FL
Taylor, Gerald W. ....Wichita Falls, TX
Taylor, Gerard ....Baltimore, MD
Taylor, Glenn Alan ....Orange Park, FL
Taylor, Glenn C. ....Hempstead, TX
Taylor, Glenn Gates ....Jackson, MS
Taylor, Gordon M.
House of Representatives,
Congressional Assistants, GV
Taylor, Gordon W. ....Fort Lauderdale, FL
Taylor, Gorman E. ....Shreveport, LA
Taylor & Graham, LLC ....Alexandria, VA
Taylor, Graham R. ....San Francisco, CA
Taylor, Gregory
Federal Deposit Insurance Corporation,
Trial Litigation Section, GV
Taylor, Gregory B. ....Plantation, FL
Taylor, Gregory C. ....Anchorage, AK
Taylor, Gregory D., (P.A.) ....Little Rock, AR
Taylor, Gregory G. ....Indianapolis, IN
Taylor, Gregory L. ....Indianapolis, IN
Taylor, Gregory M. ....Salt Lake City, UT
Taylor, Gregory S. ....Marshall, MN
Taylor, Gregory S. ....Ada, OK
Taylor, Gregory T. ....Lansing, MI
Taylor, Gretchen Wellman ....Indio, CA
Taylor & Grout ....Oakland, CA
Taylor, Grover E., II ....Tucker, GA
Taylor, Guy E. ....Oklahoma City, OK
Taylor, Guy R. ....Atlanta, GA
Taylor, Gwendolyn ....Detroit, MI
Taylor, H. Franklin, III ....Richmond, VA
Taylor, H. Gene ....Frankfort, KY
Taylor, H. George ....Norwalk, CA
Taylor, H. Kerr ....Houston, TX
Taylor, H. Wayne ....Los Angeles, CA
Taylor, Hal ....Reno, NV
Taylor, Hal W. ....Jersey City, NJ
Taylor, Hal, & W. Kathleen Baker, Ltd.
Reno, NV
Taylor, Halliburton, Ledbetter & Caldwell
Memphis, TN
Taylor & Hanlon, P.C. ....Anchorage, AK
Taylor, Harold C. ....Seminole, FL
Taylor, Harold J. ....Austin, TX
Taylor, Harp & Callier ....Phenix City, AL
Columbus, GA
Taylor, Harriett R. ....Washington, DC
Taylor, Hayes ....Chester, WV
Taylor, Hayward F., IV ....Richmond, VA
Taylor, Hazen, Kauffman & Pinchbeck, PLC
Richmond, VA
Taylor, Heather V. ....Stamford, CT
Taylor, Helene H. ....Fairhope, AL
Taylor, Hendrix Arthur, Jr. ....Pine Bluff, AR
Taylor & Henry ....Greenville, SC
Taylor, Henry H. ....West Columbia, SC
Taylor, Henry H., Jr. ....Miami, FL
Taylor, Henry, Jr. ....Temple, TX
Taylor, Herbert H., Jr. ....Tarboro, NC
Taylor, Herbert M. ....Framingham, MA
Taylor, Herman E. ....Memphis, TN
Taylor, Herman L. ....Raleigh, NC
Taylor, Hilary Sheldon ....Cleveland, OH
Taylor & Hinsdale ....Yuba City, CA
Taylor and Hladio, Law Offices
Ambridge, PA
Taylor, Hollie K. ....Mesa, AZ
Taylor, Homer R. ....El Campo, TX
Taylor, Hooper & Wiley, A Professional Corporation ....Sacramento, CA
Taylor, Howard A. ....Philadelphia, PA
Taylor, Howard H. ....San Diego, CA
Taylor, Howard Y. ....Mineola, NY
Taylor, Howell Tod ....Dyersburg, TN
Taylor, H. P., Jr. ....Wadesboro, NC
Taylor, Hugh N. ....Auburn, IN
Taylor, Hugh P. ....Marshall, TX
Taylor, Hurl R., Jr. ....Atlanta, GA
Taylor, Ian W. ....New Orleans, LA
Taylor, Ilonka Sonja ....Charleston, SC
Taylor, Ingrid B. ....Denver, CO
Taylor, Irene Churchill ....Canon City, CO
Taylor, Isabel Gereda ....Austin, TX
Taylor, J. Alton ....New Castle, IN
Taylor, J. Blan ....Naples, FL
Taylor, J. Dan ....Birmingham, AL
Taylor, J. Eric ....Tampa, FL
Taylor, J. Farrest ....Dothan, AL
Taylor, J. Frederic ....Briarcliff Manor, NY
Taylor, J. Gregory ....Dallas, TX
Taylor, J. Henk ....Phoenix, AZ
Taylor, J. Hume, Jr. ....Norfolk, VA
Richmond, VA
Taylor, J. Kirk ....Houston, TX
Taylor, J. Mark ....West Columbia, SC
Taylor, J. Michael ....Tampa, FL
Taylor, J. Michael ....Columbia, SC
Taylor, J. Morton ....Findlay, OH
Taylor, J. Robert ....Palo Alto, CA
Taylor, J. Scott, P.A. ....Tampa, FL
Taylor, J. Scott, (P.A.) ....Tampa, FL
Taylor, J. Sherrod ....Columbus, GA
Taylor, J. Spencer ....Salem, OR
Taylor, J. Van Wyck ....Charleston, SC
Taylor, Jack L. ....Yuba City, CA
Taylor, Jacqueline, Law Offices of
Houston, TX
Taylor, Jacqueline G. ....Boston, MA
Taylor, Jacqueline P. ....Lakewood, CO
Taylor, Jake A. ....Los Angeles, CA
Taylor, James A. ....Butler, PA
Taylor, James A., III ....Vero Beach, FL
Taylor, James C. ....Pensacola, FL
Taylor, James C., Jr. ....Oakland, CA
Taylor, James D. ....Claremont, CA
Taylor, James D. ....New York, NY
Taylor, James D. ....Mitchell, SD
Taylor, James E. ....Chicago, IL
Taylor, James E. ....St. Louis, MO
Taylor, James E. ....Windsor, MO
Taylor, James F. ....Baltimore, MD
Taylor, James F. ....Sherburne, NY
Taylor, James F., III ....Atlanta, GA
Taylor, James G. ....Brooklyn, NY
Taylor, James H. ....Long Grove, IL
Taylor, James H. ....Grosse Pointe Farms, MI
Taylor, James H. ....Siren, WI
Taylor, James J. ....New York, NY
Taylor, James J., Jr. ....Keystone Heights, FL
Taylor, James, Jr. ....Washington, DC
Taylor, James, Jr. ....Winston-Salem, NC
Taylor, James L. ....Las Vegas, NV
Taylor, James L. ....Watford City, ND
Taylor, James M. ....Los Angeles, CA
Taylor, James M. ....Longmont, CO
Taylor, James M. ....New Orleans, LA
Taylor, James Marlin, Jr. ....Richmond, VA
Taylor, James N. ....Elyria, OH
Taylor, James O. ....Syracuse, NY
Taylor, James Park ....Missoula, MT
Taylor, James R. ....Phoenix, AZ
Taylor, James R. ....Little Rock, AR
Taylor, James R. ....Provo, UT
Taylor, James S. ....Jacksonville, FL
Taylor, James S., Jr. ....Union City, GA
Taylor, James S., Jr. ....Houston, TX
Taylor, James W. ....Davis, CA
Taylor, James W. ....Lexington, KY
Taylor, Jamison B. ....Washington, DC
Taylor, Jana G. ....Fort Lauderdale, FL
Taylor, Jane C. ....Philadelphia, PA
Taylor, Jane Carol ....Atlanta, GA
Taylor, Jane K. ....Department of Energy,
Office of the General Counsel, GV
Taylor, Jane M. ....Department of Justice,
Civil Rights Division, GV
Taylor, Janet E. ....Atlanta, GA
Taylor, Janette ....Oneida, TN
Taylor, Janice Chenier ....New Orleans, LA
Taylor, Janice E. ....New York, NY
Taylor, Janis Nettles ....Panama City, FL
Taylor, Jarred O., II ....Birmingham, AL
Taylor, Jas. B. ....Cleveland, OH
Taylor, Jas. C. ....Salt Lake City, UT
Taylor, Jason Sean ....Tulsa, OK
Taylor, Jasper G., III ....Houston, TX
Taylor, Jasper, IV ....Bells, TN
Taylor, Jay A. ....Houston, TX
Taylor, Jay C. ....Dearborn, MI
Taylor, Jay G. ....Indianapolis, IN
Taylor, Jay R. ....Los Angeles, CA
Taylor, Jay T. ....Atlanta, GA
Taylor, Jay V. ....Lansdale, PA
Taylor, Jaye Wickham ....Wilsonville, OR
Taylor, Jean G. ....Washington, DC
Taylor, Jean H. ....Longview, TX
Taylor, Jeff S. ....Owensboro, KY
Taylor, Jeff S., P.S.C. ....Owensboro, KY
Taylor, Jefferson C. ....Miami, FL
Taylor, Jeffery D. ....Fairmont, WV
Taylor, Jeffery S., Ltd. ....Northbrook, IL
Taylor, Jeffrey ....Dayton, OH
Taylor, Jeffrey A. ....San Diego, CA
Taylor, Jeffrey A. ....Lexington, KY
Taylor, Jeffrey A. ....Lincolnton, NC
Taylor, Jeffrey A. ....Oklahoma City, OK
Addison, TX
Taylor, Jeffrey A. ....Huntington, WV
Taylor, Jeffrey C. ....Decatur, IL
Taylor, Jeffrey C. ....Baltimore, MD
Taylor, Jeffrey C. ....Knoxville, TN
Morristown, TN
Taylor, Jeffrey K.
Department of Housing and Urban
Development, GV
Taylor, Jeffrey L. ....Wells River, VT
Taylor, Jeffrey M. ....Honolulu, HI
Taylor, Jeffrey P. ....Cedar Rapids, IA
Taylor, Jeffrey S. ....Chicago, IL
Taylor, Jeffrey W. ....Wheeling, IL
Taylor, Jennifer Ann ....Dallas, TX
Taylor, Jennifer L. ....Troy, NY
Taylor, Jennifer Lee ....San Francisco, CA
Taylor, Jennifer N. ....Charleston, WV
Taylor, Jennifer Newton ....Las Vegas, NV
Taylor, Jennifer P. ....Charleston, WV
Taylor, Jeremy M. ....Chicago, IL
Taylor, Jeremy V. ....Grosse Pointe Woods, MI
Taylor, Jerome ....Philadelphia, PA
Taylor, Jerry D ....Atlantic Mine, MI
Taylor, Jerry F. ....Memphis, TN
Taylor, Jerry W. ....Nashville, TN
Taylor, Jesse, Jr. ....St. Louis, MO
Taylor, Jessica S. ....San Antonio, TX
Taylor, Jill Olsen ....Spanish Fork, UT
Taylor, Jim ....Houston, TX
Taylor, Joan Gibb ....Columbus, OH
Taylor, Joanne S. ....Benicia, CA
Taylor, Job, III ....New York, NY
Taylor, Joe D. ....Fort Worth, TX
Taylor, Joe F. ....Austin, TX
Taylor, Joe P., Jr. ....Longview, TX
Taylor, Joe T. ....Atlanta, GA
Taylor, Joel ....Little Rock, AR
Taylor, Joel B. ....Brea, CA
Taylor, Joel S. ....Columbus, OH
Taylor, John ....Indianapolis, IN
Taylor, John A. ....Orlando, FL
Taylor, John A. ....Pontiac, IL
Taylor, John A. ....Cambridge, MA
Taylor, John A., Jr. ....Los Angeles, CA
Taylor, John A., Jr. ....New York, NY
Taylor, John B. ....Charlotte, NC
Taylor, John C. ....Auburn, CA
Taylor, John C. ....Santa Monica, CA
Taylor, John C. ....Jupiter, FL
Taylor, John C. ....Champaign, IL
Taylor, John C., Jr.
Fernandina Beach, FL
Jacksonville, FL
Taylor, John C., P.A. ....Jupiter, FL

Taylor, R. Allyn ..... Palo Alto, CA
Taylor, R. Eric ..... Washington, DC
Taylor, R. Jay, Jr. ..... Indianapolis, IN
Taylor, R. John ..... Lewiston, ID
Taylor, R. Macey ..... Birmingham, AL
Taylor, R. Neil, III ..... Phoenix, AZ
Taylor, R. Peter ..... Dover, NH
Taylor, R. Scott ..... Anchorage, AK
Taylor, R. Scott ..... St. Michaels, MD
Taylor, R. Stephen ..... Tucker, GA
Taylor, Ralph A., Jr. (P.C.) Washington, DC
Taylor, Ralph C. ..... Littleton, CO
Taylor, Ralph W. ..... Salem, OR
Taylor, Randall L. ..... Sierra Madre, CA
Taylor, Randall Mark ..... San Francisco, CA
Taylor & Randolph, P.C. ..... Houston, TX
Taylor, Randolph W. ..... New York, NY
Taylor, Randy L. ..... Cleveland, OH
Taylor, Raphael (Rafe) ..... Houston, TX
Taylor, Ray ..... San Antonio, TX
Taylor, Ray A. ..... Scottsdale, AZ
Taylor, Rayford H. ..... Tallahassee, FL
Taylor, Raymond Mason ..... Raleigh, NC
Taylor, Raymond W. ..... Kingston, NH
Taylor, Reams, Tilson & Harrison Morristown, TN
Taylor, Rebecca Ann ..... Mc Comb, MS
Taylor, Rebecca C. ..... Wiggins, MS
Taylor, Rebecca L. ..... New York, NY
Taylor, Rebecca Lynn ..... Washington, DC
Taylor, Reese ..... Akron, OH
Taylor, Reese H., Jr. ..... Long Beach, CA
Taylor, Reginald K. ..... Des Plaines, IL
Taylor, Rena J. ..... West Palm Beach, FL
Taylor, Renée Beth ..... Denver, CO
Taylor, Rheubin McGhee ..... Chattanooga, TN
Taylor, Rhonda E. ..... Owensboro, KY
Taylor, Rhonda M. ..... Nashville, TN
Taylor, Richard ..... Brunswick, GA
Taylor, Richard B. ..... St. Louis, MO
Taylor, Richard C. ..... Atlanta, GA
Taylor, Richard C. ..... Crookston, MN
Taylor, Richard D. ..... Nashville, TN
Taylor, Richard D., (P.A.) ..... Little Rock, AR
Taylor, Richard E. ..... Phoenix, AZ
Taylor, Richard F. ..... Cruz Bay, St. John, VI
Taylor, Richard F., Jr. ..... Syracuse, NY
Taylor, Richard G. ..... Miami, FL
Taylor, Richard H. ..... Mobile, AL
Taylor, Richard H. ..... Pittsburgh, PA
Taylor, Richard H. C. ..... Hanover, VA
Taylor, Richard J. ..... Sarasota, FL
Taylor, Richard J. ..... New York, NY
Taylor, Richard L. ..... Irvine, CA
Taylor, Richard L. ..... Sacramento, CA
Taylor, Richard L. ..... Ventura, CA
Taylor, Richard M. ..... Spanish Fork, UT
Taylor, Richard M., III ..... San Antonio, TX
Taylor, Richard P. ..... Washington, DC
Taylor, Richard P. ..... Athens, OH
Taylor, Richard S. ..... San Francisco, CA
Taylor, Richard S. ..... Frankfort, KY
Taylor, Richard S., Jr. ..... Longwood, FL
Taylor, Richard T. ..... Atlanta, GA
Taylor, Richard T. ..... New York, NY
Taylor, Richard W. ..... Stockton, CA
Taylor, Richard W. ..... DeLand, FL
Taylor, Rick ..... Chicago, IL
Taylor, Ritchie W. ..... Raleigh, NC
Taylor, R.N. (Bo) ..... Goodlettsville, TN
Taylor, Robert ..... Riverside, CA
Taylor, Robert ..... East Orange, NJ
Taylor, Robert A. ..... Cleveland, OH
Taylor, Robert A. ..... Bethlehem, PA
Taylor, Robert A. ..... Harrisburg, PA
Taylor, Robert A. ..... Charleston, WV
Taylor, Robert A., Jr. ..... Washington, DC
Taylor, Robert B. ..... Salisbury, MD
Taylor, Robert B. ..... Forest Hills, NY
Taylor, Robert C. ..... Fort Smith, AR
Taylor, Robert C. ..... Nashville, TN
Taylor, Robert C. ..... Dallas, TX
Taylor, Robert C. ..... Seattle, WA
Taylor, Robert C., Jr. ..... Salinas, CA
Taylor, Robert D. ..... Los Angeles, CA
Taylor, Robert D. ..... Englewood, CO
Taylor, Robert D. ..... Pittsburgh, PA
Taylor, Robert E. ..... Franklin, KY
Taylor, Robert E. ..... Ridgeland, MS
Taylor, Robert E. ..... Cincinnati, OH
Taylor, Robert E., Jr. ..... Wiggins, MS
Taylor, Robert Edward ..... Charlottesville, VA
Taylor, Robert G. ..... Buena Park, CA
Taylor, Robert G. ..... Los Angeles, CA
Taylor, Robert G. ..... Riverside, CA
Taylor, Robert G. ..... Seattle, WA
Taylor, Robert G., II, (P.C.) ..... Galveston, TX
Houston, TX
Taylor, Robert G., III ..... Galveston, TX
Taylor, Robert H. ..... Gadsden, AL
Taylor, Robert H. ..... Columbus, OH
Taylor, Robert H. ..... Tulsa, OK
Taylor, Robert H. ..... Dallas, TX
Taylor, Robert H., Jr. ..... Jackson, MS
Taylor, Robert J. ..... Dover, DE
Taylor, Robert J. ..... Chicago, IL
Taylor, Robert J. ..... Lansing, MI
Taylor, Robert J. ..... Ambridge, PA
Taylor, Robert J., Jr. ..... Sacramento, CA
Taylor, Robert Jefferson ..... Searcy, AR
Taylor, Robert, Jr. ..... Baltimore, MD
Taylor, Robert K. ..... Washington, DC
Taylor, Robert L. ..... Pleasanton, CA
Taylor, Robert L. ..... Orlando, FL
Taylor, Robert L. ..... Griffith, IN
Taylor, Robert L. ..... Covington, KY
Taylor, Robert L. ..... Stone Harbor, NJ
Taylor, Robert L. ..... Boerne, TX
Taylor, Robert L., P.C. ..... Stone Harbor, NJ
Taylor, Robert Lemuel, Jr. ..... Dallas, TX
Taylor, Robert Lynn ..... Denver, CO
Taylor, Robert M. ..... Kalamazoo, MI
Taylor, Robert M. ..... Salt Lake City, UT
Taylor, Robert M. ..... Seattle, WA
Taylor, Robert M., III ..... Hartford, CT
Taylor, Robert M., Jr. ..... Irvine, CA
Taylor, Robert P. ..... Menlo Park, CA
Taylor, Robert P. ..... Atlanta, GA
Taylor, Robert P., III ..... Dallas, TX
Taylor, Robert Parkinson, Law Offices of Huntington Beach, CA
Taylor, Robert R. ..... Honolulu, HI
Taylor, Robert S. ..... Department of Defense, Office of the General Counsel, GV
Taylor, Robert Samuel, III ..... Lexington, NC
Taylor, Robert T. ..... Little Rock, AR
Taylor, Robert T. ..... Washington, DC
Taylor, Robert W. ..... New York, NY
Taylor, Robert W. ..... Houston, TX
Taylor, Robert W., Jr. ..... Towson, MD
Taylor, Roberta "Bobbi" ..... Victorville, CA
Taylor, Robertson B. ..... Bethlehem, PA
Harrisburg, PA
Taylor, Robin A. ..... Anchorage, AK
Taylor, Robin L. ..... Wrangell, AK
Taylor, Rodney J. ..... Chicago, IL
Taylor, Rodney V. ..... Indianapolis, IN
Taylor, Roger D. ..... Atlanta, GA
Taylor, Roger L. ..... Chicago, IL
Taylor, Roger W. ..... Tucson, AZ
Taylor, Ronald ..... Dallas, TX
Taylor, Ronald E. ..... St. Joseph, MO
Taylor, Ronald G. ..... Jackson, MS
Taylor, Ronald J. ..... St. Joseph, MI
Taylor, Ronald L. ..... Cypress, CA
Taylor, Ronald L. ..... Riverside, CA
Taylor, Ronald L. ..... Denver, CO
Taylor, Ronald L. ..... Southaven, MS
Taylor, Ronald R. ..... Dana Point, CA
Taylor, Ronald S. ..... Oakton, VA
Taylor, Ronald T. ..... Albuquerque, NM
Taylor, Ronald W. ..... Baltimore, MD
Taylor, Roslyn G. ..... New Orleans, LA
Taylor, Ross D. ..... Chicago, IL
Taylor, Ross E. ..... Tacoma, WA
Taylor, Rowan H. ..... Jackson, MS
Taylor, Rowan H., Jr. ..... Jackson, MS
Taylor, Roy L. ..... Miami, FL
Taylor, Royce ..... Murfreesboro, TN
Taylor, R. U. ..... Raleigh, NC
Taylor, Rufus C. "Butch", Jr. ..... Denver, CO
Taylor, Rufus C., III ..... Washington, DC
Taylor, Russell B. ..... Eskridge, KS
Taylor, Russell B. ..... Las Vegas, NV
Taylor, Russell W. ..... Oakland, CA
Taylor, Ruth Anne ..... Burbank, CA
Taylor, Ruthie L. ..... Washington, DC
Taylor, Ryan J. ..... Orem, UT
Taylor, S. Brooke ..... Port Angeles, WA
Taylor, S. Nicole ..... Raleigh, NC
Taylor, Sally A. ..... New Buffalo, MI
Taylor, Sam E. ..... Oklahoma City, OK
Taylor, Sam E., II ..... Fort Worth, TX
Taylor, Sam E., Jr. ..... Dallas, TX
Taylor, Sam M. ..... Taylorville, IL
Taylor, Sam W. ..... Montgomery, AL
Taylor, Sammye L. ..... Little Rock, AR
Taylor, Samuel B. ..... Durham, NC
Taylor, Samuel C. ..... Los Angeles, CA
Taylor, Samuel D. ..... Anderson, IN
Taylor, Samuel E ..... Frederick, MD
Taylor, Samuel M. ..... Raleigh, NC
Taylor, Sandra ..... Key West, FL
Taylor, Sandra L. ..... Jackson, MS
Taylor, Sarah E. ..... Washington, DC
Taylor, Sarah L. ..... Chicago, IL
Taylor & Schockemoehl, P.C. Richmond, VA
Taylor & Scholl, Law Office of Greensburg, IN
Taylor, Scott ..... Woodland Hills, CA
Taylor, Scott ..... New York, NY
Taylor, Scott A. ..... Austin, TX
Taylor, Scott B. ..... Milwaukee, WI
Taylor, Scott C. ..... Cupertino, CA
Taylor, Scott C. ..... San Diego, CA
Taylor, Scott C. ..... Pascagoula, MS
Taylor, Scott E. ..... Atlanta, GA
Taylor, Scott G. ..... Springfield, MO
Taylor, Scott L. ..... Tucson, AZ
Taylor, Scott P. ..... New York, NY
Taylor, Scott R. ..... Tulsa, OK
Taylor, Scott S. ..... Kansas City, MO
Taylor, Sean F. ..... Chicago, IL
Taylor, Sean McCarty ..... Warren, MI
Taylor, Septtimous ..... Owensboro, KY
Taylor, Shannon Zachary ..... New York, NY
Taylor, Sharon Gibney ..... Plano, TX
Taylor, Sharon L. ..... Washington, DC
Taylor, Sharon O. ..... Brooksville, FL
Taylor, Shereen ..... Chicago, IL
Taylor, Sheryl A. ..... Phoenix, AZ
Taylor, Sidney H. ..... DeLand, FL
Taylor, Simon ..... New York, NY
Taylor, Simonson & Winter, LLP Claremont, CA
Taylor & Smith, P.C. ..... Birmingham, AL
Taylor, Spencer M. ..... Birmingham, AL
Taylor, Stacy Colvin ..... Richmond, VA
Taylor, Stacy L. ..... San Diego, CA
Taylor, Stafford, Woody, Clithero & FitzGerald, LLP ..... Joplin, MO
Springfield, MO
Taylor, Stanley N. ..... Eugene, OR
Taylor, Stanley S., III ..... San Francisco, CA
Taylor, Stanley W. ..... New York, NY
Taylor, Stanton M. ..... Ogden, UT
Taylor, Stephan L. ..... Lexington, KY
Taylor, Stephanie ..... Baltimore, MD
Taylor, Stephanie A. ..... Washington, DC
Taylor, Stephanie A. ..... Pensacola, FL
Taylor, Stephanie Barnes ..... Houston, TX
Taylor, Stephen B. ..... Statesboro, GA
Taylor, Stephen C. ..... Los Angeles, CA
Taylor, Stephen C. ..... Wilmington, NC
Taylor, Stephen D. ..... Charleston, WV
Taylor, Stephen Glenn ..... Kansas City, MO
Taylor, Stephen J. ..... Newark, NJ
Taylor, Stephen J. ..... Pittsburgh, PA
Taylor, Stephen K. ..... Kansas City, MO
Taylor, Stephen L. ..... Sikeston, MO
Taylor, Stephen M. ..... Long Beach, CA
Taylor, Stephen T. ..... Greensburg, IN
Taylor, Stephen W. ..... Orland Park, IL
Taylor, Steve ..... Memphis, TN
Taylor, Steve D. ..... New Braunfels, TX
Taylor, Steven B. ..... Louisville, KY
Taylor, Steven B. ..... Beaverton, OR
Taylor, Steven E. ..... Fort Lauderdale, FL
Taylor, Steven H. ..... Los Angeles, CA
Taylor, Steven H. ..... Coraopolis, PA
Taylor, Steven J. M. ..... New City, NY
Taylor, Steven L. ..... Salt Lake City, UT
Taylor, Steven P. ..... San Diego, CA
Taylor, Steven T. ..... Moundsville, WV
Taylor, Steven W. ..... McAlester, OK
Taylor, Stratton ..... Claremore, OK
Taylor, Stuart S., Jr. ..... Washington, DC
Taylor, Susan C. ..... Summit, NJ
Taylor, Susan Chandler ..... Wadesboro, NC
Taylor, Susan Eleanor ..... New Bedford, MA
Taylor, Susan J. ..... Houston, TX
Taylor, Susan L. ..... Albany, NY
Taylor, Susan M. Treasury Department, GV
Taylor, Susan Marie ..... Mishawaka, IN
Taylor, Susan R. ..... Seattle, WA
Taylor, Susan Ribeiro ..... Holyoke, MA
Taylor, Susan T. ..... Houston, TX
Taylor, Suzanne ..... San Francisco, CA
Taylor, Suzanne K. ..... Salem, OR
Taylor, Suzanne Katherine ..... Buffalo, NY
Taylor & Swope ..... Tampa, FL
Taylor, T. Kevin ..... Orlando, FL
Taylor, T. Stephen Cameron Nashville, TN
Taylor, Tad M. ..... Salt Lake City, UT
Taylor, Tatiana ..... Denver, CO
Taylor & Taylor ..... Birmingham, AL
Montgomery, AL
Prattville, AL
Taylor & Taylor ..... Wiggins, MS
Taylor & Taylor ..... St. Louis, MO
Taylor & Taylor ..... Morehead City, NC
Taylor & Taylor ..... Dayton, OH
Taylor & Taylor ..... Houston, TX
Taylor & Taylor ..... Mount Pleasant, TX
Taylor, Taylor, Lannom & Williams, P.L.L.C. Lebanon, TN
Taylor, Taylor & Olizi ..... Camden, NJ
Taylor & Taylor, P.A. ..... Keystone Heights, FL
Taylor, Taylor & Taylor, Inc. ..... Richmond, VA
Taylor, Ted ..... Birmingham, AL
Prattville, AL
Taylor, Terence L. ..... Greenville, NC
Taylor, Terri Wilson ..... Atlanta, GA
Taylor, Terry A. ..... Dallas, TX
Taylor, Terry G. ..... Los Angeles, CA
Taylor, Terry M. ..... Hickory, NC
Taylor, Theodore N. ..... Plant City, FL
Taylor, Theodore N., P.A., Law Office of Plant City, FL
Taylor, Thomas Alan ..... Dallas, TX
Taylor, Thomas A. T. ..... Tampa, FL
Taylor, Thomas B. ..... Houston, TX
Taylor, Thomas B., Jr. ..... Bradenton, FL
Taylor, Thomas C. ..... Washington, DC
Taylor, Thomas C. Hilton Head Island, SC
Taylor, Thomas C., Jr. ..... Santa Rosa, CA
Taylor, Thomas D. ..... Warsaw, VA
Taylor, Thomas E. ..... Syracuse, NY
Taylor, Thomas E. ..... Charlotte, NC
Taylor, Thomas E. ..... Cincinnati, OH
Taylor, Thomas G. ..... Boston, MA
Taylor, Thomas H. ..... Madison, WI
Taylor, Thomas J. ..... Plainsboro, NJ
Taylor, Thomas J., III ..... Tumwater, WA
Taylor, Thomas L., III ..... Los Angeles, CA
Taylor, Thomas R. ..... Salt Lake City, UT
Taylor, Thomas S. ..... Provo, UT
Taylor, Thomas W. ..... Department of the Army, Office of the General Counsel, GV
Taylor, Thomas W. ..... Boston, MA
Taylor, Thomas W. ..... St. Louis, MO
Taylor, Thomas W. ..... Houston, TX
Taylor, Timothy A. ..... Lincoln, MA
Taylor, Timothy A. ..... Rocky River, OH
Taylor, Timothy B. ..... San Diego, CA
Taylor, Timothy C. ..... Austin, TX
Taylor, Timothy E. ..... Dallas, TX
Taylor, Timothy J. ..... Mount Pleasant, MI
Taylor, Timothy L. ..... Holland, MI
Taylor, Timothy M. ..... Sacramento, CA
Taylor, Timothy P. ..... Memphis, TN
Taylor, Timothy R. ..... Mount Pleasant, TX
Taylor, Timothy Roy ..... Tampa, FL
Taylor, Timothy S. ..... Albany, NY
Taylor, Timothy S. ..... Houston, TX
Taylor, Tina M. ..... Buffalo, NY
Taylor, Tobin J. ..... Peoria, IL
Taylor, Todd ..... Oklahoma City, OK
Taylor, Todd ..... Sugar Land, TX
Taylor, Todd A. ..... Minneapolis, MN
Taylor, Todd C. ..... Charlotte, NC
Taylor, Todd E. ..... Memphis, TN
Taylor, Todd T. ..... Fort Wayne, IN
Taylor, Todd W. ..... Houston, TX
Taylor, Tom A. ..... San Angelo, TX
Taylor, Tommy W. ..... Kansas City, MO
Taylor, Toni ..... El Dorado, AR
Taylor, Tony ..... Lawrenceville, GA
Taylor, Tory ..... Houston, TX
Taylor, Tracey L. ..... Boston, MA
Taylor, Tracy Doherty ..... Washington, DC
Taylor, Tracy Lynn ..... Charlottesville, VA
Taylor, Trent J. ..... Indianapolis, IN
Taylor, Trevor A. ..... Houston, TX
Taylor, Triscilla P. Department Of The Interior, Office of the Solicitor, GV
Taylor, Trisha S. ..... Houston, TX
Taylor & Trosclair ..... Opelousas, LA
Taylor, Troy R. ..... Northville, MI
Taylor, Tyra L. ..... Newark, OH
Taylor, Valerie Ullman ..... New York, NY
Taylor, Van B. ..... Dardanelle, AR
Taylor & Van Matre, P.A. ..... Pensacola, FL
Taylor, Vannie, III ..... Washington, DC
Taylor, Varley H., Jr. ..... Tulsa, OK
Taylor, Vaughan E. ..... Jacksonville, NC
Taylor, Velma C. ..... Department of Justice, Office of Legislative Affairs, GV
Taylor, Vernon A. ..... Wilmington, DE
Taylor, Victor ..... Camden, NJ
Taylor, Victor A. ..... Salt Lake City, UT
Taylor & Viers ..... Atlanta, GA
Taylor, Vikki J. ..... Greenville, MS
Taylor, Vincent S. ..... Bloomington, IN
Taylor, Virginia J. ..... Sacramento, CA
Taylor, Virginia S. ..... Atlanta, GA
Taylor, W. Brett ..... Brooklyn, NY
Taylor, W. Earl, Jr. ..... Wilson, NC
Taylor, W. Frank ..... Seattle, WA
Taylor, W. Kirkland ..... Seattle, WA
Taylor, W. Morris ..... St. Louis, MO
Taylor, W. Morris, P.C. ..... St. Louis, MO
Taylor, W. Nowlin ..... Shelbyville, TN
Taylor, W. Roberts, Jr. ..... Houston, TX
Taylor, Wakefield ..... Martinez, CA
Taylor, Walker C. ..... San Ramon, CA
Taylor & Walker, P.C. ..... Norfolk, VA
Richmond, VA
Virginia Beach, VA
Taylor, Wallace L. ..... Cedar Rapids, IA
Taylor, Waller, III ..... Seattle, WA
Taylor, Walter A. ..... San Diego, CA
Taylor, Walter C., Jr. ..... Indianapolis, IN
Taylor, Walter C., Jr. ..... Philadelphia, PA
Taylor, Walter J. ..... St. Louis, MO
Taylor, Walter L., Law Offices of Austin, TX
Taylor, Walter W. ..... Sacramento, CA
Taylor, Warner (W. H.) ..... Fayetteville, AR
Taylor, Warren A. ..... Hazard, KY
Taylor, Warren K. ..... Davis, CA
Taylor and Warren, LLP ..... Houston, TX
Taylor, Warren R. ..... Houston, TX
Taylor, Wayne D. ..... Atlanta, GA
Taylor, Wayne F. ..... Cincinnati, OH
Taylor, Wayne S. ..... Memphis, TN
Taylor, Wellons & Politz, APLC Metairie, LA
New Orleans, LA
Taylor, Wendell C. ..... Boston, MA
Taylor, Wendell L. ..... Richmond, VA
Taylor, Wendy J. ..... Providence, RI
Taylor, Wendy S. ..... Pittsburgh, PA
Taylor, Wesley L, Jr ..... Cambridge, MA
Taylor, Wilford L. ..... Mesa, AZ
Taylor, Wilford L., P.C. ..... Mesa, AZ
Phoenix, AZ
Taylor and Wilkerson, P.A. ..... Port Richey, FL
Taylor, Willard B. ..... New York, NY
Taylor, William A. ..... Bloomfield, CT
Taylor, William A., III ..... Winfield, KS
Taylor, William B., IV ..... Tampa, FL
Taylor, William C. ..... Phoenix, AZ
Taylor, William C. ..... San Francisco, CA
Taylor, William C. Department Of Health And Human Services, Social Security Administration, GV
Taylor, William D. ..... San Francisco, CA
Taylor, William D. ..... Elyria, OH
Taylor, William E. ..... Paducah, KY
Taylor, William E. ..... Portland, ME
Taylor, William E., III ..... Houston, TX
Taylor, William Edward ..... St. Louis, MO
Taylor, William F. ..... Wilmington, DE
Taylor, William F. ..... Hampton, VA
Taylor, William F., Jr. ..... Wilmington, DE
Taylor, William Fayette ..... Berkeley, CA
Taylor, William G. ..... Sioux Falls, SD
Taylor, William H. ..... Bonita, CA
Taylor, William H. ..... Milwaukee, WI
Taylor, William H., II ..... Chicago, IL
Taylor, William, IV ..... Baltimore, MD
Taylor, William J. ..... New York, NY
Taylor, William J. ..... Thornville, OH
Zanesville, OH
Taylor, William J. ..... Philadelphia, PA
Taylor, William J. ..... Philadelphia, PA
Taylor, William J., Jr. ..... Philadelphia, PA
Taylor, William L. ..... Washington, DC
Taylor, William L. ..... New York, NY
Taylor, William L. ..... Alexandria, VA
Taylor, William L. ..... Richmond, VA
Taylor, William L., Jr. ..... Chattanooga, TN
Taylor, William Lake, Jr. ..... Richmond, VA
Taylor, William Lewis ..... Washington, DC
Taylor, William M. ..... Springfield, IL

Teeters, Jeffrey R. ... **Cincinnati, OH**
Teeters, Ralph N. ... **Philadelphia, PA**
Teetor, J. Stephen ... **Columbus, OH**
Teets, Charles E. ... Clearwater, FL
Teets, George W. ... Moscow, PA
Teets, John W. ... **Austin, TX**
Teets, Scott D. ... Indianapolis, IN
Teeuwissen, Peter A. ... Hartford, CT
Teeuwissen, Pieter ... Jackson, MS
Teevan, Connie M. ... **San Francisco, CA**
Teevan, John M. ... **Chicago, IL**
Teevan, Ronald P. ... Clearwater, FL
Teevan, Ronald P., P.A. ... Clearwater, FL
Teevans, James W. ... Oakland, CA
Teeven, Kevin M. ... Washington, IL
Teffeteller, Robert Glenn ... Albany, CA
Teffner, Donald R. ... Mansfield, OH
Tefft, Christine M. ... **New York, NY**
Tefft, Roger H. ... **Costa Mesa, CA**
Tefft, Stanton E. ... Bedford, NH
Tefft, Steven M. ... Chicago, IL
Tefft, Traci ... Simsbury, CT
Tefteller, Ronald G. ... San Antonio, TX
Tefteller, Todd ... Gilmer, TX
Tegeler, David F. ... **Orlando, FL**
Tegeler, David W. ... **Boston, MA**
Tegeler, Tamara Christine ... Eagan, MN
Tegeler, W. Charles, Jr. ... Tulsa, OK
Tegenkamp, Gary E. ... Roanoke, VA
Teger, Stuart H. ... **Detroit, MI**
Tegfeldt, Jennifer A. ... Cambridge, MA
Teggelaar, Michelle R. ... **Chicago, IL**
Tegger, Karen A. ... Cypress, CA
Tegland, Karl B. ... Bothell, WA
Tegland, Leighton B. ... **Palm Desert, CA**
Tegland & Plott, LLP ... **Palm Desert, CA**
Redlands, CA
Tegnazian, Terry A. ... Los Angeles, CA
Tegreene, Casey T. ... Seattle, WA
Tegreene, Joseph G. ... **Cleveland, OH**
teGroen, Tristan ... Westlake Village, CA
TeGrotenhuis, Theodore A. ... Cleveland, OH
Tegtmeier, Dennis C. ... Lincoln, NE
Tegtmeier, James W.
Department of Transportation, Federal Aviation Administration, GV
Tegtmeier Law Firm, P.C.
Colorado Springs, CO
Tegtmeier, Richard L.
Colorado Springs, CO
Tegtmeyer, Rene D. ... **Washington, DC**
Tehan, Aaron J. ... **New York, NY**
Tehan, David George ... Auburn, NY
Tehan, John B. ... **New York, NY**
Tehan, John N. ... Springfield, OH
Tehan, Joseph L., Jr. ... **Boston, MA**
Tehan, Kevin T. ... **Scottsdale, AZ**
Tehan, Martha V. ... Oklahoma City, OK
Tehan & Stoll ... Springfield, OH
Tehan, Timothy P., (P.C.) ... **Dallas, TX**
Tehan, Valerie ... Anchorage, AK
Tehan, William R. ... **Wausau, WI**
Tehas, Donna Beck ... Metairie, LA
Tehin, Nikolai ... **San Francisco, CA**
Tehin +Partners, A Professional Corporation
San Francisco, CA
Teholiz, Peter A. ... **Lansing, MI**
Tehrani, Farinaz S. ... **Washington, DC**
Teibloom, Joel D. ... **Chicago, IL**
Teich, Genise W. ... Newark, NJ
Teich, Groh and Frost ... **Hamilton, NJ**
Lawrenceville, NJ
Princeton, NJ
Trenton, NJ
Teich, Henry E. ... Asheville, NC
Teich, Howard B. ... New York, NY
Teich, Jeffrey A. ... Stratham, NH
Teich, Jerome ... Jupiter, FL
Teich, Jill Funtleyder ... **New York, NY**
Teich, Joan F. ... Washington, DC
Teich, Katherine M. Blakeley
Norwalk, CT
Teich, Michael L. ... Chicago, IL
Teich, Morris ... Bayonne, NJ
Teich, Scott M. ... Hollywood, FL
Teich, Stanley J. ... New City, NY
Teich, Steve Emery ... San Francisco, CA
Teich, Susan Froehly ... Houston, TX
Teichberg, Arthur J. ... **New York, NY**
Teichberg, Arthur J., A Professional Corporation ... **New York, NY**
Teicher, Bruce J. ... Cleveland, OH
Teicher, David L. ... New York, NY
Teicher, Gayle R.
Federal Communications Commission, Common Carrier Bureau, GV
Teicher, Irving M. ... Long Branch, NJ
Teicher, Julie Beth ... **Southfield, MI**
Teicher, Mark L. ... Southfield, MI
Teicher, Martin A. ... Melville, NY
Teicher, Milton S. ... New York, NY
Teicher, Robert L. ... **Southport, CT**
Teicher, Stephanie L. ... **New York, NY**
Teicher, Stuart I. ... **Portland, OR**
Teichert, A. Annette ... **Atlanta, GA**
Teichert, Eileen Monaghan ... Riverside, CA
Teichert, Henry ... Sacramento, CA
Teichert, Lorie J. ... Sacramento, CA
Teichgraeber, Thomas G. ... Chicago, IL
Teichholz, Andrew D. ... **New York, NY**
Teichler, Stephen L. ... **Washington, DC**
Teichman, Andrea M. ... **Boston, MA**
Teichman, Harry P ... **Tampa, FL**
Teichman, Howard A. ... **Lawrenceville, NJ**
Teichman, J. Bruce ... Omaha, NE
Teichman, Joseph ... Hallandale Beach, FL
Teichman, Judith L. ... San Francisco, CA
Teichman, Michael W. ... **Wilmington, DE**
Teichman, Randi S. ... San Francisco, CA
Teichman, Steven ... **New York, NY**
Teichmann, David L. ... Milpitas, CA
Teichner, Bruce A. ... **Northbrook, IL**
Teichner, Howard R. ... Syosset, NY
Teichner, Lee Philip ... **Miami, FL**
Teichner, Leon J., & Associates
Chicago, IL
Teichner, Marcus S. ... St. Paul, MN
Teicholz, Barry B. ... **Boston, MA**
Teicholz, Thomas ... New York, NY
Teig, Arthur E. ... East Weymouth, MA
Teig, Brenda L. ... Las Vegas, NV
Teig, Joe M., (P.C.) ... **Jackson, WY**
Teig, Morris ... Stamford, CT
Teigen, Henry C. ... Denver, CO
Teigen, Pamela J. ... Chicago, IL
Teigen, Philip J. ... Englewood, CO
Teigen, Richard L. ... **Milwaukee, WI**
Teiger, Larry ... Atlanta, GA
Teiger, Lawrence T.
Pension Benefit Guaranty Corporation, Office of the General Counsel, GV
Teigland, Lauren A. ... **New York, NY**
Teiken, Patricia R. ... St. Paul, MN
Teilborg, James A. ... **Phoenix, AZ**
Teilborg, Sanders & Parks, Professional Corporation ... **Phoenix, AZ**
Teilh, Paul R. ... San Jose, CA
Teillon, L. Pierre, Jr. ... **Philadelphia, PA**
West Conshohocken, PA
Teiman, Richard B. ... **New York, NY**
Teimourian, Sheila M. ... **Washington, DC**
Tein, Michael ... Miami, FL
Teipel, John L. ... Macon, GA
Teir, Robert ... Washington, DC
Teis, Lawrence B. ... Graham, TX
Teisher, Sheila A. ... Los Angeles, CA
Teismann, Kevin P. ... Redmond, WA
Teitcher, Carrie W. ... Brooklyn, NY
Teitel, Jeffrey H. ... New York, NY
Teitel, Leah ... Elizabeth, NJ
Teitel, Louis E. ... New York, NY
Teitel, Richard ... Baltimore, MD
Teitel, Richard D. ... Los Angeles, CA
Teitel, Ruti G. ... New York, NY
Teitelbaum, Aaron ... New York, NY
Teitelbaum, Alan D. ... Bridgeton, MO
Teitelbaum, Braverman & Borges, P.C.
New Hyde Park, NY
Teitelbaum & Caccavale, P.C. ... Clifton, NJ
New York, NY
Teitelbaum, Carol ... Louisville, KY
Teitelbaum, David ... **Washington, DC**
Teitelbaum, David ... New York, NY
Teitelbaum, Edward M. ... Clifton, NJ
New York, NY
Teitelbaum, Eliot L. ... **Los Angeles, CA**
Teitelbaum, George A. ... **Washington, DC**
Teitelbaum, Herbert ... **New York, NY**
Teitelbaum, Hugh E. ... Pittsburgh, PA
Teitelbaum, Isidore ... East Brunswick, NJ
Teitelbaum, Israel ... Silver Spring, MD
Teitelbaum, Jay ... **New York, NY**
Teitelbaum, Jill ... **Los Angeles, CA**
Teitelbaum, Joshua C. ... New York, NY
Teitelbaum, Joshua S. ... **New York, NY**
Teitelbaum, Lawrence ... **New York, NY**
Teitelbaum, Lloyd H. ... **Boston, MA**
Teitelbaum, Marc D. ... **New York, NY**
Teitelbaum, Marilyn Schaffner
St. Louis, MO
Teitelbaum, Martin H. ... Westlake Village, CA
Teitelbaum, Martin J. ... Smithtown, NY
Teitelbaum, Melvin ... Los Angeles, CA
Teitelbaum, Miriam ... New Hyde Park, NY
Teitelbaum, Noah E. ... New York, NY
Teitelbaum, Ozer ... Dearborn, MI
Teitelbaum, Rhonda G. ... Denver, CO
Teitelbaum, Robert J. ... New York, NY
Teitelbaum, Robert W. ... Flushing, NY
Teitelbaum, Shelley ... New York, NY
Teitelbaum, Steven A. ... **Washington, DC**
Teitelbaum, Steven U. ... Albany, NY
Teitelbaum, Terri W. ... Philadelphia, PA
Teitelbaum, William J. ... **Dallas, TX**
Teitelbaum, William J., P.C., Law Office of
Dallas, TX
Duncanville, TX
Teitell, Catherine E. ... Bridgeport, CT
Teitell, Conrad ... **Stamford, CT**
Teitell, Ernest F. ... **Stamford, CT**
Teitell, Jamey A. ... Los Angeles, CA
Teitelman, Richard B. ... St. Louis, MO
Teitelman, Robert B. ... Hartford, CT
Teitelman, S. Robert ... Collingswood, NJ
Teitelman, Samuel
Equal Employment Opportunity Commission, Office of Federal Operations, GV
Teitelman, Saul ... Cherry Hill, NJ
Teitelman & Teitelman ... Collingswood, NJ
Teitenberg, John ... **Louisville, KY**
Teitenberg, Robert A. ... West Hartford, CT
Teitenberg & Wallace ... West Hartford, CT
Teitge, Carl D. ... Tacoma, WA
Teitge, Carl, Inc., P.S. ... Tacoma, WA
Teitle, Morton A. ... Davenport, IA
Teitler, John M. ... **New York, NY**
Teitler, Jules R. ... Mount Laurel, NJ
Teitler, Michael F. ... **New York, NY**
Teitler, Paul H. ... Camden, NJ
Teitler, Robert L. ... **Miami, FL**
Teitler, Stanley A. ... **New York, NY**
Teitler, Stanley A., P.C. ... **New York, NY**
Teitler & Teitler ... **New York, NY**
Teitz, Alexandra
Environmental Protection Agency, Office of the General Counsel, GV
Teitz, Andrew M. ... Providence, RI
Teitz, Elisheva S. ... **New York, NY**
Teixeira, Charles P. ... **San Francisco, CA**
Teixeira, Charles S. ... New York, NY
Teixeira, Elizabeth ... Taunton, MA
Teixeira, J. Stanley ... Fresno, CA
Teixeira, James C. ... Riverside, CA
Teixeira, Luciana Santos ... **New York, NY**
Teja, G. Dave ... Yuba City, CA
Tejani, Sonal ... Atlanta, GA
Tejani, Zohra T. ... **McLean, VA**
Tejeda, Roderick Anibal ... Monticello, KY
Tejeiro, Joseph V. ... New York, NY
Tejera, Richard E. ... Coral Gables, FL
Tejml, Sue Rosson ... Argyle, TX
Tek, Laura ... Madison, TN
Tekavec, James W. ... Cleveland, OH
Tekell, Angela Eads ... Waco, TX
Tekell, Book, Matthews & Limmer, L.L.P.
Corpus Christi, TX
Houston, TX
Tekell, David G. ... **Waco, TX**
Tekell, Kenneth ... **Houston, TX**
Tekell, Kenneth L., Jr. ... **Houston, TX**
Teker, Lawrence J. ... **Hagåtña, GU**
Tekerian, Elaine M. ... Corte Madera, CA
Tekiel, Leo ... Westbury, NY
TeKippe, Jeffrey R. ... Clarion, IA
TeKippe, Richard P. ... New Hampton, IA
Teklinski, Chester A. ... San Diego, CA
Teklits, David J. ... **Wilmington, DE**
Teklits, Joseph A. ... **Blue Bell, PA**
Te Kolste, Dale ... Omaha, NE
TeKolste, H. Kim ... Indianapolis, IN
Tekosky, Steven R. ... **Los Angeles, CA**
Teks, Arnold ... Florence, AL
Tekulsky, Joseph D. ... Los Angeles, CA
Tekulsky, Steven ... **New York, NY**
Tekunoff, Daniel J. ... **Fresno, CA**
Tela, Donald A. ... Albertson, NY
New York, NY
Telan, Patrick H. ... **Orlando, FL**
Telander, Bruce E. ... Miami, FL
Telanoff, Adam J. ... Santa Monica, CA
Telchin, Joseph G. ... Sarasota, FL
Telecki, Claire R. ... Malverne, NY
Telecki, Nicole ... **Washington, DC**
Telegadas, Francis E. ... **Richmond, VA**
Telegadis, George S. ... Los Angeles, CA
Telegen, Arthur G. ... **Boston, MA**
Telehany, Paul P. ... **Montgomery, AL**
Teleisha, William C. ... Hempstead, NY
Teleky-Petrella, Lorraine ... Hackensack, NJ
Telemaque, Yves-Merry
Cambria Heights, NY
Telep, Jeffrey M. ... **Washington, DC**
Telep, Michael T., Jr. ... Yuma, AZ
Telepas, George P., (P.A.) ... Vail, CO
Telepman, James S.
North Palm Beach, FL
Telerant, David ... Encino, CA
Telerant, Michael M. ... Beverly Hills, CA
Telesca, Michael A. ... Rochester, NY
Telese, Lina G. ... **New York, NY**
Telesford, Cyrena Ann ... Brooklyn, NY
Telesko, Tamara G. ... New York, NY
Telfair, Brian K. ... **Richmond, VA**
Telfair, Charles W., IV ... **Sarasota, FL**
Telfer, Grant Richard ... San Diego, CA
Telfer, James S. ... Indianapolis, IN
Telfer, James V. ... **San Francisco, CA**
Telfer, Jill P. ... Carmichael, CA
Telfer, Philip A. ... Raleigh, NC
Telfer, Robert J., III
West Palm Beach, FL
Telfer, Robert J., Jr. ... **Melbourne, FL**
Telfeyan, Stephen J. ... Chesapeake, VA
Telford, Charles E., III ... **Buffalo, NY**
Telford, John L., Jr ... **Atlanta, GA**
Telford, Larry W. ... **San Francisco, CA**
Telford, Leslie ... Sarasota, FL
Telford, Ned P. ... **Sacramento, CA**
Telford, Q. Ellis ... **Boston, MA**
Telford, Stephen H. ... **Idaho Falls, ID**
Telge, Timothy E. ... Houston, TX
Telgenhof, Allen R. ... **Charlevoix, MI**
Telias, Albert R. ... Bronx, NY
Telias, Albert R ... New York, NY
Telias, Henry ... Long Beach, NY
Telich, Mark S. ... Cleveland, OH
Teliska, John J., Jr. ... Troy, NY
Telisman, Alan ... Miami, FL
Telkamp, Bruce A. ... Palo Alto, CA
Telke, Johanna F. ... **Kansas City, MO**
Telken, Stephen J. ... **St. Louis, MO**
Telker, Ellen M. ... Milford, CT
Tell, A. Charles ... **Columbus, OH**
Tell, Cheser & Breitbart, L.L.P.
Morristown, NJ
Mountainside, NJ
Brooklyn, NY
Garden City, NY
New York, NY
White Plains, NY
Tell, Franklin D. ... **Garden City, NY**
New York, NY
Tell, Gary S. ... **Washington, DC**
Tell, M. David ... **New York, NY**
Tell, Meah Rothman ... Boca Raton, FL
Tell, Meah Rothman, P.A. ... Boca Raton, FL
Tell, Robert H. ... **Mountainside, NJ**
Tell, William K. ... Palm Beach, FL
Tell, William K., Jr. ... White Plains, NY
Tellalian, Aram H., Jr. ... **Bridgeport, CT**
Tellalian, Robert S. ... **Bridgeport, CT**
Tellalian & Tellalian ... **Bridgeport, CT**
Tellam, Bradley F. ... **Portland, OR**
Tellam, Frederick G. ... San Diego, CA
Tellam, Leanne Frazee ... **Miami, FL**
Tellarico, Paul J. ... **Alexandria, LA**
Telle, Jack M. ... Benton, KY
Telle, Michael S. ... **Houston, TX**
Tellechea, Albert F. ... **Orlando, FL**
Telleen, Braendle, Horberg & Smith, P.C.
Cambridge, IL
Telleen, David R. ... Department of State, Foreign Service Officers (Overseas), GV
Telleen, John D. ... **Rock Island, IL**
Davenport, IA
Telleen, John M. ... Rock Island, IL
Telleen, Kenneth L. ... **Cambridge, IL**
Telleen, L. Michael ... **Burlingame, CA**
Telleen, Philip R. ... Lombard, IL
Tellefsen, Charmaine ... Chicago, IL
Tellefsen, Ralph F., III ... Elmhurst, IL
Tellegen, W. Martin ... **San Francisco, CA**
Tellekson, David K. ... **Minneapolis, MN**
Tellem, Arn H., (P.C.) ... Santa Monica, CA
Tellem, Nancy R. ... Culver City, CA
Teller, Adam J. ... **East Hartford, CT**
Teller, B. Blake ... **Vicksburg, MS**
Teller, Barry J. ... Forest Hills, NY
Teller, Bonnie A. ... **Miami, FL**
Teller, Chaney, Hassell & Hopson, LLP
Vicksburg, MS
Teller, Ellen G. ... Houston, TX
Teller, Herbert J. ... Spruce Pine, NC
Teller, Howard B. ... Annapolis, MD
Rockville, MD
Teller, Jerome S. ... **Cincinnati, OH**
Teller, Jonathan C. ... New York, NY
Teller, Kathryn G.
General Services Administration, Office of Regional Counsel, GV
Teller & Keller ... Wilkes-Barre, PA
Teller, Landman ... Vicksburg, MS
Teller, Landman, Jr. ... **Vicksburg, MS**
Teller, Levit & Silvertrust, P.C.
Chicago, IL
Teller, Mayrav ... New York, NY
Teller, Michael W. ... **New York, NY**
Teller, Philip ... Rockaway Park, NY
Teller, Ralph P. ... Seattle, WA
Teller, Richard ... **Boston, MA**
Teller, Samuel H. ... Bolton, CT
Teller, Stephen A. ... Wilkes-Barre, PA
Teller, Stephen A. ... **Tacoma, WA**
Teller, Stephen L. ... **Los Angeles, CA**
Teller, Stuart A. ... Hollywood, FL
Teller, Susan E. ... Portland, OR
Teller, Walter S. ... Beverly Hills, CA
Teller, Wendy A. ... **Scarsdale, NY**
Telleria, Anthony F. ... Pasadena, CA
Tellerine, Philip J. ... South Pasadena, CA
Tellerman, Glenn Harris ... Mineola, NY
Tellerman Paticoff Greenberg & Taubman
New York, NY
Tellerman, Stanley V. ... **New York, NY**
Telles, Bruce ... **Beverly Hills, CA**
Telles, Jess P., Jr. ... **Dos Palos, CA**
Telles, Jess Port, IV ... **Sacramento, CA**
Telles & Kochenderfer, LLP
Sacramento, CA
San Francisco, CA
Walnut Creek, CA
Telles, Robert L. ... **Walnut Creek, CA**
Telley, Murlene Worth ... Norman, OK
Telleysh, Gail H. ... New York, NY
Tellez, Debra ... Houston, TX
Tellez, Jose S. ... Laredo, TX
Tellez, Julio G. ... Chicago, IL
Tellez, Raul E. ... **Cincinnati, OH**
Tellie, Nicholas D. ... Dunmore, PA
Tellier, Deborah K. ... **San Francisco, CA**
Tellier, John R. ... **Scottsdale, AZ**
Tellier, Paul E. ... Treasury Department, Internal Revenue Service, GV
Telling, Edward R., III ... **Rockford, IL**
Tellinghuisen, Roger A. ... **Lead, SD**
Spearfish, SD
Tellini, Mark P.
Securities and Exchange Commission, Executive Staff, GV
Tellio, Russell R. K. ... Honolulu, HI
Tellis, Robert E. ... Sudbury, MA
Tellis, Roland K. ... **Los Angeles, CA**
Tellis-Warren, Patricia A. ... Cambridge, MA
Tello, Carol P. ... **Washington, DC**
Tello, James W. ... **Washington, DC**
Tello, John A. ... **Bakersfield, CA**
Tellstrom, Joyce A. ... **Greenwood, IN**
Telman, Deborah H. ... **Chicago, IL**
Telman, H. James ... Grand Rapids, MI
Telman, Nigel F. ... **Chicago, IL**
Telman, Raymond S. ... Lansing, MI
Telpner, Brian J. ... **Washington, DC**
Telpner, Maynard S. ... **Council Bluffs, IA**
Telpner, Peterson, Smith & Ruesch
Council Bluffs, IA
Omaha, NE
Telquist, George E. ... **Kennewick, WA**
Telscher, Margaret A. ... Ridgewood, NJ
Telscher, Rudolph A., Jr. ... St. Louis, MO
Telsey, Albert I. ... Newark, NJ
Telsey, Andrew I. ... Aurora, CO
Telsey, Andrew I., P.C. ... Aurora, CO
Telsey, Suzanne Lisa ... New York, NY
Telson, Scott A. ... Edison, NJ
Telstad, Cindy K. ... **Winona, MN**
Telstad, Harold O. ... Newport News, VA
Telthorst, James A. ... **Edwardsville, IL**
Telthorst, Robert M. ... Topeka, KS
Telthorst, Thomas R. ... Kansas City, KS

Tenney, Barbara K.
Greenwood Village, CO
Tenney & Bentley, LLC ... **Chicago, IL**
Tenney, Beth C. ... **Burlingame, CA**
Tenney, Carl J. ... **Decatur, IL**
Tenney, Charles H. ... New York, NY
Tenney, Charles W. ... Boston, MA
Tenney, Cornelia R. ... **Boston, MA**
Tenney, Dudley B. ... Port Washington, NY
Tenney, Eugene C. ... **Buffalo, NY**
Tenney, George W. ... Walnut Creek, CA
Tenney, Harold F. ... Decatur, IL
Tenney, James F. ... **Atlanta, GA**
Tenney, James H. ... Alexandria, VA
Tenney, James P. ... **New York, NY**
Tenney, John M. ... **Houston, TX**
Tenney, John R. ... Utica, NY
Tenney, Juliann ... Raleigh, NC
Tenney, M. Blair ... Troy, MI
Tenney, Marc A. ... St. Petersburg, FL
Tenney, Michael P. ... Austin, TX
Tenney, Robert C. ... **Yakima, WA**
Tenney, Rockwell ... Cold Spring, NY
Tenney, Sally G. ... Seattle, WA
Tennille, Ben F. ... Greensboro, NC
Tennis, Cabell ... Seattle, WA
Tennis and Collins, P.A. ... **Forest Lake, MN**
Tennis, Diana M. ... **Orlando, FL**
Tennis, Diana M., P.A. ... **Orlando, FL**
Winter Park, FL
Tennis, Garold Edward ... Philadelphia, PA
Tennis, Greig R. ... **Forest Lake, MN**
Tennis, Stephen M. ... San Jose, CA
Tennis, William J. ... **Washington, DC**
Tennison, Mark N. ... Kansas City, MO
Tennison, Mary Christine ... **San Diego, CA**
Tennison, Pamela J. ... San Francisco, CA
Tenno, Winifred Y. ... **Honolulu, HI**
Tenny, Barron M. ... New York, NY
Tenny, Scott W. ... **Colorado Springs, CO**
Tennyson, D. Kay ... **Columbia, SC**
Tennyson, Gary W. ... Panama City, FL
Tennyson, Jeffrey A. ... **Jackson, WY**
Tennyson, Joseph L. ... Charleston, MS
Tennyson, Katherine E. ... **Portland, OR**
Tennyson, Mary M. ... Olympia, WA
Tennyson, Peter J. ... **Costa Mesa, CA**
Tennyson, Rod ... West Palm Beach, FL
Tennyson, Rod, P.A. ... West Palm Beach, FL
Tennyson, Susan E. ... Wimberley, TX
Tennyson & Winemiller ... **Portland, OR**
Ten Oever, Jonathan E.A. ... **New York, NY**
Tenoever, Kathleen M. ... Washington, DC
Tenold, Ronald C. ... Monmouth, IL
Tenopir & Huerter ... **Topeka, KS**
Tenopir, Lawrence L. ... **Topeka, KS**
Tenorio, Christopher Paul
Department of Justice,
Office of the Deputy Attorney General, GV
Tenorio, Gregory A. ... Sacramento, CA
Tenorio, Sylvia ... Department of Justice,
Criminal Division, GV
Ten Pas, Paul H. ... **Kohler, WI**
Tenpas, Ronald J. ... Tampa, FL
Tenpenny, Chad David ... United States Senate,
Senatorial Assistants, GV
Tenser, Arthur S. ... **New York, NY**
Tenser, Charles H., III ... **Boca Raton, FL**
Ten State International, L.L.P.
Charleston, SC
Tentindo, Vincent M. ... **Boston, MA**
Tentinger, Jay A. ... Minneapolis, MN
Tentler, Leslie A. ... **Johnson City, TN**
Kingsport, TN
Tentler, Richard W. ... Oxnard, CA
Santa Barbara, CA
Tentser, Irina F. ... **Los Angeles, CA**
Tenuta, Frank Cal ... Sioux City, IA
Tenuta, Luigia ... Columbus, OH
Tenuta, Rhoda Marie ... Sioux City, IA
Tenuto, Mary Ann ... Palo Alto, CA
Tenuto, V. James ... Maywood, IL
Tenwick, Thomas J. ... Rocky River, OH
Tenwick, William A. ... North Fort Myers, FL
Tenyak, Carol L. ... Chicago, IL
Tenzer, Ana Lazo ... **Denver, CO**
Tenzer, Andrew V. ... **New York, NY**
Tenzer, Babette ... Millburn, NJ
Tenzer, Barry ... New York, NY
Tenzer, Bruce M. ... **New York, NY**
Tenzer, David E. ... **Denver, CO**
Tenzer, David I. ... **Roanoke, VA**
Tenzer, David S. ... Beverly Hills, CA
Tenzer Greenblatt LLP ... **New York, NY**
Tenzer, Greenblatt & Zunz, P.A.
Hackensack, NJ
Tenzer, Jerrold A. ... Coral Springs, FL
Tenzer and Lunin LLP ... **New York, NY**
Tenzer, Marvin L. ... **New York, NY**
Tenzer, Michael A. ... Burbank, CA
Tenzer, Michael L. ... Fort Lauderdale, FL
Tenzer, Michael L., P.A.
Fort Lauderdale, FL
Tenzer, Mitchell C. ... **Los Angeles, CA**
Tenzer, Steven J. ... Chicago, IL
Tenzer, Stuart Richard ... Beverly Hills, CA
Tenzer, Wendy L. ... New York, NY
Tenzer-Gross, Ronit ... New York, NY
Teo, Faith T. ... **New York, NY**
Teobaldi, Darci D. ... **Oxnard, CA**
Teodori, Thomas ... Greenbelt, MD
Teodosio, Alexander E. ... Akron, OH
Teodosio, Cherpas. Manos & Ward
Akron, OH
Teodosio, Francis A. ... Shelton, CT
Teodosio, Linda Tucci ... Akron, OH
Teodosio, Thomas Alan ... Akron, OH
Teofan, Vernon O. ... **Dallas, TX**

Teofan, Yvette P. ... **New York, NY**
Teoli, William A. ... **Latham, NY**
Tepas, Kevin M. ... **Stamford, CT**
TePaske, John D. ... Orange City, IA
TePaske, Rens, Rensink & Pluim
Orange City, IA
Tepe, John B., Jr. ... **Wilmington, DE**
Tepe, R. Edward ... **Cincinnati, OH**
Tepe, Thomas M. ... **Cincinnati, OH**
Tepe, Timothy A. ... **Cincinnati, OH**
Tepe, Timothy N. ... Cincinnati, OH
Tepe, Timothy N. ... **Franklin, OH**
Springboro, OH
Tepedino, Francis J. ... San Diego, CA
Tepedino, Michael V. ... Albany, NY
Teper, Helene R. ... **New York, NY**
Teper, James M. ... **Chicago, IL**
Teper, Robert A. ... **Milwaukee, WI**
Teper, Terry D. ... Milwaukee, WI
Teperman, Bruce Roy ... New York, NY
Teperman, Jos. H. ... New York, NY
Teperman & Teperman ... New York, NY
Teperson, Jonathan B. ... **Santa Monica, CA**
Tepfer, Elizabeth M. ... Houghton, MI
Tepfer, Herbert ... Brooklyn, NY
Tepfer, Joseph ... Brooklyn, NY
Tephly, Annette M. ... **Rock Island, IL**
Tepikian, Bruce R. ... **Kansas City, MO**
Teple, Edwin R. ... Willoughby, OH
Teplen, Philip H. ... **New York, NY**
Tepler, Sheldon Joel ... Lewiston, ME
Tepley, Adelbert T. ... Windsor, CT
Tepley, Eugene H. ... Denver, CO
Tepley, Stephen O. ... Chattanooga, TN
Teplin, Lawrence ... **Los Angeles, CA**
Teplinsky, Allan D. ... Northridge, CA
Teplinsky, Howard L. ... **Chicago, IL**
Teplinsky, Scott A. ... **Minneapolis, MN**
Teplinsky, Steven B. ... **Washington, DC**
Teplinsky, Steven J. ... **Chicago, IL**
Teplitz, Jack B. ... Peoria, IL
Teplitz, Jerome M. ... Tucson, AZ
Teplitz, Mary Sue ... **Pittsburgh, PA**
Teplitz, Steven N. ... Washington, DC
Teplitzky, Joshua A. ... Woodbridge, CT
Teplitzky, Ronald J. ... **Cleveland, OH**
Teplitzky, Sanford V. ... **Baltimore, MD**
Teply, Ruth Elizabeth ... Phoenix, AZ
Tepp, Heidi S. ... **Madison, WI**
Tepp, Steven M. ... United States Senate,
Committee Legal Personnel, GV
Tepper, Alan M. ... Cherry Hill, NJ
Tepper, Andrew ... Cherry Hill, NJ
Tepper, Arthur L. ... Brooklyn, NY
Tepper, Benjamin B. ... Miami, FL
Tepper, Bradley D. ... **Albuquerque, NM**
Tepper, Cary S. ... Washington, DC
Tepper & Dardeck ... **Ludlow, VT**
Rutland, VT
Tepper, E. Clothier ... **Boston, MA**
Tepper, Edward P. ... Champaign, IL
Tepper, Eric A. ... **Glenville, NY**
Tepper, Foster ... Beverly Hills, CA
Tepper, Foster, Inc., A Professional Corporation
Beverly Hills, CA
Tepper, Frank J. ... Ormond Beach, FL
Tepper, Gary C. ... **Washington, DC**
Tepper & Gwinn, A Professional Corporation ... **Urbana, IL**
Tepper, H. Marc ... **Philadelphia, PA**
Tepper, Herbert S. ... Flushing, NY
Tepper, Ivan H. ... Waukegan, IL
Tepper, Jacqueline G. ... Stamford, CT
Tepper, Jean P. ... San Francisco, CA
Tepper, Jeffrey A. ... San Jose, CA
Tepper, Jerome A. ... Milwaukee, WI
Tepper, Julian, (P.C.) ... Bethesda, MD
Tepper, Kenneth L. ... **Blue Bell, PA**
Tepper, Lewis ... New York, NY
Tepper, Lynn ... Dade City, FL
Tepper, Mark A. ... **Fort Lauderdale, FL**
Tepper, Mark A., P.A.
Fort Lauderdale, FL
Miami, FL
Tepper, Mark S. ... Livingston, NJ
Tepper, Marla Anne ... New York, NY
Tepper, Marvin B. ... Great Neck, NY
Tepper, Maury M. ... Cincinnati, OH
Tepper, Maury M., III
Research Triangle Park, NC
Tepper, Michael ... **Urbana, IL**
Tepper, Michael A. ... Skokie, IL
Tepper, Michael A., & Associates, P.C.
Skokie, IL
Tepper, Michael S. ... **Chicago, IL**
Tepper, Miles M. ... West Orange, NJ
Tepper, Nancy Boxley ... Laguna Hills, CA
Tepper, Nancy Boxley, A Professional Corporation ... Laguna Hills, CA
Tepper, Noel ... Poughkeepsie, NY
Tepper, Pamela R. ... Dallas, TX
Tepper, Paul S. ... Los Angeles, CA
Tepper, R. Bruce, Jr. ... **Los Angeles, CA**
Tepper, Rebecca L. ... **Boston, MA**
Tepper, Robert D. ... **Chicago, IL**
Tepper, Robert I. ... **Rutland, VT**
Tepper, Robert J. ... Santa Fe, NM
Tepper, Robert R. ... Chicago, IL
Tepper, Roberta L. ... Charlotte, NC
Tepper, Rubin ... Palo Alto, CA
Tepper, Scott C., (P.A.) ... Ormond Beach, FL
Tepper, Scott J. ... Los Angeles, CA
Tepper, Sharyn A. ... Chicago, IL
Tepper, Sherrie L. ... Albuquerque, NM
Tepper, Steven G. ... **New York, NY**
Tepperman, Ellen M. ... New York, NY
Tepperman, H. Peter ... Kenilworth, NJ
Tepperman, Lynda ... **New York, NY**

Teppert, Laurel S. ... Elmhurst, IL
Teppert, Robert A. ... Chicago, IL
Teppler, Steven W. ... Washington, DC
Teppola, Susan Ertle ... Beaverton, OR
Tepps, Jerome Lewis ... Fort Lauderdale, FL
Tepstein, Daniel C. ... **Los Angeles, CA**
Teraberry, Kimberly K. ... **Seattle, WA**
Terada, Bonnie Y. ... Vancouver, WA
Terada, Suzanne T. ... Honolulu, HI
Teragawa, Karen Y. ... **Pasadena, CA**
Terai, Cheryl J. ... **Pittsburgh, PA**
Terai, Tsunemasa ... **New York, NY**
Terakawa, Alan K. ... Los Angeles, CA
Terakedis, J. Troy ... **Columbus, OH**
Terakedis, John, Jr. ... **Columbus, OH**
Teran, Carlos M. ... Claremont, CA
Teran, Diana M. ... Los Angeles, CA
Teran, Rina Elizabeth ... **New York, NY**
Teran, Ruben S. ... Douglas, AZ
Teranes, Paul S. ... Detroit, MI
Terango, Ivana ... Treasury Department,
Office of Thrift Supervision, GV
Teraoka & Associates, A Law Corporation
San Francisco, CA
Teraoka, Steven G. ... **San Francisco, CA**
Terapak, Richard G. ... **Columbus, OH**
Teras, Christopher A. ... **Washington, DC**
Terasaki, Carey W.
Department of Transportation,
Federal Aviation Administration, GV
Terauchi, Terrence S. ... Los Angeles, CA
Terbeek, Jeffrey L. ... Columbus, OH
Ter Beek, John E. ... Wyoming, MI
Terbeek, Marc Lawrence ... **Oakland, CA**
Terbush, Janice V. ... Detroit, MI
Terbush, Theron L. ... Washington, DC
Terc, Joseph A. ... Chicago, IL
Tercero, Napoleon G., III
Los Angeles, CA
Tercero, Roberto A. ... Los Angeles, CA
Tercha & Daavettila ... Houghton, MI
Tercha, James F. ... Houghton, MI
Tercilla, Fernando O. ... Miami, FL
Teren, Pamela McKibbin
Los Angeles, CA
Terens, Lori E. ... Jacksonville, FL
Terenzi, Ronald M. ... **Garden City, NY**
Terenzio, Celia A. ... West Palm Beach, FL
Terenzio, Joseph V. ... Miami, FL
Terenzio, Lisa ... Manchester, CT
Terenzio, Robert T.
Altamonte Springs, FL
Terepka, John H. ... New York, NY
Teresi, Joseph C. ... Albany, NY
Teresinski, Jerome J. ... Philadelphia, PA
Tereskerz, Patricia M. ... Charlottesville, VA
Tereskerz, Terry L. ... Charlottesville, VA
Teresso, Amy R. ... **Costa Mesa, CA**
Teret, Stephen P. ... Baltimore, MD
Terez, Dennis G. ... Cleveland, OH
Terflinger, Curtis D. ... Wichita, KS
Terhaar, Archibald, Pfefferle & Griebel, LLP
Minneapolis, MN
Ter Haar, F. Wiete ... Sacramento, CA
Terhaar, Robert J. ... **Minneapolis, MN**
Terhar, Michael J. ... **Los Angeles, CA**
Terheyden, William F. ... **San Francisco, CA**
Terhoeve, Henry G. ... **Baton Rouge, LA**
ter Horst, Eleanor ... Tucson, AZ
Terhune, Cassandra Lyn ... Kansas City, MO
Terhune, Charles P., Jr. ... Middletown, OH
Terhune, Hannah ... Toms River, NJ
Terhune, Henry A. ... **Washington, DC**
Terhune, John J. ... DeLand, FL
Terhune, Karen L. ... Washington, DC
Terhune, Kristine E. ... **Boston, MA**
Terhune, Stella ... Yorktown Heights, NY
Terhune, Wm. Peter, II
San Luis Obispo, CA
Terilla, J. Anthony ... Cuyahoga Falls, OH
Terilli, Samuel A., Jr. ... **Miami, FL**
Teringo, James K., Jr. ... Houston, TX
Terino, Raffaele M.
White River Junction, VT
Terio, B. Cheryl ... **Washington, DC**
Terjak, Maureen ... Chicago, IL
Terjesen, Barry E. ... Akron, OH
Terk, Lauren M. ... **Larkspur, CA**
San Francisco, CA
Terk, Robert E. ... Fitchburg, MA
Terkanian, Harry Sarkis ... **Orleans, MA**
Terkell, Joseph I ... White Plains, NY
Terl, Allan H. ... Fort Lauderdale, FL
Terlaje, Deborah M. ... Hagåtña, GU
Terlaje, Edward S. ... Hagåtña, GU
Terlaje, Therese M. ... Hagåtña, GU
Terlecky, Myron N. ... Columbus, OH
Terlecky, Theodore N. ... Davis, CA
Terlep, Anthony J., Jr. ... South Bend, IN
Terlep, Bruce S. ... **Wheaton, IL**
Terlep, Susan H. ... **Towson, MD**
Terlep, Vincent B., Jr.
Department of Justice, Civil Division, GV
Terlisner, Laura ... **Dallas, TX**
Terlizzese, Paul T. ... Vero Beach, FL
Terlizzi, Eric L. ... Salem, IL
Terlizzi, James D. ... West Palm Beach, FL
Terlizzi, Lewis W. ... **Elgin, IL**
Terlizzi, Raymond T. ... Tucson, AZ
TerMaat, Thomas R. ... **Grand Rapids, MI**
Terman, Donna L. ... Menlo Park, CA
Terman, Earl ... Phoenix, AZ
Terman, James L. ... Chicago, IL
Terman, Mark E. ... **Los Angeles, CA**
Terman, Stephen D. ... **Washington, DC**
Terminello, Louis J. ... **Miami, FL**
Terminello, Nancy ... **Miami, FL**
Terminello & Terminello, P.A. ... **Miami, FL**

Termini, Charles ... New York, NY
Termini, Chris P. ... **Mineola, NY**
Termini, James T. ... Houston, TX
Termini, Mark M. ... Cleveland, OH
Termini, Michael ... Northridge, CA
Termini, Raymond J. ... **Dallas, TX**
Termohlen, Susan ... Palo Alto, CA
Ter Molen, Mark R. ... **Chicago, IL**
Termondt, M. Jas. ... Chicago, IL
Termunde, Tedd T. ... **Chicago, IL**
Ternan, Lawrence R. ... **Bloomfield Hills, MI**
Ternent, Allen A. ... Atchison, KS
Terner, Andor D. ... **Newport Beach, CA**
Terner, Benjamin B. ... Silver Spring, MD
Terner, Daniel Alan ... Miami, FL
Terner, Linda M. Johnson ... Westfield, NJ
Ternes, John P. ... Petoskey, MI
Ternes, Joseph E., Jr. ... **Henderson, KY**
Ternes, Lisa McGuire ... Nashville, TN
Ternes, Mary Ellen ... **Little Rock, AR**
Ternes, Stephen J. ... Wichita, KS
Terney, Philip B. ... Greenville, MS
Terney, Risé J. ... **Chicago, IL**
Ternlund, David J. ... Boulder, CO
Ternullo, Kelly I. ... **Santa Rosa, CA**
Ternus, Marsha K. ... Des Moines, IA
Teros, James T. ... Rock Island, IL
Terp, Karl T. ... San Diego, CA
Terp, Thomas T. ... **Cincinnati, OH**
Terpak, Nan E. ... **Arlington, VA**
Terpak, Paul B. ... **Fairfax, VA**
Terpening, Armand T. ... Garden City, NY
Terpinas, William, Jr. ... **Skokie, IL**
Terpolilli, Maria ... Philadelphia, PA
Terpstra, Anita J. ... **Chicago, IL**
Terpstra & Epping ... **Cedar Rapids, IA**
Terpstra, H. Raymond, II
Cedar Rapids, IA
Terpstra, John H. ... Grinnell, IA
Newton, IA
Sully, IA
Terpstra, John W. ... Elk River, MN
Terpstra, Thomas H. ... **Stockton, CA**
Terputac, Thomas J. ... Washington, PA
Terr, Leonard B. ... **Washington, DC**
Terr, Lewis J. ... Santa Fe, NM
Terra, Anne M. ... **Newport Beach, CA**
Terra Law LLP ... Burlingame, CA
San Francisco, CA
San Jose, CA
Terra, Sharon Ecker ... Pittsburgh, PA
Terracciano, Peter John ... Syosset, NY
Terrace, Sarah E. ... St. Louis, MO
Terraciano, Annmarie ... **New York, NY**
Terral, Cinda Sistrunk ... Baton Rouge, LA
Terrall, Scott H. ... Portland, OR
Terrana, Angelo C., Jr. ... **Kingston, PA**
Terrana, Angelo C., Jr. ... **Wilkes-Barre, PA**
Terrana, John Joseph ... Kingston, PA
Terrana, John V. ... Melville, NY
Mineola, NY
Terrana, Joseph J. ... Wilkes-Barre, PA
Terrana, Michael J., P.A. ... Tampa, FL
Terrando, Thomas Joseph ... Houston, TX
Terranella, Frank ... Pennington, NJ
Terranella, Mary Ellen ... Hillsborough, CA
Terranova, Cathy Schwartz ... Buffalo, NY
Terranova, Domenic S. ... North Andover, MA
Terranova, Frank M. ... Hasbrouck Heights, NJ
Terranova, Greg ... Portland, OR
Terranova, James M.
Englewood Cliffs, NJ
Terranova, Joseph ... Garden City, NY
Terranova, Leah J. ... **Stamford, CT**
New York, NY
Terranova, Pamela S. ... Fort Lauderdale, FL
Terranova, Patrick J. ... **Santa Clara, CA**
Terranova, Paul ... **New York, NY**
Terranova, Pina Marie ... Bronx, NY
Terranova, Susan S. ... Treasury Department,
Office of Regulations and Rulings, GV
Terrar, Edward T. ... Silver Spring, MD
Terras, Alexander ... **Chicago, IL**
Terrasa, Gabriel Antonio ... Baltimore, MD
Terrasa, Jennifer R. ... Columbia, MD
Terrazas, Alfredo ... Oakland, CA
Terrazas, Robert, (P.C.) ... Missoula, MT
Terrazino, Imelda R. ... **Chicago, IL**
Terrazone, Rodney L. ... **Los Angeles, CA**
Terrazzano, Jeann R. ... **Guilford, CT**
Terre, Joseph, Jr. ... Memphis, TN
Terrebonne, Dale E. Greer ... Jackson, MS
Terrebonne, Joel N. ... **New Orleans, LA**
Terrebonne, Lynn M. ... **Metairie, LA**
Terrebonne, Perry Walker
Pointe a la Hache, LA
Terrell, A. Dennis ... **Florham Park, NJ**
Terrell, Allen M., Jr. ... **Wilmington, DE**
Terrell, Andrew J. ... **Washington, DC**
Terrell, B. Adam ... **Beaumont, TX**
Terrell, Baugh, Salmon & Born, LLP
Evansville, IN
Terrell, Beth E. ... **Seattle, WA**
Terrell, Buford C. ... Houston, TX
Terrell, Burke B. ... **Paducah, KY**
Terrell, Butterworth and Associates
Prague, OK
Terrell, C. Matthew ... **Fort Worth, TX**
Terrell, Christopher T. ... Atlanta, GA
Terrell & Crowden, P.C. ... Waco, TX
Terrell, David A.
Commodity Futures Trading Commission,
Division of Enforcement, GV
Terrell, Don T. ... Huntsville, AL
Terrell, Donald B., & Associates
Washington, DC
Terrell, Donna B.D. ... Lexington, KY
Terrell, Dorothy E. ... **Vienna, VA**

Terrell, Dove ... Jacksonville, FL
Terrell, Francis D. ... New York, NY
Terrell, G. Irvin ... Houston, TX
Terrell, Gary R. ... Lubbock, TX
Terrell, George W. ... Wayne, PA
Terrell, George W., Jr. ... Valparaiso, IN
Terrell, Isaac ... Orlando, FL
Terrell, Isaac, P.A. ... Orlando, FL
Terrell, J. Anthony ... New York, NY
Terrell, J. David ... Prague, OK
Terrell, James D. ... Hannibal, MO
Terrell, James M. ... Birmingham, AL
Terrell, James O. ... Waco, TX
Terrell, James T. ... Jacksonville, FL
Terrell, K. Lindsay ... Beaufort, SC
Terrell, Karl M. ... Atlanta, GA
Terrell, Kathleen ... Navasota, TX
Terrell, Kenneth C. ... Washington, DC
Terrell, Lawrence P. ... Evergreen, CO
Terrell, Lawrence W., Sr. ... Maywood, IL
Terrell, Linda H. ... Paducah, KY
Terrell, Louisa McKay ... Boston, MA
Terrell, Lurese A. ... Bedford, TX
Terrell, Mark T. ... Wilmington, NC
Terrell, Michael ... Conyers, GA
Terrell, Michael C. ... Indianapolis, IN
Terrell, Randall Dean ... Austin, TX
Terrell, Richard C. ... Alice, TX
Terrell, Sarah B. ... Atlanta, GA
Terrell, Sarah B. & Assoc., P.C. ... Atlanta, GA
Terrell, Scott L. ... Golden, CO
Terrell, Seymour A. ... Gates Mills, OH
Terrell, Stephen M. ... Indianapolis, IN
Terrell, Suzanne Haik ... New Orleans, LA
Terrell, Terry D. ... Pensacola, FL
Terrell, Thomas E., Jr. ... High Point, NC
Terrell, Thomas H. ... Evansville, IN
Terrell, Thomas S. ... Kerrville, TX
Terrell & Thrall ... Valparaiso, IN
Terrell, Timothy P. ... Atlanta, GA
Terrell, Timothy W. ... Anchorage, AK
Terrell, William T. ... Little Rock, AR
Terrell-Collier, Tanya N. ... Bowie, MD
Terrelonge, Lynn R. ... Brooklyn, NY
Terrelonge, Pauline C.
Department of Justice, Civil Division, GV
Terrence, Jackye Savage ... Encino, CA
Terreni, Charles L. A. ... Columbia, SC
Terrenzi, Marisa C. ... Washington, DC
Terreri, Frank J. ... Newport Beach, CA
Terreri, Howard C. ... Scranton, PA
Terres, Joyce L. ... High Point, NC
Terres, Nora Todd ... Department of Justice, Antitrust Division, GV
Terres, Samantha H. ... Belmont, NC
Terriah, Peter R. ... Ogdensburg, NY
Terriberry, Carroll & Yancey, L.L.P.
New Orleans, LA
Terribile, Charles L. ... Charlotte, NC
Terribile, Michael ... Phoenix, AZ
Terribile, Michael, P.C. ... Phoenix, AZ
Terrien, Jeb Thomas ... Accomac, VA
Terrien, Michael S. ... Chicago, IL
Terril, Ryan G. ... Kansas City, MO
Terril, Vince ... Denver, CO
Terrile, Stephen A. ... Austin, TX
Terrill, Delbert R., Jr.
Federal Energy Regulatory Commission, Office of the Administrative Law Judges, GV
Terrill, G. Sherman
San Juan Capistrano, CA
Terrill, Gary R. ... Overland Park, KS
Terrill, H. Grady, III ... Lubbock, TX
Terrill & Hege Law Offices ... Ames, IA
Terrill, James S. ... Syracuse, KS
Terrill, Jeffrey P. ... Fort Wayne, IN
Terrill, Jerry A. ... New York, NY
Terrill, John A., II ... Philadelphia, PA
West Conshohocken, PA
Terrill, John E. ... Stephenville, TX
Terrill, Kay ... Lawton, OK
Terrill, Linda A. ... Lenexa, KS
Terrill, Nancy French ... Macon, GA
Terrill, Paul M., III ... Austin, TX
Terrill, Philip R. ... Fort Wayne, IN
Terrill, Richard D. ... Topeka, KS
Terrill, Richard W. ...
Department of State, GV
Terrill, Shaun Leland ... Washington, DC
Baltimore, MD
Terrill, Stephen M. ... Ames, IA
Terrill & Westblade ... Syracuse, KS
Terrill, William K., II ... New Orleans, LA
Terrillion, Andrea M. Basile ... Rochester, NY
Terrillion, Scott M. ... Ridgefield, CT
Terrill-Spieler, Kellie ... San Jose, CA
Terrinoni, Vaughn A. ... Bethlehem, PA
Terrio, Francis C. ... New York, NY
Terrion, Halle Fine ... Cleveland, OH
Terris, Bruce J. ... Washington, DC
Terris, Nicholas G. ... Washington, DC
Terris, N.J. ... Miami, FL
Terris, Peter S. ... Boston, MA
Terris, Pravlik and Wagner ... Washington, DC
Terris, Sharon R. ... San Francisco, CA
Territo, Salvatore ... Tampa, FL
Terrizzi, Joseph G. ... Boston, NY
Terrizzi, Lisa ... Wellesley, MA
Terrizzi, Michael P. ... San Rafael, CA
Terrizzi, Morris M. ... Huntingdon, PA
Terronez, Jeff ... Rock Island, IL
Terruso, John C. ... Princeton, NJ
Terry, Alicia A. ... Washington, DC
Terry, Alisa W. ... Atlanta, GA
Terry, Alleather ... Boston, MA
Terry, Andrew J. ... Chicago, IL
Terry, Angela Dawson ... Florence, AL
Terry, Anne C. ... Tallahassee, FL
Terry, Anthony D. ... Tucson, AZ
Terry, Anthony L. ... Fresno, CA
Terry, Anthony L., A Prof. Corp.
Fresno, CA
Terry, B. Brent ... Atlanta, GA
Terry, Baker O., Jr. ... Encino, CA
Terry, Benjamin H. ... Atlanta, GA
Terry, Billy C. ... Spartanburg, SC
Terry, Brad X. ... Princeton, NJ
Terry, Brent W. ... Glen Ellyn, IL
Terry, Brian K. ... Las Vegas, NV
Terry, C. Morris ... Como, MS
Terry, Charles L., III ... Columbia, SC
Terry, Charles R. ... Morristown, TN
Terry, Christopher L. ... Detroit, MI
Terry, Clay A. ... Lake Wales, FL
Terry, Craig B. ... Salt Lake City, UT
Terry, D. Lewis, Jr. ... Dothan, AL
Terry, Daniel A. ... Charlotte, NC
Terry, David ... Dallas, TX
Terry, David E. ... Orlando, FL
Terry, David G. ... Roseburg, OR
Terry, David G., P.C. ... Roseburg, OR
Terry, David L. ... Charlotte, NC
Terry, David R. ... Tallahassee, FL
Terry, David T. ... Arlington, VA
Terry, David W. ... St. Louis, MO
Terry, Deanne ... Austin, TX
Terry, Diana L. ... Denver, CO
Terry, Douglas A. ... Oklahoma City, OK
Terry, Douglas D. ... St. George, UT
Terry, D'wana
Federal Communications Commission, Wireless Telecommunications Bureau, GV
Terry, Edwin J. (Ted), Jr., Law Offices of
Austin, TX
Terry, Elizabeth Davis ... Irvine, CA
Terry, Elmer L. ... Provo, UT
Terry, Eric ... Dallas, TX
Terry, Ernest C. ... Houston, TX
Terry, Eugene ... Highland Park, IL
Terry, Eugene ... Detroit, MI
Terry, Evelyn B. ... Bahama, NC
Terry, F. Braxton ... Morristown, TN
Terry, Floyd R. ... Kingsport, TN
Terry and Frazier, P.A. ... Orlando, FL
Terry, Frederick A., Jr. ... New York, NY
Terry, Gary A. ... St. George, UT
Terry, Gene S. ... Jefferson, TX
Terry, Gerard ... Westbury, NY
Terry, Glenn ... Miami, FL
Terry, Griffin ... Louisville, KY
Terry, Guyton O., III ... Kingsport, TN
Terry, H. Edward ... Shawnee, OK
Terry, Harry K. F. ... Dover, DE
Harrington, DE
Terry, Harry K. F., Professional Association
Dover, DE
Harrington, DE
Terry, Henry C., III ... Richmond, VA
Terry, Howard Paul ... Chestnut Hill, MA
Terry, J. Blake ... Kansas City, MO
Terry, J. Stanford ... Vicksburg, MS
Terry, Jack C. ... Independence, MO
Terry, Jacqueline ... Raleigh, NC
Terry, James D. ... Tuscaloosa, AL
Terry, James E. ... St. Louis, MO
Terry, James J. ... New York, NY
Terry, James L. ... Boston, MA
Terry, James P. ... Annandale, VA
Terry, James W. ... Napa, CA
Terry, Jana K. ... Victoria, TX
Terry, Jay D. ... Dallas, TX
Houston, TX
Terry, Jaye Ann ... Tampa, FL
Terry, Jennifer Wheeler ... Indianapolis, IN
Terry, Jerry O. ... Gulfport, MS
Terry, John A. ... Washington, DC
Terry, John H. ... Syracuse, NY
Terry, John O. ... Fort Myers, FL
Terry, Jon B. ... Bessemer, AL
Terry, Jon P. ... Denver, CO
Terry, Jonathan C. ... Irvine, CA
Terry, Joseph Denney ... Houston, TX
Terry, Joseph H. ... Lexington, KY
Terry, Joseph R., Jr. ... Memphis, TN
Terry, Julia Haynes ... New Orleans, LA
Terry, Julie Harris ... Miami, FL
Terry, Karen E. ... West Palm Beach, FL
Terry, Kathleen R. ... Minneapolis, MN
Terry, Kathryn D. ... Oklahoma City, OK
Terry, Kathryn E. ... Orange, CA
Terry, Keeva L. ... New York, NY
Terry, Ken B. ... Metropolis, IL
Terry & Kratville ... Omaha, NE
Terry, L. Timothy ... Carson City, NV
Terry, Laurel S. ... Carlisle, PA
Terry, Lawrence F. ... San Jose, CA
Terry, Lee Ellen ... Norwich, CT
Terry, Lee R. ... Omaha, NE
Terry, Lenette ... Angleton, TX
Terry, Linda M. ... Bloomfield, CT
Terry, Lisa V. ... Washington, DC
Terry, Lori A. ... Seattle, WA
Terry, M. Margaret ... New York, NY
Terry, Malcolm P. ... Minneapolis, MN
Terry, Marc L. ... Worcester, MA
Terry, Marianne W. ... Mobile, AL
Terry, Mark F. ... Sacramento, CA
Terry, Martha V. ... Austin, TX
Terry, Mary Ross ... Louisville, KY
Terry, Mary S. ... Richmond, VA
Terry, Mason L. ... Austin, TX
Terry, Matson C., II ... Irvington, VA
Terry, Michael B. ... Atlanta, GA
Terry, Michael D. ... Lindon, UT
Terry, Michael E. ... Nashville, TN
Terry, Michael F. ... Moulton, AL
Terry, Michael H. ... Savannah, GA
Terry, Michael H. ... Richmond, VA
Terry, Michael K. ... Braintree, MA
Terry, Michael L. ... Grover Beach, CA
Terry, Michael W. ... Augusta, GA
Terry, Mimzel ... Boise, ID
Terry, Mozella ... Memphis, TN
Terry, Pamela E. ... Mashpee, MA
Terry, Pamela G. ... Wallingford, VT
Terry, Patricia A. ... Providence, RI
Terry, Patrick M. ... San Francisco, CA
Terry, Paul P., Jr. ... Sacramento, CA
Walnut Creek, CA
Terry, Paul W. ... Washington, DC
Terry, Peter A. ... Phoenix, AZ
Terry, Philip D., III ... West Monroe, LA
Terry, Philip J. ... Petaluma, CA
Terry, Phillip A. ... Indianapolis, IN
Terry, Preston L., III ... Louisville, KY
Terry, R. Todd ... Las Vegas, NV
Terry, Rachel ... New York, NY
Terry, Renee
Federal Communications Commission, Common Carrier Bureau, GV
Terry, Rex M. ... Fort Smith, AR
Terry, R. G., Jr. ... Southold, NY
Terry, Richard Call ... Salt Lake City, UT
Terry, Richard R. ... Ray Brook, NY
Terry, Robert B. ... Kansas City, MO
Terry, Robert E. ... Boston, MA
Terry, Robert J. ... Costa Mesa, CA
Terry, Robert J. ... Dearborn, MI
Terry, Robin H. ... Raleigh, NC
Terry, Roy M., Jr. ... Richmond, VA
Terry, Royall P. ... Tallahassee, FL
Terry, Russell S. ... Mobile, AL
Terry, S. Jay ... Seattle, WA
Terry, S. Lee, Jr. ... Denver, CO
Terry, S. Patrick ... Lexington, KY
Terry, Scott A. ... Summit, NJ
Terry, Stephen W., Jr. ... Indianapolis, IN
Terry, Steven J. ... Minneapolis, MN
Terry, Steven K. ... Dallas, TX
Terry, Steven L. ... Mobile, AL
Terry, Steven W. ... Morristown, TN
Terry, Susan F. ... Batavia, NY
Terry, T. Rankin, Jr. ... Fort Myers, FL
Terry, Tai C. ... New York, NY
Terry, Terry and Stapleton
Morristown, TN
Rogersville, TN
Terry, Thomas D. ... Washington, DC
Terry, Thomas H., III ... Cleveland, OH
Terry, Timothy W. ... Orlando, FL
Terry, Tony ... Las Vegas, NV
Terry, Travis B. ... Sugar Land, TX
Terry, Vic ... Dallas, TX
Terry, Vic, A Prof. Corp., Law Office of
Dallas, TX
Terry, W. Burks ... Dallas, TX
Terry, W. Burks, Jr. ... Rolling Meadows, IL
Terry, Walter L., III ... Oneonta, NY
Terry, Ward E., Jr. ... Denver, CO
Terry, Warden ... San Saba, TX
Terry, Wayne R. ... Los Angeles, CA
Terry, Willard R., Jr. ... San Diego, CA
Terry, William B. ... Las Vegas, NV
Terry, William B., Chartered
Las Vegas, NV
Terry, William C. ... Bonham, TX
Terry, William J. ... Tampa, FL
Terry, William J. ... Angleton, TX
Terry, William Kevin, Jr ... Coral Gables, FL
Terry, William L. ... Little Rock, AR
Terry, William W., III ... Roanoke, VA
Terry-Crawford, Sandra D.
Philadelphia, PA
Terschan, Frank R. ... Milwaukee, WI
Terschan, Steinle & Ness ... Milwaukee, WI
Terschluse & Sandcork ... St. Louis, MO
Terschluse, Val ... St. Louis, MO
Terselic, John A. ... Waukegan, IL
Tershakovec, Christina G.
Philadelphia, PA
Tershel & Associates ... Washington, PA
Tershel, Paul A. ... Washington, PA
Tersigni, Anthony L. ... New York, NY
Tersigni, Vincent J. ... Akron, OH
Tersillo, Michael ... St. Louis, MO
Tersol, Teresa A. ... Carmel, CA
Terterian, George ... Encino, CA
Tertocha, Louis ... Miami, FL
Tertocha, Louis, P.A. ... Miami, FL
Tertzag, Kaye ... Detroit, MI
Teruya, Darryl S. ... Honolulu, HI
Teruya, Mia Y. ... Honolulu, HI
Tervala, Debra J. ... Baltimore, MD
Tervalon, Harry S., Jr. ... New Orleans, LA
Tervo, Calif K. ... San Diego, CA
Tervo, James M. ... San Francisco, CA
Tervooren, Steven S. ... Anchorage, AK
Terwedo, James A. ... New Prague, MN
Terwelp, Jeffrey A. ... Mendon, IL
Terwilleger, Kenneth B. ... Columbus, OH
Terwilliger, Anne P. ... Dallas, TX
Terwilliger, Carol Hitchings ... Oakton, VA
Terwilliger, Connie L. F. ... Beaverton, OR
Terwilliger, Emmett W. ... Lancaster, WI
Terwilliger, Francis C. ... Charlottesville, VA
Terwilliger, George J., III
Washington, DC
Terwilliger, Kurt W. ... Franklin, MA
Terwilliger, Michael T. ... Merrillville, IN
Terwilliger, Molly A. ... Olympia, WA
Terwilliger, Robert A. ... Everett, WA
Terwilliger, W. Thomas ... Wausau, WI
Terwilliger, Wakeen, Piehler & Conway, S.C.
Wausau, WI
Terz, Joseph J. ... Mechanicsburg, PA
Terzaken, Ann Marie ... Washington, DC
Baltimore, MD
Rockville, MD
Terzano, John ... Carteret, NJ
Terze Esch, Patricia ... Grand Rapids, MI
Terzenbach, Ronald B. ... Eugene, OR
Terzian, Annabelle G. ... Whitman, MA
Terzian, Barbara A. ... Columbus, OH
Terzian, Berj A. ... New York, NY
Terzian, Christopher A. ... Mineola, NY
New York, NY
White Plains, NY
Terzian, David L. ... Department of Justice, Civil Division, GV
Terzian, George Anthony ... New York, NY
Terzian, J. Garrett ... Whitman, MA
Terzian, Louise A. ... Silver Spring, MD
Terzian, Richard R. ... Los Angeles, CA
Terzian, Robert P. ... Department of Defense, Defense Legal Services Agency, GV
Terzian, Sandra ... Fairfax, CA
Terzian & Terzian ... Whitman, MA
Terzich, Milos ... Gardnerville, NV
Terzino, Mary H. ... Freeport, TX
Terzis, John E. ... Washington, DC
Terziu, John, III ... Baltimore, MD
Terzo, Carol Lynn ... Indianapolis, IN
Terzo, Frank P. ... Miami, FL
Terzola, Mark C. ... Akron, OH
Tesanovich, Milan D. ... Tucson, AZ
Tesanovich, Milan D., P.C. ... Tucson, AZ
Tesar, Christopher ... Los Angeles, CA
Tesar, J. Michael ... Omaha, NE
Tesch, Donald T. ... Edmonds, WA
Tesch, Joseph E. ... Park City, UT
Tesch, Tamara D. ... Bloomington, MN
Tesch, Thompson & Vance, LLC
Heber City, UT
Park City, UT
Tesch, Tim ... Austin, TX
Tesch, Tim, The Law Offices of
Austin, TX
Tesch, Walter F. ... Milwaukee, WI
Tesche, Allan E. ... Anchorage, AK
Tesche, Caroline J. ... Tampa, FL
Teschendorf, Benita P. ... Brighton, MI
Tescher Chaves Rubin & Forman, P.A.
Boca Raton, FL
Miami, FL
Tescher, Donald R. ... Boca Raton, FL
Miami, FL
Tescher, Howard A. ... Fort Lauderdale, FL
Tescher, Maynard K., Jr. ... Redding, CA
Teschner, Charles F., Jr. ... St. Louis, MO
Teschner, David ... New York, NY
Teschner, John H. ... New York, NY
Teschner, John S. ... Wheaton, IL
Teschner, Michael H. ... Westfield, NJ
Teschner, Susan A. ... Charleston, SC
Teschon Riccobene & Siss, P.A.
Midland Park, NJ
Teschon, Russell B. ... Midland Park, NJ
Tesdahl, Douglas Benson ... Washington, DC
Tesdahl, Edward M. ... Spokane, WA
Tesdell, Kerwin E. ... New York, NY
Teso, Carmelo C. ... Massapequa Park, NY
Tesei, John P. ... Greenwich, CT
New York, NY
Te Selle, David K. ... Englewood, CO
TeSelle, John ... Oklahoma City, OK
Tesh, Tim Rolland ... Seattle, WA
Teshima, Daryl T. ... Los Angeles, CA
Teshima, Donna J. ... San Francisco, CA
Teshoian, Sarkis ... Uxbridge, MA
Teshome, Hanna Tedla ... Washington, DC
Tesija, John I. ... Southfield, MI
Tesio, Mike, Jr. ... Midwest City, OK
Teska, Kirk ... Waltham, MA
Teska, Lora E. ... Wellesley, MA
Teske & Associates, Ltd. ... Edmonds, WA
Teske, Christopher S. ... Pasadena, CA
Teske, David S. ... Atlanta, GA
Teske, David S. ... Edmonds, WA
Teske, Jeffrey M. ... Chicago, IL
Teske, Max R., Jr. ... Waterloo, IA
Teske, Melvin C. ... Brookfield, WI
Teske, Paula S., & Associates
Los Angeles, CA
Teskin, Robin L. ... Alexandria, VA
Te Slaa, Orlin D. ... Minneapolis, MN
Tesler, Jamey L. ... Boston, MA
Tesler, Pauline H. ... Mill Valley, CA
San Francisco, CA
Tesler, Richard E. ... New York, NY
Tesler, Robert S. ... Palo Alto, CA
Tesler, Roy ... Falls Church, VA
Tesler, Sandmann & Fishman
Mill Valley, CA
San Francisco, CA
Tesler & Werblood ... Falls Church, VA
Teslik, Sarah A. B. ... Washington, DC
Teslik, W. Randolph, (P.C.)
Washington, DC
Teslow, Philip B. ... St. Paul, MN
Tesmer, Louise M. ... Milwaukee, WI
Tesmer, Stephen K. ... Indianapolis, IN
Tesnakis, Costa N. ... Staten Island, NY
Tesner, Michael A. ... Bloomfield Hills, MI
Tesno, James A. ... Celina, OH
Teson, Susan B. ... Kansas City, MO
Tesone, Mark F. ...
Department of State, GV
Tesone, Robert J. ... Hermitage, PA
Tesoriero, John V. ... New York, NY
Tesoriero, Joseph J. ... New York, NY
Tesoriero, Joyce R. ... Laurel, MD
Tesoro, Claudia M. ... Philadelphia, PA

Tesoro, Gregory L. ....New York, NY
Tesreau, Dennis H. ....Hillsboro, MO
Tess, David D. ....Rochelle, IL
Tess, David J. ....Washington, DC
Tess, Kristin L. ....New York, NY
Tessar, Joseph H. ....Riverside, RI
Tessari, Joseph A. ....Wilmington, DE
Tessaro, Donna R. ....New Castle, PA
Tessaro, Edward A. ....Butler, PA
Tessaro, Robert T. ....Fort Lee, NJ
Tessel, Stanley ....New York, NY
Tessendorf, Gale D. ....Columbus, NE
Tessendorf, Gale D., P.C. ....Columbus, NE
Tessener, Hoyt G. ....Durham, NC
Raleigh, NC
Tesser & Cohen ....Hackensack, NJ
New York, NY
Tesser, Lee M. ....Hackensack, NJ
Tesser, Lewis ....New York, NY
Tesser, Samantha Nicole
Fort Lauderdale, FL
Tesseris, George ....East Lansing, MI
Tesseris, George, P.C. ....East Lansing, MI
Tesseyman, Francis Wm., Jr.
West Seneca, NY
Tessicini, Cesidia T. ....Vallejo, CA
Tessier, Frank A. ....New Orleans, LA
Tessier, G. Anthony, Jr.
Rancho Cordova, CA
Tessier, James P. ....San Francisco, CA
Tessier, John O. ....Locust Valley, NY
Tessier, Margaret C. ....Washington, DC
Tessier, Marti ....Mandeville, LA
Tessier, Robert M. ....Encino, CA
Tessier, Terri D. ....Encino, CA
Tessier, Thomas J. ....Manchester, NH
Tessier, Troy A. ....Greenville, SC
Tessier, Victor G. ....Pomona, CA
Tessitore, Christopher ....Orlando, FL
Tessitore, Michael A. ....Orlando, FL
Tessler, Barry A. ....New York, NY
Tessler, Barry A., P.C. ....New York, NY
Tessler, Benjamin ....Lynn, MA
Tessler, Bonnie Schindel ....South Orange, NJ
Tessler, Brett ....Philadelphia, PA
Tessler, Carl H. ....Denver, CO
Tessler, Carl H., P.C. ....Denver, CO
Tessler, Corey A. ....New York, NY
Tessler, Craig L. ....New York, NY
Tessler, David Alan ....New York, NY
Tessler, Edward ....New York, NY
Tessler, Irwin H. ....Fair Lawn, NJ
Tessler, Isaac ....New York, NY
Tessler & Levin ....Lynn, MA
Tessler, Mark H.
Department of Transportation, Federal Railroad Administration, GV
Tessler, Robert L. ....New York, NY
Tess-Mattner, Kent A. ....Brookfield, WI
Tess-Mattner, Marna M. ....Milwaukee, WI
Tessmer, Charles W. ....Dallas, TX
Tessmer, Scott ....Houston, TX
Tessner, John ....St. Paul, MN
Test, Aldo J. ....Palo Alto, CA
Test, E. Allen ....Altaville, CA
Test, George S., Jr. ....Philipsburg, PA
Test, Louis S. ....Reno, NV
Test, Mary Lawrence ....Los Angeles, CA
Test, Sandra L. ....Miami, FL
Test, Stephen G. ....Virginia Beach, VA
Testa, Adena W. ....Baltimore, MD
Testa, Albert J. ....New York, NY
Testa, Alfred ....Pasadena, CA
Testa & Associates, A Professional Corporation ....Vista, CA
Testa, Bainbridge D. ....Worcester, MA
Testa, Cathy J. ....Newark, DE
Testa, Chas. R. ....Toledo, OH
Testa, D'Jean E. ....Phoenix, AZ
Testa, Frank C. ....Princeton, NJ
Testa, Frank J. ....Vineland, NJ
Testa, Gregory J. ....Vista, CA
Testa, Hurwitz & Thibeault, LLP
Boston, MA
Testa, James A. ....Princeton, NJ
Testa, James A., (P.C.) ....Vista, CA
Testa, Jean K. ....Schenectady, NY
Testa, Joseph B. ....Atlanta, GA
Testa, Kelly A. ....Cherry Hill, NJ
Testa, Louis J. ....Albany, NY
Testa, Michael ....Houston, TX
Testa, Michael H. ....New York, NY
Testa, Michael L. ....Vineland, NJ
Testa, Muriel L. D. ....Newark, DE
Testa, Paul A. ....Solon, OH
Testa, Richard J. ....Boston, MA
Testa & Testa, P.C. ....Houston, TX
Testa, Thomas A. ....Houston, TX
Testa, Thomas J. ....Sausalito, CA
Testa, Vicki Lynn ....Watsonville, CA
Testa, Wendy D. ....Westmont, NJ
Testagrossa, Charles A., Jr.
Kew Gardens, NY
Testaguzza, Louis ....Morgan Hill, CA
Testaiuti, John A. ....New York, NY
Testan, Joseph S. ....Department of Defense, Defense Legal Services Agency, GV
Testani, Carla G. ....Livonia, MI
Testani, Rocco E. ....Atlanta, GA
Testani, Rosa A. ....New York, NY
Testaverde, Paul ....Elmhurst, NY
Tester, Albert H. ....Waycross, GA
Tester, Bruce A. ....Costa Mesa, CA
Tester, Cynthia C. ....Glenwood Springs, CO
Tester, Kent ....Clinton, AR
Testerman, Kyle C. ....Knoxville, TN
Testerman, Mary Margaret ....San Diego, CA
Testerman, Michael D. ....Sacramento, CA
Testerman, Michael R. ....Branson, MO
Testerman, Thomas V. ....Newport, TN
Testerman, Warren & Roden, PLLC
Knoxville, TN
Testiani, Jacqueline P. ....Syosset, NY
Testino, Edward ....Matawan, NJ
Testo, Robt. J. ....Bridgeport, CT
Testoff, Robert Allen ....Treasury Department, Internal Revenue Service, GV
Testolin, Kelly ....Las Vegas, NV
Reno, NV
Testone, Michael G. ....Hartford, CT
Testoni, Maureen A. ....Washington, DC
Tesznar, Cynthia Godbey ....Toledo, OH
Tête, Robert J. ....Lake Charles, LA
Tête, Susan Snowden ....New Orleans, LA
Tête, William R. ....Lake Charles, LA
Tête, W. T. ....New Orleans, LA
Telelman, Larry ....New York, NY
Tetenbaum, Elliot S., (P.C.)
Newburgh, NY
Tetenbaum, Irving ....Bayside, NY
Tetenbaum, Jeffrey A. ....Omaha, NE
Teter, Harry ....Washington, DC
Teter, Jeanne M. ....Marion, IL
Teter, John D. ....San Jose, CA
Teter, Katharine J. ....Boulder, CO
Teter, Kenneth L., Jr. ....Lansing, MI
Teter, Michael L. ....Cushing, OK
Teter, Thomas N. ....Clarksburg, WV
Teter, Timothy S. ....Palo Alto, CA
Teteris, Jean Yingling ....Columbus, OH
Teters, Sandra L. ....San Francisco, CA
Tether, Ivan J. ....Los Angeles, CA
Tether, Thomas E. ....New York, NY
Teti, Catherine Power ....Tampa, FL
Teti, Frank A. ....Brooklyn, NY
Teti, Louis N. ....Exton, PA
Teti, Ralph J. ....Harrisburg, PA
Philadelphia, PA
Tetirick, Dean A. ....Fort Worth, TX
Tetlak, Edw. J. ....Middleburg Heights, OH
Tetlak, Thomas E. ....Cleveland, OH
Tetler, George W., III ....Worcester, MA
Tetlow, Alfred J. ....Tampa, FL
Tetlow, Elisabeth M. ....New Orleans, LA
Tetlow & Johnson ....Cleveland, OH
Tetlow, Tania ....New Orleans, LA
Tetlow, Wallace H. ....Anchorage, AK
Tetlow, William J. ....Cleveland, OH
Tetmeyer, Robert G. ....Floral Park, NY
Teton, Alfred B. ....Chicago, IL
Tetrault, Charles D. ....Washington, DC
Tetrault, Richard J. ....Boston, MA
Tetreault, Edward R. ....Waterford, NY
Tetreault, Frederick P. ....Bourbonnais, IL
Tetreault, Lori A. ....Gainesville, FL
Tetreault, Paul L. ....Los Angeles, CA
Tetreault, Renée E. ....Phoenix, AZ
Tetreault, Richard J. ....Las Vegas, NV
Tetreault, Robert D. ....St. Petersburg, FL
Tetreault, Robert D., P.C., Law Offices of
St. Petersburg, FL
Tetreault, Suzanne M.
Federal Communications Commission, Office of the General Counsel, GV
Tetreault, Victor J. ....Savannah, GA
Tetrick, Charles B. ....Bixby, OK
Tulsa, OK
Tetrick, David, Jr. ....Orlando, FL
Tetro, Stephen R., II ....Chicago, IL
Tetro, Valerie L. ....Washington, DC
Tettelbaum, Richard M. ....Washington, DC
Tettemer, Stephanie ....Succasunna, NJ
Tetterton, Patricia Hurst ....Columbia, SC
Tetterton, William S. ....Camden, SC
Tettlebaum, Harvey M.
Jefferson City, MO
Tetunic, Fran L. ....Fort Lauderdale, FL
Tetwiler, Lee H. ....Paola, KS
Tetzeli, Helena ....Miami, FL
Tetzlaff, Barbara ....San Francisco, CA
Tetzlaff, Charles R. ....Burlington, VT
Tetzlaff, Glenn R. ....Marion, IL
Tetzlaff, Janna D. ....Chicago, IL
Tetzlaff, Susanne L. ....Austin, TX
Tetzlaff, Theodore R. ....Chicago, IL
Teu, C. Alexander ....New York, NY
Teu, Jennifer T. ....New York, NY
Teufel, Gregory H. ....Pittsburgh, PA
Teufel, Hugo, III ....Denver, CO
Teufel, Paul J. ....Jonesboro, AR
Teufel, Roger C. ....Irving, TX
Teumer, Peter A. ....Fairfax, VA
Teune, David A. ....Wheaton, IL
Teunisse, Patricia A. ....San Dimas, CA
Teurlings, Denise M. ....St. Petersburg, FL
Teuscher, Julie A. ....Chicago, IL
Teuschler, Katharine ....Cincinnati, OH
Teuton, Jodie ....Houma, LA
Teuton, Mark Christopher
Newport Beach, CA
Teutsch, Miriam ....Pasadena, CA
Teutsch, Robert E. ....Memphis, TN
Teutsch, Robert E., Jr. ....Memphis, TN
Tevebaugh, Mary Lou ....Longview, TX
Tevelin, David I. ....Alexandria, VA
Tevelowitz, Harold B. ....Valhalla, NY
Teveni, Frank M. ....San Antonio, TX
Teveni, Marcelina ....San Antonio, TX
Teverow, Joshua ....Providence, RI
Teves, Stephen M. ....Honolulu, HI
Tevis, Gregory C. ....New York, NY
Tevis, Jeff T. ....Wichita, KS
Tevis, Jeffrey B. ....San Francisco, CA
Tevis, Lloyd ....Los Osos, CA
Tevlin, Beth A. Ahlemeyer ....Terre Haute, IN
Tevlin, Joseph F. ....Wyoming, MI
Tevlowitz, Steven M. ....
Administrative Office Of The United States Courts, GV
Tevnan, Charles R. ....Boston, MA
Tevrizian, Dickran, Jr. ....Los Angeles, CA
Tew, Allen R. ....Clayton, NC
Tew & Atchison, P.A. ....Clayton, NC
Raleigh, NC
Tew, Brian ....Houston, TX
Tew Cardenas Rebak Kellogg Lehman DeMaria & Tague, L.L.P. ....Miami, FL
West Palm Beach, FL
Tew, Jeffrey ....Miami, FL
Tew, Joel R. ....Clearwater, FL
Tew, Katherine ....New York, NY
Tew, Michael F. ....Fort Myers, FL
Tew & Nowak ....Fort Lauderdale, FL
Miami, FL
West Palm Beach, FL
Tew, Robert Stephen ....Monroe, LA
Tew, Roger O. ....Salt Lake City, UT
Tew, Ryan M. ....Gillette, WY
Tew, Sheila ....Cleveland, OH
Tew, Sherry L. ....New Orleans, LA
Tew, Thomas ....Miami, FL
West Palm Beach, FL
Tew, Zinober, Barnes, Zimmet & Unice
Clearwater, FL
Spring Hill, FL
Tewarson, Hemi D. ....Washington, DC
Tewary, Kamlesh ....Edison, NJ
Tewel, Eva B. ....Treasury Department, Internal Revenue Service, GV
Tewell, David ....Seattle, WA
Tewell, Duane L. ....Seattle, WA
Tewes, Donald E. ....Waukesha, WI
Tewes, Ellen C. ....Nashville, TN
Tewes, R. Scott ....Atlanta, GA
Tewey, Julie Lynn ....Baltimore, MD
TeWinkle, Garrett J. ....Newport Beach, CA
TeWinkle, Laurie C. ....Erie, PA
TeWinkle, L.C. ....Erie, PA
Te Winkle, William P. ....Sheboygan, WI
Tewkesbury, Alan M., Jr.
Spartanburg, SC
Tewkesbury, Edward P. ....Greensboro, SC
Tewkesbury Law Offices ....Greensboro, NC
Tewksbury, David G. ....Washington, DC
Tewksbury, Jane E. ....Boston, MA
Tewksbury, John B. ....Boston, MA
Tewksbury • Kerfeld • Zimmer, A P.A.
Minneapolis, MN
Tewksbury, Michael D. ....Minneapolis, MN
Tewksbury, Zan E. ....Portland, OR
Tews, Donald A. ....Pontiac, MI
Tews, Herbert R. ....Chicago, IL
Tews, J. Dixon ....Minneapolis, MN
Tews, Janice M. ....Orlando, FL
Tews, Theisen & Theisen ....Chicago, IL
Glenview, IL
Tex, James M. ....Cedar Hill, TX
Texada, Andrew P. ....Alexandria, LA
Texel, Timothy J. ....Lincoln, NE
Texidor, Francisco R. ....Boston, MA
Texier, Matthew T. ....St. Louis, MO
Textor, James M. ....New York, NY
Textor, Melinda Rose ....New York, NY
Textor, Michael D. ....Springfield, MO
Textor, Ralph G., Jr. ....Shawnee, KS
Teykl, James S. ....Homewood, IL
Teykl, James S., Law Offices, P.C.
Homewood, IL
Teynier, Eric ....New York, NY
Teynor, Ann Hyams ....Minnetonka, MN
Teysen, Marsha Jean ....Sault Ste. Marie, MI
Teyssier, Paul ....National City, CA
Tezak, Edward L. ....Everett, WA
Tezak, Frank Louis ....Littleton, CO
Tezak, Kandice G. ....Seattle, WA
Tezak, Margaret McNamara ....Denver, CO
Thabault, Isabelle M. ....Department of Justice, Civil Rights Division, GV
Thabes, John A. ....Fort Lauderdale, FL
Thabit, Bruce A. ....Encino, CA
Thabit, Janet E. Byrne ....Chicago, IL
Thabit, Robert W. ....New York, NY
Thacher, Albrecht & Ratcliff
San Francisco, CA
Thacher, Carol L. ....Minneapolis, MN
Thacher, Carter P. ....San Francisco, CA
Thacher, George C. ....Pacific Grove, CA
Thacher, James F. ....San Francisco, CA
Thacher, John B., III ....Hartford, CT
Thacher, Jonathan C. ....Fairfax, VA
Thacher & Maurer ....Minneapolis, MN
Thacher, Penne L. ....El Cajon, CA
Thacher Proffitt & Wood
Washington, DC
Jersey City, NJ
New York, NY
White Plains, NY
Thacher, Swiger & Day ....Fairfax, VA
Thacher, Thomas ....New Canaan, CT
Thacher, Thomas D., II ....New York, NY
Thacker, Andrew E. ....Farmers Branch, TX
Thacker, Bickel, Hodskins & Thacker, L.L.P.
Owensboro, KY
Thacker, Bob E. ....El Toro, CA
Thacker, C. Jane ....Denton, TX
Thacker, Charlotte Carlisle ....Griffin, GA
Thacker, Connie R. ....Grand Rapids, MI
Thacker, Don ....Vancouver, WA
Thacker, George ....Owensboro, KY
Thacker, George W., III ....Louisville, KY
Thacker, Holliday Hopkins ....Louisville, KY
Thacker, J. Mark ....San Jose, CA
Thacker, J. Russell ....Vero Beach, FL
Thacker, Jeffrey C. ....San Diego, CA
Thacker, Jennifer ....Clarkesville, GA
Thacker, Jess W., (Mrs.) ....Clearwater, FL
Thacker, Jo Overstreet ....Kissimmee, FL
Thacker, John G. ....Owensboro, KY
Thacker, John R. ....Roseville, CA
Thacker, Joseph P. ....Findlay, OH
Toledo, OH
Thacker, Kyle L. ....Fort Collins, CO
Thacker, Lester L. ....Kankakee, IL
Thacker, Loren R. ....St. Paul, MN
Thacker, Louis Crawford ....Griffin, GA
Thacker, Michael J. ....Cleveland, OH
Thacker, Mickey R. ....Cartersville, GA
Thacker, O. Stephen ....Clearwater, FL
Thacker & Pennick, P.A.
Hot Springs National Park, AR
Thacker, Robert L. ....Conway, AR
Thacker, Robert M., Jr. ....Framingham, MA
Thacker, Robert P. ....Bellaire, TX
Thacker, Robert W. ....Monticello, IN
Thacker, Robt. W. ....Wichita Falls, TX
Thacker, Russell S. ....Kissimmee, FL
Thacker, Sara A. ....Phoenix, AZ
Thacker & Smitherman, P.A.
Clearwater, FL
Thacker, Stephanie D. ....Charleston, WV
Thacker, Stephen M. ....Chicago, IL
Thacker & Thacker ....Griffin, GA
Thacker, Todd M. ....Los Angeles, CA
Thacker, William M. ....Ann Arbor, MI
Thacker, Wm. M., Jr. ....Wichita Falls, TX
Thackeray, Gail ....Phoenix, AZ
Thackeray, Jonathan E. ....New York, NY
Thackery, Franklin T. ....St. Joseph, MO
Thackery, Hope Ann ....Miamisburg, OH
Thackery, Joseph C. ....Washington, DC
Thackray, Gillian W. ....San Francisco, CA
Thackston, Adam ....Houston, TX
Thackston, Franklin S., Jr.
Greenville, MS
Thackston, G. William, Jr., (P.C.)
Atlanta, GA
Thackston, Mark C. ....South Boston, VA
Thackston, Robert E. ....Dallas, TX
Thackston, Thomas P. ....Newark, NJ
Thaddeus, A. Peter, Jr. ....Brownsville, TX
McAllen, TX
Thaden, Gary K. ....St. Paul, MN
Thadhani, Reena I. ....Boston, MA
Thaeler, Kent H. ....La Mesa, CA
Thagard, James B. ....Valdosta, GA
Thagard, Kristine A. ....Costa Mesa, CA
Thagard, Leonard W. ....Clinton, NC
Thagard, Thomas W., III
Birmingham, AL
Thagard, Thomas W., Jr. ....Montgomery, AL
Thaggard, Lee ....Meridian, MS
Thaggard, Taylor D. ....Dallas, TX
Thaheld, Johann F. ....Lake Oswego, OR
Thai, Duy ....San Francisco, CA
Thai, Rebecca ....Huntsville, AL
Thain, Gerald J. ....Madison, WI
Thakar, Nicolas L. ....Gold River, CA
Thakar, Todd R. ....Woodland Hills, CA
Thakkar, Pinakini ....New York, NY
Thakur, Amar L. ....La Jolla, CA
Thakur, Nirakar C. ....Toledo, OH
Thal, Debra Romero ....Albuquerque, NM
Thal, John S. ....Albuquerque, NM
Thal, Michael L. ....Cleveland, OH
Thal, Steven C. ....Minneapolis, MN
Thal, Steven C., P.A. ....Minneapolis, MN
St. Louis Park, MN
Thal, Steven H. ....New York, NY
Thal, Susan ....Hackensack, NJ
Thalacker, Arbie R. ....New York, NY
Thalacker, Karen L. ....Waverly, IA
Thalacker, Laura J. ....Las Vegas, NV
Thalasinos, Nicholas ....New York, NY
Thalblum, Donna E. ....Kansas City, MO
Thale, Melvin B. ....Northridge, CA
Thalen, Stanley ....Woodmere, NY
Thalenberg, Evan K. ....Baltimore, MD
Thalenberg, Evan K., P.A. ....Baltimore, MD
Thaler, Alan V. ....Irvine, CA
Thaler, Andrew M. ....Westbury, NY
Thaler, Carolyn H. ....Towson, MD
Thaler, Craig H. ....New York, NY
Thaler, Dena Rosenberg, Law Office of
Oakland, CA
Thaler, Douglas S. ....Farmingdale, NY
Thaler, Elizabeth K. ....Encino, CA
Thaler, Frederick R., Jr.
Salt Lake City, UT
Thaler & Gertler, LLP ....Westbury, NY
Thaler, Herbert A., Jr. ....Baltimore, MD
Thaler, Howard L. ....Beverly Hills, CA
Thaler, Jason S. ....Miami, FL
Thaler, Jeffrey A. ....Portland, ME
Thaler, Jeffrey H. ....Los Angeles, CA
Thaler, Joanne F. ....Fort Lauderdale, FL
Thaler, John H. ....Beverly Hills, CA
Thaler & Liebeler ....Washington, DC
Bethesda, MD
Fairfax, VA
Thaler, Louis ....Miami, FL
Thaler, Manley Hugh ....Boca Raton, FL
Stuart, FL
West Palm Beach, FL
Thaler, Melinda B. ....Basking Ridge, NJ
Thaler, Nancy K. ....Villanova, PA
Thaler, Olive Lee ....San Francisco, CA
Thaler, Paul S. ....Washington, DC
Bethesda, MD
Fairfax, VA
Thaler, Richard B. ....Ithaca, NY
Thaler, Richard D. ....Seattle, WA
Thaler, Robert ....Bronx, NY

Thaler, Robert B. ... Red Bank, NJ
Thaler, Robert S. ... New York, NY
Thaler, Robert S., Law Office of
New York, NY
Thaler, Stanley ... Westbury, NY
Thaler, Steven ... New York, NY
Thaler & Thaler ... Ithaca, NY
Thaler & Thaler, P.A. ... Boca Raton, FL
Stuart, FL
West Palm Beach, FL
Thalgott, Joe H. ... Dublin, GA
Thalhammer, Richard M. ... Sacramento, CA
Thalheim, Peter A. ... Old Greenwich, CT
Thalheim, Richard A., Jr. ... Thibodaux, LA
Thalheimer, Bernard J. ... Northridge, CA
Thalheimer, David S. ... Philadelphia, PA
Thalheimer, Gail M. ... Brockton, MA
Thalheimer, Jonathan ... Dallas, TX
Thalheimer, Laura B. ... New York, NY
Thalheimer, Lee S. ... Little Rock, AR
Thalheimer, Louis B. ... Baltimore, MD
Thalheimer, Richard J. ... San Francisco, CA
Thalhofer, Jos. J. ... Bend, OR
Thalken, Thomas D. ... Omaha, NE
Thall, Bruce L. ... Philadelphia, PA
Thall, Linda B. ... Rockville, MD
Thall, Peter M. ... New York, NY
Thall, Robert E. ... Kalamazoo, MI
Thallemer, John D. ... Bridgewater, NJ
Thalley, Corliss G. ... Santa Fe, NM
Thallner, Karl A., Jr. ... Philadelphia, PA
Thalman, John ... Shaker Heights, OH
Thalman, M. A. ... Platte City, MO
Thalman, Richard ... Highland Park, IL
Thalwitzer, Kurt E. ... Orlando, FL
Tham, Khai Lawrence ... Mineola, NY
Tham, Marilynn ... San Francisco, CA
Thaman, Stephen Christie ... St. Louis, MO
Thamer, Michael D. ... Yreka, CA
Thamer, Richard H. ... Amarillo, TX
Thames, B. Jackson, Jr. ... Newton, MS
Thames, Bryan A. ... Mobile, AL
Thames, Clement, Jr. ... Buchanan Dam, TX
Thames, Donna Houghton ... Jacksonville, FL
Thames, E. Glenn, Jr. ... Tyler, TX
Thames, Gerry G. ... Tulsa, OK
Thames, Joel P. ... Dalton, GA
Thames, Jon P. ... Columbia, SC
Thames, Jonathan W. ... New Orleans, LA
Thames, Lee Davis ... Jackson, MS
Thames, Lee Davis, Jr ... Vicksburg, MS
Thames, M. Elizabeth ... Atlanta, GA
Thames, Rebecca L. ... Jackson, MS
Thames, Richard R. ... Jacksonville, FL
Thames, Stephen R. ... Irvine, CA
Thames, Tammy A. ... Fort Lauderdale, FL
Thames, William G., Jr. ... Tallahassee, FL
Thames, William K., II ... Pensacola, FL
Thamm, Lee Ann ... San Antonio, TX
Thamm, Rick W. ... Houston, TX
Thampoe, Immac J. ... Kenilworth, NJ
Than, H.T. ... Washington, DC
Than, Patrick A. ... San Francisco, CA
Thanas, Thomas A. ... Joliet, IL
Thanasides, Paul B. ... Tampa, FL
Thanasoulis, Triantafyllos ... Astoria, NY
Thane, Jeremy G. ... Missoula, MT
Thane, Nancy Lee ... Caro, MI
Thane, Richard M. ... Smyrna, GA
Thanheiser, Charles A., Jr. ... Houston, TX
Thanheiser, Ford C. ... Houston, TX
Thanheiser, Lauri De Brie ... Houston, TX
Thanheiser, Matthew A. ... Houston, TX
Thankachen, Sam ... Boca Raton, FL
Thanner, Christopher J. ... New Bern, NC
Thanos, Mary Kay ... Crown Point, IN
Thao, Le Chi ... Arlington, VA
Thao, T. Chris ... Minneapolis, MN
Thapar, Amul R. ... Washington, DC
Thapedi, André Martin ... Chicago, IL
Thar, Anne E. ... Chicago, IL
Thar, John J. ... Indianapolis, IN
Tharaud, L. Rostaing ... Philadelphia, PA
Tharel, Kent L. ... Fayetteville, AR
Tharney, Laura C. ... East Brunswick, NJ
Tharnish, Deborah M. ... Des Moines, IA
Tharp & Berg ... Los Angeles, CA
Tharp, Bradley L. ... Raleigh, NC
Tharp, Cathlene A. ... Washington, DC
Tharp, Charles Andrew
Fort Lauderdale, FL
Tharp, Christine M. ... San Antonio, TX
Tharp, David K., (P.A.) ... Miami, FL
Tharp, David Kirk ... Batesville, MS
Tharp, Debra J. ... Marshalltown, IA
Tharp, Dennis J. ... Boulder, CO
Tharp, Donald R. ... Platte City, MO
Tharp, Fred C., Jr. ... Clovis, NM
Tharp, J. Greg ... Dawsonville, GA
Tharp, J. Scott ... Fairmont, WV
Tharp, James W. ... Honolulu, HI
Tharp, Jim ... Kansas City, MO
Tharp, John B. ... Tustin, CA
Tharp, John B., A Prof. Corp. ... Tustin, CA
Tharp, John F. ... Springfield, IL
Tharp, John J., Jr. ... Chicago, IL
Tharp, John R. ... Baton Rouge, LA
Tharp, John Stewart ... Baton Rouge, LA
Tharp, Kathleen K. ... Falls Church, VA
Tharp, Liotta, Janes & Yokum, LLP
Fairmont, WV
Tharp, Lorraine Power ... Albany, NY
Tharp, Mary E. ... Baton Rouge, LA
Tharp, Michael B. ... Los Angeles, CA
Tharp, Michael T. ... Overland Park, KS
Tharp, Michele K. ... Denver, CO
Tharp, Paul A. ... Norman, OK
Tharp, Philip A. ... Orlando, FL
Tharp, Richard Lee ... Sulphur, LA
Tharp, Robert M., Jr. ... Mesquite, TX
Tharp, Robin ... San Diego, CA
Tharp, Ronny R. ... Los Angeles, CA
Tharp, Ross G. ... San Diego, CA
Tharp, Russell C., Jr. ... Glens Falls, NY
Tharp, Sammye S. ... Oxford, MS
Tupelo, MS
Tharp, Stanley J. ... Boise, ID
Tharp, Terrill R. ... Gillette, WY
Tharp, W. Glenn ... Fayetteville, GA
Tharp, William D. ... Yukon, OK
Tharpe, Chet A. ... Tampa, FL
Tharpe, D. Tyler ... Fresno, CA
Tharpe, Edgar A., III ... Los Angeles, CA
Tharpe, Henry C., Jr. ... Dalton, GA
Tharpe & Howell ... Irvine, CA
Los Angeles, CA
Newport Beach, CA
Oxnard, CA
San Jose, CA
Santa Barbara, CA
Santa Maria, CA
Tharpe, J. Kevin ... Gainesville, GA
Tharpe, Lisa L. ... Chicago, IL
Tharpe, Morgan, III ... Miami, FL
Tharpe, Wilmer R. ... Newton, AL
Tharp-Farrar, Tonna K.
Kansas City, MO
Tharrington, Betty M. ... Norfolk, VA
Tharrington, Harriet Powell ... Raleigh, NC
Tharrington, J. Cary, IV ... Charlotte, NC
Tharrington, J. Harold ... Raleigh, NC
Tharrington, Joseph C. ... Charlotte, NC
Tharrington, Nicole Lehmann
Charlotte, NC
Tharrington Smith ... Cary, NC
Chapel Hill, NC
Durham, NC
Raleigh, NC
Research Triangle Park, NC
Thatch, David W. ... New York, NY
Thatch, Gregory D., Law Offices of
Sacramento, CA
Thatch, John S. ... Cincinnati, OH
Thatch, Wm. R. ... Lovell, WY
Thatcher, Allison Lynn ... Lawrenceville, GA
Thatcher, Andrea L. ... Reno, NV
Thatcher, Anna Marie ... Rapid City, SD
Thatcher, Catherine R. ... Minneapolis, MN
Thatcher, Charles M. ... Vermillion, SD
Thatcher, Christopher L. ... Sierra Madre, CA
Thatcher, David A. ... Runnemede, NJ
Thatcher, David G. ... Denver, CO
Thatcher, David P. ... Atlanta, GA
Thatcher, Dickinson ... Ojai, CA
Thatcher, Frank W. ... Runnemede, NJ
Thatcher, Gordon S. ... Rexburg, ID
Thatcher, Joanne V. ... Huntington Beach, CA
Thatcher, John C. ... Mt. Vernon, OH
Thatcher, John W. ... Flemington, NJ
Thatcher, John W. ... Portsmouth, OH
Thatcher, Judith ... New York, NY
Thatcher, K. Blake ... Mount Prospect, IL
Thatcher, Karen J. ... Asheville, NC
Thatcher, Katherine A. ... Boston, MA
Thatcher & Lanza ... Flemington, NJ
Somerville, NJ
South Plainfield, NJ
Thatcher, Laura Glover ... Atlanta, GA
Thatcher, Laura L. ... Long Beach, CA
Thatcher Law Firm, LLC ... Largo, MD
Thatcher, Linda Hitt ... Largo, MD
Thatcher, Lonabaugh, Thatcher & Passarella, P.C. ... Runnemede, NJ
Thatcher, Mark T. ... Providence, RI
Thatcher, Matthew E. ... Tampa, FL
Thatcher & Miller ... Lewistown, PA
Thatcher, Pamela A., Law Office of
Corona, CA
Thatcher, Patricia A. ... Denver, CO
Thatcher, Peter S. ... Fort Myers, FL
Thatcher, Richard M. ... Seattle, WA
Thatcher, Scott D. ... Phillipsburg, NJ
Thatcher, Stephen A. ... New York, NY
Thatcher, Wayne ... Poughkeepsie, NY
Thatcher, William ... Quakertown, PA
Thatcher, William J. ... Fort Dodge, IA
Thater, William C. ... Garden City, NY
Thau, Clifford ... New York, NY
Thau, Howard R. ... New York, NY
Thau, Jonathan C. ... New York, NY
Thau, Paul ... Valley Stream, NY
Thau, Robert H. ... Beverly Hills, CA
Thau, Shirley P. ... Boca Raton, FL
Thau, Stephen B. ... Menlo Park, CA
Thau, Theodore L. ... Salinas, CA
Thau, William A. ... Dallas, TX
Thav, Charles R. ... Birmingham, MI
Thav, Gross, Steinway & Bennett, P.C.
Birmingham, MI
Thavis, Robert P. ... Minneapolis, MN
Thaviu, Lisa ... Chicago, IL
Thaw, Bruce R. ... Farmingdale, NY
Thaw, Bruce R., Law Offices of
Farmingdale, NY
Thaw, Clifton B., III ... Salisbury, MD
Thaw, Geoffrey ... Brooklyn, NY
Thaw, Russell H. ... Van Nuys, CA
Thawley, Barbara E. ... Department of Justice, Civil Rights Division, GV
Thawley, William G. ... Dallas, TX
Thaxter, Deborah L., (P.C.) ... Boston, MA
Thaxter, Gertrude G. ... Palm Desert, CA
Thaxter, James F. ... Fresno, CA
Thaxter, Sidney St. F., II ... Portland, ME
Thaxter, Thomas E. ... Pasadena, CA
Thaxton, Anthony L. ... Laurel, MS
Thaxton, Everette F. ... Charleston, WV
Thaxton, Forrest F. ... Columbus, OH
Thaxton, Frank H., III ... Shreveport, LA
Thaxton, Hout & Howard ... Jonesboro, AR
Newport, AR
Thaxton, James E. ... Cincinnati, OH
Thaxton & Johnstone ... Charleston, WV
Thaxton, Marvin D. ... Newport, AR
Thaxton, Robert C., Jr. ... San Diego, CA
Thaxton, Sherri A. ... Richmond, VA
Thayer, Abbot A. ... Cincinnati, OH
Thayer, Alan J., Jr. ... Eugene, OR
Thayer, Alexandra N. ... Waterbury, VT
Thayer, Anita ... Albany, NY
Thayer, Bernstein & Bass, P.C.
Kansas City, MO
Thayer, Brooke H. ... Cleveland, OH
Thayer, Brooks S. ... Orleans, MA
Thayer, Charlotte P. ... Kansas City, MO
Thayer, Christopher L. ... Seattle, WA
Thayer, Dale H. ... Modesto, CA
Thayer, Daniel J. ... Grand Island, NE
Thayer, David A. ... Denver, CO
Thayer, Dennis A. ... Riverside, CA
Thayer, Edwin ... Americus, GA
Thayer, Eleanor M. ...
United States Court Of Appeals For The Federal Circuit, GV
Thayer, Ernest M. ... Oakland, CA
Thayer, Ernest M., A Professional Corporation
Oakland, CA
Thayer, Fred A. ... Oakland, MD
Thayer, Gregory C. ... Oakland, CA
Thayer, Harvey, Hodder & Gregerson, A Professional Law Corporation
Modesto, CA
Thayer, Heather B. ... Minneapolis, MN
Thayer, Henry H. ... Boston, MA
Thayer, James M. ... Union, NJ
Thayer, Janet M. ... Albany, NY
Thayer, Jody Tabner ... Washington, DC
Thayer, John R. ... Bella Vista, AR
Thayer, Joshua M. ... Boston, MA
Thayer, Lawrence W. ... Spokane, WA
Thayer, Linda Jean ... Palo Alto, CA
Thayer, Louis A. ... St. Paul, MN
Thayer, M. Patricia ... San Francisco, CA
Thayer, Mark M. ... Newport, RI
Thayer, Mark W. ... Houston, TX
Thayer, Nathaniel S. ... Pawtucket, RI
Thayer, Nelson S., Jr. ... Philadelphia, PA
Thayer, Norman S., Jr. ... Albuquerque, NM
Thayer, Richard E. ... Jacksonville, FL
Thayer, Robert W. ... San Jose, CA
Thayer, Roger E. ... Kingsport, TN
Thayer, Rufus G., Jr. ... San Francisco, CA
Thayer, Samantha ... Washington, DC
Thayer, Scott D. ... Pittsburgh, PA
Thayer, Sidney A., Jr. ... Washington, MO
Thayer, Stanley G. ... Southfield, MI
Thayer, Stella Ferguson ... Tampa, FL
Thayer, Stephen C. ... Chicago, IL
Thayer, Steven W. ... Vancouver, WA
Thayer, Steven W., P.S. ... Vancouver, WA
Thayer, Ted J. ... Phoenix, AZ
Thayer, Teresa S. ... Phoenix, AZ
Thayer & Thayer, P.C. ... Phoenix, AZ
Thayer, Tracey ... Newark, NJ
Thayer, Travis J. ... Atlanta, GA
Thayer, W. Stephen, III ... Concord, NH
Thayer, Walter E. ... Conneaut, OH
Thayer, Wayne H. ... Uniontown, OH
Thayer, Wendy L. ... Cohasset, MA
Thayer, Wilbur ... Vancouver, WA
Thayer, William K. ... Vancouver, WA
The Barbknecht Firm, A Professional Corporation ... Dallas, TX
The Funk Law Firm, P.S., Inc.
Bellevue, WA
The Louderback Law Firm
San Francisco, CA
The Mulkey Attorneys Group, P.A.
Rogers, AR
The Pacer Group, L.L.C. ... Duluth, GA
Thé, Roland Ernest ... San Francisco, CA
Thea, Jane ... Scarsdale, NY
Thea, Peter B. ... New York, NY
Theado, Thomas R. ... Lorain, OH
Theaker, Stephen B. ... Wethersfield, CT
Theall & Fontana ... Abbeville, LA
Theall, Gary E. ... Abbeville, LA
Theall, Julianna C. ... Greensboro, NC
Theall, Susan L., A Prof. Law Corp.
Lafayette, LA
Theall, Susan Lorna ... Lafayette, LA
Theard, Brad G. ... Metairie, LA
Theard, Harold E., Jr. ... New Orleans, LA
Theban, Stephanie L. Jones ... Tulsa, OK
Thebaud, Charles C., Jr. ... Washington, DC
Thebeau, Cheri A. ... Oklahoma City, OK
Theberge, John E. ... Washington, DC
Theberge, Leonard J. ... Centerville, MA
Theberge, Maurice G. ... Haverhill, MA
Thebner, Emanuel ... Lynbrook, NY
Thebo, Walter K. ... Lowell, MI
Thede, David M. ... Los Altos, CA
Thede, Gerald S. ... Santa Barbara, CA
Thede, Jeffrey C., P.C. ... Portland, OR
Thede, John C. ... Detroit, MI
Thede, Maureen P. ... Dallas, PA
Thedens, Edgar O. ... Los Angeles, CA
Thedford, David W. ... Abilene, TX
Thedford, Jon G. ... Corpus Christi, TX
Thedford, Larkin T. ... Edna, TX
Thedinga Law Firm ... Menomonie, WI
Thedinga, William H. ... Menomonie, WI
Thedinger, Robert S. ... St. Joseph, MO
Theeler, Jack ... Huron, SD
Mitchell, SD
Theemling, Fred J., Jr. ... North Bergen, NJ
Theep, Raymond T. ... San Diego, CA
Theesfeld, Phillip C. ... Milwaukee, WI
Theesfeld, Steven L. ... Minneapolis, MN
Theg, Jill Miller ... Davis, CA
Theibert, Richard L. ... Madison, WV
Theibert, Richard W. ... Birmingham, AL
Theil, Kenneth H. ... New York, NY
Theile, Michael J. ... Flint, MI
Theiler, Charles E., II ... Louisville, KY
Theiler Douglas Drachler and McKee
Seattle, WA
Theiler, Mary Alice ... Seattle, WA
Theilmann, Laura Hodges ... Louisville, KY
Theim, Raymond P. ... Bethesda, MD
Theimer, Jack West ... San Francisco, CA
Thein, James R. ... Arlington, VA
Thein, Jason P. ... St. Louis, MO
Thein, Pamela A. ... Minneapolis, MN
Thein, Rodney T. ... St. Paul, MN
Theios, George S. ... San Bernardino, CA
Theirbah, Thomas C. ... Paoli, IN
Theirl, John M. ... Dallas, TX
Theis, B. Lawrence ... Denver, CO
Theis, Brenda Lou ... St. Paul, MN
Theis, Charles R. ... Milwaukee, WI
Theis, Colin C. ... Kansas City, MO
Theis, Donald E. ... Toledo, OH
Theis, Gerald N. ... Milwaukee, WI
Theis, Gwendoline S. ... Sacramento, CA
Theis, Jill J. ... Minneapolis, MN
Theis, John H. ... Little Rock, AR
Theis, John H., Jr. ... Denver, CO
Theis, John T. ... Chicago, IL
Theis, Joseph G.
Environmental Protection Agency, Office of Enforcement and Compliance Assurance, GV
Theis, K. C. ... Fond du Lac, WI
Theis, Linda J. ... Minneapolis, MN
Theis & Long, P.A. ... Glencoe, MN
Theis, Marcelle M. ... Pittsburgh, PA
Theis, Mary Jane W. ... Chicago, IL
Theis, Paul F. ... Glencoe, MN
Theis, Peter F. ... McHenry, IL
Theis, Phillip A., Jr. ... Granite City, IL
Theis, Phillip A., Sr. ... Granite City, IL
Theis, Richard P. ... Department of Justice, Justice Management Division, GV
Theis, Roger A. ... Naperville, IL
Theis, Roger L. ... Wichita, KS
Theis, Roger M. ... Wichita, KS
Theis, Stuart H. ... Cleveland, OH
Theis, Terie M. ... San Diego, CA
Theis, Thomas L. ... Topeka, KS
Theise, Jay F. ... Boston, MA
Theise, Tod A. ... Newark, NJ
Theisen, Brock, Frye, Erb & Leeper Co., L.P.A. ... Marietta, OH
Parkersburg, WV
Theisen, Catherine C. ... Dallas, TX
Theisen, Christopher Thomas ... Wheaton, IL
Theisen, David D. ... St. Paul, MN
Theisen, Henry W. ... Ithaca, NY
Theisen, Herbert J. ... Chicago, IL
Theisen, Joel A. ... Burnsville, MN
Theisen, John C. ... Fort Wayne, IN
Theisen, Kenneth F. ... Chicago, IL
Glenview, IL
Theisen, Lank, Mulford & Goldberg, P.A.
Wilmington, DE
Theisen, Mark D. ... Omaha, NE
Theisen, Paul T. ... Marietta, OH
Theisen, Richard T. ... Detroit, MI
Theisen, Rita M. ... Washington, DC
Theisen, Ronda M. ... Oakland, CA
Theisen, Steven H. ... Richmond, VA
Theisen, Susan Marie ... Austin, TX
Theisen, Thomas D. ... Seattle, WA
Theisen, Vincent A. ... Wilmington, DE
Theisen, Virginia Bidwell ... Richmond, VA
Theising, David J. ... Indianapolis, IN
Theiss, Benét S. ... Knoxville, TN
Theiss, Douglas J. ... Columbus, OH
Theiss, James L. ... La Grange, KY
Theiss, James R., Jr. ... Chicago, IL
Theiss, John C. ... Seattle, WA
Theiss, Mary Anne ... Manlius, NY
Theiss, Paul W. ... Chicago, IL
Theiss, Raymond E. ... Cleveland, OH
Theiss, Susan L. ... Wilmette, IL
Theiss, Viktor A. ... Boston, MA
Theiss, Walter L. ... Houston, TX
Theiss, Walter O. ... Dallas, TX
Theiss, William R. ... Chicago, IL
Theissen, Gilbert E. ... Fort Lauderdale, FL
Theissen, Nancie R. ... Anoka, MN
Theissen, Paul J. ... Covington, KY
Theissen, Timothy B. ... Covington, KY
Theisz, Jacqueline ... Allen Park, MI
Theivagt, Charles E. ... Carrollton, IL
Thek, Raymond P. ... New York, NY
Thel, Albert J., Jr. ... Newport Beach, CA
Thel, Steven Scott ... New York, NY
Thelander, Donald T. ... Newark, NJ
Thelander, Fred G. ... North Aurora, IL
Thelander, Kenneth ... Houston, TX
Thelander, Robert C. ... Summit, NJ
Theleen, Ronald J. ... White Plains, NY
Thelen, A. A. ... Miami, FL
Thelen, Alan M. ... Omaha, NE
Thelen, Bruce C. ... Detroit, MI
Thelen, Carl E. ... Lake, MI
Thelen, Dennis C. ... Washington, DC
Thelen, Dennis R. ... Bakersfield, CA
Thelen, James B. ... Kalamazoo, MI

Thelen, Jennifer A. .... **New York, NY**
Thelen, John A. .... Grand Forks, ND
Thelen, John F. .... Des Moines, IA
Thelen, Julie F. .... **Grand Rapids, MI**
Thelen, Larry A. .... Sacramento, CA
Thelen, Monnica L. .... Los Angeles, CA
Thelen Reid & Priest LLP
Los Angeles, CA
San Francisco, CA
San Jose, CA
Washington, DC
New York, NY
Thelen, T. David .... **Lovingston, VA**
Thelen, Timothy A.
Research Triangle Park, NC
Thelen, Trisha A. .... **Wichita, KS**
Thelin, Calvin B. .... **Aurora, IL**
Thelin, Ellen Hoving .... Montclair, NJ
Thelin, Howard J. .... Glendale, CA
Thelin, Paul E. .... South Portland, ME
Thelin, Stephen R. .... Erie, PA
Themeles, Stephen E. .... Dracut, MA
Themelis, John C. .... Baltimore, MD
Themelis, Nicholas M. .... Hillsborough, CA
Thenell, Heather .... Appleton, WI
Thennisch, Jeffrey P. .... **Barrington, IL**
Ann Arbor, MI
Thenor, Leonid D. .... **Washington, DC**
Thensted, C. F., Ltd., A Law Corporation
New Orleans, LA
Thensted, Charles F. .... New Orleans, LA
Theobald, Andrew T. .... **Pittsburgh, PA**
Theobald, Dani S. .... **Orlando, FL**
Theobald, Edward R. .... Chicago, IL
Theobald, Forrest D. .... **Riverside, CA**
Theobald, Frederick T. .... **Lancaster, PA**
Theobald, Gregg S. .... **Michigan City, IN**
Theobald, James W. .... **Richmond, VA**
Theobald, Jane E. .... Dallas, TX
Theobald, John O., II .... Phoenix, AZ
Theobald, Jon A. .... St. Paul, MN
Theobald, Kimberly A. .... Waukesha, WI
Theobald, Mark A. .... Roseville, MN
Theobald, Michele E. .... Smithtown, NY
Theobald, Raymond M. .... Duluth, MN
Theobald, Scott M. .... **Phoenix, AZ**
Theodocion, J. Pete .... Morrow, GA
Theodor, Christ .... Xenia, OH
Theodora, Dawn S. .... Huntington Beach, CA
Theodora, Todd C. .... **Costa Mesa, CA**
Theodorakis, D. John .... Milpitas, CA
Theodore, Ann H.
Commodity Futures Trading Commission, Division of Enforcement, GV
Theodore, Anthony J. .... Madison, WI
Theodore, Carol N. .... **Washington, DC**
Theodore, Catelli Ronald, Jr. .... Red Bank, NJ
Theodore, Eleanor .... Syracuse, NY
Theodore, Gary L. .... Long Branch, NJ
Theodore, Guilene Francisque .... Tampa, FL
Theodore, Jasmina A. .... Newport Beach, CA
Theodore, Marcus G., P.C.
Salt Lake City, UT
Theodore, Mark .... **San Francisco, CA**
Theodore, Michael H. .... **Boston, MA**
Theodore, Philip A. .... **Atlanta, GA**
Theodoredis, Roger E. .... **Cincinnati, OH**
Theodore-Lewis, Sharon I. .... Albany, NY
Theodores, Thomas .... **Redwood City, CA**
Theodorides, Electra .... Tallahassee, FL
Theodoroff, B. James .... Beverly Hills, MI
Theodoroff, Douglas .... **Flint, MI**
Theodoros, Karin .... Lowell, MA
Theodoros, Perry W. .... Merrillville, IN
Theodoros, Theodoros & Rooth, P.C.
Merrillville, IN
Theodoros, William .... Merrillville, IN
Theodorou, George .... Lowell, MA
Theodorou, Nicholas C. .... **Boston, MA**
Theodosen, John M. .... Sioux Falls, SD
Theodosiou, Andreas E. .... **New York, NY**
Theodosopoulos, David J. .... Hollywood, CA
Theodosopoulos, James .... Manchester, NH
Theodosopoulos, Randi J. .... Los Angeles, CA
Theodoss, Harry Joseph
East Hartford, CT
Worcester, MA
Theofan, Charles T. .... Mineola, NY
Theofanidis, Paris .... **Houston, TX**
Theofanis, George M. .... Encino, CA
Theofanis, Roula .... **New York, NY**
Theofel, George R. .... San Rafael, CA
Theofel, Katherine Futscher
San Francisco, CA
Theofilos, Gus K. .... Youngstown, OH
Theofilos, Kathryn K. .... West Palm Beach, FL
Theoharis, Stephen C. .... **San Francisco, CA**
Theokas, Gregory P. .... Mount Clemens, MI
Theologides, Stergios .... Irvine, CA
Theophelis, James L. .... Charlotte, MI
Theophilos, Anthony .... **San Francisco, CA**
Theophilos, Peter E. .... **San Francisco, CA**
Theophilos, Theodore J. .... Schaumburg, IL
Theophilos, Thomas P. .... Buffalo, NY
Theos, Barbara A. .... New York, NY
Theos, Christina M. .... Charleston, SC
Theos, Gregory O. .... Charleston, SC
Theos, Jerry N. .... **Charleston, SC**
Theriac, James S., III .... **Cocoa, FL**
Theriaque, David A. .... **Tallahassee, FL**
Theriaque, David A., P.A. .... **Tallahassee, FL**
Theriault & Joslin, P.C. .... **Montpelier, VT**
Theriault, Stephen M. .... Plantsville, CT
Theriault, Wayne R. .... Waterville, ME
Therien, Roger W. .... Riverside, CA
Theriot, Barbara D. .... Overland Park, KS
Theriot, Donald E. .... New Orleans, LA
Theriot, Glenn .... Denver, CO
Theriot, Janice M. .... Louisville, KY
Theriot, Kimberly A. .... **Thibodaux, LA**
Theriot, Lesley J. .... Marrero, LA
Theriot, Melissa L. .... **Lafayette, LA**
Theriot, Robert L. .... **New Orleans, LA**
Theriot, Terry E., (A Prof. Law Corp.)
Lafayette, LA
Theriot, Wanda L. .... **New Orleans, LA**
Therkildsen, Don E. .... **West Hartford, CT**
Therkorn, Ernest G.
Department of Commerce, Patent and Trademark Office, GV
Therman, Thomas E. .... Stanwood, MI
Thermes, Frank J. .... Homestead, FL
Thernes, Bryon A. .... **Savannah, GA**
Thernes, Linda Jane .... Columbus, OH
Theroff, Dennis Paul .... Kansas City, KS
Theroff, Ellen L. .... **St. Louis, MO**
Theroff, Eric T. .... **Kansas City, MO**
Therolf, Wanda M. .... Tonawanda, NY
Theros, Louis .... **Detroit, MI**
Theroux, Eugene .... **Washington, DC**
Theroux, Linda Ann .... Merrimack, NH
Theroux, William G. .... Princeton, NJ
Therrel Baisden, P.A. .... **Miami, FL**
Miami Beach, FL
Therrell, Connie J. .... Atlanta, GA
Therriault, Roger R. .... Bath, ME
Therriault, Theodore M. .... Bellevue, WA
Therrien, Keith R. .... Yakima, WA
Therrien, Kenneth D. .... Yakima, WA
Therrien, Richard F. .... Manchester, NH
Therrien, Richard R. .... Costa Mesa, CA
Therrien, Scott J. .... El Monte, CA
Therrien, Valerie M. .... Fairbanks, AK
Therrien, Valerie M., P.C. .... Fairbanks, AK
Thesing, Christopher J. .... Chicago, IL
Thesing, J. Richard .... San Francisco, CA
Thesing, James D. .... Bellevue, KY
Thesing, W. Joseph, Jr. .... **Atlanta, GA**
Thesling, William H. .... Cleveland, OH
Thesman, Aaron S. .... **Addison, TX**
Thessin, James H. .... Department of State, Office of the Legal Adviser, GV
Thessin, Mark G. .... Brentwood, TN
Thesz, J. Michael, Jr. .... **Washington, DC**
Thetford, Christopher L. .... **Houston, TX**
Thetford, F. William .... Oklahoma City, OK
Thetford, F. William, P.C.
Oklahoma City, OK
Thetford, Gale S. .... Springfield, IL
Thetford, John Michael .... **Tulsa, OK**
Thetford, Joseph D. .... **Mobile, AL**
Thetford, Mark S. .... **Muskogee, OK**
Thetford, Robin Brigham .... **Mobile, AL**
Thetford & Thetford .... **Mobile, AL**
Thetford, Thomas C. .... Lake Oswego, OR
Thetford, William Dale .... Los Angeles, CA
Theuer, Fred G. .... Saginaw, MI
Theuer, Jeffrey S. .... **Lansing, MI**
Theuerkauf, Harry W. .... Wauwatosa, WI
Theulen, Jeffrey J. .... **Harlan, IA**
Panama, IA
Theune, Mark D. .... **Oak Harbor, WA**
Theune, Philipp C. .... Denver, CO
Theunissen, Kay A. .... **Lafayette, LA**
New Orleans, LA
Theunissen, Randall K. .... **Lafayette, LA**
Theurer, Gary L. .... Bethesda, MD
Theus, Edwin K., Jr. .... **Monroe, LA**
Theus, Grisham, Davis & Leigh, L.L.P.
Monroe, LA
Theus, Harold C. .... Yukon, OK
Theus, Matthew W. .... Birmingham, AL
Theus, Reese E. .... Atlanta, GA
Theus, Roma W., II .... **Fort Lauderdale, FL**
Theus, Virgil Ted .... **Columbus, GA**
Theus, Walter W., Jr. .... Columbia, SC
Theut, Brian J. .... Phoenix, AZ
Theut, C. Peter .... **Detroit, MI**
Theut, Christopher P. .... Phoenix, AZ
Theut, David M. .... Phoenix, AZ
Theut, Kristin C. .... **West Bloomfield, MI**
Theut, Mark J. .... Phoenix, AZ
Theut, Paul J. .... Phoenix, AZ
Theut, Theut and Theut, P.C. .... Phoenix, AZ
Thevenet, Susan M. .... Louisville, CO
Thevenin, Nancy M. .... **Miami, FL**
Theveny, Daniel C. .... **Seattle, WA**
Théver, Shan K. .... **Los Angeles, CA**
Théver, Shan K., & Associates, A Prof. Corp.
Los Angeles, CA
Thew, Michael E. .... Lincoln, NE
Thews, Albert W. .... Oakland, CA
Thexton, Arthur .... Madison, WI
Thiagarajan, Anuradha .... **Atlanta, GA**
Thibadeau, Paul .... **Jupiter, FL**
Thibadeau, Paul, P.A. .... **Jupiter, FL**
Palm Beach, FL
Thibadeau, Richd. A. .... Decatur, GA
Thibau, Janelle M. .... Washington, DC
Thibault, Alice O. .... Huntington Beach, CA
Thibault, Arthur R., Jr. .... **Flemington, NJ**
Thibault, Harry G. .... Foster City, CA
Thibault, Lisa M. .... Bourne, MA
Thibault, Robert P. .... **Denver, CO**
Thibaut, Charest, III .... **Baton Rouge, LA**
Thibaut, Charles H. .... **Chapel Hill, NC**
Thibaut, John S., Jr. .... **Baton Rouge, LA**
Thibaut, Joseph Major, Sr.
Baton Rouge, LA
New Roads, LA
Thibaut, Sylvia H. .... Raleigh, NC
Thibaut, Thibaut, Bacot, Latchem & Vogt, L.L.P. .... **Baton Rouge, LA**
Thibbitts, John F. .... Centerville, MA
Thibeau, Marina E. .... Augusta, ME
Thibeau, Susan C. .... Berwick, ME
Thibeault, George W. .... Boston, MA
Thibeault, Paul G. .... Cass Lake, MN
Thibeault, Sharon J. .... Barnstable, MA
Thibeaux, Robert P. .... **New Orleans, LA**
Thiberville, Gretchen S. .... New Orleans, LA
Thibodaux, Diana Monson .... **Knoxville, TN**
Thibodeau, Alfred G., Law Offices of
Providence, RI
Thibodeau, David J., Jr. .... **Lexington, MA**
Thibodeau, Evelyn Hunt .... Flint, MI
Thibodeau, Gregory S. .... Faribault, MN
Thibodeau, James D. .... La Crosse, WI
Thibodeau, Joseph H. .... **Denver, CO**
Thibodeau, Joseph H., P.C., Law Offices of
Denver, CO
Thibodeau, Mary Ellen .... **Hartford, CT**
Thibodeau, Paul E. .... Topeka, KS
Thibodeau, Richard E. .... West Hartford, CT
Thibodeau, Thomas R. .... **Duluth, MN**
Thibodeaux, Albert A. .... New Orleans, LA
Thibodeaux, Harold L. .... Lake Charles, LA
Thibodeaux, Keith Edward
St. Martinville, LA
Thibodeaux, Lee D. .... **Houston, TX**
Thibodeaux, Michael Jared .... **Houston, TX**
Thibodeaux, Ronald P. .... Gretna, LA
Thibodeaux, Sharon Patterson .... Jackson, MS
Thibodeaux, Staci Reeves .... Lake Charles, LA
Thibodeaux, Terry .... **Lake Charles, LA**
Thibodo, Todd D. .... **Los Angeles, CA**
Thick, George E., II .... Saginaw, MI
Thickstun, John E. .... San Diego, CA
Thickstun & Stern .... San Diego, CA
Thie, Bonnie L. .... Seattle, WA
Thiebaud, Stan .... **Dallas, TX**
Thiebaut, William, Jr. .... Pueblo, CO
Thieben, H. Dale, Jr. .... Madison, WI
Thieblot, Robert J. .... Baltimore, MD
Thieblot, Ryan & Miller, P.A.
Baltimore, MD
Thiede, Ann E. .... **Janesville, WI**
Thiede, Brian E. .... Parma, MI
Thiede, Edmond G. .... Walnut Creek, CA
Thiede, Marianne Mancino
Washington, DC
Thiedmann & Edler .... **Chicago, IL**
Thiedmann, Klaus U. .... **Chicago, IL**
Thieffry et Associés .... **New York, NY**
New York, NY
Thiel, Adrian .... Danville, CA
Thiel, Alan C. .... **Minneapolis, MN**
Thiel, Albert N., Jr. .... **Albuquerque, NM**
Thiel, Anthony M. .... **Norfolk, VA**
Thiel, Campbell, Gunderson & Anderson, P.L.L.P. .... **Minneapolis, MN**
Thiel, Christopher J. .... New Port Richey, FL
Thiel, Clark T. .... **San Francisco, CA**
Thiel, Cynthia K. .... **Missoula, MT**
Thiel, Dale H. .... **Kalamazoo, MI**
Thiel, Denise L. Snyder .... Ligonier, PA
Thiel, Donna K. .... **Washington, DC**
Thiel, Douglas J. .... Coral Gables, FL
Thiel, Edward R. .... Lockport, NY
Thiel, James S. .... Madison, WI
Thiel, John D. .... Merrill, WI
Thiel, John E. .... **Appleton, WI**
Thiel, John W. .... **Minneapolis, MN**
Thiel, Kathryn E. .... Oakton, VA
Thiel, Linda A. .... Eden Prairie, MN
Thiel, Matthew B. .... Missoula, MT
Thiel, Michael F. .... Chicago, IL
Thiel, Roy W., Jr. .... Manitowish Waters, WI
Thiel, Stuart E. .... **Chicago, IL**
Thiel, Thomas E. .... San Jose, CA
Thiel, Timothy D. .... McComb, OH
Thiel, W. John, Jr. .... **Boise, ID**
Thiel, Walter R. .... Santa Monica, CA
Thiel, W. F. .... **Minneapolis, MN**
Thiel, William G. .... **Eau Claire, WI**
Thiele, Alan R. .... **San Antonio, TX**
Thiele, Alexander .... **Santa Rosa, CA**
Thiele, Alexander, Inc. .... **Santa Rosa, CA**
Thiele, Christopher C. .... **Austin, TX**
Thiele, David F. .... Everett, WA
Thiele, Derek G. .... Santa Barbara, CA
Thiele, Douglas .... **Santa Rosa, CA**
Thiele, Herbert William Albert
Tallahassee, FL
Thiele, Howard N., Jr. .... Dayton, OH
Thiele, Leslie K.L. .... **Albany, NY**
Thiele, Lisa J. .... Houston, TX
Thiele, Richard C. .... Pittsburgh, PA
Thiele, Richard H. .... Somerville, NJ
Thiele, Steven J. .... Olympia, WA
Thiele, Terry V. .... Cleveland, OH
Thielemann, Elizabeth N. .... Evanston, IL
Thielemann, Troy A. .... **Santa Barbara, CA**
Thielen, Barbara J. .... Omaha, NE
Thielen, Brian P. .... Bloomington, IL
Thielen, James E. .... Waterloo, IA
Thielen, Joseph E. .... Newport Beach, CA
Thielen, Laura H. .... Kailua, HI
Thielen, Mary K. .... Omaha, NE
Thielen, Raymond J. .... Sacramento, CA
Thielen, Raymond J., II .... Sacramento, CA
Thieler, Alan H. .... Quincy, CA
Thieler, Hilary K. .... Orlando, FL
Thieler, Lisa A. .... **Atlanta, GA**
Thielhelm, Robert W., Jr. .... **Orlando, FL**
Thielke, Craig W. .... Robbinsdale, MN
Thielking, Paul M. .... Des Moines, IA
Thiella, John A. .... San Francisco, CA
Thielman, Gerhard W. .... **San Jose, CA**
Thielman, Hans H. .... Seattle, WA
Thielman, John P. .... St. Petersburg, FL
Thielman, Paul H. .... Buffalo, NY
Thielman, Phillip A. .... Buffalo, NY
Thielmann, Ilze C. .... New York, NY
Thielmann, William D. .... Sun Prairie, WI
Thiem, Matthew D. .... **Houston, TX**
Thiem, Rebecca S., P.C. .... **Bismarck, ND**
Thiem, Susan C. .... Lincolnville, ME
Thieman, Charlene .... Albany, NY
Thieman, Charles Kevin .... Louisville, KY
Thieman, Frederick W. .... **Pittsburgh, PA**
Thieman, James L. .... **Sidney, OH**
Thieman, Joan M. .... Minneapolis, MN
Thieman & Kaufman .... **Pittsburgh, PA**
Thieman, Peter P. .... **Washington, DC**
Thieman, Robert E. .... **Louisville, KY**
Thieman, Sally L. .... Overland Park, KS
Thieman, Shari D. .... **Albuquerque, NM**
Thiemann & Aitken, L.C. .... **Alexandria, VA**
Thiemann, Alan J. .... **Alexandria, VA**
Thiemann, Bruce .... Peoria, IL
Thiemann, Frank H., III .... Louisville, KY
Thiemann, Frank H., Jr. .... Louisville, KY
Thiemann, Jill .... Toms River, NJ
Thiemann, Kathleen A. .... Milwaukee, WI
Thiemann, Kevin B. .... **Hudson, NY**
Thiemann, Nicholas W. .... **Westport, CT**
Thiemann & Novak, LLC .... **Westport, CT**
Thiemann, Paul P., Jr. .... Cincinnati, OH
Thiemann & Thiemann .... Louisville, KY
Thieme, Daniel L. .... **Seattle, WA**
Thieme, Philip R. .... Fort Wayne, IN
Thieme, R. Kevin .... Grand Rapids, MI
Thieme, R. Kevin, P.C. .... Grand Rapids, MI
Thieme, Raymond G., Jr. .... Annapolis, MD
Thiemonge, Frank L., III .... Mobile, AL
Thieneman, Kevin R. .... Peoria, IL
Thienhaus, Teresa J. .... Reno, NV
Thier, Carl-Christian .... **Orlando, FL**
Thier, Clifford S., Law Offices of
West Hartford, CT
Thier, Holli P. .... San Francisco, CA
Thier, Jerome .... Loudonville, NY
Thier, Jonathan D. .... **New York, NY**
Thier, Sarah M. .... **Minneapolis, MN**
Thier, Stephanie E. .... Philadelphia, PA
Thier, Whitney .... **Las Vegas, NV**
Thierbach, Christian F., III .... Riverside, CA
Thierbach, Marlene L. .... Santa Ana, CA
Thierfelder, Erhard B. .... Flanders, NJ
Thierfelder, Mark E. .... **New York, NY**
Thierman, David R. .... Somers Point, NJ
Thierman Law Firm .... San Francisco, CA
Thierman, Mark R. .... San Francisco, CA
Thierolf, Richard B., Jr. .... **Medford, OR**
Thierry, James E. .... Port Clinton, OH
Thierry, John A. .... Hill, NH
Thierstein, Joan Voth .... Hillsdale, MI
Thierstein, Joel P. .... Edwardsville, IL
Thies, David C. .... **Urbana, IL**
Thies, David Jonathan .... Foley, AL
Thies, J. Eric .... Rahway, NJ
Thies, James R., Sr. .... Orange Park, FL
Thies, John E. .... **Urbana, IL**
Thies, Lee M. .... **Anaheim, CA**
Thies, Mary Jane .... **Pensacola, FL**
Thies, Pamela McCarroll .... Portland, OR
Thies, Randy L. .... **Wenatchee, WA**
Thies, Richard B. .... **Chicago, IL**
Thies, Richard L. .... **Urbana, IL**
Thies, Roger C. .... **Washington, DC**
Thiesen, Thomas A. .... San Francisco, CA
Thiesing, Matthew J. .... **Lenexa, KS**
Thiesing, Robert A. .... Ellington, CT
Thiesmeyer, Kirtley M. .... **Los Angeles, CA**
Thiess, Gregory G. .... **Broadview, IL**
Thiess, Kenneth C. .... Pittsburgh, PA
Thiessen, Brian D., Law Offices of
Alamo, CA
Thiessen, David W. .... St. Cloud, MN
Thiessen, Eric R. .... **Abingdon, VA**
Thiessen, Guy A. .... Tulsa, OK
Thiessen, Guy A., P.C. .... Tulsa, OK
Thiessen, Jacob G. .... **Washington, DC**
Thiessen, Kendall I. .... **Palo Alto, CA**
Thiessen, Michael R. .... **Kansas City, MO**
Thiessen, Patrick H. .... Wichita, KS
Thiessen, Robert A. .... Wichita, KS
Thiessen, Robert T. .... Sacramento, CA
Thiessen, Rose Marie .... **Newport Beach, CA**
Thietje, Timothy L. .... Lincoln, NE
Thiewes, Ronald C. .... **Kansas City, MO**
Thiewes, Ronald C., P.C.
Kansas City, MO
Thifault, Ernest G. .... New Hyde Park, NY
Thigpen, Al D. .... Tyler, TX
Thigpen, Bernita L. .... Treasury Department, Internal Revenue Service, GV
Thigpen, Blue, Stephens & Fellers
Raleigh, NC
Thigpen, Charles A. .... Montgomery, AL
Thigpen, Christopher A. .... **Tuscaloosa, AL**
Thigpen, Cressie H., Jr. .... Raleigh, NC
Thigpen, Douglas O. .... **Asheville, NC**
Thigpen, E. Eugene .... Houston, TX
Thigpen, Elijah Jacob, Jr. .... Lakewood, CO
Thigpen, Frank C. .... Robbins, NC
Thigpen, Helen .... **Dallas, TX**
Thigpen, Jeffrey A. .... Bellingham, WA
Thigpen, Jimmy E. .... Temple, TX
Thigpen, Joe K. .... **Tyler, TX**
Thigpen, John R., Jr. .... Blackshear, GA
Thigpen, Joseph .... Haskell, TX
Thigpen, Mark V. .... **Charlotte, NC**
Thigpen, Norman J. .... Lake Charles, LA
Thigpen, Randy K. .... Florence, AL
Thigpen & Raney .... **Tyler, TX**
Thigpen, Richard A. .... Tuscaloosa, AL
Thigpen, Richard M. .... Charlotte, NC
Thigpen, Wanda Douglas
New Brunswick, NJ
New York, NY

Thigpen, William M., III ... Atlanta, GA
Thikoll, Leon A. ... Tucson, AZ
Thill, Bruce G. ... Palatine, IL
Thill, David W. ... San Francisco, CA
Thill, Favaro, Buzek & Gorman, Ltd. Broomfield, CO; Palatine, IL
Thill, Jeffrey D. ... St. Louis Park, MN
Thill, John H. ... St. Paul, MN
Thill, Julie Ann ... Brooklyn Park, MN
Thill Law Firm,, P.A. ... St. Louis Park, MN
Thill, Michael A. ... Crown Point, IN
Thill, Peter J. ... Davenport, IA
Thill, Timothy J. ... Chicago, IL
Thill, Timothy J., P.C. ... Chicago, IL
Thillman, Joseph L. ... Palm Beach, FL
Thilly, J. Leroy ... Sun Prairie, WI
Thilmany, Mary Ann ... Schaumburg, IL
Thilmany & Neis ... Schaumburg, IL
Thiltgen, Bart J. ... Bakersfield, CA
Thiltgen, Christine P. ... Sacramento, CA
Thimesch, Michelle L. ... Walnut Creek, CA
Thimesch, Timothy S. ... Danville, CA
Thimke, Dolores T. ... Madison, WI
Thimke, Mark A. ... Milwaukee, WI
Thimke, Raymond C. ... Monona, WI
Thimmaiah, Maletira B. ... Staten Island, NY
Thimmesch, Victoria M. ... Reno, NV
Thimmesh, Elizabeth A. ... St. Paul, MN
Thimmig, David M. ... Chicago, IL
Thimmig, Diana M. ... Cleveland, OH
Thimmig, Michael B. ... Austin, TX
Thimmig, Paul J. ... San Francisco, CA
Thimsen, Gary P. ... Sioux Falls, SD
Thimsen, Jeffrey J. ... Spokane, WA
Thind, Aman ... San Francisco, CA
Thing, R. Steven ... Portland, ME
Thinnes, David G. ... Cedar Rapids, IA
Thinnes & Liesveld, L.C. ... Cedar Rapids, IA
Thinnes, Mary Ann ... Dayton, OH
Thinnes, Thomas A. ... Phoenix, AZ
Thinnes, Thomas A., P.A. ... Phoenix, AZ
Thinschmidt, Donald M. ... Kalamazoo, MI
Thinschmidt, Donald M., P.C. Kalamazoo, MI
Thirard, Joline Tessa ... Houston, TX
Thirer, Martin ... Fort Lauderdale, FL
Thirer, Martin, P.A. ... Fort Lauderdale, FL
Thirkell & Cretan ... San Mateo, CA
Thirkell, Edward D. ... San Mateo, CA
Thirkell, John Anton ... Golden, CO
Thirolf, Eugene M. ... Department of Justice, Civil Division, GV
Thiron, Mark W. ... Grand Blanc, MI
Thiron, Mark W., P.C. ... Grand Blanc, MI
Thiros, Andrew G. ... Pittsburgh, PA
Thiros, James N. ... Merrillville, IN
Thiros, Mark A. ... Merrillville, IN
Thiros, Nick J. ... Merrillville, IN
Thiry & Caddell ... Mobile, AL
Thiry, Richard L. ... Mobile, AL
This, Jason E. ... New Bremen, OH
Thissell, Charles William ... Diamondhead, MS
Thissen, Paul C. ... Minneapolis, MN
Thistle, Dale F. ... Newport, ME
Thistle, Daniel L. ... Philadelphia, PA
Thistle, Daniel L., P.C., Law Offices of Philadelphia, PA
Thistle, J. Jeffrey ... Delray Beach, FL
Thistle, Michael G. ... Villanova, PA
Thistle, Moore, Rosser & Tull Philadelphia, PA
Thistle, Patrick J. ... Los Angeles, CA
Thistle, Raymond A., Jr. ... Willow Grove, PA
Thistle, Scott R. ... Pittsburgh, PA
Thistle, Thomas M., III ... Philadelphia, PA
Thistle, Thomas M., Jr. ... Philadelphia, PA
Thistlethwaite, Hugh W. ... Opelousas, LA
Thistlethwaite, Jamie Olsen ... Santa Rosa, CA
Thistlethwaite, William H. ... Centreville, MI
Thistlethwaite, William H. ... Centreville, MI
Thivener, Jennifer K. ... Columbus, OH
Thoburn, Stephen B. ... Detroit, MI
Thoburn, Thomas E., (P.A.) ... Cocoa, FL
Thode, Alice Clark ... Wheaton, IL
Thode, Anna C. ... Department of Justice, Environment and Natural Resources Division, GV
Thode, Mary Ann ... San Francisco, CA
Thode, Thomas A. ... Yuma, AZ
Thode, William D. ... Denver, CO
Thoe, Marla K. ... Montrose, CO
Thoele, James C. ... St. Louis, MO
Thoelke, David J. ... Roseville, MN
Thoeming, Charles L., Law Offices of Walnut Creek, CA
Thoemmes, Boguslawa B. Department of Commerce, Office of the General Counsel, GV
Thoen, Paul M. ... Mount Clemens, MI
Thoene, Alika, Jr. ... Hilo, HI
Thoene, Christine Graves ... San Diego, CA
Thoenen, James A. ... Edwardsville, IL; St. Louis, MO
Thoenig, Raymond H. ... Seattle, WA
Thoen Levin, Claire ... Minneapolis, MN
Thofner, Jeffrey P. ... Tampa, FL
Thogersen, Gary J. ... Seattle, WA
Thoits, Edward C. ... Santa Barbara, CA
Thoits, Jeanine R. ... Hastings, MI
Thoits, Jonathan F. ... Grand Rapids, MI
Thoits, Love, Hershberger & McLean, A Professional Corporation ... Palo Alto, CA
Thoits, Michael E. ... Troy, MI
Thoits, Warren R. ... Palo Alto, CA
Thole, Eric C. ... Stillwater, MN
Thole, Lori D. ... Cincinnati, OH
Thole, Michael E. ... Sibley, IA
Thole, Thomas J. ... Cincinnati, OH
Tholen, Sandra L. ... Los Angeles, CA
Thollander, David C. ... Evanston, IL
Tholstrup, Richard Joseph ... Houston, TX
Thom, Cameron C. ... Coos Bay, OR
Thom, Charles R. ... Port Jefferson, NY
Thom & DeMotte ... Jasper, IN
Thom, Gerald R. ... Jasper, IN
Thom, Gregory W. ... Minnetonka, MN
Thom, Hendrick & Doak, P.C. Oklahoma City, OK
Thom, Jeff ... Sacramento, CA
Thom, Laurelle ... Walnut Creek, CA
Thom, Michael W. ... Oklahoma City, OK
Thom, Neil C. ... Columbus, GA
Thom, Norman R. ... Colorado Springs, CO
Thom, Phillip L. ... Seattle, WA
Thom, Roland Q. F. ... Honolulu, HI
Thom, Susan M. ... Seal Beach, CA
Thom, Terrence C. ... Milwaukee, WI
Thom, W. Scott ... Kenosha, WI
Thom, William J. ... New York, NY
Thom, Winfield S. ... Chicago, IL
Thoma, Clifford H. ... Brookfield, WI
Thoma, Corinth ... Department of Labor, Office of Secretary, GV
Thoma, James O. ... Los Angeles, CA
Thoma, Jeffrey E. ... Ukiah, CA
Thoma, John M. ... Galveston, TX
Thoma, Klaus D. ... Houston, TX
Thoma, Laurence G. ... Red Bank, NJ
Thoma, Mark A. ... Fort Wayne, IN
Thoma, Paul K. ... Kansas City, KS
Thoma, Peter J. ... Dallas, TX
Thoma, Richard A. ... Bronxville, NY
Thoma, Richard J. ... Detroit, MI
Thoma, Steven G. ... Southfield, MI
Thoma-Isgur, Shoshana L. Fort Worth, TX
Thomajan, Robert ... Austin, TX
Thoman, Charles N. ... Sioux City, IA
Thoman, Eric J. ... Renton, WA
Thoman, Henry N. ... Amelia, OH
Thoman, Mark ... New York, NY
Thomás, A. Jan, Jr. ... West Memphis, AR
Thomas, Aaron Craig ... Detroit, MI
Thomas, Adrian P. ... Pompano Beach, FL
Thomas, Aelicia L. ... Cleveland, MS
Thomas, A. J., Jr. ... Fort Lauderdale, FL
Thomas, Alan A. Federal Communications Commission, Common Carrier Bureau, GV
Thomas, Alan C. ... Newark, NJ
Thomas, Albert J., III ... Little Rock, AR
Thomas, Albert S., Jr. ... Wilson, NC
Thomas, Alexander G. ... Columbus, OH
Thomas, Alexander Y. ... McLean, VA
Thomas, Alexandra K. ... Baltimore, MD
Thomas, Alfred B. ... Grosse Pointe Park, MI
Thomas, Alice Palmer ... San Rafael, CA
Thomas, Alice R. ... New York, NY
Thomas, Allan D. ... Manchester, CT
Thomas, Allen G. ... Wilson, NC
Thomas, Allen L. ... Long Beach, CA
Thomas, Allison K. ... Lansing, MI
Thomas, Allisyn L. ... San Diego, CA
Thomas, Alvin L. ... Houston, TX
Thomas, Amos P. ... Brazil, IN
Thomas, Amy C. ... Mexia, TX
Thomas, Amy E. ... Department of Commerce, Patent and Trademark Office, GV; Davidsonville, MD
Thomas, Amy L. ... Oklahoma City, OK
Thomas, Amy S. ... Salt Lake City, UT
Thomas, Anastasia E. ... San Diego, CA
Thomas, Andrea Kojm ... Corning, NY
Thomas, Andrew A. ... Middletown, RI
Thomas, Andrew B., (P.A.) ... Orlando, FL
Thomas, Andrew D., Law Office of Evansville, IN
Thomas, Andrew E. ... Washington, DC
Thomas, Andrew J. ... Los Angeles, CA
Thomas, Andrew J. ... Los Angeles, CA
Thomas, Andrew J. ... Las Vegas, NV
Thomas, Andrew J., Jr. ... Fairfield, CT
Thomas, Andrew M. ... Evanston, IL
Thomas, Andrew P. ... Phoenix, AZ
Thomas, Andrew P. ... Brazil, IN
Thomas, Andrew R. ... New Orleans, LA
Thomas, Angela C. ... Chicago, IL
Thomas, Anita Wallace ... Atlanta, GA
Thomas, Ann ... Miami, FL
Thomas, Ann F. ... New York, NY
Thomas, Ann Lyter ... Las Vegas, NV
Thomas, Ann Victoria ... Lawrence, KS
Thomas, Ann V.W. ... Pottsboro, TX
Thomas, Anne B. ... Bentleyville, OH
Thomas, Anne Cavanaugh ... Evansville, IN
Thomas, Anne T., (P.C.) ... Riverside, CA
Thomas, Anthony ... St. Petersburg, FL
Thomas, Anthony S. ... Torrance, CA
Thomas, Antonio L. ... Atlanta, GA
Thomas, April C. ... Cincinnati, OH
Thomas, Arcelia ... Baltimore, MD
Thomas and Archer ... Nashville, TN
Thomas, Archibald J., III, Law Offices of Jacksonville, FL
Thomas, Arthur E. ... Seattle, WA
Thomas, Arthur R. ... Harrisburg, PA
Thomas Arvin and Fleming Hopkinsville, KY
Thomas, B. Brooks ... New York, NY
Thomas, B. David ... Bellevue, WA
Thomas, B. David ... Kirkland, WA
Thomas & Bailey, P.C. ... Hyannis, MA
Thomas, Ballenger, Vogelman and Turner, P.C. ... Alexandria, VA
Thomas, Barbara A. ... Chicago, IL
Thomas, Barbara A. ... Doylestown, PA
Thomas, Barbara Jean ... New York, NY
Thomas, Bart T. ... Dallas, TX
Thomas, Basil A. ... Baltimore, MD
Thomas, Ben S. ... Mooresville, NC
Thomas, Beneba J. ... San Francisco, CA
Thomas, Benjamin C. ... Phoenix, AZ
Thomas, Benjamin E. ... Fargo, ND
Thomas & Bennett ... Kernersville, NC
Thomas, Bernard R. ... Atlanta, GA
Thomas, Bertrand S. ... Washington, DC
Thomas, Beth A. ... Orlando, FL
Thomas, Beth Lynn ... Philadelphia, PA
Thomas, Bette M. ... Pensacola, FL
Thomas, Bette M., P.A. ... Pensacola, FL
Thomas, Beverly J. Federal Trade Commission, Bureau of Consumer Protection, GV
Thomas, Birdsong & Becker, P.C. Rolla, MO
Thomas, Blacknall & Thomas Waycross, GA
Thomas & Boles ... Chagrin Falls, OH
Thomas, Boris B. ... New York, NY
Thomas, Bradford A. ... Miami, FL
Thomas, Bradford W. ... Atlanta, GA
Thomas, Bradley Kim ... Waterloo, IN
Thomas, Bradley S. ... Sacramento, CA
Thomas, Bren K. ... Fresno, CA
Thomas, Brenda L. ... Westlake Village, CA
Thomas, Brett ... Los Angeles, CA
Thomas, Brett S. ... Beaumont, TX
Thomas, Brian D. ... Sterling, CO
Thomas, Brian G. ... Columbia, MO
Thomas, Brian J. ... Topeka, KS
Thomas, Brian J. ... Cincinnati, OH
Thomas, Brian N. ... Winchester, KY
Thomas, Brian R. ... Camden, NJ; Philadelphia, PA
Thomas, Brian S. ... Atlantic City, NJ; Pleasantville, NJ
Thomas, Brooke E. ... Washington, DC; Baltimore, MD
Thomas, Bruce A. ... Grand Ronde, OR
Thomas, Bruce A. ... Easton, PA
Thomas, Bruce G. ... Sioux City, IA
Thomas, Bruce L. ... Boise, ID
Thomas, Bruce M. ... Middletown, OH
Thomas, Bruce V. ... Richmond, VA
Thomas, Bryan M. ... Winter Park, FL
Thomas, Bryce O., Jr. ... Hickory, NC
Thomas, Burns & Holliday, P.C. St. Joseph, MO
Thomas, Byron A. ... Houston, TX
Thomas, C. Bruce ... Paradise Valley, AZ
Thomas, C. Douglass ... Mountain View, CA
Thomas, C. Greg ... Mobile, AL
Thomas, C. Howard, Jr. ... Lumberville, PA
Thomas, C. Sam, (P.C.) ... Atlanta, GA
Thomas, C. Siri ... New York, NY
Thomas, C. Teigue ... San Diego, CA
Thomas, C. Terrell, Jr. ... Wendell, NC
Thomas, C. William, Jr. ... Boston, MA
Thomas, Calhoun, III ... Blythewood, SC
Thomas, Calhoun, Jr. Hilton Head Island, SC
Thomas, Calvert ... Hartford, CT
Thomas, Cardell A. ... New Orleans, LA
Thomas, Caren D. ... Glencoe, IL
Thomas, Carl ... Los Angeles, CA
Thomas, Carl O. ... Rochester, NY
Thomas, Carla J. ... Easton, PA
Thomas, Carolyn, (Ms.) ... Chicago, IL
Thomas, Cassandra C. Federal Communications Commission, International Bureau, GV
Thomas, Catherine J. F. ... San Jose, CA
Thomas, Cecilia Anne ... Fort Worth, TX
Thomas, Charles A., Jr. ... Temple, GA
Thomas, Charles B. ... Washington, DC
Thomas, Charles C. ... Woodbury, NJ
Thomas, Charles D. ... Chicago, IL
Thomas, Charles D. ... Pontotoc, MS
Thomas, Charles E. ... Joliet, IL
Thomas, Charles E., Jr. ... Harrisburg, PA
Thomas, Charles F. ... Rockford, IL
Thomas, Charles G. ... Cambridge, MA; New York, NY
Thomas, Charles H. ... Santa Monica, CA
Thomas, Charles H. ... Mankato, MN
Thomas, Charles J. ... Kew Gardens, NY
Thomas, Charles L. ... Tacoma, WA
Thomas, Charles M. ... Phoenix, AZ
Thomas, Charles M. ... Kansas City, MO
Thomas, Charles M., Jr. ... Eureka, CA
Thomas, Charles M., Ltd. ... Phoenix, AZ
Thomas, Charles O. ... Bonner Springs, KS
Thomas, Charles R., (P.C.) ... Pekin, IL
Thomas, Charles W. ... Troy, NY
Thomas, Charlotte E. ... Philadelphia, PA
Thomas, Chas. F. ... Belleville, IL
Thomas, Cherry L. ... Tuscaloosa, AL
Thomas, Cheryl A. ... Minneapolis, MN
Thomas, Cheryl S. ... Virginia Beach, VA
Thomas, Christina M. ... Newark, NJ
Thomas, Christine C. ... Houston, TX
Thomas, Christopher D. ... Phoenix, AZ
Thomas, Christopher D. ... Los Angeles, CA
Thomas, Christopher D. ... Rochester, NY
Thomas, Christopher J. ... Conifer, CO
Thomas, Christopher J. ... North Canton, OH
Thomas, Christopher L. ... Riverside, CA; Santa Ana, CA
Thomas, Christopher L. ... Nicholasville, KY
Thomas, Christopher P. ... Portland, OR
Thomas, Cindy-Ann ... Cincinnati, OH
Thomas, C. J. Steuart, III ... Staunton, VA
Thomas, Claire A. ... Brooklyn, NY
Thomas, Clarence ... Supreme Court Of The United States, GV
Thomas, Clarence M. ... Timonium, MD
Thomas, Claudia Medina ... Tampa, FL
Thomas, Clayton B. ... Evanston, WY
Thomas, Clayton H., Jr. ... Doylestown, PA
Thomas, Clayton H., Jr. ... Philadelphia, PA
Thomas, Cleophus, Jr. ... Anniston, AL; Birmingham, AL
Thomas, Clint C. ... Alabaster, AL
Thomas, Clyde E. ... Cleveland, OH
Thomas, Clyde E., III ... Big Spring, TX
Thomas & Colaneri, P.C. ... Linwood, NJ
Thomas, Colin J. S., Jr. ... Staunton, VA
Thomas, Collin N. ... Columbus, OH
Thomas, Collison & Meagher ... Endicott, NY
Thomas, Constance L. ... Savannah, GA
Thomas, Craig A. ... Jacksonville, FL
Thomas, Craig A. ... Cincinnati, OH
Thomas, Craig G. ... Albuquerque, NM
Thomas, Craig N. ... Fairfax, VA
Thomas, Craig P. ... Rockford, IL
Thomas, Craig S. ... Washington, DC
Thomas, Crawford H. ... Sacramento, CA
Thomas & Culp, L.L.P. ... Dallas, TX
Thomas, Curtis H. ... Buena Park, CA
Thomas, Cynthia ... Seattle, WA
Thomas, Cynthia G. ... Detroit, MI
Thomas, Cynthia J. ... New Orleans, LA
Thomas, Cynthia R. ... White Plains, NY
Thomas, D. Alan ... Birmingham, AL
Thomas, D. Camille ... Billings, MT
Thomas, D. Dirk ... Birmingham, AL
Thomas, D. Gray ... Jacksonville, FL
Thomas, D. Keith ... Clearwater, FL
Thomas, D. Kelly, Jr. ... Maryville, TN
Thomas, D. Lee, Jr. ... Fort Worth, TX
Thomas, D. Mark ... Harrisburg, PA
Thomas, D. Russell ... Murfreesboro, TN
Thomas, Dale E. ... Chicago, IL
Thomas, Dale Robert ... Peoria, IL
Thomas, Dale V. ... San Francisco, CA
Thomas, Damian E. ... Port St. Lucie, FL
Thomas, Damon C. ... Huntsville, TX
Thomas, Damon T. ... Haverhill, MA
Thomas, Dan C. ... Tulsa, OK
Thomas, Daniel Department of the Air Force, Office of the Judge Advocate General, GV
Thomas, Daniel A. ... West Palm Beach, FL
Thomas, Daniel A. ... Warren, OH
Thomas, Daniel Albert ... Great Neck, NY
Thomas, Daniel C. ... Mayfield, KY
Thomas, Daniel F. ... Baltimore, MD
Thomas, Daniel H. ... Mobile, AL
Thomas, Daniel J. ... Avon, OH
Thomas, Daniel N. ... Hopkinsville, KY
Thomas, Daniel P. ... Warren, OH
Thomas, Daron J. ... Bakersfield, CA
Thomas, Darrell G. ... Houston, TX
Thomas, Darryl K. ... Westchester, IL
Thomas, Daryl M. ... Sacramento, CA
Thomas, Dave, and Associates, P.C. Albuquerque, NM
Thomas, David ... Boston, MA
Thomas, David ... Carrollton, MO
Thomas, David A. ... Athens, AL
Thomas, David A. ... Los Angeles, CA
Thomas, David A. ... Newton, MA
Thomas, David A. ... Newark, NJ
Thomas, David A. ... Akron, OH
Thomas, David A. ... Provo, UT
Thomas, David Abboud ... Baton Rouge, LA
Thomas, David B. ... Provo, UT
Thomas, David B. ... Charleston, WV
Thomas, David C. ... New York, NY
Thomas, David E. ... Bronx, NY
Thomas, David E. ... Dallas, TX
Thomas, David G. ... Elkhart, IN
Thomas, David H., III ... Albuquerque, NM
Thomas, David, III ... Denver, CO
Thomas, David J. ... Sauk Rapids, MN
Thomas, David L. ... Huntsville, AL
Thomas, David L. ... DeLand, FL
Thomas, David L. ... Overland Park, KS
Thomas, David L. ... Las Vegas, NV
Thomas, David L. ... Whiteville, NC
Thomas, David L. ... Oklahoma City, OK
Thomas, David L. ... Greenville, SC; West Columbia, SC
Thomas, David M. ... Englewood, CO
Thomas, David M. ... Norcross, GA
Thomas, David M. ... Ellicott City, MD
Thomas, David M. ... Rockville, MD
Thomas, David M. ... Boston, MA
Thomas, David M. ... Detroit, MI
Thomas, David M. ... Morgantown, WV
Thomas, David M., II ... Jackson, MS
Thomas, David M., P.A. ... Ellicott City, MD
Thomas, David P. ... Cleveland, OH
Thomas, David R. ... Altus, OK
Thomas, David R. ... Dallas, TX
Thomas, David Robert De Funiak Springs, FL
Thomas, David S. ... Pine Grove, CA
Thomas, David U. ... Washington, DC
Thomas, David W. ... Nicholasville, KY
Thomas, Dawn C. ... Riverhead, NY
Thomas, Dawn M. ... Bangor, ME
Thomas, Dawn M. ... New York, NY
Thomas, Dawn S. ... St. Louis, MO
Thomas, Dayton L. ... Ridgway, IL
Thomas, D. C., Law Firm Oklahoma City, OK
Thomas, Deanna D. ... Morris Plains, NJ
Thomas, Deborah A. ... Parsippany, NJ
Thomas, Debra A. ... Chicago, IL
Thomas, Debra A. ... Oak Brook, IL

Thomas, Debra B. ......**Boston, MA**
Thomas, Debra Kay ......**Dallas, TX**
Thomas, Debra Tourtelotte ......Dallas, TX
Thomas, Deirdre C. ......**Seattle, WA**
Thomas, Delaney & Wittbrodt, P.C.
Grand Blanc, MI
Thomas, Delbert A. ......Temple City, CA
Thomas, Denise McLeod ......Decatur, GA
Thomas, Dennis Dee ......Omaha, NE
Thomas, Dennis K. ......**Little Rock, AR**
Thomas, Dennis L. ......Louisville, KY
Thomas, Denton N. ......**Houston, TX**
Thomas, DeRoy C. ......New York, NY
Thomas, Derric Ernest ......McLean, VA
Thomas, Derrick ......**Richmond, VA**
Thomas, Devin Ferree ......**Raleigh, NC**
Thomas, Diana D. ......Butler, MO
Thomas, Diane E. ......**Overland Park, KS**
Thomas, Dirk D. ......**Washington, DC**
Thomas, Dixie ......Pensacola, FL
Thomas, Dixie S. ......Woodbridge, VA
Thomas, Dixon ......Fort Pierce, FL
Thomas, Dodson & Wolford
Louisville, KY
Thomas, Dominick J., Jr. ......**Derby, CT**
Thomas, Donald A. ......Liberty, KY
Thomas, Donald C. ......**Anchorage, AK**
Thomas, Donald E ......Benton, KY
Thomas, Donald Joseph ......**Boca Raton, FL**
Thomas, Donald O. ......Elk Grove, CA
Thomas, Donald S., Jr. ......**Austin, TX**
Thomas, Donna ......Deer Park, TX
Thomas, Donna M.D. ......**Baltimore, MD**
Thomas, Dorothy D. ......Baton Rouge, LA
Thomas, Douglas A. ......**Denver, CO**
Thomas, Douglas B. ......Layton, UT
Ogden, UT
Thomas, Douglas E. ......**Phoenix, AZ**
Thomas, Douglas G. ......Hatboro, PA
Thomas, Douglas M. ......Hartford, CT
Thomas, Douglas P. ......Scranton, PA
Tunkhannock, PA
Thomas, Douglas R. ......Beltsville, MD
Thomas, Douglas R., & Associates, P.C.
Beltsville, MD
Thomas, Duane E. ......Lake City, FL
Thomas, Duane M. ......Victorville, CA
Thomas, Duke W. ......**Columbus, OH**
Thomas, Dunahoe & Thomas ......**Many, LA**
Natchitoches, LA
Thomas, Dustin N. ......**Hattiesburg, MS**
Thomas, Dynda A. ......**Cleveland, OH**
Thomas, E. Michael Paul ......**Boston, MA**
Thomas, E. Rue ......Houston, TX
Thomas, Earl E. ......Los Angeles, CA
Thomas, Earl G. ......**Alexandria, VA**
Thomas, Earlyne McCalister ......St. Louis, MO
Thomas, Eddie C., Jr. ......Redwood City, CA
Thomas, Edith S. ......Brighton, MI
Thomas, Edmund M., A Prof. Law Corp.
Shreveport, LA
Thomas, Edward D. ......New York, NY
Thomas, Edward J. ......**Bakersfield, CA**
Thomas, Edward J., A Professional Corporation ......**Bakersfield, CA**
Thomas, Edward M. ......Detroit, MI
Thomas, Edwin C., III ......**Chicago, IL**
Thomas & Elardo, P.C. ......**Phoenix, AZ**
Thomas, Elizabeth ......**Seattle, WA**
Thomas, Elizabeth Ann ......Little Rock, AR
Thomas, Elizabeth Aundrea ......Miami, FL
Thomas, Elizabeth E. ......**Tupelo, MS**
Thomas, Elizabeth T. ......**Charleston, SC**
Thomas, Ella C. ......Longboat Key, FL
Thomas, Ellen K. ......Evansville, IN
Thomas & Elliott ......Los Angeles, CA
Thomas, Elroy S. ......**Joplin, MO**
Thomas, Elvira Sorrentino ......Valhalla, NY
Thomas, Erika ......**McHenry, IL**
Thomas, Ernest V., III ......Newport, KY
Cincinnati, OH
Cleveland, OH
Columbus, OH
Thomas, Ernest V., Jr. ......**Cincinnati, OH**
Thomas, Eugene C. ......**Boise, ID**
Thomas, Eunice W. ......Department of Defense, Armed Services Board of Contract Appeals, GV
Thomas, Evelyn B. ......Boise, ID
Thomas, Evora A. ......Hampton, VA
Thomas, F. Duncan ......Greenville, TX
Thomas, F. Scott ......**Winston-Salem, NC**
Thomas, F. Vaughn ......**Albuquerque, NM**
Thomas, F. Vaughn, & Associates, P.A.
Albuquerque, NM
Thomas & Farris, P.A. ......Wilson, NC
Thomas, Fayes F., Jr. ......Miami, FL
Thomas, Feldman & Wilshusen, L.L.P.
Dallas, TX
Thomas Firm, The, L.L.C. ......**Atlanta, GA**
Thomas, F. L. "Tom", Jr. ......St. George, UT
Thomas, Fletcher ......Denver, CO
Thomas, Floyd K. ......Shreveport, LA
Thomas, Floyd M., Jr. ......**El Dorado, AR**
Thomas, Frank ......Hollywood, FL
Thomas, Frank ......Ardmore, OK
Thomas, Frank ......**Nashville, TN**
Thomas, Frank A., III ......**Culpeper, VA**
Orange, VA
Thomas, Frank D., Jr., (P.C.) ......Waco, TX
Thomas, Frank M., Jr. ......**Philadelphia, PA**
Thomas, Franklin Dean ......San Francisco, CA
Thomas, Fred, Jr. ......Columbus, OH
Thomas, Fred M. ......New Bedford, MA
Thomas, Frederick B. ......**Chicago, IL**
Thomas, Frederick L., Jr.
Charleston, WV
Thomas, Fredrick Rossiter ......Raleigh, NC

Thomas, Fregiato, Myser, Hanson & Davies
Bridgeport, OH
St. Clairsville, OH
Thomas, G. Mark ......Vernal, UT
Thomas, G. Scott ......**Nashville, TN**
Thomas, G. Scott ......**Austin, TX**
Thomas, G. Wendell, Jr. ......**Knoxville, TN**
Thomas, Gail Ann ......Brooklyn, NY
Thomas, Galen B. ......Springfield, MO
Thomas, Galen C. ......New York, NY
Thomas, Garvey and Garvey, Professional Corporation ......St. Clair Shores, MI
Thomas, Gary D. ......Hanover, MA
Thomas, Gary E. ......**Atlanta, GA**
Thomas, Gary Rowe ......Red Lodge, MT
Thomas, Gary Rowe, P.C., Law Office of
Red Lodge, MT
Thomas, Gary W. ......San Rafael, CA
Thomas, Gary W. ......Statesville, NC
Thomas, Gaye J. ......**Brentwood, TN**
Thomas, Gennie L., Jr. ......Austin, TX
Thomas, Geo. M. ......New Bedford, MA
Thomas, Geoffrey C.
Treasury Department, GV
Thomas, Geoffrey L., (P.C.)
Los Angeles, CA
Thomas, George ......Waleska, GA
Thomas, George A. ......**Houston, TX**
Thomas, George C. ......Dresden, TN
Thomas, George C., III ......Newark, NJ
Thomas, George J. ......Lancaster, PA
Thomas, George J., III ......Joplin, MO
Thomas, George M. ......**Atlanta, GA**
Thomas, George M. ......New York, NY
Thomas, George M., Jr. ......**Troy, MI**
Thomas, George M., (P.A.)
Fort Lauderdale, FL
Thomas, George P., Jr. ......Morgan Hill, CA
Thomas, George R. ......**Jackson, MS**
Thomas, George R., II ......**Pittsburgh, PA**
Thomas, George S. ......**St. Louis, MO**
Thomas, George S. ......**Winston-Salem, NC**
Thomas, George W. ......**Montgomery, AL**
Thomas, George W. ......**Washington, DC**
Thomas, George W. M. ......**Stamford, CT**
Thomas, Georgia ......Miami, FL
Thomas, Gerald D. ......Sacramento, CA
Thomas, Gerald H. ......Sacramento, CA
Thomas, Gerald W. ......Mooreland, OK
Thomas, Gerard ......**Kalamazoo, MI**
Thomas, Gerard F., Jr. ......**Natchitoches, LA**
Thomas, Gerhild Barbara
Woodland Hills, CA
Thomas, Gihan L. ......Los Angeles, CA
Thomas & Gilbert, P.C. ......Traverse City, MI
Thomas, Gilda M.
Research Triangle Park, NC
Thomas, Gillian L. ......**Philadelphia, PA**
Thomas, Glass, Atkinson, Haskins, Nellis & Boudreaux ......**Tulsa, OK**
Thomas, Gloria J. ......Madison, WI
Thomas, Godley & Childers, P.A.
Mooresville, NC
Thomas, Gordon A. ......Norwich, VT
Thomas, Gordon M. ......Washington, DC
Thomas, Gordon W. ......Grand Rapids, MI
Thomas, Grace W., (Mrs.) ......Atlanta, GA
Thomas, Greg ......Dallas, TX
Thomas, Gregg Darrow ......**Tampa, FL**
Thomas, Gregg Harrison ......Overland Park, KS
Thomas, Gregory A. ......San Francisco, CA
Thomas, Gregory C. ......Houston, TX
Thomas, Gregory D. ......Elizabeth, CO
Thomas, Gregory M. ......**Derby, CT**
Thomas, Gregory M. ......**Omaha, NE**
Thomas, Gregory S. ......**Newark, NJ**
Thomas, Gretchen W. ......Olympic Valley, CA
Thomas, Gretta ......Albuquerque, NM
Thomas, Griffith David ......Sherman Oaks, CA
Thomas, Griffith V. ......Youngstown, OH
Thomas, Gwendolyn J. ......Cleveland, MS
Rosedale, MS
Thomas, H. Barton
United States Tax Court, GV
Thomas, H. Byron ......Dallas, TX
Thomas, H. Conner ......Nome, AK
Thomas, H. David ......Pittsburgh, PA
Thomas, H. Evans, V ......Appomattox, VA
Thomas, H. Suzanne ......Houston, TX
Thomas, H. Victor ......**Houston, TX**
Thomas, Hal W. ......**Louisville, KY**
Thomas and Hardy ......Lake Charles, LA
Thomas, Hardy L. ......**Los Angeles, CA**
Miami, FL
Thomas, Harley W. ......**Tulsa, OK**
Thomas, Harold A. ......**New Orleans, LA**
Thomas, Harold A. ......Corpus Christi, TX
Thomas, Harrington & Biedler
Monroe, NC
Thomas, Harry K. ......**Erie, PA**
Thomas, Harry Lee ......Arlington, VA
Thomas, Harry O. ......**Tallahassee, FL**
Thomas, Harvey D. ......Cookeville, TN
Thomas, Heather ......Louisville, KY
Thomas, Heather A. ......**Washington, DC**
Thomas, Heather E. ......**Burlington, VT**
Thomas, Hedrick R. ......Stephenville, TX
Thomas, Heidi M. ......Treasury Department, Office of the Comptroller of the Currency, GV
Thomas, Henderson & Pate
Murfreesboro, TN
Thomas, Henry A. ......Alexandria, VA
Thomas, Henry I. ......Chicago, IL
Thomas, Henry R. ......Atlanta, GA
Thomas, Herbert C. ......**Washington, DC**
New York, NY
Thomas, Herbert H. ......Dallas, TX

Thomas, Herman Y. ......Mobile, AL
Thomas, H. O., Jr. ......Mountain Brook, AL
Thomas, Hoke J., Jr. ......La Grange, GA
Thomas, Holly H. ......Clarksville, MD
Thomas, Howard C., Jr. ......Chicago, IL
Thomas, Howard J. ......Silver Spring, MD
Thomas, Howard Vincent ......Galesburg, IL
Peoria, IL
Thomas, H. R. ......Albuquerque, NM
Thomas, Hugh B. ......**Detroit, MI**
Thomas, Hugh R. ......**Rochester, NY**
Thomas, Ira M. ......Memphis, TN
Thomas, Isobel S. ......**Chicago, IL**
Thomas, Ivor F. ......Carlsbad, CA
Thomas, J. Cliff, Jr. ......**Hazlehurst, MS**
Thomas, J. Dewayne ......**Jackson, MS**
Thomas, J. Floyd ......**Waycross, GA**
Thomas, J. Jackson ......**Myrtle Beach, SC**
Thomas, J. Michael ......Grand Rapids, MI
Thomas, J. Michael ......**Greensboro, NC**
Thomas, J. Michael ......**Reidsville, NC**
Thomas, J. Nelson ......**Rochester, NY**
Thomas, J. Nicholson ......**Los Angeles, CA**
Thomas, J. Norman ......Corpus Christi, TX
Thomas, J. Patrick ......**Columbus, OH**
Thomas, J. Randall ......Pittsburgh, PA
Thomas, J. Richard ......Bakersfield, CA
Thomas, J. Steven ......Snohomish, WA
Thomas, J. Wayne ......Nashville, TN
Thomas, Jack Edward, Jr. ......St. Louis, MO
Thomas, Jack N. ......Amory, MS
Thomas, Jack N. ......**New York, NY**
Thomas, Jacob ......**New York, NY**
Thomas, Jacqueline E. ......Chicago, IL
Thomas, Jacqueline M. ......**Rochester, NY**
Thomas, Jacquelyn Lee ......Pittsburgh, PA
Thomas, Jacquelyn R.
North Hollywood, CA
Thomas, Jaime B. ......**Troy, NY**
Thomas, James A. ......New Haven, CT
Thomas, James A. ......Miami, FL
Thomas, James A. ......Chicago, IL
Thomas, James A. ......**Council Bluffs, IA**
Thomas, James A., Jr. ......**Denver, CO**
Thomas, James B. ......Boca Raton, FL
Thomas, James C. ......Detroit, MI
Thomas, James C. ......Winchester, TN
Thomas, James C., A Professional Corporation
Detroit, MI
Thomas, James C., III ......**Kansas City, MO**
Thomas, James C., Jr. ......McLean, VA
Thomas, James D.
Department of Commerce, Patent and Trademark Office, GV
Thomas, James D. ......**Cleveland, OH**
Thomas, James D. ......Oklahoma City, OK
Thomas, James D., II ......Baton Rouge, LA
Thomas, James D., P.C. ......Oklahoma City, OK
Thomas, James Don, II, A Law Corporation
Baton Rouge, LA
Thomas, James E. ......Hartford, CT
Thomas, James E. ......**Boston, MA**
Thomas, James E. ......Rocky River, OH
Thomas, James Edward ......Atlanta, GA
Thomas, James F., Jr. ......**Waycross, GA**
Thomas, James G. ......Anamosa, IA
Thomas, James G. ......**Nashville, TN**
Thomas, James H. ......**Lancaster, PA**
Thomas, James H. C., Jr. ......Hattiesburg, MS
Thomas, James J. ......**New York, NY**
Thomas, James J., II ......**Atlanta, GA**
Thomas, James K. ......Bethlehem, PA
Harrisburg, PA
Thomas, James K., II ......Bethlehem, PA
Harrisburg, PA
Thomas, James L. ......Montello, WI
Thomas, James M. ......**Augusta, GA**
Thomas, James M. ......Chicago, IL
Thomas, James M. ......**Seattle, WA**
Thomas, James N. ......Troy, AL
Thomas, James P. ......**Pittsburgh, PA**
Thomas, James Patrick ......**Milwaukee, WI**
Thomas, James R. ......Okanogan, WA
Thomas, James S. ......Cynthiana, KY
Jonesville, VA
Thomas, James S., Jr. ......Atlanta, GA
Thomas, James T., IV ......**Jackson, MS**
Thomas, James W. ......**Eaton, OH**
Thomas, James W. ......Girard, OH
Thomas, James W. ......**Charleston, WV**
Thomas, James W., (Co., L.P.A.)
Girard, OH
Thomas, Jamie Ann ......**Troy, MI**
Thomas, Jane L. ......San Francisco, CA
Thomas, Janet M. C. ......Washington, DC
Thomas, Janet Singletary ......**Richmond, VA**
Thomas, Jas. J. ......Chicago, IL
Thomas, Jason L. ......Chattanooga, TN
Thomas, Jason N. ......**Dallas, TX**
Thomas, Jason P. ......**Louisville, KY**
Thomas, Jason S. ......**Raleigh, NC**
Thomas, Jay ......**Olathe, KS**
Thomas, Jay W. ......Richardson, TX
Thomas, J. C. ......Austin, TX
Thomas, Jeane A. ......**Washington, DC**
Thomas, Jeanette M. ......Woodland Hills, CA
Thomas, Jeanne A. ......Irvine, CA
Thomas, Jeanne Casstevens ......Nashville, TN
Thomas, Jeff ......**Menlo Park, CA**
Chicago, IL
Thomas, Jeff M. ......Clinton, IN
Thomas, Jeffrey B. ......San Francisco, CA
Thomas, Jeffrey B. ......Dallas, TX
Thomas, Jeffrey D. ......Mt. Pleasant, IA
Thomas, Jeffrey E. ......Santa Barbara, CA
Thomas, Jeffrey F. ......**Stuart, FL**
Thomas, Jeffrey Gray ......Los Angeles, CA
Thomas, Jeffrey H. ......**Natchitoches, LA**

Thomas, Jeffrey Hale ......**Little Rock, AR**
Thomas, Jeffrey K. ......**Pontiac, MI**
Thomas, Jeffrey M. ......**Seattle, WA**
Thomas, Jeffrey Robert
Greenwood Village, CO
Thomas, Jeffrey S. ......Los Angeles, CA
Thomas, Jeffrey T. ......**Irvine, CA**
Thomas, Jeffrey W. ......Seattle, WA
Thomas, Jenna B. ......**Raleigh, NC**
Thomas, Jennifer H. ......**Rochester, NY**
Thomas, Jennifer Rusk ......Waukegan, IL
Thomas, Jeremiah L., III ......**New York, NY**
Thomas, Jerri Lynn ......Olympia, WA
Thomas, Jerry K. ......Sparta, IL
Thomas, Jerry N. ......Flagstaff, AZ
Thomas, Jettie K. ......New York, NY
Thomas, Jewel M. ......Houston, TX
Thomas, Jill A. ......Encino, CA
Thomas, Jill Nelson ......Tulsa, OK
Thomas, Jill Thomas ......St. Petersburg, FL
Thomas, Jim, Law Office, The ......Atlanta, GA
Thomas, Joan Mann ......San Francisco, CA
Thomas, Jodi M. ......**Hartford, CT**
Thomas, Joe L. ......Brenham, TX
Thomas, Joel J. ......Long Beach, CA
Thomas, Joel T. ......Washington, DC
Thomas, John ......Center, NE
Thomas, John ......Chickasha, OK
Thomas, John A. ......Arkadelphia, AR
Thomas, John A. ......Knoxville, TN
Thomas, John A. ......**Dallas, TX**
Thomas, John A. ......**Evanston, WY**
Thomas, John A. ......**Green River, WY**
Thomas, John B. ......**Houston, TX**
Thomas, John C. ......Newbury Park, CA
Thomas, John C. ......Boca Raton, FL
Thomas, John C. ......**Minneapolis, MN**
Thomas, John C. ......Conway, SC
Thomas, John C., P.A. ......Conway, SC
Thomas, John Charles ......**New York, NY**
Thomas, John Charles ......**Richmond, VA**
Thomas, John D. ......Rocky Hill, CT
Thomas, John D. ......Cross City, FL
Thomas, John D., Jr. ......**Honolulu, HI**
Thomas, John Davidson ......**Washington, DC**
Thomas, John E. ......**Washington, DC**
Thomas, John E. ......**Plymouth, MI**
Thomas, John E. ......St. Paul, MN
Thomas, John E. ......Rochester, NY
Thomas, John E. "Jed" ......**Tampa, FL**
Thomas, John Edward ......Toledo, OH
Thomas, John F. ......**Omaha, NE**
Thomas, John F., Jr. ......New Castle, DE
Philadelphia, PA
Thomas, John G. ......Scottsdale, AZ
Thomas, John H. ......**La Jolla, CA**
Thomas, John H. ......Miami, FL
Thomas, John H. ......New Orleans, LA
Thomas, John H. ......Frackville, PA
Thomas, John H. ......**Arlington, VA**
Richmond, VA
Thomas, John H. ......Chesterfield, VA
Thomas, John H. ......Charleston, WV
Thomas, John H., Jr. ......**Walden, NY**
Thomas, John H., P.A. ......Miami, FL
Thomas, John J. ......Lutz, FL
Thomas, John J. ......Brazil, IN
Thomas, John J. ......St. Louis, MO
Thomas, John J. ......Wilkes-Barre, PA
Thomas, John K. ......St. Joseph, MO
Thomas, John L., II ......Orlando, FL
Thomas, John M. ......Palo Alto, CA
Thomas, John M. ......**Boston, MA**
Thomas, John M. ......**Dearborn, MI**
Thomas, John M. ......Holland, MI
Thomas, John M. ......Binghamton, NY
Thomas, John M. ......Yanceyville, NC
Thomas, John P. ......Bakersfield, CA
Thomas, John P. ......Redwood City, CA
Thomas, John P. ......Allentown, PA
Thomas, John R. ......Birmingham, AL
Thomas, John R. ......Minneapolis, MN
Thomas, John R. ......**Columbus, OH**
Thomas, John R. ......**Portland, OR**
Thomas, John R. ......Philadelphia, PA
Thomas, John R. ......**Greenville, SC**
Thomas, John Ralph ......**San Rafael, CA**
Thomas, John S. ......Enid, OK
Thomas, John S. ......Portland, OR
Thomas, John S., P.C. ......Enid, OK
Thomas, John V.
Federal Deposit Insurance Corporation, Professional Liability Section, GV
Thomas, John W. ......**Washington, DC**
Thomas, John W. ......**Boston, MA**
Thomas, John W. ......Hamilton, OH
Thomas, John W. ......**Austin, TX**
Thomas, John Waties ......Columbia, SC
Thomas, John William
New Smyrna Beach, FL
Grand Blanc, MI
Thomas, Johnny W., Jr. ......San Antonio, TX
Thomas, Jon C. ......**Colorado Springs, CO**
Thomas, Jon C., P.C.
Colorado Springs, CO
Thomas, Jonathan Y. ......Santa Monica, CA
Thomas, Joseph A. ......Indianapolis, IN
Thomas, Joseph E. ......**Irvine, CA**
Thomas, Joseph N. ......Portage, IN
Thomas, Joseph P. ......**Cincinnati, OH**
Thomas, Joseph R. ......**Oak Brook, IL**
Thomas, Joseph R. ......Madison, WI
Thomas, Joseph W. ......New Orleans, LA
Thomas, Joseph W. ......**Troy, MI**
Thomas, Joseph W., II ......**Casselberry, FL**
Thomas, Joseph W., II, P.A.
Casselberry, FL
Thomas, Joshua D. ......Palo Alto, CA

Thomas, Joy Heath .... Raleigh, NC
Thomas, Joyce L. .... Seattle, WA
Thomas, J. T. .... Hilo, HI
Thomas, Juan R. .... Aurora, IL
Thomas, Juanita M. .... Long Grove, IL
Thomas, Judith Thomson .... Schaumburg, IL
Thomas, Judy .... Philadelphia, PA
Pittsburgh, PA
Thomas, Julia A. .... Highlands Ranch, CO
Thomas, Julie .... Mayfield Heights, OH
Thomas, Julie A. .... Salt Lake City, UT
Thomas, Julie Hird .... Tulsa, OK
Thomas, J. W., Jr. .... San Antonio, TX
Thomas, K. Blair .... Oakland, CA
Thomas, K. Brooks .... Atlanta, GA
Thomas, Kaaran E. .... Las Vegas, NV
Thomas & Kalichman, P.A. .... Baltimore, MD
Thomas, Karen Gilpin .... Lawrenceville, GA
Thomas, Karen Hudson .... Columbia, SC
Thomas, Karen L. .... San Diego, CA
Thomas, Karina M. .... Denver, CO
Thomas, Karl L. .... Spring, TX
Thomas, Karol Ann .... Tyler, TX
Thomas, Katharine M. .... Toledo, OH
Thomas, Kathleen M. .... Ambler, PA
Thomas, Kathryn .... Columbia, SC
Thomas, Kathryn A. .... Randolph, MA
Thomas, Kathryn A. .... Columbus, OH
Thomas, Kathryn C. .... Chicago, IL
Thomas, Kathryn J. .... Carrboro, NC
Thomas, Katlyn .... Indianapolis, IN
Thomas, Kayden, Horstemeyer & Risley, L.L.P. .... Atlanta, GA
Marietta, GA
Thomas, Kaye A. .... Chicago, IL
Thomas, Keith .... Newport Beach, CA
Thomas, Keith R. .... Memphis, TN
Thomas, Kelly, Habermehl & Mays, S.C.
Madison, WI
Thomas, Kelly M. .... York, NE
Thomas, Kelly S. .... Charlotte, NC
Thomas, Kennedy, Sampson & Patterson
Atlanta, GA
Thomas, Kenneth .... Columbia Falls, MT
Thomas, Kenneth .... New York, NY
Thomas, Kenneth C. .... Quincy, IL
Thomas, Kenneth L. .... Birmingham, AL
Thomas, Kenneth L. .... West Haven, CT
Thomas, Kenneth P. .... Houston, TX
Thomas, Kenneth R. .... Library of Congress, Congressional Research Service, GV
Thomas, Kenneth Wesley .... Lebanon, NJ
Thomas, Kent B. .... Nashville, TN
Thomas, Kevin B. .... Manahawkin, NJ
Thomas, Kevin D. .... Tampa, FL
Thomas, Kevin S. .... Portland, OR
Thomas, Kim Purdy .... Shreveport, LA
Thomas, Kimberley L. .... Harrisburg, PA
Thomas, Kimberly D. .... Kansas City, MO
Thomas, Kirby J. .... Thousand Oaks, CA
Thomas, Kirk C. .... Los Angeles, CA
Thomas, Kris J. .... Madison, WI
Thomas, Kristina E. .... Santa Barbara, CA
Thomas, Kristine M. .... Omaha, NE
Thomas, Kurt M. .... Carrollton, GA
Thomas, Kyle M. .... St. Paul, MN
Thomas, L. Jackson, II .... Washington, DC
Thomas, L. A. .... Bismarck, ND
Thomas, Lance K. .... Houston, TX
Thomas, Lane J. .... Pasadena, CA
Thomas, Larriet E. .... Dallas, TX
Thomas, Larry A. .... Dallas, TX
Thomas, Larry C. .... Clinton, IN
Thomas, Larry D. .... Tulsa, OK
Thomas, Larry E. .... Missouri City, TX
Thomas, Larry W. .... Washington, DC
Thomas, Laura Austin .... Stillwater, OK
Thomas, Laura K. .... Nashville, TN
Thomas, Laura M. .... Minneapolis, MN
Thomas, Laurie J. .... Buffalo, NY
Thomas Law Firm .... Long Beach, CA
Thomas Law Firm .... Cleveland, MS
Rosedale, MS
Thomas Law Firm .... Minot, ND
Thomas Law Firm, P.C. .... Dallas, TX
Thomas Law Firm, The .... Albuquerque, NM
Los Lunas, NM
Thomas Law Firm, The, P.C. .... Adel, GA
Thomas Law Office .... Indianapolis, IN
Thomas Law Offices .... Charleston, WV
Thomas Law Offices, PC .... Dallas, TX
Thomas, Lawrence W. .... Bradenton, FL
Thomas, Lawrence W. .... Fishkill, NY
Scarsdale, NY
Thomas, Lee Daniel .... Metairie, LA
Thomas, Leigh E. .... Sarasota, FL
Thomas, Leo A. .... Pensacola, FL
Thomas, Leon J. .... Albuquerque, NM
Thomas, Leona A. .... Seattle, WA
Thomas, Leslie .... Crowell, TX
Thomas, Leslie Jones .... New York, NY
Thomas, Lewis Proctor .... Houston, TX
Thomas & Libowitz, P.A.
Washington, DC
Baltimore, MD
Columbia, MD
Towson, MD
Thomas, Liisa M. .... Chicago, IL
Thomas, Linda B. .... Bowling Green, KY
Thomas, Linda D. .... Miami, FL
Thomas, Linda K. .... Los Angeles, CA
Thomas, Linda K. .... Bradenton, FL
Thomas, Linda K. .... Springfield, MO
Thomas, Linda M. .... Concord, NC
Thomas, Linda Marotta .... Baltimore, MD
Thomas, Linda McDonald .... East Orange, NJ
Thomas, Linda Mitchell .... Cumberland, MD
Thomas, Linda S. .... Anchorage, AK
Thomas, Linda S. .... Clifton, VA
Thomas, Lisa .... Fort Lauderdale, FL
Thomas, Lisa A. .... Conway, SC
Thomas, Lizanne .... Atlanta, GA
Thomas, Llewellyn C. .... Charlottesville, VA
Thomas, Lloyd H., III .... Atlanta, GA
Thomas, Lois K. .... Berkeley, CA
Thomas, Lola Bohn .... Miami, FL
Thomas, Lonny D. .... Woodbury, MN
Thomas, Lori R. .... Fort Worth, TX
Thomas, Lott H. .... Champaign, IL
Thomas, Louis C. .... Miami, FL
Thomas, Louise Carnley .... Jonesboro, GA
Thomas, Louise K. .... Portland, ME
Thomas, Lowell David .... Seattle, WA
Thomas, Lowell S., Jr. .... Philadelphia, PA
Thomas, Loyd K. .... Shreveport, LA
Thomas & Lucas .... Phoenix, AZ
Thomas, Lucie-Anne Dionne
Middletown, RI
Thomas, Lucile C. .... Canton, GA
Thomas, Lynn .... San Diego, CA
Thomas, Lynn A. .... South Easton, MA
Thomas, Lynn E. .... Boise, ID
Thomas, M. Antoinette .... New York, NY
Thomas, M. Kemmerly .... Tallahassee, FL
Thomas, M. Regina .... Atlanta, GA
Thomas, Mack L. .... Fargo, ND
Thomas, Madeleine A. .... Traverse City, MI
Thomas, Mamer & Haughey
Champaign, IL
Urbana, IL
Thomas, Marc E. .... Detroit, MI
Thomas, Marcia Lee .... Burlington, KY
Thomas, Margot E. .... Northampton, MA
Thomas, Marguerite Neill .... Frankfort, KY
Thomas, Maria Isabel Arantes De Noronha
New York, NY
Thomas, Mariclare .... Lincoln, NE
Thomas, Marie
Charlotte Amalie, St. Thomas, VI
Thomas, Marion F., Jr. .... Nashville, TN
Thomas, Marjorie Bekaert .... Orlando, FL
Thomas, Marjorie L. .... Butte, MT
Thomas, Mark A. .... Denver, CO
Thomas, Mark A. .... Boaz, KY
Thomas, Mark A. .... St. Clairsville, OH
Thomas, Mark C. .... Somers, NY
Thomas, Mark D. .... Hagerstown, MD
Thomas, Mark E., Jr. .... San Jose, CA
Thomas, Mark H. .... Englewood, CO
Thomas, Mark K. .... Chicago, IL
Thomas, Mark S. .... Raleigh, NC
Thomas, Mark W. .... Atlanta, GA
Thomas, Mark W. .... Des Moines, IA
Thomas, Mark W. .... Albany, NY
Thomas, Martha Q. .... Lafayette, LA
Thomas, Martha Ross .... Jackson, MS
Thomas, Martha Taylor, (Ltd.)
Paradise Valley, AZ
Thomas, Martin A. .... Norfolk, VA
Thomas, Martin K. .... Dallas, TX
Thomas, Marvin R. .... Dallas, TX
Thomas, Mary Ann .... Cleveland, OH
Thomas, Mary B. .... Minneapolis, MN
Thomas, Mary Bobko .... Stuart, FL
Thomas, Mary Lucinda .... Washington, DC
Thomas, Mary Sikra .... Los Angeles, CA
Thomas, Mason P., Jr. .... Raleigh, NC
Thomas, Matry G. .... St. Clair Shores, MI
Thomas, Matt L. .... Odessa, TX
Thomas, Matthew H. .... Billings, MT
Thomas, Matthew H. .... Tacoma, WA
Thomas, Matthew J.
Federal Maritime Commission, Office of the General Counsel, GV
Thomas, Matthew J. .... Chicago, IL
Thomas, Matthew J. .... New Bedford, MA
Thomas, Maureen E. .... Bloomfield Hills, MI
Thomas, Maureen F. .... Glendale, CA
Ventura, CA
Thomas, Maureen Meritt .... Chicago, IL
Thomas, Maurice C. .... Macon, GA
Thomas, Maxine S. .... Dayton, OH
Thomas, Means, Gillis, Devlin, Robinson & Seay, P.C. .... Birmingham, AL
Eutaw, AL
Hayneville, AL
Montgomery, AL
Tuskegee, AL
Atlanta, GA
Thomas, Meg Marshall .... St. Louis, MO
Thomas, Megan E. .... Princeton, NJ
Thomas, Melissa A. .... Bakersfield, CA
Thomas, Melissa B. .... Phenix City, AL
Thomas, Melody G. .... Beaumont, TX
Thomas, Melvin C., Jr.
Joint Committees And Commissions, GV
Thomas, Melvin D. .... Laguna Hills, CA
Thomas, Michael .... Glendale, CA
Ventura, CA
Thomas, Michael .... Mexia, TX
Thomas, Michael A. .... Cleveland, OH
Thomas, Michael A. .... Lubbock, TX
Thomas, Michael D. .... Saginaw, MI
Thomas, Michael D. .... Miamisburg, OH
Thomas, Michael D. .... Richmond, VA
Thomas, Michael E. .... Boise, ID
Thomas, Michael E. .... Flint, MI
Thomas, Michael E., P.C. .... Flint, MI
Thomas, Michael G. .... San Francisco, CA
Thomas, Michael G. .... Denver, CO
Thomas, Michael G. .... Rockleigh, NJ
Thomas, Michael J. .... Sacramento, CA
Thomas, Michael J. .... Tallahassee, FL
Thomas, Michael J. .... Detroit, MI
Thomas, Michael J. .... Redmond, WA
Thomas, Michael Joseph .... St. Louis, MO
Thomas, Michael M. .... Fargo, ND
Thomas, Michael Paul .... Beverly Hills, CA
Newport Beach, CA
Thomas, Michael Paul, A Prof. Corp., Law Offices of .... Beverly Hills, CA
Newport Beach, CA
Thomas, Michael R. .... Bridgeport, OH
Thomas, Michael R. .... Columbus, OH
Thomas, Michael R. .... Middletown, OH
Thomas, Michael R. .... Fort Worth, TX
Thomas, Michael S. .... Detroit, MI
Thomas, Michael W. .... San Francisco, CA
Thomas, Michael W. .... Honolulu, HI
Kamuela, HI
Thomas, Michele K. .... Newark, NJ
Thomas, Michele M. .... Pompano Beach, FL
Thomas, Milton C., II .... Stamford, CT
Thomas, Molly P. .... Corpus Christi, TX
Thomas, Morgan E. .... Linwood, NJ
Thomas, Morton .... Philadelphia, PA
Thomas, Mottaz, Eastman & Erthal
Alton, IL
Thomas, Myles J. .... Billings, MT
Thomas, N. David .... San Jose, CA
Thomas, N. John .... Waynesville, NC
Thomas, Nancie A. .... Washington, DC
Thomas, Nancy A. .... Dallas, TX
Thomas, Nancy Bausch .... Evanston, IL
Thomas, Nancy C. .... Olympia, WA
Thomas, Nancy Davis .... Vicksburg, MS
Thomas, Nancy L. .... Glastonbury, CT
Thomas, Nanette S. .... Franklin Lakes, NJ
Thomas, Nathan R. .... Issaquah, WA
Thomas, Neal B. .... Phoenix, AZ
Thomas, Neal L. .... Washington, DC
Thomas, Neal S. .... El Paso, TX
Thomas & Neilon, P.C. .... Dallas, TX
Thomas, Nicholas D. .... Raleigh, NC
Thomas, Nicole .... Denver, CO
Thomas, Nix & McIntyre
Oklahoma City, OK
Thomas, Norm .... Corpus Christi, TX
Thomas, Norman A. .... Norfolk, VA
Thomas, O. Gordon .... Santa Rosa, CA
Thomas, Oliver S. .... Maryville, TN
Thomas, Oren R., III .... Collingswood, NJ
Thomas, Oscar L. .... Memphis, TN
Thomas, P. Richard .... Meadville, PA
Thomas, Pamela A. .... New York, NY
Thomas, Pamela Anne .... Tallahassee, FL
Thomas, Patricia A. .... Abbeville, LA
Thomas, Patricia Ann .... Burkesville, KY
Thomas, Patricia D. .... Middleburg, VA
Thomas, Patricia Elizabeth .... Short Hills, NJ
Thomas, Patricia H. .... Lake St. Louis, MO
Thomas, Patricia M. .... Somerset, KY
Thomas, Patricia Percival .... Atlanta, GA
Thomas, Patricia Sullivan .... Medfield, MA
Thomas, Patrick M. .... Nashville, TN
Thomas, Paul A., Jr. .... Albuquerque, NM
Thomas, Paul Everette .... Virginia Beach, VA
Thomas, Paul F. .... Bridgeport, CT
Thomas, Paul G. .... New York, NY
Thomas, Paul M. .... Washington, DC
Thomas, Paul R. .... Tulsa, OK
Thomas, Paul W. .... Carlsbad, CA
Thomas, Paula H. .... Georgetown, SC
Thomas, Peter C. .... New York, NY
Thomas, Peter H. .... Norristown, PA
Thomas, Peter J. .... New Bedford, MA
Thomas, Peter O., Jr. .... Little Rock, AR
Thomas, Peter W. .... Washington, DC
Thomas, Peter W. .... Atlantic City, NJ
Thomas, Peter William, Jr. .... Aspen, CO
Denver, CO
Thomas, Peter William, LLC .... Aspen, CO
Denver, CO
Thomas, Petersen S. .... Louisville, KY
Thomas, Philip H. .... New York, NY
Thomas, Philip W. .... Jackson, MS
Thomas, Preston G. .... Pontiac, MI
Thomas & Price .... Glendale, CA
Ventura, CA
Thomas, Prince Altee .... Philadelphia, PA
Thomas, R. Charles .... Meadville, PA
Thomas, R. Dale .... Jackson, TN
Thomas, R. Davis, Jr. .... Tallahassee, FL
Thomas, R. Keith .... Department of Justice, Office of Professional Responsibility, GV
Thomas, R. Lar .... Albuquerque, NM
Los Lunas, NM
Thomas, R. Lon .... Marietta, GA
Thomas, R. Mark .... Mechanicsburg, PA
Thomas, Ralph C. .... Tulsa, OK
Thomas, Ralph I. .... Kirkland, WA
Thomas, Ralph L. .... Madison, WI
Thomas, Ralph W. .... Atlanta, GA
Thomas, Randal H. .... Fort Myers, FL
Thomas, Randall .... Montgomery, AL
Thomas, Randall S. .... Iowa City, IA
Thomas, Randy E. .... Woodbridge, CA
Thomas, Randy W. .... Treasury Department, Office of Thrift Supervision, GV
Thomas, Ray L. .... Salt Lake City, UT
Thomas, Raymon E. .... Seattle, WA
Thomas, Raymond A. .... Bristol, RI
Thomas, Raymond C. .... Department of Justice, Federal Bureau of Investigation, GV
Thomas, Raymond D. .... Kernersville, NC
Thomas, Raymond F. .... Portland, OR
Thomas, Raymond L. .... McAllen, TX
Thomas, Raymond W. .... Los Angeles, CA
Thomas, Rea Boylan .... Doylestown, PA
Thomas, Reba W. .... Los Angeles, CA
Thomas, Rebecca .... Nashville, TN
Thomas, Rebecca L. .... Mount Clemens, MI
Thomas, Rebecca L. .... Charlotte, NC
Thomas, Rebecca M. .... Mansfield, OH
Thomas, Reese K. .... Knoxville, TN
Thomas, Regina O'Brien
Philadelphia, PA
Thomas, Reginald D. .... Colorado Springs, CO
Thomas, Reginald L. .... Lexington, KY
Thomas Ré & Partners .... New York, NY
Thomas, Rexford M., Jr. .... Sacramento, CA
Thomas, Reynolds B. .... Fort Dodge, IA
Thomas & Reynolds,, P.C. .... Portland, OR
Thomas, R. G. .... Washington, DC
Thomas, Rhonda C. .... St. Louis, MO
Thomas, Rhonda J. .... Jefferson, LA
Thomas, Rhonda L Payne .... Philadelphia, PA
Thomas, Rhonda Payne .... Philadelphia, PA
Thomas, Richard B. .... Minot, ND
Thomas, Richard Banks, Jr. .... Morristown, NJ
Thomas, Richard C. .... Columbia, MO
Thomas, Richard C. .... Columbia, SC
Thomas, Richard D. .... Burlington, CO
Thomas, Richard D. .... Arlington Heights, IL
Thomas, Richard D. .... Canton, MI
Thomas, Richard D., P.C. .... Burlington, CO
Thomas, Richard E. .... West Palm Beach, FL
Thomas, Richard E. .... Augusta, GA
Thomas, Richard F.G. .... Hermosa Beach, CA
Thomas, Richard G. .... Orinda, CA
Thomas, Richard Gary .... Dallas, TX
Thomas, Richard H. .... Cleveland, OH
Thomas, Richard H. .... Williston, VT
Thomas, Richard I. .... Pittsburgh, PA
Thomas, Richard J. .... St. Paul, MN
Thomas, Richard J. .... Marietta, OH
Thomas, Richard J. .... Youngstown, OH
Thomas, Richard M.
Department Of Health And Human Services, Office of the General Counsel, GV
Thomas, Richard M. .... Detroit, MI
Thomas, Richard M. .... Roanoke, VA
Thomas, Richard O. .... Portland, OR
Thomas, Richard P. .... Covington, KY
Thomas, Richard, P.C. .... Canton, MI
Thomas, Richard R. .... Phoenix, AZ
Thomas, Richard S. .... Baton Rouge, LA
Thomas, Richard V. .... Cheyenne, WY
Thomas, Rick L. .... Lexington, KY
Thomas & Rindlisbacher .... Fresno, CA
Thomas, Rita E. .... Salem, OR
Thomas, Ritchie T. .... Washington, DC
Thomas, Robert B. .... Endicott, NY
Thomas, Robert B., Jr.
Virginia Beach, VA
Thomas, Robert C. .... Natchitoches, LA
Thomas, Robert C., Jr. .... Alabaster, AL
Thomas, Robert D. .... Palo Alto, CA
Thomas, Robert D. .... Austin, TX
Thomas, Robert E. .... Santa Ana, CA
Thomas, Robert E. .... New Orleans, LA
Thomas, Robert E. .... Newton, NC
Thomas, Robert E. .... Johnstown, PA
Thomas, Robert E., Jr. .... Atlanta, GA
Thomas, Robert F. .... Cherry Hill, NJ
Thomas, Robert G. .... New York, NY
Thomas, Robert H. .... Honolulu, HI
Thomas, Robert H. .... Brentwood, TN
Thomas, Robert H. .... Houston, TX
Thomas, Robert Hyer, (P.C.) .... Dallas, TX
Thomas, Robert J. .... Denver, CO
Thomas, Robert J. .... Montrose, CO
Thomas, Robert J. .... Columbia, SC
Thomas, Robert J. .... Houston, TX
Thomas, Robert J. .... Seattle, WA
Thomas, Robert J., Jr. .... Oklahoma City, OK
Thomas, Robert K. .... Albuquerque, NM
Thomas, Robert L. .... Wilmington, DE
Thomas, Robert L. .... Fort Walton Beach, FL
Thomas, Robert L. .... Mitchellville, MD
Thomas, Robert L. .... Philadelphia, MS
Thomas, Robert L. .... North Bend, OR
Thomas, Robert L. .... Sioux Falls, SD
Thomas, Robert L., III .... Beaumont, TX
Thomas, Robert L., Jr. .... Houston, TX
Thomas, Robert M. .... Salinas, CA
Thomas, Robert M., Jr. .... Boston, MA
Thomas, Robert M., Jr. .... New York, NY
Thomas, Robert M., (P.C.)
Baltimore, MD
Thomas, Robert O. .... Austin, TX
Thomas, Robert P. .... Indianapolis, IN
Thomas, Robert P. .... Cincinnati, OH
Thomas, Robert P. .... Nashville, TN
Thomas, Robert P., III .... San Antonio, TX
Thomas, Robert R. .... Indianapolis, IN
Thomas, Robert S. .... Birmingham, AL
Thomas, Robert S. .... Arlington Heights, IL
Thomas, Robert S. .... Minot, ND
Thomas, Robert W. .... Santa Monica, CA
Thomas, Robert W. .... Washington, DC
Thomas, Robert W. .... Joliet, IL
Thomas, Robert W. .... Lake Charles, LA
Thomas, Robert W. .... Lapeer, MI
Thomas, Robert W. .... Pittsburgh, PA
Thomas, Robert W., Jr. .... Philadelphia, PA
Thomas, Robt. F. .... Asheville, NC
Thomas, Robt. L. .... San Diego, CA
Thomas, Robt. M. .... Covington, LA
Thomas, Rodney P. .... New Bedford, MA
Thomas, Roger C. .... Upper Marlboro, MD
Thomas, Roger Jaye
General Accounting Office, Office of the General Counsel, GV
Thomas, Roger M. .... Weston, MA
Thomas, Roger W. .... Billings, MT
Thomas, Roger W. .... Blairstown, NJ
Newton, NJ
Thomas, Roger W. .... Cranford, NJ
Thomas, Roger W. .... New York, NY
Thomas, Roger W. .... Nashville, TN
Thomas, Ronald B. .... Waycross, GA

Thomas, Ronald & Cooper, P.A.
Towson, MD
Thomas, Ronald Glen ... Angola, IN
Thomas, Ronald J. ... Darien, CT
Thomas, Ronald William, Jr ... New York, NY
Thomas, Roosevelt ... Dowagiac, MI
Thomas, Rosemarie P. ... Wayne, PA
Thomas, Rosemary Pickering ... Atlanta, GA
Thomas, Roy E. ... Batesville, AR
Thomas & Rozas ... Baton Rouge, LA
Thomas, Ruby J. ... Decatur, GA
Thomas, Russell J., Jr. ... Newport Beach, CA
Thomas, Russell S. ... Atlanta, GA
Thomas, Russell S., (P.A.) ... Tampa, FL
Thomas, Ruth J. ... Salem, OR
Thomas, S. Deann ... Jackson, MS
Thomas, S. Gregory ... Cheyenne, WY
Thomas, S. Jay ... Baton Rouge, LA
Thomas, S. Michael ... Leawood, KS
Kansas City, MO
Thomas, S. Pamela ... Washington, DC
Thomas, S. Perry, Jr. ... Atlanta, GA
Thomas, Sally A. ... Los Angeles, CA
Thomas, Salter & Lyding ... San Jose, CA
Walnut Creek, CA
Thomas, Sam E. ... Atlanta, GA
Thomas, Sam Starnes ... Jackson, MS
Thomas, Sam W. ... Detroit, MI
Thomas, Sam W., P.C. ... Detroit, MI
Thomas, Samantha A. ... Jackson, MS
Thomas, Samuel A. ... West Palm Beach, FL
Thomas, Samuel H. ... Tallulah, LA
Thomas, Samuel J. ... Florham Park, NJ
Thomas, Sandra Lee ... San Bernardino, CA
Thomas, Sandra M. ... Los Angeles, CA
Thomas, Sandra S. A.
Administrative Office Of The United States Courts, GV
Thomas, Sara L. ... Chicago, IL
Thomas, Sarah ... New York, NY
Thomas, Scott A. ... Baltimore, MD
Thomas, Scott Christopher ... Englewood, CO
Thomas, Scott E.
Federal Election Commission, Offices of the Commissioners, GV
Thomas, Scott E. ... New Bern, NC
Thomas, Scott G. ... Milwaukee, WI
Thomas, Scott G., Law Offices of
Milwaukee, WI
Thomas, Scott H. ... Phoenix, AZ
Thomas, Scott J. ... Houston, TX
Thomas, Scott R. ... Cincinnati, OH
Thomas, Scott S. ... Irvine, CA
Thomas, Scott S. ... Washington, DC
Thomas, Seana B. ... Santa Barbara, CA
Thomas & Self, A Professional Corporation
Dallas, TX
Thomas, Sergei B ... Golden, CO
Thomas and Settle ... Nahunta, GA
Waycross, GA
Thomas, Shannon R. ... Weston, WV
Thomas, Sharon A.
Colorado Springs, CO
Thomas, Sharon E. ... Broomfield, CO
Thomas, Sharon M. ... Tampa, FL
Thomas, Sharon T. ... Oklahoma City, OK
Thomas, Shawn Allen ... Springfield, OH
Thomas, Sheila Dawn ... Orange, NJ
Thomas, Sheila Y. ... Oakland, CA
Thomas, Shelley B. ... Tulsa, OK
Thomas, Sherry Carden ... Bingham Farms, MI
Thomas, Sherry H. ... Birmingham, AL
Thomas, Sherry S. ... Houston, TX
Thomas, Sideney R. ... Wichita, KS
Thomas, Sidney R. ... Billings, MT
Thomas & Snell, A Professional Corporation
Fresno, CA
Hanford, CA
Merced, CA
Visalia, CA
Thomas, Soranno, Jacobson & Radke
Manchester, CT
Thomas, Spadafore, Walker & Keenan
Meadville, PA
Thomas, Stacy E. ... Jackson, MS
Thomas, Stacy P. ... Dearborn, MI
Thomas, Stanley B. ... New York, NY
Thomas, Stanton E. ... Milwaukee, WI
Thomas, Stephanie Johnston ... Atlanta, GA
Thomas, Stephen A. ... Tucson, AZ
Thomas, Stephen A. ... Detroit, MI
Thomas, Stephen A., P.C. ... Detroit, MI
Thomas, Stephen D. ... St. Petersburg, FL
Thomas, Stephen G. ... Monterey, CA
Thomas, Stephen G. ... Chagrin Falls, OH
Thomas, Stephen Hensleigh
Evansville, IN
Thomas, Stephen J. ... Napa, CA
Thomas, Stephen J. ... Peoria, IL
Thomas, Stephen K. ... Hattiesburg, MS
Thomas, Stephen L. ... Los Angeles, CA
Thomas, Stephen L. ... Greenville, MS
Thomas, Stephen Mason ... Hickory, NC
Thomas, Stephen P. ... Chicago, IL
Thomas, Stephen R. ... Boise, ID
Thomas, Stephen R. ... Seattle, WA
Thomas, Stephen S. ... Siloam Springs, AR
Thomas, Stephen T. ... Port Huron, MI
Thomas, Stephen W. ... Danville, CA
Thomas, Steven ... New York, NY
Thomas, Steven A. ... Jasper, AL
Thomas, Steven Anargyros
Baltimore, MD
Thomas, Steven D. ... Nashville, TN
Thomas, Steven E. ... Los Angeles, CA
Thomas, Steven E. ... Honolulu, HI
Thomas, Steven E. ... Boston, MA
Thomas, Steven H. ... Dallas, TX

Thomas, Steven J. ... Enumclaw, WA
Thomas, Steven J. ... Menomonee Falls, WI
Thomas, Steven L. ... Charleston, WV
Thomas, Steven M. ... Kansas City, MO
Thomas, Steven M. ... Dallas, TX
Thomas, Steven N. ... Pendleton, OR
Thomas, Steven R. ... Mansfield, LA
Thomas, Steven R. ... Beaumont, TX
Thomas, Steven W. ... Los Angeles, CA
Thomas, Stewart H. ... Dallas, TX
Thomas, Stewart M. ... Jennings, LA
Thomas, Stuart D. ... Colorado Springs, CO
Thomas, Sunila Juliet ... Springfield, MA
Thomas, Susan B. ... Minneapolis, MN
Thomas, Susan D. ... Portland, ME
Thomas, Susan J. ... Lakewood, CO
Thomas, Susan J. ... Washington, DC
Thomas, Susan J. ... Moorhead, MN
Thomas, Susan K. ... Palo Alto, CA
Thomas, Susan Kay ... Missouri City, TX
Thomas, Susan Marie ... Oakland, CA
Thomas, Susan Schneider
Philadelphia, PA
Thomas, Susan Stuermer ... Palo Alto, CA
Thomas, Susan Warnock ... Philadelphia, PA
Thomas, Suzan Barnes ... New York, NY
Thomas, Suzanne J. ... Seattle, WA
Thomas, Suzanne J., P.S. ... Seattle, WA
Thomas, Sydney A. ... Waterloo, IA
Thomas, T. Michael ... Denver, CO
Thomas, T. Neil ... Houston, TX
Thomas, Taliaferro, Forman, Burr & Murray ... Birmingham, AL
Thomas & Talley ... Joplin, MO
Thomas, Talmage Hardy, Jr. ... Arlington, TX
Thomas, Tamberley Kennedy ... Bellaire, TX
Thomas & Teaff ... La Jolla, CA
San Diego, CA
Thomas, Ted ... Little Rock, AR
Thomas, Terence A. ... Detroit, MI
Thomas, Terence L. ... Cleveland, OH
Thomas, Teresa Scott ... Nashville, TN
Thomas, Teretha Lundy ... Miami, FL
Thomas, Terrence R. ... White Cloud, MI
Thomas, Terri Willingham ... Cullman, AL
Thomas, Terry John ... Truckee, CA
Thomas, Terry L. ... Torrance, CA
Thomas, Terry M. ... Tulsa, OK
Thomas, Terry-Dawn Marie ... Atlanta, GA
Thomas, Theodore W. ... Slatington, PA
Thomas, Theresa L. ... Berkeley, CA
Thomas & Thomas ... Salinas, CA
Thomas & Thomas ... Colorado Springs, CO
Thomas and Thomas ... Boca Raton, FL
Thomas and Thomas ... Hollywood, FL
Thomas & Thomas ... Brazil, IN
Thomas & Thomas ... Clinton, IN
Thomas and Thomas ... Waterloo, IN
Thomas & Thomas ... Newport, KY
Thomas & Thomas ... Shreveport, LA
Thomas & Thomas ... New Bedford, MA
Thomas and Thomas ... Hattiesburg, MS
Thomas, Thomas ... Fayetteville, NY
Thomas & Thomas ... Cincinnati, OH
Cleveland, OH
Columbus, OH
Thomas & Thomas ... Easton, PA
Thomas & Thomas ... Hilton Head Island, SC
Thomas & Thomas ... Memphis, TN
Thomas, Thomas A. ... Hollywood, FL
Thomas, Thomas A. ... Dresden, TN
Thomas, Thomas A. ... Beaumont, TX
Thomas, Thomas A., Jr. ... Hollywood, FL
Thomas, Thomas, Armstrong & Niesen
Harrisburg, PA
Thomas, Thomas C. ... Palo Alto, CA
Thomas, Thomas D. ... Los Angeles, CA
Thomas, Thomas G. ... Tallahassee, FL
Thomas, Thomas & Hafer, LLP
Bethlehem, PA
Harrisburg, PA
Thomas, Thomas J. ... Atlanta, GA
Thomas, Thomas J., Jr. ... Manchester, NH
Thomas & Thomas, L.L.P.
Santa Barbara, CA
Thomas, Thomas R. ... Atlanta, GA
Thomas, Thomas R. ... Jeffersonville, IN
Thomas, Thomas W. ... Lancaster, SC
Thomas, Thomasina ... Amarillo, TX
Thomas, Thorp S. ... Little Rock, AR
Thomas, Thorp S., P.A. ... Little Rock, AR
Thomas, Tilman R., Jr. ... San Antonio, TX
Thomas, Timothy A. ... Minneapolis, MN
Thomas, Timothy L. ... Rapid City, SD
Thomas, Timothy N. ... Indianapolis, IN
Thomas, Timothy P. ... Las Vegas, NV
Thomas, Timothy R. ... Costa Mesa, CA
Thomas, Timothy R. ... Ravenna, OH
Thomas, Timothy S. ... San Diego, CA
Thomas, Tina A. ... Sacramento, CA
Thomas, Tina Nelson ... Minneapolis, MN
Thomas, Tina S. ... Pittsburgh, PA
Thomas, Todd H. ... Skokie, IL
Thomas, Tom ... Dallas, TX
Thomas, Tom W., Jr. ... Adel, GA
Thomas, Tom W., Sr. ... Adel, GA
Thomas, Tommy A. ... Irmo, SC
Thomas, Torrence R., Jr. ... Seattle, WA
Thomas, Tracey R. ... Chicago, IL
Thomas, Tracy A. ... Washington, DC
Thomas, Tracy J. ... St. Petersburg, FL
Thomas, Tracy S. ... Plymouth, MI
Thomas, Tricia A. ... Doylestown, PA
Thomas, Trina M. ... New Orleans, LA
Thomas, Troy ... Irvine, CA
Thomas, Tyrone ... Fairfax Station, VA
Thomas, Valeria Bland ... Miami, FL
Thomas, Vanessa ... Ocala, FL

Thomas, Vernon B., Jr. ... Chicago, IL
Thomas, Vernon P. ... New Orleans, LA
Thomas, Vicki Whitlow ... Houston, TX
Thomas, Victoria W. ... Jackson, MS
Thomas, Vida L. ... Sacramento, CA
Thomas, Vincent D., Jr.
Silver Spring, MD
Thomas, Vincent E. ... Cincinnati, OH
Thomas, W. Bruce ... Sewickley, PA
Thomas, W. Daniel, III ... Dallas, TX
Thomas, W. David ... Washington, DC
Thomas, W. Glenn, Jr. ... Jesup, GA
Thomas, W. John ... Hamden, CT
Thomas, W. Keith ... Stillwater, OK
Thomas, W. Lee ... Towson, MD
Thomas, W. Miller ... Houston, TX
Nacogdoches, TX
Thomas, W. Neil, III ... Chattanooga, TN
Thomas, W. Neil, Jr. ... Chattanooga, TN
Thomas, W. Scott ... San Francisco, CA
Thomas, W. Todd ... Washington, DC
Thomas, Wade P., Jr. ... Annapolis, MD
Thomas, Walke & Houle ... Port Huron, MI
Thomas, Walter E. ... Oakland, CA
Thomas, Walter, Jr. ...
Department of Defense, GV
Thomas, Walter P. ... Council Bluffs, IA
Thomas & Walton LLP ... Los Angeles, CA
Thomas, Ward H., Jr. ... Corpus Christi, TX
Thomas, Warlick, (P.C.) ... Amarillo, TX
Thomas, Warner M., Jr. ... Columbus, OH
Thomas, Warren E. ... Jacksonville, FL
Thomas, Wayne D. ... San Diego, CA
Thomas, Wayne E. ... Chattanooga, TN
Thomas, Wayne H. ... San Jose, CA
Thomas, Wayne H., Jr. ... Fresno, CA
Thomas, Wayne Lee ... Tampa, FL
Thomas, Wayne M. ... Philadelphia, PA
Thomas, Wendy L. ... Los Angeles, CA
Thomas, W. H. ... Gadsden, AL
Thomas, W.H. ... Alton, IL
Thomas, W. H. (Tom), Jr. ... Rolla, MO
Thomas & White ... New York, NY
Thomas Whittington Bergan ... Issaquah, WA
Thomas, Wiley ... Angleton, TX
Thomas, Wilkin E., Jr. ... Wilmington, DE
Thomas, William A. ... Clifton Park, NY
Thomas, William A. ... Oak Ridge, TN
Thomas, William A. ... Fort Worth, TX
Thomas, William A., Jr. ... Elizabeth, NJ
Thomas, William A., Jr. ... Abilene, TX
Thomas, William A., Jr. ... Eastville, VA
Virginia Beach, VA
Thomas, William B. ... Tallahassee, FL
Thomas, William C., Jr. ... Alexandria, VA
Thomas, William D. ... Des Moines, IA
Pocahontas, IA
Thomas, William E. ... Riverside, CA
Thomas, William E., Jr.
Department Of Veterans Affairs, Board of Contract Appeals, GV
Thomas, William F., Jr. ... Pulaski, VA
Thomas, William Griffith
Falls Church, VA
Thomas, William H. ... Beverly Hills, CA
Thomas, William H. ... Boise, ID
Thomas, William H., A P.L.C.
Beverly Hills, CA
Thomas, William H., III ... Greenville, SC
Thomas, William H., III, P.A.
Greenville, SC
Thomas, William H., Jr. ... Memphis, TN
Thomas, William J. ... Jacksonville, FL
Thomas, William J. ... Peoria, IL
Thomas, William J. ... Baltimore, MD
Thomas, William J. ... Princeton, NJ
New York, NY
Thomas, William J., II ... Durham, NC
Thomas, William J., Jr. ... Sacramento, CA
Thomas, William, Jr. ... Greenville, MS
Thomas, William K. ... Birmingham, AL
Mobile, AL
Thomas, William L. ... Washington, DC
Thomas, William L. ... Cedar Rapids, IA
Thomas, William L. ... Martins Ferry, OH
Thomas, William M. ... Binghamton, NY
Thomas, William M., Jr. ... Miami, FL
Thomas, William P. ... Wilton Manors, FL
Thomas, William P. ... Cruger, MS
Thomas, William P., Jr. ... Waynesburg, PA
Thomas, William R. ... Walnut Creek, CA
Thomas, William R. ... Chicago, IL
Thomas, William R. ... Madisonville, KY
Thomas, William R. ... Cincinnati, OH
Columbus, OH
Thomas, William R. ... Lebanon, OR
Thomas, William R. ... Seattle, WA
Thomas, William R., P.S. ... Seattle, WA
Thomas, William S. ... St. Louis, MO
Thomas, William S. ... Austin, TX
Thomas, William S., Jr. ... Rochester, NY
Thomas, William W. ... Hyannis, MA
Thomas, Willie T.C. ... Department of Labor, Office of Secretary, GV
Thomas, Wm. F. ... Portland, OR
Thomas, Wm. Lanier ... Fresno, CA
Thomas, Wm. M., Jr. ... Pryor, OK
Thomas, Wm. N., Sr. ... Toledo, OH
Thomas and Worthy ... Irmo, SC
Thomas, Yanic L.
Federal Communications Commission, Wireless Telecommunications Bureau, GV
Thomas, Yvette E. Taylor ... Holmdel, NJ
Thomas-Boehnlein, Karen M.
Cuyahoga Falls, OH
Thomasch, Daniel J. ... New York, NY
Thomasch, Roger P. ... Denver, CO
Thomases, Andrew N. ... Palo Alto, CA

Thomases, Jerome ... New Hyde Park, NY
Thomases, Susan P. ... Washington, DC
Thomas-Francis, Audery
Charlotte Amalie, St. Thomas, VI
Thomasgard, Robert B., Jr. ... Madison, WI
Thomashow, Mark H. ... Beaverton, OR
Thomashower, Barbara ... Brooklyn, NY
Thomashower, William J. ... New York, NY
Thomasian, Charles A. ... Houston, TX
Thomasini, Christina Mitchell ... Boerne, TX
Thomas-Mellema, Amy ... Grand Rapids, MI
Thomas-Nuruddin, Sasha ... New York, NY
Thomason, Andrew B. ... Oakland, CA
Thomason, Benjamin Cooper
Mercer Island, WA
Thomason, Bruce A. ... Huntington Beach, CA
Thomason, Byron ... Magnolia, AR
Thomason, Charles Lee ... Red Bank, NJ
Thomason, David H. ... Henderson, KY
Lexington, KY
Thomason, Douglas N., Law Offices of
San Francisco, CA
Thomason, Evelyn Betts ... Bethesda, MD
Thomason & French ... Spartanburg, SC
Thomason, G. William ... Greenwood, SC
Thomason, Gail Harris ... Chicago, IL
Thomason, George H. ... Spartanburg, SC
Thomason, Harry E. ... Fort Washington, MD
Thomason, Hendrix, Harvey, Johnson & Mitchell ... Memphis, TN
Thomason and Hessmer, LLC
Washington, DC
Bethesda, MD
Thomason, Jacqueline ... Cuyahoga Falls, OH
Thomason, James O., Sr. ... Spartanburg, SC
Thomason, Jeffrey F. ... Odessa, TX
Thomason, John A. ... Henderson, KY
Lexington, KY
Thomason, John C. ... Anniston, AL
Thomason, John J. ... Memphis, TN
Thomason, John R. ... Houston, TX
Thomason, Karen P. ... Shreveport, LA
Thomason, Kevin J. ... Dallas, TX
Thomason Law Office ... Park Rapids, MN
Thomason, Linda J. ... Richmond, VA
Thomason, Mark ... Park Rapids, MN
Thomason, Mark R. ... Honolulu, HI
Thomason, Marlene ... Orange, CA
Thomason, Mary ... El Dorado, AR
Hampton, AR
Thomason, Matthew D., III ... Huntsville, AL
Thomason, Moser & Patterson, LLP
San Jose, CA
Red Bank, NJ
Houston, TX
Thomason, Nancy Jo ... Anderson, SC
Thomason, Neil A. ... Sonora, CA
Thomason, Rebecca Green ... Russellville, AL
Thomason, Robert I., Jr. ... Waverly, TN
Thomason & Roberts, A Prof. Corp.
Sonora, CA
Thomason, Ronald C. ... Atlanta, GA
Macon, GA
Thomason, Ronald G. ... Norton, VA
Thomason, Russell D. ... Eastland, TX
Thomason, Salli L. ... Carrollton, GA
Thomason, Terry E. ... Honolulu, HI
Thomason, Thomas E. ... San Francisco, CA
Thomason & Thomason ... Anniston, AL
Thomason, Timothy J. ... Phoenix, AZ
Thomason, Valerie Carl ... Carrollton, GA
Thomassen, James A. ... Austin, TX
Thomassen, Jane B. ... Boston, MA
Thomassen, Pieter G. V. ... Dexter, MI
Thomasson, Anthony ... Decatur, GA
Thomasson, Brian A. ... Virginia Beach, VA
Thomasson, Charles W.
Corpus Christi, TX
Thomasson, Dean A. ... Middletown, CT
Thomasson, Denise Ann ... Washington, DC
Thomasson, Donald P.
Cape Girardeau, MO
Thomasson, George B. ... Kings Mountain, NC
Thomasson, Gilbert, Cook & Maguire, L.C.
Cape Girardeau, MO
Thomasson, Greta L. ... Atlanta, GA
Thomasson, Harold H. ... Cherry Hill, NJ
Thomasson, James S. ... Akron, OH
Thomasson, James T., Jr. ... La Grange, GA
Thomasson, Jerome W. ... St. Louis, MO
Thomasson, Lauren P. ... Stockton, CA
Thomasson, Linda D. ... Philadelphia, PA
Thomasson, Michael ... Columbus, IN
Thomasson, Richard E. ... Atlanta, GA
Thomasson, Richard E., P.C. ... Atlanta, GA
Thomasson, Samuel M., III
Woodland Hills, CA
Thomasy, Beth ... San Francisco, CA
Thomay, John S. ... North Olmsted, OH
Thomay, Mark L. ... Akron, OH
Thome, Christopher W. ... Boston, MA
Thome, Dennis W. ... Lakewood, CO
Thome, James K. ... Birmingham, MI
Detroit, MI
Thome, Joni M. ... Minneapolis, MN
Thome, Joseph R. ... Madison, WI
Thome, Linda F. ... Department of Justice, Civil Rights Division, GV
Thome, Nancy A. ... Baraboo, WI
Thome, Nancy C. ... Philadelphia, PA
Thomeczek, Edward L. ... St. Louis, MO
Thomeczek Law Firm, L.L.C.
St. Louis, MO
Thomeczek, Robert J. ... St. Louis, MO
Thomen, Jeffrey M. ... Middletown, NJ
Thomen, John ... Katy, TX
Thomerson, H. Keith ... Jacksonville, FL
Thomerson, James L. ... Lexington, KY

Thomerson, Michael Jonas Savannah, GA
Thomes, Robin C. Naples, FL
Thomes, T. Nicholas Key Largo, FL
Thomes, Timothy Nicholas, P.A. Key Largo, FL; Miami, FL
Thomesen, Harland L. St. Paul, MN
Thomey, Dwight E. Elkton, MD
Thomey, J. William Rochester, NY
Thomey, Richard E., II Wauwatosa, WI
Thomforde, Fredrich H., Jr. Knoxville, TN
Thomisee, Donna F. Houston, TX
Thomisee, John H., Jr. Houston, TX
Thomison, James Edward Sarasota, FL
Thomley, Jerry J. Birmingham, AL
Thomley, Patsy W. Birmingham, AL
Thommarson, Ronald J. Costa Mesa, CA
Thompkins, Gina Bardwell Pascagoula, MS
Thompkins, Renita O. Winston-Salem, NC
Thompkins, Stephen R. Dallas, TX
Thompsen, James A. San Diego, CA
Thompson, A. Gary Fort Worth, TX
Thompson, A. Leon, Jr. Austin, TX
Thompson, A. Scott Topeka, KS
Thompson, Adam M. New York, NY
Thompson, Addison B. Richmond, VA
Thompson, Al M., Jr. New Orleans, LA
Thompson, Alan Panama City, FL
Thompson, Alan R. Department of State, Foreign Service Officers (Overseas), GV
Thompson, Alan R. Florence, KY
Thompson, Alan S. Denver, CO
Thompson, Albert L., Jr. Atlanta, GA
Thompson, Albert W. Columbus, GA
Thompson, Alexander G. Merit Systems Protection Board, Office of Appeals Counsel, GV
Thompson, Allan J. San Francisco, CA
Thompson, Allison L. Winston-Salem, NC
Thompson, Alvin W. Hartford, CT
Thompson, Amanda Pope Lexington, KY
Thompson, Amy J. Chicago, IL
Thompson, Amy J. St. Louis, MO
Thompson, Andrea Bastianelli Annandale, VA
Thompson, Andrew C. Oshkosh, WI
Thompson, Andrew, Jr. Woodland, CA
Thompson, Andrew M. Washington, DC
Thompson, Andrew M. Atlanta, GA
Thompson, Andrew Z. San Antonio, TX
Thompson, Ann Kansas City, MO
Thompson, Ann C. Venice, FL
Thompson, Ann Curry Detroit, MI
Thompson, Ann D. New York, NY
Thompson, Ann M. Glendale, CO
Thompson, Ann Marie San Diego, CA
Thompson, Anne E. Trenton, NJ
Thompson, Anne L. New York, NY
Thompson, Anne M. Beaverton, OR
Thompson, Anthony Washington, DC
Thompson, Anthony C. Richmond, CA
Thompson, Anthony J. Washington, DC
Thompson, Anthony R. Allentown, PA
Thompson, Arne B., Jr. Memphis, TN
Thompson, Arthur & Davidson Russell, KS
Thompson, Arthur J. Billings, MT
Thompson and Ashcraft, L.L.P. Boise, ID; Mountain Home, ID
Thompson & Associates Atlanta, GA
Thompson, B. Todd Louisville, KY
Thompson and Baily Waynesburg, PA
Thompson, Barbara A. Denver, CO
Thompson, Barbara A. Westlake, OH
Thompson, Barbara Botic Marina Del Rey, CA
Thompson, Barbara S. Downers Grove, IL
Thompson, Barbara W. Media, PA
Thompson, Barry J. Los Angeles, CA
Thompson, Barry L. Mobile, AL
Thompson, Barry L. Plainville, CT
Thompson, Barry R. Palo Alto, CA
Thompson, Barry S. Kingsley, IA
Thompson, Barton H., Jr. Palo Alto, CA
Thompson, Bartt G. Houston, TX
Thompson, Ben W., Jr. Boulder, CO
Thompson, Benjamin Portland, ME
Thompson, Benjamin N. Raleigh, NC
Thompson, Bernard E. Department of Justice, Federal Bureau of Investigation, GV
Thompson, Bert M. Peoria, IL
Thompson, Bert W. San Antonio, TX
Thompson, Beth S. St. Cloud, MN
Thompson, Betty A. Arlington, VA
Thompson, Betty A., Ltd. Arlington, VA
Thompson, Betty J. Winthrop Harbor, IL
Thompson, B. G., Jr. Tucson, AZ
Thompson, Bill J. Valencia, CA
Thompson, Bill L. Jefferson City, MO
Thompson, B.J. Jeanie Dallas, TX
Thompson, Blair C. Cincinnati, OH
Thompson, Blake A. Denver, CO
Thompson, Bob F. Nashville, TN
Thompson, Bonne Harris Elgin, IL
Thompson & Bowdoin Boston, MA
Thompson & Bowie Portland, ME
Thompson, Boyd A. New Orleans, LA
Thompson & Bradford L.C. Kissimmee, FL; Maitland, FL; Orlando, FL; Tavares, FL
Thompson, Bradley H. Wheeling, WV
Thompson, Bradley Merrill Indianapolis, IN
Thompson, Brenda Barnes Nashville, TN
Thompson, Brenda V. Cincinnati, OH
Thompson, Brent L. Winston-Salem, NC
Thompson, Brent M., A Prof. Corp. Santa Ana, CA
Thompson, Brent T. Washington, DC
Thompson, Brett A. Houston, TX
Thompson, Brett A. Madison, WI
Thompson, Brian Westlake, OH
Thompson, Brian K. Alexandria, VA
Thompson, Brian L. Tampa, FL
Thompson, Brian M. Eugene, OR
Thompson, Brian R. Securities and Exchange Commission, Division of Investment Management, GV
Thompson, Brook Kenneth Nashville, TN
Thompson, Bruce A. Oak View, CA
Thompson, Bruce E. Attleboro, MA
Thompson, Bruce G. Portland, OR
Thompson, Bruce H. Atlanta, GA
Thompson, Bruce R. Columbus, OH
Thompson, Bruce W. New Haven, CT
Thompson, Bryan M. Los Angeles, CA
Thompson, Bryon Alan Frankfort, KY
Thompson, Bull, Furey, Bass & MacColl, LLC, P.A. Portland, ME
Thompson, Byron Clayton Oakland, CA
Thompson, Byron M. Lucasville, OH
Thompson, Byron W. Frederick, MD
Thompson, C. Donald, Jr. Henderson, KY
Thompson, C. Everett, II Elizabeth City, NC
Thompson, C. Gerard Portsmouth, VA
Thompson, C. Richard Mansfield, OH
Thompson Calkins & Sutter Pittsburgh, PA
Thompson, Carl L., Jr. Orlando, FL
Thompson, Carla D. Salem, OR
Thompson, Carleen McElroy Memphis, TN
Thompson, Carlton Washington, DC
Thompson, Carlton F. Binghamton, NY
Thompson, Carlton L. Essexville, MI
Thompson, Carol A. Barrington, IL
Thompson, Carol A. Boston, MA
Thompson, Carol K. Chicago, IL
Thompson, Carol Lynn San Francisco, CA
Thompson, Carol S. Lincoln, NE
Thompson, Carolyn A. Sioux Falls, SD
Thompson, Carolyn S. Oklahoma City, OK
Thompson, Carolyn S. Burke, VA
Thompson, Carolyn Y. Washington, DC
Thompson, Carrie Lynn Englewood, CO
Thompson, Catalina Maree Leavenworth, KS
Thompson, Cater C. Macon, GA
Thompson, Catherine E. Charlotte, NC
Thompson, Catherine Hagerty Wilmington, DE
Thompson, Catherine M. Hartford, CT
Thompson, Cawley, Veazey & Burns, A Professional Corporation Ardmore, OK
Thompson, C. E. Marietta, GA
Thompson & Chan Honolulu, HI
Thompson, Charles A. Dallas, TX
Thompson, Charles Amos Birmingham, AL
Thompson, Charles C. Washington, DC
Thompson, Charles C., III Graham, NC
Thompson, Charles D. Corpus Christi, TX
Thompson, Charles D. Irving, TX
Thompson, Charles E. Las Vegas, NV
Thompson, Charles E. Atlanta, TX
Thompson, Charles E., Law Offices, Ltd. Las Vegas, NV
Thompson, Charles F., Jr. Aurora, IL
Thompson, Charles F., Jr. Columbia, SC
Thompson, Charles H. Syracuse, NY
Thompson, Charles H., Jr. Forest Park, GA
Thompson, Charles I., Jr. Philadelphia, PA
Thompson, Charles K. Kansas City, MO
Thompson, Charles L., IV San Francisco, CA
Thompson, Charles M. Birmingham, AL
Thompson, Charles M. San Francisco, CA
Thompson, Charles M. Pierre, SD
Thompson, Charles O. San Francisco, CA
Thompson, Charles R. Albuquerque, NM
Thompson, Charles W., Jr. Westminster, MD
Thompson, Charles W. N. Glencoe, IL
Thompson, Charles W. N., Jr. Santa Fe, NM
Thompson, Charlotte M. Lafayette, CA
Thompson, Chas. C. Madison, WI
Thompson, Cherie E. Chicago, IL
Thompson, Cheryl A. Albuquerque, NM
Thompson, Cheryl H. San Antonio, TX
Thompson, Chet M. Washington, DC
Thompson, Christian Charles Philadelphia, PA
Thompson, Christina Austin, TX
Thompson, Christina M. New York, NY
Thompson, Christopher A. Atlanta, GA
Thompson, Christopher A. Dallas, TX
Thompson, Christopher D. Houston, TX
Thompson, Christopher J. Savannah, GA
Thompson, Christopher L. Apple Valley, CA
Thompson, Christopher L. Kansas City, MO
Thompson, Christopher Sealy St. Louis, MO
Thompson, Christopher W. Dayton, OH
Thompson, Cindy L. Springfield, NJ
Thompson, Claire L. Springfield, MA
Thompson, Clark G. Houston, TX
Thompson, Clark G., Jr. Houston, TX
Thompson, Clay Peoria, IL
Thompson, Clay Tulsa, OK
Thompson, Clayton W., II Arlington, VA
Thompson, Cliff F. Madison, WI
Thompson, Clifford C. Jackson, MS
Thompson, Clifford K., Jr. San Francisco, CA
Thompson, Clifton W. Sandy, UT
Thompson, Clint P. Trinity, AL
Thompson, Clyde A. Oakland, CA
Thompson, Clyde E. Englewood, CO
Thompson Coburn LLP Washington, DC; Belleville, IL; St. Charles, MO; St. Louis, MO; Billings, MT
Thompson, Cody Dewayne Fort Smith, AR
Thompson, Coe, Cousins & Irons, L.L.P. Austin, TX; Dallas, TX
Thompson & Colegate LLP Riverside, CA
Thompson & Company, L.P.A. Cincinnati, OH
Thompson, Craig A., & Associates, P.C. Dallas, TX
Thompson, Craig Alan Dallas, TX
Thompson, Craig C. Sacramento, CA
Thompson, Craig E. Los Angeles, CA
Thompson, Craig K. Vermillion, SD
Thompson, Craig R. Knoxville, TN
Thompson, Craig S. Southfield, MI
Thompson, Crawford & Smiley Tallahassee, FL
Thompson, Curtis F. Jefferson City, MO
Thompson, Curtis G. Great Falls, MT
Thompson, Cynthia K. Huntsville, AL
Thompson, Cynthia R. Santa Monica, CA
Thompson, D. Olcott Salem, OR
Thompson, Dahl C. Houston, TX
Thompson, Dale A. Mansfield, OH
Thompson, Dale R. Madison, WI
Thompson, Dan Madison, WI
Thompson, Dana M. Canton, GA
Thompson, Daniel H. Tallahassee, FL
Thompson, Daniel J., Jr. Atlanta, GA
Thompson, Daniel K. Sidney, OH
Thompson, Daniel R. Washington, DC
Thompson, Daniel R., P.C. Washington, DC
Thompson, Darin G. Cleveland, OH
Thompson, Darrell Los Angeles, CA
Thompson, Darrell T. Oakland, CA
Thompson, Darrow M. Phoenix, AZ
Thompson, Darryl L. Anchorage, AK
Thompson, Darryl L., P.C. Anchorage, AK
Thompson, Daryl B. Orange, CA
Thompson, Daryl B., A Professional Law Corporation Orange, CA
Thompson, David Philipsburg, PA
Thompson, David A. Westminster, CA
Thompson, David A. Chicago, IL
Thompson, David A. Northfield, MN
Thompson, David A. Dallas, TX
Thompson, David A. Yakima, WA
Thompson, David Ayers San Francisco, CA
Thompson, David B. Park City, UT
Thompson, David C. Austin, TX
Thompson, David D. Indianapolis, IN
Thompson, David E. Elkins, WV
Thompson, David F. Lake Forest, IL
Thompson, David H. Washington, DC
Thompson, David I. Phoenix, AZ
Thompson, David J. Bloomfield Hills, MI
Thompson, David J. Ashland, OR
Thompson, David J., Jr. Louisville, KY
Thompson, David K. Burbank, CA
Thompson, David L. Hartford, CT
Thompson, David L. Washington, DC
Thompson, David L. Jacksonville, FL
Thompson, David L. Independence, KS
Thompson, David M. Department of Justice, Environment and Natural Resources Division, GV
Thompson, David O. Seattle, WA
Thompson, David P. Lincoln, NE
Thompson, David P. New York, NY; Philadelphia, PA
Thompson, David R. Carlsbad, CA
Thompson, David R. San Diego, CA
Thompson, David R. Easton, MD
Thompson, David T. Elizabethtown, KY
Thompson, David W. New York, NY
Thompson, David W. Cleveland, OH
Thompson, Davis D. Cerritos, CA
Thompson, Dean D. Anchorage, AK
Thompson, Debbie J. Trenton, NJ
Thompson, Deborah A. Gulfport, MS
Thompson, Deborah A., P.A. Gulfport, MS
Thompson, Deborah W. Detroit, MI
Thompson, Debra A. Knoxville, TN
Thompson, Debra Jean Mansfield, MA
Thompson, Debra M. Atlanta, GA
Thompson, Delores Ellen Department of Defense, Defense Legal Services Agency, GV
Thompson, Denise E. Jefferson City, MO
Thompson, Dennis P. Clearwater, FL
Thompson, Dennis R. Des Moines, IA
Thompson, Dennis R. Akron, OH
Thompson & DeVeny Co., L.P.A. Dayton, OH
Thompson, DeWitte Norcross, GA
Thompson, Diana F. Bellevue, WA
Thompson, Diane A. Los Angeles, CA
Thompson, Diedra M. Fairfax, VA
Thompson, Dionne Washington, DC
Thompson, Disney D. Miami, FL
Thompson, D. Olcott, P.C. Salem, OR
Thompson, Don New York, NY
Thompson, Don A. Mauldin, SC
Thompson, Don Wesley Summerville, GA
Thompson, Donald D. Sapulpa, OK
Thompson, Donald E., II Boca Raton, FL
Thompson, Donald G. Cedar Rapids, IA
Thompson, Donald H. Tacoma, WA
Thompson, Donald L., Jr. Little Rock, AR
Thompson, Donald M. Irvine, CA
Thompson, Donald M. Chicago, IL
Thompson, Donald M. Rochester, NY
Thompson, Dorothy Marina Del Rey, CA
Thompson, Dorothy H. Easton, MD
Thompson, Douglas A. Calabasas, CA
Thompson, Douglas A. McLean, VA
Thompson, Douglas Alan Pittsburgh, PA
Thompson, Douglas E. West Palm Beach, FL
Thompson, Douglas G. Abilene, KS
Thompson, Douglas G., Jr. Washington, DC
Thompson, Douglas M. Paramount, CA
Thompson, Douglas M. Portland, OR
Thompson, Douglas P. Kansas City, MO
Thompson, Douglas R. Atlanta, GA
Thompson, Drury Blair Atlanta, GA
Thompson, Duane Dale Rock Island, IL
Thompson, Duane K. Washington, DC
Thompson, Dudley E., Jr. Washington, DC
Thompson, Dudley M. Staten Island, NY
Thompson, Dunlap, Heydinger, MacDonald, Watkins & Traul, Ltd. Bellefontaine, OH
Thompson, Durke G. Rockville, MD
Thompson, E. Brett Rome, GA
Thompson, E. Bruce Los Angeles, CA
Thompson, E. Buddy Baton Rouge, LA
Thompson, E.C., III, P.C. Warsaw, NC
Thompson, E. Danielle Winston-Salem, NC
Thompson, E. Diane Norfolk, VA
Thompson, E. James, Jr. Severna Park, MD
Thompson, E. C., III Warsaw, NC
Thompson, Eckhart A. Fresno, CA
Thompson, Edgar R. Cabot, AR
Thompson, Edith Tampa, FL; Laurel, MD
Thompson, Edmonstone F. St. Louis, MO
Thompson, Edward Babylon, NY
Thompson, Edward F. Delavan, WI
Thompson, Edward J., Sr. Linthicum, MD
Thompson, Edward, Jr. East Moriches, NY
Thompson, Edward L. Oklahoma City, OK
Thompson, Edward M. Lexington, KY
Thompson, Edward M. Atlantic City, NJ
Thompson, Edward P. Sherborn, MA
Thompson, Edward P. Kalamazoo, MI
Thompson, Edward P. Eugene, OR
Thompson, Edward Steven Atlanta, GA
Thompson, Elaine Harriette Pembroke, MA
Thompson, Elaine L. West Palm Beach, FL
Thompson, Eleanor D. Philadelphia, PA
Thompson, Eleanor Joyce Darden Oklahoma City, OK
Thompson, Eley O. Chicago, IL
Thompson, Elgin M., Jr. Chicago, IL
Thompson, Elizabeth A. San Francisco, CA
Thompson, Elizabeth A.C. Honolulu, HI
Thompson, Elizabeth F. Macon, GA; Savannah, GA
Thompson, Elizabeth L. Denver, CO; Chicago, IL
Thompson, Elizabeth Lee Lexington, KY
Thompson, Elizabeth M. Beverly, MA
Thompson, Ellis W. Sulphur, LA
Thompson, Elsie Dunn Wilson Charlottesville, VA
Thompson, Elton E. Poteau, OK
Thompson, Emerson M., III Raleigh, NC
Thompson, Emily A. Walnut Creek, CA
Thompson, Eric Treasury Department, Office of the Comptroller of the Currency, GV
Thompson, Erica Chicago, IL
Thompson, Erik J. Chicago, IL
Thompson, Erin Tuckahoe, NJ
Thompson, Ernest W. Cleveland, OH
Thompson, Errol R. Silver Spring, MD
Thompson, Eugene H. Newark, NJ
Thompson, Eugene M. Roseburg, OR
Thompson, Eugene R. Madison, WI
Thompson, Eugene S. San Diego, CA
Thompson, Eugenia M. Kansas City, MO
Thompson, Evan L. Forest, MS
Thompson, Evania A. New York, NY
Thompson, Everald F. Columbia, MD
Thompson, Faith Indian Orchard, MA
Thompson, F. L. (Tommy) Kansas City, MO
Thompson, Fletcher Atlanta, GA
Thompson, Fletcher D. Spartanburg, SC
Thompson, Fletcher P. Cambridge, MD
Thompson, Flora L. Mobile, AL
Thompson & Foote, P.A. Clearwater, FL
Thompson, Ford L. Tallahassee, FL
Thompson & Fourqurean Fairfax, VA
Thompson, Frances H. Moscow, ID
Thompson, Frank J. Stamford, CT
Thompson, Frank L. Tulsa, OK
Thompson, Frank M. Escondido, CA
Thompson, Frank M. Chattanooga, TN
Thompson, Frank P. Houston, TX
Thompson, Frank W. Reno, NV
Thompson, Fred A., II Upper Marlboro, MD
Thompson, Fred A., P.C. Upper Marlboro, MD
Thompson, Fred C., Jr. Charlotte, NC
Thompson, Fred D., Jr. Nashville, TN

Thompson, Fred D., Law Offices of ... Nashville, TN
Thompson, Fred, III ... Charleston, SC
Thompson, Frederick ... Woodbury, NJ
Thompson, Frederick ... Rochester, NY
Thompson, Frederick D. ... Omaha, NE
Thompson, Frederick G., IV ... Kansas City, MO
Thompson, Frederick J. ... Scottsdale, AZ
Thompson, Frederick J. ... Mount Clemens, MI
Thompson, Frederick T. ... North Adams, MA
Thompson, Frederick W. ... Sacramento, CA
Thompson, Fredk. D. ... New York, NY
Thompson, G. Douglas ... Vacaville, CA
Thompson, G. Gaye ... Austin, TX
Thompson, G. Mark ... Orlando, FL
Thompson, G. Nanette ... Anchorage, AK
Thompson, G. Patrick ... Corydon, IN
Thompson, G. Roger ... Atlanta, GA
Thompson, G. Scott ... Atlanta, GA
Thompson, Gabrielle M. ... Manhattan, KS
Thompson, Gail Kinsey ... Omaha, NE
Thompson, Garrett & Hines ... Atmore, AL
Brewton, AL
Evergreen, AL
Monroeville, AL
Thompson, Gary ... Washington, DC
Thompson, Gary A. ... Minnetonka, MN
Thompson, Gary B. ... Englewood, CO
Thompson, Gary D. ... Las Vegas, NV
Thompson, Gary D. ... Pitman, NJ
Thompson, Gary E. ... Tulsa, OK
Thompson, Gary E. ... Philadelphia, PA
Thompson, Gary E. ... Richmond, VA
Thompson, Gary Edward ... Rockville, MD
Thompson, Gary G. ... Beatrice, NE
Thompson, Gary L. ... Marion, IN
Thompson, Gary R. ... Gurnee, IL
Thompson, Gary R. ... Kearny, NJ
Thompson, Gary R. ... Nashville, TN
Thompson, Gary S. ... Prineville, OR
Thompson, Gary W. Department Of Veterans Affairs, Board of Veterans Appeals, GV
Thompson, Gary W. ... Milwaukee, WI
Thompson, Gayla ... Indianapolis, IN
Thompson, Gene ... Pampa, TX
Thompson, Gene ... Pampa, TX
Thompson, Geo. C., Jr. (Inc.) ... Fort Worth, TX
Thompson, George ... Washington, DC
Thompson, George ... Fort Worth, TX
Thompson, George A. ... Omaha, NE
Thompson, George A. ... Papillion, NE
Thompson, George Benjamin, IV ... Statesboro, GA
Thompson, George C. ... New York, NY
Thompson, George D. ... Santa Ana, CA
Thompson, George E. ... Houston, TX
Thompson, George G. ... North Baltimore, OH
Thompson, George G. ... Franklin, PA
Thompson, George H. ... Pittsburgh, PA
Thompson, George H., III ... Nashville, TN
Thompson, George H., Jr. ... Nashua, NH
Thompson, George L., III ... Lubbock, TX
Thompson, George M., Jr. ... Worcester, MA
Thompson, George R. ... Traverse City, MI
Thompson, George S. ... Salisbury, MD
Thompson, George S. ... Tulsa, OK
Thompson, Gerald L. ... Kansas City, MO
Thompson, Gerald R. ... Novi, MI
Thompson, Gerard F. ... New York, NY
Thompson, Gilbert G. ... Juneau, WI
Thompson, Gilda Ena Federal Energy Regulatory Commission, Office of the General Counsel, GV
Thompson, Glen W. ... Virginia Beach, VA
Thompson, Glenn A. W. ... Meadville, PA
Thompson, Glenn E. ... Decatur, AL
Thompson, Glenn E. ... Poteau, OK
Thompson Goodis & Thompson, A Professional Association ... Orlando, FL
St. Petersburg, FL
Thompson, Gordon C. ... Williston, ND
Thompson, Gordon E. ... Binghamton, NY
Owego, NY
Thompson, Gordon, Jr. ... San Diego, CA
Thompson, Grace H. ... Fairfield, OH
Thompson, Grace Patricia ... Brooklyn, NY
Thompson, Grady R. ... McKinney, TX
Thompson, Grant P. ... Washington, DC
Thompson, Greg ... Beaumont, TX
Thompson, Gregory A. ... Jackson, MS
Thompson, Gregory E. ... Washington, DC
Thompson, Gregory I. ... Elizabethtown, KY
Thompson, Gregory J. ... White Plains, NY
Thompson, Gregory L. ... Fargo, ND
Thompson, H. Dale ... Dublin, GA
Thompson, H. Jerome ... Moulton, AL
Thompson, H. Lee ... Columbus, OH
Thompson, H. Michael ... Fairview Heights, IL
Thompson, H. Reginald ... Swainsboro, GA
Thompson, Hannah L. ... Pittsburgh, PA
Thompson, Hardy E., III ... Dallas, TX
Thompson, Harold B. ... Reno, NV
Thompson, Harriet ... Brooklyn, NY
Thompson, Harriet S. ... Bolivar, TN
Thompson, Harry A., II ... Pittsburgh, PA
Thompson, Harry J. ... Severna Park, MD
Thompson, Harry L. ... Richmond, VA
Thompson, Heather Walters ... Memphis, TN
Thompson & Heidrick ... Salina, KS
Thompson, Helen A. ... Cleveland, OH
Columbus, OH
Thompson, Helen B. Department of the Navy, Office of the Judge Advocate General, GV
Thompson, Helen M. ... Hempstead, NY
Thompson, Henry ... Miami, FL
Thompson, Henry L. ... Birmingham, AL
Thompson & Hensley, P.A. ... St. Petersburg, FL
Thompson, Herman G. House of Representatives, Committee on Post Office & Civil Service, GV
Thompson Hine & Flory LLP ... Washington, DC
Palm Beach, FL
Cincinnati, OH
Cleveland, OH
Columbus, OH
Dayton, OH
Thompson, Holley M. ... New Providence, NJ
Thompson & Hollingsworth, P.A. ... Forest, MS
Thompson, Hollis C., Jr. ... Gulfport, MS
Thompson, Holly Lincoln ... Columbia, MD
Thompson, Homer B. ... San Jose, CA
Thompson, Horace S. ... Cleveland, OH
Thompson, Houston I. ... Silsbee, TX
Thompson, Howard ... Houston, TX
Thompson, Howard F. ... Phoenix, AZ
Thompson, Howard O. ... Lansing, MI
Thompson, Howard O. ... Newark, NJ
Thompson, Howard S. ... Chicago, IL
Thompson, Hubert O. ... Chicago, IL
Thompson, Hugh P. ... Atlanta, GA
Thompson, Hugh R., Jr. ... Richmond, VA
Thompson, Hurley E., Jr. ... Carthage, NC
Thompson, Hurley E., Jr. ... Pinehurst, NC
Southern Pines, NC
Thompson Hutsler & Carson ... Birmingham, AL
Thompson, Hydee C. ... Salt Lake City, UT
Thompson, I. Matt, II ... Monroe, GA
Thompson, Ian S. ... Washington, DC
Thompson, India S. ... Los Angeles, CA
Thompson, J. Alston, Jr. ... Atlanta, GA
Thompson, J. Brent ... Hamilton, AL
Thompson, J. Carole ... Atlanta, GA
Thompson, J. Carter, Jr. ... Jackson, MS
Thompson, J. Charles ... Las Vegas, NV
Thompson, J. David, III ... Austin, TX
Houston, TX
Thompson, J. Edward ... Northfield, IL
Thompson, J. Frank ... Fort Worth, TX
Thompson, J. Garrison ... Selma, AL
Thompson, J. Ken ... Birmingham, AL
Thompson, J. Kevin ... Dallas, TX
Thompson, J. Matthew ... Oklahoma City, OK
Thompson, J. Patrick, (P.C.) ... Tulsa, OK
Thompson, J. Peter ... Lewiston, ME
Thompson, J. Roger ... Ellijay, GA
Thompson, Jack ... Oak Hill, WV
Thompson, Jack A. ... Encino, CA
Thompson, Jack A. ... Fayetteville, NC
Thompson, Jack A., Inc. ... Encino, CA
Thompson, Jack C. ... Fullerton, CA
Thompson, Jack R., Jr. ... Birmingham, AL
Thompson, Jack W. ... Houston, TX
Thompson, Jacobsen & Potts, P.C. ... Great Falls, MT
Thompson, James ... Louisville, KY
Thompson, James A. ... Santa Rosa, CA
Thompson, James A. ... McCall, ID
Thompson, James A., Jr. ... Hartford, CT
Thompson, James A., Law Offices of ... Redwood City, CA
Thompson, James B. ... Sacramento, CA
Thompson, James B. ... Orlando, FL
St. Petersburg, FL
Thompson, James B., III ... Baton Rouge, LA
Thompson, James B., Jr. ... Orlando, FL
St. Petersburg, FL
Thompson, James C. ... Santa Cruz, CA
Thompson, James C. ... Loves Park, IL
Thompson, James C. ... Reed City, MI
Thompson, James C. ... Richmond, MO
Thompson, James C. ... Columbus, OH
Groveport, OH
Thompson, James C. ... Reynoldsburg, OH
Thompson, James D. ... St. Louis, MO
Thompson, James D., III ... Houston, TX
Thompson, James E. ... Cullman, AL
Thompson, James E. ... Phoenix, AZ
Thompson, James E. ... Sacramento, CA
Thompson, James E. ... Tampa, FL
Thompson, James E. ... Richmond, KY
Thompson, James E. ... Ada, MI
Thompson, James E. ... Ardmore, OK
Thompson, James E. ... Crossville, TN
Thompson, James E., Jr. ... Centreville, MD
Thompson, James E., Jr. ... Belton, MO
Harrisonville, MO
Thompson, James F. ... Bloomington, IN
Thompson, James F. ... Boston, MA
Thompson, James F. ... Kansas City, MO
Thompson, James Fletcher ... Spartanburg, SC
Thompson, James Grant, III ... Waterbury, VT
Thompson, James H. ... Tampa, FL
Thompson, James H. ... Atlanta, GA
Thompson, James H. ... Reno, NV
Thompson, James Harold ... Tallahassee, FL
Thompson, James J. ... Chico, CA
Thompson, James J. ... Los Angeles, CA
Thompson, James J. ... San Leandro, CA
Thompson, James J. ... Roslyn, PA
Thompson, James J., Jr. ... Birmingham, AL
Thompson, James L. ... Chicago, IL
Thompson, James L. ... Rockville, MD
Thompson, James L. "Lin" ... Tyler, TX
Thompson, James M. ... Tampa, FL
Thompson, James M. ... Augusta, GA
Thompson, James M. ... Kansas City, MO
Thompson, James O. ... Mill Valley, CA
Thompson, James P. ... Los Angeles, CA
Thompson, James P. ... San Diego, CA
Nashville, TN
Thompson, James P. ... San Pedro, CA
Thompson, James P. ... Baton Rouge, LA
Thompson, James P. ... Princeton, NJ
Thompson, James P. (Casey) ... Bellingham, WA
Thompson, James P., Jr. ... Avondale, LA
Thompson, James R. ... Berkeley, CA
Thompson, James R. ... Los Angeles, CA
Thompson, James R. ... Fort Myers, FL
Thompson, James R. ... Atlanta, GA
Thompson, James R. ... Boise, ID
Thompson, James R. ... Haddonfield, NJ
Thompson, James R. ... Gaffney, SC
Thompson, James R. ... Copperas Cove, TX
Thompson, James R., Jr. ... Chicago, IL
Thompson, James S. ... New Orleans, LA
Thompson, James S. ... New York, NY
Thompson, James S. ... Cleveland, TN
Thompson, James T. ... Kansas City, MO
Thompson, James V. ... Ludlow, MA
Thompson, James W. ... Raymore, MO
Thompson, James W. ... Billings, MT
Thompson, James W. ... Morehead City, NC
Thompson, James W. ... Cincinnati, OH
Thompson, James W. ... Miami, OK
Thompson, Jan H. ... Lexington, KY
Thompson, Jan Steinour ... Austin, TX
Thompson, Jane Ann ... Pittsburgh, PA
Thompson, Jane E. ... Boulder, CO
Thompson, Jane W. ... Pittsburgh, PA
Thompson, Janet C. ... Lexington, KY
Thompson, Janet M. ... Columbia, MO
Thompson, Janette R. ... Fort Worth, TX
Thompson, Jason J. ... San Antonio, TX
Thompson, Jay A. ... Austin, TX
Thompson, Jay M. ... Dallas, TX
Thompson, Jay T. ... Costa Mesa, CA
Thompson, Jayne A. ... Tucson, AZ
Thompson, Jeanne L. ... Springfield, MA
Thompson, Jeff ... Greensboro, FL
Thompson, Jeff R. ... Bossier City, LA
Thompson, Jeffery L. ... Macon, GA
Thompson, Jeffrey A. ... Red Bluff, CA
Thompson, Jeffrey B. ... Alto, NM
Austin, TX
Thompson, Jeffrey C. ... Brooklyn Center, MN
Thompson, Jeffrey C. ... Armonk, NY
Thompson, Jeffrey C. ... Charlotte, NC
Thompson, Jeffrey D. ... Irvine, CA
Thompson, Jeffrey D. ... Evansville, IN
Thompson, Jeffrey D. ... Louisville, KY
Thompson, Jeffrey E. ... Centreville, MD
Thompson, Jeffrey E. ... Lansing, MI
Thompson, Jeffrey E. ... Rochester, MN
Thompson, Jeffrey E. ... Memphis, TN
Thompson, Jeffrey G. ... Melbourne, FL
Thompson, Jeffrey G. ... Columbus, OH
Thompson, Jeffrey L. ... Scandia, KS
Thompson, Jeffrey M. ... Winter Park, FL
Thompson, Jeffrey M. ... Minneapolis, MN
Thompson, Jeffrey M. ... Butler, PA
Thompson, Jeffrey M., Law Offices, P.C. ... Butler, PA
Thompson, Jeffrey P. ... Santa Ana, CA
Thompson, Jeffrey S. ... Houston, TX
Thompson, Jeffrey W. ... Columbia, MD
Thompson, Jennifer ... Riverside, CA
Thompson, Jennifer K. ... Indianapolis, IN
Thompson, Jennifer Lynn ... Nashville, TN
Thompson, Jennings B. ... Houston, TX
Thompson, Jere G. ... Philadelphia, PA
Thompson, Jesse W. ... Conway, AR
Thompson, Jill A. ... San Francisco, CA
Thompson, Jill R. ... Homestead, FL
Thompson, Jill Shipley ... Macon, GA
Thompson, Jim F. ... Atlanta, TX
Thompson, Jimmie N. ... Paris, TX
Thompson, J. L., III ... Nashville, TN
Thompson, Joan A. ... Hempstead, NY
Thompson, Jocelyn Niebur ... Los Angeles, CA
Thompson, Jodee Rowe ... Enterprise, AL
Thompson, Joe A. ... Hattiesburg, MS
Thompson, Joe B., Jr. ... Atmore, AL
Brewton, AL
Thompson, Joe E. ... Baton Rouge, LA
Thompson, Joe E. ... Willmar, MN
Thompson, Joe Glenn ... Houston, TX
Thompson, Joe L. ... Houston, TX
Thompson, Joe R. ... Minneapolis, MN
Thompson, Joel C. ... Houston, TX
Thompson, Joel Erik ... Phoenix, AZ
Thompson, Joel Erik, Ltd. ... Phoenix, AZ
Thompson, Joel H. ... Portland, ME
Thompson, Joel S. ... Steamboat Springs, CO
Thompson, John A. ... Pebble Beach, CA
Thompson, John A., Jr. ... Coral Gables, FL
Thompson, John Andrew ... Cranston, RI
Thompson, John B. ... Coral Gables, FL
Thompson, John B. ... Richmond, VA
Thompson, John C. ... Williamsville, NY
Thompson, John C. ... Conway, SC
Thompson, John D. ... Evergreen, CO
Thompson, John D. ... Minneapolis, MN
Thompson, John D. ... Kirkland, WA
Thompson, John D., Jr. ... Lafayette, LA
Thompson, John E. ... Atlanta, GA
Thompson, John E. ... Lincolnwood, IL
Thompson, John F. ... Denver, CO
Thompson, John F. ... Leavenworth, KS
Thompson, John F., Jr. ... Santa Ana, CA
Thompson, John G. ... Tarpon Springs, FL
Thompson, John G. ... Mount Clemens, MI
Thompson, John G., & Associates, P.A. ... Tarpon Springs, FL
Thompson, John H. Department Of Veterans Affairs, Office of the General Counsel, GV
Thompson, John H., IV ... St. Petersburg, FL
Thompson, John J. ... Wilmington, DE
Thompson, John L. ... Augusta, GA
Thompson, John L. ... Dallas, TX
Thompson, John L., Jr. ... Walkersville, MD
Thompson, John L., Jr. ... Detroit, MI
Thompson, John L., P.C. ... Augusta, GA
Thompson, John Larkin ... Boston, MA
Thompson, John M. ... Springfield, MA
Thompson, John M. ... Oklahoma City, OK
Thompson, John M., IV ... Green Bay, WI
Thompson, John Michael ... Nashville, TN
Thompson, John R. ... Lincoln, NE
Thompson, John R. ... Oklahoma City, OK
Thompson, John R. ... Salt Lake City, UT
Thompson, John Randolph, Jr. ... Fort Worth, TX
Thompson, John Rex ... Tyler, TX
Thompson, John Rex, P.C. ... Tyler, TX
Thompson, John Robert ... Swainsboro, GA
Thompson, John S. ... Tinley Park, IL
Thompson, John T., Jr. ... Woodridge, IL
Thompson, John W. ... Sunnyvale, CA
Thompson, John W. ... Phippsburg, ME
Thompson, John W. ... O'Fallon, MO
Thompson, John W. ... Ruidoso, NM
Thompson, John W., II ... Butler, AL
Thompson, John W., Jr. ... York, PA
Thompson, Jo-Linda ... Sacramento, CA
Thompson, Jon W. ... Phoenix, AZ
Thompson, Jos. R. ... Philadelphia, PA
Thompson, Joseph A., Jr. ... Boston, MA
Thompson, Joseph D., III ... Charleston, SC
Thompson, Joseph G. ... Wayzata, MN
Thompson, Joseph G., III ... Houston, TX
Thompson, Joseph P. ... Gilroy, CA
Thompson, Joseph S. ... Columbus, IN
Thompson, Joseph S. ... Miami, OK
Thompson, Joseph T. ... Los Angeles, CA
Thompson, Joy Gaines ... Philadelphia, PA
Thompson, Judith ... Birmingham, AL
Thompson, Judith ... New York, NY
Thompson, Judith J. ... Oklahoma City, OK
Thompson, Judy D. ... Charlotte, NC
Thompson, Julia Duchow ... Farmington, CT
Thompson, Julia Treacy ... Denver, CO
Thompson, Julio A. ... Los Angeles, CA
Thompson, Justin X. ... Irvine, CA
Jeffersonville, IN
Thompson, Justine I. ... Atlanta, GA
Thompson, Juul H. ... Batavia, IL
Thompson, Karen G. ... Atlanta, GA
Thompson, Karen Gillison ... Portland, OR
Thompson, Karen M. ... Houston, TX
Thompson, Karen R. ... Portland, OR
Thompson, Karen S. ... Salt Lake City, UT
Thompson, Katherine G. ... New York, NY
Thompson, Katherine Kole ... Bel Air, MD
Thompson, Katherine M. ... Los Angeles, CA
Thompson, Kathleen Crowdus ... Louisville, KY
Thompson, Kathleen M. ... Spokane, WA
Thompson, Kathleen O'Flaherty ... Washington, DC
Thompson, Kathryn Angela ... Chicago, IL
Thompson, Kathryn Leola ... Chandler, OK
Thompson, Kathryn S. ... Red Bluff, CA
Thompson, K.C. ... Dallas, TX
Thompson, Keith C. ... Manhasset, NY
Thompson, Keith G. ... Sheldon, IA
Thompson, Keith W. ... Junction City, OR
Thompson, Kelli L. ... Knoxville, TN
Thompson, Kelly A. ... Arlington, VA
Thompson, Kelly, Jr. ... Bowling Green, KY
Thompson, Kendra F. ... Dayton, OH
Thompson, Kenley J. ... Neodesha, KS
Thompson, Kenneth E. ... Traverse City, MI
Thompson, Kenneth E. ... Newark, NJ
Thompson, Kenneth F. ... Marshfield, MO
Thompson, Kenneth K. ... Lehigh Acres, FL
Thompson, Kenneth L. ... Baltimore, MD
Thompson, Kenneth L., Jr. ... Bronx, NY
Thompson, Kenneth L. S. ... Bronx, NY
Thompson, Kenneth P. ... Brooklyn, NY
Thompson, Kenneth R., II ... Cincinnati, OH
Thompson, Kenneth R. M. ... Chicago, IL
Thompson, Kenneth W. ... Torrance, CA
Thompson, Kent ... San Antonio, TX
Thompson, Kent C. ... San Diego, CA
Thompson, Kent L. ... Overland Park, KS
Thompson, Kent L. ... Wichita, KS
Thompson, Kerri E. ... Washington, DC
Thompson, Kerry L. ... Scottsburg, IN
Thompson, Kevin A. ... San Francisco, CA
Thompson, Kevin S. ... Madison, WI
Thompson, Kim A. ... San Francisco, CA
Thompson, Kim D. ... Costa Mesa, CA
Thompson, Kim K. ... San Francisco, CA
Thompson, Kim Kiel ... Atlanta, GA
Thompson, Kimberley E. ... Alexandria, VA
Thompson, Kimberly O'Dawn ... Dallas, TX
Thompson, Kimberly R ... Chicago, IL
Thompson & King ... Valencia, CA
Thompson & King Law Firm ... Anderson, SC
Thompson, Kirk ... Glendale, AZ
Thompson, Kirk C. ... Minneapolis, MN
Thompson, Kirk M. ... Pittsburgh, PA
Thompson, Kirsten E. ... Hillsboro, OR
Thompson Knight Brown Parker & Leahy L.L.P. ... Houston, TX

Thompson & Knight L.L.P. ... Austin, TX
Dallas, TX
Fort Worth, TX
Thompson, Krilich, LaPorte, Tucci & West, P.S. Tacoma, WA
Thompson, Kris P. ... San Diego, CA
Thompson, Kristen R. ... Boise, ID
Thompson, Kristin L. ... Philadelphia, PA
Thompson, Kristine L. ... Columbia, SC
Thompson, Kushner & Rhoades, LLP Albuquerque, NM
Thompson, Kyle A. ... Honolulu, HI
Thompson, Laja K ... Denver, CO
Thompson, Lamont, Flaherty & Masur, A Professional Corporation ... Aurora, IL
De Kalb, IL
Thompson, Lance E. ... Columbus, OH
Thompson, Lance S. ... Victorville, CA
Thompson, Larry A. ... Beverly Hills, CA
Thompson, Larry D. ... Atlanta, GA
Thompson, Larry D. ... Houston, TX
Thompson, Larry E. ... New York, NY
Thompson, Larry E. ... Williamson, WV
Thompson, Larry J. ... Rogers, AR
Thompson, Larry M. ... Fort Worth, TX
Thompson, Laura ... Toms River, NJ
Thompson, Laura E. ... Southport, NC
Thompson, Laura Hartman Ludington, MI
Thompson, Laura K. ... Ogden, UT
Thompson, Laura M. ... Boston, MA
Thompson, Lauri S. ... Las Vegas, NV
Thompson, Laurie A. ... Miami, FL
Thompson & Lavender ... New Orleans, LA
Thompson Law Firm, The ... Beaverton, OR
Thompson Law Firm, The, P.A. Conway, SC
Myrtle Beach, SC
Thompson Law Office ... Havre, MT
Thompson Law Office, Ltd. ... La Crosse, WI
Thompson Law Office, P.C. ... Reinbeck, IA
Thompson Law Office, The ... Monterey, CA
Salinas, CA
Thompson, Lawrence A. ... Studio City, CA
Thompson, Lawrence B. ... New York, NY
Thompson, Lawrence E. ... Phoenix, AZ
Thompson, Lawrence E., II ... Highlands, NC
Thompson, Lawrence H. ... Los Angeles, CA
Thompson, Lawrence L. ... Atlanta, GA
Thompson, Lawrence M., Jr. Wyomissing, PA
Thompson, Layne A. ... Houston, TX
Thompson, Leah D. Embry Treasury Department, GV
Thompson, Lee ... Wichita, KS
Thompson, Lee A. ... Redwood City, CA
Thompson, Lee A. ... Lancaster, OH
Thompson, Leonard C. ... Kansas City, MO
Thompson, Lester R. ... Dayton, OH
Thompson, Lewis A., III ... Warrenton, NC
Thompson, Lewis D. ... New York, NY
Thompson, Lewis J. Grosse Pointe Farms, MI
Thompson, Lily ... Chicago, IL
Thompson, Linda ... Atlanta, GA
Thompson, Linda A. ... Jackson, MS
Thompson, Linda Frederick ... Omaha, NE
Thompson, Linda J. ... Springfield, MA
Thompson, Lindsay T. ... Seattle, WA
Thompson, Lindsay T., P.C. ... Seattle, WA
Thompson, Linnea E. ... Moline, IL
Thompson, Lisa A. ... New York, NY
Thompson, Lisa A. ... Reading, PA
Thompson, Lisa C. ... Tucson, AZ
Thompson, Lisa Chadwick ... Fairfield, NJ
Thompson, Lisa D. ... St. Louis, MO
Thompson, Lisa Fields ... Columbus, OH
Thompson, Lisa M. ... Fort Dodge, IA
Thompson, Lisa N. ... Vero Beach, FL
Thompson, Llewellyn E., II ... Oakland, CA
Thompson and Llewellyn, P.A. Fort Smith, AR
Thompson, Lloyd D. ... Staten Island, NY
Thompson, Lois D. ... Los Angeles, CA
Thompson, Lonna M. ... Washington, DC
Thompson, Loran T. ... New York, NY
Thompson, Loren G. Federal Trade Commission, Bureau of Consumer Protection, GV
Thompson, Lori D. ... Roanoke, VA
Thompson, Lorri M. ... Manhattan Beach, CA
Thompson, Lou ... Dallas, TX
Thompson, Loudoun L. ... Romney, WV
Thompson, Louis A., Jr. ... Irvington, NY
Thompson, Louise Seelinger Conshohocken, PA
Thompson, Luanne Stark ... Aberdeen, MS
Thompson, Luke D. ... Los Angeles, CA
Thompson, Lundquist & Sicoli, Ltd. Minneapolis, MN
Thompson, Luther C., Jr. ... Farwell, TX
Thompson, Luther M. ... Jackson, MS
Thompson, Lynn Alan ... Tallahassee, FL
Thompson, Lynn C. ... Petrolia, PA
Thompson, Lynn Cresalia ... Reno, NV
Thompson, Lynn E. ... Pittsburgh, PA
Thompson, Lynn K. ... Santa Monica, CA
Thompson, Lynn M. ... St. Louis, MO
Thompson, Lynne R. ... Melbourne, FL
Thompson, Lynne R., P.A. ... Melbourne, FL
Thompson, M. Allison ... Nashville, TN
Thompson, M. Brian ... Baltimore, MD
Thompson, M. Karen ... Somerville, NJ
Thompson, M. Lee, P.A. West Palm Beach, FL
Thompson, M. Shane ... Dallas, TX
Thompson, M. Wayne ... Laurel, MS
Thompson, Malone & Conti Los Angeles, CA
Thompson, Mara R. ... Minneapolis, MN
Thompson, Marc C. ... Cody, WY
Thompson, Marc R. ... New York, NY
Thompson, Marcia K. ... Alexandria, VA
Thompson, Marcus L. ... Houston, TX
Thompson, Mardi Ruth Department of Transportation, Federal Aviation Administration, GV
Thompson, Margaret Gallagher Philadelphia, PA
Thompson, Margaret O. ... Austin, TX
Thompson, Maria Matteo Philadelphia, PA
Thompson, Marilyn ... San Rafael, CA
Thompson, Marjorie L. ... San Jose, CA
Thompson, Mark ... New York, NY
Thompson, Mark A. ... Englewood, CO
Thompson, Mark A. ... Bronx, NY
Thompson, Mark Alexander Washington, DC
Thompson, Mark B. ... Watseka, IL
Thompson, Mark D. ... Breckenridge, CO
Thompson, Mark E. ... Lancaster, CA
Thompson, Mark E. ... Atlanta, GA
Thompson, Mark E., A Professional Corporation ... Lancaster, CA
Thompson, Mark G. ... Hartford, CT
Thompson, Mark R. ... Venice, FL
Thompson, Mark R. ... Kansas City, MO
Thompson, Martha B. ... Miami, OK
Thompson, Martha Leach Birmingham, AL
Thompson, Martha R. ... Gastonia, NC
Thompson, Martin F. ... Memphis, TN
Thompson, Martin J. ... Costa Mesa, CA
Thompson, Martin J. ... Hauppauge, NY
Thompson, Marttie Louis ... New York, NY
Thompson, Marvic Gonzalez Metairie, LA
Thompson, Marvin E. ... Russell, KS
Thompson, Mary Anne ... Long Beach, CA
Thompson, Mary C. ... Homewood, IL
Thompson, Mary C. ... Houston, TX
Thompson, Mary Davis ... Raleigh, NC
Thompson, Mary Ellen ... Brockton, MA
Thompson, Mary Grubb ... Washington, DC
Thompson, Mary H. ... Birmingham, AL
Thompson, Mary H. ... Baton Rouge, LA
Thompson, Mary Holmes ... Houston, TX
Thompson, Mary Jane ... Schaumburg, IL
Thompson, Mary O. ... Overland Park, KS
Kansas City, MO
Thompson, Mary Penny ... Raleigh, NC
Thompson, Marylyn Harty Farmington Hills, MI
Thompson, Matthew C. ... Los Angeles, CA
Thompson, Matthew G. ... Houston, TX
Thompson, Matthew J. ... Columbus, OH
Thompson, Matthew L. ... Minneapolis, MN
Thompson, Maureen A. ... Takoma Park, MD
Thompson, Maureen F. ... New York, NY
Thompson, Maury C. ... Bismarck, ND
Thompson, Mavis T. ... St. Louis, MO
Thompson, Mayo J., (P.C.) ... Houston, TX
Thompson & McMullan, A Professional Corporation ... Chester, VA
Chesterfield, VA
Hanover, VA
Richmond, VA
Thompson, M. E., Jr. ... Valdosta, GA
Thompson, Meier & Dersom ... Columbus, OH
Thompson, Melanie J. ... Wilmington, DE
Thompson, Melicent B. ... New Haven, CT
Thompson, Melisa G. ... Chicago, IL
Thompson, Melissa C. ... Phoenix, AZ
Thompson, Melissa K. ... Denver, CO
Thompson, Melissa M. ... Lexington, MA
Thompson, Melvin E., Jr. ... Valdosta, GA
Thompson, Melvin J. ... Bakersfield, CA
Thompson, Merrill S. ... Bridgeton, IN
Indianapolis, IN
Thompson, Merrill S., P.C. ... Bridgeton, IN
Thompson, Merton E., IV ... Boston, MA
Thompson, Mia D. ... Los Angeles, CA
Thompson, Michael ... Kansas City, MO
Thompson, Michael ... Denison, TX
Thompson, Michael ... San Antonio, TX
Thompson, Michael A. ... Ketchikan, AK
Thompson, Michael A. ... Canton, OH
Salem, OH
Thompson, Michael, and Associates, L.L.P. Denison, TX
Thompson, Michael B. ... Roanoke, IL
Thompson, Michael B. ... Sioux Falls, SD
Thompson, Michael B., P.C. Sioux Falls, SD
Thompson, Michael C. ... Denver, CO
Thompson, Michael C. ... Plattsburgh, NY
Thompson, Michael D. ... Atlanta, GA
Newark, NJ
Thompson, Michael D. ... Helena, MT
Thompson, Michael D. ... Charles Town, WV
Martinsburg, WV
Thompson, Michael E. ... Mount Laurel, NJ
Thompson, Michael G. ... New Orleans, LA
Thompson, Michael G. ... Spokane, WA
Thompson, Michael J. ... Los Angeles, CA
Thompson, Michael J. ... Washington, DC
Thompson, Michael J. ... Litchfield, MN
Thompson, Michael J. ... Easton, PA
Thompson, Michael, Jr. ... Austin, TX
Thompson, Michael L. ... Houston, TX
Thompson, Michael M. Hendersonville, NC
Thompson, Michael P. ... Hartford, CT
Thompson, Michael T. ... Staten Island, NY
Thompson, Michael V. ... Nashville, TN
Thompson, Michael W. ... Sacramento, CA
Thompson, Michael W. ... Kansas City, MO
Thompson, Micheal A. ... Vallejo, CA
Thompson, Michel A. ... Kansas City, MO
Thompson, Michele Barbero ... Austin, TX
Thompson, Michelle ... Charlotte, NC
Thompson, Michelle Farrar ... Chicago, IL
Thompson, Michelle K. ... St. Louis, MO
Thompson, Mike ... El Paso, TX
Thompson, Mike Kevin ... New Haven, CT
Thompson, Miki ... Williamson, WV
Thompson & Miller PLC ... Louisville, KY
Thompson, Milton O. ... Indianapolis, IN
Thompson, Miriam M. ... Wilmington, NC
Thompson & Mitchell ... Washington, DC
Belleville, IL
St. Charles, MO
St. Louis, MO
Thompson, Mitchell F. ... Hagåtña, GU
Thompson, Mitchell S. ... Cleveland, OH
Thompson, Molly M. ... Cincinnati, OH
Thompson, Monica L., (P.C.) ... Chicago, IL
Thompson, Monica S. ... Dallas, TX
Thompson, Monte D. ... Salt Lake City, UT
Thompson, Montgomery & Cahill Globe, AZ
Thompson Morello, Professional Corporation Detroit, MI
Farmington Hills, MI
Southfield, MI
Wyandotte, MI
Thompson, Morley P. ... New York, NY
Thompson, Mozelle W. Federal Trade Commission, Offices of Commissioners, GV
Thompson, M.R. ... San Diego, CA
Thompson, M. T., Jr. ... Saginaw, MI
Thompson, Myron H. ... Montgomery, AL
Thompson, N. David ... New York, NY
Thompson, Nancy A. ... Los Gatos, CA
Thompson, Nancy C. ... San Diego, CA
Thompson, Nancy L. ... Walthill, NE
Thompson, Nancy L. ... New York, NY
Thompson, Naomi R. ... Boston, MA
Thompson, Neal B., Jr. ... Long Beach, CA
Thompson, Neal L. ... Chattanooga, TN
Thompson, Neela Kartha ... Miami, FL
Thompson, Neil ... Devils Lake, ND
Thompson, Neil D. ... Salt Lake City, UT
Thompson, Neils L. ... Albuquerque, NM
Thompson, Nicholas ... Little Rock, AR
Thompson, Nicholas S. ... Santa Ana, CA
Thompson, Nichole A. ... Simsbury, CT
Thompson, Nick C. ... Louisville, KY
Thompson, Nicola Anne ... Houston, TX
Thompson, O'Brien, Kemp & Nasuti, P.C. Atlanta, GA
Norcross, GA
Thompson, O'Donnell, Markham, Norton & Hannon ... Washington, DC
Thompson, Oliver A. ... Cleveland, OH
Thompson, O'Neil & VanderVeen, P.C. Traverse City, MI
Thompson, Orval N. ... Albany, OR
Thompson, Otho M. ... Baltimore, MD
Thompson, Overton, III ... Nashville, TN
Thompson, P. Mark ... Boise, ID
Thompson, Pamela J. ... Detroit, MI
Thompson, Pamela K. ... Jeffersonville, IN
Thompson, Pamela L. ... New York, NY
Thompson, Pamela S. ... San Antonio, TX
Thompson, Pandora ... Newark, NJ
Thompson, Parke G. ... Akron, OH
Thompson & Parsons ... Romney, WV
Thompson, Patricia A. ... Spokane, WA
Thompson, Patricia Ann ... St. Cloud, MN
Thompson, Patricia E. ... Bellevue, WA
Thompson, Patricia Halvorson ... Miami, FL
Thompson, Patricia J. Securities and Exchange Commission, Division of Enforcement, GV
Thompson, Patricia J. ... Chicago, IL
Thompson, Patricia L. ... Portland, OR
Thompson, Patricia McHugh ... Atlanta, GA
Thompson, Patricia S. ... Washington, DC
Thompson, Patrick A. ... Atlanta, GA
Thompson, Patrick A. ... Perkins, OK
Thompson, Patrick E. ... Stevensville, MD
Thompson, Patrick Ford ... Austin, TX
Thompson, Patrick H. ... Salina, KS
Thompson, Patrick S. ... San Francisco, CA
Thompson, Paul A. ... Minneapolis, MN
Thompson, Paul A. ... Kenilworth, NJ
Thompson, Paul B. ... Newark, NJ
Thompson, Paul E. ... Libertyville, IL
Thompson, Paul G. ... Sacramento, CA
Thompson, Paul G. ... Chevy Chase, MD
Thompson, Paul G. ... Bemidji, MN
Thompson, Paul J. ... Cleveland, OH
Thompson, Paul Joseph ... Birmingham, AL
Thompson, Paul Kevin ... Carmel, IN
Thompson, Paul L. ... Columbus, OH
Thompson, Paul M. ... Maitland, FL
Thompson, Paul M. ... Pittsburgh, PA
Thompson, Paul M. ... Richmond, VA
Thompson, Paul T. ... Baker, LA
Thompson, Pauline M. ... Pittsburgh, PA
Thompson, Peggy C. ... Wexford, PA
Thompson, Perry R. ... Wheaton, IL
Thompson, Peter ... Houston, TX
Thompson, Peter A. ... Mesa, AZ
Thompson, Peter A., P.C. ... Mesa, AZ
Thompson, Peter G. ... Washington, DC
Thompson, Peter J. ... Washington, DC
Thompson, Peter J. ... Minneapolis, MN
Thompson, Peter J. ... Syracuse, NY
Thompson, Peter J. ... Eau Claire, WI
Thompson, Peter K. ... San Francisco, CA
Thompson, Peter K. ... Charlotte, NC
Thompson, Peter L. ... Kennebunk, ME
Thompson, Peter N. ... St. Paul, MN
Thompson, Peter R. ... San Diego, CA
Thompson, Peter R. ... Addison, TX
Thompson, Peter R., Jr. ... Hazelwood, MO
Thompson, Peter R. J. ... Chula Vista, CA
Thompson, Peter S. ... Doylestown, PA
Thompson, Phil K. ... Jay, OK
Thompson, Philip A. ... Bellevue, WA
Thompson, Philip Allen ... Auburn, AL
Thompson, Philip C. ... Atlanta, GA
Thompson, Philip C. ... Conway, SC
Thompson, Philip H. ... Santa Monica, CA
Thompson, Philip J. ... Spokane, WA
Thompson, Philip R. ... Indianapolis, IN
Thompson, Phillip E. ... Fort Washington, MD
Thompson, Phyllis D. ... Washington, DC
Thompson, R. Bruce, II ... Raleigh, NC
Thompson, R. Dean ... Riverside, CA
Thompson, R. Everett ... Alpharetta, GA
Thompson, R. Keith ... El Paso, TX
Thompson, R., Law Firm, The, LLC Greenville, SC
Thompson, R. Lynn ... Claremore, OK
Tulsa, OK
Thompson, R. Michael ... Norcross, GA
Thompson, R. Patrick ... New York, NY
Thompson, R. Scott ... Roseland, NJ
Thompson, R. Waylon ... Panama City, FL
Thompson, Rachel B. ... Mission Woods, KS
Thompson, Ralph G. ... Oklahoma City, OK
Thompson, Ralph O. ... Salinas, CA
Thompson, Ralph W., III ... Monterey, CA
Thompson, Ralph W., Jr. ... Monterey, CA
Thompson, Randall D. ... Bethany, MO
Kansas City, MO
Thompson, Randall L. ... Albuquerque, NM
Thompson, Randall S. ... St. Louis, MO
Thompson, Randall Todd ... Hagåtña, GU
Thompson, Randle D. Fort Walton Beach, FL
Panama City, FL
Pensacola, FL
Thompson, Randolph C. ... Washington, DC
Thompson, Randy V. ... Minneapolis, MN
Thompson, Ray C. ... Sacramento, CA
Thompson, Ray E., Jr. ... Spartanburg, SC
Thompson, Ray M. ... Mobile, AL
Thompson, Raymond D. ... Middlebury, CT
Thompson, Raymond E. ... Ocala, FL
Thompson, R.C. ... Austin, TX
Thompson, R. E. ... Albuquerque, NM
Thompson, Rebecca A. ... Walnut Creek, CA
Thompson, Rebecca Ann ... Los Angeles, CA
Thompson, Rebecca L. United States Court Of Appeals District Of Columbia Circuit, GV
Thompson, Rebecca S. ... Batesville, MS
Hernando, MS
Thompson, Redmond, Nicolson & Ray Columbus, GA
Thompson, Reed & Boyce, P.C. Fall River, MA
Thompson, Reed W. ... North Little Rock, AR
Thompson, Regina L. ... Scandia, KS
Thompson & Reilley, P.C. ... Houston, TX
Thompson, Rex L. ... Shawnee, OK
Thompson, Rex Wade ... Tulsa, OK
Thompson, Rhonda D. ... New York, NY
Thompson, Richard ... Carmel, CA
Thompson, Richard ... Pontiac, MI
Thompson, Richard ... Lavalette, WV
Thompson, Richard A. ... Tuscaloosa, AL
Thompson, Richard A. ... New Orleans, LA
Thompson, Richard C. ... White Plains, NY
Thompson, Richard C. ... La Crosse, WI
Thompson, Richard D. ... Beverly Hills, CA
Thompson, Richard D. ... Oxnard, CA
Thompson, Richard E. ... Wilmette, IL
Thompson, Richard E. "Chip", II Atlanta, GA
Thompson, Richard E., Jr. ... Anderson, SC
Thompson, Richard H. ... Naples, ME
Thompson, Richard K. ... Wichita, KS
Thompson, Richard Kent ... Reno, NV
Thompson, Richard L. ... Westfield, MA
Thompson, Richard N. ... Lincoln, NE
Thompson, Richard N. ... Hempstead, NY
Thompson, Richard N. ... Houston, TX
Thompson, Richard P. ... Seattle, WA
Thompson, Richard S. ... Orlando, FL
Thompson, Richard S. ... Vidalia, GA
Thompson, Richard W. ... Belleville, IL
Thompson, Rick A. ... Cheyenne, WY
Thompson, Riley B. ... Victorville, CA
Thompson, Robert ... Memphis, TN
Thompson, Robert ... San Francisco, CA
Thompson, Robert A. ... Salina, KS
Thompson, Robert A. ... Boston, MA
Thompson, Robert B. ... Gainesville, GA
Thompson, Robert B. ... Chicago, IL
Thompson, Robert B. ... St. Louis, MO
Thompson, Robert C. ... San Francisco, CA
Thompson, Robert C. ... Port St. Lucie, FL
Thompson, Robert C., Jr. Indianapolis, IN
Thompson, Robert D. ... Cherry Hill, NJ
Thompson, Robert E. ... San Francisco, CA
Thompson, Robert E. ... Beaverton, OR
Thompson, Robert E. ... Dallas, TX
Thompson, Robert E. ... Fort Worth, TX
Thompson, Robert E., Jr. Oklahoma City, OK
Thompson, Robert F. ... Paragould, AR
Thompson, Robert F., III ... Little Rock, AR
Thompson, Robert Fulton ... Jackson, MS

Thompson, Robert G. .... Boca Raton, FL
Thompson, Robert G., Jr. .... Sacramento, CA
Thompson, Robert H. .... Las Vegas, NV
Thompson, Robert H .... Huntington, NY
Thompson, Robert H. .... Knoxville, TN
Thompson, Robert H. .... Seattle, WA
Thompson, Robert H., Jr. .... Spokane, WA
Thompson, Robert I., III .... Shreveport, LA
Thompson, Robert K. .... Fairfax, VA
Thompson, Robert L. .... Atlanta, GA
Thompson, Robert L. .... Concord, NH
Thompson, Robert L. .... Albuquerque, NM
Thompson, Robert L., Jr. .... Fort Wayne, IN
Thompson, Robert L., Jr. .... Summit, NJ
Thompson, Robert Lewis .... Alexandria, VA
Thompson, Robert M. .... Kansas City, MO
Thompson, Robert M., Law Offices of
Sacramento, CA
Thompson, Robert P. .... Jackson, MS
Thompson, Robert R. .... Dover, DE
Thompson, Robert R. .... Novi, MI
Thompson, Robert R. .... Corpus Christi, TX
Thompson, Robert S. .... Atlanta, GA
Thompson, Robert S. .... Southern Pines, NC
Thompson, Robert S. .... McMinnville, OR
Thompson, Robert S. .... Cleveland, TN
Thompson, Robert S. .... San Antonio, TX
Thompson, Robert S., P.A. .... Pinehurst, NC
Southern Pines, NC
Thompson, Robert Stephen .... Tyler, TX
Thompson, Robert T. .... Atlanta, GA
Greenville, SC
Thompson, Robert Thomas, Jr.
Atlanta, GA
Thompson, Robert W. .... Tustin, CA
Thompson, Robert W. .... Reinbeck, IA
Thompson, Robert W. .... Annapolis, MD
Thompson, Robert W. .... Oklahoma City, OK
Thompson, Robert W. .... Salt Lake City, UT
Thompson, Robert W. .... Salt Lake City, UT
Thompson, Roberta L. .... Marlborough, MA
Thompson, Robt. D. .... Olanta, SC
Thompson, Robt. F. .... Wheeling, WV
Thompson, Roderick M. .... San Francisco, CA
Thompson, Rodney W. .... Belleville, IL
Thompson, Roger H. .... Salt Lake City, UT
Thompson, Roger L. .... Buckhannon, WV
Thompson, Roger S. .... New York, NY
Thompson, Roger W. .... Lincoln, IL
Thompson & Rogers .... Fort Wayne, IN
Thompson, Ronald B. .... Mount Holly, NJ
Thompson, Ronald E. .... Gig Harbor, WA
Thompson, Ronald F. .... Birmingham, AL
Thompson, Ronald H. .... Denver, CO
Thompson, Ronald J. .... Las Vegas, NV
Thompson, Ronald J. .... Madison, WI
Thompson, Ronald K. .... Rincon, GA
Thompson, Ronald K., P.C. .... Rincon, GA
Thompson, Ronald P. .... Guntersville, AL
Thompson, Ronald R. .... Baton Rouge, LA
Thompson, Ronald R. .... Fairfax, VA
Thompson, Ronald S. .... Southfield, MI
Thompson, Ronnette A.
Upper Marlboro, MD
Thompson, Rose F. .... Miami, FL
Thompson, Rosemary Simota
Department of Justice,
Antitrust Division, GV
Thompson, Ross W. .... Verona, PA
Thompson, Roy E., Jr. .... Portland, ME
Thompson, Russell A. .... New York, NY
Thompson, Russell D. .... Ocean Springs, MS
Thompson, Russell M. .... Deerfield Beach, FL
Thompson, Russell X. .... Memphis, TN
Thompson, Ruth P. .... Arlington Heights, IL
Thompson, S. Brent .... Anchorage, AK
Thompson, Sabin R. .... Nashville, TN
Thompson, Sabrina M. .... Auburn, CA
Thompson, Samuel C. .... Olympia, WA
Thompson, Samuel G. .... Raleigh, NC
Thompson, Samuel S. .... Elkhart, IN
Thompson, Sandra A. .... Torrance, CA
Thompson, Sandra E. .... Atlanta, GA
Thompson, Sanford W., IV .... Raleigh, NC
Thompson, Sarah A. .... United States Senate,
Senatorial Assistants, GV
Thompson, Sarah M. .... Philadelphia, PA
Philadelphia, PA
Thompson, Sarah W. .... Columbus, OH
Thompson & Schreiber, P.A.
Fort Myers, FL
Thompson & Scott .... Yakima, WA
Thompson, Scott .... Monroe, WI
Thompson, Scott A. .... Three Rivers, CA
Thompson, Scott B., Jr. .... Dublin, GA
Thompson, Scott C. .... Orlando, FL
Thompson, Scott C. .... Philadelphia, PA
Thompson, Scott D. .... Brick, NJ
Thompson, Scott E. .... New York, NY
Thompson, Scott H. .... Dallas, TX
Thompson, Scott R. .... Devils Lake, ND
Thompson, Scott S. .... Santa Monica, CA
Thompson, Sean Y. .... Santa Barbara, CA
Thompson, Seth B. .... Cullman, AL
Thompson, Seth C. .... Riverside, CA
Thompson, Shannon E. .... Seattle, WA
Thompson, Shari A. .... Anaheim, CA
Thompson, Sharon A. .... Durham, NC
Thompson, Sharon E. .... Fairfax, VA
Thompson, Sharon, Law Group
Durham, NC
Thompson, Shaun R. .... Helena, MT
Thompson, Shawn .... Dallas, TX
Thompson, Shawn B. .... Honolulu, HI
Thompson, Shawn Roger .... Longmont, CO
Thompson, Shelley B. .... St. Paul, MN
Thompson, Sherrie B. Moses
New York, NY

Thompson, Sherry A. .... Victorville, CA
Thompson, Sherry Marie .... San Diego, CA
Thompson, Sherry P. .... Grants, NM
Thompson & Shirk .... Naples, FL
Thompson, Shirley N. .... San Francisco, CA
Thompson, Sidney H. .... Suffern, NY
Thompson, Sinclair & Anderson
Spartanburg, SC
Thompson & Singer, P.A. .... Atlanta, GA
Thompson, Sizemore & Gonzalez,
Professional Association .... Tampa, FL
Thompson, Skrobarcek & Miller
Corpus Christi, TX
Thompson & Slagle, P.C. .... Atlanta, GA
Norcross, GA
Thompson & Smith, P.C. .... Atlanta, GA
Augusta, GA
Thompson, Smithers, Newman, Wade &
Childress, L.L.P. .... Richmond, VA
Thompson & Smyth, L.L.P. .... Raleigh, NC
Thompson, Sparks, Dean & Morris
Monroe, LA
Thompson, Stafford W., (P.A.)
Red Bank, NJ
Thompson, Stanley .... Philadelphia, PA
Thompson, Stanley H. .... Owatonna, MN
Thompson, Stanley J. .... Des Moines, IA
Thompson, Stanley M. .... Richmond, MO
Thompson, Stephanie Cunningham
Marlborough, MA
Thompson, Stephanie Elaine .... Dallas, TX
Thompson, Stephanie Garner
Equal Employment Opportunity
Commission,
Office of Legal Counsel, GV
Thompson, Stephen A. .... Cottonwood, AZ
Flagstaff, AZ
Sedona, AZ
Thompson, Stephen A. .... St. Louis, MO
Thompson, Stephen C. .... Portland, OR
Thompson, Stephen D. .... Fort Myers, FL
Thompson, Stephen D. .... Ketchum, ID
Thompson, Stephen D. .... Canton, OH
Thompson, Stephen E. .... Naples, FL
Thompson, Stephen G. .... Cincinnati, OH
Thompson, Stephen L. .... Oklahoma City, OK
Thompson, Stephen L. .... Charleston, WV
Thompson, Stephen M. .... Denver, CO
Thompson, Stephen P. .... Frankfort, KY
Thompson, Stephen R. .... Franklin Lakes, NJ
Thompson, Stephen W. .... Bradenton, FL
Thompson, Stephen W. .... Camden, NJ
Thompson, Stevan H. .... Idaho Falls, ID
Thompson, Steve Bruce .... Denver, CO
Thompson, Steven C. .... Baton Rouge, LA
Thompson, Steven C. .... Minneapolis, MN
Thompson, Steven C. .... Philadelphia, PA
Thompson, Steven F. .... Tampa, FL
Thompson, Steven G. .... New York, NY
Thompson, Steven J. .... Chicago, IL
Thompson, Steven M. .... Chicago, IL
Thompson, Steven R. .... St. Paul, MN
Thompson, Stuart A. .... Naples, FL
Thompson, Stuart C. .... Buffalo, NY
Thompson, Stuart L. .... Sacramento, CA
Thompson, Sudie .... Dallas, TX
Thompson, Sue E. .... Petaluma, CA
Thompson, Susan .... Minneapolis, MN
Thompson, Susan D. .... Headland, AL
Thompson, Susan J. .... Minneapolis, MN
Thompson, Susan R. .... Sacramento, CA
Thompson, Susan S. .... Tallahassee, FL
Thompson, Susannah E. .... Temecula, CA
Thompson, Suzanne Margaret
Jacksonville, FL
Thompson & Sweeny, P.C.
Lawrenceville, GA
Thompson, Sydnor .... Charlotte, NC
Thompson, Sydnor .... Charlotte, NC
Thompson, Sylvia A. .... Miami, FL
Thompson, T. Jay .... Liberty Corner, NJ
Thompson, T. Scott .... Washington, DC
Thompson, Tanja Lueck .... Memphis, TN
Thompson, Ted E. .... Culver City, CA
Thompson, Terence W. .... Phoenix, AZ
Thompson, Teresa Ann Melcher
Missoula, MT
Thompson, Teresa D. .... Weston, CT
Thompson, Teresa K. .... Charleston, WV
Thompson, Teresa M. .... Minneapolis, MN
Thompson, Teri Firmiss .... Chicago, IL
Thompson, Terrell M. .... Lubbock, TX
Thompson, Terrence J. .... Eudora, KS
Thompson, Terri A. .... Washington, DC
Thompson, Terrie Heers .... Las Vegas, NV
Thompson, Terry A. .... Basking Ridge, NJ
Thompson, Terry P. .... Phoenix, AZ
Thompson, T. F. .... Houston, TX
Thompson, Thedlus L.
General Services Administration,
Office of the General Counsel, GV
Thompson, Theodore K. .... Havre, MT
Thompson, Theodore Q. .... Ambler, PA
Thompson, Theodore Q. .... Philadelphia, PA
Thompson, Theresa M.
National Aeronautics And Space
Administration,
Goddard Space Flight Center, GV
Thompson, Therese .... Oldwick, NJ
Thompson, Thomas A. .... Washington, DC
Thompson, Thomas A. .... Bryan, OH
Thompson, Thomas A. .... Shawnee, OK
Thompson, Thomas A. .... Seattle, WA
Thompson, Thomas A. .... Rawlins, WY
Thompson & Thomas, A Professional
Corporation .... Lubbock, TX
Thompson, Thomas C. .... Grass Valley, CA

Thompson, Thomas C., Jr.
Washington, DC
Thompson, Thomas D. .... Salisbury, NC
Thompson, Thomas D. .... Columbus, OH
Thompson, Thomas E. .... Kansas City, MO
Thompson, Thomas G. .... Wayne, PA
Thompson, Thomas J. .... Laurens, SC
Thompson, Thomas J. "Tommy"
Baton Rouge, LA
Thompson, Thomas K. .... Liberty, MO
Thompson, Thomas L. .... Hillsdale, MI
Thompson, Thomas L. .... Jackson, MS
Thompson, Thomas L., Jr. .... Columbus, GA
Thompson, Thomas M. .... Globe, AZ
Thompson, Thomas M. .... Pittsburgh, PA
Thompson, Thomas N. .... Shreveport, LA
Thompson, Thomas R. .... Tallahassee, FL
Thompson, Thomas R. .... Austin, TX
Thompson, Thomas T. .... Ludington, MI
Thompson and Thompson .... Butler, AL
Thompson & Thompson .... San Diego, CA
Thompson & Thompson .... Washington, DC
Thompson & Thompson .... Chicago, IL
Thompson & Thompson .... Ludington, MI
Thompson & Thompson .... Devils Lake, ND
Thompson and Thompson .... Miami, OK
Thompson & Thompson .... Poteau, OK
Thompson & Thompson .... Charlottesville, VA
Thompson & Thompson, A Law Corporation
Victorville, CA
Thompson & Thompson, A Professional
Corporation .... San Antonio, TX
Thompson, Thompson & Hilbun
Dublin, GA
Thompson & Thompson LLP
Centreville, MD
Thompson & Thompson, P.A. .... Scandia, KS
Thompson & Thompson, P.C. .... Novi, MI
Thompson, Thurman Q., II .... DeSoto, TX
Thompson, Thurston A. .... Rogers, AR
Thompson & Tiemann .... Austin, TX
Thompson, Tim J. .... Memphis, TN
Thompson, Tim L. .... Tulsa, OK
Thompson, Tim W. .... North Platte, NE
Thompson, Timothy .... Bridgeville, PA
Thompson, Timothy C. .... Columbia, SC
Thompson, Timothy F. .... Chicago, IL
Thompson, Timothy H. .... Chicago, IL
Thompson, Timothy J. .... Prairie Village, KS
Thompson, Timothy L. .... Fresno, CA
Thompson, Timothy L. .... New York, NY
Thompson, Timothy N. .... Los Angeles, CA
Thompson, Timothy N. .... Kansas City, MO
Thompson, Timothy R. .... Grants Pass, OR
Thompson, Todd E. .... San Francisco, CA
Thompson, Todd N. .... Lawrence, KS
Thompson, Tom .... Batesville, AR
Thompson, Tom P., Jr. .... Hartsville, TN
Thompson, Tommy F. .... Boston, MA
Thompson, Tommy G. .... Madison, WI
Thompson, Tommy L. .... Columbus, OH
Thompson, T. R., Jr. .... Aurora, NC
Thompson, Tracey Holmes .... Atlanta, GA
Thompson, Tracy .... San Francisco, CA
Thompson, Tracy A. .... Alexandria, VA
Thompson, Tracy C. .... Farmington Hills, MI
Thompson, Tracy M. .... Birmingham, AL
Thompson, Tracy M. .... Ludington, MI
Thompson, Travis J. .... Richboro, PA
Thompson, Trent .... Salem, IN
Thompson, Tricia L. .... Indianapolis, IN
Thompson, Trisa J. .... Round Rock, TX
Thompson, Troy .... San Francisco, CA
Thompson, Troy D. .... Neenah, WI
Thompson, Tucker S. .... Soldotna, AK
Thompson, Tyler S. .... Louisville, KY
Thompson, Tyrus Hugh .... Arlington, VA
Thompson, V. Bruce .... United States Senate,
Senatorial Assistants, GV
Thompson, Valerie Martinez
Alexandria, LA
Thompson, Van, Jr. .... Fort Worth, TX
Thompson, Vicki A. .... Kenilworth, IL
Thompson, Vicki C. .... Herndon, VA
Thompson, Vicki L. .... San Diego, CA
Thompson, Vickie R. .... Beaumont, TX
Thompson, Victor B. .... St. Louis, MO
Thompson, Victoria L. .... Houston, TX
Thompson, Vincent E. .... Dallas, TX
Thompson, Vincent E., P.C. .... Dallas, TX
Thompson, Virgil G. .... Weirton, WV
Thompson, Virgil Lee, Jr.
Lawrenceville, GA
Thompson, W. Carrington .... Chatham, VA
Thompson, W. Dane .... Bloomfield Hills, MI
Thompson, W. McIlwaine, Jr.
Charlottesville, VA
Thompson, W. Mote, Jr. .... Ashland, KY
Thompson, W. Paul .... Sandy, UT
Thompson, W. Shan .... Jackson, MS
Thompson, W. Wade, (P.A.)
Bradenton, FL
Thompson, Wade R. .... Post, OR
Thompson & Waldron .... Washington, DC
Alexandria, VA
Thompson, Wallace A. .... Winnebago, MN
Thompson, Walter C., Jr.
New Orleans, LA
Thompson, Walter, Law Office
Clarksdale, MS
Thompson, Walter R. .... Winona, MN
Thompson, Walter W. .... Clarksdale, MS
Thompson, Walter W. .... York, SC
Thompson, Warren B. .... Lafayette, IN
Thompson, Warren Clinton, III .... Tacoma, WA
Thompson, Warren R. .... Palmer, MA
Thompson, Wayln G. .... Beaumont, TX
Thompson, Wayne E., Jr. .... Costa Mesa, CA

Thompson, Wayne J., Jr. .... Littleton, CO
Thompson, Wayne M. .... Salem, OR
Thompson & Welsh .... Corpus Christi, TX
Thompson, Wendell L. .... Ottawa, IL
Thompson, Wendell R. .... San Gabriel, CA
Thompson, Wesley R. .... Vista, CA
Thompson, Wesley R. .... Sapulpa, OK
Thompson, Willard B. .... Wichita, KS
Thompson, Willard L., Jr. .... Wichita, KS
Thompson, Willard V. .... Vulcan, MI
Thompson, William A. .... Lynnfield, MA
Thompson, William A. .... Jackson, MI
Thompson, William A. .... Columbus, OH
Thompson, William A., III .... Atlantic City, NJ
Thompson, William A., P.C. .... Jackson, MI
Thompson, William B. .... Wheaton, IL
Thompson, William B., Jr. .... Jackson, MS
Thompson, William (Bill) .... Talladega, AL
Thompson, William C. .... Irvine, CA
Thompson, William C. .... Atlanta, GA
Thompson, William C. .... Forest, MS
Thompson, William D. .... Rockville, MD
Thompson, William D., Jr. .... Hartford, CT
Thompson, William deForest .... Naples, FL
Thompson, William deForest, Jr.
Fort Myers, FL
Naples, FL
Thompson, William deForest, P.A.
Fort Lauderdale, FL
Fort Myers, FL
Naples, FL
Thompson, William E. .... Orangevale, CA
Thompson, William F. .... Indianapolis, IN
Thompson, William F., III .... Honolulu, HI
Thompson, William G., Law Office of
Breckenridge, TX
Thompson, William H. .... Indianapolis, IN
Thompson, William H. .... Southfield, MI
Thompson, William H. .... Montclair, NJ
Thompson, William H. .... Raleigh, NC
Thompson, William H. .... Cleveland, OH
Thompson, William J. .... Atlanta, GA
Thompson, William J. .... Schaumburg, IL
Thompson, William J. .... Boston, MA
Thompson, William J. .... Haddonfield, NJ
Thompson, William J. .... Cleveland, OH
Thompson, William L. .... Douglas, GA
Thompson, William L. .... Salem, IN
Thompson, William L. .... Everett, MA
Thompson, William Lewis, Jr.
Orange Park, FL
Thompson, William Lewis, Jr., P.A.
Orange Park, FL
Thompson, William M., Jr. .... Bridgeton, NJ
Thompson, William P. .... Fort Smith, AR
Thompson, William P. .... La Grange Park, IL
Thompson, William R. .... Washington, DC
Thompson, William R. .... Mount Pleasant, MI
Thompson, William R. .... Philadelphia, PA
Thompson, William R., Jr. .... Calhoun, GA
Thompson, William Randolph
Washington, DC
Thompson, William Richard, II
Houston, TX
Thompson, William Stewart .... Madison, WV
Thompson, William W., II .... Washington, DC
Thompson, William W., IV .... Cleveland, OH
Thompson, William W., Jr. .... Moscow, ID
Thompson, William W., Jr.
Alexandria, VA
Thompson, Winfred L. .... Conway, AR
Thompson, Winthrop E. .... Hemet, CA
Thompson, Wm. L. .... Anderson, SC
Thompson, Wm. Mark .... Lubbock, TX
Thompson, Wm. S. .... Washington, DC
Thompson & Wolf, L.P.A. .... Mansfield, OH
Thompson & Young .... Philadelphia, PA
Thompson & Zall LLC .... Denver, CO
Thompson, Zane A. .... Roque Bluffs, ME
Thompson-Adams, Michelle .... Denver, CO
Thompson-Cody, Brandy .... San Diego, CA
Thompson-Collins, Aetna, Law Offices of
Rockville, MD
Thompson-Hill, Patricia .... Greenbelt, MD
Thompson III, Horace A., (P.C.)
New Orleans, LA
Thompson III, James R. .... Fayetteville, TN
Thompson-King, Sumara M.
National Aeronautics And Space
Administration,
Office of the General Counsel, GV
Thompson-Lagerberg, Elizabeth
Chehalis, WA
Thompson-Metzger, Christa D. .... Newark, DE
Thompson-Stack, Elizabeth .... Miami, FL
Thompson-Stanley, Trina L. .... Oakland, CA
Thompson-Swain, Valerie O. .... St. Louis, MO
Thoms, Allan T. .... Des Moines, IA
Thoms, David M. .... Detroit, MI
Thoms, David M., & Associates, P.C.
Detroit, MI
Thoms, Jeannine A. .... Crystal Lake, IL
Thoms, Peter W. .... Boston, MA
Thoms, William F., Jr. .... Indianapolis, IN
Thomsen, B. Scott .... Grass Valley, CA
Thomsen and Burke, LLP
Washington, DC
Baltimore, MD
Thomsen, Curt R. .... Idaho Falls, ID
Thomsen, David A. .... Ruidoso, NM
Thomsen, Donald P. .... Eugene, OR
Thomsen, Eric J. .... Davenport, IA
Muscatine, IA
Wilton, IA
Thomsen, F. Theodore .... Bellevue, WA
Thomsen, George E. .... Baltimore, MD
Thomsen & Gough .... Eugene, OR
Thomsen, Helge .... Minneapolis, MN

Thomsen, Ira H. .... Dayton, OH
Springboro, OH
Thomsen, J. Frederick .... Knoxville, TN
Thomsen, Jeffry S. .... St. Louis, MO
Thomsen, Joan M. .... Treasury Department, Internal Revenue Service, GV
Thomsen, Kristina L. .... Chicago, IL
Thomsen, Leslie A. .... Fairfax, CA
Thomsen, Lynn A. .... Nevada City, CA
Thomsen, Mark L. .... Brookfield, WI
Thomsen, Matthew H. .... Westerly, RI
Thomsen, Meghan M. .... Cherry Hill, NJ
Philadelphia, PA
Thomsen, Michael W. .... Eaton Rapids, MI
Thomsen & Nybeck, P.A.
Minneapolis, MN
Thomsen, Paul H. .... Prior Lake, MN
Thomsen, Randall .... Seattle, WA
Thomsen, Roszel C., II .... Washington, DC
Baltimore, MD
Thomsen, Sonia Gustafson .... Washington, DC
Thomsen and Stephens, P.A.
Idaho Falls, ID
Pocatello, ID
Thomsen, Steuart H. .... Washington, DC
Thomsen, Steven A. .... Pocatello, ID
Thomsen, Susan E. .... Ketchikan, AK
Thomsen, Thomas B. .... Fremont, NE
Thomsen-Reynolds, Dianna
Washington, DC
Thomson, A. Robert E. .... Federal Way, WA
Thomson, Addison H. .... Miami, FL
Thomson, Alexander D. .... Whittier, CA
Thomson, Alexander L., Jr. .... Denver, CO
Thomson, Alexander W. .... Pittsburgh, PA
Thomson, Andrew C. .... Bakersfield, CA
Thomson, Angela S. .... Northville, MI
Thomson, Anne M. .... Detroit, MI
Thomson, B. Joe .... Houston, TX
Thomson, Barbara Ellen
United States Senate, Senatorial Assistants, GV
Thomson, Barbara Susan .... Brooklyn, NY
Thomson, Basil H., Jr. .... Waco, TX
Thomson, Benjamin E. .... Raleigh, NC
Thomson, Candi L. Rawdon .... Sturgis, SD
Thomson, Carol Lynn .... Denver, CO
Thomson, Carolyn H. .... Oklahoma City, OK
Thomson, Catherine M. .... Chicago, IL
Thomson, Charles McQuillen .... Chicago, IL
Thomson, Christine .... Charlottesville, VA
Thomson, Christopher .... West Chester, PA
Thomson, Christopher C. .... Washington, DC
Thomson, Corrine Heine
Minneapolis, MN
Thomson, Curtis P. .... Edmonds, WA
Thomson, Dale P. .... Rexburg, ID
Thomson, David A. .... Phoenix, AZ
Thomson, David A., A Prof. Corp., Law Offices of .... Phoenix, AZ
Thomson, David I. C. .... Denver, CO
Thomson, David M. .... Plantation, FL
Thomson, David S. .... Athens, GA
Thomson, Dean B. .... Minneapolis, MN
Thomson, Deborah H. .... Boston, MA
Thomson, Donald E. .... Elmira, NY
Thomson, Dorothy A. .... Sacramento, CA
Thomson, Doug .... Maryville, MO
Thomson, Douglas D. .... Cincinnati, OH
Thomson, Douglas W. .... St. Paul, MN
Thomson, Douglas W. .... Milford, OH
Thomson, Douglas W., Ltd. .... St. Paul, MN
Thomson, Edward G. .... New York, NY
Thomson, Edward N. .... Sausalito, CA
Thomson, Eric A. .... La Jolla, CA
Thomson, Frances A. .... Norristown, PA
Thomson, Frank H. .... Broomfield, CO
Thomson, G. Donald, Jr.
Bonita Springs, FL
Thomson, G. Donald, P.A.
Bonita Springs, FL
Thomson, George Baker .... Coral Gables, FL
Thomson, Glenn R. .... Atlanta, GA
Thomson, Gregory A. .... Los Angeles, CA
Thomson, Harold A., Jr. .... Milford, PA
Thomson, Hugh T. .... San Jose, CA
Thomson, J. Faison, Jr. .... Goldsboro, NC
Thomson, J. Morton, Jr. .... Memphis, TN
Thomson, J. Wilmot, Jr. .... Starkville, MS
Thomson, Jack .... New Orleans, LA
Thomson, James E. .... Waukon, IA
Thomson, James E. .... Santa Fe, NM
Thomson, James J. .... Minneapolis, MN
Thomson, James M. .... Redwood City, CA
Thomson, James M. .... Richmond, VA
Thomson, James S. .... Berkeley, CA
Thomson, Jeani Dwyer .... Springfield, MO
Thomson, Jeannine M. .... Cherry Hill, NJ
Philadelphia, PA
Thomson, Jeffrey A. .... Boise, ID
Thomson, Jere Rogers (IBA) .... New York, NY
Thomson, Joe .... Alameda, CA
Thomson, John A., Jr. .... Atlanta, GA
Thomson, John C. .... Boston, MA
Thomson, John G. .... New Glarus, WI
Thomson, John M. .... Coral Gables, FL
Thomson, John N. .... Southfield, MI
Thomson, John T. .... Hanover, MA
Thomson, John W. .... Las Vegas, NV
Thomson, John W. .... Staten Island, NY
Thomson, Joseph A. .... Minneapolis, MN
Thomson, Joseph M. .... Toledo, OH
Thomson, Karen Duzan .... Wilsonville, OR
Thomson, Katherine J. .... Oakland, CA
Thomson, Kathryn B. .... Washington, DC
Thomson, Keith C. .... Seattle, WA
Thomson, Kenneth L. .... Freehold, NJ
Thomson, Kevin M. .... Jackson, MI
Thomson, Larry D. .... Salem, OR
Thomson Law Office .... Edwardsville, IL
Springfield, IL
Thomson Law Offices, Chartered
Rexburg, ID
Thomson, Leann K. .... Barre, VT
Thomson, Lee Stuart .... Towson, MD
Thomson, Leslie A. .... Kansas City, MO
Thomson, Lucy L. .... Department of Justice, Criminal Division, GV
Thomson, Margaret A.
Department of Energy, Office of the General Counsel, GV
Thomson, Maria N. .... Barstow, CA
Thomson, Marian T. .... Richmond, CA
Thomson, Mark D. .... Orlando, FL
Thomson, Marlene D. .... Dallas, TX
Thomson, Mary Beth .... Eden Prairie, MN
Thomson, Mary C. .... Boston, MA
Thomson, Mary Lee .... Sacramento, CA
Thomson, Maynard F. .... Cleveland, OH
Thomson, Michael D. .... Washington, DC
Thomson, Mitchell & McNeely, P.C.
Jacksonville, IL
Thomson Muraro Razook & Hart, P.A.
Fort Lauderdale, FL
Miami, FL
Thomson, Neil W. .... Phoenix, AZ
Thomson & Nelson, A Professional Law Corporation .... Los Angeles, CA
Santa Ana, CA
Whittier, CA
Thomson, Nina .... Sacramento, CA
Thomson & O'Brien .... Akron, OH
Thomson, Parker Davidson .... Miami, FL
Thomson, Patricia A. .... Gainesville, FL
Thomson, Paul D. .... Port Washington, NY
Thomson, Paul G.
Department Of Veterans Affairs, VA Regional Counsel Office, Washington, D.C., GV
Thomson, Paul H. .... Winchester, VA
Thomson, Paul R., III .... Roanoke, VA
Thomson, Paul R., Jr. .... Roanoke, VA
Thomson, Peter M. .... New Orleans, LA
Thomson, R. Scott .... Albany, NY
Thomson, R. Stuart .... Seattle, WA
Thomson, Ralph .... Jacksonville, IL
Thomson, Rhodes & Cowie, P.C.
Pittsburgh, PA
Thomson, Richard C. .... Sacramento, CA
Thomson, Richard J. .... Walton, NY
Thomson, Richard K. .... Erie, PA
Thomson, Richard T. .... Minneapolis, MN
Thomson, Robert B. .... Kansas City, MO
Thomson, Robert C. .... Des Moines, IA
Thomson, Robert C., Jr. .... Westfield, NJ
Sleepy Hollow, NY
Thomson, Robert E. .... Scottsdale, AZ
Thomson, Robert H. .... Portland, OR
Thomson, Robert M. .... Akron, OH
Thomson, Robert W. .... Pittsburgh, PA
Thomson, Roderick E. .... Dedham, MA
Thomson, Roger F. .... Dallas, TX
Thomson, Romin P. .... San Jose, CA
Thomson, Ronald T. P.C. .... New York, NY
Thomson, Ronald Theodore .... New York, NY
Thomson, Russell A. .... Monterey, CA
Thomson, Sara J. .... Philadelphia, PA
Thomson, Scott D. .... New York, NY
Thomson, Spencer R. .... Kansas City, MO
Thomson, Stephanie Schrimpf
Cincinnati, OH
Thomson, Stephen W. .... Edwardsville, IL
Springfield, IL
Thomson, Tamara Burchill .... Baltimore, MD
Thomson, Terry E. .... Seattle, WA
Thomson, W. Kent .... Mt. Pleasant, IA
Thomson, W. Loren .... Bloomington, IL
Thomson, W. Scott .... Louisville, KY
Thomson, Warren R. .... Manchester, MA
Thomson, Wayne H. .... Parsippany, NJ
Thomson & Weintraub .... Bloomington, IL
Thomson, Wendy S. .... Westport, CT
Thomson, William .... Washington, DC
Thomson, William D. .... Livermore, CA
Thomson, William E. .... Los Angeles, CA
Thomson, William E., Jr.
Los Angeles, CA
Thomson, William F., Jr. .... Fairless Hills, PA
Thomson, William H. .... Blue Island, IL
Thomson, William J., II .... Cheyenne, WY
Thomson, William M. .... Pittsburgh, PA
Thomson, William R. (Dick) .... Maryville, MO
Thomson, Wm. Charles .... Phoenix, AZ
Thomson-Taylor, Therese A. .... Phoenix, AZ
Thomsson, David .... Brooklyn, NY
Thomte, Dennis L. .... Des Moines, IA
Omaha, NE
Thomton, R. N. .... Litchfield, MN
Thomton, Sperry & Jensen, Ltd.
Litchfield, MN
Thomulka, Russell J. .... Encino, CA
Thomure, John C., Jr. .... Milwaukee, WI
Thomure, Pamela A. .... Boston, MA
Thon, Beck, Vanni, Phillipi & Nutt, A Professional Corporation
Los Angeles, CA
Pasadena, CA
Thon, Rhonda E. .... Rockville Centre, NY
Thon, Susan C. .... New York, NY
Thon, William M. .... Pasadena, CA
Thonander, Robert V. .... Winnetka, IL
Thone, Charles .... Lincoln, NE
Thone, Jeffrey W. .... Hopkins, MN
Thone, William J. .... St. Paul, MN
Thonert, Richard J. .... Fort Wayne, IN
Thonet, Nicole M. .... McLean, VA
Thonis, James W. .... Ventura, CA
Thonn, Jerry E. .... Seattle, WA
Thopy, Robert T. .... Shelbyville, IN
Thorbrogger, Susan .... Seattle, WA
Thorburn, Alison .... Detroit, MI
Thorburn, Bruce J. .... Bloomfield Hills, MI
Thorburn, Bruce J., P.C.
Bloomfield Hills, MI
Pontiac, MI
Thorburn, Douglas C., (P.C.) .... Boulder, CO
Thorburn, James D. .... Elizabeth, CO
Thorburn, James M. .... Southport, CT
Thorburn, James S. .... Birmingham, MI
Thorburn, Mark A. .... Point Roberts, WA
Thorburn, Sakol & Throne .... Boulder, CO
Thorburn, Wm. J. .... Woodland, CA
Thordsen, Herman .... Santa Ana, CA
Thordsen, Herman, Law Offices of
Santa Ana, CA
Thoreen, Gerald L. .... St. Cloud, MN
Thoreen, Harold A., Jr. .... Seattle, WA
Thoreen, W. Richard .... Altamonte Springs, FL
Thorell, Keith R. .... Los Angeles, CA
Thorelli & Associates .... Chicago, IL
Thorelli, Thomas H. .... Chicago, IL
Thoren, Peter L. .... Westport, CT
Thoren, Steven B. .... Denver, CO
Thoren-Peden, Deborah S.
Los Angeles, CA
Thoresen, Ahna M. .... Minneapolis, MN
Thoresen, Alice D. .... Springfield, OH
Thoresen, Jean H. .... Willimantic, CT
Thoresen, Trygve M. .... Torrance, CA
Thoreson, Bradley P. .... Seattle, WA
Thoreson, Donald L. .... Seattle, WA
Thoreson, Eric .... Seattle, WA
Thoreson, Gregory K. .... Baltimore, MD
Thoreson, Phillip L. .... Seattle, WA
Thoreson, Steven James .... Minneapolis, MN
Thoresz, Monique N. .... New York, NY
Thorfinnson & Olson, P.A.
Eden Prairie, MN
Thorfinnson, Romaine D. .... Oshkosh, WI
Thorfinnson, Ross L. .... Eden Prairie, MN
Thorfinnson, Thomas M. .... Eden Prairie, MN
Thorgaard, Terrence H. .... Fairbanks, AK
Thorguson, David M. .... Morgan City, LA
Thorie, William H. .... Ellsworth, WI
Thorin, J. Paul .... San Jose, CA
Thorington & Gregory .... Montgomery, AL
Thorington, Nancy B. .... Petaluma, CA
Thorington, Robert D. .... Montgomery, AL
Thorkelson, Mary M. .... Chicago, IL
Thorkelson, Peter .... North Haven, CT
Thorland, Charles E. D. .... Boston, MA
Thorland, Karen R. .... Los Angeles, CA
Thorleifson, Tracy S. .... Seattle, WA
Thorlton, Timothy J. .... Danville, IL
Thormaehlen, Claus E. .... Manchester, TN
Thorman, Christopher P. .... Cleveland, OH
Thorman, Lincoln R. .... Cleveland, OH
Thorman, Michael P. .... Hayward, CA
Thorman, Victoria Mertens .... New York, NY
Thorman, Walter D. .... San Antonio, TX
Thorman, William A., III .... Columbus, OH
Thorme, Melissa A. .... Sacramento, CA
Thorn, Andrea Papp .... Andover, MA
Thorn, Arthur H. .... Albany, NY
Thorn, Charles L. .... Fort Worth, TX
Thorn, Christopher Adams
Los Angeles, CA
Thorn, Dale A. .... Miami, FL
Thorn, David M. .... Spokane, WA
Thorn, Dennis W. .... Chicago, IL
Thorn, Dennis W., & Associates
Chicago, IL
Thorn, Douglas R. .... Rocklin, CA
Thorn, Elise Owens .... Honolulu, HI
Thorn, Ellen M. .... Sparta, WI
Thorn, Eric J. .... Tallahassee, FL
Thorn, Gerald A. .... Orlando, FL
Thorn and Gershon, LLP .... Albany, NY
Saratoga Springs, NY
Thorn, Gordon L., Jr. .... Kansas City, MO
Thorn, James E. .... Council Bluffs, IA
Thorn, James R. .... San Antonio, TX
Thorn, Jerry G. .... Houston, TX
Thorn, John T. .... Philadelphia, PA
Thorn, Lauren V. .... Concord, NH
Thorn, Melissa G. .... Tampa, FL
Thorn, Paul J., Jr. .... Chicago, IL
Thorn, Rachel W. .... New York, NY
Thorn, Richard D. .... San Diego, CA
Thorn, Robert .... Jacksonville, FL
Thorn, Robert C. .... San Diego, CA
Thorn, Sandra D. .... New York, NY
Thorn, Suzie S. .... San Francisco, CA
Thorn, Terry M. .... Palestine, TX
Thorn, Todd F. .... West Plains, MO
Thorn, W. Thompson, III .... Tampa, FL
Thorn, Wayne .... Birmingham, AL
Thorn, William P. .... Rushford, NY
Thornber, Judy P. .... Chicago, IL
Thornberry, Catherine L. .... McLean, VA
Thornberry, Daniel T. .... San Antonio, TX
Thornberry, Harry F. .... Dallas, TX
Thornberry, James E. .... Louisville, KY
Thornberry, John O. .... Salinas, CA
Thornberry, Megan C. .... Kansas City, MO
Thornberry, Molly .... McAllen, TX
Thornberry, Stephen C. .... Kansas City, MO
Thornberry, Thomas C. .... Craig, CO
Thornberry, Thomas C. .... New Haven, CT
Thornbladh, Kurt .... Farmington, MI
Thornborrow, Andrew .... San Francisco, CA
Thornbrugh, Jane Kristen .... Kansas City, MO
Thornbrugh, Jon E. .... Olathe, KS
Thornbrugh, Kristen .... Kansas City, MO
Thornbrugh, P. Thomas .... Tulsa, OK
Thornburg, Alan Z. .... Asheville, NC
Thornburg, Bean & Glick
St. Clairsville, OH
Woodsfield, OH
Thornburg, Douglas R. .... St. Louis, MO
Thornburg, Elizabeth G. .... Dallas, TX
Thornburg, Frederick F. .... Miami, FL
Thornburg, Jon C. .... Chula Vista, CA
Thornburg, Lacy H. .... Asheville, NC
Thornburg, Michael L. .... Ventura, CA
Thornburg, Richard A. .... Pottsville, PA
Thornburg, Richard W. .... Tallahassee, FL
Thornburg, Robin L.
West Conshohocken, PA
Thornburg, Robin L., P.C.
Philadelphia, PA
West Conshohocken, PA
Thornburg, Sarah Sparboe .... Asheville, NC
Thornburg, Thomas H. .... Chapel Hill, NC
Thornburgh, Carrie Dawn
Birmingham, AL
Thornburgh, Dick .... Washington, DC
Thornburgh, Don .... Los Angeles, CA
Thornburgh, James E. .... Birmingham, AL
Thornburgh, John R. .... Atlanta, GA
Thornburgh, John R. .... Indianapolis, IN
Thornburgh, John W. .... Menlo Park, CA
Thornburgh, Jon P. .... Las Vegas, NV
Thornburgh, Nancy .... Troy, OH
Thornburgh, Robert L. .... Santa Barbara, CA
Thornburgh, William H. .... Troy, OH
Thornbury, Herbert A. .... Chattanooga, TN
Thornbury, James R. .... Toledo, OH
Thornbury, Lee A. .... Columbus, OH
Thornbury, William M. .... Santa Monica, CA
Thorndal, Armstrong, Delk, Balkenbush & Eisinger, A Professional Corporation
Las Vegas, NV
Reno, NV
Thorndal, Helen Posnansky .... Oakland, CA
Thorndal, John L. .... Las Vegas, NV
Thorndal, Mary .... Los Angeles, CA
Thorndal, Paul W. .... San Francisco, CA
Thorndike, Alan .... Stowe, VT
Thorndike, Daniel C. .... Medford, OR
Thorndike, Peter R. .... Cherry Hill, NJ
Thorne, Brian G. .... San Bernardino, CA
Thorne, Carl F. .... Dallas, TX
Thorne, Carol E. .... Yorktown Heights, NY
Thorne, Charles M. .... Louisville, KY
Thorne, Christopher L. .... Denver, CO
Thorne and Company, A Professional Law Corporation .... Los Angeles, CA
Thorne, Creath S. .... St. Joseph, MO
Thorne, D. Eugene .... Provo, UT
Thorne, D. Larry .... Upland, CA
Thorne, David B. .... Kansas City, MO
Thorne, David C. .... Upland, CA
Thorne, David W. .... Seattle, WA
Thorne, Deborah L. .... Chicago, IL
Thorne, Elizabeth .... New York, NY
Thorne, Fred E. .... Tacoma, WA
Thorne, Frederick P., Jr. .... Marion, AR
Thorne, Frederick W. .... St. Charles, IL
Thorne, Gregory L. .... Tarrytown, NY
Thorne, Grodnik, Ransel, Duncan, Byron, Hostetler & Trippel, LLP .... Elkhart, IN
Goshen, IN
Mishawaka, IN
South Bend, IN
Thorne, Hal T. .... Grand Prairie, TX
Thorne, James L. .... Washington, DC
Thorne, James R. .... Pleasanton, TX
Thorne, J. D. .... Milwaukee, WI
Thorne, Jeff R. .... Brigham City, UT
Thorne, Jeffrey J. .... Austin, TX
Thorne, Jeffrey L. .... Michigan City, IN
Thorne, Jessica W. .... Dallas, TX
Thorne, John .... Arlington, VA
Thorne, John C., Jr. .... Lisbon, OH
Thorne, John E. .... Olympia, WA
Thorne, John M., Jr. .... Grand Prairie, TX
Thorne, John W. .... Atlantic Beach, FL
Thorne, Julie A. .... Albany, NY
Thorne, Kevin W. .... San Francisco, CA
Thorne, Kim R. .... Grand Prairie, TX
Thorne, Kim R., Law Office of
Grand Prairie, TX
Thorne, Kropf & Schlee, P.C.
Kalamazoo, MI
Thorne, Lawrence E., Jr. .... Beaumont, TX
Thorne, Mary Ellen .... Coronado, CA
Thorne, Maxim A. .... Roseland, NJ
Thorne, Michael A. .... St. Louis, MO
Thorne, Michael G. .... Tupelo, MS
Thorne, Patricia E. .... Lake Worth, FL
Thorne & Perry .... El Paso, TX
Thorne, Polly .... Grand Prairie, TX
Thorne, R. Don .... El Paso, TX
Thorne, Ralph W. "Pat" .... Williamsport, PA
Thorne, Rebecca Ann .... Charlotte, NC
Thorne, René E. .... New Orleans, LA
Thorne, Robert .... Los Angeles, CA
Thorne, Robert E. .... New Haven, CT
Thorne, Sally .... Grand Prairie, TX
Thorne, Steven G. .... Minneapolis, MN
Thorne, Steven G. .... University Park, PA
Thorne, Steven M. .... Madison, WV
Thorne, Thomas W. .... Kalamazoo, MI
Thorne, Thomas W., Jr. .... New Orleans, LA
Thorne & Thorne, Inc. .... Grand Prairie, TX
Thorne, Vail T. .... Atlanta, GA
Thorne, W. Douglas .... Elkhart, IN
Mishawaka, IN
Thorne, William A. .... Elkhart, IN
Mishawaka, IN
Thorne, William A., Jr. .... Salt Lake City, UT

Thorne, William L. ....Medina, OH
Thorneburg, J. Lynn ....Charlotte, NC
Thorne-Corke, Alisa ....Fayetteville, AR
Thornell, G. Warren ....Shreveport, LA
Thornell, G. Warren, A Professional Law Corporation ....Bossier City, LA
Shreveport, LA
Thornell, John R. ....Kansas City, MO
Thornell, Richard P. ....Washington, DC
Thorner, David A. ....Yakima, WA
Thorner, Kennedy & Gano, P.S.
Yakima, WA
Thorner, Kimberly ....Encinitas, CA
Thorner, Leonard ....Brooklyn, NY
Thorner, Richard ....Manchester, NH
Thorner, Susan L. ....Cupertino, CA
Thorner, Tom ....Kentfield, CA
Thornes, Frederick G. ....Rialto, CA
Thorne-Thomsen, Thomas ....Chicago, IL
Thornfeldt, Paul R. ....San Francisco, CA
Thornhill, Angela F. ....Birmingham, AL
Thornhill & Associates ....Encino, CA
Thornhill, Curtis Lee ....Altavista, VA
Thornhill, Dan W. ....Kittery, ME
Thornhill, Edward, III, P.A.
Waynesville, NC
Thornhill, Harold V. ....Richmond, VA
Thornhill, Herbert L., Jr. ....New York, NY
Thornhill, Ian K. ....Norfolk, VA
Thornhill, James A. ....Richmond, VA
Thornhill, Joseph M. ....San Francisco, CA
Thornhill, Kelley, Farris & Faustermann, L.C. ....New Orleans, LA
Thornhill, Kelley & Faustermann, L.C.
Slidell, LA
Thornhill, Lois Sandiford ....Boston, MA
Thornhill, Mark A. ....Kansas City, MO
Thornhill, Michael C. ....Encino, CA
Thornhill, Robert G., Jr. ....Winter Haven, FL
Thornhill, Robert Gordon, III
Winter Haven, FL
Thornhill, Thomas H. ....Muskegon, MI
Thornhill, Todd M. ....Springfield, MO
Thornhill, Tom W. ....Slidell, LA
Thornhill, W. A., III ....Beckley, WV
Thornhill, W. Routt ....Austin, TX
Thornhill, Warren A., III ....Beckley, WV
Thornhill, William T. ....Fresno, CA
Thornhill, William T., A P.C. ....Fresno, CA
Thornhill-Childress, Lori Ann ....Detroit, MI
Thornley, J. Brent ....Jasper, AL
Thornley, James D. ....Atoka, OK
Thornley, Linda Annabelle
Beverly Hills, CA
Thornley, Richard H. ....Ogden, UT
Thornley, Robert M. ....Las Vegas, NV
Thornley, Trent J. ....San Francisco, CA
Thornock, John R. ....Department of Defense, Defense Legal Services Agency, GV
Thornquist, David K. ....New York, NY
Thornsberry, Ronald E. ....Lexington, KY
Thornsbury, Michael ....Williamson, WV
Thornsbury, Staci L. ....Charleston, WV
Thornsbury & Thompson ....Williamson, WV
Thornsjo, Dale O. ....Minneapolis, MN
Thornton, A. Clifford, Jr. ....Cleveland, OH
Thornton, Allison E. ....Atlanta, GA
Thornton, Ana Kirk ....Austin, TX
Thornton, Audrey Powers ....Encinitas, CA
Thornton, Barry F. ....San Francisco, CA
Thornton, Bernard P. ....Cranford, NJ
Thornton, Bradley D. ....Dakota Dunes, SD
Thornton, Brenda Sue ....Wilmington, DE
Thornton, Brenda Y ....Southfield, MI
Thornton, Bruce M. ....Los Angeles, CA
Thornton & Burnett ....Houston, TX
Thornton & Caulfield ....Southbury, CT
Thornton, Charisse P. ....Jacksonville, FL
Thornton, Charlene B. ....Baltimore, MD
Thornton, Charles V. ....San Francisco, CA
Thornton, Christina J. ....Knoxville, TN
Thornton, Christopher A. ....St. Louis, MO
Thornton, Christopher J. ....Tallahassee, FL
Thornton, Christopher J. ....Memphis, TN
Thornton, Cleveland ....Washington, DC
Thornton, Courtney S. ....Washington, DC
Thornton, Cynthia ....Miles City, MT
Thornton, Cynthia A. ....Philadelphia, PA
Thornton, Cynthia K. ....San Diego, CA
Thornton, Cynthia Rosebaugh ....Portland, OR
Thornton, D. John ....Boise, ID
Thornton, D. Whitney, II
San Francisco, CA
Thornton, David A. ....Memphis, TN
Thornton, David B. ....Asheville, NC
Thornton, David L. ....Friendswood, TX
Thornton, David M. (Mike), Jr.
Tulsa, OK
Thornton, Davis & Murray, P.A.
Miami, FL
Thornton, Deborah ....Chicago, IL
Thornton, Debra A.
Inver Grove Heights, MN
Thornton, Dennis J. ....Hayward, CA
Thornton, Denver L. ....El Dorado, AR
Thornton, D. John, & Associates, P.A.
Boise, ID
Thornton, Domenique S. ....Middletown, CT
Thornton, Douglas A.G. ....Keene, NH
Thornton, Douglas K. ....Frederick, MD
Thornton, Douglas V. ....Fresno, CA
Thornton, E. Carroll, Jr.
Youngstown, OH
Thornton, Early & Naumes LLP
Boston, MA
Thornton, Edna L. ....Bronxville, NY
Thornton, Edward L. ....Rahway, NJ
Thornton, Edward R. ....Manchester, NH
Thornton, Edward R., Jr. ....Derry, NH
Thornton, E. H., Jr. ....Houston, TX
Thornton, Esther A. ....Princeton, NJ
Thornton, F. Allen, Jr. ....Atlanta, GA
Thornton, F. Richard ....Des Moines, IA
Thornton, Fred Howell, III ......Sikeston, MO
Thornton, Gardner S. ....Houston, TX
Thornton, Gary A. ....Austin, TX
Thornton, Gene R. ....Colorado Springs, CO
Thornton, Geo. R. ....East Lansing, MI
Thornton, George A. ....Seattle, WA
Thornton, George A., & Associates P.L.L.C.
Seattle, WA
Thornton, Gerald A. ....Knoxville, TN
Thornton, Gerald E., Jr.
Corpus Christi, TX
Thornton, Glenda L. ....Tallahassee, FL
Thornton, Gregg A. ....San Francisco, CA
Thornton, Gregg B. ....Columbus, OH
Thornton, Gregg E. ....Lexington, KY
Thornton, Gregory R. ....Syracuse, NY
Thornton, Guerry R. ....Newnan, GA
Thornton, Guerry R., Jr. ....Atlanta, GA
Thornton, Guilford F., Jr. ....Nashville, TN
Thornton, Guyton, Dorrill and Pettit
Kosciusko, MS
Thornton, H. Marie ....Decatur, AL
Thornton, H. Vincent ....Brandon, FL
Thornton, Haywood A. ....Richmond, VA
Thornton, Hegg, Reif, Dolan & Bowen, P.A.
Alexandria, MN
Thornton, H. R., Jr. ....St. Cloud, FL
Thornton, Hurd ....Orange, CA
Santa Ana, CA
Thornton, J. Dennis ....Milwaukee, WI
Thornton, J. Duke ....Albuquerque, NM
Thornton, J. Scott ....Little Rock, AR
Thornton, J. Thompson ....Miami, FL
Thornton, Jack Ewald, Jr.
Winston-Salem, NC
Thornton, Jack W., P.C. ....Susanville, CA
Thornton, James ....New York, NY
Thornton, James C. ....La Grange, GA
Thornton, James C. ....Raleigh, NC
Thornton, James D. ....Westerly, RI
Thornton, James D. ....Richmond, VA
Thornton, James F. ....San Francisco, CA
Thornton, James F., Jr. ....Newport News, VA
Thornton, James G ....Hattiesburg, MS
Thornton, James J. ....Shreveport, LA
Thornton, James P. ....Omaha, NE
Thornton, Jason R. ....San Diego, CA
Thornton, Jennifer L. ....El Dorado, AR
Thornton, Jock ....Yonkers, NY
Thornton, Joel H. ....Virginia Beach, VA
Thornton, John A. ....Fincastle, VA
Thornton, John C. ....Newport Beach, CA
Thornton, John H. ....Baltimore, MD
Thornton, John J. ....Quincy, MA
Thornton, John P. ....Eau Claire, WI
Thornton, John R. ....Wetumpka, AL
Thornton, John S., Jr. ....Madeira Beach, FL
Thornton, John T. ....Los Angeles, CA
Thornton, John T. ....Minneapolis, MN
Thornton, John V. ....New York, NY
Thornton, John W., Jr. ....Miami, FL
Thornton, John W., Jr. ....Plano, TX
Thornton, John W., Sr. ....Miami, FL
Thornton, Jonathan L. ....Norfolk, VA
Thornton, Joseph D. ....Council Bluffs, IA
Thornton, Joseph P. ....Springfield, IL
Thornton, Judith Worrell ....Bangor, ME
Thornton, Judson D. ....Jonesborough, TN
Thornton, Julia H. ....Baton Rouge, LA
Thornton, Justin A. ....Washington, DC
Thornton, Justin Allen ....Washington, DC
Thornton, K. Alec ....Norwalk, OH
Thornton, K. Douglas ....Georgetown, SC
Thornton, Karen M. Kemp ....Tampa, FL
Thornton, Karon B. ....Raleigh, NC
Thornton, Kathleen M. ....Greensboro, NC
Raleigh, NC
Thornton, Kay E. ....Kansas City, MO
Thornton, Kelly Cox ....Houston, TX
Thornton, Kenneth E. ....St. Petersburg, FL
Thornton, Kevin J. ....Atlantic City, NJ
Thornton, Kevin P. ....Southbury, CT
Thornton, Kevin W. ....Lebanon, OH
Thornton, Laura A. ....Harrisonburg, VA
Thornton, Laura H. ....Florham Park, NJ
Thornton, Leonard H. ....Naples, FL
Thornton, Linda ....Los Angeles, CA
Oakland, CA
Thornton, Linda ....Sierra Madre, CA
Thornton, Linda S. ....Las Vegas, NV
Thornton, Lucie E. ....New Orleans, LA
Thornton, Lucretia A. ....Gary, IN
Thornton, M. Kenneth ....Norwalk, OH
Willard, OH
Thornton, M. Matthew ....Memphis, TN
Thornton, M. Robert ....Atlanta, GA
Thornton, Mary E. ....Washington, DC
Thornton, Mary P. ....Birmingham, AL
Thornton, Mastrucci & Minkin
Coral Gables, FL
Fort Lauderdale, FL
Miami, FL
West Palm Beach, FL
Thornton, Megan Lake ....Lexington, KY
Thornton, Michael B.
United States Tax Court, GV
Thornton, Michael B. ....Provo, UT
Thornton, Michael G. ....San Francisco, CA
Thornton, Michael L. ....Houston, TX
Thornton, Michael P. ....Boston, MA
Thornton, Michael R. ....Raleigh, NC
Thornton, Michael T. ....Atlanta, GA
Thornton, Michael T., P.C. ....Atlanta, GA
Thornton, Monica Cruz ....Los Angeles, CA
Thornton, Nancy E. ....Casper, WY
Thornton, Nancy F. ....San Jose, CA
Thornton, O. Stanley ....Talladega, AL
Thornton, Patricia A. ....Newark, NJ
Thornton, Patricia M. ....Lanham, MD
Thornton, Patrick James ....Houston, TX
Thornton, Patrick K. ....Spring, TX
Thornton, Patrick W. ....Tulsa, OK
Thornton, P. D., Jr. ....Mineola, TX
Thornton, Peter ....Chicago, IL
Thornton, Peter W. ....Notre Dame, IN
Thornton & Price ....Olney, TX
Thornton, Randall N. ....Lake Panasoffkee, FL
Thornton, Rhonda McKinnis
Little Rock, AR
Thornton, Richard B. ....Macon, GA
Thornton, Richard H. ....Salt Lake City, UT
Thornton, Richard J. ....Miami, FL
Thornton, Robert Alan, Jr. ....Denton, MD
Thornton, Robert B. ....San Antonio, TX
Thornton, Robert D. ....Irvine, CA
Thornton, Robert E. ....Olney, TX
Thornton, Robert F. ....Norwalk, OH
Willard, OH
Thornton, Robert L. ....Pinehurst, NC
Thornton, Robert M. ....Dallas, TX
Thornton, Robert R. ....Los Angeles, CA
Thornton, Robert R. ....Peoria, IL
Thornton, Robt. Y. ....Salem, OR
Thornton, Ronald G. ....Port Richey, FL
Thornton & Rose ....Tucker, GA
Thornton, Rosemary ....Milwaukee, WI
Thornton & Rothman, P.A.
Fort Lauderdale, FL
Miami, FL
Thornton, Russell G. ....Dallas, TX
Thornton, Sandra W. ....Tucker, GA
Thornton, Sean M. ....Washington, DC
Thornton, Stephanie E. ....Monterey Park, CA
Thornton, Steven M. ....Dallas, TX
Thornton, Steven O. ....Bowling Green, KY
Thornton, Steven W. ....Indianapolis, IN
Thornton, Steven W. ....Dallas, TX
Thornton, Summers, Biechlin, Dunham & Brown, L.C. ....Austin, TX
Corpus Christi, TX
McAllen, TX
San Antonio, TX
Thornton, T. Emmet ....Los Angeles, CA
Thornton & Tanenhaus ....New York, NY
Thornton, Taylor, Downs, Becker, Tolson & Doherty ....San Francisco, CA
Thornton, Terry Lynn ....Dallas, TX
Thornton, Thomas A. ....Harrisburg, PA
Thornton, Thomas B. ....Catskill, NY
Thornton, Thomas J. ....Birmingham, AL
Thornton, Thomas S., III
Birmingham, AL
Thornton, Thomas S., Jr. ....Greensboro, NC
Thornton & Thomsen, Inc. ....Westerly, RI
Thornton and Thornton, A Professional Corporation ....Tulsa, OK
Thornton, Thornton & Harwood
Norwalk, OH
Willard, OH
Thornton & Thornton, P.A. ....Manchester, NH
Thornton, Timothy B. ....Albany, NY
Thornton, Timothy M. ....Los Angeles, CA
Thornton, Timothy M., Jr.
Santa Monica, CA
Thornton, Timothy R. ....Minneapolis, MN
Thornton, Timothy R. ....St. Louis, MO
Thornton, Torrence & Gonzales, P.A.
Port Richey, FL
Thornton, Tracey E. ....Washington, DC
Thornton, Travis S. ....Aspen, CO
Thornton, Truss, Graham ....Southfield, MI
Thornton, W. Gerald ....Raleigh, NC
Thornton, W. A. ....Jackson, MS
Thornton, Wendy N. ....Birmingham, AL
Thornton, Wendy Nix ....Birmingham, AL
Thornton, William B. ....Westerly, RI
Thornton, William C. ....Reno, NV
Thornton, William F. ....Short Hills, NJ
Thornton, William G. ....Minneapolis, MN
Thornton, William G. ....Manchester, NH
Thornton, William H. ....Los Angeles, CA
Thornton, William H. ....Chicago, IL
Thornton, William I., Jr. ....Durham, NC
Thornton, William P., Jr. ....Reading, PA
Thornton, William S. ....Bryan, TX
Thornton, William S., Jr. ....Bryan, TX
Thornton, William Thomas ....Tulsa, OK
Thornton-Fluetsch, Kristina L.
San Francisco, CA
Thornton-Green, Donna Sue ....Paducah, KY
Thornwall, Paul W. ....Glen Rock, NJ
Thoron, Gray ....Ithaca, NY
Thoroughgood, Alton B. ....Jackson, WY
Thorp, Albert B. ....Hackettstown, NJ
Thorp, Allan B. ....Memphis, TN
Thorp, Carolyn A. ....Santa Monica, CA
Thorp and Clarke ....Fayetteville, NC
Thorp, Elizabeth K. ....St. Louis, MO
Thorp, Eric C. ....Maynard, MA
Thorp and Fones ....Memphis, TN
Thorp, H. Norman, III ....Oxford, NC
Thorp, Hollis ....Fairview, OK
Thorp, Isaac L. ....Raleigh, NC
Thorp, James Stephen ....Walnut Creek, CA
Thorp, John S., Jr. ....Mineola, NY
Thorp, Justin M. ....Portland, OR
Thorp, Laurence E. ....Springfield, OR
Thorp, Margaret E. ....Louisville, KY
Thorp, Michael R. ....San Diego, CA
Thorp, Michael R. ....Seattle, WA
Thorp, Michele J. ....Bethlehem, PA
Harrisburg, PA
Thorp, Paul ....Dallas, TX
Thorp, Purdy, Jewett, Urness & Wilkinson, P.C.
Springfield, OR
Thorp Reed & Armstrong, LLP
Philadelphia, PA
Pittsburgh, PA
Wheeling, WV
Thorp, Richard B. ....San Diego, CA
Thorp, Robert L. ....San Francisco, CA
Thorp, Sheila R. ....Flint, MI
Thorp, Sullivan & Thorp, P.A.
Chapel Hill, NC
Thorp, Thomas K. ....Hackettstown, NJ
Thorp & Thorp ....Hackettstown, NJ
Thorp, William L. ....Chapel Hill, NC
Thorpe, Allen S. ....Castle Dale, UT
Thorpe, Angela J. ....Dallas, TX
Thorpe, Arthur C. ....Chicago, IL
Thorpe, Brendan J. ....Los Angeles, CA
Thorpe, Dale L. ....Delavan, WI
Thorpe, David James ....Glen Spey, NY
Thorpe, Donald A. ....Denver, CO
Thorpe, Donald A. ....Reno, NV
Thorpe, Douglas L. ....Santa Monica, CA
Thorpe, G. Lynn ....Sacramento, CA
Thorpe, Geoffrey L. ....Boise, ID
Thorpe, Gerald A. ....Albany, NY
Thorpe, Graham A. ....Macon, GA
Thorpe, Gregory A. ....Chicago, IL
Thorpe, Gregory B. ....Los Angeles, CA
Thorpe, Gregory L. ....San Diego, CA
Thorpe, Hatcher & Washington, L.L.P.
Dallas, TX
Thorpe, Jack A. ....Burbank, CA
Thorpe, James J. ....Atlanta, GA
Thorpe, James R. ....Janesville, WI
Thorpe, Jane ....Washington, DC
Thorpe, Jane Fugate ....Atlanta, GA
Thorpe, Jane Hyatt ....Nashville, TN
Thorpe, Janet Claire ....Orlando, FL
Thorpe, Jeffrey H. ....Salt Lake City, UT
Thorpe, Jeffrey R. ....Atlanta, GA
Thorpe, John G. ....Los Angeles, CA
Thorpe, John Jay ....Galveston, TX
Thorpe, John M. ....Hayward, CA
Thorpe, Joshua F. ....Atlanta, GA
Thorpe, Larry W. ....Beaumont, TX
Thorpe, Lawrence I. ....Roswell, GA
Thorpe, Lawrence W., Law Offices of
San Francisco, CA
Thorpe, Leon F. ....Pittsburgh, PA
Thorpe, Leslie Kay ....Columbus, OH
Thorpe, Linda Maney ....Orlando, FL
Thorpe, Lisa Vanston ....Bethesda, MD
Thorpe, Lynn Urkov ....Chicago, IL
Thorpe, Mara T. ....New York, NY
Thorpe, Maura F. ....Los Angeles, CA
Thorpe, Michael D. ....Atlanta, GA
Thorpe, Michael D. ....Salt Lake City, UT
Thorpe, Norman R. ....Detroit, MI
Thorpe, North & Western ....Las Vegas, NV
Sandy, UT
Thorpe, Paul W., Jr. ....Farmingdale, NY
Thorpe, R. Wayne ....Atlanta, GA
Thorpe, Richard Gordon ....New York, NY
Thorpe, Richard J. ....Everett, WA
Thorpe, Robert D. ....Corpus Christi, TX
Thorpe, Robert D., P.C. ....Corpus Christi, TX
Thorpe, Roy B., Jr. ....Christiansburg, VA
Thorpe, Sara M. ....San Francisco, CA
Thorpe, Steven B. ....Dallas, TX
Thorpe, Steven R. ....Knoxville, TN
Thorpe, Straley M. ....Merrillville, IN
Thorpe, T. Huntley, III. ....Warrenton, VA
Thorpe, Thomas B. ....Dallas, TX
Thorpe, Thomas K. ....Tygh Valley, OR
Thorpe and Thorpe, Professional Corporation ....Los Angeles, CA
Thorpe, Trevor C. ....San Francisco, CA
Thorpe, Vincent W. ....Los Angeles, CA
Thorpe, William L. ....Phoenix, AZ
Thorpe, William P. ....Detroit, MI
Thorpe-Mock, Lorna Patricia
Clarksville, TN
Thorpe-Moll, Felise ....Salt Lake City, UT
Thors, Reginald F. ....Boston, MA
Thorsen Altamore & Smith ....Rockford, IL
Thorsen & Armitage ....St. Helena, CA
Thorsen, Bradley C. ....Minneapolis, MN
Thorsen, Donald R. ....Warren, NJ
Thorsen, Eric J. ....Grand Rapids, MI
Thorsen, Eric O. ....New City, NY
Thorsen, Gregg L. ....Dallas, TX
Thorsen, Harold J. ....St. Helena, CA
Thorsen, James B. ....Richmond, VA
Thorsen, Madge S. ....Minneapolis, MN
Thorsen Marchant & Scher LLP
Richmond, VA
Thorsen, Michael Earle ....Liberty, KY
Fairfax, VA
Thorsen, Richard P. ....Mount Prospect, IL
Thorsen, Robert ....Chicago, IL
Thorsen, Robert L. ....Rockford, IL
Thorsen, Rolf Michael ....New City, NY
Thorsen & Widdel, Chartered
Grand Forks, ND
Thorsett, Ronald L. ....Eden Prairie, MN
Thorsey, A. Richard ....Vienna, VA
Thorsnes, Bartolotta, McGuire & Padilla
Imperial Beach, CA
Palm Springs, CA
San Diego, CA
Santa Ana, CA
Thorsnes, Michael T., (A.P.C., P.C.)
San Diego, CA
Thorsness, David H. ....Anchorage, AK

Thorsness, John B. .... **Anchorage, AK**
Thorsness, Kristen J. .... Oakland, CA
Thorsness, William W. .... **Oak Brook, IL**
Thorson, A. Thomas .... New York, NY
Thorson, Andrew H. .... **Los Angeles, CA**
Thorson, Becky R. .... **Minneapolis, MN**
Thorson, Bob .... **Albuquerque, NM**
Thorson, Cassandra C. .... La Mesa, CA
Thorson, Dale R. .... Mesa, AZ
Thorson, David M. .... Fairplay, CO
Thorson, Delton J. .... Augusta, WI
Thorson, Eric W. .... Costa Mesa, CA
Thorson, Frederick L. .... **Minneapolis, MN**
Thorson, James M., Jr. .... **Dayton, OH**
Thorson, John E. .... Phoenix, AZ
Thorson, John O., Jr. .... Valley City, ND
Thorson, Kenneth W. .... **Richmond, VA**
Thorson, Larry J. .... Cedar Rapids, IA
Center Point, IA
Thorson Law Office, S.C. .... Elkhorn, WI
Thorson, Lee A. .... **Seattle, WA**
Thorson, Loren I. .... Chandler, AZ
Thorson, Mary F. .... Chicago, IL
Thorson, Peter M. .... **Los Angeles, CA**
Thorson, Robert A. .... Chippewa Falls, WI
Thorson, Rodney A. .... Elkhorn, WI
Thorson, Rodney O. .... Washington, DC
Thorson, Sondra J. .... Chicago, IL
Thorson, Steven G. .... **Minneapolis, MN**
Thorson & Switala, LLP .... **Cincinnati, OH**
Dayton, OH
Springfield, OH
Thorson, Thomas J. .... Chicago, IL
Thorson, Timothy K. .... Seattle, WA
Thorsrud Cane & Paulich, Inc., P.S.
Seattle, WA
Thorsrud, Mark N. .... **Seattle, WA**
Thorsrud, Steven L. .... **Seattle, WA**
Thorstad, J. Cheryl .... Cary, NC
Thorstenn, Magnus G. .... New York, NY
Thorstenn, Susan E. .... New York, NY
Thorstenn & Thorstenn .... New York, NY
Thorstenson, Craig R. .... **Chicago, IL**
Thorstenson, Verne .... Rapid City, SD
Thorup, A. Robert .... **Salt Lake City, UT**
Thorup, Gary R. .... **Salt Lake City, UT**
Thorup, Kent D. .... Alexandria, VA
Thorup, Stanley N. .... Anoka, MN
Thorvilson, James O.
Steamboat Springs, CO
Thorwaldsen, Paul R. .... Detroit Lakes, MN
Thorwaldsen, Quam, Beeson, Malmstrom & Sorum .... Callaway, MN
Detroit Lakes, MN
Thowsen, A. Paul .... Ann Arbor, MI
Thoyer, Judith Reinhardt .... **New York, NY**
Thrailkill, Daniel B. .... **Mena, AR**
Thrailkill, Harris & Wood, PLC
Brentwood, TN
Nashville, TN
Thrailkill, Larry T. .... **Brentwood, TN**
Thrailkill, Teresa L. .... **Denver, CO**
Thrall, Charles A. .... Philadelphia, PA
Thrall, Gordon F. .... **Jacksonville, TX**
Thrall, Joseph B., II .... Windsor, CT
Thrall, Larry E. .... Valparaiso, IN
Thrall, Michael W. .... **Des Moines, IA**
Thramann, Kendra A. .... **Chicago, IL**
Thrane, Karen Kunen .... Washington, DC
Thrane, Peter H. .... **St. Paul, MN**
Thrapp, John C. .... Kendallville, IN
Thrapp, Linda Walker .... Indianapolis, IN
Thrapp, Richard J. .... **Indianapolis, IN**
Thrapp & Thrapp .... Kendallville, IN
Thrash, Charles E. .... Cedar City, UT
Thrash, Charles G., Jr. .... Brenham, TX
Thrash, Erin Moran .... Houston, TX
Thrash, Gary D. .... **Biloxi, MS**
Jackson, MS
Thrash, James R. .... Opelika, AL
Thrash, Mark S. .... **Arlington, VA**
Thrash, Melissa L. .... Newton, MS
Thrash, Roy, Jr. .... **Pine Hill, AL**
Thrash, Scott .... Lufkin, TX
Thrash, Thomas P. .... Little Rock, AR
Thrash, Thomas W. .... Atlanta, GA
Thrasher, Andrea E. .... **McLean, VA**
Thrasher, Bobby O., Jr. .... Phoenix, AZ
Thrasher, Bret T. .... **Norcross, GA**
Thrasher, Bruce .... Austin, TX
Thrasher, Chas. O., Jr. .... Sacramento, CA
Thrasher, Dana L. .... **Birmingham, AL**
Thrasher, Dinsmore & Dolan, A Legal Professional Association .... **Chardon, OH**
Thrasher, Doyle, Pelish & Franti, Ltd.
Eau Claire, WI
Rice Lake, WI
Thrasher, Elwin R., Jr. .... Tallahassee, FL
Thrasher, Frederick Elmore, Jr.
Williamsburg, VA
Thrasher Griffith & Voelkel, P.C.
Indianapolis, IN
Thrasher, H. Grady, III .... **Atlanta, GA**
Thrasher, H. Grady, IV .... **Atlanta, GA**
Thrasher, J. Martin .... Colorado Springs, CO
Thrasher, Jack H. .... **Atlanta, GA**
Thrasher, Jack H., P.C. .... **Atlanta, GA**
Thrasher, James D. .... Mansfield, MA
Thrasher, Joe .... **Rice Lake, WI**
Thrasher, John C. .... **Montpelier, VT**
Thrasher, John E. .... **Jacksonville, FL**
Thrasher, John E. .... Indianapolis, IN
Thrasher, Laura S. .... Tallahassee, FL
Thrasher, Michael A. .... **Washington, DC**
Thrasher, Philip C. .... **Indianapolis, IN**
Thrasher, Richard C.
Department Of Veterans Affairs, Board of Veterans Appeals, GV
Thrasher, Richard E. .... **Gettysburg, PA**
Thrasher, Steven W. .... **Richardson, TX**
Thrasher, Tessa M. .... **Birmingham, AL**
Thrasher, Thomas N. .... Santa Ana, CA
Thrasher, Thomas N., Jr. .... Orange, CA
Thrasher, Whitley, Hampton & Morgan, A Professional Corporation .... **Atlanta, GA**
Threadgill & Associates .... **Knoxville, TN**
Threadgill, Burney F. .... Columbus, MS
Threadgill, Dennis K. .... Tallahassee, FL
Threadgill, Edward F., Jr. .... Lakeland, FL
Threadgill, Eugene E. .... McLean, VA
Threadgill, Eugene E., P.C. .... McLean, VA
Threadgill, John O. .... **Knoxville, TN**
Threadgill, Robert H. .... Maitland, FL
Threadgill, Rodney L. .... **Atlanta, GA**
Threadgill, Timothy M. .... **Jackson, MS**
Threadgill, William A. .... New York, NY
Threadgill, William J. .... **Columbus, MS**
Tupelo, MS
Threatt, Adrianne G.
Board of Governors Of The Federal Reserve System, Office of the General Counsel, GV
Threatt, B. Beecher .... Austin, TX
Threatt, Darlene Rice .... Philadelphia, PA
Threatt, Glennon F., Jr. .... Washington, DC
Threatt, Judie .... Independence, MO
Threedy, Debora L. .... Salt Lake City, UT
Threet, Gerald L. .... Seattle, WA
Threet, J. Michael .... **Fayetteville, AR**
Threet, Martin E. .... **Albuquerque, NM**
Threet, Martin E., & Associates
Albuquerque, NM
Threet, Sterling R. .... Mesa, AZ
Threet, Toby Alaska .... Midland, MI
Threlkeld, Ann M. .... **Oklahoma City, OK**
Threlkeld, C. William
Oklahoma City, OK
Threlkeld, Harold P. .... Anderson, SC
Threlkeld, James E. .... Memphis, TN
Threlkeld, John Brent .... **Williamstown, KY**
Threlkeld, Reid A. .... **Vidalia, GA**
Threlkeld, Richard Dutton .... Miami, FL
Threlkeld, Robert C. .... **Atlanta, GA**
Threlkeld, Sheila .... Chicago, IL
Threlkeld & Threlkeld, P.S.C.
Williamstown, KY
Threlkeld, W. Brent .... **Indianapolis, IN**
Threlkeld, William F. .... **Williamstown, KY**
Thren, Christine M. .... Department of Justice, Office of Intelligence Policy and Review, GV
Thren, Kathleen L. .... Philadelphia, PA
Threston, Joseph T., III, Law Offices of
Cherry Hill, NJ
Riverton, NJ
Thriffiley, Paul J., III .... New Orleans, LA
Thriffiley, Peter S. .... New Orleans, LA
Thriffiley, Peter S., A Professional Law Corporation .... New Orleans, LA
Thriffiley, Timothy .... **Belle Chasse, LA**
Thrift, Albert A. .... Half Moon Bay, CA
Thrift, Ashley O. .... **Winston-Salem, NC**
Thrift, Michael W.
Environmental Protection Agency, Office of the General Counsel, GV
Thro, William Eugene .... Richmond, VA
Throckmartin, Chi-yong .... **Belleville, IL**
Throckmorton, A. Robert
Newport Beach, CA
Throckmorton, Beckstrom, Oakes & Tomassian LLP .... **Los Angeles, CA**
Newport Beach, CA
Pasadena, CA
Throckmorton, Bruce L. .... Trenton, NJ
Throckmorton, Charles W., IV
Miami, FL
Throckmorton, John S.
San Francisco, CA
Throckmorton, Karen P. .... Miami, FL
Throckmorton, Katherine M. .... **Wilton, CT**
Throckmorton, Keith A. .... Akron, OH
Throckmorton, Ralph R. .... Idaho Falls, ID
Throckmorton, Rex D. .... **Albuquerque, NM**
Throckmorton, Robert A. .... Cranford, NJ
Throckmorton, Robert B. .... Des Moines, IA
Throckmorton, Robert S.
Newport Beach, CA
Throckmorton, R.T., III .... Franklin, TN
Throckmorton, Susan S.
Albuquerque, NM
Throckmorton, Timothy H.
New Canaan, CT
Throckmorton, William S. .... Long Branch, NJ
Throesch, David .... Pocahontas, AR
Throesch, John C. .... Pocahontas, AR
Throgmorton, Jamie J. .... Alexandria, VA
Throgmorton, Winston C. .... Marion, IL
Thron, Phillip W. .... **Fort Lauderdale, FL**
Throndrud, Mary L. .... Minneapolis, MN
Throne, Barbara Jean .... Miami, FL
Throne, Bruce C. .... **Santa Fe, NM**
Throne, Daphne M. .... Vista, CA
Boulder, CO
Throne, Dawn R. .... **Las Vegas, NV**
Throne, Jason T. .... **Broomfield, CO**
Throne, Mary A. .... **Cheyenne, WY**
Throne, S. Thomas .... **Sheridan, WY**
Throne, Sara R. .... New York, NY
Throneburg, Patricia B. .... Charlotte, NC
Throneburg, Thad A. .... Pineville, NC
Thronson, Charles H. .... **Salt Lake City, UT**
Thronson, Charles H. .... Dayton, WA
Thronson, David B. .... Newark, NJ
Thronson, Jodean A. .... **St. Paul, MN**
Thronson, Mark J. .... **Washington, DC**
Throop, Ellen Watts .... Columbia, MD
Throop, John S., Jr. .... Water Valley, MS
Throop, William M., Jr. .... **New Canaan, CT**
New York, NY
Thrope, B. Michael .... **New York, NY**
Thrope, Bess E. .... Great Neck, NY
Thrope, Gregory A. .... Chicago, IL
Thrope, Irwin M. .... New York, NY
Thrope, Jeffrey C. .... **New York, NY**
Thrope, Jerrold A. .... **Baltimore, MD**
Thrope, Leslie De Montis .... New York, NY
Thropp, Christopher Duvall
Philadelphia, PA
Throssell, Robert R. .... **Helena, MT**
Throwe, James H. .... **East Hartford, CT**
Thrower, Alan W. .... Milledgeville, GA
Thrower, David J. .... Boulder, CO
Thrower, Greg W. .... Houston, TX
Thrower, John M. .... Nashville, TN
Thrower, Larry T. .... Farmington, NM
Thrower, Lawrence A. .... **Atlanta, GA**
Thrower, Lilly E. .... **Houston, TX**
Thrower, Pennie M. .... Auburn, MA
Thrower, Randolph W. .... **Atlanta, GA**
Thrower, Susan E. .... Chicago, IL
Thrower, V. Lynn .... Houston, TX
Thrower, Vern J. .... Houston, TX
Thrower, Vern J., & Associates, P.C.
Houston, TX
Thrower Miles, Laurie .... **Lakeland, FL**
Thrubis, Anthony P. .... **Detroit, MI**
Thrun, Howard A., Jr. .... Mount Prospect, IL
Thrun, Maatsch and Nordberg, P.C.
Lansing, MI
Thrun, Robert M. .... **Lansing, MI**
Thrun, Tallman & Cohn, Ltd.
Mount Prospect, IL
Thrush, Dale A. .... Van Nuys, CA
Thrush, Douglas L. .... Mansfield, OH
Thrush, Jennifer Lea .... Boston, MA
Thrush, John H. .... Melbourne, FL
Thrush, Larry C. .... Wabash, IN
Thrush, Rose .... Portland, OR
Thrush & Sikand .... Van Nuys, CA
Thrush, Thomas C. .... Denver, CO
Thrush, Thomas C., P.C. .... Denver, CO
Thrush, William H., Jr. .... Bowie, MD
Thruston, Armand D. .... Ontario, CA
Thrutchley, Christopher S. .... Tulsa, OK
Thudium, Jacinda A. .... **Springfield, MO**
Thue, Daniel D. .... Edina, MN
Thuemmel, Robert G. .... Portland, OR
Thuemmel & Uhle .... Portland, OR
Thuente, John F. .... **Minneapolis, MN**
Thuermer, Richard .... Mishicot, WI
Reedsville, WI
Thuesen, Donald C. .... Fresno, CA
Thuesen, Victor C. .... Petaluma, CA
Thueson, Erik B. .... **Helena, MT**
Thueson & Lamb .... **Helena, MT**
Thuet, Pugh & Rogosheske, Ltd.
South St. Paul, MN
Thuet, William F. .... Hastings, MN
Thuftedal, Dennis L. .... South Holland, IL
Thuillez, Dale M. .... **Albany, NY**
Thuillez, Ford, Gold & Johnson, L.L.P.
Albany, NY
Thul, Brian W. .... Omaha, NE
Thul, John T. .... **Minneapolis, MN**
Thul, Nicholas R. .... Flemington, NJ
Thulin, Charles H. .... **Seattle, WA**
Thulin, Gregory E. .... Bellingham, WA
Thuline, Dorn D. .... Moline, IL
Thullbery, Alfred C., Jr. .... Bartow, FL
Thullen, Henry M. .... Lake Forest, IL
Thullen, Matthew P. .... Tustin, CA
Thulman, David K. .... Tallahassee, FL
Thulson, John A. .... **Glenwood Springs, CO**
Thulson, Timothy A.
Glenwood Springs, CO
Thum, Robert B. .... **San Francisco, CA**
Thum, Terence J. .... **Kansas City, MO**
Thuma, David T. .... **Albuquerque, NM**
Thuma, William A., Jr. .... Chicago, IL
Thuman, Deborah Lee .... Lockport, NY
Thumann, Henry C. .... **Los Angeles, CA**
Thumann, Richard K. .... **Bellevue, WA**
Thumm, Lewis R. .... Mount Clemens, MI
Thumma, Earl Q., Jr. .... Harrisonburg, VA
Thumma, Samuel A. .... **Phoenix, AZ**
Thums, Raymond F. .... Wausau, WI
Thumser, Peter J. .... **New York, NY**
Thun, Todd J. .... Minneapolis, MN
Thunberg, Kurt W. .... **Albuquerque, NM**
Thunberg, Lee M. .... **Los Angeles, CA**
Rancho Cucamonga, CA
Thunder, James M. .... McLean, VA
Thune, Gary R. .... **Bismarck, ND**
Thune, Howard L. .... Merrick, NY
Thune, Paul C. .... **Des Moines, IA**
Thunen, Ronald V., Jr. .... San Francisco, CA
Thunhorst, David G. .... **Atlanta, GA**
Thunhorst, Thomas E. .... Kenyon, MN
Thunhorst, Wade A. .... Dallas, TX
Thuotte, Robert W. .... **Boston, MA**
Thur, Calvin C. .... Scottsdale, AZ
Thur & O'Sullivan .... Scottsdale, AZ
Thurau, John P. .... **San Jose, CA**
Thurau, John P., A Professional Corporation
San Jose, CA
Thurau, Robert H., II .... Sarasota, FL
Thurau, Talitha .... Gray, ME
Thurbee, Jessica E. .... Charlotte, NC
Thurber Cappell, L.L.C. .... **Hackensack, NJ**
Thurber, Claudia H. .... Department of Labor, Office of the Solicitor, GV
Thurber, Cooper C. .... **Mobile, AL**
Thurber, Dan .... New York, NY
Thurber, David K. .... Santa Barbara, CA
Thurber, Deirdre L. .... Falmouth, MA
Thurber, James Philip .... Falls Church, VA
Thurber, John A., (P.C.) .... **Troy, MI**
Thurber, John J. .... Tampa, FL
Thurber, John P. .... Trenton, NJ
Thurber, John R. .... Sacramento, CA
Thurber, Kent B. .... **Portland, OR**
Thurber, Mark .... **Boston, MA**
Thurber, Mark J. .... **Houston, TX**
Thurber, Marshall .... **La Jolla, CA**
Thurber, Mary F. .... **Hackensack, NJ**
Thurber, Michelle V. .... **Detroit, MI**
Thurber, Peter P. .... **Detroit, MI**
Thurber, Stephen F. .... **Washington, DC**
Thurbon, Robert E., Jr. .... Sacramento, CA
Thurbon, Terry L. .... **Juneau, AK**
Thurer, Carol Ellen .... **New York, NY**
Thurer, Warren N. .... Mineola, NY
Thurin, Martine M. .... New York, NY
Thuring, Joseph M. .... Jersey City, NJ
Thuring, Richard M. .... New Providence, NJ
Thurler, Daniel W. .... Boston, MA
Thurlow, Gary .... Wasilla, AK
Thurlow, Katharine .... **Baltimore, MD**
Thurlow, Louise Magnarelli .... Syracuse, NY
Thurlow & Nolan, P.A. .... **Baltimore, MD**
Thurlow, Peter G. .... **New York, NY**
Thurlow, Rachel .... Boston, MA
Thurlow, Robert S., Sr.
New Smyrna Beach, FL
Thurlow & Smith, P.A. .... Stuart, FL
Thurlow, Thomas F. .... Palo Alto, CA
Thurlow, Thomas H. .... Palm City, FL
Thurlow, Thomas H., III .... Stuart, FL
Thurlow, Thomas H., Jr. .... Stuart, FL
Thurlow, Thomas N. .... Houston, TX
Thurm & Heller, LLP .... **New York, NY**
Thurm, Mary-Ellen
National Labor Relations Board, Office of Board Members, GV
Thurm, Milton .... **New York, NY**
Thurm, Wendy J. .... **San Francisco, CA**
Thurman, Adam J. .... **Cleveland, OH**
Thurman & Andres, P.C. .... Dallas, TX
Thurman, Andrew E. .... Pittsburgh, PA
Thurman, Brett L. .... Dayton, OH
Thurman, Britt .... Abilene, TX
Thurman, Carl W., III .... **Wilmington, NC**
Thurman, Elizabeth J. .... Monroe, LA
Thurman, Frederick M., Jr.
Charlotte, NC
Thurman, Gregory A. .... **Fayetteville, AR**
Thurman, Howard, Weber, Senkel & Norrick, L.L.C. .... **Hillsboro, MO**
St. Louis, MO
Thurman, James Amery .... Virginia Beach, VA
Thurman, James U. .... Dallas, TX
Thurman, Jan R. .... Dallas, TX
Thurman, John B. .... Little Rock, AR
Thurman, John L. .... **Princeton, NJ**
Thurman, John P. .... Dunnellon, FL
Thurman, K Keith .... Virginia Beach, VA
Thurman, Kay Ellen .... St. Louis, MO
Thurman, Kelly J. .... **Dallas, TX**
Thurman, Leon .... Anson, TX
Thurman, M. B., Jr. .... Austin, TX
Thurman, Michael A. .... Los Angeles, CA
Thurman, Michael B. .... San Antonio, TX
Thurman, Milton, Jr. .... Cincinnati, OH
Thurman, Patrick S. .... Jackson, MI
Thurman, Phillips & Schaub, A Professional Corporation .... San Antonio, TX
Thurman, Ronald, & Associates
Cookeville, TN
Thurman, Rosemarie .... Hines, IL
Thurman, Ruth Fleet .... St. Petersburg, FL
Thurman, Samuel D. .... Salt Lake City, UT
Thurman, Susan Granberry
Washington, DC
Thurman, Thomas B. .... Nashville, TN
Thurman, Thomas D. .... Pittsburgh, PA
Thurman & Thurman .... Virginia Beach, VA
Thurman, Virgil A. .... Geneseo, IL
Thurman, W. David .... Charlotte, NC
Thurman, White, McCann & Anderson
Lexington, KY
Thurman, William A. .... Prairie Grove, AR
Thurman, William P., Jr. .... **Lexington, KY**
Thurman, William Taft
Salt Lake City, UT
Thurman, William Thomas
Salt Lake City, UT
Thurmer, Stephen W. .... St. Louis, MO
Thurmer, Susan D. .... **St. Paul, MN**
Thurmon, Mark A. .... **Austin, TX**
Thurmon, Monique B. .... Ruston, LA
Thurmond, A. Jacy, Jr.
Equal Employment Opportunity Commission, Office of Legal Counsel, GV
Thurmond, Candace Nicole .... **Atlanta, GA**
Thurmond, Charles J. .... Gainesville, GA
Thurmond, Cornelius B., Jr. .... Augusta, GA
Thurmond, Cornelius B., Jr., P.C.
Augusta, GA
Thurmond, George M. .... Del Rio, TX
Thurmond, Gerald P. .... Houston, TX
Thurmond, James D. .... Smyrna, GA
Thurmond, Janice M. .... Athens, GA
Thurmond, Karl S. .... **Los Angeles, CA**
Thurmond, Marikaye C. .... **Brownsville, TN**
Memphis, TN
Thurmond, Monica K. .... **New York, NY**
Thurmond, Robert H., III .... Houston, TX
Thurmond, Robert N., Jr. .... Omaha, NE
Thurmond, Thomas R. .... Vacaville, CA
Thurmond, W. Michael .... St. Augustine, FL
Thurmond, Walter B. .... Houston, TX

Thurmond, William A. ....El Paso, TX
Thurmond, Wm. E., Jr. ....Lexington, MS
Thurn, Clark ....St. Paul, MN
Thurn, Richard L. ....Sacramento, CA
Thurnau, Jeffrey A. ....Longmont, CO
Thuronyi, Victor ....Buffalo, NY
Thurow, Cutler & Batteen ....Aberdeen, SD
Thurow, Duane A. ....Aberdeen, SD
Thurow, Walter D., Law Offices of
Madison, WI
Thurrell, Roger B. ....Santa Rosa, CA
Thurrott, Hope E. ....San Antonio, TX
Thursby, Karen M. ....Boston, MA
Thursby, Nancy Magnis ....Coppell, TX
Thursby, W. Gerald ....Northbrook, IL
Thurschwell, Adam ....New York, NY
Thurschwell, Charlotte ....Wynnewood, PA
Thursland, William M. ....Houston, TX
Thurston, Adam J. ....Santa Monica, CA
Thurston, Bernays Kennedy ....Red Lion, PA
Thurston, Bradley H. ....Holmes Beach, FL
Thurston, Cathy ....Washington, DC
Thurston, Curtis A., Jr. ....Atlanta, GA
Thurston, Cynthia K. ....Minneapolis, MN
Rice Lake, WI
Thurston, Damon M. ....Oakland, CA
Thurston, David W. ....St. Paul, MN
Thurston, Earle E. ....Auburn, NY
Thurston, F. Timothy ....Columbus, OH
Thurston, Gilbert M., Jr. ....Saginaw, MI
Thurston, Gregg A. ....Phoenix, AZ
Thurston, Gregg A., P.C. ....Phoenix, AZ
Thurston, Gregory W. ....Minneapolis, MN
Thurston, Hal ....Bellingham, WA
Thurston, Heather L. ....Cincinnati, OH
Thurston, James K. ....Chicago, IL
Thurston, James P. ....San Francisco, CA
Thurston, Janet Hall ....Jacksonville, FL
Thurston, Janice L. ....Sacramento, CA
Thurston, John R. ....Marshfield, MA
Thurston Law Offices ....Atlanta, GA
Thurston, M. Alice ....Department of Justice, Environment and Natural Resources Division, GV
Thurston, Marion F., Jr. ....Columbia, MO
Thurston, Mark O. ....Tulsa, OK
Thurston, Meredith Fortune ....Clovis, CA
Thurston, Michael E. ....Department of State, GV
Thurston, Morgan Robert ....Syracuse, NY
Thurston, Morris A. ....Costa Mesa, CA
Thurston, Pamela Hackes ....Columbus, OH
Thurston, Richard L. ....Dallas, TX
Thurston, Robert C. ....Chicago, IL
Thurston, Robert S. ....Providence, RI
Thurston, Rosemarie A. ....Atlanta, GA
Thurston, Royal C., III ....East Orleans, MA
Thurston, Sally A. ....New York, NY
Thurston, Stanley P. ....Merced, CA
Thurston, Susan M. ....Providence, RI
Thurston, Thomas L. ....Overland Park, KS
Thurston, Wallace E. ....Cambridge, MA
Thurston, William L. ....Richmond, VA
Thurswell, Chayet & Weiner, P.C.
Southfield, MI
Thurswell, Gerald E. ....Southfield, MI
Thurtle, Timothy P. ....Annapolis, MD
Thuston, Linus Augustus ....Chanute, KS
Thuston, W. Lee ....Birmingham, AL
Thut, C. Jeffrey ....Libertyville, IL
Thute, Clinton W. ....Phoenix, AZ
Thvedt, Joel A. ....Los Angeles, CA
Thwaites, Ellen M. ....Santa Rosa, CA
Thwaites, Michael S. ....Greenville, SC
Thwaites, Richard S., Jr. ....Anchorage, AK
Thweatt, Albert W., II ....Richmond, VA
Thweatt, C. Harold ....Oklahoma City, OK
Thweatt, John R. ....Elmira, NY
Thwing, James B. ....Lake Oswego, OR
Thwing, Randall E. ....Eugene, OR
Thwing, Sidney E. ....Eugene, OR
Thwing & Thwing ....Eugene, OR
Thyagarajan, Lara C. ....Boston, MA
Thyberg, Gregory A. ....Glendale, CA
Thyberg, Regina Wallace ....Bowie, MD
Thyberg, Todd E. ....Walnut Creek, CA
Thyden, Freda Lippert
Federal Communications Commission, Wireless Telecommunications Bureau, GV
Thyden, Gross & Callahan
Chevy Chase, MD
Thyden, John W. ....Chevy Chase, MD
Thye, Gary A. ....Portland, OR
Thyer, Christopher R. ....Jonesboro, AR
Thyer, Cindy Grace ....Jonesboro, AR
Thyer, James W. ....Dayton, OH
Thygerson, John P. ....Norwalk, CT
Thygesen, Norman D. ....Oklahoma City, OK
Thymian, Marcus ....Chicago, IL
Thymius, William G. ....New York, NY
Thyne, Kenneth S. ....Towaco, NJ
Thyne, Rebecca J. ....Pasadena, CA
Thynne, Michael I. ....Denver, CO
Thyret, Kathryn M. ....Mill Valley, CA
Thys, Natacha ....Silver Spring, MD
Tiajoloff, Andrew L. ....New York, NY
Tian, Hui ....Phoenix, AZ
Tiangco, Kenneth T. ....Staten Island, NY
Tiano, Joseph R., Jr. ....Tysons Corner, VA
Tiano, Linda V. ....Schenectady, NY
Tiano, Sam A. ....Huntington, WV
Tiano, William M. ....Charleston, WV
Tiarks, Stephen R. ....Westborough, MA
Tibaldeo, Victor Louis, Jr.
Miami Shores, FL
Tibaldi, Charles K. ....Providence, RI
Tibaldi, Elmo J. ....Farmington Hills, MI
Tibaldi, Thomas J. ....Bronx, NY

Tiballi, Frederick P. ....Burlington, VT
Tiballi, Frederick P., & Associates, P.A.
Burlington, VT
Tiballi, Jason R ....Burlington, VT
Tibbals, James Michael ....Dallas, TX
Tibbals, Lara J. ....Tampa, FL
Tibbals, Robert L., Jr. ....Englewood, CO
Tibbals, Tracy L. ....Ontario, CA
Tibbals, Wesley D. ....Tampa, FL
Tibberts, Mark S. ....Columbus, OH
Tibbets, Gaye B. ....Wichita, KS
Tibbets, Michael R. ....Houston, TX
Tibbetts, Alfred P. ....Darien, CT
Tibbetts, Carl A.
Securities and Exchange Commission, Division of Enforcement, GV
Tibbetts, David A., Law Offices of
Annapolis, MD
Tibbetts, Deborah J. ....San Diego, CA
Tibbetts, Edward R. ....Mobile, AL
Tibbetts, Georgene K. ....Orange, CA
Tibbetts, Gregory C. ....Nashville, TN
Tibbetts, Jack H. ....Oak Park, IL
Tibbetts, Jean M. ....Boston, MA
Tibbetts & Keating ....Darien, CT
Tibbetts, Kirk E., Jr. ....Albany, OR
Tibbetts, Margery Mebane ....Janesville, WI
Tibbetts, Mary Elizabeth ....Brooklyn, NY
Tibbetts, Merle F. ....South Yarmouth, MA
Tibbetts, Robert E. ....Calais, ME
Tibbetts, Roger D. ....Lakewood, OH
Tibbetts, Stephanie P. ....West Hartford, CT
Tibbits, Gwena Kay ....Alexandria, VA
Tibbits, Gwena Kay, Law Offices of
Alexandria, VA
Tibbits, Norman A.
Grosse Pointe Farms, MI
Tibbitts, J. Brett ....Westlake Village, CA
Tibbitts, Kent F. ....Laguna Hills, CA
Tibbitts, Lewis W. ....Fair Oaks, CA
Tibbitts, Pamela Marie ....Larkspur, CA
Tibbitts, Ryan E. ....Salt Lake City, UT
Tibble, Douglas C. ....Oakbrook Terrace, IL
Tibble, Gary E. ....Kalamazoo, MI
Tibbott, David W. ....Phillipsburg, NJ
Tibbs, Don V. ....Manti, UT
Tibbs, Eugene E., Jr. ....Memphis, TN
Tibbs, Michael J. ....Peoria, IL
Tibbs, Philippa V. ....Atlanta, GA
Tibbs, Richard B. ....Honolulu, HI
Tibbs, Thurlow E. ....Washington, DC
Tibbs-Nnawulezi, Karen L. ....Omaha, NE
Tiberend, Diane E. ....Orange, CA
Tiberi, Phillip V. ....Las Vegas, NV
Tiberi, Todd J. ....New York, NY
Tiberii, David A. ....Dudley, MA
Tiberio, Michael A. ....Youngstown, OH
Tibey, Phillip E. ....Tulsa, OK
Tibiletti, Thomas Peter ....Longview, TX
Tiboni, Joseph B. ....New Providence, NJ
Tibui, Joseph L.T., Law Office of
Arlington, VA
Tiburzi, D. James ....Clayton, MO
Tiburzi, Paul A. ....Baltimore, MD
Tiburzi, Robert V., Jr. ....Scarsdale, NY
Tiburzio, Terese M. ....Cleveland, OH
Tice, Beatrice A. ....Corona Del Mar, CA
Tice, Christopher Alan ....Fort Myers, FL
Tice, Douglas O., Jr. ....Richmond, VA
Tice, Elizabeth D. ....Spring Lake Heights, NJ
Tice, Homer J. ....Beardstown, IL
Petersburg, IL
Virginia, IL
Tice, Janice C. ....Ann Arbor, MI
Tice, Jennifer J. ....Santa Barbara, CA
Tice, Jim Travis ....Anaheim, CA
Tice, John E. ....Portland, OR
Tice, Kristie M. ....Houston, TX
Tice, Laurie D. ....Austin, TX
Tice, Merton B., Jr. ....Rapid City, SD
Tice, Michael C. ....Fort Myers, FL
Tice, Richard L. ....Flemington, NJ
Tice, Richard V. B. ....Glenmont, NY
Tice, Robert C. ....Detroit, MI
Farmington Hills, MI
Tice, Robert W. ....St. Paul, MN
Tice, Ronald J. ....Toledo, OH
Tice, Royena M. ....Kalamazoo, MI
Tice, Tanya R. ....La Jolla, CA
Tice, Wallace M. ....San Francisco, CA
Ticen, Thomas E. ....Richfield, MN
Ticen, Thomas E., Ltd., Law Office
Richfield, MN
Ticer, Bernard H. ....New Orleans, LA
Ticer, Cecily Shull ....Dallas, TX
Ticer, Mark A., Law Office of ....Dallas, TX
Ticer, Wilmer R. ....Oxon Hill, MD
Tice-Wallner, Wendy L.
San Francisco, CA
Tichane, David ....Cupertino, CA
Tichanski, David M. ....Hampton, VA
Tichell, Ian G. ....Buffalo, NY
Tichenor, Amy D. ....Los Angeles, CA
Tichenor, Bonnie Sue ....Summersville, WV
Tichenor, James G. ....Des Moines, IA
Tichenor, James L. ....Philadelphia, PA
Tichenor, Kathleen R. ....San Francisco, CA
Tichenor, Keith E. ....Portland, OR
Tichenor, Michael V. ....Memphis, TN
Tichenor, M. T. ....Harlingen, TX
Tichenor, Patricia E.
Department of Agriculture, Office of the General Counsel, GV
Tichenor, Roberta A. ....Portland, OR
Tichenor, Sandra Pelle ....Sonoma, CA
Tichenor, Terri L ....Spelter, WV
Tichenor, W. B. ....Jefferson City, MO
Tichinin, Bruce ....Morgan Hill, CA

Tichnor, Michael L. ....Wayland, MA
Tichon, Michael John ....Los Angeles, CA
Tichy, George J., II ....San Francisco, CA
Tichy, Joyce ....New York, NY
Tichy, Karen ....Hartford, CT
Tick, Alan L. ....Treasury Department, Departmental Offices, GV
Tick, Daniel Jay ....Roslyn, NY
Tick, Jerome H. ....New York, NY
Tick, Stephen ....Englewood, CO
Tick, William ....Boston, MA
Ticker, Neil ....Los Angeles, CA
Tickin, Peter ....Boca Raton, FL
Tickle, Donald R. ....San Francisco, CA
Tickle, Kelly L. ....Minneapolis, MN
Tickner, Jack L. ....Dallas, TX
Tickner, Kere K. ....Orange, CA
Ticknor, Charles E., III ....Columbus, OH
Ticknor, George ....Boston, MA
Ticknor, Patrice M. ....Detroit, MI
Ticknor, Suzanne ....Phoenix, AZ
Ticktin, Baron, Koepper & Co., L.P.A.
Cleveland, OH
Ticktin, Daniel S. ....Cleveland, OH
Ticktin, Harold ....Cleveland, OH
Ticktin, Peter, Law Offices of, P.A.
Boca Raton, FL
Ticktin, Richard M. ....New York, NY
Ticktin, Robert E. ....New York, NY
Ticktin, Stanley P. ....Safety Harbor, FL
Tico, Teresa Simpson ....Kilauea, HI
Ticotin, Mark S. ....New York, NY
Ticzon, Cristeta R. ....San Francisco, CA
Tidalgo, Michelle ....San Jose, CA
Tiday, Ronald L. ....Fallbrook, CA
Tidball, Eugene C. ....Boulder, CO
Tidball, Jane A. ....Boulder, CO
Tidball, Volney J. ....San Jose, CA
Tidd, Brian L. ....Mesa, AZ
Tidd, Jonathan G. ....West Simsbury, CT
Tidd, Kat ....Dallas, TX
Tidd, Kat, P.C., Law & Legal Mgt. Offices of
Austin, TX
Dallas, TX
Tiddy, Tracy Welsh ....Greenville, SC
Tideman, Curtis L. ....Overland Park, KS
Tideman, David R. ....Wayne, NJ
Tider, David E. ....Union City, NJ
Tiderington, James ....Saginaw, MI
Tiderington, Robert H. ....Saginaw, MI
Tiderington, Thomas E.S. ....Kalamazoo, MI
Tidey, George F. ....Richmond, VA
Tidgewell, Todd M. ....Washington, DC
Tidgren, Kristine A. ....Kansas City, MO
Tidholm, Mary Johnson
Oklahoma City, OK
Tidholm, W. David ....Houston, TX
Tidman, E. Charles, III ....Worcester, MA
Tidman, Mark H. ....Washington, DC
Tidmarsh, Jay ....Notre Dame, IN
Tidmore, Candace L. ....Kingwood, TX
Tidmore, David M. ....Birmingham, AL
Tidmore, Janet B. ....Atlanta, GA
Tidmore, Johnny L. ....Nashville, TN
Tidmore, Larry M. ....Bradenton, FL
Tidmore, Phillip G.
Department of the Air Force, Office of the Judge Advocate General, GV
Tidmore, Steve M. ....Phoenix, AZ
Tidrick, Don L. ....Des Moines, IA
Tidus, Jeffrey A. ....Los Angeles, CA
Tidus, Michael L. ....Irvine, CA
Tidwall, Karen ....Milwaukee, WI
Tidwell, Al ....Hamilton, AL
Tidwell, Albert L. ....St. James City, FL
Tidwell, Bruce B. ....Little Rock, AR
Tidwell, Charles E. ....Decatur, GA
Tidwell, Clark H. ....Nashville, TN
Tidwell, G. Ernest ....Atlanta, GA
Tidwell, Gary L. ....Charleston, SC
Tidwell, Geo. H. ....North Fort Myers, FL
Tidwell, Greer C., Jr. ....Nashville, TN
Tidwell, Gwen R. ....Chattanooga, TN
Tidwell, J. Coleman ....Macon, GA
Tidwell, Jack Q. ....Odessa, TX
Tidwell, James C. ....Sherman, TX
Tidwell, John L. ....Texarkana, TX
Tidwell, Kathryn J. ....Lewisville, TX
Tidwell, Kelly B. ....Texarkana, TX
Tidwell, Mark A. ....Houston, TX
Tidwell, Michael Donovan ....Pensacola, FL
Tidwell, Michael T.
United States Postal Service, Law Department, GV
Tidwell, Moody R., III
United States Court of Federal Claims, GV
Tidwell, Ponce D., Jr. ....Indianapolis, IN
Tidwell, R. Wesley ....Paris, TX
Tidwell, Robin Reid ....Columbia, SC
Tidwell, Samuel M. ....Dallas, TX
Tidwell, Scott M. ....Odessa, TX
Tidwell, Shawn A. ....Memphis, TN
Tidwell Swaim, & Associates, P.C., The Law Firm of ....Dallas, TX
Tidwell, Thomas G. ....Atlanta, GA
Tidwell, Tiffany ....Austin, TX
Tidwell, W. Gerald, Jr. ....Chattanooga, TN
Tidwell, W. Gerald, Jr., P.C.
Chattanooga, TN
Tidwell, William C., III ....Mobile, AL
Tidwell, William DeVane ....Charlotte, NC
Tidwell, William R. ....Las Vegas, NV
Tiebauer, Eric A. ....Waynesboro, MS
Tiede, Charles R. ....North Manchester, IN
Wabash, IN
Tiede, Daniel P. ....Buffalo, NY
Tiede, David M. ....San Diego, CA
Tiede, John W. ....Joplin, MO

Tiede, Metz & Downs, P.C.
North Manchester, IN
Wabash, IN
Tiede, Peter B. ....St. Paul, MN
Tiede, Stuart L. ....Sioux Falls, SD
Tiedeken, Julie Nye ....Cheyenne, WY
Tiedeken Law Offices ....Cheyenne, WY
Tiedeken, Robert W. ....Cheyenne, WY
Tiedeman, Edward D. ....Chicago, IL
Tiedeman, Forrest G. ....Boston, MA
Tiedeman, John P., Jr. ....Omaha, NE
Tiedeman, Lynch, Smart & Kampfe
Omaha, NE
Tiedemann, Charles Welch
Washington, DC
Tiedemann, Donald C. ....Westfield, NY
Tiedemann, Edward J. ....Sacramento, CA
Tiedemann, Francis J. ....Jersey City, NJ
Tiedemann, John ....West Palm Beach, FL
Tiedemann, John J., III ....Lafayette, LA
Tiedemann, Karen M. ....San Francisco, CA
Tiedemann, Paula Savren ....Bethesda, MD
Tiedemann, Robert E., III ....New York, NY
Tiedemann, Robert J. ....Jersey City, NJ
Tieder, John B., Jr. ....Washington, DC
McLean, VA
Tiedge, John H. ....Palo Alto, CA
Tiedman, Tracey Nelson ....Denver, CO
Tiedrich, Lee J. ....San Francisco, CA
Washington, DC
Tiedt, Dennis C. ....Wausau, WI
Tiedt, Glenn F. ....Denver, CO
Tiedt, John E. ....San Bernardino, CA
Tiedt, Thao A. ....Seattle, WA
Tiefenbrun, Susan W. ....Mamaroneck, NY
Tiefenthaler, Gina M. ....Minneapolis, MN
Tiefenthaler, Gina Marie ....Minneapolis, MN
Tiefenthaler, Robert D. ....Sioux City, IA
Tiefer, Charles ....Washington, DC
Tiegel, Howard C. ....New York, NY
Tiegel, Lisa R. ....St. Paul, MN
Tieger & Bumiller, Law Offices of
Santa Ana, CA
Tieger, Harold A. ....Cincinnati, OH
Tieger, Marcy ....Santa Ana, CA
Tiegerman, Philip ....Houston, TX
Tieh, Judy W. ....New York, NY
Tiehen, Thomas M. ....Omaha, NE
Tielborg, J. Patrick, (P.C.) ....Dallas, TX
Tielle, Benjamin P., Jr. ....Kingston, PA
Tieman, Lee C. ....St. Joseph, MO
Tieman, Lyman C. ....Joliet, IL
Tieman, Shane A. ....Portsmouth, OH
Tiemann, A. Lynn ....Austin, TX
Tiemann, Carrie Parker ....Pflugerville, TX
Tiemann, M. Joseph ....Gretna, LA
Tiemann, Richard D., Jr. ....Gretna, LA
Tiemann, Robert M. ....Austin, TX
Tiemann, Shahady & Kenney, P.C.
Austin, TX
Pflugerville, TX
Tiemann, Thomas E. ....Austin, TX
Tiemeier, C. Gregory ....Denver, CO
Tiemessen, John J. ....Fairbanks, AK
Tiemeyer, Donald C. ....St. Charles, MO
Tiemeyer, Richard L. ....Jefferson City, MO
Tiemstra, James A. ....Walnut Creek, CA
Tien, Jessica C. ....Tampa, FL
Tien, Wendy S. ....San Francisco, CA
St. Paul, MN
Tiencken, John H., Jr. ....Moncks Corner, SC
Tieng, Thomas V. ....Detroit, MI
Tienken, James C. ....Louisville, CO
Tienken, James C., P.C. ....Boulder, CO
Denver, CO
Louisville, CO
Tienson, Thane W. ....Portland, OR
Tienstra, Linda M. ....Fort Myers, FL
Tier, Michael A. ....Bayville, NJ
Tier, Ronald G., Law Offices of
Gladwin, MI
Tierce, Michael G. ....Philadelphia, PA
Tierman, I. Victor ....Westlake Village, CA
Tierman, Jeffrey H. ....San Diego, CA
Tiernan, Robert D. ....New York, NY
Tiernan, Charles E., III ....New Haven, CT
Tiernan, Frank E. ....Lake Success, NY
Tiernan, Frank E. ....Staten Island, NY
Tiernan & Gmeiner ....Littleton, MA
Tiernan, Janelle ....Cambridge, MA
Tiernan, John C. ....Cleveland, OH
Tiernan, John H. ....Colusa, CA
Tiernan, Lee Kennedy ....New Haven, CT
Tiernan, Marion G. ....Flossmoor, IL
Tiernan, Mark H. ....Rochester, NY
Tiernan, Mark S. ....Seattle, WA
Tiernan, Paul J. ....Littleton, MA
Tiernan, Peter E. ....San Jose, CA
Tiernan, Raymond A. ....Washington, DC
Tiernan, Robert O. ....Providence, RI
Tiernan, Robert P. ....Walnut Creek, CA
Tiernan, Robert R. ....Lake Oswego, OR
Tiernan, Shawn G. ....New Haven, CT
Tiernan, William F., Jr. ....New Haven, CT
Tiernan, William H. ....San Diego, CA
Tiernan, William J. ....Oakland, NJ
Tiernan, William J. ....Gig Harbor, WA
Tierney, Abigail A. ....Harrisburg, PA
Tierney, Albert G., III ....Boston, MA
Tierney, Albert G., Jr. ....Norwell, MA
Tierney, Betty L. ....St. Louis, MO
Tierney, Brian P. ....Philadelphia, PA
Tierney, Carl J. ....Department of Justice, Tax Division, GV
Tierney, Charles G. ....New York, NY
Tierney, Claire C. ....Babylon, NY
Tierney, Daniel E. ....New York, NY

Tierney, David C. ... Phoenix, AZ
Scottsdale, AZ
Tierney, Erin J. ... Taunton, MA
Tierney, Eugene F. ... Columbus, OH
Tierney, Gregory J. ... Passaic, NJ
Tierney & Haughwout
West Palm Beach, FL
Tierney, J. Brian ... Butte, MT
Tierney, J. Donald ... Green Village, NJ
Tierney, J. Stephen, III ... Fort Pierce, FL
Tierney, James E. ... Lisbon Falls, ME
Tierney, James E. ... Toledo, OH
Tierney, James F. ... Victorville, CA
Tierney, James F., III ... Redlands, CA
Tierney, James F., IV ... Philadelphia, PA
Scranton, PA
Tierney, James J. ... Department of Justice,
Antitrust Division, GV
Tierney, James J., (P.C.) ... Chicago, IL
Tierney, James L., II ... Beachwood, OH
Tierney, James M. ... Albany, NY
Tierney, James P. ... Malibu, CA
Tierney, James P. ... Kansas City, MO
Tierney, James P., P.C., The Law Offices of
Malibu, CA
Tierney, Jan M.
Environmental Protection Agency,
Office of the General Counsel, GV
Tierney, Jennifer C. ... Brookfield, WI
Tierney, John A. ... Brighton, MA
Tierney, John D. ... Minneapolis, MN
Tierney, John F. ... Salem, MA
Tierney, John F. ... Salem, MA
Tierney, John F., III
West Palm Beach, FL
Tierney, John J. ... Port Jefferson Station, NY
Tierney, John J., Jr. ... Boston, MA
Tierney, John L. ... Washington, DC
Tierney, John N. ... Los Angeles, CA
Tierney, John T., III ... Pittsburgh, PA
Tierney, Joseph E., III ... Milwaukee, WI
Tierney, Joseph E., IV ... Milwaukee, WI
Tierney, Joseph E., Jr. ... Milwaukee, WI
Tierney, Joseph J., Jr. ... Charleston, SC
Tierney, Joseph M. ... Boston, MA
Tierney, Joseph W., Jr. ... Acton, MA
Tierney, June E. ... White River Junction, VT
Tierney, Justin N., Jr. ... Sacramento, CA
Tierney, Keith J. ... Las Vegas, NV
Tierney, Kent P. ... Alamo, CA
Tierney, Kevin ... Stamford, CT
Tierney, Kevin C. ... Princeton, NJ
Philadelphia, PA
Tierney, Kevin H. ... San Francisco, CA
Tierney, Kevin J. ... Portland, ME
Tierney, Kevin M. ... Boston, MA
Tierney Law Office ... New Bedford, MA
Tierney Law Offices ... Princeton, NJ
Philadelphia, PA
Tierney, Lawrence J. ... Omaha, NE
Tierney, Letitia E. ... Charleston, WV
Tierney, Margery A.
Department of Commerce,
Patent and Trademark Office, GV
Tierney, Mark R. ... Cincinnati, OH
Tierney, Martha M. ... Denver, CO
Tierney, Martin J., Jr. ... San Francisco, CA
Tierney, Mary Geraldine Duffy
Riverhead, NY
Tierney, Matthew W. ... Baton Rouge, LA
Tierney, Michael C. ... San Diego, CA
Tierney, Michael E.
Port Jefferson Station, NY
Tierney, Michael J. ... Philadelphia, PA
Tierney, Michael P. ... Washington, DC
Tierney, Michael P. ... St. Paul, MN
Tierney, Michael T. ... Duluth, MN
Tierney, O. Craig, Jr. ... Raleigh, NC
Tierney, Patrick T. ... St. Paul, MN
Tierney, Paul Richard, Jr. ... Quincy, MA
Tierney, Peter ... Dallas, TX
Tierney, Peter T. ... New York, NY
Tierney, Philip ... McLean, VA
Tierney, Philip J. ... Rockville, MD
Tierney, Philip T. ... Boston, MA
Tierney, Raymond M., Jr.
Florham Park, NJ
Tierney, Renee ... San Francisco, CA
Tierney, Robert B. ... Southfield, MI
Tierney, Robert B. ... New York, NY
Tierney, Robert E. ... Hingham, MA
Tierney, Robert E. ... Fort Edward, NY
Tierney, Scott P. ... Providence, RI
Tierney, Sheila Marie ... New Bedford, MA
Tierney, Theodore J. ... Chicago, IL
Tierney, Thomas ... Norwalk, CT
Tierney, Thomas W. ... San Diego, CA
Tierney & Tierney
Port Jefferson Station, NY
Tierney, Timothy A. ... Madison, WI
Tierney, Timothy M. ... St. Louis, MO
Tierney, Tracy M. ... San Francisco, CA
Tierney, W. Stephen ... Rochester, NY
Tierney, Walden & Watson, A Professional Corporation ... San Francisco, CA
Tierney, William J. ... West New York, NJ
Tierney, William J. ... White Plains, NY
Tierney, William J. ... Elkins Park, PA
Tierney, Zullo, Flaherty & Murphy, P.C.
Greenwich, CT
Norwalk, CT
Stamford, CT
Tierney-Sosnowski, Moira E.
New Bedford, MA
Tierno, Jean Raymond ... Swarthmore, PA
Tiers, David P. ... Tucson, AZ
Tiersky, Martin ... Chicago, IL
Tiersky, Terri S. ... Chicago, IL

Tiesen, Frank G. ... Sacramento, CA
Tiesenga, Mary Britt A. ... Chicago, IL
Tie-Shue, Gary L. ... Miami, FL
Tiesi, Angelo F. ... Chicago, IL
Tieso, Robert J. ... Plantation, FL
Tiessen, Stefan-M. ... Atlanta, GA
Tieszen Law Office, LLP ... Pierre, SD
Tieszen, Richard P. ... Pierre, SD
Tiet, Kien C. ... Pasadena, CA
Tietig, Edward C. ... Palm Bay, FL
Tietig, Edward C., P.A. ... Palm Bay, FL
Tietig, Lisa M. Kuhlman ... Merritt Island, FL
Tietig, Mark E. ... Merritt Island, FL
Tietig & Tietig ... Merritt Island, FL
Tietje, Jacob R. ... New York, NY
Tietjen, Dalton W. ... Omaha, NE
Tietjen, Herman H. ... Rhinebeck, NY
Tietjen, Randall ... Minneapolis, MN
Tietjen, Riefe ... Guilford, CT
Tietjen, Simon & Boyle ... Omaha, NE
Tietjen, Timothy G. ... San Francisco, CA
Tietjen, William ... New York, NY
Tietz, Christopher M. ... Decatur, IL
Tietz, Daniel W. ... Boston, MA
Tietz, Gerald F. ... Philadelphia, PA
Tietz, Gilbert E. ... Rockville, MD
Tietz & Goldberg, P.C. ... Rockville, MD
Tietz, Janet L. ... Port Washington, NY
Tietz, Karen E. ... Chicago, IL
Tietz, Michael F. ... New York, NY
Tietz, Paul H. ... Minneapolis, MN
Tietz & Richardson ... Decatur, IL
Shelbyville, IL
Tietze, Connie F. ... San Jose, CA
Tietze, Fred B. ... Hoffman Estates, IL
Tietze, Timothy ... Chester Springs, PA
Tietzer, Allen ... Owings Mills, MD
Tievsky, Seth H. ... Washington, DC
Tiews, Kenneth E. ... Grand Rapids, MI
Tiffany, Aleen R. ... Woodstock, IL
Tiffany, Beverly A. ... Los Angeles, CA
Tiffany & Bosco, P.A. ... Phoenix, AZ
Tiffany, Charles B. ... Kissimmee, FL
Orlando, FL
Tiffany, David V. ... Iowa City, IA
Tiffany, DeForrest N. ... Fort Worth, TX
Tiffany, F. Gile, Jr. ... Oxnard, CA
Tiffany, Gordon M. ... Weare, NH
Tiffany, Hunt & Brown, A Professional Corporation ... Oxnard, CA
Tiffany, Joseph R., II ... Palo Alto, CA
Tiffany, Katherine H. ... Greenville, SC
Greer, SC
Tiffany, Lawrence P. ... Denver, CO
Tiffany, Marcy J. K. ... El Segundo, CA
Tiffany, Matthew Wayne ... Virginia Beach, VA
Tiffany, Michael E. ... Phoenix, AZ
Tiffany, R. Ray, Jr. ... Phoenix, AZ
Tiffany, Robert D. ... Redwood Falls, MN
Tiffany, Samuel S. ... Phoenix, AZ
Tiffany & Tiffany ... Warrenton, VA
Tiffany, W. Wayne ... Virginia Beach, VA
Tiffany, Walter W. ... Madison, WI
Tiffany, William G. ... Hollister, CA
Tiffany, W. N., Jr. ... Warrenton, VA
Tiffen, Anne L. ... Phoenix, AZ
Tiffin, Barbara M. ... Greenville, SC
Tiffin, James B. ... Boston, MA
Tiffin, Jay H. ... Belleair, FL
Tiffin, Paul L. ... Milwaukee, WI
Tiffin, Thomas E., Jr. ... Birmingham, AL
Tiffin & Tiffin ... Boston, MA
Tifford, Arthur W. ... Miami, FL
Tifford, Arthur W., P.A. ... Miami, FL
Tifford, Jennifer ... New York, NY
Tifford, John M. ... Washington, DC
Tifft, Kenneth A. ... Elmira, NY
Tifft, William L. ... Globe, AZ
Tift, David L. ... Seattle, WA
Tifverman, Nicole D. ... Atlanta, GA
Tifverman, Robert T. ... Atlanta, GA
Tigani, Bruce W. ... Wilmington, DE
Tigani, James V., Jr. ... Wilmington, DE
Tigani, Janice Rowe ... Wilmington, DE
Tigano, Ernest J. ... San Diego, CA
Tigano, William ... Miami Beach, FL
Tigar, Andrea R.
Small Business Administration,
Office of the General Counsel, GV
Tigar, Jane ... Washington, DC
Tigar, Jon S. ... San Francisco, CA
Tigar, Michael E. ... Washington, DC
Tiger, Abbe R. ... New York, NY
Tiger, Alexander E. ... Morristown, NJ
Tiger, David ... Washington, DC
Tiger, Ira P. ... Philadelphia, PA
Tiger, Louis, Jr. ... Washington, DC
Tiger, Michelle ... Philadelphia, PA
Tiger, Neil H. ... New York, NY
Tiger, Ruth G. ... Washington, DC
Tigera, Antonio J. ... Miami, FL
Tigerman, Bert Z. ... Beverly Hills, CA
Tigerman, Charles S., (Professional Corporation) ... Los Angeles, CA
Tigerman, Sarah E. ... Palo Alto, CA
Tigerman, Stephen M. ... San Francisco, CA
Tigert & Ledig ... Washington, DC
Fairfax, VA
Tiggelaar, Beth Pace ... Dallas, TX
Tigges, Dale C. ... Sioux City, IA
Tigges, David J. ... Hilton Head Island, SC
Tigges, Rodney D. ... Asheville, NC
Tigges, Steven W. ... Columbus, OH
Tiggs, Marcus Gregory ... Los Angeles, CA
Tighe, Alexander W. ... Old Saybrook, CT
Tighe, Alfred Joseph, Jr. ... Washington, DC
Tighe, Ann C. ... Chicago, IL
Tighe, Austin P. ... Austin, TX

Tighe, Barry ... Los Angeles, CA
Tighe, Casey Patrick ... Denver, CO
Tighe, Charles L. ... Midland, TX
Tighe, Charles M. ... Wilmington, NC
Tighe, Cottrell & Logan, P.A.
Wilmington, DE
Towson, MD
Woodstown, NJ
Philadelphia, PA
Tighe, Craig M. ... Palo Alto, CA
Tighe, Daniel P. ... Boston, MA
Tighe, David J. ... Denver, CO
Tighe, Denise Vicente ... Kinnelon, NJ
Tighe, Dennis J. ... Great Falls, MT
Tighe, Edward J. ... Flushing, NY
Tighe, Evan, Ehrman, Schenck & Paras
Pittsburgh, PA
Tighe, Frank P., III ... Oak Brook, IL
Tighe, Frank P., III ... Oak Brook, IL
Tighe, Gail R. ... Lincoln, RI
Tighe, Gerald G. ... Florham Park, NJ
Tighe, J. Hagood ... Charlotte, NC
Raleigh, NC
Columbia, SC
Tighe, John F., Jr. ... Woodlawn, MD
Tighe, John Michael ... Pittsburgh, PA
Tighe, Joseph E. ... Chicago, IL
Tighe, Joseph E., P.C. ... Chicago, IL
Tighe, Karen A. ... Bay City, MI
Tighe, Kathleen S.
General Services Administration,
Office of Inspector General, GV
Tighe, Kevin D. ... Providence, RI
Tighe, Kevin M. ... Hartford, CT
Tighe, Kevin M. ... Londonderry, NH
Tighe, Kevin P., (P.C.) ... Washington, DC
Tighe, Laura A. ... Denver, CO
Tighe, Lisa A.P. ... Framingham, MA
Tighe, M. Joan ... Pasadena, CA
Tighe, Maureen A. ... Los Angeles, CA
Tighe, Maureen A. ... New York, NY
Tighe, Maureen N. ... Albany, NY
Tighe, Michael C. ... Midland, TX
Tighe, Michael J. ... Cold Spring, NY
Tighe, Michael K. ... Wilmington, DE
Tighe, Michael W. ... Columbia, SC
Tighe, Patton & Babbin, P.L.L.C.
Washington, DC
Tighe, Paula Christine ... Fort Lauderdale, FL
Tighe, Robert F. ... Cleveland, OH
Tighe, Robert G. ... Grosse Pointe Farms, MI
Tighe, Rodger W. ... New York, NY
Tighe, Rudolph E., Jr. ... Baltimore, MD
Tighe, Samantha A. ... San Francisco, CA
Tighe, Suzanne T. ... Scranton, PA
Tighe, Terence ... San Jose, CA
Tighe, Thomas J. ... San Diego, CA
Tighe, Thomas J. ... Fort Lauderdale, FL
Tighe, William R. ... Pittsburgh, PA
Tight, Dexter C. ... Woodside, CA
Tight, Stephen A. ... Minneapolis, MN
Tignanelli, A. Andrew ... Harleysville, PA
Tigner, Ronald E. ... Houston, TX
Tigno, Christopher B. ... Burlingame, CA
Tigno, Fiel D. ... Oakland, CA
Tignor, Kathryn L. ... West Palm Beach, FL
Tignor, Robert S. ... Washington, DC
Tigue, John J., Jr. ... New York, NY
Tigue, Mary E. ... Chicago, IL
Tigue, Randall D. B. ... Minneapolis, MN
Tigue, Thomas E. ... Nashville, TN
Tiholiz, John C. ... Dallas, TX
Tiistola, David W. ... Casper, WY
Tijerina, David A. ... Dallas, TX
Tijerina, Jaime E. ... McAllen, TX
Tijerina, Juan ... Fort Worth, TX
Tijerina, Kathryn Harris
United States Senate,
Committee Legal Personnel, GV
Tijerina & Kun, P.C. ... Dallas, TX
Tijerina, Pete ... San Antonio, TX
Tijerina, Rosaura P. ... Laredo, TX
Tikalsky, Donald J. ... Waukesha, WI
Tikalsky, Eleanor S. ... Hartland, WI
Tikalsky, J. Steven ... Waukesha, WI
Tikalsky, Raasch & Tikalsky
Waukesha, WI
Tikellis, Pamela S. ... Wilmington, DE
Tikku, Anup ... San Francisco, CA
Tikosh, Mark A. ... Long Beach, CA
Tiktin, Andrew Michael ... Houston, TX
Tiktin, Roger D. ... Cleveland, OH
Tiktin, Stephen N. ... Bend, OR
Tilaro, Laura A. ... Wakefield, MA
Tilberg, Karin R. ... Bowdoinham, ME
Tilberry, James H. ... Lady Lake, FL
Tilbrook, Stephen K.
Fort Lauderdale, FL
Tilbury, Brian ... Burke, VA
Tilchen, Alan S. ... Bloomfield Hills, MI
Tilchin, Asher N. ... Farmington Hills, MI
Tilchin, Hall & Reynolds, P.C.
Farmington Hills, MI
Tilden, Charles M. ... Minneapolis, MN
Tilden, Cynthia A. ... Porter, IN
Tilden, James C. ... Kansas City, MO
Tilden, Janice ... Denver, CO
Tilden, Jeffrey I. ... Seattle, WA
Tilden, M. William ... Riverside, CA
San Bernardino, CA
Tilden, Mark C. ... Boulder, CO
Tilden, Mark Christopher ... Boulder, CO
Tilden, Mark S. ... Framingham, MA
Tilden, Rebecca R. ... Kansas City, MO
Tilden, Robert C., (P.C.) ... Cedar Rapids, IA
Tildon, Rhonda Phoenix
Department of Justice,
Office of Justice Programs, GV

Tilem, David A. ... Glendale, CA
Tilem & Gole ... Beverly Hills, CA
Tilem, Joseph N. ... Beverly Hills, CA
Tilem, Peter H. ... New York, NY
Tilem & White LLP ... Glendale, CA
Tilén, Federico ... San Juan, PR
Tileston, Fred M., Jr. ... Hillsborough, CA
Tilev, Metodi A. ... Silver Spring, MD
Tilevitz, Orrin E. ... New York, NY
Tilewick, Robert ... New York, NY
Tiley, Stephen D. ... Carlisle, PA
Tilford, Dobbins, Alexander, Buckaway & Black ... Louisville, KY
Tilford, Thomas B. ... Spokane, WA
Tilg, Howard A. ... Wauwatosa, WI
Tilg, Koch, Ramstack & Foy, S.C.
Wauwatosa, WI
Tilgen, Burnell J. ... Brooklyn Park, MN
Tilghman, Anthony J., III ... Palo Alto, CA
Tilghman, Barbara Mary ... Baltimore, MD
Tilghman, Carl L. ... Beaufort, NC
Tilghman, Eileen L. ... Miami, FL
Tilghman, Henry R. ... Portland, OR
Tilghman, James B., Jr. ... Miami, FL
Tilghman, Joan F. ... Columbia, MD
Tilghman, Johnson ... Dunn, NC
Tilghman, Joseph F. ... Bryn Mawr, PA
Tilghman, Richard C., Jr. ... Baltimore, MD
Tilghman, Robert C. ... Miami, FL
Tilghman, S. Mark ... Salisbury, MD
Tilghman, Susan Seidel ... Salisbury, MD
Tilghman & Vieth, P.A. ... Miami, FL
Tilghman, William F. ... Washington, DC
Tilhou, John A. ... Virginia Beach, VA
Tilis, Harry F. ... Syosset, NY
Tilitsky, Lisa Michele ... Bethesda, MD
Tilker, Barbara Doblin ... Garden City, NY
New York, NY
Tilker, James A. ... Scottsdale, AZ
Tilker, James A., P.C. ... Phoenix, AZ
Scottsdale, AZ
Tilker, Kristopher R. ... Wichita Falls, TX
Till, A. Grey, Jr. ... Birmingham, AL
Till, Allen ... Houston, TX
Till, Andrea Rose ... Denver, CO
Till, Carl W. ... Sacramento, CA
Till, Gerald F. ... Bisbee, AZ
Till, Gregory J. ... Treasury Department,
Bureau of the Public Debt, GV
Till, Guy ... Denver, CO
Till, John C. ... Burlingame, CA
Till, Joseph J., III ... Superior, WI
Till, Kimberly Katherine
Birmingham, AL
Till, Laura A. ... Irvine, CA
Till, Peter W. ... Newark, NJ
Till, Peter W. ... Newark, NJ
Short Hills, NJ
Till, Quentin T. ... Jacksonville, FL
Till, Salzer & Blank, Ltd. ... Superior, WI
Tillack, Clay A. ... Chicago, IL
Tillage, Charles E. ... Burlingame, CA
Tillapaugh, Martin H. ... Owego, NY
Tillar, Mark T. ... Cincinnati, OH
Tillem, David L. ... White Plains, NY
Tillem, Jack ... New York, NY
Tillem, Jack D. ... Bronx, NY
Tillem, Jennifer B. ... New York, NY
Tillem, Jonathan Ross ... New York, NY
Tilleman, Karl M. ... Phoenix, AZ
Tilleman, Paul J. ... Milwaukee, WI
Tillemans, Paul J. ... South Bend, IN
Tiller, Ann Marie ... Houston, TX
Tiller, Calvin F. ... Richmond, VA
Tiller, Craig P. ... Lynchburg, VA
Tiller, E. Allan ... Houston, TX
Tiller, Emerson H. ... Merrillville, IN
Tiller, James E. ... Hamel, MN
Tiller, John H. ... Charleston, SC
Tiller, Laurel L. ... Centralia, WA
Tiller, Linda Gail ... St. Paul, VA
Tiller, Linda K. ... Kansas City, MO
Tiller, Marc R. ... Palm Beach Gardens, FL
Tiller, Marie C. ... Myrtle Beach, SC
Pawleys Island, SC
Tiller, Peter B. ... Centralia, WA
Tiller, Robert H. ... Raleigh, NC
Tiller, Robert M. ... Louisville, KY
Tiller, Sharon L. ... Chicago, IL
Tiller, Steven E. ... Baltimore, MD
Tiller, Warren O. ... DeLand, FL
Tiller, Wheeler & Tiller ... Centralia, WA
Tiller, William B. ... Richmond, VA
Tillers, Peter ... New York, NY
Tillery, A. Scott ... Chalmette, LA
Tillery, Allen J. ... Chalmette, LA
Tillery, Annie M. ... San Francisco, CA
Tillery, Edward T. ... Pauls Valley, OK
Tillery, Eileen Zacary ... New Orleans, LA
Tillery, James P., Jr. ... Birmingham, AL
Tillery, Jefferson R. ... New Orleans, LA
Tillery, John Gregory, III
Wilmington, NC
Tillery, Katherine J. ... East St. Louis, IL
Tillery, L. Bradford ... Wilmington, NC
Tillery, M. Kelly ... Philadelphia, PA
Tillery, Robert W. ... Hammond, LA
Tillery, Stephen M. ... Belleville, IL
East St. Louis, IL
Tillery & Tillery ... Chalmette, LA
Tilles, Alan S. ... Rockville, MD
Tilles, C. Evans ... New York, NY
Tilles, David F. ... Los Angeles, CA
Tilles, Eric A. ... Philadelphia, PA
Tilles, Gary ... Philadelphia, PA
Tilles, Gayle Podell, P.C. ... Chicago, IL
Tilles, Monty J. ... Quechee, VT
Tilles, Monty J., P.C. ... Quechee, VT

Tilles, Robert Stuart ... **Los Angeles, CA**
Tilles, Roger B. ... Woodbury, NY
Tilles, Webb, Kulla & Grant, A Law Corporation ... **Beverly Hills, CA**
Los Angeles, CA
Tillet, Rebecca ... House of Representatives, Committee on Post Office & Civil Service, GV
Tillett, Jerry R. ... Nags Head, NC
Tillett Law Offices PLLC ... **Charlotte, NC**
Tillett, S. Raymond ... **Chicago, IL**
Tillett, Thomas M. ... **Charlotte, NC**
Tilley, Allison Leopold ... **Palo Alto, CA**
Tilley, B. Scott ... **Richmond, VA**
Tilley & Chapman ... Boca Raton, FL
Tilley, Diane S. ... **Raleigh, NC**
Tilley, James W. ... **Little Rock, AR**
Tilley, John C. ... **Hopkinsville, KY**
Tilley, Laura F. Davies ... Arnold, MD
Tilley, Marcia L. ... Stillwater, OK
Tilley, Mark P. ... **Austin, TX**
Tilley, Michael R. ... Boca Raton, FL
Tilley, N. Carlton, Jr. ... Greensboro, NC
Tilley, R. Bryan ... **Heber Springs, AR**
Tilley, Rice M., Jr. ... **Fort Worth, TX**
Tilley, Sabrina Marie
Department Of Veterans Affairs, Board of Veterans Appeals, GV
Tilley, Stacey F. ... **Houston, TX**
Tilley, Stanley D. ... **Cartersville, GA**
Tilley, Velma Cowen ... **Cartersville, GA**
Tilley, Walter A., III ... **York, PA**
Tilley, William E. ... Leesville, LA
Tillim, Louis B. ... Huntington, NY
Tillinger, Christina Shropshire
Houston, TX
Tillinghast, D. Lance ... Dover, NH
Tillinghast, David R. ... **New York, NY**
Tillinghast, Edward H., III
New York, NY
Tillinghast, George E., Jr. ... Glastonbury, CT
Tillinghast, Jonathan K. ... **Juneau, AK**
Tillinghast Licht & Semonoff Ltd.
Providence, RI
Tillinghast, Margaret S.
San Francisco, CA
Tillinghast, Pamela ... Washington, DC
Tillinghast, Wayne G. ... **Norwich, CT**
Tillipman, James M. ... **Los Angeles, CA**
Tillipman, James M. ... **Santa Monica, CA**
Tillis, Andrea G. ... Drexel Hill, PA
Tillis, Barry Ira ... Cheyenne, WY
Tillis, Lenita T. ... Los Angeles, CA
Tillis, Monte J., Jr. ... Bartow, FL
Tillisch, Cal R. ... Wausau, WI
Tillitt, Laura Melissa ... Florence, SC
Tillitt, McCarten, Johnson & Haseman, Ltd.
Alexandria, MN
Tillitt, R. Stephen ... **Minneapolis, MN**
Tillitt, Ralph S. ... **Alexandria, MN**
Tillman & Anderson ... Leesville, LA
Tillman, Andrew R. ... **Knoxville, TN**
Tillman, Audrey Boone ... **Columbus, GA**
Tillman, Beatrice C. ... San Diego, CA
Tillman, Burton L. ... Atlanta, GA
Tillman, Carolyn O. ... Fairfax, VA
Tillman, Chad Dustin ... **Charlotte, NC**
Tillman, Curtis V. ... Chamblee, GA
Tillman, Daniel T. ... St. Louis, MO
Tillman, Douglas L. ... **Indianapolis, IN**
Tillman, Elva E. ... Baltimore, MD
Tillman, Eugene ... **Washington, DC**
Tillman, Fred A., Jr. ... Atlanta, GA
Tillman, Gary B. ... **Alexandria, LA**
Tillman & Gaster ... Los Olivos, CA
Tillman, George E., III ... Englewood, CO
Tillman, H. Robert ... Princeton, NJ
Tillman, John C. ... Mayfield Heights, OH
Tillman, Jonathan A. ... Los Olivos, CA
Tillman, Karen Graham ... Gainesville, FL
Tillman Law Firm ... North Charleston, SC
Tillman, Leonard Charles
Birmingham, AL
Tillman, Mark D. ... **Amarillo, TX**
Tillman, Massie ... Fort Worth, TX
Tillman, Michael ... Gainesville, FL
Tillman, Michaune D. ... **Philadelphia, PA**
Tillman, Myron E. ... Rochester, NY
Tillman, Patrick J. ... Redding, CA
Tillman, Patrick K. ... Sunnyvale, CA
Tillman, Paula S. ... Chicago, IL
Tillman, Ross D. ... **Missoula, MT**
Tillman, Samuel S. ... **Fort Worth, TX**
Tillman, Seymour ... Longmeadow, MA
Tillman, Stephanie B. ... Thomasville, GA
Tillman, Stephanie E. ... **Atlanta, GA**
Tillman, Stephen E. ... Baxley, GA
Tillman, Stephen J. ... Louisville, KY
Tillman, Todd T. ... Fremont, NE
Tillman, W. Polk ... Memphis, TN
Tillman, Wallace F. ... **Arlington, VA**
Tillman, Wendy Gaster ... Los Olivos, CA
Tillman, Wheeler M. ... North Charleston, SC
Tillman, William A. ... Houston, TX
Tillmann, Jacqueline ... **Princeton, NJ**
Tillona, Mary Anne B. ... Windsor Locks, CT
Tillona, Zina ... Amherst, MA
Tillotson, Cheryl A. ... San Francisco, CA
Tillotson, David B. ... **San Francisco, CA**
Tillotson, David, Law Office of
Washington, DC
Tillotson, Diane C. ... **Boston, MA**
Tillotson, Drew R. ... **Des Moines, IA**
Tillotson, Frank A. ... **Washington, DC**
Tillotson, Jeffrey M., (P.C.) ... **Dallas, TX**
Tillotson, John C. ... **Leavenworth, KS**
Tillotson, Madeline J. ... Worcester, MA
Tillotson, Stephen A. ... Everglades City, FL
Tillotson, Suzanne C. ... Charlotte, NC
Tillou & Johnson ... Hamburg, NY
Tillou, Julia D. H. ... Norfolk, VA
Tillou, Kenneth B. ... **Norfolk, VA**
Tillquist, Neil Leslie ... Denver, CO
Tills, Matthew W. ... **Denver, CO**
Tills, Robert W. ... **Hamburg, NY**
Tills, Ronald H. ... Buffalo, NY
Tillson, James F. ... Houston, TX
Tillson, Joseph W. ... **South Lake Tahoe, CA**
Tilly & Associates ... **Tulsa, OK**
Tilly & Graves, Professional Corporation
Denver, CO
Tilly, James W. ... **Tulsa, OK**
Tilly, John R. ... **Dallas, TX**
Tilly, Laura E. ... **Chicago, IL**
Tilly, Miles Edward ... Arnaudville, LA
Tillyard, Virginia ... **New York, NY**
Tilmon, Charles E., Jr. ... Texarkana, AR
Tilmon, Paula M. ... Newark, DE
Tilner, Mitchell C. ... **Los Angeles, CA**
Tilney, Leonard G., Jr. ... Lockport, NY
Tilove-Navatta, Sharon B. ... **Uniondale, NY**
Tils, Robert M. ... **Garden City, NY**
Tilsen, Judith M. ... St. Paul, MN
Tilsen, Kenneth E. ... St. Paul, MN
Tilsen, Scott F. ... Minneapolis, MN
Tilsley, Roy W., Jr. ... **Manchester, NH**
Tilson, Arthur R. ... **Fort Washington, PA**
Tilson, David M. ... **Morristown, TN**
Tilson, Hugh H., Jr. ... Raleigh, NC
Tilson, J. Lane ... Los Angeles, CA
Tilson, J. Lee ... **Southfield, MI**
Tilson, Joe A. ... Greeneville, TN
Tilson, John Q. ... **New Haven, CT**
Tilson, Joseph E. ... **Chicago, IL**
Tilson, Lynn & Hanson ... Homestead, FL
Tilson, Marion White ... **Atlanta, GA**
Tilson, Martin R., Jr. ... **Atlanta, GA**
Tilson, Stephen F. ... Galion, OH
Tilson, Susan Blackman ... **New York, NY**
Tilson, Thomas A. ... Homestead, FL
Tilt, Bradley Lloyd ... **Salt Lake City, UT**
Tilton, Bronwyn Burke ... **Houston, TX**
Tilton, C. Norris ... **Jensen Beach, FL**
Tilton, David S. ... Coos Bay, OR
Tilton, Dennis S. ... San Bernardino, CA
Tilton, Edwin O. ... **Buffalo, NY**
Tilton, Eric B. ... **Tallahassee, FL**
Tilton, Fallon, Lungmus & Chestnut
Chicago, IL
Tilton, Fredric F. ... Cincinnati, OH
Tilton, George H., Jr. ... **Denver, CO**
Tilton, George H., Jr., P.C. ... **Denver, CO**
Tilton & Hoffman ... Topeka, KS
Tilton, Jerry E. ... Columbus, OH
Tilton, Joshua A. ... Mandeville, LA
Tilton, Julie A. ... **Minneapolis, MN**
Tilton, Kelly R. ... **San Leandro, CA**
Tilton, Kevin W. ... Bartonville, IL
Tilton, Kirk W. ... Lavallette, NJ
Tilton, Kurt D. ... **Kansas City, MO**
Tilton, Lois ... **New York, NY**
Yorktown Heights, NY
Tilton, Louis R. ... Edina, MN
Tilton & Metzger, P.A. ... **Tallahassee, FL**
Tilton, Michelle Worrall ... Kansas City, MO
Tilton, Philip J. ... **Minneapolis, MN**
Tilton, Richard E. ... Old Bridge, NJ
Tilton, Richard J. ... Columbus, OH
Tilton, Richard N. ... **New York, NY**
Tilton, Robert E. ... Topeka, KS
Tilton, Robt. P. ... Laconia, NH
Tilton & Rosenbaum, P.L.L.P ... St. Paul, MN
Tilton, Rustine ... Elmwood Park, NJ
Tilton, Samuel O. ... **Rochester, NY**
Tilton, Stephen R., Jr. ... Hackensack, NJ
Tilton, Steven M. ... Topeka, KS
Tilton, Sumner B., Jr. ... **Worcester, MA**
Tilton, Thomas A., III ... Waterville, ME
Tilton, Thomas T. ... Tucson, AZ
Tilton, Timothy L. ... Chicago, IL
Tilton, William L. ... St. Paul, MN
Tilton-McCarthy, Lisa M. ... **Houston, TX**
Tily, Gil C. ... **Princeton, NJ**
Tily, H. Coleman ... Haddonfield, NJ
Timaeus, Dana ... **Beaumont, TX**
Timan, Richard ... Watsonville, CA
Timar, John J. ... **Atlanta, GA**
Timban, Demetrio S., Jr. ... Brooklyn, NY
Timbanard, Jeffrey R. ... Mesa, AZ
Phoenix, AZ
Timbanard Tolman & Kamper, L.L.P.
Mesa, AZ
Phoenix, AZ
Timber, Christine J. ... Troy, NY
Timberlake, Deana L.
Department of Justice, Antitrust Division, GV
Timberlake, Donald J.
Oklahoma City, OK
Timberlake, Donald J., Jr.
Oklahoma City, OK
Timberlake, George W. ... Mount Vernon, IL
Timberlake, Grace H. ... New York, NY
Timberlake, H. Kenan ... Huntsville, AL
Timberlake, Joe ... Signal Mountain, TN
Timberlake, Marshall ... **Birmingham, AL**
Timberlake, Michael Kenan
Huntsville, AL
Timberlake, Morgan E., II ... Honolulu, HI
Timberlake, Smith, Thomas & Moses, P.C.
Staunton, VA
Timberlake & Weaver, P.C. ... **Lubbock, TX**
Timberman, Wayne H. ... Bridgeton, NJ
Timbers, Briggs & Morgan, P.C.
Glastonbury, CT
Hartford, CT
Timbers, Bryan P. ... Nome, AK
Timbers, Dwight E. ... **Glastonbury, CT**
Timbers, Katharine S. ... **San Francisco, CA**
Timbers, Kerry L. ... **Boston, MA**
Timbie, Donald N. ... Alexandria, VA
Timbie, Richard E. ... **Washington, DC**
Timble, Suzanne M. ... Lake Forest, IL
Timblin, Charles ... McLean, VA
Timblin, Terence E. ... Tamuning, GU
Timbs, Chester C. ... Tyler, TX
Timbs, Chester C., P.C., Law Offices of
Tyler, TX
Timby & Dillon ... Newtown, PA
Timby, Robert Mitchell ... Houston, TX
Timby, Thomas E. ... Newtown, PA
Timby, Walter J., III ... **Philadelphia, PA**
Timby, Walter J., Jr. ... **Philadelphia, PA**
Timchak, Louis J., Jr. ... Lutz, FL
Timchak, Louis J., Jr., P.A. ... Lutz, FL
Timchula, Stephan A. ... **Westminster, MD**
Time, Fred ... Dallas, TX
Timianko, Laura F. ... Closter, NJ
Timin, Gary P. ... **Tallahassee, FL**
Timins, Arthur J. ... Roseland, NJ
Timins, Larsen, Beacham & Hughes
Roseland, NJ
Timinski, Michael J.
Department Of Veterans Affairs, Office of the General Counsel, GV
Timken, Heidi A. ... **Walnut Creek, CA**
Timken, Jane Murphy ... **Canton, OH**
Timken, Kevin C. ... **Salt Lake City, UT**
Timken, Nelson E. ... Kew Gardens, NY
Timken, Thomas R. ... Madison, WI
Timko, Andrea Ann ... **Washington, DC**
Timko Engle & Young ... New York, NY
Timko, Joseph F. ... Westbury, NY
Timko, Michael J. ... **Purchase, NY**
Timko, Michelle T. ... John Day, OR
Timko, Nicholas I. ... **New York, NY**
Timko, V. Paul ... Lorain, OH
Timlin, Jeffrey J. ... Denver, CO
Timlin, Robert J. ... Riverside, CA
Timlin, Thomas F. ... Sandwich, MA
Timm, Aaron C. ... **San Francisco, CA**
Timm, Barbara C. ... Bloomfield Hills, MI
Timm, Beth Gerstein ... **Minneapolis, MN**
St. Paul, MN
Timm, Beverly B. ... Charlotte, NC
Timm, Bruce M. ... **Sacramento, CA**
Timm, Carol A. ... **Palo Alto, CA**
Timm, Curtis J. ... **Sarasota, FL**
Timm, David J. ... Green Bay, WI
Timm, Derek J. ... **San Francisco, CA**
Timm, Donald A. ... Muscatine, IA
Timm, Gregory D. ... Colorado Springs, CO
Timm, Gregory D., LLC
Colorado Springs, CO
Timm, Kathryn M. ... Anoka, MN
Timm, Kenneth E. ... **Joliet, IL**
Timm, Lorence L. ... San Leandro, CA
Timm, Margene M. ... Lincoln, NE
Timm, Maynard L. ... **Detroit, MI**
Timm, Michael E. ... Poughkeepsie, NY
Timm, Patricia A. ... **Walnut Creek, CA**
Timm, Robert ... Watertown, SD
Timm, Roger K. ... **Detroit, MI**
Timm, Ruth M. ... **Minneapolis, MN**
Timm, Scott R. ... **Waconia, MN**
Timm, Sharon Gilbert ... Doylestown, PA
Timm, Stephen J. ... Aurora, CO
Timm, Steven B. ... Beatrice, NE
Timm, Theodore R. ... Des Plaines, IL
Timm, Walter F. ... St. Louis, MO
Timm, Walter W. ... Brentwood, MO
Timme, William H. ... **Anchorage, AK**
Timmel, John J. ... Yonkers, NY
Timmel, Richard J. ... **Chicago, IL**
Timmeny, Wallace L. ... **Washington, DC**
Timmer, Amy ... Lansing, MI
Timmer, Ann A. Scott ... **Phoenix, AZ**
Timmer, Barbara ... **Washington, DC**
Timmer, Douglas D. ... **Chicago, IL**
Timmer, Edward J. ... Kalamazoo, MI
Timmer, Gregory G. ... **Grand Rapids, MI**
Timmer, J. Scott ... **Muskegon, MI**
Timmer, James A. ... **Lansing, MI**
Timmer, Jamo & O'Leary ... **Lansing, MI**
Timmer, John J. ... **Grand Rapids, MI**
Timmer, Patrick D. ... **Lincoln, NE**
Timmer, Stephen B. ... **Chicago, IL**
Timmer, Steven J. ... **Minneapolis, MN**
Timmerman, Barbara R.
General Accounting Office, Office of the General Counsel, GV
Timmerman & Dickinson ... Watertown, NY
Timmerman, Donna L. ... San Jose, CA
Timmerman, Douglas S. ... Urbana, IL
Timmerman, Henry L. ... **Phoenix, AZ**
Timmerman, J. Todd ... **Tampa, FL**
Timmerman, James M. ... **Towson, MD**
Timmerman, Jerianne ... **Washington, DC**
Timmerman, Jodi ... Janesville, WI
Timmerman, Karl H. ... Grandview, MO
Holden, MO
Timmerman, Lawrence W. ... Nashotah, WI
Timmerman, Lewin E. ... Wichita, KS
Timmerman, Nancy Jane ... Phoenix, AZ
Timmerman, Rand R. ... Watertown, NY
Timmerman, Timothy Neal ... Dearborn, MI
Timmerman, Troy G. ... Blue Earth, MN
Timmerman, Wayne S. ... Tampa, FL
Timmerman, William P. ... Wichita, KS
Timmermans, Todd J. ... **Anchorage, AK**
Timmermeier, Cynthia P. ... Omaha, NE
Timmermier, Gross & Prentiss
Council Bluffs, IA
Omaha, NE
Timmermier, John R. ... **Omaha, NE**
Timmers, Michael G. ... **Chicago, IL**
Timmers, Richard H. ... Wyoming, MI
Timmerwilke, Charles E. ... **Rockford, IL**
Timmerwilke, Gerald L. ... Quincy, IL
Timmerwilke, Kimberly Baker ... Rockford, IL
Timmins & Associates, L.L.C.
Denver, CO
Timmins, B. H. (Tim), Jr. ... Dallas, TX
Timmins, Christian G. ... Metairie, LA
Timmins, David H. ... **Dallas, TX**
Timmins, Edward P. ... **Denver, CO**
Timmins, Janel A. ... Colorado Springs, CO
Timmins, Jo ... Denver, CO
Timmins, Mary Joanne Deziel
Denver, CO
Timmins, Megan C. ... **Pittsburgh, PA**
Timmins, Patrick F., Jr. ... Columbus, OH
Timmins, Paul V. ... **Denver, CO**
Timmins, Robert J. ... Omaha, NE
Timmins, Terrence L. ... Sioux City, IA
Timmis, David B. ... **Birmingham, MI**
Timmis, Gayle T. ... **Bingham Farms, MI**
Timmis & Inman L.L.P. ... **Ann Arbor, MI**
Detroit, MI
Grosse Pointe, MI
Mount Clemens, MI
Pontiac, MI
Timmis, Michael T. ... **Detroit, MI**
Timmis, Truman D. ... Southfield, MI
Timmons, Aletia Haynes
Oklahoma City, OK
Timmons, Bradley V. ... **The Dalles, OR**
Timmons, Brock C. ... Atlanta, GA
Tucker, GA
Timmons, Bruce A. ... Lansing, MI
Timmons, Carla Michel ... **New Orleans, LA**
Timmons, Christopher M.
Costa Mesa, CA
Timmons, Dann Sterling ... Garrettsville, OH
Timmons, Duane H. ... **Long Beach, CA**
Redding, CA
Timmons, Durward E., Jr.
Colorado Springs, CO
Timmons, Gregg K. ... Shreveport, LA
Timmons, Gregory D. ... **Pittsburgh, PA**
Timmons, Haggard & Carney ... Athens, GA
Timmons, Hal W. ... Salt Lake City, UT
Timmons, J. Scott ... Lacey, WA
Timmons, Jeanette Cook
Oklahoma City, OK
Timmons, Jeffrey L. ... Washington, DC
Timmons, Jennifer Young ... **Dallas, TX**
Timmons, Joe Blair ... Tupelo, MS
Timmons, John ... Washington, DC
Timmons, John L. ... Ames, IA
Timmons, John P., III ... Sacramento, CA
Timmons, John W., Jr. ... Athens, GA
Timmons, Joseph F. ... Akron, OH
Timmons, Joyce Terrell ... Eastpoint, FL
Timmons, Kathleen M. ... Atlanta, GA
Timmons & Kelly ... **Dallas, TX**
Timmons, Kelly Cahill ... Cincinnati, OH
Timmons, Michael J. ... **New York, NY**
Timmons, Patrick F., Jr. ... Houston, TX
Timmons, Peter ... Hauppauge, NY
Timmons, Peter J. ... **Minneapolis, MN**
Timmons, R. Brian ... **Costa Mesa, CA**
Timmons, Richard C. ... Washington, DC
Timmons, Robert C., P.C.
Grand Rapids, MI
Timmons, Samuel D. ... San Diego, CA
Timmons, Sean A. ... **Raleigh, NC**
Timmons, Stephen D., (P.C.)
Kansas City, MO
Timmons, Timothy D. ... Concord, CA
Timmons, W. Thomas ... **Dallas, TX**
Timmons, William E. ... **Des Moines, IA**
Timmons, William F. ... **Atlanta, GA**
Timmons-Goodson, Patricia ... Raleigh, NC
Timms, Charles F., Jr. ... Los Angeles, CA
Timms, Cynthia Keely ... **Dallas, TX**
Timms, Gwyn Goodson ... **San Diego, CA**
Timms, Kimberley Herson ... **Norfolk, VA**
Timms, Robert V., Jr. ... **Norfolk, VA**
Timon, Kimon Peter ... New York, NY
Timone, Denis J. ... Tuckahoe, NY
Timoner, Sharon L. ... Santa Clara, CA
Timonere, Steven ... **Toledo, OH**
Timoney, Knox, Hasson & Weand, LLP
Ambler, PA
Doylestown, PA
Fort Washington, PA
Norristown, PA
Timoney, Maria ... Marion, VA
Timoney, Maureen A. ... Nashville, TN
Timoney, Patrick C.
West Conshohocken, PA
Timoney, Thomas J. ... **Fort Washington, PA**
Timoni, Stephen A. ... **Newark, NJ**
Timony, James P. ... Federal Trade Commission, Office of Administrative Law Judges, GV
Timony, Joseph T. ... Trenton, NJ
Timothée, Ida Josefina ... **Washington, DC**
Timothy, Kathleen J. ... Port Washington, NY
Timothy, Marjory J. ... Charlotte, NC
Timothy, Michael C. ... Northbrook, IL
Timothy, Raymond J. ... Cleveland, OH
Timpane, Michael J. ... **San Francisco, CA**
Timpanelli, Chris A. ... Stratford, CT
Timpano, Anthony B., II ... Plymouth, MN
Timpe, Virgil W. ... Quincy, IL
Timpe-Brennan, Ann ... Houston, TX
Timperio, John M. ... **Charlotte, NC**
Timperio, Nicholas E. ... Uniontown, PA

Timperman, Ernest J. .... Cincinnati, OH
Timpone, Walter F. .... Morristown, NJ
Timpson, Jennifer Regina .... Pittsburgh, PA
Timroth, Valana K. .... Bakersfield, CA
Tims, Cindy .... Mount Vernon, WA
Tims, Jay .... Youngstown, OH
Tims, Lowry L. .... Dallas, TX
Tims, Marianne Marshall .... Denver, CO
Tims, Otis R. .... Columbus, MS
Tupelo, MS
Tims, Shelia Darling .... Oklahoma City, OK
Timson, Beth Ann .... Norwood, MA
Timson, Christopher G. .... Norwood, MA
Timte, Lawrence D. .... Houston, TX
Tin, Noell Peter .... Charlotte, NC
Tinagero, James D. .... Queens Village, NY
Tinagero, Margaret .... New York, NY
Tinaglia, Michael Lee .... Park Ridge, IL
Tinan, Smith & Bucher .... Mitchell, SD
Tinari, Anthony P. .... Skillman, NJ
Tinari, Christopher A. .... Philadelphia, PA
Tinari, Eugene P. .... Philadelphia, PA
Tinari, Michael V. .... Moorestown, NJ
Philadelphia, PA
Tinari, Nino V. .... Philadelphia, PA
Tinawi, Emad .... Washington, DC
Tinberg, Sidney .... Los Angeles, CA
Tinberg, Toni Lenz .... Boston, MA
Tinch, William H. .... Poughkeepsie, NY
Tincknell, Julie B. .... Kansas City, MO
Tindal, Douglas L. .... Washington, IA
Tindal, Erdahl, Goddard & Nestor, PLC
Washington, IA
Tindal, George E. .... Baltimore, MD
Tindal, Janeice B. .... Reidsville, NC
Tindal, Mark E. .... Birmingham, AL
Tindal, Steven L. .... Bradenton, FL
Tindal, William C. .... Lancaster, SC
Tindale, Christopher S. .... Jacksonville, FL
Tindall & Akers, P.C. .... Potosi, MO
Tindall, Albert G. .... Potosi, MO
Tindall, Alphonso E., Jr. .... New York, NY
Tindall Bennett & Shoup, P.C.
Anchorage, AK
Tindall, Charles S., III .... Greenville, MS
Tindall, Charles S., Jr. .... Paducah, KY
Greenville, MS
Jackson, MS
Tindall, Craig D. .... Phoenix, AZ
Tindall, Edwin W. .... Greenville, MS
Tindall, Elizabeth Steele .... Dallas, TX
Tindall & Foster, P.C. .... Houston, TX
Tindall, Harry L. .... Houston, TX
Tindall, Jennifer C. .... Tampa, FL
Tindall, John H. .... Anchorage, AK
Tindall, Joseph D., Jr. .... Atlanta, GA
Tindall, Kern E. .... Auburn, CA
Tindall, L. Diane .... Raleigh, NC
Tindall, Michael E. .... Port Huron, MI
Tindall, M.J. (Jeff) .... Pittsburgh, PA
Tindall, Richard A. .... Houston, TX
Tindall, Robert E., Jr. .... Tucson, AZ
Tindall, Steven M. .... San Francisco, CA
Tindall-O'Brien, Pamela .... Albany, NY
Tindel, Andy .... Tyler, TX
Tindel, Kay F. .... Berkeley, CA
Tindel, Seymour .... Kings Point, NY
Tindell, Chadwick B. .... Knoxville, TN
Tindell, Charles .... Daytona Beach, FL
Daytona Beach, FL
Maitland, FL
Tindell, Edward J. .... Garden City, NY
Tindell, Jeffrey W. .... New York, NY
Tindell, Verne H. .... Riverside, CA
Tinder, John D. .... Indianapolis, IN
Tinder, John G. .... Indianapolis, IN
Tinder, Thomas R. .... Charleston, WV
Tindol, M. Chad .... Enterprise, AL
Tine, Andrew J. .... Boston, MA
Tine, Richard J. .... Fortuna, CA
Tiner, Lohnes T. .... Harrisburg, AR
Tinero, Ellen-Jo Friedman .... Encino, CA
Tinero and Rauch .... Encino, CA
Ting, Angela Y. .... Department of Justice,
Antitrust Division, GV
Ting, Henry P. .... Washington, DC
Ting, Jan C. .... Philadelphia, PA
Ting, Peter D. .... Department of Defense,
Armed Services Board of Contract Appeals,
GV
Ting, Richard .... Los Angeles, CA
Ting, Theodore T. .... Oakland, CA
Ting, Vicki .... Palo Alto, CA
Ting, William K.C. .... Los Angeles, CA
Tingen, Gerald A. .... Raleigh, NC
Tingey, Brent C. .... Rupert, ID
Tingey, Bruce D. .... Las Vegas, NV
Tingey, Dean M. .... Las Vegas, NV
Tingey, Don C. .... Las Vegas, NV
Tingey, Joel E. .... Idaho Falls, ID
Tingey, Robert D. .... Salt Lake City, UT
Tingey, Stephen C. .... Salt Lake City, UT
Tingey & Tingey .... Las Vegas, NV
Ting-Hopper, Rita .... Los Angeles, CA
Tingle, Brent A. .... Worcester, MA
Tingle, Charles A., Jr. .... Lawrenceville, GA
Tingle, Charles A., Jr., P.C.
Lawrenceville, GA
Tingle, James M. .... Birmingham, AL
Tingle, James O'M. .... San Francisco, CA
Tingle, Lewis M. .... Cambridge, OH
Tingle, Michal L. .... Department of Justice,
Civil Division, GV
Tingle, Philip D.F. .... Jacksonville, FL
Tingle, Richard W. .... Huntsville, AL
Tingle, Tricia A. .... Department of Justice,
Civil Rights Division, GV
Tingle, William E. .... Oakland, CA
Tingler, David S. .... Newport Beach, CA
Tingler, Gregory Rean .... Elkins, WV
Tingler, Robert A. .... Chicago, IL
Tingley, Curtis R. .... San Jose, CA
Tingley, John B. .... Columbus, OH
Tingley, John C. .... Department of Commerce,
Patent and Trademark Office, GV
Tinglin, Karen Elaine .... Chicago, IL
Tingling, Milton F. .... New York, NY
Tinglum, Britt L. .... Seattle, WA
Tinglum, Kirsten A. .... Anchorage, AK
Tinglum & Sixel, S.C. .... River Falls, WI
Tinglum, Sverre O. .... River Falls, WI
Tingoli, Michael M. .... New York, NY
Tingstad, Anders B., Jr. .... Bessemer, MI
Tingstad, David .... Seattle, WA
Tingue, Lisa D. .... Worcester, MA
Tingum, Kirk A. .... Grand Forks, ND
Tingvall, Douglas S. .... Bellevue, WA
Tini, James J. .... Mineola, NY
Tinianow, Jerome C. .... Columbus, OH
Tinio, Ferdinand S. .... Rochester, NY
Tinker, Bill T. .... Albuquerque, NM
Tinker, Catherine E. .... Chicago, IL
Tinker, Connie J. .... Wichita, KS
Tinker, David E. .... Watertown, NY
Tinker, Donald C., Jr. .... Wichita, KS
Tinker, George H. .... Genoa, IL
Tinker, Gregg L. .... Seattle, WA
Tinker, J. Douglas .... Corpus Christi, TX
Tinker, James M. .... Audubon, IA
Tinker, John G., Jr. .... Cedar Knolls, NJ
Tinker, Julie Lynn .... Grand Rapids, MI
Tinker, Megan H. .... Washington, DC
Tinker, Nikki M. .... Birmingham, AL
Tinker, Paul M. .... Salt Lake City, UT
Tinker, Thomas P. .... Tampa, FL
Tinker, Todd D. .... Seattle, WA
Tinker, William .... Wichita, KS
Tinker, William, Jr. .... Wichita, KS
Tinkerian, Armand .... North Hollywood, CA
Tinkey, Byron L. .... Akron, IN
Tinkham, George W. .... Springfield, IL
Tinkham, J. Jeffrey .... Chesapeake, VA
Tinkham, Jeffrey G. .... Houston, TX
Tinkham, John R. .... Chicago, IL
Tinkham, Matthew H., Jr. .... Northville, MI
Tinkham, Peter B. .... Dallas, TX
Tinkham, Richard P., Jr. .... Indianapolis, IN
Tinkham, Richard P., Jr., P.C.
Indianapolis, IN
Tinkham, Robert K. .... St. Petersburg, FL
Tinkham, Thomas W. .... Minneapolis, MN
Tinkle, Lloyd L. .... Sioux City, IA
Tinkle, Marshall J. .... Portland, ME
Tinkler & Bennett .... Santa Fe, NM
Tinkler, Cornelia E .... Piqua, OH
Tinkler, David K. .... Columbia, SC
Tinkler, James C. .... Houston, TX
Tinkler, Kenneth Anthony .... Tampa, FL
Tinkler, Paul E. .... Charleston, SC
Tinkler, Samuel A., Jr. .... Fort Lauderdale, FL
Tinkler, Stephen E. .... Santa Fe, NM
Tinkler, Timothy E. .... Painesville, OH
Tinkler, Virginia W. .... Atlanta, GA
Tinkler, Virginia W. .... Decatur, GA
Tinkler, Virginia W. .... Lawrenceville, GA
Tinkler, William, Jr. .... Decatur, GA
Tinkler, William Jr., Attorney at Law, P.C.
Atlanta, GA
Decatur, GA
Tinkler-Mendez, Marisa .... Miami, FL
Tinko, Joseph W. .... Meadville, PA
Tinkoff, Bruce N. .... Chicago, IL
Tinkoff, Paysoff, Jr. .... Chicago, IL
Tinkoff, Popko & DuVal .... Chicago, IL
Tinl, Robert T. .... Brunswick, OH
Tinley, Christopher J. .... Council Bluffs, IA
Tinley, Emmet .... Council Bluffs, IA
Tinley, Jeffrey J. .... Waterbury, CT
Tinley, Nastri, Renehan & Dost, LLP
Hartford, CT
New Haven, CT
Waterbury, CT
Tinley, Pat .... Kerrville, TX
Tinley, Thomas W., III .... Augusta, GA
Tinlin, Charles J. .... St. Augustine, FL
Tinling, Nicholas G. .... Sacramento, CA
Tinnell, Robert W. .... El Paso, TX
Tinnes, Christy .... Washington, DC
Tinney, Carolyn L.E. .... Buffalo, NY
Tinney, Claire Jones .... Athens, AL
Tinney, John A. .... Roanoke, AL
Tinney, John H. .... Charleston, WV
Tinney, John H., Jr. .... Charleston, WV
Tinney, Joseph C. .... Petaluma, CA
Tinney, Joseph E. .... Petaluma, CA
Tinney, Larry L. .... Fayetteville, NC
Tinney, Lee B. .... Everett, WA
Tinney, Michael L. .... Oklahoma City, OK
Tinney, Sarah B. .... Champaign, IL
Tinney, William H. .... Tucson, AZ
Tinnin, Robert P., Jr. .... Albuquerque, NM
Tinning, William J. .... Portland, TX
Tinning, William J., P.C. .... Portland, TX
Tinnion, Antoine .... New York, NY
Tinnon, Scott E. .... Atlanta, GA
Tinnon, Scott E., P.C. .... Atlanta, GA
Tinnon, Susan Watson .... Bowling Green, KY
Tinnyo, James .... Harrisburg, PA
Tino, Carol A .... Philadelphia, PA
Tino, Rita J. .... White Plains, NY
Tinsley Bacon Tinsley, L.L.C.
Alpharetta, GA
Atlanta, GA
Tinsley, Carlos O. .... Redwood City, CA
Tinsley, Ernest D. .... Phoenix, AZ
Tinsley, Ferrell and Tinsley .... Lynchburg, VA
Tinsley, Fred .... Dallas, TX
Tinsley, Fred, Law Office of, P.C.
Dallas, TX
Tinsley, Gary W. .... Daytona Beach, FL
Tinsley, James Paul .... Jackson, MS
Tinsley, Jimmie E. .... San Francisco, CA
Tinsley, Laurence G., Jr. .... Phoenix, AZ
Tinsley, M. Patrick .... Denver, CO
Tinsley, Mansur .... Boulder, CO
Tinsley, Margaret R. .... Tempe, AZ
Tinsley, Mark B. .... Columbia, SC
Tinsley, Nancy G. .... Indianapolis, IN
Tinsley, Paul R. .... Houston, TX
Tinsley, Robert E., Jr. .... Lynchburg, VA
Tinsley, Robert E., Sr. .... Lynchburg, VA
Tinsley, Robert J. .... Greenwood, SC
Tinsley, Steven R. .... Kissimmee, FL
Tinsley, V. Randall .... Greensboro, NC
Tinsley, Walton Eugene .... Los Angeles, CA
Tinsley, Willard M. .... Houston, TX
Tinsley, William C., II .... Alpharetta, GA
Tinsley, William D., Jr. .... Greenwood, SC
Tinsley, William J., Jr. .... Newark, NJ
New York, NY
Tinsman & Houser, Inc. .... San Antonio, TX
Tinsman, Richard .... San Antonio, TX
Tinsman, Theodore Landon .... Springfield, MO
Tinstman, Dale C. .... Lincoln, NE
Tinstman, William A. .... Omaha, NE
Tintenfass, Chester S. .... Voorhees, NJ
Philadelphia, PA
Tinter, Jay A. .... New Hyde Park, NY
Tintera, Thomas J. .... Hillsboro, OR
Tinti, Steven J. .... Crystal Falls, MI
Tinti, William J., P.C. .... Salem, MA
Tintner, Leonard .... Harrisburg, PA
Tintner, Robert S. .... Philadelphia, PA
Tinubu, Babatunde G. .... Far Rockaway, NY
Tinucci, Richard C. .... Media, PA
Tinucci, Victor H., III .... New York, NY
Tiongson, Russell Tagle
New Hyde Park, NY
Tipaldo, Joseph F. .... Garden City, NY
Tiplady, Robert P. .... Detroit, MI
Tiplady, Robert P. .... Plymouth, MI
Tipler, James Harvey .... Andalusia, AL
Los Angeles, CA
Fort Walton Beach, FL
Atlanta, GA
Tipler, Steven D. .... Birmingham, AL
Tipograph, Peter S. .... New York, NY
Tipp, Bryan Charles .... Missoula, MT
Tipp, Frizzell & Buley .... Missoula, MT
Tipp, Raymond P. .... Missoula, MT
Tippens, Daphne D. .... Washington, DC
Tippens, Terry W. .... Oklahoma City, OK
Tipper, Donald G. .... Tuscaloosa, AL
Tipperman, Mark .... La Grande, OR
Tippet, Sarah Eden .... Hartford, CT
Tippett & Associates .... Boulder, CO
Tippett, C. Lewis .... Lebanon, OH
Tippett, Donald C. .... Fort Smith, AR
Tippett, J. Royall, Jr. .... Baltimore, MD
Tippett, J. Tyler .... Atlanta, GA
Tippett, Michael R. .... Atlanta, GA
Tippett, Robert S. .... Los Angeles, CA
Tippett, Scott A. .... Boulder, CO
Tippett, Scott K. .... Winston-Salem, NC
Tippett, Sherry J. .... Santa Fe, NM
Tippett, Walter L., Jr. .... Raleigh, NC
Tippetts, David R. .... Houston, TX
Tippie, Alan G. .... Los Angeles, CA
Tippin, Elizabeth A. .... San Francisco, CA
Tipping, Christopher A. .... Akron, OH
Tipping, Clayton D. .... Grand Junction, CO
Tipping, Ellen M. .... Santa Ana, CA
Tipping, Harry A. .... Akron, OH
Tipping, Harry A., Co., L.P.A., A Legal Prof. Assn. .... Akron, OH
Canton, OH
New Philadelphia, OH
Youngstown, OH
Tipping, Marla R. .... Minneapolis, MN
Tipping, Mary Jo .... Cleveland, OH
Tipping, William J. .... Minneapolis, MN
Tippins, Bedell A. .... Chicago, IL
Tippins and Cornaire, L.L.P. .... Troy, NY
Tippins, J. Rankin .... Houston, TX
Tippins, Mark E. .... Jacksonville, FL
Tippins, Mark E., P.C. .... Jacksonville, FL
Tippins, Robert M. .... Fort Walton Beach, FL
Tippins, Timothy M. .... Garden City, NY
Troy, NY
Tippit, John H. .... Boulder, CO
Tippit, John L., III .... Edinburg, TX
Tippit, Sara L. .... Weslaco, TX
Tippit, Terry R. .... Austin, TX
Tipple, Elvia N. M. .... Dallas, TX
Tipps, Dale A. .... Nashville, TN
Tipps, J. Mark .... Nashville, TN
Tipps, James R. .... Beverly Hills, CA
Tipps, Kimberli Joi .... Nashville, TN
Tipps, Maynard E. .... Charlotte, NC
Tipps, Michael D. .... Ardmore, OK
Tipps, Michael J. .... San Antonio, TX
Tipps, Shelley A. .... Yukon, OK
Tipps, Stephen Gillham .... Houston, TX
Tippy, T. Allen .... Mobile, AL
Tips & Gibson .... Tulsa, OK
Tips, Robert H. .... Tulsa, OK
Tipsord, Jennifer A. .... Los Angeles, CA
Tipsword, Marilyn J. .... Chicago, IL
Tipsword, Rolland F. .... Taylorville, IL
Tipton, Alan L. .... Phoenix, AZ
Tipton, Ann J. .... Pensacola, FL
Tipton, Ben W., Jr. .... Fort Worth, TX
Tipton, Brian R. .... Phillipsburg, NJ
Tipton, C. Anne .... Memphis, TN
Tipton, Caroline .... Washington, DC
Tipton, Carrie A. .... Leesburg, VA
Tipton, Cecil M., Jr. .... Opelika, AL
Tipton, Cheryl A. .... Honolulu, HI
Tipton, Darrel D. .... Sacramento, CA
Tipton, David J. .... Bradenton, FL
Tipton, David W. .... Bristol, TN
Tipton, David W. .... Knoxville, TN
Sevierville, TN
Tipton, Debra Gemgnani .... Monterey, CA
Tipton, Deric F. .... Loxahatchee, FL
Tipton, Deric F. .... West Palm Beach, FL
Tipton, Donald L. .... Sacramento, CA
Tipton, Drew B. .... Houston, TX
Tipton, Elaine M. .... Redwood City, CA
Tipton, Elizabeth Ann .... Decatur, GA
Tipton, Elizabeth H., & Assoc., P.L.L.C.
Houston, TX
Tipton, Elizabeth Holbert .... Houston, TX
Tipton, Ellen .... Houston, TX
Tipton, F. Paul .... Orlando, FL
Tipton, Frank P. .... San Antonio, TX
Tipton, Governor .... New York, NY
Tipton, Guy L. .... Birmingham, AL
Tipton, Henry W. .... Pensacola, FL
Tipton, Hiram G. .... Knoxville, TN
Tipton, James "Rell", Jr. .... Houston, TX
Tipton, James S., Jr. .... Knoxville, TN
Tipton, Jeffery R. .... Corbin, KY
Tipton, John M. .... Los Angeles, CA
Tipton, John M. .... Natchez, MS
Tipton and Jones .... Bristol, TN
Tipton, Joseph M. .... Knoxville, TN
Tipton, Larry R. .... Boston, MA
Tipton, LeRoy, Jr. .... Greeneville, TN
Tipton, Mark N. .... Ocala, FL
Tipton, Nicole A. .... Cincinnati, OH
Tipton, Patrick Bryan .... Princeton, NJ
Tipton, Paul W. .... Dallas, TX
Tipton, Paul W., & Associates, P.C.
Dallas, TX
Tipton, Raymond J. .... Scottsdale, AZ
Tipton, Richard D. .... Chicago, IL
Tipton, Ritchie L. .... Tuscaloosa, AL
Tipton, R. M. .... Jackson, MS
Tipton, Robert L. .... Akron, OH
Tipton, Robert R., (P.C.) .... Livermore, CA
Tipton, S. Victor .... Maitland, FL
Tipton, Senith C. .... Jackson, MS
Tipton, Sheila K. .... Des Moines, IA
Tipton, Steven M. .... Austin, TX
Tipton, Timothy D. .... Excelsior Springs, MO
Tipton, Timothy E. .... Tulsa, OK
Tipton and Tipton .... Corbin, KY
Tipton & Tipton .... Covington, TN
Tipton, Virgil .... Pauls Valley, OK
Tipton, W. Keith .... Broomfield, CO
Tipton, Walker T. .... Covington, TN
Tipton, Wesley R. .... Corbin, KY
Tipton-Downie, Sarah .... Vidalia, GA
Tipton-Downie, Sarah, P.C. .... Vidalia, GA
Tira, James J. .... Coal City, IL
Tira, John M. .... Coal City, IL
Tira, Joseph R. .... Cleveland, OH
Tira & Tira .... Coal City, IL
Tirabassi, E. Ralph .... Sarasota, FL
Tirabassi, Phillip N. .... Baltimore, MD
Bel Air, MD
Tirabasso, Victor J., Jr. .... Brooklyn, NY
Tirado, Armando J. (IBA) .... **Memphis, TN**
Tirado, Elizabeth .... Terrell, TX
Tirado-Vales, Mariangela .... San Juan, PR
Tirana, Bardyl R. .... Washington, DC
New York, NY
Tirapelle, Leon E. .... Fresno, CA
Tiras, E. Alan .... Incline Village, NV
Tiras, Mitchell A. .... Houston, TX
Tirella, Alfred J. .... Miami Shores, FL
Tirella, David T. .... Tampa, FL
Tirelli, Linda M. .... New Canaan, CT
Tirey, Patricia H. .... San Diego, CA
Tirik, Kelly J. .... Miami, FL
Tirino, Denise .... Kew Gardens, NY
Tirino, Kristin M. .... Greenwich, CT
Jericho, NY
Tiritilli, Christine M. .... West Orange, NJ
Tirola & Herring .... Stamford, CT
Westport, CT
New York, NY
Tirola, Vincent S. .... Westport, CT
New York, NY
Tirona, Roberto Tria .... Downers Grove, IL
Tirone, Anthony R. .... White Plains, NY
Tirone, Gregg M. .... Rochester, NY
Tirone, John A. .... Harper Woods, MI
Tirone, Joseph G. .... Charlotte, NC
Tirone, Vito F. .... Bronx, NY
Tirpak, Edward T. .... Buffalo, NY
Tirpak, Ronald J. .... Fort Wayne, IN
Tirre, Amy N. .... Reno, NV
Tirrell, Nancy Sue .... Santa Ana, CA
Tirrell, Philip I. .... Boston, MA
Tirrell, Richard S. .... Boston, MA
Tirro, Richard A. .... Omaha, NE
Tirschwell, Donald .... New City, NY
Tirva, Algis A. .... Lisle, IL
Tisa, Stephen R.
Agency for International Development,
Office of the General Counsel, GV
Tisano, William E. .... Ellicott City, MD
Tisch, Donna J. .... Fort Myers, FL
Tisch, Howard B. .... New York, NY
Tisch, Melinda A. .... San Francisco, CA
Tisch, Richard G. .... Danbury, CT
Tisch, Ronald I. .... Washington, DC
Tisch, Wendy J. .... Pound Ridge, NY
Tisch, William F. .... Los Angeles, CA
Tischenkel, Robert .... Miami, FL

Tischer, Arthur H. ... St. Louis, MO
Tischer, Courtenay L. ... **Danbury, CT**
Tischer, Dirk P. ... Royal Oak, MI
Tischer, Gene J. ... Tallahassee, FL
Tischer, Michelle Julia Galaska ... Parma, OH
Tischhauser, Carol Diane ... Columbia, MD
Tischleder, Edward C. ... **Eagan, MN**
Tischler, Beth S. ... Westfield, NJ
Tischler, Bruce A. ... **Cape Coral, FL**
Tischler, C. Merle ... York, PA
Tischler, David J. ... New York, NY
Tischler, Dorothy R. ... Troy, NY
Tischler, Douglas G. ... **Uniondale, NY**
Tischler, Harry S. ... Philadelphia, PA
Tischler, Keith C. ... Tallahassee, FL
Tischler, Milton ... Monroe, NY
Tischler, Robert G. ... New York, NY
Tischler, Ronald B., (P.C.)
Los Angeles, CA
Tischler, Ronni ... **Detroit, MI**
Tischler, Sarah Gentry ... Burlington, VT
Tischler, Therese ... Trumansburg, NY
Tischman, Michael B. ... **Atlantic City, NJ**
Newark, NJ
New York, NY
Tisci, Michael A. ... **Winston-Salem, NC**
Tisci, Ross M. ... **Auburn, NY**
Tisdahl, Alfred C., Jr. ... **Chicago, IL**
Tisdal, Mart ... Clinton, OK
Tisdale, Carolyn Schwarz ... **Southfield, MI**
Tisdale, Charles H., Jr. ... **Atlanta, GA**
Tisdale, Cindy V. ... **Waco, TX**
Tisdale, Dana J. ... Grafton, ND
Tisdale, Darlene ... Houston, TX
Tisdale & Davis, P.A. ... **Portland, ME**
Tisdale, Donald K. ... Winston-Salem, NC
Tisdale, Douglas M. ... **Denver, CO**
Tisdale, H. Bernard, III ... **Raleigh, NC**
Greenville, SC
Tisdale, Jeffrey A. ... **Los Angeles, CA**
Tisdale, John A. ... **Boston, MA**
Tisdale, John H. ... Frederick, MD
Tisdale, John R. ... **Little Rock, AR**
Tisdale, Jon H. ... **Los Angeles, CA**
Tisdale, Laverne S. ... Atlanta, GA
Tisdale & Lennon, LLC ... **Southport, CT**
Stamford, CT
New York, NY
Tisdale, Melanie Collins ... Niagara Falls, NY
Tisdale & Nicholson, LLP
Los Angeles, CA
Tisdale, Norwood Boyd ... **Jacksonville, NC**
Tisdale, Patricia C. ... **Denver, CO**
Tisdale, Patricia S. ... **Gulfport, MS**
Tisdale, Raphael E. ... Los Angeles, CA
Tisdale, Samuel T. ... Greenfield, MA
Tisdale, Steve ... Eudora, AR
Tisdale, Stuart W., Jr. ... **Portland, ME**
Tisdale, T. Mark ... Midland, TX
Tisdale, Thomas K. ... Cleveland, TN
Tisdale, Thomas L. ... **Southport, CT**
New York, NY
Tisdale, Thomas S., Jr. ... **Charleston, SC**
Tisdale, Warren L. ... **Norfolk, VA**
Tisdale, William E. ... Biloxi, MS
Tisdale, Wright, Jr. ... **Knoxville, TN**
Tisdall, Nancy P. ... **Denver, CO**
Tisdel, Hockersmith, Burns & Mueller, P.C.
Ouray, CO
Tisdel, Hockersmith & Burns, P.C.
Montrose, CO
Tisdel, Malcolm ... Plainview, TX
Tisdell, David L. ... Clarksdale, MS
Tisdell, Moore, Walter & Bigsby
Syracuse, NY
Tisdell, Robert L. ... Syracuse, NY
Tise, Allan Brandon ... Wilmington, NC
Tish, Elyse M. ... Northbrook, IL
Tish, Eugene C. ... Salem, OR
Tish, Martin H. ... **Chicago, IL**
Tishberg, Mark S. ... Milwaukee, WI
Tishberg, S. D. ... Milwaukee, WI
Tishelman, Edward I. ... **New York, NY**
Tishelman, Harry S. ... Nyack, NY
Tisher, C. Tim ... Columbia, TN
Tisher, Francisca P. ... Napa, CA
Tishgart, Leonard ... Philadelphia, PA
Tishkoff, Gregory C. ... Mesa, AZ
Tishkoff, Judith M. ... **Los Angeles, CA**
Tishkoff, William G. ... **Ann Arbor, MI**
Tishkowski, Julie A. ... **Boulder, CO**
Tishler, Barbara S. ... Northbrook, IL
Tishler, David F.
Department Of Health And Human Services, Food & Drug Administration, GV
Tishler, Gerald P. ... **Boston, MA**
Tishler, John C. ... **Nashville, TN**
Tishler, Leslie G. ... New York, NY
Tishler, Louis B., Jr. ... **Chicago, IL**
Tishler, Nicholas E. ... **Albany, NY**
Tishler, Nicholas E. ... **Niskayuna, NY**
Tishler, Nicholas E. ... **Schenectady, NY**
Tishler, Richard N. ... **St. Louis, MO**
Tishler & Wald, Ltd. ... **Chicago, IL**
Tishman, David G.
Federal Energy Regulatory Commission, Office of the General Counsel, GV
Tishman, Lonnie G. ... New York, NY
Tishman, Pamela ... New York, NY
Tishman, Ted ... Pittsburgh, PA
Tishok, John M. ... **Pittsburgh, PA**
Tishuk, Barbara Starke
Federal Deposit Insurance Corporation, Liquidation Branch, GV
Tisi, Christopher V. ... **Washington, DC**
Tisi, Steven A. ... **San Diego, CA**
Tisinger, Amy Beth ... Woodstock, VA
Tisinger, Billy Joe ... **Winchester, VA**
Tisinger, David H. ... **Carrollton, GA**
Tisinger, Richard G., Jr. ... **Carrollton, GA**
Tisinger, Richard G., Sr. ... **Carrollton, GA**
Tisinger, Tisinger, Vance & Greer, A Professional Corporation ... **Carrollton, GA**
Columbus, GA
Villa Rica, GA
Tisinger, Travis J. ... **Winchester, VA**
Tiska, Tracey A. ... **New York, NY**
Tisman, Russell G. ... **Carle Place, NY**
Tisman, Stephen E. ... **New York, NY**
Tismo, J. Pierre ... **Covington, KY**
Tisne, Peter B. ... **New York, NY**
Tiso, Christopher A. ... **Miami, FL**
Tiso, Christopher Paul ... Tuckahoe, NY
Tisoglu, Melda A. ... **New York, NY**
Tison, Claude H., Jr. ... Tampa, FL
Tison, Claude H., Jr., P.A. ... Tampa, FL
Tison, J. Earl ... Columbia City, IN
Tison, Julia K. ... Hartsville, SC
Tison, Krystal S. ... Harrisburg, IL
Tison, Sidney S., Jr. ... Hartsville, SC
Tisone, Raymond J. ... Warren, OH
Tissandier, Stephen J. ... Fayetteville, OH
Tisser, Doron M. ... **Calabasas, CA**
Tissi, Vincent J. ... Fenton, MO
Tissier, Theresa ... Malibu, CA
Tissot, Jeremy L. ... **Los Angeles, CA**
Tissue, John W. ... Jacksonville, FL
Tissue, Joseph N. ... **Charlotte, NC**
Tissue, Philip J. ... Oak Hill, WV
Tistaert, Lawrence C. ... **Los Angeles, CA**
Tita, Joseph L. ... Houston, TX
Tita, Kristin M. ... **Denver, CO**
Titas, Francis G. ... **Cleveland, OH**
Titchell, Haskell ... **San Francisco, CA**
Titchell, Maltzman, Mark & Ohleyer, A Professional Corporation
San Francisco, CA
Titchener, William R. ... **Raleigh, NC**
Titcher, Paul J. ... **Los Angeles, CA**
Titcomb, Judith L. ... **St. Paul, MN**
Titcomb, Martin M. ... San Francisco, CA
Titcomb, Martin McKown, Professional Corporation ... San Francisco, CA
Titcomb, Norma De Santis ... **Honolulu, HI**
Titcombe, Harry G., Jr. ... Aurora, CO
Titelbaum, Daniel E. ... **San Francisco, CA**
Titelbaum, Emily H. ... Pueblo, CO
Titelbaum, Sydney ... Oakland, CA
Titens, Michael C. ... **Dallas, TX**
Titgemeyer, Sylvia G. ... **St. Louis, MO**
Tither, W. Thomas, Jr. ... Philadelphia, PA
Titiner, Steven D. ... Aurora, IL
Title, Frederick S. ... New Brunswick, NJ
Title, Gail Migdal ... **Los Angeles, CA**
Title, Heidi ... New York, NY
Title, Julius M. ... Los Angeles, CA
Title, Lawrence H., Law Office of
Los Angeles, CA
Title, Neil I. ... **Arlington, VA**
Title, Peter S. ... **New Orleans, LA**
Titlebaum, Allen R. ... Skokie, IL
Titlebaum, Earl S. ... Hopkinton, MA
Titlebaum, Ellen R. ... **Cleveland, OH**
Titlebaum, Joseph E. ... **Canton, MA**
Titler, John M. ... Cedar Rapids, IA
Titley, Ian D. ... **Richmond, VA**
Titley, John H. ... Watertown, CT
Titley, Larry J. ... **Grand Rapids, MI**
Titley, Robert L. ... **Milwaukee, WI**
Titlow, Robert A. ... Indianapolis, IN
Titman, David A. ... Ellicott City, MD
Titmus, Janice Crosetti ... Lafayette, CA
Titmus, Thomas J. ... Lafayette, CA
Tito, Celeste L. ... Des Moines, IA
Titolo Law Offices ... **Las Vegas, NV**
Titolo, Timothy R. ... **Las Vegas, NV**
Titone, Anthony J. ... Fort Lauderdale, FL
Titone, Anthony J., P.A.
Fort Lauderdale, FL
Titone, John A. ... Mount Holly, NJ
Titone, Joseph P. ... **Baton Rouge, LA**
Titone, Vito J., Jr. ... **New York, NY**
Titoni, Frank Wm. ... Pueblo, CO
Titowsky, Michael B. ... **New York, NY**
Titrud, Blake K. ... **New York, NY**
Titrud, Jeffrey S. ... Ocala, FL
Titshaw, Scott C. ... **Atlanta, GA**
Titsworth, Daniel B. ... Cary, NC
Titsworth, Thomas D. ... Carmel, IN
Titsworth, Thomas D., Jr. ... **Chicago, IL**
Titta, Peter A. ... **Grand Rapids, MI**
Tittel, Bruce ... **Cincinnati, OH**
Tittel, Larry D. ... Ness City, KS
Tittemore, Lisa M. ... **Boston, MA**
Titterington, Joseph P.
Oklahoma City, OK
Titterton, Anne E. ... Wilmington, DE
Titterton, Edward G., III ... Philadelphia, PA
Tittle, Charles P. ... Tavernier, FL
Tittle, David O. ... **Indianapolis, IN**
Tittle, Deborah L. ... Tyler, TX
Tittle, Donald S. ... Fairview Park, OH
Tittle, Fred N., Jr. ... Key Largo, FL
Tittle & Holbrook ... Metairie, LA
Tittle, Jack A., Jr. ... Metairie, LA
Tittle, James D., Jr. ... **West Palm Beach, FL**
Tittle, Lawrence E. ... Independence, MO
Tittle, Lawrence E., P.C. ... Independence, MO
Tittle, Patrick S. ... **Peekskill, NY**
Tittle & Tittle, P.A. ... Tavernier, FL
Tittle, William P. ... Metairie, LA
Tittmann, Harold H. ... Philadelphia, PA
Tittmann, Raymond J. ... **San Francisco, CA**
Tittsworth, Clayton M. ... Brandon, FL
Tittsworth, David G. ... Washington, DC
Tittsworth, Grabbe & Spillers ... Atlanta, GA
Tittsworth, Michael W. ... Atlanta, GA
Titus, Alan D. ... **Washington, DC**
Titus, Alan J. ... **Mill Valley, CA**
Titus, Angela C. ... **Haddonfield, NJ**
Titus, Austin E., Jr. ... Brooklyn, NY
Titus, Brent A. ... **Lansing, MI**
Titus, Bruce E. ... **Vienna, VA**
Titus, Brueckner & Berry, P.C.
Phoenix, AZ
Scottsdale, AZ
Titus, Cassius C. ... Los Angeles, CA
Titus, Christina M. ... New York, NY
Titus, Christopher G. L. ... **Fort Myers, FL**
Titus, Curtis V. ... **Waterbury, CT**
Titus, D. Douglas ... Seattle, WA
Titus, David B. ... Marion, MA
Titus, Douglas Jules, Jr. ... **Tampa, FL**
Titus, Frank A. ... **Columbus, OH**
Titus, Gary L. ... Dayton, OH
Titus, Gary R. ... Independence, MO
Titus, Gerald M., Jr. ... **Parkersburg, WV**
Titus & Glasgow ... **Rockville, MD**
Titus, Harry M. ... Saginaw, MI
Titus, Herbert W. ... Virginia Beach, VA
Titus, Hillis & Reynolds, P.C. ... **Tulsa, OK**
Titus, Ilene ... Worcester, MA
Titus, J Schaad ... **Tulsa, OK**
Titus, Jack A. ... Dallas, TX
Titus, Janet K. ... New York, NY
Titus, Jeffrey A. ... Santa Rosa, CA
Titus, Jim R. ... **Lincoln, NE**
Titus, John A. ... Rochester, NY
Titus, John D. ... **Phoenix, AZ**
Titus, John E. ... **Chicago, IL**
Titus, John W. ... **Nashville, TN**
Titus, Jon A. ... **Scottsdale, AZ**
Titus, Kenneth C. ... Durham, NC
Titus, Kevin A. ... **Chicago, IL**
Titus, Lee S. ... New Haven, CT
Titus, Lewis R., Jr. ... Pasadena, CA
Titus, Margie J. ... **Denver, CO**
Titus, Marlana K. ... Washington, DC
Titus & McConomy LLP ... Pittsburgh, PA
Titus & McDonald, P.A. ... **Fort Myers, FL**
Titus, Patricia Jo ... Los Angeles, CA
Titus, Paul Allen ... Staunton, VA
Titus, Paul H. ... **Pittsburgh, PA**
Titus, Richard J. ... San Jose, CA
Titus, Richard R. ... **Westminster, MD**
Titus, Robert B. ... **San Diego, CA**
Titus, Robert B. ... Springfield, MA
Titus, Roger W. ... **Rockville, MD**
Titus, Susan B. ... San Francisco, CA
Titus, Thomas W. ... Colorado Springs, CO
Titus, Timothy C. ... Kansas City, MO
Titus, Troy A. ... Virginia Beach, VA
Titus, Troy, P.C. ... Virginia Beach, VA
Titus, Victor A. ... Farmington, NM
Titus, Warren I., Jr. ... **Melville, NY**
Titus-Rogan, Dawn ... **Alexandria, VA**
Titzler, Scott K. ... Grants Pass, OR
Tiu, James F. ... Washington, DC
Tiura, Anne B. ... **Seattle, WA**
Tius, Susan ... **Honolulu, HI**
Tive, Ralph D. ... Harrisburg, PA
Tivenan, Charles P. ... Brick, NJ
Tiveron, Diane R. ... Amherst, NY
Tivin, Barry S. ... Flushing, NY
Tivin, Mark I. ... Chicago, IL
Tivnan, Thomas F. ... New York, NY
Tivol, Thomas S. ... Kansas City, MO
Tivvis, Joseph I., Jr. ... **Baltimore, MD**
Tiwald, John R. ... Albuquerque, NM
Tiwari, Rana ... Orlando, FL
Tixier, Joseph C. ... **Itasca, IL**
Tjaden, Christopher J. ... **Omaha, NE**
Tjaden, Earl D. ... Kansas City, KS
Tjaden, John R. ... Silver Spring, MD
Tjaden, Kurt F. ... **Omaha, NE**
Tjaden, Thomas R. ... **Sarasota, FL**
Tjader, Michele A. ... **Madison, WI**
Tjan, Lawrence J. ... Los Angeles, CA
Tjandrasuwita, Ina ... Laguna Niguel, CA
Tjelmeland, Kurt Thomas ... Ely, IA
Tjioe, Roy John ... **Honolulu, HI**
Tjoflat, Gerald Bard ... Jacksonville, FL
Tjoflat, Marcia Parker ... **Jacksonville, FL**
Tjon, Lowell O. ... Lisbon, ND
Tjossem, Robert P., (P.S.) ... **Kirkland, WA**
Tkac, Tracy S. ... Lincoln Park, NJ
Tkach, John A. ... Pasadena, CA
T'Kach, Stephen J. ... Department of Justice, Criminal Division, GV
Tkacik, Douglas Jon ... **Bethlehem, PA**
Tkacik, Joseph Christopher ... Mount Airy, MD
T'Kindt, Brian J. ... **Fort Wayne, IN**
Tlapek, David L. ... Cape Girardeau, MO
Tlusty, David S. ... **New York, NY**
Tlusty, Hittner, Kennedy & Freeburg, S.C.
Birnamwood, WI
Schofield, WI
Tlusty, Jay R. ... **Abbotsford, WI**
Merrill, WI
Tlusty, Jerome P. ... Schofield, WI
Tlusty, Jessica J. ... Schofield, WI
To, Lindy Bach ... Houston, TX
To, My Chi ... **New York, NY**
Toabe and Riley ... Chatham, MA
Toadvin, William C. ... Baton Rouge, LA
Toadvine, Allen W. ... Langhorne, PA
Toadvine, J. René ... **Charlotte, NC**
Toadvine, Patricia Pritt ... **Washington, DC**
Toadvine, Wm. M. ... Baltimore, MD
Toal, Charles A. ... Tuxedo, NY
Toal, Daniel J. ... **New York, NY**
Toal, David F. ... **Pittsburgh, PA**
Toal, Helen L. ... **Chicago, IL**
Toal, Jean Hoefer ... Columbia, SC
Toal, John A. ... **Norristown, PA**
Toal, John Christopher ... Sharon, MA
Toal, John H. ... Media, PA
Toal, Margaret L. ... **Boulder, CO**
Denver, CO
Toal, William R., III ... Media, PA
Toal, William T. ... Columbia, SC
Toale, James E. ... **Sarasota, FL**
Toale, Robert S. ... **Gretna, LA**
Toaltoan, Jeffrey Sheridan ... Philadelphia, PA
Toan, Robert W. ... **New York, NY**
Toas, Joshua B. ... Albany, NY
Toates, W. Russell, (P.C.) ... Dallas, TX
Toavs, Terrance L. ... Wolf Point, MT
Toback, Alan Jay ... **Chicago, IL**
Toback, Ann B. ... **Boston, MA**
Toback, Arthur M. ... **New York, NY**
Toback & Associates ... **Dallas, TX**
Toback, David Stuart ... Orlando, FL
Toback, Hyman & Bernstein
New York, NY
Toback, Jeffrey W. ... New York, NY
Toback, Leejanice ... New York, NY
Toback, Matthew A. ... **Dallas, TX**
Toback, Monica Ann ... **Atlanta, GA**
Tobak, James W. ... **Providence, RI**
Tobak, Mark ... Pound Ridge, NY
Tobak, Michael J., III ... **Chicago, IL**
Toban, Scott B. ... **Chicago, IL**
Tobar, Laurel Gallaher ... San Diego, CA
Tobbe, L. Lee ... Monticello, KY
Tobben, Daniel G., (P.C.) ... **St. Louis, MO**
Tobben, David B. ... Union, MO
Tobe, Richard ... Buffalo, NY
Tobe, Roslyn T. ... Sacramento, CA
Tobe, Susan Bring ... Buffalo, NY
Toben, Bradley J.B. ... Waco, TX
Toben, Elizabeth A. ... Waco, TX
Tobenkin, David N. ... **Washington, DC**
Tobenkin, Michele Mercer ... Inglewood, CA
Tober, Gary P. ... **Seattle, WA**
Tober, John E. ... **Miami, FL**
Tober Law Offices, P.A. ... **Portsmouth, NH**
Tober, Peter J. ... Lakewood, NJ
Tober, Stephen J. ... Chicago, IL
Tober, Stephen L. ... **Portsmouth, NH**
Toberer, Jeffrey D. ... **Omaha, NE**
Toberman, Beth K. ... **Atlanta, GA**
Toberoff, Max ... New York, NY
Toberoff, Tessler & Schochet, L.L.P.
New York, NY
Toberty, David P. ... Newport Beach, CA
Tobey, Beverly Meeker ... Sacramento, CA
Tobey, Bruce D. ... **Los Angeles, CA**
Tobey, Carl Payne "Chip", Jr. ... Boerne, TX
Tobey, Gary H. ... **Denver, CO**
Tobey, Harold W. ... Anchorage, AK
Tobey, J. E. "Mike", III ... Davenport, IA
Tobey, Julia C. ... New York, NY
Tobey, Laurence E.
Department of State, GV
Tobey Law Firm, The ... Boerne, TX
Tobey, Margaret L. ... **Washington, DC**
Tobey, Mark B. ... Austin, TX
Tobey, McClure & Lemmon
Sacramento, CA
Tobey, Paul A. ... Chicago, IL
Tobey, Rayanne Griffin ... **Tulsa, OK**
Tobey, Robert L. ... **Dallas, TX**
Tobey & Toro, P.C. ... **Denver, CO**
Tobey, William R.
Federal Labor Relations Authority, Office of the Solicitor, GV
Tobia, Andrew L. ... Sacramento, CA
Tobia, Annette M. ... Princeton, NJ
Tobia, George N. ... Gardner, MA
Tobia, George N., Jr. ... **Boston, MA**
Tobia, James ... **Wilmington, DE**
Tobia, Jill Sorger ... Montclair, NJ
Tobia, Kathleen R. ... **Allentown, PA**
Tobia, Patrick D. ... **Morristown, NJ**
Tobia, Robert ... Philadelphia, PA
Tobia, Ronald L. ... Montclair, NJ
Trenton, NJ
Tobia, Vincent J. ... **Buffalo, NY**
Tobias, Allan D. ... Walnut Creek, CA
Tobias, Alvin S. ... Manhattan Beach, CA
Tobias, Andy M. ... Houston, TX
Tobias, Barry I. ... Irwindale, CA
Tobias, Barry L. ... **Los Angeles, CA**
Tobias, Brian S.W. ... Denver, CO
Tobias, Carl W. ... Missoula, MT
Tobias, Charles H., Jr. ... Cincinnati, OH
Tobias, Constance B.
Department Of Veterans Affairs, Board of Veterans Appeals, GV
Tobias, David E. ... Hauppauge, NY
Tobias, David G. ... **New York, NY**
Tobias, David M. ... **Dallas, TX**
Tobias, Debra S. ... Calabasas, CA
Tobias, Desmond V. ... **Mobile, AL**
Tobias, Donald J., Law Offices of
New York, NY
Tobias, Emily A. ... Southern Pines, NC
Tobias, Emily Cosner ... Birmingham, MI
Tobias, Eric L. ... Washington, DC
Tobias, Geoffrey S. ... **Baltimore, MD**
Tobias, George W. ... Southfield, MI
Tobias, Gregory J. ... **Albuquerque, NM**
Tobias, Harry J. ... Hollister, CA
Tobias, Haven ... **Oklahoma City, OK**
Tobias, Ivan M., (P.A.) ... Coral Gables, FL
Tobias, Jeffrey ... Silver Spring, MD
Tobias, Jennifer Paley ... Hackensack, NJ
Tobias, Jos. M. ... Northfield, IL
Tobias, Kara ... New York, NY
Tobias, Kathryn J. ... Sacramento, CA
Tobias, Kraus & Torchia ... Cincinnati, OH

Todd, Joseph K. .... New York, NY
Todd, Joseph M. .... Jonesboro, GA
Todd, Joseph M., P.C. .... Jonesboro, GA
Todd, Judith F. .... Birmingham, AL
Todd, Julia A. .... St. Louis, MO
Todd, K. Chris .... Washington, DC
Todd, Kae C. .... Lewisburg, TN
Todd, Kathryn Kaeble .... Denver, CO
Todd, Kenneth G. .... Bloomington, IN
Todd, Kent E. .... Woodbury, MN
Todd, Kevin J. .... Chicago, IL
Todd, Kyra A. .... Washington, DC
Todd, Larry A. .... North Platte, NE
Todd, Leo J. .... Grass Valley, CA
Todd, Leslie A. .... Miami, FL
Todd, Letitia Rei .... San Francisco, CA
Todd & Levi, LLP .... New York, NY
Todd, Linda K. .... Indianapolis, IN
Todd, Lisa Anderson .... Department of Defense, Armed Services Board of Contract Appeals, GV
Todd, Lisa Victoria .... Riverside, CA
Todd, Loraine .... Encino, CA
Todd, Loui M., III .... Memphis, TN
Todd, Lynn E. .... San Diego, CA
Todd, Marcus R. .... Thomasville, GA
Todd, Margaret Blake .... Rancho Santa Fe, CA
Todd, Marilyn Ressler .... La Jolla, CA
Todd, Mark A. .... Dallas, TX
Todd, Marsha .... Riverside, CA
Todd, Melvin (Matt) A. .... San Antonio, TX
Todd, Meredith O. .... Claremont, CA
Todd, Michael Andrew .... New Albany, MS
Todd, Michael C. .... Washington, DC
Todd, Michael E. .... Paragould, AR
Todd, Michael Edward .... Houston, TX
Todd, Michael R. .... Tuckahoe, NY
Todd, Monteith P. .... Columbia, SC
Todd, Oliver E., Jr. .... Toledo, OH
Todd Parham Harris & Dixon, PLLC
Charlotte, NC
Todd, Patricia B. .... Charlotte, NC
Todd, Randal B. .... Pittsburgh, PA
Todd, Rebecca F. .... Lake Charles, LA
Todd, Richard J. .... Anchorage, AK
Todd, Richard Temby .... Pahrump, NV
Todd, Richard W. .... Treasury Department, Internal Revenue Service, GV
Todd, Richard W. .... Portland, OR
Todd, Rob .... Houston, TX
Todd, Robert A. .... Tulsa, OK
Todd, Robert B. .... Houston, TX
Todd, Robert H. .... Richardson, TX
Todd, Robert L., IV .... Greenville, GA
Todd, Robert L., IV .... La Grange, GA
Todd, Robert M. .... Clearwater, FL
Todd, Robert M., P.A. .... Clearwater, FL
St. Petersburg, FL
Todd, Robert S., II .... Rowley, MA
Todd, Roderick M., Jr. .... Camden, SC
Todd, Roger B. .... North Bend, OR
Todd, Ronald Eugene .... Otsego, MI
Todd, Ronald G. .... New York, NY
Todd, Ronald S. .... Kokomo, IN
Todd, Ronald W. .... Madison, WI
Todd, Rucker .... Louisville, KY
Todd, Ryan Curtis .... Sacramento, CA
Todd, S. Page .... Dothan, AL
Todd, S. Thomas .... Los Angeles, CA
Todd, Sandra J. Seaton .... Richmond, VA
Todd, Sara L. .... Hilliard, OH
Todd & Schodde, Inc. .... San Bernardino, CA
Todd, Sean Garnet .... Atlanta, GA
Todd, Sherry Abbott .... Oklahoma City, OK
Todd, Stanley M. .... Lumberton, NC
Todd, Stephan E. .... Mill Creek, WA
Todd, Stephan K. .... Pittsburgh, PA
Todd, Stephen C. .... Bowling Green, KY
Todd, Stephen M. .... St. Petersburg, FL
Todd, Stephen M. .... Kansas City, MO
Todd, Stephen M. .... Seattle, WA
Todd, Stephenson .... Kingsport, TN
Todd, Steven A. .... Portland, OR
Todd, Steven M. .... Brownsville, TX
Todd, Steven O. .... Charlotte, NC
Todd, Stuart W. .... Seattle, WA
Todd, T. Michael .... Charlotte, NC
Todd, Ted R. .... Madison, IN
Todd, Teresa L. .... Indianapolis, IN
Todd, Terry .... Tulsa, OK
Todd, Terry P. .... Independence, KS
Todd, Thomas .... Pittsburgh, PA
Todd, Thomas E. .... New Port Richey, FL
Todd, Thomas E., P.A. .... New Port Richey, FL
Todd, Thomas J. .... Aspen, CO
Todd, Thomas M. .... Lexington, KY
Todd, Thomas N. .... Chicago, IL
Todd, Tom .... Daytona Beach, FL
Todd, Vanderbloemen and Brady, P.A.
Lenoir, NC
Todd, Vernon R. .... Seminole, FL
Todd, Vincent C. .... Lakewood, CO
Todd, Virginia M. .... Jackson, MS
Todd, W Michael .... New London, NH
Todd & Wakefield .... Seattle, WA
Todd, Walker F. .... Chagrin Falls, OH
Todd & Walter .... Lexington, KY
Todd, Walter B., Jr. .... Columbia, SC
Todd, Walter J. .... Salem, OR
Todd, Warren R. .... Pensacola, FL
Todd & Weld .... Boston, MA
Todd, Will .... Boston, MA
Todd, William F., Jr. .... Conyers, GA
Todd, William G. .... Nixa, MO
Todd, William G. .... New York, NY
Todd, William L. .... Columbia, SC
Todd, William L., Jr. .... San Diego, CA
Todd, William M. .... Columbus, OH
Todd, William R. .... Flora, IL
Todd, William R. .... Flora, IL
Todd, William S. .... Kingsport, TN
Todd, Winship A., Jr. .... Seattle, WA
Todderud, Eric R. .... Portland, OR
Toddy, Clayton J. .... Sanford, NC
Toddy, Joseph M. .... Philadelphia, PA
Toddy, Matthew J. .... Atlanta, GA
Todel, Mortimer .... New York, NY
Toder, Brian N. .... St. Paul, MN
Toder, Brian N., Ltd. .... St. Paul, MN
Toder, Richard S. .... New York, NY
Todes, S. Bradley .... Houston, TX
Todesco, Andrew L. .... Houston, TX
Todhunter, L. Judson .... Chicago, IL
Todhunter, Marcia C. .... Menlo Park, CA
Todia, Ellen Zopff .... Parma Heights, OH
Todia, William C. .... Berea, OH
Todisco, Amy E. .... Fairfield, CT
Todisco, John J., Jr. .... Malden, MA
Todisco, Jos. A. .... Natick, MA
Todisco, Louis B. .... New Haven, CT
Todman, Terence A., Jr. .... New York, NY
Todor, John J. .... Columbus, OH
Todoro, Peter J. .... Buffalo, NY
Todoroff, Christopher M. .... Hartford, CT
Todoroff, James G. .... Mentor, OH
Todorov, Dimiter V. .... Omaha, NE
Todorov, Lynn S.
Small Business Administration, Office of the General Counsel, GV
Todorov, Vera M.I. .... Salinas, CA
Todorovic, Elizabeth Matich .... Chicago, IL
Todorovich, John B. .... New York, NY
Todres, Debra .... New York, NY
Todres, Jacob L. .... Flushing, NY
Todres, Sidney .... New York, NY
Todrys, Steven C. .... New York, NY
Todt, Blair W. .... Albany, NY
Todt, Charles P. .... St. Louis, MO
Todt, Daniel, Firm .... Cleveland, OH
Todt, Daniel T. .... Cleveland, OH
Todt Law Firm, The, P.C. .... St. Louis, MO
Todt, Michael C. .... St. Charles, MO
Todt, Rebecca L. .... Cleveland, OH
Todt, Robert W. .... Cleveland, OH
Todtman, Martin .... New York, NY
Todtman, Nachamie, Spizz & Johns, P.C.
New York, NY
Toebben, Scott D. .... Denver, CO
Toedt, D. C., III .... Houston, TX
Toedte, Lynn W. .... Denver, CO
Toedter, Dennis L. .... Tulsa, OK
Toelke, Donna Voss .... Boston, MA
Toelke, Richard A. .... Boston, MA
Toelle, John C. .... Denver, CO
Toeller, Melissa J. .... Dublin, OH
Toenjes, Bruce J. .... Shell Rock, IA
Toenjes, Vincent G. .... Denver, CO
Toennies, Marti S. .... Little Rock, AR
Toennis, Paul E. .... Billings, MT
Toensing, Brady C. .... Washington, DC
Toensing, Elizabeth C. .... St. Paul, MN
Toensing, Victoria .... Washington, DC
Toensmeier, Arthur M. .... Philadelphia, PA
Toepel, Eugene A. .... Onalaska, WI
Toepfer, Betty Nora
Federal Energy Regulatory Commission, Office of the General Counsel, GV
Toepfer, David M. .... Ravenna, OH
Toepfer, David S. .... Minneapolis, MN
Toepfer, Leslie Gartrell .... Denver, CO
Toepfer, Louis A. .... Saxtons River, VT
Toepfer, Michael A. .... Galena, IL
Warren, IL
Toepfer, R. Elizabeth .... Milpitas, CA
Toepfer, Robert A. .... Bay Village, OH
Toepfer, Susan J. .... Miami, FL
Toepfer, Thomas L. .... Hays, KS
Toepke, Andrea E. .... Tucson, AZ
Toepke, Barbara L. .... St. Louis, MO
Toepke, Utz P. .... New York, NY
Toerek, Sharon L. .... Cleveland, OH
Toering, Douglas L. .... Troy, MI
Toering, Gordon J. .... Grand Rapids, MI
Toering, Myron D. .... Sioux Center, IA
Toering, Rick A. .... Washington, DC
Toerner, John G. .... Hammond, LA
Toerner, Julie M. .... Santa Ana, CA
Toes, Susanne M. .... New York, NY
Toevs, Thomas H. .... Albuquerque, NM
Toews, J. Christopher
San Luis Obispo, CA
Toews, J. Christopher, Inc. Law Office
San Luis Obispo, CA
Toews, Robert G. .... Chicago, IL
Toews, Ronald .... Los Angeles, CA
Tofano, Rosemarie .... Scarsdale, NY
Tofaute, George B. .... Terre Haute, IN
Tofaute, Phillip G. .... Terre Haute, IN
Tofaute & Spelman .... Terre Haute, IN
Tofel, Lawrence E. .... New York, NY
Tofel & Partners, P.C. .... New York, NY
Tofel, Robert L. .... New York, NY
Toff, Herbert .... Easton, PA
Toff, Jeffrey R., Law Offices of
Grass Valley, CA
Toff, Ronald I. .... Morgan Hill, CA
Toff, Ronald I., A Professional Corporation
Morgan Hill, CA
San Jose, CA
Toffel, André M. .... Birmingham, AL
Toffel, André M., P.C. .... Birmingham, AL
Toffel, Philip J. .... Albany, NY
Toffenetti, Judith L. .... Washington, DC
Toffenetti, William L. .... Chicago, IL
Toffler, Van E. .... New York, NY
Toffoli, Mark B. .... Oklahoma City, OK
Tofigh, Navid J. .... Washington, DC
Tofle, Marvin .... Columbia, MO
Toft, Adam Blaine .... New York, NY
Toft, Andrew M. .... Denver, CO
Toft, Dennis M. .... Roseland, NJ
Toft & Dorothy .... St. Louis, MO
Toft, Jeanne G. .... Chicago, IL
Toft, Robbye Hill .... St. Louis, MO
Toft, Thorval T. .... Sturgeon Bay, WI
Toft, Trudy A. .... Sturgeon Bay, WI
Tofte, Sandra A. .... Towson, MD
Tofte, Thomas .... Racine, WI
Tofteland, Anne M. .... Minneapolis, MN
Tofteland, Walter A. .... Luverne, MN
Toftemark, Lars E. .... Bellevue, NE
Toften, Emil F., & Associates .... Chalfont, PA
Toftey, Robert E. .... Duluth, MN
Toftness, Cecil G. .... Palos Verdes Estates, CA
Toga, Linda M. .... Melville, NY
Togasaki, Akira .... San Francisco, CA
Togioka, Leslie C. .... Honolulu, HI
Togman, Leonard S. .... Wilmington, DE
Tognarelli, Richard L. .... Collinsville, IL
Togni, Kathy M. .... New York, NY
Togni, Martin L. .... San Diego, CA
Tognino, Alexander .... Purchase, NY
Tognino, Michael A. .... White Plains, NY
Tognoni, Hale C. .... Phoenix, AZ
Tognotti, David M. .... San Jose, CA
Togonon, Jody Reynald .... Oakland, CA
Togrul, Cheryl .... Traverse City, MI
Togrul, Cheryl S., P.C. .... Traverse City, MI
Togut, Albert .... New York, NY
Togut, Segal & Segal .... New York, NY
Togut, Torin D. .... Atlanta, GA
Toher, J. Eric .... Houston, TX
Toher, J. Patrick .... Boston, MA
Toher, Kathleen .... Uniondale, NY
Tohill, Anthony B. .... Riverhead, NY
Tohill, Anthony B., P.C. .... Riverhead, NY
Tohill, Jim B. .... Jackson, MS
Tohir, Kathryn W. .... New York, NY
Tohl, Bernard G. .... Los Angeles, CA
Toia, Joseph .... Clinton Township, MI
Toigo, Michael J. .... Las Vegas, NV
Toikka, Richard S. .... Washington, DC
Toister, Dror .... Van Nuys, CA
Toister, Steven M. .... Miami, FL
Toister, Tamar Rachel .... Los Angeles, CA
Toivonen, Dennis W. .... New York, NY
Tokach, Jeffrey J. .... Pittston, PA
Tokar, Charles E. .... Chicago Ridge, IL
Tokar, Thomas .... Elkhart, IN
Tokar, Wendy L. .... Roanoke, VA
Tokarczyk, Lucyna M. .... New York, NY
Tokarski, Steve H. .... Schererville, IN
Tokarski, Susan M. .... Mineola, NY
Tokarsky, Diane M. .... Harrisburg, PA
Tokarsky, Fred R. .... Orlando, FL
Tokarz, Anthony P. .... Lexington, KY
Tokarz, Audrey Kies .... Oak Brook, IL
Tokarz, Karen L. .... St. Louis, MO
Tokarz, Mary E. .... Poughkeepsie, NY
Tokay, Alan R. .... Bristol, CT
Tokayer, Ira Daniel .... New York, NY
Tokayer, Marsi S. .... Scarsdale, NY
Toke, Lisa L. .... Walnut Creek, CA
Toke, Michael J. .... San Francisco, CA
Toker, Anne S. .... New York, NY
Toker, Donald L., Jr. .... Washington, DC
Toker, Gretal J. .... McLean, VA
Toker, H. Leonard .... New York, NY
Toker, Janmarie .... Topsham, ME
Toker, John A. .... San Francisco, CA
Tokerud, Keith .... Great Falls, MT
Toki, Alan A. .... San Diego, CA
Toko, Gale Lea .... Clayton, MO
Tokoli, John F. .... Rochester, NY
Tokoly, Stephen P. .... Dallas, TX
Tokuhama, Miko A. .... San Diego, CA
Tokumori, Gary .... Los Angeles, CA
Tokunaga, Mark D. .... Tahoe City, CA
Tokunaga, Robert D. .... Sacramento, CA
Tokunaga, Tatia M. .... Long Beach, CA
Tokus, Leonard A. .... Milwaukee, WI
Tolan, David J. .... Milwaukee, WI
Tolan, Elliott .... Philadelphia, PA
Tolan, James E. .... New York, NY
Tolan, James E., II .... New York, NY
Tolan, Paula A. .... Evanston, IL
Toland, Andrew J. .... Baltimore, MD
Toland, Bruce Jay .... Miami, FL
Toland, Bruce Jay, P.A. .... Miami, FL
Toland, Clyde W. .... Iola, KS
Toland, Howard S. .... Fort Lauderdale, FL
Toland, John R. .... Iola, KS
Toland, Marguerite J. .... Voorhees, NJ
Toland, Marilyn N. .... Waterbury, CT
Toland, Patrice A. .... Philadelphia, PA
Toland, Paul F. .... Cary, NC
Toland, Peter C. .... Boston, MA
Toland, Peter T. .... Boston, MA
Toland, Robert, II .... Philadelphia, PA
Toland & Thompson, LLC .... Iola, KS
Toland, Virginia King .... Wellesley, MA
Toland, W. Patrick, Jr. .... Scituate, MA
Tolar, Gregory Eugene .... Selma, AL
Tolar, Jane .... Easton, MD
Tolar, Jane, P.A. .... Easton, MD
Tolari, Jeffrey L. .... Farmington Hills, MI
Tolaro, Alfred J. .... Cleveland, OH
Tolber, Reed Stewart
Fort Lauderdale, FL
Tolber, Reed Stewart .... Miami, FL
Tolbert, Anthony J. .... Los Angeles, CA
Tolbert, Bruce E. .... White Plains, NY
Tolbert, C. Thomas .... Sulphur, LA
Tolbert, C. Wynne .... Arlington, VA
Tolbert, Carrie G. .... Atlanta, GA
Tolbert, Cynthia L. .... Jackson, MS
Tolbert, David S. .... Troy, MI
Tolbert, E. Lake .... Jackson, MS
Tolbert, Evonne W. J. .... New York, NY
Tolbert, Frank E. .... Logansport, IN
Tolbert, Gregory R. .... Tacoma, WA
Tolbert, H. Kenneth .... Clarkston, MI
Tolbert, H. G. .... Watonga, OK
Tolbert, J. David .... Charlotte, NC
Tolbert, James E., III .... Chicago, IL
Tolbert, Joe D. .... Fort Worth, TX
Tolbert, John T. .... Aston, PA
Tolbert, Larry K. .... Murfreesboro, TN
Tolbert, Mary Hirth .... Oklahoma City, OK
Tolbert, Ned E. .... Davis, CA
Tolbert, Richard S. .... West Palm Beach, FL
Tolbert, Roger M. .... Bellevue, WA
Tolbert, Steven M. .... Cincinnati, OH
Tolbert, Susan W. .... Maitland, FL
Tolbert, Timothy J., Law Office of
Hillsville, VA
Tolbert, Timothy J., Law Office of
Wytheville, VA
Tolbert, Valerie L. .... North Canton, OH
Tolbert, Victor P. .... Sherman, IL
Tolbin, David E. .... New York, NY
Tolboe, Christopher A. .... Salt Lake City, UT
Tolces, David N. .... Delray Beach, FL
Tolchin, Edward J. .... Fairfax, VA
Tolchin, Marsha A. .... Chicago, IL
Tolchinsky, Abby W. .... Larchmont, NY
Tolchinsky, Gary S. .... New York, NY
Tolchinsky, Harold N. .... Hackensack, NJ
Tolciss, A. Neil .... New York, NY
Tolcott, Michael B. .... Philadelphia, PA
Toldi, Francis G. .... San Francisco, CA
Toldo, Andrew A. .... Braintree, MA
Tole, Gregory G. .... Newark, NJ
Tole, Karen Loys, Law Office of
Lubbock, TX
Toledano, Benjamin C. .... Pass Christian, MS
Toledano, James .... Irvine, CA
Toledano, Rykert O., Jr. .... Covington, LA
Toledo, Alison .... Washington, DC
Toledo, Carmen R. .... Atlanta, GA
Toledo, Jonathan W. .... Farmington, NM
Toledo, Leticia G. .... Millbrae, CA
Toledo, Margaret .... Sacramento, CA
Toledo, Mark S. .... Tigard, OR
Toledo, Marlene .... New York, NY
Toledo, Osvaldo .... San Juan, PR
Toledo, Randy
Department of Justice, GV
Toledo, Richard G. .... Coral Gables, FL
Toledo-David, Miriam B. .... San Juan, PR
Toledo-De La Cruz, Omayra M.
San Juan, PR
Toledo-Rivera, Félix .... Washington, DC
Tolefree, Bryce H. .... Milwaukee, WI
Tolen, Carol A. .... Winnsboro, SC
Tolen, Eric T. .... St. Louis, MO
Tolen, Frank E. .... Kirksville, MO
Tolen, George R. .... Shelbyville, IN
Tolen, Lynda A. .... St. Joseph, MI
Tolentino, Dominador D. .... Los Angeles, CA
Tolentino, Emerito O. .... Secaucus, NJ
Tolentino, Jonar J. .... Barrington, IL
Tolentino, Shirley A. .... Jersey City, NJ
Tolentino, Sinforoso M. .... Hagåtña, GU
Tolentino, DanaLynn .... Newark, NJ
Toler, Boyd A. .... Evansville, IN
Toler, Darryl A. .... Washington, DC
Toler, Desmond B. .... Mobile, AL
Toler, Edward .... New York, NY
Toler, Eugene J. .... Mill Valley, CA
Toler, Gregory L. .... Mount Clemens, MI
Toler, Jeffrey G. .... Austin, TX
Toler, Robin R. .... Austin, TX
Toler, Timothy N. .... Atlanta, GA
Toler, Wesley F. .... Houston, TX
Toler, William A. .... Columbus, OH
Tolerico, Julia Wells .... Detroit, MI
Tolerton & Brown, P.C. .... Norfolk, VA
Tolerton, Robin L. .... Norfolk, VA
Toles, Andrew J. .... Seattle, WA
Toles & Associates, P.C. .... Phoenix, AZ
Toles, Cynthia Ann .... Houston, TX
Toles, H. Edward, III .... Dallas, TX
Toles, Henry M. .... Los Angeles, CA
Toles, Henry M., A Professional Law Corporation .... Beverly Hills, CA
Los Angeles, CA
Santa Monica, CA
Toles, J. Penrod .... Roswell, NM
Toles, M. Jeremy .... Phoenix, AZ
Toles, Perry S. .... Roswell, NM
Toles, William Marcus .... Dallas, TX
Tolford, John C. .... Washington, DC
Tolfree, Daniel E. .... Seattle, WA
Tolgyesi, Anthony L. .... Hollywood, FL
Tolgyesi, Katz, Tarr & Hankin, P.A.
Hollywood, FL
Tolhurst, Frederick L. .... Pittsburgh, PA
Tolin, David L. .... Beaumont, TX
Tolin, Donald Lee .... Casper, WY
Tolin, Gerald P. .... Department of Commerce, Patent and Trademark Office, GV
Tolin, James W., Jr. .... Roxboro, NC
Tolin, Jason E. .... San Diego, CA
Tolin, Jeffrey J. .... New York, NY
Tolin, Josh P. .... St. Louis, MO
Tolin, Richard D. .... Southfield, MI
Tolin, Seth W. .... Silver Spring, MD
Tolin, Stefen A. .... Minneapolis, MN
Tolin & Zevan, LLC .... St. Louis, MO
Tolins & Lowenfels, A Professional Corporation .... New York, NY

Tolins, Nora ..... Worcester, MA
Tolins, Robert B. ..... Lowell, MA
Tolins, Roger A. ..... New York, NY
Tolisano, Vincent P. ..... Cape Coral, FL
Tolitano, Tami A. ..... Chicago, IL
Toliver, A. Leroy, (P.C.) ..... Atlanta, GA
Toliver, Andrea Fulton ..... Atlanta, GA
Toliver, Charles H., IV ..... Wilmington, DE
Toliver, David L. ..... North Palm Beach, FL
Toliver & Davis ..... Gilmer, TX
Toliver, Dwayne M. ..... Rockville, MD
Toliver & Gainer, LLP ..... Atlanta, GA
Conyers, GA
Toliver, Jack E. ..... Lexington, KY
Toliver, Jacques A.
Department of Education, Office for Civil Rights, GV
Toliver, Shawn A. ..... San Francisco, CA
Toliver, Tolie ..... Tulsa, OK
Toliver, Walter T. ..... Philadelphia, PA
Toliver, Wayne ..... Gilmer, TX
Toljanic, Mark D. ..... Oak Brook, IL
Tolk, Bentley J. ..... Salt Lake City, UT
Tolkach, Elizabeth L. ..... Trenton, NJ
Tolkan, Howard B. ..... Milwaukee, WI
Tolkan, James ..... Milwaukee, WI
Tolkin, Jeffrey D. ..... Farmingdale, NY
Tolkin, Laurie Young ..... Bellevue, WA
Tolkoff, Andrew B. ..... New York, NY
Tolks, Arnis R. ..... Santa Barbara, CA
Toll, Alan E. ..... Wilmington, NC
Toll, Arthur ..... Los Angeles, CA
Toll, Christopher H.
Greenwood Village, CO
Toll, Christopher T. ..... Denver, CO
Toll, Curtis B. ..... Philadelphia, PA
Toll, Daniel M. ..... Los Angeles, CA
Toll, David J. ..... Lansdale, PA
Toll, Doris M. ..... Wilmington, DE
Toll, Ebby, Langer & Marvin, A Professional Corporation ..... Philadelphia, PA
Toll, Edward C. ..... Kerrville, TX
Toll, Elizabeth M. ..... New York, NY
Toll, Ellen ..... Anchorage, AK
Toll, Erin K. ..... Greenwood Village, CO
Toll, George S. ..... St. Louis, MO
Toll, Gilbert E. ..... Bala Cynwyd, PA
Bala Cynwyd, PA
Toll, Gilbert E. ..... Philadelphia, PA
Toll, Henry W., Jr. ..... Denver, CO
Toll, Jack B. ..... Golden, CO
Toll, James D. ..... Atlantic City, NJ
Toll, Jeffrey A. ..... Philadelphia, PA
Toll, Jeffrey B. ..... Cherry Hill, NJ
Toll, Jessica F. ..... Denver, CO
Toll, Joshua C. ..... Washington, DC
Toll, Martha A. ..... Washington, DC
Toll, Michelle L. ..... New York, NY
Toll, Perry M. ..... Kansas City, MO
Toll, Pollyann O. ..... Cherry Hill, NJ
Toll, Robert I. ..... Huntingdon Valley, PA
Toll, Roger W. ..... Culver City, CA
Toll, Seymour I. ..... Philadelphia, PA
Toll, Sheldon S. ..... Detroit, MI
Toll, Steven J. ..... Seattle, WA
Toll, Sullivan & Luthman ..... Cherry Hill, NJ
Tollakson, Thomas W. ..... Milwaukee, WI
Tollan, Lorraine E. ..... New York, NY
Tolle, A. Vaughn ..... Wichita, KS
Tolle, Dirk V. ..... Tampa, FL
Tolle, John B. ..... Dallas, TX
Tolle, John R. ..... McLean, VA
Tolle, Leanne S. ..... New York, NY
Tolle, Mark S. ..... Dallas, TX
Tolle, Norman L. ..... Uniondale, NY
Tolle & Parish ..... Okemah, OK
Tolle, Robert M. ..... Forest Hills, NY
Tollefsen, Adrianne L. ..... Seattle, WA
Tollefsen & Co., P.C. ..... Mill Creek, WA
Tollefsen, Gig A. ..... Bozeman, MT
Tollefsen, John J. ..... Mill Creek, WA
Tollefsen, Robert L. ..... Santa Rosa, CA
Tollefsen, Scott B. ..... El Segundo, CA
Tollefson, Brian M. ..... Tacoma, WA
Tollefson, Daniel A. ..... Foley, MN
Tollefson, Daniel H. ..... St. Cloud, MN
Tollefson, Donald G. ..... Encino, CA
Tollefson, G. Val ..... Seattle, WA
Tollefson, Gregory C. ..... Boise, ID
Tollefson, John C. ..... Dallas, TX
Tollefson, John M. ..... Dawson, MN
Madison, MN
Tollefson, Richard E. ..... Owatonna, MN
Tollefson, Ronald B. ..... Gig Harbor, WA
Tollefson, W. Donald ..... Venice, CA
Tollen, David W. ..... Palo Alto, CA
Tollen, Robert William
San Francisco, CA
Toller, Suzanne K. ..... San Francisco, CA
Tolleris, John A. ..... Treasury Department, Internal Revenue Service, GV
Tollers, Jeffery B. ..... Green Bay, WI
Tolles, Denise ..... Rye, NY
Tolles, E. Leroy ..... San Marino, CA
Tolles, Lois V. McKenna ..... Novato, CA
Tolles, Mark D. ..... Bowling Green, OH
Tolles, Stephen L. ..... Los Angeles, CA
Tolles, Theodore L. ..... Utica, NY
Tolleson & Associates ..... Austin, TX
Tolleson, James E. ..... Huntsville, AL
Tolleson, Jean Ann ..... Baton Rouge, LA
Tolleson, Julie C. ..... Phoenix, AZ
Denver, CO
Tolleson, Kim H. ..... Tomball, TX
Tolleson, R. Michael ..... Austin, TX
Tollett, Brenda L. ..... Lexington, KY
Tollett, Jason B. ..... Austin, TX
Tollett, Kenneth S., Sr. ..... Washington, DC
Tollett, Raymond L., Jr. ..... Dallas, TX
Tollette, Steven R. ..... Jenks, OK
Tolley, B. Cary, III ..... New York, NY
Tolley & Brooks ..... Fayetteville, AR
Tolley, Christopher S. ..... Boston, MA
Tolley, Edward D. ..... Athens, GA
Tolley, Edward P., III ..... New York, NY
Tolley, Edward P., Jr. ..... New York, NY
Tolley, George S., III ..... Timonium, MD
Tolley, Gerald G. ..... Colorado Springs, CO
Tolley, Jay N. ..... Fayetteville, AR
Tolley, Joyce L. ..... New York, NY
Tolley, Kenneth J. ..... Cleveland, OH
Tolley, Peter R. ..... Grand Rapids, MI
Tolley, Ramona L. ..... Miami, FL
Tolley, Randall B. ..... Memphis, TN
Tolley, Russell A. ..... Atlanta, GA
Tolley, VandenBosch, Walton, Korolewicz & Brengle, P.C. ..... Grand Rapids, MI
Tollie, Stacy O. ..... Winston-Salem, NC
Tollin, Howard M. ..... Uniondale, NY
Tollin, L. Andrew ..... Washington, DC
Tollinche, Edward W. Hill ..... San Juan, PR
Tollinger, Jane H. ..... New York, NY
Tollinger, William Preston, Jr.
New York, NY
Tollisen, Kevin J. ..... Clifton Park, NY
Tollison, Grady F., Jr. ..... Oxford, MS
Tollison, Gray ..... Oxford, MS
Tollison, L. Walter, III ..... Greenville, SC
Tollison Law Firm, P.A. ..... Oxford, MS
Tollison, Mitchell G. ..... Humboldt, TN
Tollison, Nina Stubblefield ..... Oxford, MS
Tollison, Thomas F. ..... Albuquerque, NM
Tolliver, Elkin A., Jr. ..... Philadelphia, PA
Tolliver, Kenneth D. ..... Billings, MT
Tolliver, Sheila Patricia Hale ..... Grundy, VA
Tolliver, Staci L. ..... Raleigh, NC
Tolliver, Stanley E. ..... Cleveland, OH
Tolliver, Steven C. ..... Philadelphia, PA
Tolliver, Vonda K. ..... Lexington, KY
Tollman, Martha ..... New York, NY
Tollman, Michael ..... New York, NY
Tolmach, David M. ..... New York, NY
Tolmach, Madeleine ..... Washington, DC
Tolmachoff, Innokenty, Jr. ..... Washington, DC
Tolmack & Kargman, P.C. ..... New York, NY
Tolmack, Milton ..... New York, NY
Tolman, A. Jean ..... Atlanta, GA
Tolman, David ..... Summit, NJ
Tolman, Gareth W. ..... Galveston, TX
Tolman, J. Robert ..... Phoenix, AZ
Tolman, Jeffrey L. ..... Poulsbo, WA
Tolman • Kirk ..... Poulsbo, WA
Tolman Law Office ..... Twin Falls, ID
Tolman, Lisa Giacchino ..... League City, TX
Tolman, Mitchell E. ..... Salt Lake City, UT
Tolman & Osborne, P.C. ..... Tempe, AZ
Tolman, Reed C. ..... Tempe, AZ
Tolman, Steven I. ..... New York, NY
Tolman, Steven K. ..... Twin Falls, ID
Tolman, Warren E. ..... Boston, MA
Tolmas, Ed ..... Los Angeles, CA
Tolmas, Gerson Z. ..... Metairie, LA
Tolmas, Oscar J. ..... Metairie, LA
Tolmatsky, Alexander ..... Skokie, IL
Tolmie, Donald M. ..... Norfolk, VA
Tolnai, Lester J. ..... Los Angeles, CA
Tolomei, John G. ..... Des Plaines, IL
Tolomeo, Marianne C. ..... Newark, NJ
Tolomeo, Ralph J. ..... Newark, NJ
Tolone, James J. ..... Chicago, IL
Tolosa-Ramírez, Sara E. ..... San Juan, PR
Tolosky, Mark R. ..... Cambridge, MA
Tolpa, John M. ..... Montclair, NJ
Tolpegin, Andre V. ..... San Francisco, CA
Tolpen, Farley S. ..... Mill Valley, CA
Tolpin, Jim ..... Miami, FL
Tolpin, Jonathan S. ..... Jericho, NY
Tolpin, Thomas W. ..... Chicago, IL
Tolsdorf, Maia Scott ..... Philadelphia, PA
Tolson, Greg S., (P.C.) ..... San Francisco, CA
Tolson, Jay H. ..... Warminster, PA
Tolson, John F., Jr. ..... Orange Park, FL
Tolson, Jon H. ..... San Francisco, CA
Tolson, Lance S. ..... Denver, CO
Tolson, Michael B. ..... Tulsa, OK
Tolson, Peggy L. ..... Brentwood, TN
Tolson, Robert, Jr. ..... Pine Bluff, AR
Tolstedt, Michael W. ..... Billings, MT
Tolstoi, Barry S. ..... Elizabeth, NJ
Livingston, NJ
Tolstoi, Mark J. ..... Roseland, NJ
Tolstoi & Tolstoi ..... Elizabeth, NJ
Livingston, NJ
Tolt, Lester T. ..... Cleveland, OH
Tolt, Nikki ..... Beverly Hills, CA
Tolton, Mary Carr ..... Raleigh, NC
Tolton, Rebecca S. ..... Indianapolis, IN
Tolton, William J., Jr. ..... Shalimar, FL
Tolton, Wm. Jere, III ..... Tampa, FL
Toltz, Harry H. ..... Chelsea, MA
Toltz, Steven D. ..... Denver, CO
Tolud, Jean Ernest ..... New York, NY
Tolva, Donald E. ..... Oak Brook, IL
Tolva, Maria ..... Wheaton, IL
Tolve, Vincent J. ..... Chicago, IL
Tolwin, Samuel L. ..... Los Angeles, CA
Tolz, Robert D. ..... New York, NY
Tolzman, Paul G. ..... Baltimore, MD
Tom, Albert ..... San Diego, CA
Tom, Allen W.H. ..... Olympia, WA
Tom, Beverly S. K. ..... Honolulu, HI
Tom, Carl ..... Honolulu, HI
Tom, Darryl ..... Chicago, IL
Tom, David B. ..... Palo Alto, CA
Tom, Franklin ..... Woodland Hills, CA
Tom, Gaylord G. ..... Honolulu, HI
Tom, Gregory Y.P. ..... Honolulu, HI
Tom, Henry W. ..... Phoenix, AZ
Tom, Herbert K. ..... Honolulu, HI
Tom, James F. ..... Glendale, CA
Tom, Joy ..... San Francisco, CA
Tom, Joyce A. ..... San Francisco, CA
Tom, Karen ..... Walnut Creek, CA
Tom, Kevin Brian ..... San Jose, CA
Tom, Mary ..... Totowa, NJ
Tom, Merle H. ..... Virginia Beach, VA
Tom, Michael D. ..... Honolulu, HI
Tom, Michael V. ..... Portland, OR
Tom & Petrus ..... Honolulu, HI
Tom, Quinlan S. ..... Oakland, CA
Tom, Randolph L. ..... Palo Alto, CA
Tom, Rebecca Biermann ..... Salem, OR
Tom, Reginald K. ..... Department of Justice, Antitrust Division, GV
Tom, Richard S. ..... Rosemead, CA
Tom, Roslyn ..... New York, NY
Tom, Sharlene W. Y. ..... Honolulu, HI
Tom, Stephen D. ..... Honolulu, HI
Tom, Susan M. ..... Lubbock, TX
Tom, Tenny Hoon ..... Honolulu, HI
Tom, Terrance W. H. ..... Honolulu, HI
Tom, Willard K.
Federal Trade Commission, Bureau of Competition, GV
Toma, Albert H., III ..... Green Bay, WI
Toma, Byron K. ..... Las Vegas, NV
Toma, John E., Jr. ..... St. Louis, MO
Toma, Lynn R. ..... Alameda, CA
San Jose, CA
Toma, Michael Steven ..... Westport, CT
Toma, Ray M. ..... Bingham Farms, MI
Toma, Robin S. ..... Los Angeles, CA
Toma, Sabrina R. ..... Honolulu, HI
Toma, Timothy N. ..... Euclid, OH
Tomac, Cheryl Linnette ..... Vista, CA
Tomai, Sarah J. ..... Dearborn, MI
Tomaiko, Denise K. ..... Torrance, CA
Tomain, Joseph P. ..... Cincinnati, OH
Tomaine, David J. ..... Scranton, PA
Tomaine, John J. ..... Warren, NJ
Tomaino, Joseph M. ..... Newark, NJ
Tomaino, Joseph R. ..... Murrysville, PA
Tomaino, Mark M. ..... Rochester, NY
Tomaino, Michael T. ..... Rochester, NY
Tomaino, Michael T., Jr. ..... New York, NY
Tomaino, Peter A. ..... Reno, NV
Tomak, Robert S. ..... Troy, MI
Tomaka, Eileen ..... Lackawanna, NY
Tomal, Eric X. ..... Eaton Rapids, MI
Tomalas, Roger P. ..... Newport Beach, CA
Tomalis, Matthew W. ..... Harrisburg, PA
Tomallo, Ronald P., Jr. ..... Cleveland, OH
Tomalty, Sarah E. ..... Washington, DC
Houston, TX
Toman, Amy McKeever ..... Chicago, IL
Toman, Bradley P. ..... Cleveland, OH
Toman, Brian W. ..... Sacramento, CA
Toman, Cecilia ..... San Francisco, CA
Toman, Dennis J. ..... Greensboro, NC
Toman, Gary J. ..... Atlanta, GA
Toman, John A. ..... Berwyn, IL
Toman, Richard J. ..... Elk Grove Village, IL
Toman, William J. ..... Madison, WI
Tomana, Michael J. ..... Pittsburgh, PA
Tomanek, John M. ..... Phoenix, AZ
Tomanelli, Steven N.
Department of the Air Force, Office of the General Counsel, GV
Tomann, Stephen G. ..... Cold Spring, NY
Tomanovich, Milo I. ..... Rochester, NY
Tomao, Joseph L., Jr. ..... Garden City, NY
Tomao and Marangas ..... Garden City, NY
Tomao, Peter J. ..... Garden City, NY
Tomao, Sharon Marie ..... New York, NY
Tomar, Paul A. ..... Honolulu, HI
Tomar, Richard T. ..... Washington, DC
Rockville, MD
Tomar, Simonoff, Adourian, O'Brien, Kaplan, Jacoby & Graziano
Wilmington, DE
Atlantic City, NJ
Camden, NJ
Cherry Hill, NJ
Northfield, NJ
Media, PA
Tomar, William ..... Atlantic City, NJ
Cherry Hill, NJ
Northfield, NJ
Tomaras, Brenda L. ..... San Diego, CA
Tomaras, Peter A. ..... Chicago, IL
Tomarchio, Jack Thomas ..... Philadelphia, PA
Tomari, Anthony J. ..... New York, NY
Tomaro, Anthony A. ..... Manchester, CT
Tomaro, James ..... Bloomfield Hills, MI
Tomaro, Robert B. ..... Cleveland, OH
Tomas, Christine ..... Lake Geneva, WI
Tomas, Mark ..... Mukilteo, WA
Tomasco, Jean E. ..... Hartford, CT
Tomasco, Mary Ellen ..... Phoenixville, PA
Tomasco, Patricia Baron ..... Austin, TX
Tomasek, Bryan J. ..... Washington, DC
Tomasek, Joseph J., Law Offices of
Somerville, NJ
Tomasek, Michael F. ..... Chicago, IL
Tomasella, Louis C. ..... Hackensack, NJ
Tomasella, Victoria L. ..... Hackensack, NJ
Tomaselli, Anthony A. ..... Madison, WI
Tomaselli, Charles M. ..... New York, NY
Tomaselli, Eugene A. ..... Pearl River, NY
Tomaselli, Joe W., Jr. ..... Dallas, TX
Tomaselli, John J. ..... New York, NY
Tomaselli, Linda A. ..... Nashua, NH
Tomaselli, Michael V. ..... Washington, DC
Tomaselli, Patrick J. ..... Troy, NY
Tomaselli, Traci M. ..... New York, NY
Tomasello, Charles ..... Hauppauge, NY
Tomasello, Francis A. ..... Ocean City, NJ
Tomasello, John ..... Woodbury, NJ
Tomasello, Louis ..... North Andover, MA
Tomasetti, Dorothy H. ..... Littleton, CO
Tomasetti, Raymond E., Jr.
Fenwick Island, DE
Newport, DE
Tomasetti, Robert J. ..... Stamford, CT
Tomasevich, Jeffery A. ..... Washington, DC
Tomasevich, Kerry John ..... Boston, MA
Tomashefsky, C. Steven ..... Chicago, IL
Tomashek, Thomas N. ..... Seattle, WA
Tomashoff, Mortimer J.
Westlake Village, CA
Tomasi, James C. ..... Salem, NY
Tomasi, Paul J. ..... Calumet, MI
Houghton, MI
Tomasi, Torrey R. ..... San Diego, CA
Tomasic, Denise E. ..... Kansas City, KS
Tomasic, Nicholas A. ..... Kansas City, KS
Tomasiello, Anthony N. ..... Shrewsbury, MA
Tomasiello, Anthony N., Jr.
Worcester, MA
Tomasik, Annie M. ..... Vista, CA
Tomasik, Joseph E. ..... Berkeley, CA
Tomasik, Timothy S. ..... Chicago, IL
Tomasin, John ..... West New York, NJ
Tomasino, Justin D. ..... New York, NY
Tomaska, Melissa M. ..... Wheaton, IL
Tomasko & Koranda, P.C. ..... Harrisburg, PA
Tomasko, Ronald T. ..... Harrisburg, PA
Tomasky, Maria T. ..... Westport, CT
Tomasky, Susan ..... Columbus, OH
Tomaso, Alphonse R. ..... Chicago, IL
Tomaso, Robert J. ..... St. Louis, MO
Tomaso, Toney J. ..... Urbana, IL
Tomasone, Frederick S.
Franklin Square, NY
Tomasseti, Lisa J. ..... Arlington, VA
Tomassetti, A. Jeffrey ..... Fernandina Beach, FL
Tomassetti, Daniel A. ..... Wheeling, WV
Tomassetti, Terrence E. ..... Altoona, PA
Tomassi, Craig A. ..... Chicago, IL
Tomassi, John A. ..... Cleveland, OH
Tomassi, Marie ..... St. Petersburg, FL
Tampa, FL
Tomassi, Radogno, Cameli & Hoag, P.C.
Chicago, IL
Tomassi, Robert S., Jr. ..... Pittsburg, KS
Tomassi, Scott C. ..... Chicago, IL
Tomassi, Stephen J. ..... Milwaukee, WI
Tomassian, Gerald M. ..... Fresno, CA
Tomassian, Martin V., Jr. ..... Edgartown, MA
Tomassian, Pimentel & Shapazian
Fresno, CA
Tomassian, Serge ..... Newport Beach, CA
Tomassian & Tomassian ..... Edgartown, MA
Tomasso, John J. ..... Coral Gables, FL
Tomasso, John P. ..... Providence, RI
Tomasso, Michelle J. ..... New Brunswick, NJ
Tomasso, Raymond A. ..... Providence, RI
Tomasso, Raymond J. ..... Providence, RI
Tomasso & Tomasso ..... Providence, RI
Tomasu, Bert M. ..... Honolulu, HI
Tomasulo, Daniel A. ..... West Trenton, NJ
Tomasulo, Jason C. ..... Vienna, VA
Tomasulo, Michael A. ..... Los Angeles, CA
Tomaszczuk, Alexander D. ..... McLean, VA
Tomaszczuk, Carol M. ..... Washington, DC
Tomaszek, Mark E. ..... Greenville, SC
Tomaszewski, Barbara ..... Bellevue, WA
Tomaszewski, Anthony J., Jr. ..... Flint, MI
Tomaszewski, David P. ..... Wilkes-Barre, PA
Tomaszewski, John ..... New York, NY
Tomaszewski, John J. ..... New Haven, CT
Tomaszewski, John Paul ..... Jacksonville, FL
Tomaszewski, Raymond G. ..... Linden, NJ
Tomaszewski, William L., Jr. ..... Montclair, NJ
Tomaszycki, Christopher
Sterling Heights, MI
Tomaszycki, Christopher, P.C.
Sterling Heights, MI
Tomaw, James G. ..... Newton, IL
Tomaw, Patricia ..... Newton, IL
Tomayko, Lauren M. ..... Warren, MI
Tomazin, Thomas J. ..... Englewood, CO
Tomazin, Thomas J., P.C. ..... Denver, CO
Englewood, CO
Tomb, David R., Jr. ..... Indiana, PA
Tomb, Heather L. ..... Blue Bell, PA
Tomb, Karen A. ..... Denver, CO
Tomb, Mack and Kauffman ..... Indiana, PA
Tomb, Myron Hay ..... Indiana, PA
Tomb, Stacey E. ..... Chicago, IL
Tomb and Tomb ..... Indiana, PA
Tomback, Andrew E. ..... New York, NY
Tomback, Jay L. ..... Phoenix, AZ
Tomback, Jay L., Ltd. ..... Phoenix, AZ
Tomback, Peter A. ..... Scarsdale, NY
Tombak, Ivy ..... Los Angeles, CA
Tombalakian, Steven R. ..... Newark, NJ
Tombari, Robert J., Jr. ..... Quincy, MA
Tombari, William A., Jr. ..... Spokane, WA
Tombaugh, Wendell C. ..... Rochester, IN
Tomberg, Jeff ..... Boynton Beach, FL
Tomberg, Joseph ..... Boynton Beach, FL
Tomberg, Michael A. ..... San Antonio, TX
Tomberg & Spall, P.A. ..... Boynton Beach, FL
Tomberlin, George E., Jr. ..... Oakland, CA
Tomberlin, Lucy ..... Valdosta, GA
Tomberlin, Phillip Yeates, Jr.
Jacksonville, FL
Tomberlin, Richard H. ..... Charlotte, NC
Tomberlin, Rollin E. ..... Ocala, FL
Tomberlin, Ronald D. ..... Wichita Falls, TX
Tombers, Evelyn C. ..... Southfield, MI

Tombini, Michele M. ....Scarsdale, NY
Tomblin, A. Clyde ....Spindale, NC
Tomblin, Anthony "Lucky" ....Austin, TX
Tomblin, Carnes & McCormack, L.L.P.
Austin, TX
Tomblin and Perry ....Spindale, NC
Tomblin, William D ....East Lansing, MI
Tombrink, Richard, Jr. ....Brooksville, FL
Tombs, Susan M. ....Greenfield, MA
Tomburrini, Debra M. ....Lansing, MI
Tomc, Richard W. ....Middletown, CT
Tomc, Richard W., & Associates, P.C.
Middletown, CT
Tomcal, Barbara J. ....Saginaw, MI
Tomchin, David L. ....Washington, DC
Tomchin, Eric R. ....Asheville, NC
Tomchin, Harold ....Princeton, WV
Tomchin, Jennifer Brooke
Washington, DC
Tomchin, Kenneth A. ....Jacksonville, FL
Tomchin & Odom, P.A. ....Jacksonville, FL
Tomchin, R. Gregory ....Charlotte, NC
Tomcho, Kathleen M. ....Atlanta, GA
Tomcik, David J. ....Pleasanton, CA
Tomcik, James R. ....Pleasanton, CA
Tomczak & Haney ....Joliet, IL
Tomczak, Jeffery J. ....Joliet, IL
Tomczak, Judy Anne ....Fitchburg, WI
Tomczak, Starr L. ....New York, NY
Tomczak, Thomas N. ....Toledo, OH
Tomczuk, Paul J. ....State College, PA
Tomczyk, Deborah C. ....Milwaukee, WI
Tome, Christopher J. ....Austin, TX
Tome, Jay R. ....Ocala, FL
Tomeczko, Michael G. ....Chicago, IL
Tomei, Albert ....Brooklyn, NY
Tomei, Eugene A. ....Brooklyn, NY
Tomei, Gary A. ....New York, NY
Tomei, Jeffrey E. ....Brooklyn, NY
Tomei, John A. ....Raleigh, NC
Tomei, Marilyn Ellison ....Raleigh, NC
Tomei, Richard K. ....Chicago, IL
Tomek, David W. ....Austin, TX
Tomenga, Michael K. ....Washington, DC
Tomenson, Leslie A. ....New York, NY
Tomeny, Frank, III ....Baton Rouge, LA
Tomeny, Jennifer A. ....New York, NY
Tomeny Law Firm, A Professional Law
Corporation ....Baton Rouge, LA
Tomeny, Lynne J. ....Muskegon, MI
Tomeny, Richard J., Jr. ....Metairie, LA
Tomeny, Richard J., Jr., A Professional
Corporation ....Metairie, LA
Tomeo, David G. ....Roseland, NJ
Tomeo, Kathleen A. ....La Mirada, CA
Tomeo, Richard W. ....Hartford, CT
Tomer, Clifford W. ....North Chili, NY
Tomer, Michele A. ....Akron, OH
Tomerlin, Granville ....Oklahoma City, OK
Tomerlin, High & High ....Oklahoma City, OK
Tomes & Dvorak ....Leawood, KS
Overland Park, KS
Kansas City, MO
Tomes, Frances ....East Brunswick, NJ
Tomes, Jonathan P. ....Leawood, KS
Tomes, Kenda K. ....Kansas City, MO
Tomey Charitable Law ....Wynnewood, PA
Tomey, Kim A. ....Honolulu, HI
Tomey, Wendy C. ....Liberty Corner, NJ
Wynnewood, PA
Tomich, Deborah ....St. Charles, MO
Tomich, Jane Ellen ....St. Charles, MO
Tomich, John A. ....Meriden, CT
Tomich, Lillian, Law Offices of
San Marino, CA
Tomich, Martha J.
United States Court Of Appeals District Of
Columbia Circuit, GV
Tomich, Mary T. ....Philadelphia, PA
Tomich, Philip L ....Mineola, NY
Tomicich, Mark A.
Department of Transportation,
Federal Aviation Administration, GV
Tomiello, Steven J. ....Chicago, IL
Tomilowitz, Rebecca M. ....Los Angeles, CA
Tomin, Harold J. ....Los Angeles, CA
Tominberg, Carl S. ....Chicago, IL
Tomine, Eugene ....Oakland, CA
Tomino, Carla A. ....Chicago, IL
Tomino, Michael A., Jr. ....Lafayette, LA
Tomino, Nick C. ....Cleveland, OH
Tomioka, June I. ....Honolulu, HI
Tomita, Derek K. ....Honolulu, HI
Tomita, Kimilyn C. ....Honolulu, HI
Tomita, Paul K. ....San Francisco, CA
Tomita & Simpson, P.C.
Albuquerque, NM
Tomita, Stanley T. ....San Jose, CA
Tomita, Susan K. ....Albuquerque, NM
Tomita, Susan L. ....Philadelphia, PA
Tomkiel, Stanley A. ....Yonkers, NY
Tomkiel, Stanley A., III ....Yonkers, NY
Tomkies, Michael C. ....Mandeville, LA
Columbus, OH
Tomkies, Suzanne E. ....Houston, TX
Tomkiewicz, Joseph A. ....Fairfax, VA
Tomkins, Ann M. ....Irwindale, CA
Tomkins, D. Michael ....Seattle, WA
Tomkins, David N. ....San Jose, CA
Tomkins, Eileen ....Croton-On-Hudson, NY
Tomkins, Frank S. ....Phoenix, AZ
Tomkins, James R. ....Nashville, TN
Tomkins, Juliet M. ....St. Paul, MN
Tomkins, Katherine F. ....Glastonbury, CT
Tomkins, Richard M. ....Northbrook, IL
Tomkins, Sharon L. ....Los Angeles, CA
Tomkins, Suzanne E. ....Getzville, NY
Tomkiw, Andrey T. ....Royal Oak, MI
Tomkiw & Associates, PLLC
Royal Oak, MI
Tomko, Brian S. ....New York, NY
Tomko, Edwin J. ....Dallas, TX
Tomko, Janet Levis ....Atlanta, GA
Tomko, Kenneth F. ....Binghamton, NY
Tomko, Michael J. ....Salt Lake City, UT
Tomko, Stephen T. ....Wilmerding, PA
Tomko, Thomas J.
Macomb Township, MI
Mount Clemens, MI
Shelby Township, MI
Tomko, Thomas J. ....Sterling Heights, MI
Tomko, Thomas J. ....Warren, MI
Tomko, W. Edward, III ....Emporia, VA
Tomkovicz, James J. ....Iowa City, IA
Tomkovitch, Michael J.
Hopewell Junction, NY
Tomkowiak, Edward R. ....Chicago, IL
Tomkowicz, Sandra M. ....West Chester, PA
Tomlan, John R. ....St. Clairsville, OH
Tomlin, Brian ....Greensboro, NC
Tomlin, D. David ....Rome, GA
Tomlin, Gary A. ....Montgomery, AL
Tomlin, Ginger ....Birmingham, AL
Tomlin, Henry H., III ....Haddonfield, NJ
Tomlin, Hewitt P., Jr. ....Jackson, TN
Tomlin, Hopkin & Montemurro
Haddonfield, NJ
Tomlin, J. Warren ....Virginia Beach, VA
Tomlin, James M. ....Peoria, IL
Tomlin, Judson Eugene, Jr. ....Birmingham, AL
Tomlin, Michael E. ....Bentonville, AR
Tomlin, Michael K. ....Santa Fe Springs, CA
Tomlin, Michael T., (P.A.) ....Miami, FL
Tomlin, Richard A. ....Fort Lauderdale, FL
Tomlin, Richard Alan ....Houston, TX
Tomlin, Ruth C. ....Haddonfield, NJ
Tomlin, Shelly ....Dallas, TX
Tomlin, Timothy J. ....Santa Rosa, CA
Tomlin, Tracy E. ....Charlotte, NC
Tomlins, Edward E., Jr. ....Tulsa, OK
Tomlins & Goins, A Professional
Corporation ....Tulsa, OK
Tomlins, Neal ....Tulsa, OK
Tomlins, Ronald R. ....Poughkeepsie, NY
Tomlinson, A. Kathleen ....Uniondale, NY
Tomlinson, Allen K. ....East Greenville, PA
Tomlinson, Allen R.
West Palm Beach, FL
Tomlinson, Andrew L. ....Cherry Hill, NJ
Tomlinson, Angela E. ....Houston, TX
Tomlinson & Associates, P.C.
Stone Mountain, GA
Tomlinson, Aubrey S., Jr. ....Louisburg, NC
Tomlinson, Barry J. ....East Greenville, PA
Tomlinson, Benson C. ....St. Louis, MO
Tomlinson, D. Neal ....Las Vegas, NV
Tomlinson, David A. ....Fort Worth, TX
Tomlinson, David Allen ....Florence, AL
Tomlinson, David C. ....Colon, MI
Tomlinson, David E. ....Bethlehem, PA
Tomlinson, David J. ....San Francisco, CA
Tomlinson, Denise P. ....Austin, TX
Tomlinson, Diane A. ....Gainesville, FL
Tomlinson, Don E. ....College Station, TX
Tomlinson, Donald R. ....Pittsburgh, PA
Tomlinson, Edward B., II ....Garland, TX
Tomlinson, Ephraim, 2nd ....Medford, NJ
Tomlinson, F. Hilton-Green
Birmingham, AL
Tomlinson, Faye L. ....Seattle, WA
Tomlinson, George J. ....Santa Barbara, CA
Tomlinson & Gerhart ....East Greenville, PA
Tomlinson, Guy P. ....Fonda, NY
Tomlinson, H. Weston ....Media, PA
Tomlinson & Hatch ....Andover, MA
Tomlinson, J. Kenneth, Sr. ....Columbia, SC
Tomlinson, Jack H. ....San Francisco, CA
Tomlinson, James A. ....Jacksonville, FL
Tomlinson, James R. ....Tacoma, WA
Tomlinson, Janet M. ....Los Angeles, CA
Tomlinson, John ....San Francisco, CA
Tomlinson, John D. ....Port Huron, MI
Tomlinson, John E. ....Stone Mountain, GA
Tomlinson, John G., Jr. ....Miami, FL
Tomlinson, John R. ....Seattle, WA
Tomlinson, John R., Jr. ....Seattle, WA
Tomlinson, Kenneth B. ....Dallas, TX
Tomlinson, Madaline B. ....Media, PA
Tomlinson, Malcolm ....Hadley, NY
Tomlinson, Max Stanford
San Bernardino, CA
Tomlinson, Nellie Shipley ....Raleigh, NC
Tomlinson, Norman B., Jr. ....Morristown, NJ
Tomlinson, Nydam & Prince
San Bernardino, CA
Tomlinson, Peter W. ....New York, NY
Tomlinson, Philip V. ....Berkley, MI
Tomlinson, R. (Richard) Sande
Eugene, OR
Eugene, OR
Tomlinson, R. Sande, P.C. ....Eugene, OR
Tomlinson, R. Tyler ....Morristown, NJ
Tomlinson, Ray A. ....Madison, WI
Tomlinson, Richard ....Houston, TX
Tomlinson, Richard B. ....Troy, MI
Tomlinson, Robert D.
Oklahoma City, OK
Tomlinson, Robert J. ....Seattle, WA
Tomlinson, Robert L., II ....Arlington, VA
Tomlinson, Rodney G. ....Pasadena, CA
Tomlinson, Stanley R. ....Carlsbad, CA
Tomlinson, Stephen G. ....Chicago, IL
Tomlinson, Teresa Pike ....Atlanta, GA
Columbus, GA
Tomlinson, Thomas M. ....Chula Vista, CA
Tomlinson, Thomas M. ....Houston, TX
Tomlinson, Timothy ....Palo Alto, CA
Tomlinson, Tracy L. ....Raleigh, NC
Tomlinson, Tyler ....Philadelphia, PA
Tomlinson, Wade H., III ....Atlanta, GA
Columbus, GA
Tomlinson, Warren L. ....Vail, CO
Tomlinson, Wilbur L., (P.C.)
St. Louis, MO
Tomlinson, Will ....Santa Barbara, CA
Tomlinson, William M. ....Portland, OR
Tomlinson Zisko Morosoli & Maser LLP
Palo Alto, CA
Tomlinson Lorenz, Alice
Albuquerque, NM
Tomljanovich, Esther M. ....St. Paul, MN
Tomm, Charles B. ....Jacksonville, FL
Tommaney, Elizabeth M.
East Aurora, NY
Tommaney, John J. ....New York, NY
Tommaney, Mary Anne ....Albany, NY
Tommaney, Michael J. ....Albany, NY
Tommas, Jacqueline A. ....Estacada, OR
Tommasino & Tommasino ....Boston, MA
Tommasino, William P. ....Boston, MA
Tomme, Alan W. ....Fort Worth, TX
Tomme, Curtis R. ....Abilene, TX
Tommelleo, Nancy L. ....Atlanta, GA
Tommlinson, Barry J. ....Norristown, PA
Tomney, Robin D. ....St. Paul, MN
Tomola, James D. ....Jacksonville, FL
Tomola, Natalie T. ....Jacksonville, FL
Tomomatsu, Christine A.
Menlo Park, CA
Tomon, Bert R. ....Cleveland, OH
Tomorsky, Dennis F. ....Milwaukee, WI
Tomovic, Patrick M. ....Buffalo, NY
Tompa, Peter K. ....Washington, DC
Tompert, James E. ....Washington, DC
Tompkins, A. Stuart ....Southfield, MI
Tompkins, Alan W. ....Dallas, TX
Tompkins, Arlen M. ....Philadelphia, PA
Tompkins, Ben H. ....Fort Worth, TX
Tompkins, Benjamin F. ....Falls Church, VA
Tompkins, Bruce H. ....Bloomington, IL
Tompkins, Bruce M. ....Portland, ME
Tompkins, Catherine Corrigan
Cleveland, OH
Tompkins, Charles E. ....Washington, DC
Tompkins, Charles V., Jr. ....Charlotte, NC
Tompkins, Christopher ....New Orleans, LA
Tompkins, Christopher W. ....Seattle, WA
Tompkins, Clough, Hirshon & Langer, P.A.
Portland, ME
Tompkins, Darryl J. ....Alachua, FL
Fort Lauderdale, FL
Tompkins, Darryl J., P.A. ....Alachua, FL
Tompkins & Davidson, LLP
New York, NY
Tompkins, Dean A. ....Oakland, CA
Tompkins, Donald F. ....North Bergen, NJ
Tompkins, Dwight Edward ....Downey, CA
Tompkins, Edwin W., II ....Emporium, PA
Tompkins, Edwin W., III ....Emporium, PA
Tompkins, Elena ....Department of Justice,
Office of Justice Programs, GV
Tompkins, Elizabeth Anne
Walnut Creek, CA
Tompkins, Emmett A., Jr. ....Alhambra, CA
Tompkins, George N., III ....New York, NY
Tompkins, George N., Jr. ....New York, NY
Tompkins, Harold ....New York, NY
Tompkins, James E. ....Lake Placid, FL
Tompkins, James E. ....Seattle, WA
Tompkins, James L., III ....Hillsville, VA
Tompkins, James M. ....Houston, TX
Tompkins, James R. ....Jacksonville, FL
Tompkins, James R. ....Livingston Manor, NY
Tompkins, Jeffery G. ....Camden, NY
Tompkins, Jeffrey E. ....Atlanta, GA
Tompkins, Jeffrey I. ....Colorado Springs, CO
Tompkins, Jeffrey I., P.C.
Colorado Springs, CO
Tompkins, Jeffrey J. ....Houston, TX
Tompkins, Jerry B. ....Grand Junction, CO
Tompkins, John T., III
Newport News, VA
Tompkins, Joseph B., Jr. ....Washington, DC
Tompkins, Julie F. ....Oakland, CA
Tompkins, Kevin B. ....Houston, TX
Tompkins, Kristina Pride ....Fairfax, VA
Tompkins, Leah L. ....Philadelphia, PA
Tompkins, Linda G. ....Spokane, WA
Tompkins, Lisa M. ....New Orleans, LA
Tompkins, Marguerite M. ....Chicago, IL
Tompkins, Mark H. ....Lafayette, LA
Tompkins, Mary Evangeline ....Richmond, VA
Tompkins, McGuire, Wachenfeld & Barry
Newark, NJ
Tompkins and McMaster ....Columbia, SC
Tompkins, Michael L. ....Denver, CO
Tompkins, Michael W. ....Alexandria, VA
Tompkins, N. Pride ....Tuscumbia, AL
Tompkins, Nancy L. ....San Francisco, CA
Tompkins & Parrington ....Alhambra, CA
Los Angeles, CA
Pasadena, CA
Tompkins, Paul Kelly ....Medina, OH
Tompkins, Peter B. ....New Orleans, LA
Tompkins, Randi S. ....Boca Raton, FL
Tompkins, Randi S., P.A. ....Boca Raton, FL
Tompkins, Raymond E.
Oklahoma City, OK
Tompkins, Richard J. ....St. Louis, MO
Tompkins, Richard J. ....Norristown, PA
Tompkins, Richard N., Jr. ....Mason City, IA
Tompkins, Robert J. ....Albany, NY
Tompkins, Robert K. ....Washington, DC
Tompkins, Robin ....Portland, OR
Tompkins & Root ....Livingston Manor, NY
Tompkins, Sherrill H. ....Galveston, TX
Tompkins, Sigrid E. ....Portland, ME
Tompkins, Stephen D. ....Harrisburg, PA
Tompkins, T. Daniel ....Wichita Falls, TX
Tompkins, Thomas J. ....Zanesville, OH
Tompkins, Thomas M. ....Mobile, AL
Tompkins, Timothy J. ....Seattle, WA
Tompkins & Tompkins ....Emporium, PA
Tompkins, William Clinton ....Urbana, OH
Tompkins-Smith, Isabel Lee
Floral Park, NY
Tompsett, Scott W. ....Overland Park, KS
Tompsett, William C. ....Chicago, IL
Toms, Edith Lynn ....Bethesda, MD
Toms & Evans ....Waynesboro, PA
Toms, F. Rogers, Jr. ....Baltimore, MD
Toms, Fred ....Hendersonville, NC
Toms, Frederic E., and Associates ....Cary, NC
Toms, Herbert L., Jr. ....Raleigh, NC
Toms, James E. ....New Cumberland, PA
Toms, Jerry F. ....Camden, SC
Toms, Kelly Marlaine ....Wilmington, NC
Toms, Margaret L. ....Bryson City, NC
Toms, Michael J. ....Waynesboro, PA
Toms, Nicholas R. H. ....New York, NY
Toms, Robert L., Jr. ....Pasadena, CA
Toms, Robert L., Sr. ....Pasadena, CA
Tomsche, Michael J. ....Minneapolis, MN
Tomsche, Sonnesyn & Tomsche, P.A.
Minneapolis, MN
Tomsche, Steven E. ....Minneapolis, MN
Tomse, Deanne M. ....Chicago, IL
Tomsho, Richard R. ....Allentown, PA
Tomsic, Alan ....Treasury Department,
Internal Revenue Service, GV
Tomsic, Albert J. ....Walsenburg, CO
Tomsic, Gerald A. ....Glendale, CA
Tomsic, Gerald A. ....Los Angeles, CA
Tomsic, Joseph M. ....San Francisco, CA
Tomsic, Judith J. ....San Francisco, CA
Tomsic, Peggy A. ....Salt Lake City, UT
Tomsic, Tali A. ....Danvers, MA
Tomsick, M. Lisa ....Washington, DC
Tomsick, Richard D. ....Cleveland, OH
Tomsick, Terry ....Denver, CO
Tomsky, Jan E. ....San Rafael, CA
Tomsky, John M. ....Mineola, NY
New York, NY
Tomson, M. Moran ....Johnson, KS
Tomson, William L. ....Cleveland, OH
Tomsu, Michael J. ....Austin, TX
Tomtishen, Brad M. ....Detroit, MI
Tomusko, Dale P. ....Cleveland, OH
Tonachel & Lewis, P.C. ....New York, NY
Tonachel, Pierre A. ....New York, NY
Tonagel, Diana L. ....Mandeville, LA
Metairie, LA
Tonahill, Hile, Leister & Jacobellis
Beaumont, TX
Jasper, TX
Tonahill, Joe H. ....Beaumont, TX
Jasper, TX
Tonaki, Toby M. ....Honolulu, HI
Tonaszuck, Marc J. ....Boston, MA
Toncray, Sharon L., P.C. ....Portland, OR
Tondel, Lawrence C. ....New York, NY
Tondini, John A. ....Seattle, WA
Tondre, Brice A. ....Denver, CO
Tondre & Schumacher, P.C. ....Denver, CO
Tondreau, Pamela L. ....Lafayette, CA
Tondreau, Patrick E. ....San Jose, CA
Tondro, Helle S. ....Hartford, CT
Tondro, Terry J. ....Hartford, CT
Tone, David A. ....Department of Commerce,
Patent and Trademark Office, GV
Tone, Francine R. ....Truckee, CA
Tone, Grubbe, McGory & Vermeeren
Sandusky, OH
Tone, Jeffrey R. ....Chicago, IL
Tone, Jeffry P. ....Truckee, CA
Tone, Mark B. ....Elmhurst, IL
Tone, Michael J. ....Garden City, NY
Tone, Michael P. ....Chicago, IL
Tone, Philip W. ....Chicago, IL
Tone, Sheilah Anne ....Scranton, PA
Tone & Tone ....Truckee, CA
Tone, Tygh M. ....Sandusky, OH
Tonegato, Ronald J. ....San Francisco, CA
Tonel, Wesley A. ....Santa Ana, CA
Tonella, Paul A. ....Seattle, WA
Tonelli, Carolyn ....Randolph, VT
Tonelli, Deborah A. ....Clawson, MI
Tonelli, John H. ....New York, NY
Tonelli, Michael A. ....Tampa, FL
Tonello, Anastasia ....New York, NY
Tonello, Matteo ....New York, NY
Tonelson, Emanuel D. ....New York, NY
Toner, Bridget O. ....Bay Shore, NY
Toner, David C. ....Philadelphia, PA
Toner & DiBenedetto ....Roseland, NJ
Toner, Donald L. ....Doylestown, PA
Toner, Eden Rubenstein ....Seattle, WA
Toner, Edward J. ....Florham Park, NJ
Toner, Elizabeth ....Roslindale, MA
Toner, Gerald A. ....Department of Justice,
Criminal Division, GV
Toner, Gerald R. ....Louisville, KY
Toner, Gerard H., Law Offices of
West Babylon, NY
Toner, Hugh, III ....Lewistown, IL
Toner, James J. ....Harwich Port, MA
Toner, James M. ....Ann Arbor, MI
Toner, Jeffrey E. ....Doylestown, PA
Toner, Joanne M. ....Orlando, FL
Toner, John F. ....Columbia, MD

Toner, John J.
National Labor Relations Board, Office of Executive Secretary, GV
Toner, John J. .... Lakewood, OH
Toner, Justin J. .... New York, NY
Toner, Kathleen M. .... New York, NY
Toner, Kevin Joseph .... New York, NY
Toner, Kevin M. .... Indianapolis, IN
Toner, Lisa K. .... Scarborough, ME
Toner, Mary A. .... Bay Shore, NY
Toner, Nelson A. .... Portland, ME
Toner, Patrick G. .... Lake Success, NY
Toner, Paul Francis .... Boston, MA
Toner, Roger L. .... Roseland, NJ
Toner, Stephen B. .... New York, NY
Toner, Susan Jones .... Nantucket, MA
Toner, Terrance Nicholas .... New York, NY
Toner, Tom C. .... Sheridan, WY
Toner & Toner .... Bay Shore, NY
Tonery, John .... Santa Ana, CA
Tonery, Lisa M. .... New York, NY
Tonetta, Richard P. .... Vineland, NJ
Tonetti, Joseph C. .... Riverhead, NY
Tonetti, Lawrence J. .... Bronx, NY
Toney, Bruce A. .... Huntington, WV
Toney, Causton A. .... Washington, DC
Toney, David .... Houston, TX
Toney & Douglass .... Liberty, IN
Toney, J. .... Woodland, CA
Toney, Jay L. .... Winchester, IN
Toney, Jeffrey J. .... Atlanta, GA
Toney, Keenya .... Chapel Hill, NC
Toney, Marcy A. .... Washington, DC
Toney, Steven L. .... New London, WI
Toney, William D. .... Tulsa, OK
Toney, Willis L. .... Kansas City, MO
Tong, Adrianne .... Pasadena, CA
Tong, Daron D. .... San Francisco, CA
Tong, David J. .... Tampa, FL
Tong, Elizabeth Bagby .... Easton, MD
Tong, Geoffrey T. .... Los Angeles, CA
Tong, Harry W. .... Redwood City, CA
Tong, Kin-Wah .... Red Bank, NJ
Tong, Kirk .... New York, NY
Tong, Lawrence L. .... Honolulu, HI
Tong, May Lee .... Oakland, CA
Tong, Michelle .... New York, NY
Tong, Nancy Yi-Pei .... New York, NY
Tong, Penelope Wat .... Honolulu, HI
Tong, Peter .... San Francisco, CA
Tong, Ronald G. .... San Francisco, CA
Tong-Florczak, Yen .... St. Paul, MN
Tongg, David B. .... Honolulu, HI
Tongg, Michael A. .... Honolulu, HI
Tongg, Ronald P. .... Honolulu, HI
Tongg, Tenney Z. .... Honolulu, HI
Tongg & Tongg .... Honolulu, HI
Tongg, Trudie Lee .... Honolulu, HI
Tongier, Glen L. .... Coffeyville, KS
Tongier, John D. .... Merriam, KS
Tongren, B. R. .... Peotone, IL
Tongren, Robert S. .... Columbus, OH
Tongren, Steven Hale .... Peotone, IL
Tongsuthi, Janet L. .... Los Angeles, CA
Tongue, Dorothy P. .... Westport, MA
Tongue, James W. .... Shalimar, FL
Tongue, Thomas Healy .... Portland, OR
Tonies, Theresa Mary .... Akron, OH
Tonigan, Henry C., III .... Waukegan, IL
Tonini, Melio A. .... Des Moines, IA
Toniolo and Kaplan .... Fort Lee, NJ
Toniolo, Richard J. .... Fort Lee, NJ
Tonjes, John C. .... Fond du Lac, WI
Tonkavich, Christine E. .... Lawrence, KS
Tonken, Neal J. .... Washington, DC
Tonkin, Edward C. .... Portland, OR
Tonkin, Elissa .... Boston, MA
Tonkin, Mary McGrath .... St. Louis, MO
Tonkin & Mondl, L.C. .... St. Louis, MO
Tonkin, Richard J. .... Detroit, MI
Tonkin, Simon .... St. Louis, MO
Tonkin, William G. .... Seattle, WA
Tonkinson, J. Stuart .... Dallas, TX
Tonkon Torp LLP .... Portland, OR
Tonkonow and Kendzior .... Meriden, CT
Tonkonow, Sherman M. .... Meriden, CT
Tonkonow, Sherry Rippel .... Doylestown, PA
Tonkovich, Christine Kenney .... Lawrence, KS
Tonkovich, E. Paul .... Santa Ana, CA
Tonkovich, E. Paul, A Professional Law Corporation .... Santa Ana, CA
Tonkovich, Emil A. .... Lawrence, KS
Tonkovich, Matthew L. .... Santa Ana, CA
Tonkovich, Stephen J. .... Boston, MA
Tonks, Bruce L. .... Seattle, WA
Tonks, Paul H. .... Middletown, OH
Tonks, Ronald R. .... Grosse Pointe, MI
Tonn, A. Lance .... Miles City, MT
Tonn, Boshadis L. .... Newark, NJ
Tonn, Colleen E. .... Fort Wayne, IN
Tonn, Robert E. .... San Francisco, CA
Tonneman, Noel S. .... Eatontown, NJ
Tonner, Gregory J. .... Merrillville, IN
Tonner, Jeffrey J. .... Phoenix, AZ
Tonner, Jeffrey J., P.C. .... Phoenix, AZ
Tonner, Leo L. .... Chester, NJ
Tonner, Ned J. .... Rensselaer, IN
Tonner, Ned J., P.C. .... Rensselaer, IN
Tonner, Thomas P. .... Aberdeen, SD
Tonner, Tobin & King .... Aberdeen, SD
Tonnessen, David W. .... Baltimore, MD
Tonnessen, Peter Trygve
Colorado Springs, CO
Tonnon, Alan N. .... Bellevue, WA
Tonnsen, John J. .... Billings, MT
Tonogbanua, Arobert C. .... Westmont, NJ
Tonomura, Lawrence N. .... San Francisco, CA
Tonon & Associates .... Truckee, CA
Tonon, Gayle K. .... Truckee, CA
Tonon, Margaret A. .... Missoula, MT
Tonore, Edward E., Jr. .... Jackson, MS
Tonore, Gregory E. .... Lafayette, LA
Tonos, Robert J. .... Chicago, IL
Tonozzi, Arthur P. .... Uniontown, PA
Tonozzi, Thomas A. .... Spring Valley, IL
Tonrey, James E., Jr. .... Woodbridge, NJ
Tonry, Dylan Tyson .... Boston, MA
Tonry, Eugene A. .... Elyria, OH
Tonry and Ginart .... Chalmette, LA
Tonry, Michael H. .... Minneapolis, MN
Tonry, Richard A. .... Chalmette, LA
Tonsfeldt, Steven J. .... Menlo Park, CA
Tonsich, Nicholas G. .... San Pedro, CA
Tonsing, Heather L. .... Cleveland, OH
Tonsing, Jon P. .... Walnut Creek, CA
Tonsing, Michael J. .... San Francisco, CA
Tonsmeire, George A. .... Mobile, AL
Tonti, A. Patk. .... Columbus, OH
Tonti, Amy M. .... Pittsburgh, PA
Tontz, Daniel D. .... Wichita, KS
Tontz, Gregory T. .... Norman, OK
Tonucci, Anthony A. .... New York, NY
Tonucci, Darlene M. .... Miami, FL
Tonucci, Studio Legale .... New York, NY
New York, NY
Tonuzi, Drita .... New York, NY
Tonya, Michael A. .... Los Angeles, CA
Tonzillo, Nicholas V., Jr. .... Wayne, NJ
Toobin, Jeffrey Ross .... New York, NY
Toobin, Michael D. .... Fairfax, VA
Tooby, Norton .... Oakland, CA
Tooby, Norton .... Oakland, CA
Tooch, Daron L. .... Los Angeles, CA
Tooch, Melinda J. .... Los Angeles, CA
Toof, Jonathan A. .... Portland, ME
Toogood, Arthur C. .... Hastings, NE
Tooher, Joseph J., Jr. .... Stamford, CT
Tooher, Meave M. .... Albany, NY
Tooher & Wocl, L.L.C. .... Fairfield, CT
Stamford, CT
Toohey, Ann C.
Environmental Protection Agency, Office of the General Counsel, GV
Toohey, Aylice M. .... Chicago, IL
Toohey, Brian F. .... Cleveland, OH
Toohey, Daniel W. .... Washington, DC
Toohey & DiMaggio, P.C. .... Perryville, MO
Ste. Genevieve, MO
Toohey, Francis, Jr. .... Perryville, MO
Ste. Genevieve, MO
Toohey, Gerard E., Jr .... Fairfield, NJ
Toohey, James B. .... Fairfax, VA
Toohey, James F. .... Erie, PA
Toohey, James K. .... Chicago, IL
Toohey, Janice E. .... Plano, TX
Toohey, John S. .... Mount Pleasant, PA
Toohey, Mark H. .... Kingsport, TN
Toohey, Michael J. .... Saratoga Springs, NY
Toohey, Paul E. .... Mount Pleasant, PA
Toohey, Philip S. .... Buffalo, NY
Toohey, Richard F. .... Santa Ana, CA
Toohey, Robert E. .... Bloomfield Hills, MI
Toohey, Timothy J. .... Los Angeles, CA
Toohey, Valerie D. .... Philadelphia, PA
Toohill, Clement M .... Heyworth, IL
Toohill, Donald J. .... Peoria, IL
Toohill, Jos. V. .... Farmington, IL
Toohill, Joseph V., Jr. .... Farmington, IL
Toohill, Judith A. .... Farmington, IL
Toohill, Stephen T. .... San Diego, CA
Toohill, Toohill & Toohill .... Farmington, IL
Toohy, William J. .... New York, NY
Tooke, Casper A., Jr. .... Shreveport, LA
Tooke, Margaret L. .... Baton Rouge, LA
Tooke, S. Judd .... Shreveport, LA
Tooke, William P. .... San Bernardino, CA
Tooker, David W. .... Sumter, SC
Tooker, Dean .... Okeechobee, FL
Tooker, Eric S. .... Phoenix, AZ
Tooker, Mary Hull .... New Orleans, LA
Tookey, Thomas E. .... Coral Springs, FL
Tookey, Thomas E., P.A. .... Coral Springs, FL
Tookey, William Anderson .... San Marino, CA
Tooks, Lloyd E. .... San Diego, CA
Tool, H. Warren, Jr. .... Charlotte, NC
Toolan, John T. .... New York, NY
Toolan, Kathleen Patricia .... Tallahassee, FL
Toolan, Michael J. .... New York, NY
Toolan, P. James .... Blue Bell, PA
Toolan, Paul F. .... Blue Bell, PA
Toole, Allan H. .... Spokane, WA
Toole, Arnold E. .... Chicago, IL
Toole & Breznik .... Shenandoah, PA
Toole, Bruce R. .... Billings, MT
Toole, Cecilia A. .... Augusta, GA
Toole, Charles K. .... The Dalles, OR
Toole, Cornelius E. .... Chicago, IL
Toole, Dana G. .... Dade City, FL
Toole, Daniel A. .... Cincinnati, OH
Toole, Daniel F. .... McLean, VA
Toole, Edward C., Jr. .... Philadelphia, PA
Toole, Elizabeth .... San Francisco, CA
Toole, Frampton W., III .... Aiken, SC
Toole, Frampton W., Jr. .... Aiken, SC
Toole, Frances M. .... Department of Justice, Civil Division, GV
Toole, Frank J., Jr. .... Shenandoah, PA
Toole, Frederick M. .... Geneva, NY
Toole, Gasper L., III .... Aiken, SC
Toole, J. Howard .... Missoula, MT
Toole, Janice Lenczycki .... Worcester, MA
Toole, Jeffrey C. .... Cleveland, OH
Toole, Jeffrey S. .... Indianapolis, IN
Toole, John H. .... McLean, VA
Toole, Kevin R. .... New York, NY
Toole, M. Gary .... Orlando, FL
Toole, Mary C. .... Portland, ME
Toole, Merrill L. .... Los Angeles, CA
Toole, Merrill L. .... Monrovia, CA
Toole & Palubinsky, P.C. .... Shenandoah, PA
Toole, Patrick D. .... Fresno, CA
Toole, Patrick J., Jr. .... Wilkes-Barre, PA
Toole, Richard H. .... St. Louis, MO
Toole, Steven G. .... Bellevue, WA
Toole, Thomas F. .... Shenandoah, PA
Toole and Toole .... Aiken, SC
Toole, William W. .... Charlotte, NC
Toolen, Robert L. .... Costa Mesa, CA
Tooley, Brian S. .... Denver, CO
Tooley, Janet M. .... Detroit, MI
Tooley, Joe C. .... Dallas, TX
Tooley, John F., Jr. .... Houston, TX
Tooley, Keith D. .... Denver, CO
Tooley, Michael L. .... Indianapolis, IN
Tooley, Patrick D. .... Denver, CO
Tooley, Thomas C. .... Lakewood, CO
Tooley & Voss .... Dallas, TX
Tooliatos, Nickolas P., II .... Pleasanton, CA
San Jose, CA
Toolin, Wendy Lee .... Chicago, IL
Toolis, Shannon A. .... Chicago, IL
Toolson, Stewart T. .... Green River, WY
Tooma, Farnoush H. .... New York, NY
Toomajian, William M. .... Cleveland, OH
Tooman, Lester J. .... Allegan, MI
Tooman, Marci B.H. .... Des Moines, IA
Tooman, Steven A. .... Detroit, MI
Toombs, Alfred Lawrence .... Alexandria, VA
Toombs, Charles E. .... Oakland, CA
Toombs, Clara E. .... New Orleans, LA
Toombs, Helen Lawrence .... Houston, TX
Toombs, James R. .... Carmel, IN
Toombs, Nancy Pechar .... New York, NY
Toomer, Anne P. .... Pasadena, CA
Toomer, Bruce M. .... Pasadena, CA
Toomer, Pinkie J. Turner .... Atlanta, GA
Toomey, A. Katherine .... Washington, DC
Toomey, Alison Graham
North Dartmouth, MA
Toomey, Allan A. .... Department of the Army, U.S. Army Court of Criminal Appeals, GV
Toomey, C. Scott .... Philadelphia, PA
Toomey, Christopher John .... Medford, MA
Toomey, Daniel E. .... Washington, DC
Toomey, Daniel F. .... Worcester, MA
Toomey, Daniel L. .... Merrillville, IN
Toomey, David C. .... Philadelphia, PA
Toomey, David F., Jr. .... Oradell, NJ
Toomey, David J. .... Washington, DC
Toomey, Frances H. .... Tampa, FL
Toomey, George E. .... Saratoga Springs, NY
Toomey, Gregg A. .... Fort Lauderdale, FL
Toomey, James A. .... Quincy, MA
Toomey, James C. .... Bethesda, MD
Toomey, Joan Dungey .... Kansas City, MO
Toomey, Joel B. .... Jacksonville, FL
Toomey, John F. .... Boston, MA
Toomey, John J. .... Chicago, IL
Toomey, John J. .... Houston, TX
Toomey, John J., Jr. .... Smithtown, NY
Toomey, John M. .... Ann Arbor, MI
Toomey, Joseph P. .... Brighton, MA
Toomey, Joyce M. .... Cambridge, MA
Toomey, Kenneth J. .... Albany, NY
Toomey, Kevin J. .... Boston, MA
Toomey, Larry D. .... Wichita, KS
Toomey, Mary Kate .... Salt Lake City, UT
Toomey, Michael J. .... Glens Falls, NY
Toomey, Michael V. .... Houston, TX
Toomey & Murray .... Oradell, NJ
Toomey, Neil J. .... Bayside, NY
Brooklyn, NY
New York, NY
Toomey, Patrick C. .... Boston, MA
Toomey, Patrick J., Jr.
Fort Lauderdale, FL
Toomey, Philip A. .... Torrance, CA
Toomey, Priscilla R. .... Stamford, CT
Toomey, Raymond D. .... Boston, MA
Toomey, Richard A., Jr. .... Boston, MA
Toomey, Robert B. .... New York, NY
Toomey, Robert L. .... Bethesda, MD
Toomey, Robert S. .... Rome, GA
Toomey, Robert S., P.C. .... Calhoun, GA
Cartersville, GA
Cedartown, GA
Dallas, GA
La Fayette, GA
Rome, GA
Summerville, GA
Toomey, Rory S. .... Honolulu, HI
Toomey, Rose M. .... Castro Valley, CA
Toomey, Russell, Pilgreen & Innes, L.L.C.
Wichita, KS
Toomey, Sarah Y. .... Huntington, WV
Toomey, Stephen E. .... Houston, TX
Toomey, Stephen J. .... Treasury Department, Internal Revenue Service, GV
Toomey & Stewart .... Ann Arbor, MI
Toomey, T. Murray .... Bethesda, MD
Toomey, Terry Alvin .... Meadville, PA
Toomey, Thos. A., Jr. .... San Francisco, CA
Toomey, Vincent .... Lake Success, NY
Toomey, V. M., Jr. .... Houston, TX
Toomey, William Augustus, III .... Albany, NY
Toomey, William E.
Securities and Exchange Commission, Division of Corporation Finance, GV
Toomey & Yudysky LLP .... Boston, MA
Toomi, Juri .... Mineola, NY
Toomim, David R. .... Houston, TX
Toomin, Michael P. .... Chicago, IL
Tooms & House .... London, KY
Tooms, R. William .... London, KY
Toomsoo, Samantha B. .... Bridgewater, NJ
Toon, Cassius H. .... Charleston, WV
Toon, Jason B. .... Tulsa, OK
Toone, Barry C. .... Phoenix, AZ
Toone, D. William, Jr. .... Seattle, WA
Toone, David F. .... Tucson, AZ
Toone, David G. .... Marlborough, MA
Toone, James R. .... San Diego, CA
Toone, Katherine B. .... Richmond, VA
Toone, Robert E., Jr. .... Atlanta, GA
Toone, Thomas E. .... Temple, TX
Toone, Thomas L. .... Phoenix, AZ
Toop, Diane Rowley .... White Plains, NY
Toop, R. Scott .... Louisville, KY
Toor, Bruce A. .... Los Angeles, CA
Toor, Francine H. .... Parsippany, NJ
Toor, Helen M. .... New York, NY
Toor, Joyce Hendricks .... Treasury Department, Internal Revenue Service, GV
Toornman, Mary E. .... Denver, CO
Toorock, Michael S. .... New York, NY
Toot, Christopher L. .... Flint, MI
Toot, Douglas M. .... Canfield, OH
Tootalian, Deborah A. .... Brookline, MA
Toote, Gloria E. A. .... New York, NY
Tootell, Megan .... San Francisco, CA
Toothacre & Pederson .... San Diego, CA
Toothacre, Rod M. .... San Diego, CA
Toothacre, Scott H. .... San Diego, CA
Toothaker, George R., Jr. .... Wellesley, MA
Toothaker, Stephanie J.
Fort Lauderdale, FL
Toothaker, Thomas R. .... New York, NY
Toothman, Arthur H. .... Miami, FL
Toothman, Glenn R., Jr. .... Waynesburg, PA
Toothman, James E. .... Los Gatos, CA
Toothman, John W. .... Alexandria, VA
Toothman, Richard D. .... Boise, ID
Toothman & White, P.C. .... Alexandria, VA
Tootle, Carl M. .... Tucson, AZ
Tootle, John S. .... Manhattan Beach, CA
Tootle, Kenneth L. .... Beaufort, SC
Tootle, Thomas .... Columbus, OH
Tootle, Thomas F. .... Circleville, OH
Tootooian, Michael W. .... Chicago, IL
Tooze Duden Creamer Frank & Hutchison
Portland, OR
Top, Franklin H., III .... Chicago, IL
Top, Thomas W. .... Seattle, WA
Topac, Jack .... New York, NY
Topacio, Teodoro B. .... New York, NY
Topakas, Alexander G. .... Boulder, CO
Topal, Steven L. .... New York, NY
Topalian, Hripsema R. .... Whittier, CA
Topalis, Panos T. .... Chicago, IL
Topas, Reuel E. .... Jackson, NJ
Topaz, Howard M. .... New York, NY
Topazi, Gerald S. .... Birmingham, AL
Topazian, Jonathan R. .... Washington, DC
Topazio, Andrew Robert .... Hoboken, NJ
Topazio, Elizabeth A. .... Pearl River, NY
Topazio, Steven J. .... Boston, MA
Topchik, L. John .... Portland, ME
Topczewski, David .... Milwaukee, WI
Topczewski, Peter L. .... Milwaukee, WI
Tope, Donna K. .... Ann Arbor, MI
Tope, Jacqueline A. .... Garner, NC
Tope Law Offices, PLLC .... Garner, NC
Topek, D. Aaron .... Houston, TX
Topek, E. Stanley .... Houston, TX
Topek & Topek .... Houston, TX
Topel, David L. .... Philadelphia, PA
Topel, Dorothy Nelson .... Marinette, WI
Topel, Eugene .... Los Angeles, CA
Topel & Goodman, A Professional Corporation .... San Francisco, CA
Topel, Howard A. .... Washington, DC
Topel, Jodi L. .... Minneapolis, MN
Topel, Marcus S. .... San Francisco, CA
Topel, Thomas F. .... Billings, MT
Topelius, Kathleen E. .... Washington, DC
Topelsohn, Lauren .... New York, NY
Toperzer, Robert S. .... Tucson, AZ
Topete, Diego .... San Diego, CA
Topetzes, James G. .... Milwaukee, WI
Topetzes, Stephen G. .... Washington, DC
Topf, Ian Spencer .... Columbia, MO
Topf, Morris .... Bethesda, MD
Topf, William L., III .... Phoenix, AZ
Topham, Lee E. .... Concord, NH
Topham, Leslie .... Boston, MA
Topham, Matthew S. .... Seattle, WA
Topham, Reed W. .... Salt Lake City, UT
Topham, Terry .... San Antonio, TX
Topham, Verl R. .... Salt Lake City, UT
Topham, Wm. Shane .... Salt Lake City, UT
Topiel, Amy .... Chappaqua, NY
Topiel, Fred N. .... Huntington, NY
Topinka, James E. .... San Francisco, CA
Topinka, Ralph V. .... Madison, WI
Topkin, Sanford R. .... Deerfield Beach, FL
Orlando, FL
Topkins & Bevans .... Braintree, MA
Waltham, MA
Topkins, Elliott S. .... Waltham, MA
Topkins, Elyse Michelle .... Lenoir, NC
Topkis, Jay .... New York, NY
Topletz, Bruce I. .... Franklin, IN
Topletz, Jack M. .... Dallas, TX
Topliff, James F. .... Spokane, WA
Topliff, Mary Lenox .... Oakland, CA
Topliffe, Elizabeth M. .... Grand Rapids, MI
Toplitt, Sheldon C. .... Needham, MA
Toplitz, George N. .... New York, NY
Topman, Bruce .... New York, NY
Topodas, Jonathan M. .... Hartford, CT
Topol, Allan J. .... Washington, DC
Topol, Clive M. .... Chicago, IL

Topol, David H. ....Department of Justice, Environment and Natural Resources Division, GV
Topol, Gary N. ....Elgin, IL
Topol, Morris ....Northbrook, IL
Topol, Noel Stephen ....Reno, NV
Topol, Robin A. Levitt ....White Plains, NY
Topoleski, Marc A. ....Southfield, MI
Topolnicki, John A., Jr. ....Englewood, CO
Topolosky, Gary P. ....Alcoa Center, PA
Topolski, Douglas M. ....Baltimore, MD
Topolski, Joseph ....New York, NY
Topolsky, Anthony T. ....San Francisco, CA
Topoluk, R. Elizabeth ....Chicago, IL
Topor, Joseph W., Jr. ....Springfield, MA
Topor, Thomas K. ....Fort Lauderdale, FL
Topor, Walter S. ....Palmer, MA
Toporek, Alan David ....Charleston, SC
Toporek, Jacob C. ....Newark, NJ
Toporek, Julian H. ....Savannah, GA
Toporoff, Steven .....Federal Trade Commission, Bureau of Consumer Protection, GV
Topp, Claire H. ....Minneapolis, MN
Topp, Jason D. ....Minneapolis, MN
Topp, John R. ....Sandpoint, ID
Topp, Joyce M. ....Miami, FL
Topp, Michael A. ....San Francisco, CA
Topp, Susan Hlywa ....Gaylord, MI
Toppel, Harold S. ....Mountain View, CA
Toppel, Heidi J. ....Fort Lee, NJ
Toppelberg, Alan S. ....Washington, DC
Toppen, Jon P. ....Louisburg, NC
Toppenberg & Burke, P.C. ....Knoxville, TN
Toppenberg, Douglas J. ....Knoxville, TN
Topper, Brian ....New York, NY
Topper, Daniel L. ....Brooklyn, NY
Topper, Daniel S. ....New York, NY
Topper, Elliot F. ....New York, NY
Topper, Mark R.
Charlotte Amalie, St. Thomas, VI
Topper, Philip D., Jr. ....Middletown, MD
Topper, Richard D. ....Columbus, OH
Topper, Robert ....Melville, NY
Topper, Robert, P.C. ....Melville, NY
Topper, Susan M. ....Rochester, NY
Toppeta, Debra J. ....New York, NY
Toppeta, Rita ....Schenectady, NY
Toppeta & Toppeta ....Schenectady, NY
Toppila, W. Brian ....Los Angeles, CA
Toppin, Bruce J. ....Tupelo, MS
Toppin, C. Thomas ....Bloomfield Hills, MI
Toppin, C. Thomas and Associates, P.C. Bloomfield Hills, MI
Toppin, Sherman C. ....Richmond, VA
Topping, Andrew C. ....Malvern, PA
Topping, Catherine Ray Federal Deposit Insurance Corporation, Professional Liability Section, GV
Topping, Gloria W. ....Washington, DC
Topping, Joanna M. ....Westbury, NY
Topping, John C., Jr. ....Washington, DC
Topping, John L., Jr. ....Flint, MI
Topping, Linda M. ....: Department of State, GV
Topping, Mara E. R. ....Washington, DC
Topping, Petra H. ....Rochester, NY
Topping, Robt. L. ....St. Louis, MO
Topping, Thomas S. ....Atlanta, GA
Toppins, Paul E. ....Birmingham, AL
Toppins, Roger K. ....Oklahoma City, OK
Toppo, Christopher R. ....New York, NY
Topps, Margaret M. ....Washington, DC
Topsfield, Zoë A. ....Philadelphia, PA
Toptani, Edward G. ....New York, NY
Tor, A. Deniz ....Corpus Christi, TX
Torack, Edward V. ....Franklin Lakes, NJ
Torain, Ernest W., Jr. ....Chicago, IL
Torain, Karin S. ....Chicago, IL
Torak, Joseph L. ....Limerick, PA
Torál, Todd C. ....Oakland, CA
Toran, Janice A. ....Skokie, IL
Toran, John, Jr. ....Portland, OR
Toran, Philip B. ....Philadelphia, PA
Toran, Ross P. ....Wheaton, IL
Toran, William J. ....New York, NY
Toraño, Carlos O. ....Fort Lauderdale, FL
Toranto, Lauren S. ....Houston, TX
Toras, Christina A. ....Bridgeville, PA
Toras, James ....Bridgeville, PA
Toras and Toras, P.C. ....Bridgeville, PA
Toray, Eric R. ....Denver, CO
Toraya, David R. ....New York, NY
Torbati, Melody N. ....Los Angeles, CA
Torbenson, Dane ....Denver, CO
Torbenson, Daniel L. ....Washington, DC
Torbert, C. Clay, III ....Montgomery, AL
Torbert, C. C., Jr. ....Montgomery, AL
Torbert, Cynthia H. ....Montgomery, AL
Torbert, Jack W. ....Gadsden, AL
Torbert, Jack W., Jr. ....Gadsden, AL
Torbert, Mary Dixon ....Montgomery, AL
Torbert, Patricia Kinney ....Sacramento, CA
Torbert, Preston M. ....Chicago, IL
Torbert, Richard C. ....New York, NY
Torbert, Ronald J. ....Detroit, MI
Torbert & Torbert, P.A. ....Anniston, AL
Fort Payne, AL
Gadsden, AL
Guntersville, AL
Torbert, Vance W., III ....Lakewood, NJ
Torbet, Hugo ....San Francisco, CA
Torbet, John Randolph
Colorado Springs, CO
Torbett, Gilbert E. ....Bristol, TN
Torbett, Thomas H. ....Kingsport, TN
Torbett & Torbett ....Kingsport, TN
Torbit, Kathleen E. ....Philadelphia, PA
Torborg, David S. ....Columbus, OH
Torborg, Gregory S. ....New York, NY
Torborg, Martin P. ....Fort Wayne, IN
Torcellini, Edmund ....Hamtramck, MI
Torch, Glenn F. ....Akron, OH
Torchalski, Michael J. ....Crystal Lake, IL
Torchia, David G. ....Cincinnati, OH
Torchia, Michael J. ....Redlands, CA
Torchia, Michael J. ....Jenkintown, PA
Torchia, William A., Jr. ....Philadelphia, PA
Torchiana, William D. ....New York, NY
Torchin, David ....Hackensack, NJ
Torchin, Norman G. ....Washington, DC
Torchinsky, David B. ....Washington, DC
Chevy Chase, MD
Torchio, Daniel S. ....New York, NY
Torcicollo, Peter J. ....Newark, NJ
Torcivia, Glen J. ....West Palm Beach, FL
Torcivia, Glen J., P.A. .....West Palm Beach, FL
Torcivia, Joseph A. ....Westfield, NJ
Torcivia, Paulette ....West Palm Beach, FL
Torczon, Andrea G. Department of Commerce, Office of the General Counsel, GV
Torczyner, Harry ....New York, NY
Torczyner, Neil S. ....Mineola, NY
Torda, Janine M. ....Scranton, PA
Torda, Joseph R. ....Toledo, OH
Tordai, Nancy K. ....Chicago, IL
Tordella, Daniel F. ....Fort Lauderdale, FL
Tordella & Kane, P.C. ....Paoli, PA
Philadelphia, PA
Tordella, Philip A. ....Paoli, PA
Torell, Julie ....Foley, MN
Torell Law Office ....Foley, MN
Torell, Mark C. ....Foley, MN
Torelli, Helen ....New Brunswick, NJ
Torelli, Janna Honig ....New York, NY
Torem, Adam E. ....Tacoma, WA
Torem, Christopher C. H. ....Chicago, IL
Torem, Ron ....Encino, CA
Toren, Bellanne M. ....Dallas, TX
Toren, David ....New York, NY
Toren, J. R. ....Edina, MN
Toren, Peter J. ....New York, NY
Toreno, Vincent A. ....Atlanta, GA
Toreson, Arthur H., Jr. ....Spokane, WA
Toretti, Michael J. ....Indiana, PA
Toretto, Stephen J. ....Newport Beach, CA
Torf, Jason M. ....Chicago, IL
Torf, Jeffrey S. ....Chicago, IL
Torf, Philip R. ....Northbrook, IL
Torgan, Bradly S. ....Irvine, CA
Torgelson, David J. ....Olivia, MN
Torgen & Callaghan ....North Kingstown, RI
Torgen, Edward H. ....North Kingstown, RI
Torgenrud, Don ....St. Ignatius, MT
Torgersen, Eric E. ....Golden, CO
Torgerson, Alan C. ....Albuquerque, NM
Torgerson, Andrew H. ....Mason City, IA
Rockwell, IA
Torgerson, James E. ....Anchorage, AK
Torgerson, Karin B. ....Dallas, TX
Torgerson, Kenneth A. ....Cleveland, OH
Torgerson Law Offices ....Mason City, IA
Rockwell, IA
Torgerson, Lynne A. ....Minneapolis, MN
Torgerson, Mark R. ....Juneau, AK
Torgerson, Noel K. ....Costa Mesa, CA
Torgerson, Paul M. ....Minneapolis, MN
Torgerson, R. Thomas ....Duluth, MN
Torgerson, Ray Thomas ....Houston, TX
Torgerson, Robert H. ....Minneapolis, MN
Torgerson, Susan E.
Mendota Heights, MN
Torgerson, William T. ....Washington, DC
Torgeson, Penelope H. ....Irvine, CA
Torgovitsky, Harry ....Larkspur, CA
Torgovitsky, Stanislav ....Washington, DC
Torgow, Gary H. ....Detroit, MI
Torgow, Martha A. ....Los Angeles, CA
Torgrimson, Christian F. ....Atlanta, GA
Torhorst, Allan B. ....Burlington, WI
Torhorst, Richard W. ....Lake Geneva, WI
Torian, Mary Ann ....Columbus, OH
Torian, Michael H. ....Nashville, TN
Torian, Robert E., (P.C.) ....Lafayette, LA
Torian, Roberta Griffin ....Philadelphia, PA
Toribiong, Johnson ....Koror, TT
Torielli, Gina M. ....Peoria, IL
Bloomfield Hills, MI
Kalamazoo, MI
Lansing, MI
Toriello, Albert F. ....Yonkers, NY
Toriello, Christina A. ....Marlton, NJ
Philadelphia, PA
Toriello, Denise S. ....Nanuet, NY
Toriello, John M. ....New York, NY
Torigian, John S., (P.C.) ....Austin, TX
Houston, TX
Torigian, Mark S. ....Farmington Hills, MI
Torigian, Victoria K. ....Pasadena, CA
Torigiani, Steven M. ....Bakersfield, CA
Torii, Dennis R. ....Bensenville, IL
Torii, Dennis R., P.C. ....Bensenville, IL
Torii, John S. ....Torrance, CA
Torina, Samuel J. ....Grosse Pointe Park, MI
Torino, Bruce A. ....Mineola, NY
Torino, Helen V. ....Burlington, VT
Torino, Helen V. ....Colchester, VT
Torino & Singer, P.C. ....Mineola, NY
Torinus, Louis E. ....Stillwater, MN
Torjesen, John C. ....Los Angeles, CA
Torjesen, John C., & Associates Los Angeles, CA
Torke, David R. ....Boulder, CO
Torke, James W. ....Indianapolis, IN
Torkelsen, Elizabeth Stebbins
Stamford, CT
Torkelsen, Steven M. ....Stamford, CT
Torkelson, Christopher E. ....Trenton, NJ
Torkelson, Daniel J. ....Salt Lake City, UT
Torkelson, Eric J. ....New York, NY
Torkelson, John S. ....Dallas, TX
Torkelson, Kenric P. ....Placerville, CA
Torkelson, Loren H. ....Billings, MT
Torkelson, Merle A. ....Washburn, ND
Torkelson, Nelda ....Catoosa, OK
Torkelson, William E. ....Madison, WI
Torkildson, Katz, Fonseca, Jaffe, Moore & Hetherington, Attorneys At Law, A Law Corporation ....Hilo, HI
Honolulu, HI
Lihue, HI
Wailuku, HI
Torkildson, Patricia A. ....Madison, WI
Torkildson, Raymond M. ....Honolulu, HI
Torkildson, Steven V. ....Honolulu, HI
Torkildson, Thomas Miles ....El Paso, TX
Torkington, Anne Beytin ....Downey, CA
Torline, Karen L. ....Olathe, KS
Torline, Paul B. ....Kansas City, MO
Torline, Stephen J. ....Overland Park, KS
Torline, Terry J. ....Wichita, KS
Torma, Mary D. ....Amherst, OH
Torman, Susan ....Boston, MA
Tormay, Anne Marie ....New York, NY
Tormey, Beatrice B. ....Madison, WI
Tormey, Christine E. ....New York, NY
Tormey, Denise M. ....New York, NY
Tormey, Dennis M. ....San Diego, CA
Tormey, Edmund J. ....Columbus, OH
Tormey, James C., III ....Syracuse, NY
Tormey, James R., Jr. ....San Mateo, CA
Tormey, Jeff ....Amarillo, TX
Tormey, John J., III ....New York, NY
Tormey, John J., III, P.C. ....New York, NY
Tormey, John R. R. ....Washington, DC
Tormey, Kevin M. ....Boston, MA
Tormey, Matthew F. ....New York, NY
Tormey, Michael T. ....Morris Plains, NJ
Tormey, Thomas J. ....Tucson, AZ
Tormey, William G. ....Hampton Bays, NY
Tormohlen, Robert W. ....Kansas City, MO
Tormos y Blandino, Hector S. ....San Juan, PR
Torn, Marsha ....New York, NY
Torn, R. Sam ....Houston, TX
Torna, Vincent John ....New York, NY
Tornabene, Charles J. ....Missoula, MT
Tornari, Joel Lewis ....Baltimore, MD
Tornatore, Gina Gabriella
Upper Marlboro, MD
Tornatore, Salvatore J. ....Schaumburg, IL
Tornatta, Robert Jeffrey ....Evansville, IN
Tornay, Peter C. ....Orange, CA
Tornay, Suellyn P. ....Atlanta, GA
Torneby, R. Wayne, Jr. ....Longview, WA
Tornehl, W. Ted ....Milwaukee, WI
Tornell, Edward A. ....Santa Ana, CA
Tornetta, David Andrew ....Norristown, PA
Tornetta, Paul Anthony ....Norristown, PA
Tornetta, Philip A. ....Wyckoff, NJ
Tornetta, Stephen A. ....Blue Bell, PA
Tornga, David L. ....Birmingham, MI
Tornga, David L., P.C. ....Birmingham, MI
Tornga, Timothy J. ....Grand Rapids, MI
Torngren, William P. ....Palm Springs, CA
Torngren, William P. ....Sacramento, CA
Tornheim, Milton A., (Ltd.) ....Chicago, IL
Tornillo, Daniel A. ....Bridgeport, CT
Tornillo, Glenn C. ....Atlanta, GA
Torning, Anders K. ....Charlotte, NC
Tornow, Medley A. ....Chillicothe, IL
Peoria, IL
Tornow, Thomas T. ....Whitefish, MT
Tornow, W. McNair ....Winston-Salem, NC
Tornquist, Leroy J. ....Salem, OR
Toro, Amalia M. ....Hartford, CT
Toro, Edward L. ....Boston, MA
Toro, Eugene F. ....East Greenwich, RI
Toro, Frank, Jr. ....New Haven, CT
Toro, Jeanne M. ....Denver, CO
Toro, John A. ....Warwick, RI
Toro, José Ricardo ....San Juan, PR
Toro, Luis A. ....Denver, CO
Toro, Matthew B. ....Providence, RI
Toro, Mercedes ....San Francisco, CA
Toro, Pamela J. ....Providence, RI
Toroian, Michael T. ....Okemos, MI
Torok, Andrew F. ....San Juan Capistrano, CA
Torok, David M. ....Federal Trade Commission, Bureau of Consumer Protection, GV
Torok, John Edward ....New York, NY
Torok, Mark T. ....Erie, PA
Torok, Ruth M. ....Cincinnati, OH
Torok, William David ....Bedford, TX
Channelview, TX
Toro-Lavergne, Angélica T. ....San Juan, PR
Toro-Monserrate, Jaime E. ....San Juan, PR
Toronski, Janet B. ....Dearborn, MI
Toronyi, Kelli A. ....Chicago, IL
Torosian, Jeffrey S. ....Chicago, IL
Torosian, Kevin S. ....Fresno, CA
Toross, Nancy ....Los Angeles, CA
Toro-Suarez, Alberto Luis ....San Juan, PR
Toro Velez, Lissette ....Ponce, PR
Torp, Frederick H. ....Portland, OR
Torpats, John P. ....Broadview, IL
Torpey, Michael D. ....San Francisco, CA
Torpey, Neil A. ....New York, NY
Torpey, Richard I. ....Huntingdon Valley, PA
Torpey, Scott R. ....Farmington Hills, MI
Torphy, Frederic J. ....Fall River, MA
Torphy, Michael B., Jr. ....Madison, WI
Torphy & Sullivan LLP ....Fall River, MA
Torphy-Donzella, Elizabeth I.
Baltimore, MD
Torpin, R. Stanley ....Central City, NE
Torpoco, Mark S. ....Universal City, CA
Torpy, Gary B. ....Los Angeles, CA
Torpy, Gary B., A Prof. Corp., Law Offices of Los Angeles, CA
Torpy, Joseph R. ....Boston, MA
Torpy, Karla T. ....Melbourne, FL
Vero Beach, FL
Torpy, Richard E. ....Melbourne, FL
Torpy, William J. ....Poughkeepsie, NY
Torquato, Christopher R. ....Lewistown, PA
Torquato, Thomas M. ....Lewistown, PA
Torr, Renee Hardt ....Milwaukee, WI
Torr, Todd ....Palo Alto, CA
Torraca, Carmelo Tony ....Atlantic City, NJ
Torraca, Joseph P. ....Kingston, NY
Torrado, Laura L. ....New York, NY
Torrado, Rene A., Jr. ....Chicago, IL
Torralba, Homero ....Tucson, AZ
Torrance, Aileen T. ....Boston, MA
Torrance, Andrew W. ....Seattle, WA
Torrance, Calvin W. ....Los Angeles, CA
Torrance, Edwin G. ....Providence, RI
Torrance, Gregory S. ....Texarkana, AR
Torrance, Jerry W. ....Marion, IN
Torrance, John P. ....Simi Valley, CA
Torrance, W. Alan, Jr. ....Pittsburgh, PA
Torrance, Walter F., Jr. ....Waterbury, CT
Torrano, Marcus A. ....Los Angeles, CA
Torre, Christine M. ....Santa Monica, CA
Torre, Gregory M. ....New York, NY
Torre, James M. ....Phoenix, AZ
Torre, Joseph E. ....Freeport, NY
Torre, Joseph R. ....Hasbrouck Heights, NJ
Torre, Karen Lee ....New Haven, CT
Torre, Mark A. ....Phoenix, AZ
Torre, Michael S. ....Jericho, NY
Torre, Nelson S. ....Buffalo, NY
Torre, Philip A. ....San Francisco, CA
Torre, Richard J. ....San Francisco, CA
Torre & Torre ....Hasbrouck Heights, NJ
Torre, William J. ....Hasbrouck Heights, NJ
Torreano, John A. ....Iron Mountain, MI
Torregano, Kathy Lee ....New Orleans, LA
Torregrossa, Ann Gormally ....Philadelphia, PA
Torregrossa, Brennan J. ....Philadelphia, PA
Torregrossa, Joseph A. ....Philadelphia, PA
Torrell, Gary F. ....Los Angeles, CA
Torrellas, Miguel A. ....New York, NY
Torrence, Alfred W., Jr. ....Port Richey, FL
Torrence, Charlton K., III ....Gastonia, NC
Torrence, Daniel M. ....Seattle, WA
Torrence, Edward R. ....San Diego, CA
Torrence, Francis J. ....San Francisco, CA
Torrence, John M. ....Kansas City, MO
Torrence, Mary Ann ....Topeka, KS
Torrence, Michael R. ....St. Louis, MO
Torrens, Daniel ....Phoenix, AZ
Torrens, Mary-Elizabeth ....New Orleans, LA
Torrent, Karen E. ....Department of Justice, Environment and Natural Resources Division, GV
Torrente, John J. ....New York, NY
Torrente, Josephine M. ....Washington, DC
Torrente, Patricia E. ....Armonk, NY
Torrenti, R. Eugene ....Hamden, CT
Torres, Abel ....Barrington, RI
Torres, Abel B. ....Bay City, MI
Torres, Ada Lil ....New York, NY
Torres, Alberto ....New York, NY
Torres, Alejandro C. ....Seattle, WA
Torres, Ana Delia ....New York, NY
Torres, Analisa ....New York, NY
Torres, Anna D. ....Lake Worth, FL
Torres, Annette ....Miami, FL
Torres, Anthony N. ....Treasury Department, Bureau of Alcohol, Tobacco and Firearms, GV
Torres, Arturo D. ....McAllen, TX
Torres & Associates, P.C. ....New York, NY
Torres, Austin ....Bronx, NY
Torres, Bayardo I. ....Miami, FL
Torres, Blanca E. ....Washington, DC
Torres & Brenner ....Pasadena, CA
Torres, Brian M. ....Miami, FL
Torres, Carlos A. ....Houston, TX
Torres, Carlos E. ....Orlando, FL
Torres, Celia ....Rancho Cucamonga, CA
Torres, Charles E. ....New York, NY
Torres, Charles H. ....Denver, CO
Torres, Christopher ....Boston, MA
Torres, Debra M. ....New York, NY
Torres, Denice M. ....Grand Rapids, MI
Torres, Diana M. ....Los Angeles, CA
Torres, Dominic R ....New York, NY
Torres, Edward A. ....Alhambra, CA
Torres, Edwin G. ....Miami, FL
Torres, E.E. Yolanda ....Philadelphia, PA
Torres, Elving L. ....New Orleans, LA
Torres, Ernest C. ....Providence, RI
Torres, Felix Daniel ....San Juan, PR
Torres, Ferdinand L. ....Denver, CO
Torres, Francisco G. ....San Francisco, CA
Torres, Frank ....Bronx, NY
Torres, Frank ....New York, NY
Torres, Gilberto ....Texas City, TX
Torres, Gisela Nanson ......Hallandale Beach, FL
Torres, Gonzalo "Sal" R.
San Francisco, CA
Torres, Hector ....New York, NY
Torres, Hector J. ....McAllen, TX
Torres, Irma J. ....Los Angeles, CA
Torres, Isaias D. ....Houston, TX
Torres, Jaime L. ....Chicago, IL
Torres, James F. ....River Falls, WI
Torres, James L., P.A. ....Palm Bay, FL
Torres, Jeffrey C. ....Chicago, IL
Torres, Jesus U. ....Hagåtña, GU

Toups, Louis T. ....Thibodaux, LA
Toups, Mary Pat ....Laguna Hills, CA
Toups, Mitchell A. ....Beaumont, TX
Houston, TX
Toups, Olden C., Jr. ....Gretna, LA
Toups, Steven C. ....Beaumont, TX
Toups, W. Anthony, III ....New Orleans, LA
Tour, Jeffrey H. ....Columbus, OH
Tourangeau, Paul R. ....Lakewood, CO
Touras, George C. ....Chicago, IL
Touray, Sharif ....New York, NY
Tourchinskaya, Elena ....Stamford, CT
Tourdot, Kimberly L. ....St. Paul, MN
Touré, Alai Kimberly Ny.
San Francisco, CA
Tourek, J. Elise ....Pittsburgh, PA
Tourek, James M. ....Chicago, IL
Riverside, IL
Tourek, Katherine E. ....Albuquerque, NM
Tourek, Robert C. ....Pittsburgh, PA
Tourek, Steven C. ....Minneapolis, MN
St. Paul, MN
Tourek Muirhead, Megan A. C.
Albuquerque, NM
Tourenq, Mary S. ....Houston, TX
Tourgeman, Ramon ....North Miami Beach, FL
Tourial, Jennifer Beth ....Atlanta, GA
Tourigny, Carl W. ....Biddeford, ME
Tourino, Sherry L. ....Buena Park, CA
Tourish, Thomas J., Jr. ....Washington, DC
Tourjee, Karen M. ....Williamstown, MA
Tourk, Jessica M. ....New York, NY
Tourkantonis, Arthur C. ....Woburn, MA
Tourkin, Paul J. ....San Diego, CA
Tourkow, Crell, Rosenblatt & Johnston
Fort Wayne, IN
Tourkow, Frederick R. ....Fort Wayne, IN
Tourkow, Joshua I. ....Fort Wayne, IN
Tournay, Frederick H. ....Department of Justice, Immigration and Naturalization Service, GV
Tournour, Frank E. ....East Brunswick, NJ
Tournour, Frank E., P.C.
East Brunswick, NJ
Tour-Sarkissian, Christine
San Francisco, CA
Tour-Sarkissian Law Offices
San Francisco, CA
Tour-Sarkissian, Paul ....San Francisco, CA
Tour-Sarkissian, Tania ....San Francisco, CA
Tourse, Dennis R. ....Boston, MA
Tourtellot, Christopher T.
Department of Transportation, Office of the General Counsel, GV
Tourtellotte & Associates, P.C. ....Austin, TX
Tourtellotte, James R. ....Washington, DC
Tourtellotte, Thomas N. ....Austin, TX
Tourtelot & Butler, A Professional Law Corporation ....Los Angeles, CA
Tourtelot, Robert H. ....Los Angeles, CA
Tourtelotte, James H. ....Springfield, MA
Tourtillott, W. B. ....Denver, CO
Tourtlotte, Sabrina ....Modesto, CA
Tous, Raul F. ....Newark, NJ
Tousaw, Kirk I. ....Detroit, MI
Touschner, Anthony J. ....Cleveland, OH
Tousey, Clay B., Jr. ....Jacksonville, FL
Ponte Vedra Beach, FL
Tousey, Stephen D. ....Elgin, IL
Tousi, Cameron H. ....Washington, DC
Tousignant, Alan R. ....Department of State, Foreign Service Officers (Overseas), GV
Tousignant, Dennis ....Iron River, MI
Tousignant, Mark D. ....Iron River, MI
Tousignant, Mark D., P.C. ....Iron River, MI
Tousignant, Mary C. ....Alfred, ME
Tousignant, Richard L. ....Minneapolis, MN
Touslee, Robert D. ....Denver, CO
Tousley Brain PLLC ....Seattle, WA
Tousley, John W. ....Indianapolis, IN
Tousley, Russell F., (P.S.) ....Seattle, WA
Tousley, Thomas H. ....Department of Justice, Executive Office for Immigration Review, GV
Toussaint, Bernard J., III ....Oak Brook, IL
Toussaint & Carlson, Ltd. ....Oak Brook, IL
Toussaint, Claudia S. ....Kansas City, MO
Toussaint, Jennifer Claire ....Boston, MA
Toussaint, K. Scott ....Spartanburg, SC
Toussaint, Kristin E. ....Greenville, SC
Toussaint, Lisa M. ....Milwaukee, WI
Toussaint & Nemer, P.C. ....Evergreen, CO
Toussaint, Richard W. ....Evergreen, CO
Toussaint, Scott M. ....Palo Alto, CA
Toussaint, Sharon A. ....New York, NY
Toussaint, Sherri L ....Phoenix, AZ
Toussaint, Tamra L. ....Roswell, GA
Toussaint, Wavny ....New York, NY
Toussi, Sina ....New York, NY
Toussie, Ralph S. ....New York, NY
Toussignant, Carmen L. ....Columbus, GA
Tout, Robert E. ....Orinda, CA
Tout, William E. ....Sunriver, OR
Toutant, Linda M. ....Los Angeles, CA
Touton, Todd M. ....Las Vegas, NV
Touya, Maria C. ....San Francisco, CA
Touzel, Susannah ....Fort Worth, TX
Touzin, Dawn Marie ....Concord, NH
Tovar & Cohen ....Marina Del Rey, CA
Tovar, Enrique S. ....New York, NY
Tovar, Fernando ....Houston, TX
Tovar, Monica D. ....Kansas City, KS
Tovar, Rene ....Marina Del Rey, CA
Tovar, Tomas C. ....Palo Alto, CA
Tovares-Ashmanskas, Maria ....Quincy, MA
Tovey, Morgan W. ....San Francisco, CA
Tovino, Stacey Ann ....Houston, TX
Tovkach, Walter M. ....Gainesville, FL
Tovmassian, Henry ....Los Angeles, CA
Tovornik, Mary W. ....Georgetown, SC
Myrtle Beach, SC
Tovrea, David Anthony ....Englewood, CO
Tovrov, Jessica ....Chicago, IL
Tovsky, Robert ....Federal Trade Commission, Bureau of Competition, GV
Tovstein & Kraetzer ....Irvine, CA
Tovstein, Marc Steven ....Irvine, CA
Tow, Allan M. ....Melrose, MA
Tow, Christopher Y. ....Cranston, RI
Tow, George Anna ....Pleasanton, CA
Tow, L. Michelle ....Santee, CA
Tow, Marc R. ....Newport Beach, CA
Tow, Michael H. ....Baltimore, MD
Tow, Michael V. ....Fairmont, MN
Tow, Ted C., III ....Denver, CO
Tow, Wilson L. ....Indianapolis, IN
Toward, Ronald N. ....Bartow, FL
Towber, Preston T. ....Houston, TX
Towbin, David P. ....Chatsworth, CA
Towbin, Michele ....Miami, FL
Towbin, Rachel Reich ....Hartford, CT
Towbin, Steven B. ....Chicago, IL
Towcimak, Kenneth M. ....Tallahassee, FL
Towe, Ball, Enright, Mackey & Sommerfeld, P.L.L.P. ....Billings, MT
Miles City, MT
Towe, Donald W. ....Houston, TX
Towe, Dudley J. ....Hudson Falls, NY
Towe, Fred O. ....Indianapolis, IN
Towe, James T. ....Helena, MT
Towe, Kimberly Lewis ....Helena, MT
Towe, Rolf H. ....Greenwich, CT
Towe, Teri Noel ....New York, NY
Towe, Thomas E. ....Billings, MT
Towell, Alfred I. ....Bloomington, IN
Towell, Darryl E. ....Irvine, CA
Towell, Karyl ....Louisville, KY
Towell, S. Gilmer ....Newark, NJ
Towell, Thomas W., Jr. ....Little Ferry, NJ
Tower, Andrew P. ....Houston, TX
Tower, Bruce E. ....Roseburg, OR
Tower, Carole C. ....Austin, TX
Tower, Charles H. ....New York, NY
Tower, Crocker & Mullins, Professional Association ....Jaffrey, NH
Tower, Daniel T. ....Raleigh, NC
Tower, Danny ....Corpus Christi, TX
Tower, David E. ....Newburgh, NY
Tower, David M. ....Jaffrey, NH
Tower, Eric S. ....Washington, DC
Tower, Fiona M. ....Richmond, VA
Tower, Guy K. ....Norfolk, VA
Tower, Jay W. ....Bingham Farms, MI
Tower, Jessie M. ....Columbus, OH
Tower, John C. ....Evanston, IL
Tower, John D. ....New Milford, CT
Tower, John W. ....San Diego, CA
Tower, King F. ....Richmond, VA
Tower, Lawrence A. ....Bingham Farms, MI
Tower, Lee W. ....Rancho Palos Verdes, CA
Tower, Paul E. ....Lansing, MI
Tower, Philip C. ....Phoenix, AZ
Tower, Randolph P. ....San Antonio, TX
Tower, Stephen E. ....Bridgeport, CT
Tower, Timothy W. ....San Diego, CA
Tower, Winship C. ....Virginia Beach, VA
Towerman, Craig ....St. Louis, MO
Towerman, Michael ....St. Louis, MO
Towers, Charles D., Jr. ....Jacksonville, FL
Towers, Charles G. ....Bethpage, NY
Towers, Edward F. ....San Francisco, CA
Towers, George E. ....Montecito, CA
Towers, John G. ....Chicago, IL
Towers, John R. ....Boston, MA
Towers, Michael C. ....Atlanta, GA
Towers, Randall J. ....Philadelphia, PA
Towers, Randall S. ....Sacramento, CA
Towers, Richard S. ....High Point, NC
Towers, Russell E. ....Tiverton, RI
Towers, Scott P. ....Philadelphia, PA
Towers-Dioso, Geanine ....Brooklyn, NY
Towery, Charles David ....Houston, TX
Towery, Curtis K. ....Oklahoma City, OK
Towery, James E. ....San Jose, CA
Towery, Jeong-Hwa Lee ....Atlanta, GA
Towery, Jerrel E., (P.A.) ....Venice, FL
Towery, Mark A. ....Fairfax, VA
Towery, Matthew A. ....Atlanta, GA
Towery, Robert L. ....Austin, TX
Towery, Roger E. ....Henrietta, TX
Towey, David P. ....Washington, DC
Towey, Edward A. ....Minneapolis, MN
Towey, Harry James ....Tallahassee, FL
Towey, James P., Jr. ....St. Louis, MO
Towey, Marianne B. ....Lakewood, CO
Towey, Robert D. ....Roseland, NJ
Towfighi, Arya ....Los Angeles, CA
Towill, Polly Dennis ....Los Angeles, CA
Towle, Anne Marie ....Boston, MA
Towle, C. Griffith ....San Francisco, CA
Towle, Edmund J., III, (Professional Corporation) ....Los Angeles, CA
Towle, Guy ....Seattle, WA
Towle, Holly Keesling ....San Francisco, CA
Seattle, WA
Towle, Howie & Puvogel ....Oak Park, IL
Towle, Maureen E. ....Boston, MA
Towle, Peter J. ....Knoxville, TN
Towle, Richard E. ....Basking Ridge, NJ
Towle, Robert W. ....Worcester, MA
Towle, William B. ....Albuquerque, NM
Towle, William H. ....Oak Park, IL
Towler, Oscar A., III ....Greenville, SC
Towler, Robert W. ....San Francisco, CA
Towles, E. Colette ....Gulfport, MS
Towles, Howard E. ....Chicago, IL
Towles, James G. ....Coeur d'Alene, ID
Town, Alan S. ....Rockville, MD
Town, Michael A. ....Honolulu, HI
Towne, Bradley S., Law Offices of
Sacramento, CA
Towne, Carole K. ....Chicago, IL
Towne, Harry ....Vancouver, WA
Towne, James T., Jr. ....Albany, NY
Burnt Hills, NY
Scarsdale, NY
Towne, James T., P.C., Law Offices of
Albany, NY
Burnt Hills, NY
Saratoga Springs, NY
Scarsdale, NY
Schoharie, NY
Towne, Jeffrey P. ....Waterville, ME
Towne, Jessica R. ....Lawrenceville, GA
Towne, L. Stanton ....New York, NY
Towne, Madelene Fleischer ....New York, NY
Towne, Michael J. ....Chicago, IL
Towne, Raymond L. ....Pasadena, CA
Towne, Richard P. ....Los Angeles, CA
Towne, Richard P. ....Woodland Hills, CA
Towne, Robert E. ....Anchorage, AK
Towne, Ronald N. ....Akron, OH
Townend, David W. ....Garland, TX
Townend, Frank ....Wilkes-Barre, PA
Townend, Jeanmarie Beisel ....Dallas, TX
Townend, Jeanmarie, P.C., Law Offices of
Dallas, TX
Towner, Alan G. ....Pittsburgh, PA
Towner, Andrew T. ....East Hampton, NY
Towner, Bruce M. ....San Francisco, CA
Towner, Charles Mark ....Birmingham, MI
Detroit, MI
Towner, Charles R. ....Mount Clemens, MI
Towner, George C., Jr. ....Arlington, VA
Towner, George C., Jr., P.C.
Arlington, VA
Towner, John B. ....Pittsburg, KS
Towner Law Office ....San Francisco, CA
Towner, Porter A. ....Sacramento, CA
Townes, Gwynn ....Seattle, WA
Townes, Robert V., III ....Gardendale, AL
Townes, Virginia B. ....Orlando, FL
Townes, W. Waverley ....Louisville, KY
Townes, Woods & Roberts, P.C.
Gardendale, AL
Townley, Bruce ....Almont, MI
Townley, Christopher A. ....Rossville, GA
Townley, Danforth ....New York, NY
Townley, Dennis W. ....Boston, MA
Townley, Donald J. ....Anaheim, CA
Townley, F. Bradford ....South Natick, MA
Townley, Kenneth Michael ....New York, NY
Townley Law Office ....La Fayette, GA
Ringgold, GA
Rossville, GA
Trenton, GA
Townley, Rosemary A. ....Bronx, NY
Townley, Sam A. ....Oklahoma City, OK
Townley, Thomas W. ....Niles, OH
Townley, Wayne C., Jr. ....Normal, IL
Townley-Tilson, W. H. Dale ....Franklin, NH
Towns, Cody L. ....Oklahoma City, OK
Towns, Douglas M. ....Atlanta, GA
Towns, Eleanor S.
Department of Agriculture, Forest Service, GV
Towns, Jeffrey B. ....Gardena, CA
Towns, John W. ....Worcester, MA
Towns, Patricia A. ....Oakbrook Terrace, IL
Towns, R. Vincent ....Bedford, TX
Towns, Victoria Erin ....New York, NY
Towns, William R. ....Houston, TX
Townsdin & Associates, Chtd.
Phillipsburg, KS
Townsdin, Francis G. ....Phillipsburg, KS
Townsdin, Steven Dale ....Memphis, TN
Townsel, Andre Eugene ....Chicago, IL
Townsell, Joseph C. ....Sacramento, CA
Townsend, Alan S. ....Indianapolis, IN
Townsend & Banta ....Washington, DC
Townsend, Barbara B. ....Chambersburg, PA
Townsend, Benjamin P. ....Augusta, ME
Portland, ME
Townsend, Billy W. ....Hohenwald, TN
Townsend and Bloom, PLLC
Emporia, VA
Prince George, VA
Townsend, Bradlee Wright ....Hamburg, NY
Townsend & Brannon ....Tampa, FL
Townsend, Brian C. ....Treasury Department, Internal Revenue Service, GV
Townsend, Bruce D. ....Walden, NY
Townsend, Bruce Miller ....Tulsa, OK
Townsend, Byron E. ....Tampa, FL
Townsend, Cabell D. ....Atlanta, GA
Townsend, Camille ....Lafayette, IN
Townsend, Charles E., Jr.
San Francisco, CA
Townsend, Chester Crews
Chattanooga, TN
Townsend, Chiles E. ....Ponca City, OK
Townsend, Christina L. ....Charleston, WV
Townsend, Christopher G. ....Bethesda, MD
Townsend, Christopher J. ....Chicago, IL
Townsend, Clay M. ....Orlando, FL
Townsend, Clinton B. ....Skowhegan, ME
Townsend, Courtland K., Jr.
Ocean City, MD
Townsend, Courtland K., Jr., Chartered
Ocean City, MD
Townsend, Craig G. ....Houston, TX
Townsend, Dalton L. ....Knoxville, TN
Townsend, Darrell G. ....Nashville, TN
Townsend, David ....Dallas, TX
Townsend, David A. ....Tampa, FL
Townsend, David A. ....Manakin-Sabot, VA
Townsend, David L. ....Annapolis, MD
Townsend, David, (P.C.) ....Houston, TX
Townsend, Deborah E. ....Santa Clara, CA
Townsend, Deborah J. ....Orlando, FL
Townsend, Don D. ....Atlanta, GA
Townsend, Donald E. ....Washington, DC
Townsend, Donald J. ....Chicago, IL
Townsend, Donna F. ....Louisville, KY
Townsend, Earl C., III ....Indianapolis, IN
Townsend, Earl C., Jr. ....Indianapolis, IN
Townsend, Edward J. ....El Centro, CA
Townsend, Edwin C. ....Parsons, TN
Townsend, Edwin, Jr. ....Parsons, TN
Townsend, Elizabeth ....Atlanta, GA
Townsend, Elizabeth A. ....Knoxville, TN
Townsend, Frances ....Austin, TX
Houston, TX
Townsend, Francis James, III
Baltimore, MD
Townsend, Frank M. ....Kissimmee, FL
Townsend, George W., III ....Montross, VA
Townsend, Gerald W. ....Parkersburg, WV
Williamstown, WV
Townsend, Giles de S. ....San Diego, CA
Townsend, Gregory J. ....Pontiac, MI
Townsend, Guy Mannering ....Madison, IN
Townsend, H. Lee, III ....Emporia, VA
Townsend, Howard L. ....Seal Beach, CA
Townsend, J. Kenneth, Law Office of
New York, NY
Townsend, J. Richard ....Lumberton, NC
Townsend, Jack L. ....Temple Terrace, FL
Townsend, Jack L., Sr., P.A. ....Brandon, FL
Tampa, FL
Temple Terrace, FL
Townsend, James D. ....Grand Rapids, MI
Townsend, James E. ....Minneapolis, MN
Townsend, James E. ....Londonderry, NH
Townsend, James L., Jr. ....Clarksdale, MS
Townsend, James M., Jr. ....Doylestown, PA
Townsend, James R. ....Dallas, TX
Townsend, James T. ....Rochester, NY
Townsend, James W. ....Austin, TX
Townsend, Jane I. ....Pine Bluff, AR
Townsend, Jas. E. ....Grand Haven, MI
Townsend, Jeanne Knowles
St. Louis, MO
Townsend, Jeff E., Jr. ....Lake Charles, LA
Townsend, Jeffrey A. ....Indianapolis, IN
Townsend, Jeffrey R. ....San Francisco, CA
Townsend, Joe ....Memphis, TN
Townsend, Joel H. ....Grand Rapids, MI
Townsend, Joel Scott ....Simsbury, CT
Townsend, John ....Chicago, IL
Townsend, John A. ....Meadow Lands, PA
Townsend, John A. ....Houston, TX
Townsend, John D. ....Houston, TX
Townsend, John F. ....Indianapolis, IN
Townsend, John F. ....Dallas, TX
Townsend, John F., III ....Indianapolis, IN
Townsend, John F., Jr. ....Indianapolis, IN
Townsend, John G. ....Urbana, IL
Townsend, John M. ....Washington, DC
Townsend, John M. ....Boston, MA
Townsend, John P.
Fort Walton Beach, FL
Townsend, John P., P.A. ....Crestview, FL
Fort Walton Beach, FL
Townsend & Jones, L.L.P. ....Dallas, TX
Houston, TX
Townsend, Joseph Fabian ....Lockport, NY
Townsend, Jules A. ....Miami, FL
Townsend, Julia A. ....Jackson, MS
Townsend, Karen ....Missoula, MT
Townsend, Kathleen A. ....Springfield, MA
Townsend, Kathleen Maher
Morristown, NJ
Townsend, Kathryn Eblen ....Miami, FL
Townsend, Kim H. ....White Plains, NY
Townsend, Larry J. ....Orlando, FL
Townsend Law Firm, The
Orangeburg, SC
Townsend Law Offices, The ....San Rafael, CA
Townsend, Lawrence G.
San Francisco, CA
Townsend, Leonard ....Detroit, MI
Townsend, Lonny E. ....Tulsa, OK
Townsend, Louis R., Jr.
West Palm Beach, FL
Townsend, Luke ....Chicago, IL
Townsend, Margaret ....Atlanta, GA
Townsend, Margaret Dale ....Richmond, VA
Townsend, Mark R. ....Greensboro, NC
Townsend, Mary C. ....Houston, TX
Townsend, Mary Margaret ....Huntsville, AL
Townsend, Mary Smith ....Kissimmee, FL
Townsend, Maureen Elizabeth
Hartford, CT
Townsend, M. B., Jr. ....Elk Rapids, MI
Townsend, McWilliams & Holladay
Drew, MS
Indianola, MS
Townsend, Michael J. ....Rochester, NY
Townsend & Montross ....Indianapolis, IN
Townsend, Nathan L. ....Orlando, FL
Townsend, Neil W. ....New York, NY
Townsend, Patricia A. ....Schaumburg, IL
Townsend, Paul H. ....Summit, NJ
Townsend, Paul H., Jr. ....Detroit, MI
Townsend, Peter L. ....San Rafael, CA
Townsend, R. Bruce ....Daingerfield, TX
Townsend, R. Edward, Jr. ....New York, NY
Townsend, R. Lambeth ....Austin, TX
Townsend, R. Lewis ....Vero Beach, FL
Townsend, Rachel L. ....Jefferson City, MO
Townsend, Ramon D. ....Media, PA
Townsend, Richard C. ....Waldoboro, ME

Trafimow, A. Jonathan ... **New York, NY**
Traflet & Fabian ... **Morristown, NJ**
New York, NY
Traflet, Stephen G. ... **Morristown, NJ**
New York, NY
Trafman, Howard T. ... Chicago, IL
Traft, Michael J. ... **Boston, MA**
Traft, William R. ... Kingston, MA
Trafton, Alan P. ... Irvine, CA
Trafton, David L. ... Department of Commerce, Patent and Trademark Office, GV
Trafton, Kathleen Marie ... San Francisco, CA
Trafton, Mark E. ... Las Vegas, NV
Reno, NV
Trafton & Matzen ... **Auburn, ME**
Trafton, Richard L. ... **Auburn, ME**
Trafton, Rose ... Lakewood, NJ
Trafton, Sarah H. ... Fairport, NY
Tragarz, Nancy R. ... **Santa Ana, CA**
Tragellis, Gregory W. ... Milton, MA
Tragen, Irving G.
Agency for International Development, Other Offices of A.I.D., GV
Trager, Alan ... New York, NY
Trager, Alan S. ... **New York, NY**
Trager, David A. ... **New York, NY**
Trager, David G. ... Brooklyn, NY
Trager, Glenn A. ... **Los Angeles, CA**
Trager, Katherine J. ... New York, NY
Trager, Leslie ... New York, NY
Trager, Mark A. ... **Chicago, IL**
Trager, Marshall D. ... Lake Success, NY
Trager, Michael D. ... **Washington, DC**
Trager, Michael J. ... Wyandotte, MI
Trager, Mitchell S. ... **Atlanta, GA**
Trager, Philip ... **Westport, CT**
Trager, S. George ... Miami Beach, FL
Trager, S. George, P.A. ... Miami Beach, FL
Trager, Seymour ... West Hempstead, NY
Trager, Steven E. ... Louisville, KY
Trager, Susan M. ... **Irvine, CA**
Trager, Susan M., A Prof. Corp., Law Offices of ... **Irvine, CA**
Trager, Thomas H. ... **Peoria, IL**
Trager, Thomas R. ... Long Beach, CA
Trager, Timothy J. ... **Santa Barbara, CA**
Trager & Trager, P.C. ... **Fairfield, CT**
Tragerman, Albert ... Montebello, CA
Trageser, Robert J. ... McMurray, PA
Trageser, Stacie D. ... **Baltimore, MD**
Tragesser, Joel E. ... **Indianapolis, IN**
Tragish, Murray ... Bakersfield, CA
Tragos, George E. ... **Clearwater, FL**
Tragos, George E. ... **Tampa, FL**
Tragoutsis, Elchinoff & Basin
South San Francisco, CA
Tragoutsis, Xenophon
South San Francisco, CA
Trahan, Christopher L. ... Crowley, LA
Trahan, Christopher M.
Lake Charles, LA
Trahan, David P. ... Troy, MI
Trahan, Donald J. ... Baton Rouge, LA
Trahan, Ivan ... **San Diego, CA**
Ventura, CA
Trahan, Jennifer ... **New York, NY**
Trahan, Jeremy L. ... **Cleveland, OH**
Trahan, K. Wade ... **Abbeville, LA**
Trahan, Lee Buthod ... San Diego, CA
Trahan, Paul ... **Austin, TX**
Trahan, Thomas E. ... Dallas, TX
Traher, J. Michael, (P.C.) ... Tucson, AZ
Traher, Jacqueline K. ... Menlo Park, CA
Trahey, Stephen J. ... **Bloomfield Hills, MI**
Flat Rock, MI
Trahos, Elizabeth Carr ... **Raleigh, NC**
Traica, Robert J. ... Phoenix, AZ
Traicoff, Sandra M. ... **Peoria, IL**
Traiger, Laura Silver ... Boston, MA
Traiger, Warren W. ... **New York, NY**
Trail, Christopher D. ... Columbus, MI
Trail, E. Nicole ... **Memphis, TN**
Trail, Judith E. ... Columbus, OH
Trail, Larry G. ... Murfreesboro, TN
Trail, Mike ... **Osceola, AR**
Trail, Sandra Y. ... Murfreesboro, TN
Trail, Sebert L. ... Columbus, GA
Trail & Trail ... Murfreesboro, TN
Trail, William R. ... Waco, TX
Train, Bruce ... Palo Alto, CA
Train, John K., III ... **Atlanta, GA**
Train, John K., IV ... **Atlanta, GA**
Train, Peter V. ... Harrisburg, PA
Traina, Jack A. ... Wood Ridge, NJ
Traina, James, Jr. ... Indianapolis, IN
Traina, Jennifer Hantel ... **New Orleans, LA**
Traina, Jill Kramer ... Miami, FL
Traina, Joyce Marchione ... Wood Ridge, NJ
Traina, Patricia A. ... New Orleans, LA
Traina, Paul A. ... **Los Angeles, CA**
Traina, Paul J., Jr. ... **Teterboro, NJ**
Traina, Richard L. ... **New Orleans, LA**
Traina, Salvatore A. ... New York, NY
Traina & Traina ... Wood Ridge, NJ
Trainer, Corina M. ... Washington, DC
Trainer, John D. ... **Doylestown, PA**
Trainer, Laurie Jo ... Washington, DC
Trainer, Michael D. ... **Sacramento, CA**
Trainer, Owen A. ... Glendale, CA
Trainer, Philip, Jr. ... **Wilmington, DE**
Trainer, Ryan ... **Washington, DC**
Trainer, Thomas V. ... **Bloomfield Hills, MI**
Trainer, Timothy P. ... Washington, DC
Trainer, William A. ... **Parkersburg, WV**
Traini, Anthony M. ... Framingham, MA
Traini, Rosemary A. ... Framingham, MA
Traino, Michael L. ... **Irvine, CA**
Trainor, C. Warren ... **Philadelphia, PA**
Trainor, Charles W. ... **Sacramento, CA**
Trainor, Christopher G. ... **Uniondale, NY**
Trainor, Daniel J. ... **Chicago, IL**
Trainor, Daniel Sean ... Washington, DC
Trainor, David ... Atlanta, GA
Trainor, David E. ... **Chicago, IL**
Trainor, Diane M. ... Miami, FL
Trainor, Harry J., Jr.
Upper Marlboro, MD
Trainor, James J. ... Holmdel, NJ
Trainor, James P. ... Clifton Park, NY
Trainor, Kerry R. ... Central Islip, NY
Trainor, Kevin F. ... **Twin Falls, ID**
Trainor, Larisa Avner ... **Washington, DC**
Trainor, Lestina C. ... **Greenwich, CT**
New York, NY
Trainor, Madeline A. ... **Alexandria, VA**
Trainor, Martin M. ... New York, NY
Trainor, Michael B. ... **Bangor, ME**
Trainor, Michael J. ... Albany, NY
Trainor, Paul E. ... Allentown, PA
Trainor, Robert J. ... **Kenilworth, NJ**
Trainor, Robert N. ... Covington, KY
Trainor • Robertson ... **Sacramento, CA**
Trainor, Scott A. ... Sacramento, CA
Trainor, Sonja H. ... Arlington Heights, IL
Trainor, Virginia Yoder ... **Baton Rouge, LA**
Trainor, William R. ... Worcester, MA
Trainotti, D. Michael ... **Long Beach, CA**
Trainotti, D. Michael, A Professional Law Corporation ... **Long Beach, CA**
Los Angeles, CA
Trainum, Charles A., Jr. ... **Washington, DC**
Trainum, Snowdon & Deane, P.C.
Washington, DC
Trainum, Thomas E. ... San Francisco, CA
Traiser, Richard E. ... Freeport, ME
Traisman, Kenneth Neil ... Riverwoods, IL
Traison, Michael H. ... **Detroit, MI**
Traister, F. Brad ... Beverly Hills, CA
Traister, Michael D. ... **Portland, ME**
Traister, Michael S. ... **Boston, MA**
Traitel, David M. ... **New York, NY**
Traitz, James J. ... Miami, FL
Trakas, Andrew G. ... Gastonia, NC
Trakas, Andrew P. ... Winter Haven, FL
Trakas, Andrew P., P.A. ... Winter Haven, FL
Trakas, Arthur G. ... Long Island City, NY
Trakhtenberg, Sergey ... **Los Angeles, CA**
Trakimas, Robert G. ... Haverhill, MA
Trakinski, Amy Rae ... New York, NY
Trakinski, Esther S. ... **New York, NY**
Traktman, Laurie A. ... Los Angeles, CA
Traktman, Terry J. ... Petaluma, CA
Tralewski, Walter J. ... Niles, IL
Tralins and Associates, P.A. ... Miami, FL
Tralins, David M. ... Towson, MD
Tralins, Myles J. ... Miami, FL
Tramaloni, Dennis P. ... **Nutley, NJ**
Tramantano, Robert S. ... New York, NY
Trambley, Anthony B. ... St. Marys, PA
Trambley, C. Anthony ... **Washington, DC**
Trambley, D. Brian ... Anna, IL
Trambley, Robert J. ... Chambersburg, PA
Tramblian, Ara L. ... Arlington, VA
Trame, Robert E. ... St. Louis, MO
Tramel, Charles W. ... Evanston, IL
Tramer, Neil M. ... Cleveland, OH
Tramhel, Jeannette M. ... Washington, DC
Trammel, Gary D. ... Breckenridge, TX
Trammell, Amanda M. ... Naples, FL
Trammell, Bradley E. ... **Memphis, TN**
Trammell, Brenda H. ... Madison, GA
Trammell, Brian H. ... **Knoxville, TN**
Trammell, Christopher L. ... Albuquerque, NM
Trammell, Dan ... Denton, TX
Trammell, Dan F. ... Santa Monica, CA
Trammell, Dan, P.C. ... Denton, TX
Trammell, Dennis L. ... Cincinnati, OH
Trammell, Ernest C. ... **Anderson, SC**
Trammell & Harbin, L.L.P. ... **Anderson, SC**
Trammell, Jerry M. ... Shelby, NC
Trammell Law Firm, The ... **Little Rock, AR**
Trammell, M. Chad ... **Fort Smith, AR**
Trammell, M. Lyle ... Gresham, OR
Trammell, Martha J. ... **Smyrna, TN**
Trammell, Ray ... Fayetteville, AR
Trammell, Robert D. ... Marianna, FL
Trammell, Robert David ... **Little Rock, AR**
Trammell, Talbot W. ... Miami, FL
Trammell, Virginia C. ... **Fort Smith, AR**
Tramont, Andrew V. ... **Miami, FL**
Tramont, Andrew V., P.A., Law Office of
Miami, FL
Tramont, Bryan N. ... Washington, DC
Tramontana, J. Antonio ... Monroe, LA
Tramontano, Karen ... Washington, DC
Tramonte, Jennifer G. ... Cameron, LA
Tramonte, Sam G. ... Galveston, TX
Tramonte, Tramonte & Bastien, A Professional Corporation ... Galveston, TX
Tramonte, Vincent A., II ... **Vienna, VA**
Tramonte, Vincent J. ... Galveston, TX
Tramontine, John O. ... **New York, NY**
Tramontozzi, John N. ... Boston, MA
Tramontozzi, Marina ... Woburn, MA
Tramountanas, Athan E. ... **Seattle, WA**
Tramountanas, Cindy A. ... **Seattle, WA**
Trampe, Ferdinand M. ... Fountain Valley, CA
Tramuto, Robert M. ... Houston, TX
Tramutola, Carole ... New York, NY
Tramutola, Joseph L., Jr. ... Madison, NJ
Tramz, Stephanie C. ... Mountain View, CA
Tran, Ai Nhan M. ... Fountain Valley, CA
Tran, Anna A. ... **Los Angeles, CA**
Tran, Ba D. ... San Jose, CA
Tran, Bao Q. ... **Menlo Park, CA**
Tran, Bien C. ... **Houston, TX**
Tran, Brian ... **Los Angeles, CA**
Tran, Catherine Hong ... **Seattle, WA**
Tran, Charlotte L. ... **Mount Laurel, NJ**
Tran, Dat T. ... Houston, TX
Tran, Elaine ... **Dallas, TX**
Tran, Eric D. ... **Palo Alto, CA**
Tran, Han N. ... **San Francisco, CA**
Tran, Henry ... San Gabriel, CA
Tran, Hoang N. ... Houston, TX
Tran, Hoanh Dinh ... Washington, DC
Tran, Jason C. ... Los Angeles, CA
Tran, Jessica H. ... **Reston, VA**
Tran, John M. ... **Alexandria, VA**
Tran, Julie H. ... **New York, NY**
Tran, Khanh T. ... **Modesto, CA**
Tran, Kim Huong A. ... **New Orleans, LA**
Tran, Kim M. ... **Seattle, WA**
Tran, Kinh-Luan ... **Los Angeles, CA**
Tran Law Firm ... **Mount Laurel, NJ**
Tran, Linda ... **Los Angeles, CA**
Tran, Maria Thanh Tram ... **Miami, FL**
Tran, Michelle Margolies ... **Scottsdale, AZ**
Tran, Minh Cong ... Riverside, CA
Tran, Phong (Jacques) N.
Mount Laurel, NJ
Tran, Quynh T. ... **Burlingame, CA**
Tran, Susanna C. ... Bloomington, IL
Tran, Thi Anh Nina ... **Houston, TX**
Tran, Thien-Huong ... Los Angeles, CA
Tran, Tiffany T. ... **New York, NY**
Tran, Tom N. ... **Mission Viejo, CA**
Tran, Yen T. ... **Houston, TX**
Tran, Yvonne K. ... **New York, NY**
Trana, Roger D. ... Houston, TX
Tranbarger, Gary B. ... Riverside, CA
Tranberg, David E. ... Arcata, CA
Tranberg, John W., II ... San Marcos, CA
Trance, Jas. R. ... Albany, NY
Tranchida, Peter J. ... Warren, MI
Tranchina, Brian M. ... **Morgan City, LA**
Tranchina, Frank P., Jr. (A Prof. Law Corp.)
Metairie, LA
New Orleans, LA
Tranchina & Martinez, A Professional Law Corporation ... Metairie, LA
New Orleans, LA
Tranckino, Amy L. ... **San Diego, CA**
Trandahl, Kathleen F. ... Winner, SD
Tranel, Paul N. ... **Missoula, MT**
Tranelli, Kathleen Frensky ... Rochester, NY
Tranelli, Steven J. ... **Rochester, NY**
Tranello, Lawr. F. ... Rochester, NY
Tranen, Daniel E. ... **St. Louis, MO**
Tranen, Irving N. ... Bethesda, MD
Tranfo, Joseph A. ... **Greenwich, CT**
Jericho, NY
Tranfo, Joseph C. ... **Greenwich, CT**
Tranfo & Tranfo ... Jericho, NY
Bethel, CT
Greenwich, CT
Norwalk, CT
Stamford, CT
Tranford, Lee Ann ... **Boca Raton, FL**
Trangsrud, Cynthia A. ... **Glendale, CA**
Trangsrud, Roger H. ... Washington, DC
Traniello, David ... Boston, MA
Trani-Morris, Denise ... **San Francisco, CA**
Trank, Burgess N. ... **Maitland, FL**
Trank, Lawrence R. ... New Paltz, NY
Trankocy, Richard J., Jr. ... Pittsburgh, PA
Tranlong, Perpetua B. ... Palo Alto, CA
Tranmer, A. Dean ... Pocatello, ID
Trannel, James A. ... Dubuque, IA
Trannel, Jeffrey A. ... Dubuque, IA
Tranovich, Andrew F.
Department Of Health And Human Services, GV
Tranquilli, Mark Vinson ... Pittsburgh, PA
Transeau, Alvin S. ... Cape Girardeau, MO
Transier & Anderson ... Flagstaff, AZ
Transier, Michael L. ... Flagstaff, AZ
Transit, Roy J. ... Fraser, MI
Transtrom, Jeffrey G. ... **Bismarck, ND**
Transtrum, Terrel F. ... Idaho Falls, ID
Transtrum, Wallace M. ... Soda Springs, ID
Transue, Oliver M., Jr. ... Tucson, AZ
Trant, Charles E. ... Department of the Army, U.S. Army Court of Criminal Appeals, GV
Trant, Douglas A. ... **Knoxville, TN**
Trant, Jeffrey A. ... **Palo Alto, CA**
Trant, John T. ... Granger, IN
Trant, Sid J. ... **Birmingham, AL**
Tranter, Edwin W. ... Fort Thomas, KY
Tranter, Jack C. ... **Baltimore, MD**
Tranter, John M. ... Fort Thomas, KY
Tranter, Patrick E. ... Bel Air, MD
Tranter, Richard B. ... **Cincinnati, OH**
Tranter, Ronda S. ... **Dade City, FL**
Tranter, Terence M. ... Cincinnati, OH
Trantham, Charles S. ... Fayetteville, AR
Trantham, Hugh W. ... Piggott, AR
Trantina, Elizabeth M. ... **Hackettstown, NJ**
Morristown, NJ
Trenton, NJ
Trantina, Terry Leon ... **Roseland, NJ**
Trantolo & Trantolo, P.C. ... Hartford, CT
New London, CT
Waterbury, CT
Trantolo, Vincent J. ... Hartford, CT
New London, CT
Waterbury, CT
Tranum, D. Michael ... **Johnson City, TN**
Kingsport, TN
Trapanese, Joseph S. ... Little Falls, NJ
Trapani, Christopher M.
Fort Lauderdale, FL
Trapani, David A. ... **New York, NY**
Trapani, David M. ... Campbell, CA
Trapani, John ... Alhambra, CA
Trapani, John G. ... Garden City, NY
Trapani, Joseph R. ... Milton, NY
Trapani, Lawrence P. ... **Syracuse, NY**
Trapani, Michelle C. ... Redwood City, CA
Trapani & Molldrem ... **Syracuse, NY**
Trapani, Philip R. ... Norfolk, VA
Trapani, Philip R., Jr. ... Norfolk, VA
Trapani, Philip R., Jr., P.C. ... Norfolk, VA
Trapani, Thomas A. ... **Oakland, CA**
Trapasso, Barbara Henry ... Garden City, NY
Trapasso, Dolan & Hollander ... **Newton, NJ**
Trapasso, Jody ... Washington, DC
Trapeni, Joseph T., Jr. ... Silver Spring, MD
Fairfax, VA
Trapeni, Romero & Malouf, P.C.
Silver Spring, MD
Fairfax, VA
Traphagen, Mark ... **Washington, DC**
Trapnell, Carson Sinclair ... Houston, TX
Trapnell, Emily M. ... Jacksonville Beach, FL
Trapnell, John R. ... **Atlanta, GA**
Trapnell, L. D. ... Houston, TX
Trapnell, L. D., P.C. ... Houston, TX
Trapolin, Ivor A. ... New Orleans, LA
Trapolin Law Firm, A Professional Law Corporation ... New Orleans, LA
Trapolin, Miles G. ... New Orleans, LA
Trapp, Allen M., Jr., P.C. ... **Carrollton, GA**
Trapp, Allen Matthews, Jr.
Carrollton, GA
Trapp, Allen T. ... La Crosse, WI
Trapp, Byron Edward ... Dayton, OH
Trapp and Chastain ... **Orlando, FL**
Tampa, FL
Winter Park, FL
Trapp, Chris G. ... Buffalo, NY
Trapp, Courtney Q. ... Glen Ellyn, IL
Trapp, Cristine Marie ... **Costa Mesa, CA**
Trapp, David James ... San Jose, CA
Trapp, Frank W. ... **Jackson, MS**
Trapp, G. Kay L. ... **Tupelo, MS**
Trapp & Hartman, S.C. ... Brookfield, WI
Trapp, Howard ... Hagåtña, GU
Trapp, Howard, Incorporated ... Hagåtña, GU
Trapp, Howard M. ... Kingston, TN
Trapp, James M. ... **Chicago, IL**
Trapp, Jamie M. ... Chicago, IL
Trapp, Janet E. ... **Los Angeles, CA**
Trapp, Joseph P. ... Brookfield, WI
Trapp, Karen E. ... **New York, NY**
Trapp, Louis A., Jr. ... **New York, NY**
Trapp, Mary Jane ... **Cleveland, OH**
Trapp, Randa McDaniel ... **San Diego, CA**
Trapp, Richard, (P.A.) ... Winter Park, FL
Trapp, Robert, Jr. ... Stockton, CA
Trapp, Thomas D. ... **San Francisco, CA**
Trapp, Walter F. ... Dallas, TX
Trapp, Wendell H., Jr. ... **Corinth, MS**
Trapp, William F. ... **Springfield, IL**
Trappe & Dusseault ... **Panama City, FL**
Trappe, Stan ... **Panama City, FL**
Trasatti, Marisa A. ... **Lutherville, MD**
Trascher, Charles C., III ... **Monroe, LA**
Trask, Andrew J. ... **Washington, DC**
Trask, Anthony F. ... Myrtle Beach, SC
Trask, Anthony F., P.C. ... Myrtle Beach, SC
Trask, Arthur K., Jr. ... Lihue, HI
Trask, Britt & Rossa, A Professional Corporation ... **Salt Lake City, UT**
Trask, Carol B. ... Philadelphia, PA
Trask, D. Webster ... Wilmington, NC
Trask, David H. ... Covington, KY
Trask, David V. ... **Salt Lake City, UT**
Trask, Frances Youngblood
Wilmington, NC
Trask, George Graham ... Beaufort, SC
Trask, Gloria C. ... Riverside, CA
Trask, Gordon W. ... Los Angeles, CA
Trask, Gregory J. ... **Miami, FL**
Trask, Grover C., II ... Riverside, CA
Trask, Harold E. ... **Charleston, SC**
Trask, Harvey J. ... Boston, MA
Trask, Kimberly A. ... **Wilmington, MA**
Trask, Laura W. ... **Denver, CO**
Trask, Mary E. ... Westwood, MA
Trask, Norman G. ... Presque Isle, ME
Trask, Peter L. ... Honolulu, HI
Trask, Sara Schwab ... **Irvine, CA**
Trask, Thomas D. ... **Atlanta, GA**
Trask, Thomas J. ... Dunedin, FL
Trask, William J. ... Hamburg, NY
Traskell, Jake Paul ... Bartow, FL
Traskos, Kevin T. ... **Washington, DC**
Traster, David M. ... **Wichita, KS**
Traster, Timothy A. ... **Daytona Beach, FL**
Traster, Vernon L. ... Ada, OH
Trasvina, John D. ... Department of Justice, Civil Rights Division, GV
Trataros, Fanny ... Poughkeepsie, NY
Trathen, Barbara J. ... Indianapolis, IN
Trathen, David H. ... Bloomsburg, PA
Trathen, Marcus W. ... **Greensboro, NC**
Raleigh, NC
Tratner, Louis ... New York, NY
Tratnyek, John F. ... **Morristown, NJ**
Tratos, Mark G. ... **Las Vegas, NV**
Tratras, Nicholas G. ... Houston, TX
Tratten, Mark S. ... **Sacramento, CA**
Trattler, Larry ... Denver, CO
Trattles, Gloria ... New York, NY
Trattner & Associates ... Cleveland, OH
Trattner, Barry A. ... Cleveland, OH
Trattner, Darren M. ... **Beverly Hills, CA**
Trattner & Davis ... Oklahoma City, OK
Trattner, Gregory B. ... Los Angeles, CA
Trattner, Henry ... Oklahoma City, OK
Trattner, Ira ... Los Angeles, CA

Trattner, Jeffrey B. ... **Danbury, CT**
Trattner, Mary Lou ... Cleveland, OH
Trattner, Robert B. ... **Akron, OH**
Trattner, Stephen M. ... **Washington, DC**
Trau, David M. ... Tampa, FL
Traub, Barry M. ... Pearl River, NY
Traub, Barry N. ... San Francisco, CA
Traub, Bennett B. ... **Torrance, CA**
Traub, Bonacquist & Fox LLP
New York, NY
Arlington, TX
Traub, Doris ... New York, NY
Traub Eglin Lieberman Straus
Hackensack, NJ
Hawthorne, NY
New York, NY
White Plains, NY
Traub, Evelyn Small ... **Richmond, VA**
Traub, Felicia G. ... **New York, NY**
Traub, Freddie J. ... **Towson, MD**
Traub, Gene S. ... San Francisco, CA
Traub, Harold, (P.C.) ... New York, NY
Traub, Harvey S. ... **Fairbury, IL**
Traub, Henry L. ... Beverly Hills, CA
Traub, Herman V. ... New York, NY
Traub, Hillel ... Glen Burnie, MD
Traub, Jean K. ... Falls Church, VA
Traub, Jean R., (Mr.) ... Mountain View, CA
Traub, Jeffrey ... New York, NY
Traub, Joan ... New York, NY
Traub, Joseph Z. ... **Philadelphia, PA**
Traub, Kenneth W. ... Tucker, GA
Traub, Paul ... **New York, NY**
Traub, Richard B. ... Albuquerque, NM
Traub, Richard J. ... **Chicago, IL**
Traub, Richard K. ... **Hawthorne, NY**
Traub, Rosemary ... Albuquerque, NM
Traub, Seymour ... **Allentown, PA**
Traub, Stanley A. ... Omaha, NE
Traub, Stephen I. ... **New Haven, CT**
Traub, Terry L. ... Mount Prospect, IL
Traub & Traub ... New York, NY
Traub, Weeks & Brucker, Ltd.
Fairbury, IL
Traube, Joel M. ... Staten Island, NY
Traube, Victoria G. ... New York, NY
Trauben, Bruce K. ... **Washington, DC**
Baltimore, MD
Rockville, MD
Traubenberg, Neil D. ... Rockford, IL
Traud, Thomas F., Jr. ... Allentown, PA
Trauernicht, Carl, Jr. ... **St. Louis, MO**
Trauger, Aleta Arthur ... Nashville, TN
Trauger, Byron R. ... **Nashville, TN**
Trauger, Jeffrey G. ... **Doylestown, PA**
Trauger, Thomas C. ... **Washington, DC**
Traugh, Arthur M. ... **Sacramento, CA**
Traughber, Arlie E. ... **Columbia, IL**
Traughber, Reitz & Morris, Ltd.
Columbia, IL
Waterloo, IL
Traugott, Catherine A. ... **Denver, CO**
Traugott, Isabel ... **San Francisco, CA**
Traul, Carol Woodley ... **Overland Park, KS**
Traul, Howard A., II ... **Bellefontaine, OH**
Traul, Robert Eric ... Chicago, IL
Traulsen, Richard N ... Phoenix, AZ
Traum, David Allan ... New York, NY
Traum, Jeffrey L. ... **New York, NY**
Traum, Jerome S. ... **New York, NY**
Traum, Kenneth P. ... **Hackensack, NJ**
Traum, Sheryl Alyce ... **Walnut Creek, CA**
Traum, Sydney S. ... **Miami, FL**
Traum, Sydney S., P.A. ... **Miami, FL**
Traumueller, Gerard E. ... Laguna Hills, CA
Trauner, Bruce E. ... **New York, NY**
Trauner, Cohen & Thomas ... **Atlanta, GA**
Trauner, Robert ... **Atlanta, GA**
Traunfeld, Eugene N. ... Chicago, IL
Traupman, Mary A. ... Pittsburgh, PA
Traurig, Edward ... Southfield, MI
Traurig, Robert H. ... **Miami, FL**
Trauring, Thomas J. ... **Kokomo, IN**
Trausch, James E. ... **Chicago, IL**
Trausch, Michele K. ... **San Francisco, CA**
Trausch, William Henry ... La Mesa, CA
Trause, Janet Perlman ... Glen Cove, NY
Trause, Richard S. ... Yardley, PA
Traut, Donald L. ... De Kalb, IL
Traut, Eric Vaughn ... Santa Ana, CA
Traut, James R. ... Santa Ana, CA
Trauth, Joseph L., Jr. ... **Cincinnati, OH**
Trautman, Eileen ... **Miami, FL**
Trautman, Gerald H. ... Phoenix, AZ
Trautman, Karen Crevasse ... Bradenton, FL
Trautman, Linda K. ... San Bernardino, CA
Trautman, Pamela C. ... Nashville, TN
Trautman, Philip A. ... Seattle, WA
Trautman, Tucker K. ... **Denver, CO**
Trautman, William E. ... **San Francisco, CA**
Trautmann, Joel R. ... Fort Worth, TX
Trautmann, Richard S. ... Cincinnati, OH
Trautmann, Robert E. ... Bridgeport, CT
Trautmann, Theodore W. ... Deerfield, IL
Trautmann, Victor Franz
Oklahoma City, OK
Trautner, P. Kevin ... **Houston, TX**
Trautner, Thomas G. ... **Cadillac, MI**
Trautner, Tobias ... **New York, NY**
Trautwein, Blair J. ... **Fort Collins, CO**
Cheyenne, WY
Trautwein & Keeney PLLC
Louisville, KY
Trautwein, Mary L. ... Louisville, KY
Trautwein, Randall L. ... **Huntington, WV**
Trautwein, Richard M., (P.S.C.)
Louisville, KY
Trautwein, Theodore W. ... Franklin Lakes, NJ
Trautwig, Cathleen Catallo ... Greenvale, NY
Travaglini, Thomas ... Madison, TN
Travaline, Jeffrey ... Stoneham, MA
Travaline, Joseph T. ... Burlington, MA
Travalio, Gregory M. ... Columbus, OH
Traveland, Terry L. ... **Dallas, TX**
Travell, Wayne G. ... **Washington, DC**
Travelstead, David A. ... **Indianapolis, IN**
Travelstead, Lee C.
Lauderdale-By-The-Sea, FL
Travelsted, Brent ... Bowling Green, KY
Travelsted & Crocker
Bowling Green, KY
Travelsted, Penny ... **Bowling Green, KY**
Traver, Alfred E. ... Austin, TX
Traver, Carol G. ... Croton-On-Hudson, NY
Traver, Courtland L., Jr. ... **McLean, VA**
Traver, Daniel A. ... Port Huron, MI
Traver, David F. ... Milwaukee, WI
Traver, Dennis D. ... Dover, OH
Traver, E. C. ... Fort Lauderdale, FL
Traver, Jerry M. ... Chicago, IL
Traver, Joseph A. ... Queens Village, NY
Traver, Lynn Bonilla ... Sierra Madre, CA
Traver, Mary ... Milwaukee, WI
Traver, Robert J. ... **Pasadena, CA**
Traver, Ronald H. ... **Fort Worth, TX**
Traver, Walter J.R. ... **San Francisco, CA**
Traver, Warren L. ... Atlanta, GA
Tucker, GA
Traver, Worth & Fox ... Dover, OH
Travers, Anne M. C. ... Providence, RI
Travers, Arthur H., Jr. ... Boulder, CO
Travers, Arthur J. ... Waldoboro, ME
Travers, Bernard F., III ... Longmeadow, MA
Travers, Christopher N. ... **New York, NY**
Travers, Daniel J. ... New York, NY
Travers, Denise M. ... Hackensack, NJ
Travers, Donald E. ... San Anselmo, CA
Travers, Donald R. ... Paradise, CA
Travers, Eric B. ... **Vienna, VA**
Travers, F. Warren ... Troy, NY
Travers & Gargas, P.C. ... **Boston, MA**
Travers, Gordon ... **New York, NY**
Travers, Herbert F. ... Worcester, MA
Travers, Herbert F., Jr. ... Boston, MA
Travers, Jeanne C. Farrah ... Boston, MA
Travers, Jeffrey P. ... **New York, NY**
Travers, John G. ... Albuquerque, NM
Travers, Mack J. ... **Katy, TX**
Travers, Margaret S. ... **Boston, MA**
Travers, Martin John ... **New York, NY**
Travers, Matthew James, Jr. ... Fairfax, VA
Travers, Maura C. ... **Warwick, RI**
Travers, Michael L. ... **Washington, DC**
Travers, Murphy & O'Connor
Worcester, MA
Travers, Naomi S. ... **Washington, DC**
Travers, P. Diane ... Department of the Army,
Army Materiel Command, GV
Travers, Peter J. ... Hopewell, NJ
Travers & Rank ... Paradise, CA
Travers, Richard D. ... **Vail, CO**
Travers, Robert M. ... **Pontiac, IL**
Travers, Ronald J. ... Baltimore, MD
Travers, Russell E.
Department of Defense, GV
Travers, Sherrie Haussner ... **Katy, TX**
Travers, Sherry L. ... **Dallas, TX**
Travers, Stephen W. ... Houston, TX
Travers, Thomas G. ... **Madison, WI**
Travers, Thomas J. ... Treasury Department,
Internal Revenue Service, GV
Travers, Thomas J., Jr. ... **Youngstown, OH**
Travers, Timothy E. ... Rochester, NY
Travers, Timothy K. ... **Chicago, IL**
Travers & Travers, L.L.P. ... **Katy, TX**
Traversa, Halyna M. ... Schaumburg, IL
Traverse, Edward F. ... Eureka, CA
Traverse & Karjola ... Eureka, CA
Traverse, Katherine J. ... **Houston, TX**
Traverse, Stephen E. ... Glendale, CA
Traversi, David M. ... Kenwood, CA
Traverso, Anthony A. ... **New York, NY**
Traverso, Jeanette ... **San Francisco, CA**
Traverso, Richard J. ... **Arlington, VA**
Traverso Larson, Dawn ... Fort Myers, FL
Travia, Donna L. ... Philadelphia, PA
Travieso, Bonnie Abrams ... **Baltimore, MD**
Travieso, Vanessa S. ... Coral Gables, FL
Travieso-Diaz, Matias F., (P.C.)
Washington, DC
Traviolia, George P. ... Sells, AZ
Travis, Alan C. ... Columbus, OH
Travis, Andrew D. ... Houston, TX
Travis, Benjamin ... Oakland, CA
Travis and Bonnett ... Bedford, IA
Travis, Burr J. ... Florence, KY
Travis, Catherine S. ... **Portland, OR**
Travis, Charles M. ... Hoffman Estates, IL
Travis, Christopher L. ... **Little Rock, AR**
Travis, Cliff K. ... Bloomington, IN
Travis, Cliff M. ... Inverness, FL
Travis, Curtis S. ... Indianapolis, IN
Travis, D John ... **Cleveland, OH**
Travis, Deborah S. ... **Corpus Christi, TX**
Travis, Dianne ... **New York, NY**
Travis, Donald K. ... **Plymouth, IN**
Travis, Donald W. ... Atlanta, GA
Travis, Edmunds, Jr. ... **Washington, DC**
Travis, Francis A ... **Garden City, NY**
Travis, Gary Nicholas ... Parma Heights, OH
Travis, Geoffrey L. ... **Miami, FL**
Travis & Gooch ... **Washington, DC**
Travis, Grant C. ... **Edinboro, PA**
Travis, Hannibal ... **San Francisco, CA**
Travis, James Kearney, III
Hattiesburg, MS
Travis, James N. ... Colorado Springs, CO
Travis, Jay A., III ... **Jackson, MS**
Travis, Jayne E. ... Torrance, CA
Travis, Jeffrey M. ... **Dallas, TX**
Travis, Jeremy ... Department of Justice,
Office of Justice Programs, GV
Travis, J. K., Jr. ... **Hattiesburg, MS**
Travis, Joan Schiller ... San Diego, CA
Travis, Jodylee A. ... San Francisco, CA
Travis, Joe L. ... **Somerset, KY**
Travis, Joe Lane ... Glasgow, KY
Travis, John E. ... **Jackson, MS**
Travis, Jos. C. ... Charlotte, NC
Travis, Karen J. ... Los Angeles, CA
Travis, Kelly Lynn ... St. Joseph, MI
Travis, Kenneth D. ... Midland, TX
Travis, Kenneth L. ... Hernando, FL
Travis, Kevin C. ... Westwood, KS
Travis, Lance C. ... **Dallas, TX**
Travis, Lisa A. ... Sacramento, CA
Travis, Loyd Kelley ... Jackson, MS
Travis, Luke P. ... **Fall River, MA**
Travis, Lynn M. ... Alton, IL
Travis, Margaret A. ... Glasgow, KY
Travis, Margaret E. ... **Oklahoma City, OK**
Travis, Mark ... Roseville, CA
Travis, Mark C. ... **Cookeville, TN**
Knoxville, TN
Nashville, TN
Travis, Marsh & Forrester ... **Dallas, TX**
Travis, Mary A. ... **Oklahoma City, OK**
Travis, Mercedes, (Mrs.) ... **Palm Beach, FL**
Travis, Michael F. ... Bedford, IA
Travis, Michelle A. ... Palo Alto, CA
Travis, Monte S. ... San Francisco, CA
Travis, Norton L. ... **Great Neck, NY**
Travis, Patricia M. ... **Oklahoma City, OK**
Travis, Paul ... Columbus, OH
Travis, Philip C. ... Cincinnati, OH
Travis, Phyllis A. ... Worcester, MA
Travis & Pon ... San Francisco, CA
Travis, Pruitt & Lawless ... **Somerset, KY**
Travis, R. Blake ... New Orleans, LA
Travis, Rex K. ... **Oklahoma City, OK**
Travis, Richard E., Law Offices of
Elgin, IL
Travis, Richard L. ... **Sioux Falls, SD**
Travis, Robert C. ... Jackson, MS
Travis, Robert F. ... Kalamazoo, MI
Travis, Robert F., P.C. ... Kalamazoo, MI
Travis, Robert L., Jr. ... Quincy, FL
Travis, Robert M. ... **Atlanta, GA**
Travis, Robert S. ... Atlanta, GA
Travis, Roderick B. ... Chappaqua, NY
Travis, Roland B. ... Lake Jackson, TX
Travis, Ronald C. ... Amityville, NY
Travis, Ronald C. ... **Williamsport, PA**
Travis, Seth A. ... **Chicago, IL**
Travis, Sherrie ... **Chicago, IL**
Travis, Susan J. ... **Dallas, TX**
Travis, Susan T. ... Englewood Cliffs, NJ
Travis, T. Richard ... **Nashville, TN**
Travis, Ted L. ... **Los Angeles, CA**
Travis, Thomas A., Jr. ... Atlanta, GA
Travis, Thomas G. ... **San Francisco, CA**
Washington, DC
Miami, FL
Atlanta, GA
Chicago, IL
New York, NY
Travis, Thomas L. ... Little Rock, AR
Travis, Thomas L. ... **Lexington, KY**
Travis, Todd Andrew ... Denver, CO
Travis & Travis ... **Hattiesburg, MS**
Travis, Veda M. ... Salt Lake City, UT
Travis, W. Terry ... Montgomery, AL
Travis, William D. ... Moorpark, CA
Travis, William F. ... **Southaven, MS**
Travis, William H. ... **Los Angeles, CA**
Travis, William J. ... **St. Louis, MO**
Travis, William K. ... Decatur, GA
Travis, William R., Law Office of
Austin, TX
Travis, Wm. Clifton ... Louisville, KY
Traviss, James J. ... Winter Haven, FL
Travnicek, Ivo J. ... **Cleveland, OH**
Travostino, Joan M. ... **Anchorage, AK**
Travous, Paul Kevin ... **St. Louis, MO**
Traw, Charles T. ... **Iowa City, IA**
Traw, John M. ... Norman, OK
Traw, Karen M. ... San Bernardino, CA
Traw, Kelly L. ... McLean, VA
Traw, Russell V. ... **Myrtle Beach, SC**
Traweek, Amanda ... Bartow, FL
Traweek, Robert Scott ... **Pensacola, FL**
Traweek, Stanley T. ... Dallas, TX
Trawick, Daryl E ... Miami, FL
Trawick, Debra ... **Dallas, TX**
Trawick, Donald T. ... Birmingham, AL
Trawick, Gary E. ... Burgaw, NC
Trawick, Gary R. ... Montgomery, AL
Trawick, George H. ... Ariton, AL
Trawick, Henry P., Jr. ... Sarasota, FL
Trawick, Henry P., P.A. ... Sarasota, FL
Trawick, John B. ... **Pensacola, FL**
Trawinski, Edward A., Jr. ... Bergenfield, NJ
Trawinski, Edward John ... **Morristown, NJ**
Traxler, David H. ... Des Moines, IA
Traxler, Katherine A. ... **Los Angeles, CA**
Traxler, Malkoff, Boyd, Rummell & Zamary,
Co., L.P.A. ... Youngstown, OH
Traxler, Maureen A. ... Seattle, WA
Traxler, Norbert B. ... New Prague, MN
Traxler, Seth ... **Chicago, IL**
Traxler, Thomas W. ... **Greenville, SC**
Greer, SC
Traxler, William B., Jr. ... Greenville, SC
Trayber, Rae Ellen ... Fort Lauderdale, FL
Traycik, Louis E. ... Philadelphia, PA
Trayer, Jill E. ... **New Hope, PA**
Trayers, Paul E. ... Department of Labor,
Office of Secretary, GV
Traylor, Carol J. ... **Fort Worth, TX**
Traylor, Charles A., II ... West Monroe, LA
Traylor, Charles A., III ... West Monroe, LA
Traylor, Charles E. ... Memphis, TN
Traylor, Charles J. ... **Grand Junction, CO**
Traylor, Charles V. ... **Indianapolis, IN**
Traylor, Chet D. ... Winnsboro, LA
Traylor, Daniel M. ... Little Rock, AR
Traylor, David G., Jr. ... **Columbia, SC**
Traylor, Donald W. ... Tomball, TX
Traylor, Jack P. ... Palacios, TX
Traylor, James R. ... Hopewell, VA
Traylor, Joe R. ... Portland, OR
Traylor, Joel E., Jr. ... Alexandria, VA
Traylor, John L. ... **Denver, CO**
Traylor, Kent F. ... Duncanville, TX
Traylor, Lawrence M. ... Heathsville, VA
Traylor, Lee Clyde ... Fort Payne, AL
Traylor, Lisa L. ... **Dallas, TX**
Traylor, Martha ... Newark, NJ
Traylor, Martha ... Princeton, NJ
Traylor, Michael S. ... Los Angeles, CA
Traylor, Michelle D. ... **San Francisco, CA**
Traylor, Morris & Wornom ... **Emporia, VA**
Traylor, Orba F., (Mr.) ... New York, NY
Traylor, Patrick D. ... **Washington, DC**
Traylor, Robert ... **Grand Junction, CO**
Traylor, Robert A. ... Liverpool, NY
Traylor, Stephen A. ... Princeton, NJ
Traylor, Tompkins, Black & Gaty, P.C.
Grand Junction, CO
Traylor & Traylor ... Princeton, NJ
Traylor, W. Hamilton ... **Jacksonville, FL**
Traylor, Whitney Charles ... Denver, CO
Traylor, William H. ... Princeton, NJ
Traylor, William N. ... New York, NY
Traylor, William P., III ... **Birmingham, AL**
Trayner, Albert L., III ... Tampa, FL
Trayner, Ronald G. ... Pasadena, CA
Trayner, Stephen J. ... **Salt Lake City, UT**
Traynham, Jay C. ... **Macon, GA**
Traynham, Jerry G. ... Tallahassee, FL
Traynham, Michael W. ... **Costa Mesa, CA**
Traynham, Wayne O. ... **Duluth, GA**
Traynor, A. Rodger, Jr. ... **Miami, FL**
Traynor, Carl M. ... Fort Wayne, IN
Traynor, Christine R. ... Coral Gables, FL
Traynor, Cynthia D. ... **Chicago, IL**
Traynor, Daniel M. ... **Devils Lake, ND**
Traynor, David R. ... Wayne, PA
Traynor, Duane L. ... Springfield, IL
Traynor, Gary F. ... **Dover, DE**
Traynor, J. Patrick ... Bismarck, ND
Traynor, J. Thomas, Jr. ... **Devils Lake, ND**
Traynor, John Michael, Law Office of
St. Augustine, FL
Traynor, John T. ... **Devils Lake, ND**
Traynor, Long & Wynne, P.C., A
Professional Corporation ... **Enid, OK**
Okeene, OK
Seiling, OK
Traynor, Michael ... **San Francisco, CA**
Traynor, Michael J. ... Indianapolis, IN
Traynor, Michael R. ... Delmar, NY
Traynor, Richard J. ... Morristown, NJ
Traynor, Richard Michael ... **Dallas, TX**
Traynor, Roy T. ... Wausau, WI
Traynor, Rutten & Traynor
Devils Lake, ND
Traynor, Skehan and Marks
Rochester, NY
Traynor, Steven P. ... St. Louis, MO
Traynor, Stuart J. ... Taylorville, IL
Traynor, Susan E. ... **Indianapolis, IN**
Traynor, Tamara L. ... **Philadelphia, PA**
Traynor, Timothy R. ... **Enid, OK**
Okeene, OK
Seiling, OK
Traynor, W. Patrick ... **Tucson, AZ**
Traynor, William G. ... Atlanta, GA
Traynor, William Michael ... Skokie, IL
Traynum, Elise K. ... **Costa Mesa, CA**
Traystman, Ellen S. ... Oakdale, CT
Traystman, Gary B. ... New London, CT
Traystman, Harry R. ... New London, CT
Trazenfeld, Warren R. ... **Miami, FL**
Trazenfeld, Warren R., P.A. ... **Miami, FL**
Trazig, Sue E. ... **Las Vegas, NV**
Trazzi, A. Robert ... Baltimore, MD
Trazzi, Damon A. ... Timonium, MD
Trazzi & Grasso ... Timonium, MD
Trbovich, Ned ... Pittsburgh, PA
Trbovich, Theodore M. ... Pittsburgh, PA
Trca, Michelle G. ... Coral Springs, FL
Trca, Randy E. ... Iowa City, IA
Treace, R. Jeneane ... Decatur, GA
Treacy, Brian T. ... Rutherford, NJ
Treacy, David R. ... Tarrytown, NY
Treacy, Dennis H. ... Richmond, VA
Treacy, Gerald B., Jr. ... **Bellevue, WA**
Treacy, James W. ... Indianapolis, IN
Treacy Law Group, P.L.L.C.
Bellevue, WA
Treacy, Michael D. ... Washington, NJ
Treacy, Philip ... Anaheim, CA
Treacy, Richard F., Jr. ... South Windsor, CT
Treacy, Schaffel, Moore & Mueller
West Caldwell, NJ
New York, NY
Treacy, Thomas B. ... **New York, NY**
Treacy, Timothy E. ... San Francisco, CA
Treacy, William O. ... Fort Walton Beach, FL
Treacy, William P. ... Lake Forest, IL
Treacy-Maloney, Sheila ... Chicago, IL

Treadaway, Gordon .... Lubbock, TX
Treadaway, J. Michael .... Marietta, GA
Treadaway, Randell E. .... Metairie, LA
Treadgold, Stephen F. .... San Diego, CA
Treado, Alvin D. .... Muskegon, MI
Treado, Howard C. .... Bloomfield Hills, MI
Treadon, Thomas A. .... Akron, OH
Treadup, J. Mark .... New Bedford, MA
Treadway, Bird & Nespor, P.C. .... Albion, NE
Fullerton, NE
Treadway, Donald R. .... Fullerton, NE
Treadway, E. Scott .... Indianapolis, IN
Treadway, Edwin L. .... Johnson City, TN
Kingsport, TN
Treadway, H. Craig .... Olive Branch, MS
Treadway, J. Keith .... Olive Branch, MS
Treadway, Keith R. .... Oklahoma City, OK
Treadway, Kristi L. .... Westmont, NJ
Philadelphia, PA
Treadway, Lyman H. .... Cleveland, OH
Treadway, Marcus A., III
Hattiesburg, MS
Treadway, R. Kyle .... Salt Lake City, UT
Treadway, Robert L. .... Lexington, KY
Treadway, Rose Mary .... Gainesville, FL
Treadwell, Amy E. .... Milpitas, CA
Treadwell, Burson W. .... Nahcotta, WA
Treadwell, David M. .... Denver, CO
Treadwell, David O., Jr. .... Atlanta, GA
Treadwell, Deidre .... Houston, TX
Treadwell, DeVoe G. .... Derby, KS
Treadwell, Donald H. .... Southgate, MI
Treadwell, Frederic C. .... Seattle, WA
Treadwell, James H. .... Woodland Hills, CA
Treadwell, James K. .... Seattle, WA
Treadwell, Karin S. .... Seattle, WA
Treadwell, Lujuana W. .... Berkeley, CA
Treadwell, Marc T. .... Macon, GA
Treadwell, Mark A. .... Los Angeles, CA
Treadwell, Mark A., III .... Dadeville, AL
Treadwell, Molly A. .... Knoxville, TN
Treadwell, Ronnie J. .... Anderson, SC
Treadwell, Stetler, Erickson, Cimino & McElrath .... Naples, FL
Treadwell, Thomas L. .... Naples, FL
Treadwell-Miller, Cynthia .... Denver, CO
Treadwell-Rubin, Pamela A. .... Tucson, AZ
Treakle, James E., Jr. .... Charlottesville, VA
Treannie, Lisa M. .... Lexington, MA
Treano, Robert G. .... Taunton, MA
Treano, Robert G., P.C. .... Taunton, MA
Treanor, Claire M. .... Charlotte, NC
Treanor, Gerard .... Washington, DC
Treanor, Harvey & Sullivan .... Montclair, NJ
Treanor, James .... Plattsburgh, NY
Treanor, James A., III .... Washington, DC
Treanor, Janie L. .... Dallas, TX
Treanor, Mark C. .... Charlotte, NC
Treanor, Michael R. .... New York, NY
Treanor, Richard B. .... Washington, DC
Treanor, Richard L. .... Arlington, VA
Treanor, Sullivan & Trowbridge
New York, NY
Treanor, Timothy J. .... New York, NY
Treanor, Walter G. .... Walnut Creek, CA
Treanor, Wanden P., Law Offices of
San Rafael, CA
Treanor, William F. .... New York, NY
Treanor, William M. .... Department of Justice, Office of Legal Counsel, GV
Treas, Elizabeth A. .... Oklahoma City, OK
Trease, H. William .... Iowa City, IA
Trease, Jory L. .... Salt Lake City, UT
Treaster, Byron L. .... Santa Fe, NM
Treaster, Eugene C. .... Sacramento, CA
Treaster, Steven D. .... Overland Park, KS
Treasure, Anne J. .... Columbus, OH
Treasure, Harold B. .... Kennett, MO
Treasure, Kathleen M. .... Albany, NY
Treat, Charles Stephen
San Francisco, CA
Treat, Christine M. .... Lee's Summit, MO
Treat, David L. .... San Antonio, TX
Treat, Jeffrey S. .... Honesdale, PA
Treat, John R. .... Ann Arbor, MI
Treat, John R., and Associates, P.C.
Ann Arbor, MI
Treat, Rita G. .... Fayetteville, AR
Treat, Robert T. .... Boston, MA
Treat, Sharon Anglin .... Augusta, ME
Treat, Theodore N., Jr. .... Minneapolis, MN
Treat, William W. .... Hampton, NH
Treatman, Howard P. .... Philadelphia, PA
Trebach, Barry D. .... Washington, DC
Baltimore, MD
Rockville, MD
Trebach, Bradford .... Riverdale, NY
Trebat, Alan G. .... Norwood, MA
Trebatoski, Chris J. .... Milwaukee, WI
Trebbe, Sally K. ....
Department Of Health And Human Services, GV
Trebby, Eugene P. .... Brookfield, WI
Treber, Karen Avagliano .... Frostburg, MD
Trebert, Gary R. .... Farmers Branch, TX
Trebets, John F. .... Mentor, OH
Trebilcock, Craig T. .... Hanover, PA
Lancaster, PA
Reading, PA
York, PA
Trebilcock, Everett R. .... Lansing, MI
Trebing, Al P. .... New Canaan, CT
Ridgefield, CT
Trebing, Al P., & Associates, P.C.
New Canaan, CT
Ridgefield, CT
Trebisacci, Raymond T. .... Westerly, RI
Trebisacci & Reck .... New London, CT
Stonington, CT
Westerly, RI
Trebler, Per H. .... Newport Beach, CA
Trebler, Per H., P.C. .... Newport Beach, CA
Trebon & Fine, P.C. .... Flagstaff, AZ
Trebon, John J. .... Flagstaff, AZ
Trebon, Lawrence A. .... Milwaukee, WI
Trebon & Mayhew .... Milwaukee, WI
Treby, Stuart A.
Nuclear Regulatory Commission, Office of the General Counsel, GV
Trecartin, Constance L. .... Tucson, AZ
Trecartin, Richard F. .... San Francisco, CA
Trecek, Cathy .... Omaha, NE
Trecek, John E. .... Omaha, NE
Trecek, Timothy S. .... Milwaukee, WI
Trechel, Gary M. .... Rensselaer, NY
Trechsel, Haydn M. .... Birmingham, AL
Trechter, Charles D. .... Pueblo, CO
Treciak, James S. .... Jackson, MI
Treciokas, Charles J., Jr. .... Boston, MA
Treckelo, Richard M. .... Elkhart, IN
Trecker & Fritz .... Honolulu, HI
Trecker, Steven J. .... Honolulu, HI
Tredeau, Paula C. .... Springfield, MA
Tredemeyer, Leila Anne .... Dallas, TX
Tredennick, John C., Jr. .... Denver, CO
Tredennick, Steven B. .... Round Rock, TX
Treder, Edward A. .... Covina, CA
Tredick, Peter W. .... Washington, DC
Tredinnick, Edward J. .... San Rafael, CA
Tredway, David W. .... Oxnard, CA
Tredway, Ellen H. .... Austin, TX
Tredway, Harold T. .... Downey, CA
Irvine, CA
Tredway, Lumsdaine & Doyle, LLP
Downey, CA
Irvine, CA
Los Angeles, CA
Santa Ana, CA
Tredwell, Constance C. .... Essex, CT
Tredwell, Cynthia L. .... Portland, ME
Tredwell, Scott J. .... Philadelphia, PA
Tree, Christine M. .... Fitchburg, MA
Tree, D. James .... Yakima, WA
Treeby, William D., (P.C.)
New Orleans, LA
Treece, Aimee S. .... Oklahoma City, OK
Treece, Alfrey, Musat & Bosworth, P.C.
Denver, CO
Treece, Claude R. .... Houston, TX
Treece, Geoffrey B. .... Little Rock, AR
Springfield, MO
Treece, James M. .... Austin, TX
Treece, John W. .... Chicago, IL
Treece, Karen Gail .... Denver, CO
Treece, Lawrence W. .... Denver, CO
Treece Phillips, LLP .... Fayetteville, AR
Little Rock, AR
Kansas City, MO
St. Louis, MO
Springfield, MO
Treece, Randolph F. .... Troy, NY
Treece, Randy L. .... Paducah, KY
Treece, Richdale, Malone, Corning & Abbott, Inc., P.S. .... Seattle, WA
Treece, Robert D. .... Oklahoma City, OK
Treece, Robert S. .... Denver, CO
Treece, Roger A. .... Cincinnati, OH
Treece, T. Gerald .... Houston, TX
Treece, Thomas D., P.A. .... Jacksonville, FL
Treece, Thomas M. .... Seattle, WA
Tregoob, Warren F. .... Ardmore, PA
Treem, Joshua R. .... Baltimore, MD
Treen, Catherine Mannweiler
Indianapolis, IN
Treen, David C. .... New Orleans, LA
Treene, Eric W. .... Washington, DC
Trees, Linda C. .... Washington, DC
Treese, David M. .... Dayton, OH
Treese, Leanne Pike .... Princeton, NJ
Treese, Margaret Anderson .... Dayton, OH
Treese, Martha K. .... Pennington, NJ
Treese, Robert T., III .... Auburn, AL
Treese, Robert Thomas, Jr. .... Selma, AL
Treesh, Kevin W. .... New York, NY
Treeter, David R. .... Charlotte, NC
Treff, Leslie Carol .... Rockville, MD
Treffers, Peter A. .... New Haven, CT
Treffert, Thomas L. .... San Francisco, CA
Treffiletti, Regina K. .... Albany, NY
Treffinger, Theodore R. .... Denver, CO
Trefil, James K. .... Washington, DC
Trefry, George .... Anchorage, AK
Trefry, Keith A. .... Spokane, WA
Trefts, Walter E., Jr. .... San Francisco, CA
Tregea, Steven R. .... State College, PA
Treger, Herbert W. .... Irving, TX
Treger, Michael D. .... Seattle, WA
Treger, Tracy L. .... Chicago, IL
Tregidgo, Charles .... Fair Lawn, NJ
Tregle, Ovidem, Jr. .... Chalmette, LA
Treglia, Lawrence A., Jr. .... Irvine, CA
Tregoning, Daniel K. .... Frederick, MD
Tregub, Susan H. .... Los Angeles, CA
Trehan, Meera .... San Francisco, CA
Treharne, Andrew S. .... Milwaukee, WI
Treherne, James E. .... Englewood, OH
Trehub, Ann .... Wellesley Hills, MA
Trehub, Nancy .... Jonesboro, GA
Trehus, Carl A. .... Dallas, TX
Trehy, Jerome P., Jr. .... Raleigh, NC
Trehy, Yamile Marrero .... Hollywood, FL
Treiber, Andrea E. .... Houston, TX
Treiber, David C. .... Willimantic, CT
Treiber, Guarnaccia & Connors
Willimantic, CT
Treiber, Heidi Brooks .... Dover, MA
Treiber, Mary P. .... Ketchikan, AK
Treibick, Carol Beth .... Carlisle, MA
Treich, Diane C. .... Houston, TX
Treichel, Richard L. .... Olympia Fields, IL
Treichelt, Tim .... Sacramento, CA
Treichler, Peter B. .... Princeton, NJ
Treier, J. Bret .... Akron, OH
Treiger, Ada .... Los Angeles, CA
Treiger, Irwin L. .... Seattle, WA
Treiman, Albert H. .... Bethpage, NY
Treiman, David M. .... Endicott, NY
Treiman, David Michael .... Costa Mesa, CA
Treiman, Jaak .... Canoga Park, CA
Treiman, Janet L. .... Philadelphia, PA
Treiman, Michael E. .... Beverly Hills, CA
Treiman, Robert N. .... Los Angeles, CA
Treiman, Saul D. .... Philadelphia, PA
Treimer, Ann L. .... Chicago, IL
Treinen, Kenneth .... Bloomington, MN
Treinen, L. Nicholas .... Lake Orion, MI
Treinen, Michael D. .... Des Moines, IA
Treinin, Harry .... Elmira, NY
Treinish, Alan J. .... Cleveland, OH
Treinish, Alan J., Co., L.P.A. .... Cleveland, OH
Treinish, Nathan J. .... Kansas City, MO
Treiser, Kobza & Volpe, Chartered
Naples, FL
Treiser, Richard M. .... Naples, FL
Treisman, Douglas Owen .... Fresno, CA
Treisman, Eric .... Santa Fe, NM
Treisman, Warren .... San Diego, CA
Treister, Dana S. .... Los Angeles, CA
Treister, George M. .... Los Angeles, CA
Treister, Leonard E. .... New York, NY
Treister, Robert B. .... Cerritos, CA
Treister, William R. .... Cleveland, OH
Treistman, Carlos .... Houston, TX
Treistman, Katherine G. .... Houston, TX
Treitel, Andrew .... New York, NY
Treitel, Emanuel .... Encino, CA
Treitler, William B. .... San Diego, CA
Treitmeier-McCarthy, Monica A.
New York, NY
Treitz, John G., Jr. .... Louisville, KY
Trejo, Charles David .... Beverly Hills, CA
Trejo, George Paul, Jr. .... Newport Beach, CA
Trejo, Humberto R. .... Deer Park, TX
Trejo, Laura .... Department of Transportation, Office of the General Counsel, GV
Trejo, Maria Antonieta .... Department of State, Bureau of Legislative Affairs, GV
Trekell, Cindi L. .... Amarillo, TX
Trela, Brian P. .... Fountain Valley, CA
Trela, Constantine L., Jr. .... Chicago, IL
Treland, Linda R. .... Milwaukee, WI
Treleven, Cynthia Caine, S.C.
Green Bay, WI
Trell, Scott T. .... Miami, FL
Trell, Shawn A. .... Columbus, OH
Trella, Matthew S. .... Clifton, NJ
Trelles, Ana C. .... New Orleans, LA
Trelles, Mac .... Baton Rouge, LA
Trelles, Randy .... Baton Rouge, LA
Treloar, Harriette E. .... San Francisco, CA
Trelstad, Bergitta K. .... Seattle, WA
Trelz, Eric M. .... St. Louis, MO
Trelz, Therese Rolufs .... Belleville, IL
St. Louis, MO
Tremain, Inez K. .... Chicago, IL
Tremain, Kenneth D. .... Cincinnati, OH
Tremain, Michelle H. .... Los Angeles, CA
Tremain, Robert A. .... Birmingham, MI
Tremain, Robert A., & Associates, P.C.
Birmingham, MI
Tremain, Robert E., III .... Los Angeles, CA
Tremain, Tammy S. .... Madison, WI
Tremaine, Anne .... Truckee, CA
Tremaine, Arthur J.
Arlington Heights, IL
Tremaine, Degas G. .... Washington, DC
Tremaine, H. Stewart .... Portland, OR
Tremaine, J. Richard
Steamboat Springs, CO
Tremaine, John S. .... Sumner, IA
Tremallo, Mark van Bael .... Southbridge, MA
Treman, Charles E., Jr. .... Ithaca, NY
Treman & Clynes .... Ithaca, NY
Treman, Michael J. .... Santa Barbara, CA
Tremaroli, Christopher B.
Colorado Springs, CO
Tremaroli, Cynthia L. .... Colorado Springs, CO
Tremaroli & Tremaroli, P.C.
Colorado Springs, CO
Tremarzo, Nancy Harmon
Poughkeepsie, NY
Tremayne, Eric F. .... Clayton, MO
Tremayne, Lay, Bauer, Coleman & Grady LLP .... Clayton, MO
St. Louis, MO
Tremayne, Pamela L., Law Offices of
Atlanta, GA
Tremayne, Sterling F. .... Juno Beach, FL
Tremba, Margaret A. .... Greensburg, PA
Tremba & Morman .... Greensburg, PA
Trembath, James R. .... Martinez, CA
Trembath, Jon R. .... Minneapolis, MN
Trembath Law Offices .... Oakland, CA
Pleasanton, CA
San Francisco, CA
Trembath, Peter H. .... St. Paul, MN
Trembath, Robin Y. .... Pleasanton, CA
Trembicki, Alexander J. .... Westport, CT
Tremblatt, John Y. .... San Diego, CA
Tremblay, Denise M. .... Boston, MA
Tremblay, Donald P. .... La Jolla, CA
Tremblay & Holsenback .... La Jolla, CA
Tremblay, Janet L. .... San Diego, CA
Tremblay, Kenneth R. .... Portsmouth, RI
Tremblay, Mary Adamowicz
Manchester, CT
Tremblay, Maurice C. .... San Diego, CA
Tremblay, Maurice C., A Prof. Corp., Law Offices of .... San Diego, CA
Tremblay, Maurile J. .... San Diego, CA
Tremblay, Michael J. .... Marlborough, MA
Tremblay, Paul R. .... Newton, MA
Tremblay, Peter D. .... New York, NY
Tremblay & Smith, LLP
Charlottesville, VA
Tremblay & Tremblay .... Marlborough, MA
Tremble, Angelique .... San Francisco, CA
Trembley, Anthony H. .... Oxnard, CA
Trembley, James .... Flint, MI
Trembley, M. Bushnell .... Flint, MI
Trembley & Trembley .... Flint, MI
Trembly, Lisa J. .... Newark, NJ
Trembowicz, Richard L. .... Boston, MA
Trembulak, Alan G. .... Cranford, NJ
Tremelling, Dennis S. .... Jackson, CA
Tremer, Gary S. .... Staten Island, NY
Tremiti, Ferdinand .... Brooklyn, NY
Tremiti, Joseph F. .... Wayne, NJ
Tremko, Norbert J. .... Chicago, IL
Treml, Brenda R. .... Minneapolis, MN
Treml, Colleen G. .... Cleveland, OH
Tremols, Joaquin A. .... Washington, DC
Tremont, Jason E. .... Bridgeport, CT
Tremont, Michael A. .... Syracuse, NY
Tremont & Sheldon, P.C. .... Bridgeport, CT
Tremont, T. Paul .... Bridgeport, CT
Tremont, Treg T. .... Washington, DC
Tremor, Diane D., (P.A.) .... Tallahassee, FL
Tremp, Robert P. .... Marquette, MI
Traverse City, MI
Tremp, Robert P., P.L.C. .... Marquette, MI
Traverse City, MI
Trempe, Thomas E. .... Springfield, OH
Tremper, Barbara Dockery .... Missoula, MT
Tremper, Bechert, Leonard & Terrill, Professional Corporation .... Fort Wayne, IN
Tremper, Charles Robert .... Arlington, VA
Tremper, Glenn E. .... Great Falls, MT
Trempus, Thomas R. .... Alcoa Center, PA
Tremsky, Walter .... New York, NY
Tremsyn, John P. .... Chagrin Falls, OH
Trenam, Kemker, Scharf, Barkin, Frye, O'Neill & Mullis, Professional Association
St. Petersburg, FL
Tampa, FL
Trenaman, Laura .... Houston, TX
Trenangen, John B. .... Midland, MI
Trenary, George H. .... Seven Points, TX
Trenbeath, Thomas L. .... Cavalier, ND
Trenberth, Jerry A. .... Las Vegas, NV
Trench, Christina C. .... Dallas, TX
Trench, David W., (P.A.) .... Miami, FL
Trench, Susan E. .... Miami, FL
Trenchard & Hoskins, L.L.P.
Roswell, NM
Kermit, TX
Odessa, TX
Trenchard, Louis B., III .... Houston, TX
Trenchard, Mara L. .... Princeton, NJ
Trenchard, Robert, Jr. .... Kermit, TX
Trenchard, Robert W. .... New York, NY
Trencher, Lewis J. .... Scarsdale, NY
Trencher, William M. .... Vienna, VA
Trenchi, Peter, Jr. .... Tullahoma, TN
Trenda, Regis J. .... Chicago, IL
Trendacosta, Anthony A. .... Los Angeles, CA
Trendacosta, Patricia Yamamoto
Los Angeles, CA
Trende, Colleen M. .... Delano, MN
Trendell, William P. .... Naperville, IL
Trendl, Thomas J. .... Washington, DC
Trendle, George W., Jr. .... Honolulu, HI
Trendler, Tracey Ging .... Philadelphia, PA
Trendowski, Jan C. .... Ivoryton, CT
Treneff, A. Terrance .... Newark, OH
Treneff, Craig P. .... Chicago, IL
Columbus, OH
Treneff & Williams .... Columbus, OH
Trenerry, John H., Jr.
Hot Springs National Park, AR
Trenerry, Julie E. .... Rochester, MN
Trenga, Anthony J. .... Washington, DC
Trengove, I. Johan .... Louisville, KY
Trenholm, Michael H. .... Riverside, CA
Trenholme, Steven .... Paradise, CA
Trenk, Alice Dinah-Szok
Sherman Oaks, CA
Trenk, Jos. .... New York, NY
Trenk, Joseph .... Sherman Oaks, CA
Trenk, Richard D. .... West Orange, NJ
Trenkle, Timothy P. .... Washington, DC
Trenkle, William P., Jr. .... Dodge City, KS
Trenkle, Wm. J. .... Jamaica, NY
Trennepohl, Donald L. .... Angola, IN
Trenner, Kathryn .... Princeton, NJ
Trenor, Fred C., II .... Philadelphia, PA
Pittsburgh, PA
Trenor, John A. .... Washington, DC
Trense, Charles F., Jr. .... Atlanta, GA
Trent, Adrienne Elise .... Viera, FL
Trent, B. Keith .... Dallas, TX
Trent, Beth L. .... Stamford, CT
Trent & Cohen, A Prof. Law Corp.
New Orleans, LA
Trent, Cynthia J. .... Atlanta, GA
Trent, Danny C. .... Bonner Springs, KS
Trent, Earl W., Jr. .... Valley Forge, PA
Trent, Edmund K. .... Pittsburgh, PA
Trent, Edward .... Irvine, CA
Trent, Edward H. .... Jacksonville, FL
Trent, J. Thomas, Jr. .... Nashville, TN

Trent, Jere C. ... Athens, AL
Trent, John C. ... Sterling, VA
Trent, Julie A. ... Denver, CO
Trent, Linda L. ... Boston, MA
Trent, Louis P. ... New Orleans, LA
Trent, Lucretia ... Salisbury, NC
Trent, Melanie M. ... Houston, TX
Trent, Patricia A. ... Las Vegas, NV
Trent, Patricia A., Ltd. ... Las Vegas, NV
Trent, Patricia L. ... Pleasanton, CA
Trent, Patti F. ... Colorado Springs, CO
Trent, Paul ... New York, NY
Trent, Steven H. ... Johnson City, TN
Trent, T. Christopher ... Houston, TX
Trent, Thomas A. ... Orangeburg, SC
Trent, William B., Jr. ... Muscatine, IA
Trent, William C. ... Louisville, KY
Trenta, Thomas J. ... Bloomfield Hills, MI
Trentacosta, Jack ... Detroit, MI
Trentacosta, John R. ... Southfield, MI
Trentacosta, Robert J. ... San Diego, CA
Trentacosta, Sam F. ... Mount Clemens, MI
Trentacoste, Linda M. ... White Plains, NY
Trentacoste, Mark C. ... Moorestown, NJ
Trentadue, Jesse C. ... Salt Lake City, UT
Trentadue, Michael A. ... Indianapolis, IN
Trentalange, Michael J. ... Tampa, FL
Trentalange, Michael J., P.A.
New Port Richey, FL
Tampa, FL
Trentelman, John C. ... Ocala, FL
Trentes, John H. ... Cleveland, OH
Trentham, Robert L. ... Nashville, TN
Trenti, John A. ... Virginia, MN
Trenti Law Firm ... Cook, MN
Virginia, MN
Trentman, Brian K. ... Belleville, IL
Trentman & O'Gara ... Belleville, IL
Trenz, Alan R. ... Cincinnati, OH
Trenz, William ... New York, NY
Trenzado, Maria E. ... Miami, FL
Treole, Louis F. ... Clifton, NJ
Treon, Daniel B. ... Phoenix, AZ
Treon, Richard T. ... Phoenix, AZ
Treon, Strick, Lucia & Aguirre, A Prof. Assn. of Lawyers ... Phoenix, AZ
Trepacz, Edmund J., II
Department of Education, Office of the General Counsel, GV
Trepagnier, Chris M. ... Lafayette, LA
Trepanier, Craig W. ... Minneapolis, MN
Trepel, Anthony J. ... San Jose, CA
Trepel & Clark ... San Jose, CA
Trepel, Jeffrey M. ... Charlotte, NC
Trepel, John E. ... Chicago, IL
Trepel, Joseph J. ... Silver Spring, MD
Treperinas, George S. ... Seattle, WA
Trepinski, Kathryn M. ... Los Angeles, CA
Trepod, Gary A. ... Lansing, MI
Trepp, Howard I. ... Brooklyn, NY
Trepp, Robert M. ... Yorktown Heights, NY
Treppa, James M. ... San Francisco, CA
Treppa, Michael S. ... San Francisco, CA
Treppa, Thomas L. ... Mount Clemens, MI
Trepper, Myron ... New York, NY
Treppiedi, Rocco N. ... Spokane, WA
Treptow, John A ... Anchorage, AK
Trerice, Roger ... Bay City, MI
Trerotola, Deborah A. ... Brooklyn, NY
Tresansky, John O. ... Arlington, VA
Tresback, Jill L. ... St. Louis, MO
Tresch, Gordon D. ... Buffalo, NY
Tresch, W. Kyle ... Tulsa, OK
Trescher, Robert L. ... Haverford, PA
Trescher, Susan ... Santa Barbara, CA
Treschitta, Nora ... Monroe, CT
Trescott, Robert L. ... Miami, FL
Trese, Dolores G. ... Muskegon, MI
Trese, Maureen L. ... Franklin, MI
Treseder, Anne ... San Francisco, CA
Tresemer, Kirk D. ... Denver, CO
Tresher, Frederick H., III
Daytona Beach, FL
New Smyrna Beach, FL
Tresidder, Stephen J. ... Okemos, MI
Treska, Edward J. ... Santa Ana, CA
Treski, Alan R. ... Bensalem, PA
Tresnicky, John M. ... Austin, TX
Tresnowske, John ... New York, NY
Tresnowski, Mark B. ... Westchester, IL
Trespalacios, Mario J. ... Miami, FL
Trespasz, Theodore A. ... Syracuse, NY
Trespasz, Theodore A., Jr. ... Syracuse, NY
Tress, Madeleine ... San Francisco, CA
Tressel, Harry K. ... Northbrook, IL
Tressel, Ruth A. ... Seattle, WA
Tresselt, Thomas F. ... Hartford, CT
Tresser, Benjamin I. ... San Francisco, CA
Tresslar, John E. ... St. Louis, MO
Tressler, Daniel A., II ... Orlando, FL
Tressler, Isaac J. ... Herndon, PA
Tressler, James A. ... Westerville, OH
Tressler, James M. ... Scranton, PA
Tressler, Jonathan H. ... Brownsville, OR
Tressler, Karen L. ... Aurora, OH
Tressler, Paul W. ... Norristown, PA
Tressler, Soderstrom, Maloney & Priess
Los Angeles, CA
Chicago, IL
Libertyville, IL
Waukegan, IL
Wheaton, IL
Newark, NJ
Tressler, Terry C. ... Silver Spring, MD
Trest, Roy D. ... Calabash, NC
Shallotte, NC
Trestan, Robert O. ... Boston, MA
Trester, Fredric W. ... Los Angeles, CA
Trester, Julie L. ... Chicago, IL
Trestick, Michael L. ... San Diego, CA
Trestman, Evan F. ... New Orleans, LA
Trestman, Harris F. ... Norfolk, VA
Trestman, Marlene ... Baltimore, MD
Trestman, Robert ... Plainview, NY
Treston, Sherry S. ... Chicago, IL
Tretbar, J. Margaret ... Kansas City, MO
Tretbar, William P. ... Wichita, KS
Treter, Mark C. ... Milwaukee, WI
Tretheway, Barbara E. ... Minneapolis, MN
Tretheway, Catherine M. ... Albany, NY
Trethewey, Jeffrey Clare ... Niagara Falls, NY
Trethewey, Nancy ... Denver, CO
Trethewey, Virginia M. ... Columbus, OH
Trethewy, Barbara S. ... Phoenix, AZ
Trethewy, Chess R. ... Salem, OR
Tretiak, Philip L. ... Treasury Department, Internal Revenue Service, GV
Tretola, Christopher Scott ... Somerville, NJ
Tretschok, Dale D. ... Tucson, AZ
Tretschok, McNamara & Patten, P.C.
Tucson, AZ
Tretta, Christopher M. ... Philadelphia, PA
Tretter, Andrew G. ... New York, NY
Tretter, Anna R. ... Boston, MA
Tretter, Charles C. ... Boston, MA
Tretter, Franklin E. ... New York, NY
Tretter, Ilyse Wolfe ... Scarsdale, NY
Tretter, James G. ... Wayne, NJ
Tretter, Lyndon M. ... New York, NY
Tretter, Maxwell H. ... Scarsdale, NY
Tretter, Robb L. ... New York, NY
Tretter, Thomas C. ... Haverhill, MA
Trettin, Marcie L. ... Austin, TX
Trettin, Richard T. ... Noblesville, IN
Trettis, R. Blaise ... Rockledge, FL
Trettis, Thomas T., Jr. ... Naples, FL
Treu, Kris H. ... Cleveland, OH
Treu, Rolf M. ... West Covina, CA
Treu, Steven B. ... San Antonio, TX
Treuer, Margaret Seelye ... Bemidji, MN
Treuer, Stephen D. ... Los Angeles, CA
San Diego, CA
Treuhaft, Joel S. ... Palm Harbor, FL
Treul, David F. ... Grand Rapids, MI
Treumann, Alice M. ... St. Louis, MO
Treumann, Goba & Podbelsek, P.C.
Chicago, IL
Treusch, Bradford L., Law Offices of
Los Angeles, CA
Treusch, Paul E. ... Los Angeles, CA
Treusdell, John R. ... Buffalo, NY
Treuting, Joseph B. ... Marksville, LA
Treutlein, John R. ... Hicksville, NY
Trevarrow, Paul B. ... Pinehurst, NC
Trevarthen, Donald S. ... Bloomington, MN
Trevarthen, Robert W. ... Wheaton, IL
Trevarthen, Susan L. ... Boca Raton, FL
Trevaskis, David Keller ... Glenside, PA
Trevathan, Charles L. ... Abilene, TX
Trevathan, Karen L. ... Louisville, KY
Trevathan, Richard ... Houston, TX
Trevelise, Andrew J. ... Philadelphia, PA
Trevelline, Michael J. ... Washington, DC
Trevelyan, Fiona S. ... Boston, MA
Trevena, John H ... Largo, FL
Trevena, Matthew L. ... Austin, TX
Trevenen, Calvin O. ... Upper Montclair, NJ
Treverton, William W. ... Bellevue, WA
Treves, Joseph M. ... San Pedro, CA
Trevethan, Robert E. ... San Diego, CA
Trevett, Lenweaver & Salzer, P.C.
Rochester, NY
Trevett, Thomas N. ... Rochester, NY
Trevey, John H. ... Lexington, KY
Trevey, John L., Jr. ... Treasury Department, Internal Revenue Service, GV
Trevey, Robert F. ... Lexington, KY
Trevillian, William C. ... Severn, MD
Trevillion, Charles H ... Cambridge, MA
Trevino, A. Stephen, (P.C.) ... Houston, TX
Treviño, Anthony, Jr. ... Laredo, TX
Trevino, A. U. ... San Antonio, TX
Treviño, Eddie, Jr. ... Brownsville, TX
Trevino, Elizabeth A. ... San Diego, CA
Trevino, Fern N. ... Chicago, IL
Trevino, Isabel ... Rio Grande City, TX
Trevino, Jacques E. ... Edinburg, TX
Trevino, J. C., III ... Laredo, TX
Trevino, Jerry J. ... Corpus Christi, TX
Trevino, John T. ... Palm Springs, CA
Trevino, John Valdemar, Jr. ... Houston, TX
Trevino & Leppert, L.L.P. ... Houston, TX
Trevino, Marc R. ... New York, NY
Trevino, Mari Garric ... Seattle, WA
Trevino, Mario A. ... San Antonio, TX
Treviño, Oscar G. ... Austin, TX
Treviño, Reneé ... Harlingen, TX
Trevino, Roel R. ... Pharr, TX
Trevino, Roel R., Law Offices of, P.C.
Pharr, TX
Trevino, Sergio A. ... Houston, TX
Trevino, Tito W. ... Fort Dodge, IA
Treviño-Lane, Lucia ... Charlotte, NC
Treviranus, Lisa A. ... Sterling, IL
Trevisan, Paolo M. ... Washington, DC
Trevisan, Raymond P. ... Parsippany, NJ
Trevisan, Rolfe D. ... North Andover, MA
Trevisan, Stephen C. ... Cherry Hill, NJ
Philadelphia, PA
Trevisan, Tanya Debevetz ... Boston, MA
Trevisani, Robert A. ... Boston, MA
Treviso, Edith W. ... Fresno, CA
Trevithick, Bruce A. ... San Francisco, CA
Trevithick, John A. ... Bethesda, MD
Trevithick, Ronald L. ... Los Angeles, CA
Trevor, Clark M. ... San Francisco, CA
Trevor, Curtis L. ... Moline, IL
Trevor, David Y. ... Minneapolis, MN
Trevor, Eunice ... Philadelphia, PA
Trevor, George S. ... San Francisco, CA
Trevor, Mary Benjamin ... Bloomington, MN
Trevorrow, Robert J. ... Point Pleasant, PA
Trevorrow, William B. ... Greensboro, NC
Trevors, Ellen P. ... Somerville, NJ
Trevvett, Edward A. ... Rochester, NY
Trew, Beverly Joyce ... Tulsa, OK
Trew, H. Chris ... Athens, TN
Trew, Mary S. ... Chicago, IL
Trew, Philip H., Jr. ... Weatherford, TX
Trew & Woodford ... Phoenix, AZ
Treweek, Sally A. ... Harrisburg, PA
Trewin, Michael G. ... New London, WI
Trewitt, Michael C., Jr. ... Ponca City, OK
Trewolla, David L. ... Jackson, MS
Treworgy & Baldacci ... Bangor, ME
Treworgy, Robert C. ... Bangor, ME
Treworgy, Virginia T. ... Plymouth, MA
Trexel, Emogene L. ... Harrisburg, PA
Trexell, Brian D. ... Milwaukee, WI
Trexler, Bushnell, Giangiorgi & Blackstone, Ltd. ... Chicago, IL
Trexler, C. DeForrest ... Allentown, PA
Trexler, Holly Kay ... Lawrence, KS
Trexler, Jeffrey A. ... St. Louis, MO
Trexler, John J. ... Chesterfield, VA
Trexler, Lisa Marie ... Chambersburg, PA
Trexler, Sheila S. ... Palm Desert, CA
San Diego, CA
Trexler, Stephen H. ... Fort Wayne, IN
Trey, Jeffrey S. ... New York, NY
Treyz, Debra B. ... New York, NY
Treyz, G. Victor ... New York, NY
Treyz, Mark Samuel ... Tacoma, WA
Treyz, Paul ... Eatonville, WA
Treyz, Susan M. ... White Plains, NY
Trezevant, William Francis ... Buffalo, NY
Trezise, John D. ...
Department Of The Interior, GV
Trezise, Peter L. ... Lansing, MI
Trezise, Sara J. ... Quincy, MA
Trezise, Thomas M. ... Baltimore, MD
Trezise, Walwyn M. ... Fairbury, IL
Trezza, Albert R. ... Red Hook, NY
Trezza, Ithurburn & Steidlmayer, A Professional Corporation ... Yuba City, CA
Trezza, John J. ... Yuba City, CA
Trezza, Kane & Effron ... Red Hook, NY
Trgovac, Thomas J. ... Washington, DC
Tri, William F. ... Everett, WA
Triades, Terry S. ... Bayside, NY
Triage Mediation Services Inc.
Philadelphia, PA
Trial Lawyers, P.C. ... Roanoke, VA
Triana, Gisela D. ... Austin, TX
Triana, Mariola C. ... Coral Gables, FL
Triana, Raymond F. ... San Francisco, CA
Triandafilou, Peter A. ... Seattle, WA
Trianfo, Dominic A. ... Columbus, OH
Triano, Jane M. Owens ... Haverhill, MA
Triano, Martin F. ... San Francisco, CA
Triano, Nicholas P., III ... Boston, MA
Triant, James ... Grand Rapids, MI
Triantafillou & Guérin, P.C. ... Cambridge, MA
Triantafillou, Katherine ... Cambridge, MA
Triantafilou, Alexander M.
Fort Thomas, KY
Triantaphyllis, Anastassios ... Houston, TX
Triantos, Robert D. ... Kailua-Kona, HI
Triarhos, Efthalia T. ... Fairfax, VA
Triarsi, John S. ... Elizabeth, NJ
Triarsi, Joseph J. ... Cranford, NJ
Trías, Alexander José ... New York, NY
Trías, Arturo ... San Juan, PR
Trías, Meléndez & Garay ... San Juan, PR
Trías, Peter J. ... San Juan, PR
Trias-Fraticelli, Michael ... Baltimore, MD
Trías-Monge, Jose ... San Juan, PR
Triay, Charles A., Law Offices of
Oakland, CA
Triay, Charles A., Law Offices of
San Francisco, CA
San Jose, CA
Triay, Michael A. ... Metairie, LA
Triba, Robert J. ... Boston, MA
Tribbe, Frank C. ... Penn Laird, VA
Tribbensee, Nancy E. ... Tempe, AZ
Tribbett, Charles A., III ... Chicago, IL
Tribbett, Donald J. ... Logansport, IN
Tribbett, John R. ... Crawfordsville, IN
Tribbey, Ann B. ... Midlothian, VA
Tribbie, Scott, Plummer and Padden
Cambridge, OH
St. Clairsville, OH
Tribbie, Thomas L. ... Cambridge, OH
Tribbitt, Charles R. ... New York, NY
Tribble, Douglas R. ... San Diego, CA
Tribble, Jack L. ... Rahway, NJ
Tribble, James E. ... Miami, FL
Tribble, Mark E. ... Chattanooga, TN
Tribble, Max LaLon, Jr. ... Houston, TX
Tribble, Philip E. ... Atlanta, GA
Tribble, Phillip M. ... Albany, NY
Tribble, Robert E., Jr. ... Cordova, TN
Memphis, TN
Tribble, Tarya A. ... Tampa, FL
Tribble, Wesson H. ... Houston, TX
Tribble, William A. ... Dallas, TX
Tribble, William L. ... Dublin, GA
Vidalia, GA
Tribble-Sinke, Jolene ... St. Paul, MN
Tribby, Cynthia M. ... Bonita Springs, FL
Tribby, Mary B. ... Denver, CO
Tribe, Deborah Lynn ... Portland, OR
Tribe, Laurence H. ... Cambridge, MA
Tribeck, Robert J. ... Harrisburg, PA
Tribell, Daniel ... Middlesboro, KY
Triber, David Roger ... Palo Alto, CA
Triber, Gregory A. ... Campbell, CA
Tribken, Bennett ... Falmouth, MA
Trible, Charles K. ... Richmond, VA
Trible, Michele L. ... Louisville, KY
Trible, Paul S., Jr. ... Newport News, VA
Virginia Beach, VA
Trible, Peter L. ... Mechanicsville, VA
Tribler Orpett & Crone, A Professional Corporation ... Chicago, IL
Tribler, Willis R. ... Chicago, IL
Tribolet, Craig E. ... Boulder, CO
Tribuch, Kenneth H. ... Pompano Beach, FL
Tribuiani, Danielle ... Philadelphia, PA
Tribulato, Bradley A. ... Omaha, NE
Tribulski, Jennifer H. ... Washington, DC
Tribush, Bruce I. ... Boston, MA
Tricarichi, Carla M. ... Cleveland, OH
Tricarichi, Charles S. ... Cleveland, OH
Tricarico, Christopher J. ... Los Angeles, CA
Tricarico, Joseph A. ... New York, NY
Tricarico, Joseph J. ... Martinsville, NJ
Tricarico, Michael J. ... New York, NY
Tricarico, Michael R. ... Boca Raton, FL
Tricarico, Vincent ... Los Angeles, CA
Trice, Ashton P. ... Treasury Department, Internal Revenue Service, GV
Trice, Deborah B. ... Lafayette, IN
Trice, Elisabeth Ann ...
Department of Education, GV
Trice, Eric A ... Portland, OR
Trice, Harley N., II ... Pittsburgh, PA
Trice, J. Edward, Jr. ... Thomaston, GA
Trice, James R., III ... Alexandria, VA
Trice, John G. ... Fayetteville, AR
Trice, John R. ... Elmira, NY
Trice, Judith A. ... Richmond, CA
Trice, Mary Elizabeth ... San Francisco, CA
Trice, Russell C. ... Los Angeles, CA
Trice, Terra Y. ... Los Angeles, CA
Trice, W. Berry ... Wilmington, NC
Trice, William H., III ... Little Rock, AR
Trice, Wilson R. ... Richmond, VA
Trichak, George A. ... Seattle, WA
Triche, Jane M. ... Napoleonville, LA
Triche, Risley C. ... Napoleonville, LA
Triche, Ronald J. ... New Orleans, LA
Trichel, Neil Martin ... Shreveport, LA
Trichilo, Bancroft, McGavin, Horvath & Judkins, P.C. ... Fairfax, VA
Trichilo, Benjamin J. ... Fairfax, VA
Trichka, Stephen J. ... Vienna, VA
Trichler, Timothy R. ... Jenison, MI
Trichon, Martin L. ... Philadelphia, PA
Trichter, J. Gary ... Houston, TX
Trick, Charles Jeffrey ... Petaluma, CA
Trick, Penny L. ... Middletown, CT
Trick, William W., Jr. ... Pompano Beach, FL
Trick, William Watson, Jr., P.A.
Pompano Beach, FL
Trickel & Leigh, P.A. ... Orlando, FL
Winter Park, FL
Tricker, David R. ... Atlanta, GA
Tricker, Edward H. ... Lincoln, NE
Tricker, Richard P. ... Los Angeles, CA
Tricker, Richard P., P.C. ... Los Angeles, CA
Trickey, Charles, III ... Mount Clemens, MI
Trickey, Elizabeth ... Santa Fe, NM
Trickey, Howard S. ... Anchorage, AK
Trickey, James C. ... Overland Park, KS
Trickey, Linda J. ... Alpharetta, GA
Trickey, Michael J. ... Seattle, WA
Trickey, Timothy M. ... Austin, TX
Trickey, Vonnieta E. ... Jefferson City, MO
Tricoci, Mario M. ... Chicago, IL
Tricoli, John M. ... Buffalo, NY
Tricomi, Charles W. ... New York, NY
Tricomi, Francis A. ... Casselberry, FL
Tridico, Laura Eilers ... McLean, VA
Triebel, Charles O., Jr. ... Oakland, CA
Trieber, Edward J. ... New York, NY
Triebes, David G. ... Grand Rapids, MN
Triebes, Margaret Woolverton
New Orleans, LA
Triebold, Claudius P.R. ... New York, NY
Triebsch, Christine A. ... Atlanta, GA
Triebsch, Robert E. ... Turlock, CA
Triebwasser, Jonah ... New Paltz, NY
Triebwasser, Wilma F. ... Washington, DC
Triedman, J. Russell ... Foster City, CA
Triedman, Melissa R. ... San Francisco, CA
Trief & Olk ... New York, NY
Trief, Ted E. ... New York, NY
Trieff, Daniel M. ... Morristown, NJ
Trieger, Abraham ... Chicago, IL
Triem, Frederick W. ... Petersburg, AK
Triem, Susan M. ... Eugene, OR
Triemstra, Duane T. ... Kalamazoo, MI
Triemstra, Paul L. ... Birmingham, MI
Trien, Jay W. ... Morristown, NJ
Trien, Robert M. ... New York, NY
Trienens, Howard J. ... Chicago, IL
Trier, Carolyn M. ... Fort Wayne, IN
Trier, Dana L. ... Washington, DC
Trier, Michael G. ... Des Moines, IA
Trier, Michael P. ... Chicago, IL
Trier, William C., Jr. ... Cleveland, OH
Trierweiler, B. D. (Dick) ... Cheyenne, WY
Trierweiler, Robert L. ... Indianapolis, IN
Trierweiler, Todd A. ... Portland, OR
Triesch, Harold J. ... Spokane, WA
Triesch, James R. ... Seattle, WA
Trieschmann, Gerald ... St. Louis, MO
Trieschmann, Gerald R., Jr.
St. Louis, MO
Trieshmann, Carl H. ... Atlanta, GA

Triest, Brent S. ... Southfield, MI
Triester, Stanton L. ... Bala Cynwyd, PA
Trietsch, Dennis R.
Federal Trade Commission, Office of Inspector General, GV
Trieu, John D. ... Tustin, CA
Trieweiler, David A. ... Seattle, WA
Trieweiler, Terry N. ... Helena, MT
Trifari, Norma M. ... Providence, RI
Trifelos, Geo. H. ... Canton, OH
Triff, Brent N. ... Newport Beach, CA
Triffin, Nicholas ... White Plains, NY
Triffler, Fay L. ... Chicago, IL
Triffletti, F. Steven ... Plymouth, MA
Triffo, Eve ... Los Angeles, CA
Trifiletti, Barry ... Louisville, KY
Trifiolis, Michael C. ... West Orange, NJ
Trifiro, Richard J. ... Framingham, MA
Trifon, Malcolm ... Oakland, CA
Trifovesti, Russell ... Austin, TX
Trigero, Jane L. ... Oakland, CA
Trigg, Alvin B. ... Lexington, KY
Trigg, Amanda S. ... Paterson, NJ
Trigg, Donald C. ... Indianapolis, IN
Trigg, Edward W., Jr. ... Anaheim, CA
Trigg, Hastings S., Jr. ... Wilmington, DE
Trigg, James A. ... Atlanta, GA
Trigg, John R. ... Denver, CO
Trigg, Linda S. ... Olathe, KS
Trigg, Mark G. ... Atlanta, GA
Trigg, Nicola J. ... Santa Ana, CA
Trigg, Paul R., Jr. ... Detroit, MI
Trigg, Robert S. ... Lancaster, PA
Trigg, Thomas W. ... Missoula, MT
Trigger, Grant R. ... Detroit, MI
Trigger, Larry J. ... Sterling Heights, MI
Triggiano-Hunt, Mary E. ... Milwaukee, WI
Triggs, Alan C ... Cincinnati, OH
Triggs, Casey R.
Federal Trade Commission, Bureau of Competition, GV
Triggs, Claudia J. ... Hartford, CT
Triggs, Clyde G. ... Morganton, NC
Triggs, D. Thomas ... Santa Monica, CA
Triggs, Daniel J., Jr. ... Taunton, MA
Triggs, Dennis R. ... Peoria, IL
Triggs, Doug ... Colorado Springs, CO
Triggs, Emily J. M. ... Yorktown Heights, NY
Triggs, G. Austin, Jr. ... Nashville, TN
Triggs, John F. ... New York, NY
Triggs, Matthew H. ... Boca Raton, FL
Triggs, Ronald E. ... Cheyenne, WY
Triggs, Ronald E., P.C. ... Cheyenne, WY
Trigiani, Joel P. ... Philadelphia, PA
Trigiani, Lucia Anna ... Tysons Corner, VA
Trigilio, John L. ... Buffalo, NY
Trigilio, Timothy S. ... Lorain, OH
Trigillo, Tracey ... Springfield, IL
Trigo, Andres J. Colberg ... San Juan, PR
Trigo, Manuel, Jr. ... McAllen, TX
Trigo, Patricia A. Biaggi ... Mayaguez, PR
Trigo, Sharon S. ... Laredo, TX
Trigoboff, Craig J. ... Fort Lauderdale, FL
Miami Beach, FL
Trigonoplos, Darren S. ... Washington, DC
Trigueiro, Gary L. ... Eugene, OR
Trikeriotis, Christopher ... Baltimore, MD
Trikeriotis, Christopher, P.C., Law Offices of
Baltimore, MD
Trill, Valerie L. ... Glendale, AZ
Trillanes, Mario, Jr. ... El Paso, TX
Triller, Todd R. ... New York, NY
Trilling, Barry J. ... Pittsburgh, PA
Trilling, Frederick L. ... Brighton, MA
Trilling, Helen R. ... Washington, DC
Trilling, Joel S. ... Asheville, NC
Trillo, Joseph ... Warwick, RI
Trim, Roger L. ... Sterling Heights, MI
Trimarche, Gregory D. ... Los Angeles, CA
New York, NY
Trimarchi, Peter C. ... New York, NY
Trimarco, Vincent J. ... Smithtown, NY
Trimas, Marvin ... Westland, MI
Trimbach, James L. ... Nashville, TN
Trimber, George R. ... Fort Worth, TX
Trimber, Richard F. ... Washington, DC
Trimble, Allen C. ... Corbin, KY
Trimble, Angela Dawn ... Parsons, KS
Trimble & Associates ... Houston, TX
Trimble & Associates, Ltd.
Minnetonka, MN
Trimble, Benson ... Nashville, TN
Trimble, Carl K. ... Milwaukee, WI
Trimble, Catharine W. ... Larchmont, NY
Trimble, Dale Lee ... The Woodlands, TX
Trimble, Dan ... Alexandria, VA
Trimble, David C. ... Lexington, KY
Trimble, Don ... Little Rock, AR
Trimble, Elizabeth ... San Francisco, CA
Trimble, Elizabeth H. ... Baltimore, MD
Trimble, Ernest C. ... Towson, MD
Trimble Firm, The, P.L.L.C.
The Woodlands, TX
Trimble, Foster and Soyars
Hopkinsville, KY
Trimble, Gene F. ... Modesto, CA
Trimble, Henry W., Jr. ... Syosset, NY
Trimble, Henry Weeks, III
Cape Neddick, ME
Trimble, Howard B. ... Princeton, IL
Trimble, J. Howard ... Atlanta, GA
Trimble, J. Mark ... Toledo, OH
Trimble, J. Montjoy ... Lexington, KY
Trimble, James G. ... Parkville, MO
Trimble, James J. ... Phoenix, AZ
Trimble, James T., Jr. ... Lake Charles, LA
Trimble & Jewell, P.C. ... Evansville, IN
Trimble, John C. ... Indianapolis, IN
Trimble, John D., Jr. ... El Dorado, AR
Trimble, John Gardner
San Francisco, CA
Trimble, John, Jr. ... Philadelphia, PA
Trimble, John W. ... Blackwood, NJ
Trimble, Kathy D. ... Scott Depot, WV
Trimble, King M. ... Denver, CO
Trimble, Lindsay & Shea ... Henderson, KY
Trimble, Lynne ... New York, NY
Trimble & Mann ... Corbin, KY
London, KY
Whitley City, KY
Williamsburg, KY
Trimble, Mary Jane S. ... Jacksonville, FL
Trimble, Melissa H. ... Atlanta, GA
Trimble, Melissa M. ... Clearwater, FL
Trimble, Melissa M., P.A. ... Clearwater, FL
Trimble and Nulan, P.C. ... Denver, CO
Trimble, P. Joseph ... Irvine, CA
Trimble, Paul D. ... Oklahoma City, OK
Trimble, Preston A. ... Norman, OK
Trimble, Robert M. ... Houston, TX
Trimble, Samantha B. ... Omaha, NE
Trimble, Sandra E. ... Washington, DC
Trimble, Sarah ... Los Angeles, CA
Trimble, Sherinian, & Varanini
Sacramento, CA
Trimble, South, III ... Washington, DC
Trimble, Stacy S. Pickett ... Greenbelt, MD
Trimble, Stephen A. ... Washington, DC
Trimble, Suzanne M. ... Sacramento, CA
Trimble, Tamara L. ... Winter Park, FL
Trimble, Terry L. ... Baltimore, MD
Trimble, Thomas B. ... Washington, DC
Trimble, Thomas D. ... North Chicago, IL
Trimble, Thomas L. ... Rapid City, SD
Trimble, Thomas V. ... Evansville, IN
Trimble, Thomas W. ... Columbus, OH
Trimble, Tony P. ... Minnetonka, MN
Trimble, Travis M. ... Macon, GA
Trimble, Walls ... Little Rock, AR
Trimble, William C., Jr. ... Baltimore, MD
Trimboli, Dennis B. ... Sandusky, OH
Trimboli, Jon A. ... Mentor, OH
Trimboli, Mary G. ... Toledo, OH
Trimboli, Michael C. ... Buffalo, NY
Trimboli, Stephen E. ... Hackettstown, NJ
Morristown, NJ
Trenton, NJ
Trimboli, Thomas A. ... Washington, DC
Trimbur, Catherine ... Berkeley, CA
Trimbur, John M. ... Modesto, CA
Trimingham, Erin M. ... Seattle, WA
Trimm, Chance L. ... Sacramento, CA
Trimm, Elizabeth S. ... Sacramento, CA
Trimm, James R. ... Rockville, MD
Trimm, Thomas W. ... Pittsburgh, PA
Trimmer, David A. ... Lancaster, OH
Trimmer, Glenn W. ... Baltimore, MD
Trimmer, Harold S., Jr. ... Sausalito, CA
Trimmer, J. Francis ... Casper, WY
Trimmer, J. Kevin ... Troy, MI
Trimmer, Jeannie M. ... Maryville, MO
Rock Port, MO
Trimmer, J.W. ... Jefferson City, MO
Trimmer, Kathleen S. ... Reno, NV
Trimmer, Suanne Tiberio
Bloomfield Hills, MI
Trimmer, Vicky Ann ... Harrisburg, PA
Trimmier, C. Stephen ... Birmingham, AL
Decatur, AL
Dothan, AL
Mobile, AL
Trimmier, Chip ... West Palm Beach, FL
Trimmier Law Firm ... Birmingham, AL
Decatur, AL
Dothan, AL
Mobile, AL
Trimmier Law Firm ... Boca Raton, FL
Fort Lauderdale, FL
Panama City, FL
West Palm Beach, FL
Trimmier, Roscoe, Jr. ... Boston, MA
Trimpa, Ted J. ... Denver, CO
Trimpe, Robert T. ... Champaign, IL
Trimper, George J. ... Buffalo, NY
Trimper, George, Jr. ... Buffalo, NY
Trimper, Glen A. ... Alexandria, VA
Trimper, John S. ... West Palm Beach, FL
Trimper, Paul D. ... Watertown, NY
Trimpey, Taralyn T. ... Pittsburgh, PA
Trimpi, John G. ... Elizabeth City, NC
Trimpi & Nash ... Elizabeth City, NC
Trinchard, Clare Willis ... New Orleans, LA
Trinchard, James L. ... Abita Springs, LA
New Orleans, LA
Trinchard and Trinchard, A Professional Corporation ... Abita Springs, LA
New Orleans, LA
Trinchero, Mark P. ... Portland, OR
Trindade, Tamera C. ... Redding, CA
Trindel, Robin M. ... Tampa, FL
Trinder, Rachel B. (IBA) ... **Washington, DC**
Trindl, Rick D. ... Waukesha, WI
Trine & Metcalf, P.C. ... Boulder, CO
Trine, William A. ... Boulder, CO
Trinen, Donald T. ... Denver, CO
Triner, Jeanne E. ... Oak Park, IL
Tringali, Donald J. ... Beverly Hills, CA
Tringali, Joseph A. ... West Palm Beach, FL
Tringali, Joseph F. ... New York, NY
Tringali, Joseph J. A. ... Eastchester, NY
Tringali, Joseph J.A., Jr. ... White Plains, NY
Tringas, Allison M.
Fort Walton Beach, FL
Tringe Law Off., P.C. ... Holdrege, NE
Tringe, William A., Jr. ... Holdrege, NE
Trinh, Cam Ngoc Nguyen ... Houston, TX
Trini, Gene A. ... Honolulu, HI
Trinidad, J.C., III ... Seattle, WA
Trinidad, Joveliand S., Jr. ... Reston, VA
Trinity, Frank R.
Corporation for National and Community Service, Office of the General Counsel, GV
Trinity, Joseph F. ... Clinton, NJ
Trink, Jocelyn Posser ... Holbrook, NY
Trinka, Timothy Edward
Washington, DC
Trinker, Deborah Shur ... Boca Raton, FL
Trinker, Steven T. ... Columbia, MD
Trinker, Vincent D. ... Rochester, NY
Trinkle, Catherine A. ... Morristown, NJ
Trinkle, Daniel B. ... Boston, MA
Trinkle, Redman, Swanson, Byrd & Coton, P.A. ... Plant City, FL
Trinkle, Robert P. ... West Point, PA
Trinkle, Robert S. ... Plant City, FL
Trinkle, William J. ... Oakland, CA
Trinklein, Anne A. ... Dallas, TX
Trinklein, Jeffrey M. ... Dallas, TX
Trinkler, Michael A. ... Boca Raton, FL
Trinkler, Rebecca S. ... Aventura, FL
Trinkler, Robert M. ... Sunrise, FL
Trinkley, Caroline G. ... Buffalo, NY
Trinkley, Jane W. ... Columbia, SC
Trinkoff, Alexandra ... Great Neck, NY
Trinkoff, Paul D. ... Baltimore, MD
Trinley, Alicia ... West Palm Beach, FL
Trinley, Paul T. ... West Palm Beach, FL
Trinnaman, John E. ... Costa Mesa, CA
Trinrud, Richard J. ... Rock Island, IL
Trinz, Jeffrey A. ... Miami, FL
Trio, Edward A. ... Chicago, IL
Triola, Jane L. ... Pearl River, LA
Triolo, Frank C., (P.A.) ... Cape Coral, FL
Triolo, Margaret Ann ... Greenwich, CT
Triolo, Pamela ... New York, NY
Triolo, Priscilla J. ... River Edge, NJ
New York, NY
Triolo, Richard P. ... San Rafael, CA
Trionfini, Sandra A. ... North Canton, CT
Tripathi, Ashok K. ... Los Angeles, CA
Tripathi-Zutshi, Ira ... Milford, MA
Tripi, Cecelia A. ... Costa Mesa, CA
Tripi, Cynthia ... Alexandria, VA
Tripi, Joseph A. ... Portland, OR
Tripi, Kevin M. ... Costa Mesa, CA
Tripi, Philip G. ... Cleveland, OH
Tripician, Carl N. ... Atlantic City, NJ
Longport, NJ
Northfield, NJ
Tripidakis, John ... Bethlehem, PA
Triplet, James M. ... Spokane, WA
Triplett, Aaron R. ... Portsmouth, OH
Triplett, Anthony R.
North Wilkesboro, NC
Triplett, Charles, P.S.C. ... Louisville, KY
Triplett, Charles S. ... Washington, DC
Triplett, Constance L. ... Grand Forks, ND
Triplett, Ernest E. ... Barstow, CA
Triplett, Gary Joe ... Charleston, WV
Triplett, George R. ... Elkins, WV
Triplett, George R., L.C. ... Elkins, WV
Triplett, George V., IV ... Owensboro, KY
Triplett, Henry A. ... Louisville, KY
Triplett, James B. ... Oxford, MA
Triplett, John E., Jr. ... Marietta, OH
Triplett, John R. ... Los Gatos, CA
Triplett, John R. ... Lowmansville, KY
Triplett, Linda ... Portland, OR
Triplett, Marc S. ... Bellefontaine, OH
Triplett, Martha S. ... Meriden, CT
Triplett, Oliver B., III ... Forest, MS
Triplett, P. Garrett ... Corpus Christi, TX
Triplett, Pamela M. ... St. Louis, MO
Triplett, Rick ... Austin, TX
Triplett, Robert M. ... Thousand Oaks, CA
Triplett, Robin Queen ... Clarksburg, WV
Triplett, Rosemary A. ... Chicago, IL
Triplett, Royal T. ... Newton, NC
Triplett, Thomas C. ... Wichita, KS
Triplett, Thomas J. ... St. Paul, MN
Triplett, Thomas M. ... Bend, OR
Portland, OR
Triplett, Timothy W. ... Overland Park, KS
Kansas City, MO
Triplett, Woolf & Garretson, LLC
Wichita, KS
Triplette, Constance W. ... Jackson, MS
Tripodes, Peter L. ... Pasadena, CA
Tripodi, David E. ... New York, NY
Tripodi, Joseph ... Roseland, NJ
Tripodi, Joseph I., (Co., L.P.A.)
New Philadelphia, OH
Tripodi, Kellie A. ... Forest Hills, NY
Tripodi, Paul D., II ... Los Angeles, CA
Tripodi, Wendy C. ... Dallas, TX
Tripodis, Vasiliki L. ... Boston, MA
Pelham, NH
Tripodo, Paul A. ... Livingston, NJ
Tripodoro, John A. ... New York, NY
Tripoli, Joseph S. ... Princeton, NJ
Tripoli, Linda A. ... San Francisco, CA
Tripoli, Lori N. ... Bedford, NY
Tripoli, Louis J. ... Syracuse, NY
Tripolone, Philip ... Syracuse, NY
Tripolsky, Howard A. ... Boston, MA
Tripp, Alexander D. ... New York, NY
Tripp, Annette L. ... Houston, TX
Tripp, C. Warren, Jr. ... Jacksonville, FL
Tripp, Charles Henry ... Skiatook, OK
Tripp, David E. ... Richardson, TX
Tripp, David H. ... Hastings, MI
Tripp, David H., P.C. ... Hastings, MI
Tripp, David L. ... Detroit, MI
Tripp, David R. ... Kansas City, MO
Tripp, Delores C. ... Southfield, MI
Tripp, Delores C., P.C. ... Southfield, MI
Tripp, Dennis F. ... Portland, OR
Tripp, Dennis F., P.C. ... Portland, OR
Tripp, Douglas S. ... Cincinnati, OH
Tripp, Gregory J. ... Spokane, WA
Tripp, Guy T., III ... Richmond, VA
Tripp, Heather S. ... Fort Lauderdale, FL
Tripp, Henry Franklin ... Plano, TX
Tripp, James T. B. ... New York, NY
Tripp, Karen B. ... Houston, TX
Tripp, Laresa ... Salt Lake City, UT
Tripp, Lisa Caroline ... Atlanta, GA
Tripp, Mark L. ... Des Moines, IA
Tripp, Mary Beth ... St. Louis, MO
Tripp, Michael R. ... Columbia, MO
Tripp, Norman D. ... Fort Lauderdale, FL
Tripp, Pamela R. ... Lansing, MI
Tripp, Pamela R. ... Okemos, MI
Tripp, Patrick L., P.C. ... Omaha, NE
Tripp, Paul W. ... Tampa, FL
Tripp, Paula G. ... Los Angeles, CA
Tripp, Roger S. ... Lexington, NC
Tripp, S. Stephanie ... Lakeside, CA
Tripp, Samuel C. ... Edina, MN
Tripp Scott ... Fort Lauderdale, FL
Tripp, Steven J. ... Woodbridge, NJ
Tripp, Susan Gaden ... New York, NY
Tripp, Susan M. ... Salem, OR
Tripp, Theodore L., Jr. ... Fort Myers, FL
Tripp, Thomas G. ... Clearwater, FL
Tripp, Thomas G. ... Pinellas Park, FL
Tripp, Thomas G. ... St. Petersburg, FL
Tripp, Thomas N. ... Gahanna, OH
Tripp, Timothy N. ... Des Moines, IA
Pella, IA
Tripp, Toby G. ... Odessa, TX
Tripp, Todd D. ... Cedar Rapids, IA
Tripp, Wallace M. ... Owatonna, MN
Tripp, Warren A. ... Olympia, WA
Tripp, Wendy S. ... Centralia, WA
Tripp, William H. ... Bloomfield Hills, MI
Tripp, William V., III ... Boston, MA
Trippany, Diane M. ... Bath, NY
Trippe, Allan M. ... Birmingham, AL
Trippe, Charles M., Jr. ... Jacksonville, FL
Trippe, David R. ... Decatur, GA
Trippe, Hillery Bolt ... Crockett, CA
Trippe, Melissa L. ... Raleigh, NC
Trippe and Positano ... Brooklyn, NY
Trippeer, Allen R., Jr. ... Birmingham, AL
Trippel, Craig D. ... Fresno, CA
Trippel, Michael A. ... Elkhart, IN
Mishawaka, IN
Trippel, Philip J. ... Parkersburg, WV
Trippet and Kee ... Beaver, OK
Hooker, OK
Trippet, Richard P. ... Beaver, OK
Hooker, OK
Trippett, Lewis Paul ... New York, NY
Trippett, Lillian M. ... Bethesda, MD
Trippi, Clay ... Halifax, NC
Trippi, Maurice C. ... Hammond, LA
Tripple, Herbert M. ... St. Paul, MN
Triptow, Janice Lynn ... Chicago, IL
Triptow, Susan G. ... St. Louis, MO
Tris, Mary Severson ... Lincolnshire, IL
Trischler, Clem C., Jr. ... Pittsburgh, PA
Triscoli, Donna F. ... Baltimore, MD
Triska, Richard E. ... Lebanon, OR
Trisko, Eugene M. ... Berkeley Springs, WV
Trisler, Patsy J. ... San Diego, CA
Rockville, MD
Trismen, Raymond R. ... New York, NY
Trismen, Richard F. ... Winter Park, FL
Trissell, Stanley L., Jr. ... Dayton, OH
Trissell, Teresa Dondlinger
Department of Justice, Tax Division, GV
Tristani, Gloria
Federal Communications Commission, Office of the Commissioners, GV
Tristani, King ... Cheyenne, WY
Tristano, Ceil A. ... Hickory Hills, IL
Tristano, Michael T. ... Hickory Hills, IL
Trister, Michael B. ... Washington, DC
Tristine, Joseph R. ... New Haven, CT
Tritak, John S. ... Washington, DC
Tritell, Randolph W. (IBA)
Federal Trade Commission, Bureau of Competition, GV
Tritico, Christopher L. ... Houston, TX
Tritico, Louis A. ... Kansas City, MO
Tritico, Russell T., A P.L.C.
Lake Charles, LA
Tritico, Russell T., Jr. ... Lake Charles, LA
Tritico, Russell T., Sr. ... Lake Charles, LA
Tritsch, Bruce A. ... Livingston, NJ
Tritsch, Jerre A. ... Omaha, NE
Tritsch, Peter R. ... Centerville, MA
Tritsch, Robert G. ... New York, NY
Tritsch, Steven A. ... Livingston, NJ
Tritschler, Richard Dana ... Tallahassee, FL
Tritschler, Ronald C. ... Lexington, KY
Tritt, Arnold D., Jr. ... Jacksonville, FL
Tritt, Arnold, P.A., & Associates
Jacksonville, FL
Tritt, Cheryl A. ... Washington, DC
Tritt, Deloise E. ... Fresno, CA
Tritt, Earl F. ... San Diego, CA
Tritt, James F. ... Fresno, CA
Tritt, Lee-ford ... New York, NY
Tritt, Robert E. ... Atlanta, GA
Tritt, Roy D. ... Martinez, GA
Tritt & Tritt ... Fresno, CA
Tritt, William C. ... Cleveland, OH
Tritter, Daniel F. ... New York, NY
Tritter, David M. ... Houston, TX

Trittipo, Michael A. .... Minneapolis, MN
Trittipo, Walter E. .... Chicago, IL
Trittipo, Walter E., P.C. .... Chicago, IL
Tritto, Vincent B. .... New York, NY
Tritz, Jerry L. .... New York, NY
Trivas, Jill R. .... Bel Air, MD
Trivas, Stanley I. .... Columbia, MD
Trivedi, Harit U. .... Chicago, IL
Trivedi, Sara N. .... Los Angeles, CA
Trivella, Scott P. .... Thornwood, NY
Trivelli, Annette C. .... Cleveland, OH
Trivelli, Vincent M. .... Charleston, WV
Trivelpiece, Paul A. .... Syracuse, NY
Trivers, Oscar .... Cleveland, OH
Trivers, Patricia Anne .... Lanham, MD
Trivett, Larry M. .... Marysville, WA
Trivette, W. Sidney .... Pikeville, KY
Trivette, William S. .... Greensboro, NC
Trivisonno, Susan E. .... San Jose, CA
Triviz, Edward E. .... Las Cruces, NM
Triviz, Edward E., P.A. .... Las Cruces, NM
Trizna, Robert J. .... Chicago, IL
Trkla, Kathryn M. .... Chicago, IL
Troast, Arthur L. .... Hackensack, NJ
Trobaugh, Connie G. .... Morristown, TN
Trobaugh, Phillip J. .... Minneapolis, MN
Trobe, Peter M. .... Waukegan, IL
Troberg, John A. .... Colville, WA
Troberg Law Firm .... Colville, WA
Troberman, Richard J. .... Seattle, WA
Troberman, Richard J., P.S. .... Seattle, WA
Trobich, Robert K. .... Charlotte, NC
Trobman, Malcolm H. .... Cherry Hill, NJ
Trobman, Richard M. .... New York, NY
Trobough, Tobin J. .... Irvine, CA
Trocano, Russell P. .... Ridgewood, NJ
Trocchio, Daniel P. .... Pittsburgh, PA
Troccia, Michael .... Elmira, NY
Troch, Kathryn G. .... Jarrettsville, MD
Troche, Jose E. .... El Paso, TX
Trocheck, Christina Marie .... Salina, KS
Trocino, Craig Joseph
Fort Lauderdale, FL
Trocino, Frank P. .... Elizabeth, NJ
Trock, Alan L. .... Van Nuys, CA
Trock, Kevin C. .... Chicago, IL
Trock, Yael .... Los Angeles, CA
Trocke, Michael T. .... Tampa, FL
Trockman, Howard P. .... Evansville, IN
Trockman, Wayne S. .... Evansville, IN
Trodden, James M. .... Belmont, MA
Trodden, Nancy F. .... Boston, MA
Trodden, Richard E. .... Arlington, VA
Trodden, Selena E. .... Mineola, NY
Trodella, Robert A. .... San Francisco, CA
Troe, Charles H. .... Los Angeles, CA
Troegel, Maria B. .... Houston, TX
Troeger, J. Scott .... Elkhart, IN
Troeger, Merle M. .... Denver, CO
Troell, A. Richard .... Crestview, FL
Troelstrup, John .... Oak Park, IL
Troelstrup Law Office .... Chicago, IL
Oak Park, IL
Troemel, Michael B. .... Indianapolis, IN
Kokomo, IN
Lafayette, IN
Troemper, April Gowdy .... Springfield, IL
Troesch, Hans R. .... Menlo Park, CA
Troese, Stephen J. .... Camp Springs, MD
Troese, Stephen J., P.A., Law Offices of
Camp Springs, MD
Troesken-Koczur, Lora .... Chicago, IL
Troester, Edmund M. .... Saginaw, MI
Troester, James F. .... Frankenmuth, MI
Saginaw, MI
Troetti, Thomas J. .... Elmsford, NY
Trofa, Gretchen Anne .... Chicago, IL
Trofa, M. John .... Chicago, IL
Trofemuk, Lori J. .... La Jolla, CA
Trofemuk, Nicholas Joseph, Jr. .... Fresno, CA
Troff, Eric L. .... Los Angeles, CA
Troff, Petzke & Ammeson .... St. Joseph, MI
Troff, Theodore E. .... St. Joseph, MI
Troffkin, Howard J. .... Columbia, MD
Trofimov, Alison Dyer .... Lebanon, NJ
Trofino, Ralph J. .... Johnstown, PA
Trog, JoAnn .... St. Louis, MO
Trogan, Anthony V., Jr.
Bingham Farms, MI
Trogan, Bruce F. .... Saginaw, MI
Trogan, Jos. J. .... Saginaw, MI
Trogan, Nicholas R., III .... Saginaw, MI
Trogan and Trogan, P.C. .... Saginaw, MI
Trogani, Lari Jean .... Colorado Springs, CO
Trogdon, Benjamin K. .... Washington, DC
Trogdon, Terry A. .... Duluth, MN
Troge, Ann M. .... Charles City, IA
Troger, Jay R. .... Boston, MA
Troglia, Brian W. .... Chicago, IL
Troglin, William M. .... Norcross, GA
Troglin, William M., P.C. .... Norcross, GA
Trogolo, Robert J. .... Bartow, FL
Troha, George P. .... Joliet, IL
Troha, Jane C. .... Shaker Heights, OH
Troha, Philip A. .... Joliet, IL
Trohaugh, Dennis W. .... McKees Rocks, PA
Trohn, Jonathan B. .... Lakeland, FL
Trohn, Robert L. .... Lakeland, FL
Troia, Anthony R. .... Cleveland, OH
Troia, Anthony S. .... Omaha, NE
Troia, Antonella .... New York, NY
Troia, Carl Joseph, Jr. .... Omaha, NE
Troia, Joseph S. .... Omaha, NE
Troia Law Offices .... Omaha, NE
Troia, Richard A. .... Omaha, NE
Troiani, Dolores M. .... Paoli, PA
Troiani, James P. .... Martinsville, IN
Troiani, John .... Chicago, IL
Troiani, Michael J. .... Philadelphia, PA
Troiani, P. James .... Indianapolis, IN
Troiano, Anthony .... Charlestown, MA
Troiano, Anthony .... Charlestown, MA
Troiano, Brian L. .... Washington, DC
Troiano, D. A. .... Lakeland, FL
Troiano, Gabriele J. .... Staten Island, NY
Troiano, Gene .... Chevy Chase, MD
Troiano, James G. .... Cedar Grove, NJ
Troiano, Joann P. .... Farmington, CT
Troiano, John G. .... Longboat Key, FL
Troiano, Joseph .... Springfield, MA
Troiano, Joseph A. .... Portland, ME
Troiano, Marie L. .... Boston, MA
Troiano, Michael F. .... Brooklyn, NY
Troiano, Nicholas J. .... Lakeland, FL
Troiano & Roberts, P.A. .... Lakeland, FL
Troiano, Victor J. .... Lakeland, FL
Troidl, Frank S. .... Phillipsburg, NJ
Troidl, Robert H. .... Department of the Navy, Office of the Judge Advocate General, GV
Troike, Robert L. .... Washington, DC
Troilo, Arthur C. .... San Antonio, TX
Troilo, Frank T. .... Philadelphia, PA
Troilo, Louis M. .... Washington, DC
Troisi, James J. .... Salem, NH
Troisi, Joseph G., Jr. .... St. Marys, WV
Troisi, Michael E. .... New York, NY
Troisi Professional Association .... Salem, NH
Troisi, Ralph .... Waverly, WV
Trojack, John E. .... West St. Paul, MN
Trojan, David G. .... Enid, OK
Trojan, Edward P. .... Chicago, IL
Trojan Law Offices .... Beverly Hills, CA
Los Angeles, CA
Trojan, R. Joseph .... Beverly Hills, CA
Trojan, Thomas E. .... Las Vegas, NV
Trojanowski, Helen .... Wellesley, MA
Trojanowski, John .... New York, NY
Trojnar, Jacqueline A. .... Hartford, CT
Troka, William G. .... Joliet, IL
Trokenheim, Michael .... New York, NY
Trokey, Carolyn L. .... Santa Monica, CA
Trokey, Matthew F. .... Branson, MO
Trokie, Douglas S. .... New York, NY
Troland, Charles E., Jr. .... Roanoke, VA
Troll, F. Robert, Jr. .... Greenbelt, MD
Troll, John R., Jr. .... Ann Arbor, MI
Troll, Raymond C. .... Latham, NY
Troller, David E. .... Cincinnati, OH
Trolley, J. Daniel .... Bloomingdale, IL
Trollinger, Monica Ramirez
San Antonio, TX
Trollinger, Tona .... Olathe, KS
Trollope, Richard C. .... Panama City, FL
Trolman, David S. .... New York, NY
Trolman, Michael P. .... New York, NY
Trolson, S. Douglas .... Indianapolis, IN
Trom, C. Stanley .... Ventura, CA
Trombacco, Jeffrey M. .... Tustin, CA
Trombadore, Ann W. .... Somerville, NJ
Trombadore, David W. .... Somerville, NJ
Trombadore, J. Thomas
San Francisco, CA
Trombadore, John J. .... Somerville, NJ
Trombadore, Raymond R. .... Somerville, NJ
Trombadore, Raymond R. & David W., P.C.
Belvidere, NJ
Flemington, NJ
New Brunswick, NJ
Trombadore, Raymond R., & David W., P.C.
Somerville, NJ
Trombadore, Sarah J. .... Saratoga Springs, NY
Trombatore, Benjamin J. .... Prescott, AZ
Trombello, John W. .... Dallas, TX
Tromberg, Fred .... Jacksonville, FL
Tromberg, Jeffrey H. .... Jacksonville, FL
Trombetta, A. Peter .... Santa Rosa, CA
Trombetta, Carmine V. .... Chicago, IL
Trombetta, Christopher J. .... Boston, MA
Trombetta, I. Bernard .... Cleveland, OH
Trombetta, Patricia J. .... Cincinnati, OH
Trombetta, William L. .... Philadelphia, PA
Trombi, Heidy Berger .... Los Angeles, CA
Trombino, John J. .... Phoenix, AZ
Trombino, Lawrence P. .... Naperville, IL
Trombley, David H. .... Farmington, MI
Trombley, Edward J. .... Plattsburgh, NY
Trombley, Gary R. .... Tampa, FL
Trombley & Hanes .... Tampa, FL
Trombley, J. Kirk .... Portsmouth, NH
Trombley, J. Todd .... Houston, TX
Trombley, Lobozzo, Schommer, Disler & Accorsi, A Prtnshp. incl. Prof. Assns.
Sebring, FL
Trombley, M. Lesa .... Alvin, TX
Trombley, Michael J., (P.A.) .... Sebring, FL
Trombley, Wilson J. .... Wolcott, CT
Trombly, Amy Moss
Securities and Exchange Commission, Division of Corporation Finance, GV
Trombly, Angela M. .... Stamford, CT
Trombly, Arthur L. .... Keene, NH
Trombly, Charles W., Jr. .... Andover, MA
Trombly, Edward J. .... Albany, NY
Trombly, Joseph S. .... Andover, MA
Trombly, Kenneth M. .... Washington, DC
Trombly, Kenneth M., P.C.
Washington, DC
Trombly, Mark E. .... Bingham Farms, MI
Trombly, Richard W. .... Southfield, MI
Trombly, Ricky Alan .... Boscawen, NH
Trombly, Robert Matthew .... Parker, CO
Trombly, Sally T. .... Cambridge, MA
Trombo, Joseph L.
Department of the Air Force, Office of the General Counsel, GV
Tromello, Michael .... New York, NY
Trommald, John Eric .... Seal Beach, CA
Trompeter, Kirk .... Phoenix, AZ
Trompeter, Philip .... Salem, VA
Trompeter, Ronald J. .... Seattle, WA
Trompeter, Schiffman, Petrovits, Friedman & Hulse, L.L.P. .... Phoenix, AZ
Trompeter, Thomas R. .... Dallas, TX
Trompke, Edward H. .... Portland, OR
Trompler, Vicky Ann .... Dallas, TX
Tron, Geula Ziva .... Southfield, MI
Tron, Lanny M. .... Alamo, CA
Tron, Terry L. .... Walnut Creek, CA
Troncelliti, Manrico A., Jr. .... Norristown, PA
Pottstown, PA
Wynnewood, PA
Troncelliti & Morgan .... Norristown, PA
Wynnewood, PA
Tronco, Larry H. .... New York, NY
Troncone, Frederick R. .... Washington, DC
St. Louis, MO
Troncone, Mark A. .... Brick, NJ
Troncoso, Alberto J. .... New York, NY
Troncoso, Francisco M. .... San Juan, PR
Troncoso, Teresa B. .... Tampa, FL
Trone, Darren P. .... Riverside, CA
Trone, Darren P., A Professional Corporation
Riverside, CA
Trone, Doane Kent .... Troy, IL
Trone, Robert E. .... Edwardsville, IL
Trone, Sophia Grant .... Los Angeles, CA
Trongard, Dean Allen
Brooklyn Park, MN
Trono, James M. .... Agawam, MA
Tronolone, Carl .... Buffalo, NY
Tronolone, Daniel G. .... Buffalo, NY
Tronolone, Robert J. .... Buffalo, NY
Tronolone & Surgalla, P.C. .... Buffalo, NY
Tronquet, Michael C. .... Seattle, WA
Tronrud, Beverly G. .... Billings, MT
Tronson, Gregory W. .... Department of Labor, Office of the Solicitor, GV
Tronstein, Barbara Kahn .... Warren, MI
Tronstein, Steven L. .... Warren, MI
Tronto, Nora J. .... New Hyde Park, NY
Tronvig Law Firm .... Sacramento, CA
Tronvig, Robert C., Jr. .... Sacramento, CA
Tronvold, Jeffrey R. .... Cedar Rapids, IA
Troobnick, Mark Nathan .... Washington, DC
Trooboff, Peter D. .... Washington, DC
Troodler, Meryl Canetti .... Nanuet, NY
Trooien, Dennis J. .... Minneapolis, MN
Trook-White, Eve .... Huntsville, TX
Troop, Andrew M. .... Boston, MA
Troop, Richard E. .... Los Angeles, CA
Troop Steuber Pasich Reddick & Tobey, LLP
Los Angeles, CA
Troop, W. Michael .... Frankfort, KY
Troope, Lesley Ann .... Atlanta, GA
Trop, Adam .... Naples, FL
Trop, Gary M. .... Jamaica, NY
Trop, Harriet .... Chicago, IL
Trop, M. Marc .... North Bellmore, NY
Trop, Mark Andrew .... Miami, FL
Trop, Michael L. .... Fort Lauderdale, FL
Trop, Robert E. .... Garden City, NY
Trope, Edward C., Jr. .... Richmond, VA
Trope, Eugene L. .... Los Angeles, CA
Trope, Jack F. .... Washington, DC
Trope, James G. .... Sarasota, FL
Trope, Michael L. .... Los Angeles, CA
Trope, Sorrell .... Los Angeles, CA
Trope and Trope .... Los Angeles, CA
Tropiano, Joseph J. .... Derry, NH
Tropin, Harley S. .... Miami, FL
Tropio & Morlan .... Canoga Park, CA
Tropio, Scott T. .... Canoga Park, CA
Tropp, Arlene .... Mount Kisco, NY
Tropp, Charles R. .... Staten Island, NY
Tropp, Daniel E. .... Miami, FL
Tropp, Deborah S. .... Santa Ana, CA
Tropp, Edmund W. .... Detroit, MI
Tropp, Harvey .... Mount Kisco, NY
Tropp, Jonathan B. .... Stamford, CT
Tropp, Laurence H.
Department of Agriculture, Food and Consumer Service, GV
Tropp, Matthew E. .... New York, NY
Tropp, Richard W. .... Irvine, CA
Tropp, Robert A. .... Tampa, FL
Tropp, Stephen W. .... Sacramento, CA
Tropp, Thomas H. .... Philadelphia, PA
Tropp & Tropp .... Mount Kisco, NY
Tropper, Joshua .... Atlanta, GA
Troppmann, Susan W. .... Spokane, WA
Troppoli, Ronald J. .... Neptune, NJ
Trosch, Carl V. .... Pittsburgh, PA
Trosch, Louis A. .... Charlotte, NC
Trosch, William C. .... Charlotte, NC
Trosclair, Carlton J. .... Washington, DC
Trosclair, Frank P., Jr. .... Opelousas, LA
Trosclair, Jennifer M. .... Baton Rouge, LA
Trosen, Wallace W. .... Kirksville, MO
Trosen and Williams, P.C. .... Kirksville, MO
Troshynski, Martin J. .... North Platte, NE
Trosino, James .... Palo Alto, CA
Tross, Evangeline W. .... Newark, NJ
Tross, Roberta Lynn .... New York, NY
Tross, Scott T. .... Princeton, NJ
New York, NY
Trossello, Judith T. .... Quincy, MA
Trosset, Edward J. .... Cooperstown, NY
Richfield Springs, NY
Trosset, Michael Edward .... Boston, MA
Trossevin, Marguerite E.
Department of Commerce, Office of the General Counsel, GV
Trossman, Herbert D. .... New York, NY
Trost, Charles A. .... Columbia, TN
Nashville, TN
Trost, Eileen Bannon .... Chicago, IL
Trost, Glenn W. .... Los Angeles, CA
Trost, J. Douglas .... Boston, NY
Trost, J. Ronald .... New York, NY
Trost, Janet .... Las Vegas, NV
Trost, Jay S. .... Rockford, IL
Trost, Jonathan H. .... Rochester, NY
Trost, Kevin .... Madison, WI
Trost, Kirk E. .... Sacramento, CA
Trost, Lonn A. .... New York, NY
Trost, Michael J. .... Atlanta, GA
Trost, Randall J. .... Lynchburg, VA
Trost, Randall J., P.C. .... Bedford, VA
Danville, VA
Lynchburg, VA
Trost, Richard M. .... Brighton, MI
Trost, Richard W. .... San Diego, CA
Trost, Scott T. .... Burbank, CA
Trost, Steven R. .... New York, NY
Trost, Thomas G. .... Sacramento, CA
Trost, Timothy J. .... Buffalo, NY
Trost, Virginia V. .... Lynchburg, VA
Trosten, Leonard M. .... Washington, DC
Trostle, J. Kay .... Austin, TX
Trostle, Keith A. .... Wilmington, DE
Trostle, Mary Pat .... Wilmington, DE
Trostle, Patrick J. .... Hartford, CT
Trostle, Richard S. .... New York, NY
Trostle, Terriann .... Houston, TX
Trostle, W. M. .... Cleveland, OH
Trostler, Flora .... Los Angeles, CA
Trostorff, Alex P. .... New Orleans, LA
Trostorff, Danielle Lombardo
New Orleans, LA
Trost-Walker, Kelly Jo .... Oklahoma City, OK
Trosty, Ronald J. .... Lansing, MI
Trosvig, Derek A. .... Alexandria, MN
Troth, Glenn Hancock .... Paulding, OH
Troth, Hugh L. .... Ashland, OH
Troth, Rebecca K. .... Department of Justice, Civil Rights Division, GV
Troth, Thomas M. .... Frankfort, KY
Troth & Van Tilburg .... Ashland, OH
Trotman, John R. .... Philadelphia, PA
Trotman, Mary E. .... Falls Church, VA
Trotman, Paul F. .... Marstons Mills, MA
Trotman, Thane C.J. .... West Chester, PA
Trotner, Arvey Abraham .... Bethlehem, PA
Trotner, Robert S. .... Easton, PA
Trott, David A. .... Bingham Farms, MI
Trott, Dennis C. .... New York, NY
Trott, Emil, Jr. .... Larchwood, IA
Trott, Jack E. .... Houston, TX
Trott, John Matthew .... Los Angeles, CA
Trott, John S. .... Petaluma, CA
Trott, Kara J. .... Columbus, OH
Trott, Larry J. .... Modesto, CA
Trott, Merideth A. .... Dayton, OH
Trott, Sophia Loren .... Mount Vernon, NY
Trott, Stephen S. .... Boise, ID
Trott, Terry A. .... Hudson, MI
Trott, Thomas G. .... The Woodlands, TX
Trott, Timothy J. .... West Chester, PA
Trott & Trott, A Professional Corporation
Bingham Farms, MI
Detroit, MI
Trott, William M. .... Raleigh, NC
Trotta, Anthoney .... Baltimore, MD
Trotta, Antonio, III .... New York, NY
Trotta, Frank P., Jr. .... Cos Cob, CT
Greenwich, CT
New Rochelle, NY
Trotta, Frederick J. .... New Haven, CT
Trotta, Joseph F. .... New Haven, CT
Trotta Law Firm .... Cos Cob, CT
Greenwich, CT
New Rochelle, NY
Trotta, Louis .... New York, NY
Trotta, Marlo Ann .... Baltimore, MD
Trotta, Robert D. .... Millerton, NY
Trotta, Robert M. .... Princeton, NJ
Trotta, Thos. N. .... Ocean Park, WA
Trotta, Trotta & Trotta .... New Haven, CT
Trotter, Charles L., Jr. .... Huntingdon, TN
Trotter & Cooper .... Bethesda, MD
Trotter, Daphne .... Washington, DC
Trotter, David W. .... Walnut Creek, CA
Trotter, Donna M. .... Vernal, UT
Trotter, Elizabeth P. .... New Orleans, LA
Trotter, Frank D. .... Wichita Falls, TX
Trotter, Gayle Leslie Shafer .... McLean, VA
Trotter, Gene .... Columbia, SC
Trotter, Haynie Seay .... McLean, VA
Trotter, J. David .... Austin, TX
Trotter, J. David, A Professional Corporation
Austin, TX
Trotter, J. Jeffrey .... Jackson, MS
Trotter, Jack T. .... Washington, DC
Trotter, James R. .... Raleigh, NC
Trotter, Joel H. .... Washington, DC
Trotter, John C. .... Houston, TX
Trotter, John K., Jr. .... Santa Ana, CA
Trotter, Joseph A., Jr. .... Bethesda, MD
Trotter, Julia Anne .... Washington, DC
Trotter, Katie Murff .... Los Angeles, CA
Trotter, Lawrence R. .... Anchorage, AK
Trotter, Louis J., Jr. .... Bethesda, MD
Trotter, Mary F. .... Tampa, FL
Trotter, Mary F., P.A. .... Tampa, FL
Trotter, Matthew N. .... Long Beach, CA
Trotter, Michael H. .... Atlanta, GA
Trotter, Michael J. .... Long Beach, CA
Trotter, Patsy A. .... Oklahoma City, OK
Trotter, Rhonda Renee .... Los Angeles, CA
Trotter, Richard Clayton
San Antonio, TX

Trotter, Scott C. ...Little Rock, AR
Trotter, Stephen D. ...Fort Wayne, IN
Trotter, Steven D. ...Irvine, CA
Trotter, Thomas R. ...Akron, OH
Trotter, Virgil W. ...Kansas City, MO
Trotter, W. Stacy ...Odessa, TX
Trotter, William A., III ...Augusta, GA
Trotter, William A., III, P.C. ...Augusta, GA
Trotter, William C., III ...Belzoni, MS
Trotter, William H., Jr. ...Charlotte, NC
Trotter, William P. ...La Grange, GA
Trotter, Wilson N. ...Memphis, TN
Trotti, Isabelle ...Los Angeles, CA
Trotti, Joseph ...Bayside, NY
Trotti, Robert S. ...Dallas, TX
Trottier, Lori A. ...Boston, MA
Trottier, Mark W. ...Royal Oak, MI
Trottier, Richard O. ...Durham, NC
Trottner, Mary Ellen ...West Allis, WI
Trotto, Anthony J. ...Wood Dale, IL
Trotto, Christopher D. ...Rochester, NY
Trotto, Hertha C. ...Hauppauge, NY
Trotto, Stephen P. ...Chicago, IL
Trotz, Corey B. ...Memphis, TN
Trotz, John William ...Baltimore, MD
Trotz-Cosgrove, Christine ...Johnstown, PA
Trotzig, Marten A. ...Le Mars, IA
Trotzky, Katie ...St. Paul, MN
Troubh, Heisler & Piampiano, P.C.
Portland, ME
Troubh, Raymond S. ...New York, NY
Troubh, William B. ...Portland, ME
Troublefield, G. Glennon ...Philadelphia, PA
Trouche, J. Paul ...Charleston, SC
Troue, Gary P. ...Troy, NY
Troue, J. Paul ...Troy, NY
Troue, Sherry M. ...Troy, NY
Troughton, John D. ...Evanston, WY
Troughton, Mathew R. ...San Jose, CA
Troughton, Megaret ...San Francisco, CA
Troum, Mark S. ...Winter Park, FL
Troum & Wallsh, Chartered Law Offices of
Orlando, FL
Winter Park, FL
Troumouliaris, Michael J. ...Merrillville, IN
Troup, Christnacht, Ladenburg, McKasy & Durkin, Inc., P.S. ...Tacoma, WA
Troup, David P. ...Junction City, KS
Manhattan, KS
Troup, James U. ...Washington, DC
Troup, John B. ...Tacoma, WA
Troup, Robert R. ...Valhalla, NY
Troup, Steven ...New York, NY
Troupe, Edwina L. ...Davis, CA
Troupe, Warren L. ...Denver, CO
Troupe, William H. ...Boston, MA
Troupis, Christ T. ...Boise, ID
Troupis, Christ T. ...Mendota, IL
Troupis, James R. ...Madison, WI
Trousdale, Albert J., II ...Florence, AL
Trousdale, Elmer B. ...St. Paul, MN
Trousdale, Heath F. ...Florence, AL
Trousdale, Jeremy N. ...Birmingham, AL
Trousdale, Preston S., Jr. ...Florence, AL
Trousdale, William H. ...Newark, NJ
Trousdell, William O. ...Washington, DC
Trout, Brett J. ...Des Moines, IA
Trout, David G. ...Chicago, IL
Trout, Ellen M. ...St. Paul, MN
Trout, George I. ...Greensburg, PA
Trout, Gloria E. ...Oklahoma City, OK
Trout, Gregory C. ...Columbus, OH
Trout, Howard T., III
Cape May Court House, NJ
Trout, Jay L. ...York, PA
Trout, Jeffrey P. ...Colchester, VT
Trout, Joan D. ...Des Moines, IA
Trout, Jodi Barone ...York, PA
Trout, John T. ...Minneapolis, MN
Trout, Joseph D. ...Terre Haute, IN
Trout, Kevin K. ...Oklahoma City, OK
Trout, Kim J. ...Boise, ID
Trout, Linda Copple ...Boise, ID
Trout, Linda S. ...Kansas City, MO
Trout, Nevin J. ...York, PA
Trout, Perry, Jr. ...San Diego, CA
Trout & Raley, P.C. ...Denver, CO
Trout & Richards, P.L.L.C.
Washington, DC
Alexandria, VA
Trout, Robert L. ...Grain Valley, MO
Trout, Robert P. ...Washington, DC
Alexandria, VA
Trout, Robert V. ...Denver, CO
Trout, Scott C. ...St. Louis, MO
Trout, Stephen Walker ...Pittsburgh, PA
Trout, Stran L. ...Richmond, VA
Trout, Susan J. ...Lakewood, CO
Trout, Thomas R. ...New Albany, MS
Trout, William J. ...Des Moines, IA
Troutdale Law Firm, Richard A. Weill, P.C.
Gresham, OR
Troutdale, OR
Trouten, David S., Jr. ...St. Clairsville, OH
Troutman, Andrew Craig ...Knoxville, TN
Troutman, Anne O'Brien ...Cambridge, MA
Troutman, Becky L. ...San Francisco, CA
Troutman, Charles H., III ...Hagåtña, GU
Troutman, Conrad E., Jr. ...La Follette, TN
Troutman, Conrad M. ...Knoxville, TN
Troutman, Courtland W. ...New York, NY
Troutman, E. Mac ...Reading, PA
Troutman, Forrest N. ...Austin, TX
Troutman, Forrest N., II ...Bastrop, TX
Troutman, Frank, Jr. ...Mableton, GA
Troutman, Gayle L. ...Tulsa, OK
Troutman, Harry B. ...Louisville, KY
Troutman, Henry B., Jr. ...Atlanta, GA
Troutman, J. Gregory ...Louisville, KY
Troutman, Jay W. ...Washington, PA
Troutman, Jennifer Carson ...Louisville, KY
Troutman, John C. ...Irvine, CA
Troutman, Lori McFarlin ...Houston, TX
Troutman, Mark T. ...Kingwood, TX
Troutman, Matthew Barry ...Louisville, KY
Troutman, Michael K. ...High Point, NC
Troutman, Michael W. ...Lexington, KY
Troutman, Nancy K. ...St. Louis, MO
Troutman, Reid ...Knoxville, TN
Troutman, Richard B. ...Winter Park, FL
Troutman, Richard B., P.A. ...Orlando, FL
Winter Park, FL
Troutman, Russell ...Winter Park, FL
Troutman Sanders LLP ...Washington, DC
Atlanta, GA
Troutman, Ted A. ...Portland, OR
Troutman, William Harris ...Columbia, SC
Troutman, Williams, Irvin, Green & Helms, Professional Association ...Kissimmee, FL
Orlando, FL
Oviedo, FL
Winter Park, FL
Troutman-Cheek, Tracy L. ...Orlando, FL
Troutt Alexander Popit & Warner, P.C.
Benton, IL
Troutt, Christopher A. ...Arlington, TX
Troutt, Jeff ...Benton, IL
Troutt, Jeffery D. ...Juneau, AK
Troutt, Randy ...Wichita, KS
Troutt, Sarah Rhoads ...Salem, OR
Troutt, Shawn D. ...New York, NY
Troutwine, Gayle L. ...Portland, OR
Trovarelli, Mario J. ...Fox Island, WA
Trovarelli, Michael ...Philadelphia, PA
Trovato, David M. ...North Andover, MA
Trovato, Joseph ...New York, NY
Trovato, Lisa R. ...Washington, DC
Trovato, Mark J. ...Westerly, RI
Trovato, Nicholas F. ...Chicago, IL
Trover, Ellen Lloyd ...Thousand Oaks, CA
Trover, Stephen P. ...Chico, CA
Trovillion, D. P. ...San Diego, CA
Trovillion, Wilfred W. ...San Diego, CA
Trovini, Josephine ...New York, NY
Trovini, Michael D. ...New York, NY
Trovini, Vincent P. ...Hackensack, NJ
Trovini, Vincent P., A Professional Corporation
Hackensack, NJ
Trow, Griffith H. ...Stamford, CT
White Plains, NY
Trow, Jd ...San Francisco, CA
Trow & Kearney, P.C. ...Washington, DC
Trow, Michael Edward ...Portland, OR
Trow, Randolph E., Jr. ...Richmond, VA
Trow & Sank, P.C. ...Greenwich, CT
Stamford, CT
White Plains, NY
Trow, Stephen C. ...Washington, DC
Trow, W. Clark ...Buffalo, NY
Trowbridge, Ann L. ...Sacramento, CA
Trowbridge & Basine, P.C.
Glastonbury, CT
Trowbridge, Brett C. ...Olympia, WA
Trowbridge, C. Pfeiffer ...Stuart, FL
Trowbridge, Charles L. ...New York, NY
Trowbridge, Christopher B. ...Dallas, TX
Trowbridge, David C. ...Kansas City, MO
Trowbridge, Douglas H.
Redondo Beach, CA
Trowbridge, Fred M., Jr.
New Orleans, LA
Trowbridge, Frederick N., Jr.
Green Bay, WI
Trowbridge, George Fox, Jr. ...Fairfax, VA
Trowbridge, Glen M. W. ...Los Angeles, CA
Trowbridge, Jeffery D. ...Oakland, CA
Trowbridge, Kara A. ...Rockville, MD
Trowbridge Law Firm, P.C. ...Detroit, MI
Trowbridge, Nancy W. ...New York, NY
Trowbridge, Newman, Jr. ...Franklin, LA
Trowbridge, Paul K.
Department Of Veterans Affairs, Veterans Benefits Administration, GV
Trowbridge, Penelope C. ...Chicago, IL
Trowbridge, Robert L. ...Glastonbury, CT
Trowbridge, Susan M. ...Portland, OR
Trowbridge, Suzanne Jett
Charleston, WV
Trowbridge, Thomas R., III
New York, NY
Trower, C. Christopher ...Atlanta, GA
Trower, E. Dale ...Denver, CO
Trower, Shannon ...Ventura, CA
Trower, Suzanna L. ...Kansas City, MO
Trower, Thomas H. ...Tulsa, OK
Trowhill, Richard ...Bad Axe, MI
Troxel, John E. ...Charlotte, NC
Troxel, Theodore J. ...Pensacola, FL
Troxell, Christopher ...San Francisco, CA
Troxell, D. Chase ...New York, NY
Troxell, Elizabeth M. ...Dublin, OH
Troxell, Emily D. ...Dana Point, CA
Troxell, F. N. "Buddy" ...Houston, TX
Troxell, Gary F. ...Millburn, NJ
Troxell, James D. ...Cleveland, OH
Troxell, Keith Chase ...McLean, VA
Troxell, Kincaid & Mullin, P.L.L.C.
Leesburg, VA
McLean, VA
Troxell, Richard H H ...Columbus, OH
Troxell, Susan L. ...Philadelphia, PA
Troy, Alexander ...New York, NY
Troy, Anthony F. ...Richmond, VA
Troy, Bartley J. ...Cleveland, OH
Troy, Bernard E. ...New York, NY
Troy, Brian J. ...Buffalo, NY
Troy, Brigitta B., (Mrs.) ...Los Angeles, CA
Troy, Christian R. ...Charlotte, NC
Troy, Christopher L. ...Philadelphia, PA
Troy, Daniel E. ...Washington, DC
Troy, Denise H. ...Phoenix, AZ
Troy, F.G. (Jamie), II ...Portland, OR
Troy, Frank J., Sr. ...Akron, OH
Troy, Frank T. ...Haddonfield, NJ
Troy, Gerald A. ...Bellevue, WA
Troy, Gordon E. R. ...Warren, VT
Troy & Gould, Professional Corporation
Los Angeles, CA
Troy, Gregory R. ...Roseville, MN
Troy, James J. ...Binghamton, NY
Troy, Jeffrey D. ...Fort Myers, FL
Troy, John F. ...Hartford, CT
Troy, John F. ...Salem, NH
Troy, John G., Jr. ...Longview, TX
Troy, Joseph F. ...Los Angeles, CA
Troy, Joseph M. ...Appleton, WI
Troy, Joseph P. ...Schuylkill Haven, PA
Troy, Kathleen E. ...McLean, VA
Troy, Kathleen M. ...Brooklyn, NY
Troy Law Firm, P.S. ...Bellevue, WA
Troy, Lawrence M. ...Cranbury, NJ
Troy, Lynne Ellen ...New York, NY
Troy, Mark A. ...Dallas, TX
Troy, Mark A., A Professional Corporation
Dallas, TX
Troy, Mark E. ...Charleston, WV
Troy, Mark R. ...Los Angeles, CA
Troy, Marti A. ...Phoenix, AZ
Troy, Mary Tate ...Duxbury, MA
Troy, Matthew J. ...Department of Justice, Civil Division, GV
Troy, Matthew J., III ...Garden City, NY
Troy, Matthew J., Jr. ...Westbury, NY
Troy, Megan H. ...Washington, DC
Troy, Michael A. ...Washington, DC
Troy, Michael C. ...Durham, NC
Troy, Michael J. ...Washington, DC
Troy, Paul C. ...Norristown, PA
Philadelphia, PA
Troy, Paul E. ...Boston, MA
Troy, Paul M. ...Everett, MA
Troy, Richard H. ...Aurora, CO
Troy, Richard J. ...Chicago, IL
Troy, Richard J. ...Everett, MA
Troy, Richard L. ...New York, NY
Troy, Richard M., Jr. ...New Orleans, LA
Troy, Robert P. ...San Diego, CA
Troy, Robert Sweeney ...Sandwich, MA
Troy, Stephen C. ...New York, NY
Troy, Steven Jared ...Baltimore, MD
Troy, Steven P. ...Joliet, IL
Troy, Stuart ...New York, NY
Troy, Susan J. ...Los Angeles, CA
Troy, Terry ...Chicago, IL
Troy, Thomas C. ...Reading, MA
Troy, Timothy J. ...Midland, MI
Troy, William J., III ...Ithaca, NY
Troy & Yeslow, P.A. ...Fort Myers, FL
Naples, FL
Troyan, Francis G. ...Bethlehem, PA
Troyan, Gary M. ...Columbus, OH
Troyan, Michele McCormick
Newport Beach, CA
Troyanovich, Michael G. ...Warren, MI
Troyer, Brian ...Cleveland, OH
Troyer, Craig ...New York, NY
Troyer, Glenn T. ...Indianapolis, IN
Troyer, John ...Minneapolis, MN
Troyer, Loraine P. ...Goshen, IN
Troyer, Lucinda Rauhuff ...Bartlett, TN
Troyer, Matthew T. ...Indianapolis, IN
Troyer, Phillip J. ...Fort Wayne, IN
Troyer, Robert W. ...Ponchatoula, LA
Troyer, Steven A. ...New York, NY
Troyer, Terence M. ...Boston, MA
Troyer, Thomas A. ...Washington, DC
Troyer, Tracy L. ...Fort Wayne, IN
Troyka, William D. ...Boston, MA
Trozpek, Robin Weeks ...Claremont, CA
Trozzolillo, Anthony P. ...Mansfield, OH
Trpis, Martin ...Washington, DC
Truax, Daniel S. ...Stockton, CA
Truax, James C. ...Chicago, IL
Truax, Judd E. ...Cedar Falls, IA
Truax, Judith L. ...Boston, MA
Truax, Keely ...Chicago, IL
Truax, Kenneth M. ...Hastings, MN
Truax, Kerry A. ...Rochester, MN
Truax, Kerry A. ...Rochester, MN
Truax, Lonnie ...Monterey, CA
Truax, Louise T. ...Westport, CT
Truax, Michael H. ...Orlando, FL
Truax, SaraLloyd ...Poughkeepsie, NY
Truax, Susan K. ...Department of Commerce, Office of the General Counsel, GV
Truax, Terrence J. ...Chicago, IL
Truax, Thomas T. ...Salem, MA
Truax, Timothy M. ...Los Angeles, CA
Truax, William H. ...Columbus, OH
Truba, William L. ...Clinton, MI
Truban, John W. ...Winchester, VA
Trubatch, Sheldon L. ...Washington, DC
Trube, John E. ...Tyler, TX
Trubek, Josephine S. ...Rochester, NY
Trubek, Louise G. ...Madison, WI
Trubenbach, Jack G. ...Trenton, NJ
Trubey, Marilyn M. ...Topeka, KS
Trubiano, Mark A. ...Cleveland, OH
Trubin, Andrew J. ...New York, NY
Trubin, Edna G. ...New York, NY
Trubin, John ...New York, NY
Trubitsky, Marina ...New York, NY
Trubitt, Ari M. ...Chicago, IL
Trubitt, Hayden J. ...San Diego, CA
Trubitt, Hillard J. ...Bloomington, IN
Trubman, Howard K. ...Philadelphia, PA
Trubo, Herbert A. ...Portland, OR
Trubow, George B. ...Chicago, IL
Truby, John ...Appleton, WI
Truby, Phyllis Alden ...Los Angeles, CA
Truby, Phyllis Alden ...Santa Monica, CA
Truby, Timothy J. ...Akron, OH
Trucano, Jennifer K. ...Rapid City, SD
Trucano, Michael ...Minneapolis, MN
Trucchi, Teresa Ann ...San Diego, CA
Trucco, John A., Jr. ...Wausau, WI
Trucco, Michael T. ...Chicago, IL
Truce, W. Joseph ...Long Beach, CA
Los Angeles, CA
Truce, Walter ...Aptos, CA
Truchinski, Steven W. ...Oshkosh, WI
Trucios-Haynes, Enid ...Louisville, KY
Truck Injury Lawyers, LLP ...San Diego, CA
Truckenbrod, Donald W. ...McHenry, IL
Trucker Huss, A Professional Corporation
San Francisco, CA
Trucker, Lee A. ...San Francisco, CA
Trucks, J. Karl ...Panama City, FL
Trucks, J. Karl, P.A. ...Panama City, FL
Trucks, J. Todd ...Clare, MI
Trucks, Jacqueline A. ...Wetumpka, AL
Trucks, Jay F. ...Clare, MI
Trucks, Michael G. ...Fairfield, AL
Trucks and Trucks ...Fairfield, AL
Trucksess, Lin M. ...San Francisco, CA
Trude, Gareth P. ...Riverside, CA
Trude, William W., Jr. ...Irvine, KY
Trudeau, Daniel J. ...St. Paul, MN
Trudeau, Gerard F. ...Middlebury, VT
Trudeau, Jane A. ...Lexington, MA
Trudeau, John J., Jr. ...Rockville, MD
Trudeau, Karl Joseph ...Springfield, OR
Trudeau, Mark A. ...Cedar Knolls, NJ
Trudeau, Michael A. ...Barnstable, MA
Trudeau, Penelope D. ...New Hope, MN
Trudeau, Robert S. ...San Antonio, TX
Trudeau, Roger J. ...Bedford Park, IL
Trudeau, Ronald W. ...Dandridge, TN
Trudeau, Stephanie E. ...Cleveland, OH
Trudel, Gerard ...Allen Park, MI
Trudel, Glen P. ...Newark, DE
Trudel, James R. ...Nashville, TN
Trudel, Paul A. ...Greenfield, MA
Trudel, Valerie A. ...Toledo, OH
Trudell, Jayne G. ...Minneapolis, MN
Trudell, Jereen G. ...Auburn Hills, MI
Trudell, Kathleen A. ...Santa Ana, CA
Trudell, Patrick A. ...Kirkland, WA
Truden, Colleen D. ...Glenwood Springs, CO
Trudgen, Robert R. ...Jackson, CA
Trudgeon, Jon H. ...Oklahoma City, OK
True, Bobby Knox ...Bedford, KY
True, Calvin E. ...Bangor, ME
Blue Hill, ME
True, Edward L. ...Wichita Falls, TX
True, Gary E. ...Edwardsville, IL
True, J. Guthrie ...Frankfort, KY
True, J. Robert ...Batavia, OH
True, James R. ...Aspen, CO
True, Jenninfer O. ...Ashland, KY
True, John C. ...Chicago, IL
True, John M., III ...San Francisco, CA
True, Joi C. ...Palo Alto, CA
True, Kim Anderson ...North Yarmouth, ME
True, Lawrence Y. ...San Diego, CA
True, Mary R. ...Columbus, OH
True, Ronald C. ...Asheville, NC
True, Roy B. ...Kansas City, MO
True, Roy J. ...Dallas, TX
True, Sadhna ...Department of Justice, Civil Division, GV
True, Sally Thompson ...Ithaca, NY
True & Shackelford, LLP ...Dallas, TX
True, Walsh & Miller, LLP ...Ithaca, NY
Trueax, John W. ...Englewood, CO
Trueb, Lanning M. ...Anchorage, AK
Trueba, William R. ...Miami, FL
Truebenbach, Paul R. ...San Francisco, CA
Trueblood, Alexander B. ...Mill Valley, CA
Trueblood & Amacher ...Norristown, PA
Trueblood, Brooks G. ...Hillsboro, OH
Trueblood, Craig S. ...Seattle, WA
Trueblood, David Randall
Salt Lake City, UT
Trueblood, D. Randall, A Professional Corporation ...Salt Lake City, UT
Trueblood & Graham ...Lafayette, IN
Trueblood, J. Michael ...Lafayette, IN
Trueblood Law Firm ...Terre Haute, IN
Trueblood, Samuel J. ...Norristown, PA
Trueblood, Stephen L. ...Terre Haute, IN
Truebner, Peter L. ...Stamford, CT
Trueheart, Harry P., III ...New York, NY
Rochester, NY
Trueheart, John H., Jr. ...Houston, TX
Truel, Robert B. ...Pittsburgh, PA
Truel, Timothy M. ...Milwaukee, WI
Truell, James H. ...Grand Island, NE
Truell, Murray & Walters
Grand Island, NE
Truelove, David J. ...Morrisville, PA
Truelove, Dee Ann R. ...Livingston, AL
Truelove & Dee, LLP ...Boston, MA
Truelove, John M. ...Boston, MA
Truelsen, Charles H. ...Omaha, NE
Truelsen, Roy Lawrence ...Portland, OR
Truelson, Raymond L. ...Minneapolis, MN
Truelson, Robert B., II ...Dallas, TX
Truelson, Roy W. ...Rochester, MN
Trueman, David Lawrence ...New York, NY
Trueman, Elizabeth J. ...Palo Alto, CA
Trueman, Jeffrey A. ...Baltimore, MD

Truemper, Hollingsworth, Wojtecki, Courtin & Titiner ... Aurora, IL
Truemper, Roger Lea ... Wilmington, DE
Truemper, William J. ... Aurora, IL
Trueschler, John G. ... Lutherville, MD
Truesdale, Bruce C. ... Cherry Hill, NJ
Truesdale, Daniel C. ... Tinley Park, IL
Truesdale, John C. National Labor Relations Board, Board Members, GV
Truesdale, Michael S. ... Austin, TX
Truesdale, Nancy J. ... Princeton, NJ
Truesdale, Tracey L. ... Chicago, IL
Truesdell, Alfred ... Cocoa, FL **Orlando, FL**
Truesdell, Clifford A. ... Cambridge, MA
Truesdell, Kellean K. ... Dunnellon, FL
Truesdell, Kellean K., P.A. ... Dunnellon, FL
Truesdell, Laurie S. ... Greensboro, NC
Truesdell, Lynn G. ... Minneapolis, MN
Truesdell, Mark E. ... Des Moines, IA
Truesdell, Richard D., Jr. ... New York, NY
Truesdell, Scott ... Richmond, KY
Truesdell, Scott, P.S.C. ... Richmond, KY
Truett, Charla ... Dallas, TX
Truett, Elizabeth M. ... New Orleans, LA
Truett, William T. ... Duluth, GA
Trueworthy, Robin C. ... Kansas City, MO
Truex, A.L. ... Dallas, TX
Truex, Bruce A. ... Farmington Hills, MI
Truex and Earnest, P.A. ... Davie, FL
Truex, Mark E. ... Oklahoma City, OK
Truex, Shelley A. ... Niagara Falls, NY
Truex, Thomas A. ... Davie, FL
Trufelli, Arthur W. ... Jupiter, FL
Truffer, Keith R. ... Towson, MD
Truglia, Dunewood ... New Suffolk, NY
Truglio, Elizabeth ... Denver, CO
Truglio, Fred ... Chicago, IL
Trugman, Harry ... Miami Beach, FL
Trugman, Ina F. ... San Francisco, CA
Trugman, Richard S. ... Encino, CA
Truhe, Beardsley, Jensen, Helmers & Von Wald, A Professional L.L.C. Rapid City, SD
Truhe, Janet M. ... Towson, MD
Truhe & Maier, P.A. ... Towson, MD
Truhe, Marvin D. ... Rapid City, SD
Truhill, Robert J. ... El Paso, TX
Truhlar, Doris B. ... Littleton, CO
Truhlar, Robert J. ... Littleton, CO
Truhlar and Truhlar, L.L.P. ... Littleton, CO
Truitt, A. Brent ... New York, NY
Truitt, Andrea D. ... Columbia, SC
Truitt, Brown & Truitt ... Chicago, IL
Truitt, Christine K. ... Denver, CO
Truitt, Craig C. ... Chicago, IL
Truitt, Curtright C. ... Fort Myers, FL
Truitt, Curtright C., P.A. ... Fort Myers, FL
Truitt, Dale M. ... Virginia Beach, VA
Truitt, David F. ... Lebanon, IN Zionsville, IN
Truitt, David M. ... Chicago, IL
Truitt, Donald H., Jr. ... Silver Spring, MD
Truitt, Donald L. ... Charlottesville, VA
Truitt, G. Ken ... Juneau, AK
Truitt, Gary M. ... Pittsburgh, PA
Truitt, Gary R. ... Pittsburgh, PA
Truitt, George R., Jr. ... Fort Lauderdale, FL
Truitt & Herr ... Lafayette, IN
Truitt, J Alan ... Birmingham, AL
Truitt, Jack E. ... Metairie, LA
Truitt, Jack E. ... Metairie, LA
Truitt, James F., Jr. ... Baltimore, MD
Truitt, James L. ... Dallas, TX
Truitt, Jerry D. ... Lexington, KY
Truitt, John R. ... Rockford, IL
Truitt Law Firm, The ... Metairie, LA New Orleans, LA
Truitt, Linda J. ... Detroit, MI
Truitt, Max O., Jr. ... Washington, DC
Truitt, Patricia Peyton ... Lafayette, IN
Truitt, Raymond G. ... Baltimore, MD
Truitt, Richard B. ... Chicago, IL
Truitt, Richard T. ... Huntington, IN
Truitt, Robert D. ... South Bend, IN
Truitt, Robert R., Jr. ... Midland, TX
Truitt, Robin C. ... Mill Valley, CA
Truitt, Stephen M. ... Washington, DC
Truitt, Tracey S. ... Kansas City, MO
Truitt, Wm. Roger ... Baltimore, MD
Trujillo, Angelica M. ... Miami, FL
Trujillo, Beatrice B. ... Moline, IL
Trujillo, Benjamin A. ... St. Louis, MO
Trujillo, Bernard Roberts ... Washington, DC
Trujillo, Carol A. ... San Diego, CA
Trujillo, Christopher D. Salt Lake City, UT
Trujillo, David B. ... Selah, WA
Trujillo, Denise ... Arlington, VA
Trujillo, Doreen Y. ... Philadelphia, PA
Trujillo, Gilbert A. ... San Luis Obispo, CA
Trujillo, James A. ... Bellevue, WA
Trujillo, James A., P.S. ... Bellevue, WA
Trujillo, John ... Las Cruces, NM
Trujillo, Juan Manuel ... New York, NY
Trujillo, Kenneth I. ... Philadelphia, PA
Trujillo, Lorenzo A. ... Westminster, CO
Trujillo, Luisa F. ... Chicago, IL
Trujillo, Mark Daniel ... Estancia, NM
Trujillo, Michael H. ... Monte Vista, CO
Trujillo, Michael H., P.C. ... Monte Vista, CO
Trujillo, Olga Rosa ... Department of Justice, Office of Justice Programs, GV
Trujillo, Patricia Department Of Veterans Affairs, Office of the General Counsel, GV
Trujillo, Patricia Ann ... Harrisburg, PA
Trujillo, Paul ... Jarales, NM
Trujillo, Phillip ... Albuquerque, NM
Trujillo, Phillip A. ... Walnut Creek, CA
Trujillo, Richard J. ... Phoenix, AZ
Trujillo, Richard J., Ltd. ... Phoenix, AZ
Trujillo, Richard R. ... Phoenix, AZ
Trujillo, Robert A. ... Temecula, CA
Trujillo, Rodriguez & Richards, LLC Cherry Hill, NJ **Philadelphia, PA**
Trujillo, Sylvia J. ... Los Angeles, CA
Trujillo, Tanya M. ... Santa Fe, NM
Trujillo, Thomas G. ... Detroit, MI
Trujillo, Timothy J. ... Des Moines, IA
Trujillo, Timothy T. ... San Bernardino, CA
Trujillo, Twyla Scudder ... Frankfort, KY
Trujillo, Walquiria ... Dothan, AL
Trujillo, William G. ... Colorado Springs, CO
Truland, David W. ... Troy, NY
Truland, Kevin ... Boston, MA
Trulio, David V. ... Los Angeles, CA
Trull, Ethan E. ... North Chicago, IL
Trull, Gregory ... Walnut Creek, CA
Trull, J. Kent ... Troy, NC
Trull, Susan C. ... San Antonio, TX
Trull, William J., Jr. ... Asheville, NC
Trull, William J., Jr., P.A. ... Asheville, NC
Trullenque, Anthony L. ... Miami Beach, FL
Trulli, David P. ... Philadelphia, PA
Trullinger, Charles E. ... Phoenix, AZ
Trullinger, Kara L. ... Phoenix, AZ
Trulock, Charles R., Jr. ... Orlando, FL
Trulock, Georgina Todd ... Albany, GA
Trulock, James R., II ... Bloomington, IN
Trulock, James W. ... Muncie, IN
Trulock, Jennifer M. ... Dallas, TX
Trulock, Sharon L. ... New York, NY
Trulove, Jodi ... Washington, DC
Trulove, Lemuel B., Jr. ... Sabinal, TX
Trulsson, Kent ... Dallas, TX
Truluck, Jefferson R. ... Greenville, SC
Truly, Elizabeth A. ... New York, NY
Truly, Ethel ... Yazoo City, MS
Truly, Everette ... Natchez, MS
Truly, Richard M., Jr. ... Natchez, MS
Truly, Smith & Latham ... Gulfport, MS Hattiesburg, MS Jackson, MS Natchez, MS
Truly, Traci ... Dallas, TX
Trum, Kathleen K. ... Garden City, NY
Truman, Catharine Turk ... Owego, NY
Truman, Craig L. ... Denver, CO
Truman, Craig L., P.C. ... Denver, CO
Truman, Donald A. ... Boston, MA
Truman, Edward B. ... Phoenix, AZ
Truman, Erin Lee ... Las Vegas, NV
Truman, Gale Pearson ... Westover, WV
Truman, Gary W. ... Wheat Ridge, CO
Truman, John L. ... New York, NY
Truman, Nanette R. ... St. Louis, MO
Truman, Karl N. ... Jeffersonville, IN
Truman, Kathleen M. O'Prey Los Angeles, CA
Truman, Roberta M. ... Fairton, NJ
Truman, Ronald W. ... Las Vegas, NV St. George, UT
Truman, Spicer & Oujesky, P.L.L.C. Hurst, TX
Truman, Tim ... Hurst, TX
Truman, Tom ... Beckley, WV
Truman, Tracy James ... Las Vegas, NV
Truman-Zorr, Barbara ... San Rafael, CA
Trumbaturi, Shelly C. ... Metairie, LA
Trumbauer, Brian R. ... Detroit, MI
Trumble, Jay W. ... Anchorage, AK
Trumble, Robert W. ... Martinsburg, WV
Trumbly, Anthony S. ... Denver, CO
Trumbo, Charles Bass ... Fayetteville, AR
Trumbo, George W. ... Cleveland, OH
Trumbo, Malfourd W. ... Fincastle, VA
Trumbo, Oliver Ott, II ... New York, NY
Trumbo, Robert B., Jr. New Smyrna Beach, FL
Trumbo, Steven R. ... Cincinnati, OH
Trumbo and Tucker ... Fincastle, VA
Trumbull, Allan ... New York, NY
Trumbull, Cherry ... Sherman Oaks, CA
Trumbull, George V. ... Chicago, IL
Trumbull, John A. ... Novato, CA
Trumbull, Loyal W. ... Denver, CO
Trumbull, Patricia V. ... San Jose, CA
Trumbull, Terry A. ... San Jose, CA
Trumka, Richard L. ... Washington, DC
Trumm, Tonya A. ... Milwaukee, WI
Trummel, David P. ... Indianapolis, IN
Trummer-Napolitano, Linda ... Millburn, NJ White Plains, NY
Trump, Arthur W., Jr. ... Ellicott City, MD
Trump, C. Samuel ... Berkeley Springs, WV
Trump, Charles S., IV Berkeley Springs, WV
Trump, Douglas P. ... Parsippany, NJ
Trump, Frederick W. ... Syracuse, NY
Trump, James D. ... East Setauket, NY
Trump, James L. ... Alexandria, VA
Trump, John V. ... San Francisco, CA
Trump, Paul D. ... Los Angeles, CA
Trump, Robert C. ... Cleveland, OH
Trump, Russell G. ... Drain, OR
Trump, Timothy T. ... Tulsa, OK
Trumpbour, Jason F. ... Sparks, MD
Trumper, E. Todd ... Long Beach, CA
Trumper, Regan L. ... New York, NY
Trumpeter, William G. ... Atlanta, GA
Trumpler, Douglas R. ... Elma, NY
Trumpower, Ian N. ... Dallas, TX
Truncale, Brian K. ... Dallas, TX
Truncale, Joseph C. ... Springfield, NJ
Truncale, Michael J. ... Beaumont, TX
Trundle, Audrey S. ... New York, NY
Trundle, W. Scott ... Ogden, UT
Trundy, Christopher C. ... New Bedford, MA
Trundy, Sean Kevin ... Charleston, SC
Trunick, John R., III ... San Diego, CA
Trunk, Carl F., Jr. ... Brooklyn, NY
Trunk, Robert ... Pueblo, CO
Trunk, Robert N., P.C. ... Pueblo, CO
Trunk, Wm. L. ... Chicago, IL
Trunkenbolz, Jerry L. ... Spokane, WA
Trunkes, Thos. T. ... Brooklyn, NY
Trunkett, Kerry S. ... Chicago, IL
Trunko, Tiffany D. ... New York, NY
Trunnell, Christian W. ... Los Angeles, CA
Trunnell, J. William ... Elberton, GA
Trunnell, Richard R ... Crofton, MD
Trunzo, Christopher S. ... San Diego, CA
Trunzo, Claire E. ... Pittsburgh, PA
Trunzo, Francis J., Jr. ... St. Helena Island, SC
Trunzo, Pasquale J., III ... East Hampton, NY
Trunzo, Thomas H., Jr. ... Lebanon, NH
Trunzo, Thomas H., Jr., Law Offices of, P.A. Lebanon, NH
Truong, Bobby K. ... San Jose, CA
Truong, Jason V. ... Beverly Hills, CA
Truong, John C. ... Washington, DC
Truong, Mac ... New York, NY
Truong, Thu-Thanh T. ... Sacramento, CA
Truong, To-Quyen T. Federal Communications Commission, Common Carrier Bureau, GV
Truono, Eugene J., Jr. ... Wilmington, DE
Trupe, Sara D. ... Newton, MA
Trupiano, Martin J. ... Los Angeles, CA
Trupp, Robin S. ... Sarasota, FL
Truppe, Stephen M. ... Panorama City, CA
Truppman, Keith A. ... Miami, FL
Truscelli, Patricia Lynne ... New York, NY
Truscello, Deborah M. ... Media, PA
Trusch, Norma Levine ... Houston, TX
Truschel, Mary M. ... Harrisburg, PA
Truscott, Michael Thomas Department of Justice, Civil Division, GV
Truscott, Wesley L., Jr. ... Pebble Beach, CA
Trusdale, Scott H. ... Cozad, NE
Trusdale & Trusdale, P.C. ... Cozad, NE
Trusdell, Laurence M. ... Wood Dale, IL
Trusdell, Tharrington T. ... Honolulu, HI
Trusevich, Andrew M. ... Dallas, TX
Trush, Edward H. ... Cranford, NJ
Trush, James M. ... Newport Beach, CA
Trushel, David H. ... Pittsburgh, PA
Trushel, Dwight H. ... Weirton, WV
Trushel Law Group, The ... Pittsburgh, PA
Trushel, Timothy D. ... United States Senate, Office of the Legislative Counsel, GV
Trushin, Bradley H. ... Miami, FL
Trusiak, Robert G. ... Toledo, OH
Truske, Sharon D. ... Weston, FL
Truskey, Jeffrey J. ... San Francisco, CA
Truskol, Michael F. ... Davis, CA
Truskoski, Ryan Thomas ... Orlando, FL
Truskowski, John B. ... Chicago, IL
Truslow, Douglas N. ... Columbia, SC
Truslow, Frederic J. ... Washington, DC
Truslow, James Linklater, V Providence, RI
Truslow, John W., Jr. ... Atlanta, GA
Truslow, Robyn Ann Clark ... Charleston, SC
Truslow, Sophia LaVerdiere ... Brooklyn, NY
Truslow, Timothy Kirk North Myrtle Beach, SC
Truslow, William A. ... Boston, MA
Truss, Gloria A. ... Southfield, MI
Truss, James M. ... San Antonio, TX
Trussell, David R. ... Little Rock, AR
Trussell, Elizabeth S. ... Los Angeles, CA
Trussell & Funderburg, P.C. ... Pell City, AL
Trussell, James J. ... St. Paul, MN
Trussell, John C. ... Lake Forest, IL
Trussell, L. Weems ... Fordyce, AR
Trussell, Samuel F. ... Indio, CA
Trussell, Sara Martha ... Union Springs, AL
Trussell, William J. ... Pell City, AL
Trusso, Jennifer A. ... Newport Beach, CA
Trusso, Paul S. ... La Jolla, CA
Trust, Brian ... New York, NY
Trustan, Nola ... Toms River, NJ
Truster, Jerry E. ... Tulsa, OK
Trustin, Mark S. ... Durham, NC
Trusty, Candis ... Miami, FL
Trusty, Joan E. ... Southfield, MI
Trusty, M. J. ... Houston, TX
Trusty, Robert M. ... Atlanta, GA
Trusty, William E., (P.A.) ... Batesville, MS
Truswell, Lynn Malcolm Northampton, MA
Truszkowski, Henry C. ... Los Angeles, CA
Trutanich, Carmen A. ... San Pedro, CA
Trutanich, Dominic J. ... San Pedro, CA
Trute, Melvyn ... Bay Harbor Islands, FL
Trutenko, Nicholas N. ... Chicago, IL
Trutner, Cynthia de Nevers ... Oakland, CA
Trutner, Elizabeth E. ... Livermore, CA
Trutner, Herman A. ... Oakland, CA
Trutner, Leslie B. ... San Francisco, CA
Trutner & Trutner ... Oakland, CA
Trutt, Judith M. ... Westport, CT
Truwit, Seth I. ... New York, NY
Truxal, Ann R. ... Olympia, WA
Truxaw, John W. ... San Leandro, CA
Truxaw, Timothy J. ... San Diego, CA
Truxell, Linda C. ... Bloomfield Hills, MI
Truxillo, Douglas W. ... Lafayette, LA
Truxton, Gregg S. ... Fort Myers, FL Miami, FL
Tryban, Esther Elizabeth ... Chicago, IL
Tryboski, Thomas K. ... Chicago, IL
Trybula, Peter G. ... Elkhart, IN South Bend, IN
Trybulski, Stanley Francis ... New York, NY
Trybus, Bruce Michael Fort Lauderdale, FL
Trybus, Janice R. ... Buffalo, NY
Trybus, Ronald H. ... Tampa, FL
Trybus, Steven R. ... Chicago, IL
Trybus & Woodward, P.A. ... Tampa, FL
Trygar, John Paul Merit Systems Protection Board, Office of Appeals Counsel, GV
Trygar, Louis P. ... Encino, CA
Trygg, Lori M. ... St. Paul, MN
Trygstad, David J. ... Pipestone, MN
Trygstad, Lawrence B. ... Los Angeles, CA
Trygstad, Lawrence B., A Law Corporation Los Angeles, CA
Trygstad, Shanon ... Los Angeles, CA
Tryk, Julia Osborne ... Parma, OH
Tryloff, Paul W. ... Birmingham, MI
Tryner, Joseph J. ... Wilmington, IL
Tryniecki, Timothy J. ... St. Louis, MO
Trynor, Carl R. ... Portland, ME
Tryon & Associates, P.C. Garden City, NY New York, NY
Tryon, David C. ... Cleveland, OH
Tryon, G. Michael ... Scottsdale, AZ
Tryon, Heller & Rayes, P.C. ... Scottsdale, AZ
Tryon, Jon W. ... Lancaster, PA
Tryon, Jonathan S. ... Barrington, RI
Tryon, Kimberly ... Phoenix, AZ
Tryon Legal Group, The ... Charlotte, NC
Tryon, Michael D. ... Garden City, NY
Tryon, Ronald James ... Columbia, SC
Tryon, William J. ... Albuquerque, NM
Tryon, William J., P.A. ... Albuquerque, NM
Trysla, Patrick J. ... Kansas City, MO
Trysla, Trudi Noel ... Rochester, MN
Trytten, Steven E. ... Glendale, CA
Trytten, Steven E., A Professional Law Corporation ... Glendale, CA
Trzaskoma, Theresa ... New York, NY
Trzcinski, Diane M. ... Los Angeles, CA
Trzcinski, Stephen ... Albany, NY
Trzcinski, Thomas Joseph ... Detroit, MI
Trzuskowski, Francis J. ... Wilmington, DE
Trzuskowski, Kipp, Kelleher & Pearce, P.A. Wilmington, DE
Trzynka, Ann M. ... Fort Wayne, IN
Tsacoumis, Stephanie ... Washington, DC
Tsadok, Debra S. ... Englewood, NJ
Tsaffaras, Peter H. ... Quincy, MA
Tsaganos, Vasiliki B. ... Washington, DC
Tsagaris, Terri J. ... Boston, MA
Tsai, Andre T. ... Seattle, WA
Tsai, Beti ... Los Angeles, CA
Tsai, Edward S. ... New York, NY
Tsai, Elizabeth T. Securities and Exchange Commission, Office of Freedom of Information and Privacy Act Operations, GV
Tsai, Felix ... Menlo Park, CA
Tsai, Huai-Ching Robert Huntington Beach, CA
Tsai, James C. ... Washington, DC
Tsai, Judy, Law Office of ... San Jose, CA
Tsai, Michael I. ... Milpitas, CA
Tsai, Michael M. ... Santa Ana, CA New York, NY
Tsai, Stella M. ... Philadelphia, PA
Tsai, Stephen ... Edison, NJ New York, NY
Tsai, Tzong-Bing ... Irvine, CA
Tsai, Virginia ... Boston, MA
Tsai, Winston Wen-Hsiung ... Washington, DC
Tsakalos, T. J. ... Salt Lake City, UT
Tsakanikas, Athena R. ... Hartford, CT
Tsakas, Nicholas J. ... Los Angeles, CA
Tsaknis, Mayda Colón ... Rockville, MD
Tsakonas, Basil T. ... Danielson, CT
Tsamis, Donna R. ... White Plains, NY
Tsamoutales, Nicholas F. ... Palm Bay, FL
Tsamoutales, Nicholas F., P.A. Palm Bay, FL
Tsandikos, George S. ... New York, NY
Tsang, Alfred K. B. ... Indianapolis, IN
Tsang, Charlene H. ... Houston, TX
Tsang, Jarlon ... Los Angeles, CA
Tsang, Lori J. Federal Energy Regulatory Commission, Office of the General Counsel, GV
Tsang, Marjorie ... New York, NY
Tsang, Michael ... Brooklyn, NY
Tsang, Sandra L. ... New York, NY
Tsang, Simon ... Tampa, FL
Tsang, Vivien Y. ... Cleveland, OH
Tsang, Winnie ... New York, NY
Tsang, Y. Grace ... Houston, TX
Tsangaris, Steven Nathan ... Tampa, FL
Tsangeos, Angelo James ... Canton, OH
Tsantes, Stephanie Ann ... Georgetown, DE
Tsantiris, Susan B. ... Farmington, CT
Tsao, Alison ... Costa Mesa, CA
Tsao, Carol Meyerdierks ... Boston, MA
Tsao, Fred ... Rockford, IL
Tsao, Jennifer M. ... Rosemead, CA
Tsao, Y. Rocky ... Boston, MA
Tsapis, Callie ... Palm Harbor, FL
Tsapogas, Pericles ... College Point, NY
Tsarnas, Emanuel G. ... Brooklyn, NY
Tsarnas, George P. ... Akron, OH
Tsarnas, Lorie D. ... Merrillville, IN
Tsarouhas, Antonios P. ... Akron, OH
Tsatalis, Marina C. ... Palo Alto, CA

Tsavaris, John E., II ... New York, NY
Tsaw, Diana ... Thousand Oaks, CA
Tsay, Jennifer ... Palo Alto, CA
Tschaepe, Kurt O. E. ... Gallatin, TN
Tschantz, David Edward ... Wooster, OH
Tschantz, Mary Myers ... Akron, OH
Tschantz, Richard T. ... Brooksville, FL
Tschanz, Roger ... West Jordan, UT
Tscharner, R. L. ... Glendora, CA
Tschetter, Duane D. ... Oak Lawn, IL
Tschetter, Margo R. ... Rapid City, SD
Tschetter, Mark N. ... Aurora, CO
Tschetter, Robert L. ... Belle Fourche, SD
Tschida, Alan T. ... Woodbury, MN
Tschida, Daniel P. ... Minneapolis, MN
Tschida, James R. ... St. Paul, MN
Tschida, Joseph J. ... Maitland, FL
Tschider, David A. ... Bismarck, ND
Tschider, Gregory W., III
San Francisco, CA
Tschider, Gregory W., Jr. ... Bismarck, ND
Tschider, Ivan A. ... Bismarck, ND
Tschider, Morris A., (P.C.) ... Bismarck, ND
Tschider, Richau & Boeckel ... Bismarck, ND
Tschider & Smith ... Bismarck, ND
Tschiember, Georgia Anne ... Riverhead, NY
Tschiemer, Robert S. ... Little Rock, AR
Tschirgi, Arnold B. ... Lander, WY
Tschirgi, Glen H. ... Baltimore, MD
Tschirgi, Scott A. ... Boise, ID
Tschirhart, Daniel L. ... Lansing, MI
Tschirhart, Paul M. ... Washington, DC
Tschirhart, Scott M. ... Waco, TX
Tschirhart, Wm. ("Bill") T., Jr.
Castroville, TX
Tschirn, Darryl J. ... La Jolla, CA
Tschoepe, Andy A., II, (P.C.)
San Antonio, TX
Tschoepe, Erwin (Trey) C., III
New Braunfels, TX
Tscholl, Robert J. ... Canton, OH
Tschudy, B. Scott ... Overland Park, KS
Tschugunov, Eleanor J. ... Akron, OH
Tschura, Gerald T. ... Troy, MI
Tse, Abbie ... Oakland, CA
Tse, Alan K. ... Palo Alto, CA
Tse, Alex G.
Department of Justice, GV
Tse, Bianca Kwok-Man ... Seattle, WA
Tse, Charles Yung-Chang ... New York, NY
Tse, Frank M. ... San Francisco, CA
Tse, Jane C. W. ... New York, NY
Tse, Marian A. ... Boston, MA
Tse, Natalie ... Honolulu, HI
Tseitlin, Alexandra V. ... New York, NY
Tsekerides, Theodore E. ... New York, NY
Tselikis, Gregory A. ... Portland, ME
Tselos, Alexander G. ... Minneapolis, MN
Tseng, Elaine H. ... Menlo Park, CA
Tseng, George G. C. ... Los Angeles, CA
Tseng, Helen C. Y. ... Dearborn, MI
Tseng, Jennifer Tina ... Thousand Oaks, CA
Tseng, Kai ... Menlo Park, CA
Tseng, Shane W. ... Los Angeles, CA
Tseng, Vivian ... Concord, MA
Tsenin, Ksenia K. ... San Francisco, CA
Tsevdos, Estelle J. ... New York, NY
Tsevdos, Noelle T. ... Columbus, OH
Tse-Wong, Natalie K. ... Honolulu, HI
Tsibouris, Konstantin ... Columbus, OH
Tsien, Arthur Y. ... Washington, DC
Tsien, Christopher C. ... Columbia, MD
Tsien, Frederick R. ... Portola Valley, CA
Tsien, Winnie ... Los Angeles, CA
Tsifrin, Donna ... Oakland, CA
Tsilas, Nicos L. ... Washington, DC
Tsilas, Vicky ... Washington, DC
Tsiliacos, Narcus J. ... Westerville, OH
Tsiliacos, Olga ... Columbus, OH
Tsimbinos, Spiros A. ... Kew Gardens, NY
Tsimbinos, Steven J. ... Roseland, NJ
Tsimerman, Inna ... Chicago, IL
Tsimis, George J. ... New York, NY
Tsimortos, Susan R. ... Jackson, MS
Tsimpedes, Athan T. ... Washington, DC
Tsingos, Basilios E. ... Boston, MA
Tsingos, Helen E. ... Boston, MA
Tsintolas, Suzanne M.
Fort Washington, MD
Silver Spring, MD
Tsintolas, Suzanne M., The Law Offices of
Fort Washington, MD
Tsiolis, Lisa R. ... Phoenix, AZ
Tsiotos, Chris ... Somerville, MA
Tsipis, Constantine E. ... Mayfield Heights, OH
Tsirimokos, Thomas X. ... Nashua, NH
Tsiros, John I. ... Saginaw, MI
Tsiros, Louis K. ... Los Angeles, CA
Tsismenakis, Vasilia H.A. ... New York, NY
Tsitouris, Harry G. ... Gaithersburg, MD
Tsitsiragos, Maria ... Cranford, NJ
Tso, Diane P. ... New York, NY
Tso, Joe ... Ellenville, NY
Tso, Kerrin I. ... Los Angeles, CA
Tso, Wendy ... Bronx, NY
Tsoi, James Wei ... Richardson, TX
Tsoi, Vivian ... Honolulu, HI
Tsokanis, Constance R. ... Albany, NY
Tsonas, Constantine J. ... Sarasota, FL
Tsonis, Nikos D. ... Boston, MA
Tsoris, Stephen A. ... Chicago, IL
Tsou, Lisa ... New York, NY
Tsou, Paul ... Alexandria, VA
Tsoucalas, Nicholas ... New York, NY
Tsoucaris, Valissa A. ... Denver, CO
Tsoudis, Nicholas ... Washington, DC
Tsougarakis, George A. ... New York, NY
Tsoukalas, Maria E. ... New York, NY

Tsoulas, Diane L. ... Boston, MA
Tsoumas, Themis J. ... Belchertown, MA
Tsoumas, Theodore Joseph ... Chicago, IL
Tsouprake, Charles S. ... New Bedford, MA
Tsouprake, Ted E. ... Coral Gables, FL
Tsouros, Christopher C. ... Boston, MA
Providence, RI
Tsoutsoplides, Voula ... New York, NY
Tsoutsouris, James V. ... Valparaiso, IN
Tsu, Christina C. ... New York, NY
Tsu, Victor ... Stamford, CT
Tsuboi, Dahni K. ... Los Angeles, CA
Tsubota, Miori ... New York, NY
Tsuchida, Michael H. ... Honolulu, HI
Tsuchida, S. Fred ... Mamaroneck, NY
Tsuchiyama, Thomas ... Honolulu, HI
Tsuda, Naomi C. ... Los Angeles, CA
Tsugawa, Eric H. ... Honolulu, HI
Tsu-Hsi Fang, Kenneth ... Los Angeles, CA
Tsui, Amy Y. ... Fairfax, VA
Tsui, Biann-Sheng ... Seattle, WA
Tsui, Daisy D. ... New York, NY
Tsui, Susan ... Washington, DC
Tsui-Yip, Gloria ... New York, NY
Tsuji, Edward M. ... Honolulu, HI
Tsuji, Russell Y. ... Honolulu, HI
Tsujimoto, Trude A. ... Valencia, CA
Tsujimura, R. Brian ... Honolulu, HI
Tsukahara, Jeannine M.
San Francisco, CA
Tsukazaki, Matt A. ... Honolulu, HI
Tsukazaki, R. Ben ... Hilo, HI
Tsukiyama, Ted T. ... Honolulu, HI
Tsukiyama, Ted T., A Law Corporation
Honolulu, HI
Tsukuno, Paul A. ... Chicago, IL
Tsung, Jo Anne P. ... New York, NY
Tsunis, Andrew Charles ... New York, NY
Tsunis, George J. ... Uniondale, NY
Tsunis, John C. ... Hauppauge, NY
Tsurutani, Henry J. ... Santa Monica, CA
Tu, Amy Elizabeth ... Bentonville, AR
Tu, Anh-huong T. ... Falls Church, VA
Tu, David ... San Francisco, CA
Tu, David J. ... Miami, FL
Tu, David J. ... Miami, FL
Tu, David J., P.A. ... Miami, FL
Tu, James ... Wheaton, IL
Tu, John Y. ... Monterey Park, CA
Tu, Michael C. ... Los Angeles, CA
Tu, Nancy A. ... Los Angeles, CA
Tu, Peter ... New York, NY
Tu, Veronique H. ... Detroit, MI
Tua, Judith ... Katonah, NY
Tual, Blanchard E. ... Memphis, TN
Tual, Blanchard E., P.C. ... Memphis, TN
Tual, Diana ... Palm Bay, FL
Tuan, Han-Hsien ... New York, NY
Tuan, Kuang-Sheng ... Los Angeles, CA
Tuan, Leon Y. ... San Francisco, CA
Tuazon, Rebecca Sexton ... Portland, OR
Tubach, Cheryl J. ... Kingsport, TN
Tubach, Dorothy M. ... Omaha, NE
Tubach, Michael F. ... San Francisco, CA
Tubb, Allen R. ... Dallas, TX
Tubb, George F. ... Gainesville, FL
Tubb, J. Glynn ... Decatur, AL
Tubb, J. Richard ... Dallas, TX
Tubb, James F. ... Oklahoma City, OK
Tubb, Jeremy ... Oklahoma City, OK
Tubb, Jerry ... Oklahoma City, OK
Tubb, Mack ... Spring, TX
Tubb, Paul L. ... Dallas, TX
Tubb & Ross, P.A. ... West Point, MS
Tubb, Stevens & Morrison ... West Point, MS
Tubb, Thomas M. ... West Point, MS
Tubbesing, Michael J. ... Kansas City, MO
Tubbesing, Theodore H. ... Alexandria, VA
Tubbs, Henry W., III ... Encinitas, CA
Tubbs, Nancy Ruoff ... Berkeley Heights, NJ
Tubbs, Robert James ... Charlotte, NC
Tubbs, Robert W. ... Traverse City, MI
Tubbs, Roger M. ... Tupelo, MS
Tubbs, Steven B. ... Vancouver, WA
Tubbs, William A. (Chip), Jr. ... Atlanta, GA
Tubbs, W.W. ... Kennesaw, GA
Tuber, Barry R. ... Springfield, MA
Tuber, Harold F. ... Chicago, IL
Tuber, Hope E. ... Morristown, NJ
Tubergen, Dane L. ... Fort Wayne, IN
Tubert, Patricia V. ... Los Angeles, CA
Tubertini, Richard B. ... Gulfport, MS
Tuberville, W. Paul ... Memphis, TN
Tubesing, Angela Page ... Fort Mitchell, KY
Tubin, Bradley D. ... Long Beach, CA
Tubiolo, Richard S. ... Rochester, NY
Tubis, Schwartz & Ziegler ... Philadelphia, PA
Tublin, Melvin J. ... New York, NY
Tubman, Irwin D. ... New York, NY
Tubman, Lloyd H. ... Woodbridge, NJ
Tubman, Rogene V. ... Chicago, IL
Tubridy, James J. ... Yonkers, NY
Tubridy, Kevin G. ... Framingham, MA
Tubridy, Laurie Heap ... Baton Rouge, LA
Tucceri, Ronald ... Washington, DC
Tucceri, Vincent A. ... Pittsburgh, PA
Tucci, Alexis ... West Long Branch, NJ
Tucci, Allen C. ... Wilmington, DE
Philadelphia, PA
Tucci, Anthony J. ... Staten Island, NY
Tucci, Carl ... Campbell, CA
Tucci, Carol E. ... Media, PA
Tucci, Christopher J. ... Charlotte, NC
Tucci, Gregory E. ... Ocala, FL
Tucci, John S., Jr. ... Philadelphia, PA
Tucci, Karen H. ... New York, NY
Tucci, Louis R. ... Cleveland, OH
Tucci, Michael E. ... Washington, DC

Tucci, Michele Martine ... Southfield, MI
Tucci, Peter A., Jr. ... Teaneck, NJ
Tucci, Peter J. ... Philadelphia, PA
Tucci, Reisner & Collins, A Professional
Corporation ... West Long Branch, NJ
Tucci, Stephen J. ... San Diego, CA
Tucci & Tannenbaum, A Professional
Corporation ... Wilmington, DE
Philadelphia, PA
Tucci, Theodore J. ... Hartford, CT
Tucci, Thomas J. ... Minneapolis, MN
Tucci, Vincent John ... Huntington Beach, CA
Tucciarone, Eric G. ... Detroit, MI
Tucciarone, John M. ... Rockville Centre, NY
Tucciarone, John P. ... Pleasantville, NY
Tucciarone, Mario A. ... Glen Oaks, NY
Tuccillo, Anthony ... Akron, OH
Tuccillo, Kenneth M. ... Ardsley, NY
Tuccillo, Nicholas J. ... Springfield, MA
Tuccillo, Susana Miraballes
Department of Commerce,
Patent and Trademark Office, GV
Tuccio, William P. ... Ansonia, CT
Tucek, Gregg J. ... Phoenix, AZ
Tucek, Jennifer E. ... Ithaca, NY
Tucek, Vicki L. ... Brandon, SD
Tuch, Robert I. ... Los Angeles, CA
Tuch, Robert L. ... Columbus, OH
Tuchband, Matthew ... Treasury Department,
Office of Foreign Assets Control, GV
Tucher, Alison ... San Francisco, CA
Tucher, Francis E. ... Indianapolis, IN
Tuchi, John J. ... Phoenix, AZ
Tuchin, Michael L. ... Los Angeles, CA
Tuchin, Tali ... San Diego, CA
Tuchinsky, Joseph B. ... Great Neck, NY
Tuchler, Dennis J. ... St. Louis, MO
Tuchman, Aviv L. ... Los Angeles, CA
Tuchman, Bert ... New York, NY
Tuchman, Chester ... Syosset, NY
Tuchman, Clara ... Brooklyn, NY
Tuchman, Daniel ... Miami, FL
Tuchman, Deborah S. ... New York, NY
Tuchman, Gloria ... Syosset, NY
Tuchman, Ido ... Denver, CO
Tuchman, Isaac N. ... Brooklyn, NY
Tuchman, Joseph A. ... New York, NY
Tuchman, Katz, Schwartz, Gelles & Korngold
New York, NY
Tuchman, Kenneth I. ... New York, NY
Tuchman, Lee B. ... Owings Mills, MD
Tuchman, Louis ... New York, NY
Tuchman, Michael J. ... Chicago, IL
Tuchman, Morris ... New York, NY
Tuchman, Robert ... Denver, CO
Tuchman, Robert L. ... Denver, CO
Tuchman, Stacy C. ... Rockville Centre, NY
Tuchman, Steven L. ... Indianapolis, IN
Tuchman & Tuchman ... Brooklyn, NY
Tuchmann, Eric P. ... New York, NY
Tuchmann, Robert ... Boston, MA
Tuchow, Gerald ... Bloomfield Hills, MI
Flat Rock, MI
Tuchow, Matthew N. ... San Francisco, CA
Tuchow & Trahey ... Bloomfield Hills, MI
Detroit, MI
Flat Rock, MI
Tuchscherer, Eckert, Smith & Rudolph, S.C.,
Law Offices of ... Antigo, WI
Wausau, WI
Tuchscherer, H. James
Wisconsin Rapids, WI
Tuchscherer, Konrad T. ... Wausau, WI
Tuck, Alan D., Jr. ... Santa Ana, CA
Tuck, C. Bradley ... Springfield, MO
Tuck, Cheryl S. ... Richmond, VA
Tuck, Constance M. ... St. Paul, MN
Tuck, Cynthia K. ... Sacramento, CA
Tuck, D. Sue ... Tulsa, OK
Tuck, Desmond B., Law Offices of
San Mateo, CA
Tuck, Dillard, Nelson & Dillard
South Boston, VA
Tuck, Edward Hallam ... New York, NY
Tuck, Emily E. ... Waltham, MA
Tuck, Garrison & Moore, P.L.L.C.
Albion, MI
Tuck, Henry L., III ... Little Rock, AR
Tuck, Ira N. ... Yucca Valley, CA
Tuck, Jas. R. ... Nashville, TN
Tuck, Jerome M. ... Brookline, MA
Tuck & Johns, A Professional Corporation
Springfield, MO
Tuck, Joseph G. ... Austin, TX
Tuck, Lenard W., Jr. ... Richmond, VA
Tuck, Marsha Lynn ... Livonia, MI
Tuck, Mary Agnes ... Los Angeles, CA
Tuck, Matthew L. ... Mount Clemens, MI
Tuck, Maurice L. ... Lafayette, CO
Tuck, Michael J. ... Chatsworth, GA
Tuck, Michael J. ... Dalton, GA
Tuck, Nicholas Charles ... St. Louis, MO
Tuck, Peterson, Foreman, Gilliam & Allen
Richmond, VA
Tuck, Rachel E. ... Wilmington, DE
Tuck, Richard L. ... Brookline, MA
Tuck, Robert C. ... Albion, MI
Tuck, Robert M. ... Richmond, VA
Tuck, Roy B., Jr. ... Leesville, LA
Tuck, T. Christopher ... Charleston, SC
Tuck, Tim ... Tulsa, OK
Tuck, W. Marshall ... Richmond, VA
Tuck, William K. ... San Mateo, CA
Tucka, M. Patricia ... St. Louis, MO
Tucker, A. Michael ... Livonia, MI
Tucker, A. Thomas, Jr. ... Tunica, MS
Tucker, Alan D. ... Havana, IL
Tucker, Alan David ... Brunswick, GA

Tucker, Alan David, P.C. ... Brunswick, GA
Woodbine, GA
Tucker, Alan H. ... Oceanside, NY
Tucker, Amy McNeer ... Birmingham, AL
Tucker, Amy T. ... St. Louis, MO
Tucker, Andrea S. ... Treasury Department,
Internal Revenue Service, GV
Tucker, Andrew M. ... McLean, VA
Tucker, Ann Marie ... Buffalo, NY
Tucker, Anna K. ... Cleveland, OH
Tucker Arensberg, P.C. ... Greensburg, PA
Moon Township, PA
Pittsburgh, PA
Tucker Arensberg & Swartz
Harrisburg, PA
Lewistown, PA
Tucker, Arthur L. ... Sumiton, AL
Tucker & Associates ... Charlottesville, VA
Tucker & Associates, Incorporated
Randolph, MA
Tucker, B. Wayne ... Richmond, VA
Tucker, Barbara J. ... Billings, MT
Tucker, Barry J. ... La Jolla, CA
Tucker & Baum ... Beverly Hills, CA
Tucker, Benjamin F. ... Madison, NC
Tucker, Benny M. ... Arkadelphia, AR
Tucker, Berry K. ... Oak Lawn, IL
Tucker, Betty B. ... Jackson, MS
Tucker, Beverly Scales ... Detroit, MI
Tucker, Bill D. ... Lubbock, TX
Tucker, Billie Anne, (Mrs.) ... Lafayette, AL
Tucker, Blaine A. ... Sugar Land, TX
Tucker, Bob D. ... Baton Rouge, LA
Tucker, Bonnie P. ... Tempe, AZ
Tucker, Bowen H. ... Chicago, IL
Tucker, Bradford ... Houston, TX
Tucker, Bradley D. ... Englewood, CO
Tucker, Bradley L. ... Iowa City, IA
Tucker, Brennan B. ... Kansas City, MO
Tucker, Brian H. ... Camp Hill, PA
Tucker, Brian J. ... Los Angeles, CA
Tucker, Brian J. ... New York, NY
Tucker, Brian T. ... Concord, NH
Tucker, Brian Thomas ... Idaho Falls, ID
Tucker, Bruce G. ... Providence, RI
Tucker, C. Taylor ... Kosciusko, MS
Tucker, C. Taylor ... Louisville, MS
Tucker, Carl L. ... Dallas, TX
Tucker, Carol A. ... San Antonio, TX
Tucker, Carter H. ... Richmond, VA
Tucker, Casey R. ... Little Rock, AR
Tucker, Catherine I. ... Greensboro, NC
Tucker, Cathleen ... Fairfax, VA
Tucker, Charles E., Jr. ... Peoria, IL
Tucker, Charles F. ... Exeter, NH
Tucker, Charles F. ... Norfolk, VA
Tucker, Charles K. ... Santa Clara, CA
Tucker, Charles R. ... Ocala, FL
Tucker, Chas. I. ... Louisville, KY
Tucker, Chas. T. ... Louisville, KY
Tucker, Christian Douglas
Fort Worth, TX
Tucker, Christopher E. ... Seattle, WA
Tucker & Cinquegrana ... Boston, MA
Tucker, Clarence B. ... Detroit, MI
Tucker & Clennan, PLLC ... Stafford, TX
Tucker, Coleman R. ... Houston, TX
Tucker, Colin H. ... Tulsa, OK
Tucker, Creed D. ... Champaign, IL
Tucker, Creed T. ... Chicago, IL
Tucker, Curtis ... Middletown, OH
Tucker, Cynthia A. ... Springfield, MA
Tucker, D. Scott ... New York, NY
Tucker, D. Suzan ... McCune, KS
Tucker, Dale Paul ... Denver, CO
Tucker, Damian L. ... Rocky Mount, NC
Tucker, Damian Traviss ... Charleston, WV
Tucker, Daniel K. ... Booneville, MS
Tucker, Darren S. ... Philadelphia, PA
Tucker, David A. ... Boston, MA
Tucker, David A. ... Houston, TX
Tucker, David C. ... Kansas City, MO
Tucker, David F., Jr. ... Elizabethton, TN
Tucker, David K. ... Miami, FL
Tucker, David L., Jr. ... Albuquerque, NM
Tucker, David W. ... San Francisco, CA
Tucker & Davidson, P.C. ... Three Rivers, MI
Tucker, Deanna M. Marzian
Louisville, KY
Tucker, Debra J. ... Chicago, IL
Tucker, Debra James ... Columbus, OH
Tucker, Deron ... Jamaica, NY
Tucker, Diane E. ... San Francisco, CA
Tucker, Diane E. ... Syracuse, NY
Tucker, Diane Reese ... Harrisburg, PA
Tucker, Don E. ... Youngstown, OH
Tucker, Donald F. ... Bloomfield Hills, MI
Lansing, MI
Tucker, Donald G. ... Montgomery, AL
Tucker, Donald H., Jr. ... Raleigh, NC
Tucker, Donald L. ... Tallahassee, FL
Tucker, Donald L., P.A. ... Tallahassee, FL
Tucker, Donzell Marie ... Brooklyn, NY
Tucker, Douglas ... Fresno, CA
Tucker, Douglas A. ... Washington, DC
Tucker, Douglas J. ... Chicago, IL
Tucker, E. Glenn ... Marco Island, FL
Tucker, E. Montgomery ... Richmond, VA
Tucker, E. Randolph ... Boston, MA
Tucker, Eddie H. ... Jackson, MS
Tucker, Edmon W. ... Hollywood, FL
Tucker, Edmund J. ... Elizabeth, NJ
Tucker, Edward A. ... Stafford, TX
Tucker, Edward B. ... Mount Sterling, IL
Tucker, Edward W. ... Sandusky, OH
Tucker, Edwin E. ... Monroe, LA
Tucker, Eliot P. ... Houston, TX
Tucker, Elizabeth A. ... Brooklyn, NY

Tucker, Elton G. ... Wilmington, NC
Tucker, Emmett E., Jr. ... Roanoke, VA
Tucker, Eric E. ... Washington, DC
Tucker, Ernest C. ... Rockville, MD
Tucker, Ernest F. ... Decatur, GA
Tucker, F. Michael ... Albany, NY
Tucker, Frances I. ... Brookline, MA
Tucker, Frederick C., III ... Indianapolis, IN
Tucker & Gano ... Dallas, TX
Tucker, Garrett R., Jr. ... Houston, TX
Tucker, Gary C. ... Tucson, AZ
Tucker, Gary S. ... Houston, TX
Tucker, George H. ... Coral Springs, FL
Tucker, Gerald A. ... Oklahoma City, OK
Tucker, Gerald E. ... Jacksonville, FL
Tucker, Glen E. ... Pasadena, CA
Tucker, Gregory A. ... Summersville, WV
Tucker, Gregory M. ... Farmington, NM
Tucker, H. Allan ... Hollywood, FL
Tucker, H. Glenn ... Newark, NJ
Tucker, Harry A., Jr. ... Grand Junction, CO
Tucker, Harve D. ... Chicago, IL
Tucker, Helene Debra ... Washington, DC
Tucker, Hendryx, Taunton, Snyder & Slade, P.C. ... Houston, TX
Tucker, Henry R. ... New York, NY
Tucker, Henry T., Jr. ... Baltimore, MD
Tucker, Herbert E., IV ... Denver, CO
Tucker, Hugh ... Houston, TX
Tucker & Hughes ... Detroit, MI
Tucker, Irvin B., Jr. ... Raleigh, NC
Tucker, Isidore R. ... New Hyde Park, NY
New York, NY
Tucker, J. David ... Tifton, GA
Tucker, J. Grant ... Columbus, IN
Tucker, J. Kendrick ... Tallahassee, FL
Tucker, J. Maxwell ... Dallas, TX
Tucker, J. Randolph, Jr. ... Richmond, VA
Tucker, J. Richard ... Wilmington, DE
Tucker, J. Ronald ... Houston, TX
Tucker, J. Scott ... Washington, DC
Tucker, J. Waddy ... Shreveport, LA
Tucker, Jack L. ... Cincinnati, OH
Tucker, Jack N. ... Tunica, MS
Tucker, Jack W., Jr. ... Houston, TX
Tucker, James A. ... Montgomery, AL
Tucker, James A. ... Ocala, FL
Tucker, James B. ... Laguna Hills, CA
Tucker, James B. ... Jackson, MS
Tucker, James C. ... Boise, ID
Twin Falls, ID
Tucker, James C. ... Paoli, IN
Tucker, James D. ... Springfield, MO
Tucker, James H. ... New York, NY
Tucker, James H., Jr. ... Nashville, TN
Tucker, James L. ... Minneapolis, MN
Tucker, James L. ... Rochester, NY
Tucker, James L., III ... Minneapolis, MN
Tucker, James M. ... Charlotte, NC
Tucker, James M. ... Houston, TX
Tucker, James R. ... Sacramento, CA
Tucker, James R. ... Dallas, TX
Tucker, James R., Jr. ... Washington, DC
Tucker, James R., P.C., Law Offices of ... Dallas, TX
Tucker, James Thomas ... Phoenix, AZ
Tucker, James W., Jr. ... Rock Hill, SC
Tucker, Jane D. ... Norfolk, VA
Tucker, Janice L. ... Milwaukee, WI
Tucker, Janna ... Bradenton, FL
Tucker, Jason A. ... Boston, MA
Tucker, Jean Walker ... Mobile, AL
Tucker, Jeffrey A. ... Houston, TX
Tucker, Jeffrey D. ... Riverside, CA
Tucker, Jeffrey T. ... Doylestown, PA
Tucker, Jennifer A. ... Paoli, IN
Tucker, Jennifer Catlin ... Boston, MA
Tucker, Jerome ... Birmingham, AL
Tucker, Jerome, III ... Birmingham, AL
Tucker, Jeter, Jackson and Hickman, L.L.P. ... Shreveport, LA
Tucker, Joan Blanton
West Palm Beach, FL
Tucker, Jodi Ann ... Washington, DC
Tucker, Joe B. ... Ringgold, GA
Tucker, Joe H., Jr. ... Philadelphia, PA
Tucker, Joe L., Jr. ... Birmingham, AL
Tucker, John A. ... Jacksonville, FL
Tucker, John A., Jr. ... Los Angeles, CA
Tucker, John Essex ... Hartford, CT
Tucker, John G. ... Beaumont, TX
Tucker, John H. ... Tulsa, OK
Tucker, John M. ... Canton, OH
Salem, OH
Tucker, John P., Jr. ... Blue Ridge, GA
Tucker, John R. ... Atlanta, GA
Tucker, John R. ... Flint, MI
Tucker, John T., III ... Salem, VA
Tucker, John V. ... St. Petersburg, FL
Tucker, Jonathan D. ... Kent, OH
Tucker, Jordan W. ... Brooklyn, NY
Tucker, Joseph L. ... Birmingham, AL
Tucker, Joseph L. ... St. Louis, MO
Tucker, Joseph M. ... Lafayette, AL
Tucker, Joseph N. ... Louisville, KY
Tucker, Joseph P. ... Westport, CT
New York, NY
Tucker, Josephine Staton ... Irvine, CA
Tucker, Judson T. ... Meridian, MS
Tucker, Julia A. ... Anchorage, AK
Tucker, Julie Hills ... Jacksonville, FL
Tucker, Karen L. ... Mobile, AL
Tucker, Kathryn L. ... Seattle, WA
Tucker, Kathryn M. ... Milan, TN
Tucker, Kay E. ... Philadelphia, PA
Tucker, Kaye E. ... Beverly Hills, CA
Tucker, Kenneth ... Dallas, TX
Tucker, Kenneth C. ... Knoxville, TN
Tucker, Kenneth L. ... Phoenix, AZ
Tucker, Kenneth Robert ... Flint, MI
Tucker, Kerry ... Watertown, MA
Tucker, Kevin J. ... Phoenix, AZ
Tucker, Kevin L. ... Southfield, MI
Tucker, Kimberly Griffin ... Dallas, TX
Tucker, Kimberly J. ... Tallahassee, FL
Tucker, Kimberly Rogers ... Louisville, KY
Tucker, Kimberly Wood ... Little Rock, AR
Tucker, Kimyard H. ... St. Louis, MO
Tucker, Kirsten ... Denver, CO
Tucker & Kotler, P.A. ... Miami, FL
Tucker, L. Campbell, III ... Charlotte, NC
Tucker, L. Dan ... Dallas, TX
Tucker, Larry ... Newport Beach, CA
Tucker, Larry D. ... Charlotte, NC
Tucker, Laura Hays ... Tuscaloosa, AL
Tucker, Laura M. ... Baltimore, MD
Tucker, Laura Romeo ... Detroit, MI
Tucker, Laurence R. ... Kansas City, MO
Tucker Law Firm ... Billings, MT
Tucker Law Office ... Des Moines, IA
Tucker, Lawrence ... Cleveland, OH
Tucker, Lee ... Tucson, AZ
Tucker, Lenore W. ... New York, NY
Tucker, Leon W. ... Philadelphia, PA
Tucker, Leslie A. ... Charlotte, NC
Tucker, Linda ... Raleigh, NC
Tucker, Lisa Helpert ... Washington, DC
Tucker, Lisa M.P. ... Gaylord, MI
Tucker, Loren ... Virginia City, MT
Tucker, Louise L.M. ... Washington, DC
Tucker, Lynn M. ... Richmond, VA
Tucker, M. Jeffrey ... Chicago, IL
Tucker, M. Wayne ... San Bernardino, CA
Tucker, Marc B. ... Wilmington, DE
Tucker, Marc C. ... Southfield, MI
Tucker, Marc K. ... Newburyport, MA
Tucker, Marcus O. ... Monterey Park, CA
Tucker, Marcus R. ... Houston, TX
Tucker, Mark C. ... Southfield, MI
Tucker, Mark D. ... Tallahassee, FL
Tucker, Mark D. ... Midland, MI
Tucker, Mark D. ... Columbus, OH
Tucker, Mark M. ... San Francisco, CA
Tucker, Marna S. ... Washington, DC
Tucker, Martha ... Wallingford, PA
Tucker, Martin ... Palm Beach Gardens, FL
Tucker, Marvin L. ... Kansas City, MO
Tucker, Mary Shea ... Salt Lake City, UT
Tucker, Michael C. ... Lansing, MI
Tucker, Michael J. ... Phoenix, AZ
Tucker, Michael K. ... Cherry Hill, NJ
Tucker, Michael L. ... Bessemer, AL
Tucker, Michael L. ... Chicago, IL
Tucker, Michael L. ... Dayton, OH
Tucker, Michael R. ... Memphis, TN
Tucker, Michael S. ... Cleveland, OH
Tucker, Michelle H. ... Honolulu, HI
Tucker, Morris C. ... Fort Lauderdale, FL
Tucker, Neil R. ... New York, NY
Tucker, Norman D. ... Southfield, MI
Tucker, Pamela Wilkinson ... Scottsboro, AL
Tucker, Patricia ... Albuquerque, NM
Tucker, Patrick A. ... United States Senate,
Committee Legal Personnel, GV
Tucker, Paul A. ... Houston, TX
Tucker, Paul A. ... Fincastle, VA
Tucker, Paul T. ... Wheeling, WV
Tucker, Paula ... Dallas, TX
Tucker, Phillip James ... Edmond, OK
Tucker, Pryce G. ... Kansas City, KS
Dallas, TX
Tucker, R. Rand ... Greensboro, NC
Tucker, Ralph J. ... Paradise Valley, AZ
Tucker, Ralph L., Jr. ... Topsham, ME
Tucker, Randolph C. ... Orlando, FL
Tucker, Randolph W. ... Staunton, VA
Tucker, Ray M. S., (Mrs.)
New Hyde Park, NY
Tucker, Raymond ... New York, NY
Tucker, Rhetta Joan ... New York, NY
Tucker, Richard B., III ... Pittsburgh, PA
Tucker, Richard B., Jr.
New Brunswick, NJ
New Brunswick, NJ
Tucker, Richard D. ... Bangor, ME
Tucker, Richard G. ... Parsons, KS
Tucker, Richard M. ... Iowa City, IA
Tucker, Richard S. ... Fort Worth, TX
Tucker, Richard T. ... Worcester, MA
Tucker & Ricks ... San Bernardino, CA
Tucker, Rina C. ... Department of Justice,
Civil Division, GV
Tucker, Robert A. ... Great Falls, MT
Tucker, Robert A. ... Memphis, TN
Tucker, Robert B., Jr. ... Charlotte, NC
Tucker, Robert C. ... Baton Rouge, LA
Tucker, Robert C. ... St. Louis, MO
Tucker, Robert C. ... Cleveland, OH
Tucker, Robert D. ... Edwardsville, IL
Tucker, Robert E. ... Des Moines, IA
Tucker, Robert E. ... St. Louis, MO
Tucker, Robert E. ... Pittsburgh, PA
Tucker, Robert G. ... Chicago, IL
Tucker, Robert H. ... St. Paul, MN
Tucker, Robert H. ... Jericho, NY
Tucker, Robert K. ... Miami, FL
Tucker, Robert L. ... Chicago, IL
Tucker, Robert L. ... New York, NY
Tucker, Robert L. ... Akron, OH
Tucker, Robert L.
Christiansted, St. Croix, VI
Tucker, Robert M. ... Los Angeles, CA
Tucker, Robert M. ... Salt Lake City, UT
Tucker, Robert P. ... Toledo, OH
Tucker, Robert P., II ... Asheville, NC
Tucker, Robert T. ... Rye, NY
Tucker, Robert W., Sr. ... Baton Rouge, LA
Tucker, Robin K. ... Houston, TX
Tucker, Rodney Alan ... Merrillville, IN
Tucker, Roger S. ... St. Petersburg, FL
Tucker & Rolf, A Professional Corporation
Southfield, MI
Tucker, Ron L. ... Fairmont, WV
Tucker, Ronald A. ... Albuquerque, NM
Tucker, Ronald C. ... Denver, CO
Tucker, Ronald M. ... Indianapolis, IN
Tucker, Ronald S. ... La Quinta, CA
Tucker, Roslyn L. ... Portland, OR
Tucker, Roy W. ... Portland, OR
Tucker, S. Gail ... Tampa, FL
Tucker, Samuel E. ... Milton-Freewater, OR
Tucker, Samuel L. ... Ocean Springs, MS
Tucker, Sandra ... Dallas, TX
Tucker, Sandy T. ... Richmond, VA
Tucker, Scot D. ... Seattle, WA
Tucker, Scott H., (P.A.) ... Little Rock, AR
Tucker, Scott J. ... Boston, MA
Tucker, Scott R. ... Seattle, WA
Tucker Selden, Lawyers, P.L.L.C.
Tunica, MS
Tucker, Seth A. ... Washington, DC
Tucker, Shannon A. ... Durham, NC
Tucker, Sharon K. ... Washington, DC
Tucker, Shelley L. ... Department of Justice,
Civil Division, GV
Tucker, Sherry E. ... Raleigh, NC
Tucker, Shuford A., Jr. ... Birmingham, AL
Tucker, Slaughter & Singletary, P.A.
Albemarle, NC
Tucker, Stacey Lynn ... West Palm Beach, FL
Tucker, Stanley L. ... Carthage, IL
Macomb, IL
Tucker, Stefan F. ... Washington, DC
Tucker, Stephen ... New York, NY
Tucker, Stephen E. ... New York, NY
Tucker, Stephen T. ... Ventura, CA
Tucker, Steve A. ... Birmingham, AL
Tucker, Steven L. ... Santa Fe, NM
Tucker Strohm Miller & Tucker, P.C.
Phoenix, AZ
Tucker, Stuart A. ... Lawrenceville, NJ
Tucker, Susan B. ... New York, NY
Tucker, Susan B. ... Charleston, WV
Tucker, Susan Ellen ... Topeka, KS
Tucker, Sydney Stallard ... Boston, MA
Tucker, Tami L. ... Baton Rouge, LA
Tucker, Teresa C. ... Manchester, NH
Tucker, Terry D. ... Jefferson City, TN
Tucker, Terry G. ... Bridgeton, NJ
Tucker, Theodore B., III ... Toledo, OH
Tucker, Theodore J. ... Three Rivers, MI
Tucker, Thomas A. ... Union City, CA
Tucker, Thomas E. ... Upper Montclair, NJ
Tucker, Thomas E., P.C.
Upper Montclair, NJ
Tucker, Thomas G. ... Austin, TX
Tucker, Thomas H. ... Boston, MA
Tucker, Thomas J. ... Siloam Springs, AR
Tucker, Thomas J. ... Irvine, CA
Tucker, Thomas J. ... Ann Arbor, MI
Findlay, OH
Toledo, OH
Tucker, Thomas M. ... Sarasota, FL
Tucker, Thomas W. ... Augusta, GA
Tucker & Tighe, P.A. ... Fort Lauderdale, FL
Tucker, Tim D. ... Madison, TN
Tucker, Timi D. ... Frankfort, KY
Tucker, Timothy G. ... Wynne, AR
Tucker, Timothy N. ... Atlanta, GA
Tucker, Todd O. ... Oak Brook, IL
Tucker, Todd R. ... Cleveland, OH
Tucker & Tucker ... Tunica, MS
Tucker and Tucker, P.C. ... Paoli, IN
Tucker, Vicki Obenchain ... Richmond, VA
Tucker, W. Lee ... Bryant, AR
Tucker, Warren A. ... Anchorage, AK
Tucker, Watson B. ... Chicago, IL
Tucker, Wendell R. ... Brea, CA
Tucker, Wendy A. ... Los Angeles, CA
Tucker, Wendy F. ... Media, PA
Tucker, Wendy L. ... San Diego, CA
Tucker, William C. ... Manchester, NH
Tucker, William C. ... Albemarle, NC
Tucker, William C., Jr. ... Birmingham, AL
Tucker, William D. ... Fort Lauderdale, FL
Tucker, William D., III ... Charlottesville, VA
Tucker, William D., Jr. ... New York, NY
Tucker, William F. ... Dallas, TX
Tucker, William G. ... Redwood City, CA
Tucker, William Gareth ... Deep River, CT
Tucker, William H. ... Augusta, GA
Aiken, SC
Tucker, William H. ... Nashville, TN
Tucker, William J. ... San Diego, CA
Tucker, William J. ... Indianapolis, IN
Tucker, William J. ... Dallas, TX
Tucker, William L. ... Columbus, GA
Tucker, William M. ... Iowa City, IA
Tucker, William P. ... Garden City, NY
Tucker, William S., Jr. ... Newark, NJ
Tucker, William V. ... Ellicott City, MD
Tucker, William S. ... Springfield, MO
Tucker, Wm. F., Jr. ... Tulsa, OK
Tucker, Woodrow W. ... Atlanta, GA
Tucker, Woodrow W. ... Peace Dale, RI
Tucker, Zelda W. ... Shreveport, LA
Tuckerman, Jan ... Sunriver, OR
Tuckerman, John L. ... Cleveland, OH
Tuckerman, Richard J. ... Claremont, CA
Tuckett, Ernest A., III ... Washington, DC
Tuckett, Shannon ... Texarkana, AR
Tuckey, Stephen F. ... Gettysburg, PA
Tuckfelt, Jeffrey C. ... Washington, DC
Tuckfield, David J. ... Austin, TX
Tuckfield, Ilene Felice ... Miami, FL
Tuckler, Jorge Albert ... San Antonio, TX
Tuckman, Ellen H. ... New City, NY
Tuckman, Scott E. ... Boca Raton, FL
Tuckner, Jack B. ... New York, NY
Tuckner, Jack Bryant, P.C. ... New York, NY
Tuck-Richmond, Doletta
Oklahoma City, OK
Tuck-Smith, Cheryl L. ... Chico, CA
Tuczak, Robin M. ... Aberdeen, NC
Tuczinski, Daniel J. ... Albany, NY
Tuczinski, Marlene O. ... East Chatham, NY
Tudhope, Wallace W. ... Longwood, FL
Tudhope, Wallace W., P.A. ... Longwood, FL
Tudhope, Wallace, W., P.A. ... Orlando, FL
Tudino, Domenic ... Providence, RI
Tudino, Domenic, Esq., Inc. ... Providence, RI
Tudino, Joseph D. ... Providence, RI
Tudino, Mark ... Miami, FL
Tudisco, Astra M. ... New York, NY
Tudisco, Robert M. ... Bronx, NY
Tudor, Bynum Ellsworth, III
Nashville, TN
Tudor, Darcia Owings ... Seattle, WA
Tudor, David ... Noblesville, IN
Tudor, Deborah H. ... Lexington, KY
Tudor, Frederic M. ... Newark, NJ
New York, NY
Tudor, Gary A. ... Lake Forest, CA
Tudor, Gary A. ... Seattle, WA
Tudor, John M. ... Kenton, OH
Tudor, Joseph H. ... Rockville, MD
Tudor & Lindsey, P.C. ... Nashville, TN
Tudor, Louise I. ... New York, NY
Tudor, Michael S. ... Alexandria, LA
Tudor, Philip L. ... San Francisco, CA
Tudor, Tanya K. ... San Francisco, CA
Tudor, Thad Nathan ... Marshall, MN
Tudor, Thomas B. ... Bismarck, ND
Tudor & Tudor ... Seattle, WA
Tudruj, Roman ... Westport, CT
Tudzarov, Louise E. ... Fort Lauderdale, FL
Tudzin, Ellis L. ... Houston, TX
Tudzin, Lisa Schwartz ... Los Angeles, CA
Tudzin, Michael ... Los Angeles, CA
Tuegel, Donald W. ... St. Louis, MO
Tuel & Garman, LLP ... West Sacramento, CA
Tuel, Houston N., Jr. ... West Sacramento, CA
Tuel, Larry L. ... Des Moines, IA
Tuell & Couture, P.S. ... Tacoma, WA
Tuell, David R., Jr. ... Tacoma, WA
Tuell, Todd J. ... Tacoma, WA
Tueller, Alden B. ... Orem, UT
Tueller, Douglas R. ... Telluride, CO
Tueller, Douglas R., P.C. ... Telluride, CO
Tuepker, Max C. ... Oklahoma City, OK
Tuepker, Max C., P.C.
Oklahoma City, OK
Tuer, Jodi R. ... Washington, DC
Tuerck, Timothy T. ... Redwood City, CA
Tuerff, T. Timothy ... Washington, DC
Tuerk, Carl E., Jr. ... Baltimore, MD
Tuerk, Edward F. ... Alexandria, VA
Tuerk, Robert D. ... Chicago, IL
Tuerk, Robyn B. ... Los Angeles, CA
Tuerkheimer, Barbara W. ... Madison, WI
Tuerkheimer, Frank M. ... Madison, WI
Tuero, Sergio J. ... Staten Island, NY
Tuesley & Hall ... Elkhart, IN
South Bend, IN
Tuesley, Malcolm ... South Bend, IN
Tueth, James E. ... Decatur, IL
Tueth, Stephanie L. ... St. Louis, MO
Tueth, Thomas E. ... St. Louis, MO
Tueting, William F. ... Chicago, IL
Tuey, Soo Man ... San Diego, CA
Tuey, Wendy W. ... Boulder, CO
Denver, CO
Tufankjian, Allan H. ... Brockton, MA
Tufankjian & McDonald ... Brockton, MA
Tufano, Mary Jeanne Gaffney ... Boston, MA
Tufano, Paul A. ... Harrisburg, PA
Tufano, Richard J. ... New York, NY
Tufariello, Panagiota Betty ... Mineola, NY
Tufaro, David F. ... Baltimore, MD
Tufaro, Paul S. ... New York, NY
Tufaro, Richard C. ... Washington, DC
Tuffias, Heidi S. ... Los Angeles, CA
Tuffin, Amalie Lewis
Research Triangle Park, NC
Tuffin, James W. ... Manhasset, NY
Tuffin, Paul J. ... Cleveland, OH
Tuffley, Charles ... Bingham Farms, MI
Tuffley, F. Douglas ... Seattle, WA
Tuffnell, John B. ... Des Moines, IA
Tufford, Victor O. ... Upland, CA
Tufino, Salvatore J. ... Miami, FL
Tufo, Daniel A. ... Commack, NY
Tuft, Christine L. ... Minneapolis, MN
Tuft, Leonard W. ... Piscataway, NJ
Tuft, Mark L. ... San Francisco, CA
Tuft, Michael L. ... Englewood, CO
Tuft, Paul R. ... Paradise Valley, AZ
Tuft, Steven A. ... Burley, ID
Tuft, Thomas W. ... St. Paul, MN
Tufte, Brian N. ... Minneapolis, MN
Tufteland, James N. ... Las Vegas, NV
Tufts, Allison Corinne ... Winston-Salem, NC
Tufts, Charles E. ... Pasadena, MD
Tufts, Cynthia Ann Delaney ... Opelika, AL
Tufts, David W. ... Salt Lake City, UT
Tufts, Douglas W. ... Tacoma, WA
Tufts, Frederick J. ... New Orleans, LA
Tufts, J. David, III ... New Orleans, LA
Tufts, Marie D. ... New Orleans, LA
Tufts, Meredith Peterson ... Manchester, MA
Tufts, Robert A. ... Opelika, AL
Tufts, Robert R. ... San Francisco, CA

Tufts Stephenson & Kasper, LLP
San Francisco, CA
Tufts, T. Scott .... Orlando, FL
Tufts, Tamar A. .... Frederick, MD
Tufts, William L. .... Eugene, OR
Tufvesson Shuck, Maria .... New York, NY
Tugander, Juliette P. .... New York, NY
Tugander, Robert .... Melville, NY
Tugander, Robert .... Uniondale, NY
Tugander, Steven .... Department of Justice, Antitrust Division, GV
Tugender, Carmen I. .... Miami, FL
Tugendrajch, Lydia .... New York, NY
Tugentman, Steven .... Bedminster, NJ
Tuggey, Timothy N. .... San Antonio, TX
Tuggle, Charles T., Jr. .... Memphis, TN
Tuggle, David A. .... Danville, IL
Tuggle, David C. .... Roanoke, VA
Tuggle Duggins & Meschan, P.A.
Greensboro, NC
High Point, NC
Tuggle, James H. .... Los Angeles, CA
Tuggle, Jonathan J. .... Marietta, GA
Tuggle, Judy A. .... Edmond, OK
Tuggle, Kenneth J. .... Louisville, KY
Tuggle, Leonard M., Jr. .... Augusta, GA
Tuggle, R. Slaton, III .... Atlanta, GA
Tuggle, Richard J. .... Greensboro, NC
Tuggle, Richard J., Jr. .... Burlington, NC
Tuggle, Robert T., III .... Perry, GA
Tuggle & Schiro .... Danville, IL
Tuggle, Thomas M. .... Concordia, KS
Tuggy, Stephen A. .... Los Angeles, CA
Tugman, David F. .... Chattanooga, TN
Tugman, Richard J. .... Norfolk, VA
Tugwell, Frank B. .... Bastrop, LA
Tuholske, Jack R. .... Missoula, MT
Tuhy, Alan H. .... Kailua-Kona, HI
Tuhy, Elena V. .... Newark, OH
Tuinei, Tauivi .... Pago Pago, TT
Tuit, Frank E., II .... Northampton, MA
Tuite, Christopher P. .... Rochester, NY
Tuite, Edward J. .... Philadelphia, PA
Tuite, Edward J., & Associates
Philadelphia, PA
Tuite, Gerald F. .... Rockford, IL
Tuite, Gregory E. .... Rockford, IL
Tuite, James P. .... Washington, DC
Tuite, James R. .... Bloomington, IL
Tuite, Patrick A. .... Chicago, IL
Tuite, Rae Anne .... Oradell, NJ
Tuite, Shaw, Gesmer, Finnegan & Tuite
Rockford, IL
Tuite, Susan K. .... Ann Arbor, MI
Tujian, Tamar D. .... Los Angeles, CA
Tujios, Andrew P. .... Honolulu, HI
Tujios, Andrew P., Attorney at Law, A Law Corporation .... Honolulu, HI
Tujo, John A. .... Portland, OR
Tukdarian, Thomas H. .... Orlando, FL
Tukdarian & Uncapher, P.A. .... Orlando, FL
Tuke, Robert D. .... Nashville, TN
Tuke Yopp & Sweeney, PLC
Nashville, TN
Tukel, Daniel B. .... Detroit, MI
Tukel, Irving .... Detroit, MI
Pontiac, MI
Tukel, Irving .... Southfield, MI
Tukel, Jonathan .... Detroit, MI
Tukel, Sherwin .... West Bloomfield, MI
Tukel, Susan .... Southfield, MI
Tukesbrey, James S. .... Waukegan, IL
Tukey, Robert G. .... Norwich, CT
Tukloff, Tammara N. .... Clovis, CA
Tuku, Elisha Kidane .... New York, NY
Tulac, John W. .... Claremont, CA
Tulac, John W. .... Irvine, CA
Los Angeles, CA
Newport Beach, CA
Tulacz, Gary J. .... New York, NY
Tulafono, Talalelei A. .... Fagatogo, TT
Tulanian, Stephen D. .... Lower Lake, CA
Tulberg, Carolyn Richards .... Ventura, CA
Tulbert, David N. .... Green Bay, WI
Tulch, Robert .... Cincinnati, OH
Tulchin, David B. .... New York, NY
Tulchinsky, Guy .... Chestnut Hill, MA
Tulchinsky, Maurice M. .... South Bend, IN
Tule, Michael B. .... Manchester, NH
Tuleja, Laurine E. .... Diamond Bar, CA
Tuley, Alison .... Chattanooga, TN
Tuley, Charles M. .... Atchison, KS
Tuley, Daniel J. .... Evansville, IN
Tuley, James R. .... Columbia, MO
Tuley, Jay S. .... Montgomery, AL
Tuley, Ryan C. .... Irvine, CA
Tuley, Scarlette M. .... Montgomery, AL
Tuley, William M. .... Overland Park, KS
Tuleya, Robert Lawson
Virginia Beach, VA
Tulier, Esdras .... New York, NY
Tulin, Charles E. .... Anchorage, AK
Tulin, George C. .... Miami, FL
Tulin, George C., P.A. .... Miami, FL
Tulin, Patricia S. .... Farmington, CT
Tulin, Peter A. .... Saratoga Springs, NY
Tulin, Ronald .... Charleston, IL
Tulin, Ronald, Ltd. .... Charleston, IL
Tulin, Stephen Wise .... New York, NY
Tulinski, Pat .... Houston, TX
Tulip, Mark E. .... Brooklyn, NY
Tulipan & Conk, P.C. .... Jersey City, NJ
South Orange, NJ
Tulipan, Eileen Rhea .... Jersey City, NJ
South Orange, NJ
Tulipan, Philip .... Jersey City, NJ
Tulis, Mark S. .... Chicago, IL
Hawthorne, NY

Tulisano, Richard D. .... Rocky Hill, CT
Tulk & Deaderick .... Austin, TX
Tulk, Janet G. .... Livermore, CA
Tulk, Richard E. .... Austin, TX
Tulkoff, Myer S. .... Monsey, NY
Tull, Charles J. .... Bellingham, WA
Tull, Douglas A. .... Utica, MI
Tull, Douglas A., P.C. .... Utica, MI
Tull, H. Kenneth .... Philadelphia, PA
Tull, Jennifer .... Austin, TX
Tull, John A. .... Nederland, CO
Tull, John E., III .... Little Rock, AR
Tull, Kelly Kathleen .... Newnan, GA
Tull, Marc B. .... Denver, CO
Tull, Melvin E., III .... Richmond, VA
Tull, Robert M. .... Bellingham, WA
Tull, William F. .... Palmer, AK
Tulla, Eric A. .... San Juan, PR
Tulla, José Antonio .... San Juan, PR
Tullar, Allen I. .... Allentown, PA
Tullar, Robert S. .... Tucson, AZ
Tuller, Ronald A. .... Los Angeles, CA
Tuller, S. Mark .... Bedminster, NJ
Tuller, Tammy E. .... New York, NY
Tullett, Rodney C. .... Seattle, WA
Tulley, Angela M. .... Lawrence, MA
Tulley, Douglas H., Jr. .... Roswell, GA
Tulley, Fredrick R. .... Baton Rouge, LA
Tulley, Harold J. .... Bel Air, MD
Tulley, Jason D. .... Baltimore, MD
Tulley, Joseph P. .... Willoughby, OH
Tulley, Patrick J. .... Cleveland, OH
Tulley, Raymond D. .... Lawrence, MA
Tulley, Richard G. .... Crawfordsville, IN
Tulli, Richard A. .... Dallas, TX
Tullidge, Thomas H. .... Middlebrook, VA
Tullidge, Thomas H., Jr. .... Richmond, VA
Tullie, Richard E. .... Boca Raton, FL
Tullier, Kelly Mahon .... Plano, TX
Tullio, Christine C.A. .... Chicago, IL
Tullio, Peter A., Jr. .... Van Nuys, CA
Tullis, Charles W. .... Houston, TX
Tullis, Ernie W. .... Austin, TX
Tullis, Gary B. .... Jacksonville, FL
Tullis, Gary B., P.A. .... Jacksonville, FL
Tullis, Jeffrey A. .... Naperville, IL
Tullis, John W. .... Owensboro, KY
Tullis, Richard .... San Francisco, CA
Tullis, Robert Wood .... Chicago, IL
Tullis, Rodman C. .... Spartanburg, SC
Tullis, Timothy T. .... Columbus, OH
Tullis, William O., Jr. .... Atlanta, GA
Tullius, Russel C. .... Daytona Beach, FL
Tullius, Russel C., P.A.
Daytona Beach, FL
Tullman, Howard A. .... Chicago, IL
Tullman, Jeffrey S. .... New York, NY
Tullman, Paul L. .... Great Neck, NY
Tullo, Janet V. .... Bronx, NY
Tulloch, Elizabeth K. .... Denver, CO
Tulloch, Kathleen J. .... Brooklyn, NY
Tulloch, Rebecca W. .... Wilmington, DE
Tulloch, Robert N. .... Gig Harbor, WA
Tullock, Linda A. .... Schenectady, NY
Tullos, Edwin F. .... Raleigh, MS
Tullos, Eugene C. .... Raleigh, MS
Tullos, Hugh S., III .... Oklahoma City, OK
Tullos, John Raymond .... Raleigh, MS
Tullos, Kathryn Jane .... Austin, TX
Tullos, Mark K. .... Raleigh, MS
Tullos, Thomas .... Bay Springs, MS
Tullos, Tim A. .... Baton Rouge, LA
Tullos, Tullos & Tullos .... Raleigh, MS
Tulloss, Carl E. .... Houston, TX
Tully, Albert J. .... Mobile, AL
Tully, Andrew W., Jr.
Yorktown Heights, NY
Tully, Bernard M. .... Pittsburgh, PA
Tully, Billie M. .... Gretna, LA
Tully, Brian Brendan .... Phoenix, AZ
Tully & Burns .... Yorktown Heights, NY
Tully, Catherine T. .... Milwaukee, WI
Tully, Christopher J. .... Rockville, MD
Tully, Christopher S. .... New York, NY
Tully, Clare T. .... New York, NY
Tully, Deanne M. .... Pleasanton, CA
Tully, Dennis E. .... East Longmeadow, MA
Tully, Dorothy R. .... New York, NY
Tully, Gary D. .... Waco, TX
Tully, Griffeth E. .... Hayward, CA
Tully, Guy P. .... Boston, MA
Tully, Gwyn-Mohr .... Sacramento, CA
Tully, J. Michael .... Tucson, AZ
Tully, J. Michael, P.C. .... Tucson, AZ
Tully, James F., III .... Catonsville, MD
Tully, James H., Jr. .... Albany, NY
Tully, Jane Connolly .... New York, NY
Tully, Jeanne Noel .... Goshen, NY
Tully, John .... Tucson, AZ
Tully, John D. .... Grand Rapids, MI
Tully, John F. .... Houston, TX
Tully, John J., Jr. .... Chicago, IL
Tully, John P. .... Chicago, IL
Tully & Jolley .... Farmington, NM
Tully, Kevin J. .... San Mateo, CA
Tully, Kevin R. .... New Orleans, LA
Tully, L. Lawrence .... Syracuse, NY
Tully, Lizbeth Ann .... Lexington, KY
Tully, Marian Haycock .... Claremont, CA
Tully, Mark E. .... Andover, MA
Tully, Mark E. .... Boston, MA
Tully, Martin F. .... New Paltz, NY
Tully, Martin P. .... Wilmington, DE
Tully, Martin T. .... Chicago, IL
Tully, Mary Ellen .... West Orange, NJ
Tully, Maura K. .... New York, NY
Tully & Melbert .... New Paltz, NY

Tully, Michael D.
General Services Administration, Office of the General Counsel, GV
Tully, Michael D. .... Lorain, OH
Tully, Michael D., Co., L.P.A. .... Lorain, OH
Tully, Michael J. .... Fairfield, CT
Tully, Neal C. .... Boston, MA
Tully, Peter K. .... Flushing, NY
Tully & Philips .... Mobile, AL
Tully, Ralph H. .... Minneapolis, MN
Tully, Richard T. C. .... Farmington, NM
Tully, Robert B. .... Hilo, HI
Tully, Robert G. .... Des Moines, IA
Tully, Robert S. .... Department of the Navy, Office of the Judge Advocate General, GV
Tully, Rosemarie .... Islandia, NY
Tully, Scott L. .... Tulsa, OK
Tully, Stephen J. .... Westlake Village, CA
Tully, Stephen R. .... Baltimore, MD
Cumberland, MD
Towson, MD
Tully, Stephen W. .... Phoenix, AZ
Tully, Therese .... Chicago, IL
Tully, Thomas L. .... Fairfield, CT
Tully, W. Bradley .... Los Angeles, CA
Tully, W. Jeffrey .... Marina Del Rey, CA
Tully, Wellington W., Jr.
Minneapolis, MN
Tully, William T. .... Harrisburg, PA
Tulman, Elizabeth E. .... Columbus, OH
Tulman, Scott B., Law Offices of
New York, NY
Tulowitzki, David J. .... Ebensburg, PA
Tulsiak, Dennis C. .... Los Angeles, CA
Tulsky, Kim R. .... Berkeley, CA
Tulumello, Andrew S. .... Washington, DC
Tulupan, L. Zoe .... Chicago, IL
Tuma & Davis, P.A. .... Columbia, MD
Tuma, John A. .... Northfield, MN
Tuma, Malik J. .... Annapolis, MD
Greenbelt, MD
Tuma, Robert L. .... Cleveland, OH
Tuma, Samir J. .... San Francisco, CA
Tuma, Samuel E. .... Albuquerque, NM
Tuma & Thompson, P.L.L.P. .... Northfield, MN
Tuman, Carol A. .... Oak Lawn, IL
Tuman, Martin .... Bayonne, NJ
Tumarkin, Allan L. .... Edison, NJ
Tumarkin, Patricia Lother
Kissimmee, FL
Tumas, Michael B. .... Wilmington, DE
Tumavicus, Edward M. .... Ithaca, NY
Tumbarello, Gregory L. .... Mount Prospect, IL
Tumbarello, Phillip A. .... New York, NY
Tumbleson, J. Doyle .... Daytona Beach, FL
Tumbleson, Mark W. .... Camarillo, CA
Tumbleson, Paul A. .... Parsippany, NJ
Tumblin, Stephen M. .... Salt Lake City, UT
Tumbri, John A. .... Youngstown, OH
Tumbush, Stephen R. .... Madison, WI
Tumen, David A. .... Columbus, OH
Tumen, Harry B. .... Asbury Park, NJ
Tumey, Samuel M. .... Liberty, MS
Tumey, Tod T. .... Houston, TX
Tumilty, John J. .... Boston, MA
Tumilty, Thomas G. .... Boston, MA
Tumin, David U. .... Jacksonville, FL
Tuminaro, Dominick J. .... New York, NY
Tuminelli, Arcangelo M. .... Baltimore, MD
Tuminelli, Barry M. .... Bay Shore, NY
Tumlin, Cheryl O. .... Portland, ME
Tumlin, Edward D. .... Vestavia Hills, AL
Tumlin, R. Steve, Jr. .... Marietta, GA
Tumlin, Tracy N. .... Silver Spring, MD
Tumlin, Wayne E. .... Portland, ME
Tumlinson, Jack Maynard .... Alexandria, VA
Tumm, Brian R. .... Kalamazoo, MI
Tummelson Bryan & Knox
Champaign, IL
Urbana, IL
Tummelson, Hurshal C. .... Urbana, IL
Tumminaro, Peter M. .... Roselle, IL
Tumminelli, Jennifer A. .... Buffalo, NY
Tumminelli, Lisa .... Schenectady, NY
Tumminello, Anthony G. .... St. Louis, MO
Tumminello, Anthony P. .... Philadelphia, PA
Tumminello, Douglas B. .... Denver, CO
Tumminello, Lee Mosier .... Indianapolis, IN
Tumminia, Paul J.
Export-Import Bank of The United States, Office of the General Counsel, GV
Tummino, Barry L. .... Cleveland, OH
Tummino, Michael J. .... Lowell, MI
Tummiolo, Elisa M. .... New York, NY
Tummonds, Paul A, Jr .... Washington, DC
Tumola, Thomas J. .... Philadelphia, PA
Tumolo, John A. .... Pittsburgh, PA
Tumolo, Lisa M. .... Pittsburgh, PA
Tumolo, Michael L. .... Paramus, NJ
Tumonis, Elaine F. .... Los Angeles, CA
Tumpson, Albert J. .... Los Angeles, CA
Tumpson & Charchat, P.A. .... Miami, FL
Tumpson, Joan B. .... Miami, FL
Tumulty, James H. .... Minneapolis, MN
Tumulty, Joseph W. .... Jersey City, NJ
Tun, Harry .... Washington, DC
Tundermann, David W.
Salt Lake City, UT
Tundermann, Ren L. .... Baltimore, MD
Tundis, Mark J. .... Upland, CA
Tune, Cydney A. .... San Francisco, CA
Tune, Entrekin & White, P.C.
Nashville, TN
Tune, James F. .... Seattle, WA
Tune, Kenneth S. .... Los Angeles, CA
Tune, Mark H. .... San Francisco, CA
Tune, Merrie Kathleen .... Plano, TX
Tuneberg, James E. .... Rockford, IL

Tunell, William P., Jr. .... Tulsa, OK
Tuneski, Robert S. .... New London, CT
Tung, Arthur C. C. .... Upper Darby, PA
Tung, Cora K. .... Bangor, ME
Tung, Elaine .... Lexington, MA
Tung, Gea .... Buffalo, NY
Tung, George C. .... Irvine, CA
Tung, Hao-Yuan .... Palo Alto, CA
Tung, Jeffrey C. .... San Francisco, CA
Tung, Kim .... Los Angeles, CA
Tung, Ko-Yung .... New York, NY
Tung, Melanie H. .... Department of Commerce, Patent and Trademark Office, GV
Tungate, David E. .... Pittsburgh, PA
Tungate, James L. .... Cissna Park, IL
Watseka, IL
Tungate Law Offices, Ltd. .... Cissna Park, IL
Watseka, IL
Tungate, Mark J. .... Flora, IL
Tungate, Sherri L. E. .... Louisville, IL
Tungate, Susan R. .... Atlanta, GA
Tungol, Diane .... Marlton, NJ
Tungol, Wilfredo O. .... Honolulu, HI
Tunheim, Jon .... Olympia, WA
Tunheim, Marcia Ann .... Seattle, WA
Tunheim, Robert E. .... Minneapolis, MN
Tunick, Andrew J. .... New York, NY
Tunick, Bonnie I. .... North Chicago, IL
Tunick, Jeffrey Pierce .... Bedford Hills, NY
Tunick, Jennifer A. .... Washington, DC
Tunick Kupferman & Creadore, P.C.
New York, NY
Tunick, Lance E. .... Golden, CO
Tunick, Lisa A.
Department of Housing and Urban Development, GV
Tunick, Richard D. .... New York, NY
Tunik, Lloyd .... Spokane, WA
Tunila, John G. .... Manchester, CT
Tunink, Michael .... Monterey, CA
Watsonville, CA
Tunis, Amy S. .... New York, NY
Tunis, Eric .... West Orange, NJ
Tunis, Nancy D. .... New York, NY
Tunis, Paul .... Miami, FL
Tunis, Peter L. .... Fort Lauderdale, FL
Tunison, Ethel N. .... Saginaw, MI
Tunison, George M. .... Saginaw, MI
Tunison, James G., Jr. .... Valdosta, GA
Tunison, James G., Jr., Attorney at Law, P.C.
Valdosta, GA
Tunison, Theresa E. .... Auburn Hills, MI
Tunkel, Jacqueline .... Oceanside, NY
Tunkey, William R. .... Miami, FL
Tunkle, Richard D. .... Clayton, GA
Tunks, Elizabeth A. .... Department of Defense, Armed Services Board of Contract Appeals, GV
Tunks, Gerald C. .... Tucson, AZ
Tunley, Charles R. .... Nome, AK
Tunley, Scott J. .... White Plains, NY
Tunmer, Patricia Diane .... Metairie, LA
Tunnage, Donald L. .... Miami, FL
Tunnell, Andrew W. .... Birmingham, AL
Tunnell, Byron M. .... Austin, TX
Tunnell, Charles B. .... San Rafael, CA
Tunnell, Christine E. .... Georgetown, DE
Tunnell, Deana .... Dallas, TX
Tunnell, Gene H. .... Kingsport, TN
Tunnell, Graddy .... Plainview, TX
Tunnell, Joe .... Tyler, TX
Tunnell, Kurtis A. .... Columbus, OH
Tunnell, Mark L. .... West Chester, PA
Tunnell, Michele L. .... Topeka, KS
Tunnell, Norman D. .... White Plains, NY
Tunnell & Raysor .... Bethany Beach, DE
Rehoboth Beach, DE
Seaford, DE
Georgetown, DE
Tunnell, Robert W. .... Georgetown, DE
Tunnell, Shawna R. .... Washington, DC
Tunnell, T. R. .... Richardson, TX
Tunnell, W. Lawrence .... Oak Ridge, TN
Tunner, William W. .... Chesterfield, VA
Tunnero, Frank A. .... Flemington, NJ
Tunnessen, Anne Layton .... Macon, GA
Tunney, Anthony J. .... Chicago, IL
Tunney, Anthony P., Jr. .... Mount Holly, NJ
Tunney, Brian J. .... Brooklyn, NY
Tunney, Francis R., Jr. .... Irvine, CA
Tunney, Gene L. .... Santa Rosa, CA
Tunney, John A. .... Woodbridge, NJ
Tunney, John C. .... Bath, NY
Tunney, John V. .... Santa Monica, CA
Tunnicliff, Cynthia S. .... Tallahassee, FL
Tunno, Patricia .... Haines City, FL
Tunstall, Ava F. .... Maitland, FL
Tunstall, David M. .... Tuscaloosa, AL
Tunstall, Edw. W. .... Dearborn, MI
Tunstall, G. Taylor, Jr. .... Philadelphia, PA
Tunstall, Minnie L. .... Bessemer, AL
Tunstall, Stephen E. .... Miami, FL
Tunstall, Stephen E., P.A. .... Miami, FL
Tunstead, Schechter & Torre .... Jericho, NY
Mineola, NY
New York, NY
Tuntasit, Tony Jeera .... Clearwater, FL
Tuntland, Tom .... Mandan, ND
Tuohey, Conrad G. .... Laguna Hills, CA
Tuohey, Conrad G., A Professional Law Corporation .... Laguna Hills, CA
Tuohey, Mark H., III .... Washington, DC
Tuohey, Michael Joseph .... Rochester, NY
Tuohey, Seamus M. .... Newark, NJ
New York, NY
Tuohey, William F. .... Newark, NJ
Tuohey-Kay, Meaghan E. .... Newark, NJ
Tuohy, Brian J. .... Indianapolis, IN

Tuohy, C. Thomas ... Everett, WA
Tuohy, Catherine A. Honan ... Atlantic City, NJ
Tuohy, Cornelius F. ... Naugatuck, CT
Tuohy, Dennis M. ... Atlantic City, NJ
Tuohy, Dolores A. ... Albany, NY
Tuohy, James L. ... Chicago, IL
Tuohy, James L. ... Indianapolis, IN
Tuohy, John E. ... White Plains, NY
Tuohy, John L. ... Chicago, IL
Tuohy, John S. ... Boston, MA
Tuohy, Joseph P. ... Chicago, IL
Tuohy, Joyce A. ... Scottsdale, AZ
Tuohy, Kari Anne ... Seattle, WA
Tuohy, Martin J. ... Chatham, NJ
Tuohy & Martin, Ltd. ... Chicago, IL
Tuohy and Minor ... Everett, WA
Tuohy, Thomas R. ... Bethpage, NY
Tuohy, Thomas R., Jr. ... Phoenix, AZ
Tuohy, Thomas W. ... Chicago, IL
Tuohy, Tracey ... Orange, CA
Tuohy & Tuohy ... Atlantic City, NJ
Tuomainen, Paul M., Jr. ... San Diego, CA
Tuoriniemi, Joel C. ... Hancock, MI
Tuosto, Robert J. ... Commack, NY
Tuozzolo, John J. ... Danbury, CT
Tupi, Bradley S. ... Pittsburgh, PA
Tupitza, James S. ... West Chester, PA
Tupitza & Jordan, P.C. ... West Chester, PA
Tupitza, Thomas A. ... Erie, PA
Tupler, Anthony ... Santa Fe, NM
Tupler, David S. ... Plantation, FL
Tupler, David S., P.A. ... Plantation, FL
Tuplin, Frank P. ... Philadelphia, PA
Tupman, Wilbur C. ... Hilton Head Island, SC
Tuppen, Charles D., Jr., (P.C.) ... Buffalo, NY
Tuppen, James L. ... Buffalo, NY
Tupper, Charles A. ... Point Pleasant Beach, NJ
Tupper, Charles, Jr. ... Dallas, TX
Tupper, Gerald D. ... Phoenix, AZ
Tupper, Jeanie K ... Albany, GA
Tupper, Jill Kaplan ... Boothbay Harbor, ME
Tupper, Kent P. ... Key West, FL
Tupper, Paula G. ... San Diego, CA
Tupper, Ralph E. ... Beaufort, SC
Tupper, Richard J. ... Chicago, IL
Tupper, Stanley R. ... Boothbay Harbor, ME
Tupper, Stephen L. ... Bloomfield Hills, MI
Tupper, Timothy J. ... Davenport, IA
Tupper & Tupper ... Boothbay Harbor, ME
Tupper, Wayne P. ... Worcester, MA
Tupy, Claude W. ... De Kalb, IL
Tupy, Janis M. ... De Kalb, IL
Turaids, Mara S. ... San Jose, CA
Turaj, Julie ... New York, NY
Turak, Jonathan E. ... Moundsville, WV
Turak, Sadie Baris ... Jackson Heights, NY
Turan, Edward G. ... New York, NY
Turano, David A. ... Columbus, OH
Turano, John B. ... Garden City, NY
Turano, Joseph A. ... Dallas, TX
Turano, Lisa Moore ... Houston, TX
Turano, Margaret Valentine ... Jamaica, NY
Turano, Ralph Charles ... Lakewood, CO
Turano, Randall W. ... Stroudsburg, PA
Turano, Richard R. ... Paterson, NJ
Turano, Thomas A. ... Boston, MA
Turano-Flores, Sarah ... Dennis, MA
Turansick, Michael F. ... New York, NY
Turansky, David C. ... Shreveport, LA
Turay, Norman A. ... Seattle, WA
Turbak Law Office, P.C. ... Watertown, SD
Turbak, Nancy J. ... Watertown, SD
Turbak, Stephen Albin ... Milford, CT
Turberville, L. Dan ... Birmingham, AL
Turberville, L. Dan, P.C. ... Birmingham, AL
Turbes, Michael M. ... Atlanta, GA
Turbeville, C. Thomas, Jr. ... Williamsburg, VA
Turbeville, Elbert K. ... Lake City, SC
Turbeville Law Firm ... Little Rock, AR
Turbeville, Luther B. ... Jackson, MS
Turbeville, R. Wright ... Manning, SC
Turbeville, Richard N. ... Little Rock, AR
Turbeville, Wallace C. ... New York, NY
Turbeville, William J., II ... Boca Raton, FL
Turbin, Richard ... Honolulu, HI
Turbin, Richard, A Law Corporation, Law Offices of ... Honolulu, HI
Turbin, Ronald ... New York, NY
Turbiner, David S. ... Washington, DC
Turbis, Lisa A. ... San Francisco, CA
Turbitt, Daniel M. ... Dallas, TX
Turbitt, John R. ... Burke, VA
Turbiville, John F. ... Tampa, FL
Turbiville, Richard B. ... Dallas, TX
Turboff, Lisa Lepow ... Houston, TX
Turbow, Brent M. ... Jacksonville, FL
Turbow, Daniel W. ... Palo Alto, CA
Turbow, Ellen B. ... Palo Alto, CA
Turbow, Laurence A. ... Cleveland, OH
Turbow, Orrin H. ... Chatsworth, CA
Turbyfill, Donald L. ... Houston, TX
Turbyfill, John R. ... Virginia Beach, VA
Turbyfill, Toby A. ... North Lauderdale, FL
Turc, William ... Glen Burnie, MD
Turc, William, P.A. ... Glen Burnie, MD
Turchetta, David M. ... Norwood, MA
Turchi, Joseph L. ... Philadelphia, PA
Turchick, Alexander ... Latham, NY
Turchin, Aaron S. ... Pasadena, CA
Turchin, Carolyn ... Los Angeles, CA
Turchin, Daniel ... New York, NY
Turchin, Debra J. ... General Services Administration, Office of Regional Counsel, GV
Turchin, Florette S. ... La Canada Flintridge, CA
Turchin, George N. ... New York, NY
Turchin & Hoffman, P.C. ... New York, NY
Turchin, Morton J. ... New York, NY
Turchin, Raymond L. ... Burbank, CA
Turck, Mary C. ... St. Paul, MN
Turck, Mathias ... New York, NY
Turcke, Paul A. ... Boise, ID
Turco, Albert J. ... Wakefield, MA
Turco, Alfred A. ... Hartford, CT
Turco, Anthony J. ... Danvers, MA
Turco & Barnhart ... Omaha, NE
Turco, Cynthia L. ... New Bern, NC
Turco, John T. ... Omaha, NE
Turco, Joseph A. ... New York, NY
Turco, Mark A. ... Washington, DC; Baltimore, MD
Turco, Michael R. ... Detroit, MI
Turco, Michelle L. ... New York, NY
Turco, Misty W. ... Riverside, CA
Turco, Nicholas J. ... Newark, NJ
Turco, Nick A., Jr. ... New Castle, PA
Turco, Ralph ... Tacoma, WA
Turco, Samuel J., Jr. ... Omaha, NE
Turco, Samuel J., Sr. ... Omaha, NE
Turco, Victoria A. ... Philadelphia, PA
Turcott, Brian P. ... Tucker, GA
Turcott, Judith M. ... Signal Mountain, TN
Turcott, Robert G. ... Muskego, WI
Turcotte, Alphonse C. ... Chicopee, MA
Turcotte, Cathy Raba ... San Antonio, TX
Turcotte, Christopher B. ... New York, NY
Turcotte, Claire ... Portland, OR
Turcotte, David T. ... Fall River, MA
Turcotte, Erin Doherty ... Chelmsford, MA
Turcotte, John A., Jr. ... St. Louis, MO
Turcotte, John M. ... Manchester, NH
Turcotte, Kenneth L. ... Centralia, WA
Turcotte, Leo N. ... Brockton, MA
Turcotte, Peter J. ... San Francisco, CA
Turcotte, Raymond J., Jr ... New Orleans, LA
Turcotte, Roy C. ... Kingsville, TX
Turcotte, Susan M. ... Holyoke, MA
Turcotte, Suzanne E. ... Boston, MA
Turcotte, Thomas W. ... San Francisco, CA
Turcy, Philip E. ... Chicago, IL
Turean, Frances ... Seattle, WA
Tureau, Ralph ... Gonzales, LA
Tureck, Jeffrey ... Department of Labor, Office of Secretary, GV
Tureen, Charles M. ... St. Louis, MO
Tureen, Thomas N. ... Portland, ME
Turek, Allen M. ... New York, NY
Turek, Anton ... Lake Bluff, IL
Turek, Donald E. ... Elm Grove, WI
Turek, Douglas D. ... Houston, TX
Turek, Ernest ... Sioux City, IA
Turek, Gerald L. ... Skokie, IL
Turek, James J. ... Cleveland, OH
Turek, Katherine K. ... Baltimore, MD
Turek, Kenneth C. ... San Diego, CA
Turek, Marliss E. ... Lake Forest, IL
Turekian, Karla A. ... Hartford, CT
Turell, Russell B. ... Cleveland, OH
Turelli, Richard D. ... Castle Rock, CO
Turem, Alan R. ... Atlanta, GA
Turem, Alan R., P.C. ... Atlanta, GA
Turen, Edward D. ... Secaucus, NJ
Turen, George H. ... Oakland Gardens, NY
Turen, Louis G. ... Roslyn Heights, NY
Turen & Turen ... Roslyn Heights, NY
Turer & Feinland, L.P. ... Santa Rosa, CA
Turer, L. Stephen ... Santa Rosa, CA
Turer, Richard B. ... Ellicott City, MD
Turesky, David S. ... Portland, ME
Turesky and Howard ... Portland, ME
Turet, Charles S., Jr. ... Houston, TX
Turet, Craig F. ... Philadelphia, PA
Turet, Thomas R. ... Dallas, TX
Turetsky, Aaron ... Keeseville, NY
Turetsky, Beth E. ... Boston, MA
Turetsky, Carl ... New York, NY
Turetsky, Carl, P.C. ... New York, NY
Turetsky, Carol N. ... Los Angeles, CA
Turetsky, Cheryl J. G. ... Maple Glen, PA
Turetsky, David A. ... New York, NY
Turetsky, Gary S. ... Norristown, PA; Philadelphia, PA
Turetsky, Gerald J. ... New York, NY
Turetsky, Louis ... Garfield, NJ
Turetsky, Mark D. ... Norristown, PA
Turetsky, Matthew ... Seattle, WA
Turetsky, Norman L. ... Spring Valley, NY
Turetsky, Samuel H. ... Passaic, NJ
Turezyn, Andrew J. ... Wilmington, DE
Turfe, David D. ... St. Clair Shores, MI
Turfe, Edward M. ... Detroit, MI
Turffs, Robert E. ... Sarasota, FL
Turgeon, Jeannine ... Harrisburg, PA
Turgeon, Lawrence J. ... Barre, VT
Turgeon, Leonard A. ... St. Petersburg, FL
Turgeon, Lisa P. ... North Canton, OH
Turgeon, Marc P. ... Charleston, WV
Turgeon, Michael J. ... Tinley Park, IL
Turgeon, Roger D. ... Amesbury, MA
Turgeon, Thomas P. ... Baltimore, MD
Turi, A. Edward, III ... New York, NY
Turi, Albert J. ... Garden City, NY
Turi, Andrew S. ... New York, NY
Turi, Bernard J. ... Utica, NY
Turi, Dorothy G. ... Trenton, NJ
Turi, John C. ... Trenton, NJ
Turi, Louis A. ... Wickliffe, OH
Turian, Samantha R. ... Chicago, IL
Turici, Melinda B. ... Pittsburgh, PA
Turick, Henry H. ... San Marino, CA
Turiel, Bernard ... Woodbridge, NJ
Turiel, Bernard, P.A. ... Woodbridge, NJ
Turiel, Robinanne J. ... Bronx, NY
Turiello, Michael P. ... Wheaton, IL
Turiello, Ronald J., Jr. ... New York, NY
Turigliatto, Jon A. ... Los Angeles, CA
Turilli, M. Louise ... Washington, DC
Turim, David M. ... Waukesha, WI
Turin, John C. ... Toledo, OH
Turin, Todd T. ... Greensburg, PA
Turinas, Alice W. ... Basking Ridge, NJ
Turinchak, Arlene M. ... Somerset, NJ
Turino, Alfred C. ... Port Washington, NY
Turitz, Gilda R. ... San Francisco, CA
Turitz, Joseph ... Washington, DC
Turitz, Stanley ... Hackensack, NJ
Turitzin, John N. ... New York, NY
Turk, A. Marco ... Irvine, CA
Turk, Alan Mark ... Brentwood, TN
Turk, Alan Mark, P.C. ... Brentwood, TN
Turk, Andrew B. ... Phoenix, AZ
Turk, Arnold ... Reston, VA
Turk, C. David, III ... Dahlonega, GA
Turk, Craig Daniel ... Washington, DC
Turk, David L. ... Honolulu, HI
Turk, David L., A Law Corporation ... Honolulu, HI
Turk, D. E. ... Abbeville, GA
Turk, Elizabeth L. ... Phoenix, AZ
Turk, Eugene N. ... Brooklyn, NY
Turk, Frank J. ... Palm Springs, CA
Turk, Gary E. ... Jamaica, NY
Turk, Gene A., Jr. ... Carbondale, IL
Turk, Harold J. ... Miami, FL
Turk, Harold Preston ... Montgomery, AL
Turk, Harold Preston, A Professional Corporation ... Montgomery, AL
Turk, Harry N. ... Miami, FL
Turk, Hugh M. ... Hackensack, NJ; Mineola, NY; New York, NY
Turk, Jack J. ... Houston, TX
Turk, James C. ... Roanoke, VA
Turk, James C., Jr. ... Radford, VA
Turk, James E. ... Rochelle, GA
Turk, James H. ... Mankato, MN
Turk, Jeffrey Craig ... Braintree, MA
Turk, Julia A. ... Chicago, IL
Turk, Lisa M. ... Chicago, IL
Turk, Mark E. ... Dallas, TX
Turk, Norman ... Brooklyn, NY
Turk, Pamela M. ... Atlantic City, NJ
Turk, Paul A., Jr. ... Palm Beach, FL
Turk, Paul A., Jr., P.A. ... Palm Beach, FL
Turk, Randall J. ... Washington, DC
Turk, Robert B. ... Livingston, NJ
Turk, Robert M. D. ... Radford, VA
Turk, Robert S. ... Miami, FL
Turk, Roger L. ... Honolulu, HI
Turk, Ronald J. ... Rochester, NY
Turk, S. Maynard ... Wilmington, DE
Turk, Salim Naim ... Los Angeles, CA
Turk, Sherwin E. ... Nuclear Regulatory Commission, Office of the General Counsel, GV
Turk, Stanley ... Baltimore, MD
Turk, Stephen L. ... San Francisco, CA
Turk, Thad H. ... Albuquerque, NM
Turk, Thomas E. ... Westerville, OH
Turk, Truman, Bishop & Tillapaugh ... Owego, NY
Turkal, Donal L. ... Fort Worth, TX
Turkaly, Michael A. ... Charleston, WV
Turkat, Jennifer ... Los Angeles, CA
Turk-Borowick, Laurel ... New York, NY
Turke, Mary C. ... Madison, WI
Turke, Peter D. ... Milwaukee, WI
Turkel, Allison L ... New York, NY
Turkel, Dorothy G. ... Los Angeles, CA
Turkel Forman & Zimmerman, P.C. ... New York, NY
Turkel, Jeffrey ... New York, NY
Turkel, Jonathan ... New York, NY
Turkel, Judith E. ... New York, NY
Turkel, Kenneth G. ... Tampa, FL
Turkel, Richard Ellis ... Orange, TX
Turkel, Robert ... Los Angeles, CA
Turkell, Jeffrey A. ... Glendale, CA
Turkelson, Eugene I. ... West Branch, MI
Turkelson, Michael J. ... Bellaire, MI
Turken & Associates ... St. Charles, MO
Turken, James H. ... Los Angeles, CA
Turken, Jason D. ... New York, NY
Turken, Marvin ... New York, NY
Turken, Michael A. ... St. Charles, MO
Turken, Robert W. ... Miami, FL
Turkett, Stephen ... Kerrville, TX
Turkevich, Leon R. ... Washington, DC
Turkewitz, Bernard ... New York, NY
Turkewitz, Deborah C. ... Charleston, SC
Turkewitz, Eric M. ... New York, NY
Turkewitz, Neil ... Washington, DC
Turkewitz, Robert M. ... Charleston, SC
Turkheimer, Paul A. ... Riverdale, MD
Turkheimer, Wayne ... Sherman Oaks, CA
Turkin, Gregg R. ... Bronx, NY
Turkington, Craig Theron ... Ellicott City, MD
Turkington, Eric T. ... Falmouth, MA
Turkington, Herbert B. ... Linwood, NJ
Turkington, William W., III ... Mariposa, CA
Turkish, Andrew S. ... Morristown, NJ
Turkish, Forrest S. ... Jersey City, NJ
Turkish, William J. ... New York, NY
Turkle, Bruce J. ... New York, NY
Turko, Vicki A. ... Metairie, LA
Turkovic, Ksenija ... New York, NY
Turkowitz, Steven M. ... Beverly Hills, CA
Turkowitz, Steven M., A Professional Corporation ... Beverly Hills, CA
Turkus, Albert H. ... Washington, DC
Turland, Kathleen L. ... New York, NY
Turley, Anne ... Boston, MA
Turley, Anthony E. ... Toledo, OH
Turley, B. B. ... Rolla, MO
Turley, Brentnall P. ... Los Angeles, CA
Turley, Cynthia L. ... Rolla, MO
Turley, Donna M. ... Boston, MA
Turley, Edward W., Jr. ... Houston, TX
Turley, Elizabeth ... Chicago, IL
Turley, Elizabeth C. ... Beaumont, TX
Turley, Elizabeth J. ... Versailles, KY
Turley, F. Andrew ... Federal Election Commission, Office of the General Counsel, GV
Turley, Francis A. ... Westwood, MA
Turley, Gregory E. ... Houston, TX
Turley, Hal E. ... Dallas, TX
Turley, J. Wayne ... Phoenix, AZ
Turley, James A., Jr. ... Katonah, NY
Turley, James William ... Columbia, MO
Turley, Jonathan R ... Washington, DC
Turley, Kent E. ... Phoenix, AZ
Turley, Laura Crowe ... Houston, TX
Turley, Linda ... Dallas, TX
Turley, M. Glenn ... Charleston, WV
Turley, Michael R. ... St. Louis, MO
Turley, Murhl C. ... Charleston, WV
Turley, Patricia K. ... Montpelier, VT
Turley, Patrick W.D. ... Washington, DC
Turley, Paul W. ... Los Angeles, CA
Turley, Redmond & Rosasco ... Islandia, NY
Turley, Richard E., Jr. ... Salt Lake City, UT
Turley, Richard L. ... Auburn, CA
Turley, Robert J. ... Lexington, KY
Turley, Robert Randall ... Jefferson City, MO
Turley, Sheldon G., Jr. ... Department of Labor, Office of the Solicitor, GV
Turley, Stephen S. ... Richmond, VA
Turley & Stutz, P.C. ... Dallas, TX
Turley, Swan & Childers, P.C. ... Phoenix, AZ
Turley, Tod M. ... Calabasas, CA
Turley & Turley ... Charleston, WV
Turley, W. Todd ... Santa Barbara, CA
Turley, William J. ... Islandia, NY
Turley, Windle ... Dallas, TX
Turley, Windle, P.C., Law Offices of ... Dallas, TX
Turlik, John A. ... Philadelphia, PA
Turlington, David F. ... Wilmington, NC
Turlington, Ed ... Raleigh, NC
Turlington, R. Donald ... New York, NY
Turmaine, Roland Arthur ... Chelmsford, MA
Turman, Audrey M. ... Alameda, CA
Turman, Dean K. ... St. Cloud, FL
Turman, Gregory W. ... Corpus Christi, TX
Turman, Howard ... Kew Gardens, NY
Turman, Joseph A. ... Fargo, ND
Turman, L. Julius M. ... San Francisco, CA; New York, NY
Turman, Marc L. ... Los Angeles, CA
Turman, Robert L. ... Colorado Springs, CO
Turman, Rossie E., III ... New York, NY
Turman-Vedral, Sara K. ... Fort Worth, TX
Turnage, Allen P. ... Albany, GA
Turnage, Edwin Lake ... Greenville, SC
Turnage, Ellen Ezelle ... Santa Ana, CA
Turnage, Fred D. ... Washington, DC
Turnage, George L., Jr. ... Memphis, TN
Turnage, J. A. ... Helena, MT
Turnage, Jeffrey J. ... Columbus, MS
Turnage, John C. ... Shreveport, LA
Turnage, John F. ... Rocky Mount, NC
Turnage, Kirby L., Law Offices of ... Atlanta, GA
Turnage, Mark T. ... Denver, CO
Turnage, Patricia A. ... San Francisco, CA
Turnage, Steven D. ... Gainesville, FL
Turnage, Wallace J., Jr. ... Phoenix, AZ
Turnage, William E. ... Liberty, MO
Turnage Gatlin, Cheri ... Jackson, MS
Turnamian, Mark R. ... Hackensack, NJ
Turnbach, Edward J. ... Toms River, NJ
Turnbach, James E. ... Gadsden, AL
Turnbach & Warren, P.C. ... Gadsden, AL
Turnbaugh, Albert J., A Prof. Corp. ... Martinez, CA
Turnbaugh, Charles W. ... Baltimore, MD
Turnblom, Todd A. ... Logan, UT
Turnbo, Monica Meyers ... Wheaton, MD
Turnbow, Charles E. ... Apple Valley, CA
Turnbow, Charles E., APC ... Apple Valley, CA
Turnbow, James M. ... Hayti, MO
Turnbow, Kimberly Berkman ... Denver, CO
Turnbow, Penelope Y. ... Memphis, TN
Turnbow, R.M. ... Boise, ID
Turnbow, Robert E. ... Rantoul, IL
Turnbow, Tony L. ... Franklin, TN
Turnbow, William R. ... Eugene, OR
Turnbull, Albert R. ... Charlottesville, VA
Turnbull, Albert W. ... Washington, DC
Turnbull, Ann McKenrick ... Towson, MD
Turnbull, B. Harrison ... Norfolk, VA
Turnbull, Bruce H. ... Washington, DC
Turnbull, Charles E. ... Sterling Heights, MI
Turnbull, Cynthia J ... Springfield, MA
Turnbull, Dan F., Jr. ... Fort Myers, FL
Turnbull & Daniels ... Winter Park, FL
Turnbull, E.R. (Ned) ... Tulsa, OK
Turnbull, Eugene H. ... Southfield, MI
Turnbull, Geneith A. ... Mount Vernon, NY
Turnbull, H. Rutherford ... Lawrence, KS
Turnbull, Heather A. ... Livingston, NJ
Turnbull, J. Gregory ... Honolulu, HI
Turnbull, J. Scott ... Sacramento, CA
Turnbull, Jeffrey B. ... Matthews, NC
Turnbull, John A. ... Livingston, TN
Turnbull, John Grason, II ... Towson, MD

Turnbull, Julie M. ... Dallas, TX
Turnbull, Kathleen A. ... Chicago, IL
Turnbull, Kenneth J. ... New York, NY
Turnbull, Kent D. ... North Platte, NE
Turnbull, Lowell D. ... Washington, DC
Turnbull & McLaughlin ... Sacramento, CA
Turnbull, Michael T. ... Tacoma, WA
Turnbull, Mix & Farmer ... Towson, MD
Turnbull, Nat M. ... Winter Park, FL
Turnbull, Reginald H. ... Jefferson City, MO
Turnbull & Sanders, P.A. ... Towson, MD
Turnbull, Stephen Rice ... Richmond, KY
Turnbull, Tracey L. ... Cleveland, OH
Turnbull, William S., Sr. Sun City Center, FL
Turnbull, William Scott ... Detroit, MI
Turndorf, Michael P. ... Brunswick, ME
Turnell, Roy L. ... Cleveland, OH
Turnell, Valeria B., (Mrs.) Oklahoma City, OK
Turner, A. Brent ... Brookfield, MO; Chillicothe, MO
Turner, A. Kelly ... Chicago, IL
Turner, Abigail ... Minneapolis, MN
Turner & Able, L.L.P. ... Laurens, SC
Turner, Abril Bedarf ... Irvine, CA
Turner, Alan A. ... Philadelphia, PA
Turner, Albert F. ... Mountain Grove, MO
Turner, Alice M. ... Wellesley Hills, MA
Turner, Alison M. ... Beverly Hills, CA
Turner & Allen, A Professional Corporation Graham, TX; Jacksboro, TX
Turner, Allen C. ... Salt Lake City, UT
Turner, Allen Charles ... Redlands, CA
Turner, Allen M. ... Chicago, IL
Turner, Andrew A. ... Clark, NJ
Turner, Andrew D. ... Pasadena, CA
Turner, Andrew J. ... San Mateo, CA
Turner, Andrew J. ... Department of Commerce, National Oceanic and Atmospheric Administration, GV
Turner, Andrew R. ... South Orange, NJ
Turner, Andrew R. ... Tulsa, OK
Turner, Andrew T. ... Dallas, TX
Turner, Andy L. ... Little Rock, AR
Turner, Anita ... Austin, TX
Turner, Anna L. ... Tulsa, OK
Turner, Anne Marie ... Albuquerque, NM
Turner, Anthony J. ... Los Angeles, CA
Turner, Ari Lynn ... North Miami Beach, FL
Turner, Arnold, Jr. ... Prestonsburg, KY
Turner & Associates ... Vandalia, OH
Turner & Associates, A Professional Corporation ... Atlanta, GA; Marblehill, GA
Turner & Associates, P.A. North Little Rock, AR
Turner, Aubert & Friedman, LLP Beverly Hills, CA; Los Angeles, CA
Turner, Audrey Schumacher Baltimore, MD
Turner, A. W., Jr. ... Portland, OR
Turner, Barbara ... Los Angeles, CA
Turner, Barbara L. ... Sacramento, CA
Turner, Barry S. ... New York, NY
Turner, Ben B., Jr. ... Houston, TX
Turner, Ben B., Jr., & Associates, P.C. Houston, TX
Turner, Ben H. ... Cleburne, TX
Turner, Ben Hill, & Associates, P.C. Cleburne, TX
Turner, Benjamin M., Jr. ... Timonium, MD
Turner, Bennie L. ... West Point, MS
Turner, Bernard ... New York, NY
Turner, Beth S. ... Charlotte, NC
Turner, Betsy ... New York, NY
Turner, Betsy M. ... Mobile, AL
Turner, Betty R. ... Charlotte, NC
Turner, Beverly D., Jr. Indian Rocks Beach, FL
Turner, Beverly L. ... St. Paul, MN
Turner, Bob F. ... Roswell, NM
Turner and Boisseau, Chartered Great Bend, KS; Overland Park, KS; Wichita, KS; Kansas City, MO; Springfield, MO
Turner, Bonnie Kaye ... Los Angeles, CA
Turner, Bradford Ryan ... Atlanta, GA
Turner, Brett D. ... Gainesville, GA
Turner, Brett R. ... Charlottesville, VA
Turner, Brian D. ... Tuscaloosa, AL
Turner, Brian Dennis, Jr. ... Birmingham, AL
Turner, Brian, Law Office of ... Austin, TX
Turner, Brian S. ... Sacramento, CA
Turner, Brown & Knezevic, P.C. Cleveland, OH
Turner, Brown, McIntosh & Umeugo, P.C. New Haven, CT
Turner, Bruce E. ... Addison, TX
Turner, Bruce K. ... Baton Rouge, LA
Turner, Burton R. ... Sedona, AZ
Turner, C. David ... Irving, TX
Turner, C. Denise Y. ... New York, NY
Turner, C. A., III ... Eastville, VA
Turner, C. A., Jr. ... Eastville, VA
Turner, Calvin P. ... Lebanon, TN
Turner, Caren Z. ... Washington, DC
Turner, Carl ... Cold Spring, KY
Turner, Carl Ira ... Rockville, MD
Turner, Carl M. ... Santa Fe, NM
Turner, Carl O. ... Cherry Hill, NJ
Turner, Carl W. ... Tamarac, FL
Turner, Carol A. ... Cedar Rapids, IA
Turner, Carol Ann ... Tallahassee, FL
Turner, Carol M. ... Chicago, IL
Turner, Carolyn M. ... Boston, MA
Turner, Cecil L. ... Pueblo, CO
Turner, Charles ... Little Rock, AR
Turner, Charles A. ... Hamilton, OH
Turner, Charles B., IV ... Philadelphia, PA
Turner, Charles B., Law Office of Newark, NJ
Turner, Charles B., Law Office of South Orange, NJ
Turner, Charles C. ... Denver, CO
Turner, Charles F., Jr. ... Greenville, SC
Turner, Charles H. ... Portland, OR
Turner, Charles H., Jr. ... New Bern, NC
Turner, Charles I. ... Jersey City, NJ
Turner, Charles L. ... Shelby, MT
Turner, Charles S. ... Rochester, NY
Turner, Cheryl C. ... Los Angeles, CA
Turner, Chris ... Abbeville, AL
Turner, Chrisandrea L. ... Frankfort, KY
Turner, Christine L. ... Richmond, VA
Turner, Christopher B. ... Washington, DC
Turner, Christopher M.R. ... Chicago, IL
Turner, Christopher R. ... Dallas, TX
Turner, Cindy L. ... Cincinnati, OH
Turner, Cindy Lou ... Tampa, FL
Turner, Clark Savage ... Irvine, CA
Turner, Clem ... New York, NY
Turner, Clemons C. ... Friday Harbor, WA
Turner, Cleon H. ... Sandwich, MA
Turner, Clydia A. ... Portsmouth, NH
Turner, C. O., IV ... Memphis, TN
Turner, Craig E. ... Auburn, ME
Turner, Craig W. ... Ocala, FL
Turner, Cynthia ... Media, PA
Turner, Cynthia Dale ... Seattle, WA
Turner, D. Scott ... Irvine, CA
Turner, D. Scott ... Memphis, TN
Turner, Dale R. ... Chicago, IL
Turner, Damien Sedrick ... Atlanta, GA
Turner, Dan E. ... Topeka, KS
Turner, Dana Davis ... Columbia, SC
Turner, Daniel C., (P.C.) ... Tucson, AZ
Turner, Daniel E. ... Atlanta, GA
Turner, Daniel J. ... San Diego, CA
Turner, D'Anne L. ... San Francisco, CA
Turner, David A. ... Denver, CO
Turner, David A. ... Nampa, ID
Turner, David C., Jr. ... Bonham, TX
Turner, David E. ... Reading, PA
Turner, David H. ... Holdenville, OK
Turner, David J. ... Durango, CO
Turner, David J. ... Grand Junction, CO; Moab, UT
Turner, David J., Jr. ... Manchester, GA
Turner, David K. ... Clarksburg, WV
Turner, David L. ... Atlanta, GA
Turner, David L. ... Saginaw, MI
Turner, David Lee ... Brookline, MA
Turner, David O. ... Dallas, TX
Turner, David W. ... Salem, OR
Turner, Davidson V. ... Granada Hills, CA
Turner & Davis ... Odessa, TX; Midland, TX
Turner, Davis W. ... Brentwood, TN
Turner, Dealey & Zimmermann, P.C. Dallas, TX
Turner, Debora J. ... Miami Beach, FL
Turner, Denise Kathlene ... Portland, OR
Turner, Denise R. ... Pittsburgh, PA
Turner, Dennis J. ... Dayton, OH
Turner, Dennis R. ... Miami, FL
Turner, Dewey E. ... Palo Alto, CA
Turner, Diana Hamilton ... Little Rock, AR
Turner, Dianne ... Nashville, TN
Turner, Dick, The Law Office of Cleburne, TX
Turner, Don A. ... San Bernardino, CA
Turner, Donald A. ... Southfield, MI
Turner, Donald C. ... Roswell, GA
Turner, Donald C. ... West Chester, PA
Turner, Donald C., & Associates, P.C. Roswell, GA
Turner, Donald L. ... Salem, OR
Turner, Donesia D. ... New Orleans, LA
Turner, Dorian E. ... Jackson, MS
Turner, Douglas A. ... Golden, CO
Turner, Douglas C. ... Tampa, FL
Turner, Douglas Eugene, Jr. ... Dunn, NC
Turner, Douglass E. ... St. Paul, MN
Turner, Duncan C. ... Seattle, WA
Turner, E. Alexander, III ... Anderson, SC
Turner, E. Deane ... New York, NY
Turner, E. Fred ... Livonia, MI
Turner, E. Lee, Jr. ... Raleigh, NC
Turner, E. Russell ... Jackson, MS
Turner, E. Tatum ... Chatom, AL; Mobile, AL
Turner, Edward D. ... Mount Sterling, IL
Turner, Edward M. ... Carthage, TN
Turner, Edward M., III ... Hillsville, VA
Turner, Edward P., Jr. ... Chatom, AL; Mobile, AL
Turner, Edwin B. ... Houston, TX
Turner, Elaine Holland Colorado Springs, CO
Turner, Elaine R. ... Oklahoma City, OK
Turner, Elizabeth A. ... Atlanta, GA
Turner, Elizabeth Ann ... Torrance, CA
Turner, Elizabeth Ann ... San Antonio, TX
Turner, Elizabeth R. ... Dallas, TX
Turner, Elsie C. ... Altamonte Springs, FL
Turner, Elvin D. ... Hartford, CT
Turner, Emile L., Jr. ... New Orleans, LA
Turner Enochs & Lloyd, P.A. Greensboro, NC
Turner, Eric D. ... Media, PA
Turner, Eric F. ... Des Moines, IA
Turner, Eric M. ... Orlando, FL
Turner, Eric Peter ... Detroit, MI
Turner, Eric V. ... Hartford, CT
Turner, Eric W. ... Albuquerque, NM
Turner, Erika Pike ... Las Vegas, NV
Turner, Eugene C. ... Naples, FL
Turner, Ezra, Jr. ... Los Angeles, CA
Turner, Felicia S. ... Owensboro, KY
Turner, Felton, Jr. ... Jackson, NC
Turner, Francine Guariglia ... Syracuse, NY
Turner, Francis M., III ... Hattiesburg, MS
Turner, Frank C. ... Houston, TX
Turner, Frank E. ... Claremore, OK; Tulsa, OK
Turner, Frank K., Jr. ... Baltimore, MD
Turner, Franklin ... Oxford, MS
Turner, Franzetta Darlene ... Cleveland, OH
Turner, Fred L. ... La Grange, GA
Turner, Frederick D. ... Buffalo, NY
Turner, Frederick E. ... Irvine, CA
Turner, Frederick, Jr. ... Golconda, IL
Turner, Frederick W. ... Elmsford, NY
Turner, G. Murray ... Louisville, KY
Turner, Gail Harris ... Media, PA
Turner, Gardner L. ... Lexington, KY
Turner, Garrison F. ... Ashland, OR
Turner, Geneva Brown ... Waco, TX
Turner, George A.H. ... Newport Beach, CA
Turner, George B. ... Melbourne, FL
Turner, George M., The Law Offices of Pasadena, CA
Turner, George Robert, III ... Charlotte, NC
Turner, Gerald L. ... Vandalia, OH
Turner, Gerald R. ... Milwaukee, WI
Turner, Gerard J. ... Orlando, FL
Turner, Glenn E., III ... Los Angeles, CA
Turner, Glynda L. ... Dallas, TX
Turner, Graham A. ... Phoenix, AZ
Turner, Gregory G. ... Dallas, TX
Turner, Gregory P. ... Waltham, MA
Turner, Gregory P. ... Seattle, WA
Turner, Guy W. ... Coral Gables, FL
Turner, Guy W., P.A. ... Coral Gables, FL
Turner, H. Douglas ... Independence, VA
Turner, H. Lee ... Great Bend, KS; Overland Park, KS; Wichita, KS
Turner, H. A., IV ... La Plata, MD
Turner, Halron W. ... Chatom, AL; Mobile, AL
Turner, Harold ... Chicago, IL
Turner, Harold H. ... Borrego Springs, CA
Turner, Harold L. ... Rockford, IL
Turner, Harold L., & Associates, P.C. Rockford, IL
Turner, Harry B. ... Twin Falls, ID
Turner, Harry B. ... Lutherville, MD
Turner, Harry E. ... Burlingame, CA
Turner, Harry E. ... Mt. Vernon, OH
Turner, Harry Woodruff ... Pittsburgh, PA
Turner, Heather J. ... Brighton, CO
Turner, Henry A. ... Atlanta, GA; Marblehill, GA
Turner, Henry P. ... Easton, MD
Turner, Hester ... New York, NY
Turner, Howard E. ... Atlanta, GA
Turner, Howard M. ... Chicago, IL
Turner, Hugh J., Jr. ... Fort Lauderdale, FL
Turner, Huguet & Adams ... Martinez, CA
Turner, Ilo Henning ... Florissant, MO
Turner, Irving ... Arlington, VA
Turner, J. Douglas ... Louisville, KY
Turner, J. Eric ... Oklahoma City, OK
Turner, J. Glenn, Jr. ... Dallas, TX
Turner, J. Kennedy, III ... Philadelphia, MS
Turner, J. Michael ... Laurens, SC
Turner, J. Preston ... Towson, MD
Turner, J. Randy ... Midland, TX
Turner, J. Wirt, Jr. ... Jensen Beach, FL; New Castle, KY
Turner, Jack E. ... Alma, KS
Turner, Jack M. ... Coral Gables, FL
Turner, Jack N. ... Wichita, KS
Turner, Jack P. ... Atlanta, GA
Turner, James A. ... Tuscaloosa, AL
Turner, James A., Jr. ... Seneca, SC
Turner, James B. ... Colorado Springs, CO
Turner, James C. ... Los Angeles, CA
Turner, James C. ... Clarksburg, WV
Turner, James D. ... Tuscaloosa, AL
Turner, James D. ... Long Beach, CA
Turner, James D. ... Wichita, KS
Turner, James D. ... Lucas, OH
Turner, James D. ... Alexandria, VA
Turner, James E. ... Sacramento, CA
Turner, James E. ... Washington, DC
Turner, James E. (Ted) ... Dallas, TX
Turner, James H. ... Denver, CO
Turner, James H. ... Woodstock, GA
Turner, James H. ... Harrisburg, PA
Turner, James H., Jr. House of Representatives, Congressional Assistants, GV
Turner, James H., P.C. ... Woodstock, GA
Turner, James Howard ... Detroit, MI
Turner, James K. ... Newport Beach, CA
Turner, James L. ... Santa Ana, CA
Turner, James L. Environmental Protection Agency, Office of Enforcement and Compliance Assurance, GV
Turner, James L. ... Sarasota, FL
Turner, James L. ... Cincinnati, OH
Turner, James M., Jr. ... Philadelphia, PA
Turner, James N. ... Toledo, OH
Turner, James O. ... St. Joseph, MO
Turner, James O. ... Philadelphia, PA
Turner, James R. ... Greensboro, NC
Turner, James S. ... Washington, DC
Turner, James S. ... Bellevue, WA
Turner, James S. ... Chehalis, WA
Turner, James T. United States Court of Federal Claims, GV
Turner, James W. ... Crockett, TX
Turner, James Wade ... Charleston, WV; Huntington, WV
Turner, James Walter ... Charleston, WV
Turner, James William, Jr. ... Louisville, KY
Turner, Jan ... Eureka, CA
Turner, Janice Nystrom ... Portland, OR
Turner, Janis L. ... Encino, CA; San Diego, CA
Turner, Janis Lynn ... Nashville, TN
Turner, Jas. R. ... Spartanburg, SC
Turner, Jason C. ... Chicago, IL
Turner, Jason E. ... Santa Ana, CA
Turner, Jay S. ... Coppell, TX
Turner, Jayne E. ... Parsippany, NJ
Turner, J.D. ... San Diego, CA
Turner, Jeffrey A. ... San Ramon, CA
Turner, Jeffrey C. ... Dayton, OH
Turner, Jeffrey Joseph Department of Labor, GV
Turner, Jeffrey L. ... Washington, DC
Turner, Jeffrey L. ... Auburn, IN
Turner, Jeffrey L. ... Pittsford, NY; Rochester, NY
Turner, Jeffrey S. ... Los Angeles, CA
Turner, Jeffry F. ... Westerville, OH
Turner, Jere Dickson ... Dallas, TX
Turner, Jerold L. ... Bakersfield, CA
Turner, Jerome ... Memphis, TN
Turner, Jerry ... Miami, FL
Turner, Jerry D. ... Norwalk, CA
Turner, Jerry D. ... Chattanooga, TN
Turner, Jerry E. ... Austin, TX
Turner, Jerry L. ... Chatom, AL
Turner, Jerry M. ... Santa Rosa, CA
Turner, Jess N., III ... Graham, TX; Jacksboro, TX
Turner, Jill H. ... New York, NY
Turner, Jimmy D. ... Cordell, OK
Turner, Joan L. ... Canfield, OH
Turner, Joanne H. ... Minneapolis, MN
Turner, Job D., III ... Lexington, KY
Turner, Joe N. ... San Diego, CA
Turner, Joel B. ... Louisville, KY
Turner, John ... Colorado Springs, CO
Turner, John ... New Haven, CT
Turner, John A. ... West Palm Beach, FL
Turner, John A. ... Boone, NC
Turner, John A., P.A. ... Boone, NC
Turner, John B. ... Los Angeles, CA
Turner, John B. ... Tulsa, OK
Turner, John C. ... Dallas, TX
Turner, John E. ... Kansas City, MO
Turner, John E. ... Tacoma, WA
Turner, John G., III ... Amarillo, TX
Turner, John G., Jr. ... Albany, NY
Turner, John Henderson, III Richmond, VA
Turner, John J. ... Chicago, IL
Turner, John K. ... Dallas, TX
Turner, John M. ... San Diego, CA
Turner, John M., Jr. ... Atlanta, GA
Turner, John P. ... East St. Louis, IL
Turner, John Paul ... Bellevue, WA
Turner, John R. ... Southfield, MI
Turner, John S. ... Fort Myers, FL
Turner, John S. ... Versailles, KY
Turner, John W. ... Lincoln, IL
Turner, John W. ... Ellicott City, MD
Turner, John W. ... Oklahoma City, OK
Turner, John W. ... Houston, TX
Turner, Jon E. ... La Mirada, CA
Turner, Jon M., Jr. ... Birmingham, AL
Turner, Jon Robin ... Columbia, SC
Turner, Jonathan C. ... Sacramento, CA
Turner, Jonathan M. ... Los Angeles, CA
Turner, Jones & Bitting ... Clarinda, IA
Turner & Jordan, P.C. ... Lubbock, TX
Turner, Joseph A. ... Austin, TX
Turner, Joseph A., P.C. ... Austin, TX
Turner, Joseph D. ... Tampa, FL
Turner, Joseph D., P.A., The Law Office of Tampa, FL
Turner, Joseph E. ... Detroit, MI
Turner, Joseph E. ... Greensboro, NC
Turner, Joseph H., Jr. ... Atlanta, GA
Turner, Joseph Peter, Jr ... Pikeville, KY
Turner, Joseph S. ... Chicago, IL
Turner, Joseph T. ... Norwood, MA
Turner, Joseph W. ... Springfield, MO
Turner, Joy A. ... Detroit, MI
Turner, Judith A. ... Detroit, MI
Turner, Judith A. ... New York, NY
Turner, Julie A. ... Santa Barbara, CA
Turner, Julie A. ... Wilson, NC
Turner, Julie S. ... Cupertino, CA
Turner, Karen Blakely ... Dallas, TX
Turner, Karen D. Agency for International Development, Other Offices of A.I.D., GV
Turner, Karen Lee ... Philadelphia, PA
Turner, Karen Pailette ... Mobile, AL
Turner, Karen Roberts ... Chevy Chase, MD
Turner, Kathyrn L. R. ... Jefferson City, MO
Turner, Kay Farese, and Associates Memphis, TN
Turner, Kay Farese (Luckett) Memphis, TN
Turner, Keith A. ... Los Angeles, CA
Turner, Keith J. ... Los Angeles, CA
Turner, Keith W. ... Jackson, MS
Turner, Kelly L. ... Reno, NV
Turner, Kenneth W. ... Sacramento, CA

Turpen, John B. ....Snellville, GA
Turpen, Joseph F., Jr. ....Kingwood, TX
Turpen, Mark ....Flint, MI
Turpen, Michael C. ....Oklahoma City, OK
Turpie, Martin D. ....Springfield, MA
Turpin, Brian H. ....Danville, VA
Turpin, Brian H., P.C., Law Offices of
Danville, VA
Turpin, David C. ....Santa Barbara, CA
Turpin, Edgar A., Jr. ....Alexandria, VA
Turpin, Gregory B. ....Grundy, VA
Turpin, H. Wayne ....Evansville, IN
Turpin, John R., Jr. ....Corpus Christi, TX
Turpin, Kathleen J. ....Fort Wayne, IN
Turpin, Lee Hendricks ....Danville, VA
Turpin, Michelle ....Salt Lake City, UT
Turpin, Michelle, P.C. ....Salt Lake City, UT
Turpin, Ralph E., Jr. ....Amherst, VA
Lovingston, VA
Turpin, S. Diane ....St. Louis, MO
Turpin, Smith, Dyer, Saxe & MacDonald
Midland, TX
Turpin, Terry Lane ....Fayetteville, AR
Turpin, William J. ....Liberty, MO
Turpin, William W. ....Pleasantville, OH
Turpit, W. James ....Corona Del Mar, CA
Turpit, William J. ....Irvine, CA
Turqman, Elizabeth S. ....Washington, DC
Turra, Melissa S. ....Jacksonville, FL
Turran, Robert D. ....Honolulu, HI
Turre, James E. ....Englewood, CO
Turrentine, Howard B. ....San Diego, CA
Turrentine, J. Drake ....Washington, DC
Turrentine, R. Wood ....Louisville, KY
Turret, Andrew S. ....Hartford, CT
Turret, David B. ....New York, NY
Turret, Ira A. ....New York, NY
Turret, Jack ....New York, NY
Turri, Joseph A. ....Rochester, NY
Turrietta, J. Derek ....Norfolk, VA
Turriff, Diane E. ....Palo Alto, CA
Turrill, Michael L. ....Los Angeles, CA
Turrin, Fausto G. ....Great Falls, MT
Turrin, Robert M. ....Philadelphia, PA
Turrini, Elliot N. ....Roseland, NJ
Turrini, Julia A. ....Sacramento, CA
Turrini, Lisa ....Anchorage, AK
Turrini, Robert J. ....San Rafael, CA
Turro, Andrew J. ....Mineola, NY
Turro, Edward J. ....Cedar Grove, NJ
Turro, Elizabeth A. ....Philadelphia, PA
Turro, Stephen J. ....Austin, TX
Turrone, Richard C. ....San Jose, CA
Turrou, Edward J. ....Frisco, CO
Turschmann, Michael A. ....New York, NY
Turshen, Ethan Allen ....Arlington, VA
Tursi, Ande D. ....San Francisco, CA
Tursi, Carl T. ....New York, NY
Tursi, Dale P. ....Denver, CO
Tursi, Joseph G. ....Foster City, CA
Turso-Dembowski, Barbara L.
Jersey City, NJ
Tursone, Jos. A. ....Scarsdale, NY
Turteltaub, Adam M. ....New York, NY
Turteltaub, James M. ....Newark, NJ
Turteltaub, Leo ....Bayonne, NJ
Turteltaub, Linda A. ....River Edge, NJ
New York, NY
Turteltaub, Stanley W. ....Bayonne, NJ
Turteltaub & Turteltaub, P.A. ....Bayonne, NJ
Turtle, Joel S. ....San Francisco, CA
Turtletaub, Glenn R. ....Florham Park, NJ
Turtletaub, Sheldon J. ......Port Washington, NY
Turton, Eric R. ....San Antonio, TX
Turton, James R. ....Dallas, TX
Turton, Michael J. ....Atlanta, GA
Turtz & De Palma ....Provincetown, MA
Turtz, Evan M. ....Newark, NJ
Turtz, Judith E. ....Provincetown, MA
Turtz, Robert E. ....Edgewater, NJ
New York, NY
Turtz, Sydney Isadore ....South Dennis, MA
Turtzo, Craig H. ....Palm Harbor, FL
Turtzo, Spry, Sbrocchi, Faul & LaBarre, A
Professional Corporation ....Bangor, PA
Stroudsburg, PA
Turula, Joseph A. ....Clifton, NJ
Turung, Brian ....Cleveland, OH
Turvey, John J. ....Staten Island, NY
Turvey, Michelle S. ....Toledo, OH
Turville, Edward A. ....St. Petersburg, FL
Tury, Judith A. ....San Francisco, CA
Turyn, Richard ....New York, NY
Turza, Dale C. ....Washington, DC
Turza, Peter H. ....Washington, DC
Turzai, Michael Coyne ....Pittsburgh, PA
Turzi, Joseph A. ....Washington, DC
Tusa, Alan B. ....Metairie, LA
Tusa, Brian D. ....Jericho, NY
Tusa, Charles S. ....Greenwich, CT
New York, NY
Tusa, Dan ....Brea, CA
Tusa, Joan B. ....St. Paul, MN
Tusa, Joseph S. ....New York, NY
Tusa, Kathryn S. ....Smithtown, NY
Tusa, Michael T., Jr. ....Metairie, LA
Tusa & Richards, L.L.C. ....Metairie, LA
Tusan, Charlene
Department Of Health And Human Services,
Office for Civil Rights, GV
Tusan, Gail S. ....Atlanta, GA
Tusan, Thomas J. ....Fresno, CA
Tuscan, Michael S. ....Washington, DC
Tusch, Paul T. ....Stamford, CT
Tuschman, Chad M. ....Chicago, IL
Tuschman, Richard D. ....Miami, FL
Tusek, Tim ....Youngstown, OH
Tu-Sekine, Anthony ....Washington, DC

Tushar, Danene J. ....Omaha, NE
Tushar, Krista L. ....Denver, CO
Tushaus, David W. ....St. Joseph, MO
Tushin, Richard H. ....Washington, DC
Tushla, Dennis M. ....Dowagiac, MI
Tushman, Allan H. ....Southfield, MI
Tushman, Sol ....Cleveland, OH
Tushman, Sol, Co., L.P.A. ....Cleveland, OH
Tusk, Claude M. ....New York, NY
Tuskai, Les S. ....Mesa, AZ
Tusken, Michael ....Los Angeles, CA
Tuskey, John ....Virginia Beach, VA
Tuskey, Lawrence M. ....Richmond, VA
Tuss, Mark A. ....Dayton, OH
Tussay, Tina L. ....San Antonio, TX
Tussey, Deborah S. ....Charlottesville, VA
Tussey, Linda Ann ....Los Angeles, CA
Tussey, Phoebe J. ....Orinda, CA
Tussey, Susan P. ....Wilmington, DE
Tussing, James D. ....New York, NY
Tussman, David A. ....Berkeley, CA
Tustaniwsky, Oleh R. ....Frankfort, KY
Tustin & Harrison ....Placerville, CA
Tustin, Howard T. ....Spokane, WA
Tustin, Karen K. ....Placerville, CA
Tustin, Richelle M. ....Portland, OR
Tuszynska, Danuta W. ....Riverside, CA
Tutaj, Adam J. ....Milwaukee, WI
Tutaj, James P. ....Chicago, IL
Tutak, James J. ....Kearny, NJ
Tutalo, Joseph R. ....Providence, RI
Tutalo, Ronald A. ....Providence, RI
Tutan, G. Victor ....Miami, FL
Tutan, Jeffrey B. ....Hollywood, FL
Tutas, David Arthur ....Grand Rapids, MI
Tutek, Henry G. ....Bordentown, NJ
Tutelian, Michelle T. ....Fresno, CA
Tutelman, John ....Phoenix, AZ
Tuten, Dorcas M. ....Walterboro, SC
Tuten, Jeffrey A. ....Leesburg, VA
Tuten, John C., Jr. ....Philadelphia, PA
Tuten, Patrick Morris ....Huntsville, AL
Tuten, Robert B. ....Huntsville, AL
Tuter, Jack B., Jr. ....Fort Lauderdale, FL
Tutera, Albert D. ....Orlando, FL
Tuteur, Michael J. ....Boston, MA
Tuteur, Robert I. ....Cherry Hill, NJ
Philadelphia, PA
Tuthill, A. R. ....Montecito, CA
Tuthill, C. Scott ....Dallas, TX
Tuthill, David F. ....Pittsburgh, PA
Tuthill, Deborah L. ....Portland, OR
Tuthill, Frederick J. ....Houston, TX
Tuthill, Howard S. ....Stamford, CT
Naples, FL
Tuthill, Howard S., III ....Stamford, CT
Tuthill, J. Richard ....Minnetonka, MN
Tuthill, James M. ....West Palm Beach, FL
Tuthill, James P. ....Pleasanton, CA
Tuthill, John E. ....St. Petersburg, FL
Tuthill, John H. ....Tillamook, OR
Tuthill, Kathryn A. ....Kingman, AZ
Tuthill, Stephanie M. ....Denver, CO
Tuthill, Timothy J. ....Cortez, CO
Tuthill, Walter C. ....Wilmington, DE
Tuthill, William A., III ....Golden, CO
Tuths, Anthony J. ....New York, NY
Tuths, Susan Quinn ....Southampton, NY
Tutko, Angelia S. ....Columbia, SC
Tutnick, Paul ....Sedona, AZ
Tutoky, Ann M. ....Dallas, TX
Tutoli, Michele A. ....San Diego, CA
Tutolo, Joseph F. ....Philadelphia, PA
Tutor, Gerald ....Boston, MA
Tutor, Henry and Edwards ....Pontotoc, MS
Tupelo, MS
Tutor, James M. ....Booneville, MS
Tutor, Phillip L. ....Pontotoc, MS
Tupelo, MS
Tutrone, Ronald F. ....New York, NY
Tutsch, Elisabeth M. ....Yakima, WA
Tutt, Antoinette R. ....Los Angeles, CA
Tutt, Charles G. ....Shreveport, LA
Tutt, Diane H. ....Plantation, FL
Tutt, Evangeline V. ....Newark, NJ
Tutt, George C. ....Spokane, WA
Tutt, John M., (Inc.) ....San Antonio, TX
Tutt, Nicole A. ....San Leandro, CA
Tutt, Philip E. T. ....San Francisco, CA
Tutt, Ronald ....La Grange, IL
Tuttelman, David M. ....San Jose, CA
Tuttelman, Irving ....Fort Lauderdale, FL
Tutten, Thomas G., Jr. ....Birmingham, AL
Tutter, Antonin ....Bloomville, NY
Tutterow, Cynthia D. ....Shelby, NC
Tutterow, John Thomas ....Asheville, NC
Tutterrow, Victoria B. ....Dallas, TX
Tuttle, Allan Abbot ....Washington, DC
Tuttle, Anita R. ....Burlington, VT
Tuttle, Anne S. ....Newton, MA
Tuttle, Bart C. ....Plymouth Meeting, PA
Tuttle, Bruce R., Jr. ....New York, NY
Tuttle, Carroll D. ....Lenoir, NC
Tuttle, Charles D. ....Dallas, TX
Tuttle, Cheryl L. ....Columbus, OH
Tuttle, Clark A., III ....New Ulm, MN
Tuttle, Clifford L., Jr. ....Pittsburgh, PA
Tuttle, Dale H. ....Memphis, TN
Tuttle, Darrel S. ....Birmingham, MI
Tuttle, David P. ....Greenwich, CT
Tuttle, Dayna Summers ....Yoakum, TX
Tuttle, Deborah M. ....South Bend, IN
Tuttle, Din ....Fort Collins, CO
Tuttle, Douglas W. ....Melbourne, FL
Vero Beach, FL
Tuttle, Elbert ....Framingham, MA
Tuttle, Ernest H. ....Fresno, CA
Tuttle, F. Thomas ....Washington, DC

Tuttle, Franklin L., Jr. ....Austin, TX
Tuttle, Fred P. ....Auburn, CA
Tuttle, Garrett M. ....Denver, CO
Tuttle, George D. ....San Francisco, CA
Tuttle, George E., Jr. ....Alexandria, VA
Tuttle, George R. ....San Francisco, CA
Tuttle, George R., A Professional
Corporation ....San Francisco, CA
Tuttle, George R., III ....San Francisco, CA
Tuttle, Gerald G. ....Issaquah, WA
Tuttle, Gina Bradley ....Opelousas, LA
Tuttle & Gorham ....Issaquah, WA
Tuttle, Heidi J. ....Simsbury, CT
Tuttle, Helen E. ....New York, NY
Tuttle, James B. ....Albany, NY
Tuttle, James C., Law Offices of
New York, NY
Tuttle, James R. ....Seattle, WA
Tuttle, Jeffery L. ....Raleigh, NC
Tuttle, Jeffrey Brook ....Seattle, WA
Tuttle, Jeffrey E. ....San Andreas, CA
Tuttle, Jodi Len ....Indianapolis, IN
Tuttle, John L. ....Lansing, MI
Tuttle, John R. ....Columbus, OH
Tuttle, Jon F. ....Minneapolis, MN
Tuttle, Jonathan R. ....Washington, DC
Tuttle, Judith ....Fresno, CA
Tuttle, Kathleen J. ....Los Angeles, CA
Tuttle, Kristine M. ....Mattoon, IL
Tuttle, Lois M. ....Riverdale, MD
Tuttle, M. Slate, Jr. ....Kannapolis, NC
Tuttle, Mary Albanese ....Mahwah, NJ
Suffern, NY
Tuttle, Matthew J. ....Boston, MA
Tuttle, Milton H. ....Prospect Heights, IL
Tuttle, Monique A. ....Denver, CO
Tuttle, Niki Frangos ....Denver, CO
Tuttle, Norman K., II ....Oakland, CA
Tuttle, R. Paul ....New Orleans, LA
Tuttle, Rebecca Pearson ....Memphis, TN
Tuttle, Richard Brian ....Grand Junction, CO
Tuttle, Richard G. ....Philadelphia, PA
Tuttle, Robert C. J. ....Southfield, MI
Tuttle, Robert L. ....New York, NY
Tuttle, Roger L. ....Midlothian, VA
Tuttle, Seale W. ....Hartford, CT
Tuttle, Stacey A. ....Littleton, MA
Tuttle, Stephen ....New York, NY
Tuttle, Susan Greco ....Tampa, FL
Tuttle & Taylor, A Law Corporation
Los Angeles, CA
Tuttle, Taylor & Heron ....Washington, DC
Tuttle, Thomas N. ....West Bend, WI
Tuttle, Thomas N., Jr. ....Milwaukee, WI
Tuttle, Thomas W. ....Irvine, CA
Tuttle, Timothy N. ....Teaneck, NJ
Tuttle, Wallace H. ....Traverse City, MI
Tuttle, Wallace H., P.C. ....Traverse City, MI
Tuttle, Wendy ....Olean, NY
Tuttle, William M., II ....Miami, FL
Tuttle & Winborn ....Dallas, TX
Houston, TX
Tuttle & Zisgen ....Mahwah, NJ
Suffern, NY
Tuttleton, Malcolm ....South Gate, CA
Tuttman, Alan D. ....Somerville, MA
Tuttman, Peter M. ....Paramus, NJ
Tutton, Thomas A. ....Port Angeles, WA
Tutton, William, Jr. ....Baltimore, MD
Tuttrup, Martha K., (Mrs.) ....Paige, TX
Tutulis, Peter J. ....Union, NJ
Tutun, Marshall L. ....Boston, MA
Tutun, Paul D. ....Boston, MA
Tutunjian, Henry G. ....Troy, NY
Tutunjian, John G. ....New York, NY
Tutwiler, Amy B.F. ....Madison, WI
Tutwiler, William J. ....Fort Wayne, IN
Tuuk, Mary E. ....Grand Rapids, MI
Tuuk, Stephen M. ....Grand Rapids, MI
Tuura, Doris K. ....Minneapolis, MN
Tuve, Tammi J. ....New York, NY
Tuverson, Arthur W., (P.C.)
Los Angeles, CA
Tuverson & Hillyard ....Los Angeles, CA
Newport Beach, CA
Palm Springs, CA
Tuveson, Kay E. ....Minneapolis, MN
Tuvim, Mark B. ....Los Angeles, CA
Tuvim Amaya, Laurel ....Los Angeles, CA
Tuvlin, Jennifer G. ....Chicago, IL
Tu-Willis, Nora ....Los Angeles, CA
Tuxhorn, Leslie D. ....Sacramento, CA
Tuy, Salvador Enriquez, Jr. ....New York, NY
Tuyn, Richard M. ....Bloomfield Hills, MI
Tuytschaevers, Thomas J. ....Norwood, MA
Tuytschaevers, Thomas L. ....Schererville, IN
Tuza, Shannon E. ....Columbus, OH
Tuzi, Louis A. ....Sagamore Hills, OH
Tuzinski, James J. ....Minneapolis, MN
Tuzio, Francis X. ....Brooklyn, NY
Tuzon, Rita L. ....Beverly Hills, CA
Tuzzio, Gerard A. ....Fort Lauderdale, FL
Tuzzio, Michael K. ....Tinton Falls, NJ
Tuzzolino, Sam ....Skokie, IL
Tuzzolino and Terpinas ....Skokie, IL
Tvedt, Daniel C. ....Cedar Rapids, IA
Tvetenstrand, Paul D. ....New York, NY
Tvrdik, Penelope Benz ....Omaha, NE
Tvrdik, Ronald E. ....Kearney, NE
Twa, David J. ....Mankato, MN
Twachtman, Walter A., Jr.
Glastonbury, CT
Twaddell, David O. ....Harrisburg, PA
Twaddell, Miles E., III ....Budd Lake, NJ
Twait, Traci Justice ....Danville, IN
Twaits, Alan R. ....Miami, FL
Twardowski, Anthony R.
Philadelphia, PA

Twardowski, Eugene M. ....Philadelphia, PA
Twardowski, Ray J. ....San Antonio, TX
Twardowski, Thomas M. ....Reading, PA
Twardy, Jeffrey T., (P.C.) ....Annandale, VA
Twardy, Stan ....Oklahoma City, OK
Twardy, Stanley A., Jr. ....Stamford, CT
Twardzik, Barbara L. ....Indianapolis, IN
Twarog, Stanley A. ....Boston, MA
Twarog, Susan Savoca ....Cambridge, MA
Twarowski, Joseph A. ....Sunnyvale, CA
Tway, Faber F. ....Boise, ID
Twede, Charles R. ....Burlington, WA
Twede, Peter B. ....Orland, CA
Twede & Svaren, Inc., P.S. ....Burlington, WA
Twedt, Alexander Henry ....Columbia, SC
Twedt, Brad ....Chicago, IL
Twedt, James C. ....Roland, IA
Twedt, Margaret A. ....Carson City, NV
Twedt, Mark S. ....Gresham, OR
Twedt, Thomas D. ....Washington, DC
Tweed, Douglas S. ....Kingsport, TN
Tweed, Francis H., Jr. ....New York, NY
Tweed, Guy E., II ....Cleveland, OH
Tweed, R. Dennis ....Tampa, FL
Tweed, Roland D. ....Riverside, CA
Tweed, Sheila R. ....Houston, TX
Tweedell, Robert G. ....Delta, CO
Tweedie, Jim ....Everett, WA
Tweedie, Richard S. ....Camden, NJ
Philadelphia, PA
Tweedle, John F. ....Highland, IN
Tweedle, Robert Frederick ....Highland, IN
Tweedle & Sedia ....Highland, IN
Tweedle, Toni ....Indio, CA
Tweedt, Anne Murray ....Salem, OR
Tweedt, Darin E. ....Salem, OR
Tweedt, Jon E. ....Springfield, IL
Tweedy, Charles A. ....Gold River, CA
Tweedy, Charles E., Jr. ....Jasper, AL
Tweedy, Clare B. (IBA) ....New York, NY
Tweedy, Craig R. ....Sapulpa, OK
Tweedy, Diana M. ....Richmond, CA
Tweedy, Jackson, Beech & Fikes
Double Springs, AL
Fayette, AL
Hamilton, AL
Jasper, AL
Tweedy, James R. ....Van Nuys, CA
Tweedy, James R. ....Bloomfield, MO
Tweedy, James R., Inc. ....Van Nuys, CA
Tweedy, Jeffrey C. ....New York, NY
Tweedy, John B. ....Denver, CO
Tweedy, John B., Jr. ....Boulder, CO
Tweedy, Juli Martin ....Rockville, MD
Tweedy, Patricia, Law Offices of
Sacramento, CA
Tweedy, Penney & Crawford, A Law
Partnership ....Sacramento, CA
Tweedy, Richard B. ....Stamford, CT
Tweedy, Talbot T. ....Taunton, MA
Tweedy, Talbot T., Inc. ....Taunton, MA
Tweedy, Thomas A. ....Sacramento, CA
Tweedy, Thomas A. ....Sacramento, CA
Tweel, Donna S. ....Dayton, OH
Tweel, Lawrence J. ....Huntington, WV
Tweel, Robert G. ....Charleston, WV
Tweel, Ronald R. ....Charlottesville, VA
Tweel, Thomas M. ....Memphis, TN
Tween, Douglas M. ....Department of Justice,
Antitrust Division, GV
Tweet, Gary P. ....Chicago, IL
Tweet, Stephen G. ....Phoenix, AZ
Tweet, Stephen T. ....Portland, OR
Salem, OR
Tweet, Susan A. ....Chicago, IL
Tweeten, Christian D. ....Helena, MT
Tweeton, Timothy J. ....Phoenix, AZ
Twehues, Paul H., Jr. ....Newport, KY
Twehues & Verst ....Newport, KY
Twellman, Eugene J. ....Kansas City, MO
Twenhafel, Kourtney N.
Grosse Pointe Woods, MI
Twenhafel, Mark A. ....McAllen, TX
Twenhafel, Marvin G. ....Denver, CO
Twer, Daniel L. ....Orange, CA
Twerski, Aaron D. ....New York, NY
Twerski, Shlomo C. ....New York, NY
Twersky, Jonathan ....Brooklyn, NY
Twersky, Martin I. ....Philadelphia, PA
Twersky, Michael J. ....New York, NY
Twersky, Michael K. ....Cherry Hill, NJ
Philadelphia, PA
Twersky, Mitchell M. ....New York, NY
Twesme, Krista L. ....Minneapolis, MN
Twesme, Thomas F. ....Las Vegas, NV
Tweten, Henry G. ....East Grand Forks, MN
Tweten, Jeanne E. ....Seattle, WA
Twibell, Bert V. ....Springfield, MO
Twibell, David A. ....San Diego, CA
Twibell, Johnson, Johnson & Scott
Springfield, MO
Twibell, Ty S. ....Overland Park, KS
Twichel, Dennis J. ....Fife, WA
Twichell, Daniel R. ....West Fargo, ND
Twichell, P. David ....Syracuse, NY
Twichell, William H. ....Pinedale, WY
Twiddy, Curtis A. ....Raleigh, NC
Twiddy, Kathryn Ficklin ....Raleigh, NC
Twidwell, Joseph ....Fremont, NE
Twidwell, Kevin ....Seattle, WA
Twietmeyer, Don H. ....Rochester, NY
Twiford, Alice K. ....Williamsburg, VA
Twiford, H. Hunter, III ....Clarksdale, MS
Twiford, Morrison, O'Neal & Vincent
Elizabeth City, NC
Manteo, NC
Twiford, Russell E. ....Elizabeth City, NC
Manteo, NC

Twiford Webster & Gresham
Clarksdale, MS
Twiford, Webster & Gresham
Cleveland, MS
Twiford Webster & Gresham ...... Tunica, MS
Twigg, Alfred T. .... Glendale, CA
Twigg, Douglas R. .... Annapolis, MD
Twigg, Jay .... Ukiah, CA
Twigg, Robt. W. .... Cusick, WA
Twiggs, Abrams, Strickland & Trehy, P.A.
Cary, NC
Chapel Hill, NC
Durham, NC
Raleigh, NC
Research Triangle Park, NC
Twiggs, Howard F. .... Raleigh, NC
Twiggs, Jerome M., Jr. .... Montgomery, AL
Twight, Charlotte A. .... Boise, ID
Twilley, Joshua M. .... Dover, DE
Twilley & Street, P.A. .... Dover, DE
Twine, Barbara J.
Charlotte Amalie, St. Thomas, VI
Twine, Edgar H. .... Los Angeles, CA
Twine, Gia C. .... Los Angeles, CA
Twing, Shawn David .... Amarillo, TX
Twining, Danette H. .... Houston, TX
Twining, H. Kent .... Houston, TX
Twining, Joseph P. .... San Diego, CA
Twining, Kevin L. .... Dallas, TX
Twining, Peter P. .... Boston, MA
Twining, Rollin L. .... Binghamton, NY
Twinney, Denise D. .... Grand Rapids, MI
Twiss, Chester K. .... Greenville, ME
Twiss, Dennis M. .... Worthington, MN
Twiss, Harold L., Jr. .... Malone, NY
Twiss, Michael H. .... Detroit, MI
Twiss, Richard S. .... Seattle, WA
Twiss, Robert M. .... Sacramento, CA
Twiss, Stephen R.W. .... Central City, NE
Twiss & Twiss .... Detroit, MI
Pontiac, MI
Twiss, Yvonne Lundwall .... Columbus, OH
Twisselman, James D. .... Everett, WA
Twisselman, Kenneth C., II .... Bakersfield, CA
Twisselman, Roger P. .... Denver, CO
Twist, Betty L. .... Albuquerque, NM
Twist, Steven J. .... Phoenix, AZ
Twist, Thomas E. .... Salem, OR
Twiste, Eric .... New York, NY
Twitchell, Burton J. .... Santa Maria, CA
Twitchell, Dennis W. .... Myrtle Creek, OR
Twitchell, Laura E .... Seattle, WA
Twitchell, Lauren E. .... Temecula, CA
Twitchell, Marlyn J. .... Juneau, AK
Twitchell, Maurice F. .... Santa Maria, CA
Twitchell and Rice .... Santa Maria, CA
Twito, Scott .... Billings, MT
Twitty & Bankston .... Camilla, GA
Twitty, Diane M. .... Southfield, MI
Twitty, Frank S., Jr. .... Camilla, GA
Twitty, Sievwright & Mills .... Phoenix, AZ
Twitty, Theophlise L. .... Richmond, VA
Twitty, Thomas E., Jr. .... Mobile, AL
Twohey, Christopher J. .... Stuart, FL
Twohey, Edward L. .... Grand Rapids, MI
Twohey Maggini .... Alma, MI
Caledonia, MI
Grand Rapids, MI
Twohey, William N. .... Ottawa, IL
Twohig, Catherine B. .... Cleveland, OH
Twohig, George W. .... Chilton, WI
Twohig, John E. .... Boston, MA
Twohig, Mark M., III .... Cleveland, OH
Twohig, Peggy L.
Federal Trade Commission,
Bureau of Consumer Protection, GV
Twohig, Ray .... Albuquerque, NM
Twohig, Ray, P.C. .... Albuquerque, NM
Twohill, Frank B. .... Branford, CT
Twohy, Darneille & Frye .... Sacramento, CA
Twohy, James F. .... Brooklyn, NY
Twohy, John P. .... Hammond, IN
Twohy, John P. .... Brooklyn, NY
Twohy, Kelleher & Gallagher .... Brooklyn, NY
Twohy, Doane .... Princeton, NJ
Twombly, James Francis .... Austin, TX
Twombly, John C. .... New York, NY
Twombly, John R., Jr. .... Media, PA
Twombly, Jonathan D. .... New York, NY
Twombly, Oliver L. .... Barre, VT
Twombly, Oliver L., Law Office of
Barre, VT
Twombly, Peter S. .... Newark, NJ
Twombly, R. W. .... Sugar Land, TX
Twombly, W. Bruce .... Dallas, TX
Twomey, Bernard A. .... Brooklyn, NY
Twomey, Daniel M. .... Baltimore, MD
Twomey, David P. .... Boston, MA
Twomey, Donald .... Boston, MA
Twomey, Edward J. .... Washington, DC
Twomey, Hoppe & Gallanty LLP
New York, NY
Twomey, James F. .... Fargo, ND
Twomey, Jeannette P. .... Vienna, VA
Twomey, John A. .... Alpharetta, GA
Twomey, John J. .... Medford, MA
Twomey, John S. .... New York, NY
Twomey, Joseph G. .... Los Angeles, CA
Twomey, Joseph G. .... St. Paul, MN
Twomey, Kristopher E. .... Washington, DC
Twomey, Latham, Shea & Kelley, LLP
East Hampton, NY
Hauppauge, NY
Port Jefferson, NY
Riverhead, NY
Southampton, NY
Twomey, Lynda M. .... Palo Alto, CA
Twomey, Michael B. .... Tallahassee, FL
Twomey, Michael E. .... New York, NY
Twomey, Michael J. .... Boston, MA
Twomey, Michael R. .... Carbondale, IL
Twomey, Paul L. .... Andover, MA
Twomey, Richard J. .... Cary, NC
Twomey, Russell D., Jr. .... Los Angeles, CA
Twomey, Sigrid A. .... Santa Barbara, CA
Twomey, T. Michael .... New Orleans, LA
Twomey, Therese K. .... San Diego, CA
Twomey, Thomas A., Jr.
East Hampton, NY
Riverhead, NY
Twomey, Thomas L., II .... Medford, MA
Twomey, Thomas N. .... Auburn Hills, MI
Twomey, Timothy M. .... San Diego, CA
Twomey, William E., Jr. .... Richmond, VA
Twomey, William L. .... Irvine, CA
Twomley, Bruce C. .... Juneau, AK
Tworoger and Associates, P.A. .... Sebastian, FL
Tworoger, Kenneth F. .... Sebastian, FL
Twydell, Dawn M. .... Detroit, MI
Twyford & Donahey .... Columbus, OH
Twyford, George W. .... Columbus, OH
Twyford, Julie A. .... Spokane, WA
Twyford Law Office .... Spokane, WA
Twyford, Thomas L. .... Columbus, OH
Twyman, Jeffrey R. .... Bowling Green, OH
Twyman, Nelson, Ten Brink, Harms & Sharp
Bowling Green, OH
Twyman, Todd A. .... Charleston, WV
Twyman, Winkfield F., Jr. .... San Diego, CA
Twynham, Theodore T. .... Columbus, OH
Twyon, Bruce D. .... Wolfeboro, NH
Ty, Felipe F.
Federal Deposit Insurance Corporation,
Division of Bank Supervision, GV
Ty, Pamela .... San Francisco, CA
Tyack, Blackmore & Liston Co., L.P.A.
Columbus, OH
Tyack, Deborah A. .... Columbus, OH
Tyack, G. Gary .... Columbus, OH
Tyack, Jonathan T. .... Columbus, OH
Tyack & Kessler .... Columbus, OH
Tyack, Matthew J. .... Dublin, OH
Tyack, Thomas M. .... Columbus, OH
Tyacke, Nicholas A. .... New York, NY
Tyacke, Steven W. .... Duluth, MN
Tybout, F. Alton .... Wilmington, DE
Tybout, Redfearn & Pell .... Wilmington, DE
Tyburski, Charles J. .... Canton, OH
Tyburski, Raymond G., Jr. .... Raritan, NJ
Tyburski, Susan .... Denver, CO
Tycer, Ann-Douglas .... Brentwood, TN
Tycher, Marshall B. .... Roseland, NJ
Tychonievich, Daniel .... South Bend, IN
Tycko, Jonathan K. .... Washington, DC
Tyckoski, Martin A. .... Flint, MI
Tycksen, Steven C. .... Sandy, UT
Tyczkowski, Angela M. .... Appleton, WI
Tyczkowski, Mark J. .... Neenah, WI
Tyde, Michael S. .... Jacksonville, FL
Tyde, Stephen J., Jr. .... Lawrenceville, GA
Tydings, James M. .... Boulder, CO
Tydings, Joseph D. .... Washington, DC
Tydings, Kevin W. .... Charlotte, NC
Tydings, Patrick E. .... Rochester, NY
Tydings, Ronald W. .... Fairfax, VA
Tydings & Rosenberg LLP
Baltimore, MD
Tydings, Warren E., Jr. .... Rockville, MD
Tydlaska, Stephanie C. .... Los Angeles, CA
Tye, Anita Terry .... Birmingham, AL
Tye, Danny D. .... Portland, OR
Tye, Donald G. .... Boston, MA
Tye, Ginger A. .... Dallas, TX
Tye Law Firm, The .... Kearney, NE
Tye, Michael J. .... Kearney, NE
Tye, Michael W. .... Chicago, IL
Tye, Richard H., Law Office of
San Antonio, TX
Tye, Rose R. .... Dayton, OH
Tye, Thomas W. .... Kearney, NE
Tye, Thomas W., II .... Kearney, NE
Tye, Timothy N. .... Dayton, OH
Tye and Tye .... Dayton, OH
Tye, W. Randall .... Atlanta, GA
Tye, William G. .... Fort Pierce, FL
Tyerman, Barry W. .... Los Angeles, CA
Tygar, Neil .... Commack, NY
Tygart, Frederick B. .... Jacksonville, FL
Tygart, Robert M. .... Carlsbad, CA
Tygart, S. Thompson, Jr., The Law Offices of
Jacksonville, FL
Tygart, Travis Thompson .... Dallas, TX
Tygart, Tyler F. .... Jacksonville, FL
Tygesson, Gary L. .... Minneapolis, MN
Tygier, Nicole Sophia .... Metairie, LA
Tygrett, Howard V., Jr. .... Dallas, TX
Tyk, Roger E. .... Glenview, IL
Tyksinski, Martin J. .... Oneida, NY
Tyksinski, Terence J. .... Chicago, IL
Tykulsker, David, & Associates
Montclair, NJ
New York, NY
Tylander, Robert D. .... Hendersonville, NC
Tyle, Craig S. .... Washington, DC
Tylee, Mary C. .... Cleveland, OH
Tyler, Ahrian Davis .... Birmingham, AL
Tyler, Allison .... Eugene, OR
Tyler, B. A. .... Southfield, MI
Tyler, Barbara Jane .... Cleveland, OH
Tyler, Bartl, Burke and Albert, P.L.C.
Washington, DC
Alexandria, VA
Arlington, VA
Fairfax, VA
Tyler, Beth H. .... Norcross, GA
Tyler, Bradley E. .... Rochester, NY
Tyler, Brian .... Harrisburg, PA
Tyler, Bruce D., Sr. .... Somers, CT
Tyler, Bruce H. .... Lake Hughes, CA
Tyler, Bruce K. .... Afton, VA
Tyler, Cameron W. .... Boulder, CO
Tyler, Cassell, Jackson, Peace & Silver, L.L.P. .... Columbia, SC
Tyler, Charles G. .... Tuscaloosa, AL
Tyler, Charles K.
Architect of the Capitol, GV
Tyler, Cheever .... New Haven, CT
Stamford, CT
Tyler Cooper & Alcorn, LLP
Greenwich, CT
Hartford, CT
Madison, CT
New Haven, CT
Stamford, CT
Tyler, Das & Debes, A Professional Corporation .... Houston, TX
Tyler, David A. .... Ithaca, NY
Tyler, David M. .... Southfield, MI
Tyler, David M., Jr. .... Vienna, VA
Tyler, Dennis G., (A Professional Corporation) .... Irvine, CA
Tyler, Dennis R. .... Indianapolis, IN
Tyler, D. G. .... Shreveport, LA
Tyler & Dodge .... Rome, NY
Tyler, Donald Christopher .... Miami, FL
Tyler, Donald W. .... Columbia, SC
Tyler, Donald W. .... Columbia, SC
Tyler, Douglas Beck .... Moorestown, NJ
Tyler, Duane .... San Diego, CA
Tyler, Earle S., Jr. .... Milbridge, ME
Tyler, Edgar J. .... Conway, AR
Little Rock, AR
Tyler, Edward J., III .... St. Albans, VT
Tyler, Elizabeth Plott, & Associates
Los Angeles, CA
Tyler, F. Clayton .... Minneapolis, MN
Tyler, Frederick C., Jr.
Cleveland Heights, OH
Tyler, Gary L. .... East Lansing, MI
Tyler, Gene L. .... Freeport, TX
Tyler, Geo. G. .... Yreka, CA
Tyler, George J. .... Middletown, NJ
Trenton, NJ
Tyler, George T. .... Baltimore, MD
Tyler, Glen A. .... Accomac, VA
Tyler, H. Tyrone .... Jacksonville, FL
Tyler, Hamilton F. .... Baltimore, MD
Tyler & Hamilton, P.A. .... Jacksonville, FL
Tyler, Harold R., Jr. .... New York, NY
Tyler, Henry J. .... Moorestown, NJ
Tyler, J. Hoge, III .... Norfolk, VA
Tyler, J. Robert, III .... Raleigh, NC
Tyler, J. Russell, Jr. .... Irvine, CA
Tyler, James B., III .... Georgetown, DE
Tyler, James B., III .... Rehoboth Beach, DE
Tyler, James G. .... Tell City, IN
Tyler, James L. .... Newton, IA
Sully, IA
Tyler, James M. .... Philadelphia, PA
Tyler, Janet L. .... Laramie, WY
Tyler, Jeffrey H. .... Seattle, WA
Tyler, John .... Atlanta, GA
Tyler, John C. .... Atlanta, GA
Tyler, John C., P.C. .... Atlanta, GA
Tyler, John F. .... Girard, OH
Tyler, John J., II .... Northville, MI
Tyler, John J., II, P.C. .... Northville, MI
Tyler, John K., Law Offices of
Houston, TX
Tyler, John L. .... Baton Rouge, LA
Tyler, John O., Jr. .... Houston, TX
Tyler, John R. .... Department of Justice,
Civil Division, GV
Tyler, John R., Jr. .... Rochester, NY
Tyler & Johnson .... Shreveport, LA
Tyler, Judy-Beth C. .... New York, NY
Tyler, June Smith .... Cincinnati, OH
Tyler, Karen L. .... Seattle, WA
Tyler, Katharine Barr .... Chicago, IL
Tyler, Keith P. .... Casper, WY
Tyler, Keith W. .... Rochester, IN
Tyler, Kenneth C. .... Encino, CA
Tyler, Kenneth E. .... Council Bluffs, IA
Tyler, Kim J. .... Martell, NE
Tyler, Kimberly S. .... Hackensack, NJ
Tyler, Kristi B. .... Denver, CO
Council Bluffs, IA
Tyler, Laura H. .... Kansas City, MO
Tyler, Lee O. .... Portland, OR
Tyler & Lesyshen .... Waterloo, IA
Tyler, Lloyd J. .... Geneva, IL
Tyler, Lynn C. .... Indianapolis, IN
Tyler, M. Craig .... Austin, TX
Tyler, M. Leanne .... Davenport, IA
Tyler, Marie T. .... Idaho Falls, ID
Tyler, Marvin L. .... Rock Springs, WY
Tyler, Mary Victoria .... Rockville, MD
Tyler, Matthew Neal .... Florence, SC
Tyler, Merle L. .... Tulsa, OK
Tyler, Michael E. .... Topsfield, MA
Tyler, Michael R. .... Los Angeles, CA
Tyler, Michael W. .... Atlanta, GA
Tyler, Michele L. .... Phoenix, AZ
Tyler, Milan K. .... New York, NY
Tyler, Nancy Ellen .... Fort Worth, TX
Tyler, Natalie A. .... Minocqua, WI
Tyler, O. Jan .... McKinney, TX
Tyler, Pamela H. .... Miami, FL
Tyler, Pamela J. .... Grand Rapids, MI
Tyler, Paul D. .... Boston, MA
Tyler, Paul R. .... Des Moines, IA
Tyler, Peggy L.B.
Architect of the Capitol, GV
Tyler, Philip J. .... North Richland Hills, TX
Tyler & Possa, A Professional Law Corporation .... Baton Rouge, LA
Tyler, R. Stanley .... Carbondale, IL
Tyler, Ralph S. .... Baltimore, MD
Tyler & Reynolds, Professional Corporation
Boston, MA
Tyler, Richard .... Atlanta, GA
Tyler, Richard A. .... Santa Barbara, CA
Tyler, Richard B. .... Columbia, MO
Tyler, Richard J. .... New Orleans, LA
Tyler, Richard M. .... Little Rock, AR
Tyler, Robert .... Temecula, CA
Tyler, Robert .... Washington, DC
Tyler, Robert B. .... Columbia, MO
Tyler, Robert F. .... Northridge, CA
Tyler, Robert F. .... Sacramento, CA
Tyler, Robert H. .... Biloxi, MS
Tyler, Robert J. .... Fresno, CA
Tyler, Robert M. .... Richmond, VA
Tyler, Robert O. .... Alexandria, VA
Tyler, Ronald R. .... East Tawas, MI
Tyler, Russell J. .... Enfield, CT
Tyler, Scott L. .... New Albany, IN
Tyler, Scott M. .... Charlotte, NC
Tyler, Sharon E. .... Franklin, TN
Tyler, Sherie A. .... Los Angeles, CA
Tyler, Stephen A. .... Highland, IN
Tyler, Stephen Bret .... Paris, TX
Tyler, Stephen H. .... Redlands, CA
Tyler, Steven E. .... Salt Lake City, UT
Tyler, Steven G. .... Annapolis, MD
Tyler, Susan M. .... New Orleans, LA
Tyler, Tane T. .... Denver, CO
Tyler, Terry L. .... Encino, CA
Tyler, Terry W. .... Louisville, KY
Tyler, Thomas A., Jr. .... Flossmoor, IL
Tyler, Thomas C. .... Sarasota, FL
Tyler, Thomas E. .... Philadelphia, PA
Tyler, Thomas J. .... Enfield, CT
Tyler, Thomas L. .... Baton Rouge, LA
Tyler, Thomas Loy .... Washington, DC
Tyler, Thomas P., Jr. .... Englewood, CO
Tyler, Timothy A. .... Bellaire, TX
Tyler, Timothy J. .... Houston, TX
Tyler, Todd E. .... Dallas, TX
Fort Worth, TX
Tyler, Tracy Jon .... Denver, CO
Tyler, Travis S. .... Omaha, NE
Tyler & Tyler .... Enfield, CT
Tyler, Valerie W. .... Denver, CO
Tyler, W. David .... Waterloo, IA
Tyler, William B. .... Boston, MA
Tyler, William D. .... Tampa, FL
Tyler, Winston F. .... San Pedro, CA
Tyler-Wood, Irma .... Cambridge, MA
Tylicki, Thomas N. .... Milwaukee, WI
Tylinski, Lori K. .... Pittsburgh, PA
Tylka, Lawrence M. .... Houston, TX
Tylke, Roberta .... Orlando, FL
Tylock, James S. .... Fort Lauderdale, FL
Tylutki, Beatrice S. .... Trenton, NJ
Tylwalk, John C. .... Lebanon, PA
Tym, Ronald D. .... San Francisco, CA
Tyma, Alan J. .... Shelton, CT
Tyma, James J. .... New Haven, CT
Tyma, Stephen L. .... Chicago, IL
Tyma, Stephen L. .... Oak Park, IL
Tyma, Theodore R. .... Southport, CT
Tymann, Deirdre M. .... Hartford, CT
Tymann, Jeffrey J. .... Albany, NY
Tymann, Lisa D. .... Washington, DC
Tymann, Robert J. .... Albany, NY
Tymeson, Cynthia G. .... Miami, FL
Tyminski, Alfred R. .... Syracuse, NY
Tyminski, James T., Jr. .... Cleveland, OH
Tyminski, Steven M. .... Wayne, PA
Tymkovich, Timothy M. .... Denver, CO
Tymm, William E. .... Chicago, IL
Tymniak, Paul Martin .... Trumbull, CT
Tymoczko, William J. .... Bucksport, ME
Tynan, Colleen A. .... New Bedford, MA
Tynan, James D. .... Devon, PA
Tynan, John Patrick .... New York, NY
Tynan, Joseph P. .... New Orleans, LA
Tynan, Kevin P. .... Fort Lauderdale, FL
Tynan, Leo C., Jr. .... San Antonio, TX
Tynan, Mark Hyatt .... Phoenix, AZ
Tynan, Monica M. .... Chicago, IL
Tynan, Richard C. .... Hartford, CT
Tynan, Steven D. .... Mason City, IA
Tynan, William F. .... Wolcott, CT
Tynberg, Alexander H.
San Francisco, CA
Tynch, David R. .... Portsmouth, VA
Tyndall, Brian C. .... Milwaukee, WI
Tyndall & Cahners .... Los Gatos, CA
Tyndall, Candace Tillman .... Chicago, IL
Tyndall, David R., (P.C.) .... Moultrie, GA
Tyndall, John G., III (P.C.) .... Los Gatos, CA
Tyndall, Lee Griffin .... Birmingham, AL
Tyndall, Marvin C. .... Marion, SC
Tyndall, Richard .... Mooresville, NC
Tyndall, Steven M. .... Houston, TX
Tyndall, Susan R. .... Milwaukee, WI
Tyndall, William F. .... Washington, DC
Tyne, Barry J. .... Burlington, ME
Tyne, James Joseph .... New York, NY
Tyner, Damon G. .... Atlantic City, NJ
Tyner, Deborah G. .... Pontiac, MI
Tyner, E. David .... Brooksville, FL
Tyner, Earl L. .... Jacksonville, FL
Tyner, F. Richard .... West Bloomfield, MI
Tyner, Gordon C. .... Tyler, TX
Tyner, John J., Jr. .... Hillsboro, OR
Tyner, John Joseph, III .... Hillsboro, OR
Tyner, J. W., (P.A.) .... Tyler, TX
Tyner, Karen M. .... Spartanburg, SC
Tyner, L. Lee, Jr. .... Jackson, MS

Tyner, Lee R.
Environmental Protection Agency, Office of the General Counsel, GV
Tyner, Michael L. .... Lowell, MA
Tyner, Michaele .... Columbus, OH
Tyner, Mitchell A. .... Silver Spring, MD
Tyner, Pamela D. .... Galveston, TX
Tyner, Robert M., Jr. .... Clarksdale, MS
Tyner, Thomas W. .... Hattiesburg, MS
Tyner, Wayna Lynn .... Mangum, OK
Tynes, Douglas L. .... Pascagoula, MS
Tynes, Ed. .... Houston, TX
Tynes, M. Dianne .... Metairie, LA
Tynes, Maurice L. .... Lake Charles, LA
Tynes, Maurice L., & Associates, PLC
Lake Charles, LA
Tynes, Pamela A. .... Lafayette, LA
Tynes, Victor H., Jr.
Securities and Exchange Commission, Office of Equal Employment Opportunity, GV
Tyng, Franklin Somes .... Bel Air, MD
Tynion, James T., III .... Milwaukee, WI
Tynjala, Jon M. .... Minneapolis, MN
Tyo, John E. .... Shortsville, NY
Typadis, Archie D. .... Boston, MA
Typadis, Archie D., P.C. .... Boston, MA
Tyra, B. Scott .... Birmingham, AL
Tyra, Brent A. .... Alabaster, AL
Tyra, David W. .... Sacramento, CA
Tyra, John Foster .... Hamilton, AL
Tyra, Kenneth T. .... Minneapolis, MN
Tyra, Kevin C. .... Indianapolis, IN
Tyra, Sandra J. .... Salt Lake City, UT
Tyras, Jonathan C. .... New York, NY
Tyre, Gwendolyn R. .... Boston, MA
Tyre, James S. .... Pasadena, CA
Tyre, John Dulken .... Irwindale, CA
Tyre Kamins Katz & Granof
Los Angeles, CA
Tyre, Kendal, Jr. .... Washington, DC
Tyre, Milton S. .... Los Angeles, CA
Tyre, Norman R. .... Beverly Hills, CA
Tyre, Thomas E. .... Mohegan Lake, NY
Tyree, Colleen T. .... Chicago, IL
Tyree, D. Scott .... Huntington, WV
Tyree, David W. .... Pittsburgh, PA
Tyree, David W., P.C. .... Pittsburgh, PA
Tyree, Eskew & Roberts, L.C.
Blue Springs, MO
Kansas City, MO
Tyree, George A. .... Blue Springs, MO
TyRee, James A. .... Mansfield, OH
Tyree, Jane L. .... Stamford, CT
Tyree, Jeffrey K. .... Jackson, MS
Tyree, Karl T., Jr. .... Florence, AL
Tyree, Lana Jeanne .... Oklahoma City, OK
Tyree, Marilyn S. Nickell
Grand Rapids, MI
Tyree, Randell L. .... Knoxville, TN
Tyree, Rebecca Lynn .... Crook, CO
Tyree, Timothy W. .... Boise, ID
Tyrell, Elyse M. .... Las Vegas, NV
Tyrell, Jane E. .... Hanover, MA
Tyrell, Mary P. .... Deerfield, IL
Tyrell, Paul A. .... San Diego, CA
Tyrl, Larry J. .... Kansas City, MO
Tyrl, Sanderson & Etem
Kansas City, MO
Tyrone, Nelson Otis, III .... Atlanta, GA
Tyrpak, David M. .... Farmington Hills, MI
Tyrpak, David M., P.C.
Farmington Hills, MI
Tyrpin, Terry E. .... Des Plaines, IL
Tyrrell, David R. .... Tampa, FL
Tyrrell, Elizabeth Dalton
Oklahoma City, OK
Tyrrell, Emmet J. .... Canfield, OH
Tyrrell, James E., Jr. .... Newark, NJ
Tyrrell, Jayne B. .... Boston, MA
Tyrrell, John E. .... Philadelphia, PA
Tyrrell, Joseph C. .... Blue Bell, PA
Tyrrell, Judy M. .... Indianapolis, IN
Tyrrell, Kathleen Anne .... Marlton, NJ
Tyrrell, Kelli E. .... Columbus, OH
Tyrrell, Mary Ann .... San Jose, CA
Tyrrell & Mason, P.C. .... Bethesda, MD
Tyrrell, Michael A. .... Hartford, CT
Tyrrell, Natalie L. .... Las Vegas, NV
Tyrrell, Paul M.
Commodity Futures Trading Commission, Division of Enforcement, GV
Tyrrell, Peter J. .... Farmington, CT
Tyrrell, Robert J. .... Bethesda, MD
Tyrrell, Ross, (Ltd.) .... Chicago, IL
Tyrrell, Steven A. .... Miami, FL
Tyrrell, Terry L. .... Kansas City, MO
Tyrrell, Thomas C. .... New York, NY
Tyrrell, Thomas J. .... Chicago, IL
Tyrrell, Thomas Joseph .... Wantagh, NY
Tyrrell, Thomas M. .... Los Angeles, CA
Tysch, Gary L. .... Sherman Oaks, CA
Tyser, Wallace C., Jr. .... North Wilkesboro, NC
Tyshka, Rachelle Propson .... Detroit, MI
Tysinger, Allyson K. .... Fredericksburg, VA
Tyson, Allan S. .... Los Angeles, CA
Tyson, Alma Learetta .... Chicago, IL
Tyson, Anita Medina .... Chicago, IL
Tyson, Bart J. .... Pittsburgh, PA
Tyson, Bart J., P.C. .... Pittsburgh, PA
Tyson, Blair M. .... New York, NY
Tyson & Bromander, P.A.
Bloomington, MN
Tyson, Bryan G. .... Boston, MA
Tyson, Bryan L. .... Atlanta, GA
Tyson, Candace G. .... Dallas, TX
Tyson, Charles C. .... Treasury Department, Internal Revenue Service, GV
Tyson, Cleveland A. .... Rockford, IL
Tyson, Craig K. .... Jamaica, NY
Tyson, D. Paul, Jr. .... Kansas City, MO
Tyson, Daniel J. .... Albany, NY
Tyson, Daniel R. .... Minneapolis, MN
Tyson, David R. .... Huntington, WV
Tyson, Fred W. .... Montgomery, AL
Tyson, George H., Jr. .... Houston, TX
Tyson, H. Mac, II .... Bolivia, NC
Tyson, H. Mac, II .... Fayetteville, NC
Tyson, H. Shannon, Jr. .... Austin, TX
Tyson, Heidi M. .... Lexington, MA
Tyson & Ipswitch .... Pasadena, CA
Tyson, James F. .... Houston, TX
Tyson, James H. .... Chesterfield Township, MI
Tyson, John .... Dallas, TX
Tyson, John C., III .... Montgomery, AL
Tyson, John D., Jr. .... Silver Spring, MD
Tyson, John J. .... Orlando, FL
Tyson, John M. .... Mobile, AL
Tyson, John M. .... Fayetteville, NC
Tyson, John M., Jr. .... Mobile, AL
Tyson, Joseph B., Jr. .... Milwaukee, WI
Tyson, Karin .... Department of Commerce, Patent and Trademark Office, GV
Tyson, Kelley M. .... Clayton, CA
Tyson, Kenneth W. .... Washington, NJ
Tyson, Kevin .... Pasadena, CA
Tyson, Kim F., (Mr.) .... Midland, MI
Tyson, Kimberley H. .... Denver, CO
Tyson, Laura Lanza .... Houston, TX
Tyson, Lisa N. .... Dallas, TX
Tyson, Mark H. .... Jackson, MS
Tyson, Marqueta N. .... Cleveland, OH
Tyson, Matthew Perry .... San Diego, CA
Tyson, Melissa A. .... The Woodlands, TX
Tyson, Michael C. .... Orlando, FL
Tyson, Nancy J. .... Tucson, AZ
Tyson, Patrick R. .... Atlanta, GA
Arlington, VA
Tyson, R. Knox .... Dallas, TX
Tyson, Ralph E. .... Baton Rouge, LA
Tyson, Renny J. .... Columbus, OH
Tyson, Renny J., Co., L.P.A. .... Columbus, OH
Tyson, Richard E. .... Huntington, WV
Tyson, Richard F. .... Baileys Harbor, WI
Tyson, Richard P. B., (Inc.) .... Pasadena, CA
Tyson, Robert E., Jr. .... Cayce, SC
Tyson, Robert F., Jr. .... San Diego, CA
Tyson, Robert J. .... Los Angeles, CA
Tyson, Robert R. .... Syracuse, NY
Tyson, Robert W., Jr. .... Fort Lauderdale, FL
Tyson, Rogue .... Warren, MI
Tyson, Rosalind R. .... Los Angeles, CA
Tyson, Rose M.
Merit Systems Protection Board, Office of Appeals Counsel, GV
Tyson, Sandra Lee .... Beverly Hills, CA
Tyson, Sandra Lee, A Law Corporation
Beverly Hills, CA
Tyson, Tahl .... Seattle, WA
Tyson, Thomas B. .... Point Blank, TX
Tyson, Thomas E. .... Austin, TX
Tyson, Timothy T. .... Los Angeles, CA
Tyson, Tina R. .... Washington, DC
Tyson, Todd H. .... Coatesville, PA
Tyson & Tyson .... Florence, SC
Tyson & Tyson .... Huntington, WV
Tyson, William B., III .... Florence, SC
Tyson, William B., Jr. .... Florence, SC
Tyson, William C. .... Santa Rosa, CA
Tyson, William C. .... Philadelphia, PA
Tyson, William F., Jr. .... Camilla, GA
Tyson, William T. .... San Diego, CA
Tyson-Floyd, Angela P.
Christiansted, St. Croix, VI
Tysse, G. John .... Washington, DC
Tyssee, Kay Ann .... Costa Mesa, CA
Tyssowski, Joseph R. S., Jr.
Baltimore, MD
Tysver, Daniel A. .... Hopkins, MN
Tytanic, Christopher Alan
Oklahoma City, OK
Tytel, Howard J. .... New York, NY
Tytel, Judith E. .... New York, NY
Tytla, Lawrence J. .... Waterford, CT
Tytler, Morton M. .... Olympia, WA
Tytus, John B. .... Cincinnati, OH
Tyukody, Daniel J., Jr. .... Los Angeles, CA
Tzagournis, George .... Youngstown, OH
Tzanakis, George E. .... Elkton, MD
Tzanetopoulos, George J. .... Chicago, IL
Tzangas, George J. .... Canton, OH
Tzangas, Plakas & Mannos .... Akron, OH
Canton, OH
Tzanides, Kirk P. .... New York, NY
Tzavelis, Elias .... New York, NY
Tzeng, Bertrand J. .... New York, NY
Tzepos, George C. .... Middlebury, CT
Tzerman, Cindy E. .... New York, NY
Tzerman, Jeffrey M. .... Camden, SC
Tzetzo, Basil .... Buffalo, NY
Tzetzo, Dimitri J. .... Buffalo, NY
Tzikas, Aristides .... Sacramento, CA
Tzikas, Aristides G., A Professional Corporation
Sacramento, CA
Tzimopoulos, George .... New York, NY
Tzinberg, Harold A. .... St. Louis, MO
Tzou, Rebecca Landon .... Washington, DC

Uale, Bode A. .... Honolulu, HI
Uba, Christine Dombrowski .... Buffalo, NY
Uba, Mark R. .... Buffalo, NY
Ubaldi, Marc J. .... Cheshire, CT
Ubaldi, Michael V. .... Sacramento, CA
Ubarri, Enrique R. .... San Juan, PR
Ubarri, José Luis .... San Juan, PR
Ubarri-Baragaño, Maria Teresa
San Juan, PR
Ubarri-Nevares, Carmen T. .... San Juan, PR
Ubatuba, Mary Chenoweth .... Hinsdale, IL
Ubben, Donald .... Washington, DC
Manning, SC
Charlottesville, VA
Ivy, VA
Ubbens, David P. .... Jacksonville, FL
Ubbing, Thomas J. .... Cleveland, OH
Ubel, F. Andrew .... St. Paul, MN
Ubelaker, Michele H. .... Louisville, KY
Ubell, Donald P. .... Charlotte, NC
Ubell, Franklin D. .... Irvine, CA
Uber, Arthur E., Jr. .... Allison Park, PA
Uber, Edw. J. .... Chicago, IL
Uber, Gretchen A. .... Oconomowoc, WI
Uber, James G. .... Pittsburgh, PA
Uber, William F., Jr. .... Dunedin, FL
Ubersax, Jeffery D. .... Cleveland, OH
Ubersax, Kristin L. .... Cleveland, OH
Uberstine, Gary A. .... Santa Monica, CA
Ubert, William A. .... Mineola, NY
Uberti, Barbara Ann .... Wilmington, DE
Uberti, Steven D. .... Everett, WA
Uberuaga, Joseph H., II .... Boise, ID
Ubhaus, Frank R. .... San Jose, CA
Ubieta, Albert R. .... New York, NY
Ubinger, John W., Jr. .... Pittsburgh, PA
Ubl, Andrea J. .... Waterville, ME
Ubozoh, Ferdinand I. .... New York, NY
Ucchino, Janine F. .... Omaha, NE
Ucchino, Jeffrey Michael .... Indianapolis, IN
Ucci, Stephen R. .... Providence, RI
Uchacz, Ronald E. .... Department of Defense, Defense Legal Services Agency, GV
Uchendu, Vincent C. .... Washington, DC
Ucherek, William M., II .... Abilene, TX
Uchida, Richard Y. .... Concord, NH
Uchida, Rodney .... Honolulu, HI
Uchikura, Douglas E. .... San Ramon, CA
Uchill, Lawrence E. .... Boston, MA
Uchima, Anju .... New York, NY
Uchima, Kei .... Los Angeles, CA
Uchimoto, William W. .... Philadelphia, PA
Uchitel, W. Jason .... Decatur, GA
Uchitelle, Benjamin .... St. Louis, MO
Uchitelle, Elliot M. .... St. Louis, MO
Uchiumi, Ronald K. .... Santa Rosa, CA
Uchiyama, Karen Y. .... San Francisco, CA
Uchiyama, Mikio .... Fowler, CA
Uchizono, S. Alfred .... Westminster, CA
Uchman, Eileen A. .... Mineola, NY
Uchner, David D. .... Cheyenne, WY
Uchtmann, Donald L. .... Urbana, IL
Ucinski, Theodore W. .... Paramus, NJ
Ucker, David A. .... Columbus, OH
Ucker, Timothy J. .... Columbus, OH
Uckert, Colin W. .... Washington, DC
Ucros, Nancy .... Melbourne, FL
Ucuzoglu, Nathan .... Downey, CA
Uda, Michael J. .... Helena, MT
Udagawa, Stephen M. .... Sanford, FL
Udall, Calvin H. .... Phoenix, AZ
Udall, David K. .... Mesa, AZ
Udall, David King .... Phoenix, AZ
Udall, D. B. .... Tucson, AZ
Udall, Joseph L. .... Stevenson, WA
Udall, Joseph M. .... Mesa, AZ
Provo, UT
Udall, Kenyon .... Safford, AZ
Udall, Kimball R. .... Santa Fe, NM
Udall, Kristina C. .... Seattle, WA
Udall, Larry K. .... Phoenix, AZ
Udall, Morris K. .... Tucson, AZ
Udall, Nicholas .... Mesa, AZ
Udall, Shumway, Blackhurst, Allen & Lyons, P.C. .... Mesa, AZ
Phoenix, AZ
Willcox, AZ
Udall, Stephen G. .... St. Johns, AZ
Udall, Thomas S. .... Santa Fe, NM
Udall, William A. .... Mesa, AZ
Udashen, Gary A. .... Dallas, TX
Udashen, Robert N. .... Dallas, TX
Udden, Lauren John .... Santa Barbara, CA
Uddenberg, Laura .... Salinas, CA
Uddo, Basile J. .... Metairie, LA
Uddo, Eleanor M. .... Wayland, MA
Uddo, Frank J. .... Metairie, LA
Uddo & Milazzo .... Metairie, LA
Uddoh, Humphrey O. .... New York, NY
Udell, Barton S. .... North Miami Beach, FL
Udell, Byron J. .... Northbrook, IL
Udell, Harran E. .... Maitland, FL
Udell, Howard R. .... Norwalk, CT
Udell, Jeffrey A. .... New York, NY
Udell, Jonathan .... Los Angeles, CA
Udell, Laurie S. .... Needham, MA
Udell, Lei K. .... San Diego, CA
Udell, Louis .... Ann Arbor, MI
Findlay, OH
Toledo, OH
Udell, Maury Lorne .... Miami, FL
Udell, Michael Bennett .... Davie, FL
Udell, Michael Bennett
Pembroke Pines, FL
Udell, Nancy A. .... New York, NY
Udell, Richard .... New York, NY
Udell, Richard A. .... Department of Justice, Environment and Natural Resources Division, GV
Udell, Robert G., (P.A.) .... Stuart, FL
Udell, Ryan J. .... Philadelphia, PA
Udell, Sindy Rae .... General Accounting Office, Office of the General Counsel, GV
Udell, Walter B. .... Quakertown, PA
Udelsohn, Robert A. .... Memphis, TN
Udelson, Theodore .... Newton, MA
Udine, Michael I. .... Fort Lauderdale, FL
Udine, Morey .... Fort Lauderdale, FL
Udis, Howard B. .... Yonkers, NY
Udis, Laura E. .... Denver, CO
Udkovich, Michael H.
San Juan Capistrano, CA
Udkovich, Nikki Sanders .... Santa Ana, CA
Udland, Lisa M. .... Salem, OR
Udland, Robert J. .... Bismarck, ND
Udo, John .... Boston, MA
Udoff, Michael D. .... Washington, DC
Udoibok, Kenneth Ubong .... Minneapolis, MN
Udolf, Bruce L. .... Miami, FL
Udolf, Roy .... East Meadow, NY
Udoni, Joseph O. .... Chicago, IL
Udouj, Gary W. .... Fort Smith, AR
Udovic, Kimberly Ann .... Los Angeles, CA
Udovic, Michael J. .... Pasadena, CA
Udovic, Michael S. .... Los Angeles, CA
Udowchenko, Michael W. .... Orlando, FL
Udrys, Arunas T. .... Jackson, MI
Udrys, Linas N .... Irvine, CA
Udseth, William T. .... Bloomington, MN
Udvari, Kristin L. .... Portland, OR
Udwadia, Viraf A. .... New York, NY
Udziela, Robert K. .... Portland, OR
Uebel, Karl J. .... San Francisco, CA
Uebel, Susan K. .... Fort Thomas, KY
Uebele, Kathleen Grace .... New Orleans, LA
Uebelhack, Jodi L. .... Indianapolis, IN
Uebelhoer, Gail N. .... Utica, NY
Uebersax, Ralph T. .... Westminster, MD
Ueberschaer, Thomas F. .... Pensacola, FL
Uebler, E. Alan .... Wilmington, DE
Uebler, Julie A. .... Philadelphia, PA
Uechi, Daniel S. .... San Antonio, TX
Uecker, James C. .... Minneapolis, MN
Uecker, Roberta Jo .... Helena, MT
Uecker, Timothy Paul .... San Jose, CA
Ueckermann, Gerald W., Jr.
Greenbelt, MD
Ueda, Rikkyln S. .... Solana Beach, CA
Uehara, Joyce J. .... Waipahu, HI
Uehara, Russell H. .... Honolulu, HI
Uehara, Stacy E. .... Honolulu, HI
Uehlein, Cunningham & Machanic
Natick, MA
Uehlein, E. Carl, Jr. .... Washington, DC
Uehlein, Edward C. .... Natick, MA
Uehlein, W. Frederick .... Natick, MA
Uehling, Robert H. .... Columbia, SC
Uehling, Robert O. .... Madison, WI
Uehlinger, Gerard P. .... Baltimore, MD
Uehlinger, Gerard P. .... Towson, MD
Uehlinger, John P. .... New York, NY
Uejio, Jonathan T. .... New York, NY
Uelmen, Amelia J. .... New York, NY
Uelmen, David L. .... Green Bay, WI
Milwaukee, WI
Waukesha, WI
Uelmen, Gerald F. .... San Francisco, CA
Uelmen, John D. .... Milwaukee, WI
Uelmen, Martha A., Law and Mediation Office of .... Cupertino, CA
Ueltschey, Watts C. .... Jackson, MS
Uemura, Kazuaki .... Torrance, CA
Uemura, T. Bob .... Salinas, CA
Ueno, Chizuko S. .... New York, NY
Ueno, Takemi .... New York, NY
Ueoka, B. Ladd .... Wailuku, HI
Ueoka, Leslie Alan .... Honolulu, HI
Ueoka, Meyer M. .... Wailuku, HI
Ueoka, Paul M. .... Wailuku, HI
Ueoka, Robert A. .... Honolulu, HI
Ueoka & Ueoka .... Wailuku, HI
Uerlings, James R. .... Klamath Falls, OR
Uesato, Philip S. .... Honolulu, HI
Uetz, Jennifer L. .... Lansing, MI
Ufberg & Associates, P.C. .... Scranton, PA
Ufberg, Murray .... Wilkes-Barre, PA
Ufberg, Robert .... Scranton, PA
Ufer, Robert P. .... Bloomfield Hills, MI
Ufer & Spaniola, P.C.
Bloomfield Hills, MI
Detroit, MI
Uffelman, John E. .... Beaverton, OR
Uffelman, Richard A. .... Portland, OR
Uffelman, William H., Jr. .... Wilmington, DE
Uffelman, William R. .... Naperville, IL
Uffelmann, Darryl K. .... Kansas City, MO
Uffner, Jeffrey D. .... New York, NY
Uffner, Steven R. .... New York, NY
Ufford, Charles W., Jr. .... New York, NY
Ufford, Martin R. .... Wichita, KS
Ufford, Roberta J. .... Washington, DC
Ufholz, L. Terrence .... Akron, OH
Ufholz, Philip J. .... United States Senate, Senatorial Assistants, GV
Ufkes, Alvin J. .... Orange, CA
Ufkes, Frederick J. .... Los Angeles, CA
Ufkes, John H.F.
San Juan Capistrano, CA
Ufkes, LeRoy A. .... Carthage, IL
Ufland, Antony C. .... Santa Ana, CA
Ugai, Brian .... Oak Brook, IL
Ugai, Susan M. .... Lincoln, NE
Ugalde, Aileen M. .... Miami, FL
Ugalde, Gregory F. .... Torrington, CT
Ugan, James R. .... Cleveland, OH
Ugarte, Michael .... San Antonio, TX
Ugarte, Miguel F. .... Chicago, IL
Ugarte, Ricardo E. .... Chicago, IL
Ugarte & Ugarte .... San Antonio, TX
Ugast, Frederick B. .... Washington, DC
Ugbana, Matthew C. .... Houston, TX
Ugell, Scott Barry .... Hempstead, NY

Ugelow, Richard S. ....Department of Justice, Civil Rights Division, GV
Ugelow, Robert A. ....Brooklyn, NY
Ugelow, Robert A., P.C. ....Brooklyn, NY
Ugelow, Seymour J. ....Delray Beach, FL
Ugent, Alvin R. ....Milwaukee, WI
Uggen, Steven J. ....Minneapolis, MN
Uggeri, Paula ....Manhasset, NY
Ughetta, Edward F. ....New York, NY
Ughetta, James C. ....New York, NY
Ughetta, Robert L. ....New York, NY
Ughetta, Valerie J. ....Washington, DC
Ughetta, William C. ....Elmira, NY
Uglem, Jonal H., (Ms.) ....Hatton, ND
Uglietta, Ann Thompson ....Phoenix, AZ
Ugol, Alec I. ....Department of State, Office of the Legal Adviser, GV
Ugolini, Donald L. ....West Springfield, MA
Ugolini, Michael A. ....Springfield, MA
Ugolnik, Elaine G. ....Lancaster, PA
Ugoretz, Jeffrey E. ....Camden, NJ
Westmont, NJ
Ugoretz, Mark J. ....Washington, DC
Ugrin, Alexander, Zadick & Higgins, P.C.
Great Falls, MT
Ugrin, Neil E. ....Great Falls, MT
Ugulini, Susan J. ....Bondurant, IA
Uhalley, Charles J. ....Pomona, CA
Uhalt, Hugh C., (P.C.) ....New Orleans, LA
Uhalt & Reck, A Prtn. of Law Corps.
New Orleans, LA
Uhe, Robert A. ....Chicago, IL
Uher, David R. ....Norfolk, NE
Uher, Donald R. (Tom) ....Bay City, TX
Uher, Joel K. ....Sacramento, CA
Uher, Philip J. ....Pittsburgh, PA
Uher, Tangi C ....Pensacola, FL
Uherbelau, Judith H. ....Ashland, OR
Uhimchuk, Sarah James ....Greenville, SC
Uhl, Alva A. ....Denver, CO
Uhl, Arthur G., III ....San Antonio, TX
Uhl, Brian W. ....Corona, CA
Uhl, Christopher M. ....Worcester, MA
Uhl, Christopher M. ....Fitchburg, MA
Uhl, Edward A. ....Bothell, WA
Uhl, Edwin F. ....Grand Rapids, MI
Uhl, Eric J. ....Portland, ME
Uhl, George A. ....Belleville, IL
St. Louis, MO
Uhl, Holger ....Boise, ID
Uhl, James A. ....Decatur, IL
Uhl, Jay J. ....Cincinnati, OH
Uhl, Jill E. ....Chicago, IL
Uhl, John H. ....Grand Rapids, MI
Uhl, John W. ....Hamilton, OH
Uhl, Keith E. ....Des Moines, IA
Uhl, Michael J. ....Dallas, TX
Uhl, Robert A. ....Beverly Hills, CA
Las Vegas, NV
Uhl, Thomas T. ....New York, NY
Uhl, Virginia Wickham ....Syosset, NY
Uhl, William J. ....Pittsburgh, PA
Uhland, Suzzanne ....Los Angeles, CA
Newport Beach, CA
Uhland, Wendell A. ....Kingwood, TX
Uhlar, Rudolf F. ....Detroit, MI
Uhlarik, Michael A. ....Boston, MA
Uhlarik, Stephanie L. ....Chicago, IL
Uhle, D'Anne D. ....Batavia, OH
Uhle, Matthew ....Fort Myers, FL
Uhle, Richard B., Jr. ....Batavia, OH
Uhle, William K. ....Portland, OR
Uhlemeyer, Arthur F. ....St. Louis, MO
Uhlenbrock, Robert J., Jr. ....Florissant, MO
Uhlenhake, John I. ....New York, NY
Uhlenhop, Paul B. ....Chicago, IL
Uhlenhopp, John C. ....Boulder, CO
Uhler, Bedford B., Jr. ....Rockwood, ME
Uhler, E. Kemper, Jr. ....Annandale, VA
Uhler, Ingrid A. ....Rancho Cucamonga, CA
Uhler, John C. ....York, PA
Uhler, Lewis K. ....Newport Beach, CA
Uhler, Mary S. ....Indianapolis, IN
Uhler, Scott F. ....Chicago, IL
Uhler, Tamara J. ....Auburn, CA
Uhles, Keith N. ....Brownsville, TX
Uhlfelder, Daniel ....Miami, FL
Uhlfelder, Mark N. ....Aspen, CO
Uhlfelder, Steven J. ....Tallahassee, FL
Uhlick, Lawrence R. ....New York, NY
Uhlick, Todd J. ....Riverside, CA
Uhlig, Calvin D. ....Kaneohe, HI
Uhlig, Christine Greener ....Chicago, IL
Uhlig, James D. ....Yates Center, KS
Uhlig, Mark Adams ....Overland Park, KS
Uhlig, Mary T. ....Philadelphia, PA
Uhlik, Paul M. ....Paterson, NJ
Uhling, Terry Tomas ....Boise, ID
Uhlinger, Cullan J. ....Cleveland, OH
Uhlinger, James R. ....Piketon, OH
Uhlinger & Keis ....Cleveland, OH
Uhlir, Dennis J. ....New York, NY
Uhlir, Golby C. ....South Sioux City, NE
Uhlir, James R. ....Seattle, WA
Uhlman, Wesley C. ....Seattle, WA
Uhlmann, Beth Ann ....Dayton, OH
Uhlmann, David M. ....Department of Justice, Environment and Natural Resources Division, GV
Uhlmann, Michael M. ....Washington, DC
Uhlmann, Robert F. ....Memphis, TN
Uhlmann, Sheryl L. ....Greeley, CO
Uhorchuk, Robert J. ....Chattanooga, TN
Uhr, Rebecca G. ....Dallas, TX
Uhr, Stanley A. ....Philadelphia, PA
Uhr, Steven E. ....Minneapolis, MN
St. Paul, MN
Uhrain, Paul J. ....Youngstown, OH
Uhrich, Jeffrey P. ....Columbus, OH
Uhrich, Timothy G. ....Pittsburgh, PA
Uhrig, Daniel J. ....Glencoe, IL
Uhrig, Emily S. ....Los Angeles, CA
Uhrig, Hal G. ....Maitland, FL
Uhrig, Harold E. ....Indianapolis, IN
Uhrig & Munger ....Huntsville, AL
Uhrig, Paul L. ....Washington, DC
Uhrig, Raymond ....Huntsville, AL
Uhrig, Robert Francis ....Cincinnati, OH
Uhrlaub, Jerry W. ....Grand Junction, CO
Uhrmacher, Bette E. ....Newark, NJ
Uhrman, Walter M. ....Encino, CA
Uhry, Gustave L. ....Port Chester, NY
Uible, Frank R., Jr. ....Taylor, MI
Uible, Harold H. ....New Vienna, OH
Uilkema, John K. ....San Francisco, CA
Uipi, Filia H. ....Salt Lake City, UT
Uiterwyk, Hendrik ....Clearwater, FL
Tampa, FL
Tampa, FL
Uiterwyk, Sanchez & Associates
Tampa, FL
Uitti, Mary Beth ....San Francisco, CA
Uitz, Ronald A. ....Washington, DC
Ujczo, Dennis E. ....Warren, OH
Ujczo, Joseph E. ....Westlake, OH
Ujevich, Robert M. ....Springfield, VA
Ujifusa, Linda Lee ....Portsmouth, RI
Ujke, David M. ....Phoenix, AZ
Ujlaky, John W. ....Lansing, MI
Ukai, Clara A. M. ....Los Angeles, CA
Ukasick, Troy A. ....Fort Collins, CO
Ukeiley, Robert ....Boulder, CO
Ukeiley, Stephen L. ....Garden City, NY
Ukena, Jay W. ....Waukegan, IL
Ukishima, Daniel S. ....Honolulu, HI
Ukman, Stephen L. ....Chesterfield, MO
Ukockis, Timothy A. ....Denver, CO
Ukropina, James R. ....Los Angeles, CA
Uku, Eustace O. ....Pittsburgh, PA
Uku, Livinus R. ....Los Angeles, CA
Ukwu & Associates, Chartered
Washington, DC
Ukwu, Lloyd F. ....Washington, DC
Ulaky, Robert E. ....Forked River, NJ
Ulan, Hattie Miriam
National Credit Union Administration, Office of General Counsel, GV
Ulan, Howard C. ....Harrisburg, PA
Ulan, Janice J. ....Department of Labor, Office of Secretary, GV
Ulan, Shelby K. ....New York, NY
Ulan, Stephen P. ....Philadelphia, PA
Ulaner, Marcelle K. ....New York, NY
Ulanoff, Stuart A. ....Southfield, MI
Ulasewicz, Patricia M.
Saratoga Springs, NY
Ulasewicz, Thomas A. ....Lake Placid, NY
Saratoga Springs, NY
Ulaszek, Norbert Michael ....Chicago, IL
Ulatowski, Adrian T. ....Green Bay, WI
Ulbrich and Anderson, P.C. ....Chester, VT
Ulbrich, Louis F. ....Bloomington, IL
Ulbrich, Peter ....Cincinnati, OH
Ulbrich, Robert W. ....Chester, VT
Ulbrich, Volker R. ....Worcester, MA
Ulcickas, Simon D. ....New York, NY
Uldall, Eric R. ....Fairfield, CA
Uldrich, Lisa A. ....Omaha, NE
Uldriks, Casper Ernest
Department Of Health And Human Services, Food & Drug Administration, GV
Ulen, E. Clay ....Indianapolis, IN
Ulene, Douglas ....New York, NY
Ulery, Christopher J. ....Cleveland, OH
Ulery, Jeffrey J. ....Indianapolis, IN
Ulery, Shari L. ....Englewood, CO
Ulf, Richard S. ....Silver Spring, MD
Ulferts, Martin ....Merrillville, IN
Uliana-Murphy, Angela ....Pen Argyl, PA
Uliano, Charles J., (P.C.)
West Long Branch, NJ
Uliase, Carolyn Badger ....Woodbury, NJ
Uliase, Raymond W. ....Haddon Heights, NJ
Uliase, Thomas R. ....Haddon Heights, NJ
Uliase & Uliase ....Haddon Heights, NJ
Ulibarri, Daniel P. ....Albuquerque, NM
Ulibarri, Joe ....Pueblo, CO
Ulibarri, Joseph M., Jr. ....Las Vegas, NM
Ulich, Andrew K. ....Irvine, CA
Ulich, David C. ....Los Angeles, CA
Ulich, Pamela Conley ....Los Angeles, CA
Ulichney, Carol ....Wilkes-Barre, PA
Ulicki, Jalae A. ....Harrison, MI
Ulicny, James A. ....Detroit, MI
Ulicny, Luke ....Detroit, MI
Ulicny, Mark R. ....Detroit, MI
Ulin, Dale R. ....Seattle, WA
Ulin, David P. ....Boston, MA
Ulin, Jeffrey ....San Rafael, CA
Ulin, Jeffrey B. ....Roseland, NJ
Ulin, John C. ....Los Angeles, CA
Ulin & Lambe, A Professional Service Corporation ....Seattle, WA
Ulinski, Christopher K. ....Akron, OH
Ulishney, Mary Ann ....Duluth, MN
Ulizio, John A. ....Berkeley Springs, WV
Uljanov, Kathleen Marie ....Harpursville, NY
Ulke, Guillermo ....New York, NY
Ulkus, David H. ....O'Fallon, IL
Ulland, Sherri D. ....Minneapolis, MN
Ullberg, Alan D. ....Washington, DC
Ulle, Albin E. ....Greenville, SC
Ulleberg, Rolf ....Duluth, MN
Ullein, Beverly Jean ....Somerset, PA
Ullem, Benjamin B. ....Des Moines, IA
Ullenberg, Louis R. ....Milwaukee, WI
Princeton, WI
Ullendorff, Alison Spear ....Los Angeles, CA
Ullerich, David K. ....Paducah, KY
Ullerich, Eric A. ....Woodland Hills, CA
Ullerich, Henry G. ....Pacific Palisades, CA
Ullery, Mark S. ....New Ulm, MN
Ullian, Bernard ....Everett, MA
Ullian, John A. ....Braintree, MA
Ullian, Richard L. ....Everett, MA
Ullman, A. Daniel, II ....Washington, DC
Ullman, Alan J. ....Cincinnati, OH
Ullman, Andrew M. ....New Haven, CT
Ullman, Anthony B. ....New York, NY
Ullman, Bill ....Miami, FL
Ullman, Carl V. ....Chiloquin, OR
Ullman, Charles R. ....Raleigh, NC
Ullman, Curtis A. ....Phoenix, AZ
Ullman, David ....Westbury, NY
Ullman, Edith B. ....Sebastopol, CA
Ullman, Faith A. ....Parsippany, NJ
Ullman, Furhman, Broeman & Platt, P.C.
Morristown, NJ
New York, NY
Ullman, Gregory N. ....Miami, FL
Ullman, Harold ....New York, NY
Ullman, Howard ....San Francisco, CA
Cincinnati, OH
Ullman, Ian Charles ....New York, NY
Ullman, James A. ....Phoenix, AZ
Ullman, Jeffrey D. ....Morristown, NJ
New York, NY
Ullman, Joseph B. ....Scarsdale, NY
Ullman, Joyce ....Philadelphia, PA
Ullman, Kirsten K. ....Tampa, FL
Ullman, Lee E. ....Norristown, PA
Reading, PA
Topton, PA
Ullman, Lisa ....Albany, NY
Ullman, Lloydann ....Los Angeles, CA
Ullman, Marc S. ....New York, NY
Ullman, Michael D. ....Beverly Hills, CA
Ullman, Michael W. ....Fort Lauderdale, FL
Ullman & Painter ....Waynesboro, PA
Ullman, Pamela C. ....Collegeville, PA
Ullman, Paul H.
Federal Labor Relations Authority, Authority Member Staff, GV
Ullman, Perlmutter & Sklaver
New Haven, CT
Ullman, Peter M. ....Philadelphia, PA
Ullman, Richard A. ....Los Angeles, CA
Ullman, Robert ....Fort Lauderdale, FL
Ullman, Robert ....New York, NY
Ullman, Robert, P.A. ....Fort Lauderdale, FL
Ullman, Robert T. ....Reading, PA
Ullman, Robin Hirsh ....Baltimore, MD
Ullman, Roger R. ....Swarthmore, PA
Ullman, S. Thomas ....Fort Myers, FL
Ullman, Samuel C., (P.A.) ....Miami, FL
Ullman, Shapiro & Ullman, LLP
New York, NY
Ullman, Susan Katharine ....Madison, WI
Ullman & Ullman, P.A. ....Fort Lauderdale, FL
Ullmann, Cornelia S. ....New Orleans, LA
Ullmann, Deborah Anne Marie
Baltimore, MD
Ullmann, Frank J. ....York, PA
Ullmann, Gladys G. ....Larchmont, NY
Ullmann, Jonathan I. ....Jericho, NY
Ullmann, Lawrence T. ....Walnut Creek, CA
Ullmann, Michael ....New Brunswick, NJ
Ullmann, Robert L. ....Boston, MA
Ullmann, Thomas J. ....New Haven, CT
Ullmann, Wilmer R. ....Kansas City, MO
Ullner, Kimberlee S. ....Atlanta, GA
Ulloa, Alberto ....Elizabeth, NJ
Ulloa, Edward Richard ....Ventura, CA
Ulloa, Francisco E. ....New York, NY
Ullom, Jess W. ....Chesterfield, MO
Ullom, Marc F. ....Warrington, PA
Ullom, Paul J. ....Tampa, FL
Ullom-Morse, Norman J. ....Westerville, OH
Ullrich, David A. ....Chicago, IL
Ullrich, David A. ....Evanston, IL
Ullrich, Donald W., Jr. ....Sacramento, CA
Ullrich, Helen G. ....Goshen, NY
Ullrich Law Firm, The ....Sacramento, CA
Ullrich, Thomas E. ....Harrisonburg, VA
Ullrich-Eaton, Donna ....Harrison, MI
Ullstrom, Galen F. ....Omaha, NE
Ullstrom, Gregory ....Rutland, VT
Ullstrom, Richard N. ....Anchorage, AK
Bellevue, WA
Ullsvik, John M. ....Jefferson, WI
Ullyot, Theodore W. ....Washington, DC
Ulm, Alice L. ....New York, NY
Ulm, Anthony P. ....Galesburg, IL
Ulman, Barbara L. ....West Bloomfield, MI
Ulman, Craig H. ....Washington, DC
Ulman, Doris F. ....Suffern, NY
Ulman, Edward S. ....Los Angeles, CA
Ulman, Jennifer A. ....West Bloomfield, MI
Ulman, John M., II ....Bakersfield, CA
Ulman, Joshua A. ....Providence, RI
Ulman, Lawrence J. ....Los Angeles, CA
Ulman, Louis Jay ....Bethesda, MD
Columbia, MD
Ulman, Robert J. ....San Antonio, TX
Ulman, Stephen Van R. ....Locust Valley, NY
Ulman, Walter R. ....Phoenix, AZ
Ulmen, Peter W. ....Minneapolis, MN
Ulmen, Thomas L. ....Minneapolis, MN
Ulmer & Berne LLP ....Cleveland, OH
Columbus, OH
Ulmer, Betty J. ....Milwaukee, WI
Ulmer, Brian W. ....Lewisburg, PA
Ulmer, Carl E. ....Neptune, NJ
Ulmer, Carolijn ....New York, NY
Ulmer, David F. ....St. Louis, MO
Ulmer, Dorothy J.
Department of Transportation, Office of the General Counsel, GV
Ulmer, Douglas E. ....Fort Wayne, IN
Ulmer, Frances A. ....Juneau, AK
Ulmer, G. Bryan, III ....Jackson, WY
Ulmer, Gregory C. ....Houston, TX
Ulmer, Herman, Jr. ....Jacksonville, FL
Ulmer, Hillman, Burnett & Nagrich
Mobile, AL
Ulmer, James G. ....Houston, TX
Ulmer, Joan S. ....Department of Justice, Tax Division, GV
Ulmer, Jodi Lynn ....Buffalo, NY
Ulmer, John D. ....Goshen, IN
Ulmer, Leland G. ....Mandan, ND
Ulmer, Margaret A. ....Pottsville, PA
Ulmer, Mark R. ....Mobile, AL
Ulmer, Mark S. ....Miami, FL
Ulmer, Merrill A. ....New York, NY
Ulmer, Michael W. ....Jackson, MS
Ulmer, Murchison, Ashby & Taylor, P.A.
Jacksonville, FL
Ulmer, Ray E., Jr. ....Clearwater, FL
Ulmer, Richard B., Jr. ....San Francisco, CA
Ulmer, Richard E. ....El Dorado, AR
Ulmer, Ronald J. ....Minersville, PA
Ulmer, Thomas R. ....Van Nuys, CA
Ulmschneider, Mark D. ....Fort Wayne, IN
Uloth, Donald E. ....Dallas, TX
Uloth, J. Douglas ....Dallas, TX
Ulovec, Thomas J. ....Chula Vista, CA
Ulreich, Thomas D. ....Phoenix, AZ
Ulrey, James B., Sr. ....Oxford, AL
Ulrey, Thurl R. ....Port St. Lucie, FL
Ulrich, Bonnie P. ....Sioux Falls, SD
Ulrich, Carl E., Jr. ....Modesto, CA
Ulrich, Carl P. ....Rhinebeck, NY
Ulrich, Carl W., The Law Offices of
Washington, DC
Ulrich, Charles A. ....Mundelein, IL
Ulrich, Christopher L. ....Stamford, CT
Ulrich, Clifford A. ....Morristown, NJ
Ulrich, Corinna ....Dallas, TX
Ulrich, Dana Clarke ....Califon, NJ
Ulrich, Dennis P. ....Monroe, MI
Ulrich, Diana Dowd ....Houston, TX
Ulrich, Fred E. ....Ogden, UT
Ulrich, Gregory L. ....Livonia, MI
Ulrich, Jacquelyn Ellen ....Olathe, KS
Ulrich, John J. ....Sioux Falls, SD
Ulrich, John M. H., IV ....Birmingham, MI
Ulrich, Joseph E. ....Lexington, VA
Ulrich, Joseph R. ....Painesville, OH
Ulrich, Karl R. ....Dayton, OH
Ulrich, Kelli E. ....Evansville, IN
Ulrich, Kellie Muffoletto ....Buffalo, NY
Ulrich, Kenneth S. ....Chicago, IL
Ulrich, Kenneth T. ....Elkins Park, PA
Ulrich, Kessler & Anger, P.C.
Phoenix, AZ
Ulrich, Laura G. ....Dayton, OH
Ulrich, Laura Levin ....Chicago, IL
Ulrich, Laurence M. ....Santa Clara, CA
Ulrich, Lowell R. ....Sault Ste. Marie, MI
Ulrich, Mary Lamanna ....New York, NY
Ulrich, Melissa S. ....Canton, OH
Ulrich, Michelle J. ....St. Paul, MN
Ulrich, Parke H. ....Norristown, PA
Ulrich, Paul G. ....Phoenix, AZ
Ulrich, Peter J. ....Newark, NJ
Ulrich, Phyllis A. ....Cleveland, OH
Ulrich & Ramsey ....Modesto, CA
Ulrich, Richard A. ....Sarasota, FL
Ulrich, Richard H. ....St. Louis, MO
Ulrich, Robert B. ....Chicago, IL
Ulrich, Robert C. ....Vermillion, SD
Ulrich, Robert G. ....Kansas City, MO
Ulrich, Robert G. ....Montvale, NJ
Ulrich, Robert H. ....Reno, NV
Ulrich, Robert L. ....St. Petersburg, FL
Ulrich, Roy M. ....Santa Monica, CA
Ulrich, Stan G. ....Palo Alto, CA
Ulrich, Theodore A. ....Denver, CO
Ulrich, Timothy W. ....Houston, TX
Ulrich and Ulrich, Inc. A Professional Corporation ....Houston, TX
Ulrich, Werner ....Glen Ellyn, IL
Ulrich, William C. ....Antioch, CA
Ulrich, William J., Jr. ....Wheaton, IL
Ulrich Hansen, Rockie J. Ray
Spokane, WA
Ulrichsen, Amarel & Eory ....Skillman, NJ
Ulrichsen, Barbara ....Skillman, NJ
Ulsamer, Richard A. ....Newark, NJ
Ulsch, Edward M. ....Westminster, MD
Ulseth, George W. ....Moorhead, MN
Ulsh, James A. ....Harrisburg, PA
Ulsted, Dennis L. ....Salem, OR
Ulterino, Eugene D. ....Rochester, NY
Ultimo, Paul J. ....Santa Ana, CA
Ultsch, Wm. F. ....Cincinnati, OH
Uluatam, Aldoru ....Boston, MA
Uluer, Deborah B. ....Cleveland, OH
Ulum, Angela M. ....Chicago, IL
Ulveling, Jennifer A. ....Palo Alto, CA
Ulven, Debra A. ....Pittsburgh, PA
Ulven, Mark E. ....Pittsburgh, PA
Ulvestad, Thor P. ....Seattle, WA
Ulwelling, James K. ....Orange, CA
Ulwick, James P. ....Baltimore, MD
Ulyatt, John R. ....Altaville, CA
Um, Alice J. ....San Francisco, CA
Chicago, IL
Um, William T. ....Los Angeles, CA
Umali, Jose P. ....San Francisco, CA

Uman, Edith G. ... Tampa, FL
Uman, Frank L. ... Springfield, MA
Uman, Henry K. ... New York, NY
Uman, Jon D. ... Gainesville, FL
Uman, Jon D., P.A. ... Gainesville, FL
Umana, Christopher ... Boston, MA
Umana, John ... Washington, DC
Umanah, Ivory Sunny ... Minneapolis, MN
Umane, Frederic M. ... New York, NY
Umanoff, Adam S. ... Los Angeles, CA
Umans, Jay D. ... Uniondale, NY
Umans-Gough, Terry Ann ... New York, NY
Umansky, Barry D. ... Washington, DC
Umansky, Jay B. ... St. Louis, MO
Umansky, Michael M. ... Los Angeles, CA
Umansky, Michael S. ... San Diego, CA
Umansky, Raphael D. ... Sunrise, FL
Umansky, Zahra S. ... Orlando, FL
Umanzio, Claire-Frances ... Boston, MA
Umanzio, Dennis A. ... Yuba City, CA
Umbach, Arnold W., III ... Birmingham, AL
Umbach, Arnold W., Jr. ... Opelika, AL
Umbach, Corwin P. ... Arlington, VA
Umbarger, Alice J. ... Merced, CA
Umbarger, Stuart, P.A. ... Brandon, FL
Umbarger, Stuart W. ... Brandon, FL
Umbaugh, Craig A. ... Denver, CO
Umbaugh, David G. ... Hudson, OH
Umbaugh, Jennifer L. ... Wilmington, NC
Umbaugh & Sharp ... Hudson, OH
Umbenhauer, Richard A. ... Carlsbad, CA
Umberger, Horace M. ... Tucson, AZ
Umberger, Michelle M. ... Madison, WI
Umberger, Rodney L., Jr. ... Seattle, WA
Umberger, Scott Alexander
New Orleans, LA
Umbrecht, Charles H., Jr. ... Syracuse, NY
Umbrecht, Richard L. ... Philadelphia, PA
Umbreit, Timothy F. ... Encino, CA
Umebayashi, Clyde S. ... Honolulu, HI
Umeda, Glen S. ... Los Angeles, CA
Umeda, James O. ... Chattanooga, TN
Umeda, Judy ... Pleasanton, CA
Umeda, Mark Yoshio ... Sacramento, CA
Umeda, Sayuri ... Washington, DC
Umeda, Wesley T. ... Redwood City, CA
Umejima, Osamu ... Washington, DC
Umentum, Paul P. ... Green Bay, WI
Umerah, Chukwudi E. ... Fayetteville, NC
Umeugo & Associates, P.C.
West Haven, CT
Umeugo, Ikechukwu ... West Haven, CT
Umezono, Hiroyuki ... New York, NY
Umhey, Charles E., III ... Hamilton, MT
Umhoefer, Sharon Ann ... Piscataway, NJ
Umhofer, Donald G. ... San Luis Obispo, CA
Umholtz, Marie L. ... Chardon, OH
Umholtz, R. Robert ... Chardon, OH
Umholtz, Stewart J. ... Pekin, IL
Umholtz, Valerie Moehle ... Pekin, IL
Umin, Steven M. ... Washington, DC
Umipeg, Gareth J. ... Concord, CA
Umland, Carrie D. ... Federal Way, WA
Umland, John M. ... Forest Hills, NY
Umland, Julius C. ... Waller, TX
Umland, Scott E. ... Peoria, IL
Umlas, Stephen P. ... North Miami Beach, FL
Umlauf, Natalie Williams ... New York, NY
Umlauf, Roy A. ... Seattle, WA
Umlauf, Sheila ... Seattle, WA
Ummel, Gay B. ... Golden, CO
Ummel, Jerry L. ... Fort Wayne, IN
Ummel, T. Edward ... Culver, IN
Plymouth, IN
Ummer, James W. ... Pittsburgh, PA
Umoff, Peter A. ... Santa Barbara, CA
Umphenour, C. Geraldine ... Kansas City, MO
Umphlett, Archie W. ... Arlington, VA
Umphress, Jennifer Poe ... Addison, TX
Umphrey, Darren ... Nederland, TX
Umphrey, James M. ... Bad Axe, MI
Umphrey, Martha M. ... Amherst, MA
Umphrey, Michael D. ... Troy, MI
Umphrey, Walter ... Beaumont, TX
Umphrey, Willard L. ... Cambridge, MA
Umpierre-Ponton, Gustavo J.
San Juan, PR
Umpierre-Suarez, Enrique ... San Juan, PR
Umpleby, John I. ... Columbus, OH
Umrein, Kathleen A. ... San Anselmo, CA
Umscheid, Lisa M. ... Portland, OR
Umstattd, Kristen Coles ...
Department of the Navy, GV
Umstattd-Cope, Penny J. ... Mexico, MO
Umstead, Raymond L. ... Indianapolis, IN
Umstead, Scott B. ... Conway, SC
Myrtle Beach, SC
Umsted, Jim S., Jr. ... Memphis, TN
Umsted, Scott, Jr. ... Newport, RI
Un, Socheata ... Leavenworth, KS
Unatin, Mark L. ... Pittsburgh, PA
Unatin, Steven I. ... Ormond Beach, FL
Uncapher, Andrew G., Jr. ... Vandergrift, PA
Uncapher, Kenneth R. ... Orlando, FL
Uncapher & Uncapher ... Vandergrift, PA
Uncyk, Borenkind and Nadler
New York, NY
Uncyk, Eli ... New York, NY
Unda, Maria T. O'Connell ... Brockton, MA
Undem, John D. ... Grand Rapids, MN
Undem Law Office ... Grand Rapids, MN
Underberg, Alfred E. ... St. Petersburg, FL
Underberg, Eugene M. ... Lake Worth, FL
Underberg & Kessler LLP ... Buffalo, NY
Rochester, NY
Underberg, Mark A. ... New York, NY
Underberg, Neil ... New York, NY
Underberg, Paul D. ... Rochester, NY
Underberg, Robert L.
Rockville Centre, NY
Underberg, Sharon ... Rochester, NY
Underberger, Lori L. ... Bridgeport, CT
Underbrink, Ann E. ... Minneapolis, MN
Undercofler, Hiram K. ... Atlanta, GA
Undercofler, J. Clayton ... Philadelphia, PA
Underdal, Stephen M. ... Minneapolis, MN
Underdown, Ezell H. ... Columbus, OH
Underhill, Albert L. ... Minneapolis, MN
Underhill, Casey A. ... La Mesa, CA
Underhill, Christopher S. ... Lancaster, PA
Underhill, D. Michael ... Washington, DC
Underhill, David L. ... Washington, DC
Underhill, Dayna E. ... Portland, OR
Underhill, Diana C. ... Ann Arbor, MI
Underhill, Edward J. ... Chicago, IL
Underhill & Edwards ... Madison, TN
Underhill, Frederick H., Jr. ... Danville, IL
Underhill, G. Townsend, III ... Louisville, KY
Underhill, Gary M., Jr. ... Elizabeth City, NC
Underhill, James C., Jr. ... Denver, CO
Underhill, James R. ... Onawa, IA
Underhill, Jeanne B. ... Fort Lauderdale, FL
Underhill, Joanne Parsons ... Denver, CO
Underhill, John H. ... Sault Ste. Marie, MI
Underhill, John H., P.C.
Sault Ste. Marie, MI
Underhill, Kathryn A. ... Washington, DC
Underhill, Leann M. ... Plymouth, MI
Underhill, M. Kevin ... Kansas City, MO
Underhill, Michael J. ... New Bedford, MA
Underhill, Peter J. ... Charlotte, NC
Underhill, R. Michael
Department of Justice, Civil Division, GV
Underhill, Robert B. ... Scarsdale, NY
Underhill, Robert S. ... Woodbridge, NJ
Underhill, Stefan R. ... Stamford, CT
Underhill, Thomas H. ... Bakersfield, CA
Underhill, Thomas W. ... West Chatham, MA
Underhill & Underhill ... Denver, CO
Underhill, Wallace W. ... Wichita, KS
Underhill, Walter H. ... Boston, MA
Underhill, William Amory ... Washington, DC
DeLand, FL
Underhill, William L. ... Madison, TN
Underhill, Wingate E. ... Washington, DC
Underkofler, Paul B. ... Dallas, TX
Underkuffler, Frank M. ... Farmington, ME
Underkuffler, Laura S. ... Durham, NC
Underwald, Suzanne M. ... Washington, DC
Underweiser, Beatrice K. ... New York, NY
Underweiser, Irwin P. ... New York, NY
Underweiser, Jeffrey B. ... New York, NY
Underweiser, Marian ... New York, NY
Underweiser, Meric A. ... New York, NY
Underweiser, Rosanne ... Scarsdale, NY
Underweiser & Underweiser
New York, NY
Underwood, Alan W. ... Brooksville, FL
Spring Hill, FL
Underwood, Allen J., II ... Millburn, NJ
Underwood, Arthur C. ... Aurora, CO
Underwood & Associates ... Tampa, FL
Underwood & Associates, P.C. ... Lapeer, MI
Oxford, MI
Underwood, Barbara D. ... Brooklyn, NY
Underwood, Blake E. ... Portland, OR
Underwood, Bobby C. ... Birmingham, AL
Underwood, Bobby N. ... Monroe, LA
Underwood, Bradley S. ... Lubbock, TX
Underwood, Brian C. ... St. Louis, MO
Underwood, C. Harold ... Redding, CA
Underwood, Carey B. ... Monroe, LA
Underwood, Carl E., III ... Dothan, AL
Underwood, Catherine W. ... Jackson, MS
Underwood, Cecil W.
Federal Deposit Insurance Corporation,
Professional Liability Section, GV
Underwood, Charles D. ... Columbus, OH
Underwood, Christi L. ... Orlando, FL
Underwood, Colin A. ... New York, NY
Underwood, Daniel E.
Maryland Heights, MO
Underwood, David G. ... Parkersburg, WV
Ripley, WV
Underwood, David L. ... McLeansboro, IL
Underwood, Debra M. ... Lakeport, CA
Underwood, Decker ... San Jose, CA
Underwood, Derek ... Tampa, FL
Underwood, Douglas D. ... Tampa, FL
Underwood, Earl P., Jr. ... Anniston, AL
Huntsville, AL
Underwood & Eppley, P.A.
Brooksville, FL
Spring Hill, FL
Underwood, Eugene, Jr. ... Miami, FL
Underwood, Evelyn M. ... Del Norte, CO
Underwood, Frank C., III ... Savannah, GA
Underwood, Gary R. ... St. Louis, MO
Underwood, Gary R. ... Oklahoma City, OK
Underwood, George W. ... Tulsa, OK
Underwood, Gerald V. ... Modesto, CA
Underwood, Gregory L. ... Bowie, TX
Underwood, H. John ... Ruidoso, NM
Underwood, Henry J., Jr. ... Chicago, IL
Underwood, Herbert G. ... Clarksburg, WV
Underwood, Homer E. ... Vero Beach, FL
Underwood, Hugh W., III ... Tuscaloosa, AL
Underwood, J. Andrew ... New York, NY
Underwood, Jack L. ... El Paso, TX
Underwood, Jack R., Jr. ... Louisville, KY
Underwood, James L. ... Columbia, SC
Underwood, James M. ... Redding, CA
Underwood, James M. ... Dallas, TX
Underwood, James S., Jr. ... Boise, ID
Underwood, James S., Jr., A Professional
Association ... Boise, ID
Underwood, Jane Lindsay ... Toledo, OH
Underwood, Jason P. K. ... Louisville, KY
Underwood, Jeffrey A. ... Mansfield, OH
Underwood, Jerry D. ... Newport Beach, CA
Underwood, Joe W. ... Columbia, SC
Underwood, John C., Jr. ... Jackson, MS
Underwood, John E. ... Lilburn, GA
Underwood, John G.
Department Of Health And Human Services,
Social Security Administration, GV
Underwood, John H., III ... Portsmouth, VA
Underwood, John T. ... DeSoto, TX
Underwood, John W. ... Bellevue, WA
Underwood, Karcher & Karcher, P.A.
Miami, FL
Underwood, Kathryn E. ... Phoenix, AZ
Underwood, Kathy D. ... Baton Rouge, LA
Underwood, Kenneth L. ... Westerville, OH
Underwood, Kenneth W., Jr.
Montgomery, AL
Underwood, Kent W. ... Tacoma, WA
Underwood, Kevin F. ... Port Orchard, WA
Underwood, Kimberley A. ... Bothell, WA
Underwood Kinsey Warren & Tucker, P.A.
Charlotte, NC
Underwood, Kristen M. ... Atlanta, GA
Underwood, Laura E. ... Phoenix, AZ
Underwood, Lauren M.
Bloomfield Hills, MI
Underwood, Lauren M. ... Portland, OR
Underwood Law Firm ... Jackson, MS
Underwood Law Firm ... St. Louis, MO
Underwood Law Offices ... Albany, GA
Underwood, Malcolm S. ... Lynchburg, VA
Underwood, Margaret M.
Philadelphia, PA
Underwood, Martin E. ... Comstock, TX
Underwood, Michael J. ... Columbus, OH
Underwood, Molly K. ... Charleston, WV
Underwood, Murray S. ... Spencer, IA
Underwood, Norman L. ... Atlanta, GA
Underwood & Norwood ... Portland, OR
Underwood, Olen ... Conroe, TX
Underwood, Olen Grant ... Dallas, TX
Underwood, Otis M., Jr. ... Oxford, MI
Underwood, P. Benjamin ... Charleston, SC
Underwood, P. James ... Annapolis, MD
Underwood, Page ... Houston, TX
Underwood, Pamela A. ... San Francisco, CA
Underwood, Peter C. ... Milwaukee, WI
Underwood, R. Dannette ... Clayton, NC
Underwood, R. Michael ... Tallahassee, FL
Underwood, Randall A. ... Greensboro, NC
Underwood, Raymond P. ... Portland, OR
Underwood, Richard C. ... Phoenix, AZ
Underwood, Richard D. ... Memphis, TN
Underwood, Richard J. ... Boston, MA
Underwood, Robert H. ... Newark, NJ
Underwood, Robert L., III
Tallahassee, FL
Research Triangle Park, NC
Underwood, Robert L., P.A.
Research Triangle Park, NC
Underwood, Robert M. ... Carthage, TX
Underwood, Robyn M. ... Washington, DC
Underwood, Roger H. ... Spokane, WA
Underwood, Samuel B., Jr. ... Greenville, NC
Underwood, Sean E. ... Washington, DC
Underwood, Sloane J. ... Houston, TX
Underwood, Stephen D. ... Santa Barbara, CA
Underwood, Stephen E. ... Hopkinsville, KY
Underwood, Steven C. ... Madison, WI
Underwood, Steven D. ... New York, NY
Underwood, Steven L. ... Grand Rapids, MI
Underwood, Susan ... Boston, MA
Underwood, Susan P. ... Sacramento, CA
Underwood, T. Bryan, Jr. ... Chicago, IL
Underwood, Tamra N. ... Vail, CO
Underwood, Thomas B. ... Chicago, IL
Underwood, Thomas C. ... Washington, DC
Underwood, Thomas C. ... Omaha, NE
Underwood, Thomas G. ... Manassas, VA
Underwood, Thomas W., Jr. ... Foley, AL
Underwood, Thos. R. ... Lexington, KY
Underwood, Timothy P. ... Pulaski, TN
Underwood, Tisha P. ... San Diego, CA
Underwood & Underwood, LLP
Montgomery, AL
Underwood, Vicky ... Selma, AL
Underwood, Wilbur H., Jr. ... Perry, GA
Underwood, William B., III ... Houston, TX
Underwood, William C.B. ... Phoenix, AZ
Underwood, William D. ... Waco, TX
Underwood, William E., Jr.
Charlotte, NC
Underwood, William F. ... Reynoldsburg, OH
Underwood, William F., Jr. ... Albany, GA
Underwood, William H. ... Dallas, TX
Underwood, William J. ... Tuscumbia, AL
Underwood, William J., Jr. ... Dallas, TX
Underwood, William K.
Federal Labor Relations Authority,
Authority Member Staff, GV
Underwood, William L. ... Minneapolis, MN
Underwood, Wilson, Berry, Stein & Johnson,
P.C. ... Amarillo, TX
Underwood, Wynn ... Montpelier, VT
Underwood Smith, Carolyn ... Nashville, TN
Undlin, Thomas J. ... Minneapolis, MN
Unell, Jenna Vick ... Dallas, TX
Unell, John S. ... Plano, TX
Uney, Harold ... Oregon City, OR
Unfred, John Michael ... Lebanon, OR
Unfug, Charles S. ... Aurora, CO
Ung, Diane ... Los Angeles, CA
Ung, Euchung ... New York, NY
Ung, Sheree S. ... Culver City, CA
Ungar, Barry E. ... Philadelphia, PA
Ungar, Bertrand T. ... Denver, CO
Ungar, Bertrand T., P.C. ... Denver, CO
Ungar, David T. ... Bakersfield, CA
Ungar, Diane E. ... New York, NY
Ungar, Donald L. ... San Francisco, CA
Ungar, Jack H. ... Long Branch, NJ
Ungar, Joel A. ... Santa Barbara, CA
Ungar, John C. ... Philadelphia, PA
Ungar, Michael K. ... San Francisco, CA
Ungar, Michael N. ... Cleveland, OH
Ungar, Michael T. ... Rolling Hills Estates, CA
Ungar, Paul B. ... Edison, NJ
Ungar, Robert A. ... Garden City, NY
Ungar, Robert A., P.C. ... Garden City, NY
Ungar, Robert J. ... Washington, DC
Ungar, Robert M. ... Los Angeles, CA
Ungar, Sheri D. ... Burbank, CA
Ungar, Steven B. ... Portland, OR
Ungaretti & Harris ... Washington, DC
Chicago, IL
Ungaretti, Richard A. ... Chicago, IL
Ungarino & Eckert, L.L.C. ... Metairie, LA
New Orleans, LA
Ungarino, Julie ... Metairie, LA
Ungarino, Matthew J. ... Metairie, LA
Ungaro, Jane ... New York, NY
Ungaro, John-Robert, III ... Charleston, SC
Ungaro, Michael P. ... Hartford, CT
Ungaro-Benages, Ursula ... Miami, FL
Ungemach, Elmer P. ... Kenosha, WI
Ungemach, Frank S. ... Thousand Oaks, CA
Ungemah, Donald W. ... Denver, CO
Unger, Alan M. ... New York, NY
Unger, Allison J. ... New York, NY
Unger, Andrew S. ... Washington, DC
Chevy Chase, MD
Unger, Catherine D. ... Port Orange, FL
Unger, Charles J. ... Glendale, CA
Unger, Christopher Vincent ... Wheaton, IL
Unger, Cynda Riggins ... Suisun, CA
Unger, D. Bruce ... Marlboro, NJ
Unger, Daniel P. ... Chicago, IL
Unger, David C. ... Aurora, CO
Unger, Donald J. ... Washington, DC
Chicago, IL
Unger, Frederick L. ... Bellaire, TX
Unger, Geoffrey R. ... San Antonio, TX
Unger, H. Manning ... Charlotte, NC
Unger, H. Wayne, Jr. ... Charleston, SC
Edisto Island, SC
Walterboro, SC
Unger, Harold M. ... New York, NY
Unger, Harry, Jr. ... Albany, NY
Unger, Isadore Harry ... Flushing, NY
Unger, Jason L. ... Pompano Beach, FL
Unger, Jeanne H. ... Minneapolis, MN
Unger, Jeffrey A. ... Beverly Hills, CA
Unger, Joan M. ... Anchorage, AK
Unger, Joe N. ... Miami, FL
Unger, John F. ... Houston, TX
Unger, John T. ... Houston, TX
Unger, John W. ... Bellaire, MI
Unger, Jon N. ... Vacaville, CA
Unger, Karen L. ... Port Angeles, WA
Unger, Kimberly ... New York, NY
Unger, Langdon S., Jr. ... Martin, TN
Unger, Langdon S., Jr. ... Union City, TN
Unger, Larry R. ... New York, NY
Unger, Lawrence P. ... New York, NY
Unger, Leonard ... Beverly Hills, CA
Unger, Linda E. ... Chicago, IL
Unger, Marcel N. ... Bethesda, MD
Unger, Margaret A. ... Chicago, IL
Unger, Marilyn ... Westbury, NY
Unger, Mark Ilan ... San Antonio, TX
Unger, Martin B. ... Jacksonville, FL
Orlando, FL
Unger, Martin P. ... New York, NY
Unger, Mary Ann ... Augusta, GA
Unger, Matthew S. ... Sacramento, CA
Unger, Meryl L. ... New York, NY
Unger, Michael ... Boston, MA
Unger, Michael A. ... Chicago, IL
Unger, Michael E. ... Stamford, CT
New York, NY
Unger, Michael W. ... Minneapolis, MN
Unger, N. Rick ... Warren, MI
Unger, Neal M. ... Edison, NJ
Unger, Neal M., P.C. ... Edison, NJ
Unger, Paul J. ... Columbus, OH
Unger, Peter J. ... New York, NY
Unger, Peter V.B. ... Washington, DC
Unger, Randall D. ... Kew Gardens, NY
Unger, Rebekah Hughes ... Charlotte, NC
Unger, Richard C., Jr. ... Norristown, PA
Unger, Richard C., Jr.
West Conshohocken, PA
Unger, Richard M. ... Montevideo, MN
Unger, Richard M. ... Columbia, SC
Unger, Richard S. ... Miami, FL
Unger, Robert G. ... Henderson, NV
Unger, Robert G., Ltd. ... Henderson, NV
Unger, Robert M. ... Great Neck, NY
Unger, Robert M. ... New York, NY
Unger, Robert Stephen
San Francisco, CA
Unger, Ronald L. ... New York, NY
Unger, Ronald L. ... Seattle, WA
Unger, Sally E. ... New York, NY
Unger, Scott I. ... Princeton, NJ
Unger, Stephanie S. ... Cheltenham, PA
Unger, Steven F. ... Norwalk, CT
Unger, Steven H. ... Glendale, CA
Unger, Steven H.
Department Of Health And Human Services,
Food & Drug Administration, GV
Unger, Stuart C. ... Chicago, IL
Unger, Sue Ann ... Philadelphia, PA

Urban, Michael A. ... Bellevue, WA
Urban, Michael D. ... Wellesley, MA
Urban, Michael S. ... Akron, OH
Urban, Richard M. ... Fall River, MA
Urban, Robert A. ... Sebastian, FL
Urban, Robert C., Jr. ... New Philadelphia, OH
Urban, Robert M. ... Minnetonka, MN
Urban, Robin F.P. ... Pasadena, CA
Urban, Rodell L. ... Miami, FL
Urban, Ronald F. ... Chicago, IL
Urban, Ronald W. ... Columbia, SC
Urban, Shelly L. ... Philadelphia, PA
Urban, Stephen A. ... Florham Park, NJ
Urban, Steven Douglas ... Southfield, MI
Urban, Stuart G. ... Lancaster, WI
Urban, Suzanna ... Essex, CT
Urban, Tara C.
Small Business Administration, Office of the General Counsel, GV
Urban Taylor & Stawski, Ltd.
Milwaukee, WI
Urban, Theodore W. ... Washington, DC
Urban, Thomas F., II ... Atlanta, GA
Urban, Tod M. ... Chicago, IL
Urban, Tod M., P.C., Law Offices of
Chicago, IL
Urban, Walter R. ... Manhattan Beach, CA
Urban, William J. ... Warren, OH
Urbance, Elizabeth A. ... Springfield, IL
Urbancic, Brano ... Cleveland, OH
Urbancic, Gregory L. ... Naples, FL
Urbanczyk, Stephen L. ... Washington, DC
Urbanec, Patti J. ... San Francisco, CA
Urbani, Anthony, II ... Roseville, MI
Urbani, Pete, Jr. ... Galveston, TX
Urbania, Paul J. ... Red Bank, NJ
Urbaniak, Bethany L. ... Michigan Center, MI
Urbaniak, Irena J. ... Glastonbury, CT
Urbaniak, Joel E. ... Colorado Springs, CO
Urbanic, James ... Los Angeles, CA
Urbanic, Margaret M. ... Charleston, SC
Urbanik, Edward F. ... Carnegie, PA
Urbanik, Raymond J. ... Dallas, TX
Urbano, Debra Ann ... Bronx, NY
Urbano, Georgia M. ... New York, NY
Urbano, Gino D. ... Laguna Niguel, CA
Urbano, Lawrence B. ... Worthington, MA
Urbano, Michael J. ... Allentown, PA
Urbanos, Michael A. ... Roseville, MN
Urbanowicz, E. Peter ... New Orleans, LA
Urbanowicz-Pandos, Debra V.
Mountainside, NJ
Urbanski, Deborah Henshaw ... Houston, TX
Urbanski, Jeri A. ... La Crosse, WI
Urbanski, Mark A. ... Rochester, NY
Urbanski, Michael F. ... Roanoke, VA
Urbanski, Raymond J. ... Elmira, NY
Urbanski, Stephen K. ... Wilkes-Barre, PA
Urbas, Susan K.B. ... Chicago, IL
Urbatsch, Kevin ... San Francisco, CA
Urbauer, Dawn R. ... Gering, NE
Urbelis, Fieldsteel & Bailin, LLP
Andover, MA
Boston, MA
Urbelis, Josephine B. ... Chatham, NJ
Urbelis, Thomas J. ... Andover, MA
Boston, MA
Urberg, Konrad M. L. ... Fort Wayne, IN
Urberg, Ragna M. ... Cedar Rapids, IA
Urbigkit, Walter ... Cheyenne, WY
Urbin, Denise ... Gillette, WY
Urbin, Karen A. ... Pontiac, MI
Urbina, D. Jorge ... Denton, TX
Urbina, Lindsey A. ... Palo Alto, CA
San Francisco, CA
Urbina, Ricardo M.
United States District Court For The District Of Columbia, GV
Urbinato, Stephen R. ... West Orange, NJ
Urbis, Laura J. ... Brownsville, TX
Urbis, Michael J. ... Corpus Christi, TX
Urbis, Richard T. ... Detroit, MI
Urbom, David W. ... Arapahoe, NE
Cambridge, NE
Urbom, Kathleen R. ... Topeka, KS
Urbom, Kevin D. ... Arapahoe, NE
Cambridge, NE
Urbom Law Office, P.C. ... Arapahoe, NE
Beaver City, NE
Cambridge, NE
Urbom, Randall C. ... Scottsdale, AZ
Urbom, Ward C. ... Arapahoe, NE
Cambridge, NE
Urbom, Warren K. ... Lincoln, NE
Urbonya, Kathryn Rae ... Atlanta, GA
Urbut, Patrick J. ... Oak Lawn, IL
Urby, Heriberto, Jr. ... Del Rio, TX
Urch, Jack W. ... Auburn, CA
Urcheck, Nancy DeSimone
West Palm Beach, FL
Urchisin, Walter ... Boca Raton, FL
Urcia, Benjamin E. ... Alexandria, VA
Urcis, Jose ... Santa Ana, CA
Urciuoli, J. Arthur ... New York, NY
Urciuoli, Michael C. ... Florham Park, NJ
Urda, Laurie Ann ... Pittsburgh, PA
Urda Professional Corporation
South Bend, IN
Urda, Richard B., Jr. ... South Bend, IN
Urda, Richard P ... Ithaca, NY
Urda, Teresa J. ... Miami, FL
Urda Kassis, Cynthia E. ... New York, NY
Urdal, Ronald T. ... Connersville, IN
Urdan, James ... Milwaukee, WI
Urdan, Matthew R. ... San Francisco, CA
Urdang, Bruce S. ... Flagstaff, AZ
Urdang, Elliot W. ... Tenafly, NJ
Urdang, Ivy Paige ... Paramus, NJ
Ure, David G. ... Santa Ana, CA
Ure, Michael J. ... Redwood City, CA
Ure, Thomas B. ... Los Angeles, CA
Urech, Everett M. ... Daleville, AL
Urelius, Shawn R. ... Glen Allen, VA
Urell, Donald E. ... Albany, NY
Urello, Carlyle McCulloch ... Knoxville, TN
Uremovic, Joseph A. ... Fresno, CA
Uremovic, Joseph A., Law Offices of
Fresno, CA
U'Ren, Lisa M. ... Walnut Creek, CA
U'Ren, Matthew A.C. ... Portland, OR
U'Ren, Stephen A. ... Tucson, AZ
Uresk, Roland F. ... Roosevelt, UT
Uresti, Carlos I. ... San Antonio, TX
Uresti, Pablo C. ... San Antonio, TX
Ureta, Roberto M. ... Miami, FL
Uretz, Michael A. ... Santa Monica, CA
Urey, Paul K., III ... Upper Marlboro, MD
Urfirer, Roland M. ... Lake Placid, NY
Urga, William R. ... Las Vegas, NV
Urgell, Maria E. ... Chicago, IL
Urgenson, Laurence A. ... Washington, DC
Urgent, Allan B. ... Boston, MA
Urgo, Donald J. ... Chevy Chase, MD
Urgo, Donald J., Jr. ... Annapolis, MD
Urgo, John Francis ... Los Angeles, CA
Urgo, Steven D. ... Princeton, NJ
Urgo, Thomas ... Brooklyn, NY
Urhausen, Dianne P. ... San Francisco, CA
Urhausen, Peter A. ... Walnut Creek, CA
Uri, Lawrence R., Jr. ... Concordia, KS
Uría & Menéndez ... New York, NY
New York, NY
Urian, Jeffery H. ... St. Louis, MO
Uriarte, Luis A., Jr. ... Coral Gables, FL
Uriarte, Robert G. ... Los Angeles, CA
Urias, Christina ... Phoenix, AZ
Urias, Frank C. ... Oxnard, CA
Urias & Mora ... Oxnard, CA
Urias, Raymond ... Yuma, AZ
Urias, Victor E. ... Chula Vista, CA
Uriati, Marco P. ... Providence, RI
Uribe, Derly J. ... Laredo, TX
Uribe, J. A. ... Los Angeles, CA
Uribe, John J. ... Ormond Beach, FL
Uribe, Marcela ... Chicago, IL
Uribe, Mauricio A. ... Kansas City, MO
Uribe, Steven C. ... San Diego, CA
Uribe-Schmitt, Constance A.
San Marcos, CA
Uribie, Frank A. ... Houston, TX
Uricchio, Howe, Krell, Jacobson, Toporek & Theos, P.A. ... Charleston, SC
Uricchio, Paul N., III ... Charleston, SC
Uricchio, Paul N., Jr. ... Charleston, SC
Uricchio, Robin L. ... Orlando, FL
Urice, Stephen K. ... Philadelphia, PA
Urich, Heidi ... Boston, MA
Urich, Robert ... Miami, FL
Urick, Anna Katherine ... Muskegon, MI
Urick, Dana ... Sherman Oaks, CA
Urick, Lisa G. ... Los Angeles, CA
Urick, Richard ... Aliquippa, PA
Urick, Walter A. ... Hart, MI
Urick, Willis E., Jr.
La Canada Flintridge, CA
Urie, Gary D. ... San Diego, CA
Urie, Kimberly A. ... Venice, CA
Urie, Matthew C. ... Department of Justice, Environment and Natural Resources Division, GV
Urig, Susan L. ... Anchorage, AK
Urion, Celia A. ... Honolulu, HI
Uris, Alan M. ... New York, NY
Uris, Harvey R. ... New York, NY
Urisko, Mary Meinzinger ... Livonia, MI
Urist, Carl H. ... New York, NY
Uritz, Curt W. ... Ventura, CA
Uriu, Akiko Lynne ... Davis, CA
Uriu, Akiko Lynne, A Prof. Corp.
Davis, CA
Urizar, Oscar ... Hartford, CT
Urkovich, Ronald S. ... Sanibel, FL
Urland, Karl W. ... Santa Ana, CA
Urlik, Elissa ... Hayward, CA
Urman, David A. ... Portland, OR
Urman, Gary F. ... Tucson, AZ
Urman, Lawrence ... Wayne, NJ
Urman, Michael R. ... Tucson, AZ
Urmin, James E. ... Plano, TX
Urmston, Randolph W. ... Seattle, WA
Urmy, Kenneth W. ... Houston, TX
Urmy, Thomas V., Jr. ... Boston, MA
Urner, John H. ... Hagerstown, MD
Urner, Nairn & Boyer ... Hagerstown, MD
Urness, Craig ... Portland, OR
Urness, Gay B., (Mr.) ... St. Louis Park, MN
Urness, John C. ... Springfield, OR
Urness, Thor Y. ... Nashville, TN
Urness, Todd B. ... Minneapolis, MN
St. Paul, MN
Urofsky, Philip E. ... Department of Justice, Criminal Division, GV
Urowsky, Richard J. ... New York, NY
Urquhart, A. William ... Los Angeles, CA
Urquhart, Brian A. ... Ann Arbor, MI
Urquhart, C. Richard ... Vacaville, CA
Urquhart, Carla J. ... Washington, DC
Urquhart, Charles F., III ... Suffolk, VA
Urquhart, Clyde M. ... Woodbine, GA
Urquhart, Edward D. ... Houston, TX
Urquhart, G. Wesley ... Houston, TX
Urquhart, Gary R. ... Iselin, NJ
Urquhart & Hassell ... Houston, TX
Urquhart, Jack E. ... Houston, TX
Urquhart, John C. ... Ann Arbor, MI
Urquhart, John D., Jr. ... Spokane, WA
Urquhart, John M. ... San Diego, CA
Urquhart, John R. ... Troutdale, OR
Urquhart, Larry P. ... Brenham, TX
Urquhart, Marvin A., Jr. ... Panama City, FL
Urquhart, O'Dorisio & Wedell
San Diego, CA
Urquhart, Quentin F., Jr.
New Orleans, LA
Urquhart, Rachel Lynn
Grand Rapids, MI
Urquhart, Richard G. ... Dallas, TX
Urquhart, Stephen E. ... Lowell, MA
Urquia, Rafael B., II ... New York, NY
Urquiaga, Lilia R. ... Atlanta, GA
Urquiola, Joanne Rodriguez ... Miami, FL
Urrabazo, Donald S. ... Los Angeles, CA
Urrea, Matthew ... Albuquerque, NM
Urrizola, Lisa Marie ... Fresno, CA
Urrutia, J. Richard ... Portland, OR
Urrutia De Basora, Candida R.
San Juan, PR
Urrutia-Minguela, Julio E. ... Syracuse, NY
Urry, Pamela C. ... Salt Lake City, UT
Urry, Philip G. ... Phoenix, AZ
Urschel, Edward M. ... Mountain View, CA
Urscheler, Jack A. ... Fort Lee, NJ
Urschler, Charles F., Jr. ... St. Louis, MO
Urse, Stephen W., II ... Tallahassee, FL
Ursery, Frederick S., (P.A.)
Little Rock, AR
Ursic, Steven J. ... Memphis, TN
Ursich, Gregory L. ... Seattle, WA
Ursich, Thomasina L., PLLC ... Seattle, WA
Ursich, Thomasina (Tommi) L. ... Seattle, WA
Ursillo, David A. ... Greenville, SC
Ursillo, David R. ... Providence, RI
Ursillo, Michael A. ... Providence, RI
Ursillo, Teitz & Ritch, Ltd. ... Providence, RI
Ursin, John Erik ... Stanhope, NJ
Ursin, Theresa L. ... Freeport, IL
Ursini, Frank J. ... Modesto, CA
Ursini, Gerald ... Ottawa, IL
Ursini, Josephine L. ... Chevy Chase, MD
Urso, David M. ... Palo Alto, CA
Urso, Frank P. ... Rutland, VT
Urso, Frank W. ... Chicago, IL
Urso, Gary A. ... New Port Richey, FL
Urso, Jas. D. ... Denver, CO
Urso, John R. ... Detroit, MI
Urso, Joseph P. ... Dallas, TX
Urso, Liguori and Urso ... Westerly, RI
Urso, M. Linda ... Westerly, RI
Urso, Natale Louis ... Westerly, RI
Urso & Ross, P.C. ... Detroit, MI
Urso, Susan E. ... Providence, RI
Ursomarso, James P. ... Washington, DC
Urstadt, Lynn F. ... Glencoe, IL
Ursu, Joan Cowley ... Traverse City, MI
Ursu, John J. ... St. Paul, MN
Ursu, Philip C. ... Indiana, PA
Ursul, Mary L. ... Grand Rapids, MI
Ursulova, Nadezhda ... Bayside, NY
Brooklyn, NY
New York, NY
Ursulskis, Victoria ... Plainfield, IN
Urtes, J. Nelson ... San Marcos, CA
Urtis, James M. ... Chicago, IL
Urtnowski, J. Brian ... Newport Beach, CA
Urtuzuastegui, Charles ... Pasadena, CA
Urtz, Anastasia L. ... Syracuse, NY
Urtz, Gary P. ... Havertown, PA
Urtz, Paul G. ... Denver, CO
Urueta, Pamela ... San Francisco, CA
Urwiller, Kenneth L., II ... Detroit, MI
Urwin, Darlene Rabe ... Studio City, CA
Urwin, Gary L. ... Los Angeles, CA
Urwitz, Jay P. ... Washington, DC
Ury, Frank A. ... Vallejo, CA
Ury, Frederic S. ... Westport, CT
Ury & Moskow ... Westport, CT
Ury, Robert I. ... Chicago, IL
Ury, Steven K. ... Burbank, CA
Urzi, Carol J. ... Berkeley, CA
Usadi, Jacob M. ... White Plains, NY
Usadi, Robert ... New York, NY
Usami, Yuko ... New York, NY
Usan, Michael A. ... Fort Lauderdale, FL
Miami Beach, FL
Usan, Michael A., P.A.
Fort Lauderdale, FL
Miami Beach, FL
Usatine, Warren A. ... Hackensack, NJ
Uscher, Arthur ... Hackensack, NJ
Uscher, Quiat, Uscher & Russo
Hackensack, NJ
New York, NY
Uscher, Ronald H. ... Washington, DC
Uscher, William ... Hackensack, NJ
Uschold, James E. ... New Orleans, LA
Uscian, Paula M. ... Barrington, IL
Usdan, Dennis M. ... Plantation, FL
Usdan, Steven H. ... Los Angeles, CA
Usdin, Archie ... Union City, NJ
Usdin, Howard M. ... Fair Lawn, NJ
Usdin, Mark G. ... Jacksonville, FL
Usdin, Mark G., P.A. ... Jacksonville, FL
Usdin, Marvin ... Brooklyn, NY
Usdin, Steven D. ... Philadelphia, PA
Usdin, Steven W., (P.C.) ... New Orleans, LA
Usdin, Warren ... Livingston, NJ
Usdrowski, Kate ... New York, NY
Usell, Raymond J., Jr. ... Poway, CA
U'Sellis, Douglas A. ... Louisville, KY
Uselton, Jack E., II ... The Woodlands, TX
Uselton, Ronald W. ... Sherman, TX
Uselton, Russell G. ... McAlester, OK
Usem, Ronald H. ... Minneapolis, MN
Usen, Richard S. ... Buffalo, NY
Usera, Gregory T. ... San Juan, PR
Usera, J. Andrew ... Vienna, VA
Usera, Vincent L. ... Juneau, AK
Useted, Robert A. ... St. Louis, MO
Usher, A.J., IV ... Indianapolis, IN
Usher, Arthur J., IV ... Indianapolis, IN
Usher, Benjamin G.
Small Business Administration, GV
Usher, Crystal L. ... Cedar Rapids, IA
Usher, Harry L. ... Los Angeles, CA
Usher, Howard L. ... Fort Lauderdale, FL
Usher, Jack H. ... Savannah, GA
Usher, Michael C. ... Allentown, PA
Usher, Richard S. ... Los Angeles, CA
Ushijima, John T. ... Hilo, HI
Ushijima, Margaret S. ... Hilo, HI
Ushiroda, Gregg M. ... Honolulu, HI
Usich, James S. ... Miami, FL
Usich, James S., P.A. ... Miami, FL
Usignol, Laurence J. ... Marlton, NJ
Usinger, Edward J. ... Rochester, NY
Usitalo, Trent David ... Hutchinson, MN
Uskert, John J. ... Panama City, FL
Uskevich, Robert J. ... Southbury, CT
Uslan, Richard R. ... Raritan, NJ
Uslan, Richard R., A Professional Corporation
Raritan, NJ
Uslan, Stephen E. ... Denver, CO
Uslander, Gerald L. ... Washington, DC
Uslaner, Steven D. ... New York, NY
Usnick, John C. ... Vacaville, CA
Usnick, Lee Tatum ... Inverness, FL
Norman, OK
Usnick, Russell E. ... Inverness, FL
Norman, OK
Usoro, Anie I. ... Houston, TX
Usow, Jason S. ... Beverly Hills, CA
Usow, Jason S., A Professional Corporation
Beverly Hills, CA
Usow, Jeffrey A. ... Chicago, IL
Usow, Jody L. ... Milwaukee, WI
Usoz, Linda Larson ... San Jose, CA
Usoz, Stephen J. ... San Jose, CA
Uspal, Gary ... Reading, PA
Usprich, Bernard J. ... Metairie, LA
Usry, Mark L. ... Lexington, VA
Usry, Michael D. ... Atlanta, GA
Usry, T. Allen ... Metairie, LA
Usry & Weeks ... Metairie, LA
New Orleans, LA
Ussach, Betty I. ... New Bedford, MA
Ussai, Mark A. ... Phillipsburg, NJ
Usseglio, Frank G. ... Hartford, CT
Ussery, Albert T. ... Albuquerque, NM
Ussery, Andrew R. ... Charlotte, NC
Ussery, Bernard R. ... Los Angeles, CA
Ussery & Parrish, P.A. ... Albuquerque, NM
Usset, David J. ... Minneapolis, MN
Ussing, Carl O. ... Smyrna, GA
Ustach, Lynne A. ... New Britain, CT
Ustas, Deborah L. ... Hackensack, NJ
Ustasiewski, James J. ... Juneau, AK
Ustel, Iren J. ... Chicago, IL
Ustick, Douglas H. ... Bellaire, TX
Ustin, Martin D. ... Pine Brook, NJ
Ustin, Stuart K. ... New York, NY
Uston, Kathleen M. ... Alexandria, VA
Ustynoski, James Michael
Philadelphia, PA
Ustynoski, Joseph D. ... Hazleton, PA
Ustynoski, Joseph J. ... Hazleton, PA
Ustynoski and Marusak ... Hazleton, PA
Utacht, Edward C., II ... Dayton, OH
Utan, Edwin ... Scranton, PA
Utaski, Thomas J. ... Cincinnati, OH
Utay, Alan M. ... Dallas, TX
Utchen, Theodore M. ... Wheaton, IL
Utecht, Andrea E. ... Philadelphia, PA
Utecht, Francis A. ... Long Beach, CA
Utecht, Matthew P. ... Greenville, SC
Uteg, Mark D. ... West Dundee, IL
Utell, Mitchell P. ... Manchester, NH
Utermohle, Jeffrey J. ... Baltimore, MD
Utermohlen, William J. ... Alexandria, VA
Utevsky, Daniel ... New York, NY
Utevsky, David ... Seattle, WA
Utevsky, Michael D. ... New York, NY
Uth, Michael R. ... Mayfield Village, OH
Uthe, Hans M. ... San Francisco, CA
Uthe, Janet Kosid ... Sacramento, CA
Uthe, Lynn Klicker ... Minnetonka, MN
Uthe, Lynn Klicker, Ltd. ... Minnetonka, MN
Uthe, Zelda M. ... Albany, NY
Coeymans, NY
Uthoff, David V. ... St. Louis, MO
Uthoff, Gary Stephen ... St. Louis, MO
Uthoff, Graeber, Bobinette & O'Keefe
St. Louis, MO
Uthoff, Harold E. ... St. Louis, MO
Uthoff, Loren H., Jr. ... Southfield, MI
Uthoff, Stephen M. ... Long Beach, CA
Uthus, Don Charles ... Annapolis, MD
Utick, Andrew J. ... Helena, MT
Utick & Grosfield ... Helena, MT
Utigard, Gary N. ... Seattle, WA
Utke, Mark E. ... Westmont, NJ
Utken, Gregory J. ... Indianapolis, IN
Utkov, Mark S. ... Austin, TX
Utku, Sinan ... Washington, DC
Utley, David A. ... Wilmington, CA
Utley, David G. ... Akron, OH
Cleveland, OH
Utley, Frederick B., III ... New York, NY
Utley, James ... Minneapolis, MN
Red Wing, MN
Utley, Jay F. ... Dallas, TX
Utley, John ... Minneapolis, MN
Utley, Keith A. ... Henderson, KY

Utley & Latimer, P.C. ... Jackson, TN
Utley, Lloyd A. ... Jackson, TN
Utley, Mark S. ... San Jose, CA
Utley, Michael ... Charlotte, NC
Utley, Sue Ellen ... Sagamore Hills, OH
Utley, W. David ... Hoffman Estates, IL
Utrata, Carl I. ... Lakewood, OH
Utrecht, Carolyn ... Washington, DC
Utrecht, James D. ... Troy, OH
Utrecht, Paul F., Law Offices of
Oakland, CA
Utrecht, Paul F., Law Offices of
San Francisco, CA
Utrecht, Steven T. ... Boca Raton, FL
Utrecht, Steven T., P.A. ... Boca Raton, FL
Utrera, Natalia ... Coral Gables, FL
Utsch, Louis W. ... Pittsburgh, PA
Utset, Frank A. ... Fort Lauderdale, FL
Utset, Manuel A., Jr. ... Boston, MA
Utsey, Bert Glenn, III ... Charleston, SC
Utsey, Christopher, Newton & Utsey
Butler, AL
Utsey, J. Jefferson ... Butler, AL
Utsey, Keith James ... New York, NY
Utsey, Robert L., Jr. ... Jersey City, NJ
Utsey, William L. ... Butler, AL
Utsinger, Barry D. ... San Diego, CA
Utsinger, Kelly ... Amarillo, TX
Utsumi, Barry M. ... Honolulu, HI
Utsumi, Wendy J. ... Honolulu, HI
Utt, Daniel P. ... Cincinnati, OH
Uttal, Linda Marie Betleski ... Evanston, IL
Uttal, Susan L.
Nuclear Regulatory Commission,
Office of the General Counsel, GV
Uttaro, Ralph A. ... Rochester, NY
Utter, Anthony A. ... Wichita, KS
Utter, Daniel A. ... Edina, MN
Utter, David J. ... New Orleans, LA
Utter, Gregory M. ... Cincinnati, OH
Utter, Michelle M. ... Woodland Hills, CA
Utter, Philip H. ... Manchester, NH
Utter, Robert E. ... Mount Sterling, IL
Utter, Thomas C. ... St. Paul, MN
Utterback, Ann Maddox ... Albuquerque, NM
Utterback, James E. ... Batesville, IN
Utterback, Mary Margaret
Washington, DC
Uttermohlen, Lucille P. ... Monticello, IN
Utti, Gerald E. ... Encinitas, CA
Utting, George
Environmental Protection Agency,
Program Office Attorneys, GV
Uttinger, Louise ... Carson City, NV
Uttke, Ralph M. ... Antigo, WI
Utton, John W. ... Albuquerque, NM
Uttrich, Donald L. ... Washington, DC
Utykanski, David P. ... Troy, MI
Utz, Eugene J. ... Cincinnati, OH
Utz, John L. ... Overland Park, KS
Utz, Litvak, Summers, Powers & Manring
St. Joseph, MO
Utz, Mark E. ... Rochester, MN
Utz, Richard A. ... Columbus, OH
Utzman, Brian L. ... Rapid City, SD
Utzman, C. Howard ... Spokane, WA
Utzman, Glen G. ... Moscow, ID
Utzschneider, John R. ... Boston, MA
Uustal, John J. ... Fort Lauderdale, FL
Uva, Anthony N. ... Indianapolis, IN
Uva, Carmela Marie ... Downey, CA
Uva, Dominick M ... Danbury, CT
Uva, Kenneth J. ... New York, NY
Uva, Kim Marie ... Teterboro, NJ
Uvena, Frank J. ... Chicago, IL
Uvieghara, Chris I. ... San Diego, CA
Uviller, H. Richd. ... New York, NY
Uvino, Joseph F. ... New York, NY
Uxa, Frank J., Jr. ... Irvine, CA
Uyar, Diane ... New York, NY
Uyeda, James A. ... Los Angeles, CA
Uyeda, James S. ... Los Angeles, CA
Uyeda, Mark T. ... Los Angeles, CA
Uyehara, Craig H. ... Honolulu, HI
Uyehara, Emi R. ... San Francisco, CA
Uyehara, Paul M. ... Philadelphia, PA
Uyehara, Robert K., Jr. ... Camden, NJ
Uyekawa, David T. ... Glendale, CA
Uyekawa, Karen C. ... Los Angeles, CA
Uyemura, Dan K. ... Honolulu, HI
Uyeno, Carol A. ... Honolulu, HI
Uyeno, Naomi S. ... Honolulu, HI
Uyenoyama, Hidehiko ... Honolulu, HI
Uyesato, Daniel E. ... Durham, NC
Uygur, Nuriye C. ... Department of Justice,
Civil Division, GV
UyHam, John J. ... Atlanta, GA
Uylaki, Jill L. ... Chicago, IL
Uzdavinis, Ronald J. ... Woodbury, NJ
Uze, Barton J. ... Treasury Department,
Internal Revenue Service, GV
Uzee, Linda M. ... New Orleans, LA
Uzelac, Lauren L. ... Miamisburg, OH
Uzelac, Stevan, (P.C.) ... Detroit, MI
Uzemack, Marilyn V. ... Park Ridge, IL
Uzick, Adolph ... Houston, TX
Uziel, Leon A. ... Seattle, WA
Uzis, Alfred R. ... Highland, IN
Uzl, William Edward
Cleveland Heights, OH
Uzpen, Christopher R. ... Holland, MI
Uzych, Leo ... Wallingford, PA
Uzzell, Allen H. ... Houston, TX
Uzzell, James G. ... Chicago, IL
Uzzell, Melissa ... Normal, IL
Uzzelle, G. Hamp, III ... Mobile, AL
Uzzi, Gerard H. ... New York, NY
Uzzi, Peter ... San Jose, CA

Uzzo, Mark F. ... Mount Vernon, NY

Vaa, Galen J. ... Moorhead, MN
Vaage, Robert F. ... San Diego, CA
Vaage, Susan L. ... Glendale, CA
Vaaler, Bryn R. ... Minneapolis, MN
Vaaler, Paul M. ... Duluth, MN
Vaaler, Robert ... Grand Forks, ND
Vaaler, Zimney, Foster & Johnson,
Chartered ... Grand Forks, ND
Vaarsi, Mart ... Basking Ridge, NJ
Vabre, Nancy Ellen ... New York, NY
Vaca, Kris D. ... Walnut Creek, CA
Vaca, Monica E. ... Chicago, IL
Vaca, Nicolas C. ... Walnut Creek, CA
Vaca, Raymond, Jr. ... Phoenix, AZ
Vaca & Vaca, LLP ... Walnut Creek, CA
Vacala, Gregory G. ... Chicago, IL
Vacala, Alfred C. ... Scottsdale, AZ
Vacanti, Christopher A. ... Omaha, NE
Vacanti, Tricia A. ... Buffalo, NY
Vacanti, Vito C. ... Buffalo, NY
Vacca, Andrea T. ... Ballston Spa, NY
Vacca, Anthony ... Pawtucket, RI
Vacca, Edward D. ... Schenectady, NY
Vacca, Fred W. ... Department of Justice,
Executive Office for Immigration Review,
GV
Vacca, James P. ... Rochester, NY
Vacca, John J. ... Los Angeles, CA
Vacca, John Joseph ... Oxnard, CA
Vacca, Joseph L. ... Omaha, NE
Vacca, Matthew D. ... St. Louis, MO
Vacca, Paul J., Jr. ... Rochester, NY
Vacca, Richard J. ... Carver, MA
Vacca, Rita D. ... St. Louis, MO
Vaccarella, Louis F. ... Long Grove, IL
Vaccarella, Vincent F. ... Miami, FL
Vaccarelli, Marie C. ... Boston, MA
Vaccarello, Anthony M. ... Palos Hills, IL
Vaccarezza, Loren B. ... Stockton, CA
Vaccari, Michael A. ... New York, NY
Vaccarino, Frank M. ... Union City, NJ
Vaccarino, Patricia L. ... Las Vegas, NV
Vaccaro, Ann ... Lafayette, CA
Vaccaro, Barbara H. ... Saline, MI
Vaccaro, Carl ... King Of Prussia, PA
Vaccaro, Charles G.
Hot Springs National Park, AR
Boerne, TX
Tomball, TX
Vaccaro, Charles J. ... Hauppauge, NY
Vaccaro, Chiara (Claire) Vittoria
Woodbury, NY
Vaccaro, Christine M. ... Philadelphia, PA
Vaccaro, Christopher M.
Newport Beach, CA
Vaccaro, Christophe Mark
Newport Beach, CA
Vaccaro, Christopher R. ... Boston, MA
Vaccaro, Daniel J. ... Columbia, MD
Ellicott City, MD
Vaccaro, Donalda F. ... Marlborough, MA
Vaccaro, Enrico ... Bridgeport, CT
Vaccaro, George A. ... Hackensack, NJ
Vaccaro, Jasper D. ... South Beloit, IL
Vaccaro, Judy D. ... Los Angeles, CA
Vaccaro, L. Victor ... White Plains, NY
Vaccaro, Linda M. ... Allston, MA
Vaccaro, Lisa M. ... Uniondale, NY
Vaccaro, Michael F. ... Canton, OH
Vaccaro, Michael R. ... Syracuse, NY
Vaccaro, Pasquale ... Boston, MA
Vaccaro, Patrick L. ... White Plains, NY
Vaccaro & Prisco LLP ... Hauppauge, NY
Vaccaro, San E. ... Irvine, CA
Vaccaro, Steve W. ... New York, NY
Vaccaro, Steven R. ... New York, NY
Vaccaro, Timothy ... Tallahassee, FL
Vacchelli, Robert F. ... Hartford, CT
Vacchiano, Robert E. S. ... Wall Township, NJ
Vacchiano, Samuel J. ... Neptune, NJ
Vacchina, Leonardo J. ... Oakland, CA
Vacchio, Maria A. ... Rockville, MD
Vacchio, Michael A. ... Los Angeles, CA
Vacco, Dennis C. ... Albany, NY
Vacco, Philip J. ... La Grange, IL
Vacco, Richard P. ... Boston, MA
Vacco, Roger P. ... Boston, MA
Vacek, Albert E., Jr. ... Houston, TX
Vacek, Clifford J. ... Houston, TX
Vacek, Garry W. ... Austin, TX
Vacek, John R. ... Nome, AK
Vacek, Michael E. ... Albany, NY
Vacek, Robert F. ... Omaha, NE
Vacek, Steve J., Jr. ... San Antonio, TX
Vacek, Susan B. ... Grand Forks, ND
Vacek, Susan S. ... Houston, TX
Vacha, Mark H. ... New York, NY
Vache, Barbara M. ... Gladstone, MO
Vache, James M. ... Spokane, WA
Vachhani & Associates, Law Office of
Artesia, CA
Vachhani, Jagdish M. ... Artesia, CA
Vachier, Caroline ... Newark, NJ
Vachon, Dennis Paul ... Northwood, NH
Vachon, Genelle Tanos ... Washington, DC
Vachon, Matthew E.
Department of Transportation,
Maritime Administration, GV
Vachon, Philip ... Pittsfield, MA
Vachon, Reginald I. ... Atlanta, GA
Vachris, Scott Charles ... Fairfax, VA
Vachss, Alice S. ... Kew Gardens, NY
Vachss, Andrea H. ... Palo Alto, CA
Vachss, Andrew H. ... Newport, OR
Vachuda, Tomáš J. ... New York, NY

Vaci, Elizabeth Dienes ... Painesville, OH
Vaci, Henry A. ... Palos Heights, IL
Vacik, Paul J. ... Solon, OH
Vacketta, Carl L. ... Washington, DC
Vackicev, Alexi G. ... Oak Brook, IL
Vaclavik, Kathryn A. ... San Francisco, CA
Vacovec, Kenneth J. ... Newton, MA
Vacovec, Mayotte & Singer ... Boston, MA
Newton, MA
Vacura, Julie R. ... Portland, OR
Vacura, Richard J. ... Washington, DC
Vaczy, Edward L. ... Sayville, NY
Vadala, Caroline A. ... Binghamton, NY
Vadala, Joseph ... Las Vegas, NV
Vadala, Leonard S. ... Boston, MA
Vadala, Valerie Victoria ... Baltimore, MD
Vadas, Elaine M. ... Alexandria, VA
Vadasz, Stephanie R. ... Kansas City, MO
Vadeboncoeur, Philip J. ... Lakewood, CO
Vaden, Ann Berman ... Charlottesville, VA
Vaden, Christopher S. ... Department of Justice,
Environment and Natural Resources
Division, GV
Vaden, Donald B. ... Williamsburg, VA
Vaden, Eickenroht & Thompson, L.L.P.
Houston, TX
Vaden, Frank S., III ... Houston, TX
Vaden, Gaylene P. ... Dallas, TX
Vaden, Jeffery B. ... Houston, TX
Vaden, Peter B. ... Charlottesville, VA
Vader, Jay H. ... Kansas City, KS
Vader, Joseph N. ... Olathe, KS
Vader, Joseph N., P.A. ... Olathe, KS
Vadino, Anna R. I. ... Media, PA
Vadino, Christina ... Grosse Pointe Park, MI
Vadnais, Alfred W. ... Hilton Head Island, SC
Vadnais, Douglas R. ... Albuquerque, NM
Vadnal, Cynthia A. ... Cleveland, OH
Vadnal, Richard A. ... Cleveland, OH
Vadner, Michael ... Philadelphia, PA
Vadney, LeRoy F. ... San Francisco, CA
Vadnie, Michael R. ... St. Cloud, MN
Vadon, Marilyn C. ... Washington, DC
Vadon, Michele R. ... Irvine, CA
Vadvilavich, Juliet E. ... Los Gatos, CA
Vaessen, Nancy Menzies ... Palm Desert, CA
Vaeth, Christopher P. ... Rochester, NY
Vaeth, Michael C. ... Snow Hill, MD
Vafiades, Brountas & Kominsky
Bangor, ME
Vafiades, Lewis V. ... Bangor, ME
Vafiades, Vendean V. ... Augusta, ME
Vafides, Thomas A. ... Flushing, NY
Vafidis, Matthew P. ... San Francisco, CA
Vag, Andrea A. ... Iselin, NJ
Vagelatos, John ... New York, NY
Vagell, Jeanne ... Fort Lauderdale, FL
Vagelos, Ellen T. ... New York, NY
Vagenas, Konstantina ... Salem, MA
Vaggalis, Katherine L. ... Lakewood, CO
Vagi, Jolán Barbara ... Cleveland, OH
Vagianelis, John Nicholas ... Albany, NY
Vagianos, Paul ... Trenton, NJ
Vagins, Deborah J. ... Washington, DC
Vagle, Sheila ... Moorhead, MN
Vagle, Steven F. ... Washington, DC
Vagley, Robert E. ... Washington, DC
Vagliano, Alexander M. ... New York, NY
Vaglica & Meinhold, L.L.C.
Colorado Springs, CO
Englewood, CO
Vaglica, Phillip A. ... Colorado Springs, CO
Vaglienti, Christine S. ... Morgantown, WV
Vagnoni, Michael D. ... Malvern, PA
Vagnoni, Robert J. ... Norristown, PA
Vago, James C. ... Cincinnati, OH
Vago, Louis N. ... Aurora, IL
Vago, Michelle R. ... New York, NY
Vagotis, Angela T. ... Canton, OH
Vagotis, Angela T., Co., L.P.A. ... Canton, OH
Vagra, Anne Marie ... New York, NY
Vagstad, Donald W. ... Spokane, WA
Vagt, Craig D. ... Portland, OR
Vagt, Kathleen G. ... Arlington, VA
Vagt, Robt. R. ... St. Helens, OR
Vagts, Detlev F. ... Cambridge, MA
Vague, Fred R. ... Wichita, KS
Vague, Glen E. ... Houston, TX
Vague, Harold R. ... Denver, CO
Vahan, Randolph K. ... Los Angeles, CA
Vahdat, Lisa A. ... New York, NY
Vahey, Michael ... Chicago, IL
Vahid, Nazlee ... New York, NY
Vahl, C. Robert ... Olean, NY
Vahldiek, Cano, Grayson, Hovenkamp &
Petroski ... Houston, TX
Vahldiek, Paul R., Jr. ... Houston, TX
Vahle, Chet W. ... Quincy, IL
Vahlenkamp, Virgil, Jr. ... Denton, TX
Vahlsing, Joseph H. ... Cincinnati, OH
Vahrenwald, Jack D. ... Fort Collins, CO
Vahsholtz, George R. ... Colorado Springs, CO
Vahsholtz, George R., P.C.
Colorado Springs, CO
Vaiana, Anthony F. ... Chesterfield, MO
Vaiana, Frederick ... Indianapolis, IN
Vaiana, James H. ... Houston, TX
Vaias, Emily J. ... Silver Spring, MD
Vaid, Rachna ... Rochester, NY
Vaida, David ... Allentown, PA
Vaida, Elena C. ... Albany, NY
Vaida, M. Anthony ... Ringoes, NJ
Vaida & Manfreda, P.C. ... Washington, DC
Ringoes, NJ
Vaiden, H. Wayne, Jr. ... Memphis, TN
Vaiden, James E. ... Norfolk, VA
Vaiden, Kristi L. ... Roseland, NJ
Vaidya, Ajit J. ... Washington, DC

Vaidya, Harshad R. ... Newark, NJ
Vail, Anne Findlay ... Chicago, IL
Vail, Bernard F. ... Portland, OR
Vail, Bruce R. ... McDonough, GA
Vail, Charles S. ... Memphis, TN
Vail, Christina L. ... Palo Alto, CA
Vail, Daniel T. ... Washington, DC
Vail, David B. ... Tacoma, WA
Vail, David R. ... Minneapolis, MN
Vail, Donald ... New York, NY
Vail, Edwin H., Jr. ... Costa Mesa, CA
Vail, Eric S. ... Ontario, CA
Vail, Garrett M. ... Minneapolis, MN
St. Paul, MN
Vail, Gregory G. ... New York, NY
Vail, Howard B. ... New York, NY
Vail, James D. ... Cleveland, OH
Vail, James E., Jr. ... Toledo, OH
Vail, James N. ... Chicago, IL
Vail, Jason ... Tallahassee, FL
Vail, Jeffrey T. ... Department of Agriculture,
Office of the General Counsel, GV
Vail, Jeffrey T. ... New York, NY
Vail, John J. ... South Amboy, NJ
Vail, John P. ... Chicago, IL
Vail, Judi A. ... Vancouver, WA
Vail, Julia Barlow ... Cleveland, OH
Vail, Kenneth H. ... Department of Agriculture,
Office of the General Counsel, GV
Vail, Lee E. ... Los Angeles, CA
Vail, Loren Loving ... Gates Mills, OH
Vail, M. Richard W. ... Mantoloking, NJ
Vail, Maria R. ... Sacramento, CA
Vail, Mary E. ... Carmel, NY
Vail, Mary S. ... Roseland, NJ
Vail, Patricia ... Jacksonville, FL
Vail, Richard G. ... Greens Farms, CT
Vail, Robert E. ... Cleveland, OH
Vail, Robert E. ... Fond du Lac, WI
Vail, Robert W. ... Boise, ID
Vail, Russell O. ... Walled Lake, MI
Vail, Sarah E. ... Chester, VT
Vail, Steven W. ... Oakland, CA
Vail, Thomas V. H., Jr. ... Shaker Heights, OH
Vaile, George Q. B. ... Marengo, OH
Vail French, Lora ... Oakland, CA
Vaill, Edward Everett ... Los Angeles, CA
Vaillancourt, Diane K. ... Santa Cruz, CA
Vaillancourt, Donald C. ... Wayne, NJ
Vaillancourt, George H. ... Washington, DC
Vaillancourt, Michele D.
Minneapolis, MN
St. Paul, MN
Vaillancourt, Robin A., (P.A.) ... Largo, FL
Vaillancourt, Steven M. ... Lowell, MA
Vaillancourt, Susan A. ... Manchester, NH
Vaillant, Michele F. ... Newark, NJ
Vailliencourt, William J., Jr.
Birmingham, MI
Vainder, Steven J. ... Miami, FL
Vainikos, Jim M. ... Chicago, IL
Vainio, Kevin E. ... Butte, MT
Vainisi, Jerome R. ... Chicago, IL
Vainisi, Mark E. ... Chicago, IL
Vainisi, William A. ... Northbrook, IL
Voino, Sharon Worthing ... New York, NY
Vair, Jonathan C. ... Miami, FL
Vaira, Peter F. ... Philadelphia, PA
Vaira & Riley, P.C. ... Philadelphia, PA
Vairavan, Valli ... Milwaukee, WI
Vairo, Bonnie R. ... West Palm Beach, FL
Vairo, Georgene M. ... New York, NY
Vairo, Gerald G. ... Calumet, MI
Houghton, MI
Vairo, Mechlin, Tomasi, Johnson &
Manchester ... Calumet, MI
Houghton, MI
Vairo, Peter Edward ... Forest Hills, NY
Vairo, Susan M. ... Mamaroneck, NY
Vaisbort, Edward D. ... Los Angeles, CA
Las Vegas, NV
Vaisbort, Ronald S. ... Los Angeles, CA
Vaish, Rachna ... Old Bridge, NJ
Vaisvilas, Terrance A. ... Chicago, IL
Vajdak, Roy W. ... Houston, TX
Vajgrt, Terry S. ... Luverne, MN
Vajretti, Jolene A. ... Fresno, CA
Vajtay, Stephen M., Jr. ... Newark, NJ
Vaka, George A. ... Tampa, FL
Vaka, Larson & Johnson, P.L. ... Tampa, FL
Vakerics, Thomas V. ... Washington, DC
Vakharia, Tejal R. ... Chicago, IL
Vakil, Bijal V. ... Los Angeles, CA
Vakil, Ketan S. ... Los Angeles, CA
Vakil, Virgie M. ... Media, PA
Vakili & Leus, LLP ... Los Angeles, CA
Vakili, Lily I. ... New York, NY
Vakili, Sa'id ... Los Angeles, CA
Vaklyes, Edmond J., Jr. ... Waukesha, WI
Vaknin, Joseph ... Camilla, GA
Vakos, George W. ... Virginia Beach, VA
Vaksberg, Svetlana ... Menlo Park, CA
Vakula, Alex B. ... Mesa, AZ
Prescott, AZ
Vakula, Nicholas E. ... Phoenix, AZ
Vakulskas & Hoffmeyer, P.C. ... Sioux City, IA
Vakulskas, Thomas A. ... Sioux City, IA
Vaky, Paul S. ... Department of Justice,
Criminal Division, GV
Valacich, Christina N. ... Whitefish, MT
Valad, Bart T. ... Washington, DC
Valada, M. Christine ... Encino, CA
Valade, Alan M. ... Lansing, MI
Valadez, Leonard P. ... Riverside, CA
Valadez, Michael ... Gambrills, MD
Valadez, Robert A. ... San Antonio, TX
Valadez, Ruben ... San Antonio, TX
Valadez, Stephanie L. ... Carmel, IN

Valaik, Michael J. .... **Indianapolis, IN**
Valainis, Anita R. .... Phoenix, AZ
Valainis, LucyH. .... Davenport, IA
Valaitis, Aldona M. .... San Francisco, CA
Valance, Edward H. .... **Falls Church, VA**
Valancy, Steven S. .... **Fort Lauderdale, FL**
Valant, Edwin J. .... Tucson, AZ
Valante, Lawrence W. .... Avenel, NJ
Valanty, Burton J. .... Troy, MI
Valanzola, Donna L. .... **Plymouth, MA**
Valanzola, Edward W. .... Boston, MA
Valaoras, Nicholas Peter .... **Charlotte, NC**
Valar, Christina K. .... Augusta, ME
Valas, John C. .... **Memphis, TN**
Valas, Rory A. .... **Boston, MA**
Valasco, Glenn C. .... Riverview, MI
Valasek, Kenneth G. .... Kittanning, PA
Valasek, Ronald E. .... Lower Burrell, PA
Valashinas, Kimberly M.
Fort Lauderdale, FL
Valat, Thierry .... **New York, NY**
Valauri, John T. .... Seattle, WA
Valauskas, Charles C. .... **Chicago, IL**
Valaw, Barbara L. .... **Pittsburgh, PA**
Valayre, Roland .... **Los Angeles, CA**
San Francisco, CA
Valbh, S. I. .... **Orlando, FL**
Valbracht, James P. .... **Chillicothe, MO**
Valbrune, Alphonse .... **Chicago, IL**
Valbuena, Monique .... **Washington, DC**
Valburn, Lori M. .... Montpelier, VT
Valby, Gary L. .... **Washington, DC**
Valby, Scott R. .... Houston, TX
Valcarce, Jim .... **Bethel, AK**
Valcarce, Nancy C. .... **Miami, FL**
Valcarcel, Manuel R., IV .... **Miami, FL**
Valchine, Craig M. .... Tampa, FL
Valcic, Susan J. .... New York, NY
Valcourt, Matthew J. .... **Tampa, FL**
Valcourt, Ronald A. .... Fall River, MA
Vald, Roman .... West Des Moines, IA
Valder, Joseph B. .... Washington, DC
Valder Law Offices, P.C. .... **Phoenix, AZ**
Valder, Michael J. .... **Phoenix, AZ**
Valderas, Harold L. .... Fort Worth, TX
Valderhaug, Erik Olav .... **San Diego, CA**
Valderhaug, Harold O. .... **San Diego, CA**
Valderrabano-Marina, Fernando
San Juan, PR
Valderrama, Franklin U. .... **Chicago, IL**
Valderrama, Pamela Griffith .... **Chicago, IL**
Valderrama, Teresa S. .... **Houston, TX**
Valdés, Adolfo .... **San Juan, PR**
Valdes, Ariel Omar .... Chicago, IL
Valdes, Charles P. .... Sacramento, CA
Valdes, Ernesto .... Houston, TX
Valdes, Ernesto Amando .... Miami, FL
Valdes, Frank .... San Diego, CA
Valdes, Gilberto .... New York, NY
Valdes, Joan I. .... Coral Gables, FL
Valdes, Joanna Stern .... **Cincinnati, OH**
Valdes, John H. .... Bethesda, MD
Valdes, Jorge G. .... **Santa Ana, CA**
Valdes, Jose I. .... **Miami, FL**
Valdes, Juan E. .... Hialeah, FL
Valdes Law Offices, The .... San Jose, CA
Valdes, Leticia L. .... Tallahassee, FL
Valdes, Richard A. .... Dallas, TX
Valdes, Sonia M. .... New York, NY
Valdes, Steven W. .... San Jose, CA
Valdes, Villaverde & Godfrey, P.A.
Coral Gables, FL
Valdes Almeida, Elizabeth .... **San Juan, PR**
Valdés Alvarez, Carmen A. .... **San Juan, PR**
Valdes-Cruz, Jose Manuel .... Chicago, IL
Valdes-Cugat, J. .... Tampa, FL
Valdes-Dapena, Catalina I. .... Philadelphia, PA
Valdés-Fauli, Raúl E. .... **Miami, FL**
Valdés-Fauli, Raúl J. .... **Miami, FL**
Valdes-Fauly, Lourdes .... Palo Alto, CA
Valdespino, Andres J. .... **Tarrytown, NY**
Valdespino & Associates .... **Miami, FL**
Valdespino Copland, LLP .... **Tarrytown, NY**
Valdespino, Edward F. .... **San Antonio, TX**
Valdespino, Henry .... San Antonio, TX
Valdespino, Henry, Jr. .... **San Antonio, TX**
Valdespino, Jacqueline M. .... **Miami, FL**
Valdespino, Lillian .... Miami, FL
Valdez, Aguinaldo .... **Dallas, TX**
Valdez, Anthony D. .... Honolulu, HI
Valdez, Anthony M. .... **Twin Falls, ID**
Valdez, Carlos .... Corpus Christi, TX
Valdez, Cyndy A. .... Tucson, AZ
Valdez, David G. .... **San Francisco, CA**
Valdez, Donald J .... **Arlington, TX**
Valdez, Donna A.
United States Court of Federal Claims, GV
Valdez, Earl .... Alhambra, CA
Valdez, Edward C. .... Fresno, CA
Valdez, Ernest E. .... Santa Fe, NM
Valdez, Ernest G. .... San Antonio, TX
Valdez, Felix D. .... La Jara, CO
Valdez, Filemon, Jr. .... Boston, MA
Valdez, Frances Valdez .... Plano, TX
Valdez, Frank J. .... Santa Ana, CA
Valdez, Fred H. .... Anchorage, AK
Valdez, G. Greg .... Las Cruces, NM
Valdez, Gabrielle M. .... **Albuquerque, NM**
Valdez, Geraldine A. .... **San Diego, CA**
Valdez, Glenn Smith .... Albuquerque, NM
Valdez, Henry R. .... **Oak Brook, IL**
Valdez, Irma .... Chicago, IL
Valdez, Jake R. .... Denver, CO
Valdez, James A. .... Salt Lake City, UT
Valdez, Janice .... **St. Louis, MO**
Valdez, Julio C. .... **Elgin, IL**
Valdez Law Firm .... Santa Fe, NM

Valdez, Maria Beatrice
Department Of Health And Human Services,
Office of Community Services, GV
Valdez, Maria E. .... **Sacramento, CA**
Valdez, Marlana R. .... Washington, DC
Valdez, Michael A. .... Ocean Shores, WA
Valdez, Ramon Arellano .... Milwaukee, WI
Valdez, Raymond J. .... La Jara, CO
Valdez, Richard M. .... **San Diego, CA**
Valdez, Robert A. .... San Antonio, TX
Valdez, Robert E. .... San Antonio, TX
Valdez & Sage .... Ocean Shores, WA
Valdez, Thomas A. .... Tampa, FL
Valdez, Thomas Anthony .... Casper, WY
Valdez, Troy A. .... **Sacramento, CA**
Valdez, Victor Edmund .... Albuquerque, NM
Valdin, Guyton H., Jr. .... **Metairie, LA**
Valdina, Christopher Thomas .... Auburn, NY
Valdina, David L. .... Cataumet, MA
Valdini, David J. .... **Fort Lauderdale, FL**
Valdini & Palmer, P.A.
Fort Lauderdale, FL
Valdivia, Basil Andres .... **Orlando, FL**
Valdivia, Enrique .... San Antonio, TX
Valdivia, Jeannette E. .... **Pasadena, CA**
Valdivia, Jeannette E., A Prof. Law Corp., Law Offices of .... **Los Angeles, CA**
Pasadena, CA
Valdivia, Richard G. .... Lawrenceville, NJ
Valdivielso, John Carl .... **Newport News, VA**
Valdivieso, Jorge Lucas P., Jr. .... Ponce, PR
Valdivieso, Lawrence Andrew
Thousand Oaks, CA
Valdman, Lilya .... Malibu, CA
Valdrini, Rita R. .... Pittsburgh, PA
Vale, Anthony .... **Philadelphia, PA**
Vale, Barbara Ann .... Seattle, WA
Vale, Catherine M. .... **St. Louis, MO**
Vale, Emil .... Cincinnati, OH
Vale, John S. .... **Cambridge, MA**
Vale, Kenneth C. .... Cranston, RI
Vale, Michael D. .... Oakland, CA
Vale, Patrick G., Law Offices of
Winston-Salem, NC
Vale, Richard S. .... **Metairie, LA**
New Orleans, LA
Vale, Robert A. .... Miami, FL
Vale, Robert D. .... Palo Alto, CA
San Mateo, CA
Vale, Robert W. .... **Miami, FL**
Vale, Shannon Timothy .... **Austin, TX**
Vale, Thomas H. .... Belleville, IL
Vale, Thomas J. .... Monroe, WI
New Glarus, WI
Valeck, David J. .... **New York, NY**
Valecko, James P. .... **Pittsburgh, PA**
Valega, Thomas M., Jr. .... **Houston, TX**
Valek, Benny R. .... **Dallas, TX**
Valek, Marjorie Faucher .... Sumner, WA
Valella, Alejandro J. .... New York, NY
Valen, Anthony .... Middletown, OH
Valen, Eric W. .... St. Paul, MN
Valen, John E. .... **Walker, MN**
Valen, Kelly B. .... **San Francisco, CA**
Valen, Mark .... Jackson, CA
Valen, Michael James .... Pensacola, FL
Valen, Stephen J. .... **Oakland, CA**
Valen, Thomas R. .... **Newark, NJ**
Valencia, Adrienne L. .... **New York, NY**
Valencia, Catalina .... Berkeley, CA
Valencia, Henry C. .... West Covina, CA
Valencia, Jennifer .... Ogden, UT
Valencia, John R. .... **Sacramento, CA**
Valencia, Juan R. A. .... Santa Fe, NM
Valencia, Kathy Brown .... **Jonesboro, GA**
Valencia, Louis E. .... Albuquerque, NM
Valencia, M. Guadalupe .... Los Angeles, CA
Valencia, Mario D. .... **Las Vegas, NV**
Valencia, Mark Garrett .... **Honolulu, HI**
Valencia, Melinda S. .... East Hartford, CT
Valencia, Michael J. .... **San Bruno, CA**
Valencia, Pascual .... Jackson Heights, NY
Valencia, Patrick Samuel .... San Jose, CA
Valencia, Robert L. .... Berkeley, CA
Valencia, Robert R. .... **Los Angeles, CA**
Valencia, Ronald .... **Oakland, CA**
Valencia, Rosa Q. .... Albuquerque, NM
Valencia, Vicente, Jr. .... **Los Angeles, CA**
Valencia & Wilberding .... **Oakland, CA**
Valencia-Aponte, Angel A. .... San Juan, PR
Valenciano, Randal Grant B. .... Lihue, HI
Valencia-Weber, Gloria .... Albuquerque, NM
Valencic, Michelle R. .... **Chicago, IL**
Valensi, Rose & Magaram, Professional Law Corporation .... **Los Angeles, CA**
Valensi, Stephen G. .... **Los Angeles, CA**
Valenstein, Carl A. .... **Washington, DC**
Valenstein, Jill M. .... **Washington, DC**
Valent, Leander R. .... Rosemont, IL
Valent, Richard J. .... **Mineola, NY**
Valenta, Frank L., Jr. .... Columbia, SC
Valenta, Mary Confroy .... Leesburg, VA
Valenta-Weise, Cathy .... Carson City, NV
Valente, Angela M. .... Albany, CA
Valente, Anthony A. .... Charlottesville, VA
Valente, Anthony F. .... East Hanover, NJ
Valente, Charles A. .... **Chicago, IL**
Valente, Daniel .... **Washington, DC**
Valente, Douglas, Law Offices
Northport, NY
Valente, Edmond J. .... **Albany, NY**
Valente, Francis L., Jr. .... **New York, NY**
Valente, John William .... **Rutland, VT**
Valente, Lucia M. .... **New York, NY**
Valente, Michael W. .... **Roseland, NJ**
Valente, Miki C. .... **Palo Alto, CA**
Valente, Paul R. .... Springfield, OH
Valente, Peter C. .... **New York, NY**

Valente, Philip L., Jr.
West Palm Beach, FL
Valente, Silvio T. .... Rutland, VT
Valente, Stephen M. .... New York, NY
Valente, Susan Tribble .... **Boston, MA**
Valente, William D. .... Villanova, PA
Valenti, Alfred T. .... Chicago, IL
Valenti, Andrew F. .... Birmingham, MI
Valenti, Anthony .... Mount Laurel, NJ
Valenti, Anthony P. .... **Springfield, NJ**
Valenti, Carl T. .... New Brunswick, NJ
Valenti, Dana Ann .... **Jacksonville, FL**
Valenti, Daniel A. .... Teaneck, NJ
Valenti, David .... **Palo Alto, CA**
Valenti, David A. .... Chicago, IL
Valenti, Dennis R. .... **Ann Arbor, MI**
Valenti, Dominick A. .... Bronx, NY
Valenti, James A. .... **Rochester, NY**
Valenti, James C. .... **Lake Wales, FL**
Valenti, James K. .... Manalapan, NJ
Valenti, James Michael .... East Rochester, NY
Valenti, Jeffrey E. .... Kansas City, MO
Valenti, Jennifer F. .... **Milwaukee, WI**
Valenti, Jennifer F., S.C. .... **Milwaukee, WI**
Valenti, John A. .... Brighton, MI
Valenti, John A. .... **Cleveland, OH**
Valenti, John C. .... **St. Clair Shores, MI**
Valenti, Joseph A. F. .... **Rochester, NY**
Valenti, Joseph J. .... Tucson, AZ
Valenti, Joseph J. .... Buffalo, NY
Valenti, Joseph P. .... **Paramus, NJ**
Valenti, Linda P. .... Skokie, IL
Valenti, Lorraine A. .... **Tampa, FL**
Valenti, Lynne A. .... New York, NY
Valenti, M. Richard .... **Newton, NJ**
Valenti, Michael A. .... **Louisville, KY**
Valenti, Peter A. .... **Lakewood, NJ**
Valenti, Philip C. .... Boca Raton, FL
Valenti, Thomas J. .... Syracuse, NY
Valenti, Thomas P. .... Chicago, IL
Valenti, Thomas P., P.C. .... Chicago, IL
Valenti, Victor S. .... **Detroit, MI**
Valentic, Teresa Kathleen Polo
San Antonio, TX
Valentin, James .... **Langhorne, PA**
Valentin, Luis A. .... Jersey City, NJ
Valentín-Capeles, Dirma M.
San Juan, PR
Valentine, Adams & Lamar, L.L.P.
Nashville, NC
Valentine, Andrew .... New York, NY
Valentine, Andrew, III .... Charlotte, NC
Valentine, Andrew J. .... Chicago, IL
Winnetka, IL
Valentine, Andrew Paul .... **Palo Alto, CA**
Valentine, Anne M. .... **Columbus, OH**
Valentine, Anthony J. .... **Grand Rapids, MI**
Valentine & Associates, P.C. .... **Detroit, MI**
Troy, MI
West Bloomfield, MI
Valentine, Brian K. .... **Bellingham, WA**
Valentine, C. Braxton, Jr.
United States Senate,
Committee Legal Personnel, GV
Valentine, C. Thomas, Jr. .... **Houston, TX**
Valentine, Catherine L. .... Mountain View, CA
Valentine, Clifton G., Jr. .... Plain City, OH
Valentine, David L. .... Ridgeland, MS
Valentine, Debra A.
Federal Trade Commission,
Office of the General Counsel, GV
Valentine, Dennis E. .... Denver, CO
Valentine, Diana .... Los Angeles, CA
Valentine, Domenic J. .... Bronx, NY
Valentine, Dwight D. .... Boston, MA
Valentine, Eric W. .... La Grande, OR
Valentine, Fred Lee .... Montgomery, AL
Valentine, Frederick Lee .... Cincinnati, OH
Valentine, Gail M. .... Indianapolis, IN
Valentine, George H. .... **Sioux City, IA**
Valentine, Gregory R.
White River Junction, VT
Valentine, H. Wayne .... Dallas, TX
Valentine, Harold .... Clifton, NJ
Valentine, Itimous T., Jr. .... **Nashville, NC**
Valentine, James C. .... Pittsburgh, PA
Valentine, James E. .... Cleveland, OH
Valentine, James F. .... **Menlo Park, CA**
Valentine, James P. .... **Wilkes-Barre, PA**
Valentine, James S. .... **Schaumburg, IL**
Valentine, Janece M. .... Fort Dodge, IA
Valentine, Janet Nolan .... Pittsburgh, PA
Valentine, Jerald A. .... Las Cruces, NM
Valentine, Jerry .... Denver, CO
Valentine, Joanne S. .... Potomac, MD
Valentine, John A. .... **Philadelphia, PA**
Valentine, John C. .... Logan, WV
Valentine, John D. .... **St. Louis, MO**
Valentine, John, Jr. .... **Los Angeles, CA**
Valentine, John L. .... Treasury Department,
Office of Regulations and Rulings, GV
Valentine, John L. .... **Provo, UT**
Valentine, John W. .... **Boston, MA**
Valentine, John W. .... Cleveland, MS
Valentine, Joseph B. .... **Denver, CO**
Roslyn, NY
Valentine, Karen M. .... Department of Justice,
Civil Division, GV
Valentine, Kathleen M. .... Narberth, PA
Valentine, Kevin L. .... **Philadelphia, PA**
Valentine, Kurt P. .... **Jefferson City, MO**
Valentine, Larry D. .... St. Louis, MO
Valentine, Laurie W. .... **St. Petersburg, FL**
Valentine Law Office .... Fort Dodge, IA
Valentine, Leanne M. .... Des Moines, IA
Valentine, Linda Bryant .... Hinsdale, IL
Valentine, M. Theodore .... Lexington, KY
Valentine, Mark A. .... Miami, FL

Valentine, Mark C., Law Offices of
Stratford, CT
Valentine, Michael D.
Huntington Beach, CA
Valentine, Michael J. .... Houston, TX
Valentine, Michael J. .... Fairfax, VA
Valentine, Michael L. .... **Warsaw, IN**
Valentine & Miner .... **Warsaw, IN**
Valentine, Nancy A. .... **Canton, OH**
Valentine, Pamela S. .... **New York, NY**
Valentine, Peter S. .... Irvington, NJ
Valentine, Regis .... Old Greenwich, CT
Valentine, Richard H. .... **New York, NY**
Valentine, Robert L. .... **Lakeland, FL**
Valentine, Robert L., P.A. .... **Lakeland, FL**
Valentine, Robert S.
Manhattan Beach, CA
Valentine, Ronald C. .... Macedon, NY
Valentine, Sarah .... **Oakland, CA**
Valentine, Sherri Stabile .... Lakewood, CO
Valentine, Staci L. .... Washington, DC
Valentine, Stephen K., Jr.
West Bloomfield, MI
Valentine, Stephen M. .... **Beaufort, NC**
Valentine, Stephen W. .... Cameron Park, CA
Valentine, Steven Richards
United States Senate,
Senatorial Assistants, GV
Valentine, Susan .... Chicago, IL
Valentine, Teresa E. .... **Washington, DC**
Valentine, Teri Williams
Wellesley Hills, MA
Valentine, Theresa A. .... **Southfield, MI**
Valentine, Thomas A. .... **Topeka, KS**
Valentine, Thomas A., P.A. .... **Topeka, KS**
Valentine, Thomas C. .... Sarasota, FL
Valentine, Thomas C., P.A. .... Sarasota, FL
Valentine, Thomas D. .... Tallahassee, FL
Valentine & Valentine .... Cleveland, MS
Valentine, Vicki V. .... Maryville, TN
Valentine, Victoria A. .... West Bloomfield, MI
Valentine, William E. .... Roanoke, VA
Valentine, Wm. J. .... Long Beach, CA
Valentine-Sibert, Kimberly A.
Santa Ana, CA
Valentini, David L. .... Minneapolis, MN
Valentini, Fabio .... Chicago, IL
Valentini, Frank D. .... San Francisco, CA
Valentini, Gerald J. .... **Philadelphia, PA**
Valentini, Kenneth L. .... **Miami, FL**
Valentino, Anthony J. .... Costa Mesa, CA
Valentino, Caroline N. .... **Oakland, CA**
Valentino, Deborah L. .... Clearwater, FL
Valentino, Dunne & Stein, A Professional Corporation .... Succasunna, NJ
Valentino, Francis J. .... Jamaica, NY
Valentino, James J. .... **Washington, DC**
Valentino, John L. .... **Syracuse, NY**
Valentino, Joseph D. .... Rochester, NY
Valentino, Joseph G. .... Rockville, MD
Valentino, Joseph Paul .... **New Castle, PA**
Sharon, PA
Valentino, Joseph R. .... Succasunna, NJ
Valentino, Joseph R., (P.C.) .... **Houston, TX**
Valentino, Nicholas .... Cleveland, OH
Valentino, Nicholas Donald .... Mentor, OH
Valentino, Patrick C., The Law Offices of
San Diego, CA
Valentino, Paul G. .... Bloomfield Hills, MI
Valentino, Richard T. .... **Chicago, IL**
Valentino, Robert .... La Jolla, CA
Valentino, Victor P. .... Bloomfield Hills, MI
Valentino, Vincent .... **York, NE**
Valentino, William Rider .... Charleston, WV
Valentino, William S. .... Wheeling, WV
Valento, James J. .... Dayton, OH
Valenty, Jo Anne .... Clearwater, FL
Valentyn, Thomas E. .... Milwaukee, WI
Valentyn, Tim R. .... **Madison, WI**
Valenza, Charles R. .... Rochester, NY
Valenza, D. Gregory .... **San Francisco, CA**
Valenza, Dennis J. .... **Philadelphia, PA**
Valenza, Michael A. .... **Abington, PA**
Philadelphia, PA
Valenza, Stacey M. .... **Garden City, NY**
Valenza, Vincent L. .... **Albany, NY**
Valenziano, Nicholas J., Jr.
Winston-Salem, NC
Valenzuela, Daniel F. .... San Pedro, CA
Valenzuela, Estéban L., Law Offices of
Bakersfield, CA
Fresno, CA
Valenzuela, Estéban L., Law Offices of
Santa Maria, CA
Valenzuela, Henry E. .... **Tampa, FL**
Valenzuela, Henry E., P.A. .... **Tampa, FL**
Valenzuela, Humberto A. .... La Jolla, CA
Valenzuela, Jacqueline I. .... Irving, TX
Valenzuela, Joel M.
Rancho Cucamonga, CA
Valenzuela, Lori Irene .... San Antonio, TX
Valenzuela, Manuel A., Jr. .... Los Angeles, CA
Valenzuela, Mari I. .... **Phoenix, AZ**
Valenzuela, R. Michael .... **Phoenix, AZ**
Valenzuela, Rodolfo "Rudy" .... Tucson, AZ
Valenzuela, Sandra .... **Chicago, IL**
Valeo, James A. .... **Salt Lake City, UT**
Valer, Robert D. .... Washington, DC
Valera, Arnedo S. .... Falls Church, VA
Valera & Associates .... Falls Church, VA
Valera, Elpidio B. .... Falls Church, VA
Valera, José L., (P.C.) .... **Houston, TX**
Valera-Schutz, Beatriz .... Newark, NJ
Valerga, J. Francis .... Salt Lake City, UT
Valerga, Victoria L. .... San Antonio, TX
Valeri, Gina .... Greenwich, CT
Valeri, Jodi L. .... **Washington, DC**
Valeri, John G., Jr. .... Morristown, NJ

Valerian, Patterson, Field & McGraw Walnut Creek, CA
Valerian, Richard C. .... Walnut Creek, CA
Valerian, Robert J. .... Cleveland, OH
Valeriani, Andrew A., Jr. .... Woodbridge, NJ
Valeriano, Gary J. .... Los Angeles, CA
Valeriano, Lawrence J., Jr. .... Reading, PA
Valerino, Gary J. .... Syracuse, NY
Valerino, James Robert .... Winter Park, FL
Valerio, David A. .... Diamond Springs, CA
Valerio, Elizabeth B. .... Boston, MA
Valerio, John R. .... Andover, MA
Valerio, Lois Cullen .... Niskayuna, NY
Valerio, M. Benjamin .... Los Angeles, CA
Valerio, Mark J. .... Rochester, NY
Valerio, Matthew F. .... Rutland, VT
Valerio, Michael A. .... Washington, DC
Valerio, Stacey L. .... Washington, DC
Valerio Barrad, Catherine M. Los Angeles, CA
Valeriote, Christopher J. St. Petersburg, FL
Valerious, Randi L. .... Chicago, IL
Valerius, Margaret L. .... Lansing, IL
Valerius, Seth Gray .... Topeka, KS
Valerius, Thomas F. .... Miami, FL
Valero, Steven J. .... Plymouth, MA
Vales, Donna W. .... Atlanta, GA
Mandeville, LA
Vales, John Robert .... Southlake, TX
Vales, Joseph A. .... Princeton, NJ
Vales, Julie M. .... Watertown, NY
Vales, Robert B. .... Carlsbad, CA
Valeska, Donald G., II .... Montgomery, AL
Valet, Thomas P. .... New York, NY
Valeta, Peter J. .... Chicago, IL
Valetich, Stephanie National Labor Relations Board, Office of Board Members, GV
Valetk, Harry A. .... New York, NY
Valette, George C. .... Fulton, NY
Valette, Paul Andrew .... Washington, DC
Silver Spring, MD
Valeur-Jensen, Margaret Thousand Oaks, CA
Valgenti, Frank J., Jr. .... New Vernon, NJ
Valgenti, Victor F. .... Missoula, MT
Valiant, Carrie .... Washington, DC
Valianti, Jennifer J. .... Salem, MA
Valice, Brian E. .... Cadillac, MI
Valicek, Michael D. .... San Antonio, TX
Valicek, Michelle Lorenz .... San Antonio, TX
Valicenti, Alexandra .... Bronxville, NY
Valicenti, David .... Westbury, NY
Valicenti, Mona N. .... Los Alamos, NM
Valiente, Antonio E. .... San Juan, PR
Valier, Charles E. .... St. Louis, MO
Valier, Michelle L. .... Seattle, WA
Valigura, Keith W. .... Conroe, TX
Valihura, Karen L. .... Wilmington, DE
Valihura, Robert J., Jr. .... Wilmington, DE
Valik, Eva N. .... New York, NY
Valikonis, Steven W. .... Richmond, TX
Valimont, Michael S. .... Doylestown, PA
Valin, Donna C. .... Orlando, FL
Valinoti, Elizabeth H. .... Washington, DC
Valinoti, Jack V. .... Morristown, NJ
Valinoti, James R. .... Los Angeles, CA
Valinoti, Kenneth L. .... San Francisco, CA
Valins, Fred F. .... Cleveland, OH
Valinsky, Jay L. .... Fort Lauderdale, FL
Valiquet, Brett A. .... Chicago, IL
Valiquette, Michelle E. .... Glendale, AZ
Valis, William V. .... Cleveland, OH
Valisek, James C. .... Cleveland, OH
Valitutti, Ralph F., Jr. .... Detroit, MI
Mount Clemens, MI
Valitutto, Richard E.F. .... High Point, NC
Valiulis, Anthony C. .... Chicago, IL
Valk, Alec .... Costa Mesa, CA
Valka, Kenneth R. .... Houston, TX
Valkenburg, Melville H. .... Beaufort, SC
Valkenburgh, Christine .... Bath, NY
Valkenburgh, Roger R. .... Wilton, CT
Valkenet, Thomas C. .... Baltimore, MD
Valkevich, Thomas J. .... Saugus, MA
Valko, Terrence A. .... Altoona, PA
Valko, Terrence A., P.C. .... Altoona, PA
Valla, Antonio .... San Francisco, CA
Valla, Brenda L. .... Sarasota, FL
Vallabh, Rajesh .... Boston, MA
Vallace, Anthony E. .... New York, NY
Valladao, Gregory B. .... Phoenix, AZ
Valladares, Bruce A. .... Kalamazoo, MI
Valladares, O. Frank .... Miami, FL
Valladares, Patricia C. .... Newark, NJ
Valladeres, Karla E. .... Maitland, FL
Vallance, Laura Federal Energy Regulatory Commission, Office of the General Counsel, GV
Vallance, Mathew S. .... Santa Ana, CA
Vallandigham, Paul H. .... Urbana, IL
Vallandigham, Robert V., Jr. Los Angeles, CA
Vallandingham, Michael T. .... Austin, TX
Vallant, Paul D. .... St. Paul, MN
Vallar, Giorgio .... Daytona Beach, FL
Vallar, James M. .... Chicago, IL
Vallarelli, Joanne .... Lansing, MI
Vallari, Lauren S. .... Concord, NH
Vallarino, P. Roy .... San Rafael, CA
Vallario, George H., Jr. .... Brooklyn, NY
Vallario, Joseph F., Jr. .... Suitland, MD
Vallario, Richard W. .... Nutley, NJ
Vallarta, Malyn A. .... New York, NY
Vallarta, Theresa (Tracey) .... New York, NY
Vallarta, Vanessa W. .... Salinas, CA
Vallas, Pete J. .... Mobile, AL
Vallas, Thomas A. .... Reno, NV
Vallas, V. T. .... Jackson, MS
Vallay, Jules F. .... Allendale, NJ
Valldejuli, Richard K., Jr. .... Norcross, GA
Valldejuli, Vanessa T. .... Virginia Beach, VA
Valldejuly-Sastre, Carlos A. .... San Juan, PR
Valle, Angelina .... San Jose, CA
Valle & Craig, P.A. .... Key West, FL
Miami, FL
West Palm Beach, FL
Fort Lauderdale, FL
Valle, Frank D., Jr. .... Bloomfield Hills, MI
Valle, Gabriel B. .... Washington, DC
Valle, Jeffrey B. .... Los Angeles, CA
Valle, Joseph R., Jr. .... Boston, MA
Valle, Karen Martino .... Albany, NY
New York, NY
Valle, Laurence F. .... Miami, FL
Valle, Richard J. .... Albuquerque, NM
Valle, Robyn Ann .... Roseland, NJ
Valleau & Metz .... Indianapolis, IN
Valleau, Norma Kathryn Sass Indianapolis, IN
Valleau, Richard J. .... Cincinnati, OH
Valleau, Victor .... Santa Monica, CA
Valleau, Victor, and Associates, A Law Corporation .... Santa Monica, CA
Vallecillo, Manuel I. .... San Juan, PR
Vallecorsa, Joseph A., Jr. .... Rosemead, CA
Vallee, J. Michael .... Solana Beach, CA
Vallee, James E. .... Franklin, MA
Vallee, R. Collins .... Mandeville, LA
Vallejo, Adam C. .... Whittier, CA
Vallejo, Almudena .... New York, NY
Vallejo, Arturo S. .... Metairie, LA
Vallejo, Eleen Y. .... Camarillo, CA
Vallejo, Luis A. .... Houston, TX
Vallejo, Natalia A. .... San Antonio, TX
Vallejo, Norma .... New York, NY
Vallejo, Raymond .... Bronx, NY
Vallejo, Richard H. B. .... Oklahoma City, OK
Vallejos, William A. .... Montebello, CA
Vallejos-Nichols, Dawn M. Gainesville, FL
Vallely, Carol L. .... Petaluma, CA
Vallely, Jas. L. .... Boston, MA
Vallely, Michael P. .... Washington, DC
Vallely, Thomas J. .... Tuckahoe, NY
Vallen, Marc W. .... Berlin, CT
Vallender, Charles F., III .... Washington, DC
Vallens, Brent Edward, Law Offices of Chatsworth, CA
Vallens, Howard S., Law Offices of Los Angeles, CA
Vallens, Jeffrey S. .... Woodland Hills, CA
Vallentine, Diane F. .... Anchorage, AK
Vallerand, Patricia A. .... Eugene, OR
Vallerga, David Edward .... Belmont, CA
Vallerga, Edw. D. .... Belmont, CA
Vallerga, Leslie Jean .... Belmont, CA
Vallerie, Margaret M. .... Norwalk, CT
Valle-Riestra, Christopher P. .... Oakland, CA
Valle-Riestra, Paul M. .... Walnut Creek, CA
Vallerie-Zingaro, Colleen .... Norwalk, CT
Vallery, Ray Colton .... Fayetteville, NC
Valles, Charles E. .... Dallas, TX
Valles, David A. .... Santa Ana, CA
Valles, Fred S. .... Santa Barbara, CA
Valles, Laura A. .... Pittsburgh, PA
Valles, Noe G. .... Lubbock, TX
Valles, Raul, Jr. .... Tampa, FL
Valles, Tricia Bohenberger .... Tampa, FL
Vallet, Rita .... New York, NY
Valletta, Amy E. .... Worcester, MA
Valletta, Chryssa .... New York, NY
Valletta, William .... New York, NY
Vallette, Diane Lynn .... Glendale, CA
Vallette, Joseph L. .... Hauppauge, NY
Vallette, Kent Leeds .... Glendale, CA
Vallette, Michael J. .... Ocean Springs, MS
Valley, Doyle C. .... Boston, MA
Valley Law Center, Inc. .... Cupertino, CA
Valley, Marina S. .... Oklahoma City, OK
Valley, Mark R. .... Chicago, IL
Valley, Matthew E. .... La Crosse, WI
Valli, Andrew Henry .... Peachtree City, GA
Valli, Thomas M. .... Lansing, MI
Vallianos, Peter S. .... Great Barrington, MA
Valliant, Heather M. .... New Orleans, LA
Valliant, James Stevens .... San Diego, CA
Valliant, John P., Jr. .... Knoxville, TN
Vallien, Andrew S. .... Natchitoches, LA
Vallier, Averil D. .... Montrose, CA
Vallier, Robt. .... Encino, CA
Valliere, A. James .... Stuart, FL
Valliere, Albert E. .... Leominster, MA
Valliere, Barbara .... Washington, DC
Valliere, Charles E. .... Indianapolis, IN
Valliere, Dean R. .... Leominster, MA
Valliere, Timothy A. .... New York, NY
Valliere & Valliere .... Leominster, MA
Vallillo, Paul R. .... Waterbury, CT
Vallin, Gregory A. .... Denver, CO
Vallini, Darra James .... Lexington, SC
Vallis, George P. .... Hamilton, MA
Vallo, Joseph A. .... New York, NY
Vallo, Joseph A., P.A. .... New York, NY
Vallon, Lauralee Ann Kiely .... Orange, TX
Vallone, Barbara Ancira .... Austin, TX
Vallone, Charles J. .... New York, NY
Vallone, James J. .... Crofton, MD
Vallone, James M. .... Cheektowaga, NY
Vallone, John J., Jr. .... Cranston, RI
Vallone, John L. .... Coventry, RI
Vallone, Joseph P. .... Mount Holly, NJ
Vallone, Lewis A. .... Rochester, NY
Vallone, Louis J. .... East Greenwich, RI
Vallone, Melissa A. .... Chicago, IL
Vallone, Patrick .... New York, NY
Vallone, Paul E. .... San Francisco, CA
Vallone, Paul J. .... Buffalo, NY
Vallone, Perry C. .... Edison, NJ
Vallone, Peter F. .... Astoria, NY
Vallone, Peter F., Jr. .... Astoria, NY
Vallone, Richard T., Jr. .... Cheektowaga, NY
Vallone, Roberta A. .... Buffalo, NY
Vallone, Thomas J. .... Philadelphia, PA
Vallort, Joseph R. .... Chicago, IL
Vallorz, Sonia Chopko .... Cleveland, OH
Vallot, Angela E. .... New York, NY
Vallotton, Joseph E. .... Valdosta, GA
Vallow, Eugene C. .... Dallas, TX
Vallowe, Joseph M. Department Of Veterans Affairs, Inspector General, GV
Valls, Bart Preston .... Commerce City, CO
Valls, Kenneth A. .... Laredo, TX
Valls, Marcos O. .... San Juan, PR
Valls-Miranda, Susie .... Miami, FL
Valmond, Casandra A. .... Houston, TX
Valner, Rudy .... Los Angeles, CA
Valocchi, Beth Evans .... Wilmington, DE
Valocchi, Fischer & Gerlach Downingtown, PA
Valocchi, Jeffrey J. .... Downingtown, PA
Valocchi, Teresa M. .... Treasury Department, Office of Thrift Supervision, GV
Valof, Joseph .... Natick, MA
Valoff, Jo Lynn .... Los Angeles, CA
Valoir, Tamsen .... Houston, TX
Valois, Johanne .... Tampa, FL
Valois, Johanne, P.A., Law Offices of Tampa, FL
Valois, Richard E. .... Fort Pierce, FL
Valois, Robert A. .... Raleigh, NC
Valone, David L. .... Knoxville, TN
Valone, Kathleen Hart .... Rochester, NY
Valor, Scott H. .... Los Gatos, CA
Valore, A. Richard .... Cleveland, OH
Valore, Aurelio .... Blue Ridge Summit, PA
Valore, Beverly L. .... Linwood, NJ
Valore, Carl J. .... Atlantic City, NJ
Linwood, NJ
Valore Chartered Law Offices Atlantic City, NJ
Linwood, NJ
Valore, Joseph A. .... Fairview Park, OH
Valore, Joseph P. .... Urbana, OH
Valori, Peter F. .... Miami, FL
Valori, Raymond .... Miami, FL
Valot, Dennis A. .... Columbus, OH
Valouch, Jacqueline .... Newark, NJ
Valponi, Mark J. .... Cleveland, OH
Valsame, George T. .... Garner, NC
Valsangiacomo, Detora & McQuesten, P.C. Barre, VT
Montpelier, VT
Valsangiacomo, Oreste V., Jr. .... Barre, VT
Valsing, D. Charles .... Harrisburg, PA
Valtierra, Jose Guadalupe .... Griffith, IN
Valtorta, Laura P. .... Columbia, SC
Value, Felicia R. .... La Conner, WA
Valuet, Bonnie L. .... Clarkston, MI
Valukas, Anton J. .... Chicago, IL
Valukas, Anton R. .... Chicago, IL
Valukas, Shawn Y. .... Chicago, IL
Valvano, David A. .... Livingston, NJ
Valvano, James, II .... Suffern, NY
Valverde, Kathryn A. .... San Diego, CA
Valverde, Leo .... Phoenix, AZ
Valverde, Michael A. .... Wichita Falls, TX
Valverde, Olman J. .... Los Angeles, CA
Valvo, Carl .... Boston, MA
Valvo, Carmen J. .... Rome, NY
Valvo, Janice R. .... Buffalo, NY
Forestville, NY
Valvo, Lisa A. .... Buffalo, NY
Valvo, Robert D. .... Providence, RI
Valvo, Victoria M. .... Claremont, CA
Valvo-Walkowiak, Vicky L. .... Buffalo, NY
Valz, David Randolph .... Cincinnati, OH
Valz, Duane R. .... San Francisco, CA
Valz, Frederick M., III .... Atlanta, GA
Vames, Paul J. .... Las Vegas, NV
Vammen, Fritzie .... Conway, AR
Vamos, Florence M. .... Mishawaka, IN
Edwardsburg, MI
Vamos, Stephen J., III .... Columbus, OH
Vampola, Kenneth J. .... Arlington, NE
Vamvoras, Glen D. .... Lake Charles, LA
Van, Michael C. .... Las Vegas, NV
Van, Peter .... Boston, MA
Van, Winnie .... San Francisco, CA
Vana, Dan .... San Antonio, TX
Vana, James L. .... Milwaukee, WI
Vana, Kent J. .... Grand Rapids, MI
Vana, Peter L., III .... Littleton, CO
Vana, Robert J. .... Cleveland, OH
Van Abel, Jeffrey M. .... Anchorage, AK
Van Abel, John P. .... Canton, OH
Van Acker, Henry .... Rouses Point, NY
Van Ackeren, Joe .... Liberty, MO
Van Ackern, Cheryl Lee .... Loveland, CO
Vanacore, John G. .... Concord, NH
Van Adzin, Alex A. .... Boston, MA
van Aelstyn, Nicholas W. San Francisco, CA
van Aelstyn, Philip M. .... Burlington, VT
Vanagas, Timothy J. .... Gresham, OR
Vanagel, Gregory W. .... Savannah, GA
Vanairsdale, Carol M. .... Northbrook, IL
Van Aken, John T. .... Santa Barbara, CA
Van Aken, Withers & Webster Cleveland, OH
Vanalek, David Thomas San Francisco, CA
Van Alen, William L., Jr. .... Edgemont, PA
Van Alfen, Scott B. .... Las Vegas, NV
Van Alkemade, Sara A. .... Chicago, IL
Van Allen, Barbara Ann .... Cedar Rapids, IA
Van Allen, John E. .... Harrisburg, PA
Van Allen, Marc .... Chicago, IL
Van Allen, Peter R. .... Schenectady, NY
Van Allen, William K. .... Charlotte, NC
Van Allsburg, Jon A. .... Holland, MI
VanAllsburg, Mark .... Grand Rapids, MI
Van Allsburg, Mark A. Grand Rapids, MI
Van Almen, Joan .... Lake Oswego, OR
Van Almsick, John R. .... St. Louis, MO
Van Alsburg, J. Michael .... Tucson, AZ
Van Alst, Audrey D. .... Cadillac, MI
VanAlsten, Janet S. .... Midland, MI
Van Alstine, Michael P. .... Cincinnati, OH
van Alstyne, Abigail P. .... Birmingham, AL
Van Alstyne, Debra M. Securities and Exchange Commission, Division of Corporation Finance, GV
Van Alstyne, Philip C. .... Las Vegas, NV
Van Alstyne, W. Scott, Jr. .... Gainesville, FL
VanAlstyne, William W. .... Durham, NC
Vanaman, David C. .... Greenbelt, MD
Vanaman, Valerie .... Sherman Oaks, CA
Van Amberg, Ronald J. .... Santa Fe, NM
Van Amburg, Chackes, Carlson & Spritzer, LLP .... St. Louis, MO
Van Amburg, Lisa S. .... St. Louis, MO
Van Amburgh, Robert W. .... Addison, TX
Van Amburgh, Thomas G. .... Dallas, TX
Van Amburgh, Thomas G., P.C. .... Dallas, TX
Van Amerongen, Jan A. T., Jr. Wilmington, DE
van Amerongen, Kathryn Castiglioni Wilmington, DE
Van Andel, Peter .... West Palm Beach, FL
VanAntwerp, Howard, III .... Ashland, KY
Ironton, OH
Van Antwerp, L. Walker, III Los Angeles, CA
Van Antwerp, Malin .... Bryn Mawr, PA
Van Antwerp, Mary K. .... Indianapolis, IN
VanAntwerp, Monge, Jones & Edwards LLP Ashland, KY
Van Antwerp, Patricia A. Oklahoma City, OK
Van Antwerp, Randy L. .... Kalamazoo, MI
Van Antwerp, Richard F. .... Portland, ME
Van Antwerp, Rosemary D. .... Boston, MA
Van Antwerpen, Franklin S. .... Easton, PA
Vanarelli, Donald D. .... Westfield, NJ
Vanarelli, John .... Ventura, CA
Vanaria, Alan J. .... Springfield, MA
van Arink, Deborah .... St. Louis, MO
Van Arkel, Jon .... Springfield, MO
Van Arkel-Greubel, Linda .... Tulsa, OK
Van Arnam, Frederic D., Jr. New York, NY
Van Arsdale, Barbara J. .... Pittsford, NY
VanArsdale, Christopher J. Washington, DC
Van Arsdale, Cory H. .... Redmond, WA
Van Arsdale, Elizabeth J. .... Naples, FL
Van Arsdale, Herbert, II .... Louisville, KY
Van Arsdale, J. Corbin .... Houston, TX
Van Arsdale, Leah C. .... Lancaster, CA
Van Arsdale, Robert B. .... Norfolk, VA
Van Arsdale, Stephen R. .... Rochester, NY
VanArsdel, Andrew Paul .... Seattle, WA
Van Arsdel, Peter R. .... Celina, OH
Van Arsdel, Tom .... Houston, TX
Vanarthos, John N. .... Somerville, NJ
Van Artsdalen, Donald W. .... Philadelphia, PA
Vanasco, Gina G. .... Chicago, IL
Vanasco, Robert A. .... Chicago, IL
Vanasco, Wayne & Genelly .... Chicago, IL
Van Asdale, Lena T. .... Chicago, IL
Van Asdale, Shawn .... Chicago, IL
Vanasek, Alan R. .... Owatonna, MN
St. Paul, MN
Vanasek, Gary A. .... Memphis, TN
Vanasek, William J. .... Marysville, CA
Vanaskie, Thomas I. .... Scranton, PA
Vanasse, Charles F. .... San Jose, CA
Vanasse, Julia G. .... Lancaster, PA
Vanasse, Michael A. .... Lancaster, PA
Van Assenderp, H. Kenza .... Tallahassee, FL
Van Atta, David M. .... Palo Alto, CA
Vanatta, Dean R. .... Denver, CO
Vanatta, Lynn M. .... Colorado Springs, CO
Vanatta, Sullan, Sandgrund & Sullan, P.C. Denver, CO
Van Atta, William E. .... Ontario, OR
Van Auken, Barbara S. .... Peoria, IL
Van Auken, Bradley A. .... Columbus, OH
VanAuken, Lisa .... Houston, TX
Van Auken, Lori J. .... New York, NY
Van Aulen, Peter .... Saddle Brook, NJ
Van Ausdal, Mark R. .... Skokie, IL
VanAusdal, Rodney E. .... Chicago, IL
van Ausdall, Dirk .... San Francisco, CA
VanAusdall, Rice L. .... Harrisburg, AR
Van Baalen, Guy A. .... Buffalo, NY
Van Baalen, Jack L. .... Laramie, WY
Van Baalen, Peter T. .... Phoenix, AZ
Van Baaren, Valerie M. .... Orange, NJ
Van Baren, Todd M. .... Chicago, IL
Van Baugh, Ronnie .... Whitehouse, TX
Van Bavel, Mark A. .... Baltimore, MD
Van Beasley, Kurt .... Brentwood, TN
Van Bebber, Alleen Castellani Kansas City, MO
Van Bebber, David L. .... Springdale, AR
Van Bebber, G. Thomas .... Kansas City, KS

Van Bebber, Marion Turner (Van) Dallas, TX
Van Beber, Eric A. Overland Park, KS
Van Beckum, Thomas A., Jr. Kenosha, WI
Van Beek, Andrea Orange City, IA
Van Beek, Dana M. Sioux Falls, SD
Van Beek, James G. Beverly Hills, CA
Van Beek, John P. Washington, DC
Alexandria, VA
Van Beke, Charles W. Knoxville, TN
Van Belkum, Thomas G. Bingham Farms, MI
Van Benschoten, Birney M. Amherst, MA
Van Benschoten, Christine F. Kingston, NY
Van Benschoten, David B. Saugerties, NY
van Benschoten, Duane T. Saginaw, MI
van Benschoten, Harvey E. Saginaw, MI
van Benschoten, John H. Saginaw, MI
van Benschoten Law Offices Saginaw, MI
van Benschoten, Mark T. Saginaw, MI
van Benschoten, Maurice L. Saginaw, MI
van Benthem, John C., III San Diego, CA
VanBenthuysen, Howard E. St. Albans, VT
van Benthuysen, W. Watson, Jr. New Orleans, LA
van Berg, Joan S. Federal Deposit Insurance Corporation, Professional Liability Section, GV
Van Berg, Mark Mercedes, TX
Van Bergen, Peter G. Minneapolis, MN
Van Bergen, Peter J. Williamsburg, VA
Van Bergen, Vincent G. Milwaukie, OR
Van Bergh, Mark Washington, DC
Vanberg-Wolff, George D. San Francisco, CA
Van Berkel, Paul Kaukauna, WI
Van Berkem, David F. Bothell, WA
Van Berkom, Michael C. Minneapolis, MN
Van Berkom, Trevor Paul Toledo, OH
Van Beustring, Russell V., Law Office of, P.C. Houston, TX
Van Beveren, Theresa Oakland, CA
Van Bibber, G. Wayne Charleston, WV
VanBlarcom, Douglas J. San Diego, CA
Van Blarcom, Heather K. San Diego, CA
Van Blarcom, Ronald A. Orange, CA
Van Blarcom-Gupko, Meri J. Morristown, NJ
Van Blarcum, William A. Plano, TX
Van Blargan, Mark M. Harrisburg, PA
Van Blaricum, Kenneth Pratt, KS
Van Blerkom, Lee Washington, DC
Van Blois & Associates Livermore, CA
Oakland, CA
Pleasanton, CA
San Francisco, CA
Walnut Creek, CA
Van Blois, R. Lewis Oakland, CA
Van Blunk, Henry E. Richboro, PA
Van Bogaert, Cynthia A. Madison, WI
Van Bokkelen, Joseph S. Highland, IN
Van Bolt, John F. Detroit, MI
Van Bomel, John C. White Plains, NY
Van Boom, Joel Trabuco Canyon, CA
Van Booven, Paul C. Lexington, KY
Van Bourg, Victor J. Oakland, CA
Van Bourg, Weinberg, Roger & Rosenfeld Oakland, CA
Van Boven, H. Lee San Mateo, CA
Van Brackel, Heather L. Severna Park, MD
VanBrakle, Bryant L. Federal Maritime Commission, Other Offices of the Commission, GV
Van Brauman, Martin M., Jr. Dallas, TX
Van Bree, Frank E. Chicago, IL
Van Briggle, Larry W. Elwood, IN
Van Briggle Law Office Elwood, IN
Van Brocklin, Gary Loren Youngstown, OH
Van Brocklin, Robert D. Portland, OR
Van Brocklin, Valerie A. Anchorage, AK
van Broek, Alexander G. Oakland, CA
Van Broekhoven, Rollin A. Department of Defense, Armed Services Board of Contract Appeals, GV
Van Bruggen, Elaine T. Los Gatos, CA
Vanbrunt Juzwiak & Russo, P.C. Sayville, NY
Van Brunt, Kirk Washington, DC
Van Brunt, Richard H. Sayville, NY
Van Brunt, William A. Minneapolis, MN
Van Brussel, Mark H. Sacramento, CA
Van Buren, Carol A. Jones Charlotte, NC
Van Buren, Culver Burbank, CA
Van Buren, Cynthia Palm Beach, FL
Van Buren, Edward J., Jr. Houston, TX
Van Buren, Evans W., Jr. Portland, OR
Van Buren, George W. Honolulu, HI
Van Buren, James T. Fitchburg, MA
Van Buren, James W. Fairfax, VA
Van Buren, Marybeth Portland, OR
Van Buren, Paul B. Los Altos, CA
Van Buren, Peter D. Albany, NY
Van Buren, Stanley K. Columbus, OH
Van Buren, Stephen E. Houston, TX
Van Buren, Susan Kathryn Akron, OH
Van Buren, Tye W. Orlando, FL
Van Buren, William B., III Austin, TX
Van Buren, William R., III Norfolk, VA
VanBuskirk, Anne M. Menlo Park, CA
Van Buskirk, Austin E. Kansas City, MO
Van Buskirk, Dana Lee East Setauket, NY
van Buskirk, David W. Montgomery, AL
VanBuskirk, Gerald J. Decatur, GA
Van Buskirk, John J. Lakewood, WA
Van Buskirk, John W. Indianapolis, IN
Van Buskirk, Joseph Pittsburgh, PA
VanBuskirk, Joseph E. Canton, OH
Van Buskirk, Kurt T. Brookfield, WI
Van Buskirk, Leslie Milwaukee, WI
VanBuskirk, Margaret P. Cleveland, OH
van Buskirk, Mark Capulin, NM
Van Buskirk, Mary E. Havre, MT
Van Buskirk, Michael H. Philadelphia, PA
VanBuskirk, Nicholas Robert Warrenton, VA
VanBuskirk, Paul Alan North Brunswick, NJ
Van Buskirk, Robt. Palm Desert, CA
Van Buskirk, Ronald E. San Francisco, CA
VanBuskirk, Tedd W. New York, NY
Van Camp, Allen C. Brea, CA
Van Camp, Brian R. Sacramento, CA
Van Camp, Dale Encino, CA
Van Camp, Donald Glendale, AZ
Van Camp, Douglas L. Jefferson City, MO
Van Camp, Harry E. Madison, WI
Van Camp, Hayes & Meacham, A Professional Association Aberdeen, NC
Carthage, NC
Pinehurst, NC
Robbins, NC
Southern Pines, NC
Troy, NC
West End, NC
Whispering Pines, NC
Van Camp, James R. Carthage, NC
Pinehurst, NC
Van Camp, Jean Louis Tustin, CA
Van Camp, Julie C. Long Beach, CA
Van Camp, Margaret E. San Francisco, CA
Van Camp, Patricia L. Santa Ana, CA
Van Camp, Peter E. Glendale, AZ
Van Camp, Stephen R. Columbia, SC
Van Camp, Thomas M. Carthage, NC
Pinehurst, NC
Van Camp & Van Camp Glendale, AZ
Van Camp, Victor T. Mount Clemens, MI
VanCanagan, William K. Missoula, MT
Van Caneghan, Robert J. Staten Island, NY
Vance, Alice L. Weston, WV
Vance, Amy S. New York, NY
Vance, Andrew Hugh Westminster, MD
Vance, Andrew Joseph Washington, DC
Vance, Andrew P. New York, NY
Vance, Ann Brooks, P.C. Leesburg, VA
Vance, Anthony C. McLean, VA
Vance, Anthony N. Agency for International Development, Other Offices of A.I.D., GV
Vance, Arthur W. Tucson, AZ
Vance, Bert J. Garden City, KS
Vance, Beth Kuntz House of Representatives, Committee on Ways & Means, GV
Vance, Beverly Portland, OR
Vance, Beverly Diane Buffalo, NY
Vance and Blair Irvine, CA
Vance, Bobby T. Batesville, MS
Vance, Bradley J. King Of Prussia, PA
Vance, Brian C. Philadelphia, PA
Vance, C. Gibson Montgomery, AL
Vance, Callaway S. Edna, TX
Vance, Carol S., (Mr.) Houston, TX
Vance, Catherine A. New York, NY
Vance, Charles F., Jr. Winston-Salem, NC
Vance, Claud Eugene Albuquerque, NM
Vance, Cullen B. Edna, TX
Vance, Cynthia E. Buffalo, NY
Vance, Cyrus R. New York, NY
Vance, Cyrus R., Jr. Seattle, WA
Vance, David B. Research Triangle Park, NC
Vance, David Z. New York, NY
Vance, Dean F. Houston, TX
Vance, Dolly San Francisco, CA
Vance, Donald G. Richardson, TX
Vance, Donald L. Modesto, CA
Vance & Doney, P.A. West Palm Beach, FL
Vance, Dwayne A. Park City, UT
Vance, Eric H. Philadelphia, PA
Vance, Estil A., Jr. Fort Worth, TX
Vance, Gail A. McLean, VA
Vance, Geoffrey A. Chicago, IL
Vance, Heather Slotnick Santa Clara, CA
Vance, Heidi J. Chicago, IL
Vance, J. Burton Atlanta, GA
Vance, J. Thomas Carrollton, GA
Vance, James Cincinnati, OH
Vance, James A. Lansing, MI
Vance, James C. Nashville, TN
Vance, James J. Fort Atkinson, WI
Vance, James P. Grenada, MS
Vance, James R. Bellevue, WA
Vance, James W. West Palm Beach, FL
Vance, Janet New York, NY
Vance, Jeanne L. Sacramento, CA
Vance, Jennifer W. Bethesda, MD
Vance, Jerry L. Nashville, TN
Vance, John A. McLean, VA
Vance, John C. Dallas, TX
Vance, John R., Jr. San Francisco, CA
Vance, John T. Washington, DC
Vance, Joseph Portland, OR
Vance, Joseph A., IV Fredericksburg, VA
Vance, Joseph J. Omaha, NE
Vance, Karren M. United States Postal Service, Mid-Atlantic Office, GV
Vance, Katherine McCormick Tulsa, OK
Vance, Kathleen C. Omaha, NE
Vance, Kathleen Caswell Los Angeles, CA
Vance, Kaye K. Milwaukee, WI
Vance, Keith D. Colorado Springs, CO
Denver, CO
Vance, Kelly New York, NY
Vance, Keven C. Baltimore, MD
Vance, Kevin E. Dayton, OH
Vance, L. Alexander Cocoa, FL
Vance, L. Byron, III Chicago, IL
Vance Law Firm, P.A., The Albuquerque, NM
Vance Law Office Mt. Pleasant, IA
Vance, Lawrence H., Jr. Spokane, WA
Vance, Leon T. Juneau, AK
Vance, Lisa A. San Antonio, TX
Vance, Lynn Homes Mineola, NY
Vance, M. Kim Nashville, TN
Vance, Mary Dallas, TX
Vance, Mary Anne Seattle, WA
Vance, Mary Anne, P.S., The Law Office of Seattle, WA
Vance, Melinda T. Fort Worth, TX
Vance, Michael C. Mt. Pleasant, IA
Vance, Palmer G., II Lexington, KY
Vance, Patricia A. Omaha, NE
Vance, Patricia A. Akron, OH
Vance, Paul A. Buffalo, NY
Vance, Paul C. Jacksonville, FL
Vance, Paul N. New Orleans, LA
Vance & Phillips Seymour, IN
Vance, R. Patrick New Orleans, LA
Vance, Richard A. Louisville, KY
Vance, Richard B. Fort Worth, TX
Vance, Richard D. Pocatello, ID
Vance, Richard R. Sevierville, TN
Vance, Robert D. Maysville, KY
Vance, Robert S., Jr. Birmingham, AL
Vance, Robert T., Jr. Philadelphia, PA
Vance, Romero & Montague, P.S. Bellevue, WA
Vance, Roy N. Frankfort, KY
Vance, Sara J. Phoenix, AZ
Vance, Sarah S. New Orleans, LA
Vance, Scott W. Washington, DC
Vance, Stewart E. Camden, AL
Vance, Stewart E., P.C. Camden, AL
Vance, Susan Mahone Granger, IN
Vance, Susan Margaret Beverly Shores, IN
Vance, Susan Molero New Orleans, LA
Vance, Tara L. New York, NY
Vance, Thomas L. Irvine, CA
Vance, Todd A. Alexandria, LA
Vance, Tracy V. Boise, ID
Vance, Travis T., Jr. Vicksburg, MS
Vance, Valerie R. Houston, TX
Vance, Vanessa L. Tyler, TX
Vance, Verne W., Jr. Boston, MA
Vance, Victoria L. Cleveland, OH
Vance, Wendy Chinn Aiea, HI
Vance, Wilcox, Short & Short, S.C. Fort Atkinson, WI
Vance, William Cleveland, OH
Vance, William E. Seymour, IN
Vance, William R. Birmingham, AL
Vance, William R. Waco, TX
Vance, William W. Bryan, TX
Vanchieri & Ferrier Brooklyn, NY
Vanchieri, Jack Brooklyn, NY
Vancil, Edward C., Inc., A Professional Corporation Creve Coeur, MO
Vancil, Gary W. Kailua-Kona, HI
Vancil, Karl W. Ballinger, TX
Vancil, Leigh P. Suwanee, GA
Vancil, Paul Atlanta, GA
Vancil, Stacy Graef San Antonio, TX
Vancil, Troy L. San Antonio, TX
Vancini, Gary S. Warwick, RI
Van Cise, Edwin P. Denver, CO
Van Cise, Jerrold G. New London, NH
Van Clark, Cheryl J. Gilroy, CA
Van Cleave, Albert W., III San Antonio, TX
VanCleave, Christopher C. Biloxi, MS
Van Cleave, Frank Tullahoma, TN
Van Cleave, Jerry D. Minneapolis, MN
Van Cleave, John L. Nashville, TN
Van Cleave, Jonathan E. Irvine, CA
Vancleave, Mark D. Houston, TX
Van Cleave, Michelle Kim United States Senate, Committee Legal Personnel, GV
Van Cleave, Patricia Brennan Louisville, KY
Van Cleave, Richard N. Portland, OR
Van Cleave, Robert B. Overland Park, KS
Van Cleave, Roy M., (P.C.) Chicago, IL
Van Cleave, Thomas M., III Denver, CO
Van Cleave, Thomas M., Jr. Lenexa, KS
Van Cleef, Carol R. Washington, DC
Van Cleef, Charles Tyler, TX
Van Cleef, R. Pope, Jr. Oklahoma City, OK
Van Cleef, Robert Southfield, MI
Vancleemput, Germaine Marie Nashville, TN
Van Cleve & Associates Washington, DC
Van Cleve, Gary A. Minneapolis, MN
Van Cleve, George Washington, DC
Van Cleve, Joseph C. Basye, VA
Van Cleve, Peter D. St. Louis, MO
Van Cleve, Robert B. Seattle, WA
Van Cleve, Ruth G. Alexandria, VA
Van Cleve, S. Bradley Portland, OR
Van Cleve, William M. St. Louis, MO
Van Clief, Cyndra H. Charlottesville, VA
Van Coevering, Richard J. Buffalo, NY
Van Conas, Kendall A. Camarillo, CA
Van Coney, Christine Denver, CO
Van Cooper, Thomas R. Worcester, VT
Van Cott, Bagley, Cornwall & McCarthy, A Professional Corporation Ogden, UT
Park City, UT
Salt Lake City, UT
Van Cott, Bryan C. Melville, NY
Van Cott, Charles Phoenix, AZ
Van Cott, John San Francisco, CA
Van Cott, Joyce N. Phoenix, AZ
Van Court, Frank Austin, TX
Van Court, Laurence P., P.C. Cheyenne, WY
Van Courtlandt, Valerie San Antonio, TX
Van Couyghen, August C. Providence, RI
Van Croft, Keith H. Washington, DC
Vancrum, Robert J. Overland Park, KS
Van Culin, Greg Colorado Springs, CO
Van Daele, Patrick J. Riverside, CA
VanDagens, Kathryn A. Okemos, MI
Vandagriff, K. Jill Dallas, TX
Vandagriff, R. Ted Sherwood, AR
Van Dalen, John M. Trenton, NJ
Vandall, Donna J. Portland, OR
Van Dall, Esther T. Charleston, WV
Vandall, Frank J. Atlanta, GA
Vandall, Matthew P. San Francisco, CA
Van Dall, William W. Tulsa, OK
Van Dalsem, Bruce E. Los Angeles, CA
Van Dalsem, Neil D. Tulsa, OK
van Dam, David J. San Francisco, CA
Van Dam, Gerald H. Chestnut Hill, MA
van Dam, Jacobus K.H. Englewood Cliffs, NJ
Van Dam, James F. Grand Rapids, MI
Van Dam, James N. Denver, CO
Van Dam, James S. Irvine, CA
Van Dam, John R. Santa Ana, CA
Van Dam, Linda J. Irvine, CA
van Dam, M. Nicole Los Angeles, CA
Van Dam, Marilynn A. Los Angeles, CA
van Dam, Marta B. Boston, MA
Van Dam, Philip Midland, MI
Van Dam, T. Thomas Hackensack, NJ
Van Dam, Tina Sutow Midland, MI
Van Dam & Van Dam, A Prof. Law Corp. Irvine, CA
Vandamm, Michael J. United States Postal Service, Law Department, GV
Van Damme, Monique J. Pittsburgh, PA
Van Davis, Lynda New Orleans, LA
Vandeberg, Elvin J. Tacoma, WA
Vandeberg, James L. Seattle, WA
Vandeberg Johnson & Gandara Seattle, WA
Tacoma, WA
Van De Bogart, James A. Whitewater, WI
van de Bunt, Dirk W. Studio City, CA
Van de Bunt, Susan Stager Calabasas, CA
Vande Bunte, Jack A. Jenison, MI
Vande Bunte, James E. Haslett, MI
Van De Car, Diana L. Hilo, HI
Van de Carr, Charles R., IV Chillicothe, OH
Van de Carr, Kara New Orleans, LA
Van De Carr, Lee J., Jr. Raleigh, NC
Vande Castle, William J. Green Bay, WI
Vandecaveye, Lisa Diehl Detroit, MI
Vandeford, Darryl R. Lawrenceville, GA
Vandeginste, David R. Kansas City, MO
Van De Graaf, J. J., Sr. St. Clair Shores, MI
van de Graaf, Paul J. Philadelphia, PA
Van De Graaff, James D. Chicago, IL
Vande Griend, Douglas K. Salem, OR
Vandegrift, Bart Wenatchee, WA
Vandegrift, Bruce D. Bay City, MI
Vandegrift, Charles Frank Peoria, AZ
van de Grift, Garrett H. Atlanta, GA
Van De Grift, Jon H. San Diego, CA
Vandegrift, Kristyn J. Horsham, PA
Vandegrift, Lucian B. Magalia, CA
Vandegrift, Susan J. Reading, PA
Van de Hey, David L. Santa Clara, CA
Van De Hey, Diana Longmont, CO
Van De Hey, Robert P. Lancaster, WI
Van Deilen, Harry J., (A Professional Corporation) Houston, TX
Van De Kamp, John K. Los Angeles, CA
Van de Kerckhove, Michael E. Des Plaines, IL
Vande Krol, Douglas R. Scottsdale, AZ
VanDelinder, Charles J. Miami, FL
Vandelist, Lisa P. Fridley, MN
Vandelist, Mark C. Fridley, MN
Van Dellen, Alan W. Minneapolis, MN
Van Dellen, H. Todd Milwaukee, WI
Van Dellen, Theodore Albion, MI
Vandello, James P. Denver, CO
Vandeman, George A. Thousand Oaks, CA
Vandemark, Allan Charles Ithaca, NY
Van Demark, Carl New York, NY
Van Demark, Dale C. Danbury, CT
Washington, DC
Vandemark, Dale M. Lima, OH
Van De Mark, Julie Ann Columbus, OH
Van Demark, Margaret Wolframsdorf Minneapolis, MN
VanDemark, Ruth E., Law Offices of Chicago, IL
Van De Mark, Scott Austin, TX
Vandemark, William C. Lima, OH
Vandemoer & Carlson, P.C. Julesburg, CO
Vandemoer, Corbin Cottonwood, AZ
Flagstaff, AZ
Van De Moere, Bryce San Diego, CA
Vandenack, Joe R. Yutan, NE
Vandenack, Mary E. Yutan, NE
Vandenack, Matthew J. Yutan, NE
Vandenassem, Christian W., Jr. Agency for International Development, GV

Vandenberg, Brian D. ....Chicago, IL
Vandenberg, Christine Toohig New York, NY
Vandenberg, David M. ....Lakeview, OR
Vandenberg, David N. ....Capitola, CA
Vandenberg, Dennis A. ....Stuart, FL
West Palm Beach, FL
Vandenberg, Edward L. ....Ann Arbor, MI
van den Berg, Egerton K. ....Orlando, FL
Vandenberg, Ellie M. .... Department of State, GV
Vandenberg & Feliu, LLP ....New York, NY
Vandenberg, George H. ....Omaha, NE
Vandenberg, James A. ....Lakeland, MN
Vandenberg, John C., III ....Newton, NJ
Vandenberg, John D. ....Portland, OR
van den Berg, Kent C. ....Minneapolis, MN
van den Berg, Kent T. ....Seattle, WA
Vanden Berg, Kristin M. ....Grand Rapids, MI
Vandenberg, Newell, Curtis, Nelson & Schuur, A Professional Corporation Long Beach, CA
Vandenberg, Raymond L. ....New York, NY
VandenBerg, Ronald A. ....Palo Alto, CA
Vanden Berg, Steven C. ....Mason City, IA
Vandenberg, Susan E. ....Minneapolis, MN
Vandenberg, Thomas ....Fort Collins, CO
Vandenberg, Thomas A. ....Albuquerque, NM
Vandenberg, Thomas E. ....Green Bay, WI
VandenBerg, Timothy D. Grand Rapids, MI
Vanden Berge, Douglas P. Grand Rapids, MI
Vandenberge, Keith J. ....Denver, CO
Van Denbergh, Frederick A., Jr. Philadelphia, PA
Vandenbergh, Michael P. ....Washington, DC
Van Denbergh, Ross ....Philadelphia, PA
Vandenbergh, William H. ....Kailua, HI
Van den Boom, Peter W. ....Bartow, FL
Vanden Bos & Chapman ....Portland, OR
Vanden Bos, Lawrence H. ....Torrance, CA
Vanden Bos, Robert J ....Portland, OR
Vandenbosch, Andrew J. ....Kokomo, IN
Vanden Bosch & Avery ....Comstock Park, MI
Van den Bosch, Carlo ....Los Angeles, CA
VandenBosch, Jennifer Lynn ....El Paso, TX
Van den Bosch, John, Jr. ....Jackson, TN
VandenBosch, Lynwood P. Grand Rapids, MI
Vanden Bosch, Thomas G. Comstock Park, MI
Vanden Bosch, Virginia C. ....Miamisburg, OH
van den Bossche, Anne-Rose ....Boston, MA
Vanden, Bossche, Harold E. St. Clair Shores, MI
Vandenbrink, Marina P. ....Detroit, MI
VanDenBrink, Thomas R. ....Kalamazoo, MI
Vandenbroucke, Robert C. ....Berkley, MI
Vandenburg, Thomas F. ....Los Angeles, CA
Vandenburgh, Adele L. ....Smithfield, RI
Vandenburgh, Beverly A. ....Barrington, IL
Vandenburgh, Charles F. ....Hartford, CT
Vandenburgh, Edward C. ....Dubuque, IA
VanDenburgh, Howard F. ....Fairfield, CT
Vandenburgh, J. Derek ....Minneapolis, MN
VanDenburgh, John W. ....Albany, NY
Vandenburgh, Lynn ....Stillwater, MN
Vandenburgh, Richard W. Westhampton, NY
Vanden Busch, Gary W. ....Salem, OR
VandenBussche, Marisela ....Palm Desert, CA
Van Den Bussche, Richard A. ....Urbana, IL
VandenBussche, Thomas G. Traverse City, MI
Van den Dool, Peter C. ....Chicago, IL
Van Dendooren, Keith P. ....Tallahassee, FL
Vanden Eykel, Ike ....Dallas, TX
Plano, TX
Vanden Heuval, Roy J. ....Yuba City, CA
Vanden Heuvel & Dineen ....Slinger, WI
Van Den Heuvel, Howard G. Grand Rapids, MI
Vanden Heuvel, Kathleen M. ....Berkeley, CA
Vanden Heuvel, Linda S. ....Slinger, WI
Van Den Heuvel, Roy J. ....Yuba City, CA
vanden Heuvel, William J. ....New York, NY
VandenHombergh, John ....Kalamazoo, MI
Vandenhouten, Peter G. ....Madison, WI
Vandenhouten, Warren ....Staten Island, NY
Vandenhouter, Scott J. ....Milwaukee, WI
Van Denover, Arlo ....Houston, TX
Vandenweghe, Roland M., Jr. New Orleans, LA
Van De Poel, John F. ....Martinez, CA
Van De Poel, John F., Jr. Walnut Creek, CA
Van De Pol, Karen Lyons ....Las Vegas, NV
Van Den Aa, Douglas J. ....Grand Rapids, MI
Van Den Aa, John M. ....South Holland, IL
Van Den Aa, Lanting & Paarlberg, Ltd. South Holland, IL
Vander Arend, J. Eric ....Chicago, IL
Vander Ark, Steven J. ....Grand Rapids, MI
Van Den Aue, Kathleen M. ....Southport, CT
VanDerbeck, Colette A ....Saugerties, NY
VanDerbeck, James Scott ....LaGrange, IN
Van Den Beken, David P. ....Manchester, NH
Van der Bellen, Alexander M.R. Washington, DC
Vanderberg, Thomas S. ....Amityville, NY
Vanderberry, James G. ....Columbia, SC
Vanderbilt, Arthur T., II ....Roseland, NJ
Vanderbilt, Christine L. Santa Barbara, CA
Vanderbilt, Jim A. ....Oskaloosa, KS
Vanderbilt, Larry L. ....Columbia, SC
Vanderbilt, Tana Goodwin ....Columbia, SC
Vanderbilt, Tanya B. ....Washington, DC
Vanderbilt, Virginia Ruth ....Salem, OR
Vanderbilt-Meier, Kimberly ....Chicago, IL
Vanderbloemen, Bruce W. ....Lenoir, NC
Vanderbloemen, John A. Steamboat Springs, CO
Vander Broek, Kathryn S. ....Chicago, IL
VanderBroek, Mark S. ....Atlanta, GA
Vanderbrug, Sam G. ....Temecula, CA
Vanderburg, Ann E. ....Austin, TX
Vanderburg, Keith A. ....Cleveland, OH
Vanderburg, Lee ....Austin, TX
Vanderburg, Michael R. ....Broken Arrow, OK
Vander Byl, Wayne A. ....Williamson, NY
Vander Clute, Norman R. Washington, DC
Vandercook, Marcia ....Wauwatosa, WI
Vandercook, Nancy ....Dallas, TX
VanDercreek, William ....Tallahassee, FL
Vanderdonck, Holly J. ....Torrance, CA
Van Derdys, Fernando ....San Juan, PR
Van Deren, Kurt J ....Albuquerque, NM
Van Deren, Marywave ....Tacoma, WA
Vanderet, Robert C. ....Los Angeles, CA
Vanderford, Heather Anne ....Lexington, KY
Vanderford, Herbert T. ....Sagle, ID
Vanderford, Maile P. ....Los Angeles, CA
Vanderford, Michael P. ....Little Rock, AR
Vanderford, R. Scott ....Detroit, MI
Vanderford, Thomas H., IV Charleston, WV
Vanderford, Thomas N., Jr. Fountain Valley, CA
Vanderford, Ty S. ....Los Angeles, CA
VanDerGinst, Dennis A. ....Rock Island, IL
Van Den Graaf, Maarten J.C. New York, NY
Vandergriff, David B. ....Fort Smith, AR
Vandergriff, Mary Ann W. ....Memphis, TN
Vandergriff, Victor T. ....Arlington, TX
Vandergrift, Craig L. ....Pittsburgh, PA
VanderHaagen, David ....Lansing, MI
Vander Haar, David M. ....Minneapolis, MN
Vander Hart, Allan W. ....Independence, IA
VanderHeide, Jeanne ....Birmingham, MI
VanderHeide, Jennifer Carole ....Hoopa, CA
Van Den Heide, Martin, III ....Sussex, NJ
Vander Heide, Timothy J. ....Custer, SD
van der Heiden, Kimberly ....Lexington, KY
Vanderheiden, Marie A. ....Arvada, CO
Vanderheider, J. R. ....Anahuac, TX
Vanderheider, Nancy R. ....Plymouth, MN
Vanderheyden, David W. ....Rochester, MN
Vanderheyden & Ruffalo, P.A. Rochester, MN
Van der Hiel & Mansfield ....Mansfield, PA
Van der Hiel, Rudolph J. ....Mansfield, PA
Vanderhoef, C. Scott ....New City, NY
Vanderhoef, Jerry M. ....Florence, AL
Van Derhoef, Kenneth D. ....Seattle, WA
Vanderhoef, Philip J. ....Seattle, WA
VanDerhoef, Stephen P. ....Seattle, WA
Vanderhoef, William D. ....Troy, MI
Vander Hoff, Kenneth J., Jr. ....Cumming, GA
Van Derhoff, Richard ....Escondido, CA
Van Derhoff, Robert ....Vista, CA
Vanderhoof, Andrew M. ....Vienna, VA
Vanderhoof, Lisa A. ....Denver, CO
Vanderhoof, Martha Gower Bethesda, MD
Vanderhoof, Ryan J. ....Medford, OR
Vander Horst, Allston ....Centerville, TN
Vanderhorst, Joseph A. ....Los Angeles, CA
Van Den Horst, Laurence ....Chicago, IL
Vanderhorst, Michael A. ....Dublin, OH
Vanderhorst, Robert E. ....Porterville, CA
Van Der Hout & Brigagliano
Palo Alto, CA
San Francisco, CA
Van Den Hout, Marc ....San Francisco, CA
VanderHulst, John Charles ....Brea, CA
Vanderhye, Robert A. ....Arlington, VA
Van Den Jagt, Carolyn Federal Energy Regulatory Commission, Office of the General Counsel, GV
Vander Jagt, Guy ....Washington, DC
Vanderkam, Hank ....Houston, TX
Vanderkam & Sanders ....Houston, TX
Van Den Kamp, Roy W. ....Rock Island, IL
Van Den Karr, Philip A. ....Canandaigua, NY
Van DerKarr, Scott D. ....Columbus, OH
VanderKelen, James B. ....Midland, MI
VanderKloot, William R. Bloomfield Hills, MI
Vander Kolk, Kevin J. ....Jacksonville, FL
Vander Kooi, Benjamin, Jr. ....Luverne, MN
Vanderkooi, Douglas J. ....Pompton Plains, NJ
Vander Kooi, Lois K. ....Louisville, CO
Vanderlaan, Aaron A. ....Cincinnati, OH
VanderLaan, Ann L. ....Bloomfield Hills, MI
VanderLaan & Associates ....Grand Rapids, MI
Vanderlaan, Christopher A. Los Angeles, CA
Vanderlaan, Karen J. ....Seattle, WA
Vanderlaan, Kathryn H. ....Los Angeles, CA
Vanderlaan, Marcus ....Carmichael, CA
VanDerLaan, Maria A. ....New Haven, CT
Vander Laan, Mark A. ....Cincinnati, OH
van der Laan, Mark David Grand Rapids, MI
VanderLaan, Robert D. ....Grand Rapids, MI
Vander Lans, John A. ....Long Beach, CA
Vander Lans, Leo J. ....Long Beach, CA
Vanderlee, Johanna ....Everett, WA
Vander Leest, Kenneth F. ....Peoria, IL
VanderLeest, Kirk A. ....Chicago, IL
van der Leeuw, P. Graham Minneapolis, MN
Vanderlin, Richard A. ....Williamsport, PA
Vanderlin & Zurich, P.C. ....Williamsport, PA
Vander Linde, Joan S. Prospect Heights, IL
Van der Linde, Kristen M. Jacksonville, FL
Vander Linden, Charles E. Fitchburg, MA
Vander Linden, James G. ....Minneapolis, MN
van der Linden, Jeannine M. ....Atlanta, GA
Vander Linden, Lance J. ....Dallas, TX
Vander Linden, Leon J. ....Webster, SD
Vanderlip, Nancy L. ....Cleveland, OH
Vander Lippe, John M. ....Overland Park, KS
Vanderloo, Peter L. ....McLean, VA
Vander Loop, Robert J. ....Oshkosh, WI
Vander Lugt, Robert D. ....Washington, DC
Van Den Maaten, Andrew F. ....Decorah, IA
Vander Maazen, Lisa Beth ....Appleton, WI
Vander Male, Bellamy, Gilchrist, Vande Vusse & Cafferty ....Detroit, MI
Vanderman, Kris A. ....Charleroi, PA
McMurray, PA
Vanderman Law Associates ....Charleroi, PA
McMurray, PA
Vandermark, Edward J. ....Houston, TX
VanderMay Law Firm The ....Salem, OR
VanderMay, Maureen Callahan ....Salem, OR
VanderMay, Monty K. ....Salem, OR
VanderMeer, Abram W., Jr. Virginia Beach, VA
Vander Meer, Michael Paul Department Of Veterans Affairs, Board of Veterans Appeals, GV
VanderMeer, Wanda ....Waterford, MI
Van Der Mei Law Firm, The Sacramento, CA
Van Den Mei, William G. ....Sacramento, CA
Van Den Meid, Theodore J. House of Representatives, Congressional Assistants, GV
van der Merwe, Anton J. Minneapolis, MN
Vandermeulen, Goldman and Allen Augusta, ME
Vandermeulen, Kim M. ....Augusta, ME
van der Meulen, Pamela ....New York, NY
VanDerMolen, Harold H. ....Wheaton, IL
Vander Molen, Katherynne N. Grand Rapids, MI
Vander Molen & Malin ....Orange, CA
Van Den Molen, Mark ....Merrillville, IN
VanderMolen, Mark R. ....Grand Rapids, MI
Vander Molen, Milton J. ....Orange, CA
Vander Molen, Thomas D. Minneapolis, MN
Van Dermyden, Sue Ann ....Sacramento, CA
Vandernat, Ray F. ....Los Angeles, CA
Vander Neut, John ....Staten Island, NY
Vander Noor, Robert B. ....Bakersfield, CA
Vanderplas, James M. Indian Rocks Beach, FL
Vander Ploeg, Charles L. ....Pella, IA
Vander Ploeg, Claude L. Grand Rapids, MI
Vander Ploeg, David ....St. Joseph, MI
Vander Ploeg, Edwin J., Jr. ....Holland, MI
VanderPloeg, Frank P. ....Chicago, IL
VanderPloeg, Jill G. ....Denver, CO
Vander Ploeg, Jon D. ....Grand Rapids, MI
Vander Ploeg, Sally J. ....Ada, MI
Vanderploeg, W. Stevens Grand Rapids, MI
Vanderpol, Dolph J. ....Boston, MA
Van Den Pol, William, Jr. ....Martinsville, IN
Vanderpool, Daniel J. ....Wabash, IN
Vanderpool, David ....Melville, NY
Vanderpool, Douglas Brent ....Cypress, CA
Vanderpool, Eric S. ....San Francisco, CA
Vanderpool, Frostick & Nishanian, P.C. Manassas, VA
Vanderpool, Jon Y. ....San Diego, CA
Vanderpool, Michael R. ....Manassas, VA
Vanderpool, Phil N. ....Pampa, TX
Vanderpool, Terry ....Houston, TX
Vanderpool, Travis E. ....Dallas, TX
Vanderpool, William S., III ....Des Moines, IA
Vanderpool-Ziegler, Janna ....Florence, AZ
Vanderpuye, Kwarma ....New York, NY
Van der Reis, Melinda H. San Francisco, CA
VanderRoest, James E. ....Kalamazoo, MI
Vander Schaaf, Lyle B. ....Washington, DC
VanderSchaaff, Bertis J., IV ....Dayton, OH
Vanderschaff, Bertis J. ....Dayton, OH
van der Schee, Jan-Marc Menlo Park, CA
VanderSchoor, Vic L. ....Pasco, WA
Van Den Schyff, Rhodah ....Rolling Hills, CA
Van Derslice, Andrew L. ....New York, NY
Vanderslice, John ....San Diego, CA
Vanderslice, John Carl ....Lincoln, NE
Vanderslice, Lane W. ....Chicago, IL
Vandersloot, James E., (A Professional Corporation) ....San Pablo, CA
Vander Sluis, William R. Grand Rapids, MI
van der Smissen, Betty ....East Lansing, MI
Van Den Snick, J. Brick ....Geneva, IL
Vandersnick, Larry S. ....Cambridge, IL
Vanderstar, John ....Washington, DC
Vanderstar, Thankful Townsend Department of Justice, Civil Division, GV
van der Sterre, Kees ....Corning, NY
Vander Stoep, J. A., Jr. ....Chehalis, WA
Vander Stoep, James A. ....Chehalis, WA
Vander Stoep, Remund, Kelly & Blinks Chehalis, WA
Vandersyde, Arthur ....El Cajon, CA
Vandertoll, John J. ....Fort Smith, AR
van der Toorren, Elizabeth San Francisco, CA
Van Den Tuin, John T. ....New York, NY
van der Vaart, Sandra D. ....Raleigh, NC
Vandervalk, Margaret L. ....Dallas, TX
Vanderveen, Jeffrey T. ....Laguna Hills, CA
VanderVeen, Joel W. ....Omaha, NE
VanderVeen, John R. ....Traverse City, MI
Vander Veen, Joseph P. Grand Rapids, MI
Vander Veen, Richard F. ....Grand Rapids, MI
Vander Veen, Richard F., III Grand Rapids, MI
Vander Veen, Ronald J. ....Holland, MI
Vander Veer, C. Grant ....Holland, MI
Van der Veer, Hugh G. ....Pittsburgh, PA
Vandervelde, Jane A. ....Holland, MI
Vander Velde, Jay W. ....Emporia, KS
Vander Velde, Peter P. ....Chicago, IL
Van Den Velde, Robert J. ....Montgomery, AL
Vandervelden, Steven T. ....White Plains, NY
Van Derven, Bruce E. ....Stafford, VA
VanderVennet, Charles T. ....Buffalo Grove, IL
Vander Vennet & Motto, P.C. ....Davenport, IA
Vanderver, Timothy A., III ....Atlanta, GA
Vanderver, Timothy A., Jr. Washington, DC
Vandervest, Brian T. ....Milwaukee, WI
Vandervoort, Adam C. ....Los Angeles, CA
Vandervoort, Christ & Fisher, P.C.
Battle Creek, MI
Charlotte, MI
Coldwater, MI
Hastings, MI
Kalamazoo, MI
Marshall, MI
Vandervoort, Craig M. ....Lancaster, OH
Vandervoort, Georgia Ann ....Fort Worth, TX
Vandervoort, Jeffrey K. ....Toledo, OH
Van Dervoort, John W. ....Columbus, OH
Vandervoort, Peter ....Hackensack, NJ
Vandervoort, Peter M. ....Lancaster, OH
van der Voort, Rachel E. ....Atlanta, GA
Vandervoort, Terre L. ....Lancaster, OH
van der Voort, Thomas L. United States Senate, Senatorial Assistants, GV
Vander Voort, William E. ....Houston, TX
Van Dervort, Daina B. ....Cleveland, OH
Van Dervort, Deborah Y. ....Charleston, WV
Vandervort, Hu S. ....Morgantown, WV
Vander Vort, John W. ....San Francisco, CA
Vander Vort, Paul A. ....Minneapolis, MN
Vandervort, R. Clarke ....Charleston, WV
Van Den Waag, Robert F. Garden City, NY
VanderWaal, Shane J. ....Wausau, WI
Vander Waerdt, Lois ....St. Louis, MO
Vander Wal, Larry D. ....Grand Rapids, MI
Vanderwalde, Paul Douglas ....Palo Alto, CA
Vanderwall, Dale W. ....Virginia Beach, VA
Vander Wall, David C. ....Modesto, CA
Van Den Wall, John ....Newark, NJ
Van Den Wall, Robert J. ....Miami, FL
Tampa, FL
Vanderwarker, Peter J. Overland Park, KS
Vanderwater, Jodi M. ....Chicago, IL
VanDerway, Richard E. ....Barrington, IL
VanderWeele, Julia M. ....Kansas City, MO
VanderWeele, Mary Kay ....Portland, OR
Van Den Weele, Philip S. ....Portland, OR
VanderWeele, Sally A. ....Boston, MA
Van Den Weide, Mark E. Board of Governors Of The Federal Reserve System, Office of the General Counsel, GV
Vander Weide, Vernon J. Minneapolis, MN
Vander Weit, John, Jr. ....Homewood, IL
Vander Wel, Jacobson & Bishop, PLLC Bellevue, WA
Vander Wel, W. Theodore ....Bellevue, WA
VanderWerf, Gretchen A. ....Denver, CO
VanderWerf, Gretchen, P.C. ....Denver, CO
Vander Werff, Godfrey ....Grand Rapids, MI
Van Den Werff, Jan Peter ....West Hartford, CT
Vanderwerff, Karen J. ....Grand Rapids, MI
Vander Werff Law Office, P.C. Grand Rapids, MI
Vander Werff, Sara E. ....Grand Rapids, MI
VanDerwerken, Paul W. ....Las Vegas, NV
Vander Wert, Chad D. ....Nashville, TN
Vander Weyden, Keith A. Grand Rapids, MI
Vanderwicken, Sarah ....Chicago, IL
Vanderwilt, Lester E. ....Irvine, CA
Vanderwist, James C. ....Cleveland, OH
Vanderwist, Kathryn Kariotis Bedford Heights, OH
Vanderwold, Claude W. ....Sacramento, CA
Vanderwood, Derek J. ....Vancouver, WA
Vander Woude, John S. ....Baltimore, MD
VanDer Woude, Paul S. ....Chicago, IL
Vander Woude, Richard J. ....Waco, TX
Vander Woude, Vikki L. ....Irvine, CA
Vander Wulp, Sharon S. ....Venice, FL
Vanderzanden, Danielle Y. ....Boston, MA
Vanderzanden, Edwinna C. Hampton, NH
Vanderzanden, Julie C. ....Seattle, WA
Vanderzee, Elizabeth Lee ....Loveland, CO
van der Zee, Mary Beth ....Jacksonville, FL
Vanderziel, Kathleen M. ....Los Angeles, CA

Vanderzyl, Kari A. ... Oregon, IL
Vande Sande, George ... Washington, DC
Vande Sande, Thomas J. ... Potomac, MD
Vande Stouwe, Richard J. Williston Park, NY
Van de Streek, Nevin ... Minot, ND
Van Detta, Jeffrey A. ... Atlanta, GA
Van Detta, Kathleen J. ... Atlanta, GA
Vandetty, Michael A. ... Miami, FL
Van Deuren, Richard A. ... Milwaukee, WI
Van Deusen, Christian R. ... Santa Ana, CA
VanDeusen, Darrell R. ... Baltimore, MD
Van Deusen, Edwin H. ... Columbus, OH
Van Deusen, Katherine O'Dea ... Scranton, PA
Van Deusen, Lloyd A. ... Waukegan, IL
Van Deusen, Lois M. ... Newark, NJ
VanDeusen, Margaret H. ... Boston, MA
Van Deusen, Roger W. ... Cleveland, OH
Van Deusen, Youmans and Walmsley, P.C. Santa Ana, CA
Van Devander, Charles W. ... Denver, CO
Van De Vate, Peter D. ... Knoxville, TN
Vandeveer, Frederick R. ... La Jolla, CA
San Diego, CA
Vandeveer Garzia ... Lansing, MI
Birmingham, MI
Detroit, MI
Vandeveer, Jennifer Steen ... Memphis, TN
Van de Veer, Philip J. ... Newport, WA
VanDeveer, Wayne ... Memphis, TN
Vandeveld, Amy B. ... San Diego, CA
Vandeveld, Andrew A. ... San Francisco, CA
Van de Veld, Curtis C. ... Hagåtña, GU
Vandeveld, Darrel J. ... Erie, PA
Vandeveld, Dirk J. ... Chicago, IL
Vandeveld, Thomas J., III ... San Diego, CA
Vandevelde, John D. ... Los Angeles, CA
Van de Ven, Martha A. ... Long Lake, MN
Vandevender, Darwin L. ... Hudson, MI
Vandevender, Dwayne C Webster Springs, WV
Vandevender, Janet K. ... Madison, WI
Van Deventer, Andrea W. ... Little Rock, AR
VanDeventer, Ann M. ... Bridgeport, CT
Vandeventer Black LLP ... Kitty Hawk, NC
Norfolk, VA
VanDeventer, James D. ... Tyler, TX
Van Deventer, John Meade ... New York, NY
Van Deventer, Kenneth M. Morristown, NJ
Van Deventer, Peter B., Jr. ... Newark, NJ
VanDeventer, Susan P. ... Rumson, NJ
Van Deventer, Theodore H., Jr. Winter Garden, FL
Vandever, Gary ... Lebanon, TN
Vandever, James D. ... Los Angeles, CA
Vandever, Kay ... Rogers, AR
Vandever, Ralph A. ... Hillsboro, IL
Vandever, Wm. Dirk ... Kansas City, MO
Vandevert, Paulsen K. ... New York, NY
Van de Voorde, Mark H. ... Chicago, IL
Van De Voorde, Rene G. ... Sebastian, FL
Vandevoort, John R. ... Dallas, TX
Vande Vrede, Larry D. ... Clinton, MI
Vande Vrede & Lavigne, P.C. ... Clinton, MI
Vande Vusse, Bruce A. ... Detroit, MI
Van de Vuurst, Robert D. Johnson City, TN
Van de Walle, Charles R. ... Jericho, NY
Vande Walle, Gerald W. ... Bismarck, ND
Vande Walle, John M. ... Chicago, IL
Van de Walle, Sandra T. ... New York, NY
Van de Water, David A. ... Sheboygan, WI
Van de Water, Douglas K. ... Sheboygan, WI
Van De Water, Eric Noyes ... Atlanta, GA
Van de Water, Eric R. ... Santa Barbara, CA
Vandewater, Glenn T. Altamonte Springs, FL
Van De Water, Sandra Cho ... Atlanta, GA
Van DeWater & Van DeWater Pawling, NY
Poughkeepsie, NY
VanDeWeert, John K. ... Chicago, IL
Van de Weghe, Bart G. ... White Plains, NY
Van De Weghe, G. William (Bill), Jr.
Los Angeles, CA
San Diego, CA
Santa Ana, CA
Vandeweghe, Gary S. ... San Jose, CA
Vande Werken, Jerry ... Columbus, OH
Vandewerken, Walter ... Chicago, IL
Vandewettering, Mari E. ... Portland, OR
VandeWiele, Mark A. ... East Moline, IL
Van Dewsen, Mark C. ... Richmond, VA
Vande Wydeven, Mathew J. Long Beach, CA
VandeWyngearde, James D. ... Detroit, MI
Vande Zande, Daniel L. ... Waupun, WI
Van Dien, Pieter G. ... Naples, FL
Van Dillen & Flood, P.C. ... St. Louis, MO
Van Dillen, James L. ... St. Louis, MO
VanDine, Howard A., III ... Columbia, SC
Van Dingenen, Donald ... Winter Park, FL
Van Dis, Thomas H. ... Kalamazoo, MI
Vandiver & Bowman ... Artesia, NM
Vandiver, David R. ... Artesia, NM
Vandiver, David S., III ... Atlanta, GA
Vandiver, Donald G. ... Lubbock, TX
Vandiver, Frank A. ... Houston, TX
Vandiver, Karen A. ... Albuquerque, NM
Vandiver, Lisa R. ... Bowling Green, KY
Vandiver, S. Ernest, III ... Lavonia, GA
Vandiver, S. Ernest, Jr. ... Lavonia, GA
Vandiver, Susan W. ... Houston, TX
Vandiver, Thomas K. ... St. Louis, MO
Vandiver and Vandiver ... Carnesville, GA
Lavonia, GA
Vandivere, Jamie S. ... Amarillo, TX

Vandivier, Blair R. ... Indianapolis, IN
Vandivier, J. Suzette ... Indianapolis, IN
Vandivier, John C., Jr. ... Danville, IN
Vandivier, Richard W. ... Indianapolis, IN
Vandivier, Thomas M. ... Austin, TX
Vandivort, William Clayton ... Sikeston, MO
Vandlik, Mark J. ... Park Ridge, IL
Vandling, William H. ... Vista, CA
Van Dolsen, Stephen ... New York, NY
Van Dolsen, Randall D. ... Chattanooga, TN
Van Domelen, Gary J. ... Pittsburgh, PA
Van Domelen, Harold E. ... Indianapolis, IN
Van Dongen, Troy M. ... San Francisco, CA
Van Donsel, Richard C. ... Cortland, NY
Van Doorn, Paul K. ... Columbus, OH
Vandor, Marjorie L. ... Juneau, AK
Van Dora, Tash J. ... Atlanta, GA
Van Doren, A. Reading, Jr. New York, NY
Van Doren, Andrew J. ... Coldwater, MI
Van Doren, Charles N. ... Washington, DC
VanDoren, E. Barclay ... Department of Energy, Office of Hearings and Appeals, GV
Van Doren, Gregory M. ... Manassas, VA
Van Doren, Jeffrey A. ... Pittsburgh, PA
Van Doren, John W. ... Tallahassee, FL
Van Doren, Jon F. Federal Labor Relations Authority, Authority Member Staff, GV
Van Doren, Kieth ... Englewood, CO
Van Doren, Mark W. ... Knoxville, TN
Van Doren, Max E. ... Arcadia, CA
Van Doren, Noreen J. ... Albany, NY
van Doren, Rebecca Lee ... Phoenix, AZ
Van Doren, William O. ... Santa Maria, CA
Van Dorf, Steven, (Ltd.) ... Chicago, IL
VanDorn, Carl E. ... Kokomo, IN
Van Dorn & Cullenberg ... Orford, NH
Van Dorn, Daniel K. ... Millburn, NJ
Van Dorn, Edward M., Jr. ... Orford, NH
VanDorn, Erick E. ... Belleville, IL
Van Dorn, Frederic E. ... Fairfield, CA
Van Dorn, Robert W. ... Walla Walla, WA
Van Dorn, Walter G. ... Boston, MA
Van Dorn, Walter G., Jr. ... New York, NY
Van Dorn, Wendy S. ... Garden City, NY
Vandoros, Alexandra ... New York, NY
Van Dort, Jan ... Juneau, AK
Van Dover, James R. ... Marianna, AR
Vandover, Samuel T. ... St. Louis, MO
Vandow, Marjorie A. ... New York, NY
Van Dox, Carly R. ... Phoenix, AZ
VanDreumel, Treasure Lynn ... Phoenix, AZ
VanDreumel, Treasure, PLC, Law Office of Phoenix, AZ
Van Driel, Eugene P. ... Davenport, IA
Van Driesen, Jennifer ... Washington, DC
Vandroff, Arthur D. ... Sarasota, FL
Van Dueck, Ralph A. ... Los Angeles, CA
Van Duerm, James ... Chicago, IL
Van Duizend, Richard ... Alexandria, VA
Van Dusen, Amanda ... Detroit, MI
Van Dusen, Bruce D. ... New York, NY
Van Dusen, Donald M. ... Boca Raton, FL
Van Dusen, Donald M., Law Offices of Boca Raton, FL
Van Dusen, Francis L., Jr., P.C. Seattle, WA
Van Dusen, John G. ... Marblehead, MA
Van Dusen, John P. Bloomfield Township, MI
Van Dusen, Lewis H., Jr. Philadelphia, PA
Van Dusen, Richard A. ... New York, NY
Van Dusen, Richard W. ... El Monte, CA
Van Dusen, Susan W. ... Miami, FL
vanDusen, Theron McK. ... Raleigh, NC
Research Triangle Park, NC
Van Dusen, Thomas ... Troy, MI
Van Dusen, Timothy R. ... Troy, MI
Van Dusen, Virgil R. ... Tulsa, OK
Van Dusen, William B. ... San Diego, CA
Van Duser, John S. ... New York, NY
Van Duser, Kevin R. ... Syracuse, NY
VanDuyn, Amy L. ... Des Moines, IA
Van Duyn, Pamela C. ... Baker City, OR
Van Duyn, Pamela C., P.C. ... Baker City, OR
Van Duyne, Barbara Geddis ... Dallas, TX
Van Duyne, Richard B. ... Morris Plains, NJ
Van Duys, John K. ... Columbia, SC
Van Duzer, Gershon, Jordan, Petersen & Loeffler, A Professional Corporation Chicago, IL
Van Duzer, Jane ... Chicago, IL
Van Duzer, Jeffrey B. ... Seattle, WA
Van Duzer, John B. ... Chicago, IL
Van Duzer, John B., Jr. ... Chicago, IL
Van Duzer, Nathan H. ... Boston, MA
Van Duzer, Richard A. ... St. Helena, CA
San Francisco, CA
Van Duzer, William H. ... Lake Placid, FL
Van Dyck, Fiona J. ... Mount Laurel, NJ
Philadelphia, PA
Van Dyck, Gregory L. ... Trenton, NJ
Van Dyck, John M. ... Houston, TX
Van Dyck, Louise ... Simsbury, CT
Van Dyck, Mary Elizabeth ... Wellesley, MA
Van Dyck, Richard G. ... Chickasha, OK
Van Dyck, Sharon L. ... Minneapolis, MN
Van Dyck, Timothy P. ... Boston, MA
Van Dyk, Bruce W. ... Albany, NY
Van Dyk, Douglas V. ... Portland, OR
Van Dyk, Gloria F. ... Sherman Oaks, CA
Van Dyk, Hendrik W. ... New Richmond, WI
Van Dyk, Suzanne B. ... Minneapolis, MN
Van Dyke, Barry Alan ... Chicago, IL
Van Dyke, C. Todd ... Atlanta, GA
Van Dyke, Charlotte A. ... Seattle, WA

Van Dyke, Daniel (IBA) ... **Grand Rapids, MI**
Van Dyke, Daniel J. ... Woodburn, OR
VanDyke, David A. ... Jefferson City, MO
Van Dyke, David A. ... Bountiful, UT
Van Dyke, David C. ... Chicago, IL
Van Dyke, David J. ... Lewiston, ME
Van Dyke, David S. ... Stockton, CA
Van Dyke, Gardner, Linn & Burkhart, LLP Grand Rapids, MI
van Dyke, Henry ... New Canaan, CT
Van Dyke, Henry J. ... Schenectady, NY
Van Dyke, James C. ... Stockton, CA
Van Dyke, James C. ... Bingham Farms, MI
Van Dyke, James R. ... Carroll, IA
Van Dyke, Jeffrey R. ... Wheaton, IL
Van Dyke, Jeffrey R., P.C. ... Wheaton, IL
Van Dyke, Joe ... Irving, TX
Van Dyke, Jon M. ... Honolulu, HI
Van Dyke, Judith Croft ... Opelika, AL
Van Dyke, Karen W. ... Lewiston, ME
Van Dyke, Keith F. ... Irvine, CA
Van Dyke, Kevin D. ... Des Moines, IA
Van Dyke, Lawrence H. Roslyn Heights, NY
Van Dyke, Lindell H. ... Menlo Park, CA
VanDyke, Lindy W. ... Ogden, UT
Van Dyke, Lora L. ... Sioux Falls, SD
Van Dyke, M. Joanne ... Syracuse, NY
Van Dyke, Michael J. ... Honolulu, HI
Van Dyke, Michelle L. ... San Diego, CA
Van Dyke, Patricia A. ... Los Angeles, CA
Van Dyke, Paul C. ... Radnor, PA
Van Dyke, Paul H. ... Salt Lake City, UT
Van Dyke, Peter J. ... South Bend, IN
Van Dyke, Peter J. ... Toms River, NJ
Van Dyke, Peter T. ... Oklahoma City, OK
Van Dyke, Raymond ... Dallas, TX
Van Dyke, Richard S. ... Vista, CA
Van Dyke, Stephen A. ... Farmington, UT
Van Dyke, Susan J. ... Boone, NC
Van Dyke, Thomas H. ... Stockton, CA
Van Dyke, Thomas W. Overland Park, KS
Van Dyke & Werden, P.C. ... Carroll, IA
Van Dyken, Deborah A. ... Hillsborough, NC
VanDyne, Charles ... Ada, OH
Van Dyne, Janice K. ... Columbus, OH
Van Dyne, Mark A. ... Lima, OH
Van Dzura, Terence G. ... Edison, NJ
Vane, Jennifer A. ... Los Angeles, CA
Vane, Mark ... Austin, TX
Vane, Patrick H. ... Seattle, WA
Vane, Terence G., Jr. ... Jacksonville, FL
Van Eaton, Joseph ... Washington, DC
Van Eaton, Leonard E. ... Memphis, TN
Van Eaton, Robert H. ... Green Valley, AZ
Vanecek, Charles W. ... Tampa, FL
Vanecek, Joseph J. ... Wayne, NJ
Van Eck, Henry ... Harrisburg, PA
Van Eck, William A. ... Belding, MI
Van Eckhardt, Michael R.C. ... Seattle, WA
Vanecko, Mari-Rose McManus ... Chicago, IL
Vanecko, Mark G. ... Chicago, IL
Vanecko, Robert G. ... Chicago, IL
Van Eenenaam, John P. Grand Haven, MI
Van Eepoel, August ... Tampa, FL
Van Egeren, James L. ... Green Bay, WI
Vanek, Christine M. ... Hackensack, NJ
Vanek, James F. ... Chicago, IL
Vanek, John E. ... Yakima, WA
Vanek, Joseph M. ... Chicago, IL
Vanek, Martin J. ... Nashville, TN
Vanek, Stephen S. ... Cleveland, OH
Vanek, Traci Meakem ... Washington, DC
Vanek, Yaakov G. ... Los Angeles, CA
Vanek-Bigelow, Helen ... Treasury Department, Internal Revenue Service, GV
Van Ekeren, Jacklyn K. ... Des Moines, IA
Van Elgort, Howard M. ... Soquel, CA
Vanelli, William A. ... Bronx, NY
Van Eman, James J., III Mount Clemens, MI
Van Eman, Timothy L. ... Columbus, OH
VanEmbden, Julie ... Philadelphia, PA
Van Embden, Nathan ... Millville, NJ
Van Embden, Paul ... Vineland, NJ
Van Embden, Phillip S., (P.C.) ... Millville, NJ
Van Emburgh, Joanne ... Torrance, CA
Van Emden, Busch & Van Emden Chicago, IL
Van Emden, Geo. J. ... Chicago, IL
VanEmmerik, Allen ... Woodbine, MD
Van Engelhoven, David A. ... Phoenix, AZ
Van Engen, Brian K. ... Rock Valley, IA
Van Engen, Kurt E. ... Washington, DC
VanEnk-Giardiello, Sandra K. Morristown, NJ
van Enter, Eric C. ... Miami, FL
Van Epps, Dale L. ... Syracuse, NY
Van Epps, Diane L. ... New York, NY
Van Epps, George D. ... Muskegon, MI
Van Epps, James B. ... Maplewood, NJ
Van Epps, Mark J. ... Owosso, MI
Van Epps, Matthew J. ... Owosso, MI
Van Epps, Michael J. ... Muskegon, MI
Van Epps, Robert F. ... Elmhurst, IL
Oak Brook, IL
Van Epps, Robert F., Ltd., P.C. ... Elmhurst, IL
Van Epps, Ruth E., (Mrs.) ... Weyauwega, WI
Van Epps & Van Epps ... Owosso, MI
Van Epps and Werth ... Weyauwega, WI
Vaneria, John Sebastian ... New York, NY
Vaneria & Sesti, LLP ... New York, NY
Vanerian, Vahan C. ... Livonia, MI
Van Erp, Michael L. ... Okemos, MI
Van Ert, Wayne R. ... Milwaukee, WI
Van Es, Amy D. ... Cedar Rapids, IA

van Es, J. Pieter ... Chicago, IL
Vanesian, Kathleen S. ... Phoenix, AZ
Vaneska, Robert J. ... Milwaukee, WI
Van Ess, Barbara J. ... Seattle, WA
Van Ess, David A. ... Milwaukee, WI
Vanesse, Michel ... Chicago, IL
Van Essen, Douglas W. Grand Rapids, MI
VanEssendelft, Kimberly Rouse ... Norfolk, VA
Vanetik, Yuri ... Pittsburgh, PA
Vanett, Todd C. ... Philadelphia, PA
Van Etten, Alan ... Honolulu, HI
Van Etten, Arnold J. ... Dubuque, IA
Van Etten, C. Angela ... Rochester, NY
Van Etten, David B. ... Los Angeles, CA
Van Etten, Jeffrey K. ... Mineola, NY
New York, NY
Smithtown, NY
Van Etten, Suzumoto & Haag, LLP Los Angeles, CA
Vanetti, Henry R. ... Barre, VT
Van Euwen, Peter W., III ... Cleveland, OH
Van Evera, Richard K. ... Rockford, IL
Van Every, Peter J. ... Seabrook Island, SC
Van Every, Robert W. ... Falconer, NY
van Eyl, Diderico ... Pittsburgh, PA
VanEysden, Inga ... New York, NY
Van Fleet, Allan ... Houston, TX
Van Fleet, G. Nelson ... Wichita, KS
Van Fleet, Herbert ... Joplin, MO
Van Fleet, Jeffrey M. ... Portland, ME
VanFleet, Joseph B. ... Peoria, IL
VanFleet, Joseph B., L.L.C., Law Office of Peoria, IL
Van Fleet, Laurie ... Houston, TX
Van Fleet, Lee A. ... Dallas, TX
Van Fleet, Lisa A. ... St. Louis, MO
Van Fleet, Vicki F. ... San Francisco, CA
Van Fleet, William L. ... Houston, TX
Van Flein, Thomas V. ... Anchorage, AK
Van Fossen, Larry J. ... Columbus, OH
Van Frank, Leslie ... Salt Lake City, UT
Van Frank, Richard W. ... Ontario, CA
Vang, Koua C. ... Sun Prairie, WI
Vang, R. Michael ... Laramie, WY
Van Gaasbeck, Stephen E. ... San Antonio, TX
Van Gaasbeek, David A. ... Canton, OH
Van Gartenstein, Adley ... New York, NY
van Geel, Tyll ... Rochester, NY
VanGeest, Bruce A. ... Madison, WI
Van Geffen, Geo. H. ... Slidell, LA
VanGeison, Gregory L. ... Baltimore, MD
Vangel, Steven P. ... Houston, TX
Vangel, Thomas S. ... Boston, MA
Van Gelder, Barbara ... Washington, DC
Van Gelder, Colleen A. ... Buffalo, NY
VanGelder, Edward S. North Hollywood, CA
VanGelder, Susan E. ... Buffalo, NY
Van Gelderen, Michele R. ... Los Angeles, CA
van Geldern, Jody ... Greenwich, CT
New York, NY
Vangeli, Arthur L. ... Chatham, NJ
Vangellow, Paul P. ... Falls Church, VA
Sterling, VA
Van Gemert, Gerald J. ... Irvine, CA
Van Gemert, Mary ... Seattle, WA
Van Gemert, Robert J. ... Point Richmond, CA
Van Genderen, Sara E. ... Jackson, WY
Van Genderen-Brakke, Joni Lynn Northville, MI
Van Gent, Ronnie ... Fairfax, VA
Van Gerpen, Earl J. ... Atlanta, GA
Van Gessel, Douglas G. San Francisco, CA
Van Gessel, John T. ... Fort Lauderdale, FL
van Gestel, Allan ... Rockport, MA
Vangieson, Edward A. ... San Francisco, CA
Van Gilder, David C. ... Fort Wayne, IN
Van Gilder, Derek R., Law Office of Bastrop, TX
VanGilder, Donald N. ... North Olmsted, OH
VanGilder, Jeffrey W. ... Charleston, WV
van Ginkel, Eric ... Los Angeles, CA
Van Ginkel, James ... Atlantic, IA
Van Ginkel, J. C. ... Atlantic, IA
Van Ginkel Law Offices ... Atlantic, IA
Van Goor, Stacy Gould ... Washington, DC
Van Goor, Stephen J. ... Anchorage, AK
Van Gorder, Celia Pantle San Francisco, CA
Van Gorder, Charles H. ... Bellingham, WA
Van Gorder, Charles H., P.C., A P.S.C., The Law Offices of ... Bellingham, WA
Van Gorder, Jan, (Mr.) ... Erie, PA
Van Gorder, Jerre D. ... Anaheim, CA
Van Gorder, John F. ... Massapequa, NY
Van Gorp, Amy S. ... Chicago, IL
Van Gorp, Jon D. ... Chicago, IL
VanGraafeiland, Anne ... Rochester, NY
Van Graafeiland, Ellsworth A. Rochester, NY
Van Graafeiland, Gary P. ... Rochester, NY
Van Grack, Axelson & Williamowsky, P.C. Washington, DC
Frederick, MD
Rockville, MD
Van Grack, Jeffrey ... Bethesda, MD
Frederick, MD
Van Grack, Steven ... Rockville, MD
Van Grant, Ronald ... Honolulu, HI
VanGrinsven, Bryan ... Minot, ND
Van Grinsven, John P., III ... Minot, ND
Vangrossi, Paul C. ... Norristown, PA
Vangrossi & Recchuiti ... Norristown, PA
Van Grouw, David A. ... Roseland, NJ
Van Grover, Robert B. ... New York, NY
Van Grunsven, Paul R. ... Milwaukee, WI

Vann, Nancy S. ....New York, NY
Vann & Sheridan, LLP ....Raleigh, NC
Vann & Slavin, P.C. ....New York, NY
Vann, Stephanie ....Tampa, FL
Vann, Steven J. ....West Palm Beach, FL
Vann, Terry
Merit Systems Protection Board, Office of Board Members, GV
Vann, Terry G. ....Lenoir City, TN
Vann, Thomas H., Jr. ....Thomasville, GA
Vann, Thomas K., Jr. ....Thomasville, GA
Vann, William O. ....Birmingham, AL
Van Nagell, Jo Alice ....Lexington, KY
Vannah Costello Canepa Riedy & Rubino
Las Vegas, NV
Vannah, Ellen ....Beaumont, TX
Vannah, George A. ....Manchester, NH
Vannah, Matthew ....Las Vegas, NV
Vannah, Robert D., (Chartered)
Las Vegas, NV
Van Name, Richard ....Westlake Village, CA
Vannan, Karen M. ....Yorktown, VA
Vannatta, Bill ....Waco, TX
Van Natta, George G. ....St. Helens, OR
Vannatta, Julie Dunwell ....Columbus, OH
Vannatta, Kevin M. ....Fort Lauderdale, FL
Tampa, FL
West Palm Beach, FL
Vannatta, Mark E. ....Columbus, OH
Van Natta & Petersen ....St. Helens, OR
Vannatta, R. Timothy ....Miami, FL
VanNatta, Robert P. ....St. Helens, OR
Vannatta, Shane A. ....Missoula, MT
Van Natter, Wm. J. ....Bothell, WA
Vannella, Michael F. ....Bridgeton, NJ
Vannelli, Gail L. ....Ravenna, OH
Vannelli, Gary P. ....San Francisco, CA
Van Nelson, Patricia L. ....Washington, DC
Vanneman, Edgar, Jr. ....Evanston, IL
Vanneman, Michelle M.
Treasury Department, Bureau of Alcohol, Tobacco and Firearms, GV
Vanner, Bruce S. ....Pasadena, CA
Van Nes, Hans A. ....White Plains, NY
Van Ness, Beverly ....New York, NY
Van Ness, Carolyn J. ....Detroit, MI
Van Ness, Charles J. ....Mayfield Heights, OH
Van Ness, Charles J., & Associates
Mayfield Heights, OH
Van Ness, Denise ....Crystal River, FL
Van Ness, Diane M. ....Miami, FL
Van Ness, Diane M., P.A. ....Miami, FL
Van Ness Feldman, A Professional Corporation ....Washington, DC
Seattle, WA
Van Ness, Gretchen ....Boston, MA
Van Ness, James G. ....Department of Defense, Office of the General Counsel, GV
Van Ness, Jeremy D. ....Los Angeles, CA
Van Ness, Jesse ....San Antonio, TX
Van Ness, John E. ....Houston, TX
Van Ness, John P. ....Aspen, CO
Van Ness, Mark C. ....Denver, CO
Van Ness, Michael Greenlee ....Lexington, VA
Van Ness, Paul B. ....Dallas, TX
Van Ness, Phillip R. ....Urbana, IL
Van Ness, Robert Terry ....Laguna Hills, CA
Van Ness, Stanley C. ....Princeton, NJ
Van Ness, Thomas M., Jr.
Crystal River, FL
Van Ness & Van Ness, P.A.
Crystal River, FL
Inverness, FL
Van Ness, W. Scott ....Sarasota, FL
Van Ness, William J., Jr. ....Seattle, WA
Van Nest, Elizabeth L. ....Albany, NY
Van Nest, George S. ....Buffalo, NY
Van Nest, Jeffrey K.
United States Court Of Appeals District Of Columbia Circuit, GV
Van Nest, Joseph M. ....Houston, TX
Van Nest, Nancy L. ....Denver, CO
Van Nest, Robert A. ....San Francisco, CA
Van Neuyen, Khue ....Houston, TX
VanNevel, David Martin ....Gaithersburg, MD
Fairfax, VA
Vanney, David C. ....St. Paul, MN
Vanni, Gregory R. ....Pasadena, CA
Vanni, Lawrence J. ....Pasadena, CA
Vanni, Robert J. ....New York, NY
Van Niekerk, Marc G. ....San Jose, CA
Vannier, Ariel ....Washington, DC
Baltimore, MD
Vannier, Marvin L. ....Council Bluffs, IA
Van Nocken, Victoria J. ....Seattle, WA
Van Noord, Thomas R. ....Shingle Springs, CA
Van Noppen, Donnell, III
Charlottesville, VA
Van Noppen, Leonard H. ....Greensboro, NC
Van Norde, Peter J. ....Wayne, NJ
Van Norden, L. John ....Schenectady, NY
Van Norden, Langdon ....New York, NY
Van Norden, Robert M. ....Glen Head, NY
Van Norman, Barry Warren
Kansas City, MO
Van Norman, Beverly M. ....Lake Charles, LA
Van Norman, John L., III ....Lake Charles, LA
Van Norman, Laureen ....Lincoln, NE
Van Norman, Mark C. ....Department of Justice, Environment and Natural Resources Division, GV
Van Norman, Rayland C. ....Houston, TX
Van Norman, Robert W. ....Rapid City, SD
Van Norman, Thomas James ....Toppenish, WA
Van Norman, Warren E. ....Ballwin, MO
Vannorsdall, Hope A. ....Compton, CA
Van Norstrand, Ronald L. ....Syracuse, NY

Van Norte, Robert O. S. ....Atlanta, GA
VanNortwick, William A., Jr.
Tallahassee, FL
Van Nostrand, James M. ....Bellevue, WA
VanNostrand, LeRoy, Jr. ....Amityville, NY
VanNostrand and Martin ....Amityville, NY
Van Nostrand, Montie ....Sutton, WV
Webster Springs, WV
Van Nostrand & Morton
Webster Springs, WV
Van Nostrand & Morton PLLC ....Sutton, WV
Van Nostrand, Richard C. ....Worcester, MA
Van Note, Bruce A. ....Topsham, ME
Van Note, David A. ....Orland, CA
Van Note, Gilbert H., Jr. ....Spring Lake, NJ
Van Note, John W. ....Madison, WI
Van Noy, Allan C. ....Salinas, CA
Vannoy, Brent L. ....Houston, TX
Van Noy, Carolyn M. ....Seattle, WA
Vannoy, Colvard, Triplett & Vannoy, P.L.L.C. ....North Wilkesboro, NC
Vannoy, Douglas R. ....Fort Morgan, CO
Vannoy, J. Gary ....North Wilkesboro, NC
Vannoy, Jody Montgomery ....Cody, WY
Vannoy, John G. (Jay), Jr.
North Wilkesboro, NC
Van Noy, Kim ....Little Rock, AR
Vannoy & Reeves ....Jefferson, NC
West Jefferson, NC
Vannoy-Pineda, Kathleen D.
Fresh Meadows, NY
Vannucci, Dominic J. ....Cleveland, OH
Vannucci, John F. ....San Francisco, CA
Vannucci, John Fitzpatrick
Redwood City, CA
Vannucci, Peter S. ....New Fairfield, CT
Vannucci, Philip ....Ukiah, CA
Vannucci, Sara A. ....Scottsdale, AZ
van Nuis, Rosalie P. ....Cincinnati, OH
Van Nuland, Margarita ....La Crosse, WI
Van Nuys, Peter ....New York, NY
Van Nuys, Peter ....New York, NY
Vano, Alfred S. ....Chicago, IL
Vano, James F. ....Overland Park, KS
Van Ochten, Marjorie M. ....Lansing, MI
Van Oeveren, Edward L. ....Falls Church, VA
Van Offeren, Barbara C. ....Detroit Lakes, MN
Van Ogtrop, Bernard A. ....Wilmington, DE
van Ogtrop, Piet H. ....Newark, DE
Wilmington, DE
Van Ohlen, John ....Tacoma, WA
Vanoli, Gerald C. ....Lafayette, CA
Van Olst, Kathleen C. ....Seattle, WA
Van Oordt, Javier H. ....Irvine, CA
Van Oorschot, Marlo ....Los Angeles, CA
Van Oostenburg, Paul ....Grand Rapids, MI
Van Oosterhout, Lori A.
Redondo Beach, CA
Van Oosterhout, Peter D. ....Akron, OH
Van Oosterum, Cris J. ....Ludington, MI
Van Oot, Martha ....Hopkinton, NH
Van Oot, Peter D. ....Brattleboro, VT
Van Opdorp, Harold J. ....Geneva, NY
VanOphem, John A. ....Grand Rapids, MI
van Ophem, Mark A.E. ....New York, NY
VanOphem Meehan & VanOphem, P.C.
Toledo, OH
VanOphem, Nancy C. ....Troy, MI
VanOphem, Remy I., P.C. ....Troy, MI
VanOphem, Remy J. ....Troy, MI
Vanora, Jerome P. ....Jamaica, NY
Van Orden, Charles H. ....Belton, TX
Killeen, TX
Van Orden, Dennis J., (Ltd.)
Minneapolis, MN
Van Orden, Richard M. ....Manistee, MI
Van Order, William R. ....Hemet, CA
Vanore, Andrew A. ....Raleigh, NC
Vanore, Andrew A., III ....Raleigh, NC
Vanore, Lawrence A. ....Indianapolis, IN
Vanore, Richard L. ....Greensboro, NC
Van Orman, Kristin ....Salt Lake City, UT
Van Orman, Mary R. ....Brooklyn, NY
Van Orman, Philip ....New York, NY
Van Ormer, Darrell N., Jr.
Elizabethtown, PA
VanOrsdel, Robert A. ....Des Moines, IA
Van Orsdol, James R.
Department of the Air Force, Office of the Judge Advocate General, GV
Van Os, David ....San Antonio, TX
Van Os, George J., (P.C.) ....Houston, TX
Vanosdall, John A. ....Ashland, OH
Van Os, David, & Associates, P.C.
San Antonio, TX
Van Osdel & Miller, Ltd. ....Fargo, ND
Van Osdel, Thomas J. ....Fargo, ND
Van Osdell, James B. ....Myrtle Beach, SC
Van Osdell, Lester, Howe & Jordan, P.A.
Myrtle Beach, SC
Van Osdol, Magruder, Erickson and Redmond, P.C. ....Kansas City, MO
Van Oss, David J.
Department of the Navy, GV
Van Osselaer, Paul J. ....Austin, TX
Van Ostrand, Elvidge & Overturf
Indianapolis, IN
Van Ostrand, Shannie Bibie ....Indianapolis, IN
Van Over, C. Joel ....Washington, DC
Vanover, Hall & Bartley, P.S.C.
Pikeville, KY
Prestonsburg, KY
Vanover, Jim G. ....Pikeville, KY
Prestonsburg, KY
Vanover, Joseph W. ....Platte City, MO
Vanover, Keith P. ....Destin, FL
Vanover, Keith P., & Associates, P.A.
Destin, FL

Van Over, Perry E. ....Washington, DC
Vanover, Roger D. ....Nicholasville, KY
Van Overbeke, Michael J. ....Detroit, MI
Van Parys, David C. ....Leavenworth, KS
Van Patten, Anthony J., (P.C.)
Los Angeles, CA
Van Patten, J. Kelby ....Irvine, CA
Van Patten, Jonathan K. ....Vermillion, SD
Van Patten, Robert F., Jr. ....Grand Rapids, MI
Van Patten, Robynn L. ....Morristown, NJ
Van Patten-Poulakos, Seay ....Newnan, GA
Van Pee, Kristina M. ....Washington, DC
Van Pelt, Beth Chapman ....Boston, MA
Van Pelt, Carol ....Lakewood, CO
Van Pelt, Christian M. ....Morris Plains, NJ
New York, NY
Van Pelt, Christian M., P.C.
Morris Plains, NJ
New York, NY
Van Pelt, David T. ....Los Angeles, CA
Van Pelt, Donald C. ....Salisbury, MD
Van Pelt and Frank, P.C., Law Offices
Houston, TX
Van Pelt, George W. ....Lyndhurst, OH
Van Pelt, James A. ....Austin, TX
Van Pelt, Joan D. ....Newark, NJ
Van Pelt, Laura J. ....Dallas, TX
Van Pelt, Lee ....Los Altos, CA
Van Pelt, Lenny ....Bellevue, WA
Van Pelt, Lester, III ....Austin, TX
Van Pelt, Marcus W. ....Springdale, AR
Van Pelt, Norman D. ....Houston, TX
Van Pelt, Ralph L. ....Carrollton, GA
Van Pelt, Ralph L., Jr. ....La Fayette, GA
Van Pelt, Samuel ....Hickman, NE
Van Pelt, Traci L. ....Denver, CO
Van Pelt, Wanda Kay ....Edwardsville, IL
Topeka, KS
Van Pelt-Kurtz, Marcia L. ....Milford, OH
Van Pernis, Mark ....Kailua-Kona, HI
Van Pernis, Smith & Vancil, Attorneys at Law, A Law Corporation ....Hilo, HI
Kailua-Kona, HI
Kamuela, HI
Van Petten, H. O ....Los Angeles, CA
Van Petten & Holen ....Los Angeles, CA
Van Poolen, James P. ....Grand Haven, MI
VanPopering, Randy E., & Associates, Law Offices of ....Chicago, IL
Van Poppering, Melissa J. ....Chicago, IL
Van Pottelbergh, Véronique M.
Ridgefield Park, NJ
Van Poucke, Michael ....Naperville, IL
Van Praag, Alan ....New York, NY
Van Purnell, Ernest D. ....Baton Rouge, LA
Van Putten, Marinus W., Jr.
Minneapolis, MN
Van Putten, Mark C. ....Ann Arbor, MI
Van Puymbroeck, Rudolf V.
Washington, DC
Van Puymbrouck, Darren M. R.
Chicago, IL
Van Raalte, Brenda L. ....Luverne, MN
Van Raalte, Derk Bleckman Kekkert, IV
North Charleston, SC
Van Raalte, G. Reginald
Agency for International Development, Other Offices of A.I.D., GV
Van Raalte, Lisa Shilepsky ....Charleston, SC
Van & Ralphs, Chtd. ....Las Vegas, NV
Van Rees, Cornelius S. ....New York, NY
Van Regenmorter, Jennifer B.
Grand Rapids, MI
Van Remmen, Geoffrey ....Racine, WI
Van Remmen Law Office, S.C. ....Racine, WI
Van Remortel, Fred ....New York, NY
van Rensburg, Ramona M.
Canyon Lake, CA
VanRensler, Barry W. ....Media, PA
Van Rensselaer, Robert M. M.
Bernardsville, NJ
VanRheenen & Associates, P.C.
Indianapolis, IN
VanRheenen, Richard S. ....Indianapolis, IN
Van Riel, Nicoline ....Chicago, IL
Van Riet, Frank M. ....Stamford, CT
Van Riper, Christopher ....Knoxville, TN
Van Riper, David A. ....Orange, CA
Van Riper, Ellen M. ....Phoenix, AZ
VanRiper, Janice S. ....Helena, MT
Van Riper, Jean M. ....Oyster Bay, NY
Van Riper, Marianne ....Santa Ana, CA
Van Riper, Philip E. ....Binghamton, NY
VanRiper, Yvette Mari ....Detroit, MI
vanRoden, Christopher R. ....Bel Air, MD
Van Roekel, Tanya Denton ....Raleigh, NC
Van Roeyen, Eileen W. ....Chicago, IL
Van Ronzelen, Timothy W.
Jefferson City, MO
Van Roo, William A. ....San Jose, CA
Van Roo, William A., P.C. ....San Jose, CA
Van Rooyan, Gary J. ....Houston, TX
Van Rooyen, Craig B. ....Riverside, CA
van Rossem, Lori ....Atlanta, GA
Van Roy, Jantra ....New York, NY
VanRoy, Thomas E. ....Hayward, WI
Van Royen, William S. (Tom) ....Tampa, FL
VanRozeboom, Russell G. ....Fresno, CA
Van Runkle, Peter E. ....Columbus, OH
Van Ry, Bradley O. ....Safford, AZ
Van Rybroek, Diana ....Madison, WI
Vanryn, J Matthew ....New York, NY
Van Ryn, Leonard ....Albany, NY
Van Ryn, Paul W. ....Delmar, NY
Van Rysselberghe, Pierre C.
Palo Alto, CA
Portland, OR
Van Rysselberghe, Pierre L. ....Eugene, OR

Van Rysselberghe, Todd L. ....Portland, OR
Van Saders, William P. ....Basking Ridge, NJ
Van Saghi, Robert L. ....Oak Park, MI
Van Sambeek, Carol Marie Crandall
St. Louis, MO
Van Sambeek, Mavis J. ....Minneapolis, MN
Van Sanford, Gordon M. ....Van Nuys, CA
Van Sant, Barbara Lohr ....Lecanto, FL
Vansant, Catherine A. ....Post Mills, VT
Vansant, Corriere & McClure, P.C.
Albany, GA
Van Sant, Daniel Michael ....Nashville, TN
Van Sant, Grant ....Homer, NY
Van Sant, J. Douglas ....Stockton, CA
Vansant, John M., Jr. ....Albany, GA
Vansant, Joseph A. ....Baltimore, MD
Van Sant, Nancy J. ....Miami, FL
VanSant, Susan B. ....Durham, NC
Van Santen, James ....Chicago, IL
Arlington, VA
Van Santen, Todd M. ....Sacramento, CA
Van Santen, William A. ....Chicago, IL
van Schaick, Peter ....Glen Ridge, NJ
Van Schaik, Carolyn ....Lewiston, NY
VanSchaik, Chris R. V. ....Dayton, OH
Van Schaik, John ....General Accounting Office, Office of the General Counsel, GV
van Schie, Adrian ....New York, NY
van Schilfgaarde, Elizabeth
New York, NY
van Schoonenberg, Robert G.
Pasadena, CA
Van Schouwen, Craig R. ....Valparaiso, IN
Van Sciver, J. Gilbert, Jr. ....Mount Holly, NJ
Van Sciver, John C. ....Ship Bottom, NJ
Van Sciver, L. David ....Pacifica, CA
Van Sciver, Robert ....Bountiful, UT
Van Scoy, Donna E. ....Rockville, MD
Vanscoy, Douglas W. ....Tacoma, WA
Van Scoy, Jerry D. ....Clinton, IA
Van Scoy & Kross, P.C. ....Clinton, IA
Van Scoyk, Ward L. ....Steamboat Springs, CO
Van Scoyoc, Carol L. ....White Plains, NY
Van Scoyoc, Harry Stewart ....Washington, DC
Van Scyoc, Wilma ....Springfield, IL
Vanselow, Michael J. ....St. Paul, MN
Vansen, Lise ....San Francisco, CA
van Setter, George G. ....New York, NY
Van Shellenbeck, Glenn K. ....Austin, TX
Van Shura, John J., Jr. ....Reading, PA
VanSickel, David B. ....Des Moines, IA
Van Sickle, Barbara Z.
Santa Monica, CA
Van Sickle, Barry ....Los Angeles, CA
Van Sickle, Bruce M. ....Bismarck, ND
Van Sickle, Charles S. ....Madison, WI
VanSickle, Fred ....Spokane, WA
Van Sickle, James E. ....Canton, IL
Van Sickle, John A. ....Columbus, OH
Van Sickle, Michael S. ....Ventura, CA
Van Sickle, Peter E. ....Cumberland, WI
Van Sickle, Richard ....Thousand Oaks, CA
Van Sickle, Richard William
Minneapolis, MN
Van Sickle & Rowley ....Thousand Oaks, CA
Van Sickle, Russell F. ....Pensacola, FL
Van Sickle, Tom R. ....Scottsdale, AZ
Van Sicklen, Michael B. ....Madison, WI
Van Sicklen, Steven R. ....Los Angeles, CA
VanSickler, Kimberly T. ....Columbus, OH
Van Siclen, Robert C. ....Auburn, WA
Van Siclen, Stocks & Firkins
Auburn, WA
Bellevue, WA
Seattle, WA
Van Skike, Phyllis ....Santa Rosa, CA
Van Slambrook, Dale E. ....Charleston, SC
VanSlambrouck, John G. ....Kalamazoo, MI
VanSlingerlandt, William H. ....Detroit, MI
Van Slooten, Mark T. ....Grand Rapids, MI
Van Slooten, Nancy J. ....Sierra Madre, CA
VanSluytman, Bernard M.
Charlotte Amalie, St. Thomas, VI
Van Slyck, Annalea W.
Grosse Pointe Shores, MI
Van Slyck, Willard N., Jr. ....Tucson, AZ
Van Slyke, Albert A. ....San Diego, CA
Van Slyke, Allan D. ....Richmond, TX
Van Slyke, Clague A. ....Tucson, AZ
Van Slyke, Clague A., III ....Tucson, AZ
Van Slyke, David B. ....Portland, ME
Van Slyke, Glen ....Houston, TX
Van Slyke, J. Arby ....Pensacola, FL
Van Slyke, J. Arby, P.A. ....Pensacola, FL
Van Slyke, J. B., Jr. ....Hattiesburg, MS
Van Slyke, Leonard D., Jr. ....Jackson, MS
Van Slyke, Lester A. ....Richmond, TX
Van Slyke, Lester A., Jr. ....Richmond, TX
Vanslyke, Mary Winter ....Memphis, TN
Van Slyke, Paul C. ....Houston, TX
Van Soelen, Esther Smith ....Clovis, NM
Van Soelen, Greig & Richards, P.A.
Clovis, NM
VanSoelen, Marian B. ....Boston, MA
Van Soest, Peter D. ....Denver, CO
Van Someren, Robert A. ....Houston, TX
Van Son, Gary W. ....Rochester, NY
van Son, Paul B. ....Department of State, Foreign Service Officers (Overseas), GV
Van Son, Peter E. ....New York, NY
Vanson, William A. ....Kew Gardens, NY
Van Soye, Scott C. ....San Bernardino, CA
Vanspeybroeck, David D. ....Portland, OR
Van Steel, Lauren G. ....Lansing, MI
VanSteelandt, René J., (Mr.)
Fairfield Bay, AR

Varga, Judith Fleming .... Livonia, MI
Varga, Michael J. .... Dayton, OH
Varga, Robert C. .... Atlanta, GA
Varga, S. Gary .... Carmel, CA
Varga, Stephen A. .... Torrance, CA
Varga, William R. .... Annapolis, MD
Vargas, Amado J. .... Middletown, CT
Vargas, Debbie M. .... San Leandro, CA
Vargas, Diana M. .... New York, NY
Vargas, Donna M. .... San Francisco, CA
Vargas, Edward E. .... Covina, CA
Vargas, Edwin J. .... Cleveland, OH
Vargas, Eric R. .... Yakima, WA
Vargas, Eric S. .... Metairie, LA
Vargas, Ernest A., A Law Corporation
Pasadena, CA
Vargas, Fernando D. .... Los Angeles, CA
Vargas, Frank A., III .... Worcester, MA
Vargas, Gustavo .... Orlando, FL
Vargas, Heather B. .... San Jose, CA
Vargas, Ivanyla D. .... Newark, NJ
Vargas, James T. .... Austin, TX
Vargas, Javier E. .... Mineola, NY
Vargas, Juan M. .... Miami, FL
Vargas, Julie J. .... Albuquerque, NM
Vargas, Louis A. .... Tallahassee, FL
Vargas, Manuel D. .... Brooklyn, NY
Vargas, Naomi A. .... Mountain View, CA
Vargas, Noël E., II .... Metairie, LA
Vargas, Priscilla D. .... Miami, FL
Vargas, Rafael A. .... New York, NY
Vargas, Ramon H. .... San Juan, PR
Vargas, Ray M. .... Albuquerque, NM
Vargas, Ray M., II .... Albuquerque, NM
Vargas, Robert A. .... Pasadena, CA
Vargas, Roberto M. .... Tallahassee, FL
Vargas, Susan Victoria .... Gardena, CA
Vargas, Vanessa L. .... Chicago, IL
Vargas & Vargas .... Pasadena, CA
Vargas & Vargas .... Metairie, LA
New Orleans, LA
Vargas, Wilhelm Isaiah .... Glendale, CA
Vargas, Yvonne .... Chicago, IL
Vargas & Zion .... Miami, FL
Vargas-Flood, C. Sofia .... San Diego, CA
Vargason, James B. .... Auburn, NY
Vargas-Rodriguez, Maria C.
Los Angeles, CA
Vargas-Ruiz, Rebeca .... San Juan, PR
Vargas-Valverde, Jorge .... Salinas, CA
Vargelis, Demetrios C. .... Boston, MA
Vargelis, Jason C. .... New York, NY
Varghese, Cherian G. .... Yonkers, NY
Varghese, Lal .... Lewisville, TX
Vargish, Frank J., III .... Lancaster, PA
Vargo, Brian S. .... Philadelphia, PA
Vargo, Bruce D. .... Roseland, NJ
Vargo, Deborah J. .... Lafayette, IN
Vargo, Ernest E., Jr. .... Cleveland, OH
Vargo, Gerald P. .... Lakewood, CO
Vargo, James G. .... Columbus, OH
Vargo, Janet O. .... Indianapolis, IN
Vargo, John E. .... Washington, DC
Vargo, John F. .... Indianapolis, IN
Vargo, Joseph F. .... Mount Carmel, IL
Vargo, Kathryn B. .... Atlanta, GA
Vargo, Michelle Mercier .... Springfield, MA
Vargo, Naeem V. .... New York, NY
Vargo, Paul M. .... Chicago, IL
Vargo, Robert F. .... Huntsville, AL
Vargo, Stephen E. .... Chicago, IL
Vargo, Stephen G. .... Joliet, IL
Vargo, Stuart F. .... Birmingham, AL
Vargo, Tara L. .... Franklinville, NJ
Vargo, Thomas W. .... Columbus, OH
Vargo, Vicki M. .... Orlando, FL
Vargo-Lewandowski, Diana L. .... Joliet, IL
Vargyas, Ellen J.
Equal Employment Opportunity Commission, Office of Legal Counsel, GV
Vargyas, Joseph F.
Commodity Futures Trading Commission, Division of Enforcement, GV
Varhola, Aaron R. .... Miami, FL
Varholy, John Robert .... Atlanta, GA
Varhus, Alan P. .... Columbus, OH
Vari, Diane .... Vineland, NJ
Vari, Louann Jackson .... Dover, DE
Vari, Nicholas P. .... Pittsburgh, PA
Vari, Susan .... Lake Success, NY
Varian, Donald S., Jr. .... Akron, OH
Varian, Gregory T. .... New Rochelle, NY
Varian & Henretta .... Akron, OH
Cleveland, OH
Varian, Robert P. .... San Francisco, CA
Varian, Susan .... San Francisco, CA
Varian, William C., Jr. .... Parsippany, NJ
Varick, Steven B. .... Chicago, IL
Varidin, Diane M. .... Seminole, FL
Varie, Douglas R. .... Emmett, ID
Variel, Richard P. .... La Crescenta, CA
Varieur, Michele Viger .... Troy, NY
Varilek, Robert L. .... Rapid City, SD
Varin, John F. .... Fairfield, ID
Varin-Hommen, Alvora .... Bensalem, PA
Vario, Robert R. .... West Seneca, NY
Variola, John .... Canton, OH
Varitz, Robert D. .... Portland, OR
Varitz, Robert D., P.C. .... Portland, OR
Varjabedian, John .... Ocean City, NJ
Varkas, Alexander D., Jr. .... Boca Raton, FL
Varker, Lucy G. .... Chesapeake, VA
Varky, Susheela .... Silver Spring, MD
Varlack, Carlyle G., Jr. .... San Jose, CA
Varlan, Nicholas P. .... Rochester, NY
Varlan, Thomas A. .... Knoxville, TN
Varland, Scott J. .... Louisville, KY

Varlas-Teel, Katherine A. .... Davenport, IA
Varlese, Doris R. .... New York, NY
Varlese, Felicia M. .... New York, NY
Varlese, Rocco S. .... Long Island City, NY
Varlese, Susanne .... San Francisco, CA
Varley, Bridget M. .... New York, NY
Varley, Douglas N. .... Washington, DC
Varley, J. David .... Washington, DC
Varley, Janet M. .... St. Louis, MO
Varley, John F., III .... Livingston, NJ
Varley, John J. .... Atlanta, GA
Varley, Kenneth, Jr. .... Albany, NY
Varley, Maureen A. .... Roseland, NJ
Varley & Messer, LLP .... Montgomery, AL
Varley, Nancy A. .... Cleveland, OH
Varley, Rachelle J. .... Glendale, CA
Varley, Robert John .... Montgomery, AL
Varley, Thomas A. .... Philadelphia, PA
Varley, Val J. .... Clarksville, TX
Varley, Warren A. .... Stuart, IA
Varline, Daniel W. .... Milwaukee, WI
Wausau, WI
Varma, Anita .... Boston, MA
Varma, Anurag .... Washington, DC
Varma, Ashoka .... New York, NY
Varma, Asim .... Washington, DC
Varma, Kanakatara .... Bronx, NY
Varma, Rishi A. .... New York, NY
Varma, Sanjay K. .... Akron, OH
Varmer, Ole .... Department of Commerce, National Oceanic and Atmospheric Administration, GV
Varn, Corise P., (Miss) .... St. Augustine, FL
Varn, Craig D. .... Tallahassee, FL
Varn, Jacob D. .... Tallahassee, FL
Varn, Jessica Enciso .... Tallahassee, FL
Varn, Larry L. .... Boston, MA
Varn, Michael T. .... Gordon, NE
Varn, Russell .... Whittier, CA
Varn, Wilfred C. .... Tallahassee, FL
Varnado, Angelique L. .... Washington, DC
Varnado, Carey R. .... Hattiesburg, MS
Varnado, Gerald R. .... Athens, GA
Varnado, Harlon H. .... Jackson, MS
Varnado, Mager A., Jr. .... Gulfport, MS
Varnado, Robert Bratton .... Charleston, SC
Varnado, Robert W., Jr. .... Bogalusa, LA
Varnado, T.D., Jr. .... Gulfport, MS
Varnadoe, George L. .... Naples, FL
Varnadoe, James T. .... Atlanta, GA
Varnadore, Eddie C. .... Marietta, GA
Varnadore, M. DeWayne .... Tyler, TX
Varnadore, M. DeWayne, P.C., Law Offices of .... Tyler, TX
Varnado-Rhodes, Sharon S. .... Seattle, WA
Varnavas, Helene Andrea .... New York, NY
Varndell, Therese B. .... Alexandria, VA
Varnell, Burns & Sharp, P.C. .... Cleveland, TN
Varnell, James L. .... Seattle, WA
Varnell, John D. .... Leesburg, GA
Varnell, John D., P.C. .... Leesburg, GA
Varnell, Judy Hicks .... Albany, GA
Varnell, Lester J. (Jake), Jr.
Mineral Wells, TX
Varnell, Robert C. .... Chicago, IL
Varnen, Craig .... Los Angeles, CA
Varner, Alexandra D. .... Charleston, SC
Varner, Andrew J. .... Washington, DC
Varner, B. Douglas .... Lake Ozark, MO
Varner, Bradley L. .... South Bend, IN
Varner, Brent W. .... Baraboo, WI
Varner, Bruce D. .... Riverside, CA
Varner, Bryan J. .... Santa Rosa, CA
Varner, Carlton A. .... Los Angeles, CA
Varner, Carson H., Jr. .... Normal, IL
Varner, Chilton Davis .... Atlanta, GA
Varner, Christine Lewis .... Lubbock, TX
Varner, Christopher E. .... Hallandale Beach, FL
Varner, Christopher L.
Department of Justice, Criminal Division, GV
Varner, Christopher T. .... Chattanooga, TN
Varner, Claretta Jane .... Detroit, MI
Varner, Conrad W. .... Frederick, MD
Varner, David E. .... Houston, TX
Varner, Dewey H., Jr. .... Lake Worth, FL
Varner, Dominique M. .... Houston, TX
Varner, Donald J. .... Youngstown, OH
Varner, Donica Thomas .... Detroit, MI
Varner, Edwin S., Jr. .... Warner Robins, GA
Varner, Edwin S., P.C.
Warner Robins, GA
Varner, Herbert W. .... Houston, TX
Varner, J. Mack .... Vicksburg, MS
Varner, J. Paul .... Jackson, MS
Varner, Jack F. .... Leesburg, GA
Varner, James A. .... Clarksburg, WV
Varner, James H., Jr. .... Knoxville, TN
Varner, Jane Ann .... Abilene, TX
Varner, Joseph E., III .... Jackson, MS
Varner, Joseph H., III .... Tampa, FL
Varner, K. Morgan, III, (P.C.)
Atlanta, GA
Varner, Karl J.
Securities and Exchange Commission, Division of Market Regulation, GV
Varner, Kaslick & Goundry, A Professional Corporation .... Frederick, MD
Varner, Katrin Christiane .... Chicago, IL
Varner, Keith R. .... Augusta, ME
Varner, Kim L.
Federal Communications Commission, Mass Media Bureau, GV
Varner, Kim R., (Mr.) .... Greenville, SC
Varner, Lisa B. .... Mebane, NC
Varner, Michael A. .... Houston, TX
Varner Parker & Sessums, P.A.
Vicksburg, MS

Varner, Philip W. .... Toledo, OH
Varner, Randy L. .... Harrisburg, PA
Varner, Robert E. .... Montgomery, AL
Varner, Robert Glenn, Jr.
Washington, DC
Varner, Robert Ray, Jr. .... Dallas, TX
Varner, Saleson & Dobler LLP
Riverside, CA
Varner, Sallie Stroud .... Bentonville, AR
Varner, Sean S. .... Riverside, CA
Varner, Shannon R. .... Richmond, VA
Varner, Stephens, Humphries & White, LLC
Atlanta, GA
Varner, Thad W. .... Jackson, MS
Varner, Thomas H. .... Chicago, IL
Varnes, Donald W. .... Portland, OR
Varnes, Kelly J. .... Billings, MT
Varnet, Theresa M. .... Northborough, MA
Varney, Andrew P. .... Washington, DC
Varney, Bruce B. .... Garden City, NY
Varney, Cecil C. .... Williamson, WV
Varney, Christine A. .... Washington, DC
Varney, John .... Miami, FL
Varney, John P. .... Roanoke, VA
Varney, John R. .... Syracuse, NY
Varney, Kimberly .... Cincinnati, OH
Varney, Lana K. .... Austin, TX
Varney, Norman A., Jr. .... Philadelphia, PA
Varney, Robert C. .... Wolfeboro, NH
Varney, Robert T. .... Bloomington, IL
Chicago, IL
Varney, S. Mark .... San Francisco, CA
Varney, Steven W. .... Hartford, CT
Varni, Anthony B. .... Hayward, CA
Varni, Fraser, Hartwell & Rodgers
Hayward, CA
Varni, Fraser, Hartwell & Trutner
Livermore, CA
Varni, Frederic K. .... San Bernardino, CA
Varni, John J. .... Temecula, CA
Varni, Joseph A. .... Stockton, CA
Varnier, Lisa M. .... Detroit, MI
Varns, Kenneth E. .... Aberdeen, SD
Varnum, Riddering, Schmidt & Howlett LLP
Grand Haven, MI
Grand Rapids, MI
Kalamazoo, MI
Lansing, MI
Milwaukee, WI
Varnum, Robert V. .... Washington, DC
Varoli, David J. .... New York, NY
Varon, Harry R. .... New York, NY
Varon, James A. .... Fresno, CA
Varon, Jay N. .... Washington, DC
Varon, Joseph A. .... Hollywood, FL
Varon, Joseph J. .... New York, NY
Varon, Stanley M. .... South Orange, NJ
Varon, Sue Kisner .... Marietta, GA
Varona, Anthony E. .... Washington, DC
Varone, Anthony T. .... Bridgeport, CT
Varone, J. Curtis .... Exeter, RI
Varone, Vanessa J. .... Cranston, RI
Varone, Vince .... Milwaukee, WI
Varoutsos, George D. .... Arlington, VA
Varoutsos & Koutoulakos .... Arlington, VA
Varoutsos, Paul G. .... Arlington, VA
Varpetian, Lousine .... Manhattan Beach, CA
Varpness, John E. .... Minneapolis, MN
Varra, Robert A. .... Denver, CO
Varraveto, Dominick, Jr. .... Lockport, IL
Varrecchia, Cindy .... New York, NY
Varriale, Carla .... New York, NY
Varriale, Corinne D. .... Marlboro, NJ
Varriale, Lisa A. .... Denver, CO
Varriale, Paul R. .... Mineola, NY
New York, NY
White Plains, NY
Varriano, Richard D. .... Moorhead, MN
Varricchio, Michele A. .... Allentown, PA
Varricchio, Philip T. .... Las Vegas, NV
Varrichio, Mark A. .... Bronx, NY
Varrin, René D., (Mr.) .... Boston, MA
Varrone, Edward G., Law Office of
Washington, DC
Varrone, James A. .... North Haven, CT
Varrone, John M. .... Bridgeport, CT
Varrone, Joseph F., Jr. .... Bridgeport, CT
Varrone & Varrone .... Bridgeport, CT
Vars, Addison F., III .... Syracuse, NY
Watertown, NY
Vars, Ellen S. .... Boston, MA
Vars, Robert J. .... Encino, CA
Varsalona, Dawn M. .... Staten Island, NY
Varsalona, Peter J. .... Jersey City, NJ
Varsalona, Sal W. .... Clinton, TN
Varsam, Nick H. .... St. Louis, MO
Varsek, Lawrence E. .... Joliet, IL
Varsha, Robert A. .... Atlanta, GA
Vartabedian, Michael .... Katonah, NY
Vartabedian, Steven M. .... Fresno, CA
Vartain, Michael J. .... San Francisco, CA
Vartain, Richard G. .... Department of Justice, Civil Division, GV
Vartan, Leo R. .... Kearny, NJ
Vartan, Robert V. C. .... Fresno, CA
Vartanian, E. Christine .... Santa Ana, CA
Vartanian, Emily .... Washington, DC
Vartanian, Michael Gary .... Detroit, MI
Vartanian, Thomas P. .... Washington, DC
Vartanian, Walter G. .... Boston, MA
Vartelas, John J. .... East Hartford, CT
Vartian, Armen R. .... New York, NY
Vartio, Ryan K. .... Los Angeles, CA
Varunes, Anita M. .... Hartford, CT
Varvaro, Joseph .... Uniondale, NY
Varvaro, Marjory J. .... Springfield, MA
Varvel, Mary Ellen Thompson
Grand Forks, ND

Varveris, Nicholas M. .... Columbus, OH
Vary, George F. .... Washington, DC
Vary, Michael W. .... Cleveland, OH
Vary, Nancy L. .... New York, NY
Vary, Richard R. .... Saginaw, MI
Vasady-Kovacs, Ferenc L. .... Marathon, FL
Vasady-Kovacs, Julie R. .... Albany, NY
Vasagam, Kamala .... Washington, DC
Vasak, Stephen .... Hackensack, NJ
New York, NY
Vasaly, Charles E. .... Falls Church, VA
Vasaly, Mary R. .... Minneapolis, MN
Vasan, Vel S. .... Bridgeview, IL
Vasapoli, Dennis
Federal Energy Regulatory Commission, Office of the General Counsel, GV
Vasapoli, Joseph V. .... Washington, DC
Vasapolli, John J. .... Saugus, MA
Vasaturo, Gaylene .... Chicago, IL
Vasaturo, Laura M. .... Brooklyn, NY
Vasbinder, Susan A. .... Los Altos, CA
Vasco, Mark .... Charlotte, NC
Vasco, Mary Beth .... Denver, CO
Vascocu, Marcus F. .... Longview, TX
Vasconcellos, Danny J. .... Honolulu, HI
Vasconcellos, John B. .... San Jose, CA
Vasconcellos, Renata S. .... Washington, DC
Vasconcellos, William L. .... Boise, ID
Vasconi, Kimberly .... Washington, DC
Vasegh, Donna .... Los Angeles, CA
Vasek, Saundra S. .... Waco, TX
Vasek, Stephen J. .... Lexington, KY
Vaselaney, Missia H. .... Cleveland, OH
Vaseleck, James Michael, Jr. .... Newtown, PA
Vaseliades, Leon W. .... Houston, TX
Vasels, Nicholas C. .... Newport Beach, CA
Vaserstein, Anna L. .... Underhill, VT
Vasey, Brian K. .... Renton, WA
Vasey, Jon A. .... Des Moines, IA
Vasey, Laura Maines .... New York, NY
Vash, Bernard R. .... Kenosha, WI
Vash, Dale W. .... Tampa, FL
Vash, Serina Marie .... New York, NY
Vashak, Walter E. .... Ann Arbor, MI
Vashko, Robert E., II .... New Orleans, LA
Vasi, Valentino .... New York, NY
Vasic, Ivan .... Chicago, IL
Vasichek, Laurie A. .... Minneapolis, MN
Vasil, Christopher W.
Supreme Court Of The United States, GV
Vasil, Gregory P. .... Boston, MA
Vasil, John G. .... Campbell, CA
Vasil, Kenneth G. .... Erie, PA
Vasil, Monika .... Seattle, WA
Vasil, Walter W. .... Duluth, MN
Vasilaros & Politis, P.A.
Daytona Beach, FL
Deltona, FL
Vasilaros, Steven T. .... Daytona Beach, FL
Deltona, FL
Vasilatos, Spiros, Jr. .... Akron, OH
Vasile, James B. .... Washington, DC
Vasile, John A. .... New Rochelle, NY
Vasile, Nicholas R. .... Trenton, NJ
Vasile, Roy W. .... Merrick, NY
Vasileff, Boris A. .... Bloomfield Hills, MI
Vasileff, Nick D. .... Madison, IL
Vasiliadis, Constantine M. .... Bethlehem, PA
Vasiliadis, Stanley M. .... Bethlehem, PA
Vasilius, Charles J. .... Wheat Ridge, CO
Vasilius, Charles J., P.C. .... Wheat Ridge, CO
Vasiljevic, Vladan M. .... Chicago, IL
Vasiljevich, Thomas .... Chicago, IL
Vasiloff, Karl S. .... Waltham, MA
Vasilopoulos, Katherine .... Forest Hills, NY
Vasily, John M. .... New York, NY
Vasily-Cioffi, Joanne M. .... Boston, MA
Vasington, Paul M. .... Norwich, CT
Vasios, H. Barry .... New York, NY
Vasios, James A. .... Short Hills, NJ
Vaska, Michael K. .... Seattle, WA
Vaskas, Alan V. .... West Chester, PA
Vaske, Philip J. .... Cincinnati, OH
Vaske, Ronald K. .... Minneapolis, MN
Vaskis, Maureen F. .... Newark, NJ
Vasko, George B. .... Akron, OH
Vasko, John A. .... Chicago, IL
Vasko, Michael P. .... Columbus, OH
Vasko, Roberto & Evans, Co., L.P.A.
Akron, OH
Vaskov, John A. .... Pittsburgh, PA
Vaskov, Stephen G. .... Washington, DC
Vason, Robert F., Jr. .... Mount Dora, FL
Vason, Robert F., Jr., P.A. .... Mount Dora, FL
Vason, Wayne R. .... Atlanta, GA
Vasos, Donald W. .... Kansas City, KS
Overland Park, KS
Vasos Law Offices .... Kansas City, KS
Overland Park, KS
Vasquez, Alicia J. .... Palo Alto, CA
Vasquez, Aurora .... Los Angeles, CA
Vasquez, Carlos E. .... San Francisco, CA
Vasquez, Carmen M. .... New York, NY
Vasquez, Consuelo A. .... New York, NY
Vasquez, David A. .... Tucson, AZ
Vasquez, David A., P.C. .... Tucson, AZ
Vasquez, David R. .... Irvine, CA
Vasquez, Deirdre .... San Antonio, TX
Vasquez, Douglas V. .... Denver, CO
Vasquez, Edward T. .... Salt Lake City, UT
Vasquez, Elisa .... Galveston, TX
Vasquez, Emily E. .... Sacramento, CA
Vasquez, Eric J., Law Offices of
Marco Island, FL
Naples, FL
Vasquez, Francis A., Jr. .... Washington, DC
Vasquez, Gary D. .... Orlando, FL
Vasquez, Garye L. .... Casa Grande, AZ

Vaughn, Robt. H. ....Oklahoma City, OK
Vaughn, Scott M. ....Somerville, MA
Vaughn, Scott P. ....Charlotte, NC
Vaughn, Scott Thomas ....Little Rock, AR
North Little Rock, AR
Vaughn, Sharon Y.
Department of Transportation, National Highway Traffic Safety Administration, GV
Vaughn, Stephen P. ....Washington, DC
Vaughn, Steve C. ....Cleveland, OH
Vaughn, Stuart E. ....San Francisco, CA
Vaughn, Susan E. ....Boston, MA
Vaughn, Tamara A. ....Coral Gables, FL
Vaughn, Thomas A., Jr. ....Houston, TX
Vaughn, Thomas D. ....Jefferson City, MO
Vaughn, Thomas E. ....Chicago, IL
Vaughn, Thomas E. ....Gulfport, MS
Vaughn, Thomas L. ....Colonial Heights, VA
Vaughn, Thomas Stephen ....Detroit, MI
Vaughn, Timothy G. ....Eastman, GA
Vaughn, Todd A. ....Department of Commerce, Patent and Trademark Office, GV
Vaughn & Vaughn ....San Diego, CA
Vaughn, Victor J. ....Morristown, TN
Vaughn, Vonda Kay ....Chicago, IL
Vaughn, W. Daniel ....Galveston, TX
Vaughn, W. David ....Jacksonville, FL
Vaughn, William A. ....Los Banos, CA
Vaughn, William A. ....Tulsa, OK
Vaughn, William H. ....Dover, DE
Vaughn, William W. ....Los Angeles, CA
Vaughn, W. J. ....Melbourne, FL
Vaughn, Wm. Lewis, Law Offices of
Macon, GA
Vaughn, Wright & Stearns LLP
Atlanta, GA
Forsyth, GA
Vaughns, Katherine L. ....Baltimore, MD
Vaught, Allen R. ....Decatur, TX
Vaught, Ashlee H. ....Savannah, GA
Vaught, Cheryl A. ....Oklahoma City, OK
Vaught & Conner ....Oklahoma City, OK
Vaught, Curt J., & Associates ....Hickory, NC
Vaught, Don M. ....Edmond, OK
Vaught, Douglas S. ....Galax, VA
Vaught, Gene P., III ....Myrtle Beach, SC
Vaught, J. Barrington ....Columbus, GA
Vaught, James A. ....Austin, TX
Vaught, James S. ....Tallahassee, FL
Vaught, John M. ....Denver, CO
Vaught, Jon R. ....Oakland, CA
Vaught, Kevin S. ....Fort Smith, AR
Vaught, Larry D. ....Little Rock, AR
Vaught & Loftin, P.C. ....Galax, VA
Vaught, Randall K. ....Southfield, MI
Vaught, Richard B. ....San Jose, CA
Vaught, Ronald W. ....Warm Springs, VA
Vaught, Ronald W., PLC ....Hot Springs, VA
Warm Springs, VA
Vaught, Samuel H. ....Santa Cruz, CA
Vaught, Victoria Thomas ....Conway, SC
Vaught, Winston W. ....Conway, SC
Vaughters, Cecilie A. ....Los Altos, CA
Vaughters, Julia E. ....Philadelphia, PA
Vaupel, Wendy L. ....Pittsburgh, PA
Vaurio, Ann Marie ....Princeton, NJ
Vause, W. Gary ....St. Petersburg, FL
Vausher, George A. ....Chino, CA
Vauthier, David W. ....Baltimore, MD
Vauthy, Christopher J. ....New York, NY
Vautier, Donald F. ....Woodbury, NY
Vaux & Marscher, P.A. ....Bluffton, SC
Hilton Head Island, SC
Vaux, Roberts ....Bluffton, SC
Vavasour, Robert S. ....Mountain View, CA
Vavonese, Andrea T. ....Washington, DC
Vavonese, Daniel P.
Department of Commerce, Patent and Trademark Office, GV
Vavonese, Frank J. ....Syracuse, NY
Vavonese, Michael J. ....Syracuse, NY
Vavonese, Samuel B. ....Syracuse, NY
Vavra, John Andrew ....St. Clairsville, OH
Vavra, Richard J. ....Northbrook, IL
Vavrichek, Wayne ....Seattle, WA
Vavrick, Evangeline M. ....New Orleans, LA
Vavrina, Robert F. ....Annapolis, MD
Vavro, Edward M., Jr. ....Pittsburgh, PA
Vavroch, Mary W. ....Des Moines, IA
VavRosky, Dennis R. ....Portland, OR
Vavrosky, Joanne ....Duluth, MN
VavRosky, MacColl & Olson, P.C.
Portland, OR
Vavruska, Stasia M. ....Beachwood, OH
Vavuris, S. Lee ....San Francisco, CA
Vawrinek, Jeffrey J. ....Plano, TX
Vawter, Alison Boothby ....Washington, DC
Vawter, Jana R. ....Columbus, OH
Vawter, John K. ....San Diego, CA
Vawter, Kimberly Peck ....Redmond, WA
Vawter, Richard E. ....Merrillville, IN
Vawter, Richard H. ....Rolling Hills, CA
Vawter, Robert J. ....Albany, NY
Vawter, Robert R., Jr. ....Tampa, FL
Vax, Julia ....Palo Alto, CA
Vay, John J. ....Austin, TX
Vayda & Alloy ....Palatine, IL
Vayda, George T. ....Hertford, NC
Vayda, John P. ....New York, NY
Vayda, Terence E. ....Palatine, IL
Vayer, M. Scott ....New York, NY
Vayer, Paul S. ....New Britain, CT
Vaygen, Paul A. ....Brooklyn, NY
Vayos, Daphne R. ....Avon, CT
Vazakas, Thomas L. ....San Diego, CA
Vaziri, Emili M. ....Providence, RI
Vazmina, Shelley C. ....Akron, OH

Vaznaugh, Richard J. ....San Francisco, CA
Vazquez, Alina Maria ....Miami, FL
Vazquez, Ana I. ....Chicago, IL
Vazquez, Andrea D. ....Los Angeles, CA
Vazquez, Andrew J. ....Pasadena, CA
Vazquez, Arturo ....El Paso, TX
Vazquez, Carlos A. ....Chicago, IL
Vazquez, Cesar J. ....Kenner, LA
Vazquez, Curt ....Pittsburgh, PA
Vazquez, Daniel ....Hollywood, FL
Vazquez, Elizabeth ....Anchorage, AK
Vazquez, Francisco ....New York, NY
Vazquez, Frank R. ....Neillsville, WI
Vazquez, Gerardo A. ....Miami, FL
Vázquez, Gilbert F. ....San Antonio, TX
Vazquez, Gregory P. ....Chicago, IL
Vazquez, Gustavo ....San Juan, PR
Vázquez, Jesús M., Jr. ....Denver, CO
Vazquez, Laura T.
National Labor Relations Board, Office of the General Counsel, GV
Vazquez, Manuel ....Miami, FL
Vazquez, Manuel, P.A. ....Miami, FL
Vazquez, Maria B. ....Orlando, FL
Vazquez, Mario F. ....Los Angeles, CA
Vazquez, Martha A. ....Santa Fe, NM
Vazquez, Michael A. ....Miami, FL
Vazquez, Michael J., Jr. ....Scranton, PA
Vazquez, Moises ....Whittier, CA
Vazquez, Paul A. ....Tallahassee, FL
Vazquez, Peter J. ....Jersey City, NJ
Vazquez, René A. ....Chantilly, VA
Vazquez, Respicio F. ....Chicago, IL
Vazquez, Rosali ....New York, NY
Vazquez, Sara ....San Juan, PR
Vazquez, Sheila R. ....Portland, OR
Vazquez, Steven W. ....Tampa, FL
Vazquez, Theresa ....Brooklyn, NY
Vazquez, Timothy C. ....New York, NY
Vazquez, Tomasa Del C. ....San Juan, PR
Vazquez, Victoria ....New York, NY
Vazquez Vizcarrondo & Angelet
San Juan, PR
Vazquez-Azpiri, A. James
San Francisco, CA
Vázquez-Bello, Clemente L. ....Miami, FL
Vazquez-Bernier, Jaime L. ....San Juan, PR
Vazquez Bote, Eduardo ....San Juan, PR
Vazquez de Schwartz, Graciela
Department of Justice, Washington, D.C. District Office, GV
Vazquez-Gonzalez, Angel A. ....San Juan, PR
Vázquez-Morales, César ....San Juan, PR
Vazquez Otero, Edmundo ....San Juan, PR
Vazquez-Rodriguez, Julio D.
San Juan, PR
Vázquez Sandoval, Humberto
San Juan, PR
Vazquez-Santoni, Francisco M.
San Juan, PR
Vazzana, Bethaney J.
Christiansted, St. Croix, VI
Vazzana, James A. ....Rochester, NY
Vazzana, James G. ....Rochester, NY
Vazzana, James Leigh ....Mentor, OH
Vazzana, Nicholas S. ....Huntington, NY
Vazzana, Patricia O'Toole ....Rochester, NY
Vea, Laura L. ....New York, NY
Veach, Carson P. ....Chicago, IL
Veach & Coats-Thomas ....Hackensack, NJ
Veach, Deborah ....Hackensack, NJ
Veach, Gregory A. ....Carbondale, IL
Veach, James D. ....New York, NY
Veach, James J. ....Los Angeles, CA
Veach, James L. ....Plano, TX
Veach, John B., III ....Nashville, TN
Veach, Julie A. ....Washington, DC
Veach, Lowell N. ....Tallahassee, FL
Veach, Robert R. ....Omaha, NE
Veach, Robert R., Jr. ....Dallas, TX
Veach, Thomas W. ....Smyrna, GA
Veaco, Kristina ....San Francisco, CA
Veade, Webster, Jr. ....Metairie, LA
Veal & Associates ....Birmingham, AL
Veal, Daryl R.
Securities and Exchange Commission, Division of Enforcement, GV
Veal, Edward Thomas ....Chicago, IL
Veal, Gregory R. ....Atlanta, GA
Veal, Harlan K. ....Woodside, CA
Veal, Rex R. ....Atlanta, GA
Veal, Robert J. ....Birmingham, AL
Veal, Susan D. ....Tallahassee, FL
Veal, William C. ....Birmingham, AL
Veal, William R. ....Santa Rosa, CA
Veale, Francis J., Jr. ....Attleboro, MA
Veale, Karen M. ....Haverhill, MA
Vealey, Bruce E. ....Greenville, RI
Veals, Craig E. ....Los Angeles, CA
Veara, E. James ....Dennis, MA
Veara, Edward E. ....Dennis, MA
Wellesley, MA
Veary, Raymond P., Jr. ....New Bedford, MA
Veasey, E. Norman ....Wilmington, DE
Veasey, Glenda ....Los Angeles, CA
Veasy, Pamela M. ....Boston, MA
Veasy, Paul D. ....Salt Lake City, UT
Veatch, Alan K. ....Columbus, OH
Veatch, Carlson, Grogan & Nelson
Los Angeles, CA
Veatch, Clifford F. ....Olathe, KS
Veatch, J. William, III ....Atlanta, GA
Veatch, John C., II ....Sisters, OR
Veatch, Karin L. ....Indianapolis, IN
Veatch, Ned P. ....Wilmington, DE
Veatch, Wayne ....Los Angeles, CA
Veatch, William S. ....Palo Alto, CA

Veath, Beth Kamp ....Belleville, IL
St. Louis, MO
Veator, David L. ....Randolph, MA
Veazey, Alexander (Lex) H., III
Hendersonville, NC
Veazey, G. Andrew ....Lafayette, LA
Veazey, Gary E. ....Memphis, TN
Veazey, Jeffrey R. ....Dallas, TX
Veazey, Linda ....Abbeville, LA
Veazey, Paul L., Jr. ....Lake Charles, LA
Veazey, Randolph A. ....Nashville, TN
Veazey, Samuel J. ....Ardmore, OK
Veazey-Watson, Chrystal L. ....Newark, NJ
Veazie, Cheryl T. ....Baton Rouge, LA
Veazie, Steven A. ....Urbana, IL
Veber, Jeffrey T. ....Chicago, IL
Veblen, John ....Seattle, WA
Veblen, John Elvidge ....Seattle, WA
Vebman, Joseph ....New York, NY
Vecchi, Christa Van Anh
Federal Trade Commission, Bureau of Consumer Protection, GV
Vecchiarelli, Nancy A. ....Cleveland, OH
Vecchio, Alex B. ....Tampa, FL
Vecchio, Anthony J. ....North Syracuse, NY
Vecchio & Clark ....North Syracuse, NY
Vecchio, Eugenia M. ....Harrison, NY
Vecchio, Eugenia M., and Associates
Harrison, NY
Vecchio, Frank B. ....Birmingham, MI
Vecchio, Gwen ....Santa Ana, CA
Vecchio, Jennifer A. Huffman ....Miami, FL
Vecchio, Joseph A., Jr. ....Fort Lauderdale, FL
Vecchio, Joseph C. ....Falls Church, VA
Vecchio, Joseph G., Jr. ....Winthrop, MA
Vecchio, Lawrence M. ....Haddonfield, NJ
Vecchio, Lynn Dolan-Del ....Newark, NJ
Vecchio, Mark S. ....New York, NY
Vecchio, Philip J. ....East Greenbush, NY
Vecchio, Ralph J. ....Albany, NY
Vecchio, Richard S. ....White Plains, NY
Vecchio, Robert F. ....Arlington, TX
Vecchio, Robert J. ....Cleveland, OH
Mansfield, OH
Vecchio, Robert J., Co., L.P.A.
Cleveland, OH
Mansfield, OH
Vecchio, Steven G. ....Rockford, IL
Vecchioli, Joan M. ....Clearwater, FL
Vecchiolla, John L. ....Greenwich, CT
Vecchione, Constance V. ....Boston, MA
Vecchione, Frank J. ....Newark, NJ
Vecchione, Frank T. ....San Diego, CA
Vecchione, Michael F. ....Williston Park, NY
Vecchione, Robert M. ....New Hyde Park, NY
Vecchiotti, Maria L. ....New York, NY
Vecci, Robert J. ....Los Angeles, CA
Vecella, Frank C. ....Dallas, TX
Vecella, Frank J. ....Baltimore, MD
Vecellio, Constance M.
Federal Trade Commission, Bureau of Consumer Protection, GV
Vecera, David R. ....Arlington, VA
Vecera, Patricia ....Anchorage, AK
Vecere, Andrew Paul ....Smithtown, NY
Vechiola, Robert J. ....Chicago, IL
Vecino, Tony ....San Francisco, CA
Vedder, Andrew T. ....Minneapolis, MN
Vedder, Arthur F. ....Clay, NY
Vedder, Christopher M. ....York, PA
Vedder, Clyde Williamson ....York, PA
Vedder, David F. ....Ormond Beach, FL
Vedder, David F., P.A. ....Daytona Beach, FL
Ormond Beach, FL
Vedder, James F. ....Neenah, WI
Vedder, Karen Ann ....Fayetteville, NY
Vedder, Karen E. ....Mount Vernon, WA
Vedder, Morris A. ....Lincoln Park, MI
Vedder, Phillip ....Carpinteria, CA
Vedder, Price, Kaufman & Kammholz
Chicago, IL
Livingston, NJ
New York, NY
Vedder, Wentworth D. ....Philadelphia, PA
Vedder, Wentworth Darcy ....York, PA
Vedell, Robert L. ....Orange, CA
Vedmed, Victor ....Sarasota, FL
Vedomsky, Michael ....Easton, PA
Vedral, Steven Carl ....Dallas, TX
Vedrich, Amanda E. ....Seattle, WA
Vedrine, Kevin J. ....Wheaton, IL
Vedro, Stephen E. ....Philadelphia, PA
Vedros, George P. ....New Orleans, LA
Vedros, Philip J., III ....Vicksburg, MS
Vee, Harry ....Corona, NY
Veech, Matthew S. ....Houston, TX
Veed, Mary Cannon ....Chicago, IL
Veeder, David A. ....Billings, MT
Veeder, Jolane D. ....Billings, MT
Veeder Law Firm, P.C. A Professional Corporation ....Billings, MT
Veeder, Peter G. ....Pittsburgh, PA
Veeder, R. Bruce ....Toms River, NJ
Veen, William L. ....San Francisco, CA
Veen, William L., A Professional Corporation
San Francisco, CA
Veenendaal, Robert ....Milwaukee, WI
Veenhuis, Diana ....Los Angeles, CA
Veenhuis, Eugene H., (A Professional Corporation) ....Los Angeles, CA
Veenker, Vicki S. ....Palo Alto, CA
Veenstra, Charles K. ....Troy, MI
Veenstra, Henry R., Jr.
West Des Moines, IA
Veenstra, Joseph G. ....La Crosse, WI
Veenstra, Kevin S. ....Santa Rosa, CA
Veenstra, Yves C. ....Marlton, NJ
Veerman, Daniel J. ....Lynn, MA

Veerman, Louis R. ....Anchorage, AK
Veeser, Timothy ....Boston, MA
Vega, Adan G. ....Houston, TX
Vega, Adan G., & Associates, A Prof. Corp.
Houston, TX
Vega, Andrés ....Camden, NJ
Vega, Arthur G., The Law Offices of
San Antonio, TX
Vega, Benj. U. ....Santa Monica, CA
Vega, Benjamin C., Jr. ....Donaldsonville, LA
Vega, Bridgette ....Glendale, CA
Vega, Brown, Stanley & Burke, P.A.
Marco Island, FL
Naples, FL
Vega, Daniel R. ....Miami, FL
Vega, Eric M. ....Milwaukee, WI
Vega, George, Jr. ....Naples, FL
Vega, Guillermo, Jr. ....Brownsville, TX
Vega, Jorge ....San Antonio, TX
Vega, Juan A. ....San Antonio, TX
Vega, Julio E. ....Boston, MA
Vega, Katrina W. ....Covington, KY
Vega, Louie L. ....Bakersfield, CA
Vega, Mario D. ....Los Angeles, CA
Vega, Mark A. ....Los Angeles, CA
Vega, Matias Alfonso ....New York, NY
Vega, Matthew A. ....Spartanburg, SC
Vega, Miguel J. ....Boston, MA
Vega, Robert ....Portage, IN
Vega, Ronald J. ....Kenner, LA
Vega, Rosa M., P.A., Law Offices of
Miami, FL
Vega, Rosa Martin ....Miami, FL
Vega, Rosario Dyana ....Albuquerque, NM
Vega, Ruben J. ....San Pedro, CA
Vega, Sergio ....Miami, FL
Vega, Teresita V. ....Sacramento, CA
Vega, Valorie J. ....Las Vegas, NV
Vega, Vivian M. ....Miami, FL
Vega, Xavier J. ....Los Angeles, CA
Vega-Byrnes, Thomas J. ....Chicago, IL
Vega Couto, Marisol ....San Juan, PR
Vega-López, Edgardo A. ....San Juan, PR
Veganes, Theodore P. ....San Pedro, CA
Vega-Pacheco, Jorge E. ....Aguadilla, PR
Vega Pacheco, Roberto E. ....San Juan, PR
Vegaromero, Juan P. ....Mastic, NY
Vegas, Maria C. ....New York, NY
Vegeler, Robert Owen ....Fort Wayne, IN
Vegh, Anthony J. ....Cleveland, OH
Vegh, Mark A. ....Redding, CA
Veglia, Josephine L. ....Oxford, MA
Veglia, Margaret M. ....Walnut Creek, CA
Vegliante, David J. ....New Haven, CT
Vegliante, Steven Ernest ....Monticello, NY
Vegosen, Dean ....West Palm Beach, FL
Vegosen, Jonathan ....Chicago, IL
Vegter, J. Robert ....Merrillville, IN
Vehanen, Jerome D. ....Minneapolis, MN
Vehar Law Firm, The ....Evanston, WY
Vehar, V. Anthony ....Evanston, WY
Vehec, Kelly R. ....Pittsburgh, PA
Vehik, Joan L. ....Little Rock, AR
Vehik, Mart ....Little Rock, AR
Vehlow, John ....Kuna, ID
Vehrenkamp, Julie A. ....Palo Alto, CA
Vehrs, Kristin L. ....Arlington, VA
Vehrs, Roger K. ....Fresno, CA
Vehslage, Royce L. ....Glastonbury, CT
Veidemanis, Maris ....New York, NY
Veidenheimer, Paul S. ....Department of State, Office of the Legal Adviser, GV
Veidlinger, Rebecca L. ....Bloomington, IN
Veidt, Christopher E. ....Logan, OH
Veiga, AnaMaria ....Orlando, FL
Veiga, Jennifer L. ....Denver, CO
Veiga, Robert J. ....Concord, NH
Veigas, Keith W., Jr. ....Birmingham, AL
Veigel, Charles H. ....Seattle, WA
Veigel, Edward J. ....McKinney, TX
Veigel, Jeffrey E. ....Lakewood, CO
Veigel, Thomas L. ....Columbus, OH
Veight, Joseph W., III ....Bridgeton, NJ
Veiguela, Peter J. ....Chicago, IL
Veil, Robert C., Jr. ....Hagerstown, MD
Veil, Robert C., Jr., P.A. ....Hagerstown, MD
Veillette, James P. ....Washington, DC
Veillette, Michael R. ....Houston, TX
Veillette, Robert E. ....Westlake, OH
Veilleux, Charles H. ....Skowhegan, ME
Veilleux, David N. ....Lewiston, ME
Veilleux, Diana J. ....Washington, DC
Veilleux, Jean Wright ....Charlotte, NC
Veilleux, John E. ....Arlington, VA
Veilleux, Marc J. ....New York, NY
Veilleux, Neil Thomas ....New York, NY
Veilleux, Patricia J. ....Pittsburgh, PA
Veilleux, Paul E. ....Danielson, CT
Veillon, Denise C. ....Portsmouth, VA
Veiluva, Michael J. ....Walnut Creek, CA
Vein, Jon F. ....North Hollywood, CA
Veintraub, Martin Y. ....Cranbury, NJ
Veio, Kent C. ....Denver, CO
Veira, E. Fitzgerald ....Atlanta, GA
Veirs, Kenneth Todd ....Louisville, KY
Veis, Bryan T. ....Treasury Department, Office of Thrift Supervision, GV
Veis, David C. ....Los Angeles, CA
Veis, Kirk M. ....Olympia, WA
Veis, Mimi Yoon ....Washington, DC
Veis, Susan J. ....Santa Monica, CA
Veismanis, Modris ....Placentia, CA
Veisz, Howard S. ....New York, NY
Veit, C. Henry ....San Francisco, CA
Veit, Eric M. ....Emerald Isle, NC
Veit, Frederick C. ....Briarcliff Manor, NY
Veit, Glenn C. ....Hillsborough, NC
Veit, Hans R. ....Chardon, OH

Venino, Richard O., Jr. .... Sea Girt, NJ
Venino, Richard P. .... North Bergen, NJ
Venino, Thomas M. .... North Bergen, NJ
Venino, Thomas M., Jr. .... North Bergen, NJ
Venino and Venino .... North Bergen, NJ
Venishnick, Joseph K. .... Windsor, CT
Venit, Steven L. .... Chicago, IL
Venizelos, James C. .... Cleveland, OH
Venkatappan, Malathi .... Fort Worth, TX
Venkatesh, Vandana .... Waltham, MA
Venkatraman, Bharathi A.
Department of Justice, Executive Office for Immigration Review, GV
Venker, Paul N. .... St. Louis, MO
Venker, Thomas E., Jr. .... St. Louis, MO
Venker, Thomas J. .... Atlanta, GA
Venker, Vincent H., II .... St. Louis, MO
Venkus, Gerald A. .... Worth, IL
Venman, Deborah B. .... Middlebury, VT
Venman, James W. .... Bridgeport, CT
Southport, CT
Venn, Jerry Frederick .... Pagosa Springs, CO
Venn, John E., Jr. .... Pensacola, FL
Venn, John E., Jr., P.A. .... Pensacola, FL
Venne, Donald J. .... Anoka, MN
Venne, Vernon F. .... Dublin, OH
Venneberg, Terry A. .... Eagle River, AK
Vennema, Carey .... New York, NY
Vennemann, Jerome A. .... Cincinnati, OH
Venner, Duane J. .... Denver, CO
Venner, Jason M. .... San Francisco, CA
Venner, John O. .... Virginia Beach, VA
Venner, Troy D. .... Davenport, IA
Vennera, Kenneth R. .... Philadelphia, PA
Venney, Robert E. .... Miami, FL
Venning, Robert S. .... San Francisco, CA
Vennitti, Louis J. .... Warren, OH
Veno, Julie M. .... Woburn, MA
Venokur, Harold Ira .... Brooklyn, NY
Venokur, Sherri .... New York, NY
Venola, J. E., (Ms.) .... Ridgecrest, CA
Venora, Daniel P. .... Berlin, CT
Vensko, Nancy Ways .... San Diego, CA
Venskus, John W. .... Chambersburg, PA
York, PA
Venso, Norma .... Galveston, TX
Vent, H. Henning .... Washington, DC
Ventantonio, James B. .... Warren, NJ
Ventantonio & Wildenhain .... Warren, NJ
Vente, Robert P.
Department of Transportation, Federal Aviation Administration, GV
Venteicher, George W. .... Omaha, NE
Venteicher & Kulig .... Omaha, NE
Venters, Daniel J. .... Somerset, KY
Venters, Edgar N. .... Pikeville, KY
Venters, Harley E. .... Oklahoma City, OK
Venters, Jane Adams .... Somerset, KY
Venters, Jerry W. .... Kansas City, MO
Venters, Tracy D. .... Kansas City, KS
Venti, Gail .... Fremont, CA
Venti, Joseph A. .... Elmwood Park, NJ
Venti, Katherine .... Charleston, WV
Ventimiglia, Joseph J. .... New York, NY
Ventimiglia, Thomas F.
Hilton Head Island, SC
Ventimiglia, Tiziana M. .... Crystal Lake, IL
Ventker, David N. .... Virginia Beach, VA
Vento, Carol Ann .... Moorestown, NJ
Vento, Jill C. .... Waukesha, WI
Vento, Joan T. .... Los Angeles, CA
Vento, John Sebastian .... Tampa, FL
Vento, Joseph A. .... Colorado Springs, CO
Vento, M. Thérèse .... Miami, FL
Ventola, Catherine L. .... St. Louis, MO
Ventola, John F. .... Boston, MA
Ventola, Mark .... Boston, MA
Ventola, Pasquale J. .... Boston, MA
Ventola, Ronald J., II .... New Orleans, LA
Ventola, Samuel M. .... Denver, CO
Ventomiller, Vincent P. .... Pittsburgh, PA
Ventre, Frank, Jr. .... Syracuse, NY
Ventre, Louis, Jr. .... Oakton, VA
Ventre, Martin A. .... Syracuse, NY
Ventre, Robert D. .... Syracuse, NY
Ventre, Stephen J. .... Gilbert, AZ
Ventre, Thomas R. .... Hartford, CT
Ventrell, Camille T. .... Englewood, CO
Ventrell, Karen Hahn .... Washington, DC
Ventrell, Marvin R. .... Denver, CO
Ventrella, Jeffery J. .... Boise, ID
Ventrelle, Michael J. .... Elmhurst, IL
Ventrelli, Mario R. .... Chicago, IL
Ventrell-Monsees, Cathy .... Washington, DC
Ventres, Daniel B., Jr. .... Minneapolis, MN
Ventres, D.B., P.A. .... Minneapolis, MN
Ventres, Judith Martin .... Minneapolis, MN
Ventresca, Benita A., Law Offices of
San Jose, CA
Ventresca, Kenneth M. .... Pittsburgh, PA
Ventresca, Lisa M. .... Pittsburgh, PA
Ventresca, Riccardo D. .... Princeton, NJ
Ventress, Joseph L. .... Santa Monica, CA
Ventress, Michelle B. .... Chicago, IL
Ventress, William T., Jr. .... Enterprise, AL
Ventress, William W. .... Cincinnati, OH
Ventrice, Peter .... Metuchen, NJ
Ventricelli, Daniel J. .... New York, NY
Ventricelli, Joseph C. .... Norwalk, CT
Ventriglia, Denis L., (P.C.) .... Washington, DC
Wilmington, NC
Ventriglia, Denis L., P.C. .... Wilmington, NC
Ventrone, Mark A. .... Syracuse, NY
Ventry, Amy L. .... Garden City, NY
Ventry, Catherine V. .... New Windsor, NY
Ventry, Lynne S.K., P.A. .... Boca Raton, FL
Ventry, Lynne S.K. .... Boca Raton, FL
Ventullo, Maria Christine .... Medford, MA
Ventura, Alfred J. .... Philadelphia, PA
Ventura, Americo S. .... Danbury, CT
Ventura, Anthony F. .... San Jose, CA
Ventura, Anthony J. .... Floral Park, NY
Ventura, Brent N. .... Los Gatos, CA
Ventura, Bruce A. .... New York, NY
Ventura, Carol L. .... Sacramento, CA
Ventura, Danielle L. .... Phoenix, AZ
Ventura, Douglas M. .... Dayton, OH
Ventura, George G. .... Salt Lake City, UT
Ventura, James F. .... Honolulu, HI
Ventura, Janice A. .... Sagamore Beach, MA
Kaysville, UT
Ventura, Jerome P., (P.A.) .... Hollywood, FL
Ventura, Joanne M. .... Marlton, NJ
Ventura, John .... Brownsville, TX
Ventura, John, P.C. .... Brownsville, TX
Harlingen, TX
McAllen, TX
Ventura, Joseph, (P.C.) .... Austin, TX
Ventura, Michael .... Summit, NJ
Ventura, Miesowitz, Albano & Keough, A Professional Corporation .... Elizabeth, NJ
Morristown, NJ
Newark, NJ
Summit, NJ
Ventura, Misty M. .... Dallas, TX
Ventura, Ralph .... Miami, FL
Ventura, Robert G. .... Boston, MA
Ventura, Roderick .... Window Rock, AZ
Ventura, V. James .... Fredericksburg, VA
Venture Law Group .... Menlo Park, CA
San Francisco, CA
San Jose, CA
Kirkland, WA
Venture, Veronica A.
Equal Employment Opportunity Commission, Office of Federal Operations, GV
Venturelli, Andrew .... Passaic, NJ
Venturelli, Donald M. .... Decatur, IL
Venturelli, Lisa A. .... Charlotte, NC
Venturi, Greg J. .... Los Angeles, CA
Venturi, Jack .... New Brunswick, NJ
Venturi, Margaret Garnand .... Sacramento, CA
Venturi, Roger E. .... Gold River, CA
Venturi, Ron A. .... Sea Bright, NJ
Venturini, August C. .... New York, NY
Venturino, Anthony P. .... Washington, DC
Venturino, Lisa A. .... Lake Success, NY
Venturino, Ralph J. .... Los Angeles, CA
Venugopal, Balan .... New York, NY
Venus, Ellen R. .... Boston, MA
Venus, S. Margie .... Houston, TX
Venuti, Annmarie P. .... New York, NY
Venuti, Cynthia Weingart .... Santa Monica, CA
Venuti, Daniel E. .... Aurora, IL
Venuti, Daniel James .... Fairport, NY
Venuti, Dennis P. .... Atlantic City, NJ
Venuti, Joseph A., Jr. .... Mount Laurel, NJ
Venuti, Mark A. .... Geneva, NY
Venuti, Michael David .... Binghamton, NY
Venuto & Associates, Inc. .... Lansing, MI
Venuto, Dino I. .... New York, NY
Venuto, Frank R. .... Lansing, MI
Venuto, Stephen J. .... Menlo Park, CA
Venverloh, Sally L. .... Chicago, IL
Venvertloh, Dale J. .... Quincy, IL
Venza, Denese .... Charleston, WV
Venzer, Ellen Sue .... Miami, FL
Venzie, Howard D., Jr. .... Philadelphia, PA
Venzie, Jeffrey C. .... Philadelphia, PA
Venzie, Phillips & Warshawer, A Professional Corporation .... Philadelphia, PA
Venzke, Gene M. .... Reading, PA
Venzke, John P. .... Houston, TX
Venzke Law Firm, The, L.L.P. .... Houston, TX
Venzke, Tamera L. .... Houston, TX
Venzon, Catharine M. .... Buffalo, NY
Venzon, Joseph A. .... Chicago, IL
Veon, Leslie L., Law Offices of
Chicago, IL
Veon, Marie T. .... Franklin, PA
Veon, Richard A. .... Exton, PA
Veon, Robert .... Philadelphia, PA
Veoukas, April T. .... North Chicago, IL
Vera, Gloria Lee .... Austin, TX
Vera, Helen V. .... New York, NY
Vera, Hernan D. .... Los Angeles, CA
Vera, John B. .... Oklahoma City, OK
Vera, Jorge J. .... Berwyn, IL
Vera, Jose F. .... Seattle, WA
Vera, Joseph S. .... Boston, MA
Vera, Juan J. .... Stockton, CA
Vera, Luis R., Jr. .... San Antonio, TX
Vera, Margaret M. .... San Antonio, TX
Vera, Ronald T. .... Claremont, CA
Vera, Yasmin .... San Francisco, CA
Veracco, Karl J. .... Fort Wayne, IN
Vera-Garcia, Caridad .... Fort Lauderdale, FL
Veraldi, Dennis L. .... Pittsburgh, PA
Veraldi, Lorna .... Miami, FL
Veralrud, Clark, Duvall & Orr, Attorneys, P.C. .... Eugene, OR
Veralrud, Gregory E. .... Eugene, OR
Verani, John R. .... Boston, MA
Verano, Beverly J. .... Irvine, CA
Verano, Carina M. .... Los Angeles, CA
Verano, Hugh T. .... Quincy, MA
Verano, Hugh T., Jr. .... Irvine, CA
Verano, Roxana E. .... Temecula, CA
Verano & Verano, A Professional Law Corporation .... Irvine, CA
Veranth, Amy L. .... Salem, OR
Verardi, Anthony John .... Millburn, NJ
Verardi, Paul A. .... Pittsburgh, PA
Veras, Michael J. .... New York, NY
Verastegui, Yvette .... Santa Ana, CA
Verba, Alexander .... Fairfax, VA
Verba, Steven J. .... St. Clairsville, OH
Verbanic, John T. .... Kansas City, KS
Verbeck, Bruno J. .... La Jolla, CA
Ver Beek, Carl E. .... Grand Rapids, MI
Verbeek, Jeffrey L. .... Mount Clemens, MI
Verber, Ann G. .... Philadelphia, PA
Verber, John J. .... Oakland, CA
Verber, Robert F. .... San Francisco, CA
Verbesey, Paul .... New York, NY
Verbesey, Paul J. .... Boston, MA
Verbillis, Michael J. .... Coeur d'Alene, ID
Verbillis, Michael J., P.A.
Coeur d'Alene, ID
Verbin, Jeffrey H. .... Phoenix, AZ
Verbiski, Laura .... Cleveland, OH
Verbit, David Marc .... Houston, TX
Verbit, Gilbert P. .... Boston, MA
Verbit, Larry E. .... Beverly Hills, CA
Verbit, Stephen R. .... Miami, FL
Verbofsky, Howard I. .... Philadelphia, PA
Verbois, Brenda H. .... Baton Rouge, LA
Verbonitz, Susan .... Turnersville, NJ
Philadelphia, PA
Verboon, Gary W. .... Los Angeles, CA
Verboon, Whitaker & Peter, LLP
Los Angeles, CA
Verbos, Amy Klemm .... Milwaukee, WI
Verburg, Gary .... Williams, AZ
Verby, Dinah F. .... San Francisco, CA
Verby, Steven C. .... Sandpoint, ID
Verby, Steven C., Atty. at Law, P.A., A Prof. Corp. .... Sandpoint, ID
Vercammen, Kenneth A. .... Metuchen, NJ
Vercauteren, Keith E. .... Phoenix, AZ
Verce, Joseph J., Jr. .... Farmington, NM
Verce Law Offices, P.C. .... Farmington, NM
Vercelli, Charles E., Jr. .... Montgomery, AL
Vercelli, Patricia N. .... Reston, VA
Vercheak, Susan J. .... Newark, NJ
Vercher, Cary W. .... Morgan City, LA
Vercher, J. Ronald .... Houston, TX
Verchick, Richard .... New York, NY
Verchick, Stephen H. .... Woodland Hills, CA
Verchio, Donna Marie .... Williamstown, NJ
Verchot, Joan M. .... Cincinnati, OH
Verchota, Allen E., III .... Urbana, IL
Vercillo, Damian J. .... Ashland, OH
Vercimak, John F. .... Olympia, WA
Vercollone, Richard W. .... Hawthorne, NY
Vercruysse Metz & Murray, A Professional Corporation .... Bingham Farms, MI
Detroit, MI
Vercruysse, Robert M.
Bingham Farms, MI
Verd, George H. .... Anacortes, WA
Verde, Louis J. .... Fort Lee, NJ
Verde, Michael A. .... Bristol, CT
Verde, Michael A., P.C. .... Bristol, CT
Verde, Michael I. .... New York, NY
Verde, Richard J. .... West Caldwell, NJ
Verde, Steinberg & Pontell .... Fort Lee, NJ
Hackensack, NJ
New York, NY
Verderaime & Du Bois, P.A.
Baltimore, MD
Verderaime, Robert C. .... Baltimore, MD
Verderame, Deborah S. .... Newark, NJ
Verderame, Frank .... Phoenix, AZ
Verderame, Mary C. .... New York, NY
Verderame, Peter .... Levittown, PA
Verderber, Arlene Rose .... Westbury, NY
Verderose, Alfred J. .... Vineland, NJ
Verdery, Winslow H. .... Cornelia, GA
Verdesca, Joseph T., Jr. .... Newark, NJ
Verdesco, Annette .... Newark, NJ
Verdi, Alfred Joseph .... Beverly Hills, CA
Verdi, Frank P. .... Tampa, FL
Verdi, Gina Witalec .... Boston, MA
Verdi, Raymond W., Jr. .... Garden City, NY
Verdi, Vincent A. .... Westbury, NY
Verdiales, Miguel A. .... San Juan, PR
Verdier, Debora Lynn .... Phoenix, AZ
Verdier, Lawrence J. .... Leland, MI
Verdier, Stephen J. .... Washington, DC
Verdile, Deborah J. .... New York, NY
Verdin, Charles S., IV .... Greenville, SC
Verdin, Jesus A. .... South Pasadena, CA
Verdirame, Bart J. .... New York, NY
Verdirame, Bartholomew .... New York, NY
Verdirame, Bartholomew Michael
Brooklyn, NY
Verdirame, Karen M. .... Omaha, NE
Verdirame, Peter J. .... Baldwin, NY
Verdirame, Vincent L. .... Jersey City, NJ
Verdisco, Robert J. .... Springfield, VA
Verdoia, Carol L. C. .... Salt Lake City, UT
Verdolini, Mario J., Jr. .... New York, NY
Verdon, Anne E. .... New York, NY
Verdon, Jane K. .... Raleigh, NC
Verdon, Jeffrey M. .... Irvine, CA
Verdon, Jeffrey M., P.C. .... Irvine, CA
Verdon, Joseph P. .... New York, NY
Verdon, Karin A. .... Atlanta, GA
Verdon, Peter L. .... Islandia, NY
Verdone, R. Alisha .... Hartford, CT
Verdonik, James F. .... Raleigh, NC
Verdonk and Dunn .... South Haven, MI
Verdonk, John H. .... Bangor, MI
Verdonk, John W. .... Bangor, MI
Verdonk, Verdonk & DiStefano .... Bangor, MI
Verdonk, William J. .... South Haven, MI
Verdream, Anthony F. .... San Ramon, CA
Verdries, Annie .... Costa Mesa, CA
Verduci, Alexander C. .... Carlsbad, CA
Verduci, Paul .... West Chester, PA
Verduci, Samuel P. .... Minneapolis, MN
Ver Dught, ElGene C. .... Higginsville, MO
Independence, MO
Verdugo, Georgina C. .... Department of Justice, Office of Legislative Affairs, GV
Verdugo, Louis .... Los Angeles, CA
Verdugo, Phyllis Bowen .... Los Angeles, CA
Verduin, Timm A. .... San Francisco, CA
Verdun, Hayward A., Jr. .... Palo Alto, CA
Verdun, Helen R. .... Quincy, MA
Vere, Mary A. .... Princeton, NJ
Vereb, Glen Edward .... Treasury Department, Office of Regulations and Rulings, GV
Verebes, Joseph .... New York, NY
Vereeke, David M., Law Offices of
Dallas, TX
Vereen, Darryl S. .... El Paso, TX
Vereen, Elizabeth N. .... Columbia, SC
Veregge, Peter S. .... Los Angeles, CA
Verellen, James R. .... Seattle, WA
Verenes, James L. .... Aiken, SC
Veres, Joseph A. .... Pittsburgh, PA
Veres, Judith H. .... Charleroi, PA
Washington, PA
Veres, Patricia L. .... Denville, NJ
Veres, Richard Kimball .... Oakland, CA
Veres, Robt. L. .... Oakland, CA
Veresan, Nancy K. .... Hanover, NH
Vereschagin, Bryan W. .... San Francisco, CA
Verfurth, Donald J. .... Seattle, WA
Verga, Deborah U. .... Lexington, MA
Verga, Joseph .... Brooklyn, NY
Verga, Patricia Ann .... Jefferson City, MO
Verga, Ronald J. .... Honolulu, HI
Vergados, Anna R. .... Milford, MA
Vergados, Nicholas J. .... Boston, MA
Vergamini, Thomas P. .... Covington, KY
Vergano, Ronald J. .... Teaneck, NJ
Vergano, Sandy Kent .... Philadelphia, PA
Vergara & Associates .... Hopewell, VA
Vergara, E. Marlene .... Hanover, NH
Vergara, James J., Jr. .... Hopewell, VA
Vergara, Michael E. .... Sacramento, CA
Vergara, Rosalyn P. M. .... Arlington, VA
Fairfax, VA
Vergara, Tamara L. .... Downers Grove, IL
Vergari, Bohn C. .... Bronxville, NY
Vergari, Carl A. (IBA) .... White Plains, NY
Vergari, Cozette C. .... Marina Del Rey, CA
Vergas, Richard D. .... Oakland, CA
Verge, Douglas G. .... Manchester, NH
Verge, Thomas L. .... Mount Vernon, WA
Vergeer, Duane .... Portland, OR
Vergeer, John Teunis .... Janesville, WI
Vergeer, Vytas Varekojis .... Washington, DC
Vergelli, John C. .... Sacramento, CA
Vergeront, John G. .... Milwaukee, WI
Vergeront, Margaret J. .... Madison, WI
Vergeront, Meg .... Madison, WI
Vergeront, Robert J. .... Madison, WI
Verges, Conrad G. .... Glenview, IL
Verges, Keith R. .... Dallas, TX
Verges, Scott C. .... San Francisco, CA
Vergets, Paul R. .... Valencia, CA
Vergilii, Jennifer L. .... Des Moines, IA
Vergilio, Joseph Anthony
General Services Administration, Board of Contract Appeals, GV
Vergilis, Gerald A. .... Newburgh, NY
Poughkeepsie, NY
Wappingers Falls, NY
Vergilis, Stenger, Roberts & Pergament
Newburgh, NY
Poughkeepsie, NY
Wappingers Falls, NY
Vergillo, Marc L. .... Philadelphia, PA
Verginia, Melissa .... Moses Lake, WA
Vergne, Jorge .... New Brunswick, NJ
Vergnetti, Anthony .... Treasury Department, Bureau of Alcohol, Tobacco and Firearms, GV
Vergon, Charles B. .... Ann Arbor, MI
Vergon, Frederick P., Jr. .... Cleveland, OH
Vergos, Ellen Bronaugh .... Memphis, TN
Vergos, John C. .... Memphis, TN
Vergotz, James S. .... Pittsburgh, PA
Vergun, Lawrence M. .... Oregon City, OR
Verhaagh, Dennis J. .... Green Bay, WI
Verhaaren, Harold C. .... Salt Lake City, UT
Verhaaren, Robert C. .... New York, NY
Verhage, George E. .... Naperville, IL
Ver Halen, Joanna M. .... Oak Park, IL
Ver Halen, Peter C. .... Los Angeles, CA
Ver Halen, Peter C., Law Corporation
Los Angeles, CA
Verhamme, William A. .... Cleveland, OH
Verharen, Arthur Ward, III .... Tacoma, WA
Verheggen, Theodore F.
Federal Mine Safety and Health Review Commission, Office of the Commissioners, GV
Verheij, Richard H. .... Greenwich, CT
Verhein, Jennifer A. .... Burlington, IA
VerHeulen, Robert J. .... Grand Rapids, MI
Verhey, David M. .... Sacramento, CA
VerHey, Elizabeth Roberts
Grand Rapids, MI
Verhey, John F. .... Chicago, IL
Verheye, Julie P. .... Mishawaka, IN
Verhine, Everette .... Vicksburg, MS
Verhoef, Martin .... Salt Lake City, UT
Ver Hoef, Mary Clarke .... Sacramento, CA
Verhoeff, Karen .... Holly, CO
Verhoeff, Kim R. .... Lamar, CO
Verhoeven, Charles K. .... Palo Alto, CA
Verhoff, Catherine .... New York, NY
Verhoff, Laura Skilton .... Madison, WI
Verhoff, Timothy R. .... Madison, WI
Ver Huel, William R. .... Evanston, IL

Verhulst, Marvin P. .... Madison, WI
Verhulst, Steven L. .... Hillsboro, OR
Verhulst, Thomas C. .... Waterloo, IA
Veri, Joan D. .... Columbus, OH
Verick, William L. .... Eureka, CA
Verin, Eugene R. .... Bessemer, AL
Vering, John A., III .... Kansas City, MO
Verity, Duane P. .... Marion, IL
Verity, George L. .... Oklahoma City, OK
Verity, G. L. Jidge .... Oklahoma City, OK
Verity, Joanne LeBlanc .... Oklahoma City, OK
Verity, Neal .... Akron, OH
Verjovsky, Janice K. .... St. Paul, MN
Verkamp, Jennifer M. .... Cincinnati, OH
Verkamp, John P. .... Greenwood, AR
Verkamp, Joseph L. .... Jasper, IN
Verkamp & McConnell .... Jasper, IN
Verkamp, Stephen L. .... Flagstaff, AZ
Verkin, W. E. "Rusty", II .... Houston, TX
Verkler, Richard A. .... Chicago, IL
Verkler, Richard L., (Ltd.)
Lake Forest, IL
Verkler, Wendy E. .... Chicago, IL
Verkowitz, Charlene K.
New Hyde Park, NY
Verlander, David E., III (P.L.C.)
Monroe, LA
Verlander, Harry S. H., Jr. .... New Orleans, LA
Verlander, Linda A. .... New Orleans, LA
Verlander, Paul J. .... Monroe, LA
Verlander, Richard G., Jr. .... Metairie, LA
Verlaney, Georgia Lynn .... New York, NY
Verlaque, John W. .... Princeton, NJ
Verlasky, Richard P. .... San Diego, CA
Verlato, Cletus R. .... Arcadia, CA
Verlato, Richard Cletus .... Visalia, CA
Verlihay, George A. .... Beaver Falls, PA
Verlin, Jerome R. .... Kennett Square, PA
Verlin, Mark A. .... Bala Cynwyd, PA
Verlizzo, David J. .... Mineola, NY
Verma, Dinesh C. .... Washington, DC
Verma, Kavita .... New York, NY
Verma, Ravender K .... Fort Bragg, NC
Verma, Richard R. .... Washington, DC
Vermazen, Richard V. .... San Diego, CA
Vermeer, Barry G. .... Minneapolis, MN
Vermeer, Edward F. .... Palo Alto, CA
Vermeer, John E. .... Big Rapids, MI
Vermeeren, Barry W. .... Sandusky, OH
Vermeersch, Joyce A. .... Davis, CA
Vermeire, Richard S., (P.C.) .... Denver, CO
Ver Merris, Larry A. .... Grand Rapids, MI
Vermette, Charles E., Jr. .... Hartford, CT
Vermette, Dwight A. .... St. Louis, MO
Vermette, William M. .... Vienna, VA
Vermetten, Matthew D. .... Traverse City, MI
Vermeulen, Joan .... New York, NY
Vermeulen, Kenneth W.
Grand Rapids, MI
Vermeulen, Mark R. .... San Francisco, CA
Vermeys, Gregg R. .... Las Vegas, NV
Vermeys, Sonia C. .... Las Vegas, NV
Vermie, Craig D. .... Cedar Rapids, IA
Vermiglio, Ivan Antonio .... Chicago, IL
Vermillera, Lynn J.
Federal Communications Commission,
Common Carrier Bureau, GV
Vermillion, Claire .... Long Beach, CA
Vermillion, Daniel D. .... Billings, MT
Vermillion, Debra A. .... Overland Park, KS
Vermillion, Lois J. .... Washington, DC
Fairfax, VA
Vermillion, Mary L. .... Albuquerque, NM
Vermillion, Peter A. .... Austin, TX
Vermillion, Robert J. .... Great Falls, MT
Vermillion, Virginia M. .... Chicago, IL
Vermilyea, Jeremy T. .... Anchorage, AK
Vermont, David B. .... Brooklyn, NY
Vermont, Peter .... New York, NY
Vermont, Phillip G. .... Pleasanton, CA
San Jose, CA
Vermont, Venable, Jr. .... Anchorage, AK
Vermooten, Vincent H. .... Austin, TX
Vermut, Richard S. .... Jacksonville, FL
Verna, Catherine M. .... Piscataway, NJ
Verna, James M. .... Washington, DC
Verna, Michael P. .... Walnut Creek, CA
Vernaglia, Joshua J., Jr. .... Boston, MA
Vernaglia, Lawrence W. .... Boston, MA
Providence, RI
Vernallis, Stacey F. .... Pittsburgh, PA
Vernau, Adam K. .... Newark, OH
Vernava, Anthony M. .... Washington, DC
Vernava, Anthony M. .... Fairfax, VA
Verne, Andrew G., & Associates
San Diego, CA
Verne, Barbara A. .... Cleveland, OH
Verne, Maxine H. .... New York, NY
Vernell, Louis, Jr. .... North Miami Beach, FL
Vernen, Rod A. .... Tallahassee, FL
Verner, Andrew .... Boca Raton, FL
Verner & Brumley, A Professional
Corporation .... Dallas, TX
Verner, Charles V. .... Newberry, SC
Verner, Douglas H. .... Silver Spring, MD
Verner, James M. .... Washington, DC
Verner, James S., Jr. .... Newberry, SC
Verner, Jimmy L., Jr. .... Dallas, TX
Verner, John L. .... Houston, TX
Verner, Liipfert, Bernhard, McPherson and
Hand, Chartered .... Washington, DC
Miami, FL
Honolulu, HI
Austin, TX
Houston, TX
Verner, Paul W. .... Audubon, NJ
New York, NY
Verner, Richard B. .... New York, NY

Verner, Shawn L. .... Memphis, TN
Verner Simon LLP .... Audubon, NJ
New York, NY
Verneris, Erin M. .... Palo Alto, CA
Vernet, Jean E.
Department of Energy, GV
Vernetti, JoAnna .... Raymondville, TX
Verneuille, Jo Lynne .... Elk Grove, CA
Verney, Bernard .... Verona, NJ
Verni, John A. .... White Plains, NY
Verni, Ralph M. .... Baldwin, NY
Vernia, Benjamin J. .... Department of Justice,
Civil Division, GV
Vernick, Amy .... New York, NY
Vernick, Andrew E. .... Annapolis, MD
Baltimore, MD
Vernick, Gary B. .... Philadelphia, PA
Vernick, Kevin J. .... New York, NY
Vernick, Michael J. .... Washington, DC
Vernick, Scott L. .... Philadelphia, PA
Vernier, D. Paul, Jr. .... Hagåtña, GU
Vernier, Michael K. .... New York, NY
Vernier-Gelven, Nicole Marie
Oklahoma City, OK
Verniero, Peter G. .... Trenton, NJ
Vernieu, John T. .... Albany, NY
Vernieu, Paul D. .... Ogden, UT
Vernis & Bowling of Ft. Lauderdale, P.A.
Fort Lauderdale, FL
Vernis & Bowling of Miami, P.A.
DeLand, FL
Fort Myers, FL
Islamorada, FL
North Miami, FL
Vernis & Bowling of Palm Beach, P.A.
Jupiter, FL
Vernis & Bowling of the Gulf Coast, P.A.
Clearwater, FL
Vernis, Frank C., Jr., (P.A.)
Fort Lauderdale, FL
North Miami, FL
Vernis, G. Jeffrey .... Jupiter, FL
North Miami, FL
Verno, Michele C. .... Linwood, NJ
Vernoff, Wallace R. .... Pasadena, CA
Vernoia, Francis J. .... Livingston, NJ
Vernon, Albert E., III .... Tampa, FL
Vernon, Allen H., Jr. .... Ocean City, NJ
Vernon, Bill .... Houston, TX
Vernon, Charles A. .... Houston, TX
Vernon, Charles E. .... Kalispell, MT
Vernon, Charles W., III
Pension Benefit Guaranty Corporation,
Office of the General Counsel, GV
Vernon, Christopher T. .... Naples, FL
Vernon, Craig K. .... Coeur d'Alene, ID
Vernon, Darryl M. .... New York, NY
Vernon, David H. .... Iowa City, IA
Vernon, David W. .... Weatherford, TX
Vernon, Dean P. .... Las Vegas, NV
Vernon, Donald P. .... Berwyn, PA
Vernon & Duray, L.L.P. .... Dallas, TX
Vernon, Elliott H. .... Shrewsbury, NJ
Vernon, Eric A. .... Raleigh, NC
Vernon, George .... Chicago, IL
Monroe, WI
Vernon & Ginsburg .... New York, NY
Vernon, Glen K. .... King Salmon, AK
Vernon, Jacqueline M. .... New York, NY
Vernon, James F. .... Los Angeles, CA
Vernon, James H. .... San Ramon, CA
Vernon, James M. .... Nevada City, CA
Vernon, Jan M. .... Denver, CO
Vernon, Jennifer J. .... Sun Prairie, WI
Vernon, John C. .... Tacoma, WA
Vernon, John G. .... Marion, IA
Vernon, John H., III .... Burlington, NC
Vernon, John K. .... Des Moines, IA
Vernon, John M. .... Dallas, TX
Vernon, Judith C. .... Evant, TX
Vernon, Keith T. .... Cleveland, OH
Vernon, Kim B. .... Austin, TX
Vernon, Kirby A. .... Wichita, KS
Vernon, L. Skip .... Albuquerque, NM
Vernon, Larry S. .... Concordia, KS
Vernon, Lawson C. .... Houston, TX
Vernon, Leo .... Philadelphia, PA
Vernon, Leo, P.C. .... Philadelphia, PA
Vernon, Lillian Malley .... Remsenburg, NY
Vernon, Livingston .... Morganton, NC
Vernon, M. Catherine .... Highland Heights, OH
Vernon, Nancy P. .... Jacksonville, AL
Vernon, Page Humphrey .... Pittsboro, NC
Vernon, Paul F. .... Dallas, TX
Vernon, Richard G. .... Bethesda, MD
Vernon, Robert Bruce .... Charlotte, NC
Vernon, Ronald Eugene .... Seattle, WA
Vernon, Susan .... Key West, FL
Vernon, Terry M. .... Fort Worth, TX
Vernon, Vernon, Wooten, Brown, Andrews &
Garrett, P.A. .... Burlington, NC
Graham, NC
Vernon, W. John .... Baltimore, MD
Vernon, W. Thomas .... Columbia, SC
Vernon, William S. .... Cedar Rapids, IA
Vernone, Michael J. .... Dallas, TX
Vernon-Gann, Sherry .... Springfield, MO
Verny, Hana .... Palo Alto, CA
Vero, Anthony .... Chicago, IL
Vero, Martina Jaccarino .... Las Vegas, NV
Veron, Enid L. .... Washington, DC
Veron, Gary Lee .... Annapolis, MD
Veron, J. Michael .... Lake Charles, LA
Veron, Richard L. .... New York, NY
Verona, David A., Jr. .... Schaumburg, IL
Verona & Freeman, P.A. .... St. Petersburg, FL
Verona, Jay B. .... St. Petersburg, FL
Verona, Russell M. .... Miami, FL

Veronese, William L. .... Melville, NY
Veronica Law Offices, Ltd.
Minneapolis, MN
Veronica, Louis A. .... Haddonfield, NJ
Veronica, Meloni & Vecchio
Haddonfield, NJ
Veronis, Nicholas A. .... Lancaster, PA
Verosloff, Byron M. .... North Brunswick, NJ
Verosloff, Irving J. .... North Brunswick, NJ
Verow, Dorothy R. .... Westbury, NY
Verp, Leddy & Ranieri .... Wayne, NJ
Verp, Martin .... Wayne, NJ
Verp, Stephen A. .... Wayne, NJ
VerPlanck, Alan .... Fort Wayne, IN
Ver Ploeg, Brenton N. .... Miami, FL
Ver Ploeg, Christine D. .... St. Paul, MN
Ver Ploeg & Lumpkin, P.A. .... Key West, FL
Miami, FL
Verr, Steven R. .... Chicago, IL
Verrall, Timothy G. .... Oklahoma City, OK
Verran, Rowland E. .... Johnson City, TN
Verras, Spiro J. .... New Orleans, LA
Verrastro, Danielle M. .... Springfield, NJ
Verrastro, Gaetano J. .... Ojai, CA
Verrastro, James P. .... Buffalo, NY
Verratti, Carol McCue
United States International Trade
Commission,
Office of the General Counsel, GV
Verrelli, Anthony L. .... Bronx, NY
Verret, Chris A. .... Lafayette, LA
Verret, Mark W. .... Covington, LA
Verrett, Ann E. .... St. Louis, MO
Verrett, Timothy C. .... Anchorage, AK
Verrette, Phillip .... Tucson, AZ
Verri Law Offices .... Providence, RI
Verri, Richard G. .... Providence, RI
Verri, Robert P. .... Providence, RI
Verri, Saundra B. .... Providence, RI
Verrico, James Andrew .... Buffalo, NY
Verrier, Jo-Ann M. .... Philadelphia, PA
Verrier, Lita Monique .... San Jose, CA
Verrigni, Alexandra .... Rexford, NY
Verrill, Charles Owen, Jr.
Washington, DC
Verrill & Dana .... Washington, DC
Augusta, ME
Kennebunk, ME
Portland, ME
Verrill, Eric .... Arlington, MA
Verrill, Ralph T. .... New York, NY
Verrill, Ted W. .... Stamford, CT
Verrilli, Donald B. .... New York, NY
Verrilli, Donald B., Jr. .... Washington, DC
Verrilli, Frank J. .... Bridgeport, CT
Verrilli, John M. .... Oakhurst, NJ
Verrilli, John T. .... Clifton, NJ
Verrilli, Timothy R. .... Chicago, IL
Verrillo, Eugénie .... Greenwich, CT
Verrillo, James G. .... Bridgeport, CT
Verrillo, Maurice J. .... Rochester, NY
Verrillo, Philip .... Hartford, CT
Verron, Kathleen M. .... Wilton, CT
Verrone, Judy A. .... Teaneck, NJ
Verrone, Patric M. .... Pacific Palisades, CA
Verrue-Slater, Katherine M. .... Rocklin, CA
Versace, Kimberly M. .... Washington, DC
New York, NY
Versace, Rocco L. .... Rome, NY
Versaci, Tina Chericoni .... Albany, NY
Verscaj, James P. .... New York, NY
Verscaj, John J. .... Northbrook, IL
Versch, Werner, II .... Richmond, VA
Verschelden, Matthew J.
Kansas City, MO
Verschleiser, Jack .... Brooklyn, NY
Verschoor, Katherine Anne .... Chicago, IL
Verschoyle, James H. .... Atlanta, TX
Verschuuren, Charles L. .... Babylon, NY
Verseman, Scott
Department of Justice, GV
Verser, Craddock D. .... Port Townsend, WA
Versfelt, David S. .... New York, NY
Vershbow, Mark E. .... Boston, MA
Vershum, Mary J. .... Portland, OR
Versichelli, Michael P. .... Uniondale, NY
Verska, Kimberly A. (Yahr) .... Atlanta, GA
Versluis, Peter P. .... Grand Rapids, MI
Versnel, John C., III .... Seattle, WA
Versolato, Amy-Jo C. .... St. Paul, MN
Verson, Alan .... Northampton, MA
Verspoor, Carl J. .... Grand Rapids, MI
Verspoor, Waalkes, Lalley & Slotsema, P.C.
Grand Rapids, MI
Verst, Edward C. .... Cincinnati, OH
Verst, Justin D. .... Newport, KY
Verstandig, John D. .... Washington, DC
VerSteeg, J. Russell .... Boston, MA
Ver Steeg, John C. .... Washington, DC
Ver Steeg, Jolene .... Englewood, CO
Ver Steeg, Kristen Kay .... Treasury Department,
Office of Regulations and Rulings, GV
Versteeg, Ronald B. .... Cave Junction, OR
Ver Steegh, Jack .... Minneapolis, MN
Verstegen, Anne-Marie .... Washington, DC
Verstegen & Fobe .... Washington, DC
Verster, Martyn W. D., P.A.
Homestead, FL
Miami, FL
Verster, Martyn W. D. .... Miami, FL
Verstynen, Michael A. .... Decatur, TN
Versurah, Vincent V., Jr. .... Tampa, FL
Vert, Kenneth C. .... Department of Justice,
Tax Division, GV
Vertefeuille, Christine S. .... Waterbury, CT
Verterano, Frank G. .... New Castle, PA
Verterano & Manolis .... New Castle, PA
Vertes, William W. .... Detroit, MI

Vertesch, Michael F. .... Indianapolis, IN
Vertesch, Paul F. .... Richmond, IN
Vertetis, Thomas B. .... Bridgewater, NJ
Verticchio, Rick .... Gillespie, IL
Verticchio, Thomas J. .... Chicago, IL
Vertinsky, Liza .... Boston, MA
Vertman, Jedd B. .... Washington, DC
Vertner, Victor D. .... San Jose, CA
Vertovec, Edward J. .... Oak Brook, IL
Vertreace, Walter C. .... Woodbridge, NJ
Vertrees, John C. .... Seattle, WA
Vertrees, Ralph W. .... Austin, TX
Vertucci, Sherri L. .... Schenectady, NY
Vertun, Alan S. .... Los Angeles, CA
Vertun, Alan S., A Prof. Law Corp.
Los Angeles, CA
Vertuno, Anthony A. .... Washington, DC
Vertuno, Maria L. .... Chicago, IL
Vertz, Brian C. .... Pittsburgh, PA
Vervack, Jerry J. .... Goshen, AR
Vervaecke, Karen L. .... Omaha, NE
Vervaecke, Michael S. .... Mason City, IA
Vervaecke, Mindi M. .... Mason City, IA
Verveer, Alexandra .... Department of Justice,
Office of the Associate Attorney General,
GV
Verveer, Philip L. .... Washington, DC
Verveniotis, Steven .... New York, NY
Ververidis, Harikliа .... Malden, MA
Verville, Elizabeth G.
Department of State, GV
Verville, Jeanne M. .... Seattle, WA
Verville, Richard E. .... Washington, DC
Verville, Sarah A. .... Freeport, ME
Ver Weire, W. Todd .... Farmington, AR
Verwey, Vickey A., Jr. .... Richmond, VA
Ver Weyst, Katherine Chester .... Bismarck, ND
Verwolf, Nick S. .... Bellevue, WA
Verwys, Mark H. .... Grand Rapids, MI
Very, David P. .... Portland, ME
Very, Dennis R. .... Pittsburgh, PA
Verzaal, Gerard P. .... Cartersville, GA
Verzani, Marc E. .... Boston, MA
Verzani, Robert J. .... Federal Way, WA
Verzyl, Edwin .... Safety Harbor, FL
Vesagas, Maria Rita .... Beverly Hills, CA
Vescelus, John W. .... Mesa, AZ
Vescelus, Powell & Stock .... Wheaton, IL
Veschio, Victor H. .... Tampa, FL
Vescio, Lynda R. .... New York, NY
Vescio, Michael A. .... Lexington, KY
Vescio, Michael R. .... Racine, WI
Vesco, John A. .... El Segundo, CA
Vesco, Paul A., Jr. .... Jamul, CA
Vescovacci, Milton A. .... New York, NY
Vescovo, Anna M. .... Memphis, TN
Vescovo, Christopher L. .... Memphis, TN
Vescovo, Stephen W. .... Memphis, TN
Vesel, Beverly L. .... Fort Lauderdale, FL
Vesel, David A. .... Raleigh, NC
Vesel, Edward .... Mineola, NY
Veseli, Ralph R. .... Milpitas, CA
Veselich, Lisa A. .... Kansas City, MO
Veselka, Larry R. .... Houston, TX
Veselka, Shelburne J. .... Austin, TX
Vesely, Amy J. .... Wellesley, MA
Vesely, Brandon S. .... St. Petersburg, FL
Vesely, Edward G., Jr. .... Hinsdale, IL
Vesely, Ernest V. .... Pittsburgh, PA
Vesely, Ivan J. .... Portland, OR
Vesely, Jeffrey M. .... San Francisco, CA
Vesely, Lawrence G. .... Green Bay, WI
Vesely, Liam J. .... Boston, MA
Vesely, Miller & Steiner, P.A. .... Hopkins, MN
Vesely, Robert H. .... Williamsport, PA
Vesely, Shirin Mohammadbhoy
St. Petersburg, FL
Vesely, Thomas .... North Woodmere, NY
Vesely, Tori A. .... Baraboo, WI
Vesely, V. Lee .... Silver City, NM
Vesely, William J. .... Williamsburg, VA
Vesely, William J., Jr. .... Atlanta, GA
Veser, George B. .... Latham, NY
Vesey, Thomas A. .... Claremont, CA
Vesheco, Michael J. .... Harrisburg, PA
Veshia, Jennifer L. .... Hartford, CT
Veskauf, Thomas J. .... Springfield, OH
Veski, Vello .... Palm City, FL
Vesledahl, Kenneth Mark .... Dallas, TX
Vesmas, R. J. .... Warren, OH
Vesnaver, Paul G. .... Rockville Centre, NY
Vesneski, William M. .... Seattle, WA
Vesole, Martin K. .... Chicago, IL
Vesole, Richard I. .... Bettendorf, IA
Vespa, Adele M. .... Atlanta, GA
Vespa, Anthony L. .... Troy, MI
Vespa, Joe R. .... Peoria, IL
Vespa, John P. .... Peoria, IL
Vespa, Robert F. .... Springfield, IL
Vespa-Papaleo, J. Frank .... Livingston, NJ
Vespasiano, Louis A. .... Springfield, NJ
Vesper, Christian James .... New York, NY
Vesper, Gerald W., Law Office of
Washington, DC
Vesper, James M. .... San Francisco, CA
Vesper, Stephanie M. .... Cincinnati, OH
Vesper, Thomas J. .... Atlantic City, NJ
Vespereny, Linda E. .... Cherokee, NC
Vespia, James A. .... Warwick, RI
Vespole, Mark Robert .... West Orange, NJ
Vespoli, Leila .... Akron, OH
Vess, Bryan C. .... San Diego, CA
Vess & Carpenter .... North Little Rock, AR
Vess, Henry B., III .... Wheaton, IL
Vess, Stuart C. .... North Little Rock, AR
Vessa, Michael P. .... Mineola, NY
Vessa & Wilensky, P.C. .... Mineola, NY
Vessal, Elissa S. .... Philadelphia, PA

Vessel & Morales, P.A. ....Tampa, FL
Vessel, Robert L. ....Tampa, FL
Vesselinovitch, Alexander S. ....Chicago, IL
Vessella, Maret ....New Castle, PA
Vessels, Ann S. Irwin ......Colorado Springs, CO
Vessels, Rodney J. ....Hartford, CT
Vessenes, Katherine K. ....St. Paul, MN
Vessey, James B., (P.A.) ......Minneapolis, MN
Vest, Alan ....Sac City, IA
Vest, Becker & Murray ....Sac City, IA
Vest, David G. ....Newport Beach, CA
Vest, David G. ....Lexington, KY
Vest, G. Waverly, Jr. ....Houston, TX
Vest & Howse, P.A. ....Brooklyn Center, MN
Vest, Jefferson D. ....Sacramento, CA
Vest, Jeffrey K. ....Brooklyn Center, MN
Vest, Kenneth W. ....Morristown, NJ
Vest, Margaret E. ....Wooster, OH
Vest, Pamela Jean ....Columbus, OH
Vest, Phillip R. ....Nashville, TN
Vest, Robert E. ....St. Augustine, FL
Vestal, Allan W. ....Lexington, VA
Vestal, Barbara A. ....Portland, ME
Vestal, David D. ....Des Moines, IA
Vestal, Donald J. ....Hollywood, FL
Vestal, John H. ....Plano, TX
Vestal, Josephine B. ....Seattle, WA
Vestal, Katharine T. ....Washington, DC
Vestal, Kent Greer, Jr. ....Little Rock, AR
Vestal, L. Charles ....Yadkinville, NC
Vestal, Paul E. ....Tulsa, OK
Vestal, Peter L. ....San Francisco, CA
Vestal, R. Gerald ....Winston-Salem, NC
Vestal, Richard H. ....Houston, TX
Vestal & Simonson, P.A. ....Tulsa, OK
Vestal, Truett H. ....Houston, TX
Vestecka, Buethe & Frey ....Lincoln, NE
Vestevich, Mallender, DuBois & Dritsas, P.C.
Bloomfield Hills, MI
Vestevich, Peter ....Bloomfield Hills, MI
Vestevich, Philip ....Bloomfield Hills, MI
Vestevich, Susan A. ....Detroit, MI
Vestner, Eliot N., Jr. ....New York, NY
Vestrand, Joan P. ....Southfield, MI
Vesy, Caryl H. ....New Orleans, LA
Veta, D. Jean ....Department of Education,
Office of the General Counsel, GV
Vetere, Robert L. ....Danbury, CT
Veteri, Kathleen K. ....New York, NY
Veternick, Robin ....Appleton, WI
Veters, Frederick W. "Fritz"
New Orleans, LA
Veters, Patrick J. ....New Orleans, LA
Veteto, Thomas M. ....Memphis, TN
Veth, John J. ....Irvine, CA
Vetica, John P., Jr. ....Pittsburgh, PA
Vetne, J. Thomas ....Merrillville, IN
Vetne, John H. ....Peterborough, NH
Veto, Anthony H. ....Lakewood, CO
Veto, William R. ....New York, NY
Vetrano, Anthony J. ....King Of Prussia, PA
Vetrano, Anthony L., Jr. ....Houston, TX
Vetrano & Bravacos ....King Of Prussia, PA
Vetrano, Kathleen Bilotta
King Of Prussia, PA
Vetrano, Vincent P. ....Endicott, NY
Vetri, Barbara ....Philadelphia, PA
Vetri, Dominick R. ....Eugene, OR
Vetri, Matthew J. ....Brooklyn, NY
Vetri, Scott M. ....New York, NY
Vetrick, Joseph J. ....Tavernier, FL
Vetro, Frank ....Gloversville, NY
Vetro, Michael ....Boone, NC
Vetro, Michael, Atty. & Counsellor at Law, P.C.
Boone, NC
Vetro, Peter F. ....Garden City, NY
Vetrone, Christine Burke ....New York, NY
Vetstein, Edward M. ....Boston, MA
Vetstein, Richard D. ....Boston, MA
Vettel, Ronald W. ....Jefferson, OH
Vettel, Steven L. ....San Francisco, CA
Vetter, Adam, Jr. ....Mansfield, OH
Vetter, Bernard K. ....New Orleans, LA
Vetter, Charles T., Jr. ....Washington, DC
Vetter, Connie J. ....Charlotte, NC
Vetter, Cyril E. ....Baton Rouge, LA
Vetter, David R. ....Clearwater, FL
Vetter, Douglas G. ....Armonk, NY
Vetter, E. Russell ....Salt Lake City, UT
Vetter, George ....Providence, RI
Vetter, Gerard R. ....Baltimore, MD
Vetter, Jack ....Sacramento, CA
Vetter, James G., Jr. ....Dallas, TX
Vetter, Jan ....Berkeley, CA
Vetter, Jeffrey R. ....Palo Alto, CA
Vetter, John A. ....Wichita, KS
Vetter, John C. ....New York, NY
Vetter, John R. (Jack) ....Sacramento, CA
Vetter, Kathy Renee ....Parker, CO
Vetter, Mark F. ....Milwaukee, WI
Vetter, Melanie Hirschhorn ....Mill Valley, CA
Vetter, Michael J. ....Nashville, TN
Vetter, Norman L. ....Oceanside, CA
Vetter, Peter P. ....Butler, WI
Vetter, Richard H.
Environmental Protection Agency,
Office of the General Counsel, GV
Research Triangle Park, NC
Vetter, Roger L. ....Belleville, IL
Vetter, Roger L. P.C. ....Belleville, IL
Vetter, Stephen K. ....Washington, DC
Vetter, Thomas A. ....Jefferson City, MO
Vetter, Thomas J. ....Norwalk, CT
Vetter, Thomas J. ....New York, NY
Vetter, Todd B. ....Norfolk, NE
Vetter, Virginia R. ....Tampa, FL
Vetter & White, Incorporated
Providence, RI
Vetter, William ....Seal Beach, CA
Vetterlein, Eric H. ....Portland, OR
Vetterli, John R. ....New York, NY
Vetters, Clare I. ....Houston, TX
Vettiyil & Associates, P.C. ....Nogales, AZ
Tucson, AZ
Vettiyil, Saji ....Nogales, AZ
Tucson, AZ
Vetto, Jane E. ....Lake Oswego, OR
Vettorello, Nancy E. ....Detroit, MI
Vettori, Frank Q. ....Knoxville, TN
Vettori, Paul M. ....Baltimore, MD
Vetzner, Charles B. ....Madison, WI
Vetzner, Gretchen T. ....Madison, WI
Veugeler, Kevin T. ....Chicago, IL
Veum, Thomas J., P.C. ......Sault Ste. Marie, MI
Veurink, Gary Lee ....Muskegon, MI
Veve, Michael E. ....Washington, DC
Veve, Valerie ....San Antonio, TX
Veverka, Charles J. ....Salt Lake City, UT
Veverka, Donald J. ....Chicago, IL
Veverka, Rosen & Haugh ....Chicago, IL
Vexler, Robert Irwin ....Chappaqua, NY
Vey, Gary S. ....Suwanee, GA
Vey, Mary M. ....Pittsburgh, PA
Vey, Paul K. ....Pittsburgh, PA
Veylupek, Alex N. ....Sacramento, CA
Veyrac, Christine C. ....San Jose, CA
Veys, Richard S. ....Chicago, IL
Veysey, Michael C. ....Eastlake, OH
Vezeau, Timothy J. ....Chicago, IL
Vezeris, David J. ....New York, NY
Vezey, Bryan P. ....Houston, TX
Vezina, G. Scott ....Gretna, LA
Vezina, Kathryn L. ....Augusta, ME
Portland, ME
Vezina, Lawrence & Piscitelli, P.A.
Fort Lauderdale, FL
Orlando, FL
Tallahassee, FL
Tampa, FL
Vezina, Nel F. ....Gretna, LA
Vezina, Stacy L. ....Boston, MA
Vezina, W. Robert, III ....Tallahassee, FL
Vezino, Patrick J. ....Chicago, IL
Veznaian, Mary ....Boston, MA
Vezzani, Diane L. ....Los Angeles, CA
Vezzani, Mark B. ....San Fernando, CA
Vezzetti, Roxanne ....Department of Labor,
Office of Secretary, GV
Vezzolini, Robert M. ....San Jose, CA
Vhay, Michael D. ....Boston, MA
Vhugen, Harold F. ....Seattle, WA
Via, Bernard S., III ....Bristol, VA
Via, E. Jane ....San Diego, CA
Via, George M. ....Booneville, MS
Via, Martha L. ....Denton, TX
Via, Mikael W. ....Ventura, CA
Via, Patricia P. ....Rockville, MD
Via, Patrick I. ....Lewisburg, WV
Via, Raymond B., Jr. ....Silver Spring, MD
Via, Susan R. ....Boston, MA
Via, Tay C. ....San Francisco, CA
Via, Willard R., Jr. ....Atlanta, GA
Viada, Ramon G., III ....Houston, TX
Viadro, Christopher A.
San Francisco, CA
Viadro, Harriet Ann ....Redwood City, CA
Viaene, Axel ....Atlanta, GA
Viakley, Ellen M. ....Pittsburgh, PA
Vial, A.R., Associates, P.C. ....Portland, OR
Vial, A. Richard ....Portland, OR
Vial, Hamilton, Koch & Knox, L.L.P.
Dallas, TX
Houston, TX
Vial, Leon C., III (A P.L.C.) ....Hahnville, LA
Vial, Leslie A. ....Arlington, VA
Vial, Peter M. ....Seattle, WA
Vial, Robert Crist ....Dallas, TX
Vial, Robert G., (P.C.) ....Dallas, TX
Vialet, Fred, Jr.
Charlotte Amalie, St. Thomas, VI
Viall, Thomas R. ....Montpelier, VT
Viall, Wilton S., III ....Seattle, WA
Vian, Deborah Ann ....Orange, CA
Vian, John T. ....Atlanta, GA
Viana, Carlos ....New York, NY
Viana, Claudia T. ....New York, NY
Viana, Steven P. ....Bradenton, FL
Vianale, Kenneth J. ....Boca Raton, FL
Viani, Mark Michael ....Silver Spring, MD
Vianna, Nicholas F. ....New York, NY
Viano, Peter A. ....San Jose, CA
Viar, David B. ....Southfield, MI
Viar, Elisabeth Anne
United States Court Of Appeals District Of
Columbia Circuit, GV
Viar, Richard E. ....Roanoke, VA
Viator, Mary M. ....Palm Beach, FL
Viau, Floyd R. B. ....Del Rey, CA
Viau, James J. ....Escanaba, MI
Viau, James J., P.C. ....Escanaba, MI
Viau, Jeanette L. ....Glendale, CA
Viau, Lawrence E., Jr. ....Del Rey, CA
Vibbard, Mark ....Del Mar, CA
Vibbert, Dwight N. ....Lexington, MA
Vibhakar, Vineeta J. ....Torrance, CA
Vican, Ronald ....Stroudsburg, PA
Vicari, Anne Marie ....Gurnee, IL
Vicari, Dominick G. ....White Plains, NY
Vicari, Louis R. ....Stony Point, NY
Vicari, Matthew L. ....Grand Rapids, MI
Vicario, Joseph A., Jr. ....Dallas, TX
Vicario, Lawson ....Greenville, SC
Vicarisi, Joseph R. ....Nutley, NJ
Vicary, Henry, III ....Peoria, IL
Vicary, Lester Wm., Jr., (P.C.) ....Morton, IL
Viccaro, Patrick J. ....Pittsburgh, PA
Viccellio, Charles D. ....Lake Charles, LA
Vicellio, Susan Gay ....Lake Charles, LA
Viccora, Michael A. ....Washington, DC
Vice, Barry P. ....Houma, LA
Vice, Daniel R. ....Washington, DC
Vice, Gwen Clore ....Florence, KY
Vice, Kevin W. ....Dallas, TX
Vice, Robert B. ....Louisville, KY
Viceconte, Christopher ....Morristown, NJ
Vicedomini, Thomas J. ....Commack, NY
Vicencia, Michael P. ....Long Beach, CA
Vicencio, Fiorello J., Jr. ....Washington, DC
Vicente, Harold D. ....San Juan, PR
Vicente, Jason J. ....Brighton, MA
Vicente, Rebecca M. ....Bloomfield, CT
Vicente, Wendy S. ....Washington, DC
Vicente Colon, Harold D. ....San Juan, PR
Vichich, Jon J. ....Pittsburgh, PA
Vichness, Paul J. ....Fairfield, NJ
Vician, George, Jr. ....New York, NY
Vician, Glenn S. ....Merrillville, IN
Vicien-Milburn, R. Maria ....New York, NY
Vicinaiz, Victor V. ....McAllen, TX
Vicinanza, Gregg H.
Federal Trade Commission,
Bureau of Competition, GV
Vicinanza, Joseph J. ....New York, NY
Vicinanzo, David A. ....Concord, NH
Vicinanzo, Vincent E. ....Amsterdam, NY
Vick, Ardita L. ....Dallas, TX
Vick, B. Jim ....Waco, TX
Vick, Bruce S. ....Belleville, IL
Vick, Calvin T., Jr. ....Atlanta, GA
Vick, Chandra V. ....Bridgewater, NJ
Vick, Chrestman & Carney, L.L.P.
Weatherford, TX
Vick, Deborah L. ....Issaquah, WA
Vick, Forest B., Jr. ....Sacramento, CA
Vick, Gabe T. ....Weatherford, TX
Vick, Helen Conklin ....Ypsilanti, MI
Vick, J. Jerry, Jr. ....Jackson, NC
Vick, James D. ....Salem, OR
Vick, Jason H. ....Alexandria, VA
Vick, J. J. ....Fort Collins, CO
Greeley, CO
Vick, Joe P. ....Cincinnati, OH
Vick, John E., Jr. ....Greenville, SC
Vick, Jonathan S. ....Irvine, CA
Los Angeles, CA
Pleasanton, CA
Vick, Joseph James, III ....Fort Collins, CO
Vick, Karl A. ....Chicago, IL
Vick, L. Kevin ....Belleville, IL
St. Louis, MO
Vick, Larry D. ....Raleigh, NC
Vick, Leroy ....Cheyenne, OK
Vick, Margaret J. ....Tempe, AZ
Vick, Patricia G. ....Pasadena, CA
Vick, Paul A. ....Rochester, NY
Vick, Paul G., Law Office of
San Antonio, TX
Vick, Phillip O. ....Denton, TX
Vick, Ralph D. ....Greenville, KY
Vick, Robert E. ....Greenville, KY
Vick, Scott ....Los Angeles, CA
Vick, Susan F. ....Raleigh, NC
Vick, Wayne L. ....Circle, MT
Vick, Willard O. ....Silver Spring, MD
Vickaryous, James G. ....Orlando, FL
Vickaryous, James Gabriel ....Tampa, FL
Vicker, Thomas H. ....Minneapolis, MN
Vickerman, Lee, (Mr.) ....Shakopee, MN
Vickerman, Thomas R. ....Pierre, SD
Vickers, Alice M. ....Tallahassee, FL
Vickers, Antoinette L. ....Salem, MA
Vickers, Arlene M. ....St. Paul, MN
Vickers, Bartley K. ....Jacksonville, FL
Vickers, Brenda ....Mineral Wells, TX
Vickers, C. Wallace ....Winston-Salem, NC
Vickers, Charles M. ....Fayetteville, WV
Vickers, Damon L. ....McMinnville, OR
Vickers, Daniels & Young ....Cleveland, OH
Vickers, David J. ....Sioux Falls, SD
Vickers, David W. ....Montgomery, AL
Vickers, Don H. ....Santa Barbara, CA
Vickers, E. Newton ....Topeka, KS
Vickers, Earl M. ....Montgomery, WV
Vickers, Ellis G. ....Roswell, NM
Vickers, F. Thomas ....Cleveland, OH
Vickers, Gayle Riley ....Austin, TX
Vickers, George L. ....Montgomery, WV
Vickers, Gregory S. ....Cleveland, OH
Vickers, Harrison ....Houston, TX
Vickers, James R. ....Arleta, CA
Vickers, James W.
General Accounting Office,
Office of the General Counsel, GV
Vickers, Jay G. ....Riverside, CA
Vickers, Joe W. ....Jourdanton, TX
Vickers, John F. ....Ottawa, IL
Vickers, Karen M. ....Portland, OR
Vickers, Kay Carnley ....Houston, TX
Vickers, Kelly Dean ....Wetumpka, AL
Vickers, Kendall, P.C. ....Nevada, MO
Vickers, Kendall R. ....Nevada, MO
Vickers, Laura A. ....Austin, TX
Vickers Law Office ....Greene, IA
Vickers, Lee G. ....Austin, TX
Vickers, Lucinda A. ....Pleasanton, TX
Vickers, M. Coppley ....Sevierville, TN
Vickers Madsen & Goldman, LLP
Tallahassee, FL
Vickers, M. Coppley, & Associates, P.C.
Sevierville, TN
Vickers, Nancy Murphy ....Hershey, PA
Vickers, Noël Moran ....Evergreen, CO
Vickers, Patrick G. ....Greene, IA
Vickers, Raymond B., (P.A.) .....Tallahassee, FL
Vickers, Raymond W. ....Irvine, CA
Vickers, Richard ....Greene, IA
Vickers, Richard J. ....Columbus, OH
Vickers, Richard R. ....Tampa, FL
Vickers, Riis, Murray and Curran, L.L.C.
Mobile, AL
Vickers, Robert L. ....Concord, CA
Vickers, Robert V. ....Cleveland, OH
Vickers, Stanley M. ....Wichita Falls, TX
Vickers, Therese A. ....Irvine, CA
Vickers, Thomas A. ....Chicago, IL
Vickers, Thomas F. ....San Antonio, TX
Vickers, Thomas H. ....Los Angeles, CA
Vickers, Tonja Rene ....Tampa, FL
Vickers, Vincent H., II ....Georgetown, DE
Vickerson, William L. ....Portland, ME
Vickery, Alan Borden ....Armonk, NY
Vickery, Alan R. ....Dallas, TX
Vickery, Amy E. ....Kansas City, MO
Vickery, Ann Morgan ....Washington, DC
Vickery, Arnold Anderson (Andy)
Houston, TX
Vickery, Bruce L. ....Wellsboro, PA
Vickery, Byron ....Columbus, OH
Vickery, Charles R., Jr. ....Houston, TX
Vickery, Christine ....New York, NY
Vickery, David B. ....Leitchfield, KY
Vickery, Earl Landers (Lanny)
Austin, TX
Vickery, Edward D. ....Houston, TX
Vickery, Eugene B., Jr. ....New Orleans, LA
Vickery, Glenn ....Baytown, TX
Houston, TX
Vickery, Howard L. ....New York, NY
Vickery, Ian W. ....El Dorado, AR
Vickery, James M. ....Austin, TX
Vickery, John D., Jr. ....Pickens, SC
Vickery, Jonathan W. ....Dallas, TX
Vickery & Landers, P.L.L.C. ......El Dorado, AR
Vickery & Linebaugh ....Baytown, TX
Houston, TX
Vickery, Matthew S. ....Sleepy Eye, MN
Vickery, Peter ....Belmont, MA
Vickery, Randall G. ....Chicago, IL
Vickery, Raymond E., Jr.
Washington, DC
New York, NY
Vickery, Riehl & Alter ....Columbus, OH
Vickery, Ronald S. ....Tyler, TX
Vickery, Thomas E. ....Washington, DC
Vickery, Travis ....Houston, TX
Vickery, Van Buren ....North Miami, FL
Vickery, Virgil E. ....Houston, TX
Vickery, William A. ....Wichita, KS
Vickland, John R. ....Oakland, CA
Vickles, Heather Fox ....Denver, CO
Vicklund, Jon C. ....Houston, TX
VicklundWilson, Susan ....Morgan Hill, CA
Vickman, James A. ....Beverly Hills, CA
Vickman Law Corporation ....Encino, CA
Vickman, Lee J. ....Highland Park, IL
Vickman, Leon L. ....Encino, CA
Vicknair, Audrey Mullert
Corpus Christi, TX
Vickory, Charles B., III ....Goldsboro, NC
Vickory, Barry R. ....Vermillion, SD
Vickrey, David H. ....Dobbs Ferry, NY
Vickrey, George E. ....Valley Center, CA
Vickrey, James F., Jr. ....Troy, AL
Vickrey, Paul K. ....Chicago, IL
Vickrey, Robert S. ....Mount Clemens, MI
Vickrey • Wegmeyer ....Mount Clemens, MI
Vickroy, Nicole D. ....Dayton, OH
Vicksman, Sophia R. ....New York, NY
Vickstrom, Dwane E. ....Charlotte, NC
Vickstrom, Mark A. ....Denver, CO
Vicroy, Steven F. ....Lexington, KY
Victor, A. Paul, (P.C.) ....New York, NY
Victor, A. Rex ....San Bernardino, CA
Victor, Alan E. ....Los Angeles, CA
Victor, Arthur H. ....New York, NY
Victor & Atorthy, PLLC
Bloomfield Hills, MI
Victor, Brian K. ....New York, NY
Victor, Carol R. ....Napa, CA
Victor, Cindy Rhodes ....Bloomfield Hills, MI
Victor, Daniel ....New York, NY
Victor, David ....Phoenix, AZ
Victor, David ....Chicago, IL
Victor, David M. ....Bronx, NY
Victor, David M. ....Brookfield, WI
Victor, David W. ....Los Angeles, CA
Victor, Dolores ....Norristown, PA
Victor, Donald ....Commack, NY
Victor, Edward G. ....Los Angeles, CA
Victor, Gary M. ....Ypsilanti, MI
Victor, Gregory A. ....Miami, FL
Victor & Hall, P.L.C. ....Tempe, AZ
Victor, Howard J. ....Southfield, MI
Victor, Irving W. ....Cincinnati, OH
Victor, J. Scott ....Philadelphia, PA
Victor, Jack R. ....Republic, MO
Victor, Jeffrey L. ....Phoenix, AZ
Victor, Jennifer R. ....Huntington, WV
Victor, JoAnn Ellen ....Los Angeles, CA
Victor, Jonathan A. ....Beverly Hills, CA
Victor, Karl N., Jr. ....New Albany, IN
Louisville, KY
Victor, K.C. ....New York, NY
Victor, Kim Debra ....New York, NY
Victor, Leon A. ....Los Angeles, CA
Victor, Lewis S. ....Brockton, MA
Victor, Linda S. ....Dix Hills, NY
Victor, Marc B. ....Menlo Park, CA
Victor, Marc J. ....Tempe, AZ
Victor, Marilyn R. ....Encino, CA
Victor, Mark A. ....Pacific Palisades, CA

Victor, Marsha L. ..... Riverside, CA
Victor, Marvin M. ..... Chicago, IL
Victor, Michael T. ..... Erie, PA
Victor, Paul A. ..... New York, NY
Victor, Perri S. ..... Los Angeles, CA
Victor & Raphel, P.C. ..... Brockton, MA
Victor, Raymond J. ..... Gaylord, MI
Victor, Raymond M. ..... Norristown, PA
Victor, Raymond M., P.C. ..... Norristown, PA
Philadelphia, PA
Victor, Richard A. ..... Madison, WI
Victor, Richard S. ..... Bloomfield Hills, MI
Victor, Robbins & Devine
Bloomfield Hills, MI
Victor, Robert E. ..... Beverly Hills, CA
Victor, Robert M. ..... Encino, CA
Victor, Royall ..... Contoocook, NH
Victor, Ryan J. ..... Los Angeles, CA
Victor & Sandler ..... Los Angeles, CA
Victor, Sanford ..... New York, NY
Victor, Saul L. ..... New York, NY
Victor, Scott B. ..... Randolph, MA
Victor, Stephanie G. ..... Department of Justice,
Antitrust Division, GV
Victor, Steven I. ..... Birmingham, MI
Victor, Steven L., Law Office of
San Diego, CA
Victor, Toni L. ..... Northridge, CA
Victor & Victor ..... Los Angeles, CA
Encino, CA
Victor, William Henry ..... Akron, OH
Victoria, Richard R. ..... Belle Vernon, PA
Victoria, Richard T. ..... Pittsburgh, PA
Victoria, Rodolfo ..... Glendale, CA
Victoria, Susan L. ..... Tenafly, NJ
Victoria-Magpantay, Mara C.
La Mirada, CA
Victorian, Miriam O. ..... McAllen, TX
Victorino, Louis D. ..... Los Angeles, CA
Washington, DC
Victoroff, Gregory T. ..... Los Angeles, CA
Victorson, Larry ..... Skokie, IL
Victorson, Michael B. ..... Charleston, WV
Victory, Arjang ..... New York, NY
Victory, Jeffrey P. ..... Shreveport, LA
Victory, Kathleen ..... Washington, DC
Arlington, VA
Victory, Nancy J. ..... Washington, DC
Victory, Thomas, Jr. ..... Jupiter, FL
Victory, Thomas K. M. ..... Cleveland, OH
Vida, Behrooz P. ..... Fort Worth, TX
Vida, Carla Reed ..... Fort Worth, TX
Vida, Glen J., P.C. ..... Springfield, NJ
Vida, Marvin ..... Westminster, CA
Vida, Mary Jo ..... Dallas, TX
Vida, Scott J. ..... Los Angeles, CA
Vidakis, Irene ..... Lincolnwood, IL
Vidakis, Maria ..... Fort Lauderdale, FL
Vidal, Albert J. ..... Ocala, FL
Vidal, Ana Maria, (P.A.) ..... Miami, FL
Vidal, Angela C. ..... Somerville, NJ
Vidal, Dorothea L. ..... Dallas, TX
Vidal, Eduardo R. ..... New York, NY
Vidal, James E. ..... Kalispell, MT
Vidal, Orlando E. ..... Washington, DC
Vidal, Raquel ..... Los Angeles, CA
Vidal, Renee C. ..... Mount Laurel, NJ
Vidal, Richard W. ..... Rockford, IL
Vidal, Timothy ..... Santa Fe, NM
Vidal-Cordero, David ..... Washington, DC
Vidal-Cordero, Pedro I. ..... San Juan, PR
Vidal-Montilla, Denise ..... Bronx, NY
Vidal-Montilla, Denise, P.C. ..... Bronx, NY
Vidano, Thomas A. ..... San Diego, CA
Vidas, Arrett & Steinkraus, A Professional
Association ..... Minnetonka, MN
Vidas, Daniel F. ..... Portland, OR
Vidas, Kristen J. ..... Princeton, NJ
Vidas, Mary T. ..... Philadelphia, PA
Vidas, Robert O. ..... Minnetonka, MN
Vidas, Sandra M. ..... Federal Trade Commission,
Office of the General Counsel, GV
Vidas, Scott Q. ..... Minnetonka, MN
Vidaurreta, Marisa S. ..... Seaside, CA
Vidaurri, Celso, III ..... Denton, TX
McKinney, TX
Vidaurri, R. A. (Ralph) ..... Edinburg, TX
Vidaurri, Steven Mark ..... Edinburg, TX
Vidaurri III, Celso ..... Arlington, TX
Videan, James M. ..... Phoenix, AZ
Videbeck, James N. ..... Oakbrook Terrace, IL
Videen, Garven W. ..... Tucson, AZ
Videla, Gabriel C. ..... New York, NY
Videlock, Erik N. ..... Philadelphia, PA
Videnieks, Heinrich Leo ..... New York, NY
Vidensek, Paul D. ..... Hinckley, OH
Videon, David T. ..... Media, PA
Vider, Isreal ..... Brooklyn, NY
Viders, Elaine M. ..... Carle Place, NY
Viders, Jay R. ..... Carle Place, NY
Viders & Wiesen ..... Carle Place, NY
Videto, Stephen J. ..... Okemos, MI
Vidette, Michael P., Jr. ..... Plymouth, MA
Vidgoff, Martin B. ..... Salem, OR
Vidibor, Sheldon, (Inc.) ..... Beverly Hills, CA
Vidis, Jennifer D. ..... Chicago, IL
Vidmar, Jacqueline M. ..... Chicago, IL
Vidmar, James A., Jr. ..... Greenbelt, MD
Silver Spring, MD
Vidmar, Lisa A. ..... Los Angeles, CA
Vidmar, Stephan M. ..... Albuquerque, NM
Vidmer, Stephen D. ..... Murray, KY
Vidor, Robert W. ..... Los Angeles, CA
Vidovic, Christopher M. ..... Chicago, IL
Vidovich, Anthony ..... Philadelphia, PA
Vidovich, Kristin K. ..... Washington, DC
Vidrine, David C. ..... Baton Rouge, LA
Vidrine, Dennis J. ..... Lafayette, LA
Vidrine, John Larry ..... Ville Platte, LA
Vidrine, Richard W. ..... Ville Platte, LA
Vidrine, William C. ..... Lafayette, LA
Viducich, Anthony J. ..... Portland, OR
Viducich, Robert R. ..... New York, NY
Vidulich, Joseph P. ..... New York, NY
Vidwans, Maulin S. ..... Cherry Hill, NJ
Philadelphia, PA
Vidyarthi, Alok ..... Duluth, MN
Vie, George W., III ..... Galveston, TX
Vieau, Yvonne ..... Phoenix, AZ
Viebrock, Michael E. ..... Culver City, CA
Vieceli, James J., III ..... Los Angeles, CA
Viefhaus, Robert Manning
Huntington Beach, CA
Viegas, Stephen G. ..... Reading, MA
Vieh, Jacqueline Norton ..... Phoenix, AZ
Vieh, James E. ..... Scottsdale, AZ
Viehe-Naess, Brenda R. ..... Washington, DC
Viehman, Eric ..... Houston, TX
Viehman, J. Karl ..... Dallas, TX
Viehmann, Carol E. ..... Ashfield, MA
Vieira, Angela M. ..... Boston, MA
Vieira, Daniel J. ..... Providence, RI
Vieira, Marc W. ..... Napa, CA
Vieira, Norman ..... Carbondale, IL
Vieira-Cardoza, Yvonne ..... Boston, MA
Vieito, Lorenzo ..... Coral Gables, FL
Viel, Charles E. ..... Bridgeton, NJ
Viel, Mark W. ..... Big Rapids, MI
Traverse City, MI
Viel, Mark W., P.C. ..... Big Rapids, MI
Traverse City, MI
Viele, Terry James ..... Ventura, CA
Vieley, Jack C. ..... Bloomington, IL
Vielhaber, Robert A. ..... New Carrollton, MD
Vielhauer, Harold G. ..... Cincinnati, OH
Vielmetti, Paul G. ..... Portland, ME
Vien, Dien T ..... Maumee, OH
Viener, John D. ..... New York, NY
Viener, Joseph Brenner ..... Mineola, NY
Vienna, Anthony M. ..... Los Angeles, CA
Vienna, Darrell J. ..... Sierra Madre, CA
Vienna, Kevin R. ..... Coronado, CA
Vienna, Pattricia M. ..... Redondo Beach, CA
Vienna, Vincent ..... Brooklyn, NY
Vienneau, Robert A. ..... Woodinville, WA
Vieno, Mark J. ..... Minneapolis, MN
Viens, Gail Borjeson
Upper Marlboro, MD
Viens, Michele Marie ..... Anaheim, CA
Vient, Timothy C. ..... La Crescenta, CA
Vienuzis, Edward V. ..... Rolling Meadows, IL
Viera, Antonio T. ..... Fort Lauderdale, FL
Viera, Dino E. ..... Oklahoma City, OK
Viera, Melie ..... Miami, FL
Viera, Robert W. ..... Redwood City, CA
Viera-Canales, Roxana M. ..... San Juan, PR
Viera Martinez, Angel ..... San Juan, PR
Viera-Rabelo, Vanessa ..... San Juan, PR
Viera-Villeneuve, Harry ..... San Juan, PR
Vierbuchen, Margaret ..... Washington, DC
Viereck, Keli Crandall ..... Houston, TX
Vieregg, James D. ..... Phoenix, AZ
Vieregg, R. Todd ..... Chicago, IL
Viereggi, Arthur B., Jr. ..... Fairfax, VA
Viergever, Kimberly A. ..... Denver, CO
Viergever, William T.
West Palm Beach, FL
Viergutz, Herbert A. ..... Anchorage, AK
Viergutz, Mary E. ..... Columbus, OH
Vieri, Albert ..... Los Angeles, CA
Viering, Peter B. ..... Stonington, CT
Viering, Russell W. ..... Noank, CT
Vierk, Richard J. ..... Lincoln, NE
Vierkorn, Katherine A.
Mayfield Village, OH
Vierling, Mark J. ..... Stillwater, MN
Vierling, Thomas A. ..... Phoenix, AZ
Vierneisel, Gail M. ..... Glenview, IL
Vierow, Frederick A. ..... Columbus, OH
Vierra, Anthony A. ..... Wailuku, HI
Vierra, Donna Christine ..... Silver Spring, MD
Vierra, Eugene J. ..... Los Banos, CA
Vierra, Kenneth F., Jr. ..... San Francisco, CA
Vierra, Larry E. ..... San Francisco, CA
Vierra, Manuel N. ..... Hanford, CA
Vierra, Sheila ..... Honolulu, HI
Vierra-Boelk, Christine ..... Pleasant Hill, CA
Viers, Raye Ann ..... Atlanta, GA
Viers, W. Glenn ..... Atlanta, GA
Viert, William G. ..... Tacoma, WA
Viertel, George J. ..... Silver Spring, MD
Vierthaler, John J. ..... Littleton, CO
Viesca, Ana Maria Cristina ..... El Paso, TX
Viesca, James ..... San Antonio, TX
Vieser, Sandra L. ..... Metuchen, NJ
Vieson, Julie C. ..... Tampa, FL
Viesselman, Terry W. ..... Fairmont, MN
Viesturs, Heidi E. ..... Minneapolis, MN
Vieth, Erich V. ..... St. Louis, MO
Vieth, G. Duane ..... Washington, DC
Vieth, George W., Jr. ..... Louisville, KY
Vieth, H. Mark ..... Miami, FL
Vieth, James M. ..... Columbus, OH
Vieth, Jean M. ..... San Francisco, CA
Vieth, Laura Anderson ..... Miami, FL
Vieth, Perry J. ..... Chicago, IL
Vieth, Peter D. ..... Roanoke, VA
Vieth, Richard W. ..... Spartanburg, SC
Vieth, Robert R. ..... McLean, VA
Vietor, Harold D. ..... Des Moines, IA
Viets, Andy H. ..... Ventura, CA
Viets, Bonnie K. ..... Los Angeles, CA
Viets, Dan ..... Columbia, MO
Viets, Don W. ..... Whiteville, NC
Viets, Hamilton P. ..... Barrington, IL
Viets, James D. ..... Groveport, OH
Viets, Jon R. ..... Independence, KS
Viets, Paul R. ..... Springfield, MA
Viets, Richard L. ..... Sacramento, CA
Viets, Robert O. ..... Peoria, IL
Viets, Robert W. ..... New York, NY
Viets, Roger R. ..... Jackson, WY
Viets, William C. ..... New York, NY
Viets-Rennison, Sheila M. ..... Gulfport, MS
Vietti, Vincent A. ..... Philadelphia, PA
Vietz, Gregory J. ..... Boise, ID
Vietzen, Laurel A. ..... Elgin, IL
Vietzke, Lance L. ..... Minneapolis, MN
Vieux, Philip C. ..... Garden City, KS
Vieux, Rodney F. ..... Johnson, VT
View, James E. ..... Orlando, FL
Vieweg, David E. ..... Phoenix, AZ
Vieweg, George B., III ..... Charleston, WV
Vieweg, Mark E. ..... Wheeling, WV
Viewig, Alan R. ..... Portland, OR
Vig, Vernon Edward ..... New York, NY
Vigderman, M. Howard ..... Cherry Hill, NJ
Philadelphia, PA
Vigderman, Martin J. ..... Philadelphia, PA
Vigderson, Tal O. ..... Los Angeles, CA
Vigdor, Gregory ..... Seattle, WA
Vigdor, Justin L. ..... Rochester, NY
Vigdor, Robert M. ..... Rochester, NY
Vigdor, William R.
Federal Trade Commission,
Bureau of Competition, GV
Vigdorchik, Oleg A. ..... Belmont, CA
Vigeland, Peter K. ..... New York, NY
Vigen, Eric E. ..... Sarasota, FL
Viger, Andrew S. ..... Richardson, TX
Viger Law Offices, The ..... Troy, NY
Viggiani, Janet A. ..... Boston, MA
Viggiani, John ..... Fort Lauderdale, FL
Viggiani, Steven J.
Environmental Protection Agency,
Office of Enforcement and Compliance
Assurance, GV
Viggiano, Gregory A. ..... New York, NY
Viggiano, Stephen T. ..... Lansing, MI
Vigh, Karyn J. ..... New Orleans, LA
Vigh, Robert Alexander ..... Tampa, FL
Vighi, Melissa A. ..... St. Louis, MO
Vigil & Associates ..... Barrington, IL
Chicago, IL
Vigil, Barbara J. ..... Santa Fe, NM
Vigil Berkley Schulz & Gordon, P.C.
Chicago, IL
Vigil, Carlos Manuel ..... Chicago, IL
Vigil, Carmen ..... Los Angeles, CA
Vigil, Charles J. ..... Albuquerque, NM
Vigil, Charles S. ..... Denver, CO
Trinidad, CO
Vigil, Christina C. ..... Albuquerque, NM
Vigil, Czar ..... New York, NY
Vigil, Daniel A. ..... Boulder, CO
Vigil, David C. ..... Denver, CO
Trinidad, CO
Vigil, Donald D. ..... Albuquerque, NM
Vigil, Donald D., P.C. ..... Albuquerque, NM
Vigil, Douglas E. ..... Albuquerque, NM
Vigil, Frank G. ..... Denver, CO
Vigil, Jacob ..... Albuquerque, NM
Vigil, John J. ..... Brighton, CO
Vigil, Jorge M. ..... Coral Gables, FL
Vigil, Joseph I. ..... Phoenix, AZ
Vigil, Joyce A. ..... Pueblo, CO
Vigil, Juan E. ..... Denver, CO
Vigil, Katherine ..... Denver, CO
Vigil, Kathleen Sweeney ..... San Mateo, CA
Vigil Law Firm, P.A. ..... Albuquerque, NM
Vigil Law Offices, P.C. ..... Denver, CO
Vigil, Lisa K. ..... Albuquerque, NM
Vigil Marchiondo & Associates, P.C.
Albuquerque, NM
Vigil, Marcia K. ..... Denver, CO
Vigil, Michael Edward ..... Albuquerque, NM
Vigil, Michael Eugene ..... Santa Fe, NM
Vigil, Ramon ..... Santa Fe, NM
Vigil, Thomas R. ..... Barrington, IL
Vigil, Timothy John ..... Santa Fe, NM
Vigil, Troy ..... Los Angeles, CA
Vigil, Valerie V. ..... Albuquerque, NM
Vigil, Vincent ..... Chicago, IL
Vigil, Y. Leticia Sanchez ..... Fort Worth, TX
Vigilante, David C. ..... Atlanta, GA
Vigilante, Jacqueline M. ..... Philadelphia, PA
Vigilante, John A. ..... Norwalk, CT
Vigilante, Ted ..... Philadelphia, PA
Vigilante, Theodore J. ..... Philadelphia, PA
Vigiletti, James E. ..... Grand Blanc, MI
Vigil-Fariñas, Elena ..... Hialeah, FL
Vigil-Fariqas, Elena ..... Hialeah, FL
Vigilius, Morten ..... Wichita, KS
Vigliano, Dean J. ..... New York, NY
Vigliarolo, Frank S. ..... Jericho, NY
Viglione, Dennis L. ..... Sacramento, CA
Vigliotti, Anthony J. ..... Worcester, MA
Vigliotti, Anthony J. ..... Birmingham, MI
Vigliotti, Gina A. ..... Providence, RI
Vigliotti, James A. ..... Summit, NJ
Viglotti, Christine L. ..... Philadelphia, PA
Viglotti, Louis J. ..... Wappingers Falls, NY
Viglotti & O'Neil ..... Wappingers Falls, NY
Vigluicci, Edward J. ..... Knoxville, TN
Vigna, Anthony P. ..... Eastchester, NY
Vigna, Cheryl E. ..... Woodland Hills, CA
Vigna, David J. ..... Farmington Hills, MI
Vigna, Gary L. ..... Portland, OR
Vignali, Amy C. ..... Providence, RI
Vignali, Matthew S. ..... Burlington, WI
Kenosha, WI
Vignali, Rosario M. ..... New York, NY
Vignati, Beth A. ..... Concord, NH
Vignati, Francis C. ..... East Hartford, CT
Vignati, Francis C., Jr. ..... East Hartford, CT
Vignati & Vignati, P.C. ..... East Hartford, CT
Vigneri, Joseph W. ..... Decatur, IL
Taylorville, IL
Vigneri, Joseph W., Ltd. A Professional
Corporation ..... Decatur, IL
Taylorville, IL
Vigneron, Amy J. ..... Buffalo, NY
Vignery, Carolyn L. ..... Atlanta, GA
Vignery, J. Ronald ..... Goodland, KS
Vignery & Mason, L.L.C. ..... Goodland, KS
Vigness, Brian C. ..... Fort Myers, FL
Vignier, Anthony J. ..... Chester, NJ
Vignola, Chad A. ..... New York, NY
Vignola, Joseph C. ..... Philadelphia, PA
Vignola, Louis E. ..... Philadelphia, PA
Vignola, Michele M. ..... Washington, DC
Vignola, Paul ..... Landing, NJ
Vignola, Robert Paul ..... Fort Lauderdale, FL
Vignola, Rocco ..... Bronx, NY
Vignoles, Niall ..... San Francisco, CA
Vignolo, Anthony L. ..... Stockton, CA
Vignone, Anthony M. ..... Wrentham, MA
Vignone, John Paul ..... Wrentham, MA
Vignos, Gregg F. ..... San Francisco, CA
Vignuolo, Anthony B.
North Brunswick, NJ
Vignuolo, Lisa M. ..... North Brunswick, NJ
Vignuolo, Peter A. ..... North Brunswick, NJ
Vigoda, David ..... Sharon, MA
Vigoda, Robert A. ..... Boston, MA
Vigor, John C., Jr. ..... Ashland, KY
Vigorita, Howard ..... New York, NY
Vigorita, Louis J. ..... Ventura, CA
Vigorito, Alfred P. ..... Mineola, NY
New York, NY
White Plains, NY
Vigorito, Carmine T. ..... Paterson, NJ
Vigorito, Philip M. ..... Warren, OH
Vigue, Ronald L. ..... Berwick, ME
Vigue, Ronald R. ..... Junction City, OH
Viguerie, Joseph E., Jr. ..... New Orleans, LA
Viguerie, P. Robert, Jr. ..... Lafayette, LA
Viguet, R. Ross ..... Dallas, TX
Viguet, Robert J., Jr. ..... Houston, TX
Vigushin, Paul ..... Austin, TX
Vihlen, Sidney L., III
Altamonte Springs, FL
Vihon, Charles F. ..... Chicago, IL
Vihon, Robert S. ..... Chicago, IL
Vihstadt, John E. ..... Washington, DC
Vihtelic, James W. ..... Troy, MI
Vihtelic, James W., P.C. ..... Troy, MI
Vik, LaDonne R. ..... Fargo, ND
Vikander, Laura A. ..... Washington, DC
Viken, Jeffrey L. ..... Rapid City, SD
Viken, Linda Lea M. ..... Rapid City, SD
Viken, Viken, Pechota, Leach & Dewell, L.L.P.
Rapid City, SD
Viker, Dewel E., Jr. ..... Hillsboro, ND
Viklund, David A. ..... New York, NY
Vikmanis, Valda Maija ..... Washington, DC
Vikoren, Harold B. ..... Doylestown, PA
Vikoren, Susanne ..... New York, NY
Viksjo, Thomas M. ..... Buffalo, NY
Viksman, Irene ..... Los Angeles, CA
Viksnins, Ann S. ..... Minneapolis, MN
Viksnins, Ansis V. ..... Minneapolis, MN
Viktora, Philip R. ..... Chicago, IL
Viktora, Richard E. ..... New York, NY
Vila, George T. ..... Metairie, LA
Vila, Richard E. ..... Short Hills, NJ
Vila-Carrion & Burgos ..... San Juan, PR
Vila-Carrion, Rafael A. ..... San Juan, PR
Vila-Navarrete, Gilberto ..... San Juan, PR
Vilanova Font & Colon ..... San Juan, PR
Vilanova, Maureen E. ..... Brick, NJ
Vilaplana, Victor A. ..... San Diego, CA
Vilar, Mark F. ..... Alexandria, LA
Vilar, Patrick ..... Miami, FL
Vilarchao, Veronica ..... Fort Lauderdale, FL
Vilardi, Alice ..... Castro Valley, CA
Vilardi, Thomas S. ..... New Brunswick, NJ
Vilardo, Joseph A. ..... Houston, TX
Vilardo, Lawrence J. ..... Buffalo, NY
Vilardo, Terry Otero ..... Houston, TX
Vilardofsky, Beverly I.
Oklahoma City, OK
Vilaró Law Offices ..... San Juan, PR
Vilaró Nelms, Paul M. ..... San Juan, PR
Vilas, Mary C. ..... Apex, NC
Vilas, T. R. ..... Sonora, CA
Vilá-Sellés, Raúl J. ..... San Juan, PR
Vilbig & Associates, P.C. ..... St. Louis, MO
Vilbig, Fred L. ..... St. Louis, MO
Vilches, Sam N., Jr. ..... Dallas, TX
Vilchez, Victoria A. ..... West Palm Beach, FL
Vilchez, Victoria A., P.A.
West Palm Beach, FL
Vild, Jeffrey T. ..... Oregon, OH
Vild, Michael L. ..... Wilmington, DE
Vilders, Gregory R. ..... Treasury Department,
Office of Regulations and Rulings, GV
Vilders, Kurt R. ..... Detroit, MI
Vile, Russell E. ..... New London, CT
Vilella, Philip A. ..... Lansing, MI
Vilensky, Robert ..... New York, NY
Viles, Andrew F. ..... Boston, MA
Viles, Bruce D. ..... Corpus Christi, TX
Viles, Bruce E., (Ms.) ..... Concord, NH
Viles Law Firm, P.A. ..... Fort Myers, FL
Viles, Marcus W. ..... Fort Myers, FL
Viles, Mary Pat ..... Fort Myers, FL
Viles, Philip H., Jr. ..... Tulsa, OK
Viles-Muzzey, Susan ..... Seattle, WA
Viletto, Harold E. ..... Philadelphia, PA
Vilfer, Donald E. .....
Department of Justice, GV

Vilfroy, Ute Lindenmaier ... Cleveland, OH
Vilhauer, Jacob E., Jr. ... Portland, OR
Vilicich, Andrew J. ... San Pedro, CA
Vilicich, Stephanie M. ... Long Beach, CA
Vilim, Donald J. ... Wood Dale, IL
Vilimek, Mark S. ... Chicago, IL
Wheaton, IL
Vilinskis, Cathy Baldyga ... White Plains, NY
Viljoen, John R. ... Salinas, CA
Vilke, Kevin ... San Francisco, CA
Vilkelis, Peter J. ... Chicago, IL
Vilker, Lee H. ... New York, NY
Vilkin, Richard J. ... Huntington Beach, CA
Villa, Aristia K. ... Department of Justice, Office of Attorney Personnel Management, GV
Villa, B. Troy ... Baton Rouge, LA
New Orleans, LA
Villa, Carlos ... El Paso, TX
Villa, Clifford J. ... Denver, CO
Villa, D. James ... Baltimore, MD
Villa, David N. ... West Covina, CA
Villa, Ernest A., Jr. ... Paramus, NJ
Villa, Fernando ... Los Angeles, CA
Villa, Herbert J. ... Cleveland, OH
Villa, James D. ... Department of Justice, GV
Villa, James Gerard ... Brooklyn, NY
Villa, Jesús J. ... Milwaukee, WI
Villa, John K. ... Washington, DC
Villa, Joyce Yaple ... Albany, NY
Villa & Keith, L.L.P. ... El Paso, TX
Villa, Maria D. ... Redondo Beach, CA
Villa, Maria E. ... Albany, NY
Villa, Michael J. ... San Antonio, TX
Villa & Monaghan Nazar ... Brooklyn, NY
Villa, Richard J. ... Manchester, MA
Villa, Rita Flynn ... Burlington, VT
Villa, Robert K. ... Chicago, IL
Villa, Virginia G. ... Minneapolis, MN
Villa, Yolanda ... Rochester, NY
Villaamil, Anthony ... Miami, FL
Villaamil, Antonio P. ... Miami, FL
Villacci, Irene V. ... Hauppauge, NY
Villacci, Joseph J. ... Fort Lauderdale, FL
Villacorta, Adrian V. ... Houston, TX
Villacorta, Gilberto M. ... Washington, DC
Villacorta, James H. ... Miami, FL
Villacorta, Kathleen A. ... Tallahassee, FL
Villacorta, Zoila E. ... Palo Alto, CA
Villadolid, David M. ... Phoenix, AZ
Villafaña, A. Marie ... Minneapolis, MN
Villafana, Monica G. ... Los Angeles, CA
Villafane, Elena ... Glen Cove, NY
Villafane-Lopez, Juan ... San Juan, PR
Villafranca, Glenn D. ... Victoria, TX
Villafranco, John E. ... Washington, DC
Villafuerte, Christopher A. ... Department of Housing and Urban Development, GV
Villagomez, Ramon G. ... Saipan, TT
Villagomez, Rosa Maria ... Brownsville, TX
Villalaz, Rene A. Panama Canal Commission, Office of the General Counsel, GV
Villalba, A. J. ... Riverwoods, IL
Villalba, Jason ... Dallas, TX
Villalba, Michael A. ... Houston, TX
Villalobos, Edward A. ... Long Beach, CA
Villalobos, Hugo ... Elizabeth, NJ
Villalobos, Jesus, Jr. ... Edinburg, TX
Villalobos, Jose A. ... Miami, FL
Villalobos, Margie ... McAllen, TX
Villalobos, Michael ... Los Angeles, CA
Villalobos, P. Michael ... Fort Myers, FL
Villalobos, Pablo ... Metairie, LA
Villalobos, Rafael M., Jr. Philadelphia, PA
Villalobos, Raul ... El Paso, TX
Villalon, Isabel Maria ... Lawrence, KS
Villalon, Manuel F. ... San Juan, PR
Villalovos, Robert N. ... Sacramento, CA
Villalpando, Daniel J. ... Los Angeles, CA
Villalpando, Jesse M. ... Griffith, IN
Villalpando, Mark G. ... Scottsdale, AZ
Villalta, Cisco ... Woodland Hills, CA
Villamana, Robert L. ... Tucson, AZ
Villamaria, James K. ... Pittsburg, KS
Villamil, Arnaldo ... San Juan, PR
Villamil, Ellen ... Newburgh, NY
Villamizar, Joann ... Tarrytown, NY
Villani, Anthony J. ... Williamson, NY
Villani, Anthony W. ... Dallas, TX
Villani, Carmine R. ... Neptune, NJ
Villani, Denise Cotter ... Dallas, TX
Villani, Dino R. ... Las Cruces, NM
Villani, Francesca J. ... Hebron, CT
Villani & Grow ... Williamson, NY
Villani, Henry P. ... Mount Vernon, IL
Villani, James Joseph ... Natick, MA
Villani, James M. ... Mineola, NY
Villani, John V. ... Syracuse, NY
Villani, Michael P. ... Las Vegas, NV
Villani, Miriam E. ... Uniondale, NY
Villani, Patricia ... Morris Plains, NJ
Villani, Richard A. ... Milford, MA
Villani, Robert W. ... White Plains, NY
Villani, Theresa C. ... New York, NY
Villano, Barbara Ann ... Toms River, NJ
Villano, John A. ... Waterbury, CT
Villano, Laurie A. ... Springfield, NJ
Villano, Michael C. ... Denver, CO
Villano, Michael C. ... Golden, CO
Villano, Stephen P. ... Denver, CO
Villanova, James A. ... Pittsburgh, PA
Villanova Law Offices, P.C. ... Pittsburgh, PA
Villanti, Craig C. ... New Port Richey, FL
Villanti, Mario T. ... Bourne, MA

Villanueva, Carlos J. ... Miami, FL
Villanueva, Charles E. ... Morristown, NJ
Villanueva, J. Anthony ... Palo Alto, CA
Villanueva, Jeffrey M. ... Denver, CO
Villanueva, Jeffrey M., P.C. ... Denver, CO
Villanueva, Jocelyn A. ... Kansas City, MO
Villanueva, Orlando R. ... Pleasant Hill, CA
Villanueva, Pamela M. ... Los Angeles, CA
Villanueva, Raquel ... Chicago, IL
Villanueva, Ricardo D. ... McAllen, TX
Villanueva, Roberto C. ... Chicago, IL
Villanueva, Robin H. ... Washington, DC
Villanueva, Sarah H. ... Seattle, WA
Villanueva, Stephen R. ... Apex, NC
Villanueva, Theresa A. ... Englewood, CO
Villanueva, Valerie A. ... San Francisco, CA
Villanueva-Matkovich, Karen C. Beckley, WV
Villapol, Joseph J. ... New York, NY
Villapudua, Armando ... Stockton, CA
Villar, Barbara Beck ... Houston, TX
Villar, C. Michael ... Grand Rapids, MI
Villard, William Nichols ... Santa Ana, CA
Villare, Franceska Anestasia ... Paulsboro, NJ
Villareal, Andres ... Southlake, TX
Villareal, Bobbie R. Yowell ... Fort Worth, TX
Villareal, Dewey R., Jr. ... Tampa, FL
Villareal, Gavin R. ... Austin, TX
Villareal, Marc E. ... Corpus Christi, TX
Villareal, Patricia ... Dallas, TX
Villareale, Faust C. ... Upper Marlboro, MD
Villareale, Robert W. ... Kirkland, WA
Villari, Aurel A. ... Jersey City, NJ
Villari Golomb & Honik ... Philadelphia, PA
Villari, Leonard G. ... Philadelphia, PA
Villari, Mary Ann ... New York, NY
Villari, Peter M. ... Philadelphia, PA
Villarini and Henry, LLP ... Hamburg, NY
Villarini, Robert Mark ... Hamburg, NY
Villaronga, Luis M. ... San Juan, PR
Villarosa, Sharon Woods ... Department of State, GV
Villarosa, Sue W. ... West Trenton, NJ
Villarreal, Alejandra I. ... San Antonio, TX
Villarreal, Alejandro E., III ... Laredo, TX
Villarreal, Alfredo R., Jr. ... San Antonio, TX
Villarreal, Alma Z. ... Edinburg, TX
Villarreal & Alvarez ... Kingsville, TX
Villarreal, Arturo I. ... Yuma, AZ
Villarreal, Carlos A. ... Corpus Christi, TX
Villarreal, Clara M. ... New York, NY
Villarreal, Debra J. ... Dallas, TX
Villarreal, Elpidio ... Fairfield, CT
Villarreal, Fernando ... Waco, TX
Villarreal, Francisco R. ... McAllen, TX
Villarreal, Hector J. ... Edinburg, TX
Villarreal, Irma ... Chicago, IL
Villarreal, Joaquin, III ... Corpus Christi, TX
Villarreal, Joe, Jr. ... San Antonio, TX
Villarreal, Joe, Jr., Inc. ... San Antonio, TX
Villarreal, John D. ... Palo Alto, CA
Villarreal, Jose C. ... Houston, TX
Villarreal, Jose G. ... Los Angeles, CA
Villarreal, José H., (P.C.) San Antonio, TX
Villarreal, Judith A. ... Pahoa, HI
Villarreal Law Offices ... Tucson, AZ
Villarreal, Leo ... Kingsville, TX
Villarreal, Luis M. ... Fairfield, CA
Villarreal, Lydia ... Salinas, CA
Villarreal, Michael ... Florence, AZ
Villarreal, Moreno & Ruiz ... San Antonio, TX
Villarreal, Norma L. ... Andover, MA
Villarreal, Oscar H. ... San Antonio, TX
Villarreal, Peter ... Highland, IN
Villarreal, Raul ... San Antonio, TX
Villarreal, Raul X. ... San Antonio, TX
Villarreal, Ricardo J. ... Houston, TX
Villarreal, Richard ... Dumas, TX
Villarreal, Stephen C. ... Tucson, AZ
Villarreal, Teresa ... Lima, OH
Villarrial, Gerald R. ... Waco, TX
Villarrubia, John G. ... Metairie, LA
Villarrubia, Todd M. ... New Orleans, LA
Villarruel, Paul K. ... Bloomfield Hills, MI
Villarruel, Rafael C., Jr. ... Detroit, MI
Villas, Gary G. ... Eaton Rapids, MI
Villasana, George A. ... Miami, FL
Villasana, George V. Securities and Exchange Commission, Division of Market Regulation, GV
Villasana, Joseph P. ... Ventura, CA
Villasana, Sol ... Austin, TX
Villasana, Sol ... Dallas, TX
Villasante, Roberto ... Miami, FL
Villasenor, Lisa A. ... Los Angeles, CA
San Francisco, CA
Villasenor, Richard ... Arcadia, CA
Villasenor, Richard L. ... San Francisco, CA
Villa-Smith, Kathryn L. ... Gresham, OR
Villasuso, Raul, Jr. ... Chicago, IL
Villaume, Frank E., III ... St. Paul, MN
Villaume, Philip G. ... Edina, MN
Villaverde, Hava B. ... Miami, FL
Villaverde, Sergio ... Bronx, NY
Villaverde, Toni L. ... Coral Gables, FL
Villavicencio, Dennis R. ... Carlsbad, CA
Villazon, Daniel ... Orlando, FL
Ville, Jeffrey A., P.A. ... Palm Bay, FL
Villeck, Michael Frederick ... Mineola, NY
Villeda, Antonio ... McAllen, TX
Villee, Suzanne C. ... Providence, RI
Villegas, Anouk M. ... Miami, FL
Villegas, Carlos A. ... San Diego, CA
Villegas, Cesar G. ... San Diego, CA
Villegas, Daniel R. ... Los Angeles, CA
Villegas, Gabriel J. Charlotte Amalie, St. Thomas, VI

Villegas, Jose A. ... Montebello, CA
Villegas, M. Victoria A. ... Tonopah, NV
Villegas, Mirna ... Los Angeles, CA
Villela, Ruy S. ... New Bedford, MA
Villella, Gerald J. ... Erie, PA
Villella, Louis ... New York, NY
Villella, Margaret Zinkler ... Hollywood, FL
Villella, Patrick S. ... Albuquerque, NM
Villella, Skarsgard & Noya, P.A. Albuquerque, NM
Villemaire, Karen ... Rutland, VT
Villemarette, Warren P. ... Metairie, LA
Villemez, Jane A. ... Cheyenne, WY
Villemez Law Office ... Cheyenne, WY
Villeneuve, Joseph M. ... Berkeley, CA
Mountain View, CA
Villeneuve, Kiernan Ignacio ... Hartford, CT
Villeneuve, Michael S. ... Long Beach, CA
Villeneuve, Paul M. ... Tallahassee, FL
Villeneuve, Thomas F. ... Menlo Park, CA
Villere, Edward J. ... New Orleans, LA
Villeré, James F., Jr. ... Morristown, NJ
Villeré, Plauch éF., Jr. ... Stockton, CA
Villet, Jeffrey M. ... Washington, DC
Villeza, Rob B. ... Los Angeles, CA
Villhauer, Neal C. ... Lansing, MI
Villicana, Ann-Marie ... Pasadena, CA
Villiere, George J. ... Old Forge, NY
Villines, Floyd G. (Buddy), III Little Rock, AR
Villines, John W. ... Modesto, CA
Villines, Judith A. ... Frankfort, KY
Villios, John N. ... New York, NY
Villiotte, Richard B. ... Revere, MA
Villmoare, Edwin S., III ... Sacramento, CA
Villmow, Keith ... Chicago, IL
Villone, James R. ... Sioux City, IA
Villone, Wm. L. ... Quincy, MA
Villongco, Martin R. ... Los Angeles, CA
Villoni, Dominic A. ... Corona, NY
Villont, J.D. ... West Union, IA
Villota, Carlos P. ... Dallas, TX
Villwock, Arthur P. ... West Palm Beach, FL
Villwock, Byron J. ... Winter Park, FL
Villwock, Mary Ann ... Ukiah, CA
Vilmont, William M. ... Clinton, IA
Vilmos, Peter C. ... Orlando, FL
Viloria, Bam Marie ... New Orleans, LA
Viloria, Thomas E. ... Reno, NV
Vilos, James D. (Mitch) ... Salt Lake City, UT
Viloski, Benjamin J. ... Pittsburgh, PA
Viloski Law Firm ... Pittsburgh, PA
Vilsack, Robert D. ... Cleveland Heights, OH
Vilsoet, Richard B. ... New York, NY
Vilt and Associates ... Houston, TX
Vilt, Robert C. ... Houston, TX
Vilter, Robert M. ... New York, NY
Viltoft, Steven L. ... Hopkins, MN
Vilutis, V. Anthony ... Fort Wayne, IN
Vimont, Richard E. ... Lexington, KY
Vimont & Wills PLLC ... Lexington, KY
Vinagre, John M. ... Waltham, MA
Vinal, Gregory M. ... Buffalo, NY
Vinal, Jeanne Marie ... Buffalo, NY
Vinal & Vinal ... Buffalo, NY
Vinall, Jessica Lynn ... Poughkeepsie, NY
Vinar, Benjamin ... Garden City, NY
Vinar, Benjamin ... New York, NY
Vinar, Dov Jacob ... White Plains, NY
Vinar, Jacqueline ... New York, NY
Vinardi, Bernard E. ... Omaha, NE
Vinas, Frank J. ... Miami, FL
Vinas, Sara L. ... Davie, FL
Viñas Bueso, Ramón L. ... San Juan, PR
Vinatieri, Joseph A. ... Whittier, CA
Vinay, Louis E., Jr. ... Morganton, NC
Vinberg, Stacy L ... Canby, MN
Vince, Charles A. ... Columbus, OH
Vince, Clinton A. ... Washington, DC
Vince, George A., Jr. ... Madison, OH
Vince, George R. ... Bristol, VT
Vince, Gerard C. ... Oakhurst, NJ
Vince, Katherine D. ... Jacksonville, FL
Vince, Paul W. ... Rockville, MD
Vince, Ralph ... Cleveland, OH
Vincek, Edward K. ... Fort Lauderdale, FL
Vincelette, Daniel G. ... Latham, NY
Vincelette, Tamara K. ... Denver, CO
Vincent, Adrian R. ... Saugatuck, MI
Vincent, Alexander Craig Department of Justice, Criminal Division, GV
Vincent & Alig ... Covington, KY
Vincent, Arthur ... Plantation, FL
Vincent, Austin K. ... Topeka, KS
Vincent, B. Lance ... Tyler, TX
Vincent, Berg, Stalzer & Menendez, P.C. Atlanta, GA
Vincent, Bobby R. ... San Bernardino, CA
Vincent, Branch W. "Chip" Elizabeth City, NC
Vincent, Brian D. ... Grand Rapids, MI
Vincent, Carl, Jr. ... Tulsa, OK
Vincent, Carol Ann ... Pleasantville, NY
Vincent, Caroline C. ... Santa Monica, CA
Vincent, Catherine A. ... Yucca Valley, CA
Vincent, Charles D. ... Wellsville, KS
Vincent, Charles H. ... Eugene, OR
Vincent, Charles M. ... Greenville, NC
Vincent, Charles R. ... Kinston, NC
Vincent, Craig T. ... Salt Lake City, UT
Vincent, Cynthia Ann ... New Bedford, MA
Vincent, David A. ... Washington, DC
Vincent, David L. ... Nashville, TN
Vincent, David Lee, III ... St. Louis, MO
Vincent, Deborah Wiers ... Fort Wayne, IN
Vincent, Dirk L. ... Los Angeles, CA
Vincent, Donald ... Plano, TX

Vincent, Douglas T. ... Buffalo, NY
Vincent, Douglass F. ... Boulder, CO
Vincent, Dwight H. ... Detroit, MI
Vincent, E. Lawrence, Jr. ... Dallas, TX
Vincent, Edna Ruth ... Fairfax, VA
Vincent, Edward C. ... Tucson, AZ
Vincent, Edward W., Jr., Law Offices of Edgartown, MA
Vincent, Ernest O. ... San Bernardino, CA
Vincent, Fabrice N. ... San Francisco, CA
Vincent & Fiddler, PLLP Minneapolis, MN
Vincent, Francis T., Jr. ... New York, NY
Vincent, G. Craig ... Valparaiso, IN
Vincent, Garth T. ... Los Angeles, CA
Vincent, Gary L. ... St. Louis, MO
Vincent, George H. ... Cincinnati, OH
Vincent & Gjurgevich ... Tucson, AZ
Vincent, Gordon S. ... Accomac, VA
Vincent, Gregory R. ... Brownsville, KY
Vincent, H. Benjamin ... Emporia, VA
Vincent, Hasty, Sullivan & Elliott, P.C. Birmingham, AL
Vincent, Howard ... Napa, CA
Vincent, Howell W. ... Covington, KY
Vincent, Irving ... Florence, AZ
Vincent, J. Thomas ... Hartford, CT
Vincent, James B. ... Galena, IL
Warren, IL
Vincent, James R. ... Dallas, TX
Vincent, Jason ... New York, NY
Vincent, Jay E. ... Riverton, WY
Vincent, Jeffrey M. ... Salt Lake City, UT
Vincent, Jeffrey R. ... Pleasant Hill, CA
Vincent, Jennifer West Newport News, VA
Richmond, VA
Vincent, Jerry P. ... Catlettsburg, KY
Vincent, Jill Lolley ... Birmingham, AL
Vincent, Joel C. ... Portland, ME
Vincent, Joel M. ... Riverton, WY
Vincent, John C., Jr. ... Boston, MA
Vincent, John E., Jr. ... Columbus, OH
Vincent, John F. ... Ashland, KY
Vincent, John K. ... Sacramento, CA
Vincent, John M. ... Port Townsend, WA
Vincent, John R. ... Riverton, WY
Vincent, John S. ... Buffalo, NY
Vincent, Joseph G. ... Lakewood, CO
Vincent, Joseph M., II ... Seattle, WA
Vincent, Joshua G. ... Chicago, IL
Vincent, Judith D. ... Minneapolis, MN
Vincent, Julie Hymel ... Sacramento, CA
Vincent, K. Mark ... Dallas, TX
Vincent, Kirk F. ... Pittsburgh, PA
Vincent Law Offices ... Lincoln, NE
Vincent Law Offices ... Emporia, VA
Vincent, Lawrence M. ... Baltimore, MD
Vincent, Lawrence Y. ... New York, NY
Vincent, Leonard C. ... Parchman, MS
Vincent, Leslie Susan ... Middletown, NJ
Vincent, Lester J. ... Sunnyvale, CA
Vincent, Louis E. ... San Francisco, CA
Vincent, Luci Daley ... Boston, MA
Vincent, Maggie K. ... Barre, VT
Vincent, Mark L. ... Rushville, IL
Vincent, Mark S. ... Union, MO
Vincent, Mark S. ... Freehold, NJ
Vincent, Matthew P. ... Boston, MA
Vincent, Maxwell James ... Yakima, WA
Vincent, Melanie L. ... Houston, TX
Vincent & Meyer ... Union, MO
Vincent, Michael A. ... Mesa, AZ
Vincent, Michael J. ... Ypsilanti, MI
Vincent, Michael J., P.C. ... Ypsilanti, MI
Vincent, Musette T. ... Cleveland, OH
Vincent, Nancy A. ... Nashville, TN
Vincent, Neil G. ... Lafayette, LA
Vincent, Nicholas ... Houston, TX
Vincent, Norma Brenne ... Naples, FL
Vincent, Northam & Lewis ... Accomac, VA
Vincent, O. Kevin ... Washington, DC
Vincent, Odessa F. ... Department of Justice, Drug Enforcement Administration, GV
Vincent, Oreste ... Catskill, NY
Vincent, Patricia P. ... Chattanooga, TN
Vincent, Patricia R. ... New Orleans, LA
Vincent, Paul ... Troy, MI
Vincent, Paul M. ... Washington, DC
Vincent, Peggy S. ... Raleigh, NC
Vincent, Peter S. ... San Francisco, CA
Washington, DC
Vincent, Pierre A. ... Boston, MA
Vincent, Pierre Louis ... Philadelphia, PA
Vincent, Raymond A. ... Del City, OK
Oklahoma City, OK
Vincent, Richard A. ... San Jose, CA
Vincent, Richard B. ... Englewood, CO
Vincent, Richard H. ... Atlanta, GA
Vincent, Richard L. ... Birmingham, AL
Vincent, Robert C., Jr. ... New York, NY
Vincent, Robert E., II Department of the Navy, Office of the Judge Advocate General, GV
Vincent, Rodney K. ... Lincoln, NE
Vincent, Rodney P., (P.C.) New Orleans, LA
Vincent, Roger G., Jr. ... Lafayette, LA
Vincent & Roth, P.C. ... Galena, IL
Warren, IL
Vincent, Sampson G. ... Salisbury, MD
Vincent, Sanborn ... Hilton Head Island, SC
Vincent, Sandra Lee ... Glendale, CA
Vincent, Scott E. ... Kansas City, MO
Vincent, Scott G. ... New Orleans, LA
Vincent, Shelley D. ... Mendon, MA
Vincent, Steven P. ... New York, NY
Vincent, T. Griffin ... Houston, TX

Vincent, Terry W. ... Cleveland, OH
Vincent, Thad H. ... Charleston, SC
Vincent, Thomas L. ... Irvine, CA
Vincent, Thomas P. ... Northampton, MA
Vincent, Thomas P. ... Detroit, MI
Vincent & Vincent ... Riverton, WY
Vincent, William A. ... Bloomington, MN
Vincent, William C. ... Baltimore, MD
Vincent, William J. ... Detroit, MI
Vincent, William R. ... Topeka, KS
Vincent, William R., A Prof. Corp.
Topeka, KS
Vincent, William R., P.A. ... Topeka, KS
Vincent, William S., Jr. ... New Orleans, LA
Vincent, William Slater ... Atlanta, GA
Vincenti, Christine M. ... Dallas, TX
Vincenti, Donna D. ... Hartford, CT
Vincenti, John V. ... New York, NY
Vincenti, Leonard M. ... Clearwater, FL
Clearwater, FL
Vincenti, Leonard M., P.A., Law Offices
Clearwater, FL
Vincenti, Michael B. ... Louisville, KY
Vincenti, Paul J. ... New York, NY
Vincenti, Ross D. ... Orange, CA
Vincenti, Sheldon A. ... Moscow, ID
Vincenti & Vincenti, P.C. ... New York, NY
Vincenti, Vito R. ... New York, NY
Vincent-Kolcun, Natacha M. ... Toledo, OH
Vincenty, Ismael ... San Juan, PR
Vincenzi, Victor A. ... New York, NY
Vincenzo, Daniel M. ... Irving, TX
Vincenzo, Michael L. ... New Orleans, LA
Vinch, James J. ... Columbus, OH
Vinci, Ann F. ... New York, NY
Vinci, Benjamin D. ... Denver, CO
Vinci, Frank J. ... Blue Bell, PA
Vinci, George M., Jr. ... Moorestown, NJ
Philadelphia, PA
Vinci, Gerald F. ... Camp Hill, PA
Vinci, Janine E. ... Philadelphia, PA
Vinci, Martin F. P., III ... McKees Rocks, PA
Vinci, Patricia A. M. ... Providence, RI
Vinci, Paul J., Sr. ... Boston, MA
Vinci, Philip M. ... San Diego, CA
Vinci, Robert M. ... Florham Park, NJ
Vinci, Thomas C. ... New York, NY
Vinciguerra, Lori ... New York, NY
Vinciguerra, Ralph D. ... Sylvania, OH
Vinciguerra, Stephen P. ... Latham, NY
Vincler & Knoll ... Pittsburgh, PA
Vincler, Robert P. ... Pittsburgh, PA
Vincze, Robert J. ... Denver, CO
Vind, David A. ... Reading, PA
Vindigni, Richard G. ... Oneida, NY
Vinding, Jens ... Ukiah, CA
Vinding, Michael E. ... Sacramento, CA
Vine, Adele Ross
General Services Administration,
Office of Regional Counsel, GV
Vine, Howard A. ... Washington, DC
Vine, John M. ... Washington, DC
Vine, Kristen C. ... Long Beach, CA
Vine, Leo ... Shelton, CT
Vine, Sherwin ... Birmingham, MI
Vine, Stephen M. ... New York, NY
Vine, Suzanne E. ... Brooklyn, NY
Vinegar, Richard J.
Research Triangle Park, NC
Vinegrad, Alan ... Brooklyn, NY
Viner, Anne E. ... Chicago, IL
Viner, Jonathan T. ... Chicago, IL
Viner, Michael B. ... Chicago, IL
Viner, Monte ... Chicago, IL
Viner, Robert B. ... New York, NY
Viner, Shari R. ... Vernon Hills, IL
Viner, Spencer W. ... Providence, RI
Viner, Steven E. ... Stevens Point, WI
Viner Samborn, Hope R. ... Glenview, IL
Vines, C. Wesley ... Dallas, TX
Vines, Carlton H. ... Summerville, GA
Vines, Claude C., Jr. ... Birmingham, AL
Vines, David R. ... Charlotte, NC
Vines, Ellsworth ... Irvine, CA
Vines, Glenn Keith, Jr. ... Memphis, TN
Vines, J. Andrew ... Little Rock, AR
Vines, James K. ... Nashville, TN
Vines, Keith B. ... San Francisco, CA
Vines, Kenneth E. ... Montgomery, AL
Vines, Kenneth G. ... Cheyenne, WY
Vines, Lane L. ... Philadelphia, PA
Vines, Lanny S. ... Birmingham, AL
Vines, Leonard D. ... St. Louis, MO
Vines, Monte ... Wichita, KS
Vines, Robert I. ... Ontario, CA
Vines, Robyn ... Hollywood, FL
Vines, William D., III ... Knoxville, TN
Vines, William H. ... Wheatland, WY
Vines, William M. ... Jackson, MS
Vineski, Joseph S. ... Troy, PA
Vineski, Robert R. ... Sarasota, FL
Vinet, Denise Ann ... Baton Rouge, LA
Vinet, Raymond C., Sr. ... Baton Rouge, LA
Vinet, William C., Jr. ... Springfield, VA
Vinette, Richard H., Jr. ... Lanesborough, MA
Viney, Gretchen ... Baraboo, WI
Viney, Joseph L. ... Baraboo, WI
Viney, Lauri D. ... Batavia, OH
Viney & Viney ... Baraboo, WI
Viney, William Elliott ... Covina, CA
Vineyard, Daniel E. ... Houston, TX
Vineyard, John W. ... Los Angeles, CA
Vineyard & Minter, L.L.P. ... Dallas, TX
Vineyard, Russell G. ... Atlanta, GA
Vineyard, Timothy J. ... Dallas, TX
Vingan, Howard ... Brentwood, NY
Vingelli & Bryson ... Tucson, AZ
Vingelli, Michael J. ... Tucson, AZ
Vingiello, Arthur A. ... Baton Rouge, LA
Vingiello, J. Richard ... West Haverstraw, NY
Vingoe, D. Grant ... New York, NY
Viniar, Carl B. ... Cherry Hill, NJ
Woodbury, NJ
Vinick, Alan N. ... St. Davids, PA
Vinick & Docherty ... Newark, NJ
Roseland, NJ
Vinick, Jani Wase ... New York, NY
Vinick, Philip B. ... Roseland, NJ
Vinick, Sharon R. ... San Francisco, CA
Vinicombe, Charles J. ... Princeton, NJ
Vinik, Bart J. ... Marlborough, MA
Vinik, Grant R. ... Washington, DC
Vinik, Jack ... Delray Beach, FL
Vinik, Joshua H. ... New York, NY
Vinik, Nina E. ... Miami, FL
Vinik, Sandra K. ... Birmingham, AL
Vinikoff, Harold ... Troy, NY
Vinikoff, Jerald L. ... Albany, NY
Vinikoor, David G. ... Fort Lauderdale, FL
Vinikoor, Robert D. ... Arlington Heights, IL
Vining, Ann ... Everett, WA
Vining, Charles W. ... Somerville, MA
Vining, Hannah ... Brooklyn, NY
Vining, Janet M. ... Sacramento, CA
Vining, Joseph ... Ann Arbor, MI
Vining, Linda L. ... Atlanta, GA
Vining, Mark A. ... Wichita, KS
Vining and Meyer, P.C. ... Clayton, MO
Vining, Pamela L. ... Scottsdale, AZ
Vining, Robert B. ... Clayton, MO
Vining, Robert B., Jr. ... Clayton, MO
Vining, Robert L., Jr. ... Rome, GA
Vining, Robert P. ... New Orleans, LA
Vining, Steven J. ... Cary, NC
Vinion, Lon ... Wooster, OH
Vinitskaya, Lena I. ... Irvine, CA
Vinitsky, Elyse ... Bethesda, MD
Vinjamuri, Jill ... Omaha, NE
Vinje, Edmund G., II ... Fargo, ND
Vinje Law Office, P.C. ... Fargo, ND
Vinje, Ralph A. ... Bismarck, ND
Vinje, S. Lee ... Mayville, ND
Vink, Paul T. ... Carmel, NY
White Plains, NY
Vink, Paul T., P.C. ... White Plains, NY
Vinkels, Valdis ... Hartford, CT
Vinkemulder, H. Yvonne ... Madison, WI
Vinnacia, Jacqueline S. ... San Diego, CA
Vinnard, Gerald D. ... Fresno, CA
Vinnedge, Gafney & Gladson, Inc.
Upland, CA
Vinnick, Jeffrey A. ... Santa Monica, CA
Vinnicof, Cecil ... Los Angeles, CA
Vinnicof, Paul ... Los Angeles, CA
Vinnik, Daniel M. ... Boca Raton, FL
Vinnik, Jeffrey L. ... Treasury Department,
Internal Revenue Service, GV
Vinocur, Nancy Moss ... Simsbury, CT
Vinocur, Peter A. ... Cleveland, OH
Vinokour, Jan L. ... New York, NY
Vinokur, Howard N. ... Garden City, NY
New York, NY
Vinokur, Leon L. ... Wilmington, DE
Vinolus, Athan A. ... Dayton, OH
Vinolus, Peter A. ... Lackawanna, NY
Vinopal, Michael J. ... Eau Claire, WI
Vinovich, Daniel Blake ... Highland, IN
Vinroot, Richard A. ... Charlotte, NC
Vinsavich, Stephen M. ... Birmingham, AL
Vinsel, Jay F. ... Zanesville, OH
Vinski, Dorothy ... San Francisco, CA
Vinson, Allen R. ... Walnut Creek, CA
Vinson, B. Todd ... Nashville, TN
Vinson, Brian N. ... Department of Commerce,
Patent and Trademark Office, GV
Vinson, Carter L. ... Boston, MA
Vinson, Charles E. ... El Paso, TX
Vinson, Daniel J. ... New York, NY
Vinson, David A. ... Eugene, OR
Vinson, Elizabeth B. ... Williamsburg, VA
Vinson & Elkins L.L.P. ... Washington, DC
New York, NY
Austin, TX
Dallas, TX
Houston, TX
Vinson, Eric H. ... New York, NY
Vinson, Eric L. ... Houston, TX
Vinson, Ethan ... Livonia, MI
Vinson, Flo Lester ... Florence, SC
Vinson, Gary L. ... Sacramento, CA
Vinson, Gary M. ... Batesville, AR
Vinson, Gay Paisley ... Asheville, NC
Vinson, J. Michael ... Baton Rouge, LA
Vinson, James A., III ... Goldsboro, NC
Vinson, James C. ... Aiken, SC
Vinson, Jerry D., Jr. ... Florence, SC
Vinson, John Charles ... Concord, NH
Vinson, Kathleen Elliott ... Boston, MA
Vinson, Kenneth G. ... Dallas, GA
Vinson, Lance C. ... Houston, TX
Vinson, Laurence Duncan, Jr.
Birmingham, AL
Vinson Law Firm, The, P.A. ... Florence, SC
Vinson, Linda O. ... Lithonia, GA
Vinson, Lindsey P. ... Irving, TX
Vinson, M. Glenn, Jr. ... San Francisco, CA
Vinson, Mark ... Houston, TX
Vinson, Melanie D. ... Palo Alto, CA
Vinson, Nelson ... Hamilton, AL
Vinson, Peggy ... Seattle, WA
Vinson, Phyllisina L.
Department Of The Interior,
Office of the Solicitor, GV
Vinson, Richard A. ... Novato, CA
Vinson, Robert E. ... Wichita Falls, TX
Vinson, Robert E., Jr. ... Dallas, TX
Vinson, Robin Kenton ... Raleigh, NC
Vinson, Roger ... Pensacola, FL
Vinson, Rosalind R.
Equal Employment Opportunity
Commission,
Office of Federal Operations, GV
Vinson, Sam ... Chicago, IL
Vinson, Stephen L., Jr. ... Miami, FL
Vinson, Stephen L., Jr., P.A. ... Miami, FL
Vinson, Talley, Richardson & Cable, P.A.
Dallas, GA
Vinson, Tamra Glynn ... Baton Rouge, LA
Vinson, Thomas D. ... Austin, TX
Vinson, Timothy L. ... Hurst, TX
Vinson, Tracey Garland ... Pittsburgh, PA
Vinson, Troy C. ... Dallas, TX
Vinson, Virginia A. ... Birmingham, AL
Vinson, W. Sidney, III ... Erin, TN
Vinson, W. Sidney, III, P.C. ... Erin, TN
Vinson, William E., Jr. ... Lakeland, FL
Vinson, William L. ... Tarpon Springs, FL
Vinson, William L. ... Atlanta, GA
Vinson, William L., P.A. ... Tarpon Springs, FL
Vinson, William T. ... Westlake Village, CA
Vinson, Z. T. ... Department of Transportation,
National Highway Traffic Safety
Administration, GV
Vint, Edw. L. ... Dallas, TX
Vint, Michael J. ... Memphis, TN
Vinterella, David A. ... Metairie, LA
Vinton, George G. ... North Platte, NE
Vinton, Karri L. ... Dallas, TX
Vinton, Lori J. ... North Platte, NE
Vinton Nissler Allen & Vellone, P.C.
Denver, CO
Vinton, Norman D. ... Woodstock, IL
Vinton, Ray ... Dallas, TX
Vinton, Robert M. ... Denver, CO
Vinton, Steven P. ... North Platte, NE
Vinturella, James E. ... New Orleans, LA
Vinueza, Fausto H. ... Pompano Beach, FL
Vinyard & Associates ... Washington, DC
Vinyard, Christopher Evans
Richmond, VA
Vinyard & Curran ... Ottumwa, IA
Vinyard, George A. ... Chicago, IL
Vinyard, Henry L. ... Salisbury, MD
Vinyard, Julie A.S. ... Washington, DC
Vinyard, Michael C. ... Ottumwa, IA
Vinyard, Robert Austin ... Abingdon, VA
Marion, VA
Vinyard, Robert Austin, Attorney at Law, P.C. ... Abingdon, VA
Marion, VA
Vinyard & Spain ... Salisbury, MD
Vinyard, Walter Darnall ... Washington, DC
Vinzani, M. Jeffrey ... Charleston, SC
Viola, Anthony J. ... New York, NY
Viola, Anthony J. ... Cleveland, OH
Viola, Frank ... Springfield, NJ
Viola, Gina L. ... San Francisco, CA
Viola, Gregg E. ... Baltimore, MD
Viola, James S. ... Springfield, MA
Viola, Jane Cava ... Williston Park, NY
Viola, Jeffrey M. ... Philadelphia, PA
Viola, John L. ... Los Angeles, CA
Viola, Joseph E. ... Albany, NY
Viola, Joseph P. ... Honolulu, HI
Viola, Lawrence S. ... San Mateo, CA
Viola, Matthew J. ... Honolulu, HI
Viola, Michael J. ... Nutley, NJ
Viola, Richard W. ... Charlotte, NC
Viola, Robert ... Niagara Falls, NY
Viola, Rocco, Jr. ... Mars, PA
Viola, Roger K. ... Topeka, KS
Viola, Sharon A. ... Oak Brook, IL
Viola, Thomas J. ... Los Angeles, CA
Violand, James P. ... North Olmsted, OH
Violando, Michael D. ... Albany, NY
Violante, Lynn M. ... Geneva, IL
Violante, Mark Anthony ... Niagara Falls, NY
Violante, Martin P. ... Buffalo, NY
Violante, Michael J. ... Niagara Falls, NY
Violanti, Mary Anne ... Stockton, CA
Violanti, Michael L. ... San Francisco, CA
Violet, Timothy C. ... Mankato, MN
Violette, Elmer H. ... Caribou, ME
Violette, Jay O. ... Spokane, WA
Violette, Richard D., Jr. ... Brewer, ME
East Millinocket, ME
Violette, Timothy Paul ... Staten Island, NY
Violi, Leonard ... Iselin, NJ
New York, NY
Vioni, Edward W. ... Bridgeport, CT
Viorel, Lee J., III ... Springfield, MO
Viorst, Anthony J. ... Pueblo, CO
Viosca, Barry F. ... Metairie, LA
Viosca, Bonnie A. ... Metairie, LA
Viot, Sheryl Sutherland ... El Segundo, CA
Viot, Van H. ... Asheville, NC
Vipond, Jonathan, III ... Harrisburg, PA
Vipond, Patrick G. ... Omaha, NE
Vipond, Richard J. ... Denison, IA
Vipond, William R. ... Des Moines, IA
Vipperman, John F. ... Grand Island, NE
Vipperman, Ramona M. ... Burbank, CA
Vira, Daniel Z. ... New York, NY
Virag, Allen ... New York, NY
Virag, Peter G. ... Encino, CA
Viramontes, Daniel ... Deming, NM
Virant, Floyd C. ... Clawson, MI
Plymouth, MI
Virdeh, Abraham ... Santa Rosa, CA
Virden, Barton F. ... Morrilton, AR
Virden, Gaylord A. ... Evergreen, CO
Virden, Jeffrey W. ... Tustin, CA
Virden, Jenny M. ... Greenville, MS
Virden, R. Brittain ... Greenville, MS
Virden, Robert J. ... Kansas City, MO
Virden, Robert N. ... Dallas, TX
Virden, Robert N., P.C. ... Dallas, TX
Virdure, Louis ... St. Louis, MO
Virella Santana, Jose A. ... San Juan, PR
Virelli, Louis J., Jr. ... Bridgewater, NJ
Viren, Jack P., Jr. ... Toledo, OH
Virga, Gerard A. ... New York, NY
Virga, Jane M. ... Farm Credit Administration,
Legal Counsel Division, GV
Virga, John E., (A P.C.) ... Sacramento, CA
Virga, Michael J. ... Sacramento, CA
Virgadamo, Michael J. ... Tampa, FL
Virgalitte, Sherri A. ... Niles, OH
Virgen, Alberto ... San Antonio, TX
Virgen & Virgen ... San Antonio, TX
Virgil, Craig S. ... Middletown, NJ
Virgil, J. Eric ... Coral Gables, FL
Virgil, Michael S. ... Chicago, IL
Virgil, Steven M. ... Omaha, NE
Virgilio, John V. ... Chicago, IL
Virgilio, Joseph A. ... Santa Monica, CA
Virgin, Blake ... Norman, OK
Virgin, David A. ... Bethalto, IL
Virgin, Frank W. ... Atlanta, GA
Virginia & Ambinder ... New York, NY
Virginia, Charles R., III ... New York, NY
Virginia, Mary E. ... Williamsville, NY
Virgino, Tamera D. ... Los Angeles, CA
Virgo, Paul J. ... Los Angeles, CA
Virgona, MaryAnn ... Hackensack, NJ
Virgulak, William J., Jr. ... Washington, DC
Fairfax, VA
Virgulto, Thomas A. ... New Haven, CT
Viri, Peter A. ... Stockton, CA
Virjee, Framroze M. ... Los Angeles, CA
Virji, Arif ... San Francisco, CA
Virk, Devki K. ... Washington, DC
Virk, Rachel Lewis ... Springfield, VA
Virkar, Salil R., Sr. ... Plano, TX
Virkler, Paul Y. ... Richmond, VA
Virkler, Sarah J. ... Chateaugay, NY
Virnelli, Frank R., Jr. ... Farmington, CT
Virnich, Sean H. ... Denver, CO
Virnig, April M. ... Minneapolis, MN
Virnig, Richard S. ... Minneapolis, MN
Virnstein, Jill C. ... Washington, DC
Virostek, Janet E. ... Youngstown, OH
Virr, Thomas F. ... Austin, TX
Virrill, David C., Jr. ... New York, NY
Virruso, Michael L. ... Tucson, AZ
Virshup, Caplan & Hecht ... New Haven, CT
Virsik, Sylvia M. ... Los Angeles, CA
Virtel, James J. ... Belleville, IL
St. Louis, MO
Virtel, Lee T. ... Lemont, IL
Virtue, Crystal C. ... Sacramento, CA
Virtue, John ... Newport Beach, CA
Virtue, Melodie A. ... Arlington, VA
Virtue Najjar Bartell Matthews & Brown P.C. ... Albuquerque, NM
Santa Fe, NM
Virtue, Pamela A. ... Scottsdale, AZ
Virtue, Paul W. ... Washington, DC
Virtue, Richard L. C. ... Santa Fe, NM
Virzera, Diane L. ... New York, NY
Virzi, Michelle ... New York, NY
Virzi, Vito A. ... Winchendon, MA
Vis, Daniel W. ... Luverne, MN
Vis, David E. ... Bellingham, WA
Visalli, Joseph C.
Cape May Court House, NJ
Visani, Hernan N. ... Cleveland, OH
Visani, Sherlyn K. ... Denver, CO
Visano, Ralph M. ... Buffalo, NY
Visbaras, Kim Alexander ... Lewiston, ME
Viscardi, Dominick J. ... Ticonderoga, NY
Viscardi, Gerard C. ... Meeker, CO
Viscardi, Steinman & Basner, P.C.
Jamaica, NY
Viscarello, Kenneth A. ... Concord, NH
Manchester, NH
Visceglia, Diego R. ... Edison, NJ
Visceglia, Peter C. ... Edison, NJ
Viscelli, Stephanie ... Auburn, NY
Vischer, Robert K. ... Chicago, IL
Visci, Joseph J. J. ... Brooklyn, NY
Visciano, Frank W. ... Denver, CO
Viscione, Alfonso C. ... Glen Ridge, NJ
Visclosky, Peter J. ... Gary, IN
Visco, Alfred ... Torrance, CA
Visco, Anthony F., Jr. ... Philadelphia, PA
Visco, Frances M. ... Philadelphia, PA
Visco, Frank E., Sr. ... Cortland, NY
Visco, John M. ... Buffalo, NY
Visco, Louis Gerald ... Columbus, OH
Viscoli, Theresa ... Santa Ana, CA
Viscome, Lisa B ... West Palm Beach, FL
Viscomi, Christina M. ... Detroit, MI
Viscomi, Marianne S. ... Radnor, PA
Viscomi, Michael A.
West Palm Beach, FL
Visconsi, John ... Los Angeles, CA
Visconsi, Thomas A., Jr. ... Independence, OH
Visconte, Rachelle S. ... Los Angeles, CA
Visconte, Wade Thomas
Lake Charles, LA
Visconti, Anthony T. ... Dedham, MA
Visconti & Boren, Ltd. ... Providence, RI
Visconti, Camille T. ... Somerville, MA
Visconti, Charlene ... Brooklyn, NY
Visconti, Girard R. ... Providence, RI
Visconti, Peter C. ... Garden City, NY
Visconti, Richard A. ... Hicksville, NY
Viscount, Loretta I. ... Atlantic City, NJ
Viscount, Michael J., Jr. ... Atlantic City, NJ
Viscounty, Perry J. ... Costa Mesa, CA
Viscovich, David M. ... Washington, DC

Viscovich, William A. .... Bronx, NY
Vise, J. Wilbourn .... Jackson, MS
Vise, Joe B. .... Shawnee, KS
Visek, Franklin J. .... Philadelphia, PA
Visek, Margaret McCaskill .... Oak Park, IL
Visek, Richard C. .... Department of State, Office of the Legal Adviser, GV
Visel, Jon J. .... Newport Beach, CA
Visger, Melvin J. .... Sacramento, CA
Vish, David L. .... Louisville, KY
Vish, Donald H. .... Louisville, KY
Vishab, Stefanie .... Washington, DC
Visher, S. Chandler .... San Francisco, CA
Visher, S. Sargent .... Indianapolis, IN
Vishneski, John S., III .... Chicago, IL
Vishnick, Bernard .... Lake Success, NY
Vishno, Jeremy G. .... New Haven, CT
Vishny, Paul H. .... Chicago, IL
Visick, Christopher S. .... Deerfield, IL
Visick, H. Hal .... Provo, UT
Visingardi, Lisa M. .... Riverside, CA
Vision, Blanche Stein .... Sun City West, AZ
Visioni, Guido J. .... Clay, NY
Visk, F. Kilburn .... Chicago, IL
Viski-Hánka, Támas .... Denver, CO
Vislosky, James F., Jr. .... Newark, NJ
Visnic, Pete S. .... Weirton, WV
Visnick, Robert L. .... Gloucester, MA
Visnosky, Michael J. .... Erie, PA
Viso, Anthony .... Lodi, NJ
Viso, Corinne B. .... New Orleans, LA
Visocan, Karen A. .... Cleveland, OH
Visone, Anthony J. .... New York, NY
Visone, Thomas James .... Bayonne, NJ
Visosky, Jon A. .... Hagåtña, GU
Visotcky, Richard P. .... Manahawkin, NJ
Visovsky, Michael B. .... New York, NY
Vispi, Joseph C. .... Buffalo, NY
Visscher, Gary L. .... Occupational Safety and Health Review Commission, Office of a Commissioner, GV
Visscher, Linn M. .... Chicago, IL
Visse, Joseph M. .... San Francisco, CA
Vissenberg, Ivo .... Atlanta, GA
Vissepó Muñoz, Omar D. .... San Juan, PR
Visser & Bolhouse, A Professional Corporation .... Grandville, MI
Visser, Donald R. .... Grandville, MI
Visser, Eric J.W. .... Austin, TX
Visser, Freeman C. .... Grand Rapids, MI
Visser, Kevin J. .... Cedar Rapids, IA
Visser, Michelle L. .... Bloomfield Hills, MI
Visser, Peter Jay .... Bellingham, WA
Lynden, WA
Visser, Randolph C. .... Los Angeles, CA
Visser, Richard .... Boise, ID
Visser, Robert P. .... Washington, DC
Visser, Sandra K. .... St. Joseph, MI
Visser, Timothy B. .... Comstock Park, MI
Visser, Zender & Thurston, A Professional Service Corporation .... Bellingham, WA
Lynden, WA
Visserman, Peter .... Grand Rapids, MI
Vissers, Christian F. .... Baltimore, MD
Vissicchio, Gino .... New York, NY
Vissing and Associates LLP .... Jeffersonville, IN
Vissing, John R. .... Jeffersonville, IN
Vissman, Paul F. .... Louisville, KY
Viswanathan, Aditi .... New York, NY
Viswanathan, M. Nate .... Pasadena, CA
Viswanathan, Serena .... Washington, DC
Viswanathan, Sreelata .... Los Angeles, CA
Viswanathan, Subhash .... Syracuse, NY
Vita, Charles A. .... White Plains, NY
Vita, Jeffrey J. .... New Haven, CT
Vita, John .... Huntington Beach, CA
Vita, John B. .... Syracuse, NY
Vita, Joseph A. .... Port Chester, NY
Vita, Mark W. .... Denver, CO
Vita, Richard J. .... Boston, MA
Vita, Therese M. .... Syracuse, NY
Vita, William E. .... Garden City, NY
Vitabile, Steven .... Los Angeles, CA
Vitacco, Elene F. .... Chicago, IL
Vitacco, Guy R. .... Elmhurst, NY
Vitacco, Guy R., Jr. .... Elmhurst, NY
Vitacco & Vitacco .... Elmhurst, NY
Vitacolonna, Alison J. .... Santa Ana, CA
Vitagliano, Aldo V. .... Rye, NY
Vitagliano, Aldo V., P.C. .... Rye, NY
Vitagliano, Arthur .... Boston, MA
Vitagliano, Maria T. .... New York, NY
Vital, Adam E. .... New York, NY
Vital, Jack H., III .... Huntington, WV
Vital, Leroy P. .... Chicago, IL
Vital, Patricia Best .... Chattanooga, TN
Vital, Richard L. .... Barboursville, WV
Vital, Robert E. .... Huntington, WV
Vital, Robert M. .... Huntington, WV
Vital, Victor D. .... Dallas, TX
Vitale, Alberta A. .... Stamford, CT
Vitale, Alexander F. .... Fort Lauderdale, FL
Vitale, Angelo M. .... Sacramento, CA
Vitale, Angelo V. .... Bingham Farms, MI
Vitale, Anne T. .... New York, NY
Vitale, Anthony C. .... Miami, FL
Vitale, Anthony C., P.A. .... Miami, FL
Tampa, FL
Vitale, Cathleen Marie .... Glen Burnie, MD
Vitale, Dale T. .... Columbus, OH
Vitale, Donald N. .... Waterbury, CT
Vitale, Edward J. .... Riverhead, NY
Vitale, Jack, (P.C.) .... Monroe, MI
Vitale, John A. .... Hanson, MA
Vitale, John E. .... Millburn, NJ
Vitale, Joseph A. .... Farmington, CT
Vitale, Joseph J. .... New York, NY
Vitale, Joseph M. .... Melville, NY
Vitale, Joseph M. .... North Canton, OH
Vitale, Joseph P. .... Washington, DC
Vitale, Laureen J. .... Hartford, CT
Vitale, Linda L. .... Fort Lauderdale, FL
Vitale, Lisa Michelle .... Canton, OH
Vitale, Marc D. .... Philadelphia, PA
Vitale, Marie Cucurullo .... Bronx, NY
Vitale, Matthew J. .... Federal Communications Commission, Common Carrier Bureau, GV
Vitale, Michael A. .... St. Louis, MO
Vitale, Michael S. .... Bowling Green, KY
Vitale, Nancy .... Sacramento, CA
Vitale, Robert A., Jr. .... Chicago, IL
Vitale, Robert L. .... New York, NY
Vitale, Thomas A. .... Kenilworth, NJ
Vitale, Thomas M. .... New York, NY
Vitale, Victor S. .... West Nyack, NY
Vitale, Vincent P. .... Anchorage, AK
Vitali, Angela D. .... New York, NY
Vitali, Burt M. .... San Diego, CA
Vitali, Greg K. .... Westfield, NJ
Vitali, Gregory S. .... Havertown, PA
Vitali, John E. .... Oklahoma City, OK
Vitali, Louis .... New York, NY
Vitali, Michael Anthony .... Springfield, MA
Vitali, Richard L. .... Lynn, MA
Vitali, Richard L. .... Reno, NV
Vitali, Samuel A. .... Lynn, MA
Vitaliano, Eric N. .... Staten Island, NY
Vitalie, Carl L. .... Sandpoint, ID
Vitanvas, Gerald S. .... Lincoln, NE
Vitanza, Aaron & Fitzgerald, P.C. .... Binghamton, NY
Vitanza, Matthew A. .... Binghamton, NY
Vitanza, Matthew J. .... Binghamton, NY
Vitanza, Shabus & Fertig .... Greene, NY
Norwich, NY
Vitanza, Thomas A. .... Norwich, NY
Vitarelli, Alfred P. .... Cherry Hill, NJ
Vitarelli, Richard F. .... Hartford, CT
Vitch, Allan J. .... Niagara Falls, NY
Vitek, Anna Maria .... New York, NY
Vitek, Anne M. .... Denver, CO
Vitek, John C. .... Milwaukee, WI
Vitek, Joseph C. .... Omaha, NE
Vitek, Marina N. .... Tarzana, CA
Vitek, Marsha C. .... Baltimore, MD
Vitek, Michael G. .... Chicago, IL
Vitek, Nina M. .... Milwaukee, WI
Vitek, Reginald A. .... San Diego, CA
Vitek, Richard P. .... Troy, MI
Vitell, Joseph A. .... Chicago, IL
Vitelli, Annamaria .... Philadelphia, PA
Vitelli, James T. .... Hartford, CT
Vitelli, Kristine Hughes .... Hartford, CT
Vitelli, Mary Louise .... Washington, DC
Vitelli, Peter L. .... Tuckahoe, NY
Vitello, Edward .... Glen, NH
Vitello, Guy .... Schaumburg, IL
Vitello, Paul J. .... Derby, CT
Vitello, Ronald J. .... Indianapolis, IN
Vitenberg, Vladimir .... Cincinnati, OH
Viteo, Penelope Rhude .... San Antonio, TX
Viteretti, Robert J. .... New York, NY
Vitez, Kathleen A. .... Lancaster, PA
Vitez, Wallace A. .... Lebanon, PA
Vitez, Wallace A., P.C., Law Office of .... Lebanon, PA
Viteznik, Peter J. .... Portland, OR
Vitha, John R., II .... New York, NY
Vithoulkas, Stephanie .... Phoenix, AZ
Viti, John Thomas .... New York, NY
Viti, Kim .... Rockville, MD
Viti, Lyndia Venezia .... Bronx, NY
Viti, Norman B., Jr. .... Buffalo, NY
Vitiello, Anthony F. .... Roseland, NJ
Vitiello, Daniel J. .... Department of Agriculture, Food Safety and Inspection Service, GV
Vitiello, James M. .... Staten Island, NY
Vitiello, Louis R. .... Lexington, MA
Vitiello, Michael J. .... Morristown, NJ
Vitiello, Ralph J. .... Syracuse, NY
Vitiello, Salvatore J. .... New York, NY
Vitiello & Seltzer, P.A. .... Rahway, NJ
Vitiello, Vincent A. .... Rahway, NJ
Vitiello, Vincent A., II .... New York, NY
Vitikainen, Sybil A. .... Tacoma, WA
Vititoe, James W. .... Westlake Village, CA
Vititow, Robert Frank .... Sulphur Springs, TX
Vitkowsky, Vincent J. .... New York, NY
Providence, RI
Vitkus, Richard F. .... Glenview, IL
Vito, Christine C. .... Boston, MA
Vito, James C. .... Glenview, IL
Vito, Michael P. .... Roseland, NJ
Vito, Salvatore P.J. .... Stroudsburg, PA
Vito, Virginia A. .... Cleveland, OH
Vitola, John R. .... Brooksville, FL
Vitolo, Frank J. .... Washington, DC
Vitolo, Marc W. .... Los Angeles, CA
Vitolo, Michael J. .... White Plains, NY
Vitolo, Ralph G. .... New York, NY
Vitolo, Thomas P. .... Springfield, NJ
Vitols, Tracy A. .... Boston, MA
Vitou, John B. .... Lansing, MI
Vitou, Mark F. .... Maumee, OH
Vitousek, Betty M. .... Honolulu, HI
Vitousek, Roy A., III .... Kailua-Kona, HI
Vitrano, Paul C. .... Washington, DC
Vitrano, Peter R. .... San Francisco, CA
Vitrano, Salvatore V. .... Bristol, CT
Vitro, Sherin S. .... Phoenix, AZ
Vitsas, John L. .... Pittsburgh, PA
Vitsut, Ullar .... Los Angeles, CA
Vitt, A. Francis, Jr. .... Washington, DC
Arlington, VA
Vitt, Geoffrey J. .... Hanover, NH
Norwich, VT
Vitt, J. Thomas .... Minneapolis, MN
Vitt & Jones .... Hanover, NH
Norwich, VT
Vittal, J. Anthony .... Los Angeles, CA
Vittal and Sternberg .... Los Angeles, CA
Woodland Hills, CA
Vittands, Martin J. .... Detroit, MI
Vittek, Joseph F., Jr. .... Franklin, NH
Vitter-Thomas, Patricia .... Inverness, FL
Vittese, Mark A. .... Hammonton, NJ
Vitti, Anthony M. .... Los Angeles, CA
Vitti, Louis P. .... Pittsburgh, PA
Vitti, Louis P., and Associates, P.A. .... Pittsburgh, PA
Vitti, Patricia W. .... Washington, NJ
Vittiglio, Joseph .... Boston, MA
Vittitoe, Craig H. .... Harlingen, TX
Vittitoe, Dorothy E. .... Albuquerque, NM
Vittitow, Chester A., Jr. .... Louisville, KY
Vittitow, John K. .... Louisville, KY
Vittitow, Jon R. .... Norman, OK
Vittitow, Katherine E. .... Norman, OK
Vittitow Law Office, P.C. .... Norman, OK
Vittitow, Robert C. .... Monticello, AR
Vittone, Anthony F. .... Richmond, VA
Vittone, Eugene A., II .... Washington, PA
Vittone, John M. .... Department of Labor, Office of Secretary, GV
Vittone, Paul R. .... Pittsburgh, PA
Vittone, Tara Breslin .... Pittsburgh, PA
Vittor, Kenneth M. .... New York, NY
Vittori, Michael L. .... Chicago, IL
Vittoria, Anthony Francis .... Baltimore, MD
Vittoria & Forsythe .... New York, NY
White Plains, NY
Vittoria, Theodore J., Jr., (P.C.) .... Miami, FL
New York, NY
Vittorioso, Carol T. .... Leominster, MA
Vittorioso & Taylor .... Leominster, MA
Vittum, Daniel W., Jr. (P.C.) .... Chicago, IL
Vitu, Thomas L. .... Birmingham, MI
Columbus, OH
Vitulli, Anthony J. .... Riverside, CA
Vitullo, Anthony L. .... Dallas, TX
Vitullo, Domenick .... Philadelphia, PA
Vitullo, James A. .... Youngstown, OH
Vitullo, Louis P. .... Chicago, IL
Vitullo, Vincent F. .... Chicago, IL
Vitunac, Ann E. .... West Palm Beach, FL
Vitunac, Charles P. .... Vero Beach, FL
Vitvitsky, Bohdan .... Newark, NJ
Vitz Law Firm .... McKinney, TX
Vitz, William A. "Tony" .... McKinney, TX
Vitz, William H. .... McKinney, TX
Vitzthum, Barbara J. .... Los Angeles, CA
Viuhkola, David T. .... Milwaukie, OR
Viuker, Barry M. .... New York, NY
Vivacqua, Raymond J. .... Southfield, MI
Vivaldi, Carolynne W. .... Carlsbad, CA
Vivaldi, Walter .... Carthage, TX
Vivar, Mona Ann .... Mobile, AL
Vivas, Dorothy S. .... Mount Vernon, NY
Vivas, Ernest E. .... Folsom, CA
Vivas, Gabriel C. .... Sacramento, CA
Vivas, José Guillermo .... Ponce, PR
Vivas, José Héctor .... Ponce, PR
Vivas, Lourdes Alicea .... Ponce, PR
Vivas & Vivas .... Ponce, PR
Vivenzio, Alfredo A. .... Springfield, MA
Vivenzio, James F. .... New York, NY
Vivenzio, Lawrence F., Jr. .... Mount Arlington, NJ
Vivenzio, Raymond A. .... North Andover, MA
Viverette, William J. .... Richmond, VA
Viverito, John N. .... Houston, TX
Viverito, Lou J. .... Altamont, IL
Effingham, IL
Vivero, Frank .... New York, NY
Viveros, Octavio J., Jr. .... Westwood, KS
Vives, Joseph H. .... San Antonio, TX
Vivian, Carlson .... Los Altos, CA
Vivian, Jean A. .... St. Cloud, MN
Vivian, John R., Jr., Law Offices of .... Easton, PA
Vivian, Karen M. .... Chicago, IL
Viviani, Anthony J. .... Troy, MI
Viviani, Arthur J. .... New York, NY
Viviani, Gregory J. .... Cleveland, OH
Viviani, Louis J. .... Syracuse, NY
Viviano, Antonio P. .... Mount Clemens, MI
Viviano, Charles A. .... San Diego, CA
Viviano, Cheryl B. .... Dearborn, MI
Viviano, David F. .... Detroit, MI
Viviano, Frank J. .... Southfield, MI
Viviano, Lina M. .... New York, NY
Viviano, Louis B. .... Opelousas, LA
Viviano, Mary C. .... San Diego, CA
Viviano, Peter R. .... St. Louis, MO
Viviano, Sam A. .... Pensacola, FL
Vivino, Raymond P., Law Office .... Paterson, NJ
Wayne, NJ
Vivino, Raymond S. .... Paterson, NJ
Wayne, NJ
Vivoli, Michael W. .... San Diego, CA
Vivona, Alycia M. .... Baltimore, MD
New York, NY
Vivona, Peter J. .... Binghamton, NY
Vivona, Vincent J. .... Toms River, NJ
Vivone, Thomas J. .... Las Vegas, NV
Vix, Ann Louise .... Nashville, TN
Vix, Carol A. .... Chicago, IL
Vix, Lyndon W. .... Wichita, KS
Viz, Stephen A. .... Chicago, IL
Vizas, Robert J. .... Emeryville, CA
Vizbaras, Andris J. .... New York, NY
Vizcarra de Lopez-Lay, Ginoris, (Mrs.) .... San Juan, PR
Vizcarrondo, Paul, Jr. .... New York, NY
Vizcarrondo, Rafael R. .... San Juan, PR
Vizurraga, Michelle L. .... Washington, DC
Vizy, Nick J. .... Columbus, OH
Vizza, Mark F. .... Chicago, IL
Vizzard, Sarah L. .... Bakersfield, CA
Vizzi, John J. .... West Babylon, NY
Vizzier, Dorwan G. .... Alexandria, LA
Vizzini, Charles S. .... Washington, DC
Brooklyn, NY
Vizzini, Eugene .... New York, NY
Vizzini, Tina M. .... Brooklyn, NY
Vizzoni, Anthony M. .... Hackensack, NJ
Vlaanderen, Richard T. .... Sacramento, CA
Vlach, G. Robert .... Berwyn, IL
Vlach, Robert B. .... Dallas, TX
Vlach, Thomas J. .... Westmont, IL
Vlachos, Christopher M. .... Kalamazoo, MI
Vlachos, Dino .... Huntington Beach, CA
Vlachos, Harry J. .... Waltham, MA
Vlachos, Nicholas A. .... Kalamazoo, MI
Vlachos, Paul T. .... Kalamazoo, MI
Vlachos & Vlachos, P.C. .... Kalamazoo, MI
Vlack, Edward F., III .... River Falls, WI
Vlad, Joseph G. .... Sun Prairie, WI
Vladeck, Anne C. .... New York, NY
Vladeck, David C. .... Washington, DC
Vladeck, Judith P. .... New York, NY
Vladeck, Waldman, Elias & Engelhard, P.C. .... New York, NY
Vladimir, Bert .... North Babylon, NY
Vladimir, Bert, P.C. .... North Babylon, NY
Vladimir, Paul .... Kew Gardens, NY
Vladyka, Valerie A. .... Hackensack, NJ
Vlaeminck, Evan M. .... Addison, IL
Vlahakis, Barbara J. .... Deerfield Beach, FL
Vlahakis, Elaine B. .... New York, NY
Vlahakis, James Constantine .... Chicago, IL
Vlahakis, Patricia Ann .... New York, NY
Vlahakos, Frank G. .... Houston, TX
Vlahoplus, John C. .... New York, NY
Vlahos, Andrew .... Orlando, FL
Vlahos, Anthony .... New York, NY
Vlahos, Eugene A. .... Burlingame, CA
Vlahos, Georgia .... North Chicago, IL
Vlahos, John B. .... Burlingame, CA
Vlahos, John J. .... San Francisco, CA
Vlahos, Louis .... Uniondale, NY
Vlahos, Pete N. .... Ogden, UT
Vlahos & Vlahos .... Burlingame, CA
Vlaming, Jacqueline W. .... Oakbrook Terrace, IL
Vlaming, Michael J. .... Napa, CA
Vlamis, Georgia L. .... Schaumburg, IL
Vlasak, Arthur J. .... Milwaukee, WI
Vlasak, Britton & Konkel, S.C. .... Milwaukee, WI
Vlasaty, Louis A. .... St. Louis, MO
Vlasek, Dale R. .... Cleveland, OH
Vlasek, William A. .... Lansing, IL
Vlasek, William A., P.C. .... Lansing, IL
Vlasic, Adriana Valdes .... Bloomfield Hills, MI
Vlasic, James J. .... Southfield, MI
Vlasnik, Vicki J. .... Los Angeles, CA
Vlassakis, John M. .... Boston, MA
Vlassis, Elizabeth D. .... Phoenix, AZ
Vlassis, George P. .... Phoenix, AZ
Vlassis & Vlassis .... Phoenix, AZ
Vlastos, Brooks, Henley & Drell, P.C. .... Casper, WY
Vlastos, J. E. .... Casper, WY
Vlatas, Anthony J. .... Washington, DC
Vlatkovich, Jeffrey M. .... Hibbing, MN
Vlautin, Casey Woodburn .... Reno, NV
Vlautin, Paul .... San Francisco, CA
Vlautin, Peter P., III .... Sacramento, CA
Vlavianos, Constantine .... New York, NY
Vlavianos, Richard A. .... Stockton, CA
Vlay, Burton B. .... Skokie, IL
Vlazakis, George M. .... Oakland, CA
Vlazny, Adalbert L., III .... Naperville, IL
Vlcek, Alan Benes .... Jacksonville, FL
Vlcek, Ann Lewis .... Department of State, GV
Vlcek, David M. .... Palos Hills, IL
Vlcek, Tomas V. .... Department of Commerce, Patent and Trademark Office, GV
Vlcko, Lane, Payne & Broder, P.C. .... Bingham Farms, MI
Birmingham, MI
Vlcko, Miroslav P. .... Bingham Farms, MI
Vleerick, Howard E. .... Downey, CA
Vleisides, Gregory W. .... Kansas City, MO
Vletas, Gus G. .... Los Angeles, CA
Vletas, Katie-Pat .... Houston, TX
Vliet, Daniel G. .... Milwaukee, WI
Vliet, Walter C. .... Phillipsburg, NJ
Vlietstra, Nicholas A.J. .... Minneapolis, MN
Vlioras, Katherine D. .... Dallas, TX
Vlissides & Keisler, P.C. .... Fairfax, VA
Vlissides, Nicholas .... Fairfax, VA
Vloedman, D. Andrew .... Gainesville, FL
Vloitos, Jeanette A. .... Dallas, TX
Vlosich, Richard T. .... Roy, WA
Vlosky, Denese Ashbaug .... State College, PA
Vlosky, Edward F. .... Akron, OH
Vlosky, William M. .... San Clemente, CA
Vlossak, Stephen Peter, Sr. .... Palmerton, PA
Vo, Dang M. .... San Francisco, CA
Vo, Hien T. .... McLean, VA
Vo, Joseph A. .... San Francisco, CA
Vo, Kim D. .... Boston, MA
Vo, Mary K. .... Santa Monica, CA

Vo, Thuy-Nga Thi ... St. Paul, MN
Vobach, William F. ... Denver, CO
Vobach, William H. ... Indianapolis, IN
Voboril, Joseph S., (P.C.) ... Portland, OR
Voboril, Lorna A. ... Fair Oaks, CA
Vobornik, Donna J. ... Chicago, IL
Vocalina, Michael V. ... Bridgeport, CT
Voce, Mary F. ... New York, NY
Vocelle, Charles ... Lakeland, FL
Vocelle, Louis B., Jr., (P.A.)
Vero Beach, FL
Voces, Emmanuel D. ... Virginia Beach, VA
Vochoska, Virgil D. ... Anchorage, AK
Vocht, Michelle E. ... Bloomfield Hills, MI
Vock, Curtis A. ... Boulder, CO
Vock, R. Daniel ... White Plains, NY
Vocke, Damon N. ... Chicago, IL
Vocke, Edward C., IV ... Metairie, LA
Vocke, John C. ... San Francisco, CA
Vocke, R. Kim ... Covington, KY
Vocke, Timothy L. ... Rhinelander, WI
Vockrodt, Robert M. ... Radford, VA
Vockrodt, Thomas M. ... Aurora, CO
Vockrodt, Thomas M., P.C. ... Aurora, CO
Vodnoy, Joseph T. ... Los Angeles, CA
Vodola, Peter Joseph ... Hartford, CT
Vodonick, E. John ... Roseville, CA
Vodopia, John F. ... Garden City, NY
Vodovnik, Raymond F. ... Bloomington, MN
Vodra, John M. ... Omaha, NE
Brookfield, WI
Vodra, Richard E. ... United States Senate, Senatorial Assistants, GV
Vodra, William W. ... Washington, DC
Vodraska, Adam ... General Accounting Office, Office of the General Counsel, GV
Vodrey, Jackman Stroud
East Liverpool, OH
Vodrey, William F.B. ... New Philadelphia, OH
Voegel, Robert J. ... South Barrington, IL
Voegele, Gary L. ... Faribault, MN
Voegele, George A., Jr. ... Cherry Hill, NJ
Philadelphia, PA
Voegele, Royal J. ... Washington, DC
Voegeli & Ewald Law Offices, S.C.
Monroe, WI
Monticello, WI
Voegeli, James F. ... Minneapolis, MN
Voegeli, John E. ... Baraboo, WI
Voegeli, Paul W. ... Monroe, WI
Monticello, WI
Voegelin, Wray V. ... Wheeling, WV
Voegtle, Clayton P. ... Libertyville, IL
Voegtle, Henry J. ... Dallas, TX
Voegtle & Lichter ... Libertyville, IL
Voegtlen, Anne Reynolds
Bainbridge Island, WA
Voegtli, Naomi Abe ... Washington, DC
Voeks, Howard A. ... Chicago, IL
Voelbel, Richard L. ... Minneapolis, MN
Voelcker, Laurinda J. ... Reading, PA
Voelk, Eric K. ... Milwaukee, WI
Voelke, Marilyn S. ... San Francisco, CA
Voelkel, Dennis ... Indianapolis, IN
Voelkel-Hanssen, Marty ... Towson, MD
Voelker & Battard ... Metairie, LA
Voelker, Carla R. ... Dallas, TX
Voelker, Charles P. ... Pittsburgh, PA
Voelker, Daniel J. ... Chicago, IL
Voelker, Dirken T. ... Columbus, OH
Voelker, Dorothy E. ... Pittsburgh, PA
Voelker, Dow T. ... Columbus, OH
Voelker, Frank, Jr., (P.C.)
Lake Providence, LA
New Orleans, LA
Voelker & Gricks ... Pittsburgh, PA
Voelker, James M. ... Peoria, IL
Voelker, James Robert ... St. Louis, MO
Voelker, Jennifer Heyong ... New York, NY
Voelker, John W. ... Nebraska City, NE
Voelker, Kathleen E. ... Washington, DC
Voelker, Keith W. ... New York, NY
Voelker, Kristine ... Chicago, IL
Voelker, Liisa M. ... Minneapolis, MN
Voelker, Louis W., III ... Hammond, IN
Voelker, Martin A. ... New York, NY
Voelker, Paul ... Milwaukee, WI
Voelker, Paul K. ... Las Vegas, NV
Voelker, Raymond F. ... Cheshire, CT
Voelker, Raymond F. ... Waterbury, CT
Voelker, Richard John ... Baton Rouge, LA
Voelker, Richard L., Jr. ... Metairie, LA
Voelker, Stephen R. ... Dallas, TX
Voelker, Stephen W. ... Hampstead, NC
Voelker, Troy L. ... Round Rock, TX
Voelker & Voelker ... Columbus, OH
Voelkl, Jeffrey F. ... Buffalo, NY
Voeller, Timothy J. ... Milwaukee, WI
Voellmicke, John L. ... Franklin Lakes, NJ
Voelp, John M. ... Peekskill, NY
Voelpel, John W. ... Tampa, FL
Voelpel, Mark S. ... San Antonio, TX
Voelz, James K. ... Columbus, IN
Voelz, Scott M. ... Los Angeles, CA
Voelzke, Joel D. ... Los Angeles, CA
Voepel, Lori L. ... Phoenix, AZ
Voerman, David P. ... New Bern, NC
Voermans, Adrian J. ... Spokane, WA
Voet, Leo C. ... Los Altos, CA
Voet, Martin A. ... Irvine, CA
Voevodsky, Peter ... Tucson, AZ
Vogan, Charles E., Jr., Law Offices
Norfolk, VA
Vogan, Joseph J. ... Grand Rapids, MI
Vogdes, James M., III ... Marlton, NJ
Voge, Dennis W. ... Tupelo, MS
Voge, Elizabeth Moen ... Berkeley, CA
Voge, Jeri G. ... Bakersfield, CA
Voge, William H. ... New York, NY
Vogel, Alan Garson ... Bridgeport, CT
Vogel, Albert E. ... Altadena, CA
Vogel, Albert T., Jr. ... Mesa, AZ
Vogel, Alexander N. ... Washington, DC
Vogel, Andrea ... Chatsworth, CA
Vogel, Andrew L. ... Fort Worth, TX
Vogel, Andrew M. ... Los Angeles, CA
Vogel, Arthur A., Jr. ... Milwaukee, WI
Vogel, Barry ... Sacramento, CA
Vogel, Barry ... Ukiah, CA
Vogel, Bernard H. ... New York, NY
Vogel, Bernard J., III ... San Jose, CA
Vogel, Bernard J., Jr. ... San Jose, CA
Vogel, Blair D. ... Marshalltown, IA
Vogel, Brian I. ... Rolling Hills Estates, CA
Vogel, C. Nicholas ... Fargo, ND
Vogel, Campbell, Hoffman & Blueher, P.C.
Albuquerque, NM
Vogel, Candace K. ... Buffalo, NY
Vogel, Carla J. ... Fort Worth, TX
Vogel, Carla P.S. ... New York, NY
Vogel, Carol A. ... South Bend, IN
Vogel, Carole A. ... Jacksonville, FL
Vogel, Caryn ... Miami, FL
Vogel, Cedric ... Cincinnati, OH
Vogel, Cedric W. ... Cincinnati, OH
Vogel, Chait, Schwartz and Collins, A Professional Corporation ... Morristown, NJ
Vogel, Charles D. ... Bloomington, IL
Vogel, Charles G. ... Milwaukee, WI
Vogel, Charles N. ... Phoenix, AZ
Vogel, Charles S. ... Los Angeles, CA
Vogel, Christine K. ... Tampa, FL
Vogel, Christopher A. ... Salina, KS
Vogel & Cromwell, L.L.C. ... Roanoke, VA
Vogel, Curt M. ... Perryville, MO
Vogel, Daniel G. ... St. Louis, MO
Vogel, David A. ... Washington, DC
Vogel, David C. ... Kansas City, MO
Vogel, David Jeffrey ... New York, NY
Vogel, David L. ... Wichita, KS
Vogel, David S. ... Seattle, WA
Vogel, David S., P.L.L.C., Law Offices of
Bellevue, WA
Seattle, WA
Vogel, Denis R. ... Madison, WI
Vogel, Donald J. ... Chicago, IL
Vogel, Edward D. ... San Diego, CA
Vogel, Edward W., III ... Lakeland, FL
Vogel, Erik K. ... Philadelphia, PA
Vogel, Ernest B. ... Federal Way, WA
Vogel, Eugene L. ... New York, NY
Vogel, Frank E. ... Cambridge, MA
Vogel, Frederick W.B. ... Washington, DC
Vogel, Gary D. ... Portland, ME
Vogel, Gary R. ... Washington, DC
Vogel & Gast ... Watchung, NJ
Vogel, Gayle N. ... Des Moines, IA
Vogel, George F. ... Red Wing, MN
Vogel, George I., II ... Roanoke, VA
Vogel, George T. ... Yonkers, NY
Vogel, Harold S. ... Wildwood, NJ
Vogel, Herbert A. ... Morristown, NJ
Vogel, Hilmond O. ... Sun City, AZ
Vogel, Howard H. ... Knoxville, TN
Vogel, Howard J. ... Miami, FL
Vogel, Howard J. ... Northbrook, IL
Vogel, Howard J. ... St. Paul, MN
Vogel, Howard S. ... New York, NY
Vogel, Irwin R. ... White Plains, NY
Vogel, J. Vann ... Bedminster, NJ
Vogel, James K. ... Erie, PA
Vogel, Jay M. ... Burbank, CA
Vogel, Jennifer L. ... New York, NY
Vogel, Jennifer L. ... Houston, TX
Vogel, Jerome A. ... Hawthorne, NJ
Vogel, Joanna T. ... Orange, CA
Vogel, John D. ... Houston, TX
Vogel, John H. ... Washington, DC
Vogel, John M. ... Philadelphia, PA
Vogel, John T. ... Pittsburgh, PA
Vogel, John W. ... Dansville, NY
Vogel, Jon N., P.C. ... Scottsdale, AZ
Vogel, Jonathan A. ... Atlanta, GA
Vogel, Joni B. ... Palo Alto, CA
Vogel, Joseph A. ... New York, NY
Vogel, Joshua S. ... New York, NY
Vogel, Jules B. ... Woodland Hills, CA
Vogel, Karen ... Annapolis, MD
Vogel, Karen ... Greenbelt, MD
Vogel, Karen A. ... Department of Justice, Criminal Division, GV
Vogel, Karen M. ... Norristown, PA
Vogel, Karla Y. ... Decatur, GA
Vogel, Kenneth Alan ... Washington, DC
Vogel, Kimberly A. ... Cincinnati, OH
Vogel, Laura L. ... Madison, WI
Vogel, Laura M. ... Jefferson City, MO
Vogel, Laurence ... Honolulu, HI
Vogel, Laurie A. ... Albuquerque, NM
Vogel, Lawrence H. ... Manhattan, KS
Vogel, Lawrence M. ... Englewood, CO
Vogel, Layton & Lewis, L.L.C.
Cape Girardeau, MO
Vogel, Linda I. ... Murray Hill, NJ
Vogel, Linda J. ... Los Angeles, CA
Vogel, Lisa S. ... New York, NY
Vogel, Lisa W. ... Lynchburg, VA
Vogel, Liviu ... New York, NY
Vogel, Mark A. ... New York, NY
Vogel, Mark Joseph ... Chicago, IL
Vogel, Mark R. ... Fort Lauderdale, FL
Miami, FL
West Palm Beach, FL
Vogel, Mark R., P.A. ... Boca Raton, FL
Fort Lauderdale, FL
Miami, FL
West Palm Beach, FL
Vogel, Mart Daniel ... Fargo, ND
Vogel, Mart R. ... Fargo, ND
Vogel, Melisa A. ... Denver, CO
Vogel, Melissa C. ... New York, NY
Vogel, Michael S. ... Princeton, NJ
New York, NY
Vogel, Miriam A. ... Los Angeles, CA
Vogel & Mongelli ... Hackensack, NJ
New York, NY
Vogel, Musette H. ... Belleville, IL
St. Louis, MO
Vogel, Neil ... Philadelphia, PA
Vogel, Nelson J., Jr. ... South Bend, IN
Vogel, Netti C. ... Providence, RI
Vogel, Nicholas C. ... West Hempstead, NY
Vogel & Oleen ... Manhattan, KS
Vogel, Patricia L. ... Orange City, IA
Vogel, Paul A. ... Treasury Department, Office of the Comptroller of the Currency, GV
Vogel, Paul LeRoy ... St. Louis, MO
Vogel, Paul S. ... Whitehouse Station, NJ
Vogel, Paul T. ... Orlando, FL
Vogel, Paul William ... Sandpoint, ID
Vogel, Paul William, P.A. ... Sandpoint, ID
Vogel, Pearl Franklin ... Encino, CA
Vogel, Peter F. ... Hackensack, NJ
New York, NY
Vogel, Peter J. ... Milwaukee, WI
Vogel, Peter L. ... Little Falls, MN
Vogel, Peter R. ... Naperville, IL
Vogel, Peter S. ... Dallas, TX
Vogel, Philip Z. ... Cleveland, OH
Vogel, Rachel Terner ... Los Angeles, CA
Vogel, Ralph H. ... Washington, DC
Vogel, Randy K. ... Laguna Hills, CA
Vogel, Raymond F. ... Chicago, IL
Vogel, Raymond H. ... Cape Girardeau, MO
Vogel, Renee G. ... Barrington, RI
Vogel, Richard A. ... Darien, IL
Vogel, Richard E. ... Joliet, IL
Vogel, Richard E. ... Woodbridge, VA
Vogel, Richard J. ... Grinnell, IA
Vogel, Richard M. ... Buffalo, WY
Vogel, Robert ... Grand Forks, ND
Vogel, Robert C. ... Wilmette, IL
Vogel, Robert D. ... Los Angeles, CA
Vogel, Robert L., Law Office of
Washington, DC
Vogel, Robert, Law Office, P.C.
Grand Forks, ND
Vogel, Robert P. ... Philadelphia, PA
Vogel, Robin M. ... Richmond, VA
Vogel & Rosenberg ... New York, NY
Vogel, Sanford C. ... Watchung, NJ
Vogel, Sarah M. ... Bismarck, ND
Vogel, Stephen Brent ... Las Vegas, NV
Vogel, Stephen Joseph ... Albuquerque, NM
Vogel, Steve Gregory ... Fremont, CA
Vogel, Steven H. ... Peoria, IL
Vogel, Suzanne ... Edwardsville, IL
Vogel, Terrence L. ... San Diego, CA
Vogel, Terry O. ... Washington, DC
Vogel, Terry R. ... Pittsburgh, PA
Vogel, Theodore J. ... Jackson, MI
Vogel, Thomas & Pruitt ... Fort Worth, TX
Vogel, Thomas V. ... Wayne, NJ
Vogel, Timothy A. ... Washington, DC
Vogel, Timothy M. ... Portland, ME
Vogel, Victoria R. ... New York, NY
Vogel, Virginia ... Oakland, CA
Vogel & Vogel ... San Jose, CA
Vogel, Walter J. ... Akron, OH
Vogel, Warren ... Blue Bell, PA
Vogel, Weir, Bye, Hunke & McCormick, Ltd.
Moorhead, MN
Fargo, ND
Vogel, Willard B. ... Newhall, CA
Vogel, William ... Salt Lake City, UT
Vogel, William D. ... Groton, CT
Vogel, William W. ... Norristown, PA
Vogel (Harrison), Kathleen L.
Greensburg, PA
Pittsburgh, PA
Vogele, Allan W. ... Cleveland, OH
Vogele, Colette E. ... Los Angeles, CA
Vogele, James A. ... Cincinnati, OH
Vogele, Jim W. ... San Francisco, CA
Vogelenzang, Pierre ... Los Angeles, CA
Vogeler, Alan R. ... Cincinnati, OH
Vogeler, Alan R., Jr. ... New York, NY
Vogeler, William K. ... Irvine, CA
Vogeley, Eva A. ... Gibsonia, PA
Vogelgesang, Glenn W. ... Canton, OH
Vogelgesang, Howes, Lindamood & Brunn
Canton, OH
Columbus, OH
Vogelgesang, Janette P. ... Madison, OH
Vogelgesang, Laura J. ... Denver, CO
Vogelhut, Farrel ... Hartford, CT
Vogelhut, Jos. ... Baltimore, MD
Vogelhut, Steven M. ... Baltimore, MD
Owings Mills, MD
Vogelman, Cindy N. ... Secaucus, NJ
Vogelman, Donald ... New York, NY
Vogelman, Irving I. ... Secaucus, NJ
Vogelman, Jeffrey A. ... Alexandria, VA
Vogelman, Lawrence A. ... Exeter, NH
Vogelman, Richard P. ... Northbrook, IL
Vogelsang, Berkeley I. ... Denver, CO
Vogelsang, Curry H. ... Sherman, TX
Vogelsang, Donald A. ... Chicago, IL
Vogelsang, George C. ... Miami, FL
Vogelsang, Herbert W. ... Sapphire Valley, NC
Vogelsang, Lori M. ... Beverly Hills, CA
Vogelsang, Peter R. ... New York, NY
Vogelsang, Stephen G.
West Palm Beach, FL
Vogelsberg, Stephen J. ... Lancaster, WI
Vogelsmeier, Stuart J. ... St. Louis, MO
Vogelson, David M. ... Beloit, WI
Vogelson, Jay M. ... Dallas, TX
Vogelson, M. Allan ... Haddonfield, NJ
Vogelstein, David M. ... Mill Valley, CA
Vogelstein, Kenneth C., (P.A.)
Baltimore, MD
Vogel-Vanderson, Susan L. ... Victor, NY
Vogelzang, A. Randall ... Irving, TX
Vogelzang, Jeanne M. ... Chicago, IL
Vogelzang, Julie A. ... San Diego, CA
Vogelzang, William, Jr. ... Grand Rapids, MI
Voges, David A. ... Detroit, MI
Voges, Mickie A. ... Chicago, IL
Voges, William J. ... Daytona Beach, FL
Voght, F. Brook ... Washington, DC
Voght, G. B. McVay ... Orlando, FL
Vogl, Alan J. ... San Francisco, CA
Vogl, David R. ... San Francisco, CA
Vogl, Frank E. ... Minneapolis, MN
Vogl & Meredith ... San Francisco, CA
Vogl, Peter D. ... New York, NY
Vogl, Richard G. ... Santa Ana, CA
Vogl, Steven D. ... Rutland, VT
Vogle, Ted G. ... Tulsa, OK
Vogler, Alice M. ... Duxbury, MA
Vogler, Clifford E. ... Guide Rock, NE
Vogler, David Alan ... Lincoln, NE
Vogler, E. Edward, Jr., (P.A.)
Mocksville, NC
Vogler, Edward, II ... Bradenton, FL
Vogler, Gregory J. ... Chicago, IL
Vogler, James R. ... Chicago, IL
Vogler, Jayne M. ... Brick, NJ
Vogler Law Firm, The, P.C.
St. Louis, MO
Vogler Law Offices, P.C. ... Guide Rock, NE
Vogler, Paul J. ... Shoals, IN
Vogler, Philip W. ... Philadelphia, PA
Vogler, Robert T. ... Hagerstown, MD
Vogler, Theresa M. ... Washington, DC
Vogler, Vincent D., Jr. ... St. Louis, MO
Voglewede, Barbara E. ... Grand Forks, ND
Voglewede, Jane C. ... Fargo, ND
Vogliano, Raymond C. ... Pittsburgh, PA
Vogrin, George J., Jr. ... New York, NY
Vogrin, Joseph E., III ... Pittsburgh, PA
Vogrin & Riester, P.C. ... Pittsburgh, PA
Vogrin, Stephen L. ... Wheeling, WV
Vogt, Alan H. ... Kenmore, NY
Vogt, Andrew A. ... Denver, CO
Vogt & Associates ... Portland, OR
Vogt, Brown, Merry & Hammer
Dell Rapids, SD
Vogt, Candace L. ... Birmingham, AL
Vogt, Carl W. ... Washington, DC
Vogt, Carolyn M. ... Portland, OR
Vogt, Christopher Daniel ... Trinidad, CO
Vogt, Dani L. ... Los Angeles, CA
Vogt, David Bennett ... Westlake Village, CA
Vogt, Deborah ... Juneau, AK
Vogt, Diana J. ... Omaha, NE
Vogt, Don J. ... Mercer Island, WA
Vogt, Donald D. ... Morrison, CO
Vogt, Edward G. ... Kankakee, IL
Vogt, Edward W. ... Walnut Creek, CA
Vogt, Elizabeth E. (IBA)
Santa Barbara, CA
Vogt, Eric J. ... Rochester, NY
Vogt, Francis J. ... Kingston, NY
Vogt, Frederick W. ... Minneapolis, MN
Vogt, Gay G. ... Columbia, SC
Vogt, George F., Jr. ... Rancho Cordova, CA
Vogt, Gerald L. ... Torrance, CA
Vogt, Gregory J. ... Washington, DC
Vogt, Heidi L. ... Milwaukee, WI
Vogt, Henry R., III ... New Orleans, LA
Vogt, Henry T. ... Simsbury, CT
Vogt, James D. ... Newport Beach, CA
Vogt, James M. ... Austin, TX
Vogt, James W. ... Oklahoma City, OK
Vogt, JoAnn L. ... Denver, CO
Vogt, John A. ... Los Angeles, CA
Vogt, John C., Jr. ... Tampa, FL
Vogt, John H. ... Freeport, IL
Vogt, Karl D. ... Caldwell, ID
Vogt, Kathy J. ... Warren, MI
Vogt, Keith A. ... Chicago, IL
Vogt, Kenneth J. ... Dayton, OH
Vogt Law Offices ... Carrollton, IL
Vogt, Linda J. ... Rochester, NY
Vogt, Lisa Ann ... Louisville, KY
Vogt, Lisa Rose ... Spokane, WA
Vogt, Louis ... San Diego, CA
Vogt, Louis L. ... Jonesville, LA
Vogt, M. Diane ... Tampa, FL
Vogt, Mary Ann ... Kansas City, MO
Vogt, M. Diane, P.A., Law Office of
Tampa, FL
Vogt, Michael ... St. Louis, MO
Vogt & O'Donnell, LLP ... White Plains, NY
Vogt, Paul Michael ... New York, NY
Vogt, Peter A. ... Philadelphia, PA
Vogt, Peter W. ... Charlotte, NC
Vogt, Peter W. ... Chagrin Falls, OH
Vogt, Philip P. ... Syosset, NY
Vogt, R. Eric ... White Plains, NY
Vogt, Randall ... Portland, OR
Vogt, Renee T. ... Chicago, IL
Vogt, Richard G., (P.C.) ... Rochester, NY
Vogt, Robert P. ... Chicago, IL
Vogt, Robin Hoban ... Covington, LA
Metairie, LA
Vogt, Ronald B. ... Phoenix, AZ
Vogt, Samuel H., Jr. ... Clarksville, IN

Vogt, Stephen D. ....Woodland Hills, CA
Vogt, Stephen H. ....Baton Rouge, LA
Vogt, Theodore R. ....Toledo, OH
Vogt, Thomas J. ....Syracuse, NY
Vogt, Thomas L. ....Tulsa, OK
Vogt, Thomas M. ....Minneapolis, MN
Vogt, Valerie ....West Covina, CA
Vogt, William B. ....Janesville, WI
Vogt, William G. ....Carrollton, IL
Vogt, William H., III ....White Plains, NY
Vogt, William P. ....Dell Rapids, SD
Vogtle, Jesse S., Sr. ....Mountain Brook, AL
Vogtle, Jesse Stringer, Jr.
Birmingham, AL
Vogtner, Thomas A. ....Indianapolis, IN
Vogts, James B. ....Chicago, IL
Vogtsberger, Thomas H.
Bowling Green, OH
Vohar, Donna J. ....Baden, PA
Voharas, William N. .....Department of Defense, Defense Legal Services Agency, GV
Vohl, Anne M. ....Reno, NV
Vohl, Julia C. ....Reno, NV
Vohl, Robert C. ....Reno, NV
Vohl & Vohl ....Reno, NV
Vohland, Lewis L. ....Oakland, CA
Vohlers, Richard J. ....Cary, NC
Vohr, Mark C. ....Seattle, WA
Vohra, Robert N. ....Alexandria, VA
Vohra, Shalini ....Jericho, NY
Vohs, Cathy A. ....Treasury Department, Internal Revenue Service, GV
Vohs, Pamela Schweder ....Savannah, MO
Voice, Anne Marie Hynous ....Lansing, MI
Voich, Pamela J. ....Calabasas, CA
Voight, Jason D. ....Washington, DC
Voight, Jerry D. ....Washington, DC
Voight, Kelly J. ....Durham, NC
Voight, Leonard P. ....Miami Beach, FL
Voight, Robert J. ....Avon, CT
Voigt, Barton R. ....Douglas, WY
Voigt, Edwin E., II ....Minneapolis, MN
Voigt, Frank H. ....Minneapolis, MN
Voigt, Gregory K. ....New Orleans, LA
Voigt, Howard F. ....Pittsburgh, PA
Voigt, Hubert M. ....Omaha, NE
Voigt, J. Burk ....Fairbanks, AK
Voigt, John D., (P.C.)
Fort Lauderdale, FL
Voigt, John R. ....Nashville, TN
Voigt, Joseph F. ....Santa Monica, CA
Voigt, Julie S. ....Winona, MN
Voigt, Karl P., IV ....Bechtelsville, PA
Voigt, Kenneth L. ....Philadelphia, PA
Voigt, Lisa J. ....San Antonio, TX
Voigt, Mark W. ....Huntingdon Valley, PA
Voigt, Michael A. ....Coral Gables, FL
Voigt, Richard ....Hartford, CT
Voigt, Richard L. ....Spartanburg, SC
Voigt, Robert C. ....Wake Forest, NC
Voigt, Sarah H. ....New Orleans, LA
Voigt, Stephen F. ....Sarasota, FL
Voigt, Steven R. ....Kearney, NE
Voigt, Susan M. ....Minneapolis, MN
Voigt, Thomas J. ....Annapolis, MD
Voigt, William H. ....Covington, LA
New Orleans, LA
Voigt, W. R. ....Houston, TX
Voigtman, Timothy L. ....Milwaukee, WI
Voigtmann, Fredrick W. ....Beverly Hills, CA
Voigtmann, Mark A. ....Indianapolis, IN
Voigts, Gene E. ....Kansas City, MO
Voigts, LeRoy R. ....Des Moines, IA
Voigtsberger, John H. ....Ventura, CA
Voiland, Joseph R. ....Aurora, IL
Voiles, Carol Adamson ....Perryton, TX
Voiles, Jeffrey C. ....Perryton, TX
Voinchet, Robert G., Jr. ....Pittsburgh, PA
Voinovich, George V. ....Columbus, OH
Voisin, Christopher W. ....San Diego, CA
Las Vegas, NV
Voisin, David Paul ....Columbia, SC
Voisin, Eva E. ....San Mateo, CA
Voisin, Glynn F. ....Houma, LA
Voisin, Nancy A. ....Arlington, VA
Voisinet, Chris ....Golden, CO
Voissem, Edward R. ....Eagle River, WI
Voit, Catherine H. ....West Chester, PA
Voit, Judith L. ....East Aurora, NY
Voit, Lawrence B. ....Mobile, AL
Voit, Richard L. ....Chicago, IL
Voit, Stephen T. ....San Diego, CA
Voith, Geo. J. ....Baltimore, MD
Voitier, M. Robert, Jr. ....Lafayette, LA
Vojack, Gregory J. ....Houston, TX
Vojak, Amber J. ....Bonita Springs, FL
Vojak, Amber J., P.A. ....Bonita Springs, FL
Vojcanin, Sava Alexander ....Chicago, IL
Vojdik, John T. ....Flint, MI
Vojslavek, Timothy E. ....Valparaiso, IN
Vojslavek, Timothy E., P.C. ....Valparaiso, IN
Vojta, John C. ....Arlington Heights, IL
Vojta & Lagattuta, P.C.
Arlington Heights, IL
Vojtek, Thomas M. ....Norfolk, VA
Vojvoda, Kimberly Adams ....Tulsa, OK
Voke, Brian P. ....Portland, ME
Boston, MA
Concord, NH
Providence, RI
Voke, Patrick T. ....Boston, MA
Vokey, Kristin J. ....Fall River, MA
Vokey, Scott R. ....Phoenix, AZ
Seattle, WA
Vokins, Daniel W. ....Olathe, KS
Vokoun, Edward M. ....Edwardsville, IL
St. Louis, MO
Vokoun, Joseph F., Jr. ....San Francisco, CA

Vokulich, Richard M. ....Beverly Hills, CA
Volack, Richard R. ....New York, NY
Volaire, Claudia F. ....Dallas, TX
Volan, Douglas ....New York, NY
Volan, Gregory G. ....Chicago, IL
Voland, Richard E. ....Aurora, IL
Voland, Sally A. ....Indianapolis, IN
Voland, Samuel J. ....Indianapolis, IN
Volarich, Maria A. ....Morristown, NJ
Volat, Janet ....Los Angeles, CA
Volatile, Gerard B. ....Baltimore, MD
Volberding, James W. ....Tyler, TX
Volberg, Deborah I. ....White Plains, NY
Volberg, Jeffrey Allen ....Sacramento, CA
Volcheck, Mark J. ....Sandusky, OH
Volchko, Gerri M. ....Butler, PA
Volchok, Lester B. ....Northridge, CA
Volchok, Paul M. ....Northridge, CA
Volchok, Volchok & Zayon ....Northridge, CA
Volckhausen, William A. ....New York, NY
Volcy, Paul ....Buffalo, NY
Vold, E. Denver ....Leawood, KS
Kansas City, MO
Vold, Kevin L. ....Washington, DC
Vold, Michael ....Northbrook, IL
Vold, Morris & Hallauer, P.A.
Leawood, KS
Kansas City, MO
Vold, Tara M. ....Washington, DC
Volden, John E. ....Arlington Heights, IL
Voldness, Perry G. ....Bloomington, MN
Volejnicek, David ....Denver, CO
Volek, Stephen F. ....Reno, NV
Volentine, Richard J., Jr. ....Atlanta, GA
Voler, Frank F. ....Charlotte, NC
Volesko, Vallerie G. S. ....Garden City, NY
Volesky, Ron J. ....Huron, SD
Volet, Thomas ....New York, NY
Voleti, Aparna ....Los Angeles, CA
Voletsky, Peter ....New York, NY
Volfson, Inna ....Salem, MA
Volgenau & Bosse ....Buffalo, NY
Volgenau, Coleman ....Buffalo, NY
Volgenau, Peter ....Glastonbury, CT
Volhard, Joachim J. ....Syracuse, NY
Volin, Andrew W. ....Denver, CO
Volin, John Joseph ....Mesa, AZ
Volin, Leonard S. ....Washington, DC
Volin, Michael Laurence ....Philadelphia, PA
Volin, Richard M. ....Washington, DC
Volini, Thomas A. ....Gary, IN
Volinkaty, Richard A. ....Missoula, MT
Volinn, Sidney C. ....Seattle, WA
Volino, Nicholas ....Troy, MI
Volinski, Benjamin ....Boston, MA
Volinsky, Andru H. ....Concord, NH
Voliva, Richard L., Jr. ....Princeton, NJ
Volk, Amy E. ....San Diego, CA
Volk, Andrew M. ....Seattle, WA
Volk, Angela Dawn ....Charleston, WV
Volk, Barbara C. ....New Orleans, LA
Volk, Charles R. ....Sewickley, PA
Volk, David J. ....Melbourne, FL
Volk, David L. ....Los Angeles, CA
Volk, Deborah P. ....Burlington, VT
Volk, Edward L. ....La Porte, IN
Volk, Eugene J. ....Chicago, IL
Volk, H. Donald ....Sunnyvale, CA
Volk, Helen D. ....Albany, NY
Volk, Jane Lewis ....Sewickley, PA
Volk, Jay Garrett ....Cleveland, OH
Volk, Jean ....Edison, NJ
Volk, Jerome M., Jr. ....Kenner, LA
Volk, John Pierce ....Wethersfield, CT
Volk, Kenneth H. ....Portsmouth, NH
Volk, Larry N. ....Delmar, NY
Volk Law Firm, The, P.C. ....Pittsburgh, PA
Sewickley, PA
Volk Law Offices, P.A. ....Melbourne, FL
Volk, Mark F. ....Albany, NY
Volk, Marsha Schatz ....La Porte, IN
Volk, Mary Cecelia ....Brooklyn, NY
Volk, Michael D. ....El Paso, TX
Volk, Michael D., P.C. ....El Paso, TX
Volk, Nathan J. ....Dallas, TX
Volk, Paul S. ....Burlington, VT
Volk, Phyllis L. ....Chicago, IL
Volk, Robert ....Boston, MA
Volk, Robert F. ....Kingston, NY
Volk, Stephen R. ....New York, NY
Volk, Thomas A. ....Sacramento, CA
Volk, Thomas W. ....Louisville, KY
Volk, William ....Cummington, MA
Volk, William P. ....San Diego, CA
Las Vegas, NV
Volk, William R. ....Austin, TX
Volkart, Judith H. ....Novato, CA
Volkell, Randolph Z. ....North Bellmore, NY
Volkell, Stephanie N. ....Nyack, NY
Volkema, Daniel R. ....Columbus, OH
Volker, Dale M. ....Lancaster, NY
Volker, H. Wright ....Salt Lake City, UT
Volker, Kirk C. ....West Palm Beach, FL
Volker, Melissa ....Hialeah, FL
Volker, Odean L. ....Houston, TX
Volker, Richard F. ....San Diego, CA
Volkert, Adam N. ....Costa Mesa, CA
Volkert, Donald J., Jr. ....Newark, NJ
Volkert, Eric M. ....San Diego, CA
Volkert, Matt ....Chicago, IL
Volkert, Susan Engelman ....Teaneck, NJ
Volkheimer, Stephen H. ....Albany, NY
Volkin, David ....San Diego, CA
Volkle, Arthur J., Jr. ....Philadelphia, PA
Volkman, Janice C. ....Philadelphia, PA
Volkman, John M. ....Portland, OR
Volkman, Richard W.
Treasury Department, GV

Volkman, Scott L. ....Poughkeepsie, NY
Volkman, Steven B. ....Melrose Park, IL
Volkman, William A., Jr. ....Kensington, MD
Volkman, William W. ....Glen Ellyn, IL
Volkmann, Alfred A. ....Patchogue, NY
Volkmann, Thomas C. ....Grand Junction, CO
Volkmann, Thomas C., P.C.
Grand Junction, CO
Volkmann, Timothy R. ....Santa Cruz, CA
Volkmar, William P. ....Rochester, MN
Volkmer, Elzbieta (Ela) E. (IBA)
Princeton, NJ
Volkmer, Harold L. ....Hannibal, MO
Volkmer, Lee M. ....Lincoln, NE
Volkmer, Ronald R. ....Omaha, NE
Volkmuth, Daniel R. ....Washington, DC
Volkomer, Walter E. ....New York, NY
Volkov, Ilana ....Hackensack, NJ
Volkov, Michael L. ....Washington, DC
Volkovitsch, Michael J. ....New York, NY
Voll, Richard A. ....Franklin Lakes, NJ
Vollack, Anthony F. ....Denver, CO
Vollan, Maureen C. ....Indianapolis, IN
Volland, Philip R. ....Anchorage, AK
Volland, Stephen J. ....St. Louis, MO
Vollandt, Michael P.
Rancho Cucamonga, CA
Vollbrecht, James L. ....McLean, VA
Vollbrecht, Michael J. ....New York, NY
Vollbrecht, Thomas J. ....Minneapolis, MN
Vollen, Jeffrey S. ....Chicago, IL
Vollen, Jennifer S. ....Chicago, IL
Vollen, Robert J. ....Riverwoods, IL
Vollender, Donald W.
Fort Lauderdale, FL
Vollentine, Henry H. ....Gonzales, TX
Vollenweider, David O., III
Department of Justice, Environment and Natural Resources Division, GV
Voller, Cindy M. ....Toledo, OH
Vollers, Jim ....Austin, TX
Vollers, Peter K. ....Woodstock, VT
Vollers, Tony K. ....Madison, AL
Vollersen, Melva M. ....San Jose, CA
Vollertsen & Britt, P.C. ....Davenport, IA
Vollertsen, Nancy Brostrom
Minneapolis, MN
Vollertsen, Richard E. ....Anchorage, AK
Volles, Warren K. ....Danbury, CT
Volletz, John W. ....Green Bay, WI
Volling, James L. ....Minneapolis, MN
Vollino, A. John ....Richmond, VA
Vollins, James A. ....Cleveland, OH
Vollins, Steven L. ....New York, NY
Vollintine, Larry R. ....San Francisco, CA
Vollkommer, John J. ....New York, NY
Vollman, Carl W. ....Cincinnati, OH
Vollman, Jeffrey S. ....Fairfax, OH
Vollman, Mark C. ....Cincinnati, OH
Vollman, Paul J. ....Cincinnati, OH
Vollman, Stanton H. ....Cincinnati, OH
Vollmann, Alan P. ....Washington, DC
Vollmar, Craig L. ....Minneapolis, MN
Vollmar, James O. ....Waukesha, WI
Vollmar, Michelle S. ....Dayton, OH
Vollmar, T. Andrew ....Dayton, OH
Vollmar, Valerie J. ....Salem, OR
Vollmer, Andrew N. ....Washington, DC
Vollmer, Charles J. ....Pittsburgh, PA
Vollmer, Deborah A. ....Chevy Chase, MD
Vollmer, Lynne P. ....Bethesda, MD
Vollmer, Melinda H. ....New York, NY
Vollmer, Michael J. ....Agoura Hills, CA
Vollmer, Michael L. ....Anaheim, CA
Vollmer, Michael V. ....Irvine, CA
Vollmer, Michael V. ....Newport Beach, CA
Vollmer, Michael W. ....Atlanta, GA
Vollmer, Peter ....Uniondale, NY
Vollmer, Richard W., III ....Mobile, AL
Vollmer, Richard W., Jr. ....Mobile, AL
Vollmer Rulong & Keating, P.C.
Pittsburgh, PA
Vollmer, Sara R. ....Columbus, OH
Vollmer, Stephen J. ....Syracuse, NY
Vollmer, Steven L. ....Beloit, WI
Vollmer, Susan Dayton ....Evansville, IN
Vollmer and Tanck ....Uniondale, NY
Vollmer, Thomas E. ....New Britain, CT
Vollmer, Timothy J. ....McLean, VA
Vollor, Frank G. ....Vicksburg, MS
Vollrath, Jürgen K. ....Los Angeles, CA
Volluz, Kyle S. ....Dallas, TX
Vollweiler, Cheryl P. ....New York, NY
Volman, David Gregg ....Shelton, CT
Volman, Josef B. ....Boston, MA
Volmert, Deborah J. ....Belleville, IL
St. Louis, MO
Volmert, Elizabeth P. ....Houston, TX
Volmert, Lawrence E. ....Denver, CO
Volmert, Paul Marshall
Fort Lauderdale, FL
Volner, Ian D. ....Washington, DC
Volney, John D. ....Dallas, TX
Volo, Richard A. ....Derby, CT
Volonte, Arthur C. ....Oakland, CA
Volonte, William J. ....West Orange, NJ
Volovich, A. Blane ....Pittsburgh, PA
Volow, Mark J. ....New York, NY
Volpano, Linda ....Washington, DC
Volpe, Amedeo H. ....Schenectady, NY
Volpe, Anita Marie ....Rockland, ME
Volpe, Anthony S. ....Philadelphia, PA
Volpe Bajalia Wickes & Rogerson
Jacksonville, FL
Volpe, Bruce R. ....Newark, NJ
Volpe, Charles ....San Jose, CA
Volpe, Charles J., Jr. ....Dunmore, PA

Volpe, Edward L. ....Denver, CO
Volpe, Edward L., P.C. ....Denver, CO
Volpe, Frank R. ....Washington, DC
Volpe, Fred J. ....North Kingstown, RI
Volpe, Joseph, III ....Warrenton, VA
Volpe, Joseph, Jr. ....Washington, DC
Volpe and Koenig, P.C. ....Philadelphia, PA
Volpe, Lynda M. ....Philadelphia, PA
Volpe, Mark F. ....Wallingford, CT
Volpe, Michael J. ....Naples, FL
Volpe, Michael J. ....New York, NY
Volpe, Michael R.
General Accounting Office, Office of the General Counsel, GV
Volpe, Michele M. ....Hartford, CT
Volpe, Oliver V. ....Braintree, MA
Volpe, Richard S. ....Chicago, IL
Volpe, Robert P. ....Hartford, CT
Volpe, Timothy W. ....Jacksonville, FL
Volpe, Vincent T. ....St. Louis, MO
Volpe, William S. ....Chico, CA
Volper, Raymond C. ....White Plains, NY
Volper, Vicki E. ....Stamford, CT
Volpert, Richard S. ....Los Angeles, CA
Volpert, Timothy R. ....Portland, OR
Volpi, Donald J., Jr. ....New Orleans, LA
Volpi, James C. ....West Palm Beach, FL
Volpi, Robert ....Cincinnati, OH
Volpicelli, Stephen L. ....Philadelphia, PA
Volpintesta, Louis, Jr. ....Stamford, CT
Volsky, George ....Miami, FL
Volsky, Kerry S. ....Cleveland, OH
Volsky, Mark R. ....Cleveland, OH
Volta, Armand J., Jr. ....Baltimore, MD
Volta, Sandra E. ....Rochester, NY
Voltchenko, Maxim A. ....Philadelphia, PA
Volterra, Goldberg & Mangiaratti
Attleboro, MA
Volterra, Max ....Attleboro, MA
Volterra, Vieri Guy ....Boston, MA
Voltmer, Alicia Sienne ....Dallas, TX
Voltmer, Ralph C., Jr. ....Washington, DC
Voltolini, Bruno E. ....Columbus, OH
Voltolini, John ....Columbus, OH
Voltolini, Mathew J. ....Columbus, OH
Voltolini & Voltolini ....Columbus, OH
Voltz, Charles E. ....Burlingame, CA
Voltz, David L. ....Pittsburgh, PA
Voltz, Donald L. ....Buffalo, NY
Voltz, Gus A., III ....Alexandria, LA
Voltz, Gus, Jr. ....Alexandria, LA
Voltz, Hudson L. ....Coatesville, PA
Wayne, PA
Voltz, Robert L. ....Buffalo, NY
Voltz, Robert M.
National Labor Relations Board, Office of Board Members, GV
Voltz, Stephen M. ....Franklin, MA
Voltz & Ware ....Alexandria, LA
Voltz, William R., Law Offices of
Washington, DC
Voltz-Miller, Debra ....South Bend, IN
Voluck, David ....Anchorage, AK
Voluck, Jeffrey M., P.C. ....Philadelphia, PA
Voluck, Philip R. ....Philadelphia, PA
Volyn, Scott A. ....Wenatchee, WA
Volyn, Todd F. ....Houston, TX
Volz, Carl E. ....Chicago, IL
Volz, Charles F., Jr. ....Philadelphia, PA
Volz, Charles H., III ....Montgomery, AL
Volz, Charles H., Jr. ....Montgomery, AL
Volz, Christian ....San Francisco, CA
Volz, Edward J., Jr. ....Fort Myers, FL
Volz, Elizabeth Beebe ....Denver, CO
Volz, Frederick M. ....Englewood, CO
Volz, Gregory L. ....Evansville, IN
Volz, James ....Montpelier, VT
Volz, Joan L. ....Denver, CO
Volz, John C. ....Los Angeles, CA
Volz, Karen A. ....Cedar Rapids, IA
Volz, Karen B. ....Oklahoma City, OK
Volz, Marlin M. ....Louisville, KY
Volz, Marlin M., Jr. ....Davenport, IA
Volz, Mary Louise ....Cincinnati, OH
Volz, Prestwood & Hanan, P.C.
Auburn, AL
Clayton, AL
Hayneville, AL
Montgomery, AL
Opelika, AL
Prattville, AL
Troy, AL
Tuskegee, AL
Union Springs, AL
Wetumpka, AL
Volz, Thomas A. ....Chicago, IL
Volz, Thomas M. ....Farmingdale, NY
Volz, William H. ....Detroit, MI
Volzer, Christina A. ....McLean, VA
Volzer, Harvey J. ....Washington, DC
Vomacka, John F. ....Vancouver, WA
Vomacka, Wendy ....Orlando, FL
vom Eigen, Robert P. ....Washington, DC
Vomhof, Marion ....Coronado, CA
Vomund, Susan P. ....San Francisco, CA
Von, Irene A. ....Washington, DC
Vona, Hollie R. ....Washington, DC
Vona, Jeffrey M. ....Philadelphia, PA
Vona, P. Andrew ....Lockport, NY
Vonachen, Donald F. ....Peoria, IL
Vonachen, James C. ....Broomfield, CO
Vonachen, Lawless, Trager & Slevin
Peoria, IL
Von Ahn, John F. ....Albany, NY
VonAllmen, Kyle J. ....Rochester Hills, MI
von Ammon, Philip E. ....Phoenix, AZ
Von Ancken, Linda ....Danbury, CT
Von Arx, Brooks ....Fair Haven, NJ

Vorndran-Jones, MaCharri R. **Indianapolis, IN**
Vornehm, David B. **Indianapolis, IN**
Vornholt, Richard P. **Atlanta, GA**
Vorobiev, Jill S. **Chicago, IL**
Voron, Harvey J. Philadelphia, PA
Voros, J. Frederic, Jr. Salt Lake City, UT
Vorous, Debbie J. **Sacramento, CA**
Vorpagel, Russell E. Granite Bay, CA
Vorpahl, Brad A. Milwaukee, WI
Vorpahl, Dwight E. **Houston, TX**
Vorpahl, George Steven **Diboll, TX**
Vorpahl, Joanne Meyer **Houston, TX**
Vorpahl, Myron G. San Antonio, TX
Vorperian, John M. White Plains, NY
Vorrasi, John F. North Greece, NY
Vorrasi, Kenneth J. Rochester, NY
Vorrasi, Nicole M. **Rochester, NY**
Vorro, Elizabeth A. Boston, MA
Vorsanger, Agatha L. New York, NY
Vorsanger, Debra S. Shrewsbury, MA
Vorsanger, Robert M. New York, NY
Vorsatz, Mark L. Hillsborough, CA
Vorsatz, Paul F. Burlingame, CA
Vorspan, Rachel New York, NY
Vorsteg, J. Daniel **Baltimore, MD**
Vorster, Joan O. **Worcester, MA**
Vort, Robert A. **Tenafly, NJ**
Vortman & Feinstein **Seattle, WA**
Vortman, Marlin L. **Seattle, WA**
Vortmann, Paul Visalia, CA
Vortsch, John M. Harrison, NY
Vorwald, David Norman, OK
Vorwerck, Gregg **Orange, CA**
Vorys, Arthur I. **Columbus, OH**
Vorys, Jeanny M. Columbus, OH
Vorys, John C. **Cincinnati, OH**
Vorys, Sater, Seymour and Pease LLP **Washington, DC** **Cincinnati, OH** **Cleveland, OH** **Columbus, OH** **Alexandria, VA**
Vorys, Webb I. **Columbus, OH**
Vorys, Yolanda V. Columbus, OH
Vorzimer, Andrew W. Beverly Hills, CA
Vorzimer, Masserman & Ecoff, A Professional Corporation Beverly Hills, CA
Vorzimmer, Peter J. Philadelphia, PA
Vos, Joanne **Florham Park, NJ**
Vos, John A. San Rafael, CA
Vos, John A. Grand Rapids, MI
Vos, John F., III **Southfield, MI**
Vos, John P. Department of Agriculture, Office of the General Counsel, GV
Vos, Paul E. Mitchellville, IA; Prairie City, IA
Vosahlik, Ladd Joseph Cicero, IL
Vosbeek, Kathryn Santa Ana, CA
Vosbein, Robert A. **New Orleans, LA**
Vosbein, Robert A., Jr. **New Orleans, LA**
Vosbikian, Steven Cherry Hill, NJ
Vosburg, Bruce D. **Omaha, NE**
Vosburg, Jennifer J. **Baton Rouge, LA**
Vosburg, Roger M. Novato, CA
Vosburgh, James R. Washington, NC
Vosburgh, John A. Phoenix, AZ
Vosdingh, Rhonda J. Federal Election Commission, Office of the General Counsel, GV
Vose, Blau & Hayes **Winter Park, FL**
Vose, Charles Edward San Francisco, CA
Vose, Charles S. **Los Angeles, CA**
Vose, Donna M. Long Beach, CA
Vose, Gretchen R. H. **Winter Park, FL**
Vose, James A. **Minneapolis, MN**
Vose, Leslie Patterson **Lexington, KY**
Vose, Marvin R. Greeley, CO
Vose, Rebecca Belmont, MA
Vose, Robert **Minneapolis, MN**
Vose, William C. Orlando, FL
Vose, William G. Phoenix, AZ
Voseles, Charles A. Tulsa, OK
Vosen, Jerry H. Acton, CA
Vosepka, Richard E., Jr. Minneapolis, MN
Vosguanian, Bruce C. Agoura Hills, CA
Vosguanian, Rodney N. Agoura Hills, CA
Vosguanian & Vosguanian Agoura Hills, CA
Voshell, Gary K. **Kalamazoo, MI**
Voshell, Jack G., (P.A.) Idaho Falls, ID
Vosicky, George J. **Joliet, IL**
Vosicky, Joseph F., Jr. Wheaton, IL
Vosik, Wayne G. Newtown, PA
Vosit, Joseph G. Pittsfield, MA
Vosk, Loretta A. Olympia, WA
Vosko, Alan M. Farmington Hills, MI
Vosper, Paul A. **Greenwich, CT**
Vosper, William J., Jr. Stillwater, NJ
Voss, Alton William, Jr. Berkley, MI
Voss, Andrew J. **Minneapolis, MN**
Voss, Andrew Michael **St. Louis, MO**
Voss, Arthur T. Aurora, CO
Voss, Barbara St. Louis, MO
Voss, Bradley W. **Los Angeles, CA**
Voss, Bruce **Honolulu, HI**
Voss, Carl T. Santa Rosa, CA
Voss, Christopher J. **Seattle, WA**
Voss, Clair H. Waukesha, WI
Voss, Cook & Thel LLP **Los Angeles, CA** **Newport Beach, CA** **San Diego, CA**
Voss, David C. Topeka, KS
Voss, David C. **Baton Rouge, LA**
Voss, Donald F. Rochester, MN
Voss, Donald H. Slippery Rock, PA
Voss, Donald J. Schenectady, NY
Voss, Douglas J.M. Ferndale, MI
Voss, Edward C. Phoenix, AZ
Voss, Edwin P., Jr. **Dallas, TX**
Voss, F. James Denver, CO
Voss, Frederick J. Rhinelander, WI
Voss, George Dodge City, KS
Voss, Greg D. **Covington, KY**
Voss, Jack D. Lancaster, OH
Voss, James E. Stevens Point, WI
Voss, James M. Madison, WI
Voss, James Victor Butler, PA
Voss, Janette S. Anamosa, IA
Voss, Jayna M. **Sioux Falls, SD**
Voss, John C. Jenkintown, PA
Voss, K. Allan **Sheboygan, WI**
Voss, Kenneth E. **Brookfield, WI**
Voss, Kurt A. Washington, MO
Voss, Lanny R. **Plainview, TX**
Voss, Laurence E. Bronx, NY
Voss, Marianne Elena Newton, MA
Voss, Mark R. Manassas, VA
Voss, Mary Elizabeth Ambler, PA
Voss, Myrna J. San Francisco, CA
Voss, Nancy Bea Corporation for National and Community Service, Equal Opportunity Staff, GV
Voss, Oscar M. Federal Trade Commission, Bureau of Competition, GV
Voss, Patricia R. **Fort Lauderdale, FL**
Voss, Paul J. **Chicago, IL**
Voss, Ralph F. Linn, MO
Voss, Richard P. **Atlanta, GA**
Voss, Richard P. Cincinnati, OH
Voss, Robert C. Coon Rapids, MN
Voss, Roberta L. Phoenix, AZ
Voss, Sandra L. **Philadelphia, PA**
Voss, Susan Lee **Washington, DC**
Voss, Susan Lee Austin, TX
Voss, Theodore R. **New Haven, CT** **New York, NY**
Voss, Thomas G. Madison, WI
Voss, Thomas K. Waukesha, WI
Voss, Wendy K. **Wilmington, DE**
Voss, William A. Kansas City, MO
Voss, William Bruce Newport Beach, CA
Vossberg, Arthur E., III **Philadelphia, PA**
Vosseller, Steven Kolonia, TT
Vosskuhler, Derek B. **Long Beach, CA**
Vosskuhler, Susan K. Eden Prairie, MN
Vossler, Christopher M. **Hartford, CT**
Vossler, Colleen Kotyk **Washington, DC** **Columbia, MD**
Vossler, Karen L. **Boston, MA**
Vossler, Kathleen M. Houston, TX
Vossler, Robert J. Tallahassee, FL
Vossman, Laura A. Los Angeles, CA
Vossmeyer, M. Celeste St. Louis, MO
Vossmeyer, Steve **St. Louis, MO**
Vossnack, Herman G. Lynbrook, NY
Vossoughi, Kourosh **Irvine, CA**
Vostrejs, Robert A., Jr. **Ocala, FL**
Votava, Andrew R. Lima, OH
Votava, G. Joseph, Jr. **Rochester, NY**
Votava, Shannon M. Spokane, WA
Votaw, Catherine Philadelphia, PA
Votaw, Dow La Selva Beach, CA
Votaw, Elinor J. Laguna Beach, CA
Votaw, James G. **Washington, DC**
Votaw, Joseph W., III Lawrenceburg, IN
Votaw, Linda S., Law Offices of San Francisco, CA
Vote, C. Robert **Houston, TX**
Vote, Kurt F. **Fresno, CA**
Vote, Robert M. Ashland, OR
Votel, Anderson & McEachron St. Paul, MN
Votel, Martin P. Eaton, OH
Votel, Terrance W. St. Paul, MN
Votendahl, Jerry A. Walla Walla, WA
Voter, Warren E. **Philadelphia, PA**
Voth, Darrell H. Wasco, CA
Voth, Kent G. **Wichita, KS**
Voth, Larry I. Portland, OR
Voth, Patricia A. **Dodge City, KS**
Voth, Robert F., IV Cleveland, OH
Voth, William H. **New York, NY**
Votolato, Arthur N. Providence, RI
Votre & Associates, P.C. **New Haven, CT**
Votre, Kenneth A. **New Haven, CT**
Votruba, John F. Santa Rosa, CA
Votta, Jill S. Providence, RI
Votta, Joseph S., Jr. Providence, RI
Votta, Paul J., Jr. **Warwick, RI**
Votta, Richard J. **Greensboro, NC**
Votta, Steven Providence, RI
Votta & Votta Providence, RI
Votto, Joseph F. Whitestone, NY
Votto, Louis Smith Clinton, CT; West Haven, CT
Votto, Valerie Ann **New London, CT** **Old Lyme, CT**
Voudouris, S. Peter **Cleveland, OH**
Voudris, Stephan I. **Miami, FL**
Vouga, Richard R. **St. Louis, MO**
Vouga, Victor E. Butler, PA
Vough & Associates **Pittston, PA** **Scranton, PA** **Wilkes-Barre, PA**
Vough, Michael T. **Pittston, PA**
Vought, Kimber E. **Philadelphia, PA**
Vouis, Lynn M. Sanford, FL
Voulgarelis, Christina **New York, NY**
Vounessea, Stefan J. **Boston, MA**
Vourderis, Dennis E. Staten Island, NY
Vourlis, Simina **Columbus, OH**
Vournazos, C. Anthony Danbury, CT
Vournazos, George J. **Chicago, IL**
Vouros, James G. Philadelphia, PA
Vouros, Joseph E. Youngstown, OH
Vouté, Arthur J., Jr. **White Plains, NY**
Vouté, Lohrfink, Magro & Collins, LLP **New York, NY** **Scarsdale, NY** **White Plains, NY**
Voutsinas, Jean **New York, NY**
Vova, Cindy S. Fort Lauderdale, FL
Vova, Philip S. Miami, FL
Vovakes, Heather H. P. **Baltimore, MD**
Vovakis, Lewis H. Washington, DC
Voveris, Jeanne L. Boston, MA
Voves, Michael J. **Minneapolis, MN**
Vovos, Mark E. **Spokane, WA**
Vovos, Mark Roberts, P.S. **Spokane, WA**
Vowell & Atchley **Berryville, AR**
Vowell, Donald K. Knoxville, TN
Vowell, Fred C. Martin, TN
Vowell, J. Scott Birmingham, AL
Vowell, Mark R. **Dallas, TX**
Vowell, Stevan E. **Berryville, AR**
Vowels, Donald R. **Evansville, IN**
Vowinkel, Michael J. **Sheboygan, WI**; Sheboygan Falls, WI
Vowles, Janie Lanza **Boston, MA**
Voxman, William A. **Los Angeles, CA**
Voydat, Linda Lory San Jose, CA
Voyer, Gerard E. W. **Norfolk, VA**
Voyles, Adam **Houston, TX**
Voyles, Charles M. Fayetteville, GA
Voyles, Dale S. Alpharetta, GA
Voyles, David R. Loveland, OH
Voyles, E. Elaine Pennsville, NJ
Voyles, James H. Indianapolis, IN
Voyles, James K. Apple Valley, MN
Voyles, James R. **Louisville, KY**
Voyles & Johnson, P.S.C. **Louisville, KY**
Voyles, M. Kevin Jackson, WY
Voyles, Robb L. **Austin, TX** **Dallas, TX**
Voyles, Robert Patterson Atlanta, GA
Voyles, Shawn A. **Virginia Beach, VA**
Voyles, Stanley R. Los Gatos, CA
Voynich, John J. Columbus, GA
Voynick, John S., Jr. Cedar Grove, NJ
Voysey, James K. Santa Maria, CA
Voytek, Michael T. **Atlanta, GA**
Voytovich, Anna M. Chicago, IL
Vozar, Roberts & Matejczyk Cleveland, OH
Vozar, Thomas J. Cleveland, OH
Vozella, Harry W. Franklin, MA
Vozella, John J. Mansfield, MA
Vozella, Paul F. Worcester, MA
Vozza, Rocco Ernesto Bronx, NY
Vozzella, Carmen Delray Beach, FL
Vozzella, Lisa M. **West Hartford, CT**
Vozzo, Armand M., Jr. Doylestown, PA
Vraa, Paula Duggan **Minneapolis, MN**
Vrabel, Joseph P. J. **Framingham, MA**
Vrabel, Paul M. Adams, MA
Vrable, Michael J. Hayden, ID
Vradelis, Anthony J. Dayton, OH
Vradelis, Theodore J. Dayton, OH
Vradenburg, Alissa L. Encino, CA
Vradenburg, George, III Dulles, VA
Vragel, Kurt E., Jr. Glenview, IL
Vragel, Kurt E., P.C. Glenview, IL
Vrahas-Coleman, Lynn A. McKees Rocks, PA
Vrahoretis, Susan H. Department of Justice, Tax Division, GV
Vrana, Bruce **Durham, NC**
Vrana, Christopher Basking Ridge, NJ
Vrana, Devon Houston, TX
Vrana, Karl Taunton, MA
Vrana, Michael K. Dallas, TX
Vrana, Paul E. Houston, TX
Vrana, Rachel A. San Jose, CA
Vrana, Susan Dallas, TX
Vrana, Theo. W. Lincoln, NE
Vrana, Timothy J. **Columbus, IN**
Vrana & Vrana Houston, TX
Vranas, George Chicago, IL
Vrancik, Barbara A. New York, NY
Vranekovic, James D. General Services Administration, Regional Counsel (National Capital Region), GV
Vranesh and Raisch, L.L.P. **Boulder, CO** **Denver, CO**
Vranesic, John R. Lakewood, CO
Vranesic & Peters, P.C. Denver, CO
Vranicar, John E. **Chicago, IL**
Vranicar, Michael G. Chicago, IL
Vranjes, Mark, (Professional Corporation) **San Diego, CA**
Vranum, Peter J. New York, NY
Vraspir, Cindy **Miami, FL**
Vraspir, Todd W. **Miami, FL**
Vrastil, Timothy R. Culver City, CA
Vratil, John L. **Overland Park, KS**
Vratil, Kathryn H. Kansas City, KS
Vratis, Jim N. Crystal Beach, TX
Vrato, Elizabeth J. **Philadelphia, PA**
Vrba, Daniel L. Houston, TX
Vrba, Jeffrey A. Inola, OK
Vrbanac, Mary Foster **Seattle, WA**
Vrbancic, Joseph B. San Diego, CA
Vrdolyak, Catherine Chicago, IL
Vrdolyak, Edward R., Ltd. Chicago, IL
Vredenburgh, Fletcher R. Pawtucket, RI
Vree, Roger A. **Chicago, IL**
Vreeland, Al L. Tuscaloosa, AL
Vreeland, Albert L., II **Birmingham, AL**
Vreeland, Arthur A. **Greensboro, NC**
Vreeland, Charles Jay Del Mar, CA
Vreeland, Clayton J. **Los Angeles, CA**
Vreeland, Cynthia D. **Boston, MA**
Vreeland, Dirck New York, NY
Vreeland, Jack Casper, WY
Vreeland, John K. **Lakeland, FL**
Vreeland, Joseph A. Evansville, IN
Vreeland, L. Chandler Marietta, GA
Vreeland, Neal C. **Rutland, VT**
Vreeland, Robert M. Bloomfield, NJ
Vreeland, Theodore D. Princeton, NJ
Vreeland, Thomas O. **Charleroi, PA** **Washington, PA**
Vreeland, Victoria L. **Seattle, WA**
Vreeland, William G., III **New York, NY**
Vrejan, Sandra New York, NY
Vrevich, Barry M. **San Diego, CA**
Vrhel, Victoria M. **Chicago, IL**
Vrhovc, Richard A., Jr. Clifton, NJ; New York, NY
Vricella, Pina M. **Cherry Hill, NJ**
Vrielink, Cliff W. **Houston, TX**
Vriesman, Todd L. **Denver, CO**
Vrieze, John M. **Eureka, CA**
Vriezelaar, Kent **Sioux City, IA**
Vriezelaar, Tigges, Edgington, Rossi, Bottaro & Boden **Sioux City, IA**
Vrioni, Beth A. Kennedy Space Center, FL
Vrionis, Georgia B., Ms. Germantown, TN
Vris, Jane Lee **New York, NY**
Vrla, Mark P. **Chicago, IL**
Vrod, Shari Leigh Miami, FL
Vroegop, Susan E. **Holland, MI**
Vroman, Ann Marie **New York, NY**
Vroman, James A. **Chicago, IL**
Vroman, Margaret E. Lansing, MI
Vroman, Richard E. **Aberdeen, WA**
Vrono, Charles J. Forest Park, GA
Vroom, Cynthia A. Oakland, CA
Vroom, Marilyn Ann Clarksburg, WV
Vroom, Patricia M. Phoenix, AZ
Vroom, Ronald C. Bemidji, MN
Vrooman, David V. Sioux Falls, SD
Vrooman, Edward A. **Washington, DC** **White Plains, NY**
Vrooman, Robert B. **San Francisco, CA**
Vrooman, Thomas D. **Denver, CO**
Vrooman-Rogers, Marya Rapid City, SD
Vroome, Colin M. **Philadelphia, PA**
Vroon, Bryan A. **Atlanta, GA**
Vroon, Kimberly S. **Charleston, SC**
Vrountas, Christopher T. **Boston, MA**
Vroustouris, Alexander Chicago, IL
Vrsansky, Carla J. **Pittsburgh, PA**
Vrsecky, Anthony J. Winston-Salem, NC
Vrudhula, Kalpana **San Jose, CA**
Vryhof, John C. **Phoenix, AZ**
Vryonis, Demetrios Sacramento, CA
Vsetecka, Donald J. Colorado Springs, CO
Vsetecka, Donald J., P.C. Colorado Springs, CO
Vtipil, David E. Raleigh, NC
Vu, Hao-Nhien Q. **Costa Mesa, CA**
Vu, Hoang **Houston, TX**
Vu, Hoang Quan **Houston, TX**
Vu, Kenneth K. D. **Washington, DC**
Vu, Long T. San Jose, CA
Vu, Michael C. San Jose, CA
Vu, Minh N. **Washington, DC**
Vu, Nhan T. **Irvine, CA**
Vu, Quynh Department of Justice, Civil Division, GV
Vuagniaux, Earl L. Edwardsville, IL
Vuagniaux, Earl L., A Professional Corporation Edwardsville, IL
Vucci, Charles J. Providence, RI
Vucci, Louis A. Miami, FL
Vucic, Miki **Chicago, IL**
Vucichevich, Rad L. Phoenix, AZ
Vucinich, Jeffrey M. **Menlo Park, CA**
Vucinovich, James K. **Minneapolis, MN**
Vuckovich, Adrian M. **Chicago, IL**
Vucurovich, Mark A. Butte, MT
Vudragovich, John D. Fort Lauderdale, FL
Vue, Fue St. Paul, MN
Vuernick, Richard E. Nutley, NJ
Vugrek, Ariana A. Madison, NJ
Vugteveen, Kipp V. Sanford, FL
Vuillemin, John E. **Akron, OH**
Vuillemin, Lawrence W. **Akron, OH**
Vuillieme, Claude E. **New York, NY**
Vujasinovic, Vuk S. **Houston, TX**
Vujnovich, Sandra A. New Orleans, LA
Vujovic, Radoje A. Aurora, IL
Vujovich, George Irvine, CA
Vujovich Law Firm, P.A. Eagan, MN
Vujovich, Mary S. Eagan, MN
Vukadinovich, David M. **Los Angeles, CA**
Vukanovich, Robert M. Vancouver, WA
Vukas, Robert M. Pittsburgh, PA
Vukelic, David A. Steubenville, OH
Vukelic, James M. Bismarck, ND
Vukelja, David A. **Ormond Beach, FL**
Vukmirovits, Tom G. **Worcester, MA**
Vukovich, Joseph J. Youngstown, OH
Vukovich, Joseph M. Treasury Department, Internal Revenue Service, GV
Vukowich, William T. Washington, DC
Vuksanaj, Christine M. **Eastchester, NY**
Vuksanaj, Pashko Bronx, NY
Vuksich, Paul M. San Francisco, CA
Vuksinick, Thomas R. **Salt Lake City, UT**
Vulcan, Mark A. Baltimore, MD
Vulcan, Millicent Hempstead, NY
Vulcano, Samuel **Syracuse, NY**
Vulevich, Edward J., Jr. Mobile, AL
Vulin, Anthony J. San Pedro, CA
Vulliet, Charles Francis Mercer Island, WA
Vulliez, Marie-Noëlle **Washington, DC**
Vullo, Cynthia R. **Wilkes-Barre, PA**
Vullo, Maria T. **New York, NY**
Vullo, Richard P. Rochester, NY
Vullo, Stephanie Jamaica, NY

Vulpe, Rudolph C. ... Bingham Farms, MI
Vultaggio, Jack J., Jr. ... Mansfield, MA
Vumbacco, Joseph V. ... Naples, FL
Vunderink, Russel E. ... Philadelphia, PA
Vuocolo, Diane E. ... Cherry Hill, NJ
Philadelphia, PA
Vuocolo, Kristie Forsythe ... Trenton, NJ
Vuocolo, Salvatore J. ... Somerville, NJ
Vuong, Quoc Minh ... San Diego, CA
Vuong, Thuy-Whien ... Los Angeles, CA
Vuono & Gray, LLC ... Pittsburgh, PA
Vuono, John A. ... Pittsburgh, PA
Vuono, Mark T. ... Pittsburgh, PA
Vuoso, George ... New York, NY
Vuotto, Charles F., Jr. ... Woodbridge, NJ
Vura, Richard H., Jr. ... Weston, FL
Vural, Cheryl P., Law Office of
Washington, DC
Vural, Cheryl P., Law Office of
Silver Spring, MD
Vural, Diane L. ... Boca Raton, FL
Vural, Erol M. ... New York, NY
Vurdelja, George N., Jr. ... Chicago, IL
Vurdelja & Heaphy ... Chicago, IL
Vusich, Gloria M. ... Leawood, KS
VuTamAnh, William ... Los Angeles, CA
Vutera, David Louis ... White Plains, NY
Vutov, Angela Ann ... Iowa City, IA
Vuvunas, Emmanuel J. ... Racine, WI
Vuyk, Thomas P. ... Salt Lake City, UT
Vuylsteke, Kenneth K. ... St. Louis, MO
Vyadro, Oleg A. ... Boston, MA
Vyas, Hamel ... Buffalo, NY
Vyas, Kris G. ... Los Angeles, CA
Vyas, Nita S. ... New York, NY
Vyborny, Kathleen M. ... Chicago, IL
Vydra, Frank N. ... Riverwoods, IL
Vye, H. Kemp ... Wilmington, DE
Vyhnal, Nancy L. ... Tulsa, OK
Vyhnalek, Leonard P. ... North Platte, NE
Vynalek, John H. ... Mentor, OH
Vyneman, Gary J. ... Newport Beach, CA
Vyse, Thomas A. ... Long Beach, CA
Vyskocil, Mary Kay ... New York, NY
Vysman, Inna ... New York, NY
Vyverberg, Kerry A. ... Chicago, IL
Vyverberg, Robert W., Jr. ... Chicago, IL
Vyvyan, Dawn M. P. ... Seattle, WA
Vyvyan, Mark W. ... Minneapolis, MN
Vyzas, K. Joseph ... Jersey City, NJ
Vyzas, Vincas M. ... Jersey City, NJ

W. Wagner & G. Wagner, Co., L.P.A.
Sandusky, OH
Waack, Christopher T. ... Chicago, IL
Waack, Janelle D. ... Houston, TX
Waag, Carl ... Tucson, AZ
Waag, Christian F., Jr. ... Lakewood, OH
Waag and Co. ... San Luis Obispo, CA
Waag, Susan S. ... San Luis Obispo, CA
Waage, Jon ... Denton, TX
Waage, Lina Pitesa ... San Diego, CA
Waage, Mervin Bernard ... Denton, TX
Waage, Scott A. ... San Diego, CA
Waage, Scott A., A Professional Corporation
San Diego, CA
Waage, Shannon K. ... Portland, OR
Waage & Waage, L.L.P. ... Denton, TX
Waagmeester Law Office, P.L.C.
Rock Rapids, IA
Sioux Falls, SD
Waagmeester, Randy L. ... Rock Rapids, IA
Waagner, Brian P. ... Vienna, VA
Waak, Richard W. ... Memphis, TN
Waaler, Jack ... Champaign, IL
Waaler Law Offices ... Champaign, IL
Waaler, Robert J. ... Champaign, IL
Waalkes, Marie L. ... East Lansing, MI
Waalkes, Thomas W. ... Grand Rapids, MI
Waanders, Harriet Avner ... Carlsbad, CA
Waara, Jonny Lee ... Iron River, MI
Waara, Norman ... Fort Lauderdale, FL
Waarvick, Jeffrey D. ... Newport, OR
Waarvick, Louise Smith ... Newport, OR
Waarvick & Waarvick ... Newport, OR
Waas, Darrell G. ... Denver, CO
Waas, Gene L. ... Chicago, IL
Waas, George L. ... Tallahassee, FL
Waas, Julie Reby ... Miami, FL
Waas, Norman M. ... Coral Gables, FL
Wabaunsee, Albert J. ... La Crosse, WI
Wabby, Walter J. ... Encino, CA
Wabeke, Ross J. ... Loveland, CO
Wabich, James A. ... Chicago, IL
Wabiszczewicz, John M. ... Waterbury, CT
Wabner, H. Douglas ... Dallas, TX
Wabnik, Debra Lynne ... East Meadow, NY
Wacaser, Rebecca E. ... Chicago, IL
Wach, Martha ... Dallas, TX
Wach, Michael ... Eugene, OR
Wacha, Jason B. ... San Carlos, CA
Wachbrit, Edward ... Los Angeles, CA
Wachen, David S. ... Washington, DC
Wachen, Kimberly A. ... Washington, DC
Wachendorf, Robert H.
Whitehouse Station, NJ
Wachenfeld, Howard G. ... Newark, NJ
Wachenfeld, Margaret G.
Washington, DC
Wachenfeld, William S. ... Newark, NJ
Wachenfeld, William T. ... Newark, NJ
Wachenheim, Cynthia ... New York, NY
Wachholz, Michael S. ... Atlanta, GA
Wachholz, Nancy B. ... Wonder Lake, IL
Wachholz, Teresa Gill ... Raleigh, NC
Wachler, Andrew B. ... Royal Oak, MI
Wachler & Associates, Professional
Corporation ... Royal Oak, MI
Wachob, Charles D. ... Auburn, CA
Wacholz, Wade R. ... Minneapolis, MN
Wachowiak, Joseph Walter ... Toledo, OH
Wachowiak & Johnson, S.C.
Eau Claire, WI
Wachowski, Peter C. ... Park Ridge, IL
Wachowski, Richard L. ... Eau Claire, WI
Wachs, Alan S. ... Jacksonville, FL
Wachs, Amy L. ... St. Louis, MO
Wachs, Bryan Robert ... Baltimore, MD
Wachs, Dana J. ... Eau Claire, WI
Wachs, Elliot J. ... Albany, NY
Wachs, James S. ... Cincinnati, OH
Wachs, Jeffrey S., (P.C.)
Fort Lauderdale, FL
Wachs, Joel M. ... New York, NY
Wachs, Joel S. ... Los Angeles, CA
Wachs, Julius ... Sherman Oaks, CA
Wachs, Karen ... East Rutherford, NJ
Wachs, Kelly S. ... Santa Cruz, CA
Wachs, Melvin G. ... Baltimore, MD
Wachs, Michelle J. ... Palo Alto, CA
Wachs, Mitchell ... New York, NY
Wachs, Peggy Brenner ... Philadelphia, PA
Wachs, Ray E. ... Eau Claire, WI
Wachs, Robert E. ... Philadelphia, PA
Wachs, Sanford ... Baltimore, MD
Wachs, Scott W. ... New York, NY
Wachs, Stuart ... New York, NY
Wachsberg, Michael M.
Farmington Hills, MI
Traverse City, MI
Wachsberger, Chaim ... New York, NY
Wachsman, Elizabeth E. ... Las Vegas, NV
Wachsman, Harvey F. ... Great Neck, NY
Philadelphia, PA
Wachsman, Harvey L. ... Birmingham, AL
Wachsman, Kathryn M. ... Great Neck, NY
Wachsman, Sheila Ann ... Louisville, KY
Wachsmann, John R. ... Englewood, CO
Wachsmith, Mary L. ... Los Angeles, CA
Wachsmuth, Robert W. ... San Antonio, TX
Wachspress, Eric S. ... Chicago, IL
Wachsstock, Suzanne E. ... Stamford, CT
Wachstock, Jacob S. ... Great Neck, NY
Wacht, James R. ... New York, NY
Wacht, Thomas J. ... New York, NY
Wachta, James A. ... Boston, MA
Wachtel, Alfred F. ... Brooklyn, NY
Wachtel, Andrew G. ... Reston, VA
Wachtel, Biehn & Malm
Bullhead City, AZ
Kingman, AZ
Lake Havasu City, AZ
Parker, AZ
Wachtel, Bonnie K. ... Washington, DC
Wachtel, David M. ... Washington, DC
Wachtel, Edward W. ... Los Angeles, CA
Wachtel, Eric D. ... Millburn, NJ
New York, NY
Wachtel, Eugene H. ... Chicago, IL
Wachtel, Howard ... Hicksville, NY
Wachtel, Howard, P.C. ... Hicksville, NY
Wachtel, Jeffrey H. ... Palo Alto, CA
Wachtel, John V. ... Wichita, KS
Wachtel, Jonathan M. ... Memphis, TN
Wachtel, Kenneth R. ... San Francisco, CA
Wachtel, Lawrence I. ... Rockville, MD
Wachtel, Marcy L. ... New York, NY
Wachtel & Masyr, LLP ... New York, NY
Wachtel, Norman J. ... New York, NY
Wachtel, Rena ... New York, NY
Wachtel, Ronald W. ... Glen Ellyn, IL
Wachtel, Rosina L. ... New York, NY
Wachtel & Ross ... Chevy Chase, MD
Wachtel, Samuel A. ... New York, NY
Wachtel, Solomon ... Boca Raton, FL
Wachtel, Theodore M. ... New York, NY
Wachtel, Todd ... New Brunswick, NJ
Wachtel, William B. ... New York, NY
Wachtell, Herbert M. ... New York, NY
Wachtell, Lipton, Rosen & Katz
New York, NY
Wachtell, Marc J. ... White Plains, NY
Wachtell, Michael L. ... Los Angeles, CA
Wachter, A. J. ... Pittsburg, KS
Wachter, Andrea Teper ... San Francisco, CA
Wachter, Carol D. ... Portland, OR
Wachter, Chad S. ... Montgomery, AL
Wachter, Charles ... Tampa, FL
Wachter, Edward C., Jr. ... Pittsburgh, PA
Wachter, Fred B. ... Marietta, GA
Wachter, Howard C. ... Great Neck, NY
Wachter, Jim H. ... Madison, TN
Wachter, John H. ... Topeka, KS
Wachter, Joseph H. ... Myrtle Beach, SC
Wachter, Joseph H., P.A.
Myrtle Beach, SC
Wachter, Karl ... New York, NY
Wachter Law Firm, The, A Professional
Corporation ... Marietta, GA
Wachter, Mark F. ... St. Louis, MO
Wachter, Mark I. ... Cleveland, OH
Wachter, Pamela A. ... Durham, NC
Wachter, Robert ... San Francisco, CA
Wachter, Robert A. ... Penndel, PA
Philadelphia, PA
Wachter, Roger C. ... St. Paul, MN
Wachter, Tiffany Slack ... St. Louis, MO
Wachter, Timothy J. ... Portland, OR
Wachter, William B. ... Pittsburg, KS
Wachterhauser, Mary V. Z. ... Media, PA
Wachterman, Alison ... Seattle, WA
Wachterman, Richard M. ... Cincinnati, OH
Wachtler, Daniel R. ... St. Paul, MN
Wachtler, Lauren J. ... New York, NY
Wachtman, Kristen ... Columbus, OH
Wachtmann, Francine D. ... Boston, MA
Wachtmeister, Elizabeth Anne ... Boston, MA
Wack, David M. ... Washington, DC
Wack, Patricia ... Lexington, KY
Wack, Patrick J. ... Akron, OH
Wack, Richard G. ... Winter Park, FL
Wack, Rita R. ... Coronado, CA
Wack, Shannon L. ... Honolulu, HI
Wack, Thomas E. ... St. Louis, MO
Wack, William H. ... Altamonte Springs, FL
Wackeen, W. Thomas ... Stuart, FL
Wacker, Anthony U. ... Minneapolis, MN
Wacker, Bret S. ... Baltimore, MD
Wacker, Daniel J. ... Fairfax, VA
Wacker, Herman L. ... Seattle, WA
Wacker, Isabel J. ... New York, NY
Wacker, Michael B. ... St. Paul, MN
Wacker, Richard A. ... Indianapolis, IN
Wacker, Richard P. ... Springfield, MO
Wacker, Robert A. ... Seattle, WA
Wacker, Theodore B. ... Long Beach, CA
Wackerbarth, Tim D. ... Seattle, WA
Wackerle, Rex Brian ... Washington, DC
Wackerly, Neil P. ... Bay City, MI
Wackerman, John J. ... Palm Coast, FL
Wackerman, Joseph F.
United States Postal Service,
Law Department, GV
Wackerman, Karen P. ... Wilton, CT
Wackes, Paul ... Kansas City, MO
Wackman, Christopher H. ... Wauwatosa, WI
Wackman, John Juneau ... Minneapolis, MN
Wackowski, Bruce ... Indianapolis, IN
Wacks, Edward ... Morris Plains, NJ
Wacks, Kenneth D. ... Wakefield, MA
Wacks, Mullen, Kartzman & Loyek, LLC
Morris Plains, NJ
Wacks, Peter J., Jr. ... Chicago, IL
Wacks, Robert ... Braintree, MA
Wacksman, David M. ... Roseland, NJ
Wacksman, Jeffrey E. ... New York, NY
Wacksman, Leonard ... New York, NY
Wackwitz, Linda K. ... Denver, CO
Waclawski, James ... Columbia, MD
Waclawski, John D., Jr. ... Pittsburgh, PA
Waclawski, Steven M. ... Detroit, MI
Waco, Howard C. ... San Fernando, CA
Wactlar, Edward S. ... Jericho, NY
Wactor, Jon K. ... San Francisco, CA
Waczewski, James Paul ... Tallahassee, FL
Wada, Adonica-Jo ... San Francisco, CA
Wada, Carole M. ... Tustin, CA
Wada, James T. ... Honolulu, HI
Wada, Lori H. ... Honolulu, HI
Wada, Mark R. ... Portland, OR
Wada, Richard Y. ... Honolulu, HI
Wada, Robert S. ... Fullerton, CA
Wada, Ron ... San Francisco, CA
Wada, Ronald Y ... San Francisco, CA
Wadas, Cheryl W. ... Cheyenne, WY
Waddel, Patrick O. ... Tulsa, OK
Waddell & Barnes, P.C. A Professional
Corporation ... Newport News, VA
Norfolk, VA
Waddell, Bill ... San Diego, CA
Waddell, Cameron R. ... Baton Rouge, LA
Waddell, Christian Blue ... Gulfport, MS
Waddell, Christopher W. ... Sacramento, CA
Waddell, Cody B. ... Oklahoma City, OK
Waddell, Colleen P. ... Somerset, NJ
Waddell, Darren L. ... Mason City, IA
Waddell, David D. ... Lansing, MI
Waddell, David E. ... Akron, OH
Waddell, David W. ... Milledgeville, GA
Waddell, David W. ... Houston, TX
Waddell, Earl R., III ... Grapevine, TX
Waddell, Emerson & Buice
Milledgeville, GA
Waddell, Gail Moore ... Norfolk, VA
Waddell, George L. ... San Francisco, CA
Waddell, Gregory R. ... Richmond, VA
Waddell, Howard Glenn ... Auburndale, FL
Waddell, Jerry F. ... New Bern, NC
Waddell, John B. ... Lake Worth, FL
Waddell, John Emory ... Dothan, AL
Waddell, Julie A. ... Washington, DC
Waddell, Karen T. ... Washington, DC
Waddell, Kenneth D. ... Nashville, TN
Waddell, Lan ... Columbus, WI
Waddell, Lewis E., Jr. ... Newton, NC
Waddell, Lorna M. ... Charleston, WV
Waddell, Mark E. ... New York, NY
Waddell, Matthew C. ... Grapevine, TX
Waddell, Michael P. ... Kansas City, MO
Waddell, Paul D. ... Jonesboro, AR
Waddell, Peggy A. ... Kansas City, MO
Waddell, Phillip Dean ... Memphis, TN
Waddell, R. Todd ... Oklahoma City, OK
Waddell, Ralph W. ... Jonesboro, AR
Waddell, Ready & Bouchillon, P.A.
Auburndale, FL
Waddell, Reed S. ... Los Angeles, CA
Waddell, Robert A. ... Torrance, CA
Waddell, Robert G. ... Bloomfield Hills, MI
Waddell, Robert J. ... Atlanta, GA
Waddell, Robert L. ... Lafayette, LA
Waddell, Robert P. ... Shreveport, LA
Waddell, Roy R. ... Phoenix, AZ
Waddell, Ruchadina L. ... Madison, WI
Waddell, Russell S. ... Houston, TX
Waddell, Sandra Hughes ... Los Angeles, CA
Waddell, Susan A. ... Roanoke, VA
Waddell, Thomas A., (P.A.) ... Tallahassee, FL
Waddell, Thomas Lee, (A Professional
Corporation) ... Los Angeles, CA
Waddell, Tina M. ... Dallas, TX
Waddell, Tracy Lynn ... Grapevine, TX
Waddell, W. Charles, III
Newport News, VA
Waddell, W. Gorman ... Kingsport, TN
Waddell & Waddell, P.C. ... Grapevine, TX
Waddell, William A., Jr. (P.A.)
Little Rock, AR
Waddell, William E. ... San Francisco, CA
Waddell, William J. ... Grand Rapids, MI
Waddell, William J., P.C., Law Offices of
Grand Rapids, MI
Waddell, William R. ... Norfolk, VA
Wadden, Robert V., Jr.
Manhattan Beach, CA
Waddey, I. C. (Jack), Jr. ... Nashville, TN
Waddey & Patterson, A Professional
Corporation ... Huntsville, AL
Nashville, TN
Waddick Law Firm, The, P.C.
Indianapolis, IN
Waddick, Lawrence F. ... West Bend, WI
Waddick, Sheryl F. Bailey ... Billerica, MA
Waddick, William A. ... Indianapolis, IN
Waddill, Coby ... Abilene, TX
Waddill, Diann ... Abilene, TX
Waddingham & Peterson ... Delta, UT
Fillmore, UT
Waddingham, Richard ... Delta, UT
Waddingham, Thorpe ... Delta, UT
Waddington, Croft C. ... Lisle, IL
Waddington, James M. ... New York, NY
Waddington, Lawrence C. ... Los Angeles, CA
Waddington, Michael J.
Monterey Park, CA
Waddington, Richard F. ... Washington, DC
Waddle, Jeffrey T. ... New York, NY
Waddle, Paula S. ... Corpus Christi, TX
Waddle, Robert G. ... Jackson, MS
Waddles, Nicholas J. ... Encino, CA
Waddock, Thomas P. ... Sacramento, CA
Waddoups, Clark ... Salt Lake City, UT
Waddoups, Douglas C.
Salt Lake City, UT
Waddoups, George T. ... Salt Lake City, UT
Waddoups, Gregory L. ... Washington, DC
Waddoups, Jon E. ... Salt Lake City, UT
Waddy, Currita C. ... New Orleans, LA
Waddy, John W., Jr. ... Columbus, OH
Waddy, Victoria J. ... San Antonio, TX
Wade, Allan J. ... Memphis, TN
Wade, Allison ... Atlanta, GA
Wade, Andrew F. ... Tucson, AZ
Wade, Andrew S. ... West Chester, PA
Wade, Angela K. ... Indianapolis, IN
Wade Ash Woods Hill & Farley, P.C.
Denver, CO
Wade, Barbara Moore ... Jonesboro, GA
Wade, B. J. ... Memphis, TN
Wade, Blake K. ... Salt Lake City, UT
Wade, Briand T. ... Portsmouth, NH
Wade, Bruce K. ... Bakersfield, CA
Wade, Bryan O. ... Springfield, MO
Wade, Bryant E. ... Troy, MI
Wade, Burton L. ... St. Joseph, LA
Wade, Byron L. ... Houston, TX
Wade, Carolyn A. ... Clarksburg, WV
Wade, Carolyn E. ... Brooklyn, NY
Wade, Carolyn G. ... Eugene, OR
Wade, Charles A. ... Crestview, FL
Wade, Charles E., Jr. ... Lawton, OK
Wade, Charles F. ... Greensburg, PA
Wade, Cheryl Lyn ... Hempstead, NY
Wade, Christopher Sean ... Dallas, TX
Wade Clark Mulcahy ... Westfield, NJ
New York, NY
Wade, David ... Eugene, OR
Wade, David ... Memphis, TN
Wade, David G. ... Houston, TX
Wade, Dennis M. ... Westfield, NJ
New York, NY
Wade, Deron L. ... Dallas, TX
Wade & De Young, A Professional
Corporation ... Anchorage, AK
Wade, Diane ... New York, NY
Wade, Don M. ... New York, NY
Wade, Douglas M. ... Orange, CA
Wade, Edmond D. ... Rancho Cucamonga, CA
Wade, Edward S. ... Cleveland, OH
Wade, Ellen K. ... Boston, MA
Wade, Emily D. ... Tupelo, MS
Wade, Emmett C. ... Kansas City, MO
Wade, Enid A. ... Waco, TX
Wade, Eric D. ... Houston, TX
Wade, Faires P. ... Corpus Christi, TX
Wade, Felix C. ... Columbus, OH
Wade, Frankie E., (Ms.) ... Jackson, TN
Wade, Frederick B. ... Madison, WI
Wade, Gary R. ... Knoxville, TN
Sevierville, TN
Wade, George E., Jr. ... Brooklyn, NY
Wade, George H. ... Brooklyn, NY
Wade, George J. ... New York, NY
Wade, Gregory M. ... Alexandria, VA
Wade, Guy Alton, (P.A.) ... Little Rock, AR
Wade, Guy I., III ... Dallas, TX
Wade, H. Bryce ... Salt Lake City, UT
Wade, H. Landis, Jr. ... Charlotte, NC
Wade, Hamlin L. ... Charlotte, NC
Wade, Helene H. ... Hartford, CT
Wade, Henry M. ... Dallas, TX
Wade, Hugh G. ... Anchorage, AK
Wade & Hughes, P.C. ... Alexandria, VA
Wade, Ingrid U. ... Houston, TX
Wade, J. Kirk ... Washington, DC
Wade, Jacqueline Johnson ... Portland, OR
Wade, James A. ... Hartford, CT
Wade, James A. ... Duluth, MN
Wade, James A., Jr. ... Pasadena, CA

Wade, James C. .... Louisville, KY
Wade, James C., Jr. .... Evansville, IN
Wade, James E. .... Columbia, MO
Wade, James E., III .... Bushnell, FL
Wade, James E., III, P.A. .... Bushnell, FL
Lady Lake, FL
Wade, James H. .... Charlotte, NC
Wade, James R. .... Denver, CO
Wade, James R. .... Department of Justice, Antitrust Division, GV
Wade, Jamie A. .... Ames, IA
Wade, Jas. W. .... Altadena, CA
Wade, Jeffrey L. .... Brandenburg, KY
Wade, Jeffrey P. .... San Diego, CA
Wade, Jeffrey Pritchard, Jr.
Newport Beach, CA
Wade, Jerome S. .... Dallas, TX
Wade, Jerry D. .... Sulphur, OK
Wade, Jerry M., II .... North Palm Beach, FL
Wade, John B., III .... New York, NY
Wade, John Cogan .... Little Rock, AR
Wade, John D. .... Laurel Springs, NJ
Wade, John D., P.C. .... Laurel Springs, NJ
Wade, John E. .... Cleveland, OH
Wade, John E., Jr. .... Jackson, MS
Wade, John Franklin .... Plantation, FL
Wade, John P. .... San Bernardino, CA
Wade, Jonathan J. .... Atlanta, GA
Wade, Joyce S. .... Alexandria, VA
Wade, Kathleen M. .... Tampa, FL
Wade, Kevin A. .... Welch, WV
Wade, Kevin T. .... Red Hook, NY
Wade, L. Bruce .... Salisbury, MD
Wade, Lawrence D. .... Greenville, MS
Wade, Len Allen, Law Office of
Fort Worth, TX
Wade, Lena D .... Durham, NC
Wade, Leslie W. .... Atlanta, GA
Fayetteville, GA
Wade, Linda H. .... Pensacola, FL
Wade, Lisa A. .... Atlanta, GA
Wade, Lisa Snow .... Concord, NH
Wade, Lloyd R. .... Denver, CO
Wade, Louis J. .... Overland Park, KS
Kansas City, MO
Wade, Lynn F. .... Fayetteville, AR
Wade, Mackey & Robinson, A Professional Corporation .... Lawton, OK
Wade, Malachy J. .... Middle Village, NY
Wade, Manley B. .... Orange Park, FL
Wade, Mark G. .... New York, NY
Wade, Mark T. .... Pittsburgh, PA
Wade, Marsha Mason .... Baton Rouge, LA
Wade, Martin .... Cincinnati, OH
Wade, Mary L. .... Lebanon, NH
Wade, Matthew D. F. .... Elizabeth, NJ
Wade, Matthew L. .... Lubbock, TX
Wade, Maurice F. .... Rockaway Point, NY
Wade, Melissa .... Bryan, TX
Wade, Michael A. .... Scottsdale, AZ
Wade, Michael D. .... Grand Rapids, MI
Wade, Michael E. .... Long Beach, CA
Wade, Michael G. .... Detroit, MI
Wade, Michael M. (Mickey) .... Belton, TX
Wade, Michael T. .... Hartford, CT
Wade, Michael T. .... Atlanta, GA
Wade, Michelle M. .... Overland Park, KS
Wade, Mike .... Fort Worth, TX
Wade, M. M. (Mickey) .... Belton, TX
Killeen, TX
Wade, Neill G. .... Tallahassee, FL
Wade, Nicole Jennings .... Atlanta, GA
Wade, Patrick W. .... Eugene, OR
Wade, Paul H. .... Greer, SC
Wade, Richard A. .... Three Rivers, MI
Wade, Richard L. .... Morristown, NJ
Wade, Rick G. .... Lincoln, NE
Wade, Robert .... Washington, DC
Wade, Robert A. .... South Bend, IN
Wade, Robert B. .... Morgantown, KY
Wade, Robert E. .... Belvidere, NJ
Wade, Robert J., Jr. .... Columbus, OH
Wade, Robert Keith .... Beaumont, TX
Wade, Robert W. .... Indianapolis, IN
Wade, Rodney C. .... Atlanta, GA
Wade, Roger E. .... Treasury Department, Internal Revenue Service, GV
Wade, Roger W. .... Albany, NY
Wade, Ronald L. .... Portland, OR
Wade, Ronald T. .... Rockford, IL
Wade, Rose Marie .... Atlanta, GA
Wade, S. Blake .... Ventura, CA
Wade, Scott W. .... Hermosa Beach, CA
Denver, CO
Wade, Stephanie Karen .... Washington, DC
Wade, Stephen B. .... Auburn, ME
Wade, Stephen R. .... San Bernardino, CA
Wade, Steven T. .... Helena, MT
Wade, Suzanne Elizabeth .... Richmond, VA
Wade, Terry L. .... Minneapolis, MN
Wade, Terry L., Law Office of
Mesquite, NV
St. George, UT
Wade, Thandi .... Jackson, MS
Wade, Theresa M. .... Portland, OR
Wade, Thomas A. .... Hagerstown, MD
Wade, Thomas F. .... Baton Rouge, LA
Wade, Thomas M., III .... St. Joseph, LA
Wade, Tiffanee N. .... Jackson, MS
Wade, Timothy L. .... Indianapolis, IN
Wade, Todd N. .... Austin, TX
Wade, Tyrone C. .... Charlotte, NC
Wade, Vangela M. .... Jackson, MS
Wade, W. Burgess .... Midland, TX
Wade, Wallace J. .... Santa Ana, CA
Wade, William J. .... Wilmington, DE
Wade, William J. .... Lubbock, TX
Wade, William M., Jr. .... Fort Collins, CO

Wade, William P. .... Los Angeles, CA
Wade, Winfrey T. .... Richmond, VA
Wade, W.J., Jr. .... Lubbock, TX
Wade, Wm. Kim .... Dallas, TX
Wade, Wyman R., Jr. .... Fort Smith, AR
Wadelton, Joan S.
Department of State, GV
Waden, Melissa D. .... Austin, TX
Wadeson, Jeanine Garritano .... Chester, NY
Wadewitz, Betty M. .... North Platte, NE
Wadford, Wilder .... Weaverville, NC
Wadhams & Akridge, A Professional Corporation .... Las Vegas, NV
Wadhams, Corinne P. .... Burlington, VT
Wadhams, James L. .... Las Vegas, NV
Wadhams, Richard H., Jr. .... Burlington, VT
Wadhwa, Manohar H. .... Santa Ana, CA
Wadhwa, Sanjay .... Washington, DC
Wadhwani, Catherine V. .... Pittsburgh, PA
Wadhwani, Raj T. .... Encino, CA
Wadhwani, Tejal P. .... Charlotte, NC
Wadia, Cyrus .... Oakland, CA
Wadiche, Sandra H. .... San Antonio, TX
Wadick, Ashley K. .... Austin, TX
Wadington, Robert N., & Associates
Chicago, IL
Wadkins, Robert L. .... Columbus, GA
Wadkovsky, Basil .... Chestertown, MD
Wadkovsky & Mowell .... Chestertown, MD
Wadkowski, Gerald P. .... Columbus, OH
Wadland & Associates .... Boston, MA
Wadland, Joseph J. .... Boston, MA
Wadle, Daniel .... Huntsville, AL
Wadle, Michael J. .... Englewood, CO
Wadle, Wes E. .... Dallas, TX
Wadleigh, Ralph N. .... La Junta, CO
Wadleigh, Starr & Peters, P.L.L.C.
Concord, NH
Manchester, NH
Wadleigh, Theodore .... Manchester, NH
Wadler, Arnold L. .... East Rutherford, NJ
Wadler, Barry A. .... New York, NY
Wadler, Douglas G. .... Rockville, MD
Wadler, Larry E. .... Wharton, TX
Wadler, Larry E., P.C. .... Wharton, TX
Wadler, Linda A. .... Washington, DC
Wadler, Lisa R. .... Fleischmanns, NY
Wadler, Marie Johnson .... Washington, DC
Wadler, Michael R. .... Houston, TX
Wadler, Neal S. .... Baltimore, MD
Wadler-Shin, Abby R. .... Kew Gardens, NY
Wadley, Christopher A. .... Woodland Hills, CA
Wadley, James B. .... Topeka, KS
Wadley, Teri Chastain .... Jonesboro, AR
Wadley, W. Thomas .... St. Petersburg, FL
Wadlin, John J. .... Kingston, NY
Wadlington, Dewey R. .... McKinney, TX
Wadlington, Marlon C. .... Santa Ana, CA
Wadlington, Patrick A., Jr. .... Dallas, TX
Wadlington, Walter J., III
Charlottesville, VA
Wadlow, R. Clark .... Washington, DC
Wadman, Gary A. .... Columbus, OH
Wadrzyk, Mark Edward .... Washington, DC
Wadsack, Anne Taylor .... Madison, WI
Wadsack, Charles E. .... Norman, OK
Wadsack, John F. .... Lake Charles, LA
Wadsack, Karl L. .... Seattle, WA
Wadsack, Lawrence J. .... St. Louis, MO
Wadsworth & Balzano .... Brecksville, OH
Wadsworth, Barbara .... Irvine, CA
Wadsworth, Brent M. .... Anchorage, AK
Wadsworth, Charles A. (Tony)
Louisville, KY
Wadsworth, Christopher W.
West Palm Beach, FL
Wadsworth, Clyde J. .... San Francisco, CA
Wadsworth, David A. .... Dallas, TX
Wadsworth & Davis .... Tallahassee, FL
Wadsworth, Dexter C. .... New York, NY
Wadsworth, Donald K. .... Las Vegas, NV
Wadsworth, Douglas J. .... Madison, WI
Wadsworth, Dyer S. .... Hancock, ME
Wadsworth, Edward N. .... Boston, MA
Wadsworth, Edward W. .... Metairie, LA
Wadsworth, Fraser & Dahl .... Los Angeles, CA
Wadsworth, Glenda Lynn .... Aberdeen, MS
Wadsworth, James L. .... Las Vegas, NV
Wadsworth, James M. .... Buffalo, NY
Wadsworth, Jan D'Alessandro
San Mateo, CA
Wadsworth, Joel S. .... Atlanta, GA
Tucker, GA
Wadsworth, John V. .... Redwood City, CA
Wadsworth, John W. .... Boston, MA
Wadsworth, Keith H. .... Lakeland, FL
Lake Wales, FL
Winter Haven, FL
Wadsworth, Michael R. .... Orange, CA
Wadsworth, Murray M. .... Tallahassee, FL
Wadsworth, Murray Marvin, Jr.
Tallahassee, FL
Wadsworth, Philip R. .... San Jose, CA
Wadsworth, Roger A. .... Brecksville, OH
Wadsworth, Traver & Clarke, L.L.C.
Atlanta, GA
Tucker, GA
Wadsworth, Virginia W. .... Dearborn, MI
Wadsworth, Warren F. .... Portland, OR
Wadyka, Christina S. .... Washington, DC
Wadyka, David P. .... Roseland, NJ
Wadyka, Steven J., Jr. .... Washington, DC
Wadzinski, Kevin J. .... Washington, DC
Waechter, Arthur J., Jr. .... New Orleans, LA
Waechter, C. William, Jr. .... Richmond, VA
Waechter & Gustafson .... Willmar, MN
Waechter, James A. .... Nashville, TN
Waechter, John L. .... St. Louis, MO

Waechter, Ralph W. .... Pittsburgh, PA
Waechter, Raymond R. .... Willmar, MN
Waechter, Teresa Gianetta .... Dunedin, FL
Waechter, Thomas C. .... Akron, OH
Waechter, William .... Seattle, WA
Waecker, Mark .... Los Angeles, CA
Waeen, Nadeem A. .... New York, NY
Waeffler, Alexandra L. .... Wauwatosa, WI
Waeger, Ann M. .... Westfield, NJ
Waeger, Cindy D. .... Philadelphia, PA
Waeger, Robert W. .... Harrisburg, PA
Waehler, James F. .... Georgetown, DE
Seaford, DE
Waelder, Catherine .... New York, NY
Waelder, Sandra .... Tulsa, OK
Waeldner, Robert J. .... Westbrook, ME
Waelti, Arlin B. .... Minneapolis, MN
Waer, Robt. M. .... Grand Rapids, MI
Waerig, Brian W. .... Blue Bell, PA
Waering, Jennie L. M. .... Roanoke, VA
Waers, James R. .... Kansas City, KS
Waesche, Barbara B. .... New York, NY
Waesche, Sheinbaum & O'Regan, P.C.
New York, NY
Waestman, Robert R. .... Long Beach, CA
Wafel, Ira M. .... Irvine, CA
Waffenschmidt, Thomas .... Williamsport, PA
Wafle, Ferris B., Jr. .... Fredericksburg, VA
Wafle, Ferris Bleight, Jr.
Fredericksburg, VA
Wagaman, Charles F., Jr. .... Hagerstown, MD
Wagaman, Mary D. .... Fairfax, VA
Wagan, Carole .... Peabody, MA
Wagar, Dorothy B. .... Vestal, NY
Wagar, Harvey D., III .... New Orleans, LA
Wagar, John E., Jr. .... Crowley, LA
Wagar, Kirk W.B. .... Coral Gables, FL
Wagar, Kirk W.B. .... Coconut Grove, FL
Wagar, Nelson W., III, (P.L.C.)
Metairie, LA
Wagatsuma, Wade R. .... Cleveland, OH
Wagda, Joseph A., Jr. .... Danville, CA
Wage, Charles L.E. .... Montrose, PA
Wagemaker, James F. .... Olivia, MN
Wagemaker Law Office .... Olivia, MN
Wageman, Paul N. .... Dallas, TX
Wagenaar, Ronald James .... Mason City, IA
Wagenbach, Adam J. .... Columbus, OH
Wagenbach, Jeffrey B. .... Morristown, NJ
Wagenbach, Larry D. .... Richmond, TX
Wagenberg, Lawrence .... New York, NY
Wagenblast, Dennis F. .... Toms River, NJ
Wagener, Jason B. .... Chicago, IL
Wagener, Jeffrey R. .... St. Louis, MO
Wagener, Joan .... Tucson, AZ
Wagener, John T. .... Chicago, IL
Wagener, Larry Dean .... Bixby, OK
Wagener Law Firm .... Ankeny, IA
Wagener, Matthias H. .... Los Angeles, CA
Wagener, Renauld J. .... Ankeny, IA
Wagener, Robert R. .... Libertyville, IL
Wagener, Susan Ann .... Lake Forest, IL
Wagener, Terrance J. .... Minneapolis, MN
Wagenfuehr, Susan A. .... Houston, TX
Wagenhauser, John F. .... Dallas, TX
Wagenheim, Richard L. .... Fort Lauderdale, FL
Wagenheim, Ronald A. .... Atlantic City, NJ
Wagenius, Dwight S. .... St. Paul, MN
Wagenknecht, Valerie T. .... Great Neck, NY
Wagenlander & Heisterkamp, LLC
Denver, CO
Wagenlander, James F. .... Denver, CO
Wagenmaker, Sally R. .... Chicago, IL
Wagenman, Barton L. .... Toledo, OH
Wagenseller, David, III .... Ephrata, PA
Lancaster, PA
Lititz, PA
Quarryville, PA
Wagenseller, Judson B. .... Louisville, KY
Wager, Charlotte L. .... Chicago, IL
Wager, Donald R. .... Los Angeles, CA
Wager, Eli .... Uniondale, NY
Wager, Henry W. .... Olympia, WA
Wager, Jerome A. .... Los Angeles, CA
San Diego, CA
San Francisco, CA
Santa Ana, CA
Santa Barbara, CA
Wager, Joseph S. .... Washington, DC
Wager, Lisa Klein .... New York, NY
Wager, Michael .... Cleveland, OH
Wager, Nancy Ellen .... New York, NY
Wager, Nathan
Commodity Futures Trading Commission, Division of Enforcement, GV
Wager, Patricia London .... Tarrytown, NY
Wager, Ronald A. .... Aberdeen, SD
Wager, Taylor, Howd & Brearton
Troy, NY
Wager, William F., Jr. .... Panama City, FL
Wagerman, Howard L. .... Memphis, TN
Wagers, Alan C. .... Harlan, KY
Wagers, Gardner D. .... Winchester, KY
Wagers & Keeton, Law Offices of, P.S.C.
Winchester, KY
Wagers, Margaret H. .... Charlotte, NC
Wagers, Stanton, Jr. .... Deer Park, TX
Wager-Zito, Adrian .... Washington, DC
Wages & Benham, Attorneys .... Memphis, TN
Wages, Benjamin T. .... Memphis, TN
Wages, Benjamin T., Jr. .... Memphis, TN
Wages, Harold J. .... Dallas, TX
Wages, Josh B. .... Athens, GA
Wages, Nathaniel D. .... Winder, GA
Wagg, Richard L. .... Anchorage, AK
Wagg, Thomas E., III .... Greensboro, NC
Waggal, John G. .... Cincinnati, OH
Waggaman, Douglas S. .... San Diego, CA

Waggaman, John L., IV .... Dunwoody, GA
Waggener, Arterburn & Standiferd
Topeka, KS
Waggener, Donald D. .... Lexington, KY
Waggener, Julia T. .... Denver, CO
Waggener, Robert F. .... San Francisco, CA
Waggener, Sterling S. .... Topeka, KS
Waggener, William P. .... Denver, CO
Waggener, William P., P.C. .... Denver, CO
Waggle, Catherine L. .... Pittsburgh, PA
Waggner, Nancy .... Boston, MA
Waggner, Sharon A. .... Houston, TX
Waggoner, Amy K. .... Jonesboro, GA
Waggoner, Anne-Marie .... San Jose, CA
Waggoner & Associates, P.C.
Rio Rancho, NM
Waggoner, Bobby J. .... San Antonio, TX
Waggoner, Boyd .... Dallas, TX
Waggoner, Brenda Jean .... Knoxville, TN
Waggoner, Bruce P. .... Sacramento, CA
Waggoner & Bruehl, P.A. .... Bokeelia, FL
Waggoner, Carl O. .... Modesto, CA
Waggoner, Cathy M. .... D'Iberville, MS
Waggoner, Charles E. .... New Castle, IN
Waggoner, Charles R. .... Warsaw, IN
Waggoner, Charles S., II .... Gulf Breeze, FL
Waggoner, Daniel .... Washington, DC
Seattle, WA
Waggoner, Darren G. .... Boston, MA
Waggoner, David L. .... Crystal Lake, IL
Waggoner, Debra O. .... Reno, NV
Waggoner, Dennis P. .... Tampa, FL
Waggoner, Dianna Minton
San Francisco, CA
Waggoner, Donald E. .... Centerville, OH
Waggoner, Elaine A. .... Lincoln, NE
Waggoner and Ferens .... Uniontown, PA
Waggoner, Gage A. .... Dallas, TX
Waggoner, Gary W. .... Denver, CO
Waggoner, Geoffrey .... Maumee, OH
Waggoner, Geoffrey H. .... Charleston, SC
Waggoner, Glenn D. .... Cleveland, OH
Waggoner, Gregory L. .... Crystal Lake, IL
Waggoner, Hamrick, Hasty, Monteith & Kratt, PLLC .... Charlotte, NC
Waggoner, James C. .... Portland, OR
Waggoner, James L. .... Rapid City, SD
Waggoner, Joe A. .... Jackson, MS
Waggoner, John M. .... Madison, WI
Waggoner, Jon R. .... Amarillo, TX
Waggoner, Justin M. .... Houston, TX
Waggoner, Kenneth L. .... Los Angeles, CA
Waggoner, Kristen K. .... Seattle, WA
Waggoner, Lanny P. .... Los Angeles, CA
Waggoner Law Firm, The, P.C.
Crystal Lake, IL
Waggoner Law Office .... Oconto Falls, WI
Waggoner, Lawrence L. .... Layton, UT
Waggoner, Lisa A. .... Rio Rancho, NM
Waggoner, Lisa M. .... Crystal Lake, IL
Waggoner & Loeffler, Law Offices of
Modesto, CA
Waggoner & Malouf, L.L.P. .... Dallas, TX
Waggoner, Marinell R. .... Alcoa, TN
Waggoner, Mark T. .... Birmingham, AL
Waggoner, Melanie .... Houston, TX
Waggoner, Michael J. .... Boulder, CO
Waggoner, Paul H. .... Bokeelia, FL
Waggoner, Paul W. .... Anchorage, AK
Waggoner, Richard L. .... Dallas, TX
Waggoner, Steven M. .... Springfield, IL
Waggoner, Ted A. .... Rochester, IN
Waggoner, Thomas Francis
St. Joseph, MI
Waggoner, Tracy G. .... Mill Creek, WA
Waggoner, Vance M. .... Oconto Falls, WI
Waggoner, William J. .... Santa Fe, NM
Waggoner, William J. .... Charlotte, NC
Waggoner, William S. .... Knoxville, TN
Waggonner, Kelly Rae .... San Diego, CA
Waggpmer, Benny B. .... Fairfield, IA
Waghelstein, Alan Neal .... Rockville, MD
Wagher, Harold .... Joliet, IL
Waghorn, Andrew J.
Department of the Navy, GV
Waghorne, John E. .... Bloomingdale, IL
Waghorne, Mary C. .... Chicago, IL
Wagle, Jamie L. .... Wichita, KS
Wagle, Jennifer A. .... Wichita, KS
Wagle, M. Steven .... Wichita, KS
Wagle, Sanjay .... Los Angeles, CA
Wagler, Ira .... Lancaster, PA
Wagley, William M. .... Lafayette, CA
Wagman, Arthur M. .... Rockville, MD
Wagman, Ashworth, Kreider & Wright
Lancaster, PA
Wagman, Beatriz M. Carta .... Tampa, FL
Wagman, Bruce A. .... San Francisco, CA
Wagman, David A. .... San Francisco, CA
Wagman, Gregg W. .... New London, CT
Wagman, Harley Israel
Hot Springs National Park, AR
Wagman, Harold L. .... Skokie, IL
Wagman, Heidi A. .... Chicago, IL
Wagman, James M. .... Catskill, NY
Wagman, Joel W. .... New York, NY
Wagman, Julian H. .... Tarrytown, NY
Wagman, Leonard M.
National Labor Relations Board, Division of Administrative Law Judges, GV
Wagman, Leonard W. .... New York, NY
Wagman, Marjorie C. .... Palo Alto, CA
Wagman, Michael W. .... Lancaster, PA
Wagman, Nancy D. .... Philadelphia, PA
Wagman, Philip R. .... New York, NY
Wagman, Robert D. .... Rockville, MD
Wagman, Roger A. .... Albuquerque, NM
Wagman, Sandra D. .... Chicago, IL

Wagner, Robert R. ... Boston, MA
Wagner, Robert S. ... Portland, OR
Kirkland, WA
Wagner, Robin ... New York, NY
Wagner, Roger B. ... Washington, DC
Wagner, Ronald A. ... Oakland, CA
Wagner, Ronald E. ... Detroit, MI
Wagner, Roy E. ... Menomonee Falls, WI
Wagner, Russell B. ... Rancho Santa Fe, CA
Wagner, Ruth ... Park City, UT
Wagner, Ruth Whetstone ... Tampa, FL
Wagner, S. Edward ... St. Paul, MN
Wagner, Sandra F. ... Oakland, CA
Wagner, Sandra M. ... San Diego, CA
Wagner, Scott Gregory ... Atlanta, GA
Wagner, Seymour C. ... Philadelphia, PA
Wagner, Sherri R. ... Houston, TX
Wagner, Stanley P., Jr. ... Federal Way, WA
Wagner, Stephan C. ... San Francisco, CA
Wagner, Stephanie L. ... Baltimore, MD
Wagner, Stephen ... New York, NY
Wagner, Stephen E. ... Blacksburg, VA
Wagner, Stephen G. ... Louisville, KY
Wagner, Stephen H. ... Calabasas, CA
Wagner, Stephen James, (A Law Corporation) ... Sacramento, CA
Wagner, Stephen M. ... Indianapolis, IN
Wagner, Steve R. ... Des Moines, IA
Wagner, Steven A. ... Fort Lauderdale, FL
Wagner, Steven A., P.A.
Fort Lauderdale, FL
Wagner, Steven E. ... Washington, DC
Wagner, Steven M. ... Chicago, IL
Wagner, Steven R. ... New York, NY
Wagner, Stuart & Cannon ... Tulsa, OK
Wagner, Sue ... New York, NY
Wagner, Susan Debra ... Madison, NJ
Wagner, Susan L. ... Canton, OH
Wagner, Susan M. ... Chicago, IL
Wagner, Susan S. ... Birmingham, AL
Wagner, Sylvia N. ... Rockville, MD
Wagner, T. Craig, II ... Dallas, TX
Wagner, Tamara L. ... Fullerton, CA
Wagner, Teresa J. ... Washburn, WI
Wagner, Theodore R. ... New York, NY
Wagner, Thomas A. ... Encinitas, CA
Wagner, Thomas C. ... Cleveland, OH
Wagner, Thomas C. ... Virginia Beach, VA
Wagner, Thomas E. ... Juneau, AK
Wagner, Thomas E. ... Cleveland, OH
Wagner, Thomas F. ... Michigan City, IN
Wagner, Thomas G. ... St. Marys, PA
Wagner, Thomas G. ... The Woodlands, TX
Wagner, Thomas J. ... New Orleans, LA
Wagner, Thomas J. ... Cherry Hill, NJ
Philadelphia, PA
Wagner, Thomas J. ... Cleveland, OH
Wagner, Thomas J. ... Philadelphia, PA
Wagner, Thomas P. ... Philadelphia, PA
Wagner, Tiffanie ... Arvada, CO
Wagner, Timothy J. ... Indianapolis, IN
Wagner, Timothy S. ... Irvine, CA
Wagner, Todd A. ... New York, NY
Wagner and Tomlin ... Virginia Beach, VA
Wagner, Ulrich ... New York, NY
Wagner, Valerie M. ... Palo Alto, CA
Wagner, Vaughan & McLaughlin, P.A.
Tampa, FL
Wagner, Vernon R. ... Tampa, FL
Wagner, Vincent O. ... Indianapolis, IN
Wagner, W. Richard ... San Antonio, TX
Wagner & Wagner, A Professional Corporation
Fresno, CA
Wagner, Walter C. ... Everett, WA
Wagner, Walter L., Jr. ... Dunbar, WV
Wagner, Walter P. ... Rockville Centre, NY
Wagner, Walter R. ... Sandusky, OH
Wagner, Ward, Jr. ... West Palm Beach, FL
Wagner, Wayne ... Manila, AR
Wagner & Wells ... Alexandria, LA
Wagner, Wendy E. ... Cleveland, OH
Wagner, William B. ... Austin, TX
Wagner, William C. ... Indianapolis, IN
Wagner, William C. ... Reading, MA
Wagner, William C. ... Erie, PA
Wagner, William C., II ... Dover, DE
Wagner, William Day ... Worcester, MA
Wagner, William H. ... Valparaiso, IN
Wagner, William J.
Department of Transportation, Office of the General Counsel, GV
Wagner, William J. ... Cincinnati, OH
Wagner, William O. ... Newport Beach, CA
Wagner, William O., Inc., A Law Corporation
Newport Beach, CA
Wagner, William R. ... Gainesville, FL
Wagner, William R. ... New York, NY
Wagner, William T. ... Missoula, MT
Wagner, W. J. ... Troy, MI
Wagner, Wm. Hulse ... Houston, TX
Wagner & Zamow ... Logan, WV
Wagner Cammarano, Terri
Los Angeles, CA
Wagner-Findeisen, Anne ... New York, NY
Wagner-Gutkowski, Michele M.
Saginaw, MI
Wagner-Hilliard, Diana ... St. Louis, MO
Wagner-Malloy, Mary K. ... Kenosha, WI
Wagner-Wells, Sharon ... Los Angeles, CA
Wagnild, Craig P. ... Honolulu, HI
Wagnild, Zachary C. ... Seattle, WA
Wagnitz, John H. ... Pinehurst, NC
Wagnon, Deborah Lanora ... Stateline, NV
Nashville, TN
Wagnon, J. Mark ... Lubbock, TX
Wagnon, Jeffery D. ... Plano, TX
Wagnon, Jeffery D., P.C. ... Plano, TX
Wagnon, Macbeth, Jr. ... Birmingham, AL

Wagnon, Todd Jason ... Washington, DC
Wagoner, Anna Gregory ... Greensboro, NC
Wagoner, Anna Mills S. ... Salisbury, NC
Wagoner, Ayer & Hargis ... Rockport, IN
Wagoner, David E. ... Seattle, WA
Wagoner, E. Lee, Jr. ... Akron, OH
Wagoner, F. Nan Todd ... Houston, TX
Wagoner, Jack, III ... Little Rock, AR
Wagoner, James A. ... Grand Island, NE
Wagoner, James A., III ... Point Clear, AL
Wagoner, James P. ... Fresno, CA
Wagoner, James R. ... Louisville, KY
Wagoner, Jeffrey L. ... Kansas City, MO
Wagoner, Jen Broderick ... Torrance, CA
Wagoner, John A. ... Grand Island, NE
Wagoner, John E. ... Holland, OH
Wagoner, Joseph P. ... Boca Raton, FL
Wagoner, Joseph W. ... Weston, WV
Wagoner, Judith A. ... Grand Island, NE
Wagoner, Kenneth A. ... West Plains, MO
Wagoner, Mark D. ... Holland, OH
Wagoner, Mark D., Jr. ... Toledo, OH
Wagoner, Mary M. ... Graham, NC
Wagoner, Mary Pauline ... Sacramento, CA
Wagoner, Robert J. ... Columbus, OH
Wagoner, Robert J. ... Houston, TX
Wagoner, Robert William ... Grand Island, NE
Wagoner, Ruth A. ... Dallas, TX
Wagoner & Steinberg ... Holland, OH
Wagoner, Thomas A. ... Grand Island, NE
Wagoner & Wagoner ... Grand Island, NE
Wagoner, Walter D., Jr. ... New Haven, CT
Wagonheim & Cummins ... Hanover, MD
Wagonheim, Ira J. ... Hanover, MD
Wagonheim, Sylvia S. ... Towson, MD
Wagonhurst, Cheryl ... Santa Barbara, CA
Wagonseller and Cobb ... Lubbock, TX
Wagshal, Marc R. ... Chevy Chase, MD
Wagshal & Sher ... Chevy Chase, MD
Wagshul, Bradley ... Miami, FL
Wagshul, Karen ... Hartford, CT
Wagstaff, Alvis, Stubbeman, Seamster & Longacre, L.L.P. ... Abilene, TX
Dallas, TX
Wagstaff & Cartmell, LLP
Kansas City, MO
Wagstaff, E. Wesley ... Granada Hills, CA
Wagstaff, George D. ... Topeka, KS
Wagstaff, John S. ... Tarpon Springs, FL
Wagstaff Law Office, P.A. ... Largo, FL
Wagstaff, Mary Lou Miller ... Largo, FL
Wagstaff, Richard H., III
Kansas City, MO
Wagstaff, Robert B. ... Abilene, TX
Wagstaff, Robert H., Law Offices of
Anchorage, AK
Wagstaff, Thomas L. ... Kansas City, MO
Wagstaff, Thomas W. ... Kansas City, MO
Wagstaffe, Dennis G. ... Redwood City, CA
Wagstaffe, James M. ... San Francisco, CA
Wagstaffe, Paul J. ... Sacramento, CA
Wagstaffe, Schwarzkopf & Allin
Sacramento, CA
Wagstaffe, Stephen M. ... Redwood City, CA
Wagstaffe & Wagstaffe
Redwood City, CA
Wagster, John W. ... Nashville, TN
Waguespack, Barry E. ... Baton Rouge, LA
Waguespack, Barry E., A Law Corporation
Baton Rouge, LA
Waguespack, David A. ... Baton Rouge, LA
Waguespack, David F. ... New Orleans, LA
Waguespack, Herbert W., Jr. ... Harahan, LA
Waguespack, Jason P. ... New Orleans, LA
Waguespack, Jess J. ... Napoleonville, LA
Waguespack, Michael O.
New Orleans, LA
Waguespack, Seago & Carmichael, A Professional Law Corporation
Baton Rouge, LA
Wah, Angela C. ... Chicago, IL
Wah, Carolyn R. ... Brooklyn, NY
Wah, Douglas G. ... San Francisco, CA
Wahab, Muslim, (P.C.) ... Fresno, CA
Wahab, Robt. S., Jr. ... Virginia Beach, VA
Wahab, William R. ... Virginia Beach, VA
Wahba, Sylvia ... San Francisco, CA
Wahl, Al. ... Bismarck, ND
Wahl, Anthony G. ... Morristown, NJ
Wahl & Ast, P.C. ... Morristown, NJ
Wahl, Avron J. ... Woodbridge, NJ
Wahl, Barbara S. ... Washington, DC
Wahl, Beth Ann ... Berwyn, PA
Wahl, Betsy J. ... Philadelphia, PA
Wahl, Blanche G. ... Baltimore, MD
Wahl, Bradley E. ... Atlanta, GA
Wahl, Cheryl Forino ... Louisville, KY
Wahl, David C. ... Alton, IL
Wahl, Douglas G. ... Detroit, MI
Wahl, Edward T. ... Minneapolis, MN
Wahl, Elmer B., Jr. ... Muskegon, MI
Wahl, Eric J. ... Eau Claire, WI
Wahl, Eugene A., Jr. ... Fort Smith, AR
Wahl, Gerald F. ... Ontario, NY
Wahl, James A. ... Minneapolis, MN
Wahl, James D. ... St. Louis, MO
Wahl, Janice Krempin
Bloomfield Hills, MI
Wahl, Jeffrey J. ... Tigard, OR
Wahl, JoAnn Meo ... Buffalo, NY
Wahl, John E. ... Palm Springs, CA
Wahl, John R. ... Denver, CO
Wahl, Julia L. ... Treasury Department, Internal Revenue Service, GV
Wahl, Karla Rae ... Minneapolis, MN
Wahl, Karla Rae, P.A. ... Minneapolis, MN
Wahl, Leland A. ... Los Angeles, CA
Wahl, Marvin C. ... Baltimore, MD

Wahl, Mary Carroll ... Minneapolis, MN
Wahl, Michael R. ... Mount Vernon, WA
Wahl, Nicholas P. ... Milwaukee, WI
Wahl, Phillip R. ... Houston, TX
Wahl, Richard W. ... Concordia, KS
Wahl, Robert J. ... St. Petersburg, FL
Tampa, FL
Wahl, Robert W. ... Bellevue, WA
Wahl, Rosalie E. ... St. Paul, MN
Wahl, Stephen F. ... Syosset, NY
Wahl, Timothy S. ... Irvine, CA
Wahl, Travis J. ... Columbus, OH
Wahl, Victor J., II ... Sunnyvale, CA
Wahl, William C., Jr. ... Sun City, AZ
Wahlberg, D. Karl ... Marysville, CA
Wahlberg, P. David ... Austin, TX
Wahlberg, Paul Joseph ... Boston, MA
Wahlberg, Stephen W. ... Denver, CO
Wahlberg, Wendy ... Albany, NY
Wahlbrink, J. Kurtis ... St. Louis, MO
Wahlder, Thomas B. ... Alexandria, LA
Wahle, Ingrid E. ... Englewood Cliffs, NJ
Wahle, Karen Mary ... Washington, DC
Wahlen, Bruce R. ... Troy, MI
Wahlen, Edwin A. ... Chicago, IL
Wahlen, J. Jeffry ... Tallahassee, FL
Wahler, Pecyna & Fleming ... Chicago, IL
Wahlers, John L. ... Chicago, IL
Wahlers, Kristopher ... Cleveland, OH
Wahlfors, James L. ... Burnsville, MN
Wahlgren, Sharna A. ... Minneapolis, MN
Wahlheim, Cary Tynes ... Birmingham, AL
Wahlheim, William B., Jr.
Birmingham, AL
Wahlig, Michael J. ... Minneapolis, MN
Wahlin, John D., (P.C.) ... Riverside, CA
Wahlin, Timothy J. ... Mandan, ND
Wahlquist, Charles R. ... Starbuck, MN
Wahlquist, David M. ... Salt Lake City, UT
Wahlquist, Duke ... Costa Mesa, CA
Wahlquist, Erik K. ... Wenatchee, WA
Wahlquist, Jack R. ... Dallas, TX
Wahls, Myron H. ... Detroit, MI
Wahlstedt, Arthur C., Jr.
Newport Beach, CA
Wahlster, Michael A. ... Cleveland, OH
Wahlstrand, M. A. ... Willmar, MN
Wahlstrom, Leslie A. ... Bellevue, WA
Wahlstrom, Marlene F. ... Wausau, WI
Wahlstrom, Nelsen R. ... De Pere, WI
Wahl-Taylor, Kimberly ... Council Bluffs, IA
Wahnon, Janice I. ... Chicago, IL
Wahnsiedler, Kenneth M. ... Indianapolis, IN
Wahoff, William J. ... Columbus, OH
Wahoske, Michael J. ... Minneapolis, MN
Wahowiak, Marlene Mary
Department of Justice, Office of Professional Responsibility, GV
Wahr, David J. ... Woburn, MA
Wahrenberger, Gail N. ... Seattle, WA
Wahrenberger, Judith A. ... Roseland, NJ
Wahrenbrock, Howard E. ... McLean, VA
Wahrenbrock, Scott A. ... Green Bay, WI
Wahrhaftig, Jack ... Oakland, CA
Wahrhaftig, Marc ... Oakland, CA
Wahrlich, Fred ... Houston, TX
Wahrman, C. J., III ... Boca Raton, FL
Wahrman, Harvey L. ... New York, NY
Wahrman, Miriam L. ... Purchase, NY
Wahtola, Charles Henry, III ... Chicago, IL
Wai, Bonnie Y. ... Los Angeles, CA
Wai, Louis K. ... Honolulu, HI
Wai, Minh C. ... Milwaukee, WI
Waian, James G. ... San Diego, CA
Waibel, Kirk C. ... Traverse City, MI
Waible, William ... Amherst, NY
Waichman, Herbert L. ... Great Neck, NY
New York, NY
Waicukauski, Ronald J. ... Indianapolis, IN
Waid, A. Clark, III ... Schaumburg, IL
Waid, Barry K. ... Lincoln, NE
Waid, Brian J. ... Buras, LA
Waid, Elizabeth O. ... Columbus, OH
Waid, Gerald L. ... Washington, DC
Waid, Jas B. ... Gadsden, AL
Waid, John L. ... Sacramento, CA
Waid, Phillip A. ... Dublin, OH
Waid, Richard Scott ... Sarasota, FL
Waid, Victor, Law Office of
Sacramento, CA
Waid, Walter J. ... Gadsden, AL
Waide, James D., III ... Tupelo, MS
Waide Law Office ... Tupelo, MS
Waidner, Stephanie J. ... Jacksonville, FL
Waier, Randall S. ... Newport Beach, CA
Waier & Urtnowski ... Newport Beach, CA
Waihee, John D., III ... Honolulu, HI
Waikart, Douglas O. ... Washington, DC
Wailand, Adele R. ... New York, NY
Wailand, George ... New York, NY
Wailes, C. Carter ... Richmond, VA
Wailes, W. George ... Burlingame, CA
San Francisco, CA
Wailgum, Andrew G. ... Hartford, CT
Waimey, Stephen T. ... Costa Mesa, CA
Waimon, David A. ... Chicago, IL
Wain, Alan P. ... Hackensack, NJ
Wain, Douglas C., Jr. ... Freehold, NJ
Wain, Lita ... Potomac, MD
Wain, Royce L. ... New York, NY
Wainblat, Larry R. ... Palo Alto, CA
Wainblat, Neal B. ... Cleveland, OH
Wainczak, Stacy D. ... Short Hills, NJ
Waine, Robert J. ... Pittsburgh, PA
Wainer, David S., III ... Jacksonville, FL
Wainer, Jonathan J. ... Boston, MA
Wainer, Larry A. ... Houston, TX
Wainer, Robert J. ... Woodbury, NY

Wainer, Stephen P. ... Bakersfield, CA
Wainess, Robert L. ... San Francisco, CA
Wainess, Steven R. ... Los Angeles, CA
Wainey, Deborah A. ... Cleveland, OH
Wainfeld, Gabriel H. ... Los Angeles, CA
Wainger, Mark A. ... New York, NY
Wainger, Robert A. ... Miami, FL
Wainger, Shepherd D. ... Norfolk, VA
Wainger, Stephen ... Virginia Beach, VA
Wainio, John C. ... Durham, NC
Wainman, Garth M. ... Falls Church, VA
Wainman, R. Michael ... Los Angeles, CA
Wainman, Teresa M. ... Santa Monica, CA
Wainrib, Diana L. ... Stoughton, MA
Wainrib, Ronald E. ... Franklin, MA
Wainright, R. Gary ... Saint Simons Island, GA
Wainscott, Edwin Baird ... Phoenix, AZ
Wainscott, Timothy H. ... Covington, KY
Wainstein, Arnold L. ... Philadelphia, PA
Wainstein, Kenneth L. ... Washington, DC
Wainstein, Richard ... Philadelphia, PA
Wainstein, Robert E. ... Greenfield, MA
Waintroob, Andrea R. ... Chicago, IL
Wainwright, Allan L. ... Albuquerque, NM
Las Cruces, NM
Wainwright, Allan L., P.A., Law Offices of
Albuquerque, NM
Las Cruces, NM
Wainwright, Andrew S. ... Boston, MA
Wainwright, C. Brian ... Palo Alto, CA
Wainwright, Carroll L., Jr.
New York, NY
Wainwright, Daniel L. ... Fresno, CA
Wainwright, Dianne S. ... Pittsburgh, PA
Wainwright, Duncan J.
Department of Justice, Federal Bureau of Investigation, GV
Wainwright, George L., Jr. ... Beaufort, NC
Wainwright, J. Dale ... Houston, TX
Wainwright, J. Kenneth, Jr. ... Troy, MI
Wainwright, James A. ... Dinuba, CA
Visalia, CA
Wainwright, Jonathan M. ... New York, NY
Wainwright, Lonnie D., Jr.
Birmingham, AL
Wainwright, Mark E. ... Salt Lake City, UT
Wainwright, Michael H. ... Shreveport, LA
Wainwright, Ona G. ... Brockton, MA
Wainwright, Paul S. ... Albuquerque, NM
Wainwright, Paul S., P.A. ... Albuquerque, NM
Wainwright & Pope, P.C.
Birmingham, AL
Wainwright, Richard L. ... Brockton, MA
Wainwright, Ronnie A.
United States Postal Service, Postal Inspection Service, GV
Wainwright, Stephen Reed ... Brockton, MA
Wainwright, Stuyvesant, II ... Wainscott, NY
Wainwright, Stuyvesant, IV
East Hampton, NY
Wainwright and Wainwright
Brockton, MA
Wainwright Wainwright Wainwright
Brockton, MA
Wainwright, William M. ... Brockton, MA
Wais, Gary A. ... Baltimore, MD
Wais, Michael F. ... Detroit, MI
Waisblum, Phillip L. ... Cincinnati, OH
Waisbren, Avery S. ... Los Angeles, CA
Waisbren, Benjamin ... Chicago, IL
Waisbren, Suzanne D. ... Winnetka, CA
Waisbrot, Morris ... New York, NY
Waisel, Donald R. ... Harrisburg, PA
Waisman, Andrea E. ... New York, NY
Waisman, Shai Y. ... New York, NY
Waisman, Sonia S. ... San Diego, CA
Waissar, M. Linda ... Palo Alto, CA
Wait, Christopher D. ... Rochester, NY
Wait, Coleman F. "Jeb" ... Houston, TX
Wait, Conant ... Topeka, KS
Wait, David A. ... Ballston Spa, NY
Wait, Eugene J., Jr. ... Reno, NV
Wait, Jeffrey D. ... Albany, NY
Wait, John A. ... Philadelphia, PA
Wait, Judith Best ... Wayne, PA
Wait, Patrick D. ... Milwaukee, WI
Wait, Richard P. ... Reno, NV
Wait & Shaffer, A Professional Corporation
Las Vegas, NV
Reno, NV
Wait, Thomas B. ... Claremont, CA
Wait, William B. ... Los Altos, CA
Waite, Ann Elizabeth
Huntington Woods, MI
Waite, Barbara L. ... Washington, DC
Waite, Blakeley R. ... Jacksonville, FL
Waite, Brent A. ... Gunnison, CO
Waite, C. Barry ... Holyoke, MA
Waite, C. Jeffrey ... Cincinnati, OH
Waite, Carla P. ... Philadelphia, PA
Waite, Carol ... Oakton, VA
Waite, Charles E. ... Jacksonville, FL
Waite, Cheryl Lynne ... Youngstown, OH
Waite, Clyde W. ... Newtown, PA
Waite, D. Lanny ... Las Vegas, NV
Waite, Dan R. ... Las Vegas, NV
Waite, Daren B. ... Philadelphia, PA
Waite, David M. ... Craig, CO
Waite, David P., (P.C.) ... Los Angeles, CA
Waite, Edward J., III ... Parsippany, NJ
Waite, Frederick P. ... Washington, DC
Waite, G. Graham ... Washington, DC
Waite, Gary L. ... Paris, TX
Waite, Gerald D. ... Las Vegas, NV
Waite, James R. ... Denver, CO
Waite, Jason M. ... Atlanta, GA
Waite, Jocelyn K. ... Columbia, MD
Waite, Joel A. ... Wilmington, DE

Waite, Kenneth J. ... Indianapolis, IN
Waite, Kevin J. ... Coeur d'Alene, ID
Waite, Kevin J., P.C. ... Coeur d'Alene, ID
Waite, Kevin W. ... New York, NY
Waite, Kirk C. ... Brentwood, TN
Waite, Leslie S., III ... Great Falls, MT
Waite, Linda M. ... Richland, WA
Waite, Loren H., Jr. ... Mound City, IL
Waite, Mark A. ... Houston, TX
Waite, Mark E. ... San Jose, CA
Waite, Mary Beth A. ... Boston, MA
Waite, Michael J. ... Leavenworth, KS
Waite, Norman ... Chicago, IL
Waite, Norman, Jr. ... Chicago, IL
Waite, P. Dean, Jr. ... Mobile, AL
Waite, Pamela Willis ... Augusta, ME
Waite, Peter S. ... San Jose, CA
Waite, Richard R. ... San Diego, CA
Waite, Richard W. ... Flagstaff, AZ
Waite, Sarita C. ... Berkeley, CA
Waite, Schneider, Bayless & Chesley Co., L.P.A. ... Lawrenceburg, IN
Covington, KY
Florence, KY
Newport, KY
Batavia, OH
Cincinnati, OH
Dayton, OH
Hamilton, OH
Lebanon, OH
Middletown, OH
Waite, Snapp & Doll ... Dodge City, KS
Waite, Stephen H. ... Rochester, NY
Waite, Stephen J. ... Albany, NY
Waite, Stephen K. ... New York, NY
Waite, Stuart M. ... Binghamton, NY
Waite, Terrance O. ... North Platte, NE
Waite, Thomas A. ... Seattle, WA
Waite, Virginia Fournier ... San Francisco, CA
Waite, Wayne E. ... Dayton, OH
Waite, William L., III ... Provo, UT
Waiter, Brenda A. ... Philadelphia, PA
Waiter, Joseph J. ... Greenwich, CT
Waites, Brad ... Dallas, TX
Waites, C. Patrick ... Houston, TX
Waites, Gerard M. ... Washington, DC
Waites, John E. ... Columbia, SC
Waites, Michelle ... New York, NY
Waites, Richard C. ... Houston, TX
Waites, S. Judson, II ... Norcross, GA
Waites, Wesley W., Jr. ... West Columbia, SC
Waitkus, Edward S., Jr. ... Boulder, CO
Waitman, Adam G. ... New York, NY
Waitman, Barbara E.
West Palm Beach, FL
Waitman, Gregory K. ... San Bernardino, CA
Waitman, James H. ... Owensboro, KY
Waitman, Jennifer R. ... New York, NY
Waitman, Lemuel R. ... Lewisport, KY
Waitrovich, Mary E. ... Madison, WI
Waits, Anthony Allen ... Louisville, KY
Waits, Bruce E. ... Bartlesville, OK
Waits, Burl W. ... Sacramento, CA
Waits, Dennis R. ... Independence, MO
Waits, Douglas L. ... Houston, TX
Waits, J. Kirk ... Tulsa, OK
Waits, James A. ... Kansas City, MO
Waits, John A. ... Jackson, MS
Waits, John A., II ... Washington, DC
Waits, Kathleen ... Albany, NY
Waits, Lisa M. ... Ann Arbor, MI
Waits, Myron B. ... Talladega, AL
Waits, Randolph J. ... New Orleans, LA
Waits, Sam ... Grenada, MS
Waits, Va Lita F. ... Houston, TX
Waitsman, Frederick R. ... Atlanta, GA
Waitsman, Mindy C. ... Atlanta, GA
Waitt, Robert K. ... Issaquah, WA
Waitt, Sara Shiplett ... Austin, TX
Waitt, Stephen P. ... Tucson, AZ
Waitz & Downer, P.C. ... Houma, LA
Waitz, Joseph L., Jr. ... Houma, LA
Waitz, Joseph L., (P.C.) ... Houma, LA
Waitz, Stephanie B. ... Middlebury, VT
Waitzer, Edwin S. ... Norfolk, VA
Waitzkin, Michael B. ... Washington, DC
Waitzman, Gary R. ... Buffalo Grove, IL
Waitzman, Jay L. ... New York, NY
Waitzman, Martin J. ... Wauconda, IL
Waitzman, Martin J., Law Offices of, P.C.
Wauconda, IL
Waitz-Moskowitz, Rachelle A.
Cherry Hill, NJ
Waizer, David M. ... Morristown, NJ
Waizer, Harry ... New York, NY
Wajert, Sean P. ... Philadelphia, PA
Wakatsuki, Jill K. ... Honolulu, HI
Wakayama, Gloria Lung
Port Townsend, WA
Seattle, WA
Wake, A. Norrie ... Monticello, KY
Wake, Charles K., Law Offices of
Beverly Hills, CA
Wake, Charles K., Law Offices of
Los Angeles, CA
Wake, Daniel F. ... Denver, CO
Wake, James S. ... Seward, NE
Wake, Kenneth R. ... Chicago, IL
Normal, IL
Wake, Neil Vincent, Law Offices of
Phoenix, AZ
Wake, Paul David ... Provo, UT
Wake, Robert Alan ... Augusta, ME
Wake, See, Dimes & Bryniczka
Bridgeport, CT
Darien, CT
Fairfield, CT
New Canaan, CT
Norwalk, CT
Stamford, CT
Westport, CT
Wakeen, Emil A. ... Wausau, WI
Wakeen, Linda M. ... Chicago, IL
Wakefield Browning & McCobb, A Professional Corporation ... Portland, OR
Wakefield, Charles P. ... Houston, TX
Wakefield, Charles S., Jr. ... Leesburg, VA
Wakefield, Elizabeth Petersen
Vermilion, OH
Wakefield, Frank H., II ... Franklin, KY
Wakefield, George H., Jr. ... Montgomery, AL
Wakefield, Jacqueline ... Twin Falls, ID
Wakefield, James H. ... Fort Lauderdale, FL
Wakefield, James H., & Associates, P.A.
Fort Lauderdale, FL
Wakefield, James M. ... Los Angeles, CA
Wakefield, James R. ... Newport Beach, CA
Wakefield, Jedediah ... Palo Alto, CA
Wakefield, Jeffrey M. ... Charleston, WV
Wakefield, Joel ... Seattle, WA
Wakefield, Kay B. ... Portland, OR
Wakefield, Kim S. ... Seattle, WA
Wakefield, Laura A. ... Millersburg, OH
Wakefield, Margie ... Lawrence, KS
Wakefield, Mark L. ... Cleveland, OH
Wakefield, Matthew T.
Universal City, CA
Wakefield, Pamela Gorden ... Englewood, CO
Wakefield, Paul G. ... Detroit, MI
Wakefield, Philip St. John ... Seattle, WA
Wakefield, Randy ... Carthage, TN
Wakefield, Robert N. ... Houston, TX
Wakefield, Robert T. ... Metairie, LA
Wakefield, Robert W. ... Wilmington, DE
Wakefield, S. Craig ... Kissimmee, FL
Wakefield, S. Craig, Professional Association
Kissimmee, FL
Wakefield, Scott Channing ... Seattle, WA
Wakefield, Scott D. ... Salt Lake City, UT
Wakefield, Scott S. ... Phoenix, AZ
Wakefield, Stephan ... Seattle, WA
Wakefield, Stephen A. ... Atlanta, GA
Wakefield, Stephen D. ... Memphis, TN
Wakefield, Stephen N. ... Dallas, TX
Wakefield, Thomas H. ... Key Biscayne, FL
Miami, FL
Wakefield, Tommie W. ... Wichita, KS
Wakeland, John T. ... Greenwood, MS
Wakelee, George N. ... Newtown, CT
Wakelee & Isaac ... Newtown, CT
Wakeley, Ellen ... San Leandro, CA
Wakeley, Joan M. ... San Jose, CA
Wakelin, David S. ... Portland, ME
Wakelin, Hallock & O'Donovan, LLP
Portland, ME
Wakely, David N. ... Clearwater, FL
Wakely, Nancy K. ... Oklahoma City, OK
Wakely, Thomas M. ... Oklahoma City, OK
Wakelyn, Catherine Carl
Washington, DC
Wakeman, April A. ... Tulsa, OK
Wakeman, Charles H., Jr. ... Tavernier, FL
Wakeman, Elizabeth Felt ... Woodstock, IL
Wakeman, Ellen Good ... Golden, CO
Wakeman, George E., Jr. ... Boston, MA
Wakeman, J. Peter ... Westlake Village, CA
Wakeman, Marjorie Olencki
Woodbridge, CT
Wakeman, Mary Lalley ... Tallahassee, FL
Wakeman, Robert G. ... Albany, NY
Wakeman, Scott T. ... Arlington, VA
Wakeman, Shelly R. ... Kansas City, MO
Wakeman, Sherwood G. ... Oakland, CA
Wakeman, Steven A. ... Peoria, IL
Wakeman, Thomas O. ... Lake Mills, WI
Wakenight, Mark T. ... Oak Park, IL
Wakerley, J. Charles ... Philadelphia, PA
Wakham, Elvin James ... Spring Valley, CA
Wakhariya, Shabbir S. ... New York, NY
Waki, Fred I. ... Honolulu, HI
Wakida, Lisa K. ... Chicago, IL
Wakild, Chris C. ... Prospect, KY
Wakim, James E. ... West Hartford, CT
Wakim, Kimberly Luff ... Pittsburgh, PA
Wakimura, Mary Lou ... Lexington, MA
Wakin, Alysa Beth ... Washington, DC
Wakino, Brett P. ... Alhambra, CA
Wakino, Michelle A. ... Irvine, CA
Wakiyama, Peter T. ... Philadelphia, PA
Waknine, Elissa K. ... Union, NJ
Waks, Amy M. ... Decatur, IL
Waks, Andrew "Andy" L. ... Melbourne, FL
Waks, David A. ... Paterson, NJ
Waks, Dennis S. ... Sacramento, CA
Waks, Jay W. ... New York, NY
Waks, Joan G. ... Totowa, NJ
Waks Law Corporation ... Sacramento, CA
Waks, Lawrence A. ... Austin, TX
Waks, Michael D. ... Carson, CA
Waks & Pollard, A Professional Corporation
Totowa, NJ
Waks, Randall D. ... Clinton, IL
Waks, Stephen H. ... Sacramento, CA
Waksbaum, Sherry ... New York, NY
Wakschlag, Milton S. ... Chicago, IL
Wakser, Barry T. ... Canton, OH
Wakshlag, Stanley H. ... Miami, FL
Wakshull, Robin B. ... San Jose, CA
Wakslak, Avigail ... New York, NY
Waksler, Craig R. ... Boston, MA
Waksler, Geri L. ... Punta Gorda, FL
Waksman, David ... Princeton, NJ
Waksman, David M. ... Miami, FL
Waksman, Jeffrey S. ... Philadelphia, PA
Waksman, Ted S. ... New York, NY
Wakuzawa, Bruce H. ... Honolulu, HI
Wal, Stanley A. ... Arlington, VA
Wala, Laurel I. ... Scottsdale, AZ
Walanka, Daniel M. ... Los Angeles, CA
Walasinski, Kevin J. ... Milan, MI
Walaski, Joni L. ... New York, NY
Walaszek, Roger A. ... Northampton, MA
Walawender, Norman F. ... Buffalo, NY
Walawender, Richard A. ... Detroit, MI
Walbaum, Gerard E. ... Bakersfield, CA
Walbaum, Robert C. ... Springfield, IL
Walber, John W. ... New York, NY
Walberg, Catherine M. ... Topeka, KS
Kansas City, MO
Walberg, Dagner & Tucker, P.C.
Englewood, CO
Walberg, John E. ... Denver, CO
Walberg, Kurt E. ... Littleton, CO
Walberg, Leonard D. ... South Holland, IL
Walberg, Loretta J. ... Grand Forks, ND
Walberg, Robert F. ... Coquille, OR
Walberg, Teresa J.
Department of Commerce, Patent and Trademark Office, GV
Walberg, Wendelyn K. ... Englewood, CO
Walbert, David F. ... Atlanta, GA
Walbert, Thomas D.
Hot Springs National Park, AR
Walbolt, Daniel R. ... Tampa, FL
Walbolt, Sylvia H. ... St. Petersburg, FL
Walborsky, Edwin ... Pensacola, FL
Walborsky, Paula L. ... Tallahassee, FL
Walbourn, Edwin J., III ... Covington, KY
Walbran, Furness & Leuning, Chartered
Owatonna, MN
Walbran, John W. ... St. Louis, MO
Walbran, Joseph T. ... Minneapolis, MN
Walbran, Mark Moonan ... Owatonna, MN
Walbridge, Donald J. ... Battle Creek, MI
Walbridge, Jeffrey W.
Newport Beach, CA
Walbridge, LeRoy T. ... Saratoga Springs, NY
Walbroel, Julie E. ... Orlando, FL
Walbrun, William R. ... Milwaukee, WI
Walburn, Allen B. ... San Diego, CA
Walburn, Roberta B. ... Minneapolis, MN
Walburn, Steven E. ... Church Hill, TN
Walcek, Stanley J. ... Bethany Beach, DE
Walcer, John ... Massapequa, NY
Walch, Andrew F. ... Denver, CO
Walch, Gary K. ... Calabasas, CA
Walch, Gary K., A Law Corp.
Calabasas, CA
Walch, Gregory J. ... Las Vegas, NV
Walch, John Douglas ... Portland, OR
Walch, Mary J. ... Columbia, MD
Walch, Matthew W. ... Chicago, IL
Walch, Richard ... Los Angeles, CA
Walch, Spencer D. ... Pasadena, CA
Walch, Thomas M. ... Fredericksburg, TX
Walch, Victor L. ... Burbank, CA
Walch, W. Stanley ... St. Louis, MO
Walcher, Alan E. ... Los Angeles, CA
Walchirk, Victor L. ... Chicago, IL
Walck, Richard E. ... Williamsburg, VA
Walcoff, Andrew H. ... Atlanta, GA
Walcoff, Victor ... Trenton, NJ
Walcott, Christopher ... New York, NY
Walcott, Claudette ... Brooklyn, NY
Walcott, Donald A. ... Santa Fe, NM
Walcott, Gina Y. ... Boston, MA
Walcott, H. Sage ... Gloucester, MA
Walcott, Justin H. ... Los Angeles, CA
Walcott, Melody Moss
Christiansted, St. Croix, VI
Walcott, Peter W. ... Bedford, MA
Walcott, Terry M. ... Minneapolis, MN
Walcott, Thomas A. ... Tempe, AZ
Walcott, Thomas R. ... Hazel Park, MI
Walcott, Wanji ... New York, NY
Walczak, Alexander M. ... Topeka, KS
Walczak, David ... Chicopee, MA
Walczak, Gerard T. ... Oshkosh, WI
Walczak, James R. ... Erie, PA
Walczak, Joseph J. ... Orland Park, IL
Walczak, Lisa A. ... Worthington, OH
Walczak, Stephen E. ... Wisconsin Rapids, WI
Walczak, Witold Jan ... Pittsburgh, PA
Walczyk, Christine M. ... Raleigh, NC
Walczyk, Leonard C. ... Millburn, NJ
Wald, Alexandra ... New York, NY
Wald & Associates, P.C. ... Plano, TX
Richardson, TX
Wald, B. Craig ... Glen Burnie, MD
Wald, Barbara Anderson ... Chicago, IL
Wald & Bendes ... Oakland, CA
Wald, Bernard A. ... Annapolis, MD
Wald, Bernard J. ... New York, NY
Wald, Bernard P. ... New York, NY
Wald, Bruce L. ... Chicago, IL
Wald, Carl J. ... Jupiter, FL
Wald, David E. ... Irvine, CA
Wald, David S. ... Chicago, IL
Wald & Del Vento ... West Orange, NJ
Wald, Dennis E. ... Miami, FL
Wald, Donnita A. ... Bismarck, ND
Wald, Douglas L. ... Washington, DC
Wald, Eileen M. ... St. Louis, MO
Wald, Elliot ... Cliffwood, NJ
Wald, Emil W. ... Rock Hill, SC
Wald, Gerald B. ... Miami, FL
Wald, Ginger E. ... Fort Lauderdale, FL
Baton Rouge, LA
Wald, Gregory A. ... Miami, FL
Wald, Gregory J. ... St. Paul, MN
Wald, James F. ... Seattle, WA
Wald, Jane Shay ... Los Angeles, CA
Wald, Jennifer F. ... Palo Alto, CA
Wald, Jenny ... San Francisco, CA
Wald, Jerome S. ... Chicago, IL
Wald, Jerry ... Fairfield, CT
Wald, Johanna H. ... San Francisco, CA
Wald, John R. ... Eden Prairie, MN
Wald, Jonathan D. ... Miami, FL
Wald, Jonathan D.
Palm Beach Gardens, FL
Wald, Julia P. ... Larkspur, CA
San Francisco, CA
Wald, Kathryn S. ... Dayton, OH
Wald & Kramer, LLP ... Larkspur, CA
San Francisco, CA
San Rafael, CA
Wald, Martin ... Philadelphia, PA
Wald, Matthew J. ... Miles City, MT
Wald, Mellor & Gregory ... Irvine, CA
Wald, Michael E. ... Oakland, CA
Wald, Michael H. ... Richardson, TX
Wald, Michael J. ... New York, NY
Wald, Mitchel A. ... Alexandria, VA
Wald, Mortimer ... West Orange, NJ
Wald, Nathan ... Randolph, MA
Wald, Patricia M.
United States Court Of Appeals District Of Columbia Circuit, GV
Wald, Peter A. ... San Francisco, CA
Wald, Phyllis Zelermyer ... Boston, MA
Wald, Ralph Lewis ... Brandon, FL
Wald, Robert L. ... Washington, DC
Wald, Russell L. ... San Francisco, CA
Wald, Sarah E. ... Cambridge, MA
Wald, Shelly A. ... Boca Raton, FL
Fort Lauderdale, FL
Wald, Sherri Sundem ... Pierre, SD
Wald, Stephanie ... San Francisco, CA
Wald, Stephen ... Boston, MA
Wald, Steven M. ... St. Louis, MO
Wald, Stuart J. ... Los Angeles, CA
Wald, Valerie J. ... New York, NY
Wald & Wald ... New York, NY
Wald, Wayne A. ... New York, NY
Wald, William G. ... Indianapolis, IN
Walda, John D. ... Fort Wayne, IN
Waldau, Marsha E. ... San Diego, CA
Waldau, Paul Francis ... Anaheim, CA
Waldau, William G. ... Darien, CT
Waldauer, Marc ... Syracuse, NY
Waldbaum, Corn, Koff and Berger, P.C.
Denver, CO
Waldbaum, Leonard N. ... Denver, CO
Waldbaum, Maxim H. ... New York, NY
Waldbaum, Rodney J. ... Seattle, WA
Waldbaum, Scott Ian ... New York, NY
Waldbaum, Shari R.
Department of Labor, GV
Waldbaum, Stanley L. ... Spring Valley, NY
Waldbillig, Deborah A. ... Boca Raton, FL
Waldbillig, Gainer M. ... Salt Lake City, UT
Waldburger, Elisabeth G. ... New York, NY
Waldburger, Frank J. ... Plattsburgh, NY
Waldeck, Cecelia M.
Federal Trade Commission, Bureau of Competition, GV
Waldeck, John H. ... Ann Arbor, MI
Waldeck, John J. ... Canton, OH
Waldeck, John M. ... Kansas City, MO
Waldeck, John W., Jr. ... Cleveland, OH
Waldeck & Lind, P.A. ... Minneapolis, MN
Waldeck, Michael E. ... Kansas City, MO
Waldeck, Patricia S. ... Los Angeles, CA
Las Vegas, NV
Waldeck, Timothy W. ... Minneapolis, MN
Waldeck, William G.
Grand Junction, CO
Waldecker, Charles J. ... Broomall, PA
Waldemer, Dean P. ... Clayton, MO
Walden, C. Curtis ... Cincinnati, OH
Walden, Charles A. ... Forest Park, GA
Walden, Clarence ... Woodland, CA
Walden, Clarke ... Hollywood, FL
Walden, Cole, Ohlsen & Coryell ... Decatur, IL
Walden, Daniel C. ... Montvale, NJ
Walden, Daniel S. ... Winston-Salem, NC
Walden, David L. ... Atlanta, GA
Walden, David V. ... Chicago, IL
Walden, Ennis E. ... Dallas, TX
Walden, Franklin T. ... Altamonte Springs, FL
Walden, Gatewood A. ... Montgomery, AL
Walden, Gregory S. ... Washington, DC
Walden, Harold E. ... Alabaster, AL
Walden, James R., Jr. ... Waukesha, WI
Walden, James T. ... New Hope, MN
Walden, Janet C. ... New York, NY
Walden, Janice Stanley ... Nashville, TN
Walden, Jay D. ... Grayville, IL
Walden, John C. ... Atlanta, GA
Walden, Joseph E. ... Alabaster, AL
Walden, Judith G. ... Frankfort, KY
Walden, Keith E. ... Tustin, CA
Walden, Kenneth E. ... McLean, VA
Walden, Kennon C., Jr. ... Blackstone, VA
Walden, Kevin L. ... Carrollton, MO
Walden, Kimberly A. ... Issaquah, WA
Walden Law Firm, The, LLC
Atlanta, GA
Walden, Lawrence C. ... Portland, ME
Walden, Leslie A. ... Santa Monica, CA
Walden, Lisa ... Seattle, WA
Walden, Margaret D. ... Winston-Salem, NC
Walden, Marvin R., Jr. ... West New York, NJ
Walden, Philip C. ... San Diego, CA
Walden, Raymond E. ... Omaha, NE
Walden, Rebecca A. ... San Francisco, CA
Walden, Richard E. ... Los Angeles, CA
Walden, Richard M. ... Los Angeles, CA
Walden, Richard W. ... Okmulgee, OK
Walden, Ron William ... New York, NY
Walden, Ruth ... New York, NY

Walden, Samuel C. ....New York, NY
Walden, Scott H. ....Quincy, IL
Walden, Susan ....West New York, NJ
Walden, T. Lynn ....Beaumont, TX
Walden & Walden ....Winston-Salem, NC
Walden & Walden, P.C. ....Blackstone, VA
Walden, Windley Hofler ....Norfolk, VA
Waldenberg, Alan S. ....New York, NY
Walder, David Gordon ....Boulder, CO
Walder, Jeannette M. ....Chicago, IL
Walder, Jeffrey A. ....Roseland, NJ
Walder, Justin P. ....Roseland, NJ
Walder, Lewis A. ....Langhorne, PA
Walder, Loretta ....Rocky Point, NY
Walder, Lynne ....Tampa, FL
Walder, Noeleen G. ....New York, NY
Walder, Robert A. ....New York, NY
Walder, S. Robert ....Vista, CA
Walder, Sondak & Brogan, A Professional Corporation ....Elizabeth, NJ
Morristown, NJ
Newark, NJ
Paterson, NJ
Roseland, NJ
Walder, Stephen J., Jr. ....Dallas, TX
Walder & Zaslow, P.C. ....Langhorne, PA
Waldera, Christopher B.
Fort Lauderdale, FL
Walderman, Howard ....Rockville, MD
Walderman, Richard A. ....New York, NY
Walderman, William J. ....Washington, DC
Walders, Lawrence R. ....Washington, DC
Walderzak, Cathy L. ....Lansing, MI
Waldfogel, David H. ....Holyoke, MA
Waldhauser, James R. ....Minneapolis, MN
Waldheger • Coyne, A Legal Professional Association ....Cleveland, OH
Waldheger, Martha J. ....Greenwich, CT
Waldheger, Ronald J. ....Cleveland, OH
Waldherr, Anna ....Norristown, PA
Waldherr, David P. ....Des Plaines, IL
Waldhof, Sharka Eva ....Uniondale, NY
Waldhorn, Morris ....Yonkers, NY
Waldie, Kandy F. ....Woodland Hills, CA
Waldie, Ronald R. ....Seven Points, TX
Waldier, Lowell J. ....Sutherlin, OR
Waldier, Sandra L. ....Chicago, IL
Waldin, Earl D., Jr. ....Miami, FL
Walding, Andrew L. ....Oklahoma City, OK
Walding, Jack H. ....Dallas, TX
Walding, Kevin ....Dothan, AL
Walding, Lynn M. ....Des Moines, IA
Waldinger, Arthur R., (P.C.) ....Denver, CO
Waldinger, Harlan A. ....Northbrook, IL
Waldinger, Jesse S. ....New York, NY
Waldinger, Kyle F. ....Chicago, IL
Waldinger, Lawrence J. ....Los Angeles, CA
Waldinger, Steven E. ....Mount Kisco, NY
Waldman, Aleida ....Fort Lauderdale, FL
Waldman, Ayelet ....Santa Ana, CA
Waldman, Barry J. ....Fairfax, VA
Waldman, Barry P. ....Detroit, MI
Waldman, Bart ....Seattle, WA
Waldman, Benjamin J. ....Millburn, NJ
Waldman, Beth E. ....Boston, MA
Waldman, Brian P. ....Washington, DC
Waldman, Bruce ....New Castle, PA
Waldman, Bruce J. ....Chicago, IL
Waldman, Bryan J. ....Lansing, MI
Waldman, Carl ....Beaumont, TX
Houston, TX
Nederland, TX
Waldman, Carl R. ....Los Angeles, CA
Westlake Village, CA
Waldman, Carol A. ....Chicago, IL
Waldman, Charles E. ....Memphis, TN
Waldman, Chet B. ....New York, NY
Waldman, Craig A. ....New York, NY
Waldman, Cynthia Sonns ....Fullerton, CA
Waldman, Daniel ....Washington, DC
Waldman, Daniel M. ....Red Bank, NJ
Waldman, David ....Hawthorne, NJ
Waldman, David M. ....New York, NY
Waldman, David S. ....New York, NY
Waldman & Diamond, Chartered
Kensington, MD
Waldman, Donald A. ....Phoenix, AZ
Waldman, Donald A., Professional Corporation
Phoenix, AZ
Waldman, Edward J. ....Merrick, NY
Waldman, Edward M. ....Philadelphia, PA
Waldman, Emily Rebecca ....New York, NY
Waldman Feluren & Trigoboff, P.A.
Fort Lauderdale, FL
Miami, FL
Miami Beach, FL
Waldman, Gary ....Monticello, NY
Waldman, Gary A. ....Los Angeles, CA
Waldman, Gilbert D. ....Tulsa, OK
Waldman, Glen H. ....Miami, FL
Waldman, Glenn J. ....Fort Lauderdale, FL
Miami Beach, FL
Waldman, Hal K. ....Pittsburgh, PA
Waldman, Herbert I. ....Maplewood, NJ
Waldman, Herbert L., Law Offices of
Henderson, NV
Waldman, Ira J. ....Los Angeles, CA
Waldman, Irving J. ....Providence, RI
Waldman, Irwin, (A P.C.)
Los Angeles, CA
Waldman, James W. ....Fort Lauderdale, FL
Waldman, Jay C. ....Philadelphia, PA
Waldman, Jay L. ....Brooklyn, NY
Waldman, Jay W. ....New Castle, DE
Voorhees, NJ
Philadelphia, PA
Wyomissing, PA
Waldman, Jeffrey J. ....Linwood, NJ

Waldman, Jill ....Kansas City, MO
Waldman, Joel A. ....Pittsburgh, PA
Waldman, John J. ....Bloomington, IL
Macomb, IL
Peoria, IL
Quincy, IL
Rushville, IL
Springfield, IL
Waldman, Jonathan M. ....Philadelphia, PA
Waldman, Judith A. ....Staten Island, NY
Waldman, Judith S. ....Gainesville, FL
Waldman, Julie ....Miami, FL
Waldman, Julie B. ....Beverly Hills, CA
Waldman, Keith ....Mount Laurel, NJ
Waldman Law Corporation ....Metairie, LA
Waldman, Lawrence ....Atlantic Beach, NY
Waldman, Lawrence Alan
East St. Louis, IL
Waldman, Leo, (Co., L.P.A.)
Youngstown, OH
Waldman, Lester J. ....New York, NY
Waldman, Lisa A. ....Reading, PA
Waldman, Lois C. ....New York, NY
Waldman, M. Toni ....Washington, DC
Waldman, Marian ....New York, NY
Waldman, Mark ....Beverly Hills, CA
Waldman, Martin G. ....Southfield, MI
Waldman, Marvin M. ....Kensington, MD
Waldman, Melvin ....East Rockaway, NY
Waldman, Merle Y. ....Towson, MD
Waldman, Merle Y., P.A. ....Towson, MD
Waldman, Michael Alan ....Washington, DC
Waldman, Michael J. ....New York, NY
Waldman, Michael L. ....Washington, DC
Waldman, Mitchell ....Atlantic City, NJ
Pleasantville, NJ
Waldman, Moriarty & Halfacre
Red Bank, NJ
Waldman, Murry J. ....San Francisco, CA
Waldman, Nancy S. ....Seattle, WA
Waldman, Nathan J. ....Kingston, NY
Waldman, Paul F. ....Providence, RI
Waldman, Paul H. ....Metairie, LA
Waldman, Paul R. ....New York, NY
Waldman, Randee J. ....New York, NY
Waldman, Renda & McKinney, P.A.
Hawthorne, NJ
Waldman, Robert Allan ....Dallas, TX
Waldman, Robert D. ....Baltimore, MD
Waldman, Robert J. ....Washington, DC
Waldman, Robert L. ....Baltimore, MD
Waldman, Roger L. ....New York, NY
Waldman, Ronald Lee ....New York, NY
Waldman, Sarah A. ....Omaha, NE
Waldman, Scott B. ....New York, NY
Waldman, Scott M. ....Philadelphia, PA
Waldman, Seymour M. ....New York, NY
Waldman & Smallwood, P.C.
Beaumont, TX
Houston, TX
Nederland, TX
Waldman, Stanley L. ....North Charleston, SC
Waldman, Stephen L. ....San Diego, CA
Waldman, Steve ....Beaumont, TX
Houston, TX
Waldman, Susan K. ....Greenbrae, CA
Waldman, Thomas A. ....Los Angeles, CA
Waldman, Thomas A. ....West Paterson, NJ
Waldman, Thomas D. ....Omaha, NE
Waldman, Todd E. ....Department of the Army, Office, Chief of Engineers/Headquarters, U.S. Army Corps of Engineers, GV
Waldman, Vincent M. ....Los Angeles, CA
Waldman, William L. ....Hackensack, NJ
Waldman, William R. ....Los Angeles, CA
Waldmann, Carolyn A. ....Boston, MA
Waldmann, Christine C. ....Washington, DC
Waldmann, Clement J. ....Lake Orion, MI
Waldmann, Daniel R. ....Washington, DC
Waldmann & Harrington ....Gretna, LA
Waldmann, Lester J. ....Gretna, LA
Waldmann, Lester J., A.P.L.C.
Gretna, LA
Waldmann, Paul J. ....Omaha, NE
Waldmeir, Peter W. ....Detroit, MI
Waldner, Cydni Jo ....Boise, ID
Waldner, Jennifer J. ....Los Angeles, CA
Waldner, Louisa B. ....Napa, CA
San Francisco, CA
Waldner, Paul F. ....Houston, TX
Waldo, Ann B. ....Raleigh, NC
Waldo, Burton C. ....Seattle, WA
Waldo, Carolyn S. ....Carrollton, TX
Waldo, David W. ....Columbus, OH
Waldo, Georgia J. ....Newport Beach, CA
Waldo, James C. ....Seattle, WA
Tacoma, WA
Waldo, James M. ....Ironton, OH
Waldo, James R. ....Oklahoma City, OK
Waldo, Jas. E. ....Ironton, OH
Waldo, John F. ....Salt Lake City, UT
Waldo, Joseph T. ....Norfolk, VA
Waldo, Joseph T., P.C., The Law Firm of
Norfolk, VA
Waldo, Kevin J. ....Ironton, OH
Waldo, Kurt R. ....Pittsburgh, PA
Waldo, Laird D. ....Mankato, MN
Waldo & McCormick ....Lee's Summit, MO
Waldo, Myrtice R. ....Gainesville, FL
Waldo, Robert D. ....Spokane, WA
Waldo, Robert K. ....Lee's Summit, MO
Waldo, Robert L. ....Madison, WI
Waldo, Robert M. ....Greeley, CO
Waldo, Robert R. ....Barnstable, MA
Waldo, Robert S. ....Camarillo, CA
Waldo & Schweda, P.C. ....Spokane, WA
Waldo, Thomas S. ....Juneau, AK
Waldo & Waldo ....Greeley, CO

Waldo, William Stewart ....Los Angeles, CA
Waldoch, Lauchlin T. ....Tallahassee, FL
Waldoch, Laurence R. ....Minneapolis, MN
Waldock, Frederick D. ....Sandusky, OH
Waldock, Thomas J. ....Anchorage, AK
Waldoks, Phillip H. ....New York, NY
Waldon, Alton R., Jr. ....Woodmere, NY
Waldon, Dennis C. ....Chicago, IL
Waldon, Grover H. ....Bakersfield, CA
Waldon, James M ....St. Louis, MO
Waldon, R. Forrest ....Wilmington, NC
Waldon, Russell D. ....Atlanta, GA
Waldor, Cathy L. ....West Orange, NJ
Waldorf, Angela S. ....Raleigh, NC
Waldorf, Barry C. ....New York, NY
Waldorf, Douglas L. ....Fort Myers, FL
Waldorf, Douglas L., Jr. ....Fort Myers, FL
Waldorf, Ellen R. ....Washington, DC
Waldorf, Geraldine P. ....Nanuet, NY
Waldorf, James J., (P.C.) ....Glendale, CA
Waldorf, Joseph F. ....Allendale, NJ
Waldorf, Lars ....Department of Justice, Civil Rights Division, GV
Waldorf, Michael ....New York, NY
Waldorf, Michael E. ....Los Angeles, CA
Waldorf, Pamela J. ....Palm Beach, FL
Waldorf, Terence W. ....Houston, TX
Waldow, Roburt J. ....San Francisco, CA
Waldrep, Charlie D. ....Montgomery, AL
Waldrep, Joseph L. ....Columbus, GA
Waldrep, Kenneth R. ....Atlanta, GA
Waldrep, Marvin L. ....Atlanta, GA
Waldrep, Robert L., Jr. ....Anderson, SC
Waldrep & Stoddard ....Anderson, SC
Waldrep, Thomas W., Jr.
Winston-Salem, NC
Waldrep, Wm. Gregory ....Phenix City, AL
Waldrip, Dibrell W. ....Amarillo, TX
Waldrip, Glenn J., Jr. ....New York, NY
Waldrip, Stuart T. ....Santa Ana, CA
Waldrip, Wade E. ....Rawlins, WY
Waldrom, Wm. M. ....Mesa, AZ
Waldron, A. Burch, III ....Fort Worth, TX
Waldron, Andrew J. ....Oklahoma City, OK
Waldron, Ann Marie ....Lafayette, IN
Waldron, Arthur B., Jr. ....Fort Worth, TX
Waldron, Austin J. ....Chicago, IL
Waldron, Brian M. ....Chicago, IL
Waldron, Cheryl L. ....San Antonio, TX
Waldron, Craig L. ....Somerville, MA
Waldron, Deanna R. ....New York, NY
Waldron, Dennis J. ....New Orleans, LA
Waldron, Donald ....Lansing, MI
Waldron, Edward ....Nutley, NJ
Waldron, Edward J. ....Coral Gables, FL
Waldron, Edward J., P.A. ....Coral Gables, FL
Waldron, Elissa Griffith ....Allentown, PA
Waldron, Elissa Griffith ....Bethlehem, PA
Waldron, Eugene E., Jr. ....Arcadia, FL
Waldron and Fann ....Murfreesboro, TN
Waldron, Francis T. ....Clifton, NJ
Waldron, Gary A. ....Newport Beach, CA
Waldron, George A. ....Hamden, CT
Waldron, George B., Jr. ....New London, NH
Waldron, Gerard J. ....Washington, DC
Waldron, Holly ....Oklahoma City, OK
Waldron, Holly, P.C. ....Oklahoma City, OK
Waldron, James F. ....Haverhill, MA
Waldron, James P. ....Omaha, NE
Waldron, James T. (Jay) ....Portland, OR
Waldron, Jeffrey P. ....Wayne, PA
Waldron, Jennifer M. ....Sonoma, CA
Waldron, John B. ....Wayzata, MN
Waldron, John J. ....Chicago, IL
Waldron, John J. ....Allentown, PA
Waldron, John J., Jr. ....Chicago, IL
Waldron, John T., III ....Pittsburgh, PA
Waldron, Jonathan K. ....Washington, DC
Waldron, Kathleen G. ....Trenton, NJ
Waldron, Kelly B. ....Allentown, PA
Waldron, Kimberly ....Newark, NJ
Waldron Law Offices, Ltd. ....Wayzata, MN
Waldron, Lori M. ....Newark, NJ
Waldron, Malcolm H., Jr. ....Philadelphia, PA
Waldron, Mark D. ....Tacoma, WA
Waldron, Martin Courtney
Castro Valley, CA
Waldron, Mary V. ....Woodmere, NY
Waldron, Meg A. ....Middletown, CT
Waldron, Michael S. ....Washington, DC
Waldron, Michael W. ....Washington, DC
Waldron, Nancy L. ....Exeter, NE
Waldron & Olson ....Newport Beach, CA
Waldron, Patrick V. ....Des Moines, IA
Waldron, Paul L. ....Alexandria, VA
Waldron, R. Steven ....Murfreesboro, TN
Waldron, Richard G. ....Cleveland, OH
Waldron, Richard L. ....Anaheim, CA
Waldron, Robbye R. ....Corpus Christi, TX
Houston, TX
Waldron, Robert E. ....Okemos, MI
Waldron, Robert J. ....Wolfeboro Falls, NH
Waldron, Schneider & Todd, P.C.
Corpus Christi, TX
Houston, TX
Waldron, Stephen M. ....Bel Air, MD
Waldron, Stephen R. ....Salt Lake City, UT
Waldron, Susan Roark ....Tampa, FL
Waldron, Suzanne M. ....Wooster, OH
Waldron, Thomas F. ....Dayton, OH
Waldron, William A. ....Cambridge, MA
Waldron, Xiaowei ....Bryn Mawr, PA
Waldron Perrine, Karen D. ....Richmond, VA
Waldrop, Allister M., Jr. ....Houston, TX
Waldrop and Associates, P.C.
Huntsville, AL
Waldrop, Byron N. ....Guntersville, AL
Waldrop, Cynthia F. ....Houston, TX

Waldrop, David M. ....Memphis, TN
Waldrop, E. Glenn, Jr. ....Birmingham, AL
Waldrop, Ewalde M. ....Allentown, PA
Waldrop, G. Alan ....Austin, TX
Waldrop & Hall, A Professional Association
Jackson, TN
Nashville, TN
Waldrop, Howard ....Texarkana, TX
Waldrop, Jerry E. ....Emporia, VA
Waldrop, Kathy Hyatt ....Helotes, TX
Waldrop, Keith H. ....Goochland, VA
Waldrop, Kenneth S. ....Marietta, GA
Waldrop, Norman E., Jr. ....Mobile, AL
Waldrop, Phil A. ....Houston, TX
Waldrop, R. Loy, Jr. ....Knoxville, TN
Waldrop, Raymond D., Jr. ....Huntsville, AL
Waldrop, Robert L. ....Humble, TX
Waldrop, Shaw, Minton & Brown
Henderson, TX
Waldrop, Teresa J. ....Houston, TX
Waldrop, W. Ronald ....Birmingham, AL
Waldrop, William R. ....Marietta, GA
Waldrop, Wilton ....League City, TX
Waldrop, Yvonne P. ....Laurens, SC
Waldrum, Charles L. ....Paris, TX
Waldrup, Dorothy F. ....New Orleans, LA
Waldrup, J. Charles ....Chapel Hill, NC
Waldrup, Scott D. ....Gadsden, AL
Waldrup, Steven E. ....Greenwood, MS
Waldschmidt, David A. ....Tempe, AZ
Waldschmidt, Robert H. ....Nashville, TN
Waldschmidt & Werner ....Cannelton, IN
Tell City, IN
Waldschmidt, William E. ....Indianapolis, IN
Waldschmidt, William H. ....Tell City, IN
Waldschmuidt, William E. ....Indianapolis, IN
Waldsmith, R.J. ....San Francisco, CA
Waldspurger, Michael J.
Minneapolis, MN
Waldstein, Arthur S. ....Boston, MA
Waldstein, George ....Los Angeles, CA
Boston, MA
Waldstein, Mark B ....New York, NY
Waldstein, Thomas G. ....Framingham, MA
Waldt, Dean C. ....Cherry Hill, NJ
Waldt, Richard E. ....Baltimore, MD
Waldum, George R. ....Portland, OR
Waldvogel, James R. ....Troy, MI
Walek, David B. ....Boston, MA
Walek, Kevin P.
Commodity Futures Trading Commission, Division of Trading and Markets, GV
Walen, David P. ....Wilmington, NC
Walen, David P., P.A. ....Wilmington, NC
Walen, James D. ....Billings, MT
Walen, James M. ....Fayetteville, NC
Walen & McEniry, P.A. ....Fayetteville, NC
Walenda, Kelly A. ....Philadelphia, PA
Walenta, Arthur W., Jr. ....Martinez, CA
Walentine, O'Toole, McQuillan & Gordon
Omaha, NE
Walentine, Richard L. ....Omaha, NE
Walentowicz, Henry ....Clifton, NJ
Walentynowicz, Leonard F. ....Buffalo, NY
Walerius, Robert J. ....Seattle, WA
Walerstein, Donald P. ....Los Angeles, CA
Walerstein, Robert J. ....Brooklyn, NY
Wales, Allan R. ....Seattle, WA
Wales, Darwin R. ....Binghamton, NY
Wales, David L. ....New York, NY
Wales, David P., Jr. ....Washington, DC
Wales, Deborah T. ....Middlebury, VT
Wales, Diana ....Roseburg, OR
Wales, Diana., P.C. ....Roseburg, OR
Wales, H. Elliot ....New York, NY
Wales, Herbert V. ....Midland, TX
Wales, Jason H. ....Fayetteville, AR
Wales, John Derek ....Atlanta, GA
Wales, Kelly A. ....Syracuse, NY
Wales, Linda G. ....Annapolis, MD
Baltimore, MD
Wales, Michael G. ....Phoenix, AZ
Wales, Michele Makos ....Rockville, MD
Wales, Natalie D. ....San Mateo, CA
Wales, Owen J. ....Seattle, WA
Wales, Peter G. ....Virginia Beach, VA
Wales, Peter G., P.C. ....Virginia Beach, VA
Wales, R. Scott ....San Francisco, CA
Wales, Robert B. ....El Paso, TX
Wales, Ross E. ....Cincinnati, OH
Wales, Scott A. ....Milwaukee, WI
Wales, T. Cody ....Ashland, KY
Wales, Thomas C. ....Seattle, WA
Wales, William W. ....Indianapolis, IN
Waleski, Blaze D. ....New York, NY
Walet, Sheila T. ....New Orleans, LA
Walfield, Paul ....Laguna Hills, CA
Walfish, John ....Cherry Hill, NJ
King Of Prussia, PA
Royersford, PA
Walfish, Mark ....New York, NY
Walfish & Noonan, P.C. ....Cherry Hill, NJ
King Of Prussia, PA
Walfoort, Martha ....Washington, DC
Walford, Berkley D. ....Abilene, TX
Walford, Craig W. ....Houston, TX
Walfred, Hugo A. ....Harrisburg, PA
Walgren, Gordon L. ....Silverdale, WA
Walgren, Kent L. ....Salt Lake City, UT
Walheim, Donald J. ....San Antonio, TX
Walheim, Joseph A. ....Havertown, PA
Walheim, Joseph A., & Associates, A Prof. Corp. ....Havertown, PA
Walheim, Raymond K. ....Cherry Hill, NJ
Philadelphia, PA
Walhood, Kenneth L. ....Portland, OR
Walia, Diane M. ....Clearwater, FL
Walicek, Lara ....Hanover Park, IL

Walick, Joseph A. ... Parma, OH
Waliczek, Mishca ... Kansas City, MO
Walier, Paul ... Buffalo, NY
Waligore, John Philip ... Springfield, IL
Walin, Karen ... Orland Park, IL
Walinskas, Michael A.
Securities and Exchange Commission, Division of Market Regulation, GV
Walinski, Richard S. ... Findlay, OH
Toledo, OH
Walinski, Robert J. ... Chicago, IL
Walinski, Thaddeus N. ... Toledo, OH
Walinski & Trunkett, P.C. ... Chicago, IL
Walinsky, Adam ... New York, NY
Walinsky, Edward J. ... Fairfax, VA
Waliser, Vance M. ... Medford, OR
Walizer, Michael H. ... Los Angeles, CA
Walji, Khudabuksh ... Houston, TX
Walk, Bryan S. ... Harrisburg, PA
Walk, Donald Willard ... Phillipsburg, NJ
Walk, Frank H., Jr. ... New Orleans, LA
Walk, Gary ... West Palm Beach, FL
Walk, John R. ... Richmond, VA
Walk, Mark L. ... Osage, IA
Walk, R. David, Jr. ... Philadelphia, PA
Walk, Rochelle Friedman ... Cleveland, OH
Walk, Rodger N. ... Cincinnati, OH
Walk, Steven M. ... Cleveland, OH
Walk, Thomas D. ... Salt Lake City, UT
Walk, Thomas P. ... Tazewell, VA
Walkama, Mary Ellen G. ... Hartford, CT
Walkauskas, Gregory W. ... Pittsburgh, PA
Walkden, John L. ... Fort Lauderdale, FL
Walke, Geary L. ... Oklahoma City, OK
Walke, Geary L., P.C. ... Oklahoma City, OK
Walke, Jason D. ... Des Moines, IA
Walke, John D.
Environmental Protection Agency, Office of the General Counsel, GV
Walke, John R. ... Port Huron, MI
Walke, Lawrence A. ... Washington, DC
Walke, Ralph M. ... Dublin, GA
Walke, Steffanie F. ... Atlanta, GA
Walke, Stephen C., Jr. ... Montpelier, VT
Walkenhorst, Daniel Joseph ... St. Louis, MO
Walkenhorst, Steven K. ... Salt Lake City, UT
Walkenhorst, Walter (Ted), III
Jenkintown, PA
Walker, A. Don, III ... Dyersburg, TN
Walker, Addison E. ... St. Cloud, FL
Walker, Adron H. ... Bradenton, FL
Walker, Alan D. ... Granite City, IL
Walker, Albert G., Jr. ... Austin, TX
Walker, Albert M. ... San Marcos, TX
Walker, Alexander H., III
Salt Lake City, UT
Walker, Alexander H., Jr.
Salt Lake City, UT
Walker, Alexander J., Jr. ... Manchester, NH
Walker, Alfred M. ... New York, NY
Walker, Alfred W. ... Austin, TX
Walker, Alice E. ... Boulder, CO
Walker, Allen P. ... Chicago, IL
Walker, Allison Michelle ... Visalia, CA
Walker, Alyse ... Uniondale, NY
Walker, Amber A. ... Austin, TX
Walker, Amy W. ... Atlanta, GA
Walker, Andrew R. ... Washington, DC
Walker, Andrew S. ... Bloomfield Hills, MI
Walker, Andrew S. ... New York, NY
Walker, Ann Adele ... Meadville, PA
Walker, Ann Marie ... West Roxbury, MA
Walker, Ann Yvonne ... Palo Alto, CA
Walker, Anne K. ... Richmond, VA
Walker, Anne M. ... Westfield Center, OH
Walker, Anne McBride ... Washington, DC
Walker, Anne Noble ... Hartford, CT
Walker, Anne Stark ... Denver, CO
Walker, Anthony ... Newport Beach, CA
Walker, Anthony L. ... Mamou, LA
Walker, Arthur C., Jr. ... Washington, DC
Walker, Arthur L. ... Sandersville, GA
Walker, Arthur L., Jr. ... Austin, TX
Walker and Associates, Attorneys, P.A.
Maitland, FL
Orlando, FL
Sanford, FL
Walker, B. Franklin ... Sacramento, CA
Walker & Bailey ... New York, NY
Walker, Barbara Burch ... Treasury Department, Internal Revenue Service, GV
Walker, Barbara J. ... Columbia, TN
Walker, Barbara J. ... Alexandria, VA
Walker, Barbara L. ... Arlington, VA
Walker, Barbara Webb ... Alexandria, VA
Walker, Barry J. ... Tupelo, MS
Walker, Barry J. ... Manchester, NH
Walker, Barry M. ... Corona, CA
Walker, Barry N. ... Palm Beach Gardens, FL
Walker, Barth P. ... Oklahoma City, OK
Walker, Barwick, Clark & Allen, L.L.P.
Goldsboro, NC
Walker, Bernice L. ... Cincinnati, OH
Walker, Berry J., Jr. ... Maitland, FL
Walker, Bert H. ... Jackson, MI
Walker, Bertha E. ... Roseland, NJ
Walker, Betty S. ... Washington, DC
Walker, Beverly Anthony ... Detroit, MI
Walker, Billy ... Bandera, TX
Walker, Billy, P.C. ... Bandera, TX
Walker, Bishop K., Jr. ... Blountsville, AL
Walker & Black ... Little Rock, AR
Walker, Boyd H. ... Allentown, PA
Walker, Bradford H. ... Metairie, LA
Walker, Bradley A. ... Harrisburg, PA
Walker, Bradley C. ... Mankato, MN
Walker, Bradley D. ... Santa Ana, CA
Walker & Bradshaw, P.S. ... Tacoma, WA
Walker, Brehn & Norton ... Conway, SC
Walker, Brian A. ... Columbus, OH
Walker, Brian A. ... Vancouver, WA
Walker, Brian A. ... Wenatchee, WA
Walker, Brian D. ... Dallas, TX
Walker, Brian R. ... Athens, OH
Walker, Brian Wade ... Lafayette, IN
Walker, Bright K. ... Baltimore, MD
Walker, Bright & Whittenton, P.C.
Austin, TX
Dallas, TX
Walker, Brooke U. ... Phoenix, AZ
Walker, Brown & Brown, P.A.
Hernando, MS
Walker, Bruce A. ... Indianapolis, IN
Walker, Bruce L. ... Iowa City, IA
Walker, Bruce M. ... Waycross, GA
Walker, Bruce Ray ... Charleston, WV
Walker, Bruce Z. ... Atlanta, GA
Walker, Bryan K. ... Caldwell, ID
Walker, Byron F. ... Harrisburg, PA
Walker, C. Douglas ... Monroe, LA
Walker, C. Edwin ... Peoria, IL
Walker, C. Harvey ... Laurel, MS
Walker, C. Michael ... New London, CT
Walker, C. Michael ... Covington, GA
Walker, Cameron S. ... Casper, WY
Walker, Campbell & Campbell, PLC
Harrison, AR
Walker, Candace S. ... Indianapolis, IN
Walker, Caren E. ... Houston, TX
Walker, Carl Anthony ... Chicago, IL
Walker, Carl J. ... San Antonio, TX
Walker, Carl, Jr. ... Houston, TX
Walker, Carlon B. ... Chicago, IL
Walker, Carol A. ... Gainesville, GA
Walker, Carol J. ... Davenport, IA
Walker, Carol L. Evans ... Decatur, IL
Walker, Caroline ... Birmingham, AL
Walker, Carolyn D. ... Portland, OR
Walker, Carolyn E. ... San Antonio, TX
Walker, Carrie Hollister ... Los Angeles, CA
Walker, Casey ... Vero Beach, FL
Walker, Catherine Guthrie ... Memphis, TN
Walker, Catherine L. ... Seattle, WA
Walker, Chad Elisha ... Chicago, IL
Walker, Charles A. ... Fort Dodge, IA
Walker, Charles B., Jr. ... Houston, TX
Walker, Charles D. ... Indianapolis, IN
Walker, Charles F. ... Washington, DC
Walker, Charles H. ... Oxford, MS
Walker, Charles H. ... Columbus, OH
Walker, Charles L. ... New York, NY
Walker, Charles M. ... Hope, AR
Walker, Charles M. ... Los Angeles, CA
Walker, Charles M. ... Nashville, TN
Walker, Charles N. ... Houston, TX
Walker, Charles R. ... Omaha, NE
Walker, Charlie H. ... Lexington, TN
Walker, Chauncey L. ... White Plains, NY
Walker, Chauncey Randall ... New York, NY
Walker, Cheri G. ... Denver, CO
Walker, Cheryl D.S. ... St. Louis, MO
Walker, Cheryl J. ... Washington, DC
Walker, Chrisna Jones ... Atlanta, GA
Walker, Christopher A.
Yellow Springs, OH
Walker, Christopher J. ... Jackson, MS
Oxford, MS
Walker, Christopher J., III
Gainesville, GA
Walker, Christopher A. ... Dayton, OH
Walker, Christopher W. ... Reston, VA
Walker, Christy Joynor ... Ruston, LA
Walker, Cindra K. ... Lexington, KY
Walker, Cindy M. ... Los Angeles, CA
Walker, Clarence W. ... Charlotte, NC
Walker, Claude R. ... Tallahassee, FL
Walker, Clayton Harold, Jr. ... Fort Worth, TX
Walker, Clinton P. ... Modesto, CA
Walker, Clinton W. ... Wilmington, DE
Walker, Clinton W., III ... Greenville, MS
Walker, Clyde, Jr. ... Woodbury, NJ
Walker, Colin A. ... Denver, CO
Walker, Colleen B. ... Milford, MA
Walker, Connie Othella ... Rochester, NY
Walker, Constance C. ... Montgomery, AL
Walker, Constance M. ... Houston, TX
Walker, Cora T. ... New York, NY
Walker, Corey J. L. ... Newton, IA
Walker, Cornel W. ... Dallas, TX
Walker, Cornelius F. ... Atlanta, GA
Walker, Craig A. ... Treasury Department, Office of Regulations and Rulings, GV
Walker, Craig M. ... New York, NY
Walker, Craig W. ... San Francisco, CA
Walker, Cristi C. ... Meriden, CT
Walker, Curtis K. ... Minneapolis, MN
Walker, Cuyler H. ... Berwyn, PA
Walker, Cythnia D. ... Saginaw, MI
Walker, D. Elizabeth ... Rockville, MD
Walker, D. Reid ... Houston, TX
Walker, Dahlia A. ... North Miami, FL
Walker, Dale Elizabeth ... Kansas City, MO
Walker, Dan, Jr., (P.C.) ... Hinsdale, IL
Walker, Dana M. ... St. Louis, MO
Walker, Daniel ... Denver, CO
Walker, Daniel A. ... Bloomfield, CT
Walker, Daniel J. ... Houma, LA
Walker, Daniel W. ... Salt Lake City, UT
Walker & Dansky ... Woodbury, NJ
Walker, Darrell D. ... Eugene, OR
Walker, Darrell E. ... Burbank, CA
Walker, Darren C. ... Portland, OR
Vancouver, WA
Walker, Darren L. ... New York, NY
Walker, Darrin M. ... Lufkin, TX
Walker, Daryl J. ... Savannah, GA
Walker, Daryle A. ... Sumter, SC
Walker, David ... Stuart, FL
Walker, David ... Lufkin, TX
Walker, David A. ... Oklahoma City, OK
Walker, David A. ... Philadelphia, PA
Walker, David B. ... Grover Beach, CA
Walker, David B. ... Modesto, CA
Walker, David C. ... Tustin, CA
Walker, David C. ... Pembroke, GA
Walker, David D. ... Salem, VA
Walker, David D., P.C. ... Salem, VA
Walker, David E. ... Chicago, IL
Walker, David E. ... Metairie, LA
Walker, David E. ... Valley City, ND
Walker, David F. ... Mobile, AL
Walker, David G. ... Perry, GA
Walker, David, III ... Brooklyn, NY
Walker, David J. ... Washington, DC
Walker, David J. ... Jonesboro, GA
Walker, David J. ... Chicago, IL
Walker, David J. ... Charlotte, NC
Walker, David K. ... Conroe, TX
Walker, David M. ... Detroit, MI
Walker, David M. ... New York, NY
Walker, David O., (Law Corporation)
Alexandria, LA
Walker, David P. ... Galveston, TX
Walker, David P. ... Oak Harbor, WA
Walker, David P., P.C. ... Galveston, TX
Walker, David, P.A. ... Stuart, FL
Walker, David R. ... Duxbury, MA
Walker, David R. ... Houston, TX
Walker, David S. ... Des Moines, IA
Walker, David S., Jr. ... Lilburn, GA
Walker, David Seth ... St. Petersburg, FL
Walker, David Shepherd ... Memphis, TN
Walker, David T. ... Juneau, AK
Walker, David T. ... Philadelphia, PA
Walker, David W. ... Boston, MA
Walker, David W. ... Columbia, MO
Walker, Dawn R. ... Kansas City, MO
Walker, Dean Craig ... Los Angeles, CA
Walker, Deborah A. ... Mount Vernon, KY
Walker, Deborah Byrd ... Birmingham, AL
Walker, Deborah L. ... Pittsburgh, PA
Walker, Deborah M. ... Troy, MI
Walker, Debra B. ... Chicago, IL
Walker, Dee Brown ... Dallas, TX
Walker, Denise S. ... Le Roy, NY
Walker, Dennis P. ... Denver, CO
Walker, Derek Anthony ... New Orleans, LA
Walker, Derex ... New York, NY
Walker, Diana L. ... Los Angeles, CA
Walker, Diane F. ... Dallas, TX
Walker, Diane H. ... Villanova, PA
Walker, Diane J. ... Indianapolis, IN
Walker, Diane L. ... Glendale, CA
Walker, Dirk P. ... Houston, TX
Walker, D. J., Jr. ... Graham, NC
Walker, Dolores D. ... New York, NY
Walker, Donald ... Orlando, FL
Walker, Donald B. ... Atlanta, GA
Walker, Donald B., P.C. ... Atlanta, GA
Walker, Donald C. ... Portland, OR
Walker, Donald E. ... Clawson, MI
Plymouth, MI
Walker, Donald G. ... Troy, MI
Walker, Donald J. ... Albany, NY
Walker, Donald N. ... Austin, TX
Walker, Donald R. ... Concord, CA
Walker, Donald S. ... Detroit, MI
Walker, Donis G. ... Colorado Springs, CO
Denver, CO
Walker, Donna J. ... New York, NY
Walker, Donna P. ... Anchorage, AK
Walker, Doris B. ... San Francisco, CA
Walker, Dorman ... Montgomery, AL
Walker, Dorothy A. ... Lincoln, NE
Walker, Douglas A. ... Fort Lauderdale, FL
Walker, Douglas A. ... St. Louis, MO
Walker, Douglas A. ... Cincinnati, OH
Walker, Douglas A., Law Offices of
Gainesville, FL
Walker, Douglas A., Law Offices of
Ocala, FL
Walker, Douglas C. ... Ware, MA
Walker, Douglas D. ... Reston, VA
Walker, Douglas J., Jr. ... Overland Park, KS
Mead, WA
Walker, Douglas K. ... Highland, IN
Walker, Douglas M. ... Seattle, WA
Walker, Douglas R. ... Rock Island, IL
Walker, Douglas R. ... Alma, NE
Walker, Douglas W. ... Chicago, IL
Walker, Duke W. ... Sherman, TX
Walker, Duncan D., III ... Macon, GA
Walker & Dunklin ... Little Rock, AR
Walker, Dwyla J. ... St. Louis, MO
Walker, Dylia J. ... Philadelphia, PA
Walker, E. Allen ... Tacoma, WA
Walker, E. Ellison ... Columbia, SC
Walker, E. Garrett ... Greensboro, NC
Walker, E. Ralph ... Des Moines, IA
Walker, E. Richard ... Sequim, WA
Walker, Earle H. ... Bloomfield, CT
Walker, Eddie H., Jr. ... Fort Smith, AR
Walker, Edgar G. ... New York, NY
Walker, Edmund J. ... Biloxi, MS
Walker, Edward B. ... Roanoke, VA
Walker, Edward F. ... Dallas, TX
Walker, Edward N. ... New York, NY
Walker, Edward P. ... Alexandria, VA
Walker, Edwin J., Jr. ... Durham, NC
Walker, Edwin M. ... Nashville, TN
Walker, Egan Kirk ... Reno, NV
Walker, Elisabeth A. ... Little Rock, AR
Walker, Elizabeth F. ... King Of Prussia, PA
Walker, Elizabeth J. ... Detroit, MI
Walker, Elizabeth S. ... Denver, CO
Walker, Elizabeth S. ... Chicago, IL
Walker, Elizabeth W. ... Los Angeles, CA
Walker, Elizabeth W. ... Oakland, CA
Walker, Ellen M. ... New York, NY
Walker, Ellen S. ... Rockville, MD
Walker, Elwood M. ... Brookfield, OH
Walker, Emily N. ... Franklin, TN
Walker Emmons & Shannon
Richmond, KY
Walker & England ... Dallas, TX
Walker, Erik B. ... Houston, TX
Walker, Ernest J. ... Detroit, MI
Walker, Ernest R. ... Johnstown, PA
Walker, Etta L. ... Reno, NV
Walker, Eva L. ... Paducah, KY
Walker, F. Mitchell, Jr. ... Nashville, TN
Walker & Fairbanks, P.A.
Jacksonville, FL
Ponte Vedra Beach, FL
Walker, Farrah Lyn ... Philadelphia, PA
Walker, Ferguson & Ferguson
Oklahoma City, OK
Walker, Floyd L. ... Tulsa, OK
Walker, Francis J. ... Olympia, WA
Walker, Frank B. ... Bangor, ME
Walker, Frank B. ... Ellsworth, ME
Walker, Frank C. ... Fort Lauderdale, FL
Walker, Frank D. ... San Diego, CA
Walker, Frank H., Jr. ... Charlotte, NC
Walker, Frank M., Jr. ... Lake Charles, LA
Walker, Frank S., Jr. ... Orange, VA
Walker, Franklin M., Jr., Law Offices of
Damariscotta, ME
Walker, Fred H. ... Valdosta, GA
Walker, Fred H. ... Gulfport, MS
Walker, Frederick X. ... El Paso, TX
Walker, G. Perrin ... Tacoma, WA
Walker, G. Trenholm ... Charleston, SC
Walker, Gabrielle L. ... Menlo Park, CA
Walker, Gary ... Tampa, FL
Walker, Gary E. ... Warren, NJ
Walker, Gary L. ... Marquette, MI
Walker, Gary Louis ... Bloomfield Hills, MI
Walker, Gary R. ... Pittsburgh, PA
Walker, Gary T. ... San Francisco, CA
Walker, Geo. W. ... Albuquerque, NM
Walker, Geoffrey H. ... Phoenix, AZ
Walker, Geoffrey K. ... Houston, TX
Walker, Geoffrey P. ... Dayton, OH
Walker, Geoffrey S. ... Detroit, MI
Walker, George D., Jr. ... Philadelphia, PA
Walker, George E. ... Philadelphia, PA
Walker, George G. ... San Francisco, CA
Walker, George G., Inc.
San Francisco, CA
Walker, George James ... Lufkin, TX
Walker, George K. ... Winston-Salem, NC
Walker, George M. ... Mobile, AL
Walker, George R. ... Monterey, CA
Walker, George R. ... Concord, NH
Walker, George W. ... Wolfeboro, NH
Walker, George Walton, III
Montgomery, AL
Walker, Gerald R. ... Painesville, OH
Walker, Gilbert ... Providence, RI
Walker, Glenn E. ... Shreveport, LA
Walker, Goldie V.
Federal Trade Commission, Bureau of Competition, GV
Walker, Gordon J. ... Birmingham, MI
Walker, Gordon M. ... Springville, UT
Walker, Gordon T. ... Boston, MA
Walker, Greg ... Hilton Head Island, SC
Walker, Greg A. ... Englewood, CO
Walker, Gregg M. ... San Francisco, CA
Walker, Gregory D. ... Oakland, CA
Walker, Gregory D. ... New York, NY
Walker, Gregory W. ... Chicago, IL
Walker, Greta Backstrom ... Los Angeles, CA
Walker, Grissim H. ... Sarasota, FL
Walker, Grover P. ... Los Angeles, CA
Walker, G.T. Franklin, Jr.
Washington, DC
Walker, Guy M. ... Laurel, MS
Walker, H. Carey, III ... Huntsville, AL
Walker, H. Clayton, Jr. ... Columbia, SC
Walker, H. Gregory, Jr. ... Alexandria, LA
Walker, H. Jay, III ... Warner Robins, GA
Walker, H. Lawson, II ... Covington, KY
Walker, H. Reed ... Kansas City, KS
Walker, H. Reed ... Mission, KS
Walker, Hale M. ... Ruston, LA
Walker & Hamilton ... San Francisco, CA
Walker, Hans, Jr. ... Washington, DC
Walker, Harold H., Jr. ... Dallas, TX
Walker, Harrington and Cheatham
St. Petersburg, FL
Walker, Harry C. ... Greenville, SC
Walker, Harry G. ... Jackson, MS
Walker, Harry R., Jr. ... Cape May, NJ
Walker, Harvey Bradley ... Little Rock, AR
Walker, Harvey D. ... Saginaw, MI
Walker, H. E., Jr. ... Dallas, TX
Walker, Helene McG. ... New Orleans, LA
Walker, Helgi
Federal Communications Commission, Office of the Commissioners, GV
Walker, Henry C. ... Shreveport, LA
Walker, Henry M. ... Nashville, TN
Walker, Herbert H. ... New York, NY
Walker, Herbert W. ... Napa, CA
Walker, Herman B. ... Exmore, VA
Walker, Herman G., Jr. ... Anchorage, AK
Walker, Hill, Adams, Umbach, Meadows & Walton ... Auburn, AL
Dadeville, AL
Lafayette, AL

Walker, Hill, Adams, Umbach, Meadows & Walton—Continued
Opelika, AL
Phenix City, AL
Walker, Hilman P. .... San Francisco, CA
Walker, Homer Lee .... Atlanta, GA
Walker, Horace A. .... Little Rock, AR
Walker, Howard .... Chicago, IL
Walker, Howard C., Jr. .... Akron, OH
Walker, Howard D. .... Houston, TX
Walker, Howard E. .... Boston, MA
Providence, RI
Walker, Howard L., Jr. .... Scarsdale, NY
Walker, Howard P. .... Warrenton, VA
Walker, Howard W. .... Dallas, TX
Walker, Hulbert, Gray & Byrd, L.L.P.
Perry, GA
Walker, Ian K. O. .... New York, NY
Walker, Imogene L. .... Decatur, GA
Walker, Irby E., Jr. .... Conway, SC
Walker, Irving E. .... Baltimore, MD
Walker, J. Allen .... Leesburg, VA
Walker, J. Brent .... Washington, DC
Walker, J. Davis .... Forest Grove, OR
Walker, J. Frost, III .... Coral Gables, FL
Walker, J. Grant .... Mesa, AZ
Walker, J. Henry, IV .... Atlanta, GA
Walker, J. Kelly .... Salt Lake City, UT
Walker, J. Kenneth .... Macon, GA
Walker, J. Kimball .... Norwalk, CA
Walker, J. Robert .... Knoxville, TN
Walker, J. Ross .... Willits, CA
Walker, J. Stephen .... Chicago, IL
Walker, J. Stephen .... Paris, TX
Walker, J. Stephen, & Associates, Ltd.
Chicago, IL
Walker, J. Taylor .... Chattanooga, TN
Walker, J. Tracy, IV .... Richmond, VA
Walker, Jack D. .... Madison, WI
Walker, Jackson .... Franklin, TN
Walker, Jacob .... Opelika, AL
Walker, Jacqueline S. .... San Diego, CA
Walker, James .... Bloomington, IL
Walker, James A. .... Auburn, CA
Walker, James A. .... Miami, FL
Walker, James A. .... Wichita, KS
Walker, James A. .... Logan, WV
Walker, James A., Jr. .... Atlanta, GA
Walker, James A., P.A. .... Miami, FL
Walker, James C. .... Perkasie, PA
Walker, James C., Jr. .... Houma, LA
Walker, James D. (Dee) .... Albertville, AL
Walker, James D., Jr. .... Macon, GA
Walker, James D., P.C. .... Albertville, AL
Boaz, AL
Guntersville, AL
Walker, James Dean, Jr. .... Kansas City, MO
Walker, James E. (Jim)
Oklahoma City, OK
Walker, James E., Jr. .... White Plains, NY
Walker, James E. Paschal
Roanoke Rapids, NC
Walker, James Edward, II .... Chicago, IL
Walker, James Edward, III .... Montgomery, AL
Walker, James F. .... Washington, DC
Walker, James F. .... Wellesley, MA
Walker, James F. .... Gibsonville, NC
Walker, James F. .... Seattle, WA
Walker, James F., Law Offices of
Wellesley, MA
Walker, James F., P.A. .... Gibsonville, NC
Walker, James G. .... Manchester, NH
Walker, James G. .... Dallas, TX
Walker, James H. .... Cleveland, MS
Walker, James, IV
Walker, James K. .... Levelland, TX
Walker, James K. .... Anchorage, AK
Walker, James L. .... San Antonio, TX
Walker, James L., IV .... San Rafael, CA
Walker, James, Ltd. .... Bloomington, IL
Walker, James M. .... Miami, FL
Walker, James M. .... Westfield Center, OH
Walker, James M., III .... Tifton, GA
Walker, James O., III .... Fort Lauderdale, FL
Walker, James Q. .... New York, NY
Walker, James R. .... Denver, CO
Walker, James R. .... Terre Haute, IN
Walker, James R. .... St. Paul, MN
Walker, James R. .... Eden, NC
Walker, James R. .... Pittsburgh, PA
Walker, James R. .... Houston, TX
Walker, James Stephen .... Salisbury, NC
Walker, James T. .... Fort Pierce, FL
Walker, James T. .... Merrillville, IN
Walker, James T., Professional Corporation
Merrillville, IN
Walker, James V. .... Ponte Vedra Beach, FL
Walker, James V. .... Pittsburg, KS
Walker, James W. .... Kings Park, NY
Walker, James W. .... Hamlin, PA
Walker, James W. .... Philadelphia, PA
Walker, James W. .... Richmond, VA
Walker, James Wm. .... Dallas, TX
Walker, Jan .... Dodgeville, WI
Walker, Jan A. .... Dade City, FL
Walker, Jan C. .... Parsippany, NJ
Walker, Jana L. .... Placitas, NM
Walker, Jane H. .... Cincinnati, OH
Walker, Jane L. .... Waukesha, WI
Walker, Janet Baker .... Washington, DC
Walker, Janice L. .... Cincinnati, OH
Walker, Janna S. .... New Braunfels, TX
Walker, Jas. B., Jr. .... Centerville, TN
Walker, Jay Stanley .... Lawton, OK
Walker, Jayme S. .... Department of Justice, Drug Enforcement Administration, GV
Walker, Jean T. .... Manchester, CT
Walker, Jean-Cyril .... Silver Spring, MD
Walker, Jeanne E. .... Chicago, IL
Walker, Jearl D. .... Fort Worth, TX
Walker, Jeff K. .... Springfield, TN
Walker, Jeffrey .... New York, NY
Walker, Jeffrey A. .... Jackson, MS
Walker, Jeffrey Alan .... Redlands, CA
Walker, Jeffrey C. .... Woodland Hills, CA
Walker, Jeffrey C. .... Washington, DC
Walker, Jeffrey J. .... Fort Lauderdale, FL
Walker, Jeffrey J., P.A., Law Offices
Fort Lauderdale, FL
Walker, Jeffrey K.
Department of the Air Force, Office of the Judge Advocate General, GV
Walker, Jeffrey N. .... Sandy, UT
Walker, Jeffrey R. .... Lexington, KY
Walker, Jennet S. .... New York, NY
Walker, Jennifer A. .... Chicago, IL
Walker, Jennifer B. .... San Diego, CA
Walker, Jennifer E. .... Newport Beach, CA
Walker, Jennifer E. .... Secaucus, NJ
Walker, Jenny L. .... Anoka, MN
Walker, Jeremy T. .... Manchester, NH
Walker, Jerome .... New York, NY
Walker, Jerry L. .... Rancho Cucamonga, CA
Walker, Jerry V. .... Houston, TX
Walker, Jimmy .... Houston, TX
Walker, Joan F. .... Beverly Hills, CA
Walker, Joan H. .... Miami, FL
Walker, Joan LoBianco, (P.A.)
St. Petersburg, FL
Walker, Joanna B. .... Houston, TX
Walker, Joanne M. .... Cherry Hill, NJ
Wynnewood, PA
Walker & Jocke, L.P.A. .... Akron, OH
Cleveland, OH
Medina, OH
Walker, Jodi L. .... Boston, MA
Walker, Jodi L. .... Toledo, OH
Walker, Joe .... Ozark, AL
Walker, Joe H., Jr. .... Ripley, TN
Walker, Joel M. .... New York, NY
Walker, Joel M. .... Pittsburgh, PA
Walker, Joel P. .... Hernando, MS
Walker, John .... Center, TX
Walker, John A. .... Miami, FL
Walker, John A., Jr. .... Knoxville, TN
Walker, John C. .... Treasury Department, Internal Revenue Service, GV
Walker, John C. .... Portland, ME
Walker, John C., P.A., Law Office of
Portland, ME
Walker, John Craig .... Chicago, IL
Walker, John D. .... Houston, TX
Walker, John E. .... Los Angeles, CA
Walker, John F. (Jack), III .... Tyler, TX
Walker, John F., Jr. .... Los Angeles, CA
Walker, John G. .... Charlotte, NC
Walker, John L. .... Camdenton, MO
Osage Beach, MO
Walker, John L. .... St. Louis, MO
Walker, John L. .... Albuquerque, NM
Walker, John L. .... New York, NY
Walker, John L. .... Houston, TX
Walker, John L., III .... Richmond, VA
Walker, John L., Jr. .... Jackson, MS
Walker, John L., Jr. .... Beaver, PA
Walker, John M. .... Millbrae, CA
Walker, John M. .... Woodland Hills, CA
Walker, John M. .... Washington, DC
Walker, John M. .... Cheyenne, WY
Walker, John M.V. .... San Francisco, CA
Walker, John N. .... Chicago, IL
Walker, John O., Professional Corporation
Fort Collins, CO
Walker, John Oliver .... Fort Collins, CO
Walker, John R. .... Berkeley, CA
Walker, John R. .... Houma, LA
Walker, John R. .... Lafayette, LA
Walker, John R. .... Chambersburg, PA
Walker, John R. .... Houston, TX
Walker, John R., Jr. .... Waterloo, IA
Walker, John S., P.C. .... Center, TX
Walker, John T. .... Fresno, CA
Walker, John W., (A Professional Corporation) .... Moscow, ID
Walker, John W., (P.A.) .... Little Rock, AR
Walker & Johnson .... Exmore, VA
Walker, Jonathan E. .... Pensacola, FL
Walker, Jonathan H. .... Newport News, VA
Walker, Jones, Lawrence, Duggan & Savage, P.C. .... Fairfax, VA
Rappahannock, VA
Warrenton, VA
Walker, Jonette M. .... Lubbock, TX
Walker, Jordan C. .... Sacramento, CA
Walker, Joro .... Salt Lake City, UT
Walker, Joseph A. .... Newport Beach, CA
Walker, Joseph Brent .... Memphis, TN
Walker, Joseph D. .... Columbia, SC
Walker, Joseph G. .... Dallas, TX
Walker, Joseph H. .... Longwood, FL
Walker, Joseph H., III .... Ripley, TN
Walker, Joseph M. .... Doylestown, PA
Walker, Joseph M., III .... Clearwater, FL
Walker, Joseph V. .... Chicago, IL
Walker, Joseph V. .... Southfield, MI
Walker, Joseph W. .... Dayton, OH
Walker, Josephine .... Cleveland, OH
Walker, J. T. .... Dallas, TX
Walker, Judith C. .... Charlotte, NC
Walker, Judith M. .... St. Paul, MN
Walker, Jules Scott .... Marion, IN
Walker, Julian W., Jr. .... Columbia, SC
Walker, Julie M. .... Denver, CO
Walker, J. W. .... Mendenhall, MS
Walker, Karen .... Lexington, KY
Walker, Karen B. .... Bentonville, AR
Walker, Karen D. .... Tallahassee, FL
Walker, Karen Natalie .... Washington, DC
Walker, Karl F. .... Greensburg, IN
Walker, Karla .... Valdosta, GA
Walker, Karol Corbin .... Newark, NJ
Walker, Karon S. .... New York, NY
Walker, Kathleen Campbell .... El Paso, TX
Walker, Kathleen G. .... Framingham, MA
Walker, Kathleen M. .... Los Angeles, CA
Walker, Kathleen M. .... San Diego, CA
Walker, Kathryn A. .... Palo Alto, CA
Walker, Kathryn M. .... Minneapolis, MN
Walker, Kay B. .... Corpus Christi, TX
Walker, Keeling & Carroll, L.L.P.
Port Lavaca, TX
Victoria, TX
Walker, Keith M. .... St. Anthony, ID
Walker, Keith M. .... Warren, OH
Walker, Keith P. .... Grand Rapids, MI
Walker, Keith S. .... Claremont, CA
Walker, Kelli D. .... Sterling, IL
Walker, Kelly J. .... Santa Cruz, CA
Walker, Kellye L. .... New Orleans, LA
Walker, Kendall R. .... Columbia, SC
Walker, Kenneth E. .... Dallas, TX
Walker, Kenneth J. .... Longview, TX
Walker, Kenneth J., P.C. .... Longview, TX
Walker, Kenneth L. .... Trinity, NC
Walker, Kenneth L. .... Lexington, TN
Walker, Kenneth R. .... Portland, OR
Walker, Kent .... Mountain View, CA
Walker, Kent .... Philadelphia, PA
Walker, Kent M. .... San Diego, CA
Walker, Kent William .... Atlanta, GA
Walker, Kevin B. .... Florham Park, NJ
Walker, Kevin C. .... New York, NY
Walker, Kevin E. .... Dallas, TX
Walker, Kevin J. .... Seminole, OK
Walker, Kim A. .... New York, NY
Walker, Kimberly J .... Des Moines, IA
Walker, Kimberly Page .... Sarasota, FL
Walker, Kimberly R. .... Brookfield, WI
Walker, Knopf & Billingsley .... Baxter, IA
Newton, IA
Walker, L. Mark .... Oklahoma City, OK
Walker, Laine Spears .... Atlanta, GA
Walker, Laleshia A .... Shreveport, LA
Walker, Lamont D. .... Round Rock, TX
Walker, Larry .... San Bernardino, CA
Walker, Larry .... Perry, GA
Walker, Larry C. .... New Cumberland, PA
Walker, Lary C. .... Weiser, ID
Walker, Laura C. .... Montgomery, AL
McLean, VA
Walker, Laura E. .... Washington, DC
Walker, Laura M. .... Bel Air, MD
Walker, Laurence N. .... Berkeley, CA
Walker Law Firm .... Dyersburg, TN
Walker Law Firm, The .... Des Moines, IA
Walker Law Firm, The, A Professional Corporation .... Newport Beach, CA
Walker Law Office .... Cobb, WI
Walker Law Office, P.C. .... Fort Dodge, IA
Walker, Lawrence .... Batavia, OH
Walker, Lawrence D. .... Columbus, OH
Walker, Lawrence R. .... Detroit, MI
Walker, L.D. "Dee", III .... Montgomery, AL
Walker & Leavitt .... Forest Grove, OR
Walker, Lee .... North Las Vegas, NV
Walker, Lee Ann .... Branson, MO
Walker, Lee, Ltd. .... North Las Vegas, NV
Walker, Lee M. .... Baxter, IA
Newton, IA
Walker, Lenora .... Minneapolis, MN
Walker, Leroy S. .... Los Angeles, CA
Walker, Leslie .... Boston, MA
Walker, Leslie Dillon .... Fort Worth, TX
Walker, Linda C. .... Fowlerville, MI
Walker, Linda Farrell .... Warren, NJ
Walker, Linda Lee .... Newark, NJ
Walker, Linda Mather .... New Orleans, LA
Walker, Lindsey .... Beaumont, TX
Walker, Lisa .... Manchester, NH
Walker, Lisa L. .... Baltimore, MD
Walker, Lloyd J. .... Twin Falls, ID
Walker & Long .... Dallas, TX
Walker, Lori A. .... Daytona Beach, FL
Walker, Lori E. .... Cincinnati, OH
Walker, Lorna A. .... San Francisco, CA
Walker, Lucile J. .... Oklahoma City, OK
Walker, Lyn Gammill .... Hartford, CT
Walker, Lynn, (Mr.) .... Los Angeles, CA
Walker, M. Richard .... Salt Lake City, UT
Walker, Mabin Andrew, III .... Conroe, TX
Walker, Marc .... Bayonne, NJ
Walker, Marcia Marie .... San Bernardino, CA
Walker, Margaret Ann B. .... Richmond, VA
Walker, Margaret E. .... Denver, CO
Walker, Margaret H. .... Morristown, NJ
Walker, Margaret (Molly) Bergelin
Salida, CO
Walker, Marian L. .... San Diego, CA
Walker, Marianne J. .... Rock Hill, NY
Walker, Marianne McGettigan
Philadelphia, PA
Walker, Marilyn D. .... Pontiac, MI
Walker, Marion F. .... Birmingham, AL
Walker, Mark A. .... New York, NY
Walker, Mark C. .... Stockbridge, GA
Walker, Mark C. .... El Paso, TX
Walker, Mark C., P.C. .... Stockbridge, GA
Walker, Mark E. .... Fort Walton Beach, FL
Walker, Mark E. .... Indianapolis, IN
Walker, Mark L. .... New York, NY
Walker, Mark Leonard .... Augusta, ME
Walker, Mark R. .... Dallas, TX
Walker, Mark S. .... San Diego, CA
Walker, Mark S. .... Maitland, FL
Walker, Mark W. .... McAllen, TX
Walker, Marlan C. .... Phoenix, AZ
Walker, Martha B. .... Chambersburg, PA
Walker, Marvin B. .... Paintsville, KY
Walker, Mary Ann .... Washington, DC
Walker, Mary E. .... Memphis, TN
Walker, Mary E. .... Nashville, TN
Walker, Mary L. .... San Diego, CA
Walker, Mary LaRue .... Gilbert, AZ
Walker, Mary Oates .... Washington, DC
Walker, Mary Trueheart .... Houston, TX
Walker, Matthew D. .... Chicago, IL
Walker, Matthew R. .... Philadelphia, PA
Walker, Matthew S. .... San Diego, CA
Walker, Maureen O. .... Department of State, Bureau of Oceans, International Environmental & Scientific Affairs, GV
Walker, McKenzie & Walker, A Professional Corporation .... Memphis, TN
Walker & McPhail .... Monterey, CA
Santa Cruz, CA
Walker, Melford W., Jr. .... Atlanta, GA
Walker, Melissa P. .... Atlanta, GA
Walker Melvin & Berger .... Eden, NC
Walker, Michael .... Phoenix, AZ
Walker, Michael .... Ringwood, NJ
Walker, Michael A. .... Denver, CO
Walker, Michael A. .... Princeton, NJ
New York, NY
Walker, Michael A. .... Charleston, SC
Walker, Michael B. .... Miami, FL
Walker, Michael B. .... Austin, TX
Walker, Michael C. .... Des Moines, IA
Walker, Michael C. .... Huntington, WV
Walker, Michael D. .... Hamlin, PA
Walker, Michael D., (P.C.) .... Portland, OR
Walker, Michael G. .... Ventura, CA
Walker, Michael J.
Environmental Protection Agency, Office of Enforcement and Compliance Assurance, GV
Walker, Michael J. .... Devils Lake, ND
Walker, Michael J. .... Spokane, WA
Walker, Michael K. .... Los Angeles, CA
Walker, Michael L. .... Denver, CO
Walker, Michael L. .... Palm Harbor, FL
Walker, Michael M. .... Topeka, KS
Walker, Michael W. .... Kansas City, MO
Walker, Michelle R. .... Encino, CA
Walker, Mickey .... Riverside, CA
Walker, Miller B., Jr. .... Houston, TX
Walker & Miller, P.C. .... Allentown, PA
Walker, Milton .... Houston, TX
Walker, Molly L. .... Pasadena, CA
Walker, Monica J. .... Glendale, CA
Walker, Monique R. .... Atlanta, GA
Walker, Morgan & Kinard .... Aiken, SC
Columbia, SC
Lexington, SC
Newberry, SC
Walker, Morley .... Oakland, CA
Walker, M. Richard & Assoc., P.C.
Salt Lake City, UT
Walker, Myron A., Jr. .... Baton Rouge, LA
Walker, Myron D. .... Washington, DC
Walker, Nancy
Department Of Veterans Affairs, GV
Walker, Nancy Dietz .... Philadelphia, PA
Walker, Nancy E. .... Charlotte, NC
Walker, Nancy Krispen .... Orange, TX
Walker, Nancy L. .... New Haven, CT
Walker, Nathan L. .... Dallas, TX
Walker, Nathaniel .... Selma, AL
Walker, Neal .... Roseburg, OR
Walker, Nelson L. .... Oregon City, OR
Walker, Noah .... Clearwater, FL
Walker, Nona B. .... Dallas, TX
Walker, Nona E. .... Boston, MA
Walker, Norbert S. .... San Antonio, TX
Walker, Norbert S., P.C. .... San Antonio, TX
Walker & O'Malley, P.C. .... Scranton, PA
Walker, Orrin M. .... Woodstock, GA
Walker, Orville C. .... San Antonio, TX
Walker, Owen F. .... Cleveland Heights, OH
Walker, Owen S. .... Boston, MA
Walker, P. Craig .... Richland, WA
Walker, P. Michael .... Wilmington, DE
Walker, Pamela D. .... Little Rock, AR
Walker, Pamela D., P.A. .... Little Rock, AR
Walker, Passman & Michiels
Alexandria, LA
Walker, Pat N. .... Post, TX
Walker, Patricia A. .... Medina, OH
Walker, Patricia Boleyn "Lynn"
Denver, CO
Walker, Patricia L. .... Menlo Park, CA
Walker, Patricia Stroman .... Buffalo, NY
Walker, Paul A. .... Washington, DC
Walker, Paul E. .... New York, NY
Walker, Paul G. .... Pittsburgh, PA
Walker, Paul H. .... Brookline, MA
Walker, Paul J. .... Scranton, PA
Walker, Paul R. .... Los Angeles, CA
Walker, Paul R. H. .... San Francisco, CA
Walnut Creek, CA
Walker, Paula D. .... Nashville, TN
Walker, Peggy .... Douglasville, GA
Walker, Perry N. .... Greensboro, NC
Walker, Peter A. .... New York, NY
Walker, Phil N. .... San Francisco, CA
Walker, Philip M. .... McLean, VA
Walker, Philip N. .... New Hartford, CT
Walker, Philip S. .... Hartford, CT
Walker, Philip S. .... Newport News, VA
Walker, Phillip E. .... Miami Beach, FL
Walker, Phillip R. .... Memphis, TN
Walker, Pierre G., III .... Fayetteville, AR

Walker, R. Alfred ... Albuquerque, NM
Walker, R. Scott ... Dallas, TX
Walker, Ralph B. ... Fort Wayne, IN
Walker, Ralph C. ... San Francisco, CA
Walker, Ralph G. ... Canton, GA
Walker, Ralph W., III ... Woodstock, GA
Walker, Randall W. ... Wichita Falls, TX
Walker, Randolph ... Atlanta, GA
Walker, Ray ... Dallas, TX
Walker, Raymond A., Jr. ... Windsor, CT
Walker, Rebecca A. ... Gadsden, AL
Walker, Rebecca E. ... Indianapolis, IN
Walker, Rebecca Ruth McCrary
Birmingham, AL
Walker, Reuben G., Jr. ... Richmond, KY
Walker, Rex M. ... Seattle, WA
Walker, Rhonald D. ... Garland, TX
Walker, Richard ... San Francisco, CA
Walker, Richard A. ... Savannah, GA
Walker, Richard A. ... Chicago, IL
Walker, Richard B. ... Anderson, IN
Walker, Richard B. ... Newton, KS
Walker, Richard B. ... Albuquerque, NM
Walker, Richard B., P.A. ... Albuquerque, NM
Walker, Richard E. ... Seattle, WA
Walker, Richard G. ... Chicago, IL
Walker, Richard H. ... New Canaan, CT
Walker, Richard H.
Securities and Exchange Commission,
Office of the General Counsel, GV
Walker, Richard K. ... Phoenix, AZ
Walker, Richard K. ... Sylva, NC
Walker, Richard L., II ... Philadelphia, PA
Walker, Richard P. ... San Francisco, CA
Walker, R. L. ... Houston, TX
Walker, Robert ... Memphis, TN
Walker, Robert A. ... Riverside, CA
Walker, Robert A., Jr. ... Treasury Department,
Internal Revenue Service, GV
Walker, Robert B. ... Sacramento, CA
Walker, Robert B. ... Washington, DC
Walker, Robert B. ... Herndon, VA
Walker, Robert B., Jr. ... Carson City, NV
Walker, Robert C. ... Hartford, CT
Walker, Robert C. ... Houston, TX
Walker, Robert D. ... Fairmont, MN
Walker, Robert D. ... Findlay, OH
Walker, Robert D., II ... Louisville, KY
Walker, Robert D., Jr. ... Goldsboro, NC
Walker, Robert Dee ... Argyle, TX
Walker, Robert E. ... Fort Dodge, IA
Walker, Robert F. ... Los Angeles, CA
Walker, Robert G. ... Westport, CT
Walker, Robert G. ... Princeton, NJ
Walker, Robert G., Jr. ... Clearwater, FL
Walker, Robert H. ... Apopka, FL
Walker, Robert H. ... Houston, TX
Walker, Robert Harry ... Gulfport, MS
Walker, Robert J. ... Mineola, NY
Walker, Robert J. ... Nashville, TN
Walker, Robert Kirk ... Chattanooga, TN
Walker, Robert L. ... San Francisco, CA
Walker, Robert L.
Equal Employment Opportunity
Commission,
Office of Federal Operations, GV
Walker, Robert L. ... Louisville, KY
Walker, Robert L. ... Lynchburg, VA
Walker, Robert Luke ... Rochester, NY
Walker, Robert Michael ... New York, NY
Walker, Robert P. ... Beaumont, TX
Walker, Robert S. ... Boston, MA
Walker, Robert S. ... Cleveland, OH
Walker, Robert S., III ... Lexington, KY
Walker, Robert Scott ... Fort Lauderdale, FL
Walker, Robert W. ... Florence, AL
Walker, Robert W. ... San Francisco, CA
Walker, Robert W. ... Department of Justice,
Drug Enforcement Administration, GV
Walker, Robert W. ... Midwest City, OK
Walker, Robert William ... Concord, MA
Walker, Robert Z. ... Montague, CA
Walker & Robertson ... Canton, GA
Jasper, GA
Woodstock, GA
Walker Robinson, P.C. ... Richmond, VA
Walker, Robt. E. ... Los Angeles, CA
Walker, Rodney L. ... Hemet, CA
Walker, Roger E. ... Redlands, CA
Walker, Roger J. (Jeff) ... Fort Worth, TX
Walker, Roland ... Baltimore, MD
Walker, Roland E., Jr. ... Oakland, CA
Walker, Roland P. ... Columbia, MO
Walker & Romm ... Currituck, NC
Walker, Ron L., Jr. ... Lexington, KY
Walker, Ronald B. ... Victoria, TX
Walker, Ronald E. ... San Francisco, CA
Walker, Ronald E., Jr. ... Amarillo, TX
Walker, Ronald Eugene ... Detroit, MI
Walker, Ronald F. ... Knoxville, IA
Walker, Ronald J. ... Austin, TX
Walker, Ronald L. ... Oklahoma City, OK
Walker, Ronald L. ... Beaumont, TX
Walker, Ronald N. ... Cobb, WI
Walker, Ronald R. ... Lovington, NM
Walker, Rondal A. ... Boston, MA
Walker, Ronnie H. ... Orlando, FL
Walker, Ronnie H., P.A. ... Orlando, FL
Walker, Rose Ann M. ... Brooklyn, NY
Walker, Ross P. ... Indianapolis, IN
Walker, Ruel ... Oakland, CA
Walker, Ruel C. ... Austin, TX
Walker, Rufus F., Jr. ... Hickory, NC
Walker, Rufus F., Jr. ... Statesville, NC
Walker, Russell G., Jr. ... Asheboro, NC
Walker, Russell H. ... Memphis, TN
Walker, Russell James
Oklahoma City, OK
Walker, Russell S. ... Salt Lake City, UT
Walker Ryan, P.L.C. ... Phoenix, AZ
Walker, Ryan Z. ... Los Angeles, CA
Walker, S. Lynn, A Professional Law
Corporation ... Shreveport, LA
Walker, Salliann Parker ... Norman, OK
Walker, Sally M. ... Newton, MA
Walker, Sally M. ... Columbia, SC
Walker, Salveter, Lee & Graff
Springfield, MO
Walker, Sam ... Oakland, CA
Walker, Samuel A. ... Princeton, NJ
Walker, Samuel D. ... Washington, DC
Walker, Samuel R. ... Culpeper, VA
Walker, Sandra L. ... Cleveland, OH
Walker, Sandra Lynn ... Shreveport, LA
Walker, Sara A. ... Boston, MA
Walker, Scott C. ... Columbus, OH
Walker, Scott C. ... Provo, UT
Walker, Scott E. ... Rockville, MD
Walker, Scott K. ... Bellingham, WA
Walker, Sean C. ... Salisbury, NC
Walker, Sharyl ... Palm Springs, CA
Walker, Sheldon R. ... Willoughby, OH
Walker, Shirley A. ... Tallahassee, FL
Walker, Shock, Harp & Hill, P.L.L.C.
Fort Smith, AR
Walker, Shonn W. ... Cullman, AL
Walker, Sidney J. ... Clute, TX
Walker, Sonja Caprice ... Harrisburg, PA
Walker, Spencer B. ... Grove Hill, AL
Walker, Stanley G., Jr. ... Albany, NY
Walker, Stanley M. ... Houston, TX
Walker, Stanley P. ... Enterprise, AL
Walker, Stephan Cotton ... Jefferson City, MO
Walker, Stephan L. ... New York, NY
Walker, Stephen A. ... West Palm Beach, FL
Walker, Stephen Christopher ... Decatur, GA
Walker, Stephen G. ... San Francisco, CA
Walker, Stephen L. ... Pensacola, FL
Walker, Stephen L. ... Plano, TX
Walker, Stephen M. ... Sarasota, FL
Walker, Stephen M., P.A. ... Sarasota, FL
Walker, Stephen O. ... Cleveland, OH
Walker, Stephen S. ... Portland, OR
Walker, Stephen W. ... Cincinnati, OH
Walker, Steven R. ... San Francisco, CA
Walker, Steven R. ... Atlanta, GA
Walker, Steven R. ... Memphis, TN
Walker, Stewart H. ... New York, NY
Walker, Stewart H., P.C. ... New York, NY
Walker, Stuart Scott ... Gainesville, FL
Walker, Sue ... Fort Worth, TX
Walker, Susan ... Boca Raton, FL
Walker, Susan C. ... Shreveport, LA
Walker, Susan C. ... Columbus, OH
Walker, Susan Hicks ... Englewood, CO
Walker, Susan L. ... Chicago, IL
Walker, Susan M. ... Los Angeles, CA
Walker, Susan P. ... Honolulu, HI
Walker, Susan Russ ... Montgomery, AL
Walker, Susan S. ... Virginia Beach, VA
Walker, Susan S. Hahm
San Francisco, CA
Walker, Suzanne A. ... Washington, DC
Walker & Sweat ... Waycross, GA
Walker, T. Cy ... Washington, DC
Walker, Templeton S. ... Atlanta, GA
Walker, Teresa Bates ... San Francisco, CA
Walker, Terry David ... Longmont, CO
Walker, Terry John ... San Diego, CA
Walker, Theodore F. ... Nashville, TN
Walker, Theodore L. ... Eugene, OR
Walker, Thomas A. ... Minneapolis, MN
St. Paul, MN
Walker, Thomas C. ... Lexington, KY
Walker, Thomas D. ... Fair Oaks, CA
Walker, Thomas D. ... Albuquerque, NM
Walker, Thomas E. ... Birmingham, AL
Walker, Thomas E. ... Greenbelt, MD
Walker, Thomas F., Jr. ... Milwaukee, WI
Walker, Thomas G. ... Charlotte, NC
Walker, Thomas G., Jr. ... Boise, ID
Walker, Thomas L. ... Tucker, GA
Walker, Thomas L. ... Baton Rouge, LA
Walker, Thomas L. ... Fort Worth, TX
Walker, Thomas M. ... Los Angeles, CA
Walker, Thomas R. ... Atlanta, GA
Walker, Thomas R. ... Wolfeboro, NH
Walker, Thomas S. ... Ardmore, OK
Walker, Timothy A. ... Honolulu, HI
Walker, Timothy B. ... Lafayette, CA
Walker, Timothy B., (P.C.) ... Littleton, CO
Steamboat Springs, CO
Walker, Timothy J. ... Des Moines, IA
Walker, Timothy J. ... London, KY
Walker, Timothy J. ... Buffalo, NY
Walker, Timothy J., P.S.C. ... London, KY
Walker, Timothy L. ... Long Beach, CA
Walker, Timothy P. ... San Francisco, CA
Walker, Timothy P. ... Las Cruces, NM
Walker, Todd ... San Antonio, TX
Walker, Todd D. ... Orlando, FL
Walker, Tom E. ... Tampa, FL
Walker, Tom J. E. ... Dayton, OH
Walker, Tooke, Lyons & McKeithen, L.L.P.
Shreveport, LA
Walker, Trent L. ... Jackson, MS
Walker, Troy K. ... Sandy, UT
Walker, Trudie Katz ... Melville, NY
Walker, Ulvester ... Henderson, KY
Walker, V. Carl ... New York, NY
Walker & van Heijenoort, P.C.
Albuquerque, NM
Walker, Van Horn & MacBride
Chambersburg, PA
Walker & Varney, P.C. ... Wolfeboro, NH
Walker, Vaughn R. ... San Francisco, CA
Walker, Vern R. ... Hempstead, NY
Walker, Vernetta L. ... Orlando, FL
Walker, W. David ... Danville, CA
Walker, W. Evelyn ... West Chester, PA
Walker, W. Kent ... Charlotte, NC
Walker, W. Michael ... Fredericksburg, VA
Richmond, VA
Walker & Walker ... Monroe, LA
Jackson, MS
Charlotte, NC
Walker & Walker ... Oklahoma City, OK
Walker & Walker ... Ripley, TN
Walker & Walker Co., L.P.A. ... Athens, OH
Walker & Walker, P.C. ... Knoxville, TN
Walker Walker Wendlandt & Osowski, LLC
Anchorage, AK
Valdez, AK
Walker, Wallace W., Jr. ... Naples, FL
Akron, OH
Walker, Walter ... Neosho, MO
Walker, Walter H., III ... San Francisco, CA
Walker, Walter Ray ... Salt Lake City, UT
Walker & Warren ... Portland, OR
Walker, Watts, Jackson & McFarland
Adrian, MI
Walker, Wayne ... Gretna, LA
Walker, Wayne ... Detroit, MI
Walker, Wayne R. ... Wilmington, DE
Walker, Webb, III ... Burnet, TX
Walker, Wendy S. ... New York, NY
Walker, Wesley M. ... Greenville, SC
Walker, Weslynn W. ... Richardson, TX
Walker & Wiehaus ... Monticello, FL
Tallahassee, FL
Walker, Willard ... Longview, WA
Walker, William ... Batavia, OH
Walker, William A. ... Chicago, IL
Walker, William A. ... Richardson, TX
Walker, William A., II ... Orlando, FL
Winter Park, FL
Walker, William A., Jr. ... Las Cruces, NM
Walker, William Anthony ... Gary, IN
Walker, William B. ... San Jose, CA
Walker, William C. ... Garnett, KS
Walker, William C. ... Norfolk, VA
Walker, William C., Jr. ... Melbourne, FL
Walker, William C., Jr. ... Oxford, MS
Walker, William E., Jr. ... Hartford, CT
Washington, DC
Walker, William G. ... Tucson, AZ
Walker, William G. ... Albuquerque, NM
Walker, William G., P.C. ... Tucson, AZ
Walker, William H. ... St. Petersburg, FL
Walker, William H. ... Adrian, MI
Walker, William H. ... St. Louis, MO
Walker, William H., Chartered, Law Office
of ... St. Petersburg, FL
Tampa, FL
Walker, William H., Jr. ... East Rochester, NY
Walker, William J. ... Tempe, AZ
Walker, William J., P.C. ... Tempe, AZ
Walker, William Jason ... Houston, TX
Walker, William, Jr. ... Jackson, MS
Walker, William K. ... Anchorage, AK
Walker, William L. ... Gold River, CA
Roseville, CA
Walker, William L. ... St. Petersburg, FL
Walker, William L. ... Meadville, PA
Walker, William M. ... Anchorage, AK
Valdez, AK
Walker, William M. ... Los Angeles, CA
Walker, William M. ... Santa Ana, CA
Walker, William M. ... Rock Island, IL
Walker, William M. ... Nashville, TN
Walker, William P. ... Lynchburg, VA
Walker, William P., Jr. ... Roswell, GA
Walker, William P., Jr. ... Lexington, SC
Walker, William R. ... Athens, OH
Walker, William R. ... Blacksburg, VA
Walker, William R. ... Clarksburg, WV
Walker, William T. ... Akron, OH
Walker, William T. ... Tulsa, OK
Walker, William Vincent ... Houston, TX
Walker, William W. ... Winston-Salem, NC
Walker, William W., Jr. ... Tuscaloosa, AL
Walker & Williams, Professional
Corporation ... Belleville, IL
Benton, IL
Edwardsville, IL
St. Louis, MO
Walker, Willie J. ... Jacksonville, FL
Walker, Willis ... Piketon, OH
Walker, W. J. ... Little Rock, AR
Walker, Woodrow W. ... Washington, DC
Walker, Woodrow W. ... Arlington, VA
Walker, Woodson D. ... Little Rock, AR
Walker, Wright, Tyler & Ward, LLP
Los Angeles, CA
Walker-Bright, Paul R. ... Chicago, IL
Walker-Chyle, Mary K. ... Galveston, TX
Walkerdene, James ... Detroit, MI
Walker-Dewitt, Deborah A. ... Lockport, NY
Walker Elrod, Jennifer L. ... Houston, TX
Walker-Foster, Julie M. T. ... Atlanta, GA
Walker-Johnson, Nancy J. ... Norman, OK
Walker-Jones, Joyce
Equal Employment Opportunity
Commission,
Office of Federal Operations, GV
Walker-Lee, Robin ... Detroit, MI
Walkerman, Betsy J. ... Waltham, MA
Walker-Merino Law Office ... San Juan, PR
Walker-Suchyta, Janice M. ... Houghton, MI
Walkes, Staci B. ... Fairless Hills, PA
Walkey, Deedra Smith ... Tacoma, WA
Walkey, Jack L. ... Lafayette, IN
Walkey, John R., (P.C.) ... Boston, MA
Walkey, Jonathan D. ... Lemon Grove, CA
Walkey, Theodore J. ... Atlanta, GA
Walking, Albert M. ... Decatur, MI
Walkins, Arimentha R. ... Miami, FL
Walkinshaw, Walter ... Seattle, WA
Walkley, Bryan K. ... Norman, OK
Walkley, John T. ... Monroe, CT
Walkley & Kennedy Co., L.P.A.
Norton, OH
Walkley, Nancy L. ... Stamford, CT
Walkley, Robert E. ... Redmond, WA
Walkley, Thomas L. ... Norton, OH
Walko, Andrew J. ... Trenton, NJ
Walko, Lee S. ... Akron, OH
Walko, Matthew J. ... Boston, MA
Walko, Robert V. ... Memphis, TN
Walkoe, Albert E. ... San Diego, CA
Walkoff, Judith A. ... New York, NY
Walkon, Clifford B. ... Southfield, MI
Walkon, Craig S., Law Offices of
Laguna Hills, CA
Walkovik, Donald C. (IBA) ... New York, NY
Walkow, Alan Nathan ... New York, NY
Walkow, Moujan M. ... Ontario, CA
Walkow, Ronald H. ... Pittsburgh, PA
Walkowiak, Robt. J. ... Cleveland, OH
Walkowiak, Vincent S. ... Dallas, TX
Walkowicz, Victoria A. ... Chicago, IL
Walkowski, Barbara A. ... San Mateo, CA
Walkowski, Joseph A. ... Salt Lake City, UT
Walkowsky, Joan G. ... Anderson, SC
Walkup, Amanda Tracey ... Eugene, OR
Walkup, April R. ... Chicago, IL
Walkup, Brian L. ... Sacramento, CA
Walkup & Good, Ltd. ... Palatine, IL
Walkup, Homer A. ... Alexandria, VA
Walkup, J. William "Bill" ... Coppell, TX
Walkup, John B., Jr. ... Ocala, FL
Walkup, John Knox ... Nashville, TN
Walkup, Kenneth A. ... Nashville, TN
Walkup, Melodia, Kelly & Echeverria, A
Professional Corporation
San Francisco, CA
Walkup, Michael J. ... Palatine, IL
Wall, Alex W., Jr. ... Baton Rouge, LA
Wall, Alex W., Sr. ... Baton Rouge, LA
Wall, Allen J. ... Southfield, MI
Wall, Alvin R. ... Holyoke, CO
Wall, Amanda Patrice ... Miami, FL
Wall, Ann B. ... Raleigh, NC
Wall, Anthony J. ... Santa Barbara, CA
Wall, Barbara A. ... Carson City, NV
Wall, Barbara Wartelle ... Arlington, VA
Wall, Barrye L. ... Los Angeles, CA
Wall, Bart D. ... St. Louis, MO
Wall, Bernard T., P.C. ... Chicago, IL
Wall, Bevin W. ... Newport, NC
Wall, Bradley N. ... Colonial Heights, VA
Wall, Bradley R. ... Portland, OR
Wall, Brant H. ... Salt Lake City, UT
Wall, Brett A. ... Cleveland, OH
Wall, Brian A., Jr. ... Philadelphia, PA
Wall, Brian J. ... Sandwich, MA
Wall, Bruce M. ... Chicago, IL
Wall, Carey L. ... Colorado Springs, CO
Wall, Carroll C., III ... Lexington, NC
Wall, Catherine Wynne ... St. Louis, MO
Wall, Charles D., Jr. ... Polson, MT
Wall, Charles E. ... Richmond, VA
Wall, Charles R. ... New York, NY
Wall, Christina ... Atlanta, GA
Wall, Christopher D. ... Washington, DC
Wall, Christopher G. ... Torrington, CT
Wall, Christopher R. ... Washington, DC
Wall, Cory R. ... Salt Lake City, UT
Wall, D. Keith ... Jennings, LA
Wall, Daniel E. ... Albany, NY
Wall, Daniel G. ... St. Paul, MN
Wall, Daniel M. ... San Francisco, CA
Wall, David Garrett ... Elizabethtown, NC
Wall, David H. ... Bassett, VA
Wall, David N.
Federal Deposit Insurance Corporation,
Liquidation Branch, GV
Wall, David R. ... Brooklyn, NY
Wall, David T. ... Las Vegas, NV
Wall, Dawn L. ... Bloomington, IL
Wall, Debra A. ... Clarksville, TN
Wall, Dennis J. ... Orlando, FL
Wall, Dennis J., Attorney at Law, A Prof.
Assoc. ... Orlando, FL
Wall, Dennis R. (Joe) ... Victoria, TX
Wall, Don D. ... San Diego, CA
Wall, Donald A. ... Phoenix, AZ
Wall, Donald I. ... Philadelphia, PA
Wall, Donald J. ... Chicago, IL
Wall, Donald J. ... Baton Rouge, LA
Wall, Donald R. ... New York, NY
Wall, Douglas ... Norman, OK
Wall, Douglas J. ... Flagstaff, AZ
Wall, Duane D. ... New York, NY
Wall, Eamon J. ... Red Bank, NJ
Wall, Earl F. ... Winston-Salem, NC
Wall, Edward M. ... West Simsbury, CT
Wall, Eileen J., (Miss) ... Franklin, NC
Wall, Elizabeth A. ... New York, NY
Wall & Elliott, LLP ... Macon, GA
Warner Robins, GA
Wall, Elton L. ... Macon, GA
Wall, F. Marshall ... Raleigh, NC
Wall, Frank ... Portland, OR
Wall and Gawrych ... Torrington, CT
Wall, Genevieve ... Laguna Hills, CA
Wall, Genevieve, A Law Corporation
Laguna Hills, CA
Wall, George J. ... Irvine, CA
Wall, Georgia ... Bronxville, NY
Wall, Glenn M. ... Atlanta, GA
Wall, Gregory B. ... Salt Lake City, UT

Wall, Gregory J. ....Port Orchard, WA
Wall, Guy E. ....New Orleans, LA
Wall, Henry J., Jr. ....Brooklyn, NY
Wall, Henry P. ....Columbia, SC
Wall, Howard T., III ....Brentwood, TN
Wall, Hugh E., III ....Dayton, OH
Wall, Irvin ....Amarillo, TX
Wall, Irving M. ....Freeport, NY
Wall, J. David ....Fayetteville, AR
Wall, J. Edward ....Atlanta, GA
Wall, J. Joseph, Jr. ....San Jose, CA
Wall, James A. ....Honolulu, HI
Wall, James B., (P.C.) ....Augusta, GA
Wall, James D. ....Winston-Salem, NC
Wall, James J. ....Wilmington, NC
Wall, Jamie R. ....Dallas, TX
Wall, Jay J. ....Lower Lake, CA
Wall, Jean Margaret ....San Francisco, CA
Wall, Jeanine M. ....Chicago, IL
Wall, Jeffrey J. ....Knoxville, TN
Wall, Jeffrey L. ....Fresno, CA
Wall, Jeffrey P. ....Huntington Beach, CA
Wall, Jennifer M. ....Waukesha, WI
Wall, J.K. "Rusty" ....Midland, TX
Wall, Joanne Foster
Federal Communications Commission,
Office of the General Counsel, GV
Wall, Joel ....Westborough, MA
Wall, John A. ....Windsor, CT
Wall, John C. ....Terre Haute, IN
Wall, John E., Jr. ....Dallas, TX
Wall, John E., Jr., Law Offices of
Dallas, TX
Wall, John Edward ....Pittsburgh, PA
Wall, John G. ....Pittsburgh, PA
Wall, John J. ....Manassas, VA
Wall, John J., III ....Portland, ME
Wall, John J., Jr. ....Lyndonville, VT
Wall, John J., P.C. ....Manassas, VA
Wall, John, Law Office of ....Boston, MA
Wall, John M. ....Sedan, KS
Wall, John S. ....Bakersfield, CA
Wall, John W. ....Phoenix, AZ
Wall, John W. ....Stamford, CT
Wall, John W., Jr. ....Greensboro, NC
Wall, Jolynn ....Dunedin, FL
Wall, Jonathan ....Greensboro, NC
Wall, Joseph E. ....Raleigh, NC
Wall, Joseph R. ....Milwaukee, WI
Wall, Joshua ....Westmont, NJ
Philadelphia, PA
Wall, Judith M. ....Treasury Department,
Internal Revenue Service, GV
Wall, Julius F. ....Clinton, MO
Wall, Karen E. ....Hoopeston, IL
Wall, Karen M. ....Raleigh, NC
Wall, Kathleen A. ....Buffalo, NY
Wall, Kathleen R. ....Manasquan, NJ
Wall, Kelly C. ....Norristown, PA
Wall, Kenneth E. ....Houston, TX
Wall, Kenneth S. ....Houston, TX
Wall, Kenneth W. ....Louisville, KY
Wall, Kirk M. ....Columbus, OH
Wall, Kristin Welch ....Baton Rouge, LA
Wall, Larry, & Associates ....Wichita, KS
Wall, Laura Kay Robbins ....Eufaula, OK
Wall, Lawrence J., Jr.
Greenwood Village, CO
Wall, Lee E. ....Crookston, MN
Wall, Lewis D., III ....Fort Worth, TX
Wall, Lisa N. ....New York, NY
Wall, Lisa Yussman ....Louisville, KY
Wall, Lucy A. ....Boston, MA
Wall, Maggie Kincaid ....Charleston, WV
Wall, Marc R. ....San Francisco, CA
Wall, Margaret Conlon ....Lincolnshire, IL
Wall, Margaret M. ....Englewood, CO
Wall, Marilyn Moylan ....Portland, OR
Wall, Marjama, Bilinski & Burr
Syracuse, NY
Wall, Marjorie L. ....Williamsburg, VA
Wall, Mark H. ....Charleston, SC
Wall, Mark M. ....St. Petersburg, FL
Wall, Mark M., P.A., Law Offices of
St. Petersburg, FL
Wall, Mark W. ....Middletown, OH
Wall, Marlin D. ....Woodland Hills, CA
Wall, Martin E. ....Vero Beach, FL
Wall, Martin J. ....Santa Ana, CA
Wall, Mary E. ....Washington, DC
Wall, Mary K. ....Silver Spring, MD
Wall, Mary K. ....Austin, TX
Wall, Matthew T. ....Austin, TX
Wall & McCormack, P.C. ....Windsor, CT
Wall, McCormick & Baroldi, A Prof. Corp.
Santa Ana, CA
Wall, Michael E. ....San Francisco, CA
Wall, Michael J. ....Santa Rosa, CA
Wall, Michael J. ....Chicago, IL
Wall, Michael J. ....Boston, MA
Wall, Michael J., Law Office of
Santa Rosa, CA
Wall, Michael K. ....Las Vegas, NV
Wall, Michelle ....Paramus, NJ
Wall, Michelle L. ....Indianapolis, IN
Wall, Mike R. ....Oxford, MS
Wall, Mitchell C. ....Portland, OR
Wall, N. Madison, II ....Burlington, NC
Wall, Natalie C. ....San Luis Obispo, CA
Wall & Noonan ....Roswell, GA
Wall, Patricia Kehau ....Honolulu, HI
Wall, Patrick J. ....Harwinton, CT
Wall, Patrick M. ....New York, NY
Wall, Percy L. ....Greensboro, NC
Wall, Peter J. ....Denver, CO
Wall, Peter T. ....Chicago, IL
Wall, Peter V. ....Greenwich, CT
New York, NY

Wall, Philip J. ....Rocky River, OH
Wall, Philip T. ....Greensboro, NC
Wall, R. Anthony, Jr. ....Torrington, CT
Wall, Ralph H. ....New Orleans, LA
Wall, Randall B. ....Jackson, MS
Wall, Randall D. ....Huntington, WV
Wall, Rebecca Roark ....Daytona Beach, FL
Wall, Richard ....Norman, OK
Wall, Richard A. ....Santa Ana, CA
Wall, Richard A. ....Lexington, MA
Wall, Richard F. ....Orlando, FL
Wall, Richard H. ....Radford, VA
Roanoke, VA
Wall, Richard J. ....San Francisco, CA
Wall, Richard J., Jr. ....Kansas City, MO
Wall, Richard L. ....Vergennes, VT
Wall, Richard Manning ....Spencer, MA
Wall, Robert A. ....Lexington, MA
Wall, Robert B. ....New York, NY
Wall, Robert C. ....Portland, OR
Wall, Robert E., III ....Watsonville, CA
Wall, Robert F. ....Chicago, IL
Wall, Robert F. ....Hudson, WI
Wall, Robert T. ....Warren, MI
Wall, Roberta ....New York, NY
Wall, Roger ....Ava, MO
Wall, Ronald C., Jr. ....Birmingham, AL
Wall, Ronald W., (A Prof. Corp.) ....Baker, LA
Wall, Ronny H. ....Amarillo, TX
Wall, Rosemary Pierce ....Nutley, NJ
Wall, Sandra J. ....Hoffman Estates, IL
Wall, Sarah F. ....Eastman, GA
Wall, Scott W. ....San Luis Obispo, CA
Wall, Sharon Kay Vander ....Grand Rapids, MI
Wall, Stacy M. ....Norwood, OH
Wall, Stefan T. ....Chadron, NE
Wall, Stephanie D. ....Pittsburgh, PA
Wall, Stephanie Waguespack
Baton Rouge, LA
Gonzales, LA
Wall, Stephen E. ....Bakersfield, CA
Wall, Steven B. ....Salt Lake City, UT
Wall, Steven R. ....Philadelphia, PA
Wall, Steven S. ....San Diego, CA
Wall, Sue Domingue ....Austin, TX
Wall, Susan J. ....Media, PA
Wall, Susan P. ....Boston, MA
Wall, Susan Taylor ....Charleston, SC
Wall, T. Michael ....Houston, TX
Wall, Tara M. ....Clearwater, FL
Wall, Terry J. ....Roeland Park, KS
Wall, Thomas Edward
Rancho Palos Verdes, CA
Wall, Thomas F. ....Torrington, CT
Wall, Thomas F., Jr. ....Torrington, CT
Wall, Thomas H. ....Washington, DC
Wall, Thomas J. ....Edgewater, NJ
Wall, Thomas J. ....Syracuse, NY
Wall, Thomas J., Jr. ....Detroit, MI
Wall, Thomas M. ....White Plains, NY
Wall, Thomas P., III ....Madison, TN
Wall, Tom O. ....Jefferson City, TN
Wall, Tracie ....Seattle, WA
Wall, Travis R. ....San Francisco, CA
Wall, Tyler E. ....Cupertino, CA
Wall, Victoria Gardner ....Houston, TX
Wall, Virginia ....Toledo, OH
Wall, W. Alford ....Jefferson, GA
Roswell, GA
Wall & Wall ....Salt Lake City, UT
Wall, Wall & Frauenhofer ....Torrington, CT
Wall & Wall, P.C. ....Portland, OR
Wall, Wall & Peake, A Professional Corporation
Bakersfield, CA
Wall, Walter F. ....Altoona, PA
Wall, Walter W. ....Fresno, CA
Wall, William Alford, P.C. ....Jefferson, GA
Wall, William D. ....Uniondale, NY
Wall, William D. ....Pittsburgh, PA
Wall, William E. ....Seattle, WA
Wall, William F. ....Fairfax, VA
Wall, William J. ....Yardley, PA
Wall, William P. ....Boston, MA
Wall, Willis W. ....Wichita, KS
Wall, Wintroub & Weiner ....Omaha, NE
Walla, Beth Adrienne ....Nashville, TN
Walla, Douglas M. ....Houston, TX
Walla, Jacob J. ....Bellaire, TX
Walla, Michael E. ....Lincoln, NE
Walla, Nancy A. ....Lakewood, CO
Walla, Sharon Clayton ....Elkton, MD
Wallace, A. Stephenson ....Augusta, GA
Wallace, A. Stephenson, P.C.
Augusta, GA
Wallace, Alaiyo C. ....Toluca Lake, CA
Wallace, Alan L. ....Seattle, WA
Wallace, Albert B. ....Jonesboro, GA
Wallace, Albert Bailey, P.C. ....Jonesboro, GA
Wallace, Alec S. ....Miami, FL
Wallace, Alexander W. ....Long Beach, CA
Wallace, Allan E. ....Minneapolis, MN
Wallace, Allen F. ....Rome, GA
Wallace, Allen W. ....Waverly, TN
Wallace, Amy E. ....Omaha, NE
Wallace, Amy J. ....San Diego, CA
Wallace & Anderson ....Bremerton, WA
Wallace, Anderson, Jr. ....Dallas, TX
Wallace, Anderson, Jr., P.C. ....Dallas, TX
Wallace, Andrew J. ....Albany, NY
Wallace, Andrew J. ....Hicksville, NY
Wallace, Andrew R. ....Hartford, CT
Wallace, Ann T. ....Department of Justice,
Criminal Division, GV
Wallace, Anne M. ....Saddle Brook, NJ
Wallace, Anthony A. ....New Haven, CT
Wallace, Archibald, III ....Richmond, VA
Wallace, Archie O. ....Greenville, PA
Wallace, Arthur E. ....Bakersfield, CA

Wallace, Arthur L., III ....Orlando, FL
Wallace, Arthur M., Jr. ....Benton, LA
Wallace, Barbara Childs ....Jackson, MS
Wallace, Barbara K. ....Rock Island, IL
Wallace, Barbara W. ....Clayton, MO
Wallace, Barron F. ....Houston, TX
Wallace, Bass C. ....Houston, TX
Wallace, Bass C., Jr. ....The Woodlands, TX
Wallace, Bauman, Legon, Fodiman &
Shannon, P.A. ....Coral Gables, FL
Wallace, Bauman, Legon, Fodiman &
Shannon, P.A. ....Miami, FL
Wallace, Ben B. ....Corpus Christi, TX
Wallace, Beverly A. ....Towson, MD
Wallace, Brantley & Shirley ....Scott City, KS
Wallace, Brennan & Folan ....Torrance, CA
Wallace, Brett D. ....Phoenix, AZ
Wallace, Brian D. ....Denver, CO
Wallace, Brian D. ....New Orleans, LA
Wallace, Brian L. ....Baltimore, MD
Wallace, Browning & Krawetz
Bradenton, FL
Sarasota, FL
Wallace, Bruce D. ....Mission Viejo, CA
Wallace, Bruce M., Jr. ....San Diego, CA
Wallace, Bruce R. ....San Diego, CA
Wallace, Bruce Sanford ....Mt. Orab, OH
Wallace, Bruce T. ....Ann Arbor, MI
Wallace, Bruce T. ....Patchogue, NY
Wallace Campbell Bunch Shambach Rennick &
Orr ....Covington, IN
Wallace, Campbell Edington
Metairie, LA
Wallace, Carl E., Jr. ....Chapel Hill, NC
Wallace, Catherine Bond ....Princeton, WV
Wallace, Charles G. (C.G.), III ....Kimball, NE
Wallace, Charles W. ....Killeen, TX
Wallace, Cheryl Y. ....United States Senate,
Committee Legal Personnel, GV
Wallace, Chester J. ....Garfield, NJ
Wallace, Christine M.
Milton-Freewater, OR
Wallace, Christopher B. ....Utica, NY
Wallace, Christopher J. ....New York, NY
Wallace, Christopher J. ....Cleveland, OH
Wallace, Christopher B. ....Corning, NY
Wallace, Codette G. ....Los Angeles, CA
Wallace, Connie J. ....Houston, TX
Wallace, Craig ....Poughkeepsie, NY
Wallace, Craig F. ....Tulsa, OK
Wallace, Craig W. ....San Francisco, CA
Wallace, Creech & Sarda, L.L.P.
Raleigh, NC
Wallace, Cynthia A. ....Greenwood Village, CO
Wallace, D. Fleet ....Richmond, VA
Wallace, Daniel J. ....Santa Barbara, CA
Wallace, Daniel S., (P.A.)
Daytona Beach, FL
Wallace, Darren Kendrick ....Clayton, MO
Wallace, Darren M. ....Hartford, CT
Wallace, David ....Southfield, MI
Wallace, David ....Montague Township, NJ
Glen Spey, NY
Wallace, David A. ....Sarasota, FL
Wallace, David A. ....Framingham, MA
Wallace, David A. ....Saginaw, MI
Wallace, David A. ....Winston-Salem, NC
Wallace, David A. ....Columbus, OH
Wallace, David C. ....Evanston, IL
Wallace, David C. ....Houston, TX
Wallace, David G. ....Bath, NY
Wallace, David H. ....Cleveland, OH
Wallace, David J. ....Charlotte, MI
Wallace, David L. ....Sarasota, FL
Wallace, David L. ....New York, NY
Wallace, David R. ....Anchorage, AK
Wallace, David S. ....Walnut Creek, CA
Wallace, David S. ....Muncie, IN
Wallace, David S. ....Milwaukee, WI
Wallace, David T. ....Cincinnati, OH
Wallace, David W. ....Chattanooga, TN
Wallace, David W. ....Sonora, TX
Wallace, Dean W. ....Omaha, NE
Wallace, Deborah Siri ....San Mateo, CA
Wallace & De Mayo, P.C. ....Atlanta, GA
Norcross, GA
Wallace, Dennis M. ....Spokane, WA
Wallace, Dennis P. ....Shoreham, NY
Wallace, Diana K. ....Tampa, FL
Wallace, Don, Jr. ....Washington, DC
Wallace, Donald B. ....Torrance, CA
Wallace, Donald C., Jr. ....Long Beach, CA
Wallace, Donald E. ....Salt Lake City, UT
Wallace, Donald J. ....Grand Rapids, MI
Wallace, Donald J. ....New York, NY
Wallace, Donald L. ....New York, NY
Wallace, Donna B. ....Oak Brook, IL
Wallace, Douglas ....Little Rock, AR
Wallace, Douglas A. ....Bradenton, FL
Wallace, Douglas A. ....Sarasota, FL
Wallace, Douglas K. ....Newport Beach, CA
Wallace, Douglas K. ....Santa Ana, CA
Santa Ana, CA
Hamilton, MT
Wallace, Douglas S. ....Colorado Springs, CO
Wallace, Douglas W. ....Norcross, GA
Wallace, Dwight D ....Wichita, KS
Wallace, E. Gregory ....Buies Creek, NC
Wallace, Earl R. ....Newport Beach, CA
Wallace, Edgar A. ....Kerrville, TX
Wallace, Edward C., Jr. ....New York, NY
Wallace, Edward E. ....Beverly Hills, CA
Wallace, Edwin L. ....Boston, MA
Wallace, Elaine ....Palo Alto, CA
Wallace, Eleanor E. ....Salem, OR
Wallace, Elisabeth F. ....Morgantown, WV
Wallace, Elizabeth A. ....Chicago, IL

Wallace, Elizabeth Patterson
Woodstock, AL
Wallace, Elizabeth Wilson ....Sonora, TX
Wallace, Ellen N. ....Boston, MA
Wallace, Ellen S. ....Tyrone, PA
Wallace, Ellis, Fowler and Head
Columbiana, AL
Wallace, Elva C. ....Anaheim, CA
Wallace, Erik X ....Greenwich, CT
Wallace, Ferlanda Fox ....Livingston, NJ
Wallace, Fitzhugh E., Jr. ....Kinston, NC
Wallace, Francis X. ....Altamont, NY
New Bern, NC
Wallace, Frank P. ....Tarrytown, NY
Wallace, Franklin S. ....Rock Island, IL
Wallace, Fred ....New York, NY
Wallace, Freda I. ....Rock Hill, SC
Wallace, Gail H. ....Cleveland, OH
Wallace, Gary C. ....Dallas, TX
Wallace, Gary G. ....Shelbina, MO
Wallace, Gary J. ....Chicago, IL
Wallace, Gary R. ....Santa Monica, CA
Wallace, George B. ....Sanford, FL
Wallace, George B., P.A. ....Sanford, FL
Wallace, George C. ....Montgomery, AL
Wallace, George Early ....Albany, NY
Wallace, George J. ....Washington, DC
Wallace, George K. ....Springville, UT
Wallace, George S. ....Holden, MA
Wallace, Glen H. ....Yuba City, CA
Wallace, Graehm C. ....Seattle, WA
Wallace and Graham, P.A. ....Salisbury, NC
Wallace, Gregory G. ....Philadelphia, PA
Wallace, H. David ....Fort Wright, KY
Wallace, Hank ....Washington, DC
Wallace, Harold E. ....Ann Arbor, MI
Wallace, Harold W., III ....Thomson, GA
Wallace, Harry A. ....Orange, CA
Wallace, Harry B. ....Mastic, NY
Wallace, Harry L. ....Milwaukee, WI
Wallace, Harvey B., II (PLLC)
Detroit, MI
Wallace, Heather L. ....Cupertino, CA
Wallace, Henry J., Jr. ....Pittsburgh, PA
Wallace, Henry S. ....United States Senate,
Committee Legal Personnel, GV
Wallace, Herbert N. ....Poughkeepsie, NY
Wallace, Holly Salop ....Syracuse, NY
Wallace, Howard P. ....Griffin, GA
Wallace, J. Clifford ....San Diego, CA
Wallace, J. Gregory ....Raleigh, NC
Wallace, J. McLain, Jr.
Rocky Mount, NC
Wallace, J. Randolph ....San Rafael, CA
Wallace, J. Stuart ....Mobile, AL
Wallace, Jack R. ....Burlington, WA
Wallace, Jack R., A Professional Corporation
Burlington, WA
Wallace, Jack W. ....Eufaula, AL
Wallace, Jack W., Jr. ....Montgomery, AL
Wallace, Jaime L. ....Sarasota, FL
Wallace, James A. ....Athens, OH
Wallace, James B. ....Park Rapids, MN
Wallace, James B., Jr. ....New York, NY
Wallace, James C. ....Salem, OR
Wallace, James D. ....Burlington, NJ
Wallace, James E. ....Wilmington, NC
Wallace, James E. ....Grove, OK
Wallace, James E., Jr. ....Worcester, MA
Wallace, James G. ....Charlotte, NC
Wallace, James H., Jr. ....Washington, DC
Wallace, James J. ....San Diego, CA
Wallace, James J. ....Syracuse, NY
Wallace, James M. ....San Diego, CA
Wallace, James M. ....Bradenton, FL
Wallace, James P. ....Austin, TX
Wallace, James P., Jr. ....Georgetown, TX
Houston, TX
Wallace, James P., Jr., A Professional
Corporation ....Georgetown, TX
Houston, TX
Wallace, James R., & Associates
Little Rock, AR
Wallace, James W. ....Pittsburgh, PA
Wallace, Jay B. ....Costa Mesa, CA
Wallace, Jay M. ....Dallas, TX
Wallace, Jay S. ....San Francisco, CA
Wallace, Jeffrey D. ....Dallas, TX
Wallace, Jeffrey E. ....Louisville, KY
Wallace, Jeffrey J. ....Newport Beach, CA
Wallace, Jeffrey M. ....Hermiston, OR
Wallace, Jenni R. ....Washington, DC
Wallace, Jerry R. ....El Paso, TX
Wallace, Jerry W. ....Parsons, TN
Wallace, Jessica A. ....Washington, DC
Wallace, J. F. ....McGehee, AR
Wallace, Jodi M. ....Cleveland, OH
Wallace, Joe R. ....Birmingham, AL
Wallace, John ....Winters, CA
Wallace, John ....Buffalo, NY
Wallace, John A. ....Atlanta, GA
Wallace, John B. ....Agoura Hills, CA
Wallace, John B. ....Los Angeles, CA
Wallace, John B. ....Houston, TX
Wallace, John C. ....Pasadena, CA
Wallace, John D. ....Seattle, WA
Wenatchee, WA
Wallace, John E., Jr. ....Westmont, NJ
Wallace, John F. ....Bridgeport, CT
Wallace, John Foster ....Fairbanks, AK
Wallace, John H. ....Boston, MA
Wallace, John H., III ....Oshkosh, WI
Wallace, John H., Jr. ....Oshkosh, WI
Wallace, John K., III
Department of Justice, GV
Wallace, John L. ....Lewisburg, TN
Wallace, John P. ....Ridgewood, NJ
Wallace, John P. ....Syracuse, NY

Wallace, John R. ....San Francisco, CA
Wallace, John R. ....Raleigh, NC
Wallace, John R. ....Houston, TX
Wallace, John T. ....Boston, MA
Wallace, John T. ....Logan, OH
Wallace, John W. ....Sacramento, CA
Wallace, John W. ....Denver, CO
Wallace, John W., Jr. ....Atlanta, GA
Wallace & Jones ....Sevierville, TN
Wallace, Joni M. ....Missoula, MT
Wallace, Jordan, Ratliff & Brandt, L.L.C. Birmingham, AL; Montgomery, AL
Wallace, Joseph M. ....O'Fallon, MO
Wallace, Joseph V. ....Florham Park, NJ
Wallace, Joyce Pulliam ....Altamont, NY; New Bern, NC
Wallace, K Michelle ....Kansas City, MO
Wallace, K. Todd ....New Orleans, LA
Wallace, Karen C. ....Chicago, IL
Wallace, Karen D. ....Manchester, CT
Wallace, Karen Virginia ....Benton, AR
Wallace & Karo ....Miami, FL
Wallace, Katherine T. ....Washington, DC
Wallace, Kathleen M. ....New York, NY
Wallace, Kathleen M. ....Philadelphia, PA
Wallace, Keith D. ....Alpena, MI
Wallace, Keith M. ....Evansville, IN
Wallace, Kenneth D. ....New Canaan, CT
Wallace, Kerry H. ....Avon, CO
Wallace, Kevin ....Seattle, WA
Wallace, Kevin P. ....Auburn, IN
Wallace, Kimberly ....Houston, TX
Wallace, Kimberly Paige ....Jackson, MS
Wallace King Marraro & Branson, PLLC Washington, DC
Wallace, Kirk ....Los Angeles, CA
Wallace & Kling, P.C. ....Fort Collins, CO
Wallace, Klor & Mann, P.C. Portland, OR; Seattle, WA
Wallace, L. Jim ....Houston, TX
Wallace, Lacey P. ....Shreveport, LA
Wallace, Larry ....New York, NY
Wallace, Larry A., Jr. ....Lafayette, LA; New Orleans, LA
Wallace, Larry C. ....Little Rock, AR; Washington, DC
Wallace, Larry C., P.A. ....Little Rock, AR
Wallace, Larry F, Jr ....La Vergne, TN
Wallace, Larry J. ....Indianapolis, IN
Wallace, Laurie ....Columbia Falls, MT
Wallace, Lawrence G. ....Department of Justice, Office of the Solicitor General, GV
Wallace, Lee Tarte ....Atlanta, GA; Columbus, GA
Wallace, LeMaistre & Reeves, P.C. Eufaula, AL
Wallace, Leonard F. ....New York, NY
Wallace, Leslie R. ....Los Angeles, CA
Wallace, Lisa A. ....Boston, MA
Wallace, Lisa R. ....Warren, OH
Wallace & Long, LLC ....Shreveport, LA
Wallace, Loren D. ....Key West, FL
Wallace, Lucius James ....Tulsa, OK
Wallace, M. Kristi ....Atlanta, GA
Wallace, Manuel B. ....Falls Church, VA
Wallace, Marc E. ....Coeur d'Alene, ID
Wallace, Marcia ....New York, NY
Wallace, Marcy S. ....Minneapolis, MN
Wallace, Marianne Monti ....Glastonbury, CT
Wallace, Marjorie A. ....Orinda, CA
Wallace, Mark D. ....Miami, FL
Wallace, Mark S. ....Los Angeles, CA
Wallace, Marshall A. ....West Bloomfield, MI
Wallace, Marshall Clark ....Oakland, CA
Wallace, Mary A. ....Washington, DC
Wallace, Matthew M. ....Port Huron, MI
Wallace, Matthew M., P.C. Port Huron, MI
Wallace, Matthew W. ....Savannah, GA
Wallace, Michael B. ....Jackson, MS
Wallace, Michael E. ....Birmingham, AL
Wallace, Michael E. ....Philadelphia, PA
Wallace, Michael J. ....Chicago, IL
Wallace, Michael J. ....Fayetteville, NY
Wallace, Michael J., Jr ....Westfield, NJ
Wallace, Michael K. ....South Charleston, WV
Wallace, Michael L. ....Springfield, IL
Wallace, Michael P. ....Buffalo, NY
Wallace, Michael P. ....Tyler, TX
Wallace, Michael R. ....Overland Park, KS
Wallace, Miller ....Midland, TX
Wallace, Milton J. ....Miami, FL
Wallace, Mitzi S. ....Dallas, TX
Wallace, Mona Lisa ....Salisbury, NC
Wallace, Monte J. ....Boston, MA
Wallace, Morris & Barwick, P.A. Goldsboro, NC; Greenville, NC; Jacksonville, NC; Kenansville, NC; Kinston, NC; New Bern, NC
Wallace, Mosty, Machann, Jackson & Williams, A Professional Corporation ....Kerrville, TX
Wallace, Nancy G. ....Murfreesboro, TN
Wallace, Nancy J. ....San Bernardino, CA
Wallace, Nancy L. ....Fort Collins, CO
Wallace, Nancy S. ....San Francisco, CA
Wallace, Neal C. ....Syracuse, NY
Wallace, Neal J. ....St. Louis, MO
Wallace, Neil E. ....Pontiac, MI
Wallace, Neil T. ....Ithaca, NY
Wallace, Neil W. ....Boston, MA
Wallace, Nianza E., II ....Virginia Beach, VA
Wallace, Nora Ann ....New York, NY
Wallace, Owens, Landers, Gee, Morrow, Wilson, Watson & James, A Professional Corporation ....Jay, OK; Miami, OK
Wallace, Patricia ....Lebanon, NH
Wallace, Patricia A. ....New York, NY
Wallace, Patrick E. ....Redding, CA
Wallace, Paul A. ....Mount Kisco, NY
Wallace, Paul J. ....Evansville, IN
Wallace, Paul L. ....Columbus, OH
Wallace, Paul R. ....Wilmington, DE
Wallace, Paul R. ....Miami, FL
Wallace, Paul S., Jr. ....Library of Congress, Congressional Research Service, GV
Wallace, Peggy C. ....Chicago, IL
Wallace, Perry E., Jr. ....Baltimore, MD
Wallace, Peter P. ....Los Angeles, CA
Wallace, Peter R. ....Tallahassee, FL
Wallace, Philip A. ....Bedford, VA
Wallace, Phillip K. ....Slidell, LA
Wallace, Phyllis E. ....New York, NY
Wallace, R. Brown ....Oklahoma City, OK
Wallace, R. Bruce ....Key West, FL
Wallace, R. Bruce, P.A. ....Key West, FL
Wallace, R. Byron ....Cleveland, OH
Wallace, R. Dale, Jr. ....Birmingham, AL
Wallace, R. David ....Charlotte, NC
Wallace, Randell D. ....Springfield, MO
Wallace, Randy Joseph Farmington Hills, MI
Wallace, Rebecca P. ....Henderson, NV
Wallace, Renee Pipe ....Springfield, NJ
Wallace, R. H., Jr. ....Fort Worth, TX
Wallace, Rhonda Oneita ....Chester, SC
Wallace, Richard A. ....West Hartford, CT
Wallace, Richard B. ....Miami, FL
Wallace, Richard C. ....Lenexa, KS
Wallace, Richard E., Jr. ....Washington, DC
Wallace, Richard G. ....Los Angeles, CA
Wallace, Richard G. ....Washington, DC
Wallace, Richard H. ....Sidney, OH
Wallace, Richard J. ....San Francisco, CA
Wallace, Richard J., III ....Dallas, TX
Wallace, Richard L. ....New York, NY
Wallace, Richard M. ....Ithaca, NY
Wallace, Richard P. ....Coeur d'Alene, ID
Wallace, Richard P. ....Troy, NY
Wallace, Richard T. ....Sevierville, TN
Wallace, Rickey D. ....Merced, CA
Wallace, Robert A. ....Stamford, CT
Wallace, Robert A. ....Boise, ID
Wallace, Robert A. ....Poteau, OK
Wallace, Robert A. ....Dallas, TX
Wallace, Robert B. ....Washington, DC
Wallace, Robert B. ....Jacksonville, FL
Wallace, Robert B. ....Pembroke Pines, FL
Wallace, Robert B. ....Charleston, SC
Wallace, Robert B., Jr. Corpus Christi, TX
Wallace, Robert Bruce ....Charleston, SC
Wallace, Robert C., Jr. ....Lafayette, AL
Wallace, Robert Craig Newport Beach, CA
Wallace, Robert E. ....Department of Justice, Criminal Division, GV
Wallace, Robert E. ....Marietta, GA
Wallace, Robert E., Jr. ....Philadelphia, PA
Wallace, Robert F. ....Oakland, CA
Wallace, Robert G. ....Seattle, WA
Wallace, Robert, III ....Tampa, FL
Wallace, Robert J. ....Buckhannon, WV
Wallace, Robert J., Sr. ....Troy, MI
Wallace, Robert L., Jr. Boothbay Harbor, ME
Wallace, Robert M. ....Ventura, CA
Wallace, Robert, P.A. ....Tampa, FL
Wallace, Robert R. ....Salt Lake City, UT
Wallace, Robert T. National Labor Relations Board, Division of Administrative Law Judges, GV
Wallace, Robert T. ....Sugar Land, TX
Wallace, Robin ....Washington, DC
Wallace, Robt. P. ....Corpus Christi, TX
Wallace, Ronald L. ....Oklahoma City, OK
Wallace, Royce E. ....Wichita, KS
Wallace, Russell C., P.C. ....Valdosta, GA
Wallace, Russell Cotter ....Valdosta, GA
Wallace, Russell W. ....Tulsa, OK
Wallace, Russell W., Inc. ....Tulsa, OK
Wallace, S. James ....Pittsburgh, PA
Wallace, Samuel E. ....Nashville, TN
Wallace, Samuel E., Jr. ....Nashville, TN
Wallace, Sandra ....St. Paul, MN
Wallace, Sandra L. ....Kansas City, MO
Wallace, Saunders, Austin, Brown & Enochs, Chartered ....Overland Park, KS; Wichita, KS; Kansas City, MO; Springfield, MO
Wallace, Schuyler T., Jr. ....Portland, OR
Wallace, Scott C. ....Silver Spring, MD
Wallace, Scott C. ....Dallas, TX
Wallace, Scott E. ....Darien, IL
Wallace, Scott G. ....Boca Raton, FL
Wallace, Sean D. ....Upper Marlboro, MD
Wallace, Selden Anne ....Austin, TX
Wallace, Shawn Daughtridge Charleston, SC
Wallace, Shelley L ....Hartford, CT
Wallace, Sherri L. ....Dallas, TX
Wallace, Shirley M. ....Port Neches, TX
Wallace, Sidney A. ....Washington, DC
Wallace, Sondra S. Department Of Health And Human Services, Office of the General Counsel, GV
Wallace, Sonya Opal ....Missouri City, TX
Wallace and Southerland ....Benton, LA
Wallace, Stacie A. ....San Francisco, CA
Wallace, Stephan W. ....Dallas, TX
Wallace, Stephen ....Houston, TX
Wallace, Stephen B. ....Kodiak, AK
Wallace, Stephen Bailey, II ....Jonesboro, GA
Wallace, Stephen C. ....Chesterfield, SC
Wallace, Stephen J. ....Washington, DC
Wallace, Steven ....Orlando, FL
Wallace, Steven C. ....Milwaukee, WI
Wallace, Steven C., Sr. ....Philadelphia, MS
Wallace, Steven J. ....West Bloomfield, MI
Wallace, Steven M. ....East St. Louis, IL
Wallace, Stratford C. ....Greenwich, CT
Wallace, Stuart C. ....Chicago, IL
Wallace, Susan Collier ....Sacramento, CA
Wallace, Susan Davis ....Carmel Valley, CA
Wallace, Ted James ....Bettendorf, IA
Wallace, Teri A. ....Cincinnati, OH
Wallace, Terrence Joseph ....Joliet, IL
Wallace and Tetreault, LLC ....Savannah, GA
Wallace, Theodore I., Jr. (P.C.) Costa Mesa, CA
Wallace, Thomas A. ....Oklahoma City, OK
Wallace, Thomas E. ....Memphis, TN
Wallace, Thomas G. ....Columbus, MS
Wallace, Thomas H. ....Columbus, OH
Wallace, Thomas J., Jr. ....Pearland, TX
Wallace, Thomas W. ....San Antonio, TX
Wallace and Tinkler ....Charleston, SC
Wallace, Todd ....Dallas, TX
Wallace, Tommy W. ....Canton, TX
Wallace, Vicky ....Frazier Park, CA
Wallace, Victor L., II ....Denver, CO
Wallace, W. Bruce ....York, PA
Wallace, W. Clayton ....Gulf Shores, AL
Wallace, W. Clinton ....Lakeland, FL
Wallace, W. Clinton, P.A. ....Lakeland, FL
Wallace, W. Creekmore, II ....Sapulpa, OK
Wallace, W. David ....Washington, DC
Wallace, W. Kirk ....New York, NY
Wallace, W. Scott ....Dallas, TX
Wallace & Wallace ....San Diego, CA; West Bloomfield, MI; Nashville, TN
Wallace & Wallace, S.C. ....Oshkosh, WI
Wallace & Warner, Co., L.P.A. Columbus, OH
Wallace, Wayne W ....Wichita, KS
Wallace, Wendy J. ....San Francisco, CA
Wallace, Wesley L. ....Jacksonville, FL
Wallace & Wheeler, L.L.P. Corpus Christi, TX
Wallace, William B. ....Charlotte, NC
Wallace, William C. ....Metairie, LA
Wallace, William D. ....Washington, DC
Wallace, William D. ....Dawsonville, GA
Wallace, William E., III ....Washington, DC
Wallace, William E., Jr. ....New York, NY
Wallace, William F. ....Hingham, MA
Wallace, William G. ....White Plains, NY
Wallace, William H. ....St. Charles, MO
Wallace, William H., Jr. ....Tyler, TX
Wallace, William J. ....Stockton, CA
Wallace, William J. ....West Palm Beach, FL
Wallace, William J. ....West Orange, NJ
Wallace, William J., P.A. West Palm Beach, FL
Wallace, William K., III ....Honolulu, HI; Laie, HI
Wallace, William L. ....Washington, DC
Wallace, William M. ....Los Angeles, CA
Wallace, William M. ....San Diego, CA
Wallace, William N. ....Gold Beach, OR
Wallace, William P., Jr. ....Roanoke, VA
Wallace, William R., III ....Princeton, IN
Wallace & Wyatt, P.C. ....Birmingham, AL
Wallace-Cody, Tracey ....Chelmsford, MA
Wallace-Curry, Virginia ....Cleveland, OH
Wallace-Fischler, Lori ....New York, NY
Wallace-Jackson, David J. Minneapolis, MN
Wallace-Jackson, Emily ....Edina, MN
Wallace Post, Carole Palm Beach Gardens, FL
Wallach, Alan V. ....Appleton, WI
Wallach, Alex B. ....Forest Park, GA
Wallach, Brian D. ....Washington, DC
Wallach, Cheryl L. ....Woodland Hills, CA
Wallach, Cynthia M. ....Chicago, IL
Wallach, D. Michael ....Fort Worth, TX
Wallach, Daniel L. ....New York, NY
wallach, e. robert (bob) San Francisco, CA
Wallach, Edward S. ....Scarsdale, NY
Wallach, Eric J. ....New York, NY
Wallach, Frederick E. ....Lexington, MA
Wallach, Frederick K. ....New York, NY
Wallach, Gail B. ....New York, NY
Wallach, George C. 'Skip' ....Scottsdale, AZ
Wallach, George C. 'Skip' ....Phoenix, AZ
Wallach, Gilbert ....New York, NY
Wallach & Gordon, P.A. ....Sarasota, FL
Wallach, Henry James ....New York, NY
Wallach, Howard I. ....Dearborn Heights, MI
Wallach, Ira M. ....Boston, MA
Wallach, Jack S. ....Atlanta, GA
Wallach, Jason ....Los Angeles, CA
Wallach, Jason D. ....Washington, DC
Wallach, Jeffrey J. ....New York, NY
Wallach, Jerome ....St. Louis, MO
Wallach, John M., Law Office of South Portland, ME
Wallach, John S. ....St. Louis, MO
Wallach, Jonathan D. ....New York, NY
Wallach, Jordan L. ....Sarasota, FL
Wallach, Kenneth A. ....Woodbridge, NJ
Wallach, Kenneth B. ....New York, NY
Wallach, Kevin G. ....Western Springs, IL
Wallach, Laurie R. ....Boston, MA
Wallach Law Firm, The ....St. Louis, MO
Wallach, Lawrence S. ....Tukwila, WA
Wallach, Lawrence S., P.S. ....Tukwila, WA
Wallach, Mark I. ....Cleveland, OH
Wallach, Mark S. ....Buffalo, NY
Wallach, Marlin S. ....San Jose, CA
Wallach, Melinda K. ....St. Louis, MO
Wallach, Michael H. ....Paramus, NJ
Wallach, Michael J. ....Los Angeles, CA
Wallach, Michelle C. ....New York, NY
Wallach, Mindy Anne ....Fairfield, NJ; Carle Place, NY
Wallach, Miriam G. ....New York, NY
Wallach and Moore, P.C. ....Fort Worth, TX
Wallach, Neal L. ....Houston, TX
Wallach, Paul G. ....Washington, DC
Wallach, Paul H. ....New York, NY
Wallach, Richard E. ....Dallas, TX
Wallach, Richard W. ....New York, NY
Wallach, Rita M. ....Fort Lauderdale, FL
Wallach, Roger W. ....St. Louis, MO
Wallach, Stacy L. ....New York, NY
Wallach, Stanley J. ....St. Louis, MO
Wallach, Steven ....Princeton, NJ
Wallach, Steven E. ....Fort Lauderdale, FL
Wallach, Steven I. ....New York, NY
Wallach, Stuart L. ....Newport Beach, CA
Wallach, Susan S. ....New York, NY
Wallach, William D. ....Newark, NJ; New York, NY
Wallack, Alan M. ....Princeton, NJ
Wallack, Barry Z. ....Indianapolis, IN
Wallack, Carol Lynn ....Department of Justice, Civil Division, GV
Wallack, Edward L. ....Cambridge, MA
Wallack, Gordon Reid, A Law Corporation Encino, CA
Wallack, Gordon Reid, A Law Corporation Encino, CA
Wallack, James F. ....Boston, MA
Wallack, Jeffrey Paul ....Philadelphia, PA
Wallack, Jerry B. ....Chicago, IL
Wallack, Kenneth L. ....Anchorage, AK
Wallack, Lisa Fishbone ....Boston, MA
Wallack, Marc G. ....New York, NY
Wallack, Margo Haist ....Needham, MA
Wallack, Michael M. ....Sarasota, FL
Wallack, Michael S. ....Indianapolis, IN
Wallack Somers & Haas, P.C. Indianapolis, IN
Wallack, Susan Lee ....Philadelphia, PA
Wallacker, Gretchen M. ....San Mateo, CA
Wallack-Roselli, Rina E. ....Los Angeles, CA
Wallaert, Ellen C. ....Eastpointe, MI
Wallahan & Eicher, P.C. ....Rapid City, SD
Wallan, James A. ....Medford, OR
Wallan, Kimberly D. ....Medford, OR
Wallan, Robert L. ....Los Angeles, CA
Wallance, Gregory J. ....New York, NY
Wallander, Gregg M. ....Indianapolis, IN
Wallander, Tonia ....Los Angeles, CA
Wallander, William L. ....Dallas, TX
Wallar, Richard M. ....Logan, OH
Wallas, Jonathan ....Charlotte, NC
Wallbaum, Linda J. ....Louisville, KY
Wallberg, Arthur C. ....Tallahassee, FL
Wallbillich, James P. ....Pottsville, PA
Wallbillich, John J., III ....Detroit, MI
Walle, David E. ....New Orleans, LA
Walle, James P. ....Troy, MI
Wallemann, Frank E. ....Jefferson City, MO
Wallen, Alan H. ....Philadelphia, PA
Wallen, Barbara A. ....Gallipolis, OH
Wallen, Daniel ....New York, NY
Wallen, David L. ....Atlantic City, NJ
Wallen, Ed ....Pine Bluff, AR
Wallen, Erik S.H. ....Bay City, MI
Wallen, John C. ....Rochester, NY
Wallen, John W., III ....Rahway, NJ
Wallen, Joseph E., III ....Oswego, NY
Wallen, Kate Rabassa ....Atlantic City, NJ
Wallen, Richard A. ....Los Angeles, CA
Wallen, Roy L. ....Los Angeles, CA
Wallen, Scott L. ....Erie, PA
Wallen and Wallen ....Atlantic City, NJ
Wallen, Wesley G. ....Bronx, NY
Wallenberg, David O. ....Washington, DC
Wallender, Michael T., Law Offices of Albany, NY
Wallendorf, Chris ....Comfort, TX
Wallenfang, Ronald L. ....Milwaukee, WI
Wallenfels, Helmut ....Tacoma, WA
Wallen-Friedman Law Office, P.A. Minneapolis, MN
Wallen-Friedman, Leny K. Minneapolis, MN
Wallenius, Rena ....Encinitas, CA
Wallens, William M. ....Albany, NY
Wallenstein, Arnold R. ....Waltham, MA
Wallenstein, Helene S. ....Newark, NJ
Wallenstein, Herbert J. ....Garden City, NY
Wallenstein, James H. ....Dallas, TX
Wallenstein, Joel M. ....Los Angeles, CA
Wallenstein, John S. ....Hempstead, NY
Wallenstein, Laura B. ....Cherry Hill, NJ
Wallenstein, Martin A. ....New York, NY
Wallenstein, Raymond ....Los Angeles, CA
Wallenstein, Robert L. ....San Diego, CA
Wallenstein, Sidney ....Chicago, IL
Wallenstein & Simmons ....San Diego, CA
Wallenstein, Stephen M. ....Washington, DC
Wallenstein & Wagner, Ltd. ....Chicago, IL
Wallentin, Helena ....San Diego, CA
Waller, Adele A. ....Chicago, IL
Waller, Antoinette S. ....Los Angeles, CA
Waller, Ashton C. ....Charleston, IL
Waller, Barry A. ....Columbus, OH
Waller, Benjamin Earl ....Birmingham, AL

Waller, Betty S. .... **Raleigh, NC**
Waller, Bill .... Jackson, MS
Waller, Bill, Jr. .... Jackson, MS
Waller, Bob .... Jackson, MS
Waller, Bradley J. .... **Sycamore, IL**
Waller, Brian .... Joplin, MO
Waller, Brian D. .... **New York, NY**
Waller, Carolyn .... Washington, DC
Waller, Charles D. .... **Dade City, FL**
Waller, Charles D., P.A. .... **Dade City, FL**
Waller, Dan F. .... Mount Clemens, MI
Waller, Dan R., P.C. .... **Dallas, TX**
Waller, Dana M.
Federal Emergency Management Agency, Office of the General Counsel, GV
Waller, David .... Washington, IN
Waller, David B. .... **Houston, TX**
Waller, David G. .... **Los Angeles, CA**
Torrance, CA
Waller, Deborah W. .... Jackson, MS
Waller, Deeann Boatright .... **Atlanta, GA**
Waller, Diane E. .... **New York, NY**
Waller, Donald Lee .... Wheeling, IL
Waller, Edmund A. .... Gainesville, GA
Waller, Edward M., Jr. .... **Tampa, FL**
Waller, Edward Pendleton, Jr.
San Antonio, TX
Waller, F. Earl .... Bloomingdale, GA
Waller, Greg .... **Houston, TX**
Waller, Gregory L. .... Wichita, KS
Waller, Harvey Jack .... Chicago, IL
Waller, Henry A. .... **Chicago, IL**
Waller, J. Michael .... St. Louis, MO
Waller, James H. .... Camden, NJ
Philadelphia, PA
Waller, James P. .... Kearny, NJ
Waller, Jane D. .... Waukegan, IL
Waller, Janet .... **Minneapolis, MN**
Waller, Jeffrey W. .... **Hauppauge, NY**
Waller, Joan Conway, P.C. .... **Dallas, TX**
Waller, John A. .... Washington, DC
Waller, John A. .... Austin, TX
Waller, John D. .... **Indianapolis, IN**
Waller, John D. .... Grand Forks, ND
Waller, John E. .... Temple City, CA
Waller, John H., Jr. .... Marion, SC
Waller, John J. .... Buena Park, CA
Waller, John J., Jr. .... **Los Angeles, CA**
Waller, John T. .... Akron, OH
Waller, John W. .... Sullivan, MO
Waller, Jonathan C. .... **Philadelphia, PA**
Waller, Jonathan H. .... **Birmingham, AL**
Waller, Joseph W. .... **Minneapolis, MN**
Waller, Karen K. .... **Harrisburg, PA**
Waller Lansden Dortch & Davis
Columbia, TN
Nashville, TN
Waller, Leonard, Chambers & Hanson
Washington, IN
Waller, Lorraine E. .... St. Louis Park, MN
Waller, Marcie R. .... Cleveland, OH
Waller, Marilyn A. .... **San Francisco, CA**
Waller, Mark Alston .... **Tulsa, OK**
Waller, Mark N. .... Little Rock, AR
Waller and Mark, P.C. .... **Denver, CO**
Waller, Marshall W., II .... Encino, CA
Waller, Michael C. .... **Dickinson, ND**
Waller, Michael E. .... **Morristown, NJ**
Waller, Michael J. .... Waukegan, IL
Waller, Michael M. .... **Oak Harbor, WA**
Waller, Michael R. .... **Houston, TX**
Waller, Michelle W. .... **Cleveland, OH**
Waller, Mickey E. .... **Moultrie, GA**
Waller and Mitchell .... **New Port Richey, FL**
Waller, Nancy C. .... Tallahassee, FL
Waller, Paul P., III .... **Belleville, IL**
Waller, Paul P., Jr. .... Belleville, IL
Waller, Pete H. .... Lubbock, TX
Waller, Richard A., Jr. .... Macon, GA
Waller, Richard A., Jr., LLC .... Macon, GA
Waller, Richard L. .... **Anchorage, AK**
Waller, Richard W., (P.C.) .... Chicago, IL
Waller, Robert E. .... Coweta, OK
Waller, Robert J. .... Billings, MT
Waller, Robert L. .... Lawrenceville, GA
Waller, Robin W., (Mr.) .... Niantic, CT
Waller, Roland D. .... **New Port Richey, FL**
Waller, Ruth A. Warden .... Decatur, IL
Waller, Seth .... Hewlett Harbor, NY
Waller, Smith & Palmer, P.C.
Hartford, CT
New London, CT
Old Lyme, CT
Waller, Spencer Weber .... **New York, NY**
Waller, Stephen M. .... Shreveport, LA
Waller, Thomas Alan .... **Gulfport, MS**
Waller, Tonya L. .... **Washington, DC**
Waller, Virginia Maxwell .... Washington, DC
Waller & Waller .... Jackson, MS
Waller, Wayne M. .... Chicago, IL
Waller, William A. .... New York, NY
Waller, William C. .... **Washington, DC**
Waller, William C., Jr. .... **Denver, CO**
Waller, William L., Jr. .... Jackson, MS
Waller, William M. .... Wheaton, IL
Waller, William S. .... **Los Angeles, CA**
Waller, William W. .... Gaithersburg, MD
Waller & Womack, P.C. .... Billings, MT
Waller-Little, Misheal .... **Guthrie Center, IA**
Wallerstein, David D. .... New York, NY
Wallerstein, Larry I. .... Los Gatos, CA
Wallerstein, Les .... Lexington, MA
Wallerstein, Lori R.byn .... San Francisco, CA
Wallerstein, Martin B. .... Fanwood, NJ
Wallerstein, Melvin J. .... **West Orange, NJ**
Wallerstein, Melvin J., P.A. .... **Newark, NJ**
West Orange, NJ
Wallerstein, Richard S., Jr. .... Richmond, VA

Wallerstein, Robert H. .... Los Angeles, CA
Wallerstein, Robert S. .... **Los Angeles, CA**
Wallerstein, Stanley N. .... **Newton, MA**
Walleser, Helenjean .... Des Moines, IA
Wallet, Andrew M. .... **Los Angeles, CA**
Walley, James M. .... **Metairie, LA**
Walley, John C. .... Las Vegas, NV
Walley, Noah J. .... New York, NY
Walley, Paul David .... Richton, MS
Walley, Thomas E. .... **Newport Beach, CA**
Wallfisch, M. Charles .... New Orleans, LA
Wallgren, Anita L.
Federal Communications Commission, Office of the Commissioners, GV
Wallgren, Lara Christine .... Virginia, MN
Wallhausen, E. Wayne
Fort Lauderdale, FL
Walli, Karl T. .... **Washington, DC**
Walli, Kevin T. .... **St. Paul, MN**
Wallick, David M. .... Diamond, IL
Wallick, Marc D. .... East Providence, RI
Wallick, Robert D. .... **Washington, DC**
Wallick, Ruth Brewer
Joint Committees And Commissions, GV
Wallick, Sandra M. .... Oak Park, IL
Wallin, Allison S. .... **Seattle, WA**
Wallin, Debra M. .... **Princeton, NJ**
Wallin, Dennis K. .... Moriarty, NM
Wallin, Dennis K., P.C., Law Offices of
Moriarty, NM
Wallin, Edward J. .... Santa Ana, CA
Wallin, Elizabeth Lacalli .... **Dallas, TX**
Wallin, Gary A. .... Grand Rapids, MI
Wallin, Gerald E. .... St. Paul, MN
Wallin, Howard E. .... Baltimore, MD
Wallin, James P. .... New York, NY
Wallin, Janet L., (Mrs.) .... Toledo, OH
Wallin, Joe M. .... **Seattle, WA**
Wallin, K. Erik .... Block Island, RI
Wallin, Kermit J. .... Minneapolis, MN
Wallin & Klarich, A Law Corporation
Laguna Hills, CA
Los Angeles, CA
Pasadena, CA
Pomona, CA
Rancho Cucamonga, CA
Riverside, CA
San Bernardino, CA
Santa Monica, CA
Temecula, CA
Torrance, CA
Tustin, CA
Valencia, CA
Van Nuys, CA
Victorville, CA
Whittier, CA
Woodland Hills, CA
Wallin, Kress, Reisman & Kranitz
Santa Monica, CA
Wallin, Leonard A., II .... Newport News, VA
Wallin, Paul J. .... **Tustin, CA**
Wallin, Paula Tipton .... **Wheaton, IL**
Wallin, Peter L. .... Santa Monica, CA
Wallin, R. E. "Skip" .... West Memphis, AR
Wallin, Scott F. .... Scottsdale, AZ
Wallin, Stephen R. .... Washington, DC
Wallin, Tad .... Fort Collins, CO
Wallin, Terry J. .... **New York, NY**
Wallin, Thomas G. .... Brooklyn, NY
Wallin, Thomas N. .... Gulf Breeze, FL
Wallin, Troy A. .... **Las Vegas, NV**
Wallin, William R. .... Chicago, IL
Walline, Megan J.
Department Of The Interior, Office of the Solicitor, GV
Walling, B. Haven, Jr. .... Oakton, VA
Walling & Berg, P.A. .... Minneapolis, MN
Walling, David L. .... Edmond, OK
Walling, Eric J. .... Walnut Creek, CA
Walling, G. Scott .... Fort Edward, NY
Walling, Gerald D. .... **Atlanta, GA**
Walling, Glenn P. .... **Walnut Creek, CA**
Walling, Greg B. .... **Atlanta, GA**
Walling, Kimberly S. .... Oak Ridge, TN
Walling, Mark R. .... **Buffalo, NY**
Walling, Mary Anne Webb
East Northport, NY
Walling, Meredith A. .... **Morristown, NJ**
Walling, Michael I. .... Warren, OH
Walling, Miller & Waters .... **Knoxville, TN**
Walling, Philip X. .... Detroit, MI
Walling, Robert H. .... Decatur, GA
Walling, Robert J. .... Costa Mesa, CA
Walling, Stephen C. .... **Knoxville, TN**
Walling, W. Challen .... **Abingdon, VA**
Bristol, VA
Walling, Wright S. .... Minneapolis, MN
Wallinger, M. Bruce .... **Harrisonburg, VA**
Wallinger, Marta .... Cuyahoga Falls, OH
Wallinger, Ralph Scott, Jr. .... Columbia, SC
Wallingford, Brett .... **Dallas, TX**
Wallingford, David A. .... Bellevue, OH
Wallingford, J. Whitney, II
Lexington, KY
Wallingford, J. Whitney, PSC
Lexington, KY
Wallingford, Jayne L. .... Anchorage, AK
Wallingford, Jerome Paul .... San Diego, CA
Wallingford, Katharine T. .... Houston, TX
Wallingford, Nancy Stuver .... Kansas City, MO
Wallingford, Roger D. .... Portland, OR
Wallingford, Rufus .... **Houston, TX**
Wallingford, Thomas A. .... Kansas City, MO
Wallington, James F. .... **Washington, DC**
Wallis, Albert W. .... Boston, MA
Wallis, Ben A., Jr. .... San Antonio, TX
Wallis, Bruce M., (P.C.) .... **Hemet, CA**
Sun City, CA

Wallis, C. Robert .... Olympia, WA
Wallis, Christina M. .... Santa Cruz, CA
Wallis, Danny J. .... Abilene, TX
Wallis, Darren C. .... **New York, NY**
Philadelphia, PA
Wallis, David L. .... **Phoenix, AZ**
Wallis, Diane A. .... Raleigh, NC
Wallis, Donald des G. .... Hixson, TN
Wallis, Donald W. .... **Jacksonville, FL**
Wallis, Douglas J. .... Los Angeles, CA
Wallis, Edward B. .... Lafayette, IN
Wallis, Edwin E., Jr. .... **Jackson, TN**
Wallis, Eric G. .... **Oakland, CA**
Wallis, Estalie .... Dallas, TX
Wallis, F. Rand .... **Orlando, FL**
Wallis, F. A. .... New Orleans, LA
Wallis, Franklin F. .... **St. Louis, MO**
Wallis, Garyland .... Houma, LA
Wallis, James S., Jr. .... **Houston, TX**
Wallis, James W., Jr. .... Carrollton, GA
Wallis, Jonny D. .... Goleta, CA
Wallis, Julie Marie .... Dallas, TX
Wallis, Kai A. .... Novato, CA
Wallis, Kenneth D., II .... Montgomery, AL
Wallis, Kimberly Ann .... **Raleigh, NC**
Wallis, Leslie E. .... **Los Angeles, CA**
Wallis, Leslie S. .... Seattle, WA
Wallis, Marc S. .... **St. Louis, MO**
Wallis, Michael L. .... Flint, MI
Wallis, Michael M. M. .... **Melbourne, FL**
Wallis, Olney G. .... Houston, TX
Wallis, Peter E. S. .... Boca Raton, FL
Wallis, Richard J. .... **Redmond, WA**
Wallis, Robert B. .... **Houston, TX**
Wallis, Rosalie .... **Rock Hill, NY**
Wallis, Roy C. .... Englewood, CO
Wallis, Sharon K. .... Philadelphia, PA
Wallis, Shelby D., (P.A.)
Pompano Beach, FL
Wallis & Short .... Houston, TX
Wallis, Wendie R. .... **Brookline, MA**
Wallis, William L. .... **Tallahassee, FL**
Wallisch, Louis, Jr. .... West Milford, NJ
Wallisch, Mark A. .... Brookville, PA
Wallisch, Martha Braun .... Goddard, KS
Wallisch, Michael A. .... Pittsburgh, PA
Wallisch & Wallisch .... West Milford, NJ
Wallison, Frieda K. .... Washington, DC
Wallison, Peter J. .... **Washington, DC**
Wallitsch & Figore, LLP .... Allentown, PA
Wallitsch, Nancy Perpall .... Allentown, PA
Wallitsch, Thomas A. .... Allentown, PA
Wallman, Barry J. .... West Hills, CA
Wallman, D. Michael .... Indianapolis, IN
Wallman, David J. .... **Hackensack, NJ**
Wallman, David M. .... **Stamford, CT**
Wallman, Greenberg, Gasman & McKnight, LLP .... **New York, NY**
Wallman, Jay A. .... New York, NY
Wallman, Lester .... **New York, NY**
Wallman, Marc A., (P.C.) .... **New Haven, CT**
Wallman, Mitchell J. .... Peabody, MA
Wallman, Nathaniel B. .... Stamford, CT
Wallman, Steven M.H.
Securities and Exchange Commission, Executive Staff, GV
Wallman, Suzanne M. .... **Chicago, IL**
Wallman & Wechsler, P.C. .... New York, NY
Wallmann, James L. .... San Ramon, CA
Wallmark, Gary T. .... Salem, OR
Wallner, Maggie R.
Mendota Heights, MN
Wallner, Robert A. .... **New York, NY**
Wallner, Robert M. .... Bemidji, MN
Wallner, Robt. T. .... St. Paul, MN
Wallner, Thomas .... Carmichael, CA
Walloch, Heather M. .... **Washington, DC**
Walloch, Richard L. .... Denver, CO
Wallock, Joel A. .... Oakland, CA
Wallock, Terrence J. .... Los Angeles, CA
Wallor, Kyle .... **Omaha, NE**
Wallor, Michael T. F. .... **Providence, RI**
Wallor, Robert Kurt .... Muskegon, MI
Wallover and Steff .... Beaver, PA
Wallraff, John C. .... St. Paul, MN
Wallrich, Nancy Cross .... Minnetonka, MN
Wallrichs, Brenda K. .... **Cedar Rapids, IA**
Walls, C. Michael .... Laurel, MD
Walls, Charles M. .... **Abilene, TX**
Walls, Charlotte A. .... **Jackson, MI**
Walls, Chas. A., Jr. .... Lonoke, AR
Walls, David A. .... **Oklahoma City, OK**
Walls, David S. .... **Charlotte, NC**
Walls, Daylene Brody .... Caney, KS
Walls, Donald G. .... Binghamton, NY
Walls, Elizabeth Rolle .... Atlanta, GA
Walls, Forrest W. .... **Seattle, WA**
Walls, George R. .... Charlotte, NC
Walls, Gerard J. .... New York, NY
Walls, Glenn P., Jr. .... Binghamton, NY
Walls, Homer B. .... San Antonio, TX
Walls, J. Michael .... **St. Petersburg, FL**
Walls, J. Michael, (P.C.) .... **Atlanta, GA**
Walls, Jackson .... Amarillo, TX
Walls, Jackson, P.C. .... Amarillo, TX
Walls, Janetta S. .... **Cincinnati, OH**
Walls, Johnnie E., Jr. .... Greenville, MS
Walls, Jonni S. .... **Dallas, TX**
Walls, Marshal G. .... Welch, WV
Walls, Matthew S. .... Frederick, MD
Walls, Michael J. .... Concord, NH
Walls, Michael P. .... Arlington, VA
Walls, Molly B.F. .... **Washington, DC**
Walls, Orville R., III .... Philadelphia, PA
Walls, Patrick K. .... Ridgeland, MS
Walls, Peter J. .... Santa Rosa, CA
Walls, Richard L. .... **Owensboro, KY**
Walls, Robert H. .... **Houston, TX**

Walls, Robert H., Jr. .... **Houston, TX**
Walls, Robert T., Jr. .... Dallas, TX
Walls, S. Marc .... Oklahoma City, OK
Walls, Sarah .... **Fort Worth, TX**
Walls, Shereen M. .... Atlanta, GA
Walls, Stephanie Crotty .... Great Falls, MT
Walls, Stewart E. .... Johnson City, NY
Walls, Thomas F. .... United States Senate, Senatorial Assistants, GV
Walls, Tina M. .... **Las Vegas, NV**
Walls, Tobin R. .... **Atlanta, GA**
Walls, W. Casey .... **Long Beach, CA**
Walls, William B. .... **Los Angeles, CA**
Walls, William H. .... Newark, NJ
Walls, William J. .... **Pittsburgh, PA**
Walls, William M. .... Dunbar, WV
Wallsh, Richard I. .... **Winter Park, FL**
Wallshein, William .... Lake Worth, FL
Wallshein, William, P.A. .... Lake Worth, FL
Wallsmith, David J. .... **Knox, IN**
Wallstein, Michael B. .... **Paramus, NJ**
Wallstrom, Paul Arnold .... **Seattle, WA**
Wall-Swedberg, Brenda .... **Kirksville, MO**
Walluck, Jon Scott .... Simi Valley, CA
Walluck, Vickie L. .... Simi Valley, CA
Walluk, Anthony W., Jr. .... San Antonio, TX
Wallum, Curtis E. .... Dallas, TX
Wallwork, John G. .... Lexington, MA
Wallwork, Nicholas J. .... **Phoenix, AZ**
Wally, Barry M. .... Huntington Beach, CA
Walma, Kenneth D. .... **Wilmington, DE**
Walman, A. Terry .... Crofton, MD
Walman, Beth V. .... New York, NY
Walmer, Edwin Fitch .... **Milwaukee, WI**
Walmer, James L. .... **Warsaw, IN**
Walmer, Mark F. .... Lancaster, PA
Walmer, Robert G. .... Overland Park, KS
Walmsley, Bill H. .... **Batesville, AR**
Walmsley, Lloyd A. .... Peabody, MA
Walmsley, Robert M., Jr.
New Orleans, LA
Walmsley, Robert R., Jr. .... **Santa Ana, CA**
Walmsley, Timothy R. .... **Savannah, GA**
Walmsley & Weaver .... **Batesville, AR**
Newport, AR
Walner, Lawrence .... Chicago, IL
Walner, Lawrence, & Associates, Ltd.
Chicago, IL
Walner, Robert J. .... Northbrook, IL
Walnofer, Joseph E. .... York, NE
Walos, Kevin Michael .... Oklahoma City, OK
Walovich, John P. .... **San Francisco, CA**
Walowski, Raymond J. .... Omaha, NE
Walowski, Raymond J., P.C. .... Omaha, NE
Walp, Maria McNamee .... **Beverly Hills, CA**
Walp, Winston W., II .... **Dallas, TX**
Walper, Robert A. .... **Lansdale, PA**
Walper, Thomas B. .... **Los Angeles, CA**
Walpert, Alfred M. .... Baltimore, MD
Walpert, Gary A. .... **Boston, MA**
New York, NY
Walpert, Roberta S. .... **Paramus, NJ**
Walpin, Bernard G. .... New York, NY
Walpin, Gerald .... **New York, NY**
Walpole, Bryan L., III .... **Charleston, SC**
Walpole, Charles E. .... Dallas, TX
Walpole, Daniel M. .... Akron, OH
Walpole, James R. .... **Hoffman Estates, IL**
Walpole, Robert J. .... Tulsa, OK
Walrath, Christopher F. .... **Chicago, IL**
Walrath, Christopher M. .... **Trenton, NJ**
Walrath & Coolidge .... Wellsboro, PA
Walrath, Deborah B. .... **Pittsburgh, PA**
Walrath, James A. .... Milwaukee, WI
Walrath, Jerry L. .... Flint, MI
Walrath, Louis L. .... **Thermopolis, WY**
Walrath, Priscilla M. .... Wellsboro, PA
Walrath, Robert E. .... Stow, MA
Walrath, Thomas A., Jr. .... Wellsboro, PA
Walraven, Berneta .... Seattle, WA
Walraven, Eric G. .... **Lubbock, TX**
Walraven, Larry A. .... **Newport Beach, CA**
Walraven, Richard .... **Prescott, AZ**
Walraven & Roberts .... **Prescott, AZ**
Walraven, Sharon Kraft .... Laguna Niguel, CA
Walraven, Stephen E. .... **San Antonio, TX**
Walravens, Patrick .... San Francisco, CA
Walro, Michael J. .... Madison, IN
Walro, Ronald A. .... Eugene, OR
Walrod, Kathleen A. .... Union City, NJ
Walrod, Sherman E. .... Holyoke, CO
Walrond, Karen .... **Houston, TX**
Walroth-Sadurní, Stephen P. .... **Miami, FL**
Wals, Erik .... **New York, NY**
Walschlager, Jill S. .... **Indianapolis, IN**
Walschlager, Raymond J. .... Chicago, IL
Walsdorf, Douglas C. .... San Antonio, TX
Walsen, Paul J. .... **Chicago, IL**
Walser, Albert F. .... Statesville, NC
Walser, Donald H. .... **Hutchinson, MN**
Olivia, MN
Renville, MN
Walser, Gaither S. .... **Lexington, NC**
Walser, Jason A. .... Hendersonville, NC
Walser, Kathleen .... **New York, NY**
Walser, Mary Anne .... **Atlanta, GA**
Walser, Mikki Graves
Department of Justice, Civil Division, GV
Walser, Richard W. .... East Islip, NY
Walser, Robert J. .... San Juan, PR
Walser, Thomas C. .... Boca Raton, FL
Walseth, Daniel G. .... Simsbury, CT
Walseth, James Patrick .... Cedar Rapids, IA
Walseth, Nancy R. .... Portland, OR
Walsey, Craig M. .... San Leandro, CA
Walsey, David A. .... New York, NY
Walsh, A.D., & Associates .... St. Paul, MN
Walsh, Adam M. .... **New York, NY**

Walsh, Adam W. ..... **Washington, DC**
Walsh, Aimée S. ..... **Milwaukee, WI**
Walsh, Akins & Davis, A Professional Corporation ..... Georgetown, TX
Round Rock, TX
Walsh, Albert A. ..... **New York, NY**
Walsh, Albert C. ..... Papillion, NE
Walsh, Alexander G. ..... Newport, RI
Walsh, Alfred C., Jr. ..... Coquille, OR
Walsh, Alice G. ..... Marshfield, MA
Walsh, Allan O. ..... **Salt Lake City, UT**
Walsh, Allison M. ..... New York, NY
Walsh & Amicucci LLP ..... New York, NY
Purchase, NY
Walsh, Amy E. ..... Dexter, MI
Walsh, Anderson, Brown, Schulze & Aldridge, P.C. ..... **Austin, TX**
Irving, TX
San Antonio, TX
Walsh, Andrew C. ..... St. Louis, MO
Walsh, Andrew M. ..... **Stamford, CT**
Walsh, Andrew M. ..... Atlanta, GA
Walsh, Andrew S. ..... Philadelphia, PA
Walsh, Angela Lui ..... **Los Angeles, CA**
San Diego, CA
Walsh, Ann Briks ..... Charleston, SC
Walsh, Ann L. ..... Norwell, MA
Walsh, Ann Marie ..... **Chicago, IL**
Walsh, Anna Jo ..... Santa Ana, CA
Walsh, Anne K. ..... Morristown, NJ
Walsh, Anthony A. ..... Cleveland, OH
Walsh, Anthony C. ..... **Atlanta, GA**
Walsh, Anthony F. ..... **New York, NY**
Philadelphia, PA
Walsh, Ardena L. ..... Lansing, MI
Walsh, Aristea N. ..... **New York, NY**
Walsh, Arthur B. ..... Los Angeles, CA
Walsh, Arthur D. ..... St. Paul, MN
Walsh, Arthur Robert, III
Department of Justice,
Federal Bureau of Investigation, GV
Walsh, Arthur T. ..... **Garden City, NY**
Walsh & Associates ..... **Santa Ana, CA**
Walsh & Associates ..... Brownsville, TX
Walsh, B. Lynn ..... **Atlanta, GA**
Walsh, Barbara A. ..... **Santa Rosa, CA**
Walsh, Barbara A. ..... **Boston, MA**
Walsh, Barbara E. ..... Mineola, NY
Walsh, Barbara J. ..... Braintree, MA
Walsh, Basil S., III ..... Pottsville, PA
Walsh, Bernadette M. ..... **Berwyn, PA**
Walsh, Bernard F. ..... Bradenton, FL
Sarasota, FL
Walsh, Bernard F., P.A. ..... Bradenton, FL
Walsh, Bernard F., P.A. ..... **Sarasota, FL**
Walsh, Brenda J. M. ..... Pleasanton, CA
Walsh, Bret T. ..... Baton Rouge, LA
Walsh, Brian C. ..... San Jose, CA
Walsh, Brian C. ..... **Atlanta, GA**
Walsh, Brian F. ..... **Washington, DC**
Chicago, IL
Walsh, Brian J. ..... **Fort Lauderdale, FL**
Walsh, Brian J. ..... Chicago, IL
Walsh, Brian J. ..... **St. Louis, MO**
Walsh, Brian J. ..... New York, NY
Walsh, Brian J. ..... **Scranton, PA**
Walsh, Brian P. ..... Bronx, NY
Walsh, Brian T. ..... New Britain, CT
Walsh, Bruce H. ..... Staten Island, NY
Walsh, Brule & Soboda, P.C.
Cumberland, RI
Walsh, Burt & Walsh ..... New Haven, CT
Walsh, C. Michael ..... Akron, OH
Walsh, Cari F. ..... **Kansas City, MO**
Walsh, Carl M. ..... **Chicago, IL**
Walsh, Carla Perantoni ..... Washington, DC
Walsh, Carolyn ..... Cabin John, MD
Walsh, Carolyn M. ..... **New York, NY**
Walsh, Carrol S., Jr. ..... Johnstown, NY
Walsh, Catherine A. ..... Concord, CA
Walsh, Catherine A. ..... Bronx, NY
Walsh, Catherine A. ..... Brooklyn, NY
Walsh, Catherine B. ..... **Blue Bell, PA**
Walsh, Cecilia ..... Western Springs, IL
Walsh, Charlene A. ..... Ocala, FL
Walsh, Charles E. ..... Lake Placid, NY
Walsh, Charles J. ..... Newark, NJ
Walsh, Charles S. ..... **Washington, DC**
Walsh, Chas. E. ..... Indianapolis, IN
Walsh, Chas. G., Jr. ..... Oakbrook Terrace, IL
Walsh, Cheryl Hardt ..... Woodland Hills, CA
Walsh, Cheryl Harner ..... Gilroy, CA
Walsh, Cheryl K. ..... Phoenix, AZ
Walsh, Christine ..... New York, NY
Walsh, Christopher ..... **Chicago, IL**
Walsh, Christopher ..... **Somerset, NJ**
Walsh, Christopher G., Jr. ..... **Chicago, IL**
Walsh, Christopher J. ..... Shelton, CT
Walsh, Christopher J. ..... Nyack, NY
Walsh, Christopher M. ..... **Jenkintown, PA**
Walsh, Christopher R. ..... Minneapolis, MN
Walsh, Christopher R. ..... **Columbus, OH**
Walsh, Christopher T. ..... Albany, NY
Walsh, Colleen Conti ..... Underhill, VT
Walsh, Colucci, Stackhouse, Emrich & Lubeley, P.C. ..... **Arlington, VA**
Leesburg, VA
Woodbridge, VA
Walsh, D. Bradley ..... **Oxford, MS**
Memphis, TN
Walsh, Daniel D. ..... **Omaha, NE**
Walsh, Daniel G. ..... **New York, NY**
Walsh, Daniel J. ..... Chicago, IL
Walsh, Daniel J. ..... De Pere, WI
Walsh, Daniel J., Jr. ..... Urbana, IL
Walsh, Daniel R. ..... **Carson City, NV**
Walsh, Daniel R., The Law Office of
Carson City, NV
Reno, NV
Walsh, David ..... **Corpus Christi, TX**
Walsh, David A. ..... **Reston, VA**
Walsh, David E. ..... Olympia, WA
Walsh, David G. ..... **Madison, WI**
Walsh, David H., IV ..... **Rochester, NY**
Walsh, David I. ..... Bethany Beach, DE
Wilmington, DE
Walsh, David I. ..... Harrisonburg, VA
Walsh, David J. ..... **Armonk, NY**
Walsh, David L. ..... Indianapolis, IN
Walsh, David L. ..... **Spartanburg, SC**
Walsh, David M. ..... **Los Angeles, CA**
Walsh, David M. ..... **East Meadow, NY**
Walsh, David M., IV ..... **Dallas, TX**
Walsh, David S. ..... Salt Lake City, UT
Walsh, David W. ..... Somerville, MA
Walsh, David W., III ..... Somerville, MA
Walsh, Deborah Bates ..... Windham, NH
Walsh, Debra M. ..... Salem, NH
Walsh & Declues, LLP ..... **Encino, CA**
Santa Ana, CA
Walnut Creek, CA
Walsh, Delaney & Yep ..... Lancaster, CA
Walsh, Dennis G. ..... Chicago, IL
Walsh, Dennis J. ..... **Encino, CA**
Walsh, Dennis P.
National Labor Relations Board,
Office of Board Members, GV
Walsh, Diana ..... Morristown, NJ
Walsh, Diane B. ..... Cody, WY
Walsh, Diane N. ..... Chicago, IL
Walsh, Dianne E. ..... **Minneapolis, MN**
Walsh, Donald ..... Castleton-on-Hudson, NY
Walsh, Donald G. ..... New Haven, CT
Walsh, Donald G., Jr. ..... New Haven, CT
Walsh, Donald J. ..... Baltimore, MD
Walsh, Donald O. ..... **Addison, TX**
Walsh, Donald P. ..... Villanova, PA
Walsh, Donna A. ..... **Scranton, PA**
Walsh, Donovan & Keech, LLP
San Francisco, CA
Walsh, Douglas D. ..... Olympia, WA
Walsh, Douglas L. ..... **Los Angeles, CA**
Walsh, E. Eugene ..... Torrance, CA
Walsh, E. Jeffrey ..... **Phoenix, AZ**
Walsh, Edgar P. ..... **Mobile, AL**
Walsh, Edmund J. ..... **Boston, MA**
Walsh, Edw. A. ..... Denver, CO
Walsh, Edward ..... **Whippany, NJ**
Walsh, Edward F. "Chip", IV
Kansas City, MO
Walsh, Edward J. ..... Denver, CO
Walsh, Edward J. ..... Department of Justice,
Criminal Division, GV
Walsh, Edward J. ..... Dunwoody, GA
Walsh, Edward J. ..... **Wheaton, IL**
Walsh, Edward J. ..... Georgetown, TX
Round Rock, TX
Walsh, Edward J., Jr. ..... **New York, NY**
Walsh, Edward L. ..... New Haven, CT
Walsh, Edward V. ..... **Bridgeport, CT**
Walsh, Edward V., III ..... **Chicago, IL**
Walsh, Edward V., Jr. ..... **Hempstead, NY**
Walsh & Edwards ..... Malone, NY
Walsh, Eileen H. ..... Burbank, CA
Walsh, Eileen M. ..... **Louisville, KY**
Walsh, Eileen M. ..... **Kenilworth, NJ**
Walsh, Elaine M. ..... St. Louis, MO
Walsh, Elaine Rogers ..... **Atlanta, GA**
Walsh, Elia C. ..... **Hartford, CT**
Walsh, Elizabeth Marie ..... Troy, NY
Walsh, Elmer Michael, Jr. ..... Winnetka, IL
Walsh, Eugene J. ..... Grove City, OH
Walsh, Eugene P. ..... **St. Louis, MO**
Walsh, Evangeline A. ..... Oakland, CA
Walsh & Fisher, A Professional Association
Westminster, MD
Walsh, Francis M. ..... Jericho, NY
Walsh, Francis M. ..... **Pottstown, PA**
Walsh, Francis R. ..... San Francisco, CA
Walsh, Francis X., Jr. ..... Westminster, MD
Walsh, Frank B., Jr. ..... Annapolis, MD
Walsh, Frank B., Jr., P.A. ..... Annapolis, MD
Walsh, Frank K. ..... Albany, NY
Walsh, Frank V., Jr.
Frederiksted, St. Croix, VI
Walsh & Friedman, Ltd. ..... **Las Vegas, NV**
Walsh, Fullenkamp & Doyle ..... **Omaha, NE**
Walsh & Furcolo, L.L.P. ..... San Diego, CA
Walsh, G. Allen ..... Baton Rouge, LA
Walsh, Gary E. ..... **Morristown, NJ**
Walsh, Gary William ..... Pittsburgh, PA
Walsh, George J., III ..... **New York, NY**
Walsh, Gerald M. ..... Birmingham, AL
Walsh, Gerald M. ..... Fort Lauderdale, FL
Walsh, Gerald R. ..... **Baltimore, MD**
Walsh, Gerald R. ..... **Fairfax, VA**
Walsh, Gerald R., P.A. ..... **Baltimore, MD**
Walsh, Gerald R., P.C. ..... **Fairfax, VA**
Walsh, Gerald S. ..... **Milwaukee, WI**
Walsh, Gerald T. ..... **Buffalo, NY**
Walsh, Gerald V. ..... Coral Springs, FL
Walsh, Gerald V., P.A. ..... Coral Springs, FL
Walsh, Gerald W. ..... Chelmsford, MA
Walsh, Geraldine M.
Securities and Exchange Commission,
Division of Enforcement, GV
Walsh, Gerard J. ..... **Los Angeles, CA**
Walsh, Gerry O'Malley, (Miss) ..... Houston, TX
Walsh, Grail Peyton ..... **Washington, DC**
Walsh, Gregory J. ..... **New Orleans, LA**
Walsh, Gretchen Henry ..... St. Petersburg, FL
Walsh, H. Vincent ..... Hamilton, OH
Walsh & Hacker ..... **Albany, NY**
Walsh, Harry M. ..... St. Paul, MN
Walsh, Harry M., Jr. ..... **Easton, MD**
Walsh, Henry A., Jr. ..... **New Hope, PA**
Walsh, Henry J. ..... Oxnard, CA
Walsh, Henry J. ..... **Newark, NJ**
Walsh, Holiday ..... San Francisco, CA
Walsh, J. Brian ..... **Philadelphia, PA**
Walsh, J. David ..... **Daytona Beach, FL**
Walsh, J. Joseph ..... Dayton, OH
Walsh, Jacqueline F. ..... **Boston, MA**
Walsh, James ..... **New York, NY**
Walsh, James A. ..... Brooksville, FL
Walsh, James C., Jr. ..... Palm Springs, CA
Walsh, James D. ..... **Columbia, MD**
Walsh, James D. ..... New York, NY
Walsh, James E. ..... **Cumberland, MD**
Walsh, James E. ..... Roanoke, VA
Walsh, James E., III ..... San Antonio, TX
Walsh, James E., Jr. ..... **Waterloo, IA**
Walsh, James F. ..... **Birmingham, AL**
Walsh, James F. ..... Canton, MA
Walsh, James F. ..... Seattle, WA
Walsh, James F., III ..... **San Diego, CA**
Walsh, James F., Jr. ..... **Orangeburg, SC**
Walsh, James F., Jr. ..... Nashville, TN
Walsh, James F., Metro Law Center of, P.C.
Canton, MA
Walsh, James G., Jr. ..... Kansas City, MO
Walsh, James H. ..... **Richmond, VA**
Walsh, James J. ..... San Francisco, CA
Walsh, James J. ..... **Boston, MA**
Walsh, James J. ..... **Detroit, MI**
Walsh, James J. ..... Elizabeth, NJ
Walsh, James K. ..... New York, NY
Walsh, James L. ..... Vermilion, OH
Walsh, James M. ..... Sycamore, IL
Walsh, James M. ..... **Reno, NV**
Walsh, James N. M. ..... Clearwater Beach, FL
Walsh, James O. ..... New Haven, CT
Walsh, James P. ..... Phoenix, AZ
Walsh, James P. ..... **San Francisco, CA**
Walsh, James P. ..... Chicago, IL
Walsh, James P. ..... Albany, NY
Walsh, James P. ..... Warminster, PA
Walsh, James P. ..... **Greenville, SC**
Walsh, James P., Jr. ..... **Los Angeles, CA**
Walsh, James Patrick ..... **Cincinnati, OH**
Walsh, James R. ..... San Diego, CA
Walsh, James R. (IBA) ..... **San Francisco, CA**
Walsh, James R. ..... **St. Louis, MO**
Walsh, James R. ..... **Great Falls, MT**
Walsh, James R. ..... Blasdell, NY
Walsh, James R. ..... **Buffalo, NY**
Walsh, James R. ..... **Johnstown, PA**
Walsh, James R. ..... Lynnwood, WA
Walsh, James T. ..... **Washington, DC**
Walsh, James W. ..... Ansonia, CT
Walsh, James W. ..... White Plains, NY
Walsh, Jane ..... Pittsburgh, PA
Walsh, Janet C. ..... **Lyndon, KS**
Osage City, KS
Walsh, Janet C. ..... **New York, NY**
Walsh, Janet M. ..... Phoenix, AZ
Walsh, Jas. J. ..... Scranton, PA
Walsh, Jason Matthew ..... Charleroi, PA
Donora, PA
Walsh, Jason R. ..... Riverside, CA
Walsh, Jean L. ..... Sanford, ME
Walsh, Jeanne M. ..... Nutley, NJ
Walsh, Jeffrey G. ..... **Mineola, NY**
Walsh, Jeffrey R., Law Offices of
San Francisco, CA
Walsh, Jeffrey T. ..... Manchester, CT
Walsh, Jerome K. ..... **New York, NY**
Walsh, Jillian ..... **New York, NY**
Walsh, Jim ..... **Austin, TX**
Walsh, Jo Frances ..... **Denver, CO**
Walsh, Joan M. ..... **La Mesa, CA**
Walsh, John ..... Boston, MA
Walsh, John ..... **Madison, WI**
Walsh, John A. ..... **Raynham, MA**
Walsh, John A., Jr. ..... Boston, MA
Walsh, John A., Jr. ..... St. Louis, MO
Walsh, John B. ..... **Brea, CA**
Walsh, John B. (J.B.) ..... Buffalo, NY
Walsh, John Burgess, Jr. ..... **Rockville, MD**
Walsh, John C. ..... Baton Rouge, LA
Walsh, John C. ..... **Portland, OR**
Walsh, John E. ..... **Danvers, MA**
Walsh, John E. ..... Stillwater, MN
Walsh, John F. ..... **Riverside, CA**
Walsh, John F. ..... Denver, CO
Walsh, John F. ..... Miami, FL
Walsh, John F. ..... **New York, NY**
Walsh, John F. ..... **New York, NY**
Walsh, John F. ..... Blue Bell, PA
Walsh, John F., Jr. ..... Palm Beach, FL
New York, NY
Walsh, John H. ..... San Diego, CA
Walsh, John H.
Securities and Exchange Commission,
Office of Compliance Inspections and
Examinations, GV
Walsh, John J. ..... Farmington Hills, MI
Walsh, John J. ..... Brooklyn, NY
Walsh, John J. ..... New York, NY
Walsh, John J. ..... **New York, NY**
Walsh, John J. ..... Utica, NY
Walsh, John J. ..... Reston, VA
Walsh, John J. ..... Madison, WI
Walsh, John J., II ..... **White Plains, NY**
Walsh, John J., III ..... **Chicago, IL**
Walsh, John J., Jr. ..... Jamaica Plain, MA
Walsh, John K. ..... Hackensack, NJ
Walsh, John K., Jr. ..... Hackensack, NJ
Walsh, John Kevin ..... **Memphis, TN**
Walsh, John L. ..... Northport, NY
Walsh, John L., (P.A.)
Fort Lauderdale, FL
Walsh, John M. ..... Washington, DC
Walsh, John M.
Department of Transportation,
Federal Aviation Administration, GV
Walsh, John M. ..... Buffalo, NY
Walsh, John P. ..... Pasadena, CA
Walsh, John P. ..... **St. Louis, MO**
Walsh, John P. ..... **Baldwin, NY**
Walsh, John P. ..... New York, NY
Walsh, John P. ..... Seattle, WA
Walsh, John P., Sr. ..... Havre de Grace, MD
Walsh, John Patrick, Jr. ..... Fairfax, VA
Walsh, John R., II ..... Naples, FL
Walsh, John T. ..... Salt Lake City, UT
Walsh, John T. "Jack" ..... **St. Louis, MO**
Walsh, John T., Jr. ..... Cumberland, RI
Walsh, John T., Jr. ..... **Providence, RI**
Walsh, John W. ..... Boston, MA
Walsh, Jonathan J. ..... **New York, NY**
Walsh, Jonathan M. ..... New Orleans, LA
Walsh, Joni M. ..... Philadelphia, PA
Walsh, Joseph A., II ..... **Long Beach, CA**
Walsh, Joseph A., Jr. ..... **Chicago, IL**
Walsh, Joseph E., Jr. ..... **St. Louis, MO**
Walsh, Joseph F. ..... Los Angeles, CA
Walsh, Joseph F. ..... Minot, MA
Walsh, Joseph F. ..... Scranton, PA
Walsh, Joseph F., Jr. ..... Yorkville, IL
Walsh, Joseph F., Jr. ..... Farmington Hills, MI
Walsh, Joseph G. ..... Oakland, CA
Walsh, Joseph G. ..... **Danbury, CT**
Walsh, Joseph G. ..... **Scarsdale, NY**
Walsh, Joseph G., Jr. ..... San Francisco, CA
Walsh, Joseph H. ..... **Boston, MA**
Walsh, Joseph J. ..... **Boston, MA**
Walsh, Joseph L., III ..... **St. Louis, MO**
Walsh, Joseph L., P.C. ..... **St. Louis, MO**
Walsh, Joseph M. ..... Ridgewood, NY
Walsh, Joseph M. ..... **Saratoga Springs, NY**
Walsh, Joseph M. ..... Toledo, OH
Walsh, Joseph M., III ..... **Erie, PA**
Walsh, Joseph M., Jr. ..... **Los Angeles, CA**
Walsh, Joseph P. ..... Babylon, NY
Walsh, Joseph R. ..... **San Francisco, CA**
Walsh, Joseph T. ..... Wilmington, DE
Walsh, Joseph T., III ..... **Chatham, NJ**
Toms River, NJ
Walsh, Joseph T., Jr. ..... Bangor, ME
Walsh, Joseph T., Jr. ..... **Audubon, NJ**
Walsh, Joseph W. ..... **Providence, RI**
Walsh & Joyce, P.A. ..... **Columbia, MD**
Walsh, Jude T. ..... Harrisburg, PA
Walsh, Judith B. ..... **San Francisco, CA**
Walsh, Justin M. ..... **Pittsburgh, PA**
Walsh, Karen Carden ..... **Tulsa, OK**
Walsh, Karen J. ..... New York, NY
Purchase, NY
Walsh, Katherine H. ..... Vermilion, OH
Walsh, Katherine S. ..... **St. Louis, MO**
Walsh, Kathleen A. ..... **New York, NY**
Walsh, Kathleen A. ..... **Scranton, PA**
Walsh, Kathleen Anne ..... **New York, NY**
Walsh, Kathleen G. ..... **Alexandria, VA**
Walsh, Kathleen J. ..... Dearborn, MI
Walsh, Kathleen M. ..... Lyons, IL
Walsh, Kathryn ..... Potomac, MD
Walsh, Kathryn J. ..... **Greenville, SC**
Walsh & Keating, S.C. ..... **Milwaukee, WI**
Walsh and Keegan ..... Staten Island, NY
Walsh, Keirsten L. ..... Lemoyne, PA
Walsh, Kelli M. ..... **Dallas, TX**
Walsh, Kelly M. ..... Eureka, CA
Walsh, Kenneth G. ..... **New York, NY**
Walsh, Kenneth G. ..... New York, NY
Walsh, Kenneth J. ..... **Cleveland, OH**
Walsh, Kenneth P. ..... Williamsport, PA
Walsh, Kevin ..... **New York, NY**
Walsh, Kevin A. ..... **Greenwich, CT**
Walsh, Kevin B. ..... Goshen, NY
Walsh, Kevin C. ..... **Garden City, NY**
Walsh, Kevin D. ..... Buffalo, NY
Walsh, Kevin D. ..... New York, NY
Walsh, Kevin E. ..... Wilmington, DE
Walsh, Kevin J. ..... **Simsbury, CT**
Walsh, Kevin J. ..... Atlanta, GA
Walsh, Kevin J. ..... **Boston, MA**
Walsh, Kevin J. ..... **New York, NY**
Walsh, Kevin J. ..... Pittsburgh, PA
Walsh, Kevin M. ..... San Francisco, CA
Walsh, Kevin M. ..... **Atlanta, GA**
Walsh, Kevin M. ..... Boston, MA
Walsh, Kevin M. ..... Richland, MI
Walsh, Kevin M. ..... Kingston, PA
Walsh, Kevin P. ..... **North Haven, CT**
Walsh, Kevin P. ..... **Carson City, NV**
Walsh, Kevin P. ..... Brooklyn, NY
New York, NY
Walsh, Kevin W. ..... **Philadelphia, PA**
Wayne, PA
Walsh, Kimberly A. ..... Redwood City, CA
Walsh, Knippen, Knight & Diamond, Chartered ..... **Wheaton, IL**
Walsh, Lauren M. ..... Washington, DC
Walsh, Laurie E. ..... San Jose, CA
Walsh Law Firm, The, L.L.P.
Greenville, SC
Simpsonville, SC
Walsh Law Office ..... **New Hope, PA**
Walsh Law Offices ..... Bangor, ME
Walsh, Lawr. J. ..... Akron, OH
Walsh, Lawrence A. ..... Brownsville, TX
Walsh, Lawrence E. ..... **Oklahoma City, OK**
Walsh, Lawrence J. ..... Wolfeboro, NH
Walsh, Leatrice ..... Cranston, RI
Walsh and Levine ..... **Mount Vernon, NY**
New York, NY
Yonkers, NY
Walsh, Linda L. ..... **Washington, DC**

Walsh, Liza M. ....Roseland, NJ
Walsh, Louise T. ....Chicago, IL
Walsh, Luanne ....Glendale, CA
Walsh, M. Bridget ....Chicago, IL
Walsh, M. Coleman, Jr. ....Newport News, VA
Walsh & Maier ....Troy, NY
Walsh, Marcia K. ....Kansas City, MO
Walsh, Margaret Gerry ....Atlanta, GA
Walsh, Margaret J. ....Belleville, IL
Walsh, Margaret T. ....Albany, NY
Walsh, Marguerite S. ....Philadelphia, PA
Walsh, Maria C. ....New York, NY
Walsh, Marian Wait
Saratoga Springs, NY
Walsh, Marie Patricia ....Harrisburg, PA
Walsh, Marilana S. "Marnie"
Golden, CO
Walsh, Marion M. ....New York, NY
Walsh, Mark A. ....Santa Ana, CA
Walsh, Mark A. ....Boston, MA
Walsh, Mark C. ....Scranton, PA
Walsh, Mark G. ....New York, NY
Walsh, Mark T. ....Albany, NY
Walsh, Marshall T. ....Spartanburg, SC
Walsh, Martin D. ("Art") ....Arlington, VA
Walsh, Mary A. ....Binghamton, NY
Walsh, Mary D. ....Washington, DC
Walsh, Mary Elizabeth ....New York, NY
Walsh, Mary Ellen ....Lyons, NY
Walsh, Mary J. ....Chicago, IL
Walsh, Mary Karen ....Cleveland, OH
Walsh, Mary McCabe ....Riverdale, NY
Walsh, Mary Rita D. ....Blue Bell, PA
Walsh, Mary V. G. ....Cleveland, OH
Walsh, Matthew, Jr. ....Chicago, IL
Walsh, Matthew M. ....Los Angeles, CA
Walsh, Matthew P. ....Palos Heights, IL
Walsh, Matthew P. ....Whitestone, NY
Walsh, Matthew P., & Associates, P.C.
Palos Heights, IL
Walsh, Matthew T. ....Chicago, IL
Walsh, Maura ....San Francisco, CA
Walsh, Maureen ....New York, NY
Walsh, Maureen T. ....Annandale, VA
Walsh, Maurice A., Jr. ....Jersey City, NJ
Walsh & McKenna, P.C. ....Bozeman, MT
Helena, MT
Walsh, Meghan E. ....Parsippany, NJ
Walsh, Melissa Lennon ....Philadelphia, PA
Walsh & Menapace ....Sunbury, PA
Walsh, Meredith ....Newark, NJ
Walsh, Michael ....Mineola, NY
Walsh, Michael ....Oklahoma City, OK
Walsh, Michael A. ....Decatur, IL
Walsh, Michael A. ....Dallas, TX
Walsh, Michael Arthur, (P.C.)
Boston, MA
Walsh, Michael C. ....Buffalo, NY
Walsh, Michael D. ....Palos Heights, IL
Walsh, Michael D. ....West Linn, OR
Walsh, Michael F. ....Upland, CA
Walsh, Michael F. ....Boston, MA
Walsh, Michael F. ....Lansing, MI
Walsh, Michael F. ....New York, NY
Walsh, Michael G. ....Southampton, NY
Walsh, Michael G. ....Water Mill, NY
Walsh, Michael G. ....Villanova, PA
Walsh, Michael J. ....Santa Ana, CA
Walsh, Michael J. ....Groton, CT
Hartford, CT
Walsh, Michael J. ....Department of Labor, Office of Secretary, GV
Walsh, Michael J. ....Worcester, MA
Walsh, Michael J. ....Morristown, NJ
Walsh, Michael J. ....Newport News, VA
Walsh, Michael M. ....Los Angeles, CA
Walsh, Michael P. ....Oakland, CA
Walsh, Michael P. ....San Francisco, CA
Walsh, Michael P. ....West Palm Beach, FL
Walsh, Michael P. ....Boston, MA
Walsh, Michael P. ....Philadelphia, PA
Walsh, Michael P., P.A.
West Palm Beach, FL
Walsh, Michael R. ....Orlando, FL
Walsh, Michael S. ....Campbell, CA
Walsh, Michael S. ....Chicago, IL
Walsh, Michael S. ....Carmel, IN
Walsh, Michael S. ....Sioux City, IA
Walsh, Michael S. ....Baton Rouge, LA
Walsh, Michael S., P.C. ....Carmel, IN
Walsh, Michael Sundance ....Miami, FL
Walsh, Michael T. ....Newport Beach, CA
Walsh, Michael T. ....Chicago, IL
Walsh, Michael T. ....New York, NY
Walsh, Michelle K. ....Richmond, VA
Walsh, Miller H. ....Houston, TX
Walsh, Milton I. ....Manchester, CT
Walsh, Moira C. ....Burlingame, CA
San Francisco, CA
Walsh Monzack and Monaco, P.A.
Georgetown, DE
Wilmington, DE
Walsh and Monzack, P.A.
Bethany Beach, DE
Walsh, Morgan ....Novato, CA
Walsh, Nancy E. ....Albany, NY
Walsh, Nancy L. ....Washington, DC
Walsh, Natalie A. ....Chicago, IL
Walsh, Neilli Mullen ....Wilmington, DE
Walsh, Nicholas H. ....Portland, ME
Walsh, Nina G. ....Captain Cook, HI
Walsh, O'Neal ....Baton Rouge, LA
Walsh, O'Neal, & Associates
Baton Rouge, LA
Walsh & O'Neill ....New Haven, CT
Walsh, Owen B. ....Mineola, NY
Walsh, P. Jerold ....Irvine, CA
Walsh, Pamela Johnstone ....Santa Ana, CA

Walsh, Patricia ....San Francisco, CA
Walsh, Patrick ....Bellevue, WA
Walsh, Patrick B. ....Carson City, NV
Walsh, Patrick D. ....Milwaukee, WI
Walsh, Patrick F. ....Atlanta, GA
Walsh, Patrick G ....Lyndon, KS
Osage City, KS
Walsh, Patrick J. ....Newport, KY
Walsh, Patrick J. ....Richmond, KY
Walsh, Patrick M. ....Kalamazoo, MI
Walsh, Patrick T. ....Chicago, IL
Walsh, Patrick T. ....New Bedford, MA
Walsh, Patrick W. ....Los Angeles, CA
Walsh, Patrick W. ....Madison, WI
Walsh, Paul B. ....Walnut Creek, CA
Walsh, Paul F., Jr. ....Boston, MA
Walsh, Paul J. ....Burgettstown, PA
Walsh, Paul J., & Assoc. ....Burgettstown, PA
Walsh, Paul J., III ....Pittsburgh, PA
Walsh, Paul M. ....Waltham, MA
Walsh, Paula J. ....Dallas, TX
Walsh, Peter A. ....Chicago, IL
Walsh, Peter C. ....Las Vegas, NV
Walsh, Peter C. ....Sound Beach, NY
Walsh, Peter G. ....Miami, FL
Walsh, Peter H. ....Denver, CO
Walsh, Peter J. ....Wilmington, DE
Walsh, Peter J. ....Albany, NY
Walsh, Peter J. ....Ithaca, NY
Walsh, Peter J. ....Milwaukee, WI
Walsh, Peter J., Jr. ....Wilmington, DE
Walsh, Peter M., (P.A.) ....St. Petersburg, FL
Walsh, Peter P. ....Grand Rapids, MI
Walsh, Phil ....Atlanta, GA
Walsh, Philip F. ....Bozeman, MT
Walsh, Philip J. ....New York, NY
Walsh, Philip J. ....Falls Church, VA
Walsh & Phillips, P.A. ....Easton, MD
Walsh, Prena and Fitchett
Farmington Hills, MI
Walsh, R. William ....Great Falls, MT
Walsh, Raymond J. ....Springfield, VA
Walsh, Raymond P. ....Westland, MI
Walsh, Rebecca Epstein ....St. Louis, MO
Walsh, Rebecca J. ....Carlsbad, CA
Walsh, Rebecca S. ....Southfield, MI
Walsh, Regina M. ....Oklahoma City, OK
Walsh, Regina Marie ....Greeley, CO
Walsh, Richard A. ....Chicago, IL
Walsh, Richard A. ....Green Brook, NJ
Walsh, Richard B. ....Chelmsford, MA
Walsh, Richard B., Jr. ....St. Louis, MO
Walsh, Richard C. ....Kalamazoo, MI
Walsh, Richard D. ....Cambridge, MA
Walsh, Richard F. ....Department of the Navy, Office of the Judge Advocate General, GV
Walsh, Richard F. ....Bowie, MD
Walsh, Richard F. ....Cleveland, OH
Walsh, Richard J. ....Chicago, IL
Walsh, Richard J. ....Manchester, NH
Walsh, Richard J. ....Waynesboro, PA
Walsh, Richard K. ....Colorado Springs, CO
Walsh, Richard L. ....Boston, MA
Walsh, Richard L. ....Center Sandwich, NH
Walsh, Richard L., III ....North Kingstown, RI
Walsh, Richard M. ....Salem, OR
Walsh, Richard P. ....Poplar Grove, IL
Walsh, Richard P., Jr. ....Albany, NY
Walsh, Richard T. ....New York, NY
Walsh, Richard T. ....New York, NY
Walsh, Richard T. ....Lansdale, PA
Walsh, Richard W. ....Bellmore, NY
Walsh, Robert A. ....Concordia, KS
Walsh, Robert A. ....Essex Junction, VT
Walsh, Robert E. ....West Hartford, CT
Walsh, Robert E. ....Malone, NY
Walsh, Robert E. ....Norfolk, VA
Walsh, Robert F. ....Jersey City, NJ
New York, NY
Walsh, Robert F. ....Brooklyn, NY
Walsh, Robert G. ....Blasdell, NY
Walsh, Robert J. ....Las Vegas, NV
Walsh, Robert K. ....North Haven, CT
Walsh, Robert K. ....Cedar Grove, NJ
Walsh, Robert K. ....Winston-Salem, NC
Walsh, Robert L. ....New Orleans, LA
Walsh, Robert L. ....Silver Spring, MD
Walsh, Robert L. ....Sunbury, PA
Walsh, Robert M.
Treasury Department, GV
Walsh, Robert M., III ....Boston, MA
Walsh, Robert P. ....Battle Creek, MI
Walsh, Robert P., Jr. ....Chicago, IL
Walsh, Robert R. ....Brooklyn, NY
Walsh, Robert (Robin) O. ....Porterville, CA
Walsh, Roberts & Grace ....Buffalo, NY
Walsh, Rodger J. ....Kansas City, MO
Walsh, Roger C. ....Seattle, WA
Walsh, Roger E. ....Milwaukee, WI
Walsh, Ronald E. ....Stamford, CT
Walsh, Rondi ....Los Angeles, CA
Walsh, S. Gray ....Greenville, SC
Walsh, Sara K. ....Princeton, NJ
Walsh, Sara L.
Federal Labor Relations Authority, Federal Service Impasses Panel, GV
Walsh, Sara P. ....Augusta, MT
Walsh, Scott A. ....McAllen, TX
Walsh, Sean M. ....Detroit, MI
Walsh, Sean M. ....Bronx, NY
Walsh, Sean P. ....New York, NY
Walsh, Shannon L. ....Chicago, IL
Walsh, Shaun ....Lakeville, MA
Walsh & Sheehan, LLP ....New York, NY
Walsh, Sheila E. ....Livonia, MI
Walsh, Stanley ....Sonoma, CA
Walsh, Stephanie A. ....Knoxville, TN

Walsh, Stephen ....Department of Commerce, Patent and Trademark Office, GV
Walsh, Stephen Andrew ....Birmingham, AL
Walsh, Stephen D. ....Danvers, MA
Walsh, Stephen D. ....Kansas City, MO
Walsh, Stephen E. ....Poplar Bluff, MO
Walsh, Stephen R. ....East Providence, RI
Walsh, Steven ....Hamden, CT
Walsh, Steven J. ....Buffalo Grove, IL
Walsh, Susan A. ....Oakland, CA
Walsh, Susan Horn ....Tampa, FL
Walsh, Susan L. ....Rochester, NY
Walsh, Susan M. ....Bethel Island, CA
Walsh, Susan M. ....Boston, MA
Walsh, Susanne M. ....Boston, MA
Walsh, Suzanne Brown ....Hartford, CT
Walsh, Suzanne E. ....Los Angeles, CA
Walsh, Suzanne M. ....River Grove, IL
Walsh & Sweeney, LLP ....Braintree, MA
Walsh, Terrence M. ....Chicago, IL
Walsh, Terrence M. ....Johnstown, NY
Walsh, Theresa M. ....Cleveland, OH
Walsh, Thomas A. ....Golden, CO
Walsh, Thomas A. ....Indianapolis, IN
Walsh, Thomas B., IV ....Dallas, TX
Walsh, Thomas C. ....Chicago, IL
Walsh, Thomas C. ....Boston, MA
Walsh, Thomas C. ....Lansing, MI
Walsh, Thomas C. ....St. Louis, MO
Walsh, Thomas C. ....Johnstown, NY
Walsh, Thomas C., Jr. ....Baton Rouge, LA
Walsh, Thomas E., II ....Congers, NY
Walsh, Thomas E., Jr. ....Westfield, NJ
Walsh, Thomas F. ....Rochester, NY
Walsh, Thomas G. ....Long Beach, CA
Walsh, Thomas G. ....Baltimore, MD
Walsh, Thomas H., Jr. ....Boston, MA
Walsh, Thomas J. ....Kansas City, MO
Walsh, Thomas J. ....Lee's Summit, MO
Walsh, Thomas J. ....Omaha, NE
Walsh, Thomas J. ....Cranford, NJ
Walsh, Thomas J. ....Albany, NY
Walsh, Thomas J. ....Manhasset, NY
Walsh, Thomas J. ....De Pere, WI
Walsh, Thomas J., Jr. ....Southport, CT
Walsh, Thomas J., Jr. ....Omaha, NE
Walsh, Thomas J., Jr.
New Brunswick, NJ
Walsh, Thomas J., Jr. ....Memphis, TN
Walsh, Thomas L. ....Roseville, CA
Walsh, Thomas M.
Department of Agriculture, Office of the General Counsel, GV
Walsh, Thomas M. ....Downers Grove, IL
Walsh, Thomas M. ....St. Louis, MO
Walsh, Thomas M. ....Marlton, NJ
Walsh, Thomas M. ....Seattle, WA
Walsh, Thomas P. ....Chicago, IL
Walsh, Thomas P. ....Binghamton, NY
Walsh, Thomas P. ....Beaverton, OR
Walsh, Thomas V. ....White Plains, NY
Walsh, Timothy ....New York, NY
Walsh, Timothy C. ....New York, NY
Walsh, Timothy J. ....Fairfield, CA
Walsh, Timothy J. ....Watsonville, CA
Walsh, Timothy J. ....Mishawaka, IN
Walsh, Timothy J. ....Pelham Manor, NY
Walsh, Timothy M. ....Washington, DC
Walsh, Timothy M. ....St. Paul, MN
Walsh, Timothy P. ....Chicago, IL
Walsh, Timothy P. ....Garnerville, NY
Walsh, Tracy A. ....Philadelphia, PA
Walsh, Valerie A. ....Concord, NH
Walsh, Vincent J., Jr. ....Philadelphia, PA
Walsh, W. Terence ....Atlanta, GA
Walsh, W. Urie ....San Francisco, CA
Walsh & Walsh ....Los Angeles, CA
Walsh & Walsh ....Lansing, MI
Walsh & Walsh ....Hackensack, NJ
Walsh & Walsh, LLC ....Blasdell, NY
Walsh & Walsh, LLP
Saratoga Springs, NY
Walsh & Walsh, P.C. ....Kalamazoo, MI
Walsh, Walsh & Reinhart, P.C.
Cumberland, MD
Oakland, MD
Walsh & Walsh, S.C. ....De Pere, WI
Walsh, Walter V., Jr. ....New York, NY
Walsh, Wendell W. ....South Bend, IN
Walsh, Wendy W. ....St. Louis, MO
Walsh White & Tompkins, P.C.
Houston, TX
Walsh, Wicks & Salisbury
Poughkeepsie, NY
Walsh, William A. ....White Plains, NY
Walsh, William A. ....West Chester, PA
Walsh, William A., Jr. ....Yonkers, NY
Walsh, William A., Jr. ....Richmond, VA
Walsh, William A., P.C. ....West Chester, PA
Walsh, William C. ....Washington, DC
Walsh, William C. ....Roseland, NJ
Walsh, William C., P.A. ....Roseland, NJ
Walsh, William D. ....Syracuse, NY
Walsh, William D., P.C. ....Syracuse, NY
Walsh, William E. ....Spartanburg, SC
Walsh, William F. ....Chicago, IL
Walsh, William G. ....Greenville, SC
Walsh, William, IV ....Lancaster, CA
Walsh, William J. ....Lakewood, CO
Walsh, William J. ....Washington, DC
Walsh, William J. ....Boston, MA
Walsh, William J. ....Poughkeepsie, NY
Walsh, William J. ....Charlotte, NC
Walsh, William J., IV ....Louisville, KY
Walsh, William L., Jr. (P.C.) ....McLean, VA
Walsh, William M. ....Riverside, RI
Walsh, William M. ....Memphis, TN
Walsh, William P. ....Mineola, NY

Walsh, William T. ....Agawam, MA
Walsh, William T. ....Boston, MA
Walsh, William T. ....Wayne, PA
Walsh, Wm. J. ....Chicago, IL
Walsh-Dempsey, Mary D. ....Scranton, PA
Walshe, John ....New York, NY
Walshe, Kevin J. ....Camden, NJ
Walshe, Michael Q., Jr. ....New Orleans, LA
Walshe, P. Joseph ....Brinklow, MD
Walsh III, Thomas J. ....Newtown, PA
Walsh-Rogalski, Mary Ellen
Marblehead, MA
Walsh Sullivan, Brenda E. ....Mattapan, MA
Walsingham, Carl B., Jr.
Oklahoma City, OK
Walsleben, Jennifer L. ....Los Angeles, CA
Walsma, Pamela ....Yuma, AZ
Walson, Jeffrey M. ....Winchester, KY
Walstad & Associates ....Provo, UT
Walstad, John M. ....Bismarck, ND
Walstad, Paul J., (P.C.) ....Provo, UT
Walstad, Peter F. ....Excelsior, MN
Walstead, Mertsching, Husemoen, Donaldson & Barlow, P.S. ....Longview, WA
Walster, K. Randlett, (Ms.) ....Roxbury, NY
Walston, David B. ....Birmingham, AL
Walston, E. Hoyt ....Gainesville, FL
Walston, James R. ....Mendota Heights, MN
Walston, Jeannie Bugg ....Birmingham, AL
Walston, John T. ....Goldsboro, NC
Walston, Martha K. ....Raleigh, NC
Walston, Richard H. ....Birmingham, AL
Walston, Robert H. ....Birmingham, AL
Walston, Roderick E. ....Sacramento, CA
Walston, Tammy Daley ....Plano, TX
Walston, Thomas H. ....Johnson City, TX
Walston, W. Kent ....Beaumont, TX
Walston, W. Wayne ....Mansfield, OH
Walston, Wells, Anderson & Bains, LLP
Birmingham, AL
Walston, William G., Inc. ....Rockport, TX
Walston, William G., Jr. ....Rockport, TX
Walston, William G., Sr. ....Rockport, TX
Walstrom, LaTesha L. ....Phoenix, AZ
Walstrom, Lea Harpster ....St. Paul, MN
Walsworth, Craig T. ....Easton, MD
Walsworth, Franklin, Bevins & McCall
Orange, CA
San Francisco, CA
Santa Barbara, CA
Houston, TX
Walsworth, James H. ....Newport Beach, CA
Walsworth, Jeffrey P. ....Orange, CA
Santa Barbara, CA
Walt, Alan ....Southfield, MI
Walt, Bonnie G. ....Chicago, IL
Walt, Christopher J. ....La Jolla, CA
Walt, Gary Irwin ....Chicago, IL
Walt, James A. ....Milwaukee, WI
Walt, Jennifer J. ....San Francisco, CA
Reno, NV
Walt, John D., Jr ....Wilmore, KY
Walt, John Dabney ....Memphis, TN
Walt, Linda L. ....De Kalb, IL
Walta, J. Gregory ....Colorado Springs, CO
Walta, J. Gregory, P.C.
Colorado Springs, CO
Walta, Mary E. ....Santa Fe, NM
Waltar, Stephen M. ....Seattle, WA
Waltari, Mary L. ....San Diego, CA
Waltcher, Barri G. ....New York, NY
Waltcher, Daniel R. ....New York, NY
Waltemade, Leo J. ....St. Louis, MO
Waltemath, Tamra K. ....Denver, CO
Waltemyer, Roger L. ....Fort Myers, FL
Walten, Edwin A., Jr. ....Baltimore, MD
Waltensperger, George R. ....Dayton, OH
Walter, A.P., Jr., P.A. ....Coral Gables, FL
Walter, Alan N. ....New York, NY
Walter, A. P., Jr. (P.A.) ....Coral Gables, FL
Walter, April L. ....Costa Mesa, CA
Walter, Arlene M. ....Ridgewood, NY
Walter, Bernard David ....San Francisco, CA
Las Vegas, NV
Dallas, PA
Shavertown, PA
Walter & Bornholdt
San Luis Obispo, CA
Santa Barbara, CA
Walter, Brad L. ....San Ramon, CA
Walter, Brent W. ....Plainwell, MI
Walter, Brian ....Los Angeles, CA
Walter, Bryan L. ....Fort Worth, TX
Walter, Burdzinski & Company, L.L.P.
Houston, TX
Walter, Byron D. ....Detroit, MI
Walter, Charles D. ....Paducah, KY
Walter, Charles F. ....Houston, TX
Walter, Christopher G. ....Nappanee, IN
Walter, Clark E. ....New York, NY
Walter, Conston, Alexander & Green, P.C.
Darien, CT
New York, NY
Walter, Daniel C. ....Norton, KS
Walter, Daniel M. ....Louisville, KY
Walter, David D. ....Macon, GA
Walter, David H. ....Austin, TX
Walter, David M. ....Springfield, IL
Walter, David M. ....Austin, TX
Walter, Dawn E. ....San Diego, CA
Walter, Delmar ....Sioux Falls, SD
Walter, Denise ....Los Angeles, CA
Walter, Donald E. ....Shreveport, LA
Walter, Donald E. ....Maryland Heights, MO
Walter, Donald F. ....Niles, MI
Walter, Donald S. ....Sacramento, CA
Walter, Douglas G. ....Houston, TX
Walter, Douglas H. ....Chicago, IL

Walther, Mark A. ... **San Francisco, CA**
San Mateo, CA
Walther, Mark A. ... San Mateo, CA
Walther, Michael C. ... St. Louis, MO
Walther, Milton M. ... New Orleans, LA
Walther, Muriel A. ... Pasadena, CA
Walther, P. Kevin ... Atlanta, GA
Walther, Pamela D. ... **Washington, DC**
Walther, Paul R. ... Culpeper, VA
Walther, Peter D. ... Malvern, PA
Walther, Roark, Gay & Todd, PLC
Lexington, KY
Versailles, KY
Walther, Robert G. ... Rome, GA
Walther, Roy A., III ... St. Louis, MO
Walther, Steven T. ... **Reno, NV**
Walther, Stevia M. ... **New Orleans, LA**
Walther/Glenn ... St. Louis, MO
Walther-Meade, Caroline V.
New York, NY
Walthers, Kal J. ... Burbank, CA
Walthew, Marshall J. ... **Philadelphia, PA**
Walthew, Warner, Costello, Thompson & Eagan, P.S. ... **Seattle, WA**
Walthier, John T. ... San Jose, CA
Walthour, Bess L. ... Decatur, GA
Walthour, Carrie L. ... San Francisco, CA
Walthour, Christ. C., Jr. ... Greensburg, PA
Walthour and Garland ... Greensburg, PA
Walthour, Nicole Marie ... **Memphis, TN**
Walti, J. Randall ... **Plano, TX**
Walti, Paul J., Jr. ... **San Bruno, CA**
Waltke, Tina L. ... **New York, NY**
Waltman, Albert R. ... Millville, NJ
Waltman, Bruce L. ... Orwigsburg, PA
Waltman & Cohen ... Miami, FL
Waltman, Guy S. ... New York, NY
Waltman, Irving ... Miami, FL
Waltman, John R. ... **Millersburg, OH**
Waltman, Judson ... **Lubbock, TX**
Waltman, Laura ... **Hartford, CT**
Waltman, Naomi Brufsky ... **New York, NY**
Waltman, O. L., Jr. ... Ruston, LA
Waltman, P. Dean ... Orrville, OH
Waltman & Reilly ... Millville, NJ
Waltman, Robert B. ... Bryan, TX
Waltman, Susan C. ... New York, NY
Waltner, Alan C. ... San Francisco, CA
Waltner, Paul ... Ann Arbor, MI
Walto, Catherine N. ... **Fort Washington, PA**
Walton, A. Brand ... **Birmingham, AL**
Walton & Adams, P.C. ... **McLean, VA**
Tysons Corner, VA
Walton, Alan D. ... Bay City, MI
Walton, Alfred G. ... Warren, NJ
Walton & Associates ... **San Diego, CA**
Walton & Associates ... Santa Monica, CA
Walton, Avis G. ... Atherton, CA
Walton, Barbara J. ... Meadville, PA
Walton, Barry B. ... Knoxville, TN
Walton, Benton H., III ... Whiteville, NC
Walton, Brian ... Los Angeles, CA
Walton, Brown, Walton, Seilheimer & Reid
Granbury, TX
Walton, C. Lewis, III ... Knoxville, TN
Walton, Callie E. ... **Louisville, KY**
Walton, Christine Candace ... Saginaw, MI
Walton, Christopher D. ... Santa Monica, CA
Walton, Christopher J. ... **New York, NY**
Walton, Clayton L. ... **Richmond, VA**
Walton, D. Bailey ... Bowling Green, KY
Walton, D. Gibson ... **Houston, TX**
Walton, D. Raymond ... Waterloo, IA
Walton, Dan E. ... Houston, TX
Walton, Dandridge F. ... Frankfort, KY
Walton, Daniel J. ... Gastonia, NC
Walton, Danna Moore ... Houston, TX
Walton, David A. ... **San Francisco, CA**
Walton, David Conrad ... San Diego, CA
Walton, David J. ... **Richmond, VA**
Walton, Deanna ... Treasury Department, Internal Revenue Service, GV
Walton, Debra P.
Research Triangle Park, NC
Walton, Donald C., III ... **Lexington, KY**
Walton, Donald D. ... **Los Angeles, CA**
Walton, Donald F. ... Atlanta, GA
Walton, Donald G., Jr. ... Jacksonville, NC
Walton & Donnelly, P.C. ... **Detroit, MI**
Walton, E. Andrew
Department of State, GV
Walton, E. Spencer ... Mishawaka, IN
Walton, E. Spencer, Jr. ... **South Bend, IN**
Walton, Earl D. ... **Demotte, IN**
Rensselaer, IN
Walton, Edmund L., Jr. ... **McLean, VA**
Walton, Edward C. ... **San Diego, CA**
Walton, Eileen ... New York, NY
Walton, Elbert A., Jr. ... St. Louis, MO
Walton, F. Dana ... **Mariposa, CA**
Walton, Frederick H., Jr. ... Chevy Chase, MD
Walton, Frederick M., Jr.
Philadelphia, PA
Walton, G. Douglas ... Grand Rapids, MI
Walton, Garrett W. ... Pensacola, FL
Walton, Garry L. ... **Washington, DC**
Kalamazoo, MI
Walton, Gene C. ... Albuquerque, NM
Walton, George B. ... Louisville, KY
Walton, George K. ... Frenchtown, NJ
Walton, George R. ... Richmond, VA
Walton, Gerald R. ... Cleveland, OH
Walton, Gerald R., Co., L.P.A.
Cleveland, OH
Walton, Gina Zadra ... **Seattle, WA**
Walton, Gordon K. ... **Chicago, IL**
Walton, Gus B., Jr. ... Little Rock, AR
Walton, H. Steven (IBA) ... Cypress, TX
Walton, Herbert K., Jr. ... San Rafael, CA
Walton, Herbert W. ... Olathe, KS
Walton, Homer L. ... **Pittsburgh, PA**
Walton, Howard J. ... Akron, OH
Walton, J. Richard ... Birmingham, AL
Walton, James ... **Las Vegas, NV**
Walton, James B. ... Norcross, GA
Walton, James E. ... Springfield, TN
Walton, James R. ... Sanger, CA
Walton, Jessica S. ... **Washington, DC**
Walton, Joan P. ... Vienna, VA
Walton, John A. ... De Kalb, IL
Walton, John J. ... **St. George, UT**
Walton, John R. ... **Los Angeles, CA**
Walton, John W. ... Elizabethton, TN
Walton, Jon D. ... **Pittsburgh, PA**
Walton, Jonathan R. ... New York, NY
Walton, Jonathan T., Jr. ... **Detroit, MI**
Walton, Judy L. ... **Grand Rapids, MI**
Walton, Julie A. ... Davenport, IA
Walton, Karen S. ... Findlay, OH
Walton, Kelly Diane ... **Austin, TX**
Walton, Kenneth
Department of Justice, GV
Walton, Kenneth A. ... **Sacramento, CA**
Walton, Kenneth B. ... **Boston, MA**
Walton, Kenneth R. ... **Rahway, NJ**
Walton, Kimberly M. Hubbard
Department of Commerce, GV
Walton, Kristen D. ... **Carlsbad, CA**
Walton, L. Kent ... **Traverse City, MI**
Walton, Lamont M. ... Lansing, MI
Walton & Langford ... **Las Vegas, NV**
Walton Lantaff Schroeder & Carson
Fort Lauderdale, FL
Miami, FL
West Palm Beach, FL
Walton, Laurence H. ... Sacramento, CA
Walton, Leigh ... **Nashville, TN**
Walton, Leigh S. ... Memphis, TN
Walton, Lewis R. ... Bakersfield, CA
Walton, Linda D. ... **Seattle, WA**
Walton, Linda L. ... Kealakekua, HI
Walton, Linda M. ... Washington, DC
Walton, Linus W. ... Oneida, NY
Walton, M. Lauck
Federal Deposit Insurance Corporation, Professional Liability Section, GV
Walton, Margaret B. ... Sacramento, CA
Walton, Marie ... Boulder, CO
Walton, Mark D. ... Chicago, IL
Walton, Mary Ellen ... Silverdale, WA
Walton, Matthew G. ... Tempe, AZ
Walton, Matthew M. ... Mount Clemens, MI
Walton, Maurice G. ... Granbury, TX
Walton, Merrick C. ... Houston, TX
Walton, Michael C. ... **Grand Rapids, MI**
Walton, Michael J. ... Davenport, IA
Walton, Michael L. ... **St. Louis, MO**
Walton, Michael L. ... Cincinnati, OH
Walton, Michele M. ... Asheville, NC
Walton, Mildred H. ... Houston, TX
Walton, Monty L. ... **Knoxville, TN**
Walton, Nilsen, Johnson & Guerra, P.C.
Roseburg, OR
Walton, Pamela A. ... **Tampa, FL**
Walton, Patricia A.V. ... Lewistown, IL
Walton, Paul N. ... Fremont, CA
Walton, Peter L. ... **Watertown, NY**
Walton, R. Brent ... **Seattle, WA**
Walton, R. Scott ... San Bernardino, CA
Walton, Ralph H., Jr. ... Granbury, TX
Walton, Randall K. ... Modesto, CA
Walton, Randall R. ... **Escondido, CA**
Walton, Randolph B. ... Mobile, AL
Walton, Ray H. ... Southport, NC
Walton, Ray H. ... Bismarck, ND
Walton, Ray H., P.C. ... Bismarck, ND
Walton, Raymond T. ... Davenport, IA
Walton, Reggie Barnett ... Washington, DC
Walton, Reginald Keith ... Decatur, GA
Walton, Rhondetta Goble
Bowling Green, KY
Walton, Richard A. ... Los Angeles, CA
Walton, Richard J. ... Oak Bluffs, MA
Walton, Richard P. ... Ashby, MN
Walton, Ritchie & Green, L.L.C.
Mobile, AL
Walton, R. L., Jr. ... Richmond, VA
Walton, Robert E. ... **Blue Bell, PA**
Walton, Robert J. ... Phoenix, AZ
Walton, Robert M., Jr. ... Rockaway, NJ
Walton, Robert N. ... **Vienna, VA**
Walton, Robert P. ... **Minneapolis, MN**
Walton, Robert P. ... New York, NY
Walton, Robert S. ... **Chicago, IL**
Walton, Robert S., III ... **Tampa, FL**
Walton, Robert W. ... Rock Island, IL
Walton, Roger D. (Rocky) ... **Arlington, TX**
Walton, Ronnie L. ... **Meridian, MS**
Walton, S. Robson ... Bentonville, AR
Walton, S. Thomas ... Asheville, NC
Walton, Sharon D. ... Albuquerque, NM
Walton, Simon K. ... **Baltimore, MD**
Walton, Smith, Phillips & Dixon, P.C.
Traverse City, MI
Walton, Southy E. ... Fairfax, VA
Walton & Stafford, P.C. ... **Detroit, MI**
Walton, Stanley A. ... **Las Vegas, NV**
Walton, Stephen W. ... **Flint, MI**
Walton, Thomas H. ... **Des Moines, IA**
Walton, Timothy C. ... Boise, ID
Walton, Timothy J. ... **San Francisco, CA**
Walton & Townsend, P.A. ... **Palatka, FL**
Walton, Trina M. ... **Cincinnati, OH**
Walton, Tyria B., Law Office of ... Chicago, IL
Walton, Victor A., Jr. ... **Cincinnati, OH**
Walton, Victor B. ... Lakeside, CA
Walton, W. Richard ... Ironton, OH
Walton, W. Todd, II ... Flemingsburg, KY
Walton & Walton ... Davenport, IA
Walton, Wesley S. ... **Chicago, IL**
Walton, Will O. (Trip), III ... **Opelika, AL**
Walton, William O., Jr. ... Lafayette, AL
Walton, William S. ... **Nashville, TN**
Walton, William Todd ... Flemingsburg, KY
Walton, Woodrow R. ... Shattuck, OK
Walton, Zachary R. ... **San Francisco, CA**
Walton-Everett, Laura ... Los Angeles, CA
Walton-McFalls, Rebecca S. ... Marietta, GA
Walton-Pratt, Tanya ... Indianapolis, IN
Waltrip, Bill ... Arlington, TX
Waltrip, David G. ... **St. Louis, MO**
Waltrip, T. Bradford ... **Belleville, IL**
Waltrous, Clarence L. ... Brooklyn, NY
Waltrous, Dolores L. ... New York, NY
Waltrous, Evelyn Fleuretta ... Brooklyn, NY
Walts, C. Alan ... Chicago, IL
Walts, Michael J. ... Great Bend, KS
Walts, T. Clayton ... **Atlanta, GA**
Walts, W. Edward, II, (P.C.) ... **Dallas, TX**
Waltuch, Barbara ... New York, NY
Waltuch, Benjamin ... **New York, NY**
Waltuch, Denise J. ... **Englewood Cliffs, NJ**
Waltuch, Hy A. ... St. Louis, MO
Waltuch, Joseph L. ... Newport Beach, CA
Waltuch, Robert H. ... **Tampa, FL**
Waltz, Christine Embery ... Rockledge, PA
Waltz, Daniel E. ... **Washington, DC**
Waltz & D'Antuono ... **Denver, CO**
Waltz, David Michael ... San Diego, CA
Waltz, Debora Jo ... **Indianapolis, IN**
Waltz, Donald A. ... **Philadelphia, PA**
Waltz, F. Randall, III ... Jefferson City, MO
Waltz, Fred J. ... Taos, NM
Waltz, Galen R. ... Harrisburg, PA
Waltz, James F. ... Norwalk, IA
Waltz, James Frederick
Cape Girardeau, MO
Waltz, Jon R. ... North Palm Beach, FL
Chicago, IL
Waltz, Judith A. ... San Francisco, CA
San Francisco, CA
Waltz, Kristine L. ... **Williamsport, PA**
Waltz, Peter J. ... Mount Horeb, WI
Waltz, Richard A., (P.C.) ... **Denver, CO**
Waltz, Stanley J. ... Spokane, WA
Waltz, Thomas A. ... Arlington, VA
Waltz, William M. ... Greenwood, IN
Waltzer & Associates ... **New Orleans, LA**
Waltzer, Brenda W. ... New Orleans, LA
Waltzer, Bruce C. ... **New Orleans, LA**
Waltzer, Garrett J. ... **Palo Alto, CA**
Waltzer, Joel R. ... **New Orleans, LA**
Waltzer, Miriam G. ... New Orleans, LA
Waluch, Paula G. ... **Pasadena, CA**
Walutes & Bedford ... **Annandale, VA**
Fairfax, VA
Walutes, Helen F. ... Mount Vernon, VA
Walutes, Michael P. ... **New York, NY**
Walutes, Ronald L., Jr. ... Washington, DC
Walvick, Walter J. ... **Washington, DC**
Walvoord, Al ... Midland, TX
Walvoord, David J. ... **Peoria, IL**
Walvoord, Laura E. ... **Minneapolis, MN**
Walwer, Frank K. ... Fort Worth, TX
Walwick, Robert S. ... Oceanside, CA
Walworth, Carla R. ... **Stamford, CT**
Walworth, Deborah R. ... **New Orleans, LA**
Walworth, Janet R. ... **San Jose, CA**
Walwyn, Lloyd Alexis ... Madison, TN
Walwyn, Marc A. ... Chicago, IL
Walwyn, Mark A. ... Chicago, IL
Walwyn, Melville G.M., P.C. ... Harrisburg, PA
Walwyn, Melville G. M. ... Harrisburg, PA
Walwyn, Stephen J. ... San Jose, CA
Walz, Alison M. ... **Beverly Hills, CA**
Walz & Associates ... Albuquerque, NM
Walz, Brad Paul ... Waterloo, IA
Walz, Brent Eliot ... **Wadena, MN**
Walz, Carlene G. ... Jackson, MI
Walz, Corenia Kollasch ... **Fergus Falls, MN**
Walz, Erin H. ... **Big Rapids, MI**
Traverse City, MI
Walz, Frank J. ... **Minneapolis, MN**
Walz, Gregory S. ... **St. Cloud, MN**
Walz, Herman J. ... Rochester, NY
Walz, Hermann P. ... New York, NY
Walz, Jerry A. ... Department of Commerce, Office of the General Counsel, GV
Walz, Jerry A. ... Albuquerque, NM
Walz, John M. ... Burlington, IA
Walz, Judith Carroll ... Lewisburg, WV
Walz, Judith Twigg, (Mrs.) ... Newport, PA
Walz, Karl M. ... **Louisville, KY**
Walz, Kathleen
Department of State, GV
Walz, Kenneth P. ... **Big Rapids, MI**
Traverse City, MI
Walz, Kenton E. ... Albuquerque, NM
Walz Law Office ... Redwood Falls, MN
Walz, Mark D. ... **Des Moines, IA**
Walz, Martha M. ... Chestnut Hill, MA
Walz, Mary Beth ... Bow, NH
Walz, Mary E. ... Bow, NH
Walz, Mary K. ... Los Alamos, NM
Walz, Mary K., P.A. ... Los Alamos, NM
Walz, Michael K. ... Minneapolis, MN
Walz, Monte R. ... **Sioux Falls, SD**
Walz, Pamela ... Philadelphia, PA
Walz, Raymond O. ... Redwood Falls, MN
Walz, Richard A. ... **New York, NY**
Walz, Shaubut C., III ... Newport, PA
Walz, Tamra ... Papillion, NE
Walz, Thomas M. ... **South Bend, IN**
Walz & Warba, P.C. ... **Big Rapids, MI**
Traverse City, MI
Walz, William R. ... Irvine, CA
Walzel, Michael R. ... **Beaumont, TX**
Walzel, Nancy Kersh ... Beaumont, TX
Walzer, Arline Nudell ... Roslyn Heights, NY
Walzer, Barbara T. ... Syracuse, NY
Walzer, James H. ... Boonton, NJ
Walzer, Joel ... Boston, MA
Walzer, Lee I. ... Treasury Department, Office of the Comptroller of the Currency, GV
Walzer, Martin J. ... New York, NY
Walzer, Peter M., Law Offices of
Woodland Hills, CA
Walzer, Richard L. ... St. Paul, MN
Walzer, Robert S. ... Stamford, CT
Walzer, Roy S. ... Litchfield, CT
Walzer, Sarah E. ... Trenton, NJ
Walzer, Seymour B. ... Roslyn Heights, NY
Walzer, William P. ... New York, NY
Walzl, L. Jody ... Napa, CA
Wambach, Andrew J., Jr. ... Mahnomen, MN
Wambach, Douglas E. ... **Chicago, IL**
Wambach, Heidi K. ... **Dallas, TX**
Wambach, Ronald J. ... West Allis, WI
Wambaugh, Cassandra M. ... **Phoenix, AZ**
Wambeke, Ann Marie ... Detroit, MI
Wamble, David Reid ... Holly Springs, MS
Wamble, Keena V. ... Little Rock, AR
Wambold, John D. ... **Minneapolis, MN**
Wambold, Judson J. ... Radnor, PA
Wambold, Karen Norton ... San Rafael, CA
Wambold, William C. ... Tacoma, WA
Wambsgans, Anthony W. ... Metairie, LA
Wambsgans, Katherine L. ... Cleveland, OH
Wambsganss, Andrew L. ... **Fort Worth, TX**
Wambsganss, Richard E. ... Birmingham, AL
Wamer, Gary L. ... Danbury, CT
Wamhoff, Fredrick C. ... **Houston, TX**
Wammen, Kristi K. ... **Rapid City, SD**
Wampler, Atlee W., III ... **Miami, FL**
Wampler, Buchanan & Breen, A Professional Association ... **Miami, FL**
Wampler, C. Howard ... Princeton, IL
Wampler, Christopher R. ... Beltsville, MD
Wampler, Dee ... **Springfield, MO**
Wampler, E. James (Jim) ... Dayton, OH
New Lebanon, OH
Wampler, G. S. ... Mentor, OH
Wampler, Jeffery B. ... **Champaign, IL**
Wampler, Lloyd C. ... Indianapolis, IN
Wampler, Michael H. ... Redford, MI
Wampler, Pierce & Siegel, P.C.
Memphis, TN
Wampler, Robert A. ... Memphis, TN
Wampler, Robert J. ... **Indianapolis, IN**
Wampler, Robert M. ... Helena, MT
Wampler, Sherry ... Dayton, OH
New Lebanon, OH
Wampler, Wampler & Catt
Springfield, MO
Wampold, Charles H., III ... **Princeton, NJ**
Wampold, Charles H., Jr. ... Birmingham, AL
Wampold, Michael S. ... **Seattle, WA**
Wampold, Thomas S. ... Seattle, WA
Wamser, Jerry B. ... St. Louis, MO
Wamser, Stephen E. ... Las Vegas, NV
Wamsley, Brent ... Salt Lake City, UT
Wamsley, Brian L. ... New York, NY
Wamsley, Douglas W. ... **Montvale, NJ**
Wamsley, Herbert C. ... Washington, DC
Wamsley, James L., III ... **Cleveland, OH**
Wamsley, Michael R. ... **Gadsden, AL**
Wamsley, Thomas F., Jr. ... **Atlanta, GA**
Wamsted, Jan M. ... Cleveland, OH
Wamsted, Michael L. ... Aiken, SC
Wamsted, Ronald D. ... **Austin, TX**
Wan, Bonnie B. ... Washington, DC
Wan, Danny W. ... **San Francisco, CA**
Wan, Helen C. ... **New York, NY**
Wan, Lee ... Tucker, GA
Wan, Pauline T. ... San Francisco, CA
Wan, Phyllis V. ... **Denver, CO**
Wanamaker, Bruce D. ... **Atlanta, GA**
Wanamaker, Caroline P. ... Seattle, WA
Wanamaker, Giles A. ... Syracuse, NY
Wanamaker, Laura H. ... **Macon, GA**
Wanamaker, Wayne M., II ... Orlando, FL
Wanasek, Brian R. ... **Milwaukee, WI**
Wanat, Christopher F. ... **New Haven, CT**
Wanat, Daniel E. ... Memphis, TN
Wancel, Linda R. ... Brooklyn, NY
Wanchak, Wendy W. ... Avon, CT
Wanchoo, Rahul ... **New York, NY**
Wand, Barbara Freedman ... **Boston, MA**
Wand, Carl F., & Associates
Huntington, NY
Wand, Carl F., & Associates
New York, NY
Wand, Mary E. ... **San Francisco, CA**
Wand, Philip E. ... **Crystal Lake, IL**
Wanda, Mark J. ... Deerfield, IL
Wandel, Josephine Walsh ... Omaha, NE
Wandel Law Offices, P.C. ... Omaha, NE
Wandell, David ... Margate, FL
Wander, Daniel M. ... New York, NY
Wander, David H. ... New York, NY
Wander, Elyse G. ... Washington, DC
Wander, Fred B. ... **Albany, NY**
Wander & Golden, LLP ... New York, NY
Wander, Herbert S., (P.C.) ... **Chicago, IL**
Wander, Howard L. ... West Palm Beach, FL
Wander, Jeffrey J. ... Honesdale, PA
Wander, John C. ... **Dallas, TX**
Wander, Lawrence A. ... Metuchen, NJ
Wander, Marc H. ... Pontiac, MI
Wander, Mose ... Baton Rouge, LA

Ward, Dallas S. ....Prince Frederick, MD
Ward, Damon, Beverly, Tittle & Posner, P.A.
Stuart, FL
West Palm Beach, FL
Ward, Daniel A. ....**Cleveland, OH**
Ward, Daniel I. ....**Cherry Hill, NJ**
Bensalem, PA
Ward, Daniel J. ....Collegeville, MN
Ward, Daniel J. ....Camden, NJ
Ward, Daniel J. ....Buffalo, NY
Ward, Daniel T. ....Bethesda, MD
Ward, Daryl ....Dayton, OH
Ward, David A. ....Chicago, IL
Ward, David A. ....**Keene, NH**
Brattleboro, VT
Ward, David A. ....**Hackensack, NJ**
New York, NY
Ward, David A. ....**Toledo, OH**
Ward, David A., Jr. ....**Houston, TX**
Ward, David B. ....Washington, DC
Ward, David B. ....Chester, NJ
Ward, David B. ....**Greenville, SC**
Ward, David B., P.C. ....Chester, NJ
Ward, David D. ....**Raleigh, NC**
Ward, David E., Jr. ....**Tampa, FL**
Ward, David H. ....**Homewood, AL**
Ward, David H. ....Garrison, NY
Ward, David H. ....Harrisburg, PA
Ward, David J. ....**Chattanooga, TN**
Ward, David J. ....Seattle, WA
Ward, David L. ....Fort Myers, FL
Ward, David L. ....**Boston, MA**
Ward, David L., Jr. ....**New Bern, NC**
Raleigh, NC
Ward, David M. ....**Thousand Oaks, CA**
Ward, David M. ....Austin, TX
Ward, David O.
Federal Communications Commission,
Common Carrier Bureau, GV
Ward, David P. ....Albany, GA
Ward, David R. ....Salt Lake City, UT
Ward, David S. ....Rego Park, NY
Ward, David T. ....**La Habra, CA**
Ward, Dawn J. ....**Holland, MI**
Ward, Dean M. ....Beverly Hills, CA
Ward, Deborah ....Tucson, AZ
Ward, Debra Nicholson ....**Tahoe City, CA**
Ward, DeLoris B. Narvasa ....Tigard, OR
Ward, Denise P. ....Rye, NY
Ward, Dennis E. ....Williamsville, NY
Ward, Dennis J. ....**San Jose, CA**
Ward, Dennis P. ....Chicago, IL
Ward, Dennis R. ....Cincinnati, OH
Ward, Derek William ....Lynn, MA
Ward, Derryberry & Thompson
Nashville, TN
Ward, Diane A. ....Los Angeles, CA
Ward, Diane V. ....Miami, FL
Ward, Donald E. ....Bethesda, MD
Ward, Donald J. ....Pittsburgh, PA
Ward, Donald W. ....Belleville, IL
Ward, Donald W. ....**Indianapolis, IN**
Ward, Donna Bostic ....**Houston, TX**
Ward, Dorothy Voss ....**Chicago, IL**
Lincolnwood, IL
Ward, Douglas A. ....**St. Augustine, FL**
Ward, Douglas B. ....Little Rock, AR
Ward, Douglas H. ....**Albany, NY**
Ward, Earl E. ....Hamtramck, MI
Ward, Earl S. ....New York, NY
Ward, Edmond C. ....Kentfield, CA
Ward, Edmund M. ....Cockeysville, MD
Ward, Edward ....Fort Smith, AR
Ward, Edward H. ....Tampa, FL
Ward, Edward P. ....New York, NY
Ward, Edward T., Jr. ....Wheaton, IL
Ward, Eileen K. Kelly ....Stow, OH
Ward, Eileen M. ....White Plains, NY
Ward, Elaine Neal ....Austin, TX
Ward, Elizabeth C. ....**Palo Alto, CA**
Ward, Ellen Brewster ....Washington, DC
Ward, Elsa M. ....**Los Angeles, CA**
Ward, Emmet G. ....Redwood City, CA
Ward, Eric J. ....**Rochester, NY**
Ward, Eric N. ....**New York, NY**
Ward, Erica A. ....**Washington, DC**
Ward, Erik M. ....Layton, UT
Ogden, UT
Ward, Erwin C. ....Jackson, MS
Ward, Ettie ....Jamaica, NY
Ward, Eugene A. ....New York, NY
Ward, Eugene J., III ....South Burlington, VT
Ward, Eugene W. ....Nashville, TN
Ward, Eunice ....**Chicago, IL**
Ward, Eva A. Bilodeau ....New Milford, CT
Ward, Everett S. ....**Chicago, IL**
Ward, F. Cooper ....**Washington, DC**
Ward, F. Elgin ....Salt Lake City, UT
Ward, F. Jefferson, Jr. ....**Sanford, NC**
Ward, Felker W., Jr. ....Atlanta, GA
Ward, Francesca Tosi ....**Columbus, OH**
Ward, Francine D. ....Mill Valley, CA
Ward, Francis J. ....Winchester, KY
Ward, Francis R. ....Audubon, NJ
Ward, Frank A., II ....Syracuse, NY
Ward, Frank P., Jr. ....**Raleigh, NC**
Ward, Franklin M. ....Columbia, MD
Ward, Fred J., (P.A.) ....Dania, FL
Ward, Frederick F., II ....West Hartford, CT
Ward, G. Benjamin ....**New Orleans, LA**
Ward, G. Fletcher, Jr. ....Abingdon, MD
Ward, G. Thomas, Jr. ....**Jasper, AL**
Ward, Galen E. ....**Norman, OK**
Ward, Gary A. ....Lubbock, TX
Ward, Gaunt & Raskin ....Torrance, CA
Ward, Gene R. ....**Corpus Christi, TX**
Ward, Geo. ....Norwood, MA
Ward, Geo. A. ....Spring Hill, FL

Ward, Geoffrey H. ....**New York, NY**
Ward, George C. ....**Toledo, OH**
Ward, George E. ....Detroit, MI
Ward, George W., Jr. ....Fort Lauderdale, FL
Ward, Gráinne ....Newport Beach, CA
Ward, Grant David ....Boston, MA
Ward, Gregory ....Lexington, KY
Ward, Gregory C. ....**Miami, FL**
Ward, Gregory C. ....**Chicago, IL**
Ward, Guy G. ....**Chicago, IL**
Ward, H. Clay, III ....**Lake Charles, LA**
Ward, H. William ....Lake Buena Vista, FL
Ward, Hallett S., III ....Beaufort, NC
Ward, Hamilton, IV ....Arcade, NY
Ward, Harold A., III ....**Orlando, FL**
Winter Park, FL
Ward, Harold R. ....Providence, RI
Ward, Harry N., Jr. ....Fort Worth, TX
Ward, Helene S. ....Williamsburg, VA
Ward, Henry B., III ....**Charlotte, NC**
Ward, Henry V., Jr. ....Raleigh, NC
Ward, Hiram H. ....Winston-Salem, NC
Ward, Horace T. ....Atlanta, GA
Ward, Howard A. ....Royal Oak, MI
Ward, Howard L. ....Chicago, IL
Ward, Howard N. ....Topeka, KS
Ward, H.S., Jr. ....**Waynesville, NC**
Ward, Hugh B. ....Knoxville, TN
Ward, Hugh T. ....**Shreveport, LA**
Ward & Huysentruyt ....San Francisco, CA
Ward, J. Alex ....**Washington, DC**
Ward, J. Andrew ....**New York, NY**
Ward, J. Katharine ....Water Valley, MS
Ward, J. Marc ....**Des Moines, IA**
Ward, J. Mark ....Salt Lake City, UT
Ward, J. Randolph ....Raleigh, NC
Ward, J. Ronald, Jr. ....**New Orleans, LA**
Ward, J. Tracy ....**Dalton, GA**
Ward, J. Walter, Jr. ....**New Orleans, LA**
Ward, Jack D. ....**Rockford, IL**
Ward, Jack W. ....Cumming, GA
Ward, James ....Wichita, KS
Ward, James ....San Antonio, TX
Ward, James A. ....Waukesha, WI
Ward, James A., III ....Mobile, AL
Ward, James D. ....Riverside, CA
Ward, James E., IV ....Department of Justice,
Civil Division, GV
Ward, James F. ....Lake Forest, IL
Ward, James G. ....**Boston, MA**
Ward, James H., Jr. ....Saluda, VA
Ward, James J. ....Country Club Hills, IL
Ward, James J., Jr. ....Fort Myers, FL
Ward, James J., Jr. ....**Houston, TX**
Ward, James K. ....**Sacramento, CA**
Ward, James L., Jr. ....**Columbia, SC**
Ward, James M. ....**Eau Claire, WI**
Ward, James O. ....Little Rock, AR
Ward, James Patrick ....Des Moines, IA
Ward, James R. ....Topeka, KS
Ward, James R. ....Ionia, MI
Ward, James R. ....**Kansas City, MO**
Ward, James S. ....**Birmingham, AL**
Ward, James T. ....**Galax, VA**
Hillsville, VA
Ward, Jamye Boone ....Las Cruces, NM
Ward, Jane M. ....**Philadelphia, PA**
Ward, Janet ....San Bernardino, CA
Ward, Janet E. ....Minneapolis, MN
Ward, Janet Huck ....**Wichita, KS**
Ward, Janice Diane ....Norcross, GA
Ward, Jason G. ....**Elkhart, IN**
Ward, Jay T. ....Treasury Department,
Office of the Comptroller of the Currency,
GV
Ward, Jeffery Kurt ....Idaho Falls, ID
Ward, Jeffery R. ....St. Petersburg, FL
Ward, Jeffrey A. ....Minneapolis, MN
Ward, Jeffrey A. ....**Waynesboro, VA**
Ward, Jeffrey B. ....Danvers, MA
Ward, Jeffrey J. ....**Washington, DC**
Ward, Jeffrey J. ....Belle Glade, FL
Ward, Jeffrey J. ....**Chicago, IL**
Ward, Jeffrey L. ....Rockville, MD
Ward, Jeffrey M. ....**Greeneville, TN**
Ward, Jeffrey P. ....**Pittsburgh, PA**
Ward, Jeffrey R. ....Sherman Oaks, CA
Ward, Jeffrey R. ....**Walnut Creek, CA**
Ward, Jeffrey R. ....**Dallas, TX**
Ward, Jeffrey S. ....**Madison, WI**
Ward, Jennifer ....**Salt Lake City, UT**
Ward, Jerri Lynn ....**Austin, TX**
Ward, Jerry J. ....Lisbon, OH
Ward, Jerry M. ....**Boise, ID**
Ward, Jerry M. ....Great Bend, KS
Ward, Jill Lallier ....Richmond, VA
Ward, Joe H., Jr. ....Washington, DC
Ward, Joel M. ....Beverly Hills, CA
Ward, John ....**Boston, MA**
Ward, John ....Racine, WI
Ward, John A. ....Chicago, IL
Ward, John A. ....Ithaca, NY
Ward, John A., III ....Sonora, TX
Ward, John A. J. ....**New Bern, NC**
Ward, John Andrew ....Chicago, IL
Ward, John B., Jr. ....**Baltimore, MD**
Ward, John C. ....Little Rock, AR
Ward, John C. ....**Boise, ID**
Ward, John D. ....Vernon, CT
Ward, John D. ....**Washington, DC**
Ward, John F. ....Washington, DC
Gaithersburg, MD
Greenbelt, MD
Arlington, VA
Ward, John F. ....Chicago, IL
Ward, John F. ....**Summit, NJ**
New York, NY
Ward, John F. ....**Philadelphia, PA**

Ward, John F., Jr. ....Chicago, IL
Ward, John F., Jr., (P.C.) ....**Chicago, IL**
Ward, John G., Jr. ....**Purchase, NY**
Ward, John H. ....**Orlando, FL**
Ward, John H. ....Sedro Woolley, WA
Ward, John Hester ....**Chicago, IL**
Ward, John N. ....Greensburg, PA
Ward, John P. ....**Sunnyvale, CA**
Ward, John P. "Jack" ....**Houston, TX**
Ward, John R. ....New Haven, CT
Ward, John R. ....Des Moines, IA
Ward, John S. ....**Los Angeles, CA**
Ward, John S. ....New York, NY
Ward, John T. ....Tahoe City, CA
Ward, John T. ....**Des Moines, IA**
Ward, John T. ....**Baltimore, MD**
Ward, John T., Jr. ....Mayville, NY
Ward, John W. ....Wilmington, DE
Ward, John Wesley, Jr. ....Hampton, VA
Ward & Johnson, L.L.P. ....Austin, TX
Ward, Jon A. ....**Riverhead, NY**
Ward, Jonathan D. ....Cincinnati, OH
Ward, Joseph C., Jr. ....Lumberton, NC
Ward, Joseph Jason ....West Palm Beach, FL
Ward, Joseph L. ....Biloxi, MS
Ward, Joseph L. ....Las Vegas, NV
Ward, Joseph M. ....**Atlanta, GA**
Ward, Joseph R., Jr. ....**New Orleans, LA**
Ward, Joshua J. ....Chatham, NJ
Ward, Joyce M. ....Hempstead, NY
Ward, Joyce M. ....Morristown, TN
Ward, Julie A. ....**Peoria, IL**
Ward, Julie M. ....**Los Angeles, CA**
Ward, Julie Pateman ....**New York, NY**
Ward, Kaps, Bainbridge, Maurer & Melvin
Columbus, OH
Ward, Karen J. ....Arlington, VA
Ward, Karen K. ....**Orlando, FL**
Ward, Katherine J. ....Las Vegas, NV
Ward, Katherine T.E. ....**New York, NY**
Ward, Kathleen R. ....Chicago, IL
Ward, Kathryn Brown ....**Houston, TX**
Ward, Kathryn G. ....Pleasantville, NY
Ward, Kathryn L.
Federal Deposit Insurance Corporation,
Corporate Affairs Section, GV
Ward, Kathryn L. ....Houston, TX
Ward, Keenan & Barrett, P.C. ....Phoenix, AZ
Ward, Keith A. ....**Tulsa, OK**
Ward, Keith A. ....**Austin, TX**
Ward, Kelly A. ....**Los Angeles, CA**
Ward, Kennedy W. ....New Bern, NC
Ward, Kennedy W., P.A. ....New Bern, NC
Ward, Kenneth C. ....**Walnut Creek, CA**
Ward, Kenneth D.
Department of State, GV
Ward, Kenneth T. ....**Houston, TX**
Ward, Kenneth V. ....Fernley, NV
Ward, Kenneth W. ....Geneva, FL
Ward, Kenneth W. ....**Knoxville, TN**
Ward, Kerry J. ....Brooklyn, NY
Ward, Kershaw & Minton, A Professional Association ....**Baltimore, MD**
Ward, Kevin C., Law Offices of
Southgate, KY
Ward, Kevin J. ....Galena, IL
Ward, Kevin L. ....**Atlanta, GA**
Ward, Kevin L. ....**Tulsa, OK**
Ward, Kevin M. ....**Denver, CO**
Ward & Klein, Chartered ....Washington, DC
Gaithersburg, MD
Greenbelt, MD
Arlington, VA
Ward, Kroll & Jampol, A Law Corporation
Beverly Hills, CA
Ward & Kutzuba ....Arcade, NY
Ward, L. Dale ....**Wichita, KS**
Ward, L. Graham ....Bloomfield Hills, MI
Saginaw, MI
Ward, L. Preston, Jr. ....Williamson, WV
Ward, L. Taylor, III ....**Deerfield Beach, FL**
Ward, Lafe P. ....Williamson, WV
Ward, Laraine Morse ....Seattle, WA
Ward, Larry A. ....Springdale, AR
Ward, Larry D. ....Iowa City, IA
Ward, Larry G. ....Department of Justice,
Civil Rights Division, GV
Ward, Lateesa ....Minneapolis, MN
Ward, Laura A. ....**Santa Fe, NM**
Ward, Laurence F. ....Boston, MA
Ward, Laurence F. ....Reading, PA
Ward Law Firm, The, P.A. ....**Gaffney, SC**
Spartanburg, SC
Union, SC
York, SC
Ward Law Group, The, P.A.
Clearwater, FL
Tampa, FL
Ward Law Office ....Great Bend, KS
Ward, Lawrence D., Jr. ....Houma, LA
Ward, Lawrence D., Jr., A P.L.C.
Houma, LA
Ward, Lawrence M. ....Baltimore, MD
Ward, Lawrence S. ....Oakland, CA
Ward, Lawson L. ....Hartford, CT
Ward, Lena A. ....Cheyenne, WY
Ward, Leo R. ....Cleveland, OH
Ward, Leo S. ....**Helena, MT**
Ward, Liliana E. ....**Washington, DC**
Vienna, VA
Ward, Linda C. ....Greenwood, AR
Ward, Linda K. ....Raleigh, NC
Ward, Lisa ....Washington, DC
Ward, Lisa C. ....**Los Angeles, CA**
Ward, Lisa C. ....Lansing, MI
Ward, Lisa M. ....**Hutchinson, KS**
Ward, Lloyd, & Associates, P.C. ....Dallas, TX
Ward, Lloyd E. ....Dallas, TX

Ward, Lori Anne ....**Chicago, IL**
Ward, Lori Ellen ....**Destin, FL**
Ward, Lori M. ....Santa Ana, CA
Ward, Lyle G. ....**Minneapolis, MN**
Ward, Lyle M. ....Salt Lake City, UT
Ward, Lynn D. ....**Dallas, TX**
Ward, Lynn M. ....Bowling Green, OH
Ward & Maglaras, Ltd. ....Las Vegas, NV
Ward, Marc R. ....San Luis Obispo, CA
Ward, Marcia Ann ....Milford, OH
Ward, Marcus D. ....Memphis, TN
Ward, Maretta D. ....San Francisco, CA
Ward, Margaret A. ....**Washington, DC**
Ward, Margaret Anne ....San Angelo, TX
Ward, Margaret Fonshell ....**Towson, MD**
Ward, Margaret M. ....St. Paul, MN
Ward, Marie Catherine
Albuquerque, NM
Ward, Marilyn A. ....San Mateo, CA
Ward, Marilyn Kay ....Santa Monica, CA
Ward, Mark ....Chanute, KS
Ward, Mark A. ....Biloxi, MS
Ward, Mark B. ....Burlington, VT
Ward, Mark D. ....Edwardsville, IL
Ward, Mark S.
Agency for International Development,
Other Offices of A.I.D., GV
Ward, Marquis L. ....Montevideo, MN
Ward, Marsha A. ....Atlanta, GA
Ward, Martin J. ....Boston, MA
Ward, Martin J. ....Marshall, MO
Ward, Mary C. ....Ventura, CA
Ward, Mary E. ....**Winston-Salem, NC**
Ward, Mary Elizabeth ....Department of Justice,
Environment and Natural Resources
Division, GV
Ward, Mary Livingston ....Albany, GA
Ward, Matthew W. ....**Washington, DC**
Ward, Maureen A. ....Costa Mesa, CA
Ward, Maureen O'Keefe ....**Washington, DC**
Ward, Megan A. ....Newton, NJ
Ward, Megan E. ....**Wilmington, DE**
Ward, Melinda Ramsey ....**Stephenville, TX**
Ward, Melvyn ....Matawan, NJ
Ward & Metti ....Chicago, IL
Ward, Michael A. ....**Alexandria, VA**
Fairfax, VA
Ward, Michael A. ....Charlottesville, VA
Ward, Michael D. ....Benton, KY
Ward, Michael D. ....**Grand Rapids, MI**
Ward, Michael D. ....Philadelphia, PA
Ward, Michael E. ....**Washington, DC**
Ward, Michael E. ....El Dorado, KS
Ward, Michael F. ....New Albany, IN
Ward, Michael F. ....Boston, MA
Ward, Michael F. ....Kalamazoo, MI
Ward, Michael H. ....Ann Arbor, MI
Ward, Michael H. ....Gulfport, MS
Ward, Michael J. ....**Santa Ana, CA**
Ward, Michael J., IV ....Voorhees, NJ
Ward, Michael K. ....**Sacramento, CA**
Ward, Michael L. ....**New York, NY**
Ward, Michael M. ....Minot, ND
Ward, Michael P. ....Newark, DE
Ward, Michael R. ....**San Francisco, CA**
Ward, Michael R. ....Salt Lake City, UT
Ward, Michael R. ....**Richmond, VA**
Ward, Michael S. ....**Oakland, CA**
Ward, Michael T. ....**Baltimore, MD**
Ward, Michael V. ....San Clemente, CA
Ward, Michael V. ....Canton, MS
Ward, Michael W. ....Buffalo Grove, IL
Ward, Michael W. ....Minneapolis, MN
Ward, Michael W. ....Athens, OH
Ward, Michelle A. ....**Burlingame, CA**
Ward, Michelle L. ....**Pascagoula, MS**
Ward, Milburn R., Jr. ....El Monte, CA
Ward, Miles A. ....Oregon City, OR
Ward, Molly Joseph ....Newport News, VA
Ward, Murray, Pace & Johnson, P.C.
Dixon, IL
Milledgeville, IL
Morrison, IL
Sterling, IL
Ward, N. Curtis ....**King Of Prussia, PA**
Ward, Nancy Ann ....Dixon, IL
Ward, Nathaniel P., IV ....San Diego, CA
Ward Nelson, LLC ....**New Orleans, LA**
Ward, Nicholas D. ....**Washington, DC**
Ward, Nolan F. ....Austin, TX
Ward & Oehler, Ltd. ....Rochester, MN
Ward, Oliver H., Jr. ....Fort Lauderdale, FL
Ward, Oliver O. ....Andover, MA
Ward & Olivo ....**Summit, NJ**
New York, NY
Ward, P. Michael ....Cleveland, OH
Ward, Patricia Hendrix ....Mesa, AZ
Ward, Patrick E. ....Dixon, IL
Ward, Patrick J. ....**Bismarck, ND**
Ward, Patrick W. ....Lancaster, PA
Ward, Paul Anthony, Jr. ....Providence, RI
Ward, Paul B. ....**Vienna, VA**
Ward, Paul C. ....**Irvine, CA**
Ward, Paul F. ....Columbus, OH
Ward, Paul J. ....Tempe, AZ
Ward, Paul J. ....Little Rock, AR
Ward, Paul J. ....**Latrobe, PA**
Ward, Peter ....Gainesville, FL
Ward, Peter C. ....**San Diego, CA**
Ward, Peter C. ....**Nashville, TN**
Ward, Peter D. ....Ann Arbor, MI
Ward, Peter Hamilton ....Gainesville, FL
Ward, Peter Hay ....Gainesville, FL
Ward, Peter M. ....**New York, NY**
Ward, Peter O., Jr. ....**Lynchburg, VA**
Ward, Philip E. ....**Fort Lauderdale, FL**
Ward, Philip H., III
West Palm Beach, FL

Ware, Robert L. ....Fitchburg, MA
Ware, Robt. F., Jr. ....Millry, AL
Ware, Ronald B. ....Pawtucket, RI
Ware, Russell M. ....Milwaukee, WI
Ware, Samuel G. ....San Francisco, CA
Ware, Sandra J. ....Haddonfield, NJ
Ware, Sandra J. ....Fort Worth, TX
Ware, Sheila M. ....Waterbury, VT
Ware, Snow, Fogel & Jackson, L.L.P.
Houston, TX
Ware, Stephen J. ....Birmingham, AL
Ware Streitz and Thompson ....Pitman, NJ
Ware, Sue A. ....Kansas City, MO
Ware, Susan Stoll ....San Jose, CA
Ware, T. Kirkland, III ....Acton, MA
Ware, Thaddeus V.
Department of Transportation, Board of Contract Appeals, GV
Ware, Thomas H. ....Nashville, TN
Ware, Thomas K. ....South Burlington, VT
Ware, Thomas M., II ....Beverly Hills, CA
Ware, Travis S. ....Lubbock, TX
Ware, Virginia L. ....Englewood, CO
Ware & Ware ....Millry, AL
Ware & Ware ....Acton, MA
Fitchburg, MA
Ware, Wellford H. ....Pitman, NJ
Ware, William B. ....Birmingham, AL
Ware, William D. ....Mill Valley, CA
Ware, William D. ....Westwood, NJ
Wareh, Rashad ....Washington, DC
Wareham, James D. ....Washington, DC
Wareham, Kathleen A. ....Seattle, WA
Wareheim, Robert B. ....Topeka, KS
Wareing, Richard F. ....Hartford, CT
Wareing, Tracy Lorenz ....Phoenix, AZ
Waren & Cundiff, P.C. ....Poteau, OK
Waren, Drucilla E. ....Poteau, OK
Warenda, John J. ....Morrisville, PA
Warenski, Paul D. ....San Francisco, CA
Wares, William A. ....Farmington Hills, MI
Warf, Shannon L. ....Winston-Salem, NC
Warfel, Debra Hartman ....Los Angeles, CA
Warfel, Goldberg, Dariotis, Waldoch & Olive, P.A. ....Tallahassee, FL
Warfel, Mark J. ....Arcadia, CA
Warfel, Russell E. ....Annapolis, MD
Riverdale, MD
Warfel, Timothy J. ....Tallahassee, FL
Warffuel, Heidi Lynn ....Costa Mesa, CA
Warf-Gress, Elizabeth M. ....Sacramento, CA
Warfield, Alan Michael ....Birmingham, AL
Warfield, Charles H. ....Nashville, TN
Warfield, David A. ....St. Louis, MO
Warfield, Dawn E. ....Charleston, WV
Warfield, J. Alan ....Santa Monica, CA
Warfield, James J. ....Scarsdale, NY
Warfield, Janet Smith ....Atlantic City, NJ
Warfield, Mark R. ....New Brunswick, NJ
Warfield Meredith & Darrah, P.C.
Annapolis, MD
Baltimore, MD
Severna Park, MD
Towson, MD
Warfield, Richard D. ....Dallas, TX
Warfield, Richard P. ....Pensacola, FL
Warfield, Richard P., P.A. ....Pensacola, FL
Warfield, Robert W. ....Severna Park, MD
Warfman, Maris ....New Hyde Park, NY
Warford, Robert K. ....Riverside, CA
Warford, Tommy G. ....Eastland, TX
Warg, David L. ....St. Paul, MN
Warg, Elizabeth Ann ....Canton, OH
Warga, Jon E. ....Columbus, OH
Warganz, Joseph F., Jr. ....New York, NY
Warger, Vincent J., Jr. ....Miami, FL
Wargo, Elmer ....Dayton, OH
Wargo, John J. ....Racine, WI
Wargo, John J., Jr. ....Berea, OH
Wargo, Joseph D. ....Atlanta, GA
Wargo, Kenneth W. ....Erie, PA
Wargo, Louis P., III ....Port Clinton, OH
Wargo, Michael E. ....Boca Raton, FL
Wargo, Robert P. ....Los Angeles, CA
Wargo, Ronald P., II ....Santa Rosa, CA
Wargo and Wargo Co., L.P.A. ....Berea, OH
Wargo, William A. ....Los Angeles, CA
Wargowsky, Donald S. ....Aiken, SC
Wargula, David A. ....Chicago, IL
Wargula, Michael A. ....Buffalo, NY
Warhaftig, Jeri L. ....Newark, NJ
Warhaftig, Solomon L. ....New York, NY
Warhall, Lawrence F. ....Derry, NH
Warhank, Rodney D. ....Davenport, IA
Warheit, Melissa A. ....Columbus, OH
Warheit, Neil A. ....Los Angeles, CA
Warhit, Barry E. ....New Rochelle, NY
Warhola, Andrew J. ....Lorain, OH
Warhola, Andrew J., Jr. ....Cambridge, OH
Warhola, Robert Thomas, II ....Houston, TX
Warhola, Stephen ....Palo Alto, CA
Warhurst, William R. ....San Francisco, CA
Warin, Edward G. ....Omaha, NE
Warin, Elizabeth Nicole ....New York, NY
Warin, F. Joseph ....Washington, DC
Warin, Roger E. ....Washington, DC
Warin, William M. ....Mesa, AZ
Waring, Bradish J. ....Charleston, SC
Waring, Cindy L. ....Walla Walla, WA
Waring Cox, PLC ....Memphis, TN
Waring, James T. ....San Diego, CA
Waring, Kathy P. ....San Diego, CA
Waring, Laura Campbell ....Columbia, SC
Waring, Richard E. ....Boston, MA
Waring, Roane, Jr. ....Memphis, TN
Waring, Robert L. ....San Francisco, CA
Waring, Star L. ....Denver, CO
Waring, Thomas ....Charleston, SC

Waring, Thomas Roane, III .....Memphis, TN
Waring, William W., Jr. ....New Orleans, LA
Waris, Michael, Jr. ....Bethesda, MD
Waris, Richard M. ....Chicago, IL
Wark, Allen W. ....Franklin Lakes, NJ
Wark, Jerry W. ....Phoenix, AZ
Wark, Mary Ann Barrows ....St. Paul, MN
Wark, Patricia M. ....West Columbia, SC
Wark, Patricia M., P.C. ....West Columbia, SC
Wark, R. Bruce ....Dallas, TX
Warkall, Michael A.
New Philadelphia, OH
Warke, Elizabeth A. ....Irvine, CA
Warkentine, Brent ....Broomfield, CO
Warkentine, Edith R. ....Temecula, CA
Warkentine, Lee D. ....Broomfield, CO
Warkentine, Lee, P.C. ....Broomfield, CO
Warkoczeski, Larry ....Charleston, IL
Warkow, Paul J. ....Bellmore, NY
Warlaumont, James L.
Salt Lake City, UT
Warlen, Yvonne M. ....Kansas City, MO
Warley, John C., Jr. ....Richmond, VA
Warlich, Eugene M. ....Minneapolis, MN
Warlick, Alex, Jr. ....Jacksonville, NC
Warlick, Dan ....Nashville, TN
Warlick, Diane Trace ....Dallas, TX
Christiansted, St. Croix, VI
Warlick, Douglas B. ....Roselle, IL
Warlick, Douglas B., & Associates, P.A.
Roselle, IL
Warlick, George W. ....Atlanta, GA
Warlick, Hal J. ....Easley, SC
Warlick, J. Thomas, IV ....Charlotte, NC
Warlick, John D., Jr. ....Jacksonville, NC
Warlick, Lana S. ....Jacksonville, NC
Warlick Law Office ....Easley, SC
Warlick Milsted Dotson & Carter
Jacksonville, NC
Warlick & Quigley, P.C.
Christiansted, St. Croix, VI
Warlick, Robert A. ....Jacksonville, NC
Warlick, Thomas H. ....Orlando, FL
Warlick, Thomas H., P.A. ....Orlando, FL
Warlick, Thomas W. ....Newton, NC
Warlick, Tritt & Stebbins, L.L.P.
Appling, GA
Augusta, GA
Martinez, GA
Warlick, William Byrd ....Augusta, GA
Warlow, Michael C. ....Baltimore, MD
Warlow, Michael C. ....Towson, MD
Warm, Elliot L. ....Chatham, NJ
Warm, Steven ....Boca Raton, FL
Warm, Steven Gary ....Baltimore, MD
Warmack, A. Jackson, Jr. ....Rich Square, NC
Warman, Cheryl L. ....Morgantown, WV
Warman, Daniel R. ....Norfolk, VA
Warman, Guy L. ....Pittsburgh, PA
Warman, Jessie B.
Department of Commerce, Patent and Trademark Office, GV
Warman, Lynnette R. ....Dallas, TX
Warman, Mark A. ....Tulsa, OK
Warman, Michele S. ....New York, NY
Warman, Peter C. ....Chicago, IL
Warman, Philip T. ....Pittsburgh, PA
Warman, Philip T. ....Houston, TX
Warman, Philip V. ....North Beach, MD
Warman, Ray ....Stamford, CT
Warmann, Richd. C. ....St. Louis, MO
Warmath, Allen L. ....Paragould, AR
Warmath and Boyte ....Humboldt, TN
Warmbold, David A. ....St. Louis, MO
Warmbrandt, Kevin J. ....Miami, FL
Warmbrod, Monica L. ....Birmingham, AL
Warmbrodt, James C. ....Pittsburgh, PA
Warme, James E. ....Kelso, WA
Warmeling, Jonathan R. ....Eastlake, OH
Warmer, Richard C. ....San Francisco, CA
Warmerdam, Peter A. ....Bakersfield, CA
Warmflash, David ....New York, NY
Warmington, Courtney K.
Oklahoma City, OK
Warmington, Robert A. ....Paterson, NJ
Warmke, Carter ....Stockton, CA
Warmke & Warmke ....Stockton, CA
Warmoth, William J. ....Charleston, IL
Warmsley, Beulow W. ....Los Angeles, CA
Warmund, Stephanie ....Kansas City, MO
Warmuth, Paula Jean ....Huntington, NY
Warmuth, Scott, Law Offices of
Los Angeles, CA
Warmuth, Scott, Law Offices of
Monterey Park, CA
Westminster, CA
Warmuth, Scott, Law Offices of
Westminster, CA
Warn, Philip R. ....Troy, MI
Warn, Tamara L. ....Chicago, IL
Warnagieris, Gregory R. ....Orange, CA
Warnberg, Alvin H. ....Northridge, CA
Warncke, Daniel R. ....Cincinnati, OH
Warncke, Jeffrey S. ....Atlanta, GA
Warncke, Marc F. ....Defiance, OH
Hicksville, OH
Warncke, Richard E. ....San Antonio, TX
Warne, Douglas C. ....Houston, TX
Warne, Frederick P. ....North Branford, CT
Warne, Judy L. ....Houston, TX
Warne, Richard B. ....Lexington, KY
Warne, William R. ....Sacramento, CA
Warneck, Stephen C. ....Boston, MA
Warnecke, A. Michael ....Dallas, TX
Warnecke, Andrew C. ....Chicago, IL
Warnecke, Diana R. ....Dallas, TX
Warnecke, Kathryn ....Lexington, KY
Warnecke, Michael D. ....Chicago, IL

Warnecke, Michael O. ....Chicago, IL
Warneka, Brenda K. ....Phoenix, AZ
Warnement, Pamela Pearson ....Charlotte, NC
Warnement, Robert W. ....Washington, DC
Warnement, Thalia V. ....Washington, DC
Warnement, Victor A. ....Charlotte, NC
Warnemunde, David J. ....Madison, NE
Norfolk, NE
Warner, Alice ....San Francisco, CA
Warner, Alice ....Newport, OR
Warner, Amberly A. ....Charleston, WV
Warner, Amy B. ....Wellesley, MA
Warner Angle Roper & Hallam PLC
Phoenix, AZ
Warner, Anita M. ....New Orleans, LA
Warner, Anne H. ....McLean, VA
Warner, Anne T. ....Waltham, MA
Warner, B. Kent ....Santa Ana, CA
Warner, Benjamin T. ....Carlisle, PA
Warner & Berlanstein ....Memphis, TN
Warner, Bethany C. ....Lansing, MI
Warner, Boyd L. ....Clarksburg, WV
Warner, Bradley C. ....St. Paul, MN
Warner, Brainard H., III ....Washington, DC
Warner, Bruce, (P.C.) ....Los Angeles, CA
Warner, Burton E. ....Niagara Falls, NY
Warner, C. Wilbur, Jr. ....Atlanta, GA
Warner, Carlos ....Cleveland, OH
Warner, Carol I. ....Seattle, WA
Warner, Charles C. ....Birmingham, MI
Warner, Charles C. ....Columbus, OH
Warner, Charles C., P.C. ....Birmingham, MI
Warner, Charles E. ....Savannah, GA
Warner, Charles F. ....Seattle, WA
Warner, Charles G., Law Offices of
Monterey, CA
Warner, Charles L., II ....Atlanta, GA
Warner, Christopher J. ....San Bernardino, CA
Warner, Christopher J.
San Francisco, CA
Warner, Clay ....Herndon, VA
Warner, Constance M. ....St. Louis, MO
Warner, C. R., Jr. ....Fort Smith, AR
Warner, Craig D. ....Burlington, IA
Warner, Dale ....Tulsa, OK
Warner, Dale, Inc. ....Tulsa, OK
Warner, Daniel E. ....Eagan, MN
Warner, Daniel M. ....Bellingham, WA
Warner, Darrell E. ....Baytown, TX
Warner, Darren J. ....Tucson, AZ
Warner, David D. ....Detroit, MI
Warner, David P. ....Lodi, CA
Warner, David P. ....Department of Justice, Criminal Division, GV
Warner, David Patrick ....New York, NY
Warner, David R. ....Rockville, MD
Warner, David R., Jr. ....Ada, OH
Warner, David S. ....San Francisco, CA
Warner, David W. ....Indianapolis, IN
Warner, Deborah Gallagher ....Orlando, FL
Warner, Deborah P. ....Cleveland, OH
Warner, Denise Marie ....Atlanta, GA
Warner, Donald E., Jr. ....Los Angeles, CA
Warner, Douglas B. ....Peachtree City, GA
Warner, Douglas B., P.C.
Peachtree City, GA
Warner, Douglas L. ....Scottsbluff, NE
Warner, E. Parry ....Philadelphia, PA
Warner, E. Waide, Jr. ....New York, NY
Warner, Eben D., III ....Odessa, TX
Warner, Edward W. ....St. Louis, MO
Warner, Edwin E. ....Muncie, IN
Warner, Edwin M. ....Geneva, OH
Warner, Edwina Daum ....Benton, IL
Warner, Elizabeth F. ....Bala Cynwyd, PA
Philadelphia, PA
Warner, Elizabeth Henry ....Charleston, SC
Warner, Eric ....Bronx, NY
Warner, Farley W. ....Falls Church, VA
Warner & Finley ....Albuquerque, NM
Warner & Finney ....Pampa, TX
Warner, Fox, Wackeen, Dungey Seeley, Sweet & Wright, L.L.P.
Port St. Lucie, FL
Stuart, FL
Warner, Frank J., Jr. ....Albany, NY
Warner, Frank S. ....Ogden, UT
Warner, Frank W. ....Beeville, TX
Warner, Franklin H. ....Conroe, TX
Warner, Frederick P. ....Cherry Hill, NJ
Harrisburg, PA
King Of Prussia, PA
Warner, G. Harris, Jr. ....Roanoke, VA
Warner, G. Leroy, Jr. ....Wichita, KS
Warner, George D., Jr. ....Lauderdale, MS
Warner, Gerald D. ....Mount Clemens, MI
Warner, Glenda R. ....Chelsea, MI
Warner, Glenn ....Los Angeles, CA
Warner, Gregg L. ....Harrisburg, PA
Warner, Gregory H. ....Great Falls, MT
Warner, Gregory H., P.C. ....Great Falls, MT
Warner, Gregory S. ....Malvern, PA
Warner, Harold L., Jr. ....New York, NY
Warner, Harry P. ....Los Angeles, CA
Warner, Hart & Tomal, P.C.
Eaton Rapids, MI
Warner, Howard S. ....Memphis, TN
Warner, Howard S., II ....San Marcos, TX
Warner, J. Steven ....Memphis, TN
Warner, Jack C. ....Phoenix, AZ
Warner, Jacqueline J. ....White Plains, NY
Warner, James C. ....Washington, DC
Warner, James C. ....Memphis, TN
Warner, James H. ....Fairfax, VA
Warner, James J. ....San Diego, CA
Warner, James M. ....Louisville, KY
Warner, James M. ....St. Louis, MO
Warner, James R. ....Columbus, GA

Warner, James R., Jr. ....Norfolk, VA
Warner, Jeannette S. ....New York, NY
Warner, Jerome F. ....Buffalo, NY
Warner, Jessica Layne ....Canyon, TX
Warner, Jill ....Atlanta, GA
Warner, Jill Hartzler ....Rockville, MD
Warner, John ....Havre, MT
Warner, John D., Jr. ....St. Louis, MO
Warner, John F. ....Kent, WA
Warner, John G. ....Corte Madera, CA
Warner, John J., Jr. ....Schenectady, NY
Warner, John L. ....Cleveland, OH
Warner, John L., III ....Union City, TN
Warner, John L., Jr. ....Union City, TN
Warner, John P. ....Washington, DC
Warner, John R. ....Norristown, PA
Warner, John W., (P.C.) ....Pampa, TX
Warner, Jonathan H. (Jason) ....Miami, FL
Warner, Jonathon D. ....New York, NY
Warner & Joselson ....New York, NY
Warner, Joseph E., III ....Greensboro, NC
Warner, Joseph H. ....Livingston, NJ
Warner, Joseph, III ....Albuquerque, NM
Warner, Joseph P. ....Boston, MA
Warner, Josephine P. ....Atlanta, GA
Warner, Julian R. ....Los Angeles, CA
Warner, Karen C. ....Liberty, MO
Warner, Kate ....San Rafael, CA
Warner, Katherine M. ....Dallas, TX
Warner, Kathleen D. ....New York, NY
Warner, Kenneth E. ....New York, NY
Warner, Kenneth M. ....Olathe, KS
Warner, Kenneth R. ......Westlake Village, CA
Warner, Kenneth Wesley
Grand Junction, CO
Warner, Kirk G. ....Raleigh, NC
Warner, Kristi K. ....Minneapolis, MN
Warner, Larry ....Brownsville, TX
Warner, Larry M. ....Crossville, TN
Warner Law Office, P.A. ....Eagan, MN
Warner, Lawrence A. ....Louisville, KY
Warner, Linda R. ....Pomeroy, OH
Warner, Lisa Ann ....Madison, WV
Warner, Lori ....Houston, TX
Warner, M. Richard ....Diboll, TX
Warner, Marc ....Tampa, FL
Warner, Marc E. ....Seattle, WA
Warner, Margaret H. ....Washington, DC
Warner, Margaret M. ....Riverside, CA
Warner, Marilyn Sue ....Des Moines, IA
Warner, Mark J. ....Boston, MA
Warner, Martha C. ....West Palm Beach, FL
Warner, Martha Warren ....Beeville, TX
Warner, Mary Elizabeth ....Morristown, NJ
Warner, Mary R. ....Alexandria, VA
Warner, Matthew H. P. ....Little Rock, AR
Warner, Mayoue & Bates, P.C.
Atlanta, GA
Marietta, GA
Warner, Michael A. ....Chicago, IL
Warner, Michael A. ....Pampa, TX
Warner, Michael A., Jr. ....Chicago, IL
Warner, Michael D. ....Fort Worth, TX
Warner, Michael J. ....Rock Island, IL
Warner, Michelle M. ....Chicago, IL
Warner, Miles ....West Chester, PA
Warner, Mimi Gerdes ....Seattle, WA
Warner, Molly Abel ....Monterey, CA
Warner, Myra ....Hoboken, NJ
Warner, Nanette M. ....Tucson, AZ
Warner Norcross & Judd LLP
Grand Rapids, MI
Holland, MI
Muskegon, MI
Southfield, MI
Warner, Olive Magee ....Glendale, CA
Warner, Pamela R. ....San Mateo, CA
Warner, Patricia D. ....Montgomery, AL
Warner, Patrick G. ....Sandusky, OH
Warner, Paul J. ....Eureka, CA
Warner, Paul L. ....San Francisco, CA
Warner, Paul T. ....Beaumont, TX
Houston, TX
Warner, Peter C. ....Scottsdale, AZ
Warner, Philip C. ....Minneapolis, MN
Warner, Philip G. ....Houston, TX
Warner, R. Bart ....Boston, MA
Warner, R. Craig ....Dallas, TX
Warner, R. Scott ....Columbus, OH
Warner, Ralph W. ....Hudson, MA
Warner, Randall H. ....Phoenix, AZ
Warner, Richard E. ....Marathon, FL
Warner, Richard E., P.A. ....Marathon, FL
Warner, Richard W. ....Troy, MI
Warner, Rita Wasserstein ....New York, NY
Warner, Robert B. ....Charleston, WV
Warner, Robert D. ....Cleveland, OH
Warner, Robert E. ....Honolulu, HI
Warner, Robert E., Attorney at Law, A Law Corporation ....Honolulu, HI
Warner, Robert H. ....Eaton Rapids, MI
Warner, Robert J. ....Brooklyn, NY
Warner, Robert J., Jr. ....Nashville, TN
Warner, Robert M. ....Addison, TX
Warner, Robert O. ....Chandler, AZ
Warner, Robert W. ....Bloomfield Hills, MI
Warner, Roger ....Columbus, OH
Warner, Ronald ....Los Angeles, CA
Warner, Roy M. ....Lake Success, NY
Warner, Russell S. ....Erie, PA
Warner, S. Rogers, Jr. ....Charlotte, NC
Warner, Samuel W. ....Long Beach, CA
Warner, Scot D. ....Orlando, FL
Warner, Scott ....Salisbury, CT
Warner, Scott G. ....Seattle, WA
Warner, Scott K. ....Ontario, OR
Warner, Scott L. ....Chicago, IL
Warner, Seth M. ....Washington, DC

Warner, Sharon L. ....Austin, TX
Warner, Sidney R. ....Charlotte, NC
Warner, Smith & Harris, PLC
Clarksville, AR
Fort Smith, AR
Warner & Stackpole LLP ....Boston, MA
Warner, Stephen ....Wheeling, WV
Warner, Stephen M. ....Minneapolis, MN
Warner, Stephen M. ....New York, NY
Warner, Steven E. ....Washington, DC
Warner, Steven K. ....Summit, NJ
Warner, Susan ....Philadelphia, PA
Warner, Susan L. ....Enfield, CT
Warner, Susan Shaheen ....Cleveland, OH
Warner, Susanna A. ....Fullerton, CA
Warner, Suzanne ....Salt Lake City, UT
Warner, Suzanne Cannella ....Tampa, FL
Warner, Suzanne M. ....Louisville, KY
Warner, T. Deon ....Houston, TX
Warner, Ted F. ....Phoenix, AZ
Warner, Teresa R. ....Norfolk, VA
Warner, Theodore K., Jr.
Philadelphia, PA
Warner, Thomas A., III ....Baton Rouge, LA
Warner, Thomas D. ....Davenport, IA
Warner, Thomas E. ....Stuart, FL
Warner, Thomas M., Jr. ....Wichita, KS
Warner, Timothy G. ....Greensboro, NC
Warner, Timothy G. ....Cleveland, OH
Warner, Timothy M. ....Panama City, FL
Warner, Timothy R. ....Indianapolis, IN
Warner, Tom B. ....Centralia, IL
Warner, Trinh P. ....Seattle, WA
Warner, Valerie M. ....Tulsa, OK
Warner, Vicki C. ....Shreveport, LA
Warner, Vickie A. ....Batesville, AR
Warner, Vivian E. ....Crossville, TN
Warner, W. Ann ....Detroit, MI
Warner, Wallace E. ....Green Valley, AZ
Warner, Wallace, McLaren & Dague
Muncie, IN
Warner & Warner ....Beeville, TX
Warner & Warner, PLC ....Union City, TN
Warner, Whitney ....Albuquerque, NM
Warner, William G. ....Panama City, FL
Warner, William H. G. ....Mount Gretna, PA
Warnes, Dan ....Guntersville, AL
Warnes, James C. ....Athens, GA
Warnes, James C., P.C. ....Athens, GA
Warnes, John T. ....Daly City, CA
Warnes, William C. ....Papillion, NE
Warnica, James M. ....Houston, TX
Warnick, Carol ....Casper, WY
Warnick, Darlene Dorn ....St. Louis, MO
Warnick, Elizabeth B. ....Clarksburg, WV
Warnick, Hazel A. ....Baltimore, MD
Warnick, Jeffrey L. ....Chicago, IL
Warnick, John A. ....Denver, CO
Warnick, J. Q., Jr. ....Lubbock, TX
Warnick, Kelly N. ....Chicago, IL
Warnick, Mark R. ....Kansas City, MO
Warnick, Michael P. ....Chicago, IL
Warnick, Reed T. ....Salt Lake City, UT
Warnick, Spencer K. ....Albany, NY
Warnick, Whitney B. ....Las Vegas, NV
Warnick, William F., Law Offices of
Lubbock, TX
Warnicke & Littler, P.L.C. ....Phoenix, AZ
Warnicke, Robert C. ....Phoenix, AZ
Warnicke, Ronald E. ....Phoenix, AZ
Warnicke, Rosemarie ....Pontiac, MI
Warnicke, Thomas R. ....Pontiac, MI
Warnicke & Wigent ....Detroit, MI
Keego Harbor, MI
Pontiac, MI
Warning, Brett L. ....Chicago, IL
Warning, Kiersten Elise ....Baltimore, MD
Warning, Sharon M. ....Chicago, IL
Warning, Stephen M. ....Longview, WA
Warnisher, Raymond A. ....Fullerton, CA
Warnix, Stacey Alison ....San Antonio, TX
Warnke, Albert A., III ....Schaumburg, IL
Warnke, Gordon E. ....New York, NY
Warnke, Mark R. ....Walnut Creek, CA
Warnke, Paul C. ....Department of State, Office of the Legal Adviser, GV
Warnke, Stephen A. ....New York, NY
Warnke, Thomas ....Sea Girt, NJ
Warnken, Chad ....Freehold, NJ
Warnken, Wayne L. ....New York, NY
Warnkle, Paul C. ....Washington, DC
Warnlof, John S. ....Walnut Creek, CA
Warnock, Brian R. ....Phoenix, AZ
Warnock, Curt L. ....Houston, TX
Warnock, Douglas W. ....Delaware, OH
Warnock, Douglas W., Co., L.P.A., Law Office of ....Delaware, OH
Warnock, Frank E ....Cincinnati, OH
Warnock, Frank H. ....Greenup, KY
Warnock, Frank K. ....Greenup, KY
Warnock, J. Carlton ....Soperton, GA
Warnock, Jeffrey H. ....New York, NY
Warnock, John P. ....Tucson, AZ
Warnock, John W. ....Santa Barbara, CA
Warnock, Joseph Edward ....Orange Park, FL
Warnock, Keith C. ....Daytona Beach, FL
Warnock, Keith C., P.A.
Daytona Beach, FL
Palm Coast, FL
Warnock, Rebecca D. ....Seattle, WA
Warnock, Russell W. ....Greenville, SC
Warnock, Timothy L. ....Nashville, TN
Warnock, W. Matthew ....Gilroy, CA
Warnock & Warnock ....Greenup, KY
Warnock, William F. ....Bayonne, NJ
Warnock, William R., (P.C.) ....La Grange, IL
Warnot, James R., Jr. ....New York, NY
Warns, Carl A., Jr. ....Louisville, KY
Warns, Howard E. ....St. Petersburg, FL
Warns, James T. ....Arlington, VA
Warns, Raymond H., Jr. ....Seattle, WA
Warnstadt, Kenneth L. ....Brooksville, FL
Warns-Tunstead, Alonna J.
Minneapolis, MN
Warokomski, Henry A., Jr.
East Meadow, NY
Waroway, Julie E. ....Newport, TN
Warp, George A. ....Minneapolis, MN
Warp, John M. ....Moose Lake, MN
Warpinski, Mark A. ....Green Bay, WI
Warpinski, Ted A. ....Milwaukee, WI
Warpinski & Vande Castle, S.C.
Green Bay, WI
Warpula, Christian C. ....Raleigh, NC
Warr, Alastair J. ....Indianapolis, IN
Warr, Amy ....Austin, TX
Warr, Brian L. ....Independence, MO
Warr, Eugene P., Jr. ....Hartsville, SC
Warr, Irene ....Salt Lake City, UT
Warr, Jeffrey A. ....Twin Falls, ID
Warr, Mary Lenore ....Memphis, TN
Warr, Ronald R. ....Bristol, RI
Warram, Robert A. ....Tampa, FL
Warran, Jason R. ....Kensington, MD
Warrecker, Janis Lynn ....New Haven, CT
Warrell, Michael J. ....Cleveland, OH
Warren, Adria E. ....Boston, MA
Warren, Allen, King, O'Hara & Bennett
Portland, OR
Warren, Alvin C., Jr. ....Cambridge, MA
Warren, Andrew ....Chicago, IL
Warren, Andrew J. ....Hyde Park, MA
Warren, Anjanette Rodzinak ....Boston, MA
Warren, Ann Monaco ......Jefferson City, MO
Lake Ozark, MO
Warren, Anne Schaefer ....Gulfport, MS
Warren, Arthur A. ....Department of Commerce, Office of the General Counsel, GV
Warren, Arthur D. ....Beverly Hills, CA
Warren, Barry E. ....Overland Park, KS
Warren, Barry L. ....Smithtown, NY
Warren, Benjamin S., III
Washington, DC
Warren, Bill ....Fort Smith, AR
Warren, Billie L. ....Cincinnati, OH
Warren, Bradford L. ....Indianapolis, IN
Warren, Bradley S. ....Findlay, OH
Warren, Brian K. ....Knoxville, TN
Warren, Brinton T. ....Arlington, VA
Warren, Bruce ....Thomasville, GA
Warren, Bruce Brownfield ......Waynesville, MO
Warren, Bruce E. ....Champaign, IL
Warren, Bruce G. ....Laguna Beach, CA
Warren, Bruce M. ....Los Angeles, CA
Warren, Bruce N. ....Colorado Springs, CO
Warren, Bruce W. ....Niwot, CO
Warren, C. Jeff ....Charlotte, NC
Warren, C. Mark ....Chattanooga, TN
Warren Cameron Faust & Asciutto, P.C.
Lansing, MI
Okemos, MI
Warren & Carlson, LLP ....Longmont, CO
Niwot, CO
Warren, Carlton D. ....Portland, OR
Warren, Carol Godfrey ....Portland, ME
Warren, Carol S. ....New York, NY
Warren, Carter & Hunter ....Charlotte, NC
Warren, Charles ....Sacramento, CA
Warren, Charles A. ....Denver, CO
Warren, Charles D. ....Athens, OH
Warren, Charles Edwin, Jr. ....Huntsville, AL
Warren, Charles F. ....Washington, DC
Warren, Charles F.
Department of Commerce, Patent and Trademark Office, GV
Warren, Charles H. ....South Hill, VA
Warren, Charles L. ....Washington, DC
Warren, Charles L. ....Naperville, IL
Warren, Charles M. ....Fort Scott, KS
Warren, Charles O., Jr. ....Columbia, SC
Warren, Charles Rollin ....Conway, AR
Warren, Charles S. ....New York, NY
Warren, Charles S. ....Pittsburgh, PA
Warren, Charles W. ....Oquossoc, ME
Warren, Charlotte L. ....Orlando, FL
Warren, Cheri Hodges ....Richmond, VA
Warren, Christine J. ....Baltimore, MD
Warren, Christine Marshall ....Orlando, FL
Warren, Christopher Churchman
Stamford, CT
Warren, Christopher D. ....Cherry Hill, NJ
Philadelphia, PA
Warren, Christopher S. ....Atlanta, GA
Warren, Christopher W. ....West Covina, CA
Warren, Claude M., Jr. ....Indianapolis, IN
Warren, Clifford M. ....New York, NY
Warren & Cruzcosa, L.L.P. ....Austin, TX
Warren, Currier & Buchanan, A Limited Liability Company, P.A. ....Portland, ME
Warren, Cynthia J. ....Providence, RI
Warren, Dan R. ....Daytona Beach, FL
Warren, Dana M. ....Westlake Village, CA
Warren, Daniel J. ....Atlanta, GA
Warren, Daniel R. ....Scarborough, ME
Warren, Daniel R. ....Cleveland, OH
Warren, David ....Pearl River, NY
Warren, David C. ....Denver, CO
Warren, David E. ....Portland, ME
Warren, David G. ....Durham, NC
Warren, David Gregory ....Waynesville, MO
Warren, David L. ....Portland, OR
Warren, David L., Jr. ....Birmingham, AL
Warren, David M. ....Fairfield, CT
Warren, David M. ....New York, NY
Warren, David M. ....Rocky Mount, NC
Warren, David P. ....Pasadena, CA
Warren, David S. ....Cincinnati, OH
Warren, David W. ....Farmington Hills, MI
Warren, Dean A. ....Charlotte, NC
Warren, Dean E. ....Poteau, OK
Warren, Delores W. ....Tulsa, OK
Warren, Dennis E. ....Queens Village, NY
Warren, Dennis M. ....Sacramento, CA
Warren, Dennis M., A Professional Corporation ....Sacramento, CA
Warren, Diane Bartsch ....Fayetteville, AR
Warren & Dickert ....Bristol, VA
Warren, Donald ....Boca Raton, FL
Warren, Donald R. ....San Diego, CA
Warren, Dorothea G. ....Topeka, KS
Warren & Duggan ....Seattle, WA
Warren, Dwight A. ....St. Louis, MO
Warren, Dyla L. ....Palm Beach Gardens, FL
Warren, E. Terry ....Ashtabula, OH
Warren, Earl, Jr. ....Sacramento, CA
Warren, Earl W., (P.C.) ......Beverly Hills, CA
Warren, Edie Wittick ....Beverly Hills, CA
Warren, Edward H. ....Salem, OR
Warren, Edward W., (P.C.)
Washington, DC
Warren, Edwin B. ......Rancho Palos Verdes, CA
Warren, Edwin B., Law Offices of, A Prof. Corp. ....Rancho Palos Verdes, CA
Warren, Elizabeth A. ....Houma, LA
Warren, Elizabeth A. ....Cambridge, MA
Warren, Elizabeth F. ....Columbia, SC
Warren, Elizabeth M. ....Dallas, TX
Warren, Elizabeth Salisbury
Nashville, TN
Warren, Elliot R. ....Bridgeport, CT
Stamford, CT
Warren, Elliot R. ....Westport, CT
Warren, Erik A. ....Flint, MI
Warren, Ernest, Jr. ....Portland, OR
Warren, Ethan ....Boston, MA
Warren, Euphemia B. ....New York, NY
Warren, Frances H. ....Charlottesville, VA
Warren, Franklin E. ....Louisville, KY
Warren, Frederick L., III ....Atlanta, GA
Warren, G. Martin, Jr. ....Gulfport, MS
Warren, Gail ....Richmond, VA
Warren, Gale ....Stephenville, TX
Warren, Geoffrey M.
Rolling Hills Estates, CA
Warren, George ....Lawrenceville, NJ
Warren, George M., Jr. ....Bristol, VA
Warren, Gerald M. ....Gulfport, MS
Warren, Gina Simone ....Kansas City, MO
Warren, Gordon H. ....Las Vegas, NV
Warren, H. Michael ....Dallas, TX
Warren, Hal ....Fulton, KY
Warren, Hal B. ....Evergreen, CO
Warren, Hanna M. ....Englewood, CO
Warren, Harland D. ....Ottawa, IL
Warren, Harland D., & Associates, P.C.
Ottawa, IL
Warren, Harold J. ....
Joint Committees And Commissions, GV
Warren, Harry E. ....Lawrence, KS
Warren, Harvey L., III ....Beaumont, TX
Warren, Herbert A., P.A. ....Miami, FL
Warren, Herbert L. ....Louisville, KY
Warren & Herman ....Los Angeles, CA
Warren, Howard B. ....Gadsden, AL
Warren, Ian J. ....New York, NY
Warren, Ida K. ....Springfield, VA
Warren, Ingrid M. ....Dallas, TX
Warren, Irwin Howard ....New York, NY
Warren, J. Barton ....Huntsville, AL
Warren, J. Benjamin, Jr. ....Shreveport, LA
Warren, J. Michael ....Okemos, MI
Warren, J. Robert, II ....Baltimore, MD
Warren, J. Steve ....Greenville, SC
Warren, Jack L. ....Coconut Creek, FL
Warren, Jack W. ....Mason, MI
Warren, Jacqueline M. ....New York, NY
Warren, James F. ....Washington, DC
Warren, James G. ....Oklahoma City, OK
Warren, James H. ....Fulton, KY
Warren, James H. ....Tyler, TX
Warren, James I. ....New York, NY
Warren, James I., III .....Warner Robins, GA
Warren, James I., III ....Greenville, SC
Warren, James L. ....Narrows, VA
Warren, James L, III ....Jackson, MS
Warren, James M. ....Santa Barbara, CA
Warren, James R. ....Springfield, OH
Warren, James S. ....Wake Forest, NC
Warren, James T. ....Riverside, CA
Warren, James W. ....Coxsackie, NY
Warren, James W., Jr. ....Oxford, MS
Warren, Jane Kimball ....Hartford, CT
Warren, Jeanne M. ....Dallas, TX
Warren, Jeffrey D. ....Los Angeles, CA
Warren, Jeffrey D. ....Chicago, IL
Warren, Jeffrey W. ....Tampa, FL
Warren, Jerome E. ....Oroville, CA
Warren, Jerry A. ....Oklahoma City, OK
Warren, Jesse L. ....Greensboro, NC
Warren, Jessica Mendes ....Austin, TX
Warren, Jill ....Austin, TX
Warren, Jill M. ....Hattiesburg, MS
Warren, Jimmye S. ....Department of Justice, Criminal Division, GV
Warren, Joan ....Buffalo, NY
Warren, Joel ....Beverly Hills, CA
Warren, John C. ....Columbia, SC
Warren, John C. ....Houston, TX
Warren, John D. ....Charlotte, NC
Warren, John E. ....Harwich, MA
Warren, John E., III ....Jasper, AL
Warren, John H., III ....Charleston, SC
Warren, John, Jr. ....Red Bank, NJ
Warren, John K. ....Ashland, AL
Warren, John L. ....Carmel, CA
Warren, John L. ....St. Petersburg, FL
Warren, John M. ....Waterloo, IA
Warren, John M. ....St. Joseph, MO
Warren, John N. ....Dallas, TX
Warren, John P., Jr. ....Sealy, TX
Warren, John Ray ....Montgomery, AL
Warren, John S. ....Los Angeles, CA
Warren, John S. ....Dillon, MT
Warren, John S. ....Corpus Christi, TX
Warren, John W. ....Eureka, CA
Warren, Johnny W. ....Dublin, GA
Warren, Jon G. ....Moscow, ID
Warren, Jonathan T. ....Norristown, PA
Warren, Joseph ....Larchmont, NY
Warren, Joseph A., III ....Lansing, MI
Warren, Joseph C. ....Daytona Beach, FL
Warren, Joseph, III ....Charlotte, NC
Warren, Joseph W. ....Montgomery, AL
Warren, Joseph W. C. ....Washington, DC
Warren, Joy A. ....Modesto, CA
Warren, Judith ....Los Angeles, CA
Warren, Junius P. ....Martinsville, VA
Warren, K. Brent ....Atlanta, GA
Warren & Kallianos ....Charlotte, NC
Warren, Keith A. ....Memphis, TN
Warren, Kellogg, Barber, Dean & Fontes, P.S.
Renton, WA
Warren, Kelly ....Covina, CA
Warren, Kenneth G., Jr. ....Pittsfield, MA
Warren, Kenneth J. ....Bala Cynwyd, PA
Warren, Kerr, Walston & Taylor, L.L.P.
Goldsboro, NC
Warren, Kevin F. ....Kansas City, MO
St. Louis, MO
Warren, Kirk S. ....Lakeland, FL
Warren, Kristina F. ....Tiburon, CA
Warren, Lamar ....Fort Lauderdale, FL
Warren, Larry D. ....San Antonio, TX
Warren, Larry F. ....Anniston, AL
Warren, Larry H. ....Birmingham, AL
Warren, Larry L. ....Minneapolis, MN
Warren, Lashawn Y. ....Olympia, WA
Warren, Laura Daria ....Philadelphia, PA
Warren, Laura L. ....Cincinnati, OH
Warren, Laurie A. ....Hyannis, MA
Warren, LaVone R. ....Birmingham, AL
Warren Law Office, S.C. ....Kenosha, WI
Warren, Lawrence ....Southfield, MI
Warren, Lawrence J. ....Renton, WA
Warren, Leonard H. ....Coxsackie, NY
Warren, LeRoy R. ....Los Alamos, NM
Warren, Lewis R. ....Santa Rosa, CA
Warren, Linda A. ....Rockville, MD
Warren, Linda Lyons ....New York, NY
Warren, Lindsay C., Jr. ....Goldsboro, NC
Warren, Linwood, Jr. ....Los Angeles, CA
Warren, Lisbeth A. ....New Brunswick, NJ
Warren, Lora Faye ....Austin, TX
Warren, Loretta Keimes ....Durham, NC
Warren, Loucile ....Fort Worth, TX
Warren, Louise Stanton ....Jacksonville, FL
Warren, Loyde H. ....Oklahoma City, OK
Warren, Loyde H., P.C. ......Oklahoma City, OK
Warren, Lucinda J. ....Crystal Beach, FL
Warren, Lynn K. ....Los Angeles, CA
Warren, Manning Gilbert, III .....Louisville, KY
Warren, Marc G. ....Carson City, NV
Warren, Maria ....Wilmington, NC
Warren, Marianne T. ....Austin, TX
Warren, Mark E. ....Washington, DC
Warren, Mark E. ....Boston, MA
Warren, Mark G. R. ....Jefferson City, MO
Lake Ozark, MO
Warren, Mark L. ....Los Gatos, CA
Warren, Mark W. ....Buffalo, NY
Warren, Martha S. ....Kansas City, MO
Warren & Martzin, L.L.C. .....Greenville, SC
Warren, Marvin ....Santa Ana, CA
Warren, Mary K. ....New York, NY
Warren, Mary Lee ....Department of Justice, Criminal Division, GV
Warren, Mathew C. ....Overland Park, KS
Warren, Matthew S. ....Cambridge, MA
Warren, Maureen E. ....
Department of Housing and Urban Development, GV
Warren, Melissa Allison ....Baltimore, MD
Warren, Melvin W. ....Morganville, NJ
Warren, Merritt C. ....Creighton, NE
Warren, Mervin W., Jr. ....St. Louis, MO
Warren, Michael A. ....Placentia, CA
Warren, Michael David, Jr. ....Detroit, MI
Warren, Michael E. ....Chapel Hill, NC
Warren, Michael E. ....Torrington, WY
Warren, Michael J. ....New York, NY
Warren, Michael J. ....Seattle, WA
Warren, Michael P. ....Austin, TX
Warren, Michael W. ....Brooklyn, NY
Warren, Michael Wm. ....New Albany, IN
Cincinnati, OH
Warren, Michelle L. ....New York, NY
Warren, Mike ....Hollis, OK
Warren, Monty R. ....West Palm Beach, FL
Warren, Morrison C. ....Chicago, IL
Warren, Mundt & Martin, P.C.
Colorado Springs, CO
Warren, Noel Edward ....New Orleans, LA
Warren, Norma ....Des Moines, IA
Warren, Patricia S. ....Fort Walton Beach, FL
Warren, Patrick D. ....Albany, NY
Warren, Paul D. ....Austin, TX
Warren, Paul L. ....Portsmouth, VA
Warren, Paul M. ....Billings, MT
Warren, Paul R. ....Rochester, NY
Warren, Penny R. ....Lexington, KY
Warren & Perez ....Dallas, TX

Warren, Perry, Anthony & Cook Wake Forest, NC
Warren, Perry D. ... Goodland, KS
Warren, Perry S. ... Princeton, NJ
Warren, Peter G. ... Camden, ME
Warren, Philip M. ... Pompano Beach, FL
Warren, Philip M., P.A. ... Pompano Beach, FL
Warren, Phillip H. ... San Francisco, CA
Warren, R. Dale ... Louisville, KY
Warren, R. Earl ... Englewood, FL
Warren, R. Earl, P.A., Law Offices of Englewood, FL
Warren, R. Kent ... Bloomington, IN
Warren, Rachel L. ... New York, NY
Warren, Randall B. ... Beverly, MA
Warren, Randi B. ... Fairfax, VA
Warren, Raymond Allan ... Charlotte, NC
Warren, Raymond J. ... Schaumburg, IL
Warren, Raymond M. ... Daytona Beach, FL
Warren, Reba H. ... Winston-Salem, NC
Warren, Richard A. ... Miami, FL
Warren, Richard B. West Palm Beach, FL
Warren, Richard D. ... San Francisco, CA
Warren, Richard D. ... Salisbury, MD
Warren, Richard F., Jr. ... Nashville, TN
Warren, Richard G. ... New York, NY
Warren, Richard J. ... Atlanta, GA
Warren, Richard J. ... Boonville, NY
Warren, Richard K. ... Lima, OH
Warren, Richard L., Jr. ... Cleveland, OH
Warren, Robert B. ... Colorado Springs, CO
Warren, Robert C., Jr. ... Washington, DC
Warren, Robert E. ... Jacksonville, FL
Warren, Robert E., Jr. ... Denver, CO
Warren, Robert J. ... Gainesville, FL
Warren, Robert J. ... Oneida, NY
Warren, Robert J. ... Enid, OK
Warren, Robert, Jr. ... Cleveland, OH
Warren, Robert L. ... Fort Worth, TX
Warren, Robert P. ... Washington, DC
Warren, Robert S. ... Los Angeles, CA
Warren, Robert W. ... Milwaukee, WI
Warren, Roberta A. ... St. Louis, MO
Warren, Robin K. ... Charlotte, NC
Warren, Rodney C. ... Annapolis, MD
Warren, Roger ... Kansas City, MO
Warren, Roger R. ... Salem, OR
Warren, Ronald M. ... Haddonfield, NJ
Warren, Ronda C. ... Milwaukee, WI
Warren, Roseline A. ... Laguna Beach, CA
Warren, Russell A. ... St. Louis, MO
Warren, Russell S., Jr. ... Englewood Cliffs, NJ
Warren, Ryan E. ... Department of Justice, Civil Rights Division, GV
Warren, S. Reed ... Goldsboro, NC
Warren, Sallie Estep ... San Diego, CA
Warren, Sally ... Fort Lauderdale, FL
Warren, Sally B. ... Bay City, MI
Warren, Sally B., P.C. ... Bay City, MI
Warren and Samplin ... Wantagh, NY
Warren, Samuel M. ... Missoula, MT
Warren, Sandra J. ... New York, NY
Warren, Sanford E., Jr. ... Dallas, TX
Warren, Sarah Elizabeth ... Sarasota, FL
Warren & Scheid, P.C. ... Narrows, VA
Warren, Sean C. ... New York, NY
Warren, Shannon T. ... Houston, TX
Warren, Sharon Lynn Charlotte Amalie, St. Thomas, VI
Warren, Sheldon J. ... Los Angeles, CA
Warren & Sinkler, L.L.P. ... Charleston, SC
Warren, Stacey N. ... Des Moines, IA
Warren, Stasia ... Daytona Beach, FL
Warren, Stephen A. ... Sunnyvale, CA
Warren, Stephen H. ... Los Angeles, CA
Warren, Stephen P. ... Beverly Hills, CA
Warren, Steve Ray ... Asheville, NC
Warren, Steven M. ... Norwalk, CT
Warren, Stewart D. ... Trenton, NJ
Warren, Stuart E. ... Owensboro, KY
Warren, Stuart M. ... Las Vegas, NV
Warren, Susan ... Wantagh, NY
Warren, Susan M. ... Shiprock, NM
Warren, Sydney J. ... Winston-Salem, NC
Warren, Tasheaya L. ... Los Angeles, CA
Warren, Terry D. ... Scottsdale, AZ
Warren, Terry D., P.C. ... Scottsdale, AZ
Warren, Terry T., & Associates, P.C. Okemos, MI
Warren, Terry Tabackman ... Okemos, MI
Warren, Thomas A. ... Tallahassee, FL
Warren, Thomas B. ... Fort Worth, TX
Warren, Thomas C. ... Wenatchee, WA
Warren, Thomas D. ... Augusta, ME
Warren, Thomas D. ... Lansing, MI
Warren, Thomas H. ... Atlanta, GA
Warren, Thomas J. ... Red Bank, NJ
Warren, Thomas V. ... Nottoway, VA
Warren, Timothy L. ... Chicago, IL
Warren, Tyler B. ... Greenville, NC
Warren, W. Gerald ... Detroit, MI
Warren, Walter E. Department of Housing and Urban Development, Office of General Counsel, GV
Warren & Warren ... Fulton, KY
Warren and Warren ... Waynesville, MO
Warren & Warren, PA Daytona Beach, FL
Warren, Wendy Barrett ... Washington, DC
Warren, Wendy Elizabeth ... Richmond, VA
Warren, Wesley B., Jr. Hilton Head Island, SC
Warren, Wilbur W., III ... Kenosha, WI
Warren, William B. ... New York, NY
Warren, William C. ... Department of State, Foreign Service Officers (Overseas), GV
Warren, William C. ... New York, NY
Warren, William C., Jr. ... Fort Smith, AR
Warren, William D. ... Los Angeles, CA
Warren, William F. ... Providence, RI
Warren, William J. ... Grand Rapids, MI
Warren, William L. ... Washington, DC
Warren, William L. ... Atlanta, GA
Warren, William L. ... Princeton, NJ
Warren, William M. ... Fort Worth, TX
Warren, William M., Jr. ... Birmingham, AL
Warren, William N. ... Fort Worth, TX
Warren, William P. ... New City, NY
Warren, William Rick ... Minden, LA
Warren, William S. ... Austin, TX
Warren, William W. ... Carlyle, IL
Warren, William W., III ... Minneapolis, MN
Warren, William W., Jr. ... Harrisburg, PA
Warren, William Z. ... Bethel, PA
Warren, Wm. Franklin, III Greenville, SC
Warren, Wm. H. ... Holdenville, OK
Warren, Wm. M. ... Cleveland, OH
Warren and Young PLL ... Ashtabula, OH Jefferson, OH
Warrenbrand, Neil D. ... Boston, MA
Warrenfeltz, Susan M. ... Gaithersburg, MD
Warren-Reed, Dollie I. ... Chicago, IL
Warrick, Benjamin R. ... Clinton, NC
Warrick & Boyn ... Elkhart, IN
Warrick, Bradley Alan ... Michigan City, IN
Warrick, Daniel J. ... Lubbock, TX
Warrick, Douglas B. ... Martinez, CA
Warrick, G. Scott ... Columbus, OH
Warrick, Kelly C. H. ... Stamford, CT
Warrick, Lance A. ... New York, NY
Warrick, Michael E. ... Houston, TX
Warrick, Royce A. ... Philadelphia, PA
Warrick, Stephen K. ... Omaha, NE
Warrick, Thomas E. ... Elkhart, IN
Warrick, W. Brant ... Fort Smith, AR
Warriner, C. Calvin, III West Palm Beach, FL
Warriner, Daniel C. ... Riverside, CA
Warriner, Martha A. ... Los Angeles, CA
Warriner, Melva Menzies Sacramento, CA
Warriner, Pauline M. ... New Orleans, LA
Warriner, Rhett P. ... Glendale, CA
Warriner, Thomas E. ... Woodland, CA
Warriner, Timothy E. ... Sacramento, CA
Warring, Carl N. ... Moses Lake, WA
Warring, Carl Perry ... Moses Lake, WA
Warring, Paul D. Department of the Air Force, Office of the Judge Advocate General, GV
Warring, Wendy E. ... Boston, MA
Warrington, Alfred C., V, (P.A.) Alachua, FL
Warrington, Diana L. ... Honolulu, HI
Warrington, James K. ... Greenwood, MS
Warrington, Joan P. ... Long Island City, NY
Warrington, Richard C., Jr. ... Springfield, IL
Warrington, Robert N. ... Greenville, MS
Warrum, Ronald ... Evansville, IN
Warsawsky, Jack ... Kew Gardens, NY
Warsawsky, Samuel N. ... Chicago, IL
Warsch, Barry Jay ... Cooper City, FL
Warschauer, Murray H. ... St. Louis, MO
Warsco Brogan ... Fort Wayne, IN
Warsco, Mark A. ... Fort Wayne, IN
Warsh, Jeffrey A. ... Neptune, NJ
Warsh, Richard L. ... Southfield, MI
Warsh, Sheri E. ... Chicago, IL
Warshafsky, Rotter, Tarnoff, Reinhardt & Bloch, S.C. ... Milwaukee, WI
Warshafsky, Ted M. ... Milwaukee, WI
Warshal, Stephanie M. ... Atlanta, GA
Warshauer, Alan M. ... New York, NY
Warshauer, Andrew Marc Garden City, NY
Warshauer, Bernard J. ... Sumter, SC
Warshauer, David R. ... Indianapolis, IN
Warshauer, Donald B. ... Houston, TX
Warshauer, Holly Demarest ... Fort Wayne, IN
Warshauer, Irene C. ... New York, NY
Warshauer, Irving J. ... New Orleans, LA
Warshauer, Mark J. Huntingdon Valley, PA
Warshauer, Michael J. ... Atlanta, GA
Warshauer Woodruff & Thomas Atlanta, GA
Warshavsky, Lee, (Mr.) ... New York, NY
Warshavsky, Oren J. ... New York, NY
Warshaw, Adam S. ... Burbank, CA
Warshaw, Allen C. ... Harrisburg, PA
Warshaw & Barnes ... Red Bank, NJ
Warshaw Burstein Cohen Schlesinger & Kuh, LLP ... New York, NY
Warshaw, Daniel L. ... Tarzana, CA
Warshaw, David ... Montville, NJ
Warshaw, David T. ... Wassaic, NY
Warshaw, Eileen ... Mount Clemens, MI
Warshaw, George J. ... Boston, MA
Warshaw, Jean ... New York, NY
Warshaw, Jeff D. ... Atlanta, GA
Warshaw, Jordan D. ... Blue Bell, PA
Warshaw, Laurence Stuart ... New York, NY
Warshaw, Lawrence P. ... Kansas City, MO
Warshaw, Mark D. ... Hermosa Beach, CA
Warshaw, Maureen Nesbitt Florham Park, NJ
Warshaw, Melvin ... Washington, DC
Warshaw, Melvin A. ... Boston, MA
Warshaw, Melvin S. ... Needham, MA
Warshaw, Michael Stuart ... Baltimore, MD
Warshaw, Michael T. ... Red Bank, NJ
Warshaw, Milton ... New York, NY
Warshaw, Peter E., Jr. ... Freehold, NJ
Warshaw, Robert G. ... Los Angeles, CA
Warshaw, Robert S., (P.C.) ... New York, NY
Warshawer, Sam L., Jr. ... Philadelphia, PA
Warshawsky, Anita ... West Bloomfield, MI
Warshawsky, Daniel A. ... Washington, DC
Warshawsky, Ira B. ... Jamaica, NY
Warshawsky, John ... Department of Justice, Civil Division, GV
Warshawsky, Mark ... Gastonia, NC
Warshawsky, Meyer ... Paw Paw, MI
Warshawsky, Reuben C. ... Chicago, IL
Warshawsky, Robert Q. ... Pittsburg, CA
Warshawsky, Steven M. ... Baltimore, MD
Warshell, Elaine R. ... Hanover, NH
Warshell, Elaine R. ... Norwich, VT
Warshof, Douglas A. ... Library of Congress, Congressional Research Service, GV
Warshofsky, Jason ... Coral Gables, FL
Warshofsky, Jason, P.A. ... Coral Gables, FL Miami, FL
Warshofsky, Keith A., P.A. ... Tampa, FL
Warshofsky, Keith Adam ... Tampa, FL
Warshowsky, Abby L. ... Brooklyn, NY
Warshowsky, Cassandra ... Boston, MA
Warshowsky, Paul S. ... Columbia, MD
Warso, Barbara Bauman ... Tustin, CA
Warso, David M. ... Las Vegas, NV
Warso, Sherman ... Lincolnwood, IL
Warsowe, Marc ... Redwood City, CA
Warstadt, Anne S. ... Boston, MA
Warszawski, Henry Sol ... Philadelphia, PA
Warta, Darrell L. ... Wichita, KS
Wartel, Matthew ... Alexandria, VA
Wartel, Powel F. ... Westbury, NY
Wartell, C. Robert ... Southfield, MI
Wartell, Douglas ... Southfield, MI
Wartelle, Douglas M. ... Everett, WA
Wartelle, John B. ... Lafayette, LA
Wartelle, Patrick M. ... Lafayette, LA
Wartelle, Paul F. ... San Francisco, CA
Wartelle & Weaver ... San Francisco, CA
Wartels, Edmund S., (P.C.) New York, NY
Warten, Fisher, Lee & Brown, L.L.C. Joplin, MO
Warten, Henry ... Joplin, MO
Wartenbe, Robert S. ... Fort Wayne, IN
Warth, Joseph A. ... Ocean City, MD
Warth, Thomas J. ... Rochester, NY
Warthen, Benjamin P. A. ... Richmond, VA
Warthen, George A., II ... Richmond, VA
Warthen, Harry J., III ... Richmond, VA
Warthen, John R. ... Columbia, MD
Warthen, Robert Lee ... Salt Lake City, UT
Warthen, Sally T. ... Manakin-Sabot, VA
Warthen, Vera Speakes ... Richmond, VA
Warthen, Wade D. ... Wichita, KS
Warther, Richard K. ... Orlando, FL
Wartinbee, David C. ... Soldotna, AK
Wartman, Bradley J. ... Chicago, IL
Wartman, Carl H. ... Wisconsin Rapids, WI
Wartman, John D. ... Milwaukee, WI
Wartman, Michael D. ... Ashland, WI
Wartner, Laura L. ... Atlanta, GA
Wartnick, Chaber, Harowitz, Smith & Tigerman, A Professional Corporation San Francisco, CA
Wartnick, Harry F. ... San Francisco, CA
Wartnik, Anthony P. ... Seattle, WA
Wartnik, Felicia A. ... Seattle, WA
Warton, John F., Jr. ... New Fairfield, CT
Warton, John F., P.C. ... New Fairfield, CT
Wartzman, Omansky, Blibaum, Simons, Cassin, Sachs & Sagal, P.A. ... Towson, MD
Wartzman, Paul ... Towson, MD
Warwar, Mona E. ... Plano, TX
Warwar, Sam ... Dayton, OH
Warwick, Alice E. ... Coral Gables, FL
Warwick, Alice E., P.A. ... Coral Gables, FL Miami, FL
Warwick & Banister, P.A. Palm Beach, FL
Warwick, Charles H., III ... Palm Beach, FL
Warwick, David R. ... Santa Rosa, CA
Warwick, Donald K. ... Southfield, MI
Warwick, E. Joseph ... Vicksburg, MS
Warwick, George W., Jr. ... Brevard, NC
Warwick, James G. ... Baltimore, MD
Warwick, Jeffrey K. ... Metairie, LA New Orleans, LA
Warwick, Katherine Butts ... Los Angeles, CA
Warwick, Kathleen A. ... New York, NY
Warwick, L. Alan ... Sacramento, CA
Warwick, Lisa T. ... Milwaukee, WI
Warwick, Michael E. ... Marshall, TX
Warwick, Michael P. ... Shawnee, OK
Warwick, Michael P., Inc. ... Shawnee, OK
Warwick, Robert A. ... Richmond, VA
Warwick, Scott L. ... Pennsauken, NJ
Warwick, Thomas J., Jr. ... San Diego, CA
Waryjas, Maryann A. ... Chicago, IL
Warzala, Stanley W. ... Chicago, IL
Warzecha, Gene ... Utica, NY
Warzecha, Mark F. ... New York, NY
Warzynski, Cheryl A. ... Chicago, IL
Warzynski, Deborah M. ... Paradise Valley, AZ
Warzynski, Juli Springborn ... Phoenix, AZ
Warzynski, Richard E. ... Tulsa, OK
Was, Christopher M. ... Nashville, TN
Wasacz, Mark ... San Francisco, CA
Wasatonic, John J. ... Duncan, SC
Wasch, Joseph C. ... Fort Lauderdale, FL
Wasch, Kathleen A. ... Decatur, GA
Wasch, Michelle Gruder ... Boca Raton, FL
Wasch, Nancy L. ... Pennsauken, NJ
Wasch, Tida K. ... Sylvania, OH
Wascha, Donald A., (P.C.) ... Flint, MI
Wascha, James J. ... Grand Blanc, MI
Waschak, Mark A. ... Atlanta, GA
Wasche, John E. ... Golden Valley, MN
Waschek, Pauline E. ... Redondo Beach, CA
Wascher, James D. ... Chicago, IL
Wascher, Rick R. ... McMinnville, TN
Wasden, H. William ... Mobile, AL
Wasden, Mark T. ... Washington, DC
Wasden, Wiley A., III ... Savannah, GA
Wasdin, John T. ... Bremen, GA
Wase, Ellen R. ... Philadelphia, PA
Wase, Gary S. ... Lutherville, MD
Wase, Gordon M. ... Philadelphia, PA
Wase, Joseph J. ... Towson, MD
Wase, Randy S. ... Lutherville, MD
Wase & Wase ... Lutherville, MD
Wasem, Larry L. ... Santa Rosa, CA
Wasem, Mark R. ... Dallas, TX
Wasem, Peter A. ... Barrington, IL
Waserstein, Aida ... Wilmington, DE
Waserstein, Steve L. ... Fort Lauderdale, FL
Wash, Danny C., (P.C.) ... Waco, TX
Wash, J. Lauchlan ... Los Angeles, CA
Wash, Lisa R. ... Albany, CA
Wash, Merryl L. ... Waco, TX
Wash, Michael A., Law Offices of Austin, TX
Wash, R. Bradford ... Birmingham, AL
Wash & Thomas ... Waco, TX
Washam, Scott A. ... Canton, OH
Washauer, Hal ... Danville, CA
Washauer, William W. ... San Francisco, CA
Washburn, A. Lawrence, Jr. ... New York, NY
Washburn, Alan V. ... Washington, DC
Washburn, Amy Irene ... Washington, DC
Washburn, Anderson L. ... Costa Mesa, CA
Washburn, Anne ... San Bernardino, CA
Washburn, Barbara J. ... United States Senate, Senatorial Assistants, GV
Washburn, Ben W., Jr. ... Detroit, MI
Washburn, Berk W. ... Troy, MI
Washburn, Brenda K. ... Sioux City, IA
Washburn, Briscoe & McCarthy, A Professional Corporation ... Juneau, AK Fresno, CA Sacramento, CA San Francisco, CA Tahoe City, CA
Washburn, Bruce ... Phoenix, AZ
Washburn, Burton A., III ... Paducah, KY
Washburn, Charles E., Jr. Los Angeles, CA
Washburn, Chuck E. ... Harrisburg, PA
Washburn, David M. ... Houston, TX
Washburn, David T. ... New York, NY
Washburn, Dean R. ... Marion, OH
Washburn, Dexter A. ... Seattle, WA
Washburn, Donald L. ... Nashville, TN
Washburn, Dorothy M. ... Denver, CO
Washburn, Douglas S. ... Saginaw, MI
Washburn, Edgar B. ... San Francisco, CA
Washburn, Elisabeth ... Chicago, IL
Washburn, Frederic C. ... Tonawanda, NY
Washburn, Frieda V. H. ... Kalamazoo, MI
Washburn, Gina G. ... St. Paul, MN
Washburn, Gordon W. ... Houston, TX
Washburn, J. David ... Dallas, TX
Washburn, J. Tayloe ... Seattle, WA
Washburn, Jack ... Houston, TX
Washburn, James A. ... Atlanta, GA
Washburn, James C. ... Winter Park, FL
Washburn, James Kent ... Burlington, NC
Washburn, Jeanne Cameron Albuquerque, NM
Washburn, Jeanne H. ... Raleigh, NC
Washburn, Jeffrey S. ... Columbus, IN
Washburn, John A. ... Chicago, IL
Washburn, John H. ... Dallas, TX
Washburn, John J. ... Westchester, IL North Reading, MA
Washburn, John L. ... Department of State, Foreign Service Institute, GV
Washburn, John U. ... Gansevoort, NY
Washburn, Jonathan W. ... Wilmington, NC
Washburn, Jonathan W., P.C. Wilmington, NC
Washburn, Kent G. ... Santa Cruz, CA
Washburn, Key & Lowry, PLLC Paducah, KY
Washburn, Kraig S. ... Chicago, IL
Washburn, Laura P. ... Birmingham, AL
Washburn, Lawrence L., III Lawrenceville, GA
Washburn, Margaret Gettle Lawrenceville, GA
Washburn, Margaret Gettle, P.C. Lawrenceville, GA
Washburn, Marilyn J. ... St. Louis, MO
Washburn, Melville W. ... Chicago, IL
Washburn, Michael C. ... Omaha, NE
Washburn, Michael W. ... Raleigh, NC
Washburn, Philip J. ... Roseburg, OR
Washburn, Philip L. ... Cooperstown, NY
Washburn, Robert B. ... Philadelphia, PA
Washburn, Robert L., Jr. ... Columbus, OH
Washburn, Robert M. ... Skowhegan, ME
Washburn, Robert M. ... Pennsauken, NJ
Washburn, Robert S. ... Palo Alto, CA
Washburn, Rodney H. ... Atherton, CA
Washburn, Rodney L. ... St. Charles, MO
Washburn, Russell D. ... Encino, CA
Washburn, Sarah M. ... Asheville, NC
Washburn, Tamera Cain ... Morgan City, LA
Washburn, Thomas D. ... Dallas, TX
Washburn, Thomas P. ... Austin, TX
Washburn, Timothy F. ... Northampton, MA
Washburn, Timothy N. ... Sacramento, CA
Washburn, Whitney F. ... Gold River, CA
Washburn, William F. ... Eldon, MO

Wasserman, Susan R. ....Los Angeles, CA
Wasserman, Susan R. ....Columbus, OH
Wasserman, Sylvia K. ....Sheboygan, WI
Wasserman, Terry K. ....Manhattan Beach, CA
Wasserman & Walters
Daytona Beach, FL
Orlando, FL
Winter Park, FL
Wasserman, Wendy J. ....Princeton, NJ
Wasserman, William E. ....New York, NY
Wasserman, William P., (A P.C.)
Los Angeles, CA
Wassermann, Ann L. ....Salt Lake City, UT
Wassermann, Edward H. ....Albany, NY
Wassermann, Marc D. ....Washington, DC
Wasserson, Samuel R. ....Upland, CA
Wasserson, Samuel R., Inc., A Prof. Law Corp.
Upland, CA
Wasserstein, Bruce ....New York, NY
Wasserstein, Henry P. ....New York, NY
Wasserstein, Jeffrey A. ....Madison, NJ
Wasserstein, Nathaniel Seth
White Plains, NY
Wasserstrom, Alfred H. ....Hartsdale, NY
Wasserstrom, David E. ....Elkins Park, PA
Wasserstrom, Ellen ....Atlanta, GA
Wasserstrom, Jessica L. ....Miami, FL
Wasserstrom, Keith ....Miami, FL
Wasserstrom, Mark D. ....Overland Park, KS
Wasserstrom, Neil A. ....Houston, TX
Wasserstrom, Richard A. ....Santa Cruz, CA
Wasserstrom, Richard L. ....Silver Lake, KS
Wasserstrom, Richard S. ....Washington, DC
Wasserstrom, Sara E. ....Los Angeles, CA
Wasserstrom, Silas J. ....Washington, DC
Wasserstrum, Bennett ....Clifton, NJ
Wasserstrum, Louis ....Clifton, NJ
Wasserstrum, Seymour ....Vineland, NJ
Wassil, Gerald J. ....Wilkes-Barre, PA
Wassink, Mark J. ....Grand Rapids, MI
Wassler, Jane Frances ....Cincinnati, OH
Wassmann, Michael G. ....Birmingham, MI
Wassmann, Pamela P. ....Dover, MA
Wassmer, Daniel S. ....Doylestown, PA
Wassmer, Webb L. ....Cedar Rapids, IA
Wassmuth, Laura M. ....Denver, CO
Wassmuth, Michele M.
Fort George G. Meade, MD
Wassner, Donald R. ....Muscle Shoals, AL
Wassner, Kenneth B. ....Irvine, CA
Wassom, Arley J. ....Sioux Falls, SD
Wasson, Andrea Lynn ....Jeffersonville, IN
Wasson, Carla S. ....Siloam Springs, AR
Wasson, Christopher E. ....Columbus, OH
Wasson, Christopher W. ....Philadelphia, PA
Wasson, David B. ....Irvine, CA
Wasson, Edward H., Jr. ....Atlanta, GA
Wasson, Egan & Wilson ....Franklin, PA
Wasson, Eugene R. ....Jackson, MS
Wasson, Geoffrey S. ....Denver, CO
Wasson, George W. ....Lafayette, CA
Wasson, Gerard Jeffrey ....San Diego, CA
Wasson, Gordon M. ....Phoenix, AZ
Wasson, James D. ....Kerrville, TX
Wasson, James E. ....Fresno, CA
Wasson, James E., Inc. ....Fresno, CA
Wasson, John A. ....Kosciusko, MS
Wasson, John C. ....Dayton, TN
Wasson, Karen Reed ....Orlando, FL
Wasson, Karl C. ....Duluth, MN
Wasson, Mitchell B. ....Arlington, VA
Wasson, Monica V. ....Spokane, WA
Wasson, Paul J. ....Spokane, WA
Wasson, Robert D. ....Palo Alto, CA
Wasson, Robert P., Jr. ....Boston, MA
Wasson, Robert V. ....San Pedro, CA
Wasson, Rodger D. ....Greenville, MS
Wasson, Roy D. ....Miami, FL
Wasson, Sours & Harris, A Professional Corporation ....Atlanta, GA
Wasson, T. Lynne ....Honolulu, HI
Wasson, William B. ....Avondale Estates, GA
Wassweiler, William P. ....Minneapolis, MN
Wasula, Christine A. ....Orlando, FL
Wasung, John Stephen ....Toledo, OH
Waswo, Charles R. ....Cashion, OK
Wasylenki, Joan ....Los Angeles, CA
Wasylik, Michael Alex ....Jacksonville, FL
Wasylik, Robert M. ....Columbus, OH
Wasylik, Wesley M. ....Orlando, FL
Wasylyshyn, John B. ....Camarillo, CA
Waszak, Ralph R., Jr. ....Akron, OH
Waszkiewicz, Kenneth P., LLC, Law Office of
Crofton, MD
Waszkiewicz, Kenneth Philip ....Crofton, MD
Wasznicky, Diane ....Sacramento, CA
Wataha, Jay ....Austin, TX
Watai, George ....Gardena, CA
Watai, Madge S., (Mrs.) ....Los Angeles, CA
Watanabe, Arleen Y. ....Wailuku, HI
Watanabe, Corinne K. A. ....Honolulu, HI
Watanabe, Douglas ....San Jose, CA
Watanabe, Hisashi David ....Racine, WI
Watanabe, Ing & Kawashima
Honolulu, HI
Watanabe, Jeffrey N., (Atty. At Law, A Law Corp.) ....Honolulu, HI
Watanabe, Kathleen N. Aqui ....Kapaa, HI
Watanabe, Laura A. ....New York, NY
Watanabe, Michael J. ....Denver, CO
Watanabe, Osamu ....Los Angeles, CA
Watanabe, Roy N. ....New York, NY
Watanabe, Shigeru ....Los Angeles, CA
Watanabe, Tsugumichi D. ....New York, NY
Watanabe, Wendy Y. ....Los Angeles, CA
Watanabe, Wilfred K. ....Honolulu, HI
Watanuki, Debra L. ....Fremont, CA
Watase, Kenneth D. ....Riverside, CA

Watches, Chauncey J. ....Canisteo, NY
Watchman, Abbie-Sue ....Tucson, AZ
Watchman, Gregory R. ....Washington, DC
Watchman, Hal G., Law Offices of
Pasadena, CA
Watchman, Shari ....Shrewsbury, NJ
Watchman, Susan L. ....Phoenix, AZ
Watchous, R. Owen, Chtd. ....Olathe, KS
Watchous, Robert O. ....Olathe, KS
Watel, Kathleen Finck ....San Antonio, TX
Watenmaker, Alan S. ....Los Angeles, CA
Waterbury, Charles E. ....Dallas, TX
Waterbury, James M., Jr. ....Atlanta, GA
Waterbury, Stephen C.
Grand Rapids, MI
Waterbury, Thos. L. ....Minneapolis, MN
Waterfall, Economidis, Caldwell, Hanshaw & Villamana, P.C. ....Tucson, AZ
Waterfall, Eve L.R. ....Boston, MA
Waterfall, Gordon G. ....Tucson, AZ
Waterfall, R. Scott ....Ogden, UT
Waterfield, Charles W. ....Sandusky, OH
Waterfield, Elizabeth M. ....Boston, MA
Waterfield, Steven C. ....Columbus, OH
Waterfill, Mark R. ....Indianapolis, IN
Waterhouse, Bruce L., Jr. ....Cleveland, OH
Waterhouse, Cheryl A. ....Boston, MA
Waterhouse, Homer ....Biddeford, ME
Waterhouse, Jos. P. ....Bethlehem, WV
Waterhouse, Kimberlee A. ....Lenoir City, TN
Waterhouse, Kimberly ....San Angelo, TX
Waterhouse Law Offices ....Biddeford, ME
Waterhouse, Linton S. ....Orlando, FL
Waterhouse, Rachel L. ....Nashville, TN
Waterhouse, Rick ....Corpus Christi, TX
Waterland, Laura J. ....Wilmington, DE
Waterloo, Dale Bec ....Phoenix, AZ
Waterman, A. Joseph ....Columbus, OH
Waterman, Andrew J. ....Irvine, CA
Waterman, Andrew Scott ....Olean, NY
Waterman, Avery Tillinghast "Sandy", Jr.
Newport News, VA
Richmond, VA
Waterman, Bradley S. ....Washington, DC
Waterman, C. Dana, III ....Davenport, IA
Waterman, Cathy H. ....Santa Monica, CA
Waterman, Cecily A. ....San Francisco, CA
Waterman, Charles ....Las Vegas, NV
Waterman, Charles H., III
Columbus, OH
Waterman, Christopher M. ....Boston, MA
Waterman, Christopher M.
New York, NY
Waterman, David F. ....Toledo, OH
Waterman, David L. ....Louisville, KY
Waterman, David M., Law Offices of
Tucson, AZ
Waterman, Deborah A. ....Waverly, OH
Waterman, Elizabeth Fredricey
Lexington, NE
Waterman, Gerald H. ....Columbus, OH
Waterman, Gregg E. ....Dodgeville, WI
Waterman, Irwin G. ....Louisville, KY
Waterman, James B. ....Fresno, CA
Waterman, Jane ....Los Angeles, CA
Waterman, Jennifer M. ....Denver, CO
Waterman, Jerome F. X. ....Kansas City, MO
Waterman, Joseph ....Tucson, AZ
Waterman, K. Krasnow
Department of Justice,
Federal Bureau of Investigation, GV
Waterman, Kenneth M. ....Fort Wayne, IN
Waterman, Linette M.
West Palm Beach, FL
Waterman, Louis I. ....Louisville, KY
Waterman, Lynn S. ....Miami, FL
Waterman, Marcie L. ....New York, NY
Waterman, Maria Mihalakis
Davenport, IA
Waterman, Mark C. ....Irvine, CA
Waterman, Mark W. ....Los Angeles, CA
Waterman, Martin B. ....West Hartford, CT
Waterman, Mary Ann ....Detroit, MI
Waterman, Matthew R.K. ....Tucson, AZ
Waterman, Melinda D. ....Irvine, CA
Waterman, Michael A. ....Encino, CA
Waterman, Michael D. ....San Diego, CA
Waterman, Patrick B. ....Fresno, CA
Waterman, R. Michael ....Hudson, WI
Waterman, Richard K. ....San Francisco, CA
Waterman, Rick Truman ....Sarasota, FL
Waterman, Robert A. ....Nashville, TN
Waterman, Robert V. ....Louisville, KY
Waterman, Robert V. P. ....Davenport, IA
Waterman, Robert V. P., Jr.
Rock Island, IL
Davenport, IA
Waterman, Ronald F. ....Helena, MT
Waterman, Sallee Fry ....Cincinnati, OH
Waterman, Sallee Fry, Co., L.P.A.
Cincinnati, OH
Waterman, Samantha R. ....Los Angeles, CA
Waterman, Samuel B. ....Hallandale Beach, FL
Waterman, Scott F. ....Media, PA
Waterman, Stephen P. ....Secaucus, NJ
Waterman, Steven T. ....Salt Lake City, UT
Waterman, T. Preston ....Bellport, NY
Waterman, Thomas B. ....Ponchatoula, LA
Waterman, Thomas D. ....Davenport, IA
Waterman, W. D. "Michael", Jr.
San Diego, CA
Waterman, William ....Pontiac, MI
Waterman, William B. ....Walnut Creek, CA
Waterman, William, Jr. ....New York, NY
Waterman, Wm. B. ....Davenport, IA
Watermeier, David W. ....Lincoln, NE
Waters, Arthur L. ....Roswell, GA
Waters, B. Nolan ....North Hollywood, CA

Waters & Barry, Chartered
Junction City, KS
Waters, Barry J. ....New Haven, CT
Waters, Bill W. ....Pampa, TX
Waters, Billy J. ....Covington, GA
Waters, Brian J. ....Denver, CO
Waters, Brian J. ....Woodbridge, NJ
Waters, Bruce B., P.C. ....Laramie, WY
Waters, C. Andrew ....Dallas, TX
Waters, C. Scott ....Williamsport, PA
Waters, Carolyn L. ....Las Vegas, NV
Waters, Charles A. ....Schnecksville, PA
Waters, Charles B., Jr. ....Atlanta, GA
Waters, Charles L. ....United States Senate,
Senatorial Assistants, GV
Waters, Charles M. ....Boston, MA
Waters, Charles W. ....Dallas, TX
Waters, Cody W. ....Tampa, FL
Waters, Daniel H., Jr. ....Birmingham, AL
Waters, David ....Honolulu, HI
Waters, David Fite ....Norwalk, CT
Waters, David H. ....Oakland, CA
Waters, David M. ....Washington, DC
Waters, David W. ....San Diego, CA
Waters, Deborah C. ....Norfolk, VA
Waters, Diane L. ....Kansas City, KS
Waters, Don L. ....Atlanta, GA
Savannah, GA
Waters, Donald D. ....Cranford, NJ
Waters, Doris A. ....Denver, CO
Waters, Dorothy J. ....Lawrence, KS
Waters, Dorothy R. ....Newtown Square, PA
Waters, Douglas G. ....Leavenworth, KS
Waters, Duane E. ....Montrose, CA
Waters, Edmund J., Jr., Law Offices of
Concord, NH
Waters, Edward T. ....Washington, DC
Waters, Elizabeth A. ....Tampa, FL
Waters, Frank J. ....Los Angeles, CA
Waters, George ....Sacramento, CA
Waters, George A. ....Richmond Hill, GA
Waters, Gerald T. ....Dallas, TX
Waters, Gola E. ....Carbondale, IL
Waters, Gregory K. ....Bluffton, IN
Waters, H. Franklin ....Fayetteville, AR
Waters, Hank T. ....Hamilton, MT
Waters, Harold L. ....Jacksonville, NC
Waters, Henrietta Davis ....Brooklyn, NY
Waters, Holt & Fields ....Pampa, TX
Waters, J. Conrad, Jr. ....Fairfax, VA
Waters, J. Keith ....Department of Justice,
Executive Office for Immigration Review,
GV
Waters, J. Michael, Jr. ....Arlington, TX
Dallas, TX
Waters, J. Scott, IV ....Flower Mound, TX
Waters, J. Thomas
Department of Transportation,
Federal Aviation Administration, GV
Waters, Jacqueline A. ....Chicago, IL
Waters, Jaime Crow ....New Orleans, LA
Waters, James E. ....Indianapolis, IN
Waters, James F., III ....Jacksonville, FL
Waters, James H. ....Des Moines, IA
Waters, James H., III ....St. George, UT
Waters, James L. ....Muskegon, MI
Waters, James L. ....New York, NY
Waters, James P. D. ....Newton, MA
Waters, James T.
Department of Transportation,
Federal Aviation Administration, GV
Waters, Jane E. ....Houston, TX
Waters, Jennifer N. ....Washington, DC
Waters, Jill E.
National Labor Relations Board,
Office of Board Members, GV
Waters, John A. ....Grand Rapids, MI
Waters, John B. ....Chicago, IL
Lincolnwood, IL
Waters, John B., Jr. ....Knoxville, TN
Waters, John D. ....Philadelphia, PA
Waters, John E. ....Des Moines, IA
Waters, John J. ....Minneapolis, MN
Waters, John J., Jr. ....Diamond Bar, CA
Waters, John L. ....Grafton, WV
Waters, John M., Jr. ....Salem, NJ
Waters, John R., Jr. ....Alexander City, AL
Waters, John S. ....Ozark, MO
Waters, John W., Jr. ....Montgomery, AL
Waters, John W., Jr. ....New Orleans, LA
Waters, Julia Sullivan ....Tampa, FL
Waters, Julie A. ....Los Angeles, CA
Waters, Karen M. ....Chicago, IL
Waters, Katherine M. ....Woodbridge, VA
Waters, Kathleen MacFarlane
Los Angeles, CA
Waters, Kermitt L. ....Las Vegas, NV
Waters, Kim ....Sacramento, CA
Waters, King ....Houston, TX
Waters & Kraus ....Dallas, TX
Waters, Laughlin E. ....Los Angeles, CA
Waters, Laurie D. ....Fairfax, VA
Waters, Leland W. ....Pampa, TX
Waters, Liberty ....Oakland, CA
Waters, M. Daniel ....Des Moines, IA
Waters, M. George, IV ....Atlanta, GA
Waters, M. Michael ....Peoria, IL
Waters, Mark G. ....Carrollton, TX
Waters, Martha M. ....Poughkeepsie, NY
Waters, Martin J., III ....Palo Alto, CA
Waters, Martin V. ....New York, NY
Waters, Mary Kirtley ....Washington, DC
Waters, Matthew L. ....Metter, GA
Millen, GA
Waters, McCluskey & Boehle
Los Angeles, CA
Santa Ana, CA
Santa Monica, CA

Waters, McPherson, McNeill, P.C.
Secaucus, NJ
Trenton, NJ
New York, NY
Waters, Michael A. ....Department of the Navy,
Office of the Judge Advocate General, GV
Waters, Michael D. ....Montgomery, AL
Waters, Michael J. ....New York, NY
Waters, Michael R. ....Colorado Springs, CO
Waters, Michael S. ....Newark, NJ
Waters, Miriam Bennett ....Brooklyn, NY
Waters, Monty M. ....Austin, TX
Waters & Morse, P.C. ....Grand Rapids, MI
Waters, Nathan H., Jr. ....Harrisburg, PA
Waters, Nicole E. ....Los Angeles, CA
Waters, Noel S. ....Carson City, NV
Waters, Paige D. ....Chicago, IL
Waters, Patrick G. ....Boston, MA
Waters, Patrick T. ....Los Angeles, CA
Waters, Paul V. ....Washington, DC
Waters, Peyton D., Jr. ....Houston, TX
Waters & Puma, P.A. ....Salem, NJ
Waters, R. Charles ....Hendersonville, NC
Waters, Ray A., Jr. ....Augusta, AR
Waters, Rebecca A. ....Raleigh, NC
Waters, Richard F. ....Junction City, KS
Waters, Richard J. ....Phoenix, AZ
Waters, Richard J., P.C. ....Phoenix, AZ
Waters, Richard L. ....St. Louis, MO
Waters, Richard L., Jr. ....Camilla, GA
Waters, Richard T. ....Glen Ridge, NJ
Waters, Richd. J. ....Bellingham, WA
Waters, Robert A. ....Parkersburg, WV
Waters, Robert Craig ....Tallahassee, FL
Waters, Robert G. ....Granite City, IL
Waters, Robert J. ....Washington, DC
Waters, Robert R. ....Huntington, WV
Waters, Robert S. ....Washington, DC
Waters, Robert T. ....Stockton, CA
Waters, Ronald ....Los Angeles, CA
Waters, Russell D. ....St. Louis, MO
Waters, Samuel C. ....Columbia, SC
Waters, Samuel Creighton ....Columbia, SC
Waters, Samuel D. ....Des Moines, IA
Waters, Sandy ....Golden, CO
Waters, Sharon J. ....Riverside, CA
Waters, Shelly Slate ....Decatur, AL
Waters, Stephen L. ....Denver, CO
Waters, Stephen M. ....Chicago, IL
Waters, Steven A. ....San Antonio, TX
Waters, Steven G. ....Goodlettsville, TN
Waters, Stuart R. ....Clarksburg, WV
Waters, Stuart R., Jr. ....Monroeville, PA
Waters, Susan Corey ....St. Louis, MO
Waters, Thomas E., Jr. ....Blue Bell, PA
Waters, Thomas J. ....Lansing, MI
Waters, Thomas Wilson ....Oak Brook, IL
Waters, Timothy Doyle ....San Diego, CA
Waters, Timothy J. ....Washington, DC
Waters, Twyla J. ....Memphis, TN
Waters, Vaughan E. ....Corpus Christi, TX
Waters, Vivian H. ....St. Louis, MO
Waters, Voula D. ....Los Angeles, CA
Waters, Warner & Harris, PLLC
Clarksburg, WV
Waters, Warren E. ....Largo, FL
Waters, William E. ....Topeka, KS
Waters, William F. ....Universal City, CA
Waters, William J. ....Simi Valley, CA
Waters, William J., A Prof. Corp., Law Offices of ....Simi Valley, CA
Waters, William L. ....Knoxville, TN
Waters, William R., Jr. ....Tallahassee, FL
Waters, Zondra Hutto ....Tuscaloosa, AL
Waters III, John B. ....Knoxville, TN
Waterson, David M., Jr. ....San Antonio, TX
Waters-Schwartz, Diane A.
San Francisco, CA
Waterston, Gregory G. ....Salem, NJ
Waterston, Marilyn K. ....Germantown, MD
Waterston, Marilyn K., LLC
Germantown, MD
Rockville, MD
Waterston, Tass Dever ....Dallas, TX
Waterstone, Alan R. ....Troy, MI
Waterstone, Mary M. ....Detroit, MI
Waterstone, Stuart I. ....Northridge, CA
Waterstradt, David E. ....Muskegon, MI
Waterval, Richard A., Ltd. ....Falls Church, VA
Waterway, Kenneth W.
Fort Lauderdale, FL
Watford, Rebecca B. ....Miami, FL
Wathen, Alexander B. ....Houston, TX
Wathen, Angela L. ....Owensboro, KY
Wathen, Charles F. ....Northbrook, IL
Wathen, Daniel E. ....Augusta, ME
Wathen, Douglas L. ....Birmingham, MI
Wathen, Frank J. ....Dallas, TX
Wathen, Joseph J. ....Augusta, ME
Wathen, Lissa ....Lexington, KY
Wathen, Michael Charles ....Aurora, CO
Wathen, Richard A. ....Louisville, KY
Wathen, Richard B. ....Jeffersonville, IN
Wathen, Rick J. ....Seattle, WA
Wathen-Dunn, Peter W.
Department of Education,
Office of the General Counsel, GV
Wathey, Lisa J. ....Birmingham, AL
Waties, Carol ....Philadelphia, PA
Waties, David W. ....Collingswood, NJ
Philadelphia, PA
Waties & Waties ....Collingswood, NJ
Philadelphia, PA
Watiker, Jeffrey A. ....Washington, DC
Watje, Galen E. ....Minneapolis, MN
Watkin, Clark W., Jr. ....Phoenix, AZ
Watkin, Jeffrey ....Miami, FL
Watkin, Nancy K. ....Miami, FL

Watson, Caroline N. .... **Columbia, SC**
Watson, Cary S. .... Houston, TX
Watson, Catherine Jane .... Kansas City, KS
Watson, Catherine Kunkel .... Los Angeles, CA
Watson, Charles A. .... **Houston, TX**
Watson, Charles D., Jr. .... **Drumright, OK**
Watson, Charles E. .... Wellington, KS
Watson, Charles K., Jr. .... Richmond, VA
Watson, Charles L. .... Memphis, TN
Watson, Charles M., Jr. .... Greenwood, SC
Watson, Charles R. .... Ashland, OR
Watson, Charles R., Jr. .... **Amarillo, TX**
Watson, Charles S. .... **Springfield, IL**
Watson, Charles W. .... Connellsville, PA
Watson, Chas. A. .... Cambridge, MA
Watson, Cheryl Anne .... Boston, MA
Watson, Christyne A. .... **Torrance, CA**
Watson & Clayborne .... Oklahoma City, OK
Watson, Clyde W. .... Camden, TN
Watson Cole Grindle Watson, P.L.L.C.
Washington, DC
Watson, Constance W. .... Alexandria, VA
Watson, Corey C. .... **Los Angeles, CA**
Watson, Craig L. .... **Seattle, WA**
Watson, Craig R. .... Buffalo, NY
Watson, Craig R. .... Seattle, WA
Watson, Craig S. .... Baton Rouge, LA
Watson, Craig W. .... **Sherman, TX**
Watson, Cyndi L. .... **Dallas, TX**
Watson, Cynthia Dionne .... **New York, NY**
Watson, Cyril J. .... Chicago, IL
Watson, D. Dewey .... **San Francisco, CA**
Watson, D. Maria .... New York, NY
Watson, D. Scott .... **Chicago, IL**
Watson, Dale E. .... Salisbury, MD
Watson & Dameron .... Kansas City, MO
Watson, Damon C. .... Los Angeles, CA
Watson, Dana Dean .... Springdale, AR
Watson, Dana & Gottlieb, LLP
La Fayette, GA
Watson, Daniel B. .... La Crosse, WI
Watson, Daniel C. .... Troy, MI
Watson, Darryl T. .... **San Antonio, TX**
Watson, David A. .... San Francisco, CA
Watson, David C., Jr. .... Worthington, OH
Watson, David D. .... **Cleveland, OH**
Watson, David E. .... **San Diego, CA**
Watson, David E. .... **Boston, MA**
Watson, David J. .... **Pittsburgh, PA**
Watson, David L. .... Alhambra, CA
Watson, David L. .... **Atlanta, GA**
Watson, David L. .... St. George, UT
Watson, David L. .... **Charleston, WV**
Watson, David M. .... **Boston, MA**
Watson, David M. .... Tyler, MN
Watson, David O. .... **Cincinnati, OH**
Watson, David R. .... **Longview, TX**
Watson, David S. .... **Sarasota, FL**
Watson, David W. .... **Boston, MA**
Watson, Davis .... Austin, TX
Watson, Dawn .... Hempstead, NY
Watson, D. E. .... Salina, KS
Watson, Deborah .... Department of Justice, Criminal Division, GV
Watson, Debra D. .... Rapid City, SD
Watson, deGraffenried & Hardin, LLP
Birmingham, AL
Montgomery, AL
Tuscaloosa, AL
Watson, Denise M. .... Poughkeepsie, NY
Watson, Dennis A. .... **Pittsburgh, PA**
Watson, Dennis D. .... **La Fayette, GA**
Watson, Dennis D. .... Conroe, TX
Watson, Dennis J. .... **Clearwater, FL**
Watson, Dennis J. .... **Miami, OK**
Watson, Derrick K. .... San Francisco, CA
Watson, Don E., (P.C.) .... Englewood, CO
Watson, Donald C. .... Reading, PA
Watson, Donald M., Jr. .... **Boone, NC**
Watson, Donald N. .... Stuart, FL
Watson, Dorothea C. .... Orlando, FL
Watson, Dorothy P. .... **East Hanover, NJ**
Watson, Douglas K. .... Keene, NH
Watson, Douglas M. .... Newburyport, MA
Watson, Dovey E., Jr. .... Wilson, NC
Watson, Doyle .... **Drumright, OK**
Watson, E. Steve .... Dallas, TX
Watson, E. Thomas .... **Charlotte, NC**
Watson, Edward J. .... **San Francisco, CA**
Watson, Edward M. .... Providence, RI
Watson, Edwin P. .... Honolulu, HI
Watson, Elaine .... Albuquerque, NM
Watson, Elisabeth C. .... **Los Angeles, CA**
Watson, Elizabeth .... **Los Angeles, CA**
Watson, Elmer L., Jr. .... Dallas, TX
Watson, Eric J. .... **New York, NY**
Watson, Eugene B. .... Mission Viejo, CA
Watson, Evolea C. .... **Cherry Hill, NJ**
Watson, Farley & Williams
New York, NY
Watson, Felicia B. .... Fairfield, CT
Watson, Felicia K .... **Washington, DC**
Watson, Fletcher B., IV .... Roanoke, VA
Watson, Fletcher D. .... **Covington, VA**
Watson, Folds, Steadham & Walker, A Professional Association .... **Gainesville, FL**
Watson, Forrest A., Jr. .... Barnesville, GA
Watson, Francis A., Jr. .... **Richmond, CA**
Watson, Frank .... Paterson, NJ
Watson, Frank B., Jr. .... Fort Myers, FL
Watson, Frank, Jr. .... Des Moines, IA
Watson, Frank L., III .... **Memphis, TN**
Watson, Frank L., Jr. .... **Memphis, TN**
Watson, Franklin H. .... **Seagrove Beach, FL**
Watson, Franklin H., P.A. .... **Destin, FL**
Panama City Beach, FL
Seagrove Beach, FL
Watson, Franklin T. .... **Sacramento, CA**
Watson, Fred A. .... Carlsbad, NM
Watson, G. Andrew .... **Chicago, IL**
Watson, G. Dennis .... **Memphis, TN**
Watson, G. Norris .... **Washington, DC**
Watson, G. Patrick .... **Atlanta, GA**
Watson, G. Stuart .... **Albany, GA**
Watson, G. A. (Butsba), III
New Orleans, LA
Watson, Gail .... New York, NY
Watson, Gail G. .... **New York, NY**
Watson, Gary W. .... **Stamford, CT**
Watson, Gene D. .... Lincoln, NE
Watson, Georg-Ann .... Raleigh, NC
Watson, George .... Grand Prairie, TX
Watson, George A., III .... Metairie, LA
Watson, George C. .... Port Huron, MI
Watson, George D., Jr. .... Chadron, NE
Watson, Gerald D. .... Lockport, NY
Watson, Gerald G. .... Keizer, OR
Watson, Gerald G., P.C. .... Keizer, OR
Watson, Gerard P. .... Brooklyn, NY
Watson, Gillis & Carver, P.C.
Fort Payne, AL
Watson, Glenn R. .... **Los Angeles, CA**
Watson, Gregory E. .... Louisville, KY
Watson, H. Camilla .... Newark, DE
Watson, H. Lee .... San Francisco, CA
Watson, H. Thomas .... **Los Angeles, CA**
Watson, Harold K. .... **Houston, TX**
Watson, Harry J. .... **Dallas, TX**
Watson, Harry J., III .... Indianapolis, IN
Watson, Hathaway, III .... **San Francisco, CA**
Watson, H. B., Jr. .... **Oklahoma City, OK**
Watson, Henri J. .... Kansas City, MO
Watson, Henry, III .... Cynthiana, KY
Watson, Herman A., III .... Smyrna, GA
Watson, Herman, Jr. .... **Huntsville, AL**
Watson, Hiram G. .... Jefferson City, MO
Watson, Hiffe & Hass .... **Richmond, CA**
Watson, Hollow & Reeves, P.L.C.
Knoxville, TN
Watson, Houston M., II .... **Orange, CA**
Watson, Hoyt Thomas .... Houston, TX
Watson, Hugh .... Indianapolis, IN
Watson & Hunt, P.A. .... **Spruce Pine, NC**
Watson, Hunter H. .... Laurium, MI
Watson, Ingrid Ashe .... **Richmond, VA**
Watson, J. Andrew, III .... **Huntsville, AL**
Watson, J. Calhoun .... **Columbia, SC**
Watson, J. Casey .... **Williamsport, PA**
Watson, J. David .... Dillon, SC
Watson, J. Davis .... **Austin, TX**
Watson, J. Elaine .... Houston, TX
Watson, J. Kevin .... **Jackson, MS**
Watson, J. Lynn .... Murfreesboro, TN
Watson, J. Michael .... Houston, TX
Watson, J. Scott .... **Glen Mills, PA**
Watson, J. Tom .... **Atlanta, GA**
Watson, J. Warren .... Pittsburgh, PA
Watson, J. William, Jr. .... **Halifax, VA**
Watson, Jack C. .... New Orleans, LA
Watson, Jack H., Jr. .... **Washington, DC**
Watson, Jack L. .... **Chicago, IL**
Watson, Jacqueline J. .... Houston, TX
Watson, James A. .... **Lake Charles, LA**
Watson, James A., II .... **Fairfax, VA**
Watson, James B. .... **Los Angeles, CA**
Watson, James B. .... Leakesville, MS
Watson, James Bruce .... Little Rock, AR
Watson, James F. .... Elizabeth, NJ
Watson, James F. .... Athens, TN
Watson, James Frederick .... **Lynchburg, VA**
Watson, James H. .... **Atlanta, GA**
Watson, James H. .... **Greenville, SC**
Watson, James J. .... New York, NY
Watson, James L. .... Tampa, FL
Watson, James L. .... New York, NY
Watson, James M. .... **Edwardsville, IL**
Watson, James N., Jr. .... Tallahassee, FL
Watson, James P. .... **San Francisco, CA**
Watson, James R. .... Greenbelt, MD
Watson, James R. .... Mineola, NY
Watson, James R. .... Kent, OH
Watson, James R. .... **Charleston, WV**
Watson, James R., Jr. .... **Houston, TX**
Watson, James S. .... Owensboro, KY
Watson, James Scott
Federal Deposit Insurance Corporation, Appellate Litigation Section, GV
Watson, James W., (P.C.) .... **Fort Worth, TX**
Watson, Janet L. .... Wheaton, IL
Watson, Janet M. .... Seattle, WA
Watson, Jason H. .... **Atlanta, GA**
Watson, Jason L. .... **Fayetteville, AR**
Watson, Jay Don .... **Bryan, TX**
Watson, Jean M. Otey
Equal Employment Opportunity Commission, Office of the General Counsel, GV
Watson, Jean S. .... Lakewood, CO
Watson, Jeffrey A. .... Washington, PA
Watson, Jeffrey H. .... Springdale, AR
Watson, Jeffrey L. .... **Minneapolis, MN**
Watson, Jeffrey P. .... **Jacksonville, FL**
Watson, Jennifer M. .... **Orange, CA**
Watson & Jernigan, P.A. .... **Jackson, MS**
Watson, Jerome R. .... **Detroit, MI**
Watson, Jerry L. .... Bloomfield Hills, MI
Watson, Jerry W. .... **Austin, TX**
Watson, Jessica A. .... San Diego, CA
Watson, Jeter M. .... **Richmond, VA**
Watson, Jim A. .... **Dallas, TX**
Watson Jimmerson, P.C. .... **Decatur, AL**
Huntsville, AL
Watson, Joanne C. .... **Garden City, NY**
Watson, Joe F. .... Tipton, IN
Watson, Joel C. .... Alabaster, AL
Watson, John A. .... Fort Lauderdale, FL
Watson, John A. .... **Houston, TX**
Watson, John B. .... Irving, TX
Watson, John D., III .... **Birmingham, AL**
Watson, John D., Jr. .... **Washington, DC**
Watson, John Dewey, (P.A.)
Little Rock, AR
Watson, John E. .... Los Angeles, CA
Watson, John F. .... **Mattoon, IL**
Watson, John F. .... Memphis, TN
Watson, John H. .... Batesville, IN
Watson, John H. (Chuck) .... Marietta, GA
Watson, John H., Jr. .... East Orange, NJ
Watson, John J. .... Sunman, IN
Watson, John James .... **Seattle, WA**
Watson, John K., Jr. .... St. Bonaventure, NY
Watson, John L. .... Cincinnati, OH
Watson, John L., Jr. .... Jonesboro, GA
Watson, John Leonard .... **Denver, CO**
Watson, John M. .... Santa Ana, CA
Watson, John M. .... Langley, WA
Watson, John S. .... **Minneapolis, MN**
Watson, John S. .... **Houston, TX**
Watson, John W. .... Hartford, CT
Watson, John W., III .... Daytona Beach, FL
Watson, John W., III .... Miami, FL
Watson, John W., III .... **Chicago, IL**
Watson, John W., Jr. .... **Oxford, NC**
Watson, Joseph .... Tucson, AZ
Watson, Joseph Guild .... Oregon City, OR
Watson, Joseph Jerrold .... Greenville, SC
Watson, Joseph L. .... **Buffalo, NY**
Watson, Joy M. .... Mineola, NY
Watson, Julie B. .... Tacoma, WA
Watson, Julie M. .... **Wilson, NC**
Watson, Julie R. .... Encino, CA
Watson, Julie Williams .... Chattanooga, TN
Watson, K. Bert .... Amarillo, TX
Watson, Kari Lee .... Southfield, MI
Watson, Kathleen .... New York, NY
Watson, Kathryn D. .... **Dallas, TX**
Watson, Kathryn E. .... Atlanta, GA
Watson, Katie .... **Chicago, IL**
Watson, Keith .... Ponte Vedra Beach, FL
Watson, Keith H. .... Los Angeles, CA
Watson, Keith S. .... **Washington, DC**
Watson, Kelly F. .... **Sacramento, CA**
Watson, Kelly G. .... **Las Vegas, NV**
Reno, NV
Watson, Kenneth A. .... **Mobile, AL**
Watson, Kenneth C. .... Oklahoma City, OK
Watson, Kenton J. .... Henderson, KY
Watson, Kevin B. .... **Harrisburg, PA**
King Of Prussia, PA
Watson, Khachadourian, Re & Iams, LLP
Sacramento, CA
Watson, Kimberly A. .... **Seattle, WA**
Watson, Kimberly B. .... **Knoxville, TN**
Watson, Kira P. .... **New York, NY**
Watson, Kirk P. .... **Austin, TX**
Watson, Kirstin M. .... **Los Angeles, CA**
Watson, Kristie L. .... Louisville, KY
Watson, Kyle C. .... **San Antonio, TX**
Watson, L. Allison .... Englewood, CO
Watson, L. Andrew .... Atlanta, GA
Watson, L. Chandler, Jr. .... Anniston, AL
Watson, Lane T. .... **Hartford, CT**
Watson, Larry B. .... Clarksville, TN
Watson, Laurence M. .... Santa Ana, CA
Watson Law Firm .... **Houston, TX**
Watson Law Office .... Minneapolis, MN
Watson Law Office .... Rapid City, SD
Watson Law Offices .... **Boston, MA**
Watson, Lawrence F.
National Aeronautics And Space Administration, Goddard Space Flight Center, GV
Watson, Lawrence M., Jr.
Daytona Beach, FL
Maitland, FL
Watson, Lawrence R. .... **Sacramento, CA**
Watson, Lawrence R. .... **Tulsa, OK**
Watson and Leatherbury .... Indianapolis, IN
Salem, IN
Watson, Lee Ann .... Department of Justice, Office of Professional Responsibility, GV
Watson, Lee R. .... Fort Smith, AR
Watson, Leila Hirayama .... **Birmingham, AL**
Watson, Leland S. .... Minneapolis, MN
Watson, Leo A., Jr. .... Walters, OK
Watson, Leslie R. .... **Virginia Beach, VA**
Watson, Leticia Maria .... Silver Spring, MD
Watson, Lex A., II .... **Atlanta, GA**
Watson, Linda M. .... **Detroit, MI**
Watson, Lisa Carol .... Madisonville, KY
Watson, Lisa M. .... Minneapolis, MN
Watson, Lois .... **Luling, TX**
Watson, Loren A. .... Wichita, KS
Watson, Lori A. .... **Dallas, TX**
Watson, Lori H. .... **Boston, MA**
Watson, Louis H. .... **Jackson, MS**
Watson, Louis H., Jr. .... **Jackson, MS**
Watson, Louis S., Jr. .... Raleigh, NC
Watson, Loyall G. .... Port Huron, MI
Watson, Lynn M. .... **Louisville, KY**
Watson, Lyons & Bosen, P.A.
Portsmouth, NH
Watson, M. Bradley .... **Prairie Village, KS**
Watson, M. Kirby .... **St. Petersburg, FL**
Watson, M. Susan .... **Santa Ana, CA**
Watson, Maelissa .... Dallas, TX
Watson, Marc M. .... Miami, FL
Watson, Margaret Easton .... **Boston, MA**
Watson, Margaret L. .... **New York, NY**
Watson, Marilou E. .... **Philadelphia, PA**
Watson, Marilyn Wynne .... Omaha, NE
Watson, Marjorie H.
National Labor Relations Board, Office of the General Counsel, GV
Watson, Mark .... Burlingame, CA
Watson, Mark A. .... **Alexandria, LA**
Watson, Mark A. .... Zanesville, OH
Watson, Mark D. .... **Yakima, WA**
Watson, Mark E., III .... San Antonio, TX
Watson, Mark H. .... Haddon Heights, NJ
Watson, Mark L. .... **Sunnyvale, CA**
Watson, Mark L. .... **Dallas, TX**
Watson, Mark P. .... San Jose, CA
Watson, Mark Shand .... **Macon, GA**
Watson & Marshall L.C. .... Olathe, KS
Kansas City, MO
Watson, Marvin H., Jr. .... Anniston, AL
Watson, Marvin R. .... Greenwood, SC
Watson, Mary A. .... **Orange, CA**
Watson, Mary Elizabeth .... Boise, ID
Watson, Mary P. .... **New York, NY**
Watson, Mary R. .... **Minneapolis, MN**
Watson, Matthew E. .... **Las Vegas, NV**
Watson, Matthew S. .... **Washington, DC**
Watson, Maurice A. .... **Kansas City, MO**
Watson, Maurice T. .... **San Diego, CA**
Watson, Maxey G. .... Orangeburg, SC
Watson, Melville E. .... Greenfield, IN
Watson, Michael A. .... **Dallas, TX**
Watson, Michael B. .... Abilene, TX
Watson, Michael H. .... Columbus, OH
Watson, Michael K. .... **Atlanta, GA**
Watson, Michael T. .... **Fort Worth, TX**
Watson, Michael Troy .... Cleveland, OH
Watson, Micheal D. .... **Atlanta, GA**
Watson, Millicent McClure .... Madill, OK
Watson, M. Kirby, P.A.
St. Petersburg, FL
Watson, Mundorff & Brooks
Connellsville, PA
Watson and Murphy .... Eldorado, IL
Watson, Murray, Jr. .... Waco, TX
Watson, Myron Parnell .... Cleveland, OH
Watson, Nancy Belcher .... Rancho Mirage, CA
Watson, Nancy E. .... Santa Rosa, CA
Watson, Nancy M. .... Fremont, CA
Watson & Nelson, P.C. .... **Boydton, VA**
Clarksville, VA
Halifax, VA
Watson, Neva R.
United States Postal Service, Law Department, GV
Watson, P. Kimberly .... Dayton, OH
Watson & Parker, A Professional Corporation .... **Fort Worth, TX**
Watson, Patricia A. Ward .... Gloucester, MA
Watson, Patricia L. .... Denver, CO
Watson, Patricia M. .... Newburyport, MA
Watson, Patricia M. .... **Providence, RI**
Watson, Patricia Taylor .... Emporia, VA
Watson, Paul B. .... North Windham, ME
Watson, Paul D. .... **Tampa, FL**
Watson, Paul E. .... Bartow, FL
Watson, Paul G., IV .... **Richmond, VA**
Watson, Paul L. .... St. Louis, MO
Watson, Paula R. .... **Portland, ME**
Watson, Percy W. .... Hattiesburg, MS
Watson, Peter .... **Denver, CO**
Watson, Peter H. .... Minneapolis, MN
Watson, Peter S. .... **Washington, DC**
Watson, Phil .... **Des Moines, IA**
Watson, Phil, P.C. .... **Des Moines, IA**
Watson, Philip B., Jr. .... St. Joseph, LA
Watson, Philip B., Jr. .... Whispering Pines, NC
Watson, Philip G. .... **Eureka, CA**
Watson, R. Scott .... Joplin, MO
Watson, Raymond J., Jr. .... Springfield, IL
Watson, Rebecca W. .... **Helena, MT**
Watson, Reelia R. .... Abingdon, VA
Watson, Regina .... **Springfield, OH**
Watson & Renner .... **Washington, DC**
Watson, Rexford S. .... Madison, WI
Watson, Rhonda J. .... Englewood, CO
Watson, Richard .... Tallahassee, FL
Watson, Richard A. .... **New York, NY**
Watson, Richard B. .... **Charleston, SC**
Watson, Richard C. .... Jacksonville, FL
Watson, Richard J. .... St. Louis, MO
Watson, Richard M. .... **Atlanta, GA**
Watson, Richard N. .... **Durham, NC**
Watson, Richard O. .... St. Augustine, FL
Watson, Richard P. .... Indianapolis, IN
Salem, IN
Watson, Richard T. .... **Cleveland, OH**
Watson, Richd. T. .... Natchez, MS
Watson, Rob, Jr. .... **Fort Worth, TX**
Watson, Robert A. .... Providence, RI
Watson, Robert A. .... **Fort Worth, TX**
Watson, Robert A. .... **Waco, TX**
Watson, Robert C.
Department of Commerce, Patent and Trademark Office, GV
Watson, Robert C. .... Nashville, TN
Watson, Robert C. .... Fairfax, VA
Watson, Robert E. .... **Colorado Springs, CO**
Watson, Robert E. .... **Oakland, MD**
Watson, Robert E. .... Moncks Corner, SC
Watson, Robert F. .... **Fort Worth, TX**
Watson, Robert F. .... Mineral Wells, TX
Watson, Robert Harmon, Jr.
Knoxville, TN
Watson, Robert J. .... Overland Park, KS
Watson, Robert J., Jr. .... **Orlando, FL**
Watson, Robert J., (P.A.) .... **Stuart, FL**
Watson, Robert L. .... Brighton, IL
Bunker Hill, IL
Watson, Robert L., Jr. .... Phoenix, AZ
Watson, Robert R. .... **Chicago, IL**
Watson, Robert R. .... Beaver, PA
Watson, Robert T. .... **Louisville, KY**
Watson, Robert Terence .... Columbus, OH
Watson, Robert W., Jr. .... **Charlotte, NC**

Watson, Roberta Casper ... Tampa, FL
Watson, Roger ... Naples, FL
Watson, Roland, (P.A.) ... Coeur d'Alene, ID
Watson, Rom P. ... Boston, MA
Watson, Romulus S. ... Charlotte, NC
Watson, Ronald A. ... Novi, MI
Watson, Ronald A. ... Portland, OR
Watson, Ronald D. ... Wichita, KS
Watson, Ronald H. ... Eustis, FL
Watson, Ronald L. ... Harrisburg, PA
Watson, Roy J., Jr. ... Boston, MA
Watson, Roy R. ... West Palm Beach, FL
Watson, Russell J. ... Bay Minette, AL
Watson, S. Derrin ... Goleta, CA
Watson, S. A. "Bud", Jr. ... Huntsville, AL
Watson, Sanford E., II ... Cleveland, OH
Watson, Sara Beth ... Washington, DC
Watson, Sarah ... New York, NY
Watson, Scott C. ... Woodbury, NY
Watson, Scott M. ... Cleveland, OH
Watson, Scribner & Burrows ... Provo, UT
Watson, Seth W., Jr. ... Media, PA
Watson, Sharon R. ... Minneapolis, MN
Watson, Sheri L. ... Dallas, TX
Watson, Sidney D., (Mrs.) ... Macon, GA
Watson, Slade, Law Offices of ... Mobile, AL
Watson, Soileau, DeLeo, Burgett & Pickles, P.A. ... Cocoa, FL
Watson, Solomon B., IV ... New York, NY
Watson & Speight, P.A. ... Red Wing, MN
Watson, Spence, Lowe and Chambless, L.L.P. ... Albany, GA
Watson & Spradling ... Anniston, AL
Watson, Stacy Lynn ... Jacksonville, FL
Watson, Stanley B. ... Oakland, CA
Watson, Stanley R. ... Quanah, TX
Watson, Stanley R., P.C. ... Quanah, TX
Watson, Stephen A. ... Los Angeles, CA
Watson, Stephen C. ... Lakeland, FL
Watson, Stephen C. ... Seattle, WA
Watson, Stephen D. ... Doylestown, PA
Watson, Stephen G. ... Eureka, CA
Watson, Stephen K. ... Greenwood, IN
Watson, Stephen L. ... Jacksonville, FL
Watson, Stephen M. ... New York, NY
Watson, Stephen M. ... Richmond, VA
Watson & Stephenson ... Covington, VA
Watson, Steve O. ... Seymour, TN
Watson, Steven H. ... Pago Pago, TT
Watson, Steven J. ... Elkhorn, WI
Watson, Steven J., Law Office
Elkhorn, WI
Watson, Steven M., (P.C.) ... Omaha, NE
Watson, Stevens, Fiorilla & Rutter, LLP
New Brunswick, NJ
New York, NY
Watson, Stuart ... Richardson, TX
Watson, Sue A. ... Columbus, OH
Watson, Susan A. ... San Francisco, CA
Watson, Susan B. ... Treasury Department, Internal Revenue Service, GV
Watson, Susan V. ... Washington, DC
Watson, T. Jeremy ... Dallas, TX
Watson, Terence D. ... New York, NY
Watson, Tharesa C. ... Severna Park, MD
Watson, Theresa L. ... Washington, DC
Watson, Thomas ... Alexandria, VA
Watson, Thomas Bernard
Los Angeles, CA
Watson, Thomas C. ... Washington, DC
Watson, Thomas E. ... Philadelphia, PA
Watson, Thomas J. ... Kearney, NE
Watson, Thomas L. ... New Orleans, LA
Watson, Thomas R. ... Topsham, ME
Watson, Thomas R. ... Portsmouth, NH
Watson, Thomas Todd ... Visalia, CA
Watson, Thomas W. ... Angleton, TX
Watson, Thos. S. ... Cleveland, OH
Watson, Timothy F., Sr. ... Newport, AR
Watson, Timothy J. ... Phoenix, AZ
Watson, Timothy J. ... Los Angeles, CA
Watson, Timothy M. ... Houston, TX
Watson, Todd M. ... Plano, TX
Watson, Todd W. ... Orlando, FL
Watson, Tony J. ... Bartlesville, OK
Watson, Tracy J. ... Los Angeles, CA
Watson, Tricia A. ... Philadelphia, PA
Watson, Victor M. ... Cocoa, FL
Watson, Victoria ... Kettering, OH
Watson, Virginia ... Tampa, FL
Watson, Virginia Dale ... Dallas, TX
Watson, W. Bruce ... Eureka, CA
Watson, W. Clark ... Birmingham, AL
Watson, W. G., Jr., Law Firm of
Arcata, CA
Eureka, CA
Watson, Wade H., III ... Atlanta, GA
Watson, Wade T. ... Bluefield, WV
Watson & Watson ... St. Joseph, LA
Cleveland, OH
Watson & Watson ... Drumright, OK
Watson & Watson Attorneys, P.A.
Orlando, FL
Watson & Watson, L.L.P. ... Luling, TX
Watson & Watson, P.C. ... Newburyport, MA
Watson, Wayne ... Anchorage, AK
Watson, Wayne B. ... Provo, UT
Watson, Wayne C. ... Fort Worth, TX
Watson, Welcom H., Jr.
Fort Lauderdale, FL
Watson, Welcom H., Sr.
Fort Lauderdale, FL
Watson, Wells T. ... Lake Charles, LA
Watson, Wesley, Jr. ... Seattle, WA
Watson, William A. ... Middlesboro, KY
Watson, William A., P.S.C.
Middlesboro, KY
Watson, William B., III ... Gainesville, FL
Watson, William Brooks ... Monroe, LA
Watson, William D. ... Los Angeles, CA
Watson, William D. ... Pleasant Ridge, MI
Watson, William E. ... Campbell, CA
Watson, William E., & Associates
Follansbee, WV
Watson, William E., & Associates
Wellsburg, WV
Watson, William E., Jr. ... Luling, TX
Watson, William G. ... Fullerton, CA
Watson, William H. ... Greenville, NC
Watson, William J. ... Ortonville, MN
Watson, William Joseph ... Lockport, NY
Watson, William L. ... West Palm Beach, FL
Watson, William M., Jr. ... Columbia, SC
Watson, William R. ... White Plains, NY
Watson, William R. ... Norman, OK
Watson, William T. ... Tuscaloosa, AL
Watson, William T. ... Huntington, WV
Watson, William W. ... Villa Park, CA
Watson, William W. ... St. Joseph, LA
Watson, W. N. (Rocky) ... Fort Payne, AL
Watson, Zane D. ... Kaneohe, HI
Watson-Wesley, Denise J. ... St. Louis, MO
Watstein, Herbert ... Bristol, CT
Cheshire, CT
Watstein, Julius ... Bristol, CT
Cheshire, CT
Watstein, Raymond B. ... Boston, MA
Watstein & Watstein, P.C. ... Bristol, CT
Cheshire, CT
Watt, Bevan M. ... New Brunswick, NJ
New York, NY
Watt, Bryan S. ... Tulsa, OK
Watt, Cameron D. ... San Jose, CA
Watt, Carrie E. ... Philadelphia, PA
Watt, Castro & Houser, P.C. ... Austin, TX
Watt, Charles H., III ... Thomasville, GA
Watt, Clarence L. ... Winfield, WV
Watt, David C. ... Costa Mesa, CA
Watt, David W., Jr. ... Murphysboro, IL
Watt, Dennis R. ... Albany, CA
Watt, Donald I. ... Portland, OR
Watt, E. Blake ... Nashville, TN
Watt, Edward P. ... Austin, TX
Watt, Evette Loper ... Akron, OH
Watt, Flint C., III ... Lansing, MI
Watt, Garland W. ... Chicago, IL
Watt, Gary Alan ... San Leandro, CA
Watt, Howard D. ... Tucson, AZ
Watt, Howard E. ... Denton, TX
Watt, J. Alexander ... Barnstable, MA
Watt, James D., Jr. ... Pottsville, PA
Watt, James G. ... Allentown, PA
Watt, Jim ... West Palm Beach, FL
Watt, John ... Wamego, KS
Watt, John H., Jr. ... Rochester, NY
Watt, Joseph A. ... San Rafael, CA
Watt, Joseph C., Jr. ... Syracuse, NY
Watt, Joseph M. ... Oklahoma City, OK
Watt, Kenneth Benjamin ... Tulsa, OK
Watt, Kristin L. ... Columbus, OH
Watt, Kymberly J. ... Tulsa, OK
Watt, Lana C. ... Los Altos, CA
Watt, Lucile ... Los Angeles, CA
Watt, Margaret A. ... Milwaukee, WI
Watt, Margot L. ... Buffalo, NY
Watt, Mark Joseph ... Laramie, WY
Watt, Melvin L. ... Charlotte, NC
Watt, Patrick R. ... Great Falls, MT
Watt, Paul H. ... Olympia, WA
Watt, Ralph H. ... Royal Oak, MI
Watt, Richard D. ... Houston, TX
Watt, Richard F. ... Chicago, IL
Watt, Richard S. ... Lansdale, PA
Watt, Robert D. ... Providence, RI
Watt, Robert G. ... McLean, VA
Watt, Robert L., III ... Reidsville, NC
Watt, Robert M., III ... Lexington, KY
Watt & Sawyier ... Chicago, IL
Watt, Sharon A. ... Ojai, CA
Watt, Stephen C. ... Ionia, MI
Watt, Stuart L. ... Thousand Oaks, CA
Watt, Susan Lynn ... Norfolk, VA
Watt, Terry L. ... Tulsa, OK
Watt, Theodore M. ... Paso Robles, CA
Watt, Thomas J. ... Vista, CA
Watt, Tieder, Hoffar & Fitzgerald, L.L.P.
Irvine, CA
Washington, DC
Fairfax, VA
McLean, VA
Watt, Timothy A. ... San Antonio, TX
Watt, Tobin N. ... Atlanta, GA
Watt, W. Lee ... Biloxi, MS
Pascagoula, MS
Watt, William A. ... Ormond Beach, FL
Watt, William C. ... Missoula, MT
Watt, William W. ... Little Rock, AR
Wattel, David E. ... Mesa, AZ
Watten, Discoe & Bassett ... Santa Ana, CA
Watten, Steven P. ... Dallas, TX
Watten, Wayne W. ... Santa Ana, CA
Wattenbarger, Sherri ... Department of Justice, Civil Division, GV
Wattenberg, Carl A., Jr. ... St. Louis, MO
Wattenberg, Mark H. ... Bath, NY
Wattendorf, George E. ... Dover, NH
Wattengel, Jerald A. ... Niagara Falls, NY
Wattenmaker, Glenn D. ... Philadelphia, PA
Watter, Paul N. ... Lawrenceville, NJ
Watters, Adam W ... Tucson, AZ
Watters, Caitlin Cass ... Los Angeles, CA
Watters, Catherine Neale ... Sarasota, FL
Watters, Connell J. ... Weehawken, NJ
Watters, D. J. ... Detroit, MI
Watters, Donna T. ... Dallas, TX
Watters, Edward M., III ... Berwyn, PA
Watters, Elizabeth Jean ... Columbus, OH
Watters, F. Elaine Malisch ... Santa Rosa, CA
Watters, Jacqueline A. ... Merrick, NY
Watters, Joan A. ... Visalia, CA
Watters, Keith W. ... Washington, DC
Watters, Kyle B. ... Bronx, NY
Watters, Mark M. ... Columbus, OH
Watters, Michael G. ... Santa Rosa, CA
Watters, Michael R. ... Indianapolis, IN
Watters, Richard C. ... Fresno, CA
Watters, Richard D. ... St. Louis, MO
Watters, Richard L. ... Mobile, AL
Watters, Robert L. ... Houston, TX
Watters, Russell F. ... St. Louis, MO
Watters, Sherry ... New Orleans, LA
Watters, Stephen P. ... Minneapolis, MN
Watters, Susan P. ... Billings, MT
Watters, Thomas L. ... Los Angeles, CA
Watters, Vernon C. ... San Francisco, CA
Watters, W. Robinson ... Columbus, OH
Watters, Walker L. ... Jackson, MS
Watters, William C. ... Las Vegas, NV
Watterson, Alfred V., Jr. ... Pittsburgh, PA
Watterson, Alfred V., Sr. ... Pittsburgh, PA
Watterson, Hyland & Klett, P.A.
Palm Beach Gardens, FL
Watterson, James G. ... Cleveland, OH
Watterson, James S. ... Lakewood, CO
Watterson, Kim M. ... Pittsburgh, PA
Watterson, Margaret
Department Of Health And Human Services, Social Security Administration, GV
Watterson, Paul N., Jr. ... New York, NY
Watterson & Singer, Attorneys at Law, P.C.
Birmingham, AL
Watterson, Susan J. ... Birmingham, AL
Watterson, Terence J.
Palm Beach Gardens, FL
Watterson, Wayt T. (Tim) ... Seattle, WA
Watterworth, Gayle M. ... Avon, CT
Watterworth, Larry Gene ... Lansing, MI
Wattier, Jerry L. ... Pierre, SD
Wattigny, Dean M. ... New Iberia, LA
Wattigny, Gerard B. ... New Iberia, LA
Wattigny, James ... Lafayette, LA
Wattles, Frank ... Manhattan Beach, CA
Wattles, Joshua S. ... Los Angeles, CA
Wattles, Kevin S. ... Los Angeles, CA
Wattles, Robert C. ... Orlando, FL
Wattleworth, C. Andrew
Winston-Salem, NC
Wattley, Mark A. ... Deerfield, IL
Wattman, Malcolm P. ... New York, NY
Watt-Morse, Peter M. ... Pittsburgh, PA
Watts, Alan R. ... Anaheim, CA
Watts, Alfred Delonzo ... White Plains, NY
Watts, Alice Apps ... Little Rock, AR
Watts, Andrew W. ... Cleveland, OH
Watts, Barbara G. ... Cincinnati, OH
Watts, Barton D. ... Stockbridge, GA
Watts & Benham, P.C.
Charlotte Amalie, St. Thomas, VI
Watts, Benjamin H. ... Champaign, IL
Watts, Bernard G. ... Louisville, KY
Watts, Beverley Q. ... Oklahoma City, OK
Watts, Bradford K. ... Boston, MA
Watts, Bradley D. ... Lafayette, LA
Watts, C. Allen ... Daytona Beach, FL
Watts, C. Gregory ... Flemington, NJ
Watts, C. William ... Medford, NJ
Watts, Caroline ... Madison, VA
Watts, Charles D., Jr. ... Durham, NC
Watts, Charles E. ... Bellevue, WA
Watts, Charles Gordon ... El Paso, TX
Watts, Charles J. ... Oklahoma City, OK
Watts, Charles K. ... Baton Rouge, LA
Watts, Charles R. ... Washington, DC
Watts, Charles T. ... Latham, NY
Watts, Clark ... Austin, TX
Watts, Cynthia A. ... Glastonbury, CT
Watts, Cynthia G. ... Chatsworth, CA
Watts, Dabney W. ... Winchester, VA
Watts, Dale J. ... West Bloomfield, MI
Watts, Dana J. ... Sarasota, FL
Watts, Daniel Gerard ... Chicago, IL
Watts, Daron ... Los Angeles, CA
Watts, Darren B. ... Chicago, IL
Watts, David ... Burlington, VT
Watts, David A.
Department Of The Interior, Office of the Solicitor, GV
Watts, David D. ... Los Angeles, CA
Watts, David E. ... New York, NY
Watts, David J. ... Detroit, MI
Watts, David M., Jr. ... Harrisburg, PA
Watts, Dey W. ... Glencoe, IL
Watts, Douglas E. ... Oakland, CA
Watts, Dwayne A. ... Vallejo, CA
Watts, Edward E., III ... Boston, MA
Watts, Elisabeth ... Phoenix, AZ
Watts, Elizabeth H. ... Columbus, OH
Watts, Fern S. ... Miami, FL
Watts, Frederick G.
Charlotte Amalie, St. Thomas, VI
Watts, Gary E. ... Beloit, WI
Watts, George E. ... Fitchburg, MA
Watts, George R. ... Greensburg, IN
Watts, Grant E. ... Anchorage, AK
Watts, Gregory Dean ... San Augustine, TX
Watts, Gregory Lewis ... Palo Alto, CA
Watts, Gregory Stanton ... Brooklyn, NY
Watts, Guy L. ... Corpus Christi, TX
Watts, Harry T. ... Des Moines, IA
Watts, H. B. "Scott" ... Fayetteville, GA
Jonesboro, GA
Watts, Heather Land ... San Augustine, TX
Watts & Hendrickson, P.C. ... Aurora, CO
Watts, Hoffmann, Fisher & Heinke Co., L.P.A. ... Cleveland, OH
Watts, Jackson W. ... Versailles, KY
Watts, James F., (A Law Corp.)
San Diego, CA
Watts, James H., III ... Reading, MA
Watts, James I. ... Salt Lake City, UT
Watts, James O., III ... Atlanta, GA
Watts, James O., IV ... Lynchburg, VA
Watts, James P. ... Minneapolis, MN
Watts, James R. ... Portland, OR
Watts, James W. ... Detroit, MI
Watts, Janet G. ... Fayetteville, GA
Jonesboro, GA
Watts, Janis Ernst ... Nashville, TN
Watts, Jas. R. ... Brandenburg, KY
Watts, Jay M. ... Decatur, IL
Watts, J. D. ... Milwaukee, WI
Watts, Jeffrey D. ... Honolulu, HI
Watts, Jerald L. ... Columbus, GA
Watts, JoEllen J. ... Des Moines, IA
Watts, John A. ... Allegan, MI
Watts, John A., P.C. ... Allegan, MI
Hastings, MI
Paw Paw, MI
Watts, John Charles, Jr. ... Savannah, GA
Watts, John D. ... Essex, CT
Watts, John D., III ... Greenville, SC
Watts, John Griffin ... Birmingham, AL
Watts, John L. ... Norfolk, VA
Watts, John S. ... Portland, OR
Watts, John S., III ... Duluth, GA
Watts, John W. ... Department of Justice, Environment and Natural Resources Division, GV
Watts, Karen S. ... Belgrade, MT
Watts, Kathleen C. ... Oak Brook, IL
Watts, Keith A. ... Atlanta, GA
Watts, Kellie J. ... Gahanna, OH
Watts, Kenneth K. ... Spokane, WA
Watts, Kenneth K., P.S. ... Spokane, WA
Watts, Laura E. ... San Francisco, CA
Watts, Lucile ... Detroit, MI
Watts, Lynda Cleek ... St. Louis, MO
Watts, Lynn A. ... Spokane, WA
Watts, M. Williamson ... Madison, VA
Watts, Marcus A. ... Houston, TX
Watts, Marianne R.
Federal Trade Commission, Office of the General Counsel, GV
Watts, Mark A. ... Daytona Beach, FL
Watts, Mark H. ... Pascagoula, MS
Watts, Mary Hamilton ... Indianapolis, IN
Watts, Mary S. ... Naperville, IL
Watts, Meredith J. ... San Francisco, CA
Watts, Michael N. ... Oxford, MS
Watts, Mikal C. ... Corpus Christi, TX
Watts, Ngozi A. ... North Chicago, IL
Watts, Oscar F., Jr. ... Jackson, GA
Watts, Pamela B. ... Redwood City, CA
Watts, Pat H., Jr. ... Pascagoula, MS
Watts, Patrick ... Schaumburg, IL
Watts, Patrick Robert ... Summerville, SC
Watts, Paul J. ... Spencer, IN
Watts, Peggy C. ... Charlotte, NC
Watts and Pepicelli, P.C. ... Meadville, PA
Watts, Philip O. ... Oklahoma City, OK
Watts, Phillip M. ... Santa Cruz, CA
Watts, PrincinaStone ... Bronx, NY
Watts, Prosser M., Jr. ... Adrian, MI
Watts, R. Gregory ... Mobile, AL
Watts, Randolph Harrison
Alexandria, VA
Watts, Raymond D. ... Washington, DC
Watts, Raymond E., Jr. ... Orlando, FL
Watts, Raymond N. ... Sandusky, OH
Watts, Rebecca K. ... Hillsborough, NC
Watts, Richard A. ... Atlanta, GA
Watts, Richard C. ... Santa Ana, CA
Watts, Richard K. ... Osceola, NE
Watts, Richard N. ... Little Rock, AR
Watts, Richard N. ... St. Petersburg, FL
Watts, Richard S. ... Humble, TX
Watts, Richard W. ... Franklinton, LA
Watts, Richard W., A Professional Law Corporation ... Franklinton, LA
Watts, R. J., II ... Dallas, TX
Watts, Robert B. ... Baltimore, MD
Watts, Robert C. ... Houston, TX
Watts, Robert C., Jr. ... Richmond, VA
Watts, Robin Denise ... Champaign, IL
Watts, Rodney ... Southfield, MI
Watts, Rodney, P.C. ... Southfield, MI
Watts, Roger H. ... Stamford, CT
Watts, Ronald E. ... Los Angeles, CA
Watts, Ronald J. ... Oakland, CA
Watts, Rosalyn A. ... Little Rock, AR
Watts, Roscoe E. ... Portland, OR
Watts, Ryan James ... Exton, PA
Watts, Sally Warner
Department of Housing and Urban Development, Office of General Counsel, GV
Watts, Sandra L., & Associates, P.C.
Corpus Christi, TX
Watts, Sandra Lee ... Corpus Christi, TX
Watts, Sandra S. ... Overland Park, KS
Kansas City, MO
Watts, Shannon & Mitts ... Meridian, MS
Watts, Sheri M. ... Los Angeles, CA
Watts, Stanley R. ... Phoenix, AZ
Watts, Stephen G., (P.A.) ... Clearwater, FL
Watts, Stephen H., II ... Richmond, VA
Watts, Steven A. ... New Orleans, LA
Watts, Steven R. ... Galesburg, IL
Watts, Steven R. ... Dayton, OH
Watts, Susan Anderson ... Lexington, MA
Watts, Susan E. ... Portland, OR

Watts, T. Kenneth ... Meridian, MS
Watts, Talmage M. ... New Orleans, LA
Nashville, TN
Watts, Theodore H. ... **Meadville, PA**
Watts, Thomas E., Jr. ... Nashville, TN
Watts, Thomas H. ... Baton Rouge, LA
Watts, Thomas Larry ... **Los Angeles, CA**
Watts, Thomas T. ... Honolulu, HI
Watts, Valeria W. ... Dalton, GA
Watts, Vicki Ballou ... Baltimore, MD
Watts, W. Glenn ... Jackson, MS
Watts, W. Graham ... Greensboro, NC
Watts & Watts ... Fayetteville, GA
Jonesboro, GA
Watts & Watts ... Portland, OR
Watts and Watts ... San Augustine, TX
Watts & Watts ... Madison, VA
Watts & Watts, P.A. ... Oklahoma City, OK
Watts, Wayne ... San Antonio, TX
Watts, Wendy M. ... Lawrenceville, GA
Watts, William A. ... Charlotte, NC
Watts, William D. ... **Oklahoma City, OK**
Watts, William S., Jr. ... Lexington, KY
Watts, William T., Jr. ... **Atlanta, GA**
Watts, William W., III ... **Mobile, AL**
Watts-Bazan, Karin L. ... Riverside, CA
Watts-FitzGerald, Abigail C., (P.A.)
Miami, FL
Watts-Jackson, Genelle R. ... Sparks, MD
Wattson, James A. ... San Francisco, CA
Wattson, Peter S. ... St. Paul, MN
Wattson, Robert M. ... **Minneapolis, MN**
Watts-Wilkie, Mary Elizabeth
Tallahassee, FL
Wattwood, Robert W. ... **Melbourne, FL**
Watwood, Lynn M., Jr. ... Lakewood, CO
Watz, Donna M. ... St. Paul, MN
Watz, James H. ... **Buffalo, NY**
Watz, John P. ... **Lexington, KY**
Watza, Michael J. ... **Detroit, MI**
Watzke, Garry ... Boston, MA
Watzman, Ronald N. ... Pittsburgh, PA
Waud, Charles B. ... San Mateo, CA
Waud, Edward M. ... Petoskey, MI
Waud, Morrison ... Chicago, IL
Waud, Robert M. ... New Berlin, WI
Waudby, Sally Broatch ... **Birmingham, AL**
Waudby, William L. ... **Birmingham, AL**
Waugaman, Edward R., II
Newport News, VA
Waugaman, William J. ... **Troy, MI**
Waugh, Alexander P., Jr. ... Trenton, NJ
Waugh, Alexander P., Sr. ... Chatham, NJ
Waugh, Andrew J. ... **Quincy, MA**
Waugh, Bradley R. ... **Toledo, OH**
Waugh, Bruce B. ... **Kansas City, MO**
Waugh, Chas. M. ... Muskegon Heights, MI
Waugh, Chas. W. ... Eskridge, KS
Waugh, Curtis J. ... **Topeka, KS**
Waugh, Daniel C. ... **Providence, RI**
Waugh, David K., Jr. ... Jefferson City, MO
Waugh, Emily S. ... **Tallahassee, FL**
Waugh, Frederick F. ... Norwalk, OH
Waugh, Gregory L. ... Greenville, IL
Waugh, H. Bernard ... Concord, NH
Waugh, James H. ... Richmond, MI
Waugh, John S. ... Plano, TX
Waugh, R. Hamish ... Riverdale, MD
Waugh, Raymond G., Jr. ... Wilton, CT
Waugh, Richard D. ... Sacramento, CA
Waugh, Richard M. ... Phoenix, AZ
Waugh, Richard M., Ltd. ... Phoenix, AZ
Waugh, Sharon Pearse ... **Kewanee, IL**
Waugh, William K., III
Overland Park, KS
Waugh, William K., Jr. ... Kansas City, MO
Waugh-Farretta, Robin ... **Washington, DC**
Waun, Christine A. ... **Flint, MI**
Waun, Thomas W. ... Grand Blanc, MI
Waupotic, Annmarie ... **New York, NY**
Wauro, Darlene M. ... **Phoenix, AZ**
Wauson & Associates, P.C. ... **Houston, TX**
Wauson, John Wesley ... **Houston, TX**
Wauters, Stephanie Mongiello
Toms River, NJ
Wavers, Nick A. ... Oklahoma City, OK
Wavle, James E., Jr. ... Stockton, NJ
Wavle, Tammy R. ... **Houston, TX**
Wavpotich, Susan Anne ... Somerville, MA
Wavrek, Robert ... Cleveland, OH
Wawra, Steven A. ... Los Angeles, CA
Wawro, David W. R. ... **New York, NY**
Oneonta, NY
Wawro, James ... **Los Angeles, CA**
Wawro, Mark L. D. ... **Houston, TX**
Wawro, Mary F. ... Los Angeles, CA
Wawro, R. William ... Fort Collins, CO
Wawrose, Susan C. ... Dayton, OH
Wawrzyn, Ronald M. ... **Milwaukee, WI**
Wawrzyniak, Jeffery J. ... **Toledo, OH**
Wawrzyniak, Richard E. ... San Bruno, CA
Wawzenski, Linda A. ... Chicago, IL
Wax, Abraham L., (P.C.) ... **New York, NY**
Wax, Alan J. ... **Glendale, CA**
Wax, Albert J. ... Berkeley, CA
Wax, Alvin D. ... Louisville, KY
Wax, Ari N. ... New York, NY
Wax, Barbara R. ... Rockville, MD
Wax, Barry Arlen ... Treasure Island, FL
Wax, Barry M. ... Miami, FL
Wax, Brandt A. ... Camarillo, CA
Wax, Daniel E. ... Los Angeles, CA
Wax, Elliot ... Los Gatos, CA
Wax, Erica Tukel ... White Plains, NY
Wax, Geo. L. ... New Orleans, LA
Wax, Harold W. ... **Glendale, CA**
Wax, Harry ... New Orleans, LA
Wax, Harvey ... Cleveland, OH
Wax, Harvey I. ... **Farmington Hills, MI**
Wax, Howard A. ... **Chicago, IL**
Wax, James A., Jr. ... Memphis, TN
Wax, Jeffrey Scott ... **San Francisco, CA**
Wax, Jonathan I. ... Atlanta, GA
Wax, Marjorie H. ... **Baltimore, MD**
Wax, Michael Kevin ... **San Diego, CA**
Wax, Nancy E. ... Los Angeles, CA
Wax, Randal W. ... **Washington, DC**
Wax, Robert Lawrence ... **Philadelphia, PA**
Wax, Robert P. ... Hartford, CT
Wax, Ronnie D., (Ms.) ... Forest Hills, NY
Wax, Steven H. ... Encino, CA
Wax, Steven T. ... Portland, OR
Wax & Wax ... **Glendale, CA**
Waxberg, Myron D. ... **Carteret, NJ**
Waxberg, Stanley D. ... New York, NY
Waxdeck, Brett R. ... **San Francisco, CA**
Waxenberg, Cathy G. ... New York, NY
Waxenberg, Jay D. ... **New York, NY**
Waxenberg, Michael ... **St. Louis, MO**
Waxenberg, Susan A. ... **New York, NY**
Waxenfeld, Milton ... Hartsdale, NY
Waxler, Andrew J. ... **Los Angeles, CA**
Waxler, Carol S. ... Stuart, FL
Waxler, David H. ... **New Bedford, MA**
Waxler, Jerome ... San Diego, CA
Waxler & Smith, Chartered ... Stuart, FL
Waxman, Alan N. ... **New York, NY**
Waxman, Allen P. ... **Washington, DC**
Waxman, Avrom S. ... East Hampton, NY
Waxman, Barbara Baer ... Baltimore, MD
Waxman, Barry ... Putney, VT
Waxman, Ben ... Delray Beach, FL
Waxman, Benjamin S. ... **Miami, FL**
Waxman, Brent R., Law Offices of
St. Louis, MO
Waxman, Brian K.
Palm Beach Gardens, FL
Waxman, Bruce I. ... Department of Commerce, Office of the General Counsel, GV
Waxman, Carol S. ... Cocoa, FL
Waxman, Christopher J. ... **Philadelphia, PA**
Waxman & Company ... Cleveland, OH
Waxman, Daniel ... Woodbury, NY
Waxman, Daniel Philip ... **New York, NY**
Waxman, David B. ... Cleveland, OH
Waxman, David S. ... **Chicago, IL**
Waxman, Denise C. ... New York, NY
Waxman, Eric G., III ... **Garden City, NY**
Waxman, Eric S. ... **Los Angeles, CA**
Waxman, Fran S. ... New York, NY
Waxman, Gary
Executive Office Of The President, Office of Management and Budget, GV
Waxman, H. Stuart ... Encino, CA
Waxman, Henry A. ... Los Angeles, CA
Waxman, Herbert S. ... Chicago, IL
Waxman, Irving I. ... Albany, NY
Waxman, J. Mark ... **Los Angeles, CA**
Washington, DC
Waxman, Jeffrey J. ... Miami Beach, FL
Waxman, Jerry J. ... Jacksonville, FL
Waxman, Jon M. ... New York, NY
Waxman, Jonathan H. ... Department of Labor, Office of the Solicitor, GV
Waxman, Joseph C. ... San Francisco, CA
Waxman, Joshua B. ... **New York, NY**
Waxman, Judith G.
Department Of Health And Human Services, Public Health Service, GV
Waxman, Lawrence D. ... New York, NY
Waxman, Leigh V. ... New York, NY
Waxman, Lynn G. ... **West Palm Beach, FL**
Waxman, Mark Z. ... New York, NY
Waxman, Marvin ... Flemington, NJ
Waxman, Michael D. ... Philadelphia, PA
Waxman, Michael J. ... Portland, ME
Waxman, Michael P. ... **Milwaukee, WI**
Waxman, Nathan A. ... **New York, NY**
Waxman, Ned W. ... Williamsburg, VA
Waxman, Randi ... Bethesda, MD
Waxman, Richard H. ... **Boca Raton, FL**
New York, NY
Waxman, Richard P. ... **Oakland, CA**
Waxman, Robert I. ... Department of Energy, Office of the General Counsel, GV
Waxman, Robert M. ... **Beverly Hills, CA**
Waxman, Ruth Iles ... Slingerlands, NY
Waxman, Scott E. ... **Wilmington, DE**
Waxman, Seth B. ... **Washington, DC**
Waxman, Seth P. ... Department of Justice, Office of the Solicitor General, GV
Waxman, Sheldon R. ... South Haven, MI
Waxman, Shelley ... Atlantic City, NJ
Waxman & Siemer, P.A. ... Jacksonville, FL
Waxman, Stanley R. ... Mineola, NY
Waxman, Stanley R., P.C. ... Mineola, NY
Waxman, Steven R. ... **Philadelphia, PA**
Waxman, Stuart ... **Fishkill, NY**
Waxman, Tobie B. ... **Los Angeles, CA**
Waxman, Tracie Dudley ... Fresno, CA
Waxman & Waxman, P.C. ... New York, NY
Waxse, David J. ... **Overland Park, KS**
Waxstein, Bernard A., Jr.
Citrus Heights, CA
Waxter, Dixon Gibbs ... Baltimore, MD
Waxter, Ruth Allison ... Frederick, MD
Waxter, Thomas J. S., III ... **Baltimore, MD**
Waxter, Thomas J. S., Jr. ... Baltimore, MD
Way, Barbara E. ... New York, NY
Way & Belasco ... Wildwood, NJ
Way, Brian H. ... **New York, NY**
Way, Charles S., Jr. ... Charleston, SC
Way, Charlotte H. ... **Hawkinsville, GA**
Way, Chas. R. ... San Leandro, CA
Way, Christine ... Stow, MA
Way, Cory T. ... **New York, NY**
Way, Daniel C. ... Cedar Rapids, IA
Way, Donald A. ... **Los Angeles, CA**
Way, Ethan Andrew ... Apalachicola, FL
Way, Field & Bodron ... Vicksburg, MS
Way, Fred D., III ... Brooklyn, NY
Way, G. Larison ... Redwood City, CA
Way, Gary D. ... Beaverton, OR
Way, Geoffrey G. ... Boston, MA
Way, Geoffrey S. ... Sacramento, CA
Way, Griffith ... **Seattle, WA**
Way, Jan A. ... Kansas City, KS
Way, John E., Jr. ... Morehead City, NC
Way, Karen ... **Chicago, IL**
Way, Kevin E. ... **New York, NY**
Way, Mark J. ... Cary, NC
Way, Michael J. ... Detroit, MI
Way, P. Martin, III ... Wildwood, NJ
Way, Palmer M., Jr. ... Wildwood Crest, NJ
Way, Ramsey T., Jr. ... **Hawkinsville, GA**
Way, Richard L. ... Bloomfield Hills, MI
Way, Richard L., P.C. ... Bloomfield Hills, MI
Way, Roger A., Jr. ... **Columbia, SC**
Way, Ronald R. ... Denver, CO
Way, Scott E. ... **New York, NY**
Way, Sherri D. ... **Denver, CO**
Way, Stephen C. ... Olympia, WA
Way & Way, LLP ... **Hawkinsville, GA**
Way, Wendy Alice ... Trenton, NJ
Way, Wren C. ... Vicksburg, MS
Waybourn, Ann M. ... Succasunna, NJ
Wayburn, Robert F. ... **New York, NY**
Waycaster, J. Todd ... **Natchez, MS**
Waycaster, JoAnn Allred ... **Natchez, MS**
Waycaster, Mary Margaret ... **Natchez, MS**
Waycaster, Morris, Johnson & Dean
Dalton, GA
Waycaster, R. Leslie, Jr. ... **Dalton, GA**
Waycaster, Tim ... **Natchez, MS**
Waycaster & Waycaster, L.L.P.
Natchez, MS
Wayda, Andrea L. ... **New York, NY**
Waye, J. Victor ... Gaithersburg, MD
Wayerski, Kip ... Bellingham, WA
Waygood, Charles M. ... St. Petersburg, FL
Wayland, Alan C. ... Grapevine, TX
Wayland, Carole Masters ... Concord, MA
Wayland, Edward W. ... **Newton, MA**
Wayland, Heather L. ... **Beverly Hills, CA**
Wayland, Howard M. ... Houston, TX
Wayland, Joseph F. ... **New York, NY**
Wayland, Land ... Chino, CA
Wayland, R. Eddie ... **San Diego, CA**
Nashville, TN
Wayland, Randall S. ... Cary, NC
Wayland, Steven ... **New York, NY**
Wayland, Susan Martz ... Albuquerque, NM
Wayland, Wendy Diane ... **Santa Ana, CA**
Wayland-Smith, Tina M. ... Oneida, NY
Waylett, Kathleen M. ... Raleigh, NC
Waylonis, Philip L. ... Valhalla, NY
Wayman, David J. ... San Diego, CA
Wayman, Donna L. ... Fairfield, CA
Wayman, Irvin & McAuley ... **Beaver, PA**
Butler, PA
Greensburg, PA
Pittsburgh, PA
Wayman, Jonathan N.
Grosse Pointe Park, MI
Wayman, Kenneth L. ... **Santa Ana, CA**
Wayman, Kevin D. ... St. Louis, MO
Wayman, Merl H. ... Columbus, OH
Wayman, Richard A. ... Minneapolis, MN
Wayman, Sarah Mallas ... Atlanta, GA
Wayman, Sarah Mallas, P.C. ... Atlanta, GA
Wayman, W. Russell ... Louisville, CO
Wayment, Justin W. ... **Cedar City, UT**
Wayne, Abby B. ... **Los Angeles, CA**
Wayne, Alvin ... Bay Shore, NY
Wayne, Arnold ... Northridge, CA
Wayne, Arnold, A P.C. ... Northridge, CA
Wayne, Barry M. ... **Miami, FL**
Wayne, Beth ... **Cincinnati, OH**
Wayne, Charles ... Lake Worth, FL
Wayne, Charles B. ... **Washington, DC**
Wayne, Daniel C. ... Juneau, AK
Wayne, David S. ... **Chicago, IL**
Wayne, Deborah H. ... **Mamaroneck, NY**
Wayne, Desiree Welborn ... Houston, TX
Wayne, Diane ... Los Angeles, CA
Wayne, Douglas ... Doylestown, PA
Wayne, Elisa Levin ... Los Angeles, CA
Wayne, Eric J. ... Los Angeles, CA
Wayne, Gary T. ... Ventura, CA
Wayne, Geoffrey M. ... Miami, FL
Wayne, George C. ... El Paso, TX
Wayne, Hope ... New York, NY
Wayne, Howard J. ... **Boston, MA**
Wayne, Howard W. ... Berkeley, CA
Wayne, Howell ... Westfield, NJ
Wayne, Jennifer M. ... New York, NY
Wayne, Jonathan ... **Newark, NJ**
Wayne, Jonathan ... Albany, NY
Wayne, Judith A. ... Lynn, MA
Wayne, Larry D. ... **Canoga Park, CA**
Wayne, Lawrence ... Schenectady, NY
Wayne & Le Vine ... Chicago, IL
Wayne, Linda A. ... Martinez, CA
Wayne, Lisa Monet ... **Denver, CO**
Wayne, Lisa Rose ... Staten Island, NY
Wayne, M. Howard ... San Diego, CA
Wayne, Matthew D. ... **Chicago, IL**
Wayne, Michael I. ... **Los Angeles, CA**
Wayne, Milton J. ... New York, NY
Wayne, Paul V. ... **Los Angeles, CA**
Wayne, Paula L. ... Youngstown, OH
Wayne, R. Bruce, (A P.C.) ... **San Diego, CA**
Wayne, Richard D. ... **Boston, MA**
Providence, RI
Wayne, Richard, Hurwitz & McAloon
Boston, MA
Providence, RI
Wayne, Richard, (P.C.) ... Boston, MA
Wayne, Richard S. ... **Cincinnati, OH**
Wayne, Robert ... Miami, FL
Wayne, Robert A. ... **Newark, NJ**
Wayne, Robert B. ... **Williamsport, PA**
Wayne, Robert J. ... **Seattle, WA**
Wayne, Robert J., P.S. ... **Seattle, WA**
Wayne, Robert S. ... **Atlanta, GA**
Wayne, Roger L. ... Madera, CA
Wayne, Ronald F. ... **Cleveland, OH**
Wayne, Stewart ... **Dallas, TX**
Wayne, Tamala M. ... Chesapeake, VA
Wayne, Wendy S. ... Cambridge, MA
Wayner, Stephen A. ... Miami, FL
Wayner, William E.
Department of Commerce, Patent and Trademark Office, GV
Wayne-Spindler, Kathryn M. ... Canton, MI
Waynick, David J. ... Nashville, TN
Waynick, Denelle J. ... **Newark, NJ**
Ways, Charles ... Dallas, TX
Ways, Jennifer M. ... **San Francisco, CA**
Waysdorf, Julia A. ... Washington, DC
Waysdorf, Richard H. ... Englewood, CO
Wayser, Joshua D. ... **Santa Monica, CA**
Waysman, Janice ... Pierre, SD
Way-Smith, Linda ... **Washington, DC**
Wayson, Amy M. ... **Portland, OR**
Wayson, Edward O., Jr. ... **Annapolis, MD**
Waystack, Edward W. ... **Boston, MA**
Waystack & King ... Colebrook, NH
Waystack, Paul J. ... Boston, MA
Waystack, Philip R., Jr. ... Colebrook, NH
Wayte, Alan ... **Los Angeles, CA**
Wayte, Lawrence E. ... **Fresno, CA**
Waz, Deidre J. ... **Boston, MA**
Wazeter, Alexander J., Jr. ... Millville, NJ
Wazlawek, Michael A. ... **St. Louis, MO**
Wazzan, Natasha ... Los Angeles, CA
We, Insun ... Baltimore, MD
Weaber, John F. ... Harleysville, PA
Weaber, Kristi R. ... **Amarillo, TX**
Wead, Anderson, Phipps & Aultman
Xenia, OH
Wead, Edward R. ... Bucyrus, OH
Wead, John H. ... Washington C. H., OH
Wead, Richard A. ... Xenia, OH
Wead, Shannon D. ... **Wichita, KS**
Weader, David J. ... **Washington, DC**
Weadick, Mark J. ... Cincinnati, OH
Weadon & Associates ... **Washington, DC**
Weadon, Donald Alford, Jr.
Washington, DC
Weady, Barbara N. ... **Hartford, CT**
Weagant, Lance M. ... **Los Angeles, CA**
Weage, Deborah ... Lake Mary, FL
Weagle, John G. ... Cambridge, MA
Weagly, Susan ... **Chicago, IL**
Weakland, Alan Wade ... **Los Angeles, CA**
Weakland, Brian L. ... **Tampa, FL**
Weakland, Lewis F. ... Los Angeles, CA
Weakland, Shawn Michael ... New York, NY
Weakley, Caren R. ... **Los Angeles, CA**
Weakley, Elise D. ... **Miami, FL**
Weakley, Heather L. ... **Los Angeles, CA**
Weakley, James D. ... Fresno, CA
Weakley, Kevin D. ... **Liberal, KS**
Weakley, Leonard A., Jr. ... **Cincinnati, OH**
Weakley, Mark ... **Seattle, WA**
Weakley & Ratliff, LLP ... Fresno, CA
Weakley, Steve ... **San Antonio, TX**
Weakley, Suzanne L. ... **Los Angeles, CA**
Weakley, Thomas E. ... Dyersburg, TN
Weakley, Wallace E. ... Noblesville, IN
Weaks, Gary L. ... Troy, OH
West Milton, OH
Weaks, Jerry M. ... Louisville, KY
Weal, Michael A. ... Ellicott City, MD
Wealleans, Robert-Grant ... Laguna Niguel, CA
Weals, Christopher A. ... **Washington, DC**
Wean, Paul L. ... Orlando, FL
Weand, Mark E., Jr.
Fort Washington, PA
Weaner, James K. ... **Defiance, OH**
Weaner, John W. ... **Defiance, OH**
Weaner, Zimmerman, Bacon, Yoder & Hubbard, Ltd. ... **Defiance, OH**
Hicksville, OH
Weant, Edward O., Jr. ... Westminster, MD
Wear, C. Victor ... **San Bernardino, CA**
Wear, Charles E., Jr. ... Arlington, TX
Wear, Charles E., Jr., P.C. ... Arlington, TX
Wear, Cheryl A. ... Warren, OH
Wear, David C. ... **Fort Payne, AL**
Wear, George M. ... Monroe, LA
Wear, George M., Jr. ... **Monroe, LA**
Wear, Gerald L. ... Vancouver, WA
Wear, James R. ... **Vail, CO**
Wear, John C. ... Fort Payne, AL
Wear, Michael L. ... **Akron, OH**
Wear, Nancy C. ... **Miami, FL**
Wear, Nelms & Sharp ... Springfield, MO
Wear, Robert Sean ... Arlington, TX
Wear, Teresa M. ... Shawnee, KS
Wear, Terrance J. ... Washington, DC
Wear, Travers & Davis, A Professional Corporation ... **Avon, CO**
Vail, CO
Wear, William A. ... Springfield, MO
Wear, William A., Jr. ... Springfield, MO
Wear, Wilson & Scott, P.A.
Fort Payne, AL
Wearin, Josiah C. ... **Red Oak, IA**
Wearing, Thomas V. ... San Francisco, CA

Webb, Bradford I. ... Westminster, MD
Webb, Bradley N. ... **Sacramento, CA**
Webb, Brenden W. ... **Overland Park, KS**
Webb, Brian D. ... **Tampa, FL**
Webb, Brian L. ... **Dallas, TX**
Webb, Brian R. ... New York, NY
Webb, Bryan ... **New York, NY**
Webb, Burke H. ... Marcellus, MI
Webb, Burnett, Jackson, Cornbrooks, Wilber, Vorhis & Douse, LLP
Cambridge, MD
Ocean City, MD
Salisbury, MD
Webb, C. Rena ... Scottsboro, AL
Webb, Calvin J., II ... **Ebensburg, PA**
Webb, Camden R. ... **Raleigh, NC**
Webb & Carey ... San Diego, CA
Webb, Carlock, Copeland, Semler & Stair, LLP ... **Atlanta, GA**
Webb, Charles ... Austin, TX
Webb, Charles C., Jr. ... Corpus Christi, TX
Webb, Charles "Chuck" H.
Port Charlotte, FL
Webb, Charles D., Jr. ... **Lexington, KY**
Webb, Charles E. ... **San Francisco, CA**
Webb, Charles E. ... Duluth, GA
Webb, Charles E. ... Fort Worth, TX
Webb, Charles H. ... **Bradenton, FL**
Webb, Charles, Law Office
Clarkston, WA
Webb, Charles R. ... **Charleston, WV**
Webb, Charles R., Jr. ... Kailua, HI
Webb, Charles S., III ... **New York, NY**
Webb, Charles V. ... **Washington, DC**
Webb, Charles V., Jr. ... Mantoloking, NJ
Webb, Charles W. ... Sarasota, FL
Webb, Charlotte ... Atlanta, GA
Webb, Christian Scott ... Olathe, KS
Webb, Christine B. ... Burnet, TX
Webb, Christopher J. ... Farmington Hills, MI
Webb, Corinne M. ... Camden, NJ
Webb, Curtis R., (Chartered)
Twin Falls, ID
Webb, Cynthia ... New York, NY
Webb, D. Eugene, Jr. ... **Richmond, VA**
Webb, D. Timothy ... Fairfax, VA
Webb, Dale W. ... **Roanoke, VA**
Webb, Dan K. ... **Chicago, IL**
Webb, Dan W. ... **Oxford, MS**
Tupelo, MS
Webb, Daniel A. ... **New Orleans, LA**
Webb, Daniel Clinton ... Palo Alto, CA
Webb, Daniel F. ... Chicago, IL
Webb, Daniel M. ... **Tulsa, OK**
Webb, Danne W. ... **Kansas City, MO**
Webb, Daphne ... **Madison, WI**
Webb, David A. ... Broken Bow, OK
Webb, David B. ... Philadelphia, PA
Webb, David C. ... Bryn Mawr, PA
Webb, David C., P.C. ... Bryn Mawr, PA
Webb, David E. ... **New York, NY**
Webb, David F. ... **Houston, TX**
Webb, David G. ... Lawrenceburg, KY
Webb, David J. ... **New York, NY**
Webb, David P. ... **Jackson, MS**
Webb, David R. ... **Lincoln, NE**
Webb, David T., Jr. ... New Orleans, LA
Webb, Deborah L. ... **Bethesda, MD**
Webb, Debra M. ... Indianapolis, IN
Webb, Dennis D. ... Wichita, KS
Webb, Dennis J., Jr. ... **Atlanta, GA**
Webb, Dennis J., (P.C.) ... **Atlanta, GA**
Webb, Dennis L. ... **Fort Myers, FL**
Webb, Diane ... **Albuquerque, NM**
Webb, Diane, Attorney At Law, P.C.
Albuquerque, NM
Webb, D. J. Harry ... New Britain, CT
Webb and Doerpinghaus ... Benton, AR
Webb, Donald W. ... **Lexington, KY**
Webb, Donald Woodford, Jr.
Lexington, KY
Webb & D'Orazio ... Atlanta, GA
Webb, Dorothy M. ... Houston, TX
Webb, Douglas F. ... San Diego, CA
Webb, Doyle L., II ... Benton, AR
Webb, Drew D. ... **Oklahoma City, OK**
Webb, Dudley ... **Lexington, KY**
Webb, E. Adam ... **Atlanta, GA**
Webb, Edward Jennings, Jr.
Johnson City, TN
Kingsport, TN
Webb & Eley, P.C. ... **Hayneville, AL**
Luverne, AL
Montgomery, AL
Prattville, AL
Troy, AL
Tuskegee, AL
Wetumpka, AL
Webb, Elizabeth A. ... **Austin, TX**
Webb, Elizabeth E. ... Beverly Hills, CA
Webb, Elizabeth Hogan ... Gainesville, FL
Webb, Elizabeth Kalogeros
Johnson City, TN
Webb, Elizabeth S. ... Birmingham, AL
Webb, Eric L. ... **Newport Beach, CA**
Webb, Erin A. ... **Miami, FL**
Webb, Eugene M. ... Pacific Palisades, CA
Webb, Faron Ross ... Weehawken, NJ
Webb, Frank B. ... **Columbus, MS**
Webb, Frank C. ... New Orleans, LA
Webb, G. Stewart, Jr. ... **Baltimore, MD**
Webb, Gary A. ... **Cincinnati, OH**
Webb, Gary B. ... Houston, TX
Webb, Gary R. ... **Knoxville, TN**
Webb, G. D. ... Chapel Hill, NC
Webb, George D., II ... Baltimore, MD
Webb, George S., III ... Madison, VA
Webb, George Walton, III ... **Houston, TX**
Webb, Gilbert ... Chicago, IL
Webb, Glenn L. ... Denver, CO
Webb, Gordon ... Harrison, AR
Webb & Graves, P.L.L.C. ... **Aberdeen, NC**
Wilmington, NC
Webb, Gwendolyn Hill ... Austin, TX
Webb, Harold ... New York, NY
Webb, Harry ... Lansing, MI
Webb, Heather C. ... **Memphis, TN**
Webb, Heather Duncan ... **Amarillo, TX**
Webb, Henley R. ... Cincinnati, OH
Webb, Henry Winder, III ... Tacoma, WA
Webb, Herbert M. ... Gainesville, FL
Webb, Hoskins, Glover & Thompson, P.S.C.
Lexington, KY
Webb, Hoyt K. ... New York, NY
Webb & Humberd ... Cleveland, TN
Webb, J. Bradley ... Wheaton, IL
Webb, J. Chester ... Lincoln, MA
Webb, J. David ... Paulding, OH
Webb, J. Duncan, IV ... Plano, TX
Webb, J. Gregory ... **Charlottesville, VA**
Richmond, VA
Webb, J. Lee ... **Atlanta, GA**
Webb, Jackson S. ... Elgin, TX
Webb, James B. ... St. Charles, IL
Webb, James Belew ... **Milan, TN**
Webb, James D., III ... Plano, TX
Webb, James E. ... Smyrna, GA
Webb, James E. ... **Fort Worth, TX**
Webb, James H., Jr. ... **McLean, VA**
Webb, James Hugh, Jr. ... **Atlanta, GA**
Webb, James J. ... **Fort Lauderdale, FL**
Webb, James J., Jr. ... **Memphis, TN**
Webb, James L. ... Atlanta, GA
Webb, James N. ... Melbourne, FL
Webb, James R. ... Juneau, AK
Webb, James R. ... **Oklahoma City, OK**
Webb, James S., (P.C.) ... Cleveland, TN
Webb, James W. ... **Montgomery, AL**
Webb, James W. ... **Elberton, GA**
Webb, Janet D. ... Rockville, MD
Webb, Janine Janas ... Penfield, NY
Webb, Jeffrey F. ... **Beverly Hills, CA**
Webb, Jeffrey O. ... Richmond, TX
Webb, Jeffrey T. ... Carthage, MS
Webb, Jere M. ... **Portland, OR**
Webb, Jerome J. ... Chicago, IL
Webb, Jerome William, Jr. ... **Miami, FL**
Webb, Jerry L. ... Tarzana, CA
Webb, John ... Northbrook, IL
Webb, John ... Raleigh, NC
Webb, John A. ... Moreno Valley, CA
Webb, John A. ... **Ashland, KY**
Webb, John C. ... Leland, MS
Webb, John C., Jr. ... **College Station, TX**
Webb, John D. ... Jacksonville, FL
Webb, John F., Jr. ... Englewood, CO
Webb, John F., Jr., P.C. ... Englewood, CO
Webb, John G., III ... Mount Olive, NJ
Webb, John Keith ... Seattle, WA
Webb, John L. ... Houston, TX
Webb, John M. ... Princeton, NJ
Webb, John Micheal ... Houston, TX
Webb, John P. ... **Stockbridge, GA**
Webb, John P. ... Scituate, MA
Webb, John R. ... **Denver, CO**
Webb, John S. ... Shreveport, LA
Webb, John Scott ... **Saco, ME**
Webb, John Thomas ... Department of Justice, Environment and Natural Resources Division, GV
Webb, Jonathan B. ... Dallas, TX
Webb, Jones ... **Lawrenceville, GA**
Webb, Joseph ... St. Louis, MO
Webb, Joseph G. ... **Denver, CO**
Webb, Joseph H., Jr.
Department of Commerce, Patent and Trademark Office, GV
Webb, Joy Rhyne ... Creedmoor, NC
Durham, NC
Greensboro, NC
Raleigh, NC
Webb, Julia D. ... Hartford, CT
Webb, Julian ... Donalsonville, GA
Webb, Julian, P.C. ... Donalsonville, GA
Webb, Julie A. ... **Mount Vernon, IL**
Webb, J. W. Thompson ... **Baltimore, MD**
Webb, Karen E. ... Yakima, WA
Webb, Karen F. ... **Jacksonville, FL**
Webb, Karri J. ... **Houston, TX**
Webb, Kaye R. ... Durham, NC
Webb, Kelley W. ... Trumann, AR
Webb, Kendrick E. ... **Montgomery, AL**
Webb, Kenn W. ... **Dallas, TX**
Webb, Kenneth A. ... Pittsburg, KS
Webb, Kenneth A. ... Troy, MI
Webb, Kenneth A., P.C. ... Troy, MI
Webb, Kenneth E., Jr. ... **Charleston, WV**
Webb, Kent Randall ... Tulsa, OK
Webb, Kevin J. ... **New Orleans, LA**
Webb, Kevin Stark ... **Richmond, VA**
Webb, Kimberly ... **Little Rock, AR**
Webb, L. Kent ... **Atlanta, GA**
Webb, L. Rodger ... Detroit, MI
Webb, L. Suzanne ... **New York, NY**
Webb, Lance E. ... Union City, TN
Webb, Lane E. ... **San Diego, CA**
Webb, Laura C. ... **Knoxville, TN**
Webb, Laurie A. ... **Sunnyvale, CA**
Webb & Lauterbach, P.C. ... Houston, TX
Webb Law Firm ... Roanoke Rapids, NC
Webb, Lawrence L. ... New Orleans, LA
Webb, Lee Ann ... Prestonsburg, KY
Webb, Lenita M. ... Roanoke Rapids, NC
Webb, Leo A.
United States International Trade Commission, Office of Tariff Affairs & Trade Agreements, GV
Webb, Leonard G. ... Knoxville, TN
Webb, Leslie A. ... Austin, TX
Webb, Leslie Miller ... **Charlotte, NC**
Webb, Lewis W., III ... **Norfolk, VA**
Webb, Linda Anna ... Anchorage, AK
Webb, Linda Smith ... Montgomery, AL
Webb, Lloyd J., (Chartered)
Twin Falls, ID
Webb, Lloyd J. and Curtis R.
Twin Falls, ID
Webb, Lorraine J. ... **Greenbelt, MD**
Waldorf, MD
Webb, Louis C. ... **Phoenix, AZ**
Webb, Louis C., P.C. ... **Phoenix, AZ**
Webb, Lucie Frost ... **San Antonio, TX**
Webb, M. Kathryn ... **Wichita, KS**
Webb, M. Sharon ... **Boston, MA**
Webb, Marcia Lee ... Pittsburgh, PA
Webb, Margaret Nell ... Durango, CO
Webb, Mark Charles ... Indianapolis, IN
Webb, Mark L. ... San Francisco, CA
Webb, Mark L., Law Offices of
San Francisco, CA
Webb, Mark M. J. ... **Rome, GA**
Webb, Mark O. ... Richmond, VA
Webb, Mark S.
Securities and Exchange Commission, Division of Corporation Finance, GV
Webb, Mark W. ... Fort Smith, AR
Webb, Marland O. ... **Chicago, IL**
Webb, Mary Jane R. ... Vienna, IL
Webb, Mary McHugh ... **Raleigh, NC**
Webb, Matthew J. ... Oakland, CA
Webb, Max A.
Securities and Exchange Commission, Division of Corporation Finance, GV
Webb, Melissa ... **Dallas, TX**
Webb, Michael J. ... Bakersfield, CA
Webb, Michael L. ... Sacramento, CA
Webb, Michael S. ... Orlando, FL
Webb, Michael S. ... Duluth, GA
Webb, Michael W. ... Redondo Beach, CA
Webb, Micheal C. ... Honolulu, HI
Webb, Michelle ... Levelland, TX
Webb, Morrison DeS. ... New York, NY
Webb, Nathaniel J., III ... Hampton, VA
Webb, Neil E.
Department of Justice, GV
Webb, Nichole C. ... Chicago, IL
Webb, Nina Ilene ... Columbus, OH
Webb, Norriss M. ... Lake Oswego, OR
Webb & O'Quinn, Professional Association
Jacksonville, FL
Webb, P. Jennifer ... Newport Beach, CA
Webb, Pamela B. ... Rochester, NY
Webb, Patricia H. ... **Houston, TX**
Webb, Patrick D. ... **Escondido, CA**
San Diego, CA
Webb, Patterson and Tapella
Sacramento, CA
Webb, Paul ... Wharton, TX
Webb, Paul C. ... **Dallas, TX**
Webb, Paul H. ... **Birmingham, AL**
Webb, Paul, Jr. ... **Atlanta, GA**
Webb, Paul R., II ... Schenectady, NY
Webb, Paul V., Jr. ... **Jamestown, NY**
Webb, Peter G. ... **Nashua, NH**
Webb, Philip A., III ... **Jacksonville, FL**
Webb, Philip D. ... Dallas, TX
Webb, Rachael Howell ... **Oxford, MS**
Tupelo, MS
Webb, Rebecca M. ... Boston, MA
Webb, Reginald D. ... **New Orleans, LA**
Webb, Richard C. ... **Charleston, SC**
Webb, Richard F. ... Hartford, CT
Webb, Richard J. ... **Newark, NJ**
Webb, Richard L. ... **Boulder, CO**
Webb, Richard L., Jr. ... **Keene, NH**
Brattleboro, VT
Webb, Richard S., IV ... **Sarasota, FL**
Webb, Richard W. ... Jim Thorpe, PA
Webb, Robert A., Law Office of
Austin, TX
Webb, Robert B., III ... **McLean, VA**
Webb, Robert C. ... **Louisville, KY**
Webb, Robert D. ... **Boston, MA**
Webb, Robert D. ... Medford, MA
Webb, Robert D. ... Geneva, OH
Webb, Robert E., Jr. ... Louisville, KY
Webb, Robert F. ... Atlanta, GA
Webb, Robert J. ... **Orlando, FL**
Webb, Robert W. ... **Chicago, IL**
Webb, Robert W., Jr. ... **Atlanta, GA**
Webb, Robt. L. ... Los Gatos, CA
Webb, Robt. S., III ... Houston, TX
Webb, Robyn Oliver ... **Atlanta, GA**
Webb, Rodney S. ... Fargo, ND
Webb, Ronald R. ... San Diego, CA
Webb, Russell E., III ... Idaho Falls, ID
Webb, Russell M., Jr. ... Plainfield, IN
Webb, Ruth ... Lexington, KY
Webb, Sallye Goodwin ... **New Orleans, LA**
Webb & Salyer, P.C. ... Corpus Christi, TX
Webb, Sanders, Balducci & Smith, P.L.L.C.
Oxford, MS
Tupelo, MS
Webb, Sandra K. ... **Amarillo, TX**
Webb & Scarmozzino, P.A.
Fort Myers, FL
Webb, Scott L. ... Anderson, IN
Webb, Shannon W. ... **Dallas, TX**
Webb, Sharon Cohen ... New Haven, CT
Webb, Sharon D. ... Stamford, CT
Webb, Shelley A. ... Hood River, OR
Webb, Stacey ... **Houston, TX**
Webb, Stanley M. ... Phoenix, AZ
Webb, Stephen P. ... **Beverly Hills, CA**
Webb, Stephen P. ... Austin, TX
Webb, Steven K. ... Richmond, VA
Webb, Stokes & Sparks ... **San Angelo, TX**
Webb, Stuart G. ... **Minneapolis, MN**
Webb, Stuckey & Lindsey, LLC
Atlanta, GA
Fairburn, GA
Peachtree City, GA
Webb, Suzanne ... San Pedro, CA
Webb, Suzanne V. ... Marlton, NJ
Webb, T. Coyt (Cody) ... **Amarillo, TX**
Webb, Tanner & Powell, LLP
Atlanta, GA
Lawrenceville, GA
Norcross, GA
Snellville, GA
Winder, GA
Webb, Thomas A. ... **Jackson, MS**
Webb, Thomas B. ... McAlester, OK
Webb, Thomas E. ... Lutherville, MD
Webb, Thomas E. ... **Buffalo, NY**
Eden, NY
Westfield, NY
Webb, Thomas E., Jr. ... Williamsville, NY
Webb, Thomas I. ... Monclova, OH
Webb, Thomas I., Jr. ... **Toledo, OH**
Webb, Thomas L. ... **Meridian, MS**
Webb, Thomas L., PLLC ... **Meridian, MS**
Webb, Thomas R. ... West Hartford, CT
Webb & Tiholiz, LLP ... **Dallas, TX**
Webb, Timothy D. ... St. Paul, MN
Webb, Todd S. ... Moorhead, MN
Webb, Tracy ... Pasadena, CA
Webb, Tracy L. ... **Charleston, WV**
Webb, Tyler G. ... Edgewater, MD
Webb, Valerie M. ... **Nashville, TN**
Webb, Vanedda Price ... Gallatin, TN
Webb, Vicki E. ... Laurel, MD
Webb, Virginia ... Columbus, GA
Webb, W. Edward ... **Chicago, IL**
Webb, W. Hollis, Jr. ... Lubbock, TX
Webb, W. Perry ... **Birmingham, AL**
Webb, W. Ray, Jr. ... Chattanooga, TN
Webb, W. Roger ... Edmond, OK
Webb, Wade Lykken ... Fargo, ND
Webb, Wayne E. ... Shreveport, LA
Webb & Webb ... Duluth, GA
Webb & Webb ... Austin, TX
Webb & Webb, P.C. ... Plano, TX
Webb, Wilbur D. ... Spencer, WV
Webb, William A. ... **Chicago, IL**
Webb, William B., Jr. ... Charlotte, NC
Webb, William Curtis ... **Houston, TX**
Webb, William D. ... Gardner, KS
Webb, William G. ... Colorado Springs, CO
Webb, William G. ... Dallas, TX
Webb, William Gregory ... **Memphis, TN**
Webb, William H., Jr ... **Chattanooga, TN**
Webb, William J. ... Cleveland, OH
Webb, William M. ... El Paso, TX
Webb, William O. ... Seattle, WA
Webb, William R. ... New Port Richey, FL
Webb, William R., Jr. ... **Hamlet, NC**
Rockingham, NC
Webb, William T. ... **Denver, CO**
Webb, William T., Jr. ... Virginia Beach, VA
Webb, William W. ... **Los Angeles, CA**
Webb, William W. ... San Francisco, CA
Webb, William W. ... Birmingham, MI
Webb, William Woodward, (P.C.)
Raleigh, NC
Webb, William Y. ... **Philadelphia, PA**
Webb, Wm. A. ... Hartford, CT
Webb, Wm. David ... Wyncote, PA
Webb, W. S., Jr. ... Tallahassee, FL
Webb, W. Y. Alex ... **Aberdeen, NC**
Webb Ziesenheim Logsdon Orkin & Hanson, P.C. ... **Harrisburg, PA**
Pittsburgh, PA
Webbe, Peggy J. ... Farmington, CT
Webber, A. Duane ... **Washington, DC**
Webber, Albert G., III ... **Decatur, IL**
Webber, Albert G., IV ... **Decatur, IL**
Webber, Alvin R. ... Sacramento, CA
Webber, Arthur L. ... New Milford, CT
Webber, Barry S. ... Pembroke Pines, FL
Webber, Beth A. ... **Fort Wayne, IN**
Webber, Beth K. ... **New York, NY**
Webber, Carl M. ... **Urbana, IL**
Webber, Charles F. ... **Minneapolis, MN**
Webber, Christine E. ... **Washington, DC**
Webber, Christopher A., Jr.
Wallingford, VT
Webber, Christopher A., Jr. ... **Rutland, VT**
Webber, Cori-Lynn S. ... West Hartford, CT
Webber, Curtis ... **Auburn, ME**
Webber, Dale S. ... **Tampa, FL**
Webber, Daniel G. ... Oklahoma City, OK
Watonga, OK
Webber, Daniel Patrick ... **Flint, MI**
Webber, David D. ... Camano, WA
Webber, David F. ... **Houston, TX**
Webber, David W. ... Philadelphia, PA
Webber, Don L. ... Stamford, CT
Webber, Donna Avergun
East Brunswick, NJ
Webber, Douglas G. ... Omak, WA
Webber, E. Richard ... St. Louis, MO
Webber, Emalyn H. ... West Palm Beach, FL
Webber, Eric A. ... **Los Angeles, CA**
Webber, Erin A. ... **St. Joseph, MO**
Webber, Gary A. ... **Urbana, IL**
Webber, Gaumer, Emanuel & Daily, P.C.
Ottumwa, IA
Webber, Ginger M. ... **Fort Worth, TX**
Webber, Glenn J. ... Fort Lauderdale, FL

Weber, Seth ... Philadelphia, PA
Weber, Seth I. ... Greenbelt, MD
Weber, Sharon A. ... Coram, NY
Weber, Sheila E. ... Bronx, NY
Weber, Shelton R. ... Louisville, KY
Weber, Sophie R. ... New Rochelle, NY
Weber, Stan M. ... New Orleans, LA
Weber, Stanley E. ... Portland, OR
Weber, Stephen A. ... Charleston, WV
Weber, Stephen K. ... Glenview, IL
Weber, Stephen L. ... Detroit, MI
Weber, Stephen Lee ... Irvine, CA
Weber & Sterling, LLC
Bowling Green, OH
Maumee, OH
Toledo, OH
Weber, Steven D. ... Charlotte, NC
Weber, Steven J. ... McLean, VA
Weber, Steven J., (Professional Corporation)
San Francisco, CA
Weber, Steven R. ... San Bernardino, CA
Weber, Susan A. ... Chicago, IL
Weber, Susan F. ... Albany, NY
Weber, Susan N. ... Sacramento, CA
Weber, Sylvia ... New York, NY
Weber, Terri ... Madison, WI
Weber, Theodore V. ... Aurora, IL
Weber, Thomas J. ... New York, NY
Weber, Thomas J. ... Harrisburg, PA
Weber, Thomas L. ... Gahanna, OH
Weber, Thomas M. ... Austin, TX
Weber, Thomas W. ... Chicago, IL
Weber, Timothy Wayne
St. Petersburg, FL
Weber, Tina Marcy ... Philadelphia, PA
Weber, Todd W. ... Saranac Lake, NY
Weber, Tom L. ... Olney, IL
Weber, Tracy M. ... Terre Haute, IN
Weber, V. Mia ... San Jose, CA
Weber, Victoria L. ... Tallahassee, FL
Weber, Vince ... Bethel, AK
Weber, Virginia L. ... San Diego, CA
Weber, W. Erik ... Auburn, IN
Weber, Walter M. ... Washington, DC
Weber, Walter U. ... Tucson, AZ
Weber, Walter W., Jr. ... Ramsey, NJ
Weber, Wayne D. ... Houston, TX
Weber & Weber ... St. Louis, MO
Weber & Weber ... Weston, WV
Weber & Weinhold, P.C. ... Lexington, NE
Weber, Wendy Lynne ... Boston, MA
Weber, William A. ... Miami, FL
Weber, William D. ... Houston, TX
Weber, William J. ... Signal Mountain, TN
Weber, William J., Jr. ... Cherry Hill, NJ
Paoli, PA
Philadelphia, PA
Weber, William L. ... Milwaukee, WI
Weber, William L., Jr. ... Kansas City, MO
Weber, William M. ... Utica, NY
Weber, William M. ... Chagrin Falls, OH
Weber, William R. ... Washington, DC
Weber, William W. ... New Britain, CT
Weber, Wm. H., Jr. ... Orchard Park, NY
Weber, Wm. Randolph ... St. Charles, MO
Weber, W. T., III ... Weston, WV
Weber, W. T., Jr. ... Weston, WV
Weberg, Arlene F. ... New York, NY
Webering, James C. ... Glenwood, IA
Red Oak, IA
Webering, James C., A Prof. Law Corp.
Red Oak, IA
Glenwood, IA
Weberman, Bernard H. ... Treasury Department, Internal Revenue Service, GV
Weberman, Daniel I. ... West Bloomfield, MI
Weberman, Paula Silverman
Farmington Hills, MI
Weberman, Philip ... Beachwood, OH
Webernick, Jack N. ... Georgetown, TX
Weberpal, Mike ... Houston, TX
Webert, C. Stanley ... Seattle, WA
Webking, Catherine J.
Dripping Springs, TX
Webley, Gregory S. ... Puyallup, WA
Webman, Susan M. ... Department of Labor, Office of the Solicitor, GV
Webne, Ronald L. ... Washington, DC
Webner, Corinne Palmer ... Washington, DC
Webner, Dale F. ... Miami, FL
Webner, Robert N. ... Columbus, OH
Webner, William Mack ... Washington, DC
Webostad, Wesley Eric ... Waltham, MA
Webre, G. Patrick ... Metairie, LA
Webre, Gerald P. ... Metairie, LA
Webre, Harold J., III ... Naples, FL
Webre, Jane M. N. ... Austin, TX
Webster, A. Timothy ... Buffalo, NY
Webster, Aen W. ... Washington, DC
Webster, Allen D. ... Burlington, VT
Webster, Allison D. ... Boston, MA
Webster, Amy E. ... Hollidaysburg, PA
Webster & Anderson ... Oakland, CA
Webster, Andrew C. ... Metairie, LA
Webster, Anita A. ... Las Vegas, NV
Webster, Ann Adams ... Richmond, VA
Webster, Annmarie ... Northbrook, IL
Webster, Ben H. ... Flat Rock, NC
Webster, Benjamin L. ... Sacramento, CA
Webster, Bennett A. ... Des Moines, IA
Webster, Bonnie ... Johnson City, TN
Webster, Bonnie Pearce ... Pittsburgh, PA
Webster, Brannon & Bisodi, P.A.
Fort Walton Beach, FL
Webster, Brannon & Bisordi, P.A.
Shalimar, FL
Webster, Bruce A. ... Sacramento, CA
Webster, Bruce A. ... St. Paul, MN
Webster, Bruce A., P.A., & Associates
St. Paul, MN
Webster, Bryant D. ... Asheville, NC
Webster, C. Edward, II ... Cody, WY
Webster, Carrie L. ... Charleston, WV
Webster & Cassidy ... Madison, NC
Webster, Chamberlain & Bean
Washington, DC
Bethesda, MD
Fairfax, VA
Webster, Charles E. ... Clarksdale, MS
Webster, Charles K. ... Cleveland, OH
Webster, Charles W. ... Chicago, IL
Webster, Christine E. ... Springfield, MA
Webster, Christopher W. ... Ridgeland, MS
Webster, Clifford A. ... Seattle, WA
Webster, D. Robert ... Indianapolis, IN
Webster, Dale P. ... Vincennes, IN
Webster, Dan G., III ... San Antonio, TX
Webster, Daniel J. ... Daytona Beach, FL
Webster, Daniel J., P.A.
Daytona Beach, FL
Webster, Daniel L. ... Uniontown, PA
Webster, Darrell E. ... Roseville, CA
Webster, David A. ... Longwood, FL
Webster, David A. (IBA) ... Orlando, FL
Webster, David A. ... Atlanta, GA
Webster, David A., P.A. ... Orlando, FL
Webster, David B. ... Cleveland, OH
Webster, David B. ... Philadelphia, PA
Webster, David E. ... San Francisco, CA
Webster, David H. ... Gadsden, AL
Webster, David John ... Trinidad, CO
Webster, David M. ... Chicago, IL
Webster, David N. ... Washington, DC
Webster, David R. ... Tampa, FL
Webster, David S. ... Oakland, CA
Webster, David Z. ... Boston, MA
Webster, Deirdré L. ... Trenton, NJ
Webster, Denise ... Department of Defense, Defense Legal Services Agency, GV
Webster, Diane ... Pittsburg, CA
Webster, Diane T. ... White Plains, NY
Webster, Donald B. ... Red Bluff, CA
Webster, Donald D. ... Chevy Chase, MD
Webster, Douglas E. ... San Diego, CA
Webster, Douglas L. ... Southfield, MI
Webster Dyrud Mitchell ... Miami, FL
Webster, Edith F. ... Baltimore, MD
Webster, Edward D. ... Riverside, CA
Webster, Elnardo J., II ... Newark, NJ
Webster & Engel ... Bismarck, ND
Webster, Felice A. ... Los Angeles, CA
Webster, Frank A. ... Fort Wayne, IN
Webster, Frank R. ... Rochester, NY
Webster, Fredric L. ... Pittsburg, CA
Webster, Fredrickson & Brackshaw
Washington, DC
Fairfax, VA
Webster, Garth A., (P.A.) ... Miami, FL
Webster, Geoffrey E. ... Columbus, OH
Webster, George C., II ... Los Angeles, CA
Webster, Guy N. ... Los Angeles, CA
Webster, Harold W. ... North Vernon, IN
Webster, H.M., III ... Los Angeles, CA
Webster, Hollis L. ... Wheaton, IL
Webster, Hugh K. ... Washington, DC
Webster, J. Aldean, III ... Raleigh, NC
Webster, J. Lance ... Birmingham, AL
Webster, J. Michael ... Los Angeles, CA
Webster, James A. ... Anchorage, AK
Webster, James C. ... New Orleans, LA
Houston, TX
Webster, James E. ... Madison, WI
Webster, James H. ... Pittsburgh, PA
Webster, James H. ... Seattle, WA
Webster, James J. ... Los Angeles, CA
Webster, James L. ... Chicago, IL
Webster, James M. ... Oak Ridge, TN
Webster, James M., III ... Baltimore, MD
Webster, James R. ... Mountain View, CA
Webster, James W. ... Sonora, CA
Webster, James W., (P.C.) ... Providence, RI
Webster, Jan H. ... San Diego, CA
Webster, Jean Louise ... Oxnard, CA
Webster, Jennifer L. ... Dallas, TX
Webster, Jess G. ... Seattle, WA
Webster, Joe C. ... Clarksdale, MS
Webster, Joe L. ... Pittsboro, NC
Webster, John A. ... Selma, AL
Webster, John B. ... Toledo, OH
Webster, John B. ... Warwick, RI
Webster, John B. ... Dallas, TX
Webster, John C. ... Alton, IL
Webster, John C., III ... Hanson, MA
Webster, John D. ... Saratoga, CA
Webster, John F. ... St. Albans, VT
Webster, John M. ... Manitowoc, WI
Webster, John R. ... Ventura, CA
Webster, John R., Jr. ... Clinton, MD
Webster, John W. ... Albemarle, NC
Webster, Jon O. ... Rochester, NY
Webster, Jon P. ... Pleasant Hill, CA
Webster, Joseph H. ... Washington, DC
Webster, Joy R. ... Macon, GA
Webster, Karen D. ... Memphis, TN
Webster, Kathleen P. ... Conshohocken, PA
Webster, K. C. ... Redmond, WA
Webster, Kenneth C. ... San Francisco, CA
Webster & Knerly, P.A. ... Tampa, FL
Webster Law Firm ... Sacramento, CA
Webster, Lawrence R. ... Pikeville, KY
Webster, LeeAnn M. ... Los Angeles, CA
Webster, Lesley Douglass ... Albany, NY
Webster, Lori B. ... Hollidaysburg, PA
Webster, Louis I. ... Noblesville, IN
Webster, Lucas F. ... Silver Spring, MD
Webster, Luther Ira ... Rochester, NY
Webster, Mark C. ... Louisville, KY
Webster, Martial A., Jr.
Frederiksted, St. Croix, VI
Webster, Martin H. ... Los Angeles, CA
Webster, Mary F. ... Southfield, MI
Webster, Matthew B. ... Joplin, MO
Webster, Melanie L. ... Albuquerque, NM
Webster, Melvin L. ... Bismarck, ND
Webster, Michael E. ... Billings, MT
Webster, Michael T. ... Shalimar, FL
Webster & Moore, P.A. ... Salisbury, MD
Webster Mrak & Blumberg ... Seattle, WA
Webster, Nancy L. ... Los Angeles, CA
Webster, Nannette W. ... San Antonio, TX
Webster, Noah E. ... Arlington, TX
Webster, Norma Stamps ... Kansas City, MO
Webster, Norris L. ... Medina, NY
Webster, Norton R. ... Columbus, OH
Webster, Palmavon J. (IBA) ... Miami, FL
Webster, Pamela Kohlman
Los Angeles, CA
Webster, Paula P. ... Buffalo, NY
Webster, Peter ... Magna, UT
Webster, Peter B. ... Portland, ME
Webster, Peter D. ... Tallahassee, FL
Webster, Peter H. ... Detroit, MI
Webster, Phyllis K. ... El Dorado, KS
Webster, R. Daniel ... Detroit, MI
Webster, R. Daniel, P.C. ... Detroit, MI
Webster, R. Kenly ... Washington, DC
Webster, R. Kenly, P.C. ... Washington, DC
Webster, Reid G. ... Huntsville, AL
Webster, Richard ... Iowa City, IA
Webster, Richard C. ... Cascade, CO
Webster, Robert B. ... Birmingham, MI
Webster, Robert C. ... San Francisco, CA
Webster, Robert D. ... New York, NY
Webster, Robert J.
Department of Commerce, Patent and Trademark Office, GV
Webster, Robert L. ... San Mateo, CA
Webster, Robert L. ... Uniontown, PA
Webster, Robert L. ... Dallas, TX
Webster, Robert L. ... Milwaukee, WI
Webster, Robert L., Jr. ... Uniontown, PA
Webster, Robert O. ... Portola Valley, CA
Webster, Robert T. ... Detroit, MI
Webster & Robison ... Durant, OK
Webster, Ronald A. ... Knoxville, TN
Webster, Ronald B. ... Colfax, WA
Webster, Ronald S. ... Marco Island, FL
Webster, Ronald S. ... Orlando, FL
Webster, Ronald S. ... Houston, TX
Webster, Ruth Ann ... New Ulm, MN
Webster, Samuel J. ... Norfolk, VA
Webster, Sara M. ... Doylestown, PA
Webster & Schubel ... Medina, NY
Webster, Scott A. ... Boston, MA
Webster, Scott M. ... Barbourville, KY
Webster, Shane W. ... Dallas, TX
Webster, S. J., Jr. ... Madison, NC
Webster, Stephanie Ann ... Baltimore, MD
Webster, Stephanie H. ... Atlanta, GA
Webster, Stephen D. ... Cleveland, OH
Webster, Stephen W. ... Fresno, CA
Webster, Stephen W. ... Randolph, VT
Webster, Steven M. ... Department of Justice, Tax Division, GV
Webster, Steven R. ... Atlanta, GA
Webster, Steven T. ... Falls Church, VA
Webster, Susan ... New York, NY
Webster, Susan Hovey ... Chicago, IL
Webster Szanyi LLP ... Buffalo, NY
Webster, Thomas Campbell
Sunnyvale, CA
Webster, Thomas D. ... Indianapolis, IN
Webster, Thomas M. ... Palo Alto, CA
Webster, Thomas P. ... Belpre, OH
Marietta, OH
Webster & Thompson, LLC ... Cody, WY
Webster, Tim R. ... Durant, OK
Webster, Timothy J. ... Akron, OH
Webster, Timothy Kenly
Department of Justice, Environment and Natural Resources Division, GV
Webster, Vanessa ... Elmwood Park, NJ
Webster, Victoria ... Cypress, CA
Webster, Victoria G. ... Columbus, OH
Webster, W. Terrell, Jr. ... Aberdeen, NC
Webster, Wade P. ... New Orleans, LA
Webster, Wallace H., Jr. ... Schnecksville, PA
Webster, Walter D. ... Mission Viejo, CA
Webster, Walter D. ... Salisbury, MD
Webster, Walter E., Jr. ... Seattle, WA
Webster & Webster ... Pittsburg, CA
Webster & Webster, P.C. ... Uniontown, PA
Webster, Wendell W. ... Washington, DC
Webster, W.F. Bill ... Jonesboro, AR
Webster, William A. ... Minneapolis, MN
Webster, William E. ... Pierce, NE
Webster, William F. ... Sacramento, CA
Webster, William H. ... Montgomery, AL
Webster, William H. ... Oakland, CA
Webster, William H. ... Washington, DC
Webster, William H. ... Crawfordville, FL
Webster, William H. ... Perrysburg, OH
Webster, William R. ... Stockton, CA
Webster, William V., Jr. ... Marlton, NJ
Webster, William W. ... Denver, CO
Webster, Wm. W., P.C. ... Denver, CO
Webster-Brady, Diane ... Plattsburgh, NY
Webster-O'Keefe & Pomerantz
New Milford, CT
Webster-O'Keefe, M. Katherine
New Milford, CT
Wechkin, John M. ... Seattle, WA
Wechkin, Robin ... Seattle, WA
Wechselblatt, Eric S. ... Washington, DC
Wechselblatt, Jeffrey ... New York, NY
Wechser, Nancy Ferraro ... New York, NY
Wechsler, Alan L. ... New York, NY
Wechsler, Alfred F. ... West Hartford, CT
Washington, DC
Wechsler, Amy ... Warren, NJ
Wechsler, Becker, Erickson, Ross, Roubik and Hunter, LLP ... Seattle, WA
Wechsler, Bruce C. ... Roseland, NJ
Wechsler Bursky & Cohen, L.L.P.
New York, NY
Wechsler, Burton D. ... Washington, DC
Wechsler, Dale E. ... Boston, MA
Wechsler, Daniel ... New York, NY
Wechsler, David A. ... Bethesda, MD
Wechsler, David B. ... New York, NY
Wechsler, David N. ... New York, NY
Wechsler, David W. ... Burbank, CA
Wechsler, Doris ... New York, NY
Wechsler, Eric M. ... Stuart, FL
Wechsler, Ernest S. ... New York, NY
Wechsler & Friedman ... Rockville, MD
Wechsler, Gail A. ... St. Louis, MO
Wechsler, Glenn H. ... Walnut Creek, CA
Wechsler Harwood Halebian & Feffer LLP
New York, NY
Wechsler, Herbert ... New York, NY
Wechsler, James J. ... Santa Fe, NM
Wechsler, James M. ... Farmington Hills, MI
Wechsler, Jeri Pharis ... Houston, TX
Wechsler, Joshua ... New York, NY
Wechsler, Lawrence H. ... Washington, DC
Wechsler, Lawrence I. ... New York, NY
Wechsler, Maribeth Bohs ... Philadelphia, PA
Wechsler, Mark ... Cherry Hill, NJ
Wechsler, Mary H. ... Seattle, WA
Wechsler, Mercedes R. ... Orlando, FL
Wechsler, Michael G. ... Rockville, MD
Wechsler, Michael Harris ... San Francisco, CA
Wechsler, Nancy F. ... New York, NY
Wechsler, Nick ... Los Angeles, CA
Wechsler, Pamela J. ... Boston, MA
Wechsler, Perry J. ... New York, NY
Wechsler, Peter L. ... Miami, FL
Wechsler, Robert E. ... Great Neck, NY
Wechsler, Robert M. ... Stamford, CT
Wechsler, Selzer & Gurvitch, Chartered
Washington, DC
Bethesda, MD
Wechsler, Steven ... Syracuse, NY
Wechsler, Steven W. ... St. Albans, VT
Wechsler, Stuart D. ... New York, NY
Wechsler, Susan P. ... Sharon, MA
Wechsler, William A. ... West Hartford, CT
Wechsler, Zachary D. ... Los Angeles, CA
Wecht, Cyril H. ... Pittsburgh, PA
Wecht, David N. ... Pittsburgh, PA
Wecht Law Firm, The ... Pittsburgh, PA
Wecht, Ronald H. ... San Francisco, CA
Wecht, Sigrid R. ... Pittsburgh, PA
Wechter, Diane J. ... Grand Rapids, MI
Wechter, Kathleen A. ... New York, NY
Wechter, Kevin ... La Jolla, CA
Wechter, Lawrence D. ... Batavia, IL
Wechter, Richard J. ... New York, NY
Wechter, Thomas R. ... Chicago, IL
Wechtler, Janet M. ... Allentown, PA
Weck, James A. ... Fort Lauderdale, FL
Weck, Patricia L. ... Fort Lauderdale, FL
Weck, Warren F., Jr. ... Minnetonka, MN
Weck & Weck, P.A. ... Fort Lauderdale, FL
Weckbacher, Joseph H. ... Canton, OH
Weckel, John ... Salina, KS
Wecker, Andrew P. ... Columbus, OH
Wecker, Barbara Byrd ... Elizabeth, NJ
Wecker, Bruce J. ... San Francisco, CA
Wecker, David A. ... Silverdale, WA
Wecker & Hunko ... Silverdale, WA
Wecker, Rita L. ... Washington, DC
Wecker, Terri L. ... Atlanta, GA
Weckerly, Paul D. ... Irvine, CA
Weckesser, Sandra W. ... Philadelphia, PA
Weckesser, Susan O. ... Santa Fe, NM
Weckstein, Alyson R. ... Brooklyn, NY
Weckstein, Clifford R. ... Roanoke, VA
Weckstein, Daniel R. ... Norfolk, VA
Weckstein, Donald ... Xenia, OH
Weckstein, Kenneth B. ... Washington, DC
Weckwert, Heidi E.
Department of Justice, GV
Weckworth, Robert N. ... Greensboro, NC
Weclew, Robt. G. ... Chicago, IL
Weddel, Frederick R. ... Bemidji, MN
Weddell, Bruce B. ... Atlanta, GA
Weddell, Douglas A. ... Colorado Springs, CO
Weddell, Laura J. ... Treasury Department, U.S. Customs Service, GV
Weddell, Margaret F. ... Portland, OR
Weddell, Pamela Malakinian ... Southfield, MI
Weddell, Russell R. ... North Andover, MA
Weddell, Willard L. ... Bakersfield, CA
Wedderburn, Norman E. ... Miami, FL
Wedding, David S. ... Indianapolis, IN
Wedding, Donald K. ... Toledo, OH
Wedding and Hughey ... Marshall, TX
Wedding, James V. ... Marshall, TX
Wedding, Jo Ann M. ... Ventura, CA
Wedding, Mary Jo Hunter
Indianapolis, IN
Wedding & McNair, LLP ... Ventura, CA
Weddington, Elizabeth L. ... Raleigh, NC
Weddington, James R. (Ron) ... Austin, TX
Weddington, Keith M. ... Charlotte, NC
Weddington, Larry S. ... Bristol, TN
Weddington, Mary Margaret ... Memphis, TN
Weddington, Michael E. ... Raleigh, NC
Weddle, Alvin L., Jr. ... New Orleans, LA

Wegner, Scott D. .... Bismarck, ND
Wegner, Steven D. .... Beverly Hills, CA
Wegner, Steven G., Law Offices of
Saratoga, CA
Wegner, Susan F. .... Palo Alto, CA
Wegner, Timothy J. .... Dickinson, ND
Wegner, Wayne G.
Grosse Pointe Woods, MI
Wegner & Wegner, P.C. .... Totowa, NJ
Wegner, William Edward
Los Angeles, CA
Wegryn, Heidi M. .... Knoxville, TN
Wegryn, Richard E., Jr. .... Trenton, NJ
Wegrzyn, Edward J. .... Chicago, IL
Wegrzyn, Lisa E. .... Tampa, FL
Wegs, Thomas J. .... Denver, CO
Wehage, Patrick J. .... Mission Viejo, CA
Wehbe, A. Emily .... Mission Viejo, CA
Wehby, Alfred E. .... Madison, TN
Wehby, Joseph K. .... Fort Wright, KY
Cincinnati, OH
Wehby, Joseph M. .... Miami, FL
Wehby, Vincent E. .... Nashville, TN
Wehde, Albert Edward .... Santa Clara, CA
Wehde, Christin J. .... Ingleside, IL
Wehde, Mark .... Broomfield, CO
Wehde, Shawn .... Waterloo, IA
Wehener, Ann Lynn .... Akron, OH
Wehland, Charles E. .... Ellicott City, MD
Wehland, Charles E., P.A.
Ellicott City, MD
Wehland, Charles T. .... Chicago, IL
Wehlburg, Susan B. .... Gainesville, FL
Wehle, Jonathan Field .... New York, NY
Wehling, Caroline H.
Environmental Protection Agency,
Office of the General Counsel, GV
Wehling, Catherine .... Phoenix, AZ
Wehling, Ralph J. .... Phoenix, AZ
Wehmer, Brenda K. .... Cincinnati, OH
Wehmer, M. Jill .... St. Louis, MO
Wehmeyer, Richard L. .... Corvallis, OR
Wehmeyer, Robert E. .... Bandera, TX
Wehmeyer-Homoya, Sharon A. .... Austin, TX
Wehmhoefer, Richard A. .... Denver, CO
Wehn, Kelli M. .... La Canada Flintridge, CA
Wehner, Charles C., (P.C.)
Los Angeles, CA
Wehner, Charles V. .... Kingwood, WV
Wehner, D.K. Rudy .... Dayton, OH
Wehner, James P. .... Washington, DC
Wehner, Karen A. .... Department of Justice,
Tax Division, GV
Wehner, Karen C. .... Houston, TX
Wehner Law Offices .... Kingwood, WV
Wehner and Perlman LLP
Los Angeles, CA
Wehner, Richard H. .... Fond du Lac, WI
Wehner, Richard K. .... Kingwood, WV
Wehner, Stephen V. .... Washington, DC
Bridgeport, WV
Wehner, Thomas J. .... Philadelphia, PA
Wehner, Timothy G. .... Jackson, TN
Wehner & York .... Washington, DC
Bridgeport, WV
Fairmont, WV
Wehr, Berger, Lane & Stevens
Davenport, IA
Wehr, Daniel J. .... Little Rock, AR
Wehr, Edward N. .... Davenport, IA
Wehr, Howard F. .... Columbus, OH
Wehr, John N. .... Sigourney, IA
Wehr, Karl C. .... Annapolis, MD
Wehr, Karl C., P.A. .... Annapolis, MD
Wehr, William J. .... Newport, KY
Wehrel, Richard L. .... Appleton, WI
Wehren, Lisa D. .... Garden Grove, CA
Wehrenberg, Dan .... Atlanta, GA
Wehrenberg, Ralph A. .... Kenilworth, IL
Wehrer, Greg .... Columbus, OH
Wehrle, Donald L. .... Elgin, IL
Wehrle, J. Christopher .... St. Louis, MO
Wehrle Law Firm, P.C. .... Denver, CO
Wehrle, Paul L. .... Fairfax, VA
Wehrle, Richard M. .... Lexington, KY
Wehrle, Richard T. .... Denver, CO
Wehrle, Royellen M. .... Orlando, FL
Wehrle, Thomas W. .... St. Louis, MO
Wehrle, William H. .... Martinsville, IN
Wehrli, John E. .... San Diego, CA
Wehrli, Martin G. .... Los Angeles, CA
Wehrli, Win .... Naperville, IL
Wehrly, Mark C. .... San Francisco, CA
Wehrman & Colantuono, L.L.C.
Leawood, KS
Kansas City, MO
Wehrman, J. Gregory .... Covington, KY
Wehrman, R. Barry .... Covington, KY
Wehrman, Robert L. .... Kansas City, MO
Wehrman and Wehrman, Chartered
Covington, KY
Wehrman, William E., Jr. .... Covington, KY
Wehrman, William E., Sr. .... Covington, KY
Wehrmann, Henry .... Dallas, TX
Wehrmann, Paul A. .... Dallas, TX
Wehrmeister, Elizabeth A.
Woodland Hills, CA
Wehrum, William L. .... Washington, DC
Wehrwein, Frederick .... Fort Wayne, IN
Wei, Andrea C. .... New York, NY
Wei, Christopher J. .... San Francisco, CA
Wei, Jerray .... San Jose, CA
Wei, Jun .... New York, NY
Wei, Li .... Salem, OR
Wei, Timothy P. .... New York, NY
Wei, Virginia W. .... Palo Alto, CA
Wei, Wen-Chi .... Flushing, NY
Weians, Barbara M. .... Kansas City, KS

Weiant, Bruce E. .... Waterbury, CT
Weiant, Clarissa L. .... Washington, DC
Weibel, Carol J. .... Everett, WA
Weibel, David G. .... Cleveland, OH
Weibel, Irene .... Springfield, MA
Weibel, Mark .... Dallas, TX
Weibel, Thomas M. .... Grand Rapids, MI
Weiberg, Edwin T. .... Sacramento, CA
Weible, George A. .... Livonia, MI
Weible, Robert A. .... Cleveland, OH
Weibling, Dennis M. .... Bellevue, WA
Weiby, David M. .... Superior, WI
Weich, Cecile C. .... Washington, DC
Bronx, NY
Weich, Paul, Law Offices of .... Phoenix, AZ
Weich, Ronald H. .... Washington, DC
Weichbrod, Morris D. .... Brooklyn, NY
Weichbrodt, Karen S. .... Oklahoma City, OK
Weichbrodt, Tom .... Alexandria, VA
Weichel, J. Alden, Jr. .... Bradenton, FL
Weicher, Richard E. .... Schaumburg, IL
Fort Worth, TX
Weichert, Glenn K. .... Austin, TX
Weichert, Stephen I. .... Livingston, NJ
Weichler, William P. .... Erie, PA
Weichman, David E. .... Newhall, IA
Weichman, Jack A. .... Santa Monica, CA
Weichman, Stephen .... Jackson, WY
Weichsel, John L. .... Hackensack, NJ
Weichsel, John L. .... New York, NY
Weichselbaum, Mark P. .... Hollywood, FL
Weicht, David .... Pittsburgh, PA
Weick, David C. .... Cuyahoga Falls, OH
Weick, Gibson & Lowry
Cuyahoga Falls, OH
Weick, James K., Jr. .... Lima, OH
Weick, Paul A. .... Cleveland, OH
Weick, Paul A. .... Cuyahoga Falls, OH
Weick, Walter .... Bridgewater, NJ
Weickhardt, George G.
San Francisco, CA
Weickhardt, Karl F. .... Alexandria, VA
Weida, Bruce W. .... Allentown, PA
Weida, Jane Davis .... Milwaukee, WI
Weidaw, Kenneth M., III .... McMurray, PA
Weidberg, Bertrand H. .... Irvine, CA
Weide & Associates .... Las Vegas, NV
Weide, Randal Scott .... Las Vegas, NV
Weideman, Carl, III
Grosse Pointe Woods, MI
Weideman, Carl M., Jr.
Grosse Pointe Woods, MI
Weideman, John Wayne, (P.C.) .... Phoenix, AZ
Weideman, Mark D. .... San Francisco, CA
Weideman, Robin .... Sacramento, CA
Weideman & Weideman, P.C.
Grosse Pointe Woods, MI
Weidemann, Bradley J. .... Winston-Salem, NC
Weidemann, Danae .... Roseville, MN
Weidemann, Hartmut .... Albuquerque, NM
Weidemann, Todd W. .... Omaha, NE
Weidemeyer, Carleton L. .... Clearwater, FL
Weidemeyer, Thomas H. .... New York, NY
Weidemier, B. Jean .... Cambridge, MA
Weidemier, Jean .... Boston, MA
Weidemier, Larry E. .... Unionville, CT
Weiden, Jared .... Washington, DC
Weiden, Michael S. .... Madison, WI
Weidenaar, Amy L. .... Sioux Falls, SD
Weidenaar, Bram .... Sioux Falls, SD
Weidenaar, William B. .... Chicago, IL
Weidenbach, Joseph L. .... Detroit, MI
Weidenbach, Mary Ledwell .... Boston, MA
Weidenbach, Mitchell L. .... San Antonio, TX
Weidenbaum, Walter .... Boca Raton, FL
Weidenbenner, Patrick H. .... Tallahassee, FL
Weidenbruch, John F.
Thousand Oaks, CA
Weidenbruch, Peter P., III .... Plano, TX
Weidenfeld, David .... Oak Brook, IL
Weidenfeld, Edward L. .... Washington, DC
Weidenfeld, Harold M. .... Newark, NJ
New York, NY
Weidenfeld, Jason E. .... Washington, DC
Weidenfeld Law Firm, The, P.C.
Washington, DC
Weidenfeld, Paul S. .... New Orleans, LA
Weidenfeller, Anne M. .... New Brunswick, NJ
Weidenfeller, George L.
Department of Housing and Urban
Development,
Office of General Counsel, GV
Weidenkopf, Jerold .... Tacoma, WA
Weider, Douglas R. .... New York, NY
Weider, John R. .... Buffalo, NY
Rochester, NY
Weider, Norman S. .... Miami, FL
Weidert, Richard J., Jr. .... St. Louis, MO
Weidhaas, Andrew J. .... Boston, MA
Weidig, W. Paul .... Metairie, LA
Weidinger, G. P. .... Ocala, FL
Weidinger, Michael A. .... Wilmington, DE
Weidle, William T., Jr. .... St. Louis, MO
Weidler, David H. .... Pottsville, PA
Weidler, Jerry L. .... Montgomery, AL
Weidlich, H. Edward, Jr. .... New Orleans, LA
Weidlich, Paul S. .... Chattanooga, TN
Weidling, Frank .... Kansas City, KS
Weidling, Katharine J. .... Kansas City, KS
Weidling, Kevin H. .... Princeton, NJ
Weidling & Weidling .... Kansas City, KS
Weidman, Andrew J. .... Pittsford, NY
Weidman, Arnold .... Banks, ID
Weidman, Carole L. .... New York, NY
Weidman, Charles R. .... Chatham, MA
Weidman, Charles S. .... Richmond, VA
Weidman, David J. .... Dover, DE
Weidman, Debra B. .... Lafayette Hill, PA

Weidman, Edwin N. .... New York, NY
Weidman, James W. .... Rochester, NY
Weidman, Jennifer .... New York, NY
Weidman, John C. .... Placerville, CA
Weidman, John David .... Tulsa, OK
Weidman, Jonathan D. .... Newport, NH
Weidman, Leon W. .... Los Angeles, CA
Weidman, Linda Mar .... Washington, DC
Weidman, Misha David .... San Francisco, CA
Weidman, Peter J. .... Philadelphia, PA
Weidman, Richard .... New York, NY
Weidman & Spatz, P.C. .... New York, NY
Weidman, Susan Pittard .... Georgetown, DE
Weidman & Weidman .... Pittsford, NY
Weidman, William B. .... Pittsford, NY
Weidmann, Daniel J. .... Orlando, FL
Weidner, Brant C. .... Chicago, IL
Weidner, Brian J. .... Buffalo, NY
Weidner, Brock M. .... Juneau, AK
Weidner, C. Roy, Jr. .... Lemoyne, PA
Weidner, Carole L. .... Capitola, CA
Weidner, Charlotte J., (P.A.) .... Bronson, FL
Weidner, Dean A. .... Harrisburg, PA
Weidner, Donald J. .... Tallahassee, FL
Weidner, Donald W. .... Jacksonville, FL
Weidner, Donald W., Professional Association
Jacksonville, FL
Weidner, Ebert .... Cleveland, OH
Weidner, Gary R. .... Green Bay, WI
Weidner, Gerald D. .... Kansas City, MO
Weidner, James B. .... New York, NY
Weidner, James C. .... Clarksville, GA
Weidner, James S., Jr. .... Charlotte, NC
Weidner, Kathleen E. .... Omaha, NE
Weidner, Larry W., II .... Beaufort, SC
Weidner, Lauren F. .... San Diego, CA
Weidner, Loren B. .... Los Angeles, CA
Weidner, Michael J. .... Minneapolis, MN
Weidner, Neil J. .... New York, NY
Weidner, Pagels & Cady .... Milwaukee, WI
Weidner, Phillip Paul .... Anchorage, AK
Weidner, Phillip Paul, & Associates, P.C.
Anchorage, AK
Weidner, Robert B. .... Cincinnati, OH
Weidner, Robert P. .... Scottsdale, AZ
Weidner, Robert W., Jr. .... Westmont, NJ
Philadelphia, PA
Weidner, Steven A. .... Waterloo, IA
Weidner, Thomas B., IV .... Richmond, VA
Weidner, Thomas J. .... Stillwater, MN
Weidner, Thomas P. .... Princeton, NJ
Weidner & Wegmann, LLC .... Beaufort, SC
Weido, Kevin V. .... Houston, TX
Weidt, David L. .... Duluth, MN
Weier, Charles E. .... St. Paul, MN
Weier, G. William .... St. Louis, MO
Weier, Hockensmith & Sherby, P.C.
St. Louis, MO
Weier, James D., Jr. .... Chicago, IL
Weier, Michael H. .... Seattle, WA
Weiermiller, Everett C. .... Elmira, NY
Weiermiller, Mark A. .... Elmira, NY
Weiers, Thomas E., Jr. .... Pittsburgh, PA
Weierstall, Eric J. .... Washington, DC
Weiffenbach, Diane V. .... Santa Ana, CA
Weiffenbach, E. Jon, Jr. .... Bradenton, FL
Weiffenbach & Thomas, P.A. .... Bradenton, FL
Weig, Brian Joseph .... Grand Forks, ND
Weig, John A. .... Palm Beach, FL
Weig, Robert W. .... Albuquerque, NM
Weigand, Clarke M. .... El Cerrito, CA
Weigand, Dale F. .... Chicago, IL
Weigand & Dodd .... Houma, LA
Weigand, John K. "Jack" .... Spokane, WA
Weigand, Joseph F., Jr. .... Meriden, CT
Weigand, Joseph J., Jr. (P.C.) .... Houma, LA
Weigand, Judith Lynch .... Olympia, WA
Weigand, Kathleen A. .... Cleveland, OH
Weigand, Kenneth R. .... Deerfield, IL
Weigand, Lesley A. .... Akron, OH
Weigand & Levenson .... New Orleans, LA
Weigand, Mahon and Adelman, Attorneys At Law, P.C. .... Meriden, CT
Weigand, Mark A. .... Troy, MI
Weigand, Michael L. .... Barberton, OH
Weigand, Penny D. .... Jamul, CA
Weigand, Richard A., (A Professional Law Corporation) .... New Orleans, LA
Weigand, Richard G. .... Barberton, OH
Weigand, Tory A. .... Boston, MA
Weigand, Wendy N. .... Phoenix, AZ
Weigand, William E. .... Seattle, WA
Weigand, William L., III .... Seattle, WA
Weigand, William L., Jr. .... Yakima, WA
Weigandt, Don R. .... Los Angeles, CA
Weigant, Kasper J. .... Portland, TX
Weigel, Blair A. .... Sarasota, FL
Weigel, Charles A., Jr. .... Wilmington, DE
Weigel, Charles T. .... Dallas, TX
Weigel, Cynthia J. .... Cambridge, MA
Weigel, David C. .... Fort Lauderdale, FL
Weigel, Douglas Kenneth .... Seattle, WA
Weigel, John J. .... New Orleans, LA
Weigel, John R. .... Princeton, NJ
Weigel, John T., Jr. .... Greensboro, NC
Weigel, Kenneth G. .... Washington, DC
Weigel, Rainer R. .... Chicago, IL
Weigel, Robert A. .... Lincoln, NE
Weigel, Robert L. .... New York, NY
Weigel, Russell C., III .... Miami, FL
Weigel, W. Breck .... Cincinnati, OH
Weigel, William H. .... New York, NY
Weigel, William J. .... Madison, WI
Weigel, William J., Jr. .... Pittsburg, KS
St. Joseph, MO
Weigell, Charles T.J., III .... Los Angeles, CA
Weigelt, Patricia M. .... Edmonds, WA
Weigend, Robert E., Jr. .... Fairfax, VA

Weigert, David L. .... Department of Justice,
Environment and Natural Resources
Division, GV
Weigert, James R. .... Bronx, NY
Weigert, Lillian S. .... Poughkeepsie, NY
Weight, Gary H. .... Provo, UT
Weight, Michael A. .... Honolulu, HI
Weight, Michael A., Attorney at Law, A Law
Corporation .... Honolulu, HI
Weight, Michael E. .... Everett, WA
Weight, Wayne V.
Federal Deposit Insurance Corporation, GV
Weigl, Christopher G. .... Hackensack, NJ
Weigl, William .... Troy, OH
Weigle, Charles H. .... Augusta, GA
Aiken, SC
Weigle, Douglas S. .... Covington, KY
Cincinnati, OH
Weigle, Gerald F. .... Fairfax, VA
Weigle, Gerald V., Jr. .... Cincinnati, OH
Weigle, Jerry A. .... Shippensburg, PA
Weigle, Jill Bernson .... Grand Rapids, MI
Weiglein, A. J. .... Sacramento, CA
Weiglein, Lorenz K. .... Tuckahoe, NY
Weigler, Jerard S. .... Portland, OR
Weigler, Steven H. .... Denver, CO
Weigler, Wendy E. .... Denver, CO
Weigley, D. Andrew .... St. Louis, MO
Weigley, Mariane E. .... Milwaukee, WI
Weigly, Mary B. .... Tallahassee, FL
Weigman, David L. .... Minnetonka, MN
Weigman, Joseph M. .... Thurmont, MD
Weigold, Ursula H. .... Houston, TX
Weihe, Bruce A. .... Fort Lauderdale, FL
Weihe, Thomas C. .... Denver, CO
Weiher, Roger R. .... Toledo, OH
Weihert, Gina M. .... Glendale, CA
Weihing, Thomas J. .... Bridgeport, CT
Weihl, Donald E. .... Belleville, IL
Weihmuller, John W. .... Tampa, FL
Weihrauch & Coblentz .... Worcester, MA
Weihrauch, Robert .... Worcester, MA
Weihrouch, Steven P. .... Arlington, VA
Weihs, Gerald August .... Vergennes, VT
Weihs, Jerome F. .... Worcester, MA
Weik, Joseph W. .... Wilmington, DE
Weik, Nitsche & Dougherty
Wilmington, DE
Weik, Teresa (Terri) Marie .... Birmingham, MI
Weikart, Kirk A. .... Richmond, IN
Weikart, Neil A. .... Minneapolis, MN
Weikel, Joseph W. .... Hunt Valley, MD
Weikel, Lisa J. .... Newtown, PA
Weikel, Sharon L. .... Englewood, CO
Weikel, Vaughan K. .... Baltimore, MD
Weiker, Daniel L. .... New York, NY
Weikers, Ronald N. .... Philadelphia, PA
Weikert, Michael J. .... Bloomfield Hills, MI
Weikert, Robert A. .... San Francisco, CA
Weikert, William E. .... Jasper, IN
Weiksnar, Linda L. .... Stuart, FL
Weiksnar, Thomas E. .... Stuart, FL
Weiksner, Sandra S. .... New York, NY
Weikum, Amanda .... Los Angeles, CA
Weikum, Jeffrey S. .... Bismarck, ND
Weikum, Ronald J. .... Elgin, ND
Weil, Adrienne D. .... San Francisco, CA
Weil, Alan Jay .... Los Angeles, CA
Weil, Alan R. .... Boston, MA
Weil, Alan S. .... New York, NY
Weil, Amy J. .... Wellesley, MA
Weil, Andrew L. .... Chicago, IL
Weil, Andrew L. .... Pittsburgh, PA
Weil, Arthur S. .... Menlo Park, CA
Weil & Associates .... Houston, TX
Weil, Brent R. .... Evansville, IN
Weil, Bruce A. .... Miami, FL
Weil, Cass S. .... Minneapolis, MN
Weil, Catherine S. .... Arlington, TX
Weil, Christopher M. .... Dallas, TX
Weil, Daniel W. .... Chicago, IL
Weil, David .... Long Beach, CA
Weil, David A. .... Nashville, TN
Weil, David G., Law Offices of
Long Beach, CA
Weil, David I. .... Los Angeles, CA
Weil, David J. .... Cheshire, CT
Weil, Diane C. .... Los Angeles, CA
Weil, Edward G. .... Oakland, CA
Weil, Edward S. .... Chicago, IL
Weil, Elissa L. .... Santa Monica, CA
Weil, Floyd S. .... New York, NY
Weil, Frank A. .... Washington, DC
New York, NY
Weil, Fred B. .... San Francisco, CA
Weil, Frederick J. .... Redding, CA
Weil, Freiburg, Thomas & Petersen, P.C.
Chicago, IL
Weil, Gary L. .... Greenwood Village, CO
Weil, Gilbert H. .... New York, NY
Weil, Gotshal & Manges LLP
Menlo Park, CA
Washington, DC
Miami, FL
New York, NY
Dallas, TX
Houston, TX
Weil, Guttman & Malkin, LLP
New York, NY
Weil, Harry H. .... Pittsburgh, PA
Weil, Henry E. .... Rockville, MD
Weil, Isabel S. .... Newark, NJ
Weil, Jay Howard .... New York, NY
Weil, Jean A. .... Orange, CA
Weil, Jeffrey G. .... Philadelphia, PA
Weil, Joanne F. .... New York, NY
Weil, John A. .... Washington, DC
Weil, John A., Law Office of .... Yuma, AZ

Weil, John W. ... **Portland, OR**
Weil, Jonas, III ... San Francisco, CA
Weil, Jonathan L. ... **Palo Alto, CA**
Andover, MA
Weil, Judith H. ... **New York, NY**
Weil, Karen K. ... Chicago, IL
Weil, Karen Vogel ... **Newport Beach, CA**
Weil, Kelly Allegra ... **Los Angeles, CA**
Weil, Kenneth C. ... Seattle, WA
Weil, Kenneth J. ... **Miami, FL**
Weil & Kestenbaum ... Bayside, NY
Weil, L. James, Jr. ... Birmingham, AL
Weil, Lance T. ... Saratoga, CA
Weil, Lauren J. ... Sacramento, CA
Weil, Leah E. ... Culver City, CA
Weil, Lisa D. ... **Walnut Creek, CA**
Weil, Loren A. ... **Chicago, IL**
Weil, Lorraine Murphy ... Hartford, CT
Weil, Martin A. ... Newark, NJ
Weil, Matthew Francis
Newport Beach, CA
Weil, Michael A. ... Detroit, MI
Weil, Michael D. ... New York, NY
Weil, Murray B., Jr. ... Miami Beach, FL
Weil, Nancy S. ... Seattle, WA
Weil, Norman I. ... Hillsborough, CA
Weil, Norman I. ... **Miami, FL**
Weil, Paul M. ... **San Diego, CA**
Weil, Paul P. ... **St. Louis, MO**
Weil, Peter H. ... **New York, NY**
Weil, Peter M. ... **Los Angeles, CA**
Weil & Petrocchi, A Professional Corporation ... **Dallas, TX**
Weil, Rex ... Cincinnati, OH
Weil, Richard ... Saipan, TT
Weil, Richard B. ... Chicago, IL
Weil, Richard G. ... San Antonio, TX
Weil, Richard L. ... **New Orleans, LA**
Weil, Richard L. ... Portland, OR
Weil, Richard S. ... **San Francisco, CA**
Weil, Robert ... Los Angeles, CA
Weil, Robert B. ... Chicago, IL
Weil, Robert J. ... **Washington, DC**
Weil, Roger J. ... Middlesex, NJ
Weil, Ronald P. ... **Miami, FL**
Weil, Russell T. ... **Washington, DC**
Weil, Ruth M. ... Los Angeles, CA
Weil, Sarah Marion ... **Chicago, IL**
Weil, Sherrill Lang ... Washington, DC
Weil, Sidney ... **Cincinnati, OH**
Weil, Stephan G. ... **Washington, DC**
Weil, Stephen E. ... Washington, DC
Weil, Stephen I. ... **Houston, TX**
Weil, Steven D. ... **Boston, MA**
Weil, Steven S. ... **Alamo, CA**
Weil, Thomas E., Jr. ... **Houston, TX**
Weil, Toby Alan ... New York, NY
Weil & Weil ... Saratoga, CA
Weil, Wendy T. ... **Oakland, CA**
Weilacher, Robert G. ... **Washington, DC**
Weiland, Anne L. ... Menomonee Falls, WI
Weiland, Bruce P. ... Bainbridge Island, WA
Weiland, Charles H. ... Aurora, IL
Weiland, David J. ... **Fresno, CA**
Weiland, Donald G. ... Chicago, IL
Weiland, Herbert ... Florham Park, NJ
Weiland, Herbert E. ... Lebanon, NJ
Weiland, Jennifer Jo ... Dell Rapids, SD
Weiland, Karlene K. ... Bellingham, WA
Weiland, Kenneth J., Jr. ... Des Moines, IA
Weiland, Kurt H. ... Columbus, OH
Weiland, Lisa A. ... Chicago, IL
Weiland, Marcel P. ... **Gold River, CA**
Weiland, Mark B. ... Lombard, IL
Weiland, Melissa A. ... **Washington, DC**
Weiland, Michael A. ... Wheaton, IL
Weiland, Michael J. ... **Costa Mesa, CA**
Weiland, Richard F. ... Geneva, IL
Weiland, Robert A. ... **Boston, MA**
Weiland, S. Cass ... **Dallas, TX**
Weiland, William G. ... Elkhorn, WI
Weiland, William H. ... **Houston, TX**
Weilandt, Timothy E. ... **Chicago, IL**
Weilbacher, David P ... Arroyo Grande, CA
Weilbacher, William John ... Ventura, CA
Weilbaecher, Michelle ... Metairie, LA
Weild, David, III ... **New York, NY**
Weilding, Douglas B. ... Attleboro, MA
Weilein, George L. ... **Waterloo, IA**
Weiler, Alan G. ... New York, NY
Weiler, Anthony J. ... Bismarck, ND
Weiler, Barbara C. ... New York, NY
Weiler, Bernard K. ... **Aurora, IL**
Weiler & Borst, LLP ... **Martinez, CA**
San Ramon, CA
Walnut Creek, CA
Weiler & Brandman ... Cranford, NJ
Weiler, Claire A. ... **Chicago, IL**
Weiler, Clifford D. ... **San Diego, CA**
Weiler, Daniel A. ... West Dundee, IL
Weiler, Darcy A. ... Edina, MN
Weiler, David J. ... **Washington, DC**
Weiler, Elizabeth A. ... Cranford, NJ
White Plains, NY
Weiler, Fred M. ... **New York, NY**
Weiler, Geo. A. ... New York, NY
Weiler, Gregory N. ... **Irvine, CA**
Weiler, James F. ... Houston, TX
Weiler, Jeffry L. ... **Cleveland, OH**
Weiler, John J. ... **New Orleans, LA**
Weiler, Joseph F. ... Houston, TX
Weiler, Joseph M. ... **Topeka, KS**
Weiler, Kevin P. ... Brecksville, OH
Weiler, Kristen R. ... Germantown, OH
Weiler, Leonard A. ... St. Cloud, MN
Weiler, Leonard D., (PC) ... **San Ramon, CA**
Weiler, Linda ... Denver, CO
Weiler, Mark Stephen ... **Charleston, WV**
Weiler, Mary P. ... Portland, OR
Weiler, Michael P. ... Ladysmith, WI
Weiler & Noble, P.C. ... Geneva, IL
Weiler, Peter M. ... **Locust Valley, NY**
Weiler, Robert J. ... Columbus, OH
Weiler, Robert K. ... **Syracuse, NY**
Weiler, Roger A. ... Schiller Park, IL
Weiler, Rory T. ... Geneva, IL
Weiler, Sonya ... **Short Hills, NJ**
Weiler, Steven A. ... **Washington, DC**
Weiler, Terry D. ... **Reading, PA**
Weiler, Thomas R. ... **Chicago, IL**
Wheaton, IL
Weiler, Timothy J. ... **Wilmington, DE**
Weiler, Todd David ... **Salt Lake City, UT**
Weiler, Wayne F. ... Aurora, IL
Weiler, William A. ... Pittsburgh, PA
Weiler, William Blake ... **Wheaton, IL**
Weiler, William S. ... Detroit, MI
Weiler, William S. ... Southfield, MI
Weilert, Thomas J. ... Wichita, KS
Weilgus, Stanley R. ... Livingston, NJ
Weilheimer, Laurence ... Philadelphia, PA
Weil-Herrera, Gloria ... Los Angeles, CA
Weill, Andrew J. ... **San Francisco, CA**
Weill, David A. ... **Omaha, NE**
Weill, Douglas B. ... Sacramento, CA
Weill, Elizabeth A. ... **Mount Laurel, NJ**
New York, NY
Philadelphia, PA
Weill, Felix R. ... **Baton Rouge, LA**
Weill, Flossie ... **Chattanooga, TN**
Weill, Harry ... **Chattanooga, TN**
Weill, James D. ... Washington, DC
Weill, Jay R. ... San Francisco, CA
Weill, Jeff ... Jackson, MS
Weill, Jeffrey J. ... **Minneapolis, MN**
Weill, Judy A. ... Mount Kisco, NY
Weill, Karl S., Jr. ... Abbeville, LA
Weill, L., III ... New Orleans, LA
Weill, Leo ... Brimfield, OH
Weill, Randall B. ... **Portland, ME**
Weill, Richard A. ... **Troutdale, OR**
Weill, Richard E. ... White Plains, NY
Weill, Richard L. ... Armonk, NY
Weill, Robert C. ... **Tampa, FL**
Weill, Robert J. ... Santa Barbara, CA
Weill, Terry Paul ... Memphis, TN
Weill & Weill ... **Chattanooga, TN**
Weills, Anne Butterfield ... Oakland, CA
Weilmuenster, J. Michael ... Belleville, IL
Weiman, Edward E. ... **Los Angeles, CA**
Weiman, Enrique W. ... Stone Mountain, GA
Weiman, E. W. ... Stone Mountain, GA
Weiman, Herbert R. ... **Philadelphia, PA**
Weiman, Herbert R., Jr. ... **Philadelphia, PA**
Phoenixville, PA
Weiman and Perry, P.C.
Stone Mountain, GA
Weiman, S. Wyle ... Irvine, CA
Weiman, Sidney ... **Baltimore, MD**
Weiman and Weiman ... **Philadelphia, PA**
Weimar, John A. ... Orland Park, IL
Weimar, Karen M. ... **Nashville, TN**
Weimar, Linda M. ... **Portland, OR**
Weimer, A. R. ... Freeport, IL
Weimer, Beth E. ... Washington, DC
Weimer & Boyce ... Manassas, VA
Weimer, Brian D. ... **Washington, DC**
Weimer, Britton D. ... **Minneapolis, MN**
Weimer, Carroll A., Jr. ... Manassas, VA
Weimer, David J. ... **Kansas City, MO**
Weimer, David P. ... **Akron, OH**
Weimer, Douglas R. ... Library of Congress, Congressional Research Service, GV
Weimer, Elizabeth ... **Washington, DC**
Weimer, Elizabeth Patricia ... Clearwater, FL
Weimer, Francis P. ... **Buffalo, NY**
Weimer, Gregory A. ... **Burlington, VT**
Weimer, John B. ... **Columbus, OH**
Weimer, John L., III ... Thibodaux, LA
Weimer, Joseph S. ... Pittsburgh, PA
Weimer, Karen V. ... Anchorage, AK
Weimer, Leslee Ellen ... Orlando, FL
Weimer, Marilyn H.
Securities and Exchange Commission, Division of Enforcement, GV
Weimer, Mary ... **Santa Monica, CA**
Weimer, Paul E. ... **Akron, OH**
Weimer, Richard P. ... Lafayette, LA
Weimer and Roland ... Youngstown, OH
Weimer, Sheila Q. ... Buffalo, NY
Weimer, Shelia Jane ... Marion, VA
Weimer, William A. ... Youngstown, OH
Weimer, William K. ... Oakdale, MN
Weimers, Eric H. ... **Chicago, IL**
Weimorts, Michael L. ... Milton, FL
Wein, Alan ... West Hartford, CT
Wein, Aliza F. ... **New York, NY**
Wein, Barry D. ... Passaic, NJ
Wein, Bradley D. ... Richmond, VA
Wein, Bruce J. ... **New York, NY**
Wein, Dale A. ... Aberdeen, SD
Wein, Daren G. ... **San Jose, CA**
Wein, Frederick ... Princeton, NJ
Wein, Gale B. ... New York, NY
Wein, Gerald J. ... Rochester, NY
Wein, Grace E. ... Chicago, IL
Wein, Hershel ... **New York, NY**
Wein, Howard J. ... **Pittsburgh, PA**
Wein, Jack I. ... East Lansing, MI
Wein, Kevin M. ... **Denver, CO**
Wein, Leon E ... Brooklyn, NY
Wein, Marjorie D. (Wiener) ... New York, NY
Wein, Matthew L. ... **Los Angeles, CA**
Wein & McDonald, P.C. ... Richmond, VA
Wein, Nancy J. ... **New York, NY**
Wein, Paul H. ... Guilderland, NY
Wein, Phillip L. ... **Clarion, PA**
Wein, Rifka ... **New York, NY**
Wein, Stacy E. ... Plantation, FL
Wein, Stephen J. ... **St. Petersburg, FL**
Wein, Steven A. ... **Providence, RI**
Weinacht, J. William ... Pecos, TX
Weinacker, Robert Machel, III ... Tazewell, VA
Weinand, Bernard F. ... **Kansas City, MO**
Weinandy, James R. ... Bowling Green, OH
Weinard, John, Jr. ... Bloomington, MN
Weinbach, Elia, (A Professional Corporation)
Los Angeles, CA
Weinbaum & Abbo, P.C.
Farmington Hills, MI
Weinbaum, Barbara ... Roslyn, NY
Weinbaum, Chet E. ... Fort Pierce, FL
Weinbaum, George ... White Plains, NY
Weinbaum, Michael A. ... **Chicago, IL**
Weinbaum, Peter M. ... Montpelier, VT
Weinbaum, Richard ... Brooklyn, NY
Weinbaum, Robert C. ... **Detroit, MI**
Weinbaum, Samuel ... Brooklyn, NY
Weinbaum, Stephen J. ... Jacksonville, FL
Weinberg, A. Brian ... Los Angeles, CA
Weinberg, Aaron D. ... **Houston, TX**
Weinberg, Alan G. ... Brooklyn, NY
Weinberg, Alan H. ... **Cleveland, OH**
Weinberg, Alan M. ... New York, NY
Weinberg, Alexander M. ... Miami, FL
Weinberg, Allen ... **Philadelphia, PA**
Weinberg, Allen G. ... Beverly Hills, CA
Weinberg, Amos ... Great Neck, NY
Weinberg, Andrew L. ... **New York, NY**
Weinberg, Annette Ballou ... Cleveland, OH
Weinberg, Arden K. ... Burlingame, CA
Weinberg, Arnold ... **Chicago, IL**
Weinberg, Barbara ... **Philadelphia, PA**
Weinberg, Barry H. ... Department of Justice, Civil Rights Division, GV
Weinberg, Barry M. ... Cherry Hill, NJ
Weinberg & Bell, Attorneys at Law, A Law Corporation ... Honolulu, HI
Weinberg, Ben L., Jr. ... **Atlanta, GA**
Weinberg, Benjamin C. ... **Chicago, IL**
Weinberg, Brett A. ... **Coral Gables, FL**
Weinberg, Brown & Curtis ... **Sumter, SC**
Weinberg, Campbell, Slone & Slone, P.S.C.
Hindman, KY
Weinberg & Capello ... Lexington, KY
Weinberg, Carl David ... New York, NY
Weinberg, Charles B. ... Norwich, NY
Weinberg, Charles H. ... **New York, NY**
Weinberg, Craig A. ... **Boulder, CO**
Weinberg, David ... Dallas, TX
Weinberg, David A. ... Lexington, KY
Weinberg, David B. ... **Washington, DC**
Weinberg, David C. ... **Palo Alto, CA**
Weinberg, David C. ... **Philadelphia, PA**
Weinberg, David S. ... Chicago, IL
Weinberg, David S. ... Frederick, MD
Weinberg, Debra E. ... Columbus, OH
Weinberg, Denice ... Columbus, OH
Weinberg, Diane L. ... **New York, NY**
Weinberg, Donald C. ... **Bethesda, MD**
Weinberg, Donald L. ... Quincy, IL
Weinberg, Doron ... **San Francisco, CA**
Weinberg, Douglas D. ... **Chicago, IL**
Weinberg, Edward B. ... **Louisville, KY**
Weinberg, Edward H. ... Great Neck, NY
Weinberg, Edwin W. ... **New York, NY**
Weinberg, Elaine J. ... Irvine, CA
Weinberg, Ellsworth A., Jr. ... Dallas, TX
Weinberg, Eric H. ... New Brunswick, NJ
Weinberg, Erika ... **New York, NY**
Weinberg, Ethel E. ... Lexington, SC
Weinberg, Frederic I. ... **Voorhees, NJ**
Norristown, PA
Philadelphia, PA
Weinberg, Gale B. ... Hackensack, NJ
Weinberg, Gary ... **Westmont, NJ**
Weinberg, Gary R. ... Brooklyn, NY
Weinberg, Gayle L. ... Palatine, IL
Weinberg, Gerald ... Albany, NY
Weinberg, Glenn L. ... **Baltimore, MD**
Weinberg, Gregg G. ... **Houston, TX**
Weinberg, Gregg M. ... **Annapolis, MD**
Weinberg, Harold G. ... Seattle, WA
Weinberg, Harold R. ... Lexington, KY
Weinberg, Harris E. ... San Francisco, CA
Weinberg, Harvey ... **Garden City, NY**
Weinberg, Herbert ... **Boston, MA**
Weinberg, Herbert L. ... **Los Angeles, CA**
Weinberg, Herman P. ... **Philadelphia, PA**
Weinberg, Herschel M. ... **New York, NY**
Weinberg, Hillel ... House of Representatives, Committee Legal Personnel, GV
Weinberg, Hoffman, Casey & Ropers
Larkspur, CA
Weinberg, Howard N. ... Los Angeles, CA
Weinberg, Howard S. ... Bal Harbour, FL
Weinberg, Hugh B. ... New York, NY
Weinberg, Idele L. ... Chicago, IL
Weinberg, Irwin ... Springfield, NJ
Weinberg, Ivan ... **Larkspur, CA**
Weinberg, Jack ... Los Angeles, CA
Weinberg, Jack ... **New York, NY**
Weinberg, Jack L. ... Camden, NJ
Weinberg & Jacobs, LLP ... **Rockville, MD**
Weinberg, James L. ... **Pittsburgh, PA**
Weinberg, James L. ... **Richmond, VA**
Weinberg, James M. ... Santa Monica, CA
Weinberg, Jan M. ... Honolulu, HI
Weinberg, Jane C. ... **New York, NY**
Weinberg, Jay M. ... **Richmond, VA**
Weinberg, J. D. ... **New York, NY**
Weinberg, Jed L. ... **San Diego, CA**
Weinberg, Jeffery T. ... Baltimore, MD
Weinberg, Jeffrey A.
Executive Office Of The President, Office of Management and Budget, GV
Weinberg, Jeffrey J. ... **New York, NY**
Weinberg, Jeffrey S. ... Braddock, PA
Weinberg, Jerrold G. ... **Norfolk, VA**
Weinberg, Jerry V. ... New York, NY
Weinberg, Jesse S. ... Baltimore, MD
Weinberg, Jill J. ... **Dallas, TX**
Weinberg, Joanna K. ... Berkeley, CA
Weinberg, Joel B. ... Woodland Hills, CA
Weinberg, John Lee ... Seattle, WA
Weinberg, Jolie G. ... Columbia, MD
Weinberg, Jon L. ... Marietta, GA
Weinberg, Jonathan D. ... **Washington, DC**
Weinberg, Jonathan R. ... New York, NY
Weinberg, Joseph I. ... Atlanta, GA
Weinberg, Joseph M. ... **Haddonfield, NJ**
Weinberg, Joseph, P.C. ... Atlanta, GA
Weinberg, Joshua D. ... **Washington, DC**
Weinberg, Julien ... Manning, SC
Weinberg, Kaley, Gross & Pergament, L.L.P.
Garden City, NY
Mineola, NY
Weinberg, Kathy Coleman ... **Dallas, TX**
Weinberg, Kenneth G. ... Shaker Heights, OH
Weinberg & Kert ... Garden City, NY
Weinberg, Larry P. ... Washington, DC
Weinberg, Laura B. ... **Chicago, IL**
Weinberg, Laurel J. ... **New York, NY**
Weinberg, Lawrence I. ... Santa Monica, CA
Weinberg, Lee M. ... **Los Angeles, CA**
Weinberg, Lee S. ... Pittsburgh, PA
Weinberg Legal Group ... **Phoenix, AZ**
Weinberg, Leonard D. ... Los Angeles, CA
Weinberg, Linda M. ... **Washington, DC**
Weinberg, Lisa A. ... **Woodland Hills, CA**
Weinberg, Louis Howard ... Great Neck, NY
Weinberg, Lynn ... **Baltimore, MD**
Weinberg, Lysa M. ... Brooklyn, NY
Weinberg, Marc ... Philadelphia, PA
Weinberg, Marc A. ... Jenkintown, PA
Weinberg, Marc D. ... **Philadelphia, PA**
Weinberg, Marc P. ... St. Louis, MO
Weinberg, Margot D. ... Glencoe, IL
Weinberg, Mark ... **North Miami Beach, FL**
Weinberg, Mark B., (P.C.)
Washington, DC
Rockville, MD
Weinberg, Mark D. ... **Hackensack, NJ**
New York, NY
Weinberg, Mark D. ... Toledo, OH
Weinberg, Marshall R. ... Chicago, IL
Weinberg, Martin ... **Harrisburg, PA**
Philadelphia, PA
Weinberg, Martin B. ... Irvine, CA
Weinberg, Martin G. ... **Boston, MA**
Weinberg, Martin R. ... Roslyn Heights, NY
Weinberg, Martin S. ... **Louisville, KY**
Weinberg, Marvin L. ... **Philadelphia, PA**
Weinberg, Maryellen ... Brooklyn, NY
Weinberg, Matthew B. ... San Francisco, CA
Weinberg, Matthew B., Professional Corporation ... San Francisco, CA
Weinberg, Maynard H. ... **Omaha, NE**
Weinberg, McCormick, Chatzinoff and Paul, A Professional Association
Haddonfield, NJ
Weinberg, Melissa Ann ... **New York, NY**
Weinberg, Melvin ... **New York, NY**
Weinberg, Michael ... **Boston, MA**
Weinberg, Michael ... **Dallas, TX**
Weinberg, Michael ... **Houston, TX**
Weinberg, Michael A. ... **Chicago, IL**
Weinberg, Michael A. ... **Haddonfield, NJ**
Weinberg, Michael D. ... Denver, CO
Weinberg, Michelle A. ... Chicago, IL
Weinberg, M. M., III ... **Sumter, SC**
Weinberg, M. M., Jr. ... **Sumter, SC**
Weinberg, Morri ... **New York, NY**
Weinberg, Morris, Jr. ... **Tampa, FL**
Weinberg, Morton ... Brooklyn, NY
Weinberg, Morton M. ... Los Angeles, CA
Weinberg, Myron ... **New York, NY**
Weinberg, Neal ... Albany, GA
Weinberg, Neal, P.C. ... Albany, GA
Weinberg, Neil ... Buffalo, NY
Weinberg, Neil H. ... **Chicago, IL**
Weinberg, Norman S. ... Brighton, MA
Weinberg, Paul ... Beverly, MA
Weinberg, Paul S. ... **Springfield, MA**
Weinberg, Paul S. ... Philadelphia, PA
Weinberg, Peter A. ... **New York, NY**
Weinberg, Peter F. ... **Denver, CO**
Weinberg, Peter Michel ... Melville, NY
Weinberg, Philip S. ... Pascagoula, MS
Weinberg, Rand D. ... Frederick, MD
Weinberg, Richard A. ... **Wayne, NJ**
Weinberg, Richard B. ... Wayne, MI
Weinberg, Richard D. ... **New York, NY**
Weinberg, Richard G. ... St. Augustine, FL
Weinberg, Richard J. ... Garden City, NY
Weinberg, Richard M. ... New York, NY
Weinberg, Richard S. ... **Chicago, IL**
Weinberg, Robert ... **Washington, DC**
Weinberg, Robert A. ... **Long Beach, CA**
Weinberg, Robert B. ... **Sioux City, IA**
Weinberg, Robert E. ... Davenport, IA
Weinberg, Robert J. ... **Philadelphia, PA**
Weinberg, Robert Jay ... Santa Monica, CA
Weinberg, Robert L. ... Washington, DC
Weinberg, Robert L. ... Baltimore, MD
Weinberg, Robert L. ... Gaithersburg, MD
Weinberg, Robert M. ... **Washington, DC**
Weinberg, Robert P. ... Bayonne, NJ
Weinberg, Robin S. ... **New York, NY**
Weinberg, Roger ... **Towson, MD**
Weinberg, Roger S., P.A. ... **Towson, MD**

Weinberg, Ronald E., Jr ....Cleveland, OH
Weinberg, Sam T., (P.C.) ....Mary Esther, FL
Weinberg, Samuel ....New York, NY
Weinberg, Sanford I.
West Palm Beach, FL
Edison, NJ
Great Neck, NY
Rockville Centre, NY
Merion, PA
Weinberg, Sara C. ....Washington, DC
Weinberg, Scott A. ....New York, NY
Weinberg, Shelley Rice ....Chicago, IL
Weinberg, Sidney ....Boston, MA
Weinberg, Stacy K. ....Charlotte, NC
Columbia, SC
Spartanburg, SC
Weinberg, Stanley ....Bradenton, FL
Weinberg, Stanley ....Philadelphia, PA
Weinberg, Stanley I. ....Dallas, TX
Weinberg, Stanley L. ....Shrewsbury, MA
Weinberg & Stein, A Professional Corporation ....Norfolk, VA
Weinberg, Steve G. ....Oakland, CA
Weinberg, Steven ....Washington, DC
Weinberg, Steven ....New York, NY
Weinberg, Steven A. ......Fort Lauderdale, FL
Weinberg, Steven A. ....Dallas, TX
Weinberg, Steven D. ....Los Angeles, CA
Weinberg, Steven J. ....Chicago, IL
Weinberg, Steven J., Law Office of
Palm Desert, CA
Weinberg, Steven J., Law Office of
Palm Springs, CA
Weinberg, Steven K. ....New York, NY
Weinberg, Steven L. ....Pasadena, CA
Weinberg, Steven L. ....New York, NY
Weinberg, Steven Marc ....Phoenix, AZ
Weinberg, Stewart ....Oakland, CA
Weinberg & Ustas, P.C. ....Hackensack, NJ
Weinberg, Walter S. ....Chicago, IL
Weinberg & Weinberg ....Quincy, IL
Weinberg & Weinberg ....Frederick, MD
Weinberg & Weinberg, P.C. ....Omaha, NE
Weinberg, Wheeler, Hudgins, Gunn & Dial, LLC ....Atlanta, GA
Weinberg & Wilder ....San Francisco, CA
Weinberg, William A. ....New York, NY
Weinberg, William R. ....Hindman, KY
Weinberg, William R. ....Dallas, TX
Weinberg, Zelma Berger ....Chicago, IL
Weinberg, Ziff & Miller ....Palo Alto, CA
Redwood City, CA
San Jose, CA
Weinberg-Brodt, Chaya F. ......New York, NY
Weinberger, Alan Dean ......New Orleans, LA
Weinberger, Alan M. ....St. Louis, MO
Weinberger, Barrett N. ....Cincinnati, OH
Weinberger, Benjamin David ....Chicago, IL
Weinberger, Berman & Singer, P.C.
New York, NY
Weinberger, Brian A. ....Phoenix, AZ
Weinberger, Brian S. ....Encino, CA
Weinberger, Caspar W. ....Washington, DC
Weinberger, Charles H. ....Santa Clara, CA
Weinberger, Daniel ....Winnetka, IL
Weinberger, David ....New York, NY
Weinberger, David J. ....New York, NY
Weinberger, David P. ....Miami, FL
Weinberger, Donald ....New York, NY
Weinberger, Eleanor ....Rockville, MD
Weinberger, Elizabeth Alice ....New York, NY
Weinberger, Emanuel ....Tampa, FL
Weinberger, Gregory L. ....New York, NY
Weinberger, Harold P. ....New York, NY
Weinberger, Howard A. ....Dallas, TX
Weinberger, Jack ....New York, NY
Weinberger, James W. ....Argonne, IL
Weinberger, Janet Brauer ....Newton, MA
Weinberger, Jeff A. ....New City, NY
Weinberger, Jeffrey I. ....Los Angeles, CA
Weinberger, Jerry J. ....Scranton, PA
Weinberger, Joe, Jr. ....Roxboro, NC
Weinberger, Jonathan D. ....New York, NY
Weinberger, Joseph ....Hialeah, FL
Weinberger, Joseph A. ....New York, NY
Weinberger, Joseph B. ....Elk Grove, CA
Roseville, CA
Weinberger, Joseph B. ....Sacramento, CA
Weinberger, Julie F. ....Kissimmee, FL
Weinberger & Kanan, A Professional Corporation ....Denver, CO
Weinberger, Laurence A. ....Media, PA
Weinberger, Lawrence ....Roslyn Heights, NY
Weinberger, Lawrence Law Offices of
Roslyn Heights, NY
Weinberger, Leo ....New York, NY
Weinberger, Leonard A. ....Kew Gardens, NY
Weinberger, Marc J. ....Washington, DC
Weinberger, Mark Alan ....Washington, DC
Weinberger, Mark I. ....San Francisco, CA
Weinberger, Mark S. ....Cuyahoga Falls, OH
Weinberger, Martin R. ....Simi Valley, CA
Weinberger, Mel S. ....Washington, DC
Weinberger, Michael ....New York, NY
Charlotte, NC
Weinberger, Michael A.
Cuyahoga Falls, OH
Weinberger, Michael D. ....New York, NY
Weinberger, Michael J. ....New York, NY
Weinberger, Michael L. ....Avenel, NJ
Weinberger, Michael S. ....Roslyn Heights, NY
Weinberger, Paul I. ....Poughkeepsie, NY
Weinberger, Peter H. ....Cleveland, OH
Weinberger, Peter L. ....Los Angeles, CA
Weinberger, Richard ....New York, NY
Weinberger, Robert A. ....Denver, CO
Weinberger, Robert F. ....Daly City, CA

Weinberger, Robert M.
North Palm Beach, FL
Weinberger, Robin Janick ....St. Louis, MO
Weinberger, Seth J. ....Chicago, IL
Weinberger, Sheila N. ....Menlo Park, CA
Weinberger, Sheive & Tinsley, P.A.
Kissimmee, FL
Weinberger, Stanley J., Jr. ......St. Cloud, MN
Weinberger, Stanley R. ....Chicago, IL
Weinberger, Steven ....Hartford, CT
Weinberger, Steven E. ....Pasadena, CA
Weinberger, Steven H. ....Clearwater, FL
Weinberger, Steven I. ....Stamford, CT
Weinberger, Steven I.
Fort Lauderdale, FL
Weinberger, Thomas R. ....New York, NY
Weinberger, William E., (Professional Corporation) ....Los Angeles, CA
Weinblatt, Alan W. ....St. Paul, MN
Weinblatt, Amy J. ....Washington, DC
Weinblatt, Anita J. ....Massapequa Park, NY
Weinblatt & Gaylord, P.C. ....St. Paul, MN
Weinblatt, Henry J. ....Los Angeles, CA
Weinblatt, Marc D. ....Mineola, NY
Weinblatt, Richard A. ....Hauppauge, NY
Weinblatt, Seymour S. ....Fort Myers, FL
Weinbren, Don B. ....Tampa, FL
Weinbrenner, Neil E. ....Las Cruces, NM
Weinbrenner, Neil E., P.A., Law Offices of
Las Cruces, NM
Weincroft, Alfred S. ....Stoughton, MA
Weindler, John P. ....New York, NY
Weindling, Susan L. ....Denver, CO
Weindorf, Sherry L. ....New York, NY
Weindruch, Linda S. ....Des Moines, IA
Weine, Nelson S. ....Milwaukee, WI
Weine, Nelson S., S.C. ....Milwaukee, WI
Weiner, A. Keith ....Baltimore, MD
Weiner, A. Kenneth ....East Brunswick, NJ
Weiner, Aaron D. ....Omaha, NE
Weiner, Abby E. ....Teaneck, NJ
New York, NY
Weiner, Adam T. ....Cameron Park, CA
Weiner, Alan E. ....Melville, NY
Weiner, Alan R. ....New York, NY
Weiner, Alan S. ....New Carrollton, MD
Rockville, MD
Weiner, Alan S. ....New York, NY
Weiner, Alfred J. ....New City, NY
Weiner, Alice D. ....New York, NY
Weiner, Allan J. ....Washington, DC
Weiner, Allen S. ....Department of State,
Office of the Legal Adviser, GV
Weiner, Allison E. ....Atlantic City, NJ
Weiner, Allison Hope ....Los Angeles, CA
Weiner, Andrew B. ....Seattle, WA
Weiner, Andrew E. ....Haddonfield, NJ
Weiner, Andrew J. ....New York, NY
Weiner & Argo, P.A. ....Ocala, FL
Weiner, Arnold L. ....Plainview, NY
Weiner, Arnold M. ....Miami, FL
Weiner, Arnold M. ....Baltimore, MD
Weiner, Aron G. ....Savannah, GA
Weiner & Aronson, P.A.
Delray Beach, FL
Weiner, Arthur L. ....Barnstable, MA
Weiner, Arthur S. ....New York, NY
Weiner and Associates ....West Orange, NJ
Weiner, Barbara A. ....Highland Park, IL
Weiner, Barbara E. ....Albany, NY
Weiner, Barry A. ....Montclair, NJ
Weiner, Barry M. ....Cedarhurst, NY
Weiner, Barry Ross ....New York, NY
Weiner, Barry Ross, P.C. ....New York, NY
Weiner, Barry Y. ....Boston, MA
Weiner, B. C., (Ms.) ....Albuquerque, NM
Weiner, Benjamin ....North Brunswick, NJ
Weiner, Bennett I. ....New York, NY
Weiner, Bertram I. ....Silver Spring, MD
Weiner, Beryl H., (P.C.) ....Atlanta, GA
Weiner, Beryl, (Professional Corporation)
Los Angeles, CA
Weiner, Brodsky, Sidman & Kider, P.C.
Washington, DC
Weiner, Bruce ....Brooklyn, NY
Weiner, Bruce B. ....Pittsburgh, PA
Weiner & Burt, P.C. ....Harrisville, MI
Weiner, Cappy ....Kingston, NY
Weiner, Carl N. ....Lansdale, PA
Weiner, Carole M. ....Philadelphia, PA
Weiner, Charles ....Cincinnati, OH
Weiner, Charles ....Dresher, PA
Weiner & Charny, P.A. ....Haddonfield, NJ
Weiner, Chas. R. ....Philadelphia, PA
Weiner, Cheryl A. ....Santa Ana, CA
Weiner, Christine C. ....Newport Beach, CA
Weiner, Conna A. ....East Hanover, NJ
Weiner, Craig ....New York, NY
Weiner, Cummings & Vittoria ....Miami, FL
Weiner, Cyril V. ....Southfield, MI
Weiner, D. A. ....Chicago, IL
Weiner, Dain P. ....Cameron Park, CA
Weiner, Dan D. ....Dayton, OH
Weiner, Daniel H. ....New York, NY
Weiner, Daniel J. ....Bloomfield Hills, MI
Weiner, Daniel P. ....Stamford, CT
Weiner, David ....Shingle Springs, CA
Weiner, David C. ....Cleveland, OH
Weiner, David F. ....Pittsburgh, PA
Weiner, David M. ....Chicago, IL
Weiner, David M. ....Saugus, MA
Weiner, David M. ....New York, NY
Weiner, David P., (P.C.) ....Portland, OR
Weiner, David R. ....Dallas, TX
Weiner, David V. ....Springfield, NJ
Weiner, Dean M. ....Los Angeles, CA

Weiner, Debra A.
Federal Communications Commission,
Office of the General Counsel, GV
Weiner, Debra F. ....Chicago, IL
Weiner, Diana ....Sarasota, FL
Weiner, Diana M. ....New York, NY
Weiner, Don ....Manhattan, KS
Weiner, Douglas ....New York, NY
Weiner, Earl D. ....New York, NY
Weiner, Edna ....New York, NY
Weiner, Edward A. ....San Francisco, CA
Weiner, Edward G. ....Pine Brook, NJ
Weiner, Edward I. ....New York, NY
Weiner, Edward L. ....Fairfax, VA
Weiner, Edwin S. ....Cleveland, OH
Weiner, Eileen J. ....Pittsburgh, PA
Weiner, Eleanor S. ....Green Village, NJ
Weiner, Elissa A. ....Stamford, CT
Weiner, Elizabeth ....New York, NY
Weiner, Ellen Goldberg ....Philadelphia, PA
Weiner, Ernest J. ....Bloomfield Hills, MI
Weiner, Frank J. ....Boston, MA
Weiner, Gary D. ....Deerfield Beach, FL
Weiner, Gary M. ....Niles, IL
Weiner, Gary M. ....Springfield, MA
Weiner, George A. ....Fairfax, VA
Weiner, George J. ....Washington, DC
Weiner, Gerald B. ....Los Angeles, CA
Weiner, Gerald B. ....Rochester, NY
Weiner, Gerald T. ....Bridgeport, CT
Weiner, Gilbert B. ....Phoenix, AZ
Weiner, Gilbert J. ....Boston, MA
Weiner, Gilbert P. ....East Hills, NY
Weiner, Glass & Reed ....Dallas, TX
Weiner, Glenn A. ....Philadelphia, PA
Weiner, Gordon M. ....Gloucester, MA
Weiner, Gregg L. ....New York, NY
Weiner, Hadassah R. ....New York, NY
Weiner, Hal David ....New York, NY
Weiner, Harold M. ....New York, NY
Weiner, Harris K. ....Providence, RI
Weiner, Harvey ....Boston, MA
Weiner, Harvey E. ....Washington, DC
Weiner, Heather L. ....Washington, DC
Weiner & Hendler, Counsellors at Law, P.A.
North Brunswick, NJ
Weiner, Herbert R. ....Baltimore, MD
Weiner, Howard ....New York, NY
Weiner, Howard A. ....Wayne, NJ
Weiner, Howard M. ....Tulsa, OK
Weiner, Howard N. ....Bloomfield Hills, MI
Weiner, Ira E. ....Parsippany, NJ
Weiner, Ira Elloit ....Millburn, NJ
Weiner, Irving J. ....Miami, FL
Weiner, Irving M. ....Harrisville, MI
Weiner, Irwin J. ....Ocala, FL
Weiner, Irwin P. ....Dallas, TX
Weiner, Jack D. ....Philadelphia, PA
Weiner, Jack H. ....New York, NY
Weiner, James ....Philadelphia, PA
Weiner, James L.
Department Of The Interior,
Office of the Solicitor, GV
Weiner, James T. ....Bingham Farms, MI
Weiner, James T., P.C.
Bingham Farms, MI
Weiner, Jane M. ....Miami, FL
Weiner, Janice L. ....Washington, DC
Baltimore, MD
Weiner, Janice M. ....Chicago, IL
Weiner, Jay L. ....Brooklyn, NY
Weiner, Jeffery L. ....Miami, FL
Weiner, Jeffrey A. ....Cherry Hill, NJ
Weiner, Jeffrey I. ....New York, NY
Weiner, Jeffrey M. ....Los Angeles, CA
Weiner, Jeffrey M. ....Wilmington, DE
Weiner, Jeffrey M. ....Overland Park, KS
Weiner, Jeffrey M., A Prof. Corp., The Law Offices of ....Wilmington, DE
Weiner, Jeffrey S. ....Boca Raton, FL
Miami, FL
Weiner, Jeffrey S., Attorneys at Law, P.A.
Boca Raton, FL
Fort Lauderdale, FL
Miami, FL
Weiner, Jerome ....Towson, MD
Weiner, Jerry ....Columbus, OH
Weiner, Jessica ....New York, NY
Weiner, Jessica M. ....Miami, FL
Weiner, Joan ....Philadelphia, PA
Weiner, Joan B. ....Flagstaff, AZ
Weiner, Jody C. ....San Francisco, CA
Weiner, Joel R. ....Los Angeles, CA
Weiner, Joel R. ....Martinsville, NJ
Weiner, John B. ....Washington, DC
Weiner, John S. ....Leonardtown, MD
Weiner, Jonathan D. ....Trenton, NJ
Weiner, Joseph D. ....Leonardtown, MD
Weiner, Karen Colby ....Bloomfield Hills, MI
Weiner, Karen J. ....Wilmington, DE
Weiner, Karin ....Stamford, CT
Weiner, Keith D. ....Cleveland, OH
Weiner, Keith D., & Associates Co., L.P.A.
Akron, OH
Cleveland, OH
Youngstown, OH
Weiner, Kenneth B. ....Washington, DC
Weiner, Kenneth P. ....Omaha, NE
Weiner, Kenneth R. ....Newark, NJ
New York, NY
Weiner, Kenneth R. ....Fairfax, VA
Weiner, Kenneth S. ....Seattle, WA
Weiner, Laurence H. ....Chicago, IL
Weiner, Lauri L. ....Oakland, CA
Weiner & Laurin, L.L.P. ....Encino, CA
Weiner, Lawrence ....Miami, FL
Weiner, Lawrence C. ....Trenton, NJ
West Orange, NJ

Weiner, Lawrence and Ferris, P.C.
East Rochester, NY
Weiner, Lawrence Jay ....Chicago, IL
Weiner, Lee M. ....Bethesda, MD
Weiner, Leonard H. ....Detroit, MI
Weiner, Leonard J. ....Three Rivers, MI
Weiner, Leonard M. ....New York, NY
Weiner Lesniak ....Parsippany, NJ
Weiner, Lester ....Roselle Park, NJ
Weiner, Marc ....Brooklyn, NY
Weiner, Marc D. ....Denver, CO
Weiner, Marc S. ....Falls Church, VA
Weiner, Marcel M. ....Dallas, TX
Weiner, Marcia B. ....Boston, MA
Weiner, Marcia L. ....Norristown, PA
Weiner, Marcia S. ....San Antonio, TX
Weiner, Margaret Armstrong
White Plains, NY
Weiner, Marie Seth ....Burlingame, CA
Weiner, Mark A. ....Thousand Oaks, CA
Weiner, Mark B. ....Chicago, IL
Weiner, Mark R. ....Glendale, CA
Weiner, Maury S. ....Birmingham, AL
Weiner, Merle H. ....Iowa City, IA
Weiner, Michael C. ....Freeport, NY
Weiner, Michael F. ....New Orleans, LA
Weiner, Michael J. ....Newark, NJ
New York, NY
Weiner, Michael L. ....Palo Alto, CA
Weiner, Michael L. ....Minneapolis, MN
Weiner, Michael L. ....Minneapolis, MN
Weiner, Michael L. ....New York, NY
Weiner, Michael P. ....Princeton, NJ
Weiner, Michael R. ....Chicago, IL
Weiner, Michael R. ....Chicago, IL
Weiner, Michael S. ....Delray Beach, FL
Weiner, Michael S. ....New York, NY
Weiner, Michelle T. ....Brooklyn, NY
Weiner & Millo ....New York, NY
Weiner, Monique M. ....New Orleans, LA
Weiner, Monroe B. ....Woodland Hills, CA
Weiner, Morton J. ....New York, NY
Weiner, Murray I. ....Colorado Springs, CO
Weiner, Nancy Kolodny
Bloomfield Hills, MI
Weiner, Nancy R. ....Garden City, NY
Weiner, Nathaniel I. ....Los Angeles, CA
Weiner, Nathaniel S. ....Norwood, MA
Weiner, Nathaniel (Tani) ....New York, NY
Weiner, Neil S. ....Louisville, KY
Weiner, Neil S. ....Clifton Park, NY
Weiner, Nevin A. ....Sarasota, FL
Weiner, Nicholas ....Los Angeles, CA
Weiner, Paul D. ....Philadelphia, PA
Weiner, Paul G. ....Red Hook, NY
Weiner, Paul I. ....West Orange, NJ
Weiner, Paul J. ....Los Angeles, CA
Weiner, Paul L. ....Cleveland, OH
Weiner, Paul M. ....Parsippany, NJ
Weiner, Paul S. ....Jonesboro, GA
Weiner, Perrie M. ....Los Angeles, CA
Weiner, Peter H. ....San Francisco, CA
Weiner, Philip A. ....Shepherdstown, WV
Weiner, R. Leonard ....Houston, TX
Weiner, Randall M. ....Boulder, CO
Weiner, Richard A. ....Englewood, CO
Weiner, Richard E. (IBA) ....Minneapolis, MN
Weiner, Richard H. ....Hackensack, NJ
Weiner, Richard H. ....Albany, NY
Weiner, Richard L. ....Encino, CA
Weiner, Richard M. ....Hicksville, NY
Weiner, Richard N. ....Philadelphia, PA
Weiner, Richard S. ....Beverly Hills, CA
Weiner, Richard S. ....Los Angeles, CA
Weiner, Rick S. ....Irvine, CA
Weiner, Rickie T. ....Boston, MA
Weiner, Robert ....Springfield, IL
Weiner, Robert ....East Rochester, NY
Weiner, Robert A. ....New York, NY
Weiner, Robert E. ....Los Angeles, CA
Weiner, Robert F. ....Coral Gables, FL
Weiner, Robert F., P.A. ....Coral Gables, FL
Weiner, Robert H. ....West Orange, NJ
Weiner, Robert J. ....Philadelphia, PA
Weiner, Robert L. ....Minneapolis, MN
Weiner, Robert N. ....Washington, DC
Weiner, Robert N. ....Northfield, IL
Weiner, Robert P. ....Cherry Hill, NJ
Weiner, Robert S. ....Wilmington, DE
Weiner, Roberta Lynne ....Glendale, CA
Weiner, Robin R. ....Fort Lauderdale, FL
Weiner, Roger G. ....Department of Justice,
Criminal Division, GV
Weiner, Ronald A. ....Atlanta, GA
Weiner, Ronald S. ....Detroit, MI
Weiner, Ronald W. ....White Plains, NY
Weiner, Ross M. ....Los Angeles, CA
Weiner & Rothschild, P.C.
Springfield, MA
Weiner, Rubin D. ....Los Angeles, CA
Weiner, Saml. S. ....Yonkers, NY
Weiner, Samuel ....Hackensack, NJ
Weiner, Samuel ....Columbus, OH
Weiner, Samuel B., Co., L.P.A.
Columbus, OH
Weiner, Samuel H. ....New York, NY
Weiner, Samuel K. ....Highland Park, IL
Weiner, Samuel R. ....Los Angeles, CA
Weiner, Sanford A. ....Houston, TX
Weiner, Schiller and May, P.C.
Englewood, CO
Weiner, Scott A. ....Trenton, NJ
Weiner, Sharon L. ....Roseland, NJ
Weiner, Sharon V. ....Jersey City, NJ
Weiner, Shearouse, Weitz, Greenberg & Shawe, L.L.P. ....Savannah, GA
Weiner, Sheila C. ....Pittsburgh, PA
Weiner, Sigmund T. ....Washington, DC

Weiner, Stanley .... Spring Valley, NY
Weiner, Stanley .... Dallas, TX
Weiner, Stanley P. .... Kansas City, MO
Weiner, Stephen A. .... Long Beach, CA
Weiner, Stephen A. .... New York, NY
Weiner, Stephen D. .... Framingham, MA
Weiner, Stephen H. .... New York, NY
Weiner, Stephen L. .... New York, NY
Weiner, Stephen L., P.C. .... New York, NY
Weiner, Stephen M. .... Boston, MA
Weiner, Steven A. .... West Orange, NJ
Weiner, Steven D. .... New York, NY
Weiner, Steven R. .... Springfield, MA
Weiner, Steven S. .... Mountain View, CA
Weiner, Stewart C. W. .... Southfield, MI
Weiner, Stewart M. .... Detroit, MI
Weiner & Strother, P.C. .... Houston, TX
Weiner, Stuart R. .... Pearl River, NY
Weiner, Stuart S. .... Detroit, MI
Weiner & Suit .... Cleveland, OH
Weiner, Susan E. .... New York, NY
Weiner, Susan Forgue .... New Bedford, MA
Weiner, Susanne B. .... New Orleans, LA
Weiner, Theodore M. .... Rochester, NY
Weiner, Theodore P. .... Leonardtown, MD
Weiner, Tracy B. .... Gladstone, MO
Weiner, Victor I. .... Washington, DC
Silver Spring, MD
Weiner, W. Joseph .... West Paterson, NJ
Weiner, Wayne H. .... Parsippany, NJ
Weiner, Weiner & Weiner
Leonardtown, MD
Weiner, Weiner & Weiner, P.C.
Alexandria, VA
Arlington, VA
Fairfax, VA
Leesburg, VA
Manassas, VA
Warrenton, VA
Weiner, William .... San Francisco, CA
Weiner, William H. .... Akron, OH
Weiner, William L. .... Trenton, NJ
Weiner, William P. .... Lansing, MI
Weiner, Yancey, Dempsey & Diggs, LLP
Atlanta, GA
Weiner-Howell, Julliann .... Woodland Hills, CA
Weinerman, Craig E. .... San Diego, CA
Weinerman, Lloyd M. .... Washington, DC
Weinerman, Marsha .... Boston, MA
Weinert, Barry J. .... Mountain View, CA
Weinert, Herf M. .... Beaumont, TX
Weinert, James Joseph .... Jersey City, NJ
Weinert, Kirk W. .... Houston, TX
Weinert, Robt. A. .... Allentown, PA
Weinert-Landrith, Diana .... Scottsdale, AZ
Weinewuth, Craig Steven
Hoffman Estates, IL
Weinfeld, Andrew M. .... New York, NY
Weinfeld, Daniel R. .... New York, NY
Weinfeld, David A. .... Costa Mesa, CA
Weinfeld, Gary D. .... Miami, FL
Weinfeld, Gary D., P.A. .... Miami, FL
Weinfeld, Laura R. .... Miami, FL
Weinfeld, Roy L. .... Miami, FL
Weinfeld, Scott M. .... Goldens Bridge, NY
Weinfield, Douglas B. .... Washington, DC
Weinfield, Kenneth M. .... San Francisco, CA
Weinfield, Neal H. .... Chicago, IL
Weinflash, Bernard .... New York, NY
Weinflash, Elahna Strom .... New Hope, PA
Weinflash, Jeffrey A. .... Red Bank, NJ
Weinfurtner, Ellen .... Riverside, CA
Weingaertner, Scott T. .... Iselin, NJ
Weingard, Darren S. .... San Mateo, CA
Weingard, Joshua B. .... Miami, FL
Weingard, Laurence Jeffrey
Great Neck, NY
Weingard, Marc J. .... Garden City, NY
Weingarden, Harvey R. .... Birmingham, MI
Weingarden, Larry A. .... Bloomfield Hills, MI
Weingarden, Larry A., P.C.
Bloomfield Hills, MI
Weingarden, Mitchell I. .... White Plains, NY
Weingarden, Paul A. .... Minneapolis, MN
Weingarden, Stanley M. .... Detroit, MI
Weingart, Bertram H. .... Massapequa, NY
Weingart, Bruce J. .... St. Louis, MO
Weingart, Edward .... Pittsburgh, PA
Weingart, Gail C. .... Los Angeles, CA
Weingart, Gerald .... Wayne, NJ
Weingart, Gregory A. .... Pittsburgh, PA
Weingart, Gregory J. .... Los Angeles, CA
Weingart, James W. .... Walla Walla, WA
Weingart, Jeffrey P. .... New York, NY
Weingart, John L. .... Hiawatha, KS
Weingart, Karin L. .... Cleveland, OH
Charleston, WV
Weingart, Mark N. .... Tempe, AZ
Weingart, Marvin .... Forest Hills, NY
Weingart & Penrod .... Phoenix, AZ
Tempe, AZ
Weingart, Ronald C. .... Agoura Hills, CA
Weingart, Scott .... Northbrook, IL
Weingart, Wendy S. .... New York, NY
Weingarten, Allen L. .... New York, NY
Weingarten, David .... Washington, DC
Weingarten, David .... Boston, MA
Weingarten, George .... San Diego, CA
Weingarten, I. Jacob .... Butler, NJ
Weingarten, Ilan S.
Securities and Exchange Commission,
Division of Market Regulation, GV
Weingarten, J. Douglas .... Chicago, IL
Weingarten, Joel C. .... Washington, DC
Weingarten, Marc .... New York, NY
Weingarten, Marc P. .... Philadelphia, PA
Weingarten, Mark P. .... White Plains, NY
Weingarten, Martin S. .... Rochester, NY
Weingarten, Max .... San Francisco, CA
Weingarten, Mollie .... Rockville, MD
Weingarten, Morris .... Sun City, AZ
Weingarten, Myrna M. .... Malibu, CA
Weingarten, Reid H. .... Washington, DC
Weingarten, Rhonda .... New York, NY
Weingarten, Richard L. .... Yonkers, NY
Weingarten, Saul M. .... Seaside, CA
Weingarten, Saul M., & Associates
Seaside, CA
Weingarten, Schurgin, Gagnebin & Hayes LLP .... Boston, MA
Weingarten, Sheryl Ann .... Woodbridge, NJ
Weingarten, Stephen C. .... Secaucus, NJ
Weingarten, Steven A. .... Great Neck, NY
Weingarten, Steven B. .... Albany, NY
Weingarten, Steven E.
Federal Communications Commission,
Wireless Telecommunications Bureau, GV
Weingarten, Steven J. .... Harrisburg, PA
Weingarten, Susan B. .... Las Vegas, NV
Weingartner, Arthur M. .... Fort Wayne, IN
Weingartner, David M. .... Anchorage, AK
Weingartner, Felicia C. .... Albuquerque, NM
Weingartner, John C. .... Helena, MT
Weingartner, Lucile Gray .... Cleveland, OH
Weingartner, Murray .... New Brunswick, NJ
Weingartner, Susan C. .... St. Paul, MN
Weingartz, Julie A. .... Imlay City, MI
Weingast, Aaron B. .... Elizabeth, NJ
Weingast, Jeremy N. .... Hartford, CT
Weingast, Matthew S. .... Princeton, NJ
Weingast, Sarah Wilson .... Philadelphia, PA
Weinger, Alison Colman .... Miami, FL
Weinger, Kerry R. .... Chicago, IL
Weinger, Leah R. .... Walnut Creek, CA
Weinger, Steven M. .... Miami, FL
Weinglass, Leonard I. .... Los Angeles, CA
New York, NY
Weingold, Keith J. .... Morristown, NJ
Weingold, Maurice .... Garden City, NY
Weingold, Philip R. .... New York, NY
Weingrad, Howard R. .... New York, NY
Weingrad, Saml. B. .... New York, NY
Weingrad, Stephen A. .... New York, NY
Weingrad, Stephen C. .... Cleveland, OH
Weingram, Edward R. .... Maywood, NJ
Weingram & Zall .... Maywood, NJ
Weingrow, Sheryl A. .... Toledo, OH
Weingus, Cliff .... San Francisco, CA
Weinhagen, Robert F., Jr.
House of Representatives,
Office of Legislative Counsel, GV
Weinhardt, Mark E. .... Des Moines, IA
Weinhart, Brian S. .... Santa Monica, CA
Weinhaus, Amy .... St. Louis, MO
Weinhaus, Andrew J. .... St. Louis, MO
Weinhaus and Dobson .... St. Louis, MO
Weinhaus, Jeffrey M. .... Mamaroneck, NY
Weinhaus, S. Sheldon .... St. Louis, MO
Weinheimer, Anne H. .... Indianapolis, IN
Weinheimer, Edmund A., Jr. .... El Campo, TX
Weinheimer, Gail R. .... San Anselmo, CA
Weinheimer, Jay .... Fredericksburg, TX
Weinheimer, Mark B. .... St. Louis, MO
Weinheimer, Paul J. .... Pittsburgh, PA
Weinheimer, Richard P., II .... Amsterdam, NY
Weinheimer, Robert A. .... Pittsburgh, PA
Weinheimer, Russell E.
Treasury Department,
Internal Revenue Service, GV
Weinheimer, Schadel & Haber, P.C.
Pittsburgh, PA
Weinheimer, Titus J. .... New York, NY
Weinhofer, John E. .... Flemington, NJ
Weinhold, Willard C. .... Lexington, NE
Weinholtz, John J. .... Buffalo, NY
Weinhouse, Amy Melinda .... Washington, DC
Weinhouse, Fredric N. .... Portland, OR
Weinhouse, Gary D. .... Los Angeles, CA
Weinick, Jeffrey M. .... Liberty Corner, NJ
Weinig, Gregory J. .... Newark, DE
Wilmington, DE
Weinig, Katrina .... Department of Justice,
Office of Policy Development, GV
Weinig, Lynn E. .... White Plains, NY
Weinig, Richard A. .... Anchorage, AK
Weininger, Clifford J. .... Denville, NJ
Weininger, David A. .... Chicago, IL
Weininger, Harry D. .... Berkeley, CA
Weininger, Michael .... Chicago, IL
Weininger, William P. .... Lake Success, NY
Weinischke, William A.
Department of Justice,
Environment and Natural Resources
Division, GV
Weinkam, Louis J., Jr. .... Catonsville, MD
Weinkauf, George A., Jr. .... San Rafael, CA
Weinkauf, Russell E. .... Washington, DC
Weinkauf, Steven A. .... Pacifica, CA
Weinke, Donald C. .... St. Paul, MN
Weinke, Paul H. .... Eau Claire, WI
Weinke, Steven W. .... Fond du Lac, WI
Weinkle, James A. .... Miami, FL
Weinkle, Jeffrey D. .... Miami, FL
Weinkle, Jeffrey D., P.A. .... Miami, FL
Weinkle, Jerome H. .... Miami, FL
Weinkopf, Friedrich J. .... Chicago, IL
Weinkowitz, Michael M. .... Philadelphia, PA
Weinland, Donald A. .... Sacramento, CA
Weinland, Donald J. .... Fort Collins, CO
Weinland, Thomas M. .... Indianapolis, IN
Weinland, Timothy D. .... Sacramento, CA
Weinlein, Craig W. .... Dallas, TX
Weinlood, S. Jill .... Kansas City, MO
Weinman, Ann L. .... Culver City, CA
Weinman & Associates .... Denver, CO
Weinman, Bernie .... Memphis, TN
Weinman, Bruce L. .... Wyoming, MN
Weinman, Carol Ann .... Hartsdale, NY
Weinman, Carol J. .... Tallahassee, FL
Weinman, Daryl G. .... Austin, TX
Weinman, David J. .... Los Angeles, CA
Weinman, Ellen S. .... Salem, VA
Weinman, Glenn A. .... Los Angeles, CA
Weinman, Greg M. .... Treasury Department,
United States Mint, GV
Weinman, Howard M. .... Washington, DC
Weinman, J. Bruce .... New York, NY
Weinman, Jeffrey A. .... Denver, CO
Weinman, Joshua .... San Diego, CA
Weinman, Kathy B. .... Boston, MA
Weinman, Kenneth M. .... Los Angeles, CA
Weinman, Kevin .... Morristown, NJ
Weinman, Linda Jean .... Brooklyn, NY
Weinman, Lisa A. .... Washington, DC
Weinman, Michael L. .... Henderson, TN
Weinman, Nancy M. .... Philadelphia, PA
Weinman, Reid .... New Brunswick, NJ
Weinman, Rhoda H. .... Nantucket, MA
Weinman, Sharon C. .... Philadelphia, PA
Weinman, Sidney .... New York, NY
Weinmann, Eric .... Washington, DC
Weinmann, John G. .... New Orleans, LA
Weinmann, Kurt Lee .... Hackensack, NJ
New York, NY
Weinmann, Peter Allen .... Buffalo, NY
Weinmann, Richard A. .... Great Neck, NY
Weinmann Slive, Harriet .... Cleveland, OH
Weinmeyer, James G. .... Minneapolis, MN
Weinpel, Marc J. .... Idaho Falls, ID
Weinraub, Charles J. .... Fort Wayne, IN
Weinraub, David .... Albany, NY
Weinraub, Lester G. .... Norristown, PA
Weinraub, Martin .... New York, NY
Weinraub, Michael D. .... Philadelphia, PA
Weinreb, Alan H. .... West Babylon, NY
Weinreb, Bernard .... Suffern, NY
Weinreb, Bradley A. .... San Diego, CA
Weinreb, David L. .... Philadelphia, PA
Weinreb, Dvora M. .... Cooper City, FL
Weinreb, Dvora M., P.A. .... Cooper City, FL
Fort Lauderdale, FL
Weinreb, Elliot .... New York, NY
Weinreb, Elliot L. .... Santa Fe, NM
Weinreb, Elliot L., P.C. .... Santa Fe, NM
Weinreb, Ira A. .... Los Angeles, CA
Weinreb, Jacob M. .... New York, NY
Weinreb, Lawrence A. .... Northridge, CA
Weinreb, Lisa Selbst .... San Diego, CA
Weinreb, Lloyd L. .... Cambridge, MA
Weinreb, Marnin .... Los Angeles, CA
Weinreb, Maurice .... Bay Shore, NY
Weinreb, Michael L. .... West Babylon, NY
Weinreb, Stewart D. .... Great Neck, NY
Weinreb & Weinreb .... West Babylon, NY
Weinreb, William D. .... Washington, DC
Weinreich, Amy C. .... New York, NY
Weinreich, Andrew Paul .... New York, NY
Weinreich, Dean .... Sherman Oaks, CA
Weinreich, Gadi .... Washington, DC
Weinreich, Howard B. .... New York, NY
Weinreich, Howard L. .... New York, NY
Weinreich, Lawrence Allen .... Plainview, NY
Weinreich, Marc .... Brookline, MA
Weinreich, Rebecca R. .... Los Angeles, CA
Weinrib, Harry P. .... Buffalo, NY
Weinrib, Kenneth M. .... New York, NY
Weinrib, Neil A., & Associates
New York, NY
Weinrich, A. Carin .... Seattle, WA
Weinrich & Associates .... Seattle, WA
Weinrich, Bert H., Jr. .... Seattle, WA
Weinrich, David I. .... Delray Beach, FL
Weinrich, Douglas E. .... Butler, PA
Weinrich, Gerald S. .... Rochester, MN
Weinrich, Harold R. .... Washington, DC
Weinrich, Herman J.
Fort Washington, PA
Weinrich, Johnathan E. .... New York, NY
Weinrich, Lancer R., Jr. .... Middletown, OH
Weinrich, Phyllis Page, Mrs. .... Edenton, NC
Weinrich, Thomas Wm.
North Royalton, OH
Weinrich, Walter J. .... Philadelphia, PA
Weinrieb, Steven W. .... Arlington, VA
Weinrod, W. Bruce .... Washington, DC
Weinrot, Daniel J. .... Beverly Hills, CA
Weinroth, Daryl J. .... Novato, CA
Weinroth, George J. .... Cherry Hill, NJ
Weinroth, Joseph .... Bridgeville, PA
Weinroth, Lois L. .... New York, NY
Weinroth, Margery .... Melville, NY
Weinroth, Richard K. .... Trenton, NJ
Weinroth, Richard M. .... Phoenix, AZ
Weinroth, Robert S. .... Parsippany, NJ
Weinroth, Seth A. .... Wakefield, MA
Weinryb, Rose-Michele .... Washington, DC
Weins, Jack F. .... Boca Raton, FL
Weins, Michael J. .... Lebanon, NH
Weins, Robert J. .... New Baltimore, MI
Weinschel, Alan J. .... New York, NY
Weinschenk, Alfred J. .... Scranton, PA
Weinschenk, Fritz .... New York, NY
Weinschneider, Devorah S. .... New York, NY
Weinschreider, Charles J. .... Riverhead, NY
Weinshank, Arthur C. .... New Milford, CT
Weinsheimer, G. Bradley .... Washington, DC
Weinsheimer, William C. .... Chicago, IL
Weinshel, Norman E. .... Chicago, IL
Weinshenk, Steven W. .... Encino, CA
Weinshenker, Seth B. .... Syracuse, NY
Weinshienk, Zita L. .... Denver, CO
Weinsier, Michael .... New York, NY
Weinsoff, David Jonathan .... Oakland, CA
Weinsoft, Bruce M. .... Portland, OR
Weinsteen, Larry Jordan .... Las Vegas, NV
Weinsteen, Larry Jordan, Chtd.
Las Vegas, NV
Weinstein, Aaron .... Delray Beach, FL
Weinstein, Adam B. .... Philadelphia, PA
Weinstein, Adam K.
West Palm Beach, FL
Weinstein, Adam K. .... New York, NY
Weinstein, Alan A. .... New York, NY
Weinstein, Alan C. .... Cleveland, OH
Weinstein, Alan E., Law Offices of
Miami, FL
Weinstein, Alan E., Law Offices of
Miami Beach, FL
Weinstein, Alan R.
Department of Transportation,
Surface Transportation Board, GV
Weinstein, Albert L. .... Bridgeport, CT
Weinstein, Alice P. .... Atlanta, GA
Weinstein, Alison H. .... New York, NY
White Plains, NY
Weinstein, Alvin I., (Ltd.) .... Northfield, IL
Weinstein, Alvin N. .... Fort Myers, FL
Miami, FL
Weinstein, Alvin S. .... Brunswick, ME
Weinstein, Amy Hershoff .... Boston, MA
Weinstein, Andrea I. .... New York, NY
Weinstein, Andrea J.
Federal Energy Regulatory Commission,
Office of the General Counsel, GV
Weinstein, Andrew H. .... Miami, FL
Weinstein, Andrew J. .... Washington, DC
Weinstein, Andrew J., Law Offices of
New York, NY
Weinstein, Anita B. .... Philadelphia, PA
Weinstein, Anne Spencer .... Deerfield, IL
Weinstein, Anne W. .... Boston, MA
Weinstein, Arthur I. .... New York, NY
Weinstein and Associates .... West Hartford, CT
Weinstein Associates .... Brunswick, ME
Weinstein & Bacci, Ltd. .... North Riverside, IL
Weinstein & Bagelman, P.C. .... Dallas, TX
Weinstein, Barron L. .... Larkspur, CA
Weinstein, Barry A. .... Bronx, NY
Weinstein, Barry A. .... Williamsville, NY
Weinstein, Barry L., (Ltd.) .... Chicago, IL
Weinstein, Bavly and Moon, P.A.
Fort Myers, FL
Miami, FL
Weinstein & Bergman Lawyers, A Professional Services Corp. .... Seattle, WA
Weinstein, Bernard .... Tucson, AZ
Weinstein, Bernard I. .... Howell, NJ
Weinstein, Bert I. .... Montvale, NJ
Weinstein, Boldt, Racine, Halfhide & Camel, Professional Corporation
Los Angeles, CA
Weinstein, Bonnie H. .... Washington, DC
Weinstein, Brett B. .... King Of Prussia, PA
Monroeville, PA
Weinstein, Brett B. .... Norristown, PA
Weinstein, Brian .... Seattle, WA
Weinstein, Brian S. .... New York, NY
Weinstein, Burton I. .... Chicago, IL
Weinstein, Burton M. .... Bridgeport, CT
Weinstein, Carol .... New York, NY
Weinstein, Carol .... New York, NY
Weinstein, Charlene M. .... New York, NY
Weinstein, Charles E. .... Boston, MA
Weinstein, Charles I. .... Sherwood Forest, MD
Weinstein, Chayt & Chase, P.C.
Brooklyn, NY
New York, NY
Weinstein, Christopher G. .... Seattle, WA
Weinstein, Cliff .... Kings Point, NY
Weinstein, Clifford I. .... Dallas, TX
Weinstein, Clifford I., P.C., Law Offices of
Dallas, TX
Weinstein, Craig .... Berkeley, CA
Weinstein, Craig D. .... Manhattan Beach, CA
Weinstein, Dana M. .... Eugene, OR
Weinstein, Daniel A. .... Washington, DC
Weinstein, Daniel G. .... Jamaica Plain, MA
Weinstein, Daniel H. .... San Francisco, CA
Weinstein, Daniel J. .... Buffalo, NY
Weinstein, David .... Philadelphia, PA
Weinstein, David A. .... Los Angeles, CA
Weinstein, David A. .... Denver, CO
Weinstein, David A. .... Florham Park, NJ
Weinstein, David A. .... Montville, NJ
New York, NY
Weinstein, David A. .... Ocean City, NJ
Weinstein, David A. .... New York, NY
Weinstein, David B. .... Tampa, FL
Weinstein, David B. .... Houston, TX
Weinstein, David C. .... Boston, MA
Weinstein, David C. .... Minneapolis, MN
Weinstein, David H. .... Ellicott City, MD
Weinstein, David H. .... Philadelphia, PA
Weinstein, David Ian .... Upper Marlboro, MD
Weinstein, David J. .... New York, NY
Weinstein, David L. .... Chicago, IL
Weinstein, David L. .... North Chicago, IL
Weinstein, David M. .... Los Angeles, CA
Weinstein, David N. .... St. Johnsbury, VT
Weinstein, David P. .... Scottsdale, AZ
Weinstein, David R. .... Los Angeles, CA
Weinstein, David R. .... Philadelphia, PA
Weinstein, David S. .... Miami, FL
Weinstein, David Scott .... Louisville, KY
Weinstein, Deborah .... Haddonfield, NJ
Philadelphia, PA
Weinstein, Debra Schultz .... Bryn Mawr, PA
Weinstein, Diane Gilbert ....
United States Court of Federal Claims, GV
Weinstein, Diane L. .... New York, NY
Weinstein, Donald D. .... Kansas City, MO
Weinstein, Donna M. .... Boston, MA

Weinstein, Donna Morros .... Chicago, IL
Weinstein, Douglas C. .... Knoxville, TN
Weinstein, Douglas Scott .... Atlanta, GA
Weinstein, Edward A. .... Cleveland, OH
Weinstein, Edward R.
East Brunswick, NJ
Weinstein, Edward R. .... East Windsor, NJ
Edison, NJ
Freehold, NJ
Hamilton, NJ
Marlboro, NJ
Middletown, NJ
Monroe Township, NJ
New Brunswick, NJ
North Brunswick, NJ
Old Bridge, NJ
Weinstein, Eisen & Levine, A Professional Corporation .... Los Angeles, CA
Weinstein, Elaine B. .... Seattle, WA
Weinstein, Elicia R. .... Mount Kisco, NY
Weinstein, Elise Caren
Department of Justice, Tax Division, GV
Weinstein, Elise M. .... Washington, DC
Weinstein, Elizabeth Schutz
New York, NY
Weinstein, Ellen S. .... Syracuse, NY
Weinstein, Elliot M. .... Boston, MA
Weinstein, Eric J. .... Framingham, MA
Weinstein, Eric S. .... New York, NY
Weinstein, Estee Michelle .... New York, NY
Weinstein, Fred .... Ithaca, NY
Weinstein, Fred D. .... White Plains, NY
Weinstein, Gail L. .... New York, NY
Weinstein, Gary A. .... Takoma Park, MD
Weinstein, Gary D. .... Alexandria, VA
Weinstein, Gary M. .... Culver City, CA
Newhall, CA
Weinstein, Gary P. .... New York, NY
Weinstein, Gary S. .... Minneapolis, MN
Weinstein, Gary S. .... New York, NY
Weinstein, George .... Boca Raton, FL
Weinstein, Gerald .... Atlantic City, NJ
Weinstein, Gerald A. .... Encino, CA
Weinstein, Gerald C. .... Cincinnati, OH
Weinstein, Glen D. .... Washington, DC
Weinstein, Glenn E. .... Chicago, IL
Weinstein, Goss, Schleifer, Eisenberg, Winkler & Rothweiler, P.C. .... Cherry Hill, NJ
Weinstein, Goss, Schleifer, Eisenberg, Winkler, Rothweiler & Ostroff, P.C. .... Lansdale, PA
Philadelphia, PA
Wyomissing, PA
Weinstein, Gregory M. .... Dallas, TX
Weinstein, Halee F. .... Baltimore, MD
Weinstein, Harold .... Towson, MD
Weinstein, Harris .... Washington, DC
Weinstein and Hart .... Beverly Hills, CA
Weinstein, Helene .... Brooklyn, NY
Weinstein, Henry A. .... Garden City, NY
Weinstein, Henry C. .... New York, NY
Weinstein, Henry E. .... Los Angeles, CA
Weinstein, Henry G. .... Los Angeles, CA
Weinstein, Herschel S. .... New York, NY
Weinstein, Hilary Ann .... Washington, DC
Weinstein, Howard M. .... Millburn, NJ
Weinstein, Ian S. .... New York, NY
Weinstein, Ira .... Tampa, FL
Weinstein, Ira N. .... Brooklyn, NY
Weinstein, Irvin M. .... Jacksonville, FL
Weinstein, Irwin J. .... Brooklyn, NY
Weinstein, Jack A. .... Saginaw, MI
Weinstein, Jack A., P.C. .... Saginaw, MI
Weinstein, Jack B. .... Brooklyn, NY
Weinstein, Jack M. .... Great Neck, NY
Weinstein, Jacob M. .... Brooklyn, NY
Weinstein, Jacob M. .... New York, NY
Weinstein, James .... Tempe, AZ
Weinstein, Jan S. .... Skokie, IL
Weinstein, Janell N. .... Hackensack, NJ
Weinstein, Jason M. .... Department of Justice, Office of the Inspector General, GV
Weinstein, Jay .... New York, NY
Weinstein, Jeffrey A. .... Nashua, NH
Weinstein, Jeffrey C. .... Miami, FL
Weinstein, Jeffrey D. .... Indianapolis, IN
Weinstein, Jeffrey E. .... Washington, DC
Weinstein, Jeffrey L. .... Dallas, TX
Weinstein, Jeffrey P. .... Roseland, NJ
Weinstein, Jeffrey S. .... New York, NY
Weinstein, Jennifer Robin .... New York, NY
Weinstein, Jeremy D., Law Offices of
Walnut Creek, CA
Weinstein, Jeremy S. .... Kew Gardens, NY
Weinstein, Jerome A. .... Farmington Hills, MI
Weinstein, Jerome N. .... Boston, MA
Weinstein, Jerry L. .... Fort Worth, TX
Weinstein, Jessica S. .... Mineola, NY
New York, NY
Weinstein, Jill E. .... Miami, FL
Weinstein, Jo Ann .... Denver, CO
Weinstein, Joel .... Los Angeles, CA
Weinstein, Joel H. .... New York, NY
Weinstein, Joel R. .... Rockville, MD
Weinstein, John .... Opelousas, LA
Weinstein, John R. .... San Francisco, CA
Weinstein, Jonathan A. .... Kew Gardens, NY
Weinstein, Jordan H. .... Worcester, MA
Weinstein, Jordan S. .... Arlington, VA
Weinstein, Josef A. .... Orange, CT
Weinstein, Joseph C. .... Cleveland, OH
Weinstein, Joseph D. .... Seattle, WA
Weinstein, Judith .... New York, NY
Weinstein, Judith L. .... Miami Beach, FL
Weinstein, Judy K. .... New Haven, CT
Weinstein, Julia L. .... Los Angeles, CA
Weinstein & Kahn .... New York, NY
Weinstein, Kaplan & Cohen, P.C.
Garden City, NY

Weinstein, Karen R. .... Los Angeles, CA
Weinstein, Katherine G. .... New York, NY
Weinstein, Kathleen M. .... Washington, DC
Weinstein, Kenneth J. .... Garden City, NY
Weinstein, Kenneth W. .... Washington, DC
Weinstein, Kevin .... Haddonfield, NJ
Philadelphia, PA
Weinstein & Kimmelman
Philadelphia, PA
Weinstein Kitchenoff Scarlato & Goldman Ltd. .... Philadelphia, PA
Weinstein, Laura D. .... Washington, DC
Weinstein, Laurie E. .... Worcester, MA
Weinstein, Laurie J. .... Department of Justice, Civil Rights Division, GV
Weinstein, Lawrence C. .... Wilmette, IL
Weinstein, Lawrence I. .... New York, NY
Weinstein, Lawrence M. .... Westfield, NJ
Weinstein, Lee D. .... Boulder, CO
Weinstein, Lee M. .... Atlanta, GA
Weinstein, Leonard .... Huntington, NY
Weinstein, Leonard & Lebofsky, Associates
Philadelphia, PA
Weinstein, Les
Department Of Health And Human Services, Food & Drug Administration, GV
Weinstein, Les J. .... Los Angeles, CA
Weinstein, Lisa .... Los Angeles, CA
Weinstein, Lisa .... Chicago, IL
Weinstein, Lois J. .... Mineola, NY
Weinstein, Loren Joseph .... Plano, TX
Weinstein, Louis .... Philadelphia, PA
Weinstein, Louis H. .... New York, NY
Weinstein, Louis L. .... Bloomfield Hills, MI
Weinstein, Lyle M. .... Denver, CO
Weinstein, Marc Alan .... Pendleton, OR
Weinstein, Marc E. .... Langhorne, PA
Weinstein, Marc H. .... North Riverside, IL
Weinstein, Marc J. .... Miami, FL
Weinstein, Marc S. .... Chicago, IL
Weinstein, Margery N. .... New York, NY
Weinstein, Margo .... Chicago, IL
Weinstein, Mark .... Atlanta, GA
Weinstein, Mark A. .... Los Angeles, CA
Weinstein, Mark H. .... Hartsdale, NY
Weinstein, Mark J. .... New York, NY
Weinstein, Mark J. .... New York, NY
Weinstein, Mark L. .... Miami, FL
Weinstein, Mark L., P.A. .... Miami, FL
Weinstein, Mark M. .... New York, NY
Weinstein, Mark S. .... Miami Lakes, FL
Weinstein, Marlene G. .... Walnut Creek, CA
Weinstein, Marsha .... New York, NY
Weinstein, Martin .... Garden City, NY
Weinstein, Martin .... Schenectady, NY
Weinstein, Martin A. .... New York, NY
Weinstein, Martin G. .... Minneapolis, MN
Weinstein, Martin J. .... Washington, DC
Weinstein, Martin M. .... Chicago, IL
Weinstein, Martin S. .... Cupertino, CA
Weinstein, Marvin .... Miami Beach, FL
Weinstein, Marvin W. .... New York, NY
Weinstein, Maurice A. .... Charlotte, NC
Weinstein, Maxwell D. .... Huntington, NY
Weinstein, Melvin A. .... Chicago, IL
Weinstein, Melvin D. .... Columbus, OH
Weinstein, Melvin E., (P.C.) .... Atlanta, GA
Weinstein, Merrick C. .... Manchester, NH
Weinstein, Michael B. .... Jacksonville, FL
Weinstein, Michael B. .... Chicago, IL
Weinstein, Michael B. .... Melville, NY
Weinstein, Michael C. .... New York, NY
Weinstein, Michael D. .... Tarrytown, NY
Weinstein, Michael E. .... Port Jervis, NY
Milford, PA
Weinstein, Michael L. .... Melville, NY
Weinstein, Michael P. .... Albany, NY
Weinstein, Michael P. .... Philadelphia, PA
Weinstein, Michael R. .... San Diego, CA
Weinstein & Miller, LLP .... Rochester, NY
Weinstein, Mitchell D. .... Chicago, IL
Weinstein, Mitchell J. .... Chicago, IL
Weinstein, Molly A. .... Portland, OR
Weinstein, Moses M. .... Kew Gardens, NY
Weinstein, Murray .... Brooklyn, NY
Weinstein, Murray M. .... New York, NY
Weinstein, Naomi J. .... Secaucus, NJ
Weinstein, Naomi, (Ms.) .... San Francisco, CA
Weinstein, Neal .... Tampa, FL
Weinstein, Neal A. .... New York, NY
Weinstein, Neal L. .... Old Orchard Beach, ME
Haverhill, MA
Weinstein, Neil H. .... San Francisco, CA
Weinstein, Norman .... Philadelphia, PA
Wyomissing, PA
Weinstein, Norman H. .... Cleveland, OH
Weinstein, Paul .... Fairfield, CT
Weinstein, Paul H. .... Rockville, MD
Weinstein, Paul H. .... Princeton, NJ
Weinstein, Paul T. .... Albany, NY
Weinstein, Peter D. .... New York, NY
Weinstein, Peter M. .... Fort Lauderdale, FL
Weinstein, Philip .... New York, NY
Weinstein, Philip L. .... New York, NY
Weinstein, Philip M. .... Providence, RI
Weinstein, Philip S. .... Boston, MA
Weinstein, Philip T. .... Miami, FL
Weinstein, Rebecca J. .... Morgantown, WV
Weinstein, Rebecca L. .... Denver, CO
Chicago, IL
Weinstein, Rebecca L. .... Scarsdale, NY
Weinstein, Richard A. .... Washington, DC
Weinstein, Richard A. .... Pittsburgh, PA
Weinstein, Richard B.
Belvedere-Tiburon, CA
Weinstein, Richard B., A Prof. Corp.
Belvedere-Tiburon, CA
Weinstein, Richard H. .... New York, NY

Weinstein, Richard M. .... Philadelphia, PA
Weinstein, Richard N. .... San Antonio, TX
Weinstein, Richard P. .... West Hartford, CT
Weinstein, Richard S. .... Washington, DC
West Palm Beach, FL
Weinstein, Richard S. .... Miami, FL
Weinstein, Robert .... Los Angeles, CA
Weinstein, Robert .... Boston, MA
Weinstein, Robert H .... Denver, CO
Weinstein, Robert H. .... West Hartford, CT
Weinstein, Robert M. .... Greensboro, NC
Weinstein, Robert S. .... Brooklyn, NY
Weinstein, Robert W. .... Boston, MA
Weinstein, Robin S. .... New York, NY
Weinstein, Ronald .... Los Angeles, CA
Weinstein, Ruth A. .... New York, NY
Weinstein, Ruth Joseph .... New York, NY
Weinstein, Samuel J. .... Livingston, NJ
Weinstein, Sara A. .... Los Angeles, CA
Weinstein, Sara J. .... Tamarac, FL
Weinstein, Sarah .... San Francisco, CA
Weinstein, Saul I. .... New York, NY
Weinstein, Schneider & Kannebecker
Port Jervis, NY
Milford, PA
Weinstein, Scott A. .... Miami, FL
Weinstein, Scott Wm. .... Fort Myers, FL
Weinstein, Seth .... Philadelphia, PA
Weinstein, Seth T. .... Royal Palm Beach, FL
Weinstein, Seymour .... Worcester, MA
Weinstein, Seymour .... Rochester, NY
Weinstein, Seymour B. .... Chicago, IL
Weinstein, Seymour N. .... Stamford, CT
Weinstein, Sheldon .... St. Louis, MO
Weinstein, Sheldon A. .... Wilmington, DE
Weinstein, Shelley A., Law Offices of
Encino, CA
Weinstein, Shepard M. .... Phoenix, AZ
Weinstein, Sherwin B. .... Pittsford, NY
Weinstein, Sheryl A. .... Laguna Niguel, CA
Weinstein, Sidney H. .... Atlanta, GA
Weinstein Snyder, A Professional Corporation .... Roseland, NJ
Weinstein, Solomon .... Paramus, NJ
New York, NY
Weinstein, Solomon V. .... Southampton, PA
Weinstein & Soybel .... New York, NY
Weinstein, Stacy J. .... Los Angeles, CA
Weinstein, Stanford B. .... Potomac, MD
Weinstein, Stanley H. .... Miami Beach, FL
Weinstein, Stanley R. .... Beverly Hills, CA
Weinstein, Stanton D. .... Moorestown, NJ
Weinstein, Stephen A. .... Denver, CO
Weinstein, Stephen A. .... Orlando, FL
Weinstein, Stephen A. .... New York, NY
Weinstein, Stephen F. .... Birmingham, AL
Weinstein, Stephen H. .... New York, NY
Weinstein, Stephen J. .... New York, NY
Weinstein, Stephen L. .... New York, NY
Weinstein, Stephen M. .... Fort Lauderdale, FL
Weinstein, Stephen S. .... Morristown, NJ
Weinstein, Stephen S., A Professional Corporation .... Morristown, NJ
Newark, NJ
Weinstein, Steven A. .... New York, NY
Weinstein, Steven C. .... Tucson, AZ
Weinstein, Steven D. .... Los Angeles, CA
Weinstein, Steven D. .... Cherry Hill, NJ
Trenton, NJ
Weinstein, Steven D. .... New York, NY
Weinstein, Steven H. .... Los Angeles, CA
Weinstein, Steven I. .... Clinton, NJ
Weinstein, Steven J. .... Boston, MA
Weinstein, Steven L. .... San Francisco, CA
Weinstein, Steven L. .... Summit, NJ
Weinstein, Steven M. .... Washington, DC
Weinstein, Steven M. .... St. Louis, MO
Weinstein, Steven R. .... Miami, FL
Weinstein, Steven R. .... Livingston, NJ
Weinstein, Stewart H. .... New York, NY
Weinstein, Stuart .... Compton, CA
Weinstein, Susan P. .... Alexandria, VA
Weinstein, Toni .... Dallas, TX
Weinstein, Weiner, Ignal, Napolitano & Shapiro, P.C. .... Bridgeport, CT
New Haven, CT
Weinstein & Weinstein .... Beverly Hills, CA
Weinstein & Weinstein .... Worcester, MA
Weinstein and Weinstein .... Kew Gardens, NY
Weinstein & Weinstein .... Greensboro, NC
Weinstein, Wendi L. .... Alexandria, VA
Weinstein, William I. .... Boynton Beach, FL
Weinstein, William J. .... Bloomfield Hills, MI
Weinstein, William J., P.C.
Bloomfield Hills, MI
Weinstein, William R. .... White Plains, NY
Weinstein & Wisser, P.C.
West Hartford, CT
Weinstein, Yerachmiel E. .... Milwaukee, WI
Weinstein-Bacal, Stuart A. .... San Juan, PR
Weinstein, Co., Harold, (L.P.A.)
Cleveland, OH
Weinstein-Weinfeld, Ilene Merrill
Spring Valley, NY
Weinsten, Jeffrey J. .... North Salem, NY
Weinsten, Michael E. .... Los Angeles, CA
Weinstine, Lester S. .... Morrison, IL
Mount Carroll, IL
Weinstine, Robert R. .... Minneapolis, MN
St. Paul, MN
Weinstine, Shirk and Buckwalter, P.C.
Morrison, IL
Weinstock, Andrew D. .... Metairie, LA
Weinstock, Barry C. .... Lebanon, NJ
Weinstock, Benjamin .... Mineola, NY
Weinstock, Benjamin .... New York, NY
Weinstock, Bennett P. .... Philadelphia, PA
Weinstock, Bonnie Siber .... Melville, NY

Weinstock, Brian Scott .... St. Louis, MO
Weinstock, Bruce J. .... Los Angeles, CA
Weinstock, Christopher .... Calabasas, CA
Weinstock, Craig L. .... Houston, TX
Weinstock, Daniel S. .... Philadelphia, PA
Weinstock, David S. .... Chappaqua, NY
Weinstock, David Woody .... Tucson, AZ
Weinstock, Denis A. .... Mineola, NY
Weinstock, Denise Raquel Metzger
Westlake Village, CA
Weinstock, Frances .... New York, NY
Weinstock, Gregg D. .... Hackensack, NJ
New York, NY
Weinstock, Harold .... Los Angeles, CA
Weinstock, Henry S. .... Los Angeles, CA
Weinstock, Ian .... New York, NY
Weinstock, Ira H. .... Harrisburg, PA
Millerstown, PA
Weinstock, Ira H., P.C. .... Harrisburg, PA
Millerstown, PA
Weinstock, James .... Hollywood, FL
Weinstock, Jan Lipschultz .... Philadelphia, PA
Weinstock, Jason M. .... Baltimore, MD
Weinstock, Jason M. .... Harrisburg, PA
Weinstock, Jeffrey A. .... Deer Park, NY
Weinstock, Jeffrey C. .... Washington, DC
Weinstock, Jeffrey D. .... Boca Raton, FL
Weinstock, Jeffrey S. .... Bronx, NY
Weinstock, Jerome .... Brooklyn, NY
Weinstock, Judith Gross .... Los Angeles, CA
Weinstock, Katherine M. .... Roseland, NJ
Weinstock, Kenneth M. .... Clayton, MO
Weinstock, Kenneth S. .... Hartford, CT
Weinstock, Lawrence
Environmental Protection Agency, Program Office Attorneys, GV
Weinstock, Lawrence W. .... Park Ridge, IL
Weinstock, Leon .... Brooklyn, NY
Weinstock, Leonard .... New York, NY
Weinstock, Leonard I. .... New York, NY
Weinstock, Manion, Reisman, Shore & Neumann, A Law Corporation
Los Angeles, CA
Weinstock, Marion D. Welborn
New Orleans, LA
Weinstock, Mark A. .... Tampa, FL
Weinstock, Mark S. .... Los Angeles, CA
Weinstock, Melvyn J. .... Baltimore, MD
Weinstock, Michael .... Atlanta, GA
Weinstock, Michael J. .... Santa Ana, CA
Weinstock, Michele .... Tampa, FL
Weinstock, Pamela .... New York, NY
Weinstock, Pamela J. .... Chicago, IL
Weinstock, Peter G. .... Dallas, TX
Weinstock, Richard A. .... Ventura, CA
Weinstock, Risa H. .... New York, NY
Weinstock, Rita Barbee .... Lompoc, CA
Weinstock, Robert M. .... Calabasas, CA
Weinstock, Robert N. .... Washington, DC
Weinstock, Ronald B. .... Treasury Department, Internal Revenue Service, GV
Weinstock & Scavo, P.C. .... Atlanta, GA
Weinstock, Sharon L. .... New York, NY
Weinstock, Stevan, Harris & Friedman, P.A.
Washington, DC
Baltimore, MD
York, PA
Fairfax, VA
Weinstock, Steven D. .... Farmington Hills, MI
Weinstock, Steven F. .... North Chicago, IL
Weinstock, Thomas E. .... West Orange, NJ
Weinstock, Werner .... North Hills, NY
Weinstock, William L. .... New York, NY
Weinstock-Ames, Jill A. .... New York, NY
Weinthal, Richard W. .... San Diego, CA
Weintraub, Aaron (Buz) .... Boston, MA
Weintraub, Adam Scott .... Tulsa, OK
Weintraub, Alan
Equal Employment Opportunity Commission, Office of Federal Operations, GV
Weintraub, Alan I. .... Bloomington, IL
Weintraub, Alan M. .... New York, NY
Weintraub, Albert L. .... Miami, FL
Weintraub, Alfred .... New York, NY
Weintraub, Allen L. .... White Plains, NY
Weintraub, Ann F. .... New York, NY
Weintraub, Arnold S. .... Bingham Farms, MI
Weintraub & Aver LLP .... Los Angeles, CA
Weintraub, Barbara S. .... Kalamazoo, MI
Weintraub, Barbara S., P.C.
Kalamazoo, MI
Weintraub, Beneva .... Department of Justice, Criminal Division, GV
Weintraub, Benson B. .... Miami, FL
Weintraub, Benson B., P.A., Law Offices
Miami, FL
Weintraub, Bernard A. .... New York, NY
Weintraub, Bruce Scott .... Franklin Lakes, NJ
Weintraub, Calvin L. .... Bay Shore, NY
Weintraub, Charles H. .... Delmar, NY
Weintraub, Charles H., Attorney at Law
New York, NY
Weintraub, Charles L. .... New York, NY
Weintraub, Daniel H. .... Boston, MA
Weintraub, Daniel H. .... Marlton, NJ
Weintraub, Daniel J. .... Los Angeles, CA
Weintraub, David A. .... Washington, DC
Weintraub, David A. .... Fort Lauderdale, FL
Weintraub, David A. .... New York, NY
Weintraub, David A., P.A.
Fort Lauderdale, FL
Weintraub, David B. .... Los Angeles, CA
Weintraub, David J. .... Melville, NY
Weintraub, David N. .... Vallejo, CA
Weintraub, Diana M. .... Hackensack, NJ
Weintraub, Donald J. .... Lafayette, CA
Weintraub, Edward A. .... Cleveland, OH

Weisenfeld, Paul E.
Agency for International Development, Legal Advisers-Overseas, GV
Weisenfeld, Paul M. ... New York, NY
Weisenfeld, Stacey ... Albany, NY
Weisenfeld, Sue ... Farmington Hills, MI
Weisenfelder, Wilson G., Jr.
Cincinnati, OH
Weisenfels, John R. ... Kansas City, MO
Weisenfels & Vaughan, A Professional Corporation ... Kansas City, MO
Weisenfreund, Marc ... Pound Ridge, NY
Weisenreder, Mark L. ... Mineola, NY
Weisensee, Lloyd W. ... Lake Oswego, OR
Weisensee, Patrick A. ... Navarre, FL
Weisensel, Michael D. ... Cincinnati, OH
Weisensell, John C. ... Akron, OH
Weisenthal, Bruce P. ... Chicago, IL
Weisenthal, Lee A. ... Royal Oak, MI
Weisenthal, Lee A., P.C. ... Royal Oak, MI
Weiser, Amy H.
Department Of Health And Human Services, Office of the General Counsel, GV
Weiser, Anatoly ... New York, NY
Weiser & Associates, P.C. ... Pennsauken, NJ
Philadelphia, PA
Weiser, Barry L. ... Media, PA
Weiser, Carol A. ... Washington, DC
Weiser, Cleophas B. ... Marshall, TX
Weiser, Conrad M. ... Honolulu, HI
Weiser, Daniel J. ... Los Angeles, CA
Weiser, David ... Washington, DC
Austin, TX
Weiser, David H. ... Eden Prairie, MN
Weiser, David R. ... McLean, VA
Weiser, Deborah S. ... Los Angeles, CA
Weiser, Douglas J. ... Miami, FL
Weiser, Frank A. ... Los Angeles, CA
Weiser, Gary B. ... El Paso, TX
Weiser, Gerard J. ... Pennsauken, NJ
Philadelphia, PA
Weiser, Gregg J. ... Fort Lauderdale, FL
Weiser, Hazel ... New York, NY
Weiser, Hazel I. ... Huntington, NY
Weiser, Herbert E.
National Labor Relations Board, Office of the General Counsel, GV
Weiser, Herbert M. ... Los Angeles, CA
Weiser, Hermine E. ... Boise, ID
Weiser, Howard M. ... Orinda, CA
Weiser, Jay ... Parsippany, NJ
Weiser, Joan C. ... Columbus, OH
Weiser, Larry A. ... Cleveland, OH
Weiser, Manuel ... Silver Spring, MD
Weiser, Martin J. ... New York, NY
Weiser, Mary ... New York, NY
Weiser, Michael J. ... Alexandria, VA
Weiser, Patricia ... Philadelphia, PA
Weiser, Paul D. ... Simi Valley, CA
Weiser, Paul M. ... Phoenix, AZ
Weiser, Philip Lee ... Wichita, KS
Weiser, Rachel M. ... Rocky River, OH
Weiser, Richard R. ... East Lansing, MI
Weiser, Sherwood M. ... Miami, FL
Weiser, Sidney L. ... Lompoc, CA
Weiser, Stephen J. ... Chicago, IL
Weiser, Steven S. ... New York, NY
Weiser, Theodore T. ... Boynton Beach, FL
Weiser, Wendy R. ... New York, NY
Weisert, Donald R. ... Jesup, IA
Weisert, Kent A. F. ... Montclair, NJ
Weiser-Varon, Leonard ... Boston, MA
Weisfeld & Associates, P.C.
Indianapolis, IN
Weisfeld, Donald B. ... Rockville, MD
Weisfeld, Donald B., P.C. ... Rockville, MD
Weisfeld, Heather ... Hackensack, NJ
New York, NY
Weisfeld, Lauren M. ... New Haven, CT
Weisfeld, Steven A. ... Montvale, NJ
Weisfeld, Tamara L. ... Indianapolis, IN
Weisfelner, Edward S. ... New York, NY
Weisfield, William M. ... Seattle, WA
Weisfuse, David B. ... White Plains, NY
Weisfuse, Doreen K. ... New York, NY
Weisfuse, Martin H. ... New York, NY
Weisfuse & Weisfuse ... New York, NY
Weisgall, Jonathan M. ... Washington, DC
Weisgall, Jonathan M., Chartered
Washington, DC
Weisgerber, David B. ... Westminster, MD
Weisgerber, Edward V. ... Pittsburgh, PA
Weisgerber, Jim P. ... Topeka, KS
Weisgerber, Robert G. ... Lake Lure, NC
Weisglass, Lisa M. ... New York, NY
Weisgold, Dean E. ... Westmont, NJ
Philadelphia, PA
Weisgold, Dean E., P.C. ... Westmont, NJ
Philadelphia, PA
Weishaar, Henry A. ... North Chicago, IL
Weishaar, Pamela J. ... Germantown, MD
Weishaar, Peter J. ... Rochester, NY
Weishaar, Robert A., Jr. ... Harrisburg, PA
Weishaar, Steven F. ... La Grande, OR
Weishar, Fred A. ... Westlake, OH
Weishart, Sandra I. ... Los Angeles, CA
Weishaupl, Elizabeth Ann ... Denver, CO
Weishaupt, Jeffrey C. ... Alton, IL
Weishaupt, Matthew A., III
Poughkeepsie, NY
Weishaupt, Richard P. ... Philadelphia, PA
Weishaupt, T. Christopher ... New Haven, CT
Weishaupt, William J., Jr. ... New York, NY
Weisheit, Bowen ... Bel Air, MD
Weisheit, Bowen P., Jr. ... Baltimore, MD
Weisheit, J. Elmer ... Towson, MD
Weishoff, Robert P. ... Mount Holly, NJ
Weisiger, Gene D. ... Urbana, IL

Weisinger, J. Steven ... Conroe, TX
Weisinger, Lynn A. ... Roseland, NJ
Weisinger, Merritt L. ... Walnut Creek, CA
Weisinger, Richard H. ... Englewood Cliffs, NJ
New York, NY
Weisinger, Roberta S. ... Englewood Cliffs, NJ
Weisinger, Shelli ... Hastings-On-Hudson, NY
Weiske, Stacy L. ... Fort Worth, TX
Weiske, Sue E. ... Omaha, NE
Weiskopf, Alan R. ... New York, NY
Weiskopf, Barry ... Baltimore, MD
Weiskopf, Bess Karger ... Boston, MA
Weiskopf, David A. ... California, MD
Weiskopf, David N. ... Palo Alto, CA
Weiskopf, Gilbert G. ... Colorado Springs, CO
Weiskopf, Nicholas R. ... New York, NY
Weiskopf, Richard H. ... Schenectady, NY
Weisl, Edwin L., Jr. ... New York, NY
Weisler, Arnold S. ... North Palm Beach, FL
Weisler, Erica L. ... New York, NY
Weisler, Faye L. ... New Orleans, LA
Weisler, Howard J. ... West Palm Beach, FL
Weisler, Julian E., II ... Brenham, TX
Weisler, Wendy R. ... Los Angeles, CA
Weisling, Chris G. ... Peoria, AZ
Weislogel, Stacy ... Columbus, OH
Weisman, Allen J. ... Lake Worth, FL
Weisman, Amy Joelle ... San Diego, CA
Weisman, Anne W. ... Williamstown, MA
Weisman & Associates, A Professional Corporation ... Boston, MA
Weisman Associates, Professional Corporation ... Mishawaka, IN
South Bend, IN
Weisman, Barry ... Woodmere, NY
Weisman, Barry L. ... Boston, MA
Weisman, Bonnie M. ... Houston, TX
Weisman & Calderon LLP
Mount Vernon, NY
New York, NY
Weisman, Celler, Spett & Modlin
New York, NY
Weisman, Charles M. ... Philadelphia, PA
Weisman, Cynthia L. ... Albuquerque, NM
Weisman, Dana E. ... Beverly Hills, CA
Weisman, Daniel G. ... Staten Island, NY
Weisman, Daniel L. ... Conshohocken, PA
Weisman, Daniel L. ... Norristown, PA
Weisman, David ... Hollywood, FL
Weisman, David B. ... Mishawaka, IN
Weisman, David E. ... Rockville, MD
Weisman, David S. ... Madison Heights, MI
Weisman, Deborah A. ... Cleveland, OH
Weisman, Diana R. ... Mill Valley, CA
Weisman, Diane F. ... Bronx, NY
Weisman, Donald E. ... Hartford, CT
Weisman, Donna S. ... Bakersfield, CA
Weisman, Ellen F. ... Mineola, NY
Weisman, Eric R. ... Boulder, CO
Weisman, Eugene B. ... Clayton, MO
Weisman, Eugene B., P.C. ... Clayton, MO
Weisman, Fred ... Cleveland, OH
Weisman, Gary S. ... Tallahassee, FL
Weisman, Gilbert B. ... Malvern, PA
Weisman, Goldberg & Weisman Co., L.P.A.
Cleveland, OH
Weisman Goldman Bowen & Gross LLP
Pittsburgh, PA
Weisman, Gregory N. ... Los Angeles, CA
Weisman, Gregory S. ... Philadelphia, PA
Weisman & Guzzo ... Akron, OH
Weisman, H. John ... Waterbury, CT
Weisman, Harold ... Mount Vernon, NY
Weisman, Harold H. ... Delray Beach, FL
Weisman, Harold H., P.A. ... Delray Beach, FL
Weisman, Herbert L. ... Great Neck, NY
Weisman, Hillary ... New York, NY
Weisman, Hollis Raphael ... Hyattsville, MD
Weisman, Howard ... Northbrook, IL
Weisman, Howard Dean ... Chicago, IL
Weisman, J. Scott ... Columbus, OH
Weisman, Jackie ... Rockford, IL
Weisman, Jacqueline A. ... Washington, DC
Weisman, James A. ... Boston, MA
Weisman, James L. ... Pittsburgh, PA
Weisman, James T. ... Chicago, IL
Weisman, Jana-Lyn ... Philadelphia, PA
Weisman, Jay ... Chicago, IL
Weisman, Jed ... Cleveland, OH
Weisman, Jeffrey T. ... St. Louis, MO
Weisman, Jennifer S. ... Los Angeles, CA
Weisman, Joel D. ... Chicago, IL
Weisman, Joseph H. ... Waterbury, CT
Weisman, Julie A. ... Washington, DC
Weisman, Larry E. ... Chicago, IL
Weisman, Laurie F. ... Denver, CO
Weisman, Lawrence P. ... Westport, CT
Weisman, Lisa S. ... Boston, MA
Weisman, Louis ... Lancaster, PA
Weisman & Lubell ... Westport, CT
Weisman, M. David ... Chicago, IL
Weisman, Marjorie Morris ... St. Louis, MO
Weisman, Mark B. ... Akron, OH
Weisman, Mark L. ... Santa Monica, CA
Weisman, Mark S. ... Akron, OH
Weisman, Mark W. ... St. Louis, MO
Weisman, Martin C. ... Bingham Farms, MI
Weisman, Michael A. ... Las Vegas, NV
Weisman, Michael D. ... Boston, MA
Weisman, Michael J. ... Bridgeport, CT
Weisman, Michael J. ... Bridgeport, CT
Weisman, Mitchell A. ... Cleveland, OH
Weisman, Murray ... Kettering, OH
Weisman, Nancy E. ... Skokie, IL
Weisman, Neil L. ... South Bend, IN
Weisman, Paul H., Law Offices of
Los Angeles, CA

Weisman, Paul H., Law Offices of
Sherman Oaks, CA
Weisman, Peter J. ... Hackensack, NJ
New York, NY
Weisman, Richard S. ... Mount Vernon, NY
Weisman, Robert A. ... Chicago, IL
Weisman, Robert D. ... Columbus, OH
Weisman, Robert M.
Nuclear Regulatory Commission, Office of the General Counsel, GV
Weisman, Robin Mahler ... Washington, DC
Weisman, Robyn ... New York, NY
Weisman, Roger D. ... Los Angeles, CA
Weisman, Ross ... Chicago, IL
Weisman, Ross M. ... Chicago, IL
Weisman, Scott F. ... Washington, DC
Weisman, Sheppard L. ... Boston, MA
Weisman, Shirley D., (P.A.)
Fort Lauderdale, FL
Weisman, Steven F. ... New York, NY
Weisman, Steven H. ... New York, NY
Weisman, Steven J. J. ... Cambridge, MA
Weisman, Stewart L. ... Manlius, NY
Weisman, Todd E. ... New York, NY
Weisman, Trogan, Young and Schloss, P.C.
Bingham Farms, MI
Birmingham, MI
Detroit, MI
Weisman, Walter L. ... Beverly Hills, CA
Weisman, Wayne B. ... Berwyn, PA
Weisman & Weisman ... Chicago, IL
Weisman, Wendi S. ... Delray Beach, FL
Weisman, William S. ... Boca Raton, FL
Weisman, William S. ... Leonia, NJ
Weisman-Estis, Deborah ... Goshen, NY
Weismann, Anne L. ... Department of Justice, Civil Division, GV
Weismann, Christopher T. ... Alfred, ME
Weismann, Donald J. ... Allison Park, PA
Weismann, Henry C. ... Southold, NY
Weismantel, F. Alan ... San Diego, CA
Weisneck, Jeanne M. ... New York, NY
Weisner, Aimee S. ... Irvine, CA
Weisner, Carla R., & Associates, Law Offices of ... Los Angeles, CA
Weisner, Carol C.
Environmental Protection Agency, Program Office Attorneys, GV
Weisner, John M. ... Richmond, VA
Weisner, William W. ... New York, NY
Weiss, Adam S. ... Chicago, IL
Weiss, A. J. ... Laguna Hills, CA
Weiss, A. J., & Associates ... New York, NY
Charlotte Amalie, St. Thomas, VI
Weiss, Alan J. ... New York, NY
Weiss, Alan M. ... San Francisco, CA
Weiss, Alan M. ... Jacksonville, FL
Weiss, Albert G. ... Collingswood, NJ
Bala Cynwyd, PA
Philadelphia, PA
Weiss, Alexander ... Staten Island, NY
Weiss, Alfred M. ... Glencoe, IL
Weiss, Allan ... Louisville, KY
Weiss, Allan B. ... Jamaica, NY
Weiss, Allan B., (A Prof. Corp.)
Long Beach, CA
Weiss, Allan B., and Associates
Long Beach, CA
Weiss, Allan J. ... Peapack, NJ
Weiss, Allan Joseph ... New York, NY
Weiss, Allen ... Freehold, NJ
Weiss, Allen H. ... New York, NY
Weiss, Allison H. ... New York, NY
Weiss, Allison Wertheim ... New York, NY
Weiss, Alvin ... Morristown, NJ
Weiss, Alvin L. ... Pottstown, PA
Weiss, Alyson M. ... New York, NY
Weiss, André ... New York, NY
Weiss, Andrea F. ... Los Angeles, CA
Weiss, Andrea J. ... Los Angeles, CA
Weiss, Andrea Likwornik ... New York, NY
Weiss, Andrew D. ... Aliso Viejo, CA
Weiss, Andrew G. ... Jamaica, NY
Weiss, Andrew J. ... Flushing, NY
Weiss, Andrew L. ... West Hills, CA
Weiss, Andrew M., P.C. ... Atlanta, GA
Weiss, Andrew R. ... Fresno, CA
Weiss, Andrew R. ... Maynard, MA
Weiss, Andrew S. ... Port Washington, NY
Weiss, Ann E. ... Stamford, NY
Weiss, Ann Thornburg
Fort Washington, PA
Weiss, Anton M. ... Washington, DC
Weiss, Arlene R. ... Trenton, NJ
Weiss, Arnold ... Buffalo, NY
Weiss, Arnold M. ... New York, NY
Weiss, Arnold M., Law Offices of
Memphis, TN
Weiss, Aron Egan ... New York, NY
Weiss, Arthur A. ... Detroit, MI
Weiss, Arthur B. ... Franklin Lakes, NJ
Weiss, Arthur I. ... Santa Clarita, CA
Weiss, Arthur Jay ... Farmington Hills, MI
Weiss, Arthur R. ... Austin, TX
Weiss & Associates ... Cleveland, OH
Weiss & Associates ... Carnegie, PA
Weiss & Associates, P.C. ... St. Louis, MO
Weiss & Bacalis ... Detroit, MI
Weiss, Barbara H. ... New Orleans, LA
Weiss, Barry ... Chicago, IL
Weiss, Barry A. ... Irvine, CA
Weiss, Barry F. ... Haverstraw, NY
Weiss, Barry I. ... New City, NY
Weiss, Barry R. ... Union City, NJ
Weiss, Barton J. ... New York, NY
Weiss, Baruch ... New York, NY
Weiss, Benjamin L. ... St. Paul, MN

Weiss Berrett Petty, L.C.
Salt Lake City, UT
Weiss, Berzowski, Brady & Donahue LLP
Milwaukee, WI
Weiss & Block, Chtd. ... Chicago, IL
Weiss, Brad D. ... Washington, DC
Bethesda, MD
Vienna, VA
Weiss, Bradley Scott, Law Office of
Washington, DC
Weiss, Brett ... Olney, MD
Weiss, Brett, P.C. ... Olney, MD
Weiss, Brian E. ... Indianapolis, IN
Weiss, Brian E. ... Kalamazoo, MI
Weiss, Brian M. ... Atlanta, GA
Weiss, Bryan M. ... Los Angeles, CA
Weiss, Buell & Bell ... New York, NY
Weiss, Carl ... West Conshohocken, PA
Weiss, Carol A. ... Columbus, OH
Weiss, Carol P. Newman
Securities and Exchange Commission, Division of Corporation Finance, GV
Weiss, Carole D. ... Dublin, OH
Weiss, Cary B. ... Santa Monica, CA
Weiss, Catherine ... New York, NY
Weiss, Charles ... Pittsburgh, PA
Weiss, Charles A. ... St. Louis, MO
Weiss, Charles A. ... New York, NY
Weiss, Charles D. ... Atlanta, GA
Weiss, Charles F. ... Los Angeles, CA
Weiss, Charles J. ... Stamford, CT
Weiss, Charles J. ... Fort Washington, PA
Weiss, Charles W. ... New York, NY
Weiss, Chris N. ... Jackson, MO
Weiss, Christopher J. ... Orlando, FL
Weiss, Christopher L. ... Hackensack, NJ
Weiss, Christopher N. ... Seattle, WA
Weiss, Clifford Maxwell ... Marietta, GA
Weiss, Cornelia P. ... Steamboat Springs, CO
Telluride, CO
Weiss, Cory L. ... New York, NY
Weiss, Cynthia H. ... Fairfax, VA
Weiss, Dale B. ... Garden City, NY
Weiss, Damon Ian ... Maitland, FL
Weiss, Dan M. ... Perrysburg, OH
Weiss, Daniel ... Long Beach, NY
Weiss, Daniel A. ... Miami, FL
Weiss, Daniel G. ... San Francisco, CA
Weiss, Daniel H. ... Rockville, MD
Weiss, Daniel J. ... Chicago, IL
Weiss, Daniel J. ... Milwaukee, WI
Weiss, Daniel K. ... Worthington, OH
Weiss, Daniel L. ... Woodbridge, NJ
Weiss, Daniel S. ... Sacramento, CA
Weiss, Daniel S. ... Minneapolis, MN
Weiss, Danielle L. ... Chicago, IL
Weiss, David ... Los Angeles, CA
Weiss, David A. ... Albany, NY
Weiss, David C. ... Wilmington, DE
Weiss, David E. ... San Francisco, CA
Weiss, David E. ... Whittier, CA
Weiss, David E. ... New York, NY
Weiss, David E. ... Cleveland, OH
Weiss, David E., Jr. ... Phoenix, AZ
Weiss, David H. ... New York, NY
Weiss, David H. ... Cleveland, OH
Weiss, David I. ... Miami, FL
Weiss, David J. ... Atlantic City, NJ
Weiss, David J. ... Garden City, NY
Weiss, David J., Law Offices of
Los Angeles, CA
Weiss, David J., Law Offices of
Santa Monica, CA
Weiss, David L. ... East Haven, CT
Weiss, David N. ... Downey, CA
Weiss, David N. ... Newport Beach, CA
Weiss, David P. ... St. Louis, MO
Weiss, David R. ... Denver, CO
Weiss, David R. ... Bath, ME
Weiss, David S. ... Boston, MA
Weiss, David S. ... Philadelphia, PA
Weiss, David T. ... New York, NY
Weiss Dawid Fross Zelnick & Lehrman, P.C.
New York, NY
Weiss, Deane R. ... Denver, CO
Weiss, Deborah ... Burlington, VT
Weiss, Deborah E. ... Chicago, IL
Weiss, Deborah F. ... Buford, GA
Weiss, Deborah J. ... Boston, MA
Weiss, Deborah K. ... Walnut Creek, CA
Weiss, Deirdre B.
Department Of Veterans Affairs, Board of Veterans Appeals, GV
Weiss, Deirdre D. K. ... Washington, DC
Weiss, Denise L. ... New York, NY
Weiss, Diana ... New York, NY
Weiss, Diana L. ... San Francisco, CA
Weiss, Don E. ... San Antonio, TX
Weiss, Donald J. ... Media, PA
Weiss, Donald J., Esquire, PC ... Media, PA
West Chester, PA
Weiss, Donald P. ... Shreveport, LA
Weiss, Donald S. ... Chicago, IL
Weiss, E. Max ... Meadville, PA
Weiss, Earl W. ... Skokie, IL
Weiss, Edward ... Newark, NJ
Weiss, Edward A. ... Alamo, CA
Weiss, Edward A. ... Anaheim, CA
Weiss, Edward A. ... Stamford, CT
Weiss, Edward F. ... Wayne, NJ
Weiss, Edward J. ... New York, NY
Weiss, Edward Jay ... Media, PA
Weiss, Edward L. ... Chesterfield, MO
Weiss, Edward P. ... Carnegie, PA
Weiss, Edward R. ... Bala Cynwyd, PA
Weiss, Edwin ... San Francisco, CA
Weiss, Elaine ... Washington, DC
Weiss, Elaine ... Chicago, IL

Weiss, Elaine F. ... Coral Gables, FL
Weiss, Elaine L. ... West Palm Beach, FL
Weiss, Eli ... Holmdel, NJ
Weiss, Elizabeth ... New York, NY
Weiss, Ellen M. ... Manhasset, NY
Weiss, Elliott B. ... Williamsport, PA
Weiss, Elliott J. ... Tucson, AZ
Weiss, Emanuel G. ... Wyncote, PA
Weiss, Eric A. ... Miami, FL
Weiss, Eric A. ... Philadelphia, PA
Weiss, Eric E. ... St. Louis, MO
Weiss, Eric I. ... New York, NY
Weiss, Eric M. ... Pearl River, NY
Weiss, Eric P. ... Los Angeles, CA
Weiss, Eric S. ... New York, NY
Weiss, Eric T. ... Southfield, MI
Weiss, Erica H. ... Washington, DC
Weiss, Ernest L. ... Tustin, CA
Weiss, Eugene J. ... Beverly Hills, CA
Weiss, Eugene P. ... Columbus, OH
Weiss, Eve ... New York, NY
Weiss, Farley I. ... Scottsdale, AZ
Weiss, Francine K. ... Washington, DC
Weiss, Francis P. ... Painesville, OH
Weiss, Frank J. ... Portland, OR
Weiss, Franklin R. ... Cedarhurst, NY
Weiss, Franklyn C. ... Milpitas, CA
Weiss, Frederic C. ... Boca Raton, FL
Weiss Frederick Willett & Haynes
Louisville, KY
Weiss & Freedman, LLP
Chagrin Falls, OH
Cleveland, OH
Weiss, Garry A. ... Merrillville, IN
Weiss, Gary A. ... Cleveland, OH
Weiss, Gary E. ... Menlo Park, CA
Weiss, Gary M. ... Louisville, KY
Weiss, Gary S. ... Chicago, IL
Weiss, Gayle Flanders ... Worcester, MA
Weiss, George C. ... New York, NY
Weiss, Gerald I. ... Southfield, MI
Weiss, Gerald L. ... West Bloomfield, MI
Weiss, Gerald M. ... Bronx, NY
Weiss, Gerard A. ... White Plains, NY
Weiss, Gerson A. ... New York, NY
Weiss, Glenn H. ... Gainesville, FL
Weiss, Gregg M. ... New York, NY
Weiss, Gregory A.
Federal Communications Commission,
Common Carrier Bureau, GV
Weiss, Gregory A. ... New York, NY
Weiss, Gregory C. ... New Orleans, LA
Weiss, Gregory S. ... Dallas, TX
Weiss, Gustave ... New York, NY
Weiss & Handler, P.A. ... Boca Raton, FL
West Palm Beach, FL
New York, NY
Weiss, Harlan L. ... Chevy Chase, MD
Weiss, Harold ... Memphis, TN
Weiss, Harold L. ... Paterson, NJ
Weiss, Harry ... Camden, NJ
Philadelphia, PA
Weiss, Harry J. ... Washington, DC
Weiss, Harry M. ... Scottsdale, AZ
Las Vegas, NV
Weiss, Harry M., & Associates, P.C.
Phoenix, AZ
Scottsdale, AZ
Las Vegas, NV
Weiss, Harvey ... Brooklyn, NY
Weiss, Heather Bergerson ... Torrance, CA
Weiss, Heather R. ... Philadelphia, PA
Weiss, Heidi M. ... New York, NY
Weiss, Henry ... New York, NY
Weiss, Herbert A. ... New York, NY
Weiss, Herbert B. ... Cincinnati, OH
Weiss, Herbert M. ... Boston, MA
Weiss, Holly Hexter ... New York, NY
Weiss, Honnen S. ... Minneapolis, MN
Weiss, Howard A. ... Chicago, IL
Weiss, Howard I. ... Boca Raton, FL
New York, NY
Weiss, Howard J. ... Northbrook, IL
Weiss, Howard M. ... Washington, DC
Arlington, VA
Weiss, Howard M. ... Indialantic, FL
Weiss, Howard M. ... Bayside, NY
Weiss, Howard S. ... Franklin Lakes, NJ
Weiss, Howard S. ... New York, NY
Weiss, Ira, Law Offices of ... Pittsburgh, PA
Weiss, Irene ... Las Vegas, NV
Weiss, Irwin E. ... Towson, MD
Weiss, Irwin M. ... New York, NY
Weiss, J. Mark ... Seattle, WA
Weiss, J. Mark, P.S., Law Office of
Seattle, WA
Weiss, J. Michael ... Lubbock, TX
Weiss, Jack ... Fresno, CA
Weiss, Jack A. ... St. Petersburg, FL
Weiss, Jack M. ... New York, NY
Weiss, Jack S. ... Los Angeles, CA
Weiss, Jacqueline ... Alexandria, VA
Weiss, Jacqueline A. ... New York, NY
Weiss, Jaime L. ... New York, NY
Weiss, James A. ... Wayne, PA
Weiss, James D. ... Los Angeles, CA
Weiss, James D. ... Chicago, IL
Weiss, James L. ... New Orleans, LA
Weiss, James R. ... Washington, DC
Weiss, James S. ... Cherry Hill, NJ
Weiss, Janet M. ... New York, NY
Weiss, Janice M. ... Louisville, KY
Weiss, Jason A. ... Costa Mesa, CA
Weiss, Jason G. ... San Diego, CA
Weiss, Jason S. ... West Palm Beach, FL
Weiss, Jay B. ... Miami, FL
Weiss, Jay B., P.A. ... Miami, FL
Weiss, Jay S. ... Washington, DC
Weiss, Jay S. ... Fort Lauderdale, FL
Weiss, Jay S., P.A. ... Fort Lauderdale, FL
Weiss, Jay S., P.C., Law Offices
Washington, DC
Rockville, MD
Weiss, Jeffrey ... San Francisco, CA
Weiss, Jeffrey ... New York, NY
Weiss, Jeffrey A. ... Bronx, NY
Weiss, Jeffrey E. ... Los Angeles, CA
Weiss, Jeffrey J. ... Keene, NH
Weiss, Jeffrey L. ... Scottsdale, AZ
Weiss, Jeffrey M. ... Detroit, MI
Weiss, Jeffrey P.
Securities and Exchange Commission,
Division of Enforcement, GV
Weiss, Jeffrey S. ... Woodland Hills, CA
Weiss, Jeffrey S. ... Washington, DC
Weiss, Jeffrey S. ... Orlando, FL
Weiss, Jeffrey S. ... Woodmere, NY
Weiss, Jeffrey W. ... Shreveport, LA
Weiss, Jennifer ... Cary, NC
Weiss, Jennifer B. ... Woodbridge, VA
Weiss, Jennifer Falk ... Atlanta, GA
Weiss, Jennifer Fisher ... Morristown, NJ
Weiss, Jennifer H. ... Boston, MA
Weiss, Jennifer S. ... Chicago, IL
Weiss, Jensen, Ellis & Howard, A
Professional Corporation ... Portland, OR
Seattle, WA
Weiss, Jeremy G. ... Iselin, NJ
Weiss, Jerold M. ... Brooklyn, NY
Weiss, Jerome F. ... Cleveland, OH
Weiss, Jerrie S., (Ms.) ... Westlake Village, CA
Weiss, Jerry A. ... Albany, NY
Weiss, Jerry A. ... New York, NY
Weiss, Jesse ... New York, NY
Weiss, Joanna Joyce ... Costa Mesa, CA
Weiss, Jody M. ... Los Angeles, CA
Weiss, Joel ... New York, NY
Weiss, Joel C. ... Bala Cynwyd, PA
Weiss, Joel H. ... Brooklyn, NY
Weiss, Joel R. ... Manhasset, NY
Weiss, Joel S. ... New York, NY
Weiss, John A. ... Fullerton, CA
Weiss, John A. ... Tallahassee, FL
Weiss, John A., P.A. ... Tallahassee, FL
Weiss, John B. ... San Francisco, CA
Weiss, John C., Jr. ... Baltimore, MD
Weiss, John D. ... Encino, CA
Weiss, John Robert ... Chicago, IL
Weiss, John Ward ... Montgomery, AL
Weiss, John William, Jr. ... Cincinnati, OH
Weiss, Jon ... Phoenix, AZ
Weiss, Jonathan ... Beverly Hills, CA
Weiss, Jonathan A. ... New York, NY
Weiss, Jonathan B. ... Philadelphia, PA
Weiss, Jonathan D. ... Philadelphia, PA
Weiss, Jonathan M. ... Seattle, WA
Weiss, Jonathan T. ... New York, NY
Weiss, Jordan P. ... Los Angeles, CA
Weiss, Joseph C. ... Cherry Hill, NJ
Weiss, Joseph G., Jr. ... Miami, FL
Weiss, Joseph H. ... New York, NY
Weiss, Joseph H., Jr. ... Chesterland, OH
Weiss, Joseph H., Sr. ... Lyndhurst, OH
Weiss, Joyce Ann ... Berkeley, CA
Weiss, Judith K. ... Phoenix, AZ
Weiss, Julia M. ... Brooklyn, NY
Weiss, Julius ... New York, NY
Weiss, Justin K. ... New York, NY
Weiss & Kahn, P.A. ... Coral Gables, FL
Weiss, Karen L. ... New York, NY
Weiss, Karynne G. ... Santa Monica, CA
Weiss, Kathleen G. ... Cleveland, OH
Weiss, Katie J. ... Sherman Oaks, CA
Weiss, Kelly ... New York, NY
Weiss, Kelly M. ... Lubbock, TX
Weiss, Kenneth A. ... New Orleans, LA
Weiss, Kenneth D. ... Boston, MA
Weiss, Kenneth L. ... Treasure Island, FL
Weiss, Kenneth M. ... Atlanta, GA
Weiss, Kenneth R. ... New York, NY
Weiss, Kevin B. ... Maitland, FL
Weiss, Kimberly F. ... Killingworth, CT
Weiss, Kurt C. ... Melbourne, FL
Weiss, Kwait & Associates ... Cleveland, OH
Weiss, Larry D. ... New Orleans, LA
Weiss, Larry H. ... East Meadow, NY
Weiss, Larry I. ... Cherry Hill, NJ
Weiss, Laura G. ... New City, NY
Weiss, Lauren ... New York, NY
Weiss, Laurence A. ... San Francisco, CA
Weiss, Laurie ... San Antonio, TX
Weiss Law Corporation ... Los Angeles, CA
Weiss Law Firm, The ... Houston, TX
Weiss Law Firm, The, L.L.C.
Steamboat Springs, CO
Telluride, CO
Weiss Law Office ... Bath, ME
Weiss Law Offices ... Paterson, NJ
Wayne, NJ
Weiss, Lawrence ... Chicago, IL
Weiss, Lawrence ... Elizabeth, NJ
Weiss, Lawrence ... Maspeth, NY
Weiss, Lawrence E. ... Santa Rosa, CA
Weiss, Lawrence N. ... New York, NY
Weiss, Lawrence T. ... Mansfield, MA
Weiss, Lee A. ... Chicago, IL
Weiss, Lee A. ... New York, NY
Weiss, Leesa N. ... Washington, DC
Weiss Legal Group, P.A. ... Maitland, FL
Weiss, Lenard G. ... San Francisco, CA
Weiss, Leo ... Placentia, CA
Weiss, Leon A. ... Cleveland, OH
Weiss, Leonard ... Mount Vernon, NY
Weiss, Leonard A. ... Albany, NY
Weiss, Leonard D. ... Metuchen, NJ
Weiss, Leslie J. ... Chicago, IL
Weiss, Libby E. ... Philadelphia, PA
Weiss, Lillian S. ... Philadelphia, PA
Weiss, Linda S. ... New York, NY
Weiss, Lisa ... New York, NY
Weiss, Lisa A. ... Chicago, IL
Weiss, Lita L. ... Richmond Heights, OH
Weiss, Lois J. ... New York, NY
Weiss, Loren E. ... Salt Lake City, UT
Weiss, Lori S. ... West Palm Beach, FL
Weiss, Lucinda ... Akron, OH
Weiss, M. Jannifer ... Lebanon, PA
Weiss, Madeleine E. ... Baltimore, MD
Weiss, Malcolm C. ... Los Angeles, CA
Weiss, Manuel M. ... Colorado Springs, CO
Weiss, Marilyn J. ... Chicago, IL
Weiss, Marjorie A. ... Philadelphia, PA
Weiss, Mark A. ... Los Angeles, CA
Weiss, Mark A. ... Washington, DC
Weiss, Mark A. ... Cincinnati, OH
Weiss, Mark B. ... Lawrence, NY
Weiss, Mark E. ... Royal Oak, MI
Weiss, Mark E. ... Austin, TX
Weiss, Mark F. ... Los Angeles, CA
Newport Beach, CA
Weiss, Mark H. ... Scottsdale, AZ
Weiss, Mark H. ... Commack, NY
Weiss, Mark S. ... Washington, DC
Weiss, Marley S. ... Baltimore, MD
Weiss, Marsha Solomon ... New Paltz, NY
Weiss, Marta J. ... San Rafael, CA
Weiss, Martin ... Brooklyn, NY
Weiss, Martin ... Brooklyn, NY
Weiss, Martin ... Blue Bell, PA
Weiss, Martin Alan ... Memphis, TN
Weiss, Martin L. ... New York, NY
Weiss, Marvin H. ... Los Angeles, CA
Weiss, Mary Anne ... Los Angeles, CA
San Francisco, CA
Weiss, Mary Braisted
Department of the Army,
U.S. Army Legal Services Agency, GV
Weiss, Mary H. ... Chicago, IL
Weiss, Maureen ... New York, NY
Weiss, Melissa L. ... New York, NY
Weiss, Melissa M. ... Chicago, IL
Weiss, Melvyn I. ... Boca Raton, FL
Weiss & Mercer, P.C. ... Philadelphia, PA
Weiss, Meridith Lee ... Chicago, IL
Weiss, Merrilee G. ... Philadelphia, PA
Weiss, Michael ... Los Angeles, CA
Weiss, Michael ... Los Angeles, CA
Weiss, Michael ... Wilmington, DE
Weiss, Michael ... Manville, NJ
Weiss, Michael ... New York, NY
Weiss, Michael A. ... Washington, DC
Bloomfield Hills, MI
Harrisburg, PA
Pittsburgh, PA
Weiss, Michael A. ... Fort Lauderdale, FL
Tampa, FL
West Palm Beach, FL
Weiss, Michael, & Associates, P.A.
Boca Raton, FL
Miami, FL
Weiss, Michael B. ... Milwaukee, WI
Weiss, Michael Brenner ... New York, NY
Weiss, Michael C. ... Saginaw, MI
Weiss, Michael C. ... Morristown, NJ
Weiss, Michael D. ... Meriden, CT
Weiss, Michael H. ... Los Angeles, CA
Weiss, Michael H. ... Los Angeles, CA
Weiss, Michael H. ... Gainesville, FL
Weiss, Michael H., Law Offices of
Berkeley, CA
Weiss, Michael J. ... Beverly Hills, CA
Weiss, Michael J. ... Cherry Hill, NJ
Weiss, Michael L. ... Northfield, NJ
Weiss, Michael N. ... Boca Raton, FL
Miami, FL
Weiss, Michael, P.A. ... Wilmington, DE
Weiss, Michael R. ... Los Angeles, CA
Weiss, Michael Seth ... Cleveland, OH
Weiss, Michele F. ... Los Angeles, CA
Weiss, Mikal M. ... Northampton, MA
Weiss, Miles Sanford ... Charleston, SC
Weiss, Miller & Weiss ... Memphis, TN
Weiss, Milton S. ... Mill Valley, CA
Weiss, Miriam S ... Cranbury, NJ
Weiss, Mitchel E. ... New York, NY
Weiss, Mitchell B. ... Kew Gardens, NY
Weiss, Monroe ... New York, NY
Weiss, Monte Eric ... Milwaukee, WI
Weiss, Morris D. ... Miami, FL
Weiss, Murray A. ... Brooklyn, NY
Weiss, Myron A. ... Santa Monica, CA
Weiss, Myron A., Inc. ... Santa Monica, CA
Weiss, Nancy E. ... San Marcos, CA
Weiss, Nancy E. ... Washington, DC
Weiss, Nancy L. ... Atlanta, GA
Weiss, Nancy Solomon ... New York, NY
Weiss, Nicole E. ... Clearwater, FL
Weiss, Noel ... Northridge, CA
Weiss, Noreen R. ... New York, NY
Weiss, Norman E. ... Kingston, PA
Weiss, Norman F. ... Albuquerque, NM
Weiss, Norman Paul
Huntington Station, NY
Weiss, Norman Paul, P.C.
Huntington Station, NY
Weiss, Pamela ... Franklin Square, NY
Weiss, Pamela Ann ... Lebanon, PA
Weiss, Patricia A. P. ... Sag Harbor, NY
Weiss, Patricia L.
Federal Energy Regulatory Commission,
Office of the General Counsel, GV
Weiss, Paul A. ... San Francisco, CA
Weiss, Paul B. ... Hagerstown, MD
Martinsburg, WV
Weiss, Paul D. ... Buffalo, NY
Weiss, Paul G. ... Philadelphia, PA
Weiss, Paul J., Jr. ... Greensboro, NC
Weiss, Paul M. ... Chicago, IL
Weiss, Paula ... Trenton, NJ
Weiss, Paula ... Philadelphia, PA
Weiss, Peter ... Minneapolis, MN
Weiss, Peter F. ... Wayne, NJ
Weiss, Peter N.
Executive Office Of The President,
Office of Management and Budget, GV
Weiss, Philip D. ... Los Angeles, CA
Weiss, Philip D. ... Norristown, PA
Weiss, Philip E. ... San Diego, CA
Weiss, Philip M. ... New York, NY
Weiss, Phillip A. ... Chicago, IL
Weiss, R. Joel ... Hollywood, FL
Weiss, R. Joel, P.A. ... Hollywood, FL
Weiss, Ralph M. ... Los Angeles, CA
Weiss, Randy Alan ... Fairfax, VA
Weiss, Reba ... Seattle, WA
Weiss, Renee B. ... Cleveland, OH
Weiss, Richard ... Bullhead City, AZ
Weiss, Richard ... New Rochelle, NY
Weiss, Richard ... Plainview, NY
Weiss, Richard A. ... Richardson, TX
Weiss, Richard A. ... Milwaukee, WI
Weiss, Richard B. ... Palm Desert, CA
Weiss, Richard D. ... Los Angeles, CA
Weiss, Richard D. ... Middlebury, CT
Weiss, Richard E. ... Tacoma, WA
Weiss, Richard H. ... New York, NY
Weiss, Richard J. ... New York, NY
Weiss, Richard Jay ... Miami, FL
Weiss, Richard L. ... Chicago, IL
Weiss, Richard L. (IBA) ... Pittsburgh, PA
Weiss, Richard P. ... Wayne, NJ
Weiss, Richard S. ... Boston, MA
Weiss, Richard S. ... New York, NY
Weiss, Richd. M. ... St. Louis, MO
Weiss, Ricky J. ... Tamarac, FL
Weiss, Robert ... New York, NY
Weiss, Robert A. ... Tallahassee, FL
Weiss, Robert A. ... Union, NJ
Weiss, Robert A. ... Charleston, SC
Weiss, Robert B. ... Detroit, MI
Weiss, Robert C. ... Las Vegas, NV
Weiss, Robert C., (A Professional
Corporation) ... Los Angeles, CA
Weiss, Robert E. ... Covina, CA
Weiss, Robert E. ... Flint, MI
Weiss, Robert E., Incorporated
Covina, CA
Los Angeles, CA
Pasadena, CA
Weiss, Robert G. ... Steamboat Springs, CO
Weiss, Robert G. ... Wayne, NJ
Weiss, Robert H. ... Long Beach, NY
Weiss, Robert J. ... San Francisco, CA
Weiss, Robert J. ... Marshalltown, IA
Weiss, Robert J. ... Newark, NJ
Weiss, Robert L. ... Ventura, CA
Weiss, Robert L. ... Portland, OR
Weiss, Robert M. ... Chicago, IL
Weiss, Robert M. ... New York, NY
Weiss, Robert M. ... Milwaukee, WI
Weiss, Robyn B. ... Washington, DC
Weiss, Robyn L. ... New York, NY
Weiss, Roger J. ... Chagrin Falls, OH
Weiss, Roland B. ... Fullerton, CA
Weiss, Romina ... New York, NY
Weiss, Ronald D. ... Melville, NY
Weiss, Ronald D., P.C. ... Melville, NY
Weiss, Ronald E. ... Rochester, NY
Weiss, Ronald I. ... Cleveland, OH
Weiss, Ronald J. ... Atlanta, GA
Weiss, Ronald J. ... New York, NY
Weiss, Ronald M. ... Dallas, TX
Weiss, Ronald P. ... Springfield, MA
Weiss, Ronald, (P.C.) ... Encino, CA
Weiss, Ronald S. ... West Bloomfield, MI
Weiss, Ronald S. ... Kansas City, MO
Weiss, Ronald W. ... St. Louis, MO
Weiss, Ronald W. ... New York, NY
Weiss, Ross ... West Conshohocken, PA
Weiss, Roy L. ... New York, NY
Weiss, Russell, Jr. ... Lawrenceville, NJ
Weiss, Russell L. ... New York, NY
Weiss, Ruth A. ... Irvine, CA
Weiss, Samuel ... Houston, TX
Weiss, Samuel A. ... San Bernardino, CA
Weiss, Samuel G. ... Port Washington, NY
Weiss, Samuel G., Jr. ... Lebanon, PA
Weiss, Samuel H. ... Los Angeles, CA
Weiss, Samuel J. ... Longwood, FL
Weiss, Samuel J., P.A. ... Longwood, FL
Weiss, Samuel M., (A Professional Law
Corporation) ... Los Angeles, CA
Weiss, Sandra Byster ... Chicago, IL
Weiss, Sandra Jarva ... Washington, DC
Weiss, Sanford D. ... Montgomery, AL
Weiss, Scolney, Spees, Danker & Kop
Los Angeles, CA
Weiss, Scott A. ... Chicago, IL
Weiss, Scott K. ... Phoenix, AZ
Weiss, Scott R ... Miami, FL
Weiss Serota Helfman Pastoriza & Guedes,
P.A. ... Fort Lauderdale, FL
Miami, FL
Weiss, Seth ... New York, NY
Weiss, Sharon Z. ... Los Angeles, CA
Weiss, Shelby ... United States Senate,
Senatorial Assistants, GV
Weiss, Sheldon A. ... Millburn, NJ
Weiss, Sheldon M. ... West Babylon, NY
Weiss, Shelley M. ... Groton, CT
Weiss, Sherburt S. ... Miami, FL
Weiss, Shirley H. ... Washington, DC

Weiss, Shirli Fabbri ... San Diego, CA
Weiss, Sidney D. ... Woodbridge, NJ
Weiss, Sidney N. ... New York, NY
Weiss, Sol H. ... Philadelphia, PA
Weiss, Solomon ... Miami Beach, FL
Weiss, Spencer C. ... Greenville, SC
Weiss, Spirt & Guyer ... Blue Bell, PA
Weiss, Stanley ... Washington, DC
Weiss, Stanley G. ... New York, NY
Weiss, Stefen H. ... Santa Ana, CA
Weiss & Stein ... Buffalo, NY
Weiss, Stephen A. ... New York, NY
Weiss, Stephen A. ... New York, NY
Weiss, Stephen D. ... Gaithersburg, MD
Weiss, Stephen G. ... Newark, NJ
Weiss, Stephen H. ... Los Angeles, CA
Weiss, Stephen I. ... Buckingham, PA
Weiss, Stephen J. ... Washington, DC
Weiss, Stephen J. ... Livingston, NJ
Weiss, Stephen L. ... Phoenix, AZ
Weiss, Stephen M. ... Tucson, AZ
Weiss, Stephen M. ... Calabasas, CA
Weiss, Stephen M. ... Columbus, OH
Weiss, Stephen N. ... New York, NY
Weiss, Stephen P. ... Philadelphia, PA
Weiss, Stephen S. ... Chicago, IL
Weiss, Stephen Z. ... Lisle, IL
Weiss, Steve J. ... Bloomfield Hills, MI
Weiss, Steven ... Springfield, MA
Weiss, Steven A.
Pension Benefit Guaranty Corporation, Office of the General Counsel, GV
Weiss, Steven A. ... Chicago, IL
Weiss, Steven A. ... New York, NY
Weiss, Steven C., Law Offices of
Chicago, IL
Weiss, Steven E. ... New York, NY
Weiss, Steven G. ... Greenwich, CT
Weiss, Steven J. ... Buffalo, NY
Weiss, Steven K. ... New York, NY
Weiss, Steven M. ... San Diego, CA
Weiss, Steven M.
San Juan Capistrano, CA
Weiss, Steven M. ... Boca Raton, FL
Weiss, Steven M. ... Cleveland, OH
Weiss, Steven R. ... Des Moines, IA
Weiss, Stevens H. ... Mill Neck, NY
Weiss, Stuart A., Jr. ... Highland, NY
Weiss, Stuart J. ... Detroit, MI
Weiss, Stuart L. ... Pelham, NY
Weiss, Stuart Lloyd ... New York, NY
Weiss, Susan ... Boca Raton, FL
Weiss, Susan A. ... Seattle, WA
Weiss, Susan B. ... Chicago, IL
Weiss, Susan J. F. ... Asbury Park, NJ
Weiss, Susan K. ... Santa Monica, CA
Weiss, Susan L. ... Oakland, CA
Weiss, Susan L. ... Philadelphia, PA
Weiss, Susan S. ... Brentwood, TN
Weiss, Suzanne ... Hollywood, FL
Weiss, Suzanne T. ... Burbank, CA
Weiss, Terri L. ... White Plains, NY
Weiss, Terry M. ... Longwood, FL
Weiss, Terry R. ... Atlanta, GA
Weiss, Theo. F. ... San Antonio, TX
Weiss, Theodore B. ... Philadelphia, PA
Weiss, Theodore F., Jr. ... Houston, TX
Weiss, Thomas J. ... Los Angeles, CA
Weiss, Tobias ... Stamford, CT
Weiss, Todd J. ... Phoenix, AZ
Weiss, Tova ... Huntingdon Valley, PA
Weiss, Tracy Gilstrap ... Philadelphia, PA
Weiss, Van ... King Of Prussia, PA
Weiss and Van Scoyk, LLC
Steamboat Springs, CO
Weiss, Victor ... Monsey, NY
Weiss, Victor F. ... Sheboygan, WI
Weiss, Vita O. ... New York, NY
Weiss, Walter ... Los Angeles, CA
Weiss, Walter S. ... Los Angeles, CA
Weiss, Warren A. ... New York, NY
Weiss, Warren B. ... Brooklyn, NY
Weiss & Weiss ... Franklin Lakes, NJ
Weiss & Weiss ... New York, NY
Weiss, Weiss & Weiss ... Lebanon, PA
Weiss & Weissman ... San Francisco, CA
Weiss, Wendi K. ... Portland, OR
Weiss, Wendy L. ... Cleveland, OH
Weiss, William C. ... Syracuse, NY
Weiss, William D. ... Los Angeles, CA
Weiss, William E. ... San Francisco, CA
Weiss, William J. ... New York, NY
Weiss, William J., Jr. ... Derby, NY
Weiss, William O. ... Dobbs Ferry, NY
Weiss, William R. ... St. James, MN
Weiss, Wm. L. ... St. Louis, MO
Weiss, Yvette ... Princeton, NJ
Weiss, Zeff A. ... Indianapolis, IN
Weiss, Zoe Urena ... Indianapolis, IN
Weissbach, Shari Lash ... Iselin, NJ
New York, NY
Weissbard, Deborah B. ... New York, NY
Weissbard, Harvey ... West Orange, NJ
Weissbard, Samuel H. ... Irvine, CA
Weissbard, Sarah ... Hollywood, FL
Weissbard & Wiewiorka ... West Orange, NJ
Weissbarth, Frank D. ... Santa Fe, NM
Weissbarth, Rochelle ... Santa Fe, NM
Weissbeck, William W. ... Chicago, IL
Weissberg, Ariel ... Chicago, IL
Weissberg and Associates, Ltd. ... Chicago, IL
Weissberg, Franklin R. ... New York, NY
Weissberg Gaetjens Ziegenfeuter
New York, NY
Weissberg, Judith Lee ... Salinas, CA
Weissberg, Lynn G. ... Boston, MA
Weissberg, Sheldon S. ... New York, NY
Weissblum, George A. ... Bronxville, NY
Weissblum, Herbert ... Clinton, WA
Weissbluth, Samantha ... Chicago, IL
Weissbourd, Bernard B. ... Chicago, IL
Weissbrodt, Abe W. ... Washington, DC
Weissbrodt, Arthur Samuel ... San Jose, CA
Weissbrodt, David S. ... Minneapolis, MN
Weissbrodt, I. S. ... Washington, DC
Weissbrodt & Racin ... Washington, DC
Easton, MD
Weissburg, Adam B. ... Los Angeles, CA
Weissburg, Carl ... Los Angeles, CA
Weissburg, E. Stanley ... San Clemente, CA
Weissburg, Jerry A. ... Burbank, CA
Weissburg, Robyn Meyer ... Chicago, IL
Weisse, Frederick C. ... Escanaba, MI
Weisse, John S. ... Baltimore, MD
Weisse, Leslie ... Philadelphia, PA
Weisse, Louis E. ... Sheboygan Falls, WI
Weisse, Mark V. ... Clementon, NJ
Weisselberg, Susan E. ... New Haven, CT
Weissenbach, John A. ... Chicago, IL
Weissenberg, Kenneth A. ... New York, NY
Weissenberger, Bradley R. ... Chicago, IL
Weissenberger, Harry G. ... Irvine, CA
Laguna Hills, CA
Weissenberger, Harry G., Inc., Law Offices of
Laguna Hills, CA
Weissenborn, Anne A.
Federal Election Commission, Office of the General Counsel, GV
Weissenborn, Kramer J. ... St. Louis, MO
Weissenborn, Lee ... Miami, FL
Weissenborn, Sheridan K. ... Miami, FL
Weissenstein, A. Paul, Jr. ... Sumter, SC
Weisser, Geneva H. ... Minneapolis, MN
Weisser, Jeffrey S. ... Agawam, MA
Weisser, Mark ... Cincinnati, OH
Weisserman, Jeffrey D. ... Detroit, MI
Weissert, Andrew M. ... Indianapolis, IN
Weissert, John M. ... Dallas, TX
Weissert, Martin A. ... Fort Wayne, IN
Weissfeld, Adrian R. ... Buffalo, NY
Weissfeld, Jerold C. ... Littleton, CO
Weissfeld, Joachim A. ... Boston, MA
Providence, RI
Weissfeld, Randall D. ... Akron, OH
Weissfeld, Richard ... Sarasota, FL
Weissflach, Robert C. ... Buffalo, NY
Weissglass, Jeffrey A. ... New York, NY
Weissglass, Joel S. ... Elizabeth, NJ
Weissglass, Jonathan ... San Francisco, CA
Weissgold, Nanci L. ... Washington, DC
Weisshaar, Mark G. ... Washington, DC
Weissich, Jill Elaine ... San Rafael, CA
Weissing, Charles L. ... Tampa, FL
Weissing, Matthew D. ... Boca Raton, FL
Fort Lauderdale, FL
Weissinger, Charles, Jr. ... Rolling Fork, MS
Weissinger, Edwin B. ... Dade City, FL
Weissinger, George J. ... Garden City, NY
Weissinger & Hunter ... Rolling Fork, MS
Weissinger, Ira, Jr. ... Auburn, AL
Weissinger, William J., P.S.
Friday Harbor, WA
Weisskopf, Alexander M. ... Birmingham, AL
Weisskopf, Stephen D. ... Louisville, KY
Weissler, Eric C. ... Los Angeles, CA
Weissler, Harold J. ... New York, NY
Weissler, Mark L. ... New York, NY
Weissler, Robert C. ... Treasury Department, Internal Revenue Service, GV
Weissler, Robert I. ... Miami, FL
Weissler, Ronald ... Bronx, NY
Weisslitz, Edward ... West Orange, NJ
Weiss-Malik, Linda Sue ... Phoenix, AZ
Weissman, Aaron J. ... Granada Hills, CA
Weissman, Alison B. ... Pasadena, CA
Weissman, Amy E. ... Washington, DC
Weissman, Andrew B. ... Washington, DC
Weissman, Andrew D. ... Washington, DC
Weissman, Andrew H. ... Dulles, VA
Weissman, Andrew N. ... Culver City, CA
Weissman, Andrew Seth ... New York, NY
Weissman & Associates, Ltd.
Woodland Hills, CA
Weissman, Barry Leigh ... Los Angeles, CA
Weissman, Benj. L. ... Park Ridge, IL
Weissman, Bernard ... Los Angeles, CA
Weissman, Carol A. ... Los Angeles, CA
Weissman, Charles I. ... New York, NY
Weissman, Darryl ... Roseland, NJ
Weissman, David E. ... Great Neck, NY
Weissman, David J. ... West Palm Beach, FL
Weissman, David L. ... New York, NY
Weissman, David R. ... Miami, FL
Weissman, David S. ... Atlantic City, NJ
Weissman, Dervishi, Borgo & Nordlund, P.A.
Fort Lauderdale, FL
Miami, FL
Weissman, Donald A. ... Atlanta, GA
Weissman, Donald A., A P.C. ... Atlanta, GA
Weissman, Donna Sue Levit
Los Angeles, CA
Weissman, Dwayne ... Commack, NY
Weissman, Earl M. ... Beverly, MA
Weissman, Edward E. ... San Diego, CA
Weissman, Edward, Law Office of
New York, NY
Weissman, Ellen V. ... Buffalo, NY
New York, NY
Weissman, Erica ... New York, NY
Weissman, Esther S. ... Cleveland, OH
Weissman, Esther S., Co., L.P.A.
Cleveland, OH
Weissman, Gary A. ... Minneapolis, MN
Weissman, George H. ... Albany, NY
Weissman, George M. ... Bayonne, NJ
Weissman, Harold ... Fort Lauderdale, FL
Weissman, Howard D. ... Bethesda, MD
Weissman, Howard O. ... Bethesda, MD
Weissman, I. Donald ... Woodland Hills, CA
Weissman, Ira ... Hauppauge, NY
Weissman, Irving ... New York, NY
Weissman, Irving H. ... Houston, TX
Weissman, Jacob I. ... Chilmark, MA
Weissman, Janis ... New Hyde Park, NY
Weissman, Jay A. ... Newark, NJ
Weissman, Jeffrey ... Mineola, NY
Weissman, Jeffrey A. ... Miami, FL
Weissman, Jeffrey M.
Fort Lauderdale, FL
Miami, FL
Weissman, Jennifer Candace
Liberty Corner, NJ
Weissman, Jennifer T. ... New York, NY
Weissman, Joel ... New York, NY
Weissman, Joel M. ... West Palm Beach, FL
Weissman, Joel M., P.A.
West Palm Beach, FL
Weissman, Joseph J. ... Washington, DC
Tampa, FL
Weissman, Judith D. ... New York, NY
Weissman, Julia C. ... Irvine, CA
Weissman, Karen Pauline ... Newark, NJ
Weissman, Kenneth A. ... Los Angeles, CA
Weissman, Kim I., (Mr.) ... Springfield, MA
Weissman, Kip A., (P.C.) ... Washington, DC
Weissman, Larry A. ... Memphis, TN
Weissman, Lori Starman ... Rockford, IL
Weissman, Marc ... San Francisco, CA
Weissman, Margalo A. ... San Francisco, CA
Weissman, Mark A. ... New York, NY
Weissman, Mark D. ... New York, NY
Weissman, Matthew ... New York, NY
Weissman, Matthew M. ... Woodbridge, NJ
Weissman, Michael L. ... Chicago, IL
Weissman, Michael L.
Farmington Hills, MI
Weissman, Milton H. ... Philadelphia, PA
Weissman, Morton ... Hauppauge, NY
Weissman, Myrna B. ... Mercer Island, WA
Weissman, Nancy ... Boston, MA
Weissman, Noah M. ... New York, NY
Weissman, Nowack, Curry & Wilco, P.C.
Alpharetta, GA
Atlanta, GA
Marietta, GA
Weissman, Paul A. ... Newark, NJ
Weissman, Peter S. ... Washington, DC
Weissman, Phyllis B. ... Torrance, CA
Weissman, Rande A. ... Tampa, FL
Weissman, Richard ... Los Angeles, CA
Weissman, Richard, Inc., A Prof. Corp., Law Offices of ... Los Angeles, CA
Weissman, Richard T. ... Phoenix, AZ
Weissman, Robert A. ... Westlake Village, CA
Weissman, Robert A. ... Chantilly, VA
Weissman, Roger D. ... Phoenix, AZ
Weissman, Ruth Gevertz ... Plantation, FL
Weissman, S. Jerry ... Philadelphia, PA
Weissman, Seth G. ... Atlanta, GA
Weissman, Seth I. ... Los Angeles, CA
Weissman, Seth R. ... Palo Alto, CA
Weissman, Sonja S. ... Oakland, CA
Weissman, Stanley ... Montgomery, AL
Weissman, Stanley ... Mineola, NY
Weissman, Stephen ... Washington, DC
Weissman, Stephen B. ... New York, NY
Weissman, Stephen B. ... Uniondale, NY
Weissman, Steven ... New York, NY
Weissman, Steven ... New York, NY
Weissman, Steven A. ... San Francisco, CA
Weissman, Steven H. ... Jenkintown, PA
Weissman, Steven I. ... Miami, FL
Weissman, Steven J. ... Los Angeles, CA
New York, NY
Weissman, Susan ... Playa Del Rey, CA
Weissman, Susan ... New York, NY
Weissman, Terry D. ... Chicago, IL
Weissman & Weissman ... Mineola, NY
Weissman & Weissman, A Professional Law Corporation ... Westlake Village, CA
Weissman, William Hays ... Pleasanton, CA
Weissman, William R. ... Washington, DC
Weissmann, Andrew A. ... Brooklyn, NY
Weissmann, Benj. ... San Diego, CA
Weissmann, David A. ... Atlanta, GA
Weissmann, Eric, (P.C.) ... Beverly Hills, CA
Weissmann, Henry ... Los Angeles, CA
Weissmann, Jeffrey E. ... New York, NY
Weissmann, Leanna K. ... Lawrenceburg, IN
Weissmann, Mara S. ... New York, NY
Weissmann, Mark ... Eatontown, NJ
Weissmann, Wolff, Bergman, Coleman & Silverman, LLP ... Beverly Hills, CA
Los Angeles, CA
Weissmann & Zucker, P.C. ... Atlanta, GA
Weissman-Rothman, Karen Chaya
Lawrence, NY
Weissmeier, Alicia ... New York, NY
Weissmiller, David W. ... Mount Carroll, IL
Weissmiller Law Office ... Mount Carroll, IL
Weissmiller, Robert W. ... Mount Carroll, IL
Weissmuller, Helmut ... Sherman Oaks, CA
Weissmuller, Ingrid ... Sherman Oaks, CA
Weissmuller, Kurt ... Los Angeles, CA
Weist, Cameron A. ... Santa Cruz, CA
Weist, John R. ... Overland Park, KS
Weist, Mary Margaret ... Des Moines, IA
Weist, Robert D. ... Thousand Oaks, CA
Weist, William B. ... Fowler, IN
Weist, William B. ... Lafayette, IN
Weistart, John C. ... Durham, NC
Weistein, David A. ... Ocean City, NJ
Weistling, Ripple L. ... Washington, DC
Weistrop, Harry ... Half Moon Bay, CA
Weiswasser, Elizabeth Stotland
New York, NY
Weiswasser, Gayle D. ... San Francisco, CA
Weiswasser, Howard H. ... New York, NY
Weiswasser, Stephen A. ... Washington, DC
Weisz & Associates ... Atlanta, GA
Weisz & Associates, P.C.
Plymouth Meeting, PA
Weisz, Barry M. ... Los Angeles, CA
Weisz, Belle Seitel ... Hackensack, NJ
Weisz, Daniel ... Mineola, NY
Weisz, Daniel L. ... Woodstock, IL
Weisz, David J. ... New York, NY
Weisz, Edward ... Beverly Hills, CA
Weisz, Edward M. ... New York, NY
Weisz, Frank B. ... Plymouth Meeting, PA
Weisz, George ... New York, NY
Weisz, James S., (P.C.) ... Costa Mesa, CA
Weisz, Lee M. ... Chicago, IL
Weisz, Louis J. ... Akron, OH
Weisz, Lucy A. ... Baltimore, MD
Weisz, Michael B. ... Los Angeles, CA
Weisz, Michael Gregory ... Laramie, WY
Weisz, Michael J. ... St. Petersburg, FL
Weisz, Michael Jay ... Columbus, OH
Weisz, Michel Ociacovski ... Coral Gables, FL
Weisz & Michling ... Woodstock, IL
Weisz, Mitchell R. ... Woodstock, IL
Weisz, Peter R. ... Atlanta, GA
Weisz, Richard A. ... Los Angeles, CA
Weisz, Richard L. ... Albany, NY
Weisz, Robert C. ... New York, NY
Weisz, Tiberiu ... New York, NY
Weisz, Vera A. ... Los Angeles, CA
Weisz, Virginia G. ... Los Angeles, CA
Weiszhaar, Orville L. ... Minneapolis, MN
Weiszmann, Fred, Jr. ... Northbrook, IL
Weit, Victor A. ... East Meadow, NY
Weitberg, Jordan S. ... Florham Park, NJ
New York, NY
Weitendorf, Kurt R. ... Akron, OH
Weitgenant, Roger A. ... North Judson, IN
Weith, Glenna J., Law Office of
Champaign, IL
Weithers, Mariola K. ... Chicago, IL
Weithers, Thomas M. ... Rosemont, IL
Weithman, Cathy Jo ... Urbana, OH
Weithman, Gil ... Urbana, OH
Weithman, Stephen E. ... Delaware, OH
Weithorn, Stanley S. ... Phoenix, AZ
New York, NY
Weitinger, Don A. ... Houston, TX
Weitinger & Weitinger ... Houston, TX
Weitkamp, Fredrick J. ... Granada Hills, CA
Weitkamp, Gary R. ... Louisville, KY
Weitkamp, John F. ... Granada Hills, CA
Weitkamp & Weitkamp ... Granada Hills, CA
Weitman, David ... Dallas, TX
Weitman, Dov N.
Environmental Protection Agency, Program Office Attorneys, GV
Weitnauer, John C. ... Atlanta, GA
Weitz, Aaron ... New York, NY
Weitz, Alan S. ... Washington, DC
Weitz, Andrew M. ... Los Angeles, CA
Weitz, Barbara Malett ... Elkins Park, PA
Weitz, Daniel Michael ... New York, NY
Weitz, David J. ... Palo Alto, CA
Weitz, Ellen ... Houston, TX
Weitz, Eric D. ... San Diego, CA
Weitz, Erwin K. ... Cliffside Park, NJ
Weitz, Eugene I. ... Brooklyn, NY
Weitz, Eugene M. ... Murray Hill, NJ
Weitz, Harvey ... New York, NY
Weitz, Howard, (P.C.) ... New York, NY
Weitz, Jeffrey L. ... Fort Lauderdale, FL
Weitz, Jeremy M. ... Los Angeles, CA
Weitz, Jill Garfinkle ... Cherry Hill, NJ
Philadelphia, PA
Weitz, Leonard W. ... Basking Ridge, NJ
Weitz & Luxenberg ... Cherry Hill, NJ
South Orange, NJ
New York, NY
Weitz, Mark ... Los Alamitos, CA
Weitz, Mark S. ... Minneapolis, MN
Weitz, Mark S. ... Forest Hills, NY
Weitz, Mitchell I. ... Morristown, NJ
Weitz, N. Harvey ... Savannah, GA
Weitz, Paul B. ... New York, NY
Weitz, Paul M. ... Brooklyn, NY
Weitz, Perry ... New York, NY
Weitz, Robert A. ... Sheffield, MA
Weitz, Ronald G. ... Dallas, TX
Weitz & Schwartz, P.A. ... Fort Lauderdale, FL
Weitz, Shirley ... New Brunswick, NJ
Weitz, Stephen P. ... Framingham, MA
Weitz, Steven E. ... Encino, CA
Weitz, Stuart M. ... Duluth, GA
Weitz, Ted C. ... Pacific Palisades, CA
Weitz, Theodore M. ... Parsippany, NJ
Weitz, Tim ... Austin, TX
Weitz-Clancy, Jennifer J. ... Hartford, CT
Weitzel, Daniel P. ... Washington, DC
Weitzel, Douglas ... Austin, TX
Weitzel, Harry P. ... Houston, TX
Weitzel, J. Dennis ... Dallas, TX
Weitzel, James McKay, Jr. ... McLean, VA
Weitzel, Jerome R. ... Chicago, IL
Weitzel, John P. ... Boston, MA
Weitzel, Lynne A. ... Denver, CO
Weitzel, Mark P. ... San Francisco, CA
Weitzel, Nomiki Bouloubassis, Law Office of
Baltimore, MD
Bel Air, MD
Weitzel, Nomiki Bouloubassis ... Bel Air, MD
Weitzel, Patricia S. ... Tallahassee, FL
Weitzel, Richard S. ... Boston, MA
Weitzel, Stephan E. ... Evansville, IN

Welch, Richard J. ....Providence, RI
Welch, Richard K.
Federal Communications Commission, Office of the General Counsel, GV
Welch, Richard L. ....Belmont, MA
Welch, Richard L. ....Austin, TX
Welch, Robert ....Virginia, IL
Welch, Robert C. ....Independence, MO
Welch, Robert C., Jr. ....Ridgewood, NJ
Welch, Robert D. ....Mendenhall, MS
Welch, Robert E. ....Marysville, WA
Welch, Robert F. ....Garden City, NY
Welch, Robert G. ....Media, PA
Welch, Robert H., Jr. ....Milford, OH
Welch, Robert J., Jr. ....Orlando, FL
Welch, Robert J., Jr. ....Cincinnati, OH
Welch, Robert L. ....Atlanta, GA
Welch, Robert L. ....Cleveland, OH
Welch, Robert M., Jr. ....Houston, TX
Welch, Robert S. ....Cary, NC
Welch, Robert W. ....Salem, MA
Welch, Robin W. ....McAllen, TX
Welch, Robin W., P.C. ....McAllen, TX
Welch, Rock E. ....Colorado Springs, CO
Welch, Ronald R., (P.A.) ....Jackson, MS
Welch, Roy Emerson ....Shepherdsville, KY
Welch, Russell L. ....Denton, TX
Welch, Ruston C. ....Oklahoma City, OK
Oklahoma City, OK
Welch, Samuel H., Jr. ....Monroeville, AL
Welch, Sara E. ....Kansas City, MO
Welch, Scott H. ....Tulsa, OK
Welch, Scott T. ....New Orleans, LA
Welch, Shawn T. ....Salt Lake City, UT
Welch, Sheila J. ....Wilton, CT
Welch, Sherie M. ....Atlanta, GA
Welch, Spell, Reemsnyder, Pless & Davis, LLC ....Atlanta, GA
Welch, Stephen B. ....Walnut Creek, CA
Welch, Steven C. ....Omaha, NE
Welch, Steven H., Jr. (P.C.) ....Orinda, CA
Welch, Steven R. ....Oklahoma City, OK
Welch, Steven R. ....Austin, TX
Welch, Sue Ann ....Tucson, AZ
Welch, Susan ....Millen, GA
Welch, Susan Paulsrud ....Los Angeles, CA
Welch, Suzanne Kirby ....Chevy Chase, MD
Welch, T. Patrick ....Mc Comb, MS
Welch, Teresa J. ....Madison, WI
Welch, Terrence S. ....Dallas, TX
Welch, Terry E. ....Salt Lake City, UT
Welch, Terry S. ....Mount Clemens, MI
Welch, Theodore B. ....Oil City, PA
Welch, Theodore G. ....Racine, WI
Welch, Theresa M. ....Santa Fe, NM
Welch, Thomas A. ....Kennebunk, ME
Welch, Thomas D., Jr. ....Kahului, HI
Welch, Thomas F. ....Panama City, FL
Welch, Thomas H., Jr. ....Round Rock, TX
Welch, Thomas J. ....Shelton, CT
Welch, Thomas K. ....Salt Lake City, UT
Welch, Thomas M. ....Collinsville, IL
Welch, Thomas R. ....Jacksonville, FL
Welch, Thomas W. ....North Syracuse, NY
Welch, Timothy ....Minneapolis, MN
Welch, Timothy E. ....Washington, DC
Welch, Timothy J. ....New York, NY
Welch, Todd S. ....Colorado Springs, CO
Welch, Tracy Lind ....Boston, MA
Welch, Trevor J. ....New York, NY
Welch, Troy O. ....Fort Worth, TX
Welch, Valerie M. ....Minneapolis, MN
Welch, Vincent Joseph ....Corning, NY
Welch, W. Scott, III ....Jackson, MS
Welch, Wade M. ....Boston, MA
Falmouth, MA
Welch, Walter E. ....Madison, SD
Welch, Warren ....Rochester, NY
Welch & Welch ....Corning, NY
Welch and Welch ....Oil City, PA
Welch & White, P.A. ....Dover, DE
Georgetown, DE
Wilmington, DE
Welch, White & Wulff ....Omaha, NE
Welch, William C. ....New Lenox, IL
Welch, William David ....Denver, CO
Welch, William F. ....Atlanta, GA
Welch, William F. ....Indianapolis, IN
Welch, William F. ....Boston, MA
Welch, William H. ....Northampton, MA
Welch, William H. ....Marcellus, NY
Welch, William H. ....Fairborn, OH
Welch, William L., III ....Baltimore, MD
Welch, William M. ....Denver, CO
Welch, William M. ....New Smyrna Beach, FL
Welch, William M. ....Portland, ME
Welch, William M., II
Department of Justice, GV
Welch, William R. ....La Mesa, CA
Welch, William R. ....Chicago, IL
Welch, William T. ....McLean, VA
Welchans, Paul A. ....Bakersfield, CA
Welcher, Blake A. ....Thousand Oaks, CA
Welcher, Gayle ....Norman, OK
Welcher, Ray Willis ....Reading, PA
Welcher, Roger G. ....Miami, FL
Welchli, Robert D. ....Detroit, MI
Welchman, Philip J. ....Seattle, WA
Welchman, Thomas J. ....Somerville, NJ
Welch-Rubin, David ....New Haven, CT
Welch-Rubin, Lori A. ....New Haven, CT
Welcom, Judith ....New York, NY
Weld, Christopher, Jr. ....Boston, MA
Weld, Christopher M. ....Boston, MA
Weld, Jennifer H. ....New York, NY
Weld, John C. ....Yarmouth Port, MA
Weld, Jonathan M. ....New York, NY
Weld, Konstantine H. H. ....Burlington, NC
Weld, N. Brooks ....Pasadena, CA
Weld, Parker L. ....Rochester, NY
Weld, Riley, Prenn & Ricci, S.C.
Eau Claire, WI
Weld, Stephen L. ....Eau Claire, WI
Weld, Susan Roosevelt ....Cambridge, MA
Weld, William F. ....Boston, MA
Weldele-Wade, Stacey ....Missoula, MT
Welden, Bailey M. ....Crystal River, FL
Welden, Charles V., III ....Birmingham, AL
Welden, Charles V., Jr. ....Birmingham, AL
Welden, David R. ....Kensington, CA
Welden & Harbin ....Birmingham, AL
Welden, Jacques R. ....Kensington, CA
Welden, Robert D. ....Seattle, WA
Welden, Sondra E. ....Richmond, CA
Welden & Welden ....Kensington, CA
Welden, William Bowen ....Birmingham, AL
Welder, Joel R. ....Blue Earth, MN
Welder, Leo James, Jr.
Corpus Christi, TX
Welder, Renae L. ....Minneapolis, MN
Weldin, John C., Jr. ....Bergenfield, NJ
Welding, Jennifer M. ....Philadelphia, PA
Weldon, Aubrey W.A. ....Daly City, CA
Weldon, C. Michael ....Richmond, KY
Weldon, Charles R. ....Bellflower, CA
Downey, CA
Lakewood, CA
Weldon, Charles R. ....Norwalk, CA
Weldon, Christopher B. ....Stamford, CT
Weldon, Christopher B. ....White Plains, NY
Weldon & DeGasparis ....Santa Maria, CA
Weldon, Donna S. ....Harrisburg, PA
Weldon, E. Durward ....Georgetown, KY
Weldon, Fred ....Waxahachie, TX
Weldon, George Kent, Jr. ....Flushing, NY
Weldon & Hass ....Santa Barbara, CA
Weldon, Helen L. ....Fort Worth, TX
Weldon, Huston & Keyser ....Mansfield, OH
Weldon, Jeffrey A. ....Billings, MT
Weldon, John B., Jr. ....Phoenix, AZ
Weldon, John W. ....Atlantic Beach, FL
Weldon, Kevin M. ....Waukegan, IL
Weldon, Kevin P. ....Department of Commerce, Patent and Trademark Office, GV
Weldon, Lenore T. ....Jefferson City, MO
Weldon, Lisa ....Watertown, NY
Weldon, Malcolm W. "Mac" ....Miami, FL
Weldon, Mark ....New York, NY
Weldon, Melissa M. ....Minneapolis, MN
Weldon, Natalie J. ....Owensboro, KY
Weldon, Richard D. ....Safety Harbor, FL
Weldon, Richard D., P.A. ....Safety Harbor, FL
Weldon, Richard Lee ....Chickasha, OK
Weldon, Richard N. ....Myrtle Beach, SC
Weldon, Richard P., (A Law Corporation)
Santa Maria, CA
Weldon, Robert L. ....Harrisburg, PA
Weldon, Robert M. ....Watertown, NY
Weldon, Robert M., Jr. ....Watertown, NY
Weldon, Samuel C. ....Greenville, SC
Weldon & Smith, P.C. ....Chickasha, OK
Weldon, Stefanie G.
General Accounting Office, Office of the General Counsel, GV
Weldon, Stephen A. ....Watsonville, CA
Weldon, Susan A. ....Metairie, LA
Weldon, Susanne M. ....Laconia, NH
Weldon, Terry, Law Offices of ....Austin, TX
Weldon, Thomas P. ....Columbus, OH
Weldon, Thomas P., III ....Lompoc, CA
Weldon, Tracy A. ....Carlsbad, CA
Weldon - Trimper Law Firm, P.C.
Watertown, NY
Weldon, Walter F., Jr. ....Worcester, MA
Weldon and Wilburn ....Circleville, OH
Weldon, William E. ....Austin, TX
Weldon, Wilson O., Jr. ....Thomasville, NC
Weldon-Linne, Madeleine ....Chicago, IL
Weldon-Linne & Vogt ....Chicago, IL
Weldon-Wilson, Dee Ann ....Irving, TX
Weldy, Alan L. ....Goshen, IN
Weldy, Morton E. ....Saginaw, MI
Weldy, S. Daniel, III ....Fort Wayne, IN
Weldy, Thomas P. ....Fairfield, CT
Welebir, Douglas F. ....Redlands, CA
Welebir, McCune & Jure, A Professional Law Corporation ....Barstow, CA
Hemet, CA
Needles, CA
Redlands, CA
Riverside, CA
San Bernardino, CA
Temecula, CA
Victorville, CA
Welebir, Melissa J. ....Redlands, CA
Welenken, Martin I. ....Louisville, KY
Welensky, C. Fred ....Boston, MA
Welfel, Frederick M. ....Cleveland, OH
Welfeld, Irving H.
Department of Housing and Urban Development, GV
Welfeld, Jack A. ....Maywood, IL
Welfer, Jeremy A. ....New York, NY
Welford, Jay L. ....Detroit, MI
Welford, Mary ....Manchester, VT
Welford, Robin ....St. Louis, MO
Welgat, Michael ....Elmhurst, IL
Welge, Jack H., Jr. ....Longview, TX
Welge, Jack H., Jr., Law Office of
Longview, TX
Welge, John M. ....St. Louis, MO
Welge, Mark A. ....Philadelphia, PA
Welgos, Christopher R. ....Newark, NJ
Welhouse, Anthony W. ....Appleton, WI
Welhouse, Steven D. ....Chicago, IL
Weliczka, Kenneth F. ....Gansevoort, NY
Weliever, Daun A. ....Indianapolis, IN
Weliever, Stuart K. ....Crawfordsville, IN
Weliever, Thomas P. ....Indianapolis, IN
Welikson, Jeffrey A. ....New York, NY
Welikson, Niles C. ....Forest Hills, NY
Weliky, Mark ....Fresh Meadows, NY
Welin, Craig A. ....Los Angeles, CA
Welin, Peter D. ....Columbus, OH
Welin, Susan H. ....New York, NY
Welk, Lawrence J.
Department of Justice, GV
Welk, Robert F. ....Simsbury, CT
Welk, Robt. L. ....McLean, VA
Welk, Steven R. ....Los Angeles, CA
Welk, Thomas J. ....Sioux Falls, SD
Welk, Thomas S. ....San Mateo, CA
Welke, Brent ....English, IN
Welke, Brian J. ....Mount Dora, FL
Welke, Curtis C. ....Kokomo, IN
Welke, Dale A. ....Los Angeles, CA
Welke, E. Frank ....Kokomo, IN
Welke, Penny Cameron ....Fairfax, VA
Welke, Richard ....Detroit, MI
Welke, William R. ....Chicago, IL
Welken, Craig R. ....Fargo, ND
Welker, Catherine E. ....New York, NY
Welker, Dudley S. ....Safford, AZ
Welker, H. Delbert ....Morgan Hill, CA
Welker, J. Brent ....Phoenix, AZ
Welker, James E. ....Beloit, WI
Welker, Karin ....Boston, MA
Welker, Kenneth R. ....Palatine, IL
Welker, Mark D. ....Kansas City, MO
Welker, Mark L. L. ....Quinlan, TX
Welker, Marla ....Philadelphia, PA
Welker, Mary C. ....Winamac, IN
Welker, Michael I., (PC) ....St. George, UT
Welker, Paul ....Clarksville, TN
Welker, Robert F. ....Temple Terrace, FL
Welker, William L. ....Fort Myers, FL
Welkie, James M. ....Philadelphia, PA
Welkis, Scott ....New York, NY
Welkom, Wendy D. ....Santa Barbara, CA
Welkowitz, David S. ....Costa Mesa, CA
Well, Brett E. ....Chicago, IL
Well, David M. ....Chicago, IL
Well, Ranan Z. ....Washington, DC
Welland, James A. ....Kansas City, MO
Wellar, Courtney A. ....Pittsburgh, PA
Wellbaum, Gary S. ....Columbus, OH
Wellbaum, Leslie Raissman
San Francisco, CA
Wellbaum, Robert W., Jr. ....Englewood, FL
Wellbaum & Wolff, P.A. ....Englewood, FL
Wellbery, Barbara S.
Department of Commerce, National Telecommunications & Information Administration, GV
Wellborn, Carlton J., III ....Marietta, GA
Wellborn, Charles I. ....Albuquerque, NM
Wellborn, Christopher A. ....Rock Hill, SC
Wellborn, Christopher A., P.A.
Rock Hill, SC
Wellborn, Debra ....Quincy, IL
Wellborn, Houston, Adkison, Mann, Sadler & Hill, L.L.P. ....Carthage, TX
Henderson, TX
Longview, TX
Nacogdoches, TX
Tyler, TX
Wellborn, J. Marshall, Jr. ....New York, NY
Wellborn, Jennifer G. ....Columbus, GA
Wellborn, Paul F., III ....Atlanta, GA
Macon, GA
Wellborn, Richard B. ....Englewood, CO
Wellbrock, Cynthia E. ....Denver, CO
Wellcome Cardiff-By-The-Sea Law Offices
Cardiff-By-The-Sea, CA
Wellcome, Page ....Cardiff-By-The-Sea, CA
Welle, Elaine A. ....Laramie, WY
Welle, George B. ....Bloomfield, NJ
Welle, Lawrence G. ....Trenton, NJ
Welleford, Robert C. ....Lexington, KY
Wellek, Jeffrey A. ....Chicago, IL
Wellekens, John S. ....Staten Island, NY
Wellen, C. W. ....Houston, TX
Wellen, Ira C. ....New York, NY
Wellen, Robert H. ....Washington, DC
Wellen, Serena L. ....San Francisco, CA
Wellen, Warren R. ....Glendale, CA
Wellenberger, Robert B. ....Dallas, TX
Wellenbrock, David ....Stockton, CA
Wellenkamp, Paul M. ....Hayward, CA
Wellenraiter, Beth M. ....Peoria, IL
Wellenreiter, Walter R. ....New Orleans, LA
Wellens, Albert G. ....Potomac, MD
Wellens, David R., Law Offices of
Vail, CO
Wellensiek Law Offices ....Nebraska City, NE
Syracuse, NE
Wellensiek, Otto H. ....Nebraska City, NE
Syracuse, NE
Weller, Alan H. ....Palo Alto, CA
Weller, Barbara Malik ....New Orleans, LA
Weller, Bradley E. ....Grand Rapids, MI
Weller, Cella & West ....Richmond, MI
Weller, Charles D. ....Cleveland, OH
Weller, Charles E., Jr. ....Reno, NV
Weller, Cheryl J. ....Roseland, NJ
New York, NY
Weller, Christopher W. ....Montgomery, AL
Weller, Cyrus B. ....San Antonio, TX
Weller, Douglas L. ....Santa Clara, CA
Weller & Drucker, LLP ....San Francisco, CA
Weller, Edward B. ....Irvine, CA
Weller, Elizabeth L. ....Atlanta, GA
Weller, Francis G., (P.L.C.)
New Orleans, LA
Weller, G. Alex ....New Orleans, LA
Weller, G. Joseph ....Elgin, IL
Weller, Gerald P. ....New Orleans, LA
Weller, George H. ....Lansing, MI
Weller, Giovanna Tiberii ....Waterbury, CT
Weller, Green, Toups & Terrell, L.L.P.
Tallahassee, FL
Beaumont, TX
Houston, TX
Weller, Gwendolyn S. ....Pittsburgh, PA
Weller, H. Elizabeth "Beth" ....Dallas, TX
Weller, Harry D. ....West Hartford, CT
Weller, H. N., Jr. ....Richmond, MI
Weller, Howard H. ....New York, NY
Weller, James W. ....Springfield, IL
Weller, James W. ....Garden City, NY
Weller, Janet L. ....Washington, DC
Weller, Jill A. ....Cincinnati, OH
Weller, John C. ....St. Louis, MO
Weller, John C., P.C. ....St. Louis, MO
Weller, John Craig ....Alexandria, VA
Weller, Julia ....Washington, DC
Weller, Julia J. ....Montgomery, AL
Weller, Katherine D. ....Dallas, TX
Weller, Keith ....New York, NY
Weller, Kenneth J. ....Toledo, OH
Weller, Louis S. ....San Francisco, CA
Weller, Mark D. ....Independence, OH
Weller, Mark W. ....Washington, DC
Weller, Matthew A. ....Columbus, OH
Weller, Nancy Leibowitz ....Annapolis, MD
Baltimore, MD
Weller, O. Julia ....Washington, DC
Weller, Pamela L.
Consumer Product Safety Commission, Commissioners Office, GV
Weller, Patricia M. ....Minneapolis, MN
Shakopee, MN
Weller, Paul D. ....Philadelphia, PA
Weller, Philip D. ....New York, NY
Weller, Randall W. ....Hill City, KS
Weller, Richard A. ....Montclair, NJ
Weller, Robert Y., II ....Bloomfield Hills, MI
Weller, Stevens, Jr. ....Los Angeles, CA
Weller, Susan Neuberger ....Washington, DC
Weller, Suzanne ....Anchorage, AK
Weller, Thomas R. ....Homestead, FL
Weller, Wicks and Wallace, Professional Corporation ....Pittsburgh, PA
Weller, William E. ....Cocoa Beach, FL
Weller, William M. ....Atlanta, GA
Weller, Wm. Bradford ....San Diego, CA
Redmond, WA
Wellersdieck, Frank E., Jr. ....Bay Shore, NY
Wellerson, Craig L. ....Forked River, NJ
Wellerstein, Jeffrey ....Stockton, CA
Welles, Charles H., IV ....Scranton, PA
Welles, David B. ....Wausau, WI
Welles, David H. ....Nashville, TN
Welles, G. Henry ....Rancho Mirage, CA
Welles, James B., Jr. ....New York, NY
Welles, Jonathan S. ....Dallas, TX
Welles, Lauren B. ....New York, NY
Welles, Martin R. ....New Orleans, LA
Welles & McGrath ....Scranton, PA
Welles, Neil S. ....Springfield, VA
Welles, Patricia G. ....Miami, FL
Welles, Radcliffe ....Kamuela, HI
Welles, Stephen M. ....Palo Alto, CA
Boston, MA
Wellford, Alexander ....Richmond, VA
Wellford, Alexander W., Jr. ....Memphis, TN
Wellford, B. Randolph ....Richmond, VA
Wellford, B. Randolph, Jr. ....Richmond, VA
Wellford, Buckner Potts ....Memphis, TN
Wellford, Donald R. ....Memphis, TN
Wellford, Georgiana Gekas ....Richmond, VA
Wellford, Harry W. ....Memphis, TN
Wellford, Harry W., Jr. ....St. Louis, MO
Wellford, Hill B., III ....Washington, DC
Wellford, Hill B., Jr. ....Richmond, VA
Wellford, Robin S. ....St. Louis, MO
Wellford, Shea Sisk ....Memphis, TN
Wellford, W. Harrison ....Washington, DC
Wellford, Yvonne Steenstra
Richmond, VA
Welliever, Robert J., (Ltd.) ....Phoenix, AZ
Wellikson, Elissa R. ....Milpitas, CA
Welling, Alfred F., Jr. ....Charlotte, NC
Welling, Arthur R., Jr. ....Danville, IN
Welling, Arthur R., Jr., Professional Association
Danville, IN
Welling, Charles M. ....Charlotte, NC
Welling, John J. ....Rock Island, IL
Welling, Karen B. ....Hull, MA
Welling, Marian Clare ....Clayton, MO
Welling, Peter T. ....Chadds Ford, PA
Welling, Robert L. ....Warrensburg, MO
Welling, Sarah Newcomb ....Lexington, KY
Wellinghoff, Jon ....Las Vegas, NV
Wellinghorst, Stephen ....Livingston, NJ
Wellington, Charles R. ....Bel Air, MD
Wellington, Charles R. ....Monroe, WI
Wellington, Charles R., Law Offices of, P.A.
Bel Air, MD
Wellington, Christine C ....Boston, MA
Wellington, Daniel L. ....Washington, DC
Wellington, Donald E. ....Treasury Department, Departmental Offices, GV
Wellington, Elizabeth P. ....Riverside, CT
Wellington, Harry H. ....New York, NY
Wellington, J. Douglas ....Glen Rock, NJ
Wellington, John S. ....Harrisburg, PA
Wellington, Joseph A. ....Waterbury, CT
Wellington, Kent ....Cincinnati, OH
Wellington, Michael D. ....San Diego, CA
Wellington, Peter L. ....Washington, DC
Wellington, Peter S. ....Wilmington, DE

Wells, Samuel J. ....Los Angeles, CA
Wells, Samuel J. ....Shawnee, KS
Wells, Scott A. ....Hutchinson, KS
Wells, Sean N. R. ....Miami, FL
Wells, Sharon B. ....Chicago, IL
Wells, Sharon T. ....Boston, MA
Wells, Shawn T. ....Fort Lauderdale, FL
Wells, Shelley ....Yuma, AZ
Wells, Shelley L. ....Wausau, WI
Wells, Shelly G. ....Metairie, LA
Wells, Sherry A. ....Royal Oak, MI
Wells, Singer, Rubin and Musulin, P.A.
Bordentown, NJ
Mount Holly, NJ
Robbinsville, NJ
Wells, Small, Selke & Graham, A Law Corporation ....Redding, CA
Wells, Stanley H. ....Davis, CA
Wells, Stephen E. ....Washington, DC
Wells, Stephen L. ....St. Louis, MO
Wells, Stephen M. ....Durango, CO
Wells, Steven A. ....Eden Prairie, MN
Wells, Steven J. ....Tempe, AZ
Wells, Steven J. ....Minneapolis, MN
Wells, Steven L. ....Dallas, TX
Wells, Steven M. ....Nashville, TN
Wells, Steven M. ....Fort Worth, TX
Wells, Steven W. ....Birmingham, MI
Detroit, MI
Wells, Stuart J. ....Roseland, NJ
Wells, Stuart W., III ....Norwalk, CT
Wells, Susan E. ....Phoenix, AZ
Wells, Susan G. ....Long Beach, CA
Wells, Suzanne J. ....Joliet, IL
Wells, S. W. ....Tulsa, OK
Wells, Sylvan A. ....Daytona Beach, FL
Wells, Sylvan A., P.A. ....Daytona Beach, FL
Wells, Ted L. ....Tampa, FL
Wells, Terry R. ....Paducah, KY
Wells, Theodore V., Jr. ....Roseland, NJ
Wells & Thomas ....Los Angeles, CA
Wells, Thomas B. ....
United States Tax Court, GV
Wells, Thomas B. ....Bozeman, MT
Wells, Thomas C. ....Washington, DC
Wells, Thomas Calvin ....Jackson, MS
Wells, Thomas Jeffrey ....Richmond, VA
Wells, Thomas M. ....Paramus, NJ
Wells, Thomas O. ....Miami, FL
Wells, Thomas O. ....Alexandria, LA
Wells, Thomas W. ....Beaver Dam, WI
Wells, Thomas W., (P.A.) ....Houlton, ME
Wells, Timothy H. ....Bonifay, FL
Wells, Todd H. ....Birmingham, MI
Detroit, MI
Wells, Tom D., III ....Paris, TX
Wells, Tracy Siegel ....Holliston, MA
Wells, Troward G. ....Worcester, MA
Wells, V. Keith ....Pensacola, FL
Wells, Valerie C. ....Chicago, IL
Wells, Vanessa ....Palo Alto, CA
Wells, Vernon L., II ....Birmingham, AL
Wells, W. Howard ....Yuba City, CA
Wells, W. Whitfield ....White Plains, NY
Wells, Warren L. ....Oxford, MS
Wells, Warren L. ....Kirksville, MO
Wells Warren PC ....Richmond, VA
Wells, Wayne A. ....Edmond, OK
Wells, Wayne R. ....St. Cloud, MN
Wells and Wells ....Columbus, IN
Wells Wells, P.L.C. ....Davenport, IA
Wells, Welton W. ....Franklin, TN
Wells, Wendy Ellen ....New York, NY
Wells, Wendy M. ....Chicago, IL
Wells, Wiley H. ....Memphis, TN
Wells, William A. ....Wichita, KS
Wells, William B. ....Louisville, KY
Wells, William D. ....Pensacola, FL
Wells, William G. ....Santa Monica, CA
Wells, William Iwan ....Richmond, VA
Wells, William K., Jr. ....Washington, DC
Wells, William P. ....North Miami Beach, FL
Wells, William R. ....Houston, TX
Wells, William S. ....Englewood Cliffs, NJ
Wells, William T. ....Houston, TX
Wells, William W. ....Los Angeles, CA
Wells, William W. ....Pendleton, OR
Wells, W. V. ....Anacortes, WA
Wellsand, Ingrid J. ....Long Beach, CA
Wells-Brown, Beatrice R. ....Orlando, FL
Wellschlager, Earl K. ....Severna Park, MD
Wellschlager, Earl S. ....Baltimore, MD
Wellschlager, John R. ....Baltimore, MD
Wells Demaree, Rebecca ....Nashville, TN
Wells-Foster, E. June ....Alexandria, LA
Wellsfry, Lisa A. ....Orinda, CA
Wells-Guevara, Debora Ann
Huntington Beach, CA
Wellvang, Melinda Moore
Minneapolis, MN
Wellvang, Steven A. ....Minneapolis, MN
Welmaker, Ben H., Jr. ....Houston, TX
Welmaker, Douglas B. ....Houston, TX
Welmaker, Forrest N., Jr.
San Antonio, TX
Welmaker, G. Edward ....Pickens, SC
Welmaker, Martha Smith ....Houston, TX
Welmaker, Nolan ....San Antonio, TX
Welmaker & Welmaker, P.C.
San Antonio, TX
Welmaker, Wesley T. ....Houston, TX
Welman, Hively & Godley
Caruthersville, MO
Kennett, MO
Malden, MO
Welman, Scott H. ....Kansas City, MO
Welman, William O. ....Kennett, MO
Malden, MO

Welna, James J. ....Edina, MN
Welnak, Llowell A. ....Keene, NH
Welner, Ellen R. ....Englewood, CO
Welner, Jonathan ....Sacramento, CA
Welner, Louis L. ....Forest Hills, NY
Welnhofer, William G. ....Chicago, IL
Welp, Arthur, Jr. ....Norwalk, IA
Welp, Douglas A. ....Evansville, IN
Welp & Geffe ....Marshalltown, IA
Welp, Julie C. ....Indianapolis, IN
Welp, Martin A. ....New Orleans, LA
Welp, Robert A. ....McLean, VA
Welp, William A. ....Marshalltown, IA
Welper, F. Eugene, Jr. ....Hillsdale, MI
Welper & Macdonald, P.C. ....Hillsdale, MI
Welpton, Sherman Seymour, Jr.
Los Angeles, CA
Wels, Andrew C. ....New York, NY
Wels & Zerin ....New York, NY
Welsch, Barbara J. ....Chicago, IL
Welsch, Carol A. ....Lawrenceville, NJ
Welsch, Charles N., Jr. ....St. Louis, MO
Welsch, David C. ....St. Louis, MO
Welsch, Edward J. ....New Orleans, LA
Welsch & Hall ....Danville, IL
Welsch, Heidi G. ....Minneapolis, MN
Welsch, John A., Jr. ....Jackson, MS
Welsch, Ken S.
Occupational Safety and Health Review Commission,
Administrative Law Judges, GV
Welsch, Thomas M. ....Butte, MT
Welscher, Craig ....Houston, TX
Welsch-Lehmann, Mary di Zerega
McLean, VA
Welser, Howard T., Jr. ....Kent, OH
Welsh, Alfred John ....Louisville, KY
Welsh, Allayne F. ....Solon, OH
Welsh, Allen ....Coralville, IA
Welsh, Anne T. ....Seattle, WA
Welsh, Blaine T. ....Las Vegas, NV
Welsh, Bradley W. ....Tulsa, OK
Welsh, Brenda O. ....Los Angeles, CA
Welsh, Brian F. ....Worcester, MA
Welsh, Brian J. ....Silver City, NM
Welsh, Brian R. ....Buffalo, NY
Welsh, C. Victor, III ....Jackson, MS
Welsh, Cathleen P. ....Harrisonburg, VA
Welsh, Charles R. ....Hartford, CT
Welsh, Christopher J. ....San Diego, CA
Welsh, Clifford L. ....North Myrtle Beach, SC
Welsh, David F. ....Oklahoma City, OK
Welsh, David L. ....St. Louis, MO
Welsh, Deborah Campbell ....Leesburg, VA
Welsh, Deborah Tate ....Kansas City, MO
Welsh, Debra Pierquet ....Boulder, CO
Welsh, Diane M. ....Philadelphia, PA
Welsh, Donald E. ....New York, NY
Welsh, Donald L. ....Chicago, IL
Welsh, Edward F. ....Pittsburgh, PA
Welsh, Edward Leo, Jr.,(P.C.) ....Mesa, AZ
Welsh, Edwin J. ....Lake Oswego, OR
Welsh, Eileen Eakins ....Portland, OR
Welsh, Elizabeth A. ....Department of Justice,
Civil Division, GV
Welsh, Eric D. ....Charlotte, NC
Welsh, G. Duane ....Columbus, OH
Welsh, Gary M. ....Washington, DC
Welsh, Geoffrey S. ....Augusta, ME
Welsh, George A. ....Camp Hill, PA
Welsh, Glenn D. ....Reading, PA
Welsh, Gregory ....Baltimore, MD
Welsh, H. Ronald ....Houston, TX
Welsh, Harry M. ....Mansfield, OH
Welsh & Hubble, P.C. ....St. Louis, MO
Welsh, Hugh C. ....Newark, NJ
Welsh, Hugh H. ....New York, NY
Welsh, James C. ....Newark, NJ
Welsh, James E. ....Liberty, MO
Welsh, James G. ....Staunton, VA
Welsh, James G., Jr. ....Winston-Salem, NC
Welsh, James J. ....Indian Wells, CA
Welsh, James L., III ....Pittsburgh, PA
Welsh, James N., III ....Princeton, NJ
Welsh, James R. ....Omaha, NE
Welsh, Jane ....New York, NY
Welsh, Jeannette M. ....New York, NY
Welsh, Jeffrey D. ....Fort Lauderdale, FL
Welsh, Jocelynne Deborah ....Boston, MA
Welsh, John Beresford, Jr. ....Olympia, WA
Welsh, John C. ....Albany, NY
Welsh, John F. ....Boston, MA
Welsh, John H. ....Hartford, CT
Welsh, John J. ....Los Angeles, CA
Welsh, John L. ....Arlington, VA
Welsh, John William, Jr. ....El Paso, TX
Welsh, Joseph E. ....Easton, PA
Welsh, Julie A. ....Walnut Creek, CA
Welsh, Julie T. ....Chicago, IL
Welsh & Katz, Ltd. ....Washington, DC
Chicago, IL
Arlington, VA
Welsh, Kelly R. ....Chicago, IL
Welsh, Kevin D. ....Detroit, MI
Welsh, Kevin L. ....Pittsburgh, PA
Welsh & Lanham, P.L.C. ....Leesburg, VA
Welsh Law Group, The, LLC
Atlanta, GA
Welsh, Lawrence C. ....Media, PA
Welsh, Leonard K. ....Bakersfield, CA
Welsh, Louis M. ....San Diego, CA
Welsh, Mark D. ....Duluth, GA
Welsh, Mark D., P.C. ....Duluth, GA
Welsh, Mary Ann ....Phoenix, AZ
Minneapolis, MN
Welsh, Mary Elizabeth ....San Antonio, TX
Welsh, Mary Ellene ....Douglasville, GA
Welsh & McGilvray ....Sacramento, CA

Welsh, Michael F. ....Tinley Park, IL
Welsh, Michael Shane ....Atlanta, GA
Welsh, Michelle A. ....Pacific Grove, CA
Welsh, Nancy ....New York, NY
Welsh, Nancy A. ....Minneapolis, MN
Welsh, Natalie W. ....Hartford, CT
Welsh, Norval J., III ....Corpus Christi, TX
Welsh, Patrick J. ....Louisville, KY
Welsh, Paul ....Wilmington, DE
Welsh & Recker, A Professional Corporation
Philadelphia, PA
Welsh, Regis C., Jr. ....Allison Park, PA
Welsh, Richard E. ....Anchorage, AK
Welsh, Richard J. ....Decatur, IL
Welsh, Richard M. ....North Grafton, MA
Welsh, Richard M., Jr. ....North Grafton, MA
Welsh, Robert A. ....Chesterton, IN
Welsh, Robert A., Jr. ....Orleans, MA
Welsh, Robert C., (A Professional Corporation) ....Los Angeles, CA
Welsh, Robert E., Jr. ....Philadelphia, PA
Welsh, Robert L. ....Department of Justice,
Tax Division, GV
Welsh, Robert P. ....Charleston, WV
Welsh, Robin S. ....Fort Collins, CO
Welsh, Rosemary D. ....Cincinnati, OH
Welsh, Stanley M. ....Doylestown, PA
Welsh, Stanley W. ....Boise, ID
Welsh, Stephanie D. ....Golden, CO
Welsh, Stephen M. ....Macon, GA
Welsh and Telander ....Miami, FL
Welsh & Tennery ....Rockville, MD
Welsh, Thomas A. ....Albany, NY
Welsh, Thomas J. ....Sacramento, CA
Welsh, Thomas J. ....Meriden, CT
Welsh, Tim M. ....Lincoln, NE
Welsh, Timothy E. ....Ellicott City, MD
Welsh, Timothy G. ....Cleveland, OH
Youngstown, OH
Welsh, Timothy M. ....Omaha, NE
Welsh, Vernon J. ....Elmhurst, NY
Welsh, W. Russell ....Kansas City, MO
Welsh, Walter C. ....Hartford, CT
Welshans, Wallace A., III ....Batesville, MS
Welsher, Arthur B. ....Long Beach, NY
Welshimer, Mark J. ....New York, NY
Welshmer, Robert F. ....Newark, DE
Welstead, Christine L. ....Miami, FL
Welt, David M. ....Livingston, NJ
Welt, David S. ....Cincinnati, OH
Welt, Dixon S. ....Albany, NY
Welt, Donald D. ....Rochester, NY
Welt, Gabriels, Schunk, Arndt & Daly
Albany, NY
Welt, Gerald M. ....Las Vegas, NV
Welt, Henry ....New York, NY
Welt, Philip S. ....New York, NY
Welt, Richard J. ....Columbus, OH
Welt, Stacy E. ....Boca Raton, FL
Weltchek, Amy ....Elizabeth, NJ
Weltchek, Paul R. ....East Hampton, NY
Weltchek, Robert J., (P.A.)
Baltimore, MD
Weltchek, Roy E. ....Watchung, NJ
Welte, David A. ....Kansas City, MO
Welte, Patricia A.G. ....Camden, ME
Welte, Peter D. ....Northwood, ND
Welte & Welte, P.A. ....Camden, ME
Welte, Wendy B. ....Kansas City, MO
Welte, William H. ....Camden, ME
Welter, Craig ....
Office Of Special Counsel, GV
Welter, Cynthia A. ....Worcester, MA
Welter, Daniel G. ....Bridgeview, IL
Welter, Eric A. ....McLean, VA
Welter, Frederick L. ....Rayne, LA
Welter, Gerald G. ....Los Angeles, CA
Welter, Greene, Fidler & Chaplan, LLP
Los Angeles, CA
Welter, James E. ....Chicago, IL
Welter, Jay F. ....Clarkston, MI
Welter, John W. ....Eau Claire, WI
Welter, Joseph J. ....Buffalo, NY
Welter, Mark James ....Sioux Falls, SD
Welter, Maureen A. ....Chicago, IL
Welter, Paul A. ....Minneapolis, MN
Welter, Phyllis J. ....Minneapolis, MN
Welter, Robert J. ....Denver, CO
Welther, Frederick L. ....Annandale, VA
Welti, Belinda ....Boston, MA
Weltin Law Office, P.C. ....Oakland, CA
San Francisco, CA
Weltin, Philip R. ....Oakland, CA
Weltin, Tim ....Houston, TX
Weltler, W. J. ....Temple, TX
Weltlich, Paul M. ....Chicago, IL
Weltman, David L. ....Boston, MA
Weltman, Edward S. ....New York, NY
Weltman, Eitan, Law Office of
Bloomington, IL
Weltman, Jeffrey H. ....Canton, OH
Weltman, John J. ....Boston, MA
Weltman, Jordan S. ....Long Beach, CA
Weltman, Laura ....Calabasas, CA
Weltman, Laurence D. ....New York, NY
Weltman, Lawrence H. ....St. Louis, MO
Weltman & Moskowitz, LLP
Fair Lawn, NJ
New York, NY
Syosset, NY
Weltman, Richard E. ....Fair Lawn, NJ
New York, NY
Syosset, NY
Weltman, Robert B. ....Cleveland, OH
Weltman, S. Randall ....Cleveland, OH
Weltman, Scott S. ....Cleveland, OH
Weltman, Stephen F. ....Los Angeles, CA
Weltman, Steven L. ....Sugar Land, TX

Weltman, Steven L., P.C. ....Sugar Land, TX
Weltman, Stewart M. ....Chicago, IL
Weltman, Stewart M., P.C. ....Chicago, IL
Weltman, Weinberg & Reis Co., L.P.A.
Troy, MI
Brooklyn Heights, OH
Cincinnati, OH
Cleveland, OH
Columbus, OH
Pittsburgh, PA
Weltmann, Gary F. ....Rockville, MD
Weltmer Law Office ....Mankato, KS
Weltmer, Roderick E. ....Mankato, KS
Weltner, Charles Longstreet ....Atlanta, GA
Weltner, David D. ....Bridgeton, MO
Weltner, Robert B. ....Dayton, OH
Welton, Amy Jeanne ....Austin, TX
Welton, Barbara J ....Erie, PA
Welton, Barry S. ....Midland, TX
Welton, Charles, A Professional Corporation
Denver, CO
Welton, Charles E. ....Denver, CO
Welton, Joseph D., (Prof. Corp.) ....Detroit, MI
Welton, Mark & Associates, P.A.
Crestview, FL
Welton, Mark Henzler ....Crestview, FL
Welts, David A. ....Mount Vernon, WA
Welts, Robert B. ....Nashua, NH
Welts & Welts ....Mount Vernon, WA
Welts and White, P.C. ....Nashua, NH
Weltsek, Barbara M. ....Medford, NY
Welty & Blair, P.C. ....Arlington, VA
Welty, C. Douglas ....Arlington, VA
Welty, David G. ....Allentown, PA
Welty, David W. ....
Treasury Department, GV
Welty, David W. ....Cleveland, OH
Welty, George V. ....Ligonier, PA
Welty, James N. ....Portland, OR
Welty, Jean L. ....New Haven, CT
Welty, John R. ....Wyomissing, PA
Welty, Joseph S. ....Baltimore, MD
Frederick, MD
Welty, M. Todd ....Dallas, TX
Welty, Michael H. ....Healdsburg, CA
Welty, Patricia Mary ....Silver Spring, MD
Welty, R. Vincent ....Frederick, MD
Welty, Richard E. ....St. Augustine, FL
Welty, Robert L. ....Philadelphia, PA
Welty, William A. ....Cleveland, OH
Welty, William D. ....Centreville, MI
Weltz, Allen A. ....Newton, MA
Weltz, Irwin ....New York, NY
Weltz, Kenneth L. ....Overland Park, KS
Weltz, Paul Martin ....New York, NY
Weltz, Scott A. ....Winston-Salem, NC
Weltzer, Louis A. ....Georgetown, CO
Welu, Constance ....Clive, IA
Welu, David J. ....Adel, IA
Welykyj, Christina ....New York, NY
Welytok, Daniel S. ....Milwaukee, WI
Welz, Elzbieta K. ....Boston, MA
Welz, Robert J. ....Joliet, IL
Welz, Stephen G. ....Reading, PA
Welzenbach, Mark J. ....Concord, NH
Welzenbach, William G. ....Bakersfield, CA
Welzer, Frank C. ....New York, NY
Welzien, Michael S. ....Chicago, IL
Wember, Carolyn D. ....New York, NY
Wemhoener, Carl F. ....Oklahoma City, OK
Wemhoff, David A. ....South Bend, IN
Wemhoff, Douglas G. ....Gladstone, MO
Wemmert, Judith K. ....San Antonio, TX
Wempe, Rebecca P. ....Topeka, KS
Wempe, Tara A. ....York, PA
Wemple & Daly ....Schenectady, NY
Wemple, Howard H. ....Wheaton, IL
Wemple, Peter H. ....Lisle, IL
Wemple, William ....New York, NY
Wen, Brendon Y. ....San Francisco, CA
Wen, Oliver ....San Francisco, CA
Wen, Pauline L. ....New York, NY
Wenarsky, Jack Edward ....Succasunna, NJ
Wenbourne, Robert J. ....Sacramento, CA
Wenbourne, Thomas E. ....El Cajon, CA
Wenc, David J. ....Hartford, CT
Wenc, David J. ....Windsor Locks, CT
Springfield, MA
Wenc, Stephen H. ....Northbrook, IL
Wence, Gary F. ....Omaha, NE
Wenck, Edwin O. ....Baltimore, MD
Wenck, Patricia Kelly ....Baltimore, MD
Wencl, Annette M. ....Washington, DC
Wenczel, Arthur R. ....Lawrenceville, NJ
Wenczel, Mark A. ....Nutley, NJ
Wend, Christopher P. ....Los Angeles, CA
Wendekier, Raymond J. ....Johnstown, PA
Wendel, Bruce Leland ....Kansas City, MO
Wendel, Charles A. ....Alexandria, VA
Wendel, Chritton, Parks & DeBari, Chartered ....Lakeland, FL
Wendel, Clifford D., Jr. ....Newton, IA
Wendel, David ....Hackensack, NJ
Wendel, David I. ....Oakland, CA
Wendel, David K. ....Las Cruces, NM
Wendel, Diana M. ....Denver, CO
Wendel, Edward P. ....Washington, DC
Wendel, Fred, III ....Cleveland, OH
Wendel, Fred P. ....Eufaula, OK
Wendel, Gary C. ....Niceville, FL
Wendel, Gerald ....Boca Raton, FL
Wendel, Harvey L. ....Madison, WI
Wendel, Helen R. ....Department of Commerce,
Patent and Trademark Office, GV
Wendel, Joan Dover ....Phoenix, AZ
Wendel, John F. ....Lakeland, FL
Wendel, Joyce J. ....Carrollton, MO
Wendel, Lee A. ....Columbus, OH

Wendel, Martin	**Newark, NJ**
Wendel, Patricia H.	Las Cruces, NM
Wendel, Paul E.	Dallas, TX
Wendel, Peter T.	Malibu, CA
Wendel, Richard G., II	Cincinnati, OH
Wendel, Ronald G.	Clearwater, FL
Wendel, Rosen, Black & Dean, LLP	**Oakland, CA**
Wendel, Todd E.	Santa Ana, CA
Wendelberger, Jeralyn B.	Milwaukee, WI
Wendelbo, Chris A.	Department of the Army, U.S. Army Legal Services Agency, GV
Wendelburg, Allan, Law Office of	**Hockessin, DE**
Wendelburg, Allan, Law Office of	**Wilmington, DE**
Wendelgass, James R.	Reading, PA
Wendelken, Richard J.	Akron, OH
Wendell, Bess Castle	Richmond, VA
Wendell, David S.	Boston, MA
Wendell, George B.	New York, NY
Wendell, Harlan	**Palo Alto, CA**
Wendell, Joanne M.	**Los Angeles, CA**
Wendell, Karen A.	**New York, NY**
Wendell, Laura K.	**Miami, FL**
Wendell, Michael J.	Las Vegas, NV
Wendell, Peg	**Chicago, IL**
Wendell, Roger C.	Beverly, MA
Wendell, William D.	North Canton, OH
Wendells, Arthur T.	Seattle, WA
Wendells, David T.	Whippany, NJ
Wendeln, John H.	**Dayton, OH**
Wendelowski, Karyn I.	Environmental Protection Agency, Office of the General Counsel, GV
Wendelsdorf, Scott T.	Louisville, KY
Wender, Charles	Boca Raton, FL
Wender, Edward L., (P.C.)	**Baltimore, MD**
Wender, Faith	Los Angeles, CA
Wender, Fern Z.	Beverly Hills, CA
Wender, Ira T.	**New York, NY**
Wender, Joseph A., Jr.	Sacramento, CA
Wender, Lana J.	Atlanta, GA
Wender, Randi L.	New York, NY
Wender, Richard H.	**New York, NY**
Wenderoff, Lori A.	Encino, CA
Wenderoff, Marc W.	Los Angeles, CA
Wenderoth, Lind & Ponack, L.L.P.	**Washington, DC**
Wenderoth, Stephen J.	**Washington, DC**
Wendl, Carol A.	Guthrie Center, IA
Wendland, Arvid L.	Blue Earth, MN
Wendland, Christopher S.	**Waterloo, IA**
Wendland, Craig W.	**Rochester, MN**
Wendland, Donald W.	**Houston, TX**
Wendland, James	Menomonie, WI
Wendland, Robert C., (P.C.)	**Dallas, TX**
Wendland Timmerman, P.A.	Blue Earth, MN
Wendland & Utz, Ltd.	**Rochester, MN** **Winona, MN**
Wendlandt, Dalila Argaez	**Boston, MA**
Wendlandt, John C.	Anchorage, AK
Wendlandt, Margaret L.	Springfield, MA
Wendlandt, Walter	Austin, TX
Wendler, Arthur F.	Troy, IL
Wendler, Brian M.	**Edwardsville, IL**
Wendler, Edward T., Sr.	Austin, TX
Wendler, Guy H.	Cedar Rapids, IA
Wendler, Helen E.	**Lexington, MA**
Wendler, Jeffrey Alan	**New York, NY**
Wendler, John D.	**Edwardsville, IL**
Wendler, Phyllis F.	Garden City, KS
Wendleton, Patricia A.	**San Jose, CA**
Wendling & Associates	Burnsville, MN
Wendling, Cheryl Judge	Westfield, IN
Wendling, Gregory A.	Greensboro, NC
Wendling, Patricia L.	St. Louis, MO
Wendling, Richard E.	Clifton Park, NY
Wendling, Robert J.	Burnsville, MN
Wendling, William E., Jr.	**Carmel, IN**
Wendolowski, Raymond P.	**Wilkes-Barre, PA**
Wendorf, David R.	Blue Earth, MN
Wendorf, Mark A.	**St. Paul, MN**
Wendorf, Michael J.	**Washington, DC**
Wendorf, Scott F.	**Dallas, TX**
Wendorff, Bonnie A.	**Madison, WI**
Wendorff, E. Susie	Long Beach, CA
Wendorff Ellison & David	**Wausau, WI**
Wendorff, Mark F.	**Long Beach, CA**
Wendorff, Mark P.	**Wausau, WI**
Wendorff, Mary E.	Wausau, WI
Wendorff, Roland J.	Wausau, WI
Wendover, Jas R.	Lake Kiowa, TX
Wendroff, Allan I.	Sacramento, CA
Wendrovsky, Gerry M.	New York, NY
Wendt & Abel, A Professional Law Corporation	San Luis Obispo, CA
Wendt, Barry J.	Haddon Heights, NJ
Wendt, Brett M.	**Orlando, FL**
Wendt, Bryan D.	**Dallas, TX**
Wendt, C. Morten	Sedalia, MO
Wendt, Cheryl M.	**Mineola, NY** **Riverhead, NY**
Wendt, Christopher L.	**Detroit, MI**
Wendt, David R.	Lockport, NY
Wendt, Debra	**Chicago, IL**
Wendt, Dorothy N.	Denver, CO
Wendt, Erik J.	**Orlando, FL**
Wendt, Frank	**Overland Park, KS** **Kansas City, MO**
Wendt, Hunter L.	Mount Clemens, MI
Wendt, John A. F., Jr.	**Delta, CO**
Wendt, John T.	Minneapolis, MN
Wendt, Laurel Anne	Carbondale, IL
Wendt Law Office, The, P.C.	**Delta, CO**
Wendt, Lisa M.	**Orlando, FL**
Wendt, Lynne W.	**Atlanta, GA**
Wendt, Marjorie A.	Brookfield, WI
Wendt, Meredith K.	Chalmette, LA
Wendt, Nancy R.	Olympic Valley, CA
Wendt, Norma Kay	St. Augustine, FL
Wendt, Peter M.	New York, NY
Wendt, Richard A.	**Grand Rapids, MI**
Wendt, Richard H.	Pierre, SD
Wendt, Robert D.	San Luis Obispo, CA
Wendt, Robertson H., Jr.	**Charleston, SC**
Wendt, Robertson H., P.A.	**Charleston, SC**
Wendt, Roderick C.	Klamath Falls, OR
Wendt, Rodney G.	**Chicago, IL** **Salt Lake City, UT**
Wendt, Ronald W.	**Cedar Rapids, IA**
Wendt, T. Joseph	**Indianapolis, IN**
Wendt & Temples, LLC	**Atlanta, GA**
Wendt, Teri	Valrico, FL
Wendt, Timothy M.	**Warsaw, IN**
Wendt, Tracy Q.	Columbus, OH
Wendt, Wendt, Van Eman & Candela, P.C.	Mount Clemens, MI
Wendt, William H.	Springfield, MO
Wendt, Wilson F.	**Walnut Creek, CA**
Wendt, Wm. V.	Mount Clemens, MI
Wendte, Dennis R.	**Chicago, IL**
Wendtland, Anthony T.	**Cheyenne, WY** **Sheridan, WY**
Wendtland, Debra J.	**Cheyenne, WY** **Sheridan, WY**
Wendtland, Linda S.	Department of Justice, Civil Division, GV
Wendy, Jennifer L.	**New York, NY**
Wendy, Richard A.	**Chicago, IL**
Wendzel, Karen E.	**Jacksonville, FL**
Wendzel, Peter M.	**Hartford, CT**
Wenell, Gary E.	Sioux City, IA
Wener, Lester T.	Memphis, TN
Wenerowicz, Carole	Milwaukee, WI
Weng, Garner K.	**San Francisco, CA**
Weng, Michael J.	Rock Island, IL
Wengel, Deborah L.	**Washington, DC**
Wengel, Lawrence A.	**Sacramento, CA**
Wengel, Susan M.	El Macero, CA
Wenger, Alan D.	**Youngstown, OH**
Wenger, Brian D.	**Minneapolis, MN**
Wenger, Cathrine F.	Detroit, MI
Wenger & Cronin, P.C.	Manchester, NH
Wenger, David K.	**Detroit, MI**
Wenger, David W.	**Newark, OH**
Wenger & Donovan	Harper Woods, MI
Wenger, Edward H.	Port Washington, NY
Wenger, Eric A.	New York, NY
Wenger, Fredrick W.	Muncie, IN
Wenger, George E., Jr.	**Chambersburg, PA**
Wenger, Gregory J.	**Boston, MA** **Dover, NH**
Wenger, Howard B.	Iowa City, IA
Wenger, L. Edwin	Harper Woods, MI
Wenger, Larry B.	Charlottesville, VA
Wenger, Lisa	Grosse Pointe, MI
Wenger, Lisa, P.C.	Grosse Pointe, MI
Wenger, Marc S.	**Woodbury, NY**
Wenger, Margot	**San Francisco, CA**
Wenger, Nancy J.	Los Angeles, CA
Wenger, Paul N., Jr.	Agency for International Development, Other Offices of A.I.D., GV
Wenger, Peter C.	Albany, NY
Wenger, Peter D.	Manchester, NH
Wenger, Randi E.	Williamsport, PA
Wenger, Raymond J., Jr.	Los Angeles, CA
Wenger, Renee G.	Salem, OR
Wenger, Sylvia L.	West Palm Beach, FL
Wenger, Thomas L.	**Harrisburg, PA**
Wenger, Valerie L.	**Austin, TX**
Wengert, Paul N.	**McLean, VA**
Wengerter, Christine E.	San Francisco, CA
Wengiel, Donna J.	**Newtown, PA**
Wengler, Vance W.	Colorado Springs, CO
Wenglowskyj, Bohdan	**Rochester, NY**
Wengrofsky, Michael P.	New York, NY
Wengrow, Henry R.	Columbia, SC
Wenick, George D.	**Atlanta, GA**
Wenig, Alan B.	New York, NY
Wenig, Allyson Dee	**New York, NY**
Wenig, Cindy L.	**New York, NY**
Wenig, Devin N.	New York, NY
Wenig, Howard A.	**New York, NY**
Wenig, Leonard N.	Chicago, IL
Wenig, Mary Moers	Hamden, CT
Wenig, Meryl Lisa	Brooklyn, NY
Wenig, Michael J.	**Greensboro, NC**
Wenig, Richard Jay	Binghamton, NY
Wenig, Robin	**New York, NY**
Wenig, Wesley S.	**Westlake Village, CA**
Wenige, Lynne Oliver	**Charlotte, NC**
Wenik, Jack	**Newark, NJ** **New York, NY**
Weninger, Barbara D.	**Boston, MA**
Weninger, Belle K.	Portland, OR
Weninger, John A.	Dallas, TX
Weninger, Joseph J.	**Sacramento, CA**
Weninger, Robert A.	Lubbock, TX
Weniz, Martin P.	Los Angeles, CA
Wenk, Craig R.	Wilmington, VT
Wenk, Dawn M.	Toledo, OH
Wenk, Joel Leon	Cicero, NY
Wenkam, Chiye R.	**Honolulu, HI**
Wenkart, Ronald D.	Costa Mesa, CA
Wenke, Margaret E.	**Allentown, PA** **Philadelphia, PA**
Wenke, Michael F.	Media, PA
Wenke, Robert A.	Long Beach, CA
Wenke, Teresa R.	Atlanta, GA
Wenker, Judith A.	Universal City, CA
Wenker, Mark	**Phoenix, AZ**
Wenker, Paul F.	**Cincinnati, OH**
Wenker, Randall W.	Los Angeles, CA
Wenkert, Lynn Cosma	Huntington Station, NY
Wenkstern, Grant E.	Fort Lauderdale, FL
Wennar, Jeffrey T.	College Park, MD
Wennberg, Brent	St. Paul, MN
Wenneman, Ann F.	Brooklyn Heights, OH
Wenner, Adam	**Washington, DC**
Wenner, Charles R.	**Washington, DC**
Wenner, Cheryl Garrett	Findlay, OH
Wenner, David A.	**Phoenix, AZ**
Wenner, Hillary B.	**Chicago, IL**
Wenner, Lynette M.	Canon City, CO
Wenner, Mark M.	St. Louis, MO
Wenner, Michael C.	Troy, MI
Wenner, Neil E.	**Allentown, PA**
Wenner, Nicholas M.	**Minneapolis, MN**
Wenner, Robert H.	St. Cloud, MN
Wenner, Sandra L.	Green Bay, WI
Wenner, Scott J.	**New York, NY**
Wenner, Thomas R.	St. Cloud, MN
Wenner, William E.	Findlay, OH
Wenner, William W.	Frederick, MD
Wennergren, Kenneth H.	Los Angeles, CA
Wennerholm, Klar C.	Salinas, CA
Wennerholm, Robert W.	Oakdale, IA
Wennerholm, Traci E.	**San Francisco, CA**
Wenners, Douglas J.	**Manchester, NH**
Wenners, Vincent A., Jr.	Manchester, NH
Wennes, Marilyn A.	United States Court Of Appeals For The Federal Circuit, GV
Wennet, Richard I.	West Palm Beach, FL
Wennett, Richard W.	**Boston, MA**
Wenniger, Ian M. de Buy	**Boston, MA**
Wennihan, Angela C.	**Dallas, TX**
Wenning, Edward C.	Long Beach, NY
Wenning, Jan R.	**Cincinnati, OH**
Wenning, John C.	**Appleton, WI**
Wenning, Michael J.	**Bradley Beach, NJ**
Wenning, Steven R.	Indianapolis, IN
Wenning, Thomas F.	Reston, VA
Wennlund, Donald L.	New Lenox, IL
Wennlund, Donald L., & Assoc.	New Lenox, IL
Wenof, Michael A.	Philadelphia, PA
Wenokur, Alan J.	Seattle, WA
Wenrich, George L.	Atlanta, GA
Wensel, David W.	Anchorage, AK
Wensinger, Arnold M.	Irvine, CA
Wenskay, Donald L.	**Irvine, CA**
Wensley, Danford J.	**Rochester, NH**
Wensley, David W.	**Irvine, CA**
Wenstrup, Daniel J.	**Cincinnati, OH**
Wenstrup, Rose Mary L.	**Cleveland, OH**
Wente, David O.	Burbank, CA
Wente, Leslie Ann	Fullerton, CA
Wenten, Robert P.	Oakland, CA
Wenthe, Roger W.	Chicago, IL
Wentholt, H. Frank	Belmont, CA
Wenthur & Chachas	La Jolla, CA
Wenthur, Cris John	La Jolla, CA
Wentink, Michael J.	Department of the Army, Army Materiel Command, GV
Wentker, Frederick W., Jr.	**San Francisco, CA**
Wentlandt, Arthur W.	**Syracuse, NY**
Wentley, Richard T.	**Pittsburgh, PA**
Wento, Kay S.	Inver Grove Heights, MN
Wentt, Cassandra E.	Glendale, CA
Wentworth, Andrew S.	Las Vegas, NV
Wentworth, Charles C., II	Newport News, VA
Wentworth, David L., II	**Peoria, IL**
Wentworth, Diane Nissim	Los Angeles, CA
Wentworth, E. Jeffrey	**San Antonio, TX**
Wentworth, Francis M., Jr.	**Nashville, TN**
Wentworth, Gordon H.	**Springfield, MA**
Wentworth, Jeff	San Antonio, TX
Wentworth, John	**Santa Fe, NM**
Wentworth, John D.	Coquille, OR
Wentworth, Karen A.	Newark, OH
Wentworth, Martha B.	Indianapolis, IN
Wentworth, Michelle J.	Middleboro, MA
Wentworth, Paoli & Purdy, LLP	**Newport Beach, CA**
Wentworth, Paul V.	**Phoenix, AZ**
Wentworth, Rene T.	Lebanon, CT
Wentworth, Theodore S.	**Newport Beach, CA**
Wentworth, Timothy L.	**Houston, TX**
Wentworth, Winifred L.	Tallahassee, FL
Wentworth Strickland, Elizabeth Ann	San Jose, CA
Wentz, Aaron B.	Niceville, FL
Wentz, Craig V.	**Salt Lake City, UT**
Wentz, Daniel L.	Minneapolis, MN
Wentz, David G.	**Naperville, IL**
Wentz, Douglas E.	**St. Petersburg, FL**
Wentz, Frederic M.	**Norristown, PA**
Wentz, Gregory C.	Lancaster, OH
Wentz, Jennifer C.	Overland Park, KS
Wentz, Julia A.	St. Paul, MN
Wentz, Kevin L.	**Dallas, TX**
Wentz, Pamela J.	**Pittsburgh, PA**
Wentz, Richard B.	**Calabasas, CA**
Wentz, Richard E.	**Covington, KY**
Wentz, Robert C.	Cleveland, OH
Wentz, Roy A., Jr.	Wilmington, DE
Wentz, Thomas A.	**Minot, ND**
Wentz, Thomas, Jr.	**Minot, ND**
Wentz, Weaver & Kling, LLP	New Holland, PA
Wentz, William G.	Bedford, VA
Wentz, William H.	**Oak Brook, IL**
Wentzel, Alan R.	**Bonita Springs, FL** **New York, NY**
Wentzel, Charles R.	Tinley Park, IL
Wentzel, David F.	**Chicago, IL**
Wentzel, Frederick G.	La Verne, CA
Wentzel, Karen E.	**Palo Alto, CA**
Wentzel, Suzanne	**Cincinnati, OH**
Wentzel, W.L., Jr. & Associates, PLLC	**Minneapolis, MN**
Wentzel, Willard L., Jr.	**Minneapolis, MN**
Wentzell, Joseph A.	St. Anthony, MN
Wentzell, Michael D.	**St. Paul, MN**
Wentz-Fischer, Raylene Marie	Manchester, NH
Wenz, George	White River Junction, VT
Wenz, George L., III	Miamisburg, OH
Wenz, Paul D.	Tempe, AZ
Wenz, Warren C.	**Great Falls, MT**
Wenzel, Abby M.	**New York, NY**
Wenzel, Ann F.	Madison, WI
Wenzel, Arthur W.	Schaumburg, IL
Wenzel, Daniel J.	Racine, WI
Wenzel, Donald G., Jr.	Louisville, KY
Wenzel, Donna L.	**Mount Laurel, NJ**
Wenzel, Douglas K.	Alpena, MI
Wenzel, E.W. Rick	Fresno, CA
Wenzel, Francis G., Jr.	**Scranton, PA**
Wenzel & Harms, P.C.	**Cedar Rapids, IA**
Wenzel, Helene V.	San Francisco, CA
Wenzel, Henry G.	Vero Beach, FL
Wenzel, James R.	Austin, TX
Wenzel, John H.	Wichita, KS
Wenzel, John M.	Escondido, CA
Wenzel, John R.	**Arlington, VA**
Wenzel, Karen Jo	Alpena, MI
Wenzel, Karla J.	Salem, OR
Wenzel, Keith A.	Jefferson City, MO
Wenzel, Kenneth A.	Boca Raton, FL
Wenzel, Kenneth J.	**Santa Ana, CA**
Wenzel, Kenneth L.	**Fort Worth, TX**
Wenzel, Mark Christopher	**Reno, NV**
Wenzel, Mark D.	**Los Angeles, CA**
Wenzel, Mark R.	**Indianapolis, IN**
Wenzel, Michael E.	Pasadena, CA
Wenzel, Michelle A.	Environmental Protection Agency, Environmental Appeals Board, GV
Wenzel, Richard C.	**Cedar Rapids, IA**
Wenzel, Robert D.	**San Jose, CA**
Wenzel, Robert L.	**Cerritos, CA**
Wenzel, Robin L.	New York, NY
Wenzel, Rudolph J., Jr.	Westwood, NJ
Wenzel, Stefan	**Oklahoma City, OK**
Wenzel, Steven G.	Tampa, FL
Wenzel, Todd J.	Los Angeles, CA
Wenzel, Tracy Lyn	**Jacksonville, FL**
Wenzel, Wenzel Yahne & Rhynard, P.C.	Alpena, MI
Wenzel, William J.	**Bridgeport, CT** **Hartford, CT** **Stamford, CT**
Wenzel, Wm. F.	Newtown Square, PA
Wenzell, Albert B., Jr.	San Mateo, CA
Wenzell, Lewis A.	San Diego, CA
Wenzelman, Kendall O.	Kankakee, IL
Wenzke, James F.	Dayton, OH
Wenzke, John R.	**Roseland, NJ**
Wenzke, Margaret M.	Kettering, OH
Wenzl, Mary Stoughton	Lincoln, NE
Wenzler, Marcy	Bloomington, IN
Wenzler, Mark A.	Washington, DC
Wenzler, O. F.	New Brunswick, NJ
Wenzler, Richard A.	Upper Saddle River, NJ
Wenzloff, Paul E.	Bay City, MI
Wenzloff, Warren P.	Chicago, IL
Wepfer, Carolyn L.	Mechanicsburg, PA
Wepfer, William R.	Harlingen, TX
Wepman, Joshua M.	**New York, NY**
Wepman, Warren S.	Miami, FL
Wepman & Wepman, P.A.	Miami, FL
Wepner, Roy H.	**Westfield, NJ**
Weppler, Lawrence G.	**New York, NY**
Weppler, Terry L.	Libertyville, IL
Weppner, Dale M.	**St. Louis, MO**
Weppner, Robert A.	Seattle, WA
Wepprecht, Edward J.	Holmdel, NJ
Weprin, Barry A.	**New York, NY**
Weprin, David I.	New York, NY
Weprin, Earle F.	New York, NY
Weprin, James I.	**Dayton, OH**
Weprin, Saul	New York, NY
Weprin, Todd B.	Boca Raton, FL
Werb, Dade D.	**Wilmington, DE**
Werb, Duane D.	**Wilmington, DE**
Werb, Lewis	Staten Island, NY
Werb, Marybeth Smith	**Philadelphia, PA**
Werb, Neil N.	Malibu, CA
Werb, Roseanne Malka	Rochester, NY
Werb, Tigani, Hood & Sullivan	**Wilmington, DE**
Werb, Wendy H.	Palm Beach Gardens, FL
Werbach, Johanna L.	New York, NY
Werbach, Kevin	New York, NY
Werbalowsky, Allen P.	Kingston, NY
Werbel, David R.	**New York, NY**
Werbel, Debra E.	Los Angeles, CA
Werbel, Evan Jeffrey	**Washington, DC**
Werbel, Harvey	Brooklyn, NY
Werbel, Joel N.	Rahway, NJ
Werbel, Julie S.	Indio, CA
Werbel, Linda D.	**New York, NY**
Werbel, Morton	Brooklyn, NY
Werbel, Robert H.	**New York, NY**
Werbel, Shelly Klausner	Brooklyn, NY
Werbel, Sidney K.	Maplewood, NJ
Werbel, Stephen K.	New York, NY
Werbel, Werbel & Strauss	Brooklyn, NY

Werbelow, Judson ..... Lansing, MI
Werber, Clifford L. ..... Beverly Hills, CA
Werber, David ..... New York, NY
Werber, Jill S. ..... Beverly Hills, CA
Werber, Richard S. ..... Boca Raton, FL
Werber, Steven A. ..... Jacksonville, FL
Werbicky, Robert Earl ..... Las Vegas, NV
Werbin, Barry ..... New York, NY
Werbin, Samuel N. ..... Chamblee, GA
Werblin, Carol Ann ..... Centerport, NY
Werblin, Mary E. ..... Waterbury, CT
Werblood, Mark F. ..... Falls Church, VA
Werblowsky, Harvey Z. ..... New York, NY
Werblun, Edward D. ..... Harrisburg, PA
Werbner, Mark S. ..... Dallas, TX
Werbow, Farrell R. ..... Falls Church, VA
Werby, Christopher ..... San Francisco, CA
Werby, Elisabeth ..... New York, NY
Werby, Helen C. ..... Gulfport, MS
Werchen, David ..... New York, NY
Werchick, Arne ..... Truckee, CA
Werchick & Werchick, A Law Corp.
Truckee, CA
Wercinski, Peter J. ..... San Francisco, CA
Werdal, Pamela Brown
Department Of Veterans Affairs,
Board of Veterans Appeals, GV
Werdehoff, Stephanie W. ..... Huntsville, AL
Werdehoff and Werdehoff ..... Huntsville, AL
Werdehoff, William G. ..... Huntsville, AL
Werdel, A. Alyce ..... San Francisco, CA
Werdel, Charles C. ..... Bakersfield, CA
Werdel & Shea ..... Bakersfield, CA
Werdel, Terence J., & Associates, Law Offices of ..... Bakersfield, CA
Werdel, Thomas H., Jr. ..... Bakersfield, CA
Werdel & Werdel ..... Bakersfield, CA
Werdell & Hanson ..... Medford, OR
Werdell, Lee S. ..... Medford, OR
Werden, George W. ..... Cincinnati, OH
Werden, John C., Jr. ..... Carroll, IA
Werder, Christa Cowart ..... Orlando, FL
Werder, Horst H. ..... Naples, FL
Werder, Mark R. ..... Detroit, MI
Werder, Richard I., Jr. ..... Cleveland, OH
Werderitch, Jerome J. ..... Park Ridge, IL
Werdig, Robert M., Jr. ..... Washington, DC
Werdine, Frederick S. ..... Tampa, FL
Weremblewski, Michael R. ..... Buffalo, NY
Weresch-Doornink, Eileen ..... Seattle, WA
Weresh, John A. ..... Kansas City, MO
Werfal, Jeremy F. ..... Baton Rouge, LA
Werfel, David M. ..... Hauppauge, NY
Werff, Sara E. Vander ..... Grand Rapids, MI
Wergeles, Amy Span ..... Hartford, CT
Werger, Charles J. ..... West Sand Lake, NY
Werger, Melissa G. ..... New York, NY
Werger, William D. ..... Manchester, IA
Werges, LeRoy F. ..... Ocala, FL
Werhnyak, Ronald J. ..... Mishawaka, IN
Werholtz, Jane B. ..... Kansas City, KS
Werkenthin, Conrad P. ..... Austin, TX
Werkenthin, Fred B. ..... Austin, TX
Werkenthin, Max J., III ..... Austin, TX
Werkheiser, Gregory W. ..... Wilmington, DE
Werking, Robert G. ..... Littleton, CO
Werksman, Alan J. ..... Deerfield Beach, FL
Werksman, Gerald M. ..... Newport Beach, CA
Werksman, Mark J., Law Offices of
Los Angeles, CA
Werksman, Milton ..... Clifton, NJ
Werksman, Richard S.
United States Information Agency,
Office of the General Counsel, GV
Werksman, Saffron, Cohen & Sylvester, P.A.
Clifton, NJ
Werle, Mark F. ..... Rutland, VT
Werlein, Dan K. ..... Milwaukee, WI
Werlein, Diane L. ..... Houston, TX
Werlein, Ewing, Jr. ..... Houston, TX
Werley, Elizabeth L. ..... New York, NY
Werley, S. Gary, Law Offices of
Fort Worth, TX
Werlhof, Bruce A. ..... Lake Forest, CA
Werlich, John M. ..... Los Angeles, CA
Werlin, Leslie M. ..... Los Angeles, CA
Werlin, Robert N. ..... Boston, MA
Werling, Charles J. ..... Calumet City, IL
Werling, Mark A. ..... Fort Wayne, IN
Werling, Max R. ..... Tipton, IA
Werling, Stuart P. ..... Tipton, IA
Werlin-Gorenstein, Barbara ..... Guilderland, NY
Werlinsky, Marc A. ..... King Of Prussia, PA
Werlwas, Mary Lynne ..... San Francisco, CA
Werly, Albert C. ..... St. Petersburg, FL
Wermager, Tim D. ..... Hastings, MN
Werman, Douglas M. ..... Chicago, IL
Werman, Susan ..... New York, NY
Werme, Paula J. ..... Boscawen, NH
Wermerskirchen, Mark G. ..... Willmar, MN
Wermuth, Albert R. ..... Oak Park, MI
Wermuth, Geoffrey P. ..... Quincy, MA
Wermuth, J. Michael ..... Miami, FL
Wermuth, Paul E. ..... Trenton, NJ
Wern, Charles E., Jr. ..... Warren, OH
Wern, Kelligher & Brutz ..... Warren, OH
Werne, Sharon H. ..... Princeton, IN
Wernecke, Livingston ..... Seattle, WA
Werneke, Vicki Ruth Adams
Oklahoma City, OK
Werner, A. Matt ..... Sheboygan, WI
Werner, Allan R. ..... Montgomery, AL
Werner, Andrew S. ..... San Francisco, CA
Werner, Anthony Ira ..... Wheeling, WV
Werner, Arthur Joseph ..... Philadelphia, PA
Werner & Associates ..... San Francisco, CA
San Jose, CA
Werner, Barry S. ..... Milwaukee, WI
Werner, Bernard ..... New York, NY
Werner & Blank Co., L.P.A. ..... Toledo, OH
Werner, Bronwyn E. ..... Kansas City, MO
Werner & Burke ..... Emeryville, CA
Werner, Carl A. ..... San Antonio, TX
Werner, Carol K. ..... Denver, CO
Werner, Charles A. ..... St. Louis, MO
Werner, Cheryl E. ..... Monroe, MI
Werner, Christine A. ..... Detroit, MI
Werner, Christine L. ..... Greenwich, CT
Werner, Christopher K. ..... Rochester, NY
Werner, Claudia M. ..... Chicago, IL
Werner, Clemens A. ..... Davenport, IA
Werner, Clemens A., Jr. ..... Davenport, IA
Werner, Daniel L. ..... Hebron, NE
Werner, David A. ..... Houston, TX
Werner, David C. ..... San Antonio, TX
Werner, David D. ..... Riverside, CA
Werner, David L. ..... United States Senate,
Committee Legal Personnel, GV
Werner, Dean J. ..... Mesa, AZ
Werner, Deborah Larned ..... Tampa, FL
Werner, Deborah Larned, P.A. ..... Tampa, FL
Werner, Denise Lynn ..... Voorhees, NJ
Werner, Donna M. ..... New York, NY
Werner, E. Louis, Jr. ..... Paradise Valley, AZ
Werner, Edward J. ..... Hollywood, FL
Werner, Edward O. ..... Garden City, NY
Werner, Elizabeth Krieger ..... New York, NY
Werner, Elke ..... Los Angeles, CA
Werner, Epstein & Johnson, P.L.L.C.
Cut Bank, MT
Werner, Eric J. ..... Greenville, PA
Werner, Eric Raymond .....
Securities and Exchange Commission, GV
Werner, Eric T. ..... Washington, DC
Werner & Filipek ..... South Easton, MA
Werner, Frances E. ..... Oakland, CA
Werner, Francis A. ..... New London, WI
Werner, Frederic P. ..... Hartford, CT
Werner, Gary A. ..... Hackensack, NJ
Werner, Gary F. ..... Newark, NJ
Werner, Gary F. ..... Cleveland, OH
Werner, George C., Jr. ..... Lancaster, PA
Werner, George J. F. ..... Clearwater, FL
Werner, Gregory R. ..... Colorado Springs, CO
Werner, Harald T., Jr. ..... New Orleans, LA
Werner, Harley R. ..... Portland, OR
Werner, Harry E. ..... Buffalo, NY
Werner, Hayley W. ..... New York, NY
Werner, Herman S. ..... Chicago, IL
Werner, Howard M. ..... West Hartford, CT
Werner, Ivan L. ..... Jamaica, NY
Werner, Jack ..... Washington, DC
Werner, Jack ..... North Miami Beach, FL
Werner, James Lynn ..... Atlanta, GA
Charlotte, NC
Raleigh, NC
Columbia, SC
Werner, Jan O. ..... Mill Valley, CA
Werner, Jana C. ..... Santa Fe, NM
Werner, Jas. H. ..... Tulsa, OK
Werner, Jeffery J. ..... Huntersville, NC
Werner, Jeffery J., P.A. ..... Huntersville, NC
Werner, Jeffrey R. ..... Newburgh, NY
Werner, Joanne R. ..... Seattle, WA
Werner, Jody A. G. ..... Philadelphia, PA
Werner, John ..... Des Moines, IA
Werner, John ..... Beaumont, TX
Werner, John D. ..... New Orleans, LA
Werner, John F. ..... New York, NY
Werner, John R. ..... Tell City, IN
Werner, Joseph G. ..... Dallas, TX
Werner, Joshua D. ..... South Easton, MA
Werner, Julie Levinson ..... Roseland, NJ
Werner, Karl T. ..... Albuquerque, NM
Werner, Kathleen L. ..... New York, NY
Werner, Kathleen M. ..... Fort Madison, IA
Werner, Kathleen M. ..... Leonardtown, MD
Werner, Keith B. ..... Houston, TX
Werner, Keith E. ..... Tarboro, NC
Werner, Kelley Kosow ..... Miami, FL
Werner, Kenneth E. ..... Boston, MA
Werner, Kenneth R. ..... Honey Brook, PA
West Chester, PA
Werner & Kerrigan, LLP ..... Houston, TX
Werner, Kevin A. ..... San Diego, CA
Werner, Kevin J. ..... Bay Shore, NY
Werner, Kirk G. ..... San Francisco, CA
Werner, Kristin ..... Philadelphia, PA
Werner, Kristin Denise ..... Portage, MI
Werner, L. Rob ..... Santa Clarita, CA
Werner, Lee G. ..... Irvine, CA
Werner, Lindgren & Johnson, S.C.
New London, WI
Werner, Lisa M. ..... Burlington, VT
Werner, Louis ..... Newburgh, NY
Werner, Lynn B. ..... New York, NY
Werner, Lynne R. ..... Valentine, NE
Werner, Mark A. ..... Pittsburg, KS
Werner, Martin D. ..... Toledo, OH
Werner, Mary Ann ..... Washington, DC
Werner, Mary J. ..... La Crosse, WI
Werner, Matthew J.
Colorado Springs, CO
Werner, Matthew M. ..... Portland, OR
Werner, Melvin J. ..... Kingsport, TN
Werner, Michael B. ..... Miami Beach, FL
Werner, Michael Jay ..... United States Senate,
Committee Legal Personnel, GV
Werner, Michael R. ..... Teaneck, NJ
Werner, Minda B. ..... Saratoga, CA
Werner, N. Kate ..... Topsham, ME
Werner, Nancy A. ..... South Haven, MI
Werner, Neil T.
Department Of Veterans Affairs,
Board of Veterans Appeals, GV
Werner, Norbert F. ..... Cleveland, OH
Werner, Pamela J.
National Aeronautics And Space
Administration,
Office of the General Counsel, GV
Werner, Paul W. ..... Salt Lake City, UT
Werner, Paul William ..... New York, NY
Werner, Peter R. ..... New York, NY
Werner, Philip A. ..... Houston, TX
Werner, Philip H. ..... New York, NY
Werner, Ralph ..... Washington, DC
Werner, Raymond J. ..... Chicago, IL
Werner, Richard E. ..... Denver, CO
Werner, Richard E. ..... Pittsburgh, PA
Werner, Richard K. ..... Sacramento, CA
Werner, Richard T. ..... Janesville, WI
Werner, Robert B. ..... San Antonio, TX
Werner, Robert G. ..... San Francisco, CA
San Jose, CA
Werner, Robert J. ..... Phoenix, AZ
Werner, Robert J. ..... Santa Fe, NM
Werner, Robert J. ..... Collegeville, PA
Werner, Robert J. ..... Austin, TX
Werner, Robert L. ..... New York, NY
Werner, Robert S. ..... Silver Spring, MD
Werner, Robert W. ..... Hartford, CT
Werner, Robin E. ..... San Diego, CA
Werner, Ronald B. ..... Cleveland, OH
Werner, Ronald E. ..... San Jose, CA
Werner, Ronald G. ..... Petersburg, VA
Werner, Ronald J. ..... Minnetonka, MN
Werner, Ryan L. ..... Emeryville, CA
Werner, S. Henry ..... New York, NY
Werner, S. Mark
Research Triangle Park, NC
Werner & Saffioti ..... Newburgh, NY
Werner & Schwartz, P.C. ..... Philadelphia, PA
Werner, Sean L. ..... Downey, CA
Werner, Sharon A. ..... Wichita, KS
Werner, Sidney ..... St. Petersburg, FL
Werner, Stacy Lynn ..... Stamford, CT
Werner, Stephen C., Jr. ..... Milwaukee, WI
Werner, Steven M. ..... Colorado Springs, CO
Werner, Stewart R., Law Offices of
Amarillo, TX
Werner, Suzanne Heggie ..... Hartford, CT
Werner, Suzanne Maltais ..... Beaumont, TX
Werner, Teresa S. ..... Washington, DC
Werner, Thomas C. ..... St. Louis, MO
Werner, Thomas G. ..... Waterford, MI
Werner, Thomas J. ..... Indianapolis, IN
Werner, Thomas M. ..... Des Moines, IA
Werner, Thomas W. ..... St. Louis, MO
Werner, Timothy G. ..... Atlanta, GA
Werner, Ursula ..... Department of Justice,
Office of Legal Counsel, GV
Werner, W. Leonard ..... Baton Rouge, LA
Werner, Walter E., III ..... Pittsburgh, PA
Werner, Ward D. ..... Fort Worth, TX
Werner & Werner ..... Davenport, IA
Werner, Wilbur P. ..... Cut Bank, MT
Werner, William A. ..... Munising, MI
Werner, William B. ..... Las Vegas, NV
Werner, William R. ..... St. Louis, MO
Werner, William S. K. ..... Boston, MA
Werner & Wood ..... Honey Brook, PA
Phoenixville, PA
West Chester, PA
Wernery, Linda S. ..... Department of Justice,
Civil Division, GV
Wernet, John J. ..... Fort Wayne, IN
Wernet, R. John, Jr. ..... Lansing, MI
Wernet, William R. ..... Granville, OH
Wernette, Michael R. ..... Detroit, MI
Wernette, Richard G. ..... Walla Walla, WA
Wernette, Ronald C., Jr. ..... Detroit, MI
Wernick, Alan S. ..... Chicago, IL
Wernick, Aviva L. ..... New York, NY
Wernick, Elliot H. ..... Phoenix, AZ
Wernick, Hope E. ..... East Longmeadow, MA
Wernick, Howard B. ..... Boston, MA
Wernick, Jeffrey M. ..... Burbank, CA
Wernick, Lawrence B. ..... Springfield, MA
Wernick, Lee B. ..... South Walpole, MA
Wernick, Lionel ..... New York, NY
Wernick, Mark S. ..... Minneapolis, MN
Wernick, Max A. ..... Dallas, TX
Wernick, Michael S. ..... Harrison, NJ
Wernick, Sidney W. ..... Portland, ME
Wernicke, Frederick J. ..... Sarasota, FL
Wernik, Bruce A. ..... Los Angeles, CA
Wernik, Robin T. ..... Cranbury, NJ
Matawan, NJ
Wernimont, Melanie Fisher
Cedar Rapids, IA
Wernle, Paul A., Jr. ..... Wilmington, DE
Wernle, Ristine & Ayers, L.P.C.
Crawfordsville, IN
Wernle, Robert F. ..... Crawfordsville, IN
Wernly, Robert P. ..... West Hempstead, NY
Wernow, Adam E.
Commodity Futures Trading Commission,
Division of Trading and Markets, GV
Wernsman, Brian C. ..... Centralia, IL
Wernstrom, James L. ..... Grand Rapids, MI
Wernstrom, Todd M. ..... Key West, FL
Miami, FL
Wernstrom, Todd M., P.A. ..... Key West, FL
Miami, FL
Werntz, Heide M. ..... Washington, DC
Werntz, Joseph L. ..... Albuquerque, NM
Werny, Edwin F. ..... Farmington Hills, MI
Wernz, Ann Hart ..... Minneapolis, MN
Wernz, William J. ..... Minneapolis, MN
Werra, John B. ..... Milwaukee, WI
Werre, Gregory D. ..... Los Angeles, CA
Werre, Randall A. ..... Pensacola, FL
Werrell, Judy Nuss ..... Columbia, SC
Werren, J. Curtis ..... Canton, OH
Werren, John R. ..... Canton, OH
Werren, Robert B. ..... Cadiz, OH
Werrenrath, Reinald, III ..... Orlando, FL
Werries, William F. ..... St. Louis, MO
Werring, Thomas F. ..... Uniondale, NY
Wersal, Gregory F. ..... Minneapolis, MN
Wersan, David ..... Harrisburg, PA
Wersching, James P. ..... Cincinnati, OH
Werse, Stanley F. ..... Fair Haven, NJ
Wershals, Paul L. ..... Great Neck, NY
Wershaw, Lisa B. ..... Philadelphia, PA
Wershaw, Steven L. ..... New York, NY
Wershow, Jonathan F. ..... Gainesville, FL
Wershow & Schneider, P.A. ..... Gainesville, FL
Wersinger, Peter S., III ..... Marlboro, NJ
Werson, James B. ..... San Francisco, CA
Werstak, Bruce J., III ..... Laredo, TX
Werstak, Bruce J., III, P.C., Law Office of
Laredo, TX
Werstein, Richard F. ..... Dallas, TX
Werstein & Wilson ..... Dallas, TX
Werstiuk, Allen D. ..... Mansfield, OH
Wersyn, John S. ..... Evanston, IL
Wert, Chris W. ..... Worcester, MA
Wert, James M. ..... House of Representatives,
Office of Legislative Counsel, GV
Wert, Robert C. ..... Philadelphia, PA
Wert, Robert Stevenson ..... Chicago, IL
Wert, Thomas P. ..... Orlando, FL
Wert, W. Scott ..... Seattle, WA
Wertalik, Robert J. ..... Garfield, NJ
Wertam, John E. ..... Hartford, CT
Wertelet, John L. ..... Pittsburgh, PA
Wertenteil, Aaron J. ..... New York, NY
Wertenteil, Ephrem ..... Brooklyn, NY
Werth, Andrew D. ..... Evanston, IL
Werth, Daphne ..... Denver, CO
Werth, David L. ..... Weyauwega, WI
Werth, David P. ..... Alpena, MI
Werth, Duncan S., II ..... San Diego, CA
Werth, Fred M., Jr. ..... Galax, VA
Werth, Kristin M. ..... Denver, CO
Werth, McRae ..... Blue Hill, ME
Werth, Meera ..... Chicago, IL
Werth, Michael W. ..... Chevy Chase, MD
Werth, Mitchell J. ..... Waimanalo, HI
Werth, Robert A. ..... Fresno, CA
Werth, Robert David ..... New York, NY
Werth, Robert W. ..... Columbus, OH
Werth, Steven D. ..... San Francisco, CA
Werth, Susan ..... Orlando, FL
Werthan, Betsy ..... New York, NY
Werthan, Jeffrey M., (P.C.)
Washington, DC
Werthan, Susan M. ..... Bethesda, MD
Wertheim, Andrew J. ..... New York, NY
Wertheim, David ..... Rockleigh, NJ
Wertheim, Eric ..... Millburn, NJ
New York, NY
Wertheim, Frederick W. ..... New York, NY
Wertheim, Glenn ..... Bridgewater, NJ
Wertheim, James S. ..... Cleveland, OH
Wertheim, Jay P. ..... Irvine, CA
Wertheim, Jeffrey H. ..... Birmingham, AL
Wertheim, Jerry ..... Santa Fe, NM
Wertheim, Jerry Todd ..... Santa Fe, NM
Wertheim, John V. ..... Santa Fe, NM
Wertheim, Larry M. ..... Minneapolis, MN
Wertheim, Lawrence H. ..... Woodbridge, NJ
Wertheim, Mary A. ..... New York, NY
Wertheim, Matthew ..... San Francisco, CA
Wertheim, Nancy ..... Boston, MA
Wertheim, Ram D. ..... New York, NY
Wertheim, Ronald P. ..... Washington, DC
Wertheim, Shauna Miller ..... Reston, VA
Wertheim, Walter Reinold
Richmond Heights, OH
Wertheimer, Adam ..... San Diego, CA
Wertheimer, Alan S. ..... Los Angeles, CA
Wertheimer & Associates, P.C.
Bethesda, MD
Wertheimer, Barbara ..... Princeton, NJ
Elkins Park, PA
Wertheimer, Barbara M.
San Francisco, CA
Wertheimer, Brad ..... Mays Landing, NJ
Wertheimer, David F. ..... New York, NY
Wertheimer, Donald E. ..... South Bend, IN
Wertheimer, Douglas ..... Chicago, IL
Wertheimer, Florrie L., P.C. ..... New York, NY
Wertheimer Fredman & Siegelman, LLC
New York, NY
Wertheimer, Jay W. ..... New York, NY
Wertheimer, Jeffrey ..... Costa Mesa, CA
Wertheimer, Kara D. ..... San Francisco, CA
Wertheimer, Karen A. ..... Philadelphia, PA
Wertheimer, Laura S. ..... Washington, DC
Wertheimer, Leonard, III
Birmingham, AL
Wertheimer, M. David ..... New York, NY
Wertheimer, Marc ..... Bethesda, MD
Wertheimer, Murray ..... Long Beach, NY
Wertheimer, Rachel M. ..... New York, NY
Wertheimer, Richard F. ..... Olney, MD
Wertheimer, Richard J. ..... Davidson, NC
Wertheimer, Robert A. ..... Hudson, WI
Wertheimer, Robert I. ..... Chicago, IL
Wertheimer, Robert J. ..... New York, NY
Wertheimer, Samuel ..... St. Paul, MN
Wertheimer, Spencer M. ..... Philadelphia, PA
Wertheimer, Sydney B. ..... Scarsdale, NY
Wertheimer, Sylvia F. ..... New York, NY
Wertheimer, Thomas ..... Universal City, CA
Wertheimer, Victor ..... Beachwood, OH
Wertheimer, Warren ..... Novato, CA
Wertheimer, William A. ..... Southfield, MI
Wertheimer, William L'E. ..... Elizabeth, NJ
Werther, Barbara G. ..... Washington, DC

Werther, Caroline Gittis ... Philadelphia, PA
Werther, Jonathan B. ... Dulles, VA
Werther, Kathleen L. ... Albany, NY
Werther, Paul S. ... Newark, NJ
Werthimer, Richard J. ... San Francisco, CA
Werthmann, Barbara ... Department of Labor,
Office of the Solicitor, GV
Werths, Beth K. ... Philadelphia, PA
Wertime, David C. ... Greencastle, PA
Wertime & Guyer ... Greencastle, PA
Wertime, Robinson, Ries & Van Ullen, P.C.
Cohoes, NY
Wertime, Rudolf M. ... Greencastle, PA
Wertimer, Eleanor W. ... Clinton, NY
Wertis, Richard L. ... New York, NY
Wertjes, Catherine J. ... Skokie, IL
Wertjes, J. Catherine ... Olympia, WA
Wertkin, Robin S. ... Pittsburgh, PA
Wertlieb, Harry A. ... Lawrence, NY
Wertlieb, Neil J. ... Los Angeles, CA
Wertman, Edward W. ... Philadelphia, PA
Wertman, Georgina K. ... Kenilworth, NJ
Wertman, Jeffrey Scott
Fort Lauderdale, FL
Wertman, Justin ... New York, NY
Wertman, Patricia A. ... Loudonville, NY
Wertman, Paul W. ... Muncy, PA
Wertman, Tracey Anne ... Chicago, IL
Crystal Lake, IL
Wertman, William T., Jr. ... Martinsburg, WV
Werts, Dale A. ... Kansas City, MO
Werts, J. Stephen ... Portland, OR
Werts, Kelly J. ... Humboldt, NE
Werts, Kenneth F. ... Mount Vernon, IL
Werts, Mark D. ... Tustin, CA
Wertsch, Robert A. ... San Francisco, CA
Wertsch, Robert C. ... Oshkosh, WI
Wertsching, Robert A. ... Phoenix, AZ
Wertz, Barry L. ... Houston, TX
Wertz, Barry Lee, Jr. ... Houston, TX
Wertz, Carol B. ... Gastonia, NC
Wertz, Cynthia Hinshaw
San Francisco, CA
Wertz, George R. ... Akron, OH
Wertz, Howard R. ... De Kalb, IL
Wertz, Jeanne D. ... Chesterland, OH
Wertz, John D. ... Chappell, NE
Wertz, John Ross ... San Diego, CA
Wertz, John T. ... Robesonia, PA
Wertz & Leehey ... Cedar Rapids, IA
Wertz, Mary E. ... Wilmington, NC
Wertz, Mary H. ... Bloomington, IN
Wertz & Palik ... Chappell, NE
Wertz, Phillip A. ... Charlotte, NC
Wertz, Rebecca J. ... Department of Justice,
Civil Rights Division, GV
Wertz, Robert C. ... Smithtown, NY
Wertz, Robert Randy ... San Francisco, CA
Wertz, Stephen T. ... Kansas City, MO
Wertz, Thomas M. ... Cedar Rapids, IA
Wertz, Tracy W. ... York, PA
Wertz, William W. ... Tallahassee, FL
Wertzbaugher, Jerry A. ... Anchorage, AK
Wertzberger, John J. ... Iowa City, IA
Wertzberger, Marsha C. ... Washington, DC
Wertzberger, Pina S. ... Cherry Hill, NJ
Werve, Frances Ann ... Green Valley, AZ
Werzanski, S. Paul ... Boston, MA
Wes, Edward J., Jr. ... Menlo Park, CA
Wesbrooks Firm, The, P.C.
Wichita Falls, TX
Wesbrooks, Mark D. ... Wichita Falls, TX
Wesbrooks, Perry ... Wichita Falls, TX
Wesby, Darryl K. ... Kew Gardens, NY
Wesch, Paul Charles ... Mobile, AL
Wesch, Richard W. ... Hernando, FL
Wesche, Michael J. ... Napoleon, OH
Weschler, Cecelia A. ... Norfolk, VA
Weschler, David W. ... New York, NY
Weschler, Patrick J. ... Akron, OH
Weschler, Raymond P. ... Berkeley, CA
Wescoat, John W. ... Eastville, VA
Wescoe, David B. ... Milwaukee, WI
Wescoe, James A. ... Philadelphia, PA
Wescott, Lawrence S. ... Baltimore, MD
Wescott, Lynanne B. ... Philadelphia, PA
Wescott, Millham & Dyer ... Laconia, NH
Portsmouth, NH
Wescott, Paul A. ... Bridgton, ME
Wesdock, Sandra M. ... Department of Labor,
Office of the Solicitor, GV
Wesel, Marilyn S. ... Marietta, OH
Wesel, Michael E. ... Cleveland, OH
Weseley, Laura A. ... Malibu, CA
Weseli, Roger W. ... Cincinnati, OH
Weselka, Greg L. ... Dallas, TX
Weseloh, Mary J. ... Detroit, MI
Wesely, Edwin J. ... New York, NY
Wesely, Marissa C. ... New York, NY
Wesely, Nathan ... Houston, TX
Weseman, James C. ... San Diego, CA
Weseman, Mark A. ... Broomfield, CO
Weseman, Steven D. ... Chicago, IL
Wesenberg, Eric L. ... Menlo Park, CA
Wesenberg, Richard Lee, Jr. ... Roseburg, OR
Wesendorf, Kyle Marie ... Solana Beach, CA
Weser, Matthew ... Brooklyn, NY
Wesierski, Christopher P. ... Irvine, CA
Wesierski & Zurek, LLP ... Irvine, CA
Los Angeles, CA
Newport Beach, CA
San Diego, CA
Wesighan, Frank C. ... Orlando, FL
Weskamp, Dana ... Chicago, IL
Wesker, Natasha S. ... Baltimore, MD
Hunt Valley, MD
Wesley, Beth Eddinger ... Philadelphia, PA
Wesley, Brian R. ... Irvine, CA
Wesley, Darity ... La Mesa, CA
Wesley, Gerald A. ... Department of Defense,
Defense Legal Services Agency, GV
Wesley, Gregory M. ... Milwaukee, WI
Wesley, Gretchen Snyder ... Brunswick, ME
Wesley, H. Barry ... Carbondale, IL
Wesley & Herzog ... Houston, TX
The Woodlands, TX
Wesley, J. Quentin ... Morganfield, KY
Wesley, James B. ... Houston, TX
Wesley, James H., II ... Springfield, MO
Wesley, Jane J. ... Modesto, CA
Wesley, John C. ... Paradise Valley, AZ
Wesley, John P. ... Brattleboro, VT
Wesley, John W. ... Dallas, TX
Wesley, Kenneth F., Jr. ... Hueytown, AL
Wesley, Laurie J. ... Millwood, NY
Wesley, Lynda ... Palatine, IL
Wesley, Matthew W. ... Menlo Park, CA
Wesley, Michael P. ... Monte Vista, CO
Wesley & Moore ... Morganfield, KY
Wesley, Nancy M. ... San Francisco, CA
Wesley, Nanette L. ... Memphis, TN
Wesley, Nicole A. ... San Francisco, CA
Wesley, R. Clark ... Nickerson, KS
Wesley, R. Joseph ... Seattle, WA
Wesley, Richard C. ... Geneseo, NY
Wesley, Robert ... Tallahassee, FL
Wesley, Ronald Reynolds ... Richmond, VA
Wesley, Ronnie W. ... Austin, TX
Wesley, William M. ... Chicago, IL
Wesley, Woodburn S., Jr.(P.A.)
Fort Walton Beach, FL
Wesloh, Steven M. ... Cincinnati, OH
Weslow, Norman J. ... Plano, TX
Weslowski, John L. ... Washington, DC
Wesman, Alexander G. ... Mamaroneck, NY
Wesner, Arthur G. ... Columbus, OH
Wesner & Associates ... Houston, TX
Wesner, C. Thomas, Jr. ... Dallas, TX
Wesner Coke & Clymer, P.C. ... Dallas, TX
Wesner, Frank J., Jr. ... Media, PA
Wesner, Frederick L. ... Janesville, WI
Wesner, Jacob C. ... Dallas, TX
Wesner, Jonathan L. ... Harrisburg, PA
Wesner, Kempton, Russell and Dominique
Jefferson City, MO
Sedalia, MO
Wesner, Mark Koehn ... Madison, WI
Wesner, Mark R. ... Cordell, OK
Wesner, Melinda L. ... Houston, TX
Wesner, Ronald L. ... Cordell, OK
Wesner & Wesner ... Cordell, OK
Wesnofske, Bernard J. ... Hicksville, NY
Wesoky, Jack M. ... Denver, CO
Wesolick, Stephen J. ... Houston, TX
Wesolik, Clinton J. ... Chicago, IL
Wesolowski, Allen C. ... Chicago, IL
Wesolowski, Antoni E. ... Barrington, IL
Wesolowski, Carl R. ... Chantilly, VA
Wesolowski, Dennis M. ... East Aurora, NY
Wesolowski, Frank ... Lisle, IL
Wesolowski, James J. ... Chicago, IL
Wesolowski, James R. ... San Francisco, CA
Wesolowski, Jay T. ... Rancho Cordova, CA
Wesolowski, Jesse A. ... Franklin, WI
Wesolowski, John S. ... Palo Alto, CA
Wesolowski, Karen ... River Forest, IL
Wesolowski, Ted ... Pittsburgh, PA
Wesonig, Charles B. ... Odessa, MO
Wesorick, Richard S. ... Cleveland, OH
Wesp, E. Joel ... Columbus, OH
Wesp, Patrick W. H. ... Buffalo, NY
Wess, Bonnie S. ... Rye Brook, NY
Wess, Carl K. ... Brooklyn, NY
Wess, Hartley B. ... Albuquerque, NM
Wess, Hartley B., & Associates, P.C.
Albuquerque, NM
Wessan, Sharon ... Westport, CT
Wessberg, Ann Dunn ... Minneapolis, MN
St. Paul, MN
Wessel and Associates, A Law Corporation
New Orleans, LA
Wessel, Bruce A. ... Los Angeles, CA
Wessel, Darin L. ... San Diego, CA
Wessel, David W. ... Redwood City, CA
Wessel, Douglas B. ... Reston, VA
Wessel, Henry ... Philadelphia, PA
Wessel, John D. ... West Palm Beach, FL
Wessel, Kenneth H. ... Wynnewood, PA
Wessel, Madelyn F. ... Portland, OR
Wessel, Michael R. ... Falls Church, VA
Wessel, Norman A. ... Kailua-Kona, HI
Wessel, Paul J. ... New York, NY
Wessel, Peter ... New York, NY
Wessel, Peter A. ... New York, NY
Wessel, Richard J. ... Hamilton, OH
Wessel, Robert F. ... Hamilton, OH
Wessel, Ronald B. ... Chesterfield, MO
Wessel, Ruth Rudbarg ... Philadelphia, PA
Wessel, Susan R. ... Spearfish, SD
Wessel, Thomas F. ... Washington, DC
Wessel, Tracy L. ... Minneapolis, MN
Wessel & Wessel ... Hamilton, OH
Wessel, William F. ... New Orleans, LA
Wesselhoeft, William ... Seattle, WA
Wesselhoft, Charles W. ... Chicago, IL
Wesseling & Brackmann, P.C.
Hudsonville, MI
Wesseling, James A. ... Hudsonville, MI
Wesselink, Brenda R. ... Des Moines, IA
Wessell, John C., III ... Wilmington, NC
Wessell, Julian C., III ... Philadelphia, PA
Wessell, Michael A. ... Pittsburgh, PA
Wessell, Paul F. ... Harrisburg, PA
Wessell & Raney, L.L.P. ... Wilmington, NC
Wessells, Howard C., II ... Accomac, VA
Wessells, Paul D., Jr. ... Cleveland, OH
Wesseln, Deborah Urell ... Orange, CA
Wessels, Carlo R. ... Fort Wright, KY
Wessels, Charles H. ... Savannah, GA
Wessels, Daniel L. ... Pittsburgh, PA
Wessels, DuWayne J. ... Waterloo, IA
Wessels, Jana S. Rhatigan ... Des Moines, IA
Wessels, Jennifer L. ... Culver City, CA
Wessels, John F. ... Cedar Rapids, IA
Wessels, Kai H. ... San Jose, CA
Wessels, Larry M. ... La Grange, TX
Wessels & Pautsch, P.C. ... Chicago, IL
St. Charles, IL
Davenport, IA
Minneapolis, MN
Milwaukee, WI
Wessels, Pete M. ... Rock Island, IL
Waterloo, IA
Wessels, Richard H. ... St. Charles, IL
Davenport, IA
Wessels, Robert J. ... Cedar Rapids, IA
Wessels, Shelley K. ... Menlo Park, CA
Wessels, Stanley M. ... San Francisco, CA
Wessels, Stephen R. ... Dallas, TX
Wessels, Steven Lee ... Sacramento, CA
Wessels, Stojan & Stephens P.C.
Rock Island, IL
Waterloo, IA
Wessely, Robert P. ... New York, NY
Wessendarp, Edw. M. ... Cincinnati, OH
Wessendarp, R. Joseph ... Cincinnati, OH
Wessendorf, Walter F., Jr. ... Arlington, VA
Wesser, James J. ... Oakland, CA
Wesserling 1, Charles R. ... Detroit, MI
Wessinger, Barbara Munig ... Columbia, SC
Wessinger, C. Jo Anne ... Columbia, SC
Wessinger, James B., III ... Savannah, GA
Wessler, Jack C. ... Fort Worth, TX
Wessler, John S. ... Lawrence, MA
Wessler, Stephen L. ... Augusta, ME
Wessler, Stuart G. ... Princeton, NJ
Wessler, William P. ... Gulfport, MS
Wessler, William P. ... Jackson, MS
Wessling, Carolyn ... Los Angeles, CA
Wessling, John P. ... Wichita, KS
Wessling, Katherine Harbur ... St. Louis, MO
Wessling, Robert B. ... Los Angeles, CA
Wessman, Carol Matz ... Cleveland, OH
Wessman, Henry C. ... Bismarck, ND
Wessman, Joseph H. ... Spokane, WA
Wessman, Rebecca L. ... Mankato, MN
Wessner, Marjorie ... Andover, MA
Wesson, Barry E. ... Tempe, AZ
Wesson, Felisia A. ... Chicago, IL
Wesson, Jonathan Scott ... Warrior, AL
Wesson, Julius C. ... Los Angeles, CA
Wesson, Marianne ... Boulder, CO
Wesson, Robert ... Warrior, AL
West, A. Karen ... The Woodlands, TX
West, A. R., & Associates ... San Marino, CA
West, A. Reneé ... San Marino, CA
West, Alan D. ... Castro Valley, CA
West, Albert B. ... Providence, RI
West, Alexander T. ... Garden City, NY
West, Alexander T., Jr. ... Jersey City, NJ
West, Allen G. ... Oklahoma City, OK
West, Allen L. ... Charlotte, NC
West, Alvin O. ... Arlington, VA
West, Angel ... Des Moines, IA
West, Ann G. ... Little Rock, AR
West, Ann Zuberbuhler ... Beaver, PA
West, Anne H. ... San Diego, CA
West, Arlene ... Oakland, CA
West, Arnold B. ... Hartford, CT
West, Arthur, & Associates, P.C.
Glenshaw, PA
West, Arthur H. ... Evanston, IL
West, Barbara J. ... Sunnyvale, CA
West, Barbara S. ... Oklahoma City, OK
West, Barry G. ... Los Angeles, CA
West, Barry G. ... Tulsa, OK
West, Ben B. ... Dallas, TX
West, Bill W. ... Sacramento, CA
West, Billy L., Jr. ... Natchitoches, LA
West, Bradford D. ... Orlando, FL
West, Bradley C. ... Shawnee, OK
West, Brandon A. ... Southfield, MI
West, Brian D. ... Vienna, VA
West, Brian G. ... Towson, MD
West, Bryan C. ... St. Louis, MO
West, Bryan T. ... Miami, FL
West, Burdette Bremermann
New Orleans, LA
West, Burke ... Ridgecrest, CA
West, C. Arthur, III ... Glenshaw, PA
West, Carl J. ... Burbank, CA
West, Carl J., III, (P.S.) ... Seattle, WA
West, Carl J., Jr. ... Birmingham, AL
West, Carlton T., Jr. ... Jacksonville, AR
West, Carol C. ... Jackson, MS
West, Caroline H. ... Collegeville, PA
West, Caroline S. ... Department of Commerce,
Patent and Trademark Office, GV
West, Catherine L. ... Hilton Head Island, SC
West, Catherine P. ... Houston, TX
West, Cecilia G. ... Lewisburg, TN
West, Chalmer W., Jr. ... Denver, CO
West, Chamberlain, Bennett, Bratka & Core
Bellefontaine, OH
West, Charles B. ... Henderson, KY
West, Charles E. ... Columbus, OH
West, Charles E. ... Grove, OK
Vinita, OK
West, Charles W. ... Los Angeles, CA
West Chemical Products Inc.
Port Washington, NY
West, Christoffel, Konigsberg & Zickerman,
P.C. ... Tucson, AZ
West, Christopher R. ... Woodland Hills, CA
West, Christopher R. ... Baltimore, MD
West, Claire J. ... Flagstaff, AZ
West, Clarence A. ... Houston, TX
West, Clay F. ... Redmond, WA
West, Clifton C. ... Fayetteville, NC
West, Clyde O. ... Sacramento, CA
West, Colin ... San Francisco, CA
West & Collins, P.S. ... Auburn, WA
West, Constance M. ... Cedartown, GA
West, Craig O. ... Tualatin, OR
West, Craig W. ... Wichita, KS
West, Dan E. ... Baton Rouge, LA
West, Dana Sue McFee ... Jacksonville, AR
West, Daniel A. ... Colorado Springs, CO
West, Darrell L. ... Nashville, TN
West, David ... Los Angeles, CA
West, David ... Palo Alto, CA
West, David ... Houston, TX
West, David A. ... Boston, MA
West, David A. ... Alexandria, VA
West, David B. ... San Antonio, TX
West, David C. ... Minneapolis, MN
West, David C. ... St. George, UT
West, David D. ... Tucson, AZ
West, David I. ... Bremerton, WA
West, David L. ... Durango, CO
West, David L. ... Kansas City, MO
West, David R. ... Seattle, WA
West, David S. ... Atlanta, GA
West, David Wm. ... Phoenix, AZ
West, David Wm., P.C., Law Offices of
Phoenix, AZ
West, Deborah
Pension Benefit Guaranty Corporation,
Office of the General Counsel, GV
West, Debra K. ... Des Moines, IA
West, Derek A. ... San Jose, CA
West, Desma L. ... Seminole, FL
West, Dobson ... Minneapolis, MN
West, Donald ... Stamford, CT
West, Donald H. ... Milwaukee, WI
West, Donald J. ... Harrison, AR
West, Donald J. ... Mountain View, CA
West, Donald R. ... Orlando, FL
West, Donald W., Law Office of
Stockton, CA
West, Dorian ... San Francisco, CA
West, Douglas H. ... Birmingham, MI
West, Douglas M. ... Torrance, CA
West, Duane E. ... Garden City, KS
West, Dudley M. ... Nashville, TN
West, Edward S. ... Washington, DC
West, Edwin L., III ... Greenville, NC
West, Eileen ... New York, NY
West, Ellen E. ... Boston, MA
West, Erica ... Englewood, CO
West, Ernest Ray, III ... Brownwood, TX
West, Eugene F. ... Camarillo, CA
West & Feinberg, P.C. ... Washington, DC
Bethesda, MD
West, Frank J. ... Arlington, VA
West, Franklin D. ... Richmond, MI
West, Gaines ... College Station, TX
West, Gary R. ... Newport News, VA
Richmond, VA
West, Gayle A. ... Houston, TX
West, George A. ... Florham Park, NJ
West, George B. ... Poulsbo, WA
West, George F., Jr. ... Natchez, MS
West, George F., Jr. ... Alexandria, VA
West, Gerald M. ... Chincoteague, VA
West, Gertrude C. ... Larkspur, CA
West, Glenn D. ... Dallas, TX
West, Greg ... Salem, OR
West, Gregory A. ... Syracuse, NY
West, Gregory K. ... Ponte Vedra Beach, FL
West, Gregory K., P.A. ... Jacksonville, FL
Ponte Vedra Beach, FL
West, Harold ... Miami, FL
West, Harold A. ... Elyria, OH
West, Henry W. ... Palo Alto, CA
West, Heather Ann ... Los Angeles, CA
West, Herbert H., Jr. ... Birmingham, AL
West, Herbert T. ... Lexington, KY
West, Howard P., Jr. ... Wilmington, DE
West, Hylie A. ... Damariscotta, ME
West, J. Gardner ... Covington, GA
West, J. Kevin ... Boise, ID
West, J. Thomas ... Lillington, NC
West, J. A. ... Shelby, NC
West, Jack ... Kansas City, MO
West, Jack M. ... Corpus Christi, TX
West, James A. ... Houston, TX
West, James A., P.C. ... Houston, TX
West, James B. ... Des Moines, IA
West, James B. ... New York, NY
West, James C., Jr. ... Clarksburg, WV
West, James E. ... Fort Smith, AR
West, James J. ... Harrisburg, PA
West, James M. ... Covington, KY
West, James P. ... Raleigh, NC
West, James R. ... Tucson, AZ
West, James R. ... New Albany, IN
West, James R. ... Oklahoma City, OK
West, Jan M. ... Louisville, KY
West, Jas. B. ... Bellefontaine, OH
West, Jason L. ... Chickasha, OK
Oklahoma City, OK
West, Jennifer Armstrong ... Miami, FL
West, Jeremy Michael ... Chicago, IL
West, Jock B., P.C. ... Billings, MT
West, Joel W. ... San Diego, CA
West, John ... Miami, FL
West, John ... Beeville, TX
West, John A. ... Covington, KY
West, John Andrew ... Cincinnati, OH
West, John C. ... Phoenix, AZ
West, John C. ... Hilton Head Island, SC
West, John C., Jr. ... Austin, TX

West, John C., Jr. (P.A.) ...Camden, SC
West, John Clark ...Cincinnati, OH
West, John D. ...Bellefontaine, OH
West, John E. ...Santa Ana, CA
West, John E. ...Houston, TX
West, John H.
National Labor Relations Board, Division of Administrative Law Judges, GV
West, John H. ...Middleburg Heights, OH
West, John H., III ...Baltimore, MD
West, John Kelly ...Salt Lake City, UT
West, John Kevin ...Lexington, KY
West, John L., P.C. ...Seattle, WA
West, John M. ...Washington, DC
West, John R. ...Rochester, NY
West, John S. ...Los Angeles, CA
West, John S. ...Moncks Corner, SC
West, John S. ...Richmond, VA
West, John S. ...Everett, WA
West, John T. ...Florham Park, NJ
West, John W. ...Westwood, NJ
West, John W., III ...Sarasota, FL
West, Jon William ...Houston, TX
West, Jonathan D. ...Los Angeles, CA
West, Jonathan R. ...Indianapolis, IN
West & Jones ...Bridgeport, WV
Clarksburg, WV
Fairmont, WV
Morgantown, WV
West, Joseph A. ...Oakland, CA
West, Joseph A. ...Andover, OH
West, Joseph D. ...Washington, DC
West, Joseph Frederick ...Arlington, VA
West, Joseph K. ...Baton Rouge, LA
West, Joseph K. ...White Plains, NY
West, Joseph N., (P.C.) ...Austin, TX
West, Joseph R. ...Beaver, PA
West, Joseph W. ...Portland, OR
West, Joshua M. ...Santa Rosa, CA
West, Judith L.C. ...Salt Lake City, UT
West, Judson H. ...Indianapolis, IN
West, Julia C. ...Kingsport, TN
West, June Ellen ...Georgetown, DE
West, Karen A. ...
Overseas Private Investment Corporation, GV
West, Karen E. ...Gainesville, FL
West, Karen R. ...Dublin, GA
West, Katharine L. ...Palo Alto, CA
West, Kathleen C. ...Naperville, IL
West, Kathleen D. ...Mentor, OH
West, Kathryn M. ...Milwaukee, WI
West, Katrina ...Ontario, CA
West, Keith H. ...Pittsburgh, PA
West, Kenneth E. ...Drexel Hill, PA
West, Kenneth R. ...Bethesda, MD
West, Keri L. ...Lincoln, NE
West, Kevin E. ...Omaha, NE
West, Kim Marlow, (Mr.) ...Nevada, IA
West, Kim W. ...Los Angeles, CA
San Francisco, CA
West, Kimberly E. ...Tulsa, OK
West, Kimberly R. ...Birmingham, AL
West, Kristie L. ...Troy, MI
West, Kristin A. ...Fort Lauderdale, FL
West, Kristin H. ...Atlanta, GA
West, L. Galen ...Rock Springs, WY
West, L. Hugh, Jr. ...Statesville, NC
West, Larry ...Liberty Lake, WA
West, Larry C. ...Covington, KY
West, Laurie D. ...Denver, CO
West Law Firm, P.L.L.C. ...Mooresville, NC
West Law Firm, The ...Shawnee, OK
West Law Firm, The ...Sugar Land, TX
West Law Offices, P.C. ...Raleigh, NC
West, Lawrence A.
Securities and Exchange Commission, Division of Enforcement, GV
West, Lawrence J. ...Houston, TX
West, Lawrence R. ...New Brunswick, NJ
West, Lee R. ...Oklahoma City, OK
West, Lester A. ...Santa Barbara, CA
West, Libby J. ...Bedminster, NJ
West, Linda Atkinson ...Houston, TX
West, Linda K. ...New Orleans, LA
West, Linsey W. ...Lexington, KY
West, Lisa E. ...Kansas City, KS
West, Lisa Martin ...Fort Worth, TX
West, Lon F. ...Nashville, TN
West, Lu Carole ...Indianapolis, IN
West, Lucy Wilson ...Boston, MA
West, Luther C. ...Baltimore, MD
West, M. Holland ...New York, NY
West, M. Lacy ...Kingsport, TN
West, Malcolm R. ...Richmond, VA
West, Marilyn T. ...Hartford, CT
West, Mark ...Pasadena, CA
West, Martha S. ...Davis, CA
West, Mary Beth ...Department of State, Bureau of Oceans, International Environmental & Scientific Affairs, GV
West, Mary Ellen ...Rochester, NY
West, Mathew B. ...New York, NY
West, Matthew M. ...Ann Arbor, MI
West, Matthew T. ...Washington, DC
West, Melanie Mayo ...Bloomfield Hills, MI
West, Meredith K. ...West Bridgewater, MA
West, Michael A. ...Boston, MA
West, Michael A. ...Cobleskill, NY
Worcester, NY
West, Michael A., P.C., Law Office of
Boston, MA
West, Michael D. ...Tallahassee, FL
West, Michael D. ...Greensboro, NC
West, Michael D. ...Houston, TX
West, Michael G. ...Boston, MA
West, Michael H. ...Chicago, IL
West, Michael L. ...Port Huron, MI
West, Michael P. ...Phoenix, AZ
West, Michael P. ...Los Angeles, CA
West, Michelle ...Orange, CA
West, Milton H., Jr. ...Houston, TX
West, Mitchell L. ...Des Moines, IA
West, Mitzi S. ...Atlanta, GA
West & Miyamoto ...Camarillo, CA
West, Murray ...Terre Haute, IN
West, Natalie E. ...Oakland, CA
West, Neil S. ...Lawton, OK
West, Newell E. ...Tulsa, OK
West, Nicholas S. ...Pasadena, CA
West, Norman A. ...Fairfax, VA
West, North O. ...San Antonio, TX
West, Orson B., Jr. ...Salt Lake City, UT
West, Pamela M. ...Bay St. Louis, MS
West, Pamela S. ...Department of Justice, Environment and Natural Resources Division, GV
West, Patrick A. T. ...Columbus, OH
West, Patten, Bekkedahl & Green, P.L.L.C.
Billings, MT
West, Patti Gilman ...Baltimore, MD
West, Paul B. ...New York, NY
West, Paul C. ...Chicago, IL
West, Paul G. ...Englewood, CO
West, Paul S. ...Baton Rouge, LA
West, Paula J. ...Albuquerque, NM
West, Peggy Ann ...Atlanta, GA
West, Perry Douglas ...Winter Park, FL
West, Perry Douglas, P.A. ...Winter Park, FL
West, Philip C. ...East Lansing, MI
West, Philip R. ...Treasury Department, Departmental Offices, GV
West, Philip R. ...Eastman, GA
West, Powell & Glass ...Los Angeles, CA
West, R. Angus ...Boston, MA
West, R. Gregory ...Oneida, TN
West, R. Michael ...Tucson, AZ
Sacramento, CA
West, Randall A. ...Chillicothe, IL
Peoria, IL
West, Randall R. ...Englewood, CO
West, Randolph T. ...Newport News, VA
West, Ray W., Jr. ...Oakland, CA
West, Rebecca C. ...Decatur, GA
West, Rebecca W. ...Charlottesville, VA
West, Richard A. ...Riverside, CA
West, Richard A., Jr. ...Roseland, NJ
West, Richard Barr ...Cheboygan, MI
West, Richard E. ...Springboro, OH
West, Richard H. ...Salinas, CA
West, Richard H. ...Buffalo, MN
West, Richard L. ...New York, NY
West, Richard Ray, Sr. ...Marion, AR
West, Richard T. ...Champaign, IL
West, Richard W. ...Detroit, MI
West, Richard Wright ...Newport News, VA
West, Rita A. ...Wichita, KS
West, Robert A. ...Redding, CA
West, Robert A. ...Kansas City, MO
West, Robert A. ...Winston-Salem, NC
West, Robert B. ...Point Pleasant Beach, NJ
West, Robert D. ...Brownsburg, IN
West, Robert E. ...Pueblo, CO
West, Robert E. ...Sparks, NV
West, Robert E., Jr. ...Auburn, WA
West, Robert E., P.C. ...Pueblo, CO
West, Robert G. ...Sacramento, CA
West, Robert G. ...Fort Worth, TX
West, Robert H. ...Boone, NC
West, Robert J. ...Austin, TX
West, Robert J., Jr. ...New York, NY
West, Robert T. ...St. Louis, MO
West, Robert W., III ...Birmingham, AL
West, Robert Wm. ...Ann Arbor, MI
West, Robin Page ...Baltimore, MD
Collingswood, NJ
Philadelphia, PA
West, Roderick K. ...New Orleans, LA
West, Roger E. ...Los Angeles, CA
West, Roger O. ...Dallas, TX
West, Roger Wayne ...Lexington, KY
West, Ron ...New York, NY
West, Ronald D. ...Bethesda, MD
West, Ronald D. ...Pittsburgh, PA
West, Ronald M. ...Modesto, CA
West, Ronald T. ...Spokane, WA
West & Rose ...Kingsport, TN
West, Roy Manly ...Birmingham, AL
West, Royce ...Dallas, TX
West, Russell B. ...La Grande, OR
West, Russell C., Jr. ...Brooklyn, NY
West, Ruth Clarke ...Washington, DC
West, Ruth Tinsley ...Atlanta, GA
West, S. Scott ...Sugar Land, TX
West, Samuel E. ...Greensboro, NC
West, Scott B. ...Columbus, OH
West, Shari L. ...Springfield, IL
West, Sheridan ...Santa Monica, CA
West, Sherman W. ...Upper Marlboro, MD
West & Smith, L.L.P. ...Pinehurst, NC
Southern Pines, NC
West, Soren P. ...Lancaster, PA
West, Stacey L. ...San Francisco, CA
West, Stanley L. ...Gainesville, FL
West, Stanley W. ...Southern Pines, NC
West, Stephen Ashley ...Lexington, KY
West, Stephen C. ...Breckenridge, CO
West, Stephen G. ...Pensacola, FL
West, Stephen J. ...Ottawa, IL
West, Stephen J. ...Peoria, IL
West, Stephen K. ...New York, NY
West, Stephen Kendrick ...Boston, MA
West, Stephen L. ...Mesa, AZ
West, Stephen R. ...Ketchikan, AK
West, Stephen R. ...McLean, VA
West, Steven L. ...Nashville, TN
West, Steven M. ...Encino, CA
West, Susan M. ...Los Angeles, CA
West, Susan Mendenhall ...Anchorage, AK
West, Susan Smith ...Dallas, TX
West, Suzanne ...Lake Worth, FL
West, Sydney K. L. ...Gloucester, VA
West, Tara Barrett ...Bedminster, NJ
West, Teno A. ...New York, NY
West, Terry R. ...LaVerkin, UT
West, Terry W. ...Shawnee, OK
West, Thomas C. ...Waco, TX
West, Thomas G. ...Danbury, CT
West, Thomas G. ...Galesburg, IL
West, Thomas J. ...Tacoma, WA
West, Thomas L. ...Department of Energy, Office of the General Counsel, GV
West, Thomas L. ...Daytona Beach, FL
West, Thomas L., P.A. ...Daytona Beach, FL
West, Thomas R. ...Raleigh, NC
West, Thomas S. ...Albany, NY
West, Thos. B. ...Atlanta, GA
West, Timothy H. ...Phoenix, AZ
West, Timothy J.
Department Of The Interior, Office of Legislation, GV
West, Timothy T. ...Houston, TX
West, Truett L. ...Farmerville, LA
West, Valerie ...Philadelphia, PA
West, Valerie C. ...Oakland, CA
West, Viki Melissa ...Mooresville, NC
West, Vincent ...Port Washington, NY
West, W. Brent ...Ogden, UT
West, W. Eric ...Jackson, MS
West, W. Steven ...Memphis, TN
West, Warren John ...Bend, OR
West Weaver Hepner PC ...Englewood, CO
West, Webb, Allbritton & Gentry, Professional Corporation ...Bryan, TX
College Station, TX
West, West and Yelton ...Bethel, OH
West, Wilford V. "Russ", IV
Mooresville, NC
West, William D. ...Helena, MT
West, William D. ...Springfield, OH
West, William E., Jr. ...Winston-Salem, NC
West, William F. ...Kenmore, WA
West, William G. ...Cleveland, OH
West, William H. ...Nashville, TN
West, William K., Jr. ...Washington, DC
West, William L. ...Greeley, CO
West, William L. ...Jenkintown, PA
West, William N. ...Cleveland, OH
West, William O. ...Edmond, OK
West, William O., A Professional Corporation
Edmond, OK
West, William R. ...Milwaukee, WI
West, William W. ...Jonesboro, GA
West, W. L. ...New Orleans, LA
West, Ximena O. ...Everett, WA
West & Zuberbuhler, P.C. ...Beaver, PA
Westad, John W. ...Rancho Palos Verdes, CA
Westadt, Connie L. ...Reno, NV
Westadt, Robert D. ...Schuyler, NE
Westall, Gray & Connolly, P.A.
Asheville, NC
Westall, Jack W., Jr. ...Asheville, NC
Westall, Karen Katz ...Houston, TX
Westberg, Craig S. ...Durango, CO
Westberg, Derek J. ...Palo Alto, CA
Westberg, James L. ...Moscow, ID
Westberg, John A. ...Washington, DC
Westberg, McCabe & Collins, Chartered
Boise, ID
Westberg, Paul L. (Larry) ...Boise, ID
Westberg, Robert M. ...San Francisco, CA
Westberg, Warren R. ...Dallas, TX
Westberry, B. M. ...Marion, KY
Paducah, KY
Westberry, Karen L. ...Kansas City, MO
Westberry, R. Kent ...Louisville, KY
Westblade, Wayne K. ...Syracuse, KS
Westbrock, Gerald R. ...Jacksonville, FL
Westbrock, Paul G. ...Cincinnati, OH
Westbrook, Alan William ...Las Vegas, NV
Westbrook, Anne Waters, (Mrs.)
Savannah, GA
Westbrook, Ansley S., II ...Pittsburgh, PA
Westbrook, Anthony J. ...Binghamton, NY
Westbrook, Bruce M. ...Mobile, AL
Westbrook, Carolyn D. ...Memphis, TN
Westbrook, Clay M. ...Atlanta, GA
Westbrook, Clyde O'Neal "Tres", III
Birmingham, AL
Westbrook, Colleen E. ...New York, NY
Westbrook, Connie ...Memphis, TN
Westbrook, Craig H. ...Little Rock, AR
Westbrook, Daniel J. ...Columbia, SC
Westbrook, David Albert ...Buffalo, NY
Westbrook, Deborah C.
Department of Justice, United States Marshals Service, GV
Westbrook, Douglas H. ...Charleston, SC
Westbrook, Duff H. ...Albuquerque, NM
Westbrook, Edward J. ...Charleston, SC
Westbrook, Edwin R. ...Irvine, CA
Westbrook, Gayle R. ...Columbus, OH
Westbrook, J. Don ...Longview, TX
Westbrook, James E. ...Columbia, MO
Westbrook, Jane E. ...Grand Junction, CO
Westbrook, Jay L. ...Austin, TX
Westbrook, John E. ...Midland, TX
Westbrook, K. Coleman, Jr.
Little Rock, AR
Westbrook, Kelvin R. ...St. Louis, MO
Westbrook, Larry L. ...Nashville, TN
Westbrook, Larry Neil ...Nashville, TN
Westbrook, Marc H. ...Lexington, SC
Westbrook, Margaret Rose ...Raleigh, NC
Westbrook, Mary K. ...Costa Mesa, CA
Westbrook, Melinda ...Hartford, CT
Westbrook, Melissa L. ...New York, NY
Westbrook, Paul B. ...Fort Worth, TX
Westbrook, Redge ...El Paso, TX
Westbrook, Reeves C. ...Washington, DC
Westbrook, Robert J. ...Austin, TX
Westbrook, Robert William
Los Angeles, CA
Westbrook, Robin Wright ...Great Falls, VA
Westbrook, Stephen M. ...Oakland, CA
Westbrook, Susan Marshall ...Austin, TX
Westbrook, W. Scott ...Lakeland, FL
Westbrook, William J. ...Summerville, GA
Westbrook, William L. ...Atlanta, GA
Westbrook, William V., III ...Gulfport, MS
Westbrooke, Henry W., Jr. ...Springfield, MO
Westbrooks, Robert A. ...Cleveland, OH
Westbury, James R., Jr. ...Griffin, GA
McDonough, GA
Westby, Chester & Lees, P.A. ...St. Paul, MN
Westby, Kie ...Thomaston, CT
Westby, Laura Anne ...Owatonna, MN
Westby, Mary E. ...Salt Lake City, UT
Westby, Misha E. ...Cheyenne, WY
Westby, Peter H. ...Phoenix, AZ
Westby, Ragnhild A. ...St. Paul, MN
Westby, Steven A. ...Atlanta, GA
Westby, Timothy S. ...Houston, TX
Westcott, Allan C. ...Annapolis, MD
Westcott, Barbara J. ...Evanston, IL
Westcott, David R. ...Tallahassee, FL
Westcott, David V. ...Roseville, CA
Westcott, John E. ...San Antonio, TX
Westcott, John M., Jr. ...Boston, MA
Westcott, Kay Annette ...Houston, TX
Westcott, Michael J. ...Madison, WI
Westcott, Paul L. ...Fort Pierce, FL
Orlando, FL
Westcott & Phillips ...Belmont, MA
Westcott, Rick Dalton ...Tulsa, OK
Westebbe, David B. ...Boston, MA
Westee, Philip L. ...Kennesaw, GA
Westemeier, Julie Quagliano
Washington, DC
Westemeyer, Patricia A. ...Des Moines, IA
Westen, B. Curtis, Jr.
Woodland Hills, CA
Westen, Derek A. ...Santa Barbara, CA
Westen, Marion L. ...Laguna Niguel, CA
Westen, Peter ...Ann Arbor, MI
Westen, Ronald E. ...Detroit, MI
Westen, Valerie L. ...San Francisco, CA
Westenberg, Brian S. ...Troy, MI
Westenberg, David A. ...Boston, MA
Westenberg, Lynn Gorsey ...Vienna, VA
Westenberger, Fred P. ...Metairie, LA
Westendorf, Carol G. ...Portland, OR
Westendorf, Douglas L. ...Cincinnati, OH
Westendorf, Gayl A. ...San Francisco, CA
Westendorf, Harald ...Fremont, CA
Westendorf, Roger ...Portland, OR
Westenfield, Neuman & Parry ...Niles, OH
Westenfield, Victoria A. ...Ames, IA
Westenhover, Gary F. ...Cleburne, TX
Granbury, TX
Jacksboro, TX
Mineral Wells, TX
Westenhover, Gary F. ...Weatherford, TX
Westenhover, John Mark ...Austin, TX
Westensee, John H. ...Rock Island, IL
Wester, Barbara Leibhardt ...Chicago, IL
Wester, Barry F. ...Greenbrae, CA
Wester, Denise L. ...Allentown, PA
Wester, J. Meredith ...Tampa, FL
Wester, James W. ...Amarillo, TX
Wester, John F. ...Washington, DC
Wester, John R. ...Charlotte, NC
Wester, Mark R. ...Hudson, MA
Wester, Neil ...Dalton, GA
Wester, Nelson G. ...Johnston, RI
Wester, R. H., Jr. ...Austin, TX
Wester, Robert C. ...Papillion, NE
Wester, Thomas A. ...Millburn, NJ
Wester, Wes ...Amarillo, TX
Westerbaan-Klein, Anne Marie
Rockville, MD
Westerband, Rudolph S. ...Salem, OR
Westerbeck, Daniel J. ...Schaumburg, IL
Fort Worth, TX
Westerbeck, David F. ...Cincinnati, OH
Westerbeck, Patrick Karl Short
Rockwall, TX
Westerbeck, Patti J. ...Johnston, IA
Westerberg, D. Kent ...Saratoga, CA
Westerberg, Dennis N. ...Gold River, CA
Westerberg, Dennis N., Law Corporation
Gold River, CA
Sacramento, CA
Westerberg, Gary W. ...Chicago, IL
Westerberg, Janice N. ...Fresno, CA
Westerberg, Kent ...Burlingame, CA
Westerberg, Richard M. ...Binghamton, NY
Westerberg, Scott W. ...Reisterstown, MD
Westerberg, Scott W., P.A.
Reisterstown, MD
Westerberg, Tamera D. ...Denver, CO
Westerberg, Ward W. ...Jamestown, NY
Westerburg, Cheri L. ...Columbus, OH
Westerburg, Daniel W., Law Offices of
Homer, AK
Westerburg, L. Richard, Jr.
Baton Rouge, LA
Westerburg, Robert H. ...Dallas, TX
Westerby, David A. ...Salt Lake City, UT
Westercamp, Steven J. ...Farmington, IA
Westerchil, Scott ...Leesville, LA
Westerdahl, Sylvia W. ...Aiken, SC

Westerfeld, Barclay L. ... Rancho Cordova, CA
Westerfeld, Nancy V. ... Houston, TX
Westerfeldt, Robert C. ... Washington, DC
Westerfield, Adrienne ... New York, NY
Westerfield, Andrew M. W. Cleveland, MS
Westerfield & Associates ... Carmel, IN
Indianapolis, IN
Westerfield, Divina K. ... Carmel, IN
Westerfield, Evan B. ... Chicago, IL
Westerfield Law Offices, Ltd. Albuquerque, NM
Westerfield, Mark G. ... Washington, DC
Westerfield, Patrick L. ... Albuquerque, NM
Westerfield, Rebecca ... San Francisco, CA
Westerfield, Robert I. ... Walnut Creek, CA
Westerfield, Steve Hot Springs National Park, AR
Westerfield, Thomas J. ... Cincinnati, OH
Westergaard, James R. ... Mapleton, IA
Sloan, IA
Westergaard, Steadman H. ... New York, NY
Westergaard, Terry G. ... Rapid City, SD
Westergard, Dolena T. ... Garland, TX
Westergard, Mark S. ... Dallas, TX
Westergard, W. David ... Boise, ID
Westergren, Gary ... Gilford, NH
Westergren, Mike ... Corpus Christi, TX
Westergren, Philip M. ... Corpus Christi, TX
Westergren, Sam A., Jr. ... Corpus Christi, TX
Westerhaus, Charlotte F. ... Milwaukee, WI
Westerhaus, James A. ... St. Paul, MN
Westerhaus, Michael Frank ... Strongsville, OH
Westerhaus, Victoria R. ... Kansas City, MO
Westerhausen, Tracey ... Phoenix, AZ
Westerheim, Suzanne R. ... Dallas, TX
Westerhof, Carl L. ... Wausau, WI
Westerhof, Jacob P. ... Madison, WI
Westerhoff, Richard V. ... Pittsburgh, PA
Westerkamp, Patrick ... Newark, NJ
Westerlage, Electra ... Department of Agriculture, GV
Westerlage, Lloyd W. ... Cedar Hill, TX
Westerlind, Jennifer ... Stanford, CA
Westerling, Karel ... New York, NY
Westerlund, Ashley L. ... New Orleans, LA
Westerlund, David A. ... Muncie, IN
Westerlund, Lawrence E. ... Fresno, CA
Westerlund, Robert A. ... Arlington, VA
Westerlund, William J. ... Eau Claire, WI
Westerman, Arnold R. ... Washington, DC
Westerman & Associates, P.C. Ann Arbor, MI
Westerman, Christian C. ... Alexandria, VA
Westerman, E. C., Jr. ... Fincastle, VA
Westerman, Helen K. ... Guthrie, OK
Westerman, Jeff S. ... Los Angeles, CA
San Diego, CA
Westerman, John E. ... Garden City, NY
Westerman, John R. ... Farmington, NM
Westerman, John R., Chartered Farmington, NM
Westerman, Kevin P. ... White Plains, NY
Westerman, Leslie C. ... Fayetteville, NY
Westerman, Matthew D. ... Jacksonville, FL
Westerman, Michael M. ... East Greenwich, RI
Westerman, Morris ... Red Bank, NJ
Westerman, Paul ... Ashland, OR
Westerman, Philip R. ... Columbus, OH
Westerman, Richard L. ... Rapid City, MI
Westerman, Robert J. ... Bethlehem, PA
Westerman, Robert T., II ... Gaylord, MI
Westerman Shapiro Pollack Draghi & Miller, LLP ... Garden City, NY
Westerman, Sidney ... Everett, MA
Westerman, Susan S. ... Ann Arbor, MI
Westerman, William F. ... Washington, DC
Westermann, David, Jr. ... Garden City, NY
Westermann Hamilton & Sheehy Saddle River, NJ
Garden City, NY
Westermann, Jeffrey A. ... Cloquet, MN
Westermann, Robert S. ... Richmond, VA
Westermann, Stephen X. ... Fort Worth, TX
Westermann, William S. ... Destin, FL
Westermeier, John T., Jr. ... Washington, DC
Westermeier, Marie R. ... Seattle, WA
Westermeier, Stephanie C. ... Boise, ID
Westermeyer, Daniella A. ... Cincinnati, OH
Westermeyer, Michael T. Minneapolis, MN
Western, Gary A. ... Seattle, WA
Western, M. Wayne ... Sandy, UT
Westervelt, Carol F. ... Sacramento, CA
Westervelt, C. E., Jr. ... Westerville, OH
Westervelt, Cynthia L. ... Boston, MA
Westervelt, George W., Jr. Stroudsburg, PA
Westervelt, Johnson, Nicoll & Keller Eureka, IL
Lacon, IL
Lewistown, IL
Peoria, IL
Westervelt, Marcus ... Phoenix, AZ
Westesen, Neil G. ... Billings, MT
Westfahl, Bernard C. ... Elm Grove, WI
Westfahl, Bernard J. ... Elm Grove, WI
Westfahl, Scott A. ... Washington, DC
Westfahl & Westfahl, S.C. ... Elm Grove, WI
Westfahl, Alfred R. ... Los Angeles, CA
Westfall, Beth E. ... Binghamton, NY
Unadilla, NY
Westfall, Blake Benton ... Charleston, WV
Westfall, Constance Courtney ... Dallas, TX
Westfall, Craig C. ... Glendale Heights, IL
Westfall, Curtis A. ... Sherman Oaks, CA
Westfall, David ... Cambridge, MA
Westfall, David ... Kansas City, MO
Westfall, David S. ... Ouray, CO
Westfall, Denise M. ... Denver, CO
Westfall, Donald D. ... Armonk, NY
Westfall, Donald Kenneth, III ... Olympia, WA
Westfall, Donald R. ... Carrollton, TX
Westfall, Edith Ann ... Van Meter, IA
Westfall, Elizabeth S. ... Washington, DC
Westfall, Florence J. ... Colusa, CA
Westfall, Fred B., Jr. ... Charleston, WV
Westfall, G. David ... Dallas, TX
Westfall, G. Don ... Fairfax, VA
Westfall, G. Michael, (PC) ... St. George, UT
Westfall, George R. ... Clayton, MO
Westfall, Gregory B. ... Fort Worth, TX
Westfall, James M. ... Athens, OH
Westfall, James W. ... Cleveland, OH
Westfall, Jennifer Dunn General Accounting Office, Office of the General Counsel, GV
Westfall, Lawrence S. ... El Segundo, CA
Westfall, Lee W. ... Columbus, OH
Westfall, M. Todd ... Atlanta, GA
Westfall, Matthew R. ... Louisville, KY
Westfall, Matthew R., Jr. ... Louisville, KY
Westfall, Richard A. ... Denver, CO
Westfall, Susan Whelan ... Washington, DC
Westfall, Talbott & Woods ... Louisville, KY
Westfall, Walter S. ... Rochester, NY
Westfall, Wendell L. ... Dallas, TX
Westfaul, Jay ... Batesville, MS
Westfeldt, Patrick M. ... Denver, CO
Westfield, Dawn R. ... Fort Wayne, IN
Westfield, Edward F. ... New York, NY
Westfield, Lisa A. ... St. Louis, MO
Westfield, Thomas ... Whippany, NJ
Westgard, Kristin S. ... Minneapolis, MN
Westgate, Darla ... Stockton, CA
Westgate, Gail E. ... Burlington, VT
Westgate, J. Bradford ... Nashua, NH
Westgate, Richard A. ... Middleboro, MA
Westhafer, F. Eugene ... Santa Ana, CA
Westhafer, John A. ... Greensburg, IN
Westheimer, F. Scott ... Sarasota, FL
Westheimer, Joseph M., Jr. ... San Antonio, TX
Westheimer, Michael N. Mountain View, CA
Westheimer, Robert L. ... Venice, FL
Westheimer, Vaughn L. ... Corpus Christi, TX
Westhoff, Christopher M. ... Los Angeles, CA
Westhoff, Clint ... Pittsburg, KS
Westhoff, Douglas J. ... Cypress, CA
Westhoff, Fred L. ... Monticello, MO
Westhoff, John E. ... Weatherford, TX
Westhoff, John R. ... New York, NY
Westhoff, Kim Rodgers ... Los Angeles, CA
Westhoff, Mark R. ... Chicago, IL
Westhoff, Pamela Lynne ... Los Angeles, CA
Westhoff, Sharon DuPriest Harrisonville, MO
Westholm, Larry R. ... Tacoma, WA
Westholm, William L. ... Duluth, MN
Westholz, Harold M. (Jack), Jr. New Orleans, LA
Westholz, J. Thaddeus ... New Orleans, LA
Westhouse, Edward C. ... St. Louis, MO
Westin, Claudia D. ... San Francisco, CA
Westin, Edward P. Department of Commerce, Patent and Trademark Office, GV
Westin, Howard I. ... Fort Lauderdale, FL
Westin, James C. ... Kalamazoo, MI
Westin, Jeremy S. ... New York, NY
Westin, Marvin ... Copiague, NY
Westin, Neal K. ... Des Moines, IA
Westin, Richard A. ... Lexington, KY
Westin, Richard J. ... Berkeley, CA
Westin, Sandra H. ... Portland, OR
Westine, Lezlee Hiegel ... Corte Madera, CA
Westinghouse, Robert H. ... Seattle, WA
Westjohn, Karla ... Galesburg, IL
Westlake, Blair M. ... Universal City, CA
Westlake, Ellen Carol ... San Jose, CA
Westlake, Joseph D. ... Tulsa, OK
Westlake, Mark H. ... Nashville, TN
Westlake and Marsden, P.C. Nashville, TN
Westlake, Rosalind ... North Brunswick, NJ
Westlake, Susan Eydenberg ... Fairfield, CT
Westland, Charles W. ... New York, NY
Westland, David W. ... Merrillville, IN
Westland, John A. ... Kennewick, WA
Westland, Kelle J. ... Omaha, NE
Westle, Thomas R. ... New York, NY
Westlein, Joseph C. ... Warren, NJ
Westley, Andrew E. ... San Francisco, CA
Westley, John F. ... Chicago, IL
Westley Law Offices, S.C. ... Madison, WI
Westley, Richard A. ... Madison, WI
Westling, Dale G., Sr. ... Jacksonville, FL
Westling, Deborah J. ... St. Louis, MO
Westling, Jacque Nims ... Phoenix, AZ
Westling, Oren N. ... Edina, MN
Westling, Richard W. ... New Orleans, LA
Westling, Richard W., L.L.C., Law Offices of New Orleans, LA
Westling, Wayne T. ... Eugene, OR
Westlund, Cathy J. ... Merced, CA
Westlund, R. Scott ... San Antonio, TX
Westlund, Roger W. ... Denver, CO
Westly, Dean R. ... San Jose, CA
Westly, Hollie J. ... Spokane, WA
Westlye, Brad C. ... San Francisco, CA
Westman, Carl E. ... Key West, FL
Naples, FL
Westman, Champlin & Kelly, P.A. Minneapolis, MN
Westman, Dean E. ... Cleveland, OH
Westman, James E. ... Jamestown, NY
Westman, Jan O. ... Denver, CO
Westman, Kathryn L. ... Detroit, MI
Westman & Lintz ... Cocoa, FL
Westman, Marian T. ... Media, PA
Westman, Nickolas E. ... Minneapolis, MN
Westman, Paul W. ... Waseca, MN
Westman, Robert T. ... Cocoa, FL
Westman, Rochelle Ann ... Raleigh, NC
Westman, Steven J. ... Los Angeles, CA
Westman, Timothy G. ... Clayton, MO
Westman, Victor J. ... Martinez, CA
Westmeyer, Joseph W., Jr. ... Toledo, OH
Westmeyer, Robert ... Napa, CA
Westmont, Ruth Naomi ... Madison, WI
Westmore, Kandis A. ... Oakland, CA
Westmoreland, Barbara C. Winston-Salem, NC
Westmoreland, Barton Tull ... Houston, TX
Westmoreland, Benj. L. ... Everett, WA
Westmoreland, Brad ... Dallas, TX
Westmoreland, Bradley ... Houston, TX
Westmoreland, C. Glenn ... Baton Rouge, LA
Westmoreland, Carl E. ... Macon, GA
Westmoreland, Carl E., Jr. ... Atlanta, GA
Westmoreland, Carol J. ... Houston, TX
Westmoreland, David T. ... Fort Smith, AR
Westmoreland, Edward J. ... Houston, TX
Westmoreland, Geoffrey D. Shreveport, LA
Westmoreland, J. Lofton ... Pensacola, FL
Westmoreland, J. Ray Hilton Head Island, SC
Westmoreland, James H. ... Houston, TX
Westmoreland, Jill Amanda New York, NY
Westmoreland, John W. United States Tax Court, GV
Westmoreland, Kathleen ... Bellaire, TX
Westmoreland, Kent E. ... Houston, TX
Westmoreland, Kermit ... Fort Worth, TX
Westmoreland, Mark D. ... Richmond, VA
Westmoreland, Mary Beth ... Atlanta, GA
Westmoreland, Melvin K. ... Atlanta, GA
Westmoreland, Patterson & Moseley Albany, GA
Atlanta, GA
Macon, GA
Savannah, GA
Warner Robins, GA
Westmoreland, Rudolph C. Atlantic City, NJ
Westmoreland, Samuel P. ... Atlanta, GA
Westmoreland, Tamsen ... Portland, OR
Westmoreland, Vesper & Schwartz, A Professional Corporation Atlantic City, NJ
Westmoreland, W. T. ... Tillamook, OR
Weston, Aaron ... Clarkston, MI
Weston, Amanda Jane ... Chicago, IL
Weston, Benshoof, Rochefort, Rubalcava MacCuish LLP ... Los Angeles, CA
Weston, Blake L. ... San Francisco, CA
Weston, Bradford, III ... Sacramento, CA
Weston, Bruce J. ... Columbus, OH
Weston, Burns H. ... Iowa City, IA
Weston, Burton S. ... Great Neck, NY
Weston, C. Don ... Macomb, IL
Weston, Charles H. ... Macon, GA
Weston, Cheryl Rosen ... Madison, WI
Weston, Cori Ching ... Honolulu, HI
Weston, Cori H. ... Brooklyn, NY
Weston, Cory M. ... Savannah, GA
Weston, Craig W. ... Longview, WA
Weston, Cynthia M. ... Londonderry, NH
Weston, David ... Montgomery, AL
Weston, David ... La Jolla, CA
Weston, Donna A. ... Miami, FL
Weston, E. Duane ... Flagstaff, AZ
Weston, Gary A. ... Salt Lake City, UT
Weston, Gerald L. ... Caldwell, ID
Weston, Glen E. ... San Francisco, CA
Weston, Gregory M. ... New York, NY
Weston, Hanna B. ... Cedar Rapids, IA
Iowa City, IA
Weston, Harris K. ... Cincinnati, OH
Weston, Herbert J. ... Vista, CA
Weston Hurd Fallon Paisley & Howley L.L.P. ... Cleveland, OH
Weston, J. Michael ... Cedar Rapids, IA
Weston, J. Michael ... Dallas, TX
Weston, James K. ... Chicago, IL
Weston, James K., II ... Cedar Rapids, IA
Weston, James S. V. ... Atlanta, GA
Weston, Jane Mitchell ... San Francisco, CA
Weston, Jeffrey A. ... Colorado Springs, CO
Weston, Jeffrey M. ... Chicago, IL
Weston, Jerry S. ... Greensboro, NC
Weston, John G. ... Salt Lake City, UT
Weston, John H., (A Professional Corporation) Los Angeles, CA
Weston, John I., Jr. ... Chelan, WA
Weston, John K. ... Philadelphia, PA
Weston, John L. ... Royal Oak, MI
Weston, John R. ... Omaha, NE
Weston, Joseph R. ... Charleston, SC
Weston, Joseph R., P.A. ... Charleston, SC
Weston, Kathleen K. ... Philadelphia, PA
Weston, Kelly Lynn ... Atlanta, GA
Weston, Kenneth E. ... Amarillo, TX
Weston, Kenneth F. ... Los Angeles, CA
Weston, Larry C. ... Sumter, SC
Weston Law Offices ... Boise, ID
Weston, Lindsay Anne ... Los Angeles, CA
Weston, Lysha Nicole ... San Diego, CA
Weston, Mark G. ... Missoula, MT
Weston, Maura M. ... Concord, NH
Weston & McElvain ... Los Angeles, CA
Weston, Michael C. ... Evanston, IL
Weston, O. Morton, Jr. ... Fort Lauderdale, FL
Weston, Patrick, Willard & Redding, Professional Association ... Boston, MA
Weston, Peter W. ... Houston, TX
Weston and Printzlau, P.C. Londonderry, NH
Weston, R. Timothy ... Harrisburg, PA
Weston, Ray D., Jr. ... Dallas, TX
Weston, Richard C. ... Los Angeles, CA
Weston, Richard E. ... Boise, ID
Weston, Robert B. ... Mt. Vernon, OH
Weston, Robert G. ... Mission Viejo, CA
Weston, Ross L. ... Newark, NJ
New York, NY
Weston, S. Nelson, Jr. ... Columbia, SC
Weston, Sarno, Garrou & DeWitt Los Angeles, CA
Weston, Scott N., (A Professional Corporation) ... Los Angeles, CA
Weston, Stanley M. ... Jacksonville, FL
Weston, Steven H. ... Kalamazoo, MI
Weston, Steven J. ... Deerfield Beach, FL
Weston, Steven Thomas ... Falls Church, VA
Weston, Steven W. ... Los Angeles, CA
Weston, Susan K. ... Savannah, GA
Weston, Susan P. ... Danville, KY
Weston, Susan Perkins ... Harrisburg, PA
Weston, Tod Andrew ... Fort Lauderdale, FL
Weston, Tod Andrew, P.A. Fort Lauderdale, FL
Weston, Vivian L. ... West Haven, CT
Weston, William G. ... Willoughby, OH
Weston, William P. ... Naples, FL
Weston, William S. ... Los Angeles, CA
Weston-Dawkes, Matthew ... Modesto, CA
Weston-Overbey, Kathryn D. ... Chicago, IL
Westover, Alyssa C. ... Newport Beach, CA
Westover, Barrett E. ... Newport Beach, CA
Westover, Christine ... Lexington, KY
Westover, Christopher A. San Francisco, CA
Westover, Gail L. ... Washington, DC
Westover, Harry E. ... Newport Beach, CA
Westover, John H. ... Phoenix, AZ
Yuma, AZ
Westover, Marla K. ... San Francisco, CA
Westover, Michael ... Denver, CO
Westover, Robert F. ... Palo Alto, CA
Westover, Russell C., Jr. ... San Rafael, CA
Westover, Shadle, Byrd & Carter, P.L.C. Yuma, AZ
El Centro, CA
Westover, Susan ... Irvine, CA
Westover, Wayne A., Jr. ... Martinez, CA
Westover & Westover ... Phoenix, AZ
Westover & Westover, LLP, Law Offices of Newport Beach, CA
Westover, William H. ... Phoenix, AZ
Yuma, AZ
Westphal, Bradley D. ... Seattle, WA
Westphal, David W. ... Houston, TX
Westphal, Edward E. ... Arlington Heights, IL
Westphal, Eric Scott ... Brainerd, MN
Westphal, Frederick R., II ... Weedsport, NY
Westphal, James P. ... Minneapolis, MN
Westphal, Kristin J. ... Mobile, AL
San Diego, CA
Westphal, Marjorie Lord ... Carefree, AZ
Westphal, Mary Ann ... Fayetteville, AR
Westphal, Nancy R. ... Roseland, NJ
Westphal, Ronald S. ... San Jose, CA
Westphal, Rudolph J. ... Peoria, IL
Westphal, Steven E. ... Kohler, WI
Westphal, Todd W. ... St. Peter, MN
Westphal & Warren, PLLC ... Fayetteville, AR
Westphal-Bohn, Jan ... Chicago, IL
Westphale, Wayne L. Steamboat Springs, CO
Westra, Arnold D. ... Santa Ana, CA
Westra, Clarence, Jr. ... Bakersfield, CA
Westra, David R. ... Greenwich, CT
Westra, Donald F. ... Carol Stream, IL
Westra, James R. ... Boston, MA
Westra, John J. ... Carol Stream, IL
Westra, Mark W. ... Minneapolis, MN
Westra, Nikki Ann ... Prescott, AZ
Westra, Vincent C. ... Kalamazoo, MI
Westrate & Holmstrom ... Dowagiac, MI
Westrate, Mark A. ... Dowagiac, MI
Westray, Laura L. ... Redondo Beach, CA
Westreich, Benzion J. ... Los Angeles, CA
Westreich, Glenn E. ... San Francisco, CA
San Jose, CA
Westreich, Jonathan D. ... Alexandria, VA
Westreich, Kenneth P. ... Wall, NJ
Westreich, Meir J. ... Pasadena, CA
Westreich, Neil P. ... New York, NY
Westreich, Robert D. ... Newark, NJ
Westrem, Barbara J. ... Los Angeles, CA
Westrich, Howard D. ... New York, NY
Westrich, Scott A. ... San Francisco, CA
Westrick, John G. ... St. Paul, MN
Westrick, Kimberly Ann Oklahoma City, OK
Westrick & McDowall-Nix, PLLP St. Paul, MN
Westrick, Robert C. ... La Grange Park, IL
Westrick, Timothy A. ... Toledo, OH
Westrin, Nelson W. ... Lansing, MI
Westrup, David A. ... Milwaukee, WI
Westrup, Klick & Assoc. ... Long Beach, CA
Westrup, R. Duane ... Long Beach, CA
Westveer, Mark Edward ... Missoula, MT
Westwater, D. Brooks, Jr. ... Greensboro, NC
Westwater, Douglas S. ... Carpinteria, CA
Westwick, George ... Sacramento, CA
Westwick, R. James ... Santa Barbara, CA
Westwood, James N., P.C. ... Portland, OR

Westwood, Scott E. ....Pittsburgh, PA
Westwood, Wayne H. ....Minneapolis, MN
Wetchler, Jonathan D. ....Philadelphia, PA
Wetenkamp, Jean High ....San Jose, CA
Wetenkamp, Kristin L. ....Denver, CO
Wetering, William J. ....Worthington, MN
Weterrings, Jorgen W. ....Torrance, CA
Weth, Patricia A. ....Springfield, VA
Wethekam, Marilyn A. ....Chicago, IL
Wetherald, Margaret E. ....Seattle, WA
Wetherall, Gregory M. ....Dallas, TX
Wetherall, Peter C. ....Reno, NV
Wetherall, William B. ....Nevada City, CA
Wetherbee, Charles F. ....Jourdanton, TX
Wetherbee, Charles F. ....Pleasanton, TX
Wetherbee, James R. ....Dallas, TX
Wetherbee, Margaret Baker
Jacksonville, FL
Wetherby, Terry L. ....Middletown, KY
Wetherell, Charles F. ....Lakewood, NJ
Wetherell, Joan M. ....Pleasanton, CA
Wetherell, John R., Jr. ....La Jolla, CA
Wetherell, Karen M. ....Seattle, WA
Wetherell, Michael E. ....Boise, ID
Wetherell, Raymond C. ....Cincinnati, OH
Wetherell, Robert T. ....Boise, ID
Wetherell, Stephen L. ....Tucson, AZ
Wetherell, T. Kent, II ....Tallahassee, FL
Wetherell, Weston B.
Oakbrook Terrace, IL
Wetherholt, Robt. C. ....Bothell, WA
Wetherholt, Tamara A. ....Jefferson, OH
Wetherill, Elkins ....Norristown, PA
Wetherill, Harrison B., Jr. ....Annapolis, MD
Wetherill, Jo Tewes ....Peoria, IL
Wetherill, Richard A. ....Rockport, IN
Wetherill, Schwemer, Markley & Schwemer
Kenton, OH
Wetherill, Susan Evans ....Raleigh, NC
Wetherille, Randall L. ....Minneapolis, MN
Wetherington, C. Barry
Bloomfield Hills, MI
Wetherington, Charles A., Jr.
Valdosta, GA
Wetherington, Donald L. ....Roanoke, VA
Wetherington, Gerald T. ....Miami, FL
Wetherington, Klein & Hubbart, P.A.
Miami, FL
Wetherington, LeFloch & Hamilton, P.A.
Tampa, FL
Wetherington, Melchionna, Terry, Day & Ammar, A Professional Corporation
Roanoke, VA
Wetherington, R. Wade ....Tampa, FL
Wethern, Christine A. ....Helena, MT
Wethern, Michael D. ....Cranbury, NJ
Wethern, Samuel W. ....Atlanta, GA
Wething, David S. ....Minneapolis, MN
Wething, Lori ....Bloomington, MN
Wethington, C. Kennan ....Lexington, KY
Wethington Hurt & Crosbie, PLLC
Lexington, KY
Wethington, James A., II ....Owensboro, KY
Wethington, John A., III ....Ocala, FL
Wethington, Olin L. ....Washington, DC
Wethly, Frans Christopher ....Boston, MA
Wethly, Frederick J., Jr. ....Jersey City, NJ
Wethly, Kimberly Boyle ....Boston, MA
Wethor, Angela M. ....Roseville, MN
Wetlaufer, Gerald B. ....Iowa City, IA
Wetli, John F. ....Toledo, OH
Wetmore, Floyd E. ....Midland, MI
Wetmore, John K. ....Greenwich, CT
Wetmore, Keith C. ....San Francisco, CA
Wetmore, Kenneth H. ....Perrysburg, OH
Wetmore, LaDonna S. ....Grants Pass, OR
Wetmore, Mariann ....Port Chester, NY
Wetmore, Mark R. ....Boston, MA
Wetmore, Michael H. ....St. Louis, MO
Wetmore, Michael J. ....Stroudsburg, PA
Wetmore, Robert G., Law Offices of
Wallingford, CT
Wetmore, Thomas E. ....Silver Spring, MD
Wetmore, Weeden A. ....Elmira, NY
Wetmore, William F., Jr. ....Washington, DC
Wetmore, William H., IV
Department Of Veterans Affairs, Board of Veterans Appeals, GV
Wetovick, Rodney M. ....St. Paul, NE
Wetsch, David L. ....Des Moines, IA
Wetsch, Laura J. ....Raleigh, NC
Wetsch, Sherry R. ....Houston, TX
Wetsel, John E., Jr. ....Winchester, VA
Wetsel, Roderick E. ....Sweetwater, TX
Wetstein, Harriett Wendy ....Baltimore, MD
Wetstein, Paula ....Riverhead, NY
Wetstone, Barrie K. ....Hartford, CT
Wetstone & D'Ambrosio ....Farmington, CT
Wetta, Dennis Patrick ....Wichita, KS
Wetta, Jeanne M. ....Glenview, IL
Wetta, Leo R. ....Wichita, KS
Wettach, Christine L. ....Pittsburgh, PA
Wettach, Jane R. ....Winston-Salem, NC
Wettach, John T., Jr. ....Orlando, FL
Wettach, Joseph C. L. ....Orlando, FL
Wettach, Margaret D. ....Orlando, FL
Wettach, Thomas C. ....Pittsburgh, PA
Wettan, Howard ....Palo Alto, CA
Wetteland, John A., Jr. ....Portland, OR
Wetten, Walton ....Patagonia, AZ
Wettengel, Peggy S. ....South Milwaukee, WI
Wetter, Alison Markell ....Memphis, TN
Wetter, James Michael ....Kingston, PA
Wetter, Mark A. ....Somerville, NJ
Wetterauer, Damon E., Jr. ....Westerville, OH
Wetterer, Carolyn Boswell ....Louisville, KY
Wetterer, Charles M. ....Huntington, NY
Wetterer, Robert M. ....New York, NY
Wetterer, Thomas R., Jr. ....Columbus, OH
Wetterer, Thomas W. ....Washington, DC
Wetterer, William S., III ....Louisville, KY
Wetterer, William S., Jr. ....Louisville, KY
Wetterhahn, Mark J. ....Washington, DC
Wetterlin, Rebecca A. ....Santa Rosa, CA
Wetterling, James A. ....Garner, IA
Wetterling, James E., Jr.
Fort Lauderdale, FL
Miami, FL
Wetterman, Walter N. ....Villa Park, CA
Wettermann, Thomas E. ....Chicago, IL
Wettermark, James H. ....Birmingham, AL
Jacksonville, FL
Atlanta, GA
Wettermark, Lawrence M. ....Mobile, AL
Wetteroth, Warren C. ....Bakersfield, CA
Wettersten, Nancy C. ....Madison, WI
Wettick, R. Stanton, Jr. ....Pittsburgh, PA
Wettlaufer, Catherine Talley ....Buffalo, NY
Wettlaufer, Karl F. ....Columbus, OH
Wettlaufer, Thomas J. ....Salem, OR
Wettle, Mark J. ....Louisville, KY
Wettle, Susan S. ....Louisville, KY
Wettlin, Joseph ....Myrtle Beach, SC
Wettman, Bruce W. ....Houston, TX
Wettman & Wettman ....Houston, TX
Wettre, Leda Dunn ....Newark, NJ
Wettstein, Albert ....Cincinnati, OH
Wetwiska, James R. ....Houston, TX
Wetzel, Arthur S. ....Grand Island, NE
Wetzel, B. Todd ....Princeton, KY
Wetzel, Benjamin C., III ....Wilmington, DE
Wetzel, Carol L. ....Las Vegas, NV
Wetzel, Carroll Robbins ....Philadelphia, PA
Wetzel, Cathey L. ....Harahan, LA
Wetzel, Dana L. Rayborn
Coeur d'Alene, ID
Wetzel DeFrang & Sandor ....Portland, OR
Wetzel, Don A. ....Houston, TX
Wetzel, Douglas A. ....Owensboro, KY
Wetzel, E. Scott, III ....Seattle, WA
Wetzel, Frederick S., III, P.A.
Little Rock, AR
Wetzel, Frederick S. "Tripp", III
Little Rock, AR
Wetzel, George C. ....San Diego, CA
Wetzel, George P. ....Little Falls, MN
Wetzel and Gross ....Hialeah, FL
Wetzel, Henri & Drucker, L.L.P.
Houston, TX
Wetzel, James D. ....Tampa, FL
Wetzel, James K. ....Gulfport, MS
Wetzel, James K., & Associates A Prof. Law Corp. ....Biloxi, MS
Gulfport, MS
Wetzel, James M. ....Chicago, IL
Wetzel, Jas. C. ....Southfield, MI
Wetzel, John A. ....Philadelphia, PA
Wetzel, John C. ....Bethesda, MD
Wetzel, Jonathan H. ....Columbus, OH
Wetzel, Joseph ....Portland, OR
Wetzel, Lewis W. ....Wilkes-Barre, PA
Wetzel, Lisa A. ....Chicago, IL
Wetzel, Mary Jo ....New Albany, IN
Wetzel, Michael C. ....Portland, OR
Wetzel, Michael L., & Associates
Stone Mountain, GA
Wetzel, Phillip J. ....Spokane, WA
Wetzel, Rebecca B. ....Cleveland, OH
Wetzel, Richard D., Jr. ....Columbus, OH
Wetzel, Steven C. ....Coeur d'Alene, ID
Wetzel, Steven L. ....Idaho Falls, ID
Wetzel, Susan A. ....Fort Wayne, IN
Wetzel, Susan K. ....Kew Gardens, NY
Wetzel, Thomas K. ....Baton Rouge, LA
Wetzel & Wetzel, P.L.L.C.
Coeur d'Alene, ID
Wetzel, William C. ....Bloomington, IL
Wetzel, William G., Jr. ....Hialeah, FL
Wetzel-Williams, Kimberly K.
Kansas City, KS
Wetzler, Andrew E. ....Los Angeles, CA
Wetzler, Charles E. ....Overland Park, KS
Wetzler, David C. ....Prairie Village, KS
Wetzler, Donna S. ....Chicago, IL
Wetzler, Gerald M. ....New York, NY
Wetzler, Lisa R. ....Kansas City, KS
Wetzler, Monte E. ....Hartford, CT
Wetzler, Nadia ....San Francisco, CA
Wetzler, Richard S. ....Prairie Village, KS
Wetzler, Sandra S. ....Costa Mesa, CA
Wetzstein, Tracey S. ....Hammond, IN
Weule, Broyles, Ballard & Mondo, LLP
Irvine, CA
Riverside, CA
San Diego, CA
Santa Ana, CA
Weule, M. Colleen ....Irvine, CA
Weum, Gregory J. ....Monona, WI
Wever, Michael E. ....Columbia, SC
Wever, Nancy E. ....San Francisco, CA
Wever, Paul B., Jr. ....Evansville, IN
Weverka, Philip L. ....Oakland, CA
Wewer Law Firm ....San Francisco, CA
Washington, DC
Helena, MT
Wewer, William ....San Francisco, CA
Washington, DC
Helena, MT
Wewers, Eric D. ....Dallas, TX
Wewers, Mark E. ....Dallas, TX
Wex, Terry A. ....Grand Marsh, WI
Wexberg, Marcia J. ....Cleveland, OH
Wexelbaum, Michael ....New York, NY
Wexelblat, Gray H. ....Concord, MA
Wexelblatt, Elizabeth Marx ....Boston, MA
Wexelblatt, Keith E. ....Stoughton, MA
Wexelblatt, S. R. ....Glenside, PA
Wexell & Goldsby ....Fairfax, VA
Wexell, Richard M. ....Fairfax, VA
Wexelman, Pami ....New York, NY
Wexler, Alan S. ....Buffalo, NY
Wexler, April M. ....Brooklyn, NY
Wexler, Arlene Gold ....Rye, NY
Wexler, Barbara L. ....Boston, MA
Wexler, Ben K. ....Greeneville, TN
Wexler, Brian Keith ....Aspen, CO
Wexler, Bruce J. ....New York, NY
Wexler, Bruce M. ....New York, NY
Wexler & Burkhart, P.C. ....Uniondale, NY
Wexler, Charles W., Jr. ....Spring, TX
Wexler, Daniel M. ....Minneapolis, MN
Wexler, Danniel J. ....Newport Beach, CA
Wexler, David ....St. Louis Park, MN
Wexler, David B. ....Tucson, AZ
Wexler, David D. ....Beverly Hills, CA
Wexler, David D. ....Millbrae, CA
Wexler, Donna L. ....Springfield, MA
Wexler, Douglas B. ....Chicago, IL
Wexler, Eric J. ....Southfield, MI
Wexler, Frank S. ....Mansfield, MO
Wexler, Fred G. ....New York, NY
Wexler, Gary A. ....Los Angeles, CA
Wexler, Gary D. ....Hopewell Junction, NY
Wexler, Gene L. ....Uniondale, NY
Wexler, Gregg R. ....West Palm Beach, FL
Wexler, Harry J. ....New Haven, CT
Wexler, Howard B. ....Atlanta, GA
Wexler, Howard L. ....New York, NY
Wexler, Howard M. ....San Francisco, CA
Wexler, Ilan ....Youngstown, OH
Wexler, Jacob S. ....New York, NY
Wexler, James H. ....Boston, MA
Wexler, Janet L. ....New York, NY
Wexler, Jason S. ....Memphis, TN
Wexler, Jeffrey D. ....Los Angeles, CA
Wexler, Jeffrey Stuart ....Philadelphia, PA
Wexler, Jerome E. ....Chicago, IL
Wexler, Joan G. ....Brooklyn, NY
Wexler, Joel G. ....Garden City, NY
Wexler, Jonathan A. ....New York, NY
Wexler, Jonathan E. ....Beverly Hills, CA
Wexler, Judith M. ....Chicago, IL
Wexler, Kenneth A. ....Chicago, IL
Wexler, Lawrence H. ....Atlanta, GA
Wexler, Lelia Sadat ....St. Louis, MO
Wexler, Leon C. ....Chicago, IL
Wexler, Leonard D. ....Hauppauge, NY
Wexler, Lisa K. ....Westport, CT
Wexler, Louis ....Overland Park, KS
Wexler, Marian P. ....Chicago, IL
Wexler, Marvin ....New York, NY
Wexler, Maurice ....Memphis, TN
Wexler, Maximillion M. ....Minnetonka, MN
Wexler, Michael D. ....Chicago, IL
Wexler, Michael Folz ....San Diego, CA
Wexler, Michael H. ....San Diego, CA
Wexler, Michael Irwin ....Chicago, IL
Wexler, Mitchell H. ....Chicago, IL
Wexler, Norman P. ....Chicago, IL
Wexler, Oscar S. ....Colorado Springs, CO
Wexler, Paul A. ....Englewood, CO
Wexler, Paul D. ....New York, NY
Wexler, Peter ....Boston, MA
Wexler, Raymond P., (P.C.) ....Chicago, IL
Wexler, Richard A. ....St. Paul, MN
Wexler, Richard L. ....Chicago, IL
Wexler, Robert ....Department of Education, Office of the General Counsel, GV
Wexler, Robert A. ....San Francisco, CA
Wexler, Robert E. ....North Chicago, IL
Wexler, Robert H. ....St. Louis, MO
Wexler, Robert I. ....Saddle Brook, NJ
New York, NY
Wexler, Robin L. ....Baltimore, MD
Wexler, Samuel C. ....Lancaster, OH
Wexler, Saul R. ....Beverly Hills, CA
Wexler, Seth D. ....Houston, TX
Wexler, Sidney D. ....New York, NY
Wexler, Stacey L. ....San Francisco, CA
Wexler, Stephen B. ....Uniondale, NY
Wexler, Stephen J. ....United States Senate, Committee Legal Personnel, GV
Wexler, Stuart J. ....New York, NY
Wexler, Thomas W. ....Minneapolis, MN
Wexler & Wexler ....Chicago, IL
Wexler, Wexler & Agosta ....Millbrae, CA
Wexler, William D. ....North Babylon, NY
Wexler-Wuebker, Mara ....Haddonfield, NJ
Wexley, Matthew H. ....New York, NY
Wexner, Ira H. ....Mineola, NY
Wexstten, James M. ....Mount Vernon, IL
Wexton, Jane L. ....Stamford, CT
Weyand, Alexander M.
San Francisco, CA
Weyand, Dale ....San Antonio, TX
Weyand, Erich S. ....Gowanda, NY
Weyand, Fredric F. ....Gowanda, NY
Weyand, Fredric H. ....Gowanda, NY
Weyand, Jamie ....San Francisco, CA
Weyand, John H. ....Carrollton, OH
Weyand, Karl J., Jr. ....Saginaw, MI
Weyand & Weyand ....Gowanda, NY
Weyandt, Charles J. ....State College, PA
Weyandt, Gregory M. ....Minneapolis, MN
Weyandt, Thomas J. ....St. Paul, MN
Weyant, James M. ....Torrance, CA
Weyant, Laura A. ....Yorktown Heights, NY
Weyant, Piers J. ....Fairburn, GA
Weyant Kearney, Laura ....Teaneck, NJ
Weybrew, Sydney F., Jr. ....North Chicago, IL
Weybright, Leslie S. ....Boise, ID
Weycer, Albert S. ....Houston, TX
Weycer, Kaplan, Pulaski & Zuber, P.C.
Houston, TX
Weycer, Mark A. ....Houston, TX
Weydert, James C. ....Stockton, CA
Weyer, Brenda ....Sun Prairie, WI
Weyer, David A. ....Mountlake Terrace, WA
Weyer, Eugene E. ....Sun Prairie, WI
Weyer, Frank M. ....Los Angeles, CA
Weyer, Sally A. ....Iowa City, IA
Weyerbacher, Dewey & Weyerbacher
Boonville, IN
Newburgh, IN
Weyerbacher, John W. ....Boonville, IN
Weygandt, James P. ....Collegeville, PA
Weygandt, Peter J. ....Oxford, PA
Weygandt, Richard S. ....Fairmont, WV
Weygandt, Thomas J. ....Wooster, OH
Weygant, Cynthia M. ....Gainesville, FL
Weyher, Barbara B. ....Raleigh, NC
Weyher, Harry F. ....New York, NY
Weyhing, Robert L. ....Detroit, MI
Weyhing, Sheri Beth ....Louisville, KY
Weyhing, Steven D. ....Lansing, MI
Weyhrauch, Bruce B. ....Juneau, AK
Weyhrauch, Bruce B., LLC, Law Office of
Juneau, AK
Weyhrauch, LuAnn E.B. ....Juneau, AK
Weyhrich, Joseph H. ....St. Louis, MO
Weyl, Charles F. ....Birchrunville, PA
Weyl, John A. ....Glendale, CA
Weyl, Kenneth C. ....Scottsdale, AZ
Weyl, Lewin J. ....Trenton, NJ
Weyl, Stephen E. ....Concord, NH
Manchester, NH
Weyland, John L. ....St. Paul, MN
Weyland, John L., Professional Association
St. Paul, MN
Weylandt, Elizabeth P. ....Houston, TX
Weylandt, Robert M. ....Houston, TX
Weyler, Laura ....New York, NY
Weylie, Wallace J. D.
Indian Rocks Beach, FL
Weyls, Timothy J., Jr. ....Cleveland, OH
Weyman, Mark L. ....New York, NY
Weymann, Thomas F. ....New Orleans, LA
Weymouth, Ann G. ....Elkhart, IN
Weymouth, Lucy C. ....Washington, DC
Weymouth, Richard D.
Wisconsin Rapids, WI
Weymouth, Stephen J. ....Boston, MA
Weymouth, T. Clark ....Washington, DC
Weynand, John A. ....San Antonio, TX
Weyrauch, John M. ....Minneapolis, MN
Weyrens, J. J. ....Litchfield, MN
Weyrich, Richard A. ....Mount Vernon, WA
Weyrich & Verge ....Mount Vernon, WA
Weyuker, Richard A. ....Sacramento, CA
Wezdecki, Isabella I. ....New York, NY
Wezelman, James D. ....Tucson, AZ
Wezelman, James D., P.C., Law Offices of
Tucson, AZ
Wezelman, Janice A. ....Tucson, AZ
Wezelman, Joy L. ....Bismarck, ND
Wezelman, Stanley J. ....San Diego, CA
Wezner, Michelle M. ....Detroit, MI
Whaland, Robert G. ....Manchester, NH
Whale, Arthur R. ....Indianapolis, IN
Whalen, A. Ruth ....Wilkes-Barre, PA
Whalen, Alison M. ....Los Angeles, CA
Whalen, Andrew J., III ....Griffin, GA
Whalen, Andrew J., Jr. ....Griffin, GA
Whalen, Anthony ....Kansas City, MO
Whalen, Arthur J., Jr. ....Silver Spring, MD
Whalen, B. E. (Pete) ....Goodland, KS
Whalen, Bernard J., Jr. ....South Hadley, MA
Whalen, Bradley M. ....Houston, TX
Whalen, Charles E. ....Chicago, IL
Whalen, Charles T. ....Chicago, IL
Whalen, Colleen H. ....Clifton Park, NY
Whalen & Compton, A Legal Professional Association ....Akron, OH
Whalen, Cory P. ....Minneapolis, MN
Whalen, Curtis E. ....Washington, DC
Whalen, Daniel A. ....Albany, NY
Whalen, Daniel G. ....Los Angeles, CA
Whalen, Daniel J. ....Covington, KY
Whalen, Daniel W. ....Pittsburgh, PA
Whalen, David S ....Scotia, NY
Whalen, Dean M. ....South Hadley, MA
Whalen, Deborah Lin ....Dallas, TX
Whalen, Denise ....Plandome, NY
Whalen, Denn ....Odessa, TX
Whalen, Dennis M. ....Akron, OH
Whalen, Dennis R., P.L.C.
Baton Rouge, LA
Whalen, Donald C. ....Framingham, MA
Whalen, Donna Hylarides ....Phoenix, AZ
Whalen, Edward J., Jr. ....Chicago, IL
Whalen, Elizabeth A. ....New Haven, CT
Whalen, Firestone, Landsman, Fleming & Dixon, L.L.P. ....Seattle, WA
Whalen, Frank C. ....Cleveland, OH
Whalen, Frank J., Jr. ....Washington, DC
Whalen, George E. ....Dover Plains, NY
Whalen, Gerald J. ....Buffalo, NY
Eden, NY
Whalen, J. Michael ....Wichita Falls, TX
Whalen, J. Patrick, Jr. ....Asheville, NC
Whalen, James H. ....Pittsburgh, PA
Whalen, James M. ....Boston, MA
Whalen, James M. ....Springfield, MA
Whalen, James P. ....Plano, TX
Whalen, James T. ....Cross River, NY
Whalen, James T., Jr. ....Cross River, NY
Whalen, James W. ....Pittsburgh, PA
Whalen, Jason M. ....Tacoma, WA
Whalen, Jeanmarie, (P.A.)
Palm Beach Gardens, FL
Whalen, Jeffrey B. ....Treasury Department, Office of Regulations and Rulings, GV

Whalen, Jerome D. ..... Seattle, WA
Whalen, Jerry W. ..... Syracuse, NY
Whalen, Jill B. ..... Columbus, OH
Whalen, Joanna Delgado ..... Atlanta, GA
Whalen, Joanne C. ..... Valhalla, NY
Whalen, John B., Jr. ..... Media, PA
Whalen, John L., II ..... Arlington, VT
Whalen, John M. ..... Lewiston, ME
Whalen, John M. ..... Arlington, VT
Whalen, John M., P.A. ..... Lewiston, ME
Whalen, Jon P. ..... Hamilton, OH
Whalen, Joseph P. ..... Fairview Heights, IL
Whalen, Karla D. ..... Washington, DC
Whalen, Kathleen M. ..... Nashville, TN
Whalen, Kearons J., III ..... Pittsfield, MA
Whalen, Kelley F. ..... Gonzales, TX
Whalen, Kenneth C. ..... Tampa, FL
Whalen, Kirk E. ..... Davenport, IA
Whalen, Laurence J. .....
United States Tax Court, GV
Whalen, Lawrence Michael ..... Houston, TX
Whalen, Linda L. ..... Greensburg, PA
Whalen, Linda P. ..... Akron, OH
Whalen, Lyndanne M. ..... Pittsburgh, PA
Whalen, M. Gwyneth ..... Boulder, CO
Whalen, Mark L. ..... New York, NY
Whalen, Martin J. ..... Phoenix, AZ
Whalen, Mary Kate ..... Department of Justice,
Drug Enforcement Administration, GV
Whalen, Mary Lynne ..... Washington, DC
Whalen, Maureen T. ..... Burbank, CA
Whalen, Melissa J. ..... Cincinnati, OH
Whalen, Michael C. ..... Houston, TX
Whalen, Michael D. ..... Jacksonville, FL
Whalen, Michael J. ..... Branford, CT
Whalen, Michael J. ..... Dubuque, IA
Whalen, Michael J. ..... Billings, MT
Whalen, Michael P. ..... Costa Mesa, CA
Whalen, Michael P. ..... Washington, DC
Whalen, Michael P. ..... Upper Marlboro, MD
Whalen, Michele M.
Small Business Administration, GV
Whalen, Mike ..... Knoxville, TN
Whalen, Myles V., Jr. ..... New York, NY
Whalen, Oakley R. ..... Elverta, CA
Whalen, Patricia Ann ..... Springfield, VT
Whalen, Patricia Anne ..... Boston, MA
Whalen, Patrick E. ..... Costa Mesa, CA
Whalen, Patrick E., Law Offices of
Costa Mesa, CA
Whalen, Patrick J. ..... Kansas City, MO
Whalen, Patrick J. ..... Roseland, NJ
Whalen, Paul C. ..... New York, NY
Whalen, Paul L. ..... Fort Thomas, KY
Whalen, Peter J. ..... San Francisco, CA
Whalen, Ralph S., Jr. ..... Covington, LA
New Orleans, LA
Whalen, Richard E. ..... East Hampton, NY
Whalen, Richard Gerald ..... Boston, MA
Whalen, Richard T. ..... Lighthouse Point, FL
Whalen, Robert F. ..... Endicott, NY
Whalen, Robert J. ..... Newport Beach, CA
Whalen, Robert P., Jr. ..... Boston, MA
Whalen, Ryann ..... Chicago, IL
Whalen, Stephen C. ..... Tampa, FL
Whalen, Stephen R. ..... Baton Rouge, LA
Whalen, Stephen W. ..... Branford, CT
Whalen, Suzanne T. ..... Cross River, NY
Whalen, Teresa ..... Washington, DC
Whalen, Terry Lois ..... Cynthiana, KY
Whalen, Thomas ..... Owasso, OK
Whalen, Thomas J. ..... Washington, DC
Whalen, Thomas J. ..... Dover Plains, NY
Whalen, Thomas J. ..... New York, NY
Whalen, Thomas M., III ..... Albany, NY
Whalen, Thomas P.
Manchester Center, VT
Whalen, Thomas P., Law Offices of
Bennington, VT
Manchester Center, VT
Whalen, Timothy J. ..... Billings, MT
Whalen, Timothy L. ..... West Palm Beach, FL
Whalen, Vanessa Kelly ..... Boston, MA
Whalen, Wayne W. ..... Chicago, IL
Whalen & Whalen ..... South Hadley, MA
Whalen & Whalen ..... Billings, MT
Whalen & Whalen ..... Cross River, NY
Whalen and Whalen ..... Dover Plains, NY
Whalen & Whalen ..... Arlington, VT
Whalen, William D. ..... New York, NY
Whalen, William E. ..... Treasure Island, FL
Whalen, William J. ..... Torrance, CA
Whalen, William J. ..... Asheville, NC
Whalen-Giannandrea, Kathleen
Rockland, MA
Whaley, A. Robert ..... Tallahassee, FL
Whaley, Barbara Maines ..... Frankfort, KY
Whaley, Bonnie A. ..... Orange, CA
Whaley, C. David ..... Richmond, VA
Whaley, Daniel P. ..... Sacramento, CA
Whaley, Donald H. ..... Fenton, MO
Whaley, Douglas J. ..... Columbus, OH
Whaley, E. Mitchell ..... Fort Myers, FL
Whaley, Gail Cecchettini ..... Sacramento, CA
Whaley, Gary M. ..... Durham, NC
Whaley, Hamilton H. ..... Tampa, FL
Whaley and Higgins ..... Fenton, MO
Whaley, J. Patrick ..... Los Angeles, CA
Whaley, James D. L. ..... Novato, CA
Whaley, James E. ..... St. Louis, MO
Whaley, James S. ..... San Diego, CA
Whaley, James T. ..... Palo Alto, CA
Whaley, Jayann Lambert ..... St. Louis, MO
Whaley, John Hunt ..... Spokane, WA
Whaley, John R. ..... Lafayette, LA
Whaley, John S., Jr. ..... Charleston, SC
Whaley, John V. ..... Racine, WI
Whaley, John William (Jay)
Federal Communications Commission,
Wireless Telecommunications Bureau, GV
Whaley, Joseph R. ..... Rockville, MD
Whaley, Joseph R., P.C. ..... Rockville, MD
Whaley, Kelley A. ..... Sylva, NC
Whaley, Kevin P. ..... Milwaukee, WI
Whaley, Kimberly K. ..... Brentwood, TN
Whaley, L. Alan ..... Indianapolis, IN
Whaley, Lucinda S. ..... Spokane, WA
Whaley, Lynn Ann ..... St. Louis, MO
Whaley, Michael J. ..... Omaha, NE
Whaley, Patricia M. ..... Milwaukee, WI
Whaley, Patrick Knox ..... Atlanta, GA
Whaley, Phillip G. ..... Oklahoma City, OK
Whaley, R. Michael ..... Atlanta, GA
Whaley, Richard A. ..... Salisbury, MA
Whaley, Richard C. ..... Colorado Springs, CO
Whaley, Robert D. ..... Dallas, TX
Whaley, Robert H. ..... Spokane, WA
Whaley, Thomas H. ..... Mount Vernon, NY
Whaley, Warren D. ..... Irvine, CA
Whaley, William H. ..... Hannibal, MO
Whaley, Wyletter Vatonia ..... Richardson, TX
Whalin, Dave ..... Louisville, KY
Whalin, David M.
Department Of Health And Human Services,
Social Security Administration, GV
Whaling, Allan ..... Dublin, OH
Whaling, Greg M. ..... San Francisco, CA
Whaling, Horace M. ..... Wichita Falls, TX
Whaling, Michael J. ..... Port Huron, MI
Whaling, Thomas M. ..... El Toro, CA
Whall, Robert J., (P.C.) ..... Livonia, MI
Whalley, Christopher James ..... Ellsworth, ME
Whalley, Douglas B. ..... Seattle, WA
Whallon, Christopher C. ..... Voorhees, NJ
Whall-Sudnick, Sandra A. ..... Auburn Hills, MI
Wham, Fred L., III ..... Rockford, IL
Wham, Fred L., Jr. ..... Centralia, IL
Wham, G. Mark ..... Houston, TX
Wham, James B. ..... Centralia, IL
Wham, Mark ..... Houston, TX
Wham, Robert S. ..... Denver, CO
Wham & Wham ..... Carlyle, IL
Centralia, IL
Mount Vernon, IL
Salem, IL
Vandalia, IL
Wham, William B. ..... Centralia, IL
Wham, William D. ..... Arlington, VA
Whamond, Wilbur O. ..... Park Ridge, IL
Whan, James W. ..... Maryville, MO
Whang, Edward H. ..... New York, NY
Whang, Jane ..... San Francisco, CA
Whang, Jennifer ..... Seattle, WA
Whang, Julie K. ..... Costa Mesa, CA
Whang, Jun C. ..... New York, NY
Whang, Sung Chul ..... New York, NY
Whang, Vanessa W. ..... Sacramento, CA
Whann, Keith E. ..... Dublin, OH
Whann, Richard A., (P.C.)
New Orleans, LA
Whann, Welton B. ..... Carlsbad, CA
Wharf, Inga C. ..... Portland, OR
Wharin, Marsha B. ..... Miami, FL
Wharmby, David E. ..... Knoxville, TN
Wharrie and Albers, P.A.
St. Petersburg, FL
Wharrie, Larry G. ..... Markham, IL
Wharrie, Robert E. ..... St. Petersburg, FL
Wharry, Allison D. ..... Indianapolis, IN
Whartenby, Catherine E. ..... Wellsboro, PA
Wharton, A C, Jr. ..... Memphis, TN
Wharton, Alan D. ..... Tyler, TX
Wharton Aldhizer & Weaver, PLC
Harrisonburg, VA
Wharton, Amy A. ..... Arlington, VA
Wharton, Bernard W. ..... Cincinnati, OH
Wharton, Brooke Ann ..... Los Angeles, CA
Wharton, Cathleen S. ..... Athens, GA
Wharton, Dave, III ..... San Francisco, CA
Wharton, Denver E. ..... Johnstown, PA
Wharton, Donald E. ..... Sacramento, CA
Wharton, Donald L., II ..... New Milford, CT
Wharton, Donald R. ..... Boulder, CO
Wharton, Ellan K. ..... Washington, DC
Wharton, Garry L. ..... Columbus, OH
Wharton, Gregory P. G. ..... Santa Clara, CA
Wharton, J. David ..... Kansas City, MO
Wharton, J. Thomas ..... Rockwall, TX
Wharton, J. Thomas, P.C. ..... Rockwall, TX
Wharton, James C. ..... Livermore, CA
Wharton, James L. ..... Lubbock, TX
Wharton, James T. ..... Annapolis, MD
Baltimore, MD
Wharton, Jason A. ..... Parkersburg, WV
Wharton, Jeanette H. ..... Dallas, TX
Wharton, Jenifer M. ..... Schenectady, NY
Wharton, Joan S. ..... New York, NY
Wharton, John Gill ..... Baltimore, MD
Wharton, John L. ..... Tallahassee, FL
Wharton, John M. ..... Des Moines, IA
Wharton, John V. ..... Covington, KY
Wharton, Joseph N. ..... Chicago, IL
Wharton, Joyce A. ..... San Diego, CA
Wharton, Kathleen J. ..... Chicago, IL
Wharton, L. Patricia ..... Columbia, SC
Wharton, Lawrence M. ..... Chardon, OH
Wharton, Leslie ..... Washington, DC
Wharton Levin Ehrmantraut Klein & Nash, A Professional Association
Washington, DC
Annapolis, MD
Baltimore, MD
Bethesda, MD
Easton, MD
Ellicott City, MD
Rockville, MD
Upper Marlboro, MD
Wharton, Linda J. ..... Haddonfield, NJ
Wharton, Lisa M. ..... Cincinnati, OH
Wharton, Maureen A. ..... Houston, TX
Wharton, Michael T. ..... Annapolis, MD
Baltimore, MD
Wharton, Michael W. ..... Overland Park, KS
Wharton, Michele Y. ..... Cleveland, OH
Wharton, Milton S. ..... Belleville, IL
Wharton, Patricia Hill ..... St. Louis, MO
Wharton, Paul K. ..... Anchorage, AK
Wharton, Phillip Leslie ..... Atlanta, GA
Wharton, Richard J. ..... San Diego, CA
Wharton, Robert A., Jr. ..... Rossville, GA
Wharton, Shelley E. ..... San Francisco, CA
Wharton, Stephen E. ..... Fairfax, OH
Wharton, Susan J. ..... Kansas City, MO
Wharton, Tom H., Jr. ..... Houston, TX
Wharton, V. Lane, Jr. ..... Raleigh, NC
Wharton, W. Paul ..... Salt Lake City, UT
Wharton, William B. ..... Department of State,
Bureau of Consular Affairs, GV
Wharton, William B. ..... Houston, TX
Whately, Randall P. ..... Detroit, MI
Whatley, Anne M. ..... Vancouver, WA
Whatley, David K. ..... Atlanta, GA
Whatley Drake, L.L.C. ..... Birmingham, AL
Whatley, Frederick W. ..... Cleveland, OH
Whatley, Holly O. ..... Los Angeles, CA
Whatley, Jacqueline B. ..... Tampa, FL
Whatley, James W. ..... Lakeland, FL
Whatley, Jennifer L. ..... Seattle, WA
Whatley, Jerry D. ..... Santa Barbara, CA
Whatley, Joe R., Jr. ..... Birmingham, AL
Whatley, John H. ..... Pasadena, CA
Whatley, John T. ..... Arlington, VA
Whatley, Karen S. ..... Mobile, AL
Whatley, L. McKay ..... Asheboro, NC
Whatley, Mark D. ..... San Francisco, CA
Whatley, Melba Davis ..... Austin, TX
Whatley, Michael D. ..... Charlotte, NC
Whatley, Milly ..... Bend, OR
Whatley, Nathan L. ..... Oklahoma City, OK
Whatley, Rita Beth ..... McAllen, TX
Whatley, Robert B. ..... La Grange, GA
Whatley, Robert B., P.C. ..... La Grange, GA
Whatley, Robert L. ..... Atlanta, GA
Whatley, Shelly ..... Houston, TX
Whatley, Thomas G., Jr. ..... Savannah, GA
Whatley, Thomas L.
House of Representatives,
Congressional Assistants, GV
Whatley, William Neil ..... Birmingham, AL
Whatley, William T. ..... Vidalia, GA
Whatley, William W., Jr.
Montgomery, AL
Whatley-Gould, Gale D. ..... Birmingham, AL
Whattam, James R. ..... Baltimore, MD
Whay, Henry Todd ..... Chantilly, VA
Whayland, Deadra ..... Arlington, VA
Whealan, David W. ..... New York, NY
Whealan, John M.
Department of Commerce,
Patent and Trademark Office, GV
Whealdon, Karol A. ..... San Diego, CA
Wheale, Duncan D. ..... Augusta, GA
Whealen, John T.
Department of Defense, GV
Whealen, William F., Jr. ..... St. Louis, MO
Whealy, Michael T. ..... Atlanta, GA
Whearty, John W. ..... Portland, OR
Wheary, William A., III
Virginia Beach, VA
Wheat, A. C., Jr. ..... Midland, TX
Wheat, Allen N. ..... Angola, IN
Wheat, C. Douglas ..... Houston, TX
Wheat, Cristina Romig ..... New Orleans, LA
Wheat, Dick M. ..... Lexington, KY
Wheat, Donald R. ..... Stillwater, OK
Wheat, Douglas D. ..... Dallas, TX
Wheat, Francis M. ..... Los Angeles, CA
Wheat, Fred E. ..... Chattanooga, TN
Wheat, J. Nixon ..... Liberty, TX
Wheat, J. Robert ..... Chattanooga, TN
Wheat, Jack A. ..... Louisville, KY
Wheat, James C. ..... Manchester, NH
Wheat, James E. ..... Iselin, NJ
Wheat, Joe F. ..... Houston, TX
Wheat, John Marc ..... House of Representatives,
Committee Legal Personnel, GV
Wheat, John W. ..... Houston, TX
Wheat, Josiah ..... Woodville, TX
Wheat, Josiah, Jr. ..... Beaumont, TX
Wheat, Judith L. ..... Washington, DC
Wheat, Latrealle ..... Angola, IN
Wheat, Laura Tabler ..... Dallas, TX
Wheat, Lutie A. ..... Metairie, LA
Wheat, Michael E. ..... Bozeman, MT
Wheat, Michael G. ..... San Diego, CA
Wheat, Penny L. ..... Glendale, CA
Wheat, R. David ..... Dallas, TX
Wheat, Ralph D. ..... Columbus, OH
Wheat, Sandra Jean ..... London, OH
Wheat, Smith & Beres, PLC
Louisville, KY
Wheat, Stacy Cottrell ..... Metairie, LA
Wheat, Thomas A. ..... Liberty, TX
Wheat, Tim M. ..... Dallas, TX
Wheat, Tom C. ..... Corpus Christi, TX
Wheat & Wheat ..... Houston, TX
Wheat & Wheat, P.C. ..... Liberty, TX
Wheatcraft, Jane W. ..... Gallatin, TN
Wheatcraft, William G. ..... Des Moines, IA
Wheatcroft, Gary D. ..... Pasadena, CA
Wheatcroft, John B. ..... Miles City, MT
Wheatley, Adrienne K. ..... New York, NY
Wheatley, Benton T. ..... Broken Arrow, OK
Wheatley, Carolyn J. ..... Louisville, KY
Wheatley, Carroll A., Jr. ..... Pasadena, CA
Wheatley, Charles F., Jr. ..... Annapolis, MD
Wheatley, Charles H., III ..... Severna Park, MD
Wheatley, Charles N., Jr. ..... Chicago, IL
Wheatley, Diana M. ..... Los Angeles, CA
Wheatley, Ford H., IV ..... Denver, CO
Wheatley, H. Winship, III ..... Annapolis, MD
Wheatley, Jack F. ..... Lansing, MI
Wheatley, Jay D. ..... Boca Raton, FL
Wheatley, Jennifer D. ..... Washington, DC
Wheatley, John C. ..... Columbus, OH
Wheatley, John Clark ..... Wareham, MA
Wheatley, John E. ..... Yukon, OK
Wheatley, Katherine H.
Board of Governors Of The Federal Reserve
System,
Office of the General Counsel, GV
Wheatley, Kevin P. ..... Clifton Park, NY
Wheatley, Lawrence R. ..... Danville, IN
Wheatley, Matthew L. ..... Yukon, OK
Wheatley, Myron Daniel ..... Chardon, OH
Wheatley Osaki & Associates ..... Fullerton, CA
Long Beach, CA
Wheatley & Ranquist ..... Annapolis, MD
Wheatley, Robert M. ..... Folsom, CA
Wheatley, Russell Spencer ..... Dallas, TX
Wheatley, Scott A. ..... Dallas, TX
Wheatley, Scott M. ..... Annandale, VA
Wheatley, Seagal V. ..... San Antonio, TX
Wheatley, Segler & Wheatley, P.C.
Yukon, OK
Wheatley, Seth ..... Greenwood, MS
Wheatley, Shelley A. ..... Santa Ana, CA
Wheatley, Stanley W. ..... Boston, MA
Wheatley, Susan E. ..... Cincinnati, OH
Wheatley, Thomas B. ..... Portland, ME
Wheatley, Thomas J. ..... Kansas City, MO
Wheatley, William G. ..... Eugene, OR
Wheatley, William G., Jr. ..... Solana Beach, CA
Wheatley, William L. ..... Fall River, MA
Wheatley-Liss, Deirdre R. ..... Parsippany, NJ
Wheatly, Claud R., III ..... Beaufort, NC
Wheatly, Claud R., Jr. ..... Beaufort, NC
Wheatly, R. Stephen ..... Thousand Oaks, CA
Wheatly, Ralph S. ..... Roswell, GA
Wheatly, Wheatly, Nobles & Weeks, P.A.
Beaufort, NC
Wheatly, William R. ..... Lancaster, PA
Wheaton, Barbara K. ..... Portland, ME
Wheaton, Bonnie M. ..... Wheaton, IL
Wheaton, Boyd & Horne ..... Putnam, CT
Wheaton, Carolyn White ..... Akron, OH
Wheaton, Craig B. ..... Raleigh, NC
Wheaton, David T. ..... Edison, NJ
Wheaton, Donald C., Jr. ..... Detroit, MI
Wheaton, Douglas B. ..... Milwaukee, WI
Wheaton, Dwight, II ..... Seattle, WA
Wheaton, Harry O., Jr. ..... Alliance, OH
Wheaton, James J. ..... Norfolk, VA
Wheaton, James R. ..... Oakland, CA
Wheaton, Jill M. ..... Detroit, MI
Wheaton, John R. ..... Minneapolis, MN
Wheaton, Kristin Klein ..... Buffalo, NY
Wheaton, Melvin E. ..... Seattle, WA
Wheaton & Morris ..... Alliance, OH
Wheaton, O. Andrew ..... Los Angeles, CA
Wheaton, Rena M. ..... Los Angeles, CA
Wheaton, Robin L. ..... Flint, MI
Wheaton, Scott R. ..... Lansing, IL
Wheaton, Scott R., Jr. ..... New Orleans, LA
Wheaton, Sherry W. ..... Summit, NJ
Wheaton, Willie J. ..... Brockton, MA
Wheaton, Winston A. ..... Grand Rapids, MI
Wheble, Kathryn M. ..... San Francisco, CA
Whedbee, Charles M. ..... Treasury Department,
Internal Revenue Service, GV
Whedbee, Rosbon D. B. ..... Ahoskie, NC
Whedon, Dennis E. ..... Jackson, MI
Whedon, Dennis E., P.C. ..... Jackson, MI
Whedon, Parker ..... Charlotte, NC
Wheeker, Michael J.
Palm Beach Gardens, FL
Wheeker, Thomas R. ..... Lansing, MI
Wheelahan, Harold M., III
New Orleans, LA
Wheelan, Peter John ..... Tiburon, CA
Wheelan, R. E. ..... Houston, TX
Wheeland, Amanda R. ..... Irvine, CA
Wheeland, David R. ..... Chicago, IL
Wheeland, Robert ..... San Bernardino, CA
Wheeldin, Anthony ..... Cotati, CA
Wheelehan, Kerry Mahon ..... St. Petersburg, FL
Wheeler, Albert L., III
Oklahoma City, OK
Wheeler, Alfred ..... New York, NY
Wheeler, Alison G. ..... Denver, CO
Wheeler, Allan B. ..... Brookfield, WI
Wheeler, Allan R. ..... Birmingham, AL
Wheeler, Amanda G. ..... Yorba Linda, CA
Wheeler, Ann Behlen ..... Lock Haven, PA
Wheeler, Anne M. ("Nancy")
Washington, DC
Wheeler, Anne P. ..... Birmingham, AL
Wheeler, Annette S. ..... Bronxville, NY
Wheeler & Arey, P.A. ..... Waterville, ME
Wheeler, Arthur F. ..... Philadelphia, PA
Wheeler, Asher L. ..... Washington, DC
Wheeler and Bala ..... Oklahoma City, OK
Wheeler, Bancroft R. ..... Boston, MA
Wheeler, Benj. J. ..... Haverhill, MA
Wheeler, Brian E. ..... Detroit, MI
Wheeler, Brian E. ..... Portland, OR
Wheeler, Bryan T.
Department of the Air Force,
Office of the Judge Advocate General, GV
Wheeler, Calvin W. ..... Omaha, NE
Wheeler, Candace C. ..... Biloxi, MS

Wheeler, Carla L. ..... Washington, DC
Wheeler, Carolyn L.
Equal Employment Opportunity Commission, Office of the General Counsel, GV
Wheeler, C. B. ..... Texarkana, TX
Wheeler, Charles E. ..... San Diego, CA
Wheeler, Charles E. ..... Easton, MD
Wheeler, Charles F. ..... Venice, FL
Wheeler, Charles F., P.A. ..... Venice, FL
Wheeler, Charles H. ..... Los Angeles, CA
Wheeler, Charles H. ..... Green Bay, WI
Wheeler, Charles W. ..... Madison, WI
Wheeler, Cheri Marie
Oklahoma City, OK
Wheeler, Cheryl A. ..... Elkins, WV
Wheeler, Christina M. ..... San Francisco, CA
Wheeler, Christopher ..... Washington, DC
Wheeler, Christopher ..... Indianapolis, IN
Wheeler, Christopher C. ..... Boca Raton, FL
Wheeler, Clark W. ..... Gainesville, FL
Wheeler, Claudia Jean ..... New Port Richey, FL
Wheeler, Clay C. ..... Palo Alto, CA
Wheeler, Clinton A. ..... Macon, GA
Wheeler, Clyde L. ..... Waterville, ME
Wheeler, Courtney B. ..... Washington, DC
Wheeler, Cristy S. ..... Indianapolis, IN
Wheeler, Daniel F. ..... Cleveland, OH
Wheeler, Daniel H. ..... Philadelphia, PA
Wheeler, Daniel P. ..... Kansas City, MO
Wheeler, Daniel R. ..... Lubbock, TX
Wheeler, David ..... Boston, MA
Wheeler, David A. ..... Biloxi, MS
Wheeler, David B. ..... Charleston, SC
Wheeler, David C. ..... Los Angeles, CA
Wheeler, David E. ..... Los Angeles, CA
Wheeler, David E. ..... Washington, DC
Wheeler, David E. ..... Dayton, OH
Wheeler, David H. ..... Portland, OR
Wheeler, David Keith ..... Tulsa, OK
Wheeler, David L. ..... Syracuse, NY
Wheeler, David L. ..... Cincinnati, OH
Wheeler, David W. ..... Marion, KS
Wheeler, David W., Law Offices of
Hillsboro, KS
Marion, KS
Wheeler, Deborah A. ..... Guthrie, OK
Wheeler, Deborah L. ..... Boston, MA
Wheeler, Denise L. ..... Tampa, FL
Wheeler, Denise M. Miyasaki
Honolulu, HI
Wheeler, Dennis A. ..... Seward, AK
Wheeler, Dennis E. ..... Coeur d'Alene, ID
Wheeler, Dennis K., (A Professional Corporation) ..... Santa Monica, CA
Wheeler, Diana ..... Orange, VA
Wheeler, Diana E. ..... La Grange, KY
Wheeler, Diana L. ..... Flushing, NY
Wheeler, Dolores Lori ..... Orlando, FL
Wheeler, Don ..... Center, TX
Wheeler, Don E. ..... Lisle, IL
Wheeler, Douglas E. ..... Seattle, WA
Wheeler, Douglas P. ..... Los Angeles, CA
Washington, DC
Wheeler, E. Marie ..... Akron, OH
Wheeler, Edd D. ..... Atlanta, GA
Wheeler, Edward D. ..... Decatur, GA
Wheeler, Edward J. ..... Pasadena, TX
Wheeler, Edwin H. ..... Menlo Park, CA
Wheeler, Edwin J. ..... Tacoma, WA
Wheeler, Edwin M. ..... Washington, DC
Wheeler, Edwin M., Jr. ..... Marion, KS
Wheeler, Elizabeth C. ..... Orlando, FL
Wheeler, Elizabeth M. ..... Dalton, GA
Wheeler, Elizabeth S. ..... Brandon, FL
Wheeler, Elizabeth S. ..... New Orleans, LA
Wheeler, Ellen ..... Mountain View, CA
Wheeler, Ellen K. ..... Tucson, AZ
Wheeler, Ellen M. ..... Chicago, IL
Wheeler, Emily D. ..... Emeryville, CA
Wheeler, F. Robert, III ..... Washington, DC
Wheeler, Francis R. ..... Denver, CO
Wheeler, Frank C. ..... Venice, FL
Wheeler, Frank M. ..... Dallas, TX
Wheeler, Fredk. J., Jr. ..... Medford, MA
Wheeler, Gail ..... Charlotte, NC
Wheeler, Gary R. ..... Orlando, FL
Wheeler, Gene A. ..... Indianapolis, IN
Wheeler, George A. ..... Kansas City, MO
Wheeler, George F. ..... Chicago, IL
Wheeler, George T., Jr. ..... Memphis, TN
Wheeler, George Y., III ..... Washington, DC
Wheeler, Gerald W. ..... San Diego, CA
Wheeler, Gloria H. ..... Wheaton, MD
Wheeler, Grady Joseph, Jr. ..... Graham, NC
Wheeler, Gregory A. ..... Champlin, MN
Wheeler, Gregory H. ..... Atlanta, GA
Wheeler, Hackney & Miller, P.A.
Palm Beach Gardens, FL
Wheeler, Harold A., Sr. ..... Miami, FL
Wheeler, Harold C. ..... Chicago, IL
Wheeler, Henry ..... Boston, MA
Wheeler, Holly ..... Department Of The Interior, Office of the Solicitor, GV
Wheeler, Hugh A. ..... Kirkwood, NY
Wheeler, Irving W. ..... Winter Haven, FL
Wheeler, J. Joshua ..... Charlottesville, VA
Wheeler, J. Patrick ..... Canton, MO
Wheeler, J. Stewart, III ..... Russellville, KY
Wheeler, Jack G. ..... Lake Charles, LA
Wheeler, James A. ..... Olathe, KS
Wheeler, James C. ..... Atlanta, GA
Wheeler, James G. ..... Boston, MA
Wheeler, James G., Jr. ..... St. Johnsbury, VT
Wheeler, James J., (P.A.) ..... Boca Raton, FL
Wheeler, James K. ..... Carmel, IN
Wheeler, James Paul ..... Rockwall, TX
Wheeler, James R. ..... Johnson City, TN
Wheeler, James R., Jr. ..... Lynn, MA
Wheeler, James W. ..... Columbus, OH
Wheeler, Jane Chotard ..... Los Angeles, CA
Wheeler, Janet M. ..... Oklahoma City, OK
Wheeler, Janice O. ..... Arkadelphia, AR
Wheeler, Jansson S. ..... Madison, WI
Wheeler, Jas. J. ..... Keytesville, MO
Wheeler, Jeff D. ..... Chicago, IL
Wheeler, Jeffrey B. ..... Los Angeles, CA
Wheeler, Jeffrey D. ..... Mountain View, CA
Wheeler, Jeffrey R. ..... Colorado Springs, CO
Wheeler, Jeffrey R., P.C.
Colorado Springs, CO
Wheeler, Jeffrey S.
National Labor Relations Board, Office of Board Members, GV
Wheeler, Jennifer ..... Oklahoma City, OK
Wheeler, Joe D. ..... Oklahoma City, OK
Wheeler, Joe D., Jr. ..... Oklahoma City, OK
Wheeler, Joe S., Jr. ..... Russellville, KY
Wheeler, John Boone ..... Helena, MT
Wheeler, John C. ..... Albuquerque, NM
Las Cruces, NM
Truth or Consequences, NM
Wheeler, John D. ..... Alamogordo, NM
Wheeler, John D. ..... Cleveland, OH
Wheeler, John D. ..... Cleveland, OH
Wheeler, John G. ..... Tupelo, MS
Memphis, TN
Wheeler, John H.
Environmental Protection Agency, Office of Enforcement and Compliance Assurance, GV
Wheeler, John K. ..... Seattle, WA
Wheeler, John L. ..... Denver, CO
Wheeler, John P., Jr. ..... Garden City, KS
Wheeler, John R. ..... St. Paul, MN
Wheeler, John R. ..... Dallas, TX
Wheeler, John W. ..... Uhrichsville, OH
Wheeler, John W. ..... Knoxville, TN
Wheeler, Jonathan ..... Philadelphia, PA
Wheeler, Jonathan, P.C. ..... Philadelphia, PA
Wheeler, Joseph A. ..... Uhrichsville, OH
Wheeler, Joseph J. ..... San Diego, CA
Wheeler, Joseph N. ..... Somerville, MA
Wheeler, Joseph R. ..... Nashville, TN
Wheeler, Joyce W. ..... Charlotte, NC
Wheeler, Juliet ..... New York, NY
Wheeler, K. Douglas ..... Monroe, LA
Wheeler, Karen Hannah ..... Denver, CO
Wheeler, Karen M. ..... Washington, DC
Wheeler, Katherine ..... Baton Rouge, LA
Wheeler, Keith Paul ..... Rockwall, TX
Wheeler, Kenneth B. ..... Mount Dora, FL
Winter Park, FL
Wheeler, Kenneth B., LL.M. Tax, P.A.
Mount Dora, FL
Orlando, FL
Winter Park, FL
Wheeler, Kenneth E. ..... New York, NY
Wheeler, Kevin M. (IBA) ..... New Orleans, LA
Wheeler, Kimberly A. ..... Indianapolis, IN
Wheeler, Kimberly D. ..... Washington, DC
Wheeler & Korpeck, LLP
Silver Spring, MD
Wheeler, Kristin D. ..... San Francisco, CA
Wheeler, Laura ..... San Francisco, CA
Wheeler, Laurene A. ..... San Francisco, CA
Wheeler Law Office ..... Huron, SD
Wheeler, Lawrence A. ..... New Orleans, LA
Wheeler, Lawrence D. ..... Pacific Palisades, CA
Wheeler, Leroy M. ..... Indianapolis, IN
Wheeler, Leslie W. ..... Chatsworth, CA
Wheeler, Linda M. ..... Atlanta, GA
Wheeler, Lisa Jill ..... Duluth, GA
Wheeler, Lisha A. ..... Atlanta, GA
Wheeler, M. Wayne ..... Birmingham, AL
Wheeler, Malcolm E. ..... Denver, CO
Wheeler, Malcolm L. ..... Birmingham, AL
Wheeler, Marc ..... Centralia, WA
Wheeler, Margaret A. ..... Cambridge, MA
Wheeler, Margaret K. ..... Lebanon, NH
Wheeler, Margaret S. ..... Meridian, MS
Wheeler, Mark ..... Seattle, WA
Wheeler, Mark A. ..... Tampa, FL
Wheeler, Mark Andrew ..... Clarion, PA
Reynoldsville, PA
Wheeler, Mark B. ..... Ithaca, NY
Wheeler, Mark W. ..... Des Moines, IA
Wheeler, Mary Jane Krzys ..... Dallas, TX
Wheeler, Mary Louise ..... Hagåtña, GU
Wheeler, Max D. ..... Salt Lake City, UT
Wheeler, Mercedes Z. ..... Brawley, CA
Wheeler, Merlin G. ..... Emporia, KS
Wheeler, Michael A. ..... Cambridge, MA
Wheeler, Michael A. ..... Weyers Cave, VA
Wheeler, Michael C. ..... Lexington, KY
Wheeler, Michael R. ..... Baton Rouge, LA
Wheeler, Michael V. ..... Rapid City, SD
Wheeler & Mitchelson, Chartered
Pittsburg, KS
Wheeler, Morris H. ..... Cleveland, OH
Wheeler, M. Wayne, P.C. ..... Birmingham, AL
Wheeler, N. Janine ..... Oklahoma City, OK
Wheeler, Nancy E. ..... Racine, WI
Wheeler, Neal B. ..... Sherman, TX
Wheeler, Patricia J. ..... Yarmouth, ME
Wheeler, Patrick A. ..... Denver, CO
Wheeler, Patrick C. ..... Dallas, TX
Wheeler, Patty K. ..... Knoxville, TN
Wheeler, Pelton W. ..... Holland, OH
Wheeler, Perry D. ..... Cranston, RI
Wheeler, Peter ..... Atlanta, GA
Wheeler, Peter B. ..... Lawrenceville, GA
Wheeler, Peter L. ..... Oklahoma City, OK
Wheeler, Philip D. ..... Nashville, TN
Wheeler, Priscilla ..... Palo Alto, CA
Wheeler, Quinn C. ..... Phoenix, AZ
Wheeler, R. Dewey ..... Walnut Creek, CA
Wheeler, R. Marie ..... Farmington, MI
Wheeler, Randall L. ..... Frankfort, KY
Wheeler, Raymond L. ..... Palo Alto, CA
Wheeler, Regina Jay ..... Charlotte, NC
Wheeler, Richard F. ..... Tucson, AZ
Wheeler, Richard F. ..... Brandon, FL
Wheeler, Richard F. ..... Manassas, VA
Wheeler, Richard K. ..... Streator, IL
Wheeler, Richard R. ..... Louisville, KY
Wheeler, Richard S. ..... Winter Park, FL
Wheeler, Robert A. ..... Bedminster, NJ
Wheeler, Robert A. ..... Minot, ND
Wheeler, Robert C. ..... Martinez, CA
Wheeler, Robert D., Sr. ..... Grifton, NC
Wheeler, Robert E. ..... Broken Bow, NE
Wheeler, Robert G. ..... Denver, CO
Wheeler, Robert G. ..... Treasury Department, Internal Revenue Service, GV
Wheeler, Robert G. ..... Corpus Christi, TX
Wheeler, Robert G., Jr. ..... Nashville, TN
Wheeler, Robert H. ..... Georgetown, CO
Wheeler, Robert H. ..... Chicago, IL
Wheeler, Robert L. (Duke), (P.C.)
Oklahoma City, OK
Wheeler, Robert M. ..... Finksburg, MD
Wheeler, Robert R. ..... West Palm Beach, FL
Wheeler, Robert S. ..... Tulsa, OK
Wheeler, Robert S., Inc. ..... Tulsa, OK
Wheeler, Robert W. ..... Keytesville, MO
Wheeler, Robert Wakeley ..... Eugene, OR
Wheeler, Roger D. ..... Detroit, MI
Wheeler, Ronald C. ..... Los Angeles, CA
Wheeler, Ronald J. ..... Huron, SD
Wheeler & Russell ..... Center, TX
Wheeler, R. W. ..... Mandan, ND
Wheeler, Sally Zack ..... Denver, CO
Wheeler, Sara Kay ..... Atlanta, GA
Wheeler, Sara M. ..... Los Angeles, CA
Wheeler, Sarita Suzanne
Treasury Department, Office of the Comptroller of the Currency, GV
Wheeler, Sean T. ..... Birmingham, AL
Wheeler, Sharon Elizabeth ..... Montgomery, AL
Wheeler, Sheldon M. ..... Indianapolis, IN
Wheeler, Sidney F. ..... Atlanta, GA
Wheeler & Snyder ..... New York, NY
Wheeler, Stephanie G. ..... New York, NY
Wheeler, Stephen C. ..... Indianapolis, IN
Wheeler, Stephen L. ..... Fallbrook, CA
Wheeler, Stephen M. ..... Evergreen, CO
Wheeler, Stephen M., P.C. ..... Evergreen, CO
Wheeler, Steven M. ..... Phoenix, AZ
Wheeler, Steven S. ..... Hartford, CT
Wheeler, Stuart L. ..... Lakewood, CO
Wheeler, Terrence T. ..... Columbus, OH
Wheeler, Terry D. ..... Sacramento, CA
Wheeler, Terry K. ..... Greenville, PA
Wheeler, Thomas B. ..... Potsdam, NY
Wheeler, Thomas C. ..... Washington, DC
Wheeler, Thomas E., II ..... Indianapolis, IN
Wheeler, Thomas E., Jr. ..... Pensacola, FL
Wheeler, Thomas J. ..... Duncanville, TX
Wheeler, Thomas L., Jr. ..... Dallas, TX
Wheeler, Thomas M., Ltd., A Professional Corporation ..... Decatur, IL
Wheeler, Thomas R. ..... Rockton, IL
Wheeler, Thompson, Parker & Counts, LLP
Easton, MD
Wheeler, Timothy J. ..... Santa Monica, CA
Wheeler, Toni R. ..... Kansas City, MO
Wheeler & Traviss, P.A. ..... Winter Haven, FL
Wheeler Trigg & Kennedy, P.C.
Denver, CO
Roslyn, NY
Wheeler, Troyce A. ..... Council Bluffs, IA
Wheeler, Ty Robert ..... Emporia, KS
Wheeler Upham, A Professional Corporation
Grand Rapids, MI
Wheeler, Van Sickle & Anderson, S.C.
Madison, WI
Wheeler, Vince P. ..... Wichita, KS
Wheeler, Virgil M., Jr. ..... New Orleans, LA
Wheeler, Virginia M. ..... Anchor Point, AK
Wheeler, V. M., III ..... New Orleans, LA
Wheeler, W. David ..... Fawnskin, CA
Wheeler, W. Thomas ..... Minneapolis, MN
Wheeler, Walter S., III ..... Lansing, MI
Wheeler, Warren O. ..... Atlanta, GA
Wheeler & Wheeler ..... Russellville, KY
Wheeler & Wheeler ..... Uhrichsville, OH
Wheeler, Wheeler & Bell
Oklahoma City, OK
Wheeler & Wheeler, PLLC ..... Biloxi, MS
Wheeler & Wilkinson, LLP ..... Orlando, FL
Wheeler, Willard C., Jr. ..... Jupiter, FL
Wheeler, William B. ..... Silver Spring, MD
Wheeler, William C., Jr. ..... Des Plaines, IL
Wheeler, William E. ..... High Point, NC
Wheeler, William J. ..... Philadelphia, PA
Wheeler, William J., & Associates, P.C.
Philadelphia, PA
Wheeler, William M. ..... Hemet, CA
Wheeler, William M. ..... Thomson, GA
Wheeler, William M., Jr. ..... Carmel, CA
Wheeler, William M., P.C. ..... Thomson, GA
Wheeler, William T. ..... Silver Spring, MD
Wheeler, William W. ..... Guthrie, OK
Wheeler Wolf Law Firm ..... Bismarck, ND
Wheeless, John C., Jr. ..... Vicksburg, MS
Wheeless, Shappley, Bailess & Rector
Vicksburg, MS
Wheeless, Steven D. ..... Phoenix, AZ
Wheeley, Matthew B. ..... New Port Richey, FL
Tampa, FL
Wheeling, Mary Elizabeth ..... Castlewood, VA
Wheelington, Jimmy D. ..... Plano, TX
Wheelis, James B. ..... Wolf Point, MT
Wheelis, Lee Ann ..... Dallas, TX
Wheelis & Rozanski, PLC ..... Alexandria, LA
Wheelis, Stephen D. ..... Alexandria, LA
Wheelock, Bryan K. ..... St. Louis, MO
Wheelock, Charles E. ..... Atlanta, GA
Wheelock, Corina M. ..... Buffalo, NY
Wheelock, Cullen Ann
Colorado Springs, CO
Wheelock, E. Thomas ..... Palo Alto, CA
Wheelock, Jeffrey W. ..... Houston, TX
Wheelock, Joseph A., Jr. ..... Costa Mesa, CA
Wheelock, Kenneth S. ..... Pittsfield, MA
Wheelock, Matthew H. ..... Washington, DC
Wheelock, Richard M. ..... Chicago, IL
Wheelock, Robert J. ..... Orlando, FL
Wheelock, Robert J., P.A. ..... Orlando, FL
Wheelock, Timothy S. ..... Portsmouth, NH
Wheelock, William D. ..... La Jolla, CA
Wheelus, Kyle, Jr. ..... Beaumont, TX
Wheelwright, Kevin W. ..... Pleasanton, CA
San Jose, CA
Wheelwright, Martin L. ..... Trenton, NJ
Wheelwright, Neil ..... Burlington, VT
Wheelwright, Timothy M. ..... Ogden, UT
Wheet, Michael L. ..... Washington, DC
Wheiler, J. Michael ..... Idaho Falls, ID
Wheir, John J. ..... Amarillo, TX
Whelan, Arthur W., Jr. ..... St. Clair Shores, MI
Whelan, Barbara L. ..... Hettinger, ND
Whelan, Catherine P. ..... Greenwich, CT
Whelan, Charles D., III
New Brunswick, NJ
Whelan, Charles D., III ..... Plainfield, NJ
Warren, NJ
Whelan, Charles M. ..... New York, NY
Whelan, Chas. M. ..... Washington, DC
Whelan, Cheryl L. ..... Topeka, KS
Whelan, Christopher H. ..... Gold River, CA
Whelan, D. Nicholas ..... Corte Madera, CA
Whelan, David J. ..... White Plains, NY
Whelan, Deirdre A. ..... Boston, MA
Whelan, DeMaio & Kiszkiel, P.A.
Miami, FL
Whelan, Dennis E. ..... Los Angeles, CA
Whelan, Dennis J. ..... Richmond, VA
Whelan, Dorothy P. ..... Minneapolis, MN
Whelan, Duane ..... East Hampton, NY
Whelan, Edward M. ..... Jacksonville, FL
Whelan, Elizabeth A. ..... Atlanta, GA
Whelan, Ellen H. ..... San Diego, CA
Whelan, Frederick J., III ..... Mineola, NY
Whelan, Frederick J., Jr. ..... Greenwich, CT
Whelan, Geralyn Mary ..... Edison, NJ
Whelan, Gregory E. ..... Cape May, NJ
Whelan, Helen M. ..... Rockville, MD
Whelan, J. David ..... Menomonie, WI
Whelan, J. Michael ..... Howardstown, KY
Whelan, Jacqueline D. ..... Denver, CO
Whelan, Jeffrey R. ..... New York, NY
Whelan, Jennifer A. ..... Boston, MA
Whelan, John F. ..... Rochester, MN
Whelan, John F. ..... Milwaukee, WI
Whelan, John K. ..... New York, NY
Whelan, John M. ..... Long Beach, CA
Whelan, John M. ..... Chicago, IL
Whelan, John M. ..... New York, NY
Whelan, John R. ..... Hartford, CT
Whelan, John W. ..... Mill Valley, CA
Whelan, John W. ..... Butte, MT
Whelan, Joseph D. ..... Boston, MA
Providence, RI
Whelan, Juliana N. ..... Portland, OR
Seattle, WA
Whelan, June L. ..... Saratoga, CA
Whelan, Kevin E. ..... Syracuse, NY
Whelan, Leigh ..... Houston, TX
Whelan, Leo F. ..... Novi, MI
Whelan, M. Edward, III ..... Washington, DC
Whelan, Mary Jo L. ..... Greenwich, CT
Whelan, Mary M. ..... Sag Harbor, NY
Whelan, Maureen C. ..... San Jose, CA
Whelan, Michael A. ..... San Jose, CA
Whelan, Michael D. ..... San Francisco, CA
Whelan, Michael G. ..... Miami, FL
Whelan, Paul W. ..... Seattle, WA
Whelan, Q. Nicholas ..... Corte Madera, CA
Whelan, Richard Q. ..... New York, NY
Philadelphia, PA
Whelan, Richard V., Jr. ..... Cleveland, OH
Whelan, Robert P. ..... New York, NY
Whelan, Roger M. ..... Washington, DC
Whelan & Scherr ..... Hastings, NE
Whelan, Sidney S., Jr. ..... New York, NY
Whelan, Stephen A. ..... Chicago, IL
Whelan, Stephen T. ..... New York, NY
Whelan, Susan Marren ..... New York, NY
Whelan, Theresa Bryant ..... Central Islip, NY
Whelan, Thomas D. ..... Sacramento, CA
Whelan, Thomas J. ..... San Diego, CA
Whelan, Thomas J., Jr.
National Aeronautics And Space Administration, GV
Whelan, Thomas M. ..... Dallas, TX
Whelan, Vincent E. ..... San Diego, CA
Whelan, Walter W. ..... Fresno, CA
Whelan, Walter W., A Prof. Corp., Law Offices of ..... Bakersfield, CA
Fresno, CA
Modesto, CA
Whelan, William J., III ..... New York, NY
Whelan, William Michael, Jr. ..... Denver, CO
Whelan, William S. ..... Boise, ID
Whelan, William T. ..... Boston, MA
Whelan, William V. ..... San Diego, CA
Whelan-Kapanowski, Maureen K.
Chicago, IL
Whelchel, Betty A. ..... New York, NY

Whitcomb, William G. ....Fort Myers, FL
Whitcombe, Anne E. ....Philadelphia, PA
Whitcombe, John D. ....Torrance, CA
Whitcraft, Martin ....Philadelphia, PA
Whitcup & Arce ....Chicago, IL
Whitcup, Leonard S. ....Chicago, IL
White, A. Bartlett ....Raleigh, NC
White, A. Bruce ....Chicago, IL
White, A. Ellen ....Rustburg, VA
White, A. Thomas, Jr. ....Bridgeport, CT
White, A. B. ....Houston, TX
White, Adam ....New York, NY
White, Adrian Sherwood ....Washington, DC
White, Adrienne ....New York, NY
White, Adrienne L. ....Alexandria, VA
White, Alan G. ....Montvale, NJ
White, Alan I. ....Costa Mesa, CA
White, Alan J. ....Wisconsin Dells, WI
White, Alan M. ....Philadelphia, PA
White, Aleshia M. ....Sacramento, CA
White, Alexander P. ....Chicago, IL
White, Alexander S. ....Department of Justice, Office of Professional Responsibility, GV
White, Alfred E., Jr. ....Houston, TX
White, Alfred K., Jr. ....Cincinnati, OH
White, Alfred L., Jr. ....Front Royal, VA
White, Algird F., Jr. ....Washington, DC
Albany, NY
White, Alice A. ....Denver, CO
White, Alice Blackwell ....Orlando, FL
White, Alison Anne ....Laredo, TX
White, Allan P. ....New York, NY
White & Allen, P.A. ....Kinston, NC
White, Allinder & Graham, L.L.C.
Independence, MO
Kansas City, MO
White, Alycia Gulas ....Birmingham, AL
White, Amanda E. ....St. Louis, MO
White, Amanda Nixon ....Pine Bluff, AR
White, Amy Catherine ....New York, NY
White, Amy Collins ....Dubuque, IA
White, Amy G. ....Boise, ID
White, Andrea Eaton ....Columbia, SC
White, Andrea J. ....Torrance, CA
White, Andrea Lynn ....Richmond, VA
White, Andrew ....West Palm Beach, FL
White, Andrew ....Mocksville, NC
White, Andrew B. ....Boston, MA
White, Andrew C. ....Baltimore, MD
White, Andrew J., Jr. ....Greenville, SC
White, Andrew M. ....Los Angeles, CA
White, Andrew S. ....Hamden, CT
White, Andrew S. ....Boston, MA
White, Andrew W. ....Richmond, VA
White, Anece Baxter ....Fort Benning, GA
White, Angela M. ....Shawnee, OK
White, Angela R. ....Ann Arbor, MI
White, Angela Rose ....Sherman Oaks, CA
White, Ann Campbell ....Venice, FL
White, Ann D. ....Jenkintown, PA
White, Anna Erickson ....Palo Alto, CA
White, Anne J. ....Boston, MA
White, Anne (Jan) W. ....Bethesda, MD
White, Anne Walker ....Jackson, MI
White, Anthony B. ....Hollywood, FL
White, Anthony C. ....Columbus, OH
White, Anthony M. ....Salina, KS
White, Anthony W. ....Deming, NM
White, April Sellers ....Sapulpa, OK
White, Arnold S. ....Columbus, OH
White, Arthur C. ....
Department of Labor, GV
White, Arthur E. ....
Administrative Office Of The United States Courts, GV
White, Arthur G. ....Mountain View, CA
White, Arthur M. ....Framingham, MA
White, Ashley B. ....Cary, NC
White and Associates ....Raleigh, NC
White, Augustus T. (Toby) ....Houston, TX
White, B. Joan ....Ames, IA
White & Babey, P.A. ....Coral Springs, FL
White, Barbara E. ....Omaha, NE
White, Barbara English ....Minneapolis, MN
White, Barbara Glass ....Stamford, CT
White, Barbara L. ....Charlotte, NC
White, Barrett J. ....Olympia, WA
White, Barry A. ....Chicago, IL
White, Barry A. ....South Portland, ME
White, Barry B. ....Boston, MA
White, Barry B. ....Lewisburg, TN
White, Barry F. ....Memphis, TN
White, Barry R. ....Milwaukee, WI
White, Barry S. ....New York, NY
White, Beatty J. ....Rock Hill, SC
White, Beau J. ....St. Louis, MO
White, Ben B., III ....Princeton, WV
White, Benjamin A. ....Biloxi, MS
White, Benjamin Harvey, Jr.
Greensboro, NC
White, Benjamin Jerome ....Detroit, MI
White, Benjamin T. ....Atlanta, GA
White, Benjamin V., III ....Providence, RI
White & Bentley ....Bastrop, LA
White, Bernard S. ....Washington, DC
White, Bertram C. ....Placerville, CA
White, Betty Jo ....Silverton, OR
White, Betty-Lynn ....Danbury, CT
White & Betz ....Lawrenceburg, TN
White, Beverly ....Washington, DC
White, Beverly J. ....Columbia, MD
White, Beverly M. Barr ....Norwalk, OH
White, Bill D. ....Davis, CA
White, Billy Joe ....Tazewell, TN
White, Blackburn & Conte, P.C.
Richmond, VA
White, Blair W. ....San Francisco, CA
White, Bob O. ....Oskaloosa, IA
White, Bobby D. ....Wilson, NC
White, Bonnie J. ....Houston, TX
White, Boyd B., II ....Pocatello, ID
White, Bradley R. ....Oakland, CA
White, Bradley R. ....San Bernardino, CA
White, Bradley S. ....Los Angeles, CA
White, Brandon F. ....Boston, MA
White, Brantley ....Corpus Christi, TX
White, Brenda Baldwin ....
Department of Justice, GV
White, Brenner & Feigenbaum
Albany, NY
White, Brent W. ....New York, NY
White, Brett D. ....Palo Alto, CA
White, Brian D. ....Buffalo, NY
White, Brian J. ....La Mesa, CA
White, Brian Keith ....Anderson, SC
White, Brian L. ....Wabasso, MN
White, Brian M. ....Decatur, AL
White, Brian P. ....Riverside, CA
White, Bridgit Ann ....Houston, TX
White and Bright ....San Diego, CA
Escondido, CA
Orange, CA
White, Brinda K. ....Oklahoma City, OK
White, Brinson C. ....Charlottesville, VA
White, Britton, Jr. ....Houston, TX
White, Brooke Erin ....Los Angeles, CA
White, Brooks ....New York, NY
White & Brown, P.A. ....Miami, FL
White, Bruce D. ....Fairfax, VA
White, Bruce David ....Newport Beach, CA
White, Bruce E. ....Dallas, TX
White, Bruce H. ....Dallas, TX
White, Bruce H., (A P.C.) ....Escondido, CA
Orange, CA
White, Bruce M. ....Portland, OR
White, Bruce W. ....Bend, OR
White, Bruce W. ....Richmond, VA
White, Bryan L. ....Houston, TX
White, Bryan M. ....Metairie, LA
White, Bryan S. ....Beverly Hills, CA
White, Bryan T. ....Atlanta, GA
White, Buel ....Washington, DC
White Bundy McElroy Hodges
Abingdon, VA
White, Byron E. ....Cincinnati, OH
White, Byron F. ....San Diego, CA
White, Byron R. ....
Supreme Court Of The United States, GV
White, C. Adrian, (P.C.) ....Bristol, VA
White, C. Casey ....Glendale, CA
White, C. Craig ....Burlington, NC
White, C. Denny ....Richmond, VA
White, C. Nathaniel ....Bartow, FL
White, C. Thomas ....Omaha, NE
White, C. Timothy ....Phoenix, AZ
White, C. Timothy ....Shepherdsville, KY
White, Cara F. Leahy ....Fort Worth, TX
White, Carl N. ....Toledo, OH
White, Carl W. ....Prairie Village, KS
White, Carol L. ....Milwaukee, WI
White, Carol M. ....Pinehurst, NC
White, Carol Susan ....Wooster, OH
White, Carole V. ....San Francisco, CA
White, Caroline ....Fort Lauderdale, FL
White, Caroline Alderson ....Kansas City, KS
White, Caroline, P.A.
Fort Lauderdale, FL
White, Carolyn ....Baltimore, MD
White, Carolyn A. ....Richmond, VA
White, Carolyn M. ....Washington, DC
White and Carrier ....Oklahoma City, OK
White, Carroll E. ....Tupelo, MS
White, Carson & Alliman, Attorneys At Law, P.C. ....Knoxville, TN
Madisonville, TN
White, Carter Capps ....San Juan, TX
White, Carter H. ....Meriden, CT
White & Case ....Los Angeles, CA
Palo Alto, CA
Washington, DC
Miami, FL
New York, NY
White, Catharine D. ....Shawano, WI
White, Catherine A. ....Boston, MA
White, Catherine C. ....Chattanooga, TN
White, Catherine T. ....Reston, VA
White, Cathleen Regina ....Baltimore, MD
White, Cathryn Kerby ....Livonia, MI
White, Cecil E. ....Clinton, SC
White, Charlene Lashay ....Mobile, AL
White, Charles A., Jr. ....Alexandria, VA
White, Charles B. ....Denver, CO
White, Charles E. ....River Falls, WI
White, Charles F. ....Oklahoma City, OK
White, Charles G. ....Miami, FL
White, Charles G. ....Amarillo, TX
Dallas, TX
White, Charles H. ....New Orleans, LA
White, Charles H. ....Pawtucket, RI
White, Charles H. ....Houston, TX
White, Charles Hampton ....Nashville, TN
White, Charles L. ....Roseland, NJ
White, Charles L., II ....Greensboro, NC
White, Charles M., III ....Warrenton, NC
White, Charles N. ....New Rochelle, NY
White, Charles R. ....Troy, MI
White, Charles S. ....Fort Lauderdale, FL
White, Charles S. ....Plant City, FL
White, Charles S., P.A. ....Plant City, FL
White, Charles W. ....Baton Rouge, LA
White, Charles W. ....Durham, NC
White, Cheryl Denney ....Newark, NJ
White, Cheryl L. ....San Francisco, CA
White, Cheryle M. ....Los Angeles, CA
White, Choate & Watkins ....Calhoun, GA
Cartersville, GA
White, Christen Carlson ....Portland, OR
White, Christian S.
Federal Trade Commission, Office of the General Counsel, GV
White, Christian S., IV ....Bismarck, ND
White, Christina M. ....New York, NY
White, Christine D. ....Secaucus, NJ
White, Christine L. ....Washington, DC
White, Christopher A. ....Costa Mesa, CA
White, Christopher A.
Ponte Vedra Beach, FL
White, Christopher A. ....Chicago, IL
White, Christopher J. ....Hartsdale, NY
White, Christopher J. ....New York, NY
White, Christopher L. ....Washington, DC
White, Christopher L. ....Raleigh, NC
White, Christopher L. ....San Antonio, TX
White, Christopher L. ....Waterbury, VT
White, Christopher R. ....Sanford, FL
White, Christopher A., P.A.
Jacksonville, FL
Ponte Vedra Beach, FL
White, Christopher Lewis, P.A. ....Raleigh, NC
White, Cindy Butler ....Dallas, TX
White, Cindy L. ....Long Beach, CA
White & Cirrito ....Hempstead, NY
White, Clair F. ....Shreveport, LA
White, Claire B. ....Department of Labor, Office of the Solicitor, GV
White, Claron N. ....Oceanside, CA
White, Claude E. ....Purchase, NY
White, Clay M. ....Rome, GA
White, Clay M. ....Tyler, TX
White, Clifford J., III ....
Department of Justice, GV
White, Clifton F. ....Venice, FL
White, Cline H. ....San Antonio, TX
White, Coffey, Galt & Fite, P.C.
Oklahoma City, OK
White, Colleen Toy ....Ventura, CA
White, Collis ....San Antonio, TX
White, Connie Zimmerman ....Hamilton, TX
White, Constance B. ....Salt Lake City, UT
White, Craig ....San Antonio, TX
White, Craig E. ....Leesburg, VA
White, Craig M. ....Chicago, IL
White, Craig Michael ....Akron, OH
White, Craig Owen ....Cleveland, OH
White, Craig R. ....Atlanta, GA
White & Crouch, P.A. ....Gainesville, FL
White and Crumpler ....Winston-Salem, NC
White, Cummings & Longino, P.C.
Phoenix, AZ
White, Curtis T. ....San Juan, PR
White, Curtrice M. ....Seattle, WA
White, Cynthia B. ....San Francisco, CA
White, Cynthia E. ....Harrisburg, PA
White, Cynthia L. ....Rosamond, CA
White, Cynthia Lynn ....Concord, NH
White, Cynthia R. ....Fort Lauderdale, FL
White, Cynthia R. ....Philadelphia, PA
White, D. Knox ....Gulfport, MS
White, D. Richard ....Lawrence, KS
White, D. Shawn ....Franklin, PA
White, Dale T. ....Louisville, CO
White & Dalton ....Brevard, NC
White, Dan A. ....Arlington, TX
White, Dan E. ....Atlanta, GA
White, Daniel B. ....Greenville, SC
White, Daniel Chiel ....St. Louis, MO
White, Daniel E. ....Chicago, IL
White, Daniel E. ....Cheyenne, WY
White, Daniel E., P.C. ....Cheyenne, WY
White, Daniel H. ....Scottsville, NY
White, Daniel J. ....Cardiff-By-The-Sea, CA
White, Daniel J. ....Cleveland, OH
White, Daniel L. ....Swampscott, MA
White, Daniel M. ....San Diego, CA
White, Daniel O. ....Orlando, FL
White, Daniel P. ....Walnut Creek, CA
White, Daniel R. ....New York, NY
White, Daniel R. ....Pittsburgh, PA
White, Daniel S. ....Monroe, MI
White, Daniel S. ....Cleveland, OH
White, Daniel U. ....Athens, GA
White, Daniel W. ....Alpena, MI
White, Daniel W. ....New York, NY
White, Darrell D. ....Baton Rouge, LA
White, Darryl C. ....Redondo Beach, CA
White, David ....Washington, DC
White, David A. ....Wilmington, DE
White, David A. ....New Orleans, LA
White, David A. ....Boston, MA
White, David A. ....Boston, MA
White, David A. ....Wellesley, MA
White, David A. ....Fairport, NY
White, David A. ....Dayton, OH
White, David A. ....Toledo, OH
White, David A. ....Rock Hill, SC
White, David B. ....Bloomfield Hills, MI
White, David B. ....Pittsburgh, PA
White, David C. ....Wilsonville, OR
White, David C. ....Denton, TX
White, David C. ....Charleston, WV
White, David C., P.C., Law Offices of
Wilsonville, OR
White, David D. ....Phoenix, AZ
White, David D. ....
Department Of Health And Human Services, GV
White, David D. ....Williamsville, NY
White, David Dwayne ....Haslett, MI
White, David E. ....Treasury Department, Internal Revenue Service, GV
White, David E. ....Pittsburgh, PA
White, David F. ....Englewood, CO
White, David F. ....Collingswood, NJ
Philadelphia, PA
White, David G. ....Irvine, CA
White, David G. ....Chicago, IL
White, David G. ....Roseland, NJ
White, David G. ....Spartanburg, SC
White, David H. ....Atlanta, GA
White, David H. ....Alexandria, VA
White, David J. ....West Palm Beach, FL
White, David J. ....Nashville, TN
White, David J. ....Dallas, TX
White, David J. "Jeff" ....Gulfport, MS
White, David J., Jr. ....Nashville, TN
White, David L. ....Phoenix, AZ
White, David L. ....Bossier City, LA
White, David L. ....Worcester, MA
White, David L. ....Columbus, OH
White, David L. ....Philadelphia, PA
White, David L. ....Dallas, TX
White, David L. ....Charleston, WV
White, David M. ....Harbert, MI
White, David M. ....White Plains, NY
White, David R. ....Tucson, AZ
White, David R. ....Medford, MA
White, David R. ....Canfield, OH
White, David R. ....Canfield, OH
White, David R. ....Harrisburg, PA
White, David R., Jr. ....Philadelphia, PA
White, David R., Jr. ....Uvalde, TX
White, David S. ....Beverly Hills, CA
Beverly Hills, CA
White, David S. ....Dallas, TX
White, David S. ....Seattle, WA
White, David Thurston, III
Birmingham, AL
White, David V. ....Springfield, IL
White, David W. ....Walnut Creek, CA
White, David W. ....Overland Park, KS
White, Dawn ....Martinsburg, WV
White, Dean ....Canton, TX
White, Deanna L. Staples ....Portland, ME
White, Deborah A. ....Elizabeth, NJ
White, Deborah A. ....Morristown, NJ
White, Deborah R. ....Washington, DC
White, Debra Alligood ....Washington, DC
White, Denis ....Los Angeles, CA
White, Dennis A. ....San Diego, CA
White, Dennis A. ....Washington, DC
White, Dennis A. ....Holton, KS
White, Dennis J. ....San Francisco, CA
White, Dennis J. ....Boston, MA
White, Dennis L. ....Dallas, TX
White, Dennis M. ....Madison, WI
White, Dennis R. ....Naples, FL
White, Dennis R., P.A. ....Naples, FL
White, Derek J. ....Savannah, GA
White, Dermott J. ....Blue Bell, PA
White, Diana Churchill ....Chicago, IL
White, Diane S. ....Atlanta, GA
White, Diane Virginia
Securities and Exchange Commission, Office of the General Counsel, GV
White, Diarmuid ....New York, NY
White, Don B. ....Lexington, KY
White, Don O. ....Mobile, AL
White, Don O., P.A. ....Mobile, AL
White, Don P., Jr. ....Sacramento, CA
White, Don R., Jr. ....Denton, TX
White, Donald A. ....Webster, NY
White, Donald B. ....Coronado, CA
White, Donald E. ....Covina, CA
White, Donald E. ....Bozeman, MT
White, Donald H. ....Augusta, GA
White, Donald J. ....Mineola, NY
White, Donald P. ....Riverton, WY
White, Donald S. ....Port Townsend, WA
White, Donald W. ....Batavia, OH
White, Donna M. ....Boston, MA
White, Donna Marthel Ranson
Jefferson City, MO
White, Doris Helene ....Boston, MA
White, Douglas B. ....Schaumburg, IL
White, Douglas C. ....San Francisco, CA
White, Douglas E. ....San Francisco, CA
White, Douglas F. ....Bountiful, UT
White, Douglas G. ....Conshohocken, PA
White, Douglas J., Jr. ....Portland, OR
White, Douglas N. ....Department of Labor, Office of the Solicitor, GV
White, Doyle Eugene, Jr. ....El Dorado, KS
White, Dru Samuel ....New York, NY
White, Duane M. ....Columbus, OH
White, Dudley K. ....St. Marys, WV
White, Dunn & Booker ....Birmingham, AL
White, E. Austin ....Fort Myers, FL
White, E. Ross ....Nashville, TN
White, E. A. ....Mansfield, OH
White, Earle V. ....Wilsonville, OR
White, Earle W., Jr. ....Las Vegas, NV
White, Earnest R. ....Brewton, AL
White, Edgar H. ....North St. Paul, MN
White, Edgar W. ....Elkhart, KS
White, Edith ....San Diego, CA
White, Edmund E. ....Sacramento, CA
White, Edward A. ....Jacksonville, FL
White, Edward A. ....Atlanta, GA
White, Edward A. ....Seattle, WA
White, Edward C. ....Hartford, CT
White, Edward D. ....Denver, CO
White, Edward E. ....Washington, DC
White, Edward E., Jr. ....Brookline, MA
White, Edward G., II ....Knoxville, TN
White, Edward H. ....Washington, DC
White, Edward J. ....Overland Park, KS
White, Edward J. ....New York, NY
White, Edward J., P.A. ....Overland Park, KS
White, Edward K. ....Columbia, SC
White, Edward K., III ....Nashville, TN
White, Edward L. ....Oklahoma City, OK
White, Edward L., III ....Orlando, FL

White, Edward M. ... Chicago, IL
White, Edward R. ... Chicago, IL
White, Edward R. ... Garden City, NY
White, Edward R., Jr. ... Demorest, GA
White, Edwin Dean, III ... Memphis, TN
White, Edwin H. ... Sacramento, CA
White, Edwin J. ... San Mateo, CA
White, Edwin Morton ... Hopkinsville, KY
White, Elaine Berlin ... Portola Valley, CA
White, Elisa Masterson ... Little Rock, AR
White, Elizabeth A. ... Beverly Hills, CA
White, Elizabeth A. ... Savannah, GA
White, Elizabeth Allen ... Los Angeles, CA
White, Elizabeth Ann ... Rockville, MD
White, Elizabeth L. ... Jacksonville, FL
White, Elizabeth L. ... Indianapolis, IN
White, Elizabeth L. ... Williamsburg, VA
White, Elizabeth Le Bas ... Anchorage, AK
White, Elizabeth Sloan ... San Francisco, CA
White, Elmer E. ... Ann Arbor, MI
White, Elmer E., III ... Birmingham, AL
White, Elwin H. ... Dublin, GA
White, Emmet ... Honolulu, HI
White, Emmett J. ... Charlottesville, VA
White, Emory L., Jr. ... Dallas, TX
White, Eric Barclay ... Aurora, CO
White, Eric D. ... Virginia Beach, VA
White, Eric L. ... Dallas, TX
White, Erica Denise ... Washington, DC
White, Erica Lynn ... Green Bay, WI
White, Erika Diane ... New York, NY
White, Ernest J. ... Alexandria, VA
White, Ernest L., III ... St. Joseph, MI
White, Esther M. ... Fayetteville, AR
White, Eugene B. ... Montauk, NY
White, Eugene C. ... Newport Beach, CA
White, Eugene L. ... Peoria, IL
White, Eugene T. ... Port Jefferson, NY
White, F. Lenton ... Dothan, AL
White, F. A. (Al), Jr., Law Offices of
Kansas City, MO
White & Fish, L.P.A., Inc. ... Columbus, OH
White, Fleischner & Fino ... Red Bank, NJ
Bronx, NY
Brooklyn, NY
New York, NY
Scarsdale, NY
White Plains, NY
White, Floyd W. ... Oakland, CA
White, Frances J. ... Downers Grove, IL
White, Francine Buscemi ... Rockford, IL
White, Francis L. ... Barrington, IL
White, Francis R., III ... Covington, LA
New Orleans, LA
White, Frank A. ... Washington, DC
White, Frank G. ... Houston, TX
White, Frank H. ... St. Petersburg, FL
White, Frank L. ... Memphis, TN
White, Frank L., Jr. ... Wayne, PA
White, Frank L., P.C. ... Memphis, TN
White, Frank N. ... Atlanta, GA
White, Frank R. ... Harrisburg, IL
White, Frank T. ... Farmville, VA
White, Franklin E., Jr.
Department of Justice, Civil Division, GV
White, Fred B., III ... New York, NY
White, Fred S. ... Evansville, IN
White, Frederic ... Cleveland, OH
White, Frederick G. ... Waterloo, IA
White, Frederick L. ... Chicago, IL
White & Fudala ... Lexington, MA
White, G. Edward ... Charlottesville, VA
White, G. Mason ... Savannah, GA
White, G. Michael ... Lansing, MI
White, G. Michael ... Gillette, WY
White & Gale ... Sacramento, CA
White, Gale ... Philadelphia, PA
White, Galen J., Jr. ... Louisville, KY
White, Garrett M. ... Houston, TX
White, Garrick O. ... Toledo, OH
White, Garth Hinsdale ... Rock Hill, SC
White, Gary ... Gulfport, MS
White, Gary D., Jr. ... Topeka, KS
White, Gary L. ... Dallas, TX
White, Gary M. ... Clearwater, FL
White, Gary R. ... Sacramento, CA
White, Gary R. ... Denver, CO
White, Gentes & Garcia, A Professional Corporation ... San Diego, CA
White, Geo. A. ... Plymouth, MA
White, Geo. A. ... Ogden, UT
White, Geoffrey ... Reno, NV
White, Geoffrey B. ... Northampton, MA
White, Geoffrey V., Law Office of
San Francisco, CA
White, George ... Irving, TX
White, George B., Jr. ... Gadsden, AL
White, George F., III
Federal Communications Commission, Office of Engineering & Technology, GV
White, George G., Jr. ... Brentwood, MO
White, George H. ... Vernon Hills, IL
White, George H. ... Salisbury, MD
White, George H. ... Murfreesboro, TN
White, George, Jr. ... Los Angeles, CA
White, George L., IV ... Youngstown, OH
White, George M. ... Washington, DC
White, George, P.C. ... Irving, TX
White, George R., Jr. ... Philadelphia, PA
White, George T., Jr. ... Rochester, NY
White, George W. ... Cleveland, OH
White, Gerald E. ... Grand Rapids, MI
White, Gerald F. ... Elizabeth City, NC
White, Gerald G. ... Bloomfield Hills, MI
White, Gerald K. ... Chicago, IL
White, Gerald L. ... Sacramento, CA
White, Gerald L. ... Clare, MI
White, Gerald L. ... Jackson, MS
White, Gerard A. ... New York, NY
White, Gerard W. ... Jersey City, NJ
New York, NY
White, Getgey & Meyer Co., L.P.A.
Cincinnati, OH
White, Gladys I. ... Waynesville, NC
White, Glen F. ... Houston, TX
White, Glenn A. ... Newark, OH
White, Glenn E. ... Cape Girardeau, MO
White, Glenn L. ... Petal, MS
White, Glenn M. ... Los Angeles, CA
White, Glenn M. ... Oklahoma City, OK
White, Gloria Lynn ... Diamond Bar, CA
White, Gordie R. ... New Iberia, LA
White, Gordon B. ... Alameda, CA
White, Gordon E. ... Missouri City, TX
White, Gordon E., Jr. ... Indianapolis, IN
White, Gordon E., P.C. ... Missouri City, TX
White, Gordon M. ... Baton Rouge, LA
White, Grace A., (Miss) ... Beaufort, SC
White, Grady Lee ... Washington, DC
White, Grady W. ... Melbourne, FL
White, Grant W., Jr.
Saint Simons Island, GA
White, Greg ... Waco, TX
White, Gregory A. ... Loveland, CO
White, Gregory A. ... Elyria, OH
White, Gregory D. ... Orlando, FL
White, Gregory E. ... Dallas, TX
White, Gregory L. ... Boston, MA
White, Gregory M. ... Chicago, IL
White, Gregory P. ... South Weymouth, MA
White, Gretchen ... Syracuse, NY
White, Griffith & Oakes, P.C.
Decatur, AL
White and Guesnon ... New Orleans, LA
White, H. Aubrey, III ... Lake Charles, LA
White, H. Blair ... Chicago, IL
White, H. Darrell, Jr. ... Tallahassee, FL
White, H. Glenn, III ... Cary, NC
White, H. Katherine ... Saddle Brook, NJ
White, H. Laban ... Clarksburg, WV
White, H. Ron ... Dallas, TX
White, H. Taylor ... Fort Lauderdale, FL
White, H. Thad, Jr. ... Florence, SC
White, H. Wayne ... Houston, TX
White, H. William ... Franklin, PA
White, H. William, III ... Hermitage, PA
New Wilmington, PA
Sharon, PA
White, Hall & Dixon ... Elizabeth City, NC
White Hamilton, P.C. ... Rockwall, TX
White, Harold ... Wichita Falls, TX
White, Harold F. ... Akron, OH
White, Harold L. ... Muskogee, OK
White, Harold S., Jr. ... Atlanta, GA
White, Harold W., (P.C.) ... Estherville, IA
White, Harry B. ... Calhoun, GA
Cartersville, GA
White, Harry E., III ... Fresno, CA
White, Harry E., Jr. ... New York, NY
White, Harry Faber, II ... Meadville, PA
White, Harry W. ... Bellaire, OH
St. Clairsville, OH
White, Harvey E., Jr. ... Norfolk, VA
White, Haywood E., III ... Wilmington, NC
White, Heather G. ... Los Angeles, CA
White, Heather S. ... Salt Lake City, UT
White, Heather W. ... New York, NY
White, Helen ... Glendale, CA
White, Helen J.S. ... St. Louis, MO
White, Helga A. ... Sacramento, CA
White & Henderson ... Beckley, WV
Princeton, WV
White, Henry George ... Tallahassee, FL
White, Henry J. ... Columbia, SC
White, Herbert J. ... Concord, NC
White, Hill, Sims & Wiggins, L.L.P.
Dallas, TX
White, Howard D. ... Eau Claire, WI
White, Howard E. ... Baltimore, MD
White, Howard Lee ... Jerseyville, IL
White, H. S. ... Havana, IL
White, Hugh V., Jr. ... Richmond, VA
White, Hunter H. ... Houston, TX
White, Huseman & Pletcher
Corpus Christi, TX
White, Inker, Aronson, P.C. ... Boston, MA
White, Ira ... New York, NY
White, Isaac D. ... Dallas, TX
White, J. Andrew ... New Bedford, MA
White, J. Bennett ... Tyler, TX
White, J. Mark ... Birmingham, AL
White, J. Mercer, Jr. ... Richmond, VA
White, J. Merritt, III ... Concord, NC
White, J. Morgan ... Salisbury, MD
White, J. Patrick ... Iowa City, IA
White, J. Ralph ... New Orleans, LA
White, J. Richard ... Dallas, TX
White, J. Spratt ... Fort Mill, SC
White, J. Stewart ... Reno, NV
White, J. William ... Scottsboro, AL
White, J. William, P.C. ... Scottsboro, AL
White, Jack E. A. ... Corpus Christi, TX
White, Jack H., Jr. ... Arlington, VA
White, Jack J. ... Missouri Valley, IA
White, Jack L. ... Anaheim, CA
White, Jack R., (P.C.) ... Los Angeles, CA
White, Jack S. ... Nashua, NH
White, Jack W. ... Ballwin, MO
White, Jackson S., Jr. ... Abingdon, VA
White, Jackson W. ... Lexington, KY
White, Jacqueline A. ... Chicago, IL
White, James A. ... Chicago, IL
White, James A. ... Okemos, MI
White, James A., Jr. ... Fayetteville, GA
White, James A.D. ... Seattle, WA
White, James Boyd ... Ann Arbor, MI
White, James C. ... Loganville, GA
White, James D. ... Tallahassee, FL
White, James D. ... Wichita, KS
White, James D., Jr. ... Celina, TN
White, James D., (P.C.) ... Newport Beach, CA
White, James E. ... Clarksburg, WV
White, James E., Jr. ... Charleston, WV
White, James F. ... Batavia, IL
White, James F., Jr. ... Tampa, FL
Toledo, OH
White, James G., II ... Lawrenceburg, TN
White, James H. ... Birmingham, AL
White, James H. ... Coral Gables, FL
White, James H. ... Clayton, MO
White, James H. ... Memphis, TN
White, James H., III ... Birmingham, AL
White, James H., Jr. ... Panama City, FL
White, James J. ... Redding, CA
White, James J. ... Ann Arbor, MI
White, James J. ... Buffalo, NY
White, James K. ... Department of Commerce, Office of the General Counsel, GV
White, James K. ... Department of Energy, Office of the General Counsel, GV
White, James K. ... Grand Rapids, MI
White, James Lloyd ... Seattle, WA
White, James M. ... Centreville, AL
White, James M. ... Rochester, NY
White, James M. ... Harrisburg, PA
Philadelphia, PA
White, James M., III ... Richmond, VA
Richmond, VA
White, James M., Jr. ... Boston, MA
White, James Monroe, III
New Orleans, LA
White, James N. ... Fonda, NY
White, James O., Jr. ... Los Angeles, CA
White, James P. ... Washington, DC
White, James P. ... Chicago, IL
White, James P. ... Indianapolis, IN
White, James P., Jr. ... Bridgeport, CT
White, James R. ... Bradenton, FL
White, James R. ... Evart, MI
Reed City, MI
White, James S. ... Oakland, CA
White, James Timothy, (P.C.)
Atlanta, GA
White, James U., Jr. ... Oklahoma City, OK
White, James W. ... Indianapolis, IN
White, James W. ... Nashville, TN
White, James W., Jr. ... Toledo, OH
White, Jane Larmon ... Boston, MA
White, Janet L. ... New Orleans, LA
White, Janice G. ... Columbus, OH
White, Janis P. ... Clarksburg, WV
White & Jankowski ... Denver, CO
White, Jarrod J. ... Mobile, AL
White, Jas. C. ... Omaha, NE
White, Jason C. ... Chicago, IL
White, Jason D. ... Phoenix, AZ
Newport Beach, CA
White, Jason S. ... Broken Bow, NE
White, Jay B. ... St. Louis, MO
White, Jay C. ... San Carlos, CA
White, Jay K. ... Mooresville, NC
White, Jay V. ... Seattle, WA
White, J. E. (Gene) ... Flagler Beach, FL
White, Jean L. ... Dallas, TX
White, Jeane Van Voorhis ... Dallas Center, IA
White, Jeanne P. Hammer ... Sayville, NY
White, Jeffery H. ... Canton, TX
White, Jeffery A. ... Studio City, CA
White, Jeffery L. ... Washington, DC
White, Jeffrey M. ... Portland, ME
White, Jeffrey P. ... Barrington, IL
White, Jeffrey P. ... Rutland, VT
White, Jeffrey P., and Associates, P.C.
Barrington, IL
White, Jeffrey Robert ... Washington, DC
White, Jeffrey S. ... San Francisco, CA
White, Jeffry W. ... Montpelier, VT
White, Jennifer A. N. ... New York, NY
White, Jennifer L. ... Issaquah, WA
White, Jerald L. ... New Orleans, LA
White, Jere F. ... Cartersville, GA
White, Jere F., Jr. ... Birmingham, AL
White, Jeremy E. ... Minneapolis, MN
White, Jerry M. ... Dothan, AL
White, Jerry M. ... Dallas, TX
White, Jerry R. ... Logan, WV
White, Jessica C. ... Pittsburgh, PA
White, Jill Carolyn ... Gainesville, FL
White, Jimmie F. ... Southfield, MI
White, Jimmie D. ... Los Angeles, CA
White, Jimmie L. ... Mount Pleasant, TX
White, J. M., III ... New Orleans, LA
White, Jo Fineman ... West Chester, PA
White, Jo Lynn ... Hamburg, NY
White, Joan C. ... Woonsocket, RI
White, Joane Pappas ... Price, UT
White, Joanne M. ... Latham, NY
White, Jodi Lynn ... El Cajon, CA
White, Joe E., Jr. ... Oklahoma City, OK
White, Joe L. ... Collinsville, OK
White, Joe L., P.C. ... Collinsville, OK
White, Joel R. ... Houston, TX
White, John A. ... Los Angeles, CA
White, John A. ... San Francisco, CA
White, John A.
Department Of Health And Human Services, Social Security Administration, GV
White, John A., Jr. ... Atlanta, GA
White, John A., Jr. ... Reno, NV
White, John B., Jr. ... Spartanburg, SC
Spartanburg, SC
White, John B., (P.A.) ... Miami, FL
West Palm Beach, FL
White, John B., P.A. ... Spartanburg, SC
White, John C. ... Boston, MA
White, John C. ... Austin, TX
White, John Charles ... Elizabeth City, NC
White, John D. ... Atlanta, GA
White, John D. ... Manchester, KY
White, John D. ... Kingston, NY
White, John D. ... Houston, TX
White, John E. ... Orlando, FL
White, John E. ... Chicago, IL
White, John E. ... Buffalo, NY
White, John F. ... Chicago, IL
White, John F. ... Indianapolis, IN
White, John F., Jr. ... Patchogue, NY
White, John G. ... La Mesa, CA
White, John G., III ... West Palm Beach, FL
White, John H. ... Milton, FL
White, John H. ... Council Grove, KS
White, John H. ... Pittsburgh, PA
White, John H., Jr. ... Jackson, MS
White, John H., Jr. ... Mc Comb, MS
White, John, II ... West Palm Beach, FL
White, John J. ... Skokie, IL
White, John J. ... Bethesda, MD
White, John J. ... Austin, TX
White, John J. ... Denison, TX
White, John J., III ... Philadelphia, PA
White, John J., Jr. ... Kirkland, WA
White, John K. ... Yuma, AZ
White, John L. ... Woodbury, NJ
White, John Leslie ... Arlington, VA
White, John M. ... Greenwood, IN
White, John M. ... Bethesda, MD
Arlington, VA
Arlington, VA
Leesburg, VA
White, John M., Jr. ... Lexington, MA
White, John P. ... Naples, FL
White, John P. ... Easton, MD
White, John P. ... New York, NY
White, John P. ... Houston, TX
White, John P., Jr. ... Boston, MA
White, John P., Jr. ... Fort Worth, TX
White, John Patrick ... Grand Rapids, MI
White, John R. ... Iuka, MS
White, John R. ... Gettysburg, PA
White, John R. ... Shelbyville, TN
White, John Robert, Jr. ... Jackson, MS
White, John S. ... Green Valley, AZ
White, John S. ... Taunton, MA
White, John S. ... Hempstead, NY
White, John S., Jr. ... Baton Rouge, LA
White, John T. ... Tampa, FL
White, John T. ... Borger, TX
White, John W. ... Iola, KS
White, John W. ... Boston, MA
White, John W. ... New York, NY
White & Johnson ... Indianapolis, IN
White & Johnson, P.C. ... Anamosa, IA
Cedar Rapids, IA
Manchester, IA
Vinton, IA
White, Jonathan A. ... Weston, MA
White, Jonathan D. ... Long Island City, NY
White, Jonathan E. ... Atlanta, GA
White & Jones ... Geneseo, IL
White, Joseph ... Denver, CO
White, Joseph B. ... Northfield, NJ
White, Joseph B. ... New York, NY
White, Joseph B. ... Providence, RI
White, Joseph James, II ... Houston, TX
White, Joseph L. ... Louisville, KY
White, Joseph L. ... Columbus, OH
White, Joseph M. ... Detroit, MI
White, Joseph M. ... White Plains, NY
White, Joseph Q., Jr. ... Pascagoula, MS
White, Joseph R. ... Palmer, MA
White, Joseph R. ... Oxford, MS
White, Joseph R. ... Chattanooga, TN
White, Joseph R., Jr. ... Atlanta, GA
White, Josephine Elizabeth ... Hamden, CT
White, Jude A. ... Nashville, TN
White, Judith E. ... New York, NY
White, Judith L. ... Garland, TX
White, Judith L. ... Plano, TX
White, Judith Mostyn ... Gaithersburg, MD
White, Julia Falenski ... Columbus, OH
White, K. Claire ... Birmingham, AL
White, K. Martin ... Carlsbad, CA
White, Kalimah Z. ... Philadelphia, PA
White, Karen Day ... Greenwell Springs, LA
White, Karen Fagin ... Atlanta, GA
White, Karen Kaufman ... St. Petersburg, FL
White, Karen Krajcir ... Chicago, IL
Downers Grove, IL
White, Karen Rebecca ... Atlanta, GA
White, Karen Tucker ... Houston, TX
White, Karmen Roann ... Houston, TX
White, Katherine M. ... Detroit, MI
White, Katherine P. ... New York, NY
White, Katherine R. ... Raleigh, NC
White, Katherine W. ... San Diego, CA
White, Kathleen M. ... Woodland, CA
White, Kathleen R. ... Chicago, IL
White, Kathleen R. ... Bellaire, TX
White, Keith A. ... Lawrence, KS
White, Keith E. ... Fort Wayne, IN
White, Keith F. ... Orlando, FL
White, Keith M. ... Fresno, CA
White, Kelly Bishop ... Escondido, CA
White, Kemble ... Dallas, TX
White, Kendred A. ... Loudon, TN
Madisonville, TN
White, Kenneth E. ... Phenix City, AL
White, Kenneth E. ... Fort Lauderdale, FL
White, Kenneth F. ... Nampa, ID
White, Kenneth I., Sr. ... Toledo, OH
White, Kenneth J. ... Toledo, OH
White, Kenneth R. ... Mankato, MN

White, Kenneth S. ... Lynchburg, VA
White, Kevin B. ... Tulsa, OK
White, Kevin E. ... Chicago, IL
White, Kevin P. ... Omaha, NE
White, Kevin T. ... Dallas, TX
White, Kimber L. ... Newport News, VA
White, Kimberley Slayton ... Danville, VA
White, Kimberly Ann
Manhattan Beach, CA
White, Kimberly Heshima
Department of Justice,
Civil Rights Division, GV
White, Kipling N. ... Covington, IN
White, Knox H. ... Greenville, SC
White, Koch, Kelly & McCarthy, A Professional Association ... Santa Fe, NM
White, Krista L. ... Seattle, WA
White, Kristian Erik ... Clarksburg, WV
White, Kristin Hogan ... New Orleans, LA
White, L. Alward, Jr. ... Amarillo, TX
White, L. Wayne ... Houston, TX
White, L. A. ... St. Joseph, MI
White, Lahroy Alward ... Amarillo, TX
White, Langfred W. ... Clearwater, FL
White, Lara E. ... New Orleans, LA
White, Lara L. ... Las Cruces, NM
White, Larry E. ... Norco, CA
White, Larry J. ... Atlanta, GA
White, Larry J. ... Atlanta, GA
White, Larry J. ... Austell, GA
White, Larry K. ... Tallahassee, FL
White, Larry K., P.A. ... Tallahassee, FL
White, Larry R. ... Birmingham, AL
White, Larry R. ... Salt Lake City, UT
White, Laura A. ... Chicago, IL
White, Laura D. ... Albuquerque, NM
White, Laura R. ... Richmond, VA
White, Laurel Defoe ... Sacramento, CA
White Law Chartered ... Reno, NV
White Law Firm ... Oklahoma City, OK
White Law Office ... Holton, KS
White Law Office ... Wabasso, MN
White Law Offices, P.A. ... Kinston, NC
Raleigh, NC
White, Lawrence ... Westmont, NJ
White, Lawrence E. ... Chicago, IL
White, Lawrence R. ... Las Cruces, NM
White, Lawrence W. ... Memphis, TN
White, Ledford E. ... North Richland Hills, TX
White, Lee C. ... Washington, DC
White & Lee, LLP ... Menlo Park, CA
White, Lee T. ... Hopkinsville, KY
White, Leigh A. ... Irvine, CA
White, Leland J. ... Charleston, SC
White, Leonard A. ... Bethesda, MD
White, Leslie S. ... Birmingham, AL
White, Leslie S. ... Houston, TX
White, Lesyllee Maurelia ... Chicago, IL
White, Letitia H. ... Houston, TX
White, Lewis A. ... Mount Sterling, KY
White, Lewis N., III ... New Brunswick, NJ
White, Lianne M. ... Atlanta, GA
White, Libby A. ... Berwyn, PA
White, Linda A. ... Waukegan, IL
White, Linda D. ... Chicago, IL
White, Linda S. ... Reno, NV
White, Lionel N. ... Morristown, NJ
White, Lisa Dawn ... Boston, MA
White, Lisa Holder ... Decatur, IL
White, Lisa M. ... Pensacola, FL
White, Lisa Parsons ... Buffalo, NY
White, Llynn K. ... St. Louis, MO
White, Lori L. ... Oaks, PA
White, Louise V. ... Covington, LA
White & Lowe ... Waukesha, WI
White, Lu Ann ... Des Moines, IA
White, Lucie E. ... Cambridge, MA
White, Lucien D. ... New York, NY
White, Lucille Saundra ... Burtonsville, MD
White, Lucinda E. ... Augusta, ME
White, Luke ... Covington, IN
White, Lynda S. ... Bozeman, MT
White, Lynn Alan ... San Francisco, CA
White, Lynn L. ... New Orleans, LA
White, Lynne M. ... Orlando, FL
White, M. Douglas ... Bonifay, FL
White, M. Susie ... Greenville, SC
White, Marc A. ... Washington, DC
White, Margaret E. ... San Francisco, CA
White, Margaret F. ... Council Grove, KS
White, Margaret M. ... Cheyenne, WY
White, Margaret P. ... Fairfield, ID
White, Margot ... Charlottesville, VA
White, Mari S. ... Dorset, VT
White, Marianne B. ... Orford, NH
White, Marie ... Seattle, WA
White, Mark A. ... San Francisco, CA
White, Mark A. ... Boston, MA
White, Mark A. ... Houston, TX
White, Mark C. ... Grand Rapids, MI
White, Mark Cameron ... Menlo Park, CA
White, Mark Christopher ... Lyndhurst, OH
White, Mark D. ... Amarillo, TX
White, Mark E. ... St. Louis, MO
White, Mark G. ... Boston, MA
White, Mark J. ... Austin, TX
White, Mark J. ... Riverton, WY
White, Mark N. ... San Francisco, CA
White, Mark P. ... Lexington, MA
White, Marlin A. ... Holton, KS
White, Marlow V., Jr. ... Tallahassee, FL
White, Marsh, Anderson, Vickers & Deobler
Earlville, IL
Leland, IL
Ottawa, IL
White, Marshall T. ... Anchorage, AK

White, Martin B.
Commodity Futures Trading Commission,
Office of the General Counsel, GV
White, Martin F. ... Warren, OH
White, Martin F., Co., L.P.A.
Warren, OH
Youngstown, OH
White, Marvin L., Jr. ... Jackson, MS
White, Mary B. ... Department of Justice,
Executive Office for Immigration Review,
GV
White, Mary Carol ... Birmingham, AL
White, Mary Dacey ... Boston, MA
Milton, MA
White, Mary Dinius ... Los Angeles, CA
White, Mary E. ... Yuma, AZ
White, Mary Ellen ... Plano, TX
White, Mary F. ... Ann Arbor, MI
White, Mary G. ... Cadiz, KY
White, Mary Jane ... Waukon, IA
White, Mary Jo ... New York, NY
White, Mary Modenbach
New Orleans, LA
White, Mary Pilibos ... Menlo Park, CA
White, Mary R. ... Oil City, PA
White, Mary Ray ... Denver, CO
White, Mary Ray, P.C. ... Denver, CO
White, Mary S. ... San Francisco, CA
White, Mary Stuart ... Detroit, MI
White, Matthew A. ... Philadelphia, PA
White, Matthew B. ... New York, NY
White, Matthew David ... Boston, MA
White, Matthew J. ... Houston, TX
White, Matthew K. ... Memphis, TN
White, Matthew N. ... San Rafael, CA
White, Matthew W. ... Opelika, AL
White, Maureen Leigh ... Richmond, VA
White, Maurice E.
Administrative Office Of The United States
Courts, GV
White, Maurice J. ... Pittsburgh, PA
White, Maurice O. ... Cincinnati, OH
White, Maxine L. ... White Plains, NY
White McCann & Stewart
Winchester, KY
White & McClure, P.A., Law Offices of
Naples, FL
White & McDermott, P.C. ... Boston, MA
Wellesley, MA
White McMahon Potter ... Santa Rosa, CA
White & McSpedon, P.C. ... New York, NY
White & Meany ... Reno, NV
White, Meghan E. ... Largo, MD
White, Melanie Charrise ... Grand Rapids, MI
White, Melissa J. ... Charleston, WV
White, Melissa O. ... Seattle, WA
White, Melody ... Cleveland, OH
White, Melvin ... Washington, DC
White, Melvin G. ... College Park, GA
White, Melvin G., P.C. ... College Park, GA
White & Meredith ... Bowling Green, KY
White, Michael A. ... Saipan, TT
White, Michael B. ... Coeur d'Alene, ID
White, Michael B. ... Litchfield, IL
White, Michael B. ... Kansas City, MO
White, Michael C. ... Washington, DC
White, Michael C. ... Lexington, KY
White, Michael D. ... Anchorage, AK
White, Michael D. ... Denver, CO
White, Michael D. ... Washington, DC
White, Michael D. D. ... New York, NY
White, Michael E. ... Manhattan Beach, CA
White, Michael E. ... Chicago, IL
White, Michael E. ... Garden City, NY
White, Michael F. ... Redding, CA
White, Michael H. ... Los Angeles, CA
White, Michael J. ... Burbank, CA
White, Michael J. ... Los Angeles, CA
White, Michael J. ... San Clemente, CA
White, Michael J. ... Wilmington, DE
White, Michael J. ... Cincinnati, OH
White, Michael L. ... Montgomery, AL
White, Michael L. ... Phoenix, AZ
White, Michael L.
National Archives And Records
Administration,
Office of the Federal Register, GV
White, Michael L. ... Austin, TX
White, Michael L., P.C. ... Phoenix, AZ
White, Michael M. ... Lawrenceville, GA
White, Michael N. ... Anchorage, AK
White, Michael P. ... Sacramento, CA
White, Michael P. ... Kansas City, MO
White, Michael R. ... Montgomery, AL
White, Michael R. ... Los Angeles, CA
White, Michael T. ... Kansas City, MO
White, Michael W. ... Woodbridge, NJ
White, Michael W. ... San Antonio, TX
White, Michelle ... Phoenix, AZ
White, Michelle ... Fort Worth, TX
White, Millard Calvin ... Newport News, VA
White, Miller, Kenny & Vettori, L.L.P.
Baltimore, MD
Towson, MD
White, Mitchell D. ... Huntsville, AL
White, Molly M. ... Los Angeles, CA
White, Monte ... Wichita Falls, TX
White, Morley H. ... Cleveland, OH
White, Morris E. (Trey), III
San Antonio, TX
White, Nancy ... Boston, MA
White, Nancy ... Poultney, VT
White, Nancy A. ... Washington, DC
White, Nancy A. ... Albany, NY
White, Nancy A. ... Scranton, PA
White, Nancy B. ... Miami, FL
White, Nancy J. ... College Station, TX
White, Nancy Jane ... San Francisco, CA

White, Nancy L. ... Phoenix, AZ
White, Nancy P. ... Raleigh, NC
White, Nancy Shea ... Denver, CO
White, Nathan ... Union, NJ
White, Nathan E., Jr. ... McKinney, TX
White, Neal J. ... Chicago, IL
White, Neil P. ... Beverly Hills, CA
White, Neil R. ... Baltimore, MD
White, Newton B., Jr. ... New York, NY
White, Newton B., P.C. ... New York, NY
White, Nicholas Earl ... Hawkinsville, GA
White, Nicholas J. ... Los Angeles, CA
White, Nicholas L. ... Memphis, TN
White, Nola ... Austin, TX
White, Norman ... Lake Wales, FL
White, Norman I. ... Harrisburg, PA
White, Norman J. ... Glendale, CA
White, Norman J., A Professional Law Corporation ... Glendale, CA
White, Norman M. ... Salt Lake City, UT
White, Norman W. ... Madison, WV
White, O. Miller ... Houston, TX
White O'Connor Curry Gatti & Avanzado LLP ... Los Angeles, CA
White, Octavis ... Graham, NC
White, Ori Tucker ... Fort Stockton, TX
White, Oscar A. ... Miami, FL
White, Paige W. R. ... Rosemead, CA
White, Pamela J. ... Baltimore, MD
White, Pamela K. ... Chicago, IL
White, Paralee ... Washington, DC
White, Patricia C. ... Bloomfield Hills, MI
White, Patricia Cox ... Department of Defense,
Defense Legal Services Agency, GV
White, Patricia D. ... Tempe, AZ
White, Patricia Kay ... Fort Worth, TX
White, Patricia M. Early ... New York, NY
White, Patricia P. ... San Jose, CA
White, Patrick D. ... Phoenix, AZ
White, Patrick E. ... Kansas City, MO
White, Paul D. ... Cleveland, OH
White, Paul D., Jr. ... North Little Rock, AR
White, Paul E. ... Boston, MA
White, Paul E. ... Omaha, NE
White, Paul E. ... Lufkin, TX
White, Paul E., Jr. ... Washington, DC
White, Paul G. ... Springfield, MO
White, Paul H. ... San Francisco, CA
White, Paul L. ... Rock Rapids, IA
White, Paul R. ... Ephrata, WA
White, Paul R., Sr. ... Nashville, TN
White, Paul S. ... Beverly Hills, CA
White, Paul S. ... Danville, KY
White, Paul S. ... Spokane, WA
White, Paul S., III ... Malibu, CA
White, Paul W. ... Lincoln, NE
White, Paula E. ... Stockton, CA
White, Paula Gordon ... Bloomington, IN
White, Pauline K. ... Centreville, MD
White, Peck, Carrington, Williams and Neal, LLP ... Mount Sterling, KY
White, Perry R., Jr. ... Paris, KY
White, Peter ... Santa Fe, NM
White, Peter B. ... Topsfield, MA
White, Peter C. ... Garden City, NY
White, Peter D. ... Albuquerque, NM
White, Peter H. ... Washington, DC
White, Peter M. ... Houston, TX
White, Peter S. ... Oklahoma City, OK
White, Peter V. ... Syracuse, NY
White, Peterson, Pruss, Morrow & Gigray, P.A. ... Boise, ID
Nampa, ID
White, Philip H. ... Montpelier, VT
White, Philip, Jr. ... Laramie, WY
White, Philip R. ... Newark, NJ
New York, NY
White, Philip Robert ... Wichita, KS
White, Phillip A. ... Webster Groves, MO
White, Phillip M., Jr. ... Norwalk, OH
White, Pierce, Jr. ... Saluda, SC
White, Pierce, Mailman & Nutting
Saipan, TT
White, Pollard ... Hopkinsville, KY
White & Pollard, P.C. ... Houston, TX
White, Przybylowicz, Schneider & Baird, P.C.
Okemos, MI
White, Quinlan, Staley & Ledwith
Garden City, NY
White, R. Bruce ... Parkersburg, WV
White, R. David ... Dallas, TX
White, R. Kreis ... Brentwood, TN
Knoxville, TN
Memphis, TN
White, R. Parker ... Sacramento, CA
White, R. Patrick ... Atlanta, GA
White, R. Quincy ... Chicago, IL
White, Ralph I. ... Oakland, CA
White, Ralph O., Jr.
General Accounting Office,
Office of the General Counsel, GV
White, Rand N. ... Menlo Park, CA
White, Randal S. ... Doylestown, PA
White, Randall ... Providence, RI
White, Randall Allen ... Grand Haven, MI
White, Randall D. ... Buffalo, NY
White, Randall J. ... Dallas, TX
White, Randolph E. ... Westbury, NY
White, Raquel Lisette ... Miami, FL
Pompano Beach, FL
White & Raub, LLP ... Indianapolis, IN
White, Ray B. ... Bowling Green, KY
White, Raymond A.
Federal Communications Commission,
Mass Media Bureau, GV
White, Raymond B. ... Medford, OR
White, Raymond E. ... Austin, TX
White, Raymond W. ... Palm Desert, CA

White & Reasor ... Nashville, TN
White, Rebecca Hanner ... Athens, GA
White, Rebecca Lyn ... Springfield, IL
White, Rebecca T. ... Seattle, WA
White & Reed LLP ... Los Angeles, CA
White, Regen & Garton, PLC
Dickson, TN
White, Reginald F. ... Philadelphia, PA
White, Reginald R., III ... New Orleans, LA
White, Renee A. ... New York, NY
White, Rex H., Jr. ... Austin, TX
White, Rhoda L. ... San Diego, CA
White, Richard ... Lunenburg, MA
White, Richard ... L'Anse, MI
White, Richard ... Tulsa, OK
White, Richard ... Eau Claire, WI
White, Richard A. ... Mesa, AZ
Payson, AZ
White, Richard A.
Federal Energy Regulatory Commission,
Office of the General Counsel, GV
White, Richard A. ... New York, NY
White, Richard A. ... Seattle, WA
White, Richard B. ... Spokane, WA
White, Richard C. ... Newport Beach, CA
White, Richard C. ... Washington, DC
White, Richard C. ... El Paso, TX
White, Richard C. ... Derby, VT
White, Richard D., Jr. ... Tulsa, OK
White, Richard E. ... Murphysboro, IL
White, Richard E., Chartered, Law Offices of ... Murphysboro, IL
White, Richard G. ... San Jose, CA
White, Richard G. ... Henderson, TX
White, Richard G., A Professional Corporation
San Jose, CA
White, Richard J. ... Dayton, OH
White, Richard J. ... Houston, TX
White, Richard K., Jr. ... Baltimore, MD
White, Richard M. ... Miami, FL
White, Richard M., Jr. ... Gainesville, FL
White, Richard N. ... Youngstown, OH
White, Richard P. ... Baltimore, MD
White, Richard R. ... New York, NY
White, Richard S. ... West Hartford, CT
White, Richard S. ... Seattle, WA
White, Richard T. ... Oakland, CA
White, Richard T., Jr. ... Washington, DC
White, Richard T., Jr. ... Pontiac, MI
White, Richard W. ... Atlanta, GA
White, Richard W. ... Henderson, TX
White, Richard W. ... Waukesha, WI
White, Rick A. ... Chicago, IL
White, Robert ... Maryville, TN
White, Robert A. ... San Diego, CA
White, Robert A. ... Hartford, CT
White, Robert A. ... Coral Springs, FL
White, Robert A. ... Miami, FL
White, Robert A. ... Orlando, FL
White, Robert A. ... Tazewell, VA
White, Robert Alan ... Princeton, NJ
White, Robert B. ... Miami, FL
White, Robert B., Jr. ... Orlando, FL
White, Robert B., Jr. ... Philadelphia, PA
White, Robert B., Jr., P.C., Law Offices of
Philadelphia, PA
White, Robert C. ... Hillsboro, IL
White, Robert C. ... Minden, LA
White, Robert C. ... Elyria, OH
White, Robert C. ... Dallas, TX
White, Robert C., Jr. ... Miami, FL
White, Robert D. ... Fort Worth, TX
White, Robert E. ... Ottawa, IL
White, Robert E. ... Auburn, NY
White, Robert E. ... Saranac Lake, NY
White, Robert E. ... Odessa, TX
White, Robert E., Law Offices of
San Francisco, CA
White, Robert F. ... Watertown, MA
White, Robert F. ... Waterford, MI
White, Robert G. ... San Francisco, CA
White, Robert G. ... Chicago, IL
White, Robert Glenn ... Bayfield, CO
White, Robert H. ... Geneseo, IL
White, Robert Hal, Jr. ... Seattle, WA
White, Robert I. ... Washington, DC
White, Robert I., (P.C.) ... Houston, TX
White, Robert J. ... Los Angeles, CA
White, Robert J. ... Haverhill, MA
White, Robert J. ... Minneapolis, MN
White, Robert J., Jr. ... Hudson, NY
White, Robert J., P.C. ... Haverhill, MA
White, Robert L. ... Phoenix, AZ
White, Robert L. ... Cleveland, OH
White, Robert L. ... Oklahoma City, OK
White, Robert L. ... Langhorne, PA
White, Robert L. ... Memphis, TN
White, Robert L. ... Wenatchee, WA
White, Robert L., III ... Miami, FL
White, Robert Lee ... Madison, WV
White, Robert M. ... Santa Rosa, CA
White, Robert M.
Department Of Veterans Affairs,
Veterans Benefits Administration, GV
White, Robert M. ... Albuquerque, NM
White, Robert M. ... Greenville, SC
White, Robert M. ... Richmond, VA
White, Robert P. ... Long Lake, MN
White, Robert R. ... Fayetteville, AR
White, Robert R. ... Lowell, MA
White, Robert S. ... Bloomington, IL
White, Robert S. ... Chicago, IL
White, Robert Scott ... Worcester, MA
White, Robert T. ... St. Paul, MN
White, Robert T., Jr. ... New York, NY
White, Robert W. ... Decatur, MI
White, Robin C. ... Glenside, PA

Whitehead, Marshall G., P.C. ... Phoenix, AZ
Whitehead, Matthew J., II ... Reston, VA
Whitehead, Michael E. ... Biloxi, MS
Whitehead, Michael K. ... Kansas City, MO
Whitehead, Michael L. ... El Monte, CA
Whitehead, Michael W.
Abita Springs, LA
New Orleans, LA
Whitehead, Mitchel D. ... Los Angeles, CA
Whitehead, Nancy Rader
Newport Beach, CA
Whitehead, Nigel A. ... Nipomo, CA
Whitehead, Patrick M.
West Palm Beach, FL
Whitehead, Paul ... Pittsburgh, PA
Whitehead, Porter & Gordon
San Francisco, CA
Whitehead, Priscilla Anne
Washington, DC
Whitehead, R. L., Jr., A Prof. Corp., Law Office of ... Longview, TX
Whitehead, R. Laughton, Jr.
Longview, TX
Whitehead, Robert A., Jr. ... Hartford, CT
Whitehead, Robert C. ... New York, NY
Whitehead, Robin S. ... New York, NY
Whitehead, Ronald L. ... Burnsville, MN
Whitehead, Roy, Jr. ... Conway, AR
Whitehead, S. Wayne ... Greensburg, PA
Whitehead, Sam H. ... Lexington, KY
Whitehead, Stephen Errol
Birmingham, AL
Whitehead, Steven L. ... Princeton, IN
Whitehead, Steven L. ... Salt Lake City, UT
Whitehead, Stewart ... Austin, TX
Whitehead, Susan ... Wellesley Hills, MA
Whitehead, Theodore J. ... Stamford, CT
Whitehead, Thomas J. ... Washington, DC
Whitehead, Tyler V. ... Portland, OR
Whitehead, V. Bruce ... Rocky Mount, NC
Whitehead, Wayne A. ... Knoxville, TN
Whitehead & Whitehead ... Reno, NV
Whitehead, William A., Jr.
Hattiesburg, MS
Whitehead, Wm. Catlin ... Anderson, IN
Whitehead-Taylor, Lynda ... Ahoskie, NC
Whitehill, Andrea ... Sarasota, FL
Whitehill, Andrea ... Venice, FL
Whitehill, Charles A. ... Indianapolis, IN
Whitehill, Charles H. ... Tucson, AZ
Whitehill, Clifford L. ... Orlando, FL
Whitehill, David B. ... Tulsa, OK
Whitehill, James A. ... Tucson, AZ
Whitehill, Jess ... Los Angeles, CA
Whitehill, Linden, Grynkewich & Halladay, P.C. ... Tucson, AZ
Whitehill, Michael H. ... Los Angeles, CA
Whitehill, Samuel M., Jr. ... Houston, TX
Whitehill, Tricia M. ... Minneapolis, MN
Whitehill, William G. ... Dallas, TX
Whitehill, William H., Jr.
Oklahoma City, OK
Whitehorn, Carol R. ... Washington, DC
Whitehorn, Jo-Ann H. ... New York, NY
Whitehorn, Samuel E. ... United States Senate, Committee Legal Personnel, GV
Whitehouse, George E. ... Vermillion, SD
Whitehouse, Henry ... Orange, VA
Whitehouse, Herbert A. ... Edison, NJ
Whitehouse, Jack G. ... San Luis Obispo, CA
Whitehouse, James K. ... Albion, MI
Whitehouse, John L. ... Brockton, MA
Whitehouse, John R. ... Sanford, MI
Whitehouse, Judith Ann
San Francisco, CA
Whitehouse Law Firm ... Edison, NJ
Whitehouse, Rebecca S. ... Austin, TX
Whitehouse, Richard A. ... Columbus, OH
Whitehouse, Richard W. ... San Marino, CA
Whitehouse, Samantha B. ... Chicago, IL
Whitehouse, Sheldon ... Providence, RI
Whitehouse, Stephen T. ... Shelton, WA
Whitehouse, Theodore C.
Washington, DC
Whitehouse, Thomas J. ... Portland, OR
Whitehouse, Timothy A. ... Los Angeles, CA
Whitehouse, Warren W.
Farmington Hills, MI
Whitehouse, Warren W., P.C.
Farmington Hills, MI
Whitehouse, William H. ... Jackson, MI
White-Hoxie, Lisa Jennifer
National Labor Relations Board, Office of Board Members, GV
Whitehurst, A. J. ... Thomasville, GA
Whitehurst, Alan L. ... Alexandria, VA
Whitehurst, Alfred L. ... Los Banos, CA
Whitehurst, Alfred W. ... Norfolk, VA
Whitehurst, Bill N. ... Tyler, TX
Whitehurst, Blackburn, Warren & Kelly
Thomasville, GA
Whitehurst, Carol Banna ... New Orleans, LA
Whitehurst, Charles E., Jr. ... Dover, DE
Whitehurst, Daniel K. ... Fresno, CA
Whitehurst, David W. ... Dallas, TX
Whitehurst, Diane B. ... Tyler, TX
Whitehurst, Elaine W. ... Roswell, GA
Whitehurst, Elsa Lopez ... Tallahassee, FL
Whitehurst, Harkness, Ozmun & Archuleta, A Professional Corporation ... Austin, TX
Whitehurst, J. Paul ... Tuscaloosa, AL
White-Hurst, John M. ... Boydton, VA
Whitehurst, John R., II ... Cincinnati, OH
Whitehurst, Julian E. ... Orlando, FL
Whitehurst, Julie Weaver ... Baton Rouge, LA
Whitehurst, Kenneth N., Jr.
Virginia Beach, VA
Whitehurst, Kitty ... Tuscaloosa, AL
Whitehurst, Leon, Jr. ... Clearwater, FL
Whitehurst, Roger ... Kaufman, TX
Whitehurst & Whitehurst ... Tuscaloosa, AL
Whitehurst, William O., Jr. ... Austin, TX
Whitehurst, William R.
Winston-Salem, NC
Whiteing, Jeanne S. ... Boulder, CO
Whiteing, Leslie M. ... Alameda, CA
White Jr., William H. ... Washington, DC
Parsippany, NJ
White-Kelly, Mary Jo ... Washington, DC
Whiteker, Jerry N. ... Lufkin, TX
Whitelaw, Arthur Keith, III ... Denver, CO
Whitelaw, Brian W. ... Grand Rapids, MI
Whitelaw, Donald B. ... Middlesex, NJ
Whitelaw & Fangio ... Oswego, NY
Syracuse, NY
Whitelaw, Jae ... Concord, NH
Whitelaw, James M. ... Irvine, CA
Whitelaw, Jeffrey J. ... Sacramento, CA
Whitelaw, Jennifer L. ... Naples, FL
Whitelaw, Jill Rouff ... Wilmington, DE
Whitelaw, John S. ... Philadelphia, PA
Whitelaw, Julia ... San Francisco, CA
Whitelaw, Kenneth D. ... Syracuse, NY
Whitelaw, Nicholas Spencer ... Alexandria, VA
Whitelaw, Robert I. ... Philadelphia, PA
Whiteleather, John W., Jr.
Columbia City, IN
Whiteleather, Larry W. ... Findlay, OH
Whiteleather, Tania L. ... Lakewood, CA
Whiteley, Brenda Sue ... Grants Pass, OR
Whiteley, Brian E. ... Boston, MA
Whiteley, Conlee Schell ... New Orleans, LA
Whiteley, Daniel E., Jr. ... Cincinnati, OH
Whiteley, Darrell J. ... New York, NY
Whiteley, David D. ... Sonoma, CA
Whiteley, Frank ... Metairie, LA
Whiteley, G. Andrew ... Memphis, TN
Whiteley, Kent ... Bellevue, WA
Whiteley, R. Peyton ... Fairfax, VA
Whiteley, Richard ... Houston, TX
Whiteley, Robert Scott ... Oakland, CA
Whiteley, Susan G. ... Poughkeepsie, NY
Whiteley, T. Gates ... San Antonio, TX
Whiteley, William B. ... San Diego, CA
White-Lief, David W. ... Boston, MA
Whitelock & Associates, P.A.
Fort Lauderdale, FL
West Palm Beach, FL
Whitelock, Charles T.
West Palm Beach, FL
Whitelock, Christopher J.
Fort Lauderdale, FL
Whitelock, Jack, Jr. ... Melbourne, FL
Whitelock, Joseph C. ... St. Petersburg, FL
White-Mahaffey, Virginia L.
Washington, DC
Whiteman, Andrew O. ... Raleigh, NC
Whiteman, Bankes and Chebot
Bellmawr, NJ
Philadelphia, PA
Whiteman, Blake E. ... Scottsdale, AZ
Whiteman, Brian J. ... Newark, NJ
Whiteman, Burl V. ... Portland, IN
Whiteman, Charles B. ... Kihei, HI
Whiteman, Donna L. ... Topeka, KS
Whiteman, Frances C. ... Fairmont, WV
Whiteman & Gorray ... Westbury, NY
Whiteman, Harold W., Jr. ... Atlanta, GA
Whiteman, Harvey M. ... Decatur, GA
Whiteman, John L. ... St. Augustine, FL
Whiteman, Kelly ... Indianapolis, IN
Whiteman, Kimberly J. ... Kansas City, MO
Whiteman Law Offices ... Fairmont, WV
Whiteman, M. Jane ... Atlanta, GA
Whiteman, Marian E. ... Northbrook, IL
Whiteman, Mary E. ... Newark, NJ
Whiteman, Mary Ellen C. ... Stamford, CT
Whiteman, Mary Walton ... Decatur, GA
Whiteman, Michael ... Albany, NY
Whiteman, Nancy E. ... Baltimore, MD
Whiteman Osterman & Hanna
Albany, NY
Whiteman, Richard M. ... Detroit, MI
Whiteman, Robert G. ... Westbury, NY
Whiteman, Roger M. ... Philadelphia, PA
Whiteman, Ronald George
Canoga Park, CA
Whiteman, Roy M. ... Bloomington, IL
Whiteman, Shappell & Burkett ... Portland, IN
Whiteman, Smith & Hamilton, L.L.P.
Atlanta, GA
Whiteman, Steven H. ... Las Vegas, NV
Whiteman, Thomas L. ... West Chester, PA
Whiteman, Thomas M. ... Lynchburg, VA
Whiteman & Whiteman ... Decatur, GA
Whiteman, William D. ... San Francisco, CA
White-Miholits, Terri ... Albertville, AL
White-Mink, Cheryl D. ... New Haven, CT
Whitemyer, James W. ... Encino, CA
Whiten, Charles W., Jr. ... Anderson, SC
Whiten, Marc J. ... New York, NY
Whitenack, Curt J. ... Chicago, IL
Whitenack, Shirley Berger
Morristown, NJ
Whiteneck, Jean S. ... Oklahoma City, OK
Whitener, Claud R., III ... Raleigh, NC
Whitener, E. Peyton ... Atlanta, GA
Whitener, H. Dave, Jr. ... Columbia, SC
Whitener, James F. ... Monmouth, OR
Whitener, Joe P. ... Hickory, NC
Whitener, Mark D. ... Washington, DC
Whitener, Michael L. ...
Department of Commerce, GV
Whitener, Ronald J. ... Olympia, WA
Whitener, Tommie W. ... Novato, CA
Whitener, Varina W. ... Los Angeles, CA
Whitener & Wharton, P.A. ... Columbia, SC
Whitener-Moberg, Janis M. ... Ephrata, WA
Whitenight, G. Kenneth, Jr. ... Dallas, TX
Whitenton, Dewey C. ... Bolivar, TN
Whiter, Kelley ... Fort Lauderdale, FL
White-Redmond, Marilyn S. ... Pasadena, CA
White-Rogers, Lesli A. ... Beaumont, TX
Whiters, Alfred T. ... Chicago, IL
Whitescarver, Crystal T. ... Tampa, FL
Whitescarver, David S. ... San Diego, CA
Whitescarver, Furman B., Jr. ... Salem, VA
Whitescarver, Kenneth T., III
Fredericksburg, VA
Whitesel, Cheryl E. ... Chicago, IL
Whitesel, J. Warren ... Chicago, IL
Whitesell, A. Davis ... Boston, MA
Whitesell, Angela VanLear ... Staunton, VA
Whitesell & Bicknese ... Iowa Falls, IA
Whitesell, Calvin M. ... Montgomery, AL
Whitesell, Calvin M., Jr. ... Montgomery, AL
Whitesell, Calvin M., Jr., P.C.
Montgomery, AL
Whitesell, Charles E. ... Glendale, CA
Whitesell, Darryl D. ... Lynchburg, VA
Whitesell, Edward F. ... Poughkeepsie, NY
Whitesell, Eric D. ... Tazewell, VA
Whitesell, Eugenie B. ... Nashville, TN
Whitesell, Hunter B. ... Fulton, KY
Whitesell, Hunter B., II ... Fulton, KY
Whitesell, I. W., Jr. ... Sarasota, FL
Whitesell, Jeffrey M. ... Parma, OH
Whitesell, John P. ... Iowa Falls, IA
Whitesell, Sarah
Federal Communications Commission, Office of the Commissioners, GV
Whitesell, Steven Edward ... Durham, NC
Whitesell & Stroh ... Glendale, CA
Whitesell, Thomas C. ... Pacific Palisades, CA
Whiteside, Alba L. ... Columbus, OH
Whiteside, Alexander ... Boston, MA
Whiteside, Clyde E. ... Montague, TX
Whiteside, Coyle & Bascom, P.C.
Alpharetta, GA
Whiteside, David P., Jr. ... Birmingham, AL
Whiteside, Dorothy Thompson ... Raleigh, NC
Whiteside, Elizabeth Ayres
Columbus, OH
Whiteside, Evelyn A. ... Jasper, GA
Whiteside, Fife M. ... Columbus, GA
Whiteside, Fife M., P.C. ... Columbus, GA
Whiteside, Fred W., Jr. ... Lexington, KY
Whiteside, Janice C. ... Indianapolis, IN
Whiteside, John L. ... Columbia, MO
Whiteside, Kristi J. ... Dallas, TX
Whiteside, Laura L. ... Tampa, FL
Whiteside, Laura L., P.A. ... Tampa, FL
Whiteside, Lee B. ... Alpharetta, GA
Whiteside, Sally J. ... Minneapolis, MN
Whiteside - Smith Firm, The
Spartanburg, SC
Whiteside, Stephen G. ... Washington, DC
Whiteside, Tom H. ... Lubbock, TX
Whiteside & Whiteside ... Columbus, OH
Whiteside, William A., Jr.
Philadelphia, PA
Whitesides, Ashley ... Washington, DC
Whitesides, H. Monroe, Jr. ... Charlotte, NC
Whitesides, Henry M. ... Gastonia, NC
Whitesides, James B. ... Irvine, CA
Whitesides, John A. ... Sacramento, CA
Whitesides & Kenny, L.L.P. ... Gastonia, NC
Whitesides, Pamela L.
Newport Beach, CA
Whitesides, R. Keith ... Atlanta, GA
Whitesides, Robert ... Torrance, CA
Whitesides, Robert W. ... Laurens, SC
Whitesides & Walker, L.L.P.
Charlotte, NC
White-Small, Margaret H. ... Lakeland, FL
Whitesman, Barney R. ... Flint, MI
Whitesman, Guy E. ... Fort Myers, FL
White-Sperling, Jennifer ... Irvine, CA
Whitestone, Allen ... Boston, MA
Whitestone, Brent, Young & Merril, P.C.
Fairfax, VA
Whitestone, Hunter A. ... Fairfax, VA
Whitestone, Robert C. ... Fairfax, VA
Whiteway, Melinda Marie
Walnut Creek, CA
Whitewolf, Celeste ... Tigard, OR
Whitfield, Alberta P. ... Detroit, MI
Whitfield, Anson M. ... Oxnard, CA
Whitfield, Ben, Jr. ... Detroit, MI
Whitfield & Calvert, P.S.C.
Madisonville, KY
Whitfield, Deborah Armstrong ... Austin, TX
Whitfield & Eddy, P.L.C. ... Des Moines, IA
Whitfield, George L. ... Grand Rapids, MI
Whitfield, Greg ... Charlotte, NC
Whitfield, Harley A. ... Des Moines, IA
Whitfield, Harold L., & Associates
St. Louis, MO
Whitfield, J. Charles, Jr. ... Houston, TX
Whitfield, James, Jr.
Federal Energy Regulatory Commission, Office of the General Counsel, GV
Whitfield, James R. ... Marietta, GA
Whitfield, Jeri L. ... Greensboro, NC
Whitfield, Jesse George, Jr. ... Mobile, AL
Robertsdale, AL
Whitfield, John C. ... Madisonville, KY
Whitfield, John E. ... Harrisonburg, VA
Whitfield, John H. ... Biloxi, MS
Whitfield, John L., Jr. ... Nashville, TN
Whitfield, Judith R. ... Oak Ridge, TN
Whitfield, Karen Kaler ... New Orleans, LA
Whitfield, LeCarie S. ... Riverside, CA
Whitfield, Lisa K. ... Atlanta, GA
Whitfield, M. Gregory ... Mooresville, NC
Whitfield, Marc S. ... Baton Rouge, LA
Whitfield & McAlpine, P.C. ... Mobile, AL
Robertsdale, AL
Whitfield, Michael G. ... Charlotte, NC
Whitfield, Milton B. ... Washington, DC
Whitfield & Mosley ... West Palm Beach, FL
Whitfield, Nathaniel ... Durham, NC
Whitfield, Paul L. ... Charlotte, NC
Whitfield, Paul L., Professional Association
Charlotte, NC
Whitfield, Paula Taylor ... Indianapolis, IN
Whitfield, Pinckney N. ... Los Angeles, CA
Whitfield, Robert E. ... Creedmoor, NC
Durham, NC
Greensboro, NC
Raleigh, NC
Whitfield, Theodore K., Jr.
Chattanooga, TN
Whitfield, V. Lynn, P.A.
West Palm Beach, FL
Whitfield, W. Edward ... Jacksonville, FL
Whitfield, Wenona Y. ... Carbondale, IL
Whitfield, William E., III ... Gulfport, MS
Whitfield-Lungren, Susan J. ... Lindsborg, KS
Whitfill, Cypert O. ... Bel Air, MD
Whitford, Cornelius J. ... Cleveland, OH
Whitford, Dean L. ... Charlottesville, VA
Whitford, Elaine M. ... Raleigh, NC
Whitford, Joseph P. ... Seattle, WA
Whitford, Neil B. ... Morehead City, NC
Whitford, Paul ... Arlington, TX
Whitford, Ronald O., Jr. ... Cleveland, OH
Whitford, Thomas Caleb ... New York, NY
Whitford, Timothy P. ... Cleveland, OH
Whitford, Todd W. ... Hartford, CT
Whitford, Trent T. ... Salem, OR
Whitford, William C. ... Madison, WI
Whitham, C. Lamont ... Reston, VA
Whitham, Curtis & Whitham, PLC
Reston, VA
Whitham, David N. ... Albuquerque, NM
Whitham, Heather K. ... Torrance, CA
Whitham, Larry F. ... Indianapolis, IN
Whitham, McColley & Ross, P.C.
Indianapolis, IN
Whitham, Michael E. ... Reston, VA
Whitham, Michele A. ... Boston, MA
Whitham, Timothy K. ... Elgin, IL
Whitham, Warren ... Dallas, TX
Whitham, Wayne A., Jr. ... Richmond, VA
Whitham, Wayne B. ... Fort Worth, TX
Whitice, William Dale ... Miami, FL
Whitice, William Dale, P.A. ... Miami, FL
Whiting, Alex G. ... Cambridge, MA
Whiting & Beckstead ... Suisun City, CA
Whiting, Catherine D. ... Santa Monica, CA
Whiting, David P. ... Naples, FL
Whiting, Douglas B. ... The Woodlands, TX
Whiting, Edgar M., III ... Parsippany, NJ
Whiting, Edward V. ... Mineola, NY
Whiting, Elinoff & Keefe ... Weymouth, MA
Whiting, Elizabeth D. ... Woodbridge, VA
Whiting, Fallon & Ross ... Richmond, CA
Walnut Creek, CA
Whiting, Geoffrey M. ... Bend, OR
Whiting, George L., Jr. ... Abington, MA
Whiting, Hagg & Hagg ... Deadwood, SD
Rapid City, SD
Spearfish, SD
Whiting, Harriet J. ... New York, NY
Whiting, Herbert R. ... Cleveland, OH
Whiting, Hugh R. ... Cleveland, OH
Whiting, James H. ... Antigo, WI
Whiting, Jan W. ... Weymouth, MA
Whiting, Jeffrey L. ... Buffalo, NY
Whiting, Joanne R. ... Madison, WI
Whiting, John C. ... Atlanta, GA
Whiting, John E. ... Merced, CA
Whiting, John K., IV ... Waltham, MA
Whiting, John P. ... Chicopee, MA
Whiting, John T. ... Madison, WI
Whiting, Kelly P. ... New York, NY
Whiting, Kelly R. ... Boston, MA
Whiting, Kenneth P., III ... Binghamton, NY
Whiting, Kenneth P., Jr. ... Binghamton, NY
Whiting, Kenneth R. ... Denver, CO
Whiting, Kenneth R., Jr.
San Francisco, CA
Whiting, Laura Lyle ... Dallas, TX
Whiting Law Firm, The, P.A.
Portland, ME
Whiting, Lawrence R. ... Santa Ana, CA
Whiting, Marcia ... Rapid City, SD
Whiting, Mary A. ... Staten Island, NY
Whiting, Michael H. ... Troy, MI
Whiting, Oran F. ... Chicago, IL
Whiting, R. Bruce ... Phoenix, AZ
Whiting, Reid A. ... Le Roy, NY
Whiting, Richard ... New York, NY
Whiting, Richard A. ... Washington, DC
Whiting, Richard E. ... Rumford, ME
Whiting, Richard G. ... Columbia, SC
Greenwood, SC
Whiting, Ronald G. ... Department of Labor, Office of the Solicitor, GV
Whiting, Russell G. ... Merced, CA
Whiting, Samuel R. ... Delmar, NY
Whiting, Sidney E., III ... Suisun City, CA
Whiting, Simon D. ... Dallas, TX
Whiting, Stanley E. ... Winner, SD
Whiting, Stephen C. ... Portland, ME
Whiting, Timothy M. ... Waukegan, IL
Whiting, William F. ... Walnut Creek, CA
Whiting, Willie M. ... Chicago, IL
Whitinger, John L. ... Indianapolis, IN
Whiting-Pack, Denise E. ... Atlanta, GA
Whitis, Gavin D. ... San Francisco, CA

Whitsett, Peter A. ....Milford, CT
Whitsett, Scott D.
Federal Emergency Management Agency, Office of the General Counsel, GV
Whitsett, William ....Peoria, AZ
Lake Forest, CA
Whitsitt, Christine S. ....Lebanon, IN
Whitsitt, Karla J. ....Midland, TX
Whitsitt, Michael E. ....Westwood, KS
Whitsitt, Paul K. ....Hoffman Estates, IL
Whitsitt, Shirley J. ....Tallahassee, FL
Whitsitt, Thomas A. ....Lebanon, IN
Whitsitt, Timothy E. ....Aspen, CO
Carbondale, CO
Whitsitt, Timothy J. ....McLean, VA
Whitsitt, W.R., Jr. ....Memphis, TN
Whitson, Christopher C. ....Nashville, TN
Whitson, Debra A. ....Elizabethtown, NY
Whitson, Donald T. ....San Diego, CA
Whitson, Edmund S., III ....Tampa, FL
Whitson, Edmund S., Jr. ....Clearwater, FL
Whitson, Gwen H. ....Burbank, CA
Whitson, Jane Ann ....Nashville, TN
Whitson, Jerry E. ....New York, NY
Whitson, Keith E. ....Pittsburgh, PA
Whitson, Lish ....Seattle, WA
Whitson, Mark A. ....Raleigh, NC
Whitson, Philip L. ....Newell, NC
Whitson, Richard Rogers
Daytona Beach, FL
Whitson, Susan E. ....Plano, TX
Whitson, Wendy D. ....Santa Rosa, CA
Whitson & Whitson, P.A. ....Clearwater, FL
Whitson, William F. ....Tallahassee, FL
Whitson-Owen, Eugena A. ....Chicago, IL
Whitt, Arthur F. ....Tulsa, OK
Whitt, Burt H. ....Norfolk, VA
Whitt, C. Joanne ....Corte Madera, CA
Whitt, D. Randolph ....Columbia, SC
Whitt, David L. ....Ballwin, MO
Whitt, Gerald R. ....Los Angeles, CA
Whitt, Janice West ....Fort Smith, AR
Whitt, Jeffery W. ....Philadelphia, PA
Whitt, Jeffrey B. ....Chicago, IL
Whitt, Jeremy T. ....Milwaukee, WI
Whitt, Karen D. ....Dallas, TX
Whitt, Larry H. ....Dallas, TX
Whitt, M. Jeffrey ....Knoxville, TN
Whitt, Mark A. ....Cleveland, OH
Whitt, Michael R. ....Fort Myers, FL
Whitt, Ralph L., Jr. ....Richmond, VA
Whitt, Richard L. ....Columbia, SC
Whitt, Richard S. ....Washington, DC
Whitt, Robert C. ....Mount Holly, NC
Whitt, Robert H., Jr. ....Danville, VA
Whitt, Robert K. ....Midland, TX
Whitt, Ruthanne Q. ....Louisville, KY
Whitt, Samuel W. ....Raleigh, NC
Whitt, Sharon J. ....New York, NY
Whitt, Stephen R. ....Washington, DC
Whitt, Stuart L., Law Offices of
Aurora, IL
Whitt, Toni ....Fort Smith, AR
Whittaker, Bill G. ....Matthews, NC
Whittaker, Bruce G. ....New Orleans, LA
Whittaker, Camin ....San Bernardino, CA
Whittaker, Catherine C.
Kansas City, MO
Whittaker, Christine R. ....Hopkinton, MA
Whittaker, Clayton M. ....Chattanooga, TN
Whittaker, David M. ....Columbus, OH
Whittaker, Donald E., Jr. ....Houston, TX
Whittaker, Donald S. ....Carol Stream, IL
Whittaker, G. Daniel ....Lakewood, CO
Whittaker, Heskin A. ....Orlando, FL
Whittaker, Ingrid E. ....Atlanta, GA
Whittaker, J. David, (P.C.) ....Marietta, GA
Whittaker, James A. ....Cincinnati, OH
Whittaker, John Albert, IV
Washington, DC
Whittaker, Judith ....Kansas City, MO
Whittaker, Kenneth F. ....Boston, MA
Whittaker, Kenneth W. ....North Miami, FL
Whittaker, Kent E. ....Kansas City, MO
Whittaker, Kristina B. ....Treasury Department, Office of the Comptroller of the Currency, GV
Whittaker, Laurie ....North Miami, FL
Whittaker, Lennard K. ....Rio Grande City, TX
Whittaker, Linda A. ....Muscatine, IA
Whittaker, Lori S. ....Stockton, CA
Whittaker, Lorrie E. ....York, ME
Whittaker, M. Curtis ....Concord, NH
Whittaker, Malcolm E. ....Charlotte, NC
Whittaker, Maria C. ....Columbus, OH
Whittaker, Mark R. ....Pensacola, FL
Whittaker, Martin ....Chicago, IL
Whittaker, R. Thomas ....Midland, MI
Whittaker, Richard ....Ketchikan, AK
Whittaker, Richard W. ....Enterprise, AL
Whittaker, Robert B. ....Midland, MI
Whittaker, Robert Lee ....Oklahoma City, OK
Whittaker, Robert T. ....New York, NY
Whittaker, Scott T. ....New Orleans, LA
Whittaker, Stephen D., The Law Off. of
Kailua-Kona, HI
Whittaker, Stump, Webster & Miller, P.A.
Orlando, FL
Whittaker, Susan Lea ....Orange, CA
Whittaker, Thomas F. ....Kansas City, MO
Whittaker, Thomas J. ....Grandview, MO
Whittaker, Tiffani K. ....Washington, DC
Whittaker & Whittaker, P.A.
North Miami, FL
Whittaker, William L. ....San Jose, CA
Whittaker, Zona ....Ponca City, OK
Whittall-Scherfee, Ken R.
Sacramento, CA

Whittall-Scherfee, Law Office
Sacramento, CA
Whittamore-Mantzios, Melanie J.
Lincoln, NE
Whitteaker, Amy E. ....Hackensack, NJ
Whitteaker, John F. ....Morristown, NJ
Whitted, Alan L. ....Columbus, IN
Whitted, Brooke R. ....Chicago, IL
Whitted, Charles K. ....Merrillville, IN
Whitted, John B., Jr. ....Chicago, IL
Whitted, Peter J. ....Omaha, NE
Whitted, Warren R., Jr. ....Omaha, NE
Whittelsey, C. S. ....Opelika, AL
Whittemore, Anne Marie ....Richmond, VA
Whittemore, Arthur C. ....Cleveland, MS
Whittemore, Clark, Jr. ....Greenwich, CT
Hartford, CT
Whittemore, David C. ....Las Vegas, NV
Whittemore, David O. ....Framingham, MA
Whittemore, Donald H. ....Tampa, FL
Whittemore, Edward B. ....Washington, DC
Whittemore, Edward E. ....Barnstable, MA
Whittemore, Edwin P. ....Arlington, MA
Whittemore, Edwin P., P.C., Law Offices of
Arlington, MA
Whittemore, Ellen F. ....Las Vegas, NV
Whittemore, F. Case ....Richmond, VA
Whittemore, Gail F. ....Tarrytown, NY
Whittemore, Gilbert F. ....Boston, MA
Whittemore, Harvey ....Reno, NV
Whittemore, James D. ....Tampa, FL
Whittemore, Kent G. ....St. Petersburg, FL
Whittemore Law Group, The, P.A.
St. Petersburg, FL
Whittemore, Reed P. ....Port Washington, NY
Whittemore, Richard J. ....Portland, OR
Whittemore, Richard W., (P.C.)
Virginia Beach, VA
Whittemore, Ridgway, (P.C.) ....La Jolla, CA
Whittemore & Wallace ....Framingham, MA
Whittemore, William C., III ....Ridgefield, CT
Whitten, Alice L. ....Fort Worth, TX
Whitten, Beatrice E. ....Mount Pleasant, SC
Whitten, Blake Ivy ....Tulsa, OK
Whitten, C. G. ....Abilene, TX
Whitten, Chad R. ....Tulsa, OK
Whitten, Christopher ....Phoenix, AZ
Whitten, Christopher R. ....Indianapolis, IN
Whitten, Dale F. ....Tulsa, OK
Whitten, Dan L. ....Crown Point, IN
Whitten, David E. ....Dallas, TX
Whitten & Diamond ....Washington, DC
Whitten, George S.
Department of Agriculture, Office of the General Counsel, GV
Whitten, Hal S., Jr. ....Oklahoma City, OK
Whitten, J. Gregory ....Dallas, TX
Whitten, James A. ....San Jose, CA
Whitten, James L. ....Charleston, MS
Whitten, James M. ....Corpus Christi, TX
Sinton, TX
Whitten, James R. ....Saratoga Springs, NY
Whitten, Jamie L. ....Washington, DC
Whitten, John C. ....Quincy, MA
Whitten, John W., Jr. ....Sumner, MS
Whitten, John Wallace, III ....Sumner, MS
Whitten, Layman, MacKenzie, Padgett & Whitten ....Tulsa, OK
Whitten, Leon H. ....Jonesboro, LA
Whitten, MacKenzie, Whitten & Barnhart
Tulsa, OK
Whitten, Martha C. ....North Conway, NH
Whitten, McGuire, Wood, Terry, Roselius & Dittrich, A Prof. Ltd. Liability Co.
Oklahoma City, OK
Tulsa, OK
Whitten, Megan P. ....Dallas, TX
Whitten, Meredith Ann ....New Orleans, LA
Whitten, Michael C. ....Frankfort, IL
Whitten, Michael J. ....Denton, TX
Whitten, Patricia J. ....Chicago, IL
Whitten, Phyllis A. ....Washington, DC
Whitten, Ralph U. ....Omaha, NE
Whitten, Randy D. ....Florence, AL
Whitten, Reggie N. ....Oklahoma City, OK
Whitten, Ronald D. ....Dallas, TX
Whitten, Ronald E. ....Topeka, KS
Whitten, Terence R. ....Spokane, WA
Whitten, Thomas J. ....Lafayette, CA
Whitten & Whitten ....Oklahoma City, OK
Whitten, William C. ....Knoxville, IN
Whitten, William C., Jr. ....Milwaukee, WI
Whitten & Young, P.C. ....Abilene, TX
Whittenberger, G. Randall ....Frederick, MD
Whittenburg, Burk ....Amarillo, TX
Whittenburg, George ....Amarillo, TX
Dallas, TX
Whittenburg, Ivan J. ....Morristown, NJ
Whittenburg, James S. B. ....Austin, TX
Whittenburg, Jo Ben ....Beaumont, TX
Whittenburg, Mack ....Amarillo, TX
Dallas, TX
Whittenburg, Mark Edmonds
Chattanooga, TN
Whittenburg, Mark G. ....Cincinnati, OH
Whittenburg, Nancy L. ....Spencer, IA
Whittenburg, Nicholas W.
Chattanooga, TN
Whittenburg, Russell W. ....Columbus, OH
Whittenburg, Theodore R. ....Easton, MA
Whittenburg Whittenburg & Schachter, P.C.
Amarillo, TX
Dallas, TX
Whittenton, Jesse L. ....Austin, TX
Whitters, James P., III ....Boston, MA
Whitters, Timothy J. ....Seattle, WA
Tacoma, WA
Whitticar, Michael C. ....Richmond, VA

Whitticar, Ruth M. ....Canton, OH
Whittier, Antonie L. Wells ....Dallas, TX
Whittier, Beth A. ....Colorado Springs, CO
Whittier, David Q. ....South Paris, ME
Whittier, David R. ....Waterville, ME
Whittier, Duncan A. ....Topeka, KS
Whittier, Gary L. ....Kansas City, MO
Whittier, James M. ....Overland Park, KS
Whittier, Monte R. ....Idaho Falls, ID
Whittier, R. Max ....Pocatello, ID
Whittier, Scott B. ....Washington, DC
Whittier, Souza & Naftz, Chartered
Pocatello, ID
Whittier, Thomas N. ....Spencer, WV
Whittier, Valerie M. ....Cambridge, MA
Whittingham, David K. ....Northridge, CA
Whittingham, Mark Ernest ....Madison, WI
Whittinghill, Virginia C. ....Louisville, KY
Whittington, A. Daniel ....Cleveland, OH
Whittington & Aulgur ....Odessa, DE
Wilmington, DE
Whittington, Brock, Swayze & Dale
Greenwood, MS
Lexington, MS
Whittington, C. Mark ....Fairfax, VA
Whittington, Carolyn C. ....Kirkwood, MO
Whittington, Christopher Lee
Baton Rouge, LA
Whittington, David B.
Hot Springs National Park, AR
Whittington, David E. ....Placerville, CA
Whittington, David W. ....Charleston, SC
Whittington, Edward W., Jr. ....Mullins, SC
Whittington, G. Dale ....Houston, TX
Whittington, Gary ....Cedar Rapids, IA
Whittington, Harry M. ....Austin, TX
Whittington, Howard H. ....Clearwater, FL
Whittington, J. Richard ....Dallas, TX
Whittington, Joe W. ....Bakersfield, CA
Whittington, John A. ....Middletown, OH
Whittington, John D. ....Woodbridge, VA
Whittington, John H., Jr. ....Dallas, TX
Whittington, John P. ....Birmingham, AL
Whittington, John R., Jr. ....Houston, TX
Whittington, Joseph E. ....Anniston, AL
Whittington, Joseph P. ....Nitro, WV
Whittington, Kent E. ....Idaho Falls, ID
Whittington, Marquis E. ....San Antonio, TX
Whittington Melendy & Girdwood, P.C.
Hanover, NH
Woodstock, VT
Whittington, Michael T. ....Bakersfield, CA
Whittington, Michele ....Frankfort, KY
Whittington, Miles M. ....Galveston, TX
Whittington, O. Hampton, Jr.
Benson, NC
Whittington, Randolph K. ....Harlingen, TX
Whittington, Richard A. ....Melbourne, FL
Whittington, Robert A., (P.C.)
Brownsville, TX
Whittington, Robert M., Jr. ....Akron, OH
Whittington, Ronald L. ....Mc Comb, MS
Whittington, Steven B. ....Tallahassee, FL
Whittington, Thomas D., Jr. ....Odessa, DE
Wilmington, DE
Whittington, Thomas L. ....Issaquah, WA
Whittington, Thomas W. ....Denver, CO
Whittington, vonSternberg, Emerson & Wilsher, L.L.P. ....Houston, TX
Whittington, W. E. "Ned" ....Hanover, NH
Woodstock, VT
Whittington, William H., Jr.
Sacramento, CA
Whittington, William R. ....Prescott, AZ
Whittington, W. M., Jr. ....Greenwood, MS
Whittle, Amanda F. ....Aiken, SC
Whittle, Chester E. ....Highlands, NC
Whittle, Chester E., Jr. ....Boone, NC
Whittle, D. Kimberly Brown ....Boston, MA
Whittle, Eleanor I. ....Brunswick, GA
Whittle, Elizabeth Ward ....Washington, DC
Whittle, Gonzales, Hada & Capelo, L.L.P.
Corpus Christi, TX
Whittle, Jack J. ....New York, NY
Whittle, James E., Jr. ....Aiken, SC
Whittle, James J. ....Washington, DC
Whittle, James T., Jr. ....Amelia, OH
Whittle, Jeffrey S. ....Orlando, FL
Whittle, John K. ....Louisville, KY
Whittle, Joseph A. ....Brunswick, GA
Whittle, Joseph M. ....Louisville, KY
Whittle, L. Keith ....Williston, SC
Whittle Law Firm, The, P.L.L.C.
Corpus Christi, TX
Whittle, Marcus G. ....Los Angeles, CA
Whittle, Patrick J. ....Washington, DC
Whittle, Robert L. ....Boston, MA
Whittle, Robert W. ....Nashville, TN
Whittle, Russell S. ....Fort Myers, FL
Hollywood, FL
Whittle, Sam E., Jr. ....Baltimore, MD
Whittle, Vivian L. ....Pineville, LA
Whittle, W. Jeffrey ....Newark, DE
Wilmington, DE
Kennett Square, PA
Whittle, William A. ....Corpus Christi, TX
Whittler, Edward F. ....San Diego, CA
Whittlesey, David P. ....Austin, TX
Whittlesey, Dennis J. ....Washington, DC
Whittlesey, Franklin G. ....Flemington, NJ
Whittlesey, J. Baur ....Maple Shade, NJ
Philadelphia, PA
Whittlesey, Joan Valrance ....Englewood, CO
Whittlesey, John S. ....Dent, MN
Whittlesey, John W. ....Chappaqua, NY
Whittlesey McDowell & Riga
Maple Shade, NJ
Whittlesey, Richard C. ....Burlington, VT

Whittmore, Gregory A. ....Dallas, TX
Whitton, Cindy L. ....Kansas City, KS
Whitton, David W. ....New Castle, IN
Whitton, Henry G. ....Vero Beach, FL
Whitton, James M. ....Fort Worth, TX
Whitton, Jeffrey P. ....Panama City, FL
Whitton, John C., Jr. ....Tallahassee, FL
Whitton, Jon ....Oshkosh, WI
Whitton, Kerry K. ....San Augustine, TX
Whitton & Lansinger ....New Castle, IN
Whitton, Linda S. ....Indianapolis, IN
Whitton, Michael J. ....San Diego, CA
Whittredge, Robert B. ....Naples, FL
Whittum, Donald F. ....Rochester, NH
Whittum & Leahy ....Quincy, MA
Whitty, Charles C. ....Norwich, CT
Whitty, John W. ....Coos Bay, OR
Whitty, Michael D. ....Chicago, IL
Whitty, Michael O. ....Salem, OR
Whitty, Paul B. ....Louisville, KY
Whitty, Richard K. ....Dubuque, IA
Whitus, J. Brad ....Houston, TX
Whitwell, Ben D. ....Los Angeles, CA
Whitwell, R. Quentin, Jr. ....Oxford, MS
Whitwell, Robert Q. ....Ashland, MS
Whitwell, Sanford M. ....Cincinnati, OH
Whitwell, Stephen E. ....North Little Rock, AR
Whitworth, Amy Baumann ....Houston, TX
Whitworth, Carolyn A.W. ....Pittsburgh, PA
Whitworth, Charles R. ....Davis, CA
Whitworth, Dain P. ....Austin, TX
Whitworth, Daniel D. ....Joplin, MO
Webb City, MO
Whitworth, Daniel P. ....Brownsville, TX
Whitworth, David G., Jr. ....Crofton, MD
Whitworth, David T. ....Brunswick, GA
Whitworth, F. Dixon, Jr. ....Winchester, VA
Whitworth, George E. ....Memphis, TN
Whitworth, Gregory D.
West Palm Beach, FL
Whitworth, Guy V. ....Glendora, CA
Whitworth, H. Philip, Jr. ....Austin, TX
Whitworth, Harry P. ....Austin, TX
Whitworth, Horace P., Jr. ....Westernport, MD
Whitworth, J. Bryan ....Bartlesville, OK
Whitworth, Jason G. ....Covington, TN
Whitworth, Jill Ann ....Columbus, OH
Whitworth, John F. ....Houston, TX
Whitworth, John H., Jr. ....New York, NY
Whitworth, John W. ....Camden, TN
Whitworth, Kimberly Adams
North Reading, MA
Whitworth, Lewis B., Jr. ....Summerfield, FL
Whitworth, Mark R. ....Harlingen, TX
Whitworth, Matt J. ....Kansas City, MO
Whitworth, Matthew D. ....Pittsburgh, PA
Whitworth, Randall W. ....Lansing, MI
Whitworth, Regan ....Missoula, MT
Whitworth, Richard G. ....Baton Rouge, LA
Whitworth, Richard L. ....Arvada, CO
Whitworth, Robert F. ....Sacramento, CA
Whitworth, Shannon M. ....Milwaukee, WI
Whitworth & Smith,, P.A. ....Crofton, MD
Whitworth, Stephen A. ....Laredo, TX
Whitworth, Thomas D. ....Cleburne, TX
Whitworth, Thomas M. ....Houston, TX
Whitworth, Valerie C. ....Los Angeles, CA
Wholey, Jack ....San Francisco, CA
Wholey, John J. ....Portsmouth, NH
Wholey & Pelech ....Portsmouth, NH
Wholl, Edward R. ....Orangeburg, NY
Wholley, Richard F. ....Boston, MA
Wholly, James R. ....Bangor, ME
Whomes, Roger B. ....Reno, NV
Whong, Jason A. ....Palo Alto, CA
Whonsetler & Associates, P.S.C.
Louisville, KY
Whonsetler, Scott P. ....Louisville, KY
Whooley, Cornelius Vincent
New York, NY
Whooley, Donna M. ....Palo Alto, CA
Whoriskey, Neil Q. ....New York, NY
Whoriskey, Robert D. ....New York, NY
Whorley, James M. ....Temple, TX
Whorley, James M., P.C. ....Temple, TX
Whorley, Thomas J. ....Sheldon, IA
Whorton, Anna L. ....San Antonio, TX
Whorton, B. Michael ....Moundsville, WV
Whorton, Bert Michael, L.C.
Moundsville, WV
Whorton, J. Lowell ....Gladstone, MO
Whorton, Jack T. ....New Orleans, LA
Whorton, Mark W. ....Alamogordo, NM
Whritenour, Matthew ....Syracuse, NY
Whyatt, Thomas ....White Plains, NY
Whybrew, Charles R. ....Indianapolis, IN
Whyburn, Kay Paul ....Houston, TX
Whyburn, Kenneth G. ....San Francisco, CA
Whyland, Christopher M.
North Syracuse, NY
Whyland & Richmond ....North Syracuse, NY
Whyman, Megan Rae ....Palo Alto, CA
Whynott, Philip P. ....Cheyenne, WY
Whyte, Ann von Weise ....Los Gatos, CA
Whyte, Charles L. ....Waukegan, IL
Whyte, Daniel J. ....Helena, MT
Whyte, George K., Jr. ....Milwaukee, WI
Whyte, Hartzell J. ....Kansas City, KS
Whyte Hirschboeck Dudek S.C.
Madison, WI
Manitowoc, WI
Menomonee Falls, WI
Milwaukee, WI
Whyte & Jackson ....Kansas City, KS
Whyte, James P., Jr. ....Williamsburg, VA
Whyte, Jeffrey R. ....New York, NY
Whyte, Joseph P. ....Edwardsville, IL
Whyte, Kevin J. ....Pittsburgh, PA

Whyte, Kristi M. ... **Princeton, NJ**
Whyte, Lynn K. ... Richmond, VA
Whyte, Michael J. ... **Idaho Falls, ID**
Whyte, Nicole ... **Orange, CA**
Whyte, Robert O. ... **San Jose, CA**
Whyte, Ronald M. ... San Jose, CA
Whyte, Rudyard F. ... **New York, NY**
Whyte, S. Mathew ... **Sarasota, FL**
Whyte, Stephen M. ... Bradenton, FL
Whyte, Tammie D. ... Idaho Falls, ID
Whyte, Thomas C. ... Idaho Falls, ID
Whyte, Thomas J. ... **Pittsburgh, PA**
Whytock, Christopher A.
Newport Beach, CA
Whytsell, James Eric ... **Fairmont, WV**
Wiacek, Deborah L. ... **New York, NY**
Wiacek, Raymond J. ... **Washington, DC**
Wiacek, Robt. A. ... Chicago, IL
Wiand, Burton W. ... **Tampa, FL**
Wianecki, Richard James
Fountain Valley, CA
Wianecki, Thomas G. ... **Irvine, CA**
Wiant, James L. ... **St. Cloud, MN**
Wiant, Teresa J. ... Tacoma, WA
Wiard, Darrell D. ... Clearwater, FL
Wiard, James G. ... **Chicago, IL**
Wiarda, Martin R. ... **Dallas, TX**
Wiater, Mary Ann E. ... Batavia, NY
Wibbenmeyer, Carl T. ... Austin, TX
Wibbenmeyer & Cronfel ... Austin, TX
Wibbenmeyer, Kevin L. ... **St. Charles, MO**
Wibbenmeyer, Patrick J.
Westwood Hills, KS
Wibe, John A. ... Cherokee, IA
Wiberg, John A. ... **Minneapolis, MN**
Wiberg, Patricia O. ... Dover, NH
Wiberg, Sven D. ... Dover, NH
Wiberg & Wiberg ... Dover, NH
Wibking, Timothy J. ... Franklin, TN
Wible, Catherine A. ... **New York, NY**
Wible, Charles S. ... Owensboro, KY
Wible, Charles S., P.S.C., Law Offices of
Owensboro, KY
Wible, Craig A. ... St. Paul, MN
Wible, David Jennings ... Pike Road, AL
Wible, Elizabeth C. ... **Montgomery, AL**
Wible & Gallagher ... St. Paul, MN
Wible, Jeffrey W. ... LaGrange, IN
Wible, John Francis ... Raleigh, NC
Wible, Michael V. ... Columbus, OH
Wible, Ralph W. ... **Owensboro, KY**
Wible, Sharon Conway ... San Jose, CA
Wible, William R. ... Angola, IN
Wice, Brian W. ... **Houston, TX**
Wice, David H. ... **Philadelphia, PA**
Wice, Sharon R. ... **St. Louis, MO**
Wich, Donald A., Jr. ... **Fort Lauderdale, FL**
Wich, James J. ... **Fort Lauderdale, FL**
Wich, Joseph C., Jr. ... **Towson, MD**
Wich, Scott M. ... **New York, NY**
Wich, Thomas M. ... **Fort Lauderdale, FL**
Wich, Wich & Wich, P.A.
Fort Lauderdale, FL
Pompano Beach, FL
Wichelman, Jennifer K. ... **St. Paul, MN**
Wicher, Barbara J. ... Livonia, MI
Wicher, Camille P. ... Buffalo, NY
Wichers, Christine J. ... **Boston, MA**
Wichers, William A., II ... **Detroit, MI**
Wichinsky, Glenn E. ... Boca Raton, FL
Wichler & Gobetz, P.C. ... Suffern, NY
Wichler, Ranan ... Suffern, NY
Wichman, Charles R. ... **Honolulu, HI**
Wichman, David C. ... Manchester, CT
Wichman, Linda Kay ... Barboursville, WV
Wichman, Michael W. ... Hanalei, HI
Wichman, Ross J. ... Hays, KS
Wichmann, Brian T. ... Seattle, WA
Wichmann, Frank A. ... Erlanger, KY
Wichmann, Lucinda Gardner
Charleston, SC
Wichmann, Steven C. ... **Grand Rapids, MI**
Wichmann, William J. ... Fort Lauderdale, FL
Wichmann, William T. ... Freehold, NJ
Wichmer, Daniel R. ... **Springfield, MO**
Wichmer, Timothy E. ... **St. Louis, MO**
Wichowski, Loretta J. ... Exeter, CA
Wichrowski, Janice ... Orlando, FL
Wicht, Dennis H. ... Mequon, WI
Milwaukee, WI
Racine, WI
Wicht, J. Edward ... Evansville, IN
Wicht, William W., Jr. ... Hattiesburg, MS
Wick, Arthur A. ... Santa Rosa, CA
Wick, Bonnie Epperson
Fort Walton Beach, FL
Wick, Bryan J. ... **Dallas, TX**
Wick, Campbell, Bramer, Ukasick & Trautwein, LLC ... **Fort Collins, CO**
Cheyenne, WY
Wick, Charles D. ... Providence, RI
Wick, Charles Z. ... Los Angeles, CA
Wick, Constance R. ... Milwaukee, WI
Wick, Daniel A. ... Miami, FL
Wick, David B. ... **Springfield, MA**
Wick, David W., Law Office of
West St. Paul, MN
Wick, Diane Elan ... San Francisco, CA
Wick, Donald K. ... Mt. Gilead, OH
Wick, Douglas ... Willoughby, OH
Wick, Edmund V. ... Depew, NY
Wick, Elaine Kupp ... Depew, NY
Wick, G. Michael ... Cleveland, OH
Wick, Henry M., Jr. ... **Pittsburgh, PA**
Wick, Henry S. ... Depew, NY
Wick, Hilton A. ... Burlington, VT
Wick, James H. ... Burlington, VT
Wick, John G. ... Buffalo, NY
Wick, Kevin G. ... **Milwaukee, WI**
Wick, Lawrence S. ... **Chicago, IL**
Wick, Lucille N. ... **Pittsburgh, PA**
Wick & Maddocks ... Burlington, VT
Wick, Melissa A. ... Northfield, IL
Wick, Michael G. ... Glendale, CA
Wick, Nedra L. ... **Atlanta, GA**
Wick, Raidza T. ... **Vienna, VA**
Vienna, VA
Wick, Randall G. ... Dana Point, CA
Ridgefield Park, NJ
Wick, Rando W. H. ... **Seattle, WA**
Wick, Robert ... **Washington, DC**
Wick, Robert E., Jr. ... Bristol, VA
Wick, Robert Edward ... **Charlotte, NC**
Wick, Robert F. ... Rochester, MI
Wick, Robin L. ... **Fort Collins, CO**
Wick, Ronald F. ... **Washington, DC**
Wick, Sharon L. ... **Buffalo, NY**
Wick, Streiff, Meyer, O'Boyle & Szeligo, P.C.
Pittsburgh, PA
Wick & Wick ... Depew, NY
Wick, William A. ... **Indianapolis, IN**
Wick, William D. ... **Oakland, CA**
Wick, William R. ... **Manitowoc, WI**
Wick, Yvonne L. ... Huntington Station, NY
Wicka, James C. ... **Minneapolis, MN**
Wicka, Karen K. ... Buffalo, NY
Wicka, Kevin P. ... Schenectady, NY
Wicka, Richard V. ... Fort Worth, TX
Wickenden, D. Keith ... **Naples, FL**
Wickenden, David Richard ... Norcross, GA
Wickenkamp, Mary C. ... Lincoln, NE
Wickenkamp, William W. ... North Platte, NE
Wickens, D. Bryan ... **Louisville, KY**
Wickens, Don H. ... Greensburg, IN
Wickens, Herzer & Panza, A Legal Professional Association ... **Cleveland, OH**
Elyria, OH
Lorain, OH
Wickens, James C. ... **Bloomfield Hills, MI**
Wickens & Lebow ... Los Angeles, CA
Washington, DC
Deerfield Beach, FL
Wickens, Mark S. ... Baldwin, MI
Wickens, Paul L. ... **Kansas City, MO**
Wickens, William E. ... **Washington, DC**
Wickens, William G. ... **Lorain, OH**
Wicker, Brad W. ... Ponca City, OK
Wicker, Cameron McLean ... Danvers, MA
Wicker, Cynthia ... Stamford, CT
Wicker, Dennis A. ... Raleigh, NC
Wicker, Fredericka Homberg ... Gretna, LA
Wicker, Howard J. ... Old Saybrook, CT
Wicker, J. J., II ... **West Palm Beach, FL**
Wicker, Katherine L. ... **Indianapolis, IN**
Wicker, Mark R. ... **San Diego, CA**
Wicker, Mary Jo ... Louisville, KY
Wicker, Melissa Rice ... Charleston, SC
Wicker, Phillip K. ... **Shepherdsville, KY**
Wicker, R. David, Jr. ... Durham, NC
Wicker, Ralph J. ... Monroe, LA
Wicker, Raymond K. ... Newberry, SC
Wicker, Robert A. ... Greensboro, NC
Wicker, S. Edward ... Lynnwood, WA
Wicker & Senn, P.A. ... Newberry, SC
Wicker, Smith, Tutan, O'Hara, McCoy, Graham & Ford, P.A.
Fort Lauderdale, FL
Miami, FL
Orlando, FL
Tampa, FL
West Palm Beach, FL
Wicker, T. Carey, III ... **New Orleans, LA**
Wicker, T. Fred ... Pontotoc, MS
Wicker, Thomas A. ... **Tupelo, MS**
Wicker, Thomas C., Jr. ... Gretna, LA
Wicker, Tom, Jr. ... **El Paso, TX**
Wicker, Vivianne A. ... **Fort Lauderdale, FL**
Wicker, W. Chris ... **Reno, NV**
Wickerham, Richard D. ... Schenectady, NY
Wickers, Alonzo B., IV ... **Los Angeles, CA**
Wickers, Rodney W. ... **Torrance, CA**
Wickers, Roger T. ... Boston, MA
Wickersham & Bowers ... Daytona Beach, FL
Wickersham, Bruce ... **Boston, MA**
Wickersham, Christopher W., Sr.
Daytona Beach, FL
Wickersham, Francis X. ... **Norristown, PA**
Wickersham, Grover T. ... Palo Alto, CA
Wickersham, Grover T., Prof. Corp.
Palo Alto, CA
Wickersham, Jacqueline ... Seattle, WA
Wickersham, James B. ... Alamo, CA
Wickersham, Jerry L. ... Kansas City, MO
Wickersham, Kirk, Jr. ... Anchorage, AK
Wickersham, Michael D. ... Winchester, IN
Wickersham, Peter H. ... **San Antonio, TX**
Wickersham, Ralph R. ... Jacksonville, FL
Wickersham, Richard B. ... **Harrisburg, PA**
Wickersham, Richard B., Jr.
Mount Laurel, NJ
Philadelphia, PA
Wickersham, Richard J.
Treasury Department, GV
Wickersham, S. Charles ... San Diego, CA
Wickersham, Stephen V. ... Pleasanton, CA
Wickersham, Steven K. ... Kansas City, MO
Wickersham, Theodore S. ... **New York, NY**
Wickersham, William R. ... Harrison, NE
Wickersham-Bowers, Willard L.
Daytona Beach, FL
Wickersty, William J. ... **Chicago, IL**
Wickert, Frederick P. ... Belton, MO
Wickert, Gary A. ... Green Bay, WI
Wickert, Gary A., S.C. ... Green Bay, WI
Wickert, Gary L. ... **Hartford, WI**
Wickert, John E. ... Belton, MO
Wickert, John H. ... **Chicago, IL**
Wickert & Wickert ... Belton, MO
Wickes, Donald J. ... Marina Del Rey, CA
Wickes, Jo Lee M. ... Reno, NV
Wickes, John F., Jr. ... **Indianapolis, IN**
Wickes, Leslie A. ... **Jacksonville, FL**
Wickes, Lewin W. ... Chestertown, MD
Wickes, Paul O. ... **Dallas, TX**
Wickes, R. Paul ... **New York, NY**
Wickett, Charles C. ... Bloomingdale, MI
Wickett, James ... **Washington, DC**
Wickett, Julie Marie ... Idaho Falls, ID
Wickett, William A. ... **Des Moines, IA**
Wickey, Gene A. ... Sioux City, IA
Wickey, Gene A., P.C., Law Offices of
Sioux City, IA
Wickham, Abigail A. ... **Mattituck, NY**
Wickham, Conrad A., Jr. ... Coatesville, PA
Wickham, David R. ... **Dayton, OH**
Wickham, Deborah Lynn ... Reston, VA
Wickham, Dennis J. ... **San Diego, CA**
Wickham, Donald C. ... **Hemet, CA**
Wickham, Douglas A. ... **Los Angeles, CA**
Wickham, Douglas Q. ... **Raleigh, NC**
Wickham, Frederic O. ... Kansas City, MO
Wickham, George B. ... **Richmond, VA**
Wickham, H. Christopher ... Olympia, WA
Wickham, Henry P., Jr. ... Columbus, OH
Wickham, Henry T. ... **Richmond, VA**
Wickham, John A. ... Evergreen, CO
Wickham, Leslie Oliver, Jr. ... Durham, NC
Wickham, Lizabeth J. ... Chicago, IL
Wickham, Mary C. ... Los Angeles, CA
Wickham, Nicole M.
Department of the Air Force, Office of the Judge Advocate General, GV
Wickham, Richard J. ... **St. Louis, MO**
Wickham, Richard J., Jr.
Washington, DC
Wickham, Robert O., II ... Kansas City, KS
Wickham, Sarah C. ... **Wellesley, MA**
Wickham, Thomas J., Jr.
House of Representatives, Office of Parliamentarian, GV
Wickham, W. Christopher ... **Richmond, VA**
Wickham, Wickham & Bressler, P.C.
Mattituck, NY
Melville, NY
Wickham, William ... **Mattituck, NY**
Wickham, William R. ... Atlanta, GA
Wickhem, J. Scot ... **Minneapolis, MN**
Wickhem, James D. ... **Janesville, WI**
Wickins & Ashnault ... Penfield, NY
Wickkiser, William C. ... Allentown, PA
Wickland, David E. ... **Munster, IN**
Wickland, David E., Professional Corporation ... **Munster, IN**
Wickland, J. Scott ... Kingman, AZ
Wickland, J. Scott, P.C., Law Office of
Kingman, AZ
Wickland, Paige Leslie ... **San Francisco, CA**
Wickland, Sandra G. ... Sebastopol, CA
Wickland, Stephen A. ... **Clarksburg, WV**
Wickland, Steven B. ... Madison, WI
Wickler, Jay C. ... San Jose, CA
Wickler, Robert K. ... San Jose, CA
Wickliff, A. Martin, Jr. ... **Houston, TX**
Wickliff, Aloysius M. ... Houston, TX
Wickliff & Hall, A Professional Corporation
Austin, TX
Houston, TX
San Antonio, TX
Wickliffe, Charles D. ... Frankfort, KY
Wickliffe, Charles W., III ... **Atlanta, GA**
Wickliffe, Jerry L. ... **Houston, TX**
Wickliffe, Joy D. ... Kansas City, MO
Wickliffe, Karen Jorik ... **Atlanta, GA**
Wickliffe, Kevin B. ... Kansas City, MO
Wickliffe, Melody Craig ... Atlanta, GA
Wickliffe, W. A. ... Harrodsburg, KY
Wickline, Paul O. ... **Cleveland, OH**
Wickline, Richard P. ... **Los Angeles, CA**
Wickline, Wm. Scott ... **Charleston, WV**
Wicklow, Joseph M., III ... New Haven, CT
Wicklow, S. W. ... Rohnert Park, CA
Wicklund, David W. ... **Toledo, OH**
Wicklund, Eileen W. ... Marshall, MI
Wicklund, Lisa C. ... St. Paul, MN
Wickman, Clifford L., Jr. ... New York, NY
Wickman, John E. ... **Bradenton, FL**
Wickman, Kirk P. ... **Hartford, CT**
Wickman, Steven A. ... Vista, CA
Wickman & Wyckoff, P.A. ... **Bradenton, FL**
Wickman-Bennett, Margot ... **Omaha, NE**
Wickmark, Steven Thomas ... Webster, NY
Wickouski, M. Stephanie ... **Washington, DC**
Wickre, James A. ... Medford, OR
Wicks, Alan ... **Seattle, WA**
Wicks, Ann M. ... **San Francisco, CA**
Wicks, Charles C. ... Elkhart, IN
Wicks, Clarence R. ... **Portland, OR**
Wicks, Douglas C. ... Playa Del Rey, CA
Wicks, Douglas F. ... **Poughkeepsie, NY**
Wicks, Edward E. ... **Chicago, IL**
Wicks, Glenn P. ... Washington, DC
Wicks, James M. ... **Uniondale, NY**
Wicks, James R. ... East Northport, NY
Wicks, Jeffrey ... Rochester, NY
Wicks, John F. ... **Palo Alto, CA**
Wicks, John R. ... **Rochester, MN**
Wicks, L. Michael ... Detroit, MI
Wicks, Lloyd A., Jr. ... Ralls, TX
Wicks, Martine Apollon ... **New York, NY**
Wicks, Michael J. ... Phoenix, AZ
Wicks, Robert D. ... Bloomingdale, IL
Wicks, Ronan M. ... **New York, NY**
Wicks, Rory R. ... **San Diego, CA**
Wicks, Stephen D. ... Altoona, PA
Wicks, William R., III ... **Miami, FL**
Wicksel, Edwin J. ... Syosset, NY
Wickser, John P. ... **Buffalo, NY**
Wickstead, Michael G. ... **Seattle, WA**
Wickstrom, Beverly ... **Eau Claire, WI**
Wickstrom, Daryl S. ... New York, NY
Wickstrom, John A. ... **Worcester, MA**
Wickstrom, Mark P. ... **Worcester, MA**
Wickstrom, Thomas J. ... **Worcester, MA**
Wickstrom, Timothy P. ... **Worcester, MA**
Wickstrom, Tren ... **Seattle, WA**
Wickwire, Christian ... **New York, NY**
Wickwire, David F. ... **Seattle, WA**
Wickwire Gavin LLP ... **Los Angeles, CA**
Wickwire Gavin, P.C. ... **Washington, DC**
Vienna, VA
Madison, WI
Wickwire, Greene, Crosby, Brewer & Seward ... **Juneau, AK**
Seattle, WA
Wickwire, James ... **Seattle, WA**
Wickwire, James A. ... Castle Rock, CO
Wickwire, Jon M. ... **Washington, DC**
Vienna, VA
Wickwire, Thomas ... Fairbanks, AK
Wickwire, William B. ... Uncasville, CT
Wicky, Phillip Alan ... Rockport, MA
Wicoff, Bob ... Houston, TX
Wicoff, Patricia A. ... Houston, TX
Wiczer & Associates, Chartered
Northbrook, IL
Wiczer, Bernard ... Northbrook, IL
Wiczynski, Marilyn Ann ... Hawthorne, CA
Widawski, Jerry ... Calabasas, CA
Widburg, Andrea R. ... San Francisco, CA
Widdecke, James C. ... San Diego, CA
Widdel, John E., Jr. ... Grand Forks, ND
Widder, John M. ... **Washington, DC**
Widder, Karen Elizabeth ... Cincinnati, OH
Widder, Kurt ... Port Jefferson Station, NY
Widder, Theodore C., III ... Madison, WI
Widders, Monte L. ... **Ventura, CA**
Widdes, Steven A. ... **Bethesda, MD**
Widdifield, Ann Migden ... Los Angeles, CA
Widdifield, Melissa N. ... **Los Angeles, CA**
Widdig, Rebecca L. ... **Portsmouth, OH**
Widdis, Dennis E. ... Reno, NV
Widdis, Lawrence A. ... Glendale, CA
Widdison, Harold Kearl ... Sioux City, IA
Widdison, John J. ... Boston, MA
Widdoes, David R. ... Sapulpa, OK
Widdows, P. Gae ... Tulsa, OK
Widdowson & Carpenter ... Wichita, KS
Widdowson and Dashiell, P.A.
Salisbury, MD
Widdowson, Dirk W. ... **Salisbury, MD**
Widdowson, Edmund L., Jr.
Princess Anne, MD
Widdowson, Edmund L., Jr., P.A.
Princess Anne, MD
Widdowson, John H. ... Wichita, KS
Widdowson, Logan C. ... Princess Anne, MD
Widdowson, Mary E. ... **Flagstaff, AZ**
Widdowson, Philip C., Jr.
Princess Anne, MD
Widegren, Brian D. ... West Chatham, MA
Wideikis, John R. ... Palos Heights, IL
Widelitz, Kenneth S. ... Los Angeles, CA
Widell, Alexander D. ... **New York, NY**
Widell, Gary G. ... Minneapolis, MN
Widell, Heidi L. ... Chicago, IL
Widell, John W. ... **Seattle, WA**
Widelock, Marc D. ... Bakersfield, CA
Widem, I. Milton ... **Hartford, CT**
Widem, Lawrence G. ... Hartford, CT
Wideman, Joan M. ... St. Louis, MO
Wideman, Joseph A. ... Newkirk, OK
Wideman, Richard I. ... Santa Barbara, CA
Wideman, Suellen ... Baltimore, MD
Widemon, Carol L. ... Newark, NJ
Widen, Darrell ... **Chicago, IL**
Widen, Frederick N. ... **Cleveland, OH**
Widen, Melissa S. ... **Chicago, IL**
Widen, R. Scott ... **New York, NY**
Widen, William H. ... **New York, NY**
Widenbaum, Susan F., P.C., Law Offices of
Westland, MI
Widenbaum-Vainik, Susan F.
Westland, MI
Widener, Carla M. ... United States Senate, Senatorial Assistants, GV
Widener, China L. ... Columbus, OH
Widener, H. Emory, Jr. ... Abingdon, VA
Widener, James F., III ... Irving, TX
Widener, Jas. F. ... Irving, TX
Widener, Jo S. ... Bristol, VA
Widener, John D. ... Arkadelphia, AR
Widener, Leftwich & Widener ... Irving, TX
Widener, Michael N. ... **Phoenix, AZ**
Widener, Robert L. ... **Columbia, SC**
Widener, Stannard E., Jr. ... Johnson City, TN
Widener, Susan Donnelly ... Columbia, SC
Widenhouse, Constance E. ... Durham, NC
Widenhouse, M. Gordon, Jr.
Chapel Hill, NC
Widenmann, C. Henry, Jr. ... Pine, AZ
Widenor, David S. ... **Buffalo, NY**
Widenor, Mary H. ... **Alameda, CA**
Wider, Dorinda L. ... Minneapolis, MN
Wider, Francisca J. ... Fort Lauderdale, FL
Wider, Jedd H. ... **New York, NY**
Wider, Loretta A. ... **San Francisco, CA**
Wider, Robert L. ... St. Paul, MN
Widerberg, Willard B. ... Elgin, IL
Widerberg, Sandra M. ... Chicago, IL
Widerkehr, Robert L., Jr.
Chattanooga, TN

Widerman, Steven W.
National Credit Union Administration, Office of General Counsel, GV
Wides, Burton V. ... Washington, DC
Wides, Steven A., Law Office of ... Lexington, KY
Widett and McCarthy, P.C. ... Newton, MA
Widger, Abbie J. ... Lincoln, NE
Widger, Rodric A. ... Springfield, MO
Widger, Stanley W., Jr. ... Rochester, NY
Widgren, Kristin J. ... Detroit, MI
Widick, Barbara L. ... Denver, CO
Widick, Marshall J. ... Detroit, MI
Widick, Paul ... St. Cloud, MN
Widin, Douglas R. ... Philadelphia, PA
Widin, Richard E. ... Cary, NC
Widing, Carol ... Avon, CT
Hartford, CT
Litchfield, CT
Widing, J. William, III ... Reading, PA
Widirstky, James A. ... Hauppauge, NY
Widis, Howard M. ... Charlotte, NC
Widiss, Alan I. ... Iowa City, IA
Widlak, David A. ... Sterling Heights, MI
Widlan, Sandra E. ... Seattle, WA
Widland, James J. ... Albuquerque, NM
Widland, Michael L. ... Stamford, CT
Widlaski, Douglas J. ... Houston, TX
Widlitz, Evan S. ... New York, NY
Widlitz, Paul J. ... St. James, NY
Widlitz, Stephen I. ... Huntington, NY
Widlund, Douglas S. ... Denver, CO
Widlus, Hannah B. ... Chicago, IL
Widmaier, Charles W. ... Brighton, MI
Widmaier, James L. ... Columbus, OH
Widmaier, Janet R. ... Chicago, IL
Widmaier, Kurt ... Hauppauge, NY
Widmaier, Monica A. ... Media, PA
Widmaier, Uli ... Chicago, IL
Widman, Chas L. ... Washington, DC
Widman, Cooney & Barrett
Oakhurst, NJ
Widman, Douglas J. ... Oakhurst, NJ
Widman, Gary ... San Francisco, CA
Widman, Jeffrey L. ... Chicago, IL
Widman, Jeffrey P. ... San Jose, CA
Widman, Jerry P. ... St. Louis, MO
Widman, Joel L. ... Corrales, NM
Widman, John H. ... King Of Prussia, PA
Widman, Judith ... Philadelphia, PA
Widman, Michael J. ... Los Angeles, CA
Widman, Robert C. ... Venice, FL
Widman, Stuart M. ... Chicago, IL
Widman, Thomas D. ... Boise, ID
Widman, Thomas G. ... Bucyrus, OH
Widmann, Brian E. ... Denver, CO
Widmann, Douglas J. ... New York, NY
Widmann, Edward H. ... Denver, CO
Widmann, Franklin L. ... Newark, NJ
Widmann, Harry T. ... Metairie, LA
Widmann, Harry T., & Associates, P.L.C.
Metairie, LA
New Orleans, LA
Widmann, Jonathan P. ... Altus, OK
Widmann, Michael J. ... Milwaukee, WI
Widmann, Randall M. ... Palo Alto, CA
Widmann, Wendy ... Baltimore, MD
Widmar, Joseph H. ... Beltsville, MD
Widmayer, Lawrence A., Jr. ... Vero Beach, FL
Widmayer, Ruben R. ... Highmore, SD
Miller, SD
Widmayer, Warren J. ... Ann Arbor, MI
Widmer, Albert F., Jr. ... Metairie, LA
Widmer, Jennifer A. ... Palos Heights, IL
Widmer, Patrick J. ... Bend, OR
Widmer, Robert James, Jr. ... Denton, TX
Widmer, Ted R. ... Houston, TX
Widmer, Winifred R. ... Albany, NY
Widmer-Eby, Michelle C. ... Morgantown, WV
Widmeyer, Stephan B. ... Port Charlotte, FL
Widnell, Nicholas A. ... Washington, DC
Widner, Dalford R. V. ... Huntsville, AL
Widner, Robert C. ... Denver, CO
Widner, Susan Herrera ... Albuquerque, NM
Widoff, Joshua J. ... Denver, CO
Widoff, Mark P. ... Harrisburg, PA
Widoff, Preston C. ... Tampa, FL
Widom, Barton S. ... Department of Labor, Office of the Solicitor, GV
Widom, Ellen R. ... Miami, FL
Widom, Glenn L. ... Miami, FL
Widom, Mitchell E., (P.A.) ... Miami, FL
Widom, Richard M. ... Los Angeles, CA
Widom, Stephen C. ... New York, NY
Widor, Aimee L. ... Rochester, NY
Widowski Cassidy & Steinhart, LLP
Englewood Cliffs, NJ
New York, NY
Widowski, Esther S. ... New York, NY
Widowski, Stuart H. ... New York, NY
Widre, Sheryl ... Encino, CA
Widrig, Barbara L. ... Mayville, NY
Widseth, Gregory A. ... Crookston, MN
Widtfeldt, James ... Atkinson, NE
Width, Richard R. ... Westfield, NJ
Widule, John C. ... Elm Grove, WI
Widzinski, Paul J. ... Detroit, MI
Wieand, Donald E. ... Allentown, PA
Wieand, Donald E., Jr. ... Lehigh Valley, PA
Wieand, Jeffrey S. ... Bedford, MA
Wiebalk, Wendy L. ... Rahway, NJ
Wiebe, Calvin L. ... Wichita, KS
Wiebe, Peter J., Jr. ... Denver, CO
Wiebe, Virgil O. ... New York, NY
Wiebe, Warran D. ... Lawrence, KS
Wiebel, George C. ... North Wilkesboro, NC
Wiebelt, Andrew H., II ... New Orleans, LA
Wieben, John S. ... Monterey, CA
Wieben, Pamela Shea ... Monterey, CA
Bloomfield Hills, MI
Wieben & Wieben ... Monterey, CA
Wieber, A. Christopher ... New York, NY
Wieber, Donald M. ... Lidgerwood, ND
Wieber, John E. ... St. Johns, MI
Wieber, Michael C. ... Milwaukee, WI
Wieboldt, James C. ... Charlottesville, VA
Wieboldt, Stephanie Carol ... Charlotte, NC
Wieburg, Brett ... Gig Harbor, WA
Wiebusch, John M. ... Oconto, WI
Wiebusch, Richard V. ... Boston, MA
Wiech, Benjamin A. ... North Tonawanda, NY
Wiech, Jack ... Brownsville, TX
Wiechel, David R. ... Springfield, OH
Wiechens, Eugene A. ... Belleview, FL
Ocala, FL
Wiechers, Anthony J. ... Novato, CA
Wiechman, Robert Dean ... Wichita, KS
Wiechman, Steven R. ... Topeka, KS
Wiechmann, Daniel F., Jr. ... Hampton, IA
Wiechmann, David W. ... San Antonio, TX
Wiechmann, Don E. ... Tulsa, OK
Wiechmann, Eric Watt ... Hartford, CT
Wiechmann, William N. ... Washington, DC
Wieck, Brian Douglas ... Portland, OR
Wieck, David J. ... Seattle, WA
Wieck, Paul E. ... Marshall, IL
Wieck, Paul H., II ... Des Moines, IA
Wieck, Robert D. ... Providence, RI
Wieck, Shelley R. ... Sioux Falls, SD
Wiecking, David K. ... Richmond, VA
Wieckowski, Carol A. ... Sacramento, CA
Wieckowski, Elizabeth M. ... New York, NY
Wieckowski, Robert A. ... Fremont, CA
Wieczkowski, Jeffrey A ... Buffalo, NY
Wieczorek & Associates ... Las Vegas, NV
Wieczorek, Dennis E. ... Chicago, IL
Wieczorek, Gary E. ... Pittsburgh, PA
Wieczorek, Nicholas M. ... Las Vegas, NV
Wieczorek, Stephen D. ... Batavia, NY
Wieczorek, Talbot J. ... Rapid City, SD
Wieczorek, Terry D. ... Brookings, SD
Wieczorkowski, Andrew M.
New Port Richey, FL
Wied, C. W., Professional Corporation
San Diego, CA
Wied, Charles D. ... Bakersfield, CA
Wied, Colin W. ... San Diego, CA
Wied, Elizabeth Carol ... Sacramento, CA
Wied, Peter J. ... Los Angeles, CA
Wiedabach, Jack R. ... Milwaukee, WI
Wiede, Doris J. ... Houston, TX
Wiedeback, Roger L. ... Naples, FL
Wiedeke, Frederick R., Jr. ... Bayville, NJ
Wiedel, Michael C. ... Downers Grove, IL
Wiedemann, Herbert P. ... Milwaukee, WI
Wiedemann, Jody L. ... Mount Laurel, NJ
Wiedemann, John T. ... Cleveland, OH
Wiedemann, Karen ... New Orleans, LA
Wiedemann, Karl ... New Orleans, LA
Wiedemann, Lawrence D.
New Orleans, LA
Wiedemann, Paul ... New York, NY
Wiedemann, Robert A. ... Norwalk, OH
Wiedemann & Taube ... Marion, OH
Wiedemann & Wiedemann, A Professional Law Corporation ... New Orleans, LA
Wiedemann, William ... Marion, OH
Wiedemann, William H.
Colorado Springs, CO
Wiedemer, James I. ... Bellaire, TX
Wiedemer, Mark M. ... New York, NY
Wiedenbeck, Peter J. ... St. Louis, MO
Wiedenfeld, Mark J. ... Des Moines, IA
Wiedenfeld & McLaughlin
Des Moines, IA
Wiedenman, Jere W. ... Milwaukee, WI
Wieder, Allen M. ... New York, NY
Wieder, Bruce T. ... Alexandria, VA
Wieder, Catherine Grant ... Cerritos, CA
Wieder, David L. ... Cleveland, OH
Wieder, Frederic S. ... Palm Desert, CA
Wieder, Howard L. ... Bronx, NY
Wieder, Jane M. ... Tampa, FL
Wieder, Joan ... Department of Labor, Office of Secretary, GV
Wieder, Lawrence R. ... Harrisburg, PA
Wieder, Linda Rae ... Los Angeles, CA
Wieder, Louise A. ... New York, NY
Wieder, Mary F. ... New York, NY
Wieder, Michael D. ... South Euclid, OH
Wieder, Robert E. ... Ellicott City, MD
Wieder, Stephen A. ... New York, NY
Wieder, Thomas F. ... Ann Arbor, MI
Wiederaenders, Roland P. ... Dallas, TX
Wiederhoeft, James ... Madison, WI
Wiederhold, Cecilia B. ... New Haven, CT
Wiederhold, John P.
West Palm Beach, FL
Wiederhold, Moses, Bulfin & Rubin, P.A.
Fort Lauderdale, FL
West Palm Beach, FL
Wiederholt, Marc H. ... Mercer Island, WA
Wiederkehr, Lee S. ... White Plains, NY
Yonkers, NY
Wiederrich, James M. ... Sioux Falls, SD
Wiederschall, James S., Law Offices of
Los Angeles, CA
Wiederschall, James S., Law Offices of
Woodland Hills, CA
Wiederspahn, Alvin ... Cheyenne, WY
Wiederspahn, Harry G. ... Metairie, LA
Wiederspahn & Reese, P.C.
Cheyenne, WY
Wiederstein, Barbara ... El Paso, TX
Wiederstein, Robert Khuon ... Henderson, KY
Wiedinger, Arthur R., Jr. ... Kolonia, TT
Wiedis, David ... West Chester, PA
Wiedis, Richard N. ... Department of Justice, Criminal Division, GV
Wiedman, J.N. ... Santa Barbara, CA
Wiedman, Michelle M. ... Chicago, IL
Wiedman, Richard Brian ... Castle Rock, CO
Wiedman, Richard S. ... Pittsburgh, PA
Wiedman, Vazzana & Corcoran, P.C.
Rochester, NY
Wiedmeier, Bryan Jon ... Davie, FL
Wiedner, Burk M. ... Glendale, CA
Wiedner, Frank J. ... Chicago, IL
Wiedner, Mark C. ... Chicago, IL
Wiedner & McAuliffe, Ltd. ... Chicago, IL
Wiedner, Paul W. ... Chicago, IL
Wiedorn, Kathryn T. ... Metairie, LA
Wiedt, Kacey C. ... Harrisburg, PA
Wiedt, Karl W., III ... Pittsburgh, PA
Wiedt, Patricia T. ... Harrisburg, PA
Wiegand, Barry ... Washington, DC
Wiegand, Bruce ... Pittsburgh, PA
Wiegand, Cort V. ... Modesto, CA
Wiegand, David M.
Department of Transportation, Federal Aviation Administration, GV
Wiegand, Frank L., Jr. ... Pittsburgh, PA
Wiegand, Jeffrey P. ... New Rochelle, NY
Wiegand, Marc F. ... Houston, TX
Wiegand, Margaret A.
United States Court Of Appeals District Of Columbia Circuit, GV
Wiegand, Richard A. ... Mentor, OH
Wiegand, Robert C. ... Dallas, TX
Wiegand, Robert, II ... Breckenridge, CO
Denver, CO
Wiegand, Roger C. ... Pittsburgh, PA
Wiegand, Sarah B. ... Dallas, TX
Wiegand, Scott E. ... Cincinnati, OH
Wiegand, Shirley A. ... Norman, OK
Wiegand, Thomas J. ... Chicago, IL
Wiegand, Vic ... Cumming, GA
Wiegand-Attorneys & Counselors, L.L.C.
Breckenridge, CO
Denver, CO
Wiegandt, Ralph C. ... Fincastle, VA
Wiegard, Michael A. ... Washington, DC
Wiegartner, Paul John, Jr. ... New York, NY
Wiegel, Andrew J. ... San Francisco, CA
Wiegel, David C. ... St. Clair Shores, MI
Wiegel & Fried, Law Offices of
San Francisco, CA
Wiegel, Gary L. ... Mt. Pleasant, IA
Wiegerink, Douglas H. ... Grand Rapids, MI
Wiegers, Edward F. ... Marysville, KS
Wiegers, Edward G. ... Chesterfield, MO
Wiegers, Susan Jane ... Topeka, KS
Wiegert, Robert F. ... St. Louis, MO
Wieghaus, Brian J. ... Tarrytown, NY
Wiegleb, Jennifer A. ... Washington, DC
Wiegley, James R. ... Fort Lauderdale, FL
Wiegley, Roger D. ... New York, NY
Wiegman, Linda S. ... Austin, TX
Wiegmann, J. Bradford
Department of Defense, Office of the General Counsel, GV
Wiegmann, R. Hackney ... Washington, DC
Wiegratz, Wyon F. ... Neenah, WI
Wiehaus, Donna J. ... Monticello, FL
Tallahassee, FL
Wiehe, Catherine ... San Jose, CA
Wiehl, Derald W. ... Sioux Falls, SD
Wiehl, James G. ... St. Louis, MO
Wiehl, Lis ... Washington, DC
Seattle, WA
Wiehl, Richard L. ... Yakima, WA
Wiehle, Dana Melton ... Tallahassee, FL
Wiehle, Michael S. ... Wheaton, IL
Wiejaczka, Michelle G. ... Island Lake, IL
Wieker, Frederick J. ... Upper Marlboro, MD
Wieland, Charles A. ... Fresno, CA
Wieland, Charles F., III ... Alexandria, VA
Wieland, David L. ... Springfield, MO
Wieland, Diana K. ... St. Louis, MO
Wieland, Gary R. ... White River Junction, VT
Wieland, George A., Jr. ... San Bernardino, CA
Wieland, Glen D. ... Orlando, FL
Wieland, Henry E. ... Bloomington, MN
Wieland, Herbert E. ... Raymond, WA
Wieland, Hilado & Kelley, P.A.
Kissimmee, FL
Melbourne, FL
Orlando, FL
Wieland, Hollie ... Colorado Springs, CO
Denver, CO
Wieland, J. Lee, Jr. ... Atlanta, GA
Wieland, James B. ... Baltimore, MD
Wieland, Jeffrey P. ... Orlando, FL
Wieland, Jennifer M. ... Newton, KS
Wieland, John C. ... Omaha, NE
Wieland, Lucy A. ... Minneapolis, MN
Wieland, Matthew A. ... New York, NY
Wieland, Oscar P. ... St. Louis, MO
Wieland, Rhett Gerhardt ... Waterville, ME
Wieland, Richard A. ... Wichita, KS
Wieland, Richard J. ... Austin, TX
Wieland, Robert E. ... St. Louis, MO
Wieland, Robert N. ... Falls Church, VA
Wieland, Stuart D. ... Kansas City, MO
Wieland, William A. ... Lincoln, NE
Wieland, William J. ... Orlando, FL
Wieland, Wm. M. ... Orlando, FL
Wiele, Dana Charles ... St. Louis, MO
Wiele, Martin G. ... Austin, TX
Wieleba, Joanie ... Hartford, CT
Wielebinski, Joseph J. ... Dallas, TX
Wielechowski, Tim ... Washington, DC
Wieler, Martha Anne ... Branford, CT
Wieler, Stephen E. ... Florham Park, NJ
Wielga, Mark ... Denver, CO
Wielgus, Thomas M. ... Washington, DC
Wieliczko, Matthew B. ... Cherry Hill, NJ
Wielinski & Elleraas ... St. Cloud, MN
Wielinski, Patrick J. ... Dallas, TX
Wielinski, William F. ... St. Cloud, MN
Wiellette, Julia M. ... West Hartford, CT
Wielobob, Allison E. ... Philadelphia, PA
Wieloch, Jennifer L. ... Cambridge, MA
Wieman, F. Joseph
Department Of Health And Human Services, Social Security Administration, GV
Wieman, Lawrence E. ... New York, NY
Wieman, Marc E. ... New York, NY
Wiemelt, Mark E. ... Chicago, IL
Wiemer, Becky A. ... Lincoln, NE
Wiemer, Rod W. ... Okmulgee, OK
Wiemerslage, Daniel S. ... Chicago, IL
Wiemerslage, Frank R. ... Park Ridge, IL
Wiemerslage, Frank R., Ltd. ... Park Ridge, IL
Wiemerslage, Wayne L. ... Findlay, OH
Wien, Daniel P. ... San Diego, CA
Wien, Henry ... El Centro, CA
Wien, Holly Wallack
Upper Saddle River, NJ
Wien, Howard ... Encino, CA
Wien, Howard Gary ... New York, NY
Wien, Jake M. ... New York, NY
Wien & Malkin LLP ... New York, NY
Wien, Michael S. ... New York, NY
Wien, R. Barbara ... Miami, FL
Wien, Robert W. ... Mount Kisco, NY
Wienand, Jerry W. ... Pittsburgh, PA
Wienberg, Christine ... New York, NY
Wiencek, John S. ... Hamburg, NY
Wiencek, Mark A. ... Buffalo, NY
Wiencek, Thomas J. ... Akron, OH
Wiench, Todd E. ... Washington, DC
Wienecke, Emil A., Jr. ... Tulsa, OK
Wienecke, Russell E. ... Claremore, OK
Wieneke, Daniel L. ... Norwalk, CT
Wieneke, Kathleen L. ... Phoenix, AZ
Wiener, Alan D. ... Newark, NJ
Wiener, Alan D. ... Oak Ridge, NC
Wiener, Alan H., (A Professional Corporation) ... Irvine, CA
Wiener, Alan P. ... San Diego, CA
Wiener, Allison M. ... New York, NY
Wiener, Alyssa S. ... Boston, MA
Wiener, Andrew R. ... San Francisco, CA
Wiener, Arthur G. ... Brooklyn, NY
Wiener, Arthur W. ... Greensboro, NC
Wiener, Barry J. ... Atlanta, GA
Wiener, Benjamin R. ... Santa Barbara, CA
Wiener, Bruce H. ... New York, NY
Wiener, Bruce I. ... Tallahassee, FL
Wiener, Bruce M.
Department of Housing and Urban Development, Office of General Counsel, GV
Wiener, Bruce S. ... San Francisco, CA
Wiener, Carolyn B. ... Garden City, NY
Wiener, Cary R. ... New York, NY
Wiener, Daniel Eli ... Lynbrook, NY
Wiener, David J. ... Palm Beach Gardens, FL
Wiener, Deborah Judith
San Francisco, CA
Wiener, Donald B. ... Shreveport, LA
Wiener, Eliot J ... Denver, CO
Wiener, Elliot J. ... New York, NY
White Plains, NY
Wiener, Eric S. ... Arlington, VA
Wiener, Frank J. ... Madison, WI
Wiener, Frederick B. ... Phoenix, AZ
Wiener, Frederick P. ... New York, NY
Wiener, George M. ... Woodland Hills, CA
Wiener, Gerald H. ... Los Angeles, CA
Wiener, Glen A. ... New York, NY
Wiener, Herb, (Prof. Corp.) ... Encino, CA
Wiener, Howard A. ... Treasury Department, Internal Revenue Service, GV
Wiener, Howard A. ... West Palm Beach, FL
Allentown, PA
Wiener, Howard B. ... San Diego, CA
Wiener, Howard J. ... Boca Raton, FL
West Palm Beach, FL
Wiener, Howard J., P.A. ... Boca Raton, FL
West Palm Beach, FL
Wiener, Howard N. ... Rahway, NJ
Wiener, Ian C. ... Los Angeles, CA
Wiener, Ira E. ... New York, NY
Wiener, Jack R. ... New York, NY
Wiener, Jacques L., III ... Shreveport, LA
Wiener, James A. ... Irvine, CA
Wiener, Jane L. ... Portland, OR
Wiener, Jay L. ... San Francisco, CA
Wiener, Jerome ... Chicago, IL
Wiener, Joel ... Kenilworth, NJ
Wiener, Joel B. ... West Palm Beach, FL
Allentown, PA
Wiener, Joel S. ... Brooklyn, NY
Wiener, John D. ... Boulder, CO
Wiener, Jonathan B. ... Durham, NC
Wiener, Jonathan L. ... Washington, DC
Wiener, Joseph C., Jr. ... Belton, TX
Wiener, Joseph Kenneth ... Chantilly, VA
Wiener, Joshua J. ... Jackson, MS
Wiener, Judith Mitchell ... Jackson, MS
Wiener, June W. ... Cleveland, OH
Wiener, Keith M. ... Atlanta, GA
Wiener, Larry I. ... Rockaway, NJ
Wiener, Laurence S. ... Los Angeles, CA
Wiener Law Firm ... Jackson, MS
Wiener, Leonard ... Great Neck, NY
Wiener, Lewis R. ... Corte Madera, CA
Wiener, Lewis S. ... Department of Justice, Environment and Natural Resources Division, GV

Wiggins/Garfield Associates ....Pittsburgh, PA
Wiggins-Lester, Nancy ....Atlanta, GA
Wigginton and Associates, P.C. Wichita Falls, TX
Wigginton, David Q. ....Newark, OH
Wigginton, Eric ....New York, NY
Wigginton, J. Ronald ....Tampa, FL
Wigginton, J. Ronald, II ....Tampa, FL
Wigginton, John Klein ....Tallahassee, FL
Wigginton, Kenneth W. ....Wichita Falls, TX
Wigginton, Stephen R. ....Belleville, IL
Wigglesworth, Henry ....Saipan, TT
Wigglesworth, Leonard Department of Housing and Urban Development, Office of General Counsel, GV
Wigg-Maxwell, Paul D. New Providence, NJ
Wiggs, B. Ryland ....Franklin, TN
Wiggs, Barbara B. Federal Trade Commission, Office of Executive Director, GV
Wiggs, David H., Jr. ....El Paso, TX
Wiggs, E. Marcus, III ....Jackson, MS
Wiggs, Holly Bridges ....Jackson, MS
Wiggs, Jeffrey W. ....Mount Dora, FL
Wiggs, Rebecca Lee ....Jackson, MS
Wiggs, Sara T. ....Chicago, IL
Wiggs, Steven Brent ....Phoenix, AZ
Wiggum, Karen M. ....Wenatchee, WA
Wigham, David J. ....Wooster, OH
Wigham, John T. ....Wooster, OH
Wight, Anna Lewak ....Seattle, WA
Wight, Anne Bryant ....Edina, MN
Wight, Carroll H. ....San Diego, CA
Wight, Christopher L. ....Seattle, WA
Wight, D. Russell ....Pocatello, ID
Wight, Daniel F. ....Garden City, MI
Wight, Douglas R. ....St. Petersburg, FL
Wight, John M. ....Portland, OR
Wight, John M., P.C. ....Portland, OR
Wight, Jonathan M. ....Los Angeles, CA
Wight, Larry R. ....Roswell, GA
Wight, Les D. ....Independence, MO
Wight, Linda J. ....Chicago, IL
Wight, Mark E. ....Boise, ID
Wight, Mark E., P.C., Law Office of Boise, ID
Wight, Mark T. ....Downers Grove, IL
Wight, Paul Franklin ....Washington, DC
Wight, R. Alan ....Portland, OR
Wight, Richard J. ....New York, NY
Wight, Richard W. ....Manasquan, NJ
Wight, Stephen A. ....Portland, OR
Wight, Stephen W. ....Lawrence, MA
Wight, Talbot ....Nevada, MO
Houston, TX
Wight, Todd W. ....Los Angeles, CA
Wight, Winfield E., Jr. ....St. Petersburg, FL
Wightman, Alec ....Columbus, OH
Wightman, Alysia ....Austin, TX
Wightman, Ann ....Dayton, OH
Wightman, Arnold J. ....Madison, WI
Wightman, Charlotte K. ....Salt Lake City, UT
Wightman, David F. ....Evanston, IL
Wightman, Jeffrey M. ....Lexington, NE
Wightman, John M. ....Gothenburg, NE
Lexington, NE
Wightman, John M., Jr. ....Omaha, NE
Wightman, John Rollie ....Phoenix, AZ
Wightman, Marsha K. ....Denver, CO
Wightman, Paul C. ....Barnstable, MA
Wightman, Roland C. ....Spokane, WA
Wightman, William S. ....Key Largo, FL
Wigington, Cary ....Lewisville, TX
Wigington & Dankesreiter, L.L.P. Lewisville, TX
Wigington, Jeffrey G. ....Corpus Christi, TX
Wiginton, Don F., P.C. ....Birmingham, AL
Wiginton, Donald F., Sr. ....Birmingham, AL
Wiginton, Jim D. ....Alvin, TX
Wiginton, Joel K. ....Washington, DC
Wiginton, Melissa ....Austin, TX
Wiginton & Wood ....Alvin, TX
Wigle, Bruce M., III ....Winter Park, FL
Wigle, Reamer W. ....Lansing, MI
Wigle, W. Scott ....Boise, ID
Wigler, Andrew J. ....Great Neck, NY
Wigler, David S. ....Knoxville, TN
Wigler, Nancy D. ....Hempstead, NY
Wigler, Ronald David ....Newark, NJ
Wiglesworth, James T. ....Overland Park, KS
Wigley, Charles J., III ....Youngstown, OH
Wigley, Edmund A. ....Akron, OH
Wigman, Cohen, Leitner & Myers Washington, DC
Wigman, Victor M. ....Washington, DC
Wigmore, Michael B. ....Washington, DC
Wigmore, W. Mark ....Hartford, CT
Wigner, Harry E., Jr. ....Overland Park, KS
Wigner, Preston Douglas ....Richmond, VA
Wigness, Katherine H. ....Morristown, NJ
Wigness, Kristin C. ....New York, NY
Wigod, Constance K. ....Orange, CA
Wigod, Gerald E. ....Southfield, MI
Wigod, Myrna L. ....Newark, NJ
Wigoda, Gary I. ....Chicago, IL
Wigoda, Paul T. ....Chicago, IL
Wigoda, Robert M. ....Chicago, IL
Wigoda, Susan Seligman ....Chicago, IL
Wigoda & Wigoda ....Chicago, IL
Wigoda, William S. ....Chicago, IL
Wigoda, William S., Ltd. ....Chicago, IL
Wigodsky, Gary Steven ....Santa Monica, CA
Wigodsky, Jeffrey A. ....Washington, DC
Bethesda, MD
Wigodsky, Mary A. ....San Antonio, TX
Wigon, Elizabeth S. ....Boston, MA

Wigrizer, Steven G. ....Philadelphia, PA
Wigton, Charles E., III ....Columbus, OH
Wigton, Christine A. ....Mesa, AZ
Wigton, Michael ....Arlington, TX
Wigutow, Michael ....Huntington Station, NY
Wigutow, Mindy Robin ....New York, NY
Wihbey, Linda T. ....Waterbury, CT
Wihl, Kurt ....Albuquerque, NM
Wihtol, Jeffrey B. ....Portland, OR
Wihtol, Lavinia G. ....Sherwood, OR
Wiita, Douglas P., (P.C.) Beverly Hills, CA
Wiitala, David C. ....North Palm Beach, FL
Wijas, Michael J. ....San Diego, CA
Wijewantha, Niromi L. ....Sacramento, CA
Wijsen, L.M. ....Alameda, CA
Wik, Beverly J. ....Wilmington, DE
Wik, Thomas J. ....Omaha, NE
Wike, Antoinette R. ....Raleigh, NC
Wike, Curtis L. ....Bismarck, ND
Wike, Donald D. ....Washington, DC
Wike, Mike, Law Offices of ....Houston, TX
Wike, Sidney Alfred, Jr. ....Greenville, SC
Wikenheiser, Frank J. ....Strasburg, ND
Wikfors, Marsha P. ....Fort Pierce, FL
Wikle, C. Douglas, (Inc.) Woodland Hills, CA
Wikle and Henry, A Prtnrshp. of Prof. Corps. Woodland Hills, CA
Wikle, Kenneth C. ....Calabasas, CA
Wikle, Margaret (Peggy) Jeffers Santa Fe, NM
Wikler Gottlieb & Howard ....New York, NY
Wikman, Kathryn ....New York, NY
Wikoff, David A. ....Minneapolis, MN
Wikoff, Geo. B. ....Kerrville, TX
Wikoff, Larry R. ....Chicago, IL
Wiksell, Ronald E. ....Santa Ana, CA
Wiksell & Steinfeld ....Ventura, CA
Wiksell, Willard P. ....Ventura, CA
Wikstrom, David L. ....Springfield, NJ
Wikstrom, Eric J. ....Portland, OR
Wikstrom, Francis M. ....Salt Lake City, UT
Wilamowsky, Zvi ....Brooklyn, NY
Wilan, Jonathan Michael Washington, DC
Wiland, Linda L. ....Dallas, TX
Wilansky, Nathan L. ....Silver Spring, MD
Wilansky, Wayne M. ....Bronx, NY
Wilbanks, Ann E. ....Houston, TX
Wilbanks, Charles R. ....Jackson, MS
Wilbanks, Cody ....Irving, TX
Wilbanks, Cran H., Jr. ....Holdenville, OK
Wilbanks, Deborah Lynn ....Winder, GA
Wilbanks, H. Erwin ....Houston, TX
Wilbanks, Jim E. ....Dalton, GA
Wilbanks, Jim E., P.C. ....Dalton, GA
Wilbanks, Karen Kincannon ....Atlanta, GA
Wilbanks, Marlan B. ....Atlanta, GA
Wilbanks, Richard T., III ....Tyler, TX
Wilbanks, Sim S. ....Alexander City, AL
Wilbanks, Vicki B. ....Batesville, MS
Wilbanks & Wilbanks, P.C. ....Houston, TX
Wilbar, Anne Marie ....North Andover, MA
Wilbar, William Peyton, IV ....Boulder, CO
Wilber, Adair C. ....Port Clinton, OH
Wilber, Albert R., Jr. ....West Palm Beach, FL
Wilber, Carolyn Ann ....Durango, CO
Wilber, Christopher A. ....Washington, DC
Wilber, Donald L. ....Bloomington, IL
Colfax, IL
Wilber, George C. ....Port Clinton, OH
Wilber, H. Robinson, II ....Lebanon, KY
Wilber, Hanna R. ....San Francisco, CA
Wilber, James ....Milwaukee, WI
Wilber, James E. ....Bonita Springs, FL
Wilber, Jay L. ....Binghamton, NY
Wilber, Jeffrey T. ....San Francisco, CA
Wilber, Judy Robinson ....Little Rock, AR
Wilber, Kenneth L. ....Bloomington, IL
Colfax, IL
Wilber Law Firm, The ....Bloomington, IL
Colfax, IL
Wilber, Norman C. ....Mountain Home, AR
Wilber, Norman C., P.A. Mountain Home, AR
Wilber, Paul D. ....Salisbury, MD
Wilber, Roger W. ....Tampa, FL
Wilber, Ross L. ....Troy, MI
Wilber and Wilber ....Port Clinton, OH
Wilber, William J. ....Ansonia, CT
Wilberding, Joseph C. ....Mount Kisco, NY
Wilberding, Merle F. ....Dayton, OH
Wilberding, Thomas A. ....Oakland, CA
Wilbers, L. H. ....Jefferson City, MO
Wilbers, Michelle H. ....Bellevue, IA
Wilbert, Catherine A. ....Milwaukee, WI
Wilbert, Christian W. Rancho Santa Margarita, CA
Wilbert, Dennis P. ....Kansas City, MO
Wilbert, James C. ....New Orleans, LA
Wilbert, Joel S. ....Nashua, NH
Wilbert, John W., III ....Plaquemine, LA
Wilbert, Michael E. ....Brick, NJ
Wilbert & Montenegro, A Professional Corporation ....Brick, NJ
Wilbert, Paul L. ....Pittsburg, KS
Wilbert, Randall E., II ....Washington, DC
Wilbert, Randall E., Law Offices of Nashua, NH
Wilbert and Towner, P.A. ....Pittsburg, KS
Wilbert, Warren M. ....Wichita, KS
Wilbon, Bernadette Marie ....Arlington, VA
Wilbon, Joan M. ....Washington, DC
Wilborn, Carroll E., Jr. ....Anahuac, TX
Wilborn, Derrick R. ....Rochester, NY
Wilborn, John N. ....Phoenix, AZ
Wilborn, W. Stephen ....Frankfort, KY

Wilbourn, Beverly J. ....Washington, DC
Wilbourn, Gordon M. ....Little Rock, AR
Wilbourn, James G. ....Vance, MS
Wilbourn, Jane Miller ....Vance, MS
Wilbourn, Penny Brown ....Little Rock, AR
Wilbourn, Richard E. ....Meridian, MS
Wilbourn, Richard E., III ....Jackson, MS
Wilbourn, Rogers & Scarborough Meridian, MS
Wilbraham, Edward J. ....Wilmington, DE
Haddonfield, NJ
Philadelphia, PA
Wilbraham, Lawler & Buba, A Professional Corporation ....Wilmington, DE
Haddonfield, NJ
Philadelphia, PA
Wilbrandt, Laurence A. ....Crystal Lake, IL
Wilbrandt, Robert A. ....Crystal Lake, IL
Wilbrandt, Robert A., Ltd. ....Crystal Lake, IL
Wilbrandt, Robert A., Sr. ....Crystal Lake, IL
Wilbrandt, Robert A., Sr., Ltd. Crystal Lake, IL
Wilbur & Allen ....Jacksonville, FL
Wilbur, Brent A. ....Pierre, SD
Wilbur, Byington & McPhillips Hastings, MI
Wilbur, Carl E. ....Department of Defense, Defense Legal Services Agency, GV
Wilbur, Carter W. Charlotte Amalie, St. Thomas, VI
Wilbur, David A. ....Holyoke, MA
Wilbur, Ellen S. ....Brockton, MA
Wilbur, Erin B. ....Saratoga, CA
Wilbur, John H. ....Downey, CA
Wilbur, John H., (P.A.) ....Jacksonville, FL
Wilbur, Kathryn Hilderbrand ....Miami, FL
Wilbur, Kenneth J. ....Florham Park, NJ
Wilbur, Marcia B. ....Fullerton, CA
Wilbur, Michael E. ....San Francisco, CA
Wilbur, P. Andrew ....Houston, TX
Wilbur, Peter D. ....Chicago, IL
Wilbur, R. Carl, Jr. ....Peoria, IL
Wilbur, Ralph O. ....Hastings, MI
Wilbur, Richard ....San Francisco, CA
Wilbur, Robert E. ....Dallas, TX
Wilbur, Robert L., Jr. ....Smyrna, GA
Wilbur, Thomas B. ....Parma Heights, OH
Wilbur, Warren A., III ....Doylestown, PA
Wilburn, Bernard P. ....Circleville, OH
Wilburn, Charles W. ....Circleville, OH
Wilburn, Christopher A. Fort Lauderdale, FL
Wilburn, Clinton D., II ....Los Angeles, CA
Wilburn, David N., Jr. ....Union, SC
Wilburn, Dedra L. ....Austin, TX
Wilburn, Earl B. ....St. Louis, MO
Wilburn, Elizabeth A. ....Wilmington, DE
Wilburn, John D. ....McLean, VA
Wilburn, Luke J., Jr. ....Spartanburg, SC
Wilburn, Masterson & Smiling ....Tulsa, OK
Wilburn, Melissa L. ....Columbus, OH
Wilburn, Nadine Chandler ....Washington, DC
Wilburn, Paula A. Ranallo Muskogee, OK
Wilburn, Ray H. ....Tulsa, OK
Wilburn, Rhett Henry ....Tulsa, OK
Wilburn & Suggs ....St. Louis, MO
Wilburn, William K. ....Saratoga, CA
Wilburn, William K., A P.C. ....Saratoga, CA
Wilburn, William Karl ....Washington, DC
Wilby, Mark C., (P.C.) ....Augusta, GA
Wilcenski, Edward V. ....Albany, NY
Utica, NY
Wilch, Theodore M. ....Kansas City, MO
Wilcher, LaJuana S. ....Washington, DC
Wilcher, Larry K. ....Scottsville, KY
Wilcher, Shirley J. ....Department of Labor, Employment Standards Administration, GV
Wilcher, Susan B. ....New York, NY
Wilchins, Howard M. Department of Energy, GV
Wilchins, Julie L. ....Seattle, WA
Wilchins, Stephen N. ....Wellesley, MA
Wilck, David Stephen ....New York, NY
Wilck, Michael H. ....Morristown, NJ
Wilck, Michelle Alison ....New York, NY
Wilcke, Ernest W. ....Spirit Lake, IA
Wilcke, Heinrich C. ....New York, NY
Wilcken, Michael A. ....New York, NY
Wilco, Leigh M. ....Atlanta, GA
Wilcon, Fred B. ....Wellesley, MA
Wilcots, Rosalyn L. ....Library of Congress, Office of the General Counsel, GV
Wilcott, Scott J ....Los Angeles, CA
Wilcove, Michael N. Department of Justice, GV
Wilcox, Alan Earl ....Worcester, MA
Wilcox, Alfred H. ....Philadelphia, PA
Wilcox, Allan C. ....Joplin, MO
Wilcox, Allen D. ....Redmond, WA
Wilcox, Ann E. ....Billings, MT
Wilcox, Arthur M., Jr. ....Costa Mesa, CA
La Jolla, CA
San Diego, CA
Wilcox & Associates, P.A. Minneapolis, MN
Wilcox, Barbara L. ....Chicago, IL
Wilcox, Ben H. ....Altus, OK
Wilcox, Bradford W. ....Fort Atkinson, WI
Wilcox, Brennan Lea ....Lawrence, KS
Wilcox, Bruce A. ....Norfolk, VA
Wilcox, Bryce J. ....Spokane, WA
Wilcox, Carl E. ....Portland, OR
Wilcox, Charles H., II ....Beaumont, TX
Wilcox, Charles J. ....Troy, NY
Wilcox, Charles S. ....St. Joseph, MO
Wilcox, Cheryl Jane ....New Haven, CT
Wilcox, Christina Benitez ....El Cerrito, CA

Wilcox, Christopher J. ....Madison, WI
Wilcox, Cynthia C. ....Alexandria, VA
Wilcox, Dale L. ....Terre Haute, IN
Wilcox, Darlene A. ....Rocky River, OH
Wilcox, Daryl E. ....Fort Lauderdale, FL
Wilcox, David L. ....Inverness, FL
Wilcox, David W. ....Bradenton, FL
Wilcox, David W. ....Sarasota, FL
Wilcox, Deanna M. ....Los Angeles, CA
Wilcox, Deborah A. Schaff ....Cleveland, OH
Wilcox, Debra K. ....Englewood, CO
Wilcox, Dennis R. ....Washington, DC
Cleveland, OH
Wilcox, Diane D. ....Cleveland, OH
Wilcox, Dianne E. H. ....Moneta, VA
Wilcox, Dina L. ....Kerhonkson, NY
Wilcox, Don T. ....Tampa, FL
Wilcox, Donald A. ....Benson, MN
Wilcox, Donald P. ....Austin, TX
Wilcox, Donald W., Jr. ....Bloomington, IL
Wilcox, Douglas T. ....Springfield, IL
Wilcox, Douglas V. ....Okemos, MI
Wilcox, Eileen K. ....Fairfield, CT
Wilcox, Ellen Dollase ....Kansas City, MO
Wilcox, Elwyn R. ....Dearborn, MI
Wilcox, Everett H., Jr., P.C. ....Atlanta, GA
Wilcox Firm, The ....Troy, NY
Wilcox, Francis J. ....Eau Claire, WI
Wilcox, Francis P., Jr. ....Framingham, MA
Wilcox, Gary E. ....Chicago, IL
Wilcox, Gary N. ....Newark, NJ
Wilcox, Geoffrey L. Environmental Protection Agency, Office of the General Counsel, GV
Wilcox, George H. ....Washington, DC
Wilcox, Gerald S. ....Madison, WI
Wilcox, Gordon W. ....Seattle, WA
Wilcox, Gordon W., Inc. P.S. ....Seattle, WA
Wilcox, Gregory ....Berkeley, CA
Wilcox, Gregory B. ....Des Moines, IA
Wilcox & Grimbau ....Chicago, IL
Wilcox, Gus E. ....San Antonio, TX
Wilcox, Gwynne A. ....New York, NY
Wilcox, Harvey J. ....Ivy, VA
Wilcox, J. Matthew ....Riverside, CA
Wilcox, J. Patrick ....Minneapolis, MN
Wilcox, Jack W. ....Oklahoma City, OK
Wilcox, James B., Jr. ....Washington, DC
Wilcox, James E., Jr ....Fairfax, VA
Wilcox, James L. ....North Chicago, IL
Wilcox, James L. ....Grove City, OH
Wilcox, Jamison V. V. ....Hamden, CT
Wilcox, Janice Ozzello ....Chanhassen, MN
Wilcox, Jean ....San Francisco, CA
Wilcox, Jean C. ....Costa Mesa, CA
Wilcox, Jeffrey C., (PC) ....St. George, UT
Wilcox, Jennifer C. ....Boston, MA
Wilcox, Jessica R. ....Albany, NY
Wilcox, John ....New York, NY
Wilcox, John C. ....New York, NY
Wilcox, John D. ....Parkersburg, WV
Wilcox, John F. ....Eau Claire, WI
Wilcox, John F., Jr. ....Kansas City, MO
Wilcox, John M. ....Denver, CO
Wilcox, John R., III ....Dallas, TX
Wilcox, John W. ....Tampa, FL
Wilcox, John W., Jr. ....Atlanta, GA
Wilcox, Jon P. ....Madison, WI
Wilcox, Jon Russell ....Elm Grove, WI
Wilcox, Jonathan J. ....Menlo Park, CA
Wilcox, Joseph V. ....Albion, MI
Wilcox, Justine E. ....Washington, DC
Wilcox, Katherine ....Fort Myers, FL
Wilcox, Kathleen E. ....Los Angeles, CA
Wilcox, Kenneth A. ....Elkton, MD
Wilcox, Kevin J. ....West Palm Beach, FL
Wilcox, L. Kent ....Chicago, IL
Wilcox, Leonard A., Jr. ....Troy, MI
Wilcox, Leslie C. ....Washington, DC
Wilcox, Linda ....Walnut Creek, CA
Wilcox, Linda W. ....Boston, MA
Wilcox, Lisa Palmer ....Columbia, SC
Wilcox, M. Anne ....Denver, CO
Wilcox, M. Kirby C. ....San Francisco, CA
Wilcox, Mark D. ....Chicago, IL
Wilcox, Merle Everett ....Oak Harbor, WA
Wilcox, Michael C. ....Worcester, MA
Wilcox, Michael W. ....Madison, WI
Wilcox, Nathan B. ....Salt Lake City, UT
Wilcox, Neil H. ....New York, NY
Wilcox & Ogden, P.C. ....Denver, CO
Wilcox, Owen L. ....Boston, MA
Wilcox, Pamela S. ....Galesburg, IL
Wilcox, Paul K. ....Santa Barbara, CA
Wilcox, Paul S. ....Anchorage, AK
Wilcox, Philip C., Jr. Department of State, GV
Wilcox, Polking, Gerken, Schwarzkopf, Hoyt & Copeland, P.C. ....Carroll, IA
Churdan, IA
Grand Junction, IA
Jefferson, IA
Wilcox, Reginald E. ....Vero Beach, FL
Wilcox, Richard ....Grass Valley, CA
Wilcox, Robert A. ....North Palm Beach, FL
Wilcox, Robert A. ....Oneida, NY
Wilcox, Robert B. ....Evanston, IL
Wilcox, Robert B., Jr. ....Chicago, IL
Wilcox, Robert D. ....Troy, NY
Wilcox, Robin M. ....New York, NY
Wilcox, Rochelle L. ....Los Angeles, CA
Wilcox, Roger W., Jr ....Buffalo, NY
Wilcox, Ronald A. ....New York, NY
Wilcox, Ronald G. ....Salt Lake City, UT
Wilcox, Ronald L. ....Denver, CO
Wilcox, Ronald L. ....Columbus, OH
Wilcox, Roy S. ....Eau Claire, WI
Wilcox, S. Craig ....Houston, TX

Wiley and Bonda, P.C. ...Los Angeles, CA
Wiley, Boyd S. ...**Puyallup, WA**
Wiley, C. Mark ...**Winston-Salem, NC**
Wiley, Charles A., Jr. ...**Atlanta, GA**
Wiley, Colbert, Norseng, Cray and Herrell, S.C. ...**Chippewa Falls, WI**
Eau Claire, WI
Wiley, Dale ...**Crane, MO**
Wiley, Dale M. ...Danville, VA
Wiley, Dan K. ...**Leavenworth, KS**
Wiley, David F. ...Toledo, OH
Wiley, David L. ...**Nashville, TN**
Wiley, David T. ...**Birmingham, AL**
Wiley, David W. ...**Seattle, WA**
Wiley, Dayton G. ...**San Antonio, TX**
Wiley, Denise M. ...St. Paul, MN
Wiley, Diane Karen ...Eugene, OR
Wiley, Donald L. ...Cincinnati, OH
Wiley, Donald P. ...**Canton, OH**
Wiley, Dorothy L. ...Pullman, WA
Wiley, Edwin B. ...Princeton, WV
Wiley, Edwin P. ...**Milwaukee, WI**
Wiley, Elizabeth L. ...Chicago, IL
Wiley, Elizabeth Stoebner ...**Houston, TX**
Wiley, Ericka J. ...Merced, CA
Wiley, Fletcher H. ...**Boston, MA**
Wiley, Gordon ...Weatherford, TX
Wiley, Gregory J. ...**Minneapolis, MN**
Wiley, Helen P. ...**Rochester, NY**
Wiley, Henry C., Jr. ...**Jasper, AL**
Wiley, J. Michael ...**Williamsport, PA**
Wiley, James B. ...**Sacramento, CA**
Wiley, James Bruce ...Bloomington, IL
Wiley, James F., III ...Philadelphia, PA
Wiley, James R. ...**Tampa, FL**
Wiley, James S. ...Waco, TX
Wiley, Jan M. ...**Dillsburg, PA**
Wiley, Jason R. ...**Philadelphia, PA**
Wiley, Jay D. ...**Phoenix, AZ**
Wiley, Jay Douglas, II ...**Phoenix, AZ**
Wiley, Jeffrey T. ...**Pittsburgh, PA**
Wiley, Jerry ...Los Angeles, CA
Wiley, Jill D. ...**Tucson, AZ**
Wiley, Jimmy W. ...Winnfield, LA
Wiley, John F. ...Baltimore, MD
Wiley, John H., III ...Birmingham, AL
Wiley, John, Jr. ...**Metuchen, NJ**
Wiley, John M. ...Wausau, WI
Wiley, John P. ...Albany, NY
Wiley, John Shepard, Jr. ...Los Angeles, CA
Wiley, Joseph C. ...Gonzales, LA
Wiley, Joseph E. ...**Alameda, CA**
Wiley, Joseph, Jr. ...Columbus, GA
Wiley, Joseph K. ...**Huntington, IN**
Warren, IN
Wiley, Julia Smith ...**Toledo, OH**
Wiley, Kimberly Anastasia ...Winnfield, LA
Wiley, Là Vern D. ...**Washington, DC**
Wiley, LaVern D. ...Upper Marlboro, MD
Wiley Law Firm, The ...**San Antonio, TX**
Wiley, Lenox & Colgan, P.C.
Dillsburg, PA
Wiley, Malehorn and Sirota
Morristown, NJ
Wiley, Marchèlle A. ...**Miami, FL**
Wiley, Margaret Johnson
Santa Monica, CA
Wiley, Mary Anne ...Austin, TX
Wiley, Mary Jo ...Silver Spring, MD
Wiley, Neil W. ...San Francisco, CA
Wiley, Paul Lee, Law Office of
Harlingen, TX
Wiley, Peter J. ...**Portland, ME**
Wiley, Peter M. ...Venice, FL
Wiley & Pettit ...Pullman, WA
Wiley Price & Radulovich, LLP
Alameda, CA
Wiley, Randall J. ...Shawnee, OK
Wiley, Rein & Fielding ...**Washington, DC**
Wiley, Richard A. ...**Boston, MA**
Wiley, Richard E. ...**Washington, DC**
Wiley, Richard J. ...Highland City, FL
Wiley, Rob L. ...**Houston, TX**
Wiley, Robert H. ...Denton, TX
Wiley, Robert S. ...**Crane, MO**
Wiley, Robert W. ...Lakeport, CA
Wiley, Roger ...**McAlester, OK**
Wiley, Roger C. ...Richmond, VA
Wiley, Ronald D., Jr. ...Charlottesville, VA
Wiley, R. R., Jr. ...Oakwood, TX
Wiley, S. Donald ...Pittsburgh, PA
Wiley, Sarah H. ...San Diego, CA
Wiley, Stephen B. ...**Morristown, NJ**
Wiley, Stephen C. ...**Columbus, OH**
Wiley, Stephen J. ...**Albany, NY**
Wiley, Stephen P. ...Santa Barbara, CA
Wiley, Terry Oscar ...Oakland, CA
Wiley, Theodore ...New York, NY
Wiley, Thomas J. ...Los Angeles, CA
Wiley, Thomas W. ...Santa Fe, NM
Wiley, Todd C. ...**Phoenix, AZ**
Wiley, Tossie, Jr. ...Cleveland, OH
Wiley, Traci L. ...**Charleston, WV**
Wiley, Vicki M. ...Atlanta, GA
Wiley, William B.
Merit Systems Protection Board, Office of Board Members, GV
Wiley, William B. ...**Tallahassee, FL**
Wilf, Adam D. ...**Philadelphia, PA**
Wilf, David M. ...**New York, NY**
Wilf, Frederic M. ...**Philadelphia, PA**
Wilf, Leonard A. ...Short Hills, NJ
Wilf, Marcia M. ...**Philadelphia, PA**
Wilf, Mervin M. ...**Cambridge, MA**
Philadelphia, PA
Wilf, Mervin M., Ltd. ...**Cambridge, MA**
Philadelphia, PA
Wilf & Silverman ...Short Hills, NJ
Wilf, Zygmunt ...Short Hills, NJ
Wilfand, Max ...Bethesda, MD
Wilfert, Amy K. ...**Greenwich, CT**
Stamford, CT
Wilfley, Michael ...Denver, CO
Wilfond, Arthur E. ...Marco, FL
Wilfong, Richard R. ...**Amarillo, TX**
Wilford, David A. ...**Chicago, IL**
Wilford, Frank L. ...**Lexington, KY**
Wilford, Lawrence A. ...**St. Paul, MN**
Wilford, Pamela Fraser ...Philadelphia, PA
Wilgard, Mark A. ...**New York, NY**
Wilger, Robert J. ...**San Jose, CA**
Wilgers, Steven L. ...Coos Bay, OR
Wilgers, Steven, P.C. ...Coos Bay, OR
Wilgis, Herbert E., III ...**Seattle, WA**
Wilgoren, Howard ...Lexington, MA
Wilgren, Thomas J. ...Boston, MA
Wilguess, Douglas D. ...Oklahoma City, OK
Wilgus, George, III ...**Trenton, NJ**
Wilgus, Paul C. ...Atlanta, GA
Wilgus, Van C. ...Boulder, CO
Wilgus, William B. ...Millsboro, DE
Wilhardt, Leanne C. ...Phoenix, AZ
Wilharm, John H., Jr. ...**Cleveland, OH**
Wilheim, Julian R. ...Lake Bluff, IL
Wilheim, Steven C. ...**Glendale, CA**
Wilheim, Victoria O. ...San Francisco, CA
Wilhelm, Anne M. ...Columbus, OH
Wilhelm & Associates, P.A.
St. Augustine, FL
Wilhelm, Carol M. ...**New York, NY**
Wilhelm, Charles F. ...Purchase, NY
Wilhelm, Charles H. ...Lewistown, IL
Wilhelm, Charles W. ...Lincoln, NE
Wilhelm, Daniel F. ...New York, NY
Wilhelm, Donald G. ...El Paso, TX
Wilhelm, Gayle Brian ...**Stamford, CT**
Wilhelm, Gregory O. ...Sacramento, CA
Wilhelm, Jack M. ...Midland, TX
Wilhelm, James E., (A Professional Corporation) ...**Irvine, CA**
Wilhelm, James E., Jr. ...**Columbus, OH**
Wilhelm, Jeff R. ...**Phoenix, AZ**
Wilhelm, Jenifer L. ...Dayton, OH
Wilhelm, Jerry ...Santa Rosa, CA
Wilhelm, John A. ...**McLean, VA**
Wilhelm, John F. ...Apopka, FL
Wilhelm, John H. ...Naperville, IL
Wilhelm, John R. ...University Center, MI
Wilhelm, Joseph A., III ...Northampton, MA
Wilhelm, Julian A. ...Fort Myers, FL
Wilhelm, Kari A. ...**Honolulu, HI**
Wilhelm, Kelly J. ...**Dallas, TX**
Wilhelm, Kenneth A. ...Creve Coeur, IL
Wilhelm, Kenneth A., (P.C.) ...New York, NY
Wilhelm Law Service, S.C. ...**Appleton, WI**
Wilhelm, Marc G. ...**Anchorage, AK**
Wilhelm, Margaret M. ...Arlington Heights, IL
Wilhelm, Melvin F. ...**Brookville, IN**
Wilhelm, Michael J.
Federal Communications Commission, Wireless Telecommunications Bureau, GV
Wilhelm, Michael L. ...**Fresno, CA**
Wilhelm, Michelle L. ...**New York, NY**
Wilhelm, Natalie D. ...**Pensacola, FL**
Wilhelm, R. Sherman, III ...Tallahassee, FL
Wilhelm, Rachel M. ...**St. Louis, MO**
Wilhelm, Richard A. ...**Atlanta, GA**
Wilhelm, Richard A. ...**Detroit, MI**
Wilhelm, Richard A. ...Lake Oswego, OR
Wilhelm, Richard W. ...**Dallas, TX**
Wilhelm, Robert O. ...Carmel, CA
Wilhelm, Robert O. ...St. Augustine, FL
Wilhelm, Robert O. ...Clifton Park, NY
Wilhelm, Scott M. ...**Phillipsburg, NJ**
Wilhelm, Steven H., (A P.C.)
San Diego, CA
Wilhelm, Suzanne L. ...Detroit, MI
Wilhelm, Terry J. ...Catskill, NY
Wilhelm, Thomas D. ...**Appleton, WI**
Wilhelm, Thomas V. ...Bloomfield Hills, MI
Wilhelm, Timothy C. ...Minot, ND
Wilhelm, William Banks, Jr.
Washington, DC
Wilhelm, William G. ...La Jolla, CA
Wilhelm, William W. ...Clearwater, FL
Wilhelmi, Angel Batlas ...**Baltimore, MD**
Wilhelmi, Anna M. ...St. Charles, IL
Wilhelmi, Arthur J. ...**Joliet, IL**
Wilhelmi Haynes & Boudreaux, L.L.C.
Augusta, GA
Wilhelmi, Jennifer L. ...**Menlo Park, CA**
Wilhelmi, John R. ...Keshena, WI
Wilhelmi, Kevin M. ...**Farmington Hills, MI**
Wilhelmi, Mark L., P.C. ...**Augusta, GA**
Wilhelms, Andrew J. ...**Columbus, OH**
Wilhelms, Frederick, III ...Elizabeth, NJ
Wilhelms, Tybo Alan ...**Toledo, OH**
Wilhelmsen, David K. ...**Prescott, AZ**
Wilhelmsen, H. Kempel ...Prescott, AZ
Wilhelmsen, Shannon L. ...Mesa, AZ
Wilhelmus, Holly H. ...**Evansville, IN**
Wilhelmus, R. Todd ...Mission, KS
Wilhelmy, Alan J. ...**Walnut Creek, CA**
Wilhelmy, Lisa George
Securities and Exchange Commission, Office of Compliance Inspections and Examinations, GV
Wilhelmy, Thomas R. ...**Minneapolis, MN**
Wilhite, Alan S., Chartered ...Gainesville, FL
Wilhite and Associates ...Evansville, IN
Wilhite, Barbara L. ...New Port Richey, FL
Wilhite, Byron L. ...Durant, OK
Wilhite, Connie Kay ...**Dallas, TX**
Wilhite, David E. ...**Lebanon, MO**
Wilhite, Dixie Terrell ...Wausau, WI
Wilhite, George W. ...**Houston, TX**
Wilhite, George W., & Associates, Inc.
Houston, TX
Wilhite, Jay T. ...**Houston, TX**
Wilhite, Jeffrey A. ...Evansville, IN
Wilhite, Lawrence H. ...Lansing, MI
Wilhite, Ollie, Jr. ...Memphis, TN
Wilhite, Randall B. ...**Houston, TX**
Wilhite, Samuel E. ...Washington, DC
Wilhite, Timothy W. ...**Shreveport, LA**
Wilhoft, Steven W., Law Office of
Parsons, KS
Wilhoit, Anthony A. ...London, KY
Kingsport, TN
Wilhoit, Anthony M. ...Versailles, KY
Wilhoit, George R., Jr. ...Springfield, MO
Wilhoit, Henry R., III ...Grayson, KY
Wilhoit, Henry R., Jr. ...Grayson, KY
Wilhoit, Kaiser and Weatherly ...London, KY
Kingsport, TN
Wilhoit, Richard A. ...**St. Paul, MN**
Wilhoit, Robert E. ...**Asheboro, NC**
Wilhoit, Scott C. ...**Louisville, KY**
Wilhoit, Tony ...Johnson City, TN
Wilhoit, William H. ...Grayson, KY
Wilhoite, R. Edward, Jr. ...Chicago, IL
Wilhoite, Ronald C. ...Bradenton, FL
Wilhoite, William A. ...Connersville, IN
Wilinski, Karin ...Medford, MA
Wilinsky, Thomas B. ...New York, NY
Wilion, Allan E., Inc. ...Beverly Hills, CA
Wiljamaa, David ...Minneapolis, MN
Wilk, Adam R. ...**Washington, DC**
McLean, VA
Wilk, Allan ...Venice, CA
Wilk, Barry R. ...**Encino, CA**
Palm Springs, CA
Wilk, David F. ...Williamsport, PA
Wilk, David I. ...Dallas, TX
Wilk, David M. ...**St. Paul, MN**
Wilk, David P. ...Kenosha, WI
Milwaukee, WI
Wilk, Derek W. ...**Chicago, IL**
Wilk, Frederick P. ...Sheboygan, WI
Wilk, Jack ...**New York, NY**
Wilk, Jay K. ...Woodstock, VA
Wilk, Jay K., P.C. ...Woodstock, VA
Wilk, Jeffrey C. ...Chicago, IL
Wilk, John F. ...**New York, NY**
Wilk, John S. ...Utica, NY
Wilk, Jonathan C. ...**Waltham, MA**
Wilk, Kenneth M. ...Highland, IN
Wilk Law Office ...Dallas, TX
Wilk, Lawrence A. ...Chicago, IL
Wilk, Lawrence E. ...**Phoenix, AZ**
Wilk, Mark J. ...Ontario, OR
Wilk, Martin L. ...**Brunswick, ME**
Wilk, Matthew J. ...**Chicago, IL**
Wilk, Michael B. ...**Los Angeles, CA**
Wilk, Michael S. ...**Houston, TX**
Wilk, Michele L. ...**Northbrook, IL**
Wilk, Robert G. ...**East Meadow, NY**
Wilk, S. Michael ...Kenosha, WI
Wilk, Sanford L. ...Dresher, PA
Wilk, Vincent J. ...**Bloomfield Hills, MI**
Wilk & Waller ...Chicago, IL
Wilk, Wendell Alan ...**Lansing, MI**
Wilka, Haugen & Kirby, P.C.
Sioux Falls, SD
Wilka, John M. ...**Sioux Falls, SD**
Wilka, Tamara A. ...**Sioux Falls, SD**
Wilka, Theresa A. ...**San Francisco, CA**
Wilka, Thomas K. ...**Sioux Falls, SD**
Wilka, Timothy J. ...**Sioux Falls, SD**
Wilka, Timothy J., P.C. ...**Sioux Falls, SD**
Wilka, William C. ...**San Francisco, CA**
Wilkanowski, Barbara ...Kew Gardens, NY
Wilke, Alfred W. ...St. Clair Shores, MI
Wilke, Barbara Reynolds ...Schaumburg, IL
Wilke, Cheri Binder ...Greensburg, PA
Pittsburgh, PA
Wilke, Cheryl L. ...**Fort Lauderdale, FL**
Wilke, Craig Martin ...Santa Ana, CA
Wilke, Cynthia M. ...Hot Springs Village, AR
Wilke, Daniel E. ...Clayton, MO
Wilke, David L. ...**Palo Alto, CA**
Wilke, Donn A. ...Pittsburgh, PA
Wilke, Fleury, Hoffelt, Gould & Birney, LLP
Sacramento, CA
Wilke, James A. ...**Milwaukee, WI**
Wilke, Jenifer B. ...Los Angeles, CA
Wilke, Jill L. ...Kaukauna, WI
Wilke, John J. ...Boca Raton, FL
Wilke, John M. ...**Skokie, IL**
Wilke, John W. ...**Omaha, NE**
Wilke, Kenneth M. ...Topeka, KS
Wilke, Kurt L. ...Fort Dodge, IA
Wilke Law Offices, P.C. ...**Omaha, NE**
Wilke, Liesl D. ...Richmond, VA
Wilke, Marguerite ...Ventura, CA
Wilke, Peter J. ...Los Angeles, CA
Wilke, R. Kurt ...**Springfield, IL**
Wilke, Sherman C. ...**Sacramento, CA**
Wilke, Stephen B. ...Memphis, TN
Wilke, Warren Michael ...Greensburg, IN
Wilke, Wayne F. ...Cincinnati, OH
Wilken, Alan W. ...**Los Angeles, CA**
Wilken, Alvin D. ...**Kansas City, MO**
Wilken, Claudia ...Oakland, CA
Wilken, Greg P. ...**Minneapolis, MN**
Wilken, Kristina ...**Palo Alto, CA**
Wilken, Laurence S. ...San Diego, CA
Wilken, Steven J. ...Cincinnati, OH
Wilken, Thomas A. ...Harrisburg, PA
Wilken, Tiffany Scot ...New Orleans, LA
Wilken & Villarrubia, L.L.C.
New Orleans, LA
Wilkenfeld, Ari ...**Washington, DC**
Wilkenfeld, Cecelia ...Conroe, TX
Wilkenfeld, Wendy A. ...**Washington, DC**
Wilkening, Mark D. ...**Chicago, IL**
Wilkening, Murray ...**Lakewood, CO**
Wilkening, Murray, P.C. ...**Lakewood, CO**
Wilkening, Paul Harvey ...Tulsa, OK
Wilkening, Raquel L. ...**Los Angeles, CA**
San Francisco, CA
Wilkens, Beth Ela ...**Rochester, NY**
Wilkens, James B. ...Columbus, OH
Wilkens, James F. ...Yonkers, NY
Wilkens, James K. ...**Anchorage, AK**
Wilkens, Jeffrey M. ...**Rochester, NY**
Wilkens, Kristi A. ...**Palo Alto, CA**
Wilkens, Peter M. ...Roseville, CA
Wilkens, Terry ...**Oakland, CA**
Wilkens, Timothy F. ...Albany, NY
Wilker, Gene A. ...**Redondo Beach, CA**
Wilker, Jack G. ...Northport, NY
Wilker, P. Jay ...**New York, NY**
Wilker, Steven M. ...**Portland, OR**
Wilker, William H. ...Madison, WI
Wilkerson & Associates Co., L.P.A.
Cleveland, OH
Wilkerson & Associates, PC
Anchorage, AK
Wilkerson, Brian F. ...Dallas, TX
Wilkerson, Brian S. ...**Tulsa, OK**
Wilkerson, Carl B. ...Washington, DC
Wilkerson, Carl J. ...**Arlington, TX**
Wilkerson, Cheryl A. ...Virginia Beach, VA
Wilkerson, Conley G. ...Cincinnati, OH
Wilkerson, Cullen Christie, Jr.
Atlanta, GA
Wilkerson, David Clay ...**Houston, TX**
Wilkerson, David M. ...**Columbia, SC**
Wilkerson, David N. ...Woodville, MS
Wilkerson, Deborah L. ...Overland Park, KS
Wilkerson, Douglas G. ...Charlotte, NC
Wilkerson, Douglas W. ...**Dyersburg, TN**
Wilkerson, Emory A. ...Bloomington, IL
Wilkerson, Ernest L., Jr. ...Cleveland, OH
Wilkerson, F. Craig, Jr. ...Charleston, SC
Wilkerson, Forrest C. ...Rock Hill, SC
Wilkerson, Gary C. ...Bloomington, MN
Wilkerson, Gary C. ...**Portland, OR**
Wilkerson Gauldin & Hayes
Dyersburg, TN
Wilkerson, Glen ...**Austin, TX**
Wilkerson, Hardy L. ...Big Spring, TX
Wilkerson, J. Burton, Jr. ...**Macon, GA**
Wilkerson, J. Clifton ...East Orange, NJ
Wilkerson, J. Neill ...Georgetown, TX
Wilkerson, J. Neill, P.C., Law Office of
Georgetown, TX
Wilkerson, Jack I. ...Richmond, VA
Wilkerson, James ...Eureka, CA
Wilkerson, James D., Jr.
West Palm Beach, FL
Wilkerson, Jay M. ...**Durham, NC**
Wilkerson, Jennifer L. ...Grass Valley, CA
Wilkerson, Jerald L. ...Las Vegas, NV
Wilkerson, Jerald L., A Professional Law Corporation ...Las Vegas, NV
Wilkerson, Jerry L. ...Salem, MO
Wilkerson, John A. ...Daytona Beach, FL
Wilkerson, John H., Jr. ...Montgomery, AL
Wilkerson, John P. ...Grand Island, FL
Wilkerson, John P., Jr. ...**Columbus, OH**
Wilkerson, John S., III ...**Charleston, SC**
Wilkerson, Julie R. ...Alexandria, LA
Wilkerson, Katherine B. ...**Raleigh, NC**
Wilkerson, Kimberly A. ...**Hartwell, GA**
Wilkerson, Kimberly E. ...**Lubbock, TX**
Wilkerson, Lilia ...Riverside, CA
Wilkerson, Mark A. ...**Newton, KS**
Wilkerson, Mark D. ...**Montgomery, AL**
Wilkerson, Mark E. ...**Anchorage, AK**
Wilkerson, Marshall R. ...Corpus Christi, TX
Wilkerson, Michael B. ...Gillette, WY
Wilkerson, Pinkie Carolyn ...Grambling, LA
Wilkerson, R. Gerald ...Palo Alto, CA
Wilkerson, Robert H.C. ...**Washington, DC**
Wilkerson, Robert L. ...Los Angeles, CA
Wilkerson & Seay ...Salem, MO
Wilkerson, Sheryl J.
Federal Communications Commission, Office of Legislative and Intergovernmental Affairs, GV
Wilkerson, Sonje W. ...New Orleans, LA
Wilkerson, Stephen C. ...**Tulsa, OK**
Wilkerson, Susan C. ...Port Richey, FL
Wilkerson, Susan Payor ...**Atlanta, GA**
Wilkerson, T. Rabb, III ...Warner Robins, GA
Wilkerson, Thomas D. ...Charleston, WV
Wilkerson, Timothy L.
San Luis Obispo, CA
Wilkerson, Timothy R. ...Kingsport, TN
Wilkerson, Walter J. ...New Orleans, LA
Wilkerson, Wassall & Warman, P.C.
Tulsa, OK
Wilkerson, William A. ...Lucedale, MS
Wilkerson, William R. ...Tacoma, WA
Wilkerson & Williams, P.A.
West Palm Beach, FL
Wilkerson-Barron, Yvette
Department of Justice, Environment and Natural Resources Division, GV
Wilkes, Artis, Hedrick & Lane, Chartered
Washington, DC
Annapolis, MD
Bethesda, MD
Greenbelt, MD
Waldorf, MD
Fairfax, VA
Wilkes, Baron J., Jr. ...Memphis, TN
Wilkes, Bernard J., III ...Youngstown, OH
Wilkes, Burwell B. ...Greenville, MS

Wilkes, Charles A., Jr. Highlands Ranch, CO
Wilkes, Charles A. Jr., P.C. Highlands Ranch, CO
Wilkes, Charles C. ... Bethesda, MD
Wilkes, Charles L. ... Washington, DC
Bethesda, MD
Wilkes, Christine M. ... New York, NY
Wilkes, Christopher C. ... Martinsburg, WV
Wilkes, D. Philip ... Topeka, KS
Wilkes, David C. ... Elmsford, NY
Wilkes, Diana ... Phoenix, AZ
Wilkes, Donald E., Jr. ... Athens, GA
Wilkes & Dunn ... Edwardsville, KS
Wilkes & Dyer ... Dyersburg, TN
Wilkes, E. M., III ... Hazlehurst, GA
Wilkes, Forrest Ren ... Jackson, MS
Wilkes, Galen H. ... Phoenix, AZ
Wilkes, Gene C., Jr. ... Surfside Beach, SC
Wilkes, Gilbert, III ... Martinsburg, WV
Wilkes, Gregg A. ... Shreveport, LA
Wilkes, H. Kenneth ... Opelika, AL
Wilkes, J. Falkner ... Greenville, SC
Wilkes, J. Michael ... San Antonio, TX
Wilkes, Jacque H. ... Jefferson, GA
Wilkes, James C., Jr. ... Fort Lauderdale, FL
Wilkes, James David ... Dublin, GA
Wilkes, James M. ... Tucson, AZ
Wilkes, James S., Jr. ... Dyersburg, TN
Wilkes, James Steven ... Anniston, AL
Wilkes, James T., Jr. ... Olympia Fields, IL
Wilkes, John F., III ... Lafayette, LA
Wilkes, John P. ... Fort Lauderdale, FL
Wilkes, John P., P.A. ... Fort Lauderdale, FL
Wilkes, Karen S. ... Rome, GA
Wilkes, Keith A. ... Tulsa, OK
Wilkes, Kristine L. ... San Diego, CA
Wilkes, Larry D. ... Cleveland, OH
Youngstown, OH
Wilkes, Mary Allen ... Waltham, MA
Wilkes, Mary E. ... Orlando, FL
Wilkes, McCullough & Wagner Memphis, TN
Wilkes & McHugh, P.A. ... Birmingham, AL
Mobile, AL
Little Rock, AR
Tallahassee, FL
Tampa, FL
Wilkes, Meredith M. ... Omaha, NE
Cleveland, OH
Wilkes, Michael B. T. ... Spartanburg, SC
Wilkes, Michael F. ... Rockledge, FL
Wilkes, Nicholas E. ... Columbus, OH
Wilkes and Price ... Bethesda, MD
California, MD
Wilkes, Randall ... Santa Rosa, CA
Wilkes, Richard Benjamin ... Tampa, FL
Wilkes, Richard C. ... Kenmare, ND
Wilkes, Robert D. ... Austin, TX
Wilkes, Robert L. ... Santa Ana, CA
Wilkes, Roberta L. ... Edwardsville, KS
Wilkes, Ronald L. ... Arcadia, FL
Wilkes, Roscoe H. ... Bainbridge Island, WA
Wilkes, Sharon E. ... St. Louis, MO
Wilkes, Stanley E., Jr. ... Arlington, TX
Wilkes, Ted L. ... New York, NY
Wilkes, Thomas J. ... Orlando, FL
Wilkes, W. Roy ... Sebring, FL
Wilkes, W. D., Jr. ... Guntersville, AL
Wilkes, Wendelyn ... San Antonio, TX
Wilkes & Wilkes ... Martinsburg, WV
Wilkes, Wilkes & Welsh, A Legal Professional Association ... Youngstown, OH
Wilkes, William A. ... Jacksonville, FL
Wilkes Cape, Sheri ... Tallahassee, FL
Wilkes II, James L. ... Tampa, FL
Wilkey, Angela H. ... Spokane, WA
Wilkey, Jerry V. ... Palm Beach, FL
Wilkey, Malcolm R. ... Department of State, Foreign Service Officers (Overseas), GV
Wilkey, Mark E. ... Las Vegas, NV
Wilkey, Robert D. ... Franklin, KY
Wilkey, Roscoe S. ... Encinitas, CA
Wilkey, Russ ... Owensboro, KY
Wilkie, Austin T. ... New York, NY
Wilkie, Barry L. ... Denver, CO
Wilkie, Chester R., III ... Little Compton, RI
Wilkie, Diane E. ... Hempstead, NY
St. James, NY
Wilkie & Graff, LLC ... Kingston, NY
Wilkie, Harold W. ... Madison, WI
Wilkie, Jenny L. ... Riverwoods, IL
Wilkie, Joan B. ... Fresno, CA
Wilkie, John B. ... Tucson, AZ
Wilkie, John (Ian) McN., Jr. New York, NY
Wilkie, John M. (Jack) ... Champaign, IL
Wilkie, Kim Martin ... Lexington, KY
Wilkie, Kimberly Evans ... Houston, TX
Wilkie & McMahon ... Champaign, IL
Wilkie, Richard J. ... Houston, TX
Wilkie, Robert A. ... Hempstead, NY
Wilkie, Robert C. ... Suffern, NY
Wilkie, Robert L., Jr. ... United States Senate, Senatorial Assistants, GV
Wilkie, Robin Forbes ... Chicago, IL
Wilkie, Wendy L. ... Charleston, SC
Wilkie & Wilkie ... Hempstead, NY
St. James, NY
Wilkin, David S. ... Augusta, GA
Wilkin, Edgar B., Jr. ... Albany, GA
Wilkin, Fred T., Jr. ... Independence, KS
Wilkin, Neil D., Jr. ... Richmond, VA
Wilkin, R. Charles ... Tulsa, OK
Wilkin, Stephen D. ... Independence, KS
Wilkin, William E. ... Department of State, Foreign Service Officers (Overseas), GV
Wilking, Leo F. J. ... Fargo, ND
Wilking, Richard R. ... Casper, WY
Wilkins, Alfred S. ... Weaverville, CA
Wilkins, Alisa A. ... Washington, DC
Wilkins, Bankester, Biles & Wynne, P.A. Bay Minette, AL
Fairhope, AL
Robertsdale, AL
Wilkins & Berger ... Lewistown, MT
Wilkins, Bonnie L. ... Minneapolis, MN
Wilkins, Bruce G. ... Woodstock, IL
Wilkins, C. Richard ... Mobile, AL
Wilkins, Cassandra F. ... Silver Spring, MD
Wilkins, Charles P., (P.C.) ... Raleigh, NC
Wilkins, Christina S. ... Alexandria, LA
New Braunfels, TX
Wilkins, Clifford E., Jr. ... New York, NY
Wilkins, D. Frank ... Salt Lake City, UT
Wilkins, Daniel J. ... Lowell, MA
Wilkins, David B. ... Cambridge, MA
Wilkins, David G. ... Indianapolis, IN
Wilkins, David H. ... Greenville, SC
Wilkins, David Paul ... Billings, MT
Wilkins & Davison ... Warsaw, VA
Wilkins, Deborah Potter ... St. Louis, MO
Wilkins, Deborah Tomes Bowling Green, KY
Wilkins and DeYoung ... Hyannis, MA
Wilkins, Donald J. ... San Diego, CA
Wilkins, Douglas Alan ... Toledo, OH
Wilkins, Douglas H. ... Boston, MA
Wilkins, Drolshagen & Czeshinski, LLP Fresno, CA
Wilkins, Druhan & Holtz ... Mobile, AL
Wilkins, Elizabeth A. ... Boca Raton, FL
Wilkins, Elizabeth A., P.A. ... Boca Raton, FL
Wilkins, Elizabeth R., (Mrs.) ... Redmond, WA
Wilkins, F. Stuart ... Canton, OH
Salem, OH
Wilkins, Floyd, Jr. ... San Diego, CA
Wilkins, Fred ... Kansas City, MO
Wilkins, Frederick B. ... Reidsville, NC
Wilkins, Frohlich, Jones, Hevia, Russell & Sutter, P.A. ... Port Charlotte, FL
Wilkins, Gary L. ... Port Charlotte, FL
Wilkins, Gene E. ... Indianapolis, IN
Wilkins, Gerald P. ... St. Paul, MN
Wilkins, Gordon A. ... Warsaw, VA
Wilkins, Greg C. ... Beaumont, TX
Wilkins, H. Wesley ... Jonesboro, IL
Wilkins, Hal W. ... Nashville, TN
Wilkins, Herbert P. ... Boston, MA
Wilkins & Ivey ... Brentwood, TN
Nashville, TN
Wilkins, J. Van ... Talladega, AL
Wilkins, James C., Jr. ... Lewistown, MT
Wilkins, James G. ... Baton Rouge, LA
Wilkins, James H. ... Fresno, CA
Wilkins, James H., Jr. ... Washington, DC
Wilkins, James P. ... Cleveland, OH
Wilkins, James S. ... San Antonio, TX
Wilkins, Jeffrey B. ... Westport, CT
Wilkins, Jesse T. ... Hoboken, NJ
Forest Hills, NY
Wilkins, Jimmy B. ... Jackson, MS
Wilkins, Joann N. ... Dallas, TX
Wilkins, John A. ... Sequim, WA
Wilkins, John P. ... New York, NY
Wilkins, John T. ... Lake Placid, NY
Wilkins, John W. ... Hilton Head Island, SC
Wilkins, Jon Sharp ... Washington, DC
Wilkins, Joseph T., III ... Jackson, MS
Wilkins, Karen Lewis ... New Orleans, LA
Wilkins, Kay H. ... Mesa, AZ
Wilkins, Kelly L. ... Boston, MA
Wilkins, Kevin A. ... Tampa, FL
Wilkins, Kevin A., P.A. ... Tampa, FL
Wilkins, Kimberly A. ... Chicago, IL
Wilkins, Lauren DiSimone ... Providence, RI
Wilkins, Lawrence A ... Dayton, OH
Wilkins, Lawrence P. ... Indianapolis, IN
Wilkins, Linda A. ... Westerville, OH
Wilkins, Linda Albright ... Dallas, TX
Wilkins, Linda S. ... Cleveland, OH
Wilkins, Lisa Mills ... Orlando, FL
Wilkins & Madden, P.A. ... Greenville, SC
Wilkins, Matthew E. ... Detroit, MI
Wilkins, Michael A. ... Indianapolis, IN
Wilkins, Michael D. ... Fort Wayne, IN
Wilkins, Michael J. ... Salt Lake City, UT
Wilkins & Millin, P.C. ... Kansas City, MO
Wilkins, Nancy E. ... Cincinnati, OH
Wilkins, Norma G. ... Chicago, IL
Wilkins, Octavia B. ... Louisville, KY
Wilkins, Paul B. ... Columbia, LA
Wilkins, Paul Cooke ... Penn Valley, CA
Wilkins, Paul Cooke, P.C. ... Penn Valley, CA
Wilkins, Percy, Jr. ... Brentwood, TN
Nashville, TN
Wilkins, Philip C. ... Sacramento, CA
Wilkins, Phillip D. ... Carrollton, GA
Villa Rica, GA
Wilkins, Randall D. ... Phoenix, AZ
Wilkins, Randall D. ... Houston, TX
Wilkins, Richard G. ... Washington, DC
Wilkins, Richard G. Saint Simons Island, GA
Wilkins, Richard L. ... Jackson, MI
Wilkins, Ricky E. ... Memphis, TN
Wilkins, Robert C., Jr. ... Maitland, FL
Wilkins, Robert D. ... New York, NY
White Plains, NY
Wilkins, Robert G. ... Hillsboro, MO
Wilkins, Robert H. ... St. Louis, MO
Wilkins, Robert L. ... Washington, DC
Wilkins, Robert L. ... Milwaukee, WI
Wilkins, Robert P. ... Lexington, SC
Wilkins, Robert P., Jr. ... Lexington, SC
Wilkins, Robert W. ... Jupiter, FL
Wilkins, Russell N. ... Hyannis, MA
Wilkins, Samuel H. ... Jackson, MS
Wilkins, Samuel L. ... Columbia, SC
Wilkins, Sheryl ... San Francisco, CA
Wilkins, Stanley ... New York, NY
Wilkins, Stanley N. ... Overland Park, KS
Kansas City, MO
Wilkins, Stuart A. ... West Berlin, NJ
Wilkins, Susan M. ... Baltimore, MD
Wilkins, T. Lee ... Dallas, TX
Wilkins, Taylor D., Jr. ... Bay Minette, AL
Robertsdale, AL
Wilkins, Thomas H. ... Washington, DC
Wilkins, Thomas R., Jr. ... Lubbock, TX
Wilkins & Tidd, P.C. ... Mesa, AZ
Wilkins, Timothy A. ... Houston, TX
Wilkins, Tom, Law Offices of McAllen, TX
Wilkins & Vallone, P.C. ... Mount Holly, NJ
Wilkins, Vonda L. ... Phoenix, AZ
Wilkins, W. Jon ... Chesapeake, VA
Wilkins, W. Paul ... Baton Rouge, LA
Wilkins, William J. ... Washington, DC
Wilkins, William T. ... Mount Holly, NJ
Wilkins, William T., IV ... Jackson, MS
Wilkins, William W., Jr. ... Greenville, SC
Wilkins, William Y. ... Winston-Salem, NC
Wilkinson, Albert Mims, Jr. ... Dillard, GA
Wilkinson, Alfred F. ... Randallstown, MD
Wilkinson, Alvoid and Peyton ... Dallas, TX
Wilkinson, Andrew F. ... Hagerstown, MD
Wilkinson, Ann P. ... Reno, NV
Wilkinson, Anne T. ... Raleigh, NC
Wilkinson, B. Curtis ... Terre Haute, IN
Wilkinson Barker Knauer, LLP Washington, DC
Wilkinson, Ben H. ... Tallahassee, FL
Wilkinson, Beth A. ... Washington, DC
Wilkinson, Beth D. ... Atlanta, GA
Wilkinson, Bill V. ... Tulsa, OK
Wilkinson, Billy J. ... Camp Wood, TX
Wilkinson, Bonnie ... Troy, MI
Wilkinson, Bradley Daniel ... Jackson, MS
Wilkinson, Bruce ... Fort Worth, TX
Wilkinson, Bruce M. ... Stuart, FL
Wilkinson, Carl E. ... Cincinnati, OH
Wilkinson, Carmody & Gilliam Bossier City, LA
Shreveport, LA
Wilkinson, Carol M. ... Department of Justice, Drug Enforcement Administration, GV
Wilkinson, Cathi C. ... Tallahassee, FL
Wilkinson, Charles A., Law Offices of Bethlehem, PA
Wilkinson, Charles Francis ... Marietta, GA
Wilkinson, Charles Joseph ... Miamisburg, OH
Wilkinson, Charles L., III ... Augusta, GA
Wilkinson, Charles W., Jr. ... Oxford, NC
Wilkinson, Christopher B. San Francisco, CA
Wilkinson, Christopher G. ... Boston, MA
Wilkinson, Claudia B. ... Houston, TX
Wilkinson, Conrad M. ... Claremont, CA
Wilkinson, Constance A. ... Washington, DC
Wilkinson, Curtis R. ... Littlefield, TX
Wilkinson, Cynthia F. ... Birmingham, AL
Wilkinson, Cynthia L. ... Dallas, TX
Wilkinson, Dag ... Washington, DC
Wilkinson, Dan Olson ... San Jose, CA
Wilkinson, Darla J. ... Morristown, NJ
Wilkinson, David C. ... Boulder, CO
Wilkinson, David J. ... San Ramon, CA
Wilkinson, David L. ... Hamilton, VA
Wilkinson, Deborah S. ... Wichita, KS
Wilkinson, Don C., Law Offices of Phoenix, AZ
Wilkinson, Donald A. ... Dearborn, MI
Wilkinson, Donald A. ... Sea Isle City, NJ
Wilkinson, Donald E. ... Wheaton, IL
Wilkinson, Donald H. ... Eureka, CA
Wilkinson, Donald L. ... Houston, TX
Wilkinson, Donald M., Jr. ... New York, NY
Wilkinson, Donald R. ... Kansas City, MO
Wilkinson, Dorothy L. ... Milwaukee, WI
Wilkinson, Douglas D. ... Salt Lake City, UT
Wilkinson, Douglas R. ... Springfield, OR
Wilkinson, Edward L. ... Fort Worth, TX
Wilkinson, Elise V. ... Houston, TX
Wilkinson, Ellsworth F. ... De Smet, SD
Lake Preston, SD
Wilkinson, Eric Richard ... Washington, DC
Wilkinson, Frank A. ... Orlando, FL
Wilkinson, G. Barry ... St. Petersburg, FL
Wilkinson, Gary ... Jacksonville, FL
Wilkinson, Gary P. ... Florence, AL
Wilkinson, Gary P., P.C. ... Florence, AL
Wilkinson, Gary R. ... Memphis, TN
Wilkinson, Gene A. ... Jackson, MS
Wilkinson, George A., Jr. ... Hyattsville, MD
Wilkinson, George B. ... Cincinnati, OH
Wilkinson, George B., III ... Hartford, CT
Wilkinson, George O., Jr. ... Houston, TX
Wilkinson, Geri A. ... Mequon, WI
Wilkinson, Goeller, Modesitt, Wilkinson & Drummy ... Brazil, IN
Sullivan, IN
Terre Haute, IN
Wilkinson, Gordon M. ... Winnsboro, TX
Wilkinson, Gregory K. ... Riverside, CA
Wilkinson, Guy T. ... Camden, TN
Wilkinson, Harvie B. ... Lexington, KY
Wilkinson, Henry ... Forrest City, AR
Wilkinson, H. L. ... Stamps, AR
Wilkinson, Homer F. ... Salt Lake City, UT
Wilkinson, Hugh T. ... Washington, DC
Wilkinson, J. Carter ... Baton Rouge, LA
Wilkinson, J. Henry, Jr. ... Austin, TX
Wilkinson, J. Louis ... Birmingham, AL
Wilkinson, J. Mark ... Chicago, IL
Wilkinson, J. Naomi ... Washington, DC
Wilkinson, J. Richard, Jr. ... Atlanta, GA
Wilkinson, Jack L. ... Baton Rouge, LA
Wilkinson, James A. ... Orlando, FL
Wilkinson, James A. ... Fairview, OK
Wilkinson, James B. ... Richmond, VA
Wilkinson, James H. ... Cleveland, OH
Wilkinson, James Harvie, III Charlottesville, VA
Wilkinson, James L. ... Cambridge, MA
Wilkinson, Jean ... Olympia, WA
Wilkinson, Jean M. ... Santa Ana, CA
Wilkinson, Jeffrey B. ... Portland, OR
Wilkinson, Jennifer H. ... Anniston, AL
Wilkinson, Jennifer Ingram Hattiesburg, MS
Wilkinson, John B. ... Chicago, IL
Wilkinson, John B. ... New Orleans, LA
Wilkinson, John H. ... New York, NY
Wilkinson, John, Jr. ... Columbia, MD
Wilkinson, John T., III ... Memphis, TN
Wilkinson, Joseph C., Jr. ... New Orleans, LA
Wilkinson, Karen M. ... Phoenix, AZ
Wilkinson, Katherine B. ... Camarillo, CA
Wilkinson, Kathleen A. ... El Segundo, CA
Wilkinson, Kathleen D. ... Philadelphia, PA
Wilkinson, Kelly ... Baton Rouge, LA
Wilkinson, Kevin D. ... West Palm Beach, FL
Wilkinson, Kimberly L. San Francisco, CA
Wilkinson, Kirk A. ... Los Angeles, CA
Wilkinson, Laura A. ... Washington, DC
Wilkinson, Laura N. ... Providence, RI
Wilkinson Law Firm, The ... Tulsa, OK
Wilkinson Law Office, P.C. ... Kalamazoo, MI
Wilkinson, Leigh Allred ... New Bern, NC
Wilkinson, Leslie B., Jr. ... Nashville, TN
Wilkinson, Lester F., Jr. ... Augusta, ME
Wilkinson, Lisa ... Albany, NY
Wilkinson, Marcus D. ... Hartford, CT
Wilkinson, Mary Beth ... Chicago, IL
Wilkinson, Mary Ellen ... Richmond, VA
Wilkinson, Melody McDonald Fort Worth, TX
Wilkinson, Merlin D. ... Portland, OR
Wilkinson, Michael C. ... Brandon, MS
Wilkinson, Michael O. ... Phoenix, AZ
Wilkinson, Michael R. ... Los Angeles, CA
Wilkinson, Michael R., P.A. South Pasadena, CA
Wilkinson, Michelle C. West Palm Beach, FL
Wilkinson, Monica B. Bloomfield Hills, MI
Wilkinson, Noel G. ... Annapolis, MD
Wilkinson, Norman ... Fort Smith, AR
Wilkinson, O. Jennings, Jr. ... Phoenix, AZ
Wilkinson, P. Chauvin, Jr. Baton Rouge, LA
Wilkinson, Patricia Jo ... Claremont, CA
Wilkinson, Peter ... Southport, CT
Wilkinson, Phoebe A. ... New York, NY
Wilkinson, Phyllis H. ... Buffalo, NY
Wilkinson, R. Michael ... South Pasadena, CA
Wilkinson, R. Neal ... Baton Rouge, LA
Wilkinson, Randell L. ... Santa Ana, CA
Wilkinson, Rebecca L. ... Middletown, OH
Wilkinson, Richard D. ... Roseland, NJ
Wilkinson, Richard K. ... Orange, VA
Wilkinson, Richard W. ... Bluefield, WV
Wilkinson, Robert A. ... Norcross, GA
Wilkinson, Robert D. ... Fresno, CA
Wilkinson, Robert F. ... St. Louis, MO
Wilkinson, Robert N. ... Salt Lake City, UT
Wilkinson, Robert W. ... Pascagoula, MS
Wilkinson, Rodney J. ... Provo, UT
Wilkinson, Roger W. ... Washington, DC
Wilkinson, Ronald C. ... Vancouver, WA
Wilkinson, Ronald D. ... Tulsa, OK
Wilkinson, Ronald D. ... Provo, UT
Wilkinson, Ronald J. ... Wichita, KS
Wilkinson, Ronald L. ... Dallas, TX
Wilkinson, Sandra G. ... Dallas, TX
Wilkinson & Staebler, LLC Cumberland, MD
Wilkinson, Stanley D. ... Houston, TX
Wilkinson, Stephen C. ... Cumberland, MD
Wilkinson, Susan E. ... Cedar Rapids, IA
Wilkinson, T. Barry ... Port Allen, LA
Wilkinson, Thomas C. ... Marianna, FL
Wilkinson, Thomas G. ... Gretna, LA
Wilkinson, Thomas G., A Professional Law Corporation ... Gretna, LA
Wilkinson, Thomas G., Jr. Philadelphia, PA
Wilkinson, Thomas J. ... Garden City, NY
Wilkinson, Thomas J., Jr. Cedar Rapids, IA
Wilkinson, Thomas L. ... Cherry Hill, NJ
Wilkinson, Thomas Roy ... San Diego, CA
Wilkinson, Timothy J. ... Great Falls, MT
Wilkinson, Toby C. ... Greenville, TX
Wilkinson, Todd D. ... Bryant, SD
De Smet, SD
Lake Preston, SD
Oldham, SD
Wilkinson & Vinson ... Birmingham, AL
Wilkinson, W. John ... Kalamazoo, MI
Wilkinson & Wilkinson ... Claremont, CA
Wilkinson & Wilkinson ... New Orleans, LA
Wilkinson & Wilkinson ... Bryant, SD
De Smet, SD
Lake Preston, SD
Oldham, SD
Wilkinson, William C. ... Columbus, OH
Wilkinson, William G. ... Ashland City, TN
Wilkinson, William J. ... Chicago, IL

Wilkinson, William R. ....Muncie, IN
Wilkinson, William S. ....East Lansing, MI
Wilkinson, Wm. Justus ....Fort Collins, CO
Wilkirson, David L. ....Santa Ana, CA
Wilkison, Robert P. ....Sunbury, PA
Wilkison, Tracy J. ....Sacramento, CA
Wilkison, Tracy L. ....Los Angeles, CA
Wilkison, Warren K. ....Grover Beach, CA
Santa Maria, CA
Wilkison-Stone ....Grover Beach, CA
Santa Maria, CA
Wilkniss, Peter F. ....New York, NY
Wilkof, Arthur M., (A Prof. Corp.)
Los Angeles, CA
Wilkof, Jeffrey S. ....Canton, OH
Wilkof, Richard B. ....Washington, DC
Wilkof, Sandra G. ....Washington, DC
Wilkof, Sandra G. ....Bethesda, MD
Wilkofsky, Benj. ....Springfield Gardens, NY
Wilkofsky, Friedman, Karel & Cummins
Los Angeles, CA
San Francisco, CA
Manalapan, NJ
New York, NY
Wilkofsky, Jonathan J. ....New York, NY
Wilkonson, Arthur O. ....Denver, CO
Wilkoski, Thomas C. ....West Allis, WI
Wilkov, Marcy E. ....New York, NY
Wilkov, Scott J.
Department of the Air Force,
Office of the Judge Advocate General, GV
Wilkow, Marc R. ....Chicago, IL
Wilkow, Mark H. ....New Hyde Park, NY
Wilkow & Wilkow, P.C. ....Chicago, IL
Wilkowski, Arthur R. ....Toledo, OH
Wilkowski, Eric T. ....Cincinnati, OH
Wilkowski, John P. ....Greenwood, IN
Wilkowski, Keith A. ....Findlay, OH
Toledo, OH
Wilkowski, Mary A. ....Honolulu, HI
Wilkozek, Shari Lynn ....Chicago, IL
Wilks & Alper, P.C. ....Norfolk, VA
Virginia Beach, VA
Wilks, David B. ....Woodbridge, VA
Wilks, David E. ....Wilmington, DE
Wilks, Harry T. ....Hamilton, OH
Wilks, James L. ....Sweetwater, TX
Wilks, James L., P.C. ....Sweetwater, TX
Wilks, Jay F. ....Norfolk, VA
Wilks, John Whitfield ....Charlotte, NC
Wilks, Larry D., Law Offices of
Nashville, TN
Springfield, TN
Wilks, Marylaurel E. ....Concord, NC
Wilks, Norman D. ....Topeka, KS
Wilks, Richard B. ....Phoenix, AZ
Wilks, Robert A. ....Tustin, CA
Wilks, Stuart K. ....Palo Alto, CA
Wilks, Thomas R.
National Labor Relations Board,
Division of Administrative Law Judges, GV
Wilks, Van C. ....Carrollton, GA
New York, NY
Wilks, Wayne W. ....Burbank, CA
Wilks, William L. ....Houston, TX
Will, Alfred J. ....New York, NY
Will, Candice M. ....Department of Justice,
Office of Professional Responsibility, GV
Will, Carl T. ....Trenton, NJ
Will, Christine A. ....New York, NY
Will, Clark B. ....Dallas, TX
Will, Dale Loren ....Sacramento, CA
Will, Daniel E. ....Manchester, NH
Will, David C. ....Atlanta, GA
Will, Harriette Kingoff ....Richmond, VA
Will, Henry G. ....Tulsa, OK
Will, J. Kemper ....Denver, CO
Will, John B. ....Omaha, NE
Will, John F., Jr. ....Carnegie, PA
Will, John J. ....St. Petersburg, FL
Will, Joseph G. ....Daytona Beach, FL
Will, Kenneth J. ....Houston, TX
Will, Mary L. ....Denver, CO
Will, Michele L. ....Palm Beach Gardens, FL
Will, Nora Buchanan
Department of Commerce,
Patent and Trademark Office, GV
Will, Richard H. ....Sacramento, CA
Will, Robert G. ....Minot, ND
Will, Robert J. ....St. Louis, MO
Will, Robert P. ....Washington, DC
Will, Robert P., & Associates
Waukegan, IL
Will, Robert P., Jr. ....Waukegan, IL
Will, Robert V. ....Glendale, AZ
Will, Rodger G. ....Detroit, MI
Will, Stephen P. ....Culpeper, VA
Will, Thomas A. ....Pittsburgh, PA
Will, Timothy N. ....Torrance, CA
Will, Trevor J. ....Milwaukee, WI
Willacy, Aubrey B. ....Cleveland, OH
Willacy, Hazel M. ....Cleveland, OH
Willacy & LoPresti ....Cleveland, OH
Willacy, Louis S. ....Los Angeles, CA
Willaert, Andrew A. ....Mankato, MN
Willaert, Matthew T. ....North Chicago, IL
Willamowski, John R. ....Lima, OH
Willamowski, Mona L. ....Lima, OH
Willamowski and Willamowski, Co., L.P.A.
Lima, OH
Willan, Robert M. ....Lake Charles, LA
Willard, Benedict J. ....New Orleans, LA
Willard, C. Lawson, III ....Fairfax, VA
Willard, Christopher ....Raleigh, NC
Willard, Christopher E. ....Arlington, VA
Willard, Clyde A. ....Perry, FL
Willard, Daniel S. ....Rockville, MD
Willard, Daniel S., P.C. ....Rockville, MD
Willard, David Charles ....Lafayette, LA
Willard, Deborah A. ....Boston, MA
Willard, Donald A. ....Bloomington, IL
Willard, Donna C. ....Anchorage, AK
Willard, Eric ....Santa Fe, NM
Willard, Frank L. ....Norfolk, VA
Willard, Gail Gonya ....Raleigh, NC
Willard, Geoffrey T. ....Washington, DC
Willard, Glenn ....Terre Haute, IN
Willard, Gregory D. ....St. Louis, MO
Willard, Harold L. ....Lubbock, TX
Willard, Jack ....Merrillville, IN
Willard, James G. ....Orlando, FL
Willard, James R. ....Overland Park, KS
Willard, James S. ....Topeka, KS
Willard, Jill A. ....Houston, TX
Willard, John B. ....West Hartford, CT
Willard, John M. ....Wilmington, DE
Willard, John T. ....Hamilton, OH
Willard, Jon S. ....Olathe, KS
Willard & Kellis, P.A. ....Sanford, ME
Willard, Laurie A. ....Minneapolis, MN
Willard, Linda J. ....Washington, DC
Willard, Linda L. ....Lincoln, NE
Willard & Long, A Professional Law Corporation ....Lafayette, LA
Willard, Madelon H. ....Rockville, MD
Willard, Mark A. ....Pittsburgh, PA
Willard, Martin P. ....Washington, DC
Willard, Matthew R. ....Tallahassee, FL
Willard, Michele Hilden ....Marietta, OH
Willard & Pharris, P.C. ....Fort Collins, CO
Willard, Ralph H., Jr. ....Boston, MA
Willard, Randall M. ....Fort Collins, CO
Willard, Richard K. ....Washington, DC
Willard, Robert H. ....Columbus, OH
Willard, Robert R. ....Ventura, CA
Willard, Robert W. ....New Castle, DE
Willard, Sheri L. ....Chicago, IL
Willard, Sherwood S. ....New Haven, CT
Willard, Stephen C. ....Charlottesville, VA
Willard, Steven M. ....Portsmouth, OH
Willard, Theodore DuBose, Jr.
Columbia, SC
Willard, Timothy G. ....Georgetown, DE
Willard, Todd Douglas
Bowling Green, KY
Willard, Walter I. ....New Orleans, LA
Willard & Willard, L.L.P. ....Raleigh, NC
Willard, William E. ....Baton Rouge, LA
Willard, William G., Jr. ....Clarksdale, MS
Willard, William J. ....Totowa, NJ
Willard, William R. ....Gadsden, AL
Willard, William T. ....Seattle, WA
Willard, William W. ....Portland, ME
Willardson, John S. ....Wilkesboro, NC
Willardson & Lipscomb, LLP
Wilkesboro, NC
Willardson, Niel D. ....Minneapolis, MN
Willardson, Timothy M. ....Sandy, UT
Willars, Ruth Monty ....El Paso, TX
Willatt & Flickinger ....Austin, TX
Willatt, Mike ....Austin, TX
Willbanks, Brad T. ....Florence, SC
Willbanks, Daniel L. ....Dexter, NY
Willbanks, Stephanie J. ......South Royalton, VT
Willbern, Clyde E. ....Bellaire, TX
Willbern, Roy ....San Marcos, TX
Willborn, James D. ....Tyler, TX
Willborn, Steven L. ....Lincoln, NE
Willbrand, David J. ....Boulder, CO
Willbrand, Herbert C. ....Columbia, MO
Willbrand, John C. ....Concord, CA
Willbrand, Lawrence O. ....St. Louis, MO
Willburn, Christopher J. ....Houston, TX
Willcher, Ernest M. .....Department of the Army,
Office of the General Counsel, GV
Willcockson, Kleber ....Los Angeles, CA
Willcott, Michael F. ....Leavenworth, KS
Willcox & Baird ....Norfolk, VA
Willcox, Breckinridge L. ....Washington, DC
Willcox, Buyck & Williams, Professional Association ....Columbia, SC
Florence, SC
Willcox, C. Jason ....Albany, GA
Willcox, E. Lloyd ....Charleston, SC
Willcox, E. Lloyd, II ....Florence, SC
Willcox, Edith Slafka ....Dayton, OH
Willcox, Edward R., Jr. ....Norfolk, VA
Willcox, Herbert J. ....New York, NY
Willcox, Hugh L., Jr. ....Florence, SC
Willcox, J. Taney, Jr. ....Narberth, PA
Willcox, James R. ....San Francisco, CA
Willcox, Joe C. ....Gainesville, FL
Willcox, John B. ....Narberth, PA
Willcox, Jon N. ....White Plains, NY
Willcox, Joseph Karl ....Memphis, TN
Willcox, Lawrence G. ....Bethesda, MD
Willcox, Mark, Jr. ....Philadelphia, PA
Willcox, Mary Elise ....Havertown, PA
Norristown, PA
Willcox, McFadyen and Fields
Laurinburg, NC
Raeford, NC
Willcox, Pirozzolo and McCarthy, Professional Corporation ....Boston, MA
Willcox, R. Palmer ....Raeford, NC
Willcox, Robin ....Princeton, NJ
Willcox, Roderick H. ....Columbus, OH
Willcox & Savage, P.C. ....Chesapeake, VA
Hampton, VA
Newport News, VA
Norfolk, VA
Portsmouth, VA
Virginia Beach, VA
Willcox, Susan ....Danbury, CT
Willcox, Thomas H., Jr. ....Norfolk, VA
Willcox & Valentine ....Narberth, PA
Willcox, William H. ....Washington, DC
Willcoxon, Michael ....Dublin, CA
Willcutts, Karen Brown ....Dallas, TX
Willcutts, Thomas P., & Associates
Hartford, CT
Willd, John A. ....Los Angeles, CA
Willdorf, Barry S. ....San Francisco, CA
Wille, Brian C. ....New York, NY
Wille, Carroll G. ....West Chester, PA
Wille, Daniel E. ....Pittsburgh, PA
Wille, David G. ....Dallas, TX
Wille, Gregory A. ....Santa Ana, CA
Wille, Gregory G. ....Milwaukee, WI
Wille, Gregory & Lundeen
Milwaukee, WI
Wille, Ivan ....Philadelphia, PA
Wille, James A. ....Cleveland, TN
Wille, Karin L. ....Minneapolis, MN
Wille, Leslie Ann ....El Paso, TX
Wille, Louis J. ....Bridgewater, NJ
Wille, Margaret D. ....Hebron, ME
Wille, Paul F. ....Phoenix, AZ
Willeford, Brice J., Jr. ....Concord, NC
Willeford, Brice J., Jr. ....Kannapolis, NC
Willeford, Byron L., (P.C.) ....Houston, TX
Willeford, James F. ....New Orleans, LA
Willeke & Daniels ....Minneapolis, MN
Willeke, Donald C. ....Minneapolis, MN
Willemin, Joseph M., Jr. ....St. Louis, MO
Willemin, Kathleen Marie ....Chappaqua, NY
Willemin, Louis P. ....Ellicott City, MD
Willems, Cletus R. ....Kenosha, WI
Willems, Constance Charles
New Orleans, LA
Willems, Daniel W. ....Cedar Rapids, IA
Willems, Hector ....Bronx, NY
Willems, Jay A. ....Anamosa, IA
Willems, John H. ....Detroit, MI
Willems, John S. ....New York, NY
Willems & Mercado ....Bronx, NY
Willemsen, Michael A. ....Palo Alto, CA
Willemssen, Mac R. ....Chaska, MN
Norwood, MN
Willen, Debra L. ....Washington, DC
Willen, H. Douglas ....Hopkinsville, KY
Willen, J. Mayer ....Baltimore, MD
Willen, Jules R. ....Baltimore, MD
Willen, Marija
Securities and Exchange Commission,
Division of Corporation Finance, GV
Willen, Mark T. ....Owings Mills, MD
Willen, Stephan J. ....Charlotte, NC
Willen, William R. ....Torrance, CA
Willenberg, Wayne E. ....Minneapolis, MN
Willenborg, Edward F. ....Aurora, IN
Willenborg, Thomas R. ....Covington, KY
Willenbring, Dahl, Wocken & Zimmermann
Cold Spring, MN
Willenbring, Joseph J. ....Cold Spring, MN
Willenbrink, Rose Ann ....Louisville, KY
Willenbrock, Ronald C. ....St. Louis, MO
Willenbucher, Marguerite C. ....New York, NY
Willenburg, Don ....Altadena, CA
Willence, Arnold I. ....Brooklyn, NY
Willener, Henry C. ....Portland, OR
Willener, Henry C., P.C. ....Portland, OR
Willenken, Lisa H. ....New York, NY
Willenkin, Roberta G. ....Edgeworth, PA
Sewickley, PA
Willens, D. Damon ....Glendale, CA
Willens, Daniel V. ....Woodland Hills, CA
Willens, Earl P. ....Los Angeles, CA
Willens, Jonathan A. ....New York, NY
Willens, Mark L. ....Kansas City, MO
Willens, Matthew L. ....Chicago, IL
Willens, Sidney L. ....Kansas City, MO
Willensky, Beth A. ....New Rochelle, NY
Willenzik, David S., (P.C.)
New Orleans, LA
Willer, Betsy S. ....St. Louis, MO
Willer, Douglas C. ....Franklin Lakes, NJ
Willer, Edward G. ....Chicago, IL
Willer, Laura C. ....Raleigh, NC
Willer, Michael D. .....Palos Verdes Estates, CA
Willer, Rebecca S. ....Woodmere, NY
Willert, Alan K. ....Seattle, WA
Willert, Daniel E. ....Boston, MA
Willert, Sheryl J. ....Seattle, WA
Willert, Susan Richardson ....Seattle, WA
Willert, Timothy F. ....New York, NY
Willerth, Joe F. ....Independence, MO
Willes, Elizabeth A. ....San Francisco, CA
Willes, Errol S. ....Fort Pierce, FL
Willess, Thomas N. ....Department of Defense,
Defense Legal Services Agency, GV
Willet, Debra A. ....Columbus, OH
Willet, Michael E. ....Beatrice, NE
Wymore, NE
Willett, Alfred E. ....Cedar Rapids, IA
Willett, Barry ....Louisville, KY
Willett, Beverly A. ....Brooklyn, NY
Willett, Bryce O. ....San Diego, CA
Willett, Christopher C. ....Buffalo, NY
Willett, Claire Chason ....Cairo, GA
Willett, David E. ....San Francisco, CA
Willett, Eileen Sullivan ....Phoenix, AZ
Willett, Ellis J. ....Stockton, CA
Willett, Gregory D. ....Chattanooga, TN
Willett, Henry I., III ....Richmond, VA
Willett, James A. ....Sacramento, CA
Willett, James P., III ....Bardstown, KY
Willett, Jocelyn Moselle ....Buffalo, NY
Willett, John A. ....New York, NY
Willett, John J. ....Dysart, IA
Tama, IA
Willett, John R. ....Alexandria, VA
Willett, John T. ....Orlando, FL
Willett, John T., & Associates, P.A.
Orlando, FL
Willett, Jonathan S. ....Denver, CO
Willett & Klein, S.C. ....Phillips, WI
Willett, Linda A. ....New York, NY
Willett, Lisa A.
Department Of Veterans Affairs,
Office of the General Counsel, GV
Willett, Louis J. ....Fremont, CA
Willett, Margaret Claire Chason .....Albany, GA
Willett, Mark D. ....Laredo, TX
Willett, Martin L. ....Tucson, AZ
Willett, Michael J. ....Buffalo, NY
Willett, Nicholas H. ....Buffalo, NY
Willett, Paul R. ....Tacoma, WA
Willett, R. Hillary ....Los Angeles, CA
Willett & Rathjen ....Tama, IA
Dysart, IA
Willett, Raynold L. ....Laurel, MS
Willett, Robert E. ....Los Angeles, CA
Willett, Robert E. ....Bardstown, KY
Willett, Robert S. ....Sacramento, CA
Willett, Ronald B. ....Department of Labor,
Pension and Welfare Benefits, GV
Willett, Roy B. ....Salem, VA
Willett, S. Gene ....Mount Vernon, WA
Willett, Sabin ....Boston, MA
Willett, Stephen D. ....Phillips, WI
Willett, Thomas E. ....Rochester, NY
Willett, Walter J. ....Tama, IA
Willett, Warren D. ....Alexandria, LA
Willett & Willett ....Buffalo, NY
Willett, Yeulin V. ....Grand Junction, CO
Willette, Charles, Jr. ....Brownsville, TX
Willette, Craig A. ....Rockford, IL
Willette, Diane M. ....Wilmington, DE
Willette & Guerra, L.L.P.
Brownsville, TX
Edinburg, TX
McAllen, TX
Willette, P. H. ....Unity, ME
Willette, Philip B. ....Pickerington, OH
Willette, Philip B., Co., L.P.A.
Pickerington, OH
Willette, Wayne C. ....Big River, CA
Willetts, Roger B. ....Waynesboro, VA
Willetts, William J., Jr. ....New London, CT
Willever, Kent A. ....Providence, RI
Willey, Alexis W. ....Santa Barbara, CA
Willey, Barry C. ....Galveston, TX
Willey, Benjamin L. ....Washington, DC
Willey, Benjamin L., Jr. ....Oklahoma City, OK
Willey, Bruce A. ....Cedar Rapids, IA
Willey & Chamberlain, L.L.P.
Grand Rapids, MI
Willey, Charles W., (P.C.)
Santa Barbara, CA
Willey, Craig M. ....San Jose, CA
Willey and Crooks ....Washington, DC
Willey, Don ....Jefferson, NC
Willey, Elizabeth L. ....Salt Lake City, UT
Willey, Gerald L. ....Chicago, IL
Willey, Grafton H., III ....Barrington, RI
Willey, J. Hugh, Jr. ....Houston, TX
Willey, James A. ....Washington, DC
Willey, James R. ....Indianapolis, IN
Willey, John D., Jr. ....Toledo, OH
Willey, Joseph V. ....New York, NY
Willey, Joshua W., Jr. ....New Bern, NC
Willey, Larry C. ....Grand Rapids, MI
Willey Law Firm ....Cedar Rapids, IA
Willey Law Firm, P.C. ....Cedar Rapids, IA
Willey, Lawrence A. ....Minneapolis, MN
Willey, Michael B. ....Gallatin, TN
Willey, Michel F. ....San Francisco, CA
Willey, N. Laurence, Jr. ....Brewer, ME
Willey, Ralph G., III ....Rocky Mount, NC
Willey, Ralph G., P.A. ....Greenville, NC
Kinston, NC
Plymouth, NC
Roanoke Rapids, NC
Rocky Mount, NC
Williamston, NC
Windsor, NC
Willey, Robert K. ....Ventura, CA
Willey, Sarah K. ....Boston, MA
Willey, Sarah K. ....Kalamazoo, MI
Willey, Stephen C. ....Seattle, WA
Willey, Stephen D., Law Offices of
Arlington, TX
Willey, Steven J. ....Department of Justice,
Environment and Natural Resources
Division, GV
Willey, Wythe ....Cedar Rapids, IA
Willey-Howland, Kimberly A. ....Boston, MA
Willford, Craig D. ....Whittier, CA
Willford, Erika B. ....Sacramento, CA
Willford, Gary L., Jr. ....Montgomery, AL
Willford, Laurel W., Mr. ....San Gabriel, CA
Willford, Louis J. ....Gladwin, MI
Willford, Sandford R. ....Newport Beach, CA
Willford, Thomas M. ....El Toro, CA
Willging, Kevin J. ....Baltimore, MD
Willging, Mark J. ....Dubuque, IA
Willging, Thomas E.
Federal Judicial Center, GV
Willgohs, Eric H. ....Palo Alto, CA
Willhardt, E. Gail ....Malibu, CA
Willhelm, Keith B. ....Houston, TX
Willhelm, Kevin W. ....San Antonio, TX
Willhelm, Lisa K. ....San Diego, CA
Willhight, Tracy J. ....Marina Del Rey, CA
Willhite, Anna ....Newton, MA
Willhite, J. Martin ....Los Angeles, CA
Willhite, James A., Jr. ....Philadelphia, PA
Willhite, Piper M. ....Dallas, TX
Willhite, Theodore R. ....Seattle, WA
Willhoite, J. Todd ....Claremore, OK

Willi, James N. ... Houston, TX
Willi, Kaye Pfister ... Columbus, OH
Willi, Tracy J. ... Houston, TX
Willia, N. Richard, Jr. ... Sioux City, IA
William, Patrick S. ... Minneapolis, MN
William, Susan Krehbiel ... Topeka, KS
Williamowsky, Samuel D. ... Rockville, MD
Williams, A. Dozier ... Birmingham, AL
Williams, A. Howard ... South Bend, IN
Williams, A. Jerome, Jr. ... Wilmington, NC
Williams, A. Simpson, Jr. ... Richmond, VA
Williams, A. Simpson, Jr., P.C.
Richmond, VA
Williams, A. Taylor ... Philadelphia, PA
Williams, Aaron ... Ukiah, CA
Williams, Abigail & Associates, P.C.
Worcester, MA
Williams, Abigail R. ... Worcester, MA
Williams, Adair & Ridge ... Erie, PA
Williams, Adam J., (P.A.)
Hot Springs National Park, AR
Hot Springs Village, AR
Williams, Adolphus Levi, Jr. ... Horsham, PA
Williams, Adrian S. ... Fresno, CA
Williams, Adrienne D. ... Brooklyn, NY
Williams, Agnes N. ... Potomac, MD
Williams, Aimee L. ... Lafayette, LA
Williams & Airth, P.A. ... Orlando, FL
Williams, Al Henry ... Dixon, IL
Williams, Alaine S. ... Lawrenceville, NJ
Harrisburg, PA
Philadelphia, PA
Williams, Alan D. ... Sebring, FL
Williams, Alan D., III ... Quakertown, PA
Williams, Alan D., Jr. ... Doylestown, PA
Williams, Alan G. ... Miami, FL
Williams, Alan L. ... San Diego, CA
Williams, Alan M. ... Vernal, UT
Williams, Alan R. ... St. Petersburg, FL
Williams, Alan R., & Associates
St. Petersburg, FL
Williams, Alana S. ... Tampa, FL
Williams, Albert J. ... Wrightsville Beach, NC
Williams, Aleatra ... Oklahoma City, OK
Williams, Alexander H., III
Los Angeles, CA
Williams, Alexander J., Jr.
Fort Lauderdale, FL
Williams, Alexander, Jr. ... Greenbelt, MD
Williams, Alexander S., III ... Birmingham, AL
Williams, Alexandra Nichols ... Towson, MD
Williams, Alfred C. ... San Francisco, CA
Williams, Alfred J. ... Miami, FL
Williams, Alfred T., Jr. ... Easton, PA
Williams, Alif A., & Associates
St. Louis, MO
Williams, Allan L. ... Austin, TX
Williams, Allan R. ... New York, NY
Williams, Allan S. ... Encino, CA
Williams, Allen K. ... Honolulu, HI
Williams, Allen L. ... Stamford, CT
Williams, Allen W., Jr. ... Milwaukee, WI
Williams, Allison S. ... Charleston, WV
Williams, Amanda F. ... Brunswick, GA
Williams, Amanda K. ... Chicago, IL
Williams, Amber F. ... Clearwater, FL
Williams, Ames W. ... Alexandria, VA
Williams, Amos E. ... Detroit, MI
Williams, Amy Greaves ... Houston, TX
Williams, Amy J. ... New York, NY
Williams, Amy M. ... Clearwater, FL
Williams, Amy Mc Daniel ... Richmond, VA
Williams, Amy R. ... New Orleans, LA
Williams & Anderson ... Little Rock, AR
Williams, André L. ... Miami, FL
Williams, Andrea B. ... Hackensack, NJ
Williams, Andrea B. ... Greenville, SC
Williams, Andrea C. ... Washington, DC
Williams, Andrea D. ... Washington, DC
Williams, Andres L. ... San Francisco, CA
Williams, Andrew B., II ... Nashville, TN
Williams, Andrew C. ... Atlanta, GA
Williams, Andrew C. ... Springfield, MA
Williams, Andrew J. ... Houston, TX
Williams, Andrew J. ... Humble, TX
Williams, Andrew K. ... Allentown, PA
Williams, Andrew M. ... Houston, TX
Williams, Andrew S. ... Los Angeles, CA
Williams, Andrew S. ... Chicago, IL
Williams, Angel Bentley ... McLean, VA
Williams, Angela M. ... Chicago, IL
Williams, Angela M. ... Miamisburg, OH
Williams, Angela S. ... Southfield, MI
Williams, Anita ... Springfield, IL
Williams, Anita Sarafa ... Chicago, IL
Williams, Ann C. ... Buffalo, NY
Williams, Ann Ellen ... Calumet City, IL
Williams, Ann H. ... Boston, MA
Williams, Ann M. ... Rochester, NY
Williams, Ann O. ... Houston, TX
Williams, Anna B. ... Nashville, TN
Williams, Anna M. ... Hendersonville, TN
Williams, Anne ... Palo Alto, CA
Williams, Anne J. ... Las Vegas, NV
Williams, Anne L. ... Honolulu, HI
Williams, Anne M.
Agency for International Development,
Other Offices of A.I.D., GV
Williams, Anne R. ... Clarksburg, WV
Williams, Anne-Michael ... Mesa, AZ
Williams, Annette E. ... Maitland, FL
Williams, Anthony ... New York, NY
Williams, Anthony C. ... Oak Park, IL
Williams, Anthony J. ... Albuquerque, NM
Williams, Anthony L. ... Raleigh, NC
Williams, Anthony S. ... Houston, TX
Williams, Anthony W.
Grand Junction, CO

Williams & Apple, A Legal Professional Corporation ... Salem, OH
Williams, April M. ... Columbus, OH
Williams, Archie Edward, Jr.
Department of Commerce,
Patent and Trademark Office, GV
Williams, Ardelle ... San Diego, CA
Williams & Arnold ... Ridgeland, MS
Williams, Arnold Fitger ... Beverly Hills, CA
Burbank, CA
Williams, Arnold Fitger ... Los Angeles, CA
Williams, Arnold Fitger ... Pasadena, CA
Santa Monica, CA
Williams, Arnold N. ... Dallas, TX
Williams, Art ... Haskell, TX
Williams, Arthur B. ... Newark, NY
Palmyra, NY
Williams, Arthur C. ... Southport, CT
Williams, Arthur L. ... Louisville, KY
Williams, Arthur L., Jr. ... Las Vegas, NV
Williams & Asby, PLLC ... Washington, DC
Williams and Asby, PLLC ... New Bern, NC
Williams & Associates ... Washington, DC
Williams & Associates ... Belmont, NY
Olean, NY
Williams & Associates, Law Offices of
Pacific Palisades, CA
Williams & Associates, P.A., Law Offices
Miami, FL
Williams & Associates, P.C. ... Nashville, TN
Williams & Associates, P.L.C.
Virginia Beach, VA
Williams, Aubrey ... Louisville, KY
Williams, Aubrey R. ... Waco, TX
Williams, Audrey ... San Francisco, CA
Williams, Auvergne, III ... Jackson, MS
Williams, Averill M. ... New York, NY
Williams, Avery K. ... Detroit, MI
Farmington Hills, MI
Williams, Aylmer Gene ... Little Rock, AR
Williams, B. John, Jr. ... Washington, DC
Williams, B. Keith ... Lebanon, TN
Williams, B. Wayne ... Oxford, MS
Tupelo, MS
Williams, Babette D. ... Department of Labor,
Office of Secretary, GV
Williams • Bailey Law Firm, L.L.P.
Houston, TX
Williams, Baird & Offerman, P.C.
Beaumont, TX
Williams and Ballas ... Los Angeles, CA
Palm Desert, CA
San Francisco, CA
Williams, Barbara ... West Salem, OH
Williams, Barbara Ann ... Richmond, VA
Williams, Barbara Coyle ... Evansville, IN
Williams, Barbara June ... Houston, TX
Williams, Barbara M. ... Fort Worth, TX
Williams, Barbara S. ... Leesburg, VA
Winchester, VA
Williams, Barbara Silver
Department of Justice, Civil Division, GV
Williams, Barry D. ... Albuquerque, NM
Williams, Barry G. ... Department of Justice,
Civil Rights Division, GV
Williams, Barry G. ... Casper, WY
Williams, Barry J. ... Oakland, CA
Williams, Barry L. ... San Francisco, CA
Williams, Barry L. ... Orlando, FL
Williams, Bart H. ... Los Angeles, CA
Williams, Bartley C. ... Marysville, CA
Williams & Barzee
North Kansas City, MO
Williams and Batchelder, LLP
Medina, OH
Williams, Belinda L. ... New York, NY
Williams, Ben F., Jr. ... Tucson, AZ
Williams, Bencile H., Jr. ... Tulsa, OK
Williams, Benita Y. ... Kansas City, MO
Williams, Benjamin A. ... Courtland, VA
Williams, Benjamin A., III
Newport News, VA
Williams, Benjamin E. ... St. Louis, MO
Williams, Benjamin George
Westlake Village, CA
Williams, Benjamin S. ... Atlanta, GA
Williams, Berges & Sanford
Los Angeles, CA
North Hollywood, CA
Williams, Bernard J. ... Metairie, LA
Williams, Bert ... El Paso, TX
Williams, Beth G. ... Monroeton, PA
Williams, Beth L. ... Chicago, IL
Williams, Betty Outhier ... Muskogee, OK
Williams, Beverly A. ... Roseland, NJ
Williams, Billy John ... Portland, OR
Williams, Birnberg & Andersen, L.L.P.
Houston, TX
Williams, Blackburn, Hudson & Maharry, P.L.C. ... Des Moines, IA
Williams, Bobby E. ... Fort Myers, FL
Williams, Boger, Grady, Davis & Tuttle, P.A.
Concord, NC
Kannapolis, NC
Salisbury, NC
Williams & Bolt, P.A. ... Tulsa, OK
Williams, Bonnie ... Springfield, IL
Williams, Booth & Williams ... Lancaster, OH
Williams, Boren & Associates, P.C.
Oklahoma City, OK
Williams, Box, Forshee & Bullard, P.C.
Oklahoma City, OK
Williams, Bradford J., Jr. ... Tulsa, OK
Williams, Bradford L. ... Kingman, KS
Williams, Bradley F. ... Minneapolis, MN
Williams, Bradley J ... Idaho Falls, ID
Williams, Bradley L. ... Indianapolis, IN
Williams, Bradley P. ... Dallas, TX

Williams, Brenda E. ... Seattle, WA
Williams, Brenda Renee ... Flint, MI
Williams, Brent C. ... Boxford, MA
Williams, Brent J. ... St. Louis, MO
Williams, Brett K. ... Pascagoula, MS
Williams, Brett P. ... Seattle, WA
Williams, Brian A. ... New York, NY
Williams, Brian B. ... Portland, OR
Williams, Brian D. ... Kansas City, MO
Williams, Brian D. ... Houston, TX
Williams, Brian H. ... Martinsville, IN
Williams, Brian J. ... Chicago, IL
Williams, Brian J. ... Akron, OH
Williams, Brian K. ... Baltimore, MD
Williams, Brian L. ... Minneapolis, MN
Williams, Brian P. ... Evansville, IN
Williams, Brian P. ... Des Moines, IA
Williams, Brian R. ... Toledo, OH
Williams, Brian R. ... Philadelphia, PA
Williams, Brian S. ... Chicago, IL
Williams, Brian T. ... Birmingham, AL
Williams & Brierton ... Johnstown, PA
Williams & Brink ... Lexington, SC
Williams, Brinley H., Jr. ... Cleveland, OH
Williams, Britt S. ... Montgomery, AL
Williams, Browder G. ... Harriman, TN
Williams & Brown ... Cuba, NY
Williams, Bruce C. ... Togus, ME
Williams, Bruce C. ... Millersville, MD
Williams, Bruce D. ... Houston, TX
Williams, Bruce E. ... Huntsville, AL
Williams, Bruce E. ... Memphis, TN
Williams, Bruce H. ... Haddonfield, NJ
Williams, Bruce H. ... Seattle, WA
Williams, Bruce W. ... Salem, OR
Williams, Bruce W., P.C. ... Salem, OR
Williams, Bryan K. ... Nashville, TN
Williams, Bryan M. ... Las Vegas, NV
Williams, Bryan R. ... Greenfield, IN
Williams, Bryant F., Jr. ... Ozark, AL
Williams Buckrop Malvik, and Associates, P.C. ... Rock Island, IL
Williams, Burgess ... Ukiah, CA
Williams, Burton D. ... Germantown, MD
Williams, Burton L. ... Boston, MA
Williams and Byrd ... Lufkin, TX
Williams, Byron E., Jr. ... Pryor, OK
Williams, C. Blake T. ... Los Angeles, CA
Williams, C. Bruce ... Salem, OH
Williams, C. Carter ... Old Fields, WV
Williams, C. Crawford, Jr. ... Birmingham, AL
Williams, C. Curtis, Jr. ... Raleigh, NC
Williams, C. David, Jr. ... Wilson, NC
Williams, C. Douglas ... Signal Mountain, TN
Williams, C. Gary ... Tallahassee, FL
Williams, C. Jackson ... Oxford, MS
Williams, C. Nicks ... Aiken, SC
Williams, C. Paige ... Birmingham, AL
Williams, Caliri, Miller & Otley, A Professional Corporation
Hackensack, NJ
Morristown, NJ
Newark, NJ
Paterson, NJ
Wayne, NJ
Williams, Calvin C., Jr. ... Jackson, MS
Williams, Calvin K. ... Colby, KS
Williams, Calvin K., Chartered ... Colby, KS
Williams, Cameron ... Los Angeles, CA
Williams, Cameron J. ... Nashville, TN
Williams, Camilla C. ... Atlanta, GA
Williams, Carl A. ... Tiffin, OH
Williams, Carl J. ... St. Martinville, LA
Williams, Carl V. ... New Orleans, LA
Williams, Carla K. ... Columbia, MO
Williams, Carlos ... Selma, AL
Williams, Carlos W. ... Los Angeles, CA
Williams, Carol A. ... Chicago, IL
Williams, Carol Cavan ... Los Angeles, CA
Williams, Caroline ... Akron, OH
Williams, Carolyn H. ... Washington, DC
Williams, Carolyn H. ... Kalamazoo, MI
Williams, Carolyn V. ... Philadelphia, PA
Williams, Carrington ... McLean, VA
Williams, Carter ... Great Falls, MT
Williams, Cary J. ... Tuscaloosa, AL
Williams, Cary K.
Board of Governors Of The Federal Reserve System,
Office of the General Counsel, GV
Williams, Cassandra Ann ... Indianapolis, IN
Williams, Cassandra D. ... New York, NY
Williams, Cassondra L. ... Los Angeles, CA
Williams, Catherine L. ... New Haven, CT
Williams, Catherine L. ... Atlanta, GA
Williams, Catherine M. ... Thomasville, GA
Williams, Catherine M. ... Metairie, LA
Williams, Catherine M., LLC
Thomasville, GA
Williams, Cecelia Duncan ... Denver, CO
Williams, Cecil W.
Hot Sulphur Springs, CO
Williams, Cedric F. ... Litchfield, MN
Williams, Ceri Churchill ... Denver, CO
Williams, Chad ... Seymour, TX
Williams, Charles A. ... La Mesa, CA
Williams, Charles A. ... Lake Worth, FL
Williams, Charles A. ... Melbourne, FL
Williams, Charles Allen ... Paducah, KY
Williams, Charles B. ... Marion, AR
Williams, Charles D. ... Munfordville, KY
Williams, Charles D. ... New York, NY
Williams, Charles E. ... Washington, DC
Williams, Charles E. ... Bradenton, FL
Williams, Charles E. ... Alexandria, VA
Williams, Charles E. ... Oshkosh, WI
Williams, Charles E., III ... River Edge, NJ
New York, NY

Williams, Charles E., Jr. ... Orlando, FL
Williams, Charles E., Jr.
Winston-Salem, NC
Williams, Charles F. ... Ardmore, OK
Williams, Charles G. ... Palo Alto, CA
Williams, Charles H. ... Olympia, WA
Williams, Charles H. ... West Bend, WI
Williams, Charles H., II ... Orangeburg, SC
Williams, Charles H., Jr. ... St. Paul, MN
Williams, Charles J. ... Martinez, CA
Williams, Charles J. ... Kansas City, MO
Williams, Charles J. ... Nashville, TN
Williams, Charles J., A Professional
Corporation ... Martinez, CA
Williams, Charles J., Jr. ... San Diego, CA
Williams, Charles L. ... Philadelphia, PA
Williams, Charles L. ... Richmond, VA
Williams, Charles L., Jr. ... Roanoke, VA
Williams, Charles M. ... Denver, CO
Williams, Charles M. ... Calhoun, GA
Williams, Charles M., P.C. ... Denver, CO
Williams, Charles Manning ... Houston, TX
Williams, Charles N. ... Fayetteville, AR
Williams, Charles North ... New Britain, CT
Williams, Charles S., Jr. ... Shalimar, FL
Williams, Charles Sampson ... Kennett, MO
Williams, Charles T. ... Columbus, OH
Williams, Charles T., Jr., (A Professional Law Corp.) ... Metairie, LA
New Orleans, LA
Williams, Charles V., Jr. ... Edmond, OK
Williams, Charlie J. ... Detroit, MI
Williams, Charmain ... Miami, FL
Williams, Cherry D. ... Nashville, TN
Williams, Cheryl ... Nashville, TN
Williams, Cheryl A. ... Los Angeles, CA
Williams, Cheryl J.
Securities and Exchange Commission,
Division of Enforcement, GV
Williams & Cheshire ... Tuscaloosa, AL
Williams, Chester A., Jr. ... Stockton, NJ
Williams, Chester C. ... Bluffton, SC
Hilton Head Island, SC
Williams, Chip ... Beckley, WV
Williams, Chris E. ... Malvern, AR
Williams, Christian M. ... Cleveland, OH
Williams, Christine ... Baltimore, MD
Williams, Christopher ... New York, NY
Williams, Christopher D.
San Andreas, CA
Williams, Christopher D. ... Dallas, TX
Williams, Christopher D.
Falls Church, VA
Williams, Christopher H., Jr.
Riviera Beach, FL
Williams, Christopher P. ... Edmonds, WA
Williams, Christopher S. ... San Diego, CA
Williams, Christopher S. ... Boston, MA
Williams, Christopher S. ... Cleveland, OH
Williams, Cindy H. ... Dallas, TX
Williams, Claire A. ... San Mateo, CA
Williams, Clarence T. ... Houston, TX
Williams & Clark ... Kansas City, MO
Williams, Clark B. ... Salem, OR
Williams, Clawson L., Jr. ... West End, NC
Williams, Clay R. ... Milwaukee, WI
Williams, Clemont ... Pasadena, CA
Williams, Cleveland R. ... Fullerton, CA
Williams, Clifford K. ... Basking Ridge, NJ
Williams, Clifford R. ... Elkhart, IN
Williams, Clyde E., Jr. ... Cleveland, OH
Williams, Clyde, Jr. ... Richmond, IN
Williams, Clyde M. ... Buffalo, NY
Williams, Cone & Billings ... Greenfield, IN
Williams & Connolly ... Washington, DC
Williams, Conrad S. P., III ... Houma, LA
Williams, Cooney & Sheehy
Bridgeport, CT
New Haven, CT
Stamford, CT
Williams And Cooper ... Roseboro, NC
Williams, Cordell Hull, Jr. ... Hazard, KY
Williams, Cornelis R. ... Corona, CA
Williams, Coulson, Johnson, Lloyd, Parker & Tedesco, L.L.C. ... Pittsburgh, PA
Williams, Countess C. ... Los Angeles, CA
Williams, Courtney I. ... Dulles, VA
Williams, Craig A.
Palm Beach Gardens, FL
Williams, Craig H. ... San Rafael, CA
Williams, Craig J. ... South Plainfield, NJ
Williams, Craig K. ... Phoenix, AZ
Williams, Craig L. ... Tuscaloosa, AL
Williams, Craig L. ... Corpus Christi, TX
Williams, Cranston J. ... Los Angeles, CA
Williams, Crystal L. ... Atlanta, GA
Williams & Cuker ... Cherry Hill, NJ
Philadelphia, PA
Williams, Curtis C., Jr. ... Jackson, MS
Williams, Curtis R. ... Detroit, MI
Williams, Cynthia A. ... Bloomington, IN
Williams, Cynthia A. ... Wilmington, OH
Williams, Cynthia E. ... Philadelphia, PA
Williams, Cynthia J. ... Boston, MA
Williams, Cynthia L. ... Cleveland, OH
Williams, Cynthia Marie ... Philadelphia, PA
Williams, D. Andrew ... Columbia, SC
Williams, D. Kenyon, Jr. ... Tulsa, OK
Williams, D. Kevin ... Anchorage, AK
Williams, D. Reece, III ... Columbia, SC
Williams, D. Todd ... Jonesboro, AR
Williams, Dale A. ... Amarillo, TX
Williams, Dale D. ... Waco, TX
Williams, Dale E. ... New Orleans, LA
Williams, Dale E. ... Pittsburgh, PA
Williams, Dale, Jr. ... Columbus, OH
Williams, Damien E. ... Los Angeles, CA
Williams, Damon ... Holden, MA

Williams, Damund Edsel ....Montgomery, AL
Williams, Dan ....Dallas, TX
Williams, Dan E. ....Albany, GA
Williams, Dana Cosby ....Louisville, KY
Williams, Dana L. ....Chehalis, WA
Williams, Dana O. ....Towson, MD
Williams, Dana P. ....New York, NY
Williams, Daniel ....Mehoopany, PA
Williams, Daniel B. ....Chicago, IL
Williams, Daniel C. ....Fayetteville, NY
Williams, Daniel D. ....Baytown, TX
Williams, Daniel E. ....Boise, ID
Williams, Daniel G. ....West Palm Beach, FL
Williams, Daniel H. ....Conway, AR
Williams, Daniel H., III ....Visalia, CA
Williams, Daniel J. ....Detroit, MI
Williams, Daniel K. ....Midland, TX
Williams, Daniel R. ....New York, NY
Williams, Daniel T., Jr. ....Rockford, IL
Williams, Danny C. ....Tulsa, OK
Williams, Danny C. ....Decatur, TX
Williams, Danny G. ....Sacramento, CA
Williams, Danny L. ....Houston, TX
Williams, Danny R. ....Cleveland, OH
Williams, Dara E. ....Los Angeles, CA
Williams, Darrell E. ....Tulsa, OK
Williams, Darrell J. ....Dallas, OR
Williams, Daryl L. ....Columbia, SC
Williams, Daryl M. ....Phoenix, AZ
Williams, Dauna R. ....New York, NY
Williams, Dave ....Fort Collins, CO
Williams, David ....Leitchfield, KY
Williams, David ....Meridian, MS
Williams, David ....San Saba, TX
Williams, David A. ....Riverside, CA
Williams, David A. ....Wichita, KS
Williams, David A. ....Eaton Rapids, MI
Williams, David A. ....Morrisville, VT
Williams, David A. ....Bellevue, WA
Williams, David Andrew ....Bethlehem, PA
Williams, David B. ....Tampa, FL
Williams, David B. ....Eugene, OR
Williams, David B. ....Delavan, WI
Williams, David C. ....Salem, MA
Williams, David C. ....Muskegon, MI
Williams, David C. ....New York, NY
Williams, David C. ....Concord, NC
Williams, David C. ....Lake Geneva, WI
Williams, David D. ....Laguna Beach, CA
Williams, David E. ....San Diego, CA
Williams, David E. ....Denver, CO
Williams, David E. ....Kent, OH
Williams, David E. ....Richland, WA
Williams, David F. ....Washington, DC
Williams, David F. ....Charlotte, NC
Williams, David F. ....Columbia, SC
Williams, David Felton ....Dallas, TX
Williams, David G. ....Atlanta, GA
Williams, David G. ....Chicago, IL
Williams, David G. ....Memphis, TN
Williams, David G. ....Salt Lake City, UT
Williams, David H. ....Little Rock, AR
Williams, David H. ....San Francisco, CA
Williams, David H. ....Wilmington, DE
Williams, David H. ....Atlanta, GA
Williams, David H. ....New Orleans, LA
Williams, David H. ....Southfield, MI
Williams, David H. ....Defiance, OH
Williams, David H. ....Portland, OR
Williams, David Huntington
Washington, DC
Bethesda, MD
Williams, David J. ....Lakeland, FL
Williams, David J. ....Lake Charles, LA
Williams, David J. ....Ransom Canyon, TX
Williams, David Jed ....San Antonio, TX
Williams, David K., Jr. ....Greensboro, NC
Williams, David L. ....Little Rock, AR
Williams, David L. ....Burkesville, KY
Williams, David L. ....Pikeville, KY
Williams, David L. ....New York, NY
Williams, David L. ....Philadelphia, PA
Williams, David L. ....Chesapeake, VA
Williams, David L. ....Seattle, WA
Williams, David Lee ....Greensburg, PA
Williams, David M. ....Fairfield, IL
Williams, David M. ....Chestertown, MD
Williams, David M. ....Lincoln, NE
Williams, David McClellan, Jr. ....Chester, VA
Williams, David McI., (P.C.)
Baltimore, MD
Williams, David N. ....Albuquerque, NM
Williams, David N. ....Houston, TX
Williams, David Nicol ....Wilmington, DE
Williams, David P. ....Salt Lake City, UT
Williams, David Paul ....Bellevue, WA
Williams, David R. ....Incline Village, NV
Williams, David R. ....Cleveland, OH
Williams, David R. ....Portland, OR
Williams, David R., P.C.
Incline Village, NV
Williams, David R. M. ....Metairie, LA
Williams, David S. ....Norwich, CT
Williams, David S. ....
Administrative Office Of The United States Courts, GV
Williams, David S. ....Albany, NY
Williams, David T. ....Alexandria, VA
Williams, David V. ....Martinsville, VA
Williams, David W. ....Los Angeles, CA
Williams, David Whitehurst
Simpsonville, KY
Williams, Davidson D. ....New York, NY
Williams & Davis, P.A. ....Orlando, FL
Williams, Dawn Schiller
West Palm Beach, FL
Williams, D. D. ....Cisco, TX

Williams, Deah Tonya BirdSong, Mrs.
Montgomery, AL
Williams, Dean ....Blackfoot, ID
Williams, Debbie Scott ....Houston, TX
Williams, Deborah ....Phoenix, AZ
Williams, Deborah A. ....Angleton, TX
Williams, Deborah J. ....Springfield, IL
Williams, Deborah Marie
Queens Village, NY
Williams, Debra L. ....Little Rock, AR
Williams, Delaney & Simkin ....Richmond, IN
Williams, Del-Marae ....East Chicago, IN
Williams, Denise M. ....Boston, MA
Williams, Dennis A. ....Lebanon, IN
Williams, Dennis A. ....Princeton, NJ
Williams, Dennis P. ....Maumee, OH
Williams, Dennis R. ....Atlanta, GA
Williams, Dennis R. ....Covington, KY
Williams, Dennis R. ....Bellingham, WA
Williams, Dennis V. ....Erie, PA
Williams, Diane Rubin ....Cleveland, OH
Williams, Diane Shea ....Clearwater, FL
Williams, Dirk ....Brookline, MA
Williams, Dirk A. ....Missoula, MT
Williams, Don E. ....Mount Prospect, IL
Williams, Don E. ....La Grange, KY
Williams, Don E. ....Tulsa, OK
Williams, Don E. ....Longview, TX
Williams, Don S. ....Palo Alto, CA
Williams, Donald ....Brockton, MA
Williams, Donald A. ....Los Angeles, CA
Williams, Donald A. ....Chapel Hill, NC
Williams, Donald C. ....Los Angeles, CA
Williams, Donald C. ....Cleveland, OH
Williams, Donald, (Co., L.P.A.)
Cleveland, OH
Williams, Donald D. ....Lansing, MI
Williams, Donald D. ....Kansas City, MO
Williams, Donald E. ....Indianapolis, IN
Williams, Donald E. ....New Castle, PA
Williams, Donald E. ....New Hope, PA
Williams, Donald H. ....Las Vegas, NV
Williams, Donald J. ....Philadelphia, PA
Williams, Donald L. ....El Paso, TX
Williams, Donald M. ....Charleston, SC
Williams, Donald M., Jr.
Pennington Gap, VA
Williams, Donald N. ....Orlando, FL
Williams, Donald N., P.A. ....Orlando, FL
Williams, Donald P. ....Phoenix, AZ
Williams, Donald P. ....Troy, MI
Williams, Donald R. ....Treasury Department, Internal Revenue Service, GV
Williams, Donald R. ....Tampa, FL
Williams, Donald R. ....Kansas City, MO
Williams, Donald R., Jr. ....Boston, MA
Williams, Donelle Alisse ....Philadelphia, PA
Williams, Donna J. ....Chicago, IL
Williams, Donna Lee Harpster ....Dover, DE
Williams, Doran ....Elgin, TX
Williams, Doreen S. ....Fairfax, VA
Williams, Dorian R. ....Chicago, IL
Williams, Dorothy ....Stone Mountain, GA
Williams, Douglas ....Jamaica, NY
Williams, Douglas A. ....Fort Lauderdale, FL
Williams, Douglas A. ....Pittsburgh, PA
Williams, Douglas H. ....Chicago, IL
Williams, Douglas J. ....Putnam, CT
Williams, Douglas J. ....Minneapolis, MN
Williams, Douglas K. ....Baton Rouge, LA
Williams, Douglas K. ....Arlington, TX
Williams, Douglas L. ....Miami, FL
Williams, Douglas L. ....Columbus, OH
Williams, Douglas L., P.A. ....Miami, FL
Williams, Douglas R. ....St. Louis, MO
Williams, Dudley A. ....Brookfield, WI
Williams, Dudley D., III ....Longmeadow, MA
Williams, Dwayne E. ....Miami, FL
Williams, Dwight B. ....Salt Lake City, UT
Williams, Dwight S. ....Renton, WA
Williams, E., & Associates, P.C.
Philadelphia, PA
Williams, E. Ben, Jr. ....Tucson, AZ
Williams, E. Bragg, III ....Poplarville, MS
Williams, E. H., P.A. ....Las Cruces, NM
Williams, E. Kenneth, Jr. ....Newark, NJ
Williams, E. Robert ....Jacksonville, FL
Williams, E. Robt. ....Stockton, CA
Williams, E. Stephen ....Jackson, MS
Williams, Earl G. ....Oklahoma City, OK
Williams, Earl I. ....New Haven, CT
Williams, Ebb H., III ....Martinsville, VA
Williams, Ebb H., III, P.C.
Martinsville, VA
Stuart, VA
Williams, Ed E., III ....Kingsport, TN
Williams, Eddie C. ....Gulfport, MS
Williams, Eddie C. ....Pascagoula, MS
Williams, Eddie, III ....Tallahassee, FL
Williams, Edgar Pomeroy ....Savannah, GA
Williams, Edward A. ....Chicago, IL
Williams, Edward E. ....Phoenix, AZ
Williams, Edward E. ....Exeter, NH
Williams, Edward G. ....New York, NY
Williams, Edward H. ....Chicago, IL
Williams, Edward J. ....Oshkosh, WI
Williams, Edward L. ....Stroudsburg, PA
Williams, Edward L., Jr.
Department of Justice, Federal Bureau of Investigation, GV
Williams, Edward M. ....Treasury Department, Internal Revenue Service, GV
Williams, Edward R., Jr. ....Milwaukee, WI
Williams, Edwin A. ....Washington, DC
Vienna, VA
Williams, E. H. ....Las Cruces, NM
Williams, E. H., Jr. ....Richmond, VA
Williams, Elaine ....New York, NY

Williams, Elaine L. ....Chicago, IL
Williams, Elaine M. ....Daytona Beach, FL
Williams, Elizabeth ....San Rafael, CA
Williams, Elizabeth A. ....San Diego, CA
Williams, Elizabeth Anne ....Chicago, IL
Williams, Elizabeth E. ....Richmond, VA
Williams, Elizabeth Rust ....Berryville, VA
Williams, Elizabeth Z. ....Washington, DC
Williams, Ellen C. ....Holmdel, NJ
Williams, Ellen C. ....Austin, TX
Williams & Elliott ....Birmingham, AL
Williams, Elliott G. ....Philadelphia, PA
Williams, Elliott J. ....Salt Lake City, UT
Williams, Elliott L. ....Los Angeles, CA
Williams, Elton R. ....Meriden, CT
Springfield, MA
Williams, Elvin V. ....New York, NY
Williams, Emily M. ....Washington, DC
Williams & Emm, L.L.P. ....Fallon, NV
Williams, Emmett Filmore, III
Department of Labor, Pension and Welfare Benefits, GV
Williams, Emory Otto, Jr. ....Tallahassee, FL
Williams & Eoannou, P.C.
Washington, DC
Bethesda, MD
Williams, Eric C. ....New York, NY
Williams, Eric D. ....Big Rapids, MI
Williams, Eric E. ....Oakland, CA
Williams, Eric G. ....Department of Justice, Environment and Natural Resources Division, GV
Williams, Eric T. ....Lawrence, KS
Williams, Erica R. ....Sacramento, CA
Williams, Erica Y. ....Washington, DC
Williams, Erin Denny ....Greer, SC
Williams, Erin L. ....Dallas, TX
Williams, Ernest B., III ....Memphis, TN
Williams, Ernest B., IV ....Nashville, TN
Williams, Ernest G. ....Los Angeles, CA
Williams, Ernest J. ....Locust Valley, NY
Williams, Ernest W. ....Louisville, KY
Williams, Ernest W., & Associates, Law Office of ....Franklin, TN
Williams, Esly B., Jr. ....Detroit, MI
Williams, Ethel J. ....Seattle, WA
Williams, Eugene ....Memphis, TN
Williams, Eugene E. ....Miami, FL
Williams, Eugene J. ....Little Rock, AR
Williams, Evan D. ....Sacramento, CA
Williams, Evan G. ....Los Angeles, CA
Williams, Evan S. ....Chicago, IL
Williams, Evan S. ....Troy, PA
Williams, Evan S., Jr. ....Troy, PA
Williams, Everett B., (P.C.) ....Baytown, TX
Williams, Ezekiel J. ....Denver, CO
Williams, F. Bruce
Research Triangle Park, NC
Williams, F. Palmer ....Tallahassee, FL
Williams, Faith M. ....Columbus, OH
Williams, Fay H. ....Indianapolis, IN
Williams, Felicia Toney ....Tallulah, LA
Williams, Fielding L., Jr. ....Richmond, VA
Williams, Finis E., III ....Concord, NH
Williams Firm, The, A Professional Corporation ....Flint, MI
Grand Blanc, MI
Pontiac, MI
Williams Firm, The, P.C. ....Atlanta, GA
Marietta, GA
Williams, Fitch R. ....Carlisle, PA
Williams and Fleckenstein ....Syracuse, NY
Williams, Floyd C. ....Dallas, TX
Williams & Forsythe ....Austin, TX
Williams, Frances S. ....Miami, FL
Williams, Frances W. ....Columbia, SC
Williams, Francis R. ....Providence, RI
Williams, Frank A. ....Columbia, MO
Williams, Frank B. ....Saratoga Springs, NY
Williams, Frank B., III ....Dayton, OH
Williams, Frank C., III ....Greenville, SC
Williams, Frank J. ....Paoli, PA
Williams, Frank J. ....Providence, RI
Williams, Frank J., Jr. ....Altamont, NY
Williams, Frank, Jr. ....Cullman, AL
Williams, Frank Scott ....Tampa, FL
Williams, Frank V., III ....Kingston, TN
Williams, Frank W. ....Cuba, NY
Williams, Franklin Miller
Chattanooga, TN
Williams, Fred B. ....Marlborough, MA
Williams, Fred E. ....Warren, MI
Williams, Fred G. ....Sacramento, CA
Williams, Fred I. ....Houston, TX
Williams, Fred J. ....Durham, NC
Williams, Fred M. ....Sherman Oaks, CA
Williams, Freda L. ....Oklahoma City, OK
Williams, Frederick C. ....Washington, DC
Williams, Frederick D., II ....Houston, TX
Williams, Frederick D. (Rick) ....Sparks, NV
Williams, Frederick G. ....Berea, KY
Williams, Frederick L., Jr. ....Dulles, VA
Williams, Fredrickson & Littlefield, P.C.
Portland, OR
Williams, G. Brinson, Jr. ....Hinesville, GA
Williams, G. Coke ....Anniston, AL
Williams, G. Dale ....Grand Junction, CO
Williams, G. Edward, Jr. ....Lafayette, LA
New Orleans, LA
Williams, G. Everett Burghardt, I
Jacksonville, FL
Williams, G. James ....Midland, MI
Williams, G. James, Jr. ....Boulder, CO
Williams, G. Kimball ....Albany, NY
Williams, G. Michael ....Stockton, CA
Williams, G. Patteson, III ....Cornelius, NC
Williams, G. Rainey, Jr. ....Oklahoma City, OK

Williams, G. Scott ....Department of Justice, Environment and Natural Resources Division, GV
Williams, G. Thomas ....Olathe, KS
Williams, G. Thomas ....Philadelphia, PA
Williams, G. Thomas, III
Grand Rapids, MI
Williams, Gail E. ....New York, NY
Williams, Garrett V. ....Washington, DC
Williams, Garry W. ....Canoga Park, CA
Williams, Gary ....Port Angeles, WA
Port Angeles, WA
Williams, Gary G. ....Hamden, CT
Williams, Gary G. ....Eugene, OR
Williams, Gary H. ....Little Rock, AR
Williams, Gary L. ....Bend, OR
Williams, Gary M. ....Hales Corners, WI
Williams, Gary R. ....Crestwood, IL
Williams, Gary R. ....Ogden, UT
Williams, Gary Randall ....Dallas, GA
Williams, Gary Randall, P.C. ....Dallas, GA
Williams, Gary S. ....Palo Alto, CA
Williams, Gary W. ....Norman, OK
Williams & Gautier, P.A. ....Tallahassee, FL
Williams, Gay H. ....Oswego, NY
Williams, Gaylard T. ....St. Louis, MO
Williams, Gayle Fort ....Detroit, MI
Williams & Geiger ....Brooklyn, NY
Williams, Geline W. ....Brockton, MA
Williams, Gene H. ....Tallahassee, FL
Williams, Gene H. ....Charleston, WV
Williams, Gene M. ....Beaumont, TX
Williams, Geneace ....Oak Brook, IL
Williams, Geo. A. ....Memphis, TN
Williams, George A. ....Bonita, CA
Williams, George Alan ....Lewisburg, WV
Williams, George C. ....Quitman, MS
Williams, George Charles ....Wellsboro, PA
Williams, George H. ....Chicago, IL
Williams, George H. ....Edmond, OK
Williams, George H., Jr. ....Washington, DC
Williams, George K. ....Huntsville, AL
Williams, George L. ....Arcadia, CA
Williams, George L. ....Alexandria, VA
Williams, George L., Jr.
Warner Robins, GA
Williams, George M., Jr. ....New York, NY
Williams, George R., II ....Waterville, OH
Williams, George R. D. ....Greenwich, CT
Williams, George T. ....Orlando, FL
Williams, George T. ....Clinton, NC
Williams, George T. ....Portland, OR
Williams, George W. ....Savannah, GA
Williams, George W., Jr. ....Pasadena, CA
Williams, Gerald A. ....Phoenix, AZ
Williams, Gerald A. ....Boca Raton, FL
Williams, Gerald D. ....Hamilton, MT
Williams, Gerald E. ....Peoria, AZ
Williams, Gerald E. ....Arlington, VA
Williams, Gerald G. ....Jenks, OK
Williams, Gerald J. ....Philadelphia, PA
Williams, Gerald L. ....Indianapolis, IN
Williams, Gerald O. ....Batavia, NY
Williams, Gerald O., Jr. ....Edina, MN
Williams, Gerald R. ....Provo, UT
Williams, Gerard K. ....Farmington, ME
Williams, Geri O'Brien ....Denver, CO
Williams, Gerold G. ....Newport Beach, CA
Williams, Gerold G. ....Newport Beach, CA
Williams, Gerry Lee ....Milwaukee, WI
Williams, Gilda Branch ....Montgomery, AL
Williams, Gilda R. ....Washington, DC
Williams & Gilmore ....San Diego, CA
Williams, Gino W. ....Floyd, VA
Williams, Gino W., Attorney, P.C.
Floyd, VA
Williams, Glen A. ....Cuyahoga Falls, OH
Williams, Glen D. ....San Francisco, CA
Williams, Glen M. ....Lubbock, TX
Williams, Glen M. ....Abingdon, VA
Williams, Glenn T. ....West Palm Beach, FL
Williams & Golden ....Walla Walla, WA
Williams, Gordon J. ....Colorado Springs, CO
Williams, Gordon P., Jr. ....Richardson, TX
Williams, Gordon W. ....Lakewood, CO
Williams, Grace K. ....Canyon City, OR
Williams, Grady H., Jr. ....Jacksonville, FL
Williams, Grady H., Jr. ....Orange Park, FL
Williams, Grant T. ....St. Louis, MO
Williams and Green, P.C. ....Morrisville, VT
Williams, Greg T. ....Irvine, CA
Williams, Gregg E. ....Sioux City, IA
Williams, Gregory A. ....Toledo, OH
Williams, Gregory B. ....Philadelphia, PA
Williams, Gregory D. ....Beverly, MA
Williams, Gregory D ....Sunrise Beach, MO
Williams, Gregory D., Attorney at Law
Sunrise Beach, MO
Williams, Gregory F. ....St. Martinville, LA
Williams, Gregory G. ....Cedar Rapids, IA
Williams, Gregory G. ....Columbia, SC
Williams, Gregory J. ....New Canaan, CT
Williams, Gregory L. ....Denver, CO
Cheyenne, WY
Williams, Gregory L. ....Tampa, FL
Williams, Gregory P. ....Wilmington, DE
Williams, Gregory P. ....Albuquerque, NM
Williams, Gregory P. ....Salt Lake City, UT
Williams, Gregory S. ....Phoenix, AZ
Williams, Gregory S. ....Greensboro, NC
Williams, Gregory W. ....Rehoboth Beach, DE
Williams, Gregory W. Law Office of
Rehoboth Beach, DE
Williams & Griffin ....Childress, TX
Williams, Guy C. ....Corpus Christi, TX
Williams, Guy E. ....Arthur, IL
Decatur, IL
Williams, H. Bruce ....Columbia, SC

Williams, H. Darden ... Anniston, AL
Williams, H. Dohn, Jr.
Fort Lauderdale, FL
Williams, H. Dohn, Jr., P.A.
Boca Raton, FL
Fort Lauderdale, FL
Williams, H. Evan, IV ... Wheaton, IL
Williams, H. Gregory ... Springfield, MA
Williams, H. Randolph ... Chicago, IL
Williams, H. Scott ... Nashville, TN
Williams, H. Taylor, IV ... Franklin, VA
Williams, H. Taylor, IV, A Professional Corporation ... Courtland, VA
Franklin, VA
Williams, Hammond, Moore, Shockley & Harrison, P.A. ... Berlin, MD
Ocean City, MD
Williams & Hanson ... Ellicott City, MD
Williams, Hanson L. ... Chicago, IL
Williams, Hanson, Van Blaricum & Jorns
Pratt, KS
Williams, Harlan B., Jr. ... Arlington, VA
Williams, Harley A. ... Trenton, NJ
Williams, Harley J., (P.C.)
Los Angeles, CA
Williams, Harold ... Birmingham, AL
Williams, Harold L. ... Cleveland, OH
Williams, Harold M. ... Los Angeles, CA
Williams, Harold R. ... Houston, TX
Williams, Harold V. ... Lancaster, OH
Williams, Harris Bell ... Biloxi, MS
Gulfport, MS
Williams, Harris Bell ... Pascagoula, MS
Williams, Harrison V., Jr. ... Syracuse, NY
Williams, Harry Davis ... Paintsville, KY
Williams, Harry M. ... Denver, CO
Williams, Harry M. ... Peoria, IL
Williams, Harvey S. ... Washington, DC
Williams, Heather A. ... Hollidaysburg, PA
Williams, Heather Hayes ... Dunn, NC
Williams, Helen E. ... San Jose, CA
Williams, Helena E. ... Garden City, NY
Williams, Helene G. ... Prospect, KY
Williams, Henry E. ... Greenville, OH
Williams, Henry E., Jr. ... Savannah, TN
Williams, Henry J. ... Silver Spring, MD
Williams & Henry, LLP ... Atlanta, GA
Williams, Henry N.
Selective Service System, Office of the General Counsel, GV
Williams & Henry, Professional Association
Anderson, SC
Greenville, SC
Williams, Henry R. ... New York, NY
Williams, Herbert ... North Palm Beach, FL
Williams, Herbert B. ... Knoxville, TN
Williams, Herbert H., III ... Riverside, CA
Williams, Herbert L. ... Houston, TX
Williams, Herscal P., Jr. ... Elizabeth City, NC
Williams Hewitt & Robbins, LLP
Greenwood, IN
Indianapolis, IN
Williams, Hilary ... New York, NY
Williams, Hilton S. ... San Francisco, CA
Williams, Hollis ... Fair Oaks, CA
Williams, Hollis R. ... Fair Oaks, CA
Williams, Holly A.H. ... Costa Mesa, CA
Williams, Holly B. ... Midland, TX
Williams & Holz, P.A. ... Tallahassee, FL
Williams, Horace G. ... Eufaula, AL
Williams, Horace G. "Chip", III
Eufaula, AL
Williams, Houston G. ... Casper, WY
Williams, Howard C. ... Milwaukee, WI
Williams, Howard L. ... Greensboro, NC
Williams, Howard R. ... Palo Alto, CA
Williams, Hubert Wesley, III
Jackson, MS
Williams, Hughes, Corwin & Sininger, LLP
Muskegon, MI
Williams & Hunt, A Professional Corporation ... Salt Lake City, UT
Williams, I. Seaman ... Augusta, GA
Williams, Ian R. D. ... Winchester, VA
Williams International Patent and Trademark Office ... Arlington, VA
Williams, Irene D.
Department of Commerce, Patent and Trademark Office, GV
Williams, Ivan R. ... Big Spring, TX
Williams & Iversen, P.A.
Minneapolis, MN
St. Paul, MN
Williams, J. Allen ... Atlanta, GA
Williams, J. Bryan ... Detroit, MI
Williams, J. Calvin, Jr. ... Wilmington, DE
Williams, J. Camille ... Little Rock, AR
Williams, J. Carol ... Department of Justice, Environment and Natural Resources Division, GV
Williams, J. Clare ... Salt Lake City, UT
Williams, J. Colby ... Las Vegas, NV
Williams, J. Craig ... Irvine, CA
Williams, J. Douglas ... Woodward, OK
Williams, J. Dudley ... Aberdeen, MS
Williams, J. Franklin ... Oxford, MS
Williams, J. Harley, Jr. ... Dillon, CO
Williams, J. Herbert, II ... Ocala, FL
Williams, J. Larry ... Tallahassee, FL
Williams, J. Mason, III ... Melbourne, FL
Orlando, FL
Williams, J. Maxwell ... Memphis, TN
Williams, J. McDonald (Don) ... Dallas, TX
Williams, J. Michael ... Chicago, IL
Williams, J. Michael, Sr. ... Auburn, AL
Williams, J. Mike ... Atlanta, GA
Williams, J. Mills
Board of Governors Of The Federal Reserve System, Office of the General Counsel, GV
Williams, J. Nash ... Madison, WI
Williams, J. Page ... Charlottesville, VA
Williams, J. Peter ... Newtown Square, PA
Williams, J. Richard ... Cohoes, NY
Williams, J. Richard, P.C. ... Cohoes, NY
Williams, J. Riley ... Jacksonville, FL
Williams, J. Roger, Jr. ... Philadelphia, PA
Williams, J. Roger, Jr. ... Austin, TX
Williams, J.S., & Associates, P.C.
Houston, TX
Williams, J. Samuel (Sam) ... Siler City, NC
Williams, J. Scott ... Costa Mesa, CA
Williams, J. Scott ... Irvine, CA
Williams, J. Steve ... San Bernardino, CA
Williams, J. Stockton, Jr. ... Midland, TX
Williams, J. Taylor ... Richmond, VA
Williams, J. Terrell ... Tallahassee, FL
Williams, J. Vernon ... Seattle, WA
Williams, J. William ... Memphis, TN
Williams, Jack A. ... Shreveport, LA
Williams, Jack, (A Prof. Corp.)
Glendale, CA
Williams, Jack E. ... Dunedin, FL
Williams, Jack G. ... Panama City, FL
Williams, Jack M. ... Safford, AZ
Williams, Jackie N. ... Wichita, KS
Williams, Jackson Taylor ... Chicago, IL
Williams, Jacqueline Louise ... New York, NY
Williams, Jacques R. A.
Morgantown, WV
Williams, Ja'Ethel Brown ... St. Louis, MO
Williams, James A. ... Dodge City, KS
Williams, James A. ... Birmingham, MI
Williams, James A. ... Meridian, MS
Williams, James A. ... Austin, TX
Williams, James A. ... Dallas, TX
Williams, James C. ... Jacksonville, FL
Williams, James C. ... Cleveland, OH
Williams, James C., Jr. ... Orangeburg, SC
Williams, James D., III ... Portland, ME
Williams, James D., Jr. ... New York, NY
Williams, James D., Jr. ... Durham, NC
Williams, James D., Jr., P.A., The Law Offices of ... Durham, NC
Williams, James E. ... Montgomery, AL
Williams, James E. ... Ripon, CA
Williams, James E. ... Washington, DC
Williams, James E. ... Jacksonville, FL
Williams, James E. ... Jackson, MS
Williams, James E. ... Jacksonville, TX
Williams, James E. ... Charleston, WV
Williams, James E., Jr. ... San Francisco, CA
Williams, James E., (P.C.)
Lake Charles, LA
Williams, James Fitzgerald ... Seattle, WA
Williams, James G. ... North Haven, CT
Williams, James G. ... Highland Beach, FL
Williams, James G.
Saint Simons Island, GA
Williams, James H. ... Canton, OH
Williams, James H. ... Wilmington, OH
Williams, James H., Jr. ... New York, NY
Williams, James J. ... San Francisco, CA
Williams, James J. ... Birmingham, MI
Williams, James J. ... Detroit, MI
Williams, James J. ... Remsen, NY
Williams, James J. ... Moneta, VA
Williams, James J., Jr. ... Suwanee, GA
Williams, James L. ... Seneca, SC
Williams, James L., IV ... Covington, LA
Williams, James L., Jr. ... Fort Worth, TX
Williams, James M. ... Pompano Beach, FL
Williams, James M. ... Minneapolis, MN
Williams, James M. ... New York, NY
Williams, James M., III ... Clemson, SC
Williams, James McClendon
New Orleans, LA
Williams, James N., Jr. ... Jeffersonville, IN
Louisville, KY
Williams, James O. ... Tampa, FL
Williams, James O., Jr.
West Palm Beach, FL
Williams, James P. ... Chicago, IL
Williams, James P. ... Linneus, MO
Williams, James P. ... Portland, OR
Williams, James R. ... Springfield, MA
Williams, James R. ... Suttons Bay, MI
Williams, James R. ... Minneapolis, MN
Williams, James R. ... Brightwaters, NY
Williams, James R. ... New York, NY
Williams, James R. ... Akron, OH
Williams, James R. ... Philadelphia, PA
Williams, James R. ... Pittsburgh, PA
Williams, James Roy ... Cincinnati, OH
Williams, James S. ... Los Angeles, CA
Williams, James S. ... Naperville, IL
Williams, James Sarven ... Birmingham, AL
Williams, James T. ... New York, NY
Williams, James T. ... Chattanooga, TN
Williams, James T., Jr. ... Greensboro, NC
Raleigh, NC
Williams, James Thomas, III
Chattanooga, TN
Williams, James V., III ... Washington, DC
New Bern, NC
Williams, James W. ... Troy, MI
Williams, James W. ... Ardmore, OK
Williams, James W. ... Dallas, TX
Williams, James W., III ... Stanford, KY
Williams, James W., III ... Wilmington, NC
Williams, James W., Jr. ... Beaufort, NC
Williams, James Walker ... Asheville, NC
Williams, Jamie A. ... San Diego, CA
Williams, Jane A. ... Chesterfield, MO
Pewaukee, WI
Williams, Jane M. ... Doylestown, PA
Williams, Jane Rice ... Lexington, KY
Williams, Jane W. ... Troy, NY
Williams, Janet K. ... Colorado Springs, CO
Williams, Janet L. ... St. Louis, MO
Williams, Janet M. ... Houston, TX
Williams, Janette Redd ... Long Beach, CA
Williams, Janice Clardy ... Wetumpka, AL
Williams, Janice Elaine ... King Of Prussia, PA
Williams, Janice L. ... Bethesda, MD
Williams, Janis ... Anchorage, AK
Williams, Janis R. ... Phoenix, AZ
Williams, Janov & Cooney, P.C.
Albuquerque, NM
Williams, Jared M. ... New York, NY
Williams, Jarrett ... Washington, DC
Williams, Jas. F. ... Dallas, TX
Williams, Jas. H. ... Towner, ND
Williams, Jas. R. ... Atlanta, GA
Williams, Jason E. ... London, KY
Williams, Jason R. ... New Orleans, LA
Williams, Jason T. ... Bakersfield, CA
Williams, Jay ... Chicago, IL
Williams, Jay B. ... Bentonville, AR
Williams, Jay B. ... Gentry, AR
Williams, Jay B. ... Indianapolis, IN
Williams, Jay D., III ... Pensacola, FL
Williams, Jay G., III ... Clinton, NY
Williams, Jay W. ... Miami, FL
Williams, J. D. ... Washington, DC
Williams, J. D. ... Pendleton, OR
Williams, Jean E. ... Department of Justice, Environment and Natural Resources Division, GV
Williams, Jean F. ... Phoenix, AZ
Williams, Jeffery D. ... New York, NY
Williams, Jeffery S. ... Salt Lake City, UT
Williams, Jeffrey ... San Antonio, TX
Williams, Jeffrey B. ... Dallas, TX
Williams, Jeffrey D. ... Milford, MA
Williams, Jeffrey G. ... Mesa, AZ
Williams, Jeffrey G. ... Port Washington, NY
Williams, Jeffrey G. ... Lima, OH
Williams, Jeffrey J. ... Santa Monica, CA
Williams, Jeffrey K. ... Gainesville, GA
Williams, Jeffrey L. ... Hartford, CT
Williams, Jeffrey M. ... New Hope, PA
Williams, Jeffrey M. ... San Juan, PR
Williams, Jeffrey P. ... Chicago, IL
Williams, Jeffrey R. ... San Francisco, CA
Williams, Jeffrey R.
Federal Deposit Insurance Corporation, Professional Liability Section, GV
Williams, Jeffrey S. ... Houston, TX
Williams, Jeffrey T. ... Schaumburg, IL
Williams, Jeffrey T. ... Columbus, OH
Williams, Jeffrey W. ... Baltimore, MD
Williams, Jene P. ... West Palm Beach, FL
Williams, Jennette ... New York, NY
Williams, Jennifer E. ... Carmel, IN
Williams, Jennifer E. ... Columbia, MD
Williams, Jennifer L. ... Grasonville, MD
Williams, Jennifer L. ... Columbia, SC
Williams, Jennifer Lee ... Dallas, TX
Williams, Jennifer Peters ... Conway, SC
Williams, Jennifer R. ... Atlanta, GA
Williams & Jensen, A Professional Corporation ... Washington, DC
Williams, Jent & Dockins ... Bozeman, MT
Williams, Jeremy ... Burbank, CA
Williams, Jeri Stewart ... Castle Rock, CO
Williams, Jerome ... Hayden Lake, ID
Williams, Jerry ... Indianapolis, IN
Williams, Jerry A. ... Gainesville, GA
Williams, Jerry C. ... Granbury, TX
Williams, Jerry D. ... Thermopolis, WY
Williams, Jerry J. ... San Diego, CA
Williams, Jerry L. ... Lovington, NM
Williams, Jerry L., Jr. ... Danville, VA
Martinsville, VA
Williams, Jerry L., (Mrs.) ... Los Angeles, CA
Williams, Jerry N. ... Hobbs, NM
Williams, Jesse M., III ... Montgomery, AL
Williams, Jesse P. ... Orlando, FL
Williams, Jessica Creech ... Rocky Mount, NC
Williams, Jett, III ... Houston, TX
Williams, Jilek, Lafferty, Gallagher & Scott Co., L.P.A. ... Toledo, OH
Williams, Jim R. ... Kingsport, TN
Williams, Jimmy D. ... Richmond, KY
Williams, Joan Chalmers ... Washington, DC
Williams, JoAnn ... Department of Energy, Office of the General Counsel, GV
Williams, Joanne ... Danbury, CT
Williams, JoAnne ... Mason, MI
Williams, Jody L. ... Salt Lake City, UT
Williams, Joe A. ... Sand Springs, OK
Williams, Joe A. ... Tullahoma, TN
Williams, Joe M. ... Kansas City, MO
Williams, Joe P. ... Atlanta, GA
Williams, Joe W. ... New York, NY
Williams, Joel A. ... Birmingham, AL
Williams, Joel C., Jr. ... Atlanta, GA
Williams, Joel Lee ... Troy, AL
Williams, Joel P. ... Baltimore, MD
Williams, Joel Pittman ... Mobile, AL
Williams, Joel R. ... Los Alamos, CA
Williams, Joel T., Jr. ... Dallas, TX
Williams, Johannes W. ... Washington, DC
Williams, John ... Dover, DE
Williams, John A. ... Kent, OH
Williams, John A. ... Muskogee, OK
Williams, John B. ... Washington, DC
Williams, John B. ... Baton Rouge, LA
Williams, John B. ... Kansas City, MO
Williams, John B. ... Goose Creek, SC
Williams, John B. ... Moncks Corner, SC
Williams, John B., Jr. ... Clinton, NC
Williams, John C. ... Mobile, AL
Williams, John C. ... Washington, DC
Williams, John C. ... Atlanta, GA
Williams, John C. ... Chicago, IL
Williams, John C., Jr. ... Leesburg, FL
Williams, John C., Jr. ... Spartanburg, SC
Williams, John D. ... Westlake Village, CA
Williams, John D. ... Upper Marlboro, MD
Williams, John D. ... Newton, NJ
Williams, John E. ... San Diego, CA
Williams, John E. ... Grand Junction, CO
Williams, John E. ... Washington, DC
Williams, John E. (Jay), Jr. ... Princeton, WV
Williams, John E., Jr. ... Fort Wayne, IN
Williams, John E., Jr. ... Madison, TN
Williams, John E., Jr. ... Houston, TX
Williams, John F. ... Austin, TX
Williams, John F., Jr. ... Dallas, TX
Williams, John G. ... Natchitoches, LA
Williams, John G. ... Plandome, NY
Williams, John H., II ... Bennington, VT
Williams, John H., Jr. ... Springfield, MA
Williams, John Henry, Jr. ... Salisbury, MD
Williams, John J. ... Keene, NH
Williams, John J. ... Houston, TX
Williams, John J., III ... Kansas City, MO
Williams, John, Jr. ... Wilmington, DE
Williams, John K. ... Oklahoma City, OK
Williams, John L. ... Sarasota, FL
Williams, John L. ... Atlanta, GA
Williams, John L. ... Kansas City, MO
Williams, John L. ... Huntingdon, TN
Williams, John L., (Inc.) ... San Jose, CA
Williams, John Lee ... Waverly, TN
Williams, John Leland ... San Francisco, CA
Williams, John Leslie ... Exeter, NH
Williams, John M. ... Pasadena, CA
Williams, John M. ... Atlanta, GA
Williams, John M. ... Lexington, KY
Williams, John M. ... Park Hills, MO
Williams, John M. ... Houston, TX
Williams, John M., III ... Irvine, CA
Williams, John Michael
Oklahoma City, OK
Williams, John Morris ... Norman, OK
Williams, John N. ... Boston, MA
Williams, John O. ... Tallahassee, FL
Williams, John P. ... Washington, DC
Williams, John P. ... Detroit, MI
Williams, John P. ... Royal Oak, MI
Williams, John P. ... Kansas City, MO
Williams, John P. ... Nashville, TN
Williams, John P., Jr. ... Cincinnati, OH
Williams, John P., Jr. ... Marion, SC
Williams, John, P.A. ... Wilmington, DE
Williams, John R. ... Booneville, AR
Williams, John R. ... Newport Beach, CA
Williams, John R. ... San Jose, CA
Williams, John R. ... New Haven, CT
Williams, John R. ... West Palm Beach, FL
Williams, John R. ... Honolulu, HI
Williams, John R. ... Falmouth, MA
Williams, John Robert ... Shreveport, LA
Williams, John T. ... Chicago, IL
Williams, John T. ... Chicago, IL
Williams, John T. ... Columbus, OH
Williams, John Taylor ... Boston, MA
Williams, John T. S. ... Houston, TX
Williams, John W. ... Gainesville, FL
Williams, John W. ... St. Petersburg, FL
Williams, John W., Jr. ... Birmingham, AL
Williams, John Z. ... Rolla, MO
Salem, MO
Williams, Johnell ... Houston, TX
Williams, Johnny J., Jr. ... Houston, TX
Williams, Johnny L. ... Hattiesburg, MS
Williams & Johnson ... Hobbs, NM
Williams & Johnson ... Chehalis, WA
Williams, Jon A. ... Paragould, AR
Williams, Jon E. ... Greenwood, IN
Williams, Jon R. ... San Diego, CA
Williams, Jonathan G. ... Chatham, NJ
Williams, Jonathan L. ... Teaneck, NJ
Williams, Jonathan M. ... Houston, TX
Williams, Jonathan P. ... New York, NY
Williams, Jonathan S. ... Goldsboro, NC
Williams, Jonathan S., P.C. ... Goldsboro, NC
Williams & Jordan ... Liberty, IN
Williams, Jordan & Brodersen
Visalia, CA
Williams, Jos. A. ... Pittsburgh, PA
Williams, Joseph B. ... San Francisco, CA
Williams, Joseph B. ... Brooklyn, NY
Williams, Joseph E. ... Conyers, GA
Williams, Joseph E., Jr. ... Macon, GA
Williams, Joseph G. ... New York, NY
Williams, Joseph G. ... Houston, TX
Williams, Joseph G., Jr. ... New York, NY
Williams, Joseph H. ... Winter Park, FL
Williams, Joseph Howard ... Mount Airy, NC
Williams, Joseph M. ... Plant City, FL
Williams, Joseph M. ... Tavernier, FL
Williams, Joseph M. ... St. Charles, IL
Williams, Joseph M. ... McConnelsville, OH
Williams, Joseph P. ... Hartford, CT
Williams, Joseph P. ... Bartow, FL
Williams, Joseph P., Sr. ... Natchitoches, LA
Williams, Joseph Patrick ... Jericho, NY
Williams, Joseph T. ... Baltimore, MD
Williams, Joy E. ... Anniston, AL
Williams, Joyce Henderson ... Pensacola, FL
Williams, Judith A. ... Orange, CA
Williams, Judy A. ... Billings, MT
Williams, Julia B. ... Washington, DC
Williams, Julia B. ... Atlanta, GA
Williams, Julian L. ... Pompano Beach, FL
Williams, Julie K. ... Bremen, GA

Williams, Julie L. ....Treasury Department, Office of the Comptroller of the Currency, GV
Williams, Julie Moerer ....Kansas City, MO
Williams, Julie T. ....Wilson, NC
Williams, Julius A., Jr. ....Philadelphia, PA
Williams, Julius L. ....Orlando, FL
Williams, Junius W. ....Irvington, NJ
Williams, Justin L. ....Corpus Christi, TX
Williams, Justin W. ....Alexandria, VA
Williams, K. Michele ....Long Beach, CA
Williams, Kamili Alama
San Francisco, CA
Williams, Kandy L. ....Irvine, CA
Williams, Karen A. ....St. Petersburg, FL
Williams, Karen B. ....Washington, DC
Williams, Karen Brown ....Atlanta, GA
Williams, Karen Hastie ....Washington, DC
Williams, Karen J. ....Phoenix, AZ
Williams, Karen J. ....Orangeburg, SC
Williams, Karen K. ....San Francisco, CA
Williams, Karen L. ....Darien, CT
Williams, Karen Matthews ....Anniston, AL
Williams, Karen McGlashan ....Newark, NJ
Williams, Karen S. ....Charlotte, NC
Williams, Karen S. ....West Carrollton, OH
Williams, Kari F. ....Carrollton, KY
Williams, Karie D. ....Redding, CA
Williams, Karin L. ....Middletown, NJ
Williams, Karl T. ....Chicago, IL
Williams, Karol K. ....Tampa, FL
Williams, Karol K., P.A., Law Offices of
Tampa, FL
Williams, Kasperitis & Gowan, P.C.
Corpus Christi, TX
Williams, Kastner & Gibbs PLLC
Seattle, WA
Tacoma, WA
Williams, Katherine A. ....Chicago, IL
Williams, Katherine D. ....Towson, MD
Williams, Katherine L. ....Milwaukee, WI
Williams, Kathleen J. ....Sacramento, CA
Williams, Kathleen M. ....Washington, DC
Williams, Kathleen M. ....Miami, FL
Williams, Kathleen M. ....Boston, MA
Williams, Kathryn ....Greenville, SC
Williams, Kathryn B. ....Orlando, FL
Williams, Kathryn Diggs ....Delray Beach, FL
Williams, Kathryn, P.A. ....Greenville, SC
Williams, Kathryn R. ....Philadelphia, PA
Williams, Kathryn S. ....Epping, NH
Williams, Kathy S. ....Washington, DC
Williams, Kathy S. ....Durham, NC
Williams, Kathy S., PLLC ....Durham, NC
Williams & Katzman ....Carthage, NY
Watertown, NY
Williams, Kay L., (Co., L.P.A.) ....Warren, OH
Williams, Keary R. ....Grundy, VA
Williams, Keith C. ....Miami, FL
Williams, Keith D. ....Columbia, MD
Williams, Keith J. ....Rome, GA
Williams, Keith J. ....Doylestown, PA
Williams, Keith P., Jr. ....Laguna Beach, CA
Williams, Kell Coleman, III ....Tampa, FL
Williams, Kellie F. ....Salt Lake City, UT
Williams, Kelly A. ....Pittsburgh, PA
Williams, Kelly A. ....Longview, TX
Williams, Kelly D. ....Houston, TX
Williams, Kelly G. ....Rockingham, NC
Williams Kelly & Greer ....Chesapeake, VA
Portsmouth, VA
Virginia Beach, VA
Norfolk, VA
Williams, Kelly M. ....Newark, NJ
Williams, Kelly, Waldrip & Thompson, P.C.
Rawlins, WY
Williams, Kemper Sam, Jr. ....Victoria, TX
Williams, Kendall B. ....Grand Blanc, MI
Williams, Kenneth ....Los Angeles, CA
Williams, Kenneth A. ....Portland, OR
Williams, Kenneth Anthony ....Houston, TX
Williams, Kenneth B. ....East Lansing, MI
Williams, Kenneth C. ....Akron, OH
Williams, Kenneth E. ....Indianapolis, IN
Williams, Kenneth G. ....Hartford, CT
Williams, Kenneth J. ....Marion, IN
Williams, Kenneth, Jr., Law Offices of
Ashland, KY
Williams, Kenneth Michael
Westminster, MD
Williams, Kenneth R. ....Sacramento, CA
Williams, Kenneth R. ....Baton Rouge, LA
Williams, Kenneth R. ....Doylestown, PA
Williams, Kenneth S. ....Cookeville, TN
Williams, Kenneth Wayne ....Tallahassee, FL
Williams, Kent D. ....Rancho Cucamonga, CA
Williams, Kent M. ....Minneapolis, MN
Williams, Kermit R., III ....Dallas, TX
Williams, Kerry C. ....Houston, TX
Williams, Kevin G. ....Winston-Salem, NC
Williams, Kevin J. ....St. Louis, MO
Williams, Kevin J. ....Winston-Salem, NC
Williams, Kevin L. ....Lubbock, TX
Williams, Kevin T. ....Binghamton, NY
Williams, Kevin T. ....Syracuse, NY
Williams, Kevin T. ....Glen Allen, VA
Williams & Kilkowski ....Los Angeles, CA
Williams, Kim ....Seattle, WA
Williams, Kim M. ....Trenton, MI
Williams, Kimberley A. ....Murfreesboro, TN
Williams, Kimberly A. ....New York, NY
Williams, Kimberly J. ....Fort Bragg, CA
Williams, Kirby H. ....Montgomery, AL
Williams, Kirk D. ....Denver, CO
Williams, Kirk L.
White River Junction, VT
Williams, Kirk R. ....Dallas, TX
Williams, Kit ....Fayetteville, AR

Williams, Klukowski, Fotieo & Szczytko, P.C.
Grand Rapids, MI
Williams & Korf ....Amery, WI
Barron, WI
Williams, Kurt D. ....Kansas City, MO
Williams, L. Eugene ....Anchorage, AK
Williams, L. Frederick ....San Diego, CA
Williams, L. Frederick, Jr. ....Phoenix, AZ
Williams, L. John, Jr. ....Littleton, CO
Williams, L. Kirk ....Las Vegas, NV
Williams, L. Lee, Jr. ....Tallahassee, FL
Williams, L. Marie ....Chattanooga, TN
Williams, L. Miller ....Orlando, FL
Williams, L. O'Neal, Jr. ....Poplarville, MS
Williams, L. Richard ....Phoenix, AZ
Williams, L. Vincent ....Nashville, TN
Williams, L. Wayne ....Charleston, WV
Williams, Lafayette ....Yadkinville, NC
Williams, Lakshmi N. ....Washington, DC
Williams, Lalita ....Libertyville, IL
Williams, Lampton O'Neal
Poplarville, MS
Williams, Lance Blake ....Chicago, IL
Williams, Lance E. ....Dallas, TX
Williams, Lara A. ....Palo Alto, CA
Williams, Larry A. ....Denver, CO
Williams, Larry E. ....Los Angeles, CA
Williams, Larry L. ....Alexandria, VA
Williams, Larry R. ....Nashville, TN
Williams, Larry R ....Salt Lake City, UT
Williams, Larry R., P.C., Law Offices of
Nashville, TN
Williams, Lata Bhopale ....Melrose, MA
Williams, Latham ....Chicago, IL
Williams, Laura A. ....Cleveland, OH
Williams, Laura A. ....Jackson, TN
Williams, Laura H. ....Harrisburg, PA
Williams, Laura M. ....Los Angeles, CA
Williams, Laurel C. ....Memphis, TN
Williams, Laurence K.
Department of Justice, Tax Division, GV
Williams, Laurette T. ....Texas City, TX
Williams, Laurie B. ....Wichita, KS
Williams, Laurie Jeanne ....San Francisco, CA
Williams, Laurie R. ....Ridgeland, MS
Williams, Laurie S. ....Dallas, TX
Williams, LaVetta ....Chicago, IL
Williams Law Firm ....Little Rock, AR
Williams Law Firm, The, P.A.
Wilmington, DE
Williams Law Office ....Thermopolis, WY
Williams Law Offices ....Delavan, WI
Williams, Lawrence ....San Francisco, CA
Williams, Lawrence ....Detroit, MI
Williams, Lawrence A. ....Warren, MI
Williams, Lawrence D. ....Los Angeles, CA
San Francisco, CA
Williams, Lawrence R., II ....South Bend, IN
Williams, Leah Nicole ....Charlestown, MA
Williams, Leatrice Eve ....Jacksonville, FL
Williams, Lee Ann M., Jr ....Savannah, GA
Williams, Lee B. ....Grove Hill, AL
Williams, Lee D. ....Los Angeles, CA
Williams & Lee, LLC ....Chicago, IL
Williams, Lee R. ....Douglas, GA
Williams, Lee V., Jr. ....Fort Worth, TX
Williams, Leigh A. ....De Kalb, IL
Williams & Leininger, P.A. ....Stuart, FL
West Palm Beach, FL
Williams, Leland T. ....Rochester, NY
Williams, Leo. M. ....Bloomfield, NE
Williams, Leon A. ....Philadelphia, PA
Williams, Leonard Edwin, II ....Holly Hill, FL
Williams, Leonard J. ....Landover, MD
Williams, Lesley ....Carlsbad, NM
Williams, Leslie A. ....San Mateo, CA
Williams, Leslie A. ....Clovis, NM
Williams, Leslie Gail ....Los Angeles, CA
Williams, Leslie H. ....Indianapolis, IN
Williams, Leslie H. ....Houston, TX
Williams, Leslie J. ....Baltimore, MD
Williams, Leslie Kim ....Bedford Hills, NY
Williams, Leslie T. ....New York, NY
Williams, Leslie V. ....Oklahoma City, OK
Williams, Lester L., Jr. ....Nashville, TN
Williams, Levi G., Jr ....Fort Lauderdale, FL
Williams, Lewis E. ....Columbus, OH
Williams, Lewis E., Co., L.P.A.
Columbus, OH
Williams, Lewis L. ....Austin, TX
Williams, Libby A. ....Seattle, WA
Williams, Lila Wynne ....Cherry Hill, NJ
Williams, Lillian D. ....Lexington, KY
Williams, Linda Blackwell
San Francisco, CA
Williams, Linda Brown ....San Jose, CA
Williams, Linda C. ....San Francisco, CA
Williams, Linda C. ....Atlantic City, NJ
Williams, Linda Grant ....New York, NY
Williams, Linda J. ....Boise, ID
Williams, Linda K. ....Chicago, IL
Williams, Linda Rae ....Englewood, CO
Williams, Linnie Charles ....Jacksonville, FL
Williams, Lionel C. ....Mobile, AL
Williams, Lisa A. ....San Francisco, CA
Williams, Lisa A. ....Bethesda, MD
Williams, Lisa L. ....Jackson, MS
Williams, Lloyd E., Jr. ....Chicago, IL
Williams, Lloyd R. ....Santa Cruz, CA
Williams, Locke A. ....Corvallis, OR
Williams, Logan E. ....San Diego, CA
Williams, Lois Craig ....Westville, NJ
Williams, Lois G. ....Washington, DC
Williams, Lon R., Jr. ....Dallas, TX
Fort Worth, TX
Williams, Lonna Whittington ....Kenilworth, IL
Williams, Lonnie B. ....Wilmington, NC
Williams, Lonnie B., Jr. ....Wilmington, NC

Williams, Lonnie J., Jr. ....Phoenix, AZ
Williams, Lonnie W. ....Overland Park, KS
Williams, Loren ....Albany, TX
Williams, Lorenzo ....Fort Pierce, FL
Stuart, FL
Williams, Lori L. ....Irvine, CA
Williams, Lori Tollefson ....Beverly Hills, MI
Williams, Louis D. ....Bloomington, IL
Williams, Louis J. ....Lakeland, FL
Williams, Louis L. ....West Palm Beach, FL
Williams, Louise D.
Department of Commerce, Office of the General Counsel, GV
Williams, Louise Gunter ....Englewood, CO
Williams, Louvenia W. ....Lanham, MD
Williams, Lowell E., Jr. ....Houston, TX
Williams, Luck & Williams ....Danville, VA
Martinsville, VA
Williams, Lucy A. ....Boston, MA
Williams, Lucy G. ....Grundy, VA
Williams, Luther C., Jr. ....Brooklyn, NY
Williams, Lydia Beth ....Jackson, TN
Williams, Lyle F. ....Memphis, TN
Williams, Lynch & Whitt, A Professional Corporation ....Henrico, VA
Richmond, VA
Williams, Lynda D. ....Cool, CA
Williams, Lynda S. ....Atlanta, GA
Williams, Lynn ....Little Rock, AR
Williams, Lynn A. ....Los Angeles, CA
Williams, Lynn E. ....Baton Rouge, LA
Williams, Lynn W. ....Birmingham, AL
Williams, Lynne H. ....Houston, TX
Williams, M. Binford, Jr. ....Jackson, MS
Williams, M. Elizabeth ....Pittsburgh, PA
Williams, M. Hollis ....Memphis, TN
Williams, M. Keithley ....Carthage, MO
Williams, M. Lynn ....Hagerstown, MD
Williams, M. Max, II ....Portland, OR
Williams, M. Todd ....Dallas, TX
Williams, Major, Jr. ....San Francisco, CA
Williams, Malcolm J., Jr.
Department of Transportation, U. S. Coast Guard, GV
Williams, Manley ....Washington, DC
Williams, Mara ....Philadelphia, PA
Williams, Marc E. ....Charleston, WV
Huntington, WV
Williams, Marc J. ....Washington, DC
Williams, Marc S. ....Los Angeles, CA
Williams, Marcia E. ....Boise, ID
Williams, Marcia Y. ....New York, NY
Williams, Marcus ....Department of Justice, Justice Management Division, GV
Williams, Marcus A. ....Detroit, MI
Farmington Hills, MI
Williams, Marcus D. ....Fairfax, VA
Williams, Marcus J. ....Portland, OR
Williams & Marcus, Ltd. ....Chicago, IL
Williams, Marcus P. ....Washington, DC
Williams, Marcus W. ....Wilmington, NC
Williams, Margaret A. ....Stamford, CT
Williams, Margaret H. ....Jackson, MS
Williams, Marianna ....Dyersburg, TN
Williams, Marie K. ....Austin, TX
Williams, Marilyn E. ....Newark, NJ
Williams, Marilyn H. ....Austin, TX
Williams, Marion E. ....Beeville, TX
Williams, Marisa L. ....Denver, CO
Williams, Mark ....Fort Myers, FL
Williams, Mark ....Howell, NJ
Williams, Mark A. ....Omaha, NE
Williams, Mark A. ....Roanoke, VA
Williams, Mark B. ....Portland, OR
Williams, Mark C. ....Castle Rock, CO
Williams, Mark C.
Federal Energy Regulatory Commission, Office of the General Counsel, GV
Williams, Mark D. ....Traverse City, MI
Williams, Mark D. ....Hilliard, OH
Williams, Mark E. ....Southfield, MI
Williams, Mark F. ....Springfield, MA
Williams, Mark F. ....Cleveland, OH
Williams, Mark F. ....Virginia Beach, VA
Williams, Mark I. ....Greenville, SC
Williams, Mark J. ....Houston, TX
Williams, Mark J. ....Salt Lake City, UT
Williams, Mark K. ....Knoxville, TN
Williams, Mark L. ....Kirksville, MO
Williams, Mark M. ....Pasadena, CA
Williams, Mark M. ....Portland, OR
Williams, Mark N. ....Grand Junction, CO
Williams, Mark P. ....Birmingham, AL
Williams, Mark, P.A. ....Fort Myers, FL
Williams, Mark R. ....Chicago, IL
Williams, Mark R. ....Vermilion, OH
Williams, Mark S. ....Mesa, AZ
Williams, Mark S. ....Phoenix, AZ
Williams, Mark S. ....Pleasanton, CA
Williams, Mark S. ....Olean, NY
Williams, Mark Shelton F. ....Missoula, MT
Williams, Mark T. ....Danville, VA
Williams, Mark Timothy ....Minneapolis, MN
Williams, Mark V. ....Syracuse, NY
Williams, Mark W. ....Denver, CO
Telluride, CO
Williams & Marlar, P.C. ....Claremore, OK
Williams, Marlene C. ....Houston, TX
Williams, Marlene J. ....San Francisco, CA
Williams, Marsha L. ....Dallas, TX
Williams, Marsha L. ....Charleston, WV
Williams, Marshall D. ....Baytown, TX
Williams, Marshall E. ....Indianapolis, IN
Williams, Marshall R.
Department of Justice, GV
Williams, Martha ....Asheville, NC
Williams, Martha E. ....Cullman, AL
Williams, Martha G. ....Greenville, SC

Williams, Martha Toedt ....Houston, TX
Williams, Martin W. ....Toledo, OH
Williams & Martinet, P.C. ....Los Angeles, CA
Novato, CA
Williams, Marvin ....Meridian, MS
Williams, Marvin J. ....Houston, TX
Williams, Marvin, Jr. ....Lubbock, TX
Williams, Mary B. ....Janesville, WI
Williams, Mary B., S.C. ....Janesville, WI
Williams, Mary Bullington ....Phoenix, AZ
Williams, Mary C. ....Honea Path, SC
Williams, Mary Chadwick ....Leander, TX
Williams, Mary Ellen Coster
General Services Administration, Board of Contract Appeals, GV
Williams, Mary Kathryn
Hilton Head Island, SC
Myrtle Beach, SC
Williams, Mary Kay ....Lexington, KY
Williams, Mary Lynette
Grand Rapids, MI
Williams, Mary Newcomer
Washington, DC
Williams, Mary Pearl ....Austin, TX
Williams, Mary R. ....Point Reyes Station, CA
Williams, MaryAnn O ....Spencer, IN
Williams, Mary-Lou ....San Francisco, CA
Williams, Matthew C. ....Birmingham, AL
Williams, Matthew D. ....Atlanta, GA
Williams, Matthew J. ....New York, NY
Williams, Matthew L. ....Chicago, IL
Williams, Matthew W. ....Bozeman, MT
Williams, Mattielyn B. ....Nashville, TN
Williams, Maureen H. ....Washington, DC
Williams, Maureen, Law Office of
Minneapolis, MN
Williams, Maurice L. ....Florham Park, NJ
Williams & McCarthy, A Professional Corporation ....Oregon, IL
Rockford, IL
Williams, McCullough, III ....Columbus, OH
Williams, McDaniel, Wolfe & Womack, P.C.
Memphis, TN
Williams & McIntyre ....Boonville, NY
Williams, Meg ....Library of Congress, Office of the General Counsel, GV
Williams, Megan J. F. ....Columbus, OH
Williams, Melaine Aureilia
Department of Justice, Environment and Natural Resources Division, GV
Williams, Melanie D. ....Lawrenceville, GA
Williams, Melinda Gaugler
Treasury Department, Internal Revenue Service, GV
Williams, Melinda L. ....Sacramento, CA
Williams, Melody Frye ....Albuquerque, NM
Williams, Melvin E. ....Bedford, VA
Williams, Melvin Frank, Jr.
New York, NY
Williams, Melvin O., Jr. ....Cincinnati, OH
Williams, Melvin P. ....Hartford, CT
Williams, Melvyn James ....Macon, GA
Sandersville, GA
Williams, Melvyn James, P.C. ....Macon, GA
Sandersville, GA
Williams, Meredith J.T. ....Dallas, TX
Williams, Meriwether D. (Mike)
Spokane, WA
Williams Merrick Dailey & O'Leary, P.C.
Portland, OR
Williams, Merril K. ....Russellville, AL
Williams, Michael A. ....Denver, CO
Williams, Michael A. ....Washington, DC
McLean, VA
Williams, Michael A. ....Rock Island, IL
Williams, Michael A. ....Kansas City, MO
Williams, Michael C. ....Winchester, IN
Williams, Michael C. ....Memphis, TN
Williams, Michael C. ....DeSoto, TX
Williams, Michael C. ....Seattle, WA
Williams, Michael C. ....Milwaukee, WI
Williams, Michael Courtney
Birmingham, AL
Williams, Michael Cunningham
Washington, DC
Williams, Michael D. ....Orlando, FL
Williams, Michael D. ....Stephen, MN
Warren, MN
Williams, Michael D. ....Portland, OR
Williams, Michael D. ....Houston, TX
Williams, Michael E. ....Encinitas, CA
Williams, Michael E. ....Indianapolis, IN
Williams, Michael Ernest
Los Angeles, CA
Williams, Michael F. ....Cedar Rapids, IA
Williams, Michael F., Law Office
Princeton, MN
Williams, Michael G. ....Chattanooga, TN
Williams, Michael Gardner ....New York, NY
Williams, Michael J. ....San Francisco, CA
Williams, Michael J.
Agency for International Development, Office of the General Counsel, GV
Williams, Michael J. ....Fargo, ND
Williams, Michael J. ....Cranston, RI
Williams, Michael J. ....Lemmon, SD
Williams, Michael J. ....Richmond, VA
Williams, Michael K. ....The Woodlands, TX
Williams, Michael Kendall ....San Jose, CA
Williams, Michael L.
Colorado Springs, CO
Williams, Michael L. ....Chicago, IL
Williams, Michael L. ....Columbus, OH
Williams, Michael L. ....Portland, OR
Williams, Michael L. ....El Paso, TX
Williams, Michael P. ....Jacksonville, FL
Williams, Michael P. ....Rockford, IL

Williams, Michael P. .... **Syracuse, NY**
Williams, Michael P. .... **Raleigh, NC**
Williams, Michael P. .... Philadelphia, PA
Williams, Michael P. A. .... **Milford, CT**
Williams, Michael R. .... **Irvine, CA**
Williams, Michael R. .... **Newport Beach, CA**
Williams, Michael R. .... **Sacramento, CA**
Williams, Michael R. .... **New York, NY**
Williams, Michael T. .... **Los Angeles, CA**
Williams, Michael T. .... Tampa, FL
Williams, Michael T. .... Cleveland, OH
Williams, Michael T. .... Clarksburg, WV
Williams, Michael T., P.A. .... Tampa, FL
Williams, Michel P. .... **Denver, CO**
Williams, Michelle .... **West Palm Beach, FL**
Williams, Michelle A. .... **Atlanta, GA**
Williams, Michelle M. .... Irvine, CA
Williams, Michelle M. .... **Memphis, TN**
Williams, Michelle "Shelly" R.
Mount Sterling, KY
Williams, Mikel H. .... Boise, ID
Williams and Miller .... Memphis, TN
Williams, Millie E. .... Far Hills, NJ
Williams, Milton L. .... New York, NY
Williams, Milton L., Jr. .... **New York, NY**
Williams, Minna .... Marysville, CA
Williams, Miriam .... High Point, NC
Williams, Mitchell G. .... **New York, NY**
Williams, Mitchell J. .... **Columbia, SC**
Williams, Mitchell T. .... Rochester, NY
Williams, Molly Martin .... **Sioux City, IA**
Williams, Mona K. .... Enterprise, OR
Williams & Montgomery Ltd. .... **Miami, FL**
Chicago, IL
Joliet, IL
Waukegan, IL
Wheaton, IL
Williams, Morgan & Amerson, P.C.
Houston, TX
Williams, Morgan K. .... Fort Worth, TX
Williams, Morris E. .... Hillsboro, MO
Williams, Morris L., III .... **Little Rock, AR**
Williams, Morrison, Light & Moreau
Danville, VA
Williams, Moses E. .... Tallahassee, FL
Williams, Moses, Jr. .... Tallulah, LA
Williams, Mullen, Clark & Dobbins
Norfolk, VA
Vienna, VA
Virginia Beach, VA
Washington, DC
Newport News, VA
Richmond, VA
Williams, N. Burton .... Plano, TX
Williams, N. Keith .... Kerrville, TX
Williams, Nancy .... **Seattle, WA**
Williams, Nancy A. .... Denver, CO
Williams, Nancy E. .... Cleveland, TN
Williams, Nancy G. .... **Phoenix, AZ**
Williams, Nancy J. .... Winchester, VA
Williams, Nancy L. .... Douglas, WY
Williams, Nancy Ondrovik .... Gainesville, TX
Williams, Nancy R. .... Farmington, CT
Williams, Nancy T. .... **Novato, CA**
Williams, Nanette G. .... El Paso, TX
Williams, Natalie Renee .... Roseville, CA
Williams, Neal M. .... **Palo Alto, CA**
Williams, Neal O. .... Sylmar, CA
Williams, Nedy A. .... **Los Angeles, CA**
Williams, Neil .... **Atlanta, GA**
Williams, Neil .... Austin, TX
Williams, Neil C. .... **Charlotte, NC**
Williams, Neil E. .... Ogallala, NE
Williams, Neil E., & Associates, P.C.
Ogallala, NE
Williams, Neil G. .... Chicago, IL
Williams, Neil V. .... **Morristown, NJ**
Williams & Nenney .... Los Angeles, CA
Williams, Newton A. .... **Towson, MD**
Williams, Nicholas R. .... **New York, NY**
Williams, Nick S. .... New York, NY
Williams, Nicole Sippial
National Credit Union Administration, Office of General Counsel, GV
Williams, Nona .... Los Angeles, CA
Williams, Norma J. .... **Los Angeles, CA**
Williams, Norman .... Brooklyn, NY
Williams, Norman .... **Burlington, VT**
Williams, Norman .... South Royalton, VT
Williams, Norman Cole .... Durham, NC
Williams, Norman E. .... Durham, NC
Williams, Norman J. .... Tuscumbia, MO
Williams, Norman L. .... Lake Charles, LA
Williams, Norman R., II .... **New York, NY**
Williams, O. Edgar, Jr. .... Fort Lauderdale, FL
Williams, O'Banion, III .... **Houston, TX**
Williams & O'Donnell
Westlake Village, CA
Williams, Omer S. J. .... **New York, NY**
Williams, Orlando J. .... Akron, OH
Canton, OH
Williams, Orrin R. .... Rochester, MN
Williams, Oscar .... San Francisco, CA
Williams, Osgood O. .... Atlanta, GA
Williams, Otis W., Jr. .... Tulsa, OK
Williams, Owen R. .... Amery, WI
Barron, WI
Williams, P. Scott .... Anderson, SC
Williams, Paige E. .... **Raleigh, NC**
Williams, Pamela D. .... **Beaumont, TX**
Williams, Pamela J. .... Oakland, CA
Williams, Pamela McKenzie
Silver Spring, MD
Williams, Pamela Neale .... **Beaumont, TX**
Williams, Pamela R.K. .... New York, NY
Williams, Pamela S.
Department Of The Interior, Office of the Solicitor, GV

Williams, Parham H., Jr. .... Birmingham, AL
Orange, CA
Williams, Parker, Harrison, Dietz & Getzen, Professional Association .... **Sarasota, FL**
Williams, Patricia A. .... Bronx, NY
Williams, Patricia C. .... Spokane, WA
Williams, Patricia Dare .... Oklahoma City, OK
Williams, Patricia G. .... Albuquerque, NM
Williams, Patricia K. .... **Lincoln, NE**
Williams, Patricia K. .... **Haddonfield, NJ**
Williams, Patricia L. .... Fresno, CA
Williams, Patricia Ruth .... **Jackson, MS**
Williams, Patricia Rymar .... Tampa, FL
Williams, Patrick A. .... **Tulsa, OK**
Williams, Patrick A., Inc. .... **Tulsa, OK**
Williams, Patrick J. .... Clarendon Hills, IL
Williams, Patrick S. .... **St. Paul, MN**
Williams, Patti L. .... **Fresno, CA**
Williams, Pattillo, Squires & Wren, L.L.P.
Waco, TX
Williams, Paul .... Department of Defense, Armed Services Board of Contract Appeals, GV
Williams, Paul A. .... Grand Rapids, MI
Williams, Paul A. .... **Kansas City, MO**
Williams, Paul C. .... **Montgomery, AL**
Williams, Paul D. .... **Hartford, CT**
Williams, Paul E. .... Bowling Green, MO
Williams, Paul E. .... **Austin, TX**
Williams, Paul Earl .... Fayetteville, GA
Williams, Paul J. .... Charlotte, NC
Williams, Paul L. .... Chicago, IL
Williams, Paul M. .... Edmonds, WA
Williams, Paul R. .... Washington, DC
Williams, Paul R. .... **Garden City, NY**
Williams, Paul R., Jr. .... Westfield, NJ
Williams, Paul S. .... Long Beach, CA
Williams, Paul S. .... Dublin, OH
Williams, Paul T. .... Greensboro, NC
Williams, Paul T., Jr. .... **New York, NY**
Williams, Paul X., Jr. .... Booneville, AR
Williams, Paula A.
General Accounting Office, Office of the General Counsel, GV
Williams, Paula J. .... **Denver, CO**
Williams, Paulette J. .... New York, NY
Williams, Pearré A. .... Englewood, CO
Williams, Peeler, Jr. .... Waco, TX
Williams, Peggy J. .... **Seattle, WA**
Williams, Peggy T. .... Soquel, CA
Williams, Percy D. .... **Houston, TX**
Williams, Perry L. .... Columbia Heights, MN
Williams, Peter C. .... **Washington, DC**
Williams, Peter C. .... **New York, NY**
Williams, Peter C. .... **Alexandria, VA**
Williams, Peter C. .... Madison, WI
Williams, Peter E., III .... **Palo Alto, CA**
Williams, Peter F. .... Livingston, NJ
Williams, Peter G. .... Columbus, GA
Williams, Peter H. .... Tallahassee, FL
Williams, Peter J. .... **New York, NY**
Williams, Peter J. .... Philadelphia, PA
Williams, Peter M. .... **Long Beach, CA**
Williams, Peter M. .... **Santa Rosa, CA**
Williams, Peter R. .... **Monterey, CA**
Williams, Peter R. .... Russell, KS
Williams, Peter Whitridge (IBA)
New York, NY
Williams & Petro Co., L.L.C.
Columbus, OH
Williams, Petur S. .... Washington, DC
Williams, Philip .... **Louisville, KY**
Williams, Philip D. .... **Jacksonville, FL**
Williams, Philip E. .... Roseboro, NC
Williams, Philip E. .... Williamston, SC
Williams, Philip L. .... **Seattle, WA**
Williams, Phillip H. .... **Stroudsburg, PA**
Williams, Pinelli & Cullen, LLP
San Jose, CA
Williams, Pirjo L. .... **Sherman Oaks, CA**
Williams, P. M. .... Oklahoma City, OK
Williams, Polan & Pattis, LLC
New Haven, CT
Williams, Porter, Day & Neville, P.C.
Casper, WY
Williams, Potthoff, Williams & Smith, L.L.C.
Clayton, AL
Eufaula, AL
Union Springs, AL
Williams, Price S., Jr. .... **Atlanta, GA**
Williams & Prochaska, P.C.
Memphis, TN
Nashville, TN
Williams, Quinn .... **Phoenix, AZ**
Williams, R. Craig .... Dallas, TX
Williams, R. Ellsworth
Department of Commerce, Patent and Trademark Office, GV
Williams, R. Hanson .... Frankfort, KY
Williams, R. Jamison, Jr.
Birmingham, MI
Williams, R. Keith .... Melbourne, FL
Williams, R. Keith, P.A. .... Melbourne, FL
Williams, R. Kevin .... **Chicago, IL**
Williams, R. Richard, Jr. .... Santa Rosa, CA
Williams, R. Scott .... **Birmingham, AL**
Williams, R. Scott .... Houston, TX
Williams, R. Scott .... **Salt Lake City, UT**
Williams, Rachel F. .... **Chicago, IL**
Williams, Raina .... San Francisco, CA
Williams, Ralph B. .... Springfield, OH
Williams, Ralph C. .... Bentonville, AR
Williams, Ralph E. .... Springfield, IL
Williams, Ralph, Jr. .... Atlanta, GA
Williams, Ralph L. .... **Vista, CA**
Williams, Ralph O., III .... **Los Angeles, CA**
Williams, Ramon E. .... Houston, TX

Williams, Randall L.
Hot Springs National Park, AR
Williams, Randolph .... Philadelphia, PA
Williams, Randy J. .... **Lafayette, IN**
Williams, Randy Lee .... **Loveland, CO**
Williams, Randy W. .... **Houston, TX**
Williams & Ranney, P.C. .... **Hamilton, MT**
Kalispell, MT
Missoula, MT
Polson, MT
Williams, Raquel A. .... Watertown, NY
Williams, Ray .... Milton-Freewater, OR
Williams, Ray R., Jr. .... **Greenville, SC**
Williams, Raymond A., III .... **Dallas, TX**
Williams, Raymond A., III, P.C.
Dallas, TX
Williams, Raymond A., Jr. .... Dallas, TX
Williams, Raymond C. .... **Peoria, IL**
Williams, Raymond E. .... Wheaton, IL
Williams, Raymond E. .... **Columbia, MO**
Williams, Raymond H. .... Los Angeles, CA
Williams, Raymond H. .... **Beaufort, SC**
Williams, Raymond L. .... **Ellsworth, ME**
Williams, Raymond M. .... **Los Angeles, CA**
Williams, Raymond R. .... Media, PA
Williams, Rebecca G. .... Birmingham, AL
Williams, Rebecca L. .... **Seattle, WA**
Williams, Reed G. .... **Asheville, NC**
Williams, Reed M. .... **Irvine, CA**
Williams, Reed, Weinstein, Schifino & Mangione, P.A. .... **Tampa, FL**
Williams, Reesman & Tate .... Boonville, MO
Williams, Regina C. .... **Austin, TX**
Williams, Renauld J. .... Riverside, CA
Williams, Renee .... **Tulsa, OK**
Williams, Renee S.
Hot Springs National Park, AR
Williams, Reuben S., IV .... Ocala, FL
Williams & Rhodes, LLP .... **Denver, CO**
Williams, Rhys L. .... Gainesville, FL
Williams, Richard
Department Of Veterans Affairs, Board of Veterans Appeals, GV
Williams, Richard .... Houston, TX
Williams, Richard A. .... **Little Rock, AR**
Williams, Richard A. .... Novato, CA
Williams, Richard A. .... Danbury, CT
Stamford, CT
Williams, Richard A. .... Des Moines, IA
Williams, Richard A. .... Newton, NC
Williams, Richard A. .... **Columbus, OH**
Williams, Richard A. .... **Anadarko, OK**
Williams, Richard A. .... Salt Lake City, UT
Williams, Richard A., Jr. .... **St. Paul, MN**
Williams, Richard A., Jr. .... Newton, NC
Williams, Richard A., Jr. .... **Cincinnati, OH**
Williams, Richard B. .... Sacramento, CA
Williams, Richard B. .... Dallas, TX
Williams, Richard B., Jr. .... Memphis, TN
Williams, Richard C.
New Port Richey, FL
Williams, Richard C. .... **Houston, TX**
Williams, Richard C., Jr.
New Port Richey, FL
Williams, Richard C., Jr. .... **Jackson, MS**
Williams, Richard C., Jr., P.A.
New Port Richey, FL
Williams, Richard D. .... **Los Angeles, CA**
Williams, Richard D. .... **New York, NY**
Williams, Richard G. .... Kirksville, MO
Williams, Richard G. .... **Fort Worth, TX**
Williams, Richard H. .... Department of State, Foreign Service Officers (Overseas), GV
Williams, Richard H. .... Lincoln, NE
Williams, Richard H. .... **Portland, OR**
Williams, Richard J. .... Deerfield, IL
Williams, Richard J. .... Atlantic City, NJ
Williams, Richard J., Jr. .... **Morristown, NJ**
Williams, Richard John .... Chicago, IL
Williams, Richard L. .... San Ramon, CA
Williams, Richard L. .... **Miami, FL**
Williams, Richard L. .... **Lisle, IL**
Williams, Richard L. .... Wynnewood, PA
Williams, Richard L. .... Richmond, VA
Williams, Richard L. .... Casper, WY
Williams, Richard L., III .... **Chicago, IL**
Williams, Richard M. .... **Redwood City, CA**
Williams, Richard M. .... **Arvada, CO**
Williams, Richard M. .... Albany, NY
Williams, Richard M. .... **Allentown, PA**
Williams, Richard N. .... Hoffman Estates, IL
Williams, Richard P. .... Rochelle Park, NJ
Williams, Richard P. .... Leesburg, VA
Williams, Richard Preston
Rutherfordton, NC
Williams, Richard R. .... Mobile, AL
Williams, Richard Russell, L.L.C.
Mobile, AL
Williams, Richard S. .... United States Senate, Committee Legal Personnel, GV
Williams, Richard T. .... **Los Angeles, CA**
Williams, Richard T., II .... **Rochester, NY**
Williams, Richard T., Sr. .... Johnstown, PA
Williams, Richmond L. .... **Wilmington, DE**
Williams, Rick A. .... Montgomery, AL
Williams, Rick A., P.C. .... Montgomery, AL
Williams, Rick L. .... Lincoln, NE
Williams, Rickman E., III .... **Selma, AL**
Williams, Robert .... **Sacramento, CA**
San Francisco, CA
Williams, Robert .... Tallahassee, FL
Williams, Robert A. .... Dagsboro, DE
Williams, Robert A. .... Cleveland, OH
Williams, Robert A. .... Danville, VA
Martinsville, VA
Williams, Robert A., Jr. .... Madison, WI
Williams, Robert Alwyn .... Houston, TX

Williams, Robert B. .... Treasury Department, Internal Revenue Service, GV
Williams, Robert B. .... Chicago, IL
Williams, Robert B. .... Ellicott City, MD
Williams, Robert B. .... Takoma Park, MD
Williams, Robert B. .... **New York, NY**
Williams, Robert B. .... Toledo, OH
Williams, Robert B. .... **Pittsburgh, PA**
Williams, Robert C. .... Winnetka, IL
Williams, Robert C. .... Pontiac, MI
Williams, Robert C. .... Monticello, NY
Williams, Robert C. .... Rockville Centre, NY
Williams, Robert C. .... **Houston, TX**
Williams, Robert C. .... Seattle, WA
Williams, Robert D. .... **Idaho Falls, ID**
Williams, Robert D. .... West Des Moines, IA
Williams, Robert D. .... **Boston, MA**
Williams, Robert Deland .... **Philadelphia, PA**
Williams, Robert E. .... **Los Angeles, CA**
Williams, Robert E. .... Monterey, CA
Williams, Robert E. .... New Canaan, CT
Williams, Robert E. .... **Washington, DC**
Williams, Robert E. .... Fernandina Beach, FL
Williams, Robert E. .... Bloomington, IL
Williams, Robert E. .... **Chicago, IL**
Williams, Robert E. .... Chicago, IL
Williams, Robert E. .... Philadelphia, PA
Williams, Robert E., III .... **Jerome, ID**
Williams, Robert E., IV .... **Metairie, LA**
New Orleans, LA
Williams, Robert E., Jr.
Treasury Department, Internal Revenue Service, GV
Williams, Robert E. (Ridge) .... Austin, TX
Williams, Robert F. .... **Grand Rapids, MI**
Williams, Robert F. .... Camden, NJ
Williams, Robert F. .... Alexandria, VA
Williams, Robert G. .... Fresno, CA
Williams, Robert G. .... Mooresville, NC
Williams, Robert H. .... **Haddonfield, NJ**
Williams, Robert H. .... Huntington, NY
Williams, Robert H. .... **New York, NY**
Williams, Robert H. .... Fairview Park, OH
Williams, Robert I. .... Pleasanton, CA
Williams, Robert J. .... Mill Valley, CA
Williams, Robert J. .... San Jose, CA
Williams, Robert J. .... Boise, ID
Williams, Robert J. .... Deerfield, IL
Williams, Robert J. .... **Lake Charles, LA**
Williams, Robert J. .... Buffalo, NY
Williams, Robert J. .... **Pittsburgh, PA**
Williams, Robert J., Jr. .... Suffield, CT
Williams, Robert J., Jr. .... Troy, MI
Williams, Robert J. A. .... New Orleans, LA
Williams, Robert K. .... **Washington, DC**
Williams, Robert L. .... **Birmingham, AL**
Williams, Robert L. .... **Venice, FL**
Williams, Robert L. .... Chicago, IL
Williams, Robert L. .... Hernando, MS
Williams, Robert L., Jr. .... **Lake Wales, FL**
Williams, Robert M. .... Charleston, WV
Williams, Robert M., Jr. .... **Memphis, TN**
Williams, Robert N. .... Jackson, WY
Williams, Robert O. .... Covington, IN
Williams, Robert O., Jr. .... La Quinta, CA
Williams, Robert P., II .... **Atlanta, GA**
Williams, Robert Pate .... Asheboro, NC
Williams, Robert Q. .... **Tavares, FL**
Williams, Robert Rex .... Houston, TX
Williams, Robert S. .... Bakersfield, CA
Williams, Robert T. .... San Diego, CA
Williams, Robert T. .... Aurora, OH
Williams, Robert T. .... Lexington, SC
Williams, Robert V. .... **Tampa, FL**
Williams, Robert W. .... Pacific Palisades, CA
Williams, Robert W. .... San Francisco, CA
Williams, Robert W. .... Philadelphia, PA
Williams, Robert W. .... McAllen, TX
Williams, Roberta G. .... Auburn, NY
Williams, Robin A. .... **Washington, DC**
Williams, Robin Ann .... **Minneapolis, MN**
Williams, Robinson, White, Rigler & Parker, A Professional Corporation .... **Rolla, MO**
Salem, MO
Williams, Robt. L. .... Bakersfield, CA
Williams, Roch T. .... Westfield, NJ
Williams, Rod .... Bakersfield, CA
Williams, Rod, Law Corp. of
Bakersfield, CA
Williams, Roderick B. .... **Washington, DC**
Williams, Roderick B. .... **Austin, TX**
Williams, Rodney W. .... Honolulu, HI
Williams, Roger .... Nocona, TX
Williams, Roger A. .... **Skokie, IL**
Williams, Roger A. .... Carthage, NY
Watertown, NY
Williams, Roger B. .... Syracuse, NY
Williams, Roger B. .... **Austin, TX**
Williams, Roger B., (P.C.) .... Houston, TX
Williams, Roger C. .... Tuscaloosa, AL
Williams, Roger D. .... **Charlottesville, VA**
Williams, Roger G. .... Dallas, TX
Williams, Roger H. .... Chicago, IL
Williams, Roger H. .... **Cleveland, OH**
Twinsburg, OH
Williams, Roger L. .... **Richmond, VA**
Williams, Roger R. .... Tulsa, OK
Williams, Roger T, Jr .... **Denver, CO**
Williams, Roger W. .... **Jackson, MS**
Williams, Roland B. .... **Savannah, GA**
Williams, Roland E., Jr.
Jacksonville Beach, FL
Williams, Ronald A. .... Bentonville, AR
Williams, Ronald D. .... **Bridgeport, CT**
Williams, Ronald D., Jr. .... **Bridgeport, CT**
Williams, Ronald E. .... Liberty, IN
Williams, Ronald E. .... Dallas, TX
Williams, Ronald F. .... Atlanta, GA

Williams, Ronald J. ... Montgomery, AL
Williams, Ronald J. ... Lake Oswego, OR
Williams, Ronald L. ... Boise, ID
Williams, Ronald L. ... Wayne, PA
Williams, Ronald P. ... Wichita, KS
Williams, Ronald, (P.A.) ... Charlotte, NC
Williams, Ronald W. ... Danville, VA
Williams, Ronnie Lee ... Mobile, AL
Williams, Roscoe A. ... Prattville, AL
Williams, Rose L. ... Treasury Department, Internal Revenue Service, GV
Williams, Rose Vaughn ... Goldsboro, NC
Williams, Rosemary R. ... San Antonio, TX
Williams, Ross L. ... Studio City, CA
Williams, Roswell L. ... Stone Mountain, GA
Williams, Roth & O'Keefe, LLP
Salem, MA
Williams, Roy A. ... Dayton, OH
Williams, Roy C. ... Pascagoula, MS
Williams, Roy E. ... Kingman, KS
Williams, Roy E., Jr. ... West Plains, MO
Williams, Roy V. ... Eagle River, AK
Williams, Roy W., Jr. ... Cullman, AL
Williams, Ruby E. ... Champaign, IL
Williams, Russell J. ... Fort Lauderdale, FL
Williams, Russell R. ... Seattle, WA
Williams, Ruth ... Dallas, TX
Williams, Ruth A. ... Seattle, WA
Williams, Rutstein, Goldfarb, Sibrava & Midura, Ltd. ... Chicago, IL
Williams, S. Ashby ... Houston, TX
Williams, S. Douglas, Jr. ... Birmingham, AL
Williams, S. LaRue ... Daytona Beach, FL
Williams, S. Linn ... Irvine, CA
Williams, S. Preston
North Kansas City, MO
Williams, S. Robert ... Syracuse, NY
Williams, S. Tambor ... Greeley, CO
Williams, Sager A., Jr. ... Annapolis, MD
Williams, Sallie E. ... Rockville, MD
Williams, Sally ... San Diego, CA
Williams, Sally G. ... Jonesboro, AR
Williams, Samantha M. ... Washington, DC
Williams & Sammons ... Warner Robins, GA
Williams, Samuel J. ... New Port Richey, FL
Williams, Samuel J., P.A.
New Port Richey, FL
Williams, Samuel P. ... Boston, MA
Williams, Samuel S. ... Charlotte, NC
Williams, Samuel S., P.A. ... Charlotte, NC
Williams, Sandra J. ... Chicago, IL
Williams, Sandra K. ... Los Angeles, CA
Williams, Sandra K. ... Mansfield, OH
Williams, Sandra K. ... Houston, TX
Williams, Sandra L. N. ... Davenport, IA
Williams, Sandra M. ... Shreveport, LA
Williams, Sandra P. ... New City, NY
Williams, Sandra P. ... Houston, TX
Williams, Sanford S. ... Washington, DC
Williams, Sani Ahmadu ... New York, NY
Williams, Sarah E. ... St. Petersburg, FL
Williams & Scheetz, P.C. ... Richboro, PA
Williams & Schildt, A Professional Corporation
Doylestown, PA
Quakertown, PA
Williams, Schultz & Edelstein ... Oshkosh, WI
Williams, Scott A. ... Greenbrae, CA
Williams, Scott A. ... Pittsburgh, PA
Williams, Scott A. ... Williamsport, PA
Williams, Scott Alan ... St. Louis, MO
Williams, Scott C. ... San Diego, CA
Williams, Scott C. ... Columbia, TN
Williams, Scott E. ... Scottsdale, AZ
Williams, Scott E. ... Washington, DC
Williams, Scott E. ... Columbus, OH
Williams, Scott E. ... American Fork, UT
Williams, Scott G. ... West Palm Beach, FL
Williams, Scott M. ... Chicago, IL
Williams, Scott Porter ... Orlando, FL
Williams, Scott R. ... Bakersfield, CA
Williams, Scott T. ... Dallas, TX
Williams, Scott Thayden ... Williamsport, PA
Williams, Scott V. ... Dallas, TX
Williams, Scott W. ... Fresno, CA
Williams, Scott Wilson ... Fairfield, CT
Williams, Sennett & Scully Co., L.P.A.
Akron, OH
Cleveland, OH
Twinsburg, OH
Youngstown, OH
Williams, Serena M. ... Louisville, KY
Williams, Serena M. ... Pittsburgh, PA
Williams, Shandrea P. ... University, MS
Williams, Shannon C. ... Fullerton, CA
Williams, Sharon A. ... Portland, OR
Williams, Sharon C. ... Vienna, VA
Williams, Sharon E. ... Merced, CA
Williams, Sharon L. ... Philadelphia, PA
Williams, Sharon M. ... Chalmette, LA
Williams, Sharon M. ... Kansas City, MO
Williams, Sharon S. ... Chicago, IL
Williams, Sharon S. ... Columbia, SC
Williams, Shawnell ... Columbus, OH
Williams & Shedd ... Fair Oaks, CA
Williams, Sheila Meador
Oklahoma City, OK
Williams, Sheila T. ... Overland Park, KS
Williams, Shelia Kae ... Kingwood, WV
Williams, Shelli D. ... Chicago, IL
Williams, Shelton C. ... Missoula, MT
Williams, Sheri Annette ... Kansas City, MO
Williams, Sherry D. ... Miami, FL
Williams, Sheryl Howell ... Asheville, NC
Williams, Sheryl L.
Department of Transportation, Federal Aviation Administration, GV
Williams, Shirley B. ... Brandon, FL
Williams, Shirley K. ... Lincoln, NE

Williams, Shirley M. ... Washington, DC
Williams, Sidney ... Stillwater, OK
Williams, Sidney B., Jr. ... Kalamazoo, MI
Williams, Sidney B., (P.C.) ... Houston, TX
Williams, Sidney L. ... Columbus, OH
Williams, Silas, Jr. ... Chattanooga, TN
Williams & Sloan, P.C. ... Mehoopany, PA
Williams, Smith & Stockstill ... Picayune, MS
Williams, Smith & Summers, P.A.
Tavares, FL
Williams, Spencer ... San Jose, CA
Williams, Spottswood W. H., III
Colorado Springs, CO
Williams, Squire N., Jr. ... Frankfort, KY
Williams, Stace L. ... Lubbock, TX
Williams, Stace L., P.C. ... Lubbock, TX
Williams, Stacey D. ... Shreveport, LA
Williams, Staci J. ... New York, NY
Williams, Stacy B. ... Fort Lauderdale, FL
Williams, Stacy B. ... Atlanta, GA
Williams, Stacy J. ... Tomball, TX
Williams, Stacy J., & Associates
Houston, TX
Tomball, TX
Williams, Stacy L. ... Annapolis, MD
Williams, Stacy L. ... Houston, TX
Williams, Stanley A. ... Cleveland, OH
Williams, Stanley D. ... Mission, KS
Williams, Stanley Edward ... Houston, TX
Williams, Stanley Edward, P.C., The Law Offices of ... Houston, TX
Williams, Stanley G. ... Silverdale, WA
Williams, Stanley P. ... Los Angeles, CA
Williams, Stasia Mitchell ... Macon, GA
Williams, Steele T. ... Sarasota, FL
Williams, Stephan C. ... Walnut Creek, CA
Williams, Stephan P. ... Boston, MA
Williams, Stephanie ... Austin, TX
Williams, Stephanie P. ... Greenbelt, MD
Williams, Stephanie Rae ... Los Angeles, CA
Williams, Stephen A. ... Dalton, GA
Williams, Stephen A. ... Boston, MA
Williams, Stephen B. ...
Department of State, GV
Williams, Stephen C. ... Carbondale, IL
Williams, Stephen C. ... Richmond, VA
Williams, Stephen D. ... Wilmington, DE
Williams, Stephen D. ... Flemington, NJ
Williams, Stephen D. ... Clarksburg, WV
Williams, Stephen E.
Pension Benefit Guaranty Corporation, Office of the General Counsel, GV
Williams, Stephen E. ... Indianapolis, IN
Williams, Stephen E. ... Boston, MA
Williams, Stephen E. ... Pittsburgh, PA
Williams, Stephen F. ...
United States Court Of Appeals District Of Columbia Circuit, GV
Williams, Stephen J. ... Fort Wayne, IN
Williams, Stephen J. ... Greenbelt, MD
Williams, Stephen L. ... Terre Haute, IN
Williams, Stephen M. ... Oakland, CA
Williams, Stephen M. ... Albuquerque, NM
Williams, Stephen M. ... Houston, TX
Williams, Stephen N. ... Phoenix, AZ
Williams, Stephen N. ... Beaumont, TX
Williams, Stephen P. ... Little Rock, AR
Williams, Stephen P. ... Greenville, SC
Williams, Stephen R. ... Aripeka, FL
Williams, Stephen R. ... Norcross, GA
Williams, Stephen S. ... Houston, TX
Williams, Steve G. ... Brooklyn, NY
Williams, Steven A. ... Tampa, FL
Williams, Steven G. ... Jackson, MS
Williams, Steven H. ... Phoenix, AZ
Williams, Steven J. ... Irving, TX
Williams, Steven J., P.C. ... Irving, TX
Williams, Steven L. ... Portland, OR
Williams, Steven L. ... Chattanooga, TN
Knoxville, TN
Williams, Steven M., Law Offices of
Wichita Falls, TX
Williams, Steven N. ... Burlingame, CA
Williams, Steven N. ... Dallas, TX
Williams, Steven O. ... Lancaster, OH
Williams, Steven P. ... Houston, TX
Williams, Steven R. ... Visalia, CA
Williams, Steven R. ... Bloomington, IL
Williams, Steven R. ... Harrisburg, PA
Williams, Steven R. ... Philadelphia, PA
Williams, Steven R. ... Richmond, VA
Williams, Steven T. ... Philadelphia, PA
Williams, Steven W. ... Syracuse, NY
Williams, Stevens, McCarville & Frizzell, P.C. ... Amherst, NY
Buffalo, NY
Eden, NY
Westfield, NY
Williams, Stewart D. ... Miami, FL
Williams, Strobel, Malone, Mason & Ralph, P.A. ... Dodge City, KS
Williams, Stuart A. ... Pittsburgh, PA
Williams, Stuart L. ... Richmond, VA
Williams, Stuart L., Jr. ... Richmond, VA
Williams, Stuart T. ... Minneapolis, MN
Williams, Susan ... Los Angeles, CA
Williams, Susan ... West Palm Beach, FL
Williams, Susan A. ... Palo Alto, CA
Williams, Susan A. ... Buffalo, NY
Williams, Susan B. ... Hempstead, NY
Williams, Susan B. ... Richmond, VA
Williams, Susan Catherine ... North Platte, NE
Williams, Susan G. ... Washington, DC
Williams, Susan G. ... Columbia, SC
Williams, Susan H. ... Brookline, MA
Williams, Susan Howard ... Portland, OR
Williams, Susan J. ... Los Angeles, CA

Williams, Susan L.
Merit Systems Protection Board, Office of the General Counsel, GV
Williams, Susan L. ... New Albany, IN
Williams, Susan L. ... Boston, MA
Williams, Susan M. ... Boston, MA
Williams, Susan M. ... Troy, MI
Williams, Susan M. ... Albuquerque, NM
Williams, Susan Myklebye
St. Louis Park, MN
Williams, Susan N. ... Latrobe, PA
Philadelphia, PA
Williams, Susan Reedy ... Chicago, IL
Williams, Susan Rees ... McAllen, TX
Williams, Susan S. ... King George, VA
Williams, Suzanne E. ... Madison, WI
Williams & Swee, Ltd. ... Bloomington, IL
Williams, T. Bayard, Jr. ... Towson, MD
Williams, T. Chris ... Lee's Summit, MO
Williams, T. Craig ... Birmingham, AL
Williams, T. Gregory ... Youngstown, OH
Williams, T. Raymond ... Washington, DC
Williams, Tamalou M. ... West Frankfort, IL
Williams, Tamalou M., P.C.
West Frankfort, IL
Williams, Tambor ... Greeley, CO
Williams, Tamera L. ... Seattle, WA
Williams, Tara J. ... Durham, NC
Williams, Tari L. ... Dallas, TX
Williams, Tarleton David, Jr.
Blue Bell, PA
Williams, Tatia Lynne
Department of Commerce, National Telecommunications & Information Administration, GV
Williams, Ted H. ... Syracuse, NY
Williams, Ted J. ... Washington, DC
Williams, Tedd N. ... Bradenton, FL
Williams, Teena J. ... Anchorage, AK
Williams, Terence D. ... Atlanta, GA
Williams, Terence W. ... San Mateo, CA
Williams, Teresa ... Anchorage, AK
Williams, Teresa A. ... Pacific Palisades, CA
Williams, Teresa C. ... Indianapolis, IN
Williams, Teresa P. ... St. Petersburg, FL
Williams, Terilyn Robinson
South Orange, NJ
Williams, Terrence D. ... Stockton, CA
Williams, Terry E. ... Atlanta, GA
Williams, Terry Evan ... Delavan, WI
Williams, Terry James ... Bellefonte, PA
State College, PA
Williams, Terry L. ... Kansas City, MO
Williams, Theodore J., Jr. ... Belleville, IL
St. Louis, MO
Williams, Theodore N., Jr. ... Muskegon, MI
Williams, Theresa L. ... Anchorage, AK
Williams, Thomas A. ... Oklahoma City, OK
Williams, Thomas A. ... Chattanooga, TN
Williams, Thomas A. ... Callao, VA
Williams, Thomas A. B. ... Walla Walla, WA
Williams, Thomas C. ... Sacramento, CA
Williams, Thomas C. ... Washington, DC
Williams, Thomas C. ... Oklahoma City, OK
Williams, Thomas D. ... St. Paul, MN
Williams, Thomas D. ... Batavia, NY
Williams, Thomas D. ... Memphis, TN
Williams, Thomas E. ... Eagle River, AK
Williams, Thomas E. ... Jackson, MS
Williams, Thomas E. ... Charlotte, NC
Williams, Thomas E. ... Athens, TX
Williams, Thomas E., III ... Chicago, IL
Williams, Thomas F., Jr.
Fredericksburg, VA
Williams, Thomas F., Law Office of
Quincy, MA
Williams, Thomas G. ... Little Rock, AR
Williams, Thomas H. ... Potomac, MD
Williams, Thomas H. ... Detroit, MI
Williams, Thomas H. ... Fayetteville, NC
Williams, Thomas H. ... Columbus, OH
Williams, Thomas H. ... Claremore, OK
Williams, Thomas H., Jr. ... Miami, FL
Williams, Thomas J. ... San Francisco, CA
Williams, Thomas J. ... Greenwich, CT
Williams, Thomas J. ... Hartford, CT
Williams, Thomas J. ... Columbus, OH
Williams, Thomas J. ... Carlisle, PA
Williams, Thomas J. ... Fort Worth, TX
Williams, Thomas K. ... Anchorage, AK
Williams, Thomas L. ... Chicago, IL
Williams, Thomas L. ... Branson, MO
Joplin, MO
Williams, Thomas L. ... Charleston, SC
Williams, Thomas L. ... Appleton, WI
Williams, Thomas L., Jr. ... Montecito, CA
Santa Barbara, CA
Williams, Thomas M. ... Chicago, IL
Williams, Thomas M. ... Louisville, KY
Williams, Thomas M., Jr. ... Towson, MD
Williams, Thomas N. ... Newport Beach, CA
Williams, Thomas O. ... Camp Hill, PA
Williams, Thomas P. ... Robertsdale, AL
Williams, Thomas P. ... Malverne, NY
Williams, Thomas Parker ... Philadelphia, PA
Williams, Thomas R. ... Detroit, MI
Williams, Thomas R. ... Guthrie, OK
Williams, Thomas R. ... Portland, OR
Williams, Thomas R., Jr. ... Springfield, VA
Williams, Thomas S. ... Oshkosh, WI
Williams, Thomas T. ... San Angelo, TX
Williams, Thomas V. ... Columbus, OH
Williams, Thomas W. ... Mahwah, NJ
Williams, Thomas W., Jr. ... Honolulu, HI
Williams, Thomasina H. ... Miami, FL
Williams, Thornton, and Associates
Tallahassee, FL
Williams, Tim D. ... Conway, AR

Williams, Tim F. ... Greenville, SC
Williams, Tim J. ... Twin Falls, ID
Williams, Timothy A. ... Marietta, OH
Williams, Timothy C. ... Las Vegas, NV
Williams, Timothy C., Law Offices of
Walnut Creek, CA
Williams, Timothy Chris
Kansas City, MO
Williams, Timothy E. ... Tacoma, WA
Williams, Timothy G. ... San Diego, CA
Williams, Timothy G. ... Alpine, UT
Williams, Timothy J.
Research Triangle Park, NC
Williams, Timothy K. ... San Francisco, CA
Williams, Timothy L.
Securities and Exchange Commission, Division of Corporation Finance, GV
Williams, Timothy L. ... Atlanta, GA
Williams, Timothy L.
St. Clair Shores, MI
Williams, Timothy M. ... Melbourne, FL
Williams, Timothy M. ... Cadillac, MI
Williams, Timothy M., P.C., Law Office of
Cadillac, MI
Williams, Timothy R. ... Des Moines, IA
Williams, Timothy S. ... Oakland, CA
Williams, Timothy S ... Louisville, KY
Williams, Timothy S. ... Moravia, NY
Williams, Timothy S. ... Cleveland, OH
Williams, Timothy T. ... Baltimore, MD
Williams and Tinkham ... Houston, TX
Williams, T.L., & Associates ... Houston, TX
Williams, Todd R. ... Stroudsburg, PA
Williams, Todd R., Jr. ... Chambersburg, PA
Williams, Tommie G. ... Greenwood, MS
Williams, Tommy Joe ... Roanoke, VA
Williams, Tracey A. ... Lake Charles, LA
Williams, Tracy D. ... Chicago, IL
Williams, Tracy L. ... Richmond, CA
Williams, Trae D. ... Sherman Oaks, CA
Williams, Travis E. ... Pittsburgh, PA
Williams & Trayner ... Tampa, FL
Williams, Trevor T. ... Downers Grove, IL
Williams, Trowbridge C.
East Rochester, NY
Williams, Troy A. ... Houston, TX
Williams, Troy D. ... Ozona, TX
Williams, Turner Butler ... Birmingham, AL
Williams, Turner & Holmes, P.C.
Grand Junction, CO
Moab, UT
Williams, Tyler E., III ... Keysville, VA
Williams, Tyson Lane ... Fayetteville, AR
Williams, U. Gwyn ... Boston, MA
Williams, V. Scott ... St. Charles, MO
Williams, Valarie C. ... Atlanta, GA
Williams, Valerie Palmer ... Greenville, SC
Williams, Vanessa Peterson ... Detroit, MI
Williams & Vassallo ... Suffield, CT
Williams, Vaughn C. ... New York, NY
Williams, Verna ... Washington, DC
Williams, Vernie L. ... Columbia, SC
Williams, Vernon ... Aberdeen, SD
Williams, Vernon A.
Department of Transportation, Surface Transportation Board, GV
Williams, Vernon L. ... Wichita, KS
Williams, Vernon M. ... Kingsport, TN
Norton, VA
Williams, Vernos J. ... Toledo, OH
Williams, Vesper C., II ... Toledo, OH
Williams, Vickie J. ... Seattle, WA
Williams, Victoria T. ... Martinez, CA
Williams & Vigor ... Ashland, KY
Williams, Viki A. ... Metairie, LA
Williams, Vincent C. ... San Francisco, CA
Williams, Vivian L. ... Los Angeles, CA
Williams, W. Alan ... Schuylkill Haven, PA
Williams, W. Allan ... San Diego, CA
Williams, W. Barry ... Augusta, GA
Williams, W. Bruce ... Midland, TX
Williams, W. Dakin ... Collinsville, IL
Williams, W. Earl ... Fergus Falls, MN
Williams, W. Fred ... Greensboro, NC
Williams, W. Fred, Jr. ... Nashville, TN
Williams, W. Hunter, Jr. ... Osceola, AR
Williams, W. Jackson ... Little Rock, AR
Williams, W. Keith, II ... Yeadon, PA
Williams, W. Kirk ... San Francisco, CA
Williams, W. Ray ... East Orange, NJ
Williams, W. Scott ... Solana Beach, CA
Williams, Wade ... Houston, TX
Williams, Wade A. ... Eureka Springs, AR
Williams, Wade Bruce ... Galveston, TX
Williams, Wade S. ... Washington, DC
Williams & Wagoner ... Clarksville, IN
Jeffersonville, IN
New Albany, IN
Louisville, KY
Williams, Walter B. ... Seattle, WA
Williams, Walter B., & Associates
Houston, TX
Williams, Walter E. ... Joplin, MO
Williams, Walter F. ... Chattanooga, TN
Williams, Walter F. (Trey), III
Houston, TX
Williams, Walter J. ... Bloomfield Hills, MI
Williams, Walter J., Jr. ... Woodbury, CT
Williams, Walter L. ... Seattle, WA
Williams, Walter L. ... Clarksburg, WV
Williams, Walter V. ... Austin, TX
Williams, Walton E., III ... Birmingham, AL
Williams, Ward ... Bellingham, WA
Williams, Warren A. ... Irvine, CA
Williams, Warren E. ... Orlando, FL
Williams, Warren H.
Charlotte Amalie, St. Thomas, VI
Williams, Warren J., Jr. ... Cleveland, OH

Williamson, W. Reid .... Houston, TX
Williamson, Wade H. .... Corpus Christi, TX
Williamson, Walter .... New York, NY
Williamson & Walton, L.L.P. Whiteville, NC
Williamson, Warren R. .... Denver, CO
Williamson, Wayne A. .... Portland, OR
Williamson, Webster, Groshong & Falb Alton, IL
Williamson, Wendy Woods .... Savannah, GA
Williamson, Wilburn L. .... Oklahoma City, OK
Williamson, William J. .... Louisburg, NC
Williamson & Williamson .... Greenville, AL
Williamson & Williamson .... New York, NY
Williamson & Williamson .... Marion, OH
Williamson & Williamson .... St. Helens, OR
Williamson, W. J. .... Greenville, AL
Williamson, W. J. .... Houston, TX
Williams-Robinson, Sensimone Houston, TX
Williams Scalise, Marian .... Myrtle Beach, SC
Williams-Stander, Manley .... Washington, DC
Williams-Sulkin, Alayne .... Evanston, IL
Williams-Tracy, Jeffrey Scott Charlotte, NC
Williams-Woods, Pierre T. .... Amarillo, TX
Williams-Young, Marc G. .... Toledo, OH
Willian Brinks Hofer Gilson & Lione Arlington, VA
Willian, Clyde F. .... Chicago, IL
Willian, Jeffrey L. .... Chicago, IL
Willian, Marchell M. .... Chicago, IL
Willian, Michael B. .... Chicago, IL
Williard, Robert R. .... Jackson, MS
Williard, Steve Martin .... Houston, TX
Willibey, Steven .... Chillicothe, MO
Willick, Daniel H. .... Los Angeles, CA
Willick, Marc I. .... Los Angeles, CA
Willick, Marshal S. .... Las Vegas, NV
Willick, Nelson H. .... Westport, CT
Willie, Eric M. .... Fullerton, CA
Willie, Karen A. .... Seattle, WA
Tacoma, WA
Willie, Karen A., Law Offices of Seattle, WA
Tacoma, WA
Williford, A. Kaylynn .... Houston, TX
Williford, Angela Smith .... Conway, SC
Williford, C. Todd .... Kannapolis, NC
Williford, David G. .... Orlando, FL
Williford, Donald .... Doylestown, PA
Williford, Doris H. .... Birmingham, AL
Williford, Glen E. .... Fresno, CA
Williford, James S., Jr. .... Rockville, MD
Williford, James S., Jr., P.C. .... Rockville, MD
Williford, John L. .... Oklahoma City, OK
Williford, John R. .... Houston, TX
Williford, John S., Jr. .... Rocky Mount, NC
Williford, John W., Jr. .... Huntsville, TX
Williford, Joseph W. .... Raleigh, NC
Williford, Kenneth W. .... Fort Worth, TX
Williford, McAllister & Jacobus, LLP Jackson, MS
Williford, Michael Leighton Fayetteville, NC
Williford, Rhonda G. National Labor Relations Board, Office of Board Members, GV
Williford, Robert E. .... Jackson, MS
Williford, Robin J. .... Warren, OH
Williford, Ronald E. .... Santa Barbara, CA
Williford, Steven Eugene .... Tabor City, NC
Williford, Virginia D. .... Houston, TX
Williford, Ward .... Dallas, TX
Willig, Aimee S. .... Seattle, WA
Willig, Arnold M. .... Seattle, WA
Willig, David A. .... Perth Amboy, NJ
Willig, David S. .... Miami, FL
Willig, David S., Chtd. .... Miami, FL
Willig, Deborah R. .... Harrisburg, PA
Philadelphia, PA
Willig, Edward J., III .... Burlingame, CA
Willig, Jennifer R. .... New York, NY
Willig, Joy F. .... New York, NY
Willig, Kelly M. .... Seattle, WA
Willig, Kenneth C. H. .... New York, NY
Willig, Peter F. .... Madison, CT
Willig, Ronald .... Amherst, NY
Willig, Rosette F. .... New York, NY
Willig, Stephen F. .... New York, NY
Willig, William P. .... Saratoga Springs, NY
Willig, Williams & Davidson
Lawrenceville, NJ
Harrisburg, PA
Philadelphia, PA
Williger, Marta J. .... Cuyahoga Falls, OH
Williger, Richard L. .... Akron, OH
Williger, Sheldon .... Northridge, CA
Williger, Stephen David .... Cleveland, OH
Willihnganz, Paul W., Law Offices of Santa Rosa, CA
Willihnganz, Ty C. .... Oshkosh, WI
Willimon, Henry P. .... Greer, SC
Willimon, Henry P., Jr. .... Ellisville, MO
Willin, Joan K. .... Newington, CT
Willing, Andrew Russell .... Los Angeles, CA
Willing, Charles G., Jr. .... Concord, NH
Willing, Charles R. .... Oklahoma City, OK
Willing, Jack A., Jr. .... Princess Anne, MD
Willing, Joy Marzilli .... Washington, DC
Willing, Seana Beckerman .... Austin, TX
Willinger, Alan M. .... New York, NY
Willinger, Ann Marie Kent Bridgeport, CT
Willinger, Charles J., Jr. .... Bridgeport, CT
Willinger, Jay S. .... Beverly Hills, CA
Willinger, Jay S., A Professional Law Corporation .... Beverly Hills, CA
Willinger, Lavelle A. .... Toledo, OH
Willinger, Lowell D. .... New York, NY
Willinger, Richard .... Dover, NJ
Willinger, Scott R. .... Miami, FL
Willinger, Shepro, Tower & Bucci, P.C. Bridgeport, CT
Willinger, Warren J. .... New Rochelle, NY
New York, NY
Willingham, Allen S. C. .... Atlanta, GA
Willingham, Clark S. .... Dallas, TX
Willingham & Coté, P.C.
East Lansing, MI
Lansing, MI
St. Johns, MI
Willingham, Craig A. .... Nacogdoches, TX
Willingham, Dan J. .... Cullman, AL
Willingham, David K. .... Los Angeles, CA
Willingham, Edmund .... Atlanta, GA
Willingham, George .... San Antonio, TX
Willingham, Gloria J. .... Department of Justice, Drug Enforcement Administration, GV
Willingham, Harold S. .... Marietta, GA
Willingham, Jack G. .... Hamlin, TX
Willingham, James E., Jr. .... San Antonio, TX
Willingham, James Estes, Jr. .... Maitland, FL
Willingham, James Estes, Jr. .... Maitland, FL
Willingham, Jennifer A. .... St. Louis, MO
Willingham, John D., Jr. .... College Park, GA
Willingham, Julian B. .... Augusta, GA
Willingham, Maria D. .... Birmingham, AL
Willingham, P. Edmund, Jr. .... Atlanta, GA
Willingham, R. Mark .... Houston, TX
Nacogdoches, TX
Willingham, Thomas P. .... Birmingham, AL
Willingham, Tom .... Rome, GA
Willingham, William Bartow Tallahassee, FL
Willingham, William J. .... Talladega, AL
Willingham, Wright .... Gainesville, GA
Willinghan, George A., III Washington, DC
Willink, Donald D. .... Madison, WI
Williott, Anthony J. .... Pittsburgh, PA
Willis, A. Michelle .... Atlanta, GA
Willis, A. Rexford, III .... Greenville, NC
New Bern, NC
Willis, A. Russell .... Nashville, TN
Willis, Albert L. .... Durham, NC
Willis, Ann Hester .... Atlanta, GA
Willis, Annette V. .... Middlefield, CT
Willis & Ashby .... Fredericksburg, VA
Willis, B. Duane .... Jackson, TN
Willis, B. Grant .... Falmouth, MA
Willis, B. Jill Timberlake .... Dallas, TX
Willis, Bennett, Jr. .... McLean, VA
Willis, Bennett T., Jr. .... Macon, GA
Willis, Berry D., Jr. .... Norfolk, VA
Willis, Bonnie M. .... West Palm Beach, FL
Willis, Brian M. .... Atlanta, GA
Willis, Bruce .... Lake Jackson, TX
Willis, C. Stanley, II .... Hilliard, OH
Willis, Camile E. .... Chicago, IL
Willis, Carlton G. .... Raleigh, NC
Willis, Carroll T. .... Guilford, CT
Willis, Charles A. .... Denver, CO
Willis, Charles L. .... Clinton, NJ
Willis, Charles L. .... Rochester, NY
Willis, Charles R. .... St. Louis, MO
Willis, Charles R., P.C. .... St. Louis, MO
Willis & Chattin .... Charleston, WV
Willis, Christopher S. .... Dallas, TX
Willis, Christopher W. .... Gainesville, GA
Willis, Claudia Jo .... Fort Lauderdale, FL
Willis, Claudia Jo, P.A. Fort Lauderdale, FL
Willis, Clint Grainger .... Bowling Green, KY
Willis, Craig B. .... Orlando, FL
Tallahassee, FL
Willis, Craig E. .... Cleveland, OH
Willis, Craig N. .... Iowa City, IA
Willis, Cressondra B. .... Newport News, VA
Willis, Damico & Apgar .... Roanoke, VA
Willis, Daniel K. .... St. Francisville, LA
Willis, David B. .... Providence, RI
Willis, David C. .... Orlando, FL
Willis, David C. .... Green Lake, WI
Willis, David J. .... Houston, TX
Willis, David L. .... Lake City, IA
Willis, David L. .... San Antonio, TX
Willis, David L. .... St. Johnsbury, VT
Willis, Dean .... Los Angeles, CA
Willis, DeAnn .... Phoenix, AZ
Willis, Debby Lynn .... Augusta, ME
Willis, Deborah Nelson .... Port Angeles, WA
Willis, Derek L. .... Houston, TX
Willis, Donald C. .... Paradise, CA
Willis, Donald Joe .... Bend, OR
Portland, OR
Willis, Douglas A. .... Lombard, IL
Willis, Doyle .... Fort Worth, TX
Willis, Doyle H., Jr. .... Fort Worth, TX
Willis, Dudley H. .... Boston, MA
Willis, Elizabeth Bib .... Tallahassee, FL
Willis, Everett I. .... New York, NY
Willis, F. Michael .... Washington, DC
Willis, F. L. (Larry), Jr. .... Chico, CA
Willis, Floyd, III .... Rockville, MD
Willis, Floyd, III, Law Office of Rockville, MD
Willis, Frank D. .... Paw Paw, MI
Willis, Frank L. .... Chico, CA
Willis, Gail Ann .... Independence, MO
Willis, Geo. P., III .... El Campo, TX
Willis, Geoffrey K. .... Riverside, CA
Willis, Gerald C., Jr. .... Chicago, IL
Willis, Gordon F. .... Fredericksburg, VA
Willis, Gregory Allen .... Atlanta, GA
Willis, Gregory C. .... Fairfield, CT
Willis, Gregory J. .... Fort Lauderdale, FL
Willis, Gregory M. .... Raleigh, NC
Willis, Guion Harrison, Jr. Virginia Beach, VA
Willis, Guy R. .... Millbrook, AL
Willis, H. Lamar .... Orlando, FL
Willis, Harold J. .... Stockton, CA
Willis, Harry J. .... Albany, NY
Willis, Harry M., Law Office of Mill Valley, CA
Willis, Hart, Jr. .... Dallas, TX
Willis, Henry M. .... Los Angeles, CA
Willis & Hougham .... San Antonio, TX
Willis, J. Burton .... St. Martinville, LA
Willis, J. Martin .... Norfolk, VA
Willis, Jack G. .... Hanford, CA
Willis, Jack R. .... Los Angeles, CA
Willis, James Claude .... Omaha, NE
Willis, James E. .... Naples, FL
Willis, James M. .... Farmington, MO
Willis, James R. .... Cleveland, OH
Willis, Jane E. .... Boston, MA
Willis, Jean L. .... Manassas, VA
Willis, Jean L. .... Manitowoc, WI
Willis, Jean M. .... Mount Holly, NJ
Willis, Jefferson W. .... Columbus, GA
Willis, Jeffrey .... Tucson, AZ
Willis, Jeffrey A. .... Ashland, AL
Willis, Jeffrey H. .... Tampa, FL
Willis, Jeffrey L. .... Wichita, KS
Willis, Jeffrey W. .... Atlanta, GA
Willis, Jennifer N. .... New Orleans, LA
Willis, Jere M. H., III .... Culpeper, VA
Willis, Jerry .... La Grange, GA
Willis, Jill M. .... Northbrook, IL
Willis, Jill N. .... San Diego, CA
Willis, Jill Renfro .... Dallas, TX
Willis, J. M. H., Jr. .... Fredericksburg, VA
Willis, Joe E. .... Tallahassee, FL
Willis, Joel A., Jr. .... Warner Robins, GA
Willis, John .... Ellicott City, MD
Willis, John .... Akron, OH
Willis, John A. .... Boca Raton, FL
Willis, John A. .... Knoxville, TN
Willis, John C., IV .... Orlando, FL
Willis, John F. .... Metairie, LA
Willis, John J. .... North Andover, MA
Willis, John J., Jr. .... North Andover, MA
Willis, John L. .... Orlando, FL
Willis, John M. .... Westmont, NJ
Willis, John M. .... Philadelphia, PA
Willis, John P., IV .... Birmingham, AL
Willis, John W. .... Bethesda, MD
Willis, John W. .... St. Louis, MO
Willis, Joleen S. .... Chicago, IL
Willis, Joseph Edward .... Bradenton, FL
Willis, J. R. .... Broken Arrow, OK
Willis, Judy A. .... El Segundo, CA
Willis, J. W. .... New Orleans, LA
Willis, Karen P. Pulliam .... Hammond, IN
Willis, Kathi Grant .... Chattanooga, TN
Willis, Kathleen S. .... Decatur, GA
Willis, Kathleen Tenney .... Buffalo, NY
Willis, Kaye .... Laramie, WY
Willis, Kelly A. .... Columbus, OH
Willis, Kenneth D. .... Englewood, CO
Willis, Kenneth T. .... Boston, MA
Willis, Kent B. .... Breckenridge, CO
Willis, Kent B. .... Lake City, IA
Willis, Kent B. .... Farmington Hills, MI
Willis, Kenton W. .... Salt Lake City, UT
Willis, Kerry A. .... Sacramento, CA
Willis, Kimberly J. .... Bangor, PA
Willis, Kirk D. .... Dallas, TX
Willis & Knight .... Nashville, TN
Willis, L. Joseph, III .... Louisville, KY
Willis, Larry .... Washington, DC
Willis, Larry D. .... Chesapeake, VA
Willis, Larry N. .... Tustin, CA
Willis, Larryann C. .... Santa Clarita, CA
Willis, Lauren E. .... Baltimore, MD
Willis Law Firm .... Lake City, IA
Willis Law Firm, P.A. .... Tampa, FL
Willis & Lawrence .... Martinez, CA
Willis, Lee L. .... Tallahassee, FL
Willis, Leland F. .... Upton, NY
Willis, Lewis E., Jr. .... Indianapolis, IN
Willis, Lezlie B. .... Dallas, TX
Willis, Linda A. .... Chicago, IL
Willis, Linda G. .... Bedford, VA
Willis, Linda Gibbons .... Nashville, TN
Willis, Lloyd W. .... New Braunfels, TX
Willis, Lori M. .... New York, NY
Willis, Lu .... Norman, OK
Willis, Marguerite Smith .... Washington, DC
Willis, Mark C. .... Fredericksburg, VA
Willis, Mark L. .... Key West, FL
Willis, Mark S. .... Washington, DC
Willis, Martin R. .... Roanoke, VA
Willis, Mary S. .... Englewood, CO
Willis, Matthew J. .... Glastonbury, CT
Willis, Matthew R. .... Beaumont, TX
Willis, McKenzie & Long .... La Grange, GA
Willis, Michael D. .... Baltimore, MD
Willis, Michael D. .... Green Bay, WI
Willis, Michael W. .... Whiteville, NC
Willis, Millicent .... Chicago, IL
Willis, Monte A. .... Walla Walla, WA
Willis, Myra L. .... Kalamazoo, MI
Willis, Nancy Ashbrook .... Terrace Park, OH
Willis, Nancy B. .... Iowa City, IA
Willis, Norman W. .... Plainfield, NJ
Willis, O. Henry, Jr. .... Dunn, NC
Willis, Patricia H. .... Bay St. Louis, MS
Willis, Patricia Pritchard .... Norfolk, VA
Willis, Patrick L. .... Manitowoc, WI
Willis, Patterson F., Jr. .... Opelousas, LA
Willis, Paul Marcum .... Owensboro, KY
Willis, Paul T. .... Tucson, AZ
Willis, Paula A. .... Ocala, FL
Willis, Paula A., P.A. .... Ocala, FL
Willis, Peter D. .... Denver, CO
Willis, Peter R. .... Jersey City, NJ
Willis, R. Tim .... Corvallis, OR
Willis, Rachel E. .... Tullahoma, TN
Willis, Randolph G. .... Kansas City, MO
Willis, Raymond E. .... Detroit, MI
Willis, R. G. .... Nacogdoches, TX
Willis, Richard H. .... Atlanta, GA
Willis, Richard R. .... Atlanta, GA
Willis, Richard T. .... Lynn, MA
Willis, Robert Alma .... Laramie, WY
Willis, Robert E. .... Bradenton, FL
Willis, Robert H. .... St. Petersburg, FL
Willis, Robert H., Jr. .... St. Petersburg, FL
Willis, Robert J. .... Cleveland, OH
Willis, Robert L., Jr. .... Detroit, MI
Willis, Robert M. .... Washington, DC
Willis, Robert Stuart .... Jacksonville, FL
Willis, Robin .... Houston, TX
Willis, Robin Rankin, P.C. .... Houston, TX
Willis, Ronald M. .... Chicago, IL
Willis, Ronald W. .... Enid, OK
Willis, Ros Richardson .... Virginia Beach, VA
Willis, Russell A. .... Portage, IN
Willis, Sabrina .... Baltimore, MD
Willis & Sackett .... Adel, IA
Perry, IA
Willis, Sandra Ann .... Charleston, WV
Willis, Scott Preston .... Monroe, GA
Willis & Sessions .... Whiteville, NC
Willis, Shari Renee .... Wichita, KS
Willis, Sharon A. .... Kansas City, MO
Willis, Sherman .... Albany, GA
Willis, Stephen C. .... Tallahassee, FL
Willis, Stephen L. .... Somerville, NJ
New York, NY
Willis, Sterling Scott .... New Orleans, LA
Willis, Steven M. .... Corunna, MI
Willis, Stuart W. .... Martinez, CA
Willis, Susan A. .... Marlborough, MA
Willis, Sylvia R. .... San Francisco, CA
Willis, Terence A. .... San Antonio, TX
Willis, Terry E. .... Marietta, GA
Willis, Thomas A. .... San Francisco, CA
Willis, Thomas E., II United States Tax Court, GV
Willis, Tina Michelle .... Orlando, FL
Willis, Todd L. .... Akron, OH
Willis, Tonya R. .... Knoxville, TN
Willis, Van T. .... New Albany, IN
Willis, Victoria A.B. .... Fredericksburg, VA
Willis, W. Brett .... Oklahoma City, OK
Willis, W. Reese, III .... Nashville, TN
Willis & Watson .... Cleveland, OH
Willis, Wayne G. .... Shaker Heights, OH
Willis, Wayne P. .... Pensacola, FL
Willis, Wendy Rae .... Salem, OR
Willis, Wilford D. .... La Mesa, CA
Willis, Willett Ranney, IV .... Denver, CO
Willis, William E. .... New York, NY
Willis, William J. .... Atlanta, GA
Willis, William J. .... Milwaukee, WI
Willis, William L. .... Frankfort, KY
Willis, William L., Jr. .... Columbus, OH
Willis, William Moore, IV .... Statesville, NC
Willis, William R., Jr. .... Nashville, TN
Willis, William T. .... Knoxville, TN
Willis, William T. .... Austin, TX
Willis & Willis .... Chico, CA
Iowa City, IA
North Andover, MA
El Campo, TX
Willis, Wm. G. .... Buffalo, NY
Williscroft, Beverly R. .... Concord, CA
Williscroft, Beverly R. .... San Francisco, CA
Willis-Green, Sue .... Nashville, TN
Willison, Allegra A. .... Incline Village, NV
Willison, David P. .... Midland, MI
Willison, Eric F. .... Columbus, OH
Willison, L. David, III .... Philadelphia, PA
Willison, Michael H. .... Lakeland, FL
Willison, Michael K. .... Moorestown, NJ
Philadelphia, PA
Willison, Stephen .... Grand Rapids, MI
Willisson, Robert E. .... Huntsville, AL
Williston, James S. .... Honolulu, HI
Williston, McGibbon & Kuehn Barrington, IL
Williston, Neil C. .... Waterford, MI
Willits, Barry A. .... Phoenix, AZ
Willits, Chad E. .... Cincinnati, OH
Willits, Charles W. .... Orlando, FL
Willits & Deisler .... Orlando, FL
Willits, George W. .... Wheaton, IL
Willits, John C. .... Jonesboro, GA
Willits, Phillip H. .... Edmond, OK
Willits, Richard H. .... Lake Worth, FL
Willits, Richard H., P.A. .... Lake Worth, FL
Willitt, Troy E. .... New York, NY
Willitts, Karen Tichenor .... Springfield, NJ
Willitts, Lisa M. .... Burlington, NJ
Williver, Sterling D. .... Bend, OR
Willkie Farr & Gallagher
Washington, DC
New York, NY
Willkie, Wendell L., II .... New York, NY
Willkom, Frank J. .... Sun Prairie, WI
Willman & Arnold, LLP .... Pittsburgh, PA
Willman, Charles H. .... Glenwood Springs, CO
Willman, Charles H., P.C. Glenwood Springs, CO
Willman, Don R. .... Houston, TX
Willman, George A. .... Palo Alto, CA
Willman, Hubert B. .... San Ramon, CA
Willman Law Firm .... Tucson, AZ

Wilson, Alan D. .... Kokomo, IN
Wilson, Alan K. .... Muncie, IN
Wilson, Alan M. .... Corydon, IA
Wilson, Alan R. .... Albuquerque, NM
Wilson, Alan W. .... Tempe, AZ
Wilson, Alexander D. .... York, PA
Wilson, Alexander E., III .... Atlanta, GA
Wilson, Alexander E., Jr. .... Atlanta, GA
Wilson, Allen G. .... Hot Springs, SD
Wilson, Allen T. .... Roanoke, VA
Wilson, Allison N. .... Washington, DC
Wilson, Alma .... Oklahoma City, OK
Wilson & Altschule .... Visalia, CA
Wilson, Alvin J. .... Saginaw, MI
Wilson, Amanda Ferguson .... Atlanta, GA
Wilson, Amy E. .... Midland, MI
Wilson, Amy Jardine .... Pittsburgh, PA
Wilson & Anderson .... Ashland, OH
Wilson, Andrea Gollattscheck .... Tampa, FL
Wilson, Andrew C. .... New Orleans, LA
Wilson, Andrew G., II .... Annapolis, MD
Wilson, Andrew H. .... San Francisco, CA
Wilson, Andrew H.D. .... Greenville, NC
Wilson, Andrew J. .... Omaha, NE
Wilson, Andrew J. .... Ocean Grove, NJ
Wilson, Andrew J. .... New York, NY
Wilson, Andrew P. .... Hilo, HI
Wilson, Andrew R. .... Washington, DC
Wilson, Anette Christine .... Denver, CO
Wilson, Angela M. .... Tempe, AZ
Wilson, Anita C. .... Chicago, IL
Wilson, Anita Rutkowski .... Washington, DC
Wilson, Ann .... Louisville, KY
Wilson, Ann Bell .... San Luis Obispo, CA
Wilson, Ann Carlisle .... Arlington, VA
Wilson, Ann L. .... San Francisco, CA
Wilson, Ann Michailenko .... Pittsburgh, PA
Wilson, Ann T. .... Seattle, WA
Wilson, Anne B. .... Elmdale, KS
Wilson, Anne Byrd .... Roanoke, VA
Wilson, Anne C. .... Kansas City, MO
Wilson, Anne E. .... Omaha, NE
Wilson, Anne Elizabeth .... Chicago, IL
Wilson, Anne M. .... Minneapolis, MN
Wilson, Annette R. .... St. Cloud, MN
Wilson, Anthony H. B. .... Woodbridge, VA
Wilson, Ardeth L., (Mrs.) .... Anderson, IN
Wilson, Arthur M. .... Washington, PA
Wilson, Arthur Philip, Jr. .... Dallas, TX
Wilson & Associates .... Phoenix, AZ
Tempe, AZ
Wilson & Associates .... Boulder, CO
Wilson and Associates .... St. Louis, MO
Wilson & Associates .... New York, NY
Wilson & Associates .... Memphis, TN
Little Rock, AR
Wilson & Associates, P.C. .... Houston, TX
Wilson, Aurjul H.
Charlotte Amalie, St. Thomas, VI
Wilson & Bailey .... Louisa, KY
Weston, WV
Wilson, Bakutis, Jones, Shell, McCully & Sawyer, P.C. .... Fort Worth, TX
Wilson, Bambi L. .... Baltimore, MD
Wilson, Barbara A. .... Birmingham, MI
Wilson, Barbara A. .... Seattle, WA
Wilson, Barbara Bowen .... Dallas, TX
Wilson, Barbara E. .... Kansas City, MO
Wilson, Barbara Jo .... Austin, TX
Wilson and Barrows, Ltd. .... Elko, NV
Wilson, Barry P. .... Boston, MA
Wilson, Barry S. .... San Diego, CA
Wilson, Bave, Conboy, Cozza & Couzens, P.C. .... New York, NY
White Plains, NY
Wilson, Benjamin C. .... Montgomery, AL
Wilson, Benjamin F. .... Washington, DC
Wilson, Benjamin T., P.C.
Salt Lake City, UT
Wilson, Bennett B. .... Scottsdale, AZ
Wilson, Bernard D. .... New York, NY
Wilson, Bert L., Jr. .... Williston, ND
Wilson, Beth Mezoff .... Los Angeles, CA
Wilson, Beth S. .... Palm Harbor, FL
Wilson, Betsy Warren .... Memphis, TN
Wilson, Betty K. .... Columbia, MO
Wilson, Biesecker, Tripp & Sink
Lexington, NC
Wilson, Billy .... Irvine, KY
Wilson, Billy O. .... Baton Rouge, LA
Wilson, Bob .... Sacramento, CA
Wilson, Bob, A Prof. Law Corp., Law Offices of .... Sacramento, CA
Wilson, Bob L. .... Wichita Falls, TX
Wilson, Bobbie J. .... San Francisco, CA
Wilson, Bonnie Binder .... Salinas, CA
Wilson, Bonnie C. .... Baton Rouge, LA
Wilson, Bonnie J. .... La Jolla, CA
Wilson, Bonnie L. .... Marietta, GA
Wilson, Bonum S., III .... Charleston, SC
Wilson, Borror, Dunn & Davis, LLP
Riverside, CA
San Bernardino, CA
Wilson & Bos .... Charlotte, NC
Wilson & Bowers .... Harrisonburg, VA
Wilson & Bowling .... New Orleans, LA
Gulfport, MS
Wilson & Bradley .... Murfreesboro, TN
Wilson, Bradley A. .... Franklin, TN
Wilson, Bradley L. .... Indianapolis, IN
Wilson, Bradley M. .... West Orange, NJ
Wilson, Bradley W. .... Jacksonville, IL
Wilson & Brandt, P.A. .... Baltimore, MD
Wilson & Bratt, P.A.
Hilton Head Island, SC
Wilson, Brenda Coker .... Naples, FL
Wilson, Brent L. .... Atlanta, GA
Wilson, Bret G. .... Kansas City, MO

Wilson, Brett R. .... Hagerstown, MD
Wilson, Brian A. .... Dedham, MA
Wilson, Brian C. .... Fort Mill, SC
Wilson, Brian C., P.A. .... Fort Mill, SC
Wilson, Brian R. .... Canton, OH
Wilson, Brian T. .... Orlando, FL
Wilson, Bridget J. .... San Diego, CA
Wilson, Bridgette Rhoden .... Elkins, WV
Wilson, Broadnax, Owens & Jackson
Milwaukee, WI
Wilson Brock & Irby, L.L.C. .... Atlanta, GA
Marietta, GA
Wilson & Brooks, P.C. .... Wartburg, TN
Wilson, Bruce .... Orem, UT
Wilson, Bruce A. .... Omaha, NE
Wilson, Bruce B. .... St. Davids, PA
Wilson, Bruce D. .... Ithaca, NY
Wilson, Bruce G. .... Chicago, IL
Wilson, Bruce H. .... Akron, OH
Wilson, Bruce N. .... Grove Hill, AL
Wilson, Bruce O. .... Broomfield, CO
Troy, MI
Wilson, Bruce R. .... Clarksville, AR
Wilson, Bruce Sandess .... Washington, DC
Wilson, Bruce W. .... Monroe, WI
Wilson, Bryan J. .... Palo Alto, CA
Wilson, Bunyan S., Jr. .... Ashland, KY
Wilson, C. Arthur, Jr. .... Pittsburgh, PA
Wilson, C. Darrel .... Tucson, AZ
Wilson, C. Gary .... Sylvania, OH
Wilson, C. Kelly .... Fayetteville, TN
Wilson, C. Kelly .... Shelbyville, TN
Wilson, C. Kelly .... Tullahoma, TN
Wilson, C. Martin, III .... Austin, TX
Wilson, C. Michael .... Charlotte, NC
Wilson, C. Michael, PLLC .... Charlotte, NC
Wilson, C. Richard .... Moundsville, WV
Wilson, C. Steven .... Minneapolis, MN
Wilson, C. Thomas .... Detroit, MI
Wilson, C. Thomas .... New Ulm, MN
Wilson, Cain & Acquaviva
Oklahoma City, OK
Wilson, Calvin W. .... Pensacola, FL
Wilson Campilongo, L.L.P.
San Francisco, CA
Wilson, Candace .... Jacksonville, FL
Wilson, Candace L. .... Okemos, MI
Wilson, Carin A. .... Seattle, WA
Wilson, Carl J., Jr. .... Macon, GA
Wilson, Carol .... Tucson, AZ
Wilson, Carol A. .... San Francisco, CA
Wilson, Carol A. .... Dallas, TX
Wilson, Carol J. .... Grandville, MI
St. Joseph, MI
Wilson, Carol L. .... Orinda, CA
Wilson, Carol M. .... Edina, MN
Wilson, Carole W.
Department of Housing and Urban Development,
Office of General Counsel, GV
Wilson, Caroline T. .... Charlotte, NC
Wilson, Carolyn A. .... Atlanta, GA
Wilson, Carolyn E. .... Raleigh, NC
Wilson, Carolyn Saffold .... Atlanta, GA
Wilson, Carrie R. .... San Diego, CA
Wilson, Casimir A. .... San Francisco, CA
Wilson, Cathy A. .... Paoli, PA
Wilson, Chalmers R. .... Miami, FL
Wilson, Chandra L. .... Columbus, GA
Wilson, Chandra P. .... Atlanta, GA
Wilson, Chapin E. (Shea), III .... Seattle, WA
Wilson, Chappell R. .... Cadiz, KY
Wilson, Charleene .... Wilmington, NC
Wilson, Charlene Adelle .... Baltimore, MD
Wilson, Charles Connell .... New Orleans, LA
Wilson, Charles D. .... Minneapolis, MN
Wilson, Charles E. .... Indianapolis, IN
Wilson, Charles E. .... Columbus, OH
Wilson, Charles E., III .... Atlanta, GA
Wilson, Charles E., Jr. .... Rockville, MD
Wilson, Charles Elliot, III .... Rockville, MD
Wilson, Charles F. .... Scranton, PA
Wilson, Charles F., Jr. .... Pikeville, KY
Wilson, Charles H., Jr. .... West Union, OH
Wilson, Charles J. .... Houston, TX
Wilson, Charles M. .... Toulon, IL
Wilson, Charles M. .... Sayre, OK
Wilson, Charles M., III .... Dallas, TX
Wilson, Charles R. .... Overland Park, KS
Wilson, Charles R. .... Detroit, MI
St. Clair Shores, MI
Wilson, Charles Rayburn .... Merced, CA
Wilson, Charles S., III .... Waukegan, IL
Wilson, Charles W. .... Salem, OR
Wilson, Charles W. .... Weston, WV
Wilson, Chastity K. .... Omaha, NE
Wilson, Cheryl D. .... Houston, TX
Wilson, Cheryl L. .... Chicago, IL
Wilson, Cheryl L. .... San Antonio, TX
Wilson, Chet K. .... Southfield, MI
Wilson, Christian B. .... Bel Air, MD
Wilson, Christie Milligan
Newport News, VA
Wilson, Christina Ritchey .... Newark, OH
Wilson, Christine Chambers
Washington, DC
Wilson, Christine J. .... Los Angeles, CA
Wilson, Christine L. .... Miami, FL
Wilson, Christine Sullivan .... Denver, CO
Wilson, Christopher .... Philadelphia, PA
Wilson, Christopher A. .... Costa Mesa, CA
Wilson, Christopher A. .... Los Angeles, CA
Wilson, Christopher A. .... Bethesda, MD
Wilson, Christopher B. .... Chicago, IL
Wilson, Christopher C. .... New York, NY
Wilson, Christopher F., & Associates
Torrance, CA
Wilson, Christopher G. .... Eureka, CA

Wilson, Christopher H.
Research Triangle Park, NC
Wilson, Christopher J. .... Treasury Department,
Internal Revenue Service, GV
Wilson, Christopher J. .... Cincinnati, OH
Wilson, Christopher J. .... Atoka, OK
Wilson, Christopher L. .... Phoenix, AZ
Wilson, Christopher M. .... New York, NY
Wilson, Christopher S. .... Syracuse, NY
Wilson, Christopher T. .... Overland Park, KS
Wilson, Christopher T. .... Detroit, MI
Wilson, Christopher T. .... Dallas, TX
Wilson & Chu, P.A. .... Minneapolis, MN
Wilson, Claire M. .... Channahon, IL
Wilson, Clarence B., Jr. .... College Park, GA
Wilson, Clarence S., Jr. .... Chicago, IL
Wilson, Claude R., Jr. .... Dallas, TX
Wilson, Claudette G. .... San Diego, CA
Wilson, Clay S. .... Lawrenceville, NJ
Wilson, Clayton D. .... Arcadia, CA
Wilson, Clifford .... Nashville, TN
Wilson, Clifford A. .... Houston, TX
Wilson, Clifford E. .... Madisonville, TN
Wilson, Clifford H. .... Syracuse, NY
Wilson, Clifford R. .... Walnut Creek, CA
Wilson, Clyde A., Jr. .... San Angelo, TX
Wilson, Clyde H., Jr. .... Sarasota, FL
Wilson, Clyde L., Jr. .... Houston, TX
Wilson, Coleman Kenneth .... Montgomery, AL
Wilson, Connie L. .... Harrisburg, PA
Wilson, Coquese .... Farmington Hills, MI
Wilson & Corbin, A P.L.C. .... San Diego, CA
Wilson, Corinna Vecsey .... Harrisburg, PA
Wilson, Cory Todd .... Jackson, MS
Wilson, Courtney A. .... Chicago, IL
Wilson, Courtney B. .... Miami, FL
Wilson, Craig .... New York, NY
Wilson, Craig A. .... St. Louis, MO
Wilson, Craig E. .... San Bernardino, CA
Wilson, Craig F. .... New York, NY
Wilson, Craig P. .... Harrisburg, PA
Wilson & Craig, Professional Corporation
Eldora, IA
Hubbard, IA
Wilson, Craig R. .... Cardiff-By-The-Sea, CA
Wilson, Craig R. .... North Palm Beach, FL
Wilson, Craig R., P.A.
North Palm Beach, FL
West Palm Beach, FL
Wilson, Cribbs, Goren & Flaum, A Professional Corporation .... Houston, TX
Wilson, Curt H. .... Boston, MA
Wilson, Curtis G. .... Treasury Department,
Internal Revenue Service, GV
Wilson, Curtis R. .... St. Louis, MO
Wilson and Cushman .... Springfield, OH
Wilson, Cynthia L. .... Houston, TX
Wilson, Cynthia L. .... Charleston, WV
Wilson, Cynthia P. .... Jackson, MS
Wilson, Cynthia Schmeltekopf .... Dallas, TX
Wilson, D. Edward, Jr. .... Washington, DC
Wilson, D. Hershel .... Banning, CA
Yucaipa, CA
Wilson, D. Jay .... Ogden, UT
Wilson, D. Stuart .... Wilmette, IL
Wilson, Dale .... San Antonio, TX
Wilson, Dale S. .... Green Cove Springs, FL
Wilson, Dale S., P.A.
Green Cove Springs, FL
Orange Park, FL
Wilson, Dale T. .... Florence, KY
Wilson, Dale V. .... Akron, OH
Wilson, Dan A. .... Prescott, AZ
Wilson, Dan E. .... Sun City, AZ
Wilson, Dan E. .... Grand Junction, CO
Wilson, Dan H. .... West Chester, PA
Wilson, Dana F. .... Hazel Park, MI
Rochester, MI
Wilson, Dana M. S. .... Baltimore, MD
Wilson, Daniel A. .... Boston, MA
Wilson, Daniel C. .... Rome, NY
Wilson, Daniel J. .... Boston, MA
Wilson, Daniel Joseph .... Downey, CA
Wilson, Daniel M. .... Huntsville, AL
Wilson, Daniel P. .... Centerville, IA
Wilson, Daniel T. .... Akron, OH
Wilson, Daryl Ann .... Portland, OR
Wilson, David .... Indianapolis, IN
Wilson, David A. .... Citrus Heights, CA
Wilson, David A. .... Redding, CA
Wilson, David A. .... Washington, DC
Wilson, David A. .... Highland, IN
Wilson, David A. .... Timonium, MD
Wilson, David A. .... Boston, MA
Wilson, David A. .... Greenville, SC
Wilson, David B. .... Denver, CO
Wilson, David B. .... Boston, MA
Wilson, David B. .... Salisbury, NC
Wilson, David C. .... Palo Alto, CA
Wilson, David D. .... Hartford City, IN
Wilson, David D. .... West Union, OH
Wilson, David D. .... Oklahoma City, OK
Wilson, David D. .... Lancaster, PA
Wilson, David D., Jr. .... West Union, OH
Wilson, David D., (P.A.) .... Little Rock, AR
Wilson, David E. .... Boston, MA
Wilson, David E. .... Gulfport, MS
Wilson, David E. .... Portland, OR
Wilson, David E. .... Seattle, WA
Wilson, David G. .... Washington, DC
Wilson, David G. .... Kenvil, NJ
Wilson, David G. .... Nashville, TN
Wilson, David H. .... Sonoma, CA
Wilson, David H. .... Atlanta, GA
Wilson, David H. .... Akron, OH
Wilson, David H., Jr. .... Perrysburg, OH
Wilson, David H., Jr. .... Portland, OR
Wilson, David I. .... Washington, DC

Wilson, David, II .... Houston, TX
Wilson, David, III .... Winter Haven, FL
Wilson, David, III, P.A. .... Winter Haven, FL
Wilson, David J. .... Los Angeles, CA
Wilson, David K., & Associates
Sherman, TX
Wilson, David K. W., Jr. .... Helena, MT
Wilson, David L. .... Kimball, NE
Wilson, David L. .... Stigler, OK
Wilson, David L. .... Haverford, PA
Wilson, David L., Jr. .... Winston-Salem, NC
Wilson, David M. .... Birmingham, AL
Wilson, David M. .... Camp Verde, AZ
Wilson, David M. .... Prescott, AZ
Wilson, David M. .... San Francisco, CA
Wilson, David M. .... Springfield, IL
Wilson, David M. .... Crown Point, IN
Wilson, David M. .... Montpelier, VT
Wilson, David O. .... Eugene, OR
Wilson, David P. .... Omaha, NE
Wilson, David P. .... Beaumont, TX
Wilson, David R. .... Chula Vista, CA
Wilson, David R. .... Lincoln, NE
Wilson, David R. .... Richfield, OH
Wilson, David R. .... Houston, TX
Wilson, David R. .... Seattle, WA
Wilson, David S., III .... Little Rock, AR
West Memphis, AR
Wilson, David T., II .... Radcliff, KY
Wilson, David T., Jr. .... Louisville, MS
Wilson, David V. .... Lufkin, TX
Wilson, David W. .... Phoenix, AZ
Wilson, David W. .... Buffalo, NY
Wilson, David W., Jr. .... Corsicana, TX
Wilson, Dawn .... Rosemead, CA
Wilson, Dawn A. .... Washington, DC
Wilson, Dawn M. .... New York, NY
Wilson, Dean L. .... Zanesville, OH
Wilson, Dean Robert .... Gulfport, MS
Wilson, Deanna LaShun .... Oakland, CA
Wilson, Deanne .... Morristown, NJ
Wilson, Deaundres Diez .... Minneapolis, MN
Wilson, Deborah A. .... New York, NY
Wilson, Deborah, (A Prof. Law Corp.)
New Orleans, LA
Wilson, Deborah A. J. .... Fairfax, VA
Wilson, Deborah A. K. .... Salem, OR
Wilson, Deborah J. .... Oakland, CA
Wilson, Deborah L. .... Las Vegas, NV
Wilson, Deborah M. .... Cherry Hill, NJ
Wynnewood, PA
Wilson, Debra A. .... Atlanta, GA
Wilson, Debra A. .... St. Paul, MN
Wilson, Debra Black .... Birmingham, AL
Wilson, Debra D. .... Wilson, NY
Wilson, DeCamp & Talbott, P.S.C.
Lexington, KY
Wilson Deege Dollar and Despotovich, Law Offices of .... West Des Moines, IA
Wilson, DeGraw & Miller, L.L.P.
Winston-Salem, NC
Wilson, Denise .... New York, NY
Wilson, Dennis B. .... Washington, DC
Wilson, Dennis C. .... Hawthorne, NV
Wilson, Dennis K. .... Little Rock, AR
Wilson, Dennis K. .... North Little Rock, AR
Wilson, Dennis L. .... Beverly Hills, CA
Wilson, Dennis M. .... Chicago, IL
Wilson, Dennis O. .... The Woodlands, TX
Wilson, Dennis P. .... Dexter, MO
Wilson, Dennis W. .... Schaumburg, IL
Wilson, Denny R. .... Independence, IA
Wilson, Denton J. .... San Luis Obispo, CA
Wilson, Derek H. .... Los Angeles, CA
Wilson, Derrick H. .... New Albany, IN
Wilson, Diane .... Pleasant Hill, CA
Wilson, Diane K. .... Washington, DC
Wilson, Diane Westwood .... New York, NY
Wilson, Dolores Pegram .... Freehold, NJ
Wilson, Don L. .... Abilene, TX
Wilson, Don (Randy), III .... Abilene, TX
Wilson, Donald A. .... Redwood City, CA
Wilson, Donald C. .... Eldora, IA
Wilson, Donald D. .... Los Angeles, CA
Wilson, Donald E. .... Fayetteville, AR
Wilson, Donald E. .... Denver, CO
Wilson, Donald E., P.A. .... Fayetteville, AR
Wilson, Donald H. .... Lihue, HI
Wilson, Donald H. .... Lihue, HI
Wilson, Donald H., III .... Hampstead, MD
Wilson, Donald H., Jr. .... Bartow, FL
Wilson, Donald J. .... Eugene, OR
Wilson, Donald, Jr. .... Phoenix, AZ
Wilson, Donald K., Jr. .... Los Angeles, CA
Wilson, Donald L. .... Downey, CA
Wilson, Donald L. .... Washington, DC
Wilson, Donald L. .... Bossier City, LA
Wilson, Donald L. .... Fort Worth, TX
Wilson, Donald M. .... Boulder, CO
Wilson, Donald N. .... Cedartown, GA
Wilson, Donald N. .... Chicago, IL
Wilson, Donald R. .... Phoenix, AZ
Wilson, Donald R. .... Jena, LA
Wilson, Donald R. .... St. Louis, MO
Wilson, Donald R. .... Oklahoma City, OK
Wilson, Donald R. .... Portland, OR
Wilson, Donald R. .... Salt Lake City, UT
Wilson, Donn H. .... Bakersfield, CA
Wilson, Donna .... Spokane, WA
Wilson, Donna L. .... Washington, DC
Wilson, Donna M. .... Kansas City, MO
Wilson, Donna M. .... New York, NY
Wilson, Donna M.P. .... Bethesda, MD
Wilson, Donnie E. ....
Department of Labor, GV
Wilson, Doris K. .... Chicago, IL
Wilson, Dorothy D. .... Atlanta, GA
Wilson, Dorothy Roth .... Washington, DC

Wilson, Douglas A. ... Irvine, CA
Wilson, Douglas A. ... Akron, OH
Wilson, Douglas A. ... Tulsa, OK
Wilson, Douglas A. ... Pittsburgh, PA
Wilson, Douglas A. ... Yakima, WA
Wilson, Douglas B. ... Houston, TX
Wilson, Douglas C. ... Washington, DC
Wilson, Douglas C. ... Batesville, IN
Wilson, Douglas E. ... Stockton, CA
Wilson, Douglas K. ... Pueblo, CO
Wilson, Douglas L. ... Naples, FL
Wilson, Douglas P. ... Platte City, MO
Wilson, Douglas S. ... Scottsdale, AZ
Wilson & Drinkard ... Grove Hill, AL
Wilson, Duane E. ... San Diego, CA
Wilson, D.W. ... Tuscaloosa, AL
Wilson, E. Bryan ... Tallahassee, FL
Wilson, E. Calhoun ... Tuscaloosa, AL
Wilson, E. Hamilton, Jr. ... Montgomery, AL
Wilson, E. Reynolds ... Washington, DC
Wilson, E. Tyler ... Louisville, KY
Wilson, Earl ... Medfield, MA
Wilson, Earl R. ... Jackson, MS
Wilson, Earl S., Jr. ... Lexington, KY
Wilson, Eddie W. ... Virginia Beach, VA
Wilson, Edmund A. ... Pascagoula, MS
Wilson, Edward A. ... Whittier, CA
Wilson, Edward A. ... Lebanon, KY
Wilson, Edward C. ... La Grange, IL
Wilson, Edward C., Jr. ... Washington, DC
Wilson, Edward E., Jr. ... Huntsville, AL
Wilson, Edward E., Sr. ... Blountville, TN
Wilson, Edward J. ... Newark, NJ
Wilson, Edward R., III ... Detroit, MI
Wilson, Edward Reynolds ... Washington, DC
Wilson, Edwin G., Jr. ... Eden, NC
Wilson, Edwin J. ... Long Beach, CA
Wilson, Edwin J. ... Baton Rouge, LA
Wilson, Edwin J., Jr. ... Oakland, CA
Wilson, Edwin W. ... Bakersfield, CA
Wilson, Edwin W., Inc., A Prof. Law Corp.
Bakersfield, CA
Wilson, Edwina A. ... Waukesha, WI
Wilson, Eileen ... Houston, TX
Wilson, Elaine D. ... Arcadia, CA
Wilson, Elaine Waterhouse
Indianapolis, IN
Wilson, Elisa L. ... Portland, OR
Wilson, Elizabeth ... Tucson, AZ
Wilson, Elizabeth A. ... Chicago, IL
Wilson, Elizabeth A. ... Eatontown, NJ
Wilson, Elizabeth A. ... New York, NY
Wilson, Elizabeth B. ... Redwood City, CA
Wilson, Elizabeth Davis ... Russellville, KY
Wilson, Elizabeth Ferguson ... Plano, TX
Wilson, Elizabeth L. ... New York, NY
Wilson, Elizabeth M. ... Brentwood, TN
Wilson, Elizabeth Staggs ... Los Angeles, CA
Wilson, Elser, Moskowitz, Edelman & Dicker LLP ... Los Angeles, CA
San Diego, CA
San Francisco, CA
Washington, DC
Miami, FL
Chicago, IL
Baltimore, MD
Newark, NJ
Albany, NY
Garden City, NY
New York, NY
White Plains, NY
Philadelphia, PA
Dallas, TX
Houston, TX
Wilson, Elta M. ... Los Angeles, CA
Wilson, Elwood C. ... Canton, OH
Wilson, Engstrom, Corum & Coulter
Little Rock, AR
Wilson, Eric J. ... Chicago, IL
Wilson, Eric J. ... Syracuse, NY
Wilson, Eric J. ... St. Marys, OH
Wilson, Eric L. ... Tuscaloosa, AL
Wilson, Eric M. ... Tuscaloosa, AL
Wilson, Eric R. ... Los Angeles, CA
Wilson, Eric R. ... Nashua, NH
Wilson, Eric S. ... Hazel Park, MI
Rochester, MI
Wilson, Ernest G. ... Baltimore, MD
Wilson, Ervin F. ... Elmhurst, IL
Wilson, E. S. ... Sausalito, CA
Wilson, Eugene B. ... Santa Rosa, CA
Wilson, Eugene D. ... Corpus Christi, TX
Wilson, Eugene S. ... San Marcos, CA
Wilson, Eva J. ... Atlanta, GA
Wilson, Evan Keith ... Independence, MO
Wilson, Evelyn Jo ... Houston, TX
Wilson, Evelyn L. ... Baton Rouge, LA
Wilson, Evelyn Zabel ... Topeka, KS
Wilson, F. Bradford, Jr. ... Macon, GA
Wilson, F. Scott ... East Hartford, CT
Wilson, Fad, Jr. ... Houston, TX
Wilson, Faith M. ... Seattle, WA
Wilson, Fernald & Foley ... Portland, ME
Wilson, Floyd D. ... Albuquerque, NM
Wilson, Foredonia M. ... Riverdale, MD
Harrisburg, PA
Wilson, Forrest C., III ... Mobile, AL
Wilson, Fowler & Fusco ... Indianola, IA
Wilson & Frame ... Kinsley, KS
Wilson, Frame, Benninger & Metheney
Morgantown, WV
Wilson, Francis P. ... Branford, CT
Wilson, Francis W. ... Camden, NJ
Wilson, Frank C., III ... Selma, AL
Wilson, Frank F., II ... Lexington, KY
Wilson, Frank K. ... Alamogordo, NM
Wilson, Frank L., III ... Atlanta, GA
Wilson, Frank M. ... Montgomery, AL
Wilson, Frank M., III ... San Antonio, TX
Wilson, Frank W. ... Gaithersburg, MD
Wilson, Franklin H. ... Los Angeles, CA
Wilson, Fred E. ... West Columbia, TX
Wilson, Fred P. ... Memphis, TN
Wilson, Fred S. ... Houston, TX
Wilson, Frederick J., III ... Miami, FL
Wilson, Fredrika A. ... New York, NY
Wilson, Fucillo & Shields, L.C.
Fairmont, WV
Wilson, G. Garland ... Midlothian, VA
Wilson, G. Gray ... Winston-Salem, NC
Wilson, G. Richard ... Cincinnati, OH
Wilson, G. Thomas ... West Lafayette, IN
Wilson, Gail P. ... Philadelphia, PA
Wilson, Gail S. ... New York, NY
Wilson, Galen C. ... Duluth, MN
Wilson, Garbee & Rosenberger
Lynchburg, VA
Wilson, Garth D.
Pension Benefit Guaranty Corporation, Office of the General Counsel, GV
Wilson, Gary A. ... Philadelphia, PA
Wilson, Gary D. ... Washington, DC
Wilson, Gary D. ... Maitland, FL
Wilson, Gary D. ... Boston, MA
Wilson, Gary D. ... Syracuse, NY
Wilson, Gary Edward ... Chico, CA
Wilson, Gary H. ... Albany, NY
Wilson, Gary K. ... Naples, FL
Wilson, Gary L. ... Minneapolis, MN
Wilson, Gary M. ... Grosse Pointe, MI
Wilson, Gene A. ... Louisa, KY
Wilson, Geoffrey A. ... Greenfield, MA
Wilson, Geoffrey Tyler ... Denver, CO
Wilson, George A., II ... Naples, FL
Wilson, George A., Jr. ... Des Moines, IA
Wilson, George David ... Mountain View, CA
Wilson, George E. ... Willingboro, NJ
Wilson, George H., II ... Enid, OK
Wilson, George J. ... Mineola, NY
Riverhead, NY
Wilson, George N. ... Dallas, TX
Wilson, George O., III ... Tampa, FL
Wilson, George S., III ... Owensboro, KY
Wilson, Gerald E. ... San Juan Capistrano, CA
Wilson, Gerald E. ... Providence, RI
Wilson, Gerald G. ... Irvine, CA
Wilson, Gerald G. ... Spartanburg, SC
Wilson, Gerald G., P.A. ... Spartanburg, SC
Wilson, Gerald L. ... Marinette, WI
Wilson, Gerald W. ... Boone, NC
Wilson, Gilbert H. ... Virginia Beach, VA
Wilson, Gina T. ... Henderson, NV
Wilson, Ginger F. ... Cleveland, TN
Wilson, Glen W. ... Rockford, IL
Wilson, Glenn ... Clovis, CA
Wilson, Glenn R. ... Cleveland, OH
Wilson, Gloria E. ... Chicago, IL
Wilson, Goozman, Bernstein & Markuski
Laurel, MD
Wilson, Gordon ... Washington, DC
Wilson, Gordon C. ... Washington, DC
Wilson, Gordon F., Jr., (P.L.C.)
New Orleans, LA
Wilson, Gordon P. ... New Orleans, LA
Wilson, Graves H., Jr. ... Florence, SC
Wilson, Gray W. ... Castlewood, VA
Wilson, Green & Cecere ... Greenwood, IN
Indianapolis, IN
Wilson, Greg S. ... Oklahoma City, OK
Wilson, Gregg E. ... Wilmington, DE
Wilson, Gregg H. ... Essex Junction, VT
Wilson, Gregg J. ... Boston, MA
Wilson, Gregory ... New York, NY
Wilson, Gregory D. ... St. Marys, OH
Wilson, Gregory F. ... San Francisco, CA
Reno, NV
Wilson, Gregory J. ... Des Moines, IA
Wilson, Gregory M. ... Laurel, MD
Wilson, Gregory M. ... Spokane, WA
Wilson, Gregory O. ... Baton Rouge, LA
Wilson, Gregory R. ... Cincinnati, OH
Wilson, Gregory R., Co., L.P.A.
Cincinnati, OH
Wilson, Gregory S. ... Tacoma, WA
Wilson, Greta ... Selma, AL
Wilson, Greta L. ... New Orleans, LA
Wilson Grosenheider Moore & Jacobs, L.L.P. ... Austin, TX
Wilson Group, The, Ltd. ... Minneapolis, MN
Wilson, Guay P. ... Redlands, CA
Wilson, Guy A. ... San Francisco, CA
Wilson, Guy C. ... Scottsdale, AZ
Wilson, Guy R. ... Califon, NJ
Wilson, Guy S. ...
Department of Housing and Urban Development, GV
Wilson, H. James ... Boston, MA
Wilson, H. Norman, Jr. ... Elkton, MD
Wilson, H. Norman, Jr., P.A. ... Elkton, MD
Wilson, Hajek & Shapiro, P.C.
Virginia Beach, VA
Wilson, Halbrook & Bayard, Professional Association ... Georgetown, DE
Wilson, Harold G. ... Ypsilanti, MI
Wilson, Harold J. ... Boston, MA
Wilson, Harold S. ... Clearwater, FL
Wilson, Harold S., P.A. ... Clearwater, FL
Wilson, Harold W. ... Parkersburg, WV
Wilson, Harrel, Jr. ... New Orleans, LA
Wilson, Harrell, Smith, Boles & Farrington, P.A. ... Pensacola, FL
Wilson, Harrison B., III ... Richmond, VA
Wilson, Harry A., Jr. ... Indianapolis, IN
Wilson, Harry B., Jr. ... St. Louis, MO
Wilson, Harry C., Jr. ... Sumter, SC
Wilson, Harry E. ... Raleigh, NC
Wilson, Harry K. ... Clayton, CA
Wilson, Harry L. ... Chicago, IL
Wilson, Harry M., III ... Jacksonville, FL
Wilson, Harvey A., Jr. ... Austin, TX
Wilson, Heather L. ... Indianapolis, IN
Wilson, Heather M. ... Washington, DC
Wilson, Helen T. ... Chicago, IL
Wilson, Henry ... Anchorage, AK
Wilson, Henry Hall, III ... Charlotte, NC
Wilson, Henry S. ... Trumann, AR
Wilson, Hilary B., (Mr.) ... Berea, OH
Wilson, Hillary M. ... Scotts Valley, CA
Wilson, Hinton & Wood, P.A. ... Corinth, MS
Wilson, Holly J. ... Hartford, CT
Wilson, Homer C. ... Colorado Springs, CO
Wilson, Howard ... New York, NY
Wilson, Howard D. ... Burbank, CA
Wilson, Howard D., Jr. ... Cottage City, MD
Wilson, Howard F. ... Columbus, OH
Wilson, Howard G. ... Dallas, TX
Wilson, Howard L. ... Oklahoma City, OK
Wilson, Howard W. ... Murfreesboro, TN
Wilson, Howell A. ... Surfside Beach, SC
Wilson, Hugh ... Abbeville, GA
Wilson, Hugh M. ... Lenoir, NC
Wilson, Hugh R. ... Cleveland, OH
Wilson, Hugh Steven ... Los Angeles, CA
San Diego, CA
Wilson, Hunter ... Laguna Beach, CA
Wilson, Ian J. ... Richmond, VA
Wilson, Ira ... Bloomfield Hills, MI
Wilson, Irene E. ... Salt Lake City, UT
Wilson & Iseman, L.L.P. ... Greensboro, NC
Winston-Salem, NC
Wilson, Isvara M.A. ... Charlotte, NC
Wilson, J. Ashley, Jr. ... Palo Alto, CA
Wilson, J. Charles ... Mobile, AL
Wilson, J. Christy, III ... Orlando, FL
Wilson, J. Clancy ... San Diego, CA
Wilson, J. Elizabeth ... Mobile, AL
Wilson, J. Everett ... Miami, FL
Wilson, J. Michael ... San Diego, CA
Wilson, J. Michael ... Charlotte, NC
Wilson, J. Randolph ... Washington, DC
Wilson, J. Robert ... Golden, CO
Wilson, J. Robt. ... Akron, OH
Wilson, J. Scott ... Austin, TX
Wilson, J. William ... Austin, TX
Wilson, Jack ... Anniston, AL
Wilson, Jack A. ... Vincennes, IN
Wilson, Jack L., Jr. ... Burnsville, NC
Wilson, Jack R., III ... Richmond, VA
Wilson, Jackson D., II ... Dallas, TX
Wilson, Jacqueline A. ... Clarksburg, WV
Wilson, Jacqueline Annette
Department of Justice, Environment and Natural Resources Division, GV
Wilson, Jacquelyn D. ... Laguna Niguel, CA
Wilson, Jacquelyn K. ... San Jose, CA
Wilson, James A. ... Phoenix, AZ
Wilson, James A. ... Weymouth, MA
Wilson, James A. ... Fairmont, MN
Wilson, James A. ... Greensboro, NC
Wilson, James A. ... Raleigh, NC
Wilson, James A. ... Columbus, OH
Wilson, James A. S. ... Chattanooga, TN
Wilson, James B. ... Seattle, WA
Wilson, James B., (P.C.) ... Chicago, IL
Wilson, James Bradley ... Durham, NC
Wilson, James C. ... Mission Viejo, CA
Wilson, James C. ... Department of Justice, Civil Division, GV
Wilson, James C. ... Winston-Salem, NC
Wilson, James C., Jr. ... Birmingham, AL
Wilson, James Christopher ... Muskegon, MI
Wilson, James D. ... Chicago, IL
Wilson, James D. ... Ann Arbor, MI
Wilson, James D. ... Akron, OH
Wilson, James D. ... Cleveland, OH
Wilson, James D. ... Memphis, TN
Wilson, James D., III ... Prichard, AL
Wilson, James E. ... Jasper, AL
Wilson, James E. ... Midland, MI
Wilson, James E., Jr. ... Carson City, NV
Wilson, James Eldon ... Montgomery, AL
Wilson, James F. ... Lodi, CA
Wilson, James F. ... Wartburg, TN
Wilson, James G. ... Clovis, NM
Wilson, James H. ... Merced, CA
Wilson, James H. ... Houston, TX
Wilson, James H., Jr. ... Atlanta, GA
Wilson, James I. ... Washington, DC
Wilson, James J. ... Los Angeles, CA
Wilson, James J. ... St. Louis, MO
Wilson, James J. ... Scranton, PA
Wilson, James (Jim) H. ... Birmingham, AL
Wilson, James K. ... Houston, TX
Wilson, James L. ... Surf City, NJ
Wilson, James L. ... Liberty, NC
Wilson, James Louis ... Irvine, CA
Wilson, James M. ... Pensacola, FL
Wilson, James M. ... Yorkville, IL
Wilson, James M. ... Philadelphia, PA
Wilson, James M. ... Richmond, VA
Wilson, James M. ... Clarksburg, WV
Wilson, James M., Jr. ... Houston, TX
Wilson, James McCord ... Dallas, TX
Wilson, James O. ... Cheyenne, WY
Wilson, James O., Jr. ... Fayetteville, GA
Wilson, James O., Jr. ... Marietta, GA
Wilson, James P. ... Cockeysville, MD
Wilson, James P. ... North Hampton, OH
Wilson, James P., Jr. ... Columbus, MS
Tupelo, MS
Memphis, TN
Wilson, James R. ... Tampa, FL
Wilson, James R. ... Hyannis, MA
Wilson, James R. ... Lansing, MI
Wilson, James R. ... Cleveland, OH
Wilson, James R. ... Jasper, TX
Wilson, James R. ... Salt Lake City, UT
Wilson, James S. ... Rockville, MD
Wilson, James T. ... Oakland, CA
Wilson, James T. ... Visalia, CA
Wilson, James T. ... Countryside, IL
Wilson, James T., Jr. ... Augusta, GA
Wilson, James W. ... Elwood, IN
Wilson, James W. ... Wichita, KS
Wilson, James W. ... Allen, TX
Wilson, James W. ... Houston, TX
Wilson, Jamie M. ... San Antonio, TX
Wilson, Jane A. ... Baltimore, MD
Wilson, Jane Beaver ... New York, NY
Wilson, Jane E. ... Washington, DC
Wilson, Jane P. ... Eastlake, OH
Wilson, Jane P., & Associates Co. L.P.A.
Cleveland, OH
Eastlake, OH
Wilson, Janelle C. ... Chehalis, WA
Wilson, Janet G. ... Columbia, SC
Wilson, Janet L. ...
United States Tax Court, GV
Wilson, Janet L. ... Des Moines, IA
Wilson, Janet Lee ... Palo Alto, CA
Wilson, Janet M. ... Los Angeles, CA
Wilson, Janice M. ... Boston, MA
Wilson, Janice R. ... Portland, OR
Wilson, Janis L. ... Philadelphia, PA
Wilson, Janyce M. ... Morristown, NJ
Wilson, Jas Y. ... Lake City, FL
Wilson, Jason Haruo ... Los Angeles, CA
Wilson, Jason T ... Portland, OR
Wilson, Jay Chambers ... Atlanta, GA
Wilson, Jean ... Durham, NC
Wilson, Jean Eddy, (Mr.) ... Orlando, FL
Wilson, Jean M. ... Chicago, IL
Wilson, Jean M. ... Baraboo, WI
Wilson, Jeanne Klinefelter ... Houston, TX
Wilson, Jeanne M. ... Davis, CA
Wilson, Jeffrey ... Prineville, OR
Wilson, Jeffrey B. ... Newark, NJ
Wilson, Jeffrey C. ... Bay City, MI
Wilson, Jeffrey C. ... Sherman, TX
Wilson, Jeffrey D. ... Farmington Hills, MI
Wilson, Jeffrey F. ... Nashville, TN
Wilson, Jeffrey L. ... Durham, NC
Wilson, Jeffrey L. ... Tulsa, OK
Wilson, Jeffrey M. ... Palm Desert, CA
Wilson, Jeffrey M. ... Boise, ID
Wilson, Jeffrey R. ... Susanville, CA
Wilson, Jeffrey R. ... Pittsburgh, PA
Wilson, Jeffrey S. ... Schaumburg, IL
Wilson, Jeffrey S. ... Waldwick, NJ
Wilson, Jeffrey S. ... Philadelphia, PA
Wilson, Jeffrey T. ... San Diego, CA
Wilson, Jennifer A. ... Fairfield, CA
Wilson, Jennifer Hanson ... Laguna Beach, CA
Wilson, Jennifer K. ... Kansas City, MO
Wilson, Jennifer Lynn ... Quincy, IL
Wilson, Jennifer S. ... Houston, TX
Wilson, Jennifer Treese ... San Diego, CA
Wilson, Jerald R. ... Tucson, AZ
Wilson, Jeril B. ... Provo, UT
Wilson, Jerome L. ... New York, NY
Wilson, Jerry Cord ... Oklahoma City, OK
Wilson, Jerry I. ... Honolulu, HI
Wilson, Jerry I., A Law Corporation
Honolulu, HI
Wilson, Jerry R. ... Oswego, KS
Wilson, Jesse B., III ... Fairfax, VA
Wilson, Jill G. ... Santa Cruz, CA
Wilson, Jill R. ... Greensboro, NC
Wilson, Jillian ... Baltimore, MD
Wilson, J. L., IV ... Greenwood, MS
Wilson, Joan Elizabeth ... Mobile, AL
Wilson, Joan Reed ... Palo Alto, CA
Wilson, Joanna Barratt ... Baton Rouge, LA
Wilson, Joanna Favaro ... Carson City, NV
Wilson, Joanne A. ... Cincinnati, OH
Wilson, Joanne B. ... Seattle, WA
Wilson, Jodi Givner ... Northbrook, IL
Wilson, Joe Marr ... Amarillo, TX
Wilson, Joe Morgan ... Senatobia, MS
Wilson, John ... Lincoln, ME
Wilson, John A. ... Palo Alto, CA
Wilson, John A. ... Lakewood, CO
Wilson, John A., P.C. ... Lakewood, CO
Wilson, John B. ... Salem, OR
Wilson, John B. ... Dallas, TX
Wilson, John B. ... Salt Lake City, UT
Wilson, John B., III ... Harrisburg, PA
Wilson, John B., Jr. ... Nashville, IN
Wilson, John C. ... San Francisco, CA
Wilson, John C., (P.C.) ... Austin, TX
Wilson, John D. ... Beverly Hills, CA
Wilson, John D. ... Atlanta, GA
Wilson, John D. ... Camden, NJ
Wilson, John D. ... Erie, PA
Wilson, John D., Jr. ... Seattle, WA
Wilson, John E. ... Redwood City, CA
Wilson, John E. ... Liberty Corner, NJ
Wilson, John F. ... Crestline, CA
Wilson, John F. ... Camden, NJ
Wilson, John F. ... Parsippany, NJ
Wilson, John F. ... Pittsburgh, PA
Wilson, John F. ... Dallas, TX
Wilson, John F. ... Everett, WA
Wilson, John F., III ... Houston, TX
Wilson, John F., Jr. ... Dallas, TX
Wilson, John H. ... New York, NY
Wilson, John H. ... Pittsburgh, PA
Wilson, John J. ... Santa Ana, CA
Wilson, John J. ... Department of Justice, Office of Justice Programs, GV
Wilson, John J. ... Royal Oak, MI

Wilson, John K. .... **Milwaukee, WI**
Wilson, John Kerr .... **Santa Barbara, CA**
Wilson, John L. .... Bowling Green, KY
Wilson, John L. .... Hilton Head Island, SC
Wilson, John L. .... **Austin, TX**
Wilson, John M. .... **New Orleans, LA**
Wilson, John M. .... Birmingham, MI
Wilson, John M. .... Monroe, MI
Wilson, John M. .... **New York, NY**
Wilson, John M. .... **Pittsburgh, PA**
Wilson, John M. .... Pittsburgh, PA
Wilson, John M., II .... **Rochester, NY**
Wilson, John M., III .... **Atlanta, GA**
Wilson, John Mark .... **Charlotte, NC**
Wilson, John P. .... Palo Alto, CA
Wilson, John P. .... Palo Alto, CA
Wilson, John P. .... San Francisco, CA
Wilson, John P. .... **Greenwood, IN**
Wilson, John P., III .... **Atlanta, GA**
Wilson, John R. .... **Denver, CO**
Wilson, John R. .... Louisville, KY
Wilson, John R. .... Bangor, ME
Wilson, John R. .... Troy, MI
Wilson, John R. .... Bend, OR
Wilson, John R. .... Waco, TX
Wilson, John R. .... **Tacoma, WA**
Wilson, John Richard .... Ennis, TX
Wilson, John Robert .... Sacramento, CA
Wilson, John Robert .... Concord, NH
Wilson, John S. .... Boulder, CO
Wilson, John S. .... St. Louis, MO
Wilson, John S. .... **Norfolk, VA**
Wilson, John S., III .... **Memphis, TN**
Wilson, John T. .... Elmira, NY
Wilson, John T. .... Richardson, TX
Wilson, John W., III .... Alexandria, VA
Wilson, John W., Jr. .... Atlanta, GA
Wilson, John-Douglas .... Houston, TX
Wilson & Johnson .... Marlton, NJ
Newtown, PA
Philadelphia, PA
Wilson and Johnson .... Houston, TX
Wilson, Johnson & Jaffer, P.A.
Sarasota, FL
Wilson, Johnson & Presser .... **Hartford, KY**
Owensboro, KY
Wilson, Jon Louis .... Lockport, NY
Wilson, Jon M. .... **Los Angeles, CA**
Orlando, FL
Wilson, Jon R. .... Boise, ID
Wilson, Jonathan B. .... **Atlanta, GA**
Wilson, Jonathan C. .... **Des Moines, IA**
Wilson, Jonathan C. .... **Dallas, TX**
Wilson, Jonathan M. .... **Chicago, IL**
Wilson, Joni S. .... Tempe, AZ
Wilson, Jordana W. .... Department of Labor, Office of the Solicitor, GV
Wilson, Joseph .... **Jena, LA**
Wilson, Joseph A. .... Pleasanton, CA
Wilson, Joseph A. .... **Rochester, NY**
Wilson, Joseph B. .... **Colorado Springs, CO**
Wilson, Joseph C., III .... **Chattanooga, TN**
Wilson, Joseph C., IV .... **Charleston, SC**
Wilson, Joseph Douglas
Department of Justice, Criminal Division, GV
Wilson, Joseph F. .... Muskogee, OK
Wilson, Joseph L. .... Chicago, IL
Wilson, Joseph Lopez .... Omaha, NE
Wilson, Joseph M. .... Anchorage, AK
Wilson, Joseph M. .... Baltimore, MD
Wilson, Joseph M. .... Burke, VA
Wilson, Joseph M., Jr. .... Creedmoor, NC
Durham, NC
Greensboro, NC
Raleigh, NC
Wilson, Joseph R. .... Toledo, OH
Wilson, Joslyn .... Tallahassee, FL
Wilson, Judge B., II .... **Lexington, KY**
Wilson, Judith K. .... Hawley, MN
Wilson, Julia T. .... Laurel, MD
Wilson, Juliana D. .... Anchorage, AK
Wilson, Julie L. .... New York, NY
Wilson, June Lubniewski .... Madison, WI
Wilson, Justin P. .... Nashville, TN
Wilson, K. Nicholas .... **Oklahoma City, OK**
Wilson, Karen .... **Minneapolis, MN**
Wilson, Karen L. .... Department of Justice, Office of Legislative Affairs, GV
Wilson, Karen M. .... **Winston-Salem, NC**
Wilson, Karin E. .... Columbus, OH
Wilson & Kates, P.C. .... Baldwin, MI
Ludington, MI
Scottville, MI
Wilson, Katherine L. .... Odessa, TX
Wilson, Kathleen A. .... Department of State, Office of the Legal Adviser, GV
Wilson, Kay, Jr. .... Muskogee, OK
Wilson, K. B. .... Indianapolis, IN
Wilson, Kehoe & Winingham
Connersville, IN
Indianapolis, IN
Muncie, IN
Richmond, IN
Wilson, Keith A. .... **Los Angeles, CA**
Wilson, Keith, Jr. .... Independence, MO
Wilson, Keith N. .... **Atlanta, GA**
Wilson, Keitha V. .... Round Rock, TX
Wilson, Kelly C. .... **Chicago, IL**
Wilson, Kelly M. .... Martinez, CA
Wilson, Kelly P. .... **New York, NY**
Wilson, Kemp J. .... **Billings, MT**
Wilson, Kenna & Borys, LLP
Los Angeles, CA
Wilson, Kenneth .... Albertville, AL
Wilson, Kenneth .... Sacramento, CA
Wilson, Kenneth .... Cincinnati, OH
Wilson, Kenneth A. .... **Santa Rosa, CA**
Wilson, Kenneth B. .... **Palo Alto, CA**
Wilson, Kenneth B. .... Roswell, NM
Wilson, Kenneth C. .... Newton, MA
Wilson, Kenneth J. .... **Barnwell, SC**
Wilson, Kenneth Joe, Jr. .... **Homewood, AL**
Wilson, Kenneth R. .... Philadelphia, PA
Wilson, Kenneth S. .... **Birmingham, MI**
Wilson, Kenneth W. .... Portland, OR
Wilson, Kent A. .... **Chicago, IL**
Wilson, Kent C. .... Santa Ana, CA
Wilson, Kent L. .... Houston, TX
Wilson, Kent S. .... Merrillville, IN
Wilson, Kent S. .... Clifton Forge, VA
Lexington, VA
Wilson, Kenyon J. .... Indianapolis, IN
Wilson, Kerry M. .... **Lakeland, FL**
Lake Wales, FL
Winter Haven, FL
Wilson & Kester, P.L.C. .... Traverse City, MI
Wilson, Kevin .... **Atlanta, GA**
Wilson, Kevin B. .... **Chattanooga, TN**
Wilson, Kevin L. .... **Nashville, TN**
Wilson, Kevin L. .... Odessa, TX
Wilson & Kiddy .... Stockton, CA
Wilson, Kim R. .... **Salt Lake City, UT**
Wilson, Kimber L. .... **New York, NY**
Wilson, Kimberly A. .... **Jacksonville, FL**
Wilson, Kimberly R. .... **Weirton, WV**
Wheeling, WV
Wilson, Kirby L., III .... River Rouge, MI
Wilson, Kirk Randolph
Walnut Creek, CA
Wilson, Kirtley E. .... **Decatur, IL**
Wilson & Kochheiser Co., L.P.A.
Marion, OH
Wilson, Koh Siok Tian .... Los Angeles, CA
Wilson, Kristin L. .... **Charleston, IL**
Wilson, Kristopher T. .... **New Orleans, LA**
Wilson, Kurt E. .... **Los Gatos, CA**
Wilson, Kurt E. .... Los Gatos, CA
Wilson, Kyle R. .... **Little Rock, AR**
Wilson, L. Albert .... Billerica, MA
Wilson, L. Byron .... **Houston, TX**
Wilson, L. Dean, Jr. .... **Joplin, MO**
Wilson, L. James .... **Bloomfield Hills, MI**
Wilson, L. Kay .... East Hartford, CT
Wilson, L. Lee .... Nashville, TN
Wilson, L. Matt .... **Atlanta, GA**
Wilson, L. Michelle .... Seattle, WA
Wilson, Lance D. .... **Walnut Creek, CA**
Wilson, Lanny T. .... Wilmington, NC
Wilson, Larry .... Pasadena, TX
Wilson, Larry G. .... Bakersfield, CA
Wilson, Larry G. .... Altoona, IA
Wilson, Larry J. .... Greencastle, IN
Wilson, Larry J. .... Shelby, NC
Wilson, Larry S. .... Houston, TX
Wilson, Laura E. .... **Abingdon, VA**
Wilson, Laura J. .... **Rochester, NY**
Wilson, Laura L. .... Tallahassee, FL
Wilson, Laura M. .... **Washington, DC**
Wilson, Lauren W. .... Beverly Hills, CA
Wilson, Laurence P. .... **San Francisco, CA**
Wilson, Lavona .... Little Rock, AR
Wilson Law Firm .... Edina, MN
Wilson Law Firm .... **Easley, SC**
Greenville, SC
Pickens, SC
Wilson Law Firm, The .... Naples, FL
Wilson Law Firm, The, P.C. .... **Atlanta, GA**
Wilson Law Group, LLC .... Evansville, WI
Wilson Law Offices .... **San Francisco, CA**
Wilson Law Offices .... Charleston, WV
Wilson, Lawler and Lett .... Lansing, MI
Wilson, Lawrence A., II .... **New York, NY**
Wilson, Lawrence D. .... Nashville, TN
Wilson, Lawrence E. .... **Houston, TX**
Wilson, Lawrence G., Jr. .... Danville, VA
Wilson, Lawrence L. .... Arcadia, CA
Wilson, Lawrence P. .... **Houston, TX**
Wilson, Lawrence W. .... Grand Rapids, MI
Wilson, Lawrence W., P.C.
Grand Rapids, MI
Wilson, Lazondra A. .... San Diego, CA
Wilson, Le Von E. .... Cullowhee, NC
Wilson, Leavitt & Small, P.A.
Orlando, FL
Wilson, Lee A. .... Los Angeles, CA
Wilson, Lee & Davis .... Chicago, IL
Wilson, Lee R. .... Littleton, CO
Wilson, Lee Ruffin .... **Columbia, SC**
Wilson, Lei-Chala Indee .... San Diego, CA
Wilson, Leland Dale .... Oakland Park, FL
Wilson, Lenita L. .... **Dallas, TX**
Wilson, Leon A., II .... Waycross, GA
Wilson, Leon S. .... Newark, NJ
Wilson, Leonard A. .... Las Vegas, NV
Wilson, Leonard E. .... Jamestown, KY
Wilson, Leonard E. .... **Elkton, MD**
Wilson, Leroy, Esq., Jr., A Prof. Corp.
White Plains, NY
Wilson, Leroy, Jr. .... White Plains, NY
Wilson, Lesa .... **San Diego, CA**
Wilson, Lesly P.
General Services Administration, Office of the General Counsel, GV
Wilson, Lester A. .... Charlottesville, VA
Wilson, Lewis M. .... Spokane, WA
Wilson, Lewis N. .... **Chatham, NJ**
Wilson, L.H. (Leonard H.)
Washington, DC
Tupelo, MS
Wilson, Lillian .... **Boston, MA**
Wilson, Linda A. .... Dallas, TX
Wilson, Linda J. .... Washington, DC
Wilson, Linda J. .... Eugene, OR
Wilson, Linda K. .... Anchorage, AK
Wilson, Linda P. .... Houston, TX
Wilson, Lindsay .... Portland, OR
Wilson, Lionel J. .... Walnut Creek, CA
Wilson, Lisa .... Peoria, IL
Wilson, Lisa A. .... Fort Payne, AL
Wilson, Lisa D. .... **Duluth, MN**
Wilson, Lisa G. .... **Scranton, PA**
Wilson, Lisa M. .... Anchorage, AK
Wilson, Lisa M. .... Irvine, CA
San Jose, CA
Wilson, Lisa M. .... Newton, MA
Wilson, Lisa M. .... **Milwaukee, WI**
Wilson, Lise N. .... San Diego, CA
Wilson, Lively M. .... **Louisville, KY**
Wilson, Lloyd T., Jr. .... Bloomington, IN
Wilson, Lloyd W. .... Stockton, CA
Wilson, Logan J. .... Blue Springs, MO
Wilson, Lois S. .... Atlanta, GA
Wilson, Lora L. .... **Crystal River, FL**
Melbourne, FL
Orlando, FL
Wilson, Lori .... Cocoa Beach, FL
Wilson, Lori L. Smith .... Lincoln, NE
Wilson, Lorraine K. .... Roselle, NJ
Wilson, Lorraine L. .... Olympia, WA
Wilson, Louis A. .... Appleton, WI
Wilson, Louis A., Jr. .... **New Orleans, LA**
Wilson, Lovester James, Jr. .... Detroit, MI
Wilson, L. T. .... Fort Worth, TX
Wilson, Lu Anne .... Jacksonville, FL
Wilson, Lyle K. .... Mill Creek, WA
Wilson, Lyndon .... Eden, NY
Wilson, Lyndon A. S., Jr. .... Portland, OR
Wilson, Lynn A. .... Detroit, MI
Wilson, Lynn D. .... Dover, DE
Wilson, Lynn Ellen .... Beverly Hills, CA
Wilson, Lynn M. .... Cumming, GA
Wilson, Lynn W., (Mr.) .... Barnesville, GA
Wilson, Lynn Whittlesey .... Arlington, VA
Wilson, Lynne R. .... **Orlando, FL**
Wilson, M. Gail .... **Jamestown, KY**
Wilson, M. Keith .... Salem, OR
Wilson, M. Lisa .... **New York, NY**
Wilson, M. Scott .... **Cleveland, OH**
Wilson, M. Sue .... **Plymouth, MN**
Wilson, Malcolm .... **White Plains, NY**
Wilson, Marc Lyman .... **Laguna Hills, CA**
Wilson, Marcella Matos .... Newark, NJ
Wilson, Marcia J. .... Santa Fe, NM
Wilson, Marcus .... **San Francisco, CA**
Wilson, Marcus M. .... **Jackson, MS**
Wilson, Marcus S. .... Fullerton, CA
Wilson, Margaret A. .... Brunswick, ME
Wilson, Margaret A. .... Austin, TX
Wilson, Margaret Bush .... **St. Louis, MO**
Wilson, Margaret C. .... **Newark, NJ**
Wilson, Margaret E. .... Salt Lake City, UT
Wilson, Margaret J. .... Eugene, OR
Wilson, Margaret L. .... Scottsdale, AZ
Wilson, Marguerite A.
Thousand Oaks, CA
Wilson, Mari Anne .... **Boston, MA**
Wilson, Maria Masvidal
Fort Lauderdale, FL
Wilson, Marie .... San Carlos, CA
Wilson, Marino & Bonnevie .... Newton, MA
Wilson, Marjorie Spencer .... **Cupertino, CA**
Wilson, Mark A. .... **Portola Valley, CA**
Wilson, Mark A. .... Amarillo, TX
Wilson, Mark B. .... Newport Beach, CA
Wilson, Mark B. .... **Austin, TX**
Wilson, Mark C. .... **Lexington, MA**
Wilson, Mark D. .... **Louisville, KY**
Wilson, Mark E. .... **Chicago, IL**
Wilson, Mark E. .... **Detroit, MI**
Wilson, Mark E. .... Spokane, WA
Wilson, Mark F. .... Washington, DC
Wilson, Mark G. .... Menlo Park, CA
Wilson, Mark H. .... New York, NY
Wilson, Mark J. .... **Seattle, WA**
Wilson, Mark K. .... Eastpointe, MI
Wilson, Mark K., P.C. .... Eastpointe, MI
Wilson, Mark L. .... Palm Harbor, FL
Wilson, Mark L. .... Minneapolis, MN
Wilson, Mark R. .... **Rochester, NY**
Wilson, Mark R. .... **Columbus, OH**
Wilson, Mark T. .... Greensboro, NC
Wilson, Mark V. .... **New York, NY**
Wilson, Marlene .... Oakland, CA
Wilson Marshall & Taylor .... **Palo Alto, CA**
Wilson, Marshall V. .... **Jefferson City, MO**
Wilson, Martha K. .... Marysville, CA
Wilson, Martha V. .... Sacramento, CA
Wilson, Martin A. .... Macon, GA
Wilson, Martin B. .... Saginaw, MI
Wilson, Martin J. .... Chicago, IL
Wilson, Martin M. .... **Atlanta, GA**
Wilson, Martin R. .... Lewisburg, PA
Wilson, Marvin A. .... Florence, AL
Wilson, Marvin Lynn .... **El Centro, CA**
Wilson, Mary .... Brownsville, TX
San Antonio, TX
Wilson, Mary Ann S. .... Chicago, IL
Wilson, Mary B. .... **Phoenix, AZ**
Wilson, Mary C. .... Montvale, NJ
Wilson, Mary Cecelia .... West Palm Beach, FL
Wilson, Mary Colleen .... Madison, WI
Wilson, Mary E. .... **Atlanta, GA**
Wilson, Mary E. .... Amesbury, MA
Wilson, Mary E. .... **The Woodlands, TX**
Wilson, Mary G. .... **Chicago, IL**
Wilson, Mary G. .... **Albuquerque, NM**
Wilson, Mary J. .... **Arlington, VA**
Wilson, Mary Jean .... Athens, GA
Wilson, Mary Larkin .... Washington, DC
Wilson, Mary Long .... Bedford, MA
Wilson, Mary Patricia .... Greenwich, CT
Wilson, Mary Rutherford, Law Office of
Tucson, AZ
Wilson, Mary Sue .... Olympia, WA
Wilson, Mary-Ann .... **Chicago, IL**
Wilson & Masi .... Ravenna, OH
Wilson, Matthew C. .... **King Of Prussia, PA**
Wilson, Matthew H. .... **Dayton, OH**
Wilson, Matthew J. .... **Orlando, FL**
Wilson, Matthew L. .... Philadelphia, PA
Wilson, Max A. .... Denver, CO
Wilson, Max C. .... Canon City, CO
Wilson & Mayhan, LLC
Greenwood Village, CO
Wilson, McCalla, Raymer, Barrett & Frappier
Nashville, TN
Wilson & McColl, Chartered .... **Boise, ID**
Wilson, McConnell & Associates, P.C.
Phoenix, AZ
Wilson, McCormick V. .... Jefferson City, MO
Wilson & McIlvaine .... **Chicago, IL**
Wilson, McRae, Ivy, McTyier and Strain
Memphis, TN
Wilson, Mel L. .... Fort Lauderdale, FL
Wilson, Melanie D. .... Atlanta, GA
Wilson, Melinda G. .... **Lexington, KY**
Wilson, Melissa A. .... **Lexington, KY**
Wilson, Melisssa M. .... New York, NY
Wilson, Melvin C. .... Farmington, UT
Wilson, Melvin H. .... Los Angeles, CA
Wilson, Merritt J. .... Monroe, GA
Wilson, Michael .... **Austin, TX**
Wilson, Michael .... **Dallas, TX**
Wilson, Michael A. .... Los Angeles, CA
Wilson, Michael A. .... **Rapid City, SD**
Wilson, Michael Allen .... Hagerstown, MD
Wilson, Michael B. .... Colorado Springs, CO
Wilson, Michael C. .... Russell, KY
Wilson, Michael C. .... **Dallas, TX**
Wilson, Michael D. .... **Hoboken, NJ**
New York, NY
Wilson, Michael D. .... Houston, TX
Wilson, Michael E. .... **St. Louis, MO**
Wilson, Michael E. .... **Houston, TX**
Wilson, Michael George .... **Jackson, MI**
Wilson, Michael J. .... **Washington, DC**
Wilson, Michael J. .... Bloomington, IL
Wilson, Michael K. .... Jacksonville, AR
Wilson, Michael K. .... **Orlando, FL**
Wilson, Michael L. .... **Charlotte, NC**
Wilson, Michael L. .... Galveston, TX
Wilson, Michael M. .... Watertown, CT
Wilson, Michael M. .... **Port Charlotte, FL**
Wilson, Michael M. .... **Houston, TX**
Wilson, Michael P. .... **Baton Rouge, LA**
Wilson, Michael P. .... Paris, MO
Wilson, Michael R. .... Minneapolis, MN
Wilson, Michael S. .... **Portland, ME**
Wilson, Michael W., Jr. .... **Lynchburg, VA**
Wilson, Michele L. .... **Branson, MO**
Wilson, Michelle L. .... **San Diego, CA**
Wilson, Michelle L. .... **San Francisco, CA**
Wilson, Michelle L. .... **Cherry Hill, NJ**
Wilson, Michelle M. .... Chicago, IL
Wilson, Michelle N. .... **Provo, UT**
Wilson, Mick .... Ashland, MO
Wilson, Mickey D. .... Tulsa, OK
Wilson, Mike .... Versailles, KY
Wilson, Milena A. .... Edison, NJ
Wilson, Millard S. .... Lincolnwood, IL
Wilson, Molly .... **Los Angeles, CA**
Wilson, Monsey G. .... Detroit, MI
Wilson, Montgomery J. .... Oklahoma City, OK
Wilson, Montgomery L. .... Maryville, MO
Wilson, Morrow, Broderick, O'Neill & Tompkins, L.L.P. .... **Norristown, PA**
Wilson, Morton & Downs, LLC
Atlanta, GA
Decatur, GA
Wilson, M. Sue, Law Offices, P.A.
Plymouth, MN
Wilson, Myron K. .... Larchmont, NY
Wilson, Myroslava F. .... Evanston, IL
Wilson, Nancy B. .... **Washington, DC**
Wilson, Nancy C. .... Palm Beach Gardens, FL
Wilson, Nancy G. .... St. Louis Park, MN
Wilson, Nancy J. .... San Diego, CA
Wilson, Nancy Merrill .... **Kansas City, MO**
Wilson, Natalie S. .... **Lexington, KY**
Wilson, Nathan E. .... Baton Rouge, LA
Wilson, Nathan H. .... Ponte Vedra Beach, FL
Wilson, Neal B. .... Huntington, WV
Wilson, Neal J. .... **Washington, DC**
Wilson, Ned Elnor, (Ms.) .... San Angelo, TX
Wilson, Neil R. .... Painesville, OH
Wilson, Nicholas B. .... Columbus, OH
Wilson, Nick .... Pocahontas, AR
Wilson, Nolan N. .... Richmond, VA
Wilson, Norman E. .... Wilmette, IL
Wilson, Norman L., Jr. .... St. Louis, MO
Wilson, Norman M., Jr. .... Hatboro, PA
Wilson, Novell J. .... Tulsa, OK
Wilson, O. Meredith, Jr. .... **Portland, OR**
Wilson & Orcutt, P.C. .... **Acton, MA**
Wilson, Orville R. .... Elko, NV
Wilson, Oscar, Jr. .... Sparta, WI
Wilson, Owen D. .... Enid, OK
Wilson, P. Bruce .... Seattle, WA
Wilson, P. Preston, Jr. .... Memphis, TN
Wilson, P. Scott .... **Dover, DE**
Wilson, Palmer & Lackey, P.A. .... Lenoir, NC
Wilson, Pamela A. .... **Santa Monica, CA**
Wilson, Pamela G. .... **Louisville, KY**
Wilson, Pamela J. .... **Boston, MA**
Wilson, Pamela L. .... **Houston, TX**
Wilson, Pamela Lawton .... **San Diego, CA**
Wilson, Pamela M. .... Anniston, AL
Wilson, Parker F. .... Dallas, TX
Wilson, Parker H. .... **Norristown, PA**
Wilson, Parks H., Jr. .... Belmont, NC
Wilson & Parlett .... Upper Marlboro, MD

Wilson, Thomas S., Jr. ..... Elkhart, IN
Wilson, Thomas S. (Tam), Jr. ..... Miami, FL
Wilson, Thomas W. ..... Alameda, CA
Wilson, Thomas W. ..... Washington, DC
Wilson, Thomas W. ..... New York, NY
Wilson, Thomas W. ..... Springfield, OH
Wilson, Tim J. ..... Hyden, KY
Wilson, Timothy C. ..... San Francisco, CA
Wilson, Timothy E. ..... Altus, OK
Wilson, Timothy J. ..... Hyden, KY
Lexington, KY
London, KY
Wilson, Timothy J. ..... St. Louis, MO
Wilson, Timothy K. ..... Cary, NC
Wilson, Timothy Wood ..... Rocky Mount, NC
Wilson, T. J. ..... Monticello, IL
Wilson, Todd D. ..... Elwood, NE
Wilson, Todd W. ..... Forest Lake, MN
Wilson, Tommie ..... Pell City, AL
Wilson, Tony J. ..... Houston, TX
Wilson, Tracey A. ..... Pittsburgh, PA
Wilson, Trevino, Freed, Casso & Valls, PLLC ..... Laredo, TX
Wilson, Tristi Julane ..... Eagan, MN
Wilson, Troy H. ..... Philadelphia, PA
Wilson, Troy Michael ..... Dallas, TX
Wilson, Ulmer Graydon ..... Houston, TX
Wilson, Updike & Nicely ..... Covington, VA
Wilson, Val Pleet, (Mr.) ..... Marlton, NJ
Newtown, PA
Philadelphia, PA
Wilson, Valerie D. ..... Boulder, MT
Wilson, Valorie Kay ..... Des Moines, IA
Wilson, Vanessa M. ..... Newport, NH
Wilson, Vanessa R. ..... Houston, TX
Wilson, Vernon ..... Miamisburg, OH
Wilson, Veronica M. ..... Los Angeles, CA
Wilson, Victor M. ..... Brooklyn, NY
Wilson, Virginia Burt ..... Memphis, TN
Wilson, Virginia Leanne ..... Arvada, CO
Wilson, Voyle C. ..... Chicago, IL
Wilson, W. Cassidy, III ..... Henderson, KY
Wilson, W. Harney ..... Orinda, CA
Wilson, W. Jett ..... Corinth, MS
Wilson, W. John ..... Decatur, GA
Wilson, W. Laurence ..... Lynnwood, WA
Wilson, W. Luther ..... Baton Rouge, LA
Wilson, W. Neil ..... Miami, OK
Wilson, W. Robert ..... Pawhuska, OK
Wilson, W. Roger ..... San Antonio, TX
Wilson, W. Russell ..... Cincinnati, OH
Wilson, W. Scott ..... Richmond, VA
Wilson, W. Stephen ..... San Francisco, CA
Wilson, W. Ward ..... Detroit, MI
Wilson, W. Weir ..... Fort Worth, TX
Wilson, W. Weldon ..... Stamford, CT
Wilson, W. William ..... Cockeysville, MD
Wilson, Walker & Short ..... Hope, AR
Wilson & Waller, P.A. ..... Cary, NC
Raleigh, NC
Research Triangle Park, NC
Wilson, Walter A. I. ..... Washington, DC
Wilson, Walter E. ..... Odessa, TX
Wilson, Walter N. ..... Annandale, NJ
Wilson, Walter N., P.C. ..... Annandale, NJ
Wilson, Walter D. ..... Glen Burnie, MD
Wilson, Walton M. ..... Panama City, FL
Wilson, Warner R., Jr. ..... Atlanta, GA
Wilson, Warren A., III ..... Palm Harbor, FL
Wilson, Warren B. ..... Oakland, CA
Wilson, Warren J. ..... McMinnville, OR
Wilson, Wayne C. ..... Atlanta, GA
Wilson, Wayne D. ..... Sacramento, CA
Wilson, Wayne I. ..... West Des Moines, IA
Wilson, Wayne R. ..... Hulett, WY
Wilson, Wayne W. ..... Detroit, MI
Wilson, Wayne W. ..... Evansville, WI
Wilson, W. D. ..... Colorado Springs, CO
Wilson, Wendell G., Jr., (P.C.) ..... Phoenix, AZ
Wilson, Wesley ..... Jonesborough, TN
Wilson, Wesley M. ..... Olympia, WA
Wilson & White, L.L.P. ..... Fort Worth, TX
Wilson & White, Professional Corporation
Montpelier, VT
Newport, VT
St. Johnsbury, VT
Wilson, Whitney ..... Washington, DC
Wilson & Wildesen ..... Timonium, MD
Wilson, Will ..... Austin, TX
Wilson, Will R., Jr. ..... Austin, TX
Wilson, William A. ..... Sacramento, CA
Wilson, William A. ..... Denver, CO
Wilson, William A. ..... Houston, TX
Wilson, William B. ..... Orlando, FL
Wilson, William B. ..... Iraan, TX
Wilson, William B., Jr. ..... Lancaster, OH
Wilson, William C. ..... San Diego, CA
Wilson, William D. ..... Newark, NJ
Wilson, William D. ..... Franklin, PA
Wilson, William D., Jr ..... Charleston, SC
Wilson, William E. ..... Ferndale, MI
Wilson, William E. ..... Houston, TX
Wilson, William Edgar, Jr.
Stone Mountain, GA
Wilson, William F. ..... Medford, OR
Wilson, William G. ..... Los Angeles, CA
Wilson, William H. ..... Lawton, OK
Wilson, William H. ..... Tulsa, OK
Wilson, William H., Jr. ..... Concord, NH
Wilson, William J. ..... Sacramento, CA
Wilson, William Joseph ..... Ashland, OH
Wilson, William L. ..... South Bend, IN
Wilson, William L. ..... Sapulpa, OK
Wilson, William L., Jr. ..... Owensboro, KY
Wilson, William M. ..... Greenville, SC
Wilson, William M., Jr. ..... Dallas, TX
Wilson, William N., II ..... Houston, TX
Wilson, William P. ..... Downey, CA
Wilson, William R. ..... Dallas, TX
Wilson, William R., Jr. ..... Little Rock, AR
Wilson, William R., Sr. ..... Louisville, KY
Wilson, William Randall
Chattanooga, TN
Wilson, William Roberts, Jr. ..... Jackson, MS
Wilson, William S. ..... Miami, FL
Wilson, William S. ..... Countryside, IL
Wilson, William S. ..... Grandville, MI
Wilson, William S., II ..... New Haven, CT
Wilson, William S., Jr. ..... Portland, ME
Wilson, William T. ..... Rockford, IL
Wilson, William T. ..... West Chester, PA
Wilson, William T. ..... Temple, TX
Wilson, William T. ..... Covington, VA
Wilson, William T., III ..... Winston-Salem, NC
Wilson, William W. ..... Dallas, TX
Wilson, William Warren ..... Flagstaff, AZ
Wilson, Williams & Molberg ..... Dallas, TX
Wilson & Williams, P.A. ..... Ocala, FL
Wilson & Wilson ..... Arcadia, CA
Wilson & Wilson ..... Redwood City, CA
Wilson & Wilson ..... San Luis Obispo, CA
Wilson & Wilson ..... Countryside, IL
Wilson & Wilson ..... Newark, NJ
Wilson & Wilson ..... Enid, OK
Wilson & Wilson ..... Lewisburg, PA
Wilson & Wilson ..... Chattanooga, TN
Wilson & Wilson ..... Salt Lake City, UT
Wilson and Wilson, A Professional Legal Corporation ..... Newport News, VA
Wilson, Wilson & Long, P.A.
Palm Harbor, FL
Wilson & Wilson, P.C. ..... Jasper, AL
Wilson and Wilson, P.C. ..... Hazel Park, MI
Rochester, MI
Wilson, Wilson & Perizo ..... Downey, CA
Wilson, Wilson & Plain ..... Owensboro, KY
Wilson, Wilson & Wilson ..... West Union, OH
Wilson, Winfield D. ..... Los Angeles, CA
Wilson, Wm A. ..... Edmonds, WA
Wilson, Wm. F., Jr. ..... Lake Charles, LA
Wilson, Woodrow ..... Bastrop, LA
Wilson, Woodrow P. ..... Wheeling, IL
Wilson, Worley & Gamble, P.C.
Johnson City, TN
Kingsport, TN
Rogersville, TN
Wilson, Wynnora S. (Wendy) ..... Miami, FL
Wilson, Zachary David
North Little Rock, AR
Wilson, Zachary David, P.A.
Little Rock, AR
North Little Rock, AR
Wilson, Zachary G. ..... Fort Collins, CO
Wilson, Zane D. ..... Fairbanks, AK
Wilson-Bilik, Mary Jane ..... Washington, DC
Wilson-Carr, Lauren ..... Tuscaloosa, AL
Wilson-Coker, Patricia ..... Hartford, CT
Wilson-Espinosa, Laurie W.
Los Angeles, CA
Wilson-Freelon, Sheila ..... Chicago, IL
Wilson-Gebhart, Pamela ..... Littleton, CO
Wilson-Glah, Jolene ..... Houston, TX
Wilson-Hoss & Hoss ..... Shelton, WA
Wilson-Hoss, Robert D. ..... Shelton, WA
Wilson-Moschetti, Marci ..... New York, NY
Wilson-Patton, Stuart Freeman
Tallahassee, FL
Wilson-Rice, Rhonda K. ..... Pittsburg, CA
Wilson Schillaci, Sandra C. ..... Trenton, NJ
Wilson-Steele, Constance L.
Minneapolis, MN
Wilsted, Erin ..... Martinez, CA
Wilt, Allen Jay ..... Reno, NV
Wilt, Angela Toscas ..... Chicago, IL
Wilt, Brad A. ..... Las Vegas, NV
Wilt, Daniel D. ..... Euclid, OH
Wilt, David B. ..... Akron, OH
Wilt, David L. ..... Westerville, OH
Wilt, David Ruhl ..... Jacksonville, FL
Wilt, Dennis M. ..... Westchester, IL
Wilt, James L. ..... Parkersburg, WV
Wilt, Randy ..... Rockford, IL
Wilt, Richard S. ..... Huntingdon, PA
Wilt, Scott E. ..... Orlando, FL
Wilt, Valerie R. ..... Springfield, OH
Wilt, Vincent A. ..... Hoboken, NJ
Wilt, Walter W. ..... Harrisburg, PA
Wiltanger, Matthew J.
Overland Park, KS
Wiltbank, Ronald ..... Mesa, AZ
Wiltbank, Ronald, P.C. ..... Mesa, AZ
Wiltberger, Stephen J. ..... Greenville, SC
Wiltenburg, David W. ..... New York, NY
Wiltes, Harry J., Jr. ..... Robertsdale, AL
Wiltgen, Janet S. ..... Woodland Hills, CA
Wiltgen, Joseph N. ..... Albuquerque, NM
Wiltgen, Nancy A. ..... Minneapolis, MN
Wiltgen, Yvette M. ..... Albuquerque, NM
Wiltman, William A. ..... Greensburg, PA
Wilton, Barry A. ..... Richmond, VA
Wilton, Chad L. ..... Portland, OR
Wilton, Daniel F. ..... Union, NJ
Wilton, James M. ..... Boston, MA
Wilton, Jane L. ..... New York, NY
Wilton, Kenneth L. ..... Los Angeles, CA
Wilton, Lauren M. ..... Boston, MA
Wilton, Lisa J. ..... Cambridge, MA
Wilton, Ronald D. ..... Encino, CA
Wilton, Scott W. ..... Oak Brook, IL
Wilton, Timothy ..... Boston, MA
Wilton, Wendy A. ..... Ayer, MA
Wiltrakis, John N. ..... St. Louis, MO
Wiltrakis, Thomas A. ..... Torrance, CA
Wiltrout, Irving J. ..... Marshall, MN
Wiltrout, Joel C. ..... Worthington, MN
Wiltse, James B. ..... Pittsburgh, PA
Wiltse, John C. ..... Lincoln, NE
Wiltse, Peter C. ..... Hamburg, NY
Wiltsee, Robert J. ..... Franklinville, NJ
Woodbury, NJ
Wiltshire, Ashley T., Jr. ..... Nashville, TN
Wiltshire, Courtenay L. ..... Brooklyn, NY
Wiltshire, George Andrew
Indian Harbour Beach, FL
Wiltshire, Jas. M., Jr. ..... Nashville, TN
Wiltshire, L. Markus ..... New York, NY
Wiltshire, Laura G. ..... Little Rock, AR
Wiltshire, Michelle Preston
Richmond, VA
Wiltshire, Morris H. ..... Athens, GA
Wiltshire, Thomas M. ..... Reston, VA
Wiltshire, W.H.F. ..... Pensacola, FL
Wiltshire, William M. ..... Washington, DC
Wiltsie, Daryl Ann ..... Oswego, NY
Wiltsie, David S. ..... Wailuku, HI
Wiltsie, George R. ..... Ithaca, NY
Wiltsie, Ronald J., II ..... Washington, DC
Wiltsie, Susan Frier ..... Washington, DC
Wiltsie, Timothy S. ..... Belleville, IL
Nashville, IL
Wilty, Michel P. ..... Lafayette, LA
New Orleans, LA
Beaumont, TX
Wiltz, Alicia E. ..... Los Angeles, CA
Wilutis, Karen M. ..... Commack, NY
Wilutis, Steven J. ..... Commack, NY
Wilwerding, David G. ..... Omaha, NE
Wily, Robert M. ..... Richmond, VA
Wilzbach, Matthew S. ..... Carbondale, IL
Wilzbach, Scott ..... Salem, IL
Wiman, Stephen P. ..... Los Angeles, CA
Wimberley, Carl ..... Houston, TX
Wimberley, Carl T. ..... Canyon, TX
Wimberley, James E. ..... Beaumont, TX
Wimberley, Ray P. ..... Wailuku, HI
Wimberly, Clint A. ..... Richmond, KY
Wimberly, Dorothy Hudson, (P.C.)
New Orleans, LA
Wimberly, F. Douglas ..... Lafayette, LA
Wimberly, Gerard E., Jr. ..... Phoenix, AZ
Wimberly, J. Rush, III ..... Arcadia, LA
Wimberly, James W., Jr. ..... Atlanta, GA
Wimberly, Jesse L., III ..... Mandeville, LA
Wimberly, Jesse L., III ..... New Orleans, LA
Wimberly, John E., Jr. ..... Pensacola, FL
Wimberly, Kenneth W., Jr. ..... Dallas, TX
Wimberly, Lawson, Daniels & Brandon, LLC ..... Greenville, SC
Wimberly Lawson & Seale, PLLC
Cookeville, TN
Knoxville, TN
Morristown, TN
Nashville, TN
Wimberly, Lawson, Steckel, Nelson & Schneider, P.C. ..... Atlanta, GA
Wimberly, Linda Brooks ..... Plano, TX
Wimberly, Linda Carnes ..... Richmond, KY
Wimberly, Stephen T. ..... Metairie, LA
Wimberly & Wimberly ..... Richmond, KY
Wimbiscus, James J. ..... Princeton, IL
Wimbiscus, Thomas J. ..... Chicago, IL
Wimbiscus, William J., Jr. ..... De Pue, IL
Spring Valley, IL
Wimbish, C. Bette ..... St. Petersburg, FL
Wimbish, Carlyle R., III ..... Richmond, VA
Wimbish, Gary L. ..... Atlanta, GA
Wimbish, John B. ..... Tulsa, OK
Wimbish, Mary ..... Houston, TX
Wimbish, Mary, Atty., P.C. ..... Houston, TX
Wimbish, Michael H. ..... Dallas, TX
Wimbish, Philip R. ..... Tulsa, OK
Wimbish, R. Allan ..... Virginia Beach, VA
Wimbish, Robert A. ..... Washington, DC
Wimbish, Terrence A. ..... Miami, FL
Wimbish, William L. ..... Richmond, VA
Wimbrow, Peter A., III ..... Ocean City, MD
Wimbush, F. Blair ..... Norfolk, VA
Wimer, Charles H. ..... New York, NY
Wimer, David P. ..... Glastonbury, CT
Wimer, Harpold & Associates, P.S.
Kent, WA
Wimer & Jobe ..... Dallas, TX
Wimer, Kenneth E. ..... Davis, CA
Wimer Law Offices, P.C. ..... Pittsburgh, PA
Wimer, Matthew R. ..... Pittsburgh, PA
Wimer, Michael G. ..... Dallas, TX
Wimer, Warren B. ..... Fullerton, CA
Wimer, Wayne J. ..... Kent, WA
Wimmer, Basil L. ..... Indianapolis, IN
Wimmer, David A. ..... Los Angeles, CA
Wimmer, Glen A. ..... Memphis, TN
Wimmer, James A. ..... Palmerton, PA
Wimmer, James R. ..... Chicago, IL
Wimmer, John J. ..... Hales Corners, WI
Wimmer, John R., The Law Offices of
Downers Grove, IL
Wimmer, John R., The Law Offices of
Wheaton, IL
Wimmer, Joseph E. ..... Waukesha, WI
Wimmer, Kurt A. ..... Washington, DC
Wimmer, Leland K. ..... Salt Lake City, UT
Wimmer, Lucy K. ..... Southfield, MI
Wimmer, Peter D. ..... St. Louis, MO
Wimmer, Richard S. ..... Belleville, IL
Wimmer, Richard T. ..... Chicago, IL
Wimmer & Stiehl, P.C. ..... Belleville, IL
Wimmer, Trina M. ..... Raleigh, NC
Wimmer, William G. ..... Cuba City, WI
Wimmer, William J. ..... Des Moines, IA
Wimmer, William L., III ..... Belleville, IL
Wimmershoff, Nick ..... Longmont, CO
Wimmershoff-Caplan, Sue ..... Madison, NJ
Wimpfheimer, Henry ..... New York, NY
Wimpfheimer, Jan S. ..... New York, NY
Wimpfheimer, Loren B. ..... Atlanta, GA
Wimpfheimer, Michael C. ..... New York, NY
Wimpfheimer, Steven ..... Great Neck, NY
Wimpfheimer & Wimpfheimer
New York, NY
Wims, Michael D. ..... Salt Lake City, UT
Wims, Travis Martin ..... Oklahoma City, OK
Wimsatt, Thomas C. ..... Saginaw, MI
Wimsatt, William H., (Professional Corporation) ..... Los Angeles, CA
Winakor, David S. ..... Hartford, CT
Winakur, Stacey Karen ..... Baltimore, MD
Winand, Jame M. ..... State College, PA
Winand, John H. ..... Glenview, IL
Winandy, John R. ..... Los Angeles, CA
Winans, Christopher G. ..... Danbury, CT
Winans, Christopher G., P.C.
Danbury, CT
Winans, David E. ..... Albany, NY
Winans, H. Charles ..... Garrett, IN
Winans, Jill D. ..... Tucson, AZ
Winans, John M. ..... Ashland, KY
Winans, John W. ..... Catskill, NY
Winans, Lloyd M. ..... Westwood, NJ
Winans, Nancy Ann ..... Oklahoma City, OK
Winans, Thomas J. ..... Fairfax, VA
Winard, Arthur I. ..... New York, NY
Winard, Arthur I., P.C. ..... New York, NY
Winarsky, Lewis I. ..... Washington, DC
Winarsky, Thea Ann ..... New York, NY
Winawer, Lloyd ..... Palo Alto, CA
Winay, Nora ..... Bloomfield Hills, MI
Winbauer, John P. ..... Ellensburg, WA
Winberg, Bonnie ..... Indianapolis, IN
Winberg, Charles H. ..... Richmond, VA
Winberg, Susan L. ..... New York, NY
Winberry, Lanny T. ..... Sacramento, CA
Winberry, Marcus L. ..... Conroe, TX
Winbigler, Wellington E. ..... Kansas City, MO
Winblad, Richard S. ..... Oklahoma City, OK
Winblood-Franco, Melissa ..... El Paso, TX
Winborn, Erik L. ..... Williamsburg, IA
Winborn, Johnnie Randall ..... Florence, AL
Winborn, Terry L. ..... Dallas, TX
Winborne, George O. ..... New York, NY
Winborne, John W. ..... Atlanta, GA
Winborne Law Office, P.A. ..... Raleigh, NC
Winborne, Lynn G. ..... Waxahachie, TX
Winborne, Paul Faison S. ..... Raleigh, NC
Winborne, Saml. P. ..... Atlantic, NC
Winborne, Vaughan S. ..... Raleigh, NC
Winborne, Vaughan S., Jr. ..... Raleigh, NC
Winbourn, Reed L. ..... Denver, CO
Winbourn, Hampe & Sheehan
Dedham, MA
Winbourne, Michael G. E. ..... Dedham, MA
Winburn, D. Patrick ..... Bennington, VT
Manchester, VT
Winburn, Gene Mac ..... Athens, GA
Winburn, Henry C., Jr. ..... Tulsa, OK
Winburn, John T. ..... San Jose, CA
Winburn, Lewis & Barrow, P.C.
Athens, GA
Atlanta, GA
Winburn, Mary L. ..... Racine, WI
Winburn, Rebecca Hodges ..... Benton, AR
Winburn, Russell B. ..... Fayetteville, AR
Winburn & Young ..... Bennington, VT
Manchester, VT
Winburne, Blake H. ..... Washington, DC
Winbush, Kimberly J. ..... Harrisburg, PA
Wince, Philip D. ..... Newark, OH
Wince, Philip D. Co., L.P.A. ..... Newark, OH
Wincek, Arthur T. ..... Cleveland, OH
Wincek, Christopher G. ..... Cleveland, OH
Wincek & DeRosa Co. ..... Cleveland, OH
Wincek, Donna J. ..... Chicago, IL
Wincek, Gary Alan ..... Chicago, IL
Wincek, Mark D. ..... Washington, DC
Winch, James T. ..... Mazomanie, WI
Winch, Martin T. ..... Portland, OR
Winch, Robert R. ..... San Jose, CA
Winch, Thos. H. ..... Mazomanie, WI
Winch & Winch ..... Mazomanie, WI
Winchell, Andy V. ..... Los Angeles, CA
Winchell, Bruce ..... Seattle, WA
Winchell, Bruce M. ..... Albuquerque, NM
Winchell, Byron R. ..... Chillicothe, OH
Winchell, Dan R. ..... Indianapolis, IN
Winchell, Dennis R. ..... Barberton, OH
Winchell, James D. ..... Shepherdsville, KY
Winchell, James W. ..... Elk Grove, CA
Winchell, Michael G.
Kennedy Space Center, FL
Winchell, Neal R. ..... San Mateo, CA
Winchell, Patricia A. ..... St. Louis, MO
Winchell & Pond ..... San Mateo, CA
Winchell, Sterling Scott ..... Laguna Hills, CA
Winchell, Susan A.
Department of Education,
Office of the General Counsel, GV
Winchell, V. Lee ..... Rittman, OH
Winchell, William O. ..... Royal Oak, MI
Winchenbach, Linda L. ..... Gainesville, FL
Winchester, Alan M. ..... New York, NY
Winchester, Anthony Lee ..... Dyersburg, TN
Winchester, Anthony R. ..... Wilmington, DE
Winchester & Associates, Ltd.
Las Cruces, NM
Winchester, Brian P. ..... Augusta, ME
Winchester, Brian T. ..... Cleveland, OH
Winchester, Charles C. ..... Boston, MA
Winchester, Colin R. ..... Kanab, UT
Winchester, Colleen D. ..... San Jose, CA
Winchester, David A. ..... Kirkland, WA
Winchester, David Andrew ..... La Follette, TN
Winchester & Dickinson, P.C. ..... Dallas, TX
Winchester, G. Ann ..... Jonesboro, LA

Wingate, Gregory K. .... Wilmington, DE
Wingate, Harry L., Jr. .... Albany, GA
Wingate, Henry T. .... Jackson, MS
Wingate, Jerrold K. .... Miami, FL
Wingate, Kearney & Cullen .... Brooklyn, NY
Melville, NY
Wingate, Kenneth B. .... Columbia, SC
Wingate, Kevin L. .... Rockford, IL
Wingate, Kimberly A. .... Wichita, KS
Wingate, Leon A., Jr. .... Camden, NJ
Wingate, Levan J. .... Columbia, SC
Wingate, Molly J. .... Minneapolis, MN
Wingate, Richard C. .... Park Ridge, NJ
Wingate, Ronald L. .... Toledo, OH
Wingate, Roy .... Orange, TX
Wingate, Russotti & Shapiro, LLP
New York, NY
Wingate, Thomas P. .... McAllen, TX
Wingate, W. Leonard .... Redding, CA
Wingate, William A. .... New York, NY
Winge, Robert J. .... Claverack, NY
Wingeier, Scott Alexander .... Dallas, TX
Wingenbach, Linda M. .... Majuro, TT
Wingens, Gary M. .... Roseland, NJ
Winger, Amy A. B. .... Berkeley, CA
Winger, Brian Neil .... Edmond, OK
Winger, Elmer L. .... Modesto, CA
Winger, George M. .... Kansas City, MO
Winger, Harold R. .... Chicago, IL
Winger, Holly J. .... Hartford, CT
Winger, Kathleen Delaney .... Tucson, AZ
Winger, Lawrence C. .... Portland, ME
Winger, Lisa .... Chicago, IL
Winger, Maurice, Jr. .... Enka, NC
Winger, Michael .... New York, NY
Winger, R. Gary .... Salt Lake City, UT
Winger, Ralph O. .... New York, NY
Winger, Robert K. .... Portland, OR
Winger, William J. .... Chicago, IL
Wingerd, Bruce H. .... Clay Center, KS
Wingerd, Edmund C., Jr. .... Chambersburg, PA
Wingerd, Harold R. .... St. Paul, MN
Wingerson, Mark R. .... New York, NY
Wingert, David P. .... Lebanon, PA
Wingert, G. Page .... Towson, MD
Wingert Grebing Brubaker & Ryan LLP
San Diego, CA
Wingert, Howard E. .... New Carlisle, OH
Wingert, John R., (A Professional Corporation) .... San Diego, CA
Wingert, Kathe .... Eagan, MN
Wingert, Pamela A. .... Spirit Lake, IA
Wingert, William J. .... Presque Isle, ME
Wingerter, George C., Jr. .... Saratoga, CA
Wingerter, John R. .... Erie, PA
Wingerter, Rex B. .... Hyattsville, MD
Wingerter, Robert B., Jr. .... Indianapolis, IN
Wingerter, Warren W., Jr. .... New Orleans, LA
Wingertzahn, William M.
White Plains, NY
Winget, Howard .... Springfield, MO
Winget, Joseph P. .... Springfield, MO
Winget & Kane .... Peoria, IL
Winget, Mark L. .... Chicago, IL
Winget, Patricia .... Red Wing, MN
Winget, R. Dale .... Flemington, NJ
Winget, Spadafora & Schwartzberg, LLP
Newark, NJ
New York, NY
Winget, Walter W. .... Peoria, IL
Winget, William G. .... Newark, NJ
New York, NY
Wingfield, Alan D. .... Richmond, VA
Wingfield, Donald G. .... San Bernardino, CA
Wingfield, Elizabeth A. .... Tampa, FL
Wingfield, Hugh V., III .... Milledgeville, GA
Wingfield, Jane Lindsey .... Los Angeles, CA
Wingfield, Keith W. .... Newberg, OR
Wingfield, Linda E. .... Albuquerque, NM
Wingfield, Steven F. .... La Mesa, CA
Wingfield, Thomas C. .... Falls Church, VA
Wingfield, Thomas J., III, (P.C.)
Atlanta, GA
Wingfield, W. Terrell, Jr. .... Englewood, CO
Wingfield, Walter H. .... Atlanta, GA
Wingfield, William D. .... Overland Park, KS
Wingler, Rick L. .... Dallas, TX
Wingo, Andrew J. .... Mooresville, NC
Wingo, Barbara C. .... Gainesville, FL
Wingo, Carol Lockridge .... Richmond, VA
Wingo, Douglass T. .... Dallas, TX
Wingo, Earl W. .... Goode, VA
Wingo, Harvey .... Dallas, TX
Wingo, John R. .... Nashville, TN
Wingo, Karen L. .... Washington, DC
Wingo, Lamar D. .... La Grange, GA
Wingo, Michael B. .... Daytona Beach, FL
Wingo, Steven W. .... Ocala, FL
Wingo, Tiffany M. .... Dallas, TX
Wingo, William H. .... Salt Lake City, UT
Wingo, Wm. T. .... Cincinnati, OH
Winhoven, John R. .... Floresville, TX
Winiarski, Debra A. .... Chicago, IL
Winiarski, Denise L. .... Troy, MI
Winiarski, Gregg J. .... New York, NY
Winiarski, Henry C., Jr. .... Hartford, CT
Winiarski, James J. .... Milwaukee, WI
Winiarski, John M. .... Mesa, AZ
Winiarski, Thaddeus J. .... Detroit, MI
Winiarsky, Nativ .... New York, NY
Winick, Alan C. .... New York, NY
Winick, Alfred Z. .... Des Moines, IA
Winick, Allan L. .... Mineola, NY
Winick, Bernard S. .... Akron, OH
Winick, Bruce J. .... Coral Gables, FL
Winick, Carolyn Kohn .... Chicago, IL
Winick, Ellen L. .... San Mateo, CA
Winick, Eugene H. .... New York, NY
Winick, Herbert R. .... Hewlett, NY
Winick, Jeffrey H. .... Chicago, IL
Winick, Kimberly S. .... Los Angeles, CA
Winick, Marvin .... Des Moines, IA
Winick, Paul A. .... New York, NY
Winick, Paul M.
Environmental Protection Agency,
Office of the General Counsel, GV
Winick & Rich, P.C. .... West Hartford, CT
Hackensack, NJ
New York, NY
Winick, Robert M. .... Sarasota, FL
Winick, Robert M., P.A. .... Sarasota, FL
Winick, Russel G. .... Naperville, IL
Winick, Stacy H. .... Washington, DC
Winick, Steven H. .... San Francisco, CA
Winick, Steven J. .... Syosset, NY
Winicour, Sheldon B. .... New York, NY
Winicov, Arnold H. .... Philadelphia, PA
Winicov, Theodore P. .... Philadelphia, PA
Winig, Steven L. .... West Palm Beach, FL
Winiger, Tammy Goebel .... Middletown, OH
Winik, Arthur B. .... Dallas, TX
Winik, Peter L. .... Washington, DC
Winikates, Charles J. .... Frisco, TX
Winikates, Charles J., Jr. .... Frisco, TX
Winikates & Winikates .... Dallas, TX
Denton, TX
Frisco, TX
McKinney, TX
Winiker, S. Frederick, III .... Yakima, WA
Winikka, Daniel P. .... Dallas, TX
Winikoff, Jeffrey A. .... Fort Lauderdale, FL
Winikoff, Robert L. .... New York, NY
Winikoff, Stanley Asher .... Pittsburgh, PA
Winikow, Jeffrey K. .... Los Angeles, CA
Winikow, Scott K. .... New York, NY
Winingar, Harold D., Jr.
West Sacramento, CA
Wininger, Aaron R. .... Palo Alto, CA
Wininger, D. DeLeal, Jr. .... Birmingham, AL
Wininger, David D. .... Birmingham, AL
Wininger, E. David .... Carlsbad, CA
Wininger and Wininger, P.A.
Birmingham, AL
Tuscaloosa, AL
Winingham, John L. .... San Francisco, CA
Winingham, Roberts, Fama, Kramer & Ramberg .... San Francisco, CA
Winingham, William E., Jr.
Indianapolis, IN
Winings, Mark C. .... St. Louis, MO
Wininsky, Nicholas A. .... Wheeling, WV
Winitsky, Alex .... Santa Monica, CA
Winitsky & Sellers .... Santa Monica, CA
Winitz, Edward N. .... Miami, FL
Winitz, Flora S. .... Kansas City, MO
Winitz & Minkin .... Miami, FL
Winitzer, Marcia J. .... Sharon, MA
Winjum, Ken A. .... West Des Moines, IA
Winjum, Stephen J. .... Indianola, IA
Wink, Dulcie G. .... Houston, TX
Wink, Lori A. .... Milwaukee, WI
Wink, Robin S. .... Omaha, NE
Wink, Timothy K. .... Columbus Junction, IA
Wink, Victoria H. .... Annapolis, MD
Baltimore, MD
Wink, Wayne H., Jr. .... Mineola, NY
Winkel, Daniel P. .... Omaha, NE
Winkel, David J. .... Neenah, WI
Winkel, Eldon J. .... Algona, IA
Winkel, Evelyn W. .... San Clemente, CA
Winkel, George A. .... Hemet, CA
Winkel, James R. .... Milford, CT
Winkel, Judy K. .... Dallas, TX
Winkel, Morton A. .... Portland, OR
Winkel, Richard A. .... Denver, CO
Winkel, Richard J., Jr. .... Champaign, IL
Winkel, Robert A. .... Reno, NV
Winkel, Walter W., III .... Buffalo Grove, IL
Winkel, William M. .... West Palm Beach, FL
Winkeljohn, J. Theodore .... Findlay, OH
Winkelman, Barbara Gaines .... Norwalk, CT
Winkelman, Bruce H. .... Oakland, CA
Winkelman, Cassondra M. .... Chicago, IL
Winkelman, Earl L. .... Elm Grove, WI
Winkelman, Jeffrey W. .... La Jolla, CA
Winkelman, John D. .... Wilsonville, OR
Winkelman, Johnny M. .... Alpine, CA
Winkelman, Michael J. .... Lanham, MD
Winkelman, Michael L. .... Appleton, WI
Winkelman, Nancy .... Philadelphia, PA
Winkelman, Nora .... Philadelphia, PA
Winkelman, Peter M. .... Los Angeles, CA
Winkelman, Roger E.
Farmington Hills, MI
Winkelman, Scott L. .... Washington, DC
Winkelman, Sheldon P. .... Detroit, MI
Winkelman, Sherry L. .... Winchester, MA
Winkelman, Stephen R. .... Phoenix, AZ
Winkelman, Steven A. .... Rockville, MD
Winkelmann, Susan E. .... Minneapolis, MN
Winkelmann, Wendell G. .... Urbana, IL
Winkelried, Charles A. .... Cherry Hill, NJ
Winkels, Joann D. .... St. Cloud, MN
Winkelspecht, Thomas A. .... Bensalem, PA
Winkelstein, Harris J. .... Greensboro, NC
Winkelstein, Michael .... Atlantic City, NJ
Winker, David J. .... Miami, FL
Winker, Virginia L. .... Arlington, TX
Winkfield, John C.
Department Of Veterans Affairs,
Office of Employment Discrimination
Complaints Adjudication, GV
Winkfield, Lawrence E. .... Columbus, OH
Winkhart, Thomas W. .... Canton, OH
Salem, OH
Winking, Jennifer A. .... Quincy, IL
Winkis, Michelle Caduff .... Moorhead, MN
Fargo, ND
Winkle, Cynthia L. .... Columbus, OH
Winkle, David A. .... Santa Ana, CA
Winkle, David P. .... Jonesboro, GA
Winkle, Davy L. .... Columbus, OH
Winkle, Dennis A. .... Beatrice, NE
Winkle, Eric L. .... Lancaster, PA
Winkle, John A.
Department of Transportation,
Federal Railroad Administration, GV
Winkle, Lawrence A. .... Dallas, TX
Winkle, Lyle C. .... Columbus, NE
Winkleman, Henry W. .... Wellesley Hills, MA
Winkleman, Lori V. .... Atlanta, GA
Winkleman, Mark E. .... Phoenix, AZ
Winkler, Alan .... River Edge, NJ
New York, NY
Winkler, Alice Eleanor .... New York, NY
Winkler, Allen W. .... Atlanta, GA
Winkler, Andrea J.
Federal Deposit Insurance Corporation,
Compliance and Enforcement Section, GV
Winkler, Andrew M. .... Louisville, KY
Winkler, Arthur .... Trenton, NJ
Winkler, Barbara A. .... Key Largo, FL
Winkler, Barry T. .... Hampton Bays, NY
Winkler, Bradford .... Grand Rapids, MI
Winkler, Bridgette P. .... Cleveland, OH
Winkler, Charles R. .... North Riverside, IL
Winkler, Christopher .... Detroit, MI
Winkler, Dana J. .... Wichita, KS
Winkler, Daniel A. .... Westfield Center, OH
Winkler, Daniela .... Washington, DC
Winkler, David B. .... Langhorne, PA
Winkler, David J. .... Del Mar, CA
Winkler, David J. .... Milwaukee, WI
Winkler, Deborah S. .... Columbus, OH
Winkler, Dennis W. .... Chicago, IL
Winkler, Donald J. .... Chicago, IL
Winkler, Donald M. .... Laurens, IA
Winkler, Edward .... Fort Stockton, TX
Winkler, Edward H. .... New York, NY
Winkler, Ellen M. .... Marblehead, MA
Winkler, Fred M. .... St. Augustine, FL
Winkler, Frederick F. .... New York, NY
Winkler, Gerhard O. .... Saratoga, CA
Winkler & Gorey, Ltd. .... North Riverside, IL
Winkler, H. James .... Madison, GA
Winkler, H. James, P.C. .... Madison, GA
Winkler, Ira B. .... New York, NY
Winkler, James A. .... Chicago, IL
Winkler, James H. .... Portland, OR
Winkler, James L. .... Hasbrouck Heights, NJ
Winkler, James R.
Port Jefferson Station, NY
Winkler, James R. .... Toledo, OH
Winkler, James T. .... Las Vegas, NV
Winkler, Jason S. .... Livingston, NJ
Winkler, Jeffrey M. .... Bronx, NY
Winkler, Jeffrey P. .... St. Petersburg, FL
Winkler, John F. .... Columbus, OH
Winkler, John M. .... Portland, OR
Winkler, John S., P.A. .... Jacksonville, FL
Winkler, John Sherman .... Jacksonville, FL
Winkler, John T., II .... Fairfax, VA
Winkler, Karl F. .... Rockford, IL
Winkler, Kenneth N. .... Atlanta, GA
Winkler, Kurtz, Winkler & Dolewski
Port Jefferson Station, NY
Winkler, Lee, Tetwiler and Domoney
Paola, KS
Winkler, Linda J. .... Westport, CT
Winkler, Linda M. .... Ann Arbor, MI
Winkler, M. A. .... Chicago, IL
Winkler, Mark .... Franklin Lakes, NJ
Winkler, Michael B. .... Marion, IL
Winkler, Michael R. .... Houston, TX
Winkler, Monique C. .... Indianapolis, IN
Winkler, Nancy J. .... Cherry Hill, NJ
Philadelphia, PA
Winkler, Paul W. .... Falls Church, VA
Winkler, Peter .... Belvedere-Tiburon, CA
Winkler, Peter
National Labor Relations Board,
Office of the General Counsel, GV
Winkler, Peter A. .... Phoenix, AZ
Winkler, Ralph .... Cincinnati, OH
Winkler, Ralph Edward .... Cincinnati, OH
Winkler, Richard .... Irving, TX
Winkler, Richard A. .... Douglas, AZ
Winkler, Richard D.
Port Jefferson Station, NY
Winkler, Robert D. .... San Leandro, CA
Winkler, Robert L. .... Flint, MI
Winkler, Robert L. .... Salem, OR
Winkler, Robert N. .... Towson, MD
Winkler, Robert V. .... San Leandro, CA
Winkler, Ronald C. .... Dallas, TX
Winkler, Rudolf .... Los Angeles, CA
Winkler, Scott R. .... Milwaukee, WI
Winkler, Shelley J. .... Philadelphia, PA
Winkler, Sheryl Teitel .... Mineola, NY
Winkler, Steven H. .... East Hartford, CT
Winkler, Susan G. .... Boston, MA
Winkler, Thomas E. .... Houston, TX
Winkler, Thomas W. .... Chicago, IL
Winkler, Wendell D. .... Paola, KS
Winkles, Carl .... Knoxville, TN
Winkles, D. Frank .... Tampa, FL
Winkles, James C. .... Knoxville, TN
Winkley, William L. .... Plano, TX
Winklmann, Michael .... Oakmont, PA
Winkowski, Chester J. .... Haverhill, MA
Winks, Patricia L. .... San Francisco, CA
Winks, Paul William .... Springfield, OH
Winland, Thomas W. .... Washington, DC
Winmill, B. Lynn .... Pocatello, ID
Winmill, Patricia J. .... Salt Lake City, UT
Winn, A. Robinson .... Chesapeake, VA
Winn, Alan R. .... Garland, TX
Winn, Alice G. .... Boston, MA
Winn, Allan R. .... Washington, DC
Winn, Amy Julia .... Sacramento, CA
Winn, Anna Marie .... El Cajon, CA
Winn, Ashley M., Law Office of
Santa Cruz, CA
Winn, Beaudry & Winn, LLP .... Dallas, TX
Winn, Benjamin C., Jr.
Gaithersburg, MD
Fairfax, VA
Winn, Brian N. .... Anaheim, CA
Winn, Cheryl R. .... Louisville, KY
Winn & Cleary, P.A. .... Jacksonville, FL
Winn, Dan .... Cedartown, GA
Winn, Dan Nichols "Nick"
Douglasville, GA
Winn, David A. .... San Francisco, CA
Winn, David B. .... Dallas, TX
Winn, Delbert E. .... King Of Prussia, PA
Winn, Donald D. .... Los Angeles, CA
Winn, Donald J.
Board of Governors Of The Federal Reserve System,
Office of Board Members, GV
Winn, Doreen E. .... Hackensack, NJ
Winn, Edward B., (P.C.) .... Dallas, TX
Winn, Edward L., III .... Austin, TX
Winn, Frank C. .... Douglasville, GA
Winn, Garth A. .... Portland, OR
Winn, George C. .... Tampa, FL
Winn, Gregory L. .... Laramie, WY
Winn, H. Frank, Jr. .... Pensacola, FL
Winn, Harlan F., III .... Birmingham, AL
Winn, Jack .... Tulsa, OK
Winn, Jack, Inc. .... Tulsa, OK
Winn, James A. .... Philadelphia, PA
Winn, James G. .... Lawrence, KS
Winn, James J., Jr. .... Baltimore, MD
Winn, James W. .... Kansas City, MO
Winn, Jean E. .... Hartford, CT
Winn, Jeannette Anderson .... Greenville, SC
Winn, Jeffrey M. .... New York, NY
Winn, Jennifer L. .... St. Louis, MO
Winn, John P. .... Sacramento, CA
Winn, John R. .... Granville, NY
Winn & Jorgensen, P.A. .... Tampa, FL
Winn, Joseph R. .... Sacramento, CA
Winn, Judith K. .... Sacramento, CA
Winn, Katherine Ann .... San Diego, CA
Winn, Kathryn M. .... Boston, MA
Winn, Larry, III .... Overland Park, KS
Winn Law Office .... Mercer Island, WA
Winn, Mark Alfred .... St. Petersburg, FL
Winn, Marshall .... Greenville, SC
Winn, Melinda .... Houston, TX
Winn, Michael B. .... New York, NY
Winn, Michael C. .... Libertyville, IL
Winn, Michelle A. .... Charlotte, NC
Winn, Mitchell J. .... New York, NY
Winn, Nolan S. .... Jacksonville, FL
Winn, Norman L. .... Seattle, WA
Winn, Patrick J. .... Rockford, IL
Winn, Paul B. .... Beverly Hills, CA
Winn, Peter A. .... Dallas, TX
Winn, Philip S. .... Dryden, NY
Ithaca, NY
Winn, Price & Winn .... Douglasville, GA
Winn, R. Dan .... Pharr, TX
Winn, Randall .... Mercer Island, WA
Winn, Richard W. .... Dallas, TX
Winn, Robert .... Las Vegas, NV
Winn, Robert .... Pharr, TX
Winn, Robert C. .... Los Angeles, CA
Winn, Robert E. .... New Orleans, LA
Winn, Robert M. .... Fort Edward, NY
Winn, Ross E. .... Santa Monica, CA
Winn, Roy R. .... Livonia, MI
Winn, Sara Bugbee .... Roanoke, VA
Winn and Sims, A Professional Corp.
Anaheim, CA
Winn, Stephen G. .... New Hyde Park, NY
Winn, Steven E. .... Dunwoody, GA
Winn, Thomas M., III .... Roanoke, VA
Winn, Wendall L., Jr. .... Charlottesville, VA
Winn & Winn .... Sacramento, CA
Winn, Wm. S. .... Chicago, IL
Winnan, Nord F. .... Princeton, NJ
Winnar, Eric O. .... Ashtabula, OH
Winne, Banta, Rizzi, Hetherington & Basralian, P.C. .... Hackensack, NJ
New York, NY
Winne, Charles L. .... Cherry Hill, NJ
Winne, Donald W., Jr. .... Carson City, NV
Winne, Dooley and Bole, A Professional Corporation .... Paramus, NJ
Winne, Joseph E. .... Peoria, IL
Winne, Robert F. .... Rhinebeck, NY
Winne, William Lawrence .... Los Angeles, CA
Winneg, Neal S. .... Cambridge, MA
Winner, Anne E. .... Lincoln, NE
Winner & Associates, A Professional Corporation .... Anchorage, AK
Winner, Carl .... Arlington, VA
Winner, Charles S. .... Baltimore, MD
Winner, Ellen J. .... New York, NY
Winner, Ellen P. .... Boulder, CO
Winner, Francis L. .... Omaha, NE
Winner, Fred M. .... Denver, CO
Winner, George H., Jr. .... Elmira, NY
Winner, John D. .... Madison, WI
Winner, Joseph C. .... Columbus, OH
Winner, Kathryn A. .... Toledo, OH
Winner, Larry D. .... Spokane, WA
Winner, Leslie J. .... Charlotte, NC
Winner, Leslie S. .... Baltimore, MD

Winter, John M. .... New York, NY
Winter Johnson & Hill PLLC
Charleston, WV
Huntington, WV
Winter, Joseph E. .... Pasadena, CA
Winter, Joseph M. .... Atlanta, GA
Winter, Kathleen .... Napa, CA
Winter, Kimberly Ellen Nelson
Boston, MA
Winter, Kimberly K. .... Kansas City, MO
Winter, Larry A. .... Charleston, WV
Winter Law Firm .... Jacksonville, FL
Winter Law Firm, The .... Riverton, WY
Winter, Leslie A. .... Towson, MD
Winter, Linda R. .... Geneva, IL
Winter, Lisa C. .... New Orleans, LA
Winter, Louis .... Miami, FL
Winter, M. Suzanne .... Russellville, AR
Winter, Marc J. .... Claremont, CA
Winter, Maria Lathrop .... Chico, CA
Winter, Marion Ernest (Nick) .... Parkville, MO
Winter, Marissa A. .... Garden City, NY
Winter, Mark A. .... Carson City, NV
Winter, Mark J. .... New York, NY
Winter, Mark S. .... Parsippany, NJ
Winter, Mary Davidson .... Minneapolis, MN
Winter, Mary Doerhoff .... Jefferson City, MO
Winter, Matthew E. .... Hartford, CT
Winter, Matthew F. .... Phoenix, AZ
Winter, Michael B. .... Antigo, WI
Winter, Michael J. .... Oak Brook, IL
Winter, Michael J. .... Council Bluffs, IA
Winter, Michael P. .... Tampa, FL
Winter, Michael S. .... Milwaukee, WI
Winter, Michelle .... Riverton, WY
Winter, Nelson W. .... Pittsburgh, PA
Winter, Patricia J. .... Chicago, IL
Winter, Patrick R. .... Standish, MI
Winter, Paul L. .... Muskegon, MI
Winter, Peter J. .... Northville, MI
Winter, Philip L. .... Larchmont, NY
Winter, Ralph C. .... Los Angeles, CA
Winter, Ralph H. .... Costa Mesa, CA
Winter, Raymond F. .... Troy, MI
Winter, Renee C. .... St. Louis, MO
Winter & Rhoden .... Gaffney, SC
Spartanburg, SC
Winter, Richard D. .... Livonia, MI
Winter, Richard L. .... Fairfield, CT
Winter, Richard R. .... Chicago, IL
Winter, Richard T. .... Antigo, WI
Winter, Rick .... Manitowoc, WI
Winter, Robert .... Washington, DC
Winter, Robert A. .... Atlanta, GA
Winter, Robert A., Jr. .... Fort Mitchell, KY
Winter, Robert H. .... Denver, CO
Winter, Robert H. .... Washington, DC
Winter, Robert H., Jr. .... San Diego, CA
Winter, Robert J. .... Tulsa, OK
Winter, Robert L. .... Miami, FL
Winter, Robert Mc Kenna .... Chicago, IL
Winter, Robert R. .... Greensburg, PA
Winter, Roland A. .... Edison, NJ
Winter, Ronald J. .... Lockport, NY
Winter, Sidney C. .... Sherman Oaks, CA
Winter, Sidra P. .... Tupelo, MS
Winter, Stephen A. .... Atlanta, GA
Winter, Stephen C. .... Towson, MD
Winter, Stephen Curtis .... Sacramento, CA
Winter, Steven M. .... Atlanta, GA
Winter, Susan .... New York, NY
Winter, T. Roberts .... Ann Arbor, MI
Winter, Terri S. .... Denver, CO
Winter, Thomas Q. .... Santa Rosa, CA
Winter, Thomas W. .... St. Louis, MO
Winter, Val E. .... York, PA
Winter, W. Alan .... Jacksonville, FL
Winter, W. Steven .... St. Louis, MO
Winter, W. Steven .... Houston, TX
Winter, Walker .... Chicago, IL
Winter, Warren H. .... Casper, WY
Winter, Wayne W. .... St. Louis, MO
Winter, West Worrell .... San Antonio, TX
Winter, William Alexander
Minneapolis, MN
Winter, William D. .... Albuquerque, NM
Winter, William E., Jr. .... Gaffney, SC
Winter, William F. .... Jackson, MS
Winter, William G. .... Winston-Salem, NC
Winter, William J. .... Cincinnati, OH
Winter, William T. .... Riverton, WY
Winter Winter & Wild .... Antigo, WI
Winter, Winton A. .... Ottawa, KS
Winter, Winton A., Jr. .... Lawrence, KS
Winterbauer & Diamond, P.L.L.C.
Seattle, WA
Winterbauer, Steven H. .... Seattle, WA
Winterberg, Brent L. .... Kansas City, MO
Winterberger, Marla J. .... Sacramento, CA
Winter-Black, Janett S. .... Mattoon, IL
Winterbotham, Robert G.
Yorba Linda, CA
Winterbottom, Daniel A., Jr. .... Dallas, TX
Winterbottom, Linda K. .... Vista, CA
Winterbottom, Richard A. .... Albuquerque, NM
Roswell, NM
Winterburn, Catherine H. .... Palo Alto, CA
Winterer, Kerry T. .... Omaha, NE
Winterer, Philip S. .... New York, NY
Winterfeld, Amy Printz .... Englewood, CO
Winterfeldt, Daniel K. .... New York, NY
Winterfield, Adrian Burt .... Palm Beach, FL
Winterfield, Michael A. .... Flint, MI
Winterhalter, Alan M. .... McLean, VA
Winterhalter, Alan M., P.C. .... McLean, VA
Winterhalter, Keith J. .... Toledo, OH
Winterhalter, Michael D. .... Pittsburgh, PA
Winterhalter, Paul J. .... Marlton, NJ
Philadelphia, PA
Winterhalter, Paul J. .... Dayton, OH
Winterhof, Janis J. .... Lincoln, NE
Winterhoff, William W. .... Lansing, IL
Winterholler, Kent W. .... Salt Lake City, UT
Winterholler, M. Claire .... Charleston, WV
Winterich, Shawn M. .... Decatur, GA
Wintering, Mark .... Cleveland, OH
Wintering, Michael R. .... Columbus, OH
Wintering, Therese W. .... Rochester, MN
Winterman, Craig L. .... Los Angeles, CA
Wintermantel, Richard E. .... McLean, VA
Wintermeyer, Don R. .... St. Louis, MO
Winternheimer, Kevin W. .... Evansville, IN
Winterringer, J. C. .... Shawnee, OK
Winterrowd, Dana F. .... Sacramento, CA
Winterrowd, Laurie G. .... Sacramento, CA
Winters, Alan .... New York, NY
Winters, Alan J. .... Houston, TX
Winters, Amy M. .... New Orleans, LA
Winters, Andrea .... Dallas, TX
Winters, Barbara A. .... San Francisco, CA
Winters, Barbara Kay .... Des Moines, IA
Winters, Beth L. .... Harrisburg, PA
Winters, Bradley A. .... St. Louis, MO
Winters, Brenda S. .... Bradley Beach, NJ
Winters, Brewster, Crosby & Patchett
Carbondale, IL
Marion, IL
Winters, Brian D. .... Bradley Beach, NJ
Winters, Brian D. .... Milwaukee, WI
Winters, Brigen Lee
House of Representatives,
Committee on Ways & Means, GV
Winters, Bruce .... Port Clinton, OH
Winters, C. Michael .... Metairie, LA
Winters, Caren Brandt .... Longmont, CO
Winters, Chas. W. .... Columbus, OH
Winters, Christopher .... Washington, DC
Winters, Christopher S. .... Cleveland, OH
Winters, Cipora .... Woodbridge, NJ
Winters, Daniel B. .... Philadelphia, PA
Pittsburgh, PA
Winters, Daniel J. .... Chicago, IL
Winters, Daniel J. .... Philadelphia, PA
Winters, Daniel K. .... Morristown, NJ
Winters, Daniel W. .... Burlingame, CA
Winters, David C. .... Columbus, OH
Winters, David P. .... Chicago, IL
Winters, David Wayne .... Cheshire, CT
Winters, Dennis C. .... Santa Ana, CA
Winters, Dennis N. .... Greenville, KY
Madisonville, KY
Winters, Douglas E. .... Lancaster, PA
Winters, Elise K. .... Clearwater, FL
Winters, Elise K., P.A. .... Clearwater, FL
Winters, Eric "Skip" .... Portland, OR
Winters, Ernest F. .... Sacramento, CA
Winters, Featherstun, Gaumer, Kenney,
Postlewait & Stocks .... Decatur, IL
Winters & Forte .... Cheshire, CT
New Haven, CT
Waterbury, CT
Winters, Fred Timothy .... Irvine, CA
Winters, Frederick T. .... Denver, CO
Winters, Gary A. .... Washington, DC
Winters, Glen R., Jr. .... Stillwater, OK
Winters, Glenn R. .... Williamsburg, VA
Winters, Gregory F. .... Boca Raton, FL
Winters, Gregory M. .... Chicago, IL
Winters, Guy W., Jr. .... Philadelphia, PA
Winters, H. Richard .... Lansing, MI
Winters, Harry Hall, IV .... Columbia, LA
Winters, Henry Nicholas .... Dearborn, MI
Winters, Hugh Addison, III
Fayetteville, NC
Winters, Ian R. .... New York, NY
Winters, J. Sam .... Austin, TX
Winters, Jack B., Jr. .... San Diego, CA
Winters, James C. .... Houston, TX
Winters, Jeffrey Michael .... Ionia, MI
Winters, Jerry D. .... Greeley, CO
Winters, John A. .... Crookston, MN
Winters, John E. .... Knoxville, TN
Winters, John F., Jr. .... Chicago, IL
Winters, Joyce A. .... San Rafael, CA
Winters, Juliana M. .... Atlanta, GA
Winters, Karen A. .... Columbus, OH
Winters, Kathryn J. .... Tucson, AZ
Winters, Kathryn Keating
Washington, DC
Winters, Kenneth L. .... Roseland, NJ
Winters, Kevin M. .... Seattle, WA
Winters, Krug, Delbon & Nastari
Burlingame, CA
Redwood City, CA
San Francisco, CA
San Jose, CA
San Mateo, CA
Winters, Lauren E. .... Portland, OR
Winters Law Firm, The .... Santa Ana, CA
Winters Law Office .... Crookston, MN
Winters, Lingel H. .... San Francisco, CA
Winters, Lingel H., A Professional
Corporation .... San Francisco, CA
Winters, M. Elizabeth .... Madison, WI
Winters, Marc O. .... Seattle, WA
Winters, Marilynn J. .... San Jose, CA
Winters, Mark E. .... Chicago, IL
Winters, Mary A. .... Port Townsend, WA
Winters, Mary Ann .... Benicia, CA
Winters & Masters, Co., L.P.A.
Cleveland, OH
Winters & Merkle .... Columbus, OH
Winters, Michael E. .... New Orleans, LA
Winters, Michael G. .... Raleigh, NC
Winters, Michael L. .... Anaheim, CA
Winters, Michael T. .... Lancaster, PA
Winters, Milton S. .... Lowell, MA
Winters, Nestor A. .... Bradley Beach, NJ
Winters, Pat .... Greenville, TX
Winters, Patricia .... Pasadena, CA
Winters, Paul M. .... Washington, DC
Winters, Paula M. .... Newark, NJ
Winters, R. Gary .... Cincinnati, OH
Winters, Ray H. .... Myrtle Beach, SC
Winters, Raymond L. .... Redondo Beach, CA
Winters, Rebecca .... New York, NY
Winters, Richard D. .... Norristown, PA
Winters, Richd. R. .... Pittsburgh, PA
Winters, Rikki .... Deerfield Beach, FL
Winters, Robert .... Parsippany, NJ
Winters, Robert D. .... Decatur, IL
Winters, Robert G. .... Norfolk, VA
Winters, Robert J. .... Pittsburgh, PA
Winters, Robert K. .... Benicia, CA
Winters, Ron .... Sacramento, CA
Winters, Sarah D. .... Chicago, IL
Winters, Sean M. .... Pittsburgh, PA
Winters, Sheldon E. .... Juneau, AK
Winters, Sherman D.
Department of Commerce,
Patent and Trademark Office, GV
Winters, Stephen R. .... Chicago, IL
Winters, Steven B .... Toledo, OH
Winters, Steven B. .... Seattle, WA
Winters, Steven G. .... Philadelphia, PA
Winters, Susan A. .... Las Vegas, NV
Winters, Susan Jane .... Columbus, OH
Winters, Susan L. .... Southfield, MI
Winters, Susan Reach .... Short Hills, NJ
Winters, Thomas B. .... Riverside, CA
Winters, Thomas R. .... Columbus, OH
Winters, Vernon M. .... Menlo Park, CA
Winters, Vince .... Beverly Hills, CA
Winters, W. Douglas .... Ypsilanti, MI
Winters, Wallace C., Jr. .... Taylor, MI
Winters, W. G., Jr. .... Houston, TX
Winters, William E. .... San Francisco, CA
Winters, William H. .... Tampa, FL
Winterscheid, Joseph F. .... Washington, DC
Winterscheidt, Rebecca A. .... Phoenix, AZ
Wintersheimer, Amy T. .... San Diego, CA
Wintersheimer, Donald C. .... Frankfort, KY
Winter-Smith, Mary .... Mound City, KS
Winterson, Howard M., Jr. .... Hartford, CT
Wintersteen, Charles H. .... Chicago, IL
Wintersteen, Michael D. .... Danville, PA
Winterstein, W. J., Jr. .... Philadelphia, PA
Winterton, David J. .... Las Vegas, NV
Winterton, Reed F. .... Salt Lake City, UT
Winther, Arthur P. .... Wyoming, MI
Winther, Christian M. .... San Diego, CA
Winther, Harold E. .... Puyallup, WA
Winther, Nancy J. .... West Chester, PA
Winthers, David J. .... Winfield, IL
Winthers, Melissa J. .... Denver, CO
Winthers, Wayne W. .... Orange, CA
Winthrop Couchot, Professional Corporation
Newport Beach, CA
Winthrop, Douglas A. .... San Francisco, CA
Winthrop, Edward L. .... Mission, KS
Winthrop, Griffith J. .... Canandaigua, NY
Winthrop, Griffith J., III
Winter Park, FL
Winthrop, Hope Brock .... New York, NY
Winthrop, Lawrence F. .... Phoenix, AZ
Winthrop, Marc J. .... Newport Beach, CA
Winthrop, Marilyn M. .... Beverly Hills, CA
Winthrop, Pamela G. .... Washington, DC
Winthrop, Rebecca J. .... Los Angeles, CA
Winthrop, Samuel B. .... Statesville, NC
Winthrop, Sherman .... Minneapolis, MN
St. Paul, MN
Winthrop, Stimson, Putnam & Roberts
Stamford, CT
Washington, DC
Palm Beach, FL
New York, NY
Winthrop, Warren A. .... Statesville, NC
Winthrop & Weinstine, A Professional
Association .... Minneapolis, MN
St. Paul, MN
Winthrop-Michel, Ellen .... Los Angeles, CA
Wintjen, Gayle C. .... New York, NY
Wintle & Kane .... San Jose, CA
Wintle, Roger D. .... San Jose, CA
Wintner, Bernard G. .... Evansville, IN
Wintner, Howard A. .... New York, NY
Wintner, Jack A. .... Bridgeville, PA
Wintner, Jeffrey M. .... New York, NY
Wintner, Linda .... New York, NY
Wintner, Mark S. .... New York, NY
Wintner, P. Jeffrey .... Woodbury, NJ
Winton, A. Jeffrey .... Southfield, MI
Winton, Alon R. .... Toluca Lake, CA
Winton, Christopher J. .... Charleston, WV
Winton, Daniel K. .... Irvine, CA
Winton, David S. .... San Francisco, CA
Winton, Erik J. .... Boston, MA
Winton, Frank J. .... Southfield, MI
Winton, Glen P. .... Des Plaines, IL
Winton, Gordon H., Jr. .... Los Angeles, CA
Winton, Gregory S. .... Washington, DC
Winton, James C. .... Houston, TX
Winton, James E. .... Spokane, WA
Winton, Jeffrey D. .... Jefferson, OH
Winton, Jeffrey M. .... Washington, DC
Winton, Paul A. .... Orlando, FL
Winton, Steven W. .... San Diego, CA
Winton, Thomas W. .... Glenview, IL
Winton, Walter Ferrell, Jr.
Great Barrington, MA
Winton, Ward W. .... Hayward, WI
Winton, Warren .... Shell Lake, WI
Wintory, Randall H. .... Washington, DC
Wintory, Richard M. .... Oklahoma City, OK
Wintringer, Michael M. .... San Diego, CA
Wintringham, Drew M. .... New York, NY
Wintriss, Lynn .... Baltimore, MD
Wintrob, Jay S. .... Los Angeles, CA
Wintrob, Richard M. .... Irvine, CA
Wintrode, Donald E. .... Danville, VA
Wintrode, Ralph C. .... Irvine, CA
Wintrode, Timothy J. .... Wall Township, NJ
Wintrol, John P. .... Washington, DC
Wintroub, Alene P. .... Northbrook, IL
Wintroub, Cary J. .... Chicago, IL
Wintroub, David L. .... Los Angeles, CA
Wintroub, David Scott .... Omaha, NE
Wintroub, Edward L. .... Omaha, NE
Wintroub, Ernest B. .... Omaha, NE
Wintroub & Fridkis, P.C.
Los Angeles, CA
Wintroub, Rinden, Sens & McCreary
Moline, IL
Des Moines, IA
Minneapolis, MN
Omaha, NE
Wintrub, Warren G. .... New York, NY
Wintter & Associates, P.A.
Fort Lauderdale, FL
Hollywood, FL
Miami, FL
Wintter, Christopher Q. .... Hollywood, FL
Wintter, Ernst G. .... Hollywood, FL
Wintz, Daniel J. .... Omaha, NE
Wintz, Joseph A., III .... Falls Church, VA
Winuk, Glenn J. .... New York, NY
Winvick, Darci .... Menlo Park, CA
Winward, E. Kent .... Ogden, UT
Winward, James B. .... Brighton, MA
Winward, LaMar J .... St. George, UT
Winward Law Office, P.C. .... Ogden, UT
Winward, Thomas M. V. .... Rochester, NY
Winwood Crossman & Associates
Dayton, OH
Winwood, George M. .... Springfield, OH
Winwood, Jeffrey A. .... Dayton, OH
Winzeler, Brent L. .... Archbold, OH
Winzeler, Heidi I. .... Pittsburgh, PA
Winzenburg, James H. .... Denver, CO
Winzenburg, Leff, Purvis & Payne, LLP
Denver, CO
Winzenburg, Leo G. .... Fountain Hills, AZ
Winzenburg, Robert John .... Mankato, MN
Winzenreid, James Ernest .... Bridgeport, OH
Winzer, P. J.
Merit Systems Protection Board,
Washington, D.C. Regional Office, GV
Winzerling, Mary A. .... Little Rock, AR
Wion, Ann H. .... Rockville, MD
Wion, David A. .... Harrisburg, PA
Wiora, Neena R. .... Addison, TX
Wiorski, Robert H. .... Washington, DC
Wiper, Donald W., Jr. .... Columbus, OH
Wipf & Cotton .... Wagner, SD
Wipf, Owen R. .... Wagner, SD
Wipfler, W. John .... Augusta, ME
Wipperman, Robert C. .... New York, NY
Wippermann, Stephen D. .... Newtown, CT
Wippich, William J. .... Los Angeles, CA
Wippler, Michael P. .... Los Angeles, CA
Wippman, David .... Ithaca, NY
Wippold, William M. .... Chicago, IL
Wirbel, Louis E. .... Grand Ledge, MI
Wire, Beverly J. .... Wooster, OH
Wire, Kathryn K. .... St. Louis, MO
Wire, R. Thomas .... Westlake Village, CA
Wire, R. Thomas, A Professional
Corporation .... Los Angeles, CA
Westlake Village, CA
Wire, Robert J., Jr. .... York, PA
Wire, William S., II .... Nashville, TN
Wireman, Daniel R. .... Cincinnati, OH
Wireman, Kathy A. .... Cleveland, OH
Wireman, Marcia L. .... Jackson, KY
Wirey, Mark E. .... Indianapolis, IN
Wirfel, Emanuel W. .... Huntsville, TX
Wirfel, Kenneth I. .... New York, NY
Wirick, Andrew P. .... Indianapolis, IN
Wirick, Richard E. .... Santa Monica, CA
Wirin, William Bernard .... Palm Desert, CA
Wirken, Charles W. .... Phoenix, AZ
Wirken Group, The, A Professional
Corporation .... Kansas City, MO
Wirken, James C. .... Kansas City, MO
Wirkmaa, Andres O. .... Wyckoff, NJ
Wirnowski, Lisa J. .... Palo Alto, CA
Wirries, Donald A. .... Moorhead, MN
Wirschem, Michael R. .... Anchorage, AK
Wirsching, David B. .... Canton, OH
Wirshup, Rochelle Shapell .... Berkeley, CA
Wirsing, Kevin T. .... San Diego, CA
Wirsing, Richard M. .... Washington, DC
Wirskye, William H. .... Dallas, TX
Wirt, Alexander W. .... Republic, WA
Wirt, Brian L. .... Des Moines, IA
Wirt, Clay L. .... Richmond, VA
Wirt, David W. .... Chicago, IL
Wirt, James S. .... New Lenox, IL
Wirt, John S. .... Deerfield Beach, FL
Wirt, Laurie Blossom .... Columbus, OH
Wirt, Lyle J. .... Sioux Falls, SD
Wirt, Madeline S. .... Gainesville, GA
Wirt, W. Stephen .... Dublin, OH
Wirta, Henry A., Jr. .... Los Angeles, CA
San Francisco, CA
Wirtanen, Edward R. .... West Barnstable, MA
Wirtanen, Thomas A. .... Lowell, MA
Wirtel, Sandra J. .... Kansas City, MO
Wirtenberg, Alfred I. .... Weston, CT
Wirtes, David G., Jr. .... Mobile, AL

Wirth, Andrea L. ..... Belleville, IL
Wirth, Ann C. ..... Milwaukee, WI
Wirth, Christopher Winslow ..... Boulder, CO
Wirth, David A. ..... Lexington, VA
Wirth, Douglas D. ..... Woodland, CA
Wirth, Gabrielle M. ..... Irvine, CA
Wirth, Gary Yale ..... New York, NY
Wirth, Gerald R. ..... Miamisburg, OH
Wirth, Glenda J. ..... Joliet, IL
Wirth, Gregory D. ..... Rochester, NH
Wirth & Heise, P.C. ..... Belleville, IL
Wirth, Janet L. ..... St. Petersburg, FL
Wirth, Jeff ..... Kearney, NE
Wirth, John C. ..... Staunton, VA
Wirth, John C., Jr. ..... White Plains, NY
Wirth, John M. ..... Milwaukee, WI
Wirth, John T. ..... Denver, CO
Wirth, Joseph M. ..... Milwaukee, WI
Wirth, Judy L. ..... St. Petersburg, FL
Wirth, Karen C. ..... Chicago, IL
Wirth, Kathryn Stryker ..... Las Vegas, NV
Wirth, Kenton D. ..... Wichita, KS
Wirth, Mary Anne ..... White Plains, NY
Wirth, Mary Catherine
San Francisco, CA
Wirth, Morris A. ..... New York, NY
Wirth, Peter ..... Boston, MA
Wirth, Peter F. ..... Santa Fe, NM
Wirth, Richard J. ..... Hartford, CT
Wirth, Richard O. ..... North Billerica, MA
Wirth, Robert C. ..... Commack, NY
Wirth, Roger A. ..... Las Vegas, NV
Wirth, Rosanne H. ..... Edina, MN
Wirth, Shannon L. ..... Farmington Hills, MI
Wirth, Stephen R. ..... Harrisburg, PA
Wirth, Walter A. ..... Austin, TX
Wirth, William A. ..... Houston, TX
Wirth, William J. ..... Marietta, GA
Wirthlin, J. Stephen ..... Cincinnati, OH
Wirthlin, John R. ..... Cincinnati, OH
Wirthlin, John S. ..... Cincinnati, OH
Wirthlin, Matthew T. ..... Salt Lake City, UT
Wirthlin, Michael F. ..... Cincinnati, OH
Wirthlin, Richard C. ..... Los Angeles, CA
Wirthlin, Richard L. (IBA) ..... Los Angeles, CA
Wirthlin, Susan J. ..... St. Louis, MO
Wirthlin, William M., II ..... Salt Lake City, UT
Wirtner, Michelle T. ..... Philadelphia, PA
Wirtschafter, David ..... Los Angeles, CA
Wirtschafter, Joshua S. ..... Berkeley, CA
Wirtschafter, Nathan D.
North Hollywood, CA
Wirtshafter, Donald M., Jr. ..... Guysville, OH
Wirtshafter, John M. ..... Cleveland, OH
Wirtz, Cecelia E. ..... Washington, DC
Wirtz, David M. ..... Mineola, NY
New York, NY
Wirtz, Eli J. ..... Ankeny, IA
Wirtz, Francis J. ..... Chicago, IL
Wirtz, Gregg L. ..... Jacksonville, FL
Wirtz, James H. ..... Pittsburgh, PA
Wirtz, James H., P.C. ..... Pittsburgh, PA
Wirtz, John B. ..... Canton, OH
Wirtz & Kohn, A Legal Professional
Association ..... Columbus, OH
Wirtz, Martha McMahon ..... Jacksonville, FL
Wirtz, Richard M. ..... San Diego, CA
Wirtz, Richard S. ..... Knoxville, TN
Wirtz, Robert W. ..... Bismarck, ND
Wirtz, Ryan ..... Dallas, TX
Wirtz, Stuart P. ..... Department of Justice,
Federal Bureau of Investigation, GV
Wirtz, Thomas A. ..... Sacramento, CA
Wirtz, W. Willard ..... Washington, DC
Wirtz, Wayne Anthony ..... San Antonio, TX
Wirtz, William M. ..... Sacramento, CA
Wirum, Andrea A. ..... San Francisco, CA
Wirum, John M. ..... Anchorage, AK
Wirwahn, F. Eugene ..... Aldie, VA
Wirz, James A. ..... Dallas, TX
Wirzbicki, Gregory F. ..... Brea, CA
Wirzbicki, John C. ..... Norwich, CT
Wirzbicki, Philip James
Hopewell Junction, NY
Wisbar, Rebecca Kittok ..... Baton Rouge, LA
Wisbaum, F. C. ..... Niagara Falls, NY
Wisbaum, Keith D. ..... Laguna Beach, CA
Wisbaum, Wayne D., (P.C.) ..... Buffalo, NY
Wisby, James S. ..... Des Moines, IA
Wiscarson, Diane F. ..... Portland, OR
Wisch, Andrew S. ..... New York, NY
Wisch, Charles J. ..... San Francisco, CA
Wisch, Scott ..... Fort Worth, TX
Wisch, Steven A. ..... Houston, TX
Wische, Harry ..... Newark, NJ
Wischer, Carrie A. ..... Chicago, IL
Wischer, Christopher C. ..... Owensboro, KY
Wischkaemper, Bill M. ..... Lubbock, TX
Wischkaemper, Lois A. ..... Lubbock, TX
Wischkaemper, Michael ..... Carlsbad, CA
Wischmeier, David A. ..... St. Paul, MN
Wischmeier, Traci Ranallo ..... Anoka, MN
Wischmeyer, Martha L. ..... Valparaiso, IN
Wischow, Sandra Waldorf ..... Richmond, VA
Wiscovitch, Gustavo ..... San Juan, PR
Wiscovitch, Vincent J. ..... Mineola, NY
Wiscovitch Rentas, Noreen
Fort Lauderdale, FL
Wisdom, Debra M. ..... New York, NY
Wisdom & Logan ..... Phoenix, AZ
Wisdom, Mary Kathryn ..... Phoenix, AZ
Wisdom, Michael J. ..... Peoria, IL
Wisdom, Norvell Edwin, Jr.
Plymouth Meeting, PA
Wisdom, Rachel Wendt ..... New Orleans, LA
Wisdom, Sara S. ..... Tucson, AZ
Wisdom, Stan E. ..... Wichita, KS
Wisdom, Suzanne Lacey
New Orleans, LA
Wisdom, W. Jackson ..... Houston, TX
Wise, Aaron N. ..... New York, NY
Wise, Alan M. ..... Nashville, TN
Wise, Allen B., Jr. ..... Columbia, SC
Wise, Anderson ..... Watertown, NY
Wise, Ann ..... New Orleans, LA
Wise and Associates Co., L.P.A.
Van Wert, OH
Wise, B. Chadwick ..... Huntsville, AL
Wise, Bill L. ..... San Antonio, TX
Wise, Brett D. ..... New Orleans, LA
Wise, Brian D. ..... Rockville, MD
Wise, C. Rauch ..... Greenwood, SC
Wise, Candace R. ..... Dallas, TX
Wise, Carl L. ..... Stamford, CT
Wise, Carla S. ..... Goshen, NY
Wise Carter Child & Caraway, Professional
Association ..... Jackson, MS
Wise, Charles C., III ..... Fairmont, WV
Wise, Chris A. ..... Appleton, WI
Wise, Christopher N. ..... Joliet, IL
Wise & Cole, P.A. ..... Charleston, SC
Wise, Connie Hurley ..... New Orleans, LA
Wise, Coren Jay ..... Cape May, NJ
Wise, Corey J. ..... Wildwood, NJ
Wise, D. Christian ..... Springfield, MO
Wise, D. Peter ..... Springfield, IL
Wise, D. Scott ..... New York, NY
Wise, Dan R. ..... Hattiesburg, MS
Wise, David C. ..... Chicago, IL
Wise, David E. ..... San Antonio, TX
Wise, David G. ..... Toledo, OH
Wise, David Hilton ..... Annapolis, MD
Fairfax, VA
Wise, David M. ..... Cleveland, OH
Wise, David R. ..... Poughkeepsie, NY
Wise, David S. ..... Houston, TX
Wise, Dean W. ..... Columbus, OH
Wise, Deanna C. ..... Kansas City, MO
Wise, Donald Edward, Jr. ..... Lebanon, VA
Wise, Donald G. ..... Portsmouth, VA
Wise, Donna L. ..... Seattle, WA
Wise & Dorner, Ltd. ..... Toledo, OH
Wise, Douglas C. ..... Austin, TX
Wise, Douglas J. ..... Biloxi, MS
Wise, Earl Edward, III
Silver Spring, MD
Wise, Earle E. ..... Alliance, OH
Wise, Edmund N.
Agency for International Development,
Other Offices of A.I.D., GV
Wise, Edward J. ..... Washington, DC
Wise, Edward M. ..... Detroit, MI
Wise, Edythe
Federal Communications Commission,
Mass Media Bureau, GV
Wise, Elizabeth Ann ..... Perryville, AR
Wise, Ellen J. ..... Los Altos, CA
Wise, Eric N. ..... Arlington, VA
Wise, Eric W. ..... Springfield, OH
Wise, Erich P. ..... Long Beach, CA
Wise & Ford ..... Kansas City, MO
Wise, Frank J. ..... Northbrook, IL
Wise, Franklin C. ..... Baltimore, MD
Wise, Frederic M. ..... Colorado Springs, CO
Wise, Fredric ..... Miami, FL
Wise, Gail N. ..... New Orleans, LA
Wise, George E. ..... Long Beach, CA
Wise, George G. ..... El Paso, TX
Wise, George R., Jr. ..... Little Rock, AR
Wise, George W. ..... McLean, VA
Wise, Gordon E. ..... Port Aransas, TX
Wise, Gregory K. ..... Metamora, MI
Wise, Gregory W. ..... Webster, NY
Wise, H. Lake ..... New York, NY
Wise, Harry D., Jr. ..... Williamsburg, VA
Wise, Harry H., III ..... New York, NY
Wise, Helena Sunny ..... Burbank, CA
Wise, Henry E. (Jack) ..... Dallas, TX
Wise, Howard A. ..... Boston, MA
Wise, Hugh D., III ..... Aspen, CO
Wise, Hugh D., Jr. ..... Princeton, NJ
Wise, J. Edward ..... Memphis, TN
Wise, Jack B. ..... Thibodaux, LA
Wise, Jack G. ..... Houston, TX
Wise, Jacqueline D. ..... Ventura, CA
Wise, James D., Jr. ..... Houston, TX
Wise, James E. ..... San Diego, CA
Wise, James R. ..... Bardstown, KY
Wise, Janet E. ..... Tampa, FL
Wise, Jean W. ..... Overland Park, KS
Wise, Jeffrey Mitchell ..... Oklahoma City, OK
Wise, Jo Ann ..... Lexington, KY
Wise, Joan S. ..... Washington, DC
Wise, Jody L. ..... Tuscaloosa, AL
Wise, John A. ..... Detroit, MI
Wise, John A. ..... Dallas, TX
Wise, John B. ..... Pittsburgh, PA
Wise, John Eric ..... New York, NY
Wise, John F. ..... Matawan, NJ
Wise, John P. ..... Ottawa, IL
Wise, John R. ..... Baltimore, MD
Wise, John T.
Commodity Futures Trading Commission,
Division of Enforcement, GV
Wise, John W. ..... Canton, OH
Wise, Jolene M. ..... Chicago, IL
Wise, Jon W. ..... New Orleans, LA
Wise, Jonathan A.C. ..... New York, NY
Wise, Jose A. ..... Miami, FL
Wise, Joseph G. ..... Aiken, SC
Wise, Joseph P. ..... Jackson, MS
Wise, Judith ..... New York, NY
Wise, Julian M. ..... New York, NY
Wise, Karen R. ..... Dallas, TX
Wise, Katherine J. ..... Columbus, OH
Wise, Kathleen Flinn ..... Weatherford, TX
Wise, Kellye T. ..... Tigard, OR
Wise, Kenneth A. ..... Harrisburg, PA
Wise, Kenneth P. ..... Houston, TX
Wise, Kevin D. ..... Baltimore, MD
Wise & Kuzas, Ltd. ..... Chicago, IL
Wise, L. Gene ..... Fairfax, VA
Wise, Landrum E. ..... Houston, TX
Wise, Larry ..... Chesapeake, VA
Wise, Larry W. ..... Austin, TX
Wise, Lauren A. ..... Binghamton, NY
Wise Law Firm ..... Little Rock, AR
Wise Law Firm, The, P.C. ..... Fairfax, VA
Wise & Layton ..... New Canaan, CT
Wise, Lee ..... Oklahoma City, OK
Wise, Lewis K. ..... Hartford, CT
Wise, Linda J. ..... San Francisco, CA
Wise, Linden H. ..... New York, NY
Wise, M. Christie ..... Bloomington, IN
Wise, Marc S. ..... Southfield, MI
Wise, Marcia E. ..... Arlington, TX
Wise, Mark E. ..... Houston, TX
Wise & Marsac, Professional Corporation
Ann Arbor, MI
Birmingham, MI
Detroit, MI
Wise, Martha Waters, (P.C.) ..... Dallas, TX
Wise, Marvin J. ..... Dallas, TX
Wise, Matthew Tate ..... Oklahoma City, OK
Wise, Meghan Fawcett ..... Pittsburgh, PA
Wise, Melissa M. ..... Rancho Cucamonga, CA
Wise, Michael ..... Chicago, IL
Wise, Michael B. ..... Salem, OR
Wise, Michael J. ..... Los Angeles, CA
Wise, Michael J. ..... Sacramento, CA
Wise, Michael L. ..... Neenah, WI
Wise, Miguel D. ..... Brownsville, TX
Wise, Neil ..... Philadelphia, PA
Wise, Nicholas ..... New York, NY
Wise, Noël ..... Department of Justice,
Environment and Natural Resources
Division, GV
Wise, Norman ..... New York, NY
Wise, Pamela J. ..... Wood River, IL
Wise, Parker S., Jr. ..... Philadelphia, PA
Wise, Patricia A. ..... Toledo, OH
Wise, Patricia L. Campolong ..... Marietta, GA
Wise, Perry G. ..... Van Wert, OH
Wise, Peter J. ..... White Plains, NY
Wise, Philip J. ..... Dallas, TX
Wise, Raymond T., Jr. ..... Louisville, KY
Wise & Reeves, P.C. ..... Knoxville, TN
Wise, Richard A. ..... Lexington, MA
Wise, Richard C., II ..... Los Angeles, CA
Wise, Richard G. ..... Washington, DC
Wise, Richard H. ..... San Francisco, CA
Wise, Richard L. ..... Boston, MA
Wise, Richard W. ..... Jackson, MS
Wise, Robert C. ..... Williamsport, PA
Wise, Robert E. ..... Department of Commerce,
Patent and Trademark Office, GV
Wise, Robert E., Jr. ..... Boston, MA
Wise, Robert F., Jr. ..... New York, NY
Wise, Robert G. ..... New York, NY
Wise, Robert J. ..... Simsbury, CT
Wise, Robert J. ..... Kansas City, MO
Wise, Robert K. ..... Dallas, TX
Wise, Robert L. ..... Richmond, VA
Wise, Robert P. ..... Jackson, MS
Wise, Robert S. ..... Tampa, FL
Wise, Robert S., P.A. ..... Tampa, FL
Wise, Robert W. ..... McPherson, KS
Wise, Rodney Alan ..... Springfield, IL
Wise, Roger L. ..... Pittsburgh, PA
Wise, Roger R. ..... Los Angeles, CA
Wise, Roger S. ..... New York, NY
Wise, Ronald ..... Mobile, AL
Wise, Ronald W. ..... Montgomery, AL
Wise, Ronna F. ..... Concord, NH
Wise, Roy A. ..... Aberdeen, SD
Wise, Sander L. ..... Baltimore, MD
Wise, Sandra Casber ..... Washington, DC
Wise, Sergeant W. ..... Rochester, NY
Wise, Shally O. ..... Longwood, FL
Wise & Shepard, LLP ..... Fishkill, NY
Wise, Sherwood W. ..... Jackson, MS
Wise, Stanley E. ..... Southfield, MI
Wise, Stephen A. ..... New Canaan, CT
Wise, Stephen R. ..... Knoxville, TN
Wise, Steven ..... Linden, NJ
Wise, Steven H. ..... Chicago, IL
Wise, Steven L. ..... Alpharetta, GA
Wise, Steven M. ..... Boston, MA
Wise & Stracks ..... Chicago, IL
Wise, Susan E. Anderson
Long Beach, CA
Wise, Thomas Dewey ..... Marietta, GA
Wise, Thomas M. ..... Arvada, CO
Wise, Thomas R., III ..... New York, NY
Wise, Timothy John ..... Cassville, MO
Wise, Timothy J. W. ..... Oakland, CA
Wise, Tommy C. ..... Weatherford, TX
Wise, Toni Pryor ..... Palo Alto, CA
Wise, Tracey N. ..... Lexington, KY
Wise, Vickie Lynn ..... Frankfort, KY
Wise, Virginia Jo ..... Cambridge, MA
Wise, W. Michael ..... Indianapolis, IN
Wise, Warnecke & Wise ..... Lexington, KY
Wise, Warren R. ..... Wilbraham, MA
Wise, Wiezorek, Timmons & Wise, A
Professional Corporation
Long Beach, CA
Los Alamitos, CA
Los Angeles, CA
Redding, CA
Santa Ana, CA
Wise, William A. ..... El Paso, TX
Wise, William A. D., Jr. ..... Norwood, MA
Wise, William C. ..... Boulder, CO
Wise, William D. "Buddy" ..... Birmingham, AL
Wise, William H. ..... Chicago, IL
Wise, William J. ..... Chicago, IL
Wise, William L. ..... Traverse City, MI
Wise, William R., Jr. ..... Santa Ana, CA
Wise & Wise ..... Weatherford, TX
Wise & Wise ..... Portsmouth, VA
Wise, Wise & Shealy ..... Columbia, SC
Wise, Wm. J., Jr. ..... Lake Charles, LA
Wiseberg, Alice Whitehill ..... Boston, MA
Wiseberg, Stanley Carl ..... Washington, DC
Wiseblood, David M. ..... San Francisco, CA
Wisebram, Steven R. ..... Atlanta, GA
Wisecarver and Tucker ..... Jefferson City, TN
Wise-Douciere, Penny S. ..... Rayville, LA
Wisehart, Arthur M. ..... New York, NY
Wisehart & Koch ..... New York, NY
Wisehart, Robt. F. ..... Middletown, IN
Wisehart, Troy ..... Sandusky, OH
Wisehart & Wisehart ..... Middletown, IN
Wiseheart, Malcolm B., Jr. ..... Miami, FL
Wiseheart, Malcolm B., Jr., A Professional
Association ..... Miami, FL
Wiseley, O. Lee, Jr. ..... Atlanta, GA
Wiseley, Paul J. ..... Novelty, OH
Wisell, John T., Jr. ..... New York, NY
Wisely, Jas. R. ..... Staunton, VA
Wisely, William R.
Hot Springs National Park, AR
Wiseman, Alan M. ..... Washington, DC
Wiseman, Belinda Caspi ..... Syosset, NY
Wiseman, Blackburn & Futrell
Savannah, GA
Springfield, GA
Wiseman, Brian M. ..... Somerville, MA
Wiseman, Brian O. ..... Blackwell, OK
Wiseman, Charles J. ..... Portland, OR
Wiseman, D. Zachary ..... Salt Lake City, UT
Wiseman, David A. ..... Saipan, TT
Wiseman, David B. ..... Washington, DC
Wiseman, Debra Ann ..... Northbrook, IL
Wiseman, Diane J. ..... Los Angeles, CA
Wiseman, Donald F. ..... Memphis, TN
Wiseman, Dylan W. ..... Sacramento, CA
Wiseman, Elizabeth DeVine ..... Nashville, TN
Wiseman, Ellen R. ..... New York, NY
Wiseman, G. Michael ..... Fremont, NE
Wiseman, Gary E. ..... St. Louis, MO
Wiseman, Holly Lee ..... Department of Justice,
Civil Rights Division, GV
Wiseman, Jack M. ..... San Jose, CA
Wiseman, James A. ..... Murfreesboro, TN
Wiseman, Jane P. ..... Tulsa, OK
Wiseman, Jeffrey S. ..... New York, NY
Wiseman, Judith Frame ..... Kansas City, MO
Wiseman, Kenneth L. ..... Washington, DC
Wiseman, Kent I. ..... Redding, CA
Wiseman, Kimberly Cates ..... St. Louis, MO
Wiseman, Lang ..... Memphis, TN
Wiseman, Laurence E. ..... New York, NY
Wiseman Law Offices ..... Fremont, NE
Wiseman, Lawrence R. ..... Wilmington, DE
Philadelphia, PA
Wiseman, Marci W. ..... Tarzana, CA
Wiseman, Maria K.
Department Of The Interior,
Office of the Solicitor, GV
Wiseman, Mark D. ..... Concord, NH
Wiseman, Mark N. ..... Cleveland, OH
Wiseman, Mary L. ..... Dayton, OH
Wiseman, Michael D. ..... Bingham Farms, MI
Wiseman, Michael M. ..... New York, NY
Wiseman, Michelle S. Adams
Department of Commerce,
Patent and Trademark Office, GV
Wiseman, Morris ..... Department of Commerce,
Patent and Trademark Office, GV
Wiseman, Nancy Mayer ..... New York, NY
Wiseman, Oscar ..... Los Angeles, CA
Wiseman, Paula A. ..... St. Johns, MI
Wiseman, Phillip Tippet ..... Salem, OR
Wiseman, Randolph C. ..... Columbus, OH
Wiseman, Rebecca ..... Fresno, CA
Wiseman, Rena Gardner ..... Lexington, KY
Wiseman, Richard W. ..... Fort Worth, TX
Wiseman, Rodney C. ..... Lake Jackson, TX
Wiseman, Russell B. ..... Bucyrus, OH
Wiseman, Ruth Rachel ..... Lockport, NY
Wiseman, Shaikewitz, McGivern, Wahl, Flavin,
Hesi & Mormino, P.C. ..... Alton, IL
Wiseman, Stephen M. ..... New York, NY
Wiseman, Steven G. ..... Buffalo, NY
Wiseman, Tamela Eady ..... Naples, FL
Wiseman, Terry G. ..... Houston, TX
Wiseman, Thomas A., III ..... Nashville, TN
Wiseman, Thomas A., Jr. ..... Nashville, TN
Wiseman, Thomas G. ..... Washington, DC
Wiseman, Thomas L. ..... Columbus, OH
Wiseman, Thomas R. ..... Robinson, IL
Wiseman, Timothy R. ..... Lake Wales, FL
Wiseman, Timothy W. ..... Indianapolis, IN
Wiseman, Todd S. ..... Parkersburg, WV
Wiseman, W. Plumer, Jr. ..... Louisville, KY
Wiseman, Wayne Bennett ..... New York, NY
Wiseman, William A. ..... Milwaukee, WI
Wiseman, William J., III ..... Towson, MD
Wiseman, Wm. ..... Dayton, OH
Wisenbaker, Gary M. ..... Savannah, GA
Wisenbaker, Tricia N. ..... Dallas, TX
Wisenberg, Herbert ..... Houston, TX
Wisenberg, Solomon Louis
Washington, DC
Wisener, Gary G. ..... Dallas, TX
Wisener, Linda L. ..... San Diego, CA
Wisener, Ruth Ann ..... Fayetteville, AR
Wisener, Thomas W. ..... Lawton, OK
Wiser, C. Lawrence ..... Kensington, MD

Wiser, Daniel J. .... Tallahassee, FL
Wiser, Joseph H. .... Orlando, FL
Wiser, Kathryn T. .... Spokane, WA
Wiser, Merle E. .... Clarion, PA
Wiser, Nicholas Van .... Biloxi, MS
Wiser, Ralph E., III .... Lake Oswego, OR
Wiser, Ralph E., III, P.C.
Lake Oswego, OR
Portland, OR
Wiser, Ralph L. .... Chevy Chase, MD
Wiser, Robert .... St. Davids, PA
Wiser, Steven .... Chicago, IL
Wish, Ernest Allen .... Los Angeles, CA
Wish, Ernest Allen, A Professional Law Corporation .... Los Angeles, CA
Wish, Jerrold A. .... Miami, FL
Wish, Judith B. .... Department of Justice, Office of Professional Responsibility, GV
Wish, Linda H. .... Atlanta, GA
Wishaar, James H. .... Seattle, WA
Wishard, Darryl R. .... Williamsport, PA
Wishard, Gordon D. .... Indianapolis, IN
Wishard, Tiffany Ann Winn
Montoursville, PA
Wishard, William R. .... San Francisco, CA
Wishart, Barry J. .... Brea, CA
Wishart, Lawrence D. .... Reno, NV
Wishart, Lynn .... New York, NY
Wishart, Martha .... Cambridge, MA
Wishart, Norris, Henninger & Pittman, P.A.
Burlington, NC
Charlotte, NC
Wishart, Robert J. .... Burlington, NC
Wishchuk, Chad T. .... King Of Prussia, PA
Wishchuk, James R. .... Allentown, PA
Wishek, M. Bradley .... Sacramento, CA
Wishengrad, Marcia H. .... Rochester, NY
Wishik, Heather R. .... Brookline, MA
Wishik, Jeffrey M. .... Providence, RI
Wishik, Laura B. .... Seattle, WA
Wishingrad, Annie .... Los Angeles, CA
Wishko, Jeffrey C. .... Everett, WA
Wishman, Jeffrey N. .... Los Angeles, CA
Wishnack, Stephanie B. .... Richmond, VA
Wishner, Corey Lee .... New York, NY
Wishner, Jane B. .... Albuquerque, NM
Wishner, Mark J. .... Reston, VA
Wishnev, Karen L. .... New Orleans, LA
Wishnew, John A. .... Plano, TX
Wishney, David E. .... Boise, ID
Wishnia, Bernard .... Roseland, NJ
Wishnia, Eileen .... New York, NY
Wishnick, Susan .... Chicago, IL
Wishnie, Dennis C. .... San Francisco, CA
Wishnoff, Alan M. .... Buffalo, NY
Wishnoff, Howard .... Horsham, PA
Wishnoff, Jory I. .... Chicago, IL
Wishnow, Edward C. .... Birmingham, MI
Wishnow, Steven M. .... Washington, DC
Wishod, Eugene L. .... Melville, NY
Wishod, Joseph H. .... Melville, NY
Wishon, A. Emory, III .... Fresno, CA
Wisiackas, John S. .... Fairfax, VA
Wisialowski, Thomas S. .... Los Angeles, CA
Wisinger, John E. .... Warren, NJ
Wisinski, Jennifer Thoman .... Dallas, TX
Wisinski, Matthew K. .... Oakland, CA
Wisk, Allan C. .... Dallas, TX
Wisk, Susan K. .... Dallas, TX
Wiske, Jason P. .... Pittsburg, KS
Wiskin, Jerry P. .... New York, NY
Wiskirchen, Bradley J. .... Boise, ID
Wiskow, Phillip C. .... Denville, NJ
Wisla, Gerard A. .... Hicksville, NY
Wisla, Ronald M. .... Washington, DC
Wisler, Eric D. .... Teaneck, NJ
Wisler, James L. .... Topeka, KS
Wisler, Jeffrey C. .... Wilmington, DE
Wisler, Pearlstine, Talone, Craig, Garrity & Potash, LLP .... Blue Bell, PA
Norristown, PA
Wislocki, Stephan .... Yonkers, NY
Wismann, William A. .... Patchogue, NY
Wismer, Lauren W. .... Lincoln, NE
Wismer, Shelley K. .... Salt Lake City, UT
Wismer, William P. .... Media, PA
Wisne, Gerald .... Tulsa, OK
Wisne, Pamela J. .... Santa Monica, CA
Wisner, Adams, Walker & Line, P.C.
Huntsville, AL
Wisner, Alex B. .... Los Angeles, CA
Wisner & Associates .... Houston, TX
Wisner, Donald J. .... Rochester, NY
Wisner, Douglas L. .... New York, NY
Wisner, Edwin A. .... Columbus, OH
Wisner, Erin E. .... Mattoon, IL
Wisner, Floyd A. .... Chicago, IL
Wisner, Frederick G. .... Madison, WI
Wisner, Graham G. .... Washington, DC
Wisner, John C., III .... Little Rock, AR
Wisner, Kent F. .... San Francisco, CA
Wisner, Kevin R. .... Oklahoma City, OK
Wisner, Mark R. .... Houston, TX
Wisner, Michael K. .... Huntsville, AL
Wisner, Oliver J. .... Watertown, NY
Wisner, Peter F. .... Long Beach, CA
Wisner, Richard S. .... Phoenix, AZ
Wisner, Saunders & Livingston
Watertown, NY
Wisner, Todd J.W. .... Rochester, NY
Wisner, Victor Jay .... Houston, TX
Wisner, Wilford L. .... Washington, DC
Wisner, Wilford L. .... Sun City Center, FL
Wisneski, David S. .... Harrisburg, PA
Wisneski, Edward S. .... Washington, DC
Wisneski, Kimberley Smoron .... Chicago, IL
Wisnev, Michael A. .... Los Angeles, CA
Wisnia, Howard N. .... La Jolla, CA

Wisnicki, Norman S. .... Los Angeles, CA
Wisniewski, David A. .... Atlanta, GA
Wisniewski, Eugene F. .... Philadelphia, PA
Wisniewski, Frank H. .... Cherry Hill, NJ
Wisniewski, Jenni .... Denver, CO
Wisniewski, John S. .... Baltimore, MD
Wisniewski, John S. .... Tinton Falls, NJ
Wisniewski, Joseph M., Jr. .... Manchester, NH
Wisniewski, Joseph M., Jr., P.A.
Manchester, NH
Wisniewski, Kathy A. .... St. Louis, MO
Wisniewski, Mark .... Miami, FL
Wisniewski, Mark A. .... Detroit, MI
Wisniewski, Mark A. .... Bensalem, PA
Philadelphia, PA
Wisniewski, Marshall D. .... Perrysburg, OH
Wisniewski, Milton J. .... Kingsville, MD
Wisniewski, Paul J. .... Chicago, IL
Wisniewski, Richard J.
Saratoga Springs, NY
Wisniewski, Robert E. .... Kingman, AZ
Wisniewski, Robert F. .... Joliet, IL
Wisniewski, Stanley C. .... Brookeville, MD
Wisniewski, Wayne L. .... Brooklyn, NY
Wisnik, Robert S. .... New York, NY
Wisniowski, Karen J. .... Boston, MA
Wisnom, Craig Hunter .... Tucson, AZ
Wisnom, Patricia M. .... Tucson, AZ
Wisnouse, Randy M. .... Johnstown, PA
Wisnovsky, Anna V. .... Ringwood, NJ
Wisnowski, Deborah A. .... Washington, DC
Wisoff, C. Brandon .... San Francisco, CA
Wisong, Wayne W. .... Atlanta, GA
Charlotte, NC
Raleigh, NC
Columbia, SC
Wisor, Clark E., III .... Rockville, MD
Wisor, Dee P. .... Denver, CO
Las Vegas, NV
Reno, NV
Wisor, Ronald L., Jr. .... Washington, DC
Wisot, G. Keith .... Los Angeles, CA
Wisot, Jeremy V. .... Tucson, AZ
Wisot, Marc .... Los Angeles, CA
Wisot, Valerie .... Beverly Hills, CA
Wisotsky, Alan E., Law Offices of
Oxnard, CA
Wisotsky, Audrey D. .... Princeton, NJ
Wisotsky, Bruce J. .... Roseland, NJ
Wisotsky, Gregg A. .... Wayne, NJ
Wisotsky, Lester C. .... Orlando, FL
Wisotsky, Linda N. .... Beverly Hills, CA
Wisotsky, Linda N. .... Los Angeles, CA
Wisotsky, Steven J. .... Fort Lauderdale, FL
Wisotzkey, Samuel C. .... Milwaukee, WI
Wisowaty, Edward P. .... Sturgeon Bay, WI
Wisowaty, Sigmund W. .... Baltimore, MD
Wiss, Ilona-Anne .... Miami, FL
Wiss, Marcia A. .... Washington, DC
Wiss, Mary E. .... San Francisco, CA
Wiss, Michael Jay, & Associates
Dallas, TX
Wiss, Ronald E. .... Roseland, NJ
Wiss, Scott L. .... New York, NY
Wissak, Richard J. .... Long Island City, NY
Wissbaum, Donna Cacic .... Montello, WI
Wissbrun, Kenneth M. .... Bingham Farms, MI
Wisse, William .... Warner Robins, GA
Wissehr, Mark H., (P.C.) .... St. Joseph, MO
Wissel, Kathryn M. .... Albuquerque, NM
Wissel, Nancy Gardner .... Richmond, IN
Wissel, Philip J. .... Yorktown Heights, NY
Wissel, Scott A. .... Kansas City, KS
Wissel, Walter J. .... Houston, TX
Wisselman, Jerome A. .... Great Neck, NY
Wisselman, Jerome A., P.C., The Law Firm of
Great Neck, NY
Wisser, Ellen B. .... Bridgeport, CT
Westport, CT
Wisser, Jon N. .... Austin, TX
Wisser, Kerry Marc .... West Hartford, CT
Wisser, Mark D. .... Minneapolis, MN
Wissert, David M. .... Roseland, NJ
Wisset, Barry S. .... Rochester, NY
Wissing, Gerard M. .... New York, NY
Wissing, William K. .... Summit, NJ
Wissinger, Chad Allen .... Pittsburgh, PA
Wissinger, John W. .... Camarillo, CA
Wissinger, Norman R. .... Dayton, OH
Wissing-Healy, Beth .... San Rafael, CA
Wissink, Susan M. .... Phoenix, AZ
Wissler, Richard R. .... Waterford, NY
Wissler, William W. .... Tucson, AZ
Wissley, Deborah Z. .... Van Nuys, CA
Wissman, Angela B. .... Chicago, IL
Wissmann, Suzanne M.
Fairview Heights, IL
Wissner, John K. .... Boonville, IN
Wissner, Peter A. .... Los Angeles, CA
Wissner, Reid B. .... New York, NY
Wissner-Gross, Sigmund S.
New York, NY
Wissow, Leonard S. .... Philadelphia, PA
Wist, Charles, (P.C.) .... Houston, TX
Wist, Christopher .... Charlottesville, VA
Wist, Cole A. .... Denver, CO
Wist, E. John .... Tipp City, OH
Troy, OH
West Milton, OH
Wist Holland Kehlhof & Patton, L.L.P.
Houston, TX
Wistendahl, Douglass A. .... New York, NY
Wisti, Andrew H. .... Hancock, MI
Iron Mountain, MI
Marquette, MI
Wisti, Daniel J. .... Hancock, MI
Wisti, Mark .... Hancock, MI

Wisti & Wisti, P.C. .... Escanaba, MI
Hancock, MI
Houghton, MI
Iron Mountain, MI
Marquette, MI
Munising, MI
Wistner, Charles P. .... Huntington, WV
Wistner, Rebecca A. .... Cleveland, OH
Wistner, Robert N. .... Columbus, OH
Dublin, OH
Wistow & Barylick, Incorporated
Providence, RI
Wistow, Fred .... New York, NY
Wistow, Max .... Providence, RI
Wistrand, Edwin M. .... Minneapolis, MN
Wistrand, Pamela G. .... Burton, MI
Wistreich, Carl G. .... New York, NY
Wistrom, Kevin J. .... Muskegon, MI
Wistrom, Oyvind .... Milwaukee, WI
Wiswall, Courtney W. .... Portland, OR
Wiswall, Frank L., Jr. .... Castine, ME
Wiswall, Michael J. .... Portland, OR
Kirkland, WA
Wiswall, Thomas S. .... Buffalo, NY
Wiswell, Merideth P. .... Huntington, WV
Wisz, David L. .... Bloomfield Hills, MI
Wisz, David Scott .... Raleigh, NC
Wisz, Walter A. .... Ebensburg, PA
Wiszowaty, Edwin S. .... Chicago, IL
Wiszowaty, Marion J. .... Chicago, IL
Wiszowaty & Wiszowaty .... Chicago, IL
Wit, Adam C. .... Chicago, IL
Wit, Harold M. .... New York, NY
Witaconis, Charles R. .... Scranton, PA
Witalec, Joseph M. .... Columbus, OH
Witalis, Lawrence C. .... San Francisco, CA
Witanachchi, Vinita J. .... Tampa, FL
Witanen, John E. .... Park Ridge, IL
Witaschek, Fred V. .... Lakewood, CO
Witasick, Kevin John .... Phoenix, AZ
Witasick, Kevin John, & Associates
Phoenix, AZ
Witaske, Raymond A. .... Hampshire, IL
Witbeck, George H., Jr.
East Greenbush, NY
Witchel, Milton M. .... New York, NY
Witcher, Albert .... Waco, TX
Witcher, Andrea L. .... Gardendale, AL
Witcher, Blake B. .... Dallas, TX
Witcher, Charles C. .... Newnan, GA
Witcher, Eric L. .... Elkhart, KS
Witcher, George W., Jr. .... Gardendale, AL
Witcher, Harold L. .... Atoka, OK
Witcher, Jack F. .... Bremen, GA
Witcher, Jack F. .... Buchanan, GA
Witcher, James S., III .... Birmingham, AL
Witcher, James S., Jr. .... Birmingham, AL
Witcher, Jenelda E. .... Toledo, OH
Witcher, Jim .... Austin, TX
Witcher, Mark T. .... Austin, TX
Witcher, Robert Lance .... St. Louis, MO
Witcher, Robert P. .... Atlanta, GA
Witcher, Roger K., Jr. .... Lafayette, TN
Witcher, Thomas M. .... Bremen, GA
Witcher, Thomas M. .... Decatur, GA
Witcher, William G., Jr. .... Decatur, GA
Witchger, James D. .... Indianapolis, IN
Witchko, Richard K. .... Pittsburgh, PA
Witcoff, David L. .... Chicago, IL
Witcoff, Lulu Beth .... Glencoe, IL
Witcoff, Sheldon W. .... Chicago, IL
Witcover, Henry W. .... Fayetteville, NC
Witdorchic, Lawrence I. .... New York, NY
Witdorchic, Stephen I. .... Hauppauge, NY
Witeck, Christopher M. .... Washington, DC
Witecki, Glenn J. .... Schenectady, NY
Witecki, Marybeth .... Morristown, NJ
Witek, Keith E. .... Austin, TX
Witek, Michael P. .... Seattle, WA
Witek, Robert L. .... Oceanport, NJ
Witek, Robert W. .... Carson City, NV
Witek, Thomas .... Chicago, IL
Witenberg, Bruce P. .... Seattle, WA
Witenstein, David .... Boca Raton, FL
Wites, Marc A. .... Miami, FL
Withall, John R. .... Chicago, IL
Witham, Albert V. .... Littleton, CO
Witham, Archie A. .... Carrizozo, NM
Witham, Bob A. .... New Castle, IN
Witham, Charles B. .... San Diego, CA
Witham, Francis P. .... Lincoln Park, NJ
Witham, Herb D. .... Danville, IN
Witham, Jeanmarie .... Lincoln Park, NJ
Witham, Jeffrey R. .... Los Angeles, CA
Witham, Lyle .... Bismarck, ND
Witham, Nigel R. .... Irvine, CA
Long Beach, CA
Witham, Richard T. .... Hinsdale, IL
Witham, William L., Jr. .... Dover, DE
Witham & Witham, P.A.
Lincoln Park, NJ
Withee, Douglas R. .... Palatka, FL
Withee, Stephen .... Columbus, OH
Withee, Thomas V. .... Southgate, MI
Witheft, David J. .... Raleigh, NC
Withem, Jack E. .... Houston, TX
Withem, Michael L. .... Los Angeles, CA
Witherby, Frederick R. H. .... Boston, MA
Witherby, Frederick R. H., Jr.
Fort Lauderdale, FL
Witherby, H. Reed .... Boston, MA
Withered Corrigan & Service
Lafayette, IN
Withered, Jerome L. .... Lafayette, IN
Witherel, Kovacik & Marchewka
Pittsburgh, PA
Witherel, Matthew L. .... Pittsburgh, PA
Witherel, Michael J. .... Pittsburgh, PA

Witherell, Andrew J. .... Wilmington, DE
Witherell, Dennis P. .... Toledo, OH
Witherell, Linden E. .... Boston, MA
Witherell, Martin J. .... Toledo, OH
Witherell, Victoria Roe .... Wilmington, DE
Witherill, Christine M. .... Janesville, WI
Witheringten, Laura S.
West Long Branch, NJ
Witherington, A. Thomas .... Lynchburg, VA
Witherington, Thomas W. .... Hartford, CT
Witherow, James P. .... Fresno, CA
Witherow, John A., Jr. .... Harrisburg, PA
Witherow, Paula C. .... Newark, DE
Wilmington, DE
Kennett Square, PA
Withers, Arlene Falk .... Pasadena, CA
Withers, Brant, Igoe & Mullennix, P.C.
Excelsior Springs, MO
Gladstone, MO
Kansas City, MO
Liberty, MO
Withers, Carl R. .... Cleveland, OH
Withers, Catherine M.
Federal Communications Commission, Mass Media Bureau, GV
Withers, Charles B. .... Tucker, GA
Withers, Charles E. .... Grand Junction, CO
Withers, Charles W. .... Alpine, CA
Withers, Claudia A.
Department of Education, Office of the General Counsel, GV
Withers, Cynthia .... Dallas, TX
Withers, Darius B. .... Washington, DC
Federal Communications Commission, Common Carrier Bureau, GV
Silver Spring, MD
Withers, Gary A. .... Lake Oswego, OR
Withers, Geoffrey D. .... Winter Park, FL
Withers, J. Bertron, Jr.
Federal Communications Commission, Mass Media Bureau, GV
Withers, James D. .... Atlanta, GA
Withers, James E. .... Nashville, TN
Withers, Janna Faye .... Little Rock, AR
Withers, John L. .... Chevy Chase, MD
Withers, K. Ball .... Galveston, TX
Withers, Kenneth J. .... Boston, MA
Withers, Kevin D. .... Springfield, MA
Withers, Larry A. .... Wichita, KS
Withers, Mark V. .... Nampa, ID
Withers, Mary Hayden .... Troy, MI
Withers, Marylin F. .... Littleton, CO
Withers, Melanie C. .... Georgetown, DE
Withers, Mervin C. .... Callao, VA
Withers, Michael R. .... Anderson, IN
Withers, Morris K. .... Kansas City, MO
Withers, R. Dennis .... Atlanta, GA
Withers, Richard W. .... Jacksonville, FL
Withers, Seidman & Rice, P.C.
Grand Junction, CO
Withers, Sharon M. .... Saginaw, MI
Withers, Theresa J. .... Baltimore, MD
Withers, Thomas A. .... Savannah, GA
Withers, Timothy William .... Hammond, IN
Withers, W. Wayne .... St. Louis, MO
Withers, Wayne O'Neal, Jr. .... Martinsville, VA
Withers, William D. .... Austell, GA
Witherspoon, Ashley B. .... St. George, SC
Witherspoon, Carolyn B. .... Little Rock, AR
Witherspoon & Compton .... Meridian, MS
Witherspoon, David B. .... Washington, DC
Witherspoon, Gerald S. .... San Francisco, CA
Witherspoon, Gordon H. .... Lutherville, MD
Witherspoon, James A. .... Charlotte, NC
Witherspoon, James S. .... Austin, TX
Witherspoon, Jeanne Marie .... Chicago, IL
Witherspoon, John B., Jr.
Summerville, SC
Witherspoon, John F. .... Washington, DC
Witherspoon, John G., Jr. .... Dayton, OH
Witherspoon, John McC. .... Austin, TX
Witherspoon, Jos. P. .... Austin, TX
Witherspoon, Katherine Randolph
Wilmington, DE
Witherspoon, Kelley, Davenport & Toole, P.S. .... Coeur d'Alene, ID
Spokane, WA
Witherspoon, Kenneth J. .... Alpine, CA
Witherspoon Law Offices, The
Farmington, CT
Witherspoon, Lewis S. .... Columbus, OH
Witherspoon, Lister, IV .... Miami, FL
Witherspoon, Peter A. .... Spokane, WA
Witherspoon, Sandra D. .... Atlanta, GA
Witherspoon, Thomas W., Jr.
Farmington, CT
Witherspoon, Vernon L. .... Arlington, TX
Witherspoon, Vernon L. .... Irving, TX
Witherspoon, William K. .... Columbia, SC
Witherspoon, William W. .... Lakehurst, NJ
Witherwax, Charles H. .... New York, NY
Witherwax, Wayne R. .... Poughkeepsie, NY
Withey, Carrie P. .... Scottsdale, AZ
Withey, Michael B. .... Phoenix, AZ
Withey, Michael E. .... Seattle, WA
Withey, Pamela A. .... Pasadena, CA
Withey & Tobin, P.L.C. .... Phoenix, AZ
Withiam, Diane B. .... Ithaca, NY
Withiam, Douglas .... Cushing, OK
Withiam, Sam .... Cushing, OK
Withington & Betters, P.C. .... Plymouth, MA
Withington, Beverly Jean .... Hilo, HI
Withington, Lothrop, III .... Plymouth, MA
Withington, Mary M. .... Saratoga Springs, NY
Withington, Richd. W., Jr.
Point Pleasant, NJ
Withington, Robert C. .... St. Louis, MO

Wittig, Edith A. .... Houston, TX
Wittig, Roger J. .... Williamsville, NY
Wittik-Bravmann, Ann .... Bowie, MD
Witting, Cynthia .... Phoenix, AZ
Witting, Susan H. .... Thousand Oaks, CA
Wittkamp, J. Page .... Richmond, VA
Wittkamp, Rodney A. .... Burlington, IA
Wittkamper, Gerry V. .... Akron, OH
Wittkop, Mindy L. .... Eugene, OR
Wittlake, Lenard L. .... Boise, ID
Wittler, Terry R. .... Lincoln, NE
Wittlif, Renee .... Los Angeles, CA
Wittliff, Sally B. .... Austin, TX
Wittliff, Susan Leonard .... Dallas, TX
Wittlin, Craig S. .... Buffalo, NY
Rochester, NY
Wittlin, Floyd I. .... New York, NY
Wittlin, Irwin M. .... Encino, CA
Wittlin, Lori B. .... Washington, DC
Wittlinger, Timothy D. .... Detroit, MI
Wittman, Bryan C. .... Austin, TX
Wittman, Dennis L. .... Hamilton, OH
Wittman, George P. .... Jerseyville, IL
Wittman, Joseph I. .... Topeka, KS
Wittman, L. Christopher
Kansas City, MO
Wittman, Mark J. .... Marshfield, WI
Wittman, Mark P. .... Redmond, WA
Wittman & McCord .... Alamosa, CO
Colorado Springs, CO
Denver, CO
Durango, CO
Pueblo, CO
Wittman, Michael Lee .... New York, NY
Wittman, Paul S. .... Wilmington, DE
Wittman, Randall R. .... Irvine, CA
Wittman, Sandra J. .... San Diego, CA
Wittman, Sherwin V. "Bud", II, (P.C.)
Colorado Springs, CO
Denver, CO
Wittman, Stephen E. .... San Diego, CA
Wittman, Steven F. .... Chicago, IL
Wittman, Walter T. .... Montvale, NJ
Wittman, William A. .... Dana Point, CA
Wittman, William M. .... Miami, FL
Wittmann, Edward P. .... Erie, PA
Wittmann, Phillip A. .... New Orleans, LA
Wittmayer, Chris G. .... Highland Village, TX
Wittmayer, John A. .... Portland, OR
Wittmayer, Theodore I. .... Stockton, CA
Wittmer, Carver & Pope .... Sarasota, FL
Wittmer, Cynthia Leigh .... Raleigh, NC
Wittmer, Lyn .... Miami, FL
Wittmer, Steven T. .... Sarasota, FL
Wittmeyer, Ronald F., Jr.
Arlington Heights, IL
Wittneben, Brian L. .... Dallas, TX
Wittner, Allyson P. .... Beverly Hills, CA
Wittner, Brett Lorin .... Tacoma, WA
Wittner, Gregory Nat .... St. Louis, MO
Wittner, Howard A. .... St. Louis, MO
Wittner, Loren A. .... Phoenix, AZ
Wittner, Nicholas J. .... Torrance, CA
Wittner, Poger, Spewak & Maylack, P.C.
St. Louis, MO
Wittner, Van E., Jr. .... Stafford, TX
Wittorff, H. John .... Los Angeles, CA
Wittow, Gary B. .... Frisco, CO
Wittow, Mark .... Seattle, WA
Wittrig, Robert T. .... San Bernardino, CA
Wittrock, Gregory D. .... Taylor, MI
Wittrock, John T. .... Portland, OR
Wittrock, Monica A. .... Oklahoma City, OK
Wittrock & O'Brien .... Portland, OR
Wittrock, Quentin R. .... Minneapolis, MN
Wittry, Richard G. .... Lawndale, CA
Witts, David A. .... Dallas, TX
Wittstadt, Gerard W. .... Baltimore, MD
Wittstadt, Gerard Wm., Jr. .... Baltimore, MD
Wittstadt, Mark H. .... Baltimore, MD
Wittstadt & Wittsdadt .... Baltimore, MD
Wittstein, Andrew M. .... New Milford, CT
Wittstein, Eric S. .... New York, NY
Wittstruck, Chris E. .... Jackson Heights, NY
Wittstruck, Clarke K. .... Asheville, NC
Wittstruck, Craig D. .... Lincoln, NE
Wittstruck, Roy M. .... Fort Collins, CO
Wittwer, Cara A. .... Edina, MN
Wittwer, Jonathan .... Santa Cruz, CA
Wittwer, Kris Alan .... Minneapolis, MN
Witty, Delbert A. .... Orange, MA
Witty, Joanne .... Brooklyn, NY
Witty, John V. .... Redmond, OR
Witty, Laura L. .... Detroit, MI
Witty, Noah .... New York, NY
Witty, Peter N. .... Chicago, IL
Witucki, Stephanie Ann .... Southfield, MI
Witus, Brian .... Bloomfield Hills, MI
Witus, David .... Redmond, WA
Witus, Morley .... Detroit, MI
Witwer, James S. .... Denver, CO
Witwer, Oldenburg, Barry & Bedingfield, LLP .... Greeley, CO
Witwer, Poltrock & Giampietro
Chicago, IL
Witwer, Robert E. .... Denver, CO
Witwer, Samuel W., Jr. .... Chicago, IL
Witwer, Stow L., Jr. .... Greeley, CO
Witwicki, Raymond T. .... Pittsburgh, PA
Witynski, Curtis Alan .... Madison, WI
Witz, Allen Barry .... Beverly Hills, CA
Witz, Charles J. .... Chicago, IL
Witz, Herbert E. .... Baltimore, MD
Witz, James M. .... Chicago, IL
Witz, Jean C. .... Department of Commerce, Patent and Trademark Office, GV
Witzel, Carla Stone .... Baltimore, MD
Witzel, James L. .... East Lansing, MI
Witzel, John E., II .... St. Paul, MN
Witzel, Judith Wagner .... St. Louis, MO
Witzel, Kearns, Kenney & Dimmitt
Clayton, MO
St. Louis, MO
Witzel, Kenneth J. .... Pittsburgh, PA
Witzel, Richard C., Jr. .... Chicago, IL
Witzel, Richard C., (P.C.) .... St. Louis, MO
Witzel, Steven M. .... New York, NY
Witzer, Brian D. .... Los Angeles, CA
Witzer, Brian D., Inc., Law Offices of
Beverly Hills, CA
Los Angeles, CA
Witzgall, Elizabeth B. .... Treasury Department, Departmental Offices, GV
Witzig, Hannah & Sanders, LLP
Santa Cruz, CA
Witzig, John J. .... Chicago, IL
Witzig, Marc W. .... Harrisburg, PA
Witzig, Mark P. .... Santa Cruz, CA
Witzke, Michael P. .... Farmington Hills, MI
Witzke, Randy D. .... Oklahoma City, OK
Witzling, Morton .... New York, NY
Witztum, Ruth J. .... New York, NY
New York, NY
Wivell, Bart J. .... Jacksonville, FL
Wivell, Martha K. .... Minneapolis, MN
Wiviott, Fred .... Milwaukee, WI
Wiviott, Max D. .... Rogers, AR
Wiviott, Sheryl D. .... Columbus, OH
Wivoda, Roland T. .... Hibbing, MN
Wix, David G. .... Chicago, IL
Wix, Kurtt R. .... Fort Worth, TX
Wix, Richard H. .... Harrisburg, PA
Wix, Theresa L. Shade .... Harrisburg, PA
Wix, Wenger & Weidner, A Professional Corporation .... Harrisburg, PA
Wix, William J. .... Wichita, KS
Wixler, Keith Edward .... Greenville, SC
Wixom, Gary L. .... Honolulu, HI
Wixom, Michael B. .... Las Vegas, NV
Wixom, Raymond David .... Salt Lake City, UT
Wixon, Clarke Andrew .... Palo Alto, CA
Wixon, Henry N. .... Washington, DC
Wixsom, Matthew J. .... Ashland, KY
Wixson, Charles L. .... San Francisco, CA
Wixson, Robert G. .... Madison, WI
Wixson, Roy L. .... Amherst, NY
Wixted, Dennis G. .... Camden, NJ
Wixted, Gerald D. .... Princeton, NJ
Wixted, John G. .... Philadelphia, PA
Wixted, Kevin M. .... St. Charles, IL
Wiygul, Robert B. .... Denver, CO
Wizelman, Leslie .... Towanda, PA
Wizelman, Leslie .... Wyalusing, PA
Wizmur & Gordon .... Marlton, NJ
Wizmur, Judith H. .... Camden, NJ
Wizmur, Leonard R. .... Marlton, NJ
Wizner, Andrew L. .... Hartford, CT
Wizner, Stephen .... New Haven, CT
Wiznitzer, Jane T. .... Stamford, CT
Wiznitzer, Michelle .... Chicago, IL
Wiznitzer, Stephen B. .... Orangeburg, NY
Wizorek, Dana A.F. .... Cherry Hill, NJ
Philadelphia, PA
Wizorek, Roxana .... St. Louis, MO
Wladis, Mark N. .... Syracuse, NY
Wladyka, Agnes S. .... Newark, NJ
Wlasuk, Melanie .... Syracuse, NY
Wlazlo, MaryJo .... Philadelphia, PA
Wleklinski, Joseph P., Jr. .... Merrillville, IN
Wleklinski, Mark J. .... Walnut Creek, CA
Wloch, Vincent J. .... Youngstown, OH
Wlodek, Michael A. .... Elgin, IL
Wlodek, Steven T. .... Los Angeles, CA
Wlodek, Walter M. .... Cicero, IL
Wlodkowski, John B. .... Portland, ME
Wlodkowski, Lawrence J. .... Detroit, MI
Wnek, Robert E. .... Stratford, CT
Wnorowski, A. K. (Del) .... Wakefield, MA
Wnuck, Lisa E. .... Southbury, CT
Wnuczek, Robert J. .... Chicago, IL
Wnuk, Christopher J. .... New Orleans, LA
Wo, Julia C. .... San Francisco, CA
Wobbekind, Kenneth F. .... Tarrytown, NY
Wobbekind, William E. .... West Milford, NJ
Wobber, Kathleen M. .... Towson, MD
Wobbrock, D. Lawrence .... Portland, OR
Wobbrock, Lawrence, Trial Lawyer P.C.
Portland, OR
Wobeck, Bruce A. .... Atlanta, GA
Wobensmith, Zachary T., III
Philadelphia, PA
Wobensmith, Zachary T., III
Valley Forge, PA
Woboril, Peter P., Jr. .... Delafield, WI
Wobst, Franck G. .... Columbus, OH
Wobst, Leigh Ann .... Columbus, OH
Wochner, David C. .... Bloomington, IL
Wochner, James J. .... Northbrook, IL
Wochner, William J., Jr.
Kansas City, MO
Wochok, Taras M. .... Paoli, PA
Wochok, Taras M., & Associates, Ltd.
Paoli, PA
Wochok, Thomas M. .... Fairfax, VA
Wochos, Amy E. .... Milwaukee, WI
Wochos, F. Scott .... Green Bay, WI
Wocken, Paul J. .... Cold Spring, MN
Wocl, Nicholas E. .... Fairfield, CT
Stamford, CT
Woda, Elizabeth M. .... Cleveland, OH
Wodajo, Tizeta M. .... Rockville, MD
Wodarczyk, Edward A. .... Pittsburgh, PA
Wodarski, James M. .... Boston, MA
Wodatch, John L., Jr. .... Department of Justice, Civil Rights Division, GV
Woddell, Judith J. .... Indianapolis, IN
Wodin, Marc J. .... Woodland Hills, CA
Wodinsky, Erika .... San Francisco, CA
Wodinsky, Peter H. .... Los Angeles, CA
Wodka, Nancy A. .... Washington, DC
Wodlinger, Eric W., (P.C.) .... Boston, MA
Wodlinger, Gary D. .... Vineland, NJ
Wodlinger, Marvin M. .... Millville, NJ
Wodrich, Michael A. .... Jacksonville, FL
Wodtke, Griff .... Des Moines, IA
Woeber, Andrew K. .... New York, NY
Woeber, Linda L. .... Cincinnati, OH
Woebkenberg, Thomas M.
Cincinnati, OH
Woehler, Jason L. .... Federal Way, WA
Woehling, Robert J. .... Westfield, NJ
Woehlke, James A. .... New York, NY
Woehr, Scott W. .... Arlington, VA
Woehrel, Crescy E. .... Westmont, IL
Woehrel, Joseph A. .... Pittsburgh, PA
Woehrel, Marilyn D. .... Westmont, IL
Woehrel & Woehrel .... Westmont, IL
Woehrer, Daniel Louis .... Milwaukee, WI
Woehrle, Carla M. .... Los Angeles, CA
Woehrle, Lawrence R. .... Evesham, NJ
Philadelphia, PA
Woehrle, Thomas .... Springfield, VA
Woehrle, Thomas & Assoc., P.C.
Springfield, VA
Woelber, Tonja J. .... Anchorage, AK
Woelfel, Bradford B. .... Columbus, OH
Woelfel, Dawn C. .... Dallas, TX
Woelfel, Geo. B., Jr. .... Annapolis, MD
Woelfel, Harold F., Jr. .... Middleburg, PA
Woelfel, Jana H. .... Houston, TX
Woelfel, John .... Bethalto, IL
Woelfel, John R. .... Amesbury, MA
Woelfel, Michael A. .... Huntington, WV
Woelfer, W. Todd .... South Bend, IN
Woelfle & Stevens .... Paso Robles, CA
Woelfle, Walter T. .... Milwaukee, WI
Woelfling, Frank Adam .... Wilmington, DE
Woelfling, Maxine M. .... Harrisburg, PA
Woelk & Cole .... Russell, KS
Woelk, John C. .... Russell, KS
Woelk, Sarah E. .... Austin, TX
Woelke, O'Neil L. .... Highland Park, MI
Woelkers, William G. .... Chicago, IL
Woell, Frank J. .... Casselton, ND
Woelpper, Donna M. .... Philadelphia, PA
Woeltz, Roberta C. .... Westwood, MA
Woeppel, Fred E. .... Spokane, WA
Woeppel, James R. .... Seattle, WA
Woerle, Alvin A. .... Reading, PA
Woermer, Matthew P. .... Naugatuck, CT
Woerndle, Patterson, Strain & Miller, L.L.P.
Midland, TX
Woerndle, Rudolph A., (P.C.)
Midland, TX
Woerner, Daniel E. .... Akron, OH
Woerner, H. Charles, Jr., (P.A.)
Daytona Beach, FL
Woerner, Mark Henry .... Corpus Christi, TX
Woerner, Michael .... Seattle, WA
Woerner & Parsons .... Daytona Beach, FL
Woerthwein, Charity C. .... Philadelphia, PA
Woessner, Bernard Roland .... Denver, CO
Woessner, Cynthia L. .... New Orleans, LA
Woessner, David E. .... Bowling Green, OH
Woessner, Julia T. .... St. Louis, MO
Woessner, Ronald A. .... Dallas, TX
Woessner, Thomas J. .... Minneapolis, MN
Woessner, Warren D. .... Minneapolis, MN
Woeste, Ralph T. .... Cincinnati, OH
Woeste, Richard A. .... Alexandria, KY
Woffinden, Arlen D. .... Irvine, CA
Wofford, Charles W. .... Greenville, SC
Wofford, Chas. A. .... Atlanta, GA
Wofford, Cindy Lynn .... Washington, DC
Wofford, Clinton J., Jr. .... Dallas, TX
Wofford, Hoke S., Jr. .... Atlanta, GA
Wofford, J. Huntington .... Charlotte, NC
Wofford, John G. .... Boston, MA
Wofford, M. Russell, Jr. .... Atlanta, GA
Wofford, Merritt McGarrah .... Atlanta, GA
Wofford, Michael C. .... Bartlesville, OK
Wofford, Michael K. .... Los Angeles, CA
Wofford, Michelle .... Norman, OK
Wofford, Penny Correll .... Spartanburg, SC
Wofford, Rebecca B. .... Charlotte, NC
Wofford, Robin Assaf .... San Diego, CA
Wofford, William N.
Research Triangle Park, NC
Wofsey, Carol Miller .... Fenton, MO
Wofsey, Daniel R. .... St. Louis, MO
Wofsey, Rosen, Kweskin & Kuriansky, LLP
Greenwich, CT
Hartford, CT
Norwalk, CT
Stamford, CT
White Plains, NY
Wofsy, Marshall J. .... Jersey City, NJ
Wofsy, Noah L. .... House of Representatives, Office of Legislative Counsel, GV
Wofsy, Scott D. .... Stamford, CT
Wogalter, Lance J. .... Fort Lauderdale, FL
Wogan, Cameron F. .... Klamath Falls, OR
Wogan, Geo. T. .... Metairie, LA
Wogan, Gordon L. .... New Orleans, LA
Wogan, John D. .... New Orleans, LA
Wogan, Joyce P. .... New Bedford, MA
Wogan, Maura J. .... New York, NY
Wogee, Christine A. .... Orange, CA
Woghin, Steven M. .... Islandia, NY
Woglom, Eric C. .... New York, NY
Woglom, Susan S. .... Amherst, MA
Wognum, James P. .... Chicago, IL
Wogoman, Susan E. .... Los Angeles, CA
Wohabe, Abdul W. .... New York, NY
Wohabe, David P. .... New York, NY
Wohabe Law Offices .... New York, NY
Wohabe, Omar .... New York, NY
Wohar, Christine M. .... Nashville, TN
Wohl, Alan L. .... Somerville, NJ
Wohl, Alvin R., (Inc.) .... Sacramento, CA
Wohl, Benjamin .... North Miami, FL
Wohl, Betsy .... Ithaca, NY
Wohl, Christian & Perkins .... Hollywood, CA
Wohl, Christopher F. .... Hollywood, CA
Sacramento, CA
Wohl, David .... New York, NY
Wohl, David Evan .... Riverside, CA
Wohl, Doris K. .... Toledo, OH
Wohl, Edward H. .... New York, NY
Wohl, Emil J. .... Pasadena, CA
Wohl, Frank H. .... New York, NY
Wohl & Goldstein, P.A. .... Somerville, NJ
Wohl, Jack B. .... East Meadow, NY
Wohl, Jacqueline D. .... Tucson, AZ
Wohl, James P. .... Los Angeles, CA
Wohl, Jeffrey D. .... San Francisco, CA
Wohl, Judith M. .... Portland, ME
Wohl, Lawrence C. .... Princeton, NJ
Wohl, Leila L. .... North Hollywood, CA
Wohl, Linda S. .... New Rochelle, NY
Wohl Loewe Stettner Fabricant & Deitz, P.C.
New York, NY
Wohl, Marc .... Goshen, NY
Wohl, Matthew D. .... St. Louis, MO
Wohl, Patricia J. .... Washington, DC
Wohl, Rachel A. .... Baltimore, MD
Wohl, Richard H. .... Pasadena, CA
Wohl, Ronald Gene .... New York, NY
Wohl, Russell G. .... New York, NY
Wohl Sammis Christian & Perkins
Sacramento, CA
Wohl, Sheila B. .... Philadelphia, PA
Wohl, Steven C. .... Daly City, CA
San Mateo, CA
Wohl, Steven J. .... White Plains, NY
Wohl, Steven N. .... Chicago, IL
Wohl, William M. .... Cleveland, OH
Wohlberg, David J. .... Los Angeles, CA
Wohlberg, Stephen I. .... Brooklyn, NY
Wohleb, Stephen G. .... Austin, TX
Wohlenberg, Bradley E. .... Los Angeles, CA
Wohler, Robert M. .... O'Fallon, MO
Wohlers, Donald F. .... Basking Ridge, NJ
Wohlers, Everett T. .... Boise, ID
Wohlers, Paul D. .... Department of State, Foreign Service Officers (Overseas), GV
Wohletz, Frank E. .... Winona, MN
Wohletz, Gregory A. .... Minneapolis, MN
Wohletz Law Office .... Winona, MN
Wohlfarth, Daniel S. .... New York, NY
Wohlfarth, Diane K. .... Pittsburgh, PA
Wohlfeil, Joel R. .... San Diego, CA
Wohlfeiler, Peter W. .... San Francisco, CA
Wohlfeld, Robert K. .... Miami, FL
Wohlford, Bill .... Wichita, KS
Wohlford, Chas. W. .... Buffalo, NY
Wohlford, Patricia A. .... Overland Park, KS
Wohlford, Paul R. .... Bristol, TN
Wohlforth, E. Evans, Jr. .... Newark, NJ
Wohlforth, Eric E. .... Anchorage, AK
Wohlforth, Karen F. .... New York, NY
Wohlforth, Vassar, Johnson & Brecht, A Professional Corporation
Anchorage, AK
Wohlgelernter, Ezra .... Haddonfield, NJ
Philadelphia, PA
Wohlgemuth, Ann M. .... Greensburg, PA
Wohlgemuth, Audrey J. .... Winnetka, CA
Wohlgemuth, David M. .... Woodland Hills, CA
Wohlgemuth, Ilene S. .... Boca Raton, FL
Wohlgemuth, Joel L. .... Tulsa, OK
Wohlgemuth, Julian M. .... Valley Stream, NY
Wohlgemuth, Karl A. .... Canajoharie, NY
Wohlgemuth, Kathleen N. .... Wichita, KS
Wohlgemuth, Steven H. .... Ventura, CA
Woodland Hills, CA
Wohlgemuth, Theresa A. .... Cleveland, OH
Wohlgemuth, Thomas J. .... Annapolis, MD
Wohlgenant, Richard G. .... Denver, CO
Wohlin, John F. .... Pittsburgh, PA
Wohlleber, Richard A. .... Chicago, IL
Wohlman, Barry B. .... Philadelphia, PA
Wohlmuth, Edmund J. .... Mount Prospect, IL
Wohlmuth, Elaine R. .... New York, NY
Wohlner, Elaine Ashe .... Englewood, CO
Wohlner, Eugene L. .... Pasadena, CA
Wohlner, Jeffrey S. .... Encino, CA
Wohlner Kaplon Phillips Vogel & Young
Encino, CA
Wohlpart, Bridgett A. .... Nashville, TN
Wohlrabe, Barbara L. .... Dallas, TX
Wohlschlaeger, Frederick G. .... Chicago, IL
Wohlschlegel, Ernest I. .... San Antonio, TX
Wohlsifer, William .... Daytona Beach, FL
Wohlstadter, David M. .... Washington, DC
Wohlstadter, Michael .... Oakland, CA
Wohlstatter, Rosalie .... New York, NY
Wohlstetter, Alan F. .... Washington, DC
Wohlstetter, Alan F., Jr. .... Philadelphia, PA
Wohlt, E. J., Jr. .... Montgomery, TX
Wohltman, Richard G. .... Alexandria, VA
Wohltman, Richard G., P.C.
Alexandria, VA
Wohlust, G. Charles .... Maitland, FL
Wohlwend, Wells K. .... Rancho Mirage, CA
Wohn, Kathleen M. .... Los Angeles, CA
Wohn & McKinley, P.A. .... Cocoa, FL
Wohn, Robert A., Jr. .... Cocoa, FL
Wohner, J. Collins, Jr. .... Jackson, MS
Wohnhas, Larry D. .... Pittsburgh, PA
Wohrle, Joseph P. .... Los Angeles, CA
Woida, Thomasina S. .... Alameda, CA

Wolf, Leonard H., (P.A.)
Fort Lauderdale, FL
Wolf, Leonard M. ... **Hackensack, NJ**
Wolf, Leonard S. ... Venice, CA
Wolf, Levi S. ... **Pottstown, PA**
Wolf, Lewis I. ... New York, NY
Wolf, Lillian ... **San Jose, CA**
Wolf, Liza Leidner ... **Philadelphia, PA**
Wolf, Lloyd H. ... **Fort Madison, IA**
Wolf, Lloyd S. ... Santa Monica, CA
Wolf, Lori I. ... **Hackensack, NJ**
Wolf, Louis A. ... Baldwin, NY
Wolf, Marcia Topper ... **Chicago, IL**
Wolf, Marcus A. ... Mansfield, OH
Wolf, Marcus J. ... Montgomery, AL
Wolf, Marianne T. ... **Palo Alto, CA**
Wolf, Mark A. ... Crown Point, IN
Wolf, Mark C. ... Washington, DC
Wolf, Mark D. ... Houston, TX
Wolf, Mark L. ... Boston, MA
Wolf, Mark M. ... Hauppauge, NY
Wolf, Mark S. ... **New York, NY**
Wolf, Marquette W. ... **Mesquite, TX**
Wolf, Marsha ... **Plainsboro, NJ**
Wolf, Marsha S. ... Philadelphia, PA
Wolf, Marshall J. ... **Cleveland, OH**
Wolf, Martha O. ... Pittsburgh, PA
Wolf, Martin F. ... **Bridgeport, CT**
Wolf, Martin L. ... Philadelphia, PA
Wolf, Marvin ... Valley Stream, NY
Wolf, Marvin ... **White River Junction, VT**
Wolf, Marvin H. ... Commack, NY
Wolf, Marvin H., P.C. ... Commack, NY
Wolf, Marvin I. ... Bloomfield Hills, MI
Wolf, Marvin L. ... Los Angeles, CA
Wolf, Mary Elizabeth ... Lancaster, PA
Wolf, Mary K., Law Offices of ... Austin, TX
Wolf, Mary Therese ... Indianapolis, IN
Wolf, Mathew D. ... Houston, TX
Wolf, Matthew M. ... **Washington, DC**
Wolf, Matthew S. ... **Mount Laurel, NJ**
Wolf, Maurice (IBA) ... **Washington, DC**
New York, NY
Wolf, Melvin H. ... Waterloo, IA
Wolf, Mervyn H. ... Encino, CA
Wolf, Michael ... **Washington, DC**
Wolf, Michael A. ... **Hempstead, NY**
Wolf, Michael A. ... Houston, TX
Wolf, Michael, (A Professional Corporation)
Los Angeles, CA
Wolf, Michael B. ... **Los Angeles, CA**
Wolf, Michael B. ... Philadelphia, PA
Wolf, Michael E. ... Rocky Hill, CT
Wolf, Michael H. ... North Miami Beach, FL
Wolf, Michael H., P.A.
North Miami Beach, FL
Wolf, Michael J. ... Orange, CA
Wolf, Michael J. ... Lombard, IL
Wolf, Michael J. ... San Antonio, TX
Wolf, Michael K. ... **Chicago, IL**
Wolf, Michael O. ... **Riverside, CA**
Wolf, Michael S. ... **Baton Rouge, LA**
Wolf, Michael T. ... Toms River, NJ
Wolf, Michele R. ... San Francisco, CA
Wolf, Michelle S. ... **Boston, MA**
Wolf, Mier
Department of Housing and Urban Development,
Office of General Counsel, GV
Wolf, Milton G. ... Van Nuys, CA
Wolf, Mireet S. ... **New York, NY**
Wolf, Mitchell Craig ... United States Senate,
Committee Legal Personnel, GV
Wolf, Morris H. ... Lutherville, MD
Wolf, Myron A. ... **Hamilton, OH**
Wolf, Nancy J. ... **Minneapolis, MN**
Wolf, Nancy L. ... **Washington, DC**
Wolf, Nancy Sindell ... Madison, NJ
Wolf, Natalie S. ... **Wilmington, DE**
Wolf, Nathan P. ... **Teaneck, NJ**
Wolf, Nathaniel R. ... **Grand Rapids, MI**
Wolf, Neal L. ... **San Francisco, CA**
Wolf, Neil G. ... **Chicago, IL**
Wolf, Nelson, (P.A.) ... Kenilworth, NJ
Wolf, Norman J., Jr. ... Buffalo, NY
Wolf, Paul A. ... Beverly Hills, CA
Wolf, Paul A. ... **Hugoton, KS**
Wolf, Paul Delano ... Oakland, CA
Wolf, Paul E. ... **Phoenix, AZ**
Tucson, AZ
Wolf, Paul V. ... Cleveland, OH
Wolf, Paul W. ... Buffalo, NY
Wolf, Penrose ... **Hartford, CT**
Wolf, Peter D. ... Hastings-On-Hudson, NY
Wolf, Peter H. ... Washington, DC
Wolf, Peter L., (P.A.)
Hilton Head Island, SC
Wolf, Peter M. ... Kew Gardens, NY
Wolf, Phelan ... **East Hampton, NY**
Wolf, Philip C. ... **Englewood, CO**
Wolf, Philip H. ... Toledo, OH
Wolf, Philip, (P.A.) ... Haddonfield, NJ
Wolf Popper LLP ... **New York, NY**
Wolf Professional Association
Mount Laurel, NJ
Wolf, Randi A. ... **Cherry Hill, NJ**
Wolf, Randolph H. ... Red Bank, NJ
Wolf, Rebecca J. ... Dayton, OH
Wolf, Renee I. ... **Burbank, CA**
Wolf, Rhonda J. ... **Torrance, CA**
Wolf, Richard B. ... **Los Angeles, CA**
Wolf, Richard B. ... Hyde Park, NY
Wolf, Richard C. ... **Cheyenne, WY**
Wolf, Richard H. ... New York, NY
Wolf, Richard J. ... **Parsippany, NJ**
Wolf, Richard J. ... **Parkersburg, WV**
Wolf, Richard W. ... San Antonio, TX

Wolf & Richards, A Law Corporation
Newport Beach, CA
Santa Ana, CA
Wolf, Rick P., Jr. ... **Fresno, CA**
Wolf, Rifkin & Shapiro, LLP
Los Angeles, CA
Wolf, Robert ... **White Plains, NY**
Wolf, Robert A. ... Chicago, IL
Wolf, Robert A. ... **New York, NY**
Wolf, Robert B. ... **Philadelphia, PA**
Wolf, Robert B. ... **Pittsburgh, PA**
Wolf, Robert E. ... Las Vegas, NV
Wolf, Robert H. ... **Baltimore, MD**
Wolf, Robert J. ... Munhall, PA
Wolf, Robert L. ... Crete, NE
Wolf, Robert L. ... Portland, OR
Wolf, Robert M. ... Boca Raton, FL
Wolf, Robert M. ... Harrisburg, IL
Wolf, Robert M. ... **Boston, MA**
Wolf, Robert M. ... **Short Hills, NJ**
Wolf, Robert S. ... Beverly Hills, CA
Wolf, Robert S. ... **New York, NY**
Wolf, Robert S., P.C. ... **New York, NY**
Wolf, Robert W. ... Forest City, NC
Wolf, Rodger J. ... Montville, NJ
Wolf, Roger A. ... Houston, TX
Wolf, Roger C. ... Tucson, AZ
Wolf, Roger C. ... Baltimore, MD
Wolf & Rohr, P.A. ... St. Paul, MN
Wolf, Ronald L. ... **Philadelphia, PA**
Wolf, Ronald T.
Commodity Futures Trading Commission,
Division of Enforcement, GV
Wolf, Rosalind D. ... Los Angeles, CA
Wolf, Sanford B. ... San Jose, CA
Wolf, Sara Straight ... **Cincinnati, OH**
Wolf, Sarah J. ... Roseburg, OR
Wolf, Sarah M. ... Greenfield, IN
Wolf, Scott A. ... Delaware, OH
Wolf, Seider, Abrams & Wolf, LLP
Los Angeles, CA
Wolf, Seth M. ... **Cleveland, OH**
Wolf, Shawn P. ... **Boca Raton, FL**
Wolf & Short, Professional Association
Jacksonville, FL
Wolf, Silas C. ... Norman, OK
Wolf, Silas C., Jr. ... Norman, OK
Wolf & Slatkin, Professional Corporation
Denver, CO
Wolf, Stanley
Federal Energy Regulatory Commission,
Office of the General Counsel, GV
Wolf, Stephen A. ... **Scottsdale, AZ**
Wolf, Stephen C. ... Avon-By-The-Sea, NJ
Wolf, Steven ...
Treasury Department, GV
Wolf, Steven A. ... New York, NY
Wolf, Steven A. ... Portland, OR
Wolf, Steven B. ... Chicago, IL
Wolf, Steven B., and Associates, Ltd.
Chicago, IL
Wolf, Steven C. ... Chicago, IL
Wolf, Steven D. ... **Omaha, NE**
Wolf, Steven M. ... Villanova, PA
Wolf, Steven R. ... Canonsburg, PA
Wolf, Stuart H. ... Arlington Heights, IL
Wolf, Susan A. ... **Beverly Hills, CA**
Wolf, Susan Ellen ... **Atlanta, GA**
Wolf, Susan M. ... Minneapolis, MN
Wolf, T. Lowell ... Honolulu, HI
Wolf & Taunton, P.C. ... Montgomery, AL
Wolf & Tennant ... Chicago, IL
Wolf, Thomas ... **Rochester, MN**
Wolf, Thomas A. ... **Spokane, WA**
Wolf, Thomas E. ... Sun Valley, ID
Wolf, Thomas J. ... **Denver, CO**
Wolf, Thomas J. ... Treasury Department,
Internal Revenue Service, GV
Wolf, Thomas J., Jr. ... Marion, IL
Wolf, Thomas J., Jr., P.C. ... Marion, IL
Wolf, Thomas K. ... **Lake Oswego, OR**
Wolf, Thomas K., LLC ... **Lake Oswego, OR**
Portland, OR
Wolf, Thomas M. ... **Richmond, VA**
Wolf, Thomas R. ... Cleveland, OH
Wolf & Tiedeken ... **Cheyenne, WY**
Wolf, Timothy D. ... **Tampa, FL**
Wolf, Timothy G. ... Ellicott City, MD
Wolf, Timothy J. ... **Washington, DC**
Wolf, Timothy R. ... **St. Louis, MO**
Wolf, Todd P. ... Wisconsin Rapids, WI
Wolf, Tracy Graves ... **Longview, TX**
Wolf, Troy A. ... **Moorhead, MN**
Wolf, Victor L. ... **Riverside, CA**
Wolf, Virginia ... Long Beach, CA
Wolf, Wallace J., Jr. ... Rochester, NY
Wolf, Walter E., Jr. ... **Indianapolis, IN**
Wolf, Walter F., III ... New Orleans, LA
Wolf, Walter F., Jr. ... Gallup, NM
Wolf, Walter T. ... **Mount Laurel, NJ**
Wolf, Warren Alan ... San Antonio, TX
Wolf, Warren R. ... **Providence, RI**
Wolf, Warren S. ... Mount Laurel, NJ
Wolf, Wayne A. ... **Jacksonville, FL**
Wolf, Wayne C. ... **Albuquerque, NM**
Wolf, Wendy A. ... **Los Angeles, CA**
Wolf, Wendy E. ... Trenton, NJ
Wolf, Wendy J. ... **St. Louis, MO**
Wolf, William B., Jr. ... **Washington, DC**
Wolf, William H. ... Greenfield, IN
Wolf, William J. ... Phoenix, AZ
Wolf, William J. ... **Lakewood, NJ**
Wolf, William J. ... **Durham, NC**
Wolf, William J., P.C. ... Phoenix, AZ
Wolf, William K. ... **New York, NY**
Wolf, William L. ... **Dallas, TX**
Wolf, William L., P.C. ... **Dallas, TX**
Plano, TX

Wolf & Wolf ... **Washington, DC**
Wolf & Wolf ... Hauppauge, NY
Wolf & Wolf, P.C. ... Los Angeles, CA
Wolf & Wolf, P.C. ... Norman, OK
Wolfanger, Gary A. ... Pocono Pines, PA
Wolfard, Dennis J. ... Denver, CO
Wolfard, Lisa A. ... **Seattle, WA**
Wolfard, Mary L. ... Indianapolis, IN
Wolfarth, Alwyn E. ... St. Louis, MO
Wolfarth, Mary Lou S. ... St. Louis, MO
Wolfarth, Meredith E. ... **St. Louis, MO**
Wolfarth & Wolfarth ... St. Louis, MO
Wolfberg, Brian L. ... **Chicago, IL**
Wolfberg, Douglas M. ... **Harrisburg, PA**
Wolfberg, Lawrence ... Union City, NJ
Wolfberg, Matthew C. ... Union City, NJ
Wolfberg, Stephen ... Boston, MA
Wolfberg, Theodore ... Santa Monica, CA
Wolfberg & Wolfberg, P.A. ... Union City, NJ
Wolfbiss, Denise R. ... Woodbury, NY
Wolfbrandt, William L., Jr. ... Las Vegas, NV
Wolfcale, Arthur D., Jr. ... Youngstown, OH
Wolfe, Aaron R., (P.A.)
Daytona Beach, FL
Wolfe, Adam M. ... Tampa, FL
Wolfe, Alan R. ... **Memphis, TN**
Wolfe, Albert B. ... Boston, MA
Wolfe, Alden H. ... New City, NY
Wolfe, Alexander M. ... Modesto, CA
Wolfe, Andrew M. ... **Mill Valley, CA**
Sacramento, CA
San Francisco, CA
Wolfe, Andrew P. ... Orinda, CA
Wolfe, Andrew T. ... **Paramus, NJ**
Wolfe, Andrew T. ... Oswego, NY
Wolfe, Anna Christina ... Brookline, MA
Wolfe, Arbelyn Elizabeth ... **Harrisburg, PA**
Wolfe Associates ... Boston, MA
Wolfe & Associates ... **St. Paul, MN**
Wolfe & Associates ... **Amarillo, TX**
Lubbock, TX
Wolfe, Ava R. ... New York, NY
Wolfe •Axtmann ... San Diego, CA
Wolfe, Bardie C., Jr. ... Miami, FL
Wolfe, Bari Jane ... **New York, NY**
Wolfe, Barry M. ... Atlanta, GA
Wolfe, Begoun & Pick, L.L.P.
New Orleans, LA
Wolfe & Bentley ... Ironton, OH
Wolfe, Bernard B. ... Chicago, IL
Wolfe, Bernard J., Jr. ... Woodsville, NH
Wolfe, Bernard M. ... San Mateo, CA
Wolfe, Bernard R. ... **Atlanta, GA**
Wolfe, Beth H. ... Tamarac, FL
Wolfe, Billy R. ... **Lubbock, TX**
Wolfe, Brad M. ... **Atlanta, GA**
Wolfe, Brenda ... St. Paul, MN
Wolfe, Brian H. ... **Vancouver, WA**
Wolfe, Bruce F. ... Belvedere-Tiburon, CA
Wolfe, Bruce P. ... Van Nuys, CA
Wolfe, C. Christopher ... Ann Arbor, MI
Wolfe, Cameron W. ... Piedmont, CA
Wolfe, Cameron W., Jr.
San Francisco, CA
Wolfe, Catherine L. ... Pontiac, MI
Wolfe, Catherine O'Hagan ... New York, NY
Wolfe, Charles B. ... Lansing, MI
Wolfe, Charles Holmes, Jr.
Pittsburgh, PA
Wolfe, Charles R. ... **Seattle, WA**
Wolfe, Charles R., Jr. ... **Alexandria, VA**
Wolfe, Charles S. ... San Bernardino, CA
Wolfe, Charles W. ... **Los Angeles, CA**
Wolfe, Charles W. ... **Kansas City, MO**
Wolfe, Charles W. ... **Oklahoma City, OK**
Wolfe, Cheryl Harris ... **Charleston, WV**
Wolfe, Cheryl L. ... Spokane, WA
Wolfe, Christian (Chris) E. ... **Houston, TX**
Wolfe, Christopher B. ... Newark, DE
Wolfe, Christopher D. ... Princeton, NJ
Wolfe, Christopher R. ... **Dallas, TX**
Wolfe, Christopher Sterling
Rancho Palos Verdes, CA
Wolfe, Christopher T. ... New York, NY
Wolfe, C. J., Jr. ... Kailua, HI
Wolfe, Clark, Henderson & Tidwell, L.L.P.
Bonham, TX
Denison, TX
Gainesville, TX
Sherman, TX
Wolfe, Clyde E. ... St. Augustine, FL
Wolfe and Collins, P.A. ... Kernersville, NC
Wolfe, Connie M. ... **Oklahoma City, OK**
Wolfe, Cory Andrew ... New York, NY
Wolfe, Curtis A. ... **Miami, FL**
Wolfe, Cynthia L. ... Oakland, CA
Wolfe, Daniel ... Dallas, TX
Wolfe, Daniel H. ... Beech Grove, IN
Wolfe, Daniel L. ... New York, NY
Wolfe, Daniel R. ... Houston, TX
Wolfe, Danna L. ... **Marietta, GA**
Marietta, GA
Wolfe, Darryl C. ... Houston, TX
Wolfe, David A. ... **Racine, WI**
Wolfe, David B. ... Riverside, CA
Wolfe, David D. ... Knoxville, TN
Wolfe, David E. ... **Dallas, TX**
Wolfe, David H. ... Chicago, IL
Wolfe, David J. ... **Fresno, CA**
Wolfe, David J., Jr. ... Boardman, OH
Wolfe, David L. ... **Bonita Springs, FL**
Wolfe, David L. ... **Fort Myers, FL**
Naples, FL
Wolfe, David L. ... **Chicago, IL**
Wolfe, Dean N. ... **Bowie, MD**
Wolfe, Deborah A. ... **San Diego, CA**
Wolfe, Deborah A. ... Oklahoma City, OK
Wolfe, Deborah R. ... **New York, NY**

Wolfe, Dee Jay ... Portland, OR
Wolfe, DeWitt ... Houston, TX
Wolfe, Donald J., Jr. ... **Wilmington, DE**
Wolfe, Donald Vincent Sisk ... Portland, OR
Wolfe, Douglas D. ... Mt. Vernon, IA
Wolfe, Douglas V.
Federal Trade Commission,
Bureau of Consumer Protection, GV
Wolfe, Edward ... **New York, NY**
Wolfe, Edward C. ... **Detroit, MI**
Wolfe, Edward E. ... Newhall, CA
Wolfe, Edward E. ... Seattle, WA
Wolfe, Edward M. ... New York, NY
Wolfe, Elisa B. ... Los Angeles, CA
Wolfe, Elizabeth A. ... West Palm Beach, FL
Wolfe, Elliot G. ... **Phoenix, AZ**
Wolfe, Ernest J., Jr. ... Lowville, NY
Wolfe, Ethan G. ... New York, NY
Wolfe, Eugene ... Washington, DC
Wolfe, Evan A. ... Auburn, CA
Wolfe, Evan R. ... Miami, FL
Wolfe & Farmer ... Kingsport, TN
Knoxville, TN
La Follette, TN
Bristol, VA
Charlottesville, VA
Jonesville, VA
Norton, VA
Roanoke, VA
Vansant, VA
Wolfe, Forrest F. ... **Los Angeles, CA**
Wolfe, Forrest F. ... **Ontario, CA**
Wolfe, Frani Cohen ... Rockville, MD
Wolfe, Frank B., III ... **Tulsa, OK**
Wolfe, Frank M. ... Cocoa Beach, FL
Wolfe, Frederick J. ... **Pittsburgh, PA**
Wolfe, Gary J. ... **New York, NY**
Wolfe, Gary P. ... **Huntsville, AL**
Wolfe, Gary S. ... Beverly Hills, CA
Wolfe, Gary S. ... St. Louis, MO
Wolfe, Gary W. ... Missoula, MT
Wolfe, George B. ... Rochelle Park, NJ
Wolfe, George B. ... **Columbia, SC**
Wolfe, George M. ... Columbus, OH
Wolfe, George P. ... Johnstown, PA
Wolfe, Gerald P., II ... Columbus, OH
Wolfe, Grant A. ... Columbus, OH
Wolfe & Gross, Professional Association
Miami, FL
Wolfe, Haleh Tavakol ... Tarrytown, NY
Wolfe, Harold E., Jr.
West Palm Beach, FL
Wolfe, Harold E., Jr., P.A.
West Palm Beach, FL
Wolfe, Harvey G. ... Port Washington, NY
Wolfe, Henry Paul ... Petoskey, MI
Wolfe, Herbert N. ... **Beverly Hills, CA**
Wolfe, Howard O. ... Chicago, IL
Wolfe, Howard R. ... **Greenwich, CT**
Wolfe, Hugh Kenneth ... Staten Island, NY
Wolfe, J. Douglas ... **Johnstown, PA**
Wolfe, J. Matthew ... Philadelphia, PA
Wolfe, J. Stan ... **Gillette, WY**
Wolfe, J. Troy, Jr. ... Chattanooga, TN
Wolfe, Jack B. ... Birmingham, MI
Wolfe, Jack G. ... **Lincoln, NE**
Wolfe, Jack P. ... **Longmont, CO**
Wolfe, James B., Jr. ... Greensboro, NC
Wolfe, James D. ... Akron, OH
Wolfe, James I. ... Staten Island, NY
Wolfe, James L. ... **Portland, OR**
Wolfe, James N. ... Cheyenne, WY
Wolfe, James R. ... Hugo, OK
Wolfe, James Ronald ... New York, NY
Wolfe, Jane B. ... Buffalo, NY
Wolfe, Janell M. ... Arlington, VA
Wolfe, Janice E. ... Chicago, IL
Wolfe, Jeffrey J. ... **West Palm Beach, FL**
Wolfe, Jeffrey J. ... **Providence, RI**
Wolfe, Jeffrey S. ... Tulsa, OK
Wolfe, Jennifer A. ... New York, NY
Wolfe, Jerry Allen ... Bristol, VA
Wolfe, Joanne E. ... Kent, WA
Wolfe, Joe R. ... Clearwater, FL
Wolfe, Joe R., Chartered ... Clearwater, FL
Wolfe, John ... Ironton, OH
Wolfe, John A. ... Gettysburg, PA
Wolfe, John B., Jr. ... **St. Paul, MN**
Wolfe, John C. ... St. Petersburg, FL
Wolfe, John G., III ... Kernersville, NC
Wolfe, John J. ... **Marathon, FL**
Wolfe, John J., Jr., Law Office of
Clinton, IA
Wolfe, John L. ... Akron, OH
Wolfe, John M. ... South Bend, WA
Wolfe, John W. ... Bethel, AK
Wolfe, John W. ... **Providence, RI**
Wolfe, John W. ... **Seattle, WA**
Wolfe, John W., P.S. ... **Seattle, WA**
Wolfe, Jon Christopher ... **Macon, GA**
Wolfe, Jones & Boswell ... **Athens, AL**
Guntersville, AL
Huntsville, AL
Scottsboro, AL
Wolfe, Joseph A. ... Las Cruces, NM
Wolfe, Joseph E. ... **Norton, VA**
Vansant, VA
Wolfe, Joseph H., Jr. ... Lexington, MA
Wolfe, Joseph W. ... **Sherman, TX**
Wolfe, Judith A. ... Salem, MA
Wolfe, Julie A. ... Colorado Springs, CO
Wolfe, Katherine A. ... **Louisville, KY**
Wolfe, Kathryn G. ... Oswego, NY
Wolfe, Kenneth B. ... Lowville, NY
Wolfe, Kenneth B., Jr. ... Chicago, IL
Wolfe, Kenneth C. ... Fort Collins, CO
Wolfe, Kenneth D. ... **Atlantic City, NJ**
Wolfe, Kenneth N. ... Canyon Country, CA

Wolfe, Kenneth R. ... Melville, NY
Wolfe, Kerry B. ... Chicago, IL
Wolfe, Kevin M. ... Trenton, NJ
Wolfe, Kristin Kaplan ... Milwaukee, WI
Wolfe, Kristina L. ... Beaverton, OR
Wolfe, Larry D. ... Atlanta, GA
Wolfe, Laura M. ... Winston-Salem, NC
Wolfe, Laurence N. ... Los Angeles, CA
Wolfe Law Offices ... Mt. Vernon, IA
Wolfe, Lawrence A. ... Warren, MI
Wolfe, Lawrence J., (P.C.) ... Cheyenne, WY
Wolfe, Leon J. ... Miami, FL
Wolfe, Leonard C. ... Lansing, MI
Wolfe, Louis E. ... Plattsburgh, NY
Wolfe, Marc D. ... Chicago, IL
Woodridge, IL
Wolfe, Marc D. ... Cleveland, OH
Wolfe, Marc R. ... Stroudsburg, PA
Wolfe, Mark A. ... Minneapolis, MN
Wolfe, Mark A. ... Oklahoma City, OK
Wolfe, Mark C., P.C. ... Mobile, AL
Wolfe, Mark F. ... Chicago, IL
Wolfe, Mark M. ... Golden, CO
Wolfe, Mark R. ... South San Francisco, CA
Wolfe, Mark R. ... Tampa, FL
Wolfe, Mark R. ... New Orleans, LA
Wolfe, Marla R. ... Washington, DC
Wolfe, Mary Stavish ... Cleveland, OH
Wolfe & Masid, LL.P. ... Fort Collins, CO
Wolfe, Maya M. ... Tampa, FL
Wolfe, Melvin ... Miami, FL
Wolfe, Michael ... Chicago, IL
Wolfe, Michael A. ... Wheaton, IL
Wolfe, Michael B. ... Mechanicsburg, PA
Wolfe, Michael G. ... Reading, PA
Wolfe, Michael J. ... Wheaton, IL
Wolfe, Michael L. ... Spokane, WA
Wolfe, Michelle ... Drums, PA
Wolfe, Michelle McCoy ... Los Angeles, CA
Wolfe, Michelle S. ... Bingham Farms, MI
Wolfe, Mitchell J. ... New York, NY
Wolfe, Mitchell S. ... San Francisco, CA
Wolfe, Nicole L. ... Atlanta, GA
Wolfe, Norman H. ... United States Tax Court, Special Trial Judges, GV
Wolfe, O. Douglas, Jr. ... St. Augustine, FL
Wolfe, Patricia M. ... Los Angeles, CA
Wolfe, Patrick J., Jr. ... Philadelphia, PA
Wolfe, Paul B. ... Newport, VT
Wolfe, Paul F. ... Albany, NY
Wolfe, Peter G.
Federal Communications Commission, Wireless Telecommunications Bureau, GV
Wolfe, Peter Y. ... Newport, NH
Wolfe, Philip B. ... Topeka, KS
Wolfe & Polovin ... Chicago, IL
Wolfe, R. Bradley ... Hartford, CT
Wolfe, R. Dean ... St. Louis, MO
Wolfe, R. Wayne ... Huntsville, AL
Wolfe, Randall J. ... Lake Oswego, OR
Wolfe, Randolph J. ... Tampa, FL
Wolfe, R. B. ... Mt. Vernon, IA
Wolfe, Rebecca W. ... Dallas, TX
Wolfe & Rice ... Gettysburg, PA
Wolfe, Richard A. ... Chicago, IL
Wolfe, Richard A. ... Mount Laurel, NJ
Philadelphia, PA
Wolfe, Richard A. ... New York, NY
Wolfe, Richard C. ... Miami, FL
Wolfe, Richard Ernest ... St. Petersburg, FL
Wolfe, Richard F. ... San Diego, CA
Wolfe, Richard L. ... Utica, NY
Wolfe, Richard P. ... New Orleans, LA
Wolfe, Richard P., II ... Ashland, OH
Wolfe, Richard S. ... Cape Elizabeth, ME
Wolfe, Richard W. ... Atlanta, GA
Wolfe, Robert A.
Federal Energy Regulatory Commission, Office of the General Counsel, GV
Wolfe, Robert H. ... Plainfield, IL
Wolfe, Robert J. ... Los Angeles, CA
Wolfe, Robert J. ... Danbury, CT
Wolfe, Robert L. ... White Plains, NY
Wolfe, Robert S. ... Santa Ana, CA
Wolfe, Robert S. ... Boston, MA
Wolfe, Robert W. ... Naples, FL
Wolfe, Robin Nelson ... New York, NY
Wolfe, Robt. V. ... Coral Gables, FL
Wolfe, Roger A. ... Charleston, WV
Wolfe, Roger T. ... New York, NY
Wolfe, Romano & Joyce, LLP
Melville, NY
Wolfe, Ronald R. ... Tampa, FL
Wolfe, Roy V., III ... Harrisonburg, VA
Wolfe, Roy V., Jr. ... Abingdon, VA
Wolfe, Ruth Anne ... Cincinnati, OH
Wolfe, Samuel A. ... Trenton, NJ
Wolfe, Sarah B. ... Houston, TX
Wolfe, Saul A. ... Livingston, NJ
Wolfe, Scott E. ... Richardson, TX
Wolfe, Scott N. ... San Diego, CA
Wolfe, Sheldon H. ... San Francisco, CA
Wolfe, Sheldon J. ... McLean, VA
Wolfe, Sheldon L. ... Milwaukee, WI
Wolfe, Snowden, Hurd, Luers & Ahl
Lincoln, NE
Wolfe, Stacey H. ... Freehold, NJ
Wolfe, Stacy E. ... Boston, MA
Wolfe, Stanley R. ... Philadelphia, PA
Wolfe & Steel, P.A. ... Atlanta, GA
Wolfe, Stephen C. ... Tulsa, OK
Wolfe, Stephen G. ... Los Angeles, CA
Wolfe, Stephen P. ... Marion, IN
Wolfe, Steven E. ... Holland, PA
Wolfe, Steven E. ... Marinette, WI
Wolfe, Steven W. ... New York, NY
Wolfe, Stuart B. ... Irvine, CA
Santa Monica, CA
Wolfe, Susan C. ... New York, NY
Wolfe, Susan Dumay ... Kansas City, MO
Wolfe, Susan J. ... San Jose, CA
Wolfe, Tami R. ... Fort Lauderdale, FL
Wolfe, Terrance L. ... Missoula, MT
Wolfe, Terrance Reading ... Bennington, VT
Wolfe, Terry W. ... Akron, OH
Wolfe, Thomas D. ... Towson, MD
Wolfe, Thomas F. ... Orinda, CA
Wolfe, Thomas G. ... Oklahoma City, OK
Wolfe, Thomas H. ... Irvine, CA
Wolfe, Thomas R. ... West Palm Beach, FL
Wolfe, Timothy A. ... Chicago, IL
Wolfe, Timothy D. ... Miami, FL
Wolfe, Timothy W. ... Atlanta, GA
Wolfe, Timothy W., P.C. ... Atlanta, GA
Wolfe, Todd A. ... Oakland, CA
Wolfe, Tracey L. ... Chicago, IL
Wolfe, Virginia A. ... Baraboo, WI
Wolfe, W. Allen ... Zanesville, OH
Wolfe, Wallace E. ... La Jolla, CA
Wolfe, Walter H., Jr. ... Tallahassee, FL
Wolfe, Warren I. ... Beverly Hills, CA
Wolfe, Warren I., A Prof. Corp., Law Offices of
Beverly Hills, CA
Wolfe, Wayne G. ... Johnstown, PA
Wolfe, William F., Jr. ... Camp Hill, PA
Wolfe, William M. ... Alexandria, LA
Baton Rouge, LA
Wolfe, Wolfe & Ryd ... Chicago, IL
Wolfe & Wyman LLP ... Irvine, CA
Los Angeles, CA
Santa Monica, CA
Walnut Creek, CA
Wolfe, Zachariah ... Dallas, TX
Wolfe Gower, Margaret W.
Santa Monica, CA
Wolfeld, Warren S. ... San Francisco, CA
Wolfen, Werner F., (P.C.)
Los Angeles, CA
Wolfenbarger, J. Wayne ... Rutledge, TN
Wolfendale, Theodore J. ... Punta Gorda, FL
Wolfendale, Thomas H. ... Seattle, WA
Wolfensohn, Naomi ... New York, NY
Wolfenson, Carol B. ... New York, NY
Wolfenson, James W. ... Orland Park, IL
Wolfenson, Schouten & Burke
Orland Park, IL
Wolfenzon, Bruno ... San Diego, CA
Las Vegas, NV
Wolfenzon & Volk ... Las Vegas, NV
Wolfer, Alan B. ... Jersey City, NJ
Wolfer, Cindy Ann ... Fort Wayne, IN
Wolfer, Kathryn V. ... Pflugerville, TX
Wolfersberger, Jason R. ... Atlanta, GA
Wolfersberger, Karissa ... Champaign, IL
Wolfert, Alan R. ... Armonk, NY
Wolfert, Alton S. ... Roslyn Heights, NY
Wolfert, Barbara L. ... Chappaqua, NY
Wolfert, Jonathan P. ... New York, NY
Wolfert, Mark A. ... Provo, UT
Wolfert, Marvin L. ... Walpole, MA
Wolfert, Valinda Barrett ... Dallas, TX
Wolfert-Marino, Debra B. ... New Haven, CT
Wolferts, Judith D. ... Salt Lake City, UT
Wolfertz, Roger D. ... Sacramento, CA
Wolff, Aaron S. ... Chicago, IL
Wolff, Adam John ... New York, NY
Wolff, Alan Wm. ... Washington, DC
Wolff, Alfred L.
National Labor Relations Board, Office of Board Members, GV
Wolff, Allan I., Jr. ... Highland Park, IL
Wolff, Allen R. ... Honolulu, HI
Wolff, Alvin A., Jr. ... St. Louis, MO
Wolff, A. M. "Toni" ... Elk Grove, CA
Wolff, Andrea B. ... Brooklyn, NY
Wolff Ardis, P.C. ... Memphis, TN
Wolff, Arthur M. ... Fort Lauderdale, FL
Wolff, Benjamin E., III ... Chicago, IL
Wolff, Benjamin G. ... Portland, OR
Wolff, Bennett ... Metairie, LA
Wolff, Benno F. ... St. Paul, MN
Wolff, Bert L. ... New York, NY
Wolff, Beverly M. ... New York, NY
Wolff, Bradley S. ... Atlanta, GA
Wolff, Bruce L. ... New York, NY
Wolff, Bruce S. ... Washington, DC
Wolff, C. Elizabeth ... New York, NY
Wolff, Carol Gross ... Boston, MA
Wolff, Carolyn G. ... St. Louis, MO
Wolff, Casey ... Naples, FL
Wolff, Charles P. ... San Francisco, CA
Wolff, Cheri C.
Small Business Administration, Office of the General Counsel, GV
Wolff, Cheryl F. ... Toledo, OH
Wolff, Claudio O. ... Los Angeles, CA
Wolff, Clifford A. ... Fort Lauderdale, FL
Wolff, Craig M. ... Washington, DC
Wolff, Cynthia L. ... West Palm Beach, FL
Wolff, D. Craig ... Washington, DC
Wolff and D'Agrosa, Law Offices of
Clayton, MO
St. Louis, MO
Wolff, Dale F. ... Altamont, IL
Effingham, IL
Wolff, Daniel H. ... Beverly Hills, CA
Wolff, Daniel H. ... Chicago, IL
Wolff, David ... Santa Ana, CA
Wolff, David ... Newark, NJ
Wolff, David A. ... Louisville, CO
Wolff, David A. ... Austin, TX
Wolff, David E. ... Rockville Centre, NY
Wolff, David G. ... Columbia, SC
Wolff, Deborah ... New York, NY
Wolff, Deborah H. ... Philadelphia, PA
Wolff, Donald G. ... Houston, TX
Wolff, Donald L. ... Clayton, MO
Wolff, Edward G. ... Floral Park, NY
Wolff Ellis & Clausen, LLP
San Francisco, CA
Wolff, Elroy H. ... Washington, DC
Wolff, Frank M. ... Orlando, FL
Wolff, Frank P., Jr. ... St. Louis, MO
Wolff, Gary B. ... New York, NY
Wolff, Gary B., P.C. ... New York, NY
Wolff, Gary W. ... New York, NY
Wolff, George R. ... Syracuse, NY
Wolff, George William, Law Office of
San Francisco, CA
Wolff, Georgetta A. ... El Segundo, CA
Wolff, Gerald S. ... Miami Beach, FL
Wolff, Goodrich & Goldman ... Syracuse, NY
Wolff, Gregg M. ... Mount Laurel, NJ
Wolff, Gregory E. ... San Francisco, CA
Wolff, Hal G. ... Houston, TX
Wolff, Harry W., Jr. ... San Antonio, TX
Wolff, Helies & Duggan, A Professional Corporation ... Red Bank, NJ
Wolff, Henry L. ... Wayne, NJ
Wolff, Herbert A., Jr. ... White Plains, NY
Wolff, Herman, Jr. ... Raleigh, NC
Wolff, Hill, McFarlin & Herron, P.A.
Orlando, FL
Wolff, Ira B. ... New York, NY
Wolff, Irving M. ... Miami, FL
Wolff, Jack L. ... Morristown, NJ
Wolff, Jacqueline C. ... New York, NY
Wolff, James A. ... Spokane, WA
Wolff, James G. ... Las Vegas, NV
Wolff, Jeffrey Blair ... Dallas, TX
Wolff, Jeffrey Stephen ... Houston, TX
Wolff, Jesse D. ... New York, NY
Wolff, Jessica R. ... La Jolla, CA
Wolff, Joan ... San Francisco, CA
Wolff, Joan A. ... Los Angeles, CA
Wolff, Joan Nichols
Board of Governors Of The Federal Reserve System,
Division of Banking Supervision and Regulation, GV
Wolff, Joel A. ... Roseland, NJ
Wolff, John B. ... Chicago, IL
Wolff, John H. ... Department of Commerce, Patent and Trademark Office, GV
Wolff, John H. ... Secaucus, NJ
Wolff, John P., III ... Baton Rouge, LA
Wolff, Jonathan L. ... San Francisco, CA
Wolff, Joshua M. ... Costa Mesa, CA
Wolff, Judith C. ... San Francisco, CA
Wolff, Karen B. ... New York, NY
Wolff, Karin L. ... New York, NY
Wolff, Karla M. ... Cedar Rapids, IA
Wolff, Katherine R. ... Woodland Hills, CA
Wolff, Kathleen A. ... Irvine, CA
Wolff, Kevin A. ... Washington, DC
Wolff, Kevin E. ... Morristown, NJ
Wolff, Kevin R. ... Atlanta, GA
Wolff, Kimberly K. ... Sioux City, IA
Wolff, Kirk ... West Chester, PA
Wolff, Kurt J. ... New York, NY
Wolff & Latwin, LLP ... White Plains, NY
Wolff Law Firm ... Little Rock, AR
Wolff, Lawrence K. ... New York, NY
Wolff, Leslie Stark ... Austin, TX
Wolff, Lionel E. ... Spokane, WA
Wolff, Lisa ... Harrisburg, PA
Wolff, Lori Wellbaum ... Englewood, FL
Wolff, Lyle Robt. ... Salem, OR
Wolff, Marc R. ... Akron, OH
Wolff, Margaret L. ... New York, NY
Wolff, Mark A. ... Elk Grove, CA
Wolff, Mark J. ... Miami, FL
Wolff, Marshall S. ... Washington, DC
Wolff, Martin ... Seattle, WA
Wolff, Martin A. ... Annapolis, MD
Wolff, Mary L. ... Memphis, TN
Wolff, Melvin W. ... Mineola, NY
Wolff, Michael A. ... St. Louis, MO
Wolff, Michael A. ... St. Louis, MO
Wolff, Michael David ... Goshen, NY
Wolff, Michael G. ... Rockville, MD
Wolff, Mira Susan ... Long Beach, CA
Wolff, Miriam E. ... Los Altos Hills, CA
Wolff, Monte L. ... Everett, WA
Wolff, Nancy A. ... St. Maries, ID
Wolff, Nancy E. ... Phoenix, AZ
New York, NY
Wolff, Neil Jay ... Palo Alto, CA
Wolff, Nelson G. ... St. Louis, MO
Wolff, Nicole R. ... Rancho Cordova, CA
Wolff, Norris D. ... New York, NY
Wolff, Otto Daniel ... Covington, KY
Wolff, Patrick M. ... Hagåtña, GU
Wolff, Paul L. ... Troy, MI
Wolff, Paul Martin ... Washington, DC
Wolff, Paula A. ... Department of Justice, Criminal Division, GV
Wolff, Paula Fitgerald ... Rockville, MD
Wolff, Peter C., Jr. ... Honolulu, HI
Wolff, Peter K., Jr. ... San Francisco, CA
Wolff, Philip F. ... Jekyll Island, GA
Wolff, Phillip A. ... Sarasota, FL
Wolff, Randall A. ... Chicago, IL
Wolff, Raymond A. ... Elgin, IL
Wolff, Rhett D. ... Austin, TX
Wolff, Richard ... St. Louis, MO
Wolff, Richard A. ...
Administrative Office Of The United States Courts, GV
Wolff, Richard C. ... Oak Park, IL
Wolff, Richard E. ... Toledo, OH
Wolff, Richard H. ... Rockford, IL
Wolff, Richard I. ... New York, NY
Wolff, Richard I., P.C., Law Office of
New York, NY
Wolff, Richard L. ... Blooming Prairie, MN
Wolff, Richard M. ... Mineola, NY
Wolff, Robert H. ... New York, NY
Wolff, Robert J. ... Allentown, PA
Wolff, Robert L., Jr. ... Watervliet, NY
Wolff, Robert M. ... Cleveland, OH
Wolff, Roberta Marlene ... Beverly Hills, CA
Wolff, Robin Ann ... Billings, MT
Wolff, Ruby A. ... Elk Grove, CA
Wolff, Rufus E. ... Little Rock, AR
Wolff, Russell B. ... Department of Education, Office of the General Counsel, GV
Wolff & Samson, A Professional Corporation
Hackensack, NJ
Roseland, NJ
Wolff, Samuel ... Washington, DC
Wolff, Sandra C. ... Boxford, MA
Wolff, Sanford I. ... New Canaan, CT
Wolff, Sarah R. ... Chicago, IL
Wolff, Stephen I. ... St. Louis, MO
Wolff, Steven D. ... Glendale, CA
Wolff, Steven G. ... Los Angeles, CA
Wolff, Thomas G. ... Stamford, CT
Wilton, CT
White Plains, NY
Wolff, Thomas H. ... Chesterfield, MO
Wolff, Tobias Barrington ... New York, NY
Wolff, Wallace J. ... West Dundee, IL
Wolff, Walter C., Jr. ... San Antonio, TX
Wolff, Wayne A. ... San Francisco, CA
Wolff, Wendy J. ... New York, NY
Wolff, Whorley, De Hoogh & Thompson
Sheldon, IA
Wolff, William A. ... St. Louis, MO
Wolff, William H., Jr. ... Dayton, OH
Wolff, Wm. J. ... Baltimore, MD
Wolff and Wolff ... Elk Grove, CA
Wolff & Wolff ... San Antonio, TX
Wolff, Zachary H. ... Coral Gables, FL
Wolffarth, Wm. Chris ... Dallas, TX
Wolffe, Courtney T. ... Dallas, TX
Wolffe, Franklin D. ... Washington, DC
Wolffe, Lenard L. ... Paoli, PA
Wolffe, Susan A. ... Washington, DC
Wolfgang & Day, Chtd. ... La Plata, MD
Leonardtown, MD
Prince Frederick, MD
Waldorf, MD
Wolfgang, Jayson R. ... Harrisburg, PA
Wolfgang, Kurt W. ... La Plata, MD
Wolfgang, Michael G. ... Buffalo, NY
Wolfgang, Penny M. ... Buffalo, NY
Wolfgang, Rex A. ... Cincinnati, OH
Wolfgang, Terry J. ... New York, NY
Wolfgram, Kurt E. ... St. Louis, MO
Wolfgram, Kurt E., P.C. ... St. Louis, MO
Wolfgram, Lee R. ... Minneapolis, MN
Wolfgram, Tom R. ... Port Washington, WI
Wolfin, Richard A. ... Carlstadt, NJ
Wolfingbarger, Chanin M.
Charleston, WV
Wolfinger, Charles ... San Diego, CA
Wolfinger, Ethan A. ... Prescott, AZ
Wolfinger, Gretchen M.
Department of Justice, Civil Division, GV
Wolfinger, Harold J. ... Prescott, AZ
Wolfinger, Maria B. ... Phoenix, AZ
Wolfinger, Norman R. ... Melbourne, FL
Wolfinger, Raymond ... Trenton, NJ
Wolfington, Ronald E.
Department of Commerce, Patent and Trademark Office, GV
Wolfinsohn, Arthur A. ... Chicago, IL
Wolfish & Davis, P.C. ... Addison, TX
Wolfish, Lawrence M. ... Addison, TX
Wolfish, Sally Brenner ... Dallas, TX
Wolfkiel, Sharon M. ... Tucson, AZ
Wolfkill, Jason G. ... Memphis, TN
Wolfla, Paul A. ... Columbus, OH
Wolfley, Jeanette ... Fort Hall, ID
Wolfley, L. Scott ... Trevose, PA
Wolflick, Gregory D. ... Glendale, CA
Wolflick & Simpson ... Glendale, CA
Wolf-Maloof, Faye Judith ... Cleveland, OH
Wolfman, Alexander D. ... New York, NY
Wolfman, Andrea C.
Federal Energy Regulatory Commission, Office of the General Counsel, GV
Wolfman, Andrea L. ... Washington, DC
Wolfman, Bernard ... Cambridge, MA
Wolfman, Brian S. ... Washington, DC
Wolfman, David J. ... Merritt Island, FL
Wolfman, Isaiah C. ... San Bruno, CA
Wolfman, Jonathan ... Boston, MA
Wolfman, June D. ... Stamford, CT
Wolfman, Matthew A. ... Boston, MA
Wolfman, Paul I. ... River Forest, IL
Wolfman, Stanley ... Merritt Island, FL
Wolfman, Toni G. ... Boston, MA
Wolfman & Wolfman, P.A.
Merritt Island, FL
Wolf-McKenzie, Theresia E. ... Chicago, IL
Wolfmeyer, Marianna B. ... Willingboro, NJ
Wolford, Deborah A. ... Hialeah, FL
Wolford, Dennis F. ... Beaver, PA
Wolford, Elizabeth A. ... Rochester, NY
Wolford, Jason N. ... San Francisco, CA
Wolford, Judith ... Evergreen Park, IL
Wolford & Leclair LLP ... Rochester, NY
Wolford, Matthew L. ... Meadville, PA
Wolford, Michael R. ... Rochester, NY
Wolford, Michael R., & Associates
Rochester, NY
Wolford, Roger J. ... Louisville, KY
Wolford, Sherrill D. ... Detroit, MI
Wolford, Stephen T. ... Louisville, KY

Wolford, Thomas C. ... **Chicago, IL**
Wolford, Thorp L. ... Louisville, KY
Wolford, William C. ... Madison, WI
Wolfram, Charles W. ... Ithaca, NY
Wolfram, Frederic M. ... Amarillo, TX
Wolfram Law Firm, P.C. ... Amarillo, TX
Wolfram, M. Scott ... **Walla Walla, WA**
Wolfram, Michael L. ... **Los Angeles, CA**
Wolfram, Molly Hyland ... **Louisville, KY**
Wolfram, Neil S. ... Port Washington, NY
Wolfram, Peter ... **New York, NY**
Wolfram, Phillip J. ... Denver, CO
Wolfram, Richard H. ... **New York, NY**
Wolfram, Walter ... Amarillo, TX
Wolfram, William G. ... Franklin, MI
Wolf-Rodda, Howard A. ... **Washington, DC**
Wolfrom, R. Scott ... **Houston, TX**
Wolfrum, Thomas W. ... Walnut Creek, CA
Wolfs, Denise Y. ... **Houston, TX**
Wolfsdorf, Bernard P. ... **Los Angeles, CA**
Wolfsdorf, Bernard P., A Professional Corporation ... **Los Angeles, CA**
Wolfsen, Judith A. ... Torrance, CA
Wolfsen, Thomas H. ... Garden Grove, CA
Wolfsheimer, Abbe S. ... San Diego, CA
Wolfsheimer, Louis M., (A P.C.) San Diego, CA
Wolfsie, John Louis ... Yorktown Heights, NY
Wolfslau, Amy Louise ... Beverly Hills, CA
Wolf-Smith, Risa L. ... **Denver, CO**
Wolfsohn, David J. ... **Philadelphia, PA**
Wolfsohn, Robert Ellis ... Los Angeles, CA
Wolfson, Aimée B. ... **Santa Monica, CA**
Wolfson, Alan ... **Pittsburgh, PA**
Wolfson, Alison L. ... Pittsburgh, PA
Wolfson, Amy G. ... **Nashua, NH**
Wolfson, Anne R. ... New York, NY
Wolfson, Barry M. ... Northbrook, IL
Wolfson, Bernard, (P.A.) ... Coral Gables, FL
Wolfson, Bertram ... **Philadelphia, PA**
Wolfson, Beth Anne ... Dedham, MA
Wolfson, Bluma F. ... New Orleans, LA
Wolfson, Bruce A. ... New York, NY
Wolfson, Bruce L. ... Los Angeles, CA
Wolfson, Carl S. ... **Poughkeepsie, NY**
Wolfson & Carroll ... **New York, NY**
Wolfson, Craig G. ... San Francisco, CA
Wolfson, Craig J. ... Garden City, NY
Wolfson, Daniel F. ... York, PA
Wolfson, David J. ... **New York, NY**
Wolfson, David M. ... Valdosta, GA
Wolfson, Donald ... Aurora, OH
Wolfson, Donald Jay ... **New York, NY**
Wolfson, Donald M. ... Westbury, NY
Wolfson, Donna J. ... Minneapolis, MN
Wolfson, Douglas A. ... Boston, MA
Wolfson, Douglas K. ... New Brunswick, NJ
Wolfson, Eugene ... Woodbridge, NJ
Wolfson, Evan ... New York, NY
Wolfson, Freda L. ... Trenton, NJ
Wolfson, Frederick S. ... Lebanon, PA
Wolfson, Garth S. ... **New York, NY**
Wolfson, Gerald G. ... Encinitas, CA
Wolfson & Glass ... Las Vegas, NV
Wolfson, Greller, Egitto & Kitchen **Poughkeepsie, NY**
Wolfson & Grossman ... Westbury, NY
Wolfson, Harold M. ... Los Angeles, CA
Wolfson, Henry A. ... Springfield, IL
Wolfson, Herbert M. ... Wilmington, DE
Wolfson, Herbert S. ... Philadelphia, PA
Wolfson, Howard S. ... **New York, NY**
Wolfson, Hyman ... Yorba Linda, CA
Wolfson, I. David Department Of Health And Human Services, Food & Drug Administration, GV
Wolfson, Ilse M. ... Laguna Hills, CA
Wolfson, Jack L. ... **Worcester, MA**
Wolfson, James J. ... **Atlanta, GA**
Wolfson, James M. ... Miami Beach, FL
Wolfson, Jay ... Tampa, FL
Wolfson, Jeffrey A. ... **Washington, DC**
Wolfson, Jeffrey H. ... Fort Lauderdale, FL
Wolfson, Jeffrey S. ... **Boston, MA**
Wolfson, Jerome F. ... Springfield, IL
Wolfson, Jerome H. ... Miami, FL
Wolfson, Jerome H., P.A. ... Miami, FL
Wolfson, Jo-Anne F. ... Chicago, IL
Wolfson, Joel Rothstein ... Washington, DC
Wolfson, John M. ... **Hartford, CT**
Wolfson, Joseph E. ... **Reading, PA**
Wolfson, Keenan, Cotton & Meagher, A Professional Association ... **Worcester, MA**
Wolfson, Kenneth A. ... **Costa Mesa, CA**
Wolfson, Larry M. ... **Chicago, IL**
Wolfson Law Center, The, P.C. Bullhead City, AZ
Wolfson, Lawrence ... Holyoke, MA
Wolfson, Lawrence I. ... Westbury, NY
Wolfson, Lou Anne C ... Chicago, IL
Wolfson, Mark J. ... **Tampa, FL**
Wolfson, Maxine C. ... Tampa, FL
Wolfson, Merle A. ... **Philadelphia, PA**
Wolfson, Michael G. ... **New York, NY**
Wolfson, Michael G. ... **New York, NY**
Wolfson, Michael I. ... **New York, NY**
Wolfson, Michael P. ... Longwood, FL
Wolfson, Myron L. ... Towson, MD
Wolfson, Neil I. ... Boston, MA
Wolfson, Nicholas ... Hartford, CT
Wolfson, Norman ... Columbia, MD
Wolfson & Papushkewych ... Springfield, IL
Wolfson, Paul R. Q. ... Department of Justice, Office of the Solicitor General, GV
Wolfson, Paulette S. ... **Houston, TX**
Wolfson, Peter D. ... **New York, NY**
Wolfson, Peter J. ... **Morristown, NJ**
Wolfson, Randolph D. ... Bullhead City, AZ
Wolfson, Richard M. ... **Chicago, IL**
Wolfson, Richard M. ... Minneapolis, MN
Wolfson, Richard S. ... Miami Beach, FL
Wolfson, Roger S. ... United States Senate, Senatorial Assistants, GV
Wolfson, Ronald A. ... Nevada City, CA
Wolfson, Russell M. ... **New York, NY**
Wolfson, Samuel ... Encino, CA
Wolfson, Scott A. ... **Detroit, MI**
Wolfson, Stephen A. ... Culver City, CA
Wolfson, Steven Environmental Protection Agency, Office of the General Counsel, GV
Wolfson, Steven B. ... Las Vegas, NV
Wolfson, Steven D. ... **Phoenix, AZ**
Wolfson, Susan W. ... **New Haven, CT**
Wolfson, Suzanne L. ... Haverford, PA
Wolfson, Tamara S. ... **Boston, MA**
Wolfson, Timothy C. ... **Pittsburgh, PA**
Wolfson, Tina ... Los Angeles, CA
Wolfson, Vicki Beth ... Annapolis, MD
Wolfson, William ... Folsom, CA
Wolfson, William M. ... Detroit, MI
Wolfson, William S. ... Flemington, NJ
Wolfsont, Allen ... Smithtown, NY
Wolfstone & Ellickson ... Seattle, WA
Wolfstone, Gary L. ... Seattle, WA
Wolfstone, Jeffrey C. ... **Portland, OR**
Wolfstone, Panchot & Bloch, P.S., Inc. **Seattle, WA**
Wolfteich, Paul G. ... Department of Justice, Environment and Natural Resources Division, GV
Wolfzahn, Orna ... **New York, NY**
Wolgamot, John P. ... Danville, IL
Wolgamot, Steven ... Mahtomedi, MN
Wolgamuth, Keith R. ... Cleveland, OH
Wolgast, Anna L. ... Department of Justice, Environment and Natural Resources Division, GV
Wolge, Jayne L. ... Bedminster, NJ
Wolgel, Fred A. ... Houston, TX
Wolgel, Harold H. ... **New York, NY**
Wolgel, Joseph D. ... Chicago, IL
Wolgemuth, Jennifer A. ... **New York, NY**
Wolgemuth, Kirk L. ... **Lancaster, PA**
Wolgemuth, Philip A. ... **Lancaster, PA**
Wolhandler, Steven ... El Prado, NM
Woliansky & Doyle ... Avenel, NJ
Woliansky, Marc A. ... Avenel, NJ
Wolicki, David P. ... Canton, MA
Wolin, Alan E. ... Jericho, NY
Wolin, Alfred M. ... Newark, NJ
Wolin, Amy Jane ... Morristown, NJ
Wolin, David S. ... **New York, NY**
Wolin, Debra Ruth ... New York, NY
Wolin, Eugene R. ... New York, NY
Wolin, Harris A. ... Bethlehem, PA
Wolin, Harry A. ... Austin, TX
Wolin, Harry S. ... **Chicago, IL**
Wolin, Jerold D. ... Jericho, NY
Wolin, Jonathan S. ... Washington, DC
Wolin, Les J. ... **Los Angeles, CA**
Wolin, Marc E. ... **Newark, NJ**
Wolin, Martin J. ... Boston, MA
Wolin, Marvin ... Tucson, AZ
Wolin, Michael D. ... Freehold, NJ New York, NY
Wolin, Michele National Labor Relations Board, Office of Board Members, GV
Wolin, Milton B. ... Brooklyn, NY
Wolin, Neal S. ... Treasury Department, Office of the General Counsel, GV
Wolin, Philip S. ... **Chicago, IL**
Wolin, Ridley & Miller LLP ... **Dallas, TX**
Wolin, Robert Everett ... **Dallas, TX**
Wolin, Robert M. ... **Houston, TX**
Wolin & Rosen, Ltd. ... **Chicago, IL**
Woliner, Lisa Anne ... **Fort Lauderdale, FL**
Wolinetz, Barry H. ... **Columbus, OH**
Wolinetz, Brian L. ... **West Palm Beach, FL**
Wolinetz, Gary Keith ... **Woodbridge, NJ**
Wolinetz, Milton ... Bayside, NY
Wolins, Jason K. ... Sacramento, CA
Wolinski, Theresa E. ... New York, NY
Wolinsky, Alan M. ... Lake Ronkonkoma, NY
Wolinsky, Allen Arthur ... Hollywood, FL
Wolinsky, David C. ... **New York, NY**
Wolinsky, Douglas J. ... **Burlington, VT**
Wolinsky, Gerald S. ... New York, NY
Wolinsky, Iris C. ... Los Angeles, CA
Wolinsky, Joseph A. ... New York, NY
Wolinsky, Larry ... **Walden, NY**
Wolinsky, Marc ... **New York, NY**
Wolinsky, Melvin ... College Point, NY
Wolinsky, Michael ... Voorhees, NJ
Wolinsky & Parnell ... Lake Ronkonkoma, NY
Wolinsky, Sidney M. ... Berkeley, CA
Wolinsky & Wolinsky ... College Point, NY
Wolis, David ... Hollywood, FL
Wolis, Kenneth A., (P.A.) ... Hollywood, FL
Wolis, Steven E. ... North Miami Beach, FL
Wolitarsky, Bruce W. ... Houston, TX
Wolitzer, Michael W. ... **New York, NY**
Wolitzky, Emily ... Tucson, AZ
Wolitzky, Sidney F. ... Tucson, AZ
Woliung, Martha J. ... Long Beach, CA
Woliver, John ... Batavia, OH
Woliver, Sandra ... San Rafael, CA
Wolk, Alan M. ... **Cleveland, OH**
Wolk, Allan ... **Rochester, NY**
Wolk, Andrew R. ... Hauppauge, NY
Wolk, Anthony L. ... New York, NY
Wolk, Arthur Alan ... **Philadelphia, PA**
Wolk, Brian P. ... Los Angeles, CA
Wolk, Bruce ... Davis, CA
Wolk, Christine ... Oshkosh, WI
Wolk, Edmund F. ... **New York, NY**
Wolk & Genter ... **Philadelphia, PA**
Wolk, Gregory H. ... **St. Louis, MO**
Wolk, Howard ... Boston, MA
Wolk, I. Louis ... La Jolla, CA
Wolk, Ivor C. ... New York, NY
Wolk, Janice Bowers ... Pittsburgh, PA
Wolk, Jeffrey S. ... **New York, NY**
Wolk, Jerome ... Floral Park, NY
Wolk, Lawrence Bruce ... Fort Lauderdale, FL
Wolk, Lawrence J. ... **Washington, DC**
Wolk, Leo ... Minneapolis, MN
Wolk, Marcia S. ... Coraopolis, PA
Wolk, Maurice P. ... **Chicago, IL**
Wolk, Michael B., Law Offices of **New York, NY**
Wolk, Nathan T. ... **Boston, MA**
Wolk, Neil T. ... **New York, NY**
Wolk, Peter B. ... Longmeadow, MA
Wolk, Peter C. ... Silver Spring, MD
Wolk, Reuben ... Dayton, OH
Wolk, Saundra R. ... Sacramento, CA
Wolk, Stuart R. ... Washington, DC
Wolk, Susan L. ... Tarzana, CA
Wolk, Terry J. ... Cleveland, OH
Wolk, William G. ... **Miami, FL**
Wolke, Dan ... Grants Pass, OR
Wolke and Mays ... Eugene, OR
Wolke, Milton S., Jr. ... Philadelphia, PA
Wolke, Pat ... Condon, OR
Wolke, William C. ... Eugene, OR
Wolken, George, Jr. ... **San Jose, CA**
Wolken, Jeffrey C. ... **Cherry Hill, NJ** **Philadelphia, PA**
Wolken, Norman P. ... Pittsburgh, PA
Wolken, Susan Ackerman ... Columbus, OH
Wolkenberg, Gayle N. ... **Princeton, NJ** **New York, NY**
Wolkenbreit, Jed B. ... **Albany, NY**
Wolkey, Michelle K., P.S. ... **Spokane, WA**
Wolkin, Betsy ... San Francisco, CA
Wolkin, Brandt L. ... **San Francisco, CA**
Wolkin, Douglas A. ... **Englewood, CO**
Wolkin, Paul A. ... Philadelphia, PA
Wolkin, Robert S. ... Tucson, AZ
Wolkin, Steven Edward ... Cleveland, OH
Wolkin & Timpane, LLP **San Francisco, CA**
Wolkind, Harold L. ... Farmington Hills, MI
Wolking, John L. ... El Reno, OK
Wolkoff, Eugene A. ... New York, NY
Wolkoff, Harvey J. ... **Boston, MA**
Wolkoff, Mark G. ... Philadelphia, PA
Wolkoff, Neal L. ... New York, NY
Wolkoff, Robin L. ... Chicago, IL
Wolkoff-Beall, Sherrie L. ... Fishers, IN
Wolkofsky, Evan N. ... Raleigh, NC
Wolkon, Barry ... Monsey, NY
Wolkon & Pascucci, LLP ... **Boston, MA**
Wolkon, Robert ... **Boston, MA**
Wolkon, Shari H. ... **Boston, MA**
Wolkov, Leonard A. ... Cleveland, OH
Wolkov, Sandra K. ... **Miami, FL**
Wolkove, Jason ... **New York, NY**
Wolkow, Michael C. ... Oceanside, NY
Wolkowicz, Joseph H. ... St. Paul, MN
Wolkowicz, Micheline ... New York, NY
Wolkowitz, Barry H. ... Roslyn, NY
Wolkowitz, Edward M. ... **Los Angeles, CA**
Wolkowitz, Herbert ... St. Louis, MO
Wolkowitz, Lawrence C. ... Commack, NY
Wolkowitz, Richard J. ... **St. Louis, MO**
Wolkowski, John A. ... **Nashua, NH**
Wolkowski, John A., P.C. ... **Nashua, NH**
Wolkowsky, Joseph B. ... Tavernier, FL
Wolkstein, Gary M. ... Madison, WI
Wolkstein, Leonard A. ... Westfield, NJ
Woll, Alan ... **McLean, VA**
Woll, Andrew D. ... Placerville, CA Sacramento, CA
Woll, Christopher W. ... Chicago, IL
Woll, David J. ... **New York, NY**
Woll, David L. ... Evansville, IN
Woll, Deborah ... New York, NY
Woll, Edward, Jr. ... **Boston, MA**
Woll, Glenn H. J. ... **New York, NY**
Woll, Harvey L. ... New York, NY
Woll, Jessica R. ... Southfield, MI
Woll, Lois R. ... **New York, NY**
Woll, Pauline J. ... Southfield, MI
Woll and Woll ... Southfield, MI
Wollack, Solomon ... **San Francisco, CA**
Wollam, Erik R. ... **Houston, TX**
Wollam, H. Nevin ... Greensburg, PA
Wollam, Paul A. ... Newport Beach, CA
Wollam, Sheila ... **Houston, TX**
Wollan, Dennis E. ... Los Angeles, CA
Wollan, Eugene ... **New York, NY**
Wollan, Laurin A., Jr. ... Tallahassee, FL
Wolland, Frank ... North Miami, FL
Wollangk, Sandra J. ... Orange, CA
Wollard, Eric D. ... **Denver, CO**
Wollard Law Office, The, A Professional Corporation ... **Denver, CO**
Wollard, Mary A. ... **Denver, CO**
Wollberg, Gary L. ... **San Diego, CA**
Wollbrinck, George A. ... Olathe, CO
Wollbrinck, James H. ... St. Louis, MO
Wolle, Barbara ... Stillwater, MN
Wolle, Charles R. ... Des Moines, IA
Wolle, Robert A. ... Oak Harbor, WA
Wolle, Thomas D. ... **Cedar Rapids, IA**
Wolleat, Patricia L. ... Madison, WI
Wollen, A. Ross ... New York, NY
Wollen, Carolyn S. ... **Portland, ME** **New York, NY**
Wollen, John R. ... New York, NY
Wollen, Julius M. ... Albuquerque, NM
Wollen, Teresa K. ... Lawrence, KS
Wollen, W. Foster, Jr. ... San Francisco, CA
Wollenberg, J. Roger ... **Washington, DC**
Wollenberg, John B. ... Short Hills, NJ
Wollenberg, Richard H. ... Longview, WA
Wollenberg, William L. ... Farmington, CT
Wollenberger, Gerard ... New York, NY
Wollenzien, Harold J. ... **Waukesha, WI**
Woller, Anthonie H. ... **Portland, OR**
Woller, Edward A. ... Kewanee, IL
Woller, James A. ... **Summit, NJ**
Woller, John S. ... Orange, CA
Wollerstein, Alan J. ... New York, NY
Wollerstein & Futoran ... New York, NY
Wollert, Larry E., II ... **San Francisco, CA**
Wollesen, Woodrow D. ... Potomac, MD
Wollett, Donald H. ... Sacramento, CA
Wollett, Franklyn J. ... Clearwater, FL
Wollett, Ronald L. ... Palm Beach Gardens, FL
Wollett, Ronald S. ... Columbus, OH
Wollfarth, Robert L., Jr. **New Orleans, LA**
Wollheim, Robert ... Portland, OR
Wollin, David A. ... **Boston, MA** **Providence, RI**
Wollin, Joan L. ... Leesburg, FL
Wollin, Louis ... **New York, NY**
Wollin, Matthew K. ... **Mount Vernon, IL**
Wollin, Nancy J. ... **Atlanta, GA**
Wollinka, David J. ... **Holiday, FL** **Palm Harbor, FL**
Wollinka & Wollinka ... **Holiday, FL** **Palm Harbor, FL**
Wollins, Benjamin ... Newton, MA
Wollins, David H. ... **Denver, CO**
Wollins, Hellman & Green, P.C. **Aspen, CO** **Denver, CO**
Wollitz, Howard N. ... **Los Angeles, CA**
Wollitzer, Rachel I. ... Department of Justice, Tax Division, GV
Wollman, Amy M. ... Universal City, CA
Wollman, David A. ... Medford, NJ
Wollman, Diana L. ... **New York, NY**
Wollman, Edward E. ... **Naples, FL**
Wollman, Eric ... New York, NY
Wollman, John L. ... **Palo Alto, CA**
Wollman, Joseph D. ... **Amsterdam, NY**
Wollman, Mark J. ... Jenkintown, PA
Wollman, Milton A. ... Broad Axe, PA
Wollman, Nelson H. ... Philadelphia, PA
Wollman, Paul I. ... **Mineola, NY**
Wollman, Paul L. ... **Amsterdam, NY**
Wollman, Roger L. ... Sioux Falls, SD
Wollman, Russell S. ... **Los Angeles, CA**
Wollman, Shari Mulrooney **Los Angeles, CA**
Wollman, Stacie J. ... Annapolis, MD
Wollman, Steven L. ... Swampscott, MA
Wollman, Strauss & Associates, P.A. **Naples, FL**
Wollman, Thomas R. ... **Sioux Falls, SD**
Wollman & Tracey ... Philadelphia, PA
Wollman & Wollman ... **Albany, NY** **Amsterdam, NY**
Wollmann, Mary E. ... Woodbridge, NJ
Wollmuth, David H. ... **New York, NY**
Wollmuth Maher & Deutsch LLP **New York, NY**
Wolloch, Richard D. ... **Hackensack, NJ**
Wollonciej, Thaddeus S. ... Pasadena, CA
Wollrab, James C., Jr. ... Boulder, CO
Wollschlager, Gary G. ... Fairmont, MN
Wollschlager Law Firm, P.A. ... Fairmont, MN
Wollstein, Richmond August Colonial Heights, VA
Wollstein, Stephen K. ... **Anniston, AL**
Wolly, Michael S. ... Washington, DC
Wolman, Anita Yallowitz ... **Encino, CA**
Wolman, Babitt & King, L.L.P. Jersey City, NJ New York, NY
Wolman, Benjamin R., Law Offices of **Upper Marlboro, MD**
Wolman, Benson A. ... **Columbus, OH**
Wolman, Derek A. ... **New York, NY**
Wolman, Genshaft & Gellman **Columbus, OH**
Wolman, James D. ... **Lancaster, PA**
Wolman, Jeffrey C. ... Los Angeles, CA
Wolman, Karin ... **New York, NY**
Wolman, Martin ... San Francisco, CA
Wolman, Martin ... **Hartford, CT**
Wolman, Paul C., III ... Baltimore, MD
Wolman, Philip J. ... **Los Angeles, CA**
Wolmart, Lisa Martinez ... **Woodbridge, NJ**
Wolmer, Beth R. ... **New York, NY**
Wolmer, Brent G. ... **North Palm Beach, FL**
Wolmetz, Lori B. ... **New York, NY**
Wolney, Richard T. ... Troy, MI
Wolnitzek, Rowekamp & Bonar, P.S.C. Covington, KY
Wolnitzek, Stephen D. ... **Covington, KY**
Wolny, Michael ... **Orlando, FL**
Wolock, David H. ... Detroit, MI
Wolock, Miriam Z. ... **Bloomfield Hills, MI**
Wolock, Steven M. ... **Southfield, MI**
Wolod, Kimberly E. ... Washington, DC
Wolohojian, Gabrielle R. ... **Boston, MA**
Wolok, Miriam S. ... **Oklahoma City, OK**
Wolonsky, Joseph P. ... Hoffman Estates, IL
Wolontis, Nikki ... **Los Angeles, CA**
Wolos, Michael C. ... Flint, MI
Woloshansky, I. Alexander ... Merrillville, IN
Woloshen, Daniel S. ... **Fairfield, CT**
Woloshin, Douglas ... **Washington, DC**
Woloshin, Mark Harris ... Newport, KY
Woloshin, Melvyn A. ... **Wilmington, DE**

Wong, Jeffrey M. ... **Portland, OR**
Wong, Jennifer L. ... **Palo Alto, CA**
Wong, Jenny Tamara ... Brooklyn, NY
Wong, Jim Yicklung ... Phoenix, AZ
Wong, John D. ... Wichita, KS
Wong, John Shew ... San Francisco, CA
Wong, Johnson H. ... Honolulu, HI
Wong, Jonathan M. ... **Oakland, CA**
Wong, Judith A. ... Bedford, MA
Wong, Judith L. ... **Westlake Village, CA**
Wong, Judy C. ... **New York, NY**
Wong, Judy Lee ... **McAllen, TX**
Wong, K. Matthew ... **New York, NY**
Wong, Kam ... **New York, NY**
Wong, Karen B. ... **Los Angeles, CA**
Wong, Karen C. ... New York, NY
Wong, Karen Gail Chinn ... Seattle, WA
Wong, Kathleen H. ... Seal Beach, CA
Wong, Kenneth A. ... Costa Mesa, CA
Wong, Kenneth K. P. ... Honolulu, HI
Wong, Kenneth R. ... South Padre Island, TX
Wong, Kent D. ... Los Angeles, CA
Wong, Kimberley M.L. ... **Honolulu, HI**
Wong, Kimberly ... **Long Beach, CA**
Wong, Kim-pok ... New York, NY
Wong, King Lit ... **Washington, DC**
Wong, Kit T. ... **New York, NY**
Wong, Kristin Lynn ... San Jose, CA
Wong, Lai C. ... Anchorage, AK
Wong, Larry ... Anaheim, CA
Wong, Laureen K. K. ... Honolulu, HI
Wong, Laurence Y. ... Glendale, CA
Wong, Lawrence ... Oakland, CA
Wong, Lawrence D. ... Orange, CA
Wong & Lee ... San Francisco, CA
Wong, Leighton H. C. ... Honolulu, HI
Wong, Lena ... Boston, MA
Wong, Lester G. L. ... Honolulu, HI
Wong, Libby ... **Irvine, CA**
Wong, Lily L. ... **Mountain View, CA**
Wong, Lily L. ... **New York, NY**
Wong, Linda ... **Edison, NJ**
Philadelphia, PA
Wong, Linda Jeanne ... Los Angeles, CA
Wong, Linda L. ... Dallas, TX
Wong, Linda Wai Mun ... **New York, NY**
Wong, Linnea Sciaroni ... San Carlos, CA
Wong, Lisa L. ... **New York, NY**
Wong, Lisa W. ... **Seattle, WA**
Wong, Lisa-Anne M. ... San Francisco, CA
Wong, Lulu L., Law Offices of ... **Napa, CA**
Santa Rosa, CA
Wong, Mailine ... **San Francisco, CA**
Wong, Margaret W., & Associates
Cleveland, OH
Wong, Martha T. ... San Francisco, CA
Wong, Martin J. ... **Baltimore, MD**
Wong, Mary Beth M., (A Law Corporation)
Honolulu, HI
Wong, MaryAnn ... White Plains, NY
Wong, Merilyn ... Oakland, CA
Wong, Michael J. Y. ... **Honolulu, HI**
Wong, Michael Y. ... **Austin, TX**
Wong, Michele L. ... **Redondo Beach, CA**
Wong, Mitchell L. ... Burlingame, CA
Wong, Mitchell S. ... **Honolulu, HI**
Wong, Mitchell Y. M. ... San Francisco, CA
Wong, Monica Seine ... Orange, CA
Wong, Nancy E. Fong ... Carson City, NV
Wong, Nancy Hing ... San Francisco, CA
Wong, Nena W. ... Los Angeles, CA
Wong, Nicole A. ... **San Francisco, CA**
Wong, Nora Mein Locke ... Oakland, CA
Wong, Norman Kwai-Wing
New York, NY
Wong, Norman Y. ... **Los Angeles, CA**
Wong, Oshima & Kondo, Attorneys at Law, A Law Corporation ... **Honolulu, HI**
Wong, Pak Hoy ... Oakland, CA
Wong, Patricia B. ... **New York, NY**
Wong, Patricia K. ... Harrisburg, PA
Wong, Patricia Uyehara ... Honolulu, HI
Wong, Patricia Yung ... **Boston, MA**
Wong, Patrick I. ... Wailuku, HI
Wong, Paul W. ... **Los Angeles, CA**
Wong, Paula S.C. ... Austin, TX
Wong, Peter J. ... **Palo Alto, CA**
Wong, Peter M. O. ... **San Francisco, CA**
Wong, Peter Y.F. ... San Francisco, CA
Wong, Philip ... **Chicago, IL**
Wong, Phillip S. ... **Longmont, CO**
Wong, Pollyanna T. ... New York, NY
Wong, Randy S. ... Encino, CA
Wong, Ray L. ... **San Francisco, CA**
Wong, Raymond H. ... Bound Brook, NJ
Princeton, NJ
New York, NY
Wong, Raymond H., P.C. ... Bound Brook, NJ
Princeton, NJ
New York, NY
Wong, Raymond L. ... Cleveland, MS
Wong, Regina R. ... **Los Angeles, CA**
Wong, Reuben S. F. ... **Honolulu, HI**
Wong, Richard ... Los Angeles, CA
Wong, Richard ... New York, NY
Wong, Richard C. ... **New York, NY**
Wong, Richard L. ... Monterey Park, CA
Wong, Richard L.
Department of Transportation, Federal Transit Administration, GV
Wong, Richard L., The Law Offices Of
Monterey Park, CA
Wong, Richard M. ... **Boston, MA**
Wong, Robb N. ... Gaithersburg, MD
Wong, Robb N., P.C. ... Gaithersburg, MD
Wong, Robert W. ... New York, NY
Wong, Roger R ... Hagåtña, GU
Wong, Rollin ... Irvine, CA

Wong, Rosanne ... Los Angeles, CA
Wong, Russell T. ... **Houston, TX**
Wong, Samuel ... San Jose, CA
Wong, Sandra-Ann Y. H. ... Honolulu, HI
Wong, Senta L. ... **Boston, MA**
Wong, Sharon ... **Los Angeles, CA**
Wong, Sharon L. ... **San Jose, CA**
Wong, Sherman S. M. ... Santa Monica, CA
Wong, Shirley L. ... Chicago, IL
Wong, Shirley Y. ... San Jose, CA
Wong, Sidney J. Y. ... **Honolulu, HI**
Wong, Siu P. ... Department of Justice, Washington, D.C. District Office, GV
Wong, Stanley E. ... Glendale, CA
Wong, Stanton D. ... **San Francisco, CA**
Wong, Stephen B. ... Orange, CA
Wong, Stephen H. M. ... **San Francisco, CA**
Wong, Stephen R. ... **San Francisco, CA**
Wong, Steve A. ... **Los Angeles, CA**
Wong, Steven T. ... Houston, TX
Wong & Stuman ... San Diego, CA
Wong, Suey Y. ... El Macero, CA
Wong, Susan C. ... Honolulu, HI
Wong, Susan G. ... New York, NY
Wong, Susan M. U. ... Honolulu, HI
Wong, Teresa Yiu Tak ... Hollywood, FL
Wong, Theodore D. ... Boston, MA
Wong, Thomas A. Jr. ... Santa Monica, CA
Wong, Thomas A. Jr., P.C.
Santa Monica, CA
Wong, Thomas J. ... **Honolulu, HI**
Wong, Timothy Y. ... **St. Paul, MN**
Wong, Timothy Zachary ... **Los Angeles, CA**
Wong, Todd T. ... Austin, TX
Wong, Tuen Y. ... Sacramento, CA
Wong, Vicky ... **Santa Monica, CA**
Wong, Vincent J. ... **Indianapolis, IN**
Wong, Vincent S. ... **Washington, DC**
Wong, Wallace M. ... **Los Angeles, CA**
Wong, Wayson W. S. ... Honolulu, HI
Wong, Wean Khing ... South Pasadena, CA
Wong, Wei C. ... Alhambra, CA
Wong, Wendy W. ... Alameda, CA
Wong, William J. ... San Francisco, CA
Wong, Wilson W. ... San Bernardino, CA
Wong, Wing ... Washington, DC
Wong, Winnie Wing-See ... **New York, NY**
Wong, Winston K. Q. ... Honolulu, HI
Wong & Wong, P.C. ... Austin, TX
Wong, Yanira G. ... **New York, NY**
Wong, Yin Soon ... San Francisco, CA
Wong, Zeppelin W. ... San Francisco, CA
Wong-Ames, Cicy ... Austin, TX
Wong-Chong, Nicole M. ... Los Angeles, CA
Wong-Diaz, Francisco Raimundo
Greenbrae, CA
Wongrey, Paul ... Inverness, FL
Wong-Taylor, Katty C. ... New Brunswick, NJ
Wongwai, Sheryl Schmitt ... Denver, CO
Wonio, Rand S. ... **Davenport, IA**
Wonnacott, Bert R. ... Salt Lake City, UT
Wonneberger, Robert M. ... **Stamford, CT**
Wonnell, Christopher T. ... San Diego, CA
Wonnell, Harold E. ... Columbus, OH
Wonnell, Nancy K. ... Columbus, OH
Wonnell, Thomas Burke ... Anchorage, AK
Wons, Timothy R. ... Chicago, IL
Wonsetler, Karen J. ... Orlando, FL
Wonski, Louann ... Fords, NJ
Wonstolen, Kenneth A.
Highlands Ranch, CO
Wontor, Stephen J. ... **Edina, MN**
Woo, Andrea T. ... **San Antonio, TX**
Woo, Angela M. ... **Atlanta, GA**
Woo, Ann H. ... **San Francisco, CA**
Woo, Arnold D. ... **Los Angeles, CA**
Woo & Associates, LL.P. ... San Francisco, CA
Woo, Betty C. ... New York, NY
Woo, C. Craig ... **Los Angeles, CA**
Woo, Carol A. ... **Ventura, CA**
Woo, Chin-teh ... San Leandro, CA
Woo, Christie E. ... Los Angeles, CA
Woo, Christopher S.B. ... Honolulu, HI
Woo, Cynthia Ying ... Salem, MA
Woo, Daniel D. ... **Seattle, WA**
Woo, Darryl M. ... **Palo Alto, CA**
Woo, David B. ... Baltimore, MD
Woo, David Bow ... **Los Angeles, CA**
Woo, Donna M. ... Honolulu, HI
Woo, Edwin
Department Of Health And Human Services, Office for Civil Rights, GV
Woo, Frances Mei Soo ... New York, NY
Woo, Frankie En-Long ... Whittier, CA
Woo, James C. ... **San Antonio, TX**
Woo, Jeffery P. ... San Francisco, CA
Woo, Jennifer A. ... **San Diego, CA**
Woo, Margaret Y.K. ... Boston, MA
Woo, Maxine M. ... Treasury Department, Internal Revenue Service, GV
Woo, Melissa W. ... **Los Angeles, CA**
Woo, Michael K. ... **San Francisco, CA**
Woo, Nicole L. ... **New York, NY**
Woo, Peggy L. ... Sacramento, CA
Woo, Philip W. ... **San Jose, CA**
Woo, Phillip G. ... **Houston, TX**
Woo, Richard E. ... Los Angeles, CA
Woo, Robert K., Jr. ... **Atlanta, GA**
Woo, Samuel J. ... **Los Angeles, CA**
Woo, Sarah Suzuki ... Los Angeles, CA
Woo, Shaw B. ... New York, NY
Woo, Shirley A. ... **San Francisco, CA**
Woo, Suzanne M. ... El Cerrito, CA
Woo, T. David, Jr. ... Honolulu, HI
Woo, Terry K. ... San Jose, CA
Woo, Tina ... **New York, NY**
Woo, Vernon Y. T. ... **Honolulu, HI**

Woo, Walter H. ... Treasury Department, Internal Revenue Service, GV
Woo, Warren T. ... San Francisco, CA
Woocher, Elliot D. ... Mount Kisco, NY
Woocher, Fredric Dean ... Santa Monica, CA
Woock, Sally Ann ... Lockport, IL
Wood, A. Dylan ... **Austin, TX**
Longview, TX
Rosenberg, TX
Wood, A. Kendall ... **San Diego, CA**
Wood, A. Terry ... Greensboro, NC
Wood, Aimee J. ... **Bridgeport, CT**
Wood, Alan M. ... **Lincoln, NE**
Wood, Allen ... **Washington, DC**
Wood, Allen ... Corpus Christi, TX
Wood, Allen W., III ... **Newton, NC**
Wood, Allison D. ... **Washington, DC**
Wood, Allison L. ... **Chicago, IL**
Wood, Amelia E. ... Houston, TX
Wood, Amy E. ... **Seattle, WA**
Wood, Andrew C. ... Tequesta, FL
Wood, Andrew P. ... Neosho, MO
Wood, Andrew W. ... **Maysville, KY**
Wood, Andrew W. ... **Richmond, VA**
Wood, Anita L. ... San Francisco, CA
Wood, Ann B. ... **Clearfield, PA**
Wood, Ann Bernard ... Lake Zurich, IL
Wood, Ann Whitley ... **Dallas, TX**
Wood, Anna Marie ... Houston, TX
Wood, Annalisa C. ... Palo Alto, CA
Wood, Anne M. ... North Syracuse, NY
Wood, Anne-Marie ... **New York, NY**
Wood, April C. ... Thomasville, NC
Wood, Arthur E., Jr. ... Waynesboro, MS
Wood & Associates, L.L.P. ... **Camarillo, CA**
Los Angeles, CA
Ventura, CA
Wood & Associates, L.L.P. ... Charleston, WV
Wood & Associates, P.A.
St. Petersburg, FL
Tampa, FL
Wood, Atter, & Associates, P.A.
Jacksonville, FL
Wood, B. Jeffrey ... **Winston-Salem, NC**
Wood, B. Paul ... Lansing, MI
Wood, Ballard P. ... Smithfield, VA
Wood, Barbara A. ... **New York, NY**
Wood, Bari D. ... **Chicago, IL**
Wood, Barry C. ... Ukiah, CA
Wood, Barry D. ... **Washington, DC**
Wood, Barry E. ... Pittsburgh, PA
Wood, Benton N. ... **Miami, FL**
Orlando, FL
Wood, Betty Garrett ... **Oklahoma City, OK**
Wood, Beverly ... **San Rafael, CA**
Wood, B. F. ... Graham, NC
Wood & Bierly ... McMinnville, OR
Wood, Blair C., Jr. ... **Hanover, NH**
Norwich, VT
Wood, Bobby R. ... Corinth, MS
Wood, Bohm & Francis, LLP ... **Irvine, CA**
Los Angeles, CA
Wood, Bohm, Francis & Morrison, LLP
Washington, DC
Wood, Boykin & Wolter, A Professional Corporation ... **Corpus Christi, TX**
Wood, Bradley J. ... **St. Petersburg, FL**
Wood, Branson L., III ... **Hannibal, MO**
Wood, Brent E. ... **Raleigh, NC**
Wood, Brent K. ... Rutland, VT
Wood, Brett M. ... Woodbridge, VA
Wood, Brian A. ... **Minneapolis, MN**
Wood, Brian D. ... **Fayetteville, AR**
Wood, Brian P. ... Kansas City, MO
Wood, Brian Wilson ... **Salina, KS**
Wood, Brock Richard ... Lakewood, CO
Wood, Bruce B. ... **New York, NY**
Wood, Bruce C. ... **Washington, DC**
Wood, Bruce E. ... **Syracuse, NY**
Wood, Bryan ... **Philadelphia, PA**
Wood, Byron ... Campbellsville, KY
Wood, C. Brooks ... **Kansas City, MO**
Wood, C. Daniel ... Bangor, ME
Wood, C. David ... Decatur, GA
Wood, C. Lane ... **Naples, FL**
Wood, Cara C. ... Conroe, TX
Wood & Carlton ... Corinth, MS
Wood, Carol ... Santa Monica, CA
Wood, Carol M. ... **Atlanta, GA**
Wood, Carol Whitcher ... **Sarasota, FL**
Wood, Carolyn M. ... **Sacramento, CA**
Wood, Carolyn V. ... **Boston, MA**
Wood, Carrene M. ... Belfair, WA
Wood, Carroll ... Maitland, FL
Wood, Cary L. ... **Los Angeles, CA**
Wood, Cassell, Jr. ... Plainfield, NJ
Wood, Cecil O., Jr. ... Pawhuska, OK
Wood, Celeste K. ... Pasadena, CA
Wood, Channy F. ... **Amarillo, TX**
Wood, Charles A., Jr. ... **Walnut Creek, CA**
Wood, Charles B. ... Austin, TX
Wood, Charles D. ... **Mount Kisco, NY**
Wood, Charles E. ... Southborough, MA
Wood, Charles E. ... Gulfport, MS
Wood, Charles Edward ... Laurel, MD
Wood, Charles L. ... **Atlanta, GA**
Wood, Charlot F. ... **Winston-Salem, NC**
Wood, Chauncey B. ... Boston, MA
Wood, Cheri L. ... **Beverly Hills, CA**
Wood, Cheryl A. ... Catskill, NY
Wood, Cheryl C. ... **Richmond, VA**
Wood & Christie ... Laurel, MD
Wood, Christina D. ... Wellesley, MA
Wood, Christina M. ... **New York, NY**
Wood, Christopher A. ... Oklahoma City, OK
Wood, Christopher D. ... Baltimore, MD
Wood, Christopher G. ... **Washington, DC**
Wood, Christopher H. ... **Washington, DC**

Wood, Christopher R. ... South River, NJ
Wood, Christopher A., & Associates, P.C.
Oklahoma City, OK
Wood, Christopher W. ... **Menlo Park, CA**
Wood, Christopher W. ... **Sacramento, CA**
Wood, Claire ... **Brooklyn, NY**
Wood, Clarence E. ... Indianapolis, IN
Wood, Clarence M. ... **Jacksonville, FL**
Wood, Clark S. ... Sallisaw, OK
Wood, Clayton P. ... New York, NY
Wood, Clement B. ... **New York, NY**
Wood, Constance B. ... Denver, CO
Wood, Corin A. ... Fraser, CO
Wood, Courtney L. ... **Baltimore, MD**
Wood, Craig P. ... **San Francisco, CA**
Wood Crapo LLC ... **Salt Lake City, UT**
Wood, Curtis A. ... **New York, NY**
Wood, Curtis L. ... Spring, TX
Wood, Curtis M. ... Westfield, MA
Wood, Cynthia Ruth ... Baltimore, MD
Wood, D. Craig ... **San Antonio, TX**
Wood, D. Harris ... Fayetteville, GA
Wood, D. Lyle ... Las Cruces, NM
Wood, Dale E. ... Truckee, CA
Wood, Dana R. ... Morristown, TN
Wood, Dane London ... **Phoenix, AZ**
Wood, Daniel G. ... Friendship, WI
Wood, Danny Eugene, Jr. ... Terrell, TX
Wood, Daved F. ... Ione, CA
Wood, David A. ... Dallas, TX
Wood, David C. ... West Des Moines, IA
Wood, David E. ... **Camarillo, CA**
Wood, David E. ... Camarillo, CA
Wood, David E.• ... Edinburg, TX
Wood, David E., Law Offices of
Los Angeles, CA
Wood, David F. ... **Los Angeles, CA**
Wood, David F. ... Spartanburg, SC
Wood, David J. ... **Phoenix, AZ**
San Francisco, CA
Wood, David J. ... **Little Rock, AR**
Wood, David J. ... **Farmington Hills, MI**
Wood, David J., Jr. ... Charlottesville, VA
Wood, David L. ... **Fort Collins, CO**
Wood, David L. ... Springfield, IL
Wood, David N. ... Biddeford, ME
Wood, David P. ... **Detroit, MI**
Wood, David P ... Milford, OH
Wood, David P., Jr. ... Miami, FL
Wood, David R. ... Cincinnati, OH
Wood, David S. ... **Orlando, FL**
Wood, David W. ... Columbus, OH
Wood, David W., Jr. ... **Phoenixville, PA**
West Chester, PA
Wood, Dawson & Hellman
Washington, DC
New York, NY
Wood, Deanna Plummer ... **Huntsville, AL**
Wood, Derek D. ... **Philadelphia, PA**
Wood, Diane Doidge ... Phoenix, AZ
Wood, Diane P. ... Chicago, IL
Wood, Dianne E. ... Fairfax, VA
Wood, Dick P. ... Dallas, TX
Wood, Dick P., Jr., (P.C.) ... **Dallas, TX**
Wood, D. Lyle, P.C. ... Las Cruces, NM
Wood, Don E. ... Guymon, OK
Wood, Donald C. ... **Knoxville, TN**
Wood, Donald E. ... Anaheim, CA
Wood, Donald E. ... Springfield, IL
Wood, Donald E. ... Whitehall, OH
Wood, Donald E. ... **Houston, TX**
Wood, Donald F. ... **Austin, TX**
Wood, Donald L. ... **Maysville, KY**
Wood, Donald L. ... **Troy, MI**
Wood, Donald R. ... **Ventura, CA**
Wood, Donna Bramlett ... **Baton Rouge, LA**
Wood, Donna Christine
Export-Import Bank of The United States, Office of the General Counsel, GV
Wood, Donna L. ... Surfside Beach, SC
Wood, Donna S. ... St. Louis, MO
Wood, Douglas A. ... Naples, FL
Wood, Douglas I. ... Arlington, VA
Wood, Douglas J. ... **Los Angeles, CA**
New York, NY
Wood, Douglas J. ... Riverdale, MD
Wood, Douglas K. ... San Francisco, CA
Wood, Douglas M. ... Toledo, OH
Wood, Douglas M. ... Plano, TX
Wood, Douglas S. ... Department of Justice, Immigration and Naturalization Service, GV
Wood, E. Paul ... Salt Lake City, UT
Wood, E. Weston ... Madison, WI
Wood, Edmund J. ... Seattle, WA
Wood, Edmund R. ... Dallas, TX
Wood, Edward B. ... **Pittsburgh, PA**
Wood, Edward K., Jr. ... **Birmingham, AL**
Wood, Elizabeth H. ... Hingham, MA
Wood, Elizabeth Louise ... **Birmingham, AL**
Wood, Elizabeth Scott
Oklahoma City, OK
Wood, Elliott L. ... Carrollton, TX
Wood, Eric A. ... Newton, NJ
Wood, Eric M. ... **Atlantic City, NJ**
Wood, Erskine B. ... **Portland, OR**
Wood, Everett E. ... **Milwaukee, WI**
Wood, Exall & Bonnet, LLP ... Dallas, TX
Wood, F. Daniel, Jr. ... **Birmingham, AL**
Wood and Floge ... Bensalem, PA
Langhorne, PA
Wood, Florence A. ... **Washington, DC**
Wood & Francis, PLLC ... **Durham, NC**
Raleigh, NC
Wood, Francis W. ... Walton, NY
Wood, Frank A., Jr. ... **Jackson, MS**
Wood, Frank E. ... Cincinnati, OH
Wood, Fred A. ... Little Rock, AR
Wood, Fred G., Jr. ... **Charlottesville, VA**

Wood, Fred M., Jr. ... **Charlotte, NC**
Wood, Frederic L. ... **Washington, DC**
Wood, Frederick G. ... Mammoth Lakes, CA
Wood, Frederick J. ... **Atascadero, CA**
Wood, Frederick L. ... Coldwater, MI
Wood, G. Elaine ... New York, NY
Wood, G. Geoffrey ... **Oakland, CA**
Wood, Gabrielle M. ... Warren, OH
Wood, Gael D. ... **Washington, MO**
Wood, Garth E. ... Alvin, TX
Wood, Gary A. ... **Sacramento, CA**
Wood, Gary C. ... Portland, ME
Wood, Gary D. ... Nashville, TN
Wood, Gary J. ... Woodsville, NH
Wood, Gary James ... Monte Rio, CA
Wood, Gary K. ... Edina, MN
Wood, Gary L. ... Danville, IN
Wood, Gary W. ... **Oklahoma City, OK**
Wood, Gary W. ... **Tulsa, OK**
Wood, Gaylord A., Jr. ... Fort Lauderdale, FL
Wood, Georganne ... Tiburon, CA
Wood, George C ... **Bloomington, IL**
Wood, George F. ... Mobile, AL
Wood, George G. ... Manistique, MI
Wood, George L. ... Port Angeles, WA
Wood, George N. ... **Tampa, FL**
Wood, George P. ... Norristown, PA
Wood, George R. ... **Minneapolis, MN**
Wood, George R. ... Philadelphia, PA
Wood, Gerrit W. ... **Sacramento, CA**
Wood, Gina Leigh ... **Bloomington, IL**
Wood, Glen W. ... Austin, TX
Fort Worth, TX
Houston, TX
Wood, Glenn A. ... Boston, MA
Wood Gordon, P.C. ... **Pittsburgh, PA**
Wood & Grant ... **Atlanta, GA**
Wood, Gregory A. ... Upland, CA
Wood, Gregory B. ... **Los Angeles, CA**
Wood, Gregory J. ... **Oakland, CA**
Wood, Gregory Lance ... Mount Vernon, NY
Wood, Gus L. ... **Newnan, GA**
Wood, H. Graham ... Baltimore, MD
Wood, Hal J. ... **Chicago, IL**
Wood, Harlington, Jr. ... Springfield, IL
Wood, Harold L. ... **White Plains, NY**
Wood, Harold W., Jr. ... Visalia, CA
Wood, Harris S.
Federal Energy Regulatory Commission, Office of the General Counsel, GV
Wood, Hayes G., (P.A.) ... Coral Gables, FL
Wood, Heather A. ... Wheeling, WV
Wood, Heather Beemon ... **Nashville, TN**
Wood, Heather Morgan ... **Los Angeles, CA**
Wood & Hengber ... Coral Gables, FL
Wood, Henry E., III ... Charleston, WV
Wood, Henry Harrell ... Tucson, AZ
Wood, Herron & Evans, L.L.P.
Cincinnati, OH
Wood & Hollingsworth ... Talladega, AL
Wood, Holtzworth & Seward
Gloversville, NY
Wood, Howard ... Centreville, MD
Wood, Howard M., III ... **Manchester, CT**
Wood, Hugh ... Key Biscayne, FL
Wood, Hugh C. ... **Atlanta, GA**
Wood, Hugh L., Jr. ... Miami, FL
Wood, Iris M. Croft ... Library of Congress, Office of the General Counsel, GV
Wood, Ivan, Jr. ... **Houston, TX**
Wood, J. Darby ... Goldsboro, NC
Wood, J. Emory ... **St. Petersburg, FL**
Wood, J. Fred, Jr. ... **Birmingham, AL**
Wood, J. Marie ... Atlanta, GA
Wood, J. Michael ... **Rochester, NY**
Wood, J. Ralph, Jr. ... Dallas, TX
Wood, J. Scott ... **Emeryville, CA**
San Francisco, CA
Wood, J. Warren, III ... Princeton, NJ
Wood, Jack C. ... Houston, TX
Wood, Jack D. ... Louisville, KY
Wood, Jacqueline A. ... **Seattle, WA**
Wood, Jacqueline L. ... **Austin, TX**
Wood, Jacqueline Marie ... **Baltimore, MD**
Wood, Jacquelyne A. White ... Pittsburgh, PA
Wood, Jacques M. ... **Pittsburgh, PA**
Wood, James A. ... Baton Rouge, LA
Wood, James A. ... **Pittsburgh, PA**
Wood, James C. ... Mobile, AL
Wood, James C. ... **Chicago, IL**
Wood, James C. ... Fairfax, VA
Wood, James C. ... Milwaukee, WI
Wood, James Curtis ... Harrisburg, PA
Wood, James D. ... San Francisco, CA
Wood, James D. ... **Indianapolis, IN**
Wood, James D. ... Kansas City, MO
Wood, James D. ... **Albany, NY**
Wood, James Dean ... St. Petersburg, FL
Wood, James F. ... **Denver, CO**
Wood, James F. ... **Salt Lake City, UT**
Wood, James F., III ... Charlotte, NC
Wood, James H. ... St. Paul, MN
Wood, James H. ... **Amarillo, TX**
Wood, James H., Jr. ... Arnold, MD
Wood, James J. ... San Francisco, CA
Wood, James J. ... Lansing, MI
Wood, James Jerry ... Montgomery, AL
Wood, James K. ... Pittsburgh, PA
Wood, James M. ... **Oakland, CA**
Wood, James M. ... Albany, NY
Wood, James R. ... Sacramento, CA
Wood, James R. ... Owensboro, KY
Wood, James R. ... **Albuquerque, NM**
Wood, James Roger ... **Phoenix, AZ**
Wood, James S. ... Washington, DC
Wood, James S. ... Chesterfield, MO
Wood, James Scott ... Bay City, MI
Wood, James T. ... Santa Barbara, CA
Wood, James T. ... Williamsburg, VA
Wood, Jane Marie Pine ... Dennis, MA
Cleveland, OH
Wood, Jas. A. E. ... New York, NY
Wood, Jas. H., Jr. ... Dahlonega, GA
Wood, Jeffrey B. ... **Prospect Heights, IL**
Wood, Jeffrey G. ... Jacksonville, FL
Wood, Jeffrey G., P.A. ... Jacksonville, FL
Wood, Jeffrey John ... Harrisburg, PA
Wood, Jeffrey S. ... **Fort Lauderdale, FL**
Wood, Jefri ...
Federal Judicial Center, GV
Wood, Jenna Perkins ... Wheeling, WV
Wood, Jennifer L. ... **Minneapolis, MN**
Wood, Jennifer L. ... Pawtucket, RI
Wood, Jere F. ... **Roswell, GA**
Wood, Jeremiah ... **Gloversville, NY**
Wood, Jerry L. ... Fort Worth, TX
Wood, Jerry Lynn ... Louisville, KY
Wood, Jessica L. ... **Eugene, OR**
Wood, Jill M. ... **Atlanta, GA**
Wood, Joan Jordan ... **Orlando, FL**
Wood, Joan Jordan, P.A. ... **Orlando, FL**
Wood, Joanetta Mondino ... Centralia, IL
Wood, Jodi L. ... Cleveland, OH
Wood, Jody Burig ... Greensboro, NC
Wood, Joe W. ... **Santa Fe, NM**
Wood, John B. ... **Boulder, CO**
Wood, John B. ... **New York, NY**
Wood, John C.
Board of Governors Of The Federal Reserve System, Division of Consumer and Community Affairs, GV
Wood, John C.
United States Court Of Appeals For The Federal Circuit, GV
Wood, John C. ... Kokomo, IN
Wood, John C. ... Fairfax, VA
Wood, John Christopher ... **Washington, DC**
Wood, John D. ... **Nashville, TN**
Wood, John Daniel ... Cranbury, NJ
Wood, John E. ... New York, NY
Wood, John F. ... **Washington, DC**
Wood, John G., Jr. ... Winter Haven, FL
Wood, John H. ... Montclair, NJ
Wood, John H., Jr. ... Langhorne, PA
Wood, John, II ... Cincinnati, OH
Wood, John L. ... **Wilmington, DE**
Wood, John L. ... **Baltimore, MD**
Wood, John M. ... Birmingham, AL
Wood, John M. ... **Washington, DC**
Wood, John M. ... Springfield, IL
Wood, John M., P.C. ... Birmingham, AL
Wood, John R. ... Sarasota, FL
Wood, John R. ... Manistique, MI
Wood, John T. ... Petersburg, VA
Wood, John W. ... Anchorage, AK
Wood, John W. ... **Houston, TX**
Wood, John W., Jr. ... Wayzata, MN
Wood, Jon Bolling ... La Fayette, GA
Wood, Jon C. ... **San Antonio, TX**
Wood, Jonathan ... Ithaca, NY
Wood, Jonathan D. ... **Kingsport, TN**
Wood & Jones, P.S. ... Seattle, WA
Wood, Joseph ... San Francisco, CA
Wood, Joseph D., Jr. ... **McCook, NE**
Wood, Joseph L., III (Trey) ... **Houston, TX**
Wood, Joseph M., II ... Charlottesville, VA
Wood, Joseph P. ... Naperville, IL
Wood, Joseph T. ... Quincy, MA
Wood, Joslyn V. ... Carbondale, CO
Wood, Joyce Jackson ... **Norfolk, VA**
Wood, Judith A. ... Baltimore, MD
Wood, Judith L. ... Los Angeles, CA
Wood, Judson, Jr. ... **San Antonio, TX**
Wood, Judson R. ... Houston, TX
Wood, Karen Barbara ... Upper Marlboro, MD
Wood, Karen D. ... **San Diego, CA**
Wood, Karen E. ... Toledo, OH
Wood, Karen G. ... Laguna Hills, CA
Wood, Karen K. ... Springdale, AR
Wood, Katherine L. ... **Maysville, KY**
Wood, Kathryn A. ... Houston, TX
Wood, Kathryn Ann ... Corvallis, OR
Wood, Kathryn S. ... **Detroit, MI**
Wood, Kathy L. ... St. Joseph, MO
Wood, Keith A. ... **Greensboro, NC**
Wood, Keith C. ... New York, NY
Wood, Keith N. ... Hope, AR
Wood, Kenneth ... Perrysville, OH
Wood, Kenneth A. ... Rancho Santa Fe, CA
Wood, Kenneth L. ... **Oklahoma City, OK**
Wood, Kenneth S. ... Warren, NJ
Wood, Kevin G. ... **Redondo Beach, CA**
Wood, Kevin G., A Professional Corporation
Torrance, CA
Redondo Beach, CA
Wood, Kevin W. ... Atlanta, GA
Wood, Kim ... Alamosa, CO
Wood, Kimba M. ... New York, NY
Wood, Kimberly A. ... **Watertown, NY**
Wood, Kirk ... **Los Angeles, CA**
Wood, Kirk ... **Santa Monica, CA**
Wood, Kirsten M. ... **Southfield, MI**
Wood & Klarl ... Buchanan, NY
Wood, Kristen L. ... **Atlanta, GA**
Wood, Kull, Herschfus, Lay & Kull
Farmington Hills, MI
Wood, L. Lin ... **Atlanta, GA**
Wood & Lamping, L.L.P. ... **Cincinnati, OH**
Wood, Lance D. ... Department of the Army, Office, Chief of Engineers/Headquarters, U.S. Army Corps of Engineers, GV
Wood, Larry C. ... El Paso, TX
Wood, Larry D. ... **Anchorage, AK**
Wood, Larry G. ... Fort Worth, TX
Wood, Larry K. ... Mauldin, SC
Wood, Larry R., Jr. ... **Philadelphia, PA**
Wood, Larry W. ... Jackson, MS
Wood Law Firm, The, LLP ... **Amarillo, TX**
Wood, Lawrence E. ... West Chester, PA
Wood, Lawrence M. ... Denver, CO
Wood, Lee A. ... **Irvine, CA**
Wood, Lee M. ... **Columbus, OH**
Wood, Leonard J. ... Laurel Springs, NJ
Wood, Leonard N. ... Nashville, TN
Wood, Leonard V. ... Sanford, FL
Wood, Leslie ... **Belleville, IL**
Wood, Lester T., III ... Los Angeles, CA
Wood, Letitia E. ... **Orlando, FL**
Wood, Letitia E., P.A. ... **Orlando, FL**
Wood, Linda T. ... Bath, ME
Wood, Lindsay L. ... **Kansas City, MO**
Wood, Lisa C. ... **Livingston, NJ**
Wood, Lisa Cameron ... **Boston, MA**
Wood, Lisa Godbey ... **Brunswick, GA**
Wood, Lisa Kleiner ... **Milwaukee, WI**
Wood, Lisa M. ... **St. Louis, MO**
Wood & Lockhart, PLC ... **Little Rock, AR**
Wood, Lois Anne ... Brielle, NJ
Trenton, NJ
Philadelphia, PA
Wood, Lois J. ... East St. Louis, IL
Wood, Lois M. ... Pasco, WA
Wood, Lorann B. ... **Cherry Hill, NJ**
Philadelphia, PA
Wood, Lori ... New York, NY
Wood, Louis A. ... **Portland, ME**
Wood, Louren R. ... Jefferson City, MO
Wood, Lynn ... **Decatur, GA**
Wood, Lynn T. ... Denver, CO
Wood, Lynne O. ... Tucson, AZ
Wood, M. Anne ... Santa Fe, NM
Wood, M. Douglas ... Sherwood, AR
Wood, M. Todd ... **Fayetteville, AR**
Wood, Maines & Brown, Chartered
Washington, DC
Wood, Marcus ... **Portland, OR**
Wood, Margaret M. ... Chicago, IL
Wood, Margaret M. ... **Detroit, MI**
Wood, Marilyn J. ... Chicago, IL
Wood, Marina Garcia
Fort Lauderdale, FL
Wood, Mark ... Los Angeles, CA
Wood, Mark D. ... **Chicago, IL**
Wood, Mark E. ... Las Vegas, NV
Wood, Mark I. ... Fairbanks, AK
Wood, Mark P. ... **Litchfield, MN**
Wood, Marshall B., Jr.
Palm Beach Gardens, FL
Wood, Marshall Clark ... **Texarkana, TX**
Wood, Marshall E. ... Fernandina Beach, FL
Wood, Marshall E., P.A.
Fernandina Beach, FL
Wood, Marshall R. ... Savannah, GA
Wood, Martha L. ... New York, NY
Wood, Marvin S. ... Naples, FL
Wood, Mary Anne Q. ... **Salt Lake City, UT**
Wood, Mary C. ... Jacksonville, FL
Wood, Mary C. ... Eugene, OR
Wood, Mary Elizabeth ... **Sacramento, CA**
Wood, Mary J. ... San Diego, CA
Wood, Matthew C. ... **Dallas, TX**
Wood, Matthew W. ... **Chicago, IL**
Wood & Mayberry ... Sullivan, IL
Wood, Melanie A. ... Jamestown, NC
Wood, Melissa L. ... Richmond, VA
Wood & Meredith, LLP ... **Atlanta, GA**
Wood, Mia F. ... Denver, CO
Wood, Michael B. ... Phoenix, AZ
Wood, Michael D. ... **San Mateo, CA**
Wood, Michael D. ... Plantation, FL
Wood, Michael D. ... Charleston, SC
Wood, Michael F. ... Cleveland, OH
Wood, Michael G. ... Tucson, AZ
Wood, Michael J. ... Houston, TX
Wood, Michael L. ... **New London, NH**
Wood, Michael L. ... Grafton, VA
Wood, Michael P. ... Lexington, KY
Wood, Michael T. ... **Washington, DC**
Wood, Michael W. ... Houston, TX
Wood, Molly M. ... Topeka, KS
Wood & Murphy
Palm Beach Gardens, FL
Wood, Nancy A. ... **Omaha, NE**
Wood, Nancy R. ... **Mount Holly, NJ**
Wood, Nancy Stanger ... **New York, NY**
Wood, Nancy Talavera ... **Charlotte, NC**
Wood, Natalie A. ... **Simsbury, CT**
Wood, Neuman M. ... **New York, NY**
Wood, Nicholas J. ... **Phoenix, AZ**
Wood, Odom and Edge, P.A.
Newnan, GA
Wood, Oliver Frederick ... Hamilton, AL
Wood, Pamela J. ... Boston, MA
Wood, Pamela L. ... Department of Labor, Office of Secretary, GV
Wood, Patricia ... **Gulf Shores, AL**
Wood, Patricia A. ... San Francisco, CA
Wood, Patrick H. ... **Laconia, NH**
Wood, Patrick J. ... **San Mateo, CA**
Wood, Patrick J. ... Chelmsford, MA
Wood, Paul F. ... Boston, MA
Wood, Paul G. ... **New York, NY**
Wood, Paul H. ... **Little Rock, AR**
Wood, Paul Kevin ... Costa Mesa, CA
Wood, Paul M. ... **McCook, NE**
Wood, Paul R. ... **Denver, CO**
Wood, Paula ... Oklahoma City, OK
Wood & Perry ... **Roswell, GA**
Wood, Peter A. ... Williamstown, NJ
Wood, Philip C. ... North Syracuse, NY
Wood, Philip F. ... **Grand Rapids, MI**
Wood, Phillip S. ... Aurora, IL
Wood, Phillip Shawn ... **Chicago, IL**
Wood, Phillip W. ... Prattville, AL
Wood, Phillips, Van Santen, Clark & Mortimer ... **Chicago, IL**
Wood, Quentin H. ... Findlay, OH
Wood, R. Christopher ... **Hattiesburg, MS**
Wood, R. Craig ... **Charlottesville, VA**
Wood, R. Douglas, Jr. ... Monroe, LA
Wood, R. Joilene ... **Houston, TX**
Wood, R. Scott ... **Salt Lake City, UT**
Wood, R. Thomas ... Carlsbad, CA
Wood, R. William ... **Denton, TX**
Wood & Rabil, L.L.P. ... **Lexington, NC**
Mocksville, NC
Winston-Salem, NC
Yadkinville, NC
Wood, Rae T. ... Leesburg, FL
Wood, Rafalsky & Wood ... **Brooklyn, NY**
New York, NY
Wood, Ralph E. ... **Pinedale, WY**
Wood, Ralph H. ... Concord, NH
Wood, Ralph K. ... Englewood Cliffs, NJ
New York, NY
Wood, Randall B. ... **Austin, TX**
Wood, Randall J. ... Oklahoma City, OK
Wood, Randell K. ... Springfield, MO
Wood, Randolph C. ... **Jackson, MS**
Wood, Rebbecca Lake ... **Independence, MO**
Wood, Richard A. ... Los Angeles, CA
Wood, Richard A. ... **Miami, FL**
Wood, Richard A., Jr. ... **Asheville, NC**
Wood, Richard B. ... **Harrisburg, PA**
Wood, Richard D. ... Lafayette, IN
Wood, Richard D., Jr. ... Media, PA
Wood, Richard E. ... **Pittsburgh, PA**
Wood, Richard G. ... Bellevue, WA
Wood, Richard J. ... Treasury Department, Internal Revenue Service, GV
Wood, Richard J. ... Bedford, IN
Wood, Richard L. ... **Chicago, IL**
Arlington, VA
Wood, Richard L. ... **Louisville, KY**
Wood, Richard O. ... **Chicago, IL**
Wood, Richard R. ... Lincoln, NE
Wood, Richard W. ... Bradenton, FL
Wood, Richard W. ... **Rolla, MO**
Wood, Ricky L. ... Parsons, TN
Wood, Ris & Hames, Professional Corporation ... **Denver, CO**
Wood, Robert ... New York, NY
Wood, Robert A. ... **Danville, IN**
Wood, Robert A. ... Danville, IN
Wood, Robert A. ... Cleveland, OH
Wood, Robert A. ... **Salt Lake City, UT**
Wood, Robert C. ... San Diego, CA
Wood, Robert C. ... Bedford, MA
Wood, Robert C. ... Fort Worth, TX
Wood, Robert C., III ... **Lynchburg, VA**
Wood, Robert Clayton ... Escondido, CA
Wood, Robert E. ... **Nashville, TN**
Wood, Robert E. ... **Dallas, TX**
Wood, Robert F. ... **Jackson, MS**
Wood, Robert H. ... Little Rock, AR
Wood, Robert H. ... Jacksonville, FL
Wood, Robert H. ... **New Orleans, LA**
Wood, Robert H. ... St. Johns, MI
Wood, Robert H., Jr. ... Little Rock, AR
Wood, Robert H., Jr. ... **Metairie, LA**
Wood, Robert J. ... Helena, MT
Wood, Robert J., Jr. ... **Dallas, TX**
Wood, Robert L. ... Augusta, GA
Wood, Robert L. ... Salt Lake City, UT
Wood, Robert M. ... Manasquan, NJ
Wood, Robert M. ... Columbia, SC
Wood, Robert M. ... Woodville, TX
Wood, Robert M. ... Waukesha, WI
Wood, Robert N. ... **Oakland, CA**
Walnut Creek, CA
Wood, Robert P. ... **Columbia, SC**
Wood, Robert R. ... **San Francisco, CA**
Wood, Robert V., Jr. ... **Huntsville, AL**
Wood, Robert W. ... **San Francisco, CA**
Wood, Robert W. ... Rochester, NY
Wood, Robert W., Professional Corporation
San Francisco, CA
Wood, Robert Y., III ... **Atlanta, GA**
Wood, Robt. L. ... Denver, CO
Wood, Robt. Y., Jr. ... Natchez, MS
Wood, Rock A. ... **Grand Rapids, MI**
Wood, Roderick Barry ... Gooding, ID
Wood, Roger B. ... Atlanta, GA
Wood, Roger F. ... **Philadelphia, PA**
Wood, Roger H. ... Alhambra, CA
Wood, Rollin B. ... McMinnville, OR
Wood, Ronald A. ... Dunstable, MA
Wood, Ronald D., and Associates ... Tulsa, OK
Wood, Ronald E. ... San Francisco, CA
Wood, Ronald Eugene ... Anniston, AL
Wood, Ronald P. ... **Overland Park, KS**
Wood, Ronald R. ... Kansas City, MO
Wood, Ronald S. ... New Orleans, LA
Wood, Roy L. ... Amite, LA
Wood, Roy S., Jr. ... Miami, FL
Wood, Russell J. ... **San Francisco, CA**
Cleveland, OH
Wood, Russell O. ... **Fresno, CA**
Wood, Samuel G. ... Dallas, TX
Wood, Sandra B. ... Hartford, CT
Wood, Scott B. ... **Tulsa, OK**
Wood, Scott E. ... Torrance, CA
Wood, Scott J. ... **Mount Holly, NJ**
Wood, Scott M. ... Ankeny, IA
Wood, Scott P. ... **Lancaster, OH**
Wood, Sean W. ... Cincinnati, OH
Wood & Seitl, P.A. ... Sarasota, FL
Wood, Sharolyn P. ... Houston, TX
Wood, Sharon L. ... Dallas, TX
Wood, Sherri E. ... Rochester, NY
Wood, Sherry A. ... Lawrence, MA

Wood, Sheryl G. ...West Palm Beach, FL
Wood, Shirley J. ...La Jolla, CA
Wood Smith Henning & Berman
Costa Mesa, CA
Los Angeles, CA
Rancho Cucamonga, CA
Wood & Smith, P.C. ...Syracuse, NY
Wood, Smith, Schnipper & Clay
Hot Springs National Park, AR
Wood, Spencer R. ...Chicago, IL
Wood, Stacy D. ...Tulsa, OK
Wood, Stephannie A. ...Sterling, VA
Wood, Stephen A. ...Chicago, IL
Wood, Stephen A. ...Southfield, MI
Wood, Stephen A. ...Austin, TX
Wood, Stephen B. ...Richmond, VA
Wood, Stephen C. ...Mequon, WI
Wood, Stephen F., Jr. ...Nashville, TN
Wood, Stephen G. ...Salt Lake City, UT
Wood, Stephen K. ...West Memphis, AR
Wood, Stephen K., P.A. ...West Memphis, AR
Wood, Stephen L. ...Chicago, IL
Wood, Stephen L. ...Manistique, MI
Wood, Stephen Lee ...Rogers, AR
Wood, Stephen Lee, P.A. ...Rogers, AR
Wood, Stephen P.
Department of Transportation, National Highway Traffic Safety Administration, GV
Wood, Stephen T. ...Houston, TX
Wood, Steven G. ...Pocatello, ID
Wood, Steven J. ...Stuart, FL
Wood, Steven K. ...Sullivan, IL
Wood, Steven K. ...Brentwood, TN
Wood, Steven N.H. ...Walnut Creek, CA
Wood, Steven P. ...Wilmington, DE
Wood, Stockton B. ...Maysville, KY
Wood & Stuart, P.A. ...Fort Lauderdale, FL
Wood, Susan ...Harrisburg, PA
Wood, Susan A. ...Paoli, PA
Wood, Susan D. ...Chicago, IL
Wood, Susan D. ...Maplewood, NJ
Wood, Sylvia Stanley ...Charlotte, NC
Wood, T. Jason ...Idaho Falls, ID
Wood, Tamara L. ...Redding, CA
Wood, Tammy S. ...Dallas, TX
Wood Tatum Sanders & Murphy
Portland, OR
Wood, T. B. ...Raleigh, NC
Wood, Teri Wilford ...Armonk, NY
Wood, Terri ...Eugene, OR
Wood, Terri, P.C., Law Office of
Eugene, OR
Wood, Terry ...Beaumont, TX
Wood, Terry L. ...Glendale, CA
Wood, Terry L. ...Boston, MA
Wood, Terry L. ...Corinth, MS
Wood, Thacker & Weatherly, P.C.
Denton, TX
Wood, Theodore V. ...Idaho Falls, ID
Wood, Thomas ...Muncy, PA
Wood, Thomas A. ...Wichita, KS
Wood, Thomas B. ...Palm Bay, FL
Wood, Thomas B. ...Joliet, IL
Wood, Thomas B. ...Lincoln, NE
Wood, Thomas C., Jr. ...Columbus, OH
Wood, Thomas D. ...Redlands, CA
Wood, Thomas D., Sr. ...Coral Gables, FL
Fort Lauderdale, FL
Wood, Thomas D., Sr. ...Miami, FL
Wood, Thomas D., Sr.
West Palm Beach, FL
Wood, Thomas E. ...Berwyn, PA
Wood, Thomas E. ...Harrisburg, PA
Wood, Thomas F. ...Buchanan, NY
Wood, Thomas G. ...Menlo Park, CA
Wood, Thomas G., Law Offices of
Menlo Park, CA
Wood, Thomas H. ...Longmont, CO
Wood, Thomas H. ...Staunton, VA
Wood, Thomas M. ...Tampa, FL
Wood, Thomas M., IV ...Baltimore, MD
Wood, Thomas R. ...Portland, OR
Wood, Thomas T. ...Midvale, UT
Wood, Timothy D. ...Cleveland, OH
Wood, Timothy D. ...Dayton, OH
Wood, Timothy M. ...Salem, OR
Wood, Tonya L. ...Norcross, GA
Wood, Tonya L., P.C. ...Norcross, GA
Wood, Tracey A. ...Madison, WI
Wood, Travers D. ...Los Angeles, CA
Wood, Troy J. ...Bend, OR
Wood Tuohy Gleason Mercer & Herrin, Professional Corporation
Indianapolis, IN
Wood, W. Eric ...Superior, NE
Wood, W. Fillmore, Jr. ...Buena Park, CA
Wood, W. Kip ...Fairfax, VA
Wood, W. Mark ...Los Angeles, CA
Wood, W. Swain ...Atlanta, GA
Wood, W. Wayne ...Jackson, MS
Wood, Walter F. ...Tucson, AZ
Wood, Walter F., Ltd. ...Tucson, AZ
Wood, Walter S. ...Cincinnati, OH
Wood, Warren B. ...Burlington, KS
Wood, Warren C.
Federal Energy Regulatory Commission, Office of the General Counsel, GV
Wood, Warren E. ...Boston, MA
Wood, Warren W. ...New Richmond, WI
Wood, Weldon S. ...San Jose, CA
Wood, Wendy ...Alvin, TX
Wood, Wendy A. ...Port Clinton, OH
Wood, Wendy Scholtens ...Little Rock, AR
Wood, Wheaton B. ...Washington, DC
Wood, Wiley D., II ...Lafayette, AL
Wood, William ...Nutley, NJ
Wood, William A. ...New Orleans, LA
Wood, William A., II ...Greensboro, NC
Wood, William A., III ...Houston, TX
Wood, William A., Jr. ...Houston, TX
Wood, William B. ...Atlanta, GA
Wood, William C. ...Birmingham, AL
Wood, William C. ...Richmond, VA
Wood, William C., Jr. ...Columbia, SC
Wood, William D. ...Bloomfield Hills, MI
Wood, William D. ...Houston, TX
Wood, William Duane, III ...Tampa, FL
Wood, William E. ...Whiteville, NC
Wood, William H., Jr. ...Hartford, CT
Wood, William J. ...Indianapolis, IN
Wood, William J. ...Lincoln, NE
Wood, William L. ...Coral Gables, FL
Wood, William L. ...Chicago, IL
Wood, William L., Jr. ...Scarsdale, NY
Wood, William M. ...Captiva, FL
Wood, William M. ...Seattle, WA
Wood, William R. ...Howard, KS
Wood, William R. ...Trenton, NJ
Wood, William R., II ...Wichita, KS
Wood, William T., Law Offices of
Rockville, MD
Wood, William Z., Jr. ...Winston-Salem, NC
Wood & Wininsky, P.L.L.C. ...Wheeling, WV
Wood & Wood ...Mount Holly, NJ
Wood and Wood, P.C. ...Richmond, VA
Wood, Woodson T. ...Maysville, KY
Woodacre, Linda Conner ...Wellesley, MA
Woodacre, Lorri Seibert ...Natick, MA
Woodahl, Kristen P. ...Seattle, WA
Woodahl, Robert L. ...Choteau, MT
Woodall, A. Jackson, Jr. ...Knoxville, TN
Woodall, Alice I. ...Denver, CO
Woodall, Allison M. ...San Francisco, CA
Woodall, Barbara S.
Federal Deposit Insurance Corporation, Appellate Litigation Section, GV
Woodall, Clarence A., III ...Cadiz, KY
Woodall, Clifford L. ...Modesto, CA
Woodall, Dan ...Austin, TX
Woodall, E. Marshall ...Lillington, NC
Woodall, George W. ...Albany, GA
Woodall, Jack C. ...Hillsborough, NC
Woodall, James H. ...Salt Lake City, UT
Woodall, Jefferson, Jr. ...Akron, OH
Woodall, John T. ...Savannah, GA
Woodall, John T., P.C. ...Savannah, GA
Woodall, Jon A. ...Lexington, KY
Woodall, Judy Lynn ...Washington, DC
Woodall, Kevin F. ...San Francisco, CA
Woodall, Laurie A. ...Phoenix, AZ
Woodall Law Firm, The, P.A.
Lillington, NC
Woodall, Lia A. ...Denver, CO
Woodall, Mark ...New York, NY
Woodall, Marlene ...Virginia Beach, VA
Woodall, Nancy Griffin ...Rockwall, TX
Woodall, Nick D. ...Rockwall, TX
Woodall, Paul A., Jr. ...Birmingham, AL
Woodall, Paul O. ...Birmingham, AL
Woodall & Pflepsen, P.C. ...Albany, GA
Woodall & Quinn ...Cadiz, KY
Woodall, R. Wayne ...Gulfport, MS
Woodall, R. Wayne, P.A. ...Gulfport, MS
Woodall, Rollie L. ...Nashville, TN
Woodall, S. Roy, Jr. ...Washington, DC
Atlanta, GA
Woodall, Shelby L. ...Akron, OH
Woodall, Thomas A. ...Birmingham, AL
Woodall, Thomas T. ...Dickson, TN
Woodall, Timothy S. ...Auburn, CA
Woodall, W. Dallas ...Warren, OH
Woodall, W. Robert, III
Avondale Estates, GA
Woodall, Westerbeck & Reed ...Rockwall, TX
Woodall, William O. ...Valdosta, GA
Woodard, Alan R. ...Pasadena, CA
Woodard, Allen G. ...Andalusia, AL
Woodard, Allen S. ...Rolling Fork, MS
Woodard, Allen S., P.A. ...Rolling Fork, MS
Woodard, Arthur F. ...New York, NY
Woodard, B. Ray ...Augusta, GA
Woodard, Benny M. ...Garden Grove, CA
Woodard, Beverly J. ...Upper Marlboro, MD
Woodard, Billie Colombaro, Mrs.
Lake Charles, LA
Woodard and Bohse ...Dover, OH
Woodard, Calvin ...Charlottesville, VA
Woodard, Chas. F. ...Westwood, MA
Woodard, Cheryl Anne ...Los Angeles, CA
Woodard, Cynthia T. ...Ruston, LA
Woodard, D. Eric ...Wilsonville, OR
Woodard, Daniel J. ...Pasadena, CA
Woodard, David A. ...San Antonio, TX
Woodard, David L. ...Raleigh, NC
Woodard, David W. ...Wilson, NC
Woodard, Donald M. ...Atlanta, GA
Woodard, Duane ...Denver, CO
Woodard, Elizabeth B. ...Houston, TX
Woodard, Elizabeth H.
Charlottesville, VA
Woodard, Emhardt, Naughton, Moriarty & McNett ...Indianapolis, IN
Woodard, Eva Camacho ...Lakewood, CO
Woodard, Frank A. ...Yorba Linda, CA
Woodard, George Daniel ...Los Angeles, CA
Woodard, George W. ...Alamosa, CO
Woodard, Gilbert E., Jr. ...Saluda, VA
Woodard, Glenn E., (P.C.) ...El Paso, TX
Woodard, Gregory E. ...Los Angeles, CA
Woodard, Hall & Primm, A Professional Corporation ...Houston, TX
Woodard, Harold R. ...Indianapolis, IN
Woodard, Harriet M. ...New York, NY
Woodard, Heather A. ...San Francisco, CA
Woodard, Hernandez, Roth & Day, L.L.C.
Wichita, KS
Woodard, Hughes and Robinson
Spokane, WA
Woodard, Jack Brown ...Miami, FL
Woodard, James H. ...Miami, FL
Woodard, James L., & Associates
Franklin, TN
Woodard, James V. ...Spokane, WA
Woodard, Jerry ...El Paso, TX
Woodard, Joan C. ...Roseville, CA
Woodard, John A., Jr. ...Monett, MO
Woodard, John H. ...Hillsboro, OR
Woodard, John (Ken) ...Houston, TX
Woodard, John L. ...Dover, OH
Woodard, John L., III ...Orlando, FL
Woodard, John R., III ...Tulsa, OK
Woodard, John V. ...Boston, MA
Woodard, John W. ...Indianapolis, IN
Woodard, John W., Jr. ...New Albany, IN
Woodard, Joseph L. ...St. Petersburg, FL
Woodard, Joshua R. ...Tempe, AZ
Woodard, Karen D. ...Department of Justice, Civil Rights Division, GV
Woodard, Kevin S. ...Cincinnati, OH
Woodard, Kimberly R. ...Washington, DC
Woodard, L. Duane ...Denver, CO
Woodard, Laina D. ...Jackson, MS
Woodard, Lee E. ...Syracuse, NY
Woodard, Lee H. ...Wichita, KS
Woodard, Len, II ...Fort Worth, TX
Woodard, R. Alan ...Golden, CO
Woodard, R. Bryan ...Boston, MA
Woodard, Raymond S. ...Franklin, PA
Woodard, Rhonda Sigrist ...Cheyenne, WY
Woodard, Ripley E., Jr. ...Houston, TX
Woodard, Rodney ...Loveland, CO
Woodard, Ronald L. ...Henderson, KY
Woodard, Russell A. ...Ruston, LA
Woodard, Russell A., & Cynthia T. Woodard
Ruston, LA
Woodard, S. Michael ...Indianapolis, IN
Woodard, Sharon A. ...Birmingham, AL
Woodard, Stephen C., Jr. ...Smithfield, NC
Woodard, Terri Ann ...Philadelphia, PA
Woodard, Thomas B., IV ...Carrollton, AL
Woodard, Vernon O. ...Pinehurst, NC
Woodard, W. Samuel ...Charlotte, NC
Woodard, Wade L. ...Albuquerque, NM
Woodard, Walter W. ...Punta Gorda, FL
Woodard, William E, Jr. ...Wichita, KS
Woodard, William L. ...Detroit, MI
Woodard & Woodard ...Pasadena, CA
Woodbeck, Charles A. ...Columbus, OH
Woodberry, John D. ...Danvers, MA
Woodbery, John E. ...Bellevue, WA
Woodbridge & Associates, P.C.
Princeton, NJ
Woodbridge, Benjamin H., Jr.
Fredericksburg, VA
Woodbridge, Catherine A.J.
Sacramento, CA
Woodbridge, Frederick, Jr. ...Miami, FL
Woodbridge, Maria Lucia ...Washington, DC
Woodbridge & Reamy ...Fredericksburg, VA
Woodbridge, Richard C. ...Princeton, NJ
Woodbridge, Timothy F. ...Hartford, CT
Woodburn, Chester C., III
Des Moines, IA
Woodburn, David W. ...Akron, OH
Woodburn, Douglas R. ...Amarillo, TX
Woodburn, Graig R. ...Newport Beach, CA
Woodburn, Jill L. ...Indianapolis, IN
Woodburn, John M. ...Pasadena, CA
Woodburn, R. Robert, Jr. ...Boston, MA
Woodburn, Sam S. ...Holbrook, AZ
Woodburn and Wedge ...Reno, NV
Woodburne, John S. ...Bellevue, WA
Woodbury, Alan T. ...Radnor, PA
Woodbury, Altshuler & Baer ...Tarzana, CA
Woodbury, Angela Chinn ...Austin, TX
Woodbury, Bruce L. ...Boulder City, NV
Las Vegas, NV
Woodbury, Caroline Leigh ...Dallas, TX
Woodbury, David ...Manchester, NH
Woodbury, David P. ...Prairie Village, KS
Woodbury, Ellen H. ...Washington, DC
Woodbury, Eric G. ...Boston, MA
Woodbury, Erik E.
Charlotte Amalie, St. Thomas, VI
Woodbury, Gary D. ...Elko, NV
Woodbury, Guy R. ...Salt Lake City, UT
Woodbury, J. Wayne ...Silver City, NM
Woodbury, Jeffrey K. ...Salt Lake City, UT
Woodbury, Joan ...Fort Collins, CO
Woodbury, John M., Jr. ...Los Angeles, CA
Woodbury, Judith A. Fletcher
Portland, ME
Woodbury, K. Donald ...Suncook, NH
Woodbury & Kesler, A Professional Corporation ...Salt Lake City, UT
Woodbury, Krystal K. ...Englewood, CO
Woodbury, Margaret L. ...Napa, CA
Woodbury, Marie S. ...Kansas City, MO
Woodbury, Mark, III ...York, PA
Woodbury, Mark R. ...St. Joseph, MO
Woodbury, Michael R. ...Hanford, CA
Woodbury, Michael Scott
Sacramento, CA
Woodbury, Mitchell R. ...San Diego, CA
Woodbury, Philip D. ...Cambridge, MA
Woodbury, Robert C. ...Tarzana, CA
Woodbury, Robert C. ...Dunkirk, NY
Woodbury, Robert C., P.C. ...Dunkirk, NY
Woodbury, Stephen E. ...Salem, NH
Woodbury, Thomas C. ...Hancock, NH
Woodbury, Thomas M. ...New York, NY
Woodbury, W. Richards, Jr.
Salt Lake City, UT
Woodbury, Wallace R. ...Salt Lake City, UT
Woodbury, Walter L. ...San Diego, CA
Woodbury, William F. ...Lansing, MI
Woodcock, Alan R. ...Tulsa, OK
Woodcock, Allan, Jr. ...Bangor, ME
Woodcock, Barbara L. ...Marion, IL
Woodcock, Daniel J. ...Bloomfield Hills, MI
Woodcock, Donald Fredric
Cleveland, OH
Woodcock, Elizabeth A. ...Denver, CO
Woodcock, Elizabeth C.
United States Senate, Committee Legal Personnel, GV
Woodcock, George W. ...Mount Carmel, IL
Woodcock, J. Lane ...West Palm Beach, FL
Woodcock, Jacqueline M.
Albuquerque, NM
Woodcock, John A., Jr. ...Bangor, ME
Woodcock, John J., III ...South Windsor, CT
Woodcock, John, Jr. ...Hollidaysburg, PA
Woodcock, Joseph C., Jr. ...Hackensack, NJ
Woodcock, Joseph D. ...Aurora, MO
Woodcock & Kline, P.C. ...Mount Carmel, IL
Woodcock, Margaret Ann R. ...Ann Arbor, MI
Woodcock, Raymond L. ...Long Beach, CA
Woodcock, Richard J.
Department Of The Interior, Office of the Solicitor, GV
Woodcock, Robert C. ...Portland, ME
Woodcock, Timothy C. ...Bangor, ME
Woodcock Washburn Kurtz Mackiewicz & Norris LLP ...Philadelphia, PA
Woodcock & Woodcock ...Hollidaysburg, PA
Wooddell, Allen W. ...Honolulu, HI
Wooddell, John ...Springfield, MO
Wood-Dorsey, Deborah ...Washington, DC
Wooddy, Aubrey J., III ...Mount Pleasant, SC
Wooddy, Aubrey J., Jr. ...Mount Pleasant, SC
Wooddy, Cisa & Dodds, LLP
Mount Pleasant, SC
Wooded, Ben K. ...Jacksonville, FL
Woodell, Brent G. ...Tierra Verde, FL
Woodell, Donald P. ...Independence, MO
Woodell, Jerry C. ...Wilmington, NC
Woodell, Michael H. ...Anchorage, AK
Woodell, Will ...Ketchikan, AK
Wood-Ellis, Susan K.
Colorado Springs, CO
Wooden, David J. ...West Covina, CA
Wooden, Dean B.
Department of State, GV
Wooden, John H. ...Los Angeles, CA
Wooden & McLaughlin LLP
Indianapolis, IN
Wooden, Paul F. ...Sparks, MD
Wooden, Ray & Scarborough, P.C.
Chattanooga, TN
Wooden, Sean ...Washington, DC
Wooden, Shawn T. ...Hartford, CT
Wooden, Tracy C. ...Chattanooga, TN
Wooden, William C., II ...Conway, SC
Wooden, William C., II ...Myrtle Beach, SC
Wooden, William P. ...Indianapolis, IN
Woodfield, Alexandra M.
West Palm Beach, FL
Woodfield, Gary A. ...Palm Beach, FL
Woodfield, Gary J. ...New Britain, CT
Woodfield, John V. ...Long Beach, MS
Woodfield, Nicholas Wyckoff
Birmingham, AL
Woodfill, Jared R., V ...Houston, TX
Woodfill, Lucas & Pressler, L.L.P.
Houston, TX
Woodfin, Clinton John ...Knoxville, TN
Woodfin, Jane Dee ...Lansing, MI
Woodford, Barbara Ann ...Portland, OR
Woodford, C. Bradley ...Tempe, AZ
Woodford, Catesby ...Lexington, KY
Woodford, Kelly Collins ...Mobile, AL
Woodford, L. Thomas ...Golden, CO
Woodford, Maria J. ...Boston, MA
Woodford, Michael A. ...Cincinnati, OH
Woodford, Michael J. ...Boulder, CO
Woodford, Paul A. ...Morristown, NJ
Woodford, Paul H., II ...Glenville, WV
Woodford, Peter C. ...Chicago, IL
Woodford, Randy ...Madison, WI
Woodford, Reid ...Phoenix, AZ
Woodford, Richard F., Jr. ...Alexandria, VA
Woodford, Robert E. ...Colorado Springs, CO
Woodford, Thomas J. ...Mobile, AL
Woodford, W. Alan ...Pittsburgh, PA
Woodford, William G. ...Houston, TX
Woodford, William L. ...Baltimore, MD
Woodford, Wm. R. ...Riverside, CA
Woodgate, Cecil L. ...Boulder, MT
Woodgerd, David W. ...Helena, MT
Woodhall, Amy Leopard ...Cleveland, OH
Woodhall, Blake J. ...Ontario, CA
Woodham, Charles W. ...Abbeville, AL
Woodham, David H. ...Atlanta, GA
Woodham, John F. ...Atlanta, GA
Woodham, Kathleen N. ...Chipley, FL
Woodhams, Robert E. ...Littleton, CO
Woodhead, Ben S., Jr. ...Beaumont, TX
Woodhead, Consuelo S. ...Los Angeles, CA
Woodhead, John E. ...Riverside, CA
Woodhead, Mary J. ...Salt Lake City, UT
Woodhead, Matthew E. ...Las Vegas, NV
Reno, NV
Woodhouse, Barbara B. ...Philadelphia, PA
Woodhouse, Charles F. ...Philadelphia, PA
Woodhouse, Charles F., P.C.
Philadelphia, PA
Woodhouse, Derek ...San Jose, CA
Woodhouse, Donald Edward ...Howard, PA

Woodhouse, Edward James, Jr. ... Mount Olive, NJ
Woodhouse, Enoch O., II ... Boston, MA
Woodhouse, Gay Vanderpoel ... Cheyenne, WY
Woodhouse, Jessica B. ... Salt Lake City, UT
Woodhouse, Kevin C. ... Indianapolis, IN
Woodhouse, Richard C. ... Manchester, CT
Woodhouse, Richard P. ... Elmira, NY
Woodhouse, Rubinow & Macht, P.C. ... Manchester, CT
Woodhouse, Samuel S., III ... Philadelphia, PA
Woodhouse, Susan A.P. ... San Francisco, CA
Woodhouse, Thomas Edwin ... Berkeley, CA
Woodhouse, Violet P. ... Newport Beach, CA
Woodhouse, Violet P., A Professional Corporation ... Newport Beach, CA
Woodie, Kimberley J. ... Newtown Square, PA
Woodin, Charles J. ... Wichita, KS
Woodin, David E. ... Catskill, NY
Woodin, Mervin D. ... Camanche, IA
Woodin, Mervin D., P.C. ... Camanche, IA
Woodin, Peter H. ... New York, NY
Wooding, Carol A. ... Chicago, IL
Wooding, David S. ... Wichita, KS
Wooding, Thomas L. ... Fort Wayne, IN
Woodington, Cheri Lynn ... Troy, MI
Woodington, Kenneth P. ... Columbia, SC
Woodka, Janet L. ... Washington, DC
Wood-Kahari, Brenda M. ... Washington, DC
Woodke, David M. ... Omaha, NE
Woodke, Otepka & Gibbons, P.C. ... Omaha, NE
Woodke, Robert A. ... Bemidji, MN
Woodland, F. Michael ... Santa Ana, CA
Woodland, Irwin F. ... Los Angeles, CA
Woodland, John L., Jr. ... Manahawkin, NJ
Woodland, Kimberly Logue ... Atlanta, GA
Woodland, Lee M. ... Sacramento, CA
Woodland, M. Scott ... Salt Lake City, UT
Woodland & McCoy ... Manahawkin, NJ
Woodland, Robert F., Jr. ... Atlanta, GA
Woodland, Steven D. ... Salt Lake City, UT
Woodland, Suzanne M. ... Portsmouth, NH
Woodland, Timothy M. ... Seattle, WA
Woodland, William O. ... Torrance, CA
Woodle, Gene R. ... Rapid City, SD
Woodley, Ann E. ... Akron, OH
Woodley, Cecilia C. ... New Orleans, LA
Woodley, Donna L. ... San Diego, CA
Woodley & Dudley ... Comanche, TX
Woodley, Frederick W., Jr. ... Annandale, VA
Woodley, Gordon Arthur ... Bellevue, WA
Woodley, John Paul, Jr. ... Richmond, VA
Woodley, Joseph S. ... Shreveport, LA
Woodley, Keith ... Comanche, TX
Woodley Law Office ... Clinton, MO
Woodley, Patrick A. ... Clinton, MO
Woodley, Robert A. ... Toledo, OH
Woodley, Samuel S., Jr. ... Rocky Mount, NC
Woodley, Stephen R. ... North Little Rock, AR
St. Louis, MO
Woodley, Thomas A. ... Washington, DC
Woodley, Virginia R. ... Atlanta, GA
Woodley, Williams, Boudreau, Norman, Brown & Doyle ... Lake Charles, LA
Woodlief, Alan D., Jr. ... Raleigh, NC
Woodlief, Miles Archer ... Alexandria, VA
Woodlief, Mitchel E. ... Jacksonville, FL
Woodlief, Russell W. ... Department of the Navy, GV
Woodliff, Duane A. ... Henryetta, OK
Woodliff, George Franklin ... Jackson, MS
Woodliff, Robert P. ... Dallas, TX
Woodling, George V., Jr. ... Shaker Heights, OH
Woodling, Krost & Rust ... Cleveland, OH
Woodling, Ruth W. ... Atlanta, GA
Wood-Lively, Tamara L. ... Toledo, OH
Woodlock, Donald F. ... Bay Village, OH
Woodlock, Douglas P. ... Boston, MA
Woodlock, J. William, Jr. ... Ringwood, NJ
Woodlock, Jerry W. ... Gainesville, TX
Woodlock, Lawrence T. ... Sacramento, CA
Woodlock, Michael S. ... San Diego, CA
Woodlock, Richard B. ... Phoenix, AZ
Woodlock, Rosemary D. ... Woodland Hills, CA
Woodman, Byron E., Jr. ... Concord, MA
Woodman, Catherine L. ... Norwalk, CT
Woodman, Diana M. ... Houston, TX
Woodman, Donald K. ... New York, NY
Woodman & Eaton, P.C. ... Concord, MA
Woodman & Edmands ... Biddeford, ME
Woodman, Eric E. ... Redwood City, CA
Woodman, Eric E., A P.C. ... Redwood City, CA
Woodman, G. Kent ... Washington, DC
Woodman, George B. ... Youngstown, OH
Woodman and Getman ... Waterville, NY
Woodman, James L. ... Rockledge, FL
Woodman, Jonathan A. ... Columbus, OH
Woodman, Laura A. ... San Francisco, CA
Woodman, Michael ... Hackensack, NJ
Woodman, Patrick Thomas ... Bethel Park, PA
Woodman, Ralph R., Jr. ... Portsmouth, NH
Woodman, Richard S. ... Waterville, NY
Woodman, Robert B. ... Biddeford, ME
Woodman, Roger S. ... Memphis, TN
Woodman, Thomas L. ... Dallas, TX
Woodman, Victor E. ... Orlando, FL
Winter Park, FL
Woodmansee, Charles H. ... Los Angeles, CA
Woodmansee, David A. ... Kingsport, TN
Woodmansee, Glen D. ... Irvine, CA
Woodmansee, Mark Andrew ... La Jolla, CA
Woodmansee, W. Keith, (Inc.) ... Walnut Creek, CA
Woodmansee, Webster ... Milwaukee, WI
Woodrich, George J. ... Eugene, OR
Woodrick, Ann P. ... Traverse City, MI
Woodrick, Rosemarie G. ... Oakdale, NY
Woodring, Kevin D. ... Clearwater, FL
Woodring, Michael J. ... Pittsburgh, PA
Woodring, Patricia Kay ... Evansville, IN
Woodring, Steven K. ... Wichita, KS
Woodroe, S. Clark ... Charleston, WV
Woodroof, A. R. ... Manakin-Sabot, VA
Woodroof, Charles C. ... Athens, AL
Woodroof, James W., IV ... Athens, AL
Woodroof, T. Schram ... Athens, AL
Woodroof, William E. ... Sherman Oaks, CA
Woodroof & Woodroof ... Athens, AL
Woodrough, Stephens B. ... Tampa, FL
Woodrow, Daniel ... Denver, CO
Woodrow, Frank J. ... Montrose, CO
Woodrow & Gruskin, Professional Corporation ... Denver, CO
Woodrow, Hal Brent ... New Brunswick, NJ
Woodrow, Hugh A. ... St. Clair Shores, MI
Woodrow, James M. ... Tucson, AZ
Woodrow, John G. ... Phoenix, AZ
Woodrow, Kenneth D. ... Washington, DC
Woodrow, Paul C. ... Logan, OH
Woodrow, Randall M. ... Anniston, AL
Woodrow, Robert H., III ... Birmingham, AL
Woodrow, Robin A. ... Westbury, NY
Woodrow, Robt. H., Jr. ... Birmingham, AL
Woodrow & Roushar ... Montrose, CO
Woodrow, Sumner H. ... Belmont, MA
Woodrow, Susan J. ... Phoenix, AZ
Woodrow, Susan Payne ... Waterford, MI
Woodrow, Suzanne ... Purcell, OK
Woodrow, Thomas R. ... Chicago, IL
Woodrow, Thos. H. ... Madison, MS
Woodrow, Wendy D. ... Phoenix, AZ
Woodrow, William A. ... Neenah, WI
Woodruff, A. C. ... Clovis, CA
Woodruff, Alan P. ... Seattle, WA
Woodruff, Angel M. ... Jackson, MO
Woodruff, Arlon L. ... Lake City, AR
Woodruff & Associates ... Dallas, TX
Woodruff, Bruce E., (P.C.) ... St. Louis, MO
Woodruff, Bryan B. ... Indianapolis, IN
Woodruff, Calvin E., Jr. ... Abbeville, LA
Woodruff, Carolyn J. ... Greensboro, NC
Woodruff, Casey ... Chicago, IL
Woodruff, Charles D. ... Bradenton, FL
Woodruff, Clarke ... Springfield, IL
Woodruff, C. P. ... Pearland, TX
Woodruff, Cynthia A. ... Torrance, CA
Woodruff, D. Thomas ... Sacramento, CA
Woodruff, Daniel R. ... St. Louis, MO
Woodruff, David B. ... Jacksonville, IL
Woodruff, David J. ... Albert Lea, MN
Woodruff, Deborah A. ... Kankakee, IL
Woodruff, Denise C.S. ... Danvers, MA
Woodruff, Dennis J. ... Oakland, CA
Woodruff, Elizabeth Kerr ... Jackson, MS
Woodruff, E. P. ... Brownwood, TX
Woodruff, Frank C. ... Seattle, WA
Woodruff, Fred M., Jr. ... Kalamazoo, MI
Woodruff, Frederick C. ... Irvine, CA
Woodruff, Frederick M. ... St. Louis, MO
Woodruff, Gary B. ... Baltimore, MD
Woodruff, Gordon C. ... Smithfield, NC
Woodruff, Grant Collins ... Roseville, CA
Woodruff, H. Bowen ... Charleston, SC
Woodruff, Herbert C. ... Saratoga, CA
Woodruff, Hubert W., II ... Salem, IL
Woodruff & Huckaby ... Lake City, AR
Woodruff, J. David, Jr. ... Birmingham, AL
Woodruff, Jack R. ... Spencer, IN
Woodruff, James B. ... Rosemead, CA
Woodruff, James M. ... Lincoln, NE
Woodruff, James P. ... Oklahoma City, OK
Woodruff, Jeanne K. ... Canal Winchester, OH
Woodruff, Jeffrey T. ... Hermosa Beach, CA
Woodruff, Jennifer E. ... Portland, OR
Woodruff, Johnny L. ... Chattanooga, TN
Woodruff, Joseph A. ... Nashville, TN
Woodruff, Katherine D. ... Dallas, TX
Irving, TX
Woodruff, Kathryn M. ... Department of Justice, Civil Rights Division, GV
Woodruff, Kelly A. ... Berkeley, CA
Woodruff, Kirsten ... Tampa, FL
Woodruff, Laura Ard ... Birmingham, AL
Woodruff Law ... Tampa, FL
Woodruff Law Firm ... Fayetteville, AR
Woodruff, Lawrence A. ... Westfield, NJ
Woodruff & Lena ... Berkeley, CA
Woodruff, Leslie E. ... Bethesda, MD
Woodruff, Lyle Griffin ... Atlanta, GA
Woodruff, Margaret S. ... Philadelphia, PA
Woodruff, Marsha C. ... Fayetteville, AR
Woodruff, Mason L. ... Decatur, TX
Woodruff, Matthew W. ... New York, NY
Woodruff, Michael J. ... McLean, VA
Woodruff, Michele A. ... New Orleans, LA
Woodruff, Morris L. ... Jefferson City, MO
Woodruff, Natalie L. ... New York, NY
Woodruff, Neville ... Auburn, ME
Woodruff, O'Hair & Posner, Inc. A Law Corporation ... Sacramento, CA
Woodruff, Owen E., Jr. ... San Francisco, CA
Woodruff, Patti W. ... Tampa, FL
Woodruff, Paula Kobetz ... Abbeville, LA
Woodruff & Prather ... Abbeville, LA
Woodruff, Randall L. ... Anderson, IN
Woodruff, R. N. "Rod" ... Belle Fourche, SD
Woodruff, Robert B. ... Morristown, NJ
Woodruff, Robert H. ... Louisville, KY
Woodruff, Robert T. ... Newark, NJ
Woodruff, Ronald G. ... Fayetteville, AR
Woodruff, Ronald H. ... Wilmington, NC
Woodruff, Samuel M. ... Phoenix, AZ
Woodruff, Shannon Demos ... Virginia Beach, VA
Woodruff & Singman ... Oakland, CA
Woodruff, Spradlin & Smart, A Professional Corporation ... Orange, CA
Santa Ana, CA
Woodruff, Thomas L. ... Orange, CA
Woodruff, Thomas M., (P.A.) ... St. Petersburg, FL
Woodruff, Tom G., Jr. ... Aiken, SC
Woodruff, Vaughn N. ... Salem, IL
Woodruff, W. B., Jr. ... Decatur, TX
Woodruff, William A. ... Buies Creek, NC
Woodruff, William B., (P.C.) ... Omaha, NE
Woodruff, William M. ... Houston, TX
Woodruff & Williams, P.C. ... Spencer, IN
Woodruff & Wren, LLP ... Bridgeport, TX
Decatur, TX
Woodrum, Clifton A., III ... Roanoke, VA
Woodrum, John R. ... Washington, DC
Woodrum, M. Lanier ... Roanoke, VA
Woodrum, Tammala D. ... Ann Arbor, MI
Woods, Aaron N. ... Overland Park, KS
Woods & Aitken ... Lincoln, NE
Woods, Alan ... Denver, CO
Woods, Alan C., III ... Baltimore, MD
Woods, Alton ... Department Of The Interior, Office of the Solicitor, GV
Woods, Andrea G. ... Lancaster, OH
Woods, Andrew L. ... Washington, DC
Woods, Arleigh M. ... Los Angeles, CA
Woods & Associates ... Greenville, SC
Woods and Baker ... Kane, PA
Woods, Barbara C. ... Vienna, VA
Woods, Barbara R. ... Denver, CO
Woods, Barry A. ... San Juan, PR
Woods, Barry T. ... Portland, ME
Woods & Bates ... Lincoln, IL
Woods, Beth B. ... Marco Island, FL
Woods, Brian W. ... Kansas City, MO
Woods, Bryan ... San Antonio, TX
Woods, Bryan D. ... Madison, WI
Woods, C. Craig ... Columbus, OH
Woods, C. Laurence, III ... Louisville, KY
Woods, C. Scott ... Jackson, MS
Woods, Carolyn E. ... Staten Island, NY
Woods, Carolyn T. ... Tampa, FL
Woods, Carr L. ... Monett, MO
Woods, Catherine F. ... Towson, MD
Woods, Catherine M. ... Tucson, AZ
Woods, Cecil Gerald, Jr. ... Gulfport, MS
Woods, Charles E. ... Dallas, TX
Woods, Charles L. ... Ozark, AL
Woods, Charles R. ... San Diego, CA
Woods, Charlie H. ... Newark, NJ
Woods, Christina Gayle ... Baltimore, MD
Woods, Christina S. ... Fort Worth, TX
Woods, Claudell ... Magnolia, AR
Woods, Clint L. ... Des Moines, IA
Woods, Craig A. ... Chicago, IL
Woods, Curtis A. ... Leonardo, NJ
Woods, Curtis E. ... Kansas City, MO
Woods, Cynthia A. ... Minneapolis, MN
Woods, Cynthia Stoner ... Billings, MT
Woods, D. Brett ... Denver, CO
Woods, D. Kay ... Dallas, TX
McKinney, TX
Woods, Dani Linn ... Wallingford, CT
Woods, Daniel Hon ... Little Rock, AR
Woods, Daniel J. ... Los Angeles, CA
Woods, Daniel W. ... Houston, TX
Woods, Danny R. ... Baton Rouge, LA
Woods, David ... Dallas, TX
Woods, David G. ... Center Line, MI
Woods, David M. ... Kansas City, MO
Woods, David M. ... Rochester, NY
Woods, David R. ... Orlando, FL
Woods, David W. ... Orleans, MA
Woods, Della M. ... Houston, TX
Woods, Dennis G. ... Seattle, WA
Woods, Dennis J. ... Detroit, MI
Woods, Dennis L. ... Fowler, IN
Woods, Derek L. ... Silver Spring, MD
Woods, Dexter R., Jr. ... Ada, OH
Woods, Diana D. ... Santa Monica, CA
Woods, Diane Kay ... Marshall, MI
Woods, Dick H. ... Kansas City, MO
Woods, Dick H., Jr. ... Kansas City, MO
Woods, Donald F., Jr. ... Los Angeles, CA
Woods, Donald L. ... Springfield, IL
Woods, Donald R. ... Torrance, CA
Woods, Douglas J. ... Sacramento, CA
Woods, E. Hazen, Jr. ... Austin, TX
Woods, Edward A. ... Beverly Hills, CA
Woods & Erickson ... Las Vegas, NV
Woods, Ernest H., III ... Clarkesville, GA
Woods, F. James ... Merrick, NY
Woods, Frank A. ... Nashville, TN
Woods, Fred W., Jr. ... Greenville, SC
Woods, Frederick E. ... Alexandria, VA
Woods, Fronda C. ... Olympia, WA
Woods, Fuller, Shultz & Smith, P.C. ... Sioux Falls, SD
Woods, Gary A. ... Denver, CO
Woods, Gary L. ... Pasadena, CA
Woods, Geoffrey M. ... Miami, FL
Woods, George E. ... Detroit, MI
Woods, George T. ... Los Angeles, CA
Woods, Gerald Durr ... New Orleans, LA
Woods, Gerald R. ... Research Triangle Park, NC
Woods, Gerald T. ... Atlanta, GA
Woods, Gerald W. ... Augusta, GA
Woods & Givens, L.L.P. ... Columbia, SC
Lexington, SC
Woods, Glenn A. ... Hartford, CT
Woods, Glenn D. ... Boston, MA
Woods, Glenn R. ... Lafayette, CA
Woods, Grace F. ... Atlanta, GA
Woods, Grant ... Phoenix, AZ
Woods, Greggory J. ... Minneapolis, MN
Woods, Hammond C. ... Kansas City, MO
Woods, Harry A., Jr. ... Oklahoma City, OK
Woods, Harry E. ... San Juan, PR
Woods, Harvey B. ... Cincinnati, OH
Woods, Helga Mayer ... Hartford, CT
Woods, Henry ... Little Rock, AR
Woods, Henry T. ... Rock Hill, SC
Woods, J. David ... Cedar Grove, NJ
New York, NY
Woods, J. Diane ... Marietta, GA
Woods, J. Edison, Jr. ... Shawano, WI
Wittenberg, WI
Woods, J. Michael ... Evansville, IN
Woods, Jack E. ... South Lake Tahoe, CA
Woods & Jackson, L.L.P. ... Houston, TX
Woods, James A. ... Franklin, IN
Woods, James C. ... Albany, NY
Woods, James E. ... Olive Branch, MS
Woods, James G. ... Milton, MA
Woods, James H. ... San Francisco, CA
Woods, James H. ... Hobe Sound, FL
Woods, James J. ... Red Bank, NJ
Woods, James J. ... Cortland, NY
Woods, James J., Jr. ... Wilmington, DE
Woods, James L. ... Armonk, NY
Woods, James Madison ... Shreveport, LA
Woods, James R. ... San Francisco, CA
Woods, James W. ... Irving, TX
Woods, Janet L. ... Los Angeles, CA
Woods, Jayne Ann ... Nashville, TN
Woods, Jeanne M. ... New York, NY
Woods, Jeff A. ... Lexington, KY
Woods, Jeff Chandler ... Charleston, WV
Woods, Jeffrey A. ... Knoxville, TN
Woods, Jennifer L. ... St. Louis, MO
Woods, Jennifer R. ... San Francisco, CA
Woods, Jerome F. ... Trappe, MD
Woods, John J., Jr. ... Paterson, NJ
Woods, John L. ... Richardson, TX
Woods, John M. ... New York, NY
Woods, John Oates ... Rock Hill, SC
Woods, John P. ... Indianapolis, IN
Woods, John P. ... New York, NY
Woods, John Roger ... Knoxville, TN
Woods, John W. ... Amarillo, TX
Woods, John W., III ... Charleston, WV
Woods, John W., Jr. ... Washington, DC
Woods, Joseph A., Jr. ... Oakland, CA
Woods, Joseph R. ... Indianapolis, IN
Woods, Judith A. ... North Chicago, IL
Woods, Judy L. ... Indianapolis, IN
Woods, Julie L. ... Los Angeles, CA
Woods, K. Jeannette ... Chandler, AZ
Woods, K. Shane ... Seattle, WA
Woods, Karen Ball ... Indianapolis, IN
Woods, Karen E. ... Atlanta, GA
Woods, Katherine E. ... Nashville, TN
Woods, Kathleen Kopach ... Kansas City, MO
Woods, Kay ... Cleveland, OH
Woods, Keith F. ... Denver, CO
Woods, Kent S. ... Department of Energy, Office of Hearings and Appeals, GV
Woods, Kerin M. ... Norwich, CT
Woods, Kevin Britt ... Tampa, FL
Woods, Kiana ... Detroit, MI
Woods, Kinney & Breithaupt, P.C. ... Denver, CO
Woods, Kristina M. ... Dublin, OH
Woods, L. Hallman ... New Iberia, LA
Woods, Larry D. ... Nashville, TN
Woods, Larry F. ... Oelwein, IA
Woods, Larry M. ... Columbia, MO
Woods, Larry T. ... Gardendale, AL
Woods, Lauren A. ... Federal Judicial Center, GV
Woods, LaVerne ... Seattle, WA
Woods Law Offices ... Nashville, TN
Woods, Lawrence M. ... Kane, PA
Woods, Leonard W. ... Austin, TX
Woods, Linda J. ... Richmond, VA
Woods, Lisa L. ... Birmingham, AL
Woods, Lon C. ... Indianapolis, IN
Woods, Lowell T., Jr. ... Dayton, OH
Woods, Luther E. ... Huntington, WV
Woods, Lynn C., Jr. ... Houston, TX
Woods, Lynn Simpson ... Fort Lauderdale, FL
Woods, Lynnia K. ... Portland, OR
Woods, M. Evelyn ... Louisville, CO
Woods, Margie Gunthardt ... San Diego, CA
Woods, Maria V. ... Denver, CO
Woods, Marne E. ... Des Moines, IA
Woods, Marsha M. ... Detroit, MI
Woods, Martin B. ... Fort Lauderdale, FL
Woods, Martin M. ... Forestville, CA
Santa Rosa, CA
Woods, Matthew B. ... Norwalk, CT
Woods, Matthew B. ... Columbia, MO
Woods, Matthew G. ... Council Bluffs, IA
Woods, Matthew L. ... Minneapolis, MN
Woods, Maurice G., II ... Oklahoma City, OK
Woods, Melanie J. Caw ... Ada, OH
Woods & Messina ... San Diego, CA
Woods, Michael A. ... Davenport, IA
Woods, Michael D. ... San Francisco, CA
Woods, Michael E. ... San Francisco, CA
Woods, Michael F. ... Rochester, NY
Woods, Michael G. ... Fresno, CA

Woods, Michael H. ... Shreveport, LA
Woods, Michael J. ... Department of Justice, Federal Bureau of Investigation, GV
Woods, Michael J., P.C. ... Chesapeake, VA
Woods, Michael James ... Chesapeake, VA
Woods, Michael L. ... Berkeley, CA
Woods, Michael R. ... Sonoma, CA
Woods, Michele J. ... Washington, DC
Woods, Nancy L. ... San Diego, CA
Santa Ana, CA
Woods, Nancy L. ... Tulsa, OK
Woods, Norvell Frederick, Jr. Los Angeles, CA
Woods, Nuala Sheen ... Windham, NY
Woods and O'Keefe ... Detroit, MI
Woods, Olen D. ... San Diego, CA
Woods, Oviatt, Gilman, Sturman & Clarke LLP ... Rochester, NY
Woods, Patricia M. ... Lakewood, CO
Woods, Peter C. ... Tucson, AZ
Woods, Peter C. ... St. Louis, MO
Woods, Polly ... Fort Worth, TX
Woods, Powell ... Siloam Springs, AR
Woods, R. Glen ... Las Vegas, NV
Woods, R. Kyle ... Atlanta, GA
Woods, Rebekah Anderson Virginia Beach, VA
Woods, Richard C., Jr. ... Woburn, MA
Woods, Richard D. ... Kansas City, MO
Woods, Richard D., II ... San Antonio, TX
Woods, Richard H. ... Toms River, NJ
Woods, Richard J. ... Phoenix, AZ
Woods, Richard J. ... San Antonio, TX
Woods, Richard P. ... Dothan, AL
Woods, Richard P. ... Arlington, VA
Woods, Richard S. Hilton Head Island, SC
Woods, Richard S. ... Kaufman, TX
Woods, Richard S., P.A. Hilton Head Island, SC
Woods, Rick ... Fayetteville, AR
Woods, Rick D. ... Seattle, WA
Woods & Roach ... Lakeland, FL
Woods, Robert A. ... Washington, DC
Woods, Robert B. ... Monmouth Beach, NJ
Woods, Robert C. ... Cincinnati, OH
Woods, Robert D. ... Bakersfield, CA
Woods, Robert Deane ... South Bend, IN
Woods, Robert E. ... Minneapolis, MN
Woods, Robert P. ... Ashland, KY
Woods, Robert W. ... Santa Monica, CA
Woods, Roberta E. ... Sarasota, FL
Woods, Rogers & Hazlegrove, P.L.C. Charlottesville, VA
Danville, VA
Richmond, VA
Roanoke, VA
Woods, Ronald F. ... San Diego, CA
Woods, Ronald G. ... Houston, TX
Woods, Ronald L. ... Tulsa, OK
Woods, Ronald W. ... Greeneville, TN
Woods, Rosalie ... Vallejo, CA
Woods, Russell M. ... Cranford, NJ
Woods, Samuel B. ... Marion, SC
Woods, Sarah Wharton ... Fort Pierce, FL
Woods, Scott A. ... Houston, TX
Woods, Sharon M. ... Detroit, MI
Woods, Shelley A. ... Jefferson City, MO
Woods, Sherri L. ... Los Angeles, CA
Woods and Snyder, L.L.C. Olive Branch, MS
Woods, Stacy A. ... Minneapolis, MN
Woods, Stanley C. ... Houston, TX
Woods, Stephanie B. ... Department of Justice, Federal Bureau of Investigation, GV
Woods, Stephanie B. ... Raleigh, NC
Woods, Stephanie Michelle ... Denver, CO
Woods, Stephen E. ... Norwood, MA
Woods, Stephen J. C. ... Exeter, NH
Woods, Stephen K. ... Cassopolis, MI
Woods, Stephen K., P.C. ... Cassopolis, MI
Woods, Stephen R. ... Greenville, SC
Woods, Steven R. ... West Palm Beach, FL
Woods, Steven W. ... Wenatchee, WA
Woods, Susan E. ... Chicago, IL
Woods, Suzanne H. ... Washington, DC
Woods, T. Michael ... Orlando, FL
Woods, Terrence P. ... Phoenix, AZ
Woods, Terry Jeanette ... Knoxville, TN
Woods, Therese Marie ... Washington, DC
Woods, Thomas C. ... Miami, FL
Woods, Thomas E. ... East Lansing, MI
Lansing, MI
Woods, Thomas F. ... Tallahassee, FL
Woods, Thomas F. ... Minneapolis, MN
Woods, Thomas H. ... Altamont, NY
Woods, Thomas N. ... Santa Rosa, CA
Woods, Timothy C. ... Dublin, OH
Woods, Timothy O'Connel ... Washington, DC
Woods, Timothy P. ... Addison, TX
Woods, Timothy W. ... South Bend, IN
Woods, Tina Fletcher ... Dayton, OH
Woods, Todd I. ... Jackson, MS
Woods, Tracie J. ... Philadelphia, PA
Woods & Trembulak ... Cranford, NJ
Woods, Walter Alan ... Littleton, CO
Woods, Walter G. ... Stuart, FL
Woods, Wendell ... Darien, WI
Woods, Wendy Commodity Futures Trading Commission, Division of Enforcement, GV
Woods, Wilber G., Jr. ... Liberty, TX
Woods, William ... Los Angeles, CA
Woods, William B. ... Rossville, GA
Woods, William B. ... Lexington, SC
Woods, William C. ... Norman, OK
Woods, William E., Jr. ... Parshall, ND
Woods, William F., III ... San Diego, CA
Woods, William F., III ... Houston, TX
Woods, William F., Jr. ... Marietta, GA
Woods, William H. ... Columbus, OH
Woods, William H. ... Nashville, TN
Woods, William J. ... Weaverville, CA
Woods, William K. ... Dallas, TX
Woods, William P. ... Evansville, IN
Woods, William R. ... Ocala, FL
Woods, William R. ... Grayson, KY
Woods, William R. ... San Antonio, TX
Woods, William T. General Accounting Office, Office of the General Counsel, GV
Woods, Willis A. ... Wytheville, VA
Woods, Winnifred ... East Falmouth, MA
Woods, Winton Deruyter, III ... Phoenix, AZ
Woods & Woods ... Miami, FL
Woods & Woods ... Evansville, IN
Woods & Woods ... San Juan, PR
Woods & Woods ... Marion, SC
Woods & Woods ... Rock Hill, SC
Woods & Woods Christiansted, St. Croix, VI
Woods & Woods, P.C. ... Indianapolis, IN
Woodside, Blair C., III ... Washington, DC
Alexandria, VA
Woodside & Boemanns ... Blairsville, GA
Woodside, Carolyn C. ... Waldorf, MD
Woodside, David E. ... Jefferson City, MO
Woodside, Denise K. ... St. Louis, MO
Woodside, Diana ... Harrisburg, PA
Woodside, Frank C., III ... Cincinnati, OH
Woodside Intellectual Property Law Group Woodside, CA
Woodside, J. Stephen ... Philadelphia, PA
Woodside, Jack ... Sacramento, CA
Woodside, James M. ... Sacramento, CA
Woodside, Jane Siegel ... San Francisco, CA
Woodside, John A. ... Midland, TX
Woodside, Karen Dunne ... Detroit, MI
Woodside, Keith L. ... New York, NY
Woodside, Marilyn P. ... York, ME
Woodside, R. J. ... Harrisburg, PA
Woodside, Robert N. ... Akron, OH
Woodside, Sharon Clark ... Detroit, MI
Woodside, Steven M. ... San Jose, CA
Woodside, Steven P. ... Roanoke, VA
Woodske, Bruce E. ... Beaver, PA
Woods-King, Cathleen A. ... Stamford, CT
Woodsmall, David L. ... Kansas City, MO
Woodsmall, Douglas Hurst ... Santa Ana, CA
Woodsmall, James V. ... Elkhart, IN
Woodsmall, Joan ... Raleigh, NC
Woodsome, Edwin V., Jr. Los Angeles, CA
Woodson, Anthony H. ... San Francisco, CA
Woodson, Brenda G. ... Redwood City, CA
Woodson, Charles Scott ... Drumright, OK
Woodson, Cornelius F. ... Columbia, MD
Woodson, Danny, Law Offices of Mount Pleasant, TX
Woodson, Frank ... Mobile, AL
Woodson, Heather S. ... Leawood, KS
Woodson, J. William ... Melbourne, FL
Woodson, James R., Jr. ... Louisville, KY
Woodson, John F., II ... Houston, TX
Woodson, John W. ... Carrboro, NC
Woodson, Laura E. ... Atlanta, GA
Woodson & Loftis, A Professional Association ... Norman, OK
Woodson, Mark R. ... Oklahoma City, OK
Woodson, Marshall B., Jr. ... Prospect, KY
Woodson, Michael ... Oklahoma City, OK
Woodson, Paul M. ... Fort Lauderdale, FL
Woodson, R. Duke ... Orlando, FL
Woodson, Robert G., Jr. ... Cumberland, VA
Woodson, Roderic L. ... Washington, DC
Woodson, Russell T. ... Evansville, IN
Woodson, S. Howard, III Washington, DC
Woodson, S. Patrick ... Fort Worth, TX
Woodson, Sayers, Lawther, Short, Parrott & Hudson, LLP ... Salisbury, NC
Woodson, Stephen A. ... Raleigh, NC
Woodson, Steven D. ... Stockton, CA
Woodson, Susan Melton ... Woodbury, TN
Woodson, W. Edward ... Dallas, TX
Woodson, William E. ... Norman, OK
Woodson, William H. ... Kansas City, MO
Woodson, William V., III ... Greenville, SC
Woodstock, Charles L. ... Tulsa, OK
Woodstock & McKee ... Tulsa, OK
Woodsum, Harold E., Jr. ... Portland, ME
Woodsum, Jo Ann ... San Francisco, CA
Woodul, Layton Z. ... Lubbock, TX
Woodul, Walter F., Jr. ... Austin, TX
Woodville, Mark Hot Springs National Park, AR
Woodward, Adrian T. ... Long Beach, CA
Woodward, Albert A. ... Minneapolis, MN
Woodward, Alfred E. ... Wheaton, IL
Woodward, Allan H., III ... Birmingham, AL
Woodward, Andrew ... Dallas, TX
Woodward, Anneke K. ... Atlanta, GA
Woodward, Anthony G. ... Tampa, FL
Woodward, Arthur G. ... Sacramento, CA
Woodward, Arthur V. ... Marco, FL
Woodward, Brian L. ... Nashville, TN
Woodward, C. Victoria ... Baltimore, MD
Woodward, Calvin J. ... Warren, OH
Woodward, Carl R., III ... Roseland, NJ
Woodward, Carol Dois ... Richmond, VA
Woodward, Carol L. ... Redwood City, CA
Woodward, Caroline ... Boston, MA
Woodward, Charlene L. ... Sacramento, CA
Woodward, Charles N. ... Oklahoma City, OK
Woodward, Charles W., Jr. ... Rockville, MD
Woodward, Christie A. ... Pendleton, OR
Woodward, Christopher G. ... Miami, FL
Woodward, Claude J. ... Kosciusko, MS
Woodward Cothran & Herndon Columbia, SC
Woodward, Craig R. ... Marco Island, FL
Woodward, Danae Christina Charlotte, NC
Woodward, David E. ... Merrillville, IN
Woodward, David Luther ... Pensacola, FL
Woodward, David R. ... Dallas, TX
Woodward, David Warren ... Washington, DC
Woodward, Dean T. Research Triangle Park, NC
Woodward, Donna K. ... New York, NY
Woodward, Dorothy Kibler ... Raleigh, NC
Woodward, Edmond F. ... Windham, CT
Woodward, Edna M. ... Des Moines, IA
Woodward, Edward M., Jr. Columbia, SC
Woodward, Edward M., Sr. Columbia, SC
Woodward, Edwin G. ... Seattle, WA
Woodward, Eric W. ... Melbourne, FL
Woodward, Fielden ... Louisville, KY
Woodward, Gordon S. ... Washington, DC
Woodward & Griffiths ... Chagrin Falls, OH
Woodward, Halbert O. ... Brookshire, TX
Woodward, Henry K. ... Palo Alto, CA
Woodward, Hobson & Fulton Lexington, KY
Louisville, KY
Woodward, J. Taylor, III New Brunswick, NJ
Woodward, Jacob L. ... Suffolk, VA
Woodward, James P., Jr. ... Weaverville, CA
Woodward, James W. ... Beacon Falls, CT
Woodward, Jeff D. ... Atlanta, GA
Woodward, Jennifer K. ... Omaha, NE
Woodward, Jennifer L. Department of Education, Office of the General Counsel, GV
Woodward, Jennifer M. ... Shrewsbury, NJ
Woodward, Joan M. ... Anchorage, AK
Woodward, Joe D. ... Magnolia, AR
Woodward, John A. ... Redondo Beach, CA
Englewood, CO
Woodward, John C. ... Santa Barbara, CA
Woodward, John D. ... Denver, CO
Woodward, John L. ... Cuba, MO
Woodward, John R. ... Dallas, TX
Woodward, Joseph M. ... Department of Labor, Office of the Solicitor, GV
Woodward, Joseph T. ... Miami, FL
Woodward, Katharine H. General Accounting Office, Office of the General Counsel, GV
Woodward, Katherine A. San Francisco, CA
Woodward, Kathryn J. ... Toledo, OH
Woodward, Laura ... San Francisco, CA
Woodward, Laurence H. ... Buffalo, NY
Woodward, Lawrence H., Jr. Virginia Beach, VA
Woodward, Lee, Jr. ... Belfast, ME
Woodward, Lester R. ... Denver, CO
Woodward, Lois Smith ... Birmingham, AL
Woodward, Lyn A. ... Los Angeles, CA
Woodward, M. Kenneth, Jr. Port Aransas, TX
Woodward, M. Truman, Jr., (P.C.) New Orleans, LA
Woodward, Margaret E. ... New Orleans, LA
Woodward, Mark J. ... Naples, FL
Woodward, Martin ... McKinney, TX
Woodward, Mary A. ... Albuquerque, NM
Woodward, Matthew A. ... Philadelphia, PA
Woodward, Michael ... Tulsa, OK
Woodward, Michael J. ... Downers Grove, IL
Woodward, Michael L. ... Austin, TX
Woodward, Michael S. ... Los Angeles, CA
Woodward, Michelle L. ... Bedford, IN
Woodward, Miles & Flannagan, P.C. Bristol, VA
Woodward, M. Kenneth, Jr. Port Aransas, TX
Woodward, Nick P. ... Austin, TX
Woodward, O. James, III ... Fresno, CA
Woodward, Pat Munroe, Jr. ... Washington, DC
Woodward, Patricia Anne ... Warrenton, VA
Woodward, Patrick L. ... Davenport, IA
Woodward, Patrick L. ... Rockville, MD
Woodward, Paul K. ... Enid, OK
Okeene, OK
Seiling, OK
Woodward, Philip C. ... Burlington, VT
Woodward, Philip F. ... Dalton, GA
Woodward, Philip F., P.C. ... Dalton, GA
Woodward, Pires & Lombardo, P.A. Marco Island, FL
Naples, FL
Woodward, R. Brian ... Merrillville, IN
Woodward, Rebecca Sellers ... Tulsa, OK
Woodward, Richard G. ... Atlanta, GA
Woodward, Robert G. ... Atlanta, GA
Woodward, Robert J., Jr. ... Columbus, OH
Woodward, Robert P. ... Concord, NH
Woodward, Robin E. ... Hackensack, NJ
New York, NY
Woodward, Roland C. ... Richmond, VA
Woodward, Russell S. ... Charlotte, NC
Woodward, Russell Scott ... Whittier, CA
Woodward, Sandra K. ... Brighton, MI
Woodward Shaw & Howell, A Professional Corporation ... Dallas, TX
Woodward, Sheila S. ... Yankton, SD
Woodward, Tara Sky ... Baltimore, MD
Woodward, Terry A. ... San Jose, CA
Woodward, Thomas A. ... Pittsburgh, PA
Woodward, Thomas B. ... Tallahassee, FL
Woodward, Thomas L., Jr. ... Suffolk, VA
Woodward, Thomas M. New Martinsville, WV
Woodward, Timothy ... King Of Prussia, PA
Woodward, Timothy G. ... Chelmsford, MA
Woodward, Vernon E. ... Billings, MT
Woodward, W. Steven ... Berwyn, PA
Woodward, William B., Jr. ... Huntsville, AL
Woodward, William D. ... Dallas, TX
Woodward, William F. ... Louisville, KY
Woodward, William J., Jr. ... Philadelphia, PA
Woodward, William S. ... Green Bay, WI
Woodward, Wm. H. ... Stockton, CA
Woodward, Woodward & King El Dorado, KS
Woodwell, Keith M. ... Salt Lake City, UT
Woodwell, Tishie W. ... Pittsburgh, PA
Woodworth, Alesia M. ... Kensington, MD
Woodworth, Allan James ... Eureka, CA
Woodworth, Amy ... Minneapolis, MN
Woodworth, Bradley J. ... Portland, OR
Woodworth, Brian ... Kingston, NH
Woodworth, Brian R. ... North Chicago, IL
Woodworth, Carolyn Belle Cape Elizabeth, ME
Woodworth, Dennis G. ... Quincy, IL
Woodworth, Donald C. ... Washington, DC
Woodworth, Douglas R. ... San Diego, CA
Woodworth, Fred L. ... Washington, DC
Woodworth, George W., Jr. ... Norwalk, CA
Woodworth, Glen E. ... Anchorage, AK
Woodworth, Gregory D. ... Portland, ME
Woodworth, Jacquelyn V. ... New York, NY
Woodworth, James N. ... Bad Axe, MI
Woodworth, Jane T. ... Framingham, MA
Woodworth, Jean Elizabeth ... Louisville, KY
Woodworth, Kristina M. ... Los Angeles, CA
Woodworth, Lisa A. ... Scottsdale, AZ
Woodworth, Michael G. ... Lansing, MI
Woodworth, Michael J. ... Norfolk, VA
Woodworth, Nancy J. ... Kansas City, MO
Woodworth & Neeb, P.C. ... Bad Axe, MI
Woodworth, Phillip L. ... Overland Park, KS
Woodworth, Ramsey L. ... Washington, DC
Woodworth, Richard L. ... Palo Alto, CA
Woodworth, Roger H. ... Revere, MA
Woodworth, Stanley N. Overland Park, KS
Woodworth, Stephen M.A. ... Easton, MA
Woody, Alexander ... Honolulu, HI
Woody, Alice M. ... Knoxville, TN
Woody, Charles L. ... Charleston, WV
Woody, Clyde W. ... Houston, TX
Woody, Darren G. ... El Paso, TX
Woody, Dennis ... Media, PA
Woody, Donald E. ... Springfield, MO
Woody, Dudley F. ... Roanoke, VA
Woody, Edward F. ... Silver Spring, MD
Woody & Falkenbach ... Media, PA
Woody, Julie P. ... Houston, TX
Woody, Kelley Y. ... Columbia, SC
Woody, Kristin K. ... Washington, DC
Woody, Larry D. ... Victoria, TX
Woody, Merinda Swanson ... Murphy, NC
Woody, Michael J. ... Indianapolis, IN
Woody, Robert Henley ... Omaha, NE
Woody, Robert J. ... Washington, DC
Woody, Robert J. ... Austin, TX
Woody, Robert W. ... Washington, DC
Woody, Russell ... Chicago, IL
Woody, Stacey Lynn ... New York, NY
Woody, Stephen R. Department of the Air Force, Office of the Judge Advocate General, GV
Woody, T. Clifton, II ... Macon, GA
Woody, Teresa A. ... Kansas City, MO
Woody, W. Bruce ... Dallas, TX
Woody, Wayne S. ... San Francisco, CA
Woodyard, Alice A. ... Sacramento, CA
Woodyard, Kimberley Forseth Little Rock, AR
Woodyard, Kimberly M. ... Bakersfield, CA
Woodyard, L. Wayne ... Pawhuska, OK
Woodyard, William H. L., III Little Rock, AR
Woodyshek, J. Daniel ... Natick, MA
Woofter, Andrew C., III Parkersburg, WV
Woofter, J. Robert, Jr. ... Anchorage, AK
Woofter, Perry W. ... Washington, DC
Woofter, Roy A. ... Las Vegas, NV
Woofter, Thomas H. ... San Francisco, CA
Woog, Jocelyn R. ... Dover, MA
Woog, Laurie J. ... Madison, WI
Woog, Philip M. ... Costa Mesa, CA
Wool, Frederic A. ... Woodbury, NY
Wool, Hayden S. ... Great Neck, NY
Wool, Ivan S. ... New York, NY
Wool, Jeffrey A. ... Washington, DC
Wool, Jonathan C. ... Malone, NY
Wool, Joseph S. ... Burlington, VT
Wool, Leon ... Chicago, IL
Wool, Lisa A. ... Woodland Hills, CA
Wool, Louis C. ... New London, CT
Wool, Marilynne Graboys New London, CT
Wool, Michael W., (P.C.) ... Burlington, VT
Wool, N. Richard ... Plainview, NY
Wool, Phillip David ... San Francisco, CA
Wool, Samuel F. ... Ladue, MO
Wool, Tammy F. ... St. Louis, MO
Woolam, Kristin Heller ... Fort Myers, FL
Woolard, Deirdre J. ... Concord, CA
Woolard, Denise L. ... San Diego, CA
Woolard, Diane Marie ... Vancouver, WA
Woolard, William L. ... Charlotte, NC
Woolbert, Gordon D., II ... Canton, OH

Woolbert, Marianne ... Anderson, IN
Woolbright, Brent A. ... St. Augustine, FL
Woolbright, Kristina K.
San Francisco, CA
Woolbright, Novy R., Jr. ... Enid, OK
Woolcott, Geo. N. ... Harrodsburg, KY
Woolcott, Kenneth J. ... San Diego, CA
Woolcott, Linda McKathnie ... San Diego, CA
Wooldridge, Ann A. ... Moraga, CA
Wooldridge, Brian L. ... Los Angeles, CA
Wooldridge, David M. ... Birmingham, AL
Wooldridge, Gregory D. ... Columbus, OH
Wooldridge, John Palmer ... Livermore, CA
Wooldridge, John Thomas ... Houston, TX
Wooldridge, John W. ... Shepherdsville, KY
Wooldridge, Kimberley A. ... Denver, CO
Wooldridge, Mark ... Boonville, MO
Wooldridge, Michael G.
Grand Rapids, MI
Wooldridge, Michael Kelly ... Little Rock, AR
Wooldridge, Paul M. ... Boonville, MO
Wooldridge, Robert A. ... Dallas, TX
Wooldridge, Robert B. ... Newnan, GA
Wooldridge, Robert R. ... Chicago, IL
Wooldridge, Robert W., Jr. ... Fairfax, VA
Wooldridge, Robin L. ... Atlanta, GA
Wooldridge, Roger W. ... San Antonio, TX
Wooldridge, Steven F. ... San Antonio, TX
Wooldridge, Sue Ellen ... Sacramento, CA
Wooldridge, William C. ... Norfolk, VA
Wooldridge & Wooldridge ... San Antonio, TX
Wooledge, Catherine S. ... Washington, DC
Woolen, Michael John ... Bridgeport, CT
Woolery, Benjamin Jeremy
Upper Marlboro, MD
Woolery, Christopher M. ... Topeka, KS
Woolery, Lucinda S. ... Kansas City, MO
Woolery, P. Mitchell ... Kansas City, MO
Woolery, Richard A. ... Sapulpa, OK
Woolery, Robert L., II ... Ashland, KY
Woolery-Price, Edward R. ... Austin, TX
Woolett, Joe R. ... Wenatchee, WA
Woolever, Michael H., (P.C.) ... Chicago, IL
Wooley, Andrew ... Houston, TX
Wooley, Bill W., II ... Lake Charles, LA
Wooley, David R. ... Albany, NY
Wooley, Jeff A. ... Waco, TX
Wooley, Jeffrey J. ... Austin, TX
Wooley, John B. ... Wichita, KS
Wooley, John C. ... Austin, TX
Wooley, John D. ... Manasquan, NJ
Wooley, Karen ... Anaheim, CA
Wooley, M. Eugene ... Los Angeles, CA
Wooley, Michael E. ... Bay City, MI
Wooley, Richard D. ... Pomona, CA
Wooleyhan, Alfred M. ... Quincy, IL
Wooleyhan, John C. ... Quincy, IL
Woolf, Aaron J. ... Idaho Falls, ID
Woolf, Anthony Wallace ... San Francisco, CA
Woolf, Brian J. ... East Hartford, CT
Manchester, CT
Woolf, Brian J., LLC, The Law Offices of
East Hartford, CT
Woolf, Catherine Ann ... Las Vegas, NV
Woolf, Combo & Thompson
Idaho Falls, ID
Woolf, David J. ... Philadelphia, PA
Woolf, E. Terrence ... Fresno, CA
Woolf, Jeffrey D. ... Andover, MA
Woolf, John P. ... Wichita, KS
Woolf, Leyton S., Jr. ... Litchfield Park, AZ
Woolf, Linda S. ... Baltimore, MD
Woolf, Louis C. ... Knoxville, TN
Woolf, Malcolm D.
Environmental Protection Agency,
Office of the General Counsel, GV
Woolf, Marc S. ... West Palm Beach, FL
Woolf, Marvin B. ... Boulder, CO
Woolf, McClane, Bright, Allen & Carpenter,
PLLC ... Knoxville, TN
Woolf, Michael E. ... Phoenix, AZ
Woolf, Nancy C. ... San Francisco, CA
Woolf, Richard A. ... Miami, FL
Woolf, Robert G. ... Boston, MA
Woolf, Shirley ... Miami Beach, FL
Woolf, Simpson M. ... Encinitas, CA
Woolf, Steven M. ... Bethesda, MD
Woolfall, Brian D. ... San Diego, CA
Woolfe, Terence J. ... Houston, TX
Woolfolk, Ann ... Wilmington, DE
Woolfolk, Asa Jean, (Miss) ... Little Rock, AR
Woolfolk, Edmund T. ... Orlando, FL
Woolfolk, Gary L., (P.C.) ... Dallas, TX
Woolfolk, John W., Jr. ... New Orleans, LA
Woolfolk, Keough, DuBose & DeBari, P.A.
Frostproof, FL
Orlando, FL
Woolfolk, Margaret E. ... Marion, AR
Woolfolk, Mark T. ... Houston, TX
Woolfolk, Virgil N. ... New York, NY
Woolford, Llewellyn W. ... Baltimore, MD
Woolford, Llewellyn W., Jr.
Department Of Health And Human Services,
Office of the General Counsel, GV
Woolford, Timothy J. ... Harrisburg, PA
Woolfork, Tamara Y. ... Culver City, CA
Woolfstead, Roy D. ... Redding, CA
Woolf-Willis, Jonathan
Huntington Beach, CA
Woolhiser, Philip ... Aiken, SC
Woolhouse, Arthur H. "Trey", III
Memphis, TN
Wooliver, June ... Carmel, CA
Woollacott, Cynthia A. R.
Los Angeles, CA
Woollacott Jannol & Woollacott
Los Angeles, CA
Woollacott, Jay A., (A Law Corp.)
Los Angeles, CA
Woollams, Richard C., Jr. ... Hartford, CT
Woollard, Kathryn A. ... St. Louis, MO
Woollcott, Alexander P. ... Atlanta, GA
Woollen, Michelle L. ... Chicago, IL
Woolley, Bennett L., Jr. ... Dallas, TX
Woolley, Billie Sue M. ... Lexington, KY
Woolley, Brad A. ... Indianapolis, IN
Monticello, IN
Woolley, Brian N. ... Kansas City, MO
Woolley, Byron L., (P.C.) ... Dallas, TX
Woolley, C. Mott ... Santa Fe, NM
Woolley, David E. R. ... Long Beach, CA
Port Hueneme, CA
Woolley, Edward A. ... Bedford, NY
Woolley, Helen P. ... Huntingdon, PA
Woolley, Herbert T. ... Kailua, HI
Woolley, Jacqueline M. ... Philadelphia, PA
Woolley, Janice M. ... Omaha, NE
Woolley, John C. ... Santa Ana, CA
Woolley, Keith L. ... Boston, MA
Woolley, Michael ... Kansas City, MO
Woolley, Michelle ... Boston, MA
Woolley, Pamela ... St. Petersburg, FL
Woolley, Patrick C. ... Kansas City, MO
Woolley, Peter A. ... San Diego, CA
Woolley, Reed A. ... Girard, IL
Woolley, Roger S. ... Rancho Santa Fe, CA
Woolley Russell & Johnson
Long Beach, CA
Los Angeles, CA
Newport Beach, CA
Port Hueneme, CA
Santa Ana, CA
Woolley, Scott Laurence ... Chicago, IL
Woolley, Steven J. ... Omaha, NE
Woolley, Susan M. ... Altadena, CA
Woolley, Susan M. ... Indianapolis, IN
Woolley, Tammy Cecile Murphy
Birmingham, AL
Woolley, Thomas J., Jr. ... Boynton Beach, FL
Woolley, Vance E. ... Midland, TX
Woolley, W. Allen ... Chicago, IL
Woolley, William S. ... Wichita, KS
Woolls, James ... Alexandria, VA
Woolls, Paul ... Los Angeles, CA
Woollums, Cathy Schumann ... Davenport, IA
Woollums, Mark A. ... Davenport, IA
Woolman, Alan D. ... New York, NY
Woolman, Stuart Craig ... New York, NY
Woolman, William M. ... Fresno, CA
Woolmington, Robert E. ... Bennington, VT
Manchester Center, VT
Woolner, Rolf S. ... Los Angeles, CA
Woolpert, Harry E. ... Templeton, CA
Woolpert, Mark ... San Luis Obispo, CA
Woolpert, Wendy ... Walnut Creek, CA
Woolpert, Wickson R. ... San Luis Obispo, CA
Woolrich, Willis R., III ... Houston, TX
Woolridge, David A., Jr.
Baton Rouge, LA
Woolridge, G. Ashley ... Pittsburgh, PA
Woolridge, Kyle ... Victorville, CA
Woolsey, Brenda Russo ... Fairfield, CA
Woolsey, David P. ... Lawrenceville, NJ
Woolsey, Dean F. ... Riverside, CA
Woolsey, Helene S. ... La Selva Beach, CA
Woolsey, James M., III ... New York, NY
Woolsey, James M., Jr., (P.C.) ... Albany, NY
Woolsey, John M., Jr. ... Boston, MA
Woolsey, Linda Thomas ... Greeneville, TN
Woolsey, Monty K. ... Indianapolis, IN
Woolsey, R. James ... Washington, DC
Woolsey, Richard C. ... Corpus Christi, TX
Woolsey, Robert J. ... Fort Lee, NJ
New York, NY
Woolsey, Robert W. ... Corpus Christi, TX
Woolsey, Robin E. ... Riverside, CA
Woolsey, Roger A. ... Greeneville, TN
Woolsey & Schmidt, L.L.P.
Corpus Christi, TX
Woolsey, Thomas G. ... Versailles, MO
Woolsey, Thomas R., (P.A.)
West Palm Beach, FL
Woolsey, William N. ... Corpus Christi, TX
Woolsey and Wilson ... Clarksville, AR
Woolsey & Woolsey ... Greeneville, TN
Woolsey & Yarger ... Versailles, MO
Woolslare, Alan F. ... Erie, PA
Woolson, Charles E., Jr. ... Atlantic City, NJ
Woolson, Peter A. ... Baltimore, MD
Woolson, Sheila ... Princeton, NJ
Woolson, Sutphen, Anderson & Nergaard
Somerville, NJ
Woolston, David J. ... Seattle, WA
Woolston, Derek W. ... Seattle, WA
Woolston, James R. ... Mercer Island, WA
Woolston, Michael J. ... San Francisco, CA
Woolston, Robert G. ... Seattle, WA
Woolston, Terence D. ... Phoenix, AZ
Woolston, Thomas G. ... Washington, DC
Woolston, V. L. ... Seattle, WA
Woolston & Wheeler ... Seattle, WA
Woolstrum, Jeffrey L. ... Detroit, MI
Woolums, Darrell A. ... Decatur, IL
Woolverton, Cynthia M. ... St. Louis, MO
Woolverton, Gary F. ... Susanville, CA
Woolverton, George ... Los Angeles, CA
Woolverton, Lonnie E., (P.C.)
Los Angeles, CA
Woolverton, Nicholas W., III
New Orleans, LA
Woolverton, William H. ... Boston, MA
Woolverton, William H., Jr.
Birmingham, AL
Woolway, Gilbert ... Los Angeles, CA
Woolway, Mark ... Los Angeles, CA
Woolwine, Gerald W. ... Ashland, KS
Protection, KS
Woomer & Friday, LLP ... Pittsburgh, PA
Woomer, Robert Brown ... Pittsburgh, PA
Woomer, William H., II ... Chadds Ford, PA
Woons, Lisa L. ... Grand Rapids, MI
Woosley, Carol P. ... Chicago, IL
Woosley, Christopher K. ... Tulsa, OK
Woosley, Clifford H. ... South Pasadena, CA
Woosley, Martin G. ... Birmingham, AL
Woosley, Patrick G. ... Houston, TX
Woosley, S. Kyle ... Greensboro, NC
Wooster, Allen N. ... Garden City, NY
Wooster, Clinton E. ... Reno, NV
Wooster, Edward ... Garden City, NY
Wooster, Kelly C. ... San Francisco, CA
Wooster, Mark A. ... Universal City, CA
Wooster, Richard H. ... Tacoma, WA
Wooster, Scott R. ... Garden City, NY
Wooster & Wooster, LLP ... Garden City, NY
Wootan, Brian S. ... Poughkeepsie, NY
Wootan, James M. ... Atlanta, GA
Macon, GA
Wooten, Allison R. ... North Little Rock, AR
Wooten, Andre ... Honolulu, HI
Wooten, Andrea J. ... Arlington, VA
Wooten, Charles N. ... Lafayette, LA
Wooten, Charles N., Ltd., A Professional Law
Corporation ... Lafayette, LA
Wooten, Christopher C. ... Phoenix, AZ
Wooten & Coley ... Kinston, NC
Wooten, Council, Jr. ... Orlando, FL
Wooten, Daniel K. ... Springfield, MO
Wooten, David Scott ... Visalia, CA
Wooten, David T. ... Athens, GA
Wooten, Eric D. ... Gulfport, MS
Wooten, Everette L., Jr. ... Kinston, NC
Wooten, G. Alan ... Fort Smith, AR
Wooten, Garry L. ... Columbia, SC
Wooten, George F. ... Talladega, AL
Wooten, George W. ... Roanoke, VA
Wooten & Hart, A Professional Corporation
Roanoke, VA
Wooten, Honeywell and Kest, Professional
Association ... Kissimmee, FL
Orlando, FL
Wooten, J. Patrick ... Atlanta, GA
Wooten, Jack ... San Diego, CA
Wooten, James H., Jr. ... Glenview, IL
Wooten, Jefferey A. ... San Jose, CA
Wooten, Joel O., Jr. ... Atlanta, GA
Columbus, GA
Wooten, Kenneth F. ... Raleigh, NC
Wooten, Kenneth L. ... Oxford, MS
Wooten, Kenneth R. ... New Bern, NC
Raleigh, NC
Wilmington, NC
Wooten, Kimberly ... New Orleans, LA
Wooten, Kimila Lynn ... Greenville, SC
Wooten, Leland W., Jr. ... Merritt Island, FL
Wooten, Louis E., III ... Raleigh, NC
Wooten, Marcellus, Jr. ... Duncanville, TX
Wooten, Mariah A., (Ms.) ... Nashville, TN
Wooten, Marvin R. ... Charlotte, NC
Wooten, Nancy C. ... Orangeburg, SC
Wooten, Nancy L. ... Winston-Salem, NC
Wooten, Noelle E. ... Charlotte, NC
Wooten, Norma K. ... Overland Park, KS
Wooten, Patrick Shaun ... Ridgeland, MS
Wooten, Philip R. ... Phoenix, AZ
Wooten, Rebecca J. ... Jackson, MS
Wooten, Robert A., Jr. ... Los Angeles, CA
Wooten, Roger Todd ... Little Rock, AR
Wooten, Suzanne H. ... Dallas, TX
Wooten, Terry L. ... United States Senate,
Committee Legal Personnel, GV
Wooten, Thomas S. ... Auburn, CA
Wooten, Thornton, Carpenter, O'Brien,
Lazenby & Lawrence ... Anniston, AL
Talladega, AL
Wooten, Wallace ... Shelby, MS
Wooten, Wiley P. ... Burlington, NC
Wooten, William I., Jr. ... Greenville, NC
Wooten, William P. ... Santa Ana, CA
Wooters, Thomas A. ... Boston, MA
Wooton, James R. ... Baltimore, MD
Wooton, James R., P.A. ... Baltimore, MD
Towson, MD
Wooton, John D. ... Beckley, WV
Wooton, John R. ... Springfield, MA
Wooton Law Firm, The ... Beckley, WV
Wooton, William R. ... Beckley, WV
Wootten, Ernst F. ... New Orleans, LA
Wootten, Garth E. ... Huntington Woods, MI
Wootten, John D., Jr. ... Lafayette, TN
Wootten, Kerry ... Mount Pleasant, TX
Wootten, Michael J.
General Services Administration,
Office of the General Counsel, GV
Wootton, Chad B. ... Los Angeles, CA
Wootton, Clyde A., III ... Durham, NC
Wootton, Dale ... Dallas, TX
Wootton, Eugenia Cooper
Chestertown, MD
Wootton, Noall T. ... American Fork, UT
Wootton, Richard C. ... San Francisco, CA
Wootton, Richard E. ... Austin, TX
Wootton, Richard H.
Hot Springs National Park, AR
Wootton, Richard H., P.A.
Hot Springs National Park, AR
Wootton, Richens L., (P.C.) ... Santa Rosa, CA
Ukiah, CA
Wootton, Robert R. ... Chicago, IL
Wootton Smith and Associates
American Fork, UT
Wootton, Thomas A. ... Kalamazoo, MI
Wopat, Ben A. ... Hudson, WI
Wopat, John W., III ... Red Bank, NJ
Wopat, K. Ann ... Hackensack, NJ
Wopschall, Carl E. ... Altadena, CA
Worachek, Joan T. ... New Berlin, WI
Woram, Allison M. ... Dallas, TX
Woram, Brian J. ... Dallas, TX
Worboys, Carl E. ... Liverpool, NY
Worby, Allan N. ... Garden City, NY
Worby Borowick Groner LLP ... Carmel, NY
New York, NY
White Plains, NY
Worby, David E. ... Carmel, NY
White Plains, NY
Worcester, Dean S. ... Leesburg, VA
Worcester, George A. ... Big Rapids, MI
Worcester, John P. ... Aspen, CO
Worcester, Mark K. ... Irvine, CA
Worcester, Mark P. ... Anchorage, AK
Worcester & McKay, P.C. ... Santa Fe, NM
Worcester, Mims & Atwill, P.C.
Leesburg, VA
Worcester, Nanci R. ... Auburn, CA
Worcester, Robert P. ... Santa Fe, NM
Worcester, Steven E. ... Wichita, KS
Worcester, Theodore E.
Colorado Springs, CO
Worch, Gloria A. ... Washington, DC
Worchell, Garrett Michael ... Los Angeles, CA
Word, Gerald P. ... Carrollton, GA
Word, J. Christian ... Washington, DC
Word, James P. ... Austin, TX
Word, Lynette ... Fort Worth, TX
Word, Marshall ... Arnett, OK
Word, Morgan ... Denver, CO
Word, Reuben M. ... Carrollton, GA
Word, Reuben M., & Associates, P.C.
Carrollton, GA
Word, Richard B. ... Austin, TX
Word, Robert D., III ... Scottsboro, AL
Word, Terry M. ... Albuquerque, NM
Word, Terry M., P.C. ... Albuquerque, NM
Word, Thomas S., Jr. ... Richmond, VA
Word, Thomas Scott, III ... Richmond, VA
Wordal, Milton O. ... Great Falls, MT
Wordell, Kipp C. ... Palo Alto, CA
Worden, Charles E. ... Norton, KS
Worden, Christopher J. ... Indianapolis, IN
Worden, Curtis D. ... Rockford, IL
Worden, Donovan, Jr. ... Missoula, MT
Worden, Dorothy B.A.
Department of Transportation,
Federal Aviation Administration, GV
Worden, Gregory S. ... Seattle, WA
Worden, James M. ... Scottsbluff, NE
Worden, John L., III ... Boston, MA
Worden, John S. ... San Francisco, CA
Worden, Jon M. ... Richmond, VA
Worden, Joseph R. ... Pittsburgh, PA
Worden, Larry L. ... Houston, TX
Worden, Mary-Ellen ... Riverhead, NY
Worden, Melissa ... Detroit, MI
Worden, Neil B. ... Treasury Department,
Internal Revenue Service, GV
Worden, Nicholas S. ... Lewiston, ME
Worden, Peter B., Jr. ... Traverse City, MI
Worden, Robert P., Jr. ... Melville, NY
Worden, Rolfe A. ... Minneapolis, MN
Worden, Thane & Haines, P.C.
Deer Lodge, MT
Hamilton, MT
Missoula, MT
Polson, MT
Worden, Virginia H. ... Summit, NJ
Worden, William L. ... Portland, ME
Worden, William M. ... Charlotte, MI
Wordes, Dana ... New York, NY
Wordes, Richard S. ... Aliso Viejo, CA
Wordes, Wilshin, Goren & Conner, LLP
Aliso Viejo, CA
Wordham, Deborah A. ... Sacramento, CA
Worek, Andrew K. ... Cherry Hill, NJ
Philadelphia, PA
Worel, Janet V. ... Osseo, MN
Worel, Michael A. ... Mobile, AL
Worfel, C. Christopher ... Grand Rapids, MI
Worford, Corliss L. ... Atlanta, GA
Worhatch, S. David ... Cleveland, OH
Worhatch, S. David ... Stow, OH
Worischeck, Joseph H. ... Phoenix, AZ
Worischeck, Mark G. ... Phoenix, AZ
Work, Anne D. ... Department of Justice,
Office of Information and Privacy, GV
Work, C. Renee ... Woodward, OK
Work, C. Thomas ... Reading, PA
Work, Charles R. ... Washington, DC
Work, Claudia D. ... Phoenix, AZ
Work, Cynthia L. ... Falls Church, VA
Work, Don ... Woodward, OK
Work, Don R. ... San Diego, CA
Work, Fred E., Jr. ... Billings, MT
Work, Frederick T. ... Gary, IN
Work, Gary ... Pensacola, FL
Work, J. Kelly ... Oklahoma City, OK
Work, James E. ... Oklahoma City, OK
Work, Jeffrey K. ... Houston, TX
Work, Maureen D. M. ... Sacramento, CA
Work, Michael J., Law Office of
Newport, NH
Work, Paul E. ... Tucson, AZ
Work, Peter B. ... Washington, DC
Work, Robbi J. ... Monterey Park, CA
Work, Shannon D. ... Coeur d'Alene, ID
Work, William, III ... Brockton, MA
Work & Work ... Woodward, OK
Worke, Renee L. ... Owatonna, MN
Workeneh, Debra ... Los Angeles, CA
Worker, Danny L. ... Chicago, IL
Worker, Gregory T. ... Onsted, MI

Worker & Power ... **Chicago, IL**
Workin, Peter ... Houston, TX
Workin, Peter, A Professional Corporation
Houston, TX
Workinger, Gerald G., Jr. ... Edina, MN
Workland, James J. ... **Spokane, WA**
Workland & Witherspoon, PLLC
Spokane, WA
Workman, Amos A. ... Greenville, SC
Workman, Andrew F. ... Dunbar, WV
Workman, Anne ... Decatur, GA
Workman, Anne E. ... **Minneapolis, MN**
Workman, Brian G. ... Westminster, CA
Workman, Christopher John
San Diego, CA
Workman, Dale C. ... Knoxville, TN
Workman, David A. ... Los Angeles, CA
Workman, David James ... Torrance, CA
Workman, David R. ... **Lancaster, PA**
Workman, David S. ... **Bala Cynwyd, PA**
Philadelphia, PA
Workman, Dennis D. ... Kimberton, PA
Workman, DeVon L., (Mr.) ... Rescue, CA
Workman, Donald Alan ... **Tampa, FL**
Workman, Donald D. ... Tillamook, OR
Workman, Donald R. ... Rupert, ID
Workman, Douglas J. ... **Los Angeles, CA**
Workman, H. Ross ... **Salt Lake City, UT**
Workman, Helene Plotka ... Cupertino, CA
Workman, Henry K. ... **Los Angeles, CA**
Workman, James ... Rochester, NH
Workman, James E., Jr. ... Zanesville, OH
Workman, James W., Sr. ... Union, SC
Workman, Jayne B. ... Nashville, TN
Workman, Jeffrey T. ... **Greensboro, NC**
Workman, Joan M. ... St. Paul, MN
Workman, John R. ... Columbus, OH
Workman, Joseph H. ... Union, SC
Workman, Judith A., P.A. ... Sanibel, FL
Workman, Judith A. H. ... Sanibel, FL
Workman, Leonard F. ... Longview, WA
Workman, Linda G. ... San Diego, CA
Workman, M. Toler ... Raleigh, NC
Workman, Marcia Sue Palmer
Egg Harbor, WI
Workman, Margaret L. ... Charleston, WV
Workman, Mark K. ... Fort Collins, CO
Workman, Michael E. ... **Lakeland, FL**
Workman, Nydegger & Seeley, A Professional Corporation
Salt Lake City, UT
Workman, O. Burke, Jr. ... St. Charles, MO
Workman, Paul C. ... **Los Angeles, CA**
Workman, Petula Palmer ... **Houston, TX**
Workman, R. Thomas ... **Omaha, NE**
Workman, RicKard A. ... Lima, OH
Workman, Robin G. ... **San Francisco, CA**
Workman, Russell G. ... Salt Lake City, UT
Workman, Steven W. ... Chicago, IL
Workman, Terence L. ... **New York, NY**
Workman, Thomas E. ... Columbus, OH
Workman, Thomas E., Jr. ... Los Angeles, CA
Workman, Thomas E., Jr. ... Taunton, MA
Workman, Walter E. ... **Houston, TX**
Workowski, Sean C. ... Covington, VA
Works, C. Bruce ... Topeka, KS
Works, Cynthia ... Washington, DC
Works, Donald C., III ... **Orlando, FL**
Works, Frederick J. ... **Iola, KS**
Works, John H., Jr. ... New York, NY
Works, Julia C. ... **Evanston, IL**
Works & Lentz, Inc., A Prof. Corp.
Oklahoma City, OK
Broken Arrow, OK
Tulsa, OK
Works, Mark W. ... Topeka, KS
Works, Matthew B. ... Topeka, KS
Works, Robert G. ... Lincoln, NE
Works, Sarah S. ... Phoenix, AZ
Works, Wilton W. ... **Tulsa, OK**
Works, Works and Works, P.A. ... Topeka, KS
Worland, Diane L. ... Indianapolis, IN
Worland, F. Edward, Jr. ... **Covington, KY**
Worland, John D., Jr. ... Department of Justice, Antitrust Division, GV
World International Network, LLC
Beverly Hills, CA
WorldPeace, John ... Houston, TX
Worley, Anna E. ... **Greensboro, NC**
Worley, Carol Lockard ... **Little Rock, AR**
Worley, Caroline Z. ... **Columbus, OH**
Worley, Catherine L. ... **Columbus, OH**
Worley, Charles R. ... **Asheville, NC**
Worley, David J. ... **Atlanta, GA**
Worley, David R. ... **Oxnard, CA**
Worley, Dean L. ... **Little Rock, AR**
Worley, Demetrius L. ... **Charlotte, NC**
Worley, Dennis T. ... **Tabor City, NC**
Worley, Diane G. ... **San Francisco, CA**
Worley, Donald R. ... **San Diego, CA**
Worley, Donald R. ... Ventura, CA
Worley, Douglas M. ... **St. Louis, MO**
Worley, Francis ... York Springs, PA
Worley, G. Thomas ... Columbus, OH
Worley, Harriet F. ... Raleigh, NC
Worley, Henry D. ... **Colorado Springs, CO**
Worley, J. Michael ... Fort Worth, TX
Worley, Jane E. ... Kansas City, MO
Worley, Jane Ludwig ... Wernersville, PA
Worley, Jenifer S. ... Birmingham, AL
Worley, Jesse D. ... Newport Beach, CA
Worley, John J. ... Houston, TX
Worley, Joseph M. ... Georgetown, OH
Worley, Julie Shore ... Riverwoods, IL
Worley, Kathleen A. ... Atlantic City, NJ
Worley, Kimberley A. ... **Sacramento, CA**
Worley, Kirk L. ... **Houston, TX**
Worley, L. Glenn ... **Nashville, TN**
Worley, Merry A. ... Sherman, TX
Worley, Michael T. ... **Roswell, NM**
Worley, Mike ... **Lubbock, TX**
Worley, Patricia M. ... **Memphis, TN**
Worley, Phyllis B. ... Searcy, AR
Worley, Providence ... **Seattle, WA**
Worley, Robert B., Jr. ... **New Orleans, LA**
Worley, Robert S. ... Irvine, CA
Worley, Robert W., Jr. ... **New York, NY**
Worley, S. Thomas, Jr. ... Mount Pleasant, SC
Worley, Sarah E. ... Brockton, MA
Worley, Sharon Tarr
Colorado Springs, CO
Worline, Daniel A. ... **Toledo, OH**
Worlock, Paul A. ... Rome, NY
Worly, Donald Glenn ... Delaware, OH
Worm, Darrell S. ... Kalispell, MT
Worm, Hollis D. ... Chicago, IL
Worm, Kathleen Nowack ... **Raleigh, NC**
Worman, Cheryl L. ... **Jacksonville, FL**
Worman & Dixon, P.L.C. ... **Okemos, MI**
Worman, Gary L. ... **Okemos, MI**
Worman, George R., Jr. ... Anniston, AL
Worman, Michael A., II. ... Lancaster, PA
Worman, Robert M. ... **Hollywood, FL**
Worman, Sharon B. ... Del Mar, CA
Wormer, Christiansen von
Grosse Pointe Farms, MI
Wormer, Susan L. ... Pittsburgh, PA
Wormhoudt, Gerrit H. ... **Wichita, KS**
Wormley, Craig T. ... **Santa Monica, CA**
Wormser, David A. ... **Washington, DC**
Wormser, Kiely, Galef & Jacobs LLP
New York, NY
White Plains, NY
Wormser, Peter L. ... Indianapolis, IN
Wormsley, C. Scott ... **Las Vegas, NV**
Wormuth, Francis J. ... Scranton, PA
Worner, Henry, III ... New Orleans, LA
Wornom, Boyce C. ... **Emporia, VA**
Wornom, I. Leake, Jr. ... **Newport News, VA**
Wornom, Wesley D. ... Bethesda, MD
Stafford, VA
Wornow, Scott M. ... **New York, NY**
Wornson, Clayton L. ... Mason City, IA
Wornson, Richard F. ... New Prague, MN
Worob, Jeffrey A. ... New York, NY
Worobiec, Michelle Selig ... Worthington, OH
Worobow, Gary ... New York, NY
Woron, George ... Boston, MA
Woronko, Michael F. ... Rockford, MI
Woronoff, David S. ... Fort Collins, CO
Woronoff, Michael A. ... **Los Angeles, CA**
Woronov, David L. ... Warwick, RI
Woronov, Howard J. ... **Syracuse, NY**
Worozbyt, Theodore S. ... Atlanta, GA
Worrall, Bancroft & Greear, P.C.
Worland, WY
Worrall, Douglas G. ... **Baltimore, MD**
Worrall, John (Larry) ... Kansas City, MO
Worrall, John P. ... **Worland, WY**
Worrall, Persis H. ... Burlington, VT
Worrall, Robert Jones ... **Washington, DC**
Worrall, Stephen M. ... **Atlanta, GA**
Worrall, Stephen M., P.C. ... **Atlanta, GA**
Marietta, GA
Worrel, Rodney K. ... **Fresno, CA**
Worrel & Worrel ... **Fresno, CA**
Worrell, A. Christian, III ... **Florence, KY**
Cincinnati, OH
Worrell, Andrew E. ... **Orlando, FL**
Worrell, Charles M. ... Henderson, NV
Worrell, Claudia M. ... Charlottesville, VA
Worrell, Danny G. ... **Austin, TX**
Worrell, David C. ... **Indianapolis, IN**
Worrell, David H., Jr. ... **Richmond, VA**
Worrell, David L. ... Pasadena, CA
Worrell, David W. ... Princeton, NJ
Worrell, Douglas W. ... Chicago, IL
Worrell, Glyne D. ... **Houston, TX**
Worrell, Joan ... Fairfield, CA
Worrell, John P. ... Minneapolis, MN
Worrell, Lee A. ... Providence, RI
Worrell, Mark A. ... Buffalo, NY
Worrell & Mizner, Chartered ... Chicago, IL
Worrell, Richard D. ... Providence, RI
Worrell, Robert M. ... Harrisonburg, VA
Worrell, Stephen J. ... Glenwood Springs, CO
Worsek, Karen W. ... **Chicago, IL**
Des Plaines, IL
Worsek, Richard D. ... **Chicago, IL**
Worsek & Vihon, P.C. ... **Chicago, IL**
Worsfold, Charles H. ... **Grand Rapids, MI**
Worsfold Macfarlane McDonald
Grand Rapids, MI
Worsham, Charles B. ... Bryn Mawr, PA
Worsham, Daniel A. ... Vernon, TX
Worsham & Denman, LLP ... **Bedford, TX**
Fort Worth, TX
Worsham, E. Lee ... **West Palm Beach, FL**
Worsham, Forsythe & Wooldridge, L.L.P.
Dallas, TX
Worsham, Hugh M., Jr. ... **Savannah, GA**
Worsham, Jack W. ... Greensboro, NC
Worsham, Jean M. ... Houston, TX
Worsham, Jerry D., II ... Phoenix, AZ
Worsham, John W. ... Houston, TX
Worsham, Jos. Irion ... **Dallas, TX**
Worsham, Joseph A. I. ... Dallas, TX
Worsham, Joseph I., II ... Dallas, TX
Worsham, Laura L. ... **Dallas, TX**
Worsham Law Firm, P.A.
Little Rock, AR
Worsham, Randolph S. ... Dallas, TX
Worsham, Richard ... **Bedford, TX**
Worsham, Richard B. ... Southfield, MI
Worsham, Richard E. ... **Little Rock, AR**
Worsham, Stephen M. ... **Tullahoma, TN**
Worsinger, Laura P. ... **Los Angeles, CA**
Worsley, Carolyn R. ... **New York, NY**
Worsley, David E. ... **Chicago, IL**
Worsley, James R., Jr. ... **Washington, DC**
Worsnop, Camille L. ... Fort Lauderdale, FL
Worsnop, Camille L., P.A.
Fort Lauderdale, FL
Worst, Benjamin W. ... **Ketchum, ID**
Worst, Richard John (Tug) ... Twin Falls, ID
Worstell, David L. ... Denver, CO
Worstell, Elaine M. ... Crown Point, IN
Worstell, Jennifer L. ... **Chicago, IL**
Worswick, Lisa R. ... Tacoma, WA
Worswick, Todd M. ... Puyallup, WA
Wortel, William J. ... **Chicago, IL**
Wortelboer, Robert L., Jr. ... Jacksonville, FL
Worten, Jesse J., III ... **Bartlesville, OK**
Pawhuska, OK
Worth, Allen ... Jefferson, NC
Worth, Amos R. ... Decatur, GA
Worth, Anthony L. ... Pendleton, OR
Worth, Barbara S. ... **Elizabeth, NJ**
Maplewood, NJ
Millburn, NJ
South Orange, NJ
Worth, Barbara S. ... **Union, NJ**
Worth, Beverly ... Redondo Beach, CA
Worth, Charles Curtis ... Falmouth, MA
Worth & Chun, Attys. at Law, A Law Corporation ... Honolulu, HI
Worth, Daniel P. ... Orange Park, FL
Worth, David W. ... Dover, OH
Worth, Diane S. ... **Wichita, KS**
Worth, Douglas S. ... New York, NY
Worth, Edgar R. ... Honolulu, HI
Worth, Gregory D. ... **Lenexa, KS**
Worth, Harry F., Jr. ... **Elkhorn, WI**
Worth, James A. ... Bakersfield, CA
Worth, Jill M. ... Ridgewood, NJ
Worth, John O. ... Rushville, IN
Worth, John R. ... Scottsdale, AZ
Worth, Karen V. ... Corte Madera, CA
Worth, Kimberlee A. ... **Dover, NH**
Worth Law Offices ... Rushville, IN
Worth Law Offices, A Professional Corporation ... **Allentown, PA**
Bethlehem, PA
Jim Thorpe, PA
Worth, Leonard P. ... Newton, MA
Worth, Longworth, Bamundo & London, LLP ... **New York, NY**
Worth, Margaret Dawson ... Lincoln, NE
Worth, Marion B. ... **New York, NY**
Worth, Monroe M. ... Cleveland, OH
Worth, Nancy ... Treasury Department, Office of the Comptroller of the Currency, GV
Worth & Norton ... Edgartown, MA
Worth, Pamela F. ... **Los Angeles, CA**
Worth, Patricia Goodridge ... Belfast, ME
Worth, Patricia J. ... Jackson, MI
Worth, R. Jeffrey ... **Dallas, TX**
Worth, Randall E. ... Reynoldsburg, OH
Worth, Randolph L. ... **Raleigh, NC**
Worth, Robert I. ... Phoenix, AZ
Worth, Robert P. ... **Greensboro, NC**
Worth, Stephen C. ... **New York, NY**
Worth, Steven R. ... **Chicago, IL**
Worth, Thomas A. ... Greensboro, NC
Worth, Thomas B. ... **San Francisco, CA**
Worth, Thomas C., Jr. ... Raleigh, NC
Worth, Walker Y., Jr. ... **Fayetteville, NC**
Worth, Wallace C., Jr. ... **Allentown, PA**
Bethlehem, PA
Jim Thorpe, PA
Worth, Warren ... **Irvine, CA**
Worth, William A. ... **Boston, MA**
Worth, William, Jr. ... Jackson, MI
Wortham, Bob ... **Beaumont, TX**
Wortham, Gregory L. ... New York, NY
Wortham, J. Wallace, Jr. ... Denver, CO
Wortham, Leah ... Washington, DC
Wortham, Lisa K. ... San Antonio, TX
Wortham, Mark W. ... **Atlanta, GA**
Wortham, Michael P. ... **Richardson, TX**
Worthe, Jeffrey A. ... Santa Ana, CA
Worthen, Clyde F. ... **Albuquerque, NM**
Worthen, Cynthia L. ... **Keene, NH**
Worthen, Dale L. ... **Ellsworth, ME**
Worthen, David ... **Washington, DC**
Worthen, James T. ... Tyler, TX
Worthen, John S. ... **Chicago, IL**
Worthen, Joseph W., II ... **Keene, NH**
Worthen, Kevin J ... Provo, UT
Worthen, Ronald E. ... Ardmore, OK
Worthen, Ronald E., P.C. ... Ardmore, OK
Worthen, Sidney ... Dover, MA
Worthen, William R. ... Department of Justice, Civil Rights Division, GV
Worthge, Mark K. ... Los Angeles, CA
Worthing, Cynthia J. ... **Cleveland, OH**
Worthing, Donald E. ... **Cleveland, OH**
Worthing, Douglas L. ... Rockville, MD
Worthing, Michael D. ... **Bakersfield, CA**
Worthing, Robert W. ... Hunt Valley, MD
Worthington, Ann ... **Dallas, TX**
Worthington, Bob D. ... Kinston, NC
Worthington, Brad D. ... Lubbock, TX
Worthington, Bradley Dean ... Lubbock, TX
Worthington, Brian P. ... **San Diego, CA**
Chicago, IL
Worthington, Bruce R.
San Francisco, CA
Worthington, Carole Lynch ... **Knoxville, TN**
Worthington, Chrisanne ... Atlanta, GA
Worthington, Christopher H. ... Boston, MA
Worthington, Dan K. ... **McAllen, TX**
Worthington, David L. ... Clinton, NJ
Worthington, David S. ... **Sacramento, CA**
Worthington, Donald L. ... Stillwater, OK
Worthington, Douglas S. ... Princeton, NJ
Worthington, Elisa S. ... **Fort Myers, FL**
Worthington, Elizabeth P. ... Kinston, NC
Worthington & Flournoy ... Columbus, GA
Worthington, Frank ... Napa, CA
Worthington, Gene ... Madisonville, TN
Worthington, James C. ... **Durham, NC**
Worthington, James D. ... Lexington, MO
Worthington, Joe M. ... **Tyler, TX**
Worthington, John R. ... Washington, DC
Worthington, Joseph A. ... **Louisville, KY**
Worthington, Karl McKay ... **Phoenix, AZ**
Worthington, Katherine A. ... Washington, DC
Worthington Law Firm ... Bismarck, ND
Worthington, Margherita P. ... Stroudsburg, PA
Worthington, Maria T. ... **Evansville, IN**
Worthington, Mark F. ... **Seattle, WA**
Worthington, Mark W. ... Worcester, MA
Worthington, Michael F. ... **Los Angeles, CA**
Worthington, Michael F.
San Bernardino, CA
Santa Ana, CA
Worthington, Nancy L. ... Sebastopol, CA
Worthington & Nelson ... Spokane, WA
Worthington, Pamala J.
Bullhead City, AZ
Worthington, Raymond L. ... Washington, DC
Worthington, Robert F., Jr.
Washington, DC
Huntsville, TN
Knoxville, TN
Nashville, TN
Worthington, Roger G. ... **Dallas, TX**
Worthington, Roger G., P.C. ... **Dallas, TX**
Worthington, Roy H., III ... Manhattan, KS
Worthington, Ruth M. ... Kansas City, MO
Worthington, Sally ... Tempe, AZ
Worthington, Samuel W., III ... Columbus, GA
Worthington, Sandra B. ... Jenkintown, PA
Worthington, Stacy L. ... Denver, CO
Worthington, Stayton L. ... **Longview, TX**
Worthington, Susan C. ... **Stillwater, OK**
Worthington, Thomas S. ... Salinas, CA
Worthington, Virginia ... Seattle, WA
Worthington, W. Andrew ... Bushkill, PA
Worthington, Weston W. ... **Covington, KY**
Worthington, William A. ... **Houston, TX**
Worthington, William C., Jr. ... Bismarck, ND
Worthington, William F., Jr.
San Francisco, CA
Worthington & Worthington
Hermosa Beach, CA
San Francisco, CA
Worthley, Todd R. ... Portland, OR
Worthley, Trista R. ... Danvers, MA
Worthman, Jon ... Alliance, NE
Worthman, Monroe C. ... New York, NY
Worthy, Clark H. ... **Roanoke, VA**
Worthy, Crystal M. ... Irmo, SC
Worthy, David B. ... **Martinsville, VA**
Worthy, David L. ... Gainesville, FL
Worthy, Ford S. ... Raleigh, NC
Worthy, Gregory H. ... **Atlanta, GA**
Worthy, J. Lamar ... Stone Mountain, GA
Worthy, Jerry L., Jr. ... Dallas, GA
Worthy, K. Martin ... **Washington, DC**
Worthy, Patricia M. ... Washington, DC
Worthy, Richard G. ... Dallas, TX
Worthy, Robert B. ... Grand Ledge, MI
Wortley, Alfred C., Jr. ... **Detroit, MI**
Wortley, Carl O., III ... Phoenix, AZ
Wortley, Gail F. ... Knoxville, TN
Wortley, Michael D. ... **Dallas, TX**
Wortman, Beth ... **Richmond, VA**
Wortman & Campbell ... Phoenix, AZ
Wortman, David A. ... Fairfax Station, VA
Wortman, Dennis J. ... Phoenix, AZ
Wortman, Ellen ... Philadelphia, PA
Wortman, Estle Terrell
North Little Rock, AR
Wortman, Fumuso, Kelly, DeVerna & Snyder, LLP ... Hauppauge, NY
Uniondale, NY
Wortman, Heather L. ... Minneapolis, MN
Wortman, Jeffrey A. ... **Los Angeles, CA**
Wortman, Meredith G. ... New York, NY
Wortman, Michael R. ... **West Point, NE**
Wortman, Patti M. ... Payson, AZ
Wortman, Richard M. ... **Los Angeles, CA**
Wortman, Scott J. ... Montclair, NJ
Wortman, Tara J. ... **New York, NY**
Wortman, Walter F. ... Hauppauge, NY
Wortmann, Carol T. ... Liberty Corner, NJ
Wortmann, Erik J. ... **Garden City, NY**
Wortmann, Frank A. ... Guilford, CT
Wortmann, Frederick J. ... Livingston, NJ
Wortmann, John A., Jr. ... Boston, MA
Wortmann, Steven G. ... Salina, KS
Worton, Kenneth M. ... Newark, NJ
Worton, Linda G. ... **Miami, FL**
Wortrich, Chava C. ... Long Beach, CA
Wortz, Dennis L. ... Lansing, MI
Wortz, James M. ... Riverside, CA
Wortzel, Andrea W. ... Richmond, VA
Wortzel, Kerry Robert ... **Richmond, VA**
Wortzman, Manuel S. ... Williamsville, NY
Wortzman, Marnie ... Boston, MA
Wortzman, William A. ... Pepper Pike, OH
Woryk, Mildred P. ... **Dayton, OH**
Worzalla, David J. ... Stevens Point, WI
Wos, Irene A. ... **Tempe, AZ**
Woscoboinik, Michael L. ... Washington, DC
Wosick, Crystal Webb ... Fargo, ND
Wosick, Joseph B. ... **Albuquerque, NM**
Wosik, John J. ... Henry, IL
Wosik, Joseph M. ... Chicago, IL

Wright, Dianne ....St. Paul, MN
Wright, Dianne M. ....Seattle, WA
Wright, D.K. "Kirby", Jr. ....Anchorage, AK
Englewood, CO
Wright, Donald A. ....Lake Elmo, MN
Wright, Donald C. ....Jacksonville, FL
Wright, Donald E., Jr. ....Erie, PA
Wright, Donald E., (P.C.) ....Atlanta, GA
Wright, Donald F. ....Orlando, FL
Wright, Donald G. ....Florence, AL
Wright, Donald L. ....Castroville, TX
Wright, Donald Lewis ....Washington, DC
Wright, Donald M. ....Birmingham, AL
Wright, Donald M. ....Raleigh, NC
Wright, Donald R. ....Evansville, IN
Wright, Donna H. ....Jackson, MS
Wright, Donna H. ....Richmond, VA
Wright, Donna M. ....Merrick, NY
Wright & Donovan ....Tulsa, OK
Wright, Donovan A. ....Farmington, MI
Wright, Dorothy A. ....Somers, NY
Wright, Dorothy L. ....Green Brook, NJ
Wright, Douglas A. ....Florence, AL
Wright, Douglas A. ....Tampa, FL
Wright, Douglas D. ....Troy, MI
Wright, Douglas E. ....Greensboro, NC
Wright, Douglas J. ....Erie, PA
Wright, Douglas M. ....Tupelo, MS
Wright, Douglas M., Jr. ....Tupelo, MS
Wright, Douglas R. ....Denver, CO
Wright, Douglas R. ....Department of Justice, Environment and Natural Resources Division, GV
Wright, Douglas R. ....Falmouth, KY
Wright, Douglas S. ....Topeka, KS
Wright, Douglas Wm. ....Fort Worth, TX
Wright, Douglass B. ....Hartford, CT
Wright, Dudley K. ....Santa Ana, CA
Wright, Dudley K., A Professional Corporation
Santa Ana, CA
Wright and Dunkum ....Buckingham, VA
Wright, E.C. (Scott), P.A. ....Melbourne, FL
Wright, E. David ....Dubuque, IA
Wright, E. Robert ....Fresno, CA
Wright, E. Ronald ....New Brunswick, NJ
Wright, E. C. Scott ....Melbourne, FL
Wright, Edd K. ....New Philadelphia, OH
Wright, Edith Dailey, (Mrs.) ....Columbia, MO
Wright, Edward C. ....Philadelphia, PA
Wright, Edward J., Jr. ....Sacramento, CA
Wright, Edward L. ....Little Rock, AR
Wright, Edward M. ....La Mesa, CA
Wright, Edward P. ....Jamestown, NY
Wright, Edward S. ....Palo Alto, CA
Wright, Edward T. ....Belleair Bluffs, FL
Wright, Edward T., Jr. ....Chesterfield, MO
Wright, Edwin E., III ....Dallas, TX
Wright, Eileen Santana
San Francisco, CA
Wright, Elaine S. ....Detroit, MI
Wright, Eldon S. ....Youngstown, OH
Wright, Elissa T. ....Noank, CT
Wright, Elizabeth A. ....La Crosse, WI
Wright, Elizabeth B. ....Cleveland, OH
Wright, Elizabeth C. ....Madison, WI
Wright, Elizabeth E.
United States Court of Federal Claims, Office of Special Masters, GV
Wright, Elizabeth P. ....Frankfort, KY
Wright, Elizabeth S. ....Minneapolis, MN
Wright, Elward H. ....Baton Rouge, LA
Wright, E. M., Jr. ....Buckingham, VA
Wright, Emil F., Jr. ....Opelika, AL
Wright, Eric D. ....Seattle, WA
Wright, Eric E. ....Versailles, IN
Wright, Eric Ellsworth ....Portland, ME
Wright, Eric W. ....Palo Alto, CA
Wright, Ernest B. ....Greenville, NC
Wright, Ernest J. ....Hartford, CT
Wright, Ernest J. ....Jacksonville, NC
Wright, Ernest J., P.A. ....Jacksonville, NC
Wright, Ernie E. ....Harrison, AR
Wright, Eugene A. ....Seattle, WA
Wright, Eugene B. ....Cleveland, TX
Wright, Evans and Daly ....Evansville, IN
Wright & Everett, L.L.C.
Lake Charles, LA
Wright Firm, The, P.A.
Daytona Beach, FL
Orlando, FL
Wright, Flavel A. ....Lincoln, NE
Wright, Florence F. ....Chester, PA
Wright, Frances Johnson ....Dallas, TX
Wright, Frances Johnson, P.C., Law Offices of ....Dallas, TX
Wright, Francis X. ....Baltimore, MD
Wright, Francis X., Jr. ....Malden, MA
Wright, Frank A., Jr. ....Rustburg, VA
Wright, Frank E. ....Noblesville, IN
Wright, Frank H. ....New York, NY
Wright, Frank J. ....Dallas, TX
Wright, Frank L. ....Harrisburg, PA
Wright, Frank M., Jr. ....Chicago, IL
Wright, Frank S. ....Dallas, TX
Wright, Franklin E. ....Dallas, TX
Wright, Franklin Y. ....San Antonio, TX
Wright, Fred L. ....Torrance, CA
Wright, Fred P. ....Amory, MS
Wright, Frederick C., III ....Hagerstown, MD
Wright, Frederick L. ....Atlanta, GA
Forsyth, GA
Wright, Fredric H., III ....Oklahoma City, OK
Wright, Fulford, Moorhead and Wittek, P.A.
Orlando, FL
Wright, G. Robert ....Indianapolis, IN
Wright, G. Russell ....Cordele, GA
Wright, Gail Drake ....Augusta, ME
Wright, Gail J. ....New York, NY
Wright, Gary ....Tustin, CA
Wright, Gary A. ....Aspen, CO
Wright, Gary D. ....Bethesda, MD
Wright, Gary E. ....Fairborn, OH
Wright, Gary K. ....Houston, TX
Wright, Gary S. ....Orange City, FL
Wright, Gary W. ....Knoxville, TN
Wright, Geoffrey Willis ....Burbank, CA
Wright, George ....Eagle Grove, IA
Wright, George ....Hackensack, NJ
Wright, George A., Jr. ....New York, NY
Wright, George B. ....Florham Park, NJ
Morristown, NJ
Wright, George E. ....Fort Madison, IA
Wright, George F. ....Treasury Department, Internal Revenue Service, GV
Wright, George H. ....San Antonio, TX
Wright, George Joseph ....Bloomfield, NJ
Wright, George R. ....Smyrna, DE
Wright, George S. ....Tuscaloosa, AL
Wright, George S. ....Phoenix, AZ
Wright, George T. ....Mountain City, TN
Wright, George W., Jr. ....Miami, FL
Wright, George W., Jr., P.A. ....Miami, FL
Wright, Gerald A. ....Portola Valley, CA
Wright, Gerald E. ....San Francisco, CA
Wright, Gerald R. ....Jacksonville, FL
Wright, Gerald R. ....Indianapolis, IN
Wright, Gerald W. "Ged" ....Tulsa, OK
Wright, Gerry R. ....Richmond, VA
Wright, Gesford P. ....Lakeport, CA
Wright, Gilbert G., III ....San Antonio, TX
Wright, Gilbert P., Jr. ....Sudbury, MA
Wright, Giles M. ....Wheat Ridge, CO
Wright, Gillette F. ....St. Louis, MO
Wright, Gordon B. ....Louisville, KY
Wright, Gordon K. ....Los Angeles, CA
Wright, Gordon K. ....Dallas, TX
Wright, Gordon P. ....Chicago, IL
Wright, Gordon S. ....Encino, CA
Wright, Grady J. ....Vallejo, CA
Wright, Grant A. ....Tuscumbia, AL
Wright & Gray ....Columbia, MO
Wright & Greenhill, P.C. ....Austin, TX
Wright, Gregory Jordan ....Longview, TX
Wright, Gregory L. ....Minneapolis, MN
Wright, Gregory R. ....Virginia Beach, VA
Wright, Gregory R. ....Montello, WI
Wright, Gregory R. Law Offices, S.C.
Montello, WI
Wright, Gregory S. ....Washington, DC
Wright, Grover C., Jr. ....Virginia Beach, VA
Wright, Grover C., Jr., P.C.
Virginia Beach, VA
Wright, H. Allison ....Ephrata, PA
Lancaster, PA
Lititz, PA
Wright, H. Kevin ....Seattle, WA
Wright, H. LeArthur, II ....Dublin, OH
Wright, H. Micheal ....Phoenix, AZ
Wright, Hamersley S. ....Freeland, WA
Wright, Harold S. ....Honolulu, HI
Wright, Harry B. ....Oklahoma City, OK
Wright, Harry G. ....Orlando, FL
Wright, Harry, III ....Columbus, OH
Wright, Harry, IV ....Columbus, OH
Wright, Harvey ....Chicago, IL
Wright, Heather M. ....Charleston, WV
Wright, Helene Kaplan ....San Francisco, CA
Wright, Henrietta ....Washington, DC
Wright, Henson, Somers, Sebelius, Clark & Baker, LLP ....Topeka, KS
Wright, Herbert T., Jr. ....Little Rock, AR
Wright, Herbert W., Jr. ....Bedford, TX
Wright & Herman ....Atlanta, GA
Wright, Herman ....Houston, TX
Wright, Hiram J. ....Winnfield, LA
Wright, Hollis E. ....Louisville, KY
Wright, Howell F. ....Monroe, GA
Wright, H. P. ....Port Neches, TX
Wright, Hubert G. ....El Paso, TX
Wright, Hubert H. ....Gadsden, AL
Wright, Hubert H., IV ....Cambridge, MD
Wright, Hugh L. ....Newport Beach, CA
Wright, Hugh M. ....Fort Worth, TX
Wright & Hyman ....Cordele, GA
Wright, I. Clark, Jr. ....New Bern, NC
Wright, J. Craig R. ....Columbus, OH
Wright, J. Kenneth ....Kingsport, TN
Wright, J. Kim ....Elon College, NC
Wright, J. Lawrence ....Yakima, WA
Wright, J. MacArthur ....St. George, UT
Wright, J. Ron ....Muskogee, OK
Wright, J. Stephen ....Ridgeland, MS
Wright, J. Thomas ....Tallahassee, FL
Wright, J. Ward ....Richmond, KY
Wright, Jac O'Delle Grier ....Los Angeles, CA
Wright, Jackson A. ....Columbia, MO
Wright, Jackson W., Jr. ....Boston, MA
Wright, Jacqueline D. ....Washington, DC
Wright, Jacqueline S. ....Little Rock, AR
Wright, James A. ....San Jose, CA
Wright, James A. ....Chicago, IL
Wright, James A. ....Peoria, IL
Wright, James B. ....Anchorage, AK
Wright, James B. ....Phoenix, AZ
Wright, James B. ....San Francisco, CA
Wright, James B. ....Wake Forest, NC
Wright, James B., Jr. ....Gulfport, MS
Wright, James C. ....Topeka, KS
Wright, James C. ....Knoxville, TN
Wright, James C. ....Wheeling, WV
Wright, James D. ....Atlanta, GA
Wright, James D., (P.C.) ....Baltimore, MD
Wright, James E. ....Beverly Hills, CA
Wright, James E. ....Arlington, TX
Wright, James E., III ....New Orleans, LA
Wright, James G. ....Davis, CA
Wright, James H. ....Honolulu, HI
Wright, James H. ....Boxborough, MA
Wright, James J. ....Lynden, WA
Wright, James L. ....Dothan, AL
Wright, James L. ....Long Beach, CA
Wright, James L. ....Morgan Hill, CA
Wright, James L. ....Crystal Lake, IL
Wright, James L. ....Austin, TX
Houston, TX
Wright, James M. ....Brooklyn, NY
Wright, James M., Jr. ....Houston, TX
Wright, James R. ....Washington, DC
Wright, James R. ....Columbiana, OH
Wright, James R. (Jim Bob), Jr.
Cheyenne, OK
Clinton, OK
Wright, James R., Jr. ....Cheyenne, OK
Clinton, OK
Wright, James Roland, Jr. ....Clayton, MO
Wright, James S. ....Washington, DC
Wright, James W. ....Cary, NC
Wright, James W. ....Livingston, TX
Wright, Janet A. ....Dover, DE
Wright, Janet B. ....Dallas, TX
Wright, Janet Gaffaney ....Morgan Hill, CA
Wright, Janet L. ....Fresno, CA
Wright, Janet M. ....Dallas, TX
Wright, Janice E. ....Providence, RI
Wright, Jarrell D. ....Pittsburgh, PA
Wright, Jason P. ....Atlanta, GA
Wright, Jasper K., Jr. ....Houma, LA
Wright, Jay Kelly ....Washington, DC
Wright, Jeannette J. ....Inglewood, CA
Wright, Jeff Edward ....Denver, CO
Wright, Jeff W. ....Sioux City, IA
Wright, Jefferson V. ....Baltimore, MD
Wright, Jeffery D. ....Lancaster, PA
Wright, Jeffrey C. ....Arlington, TX
Wright, Jeffrey G. ....Rochester, NY
Wright, Jeffrey L. ....Sabina, OH
Wilmington, OH
Wright, Jeffrey L. ....Stroudsburg, PA
Wright, Jeffrey W. ....St. Louis, MO
Wright, Jennifer K. ....Leadville, CO
Wright, Jennifer L. ....Seattle, WA
Wright, Jennifer Pearson
Research Triangle Park, NC
Wright, Jerel ....Overland Park, KS
Wright, Jerry ....Lexington, KY
Wright, Jerry G. ....San Francisco, CA
Wright, Jerry M. ....Portsmouth, VA
Wright, Jerry S. ....Beaumont, TX
Wright, Jim L. ....Phoenix, AZ
Wright, Jim R. ....Eastland, TX
Wright, Jimmy B. ....Tahoka, TX
Wright, Joan C. ....Carson City, NV
Wright, JoAnn S. ....Irving, TX
Wright, Joe F. ....Louisville, KY
Wright, Joe Nathan ....Richardson, TX
Wright, Joel D. ....New York, NY
Wright, Joel E. ....Amarillo, TX
Wright, Joel E. ....Seattle, WA
Wright, Joelle Meredith ....Wilmington, DE
Wright, Joey B. ....Albuquerque, NM
Wright, John ....Grand Prairie, TX
Wright, John A. ....Miami, FL
Wright, John A., Jr. ....Houston, TX
Wright, John B., II ....Wayne, PA
Wright, John C., Jr. ....Philadelphia, PA
Wright, John D. ....San Francisco, CA
Wright, John F. ....Lincoln, NE
Wright, John G. ....Covington, KY
Wright, John H. ....Toledo, OH
Wright, John Henry ....Las Vegas, NV
Wright, John J. ....Los Angeles, CA
Wright, John K. ....Birmingham, AL
Wright, John L. ....Lakewood, CO
Wright, John L., Jr. ....Bloomington, IL
Wright, John M. ....Fort Madison, IA
Wright, John M. ....Flint, MI
Wright, John M. ....Banner Elk, NC
Wright, John N. ....Mesa, AZ
Wright, John R. ....New York, NY
Wright, John T. ....New York, NY
Wright, John W. ....Washington, DC
Wright, John W. ....Sarasota, FL
Wright, John W. ....Fort Worth, TX
Wright, Jonathan A. ....Los Angeles, CA
Wright, Jonathan K. ....Wayne, PA
Wright, Jonathan K. ....Seattle, WA
Wright, Jonathan Lane ....St. George, UT
Wright, Jordan M. ....New York, NY
Wright, Joseph ....Chicago, IL
Wright, Joseph C. ....Walnut Creek, CA
Wright, Joseph G., III ....Anderson, SC
Wright, Joseph J. ....Southfield, MI
Wright, Joseph P. ....Madison, WI
Wright, Joseph S., Jr. ....Chicago, IL
Wright, Joseph T., Jr. ....Scranton, PA
Wright, Joseph W. ....North Platte, NE
Wright, Joseph W., III ....Charlottesville, VA
Wright, Josephine Rose ....Birmingham, AL
Wright, Joshua J. ....Birmingham, AL
Wright, Joyce Kline ....Phoenix, AZ
Wright, Joyce L. ....Baltimore, MD
Wright, Judd & Winckler ....Las Vegas, NV
Wright, Judith ....Batesville, IN
Wright, Judith M. ....Chicago, IL
Wright, Judy M. ....Falmouth, KY
Wright, Julia ....Rockville, MD
Wright, Julian H., Jr. ....Charlotte, NC
Wright, Julie D. ....Towson, MD
Wright, Julie P. ....Amarillo, TX
Wright, Justin B. ....Phoenix, AZ
Wright, Justin L. ....Waterloo, IA
Wright, K. A. (Tony) ....Lubbock, TX
Wright, Karen Caviness ....Shelby, NC
Wright, Karen G. ....Allentown, PA
Wright, Karen M. ....Las Vegas, NV
Wright, Karen S. ....Austin, TX
Wright, Karla ....Chicago, IL
Wright, Karla Foreman ....Bartow, FL
Wright, Karla, Ltd. ....Chicago, IL
Wright, Karon Y. ....Austin, TX
Wright, Katherine Settle ....Chapel Hill, NC
Wright, Kathi J. ....Minneapolis, MN
Wright, Kathleen A. ....Albuquerque, NM
Wright, Kathleen Biggs ....Louisville, KY
Wright, Kathleen H. ....Hartford, CT
Wright, Kathleen K. ....Hayward, CA
Wright, Kathleen M. S.
Bainbridge Island, WA
Wright, Kathleen S. ....Atlanta, GA
Wright, Katrina F. ....Roseland, NJ
Wright, Keith G. L. ....Plano, TX
Wright, Kelly ....Vernon, TX
Wright, Kelly A. ....Plymouth Meeting, PA
Wright, Kenneth A. ....Dallas, TX
Wright, Kenneth A., Jr. ....New York, NY
Wright, Kenneth B. ....Los Angeles, CA
Wright, Kenneth B. ....Jacksonville, FL
Wright, Kenneth C. ....Orlando, FL
Wright, Kenneth E. ....Maquoketa, IA
Wright, Kenneth K. ....Bay City, MI
Wright, Kenneth K. ....Columbia, MO
Wright, Kenneth M. ....Boston, MA
Wright, Kenneth Michael
Lake Charles, LA
Wright, Kenneth P. ....Shreveport, LA
Wright, Kenneth R. ....San Diego, CA
Wright, Kenneth W. ....Orlando, FL
Wright, Kevin L. ....Washington, DC
Wright, Kim J. ....Salem, MA
Wright, Kimberly ....Waukegan, IL
Wright, Kimberly D. ....Cincinnati, OH
Wright, Kimberly Smithers
Richmond, VA
Wright & King, P.A. ....Duluth, GA
Wright & Kirschbraun ....Wailuku, HI
Wright, Kristen Merrihew ....Mayville, NY
Wright, Kristi Swisher ....Portsmouth, VA
Wright, Kristin B. ....Lynchburg, VA
Wright, L. Bruce ....Lincoln, NE
Wright, L. Martin, III ....Charlotte, NC
Wright, L. Stephen, Jr. ....Birmingham, AL
Wright, Lacy W., Jr. ....Welch, WV
Wright, Larry L. ....Bakersfield, CA
Wright, Larry R. ....Plano, TX
Wright, LaTonia Denise ....Covington, KY
Wright, Laurann C. ....Marina Del Rey, CA
Wright, Laurie A. ....Chicago, IL
Wright, Laurie E. ....San Diego, CA
Wright Law Associates, Inc. ....Warren, RI
Wright Law Firm ....Fort Madison, IA
Wright Law Firm, P.A. ....Jackson, MS
Wright Law Offices ....Danville, IL
Wright Law Offices ....Anderson, SC
Wright Law Offices, P.L.L.C.
Idaho Falls, ID
Wright, Lawrence A.
United States Tax Court, GV
Wright, Lawrence C. ....Mesa, AZ
Wright, Lawrence D.
Mount Ephraim, NJ
Conshohocken, PA
Philadelphia, PA
Wright, Lawrence E. ....San Anselmo, CA
Wright, Lawrence Marion ....Ottawa, KS
Wright, Lee C. ....Washington, DC
Wright, Lennon C. ....Houston, TX
Wright, Lennon C., P.L.L.C. ....Houston, TX
Wright, Leslie E., III ....Los Angeles, CA
Wright & L'Estrange ....San Diego, CA
Wright, Linda G. ....San Antonio, TX
Wright, Lindsey & Jennings LLP
Fayetteville, AR
Little Rock, AR
Russellville, AR
Wright, Linwood C., Jr. ....Philadelphia, PA
Wright, Lisa A. Wible ....Sacramento, CA
Wright, Lisa D. ....Walnut Creek, CA
Wright, Lizbeth London ....Akron, OH
Wright & Logan Co., L.P.A. ....Dublin, OH
Wright, Lori ....Washington, DC
Wright, Louie A. ....Kansas City, MO
Wright, Louise B. ....Kalamazoo, MI
Wright, Loyd H. ....Houston, TX
Wright, Luke W. ....Greensboro, NC
Wright, Luther, Jr. ....Nashville, TN
Wright, Lynn ....Short Hills, NJ
New York, NY
Wright, Lynn Lile ....Little Rock, AR
Wright, Lynn Walker ....Orlando, FL
Wright, M. Ann ....Richmond, VA
Wright, M. Eugene, Law Office of
Danville, IL
Wright, M. Jayne ....Aberdeen, MD
Wright, M. Jerome ....Reno, NV
Wright, M. Jocelyn ....Department of Justice, Civil Division, GV
Wright, Madison B., Jr. ....Dickinson, TX
Wright & Manning ....New York, NY
Wright, Marcus S. ....Tulsa, OK
Wright, Margaret A. ....New York, NY
Wright, Margaret K. ....Gainesville, FL
Wright, Margo T. ....Universal City, CA
Wright, Marie A. ....Hammond, LA
Wright, Marilyn J. ....Houston, TX
Wright, Mark A. ....Lake Forest, CA
Wright, Mark A. ....Manchester, NH
Wright, Mark E. ....Indianapolis, IN
Wright, Mark E. ....Fishkill, NY
Wright, Mark H. ....Tampa, FL
Wright, Mark J. ....Vancouver, WA
Wright, Mark R. ....Rochester, NY
Wright, Marshal H ....Oceanside, CA

Wrobel Markham & Schatz, LLP
Larchmont, NY
New York, NY
Wrobel, Robert F. .... **Fort Lee, NJ**
Wrobel, Stanley J. .... **Washington, DC**
Wrobel, Steven F. .... **Baltimore, MD**
Wrobel, Thomas S. .... San Francisco, CA
Wrobetz, Donald R. .... **Cheyenne, WY**
Wroblak, Bernadette M. .... Madison, NJ
Wroble, Arthur G. .... **West Palm Beach, FL**
Wroble, Arthur G., P.A.
West Palm Beach, FL
Wrobleski, Chester J., (P.C.)
New York, NY
Wrobleski, Jeanne, & Associates, LLC
Philadelphia, PA
Wrobleski, Jeanne P. .... **Philadelphia, PA**
Wrobleski, Theodore W. .... **Chicago, IL**
Wroblewski, Barbara A. .... St. Paul, NE
Wroblewski, Dennis E. .... Sylvania, OH
Wroblewski, Jonathan J. .... Washington, DC
Wroblewski Law Office .... St. Paul, NE
Wroblewski, Lisa B. .... **Pittsburgh, PA**
Wroblewski, Michael Charles
New York, NY
Wroblewski, Tamara D. .... Charlotte, NC
Wroblewski, Thomas S. .... Menasha, WI
Wrobley, Ralph G. .... **Kansas City, MO**
Wroblicka, Elizabeth L. .... Northampton, MA
Wroe, Edward F. .... **Coeur d'Alene, ID**
Wrolstad, Marwin O. .... Scandinavia, WI
Wrona, Dawn C. .... **Chicago, IL**
Wrona, James S. .... Washington, DC
Wrona, John S. .... Calumet City, IL
Wrona, Joseph E. .... Fairbanks, AK
Wrona, Patricia Ann .... Chicago, IL
Wronka, Walter W. .... Belle Mead, NJ
Wronka, Walter W., P.C. .... Belle Mead, NJ
Wronko, Carl F. .... Succasunna, NJ
Wronko, James R. .... **Somerville, NJ**
West Caldwell, NJ
Wronko, Kevin D. .... Paterson, NJ
Wronko, O'Hara & Miller .... **Somerville, NJ**
West Caldwell, NJ
Wronko, Ronald J., Jr. .... **Newark, NJ**
Wronko, Terence J. .... West Caldwell, NJ
Wronski, Andrew J. .... **Milwaukee, WI**
Wroten, Joseph E. .... Aberdeen, MS
Wroten, Kippy L. .... **Santa Ana, CA**
Wroten, Walter T. .... **Sacramento, CA**
Stockton, CA
Wrotenbery, J. Preston .... **Houston, TX**
Wrotenbery, Lori .... Austin, TX
Wroth, L. Kinvin .... Portland, ME
Wroth, Peregrine .... St. Louis, MO
Wroth, Renee Bergeron .... Springfield, MA
Wrubel, Austin .... New York, NY
Wrubel, Barbara .... **New York, NY**
Wrubel, David F. .... **New York, NY**
Wrubel, Eric I. .... **New York, NY**
Wrubel, Michael .... Fort Lauderdale, FL
Wrubel, Myra G. .... **Oradell, NJ**
Wrubel, Sharon G. .... Pacific Palisades, CA
Wrubel, Wende A. .... Washington, DC
Wruble, Jeffrey S. .... **Los Angeles, CA**
Wruble, Stacey L. .... **Washington, DC**
Wruble, Stanley F., III .... **South Bend, IN**
Wruck, Ernest G. .... Patchogue, NY
Wruck, Ernest R. .... Patchogue, NY
Wruck & Wruck .... Patchogue, NY
Wry, Brann J. .... Trenton, NJ
Wry, Charles A., Jr. .... **Waltham, MA**
Wry, Ellen T. .... Trenton, NJ
Wry, Jonathan D. .... **New York, NY**
Wrycha, Paul T. .... **Chicago, IL**
Wrye, Jill Gott .... Paducah, KY
Wrynn, Brian G. .... Flushing, NY
Wrynn, Gerard M. .... **White Plains, NY**
Wrynn, James J. .... Douglaston, NY
Wrzosek, Robert A. .... **Washington, DC**
Wsterbeck, Patricia J. .... Johnston, IA
Wszolek, Dennis F. .... Trenton, NJ
Wu, Aileen G. .... **Palo Alto, CA**
Wu, Alic S. H. .... Pasadena, CA
Wu, Allen .... New York, NY
Wu, Amy .... New York, NY
Wu, Andrew H.T. .... Los Angeles, CA
Wu, Andrew J. .... Los Angeles, CA
Wu, Angela .... **Seattle, WA**
Wu, Angela E. .... Chicago, IL
Wu, Aric H. .... **New York, NY**
Wu & Black, LLP .... Irvine, CA
Wu, Cecilia S. .... Alhambra, CA
Wu, Charles C.H. .... Irvine, CA
Wu, Christopher N. .... San Francisco, CA
Wu, Daisy C. .... Los Angeles, CA
Wu, Daniel .... **Los Angeles, CA**
Wu, Darren L. .... **Honolulu, HI**
Wu, David .... Portland, OR
Wu, Derek A. .... **Chicago, IL**
Wu, Edward C. .... Cambridge, MA
Wu, Elaine T. L. .... **Washington, DC**
Wu, Erica Y. .... Huntington Beach, CA
Wu, Felix, Law Offices of .... Pasadena, CA
Wu, Frances K. .... **Washington, DC**
Wu, Frank H. .... Washington, DC
Wu, Frank S. .... **Houston, TX**
Wu, G. Perry .... **Boston, MA**
Wu, Gerald R. .... Walnut Creek, CA
Wu, Henry Che Hou .... San Francisco, CA
Wu, Hsiao-Cheng Steven .... **Houston, TX**
Wu, Jack H. .... **Palo Alto, CA**
Wu, James .... **Bridgeport, CT**
Wu, James M. .... **Sunnyvale, CA**
Wu, James Y. .... **Chicago, IL**
Wu, Jenny C. .... **Washington, DC**
Wu, Jimmy .... Seattle, WA
Wu, Jon .... Menlo Park, CA
Wu, Joseph S. .... **Los Angeles, CA**
San Diego, CA
Wu & Kao, P.L.L.C. .... New York, NY
Wu, Kathleen J. .... **Dallas, TX**
Wu, Kathryn W. Kmain .... New York, NY
Wu, Louis L. .... **Portola Valley, CA**
Wu, Margaret L. .... **San Francisco, CA**
Wu, Marian J. .... **Austin, TX**
Wu, Michael .... East Hartford, CT
Wu, Michael C. .... Reston, VA
Wu, Morris M. .... New York, NY
Wu, Niping .... **New York, NY**
Wu, Patrick A. .... Los Angeles, CA
Wu, Patti T. .... **New York, NY**
Wu, Raymond .... **Los Angeles, CA**
Wu, Raymond F. .... Rolling Hills Estates, CA
Wu, Robin C. C., (Mr.) .... New York, NY
Wu, Sheen Y. .... Portland, OR
Wu, Simone .... Washington, DC
Wu, Stephen S. .... Mountain View, CA
Wu, Susie S. .... **New York, NY**
Wu, Ted H. .... Houston, TX
Wu, Theodore W. .... Washington, DC
Wu, Tong .... **Minneapolis, MN**
Wu, Victor .... Westminster, CA
Wu, Yi-Tze Seth .... Palo Alto, CA
Wu, Yolanda S. .... New York, NY
Wu, Yu-Yee .... **San Francisco, CA**
Wuamett, Jennifer B. .... Scottsdale, AZ
Wubbel, Richard H. .... **Oak Brook, IL**
Wubbenhorst, Andrew M. .... Riverdale, NJ
Wubneh, Elizabeth .... **New York, NY**
Wucetich, Peter M. .... San Marino, CA
Wuchenich, Allen S. .... **Pittsburgh, PA**
Wuchenich, Danielle E. .... Redlands, CA
Wuchenich, Thomas .... **Palo Alto, CA**
Wuchinich, Susan A.
Department Of Veterans Affairs, Office of the General Counsel, GV
Wuchitech, Roy G. .... **Los Angeles, CA**
Wudcoski, Karen E. W. .... St. Clair, MI
Wudowsky, Claire L.
Department of Commerce, Patent and Trademark Office, GV
Wuebbeling, Ronald J. .... **St. Louis, MO**
Wuebben, Robert Paul .... **Appleton, WI**
Wuebbling, Donald J. .... Cincinnati, OH
Wuehrmann, David B.
Federal Energy Regulatory Commission, Office of the General Counsel, GV
Wuerfel & Cholakian, A Professional Corporation .... Costa Mesa, CA
San Francisco, CA
Santa Rosa, CA
Wuerfel, Mark D. .... Costa Mesa, CA
San Francisco, CA
Wuersch, Daniel A. .... **New York, NY**
Wuersch & Gering LLP .... **New York, NY**
Wuerstle, Jack D. .... **Perkasie, PA**
Wuerth, Richard O. .... **Columbus, OH**
Wuerthner, John P. .... Great Falls, MT
Wuerthner & Wuerthner .... Great Falls, MT
Wuertz, Karen .... **New York, NY**
Wuertz, Raymond R. .... Warren, NJ
Wuertz, Troy D. .... **Dallas, TX**
Wuest, Charles S. .... **Houston, TX**
Wuest, George E. .... Louisville, KY
Wuest, Harvey E., Jr. .... Austin, TX
Wueste, Ward W., Jr. .... **Irving, TX**
Wuestenfeld, William M., (P.C.)
Anchorage, AK
Wuestenhagen, Timothy E. .... St. Paul, MN
Wuestenhoefer, Albert F. .... New Rochelle, NY
Wuester, Bert E., Jr. .... **Las Vegas, NV**
Wuester, William O., III .... **Fort Worth, TX**
Wuesthoff, Noah D. .... **Portland, ME**
Wuestling & James, L.C. .... **Clayton, MO**
St. Louis, MO
Wuestling, R. C. .... **St. Louis, MO**
Wuestner, Joseph A., Jr. .... St. Louis, MO
Wuestner, Linda D. .... St. Louis, MO
Wuetcher, Gerald E. .... Frankfort, KY
Wughalter, Eric A. .... Bronx, NY
Wugmeister, Miriam .... **Palo Alto, CA**
Wuhrman, Arnold H. .... **Tustin, CA**
Wuhrman, Arnold H., P.C., Law Offices of
Tustin, CA
Wuillamey, Marianne .... Jersey City, NJ
Wuillamey, Mark T. .... **Woodbridge, NJ**
Wujcik, Patrick J. .... Philadelphia, PA
Wukitsch, David J. .... **Albany, NY**
Wukmer, Michael A. .... **Indianapolis, IN**
Wukoson, David J. .... Houston, TX
Wukovich, George N. .... Cleveland, OH
Wukovits, Steven F. .... Cranford, NJ
Wulchak, James R. .... Daytona Beach, FL
Wulf, Arthur S. .... Chicago, IL
Wulf, David M. .... Treasury Department, Bureau of Alcohol, Tobacco and Firearms, GV
Wulf, Henry S. .... **West Palm Beach, FL**
Wulf, James V. .... Dublin, OH
Wulf, Joshua M. .... **Richmond, VA**
Wulf, Julie Zitella .... **Chicago, IL**
Wulf, Manisha C. .... **Chicago, IL**
Wulf, Matthew .... Washington, DC
Wulf, Melvin L. .... **New York, NY**
Wulf, Norman A.
Department of State, GV
Wulf, Vikki Lynn .... **Boulder, CO**
Wulf, William A. .... Merrill, WI
Wulfe, Scott N. .... **Houston, TX**
Wulfekoetter, Mitchell D. .... Topeka, KS
Wulfers, David W. .... **Tulsa, OK**
Wulfers, John M. .... **Chicago, IL**
Wulff, Bart .... **Dallas, TX**
Wulff, David C. .... Roseville, MN
Wulff, Eric J. .... St. Charles, MO
Wulff, Erik B. .... **Washington, DC**
Wulff, Geo. W. .... Oklahoma City, OK
Wulff, Karl Joseph .... Collinsville, IL
Wulff, Melissa L. .... Truckee, CA
Wulff, Randall W. .... **San Francisco, CA**
Wulff, Richard A. .... **Chicago, IL**
Wulff, Richard K.
Securities and Exchange Commission, Division of Corporation Finance, GV
Wulff, Robert A. .... **St. Louis, MO**
Wulff, Robert J. .... **Belleville, IL**
St. Louis, MO
Wulff, Robert King .... Westborough, MA
Wulff, Thomas D. .... **Omaha, NE**
Wulffraat, Robert A. .... **La Habra, CA**
Wulffson, Todd R. .... **Irvine, CA**
Wulfhorst, D. Todd .... **Denver, NC**
Lincolnton, NC
Wulfman, Andrew S. .... Morristown, NJ
Wulfmeier, LeRoy H., III .... Ann Arbor, MI
Detroit, MI
Wulfmeier & Ottenwess, PLC
Ann Arbor, MI
Detroit, MI
Wulfsberg, H. James .... **Oakland, CA**
Wulfsberg Reese & Sykes, Professional Corporation .... **Oakland, CA**
San Francisco, CA
Wulfsohn, Julius G. .... Long Beach, CA
Wulfsohn, Michael Daniel .... Denver, CO
Wulfstat, Allan A. .... **Chicago, IL**
Wuliger, Fadel & Beyer .... **Cleveland, OH**
Wuliger, Frank .... Los Angeles, CA
Wuliger, Timothy F. .... Moreland Hills, OH
Wuliger, William T. .... **Cleveland, OH**
Wulkan, Donna L. .... Washington, DC
Wulkan, Jeffrey E. .... Sherman Oaks, CA
Wullbrandt, Clyde E. .... **Santa Barbara, CA**
Wullenwaber, Dean .... **Lewiston, ID**
Wuller, James H. .... St. Louis, MO
Wuller, Ransom P. .... **Belleville, IL**
Wuller, Robert G., Jr. .... **Belleville, IL**
Wuller, Ronan P. .... **St. Louis, MO**
Wulliger, Richard C. .... Pacific Palisades, CA
Wullschleger, Arnold E. .... Beatrice, NE
Wullschleger, Karen K. .... Pomona, CA
Wulsin, Lucien .... Boulder, CO
Wulsin, Lucien, Jr. .... **Los Angeles, CA**
Wulsin, Lucien, Jr. .... **Santa Monica, CA**
Washington, DC
Wulsin, Peter J. .... **Boston, MA**
Wulsin, Richard L. .... **Boston, MA**
Wulterin, Shayne L. .... **Long Beach, CA**
Wulwick, Alexander J. .... New York, NY
Wulwick, Lisa Fogel .... **New York, NY**
Wulz, Dan L. .... Las Vegas, NV
Wunder, Bernard J., Jr. .... Washington, DC
Wunder, Brian K. .... **Houston, TX**
Wunder, David Hart .... Indianapolis, IN
Wunder, Harriette D. .... Columbia, SC
Wunder, John .... Muscatine, IA
Wunder, Knight, Levine, Thelen, Forscey & DeVierno, P.L.L.C. .... Washington, DC
Wunder, Mary Ann .... Indianapolis, IN
Wunder, Michael J. .... Hickory Hills, IL
Wunder, Richard C. .... Lyons, NY
Wunder and Wunder .... Indianapolis, IN
Wunderli, John M. .... Salt Lake City, UT
Wunderli, John P. .... **Washington, DC**
Wunderli, Russ J. .... **Sacramento, CA**
Wunderlich, F. James .... Houston, TX
Wunderlich, Frances M. .... **Livingston, NJ**
Wunderlich, Gary L. .... **Joliet, IL**
Wunderlich, Howard J. .... **Central Islip, NY**
Lake Grove, NY
Wunderlich Law Offices, Ltd. .... **Joliet, IL**
Wunderlich, Richard A. .... **St. Louis, MO**
Wunderlich, Sandra J. .... **St. Louis, MO**
Wunderlich, Sandra Rybak .... Naperville, IL
Wunderlich, Walter E. .... Carmichael, CA
Wunderlich, William M. .... San Jose, CA
Wunderlich, William M. .... High Ridge, MO
Wunderlin, Gary C. .... **Claremont, CA**
Wunderly, James E. .... Kalamazoo, MI
Wundrok, Joseph F. .... Bristol, NH
Wunerlich, Lisa J. .... Grosse Pointe Woods, MI
Wunker, Robert L. .... **Boca Raton, FL**
Wunnicke, Brooke .... **Denver, CO**
Wunsch, Alan V. .... Danbury, CT
Wunsch, Albert H., III .... Englewood Cliffs, NJ
Wunsch, Charles R. .... **Kansas City, MO**
Wunsch, Duane H. .... Brookfield, WI
Wunsch, Eric J. .... **Cincinnati, OH**
Wunsch, Gerald A. .... Indianapolis, IN
Wunsch, Gerald E. .... Lincolnshire, IL
Wunsch, Geraldine .... Montrose, MI
Wunsch, John C. .... **Chicago, IL**
Wunsch, John C., P.C. .... **Chicago, IL**
Wunsch, John H. .... Walnut Creek, CA
Wunsch, Mark A. .... St. Louis, MO
Wunsch, Paulette .... **Stamford, CT**
Wunsch, Robert S. .... **Kingman, KS**
Wunsch, William C. .... **San Francisco, CA**
Wunschel Law Firm, P.C. .... Carroll, IA
Wall Lake, IA
Wunschel, Russell S. .... Carroll, IA
Wall Lake, IA
Wuori, Thomas J. .... **Kalamazoo, MI**
Wuorinen, Susan E. .... Anchorage, AK
Wupper, Andrew .... Houston, TX
Wurcel, Ira .... **New York, NY**
Wurch, William A. .... **Irvine, CA**
Wurdeman, Richard D. .... Edmonds, WA
Wurdeman, Richard N. .... Hilo, HI
Wurdeman & Tesch .... Edmonds, WA
Wurgaft, Jack .... **Springfield, NJ**
Wurglitz, Alfred M. .... **Washington, DC**
Wurl, Daniel P. .... **Champaign, IL**
Wurm, John F. .... **Minneapolis, MN**
Wurm, Mark A. .... **Washington, DC**
Wurm, Paul .... Rutherford, NJ
Wurman, Barbara I. .... Glenview, IL
Wurman & Birnbaum .... Hempstead, NY
Wurman, Franklin A. .... Elkins Park, PA
Wurman, Kenneth H. .... Hempstead, NY
Wurms, Jeffrey C. .... **Oakland, CA**
Wurms, Marcel R. .... Lodi, NJ
Wurn, Lonnie .... Jacksonville, FL
Wurreschke, David G. .... Atlanta, GA
Wurschmidt, James W. .... Fair Oaks, CA
Wurst, Harold E. .... **Los Angeles, CA**
Wurst, Jeffrey A. .... **Mineola, NY**
New York, NY
Wurst, Jerome D. .... Arlington, TX
Wurst, John E. .... **Los Angeles, CA**
Wurst & McDowell, Ltd.
Thief River Falls, MN
Wurst, Michael F. .... **Dallas, TX**
Wurst, Richd. G. .... Wichita, KS
Wurst, Robert A. .... Thief River Falls, MN
Wurst, Thomas R. .... **Grand Rapids, MI**
Wurst, Wendel W. .... Garden City, KS
Wursta, John M. .... **Philadelphia, PA**
Wurster, Joel D. .... **Petoskey, MI**
Wurster, Lisa A. .... **Toledo, OH**
Wurster, Michelle L. .... **Austin, TX**
Wurster, Phillip D. .... Toledo, OH
Wurster, Scott C. .... Whitefish, MT
Wurster, Walter C., Co., L.P.A.
Cincinnati, OH
Wurster, Walter C., II .... Cincinnati, OH
Wurster, William F. .... Indianapolis, IN
Wurtenberger, Kenneth P.
Fort Lauderdale, FL
Wurtz, John W. .... Kettering, OH
Wurtz, Edward A. .... Rochester, NY
Wurtz, James L. .... Paducah, KY
Wurtz & Logan .... Springfield, OR
Wurtz, Mark E. .... Sheboygan, WI
Wurtz, Ronald E. .... Topeka, KS
Wurtz, Stephen T. .... Philadelphia, PA
Wurtz, Thomas A. .... **Omaha, NE**
Wurtz, Thomas E. .... Springfield, OR
Wurtz, William E. .... **New York, NY**
Wurtzel, Elan .... Plainview, NY
Wurtzel, Franklin R. .... Irwindale, CA
Wurtzel, Mark K. .... San Francisco, CA
Wurtzel, Paul A. .... Tenafly, NJ
Wurtzel, Paul A., A Prof. Corp. .... Tenafly, NJ
Wurtzel, Stewart E. .... New York, NY
Wurtzler, Gail L. .... **Denver, CO**
Wurwarg, Robert D. .... **New York, NY**
Wurz, Robert Tim .... Nashville, TN
Wurz, Theodore J. .... Bristol, CT
Wurzburg, Jocelyn Dan .... Memphis, TN
Wurzburg, Sid .... Spokane, WA
Wurzburg, Stephen M.
San Francisco, CA
San Jose, CA
Wurzburger, Myron I. .... New York, NY
Wurzel, Glenn J. .... San Francisco, CA
Wurzel, Marc A. .... **New York, NY**
Wurzer, Duane F. .... **Denver, CO**
Wurzer, Marvin A. .... Houston, TX
Wurzman, Robert M. .... Beachwood, OH
Wu-Shepherd, Christine A.
Grand Rapids, MI
Wushinske, Robert P. .... New Castle, PA
Wusinich and Brogan .... **Downingtown, PA**
Reading, PA
West Chester, PA
Wusinich, Joseph F., III
Downingtown, PA
Reading, PA
West Chester, PA
Wuslich, Raymond B. .... **Washington, DC**
Wusnack, Otto A. .... Pascagoula, MS
Wuss, Maria A. .... Paterson, NJ
Wussow, Michael H. .... Chicago, IL
Wussow, Wendy Anne .... McPherson, KS
Wustenberg, John W. .... Oklahoma City, OK
Wustner, Patrick J. .... Minneapolis, MN
Wustrack, Paul K., Jr. .... **Buffalo, NY**
Wuthrich, Daniel S. .... Fresno, CA
Wuthrich, Edward E. .... El Campo, TX
Wuthrich, Steve A. .... Montpelier, ID
Wutschel, Elroy J. .... Milwaukee, WI
Wutschel, Mary P. .... Clearwater, FL
Wutscher, Ralph T. .... **Chicago, IL**
Wutt, Robert A. .... Boca Raton, FL
Wuttke, Stephen A. .... Buffalo Grove, IL
Wutzke, Jeffrey W. .... **San Francisco, CA**
Wyand, David M. .... **Baltimore, MD**
Wyand, Jeffrey A. .... **Washington, DC**
Wyand, Ralph W. .... Hagerstown, MD
Wyand, Taylor J. .... **Oklahoma City, OK**
Wyandt, Deborah Ann .... Chantilly, VA
Wyant, C. Judley .... **Racine, WI**
Wyant, David L. .... **Wheeling, WV**
Wyant, Dom H. .... Atlanta, GA
Wyant, Edward James .... Miami, OK
Wyant, Emory A., Jr.
Plymouth Meeting, PA
Wyant, Jeffrey C. .... Chicago, IL
Wyant, John M. .... Peoria, IL
Wyant Law Offices, S.C. .... **Racine, WI**
Wyant, Mary F. .... **Racine, WI**
Wyatt & Associates .... North Hollywood, CA
Wyatt, Bill .... **Fort Collins, CO**
Wyatt, Bradley D. .... Bryan, TX
Wyatt, Brent C. .... **New Orleans, LA**
Wyatt, Brian M. .... **New York, NY**
Wyatt, Brian P. .... **Baltimore, MD**
Wyatt, Bruce R. .... **Denver, CO**
Wyatt, C. Dan, III .... **Atlanta, GA**
Wyatt, Carl K., Jr. .... **Memphis, TN**

Wynn, Patricia ... Washington, DC
Wynn, Patricia Sinskey ... Santa Monica, CA
Wynn, Paul F. ... Raynham, MA
Wynn, Philip H. ... Los Angeles, CA
Wynn, R. Scott ... Fairfax, VA
Wynn, Randy J. ... Milwaukee, WI
Wynn, Richard H. ... Boston, MA
Wynn, Robert A. ... Des Moines, IA
Wynn, Robert L., III ... Spartanburg, SC
Wynn, Robert S. ... Jefferson, OH
Wynn, Ronald S. ... San Francisco, CA
Wynn, Rowe C., Jr. ... Tulsa, OK
Wynn, Sarah Woodfin ... New York, NY
Wynn, Scott W. ... Charlestown, MA
Wynn, Sharon L. ... Princeton, NJ
Wynn, Simon D. ... New York, NY
Wynn, Stanford A. ... Milwaukee, WI
Wynn, Stephen H. ... Huntsville, AL
Wynn, Thomas F. ... New York, NY
Wynn, Thomas J. ... Chicago, IL
Wynn, Thomas J. ... Boston, MA
Falmouth, MA
Hyannis, MA
Raynham, MA
Wynn, W. Scott ... Groveland, FL
Wynn, Wayne ... Harrisburg, PA
Philadelphia, PA
Wynn, William G., Jr. ... Spartanburg, SC
Wynn, Wm. Reagan ... Fort Worth, TX
Wynn & Wynn Co., L.P.A. ... Jefferson, OH
Wynn & Wynn, P.C. ... Boston, MA
Falmouth, MA
Hyannis, MA
Raynham, MA
Taunton, MA
Wynne, Alan B. ... Atlanta, GA
Wynne, Brian D. ... Culver City, CA
Wynne, Charles S. ... Gainesville, GA
Wynne, Donna E. ... Concord, CA
Wynne, Edward C. ... Glastonbury, CT
Wynne, Edward J., III ... Boston, MA
Wynne, Edward J., Jr. ... Ross, CA
Wynne, Francis J. ... Hartford, CT
Wynne, Frank O., Jr. ... Merigold, MS
Wynne, G. William ... St. Louis, MO
Wynne, Gordon R., Jr. ... Wills Point, TX
Wynne, J. David ... Jackson, MS
Wynne, James E. ... Detroit, MI
Wynne, James E. ... St. Louis, MO
Wynne, John B. ... New York, NY
Wynne, John C. ... San Diego, CA
Wynne, John Carlton ... Houston, TX
Wynne, John F. ... New Haven, CT
Wynne, John F., Jr. ... New Haven, CT
Wynne, John H. ... Staten Island, NY
Wynne, John H. ... Enid, OK
Okeene, OK
Seiling, OK
Wynne, John M. ... St. Louis, MO
Wynne, John O. ... Virginia Beach, VA
Wynne, John V. ... Jersey City, NJ
New York, NY
Wynne, John W. ... Indianapolis, IN
Wynne, Joseph A. ... Oakland, CA
Wynne, Joseph T. ... San Juan, PR
Wynne, Kathleen ... East Meadow, NY
Wynne, Kenneth R. ... Houston, TX
Wynne, Kristen Bamford ... Seattle, WA
Wynne, Kristin L. ... Newark, NJ
Wynne Law Firm, The ... St. Louis, MO
Wynne & Maney ... Houston, TX
Wynne, Margaret M. ... Bridgeport, CT
Wynne, Marguerite Stenson ... Somerset, NJ
Wynne, Marion E., Jr. ... Bay Minette, AL
Fairhope, AL
Wynne, Mary E. ... Palo Alto, CA
Wynne, Megan S. ... Los Angeles, CA
Wynne, Melissa A. ... Evanston, IL
Wynne, Michael C. ... Sherman, TX
Wynne, Michael J. ... Ridgefield, WA
Wynne, Nancy Rich ... New York, NY
Wynne, Owen E. ... Minneapolis, MN
Wynne, Patricia A. ... Vera, FL
Wynne, Patrick J. ... Bronx, NY
Wynne, Patrick L. ... Bronx, NY
Wynne, Pontillo & Lynch ... Glastonbury, CT
Wynne, Richard L. ... Los Angeles, CA
Wynne, Richard L. ... Houston, TX
Wynne, Richard L., Jr. ... Dallas, TX
Wynne, Robert J. ... Culver City, CA
Wynne, Robert J. ... St. Louis, MO
Wynne, Robert K. ... Bristol, CT
Wynne, Robert M. ... Sandersville, GA
Wynne, Robert O. ... Hartford, CT
Wynne, Robert S. ... Indianapolis, IN
Wynne, Robin F. ... Fordyce, AR
Wynne, Robt. D. ... New Orleans, LA
Wynne, Roger D. ... Seattle, WA
Wynne, Roland Brooks ... Crawfordsville, IN
Wynne, September ... Ann Arbor, MI
Wynne, Shari A. ... Los Angeles, CA
Austin, TX
Wynne Spiegel Itkin, A Law Corporation
Los Angeles, CA
Wynne, Steven E. ... Beaverton, OR
Wynne, Suzanne Kahn ... Los Angeles, CA
Wynne, Terry F. ... Pine Bluff, AR
Wynne, Thomas D., III ... Fordyce, AR
Wynne, Thomas E. ... Garden City, NY
Wynne, Thomas J. ... Everett, WA
Wynne, Thomas More ... Cleveland, OH
Wynne, V. Peter ... Houston, TX
Wynne, W. Kendall, Jr. ... Covington, GA
Wynne, William E. ... New Orleans, LA
Wynne, William F., Jr. ... New York, NY
Wynne, William J. ... El Dorado, AR
Wynne & Wynne ... Wills Point, TX
Wynne, Wynne & Wynne ... Fordyce, AR
Wynner, Robert E. ... Westlake Village, CA
Wynns, L. Pat ... Washington, DC
Wynperle, Mary Catherine
New York, NY
Wynshaw, Warren D. ... Mahopac, NY
Wynstra, Nancy A. ... Pittsburgh, PA
Wypijewski, Anne Marie
Federal Communications Commission,
Wireless Telecommunications Bureau, GV
Wypior, Oda ... New York, NY
Wypyski, Eugene M. ... Hempstead, NY
Wypyszinski, Alex W. ... New Brunswick, NJ
Wyre, James O., II ... Fayetteville, AR
Wyrick, Austin N. ... Leavenworth, KS
Wyrick, Bart M. ... Dallas, TX
Wyrick, Christopher B. ... Kansas City, MO
Wyrick, Cynthia Richardson
Sevierville, TN
Wyrick, Dianna Calaboyias
Pittsburgh, PA
Wyrick, J. Gregory ... New Orleans, LA
Wyrick, Jermaine A. ... Detroit, MI
Wyrick & Johnson ... Texarkana, AR
Wyrick, Michelle D. ... Louisville, KY
Wyrick, Milton D. ... Los Alamos, NM
Wyrick, Mitzi D. ... Louisville, KY
Wyrick Robbins Yates & Ponton LLP
Raleigh, NC
Research Triangle Park, NC
Wyrick, Ryan E. ... Norman, OK
Wyrick, Samuel T., III ... Raleigh, NC
Wyrick, Stan G. ... Muncie, IN
Wyrick, W. Kelvin ... Texarkana, AR
Wyrick, William J. ... Pittsburgh, PA
Wyrod, Patricia M. ... Palo Alto, CA
Wyron, Richard H. ... Washington, DC
Wyrough, Richard R. Page
Upper Marlboro, MD
Wyrough, William Edward, Jr.
Tallahassee, FL
Wyrsch Hobbs Mirakian & Lee, P.C.
Kansas City, MO
Wyrsch, James R. ... Kansas City, MO
Wyrsch, Martha B. ... Lakewood, CO
Wyrsch, Raymond J.
General Accounting Office,
Office of the General Counsel, GV
Wyrzykowski, Stanley L. ... Cliffside Park, NJ
Wysack, Kathryn J. ... St. Louis, MO
Wyse, Aloha L. ... West Linn, OR
Wyse, James P. ... Morristown, NJ
Wyse, Joseph E. ... Chicago, IL
Wyse, Scott C. ... Portland, OR
Wyse, Wendy L. ... San Rafael, CA
Wyse, William W. ... Portland, OR
Wyshak, Lillian Worthing ... Beverly Hills, CA
Wyshner, Mary Ann ... New York, NY
Wyshnytzky, Orlana E. ... Chicago, IL
Wysk, Tina J. ... Dallas, TX
Wyskiel, Boc & Reid ... Dover, NH
Wyskiel, Christopher A. ... Dover, NH
Wyskiel, David E. ... Meriden, CT
Wyskowski, Barbara ... Long Branch, NJ
Wysocki, Albert L. ... Lake Villa, IL
Wysocki, Albert L., A Prof. Corp.
Lake Villa, IL
Wysocki, Bernard ... Waukegan, IL
Wysocki, C. Michael ... Kearny, NJ
Wysocki, David L. ... Riverside, CA
Wysocki, F. Michael ... Philadelphia, PA
Wysocki, Gregory L. ... Detroit, MI
Wysocki, Henry V. ... New York, NY
Wysocki, Kenneth R. ... Chicago, IL
Wysocki, Lawrence Thaddeus ... Charlotte, MI
Wysocki, Marilyn L. ... Joliet, IL
Wysocki, Mark R. ... Fort Lauderdale, FL
Wysocki, Mary Kay ... Marlton, NJ
Wysocki, Paul R. ... New York, NY
Wysocki, Ronald A., (Inc.) ... Boston, MA
Wysocki, Smith & Curtis ... Waukegan, IL
Wysoglad, Kenneth J. ... Chicago, IL
Wysoglad, Kenneth J., & Associates
Chicago, IL
Wysoker, Glassner & Weingartner
New Brunswick, NJ
Wysoker, Jack ... New Brunswick, NJ
Wysoki, David ... New York, NY
Wysong, Patrick M. ... Landover, MD
Wysong, Violette Witwer ... Albion, IN
Kendallville, IN
Wysong, Wendy L. ... Washington, DC
Wysor, Philip C. ... Lynnfield, MA
Wyss, Emert L., Jr. ... Alton, IL
Wyss, James B. ... Lake Havasu City, AZ
Wyss, James O. ... Fort Worth, TX
Wyss, John B. ... Washington, DC
Wyss, Kimberly Kay ... Canton, OH
Wyss Law Offices ... Alton, IL
Wyss, Lawrence K. ... Morristown, TN
Wyss, McNellis, Riebenack & Myers
Fort Wayne, IN
Wyss, Norbert L. ... Fort Wayne, IN
Wyss, R. John, Jr. ... San Jose, CA
Wyss, Richard D., II ... Salt Lake City, UT
Wyszynski, James Edward, Jr. ... Lansing, MI
Wyszynski, Jeffrey D. ... Bellevue, WA
Wyszynski, Michael R. ... Buffalo, NY
Wyszynski, Richard M. ... Buffalo, NY
Wythe Lawyers, P.C. ... Wytheville, VA
Wytias, Betty J. ... Denver, CO
Wyton, Sarah E. ... Chicago, IL
Wytsma, Laura Ann ... Los Angeles, CA
Wytychak, Michael, III ... Coeur d'Alene, ID
Wyzanski, Charles M. ... Boston, MA
Wyzga, Diane F. ... San Clemente, CA
Wyzgoski, Paul M. ... Detroit, MI
Wyzik, John M. ... Suffield, CT
Wzorek, Lawrence E. ... Omaha, NE
Xaiz, Earl ... Salt Lake City, UT
Xakellis, George C. ... Lancaster, PA
Xakellis, Reese & Pugh, A. Prof. Corp.
Lancaster, PA
Xanders, Edward Laucks
Beverly Hills, CA
Xanders, George L. ... Cincinnati, OH
Xanders, Julie Kusske ... Los Angeles, CA
Xanders & Xanders Co., L.P.A.
Cincinnati, OH
Xanthakis, Anthony C. ... New York, NY
Xanthakos, Stella Electra ... Bay City, MI
Xanthopoulos, John S. ... Huntingdon, TN
Xanthos, Anna ... New York, NY
Xanthos, Arthur P. ... New York, NY
Xanthos, Christopherj ... Pasadena, CA
Xanthos, George ... Tarzana, CA
Xanthos, James A. ... Laurel, MD
Xanttopoulos, William ... Miami, FL
Xanttopoulos, William, P.A. ... Miami, FL
Xavier, Angela M. ... Daly City, CA
Xavier, Eduardo M. ... Union City, CA
Xavier, Gillian S. Richards ... Houston, TX
Xenopoulos, Damon E. ... Washington, DC
Xenos, Oksana O. ... Southfield, MI
Xhumallari, Ymer ... Yonkers, NY
Xia, Lin ... Washington, DC
New York, NY
Xia, Tingkang (Tim) ... Atlanta, GA
Xiang, Shaokun S. ... New York, NY
Xiao-Lin, Charlene L. ... Kohler, WI
Xides, Byron D. ... Pittsburgh, PA
Xides, Robert G., Jr. ... Pittsburgh, PA
Xidias, Eftyhia ... Brooklyn, NY
Xifaras, Margaret D. ... New Bedford, MA
Xinos, Constantine P. ... Chicago, IL
Xiques, Alberto J. ... Miami, FL
Xistris, Demetrios G. ... New York, NY
Xistris, Victor D. ... New York, NY
Xixis, George A. ... New Haven, CT
Xlander, Frederick R. ... Binghamton, NY
Xóchihua, Paul R. ... Portland, OR
Xoinis, Elena J. ... Nashville, TN
Xu, Bing ... Washington, DC
Xu, Jackie Hui ... Pittsburgh, PA
Xu, Min (Amy) Schumann
Minneapolis, MN
Xu, X. Bing ... Orlando, FL
Xu, Xiao Bing ... Orlando, FL
Xue, Feng ... Chicago, IL
Xuereb, Joseph M. ... Dearborn, MI
Xuereb, Joseph M., P.C. ... Dearborn, MI
Xylas & Associates, LLP ... New York, NY
Xylas, George M. ... New York, NY
Xylas, Michael C. ... New York, NY

Yaap, Jerry A. ... Casper, WY
Yablen, Barry A. ... Lake George, NY
Yablin, Arnold ... Hollywood, FL
Yablin, Arnold, P.A. ... Hollywood, FL
Yablok, Nina ... San Jose, CA
Yablon, Al ... Glendale, CA
Yablon, Alfred B. ... Highland Park, IL
Yablon, Asher J. ... New Rochelle, NY
Yablon, Babette ... West Hempstead, NY
Yablon, Charles M. ... New York, NY
Yablon, Jay R. ... Schenectady, NY
Yablon, Jeffery L., (P.C.) ... Washington, DC
Yablon, Lawrence T. ... New York, NY
Yablon, Marc D. ... Sacramento, CA
Yablon, Morris A. ... Paterson, NJ
Yablonovich, Mark ... Los Angeles, CA
Yablonowitz, Scott R. ... New York, NY
Yablonski, Both & Edelman
Washington, DC
Yablonski, Costello & Leckie, P.C.
Washington, PA
Yablonski, Elise A. ... New York, NY
Yablonski, Joseph A. ... Washington, DC
Yablonski, Joshua J. ... Syracuse, NY
Yablonski, Kenneth J. ... Washington, PA
Yablonski, Mark D. ... Pittsburgh, PA
Yablonski, Michael ... Pittsburgh, PA
Yablonski, Stephen C. ... Worcester, MA
Yablonski, Steven K. ... Washington, DC
Yablonski-Toll, Karen L. ... Denver, CO
Yablonsky, Daniel J. ... Millburn, NJ
Yablonsky, Eva ... Redwood City, CA
Yabrof, Mark A. ... Ventura, CA
Yabuno, Robert G. ... San Bernardino, CA
Yacano, Mark S. ... Richmond, VA
Yacavino, Ralph A. ... Clark, NJ
Yacavone, James L., III ... Clearwater, FL
Yacavone, John P., Jr. ... Wethersfield, CT
Yacawych, Rhonda Jo ... Boston, MA
Yaccarino, Chryssa ... Neptune, NJ
Yachanin, Joseph C. ... Jupiter, FL
Yaches, Barry S. ... Jenkintown, PA
Yachmetz, Philip K. ... West Orange, NJ
Yachnin, Ralph ... Mineola, NY
Yachzel, Joel S. ... Los Angeles, CA
Yackel, Juliet M. ... Chicago, IL
Yackel, Norman L. ... Hayward, WI
Yackel, Raymond H. ... Morgantown, WV
Yackel, Raymond H., Law Offices of
Morgantown, WV
Yacker, Brett D. ... New York, NY
Yacker & Granata ... Matawan, NJ
Yacker, Jay B. ... Hoboken, NJ
Yacker, Julius Y. ... Chicago, IL
Yacker, Rhonda ... New York, NY
Yacker, Stanley ... Matawan, NJ
Yackey, Allan L. ... Indianapolis, IN
Yackey, Steven J. ... Louisville, KY
Yacknin, Eileen D. ... Pittsburgh, PA
Yacknin, Ellen M. ... Rochester, NY
Yacknin, Hallie S. ... San Rafael, CA
Yacko, Keith M. ... Fairfax, VA
Yackovetsky, Dennis P. ... Garfield, NJ
Yackshaw, Matthew ... Canton, OH
Yackulic, Corrie Johnson ... Seattle, WA
Yacobi, Stephen A. ... Greenville, SC
Yacomelli, Lisa Anne ... Randolph, NJ
Yacono, Dominick George
Department of the Navy,
Office of the Judge Advocate General, GV
Yacono, Judith ... Houston, TX
Yacono, Norberto H. ... Paterson, NJ
Yacos, John G. ... New York, NY
Yacoubian, Alan J. ... New Orleans, LA
Yacoubian, Talin V. ... Los Angeles, CA
Yacoubian, Vahe ... Los Angeles, CA
Yacoubian & Zerunyan ... Washington, DC
Yacovelle, John A. ... San Diego, CA
Yacovelle, John A. ... Collingswood, NJ
Yacovelle, John A., P.C. ... Collingswood, NJ
Yacovone, Laura M. ... New York, NY
Yacubian, Lowell H., (Mrs.)
Fort Collins, CO
Yacucci, Philip J., Jr. ... Fort Pierce, FL
Yacullo, Victor F. ... Los Angeles, CA
Yacura, Gary D. ... Falls Church, VA
Yacura, Mark M. ... Washington, DC
Yacuzzo, Karen Marie ... Nashville, TN
Yacuzzo, Lisa A. ... Nashville, TN
Yacyshyn, Paul M. ... New York, NY
Yadav, Manish ... New York, NY
Yaden, Linda S.
National Labor Relations Board,
Office of the General Counsel, GV
Yadgar, Julie N. ... Chicago, IL
Yadley, Barbara M. ... Tampa, FL
Yadley, Gregory C. ... Tampa, FL
Yadlon, Robert E. ... Wharton, NJ
Yadlon, William T. ... East Brunswick, NJ
Yadlosky, Kristen A. ... Atlanta, GA
Yado, Jess J., III ... Tampa, FL
Yado, Jess J., III, P.A. ... Tampa, FL
Yadoff, Laurie ... Exeter, NH
Yadon, Laurence J., II ... Tulsa, OK
Yadon, R. B., Jr. ... Edmond, OK
Yadvish, Kenneth ... New York, NY
Yaeckel, A. Carl ... San Diego, CA
Yaeger, Bonnie ... Los Angeles, CA
Yaeger, Daniel A. ... Cincinnati, OH
Yaeger, Derrill E. ... Corona, CA
Yaeger, Elia Diaz ... Metairie, LA
New Orleans, LA
Yaeger, Gregory T. ... Minneapolis, MN
Yaeger, Jack, Jr. ... Tallahassee, FL
Yaeger, James G. ... Fort Myers, FL
Yaeger, Judith B. ... New York, NY
Yaeger, Jungbauer, Barczak & Roe, P.L.C.
Minneapolis, MN
Yaeger, Kenneth M. ... Newport Beach, CA
Yaeger, Kurtis E. ... Sacramento, CA
Yaeger, Laura L. ... Charlotte, NC
Yaeger, Nancy Ann ... Minneapolis, MN
Yaeger, Robert H. ... Sarasota, FL
Yaeger, Thomas L. ... Madison, WI
Yaeger, William J. ... Minneapolis, MN
Yaeger, William J., Jr. ... Wheeling, WV
Yaeger, William L. ... Durham, NC
Yaeli, Nancy Daru ... Tucson, AZ
Yaffa, Andrew B. ... Boca Raton, FL
Miami, FL
Sarasota, FL
Yaffa, Doreen ... West Palm Beach, FL
Yaffa, Phillip Allen ... Miami, FL
Yaffa, Samuel M. ... Boca Raton, FL
Miami, FL
Sarasota, FL
Yaffe, Alan L., (P.C.) ... Corpus Christi, TX
Yaffe, David N. ... Melville, NY
Yaffe, David P. ... Los Angeles, CA
Yaffe, David P. ... Washington, DC
Yaffe, Deborah M. P.
National Labor Relations Board,
Office of the General Counsel, GV
Yaffe, Earl D. ... Chicago, IL
Yaffe, Joseph M. ... Costa Mesa, CA
Yaffe, Michelle Rachel ... Fort Lauderdale, FL
Yaffe, Nancy ... Los Angeles, CA
Yaffe, Robert H. ... Miami Beach, FL
Yaffe, Robert J. ... Columbus, OH
Yaffe, Roy ... Philadelphia, PA
Yaffee, David A. ... Syracuse, NY
Yaffee, Wayne A. ... Houston, TX
Yaffie, Burton S. ... Bridgeport, CT
Yaffie, Burton S. ... Trumbull, CT
Yaffie, Jessica R. ... Boston, MA
Yaged, Jonathan R. ... New York, NY
Yagel, Russell A. ... Miami, FL
Yagelski, Paul R. ... Pittsburgh, PA
Yager, Anthony D. ... Chicago, IL
Yager, Brenda Lee
Department of State, GV
Yager, Clara T. ... Durham, NC
Yager, Daniel V. ... Washington, DC
Yager, David M. ... Santa Barbara, CA
Yager, Dawn M. ... Denver, CO
Yager, Donald W., Jr. ... Cortland, NY
Yager, George F. ... Cortland, NY
Yager, Laura Hope ... Yonkers, NY
Yager, Martha R. ... New York, NY
Yager, Maurie D. ... New Orleans, LA
Yager, Paul D. ... Flint, MI
Yager, Russell ... Dallas, TX
Yager, Thomas C. ... Los Angeles, CA
Yagerman, Howard W. ... New York, NY
Yagerman, Katherine S. ... New York, NY
Yagerman, Mark S. ... New York, NY
Yaggi, Tracy L. ... Pittsburgh, PA
Yaggy, Carol C. ... San Francisco, CA
Yaggy, Michael Esher ... Baltimore, MD

Yaghi, Michael ....Menlo Park, CA
Yaghmaie, Babak ....New York, NY
Yagjian, Anita P. ....La Canada Flintridge, CA
Yagjian, Michael A. ....Pasadena, CA
Yagla, Gene R. ....Waterloo, IA
Yagla, McCoy & Riley, P.L.C.
Waterloo, IA
Yagoda, Andrea R. ....Columbus, OH
Yagoda, Scott Ross ....North Caldwell, NJ
Yagura, Ryan K. ....Los Angeles, CA
Yahia, Laurance ....Boston, MA
Yahia, Terri L. ....Boston, MA
Yahiku, Robin John ....Hilo, HI
Yahn, Neil W. ....Harrisburg, PA
Yahne, Kenneth R. ....Fort Wayne, IN
Yahne, Scott E. ....Hammond, IN
Yahne, William D. ....Alpena, MI
Yahner, Ann C. ....Washington, DC
Yahner, David F. ....New York, NY
Yahner, Deborah B. ....Houston, TX
Yahng, Robert T. ....San Francisco, CA
Yahnian, D. Steven ....Visalia, CA
Yahnic, Alice Lee ....Osage Beach, MO
Yahnke, Gary L. ....Anamosa, IA
Yahoodik, Paul D. ....Everett, MA
Yahr, Alan H. ....Sherman Oaks, CA
Yahr, Alan H., A Law Corp.
Sherman Oaks, CA
Yaist, Ronald P. ....Akron, OH
Yak, Patricia ....Pelham, NY
Yakaboski, Francis J. ....Riverhead, NY
Yakaboski, Stacy ....New York, NY
Yake, Kirk ....San Diego, CA
Yakely, Heather C. ....Spokane, WA
Yaker, Barry D. ....Birmingham, MI
Yaker, Bernard ....New York, NY
Yaker, Bradford T. ....Bloomfield Hills, MI
Yaker, Joshua W. ....Detroit, MI
Yaker, Marshall I. ....El Paso, TX
Yaker, Marvin D. ....New York, NY
Yaker, Rebeca F. ....Miami, FL
Yakes, Bauer, Kindt & Phillips, S.C.
Oshkosh, WI
Yakes, Gary R. ....Oshkosh, WI
Yakes, John C. ....Palo Alto, CA
Yakey-Fogle, Cheryl C. ....New York, NY
Yakima, Boris K. ....Bloomfield Hills, MI
Yakimo, Michael, Jr. ....Overland Park, KS
Yakimovsky, Yoram ....Portland, OR
Yakimow, John W. ....Southfield, MI
Princeton, NJ
Yakimowicz, Barbara M. ....Kingston, PA
Yaklevich, John A. ....Columbus, OH
Yaklin, Saundra M. ....Philadelphia, PA
Yaklin, Stephen A. ....Marietta, GA
Yakob, Adrian F. ....Wilmington, DE
Yakopec, Stephen, Jr. ....New Kensington, PA
Yakovakis, James S. ....Manchester, NH
Yakowicz, Meredythe J. ....Harrisburg, PA
Yakowicz, Vincent X. ....Harrisburg, PA
Yakren, Aviva ....New York, NY
Yaksic, Barbara Friedman ....Cleveland, OH
Yaksic, Michael ....Chardon, OH
Yaksich, Kelly D. ....Englewood, CO
Yakutis, Alexander B. ....Piedmont, CA
Yalamanchili, Sujata ....Buffalo, NY
Yalcin, Miranda R. ....Raleigh, NC
Yalcinkaya, Seda ....New York, NY
Yalden, Olsen & Willette ....Rockford, IL
Yalden, Raphael E., II ....Rockford, IL
Yaldo, David W. ....Southfield, MI
Yaldo, Scott Salim ....Farmington Hills, MI
Yaldoo, Laith L. ....Detroit, MI
Yale, Benjamin F. ....Waynesfield, OH
Yale, Benjamin F., & Associates Co., L.P.A.
Waynesfield, OH
Yale, Beverly S. ....Columbus, OH
Yale, Debra B. ....Chicago, IL
Yale, Diane ....Bronx, NY
Yale, Diane J. ....Indianapolis, IN
Yale, Eugene P. ....San Diego, CA
Yale, Glen A. ....San Antonio, TX
Yale, Guy D. ....Hartford, CT
Yale, Harris J. ....New York, NY
Yale, Jerold S. ....New York, NY
Yale, Michelle I. ....Washington, DC
Yale, William A. ....San Diego, CA
Yale, William Dickinson, Jr. ....Houston, TX
Yale-Loehr, Stephen W. ....Ithaca, NY
Yaley, Carole J. ....Fairfax, VA
Yalkowsky, Stanley ....New York, NY
Yalkut, Kent E. ....Las Cruces, NM
Yallen, Robert B. ....Encino, CA
Yaller, Carl S. ....Media, PA
Yalman, Ann ....Santa Fe, NM
Yalof, Andrea Pierce ....Baltimore, MD
Yalowitz, Jay A. ....Chicago, IL
Yalowitz, Kenneth G. ....Seattle, WA
Yalowitz, Kent A. ....New York, NY
Yalowitz, Warren M. ....Schererville, IN
Yam, Gerald B. ....Encino, CA
Yam, John J. ....Delray Beach, FL
Yama, Elaine M. ....Fresno, CA
Yamachika, Thomas ....Honolulu, HI
Yamada, Alan H. ....Glendale, CA
Yamada, David Charles ....Boston, MA
Yamada, Dennis R. ....Honolulu, HI
Yamada, Edsel M. ....Honolulu, HI
Yamada, Gerald H. ....Washington, DC
Yamada, Harold T. ....Hanalei, HI
Yamada, John Toshio ....Playa Del Rey, CA
Yamada, Keith Y. ....Honolulu, HI
Yamada, Nancy T. ....Sacramento, CA
Yamada, Naomi Kanbara ....San Francisco, CA
Yamada, Ranko Carol ....Oakland, CA
Yamada, Stephen K. ....Honolulu, HI
Yamada, Ted Y. ....Torrance, CA
Yamada, Terence J. ....Portland, OR

Yamaga-Karns, Kevin ....Los Angeles, CA
Yamagata, Ben ....Washington, DC
Yamagata, Blaine ....Houston, TX
Yamagata, Eric S. ....Honolulu, HI
Yamagishi, Don K. ....Mission Hills, CA
Yamaguchi, Colleen S. ....Los Angeles, CA
Yamaguchi, David ....Irving, TX
Yamaguchi, Howard S. ....Los Angeles, CA
Yamaguchi, Joan M. ....Honolulu, HI
Yamaguchi, Jon F. ....Martinez, CA
Yamaguchi, Keith S. ....Chicago, IL
Yamaguchi, Lois H. ....Honolulu, HI
Yamaguchi, Michael J. ....San Francisco, CA
Yamaguchi, Nancy ....Palo Alto, CA
Yamaguchi, Ralph T. ....Honolulu, HI
Yamaguchi, Scott N. ....Los Angeles, CA
Yamaguchi, Stephen A. ....Los Angeles, CA
Yamaguchi, Vivian K. ....Chicago, IL
Yamaguchi, Yoichiro ....Washington, DC
Yamahiro, Glenn H. ....Milwaukee, WI
Yamaichi, Kelly Diane ....Sacramento, CA
Yamakawa, David K., Jr. ....San Francisco, CA
Yamaki, Michael R. ....Los Angeles, CA
Yamali, Joseph A. ....New York, NY
Yamamoto, Alan H. ....Washington, DC
Alexandria, VA
Yamamoto, Alan H. ....Fairfax, VA
Yamamoto, Allison S. ....Washington, DC
Yamamoto, Andrew J. ....Los Angeles, CA
Yamamoto, Carol Kikue ....Honolulu, HI
Yamamoto, David K. ....Torrance, CA
Yamamoto, Dean T. ....Honolulu, HI
Yamamoto, Denise Y. ....San Jose, CA
Yamamoto, Donna H. ....Honolulu, HI
Yamamoto, Eric K. ....Honolulu, HI
Yamamoto, Eric R. ....Los Angeles, CA
Yamamoto, Eugene K. ....Oakland, CA
Yamamoto, Gordon Y. ....San Francisco, CA
Yamamoto, Jerel I. ....Hilo, HI
Yamamoto, Jodi Shin ....Honolulu, HI
Yamamoto, John M. ....Pasadena, CA
Yamamoto, Kumi ....Seattle, WA
Yamamoto, Masami ....Los Angeles, CA
Yamamoto, Michael O. ....Honolulu, HI
Yamamoto, Myles T. ....Honolulu, HI
Yamamoto, Randall Y., (Atty. At Law, A Law Corp.) ....Honolulu, HI
Yamamoto, Taeko ....New York, NY
Yamamoto, Terence S. ....Honolulu, HI
Yamamoto, Tosh G. ....Sacramento, CA
Yamamoto, Tosh G., A Professional Corporation ....Sacramento, CA
Yamamoto, Victoria M. ....Sacramento, CA
Yamamoto, Wynde M. ....Honolulu, HI
Yamamoto & Yamamoto, L.L.P.
Los Angeles, CA
Yamamura, Jon T. ....Honolulu, HI
Yamanaga, Bruce K. ....Department of Justice, Antitrust Division, GV
Yamanaka, John Morgan ....Santa Ana, CA
Yamanaka, Keith Tohru ....Sacramento, CA
Yamane, Ernest Y. ....Honolulu, HI
Yamane, John D. ....Honolulu, HI
Yamane, Niall G. ....Redwood City, CA
Yamano, John Y. ....Honolulu, HI
Yamaoka, Joseph H. ....Philadelphia, PA
Yamasaki, George, Jr. ....San Francisco, CA
Yamasaki, Jean Kim ....Berkeley, CA
Yamasaki, Makoto ....Irwindale, CA
Yamase, Dennis K. ....Koloa, HI
Yamashiro, Betty O. ....Claremont, CA
Newport Beach, CA
Yamashiro, Dean M. ....Honolulu, HI
Yamashiro, Donna S. ....Torrance, CA
Yamashiro, Li-Ann ....Honolulu, HI
Yamashiro, Maureen D. ....Chicago, IL
Yamashiro, Stephen K. ....Hilo, HI
Yamashita, Brent K. ....Honolulu, HI
Yamashita, David L. ....Mount Vernon, WA
Yamashita, Francis I. ....Honolulu, HI
Yamashita, Laura E. ....Seattle, WA
Yamashita, Lynn R. ....San Francisco, CA
Yamashita, Russel H. ....Honolulu, HI
Yamashita, Stephanie J. ....Yorba Linda, CA
Yamashita, Wesley F. ....Las Vegas, NV
Yamat, Michael A. ....Milwaukee, WI
Yamatani, Micky ....Honolulu, HI
Yamate, Gordon T. ....San Carlos, CA
Yamate, Noreen ....San Francisco, CA
Yamate, Sandra ....Chicago, IL
Yamato, Junpei ....Los Angeles, CA
Yamato, Lori L. ....Newport Beach, CA
Yamauchi, Brad ....San Francisco, CA
Yamauchi, Darlene Noriko ....Honolulu, HI
Yamauchi, Robert M. ....Honolulu, HI
Yamaya, Julie M. ....Lincolnshire, IL
Yambert, Jon ....Chicago, IL
Yamin, David ....Boston, MA
Yamin, Dianne E. ....Danbury, CT
Yamin, Joseph F. ....Bloomfield Hills, MI
Yamin, Joseph P. ....Hartford, CT
Yamin, Michael G., (P.C.) ....New York, NY
Yamin, Raymond P. ....Danbury, CT
Yamin, Robert J. ....Danbury, CT
Yamin & Yamin ....Danbury, CT
Yamini, Donna ....Los Angeles, CA
Yamini, Rola Jeanne ....San Francisco, CA
Yammine, Ralph R. ....Miami, FL
Yamner, David L. ....New York, NY
Yamner, Morris ....Newark, NJ
New York, NY
Yamouti, Victor N. ....Morganton, NC
Yampell, Elliott ....Haddonfield, NJ
Yampell, Sandra E. ....Cherry Hill, NJ
Yampolsky, Edward M. ....Grand Rapids, MI
Yampolsky, Harvey A. ....Washington, DC
Yampolsky, Mace J. ....Las Vegas, NV
Yampolsky, Robert S. ....St. Joseph, MI

Yamuder, Sheryl Ann ....Washington, DC
Yan, Betty Y. ....New York, NY
Yan, James S. ....Pasadena, CA
Yan, Karol M. ....San Francisco, CA
Yan, Tina ....Las Vegas, NV
Yana, Joseph V. ....Oshkosh, WI
Yanacheck, Timothy J. ....Madison, WI
Yanagi, Emilie S. ....Santa Clara, CA
Yanagi, Hanako ....West Linn, OR
Yanagi, Richard A. ....Honolulu, HI
Yanagida & Cooper ....Wailuku, HI
Yanagida, Joy ....Wailuku, HI
Yanagihara, Daniel S. ....Sacramento, CA
Yanagisawa, Jo Anne ....San Francisco, CA
Yanagizawa, Koichi M. ....Los Angeles, CA
Yanarella, Maryann ....White Plains, NY
Yanaros, William D. ....Port Jefferson, NY
Yanas, John J. ....Albany, NY
Yanavok, Jay A. ....Denville, NJ
Yance, James A. ....Mobile, AL
Yancey, Benjamin F., III ....Charleston, WV
Yancey, Benjamin F., Jr. ....Charleston, WV
Yancey, Bruce ....Yuma, AZ
Yancey, Darla L. ....Costa Mesa, CA
Yancey, David W. ....San Francisco, CA
Yancey, Donald L. ....Montgomery, AL
Yancey, Dorothy M. ....Amarillo, TX
Yancey, Elizabeth A. ....Mesa, AZ
Yancey, George Anthony ....Portsmouth, VA
Yancey, H. Lawrence ....Little Rock, AR
Yancey, Howard E., Jr. ....Adel, GA
Yancey, Howard E., Jr., P.C. ....Adel, GA
Yancey, James A. ....Lakeland, FL
Yancey, James A., Jr. ....Brunswick, GA
Yancey, James A., Jr., P.C. ....Brunswick, GA
Yancey, Jay P. ....Kansas City, MO
Yancey, John C. ....Atlanta, GA
Yancey, Joseph B. ....Knoxville, TN
Yancey, Kyle ....Mableton, GA
Yancey, Laurel G. ....Atlanta, GA
Yancey, Mark A. ....Oklahoma City, OK
Yancey, Michael H. ....San Jose, CA
Yancey & Pool ....Marion, NC
Yancey, Quillian S. ....Lakeland, FL
Yancey, R. Lee ....Danville, VA
Yancey, Reginald R. ....Lynchburg, VA
Yancey, Richard L. ....Marietta, GA
Yancey, Robert Anthony ....Marion, NC
Yancey, Stephen R., II ....Shreveport, LA
Yancey, Thad, Jr. ....Troy, AL
Yancey, Thomas H. ....Washington, DC
Yancey, Truman E. ....Fayetteville, AR
Yancey, Virginia E. ....Brooklyn, NY
Yancey, Wayne C. ....Warner Robins, GA
Yancey, Willie T., II ....Savannah, GA
Yancey Callahan, Teri ....Columbus, GA
Yanchek, John A. ....Sarasota, FL
Yanchuck, Joel P. ....St. Petersburg, FL
Yanchunis, John A. ....St. Petersburg, FL
Tampa, FL
Yancich, Milan ....San Francisco, CA
Yanco, Glen ....Peabody, MA
Yancy, Edward L. ....Lexington, KY
Yancy, Gregory ....Bowie, MD
Yancy, Howard ....Austin, TX
Yand, James T. ....Seattle, WA
Yanda, Julie Fry ....Kansas City, MO
Yandell, Eric ....Salem, OR
Yandell, Ron L. ....Wichita Falls, TX
Yandell, William H. ....Anthony, KS
Yandle, David S. ....Charleston, SC
Yandle, Horace ....Miami, FL
Yandle, Staci M. ....East St. Louis, IL
Yandle, Stephen T. ....New Haven, CT
Yando, David A. ....Tacoma, WA
Yando & Kent, P.S. ....Tacoma, WA
Yandoli, Gabriel A. ....Montgomeryville, PA
Yandow, Joanne Vonasek ....Hartford, CT
Yandrasitz, John E. ....Madison, NJ
Yandrich, Eric J. ....Pittsburgh, PA
Yandrisevits, Frank W. ....Northampton, PA
Yanecek, Ted O. ....Iowa City, IA
Yaneff & Cosgrove ....Sioux City, IA
Yaneff, Michael G. ....Sioux City, IA
Yaneff, Paul J. ....Sioux City, IA
Yanega, Thomas ....East Meadow, NY
Yanello, Ralph ....Danville, CA
Yanes, Katherine Earle ....Tampa, FL
Yanes, Marta ....Treasury Department, Internal Revenue Service, GV
Yanes, Raul F. ....New York, NY
Yanes, Robin Jacob ....Santa Monica, CA
Yanez, Antonio, Jr. ....New York, NY
Yanez, Kerry X. ....Fort Worth, TX
Yánez, Liliana C. ....New York, NY
Yanez, Linda Reyna ....Corpus Christi, TX
Yanez, Victoria ....Santa Rosa, CA
Yang, Anders C. ....Cambridge, MA
Yang, Angela ....Los Angeles, CA
Yang, Arlene R. ....New York, NY
Yang, Christine H. T. ....Chicago, IL
Yang, Chun Y. ....Holtsville, NY
Yang, Cora G. ....Chicago, IL
Yang, David Jia-Yih ....San Francisco, CA
Yang, Edward C. ....Alhambra, CA
Yang, Elizabeth R. ....Washington, DC
Yang, Emeline ....Dallas, TX
Yang, Frank Z. ....Wilmington, DE
Yang, Grace H. ....Tampa, FL
Yang, Henry E. ....Los Angeles, CA
Yang, Iris P. ....Sacramento, CA
Yang, Jack ....Menlo Park, CA
Yang, Jaw Fong ....Brooklyn, NY
Yang, Jennifer C. ....Los Angeles, CA
Yang, Jenny R. ....Department of Justice, Civil Rights Division, GV
Yang, Jesse Jei ....Sacramento, CA
Yang, Joe Y. ....Minneapolis, MN

Yang, John C. ....Washington, DC
Yang, Joseph ....Palo Alto, CA
Yang, Joyce C. ....New York, NY
Yang, Julie ....Wilmington, DE
Yang, Jun ....New York, NY
Yang, Katie ....New York, NY
Yang, Katy H.H. ....Los Angeles, CA
Yang, Kenneth ....San Francisco, CA
Yang, Kimberly F. ....Los Angeles, CA
Yang, Leslie S. ....Washington, DC
Yang, Li ....New York, NY
Yang, Lucy ....Kalamazoo, MI
Yang, Lyndane ....Los Angeles, CA
Yang, Maile ....Los Angeles, CA
Yang, Maiya ....Fresno, CA
Yang, Margaret Y. ....New York, NY
Yang, Michael Tsung-Shun
Santa Barbara, CA
Yang, Michele Yeun ....Los Angeles, CA
Yang, Mina S. ....San Diego, CA
Yang, P. Heejong ....New York, NY
Yang, Paul ....Menlo Park, CA
Yang, Phillip Seung il ....New York, NY
Yang, Phoebe L. ....Washington, DC
Yang, Richard P. ....Los Angeles, CA
Yang, Roberta M. ....Los Angeles, CA
Yang, Shane ....Los Angeles, CA
Yang, Shin P. ....San Gabriel, CA
Yang, Stan K. ....Los Angeles, CA
Yang, Stan Y. ....Garden City, NY
Yang, Stephen N. ....San Francisco, CA
Yang, Sue Pai ....Bridgewater, NJ
Yang, Sue Pai, L.L.C., Law Offices of
Bridgewater, NJ
Yang, Terrence C. ....New York, NY
Yang, Theresa Li-Siu ....Mount Arlington, NJ
Yang, Thomas ....Dallas, TX
Yang, Thomas W. ....New York, NY
Yang, Timothy Dae ....Houston, TX
Yang, Tseming C. ....South Royalton, VT
Yang, Virginia I. ....Chicago, IL
Yang, Vivian W. ....Los Angeles, CA
Yang, Wein-ing ....Los Angeles, CA
Yang, Wesley ....Pittsburgh, PA
Yang, Xusheng ....New York, NY
Yang, Ya-Ting ....Palo Alto, CA
Yang & Yom, LLP ....New York, NY
Yang, Yuelin T. ....San Jose, CA
Yang, Yun Jung ....Wheaton, MD
Yanger & Smith ....Crystal River, FL
Tampa, FL
Yanger, Thomas R. ....Sacramento, CA
Yanger, William H., Jr. ....Crystal River, FL
Tampa, FL
Yanger, William L. ....Tampa, FL
Yangouyian, Licia Ann ....Dearborn, MI
Yang-Patyi, Josephine ....Syracuse, NY
Yanibas, Aris F. ....Chicago, IL
Yanich, Noah Eliezer ....Rochester Hills, MI
Yanick, Miles A. ....Seattle, WA
Yanik, Glenn G. ....Wilkes-Barre, PA
Yanik, Mary Kay ....Le Roy, NY
Yanikowski, James J. ....Beaver Dam, WI
Yaninek, John F. ....Harrisburg, PA
Yaninek, Kathleen Doyle ....Harrisburg, PA
Yanisch, Richard F. ....Elm Grove, WI
Yanity, Gerald J. ....Latrobe, PA
Yanity, Joseph Blair ....Athens, OH
Yanity, Robert J. ....Portland, OR
Yank, Robert W. ....San Francisco, CA
Yank, Ronald ....San Francisco, CA
Yankala, Wayne M. ....Milwaukee, WI
Yankaver, Marian P. ....Boston, MA
Yanke, Gian-Carlo M. ....La Jolla, CA
Yankee, James A. ....Port Angeles, WA
Yankelevits, Daniel M. ....Los Angeles, CA
Yankelevits, Lori M. ....Los Angeles, CA
Yankelevitz, Robert H. ....Bayside, NY
Yankelevitz, Steven B. ....Santa Monica, CA
Yankelove, Alex ....Randallstown, MD
Yankelunas, Edward ....Buffalo, NY
Yanko, Richard F. ....Scottsdale, AZ
Yankovich, Charles E. ....Baltimore, MD
Yankovich, John ....Stamford, CT
Yankoviz, Frank T. ....Monett, MO
Yankovsky, Kristine E. ....Woodside, CA
Yankow, Keith M., Law Offices
Nantucket, MA
Yankowitz, Arthur I. ....Floral Park, NY
Yankowitz, B.J. ....Los Angeles, CA
Yankowitz, David E. ....Livingston, NJ
Yankowitz, Goldsmith & Sayers, P.A.
Livingston, NJ
Yankowski, Edw. J. ....Berlin, WI
Yankowsky, Kevin W. ....Houston, TX
Yanks, Harvey A. ....Philadelphia, PA
Yanks, Murray P. ....Miami, FL
Yanks, Nancy J. ....New York, NY
Yankwich & Associates ....Boston, MA
Cambridge, MA
Yankwich, Leon R. ....Cambridge, MA
Yankwich, Richard I. ....Palo Alto, CA
Yankwitt, George B. ....New York, NY
Yankwitt, Rochelle H. ....New York, NY
Yankwitt, Russell M. ....New York, NY
Yann, Robert M. ....Louisville, KY
Yannacone, Fay, Baldo & Daly ....Media, PA
Yannacone, John J. ....Media, PA
Yannacone, Victor John, Jr. ....Patchogue, NY
Yannacone & Yannacone, P.C.
Patchogue, NY
Yannakakis, Anne Kanela ....St. Louis, MO
Yannas, Peggy P. ....New York, NY
Yannatos, Dionysios ....Hyannis, MA
Yannella, Donald J. ....New York, NY
Yannella, Philip N. ....Philadelphia, PA
Yannelli, F. Chris ....Provo, UT
Yannelli, Frank E. ....Mineola, NY

Yannelli, Zevin & Civardi ... Mineola, NY
Yannello, Judith Ann
Department of Defense, Armed Services Board of Contract Appeals, GV
Yannello, Karen M. ... Department of Defense, Office of the General Counsel, GV
Yannerella, Don A. ... Wheeling, WV
Yannett, Bruce E. ... New York, NY
Yannetti, Bernard A., Jr. ... Gettysburg, PA
Yannetti, David Ronald ... Cambridge, MA
Yannetti, Tanis M. ... Melrose, MA
Yanney, Fred G. ... Los Angeles, CA
Yanney, Margaret ... New York, NY
Yanney, Pierre R. ... New York, NY
Yanni, Amy ... Pittsfield, MA
Yanni, Catherine A. ... San Francisco, CA
Yanni, Charles J. ... Albany, NY
Yanni, Cheryl Ann ... Blue Bell, PA
Yanni, Joseph A. ... New York, NY
Yanni, Palma R. ... Washington, DC
Yanni, Rami S. ... Los Angeles, CA
Yannias, Kathleen C. ... Oak Park, IL
Yanniello, M. Vincent ... Commerce, CA
Yannis, John A. ... Brighton, MA
Yannitelli, Thomas D. ... Tampa, FL
Yanno, J. Drew ... Chestnut Hill, MA
Yannon, Albert A. ... Hilliard, OH
Yannon, Eugene J. ... Bowie, MD
Yannotti, Joseph L. ... Trenton, NJ
Yannucci, Lisa M. ... Falls Church, VA
Yannucci, Samuel A. ... Akron, OH
Yannucci, Thomas D. ... Washington, DC
Yannuzzi, Daniel N. ... La Jolla, CA
Yannuzzi, Joseph P. ... Bethlehem, PA
Yanny & Grieco ... Los Angeles, CA
Yanny, Joseph A., (P.C.) ... Los Angeles, CA
Yano, Francis H. ... Honolulu, HI
Yano, James A. ... Columbus, OH
Yano, Kent T. ... Salt Lake City, UT
Yano, Lester I. ... Los Angeles, CA
Yano, Mas ... Salt Lake City, UT
Yano, Rina ... New York, NY
Yano, Rodd H. ... Honolulu, HI
Yano, Thomas D. ... Lihue, HI
Yano, Vincent H. ... Honolulu, HI
Yanochik, Michael J. ... Houston, TX
Yanof, Michael A. ... Dallas, TX
Yanoff, Amy J. ... Washington, DC
Yanoff, David A. ... Philadelphia, PA
Yanoff, Erica Jay
Federal Energy Regulatory Commission, Office of the General Counsel, GV
Yanoff, Leo ... West Orange, NJ
Yanoff, Michael ... Lansdale, PA
Yanoff, Warren M. ... Worcester, MA
Yanofsky, Carole Jill ... Washington, DC
Yanofsky, Cindy D. ... Boston, MA
Yanofsky, Nancy E.
Commodity Futures Trading Commission, Office of the General Counsel, GV
Yanofsky, Richard M ... Boston, MA
Yanofsky, Seymour I. ... New York, NY
Yanofsky, Stuart Barry ... Miami, FL
Yanohira, Dean Ryu ... Los Angeles, CA
Yanos, Alexander A. ... New York, NY
Yanoshak, John ... Media, PA
Yanover, Frank A. ... Albany, NY
Yanover, Jody Ann ... Forest Hills, NY
Yanover, Lawrence J. ... Santa Barbara, CA
Yanover, Michael I. ... Beverly Hills, CA
Yanover, Stacy Miller ... Kew Gardens, NY
Yanow, Adam J. ... San Anselmo, CA
Yanow, Julie B. ... Burbank, CA
Yanow, Margaret Jean ... New York, NY
Yanow, Paulette B. ... Indian Creek, IL
Yanowitch Law Center ... Miami, FL
Yanowitch, Lawrence T. ... McLean, VA
Yanowitch, Michael H. ... New York, NY
Yanowitch, Paul L. ... Department of Justice, Civil Division, GV
Yanowitch, Peter J. ... Miami, FL
Yanowitz, Alan E. ... Cleveland, OH
Yanowitz, Alan J. ... Rochester, MN
Yanowitz, Bennett ... Cleveland, OH
Yanowitz, Herbert W. ... San Francisco, CA
Yanowitz, Ira S. ... Boston, MA
Yanowitz, Jeffrey Bruce ... New City, NY
Yanowitz, Mark R. ... Philadelphia, PA
Yant, Richard Demarest ... Chicago, IL
Yanta, Virgil, P.C. ... San Antonio, TX
Yanta, Virgil W. ... San Antonio, TX
Yantek, Kenneth R. ... Westlake, OH
Yanthis, George A. ... Albany, NY
Yantis, John G. ... Chattanooga, TN
Yantsos, Laura A. ... Rockville Centre, NY
Yantz, Henry J. ... Setauket, NY
Yanuck, Charles William ... New York, NY
Yanuck, Jeff Scott ... Sherman Oaks, CA
Yanulis, Jane A.
National Labor Relations Board, Office of the General Counsel, GV
Yanz, Gordon I., (P.C.) ... Glendale, CA
Yanz & Hertz ... Glendale, CA
Yao, Alice Y. ... Metuchen, NJ
Yao, Chengxi ... Washington, DC
Yao, David K. ... San Francisco, CA
Yao, Joseph T. ... Plano, TX
Yao, Vivian P. ... Washington, DC
Yap, Beesian ... San Francisco, CA
Yap, Calvin C.S. ... Irvine, CA
Yap, Caroline Vivian ... New York, NY
Yap, Frank K. L., Jr. ... Honolulu, HI
Yap, Franklin H. ... Oakland, CA
Yap, Theodore ... Santa Ana, CA
Yapchai, Kimberlee G. ... Taylor, MI
Yapko, Brian A. ... Los Angeles, CA
Yaquinto, Robert, Jr. ... Dallas, TX

Yar, Kajeer ... Dallas, TX
Yarab, Donald S. ... Cleveland, OH
Yarano, Daniel A. ... Minneapolis, MN
Yarashus, Albert L.
Securities and Exchange Commission, Division of Corporation Finance, GV
Yarashus, Valerie A. ... Boston, MA
Yarber, John F. ... Atlanta, GA
Yarber, Michael D. ... Austin, TX
Yarber, Michelle R. ... Chicago, IL
Yarber, Sharon ... Los Angeles, CA
Yarbor, Lori A. ... Evansville, IN
Yarborough, Alma L. ... Baltimore, MD
Yarborough, Bill H. ... Hurst, TX
Yarborough, Charity O'Connell
Houston, TX
Yarborough, Clinton Joseph ... Aiken, SC
Yarborough, David Butler, Jr.
Charleston, SC
Yarborough, Donald V. ... Tyler, TX
Yarborough, F. Hall ... Orangeburg, SC
Yarborough, Garris Neil ... Fayetteville, NC
Yarborough, Hubert E., III ... Columbia, SC
Greenville, SC
Yarborough, Hutto & Jackson
Lexington, SC
Orangeburg, SC
Yarborough, Jan E. ... Winston-Salem, NC
Yarborough Law Firm, The
Fayetteville, NC
Yarborough, Margaret Moore
Jacksonville, FL
Yarborough, Ray Coit, Jr. ... Timmonsville, SC
Yarborough, Richard F., Jr.
Columbia, MS
Yarborough, W. Daniel, Jr. ... Greenville, SC
Yarborough, William D. ... Knoxville, TN
Yarb-Petersen, Susan E. ... Cleveland, OH
Yarbro, Alan D. ... Baltimore, MD
Yarbro & Associates ... Cloudcroft, NM
Yarbro, Jason G. ... Dyersburg, TN
Yarbro, R. Michael ... Birmingham, AL
Yarbro, Roger E. ... Cloudcroft, NM
Yarbrough, Alex A. ... Hartselle, AL
Yarbrough, Benjamin A. ... Charlotte, NC
Yarbrough, Brian Garrett ... Austin, TX
Yarbrough, D. Coleman ... Montgomery, AL
Yarbrough, David L. ... Midland, TX
Yarbrough, Donald A. ... Fort Lauderdale, FL
Yarbrough, Edward F. ... San Antonio, TX
Yarbrough, Edward M. ... Nashville, TN
Yarbrough & Elliott, P.C. ... Dallas, TX
Denton, TX
Yarbrough, Fletcher L. ... Dallas, TX
Yarbrough, George M., Jr. ... Dallas, TX
Yarbrough, Gina M. ... Boston, MA
Yarbrough, J. Jack ... Nacogdoches, TX
Yarbrough, Jack D. ... Nashville, TN
Yarbrough, Jameson & Gray ... Galveston, TX
Yarbrough, Janis L., P.C. ... Galveston, TX
Yarbrough, Jemal K. ... Los Angeles, CA
Yarbrough, John D., Jr. ... Waterbury, CT
Yarbrough, John N. ... Whitehouse, TX
Yarbrough, John T. ... St. Louis, MO
Yarbrough, Jonathan W. ... New Bern, NC
Yarbrough, Katherine P. ... Washington, DC
Yarbrough, Kenneth E. ... Birmingham, AL
Yarbrough, Kenneth L. ... Corpus Christi, TX
Yarbrough, Kenney ... Denton, TX
Yarbrough, Kent L. ... Denver, CO
Yarbrough, Larry ... Jackson, MS
Yarbrough, Larry W. ... Marietta, GA
Yarbrough, Larry W., P.C. ... Marietta, GA
Yarbrough, Marilyn V. ... Chapel Hill, NC
Yarbrough, Maura Lynn ... Pittsburgh, PA
Yarbrough, Michael K. ... Columbus, OH
Yarbrough, Nolan Michael ... Fayetteville, AR
Yarbrough, Paul L. ... Littlefield, TX
Yarbrough, Paul T. ... Albuquerque, NM
Yarbrough, Robert E. ... Boston, MA
Yarbrough, Robert J. ... Media, PA
Yarbrough, Ron A. ... Jackson, MS
Yarbrough, Scott M. ... New York, NY
Yarbrough, Sonya D. ... Atlanta, GA
Yarbrough, Steven B. ... Tempe, AZ
Yarbrough, Steven L. ... Crescent City, CA
Yarbrough, Susan L. ... Houston, TX
Yarbrough, T. Wayne ... Beaufort, SC
Yarbrough, Trey ... Tyler, TX
Yarbrough, W. Andrew ... Waynesboro, TN
Yarbrough, William A. ... Vidalia, LA
Yarbrough, Willis R. ... Tulsa, OK
Yarbrough, Wright & Dunn, L.L.P.
Tempe, AZ
Yarc, Mariellen ... Long Beach, CA
Yarc, Mary E. ... Waukegan, IL
Yarchin, Barry S. ... Fort Lauderdale, FL
Yarcusko, Alan C. ... Cleveland, OH
Yard, Brian M. ... Greenwich, CT
Yard, Keith Elliott ... Morris, IL
Yard, Mary Julianne ... Clearwater, FL
Yarden, David ... Woodland Hills, CA
Yarden, Linda ... New York, NY
Yardley, A.C. ... Oklahoma City, OK
Yardley, Benjamin ... Yarmouth, ME
Yardley, Dan ... Livingston, MT
Yardley, Jack ... Livingston, MT
Yardley, John H. ... Nashville, TN
Yardley, Karen D. ... Santa Monica, CA
Yardley, Laurie J. ... Lincoln, NE
Yardley, Mary Jane ... Chicago, IL
Yardley, Steve N. ... Birmingham, MI
Yardley, Thomas H. ... Cocoa, FL
Yardley, Thomas P., Jr. ... Chicago, IL
Yardley & Yardley ... Livingston, MT
Yardum, LeVone A. ... Encino, CA
Yardum-Hunter, Alice M. ... Encino, CA
Yardumian, Gary E. ... Long Beach, CA

Yared, Paul D. ... Caledonia, MI
Yared, Woodrow A. ... Grand Rapids, MI
Yarema, Geoffrey S. ... Los Angeles, CA
Yarema, John M. ... Bushnell, FL
Yaremko, Karen ... Bronx, NY
Yares, Howard S. ... Philadelphia, PA
Yarett, Jordan E. ... New York, NY
Yarger, David A. ... Versailles, MO
Yarger, Jonathon M. ... Cleveland, OH
Yarger, Larry D. ... Battle Creek, MI
Yarham, Patrice R. T. ... Cleveland, OH
Yarin, James Edward ... Boston, MA
Yarington, Barbara ... Seattle, WA
Yarington, Barbara J. ... Lexington Park, MD
Yaris, Greg ... Los Angeles, CA
Yariv, Amir ... Los Angeles, CA
Yarkin, Mark R. ... New York, NY
Yarkin, Ray Ellen ... Bay Harbor Islands, FL
Yarkon, Rachel ... New York, NY
Yarlas, Stephen B. ... Warwick, RI
Yarling, Janet K. ... Livonia, MI
Yarling, Richard W. ... Indianapolis, IN
Yarling & Robinson ... Indianapolis, IN
Yarmel, Richard T. ... Rochester, NY
Yarmey, Richard A. ... Wilkes-Barre, PA
Yarmis, Derek B. ... Baltimore, MD
Yarmolinsky, Adam ... Washington, DC
Yarmosh, Linda K. ... Boothbay Harbor, ME
Yarmoshuk, Lisa M. ... Washington, DC
Yarmoski, John P. ... Los Angeles, CA
Yarmovsky, Max ... San Jose, CA
Yarmuth, Richard C. ... Seattle, WA
Yarmuth Wilsdon Calfo PLLC
Seattle, WA
Yarn, Douglas Hurt ... Atlanta, GA
Yarnall, Rick A. ... Sioux Falls, SD
Yarnell, Bryan James ... Houston, TX
Yarnell, David M. ... St. Albans, VT
Yarnell, Harold E., Jr. ... Woodland Hills, CA
Yarnell, James Scot ... Sacramento, CA
Yarnell, Jules E. ... Rye Brook, NY
Yarnell, Kathleen A. ... St. Albans, VT
Yarnell, Michael A. ... Phoenix, AZ
Yarnell, Scott F. ... Washington, DC
Yarnell, Stephen V. ... Philadelphia, PA
Yarnell, Vernon E., Jr. ... Seattle, WA
Yarnevich, Ernest N., Jr.
Kansas City, MO
Yarnevich, George W. ... Salina, KS
Yarnoff, Denise R. ... Paoli, PA
Yarnoff, Michael K. ... Jenkintown, PA
Yarnold, Barbara M. ... North Miami, FL
Yaro, John M. ... Cleveland, OH
Yaro, Michael ... Los Angeles, CA
Yaro, William ... New York, NY
Yaron & Associates ... Los Angeles, CA
Orange, CA
San Diego, CA
San Francisco, CA
Yaron, George D. ... San Francisco, CA
Yaron, Iris C. ... New York, NY
Yaros, Alma Proffitt ... Cincinnati, OH
Yaros, G. David ... Cincinnati, OH
Yaros, Neal ... New York, NY
Yaroschuk, Robert H. ... Doylestown, PA
Yarosh, David ... Boston, MA
Yarosh, David J. ... Minneapolis, MN
Yarosh, Feldman & Yarosh ... Boston, MA
Yarosh, James A. ... Minneapolis, MN
Yarosh, Laurence ... Los Angeles, CA
Yarosh, Phyllis K. ... Boston, MA
Yarosh, Steven M. ... Chicago, IL
Yaroshefsky, Ellen C. ... New York, NY
Yaroslow, Gerald M. ... Los Angeles, CA
Yarotsky, Marvin M. ... Houston, TX
Yarowsky, Jonathan R. ... Washington, DC
Yarowsky, Sol M. ... Kansas City, MO
Yarra, Robert W. ... Fresno, CA
Yarrell, Ellen A. ... Houston, TX
Yarrell, Ellen A., P.C. ... Houston, TX
Yarrington, Hugh J. ... Washington, DC
Yarrington, Robert B. ... Pensacola, FL
Yarrish, Karen Creasia ... Harrisburg, PA
Yarsky, Kenneth J., II ... Pittsburgh, PA
Yartz, Eric C. ... Houston, TX
Yarus, Claudia J. ... St. Petersburg, FL
Yarusinsky, Steven ... Newark, NJ
Yaruss, Howard S. ... Philadelphia, PA
Yarvin, Eric B. ... Bethesda, MD
Yarvis, Lori A. ... New York, NY
Yarvis, Matthew A. ... Riverside, CA
Yaryan, Timothy H. B. ... Sacramento, CA
Yas, David ... Boston, MA
Yasdick, M. Therese ... Richland, WA
Yasensky, Thomas ... Hartford, CT
Yaser, Vickie ... Indianapolis, IN
Yasgour, Abraham J. ... Bronx, NY
Yasgur, Samuel S. ... New York, NY
White Plains, NY
Yasgur, Stevan S. ... Minneapolis, MN
Yasgur, Stevan S., P.C. ... Minneapolis, MN
Yashar, Karen L. ... Minneapolis, MN
Yashar, Marjorie J. ... Providence, RI
Yashar, Susan A.
Securities and Exchange Commission, Office of the General Counsel, GV
Yashari-Becher, Carolyn ... Los Angeles, CA
Yashinsky, Jeffrey P. ... Atlanta, GA
Yashko, Gary G. ... Columbus, OH
Yashko, Michael S. ... Columbus, OH
Yasinow, Aaron ... Buffalo, NY
Yasinow, Stephen K. ... Towson, MD
Yasinski, Julianna C. ... Los Angeles, CA
Yaskin, Herbert H. ... Philadelphia, PA
Yaskin, Judith A. ... Trenton, NJ
Yaskin, Mark ... Philadelphia, PA
Yaskin, Richard E. ... Voorhees, NJ
Yaskin & Winicov ... Philadelphia, PA

Yasnogorodsky, Eugena ... Los Angeles, CA
Yass, Robert K. ... Hartford, CT
Yassa, Nadia A. ... Boston, MA
Yassaei, Neda S. ... Los Angeles, CA
Yassen, Thomas A. ... Chicago, IL
Yassin, Omar Jamal ... Los Angeles, CA
Yassky, David S. ... Brooklyn, NY
Yassky & Lederle, P.C. ... New York, NY
Yassky, Lester H. ... New York, NY
Yassky, Linda ... New York, NY
Yassky, Rachel ... Philadelphia, PA
Yasso, Jabran G. ... Southfield, MI
Yast, C. Joseph ... Chicago, IL
Yastrow, Joseph H. ... Chicago, IL
Yastrow, Shelby ... Chicago, IL
Yasuda, John P. ... Santa Ana, CA
Yasuda, Ted K. ... Chicago, IL
Yasui, Robert K. ... Los Angeles, CA
Yasui, Scott S. ... Seattle, WA
Yasunaga, Miles N. ... Honolulu, HI
Yasunaga, Milton M. ... Honolulu, HI
Yasutake, Darrel K. ... San Francisco, CA
Yaszczemski, Chester B. ... Harrison, NJ
Yatchisin, John, Jr. ... New York, NY
Yateman, Lance Ira ... Glen Burnie, MD
Yateman, Sidney H. ... Seaside, CA
Yater, Steven D. ... Louisville, KY
Yates, Alfred G., Jr. ... Pittsburgh, PA
Yates, Amy E. ... Chicago, IL
Yates, Angela M. ... San Diego, CA
Yates, Anne W. ... Sudbury, MA
Yates, Anne Winfield ... Washington, DC
Yates & Associates, P.C. ... Portland, OR
Yates, Barbara J. ... Tallahassee, FL
Yates, Bryan R. ... Seattle, WA
Yates, C. Daniel ... Indianapolis, IN
Yates, Cara ... Columbia, SC
Yates, Carl E. ... Springfield, MO
Yates, Charles ... Rockville, MD
Yates, Christine T. ... Fort Lauderdale, FL
Yates, Christopher G. ... Palo Alto, CA
Yates, Christopher S. ... San Francisco, CA
Yates, Craig W. ... Bordentown, NJ
Yates, D. Farrington ... New York, NY
Yates, Dale R. ... Weedsport, NY
Yates, Daniel Thomas ... Houston, TX
Yates, David F. ... St. Louis, MO
Yates, David J. ... Farmington Hills, MI
Yates, David P. ... New York, NY
Yates, David W. ... Chesterfield, MO
Yates, David W. ... Boone, NC
Yates, Donald A. ... San Diego, CA
Yates, Donald R., II ... Ashland, KY
Yates & Dumas ... Morrilton, AR
Yates, E. Clayton ... Vero Beach, FL
Yates, Earl E. ... Mountlake Terrace, WA
Yates, Edmund R. ... Dallas, TX
Yates, Edward E. ... Washington, DC
Yates, Edwin L. ... Montgomery, AL
Yates, Elinor K. ... Frederick, MD
Yates, Ernest F. ... Malibu, CA
Yates & Fann, P.A. ... Miami Shores, FL
Yates, G. Kenneth ... Salem, SC
Yates, Gary R. ... Lawrenceville, GA
Yates, Gary S. ... Los Angeles, CA
Yates, George Holton ... Virginia Beach, VA
Yates, George Holton, & Associates, P.C.
Virginia Beach, VA
Yates, Georges H.G. ... Seattle, WA
Yates, Gladys L. ... Roanoke, VA
Yates, Glen L., Jr. ... Burlington, VT
Yates, Greg R. ... Washington, DC
Yates, Gregory A. ... Beverly Hills, CA
Yates, Gregory A. ... Los Angeles, CA
Yates, H. Robert, III ... Charlottesville, VA
Yates, H. Wade ... Asheboro, NC
Yates, Harvey ... West Helena, AR
Yates, Herbert D. ... Houston, TX
Yates, Howard C. ... Morrilton, AR
Yates, Irene W. ... Cincinnati, OH
Yates, Jack M. ... Abilene, TX
Yates, James ... Kansas City, KS
Yates, James A., III ... Winston-Salem, NC
Yates, James B. ... Toledo, OH
Yates, James E., III ... Statesboro, GA
Yates, James M., Jr. ... Raleigh, NC
Yates, Janice E. ... Cincinnati, OH
Yates, Jeffrey A. ... Dallas, TX
Yates, Jeffrey M. ... Alexandria, VA
Yates, Jennifer C. ... New York, NY
Yates, Jennifer Sue ... Jacksonville, FL
Yates, Jerome J. ... Boca Raton, FL
Yates, Joe H. ... Florence, AL
Yates, Joel D. ... Oskaloosa, IA
What Cheer, IA
Yates, John ... Pittsfield, MA
Yates, John C. ... Atlanta, GA
Yates, John G. ... San Antonio, TX
Yates, John H. ... Victorville, CA
Yates, John J. ... Kansas City, MO
Yates, John L. ... Fort Worth, TX
Yates, John R. ... Little Rock, AR
Yates, John R., Jr. ... Los Angeles, CA
Yates, Jonah Ted ... Cape Girardeau, MO
Yates, Jonathan L. ... Charleston, SC
Yates, Joseph S. ... New Castle, KY
Yates, Joseph S., P.S.C. ... New Castle, KY
Yates, Joseph W., III ... Raleigh, NC
Yates, Julie M. ... Laramie, WY
Yates, Karen E. ... New Haven, CT
Yates, Katherine S. ... San Antonio, TX
Yates, Kathleen A. ... Sacramento, CA
Yates, Kathrin E. ... New Orleans, LA
Yates, Kathryn D. ... Key West, FL
Yates, Kathryn J. ... Greenwich, CT
Yates, Keith O. ... Dayton, WA
Yates, Kelly Monroe ... Seattle, WA
Yates, Kenneth ... Arlington, VA

Yeilding, Manly .... **Birmingham, AL**
Yeilding, Ormend G. .... **Orlando, FL**
Yeilding, Ralph Howard .... **Birmingham, AL**
Yeiser, Ted M., Jr. .... **Memphis, TN**
Yekel, Stephen R. .... Savannah, GA
Yekikian, Henry .... **Los Angeles, CA**
Yeldell, Eric B. .... Los Angeles, CA
Yeldell, James E. .... **Bastrop, LA**
Yeldezian, Gary .... Baltimore, MD
Yelen, Barry A. .... Wilkes-Barre, PA
Yelen, David .... Coral Gables, FL
Yelen, Howard Y. .... Pembroke Pines, FL
Yelen, Jan A. .... Coral Gables, FL
Yelen, Martin .... Coral Gables, FL
Yelen, Mitchell A. .... Miami, FL
Yelen, Sandor .... Wilkes-Barre, PA
Yelen, Suzanne .... **Washington, DC**
Yelen & Yelen, P.A. .... Coral Gables, FL
Yelenak, William P. .... **Cheshire, CT**
Yelenick, Mary T. .... **New York, NY**
Yelenik, Ronald G.
Consumer Product Safety Commission, Office of Compliance, GV
Yelenosky, Stephanie A. .... **Orlando, FL**
Yeley, Vicki A. .... Redwood City, CA
Yelin, David B. .... **Chicago, IL**
Yelisetty, Krishnaiah Gupta
Los Angeles, CA
Yelish, Mark L. .... Port Orchard, WA
Yelkin, Kimberly A., (P.C.) .... **Austin, TX**
Yelkovac, Peter G. .... **St. Louis, MO**
Yelland, Janet S. .... Menlo Park, CA
Yelle, J. Jeffrey .... Springfield, MA
Yelle, Patricia E. .... Simi Valley, CA
Yellen, Barry J. .... **New York, NY**
Yellen & Boland .... Buffalo, NY
Yellen, Cindy A. .... **New York, NY**
Yellen, David M. .... Lockport, NY
Yellen, David N. .... Hempstead, NY
Yellen, Dwight .... **Hackensack, NJ**
New York, NY
Yellen, James D. .... **New York, NY**
Yellen, Jeffrey A. .... Farmington Hills, MI
Yellen, Jonathan H. .... **White Plains, NY**
Yellen, Kenneth J. .... **Atlanta, GA**
Yellen, Larry I. .... Chicago, IL
Yellen, Richard D. .... Buffalo, NY
Yellen, Robert M. .... **New York, NY**
Yellen, Susan G. .... White Plains, NY
Yellig, Terry R. .... **Washington, DC**
Yellin, Barry E. .... **Atlantic City, NJ**
Yellin, C. Robert .... Chicago, IL
Yellin, Dean R. .... New Orleans, LA
Yellin & Goldner .... Newton, MA
Yellin, Harold B. .... **Savannah, GA**
Yellin, Herbert F. .... New York, NY
Yellin, Ira C. .... Westborough, MA
Yellin, Ira E. .... Los Angeles, CA
Yellin, Jacob M. .... **Burbank, CA**
Yellin, Jeffrey C. .... Encino, CA
Yellin, John D. .... Newton, MA
Yellin, Jonathan D. .... **Boston, MA**
Yellin, Marc J., (P.L.C.) .... **New Orleans, LA**
Yellin, Melvin A. .... **New York, NY**
Yellin, Stanley J. .... **Secaucus, NJ**
Yellin, Stephen I. .... Brookline, MA
Yellin, Susan Denburg .... **Manhasset, NY**
New York, NY
Yellin, Susanne J. .... Melville, NY
Yellin, William C. .... Waukesha, WI
Yellon, Donald J. .... San Francisco, CA
Yellon, Herman .... Mineola, NY
Yellowtail, James .... Helena, MT
Yelman, Tara Lynn .... San Diego, CA
Yelnick, Marc M. .... San Mateo, CA
Yelnosky, Maryann .... **Portland, OR**
Yelovich & Flower .... **Somerset, PA**
Yelovich, James B. .... **Somerset, PA**
Yelsky, Debra A. .... **Cleveland, OH**
Yelsky, Jeffrey .... Cleveland, OH
Yelsky, Jerome A. .... Los Angeles, CA
Yelsky, Leonard W. .... Cleveland, OH
Yelton, Ballard Jay, III .... **Kalamazoo, MI**
Yelton, Ernest E. .... Brazil, IN
Yelton, Farfour, McCartney & Lutz, P.A.
Lincolnton, NC
Rutherfordton, NC
Shelby, NC
Yelton, Fred G. .... Laramie, WY
Yelton, Geoffrey B. .... Anderson, IN
Yelton, James A. .... Batesville, MS
Yelton, Jennifer L. .... **Dallas, TX**
Yelton & Kehl, Ltd. .... **Chicago, IL**
Yelton, Kim G. .... Bellaire, TX
Yelton, Nancy Barrickman .... Frankfort, KY
Yelton, Paul R. .... Bethel, OH
Yelton, Robert C., III .... **Chicago, IL**
Yelton, Robert W. .... **Shelby, NC**
Yelverton, Ann-Kelley .... Washington, DC
Yelverton, Donna Vandever
Baton Rouge, LA
Yelverton, Henry L. .... Lake Charles, LA
Yelverton, James K. .... **Lake Charles, LA**
Yelverton, Ralph A. .... **Jackson, MS**
Yelverton, Stephen Thomas
Washington, DC
Yelvington, John J. .... Mattoon, IL
Yemane-Brehan, Efrem .... Alexandria, VA
Yemc, William A. .... **Wilmington, DE**
Yemen, Arpo .... Mission Viejo, CA
Yemin, Edward .... Westfield, NJ
Yempuku, Roy Y. .... **Hermosa Beach, CA**
Honolulu, HI
Yen, Alfred C. .... Newton, MA
Yen, Dominic F. .... Cleveland, OH
Yen, Elizabeth C. .... **Bridgeport, CT**
New Haven, CT
Yen, Lina .... **San Francisco, CA**
Yen, Linda .... Albuquerque, NM
Yen, Lulu .... **San Francisco, CA**
Yen, Mallun .... **Menlo Park, CA**
Yen, Marianne .... **New York, NY**
Yen & Pilch, P.L.C. .... Phoenix, AZ
Yen, Robert E. .... Phoenix, AZ
Yen, Thomas .... **San Francisco, CA**
Yen, Wen .... New York, NY
Yendes, Carl Stephen .... Springfield, MO
Yendes, Nancy Kelley .... Springfield, MO
Yenerall, Paul M. .... **Pittsburgh, PA**
Yengich, Rich & Xaiz .... **Salt Lake City, UT**
Yengich, Ronald J. .... **Salt Lake City, UT**
Yengoyan, Alan .... Fresno, CA
Yeniscavich, William W. .... Woodbridge, VA
Yenko, Lawrence J. .... Carson City, NV
Yenner, Lloyd D. .... Kalamazoo, MI
Yenor, Jay M., III .... Orlando, FL
Yenouskas, Joseph F. .... **Washington, DC**
Yenovkian, Richard H. .... Sacramento, CA
Yenowine, Donna B. .... Louisville, KY
Yens, Laura D. .... **Washington, DC**
Yenser, Nancy E. .... **Gainesville, FL**
Yenson, Lynn, Allen & Wosick, P.C.
Albuquerque, NM
Yenson, Terrance P. .... **Albuquerque, NM**
Yent, Rufus L. .... Barstow, CA
Yentz, John P. .... **Milwaukee, WI**
Yentzer, Steven R. .... **Seattle, WA**
Yeo, Derek A.
United States Court of Federal Claims, GV
Yeo, J. Stephen .... Waltham, MA
Yeo, James R. .... Fair Oaks, CA
Yeo, Matthew .... **Washington, DC**
Yeoh, Deborah Yu .... New York, NY
Yeoh, Rosemary H. .... New York, NY
Yeoman, D. Scott .... Pontotoc, MS
Yeoman, Douglas N. .... **Tustin, CA**
Yeoman, Frank J., Jr. .... Topeka, KS
Yeoman, John D. .... Tucson, AZ
Yeoman, Richard D. .... **Greensboro, NC**
Yeoman, Solomon J., II .... Baltimore, MD
Yeomans, Bonnie L. .... **Islandia, NY**
Yeomans, Charles L., III .... Hampton, SC
Yeomans, Deborah A. .... Johnson City, TN
Yeomans, E. D. .... Los Angeles, CA
Yeomans, Gayle A. .... New York, NY
Yeomans, John E. .... Cherry Hill, NJ
Yeomans & Massaro, P.C. .... Syracuse, NY
Yeomans, Patricia M. .... Cleveland, OH
Yeomans, Peter L. .... Oceanside, CA
Yeomans, Ralph L. .... Oceanside, CA
Yeomans, Richard D. .... **Albuquerque, NM**
Yeomans, Robert P. .... Ellison Bay, WI
Yeomans, Ronald R. .... Stamford, CT
Yeomans, William B. .... Syracuse, NY
Yeomans, William R. .... Department of Justice, Civil Rights Division, GV
Yeonas, George P. .... **Vienna, VA**
Yeotis, Dean T. .... **Flint, MI**
Yeotis, Thomas C. .... Flint, MI
Yep, Brian C. .... Lancaster, CA
Yep, Stanley .... Los Angeles, CA
Yepa, David R. .... **Albuquerque, NM**
Santa Fe, NM
Yera, E. J. .... Department of Justice, Antitrust Division, GV
Yerbich, Thomas J. .... **Anchorage, AK**
Yerden, Carol A. .... Concord, NH
Yeres, David J. .... **New York, NY**
Yeretsky, James M. .... **Kansas City, MO**
Yeretsky & Maher, L.L.C.
Overland Park, KS
Kansas City, MO
Yeretzian, Richard Charles .... Forest Hills, NY
Yergeau, Edgar J. .... New York, NY
Yerger, Linda K. .... Norristown, PA
Pottstown, PA
Yerger, Russell D. .... Billings, MT
Yerger, W. Swan .... Jackson, MS
Yergey, D. Arthur .... Orlando, FL
Yergey, David A. Jr. .... Orlando, FL
Yergey, Sherwood L. .... Pottstown, PA
Yergey & Yergey .... Orlando, FL
Yergin, Alan E. .... **New Castle, IN**
Yergin, James A., Jr. .... **Herndon, VA**
Yergin & Yergin .... **New Castle, IN**
Yergler, Jon C. .... **Orlando, FL**
Yerick, Martin R. .... Pago Pago, TT
Yerigan, Debra E. .... Brooklyn Park, MN
Yerigan Law Office, P.A.
Brooklyn Park, MN
Yerke, Gary L. .... Covington, KY
Yerkes, Darden M. .... **Jacksonville, FL**
Yerkes, David John .... Cheshire, CT
Yerkes, Donald E. .... Carlsbad, CA
Yerkes, Kenneth J. .... **Indianapolis, IN**
Yerkes, Lynne M. .... **Walnut Creek, CA**
Yerkes, Robert S. .... **Jacksonville, FL**
Yerkes, Wendy V. .... Indianapolis, IN
Yerkeson, Douglas Alan .... **Dayton, OH**
Yerkovich, Lisa A. .... **Salt Lake City, UT**
Yermack, David L. .... New York, NY
Yermack, Elizabeth McCoy
Gaithersburg, MD
Skillman, NJ
Yerman, Bruce A. .... **Mineola, NY**
Yerman, Fredric W. .... **New York, NY**
Yerman, John W., Jr. .... Toledo, OH
Yerman, Mark J. .... Inverness, FL
Yerman, Pamela C. .... **New York, NY**
Yerman, Robert J. .... Baltimore, MD
Yerman & Smedley, P.A. .... Baltimore, MD
Yerman, William L. .... Bel Air, MD
Yermish, Steven N. .... **Paoli, PA**
Yeroshek, Filomena M. .... Woodland, CA
Yerrakadu, Andrew Amiya .... Elmhurst, NY
Yerrick, William A. .... Culver City, CA
Yerrid, C. Steven .... **Tampa, FL**
Yerrid, Knopik & Krieger, P.A.
Clearwater, FL
St. Petersburg, FL
Tampa, FL
Yeruhim, Yelena .... **Beverly Hills, CA**
Yerushalmi & Associates, L.L.P.
New York, NY
Yerushalmi, Joseph .... **New York, NY**
Yervasi & Coltman, LLP .... Baker City, OR
Yervasi, Damien R. .... Baker City, OR
Yerxa, Charles T., Jr. .... Colusa, CA
Yerxa, Elizabeth Powell .... Raleigh, NC
Yesalonia, Dennis J. .... **Boston, MA**
Yesalonis, Brian E. .... Edison, NJ
Yesawich, Paul J., III .... **Rochester, NY**
Yesawich, Paul J., Jr. .... Cortland, NY
Yesh, David M. .... Detroit, MI
Yeshe, Mark P. .... Helena, MT
Yesk, Michael J. .... Concord, CA
Yesko, Jerome L. .... Hackensack, NJ
Yeskoo, Richard C. .... **Hoboken, NJ**
New York, NY
Yesley, Michael S. .... Los Alamos, NM
Yeslow, Mark B. .... **Fort Myers, FL**
Yeslow, Tod David .... **Plano, TX**
Yesner, Donna Lee .... **Washington, DC**
Yesner, Shawn M. .... **Miami, FL**
Yesnowitz, Gilbert .... Valley Stream, NY
Yesowitch, Irene .... Novato, CA
Yesowitch, William .... Louisville, KY
Yessayan, Raffi Nerses .... Boston, MA
Yessel, Barbara L. .... New York, NY
Yessin, Brent W. .... Frankfort, KY
Yessin, R. & Assocs., P.S.C. .... Frankfort, KY
Yessin, Rudy .... Frankfort, KY
Yesson, Katherine A. .... Del Mar, CA
Yestrumskas, Paul E. .... Westport, CT
Yesu, Frank .... Longmeadow, MA
Yesu, James .... Longmeadow, MA
Yesufu, Issa .... **New York, NY**
Yesukevich, Robert A. .... **Chicago, IL**
Yesutis, Joseph E. .... **Washington, DC**
Yeterian, Joanne Steinkamp .... Hebron, CT
Yetka, Christopher H. .... **Minneapolis, MN**
Yetka, Frank .... Cloquet, MN
Yetka, Lawrence R. .... Cloquet, MN
Yetman, Robert A.
Occupational Safety and Health Review Commission, Administrative Law Judges, GV
Yetnikoff, Michael .... **Chicago, IL**
Yett & Associates, P.C. .... **Sevierville, TN**
Yett, Charles W. .... Denver, CO
Yett, Kathryn Huff .... **Sevierville, TN**
Yette, Frederick W. .... Washington, DC
Yette, Joyce Payne .... **Washington, DC**
Yetter, Bruce .... El Paso, TX
Yetter, Charles W. .... Binghamton, NY
Yetter, David G. .... Houston, TX
Yetter, Donald W. .... Bradenton, FL
Yetter, Jerry J. .... Cincinnati, OH
Yetter, John F. .... Tallahassee, FL
Yetter, John M. .... Treasury Department, Office of the General Counsel, GV
Yetter, Katheryn .... Salem, OR
Yetter, Larry L. .... Beverly Hills, CA
Yetter, R. Paul .... **Houston, TX**
Yetter, Richard .... El Paso, TX
Yetter, Robert E. .... **Harrisburg, PA**
Yetter & Warden, L.L.P. .... **Houston, TX**
Yetter, Zalbowitz & Gartell
Binghamton, NY
Deposit, NY
Hancock, NY
Windsor, NY
Yetter and Zaremba, P.A. .... Bradenton, FL
Yettick, Keith C. .... San Jose, CA
Yetur, Sreedhar Reddy .... Downey, CA
Yetwin, Richard M. .... **Tucson, AZ**
Yetz, Marilyn A. .... Lakeville, CT
Yetzer, Jody L. .... Hartford, CT
Yeu, Susan .... **Morristown, NJ**
Yeu, Susan .... **New Paltz, NY**
Yeung, Adrienne .... **Las Vegas, NV**
Reno, NV
Yeung, Anita Ka-Wai .... **New York, NY**
Yeung, Janet T. .... **New York, NY**
Yeung, Joseph M. .... Chicago, IL
Yeung, Rowena A. W. .... **Los Angeles, CA**
Yeung, Shirley .... **New York, NY**
Yeutter, Clayton K. .... **Washington, DC**
Yeutter, Gregg S. .... **Omaha, NE**
Yevincy, Victoria L. .... **Henderson, KY**
Yevoli, Edward T. .... **Kansas City, MO**
Yevoli, Jennifer L. .... **Kansas City, MO**
Yew, Erica .... **San Jose, CA**
Yewell, David L. .... **Owensboro, KY**
Yewell, Patsey Ely .... **Lexington, KY**
Yewell, Terry L. .... Lexington, KY
Yeyati, Sandra C. .... Naples, FL
Yezak, Herman .... Bremond, TX
Yezbak, Charles P., III .... **Nashville, TN**
Yezbick, Anthony A. .... **Bloomfield Hills, MI**
Yezzi, Michael Blase .... Pittsfield, MA
Yezzi, Richard M. .... Philadelphia, PA
Yezzo, Dominick .... Garden City, NY
Yglecias, Michael A. .... Los Angeles, CA
Yguico, Carlos V. .... **Los Angeles, CA**
Yi, Christina .... New York, NY
Yi, Haywon .... Washington, DC
Yi, Jennifer J. .... **Washington, DC**
Yi, Michael M. .... **New York, NY**
Yi, Michael Y. .... Los Angeles, CA
Yi, Miwon .... **Los Angeles, CA**
Yi, Soo Kyong .... **New York, NY**
Yi, Sue C. .... **New York, NY**
Yi, Susan Chong .... **Honolulu, HI**
Yi, Susan Crystal .... Los Altos, CA
Yi, Susette S. .... Granada Hills, CA
Yi, Theodore I. .... **Chicago, IL**
Yi Tuan & Brunstein .... **New York, NY**
Yi, Yuchong C. .... Washington, DC
Yianilos, Christopher J. .... Washington, DC
Yick, Mandy F. .... Denver, CO
Yieh, Mao-Sen .... **Houston, TX**
Yih, Daniel W. .... Mount Kisco, NY
Yih, Thomas .... **New York, NY**
Yih, Thomas M. (IBA) .... **Newton, IA**
Yilek, John A. .... **St. Paul, MN**
Yilmaz, Ken .... Hempstead, NY
Yim, B. Casey, (P.C.) .... **Los Angeles, CA**
Yim, Benedict B. .... Arcadia, CA
Yim, Craig G. H. .... **Honolulu, HI**
Yim, George W. Y. .... Honolulu, HI
Yim, John J. .... **Washington, DC**
Yim, Marian M. .... Phoenix, AZ
Yim, Millicent C. .... Washington, DC
Yim, Patrick K. S. L. .... Honolulu, HI
Yim, Peter Jung-Hyon .... Phoenix, AZ
Yim, Soo J. .... **Washington, DC**
Yim, Stephen B. .... Honolulu, HI
Yim, Susan S. .... **Washington, DC**
Yin, Christopher .... **Los Angeles, CA**
Yin, Clifford E. .... **San Francisco, CA**
Yin, Dominic David .... San Francisco, CA
Yin, Flora .... Los Angeles, CA
Yin, George K. .... United States Senate, Committee Legal Personnel, GV
Yin, Jeffrey .... **New York, NY**
Yin, Mony B. P. .... **Hartford, CT**
Yin, Ronald L. .... **San Francisco, CA**
San Jose, CA
Yin, Tung .... **Los Angeles, CA**
Yin, Xiong .... **Chicago, IL**
Yindra, Lisa Andersen .... Georgetown, DE
Yindrick, Amy L. .... **Chicago, IL**
Ying, Christina .... **Princeton, NJ**
New York, NY
Ying, Evelyn S. .... Department of Justice, Environment and Natural Resources Division, GV
Ying, Howard .... San Francisco, CA
Yinger, Carl Laurence
Benton Harbor, MI
Yinger, Emily M. .... **McLean, VA**
Yinger, Jack Herman .... Santa Ana, CA
Yinger & Oldfield .... Bakersfield, CA
Yinger, Ray A. .... Bakersfield, CA
Yingling, Beth .... **Newark, NJ**
Yingling, Edward L. .... Washington, DC
Yingling, Elizabeth L. .... **Dallas, TX**
Yingling, Gary L. .... **Washington, DC**
Yingling, John H. .... Savannah, GA
Yingling, Matthew J. .... Phoenix, AZ
Yingling, Monique E. .... **Washington, DC**
Yingling, Ronald C. .... **Cleveland, OH**
Yingst, James T. .... Hanover, PA
Yingst, Paul V. .... St. Petersburg, FL
Yingst, Robert A. .... Washington, DC
Berrien Springs, MI
Yip, Alex C. H. .... **New York, NY**
Yip, Alex L. .... New York, NY
Yip, Edward C. Y. .... San Diego, CA
Yip, Gwendolyn H. .... **Boston, MA**
Yip, Jeffrey S. .... Los Angeles, CA
Yip, Loan Chu .... **New York, NY**
Yip, Philip S. .... Palo Alto, CA
Yip, Vincent K. .... **Los Angeles, CA**
Yipp, Victor .... Chicago, IL
Yirka, Carl A. .... South Royalton, VT
Yitchinsky, Antoinette J. .... **Worcester, MA**
Yitzchaki, Mikki S., P.C. .... **Phoenix, AZ**
Yitzchaki, Mikki Sue .... **Phoenix, AZ**
Yiu, JoJo H. .... **Houston, TX**
Yiu, Tien-Tin .... Los Angeles, CA
Ykema, Sandra L. .... Philadelphia, PA
Ylitalo, David L. .... **San Antonio, TX**
Ylitalo, Joe A. .... Kilgore, TX
Ylitalo Law Offices, P.A. .... St. Paul, MN
Ylitalo, Ronald O. W. .... St. Paul, MN
Ylla, Robert N., Jr. .... Oklahoma City, OK
Yngve, Albert B. .... Golden Valley, MN
Yngve, John A. .... Minneapolis, MN
Yniguez, Dennis Anthony .... Berkeley, CA
Ynostroza, Carlos G. .... Oakland, CA
Yntema, Elizabeth B. .... Lake Forest, IL
Yntema, Hessel E., III .... **Albuquerque, NM**
Ynzunza, Samuel P. .... San Francisco, CA
Yoakam, Ted G. .... Slickville, PA
Yoakum, Alice B. .... **Lakeville, CT**
Yoakum, Grant M. .... **Akron, OH**
Yoakum, Marie Ann .... Cleveland, MO
Yoakum, Martha J. .... Tazewell, TN
Yoakum, Sue E. .... Overland Park, KS
Yoars, Peter .... **White Plains, NY**
Yob, Lillian Moyano
Commission on Civil Rights, Office of the General Counsel, GV
Yob, Mary O'Reilly .... McAlester, OK
Yob, William J. .... Grand Rapids, MI
Yobski, James B. .... Redondo Beach, CA
Yocca, Christine M. .... Los Angeles, CA
Yocca, Mark W. .... **Irvine, CA**
Yocca, Nicholas J. .... **Newport Beach, CA**
Yocca, Nick E. .... **Newport Beach, CA**
Yoch, Barry A. .... **Los Angeles, CA**
Newport Beach, CA
Yoch, Michael J. .... Washington, DC
Yoch, Stephen E. .... **Minneapolis, MN**
Yochelson, Alan S. .... Los Angeles, CA
Yochelson, Arnold L. .... Upper Marlboro, MD
Yochelson, David A. .... Los Angeles, CA
Yoches, E. Robert .... **Washington, DC**
Yochim, Elisa J. .... Chicago, IL
Yochim, Joseph A. .... Erie, PA

Yochim, Raoul ... Kalamazoo, MI
Yochim, Skiba, Moore & Nash ... Erie, PA
Yochim, William J., Jr. ... Southfield, MI
Yochum, Mark D. ... Pittsburgh, PA
Yochum, Stacy Dean
Commodity Futures Trading Commission, Executive Staff, GV
Yocis, Thomas J. ... Long Beach, CA
Yock, Bradford E. ... Houston, TX
Yock, Doris E. ... Minneapolis, MN
Yock, Robert J.
United States Court of Federal Claims, GV
Yockey, Barbara L. ... Sterling Heights, MI
Yockey, Eugene H. ... Indianapolis, IN
Yockey, J. Davy ... Bordentown, NJ
Trevose, PA
Yockey, James A. ... Seattle, WA
Yockey, Kurt D. ... Farmington Hills, MI
Yockey, Michael J. ... Farmington Hills, MI
Yockey, Thomas J. ... Decatur, IL
Yockey, Wendell E. ... Topeka, KS
Yockey, Yockey & Schliem
Ann Arbor, MI
Detroit, MI
Farmington Hills, MI
Traverse City, MI
Yockim, Ronald S. ... Roseburg, OR
Yocom, Danita D. ... San Francisco, CA
Yocom, David E. ... Salt Lake City, UT
Yocom, Jack ... Springfield, MO
Yocom, Robert E. ... Goodman, MO
Yocom, Tony Lynn ... Hope, AR
Yocum, Arlene Marie ... Philadelphia, PA
Yocum, Carol K. ... Oakland, CA
Yocum, Charles E. ... Towson, MD
Yocum, Cheryl L. ... Newport Beach, CA
Yocum, Edward J., Jr. ... New York, NY
Yocum, Henry S., Jr. ... El Dorado, AR
Yocum, James A. ... Camden, NJ
Yocum, Jane M. ... Little Rock, AR
Yocum, J. G. Gordon ... Norristown, PA
Yocum, Kevin L. ... Fairview Heights, IL
Yocum, Leonard R. ... St. Louis, MO
Yocum, Lori M. ... Rancho Bernardo, CA
Yocum, Rebecca S. ... Overland Park, KS
Yocum, Richard J. ... St. Joseph, MO
Yocum, Thomas R. ... Cincinnati, OH
Yocum, Warren R., Jr. ... Huntingdon, PA
Yocum, William L. ... Kansas City, MO
Yocum & Yocum ... Camden, NJ
Yoder, Ainlay, Ulmer & Buckingham
Elkhart, IN
Goshen, IN
Yoder & Arnold, P.C. ... Kendallville, IN
Yoder, Bonita J. ... Lawrence, KS
Yoder, Christian ... Portland, OR
Yoder, Claire C. ... Plano, TX
Yoder, David E. ... Newton, KS
Yoder, David R. ... Gary, IN
Yoder, Donald H. ... Tustin, CA
Yoder, Edward W. ... Murrysville, PA
Yoder, J. Dwight ... Lancaster, PA
Yoder, J. Stephen ... Bloomington, IL
Yoder, James S. ... Wilmington, DE
Woodstown, NJ
Yoder, James W., Law Office
Bloomington, IL
Yoder, Jennifer D. ... Highland, IN
Yoder, Joanne Thorson ... Murfreesboro, TN
Yoder, John H. ... Smethport, PA
Yoder, John S. ... Billings, MT
Yoder, John W. ... Bloomington, IL
Yoder, John W., Law Firm ... Bloomington, IL
Yoder, John Wm. ... Bloomington, IL
Yoder Law Office, P.C. ... Billings, MT
Yoder, Linda L. ... Hartford, CT
Yoder, Lois Jean ... Medina, OH
Yoder, Lowell D. ... Chicago, IL
Yoder, Mark G. ... Reading, PA
Yoder, Marlene A. ... Minneapolis, MN
Yoder, Michael G. ... Newport Beach, CA
Yoder, Michael M. ... Kendallville, IN
Yoder, P. Marshall ... Charlotte, NC
Yoder, Patrick S. ... Houston, TX
Yoder, Richard L. ... Laurel, MS
Yoder, Robert R. ... Phoenix, AZ
Yoder, Robert R., P.C. ... Phoenix, AZ
Yoder, Ronnie A.
Department of Transportation, Office of Hearings, GV
Yoder, Stanley J. ... Defiance, OH
Hicksville, OH
Yoder, Starr Ilene ... Chesapeake, VA
Yoder, Stephen A. ... Birmingham, AL
Yoder, Stephen K. ... Columbus, OH
Yoder, Susan M. ... Dayton, OH
Yoder, Thomas A. ... Holland, OH
Yoder, Thomas P. ... Fort Wayne, IN
Yoder, Thomas W. ... Fort Wayne, IN
Yoder, Walton B., Jr. ... Souderton, PA
Yoder, Wanda L. ... Lynchburg, VA
Yoder, William A. ... Bloomington, IL
Yoder, William A. ... Overland Park, KS
Yoder, Worth N. ... Goshen, IN
Yodhes, David J. ... Troy, MI
Yodice, Angela M. ... Brookhaven, NY
Yodice Associates ... Washington, DC
Yodice, Christopher P. ... New York, NY
Yodice, John S. ... Washington, DC
Yodice, Kathleen Ann ... Washington, DC
Yodowitz, Edward J. ... New York, NY
Yodowitz, Joel ... San Francisco, CA
Yodowitz, Robert ... New City, NY
Yodowitz, Sheri Ann ... Pearl River, NY
Yoedicke, Patricia ... Minneapolis, MN
Yoedt, John B. ... Pittsburgh, PA
Yoeli, Michael ... New York, NY
Yoelin, Merritt S., (P.C.) ... Portland, OR
Yoerg, Norman ... Taylor, MI
Yoerges, Roger W. ... Washington, DC
Yoes, Henry E. (Gene), III
Lake Charles, LA
Yoes Law Firm, A Professional Law Corporation ... Lake Charles, LA
Yoes, Mona Allison ... Houston, TX
Yoes, Robert E. ... Fort Smith, AR
Yoes, Stuart C. ... Beaumont, TX
Yoes, William H. ... Beaumont, TX
Yoesel, Willis G. ... Falls City, NE
Yoffe, Sheldon M. ... Louisville, KY
Yoffee, Julia J. ... Atlanta, GA
Yoffee, Susan B. ... North Palm Beach, FL
Palm Beach, FL
Yoffee, William M.
Department Of Health And Human Services, Social Security Administration, GV
Yoffie, Alan S. ... Worcester, MA
Yoffie, Beth E. ... Los Angeles, CA
Yoffie, Johanna D. Drooz ... Worcester, MA
Yoffy, James S. ... Richmond, VA
Yoffy, Kenneth R. ... Newport News, VA
Yogi, Nolan K. ... Kapolei, HI
Yogman, Judith S. ... Boston, MA
Yogmour, Gus, Jr. ... Westfield Center, OH
Yogodzinski, Debra D. ... Washington, DC
Yogore, Mariano G., III ... Flossmoor, IL
Yohai, David L. ... New York, NY
Yohalem, Harry M. ... Pasadena, CA
Yohalem, Jane Bloom ... Santa Fe, NM
Yohalem, Nathaniel H. ... Westfield, NJ
Yohanan, John S. ... San Jose, CA
Yohannan, Bincy ... New York, NY
Yohannan, David R. ... Washington, DC
Yohay, Stephen C. ... Washington, DC
Yohe, D. Spencer ... Villa Park, CA
Yohe, David W. ... Jackson, MI
Yohe, Davis G. ... Washington, PA
Yohe, Douglas C. ... Harrisburg, PA
Yohe, Susan A. ... Pittsburgh, PA
Yohe, Virginia E. ... Wilbraham, MA
Yohman, Daniel G. ... Fresno, CA
Yohn, Chad ... New York, NY
Yohn, Heather ... Palo Alto, CA
Yohn, Richard L. ... Miami, OK
Yohn, William H., Jr. ... Philadelphia, PA
Yoho, Bill L. ... Lanham, MD
Yohonn, Lois Sylor ... New York, NY
Yoka & Smith, LLP ... Los Angeles, CA
Yoka, Walter M. ... Los Angeles, CA
Yokan, Michael R. ... Jacksonville, FL
Yokas-Reese, Marina Damos
Rock Island, IL
Yoke, Frank R., Jr. ... Parkersburg, WV
Yokel, David M. ... Greenville, SC
Yokell, Roger R. ... Providence, RI
Yoken, Stephen B. ... Las Vegas, NV
Yokich, Stephen A. ... Chicago, IL
Yokitis, George E. ... Pittsburgh, PA
Yoklavich, Brian D. ... Silver Spring, MD
Yoklavich & Rush ... Silver Spring, MD
Yokley, D. Blake ... Winston-Salem, NC
Yokley, D. Blake, P.A.
Winston-Salem, NC
Yokley, James A. ... New York, NY
Yokom, Andrew Patrick
Downers Grove, IL
Yokom, Mark F. ... Arlington, TX
Yokomizo, Douglas ... South Pasadena, CA
Yokomoto, Kristin L. ... San Diego, CA
Yokota, Blane T. ... Honolulu, HI
Yokovich, Barbara Ann ... Hammond, IN
Yokow, William M. ... New Haven, CT
Yokoyama, Dennis T. ... Los Angeles, CA
Yokoyama, Frank A. ... Los Angeles, CA
Yokoyama, Gary M. ... Honolulu, HI
Yokoyama, Lori S. ... Chicago, IL
Yokubaitis, Roger T. ... Houston, TX
Yokubaitis, Ronald Barron ... Austin, TX
Yokum, Karen M. ... Fairmont, WV
Yokum, Leonard E., Jr. ... Hammond, LA
Yokum & Yokum ... Hammond, LA
Yokus, Christopher D. ... Houston, TX
Yolen and Perzin, LLC ... New Haven, CT
Yolen, Timothy B. ... New Haven, CT
Yolken, Kathryn D. ... Half Moon Bay, CA
Yolles, Monty N. ... Rockville, MD
Yolles, Murray ... Southfield, MI
Yolles, Richard W. ... Denver, CO
Yolles, Robert A. ... Chicago, IL
Yolles, William A. ... Birmingham, MI
Yollick, Eric ... The Woodlands, TX
Yom, Sang Chin ... New York, NY
Yomtov, Nancie ... San Jose, CA
Yon, Charles C. ... Oklahoma City, OK
Yon, Chester A. ... Fountain Hills, AZ
Yon, Chester A., P.C. ... Fountain Hills, AZ
Yon, Daniel T ... Huntington, WV
Yon, David A. ... Tallahassee, FL
Yon & Evatt, LLP ... Anderson, SC
Yon, Steven M. ... Anderson, SC
Yon, Tamara L. ... Crookston, MN
Yon, W. Patrick ... Anderson, SC
Yonack, Robert P. ... Dallas, TX
Yonamine, Keith M. N. ... Honolulu, HI
Yonan, Marcel Elia ... Chicago, IL
Yonan, Mark E. ... Tucson, AZ
Yonano, Nicholas D. ... Turlock, CA
Yonaty, Stephen L. ... Buffalo, NY
Yonay, Guy ... New York, NY
Yonce, Harvey A. ... Orleans, MA
Yonce, Leslie K., IV ... Richmond, VA
Yonce, Thomas M. ... Orleans, MA
Yonce and Yonce ... Orleans, MA
Yonclas, Nicholas ... Eastpoint, FL
Yonco, John ... Chicago, IL
Yonco-Haines, Margaret K. ... New York, NY
Yonehiro, Bruce L. ... Palo Alto, CA
Yonek, Joe F. ... Vancouver, WA
Yonemitsu, Jon Christopher ... Martinez, CA
Yonemura, Barbara H. ... Sacramento, CA
Yonemura, Julie ... San Jose, CA
Yonemura, Mas ... Oakland, CA
Yonemura, Masatatsu ... Oakland, CA
Yonemura, Steven ... Westminster, CA
Yonemura, Yasaki and Baizer ... Oakland, CA
Yong, Alan Y. C. ... Seattle, WA
Yong, Barbara L. ... Chicago, IL
Yong, Frank J. ... Jacksonville, FL
Yong, James C. ... Chicago, IL
Yong, Jeffrey S. ... Los Angeles, CA
Yong, John S. ... New York, NY
Yong, Thomas T. ... Arcadia, CA
Yong, Yee-Yoong ... Los Angeles, CA
Yonge, James E. ... Davie, FL
Yongue, William H., IV ... Blacksburg, VA
Yonish, Brian G. ... Department of Defense, Office of the General Counsel, GV
Yonis-Sandlaufer, Robin S.
Newport Beach, CA
Yonkauski, Stanley, Jr. ... Springfield, IL
Yonke, A. Kent ... Wheaton, IL
Yonke, Albert J. ... Kansas City, MO
Yonke, Arnold & Newbold, P.C.
Kansas City, MO
Yonke, David A. ... Dallas, TX
Yonke, Michael Thomas ... Kansas City, MO
Yonkee & Toner ... Douglas, WY
Sheridan, WY
Yonker, John E. ... Minneapolis, MN
Yonkers, Charles E. ... Washington, DC
Yonkers, Robert M. ... Troy, MI
Yonkman, Fredrick A. ... Stamford, CT
Yonkman, Mark W. ... Detroit, MI
Yonkowski, William Otis ... Memphis, TN
Yonks, Michael A. ... Dallas, TX
Yonover, Bradley N. ... New York, NY
Yonover, Geri J. ... Valparaiso, IN
Yonover, Scott D. ... Los Angeles, CA
Indianapolis, IN
Yonowitz, Robert ... Newport Beach, CA
Yonteff, Andrew J. ... New York, NY
Yonts, Brent ... Beechmont, KY
Greenville, KY
Madisonville, KY
Yonts, Brent, P.S.C. ... Beechmont, KY
Greenville, KY
Madisonville, KY
Yonts, Mark E. ... Lexington, KY
Yonts, Robert B., Jr. (P.C.) ... Santa Cruz, CA
Yonts, Stewart H. ... Houston, TX
Yontz, Ivan L. ... Pekin, IL
Yontz, Randall E. ... Columbus, OH
Yoo, Aaron S.H., The Law Office of
Honolulu, HI
Yoo, Anthony S. ... Washington, DC
Yoo, Jessica ... New York, NY
Yoo, Jiyul ... Washington, DC
Yoo, Julien H. ... New York, NY
Yoo, Kame O. ... San Francisco, CA
Yoo, Lisa M. ... New York, NY
Yoo, Mary J. ... Los Angeles, CA
Yoo, Paul H. ... Minneapolis, MN
Yoo, Pauline H. ... New York, NY
Yoo, Salle E. ... San Francisco, CA
Yoo, Samuel S. ... New York, NY
Yoo, Steven R. ... Cleveland, OH
Yoo, Sung-Min Christopher ... Irvine, CA
Yoo, Susan S. ... Chicago, IL
Yoo, Thomas J. ... Los Angeles, CA
Yoo, Timothy J. ... Los Angeles, CA
Yoo, Victor J. ... Los Angeles, CA
Yoo, William J. ... New York, NY
Yoo, Young J. ... Upper Saddle River, NJ
Yood, Andrew C. ... Washington, DC
Yood, Howard L. ... Buffalo, NY
Yood, Kenneth J. ... Los Angeles, CA
Yook, Barbara M. ... San Andreas, CA
Yoon, Angie Y. ... Los Angeles, CA
Yoon, Antonio F. ... San Diego, CA
Yoon, Charles Myungsik ... New York, NY
Yoon, Cordelia M. ... New York, NY
Yoon, David W. S. ... Englewood Cliffs, NJ
Yoon, Frank ... Tulsa, OK
Yoon, Gene ... Menlo Park, CA
Yoon, Hyelee ... Philadelphia, PA
Yoon, J. Peter ... Conshohocken, PA
Yoon, James C. ... Palo Alto, CA
Yoon, John Yong-Jin ... Los Angeles, CA
Yoon, Julie ... New York, NY
Yoon, Junie ... San Francisco, CA
Yoon, Kenneth H. ... Santa Monica, CA
Yoon, Kenneth K. ... New York, NY
Yoon, Keum A. ... New York, NY
Yoon, Mi Jung ... New York, NY
Yoon, Mimi S. ... Bowling Green, OH
Yoon, Mi-Rang ... Boston, MA
Yoon, Richard Kon ... Los Angeles, CA
Yoon, Richard Suk Joon ... Kew Gardens, NY
Yoon, Stacia L. ... Merrillville, IN
Yoon, Susan ... Los Angeles, CA
Yoon, Susan J. ... Greenwood, IN
Yoon, Suzanne Chi Sook ... Baltimore, MD
Yoon, Tacie H. ... Washington, DC
Yoon, Tae-Sik ... Washington, DC
Yoon, Youngik ... Elmhurst, NY
Yoong, Akiko Nakatani ... Los Angeles, CA
Yoong, Dominic K.L. ... Los Angeles, CA
Yopes, P. Eric ... San Francisco, CA
Yopp, G. Michael ... Nashville, TN
Yopp, L. Gregory ... Louisville, KY
Yopp, Michael L. ... Lillington, NC
Yopp, Michael S. ... Raleigh, NC
Yoppolo, Louis J. ... Toledo, OH
Yoquinto, William D. ... Troy, NY
Yoran, Dafna ... New York, NY
Yordán, A. Joaquín ... New York, NY
Yordy, Eric D. ... Los Angeles, CA
Yordy, Tina M. ... Fort Wayne, IN
Yori, James August ... Georgetown, DE
Yorihiro, Akinobu ... Los Angeles, CA
Yorio, Albert E. ... New York, NY
Yorio, Edward J. ... New York, NY
Yorio, Robert J. ... Palo Alto, CA
Yorio & Roche ... Painted Post, NY
Yorio, Ronald A. ... Painted Post, NY
Yorizane, Ronald A. ... Los Angeles, CA
York, Aaron G. ... Dallas, TX
York, Alex S. ... San Diego, CA
York, Alexandra ... Kolonia, TT
York, Alvin Robert ... Bloomington, IN
York & Andersen ... Cleveland, OH
York, Arnold G. ... Malibu, CA
York, Bertina B. ... San Antonio, TX
York, Brent A. ... Presque Isle, ME
York, Christopher ... White Plains, NY
York, Christopher J. ... Atlanta, GA
York, Cinda R. ... Birmingham, AL
York, Claudia J. ... Kansas City, MO
York, D. Craig ... Louisville, KY
York, Daniel A. ... Prineville, OR
York, Daniel R. ... Whittier, CA
York, Daniel S. ... Irving, TX
York, David A. ... Menlo Park, CA
York, David L. ... Raleigh, NC
York, David P. ... Mobile, AL
York, David R. ... Berlin, NJ
York, David R. ... Salt Lake City, UT
York, David S. ... Kalamazoo, MI
York, Dennis A. ... Big Canoe, GA
York, Edward J., Jr. ... Denver, CO
York, Elizabeth Foust ... Houston, TX
York, Elizabeth S. ... Arlington, VA
York, Ellen M. ... Napa, CA
York, Frank W. ... Greensboro, NC
York, Franklin R. ... Cedar Rapids, IA
York, Frederick Jay ... San Antonio, TX
York, Gary ... Los Angeles, CA
York, Gerard ... Orlando, FL
York, Glenn T., Jr. ... Cedartown, GA
York, Gregory A. ... Santa Ana, CA
York, Gregory C. ... Charlotte, NC
York & Gregory, P.C. ... Denver, CO
York, Harley G. ... Newark, NJ
York, Harvey L. ... Toms River, NJ
York, Helene ... Fort Lauderdale, FL
York & Hinds, L.L.P. ... Houston, TX
York, James M. ... Houston, TX
York, James R. ... Los Angeles, CA
San Francisco, CA
York, James W. ... Tallahassee, FL
York, Jane Anne ... Sanger, CA
York, Jeanette Saker ... St. Petersburg, FL
York, Jeffrey G. ... Grand Rapids, MI
York, Jeffrey P. ... Wheaton, IL
York, Jeffrey S. ... Jacksonville, FL
York, Jo Ann ... Department of State, Foreign Service Officers (Overseas), GV
York, Johannah M. ... Cambridge, MA
York, John B. ... Philadelphia, PA
York, John K. ... Orange, CA
York, John S., Jr. ... Seattle, WA
York, Jon H. ... Berkeley, CA
York, Kendra ... Sacramento, CA
York, Kenneth H. ... Malibu, CA
York, Kevin M. ... Indianapolis, IN
York, L. Edward ... Cleveland, OH
York, Lance E. ... Jericho, NY
York, Larry F. ... Austin, TX
York, Larry H. ... Barbourville, KY
York, Lisa Dawn ... Nashville, TN
York, Louis B. ... New York, NY
York, Lynn F. ... Walnut Creek, CA
York, M. Keith ... Cornelia, GA
York, Marilyn D. ... Beverly Hills, CA
York, Marvin B. ... Oklahoma City, OK
York, Mary M. ... Chicago, IL
York, Michael A. ... Rochester, MN
York, Michael G. ... Irvine, CA
York, Michael H., Sr. ... Cedartown, GA
York, Michael M. ... Washington, DC
Bridgeport, WV
York, Michael W. ... Gaithersburg, MD
York, Myrth ... Providence, RI
York, Nicholas C. ... Cleveland, OH
York, Peter R. ... Atlanta, GA
York, Philip J. ... Wellsville, MO
York, Phillip G. ... Lomita, CA
York, Randall A. ... Crossville, TN
York, Rice P. ... Jackson, MS
York, Robert Alan ... Houston, TX
York, Robert Edwin ... Corsicana, TX
York, Robert T. ... Minneapolis, MN
York, Robert W. ... Indianapolis, IN
York, Robin A. ... Cave Creek, AZ
York, Schrager & Baxter ... Indianapolis, IN
York & Slater ... Oklahoma City, OK
York & Smith ... Berkeley, CA
York, Stanley ... Winnebago, WI
York, Stephen ... Houston, TX
York, Stephen G. ... Hollywood, FL
York, Stephen S. ... New York, NY
York, Steven G. ... Denver, CO
York, Thomas B. ... Harrisburg, PA
Philadelphia, PA
York, Thomas V. ... Stanwood, MI
York, Tiderington & Miller, P.C.
Kalamazoo, MI
York, Vincent A. ... St. Louis, MO
York, Wendy C. ... Sacramento, CA
York, Wendy E. ... Albuquerque, NM
York, William E. ... Houston, TX
York, William F. ... Boston, MA

York & York ....Napa, CA
York & York, P.C. ....Cedartown, GA
Yorke, Brian ....Ventura, CA
Yorke, Jay R. ....Dexter, MO
Yorke, John B. ....Charlotte, NC
Yorke, Karin L. ....Los Angeles, CA
Yorke, Marianne ....New Brunswick, NJ
Yorke, Mary Jane ....Lake Park, GA
Yorke, Rachel A. ....Boston, MA
Yorke, Randall J. ....Naperville, IL
Yorke, Richard Alan ....Detroit, MI
Yorkgitis, Edward A., Jr. ....Washington, DC
Yorko, Thomas R. ....Philadelphia, PA
Yorks, Ben J. ....Costa Mesa, CA
La Jolla, CA
Yorks, W. Brinton, Jr. ....Bothell, WA
Yorkston, David C. ....New York, NY
Yormak, Jonathon K. ....New York, NY
Yormick, Jon P. ....Troy, MI
Yorn, Kevin B. ....Santa Monica, CA
Yoro, James A. ....Bakersfield, CA
Yorozu, Kesa L. ....Portland, OR
Yorozu, Tasha A. ....San Francisco, CA
Yorra, Hubert I. ....Boston, MA
Yorra, Laurence M. ....Boston, MA
Yorston, Henry P. ....Plantation, FL
Yorsz, Stanley ....Pittsburgh, PA
Yorton, David M., Jr. ....Redding, CA
Yorton & Yorton ....Redding, CA
Yoseloff, Sarah ....Irvine, CA
Yoseph, J.R. ....Vancouver, WA
Yoset, Thomas L. ....Meadville, PA
Yosha Krahulik & Levy ....Indianapolis, IN
Yosha, Louis Buddy ....Indianapolis, IN
Yoshida, Brian Richard ....Buffalo, NY
Yoshida, Bruce T. ....Honolulu, HI
Yoshida & Ching ....Honolulu, HI
Yoshida, Daiske ....New York, NY
Yoshida, Douglas K. ....Seattle, WA
Yoshida, Gerald C. ....Honolulu, HI
Yoshida, Gerald T. ....Los Angeles, CA
Yoshida, Gerald T. ....Santa Monica, CA
Yoshida, Isamu ....San Diego, CA
Yoshida, Jason M. ....Honolulu, HI
Yoshida, Ken Ichiro ....Philadelphia, PA
Yoshida, Lisa ....Santa Rosa, CA
Yoshida, Lois H. ....San Jose, CA
Yoshida, Marianne A. P. ....St. Paul, MN
Yoshida, Michael A. ....Honolulu, HI
Yoshida, Miyuki ....New York, NY
Yoshida, Naoki ....Washington, DC
Yoshida, Nellie M. ....San Jose, CA
Yoshida, Randal ....Honolulu, HI
Yoshida, Steve K. ....Homer, AK
Yoshida, Steve K., P.C. ....Homer, AK
Yoshida, Timothy L. ....San Francisco, CA
Yoshigai, Wayne S. ....Honolulu, HI
Yoshimi, Sharyn R. ....Los Angeles, CA
Yoshimoto, Carol A. ....San Francisco, CA
Yoshimoto, Janel M.N. ....Honolulu, HI
Yoshimoto, Nathan H. ....Honolulu, HI
Yoshimura, Edwin J.
Commodity Futures Trading Commission,
Division of Enforcement, GV
Yoshimura, Gary H. ....Santa Barbara, CA
Yoshimura, Jon Curtis ....Honolulu, HI
Yoshimura, Masahiro "Max" ....Seattle, WA
Yoshimura, Renee M. ....Honolulu, HI
Yoshinaga, Darcie S. ....Honolulu, HI
Yoshinaga, Paul I. ....Los Angeles, CA
Yoshinaka, Russ K. ....Menlo Park, CA
Yoshino, Denise L. ....Los Angeles, CA
Yoshino, Kaye N. ....New York, NY
Yoshino, Troy M. ....San Francisco, CA
Yoshioka, Gary A. ....Fairfax, VA
Yoshioka, Heidi M. ....San Francisco, CA
Yoshioka, Terence T. ....Hilo, HI
Yoshitake, Alan T. ....Los Angeles, CA
Yoshitomi, Robert B. ....San Francisco, CA
Parsippany, NJ
Yoshiyama, Denah H. ....Santa Ana, CA
Yoshor, Shira R. ....Houston, TX
Yoskin, Neil ....Princeton, NJ
Yoskosky, Christopher T. ....Pittsburgh, PA
Yoskowitz, Irving B. ....Washington, DC
Yoskowitz, Jack ....New York, NY
Yoskowitz, Marlene ....Union, NJ
Yosowitz, Jeffrey S. ....Chicago, IL
Yosowitz, Sanford ....Mayfield Heights, OH
Yospin, Harry A. ....Warren, NJ
Yospin, Richard L. ....Worcester, MA
Yoss, George T. ....Miami, FL
Yoss, Harrison H. ....Dallas, TX
Yoss, Jan A. ....Los Angeles, CA
Yoss, Jeffrey Mark ....Palm Springs, CA
Yoss, Richard A. ....Woodsfield, OH
Yosses, Edward M. ....Fort Collins, CO
Yost, Agnes J. ....Willowick, OH
Yost & Associates, P.C. ....Westport, CT
Yost & Baill, LLP ....Minneapolis, MN
Yost, Brian D. ....Charleston, WV
Yost, Brian K. ....Fort Worth, TX
Yost, Byron Paul ....Westport, CT
Yost, Carl M. ....Stroudsburg, PA
Yost, Casper Scott ....St. Louis, MO
Yost, Charles H. ....Fremont, NE
Yost, Chas. K. ....Baltimore, MD
Yost, Christopher J. ....Columbus, OH
Yost, Christopher P. ....Boise, ID
Yost, Claudette L. ....Medford, OR
Yost, Colin A. ....Salem, OR
Yost, Cynthia A. ....Columbus, OH
Yost, Daniel ....San Francisco, CA
Yost, David A. ....Meridian, MS
Yost, David A. ....Delaware, OH
Yost, David S. ....Sacramento, CA
Yost & Davidson ....Hershey, PA
Yost, Dolores Ann ....Santa Ana, CA
Yost, Donald H. ....York, PA
Yost, Donna Occhipinti ....Perry, OK
Yost, Edwin B. ....Winchester, VA
Yost, Elizabeth Schuyler ....Aurora, CO
Yost, Ellen G. ....Buffalo, NY
Yost, Eric R. ....Wichita, KS
Yost, Ernest W. ....Seaside Park, NJ
Yost, Esdel B. ....Huntington, WV
Yost, Geoffrey H. ....San Francisco, CA
Yost, Gerald B. ....Minneapolis, MN
Yost, Gerard T. ....Sebring, OH
Yost, Harold S. ....Bridgeport, WV
Yost, Harry B. ....Christiana, PA
Ephrata, PA
Lancaster, PA
Quarryville, PA
Strasburg, PA
Yost, Harry H. ....Glen Burnie, MD
Yost, Harvey D., II ....Perry, OK
Yost, Jeffrey A. ....Orlando, FL
Yost, Jeffrey J. ....Frankfort, KY
Lexington, KY
Yost, Jon A. ....Hershey, PA
Yost, Joseph Timothy ....Silver Spring, MD
Yost, Karen M. ....Flushing, NY
Yost, Kent L. ....Pocatello, ID
Yost, Kimberly M. ....Baltimore, MD
Yost, Kurt G. ....Grand Rapids, MI
Yost Law Office ....Eau Claire, WI
Yost, Lawrence H. ....Fremont, NE
Yost, Layne F. ....Eau Claire, WI
Yost, LeRoy W. ....Glencoe, MN
Yost, Lisa H. ....Seattle, WA
Yost, Lloyd ....San Diego, CA
Yost, Mark J. ....Department of Justice,
Tax Division, GV
Yost, Mel E. ....Santa Fe, NM
Yost, Melvin T. ....Santa Fe, NM
Yost, Michael A., Jr. ....Huntington, WV
Yost, Nicholas C. ....San Francisco, CA
Yost & O'Connell ....Flushing, NY
Yost & O'Malley ....Johnstown, PA
Yost, Paula M. ....San Francisco, CA
Yost, Peter A. ....Minneapolis, MN
Yost, Rebecca Anne ....St. Helena, CA
Yost, Richard W. ....Philadelphia, PA
Yost & Robertson, PLC ....Franklin, TN
Yost, Sally L. ....Baltimore, MD
Yost, Schafersman, Yost, Lamme, Hillis & Mitchell, P.C. ....Fremont, NE
Yost, Stephen C. ....Phoenix, AZ
Tucson, AZ
Yost, Stephen M. ....Roanoke, VA
Salem, VA
Yost, Stephen R. ....Cary, IL
Yost, Stephen T. ....Massillon, OH
Yost, Steven A. ....Seattle, WA
Yost, Steven Ernest ....Seaside Park, NJ
Yost, Thomas A. ....Brea, CA
Yost, Thomas Frderick, Jr. ....Baltimore, MD
Yost, Tina Marie ....Grand Haven, MI
Yost & Tretta ....Philadelphia, PA
Yost, Valerie A. ....Baltimore, MD
Yost, William A., III ....Dallas, TX
Yost, William F. ....Nampa, ID
Yost, William J. ....Franklin, TN
Yost, William Richard ....Columbus, OH
Yost & Yost ....Seaside Park, NJ
Yoste, Charles T. ....Starkville, MS
Yoste, Harry M., Jr. ....Gulfport, MS
Yostembski, Robert H. ....Trenton, NJ
Yosua, Robert G. ....Philadelphia, PA
Yoswein, Leonard E. ....Brooklyn, NY
Yots, Jason A. ....Buffalo, NY
Yott, Laurie Alexandra ....Carson City, NV
You, Peter L. ....Brooklyn, NY
You, Youlee Yim ....Portland, OR
Youakim, Sam ....Tampa, FL
Youatt, William G., Jr. ....Haslett, MI
Youchah, Elayna ....Las Vegas, NV
Youck, David A. ....Watseka, IL
Youdelman, Robert ....New York, NY
Youdelman, Robert A. ....Beachwood, OH
Youdelman, Robert, P.C. ....New York, NY
Youdelman, Sharon J. ....New York, NY
Youderian, John A., Jr. ....West Caldwell, NJ
Youdin, Michael W. ....Dallas, TX
Youdorf, Milton S. ....Roselle, IL
Youell, C. Cooper, IV ....Roanoke, VA
Youell, Spencer M. ....Dublin, OH
Youhas, Edward R. ....Chicago, IL
Youhn, Stephen M.
Securities and Exchange Commission,
Division of Market Regulation, GV
Youhne, Young ....Las Vegas, NV
Youker, Jean Christine ....Tarzana, CA
Youkilis, John C. ....Cincinnati, OH
Youle, Jessica Jeanne ....Tempe, AZ
Youle, Robert E. ....Denver, CO
Youman, Alvin ....New Bedford, MA
Youman, Andrew S. ....Philadelphia, PA
Youman, Guy R. ....McHenry, IL
Youman, Kristine Pihl ....Chicago, IL
Youmans, Alice I. ....Berkeley, CA
Youmans, Douglas L., (A Law Corporation)
Sacramento, CA
Youmans, Harold W. ....Riverview, FL
Youmans, Jeffrey B. ....Seattle, WA
Youmans, Kenwood C. ....Los Angeles, CA
Youmans, Mark R. ....Columbus, GA
Youmans, Matthew H. ....Hartford, CT
Youmans, Richard F. ....Scotia, NY
Youmans, Russell O. ....Redding, CA
Youmans, Ted R. ....Santa Ana, CA
Youmans, Timothy Clayton ....Columbia, SC
Youmatz, Vincent W. ....Andover, MA
Youn, Bonnie M. ....Doraville, GA
Youn, Sooryun ....New York, NY
Younce, Charles P. ....Greensboro, NC
Younce, Patricia Kramer ....Philadelphia, PA
Younce, Robert C., Jr. ....Raleigh, NC
Youner, Sara A. ....Springfield, NJ
Younes, Habib S. ....Chicago, IL
Younes, Joseph ....Chicago, IL
Younes, Steven J. ....Stamford, CT
Younes, Van Thomas ....Harrison, AR
Younesi, John D. ....Los Angeles, CA
Youness, Dania ....Santa Monica, CA
Younessi, Ramin R. ....Los Angeles, CA
Youney, John W. ....Skowhegan, ME
Young, A. Christopher ....Philadelphia, PA
Young, A. Keller ....Denver, CO
Young, A. Raymond ....Virginia Beach, VA
Young, Aaron M. ....Harrisburg, PA
Young, Abigail B. ....New York, NY
Young, Adam J. ....New York, NY
Young, Adrian L. ....Austin, TX
Young, Alan H. ....Brooklyn, NY
Young, Alan Price ....Stroudsburg, PA
Young, Albert J. A. ....Bel Air, MD
Young, Albion J. ....Wellman, IA
Young & Alexander Co., L.P.A.
Cincinnati, OH
Dayton, OH
Hamilton, OH
Young, Alfred L. ....Helena, MT
Young, Alice ....New York, NY
Young, Alicia L. ....New York, NY
Young, Allan I. ....Morristown, NJ
New York, NY
Young, Allan T. ....Milwaukee, WI
Young, Allen I. ....New York, NY
Young, Allen K. ....Springville, UT
Young, A.M. ....San Francisco, CA
Young, Amanda A. ....Bowling Green, KY
Young, Amanda Haynes ....Nashville, TN
Young, Amy A. ....Fort Lauderdale, FL
Young, Andrea I. ....Atlanta, GA
Young, Andrew B. ....Washington, DC
Young, Andrew B. ....Philadelphia, PA
Young, Andrew J. ....Baltimore, MD
Young, Andrew M. ....Lexington, MA
Young, Andrew W. ....Doylestown, PA
Young, Ann Yaeger ....Asheville, NC
Young, Anna ....Prescott, AZ
Young, Anne Margaret ....Vienna, VA
Young, Anthony ....Marlton, NJ
Young, Anthony E. ....Chicago, IL
Young, Anthony E., Ltd. ....Chicago, IL
Young, Anthony J. ....Boston, MA
Young, Anthony L. ....Washington, DC
Young, Anthony O. ....Santa Monica, CA
Young, Anthony T. ....Okeechobee, FL
Young, Arnold C. ....Savannah, GA
Young, Arnold L. ....Sparta, NC
Young, Arnold L., P.A. ....Sparta, NC
Young, Art Charles ....Orlando, FL
Young, Artee Felicita ....Seattle, WA
Young, Arthur M. ....Roseville, MI
Young, Arthur W., III ....Boston, MA
Young & Associates, A Professional Law Corporation ....Metairie, LA
New Orleans, LA
Young & Associates, Attorneys at Law, P.A.
Pensacola, FL
Young & Associates, P.A. ....Sumter, SC
Young & Associates, P.A., Attorney at Law
Tampa, FL
Young & Associates, P.C. ....Southfield, MI
New York, NY
Young, Audrey G. ....Chicago, IL
Young, B. Richard ....Pensacola, FL
Tampa, FL
Young, Barbara A. ....Westport, CT
Young, Barbara A. ....Valparaiso, IN
Young, Barbara H. ....Louisville, KY
Young, Barbara Jeanne ....Washington, DC
Young, Barbara L. ....Philadelphia, PA
Young, Barbara Schwarz ....Temple, TX
Young, Barney T. ....Dallas, TX
Young, Barry N. ....Palo Alto, CA
Young & Basile, P.C. ....Ann Arbor, MI
Troy, MI
Young & Bayle ....Boston, MA
Young, Bennett G. ....San Francisco, CA
Young, Berman, Karpf & Gonzalez, Professional Association
North Miami Beach, FL
Young, Bernard J. ....Washington, DC
Young, Bernard L., Jr. ....Pleasant Valley, NY
Young, Beth Ann R. ....Los Angeles, CA
Young, Beverly A. ....Houston, TX
Young, Bless S. ....Park City, UT
Young, Bob F. ....Dallas, TX
Young, Bogle, McCausland, Wells & Blanchard, P.A. ....Wichita, KS
Young, Bonita ....Gainesville, FL
Young, Bradley L. ....Sonora, CA
Young, Brant Allen ....Florence, AL
Young, Brenda LaVon
North Hollywood, CA
Young, Brent B. ....Kingsport, TN
Young, Brent D. ....Provo, UT
Young, Brian D. ....Oakland, CA
Young, Brian E. ....Cleveland, OH
Young, Brian N. ....Middletown, MD
Young, Brian P. ....Los Angeles, CA
Young, Brinton O.C. ....Pasadena, CA
Young & Brooks ....Houston, TX
Young & Brown, P.C. ....Vernon, AL
Young, Bruce A. ....Ventura, CA
Young, Bruce C. ....Grand Rapids, MI
Young, Bruce C. ....Madelia, MN
St. James, MN
Young, Bruce C. ....Las Vegas, NV
Young, Bruce C. ....Austin, TX
Young, Bruce M. ....New York, NY
Young, Bruce R. ....Palm Harbor, FL
Young, Bryant L. ....San Francisco, CA
Young, Burton ....North Miami Beach, FL
Young, C. Chad ....Ringgold, GA
Young, C. Clifton ....Carson City, NV
Young, C. Edward ....Atlanta, GA
Young, C. Edward ....Tonganoxie, KS
Eldon, MO
Young, C. Eric ....Martinsville, VA
Stuart, VA
Young, C. Thomas ....New Albany, IN
Young, Caldwell & Bubp ....West Union, OH
Young, Calvin E. ....Honolulu, HI
Young, Calvin M., III ....Acton, CA
Young, Canon T. ....San Francisco, CA
Young, Cari S. ....Austin, TX
Young, Carl H., III ....Cleveland, OH
Young, Carl J. ....Cambridge, MA
Young, Carl S. ....New York, NY
Young, Carl W. ....Edmond, OK
Young, Carlton C. ....Bessemer, AL
Young, Carol A. ....Mineola, NY
Young, Carol H. ....Scotia, NY
Young, Carol J. ....Miami, FL
Young, Carol K. ....Stamford, CT
Young, Carol L. ....San Diego, CA
Young, Carol R. ....Dallas, TX
Young, Carolann A. ....Somerset, PA
Young, Caroline Lingelbach
Indianapolis, IN
Young, Carolyn A. ....Santa Rosa, CA
Young, Carolyn R. ....Los Angeles, CA
Young, Carolyn R. ....Bedford, MA
Young, Carolyn S. Cherman ....New York, NY
Young, Carrie Carnahan ....Columbus, OH
Young, Carrie Lynn ....Toledo, OH
Young, Carrington E. (Cary)
Pine Bluff, AR
Young, Cary ....Plano, TX
Young, Caryn R. ....New York, NY
Young, Catharine C. ....Louisville, KY
Young, Catherine M. ....Milwaukee, WI
Young, Catherine Murr ....Louisville, KY
Young, Charles ....Florence, SC
Young, Charles A. ....Warren, OH
Young, Charles A., III ....Waltham, MA
Young, Charles E., Jr. ....Atlanta, GA
Young, Charles Edward, III
Fayetteville, AR
Young, Charles F. ....Effingham, IL
Young, Charles G., III ....Philadelphia, PA
Young, Charles H. ....Peoria, IL
Young, Charles H. ....Raleigh, NC
Young, Charles J. ....Brooklyn, NY
Young, Charles J. ....Austin, TX
Young, Charles L. ....Knoxville, TN
Young, Charles M. ....Cleveland, OH
Young, Charles P. ....Pensacola, FL
Young, Charles R. ....Hickory, NC
Young, Charles T., Jr. ....Harrisburg, PA
Young, Charlotte D. ....McLean, VA
Young, Charlton H. ....Lexington, KY
Young, Cheryl L. ....Norristown, PA
Philadelphia, PA
Young, Chester C. ....Albuquerque, NM
Young, Chris M. ....Houston, TX
Young, Chris R. ....Havre, MT
Young, Christie Getto ....Boston, MA
Young, Christina Ann ....Los Angeles, CA
Young, Christina C. ....Tampa, FL
Young, Christina L. ....Los Angeles, CA
Young, Christine L. ....Chicago, IL
Young, Christine W. ....Tucson, AZ
Young, Christopher A. ....Minneapolis, MN
Young, Christopher B. ....St. Petersburg, FL
Young, Christopher B. ....Austin, TX
Young, Christopher D. ....Houston, TX
Young, Christopher E., (Ms.) ....Seattle, WA
Young, Christopher G. ....Metairie, LA
Young, Christopher J. ....Annapolis, MD
Young, Christopher Lockert
Ashland City, TN
Young, Christopher M. ....San Diego, CA
Young, Christopher S. ....Ellicott City, MD
Young, Christopher S. ....Haddonfield, NJ
Young, Christopher W.
National Labor Relations Board,
Office of the General Counsel, GV
Young, Clarence N. ....Natchez, MS
Young, Clarisse W. J. ....Los Angeles, CA
Young, Clark P. ....Hugoton, KS
Young, Clarke Logan ....Santa Monica, CA
Young, Clay A. ....Anchorage, AK
Young, Clement, Rivers & Tisdale, LLP
Charleston, SC
Columbia, SC
Young, Cliff, Law Offices of ....Reno, NV
Young, Cobb ....Joplin, MO
Young, Coleman ....Amarillo, TX
Young Conaway Stargatt & Taylor, LLP
Dover, DE
Georgetown, DE
Wilmington, DE
Young, Constance L. ....Charlotte, NC
Young, Cori Leonard ....Kansas City, MO
Young & Coté ....Huntington, NY
Young, Craig ....Austin, TX
Young, Craig B. ....Washington, DC
Young, Craig R. ....Yorba Linda, CA
Young, Craig S. ....Peoria, IL
Young, Curtis A.
Securities and Exchange Commission,
Office of Municipal Securities, GV
Young, Cynthia A. ....Boston, MA
Young, Cynthia E. ....Annapolis, MD
Young, Cynthia E. ....Baltimore, MD
Young, Cynthia W. ....Louisville, KY

Young, D. Bradley ... San Diego, CA
Young, D. Kelley ... South Portland, ME
Young, D. Michael ... Bellevue, WA
Young, D. Michael ... Seattle, WA
Young, D. Scott ... Rochester, NY
Young, Dallas H., Jr. ... Provo, UT
Young, Damon ... Texarkana, TX
Young, Dan Clark ... Jonesboro, AR
Young, Dan G. ... Lubbock, TX
Young, Dan R. ... Houston, TX
Young, Dan R. ... Seattle, WA
Young, Dana D. ... Tampa, FL
Young, Daniel A. ... Lawrence, KS
Young, Daniel J. ... St. Paul, MN
Young, Daniel J. ... Ocean City, NJ
Young, Daniel M. ... Stamford, CT
Young, Daniel M. ... Moorestown, NJ
Philadelphia, PA
Young, Daniel R. ... Bethesda, MD
Young, Daniel R. ... Kansas City, MO
Young, Daniel T. ... Cleveland, OH
Young, Daniel Te ... Tallahassee, FL
Young, Darren R. ... Charleston, WV
Young, David ... Los Angeles, CA
Young, David ... New York, NY
Young, David ... Sapulpa, OK
Young, David A. ... Augusta, GA
Young, David A. ... Cleveland, OH
Young, David A. ... Mason, TX
Young, David A. ... Tacoma, WA
Young, David Alexander ... Lafayette, LA
Young, David B. ... Austin, TX
Young, David C. ... San Francisco, CA
Young, David C. ... Dallas, TX
Young, David F. ... Miami, FL
Young, David F., P.A. ... Miami, FL
Young, David H. ... Miami, FL
Young, David H. ... Morris Plains, NJ
Young, David H. ... San Antonio, TX
Young, David J. ... Cincinnati, OH
Young, David J. ... Columbus, OH
Young, David L. ... Caldwell, ID
Young, David L. ... Brockway, PA
Punxsutawney, PA
Young, David M. ... Washington, DC
Young, David Michael ... Woodland, CA
Young, David P. ... Tampa, FL
Young, David P. ... Houston, TX
Young, David R. ... Leesburg, VA
Young, David R. ... Kirkland, WA
Young, David S. ... Salt Lake City, UT
Young, David T. ... Menlo Park, CA
Young, David W. ... Tallahassee, FL
Young, David W. ... Baltimore, MD
Young, David W. ... Agawam, MA
Young, David W. ... Gresham, OR
Young, Dean ... Morrow, GA
Young, Dean A. ... Hartford City, IN
Young, Dean K. ... Honolulu, HI
Young, Dean, P.C. ... Morrow, GA
Young, Debbie L. ... Los Angeles, CA
Young, Deborah A. ... Newark, NJ
Young, Deborah S. ... Rochester, NY
Young, Debra C. ... Santa Barbara, CA
Young, Debra Esther ... Pleasantville, NY
Young, Debra M. Smith ... Vero Beach, FL
Young, DeForrest O. ... Englewood, CO
Young, Delores A. ... Landover, MD
Young, Delores A., & Associates, P.C.
Landover, MD
Young, Denise K. ... Aspen, CO
Young, Dennis A. ... New York, NY
Young, Dennis B. ... Parkesburg, PA
Young, Dennis M. ... Newport Beach, CA
Young, Dennis M. ... Walnut Creek, CA
Young, Dennis S. ... Dallas, TX
Young, Denzil R. ... Baker, MT
Young, Derek William ... Cleveland, OH
Young, Dexter W. ... San Francisco, CA
Young, Diana Whipkey ... Marietta, GA
Young, Dias A. ... Jackson, MS
Young, Dickson J. ... Fairfax, VA
Young & Dietsch ... Cleveland, OH
Young, Don A. ... Ennis, TX
Young, Don J., III ... Norfolk, VA
Young, Dona Davis Gagliano
Hartford, CT
Young, Donald A. ... Saylorsburg, PA
Young, Donald B. ... Des Moines, IA
Young, Donald D. ... Rio Rancho, NM
Young, Donald N. ... Rockville, MD
Young, Donald P. ... Washington, DC
Young, Donald R. ... New York, NY
Tarrytown, NY
Young, Donald S. ... Detroit, MI
Young, Donald S. ... Macungie, PA
Young, Donald V., (P.C.) ... Chicago, IL
Young, Donna M. ... Treasury Department, Internal Revenue Service, GV
Young, Donna M. ... New Orleans, LA
Young, Donni E. ... New Orleans, LA
Young, Doreen Stone ... St. Petersburg, FL
Young, Doris H. ... New York, NY
Young, Dorothy C. ... Richmond, VA
Young, Doug ... Austin, TX
Young, Douglas C. ... San Antonio, TX
Young, Douglas H. ... Syracuse, NY
Young, Douglas M. ... San Francisco, CA
Young, Douglas R. ... San Francisco, CA
Young, Doyle L. ... Waco, TX
Young, Doyle R. ... Florence, AL
Young, Duane ... Carmel, NY
Young, Duane D. ... Springfield, IL
Young, Duane J. ... Honolulu, HI
Young, Duane K. ... Washington, DC
Young, Duncan A. ... Omaha, NE
Young, D.W. ... Rock Island, IL
Young, E. Kevin ... San Francisco, CA
Young, E. Paul, III ... Shreveport, LA
Young, E. Preston ... Louisville, KY
Young, E. Richard, Jr. ... Ephrata, PA
Young, Edgar ... Cheyenne, WY
Young, Edward ... Boston, MA
Young, Edward D., III ... Arlington, VA
Young, Edward G. ... Madison, WI
Young, Edward L., Jr. ... Valrico, FL
Young, Edward R. ... West Babylon, NY
Young, Edward R. ... Memphis, TN
Young, Edward S. ... Beaver Falls, PA
Young, Edwin Allen ... Pittsburgh, PA
Young, Edwin Allen, Law Offices of
Pittsburgh, PA
Young, Eileen Beth ... Norman, OK
Young, Elin B. ... Cleveland, OH
Young, Elizabeth Marion ... New York, NY
Young, Elizabeth S. ... Findlay, OH
Young, Elizabeth Theobald
Indianapolis, IN
Young, Emily J. ... Dallas, TX
Young, Emmett N. ... Tallahassee, FL
Young, Eric C. ... San Diego, CA
Young, Eric C. ... Belleville, IL
Collinsville, IL
Young, Eric G. ... Santa Rosa, CA
Young, Eric R. ... Los Angeles, CA
Young, Eric S.T. ... Honolulu, HI
Young, Erik G. ... San Francisco, CA
Young, Ernest A. ... Washington, DC
Young, Erwin ... Brooklyn, NY
Young, Eugene B. ... Syracuse, NY
Young, Eugene V., Jr. ... Chesterton, IN
Young, Evelyn Pulliam ... Murray Hill, NJ
Young, F. Scott ... Atlanta, GA
Young, F. Thomas ... Valdosta, GA
Young & Fezekas, Ltd., Law Offices of
Chicago, IL
Young & Finley ... Russellville, AR
Young, Finley ... Tacoma, WA
Young, Foster M. ... Shelton, CT
Young, Frances M. ... Jackson, MS
Young, Francis J., (P.C.) ... Hartsdale, NY
Young, Francis W. ... Asheville, NC
Young, Francis X. ... New York, NY
White Plains, NY
Young, Frank M., III ... Birmingham, AL
Young, Frank R. ... Danville, IL
Young, Frederick H. ... Weymouth, MA
Young, Frederick H. ... Austin, TX
Young, Frederick N. ... Dayton, OH
Young, Fredric L. ... Dayton, OH
Young, G. Rodney, II ... Harrisonburg, VA
Young, Gail L. ... Edina, MN
Young, Gareth ... New York, NY
Young, Gary Alan ... Austin, TX
Young, Gary D. ... Paris, TX
Young, Gary F. ... Hickory, NC
Young, Gary L. ... Lincoln, NE
Young, Gary M., Law Offices of
Madison, WI
Young, Gary S. ... West Orange, NJ
Young, Gaydell ... Stamford, CT
Young, Gayle Y. L. ... Littleton, CO
Young, Genevieve M. ... Washington, DC
Young, Geo. F., Jr. ... Mc Keesport, PA
Young, Geoffrey G. ... Chattanooga, TN
Young, Geoffrey P. ... New Rochelle, NY
Young, George ... Birmingham, AL
Young, George C. ... Orlando, FL
Young, George D. ... Circleville, OH
Young, George F., III ... Allison Park, PA
Young, George G., III ... Houston, TX
Young, George G., Jr. ... East Norriton, PA
Young, George Guyer, III ... East Norriton, PA
Young, George L. ... San Marino, CA
Young, George L., Jr. ... Blue Bell, PA
Young, George Parker ... Fort Worth, TX
Young, George S. ... Salt Lake City, UT
Young, George W. ... Pasadena, CA
Young, Gerald A. ... Blue Bell, PA
Young, Gerald F. ... Lansing, MI
Young, Gerald J. ... Farmington Hills, MI
Young, Gerald W. ... Steamboat Springs, CO
Young, Glen E. ... Beverly Hills, CA
Young, Glenn D., Jr. ... Wichita, KS
Young, Glenn M. ... Washington, DC
Young, Glenn W. ... Gulph Mills, PA
Young, Goldman & Van Beek, A Professional Corporation ... Washington, DC
Alexandria, VA
Young, Gordon C. ... San Francisco, CA
Young, Gordon G. ... Baltimore, MD
Young, Gordon L. ... Phoenix, AZ
Young, Gordon M. Speights ... Houston, TX
Young, Gordon W. ... Huntington, WV
Young, Grant L. ... Rexburg, ID
Young, Gray Anthony ... Boise, ID
Young, Gregg ... New York, NY
Young, Gregory A. ... Austin, TX
Young, Gregory D. ... Santa Barbara, CA
Young, Gregory E. ... Palm Beach, FL
Young, Gregory E. ... Cincinnati, OH
Young, Gregory P. ... New York, NY
Young, Gregory R. ... Reading, PA
Young, Gregory S. ... Wichita, KS
Young, Gregory S. ... Columbus, OH
Young, Gregory T. ... Birmingham, MI
Young, Guy M. ... Alturas, CA
Young, Gwen J. ... Denver, CO
Young, Gwendolyn M. ... Louisville, KY
Young, Gwynne A. ... Tampa, FL
Young, H. Alan ... Washington, DC
Alexandria, VA
Young, H. David ... Little Rock, AR
Young, H. Franklin, III ... Charleston, SC
Young, H. Lane, II ... Atlanta, GA
Young, Hal A., Jr. ... Costa Mesa, CA
Young, Hampton M., Jr. ... Minden, NV
Reno, NV
Young, Harold ... Boynton Beach, FL
Young, Harold A. ... Des Moines, IA
Young, Harold D. ... New York, NY
Young, Harold H., Jr. ... El Paso, TX
Young, Harriet R. Campbell
New Orleans, LA
Young, Harris & Harvey, P.C.
Crawfordsville, IN
Young, Harry A., Jr. ... Chicago, IL
Young, Harry H. ... Birmingham, MI
Young, Haskins, Mann, Gregory & Smith, P.C. ... Martinsville, VA
Stuart, VA
Young, Hayes ... New York, NY
Young, Heather A. ... Emeryville, CA
Young, Heather M. ... Tacoma, WA
Young, Heidi R. ... New York, NY
Young, Henrie, Humphries & Mason
Pomona, CA
Upland, CA
Young, Henry C., Jr. ... Akron, OH
Young, Henry E. ... Norwalk, OH
Young, Henry L., Jr. ... Dawsonville, GA
Young, Henry L., Jr., P.C.
Dawsonville, GA
Gainesville, GA
Young, Herbert C. ... New York, NY
Young, Herbert L. ... San Diego, CA
Young, Hilary Hughes ... Austin, TX
Young, Hillyer McD. ... Atlanta, GA
Young, Horace S. ... Corpus Christi, TX
Young, Howard A. ... Madison, WI
Young, Howard B. ... Bingham Farms, MI
Young, Howard S., Jr. ... Indianapolis, IN
Young, Hoychick & Aguillard ... Eunice, LA
Young and Hubbell ... Lebanon, OH
Young, Hubert H., Jr. ... Suffolk, VA
Young, Ira M. ... St. Louis, MO
Young, Isaac E. ... Maplewood, MO
Young, Ivor H. ... Dublin, OH
Young, J. Addison, 2nd ... New Rochelle, NY
Young, J. Bayard ... Denver, CO
Young, J. Bradley ... St. Louis, MO
Young, J. Craig ... Birmingham, AL
Young, J. David ... Indianapolis, IN
Young, J. David ... Manheim, PA
Young, J. David, Jr. ... Manheim, PA
Young, J. Dean ... Morrow, GA
Young, J. Hoyt ... Atlanta, GA
Young, J. Mark ... Washington, DC
Young, J. Michael ... Great Falls, MT
Young, J. Michael ... Houston, TX
Young, J. Nilas, (A Professional Law Corporation) ... Eunice, LA
Young, J. Owen ... Miami, FL
Young, J. Randy ... Baton Rouge, LA
Young, J. Ron ... Houston, TX
Young, J. Rutledge, Jr. ... Charleston, SC
Young, J. Stephen ... Long Beach, CA
Young, J. Talbot, Jr. ... Cleveland, OH
Young, J. Wesley ... Fort Worth, TX
Young, Jack D. ... Portsmouth, OH
Young, Jack D. ... Muleshoe, TX
Young, Jack L. ... Virginia Beach, VA
Young, Jack M. ... Waltham, MA
Young, Jacob J. ... New York, NY
Young, Jacqueline
National Labor Relations Board, Office of the General Counsel, GV
Young, James A. ... Tampa, FL
Young, James A. ... Philadelphia, PA
Radnor, PA
Young, James Alexander ... Bennington, VT
Young, James B. ... San Francisco, CA
Young, James B. ... Naples, FL
Young, James B. ... Milwaukee, WI
Young, James B., P.A. ... Naples, FL
Young, James C. ... New Orleans, LA
Young, James D. ... Wichita, KS
Young, James D. ... Elmira, NY
Young, James D. ... Harrisburg, PA
Young, James E. ... Cleveland, OH
Young, James E., Jr. ... New Orleans, LA
Young, James F. ... Elmira, NY
Young, James F. ... White Plains, NY
Young, James F. ... Philadelphia, PA
Young, James F., Jr. ... Chicago, IL
Young, James G. ... Bellaire, MI
Young, James H. ... Indianapolis, IN
Young, James H. ... Blue Springs, MO
Young, James H., II ... Portland, ME
Young, James H., Jr. ... Wayne, WV
Young, James Harvey ... Greencastle, IN
Young, James J. F. ... New York, NY
Young, James L. ... Carmel, IN
Young, James L. ... Minneapolis, MN
Young, James L., Jr. ... New London, CT
Young, James Leon ... Jackson, MS
Young, James M. ... Salem, VA
Young, James P. ... Washington, DC
Young, James P. ... Minneapolis, MN
Young, James R. ... Boulder, CO
Young, James R. ... New York, NY
Young, James R. ... Austin, TX
Young, James R., Law Office of
Houston, TX
Young, James R., P.C., Law Office of
Austin, TX
Young, James S. ... Louisville, KY
Young, James T. ... Fort Wayne, IN
Young, James T. ... Conway, SC
Young, James W., Jr. ... Jackson, MS
Young, James W., Jr. ... Pittsburgh, PA
Young, Jamie ... Los Angeles, CA
Young, Jane Ellen ... Manchester, NH
Young, Jane G. Connell ... Louisville, KY
Young, Jane O'Leary ... Champaign, IL
Young, Jane W. ... Nashville, TN
Young, Janet E. ... Lakewood, CO
Young, Janet E. ... St. Louis, MO
Young, Janet Muller ... Virginia Beach, VA
Young, Jarold M. ... Reno, NV
Young, Jas. W. ... Forest Grove, OR
Young, Jason J. ... Troy, MI
Young, Jay A. ... Chattanooga, TN
Young, Jaye A. ... Los Angeles, CA
Young, Jean Johnston ... Woodstock, GA
Young, Jeanine Maradei ... Pittsburgh, PA
Young, Jeannie ... Great Falls, MT
Young, Jeffrey A. ... Dover, DE
Young, Jeffrey A. ... Lowell, MA
Young, Jeffrey A. ... Vienna, VA
Young, Jeffrey E. ... Atlanta, GA
Young, Jeffrey M. ... Raleigh, NC
Young, Jeffrey N. ... Topsham, ME
Young, Jeffrey S. ... Santa Barbara, CA
Young, Jeffrey S. ... Texarkana, TX
Young, Jerome D. ... San Francisco, CA
Young, Jerry M. ... Houston, TX
Young, Jess W. ... San Antonio, TX
Young, Jesse A. ... Brooklyn, NY
Young, Jessica B. ... Springfield, MA
Young, Jessica K. ... Milwaukee, WI
Young, Joan E. ... Pontiac, MI
Young, Joan E. ... New York, NY
Young, Joanne W. ... Washington, DC
Young, Joe B. ... Longview, TX
Young, Joe D. ... Des Moines, IA
Young, Joe R., Jr. ... Bartow, FL
Young, John ... Los Angeles, CA
Young, John A. ... Washington, DC
Young, John A. ... Brooklyn, NY
New York, NY
Young, John A., Jr. ... Mishawaka, IN
Young, John B. ... Bakersfield, CA
Young, John C. ... Baton Rouge, LA
Young, John C. ... New York, NY
Young, John C. ... Columbus, OH
Young, John Condon ... New York, NY
Young, John D. ... Birmingham, AL
Young, John E. ... Bloomfield Hills, MI
Young, John E. ... Kansas City, MO
Young, John E. ... New York, NY
Young, John F. ... Denver, CO
Young, John F. ... New Orleans, LA
Young, John F. ... Bradford, PA
Young, John F. ... Reston, VA
Young, John G. ... Seattle, WA
Young, John G., Jr. ... St. Louis, MO
Young, John H. ... Berkeley, CA
Young, John H. ... Miami, FL
Young, John H. ... Rockford, IL
Young, John H. ... Roanoke, VA
Young, John Hardin ... Washington, DC
Young, John J. ... Des Moines, IA
Young, John K. ... Philadelphia, PA
Young, John L. ... New Orleans, LA
Young, John L. ... Pittsfield, MA
Young, John L. ... Princeton, MO
Young, John L. ... Salt Lake City, UT
Young, John M. ... Sapulpa, OK
Young, John M. ... Columbia, SC
Young, John M. ... Houston, TX
Young, John P. ... Los Angeles, CA
Young, John P. ... Indianapolis, IN
Young, John P. ... San Antonio, TX
Young, John R. ... Palm Harbor, FL
Young, John R. ... West Palm Beach, FL
Young, John R. ... Corinth, MS
Young, John R. ... New York, NY
Young, John S. ... Gurnee, IL
Young, John S. ... Sweetwater, TX
Young, John W. ... Binghamton, NY
Young, John W. ... Sapulpa, OK
Young and Johnson ... Ennis, TX
Young, Jonathan ... New York, NY
Young, Jonathan B. ... Lansdale, PA
Young, Jonathan C. ... Braintree, MA
Young, Jonathan F. ... Atlanta, GA
Young, Jonathan M. ... Coram, NY
Young, Jonathan W. ... Chicago, IL
Young, Jorge S. ... Fremont, CA
Young, Jos. K. ... Austin, TX
Young, Joseph A. ... Oklahoma City, OK
Young, Joseph B. ... Indianapolis, IN
Young, Joseph C. ... Cleveland, OH
Young, Joseph E. ... New York, NY
Young, Joseph G. ... Ventura, CA
Young, Joseph G. ... Fort Lauderdale, FL
Miami, FL
Young, Joseph H. ... Coral Gables, FL
Young, Joseph H. ... Baltimore, MD
Young, Joseph H. ... Baltimore, MD
Young, Joseph L. ... Anchorage, AK
Young, Joseph Lee ... Vesper, WI
Young, Joseph M. ... Hampton, VA
Young, Joseph Patrick ... Minneapolis, MN
Young, Joseph R., Jr. ... Youngstown, OH
Young, Joseph W. ... St. Petersburg, FL
Young, J.T. ... Portland, OR
Young, Judith H. ... Arlington Heights, IL
Young, Judith L. ... Los Angeles, CA
Young, Judy L. ... Olympia, WA
Young, Julia L. ... San Francisco, CA
Young, Julianne May ... Bryan, TX
Young, Julie A. ... Richmond, VA
Young, Julie Arias ... Los Angeles, CA
Young, Julius O., III ... Oakland, CA
Young, Kaipolani K.B. ... San Francisco, CA
Young and Kaluzny ... Bingham Farms, MI
Young, Karen ... New York, NY
Young, Karen A.
Lauderdale-By-The-Sea, FL
Young, Karen E. ... Simsbury, CT

Young, Karen J. .... **Gulfport, MS**
Young, Karen L. .... Oklahoma City, OK
Young, Karin M. .... **Detroit, MI**
Young, Katherine A. .... Knoxville, TN
Young, Katherine J. .... The Dalles, OR
Young, Katherine L. .... **Boston, MA**
Young, Kathleen A. .... Kokomo, IN
Young, Kathleen F. .... **Minneapolis, MN**
Young, Kathryn A. .... **Beverly Hills, CA**
Young, Kathryn S. .... **Fort Collins, CO**
Young, Keita A. .... **Woodbridge, NJ**
Young, Keita Archie .... Philadelphia, PA
Young, Keith K. H. .... **Honolulu, HI**
Young, Keith L. .... **Chicago, IL**
Young, Kelly Dee, Mr. .... Fairfax, OK
Young, Kelly M. .... **Charleston, WV**
Young, Kelly T. .... Gibbsboro, NJ
Young, Kenneth A. .... Philadelphia, PA
Young, Kenneth B. .... **Williamsport, PA**
Young, Kenneth C. .... Sacramento, CA
Young, Kenneth E. .... **Greenville, SC**
Young, Kenneth J. .... Dover, DE
Young, Kenneth L. .... Upper Sandusky, OH
Young, Kenneth M. .... **Beverly Hills, CA**
Young, Kenneth M. .... Wheaton, IL
Young, Kenneth P. .... Encino, CA
Young, Kenneth R., Jr. .... **Sumter, SC**
Young, Kent E. .... Red Lodge, MT
Young, Kerry W. .... Dallas, TX
Young & Kester .... Springville, UT
Young, Kevin .... Fresno, CA
Young, Kevin C. .... Philadelphia, PA
Young, Kevin E. .... **Boston, MA**
Young, Kevin G. .... Syracuse, NY
Young, Kevin J. .... **Chicago, IL**
Young, Kevin M. .... **Albany, NY**
Young, Kevin M. .... **Cleveland, OH**
Young, Kevin M. .... **San Antonio, TX**
Young, Kial S. .... **Washington, DC**
Young, Kim B. .... Waco, TX
Young, Kimberly .... **Washington, DC**
Young, Kurt A. .... Nashville, IN
Young, Kurt M. .... Toledo, OH
Young, L. Benjamin, Jr.
Department of Agriculture, Office of the General Counsel, GV
Young, L. Bennett .... Bloomfield Hills, MI
Young, L. Everett, Jr. .... Fort Worth, TX
Young, L. Geoffrey .... **St. Petersburg, FL**
Tampa, FL
Young, L. Jackson, Jr. .... **Birmingham, AL**
Young, L. Perry .... Wharton, TX
Young, Lance C. .... **Birmingham, MI**
Young & LaPuzza .... Omaha, NE
Young, Larry L. .... Tulsa, OK
Young, Laura W. .... **San Francisco, CA**
Young, Laurence .... **San Francisco, CA**
Young, Laurence A. .... Westminster, CA
Young, Laurie Briggs .... **New Orleans, LA**
Young, Lavette H. .... Knightdale, NC
Young, Lawrence A. .... **Houston, TX**
Young, Lawrence E. .... **Oklahoma City, OK**
Young, Lawrence J. .... Syracuse, NY
Young, Lawrence M. .... **New York, NY**
Young, Lawrence R. .... Salem, OR
Young, Lawrence V. .... **York, PA**
Young, LeDon, (Ms.) .... **State College, PA**
Young, Lee .... Union, MO
Young, Lee E. .... **Pascagoula, MS**
Young, Lee R., Jr. .... Los Angeles, CA
Young, LeGrande L. .... **Shelton, CT**
Young, Lela Mahoney .... **Atlanta, GA**
Young, Leo B. .... Honolulu, HI
Young, Leo F. .... Florence, OR
Young, Leo J. .... Irvine, CA
Young, Leona G. .... **Atlanta, GA**
Young, Leonard .... Cleveland, OH
Young, Leonard A. .... **New Orleans, LA**
Young, Leonard D. .... **Cleveland, OH**
Young, Lesley D. .... Santa Ana, CA
Young, Lettie .... Sacramento, CA
Young, Lias Carl .... Dallas, TX
Young, Lind, Endres & Kraft
New Albany, IN
Young, Linda C.J. .... **Tacoma, WA**
Young, Linda H. .... New York, NY
Young, Linda M. .... Boston, MA
Young, Lindsay .... **Knoxville, TN**
Young, Linwood H. .... Ellsworth, ME
Young, Lisa .... New York, NY
Young, Lisa M. .... Orlando, FL
Young, Lisa M. .... **Chicago, IL**
Young, Lisa M. .... Binghamton, NY
Young, Llewellyn P., Jr. .... New York, NY
Young, Lloyd D.
Federal Communications Commission, Cable Services Bureau, GV
Young, Logan F. .... Honolulu, HI
Young, Lori L. .... **Ponca City, OK**
Young, Louis .... **Syracuse, NY**
Young, Louisa M. .... Boulder, CO
Young, Louise O. .... St. Petersburg, FL
Young, Lowell Dale .... Seattle, WA
Young, Lucien C., III .... Caldwell, OH
Young, Lucien C., Jr. .... Caldwell, OH
Young, Lucinda H. .... San Francisco, CA
Young & Lyndaker .... Lowville, NY
Young, Lynn S. .... Napa, CA
Young, M. Don .... Tooele, UT
Young, M. Lynn .... Gainesville, GA
Young, M. Scott .... **Cleveland, OH**
Young, Madelene V. .... Roanoke, VA
Young & Madigan, S.C. .... Milwaukee, WI
Young, Malcolm D. .... **Omaha, NE**
Young, Malcolm D., Jr. .... **Atlanta, GA**
Young, Marc A. .... Beaumont, TX
Corpus Christi, TX
Houston, TX
Young, Marc D. .... **Los Angeles, CA**
Young, Margaret Helen .... **Florence, AL**
Young, Margaret M. .... **Lexington, KY**
Young, Margaret R. .... **Dayton, OH**
Young, Marianne W. .... Ithaca, NY
Young, Marilyn A. .... San Francisco, CA
Young, Marilyn A. .... **Indianapolis, IN**
Young, Marilyn Ann .... **Oklahoma City, OK**
Young, Marilyn J. .... Calabasas, CA
Young, Marjorie A. .... Gibsonia, PA
Young, Marjorie M. .... Combined Locks, WI
Young, Mark .... Brookfield, WI
Young, Mark A. .... Mason City, IA
Young, Mark A.H. .... Los Angeles, CA
Young, Mark Bennet .... Dallas, TX
Young, Mark D. .... **Washington, DC**
Young, Mark E. .... **New Orleans, LA**
Young, Mark E. .... **Boston, MA**
Young, Mark James .... **Jacksonville, FL**
Young, Mark S. .... **Milwaukee, WI**
Young, Mark T. .... Hixson, TN
Young, Mark T., Law Offices of
Los Angeles, CA
Young, Mark V. .... Ponte Vedra Beach, FL
Young, Marlene G., P.C. .... Atlanta, GA
Young, Marlene Griffith .... Atlanta, GA
Young, Marlo A. .... **New York, NY**
Young, Marlon V. .... **Santa Rosa, CA**
Young, Marshall P. .... Rapid City, SD
Young, Martha R. .... Ann Arbor, MI
Young, Martin M. .... Cincinnati, OH
Young, Marvin E. .... **Lebanon, OH**
Young, Marvin O. .... **St. Louis, MO**
Young, Mary A. .... Warrensburg, MO
Young, Mary Ann Garr
Jefferson City, MO
Young, Mary Elaine .... San Antonio, TX
Young, Mary Jane .... Irving, TX
Young, Mary McNulty .... **Indianapolis, IN**
Young, Mary S. .... Hartford, CT
Young, Mary-James .... Simpsonville, KY
Young, Maureen Ann .... **San Francisco, CA**
Young, Maureen W. .... **Albany, NY**
Young, Maurice .... Far Rockaway, NY
Young, Maurice A. .... Youngstown, OH
Young & McDade .... Franklin, TN
Young, Melissa Amos .... **Roanoke, VA**
Young, Melissa Ann .... Wayne, NJ
Young, Melissa Hope .... Berkeley, CA
Young, Melvin F. .... Cleveland, OH
Young, Mercedes W. .... Hartville, OH
Young, Merlin S. .... Boise, ID
Young, Merne E. .... Irvine, CA
Young, Meryl L. .... **San Diego, CA**
Young, Michael .... **New York, NY**
Young, Michael A. .... Atlanta, GA
Young, Michael A. .... Shakopee, MN
Young, Michael C. .... **Green Valley, AZ**
Tucson, AZ
Young, Michael D. .... **Los Angeles, CA**
Young, Michael D. .... **Westport, CT**
Young, Michael D. .... **Jackson, MS**
Young, Michael D. .... Clinton, NJ
Young, Michael David .... **Westport, CT**
Young, Michael E. .... Pottsville, PA
Young, Michael E., & Associates, P.C.
Pottsville, PA
Young, Michael F. .... Lowville, NY
Young, Michael G. .... Cedar Park, TX
Young, Michael H., (P.C.) .... Oakland, CA
Young, Michael J. .... Walnut Creek, CA
Young, Michael J. .... Minneapolis, MN
Young, Michael J. .... Hackensack, NJ
Young, Michael L. .... **Edinburg, TX**
Young, Michael P. .... **Austin, TX**
Young, Michael R. .... **Bakersfield, CA**
Young, Michael R. .... **Redlands, CA**
Young, Michael R. .... **St. Louis, MO**
Young, Michael R. .... **New York, NY**
Young, Michael V. .... **Houston, TX**
Young, Michael W. .... Bainbridge Island, WA
Young, Michaela Smith .... Atlanta, GA
Young, Michele J. .... **Boston, MA**
Young, Min H. .... Anchorage, AK
Young, Mitzi A.
Nuclear Regulatory Commission, Office of the General Counsel, GV
Young, Mona H. .... Edina, MN
Young & Monte .... Northfield, VT
Young Moore and Henderson, P.A.
Raleigh, NC
Young, Morgan & Cann .... Clarksburg, WV
Young & Moriwaki .... **New York, NY**
Tarrytown, NY
Young, Moshe A. .... Studio City, CA
Young, Nadine Kline .... **Hartford, CT**
Young, Nancy .... **New York, NY**
Young, Nancy A. .... Pasadena, CA
Young, Nancy B. .... **Columbus, OH**
Young, Nancy J. .... Redlands, CA
Young, Nancy J. .... Ithaca, NY
Young, Nancy Lighthart .... **Fredonia, NY**
Young, Nancy M. .... Columbia, SC
Young, Nancy N. .... **Washington, DC**
Young, Nancy V.
Christiansted, St. Croix, VI
Young, Naomi .... **Los Angeles, CA**
Young, Natalie K. .... **San Francisco, CA**
Young, Nathaniel J., Jr. .... Boston, MA
Young, Neal E. .... Winter Haven, FL
Young, Neal E. .... Dallas, TX
Young, Nelson P. .... Pittsburgh, PA
Young, Nevins D. .... Huntington Beach, CA
Young, Nicholas Stokes .... Lutherville, MD
Young, Noel C. .... New Orleans, LA
Young, Norman E. .... Lander, WY
Young, Norman Gregory .... Pomona, CA
Young, O. Henry (Mike) .... **Abilene, TX**
Young, O. Philip .... San Jose, CA
Young, Oglesby H. .... **Portland, OR**
Young, Oliver C. .... Buffalo, NY
Young, Oliver E., Jr. .... Vernon, AL
Young, Ouida C. M. .... Newton, MA
Young, Pamela A. .... Boulder, CO
Young, Pamela J. .... Miami, FL
Young, Pamela M. .... **Washington, DC**
Young, Pamela Nolan .... Boston, MA
Young, Pamela S. .... **Pleasanton, CA**
Young, Pamela Thorpe .... Raleigh, NC
Young, Parker D. .... **Dallas, TX**
Young, Pasquale .... **New Haven, CT**
Young, Patrice W. L. .... Evanston, IL
Young, Patricia A. .... **San Francisco, CA**
Young, Patricia G. .... Idaho City, ID
Young, Patricia N. .... Washington, DC
Young, Patricia R. .... **Nashville, TN**
Young, Patrick H. .... Paulding, OH
Young, Patrick H., Co., L.P.A. .... Paulding, OH
Young, Patrick Joseph .... Hempstead, NY
Young, Patrick M. .... Belleville, IL
Young, Patrick W. .... Gary, IN
Young, Patsy .... Houston, TX
Young, Paul .... **Fort Lauderdale, FL**
Young, Paul A., Jr. .... Enterprise, AL
Young, Paul B. .... **Pine Bluff, AR**
Young, Paul B., Jr. .... Little Rock, AR
Young, Paul D. .... **New York, NY**
Young, Paul H., Associates .... **Bensalem, PA**
Young, Paul J. .... **Edison, NJ**
Young, Paula C. .... Denver, CO
Young, Paula M. .... **St. Louis, MO**
Young, Penelope .... Tooele, UT
Young & Perez .... Whitehouse, NJ
Young & Perl, PLC .... **Memphis, TN**
Young, Perry Y. .... **Benton, AR**
Young, Peter F. .... Hudson, OH
Young, Peter F. .... **Burlington, VT**
Young, Peter F., Jr. .... Northfield, VT
Young, Peter G. .... Wenatchee, WA
Young, Peter J. .... Hopedale, MA
Young, Peter J. .... **Casper, WY**
Young, Peter Joel C. .... Washington, DC
Young, Phebe S. .... **Wilmington, DE**
Young, Philip .... Wainscott, NY
Young, Philip B. .... **San Francisco, CA**
Young, Philip J. .... **Minneapolis, MN**
Young, Philip L. .... Atlanta, GA
Young, Philip R. .... Newark, OH
Young & Pickett .... **Texarkana, AR**
Texarkana, TX
Young, Probal G. .... **Walnut Creek, CA**
Young, Pryor, Lynn & Jerardi
Dayton, OH
Young, R. Allen .... Mount Pleasant, SC
Young, R. Anthony .... **Los Angeles, CA**
Young, R. Brent .... Shreveport, LA
Young, R. Eric .... Gresham, OR
Young, R. James .... **Jackson, MS**
Young, R. Reid, III, (P.C.) .... Martinsville, VA
Young, R. Tate .... Houston, TX
Young, Rachel D. .... **Burbank, CA**
Young, Rachel H. .... St. Paul, MN
Young, Ralph C. .... Akron, OH
Young, Ralph C. .... **Oak Hill, WV**
Young, Ralph D. .... **Gulfport, MS**
Young, Ralph E., Jr. .... **Meridian, MS**
Young, Ralph M. .... **Florence, AL**
Young, Randall D. .... Kansas City, MO
Young, Randall H. .... East Providence, RI
Young, Randel R. .... **Houston, TX**
Young, Randy W. .... Fort Wayne, IN
Young, Raymond H. .... **Boston, MA**
Young, Raymond P. .... **Gresham, OR**
Young, Rebecca C. .... Madison, WI
Young, Rebecca S. .... **San Francisco, CA**
Young, Rebecca S. .... **Lake Charles, LA**
Young, Regina Alberini .... **Jacksonville, FL**
Young, Reginald E. .... Charleston, MO
Young, Reginald G., Jr. .... Chicago, IL
Young, Rene S. .... Salina, KS
Young, Reuben F. .... Cary, NC
Young, Reverman & Napier Co., L.P.A.
Cincinnati, OH
Young, Rex L. .... Department of Justice, Criminal Division, GV
Young, R. H. .... Nampa, ID
Young & Rice .... **Biloxi, MS**
Gulfport, MS
Young, Richard .... Jacksonville, FL
Young, Richard .... Van Hornesville, NY
Young, Richard A. .... **Indianapolis, IN**
Young, Richard A. .... Dearborn Heights, MI
Young, Richard A. .... **New York, NY**
Young, Richard A. "Drew"
Indianapolis, IN
Young, Richard B. .... Bala Cynwyd, PA
Young, Richard C. .... Agawam, MA
Young, Richard D. .... **Las Vegas, NV**
Young, Richard E. .... Lake Forest, CA
Young, Richard E. .... **Washington, DC**
Young, Richard E. .... **Dallas, TX**
Young, Richard G. .... **Washington, DC**
Young, Richard G. .... Rochester, NY
Young, Richard H. .... Russellville, AR
Young, Richard L. .... Yreka, CA
Young, Richard L. .... Evansville, IN
Young, Richard L. .... Albuquerque, NM
Young, Richard M. .... **Atlanta, GA**
Young, Richard M. .... La Grange, TX
Young, Richard R. .... **Colorado Springs, CO**
Young, Richard S. .... Tempe, AZ
Young, Richard S. .... San Francisco, CA
Young, Richard S. .... **Arlington, VA**
Young, Richard T. .... **Upland, CA**
Young, Richard W. .... **Chicago, IL**
Young, Richard W. .... Grand Rapids, MI
Young, Richard W. .... Reno, NV
Young, Richard W. .... Accomac, VA
Young, Richard W., A Prof. Corp., Law Offices of .... **Reno, NV**
Young, Richaud & Myers
New Orleans, LA
Young, Rickey G. .... Martinsville, VA
Young Riley & Dudley .... Indianapolis, IN
Young, Robert .... Columbia, SC
Young, Robert A. .... Auburn, CA
Young, Robert A. .... Bartow, FL
Young, Robert A. .... **Bowling Green, KY**
Young, Robert A. .... Chesterfield, MO
Young, Robert A., Jr. .... Waterloo, IA
Young, Robert Adam
Federal Energy Regulatory Commission, Office of the General Counsel, GV
Young, Robert B. .... Phoenix, AZ
Young, Robert B. .... Jewett City, CT
Young, Robert B. .... Dover, DE
Young, Robert B. .... Chicago, IL
Young, Robert B. .... **Houston, TX**
Young, Robert C. .... **Baltimore, MD**
Young, Robert C. .... Van Wert, OH
Young, Robert D. .... Department of Justice, Antitrust Division, GV
Young, Robert D. .... Fort Myers, FL
Young, Robert D., P.A. .... Fort Myers, FL
Young, Robert E. .... Paragould, AR
Young, Robert E. .... **Los Angeles, CA**
Woodland Hills, CA
Young, Robert E. .... **West Hartford, CT**
Young, Robert E. .... Baltimore, MD
Young, Robert E. .... Bloomfield, NJ
Young, Robert E. .... **New York, NY**
Young, Robert E. .... Garland, TX
Young, Robert E. Lee .... Cincinnati, OH
Young, Robert F. .... **State College, PA**
Young, Robert G. .... Toledo, OH
Young, Robert H. .... Chula Vista, CA
Young, Robert H. .... **Philadelphia, PA**
Young, Robert H., Jr. .... **Radnor, PA**
Young, Robert J. .... Annandale, NJ
Young, Robert J. .... Whitehouse, NJ
Young, Robert J. .... Silver City, NM
Young, Robert J., III .... **New Orleans, LA**
Young, Robert J., Jr. .... **New Orleans, LA**
Young, Robert K. .... North Bellmore, NY
Young, Robert K. .... Allentown, PA
Young, Robert L. .... **San Diego, CA**
Young, Robert L. .... Sherman Oaks, CA
Young, Robert L. .... Walnut Creek, CA
Young, Robert L. .... **Orlando, FL**
Young, Robert L., A Professional Corporation
Walnut Creek, CA
Young, Robert M. .... Bakersfield, CA
Young, Robert M., Jr. .... **Los Angeles, CA**
Young, Robert Milton .... Akron, OH
Young, Robert O. .... Sherman Oaks, CA
Young, Robert O. .... West Covina, CA
Young, Robert P. .... Chattanooga, TN
Young, Robert P., Jr. .... Detroit, MI
Young, Robert R. .... St. Louis, MO
Young, Robert S. .... **Knoxville, TN**
Young, Robert S., III .... Yakima, WA
Young, Robert S. K. .... Bethesda, MD
Young, Robert W. ....
Department Of Health And Human Services, GV
Young, Robert W. .... **Dayton, OH**
Young, Robin A. .... **Garden City, NY**
Young, Robin B. .... **Benton, AR**
Young, Rocky H. .... **Knoxville, TN**
Young, Rodger D. .... **Southfield, MI**
New York, NY
Young, Rodney M. .... **Cincinnati, OH**
Young, Roger A. .... Franklin, IN
Young, Roger L. .... **Sarasota, FL**
Young, Roger L. .... **Wilson, NC**
Young, Roger M. .... North Charleston, SC
Young, Roger W. .... **Long Beach, CA**
Young, Rolan J. .... **Hartford, CT**
New Haven, CT
Young, Roland F., III .... **Hartford, CT**
Young, Roland S. .... **New York, NY**
Young, Ronald D. .... Little Rock, AR
Young, Ronald Davis .... Salt Lake City, UT
Young, Ronald E. .... Lantana, FL
Young, Ronald G .... New Lexington, OH
Young, Ronald L. .... Irvine, CA
Young, Ronald T. L. .... Napa, CA
Young, Ronald W. .... Tampa, FL
Young, Ronald W. .... St. Paul, MN
Young, Ronald W., P.A. .... Tampa, FL
Young, Ronna Friedman
Fort Lauderdale, FL
Young, Rosalind M. .... Metairie, LA
Young, Rosalyn D. .... West Orange, NJ
Young, Rosen, Dolgin & Finkel, Ltd.
Chicago, IL
Young & Rosenstrach, LLP
New Rochelle, NY
White Plains, NY
Young, Rowen N. .... Honolulu, HI
Young, Rowena .... **Menlo Park, CA**
Young, Rowland L. .... Chicago, IL
Young, Roy C. .... **Tallahassee, FL**
Young, Roy Traywick .... New York, NY
Young, Rufus C., Jr. .... **Los Angeles, CA**
Young, Rush L. .... Colorado Springs, CO
Young, Russell G. .... **San Francisco, CA**
Young, Russell M. .... Department of Justice, Environment and Natural Resources Division, GV
Young, Russell R. .... **Chicago, IL**
Young, Russell S. .... Montclair, NJ
Young, Ruth Hearn .... Savannah, GA
Young, S. Alyssa .... **New York, NY**

Youngwood, Jonathan K. ....New York, NY
Younker, Barr D., Jr. ....Melbourne, FL
Younker, Norman J. ....Salt Lake City, UT
Younker, Rodney B. ....Seattle, WA
Younkin, Cindy E. ....Bozeman, MT
Younkin, Jack C. ....Danville, PA
Shamokin, PA
Younkin, Richard W. ....Richmond, CA
Younkin, Tracy Allen ....Columbus, OH
Younkins, Kathy A. ....New York, NY
Younkins & Schecter ....New York, NY
Younossi, Helena S. ....New York, NY
Yount, Alan N. ....Washington, DC
Yount, Cynthia A. ....Tustin, CA
Yount, David W. ....Corte Madera, CA
Yount, George H. ....Citrus Heights, CA
Yount, J. Herman ....North Ridgeville, OH
Yount, Jennifer S. ....Los Angeles, CA
Yount, Joseph B., III ....Waynesboro, VA
Yount, Katie ....Wenatchee, WA
Yount, Leslie M. ....Hickory, NC
Yount, Marshall V. ....Hickory, NC
Yount, Richard C., Jr. ....Houston, TX
Yount, Scott P. ....New Orleans, LA
Houston, TX
Yount, Stephen B. ....Shallotte, NC
Southport, NC
Yount, Sue Wyskiver ....Columbus, OH
Yount, Susan M. ....Los Angeles, CA
Yount & Walker ....Hickory, NC
Younts, Alford, Brown & Goodson
Fountain Inn, SC
Greenville, SC
Younts, Melvin K. ....Fountain Inn, SC
Greenville, SC
Youpa, Jennifer Ashmos ....Dallas, TX
Youra, Gregory P. ....Atlanta, GA
Yourch, Eugene A. ....New York, NY
Youree, Earl ....Wagoner, OK
Youree, Shelly A. ....Dallas, TX
Yourick, Frank E., Jr. ....Pittsburgh, PA
Yourist, Bradley Jerrod ....Los Angeles, CA
Yourist, Daniel ....Los Angeles, CA
Yourke, Steven R. ....San Francisco, CA
Yourman, Kevin J. ....Los Angeles, CA
Yourshaw, Cynthia Marie ....Falls Church, VA
Yourshaw, Michael ....Washington, DC
Yousefzadeh, Faramarz ....Los Angeles, CA
Yousefzadeh, Faramarz, A Professional Law Corporation ....Los Angeles, CA
Youso, Bernard P. ....Monroe, WI
Youso, Karyn Gimbel ....Milwaukee, WI
Yousoof, Celeste H. ....Germantown, MD
Youssef, Ehab F. ....Los Gatos, CA
Youssef, Nivin T. ....Los Angeles, CA
Youssef-Coyle, Lami ....Toledo, OH
Youssefi, David H. ....San Francisco, CA
Youssefmir, Jacques ....Santa Monica, CA
Youssefyeh, Afshin David ....Los Angeles, CA
Youssefyeh, Liza ....Los Angeles, CA
Youssi, Francis E. ....Batavia, IL
Youssi, Youssi & Bina, Ltd. ....Batavia, IL
Youssouf, Joseph D. ....Englishtown, NJ
Youst, Lawrence R. ....Dallas, TX
Yousuff, Sohni ....Dallas, TX
Youth, Thomas B. ....Kirkland, WA
Youth, Wilfred H. C., (A Law Corporation)
Honolulu, HI
Youts, Charles A. ....Waco, TX
Youtsey, Deborah A. ....Cincinnati, OH
Youtt, Michael W. ....Houston, TX
Youtz, Carol A. ....Uniontown, OH
Youtz, Chris Robert ....Seattle, WA
Youtz, Michelle L. ....Los Angeles, CA
Youtz, Shane C. ....Albuquerque, NM
Yova, Steven P. ....Durham, NC
Yovan, Leslie A. ....Columbus, OH
Yovanovic, Nicholas S. ....Jacksonville, FL
Yovanovich, Richard D. ....Naples, FL
Yoveff, John K. ....Dearborn Heights, MI
Yoviene, Wendy M. ....Washington, DC
Yovino, Anthony ....Garden City, NY
Yovino, Lynn P. ....Atlanta, GA
Yovits, Steven ....Chicago, IL
Yovovich, Michael ....Madison, WI
Yow, Charles E. ....Brighton, MA
Yow, Fox & Mannen, L.L.P.
Wilmington, NC
Yow, H. Allen ....Jacksonville, IL
Yow, Jennifer Arlene ....Wilmington, NC
Yow, Lionel L. ....Wilmington, NC
Yowell, Brian Keith ....Fort Collins, CO
Yowell, G. Kent ....Northbrook, IL
Yowell, John L. ....Cincinnati, OH
Yowell, Paul Wayne ....Houston, TX
Yowell, William R. ....Chicago, IL
Yowell, Wm. H. ....Killeen, TX
Yox, Raymond A. ....Jamestown, NY
Yoxall, Antrim & Yoxall ....Liberal, KS
Yoxall, James R. ....Liberal, KS
Yoxall, Richard R. ....Liberal, KS
Yoxall, Thomas G. ....Dallas, TX
Yoza, Susan D. ....Honolulu, HI
Yozawitz, Sophia M. ....Bronx, NY
Yozell, Emily Jeanne ....Boston, MA
Yraquen, Francisco J. ....Vale, OR
Yruegas, Jennifer E. ....Portland, OR
Yrulegui, Richard J. ....Fresno, CA
Yrulegui, Richard J., A Prof. Corp., The Law Offices of ....Fresno, CA
Ysabal, Daniel J. ....Montebello, CA
Ysasaga, Jill K. ....Dallas, TX
Ysasaga, Michael A. ....Dallas, TX
Ysebaert, Sharon Herland
Minneapolis, MN
Yslas, John G. ....Los Angeles, CA
Yslas, Stephen D. ....Linthicum, MD
Ysursa, Benito T. ....Boise, ID
Ysursa, Bernard J. ....Belleville, IL
Ysursa, Shawn Del ....Boise, ID
Ytreberg, Dag E. ....Rochester, NY
Ytterberg, Alan V. ....Houston, TX
Ytterbo, Greta ....Atlanta, GA
Yttri, Steven N. ....Jefferson City, MO
Yturbide, B. V. ....Berkeley, CA
Yturbide & Jenkins ....Berkeley, CA
Yturralde, Christopher A. ....El Centro, CA
Yturri, David P. ....Dallas, TX
Yturri, Edward M. ....Spicewood, TX
Yturri Rose, LLP ....Fruitland, ID
Ontario, OR
Pendleton, OR
Portland, OR
Yu, Aihong ....Chicago, IL
Yu, Amy A. ....Farmington Hills, MI
Yu, Bernice ....New York, NY
Yu, Carolyn Marie ....San Francisco, CA
Yu, Chan Y. ....Pasadena, CA
Yu, Chiahua George ....Palo Alto, CA
Yu, Christina ....Orange, CA
Yu, Chuck ....Portland, OR
Yu, Constance J. ....San Francisco, CA
Yu, Cyril ....Fresno, CA
Yu, David G. ....New York, NY
Yu, Diane C. ....St. Louis, MO
Yu, Elizabeth ....Department of Justice, Environment and Natural Resources Division, GV
Yu, Felicia ....Los Angeles, CA
Yu, Frederick Y. ....Denver, CO
Yu, George C. ....San Diego, CA
Yu, Grace S. ....Nashville, TN
Yu, Gregory J. ....Burlingame, CA
Yu, Harold ....Menlo Park, CA
Yu, Helen H. ....Dallas, TX
Yu, Helen W. ....Augusta, GA
Yu, Hong-Sze A. ....San Francisco, CA
Yu, Hui ....Washington, DC
Yu, Hui Hui ....Brooklyn, NY
Yu, James S. ....New York, NY
Yu, Jeannie M. ....New York, NY
Yu, Jennifer K. ....New York, NY
Yu, John T. ....Bronx, NY
Yu, John W. ....Los Angeles, CA
Yu, Jun H. ....Pittsburgh, PA
Yu, Kay Kyungsun ....Philadelphia, PA
Yu, Kwanyu Helen ....San Francisco, CA
Yu, Kyung-Don ....Newtown Square, PA
Yu, Lien C. ....Seattle, WA
Yu, Lily Shang ....New York, NY
Yu, Margaret ....Miami, FL
Yu, Marissa J. ....Houston, TX
Yu, Matthew M. ....Los Angeles, CA
Yu, Michael T. ....San Francisco, CA
Yu, Michelle M. ....Los Angeles, CA
Yu, Mina ....New York, NY
Yu, Peter, Jr. ....New York, NY
Yu, Philip K. ....Newport Beach, CA
Yu, Robert H. ....Hackensack, NJ
Yu, Rosemarie ....New York, NY
Yu, Sandy K. ....New York, NY
Yu, Spencer H.C. ....Los Angeles, CA
Yu, Stephen ....Santa Clara, CA
Yu, Steve H. ....Los Angeles, CA
Yu Stromberg Cleveland, P.C.
Denver, CO
Yu, Susan C. ....San Bernardino, CA
Yu, Susan H. ....High Point, NC
Yu, Terry V. ....Albuquerque, NM
Yu, Tong ....New York, NY
Yu, Wayne W. ....New York, NY
Yu, William ....Chicago, IL
Yu, William ....New York, NY
Yuan, Georgia ....Moscow, ID
Yuan, Grace Tsuang ....Seattle, WA
Yuan, Ignatius H. ....St. Louis, MO
Yuan, Kelly ....New York, NY
Yuan, Loretta S. ....Los Angeles, CA
Yuan, Ma Lian ....Cambridge, MA
Yuan, Nancy Y. ....New York, NY
Yuan, Shih H. ....Pasadena, CA
Yucht, Joseph S. ....Highland Beach, FL
Yuckert, Gregory H. ....Tacoma, WA
Yuda, George S. ....Hilo, HI
Yudain, Ted ....Stamford, CT
Yudanin, Eugenia ....Roseland, NJ
Yudelevich, Yana ....Los Angeles, CA
Yudell, Carl R. ....Chicago, IL
Yudell, Kenneth S. ....New York, NY
Yudelson, David S. ....New York, NY
White Plains, NY
Yudelson, Michael J. ....Omaha, NE
Yudes, Alfred E., Jr. ....New York, NY
Yudes, James P. ....Springfield, NJ
Yudes, James P., A Professional Corporation
Springfield, NJ
Yudes, Marianne R. ....Philadelphia, PA
Yudesis, Benjamin M. ....Harlingen, TX
Yudess, Lawrence Samuel ....Roslyn, NY
Yudewitz, Brian Jason ....Hauppauge, NY
Yudewitz, Gary J. ....Fort Lauderdale, FL
Yudewitz, Gary J., P.A.
Fort Lauderdale, FL
Yudien, Geoffrey A. ....Waterbury, VT
Yudien, Jordan J. ....Walnut Creek, CA
Yudien, Mary B. ....San Ramon, CA
Yudin, David E. ....Washington, DC
Yudin, John S. ....Stuart, FL
Yudin, Jon ....Monterey, CA
Yuditski, Thomas M. ....Bridgeport, CT
Yuditski, Thomas M ....Stamford, CT
Yudkin, Franklin S. ....Louisville, KY
Yudkin, Harold B. ....Shelton, CT
Yudkin & Young ....Shelton, CT
Yudkoff, Bernard L. ....Bayonne, NJ
Yudkowitz, Martin J. ....New York, NY
Yudkowsky, Alan Z. ....Los Angeles, CA
Yudson, Joel M.
Department Of The Interior, Office of the Solicitor, GV
Yudt, Michael F. ....Valparaiso, IN
Yudt, Michael F. II ....Valparaiso, IN
Yudysky, Clark W. ....Boston, MA
Yue, Deborah W. ....Cleveland, OH
Yue, Joan A. ....Philadelphia, PA
Yue, William C. ....Department of Commerce, Office of the General Counsel, GV
Yueh, Linda Y. ....New York, NY
Yueill, Timothy R. ....Chicago, IL
Yuelys, Jordan D. ....Hackensack, NJ
Yuelys, Nicholas D. ....Bronx, NY
Yuen & Associates, Law Offices of, PLLC
Houston, TX
Yuen, Barry C. ....Washington, DC
Yuen, Charles Allen ....Morristown, NJ
Yuen, Chi-Wing ....New York, NY
Yuen, Christopher J. ....Hilo, HI
Yuen, Chuie-Wei ....Irwindale, CA
Yuen, Curtis B. K. ....Honolulu, HI
Yuen, Daniel K. ....Palo Alto, CA
Yuen, David O., (P.C.) ....Wheaton, IL
Yuen, Frank W. ....San Francisco, CA
Yuen, Hannah S. ....San Francisco, CA
Yuen, Henry C. ....Pasadena, CA
Yuen, Henry C. ....Department of Commerce, Patent and Trademark Office, GV
Yuen, Karen K. ....San Francisco, CA
Yuen, Leighton J. H. S. ....Honolulu, HI
Yuen, Matthew T. ....Los Gatos, CA
Yuen, Nancy W. ....Vienna, VA
Yuen, Nicole Brown ....Oakland, CA
Yuen, Renee M. H. ....Scottsville, KY
Yuen, Renee M. L. ....Honolulu, HI
Yuen, Renee M. L., Attorney at Law, A Law Corporation ....Honolulu, HI
Yuen, Roger ....Los Angeles, CA
Yuen, Veronica Chan ....New York, NY
Yuen, Victoria A.M. ....Los Angeles, CA
Yuen, William W. L. ....Honolulu, HI
Yuen, Xenos ....Houston, TX
Yuenger, Raymond W. ....San Jose, CA
Yuengert, Anne R. ....Birmingham, AL
Yuengling, Mary Ann ....Clementon, NJ
Yuffee, Cynthia Finn ....Washington, DC
Yuffee, Michael A. ....Washington, DC
Yufik, Alex ....Rockville, MD
Yugend, Jerome S. ....Minneapolis, MN
Yugler, Richard S. ....Portland, OR
Yuh, Kyuhong ....New York, NY
Yuhas, Christine M. ....Breckenridge, CO
Yuhas, George A. ....San Francisco, CA
Yuhas, Helena A., (Ms.) ....New York, NY
Yuhas, Maureen C. ....Dayton, OH
Yuhas, Stephen P. ....Clark, NJ
Yuhas, Steven E. ....Dayton, OH
Yuhas, Thomas F. ....Santa Monica, CA
Yuhasz, Michael P. ....Baltimore, MD
Yuhl, Christopher P. ....Santa Monica, CA
Yuhl, Eric F. ....Santa Monica, CA
Yuhl, Rhames, Yuhl & St. Clair
La Jolla, CA
Los Angeles, CA
Santa Monica, CA
Yuhnke, Robert E. ....Boulder, CO
Yuill, William D. ....Fargo, ND
Yuille, Richard Bryan ....Burton, MI
Yu-Jahnes, Lock See ....New York, NY
Yukawa, Stephanie H.
Colorado Springs, CO
Yukelson, Bruce ....Port Washington, NY
Yukevich, James J. ....Los Angeles, CA
Yukevich, Marchetti, Liekar & Zangrilli, P.C. ....Pittsburgh, PA
Yukevich, Michael, Jr. ....Pittsburgh, PA
Yukevich & Sonnett ....Los Angeles, CA
Yuki, Leslie M. ....Tracy, CA
Yukich, Kelley C. ....New York, NY
Yukimoto, Tei ....Fresno, CA
Yukimura, Jo Ann ....Lihue, HI
Yukins, Christopher R. ....Falls Church, VA
Yukitomo, Robert M. ....Honolulu, HI
Yukna, Paula Jean ....New Britain, CT
Yuknis, Clifford E. ....Chicago, IL
Yuksel, Ayse ....New York, NY
Yula, Stephen ....Exton, PA
Yule, Edward J. ....Northport, NY
Yule, Roger T. ....Fountain Valley, CA
Yules, Robert B. ....Hartford, CT
Stamford, CT
New York, NY
Yules & Yules ....Hartford, CT
Stamford, CT
New York, NY
Yulish, Stanley ....Cleveland, OH
Yulish, Twohig & Associates ....Cleveland, OH
Yulsman, Michael B. ....Media, PA
Yum, Elli ....New York, NY
Yu Mak, Michael ....San Francisco, CA
Yumkas, Charles ....Baltimore, MD
Yumkas, Lawrence J. ....Baltimore, MD
Yun, Chang Hi ....Blue Bell, PA
Yun, Christopher W. ....Sacramento, CA
Yun, Conrad M. ....Rockville, MD
Yun, David H. ....Denver, CO
Yun, Edward ....New York, NY
Yun, Jinah K. ....San Francisco, CA
Yun, Johnca ....Flint, MI
Yun, Judy ....Wayne, PA
Yun, Justena Junghi ....San Francisco, CA
Yun, Kenneth Young-gak ....New York, NY
Yun, Kim, & Banks, P.C. ....Annandale, VA
Yun, Sang (Nathan) ....Los Angeles, CA
Yun, Scott H. ....Los Angeles, CA
Yun, Sindy J. ....San Francisco, CA
Yun, Stephen L. ....Sacramento, CA
Yun, Steve Y. ....Annandale, VA
Yunck, Robert J. ....Cut Bank, MT
Yund, George E. ....Cincinnati, OH
Yund, Walter J., Jr. ....Seattle, WA
Yunek, Jay P. ....St. Cloud, MN
Yunek, Joel J. ....Mason City, IA
Yung, Andrew W. ....Dallas, TX
Yung, Brian L. ....Fort Dodge, IA
Yung, Carmen C. ....Dallas, TX
Yung, Carroll John ....Washington, DC
Yung, Gerald E. ....Dayton, OH
Yung, John A., IV ....Montgomery, AL
Yung, Keith N. ....New York, NY
Yung, R. Dale ....Springfield, IL
Yung, Steven C. ....Los Angeles, CA
Yung, Yvonne A. ....Irvine, CA
Yungblut, Gibson R. ....Cincinnati, OH
Yungblut, Stephen K. ....Dallas, TX
Yungbluth, Gregory C. ....Buffalo, NY
Yungbluth, Patricia Lynn ....Buffalo, NY
Yungling, Deane J. ....Fair Oaks, CA
Yungling, Stephen N. ....Napa, CA
Yungman, Bruce A. ....Louisville, KY
Yunis, Alexander ....New York, NY
Yunis, Barbara E. ....Syracuse, NY
Yunis, Jeffery N. ....Elmira, NY
Yunis, Joel Allen ....New York, NY
Yunis, Robin ....New York, NY
Yunits, John T., Jr. ....Brockton, MA
Yunker, Katherine K. ....Lexington, KY
Yunker, Richard D. ....Batavia, NY
Oakfield, NY
Yunker & Schneider ....San Diego, CA
Yunker, Stephen F. ....San Diego, CA
Yura, Mark D. ....Chicago, IL
Yura, Saml. ....Detroit, MI
Yurachek, Wendy B. ....Falls Church, VA
Yurasek, Jason A. ....San Francisco, CA
Yurasek, Stephen J. ....Marysville, OH
Yurasko, Frank N. ....Somerville, NJ
Yuravich, Kenneth J. ....Ansonia, CT
Yurchak, Patricia Anne ....Chicago, IL
Yurchenco, Ingrid LaFleur ....Dayton, NJ
Yurcheshen, Michael J. ....Pittsburgh, PA
Yurchison, Michael ....Youngstown, OH
Yurchuck, Roger A. ....Cincinnati, OH
Yurcon, Edward A. ....Pittsburgh, PA
Yurdin, Seth M. ....Boston, MA
Yurecka, Phil S. ....Winter Park, FL
Yurek, William
Securities and Exchange Commission, GV
Yurek, Wilson ....Costa Mesa, CA
Yurenka, David A. ....St. Clair Shores, MI
Yurenka, David A., P.C.
St. Clair Shores, MI
Yurgelun, Christine W. ....Orleans, MA
Yurgine, Joseph R. ....Kankakee, IL
Yurgine, Joseph R., Professional Corporation, Law Offices of ....Kankakee, IL
Yurgovsky, Albert J. ....Troy, MI
Yurich, Robert R. ....Cleveland, OH
Yurick, Andrew N. ....Woodbury, NJ
Yurick, Andrew N., P.C. ....Woodbury, NJ
Yurick, Brenda J. ....Pittsburgh, PA
Yurick, Martin A. ....Bay Village, OH
Yurik, Stephen B. ....Columbus, OH
Yurinich, Debra L. ....Oak Brook, IL
Yurk, Mona E. ....Seattle, WA
Yurk, Russell R. ....Phoenix, AZ
Yurk, Suzanne K. ....San Francisco, CA
Yurkanin, Michael, Jr ....Washington, DC
Yurkanin, Walter J ....Chicago, IL
Yurke, Alice F. ....New York, NY
Yurkewicz, Michael W. ....Boston, MA
Yurko, Albert ....Orlando, FL
Yurko, Alison M. ....Orlando, FL
Yurko, Amy Jo Naponic ....Pittsburgh, PA
Yurko, Lyle J. ....Charlotte, NC
Yurko & Owens, P.A. ....Charlotte, NC
Yurko & Perry, P.C. ....Boston, MA
Yurko, Richard J. ....Boston, MA
Yurko, Richard M., Jr. ....Clarksburg, WV
Yurkofsky, David E ....New York, NY
Yurkonis, Mary Ann ....Santa Monica, CA
Yuro, Ronald S. ....Manasquan, NJ
Yurosko, Michael E. ....Los Angeles, CA
Yurovich, Dale R. ....Columbus, OH
Yurow, John J. ....Washington, DC
Yurow, Lois A. ....Westfield, NJ
Yurow, M. Jay ....McLean, VA
Yurow, Scott N. ....Owings Mills, MD
Yurowitz, Steven Y. ....New York, NY
Yurtchuk, Lydia Alexis ....Los Angeles, CA
Yuse, Clement F. ....Spokane, WA
Yusem, Richard S., A Professional Association ....Aberdeen, NJ
Yusem, Richard S., A Professional Association ....Somerville, NJ
Yusem, Stephen G. ....Norristown, PA
Yusem, Stuart S. ....Roseland, NJ
Yusen, Jeff H. ....Seattle, WA
Yusi, Anthony H. ....Honolulu, HI
Yusi, Jennifer M. ....Honolulu, HI
Yusick, Andrew D., Jr. ....Angola, NY
Yusim, Allan L. ....Chicago, IL
Yusim, Milton ....Woodland Hills, CA
Yusin, John E. ....Encino, CA
Yuska, George F. ....Princeton, NJ
Yuska, George P. ....Rochester, NY
Yuska, Joseph E. ....Portland, OR
Yuskis, Michael J. ....Newport Beach, CA
Yusko, David P. ....Chicago, IL
Yusman, Harvey L. ....St. Louis, MO
Yuson, Restituto E., III ....New York, NY
Yuspeh, Alan R. ....Nashville, TN
Yuspeh, Wayne W. ....Metairie, LA

Yuspeh, Wayne W., A Prof. Law Corp.
Metairie, LA
Yussman, Jefferey M. ... Louisville, KY
Yussman, Marc, & Associates
Louisville, KY
Yustas, Vincent P. ... Brandenburg, KY
Yustein, Ross L. ... New York, NY
Yut, Scott A. ... New York, NY
Yuter, Alan B. ... Los Angeles, CA
Yuter, Arthur ... Los Angeles, CA
Yuter, Seymour C. ... Briarcliff Manor, NY
New York, NY
Yuthas, G. Anthony ... Wheat Ridge, CO
Yutkin, Stephanie ... New York, NY
Yu Yeoh, Deborah ... New York, NY
Yuzek, Dean G. ... New York, NY
Yvars, Christopher D. ... Denver, CO
Yzaguirre & Chapa ... McAllen, TX
Yzaguirre, Mark R. ... Houston, TX
Yzaguirre, Roberto J. ... McAllen, TX
Yzenbaard, Caryl A. ... Highland Heights, KY
Yzurdiaga, John ... Los Angeles, CA

Zaander, Mark C. ... Chicago, IL
Zaba, Diane M. ... Norfolk, VA
Zabak, Richard M. ... Tampa, FL
Zabala-Anderson, Ana Marie
San Francisco, CA
Zaban, Robert A. ... Indianapolis, IN
Zaban, Seymour B. ... Benton Harbor, MI
Zabanal, Eduardo O. ... Honolulu, HI
Zabaneh, Samer Michael ... Austin, TX
Zabar, Carole ... New York, NY
Zabar, Lori S. ... New York, NY
Zabar, Stanley J. ... New York, NY
Zabarauskas, Bruce J. ... Mineola, NY
Zabarte, Francisco J., (P.C.)
Brownsville, TX
Zabatta, Patrick G. ... New York, NY
Zabb, Robert Michael ... Los Angeles, CA
Zabel, Allan G. ... San Francisco, CA
Zabel & Associates ... Cherry Hill, NJ
Zabel, Cynthia A. ... Vancouver, WA
Zabel, David B. ... Bridgeport, CT
Zabel, Jay ... Chicago, IL
Zabel, Jay, & Associates, Ltd. ... Chicago, IL
Zabel, Judith L. ... Albuquerque, NM
Zabel, Judith L., P.A. ... Albuquerque, NM
Zabel, K. Allan ... Pleasant Grove, UT
Zabel, Matthew A. ... Cherry Hill, NJ
Zabel, Matthew L. ... Department of Justice,
Civil Rights Division, GV
Zabel & Quail, P.C. ... Birmingham, MI
Clarkston, MI
Zabel, Richard B. ... New York, NY
Zabel, Ronald C. ... Fairfax, VA
Zabel, Sheldon A. ... Chicago, IL
Zabel, Shirley ... Fort Worth, TX
Zabel, Steven P. ... Minneapolis, MN
Zabel, Susan M. ... Rice Lake, WI
Zabel, Terry L. ... Grand Rapids, MI
Zabel, Thomas Alan ... Houston, TX
Zabel, William D. ... New York, NY
Zabel, William G. ... Clarkston, MI
Zabell, Cary J. ... Cleveland, OH
Zabelski, Richard E. ... Evanston, IL
Zaben, Lee B. ... Wilmington, DE
Zaben, Steven J. ... Hackensack, NJ
Zabenko, Arthur L. ... Kenilworth, NJ
Zabicki, Anthony F., Jr. ... Philadelphia, PA
Zabielski, Edward M. ... Schenectady, NY
Zabik, Robert D. ... Elk Grove, CA
Zabin, Albert P. ... Boston, MA
Zabin, Harold M. ... Omaha, NE
Zabin, Jonathan D. ... New Haven, CT
Zabinski, Eric ... Los Angeles, CA
Zabinski, Lawrence E. ... Chicago, IL
Zabinsky, Zachary ... Portland, OR
Zabitchuck, Suzanne M.
North Andover, MA
Zabka, Sven P. ... Atlanta, GA
Zabkar, William J. ... Columbus, OH
Zable, Norman A. ... Dallas, TX
Zable, Norman A., A Professional Corporation ... Dallas, TX
Zablen, Leslie M., (Mr.) ... Emeryville, CA
Zablocki, Kathy L. ... Toledo, OH
Zablocki, Michael A. ... Newport Beach, CA
Zablotny-Hurst, Linda A. ... Lancaster, NY
Zablotski, Joseph M. ... Washington, DC
Zablotsky, Peter A. ... New York, NY
Zablow, Robin J. ... Mount Kisco, NY
Zablow, Sheila R. ... New York, NY
Zabludowski, Daniel A., (P.A.) (IBA)
Fort Lauderdale, FL
Zabner, Jeffrey M. ... Westlake Village, CA
Zabner & Waldman, LLP
Los Angeles, CA
Westlake Village, CA
Zabo, Margaret Anne ... Pennsauken, NJ
Zaboroski, Robert B. ... El Paso, TX
Zaborowski, Henry ... Romulus, MI
Zaborsky, Richard J. ... Chicago, IL
Zabowski, Diane M. ... Collegeville, PA
Zabriskie, Jan ... Sacramento, CA
Zabriskie, John F. ... Chicago, IL
Zabriskie, Kris ... Montesano, WA
Zabriskie, Linda I.T. ... Kansas City, MO
Zabriskie, Mims Maynard
Philadelphia, PA
Zabriskie, Wendy L. ... Detroit, MI
Zabrocki, Edward J., III ... New York, NY
Zabrocki, Marie-Anne ... New York, NY
Zabronsky, Andrew ... San Francisco, CA
Zabroski, Kimberly A. ... Pittsburgh, PA
Zabrosky, Alex W. ... Chicago, IL
Zabrowski, Patrick M. ... Milwaukee, WI

Zabusky, Byron ... New City, NY
Zaby & Associates ... Dallas, TX
Zaby, Elizabeth Fagin ... Dallas, TX
Zacaroli, Alec ... Washington, DC
Zacca, Deric ... Miami, FL
Zaccagnini, Anthony Jackson
Baltimore, MD
Zaccagnini, Bruce A. ... Cleveland, OH
Zaccagnini, Giuseppe M. ... New York, NY
Zaccagnino, Brian ... Southington, CT
Zaccagnino, Leonard D. ... Hamburg, NY
Zaccagnino, Robert Joseph
Mamaroneck, NY
Zaccard, Michelle M. ... Kenosha, WI
Zaccardelli, Gino ... Washington, DC
McLean, VA
Zaccardelli, Lisa A. ... Farmington, CT
Zaccardelli, Maryelena ... Washington, DC
Zaccardi, Elizabeth Black
West Hartford, CT
Zaccardi, Henry J. ... Hartford, CT
Zaccardo, Daniel A. ... Chicago, IL
Zaccarelli, Lauren A. ... Harrisburg, PA
Zaccaria, Anthony ... New York, NY
Zaccaria, Frank V. ... Gretna, LA
Zaccaria, James M. ... Albany, NY
Zaccaria, John ... Orangeburg, NY
Zaccaria, Joseph J. ... Columbus, OH
Zaccaro, John C., Jr. ... New London, CT
Zaccaro, Thomas A. ... Los Angeles, CA
Zaccheo, Michael P. ... Salt Lake City, UT
Zaccheo, Nicole K. ... Los Angeles, CA
Zaccheo, Philip J. ... Syracuse, NY
Zacchigna, Frank J. ... Schaumburg, IL
Zacchilli, John P. ... Milford, MA
Zacchini, Rene A. ... Tampa, FL
Zaccone, Michelle Leu ... Burlingame, CA
Zaccone, Rose C. ... Boston, MA
Zaccor, Stephen J. ... Fort Lauderdale, FL
Zacek, David E. ... Whitesboro, NY
Zacek, Michael F. ... Grand Rapids, MI
Zach, Steven C. ... Madison, WI
Zachar, Christopher S. ... Phoenix, AZ
Zachar, Melinda D. ... Palo Alto, CA
Zachar, Richard A. ... Chicago, IL
Zachara, F. Michael ... Fort Lee, NJ
Zacharakis, Anthony C. ... Tappan, NY
Zacharakis, Elaine C. ... Chicago, IL
Zacharda, Andrew P. ... Chatham, NJ
Zacharellis, Wm. ... Scranton, PA
Zacharer, F. Christopher ... Lowell, MA
Zacharer, Joseph J. ... Lowell, MA
Zacharer, O'Hearn & Zacharer ... Lowell, MA
Zachari, Herbert A., Jr. ... Louisville, KY
Zacharia, Carl Bernard ... Mc Keesport, PA
Zacharia, John H. ... Washington, DC
Zacharia, Karen ... Arlington, VA
Zacharia, Michael E. ... San Francisco, CA
Zachariah, George Abe ... Washington, DC
Zacharias, Anthony M. ... New York, NY
Zacharias, C. Michael ... Tulsa, OK
Zacharias, Henry J. ... New York, NY
Zacharias, James ... Chicago, IL
Zacharias, Laszlo, Jr. ... Fords, NJ
Zacharias, Lisa A. ... Memphis, TN
Zacharias, M. David ... Wichita, KS
Zacharias, Muriel E. ... Southport, CT
Zachariasevych, Bohdan M. ... Millville, NJ
Zacharisen, David K. ... Morristown, NJ
Newark, NJ
New York, NY
Zacharkow, George R. ... Westmont, NJ
Philadelphia, PA
Zacharopoulos, Melina ... New York, NY
Zacharski, Anthony H. ... Boston, MA
Zacharski, Casimir M., Jr.
Baltimore, MD
Zacharski, Dennis E. ... Birmingham, MI
Zacharski, James C. ... Minneapolis, MN
Zachary, Anthony T. ... Tarzana, CA
Zachary, Bruce L. ... Camarillo, CA
Santa Ana, CA
Sherman Oaks, CA
Zachary, Deborah C. ... Staten Island, NY
Zachary, Donald L. ... Nashville, TN
Zachary, Edward M. ... Phoenix, AZ
Zachary, Francis T., Jr. ... Hattiesburg, MS
Zachary, Frank Curry, Sr. ... Yadkinville, NC
Zachary, Henry B. ... Hobe Sound, FL
Zachary, John J. ... Alexandria, LA
Zachary, John S. ... Staten Island, NY
Zachary, Karen Treadway ... Arlington, VA
Zachary and Leggett, P.L.L.C. ... Biloxi, MS
Gulfport, MS
Hattiesburg, MS
Jackson, MS
Zachary, Mark S. ... Abilene, TX
Zachary, Michael S. ... New York, NY
Zachary, Patrick H. ... Hattiesburg, MS
Zachary, Robert N. ... Naples, FL
Zachary & Segraves, P.A. ... Decatur, GA
Zachary, Seth M. ... New York, NY
Zachary, Sheri M. ... Miami, FL
Zachary, Stephen ... East Hartford, CT
Zachary, Stephen P. ... Washington, DC
Fairfax, VA
Zachary, Valerie Johnson ... Yadkinville, NC
Zachary, W. Lee, Jr. ... Yadkinville, NC
Zachary, William E., Jr. ... Decatur, GA
Zachary, William E., Sr. ... Decatur, GA
Zachary and Zachary ... Yadkinville, NC
Zacheiss, Carola I. ... Brooklyn, NY
Zachem, Kathryn A. ... Washington, DC
Zacher, Allan N., Jr. ... St. Louis, MO
Zacher, Dieter ... Beverly Hills, CA
Zacher, Jennifer L. ... Long Beach, CA
Zacher, Jules ... Philadelphia, PA

Zacher, P. Gerhardt ... San Diego, CA
San Francisco, CA
Zacher, Theodore D. ... Roseburg, OR
Zacherl, Francis A., III ... Miami, FL
Zacherl, John C. ... Fond du Lac, WI
Zacherl, O'Malley & Endejan, S.C.
Fond du Lac, WI
Zacherle, Hedo M. ... Des Moines, IA
Zachman, Alicia ... Fort Lauderdale, FL
Zachman, Thomas F. ... Loveland, OH
Zachman, Thomas F. ... Ripley, OH
Zachmann, Jeffrey T. ... Armonk, NY
Zachor, H. James, Jr.
Mountlake Terrace, WA
Zachos, Kimon S. ... Manchester, NH
Zachos, Susan G. ... Austin, TX
Zachow, John R. (Jack) ... Minneapolis, MN
Zachreson, Martin K. ... Mesa, AZ
Zachritz, Anne E. ... Oklahoma City, OK
Zachritz, James D. ... Xenia, OH
Zachritz, Linda J. ... Fresno, CA
Zachritz, Rebecca D. ... McLean, VA
Zachry, Alfred F. ... La Grange, GA
Zachry, Alfred F., P.C. ... La Grange, GA
Zachry, David S., Jr. ... Oak Ridge, TN
Zachry, Earl W. ... Houston, TX
Zachry, H. Campbell ... Dallas, TX
Zachry, James E. ... Decatur, IL
Zachs, Eric M. ... Hartford, CT
Zachter, Debra ... New York, NY
Zachter, Jay S. ... New York, NY
Zachter, Morton ... Princeton, NJ
Zachter, Morton, P.C. ... Princeton, NJ
Zack, Andrew M. ... Troy, MI
Zack, Arnold M. ... Boston, MA
Zack, Arthur ... Boston, MA
Zack, Carolyn Moran ... Bala Cynwyd, PA
Zack, David J. ... San Francisco, CA
Zack, Ellen S. ... Boston, MA
Zack, Elliott Noel ... North Miami Beach, FL
Zack, Ernest J. ... San Marino, CA
Zack, Everett R. ... Lansing, MI
Zack, Gerald L. ... Los Angeles, CA
Zack, James J. ... Kingman, AZ
Zack, Joanne ... Philadelphia, PA
Zack, Joseph G. ... Philadelphia, PA
Zack, Julius ... Westfield, NJ
Zack, Kosnitzky, P.A. ... Miami, FL
Zack, Leonard ... New York, NY
Zack, Marilyn G. ... Cleveland, OH
Zack, Otto J. ... New Buffalo, MI
Zack, Richard L. ... Forty Fort, PA
Zack, Robert C. ... Southfield, MI
Zack, Robert G. ... New York, NY
Zack, Robert S. ... Fort Lauderdale, FL
Zack, Ronald L. ... Philadelphia, PA
Zack, Sherry K. ... Northbrook, IL
Zack, Stephen N. ... Miami, FL
Zackem, Ronald W. ... Buffalo, NY
Zacker, David ... Oklahoma City, OK
Zacker, Edward R. ... Saint Simons Island, GA
Zackerman, Jeffrey L. ... Cincinnati, OH
Zackery, Furrer & Tezak ... Everett, WA
Zackey, Jonathan T. ... Bellevue, WA
Zackey, Jonathan T., P.S. ... Bellevue, WA
Zackheim, Ivan S. ... Portland, OR
Zackin, Gerald H. ... Mandeville, LA
Zackin, Jack M. ... Newark, NJ
New York, NY
Zackin, Leslie A. ... New Haven, CT
Zackin, Mark H. ... Hartford, CT
Zackin, Martha J. ... Boston, MA
Zackin, Richard S. ... Newark, NJ
Zackler, Allan I. ... Oakland, CA
Zackler & Associates ... Oakland, CA
Zackrison, John A. ... Los Angeles, CA
Zackrison, Mary K. ... Bridgeport, CT
Zackrison, Mary K. ... Stamford, CT
Zackrisson, Nadine M. ... Bellevue, WA
Zacks, Andrew M., Law Offices of
San Francisco, CA
Zacks, Arnold O. ... Columbus, OH
Zacks, Arthur H, ... Los Angeles, CA
Zacks, Benjamin S. ... Columbus, OH
Zacks, David M. ... Atlanta, GA
Zacks, David N. ... Detroit, MI
Zacks, JoEllen Bursinger ... Chicago, IL
Zacks, Leslie B. ... Atlanta, GA
Zacks, Paul H. ... West Palm Beach, FL
Zacks, Richard W. ... Providence, RI
Zacks-Gabriel, Zanita A. ... Erie, PA
Zackula, Sharon K. ... Washington, DC
Zacky, Hayden A. ... Los Angeles, CA
Zacour, Wayne A. ... Wooster, OH
Zacur & Graham, P.A.
St. Petersburg, FL
Zacur, Richard A. ... St. Petersburg, FL
Zaczek, Bert J. ... Chicago, IL
Zaczek, James B. (Bert) ... Wheaton, IL
Zaczek, Nancy M.
Department of Transportation,
Federal Transit Administration, GV
Zadeh, Jamshyd (Jim) M.
Fort Worth, TX
Zadeh, Mariam ... Westbury, NY
Zadeh, Tara ... Boston, MA
Zadeik, Philip J. ... Chicago, IL
Zadeikis, Donna ... McHenry, IL
Zadek, Peter S. ... New York, NY
Zadek, Robert A. ... San Francisco, CA
Zadek, Robert F. ... Chicago, IL
Zaden, Richard J. ... Wilton Manors, FL
Zaden, Richard J., P.A.
Wilton Manors, FL
Zadick, Gary M. ... Great Falls, MT
Zadina, Christopher W. ... Chicago, IL
Zadina, Richard E. ... Dallas, TX
Zadnik, Rudolph S. ... Columbus, OH

Zadoff-Krauss, Michelle S. ... Hempstead, NY
Zadora, Ronald J. ... Bloomfield Hills, MI
Zadorozny, Daniel M., III ... Plano, TX
Zadorozny, George ... Oldsmar, FL
Zadow, Aram J. ... Boston, MA
Zadra, Nolan H. ... Milwaukee, WI
Zadra-Symes, Lynda J.
Newport Beach, CA
Zadravecz, Steven M. ... Irvine, CA
Zadrazil, John B. ... Appleton, WI
Zadrozny, Michael M. ... Arlington, VA
Zadzilko, Raymond J. ... Johnstown, PA
Zaehringer, Harold F. ... Buffalo, NY
Zaelke, Edward W. ... Los Angeles, CA
Zaenger, Mark F. ... Chicago, IL
Zaenglein, William G., Jr. ... Santa Ana, CA
Zaepfel, Patrick H. ... Pittsburgh, PA
Zaepfel, Robert P. ... Manassas, VA
Zaeske, Eric W. ... Menomonee Falls, WI
Zaeske, Laurel R. ... Irvine, CA
Zaetta, Christopher R. ...
Department of Justice, GV
Zaff, Adam S. ... Boston, MA
Zaff, Arnold M. ... Boston, MA
Zaffarano, Dario D. ... Ames, IA
Zaffer, Philip J. ... Naperville, IL
Zafferano, Marc L. ... San Carlos, CA
Zaffere, Frank D., III ... Chicago, IL
Zaffern, Bernard H. ... Farmington Hills, MI
Zaffern, David J. ... Southfield, MI
Zaffern, Joseph H. ... Southfield, MI
Zaffirini, Carlos M. ... Laredo, TX
Zaffirini & Castillo ... Laredo, TX
Zaffiro, James A. ... Lyndhurst, OH
Zaffiro, Jos. ... Reading, PA
Zaffiro, Richard L. ... Milwaukee, WI
Zaffrann, Robert C. ... Boston, MA
Zaffrio, William Thomas ... Cleveland, OH
Zaffron, Andrew S. ... Foster City, CA
Zafft, Gene M. ... St. Louis, MO
Zafft, Gerald J. ... St. Louis, MO
Zaffuts, Paul J. ... Washington, DC
Zafian, Henry J. ... New York, NY
Zafiratos, James A. ... Maywood, IL
Zafiratos, Nicholas D. ... Astoria, OR
Zafiris, Gregory A. ... Portland, OR
Zafiropoulos, Michael H. ... Boston, MA
Zafiropulos, James ... Upper Marlboro, MD
Zafis, Andrew J. ... San Diego, CA
Zafis, R. Craig ... San Diego, CA
Zafman, Norman ... Los Angeles, CA
Zafonte, Albert, Jr. ... Garden City, NY
Zafrani, André L. ... Chicago, IL
Zafris, James ... Columbus, OH
Zaft, Alice E. ... Springfield, MA
Zagajeski, Edward F. ... Brooklyn, NY
Zagalis, Penny ... New York, NY
Zagami, Anthony J.
Government Printing Office,
Office of General Counsel, GV
Zagami, Thomas J. ... Towson, MD
Zagar, Bruce A. ... Salem, OR
Zagar, Keith C. ... Dallas, TX
Zagarella, Eugene, Jr. ... Bridgewater, NJ
Zagaria, Paul A. ... Woodbury, MN
Zagaris, Bruce ... Washington, DC
Zagaroli, Mark A. ... Bloomington, IL
Zagaroli, Michael A. ... Grand Rapids, MI
Zagarolo, Nicola L. ... Pompano Beach, FL
Zagat, Eugene H., Jr. ... New York, NY
Zagat, Nina S. ... New York, NY
Zagel, James B. ... Chicago, IL
Zagel, Margaret Maxwell ... Chicago, IL
Zagelmeyer, Frank L., III ... Detroit, MI
Zagelow, Robert L. ... Walla Walla, WA
Zagelow, Stephen P. ... Olympia, WA
Zager, Abraham J. ... Red Bank, NJ
Zager, Albert A. ... Asbury Park, NJ
Zager, Bruce B. ... Waterloo, IA
Zager, Chester H. ... Woodland Hills, CA
Zager, Fuchs P.C. ... Red Bank, NJ
Zager, Ira ... Coral Gables, FL
Zager, Jan G. ... Millwood, NY
Zager, Jeffrey ... Nashville, TN
Zager, Jennifer Lynn ... Long Beach, CA
Zager, Michael ... Monticello, NY
Zager, Michael L., P.C. ... Monticello, NY
Zager, Mitchel ... La Jolla, CA
Zager, Paul E. ... Tinton Falls, NJ
Zager, Pearl A. ... Chicago, IL
Zager, Raymond L. ... Los Angeles, CA
Zager, Seymour ... Jericho, NY
Zager, Steven M. ... Austin, TX
Zager, Victor ... Bristol, TN
Zagin, Timothy ... New York, NY
Zagon, Brian L. ... Lafayette, CA
Zagon, David Ryan ... New City, NY
Zagon, Melissa Lumberg ... Chicago, IL
Zagona, Helen E. ... Salado, TX
Zagone, Nicasio J. ... Villas, NJ
Zagone, Nicholas S. ... Rolling Meadows, IL
Zagone, Raymond N. ... Silver Spring, MD
Zagoras, Hercules Paul ... Waukegan, IL
Zagoras, Hercules Paul, and Associates, Ltd.
Waukegan, IL
Zagore, David A. ... Cleveland, OH
Zagorec, J. Todd ... Salt Lake City, UT
Zagoren, Jay L. ... Philadelphia, PA
Zagoria, David ... Atlanta, GA
Zagoria, Evan A. ... Bloomfield Hills, MI
Zagoria, Laura ... New York, NY
Zagoria, Robert B. ... Princeton, NJ
Zagoria, Steven E. ... Atlanta, GA
Zagorin, Mark ... Austin, TX
Zagorin, O'Brien & Graham, L.L.P.
Austin, TX
Zagorski, Maria ... Monroe, MI
Zagorski, Robin Jablo ... Miami, FL

Zagorsky, Arthur .... **New York, NY**
Zagorsky, Floyd A. .... Riverside, CA
Zagorsky, Paul E. .... Plainville, CT
Zagorsky, Peter J. .... Plainville, CT
Zagorsky, Zagorsky & Galske .... Plainville, CT
Zagraniczny, Joseph .... **Syracuse, NY**
Zagrans, Eric H. .... **Elyria, OH**
Zagrans Law Firm, A Legal Professional Association .... **Cleveland, OH**
Elyria, OH
Zagroba, Dennis A. .... **New York, NY**
Zagrocki, Eric J. .... **Pittsburgh, PA**
Zagrodzky, Matthew G. .... **Houston, TX**
Zagula & Dittmar .... Weirton, WV
Zagula, Edward A. .... Weirton, WV
Zagzebski, Sander C. .... **Los Angeles, CA**
Zagzebski, Walter R. .... **Los Angeles, CA**
Zagzoug, Randa .... New York, NY
Zahakos, Peter J. .... Staten Island, NY
Zahar, Deborah A. .... Youngstown, OH
Zaharako, Lew .... Columbus, IN
Zahare, A. Michael .... **Anchorage, AK**
Zaharek, Zachary J. .... **Irvine, CA**
Zaharewicz, Edmund J. .... **Miami, FL**
Zaharieff, Anthony J. .... Xenia, OH
Zaharis, Christopher W. .... **Mesa, AZ**
Zaharoff, Howard G. .... **Waltham, MA**
Zaharoff, Lawrence S. .... Chestnut Hill, MA
Zaharoff, Maria K. .... San Anselmo, CA
Zaharoff, Saml. .... Chestnut Hill, MA
Zaharoni, Daniel S. .... Lawndale, CA
Zaharopoulos, Pat .... San Diego, CA
Zaharris, Drake C. .... **Towson, MD**
Zahasky, Richard D. .... **Decorah, IA**
Zahay, Debra L. .... Naperville, IL
Zahaykevich, Andrew .... Chicago, IL
Zahedi, Parastoo .... **Falls Church, VA**
Zaher, Alfred W. .... **Philadelphia, PA**
Zahirsky, Linda B. .... Canal Fulton, OH
Zahka, Albert J. .... Boston, MA
Zahka, Peter A., II .... Dedham, MA
Zahler, Eileen V. .... Playa Del Rey, CA
Zahler, Eric J. .... **New York, NY**
Zahler, Glenn A. .... San Jose, CA
Zahler, Jonathan A. .... **Jacksonville, FL**
Zahler, Karen Gantz .... New York, NY
Zahler, Melvin B. .... Lake Success, NY
Zahler, Pamela Gregg .... Los Angeles, CA
Zahler, Robert E., (P.C.) .... **Washington, DC**
Zahler, Scott M. .... **Atlanta, GA**
Zahler-Gringer, Barbara A. .... New York, NY
Zahm, Douglas C., (P.A.) .... Clearwater, FL
Zahm, Michael E., Jr. .... **Irvine, CA**
Zahn, Bari .... New York, NY
Zahn, Charles W., Jr. .... Port Aransas, TX
Zahn, Daniel A. .... Holbrook, NY
Zahn, Dennis E. .... Indianapolis, IN
Zahn, Donald Jack, P.C. .... Fort Worth, TX
Zahn, F. Anthony .... **Bartlesville, OK**
Zahn, James K. .... Chicago, IL
Zahn, Kira K. .... Dallas, TX
Zahn Law Office .... **Minneapolis, MN**
Zahn, Matthew R. .... **Minneapolis, MN**
Zahn, Michael .... **Charlotte, NC**
Zahn, Peter E. .... San Diego, CA
Zahn, Richard S. .... Catonsville, MD
Zahn, Richard W., Jr. .... **Norfolk, VA**
Zahn, Roger A. .... **Minneapolis, MN**
Zahn, Victor S. .... Long Beach, CA
Zahnd, Craig C. .... Kansas City, MO
Zahnd, Eric G. .... **Kansas City, MO**
Zahnd, L. Glen .... Savannah, MO
Zahnd, Larry L. .... **Maryville, MO**
Zahnd, Richard H. .... New York, NY
Zahnd, Ross & Thomson, L.L.P.
Maryville, MO
Zahner, Carl J. .... Tallahassee, FL
Zahner, Daniel .... San Francisco, CA
Zahner, Harold E. .... Long Beach, CA
Zahner, Mark L. .... Sacramento, CA
Zahner, Michele P. .... **Baltimore, MD**
Zahner, Robert D. .... Coral Gables, FL
Zahner, Sharon A. .... Tallahassee, FL
Zahniser, David W. .... **Lexington, KY**
Zahniser, Julie A., Law Offices of
Miami, FL
Zahniser, Timothy .... Norman, OK
Zahnleuter, Linda S. .... Albany, NY
Zahnleuter, Richard J. .... Clifton Park, NY
Zahorik, Kathleen M. .... Boston, MA
Zahorik, Michael A. .... **Houston, TX**
Zahorsky, Stanley N. .... Edina, MN
Zahorsky, Timothy .... **Merrillville, IN**
Zahour, Alonzo H. .... Bolingbrook, IL
Zahour, James J. .... La Grange, IL
Zahour, Nilgün F. Aykent .... **Chicago, IL**
Zahra, Brian K. .... Detroit, MI
Zahra, E. Ellis, Jr. .... **Jacksonville, FL**
Zahradka, Joseph F. .... Lankin, ND
Zahrt, William D., II .... **Sunnyvale, CA**
Zahs, Gregory Dalton .... **New York, NY**
Zahs, Stephen F. .... Oak Park, MI
Zaiac, Manuel .... Miami, FL
Zaid, Keith E. .... Atlantic City, NJ
Zaid, Mark .... Washington, DC
Zaid, Mark S., P.C., Law Offices of
Washington, DC
Zaid, Pamela J. .... **Irvine, CA**
Zaidan, Louis .... Clinton Township, MI
Zaideman & Esrig, P.C. .... **Chicago, IL**
Zaideman, Robert J. .... **Chicago, IL**
Zaidman, Natalie F. .... **Baltimore, MD**
Zaifert, Richard S. .... Fort Lauderdale, FL
Zaifert, Richard S., P.A.
Fort Lauderdale, FL
Zaiger, Adam Michael .... **Boston, MA**
Zaiger, Brian J. .... **Noblesville, IN**
Zaiger, Mark L. .... **Cedar Rapids, IA**
Zaiger, Richard D. .... Boston, MA
Zaikis, Andrew M. .... Boston, MA
Zailckas, F. Patrick .... Waterbury, CT
Zailckas, Patrick .... Waterbury, CT
Zailckas & Zailckas .... Waterbury, CT
Zaimes, John P. .... **Los Angeles, CA**
Zaina, Lisa M.
Federal Communications Commission, Common Carrier Bureau, GV
Zainey, Jay C. .... New Orleans, LA
Zaino, Domenico, Jr. .... **Waterbury, CT**
Zaino, Laura A. .... **Hartford, CT**
Zaino, Michael J. .... Dublin, OH
Zaino, Michael J., Co., L.P.A. .... Dublin, OH
Zaino, Russell .... Louisville, KY
Zaino, Stephen E. .... **Garden City, NY**
Zaino, Thomas M. .... Gahanna, OH
Zaino, William J. .... Basking Ridge, NJ
Zaiser, George R. .... Harrisburg, PA
Zaiser, Kent A. .... **Tallahassee, FL**
Zaiss, Craig R. .... Parma, ID
Zaiss, Rolf .... **New York, NY**
Zaitlen, Richard H. .... **Los Angeles, CA**
Zaitz, Michael M. .... **New York, NY**
Zaitzeff, Roger M. .... **New York, NY**
Zaitzow, Donald J. .... San Diego, CA
Zaitzow, Rock .... San Diego, CA
Zajac, Andrew .... **Jericho, NY**
Zajac, Charles A. .... Grosse Pointe Farms, MI
Zajac, Claire M. .... Minneapolis, MN
Zajac, Craig P. .... Newton, MA
Zajac, Daniel R. .... Highland, IN
Zajac, Debby Lynne .... **Los Angeles, CA**
Zajac, Eric G. .... Philadelphia, PA
Zajac, James E. .... New York, NY
Zajac, John E. .... Taunton, MA
Zajac, John F. .... Cleveland, OH
Zajac, Kristine J. .... Plymouth, MN
Zajac, Mark A. .... New Bedford, MA
Zajac, Martin F. .... Uxbridge, MA
Zajac, Nancy A. .... **New York, NY**
Zajac, Robert L. .... **San Diego, CA**
Zajac, Ronald .... Detroit, MI
Zajac, Ronald, P.C. .... Detroit, MI
Zajac, Rudolph M. .... Whiting, IN
Zajas, J. Grant .... Angola, NY
Zajec, John .... Inglewood, CA
Zajic, Christopher A. .... Santa Barbara, CA
Zajic, Christopher J. .... Santa Barbara, CA
Zajic, Keith C. .... Burbank, CA
Zajic, Stuart J. .... Santa Barbara, CA
Zajic & Zajic .... Santa Barbara, CA
Zajicek, David E. .... **Oakbrook Terrace, IL**
Zajicek, Martha K. .... Omaha, NE
Zak & Blakely .... La Jolla, CA
Zak, Colleen A. .... **Pittsburgh, PA**
Zak, Dennis F. .... St. Clair Shores, MI
Zak, Edward A. .... Rocky River, OH
Zak, Henry S. .... Department of Commerce, Patent and Trademark Office, GV
Zak, James J. .... Westminster, CO
Zak, James T. .... East Meadow, NY
Zak, John E. .... Lexington, KY
San Antonio, TX
Zak, John J. .... **Buffalo, NY**
Zak, Jonathan M. .... Santa Ana, CA
Zak, Kenneth A. .... La Jolla, CA
Zak, Kenneth M. .... Chicago, IL
Zak, Leocadia Irine .... **Boston, MA**
Zak, Leonard E. .... Evanston, IL
Zak, Marnie J. .... **Anoka, MN**
Zak, Mary T. .... Monroe, WI
Zak, Oshrie .... New York, NY
Zak, Patricia A. .... Springfield, MA
Zak, R. Joseph .... **Charleston, WV**
Zak, S. Arieh .... Montvale, NJ
Zak, Susan E. .... **Springfield, MA**
Zak, Teresa .... **Los Angeles, CA**
Zak, Timothy J. .... Minneapolis, MN
Zakaib, Paul, Jr. .... Charleston, WV
Zakar, Barrance Q. .... San Diego, CA
Zakari, Robert V. .... **Beverly Hills, CA**
Zakaria, Jodi .... **Inverness, FL**
Zakaria, Shamoon .... San Francisco, CA
Zakariaie, Jack M. .... **Los Angeles, CA**
Zakarian, Albert .... **Hartford, CT**
Zakarian, Albert A. .... Albany, NY
Zakarian, Dana .... **Boston, MA**
Zakarin, Donald S. .... **New York, NY**
Zakarin, Harris J. .... **New York, NY**
Zakarin, Keith .... Los Angeles, CA
San Diego, CA
San Francisco, CA
Zakarin, Rachel .... **Roseland, NJ**
Zakarin, Ronald M. .... Boca Raton, FL
Zakas, Dennis L. .... **Atlanta, GA**
Zakas, Joseph C. .... **Elkhart, IN**
Zakem, Robert M. .... **New York, NY**
Zaken, Marc L. .... **Stamford, CT**
Zakens, Judith A. .... Bloomfield Hills, MI
Zakes, Albert P. .... **New York, NY**
Zakheim, Marcie H. .... **Washington, DC**
Zakheim, Rosalyn S. .... Los Angeles, CA
Zakheim, Scott C. .... Fort Lauderdale, FL
Zakheim, Sloan T. .... **New York, NY**
Zaki, Maha S. .... **Washington, DC**
Atlanta, GA
Zakia, Nelson F. .... Buffalo, NY
Zakian, Gary W. .... Wailuku, HI
Zakim, Jack S. .... **Hackensack, NJ**
Zakin, Kenneth L. .... New York, NY
Zakin, Richard J. .... **New York, NY**
Zaklukiewicz, Francis E. .... Merrick, NY
Riverhead, NY
Zaknoen, Edward G. .... **Chicago, IL**
Zaknoen, Joseph J. .... **Chicago, IL**
Zakos, Dean R. .... Racine, WI
Zakos, Stephen W. .... **Lansdale, PA**
Zakotnik, Bonnie Lynn .... New Orleans, LA
Zakoura, James P. .... **Overland Park, KS**
Zakovics, Zigismunds I. .... **Portland, OR**
Zakow, Patti A. .... New York, NY
Zakowski, John P. .... Green Bay, WI
Zakrajsheck, James D. .... Milwaukee, WI
Zakreski, Randall J. .... **Ridgefield, CT**
Zakroff & Associates, P.C. .... Washington, DC
Bethesda, MD
Alexandria, VA
Zakroff, Robert J. .... Washington, DC
Bethesda, MD
Alexandria, VA
Zakrzewski, Cheryl A. .... **Seattle, WA**
Zakrzewski, Daniel M. .... New Carlisle, IN
Zakrzewski, Rita A. .... Buffalo, NY
Zaks, Allen .... Verona, NJ
Zaks, Richard .... Long Beach, CA
Zaks, Stanley J. .... San Francisco, CA
Zakson, Laurence S. .... Los Angeles, CA
Zakupowsky, Alexander, Jr.
Washington, DC
Zal, Cyrus .... Folsom, CA
Zalaoras, Mark L. .... North Las Vegas, NV
Zalar, Charles R. .... Springfield, IL
Zalasin, Andrew L. .... **New York, NY**
Zalasky, Jeff M. .... Minneapolis, MN
Zalasky, Richard J. .... **St. Louis, MO**
Zalaznick, Barry .... **New York, NY**
Zalba, Julia .... **Los Angeles, CA**
Zalbowitz, Alan M. .... Binghamton, NY
Deposit, NY
Zalcman, Helen Myra Gotheiner
Brooklyn, NY
Zalcman, Lawrence C., (P.C.) .... Boston, MA
Zaldivar, Pascale Henn .... Kansas City, MO
Zaldivar, Rogelio A. .... **Miami, FL**
Zalduondo Viera, Juan R. .... **San Juan, PR**
Zale, Henry T. .... **Pottstown, PA**
Zale, Karen B. .... Baltimore, MD
Zale, Larry C. .... Bayport, NY
Zale, Lawrence P. .... Mansfield, MA
Zale, Matthew J. .... Paradise Valley, AZ
Zalecki, Gregory T. .... Warren, MI
Zalecki, Paul H. .... Bloomfield Hills, MI
Zalecki & Swensen, P.C. .... Warren, MI
Zaleha, D. Bernard .... Boise, ID
Zaleha Law Office .... Boise, ID
Zalel, Melvin J. .... New York, NY
Zalen, Stanley L. .... Albany, NY
Zalenski, Cheryl M. .... Battle Creek, MI
Zalenski, Thaddeus A. .... **Cleveland, OH**
Zalenski, Walter E. .... **Washington, DC**
Zales, Allison S. .... **Philadelphia, PA**
Zales, Neil .... **Southfield, MI**
Zalesin, Alicia R. .... **New York, NY**
Zalesin, Steven A. .... **New York, NY**
Zaleskas, Kristine .... **New York, NY**
Zaleski, A. Christopher .... Virginia Beach, VA
Zaleski, Aimee A. .... **Columbus, OH**
Zaleski, Allan D. .... **Norfolk, VA**
Zaleski, Charles E. .... **Harrisburg, PA**
Zaleski, Donald M. .... Lorain, OH
Zaleski, Edward M. .... Lorain, OH
Zaleski, H. Alexander .... Riverhead, NY
Zaleski, Jerome A. .... Philadelphia, PA
Zaleski, Kenneth G. .... Deerfield, IL
Zaleski, Margaret E. .... **Edison, NJ**
Zaleski, Matthew G., III .... **Wilmington, DE**
Zaleski, Michael L. .... **Madison, WI**
Zaleski, Robert M. .... **Woodbridge, NJ**
Zaleski, Steven W. .... Austin, TX
Zaleski, Terence M. .... Cold Spring, NY
Zalesne, David .... **Philadelphia, PA**
Zalesne, E. Kinney .... Department of Justice, Office of the Attorney General, GV
Zaletel, Ann Marie .... **Los Angeles, CA**
Zaletel, Robert L. .... **San Francisco, CA**
Zalevsky, Harvey A. .... Greensburg, PA
Zalewa, James D. .... **Chicago, IL**
Zalewski, Andrew J. .... Albany, NY
Zalewski, David T. .... **Minneapolis, MN**
Zalewski, Donald S. .... **Santa Ana, CA**
Zalewski, James C. .... **Lincoln, NE**
Zalewski, John D. .... **Honolulu, HI**
Zalewski, Kathryn D. .... **Chicago, IL**
Zalewski, Mary-Ellen .... Anchorage, AK
Zalewski, Philip L. .... Santa Ana, CA
Zalewski, Richard W. .... Wausau, WI
Zaleznick, Steven .... Washington, DC
Zaleznik, Ira H. .... **Boston, MA**
Zalik, Alice T. .... Department of Commerce, Patent and Trademark Office, GV
Zalimeni, Gail M. .... Columbus, OH
Zalinger Cameron & Lambek, P.C.
Montpelier, VT
Zalinger, Philip H., Jr. .... **Montpelier, VT**
Zalinski, Rhonda L. .... Dundee, IL
Zalinsky, Bertrand A. .... Manchester, NH
Zalis, Lawrence A. .... Barnstable, MA
Zalis, Leon .... Baltimore, MD
Zalk, Joseph .... Floral Park, NY
Zalk, Michael D. .... **Minneapolis, MN**
Zalk, Richard A. .... New York, NY
Zalk, Robert H. .... **Minneapolis, MN**
Zalk & Wood, P.A. .... **Minneapolis, MN**
Zalkin, Irwin M. .... San Diego, CA
Zalkin, Jonathan A. .... **New York, NY**
Zalkin, Leonard .... New York, NY
Zalkin, Monroe .... Miami, FL
Zalkin, Natasha .... Panama City Beach, FL
Zalkin, Seth R. .... New York, NY
Zalkin, Steven O. .... New York, NY
Zalkin, Steven O., P.C. .... New York, NY
Zalkind, Cecilia M. .... Newark, NJ
Zalkind, Jack I. .... Boston, MA
Zalkind, Norman S. .... **Boston, MA**
Zalkind, Rodriguez, Lunt & Duncan
Boston, MA
Zalkind, Stephen R. .... **Jackson, CA**
Zalkind, Stephen R. .... **San Andreas, CA**
Sonora, CA
Zall, Alan S. .... Tustin, CA
Zall, Barnaby W. .... Rockville, MD
Zall, Brian David .... **Denver, CO**
Zall, Charles C. .... **Philadelphia, PA**
Zall, Clifford E. .... Sacramento, CA
Zall, Darrell R. .... **Milwaukee, WI**
Zall, Jayne C. .... New Brunswick, NJ
Zall, Jon M. .... **Denver, CO**
Zall, Michael E. .... Maywood, NJ
Zall, Richard J. .... **New York, NY**
Zall, Ronald I. .... **Denver, CO**
Zall, Terri A. .... Department of Justice, Federal Bureau of Investigation, GV
Zall, William M. .... Natick, MA
Zalla, Daniel J. .... Covington, KY
Zallaps, Jeffrey J. .... Englewood, CO
Zallaps, Lori .... **Seattle, WA**
Zallar, Robert J. .... **Duluth, MN**
Zallar, Therese E. .... Chicago, IL
Zallen, Deanna L. W. .... **Denver, CO**
Zallen, Joseph .... **Fort Lauderdale, FL**
Zallen, Joseph, P.A. .... **Fort Lauderdale, FL**
Zaller, Craig Brian .... Columbia, MD
Zalma, Barry .... **Culver City, CA**
Zalma, Barry, Inc. .... **Culver City, CA**
Zalman, Benjamin .... New York, NY
Zalman, Ellen .... Sebastopol, CA
Zalman, Greta A. .... Birmingham, MI
Zalman & Schnurman .... New York, NY
Zalob, David S. .... **San Francisco, CA**
Zaloba, Edward .... Forest Hills, NY
Zalobsky, Michael D. .... **Troy, MI**
Zalon, Jules D. .... New York, NY
Zaloom, Ina .... **Hackensack, NJ**
New York, NY
Zaloom, J. Gordon .... South Hackensack, NJ
Zaloom, John A. .... **New York, NY**
Zaloom, John B. .... West Caldwell, NJ
Zalosh, Harry H. .... Morton Grove, IL
Zaloudek, Steven J. .... **Atlanta, GA**
Zaloum, Saml. E. .... Brooklyn, NY
Zalowitz, Rudolph L. .... Hackensack, NJ
Zalph, David A. .... Wilmington, NC
Zaltas, A. David .... Natick, MA
Zaltas, Arnold I. .... Natick, MA
Zaltas, Medoff & Raider .... Natick, MA
Zaltsman, David L. .... Napa, CA
Zalucki, Robert J. .... **Fairfield, CT**
Zalud, Deirdre M. .... Santa Ana, CA
Zalud, Eric L. .... **Cleveland, OH**
Zalud, Kenneth J. .... Encinitas, CA
Zaluda, Deborah Lust .... **Northbrook, IL**
Zaluda, Jeffrey A. .... **Chicago, IL**
Zaluski, Joseph J. .... **Frankfort, KY**
Zalutsky, Irwin L. .... Chicago, IL
Zalutsky & Klarquist, P.C. .... **Portland, OR**
Zalutsky, Morton H. .... **Portland, OR**
Zalutsky & Pinski, Ltd. .... Chicago, IL
Zama, Nunotte .... Washington, DC
Zamagni, Julio A. .... Lakewood, CO
Zamal, Albert J. .... Woodbury, NJ
Zaman, Claudia J. .... Woodland Hills, CA
Zaman, Karen, & Associates
Charlotte, NC
Zaman-Malik, Fauzia Zia .... **Chicago, IL**
Zamansky and Associates
White Plains, NY
Zamansky, Calvin D. .... Berkeley, CA
Zamansky, Jacob H., & Associates
New York, NY
Zamansky, Leonard D. .... **Newton, MA**
Zamansky Professional Association
Minneapolis, MN
St. Paul, MN
Zamansky, Ronald A. .... **Minneapolis, MN**
St. Paul, MN
Zamansky, Stephen .... Hartford, CT
Zamarian, Paul .... Redding, CA
Zamarin, Edward L. .... Lutherville, MD
Zamarripa, Lupe .... Austin, TX
Zamary, Gary M. .... Youngstown, OH
Zamastil, Kristine .... Chicago, IL
Zamba, Patricia .... Salem, WI
Zambardi, Victor A. .... Rochester, MI
Zambelli, Barbara Gunther
Mount Vernon, NY
Zambelli, Victor F. .... Piscataway, NJ
Zambie, Allan J. .... Cleveland, OH
Zambie, Paul J. .... Austin, TX
Zambito, Charles N. .... Rochester, NY
Zambito, Peter J. .... New York, NY
Zambito, Vincent .... Riverhead, NY
Zambo, Richard A. .... Palm City, FL
Zambo, Richard A., P.A. .... Palm City, FL
Zamboldi, Richard H. .... **Erie, PA**
Zambon, James J. .... Crystal Lake, IL
Zambon, Richard E. .... Grand Rapids, MI
Zambon, Richard E., P.C. .... Grand Rapids, MI
Zamboni, Frank J. .... Rye, NY
Zamboni, Helen A. .... Rochester, NY
Zamboni, Peter Thomas .... Seattle, WA
Zamborowski, Gerald M. .... Algonac, MI
Zamborsky, Donald A. .... **Allentown, PA**
Zamborsky, Edward J. .... **Allentown, PA**
Zamborsky, Kathryn L. .... **Philadelphia, PA**
Zambrana-Grana, Jaime L. .... Cabo Rojo, PR
Zambrano, Gabriel F.
Fort Lauderdale, FL
Zambrano, Raul A. .... Daytona Beach, FL
Zambreno, John .... Deerfield, IL
Zambri, Mary A. .... **Greenbelt, MD**
La Plata, MD
Zambri, Melissa M. .... **Albany, NY**

Zambri, Robert R. ... Kansas City, MO
Zambri, Salvatore J. ... Washington, DC
Upper Marlboro, MD
Fairfax, VA
Zambrio, Louis A. ... New York, NY
Zambrowicz, Kevin A. ... Washington, DC
Zamczyk, Bradley M. ... Oakland, CA
Zameck, Harvey J. ... Southfield, MI
Zamecki, E. Richard ... Bellaire, TX
Zamecki, E. Richard, P.C. ... Bellaire, TX
Houston, TX
Zameic, Joseph N. ... Argonne, IL
Zamek, Scott ... Melville, NY
Zamel, Stanley A. ... Los Angeles, CA
Zamelis, Douglas H. ... Syracuse, NY
Zamer, John E. ... Atlanta, GA
Zametto, Marc A. ... New York, NY
Zamir, Amy J. ... Garden City, NY
Zamis, Peter A. ... Wheaton, IL
Zamites, Matthew J. ... Philadelphia, PA
Zamler, Chad ... Southfield, MI
Zamler, Craig M. ... Southfield, MI
Zamler, Sherwin E. ... Bloomfield Hills, MI
Zamloch, Archer ... Torrance, CA
Zamlowski, Robert J. ... Hartford, CT
Zamm, Edward J. ... Norwalk, CT
Zammarelli, Louis C. ... Providence, RI
Zammiello, Michael F. ... Providence, RI
Zammit, Joseph P. ... New York, NY
Zammit, Leah J. ... Orlando, FL
Zammitti, Dawn N. ... Hartford, CT
Zammitti, Natalie A.
Englewood Cliffs, NJ
Zammuto, Carmela T. ... Skokie, IL
Zamolo, Paul R. ... San Francisco, CA
Zamora, Alejandro A., Law Offices of
Miami, FL
Zamora, Anthony N.R. ... Los Angeles, CA
Zamora, Antonio R. ... Miami, FL
Zamora, Charles ... Columbus, OH
Zamora, D. Diego ... Santa Fe, NM
Zamora, Elaine A. ... San Francisco, CA
Zamora, Elizabeth ... Cerritos, CA
Zamora, Enrique ... Coral Gables, FL
Zamora, Eugene I. ... Boston, MA
Zamora, Herman ... New York, NY
Zamora & Hoffmeier, A Professional
Corporation ... Los Angeles, CA
Zamora, Irene P. ... Baltimore, MD
Zamora, Joaquin J. ... Edinburg, TX
Zamora, John J., III ... Metairie, LA
Zamora, Joseph R. ... Los Angeles, CA
Zamora Law Firm, P.A. ... Santa Fe, NM
Zamora, Louis ... Bronx, NY
Zamora, M. Monica ... Santa Fe, NM
Zamora, Marla C. ... San Francisco, CA
Zamora, Matias A. ... Santa Fe, NM
Zamora, Oscar A. ... New York, NY
Zamora, Patricia ... Davenport, IA
Zamora, Peter A. ... Austin, TX
Zamora, Richard Jose ... Basehor, KS
Zamora, Richard M. ... El Paso, TX
Zamora, Robert M. ... Corpus Christi, TX
Zamora, Sandra C. ... San Antonio, TX
Zamorano, Andre J. ... Miami, FL
Zamorano-Reagin, Guadalupe Cecilia
Los Angeles, CA
Zamore, Eric A. ... Salem, MA
Zamore, Gisser, Turoff & Sprague
Cleveland, OH
Zamore, Joseph D. ... Cleveland, OH
Zamore, Peter H. ... South Burlington, VT
Zamore, Sharon
Securities and Exchange Commission,
Division of Enforcement, GV
Zamorski, Jerome F. ... New Hartford, NY
Zamorsky, Tania ... New York, NY
Zamos, Jerome ... Woodland Hills, CA
Zamost, Bruce H. ... Voorhees, NJ
Zamost, I. M. ... Highland Park, NJ
Zamost, Nanette Brown ... Los Angeles, CA
Zamow, Thomas ... Logan, WV
Zamoyski, James J. ... Southfield, MI
Zamoyski, Peter A. ... San Diego, CA
Zampa, David J. ... Chicago, IL
Zampano, Robert C. ... New Haven, CT
Zamparelli, Andrew J. ... Medford, MA
Zamparelli, Leo R. ... Hamilton, NJ
Princeton, NJ
Zamparelli, Leo R. ... Trenton, NJ
Zamparo and Goldstein, P.C. ... Northbrook, IL
Zamparo, Roger, Jr. ... Northbrook, IL
Zamperini, Michael A. ... San Francisco, CA
Zampetti, Cristina ... Morristown, NJ
Zampetti, Debra M. ... Las Vegas, NV
Zampini, Melanie A. ... Chambersburg, PA
Reading, PA
York, PA
Zampino, Daniel W. ... Marblehead, MA
Zampino, Edward ... Newark, NJ
Zampino, Filomena M. ... Oaklyn, NJ
Zampino, John P. ... New York, NY
Zampino, Joseph W. ... Pennsauken, NJ
Zampino, Thomas ... Boston, MA
Zamplas, Dennis ... Birmingham, MI
Zamplas, Johnson, Sopt & Cavanagh, P.C.
Birmingham, MI
Zamplas, Sheryl S. ... Rochester Hills, MI
Zampogna, Christopher A. ... Buffalo, NY
Zampol, W. Paul ... Atlanta, GA
Zamren, Allan S. ... Miami, FL
Zamsky Law Firm ... Hagåtña, GU
Zamsky, Marc S. ... Philadelphia, PA
Zamsky, Steven A. ... Hagåtña, GU
Zamudio, Gregory Q. ... Seattle, WA
Zamula, Elaine ... Brick, NJ
Zamuner, Dino F. ... Corona, NY
Zamurs, Karl ... Melville, NY

Zamzow, Susan K. ... New York, NY
Zan, Koethi ... New York, NY
Zanakos, Nicholas M. ... Bethlehem, PA
Zanan, Arthur Steven ... Norristown, PA
Zanar, Louise P. ... Washington, DC
Zanardi, David G. ... Washington, DC
Zanardi, Francis J. ... Iron Mountain, MI
Zanaty, Wadell C., Jr. ... Birmingham, AL
Zanayed, Akram Khalil ... Chicago, IL
Zanazzi, Anthony L. ... Harrison, NY
Zanca, Andrea Simpson ... Diamondhead, MS
Zanca, Michael A. ... McAllen, TX
Zanca, William S. ... Department of Defense,
Defense Legal Services Agency, GV
Zancan, Sabrina Brewster ... New York, NY
Zanck, Thomas C. ... Crystal Lake, IL
Zancolli, Mark R. ... New York, NY
Zand, J. Philip ... New Paltz, NY
Zand, Joel R. ... New York, NY
Zand, Marc J. ... New York, NY
Zand, Marcia M. ... Columbus, OH
Zand, Richard V. ... New York, NY
Zand, Steve S. ... Encino, CA
Zandecki, Thomas J.
New Port Richey, FL
Zandecki, Thomas J., P.A.
New Port Richey, FL
Zander, Alvin N. ... New Orleans, LA
Zander, Barb ... St. Johnsbury, VT
Zander, Ben J. ... Springfield, NJ
Zander, Janet Holter ... Williston, ND
Zander, Karin Kirksey ... Raleigh, NC
Zander Law Office, P.C. ... Williston, ND
Zander, Lester P. ... Great Neck, NY
Zander, Scott T. ... New Orleans, LA
Zander, Thomas K. ... Milwaukee, WI
Zander, Troy ... San Diego, CA
Zandman, Norma Rein ... New Canaan, CT
Zandona, Anthony ... Norwalk, CA
Zandrow, Leonard F., Jr. ... Boston, MA
Zandstra, Bartel ... Highland, IN
Zandstra, Charles L. ... Highland, IN
Zandstra & Muha ... Highland, IN
Zandy, Aaron L. ... Orlando, FL
Zandy, John G. ... New Haven, CT
Zane, Audra ... Garden City, NY
Zane, Caroline Rose ... Rochester, NY
Zane, Dale Edward F.T. ... Honolulu, HI
Zane, Daniel M. ... White Plains, NY
Zane, David N. ... New York, NY
Zane, Gordon ... San Francisco, CA
Zane, James B., (P.C.) ... New York, NY
Zane, Jeffery P. ... West Palm Beach, FL
Zane, Joseph A. ... Schuylkill Haven, PA
Zane, Peter L. ... Canton, MA
Zane, Phillip C. ... Washington, DC
Zane, Raymond J. ... Woodbury, NJ
Zane, Robert T. ... Barrington, NJ
Zane and Rudofsky ... New York, NY
Zane, Sheldon Sin Hee ... Honolulu, HI
Zanecchia, Paul M. ... Providence, RI
Zanecki & Associates, P.C.
Annapolis, MD
Greenbelt, MD
Zanecki, V. Paul ... Annapolis, MD
Zanella, Gilardi and Boath ... Stratford, CT
Zanella, Vincent M., Jr. ... Stratford, CT
Zanelli, Richard L. ... Westminster, CA
Zanello, Robert J. ... Boston, MA
Zanelotti, John P. ... Greenbelt, MD
Zaner, Adam J. ... Dallas, TX
Zaner, Heidi Lempert ... Atlanta, GA
Zaner, Karin M. ... Dallas, TX
Zaner, Lorin J. ... Toledo, OH
Zanercik, Gary D. ... Boston, MA
Zanetis, John M., Jr. ... Carmel, IN
Zanetta, Joseph M. ... Whittier, CA
Zanetti, J. R., Jr. ... Southfield, MI
Zanetti, Victor B. ... Dallas, TX
Zanfagna, Gary P.
Federal Trade Commission,
Policy Planning, GV
Zanfardino, Dominic P. ... Chicago, IL
Zanfini, Maria L. ... New York, NY
Zang, Edward E. ... Altoona, PA
Zang, Joseph Paul, III ... Atlanta, GA
Zang, Robert E. ... Aptos, CA
Zang, Theodore, Jr. ... New York, NY
Zanga, Catherine A. ... Alexandria, VA
Zangara, Henry A. ... New York, NY
Zangara, Kevin A. ... Taos, NM
Zangara (Kennedy), Deborah E.
New York, NY
Zangari, Carol A. ... Providence, RI
Zangari, Christopher J. ... Providence, RI
Zangari, David P. ... Liverpool, NY
Zangari, Mario J. ... New Haven, CT
Zangari, Ted ... Newark, NJ
Zanger, Andrew M. ... Santa Monica, CA
Zanger, Barbara ... San Francisco, CA
Zanger, Carl L. ... New York, NY
Zanger, Carl L., P.C. ... New York, NY
Zanger, David B. ... Boston, MA
Zanger, Hugh M. ... New York, NY
Zanger, Larry M. ... Chicago, IL
Zanger, Pamela J. ... San Francisco, CA
Zanger, Robert M. ... Department of Justice,
Justice Management Division, GV
Zanger, Sally R. ... Southfield, MI
Zangerle, Gary J. ... Moorestown, NJ
Zangerle, J. Adam ... Mentor, OH
Zangerle, John A. ... Cleveland, OH
Zangerle, Kari B. ... Phoenix, AZ
Zangerle, Willis J. ... Cleveland, OH
Zanghi, John ... San Bernardino, CA
Zanghi, John P. ... San Francisco, CA
Zanghi, John S. ... Cleveland, OH
Zanghi, Phyllis ... New York, NY

Zanghi, Stephen P. ... Mayville, NY
Zanglein, Jayne E. ... Lubbock, TX
Zanglis, Constance G.
La Canada Flintridge, CA
Zangrilli, Albert J., Jr. ... Pittsburgh, PA
Zangrilli, Joan C. ... Pittsburgh, PA
Zangrillo, Tina ... Weston, CT
Zangwill, Henry S. ... Los Angeles, CA
Zangwill, Marc D. ... Clementon, NJ
Zani, Melissa Meallo ... Portsmouth, NH
Zanic, George N. ... Huntingdon, PA
Zanic, Michael G. ... Pittsburgh, PA
Zanides, Mark N. ... Oakland, CA
Zaniel, Robert F. ... Fairfax, VA
Zaniewski, Felix J. ... Bellevue, NE
Zanini, Daniel B. ... Orlando, FL
Zanini, John P. ... Boston, MA
Zanini, Mark D. ... Boston, MA
Zank, Gloria A. ... Los Angeles, CA
Zanke, Alaina M. ... Southfield, MI
Zankel, Jeffrey A. ... Garden City, NY
Zankel, Martin I. ... San Francisco, CA
Zankich, Louis ... Palm Desert, CA
Zankowski, Doreen M. ... Boston, MA
Providence, RI
Zann, Karen M. ... Fort Lauderdale, FL
Zannelli, Sharon Ann ... Jersey City, NJ
Zanner, Kevin J. ... Buffalo, NY
Zannieri, Joseph A. ... Sandusky, OH
Zannotti, Mark A. ... Tulsa, OK
Zanobini, Mark J. ... San Francisco, CA
Zanolli, Carl M. ... San Diego, CA
Zanolli, Claire Gavin ... Salt Lake City, UT
Zanolli, Victor J., III ... Franklin, MI
Zanon, Daniel A. ... Phoenix, AZ
Zanoni, Anthony Joseph ... Hollidaysburg, PA
Zanoni, James M. ... Charlotte, NC
Zanoni, Leon J. ... Bloomington, IL
Zanoni, Marc H. ... New York, NY
Zanoni, Melinda Morris ... Charlotte, NC
Zanoni, Ronald A. ... New York, NY
Zanopoulo, Sotiri B. ... New York, NY
Zanot, Craig A. ... Flint, MI
Saginaw, MI
Zanotti, John P. ... Covington, KY
Zanotto, Fred A. ... Redding, CA
Santa Rosa, CA
Zanowic, Steven P.
Equal Employment Opportunity
Commission,
Office of Federal Operations, GV
Zansberg, Steven D. ... Denver, CO
Zansitis, Gerald D. ... Chicago, IL
Zansitis, Richard A. ... Lewisburg, PA
Zant, Jerry D. ... Midland, TX
Zanta, Jaye Bailey ... Wethersfield, CT
Zantello, Frederick A. ... Troy, MI
Zantke, Katharina ... Los Angeles, CA
Zanton, Shirley L. ... San Juan Capistrano, CA
Zanussi, Elena Lourdes ... Portland, OR
Zanville, Harry W. ... Vinton, IA
Zanze, Brian N. ... Redding, CA
Zanzig, W. Scott ... Seattle, WA
Zanzinger, Gerald J. ... San Mateo, CA
Zanzinger & Johnston ... San Mateo, CA
Zaorski, James M. ... Mountain View, CA
Zaorski, William J. ... Trenton, NJ
Zapala, Alan J. ... San Jose, CA
Zapalac, William C. ... Austin, TX
Zapata, Alberto H.
Department Of Veterans Affairs,
Board of Veterans Appeals, GV
Zapata, Eino ... Bandera, TX
Zapata, Eino, P.C. ... Bandera, TX
Zapata, Joseph R., Jr. ... Parsippany, NJ
Zapata, Julio M. ... Seattle, WA
Zapata, Kathleen M. ... San Diego, CA
Zapata, Kimberly Paul ... Palo Alto, CA
Zapata, Stephanie ... Dallas, TX
Zapater, Antonio ... Ponce, PR
Zapcic, Andrew M. ... Hazlet, NJ
Zapel, Scott O. ... Chicago, IL
Zaper, Peter D. ... Chicago, IL
Zapf, Jacqueline Trzaska ... Los Angeles, CA
Zapf, John A., II ... Bethlehem, PA
Zapf, Matthew A. C. ... Peoria, IL
Zapf, Robert D. ... Kenosha, WI
Zapf, Robert J. ... Los Angeles, CA
Zapf, Thomas R. ... New York, NY
Zapfel, Elaine B. ... New York, NY
Zaphiriou, George A. ... Rockville, MD
Zaphiriou, James A. ... Chicago, IL
Zapien, Carol L. ... Kansas City, MO
Zapiler, Steven M. ... Denver, CO
Zapinski, Robert P. ... Lake Forest, IL
Zapka, Dennis P. ... Cleveland, OH
Zapler, Leonard J. ... Pittsburgh, PA
Zapol, Nikki J. ... Boston, MA
Zapol, Rochelle ... Boston, MA
Zapolin, Sandor J. ... Wellesley, MA
Zapolsky, David A. ... Seattle, WA
Zapor, Mary L. ... Rockville, MD
Zapor, Rose Mary ... Denver, CO
Zapora, Steven R. ... Baltimore, MD
Zaporskie, Kira ... Madison, WI
Zapp, Amy ... Harrisburg, PA
Zapp, David S. ... Leonia, NJ
Zapp, James A. ... Los Angeles, CA
Zapp, Kirk M. ... Chicago, IL
Zapp, William A. ... Columbus, OH
Zappa, James M. ... Minneapolis, MN
Zappa, Joann Maria ... Garden City, NY
Zappa, Richard A. ... Wilmington, DE
Zappa, Roger W. ... Marquette, MI
Zappacosta, Jack J. ... Cherry Hill, NJ
Zappala, Alberto V. ... New Haven, CT

Zappala, Alfred M., Law Offices of
Andover, MA
Boston, MA
Zappala, Charles R. ... Pittsburgh, PA
Zappala, Fern N. ... Bethesda, MD
Zappala, Lisa A. ... McLean, VA
Zappala, Lori A. ... Washington, DC
Zappala, Ralph A. ... San Francisco, CA
Zappala, Stephen A.
Cranberry Township, PA
Zapparoni, Ceide ... Los Angeles, CA
Zappe, Linda B. ... San Diego, CA
Zappelli, Ronald J. ... Oakland, CA
Zappen, Edward F. ... Marshfield, WI
Zappen, Edward F., Jr.
Wisconsin Rapids, WI
Zappetti, Craig F. ... Philadelphia, PA
Zappettini, C. D. ... San Francisco, CA
Zappettini, Gianna C. ... Sacramento, CA
Zappi, Debra A. ... Tallahassee, FL
Zappia, Andrew P. ... Washington, DC
Rochester, NY
Zappia, Anthony M. ... South Bend, IN
Zappia, Edward P. ... Los Angeles, CA
Zappia, Joseph F. ... Indianapolis, IN
Zappia, Mario J. ... South Bend, IN
Zappia, Thomas M. ... Fridley, MN
Zappia & Zappia ... South Bend, IN
Zappitell, David J. ... Boca Raton, FL
Zappitell & Kapral, P.A. ... Boca Raton, FL
Zapple, Nicholas ... United States Senate,
Committee Legal Personnel, GV
Zappo, Daniel W. ... Woodbridge, NJ
Zappolo, Scott W.
Palm Beach Gardens, FL
Zappone, Debra J. ... Waterbury, CT
Zappone, Joseph W. ... Latham, NY
Zappulla, Louis S. ... Bronx, NY
Zappy, Mark A. ... New Brunswick, NJ
Zapruder, Henry G. ... Washington, DC
Zaprudsky, Alla R. ... Des Moines, IA
Zapson, Michael G. ... Long Beach, NY
New York, NY
Zar, Keith A. ... Horsham, PA
Zar, Parham ... Los Angeles, CA
Zara, Maurice R. ... New York, NY
Zaragoza, Carlos ... Pasadena, CA
Zaragoza, Dennis ... San Francisco, CA
Zaragoza, Gabriel James ... Los Angeles, CA
Zaragoza, Gregory R. ... New York, NY
Zaragoza, Richard R. ... Washington, DC
Zaranek, Robert E.
Grosse Pointe Farms, MI
Zaransky, Stephen P. ... Cleveland, OH
Zarapkar, Monalee ... Tampa, FL
Zarate, Albert R. ... Treasury Department,
Financial Crimes Enforcement Network, GV
Zarate, Gustavo A. ... Los Angeles, CA
Zarate, Juan C. ... Department of Justice,
Criminal Division, GV
Zaraza, Mari-Kathleen Sarno ... Chicago, IL
Zarazua, Blanca E. ... Monterey, CA
Salinas, CA
Zarb, Frank G., Jr. ... Washington, DC
Zarba, Tony L. ... Tallahassee, FL
Zarbano, John S. ... Oshkosh, WI
Zarbetski, Paul J. ... Roseland, NJ
Zarbin, Robert Julian ... Baltimore, MD
Zarbock, Glenda M. ... San Francisco, CA
Zarcaro, John J. ... San Diego, CA
Zarcaro, Lewis & Pope ... San Diego, CA
Zarco & Pardo, P.A. ... Miami, FL
Zarco, Robert ... Miami, FL
Zarcone, Carl J. ... Fort Lauderdale, FL
Zarcone, John M. ... Putnam Valley, NY
Zarcone, Kelly V. ... Buffalo, NY
Zarcone, Michael A. ... New York, NY
Zard, Steven D. ... New Prague, MN
Zarda, Kathleen Ann ... Mission, KS
Zardenetta, Antonio A. ... Laredo, TX
Zarefsky, Paul H. ... Santa Clara, CA
Zareh & Associates ... San Francisco, CA
Zareh, Elizabeth A. ... San Francisco, CA
Zareh, Omid ... New York, NY
Zarella, Nancy Dzwonczyk
West Chester, PA
Zarella, Peter T. ... Rockville, CT
Zarelli, Renée ... Lawrenceville, NJ
Zarelli, Renée, P.C., The Law Offices of
Lawrenceville, NJ
Zaremba, Allen B. ... Merrillville, IN
Zaremba, Cheryl Ann ... Austin, TX
Zaremba, Frank W. ... Bradenton, FL
Zaremba, Jerome F. ... Dearborn, MI
Zaremba, John M. ... Washington, DC
Zaremba, Kenneth ... Livingston, NJ
Zaremba, Scott W. ... Richmond, VA
Zaremba, Thomas J. ... Madison, WI
Zaremba, Thomas S. ... Toledo, OH
Zaremberg, Allen S. ... Elk Grove, CA
Zaremski, Jack ... New York, NY
Zaremski, Linda E. ... Plant City, FL
Zaremski, Miles J. ... Chicago, IL
Zaremsky, Michael L. ... Cleveland, OH
Zaret, Scott D. ... Cleveland, OH
Zaret, Thomas C., Law Offices of
Los Angeles, CA
Zaret, Thomas C., Law Offices of
Santa Monica, CA
Zaretsky, Allen ... Rochester, NY
Zaretsky, Donn ... New York, NY
Zaretsky, Esther A. ... West Palm Beach, FL
Zaretsky, Louis D. ... Miami, FL
Zaretsky, Michael J. ... Clifton, NJ
Zaretsky, Murray ... Providence, RI
Zaretsky, Richard P.
West Palm Beach, FL

Zaretsky, Richard P., P.A.
Palm Beach, FL
West Palm Beach, FL
Zarett, David A. ... Massapequa, NY
Zarfas, Louis S. ... Department of Commerce, Patent and Trademark Office, GV
Zarfes, David J. ... New York, NY
Zarfes, Marlene A. ... New York, NY
Zargarof, Pasha ... New York, NY
Zargos, Olga E. ... Cheshire, CT
Zarian, John N. ... Los Angeles, CA
Zaribaf, Vivian ... Miami, FL
Zarich, Robert ... Westbury, NY
Zarick, Gail H. ... New York, NY
Zarick, Hobson & Harlan ... Sutter Creek, CA
Zarick, Robert N. ... Sacramento, CA
Zarifes, James P. ... Los Angeles, CA
Zarillo, Anthony J., Jr. ... Morristown, NJ
Zarin, Donald ... Washington, DC
Zarin, Glenn P. ... New York, NY
Zarin, Heath B. ... New York, NY
Zarin, Ira J. ... Springfield, NJ
Zarin, Lenore ... New York, NY
Zarin, Michael D. ... White Plains, NY
Zarin, Michael S. ... Great Neck, NY
Zarin, Richard S. ... New York, NY
Zarin, Scott ... New York, NY
Zarin & Steinmetz ... New York, NY
White Plains, NY
Zarin, Todd Bennett ... New York, NY
Zaring & Gish ... Basin, WY
Zaring, James A. ... Basin, WY
Zarins, Edgar A. ... Taylor, MI
Zaris, Steven N. ... Chicago, IL
Zariski, Adrienne ... New York, NY
Zariski, Daniel A. ... Seattle, WA
Zaritsky, Howard M. ... Rapidan, VA
Zaritsky, Martha Altschuller ... Rapidan, VA
Zaritsky & Zaritsky ... Rapidan, VA
Zarka, David R. ... Gold River, CA
Zarkades, Karen L. ... Cheshire, CT
Zarkesh, Kim ... Newark, NJ
Zarkou, Russell J. ... Phoenix, AZ
Zarkou, Russell J., Chartered ... Phoenix, AZ
Zarkowski, Pamela ... Detroit, MI
Zarkowsky, Aaron B. ... Chicago, IL
Zarky, Alan ... Seattle, WA
Zarlenga, Audra J. ... Cleveland, OH
Zarlenga, Carmine R. ... Washington, DC
Zarlenga, Lisa M. ... Washington, DC
Zarlenga, Michael W. ... Washington, DC
Zarlengo, Albert E., Jr. ... Denver, CO
Zarlengo, Arthur W. ... Denver, CO
Zarlengo, Dante L. ... Denver, CO
Zarlengo, Joseph A. ... Matteson, IL
Zarlengo & Kimmell, L.L.C. ... Denver, CO
Zarlengo, Mott, Zarlengo and Winbourn, P.C. ... Denver, CO
Zarlengo Planera & Zaluda, P.C.
Chicago, IL
Matteson, IL
Northbrook, IL
Zarlengo, Richard A. ... Denver, CO
Zarlengo, Rosemary ... Denver, CO
Zarlengo, Vincent A. ... Denver, CO
Zarley, Donald H. ... Des Moines, IA
Omaha, NE
Zarley, McKee, Thomte, Voorhees & Sease
Omaha, NE
Des Moines, IA
Zarley, Timothy J. ... Des Moines, IA
Omaha, NE
Zarling, William A. ... Trenton, NJ
Zarlingo, Pamela ... Cleveland, OH
Zarlock, Diane C. ... Buffalo, NY
Zarlock, Preston L. ... Buffalo, NY
Zarmin, Audrey ... Chicago, IL
Zarne, Debra H. ... Milwaukee, WI
Zarnegar, Jennifer ... Menlo Park, CA
Zarnick, Jacklynn M. ... Lisbon, OH
Zarnoch, Robert A. ... Annapolis, MD
Zaro, David R. ... Los Angeles, CA
Zaro, Jerold L. ... Ocean Township, NJ
Zaro, Robert B. ... Sacramento, CA
Zarobsky, Lena J. ... Coldbrook, NY
Zarocostas, Michael G. ... New York, NY
Zaroda, Danuta M. ... San Francisco, CA
Zaroff, Allan R. ... New York, NY
Zaroff, Richard M. ... New York, NY
Zaron, Andrew D. ... Fort Lauderdale, FL
Zarone, Philip W. ... Pittsburgh, PA
Zarosinski, David J. ... Portland, OR
Zarosinski & Hill ... Portland, OR
Zaroski, Laura R. ... Chicago, IL
Zarotsky, Bella ... Sherman Oaks, CA
Zarou, George Robert ... Brooklyn, NY
Zaroulis, Andrew J. ... Lowell, MA
Zaroulis, Charles J. ... Lowell, MA
Zarov, Herbert L. ... Chicago, IL
Zarov, Peter D. ... Chicago, IL
Zarowitz, Ronald Seth ... Detroit, MI
Zarowny, Steven M. ... Detroit, MI
Zarpas, Crystal A. ... Tarzana, CA
Zarr, Gerald H.
Agency for International Development, Other Offices of A.I.D., GV
Zarr, Melvyn ... Portland, ME
Zarr, Thomas M. ... Salt Lake City, UT
Zarr, William W. ... Los Alamos, NM
Zarrabian, F. Michael ... Los Angeles, CA
Zarrella, James A. M. ... Harrisburg, PA
Zarrella, Maria L. ... Morristown, NJ
Zarrello, Marilyn L. ... New York, NY
Zarrett, Linda P. ... Mankato, MN
Zarrilli, Francis Leonard ... Broomall, PA
Zarrilli, Francis Louis ... Broomall, PA
Zarrilli, Michael J. ... St. Louis, MO
Zarrilli and Zarrilli ... Broomall, PA
Zarrillo, Anthony J., Jr. ... Cherry Hill, NJ
Zarrillo, James V. ... Montvale, NJ
Zarrillo & Zappacosta ... Cherry Hill, NJ
Zarro, Francis A., Jr. ... Albany, NY
New York, NY
Zarro, Janice ... Washington, DC
Zarro, Joseph N. ... New York, NY
Zarro, Michael T. ... Los Angeles, CA
Zarro, Renee ... Norfolk, VA
Zarrow, Joshua D. ... Cerritos, CA
Zarrow, Mark I. ... Worcester, MA
Zarrow, Stanton H. ... Los Angeles, CA
Zars, Reed ... Boston, MA
Zarsadias, Isidore T. ... Pittsburgh, PA
Zarshenas, Marcelle B. ... Memphis, TN
Zarski, David E. ... Chicago, IL
Zarski, Michael J. ... Chicago, IL
Zarsky, Barbara J. ... Philadelphia, PA
Zarsky, Clifford L. ... Corpus Christi, TX
Zartarian, Arsen ... Red Bank, NJ
Zartarian, Mark G. ... Birmingham, MI
Zarter, Charles F. ... Overland Park, KS
Kansas City, MO
Zartler, Stacey A. ... San Francisco, CA
Zartman, Dan A. ... Atlanta, GA
Zartman, James N. ... Chicago, IL
Zartman, Michael B. ... Beachwood, OH
Zartman, Ned K. ... Playa Del Rey, CA
Zartman, Therese M.
Rancho Cucamonga, CA
Zartner, Dana ... San Francisco, CA
Zaruba, Carleton J. ... Lisle, IL
Zaruba, Karel L. ... Morris Plains, NJ
Zaruches, Misti H. ... West Palm Beach, FL
Zarwell, Elwin J. ... Milwaukee, WI
Zarwin, Baum, DeVito, Kaplan & O'Donnell, P.C. ... Cherry Hill, NJ
Jersey City, NJ
Philadelphia, PA
Zarwin, Norman P. ... Philadelphia, PA
Zarych, John J. ... Northfield, NJ
Zarych, John J., P.A. ... Northfield, NJ
Zaryczny, Catherine A. ... Chicago, IL
Zarzana, Maxmilian V. ... San Jose, CA
Zarzaur, Ben L. ... Birmingham, AL
Zarzaur, Joseph Anthony, Jr. ... Mobile, AL
Zarzaur & Schwartz, P.C. ... Birmingham, AL
Zarzaur, Wendy Ann ... Birmingham, AL
Zarzecki, Stephen F. ... Livingston, NJ
Zarzynski, Jeffrey P. ... Milwaukee, WI
Zarzynski, John R. ... Mesa, AZ
Zas, Edward S. ... New York, NY
Zasada, John Robert ... Washington, DC
Zashin, Andrew A. ... Cleveland, OH
Zashin & Rich Co., L.P.A. ... Cleveland, OH
Zashin, Robert I. ... Cleveland, OH
Zashin, Stephen S. ... Cleveland, OH
Zaske, Dorian W. ... Minneapolis, MN
Zasky, Alan I. ... New York, NY
Zaslav & Auerbach, P.C. ... New York, NY
Zaslav, H. Gary ... New York, NY
Zaslav, Jesse ... Flushing, NY
Zaslav, Scott M. ... Fort Lauderdale, FL
Zaslav, Steven Lee ... New York, NY
Zaslavsky, Dennis M. ... Chicago, IL
Zaslavsky, Michael A. ... Chicago, IL
Zaslavsky, Morton L. ... Chicago, IL
Zaslofsky, Mary ... Bronx, NY
Zaslow, Ann M. ... New York, NY
Zaslow & Associates, P.C. ... Hollywood, FL
Cherry Hill, NJ
Philadelphia, PA
Zaslow, Darrell M. ... Langhorne, PA
Zaslow, Daryl L. ... Chatham, NJ
Zaslow, David R. ... Philadelphia, PA
Zaslow, Jerry ... Hollywood, FL
Cherry Hill, NJ
Philadelphia, PA
Zaslow, Joan Z. ... Metairie, LA
Zaslow-Silar, Heidi M. ... Philadelphia, PA
Zaslowsky, Daniel N. ... New York, NY
Zaslowsky, David ... New York, NY
Zastera, William B. ... Nebraska City, NE
Zastrow, John T. ... Tucson, AZ
Zastrow, Laurence J. ... Pierre, SD
Zastrow, Robert J. ... Arlington, VA
Zatcoff, Alicia Renee ... Richmond, VA
Zatcoff, Sanford H., (P.C.) ... Atlanta, GA
Zate, Steven E. ... Naples, FL
Zateeny, Deborah J. ... Philadelphia, PA
Zaterman, David B. ... Englewood, CO
Zatezalo, Martha A. ... Pittsburgh, PA
Zatezalo, Michael E. ... Columbus, OH
Zatina, Elizabeth A. ... Detroit, MI
Zatir, Peter T. ... New Bedford, MA
Zatkin, Richard H. ... Pinckney, MI
Zatkin, Steven R. ... Oakland, CA
Zatkin, Victoria B. ... Oakland, CA
Zatkin-Butler, Ilene B. ... New York, NY
Zatko, Matthew R. ... Somerset, PA
Zatkoff, Kenneth W. ... Troy, MI
Zatkoff, Lawrence P. ... Detroit, MI
Zatkos, John W., Jr. ... Pittsburgh, PA
Zatkowsky, Miles P. ... Rochester, NY
Zatlin, Suzanne L. ... St. Louis, MO
Zatman, Murray A. ... Santa Rosa, CA
Zatolokin, James R. ... Beverly Hills, CA
Zatopa, James R. ... Chicago, IL
Zator, Joseph A., II ... Allentown, PA
Zator Law Offices ... Allentown, PA
Zatorski, Robert D. ... Saddle Brook, NJ
Zatt, Mark E. ... San Diego, CA
Zatuchni, David ... Princeton, NJ
Zatyko, Donald R. ... Willoughby, OH
Zatz, Arthur A. ... Philadelphia, PA
Zatz, Clifford J. ... Washington, DC
Zatz, Glen M. ... Detroit, MI
Zatz, Julie ...
Department of Justice, GV
Zatz, Peter B. ... Minneapolis, MN
Zatz, Peter B., P.A. ... Minneapolis, MN
Zatzkis & Associates ... New Orleans, LA
Zatzkis, Lanny R. ... New Orleans, LA
Zatzkis, Ralph J. ... New Orleans, LA
Houston, TX
Zauberman, L. Jeffrey ... Southfield, MI
Zaucha, Jerome J. ... Washington, DC
Zauderer, Howard J. ... Melville, NY
Zauderer, Mark C. ... New York, NY
Zauderer, Philip Q. ... Girard, OH
Zauel, Pamela M. ... Ann Arbor, MI
Detroit, MI
Zaug, Justin B. ... Seattle, WA
Zaug, Mary E. ... Chicago, IL
Zaugg, Gary ... Lawton, OK
Zaugg, Julia A. ... Lake Forest, IL
Zaums, Peter M. ... Lambertville, MI
Zaun, Anne M. ... Milltown, NJ
Zaun, Lesley ... Minneapolis, MN
Zaun, William F. ... Coplay, PA
Zaunbrecher, Alan A. ... Metairie, LA
Zaunbrecher, Alan A. ... New Orleans, LA
Zaunbrecher, Christopher L.
Lafayette, LA
Zaunbrecher, Lester J. ... Lafayette, LA
Zaunbrecher, Michael H. ... Alvarado, TX
Zaunbrecher, Russell K. ... Crowley, LA
Zaunbrecher, Susan B. ... Cincinnati, OH
Zauner, Joseph F., III ... Baltimore, MD
Zausmer, Aviva R. ... Port Washington, NY
Zausmer, Gary E. ... Austin, TX
Zausmer, Mark J. ... Detroit, MI
Farmington Hills, MI
Zausmer, Morris L. ... Glen Cove, NY
Zausmer, Nathan ... Glen Cove, NY
Zausmer, Robert N. ... Mineola, NY
Zausner, Henry T. ... Kalamazoo, MI
Zausner, L. Andrew ... Washington, DC
Zautcke, Donald W. ... Cedarburg, WI
Zauzig, Charles J. ... Woodbridge, VA
Zauzmer, Robert A. ... Philadelphia, PA
Zavadil, Daniel M. ... Arlington, VA
Zavadil, Daniel M., P.C. ... Arlington, VA
Zavadil, George ... Towson, MD
Zavadil, Lawrence M. ... Denver, CO
Zavaglia, Joseph, Jr. ... Eatontown, NJ
Zavagno, Denise M. ... Rockville, MD
Zavah, Barry A. ... Buffalo, NY
Zavakos, Christ L. ... Dayton, OH
Zavala, Donald ... Phoenix, AZ
Zavala, Graciela E. ... Salinas, CA
Zavala, Paul ... Detroit, MI
Zavala, Riordan J. ... Placentia, CA
Zavala, Stacy Bearden ... El Paso, TX
Zavaleta, Claudia M. ... Houston, TX
Zavaleta, Hector M. ... El Paso, TX
Zavaleta, Hector M., P.C. ... El Paso, TX
Zavaletta, Peter M. ... Brownsville, TX
Zavaletta, Peter M., P.C. ... Brownsville, TX
Zavareei, Hassan A. ... Washington, DC
Zavarella, Gino ... Cleveland, OH
Zavarella, Paul D. ... Pittsburgh, PA
Zavarella, Paul R. ... Pittsburgh, PA
Zavarelli, Glynis L. ... Dallas, TX
Zavarello, A. William ... Akron, OH
Zavarello, A. William, Co., L.P.A.
Akron, OH
Zavatsky, Kathleen Hanson
Cincinnati, OH
Zavatsky, Michael J. ... Cincinnati, OH
Zavatsky, Peter G. ... Syosset, NY
Zavela, Thomas C.
Grosse Pointe Woods, MI
Zavell, A. Stephen ... San Francisco, CA
Zavell, Chas. M. ... Beachwood, OH
Zavell, James P. ... St. Clair Shores, MI
Zavertnik, John L. ... Miami, FL
Zaverton, Michael D. ... Cleveland, OH
Zaverzence, Denise ... Plymouth, MI
Zavesky, Joseph E. ... Roseland, NJ
Zavesky, Robert J. ... Cleveland, OH
Zavett, Errol ... Chicago, IL
Zavett, Rebecca ... Chicago, IL
Zavez, John Peter ... Boston, MA
Zavidow, Patricia Reid
Westlake Village, CA
Zavidow, Robert M. ... Long Beach, CA
Zavin, Jonathan ... New York, NY
Zavin, Theodora ... New York, NY
Zavinski, Dennis M. ... Ravenna, OH
Zavis, Michael Wm., (P.C.) ... Chicago, IL
Zavislak, John L. ... Oak Brook, IL
Zavislak & Mann, Ltd. ... Oak Brook, IL
Zavitsanos, John ... Houston, TX
Zavitz, John W. ... Albuquerque, NM
Zavoda, David P. ... La Grange, TX
Zavodnick, Allen ... Jersey City, NJ
Zavodnick, Howard B. ... Philadelphia, PA
Zavodnick, Sandra F. ... Philadelphia, PA
Zavodnick, Steven D. ... San Jose, CA
Zavodnick, Steven D., A Professional Law Corporation ... San Jose, CA
Zavodnick & Zavodnick ... Philadelphia, PA
Zavodnyik, Ernest S. ... Flossmoor, IL
Zavodnyik, Peter ... Chicago, IL
Zavoli, John R. ... Acton, MA
Zavon, Bruce P. ... Tallahassee, FL
Zavon, Dan A. ... Cincinnati, OH
Zavos, Harry N. ... Glendale, CA
Zawacki, Deanna M. ... Detroit, MI
Zawacki, Edward W. ... Westport, CT
Zawacki, Everett, Gray & McLaughlin, Law Offices of ... New York, NY
White Plains, NY
Zawacki, Martha S. ... New York, NY
Zawacki, Ronald Anthony ... East Lansing, MI
Zawacki, Stephen J. ... Casselberry, FL
Zawada, Thomas J. ... Tucson, AZ
Zawadsky, John H. ... Madison, WI
Zawadzkas, Michael A. ... Orleans, MA
Zawadzki, Paula A. ... Pittsburgh, PA
Zawadzki, Roman J. ... Los Angeles, CA
Zawahry, Hosam Kamal
Panama City, FL
Zawalich, Chet ... South Bend, IN
Zawaly, Peter P., II. ... Dublin, OH
Zawarus, Gordon ... Chicago, IL
Zawatsky, Evelyn Weiss ... Bristol, RI
Zawicki, Paul P. ... Baltimore, MD
Zawila, Joseph ... Roseland, NJ
Zawila, William L. ... Garden Grove, CA
Zawilski, Richard Ian ... Yorba Linda, CA
Zawinsy, Mark T. ... Brooklyn, NY
Zawistoski, John J. ... Rutland, VT
Zawistowski, Leonard A., Jr.
Board of Governors Of The Federal Reserve System,
Division of Banking Supervision and Regulation, GV
Zawisza, Christina A. ... Fort Lauderdale, FL
Zawitoski, Gina Monath ... Baltimore, MD
Zawitoski, JoAnne ... Baltimore, MD
Zawodniak, Bruce A. ... New Britain, CT
Zawol, Matthew G. ... Los Angeles, CA
Zawoyski, Marilyn B ... Pittsburgh, PA
Zawtocki, Marie Splees ... Phoenix, AZ
Zawtocki, Richard W. ... Casa Grande, AZ
Phoenix, AZ
Zawyrucha, Thomas S. ... Riverhead, NY
Zax, Harry ... Paterson, NJ
Zax, Helen Kemp ... Washington, DC
Zax, Lauren E. ... Los Angeles, CA
Sacramento, CA
Zax, Leonard A. ... Washington, DC
Zayachak, Joseph J. ... Los Angeles, CA
Zayas, Ange'lica Dianne ... Miami, FL
Zayas, Eduardo A. ... San Juan, PR
Zayas, Joseph A. ... New York, NY
Zayas, Louis A. ... New York, NY
Zayas & Oquendo, LLP ... New York, NY
Zayas, Richard L. ... Hartford, CT
Zayas, Richard R. ... New York, NY
Zayas-Davis, Marilyn ... New Richmond, OH
Zaydon, James J., Jr. ... Scranton, PA
Zaydon & Zaydon ... Scranton, PA
Zayed, Dean K. ... Downers Grove, IL
Zayed, Rabea J. ... Minneapolis, MN
Zayicek, Douglas M. ... Myrtle Beach, SC
Zayid, Geno, P.C., Law Offices of
Southfield, MI
Zayid, Geno T. ... Southfield, MI
Zayko, Kristine M. ... East Lansing, MI
Zayler, Stephen J. ... Lufkin, TX
Zayner, Theodore C. ... San Jose, CA
Zayon, Herman ... Northridge, CA
Zayotti, Matthew P. ... Boston, MA
Zaytoun, Robert E. ... Raleigh, NC
Zaytoun, Robert E., P.A., Law Offices of
Raleigh, NC
Zazakis, James D. ... Chicago, IL
Zazella, Alfred J. ... Wayne, NJ
Zazella & Singer ... Wayne, NJ
Zazik, Wendy B. ... Boston, MA
Zazove, Daniel A. ... Chicago, IL
Zazove, Linda L. ... East St. Louis, IL
Zazueta, Fernando R. ... San Jose, CA
Zazueta Law Office ... San Jose, CA
Zazzali, Andrew F., Jr. ... Newark, NJ
Zazzali, James R. ... Newark, NJ
Zazzali, Zazzali, Fagella & Nowak, A Prof. Corp. ... Trenton, NJ
New York, NY
Newark, NJ
Zazzaro, Frank J. ... Montclair, NJ
Zazzera, Kevin ... Staten Island, NY
Zazzo, Samantha P. ... Westmont, NJ
Zbar, Darrell ... Hollywood, FL
Zbaracki, Andrew J. ... Waukesha, WI
Z'berg, Cynthia ... Sacramento, CA
Zbiegien, John ... Blaine, MN
Zbieroski, Mark Joel ... Nevada, IA
Zbikowski, Susan J. ... Detroit, MI
Zbilut, L. Wally ... Chicago, IL
Zbinden & Curtis ... Portland, OR
Zbinden, Jodi Pearson ... Charlotte, NC
Zbinden, Jon A. ... Portland, OR
Zboray, Debra A. ... Fair Lawn, NJ
Zboray, James A. ... Baytown, TX
Zborowski, Thomas F. ... Rahway, NJ
Zboyan, JoAnne M. ... Denver, CO
Zbranek, Angela A. ... Liberty, TX
Zbranek, J. C. ... Liberty, TX
Zbranek, Zachary M. ... Liberty, TX
Zbranek, Zeb D. ... Liberty, TX
Zbrzeznj, Bernard E. ... Philadelphia, PA
Zbrzeznj, Betty Jo ... Horsham, PA
Zbur, Richard S. ... Los Angeles, CA
Zbytowski, Jennifer S. ... Detroit, MI
Zdan, Brian ... Omaha, NE
Zdan, Carole E. ... Garden City, NY
Zdancewicz, Michael J. ... Phoenix, AZ
Zdancewicz, William P. ... Memphis, TN
Zdanio, James C. ... Warren, MI
Zdarsky, Joseph E. ... Buffalo, NY
Zdarsky, Sawicki & Agostinelli
Buffalo, NY
Niagara Falls, NY
Zdatny, Sophie E. ... Morgantown, WV
Zdeb, Michael J. ... Chicago, IL
Zdebski, Charles A. ... Washington, DC
Zdimal, Janice M. ... San Jose, CA
Zdobinski, Marilyn G. ... Hackensack, NJ
Zdrahal, Katerina ... Washington, DC

Zelante, Thomas A. ... Dover, NJ
Zelasko, Bradford D. ... Cleveland, OH
Zelasko, Gregory J. ... Columbus, OH
Zelasko, Hope Patrice ... Denver, CO
Zelasko, Ted F. ... Aberdeen, WA
Zelaya, Carlos A., II ... Chalmette, LA
Zelaya, Kandace A. ... New Orleans, LA
Zelaznik, Marshall ... Los Angeles, CA
Zelazny, Eric G. ... Chicago, IL
Zelbo, Howard ... New York, NY
Zelbo, Sian E. ... New York, NY
Zelbst, John P. ... Lawton, OK
Zelbst, John P., Law Firm ... Lawton, OK
Zelcer, Harry ... New York, NY
Zelcs, George A. ... Chicago, IL
Zelden & Associates ... New Orleans, LA
Zelden, Jerome J. ... Lincolnwood, IL
Zelden, Max ... New Orleans, LA
Zeldes, Jacob D. ... Bridgeport, CT
Zeldes, Needle & Cooper, A Professional Corporation ... Bridgeport, CT
New Haven, CT
Zeldin, Adria S.
Equal Employment Opportunity Commission, Office of Federal Operations, GV
Zeldin, Andrew S. ... Trenton, NJ
Zeldin, Elizabeth A. ... Boston, MA
Zeldin, Jessica ... Wilmington, DE
Zeldin, Joel ... San Francisco, CA
Zeldin, Kim ... San Francisco, CA
Zeldin, Kim S. ... San Francisco, CA
Zeldin, Laura S., Law Office of
Columbus, OH
Zeldin, Michael F. ... Washington, DC
Zeldin, Robert B. ... Kansas City, MO
Zeldin, Robin Jeffrey ... Chicago, IL
Zeldin, Stanford A. ... Kansas City, MO
Zeldman, Karyn B. ... New York, NY
Zeldow, Edward ... Los Angeles, CA
Zele, Gregory T. ... Tampa, FL
Zele, John D. ... Washington, DC
Zele, Ronald ... Eastlake, OH
Zele, Scott J. ... Eastlake, OH
Zele & Zele, Co., L.P.A. ... Eastlake, OH
Zelechiwsky, Bohdan J. ... Bethlehem, PA
Zelechowski, Leon ... Chicago, IL
Zelechowski, Leon, Ltd. ... Chicago, IL
Zeledon, Carlos E. ... New Orleans, LA
Zelek, Eugene F., Jr. ... Chicago, IL
Zelek, Mark E. ... Miami, FL
Zelek, Robert M. ... Chicago, IL
Zelen, Garrett J. ... Los Angeles, CA
Zelenak, Edward M. ... Lincoln Park, MI
Zelenak, Lawrence A. ... Portland, OR
Zelener, Howard M. ... Redlands, CA
Zeleniak, Martha A. ... Garden City, NY
Zelenka, Daniel E., II ... Gretna, LA
Zelenka, Donald J. ... Columbia, SC
Zelenka, Michael J. ... Tinton Falls, NJ
Zelenka, Robert G. ... San Jose, CA
Zelenko, Benjamin L. ... Washington, DC
Zelenko, Norman ... New York, NY
Zelenock, Gerald B., Jr. ... Traverse City, MI
Zelenock, Katheryne L. ... Birmingham, MI
Zelenock, Michael J. ... Novi, MI
Zelenock, Michael J., P.C. ... Novi, MI
Zelenske, Ethel ... Washington, DC
Zelensky, Michael J. ... Ketchikan, AK
Zelensky, Samuel ... New York, NY
Zelenty, Michael W. ... Morristown, NJ
New York, NY
Zelenty, Paul L. ... Morristown, NJ
Zeleny, Thomas D. ... Chicago, IL
Zelermyer, B. Andrew ... Boston, MA
Zelermyer, Benjamin ... White Plains, NY
Zeleskey, Cornelius, Hallmark, Roper & Hicks, L.L.P. ... Lufkin, TX
Zeleskey, James J. ... Lufkin, TX
Zeleski, Samuel ... Grand Island, NE
Zelevansky, Howard L. ... Brooklyn, NY
Zeleznak, Cheryl C. ... Oak Forest, IL
Zeleznik, Richard G. ... Pittsburgh, PA
Zelezny, John Dean ... Clovis, CA
Zelichov, Richard ... Los Angeles, CA
Zelickson, Barry M. ... Minnetonka, MN
Zelickson, Meg ... Hastings-On-Hudson, NY
Zeliff, A. Nathan ... Moraga, CA
Zeliff, Harry J. ... Lansing, MI
Zeliger, Michael E. ... Boston, MA
Zeligs, David M. ... Long Beach, CA
Zeligson, Laurie ... Long Island City, NY
Zeligson, Samuel L. ... Tulsa, OK
Zeligson, Sheryl ... New York, NY
Zeligson, Stephen J. ... Tulsa, OK
Zelikoff, David B. ... Philadelphia, PA
Zelikovic, Allan ... New York, NY
Zelikovitz, Kelly D. ... Houston, TX
Zelikow, Nathaniel ... New York, NY
Zelikson, Alexandra ... Washington, DC
Zelikson, Jennifer ... San Francisco, CA
Zelin, M. Jason ... Los Angeles, CA
Zelin, Nicole A. ... Greenfield, IN
Zelin, Randy Scott ... Jericho, NY
Zelina, Richard S. ... Baltimore, MD
Zelinger, C. Robert ... Waterbury, CT
Zelinger, Steven L. ... San Francisco, CA
Zelinka, Elizabeth A. ... Washington, DC
Zelinski, Terry A. ... Fayetteville, AR
Zelinsky, Donald ... Los Angeles, CA
Zelinsky, Edward A. ... New York, NY
Zelinsky, Martin H. ... Colorado Springs, CO
Zelinsky, Richd. M. ... Malden, MA
Zelinsky, Yuri B.
Securities and Exchange Commission, Division of Enforcement, GV
Zelis, Bruce P. ... Walnut Creek, CA
Zelitch, Steven M. ... Elkins Park, PA

Zelizer, Carol ... Columbus, OH
Zelkind, Boris ... Minneapolis, MN
Zelkind, Donald ... Denver, CO
Zelko, Katherine M. ... Portland, OR
Zelko, Mark I. ... New York, NY
Zelkowitz, Alan S. ... Chicago, IL
Zelkowitz, Barry & Cullers
Mt. Vernon, OH
Zelkowitz, Geanne K. ... Philadelphia, PA
Zelkowitz, Jeffrey H.
United States Postal Service, Law Department, GV
Zelkowitz, Steven L. ... Hicksville, NY
Zelkowitz, Steven W. ... Miami, FL
Zell, Bernadette E. ... Lexington, KY
Zell, Bradley G. ... Miller, SD
Zell, David L. ... Houston, TX
Zell, Glenn ... Atlanta, GA
Zell, James Neil ... New York, NY
Zell, Jeffrey J. ... Macon, GA
Zell, L. Marc ... Washington, DC
Zell, Lee H. ... Birmingham, AL
Zell, Mary McNeill ... Philadelphia, PA
Zell, Michael P. ... Baltimore, MD
Zell, Michael P., Law Offices of
Baltimore, MD
Zell, Patricia S. ... Honolulu, HI
Zell, Rodney S. ... Atlanta, GA
Zell, Samuel ... Chicago, IL
Zell, Stephen H. ... Tustin, CA
Zell, Thomas B. ... Palo Alto, CA
Zell, Wayne M. ... Washington, DC
Zell & Zell, P.C. ... Atlanta, GA
Zellan, Jeffrey S. ... New York, NY
Zellar, Jay B. ... Zanesville, OH
Zellar, Ronald C. ... Lansing, MI
Zellar & Zellar ... Zanesville, OH
Zelle, Anthony R. ... Boston, MA
Zelle, Hofmann, Voelbel & Gette, LLP
Los Angeles, CA
San Francisco, CA
Waltham, MA
Minneapolis, MN
Dallas, TX
Zelle, Lawrence ... Minneapolis, MN
Zellefrow & Associates ... Indianapolis, IN
Zellefrow, Grant E. ... Indianapolis, IN
Zellen, James B. ... Bloomfield Hills, MI
Zellen, Todd R. ... Boca Raton, FL
Zeller, Allen S. ... Cherry Hill, NJ
Zeller & Bryant ... Cherry Hill, NJ
Zeller, Cathy A. ... Napa, CA
Zeller, Charles J. ... Stamford, CT
Zeller, David J. ... Skokie, IL
Zeller, Deborah Dobbs ... Peoria, IL
Zeller, Donald F. ... Lexington, KY
Zeller, Elizabeth A.
Environmental Protection Agency, Program Office Attorneys, GV
Zeller, Frank J. ... Mount Kisco, NY
Zeller, Frank J., P.C. ... Mount Kisco, NY
Zeller, Gerard A. ... Sayre, PA
Zeller, Harvey ... Parsippany, NJ
Zeller, Harvey R. ... Roseland, NJ
Zeller, Hoff & Zeller, Inc. ... Napa, CA
Zeller, Howard ... Oneida, NY
Zeller, James A. ... Torrington, CT
Zeller, James P. ... Chicago, IL
Zeller, James W. ... Arbutus, MD
Zeller, Jason J. ... San Francisco, CA
Zeller, Joseph M. ... Baltimore, MD
Zeller, Julia Smith ... Harrisburg, PA
Zeller & Keihner, L.L.P. ... Palm Beach, FL
Zeller, Louis John, Jr. ... New Orleans, LA
Zeller, M. Stephanie ... Rochester, NY
Zeller, Michael C. ... New York, NY
Zeller, Michael E. ... Charlotte, NC
Zeller, Michael R. ... Stamford, CT
New York, NY
Zeller, Michael T. ... Los Angeles, CA
Zeller, Nora Lee ... Deerfield, IL
Zeller, Paul W. ... New York, NY
Zeller, Randi E. ... New York, NY
Zeller, Robert ... Hackensack, NJ
Zeller, Robert H. ... Napa, CA
Zeller, Robert M. ... Los Angeles, CA
Zeller, Robert S. ... Cleveland, OH
Zeller, Robt. G. ... Scottsdale, AZ
Zeller, Ronald J., P.A. ... Palm Beach, FL
Zeller, Sharon L. ... Hollywood, FL
Zeller, Steven C. ... Boston, MA
Zeller, Steven McMahon ... Chicago, IL
Zeller & Strulowitz, LLP ... Newark, NJ
Roseland, NJ
West Orange, NJ
Zeller, Theodore J., III ... Allentown, PA
Zeller, Thomas M. ... Dallas, TX
Zeller, Ty ... Port Lavaca, TX
Zeller, Wendy J. ... Minneapolis, MN
Zeller, William A. ... El Segundo, CA
Zeller, William D. ... New York, NY
Zellerbach, Nancy ... San Francisco, CA
Zellerbach, Paul E. ... Riverside, CA
Zellerbach, Thomas H. ... Menlo Park, CA
Zellermayer, Reuben J. ... Chicago, IL
Zellers, Carl A. ... Cleveland, OH
Zellers, Catherine ... Weatherford, TX
Zellers, Jason A. ... Chicago, IL
Zellers, Jeffrey J. ... Concord, NH
Zellers, June D. ... Auburn, ME
Zellers, Lori Jo ... Grand Rapids, MI
Zellers, Michael C. ... Los Angeles, CA
Zellers, Richard G. ... Youngstown, OH
Zellers, Walter E. ... Weatherford, TX
Zellers & Zellers ... Weatherford, TX
Zelley, Frederick B. ... Basking Ridge, NJ
Zellhoefer, David R. ... Waterloo, IA
Zellhoefer Law Firm ... Waterloo, IA

Zellhoefer, Richard G. ... Waterloo, IA
Zellinger, Katherine J. ... New York, NY
Zellmann, Donald W. ... San Diego, CA
Zellmer, Ann E. ... Cleveland, OH
Zellmer, Charles B. ... Cleveland, OH
Zellmer, George ... McAlester, OK
Zellmer & Gruber ... Cleveland, OH
Zellmer, Jill A. G. ... Stamford, CT
Zellmer, Joseph F., III ... Auburn, CA
Zellmer, Kimberly Shell ... Kansas City, MO
Zellmer, Mark G. ... St. Louis, MO
Zellmer, Randy J. ... Mankato, MN
Zellmer, Timothy J. ... Minneapolis, MN
Zellmer, Willard A. ... Davenport, WA
Zellner, Brian K. ... Camp Hill, PA
Zellner, Kathleen T., & Associates
Naperville, IL
Zellner, Natalie ... Atlanta, GA
Zellner, Richard A. ... Cleveland, OH
Zellner, Robert J. ... Lake Forest, IL
Zells, Evette J. ... Chicago, IL
Zells, Heidi S. ... Chicago, IL
Zells, Martin B. ... Chicago, IL
Zellweger, Jake E. ... Towson, MD
Zelma, George P. ... New York, NY
Zelman, Abner T. ... New York, NY
Zelman, Andrea E. ... Tampa, FL
Zelman, Andrew ... Winter Park, FL
Zelman, Andrew E. ... New York, NY
Zelman, Arnold N. ... Buffalo, NY
Zelman, Bonita E. ... New York, NY
Zelman & Buongiorno ... Tarzana, CA
Zelman, David A. ... New York, NY
Zelman, Elizabeth Susan ... White Plains, NY
Zelman, Martha K. ... Kew Gardens, NY
Zelman, Michael ... Coral Gables, FL
Zelman, Michael H. ... Tarzana, CA
Zelman, Michael, P.A. ... Coral Gables, FL
Zelman, Nancy E. ... Ventura, CA
Zelman, Richard M. ... Miami, FL
Zelman, Stephen M. ... New York, NY
Zelman, Steven A. ... Bronx, NY
Zelman, Steven M. ... Bloomfield, CT
Zelmanoff, Marci ... New York, NY
Zelmanovitz, Joseph ... New York, NY
Zelmanovitz, Menachem O.
New York, NY
Zelmanow, Edward L. ... Nanuet, NY
Zelmanow, Jeffrey H. ... Greeley, CO
Zelmar, Michael A. ... Northbrook, IL
Zelmer, Patricia A. ... Indianapolis, IN
South Bend, IN
Zelner, Barry S. ... Beverly Hills, CA
Zelner, Martin ... New York, NY
Zelnick, Allan ... New York, NY
Zelnick, Irene ... New York, NY
Zelnick, Robert J. ... Woodbridge, VA
Zelnick, Robert W. ... Washington, DC
Zelnick, Stephen A. ... New York, NY
Zelnik, Jonathan R. ... Treasury Department, Internal Revenue Service, GV
Zelon, Allen Harvey ... New York, NY
Zelon, Laurie D. ... Los Angeles, CA
Zelonker, Regina ... Coral Gables, FL
Zelpe, Samuel ... Sheboygan, WI
Zelson, Cindy M. ... New York, NY
Zeltner, Benjamin ... Atlantic City, NJ
Zeltner, David E. ... New York, NY
Zeltner, Peter P. ... Scarsdale, NY
Zeltner, Raymond J. ... Elizabeth, NJ
Zeltonoga, William L. ... Los Angeles, CA
Zeltt, Douglas J. ... Trenton, NJ
Zeltzer, George M. ... Bloomfield Hills, MI
Zeltzer, Nancy E. ... Costa Mesa, CA
Zelvin, Jamie L. ... Chicago, IL
Zelvy, Robert, & Associates ... Sandusky, OH
Zelznick, S. Paul ... Chicago, IL
Zemah, Yigal ... New York, NY
Zemaitis, Thomas E. ... Philadelphia, PA
Zeman, Cheryl A. ... Harrisburg, PA
Zeman, Christine G. ... Springfield, IL
Zeman, David W. ... Canonsburg, PA
Zeman, Donald ... New Bedford, MA
Zeman, Francis J., Jr. ... Skokie, IL
Zeman, James C. ... Detroit, MI
Zeman, Jeffrey B. ... Hartford, CT
Zeman, Jules Solomon ... Santa Monica, CA
Zeman, Larry S. ... Irvine, CA
Zeman, Laura Herpers ... Seattle, WA
Zeman, Laura J. ... Phoenix, AZ
Zeman, Laura Weiss ... Lafayette, IN
Zeman, Michael ... New Bedford, MA
Zeman, Nicolle Y. ... Hauppauge, NY
Zeman, Robert A. ... Phoenix, AZ
Zeman, Robert L. ... Des Plaines, IL
Zeman, Robert L. ... Canonsburg, PA
Zeman, Sally Herron ... Denver, CO
Zeman, Theresa A. ... Atlanta, GA
Zeman, William S. ... Hartford, CT
Zeman and Zeman ... Canonsburg, PA
Zemanek, Jan A. ... Newport Beach, CA
Zemanek, John D. ... Los Angeles, CA
Zemanek & Mills, A Professional Corporation ... Los Angeles, CA
Zemanian, Peter G. ... Norfolk, VA
Zemanian, Rosemary Kearns ... Norfolk, VA
Zemanick, Gregory J. ... Chicago, IL
Zemanick, Peggy A. ... Chicago, IL
Zemann, Daniel, Jr. ... New York, NY
Zemba, Karen Kozak ... Independence, OH
Zemba, Mark J. ... Columbus, OH
Zembar, Stephanie Ann ... Columbus, OH
Zembek, Richard S. ... Houston, TX
Zember, Gerald S. ... Reading, PA
Zembko, Elizabeth A. ... New Britain, CT
Zemble, Karen S. ... New York, NY
Zembsch, Mark J. ... San Francisco, CA
Zemcik, Mark S. ... New York, NY

Zeme, Susan Winer ... Oakland, CA
Zemek, Elliot ... New Bern, NC
Zemel, Albert I. ... Chicago, IL
Zemel, Avital G.
Environmental Protection Agency, Office of the General Counsel, GV
Zemel, Daniel J. ... Aventura, FL
Zemel, Dean B. ... Milwaukee, WI
Zemel, Douglas E. ... Cambridge, MA
Zemel, Franklin L. ... Aventura, FL
Zemel, Fred D. ... Roseland, NJ
Zemel, Herbert C. ... Hollywood, FL
Zemel, Irina S. ... Fairfax, VA
Zemel and Kaufman, P.A. ... Hollywood, FL
Zemel, Margo R. ... West Orange, NJ
Zemel, Mitchel B. ... Pittsburgh, PA
Zemel, Morton B. ... Miami, FL
Zemel, Sharon ... Los Angeles, CA
Zemelman, Mark S. ... Oakland, CA
Zemenak, Cara E. ... Chicago, IL
Zemenak, John R. ... Wheaton, IL
Zemetis, Joseph C. ... Farmington, CT
Zemetis, Terence A. ... Wallingford, CT
Zemetra, Michael B. ... San Jose, CA
Zemil, Brian Alain ... Baltimore, MD
Zemil, Jack N. ... Baltimore, MD
Zemis, Karen K. ... San Antonio, TX
Zemis, Kristin R. ... Montgomery, AL
Zemites, Donald L. ... Kansas City, KS
Zemke, Norman L. ... Farmington, MI
Zemlicka, Ronald L. ... Milwaukee, WI
Zemlin, Raymond C., (P.C.) ... Boston, MA
Zemlock, Abraham ... New York, NY
Zemlock, Albert J. ... Miami, FL
Zemlock, Barbara A. ... Harrisburg, PA
Zemm, Sandra P. ... Chicago, IL
Zemmelman, Connie F. ... Toledo, OH
Zemmol, Allen ... Detroit, MI
Zemnickas, George T. ... Detroit, MI
Zemp, Brian L. ... Scottsdale, AZ
Zemp, F. Lachicotte, Jr. ... Juneau, AK
Zemp, Kapsal, Carpenter & Hazlewood, P.L.L.C. ... Scottsdale, AZ
Zemp, Mary H. ... Juneau, AK
Zempel, Paul C. ... Tarpon Springs, FL
Zempolich, Stephen J. ... Washington, DC
Zemprelli, Edw. P. ... Pittsburgh, PA
Zemser, Scott M. ... New York, NY
Zemsky, David E. ... Hempstead, NY
Zemsky, David E., P.C., Law Offices of
Hempstead, NY
Zemsky, Susan Jean ... San Francisco, CA
Zemyan, Mary Louise ... Wolf Point, MT
Zen, David Hen Ming ... Littleton, CO
Zen, Erik R. ... Honolulu, HI
Zen, Omar M. ... Baltimore, MD
Zena, Amendolara & Palombaro
Youngstown, OH
Zena, Thomas E. ... Youngstown, OH
Zendan, Michael F., II ... Charlotte, NC
Zendejas, M. James ... Colorado Springs, CO
Zendel, Daniel F. ... New York, NY
Zendell, David J. ... Paterson, NJ
Zendell, David J., P.A. ... Paterson, NJ
Zender, Daniel D. ... Bellingham, WA
Zender, Jan M. ... St. James, MN
Zender, Jill A. ... Salt Lake City, UT
Zender, Michael C. ... Minneapolis, MN
Zender, Philip R. ... San Francisco, CA
Zenderman, Marsha ... Albuquerque, NM
Zener, Robert V. ... Washington, DC
Zener, Thomas A. ... Santa Ana, CA
Zenere, James J. ... San Jose, CA
Zeng, Ying ... Houston, TX
Zenga, V. James ... West Palm Beach, FL
Zenge, Lorraine ... Springfield, IL
Zengel, Andrew S. ... New Orleans, LA
Zenger, H. Kenneth ... Hillsboro, OR
Zenger, Todd E. ... Salt Lake City, UT
Zengerle, Joseph C., III ... Washington, DC
Zengerle, Lynda S. ... Washington, DC
Zengilowski, Richard E. ... Gardner, MA
Zengler, David K. ... Boonville, IN
Zengler, George A. ... San Francisco, CA
Zengler, Jill Ellen ... Indianapolis, IN
Zeni, Ferdinand J., Jr. ... Chicago, IL
Zenick, Elliott ... Washington, DC
Zenk, Ann M. ... Newton, IA
Zenk, Carolyn A. ... Bridgehampton, NY
Zenk Law Office ... Elkhorn, WI
Zenk, Sandra M. ... Des Moines, IA
Zenk, W. Ryan ... Elkhorn, WI
Zenkel, Elliott L. ... New York, NY
Zenkel, Gary B. ... New York, NY
Zenker, Arnold ... Boston, MA
Zenker, Larry L. ... Honolulu, HI
Zenker, M. Patricia ... Waukegan, IL
Zenkert, Raymond W., Jr. ... Westfield, MA
Zenn, Deanna M. ... Kew Gardens, NY
Zenn, Jeffrey A. ... Hackensack, NJ
Zenna, Jeffrey J. ... Chatham, NJ
Zennaché, Charles M. ... Eugene, OR
Zenner, Albert W. ... Erie, PA
Zenner, Brian S. ... Chicago, IL
Zenner, David Michael ... Albuquerque, NM
Zenner, Ivette Iza ... Syracuse, NY
Zenner, Laurie A. ... Minneapolis, MN
Zenner, Mathew R. ... Nashville, TN
Zenner, Michael J. ... Atlanta, GA
Zenner, Sheldon T. ... Chicago, IL
Zenner, Walter F. ... Washington, DC
Zeno, G. Michael, Jr. ... Kirkland, WA
Zeno, Melvin C. ... Gretna, LA
Zeno, Thomas E. ... Washington, DC
Zenobi, Eugene F. ... Miami, FL
Zenoff, A. J. ... Chicago, IL
Zenoff, Alan H. ... Chicago, IL
Zenoff, David ... Carson City, NV

Ziegenhorn, Bart E. ....West Memphis, AR
Ziegenhorn, Eric H. ....Kansas City, MO
Ziegenhorn, Jennifer ....Memphis, TN
Zieger, Jon M. ....Bellevue, WA
Zieger, Lawrence P. ....Milwaukee, WI
Zieger, Rudolph, Jr. ....Allentown, PA
Ziegler, Alan B. ....Reading, PA
Ziegler, Alan S. ....Greenwich, CT
Ziegler, Alvin ....Orinda, CA
Ziegler, Alyson V. ....Alexandria, VA
Ziegler, Amy J. ....Buffalo, NY
Ziegler, Amy Louise ....St. Louis, MO
Ziegler, Andrea Certilman ......Woodsburgh, NY
Ziegler, Ann E. ....Chicago, IL
Ziegler, Annette K. ....West Bend, WI
Ziegler, Arnold G. ....Silver Spring, MD
Ziegler, Arnold G., P.C., Law Offices of
Washington, DC
Laurel, MD
Silver Spring, MD
Upper Marlboro, MD
Ziegler, Brandon E. ....New York, NY
Ziegler, Brian K. ....East Meadow, NY
Ziegler, Carol L. ....Brooklyn, NY
Ziegler, Catherine A. ....New York, NY
Ziegler, Chad E. ....Philadelphia, PA
Ziegler, Charles A. ....Warren, OH
Ziegler, Charles W. ....Lafayette, LA
Ziegler, Cheryl L. ....Washington, DC
Landover, MD
Ziegler, Christian J. ....Orange, CA
Ziegler, Christopher M. ....Alpharetta, GA
Ziegler, Craig E. ....Philadelphia, PA
Ziegler, David ....Pittsburgh, PA
Ziegler, David L. ....Hinton, WV
Ziegler, Deborah ....Houston, TX
Ziegler, Deborah A. ....Akron, OH
Ziegler, Donald E. ....Pittsburgh, PA
Ziegler, Edward H. ....Dayton, OH
Ziegler, Elizabeth A. ....Juneau, AK
Ziegler, E. S. ....Baltimore, MD
Ziegler, Felecia Grossman ....Orlando, FL
Ziegler, Frank J. ....Rosemont, IL
Ziegler, Frank W., III ....Brentwood, TN
Ziegler, George N. ....Chatham, NJ
Ziegler, George P. ....New York, NY
Ziegler, Geza C., Jr. ....New Haven, CT
Ziegler, Glen ....Hillsdale, MI
Ziegler, Gregory N. ....Dallas, TX
Ziegler & Gunnoe ....Hinton, WV
Ziegler, H. Jeffrey ....Baltimore, MD
Ziegler, Hal W. ....Jackson, MI
Ziegler, Harry L. ....Fairfield, IL
Ziegler, Henry S. ....New York, NY
Ziegler, Herman J. ....New York, NY
Ziegler, Jacqueline M. ....Coral Springs, FL
Ziegler, James M. ....Independence, MO
Ziegler, James P. ....Chicago, IL
Ziegler, Jamie L. ....Chicago, IL
Ziegler, Janet E. ....Chicago, IL
Ziegler, Janice Helen ....Washington, DC
Ziegler, Jay R. ....Los Angeles, CA
Ziegler, Joan A. ....Nashville, TN
Ziegler, Joel J. ....Smithtown, NY
Ziegler, Joel S. ....Maplewood, NJ
Ziegler, John A. ....Buffalo, NY
Ziegler, John A., Jr. ....Bloomfield Hills, MI
Ziegler, Jon A. ....Columbus, OH
Ziegler, Judy L. ....Wayne, PA
Ziegler, Larry J. ....Cedaredge, CO
Ziegler, Laura D. ....San Francisco, CA
Ziegler, Laurence D. ....Westbury, NY
Ziegler, Laurie ....New York, NY
Ziegler Law Firm ....Ketchikan, AK
Ziegler, Leonard ....Fresh Meadows, NY
Ziegler, M. Allen, Jr. ....Colorado Springs, CO
Ziegler, Marcie R. ....Washington, DC
Ziegler, Metzger & Miller ....Cleveland, OH
Mentor, OH
Pepper Pike, OH
Ziegler, Michael F. ....Phoenix, AZ
Ziegler, Michael L. ....New York, NY
Ziegler, Nicholas J. ....Deerfield Beach, FL
Ziegler, Paul W. ....Cleveland, OH
Ziegler, Peter F. ....Los Angeles, CA
Ziegler, Richard E. ....Detroit Lakes, MN
Ziegler, Richard F. ....New York, NY
Ziegler, Richard G. ....Chicago, IL
Ziegler, Richard P. ....Chagrin Falls, OH
Ziegler, Richard S. ....Minneapolis, MN
Ziegler, Robert C. ....Covington, KY
Ziegler, Robert E. ....Fort Lauderdale, FL
Ziegler, Robert P. ....Nashville, TN
Ziegler & Robinson ....New York, NY
Ziegler, Ronald ....Philadelphia, PA
Ziegler, Ruth A. ....New York, NY
Ziegler, Ruthann G. ....Sacramento, CA
Ziegler, S. Harvey ....Miami, FL
Ziegler, Sagal & Winters, P.C.
New York, NY
Ziegler & Schneider, P.S.C.
Covington, KY
Ziegler, Scott A. ....Chicago, IL
New York, NY
Philadelphia, PA
Ziegler, Stephen J. ....Lansing, MI
Ziegler, Stephen L. ....Fort Lauderdale, FL
Ziegler, Stephen S. ....New York, NY
Ziegler, Steven D. ....Watseka, IL
Ziegler, Steven M. ....Hollywood, FL
Ziegler, Steven M., P.A., Law Offices of
Hollywood, FL
Ziegler, Thomas F. ....Cincinnati, OH
Ziegler, Thomas Mathew
Canyon Country, CA
Ziegler, Todd L. ....Cashton, WI
Sparta, WI
Ziegler, Vikki S. ....Livingston, NJ

Ziegler Wheeler & Searles, P.L.L.P.
Minneapolis, MN
Ziegler, Wilbert L. ....Covington, KY
Ziegler, William A. ....New York, NY
Ziegler, William F. ....Woodbury, NJ
Ziegler, William J. ....San Francisco, CA
Ziegler, William J. ....Ellicott City, MD
Ziegler, William J., Jr. ....Lafayette, LA
Ziegler, William L. ....Cleveland, OH
Ziegler, William R. ....New York, NY
Ziegler, Ziegler & Altman LLP
New York, NY
Ziegler Fox, Shari ....New York, NY
Ziehl, Catherine C. ....Stamford, CT
Ziehl, Dean A. ....Los Angeles, CA
Ziehl, Joseph P. ....New Haven, CT
Ziehm, Eugene C. ....Glendale, CA
Ziehm, Ronald J. ....Cleveland, OH
Ziehmer, George P. ....Yonkers, NY
Ziehnert, Walter L. ....Mount Vernon, NY
Ziel, Susan E. ....Indianapolis, IN
Zielasko, Gus W. ....North Canton, OH
Zielaznicki, Karl M. ....New York, NY
Zielezienski, J. Stephen ....Washington, DC
Zielinski, Bryan C. ....New York, NY
Zielinski, Charles A. ....Washington, DC
Zielinski, Daniel F. ....Danville, IN
Zielinski, John D.
National Labor Relations Board,
Office of the Inspector General, GV
Zielinski, Michael A. ....North Brunswick, NJ
Zielinski, Michael E. ....Washington, DC
Zielinski, Rasha Marie ....Irvine, CA
Zielinski, Richard F. ....Flint, MI
Zielinski, Richard G. ....Tempe, AZ
Zielinski, Richard J. ....Cleveland, OH
Zielinski, Richard M. ....Boston, MA
Zielinski, Robert E. ....Omaha, NE
Zielinski, Robert F. ....Philadelphia, PA
Zielinski, Robert M. ....Greenville, SC
Zielinski, Robert T. ....Chicago, IL
Zielinski, Stephen J., Jr.
Lawrenceville, NJ
Zielinski, Stephen J., Jr. ....Princeton, NJ
Zielinski, Thomas C. ....Philadelphia, PA
Zielinski, Vernon J. ....Brook Park, OH
Zielinski, Victoria E. ....Woodland Hills, CA
Zielinski, Walt Thomas ....New York, NY
Zielinski, William S., Jr. ....Dansville, NY
Zielinsky, Bryan C. ....New York, NY
Zielke, David H. ....Bellevue, WA
Zielke, Jeremy P. ....La Crosse, WI
Zielke, Kevin M. ....Detroit, MI
Zielke, Larry A. ....Houston, TX
Zielke, Laurence J. ....Louisville, KY
Zielke, Lawrence P. ....Edina, MN
Zielke, Robert Allen ....Everett, WA
Zielke, Susan L. ....Mattoon, IL
Zielonis, Kenneth ....Harrisburg, PA
Ziem, F. C. ....Waterford, MI
Zieman, Speegle, Jackson & Hoffman, L.L.C.
Mobile, AL
Zieman, Thomas Troy, Jr. ....Mobile, AL
Ziemann, Stephen M. ....Glendale, CA
Ziemann, Timothy H. ....Manhattan Beach, CA
Ziemba, Andrew A. ....Mount Prospect, IL
Ziemba, Carl ....Detroit, MI
Ziemba, Charles S. ....Houston, TX
Ziemba, Christopher Joseph ....Joliet, IL
Ziemba, Daniel E. ....Deerfield, IL
Ziemba, Dennis P. ....Mount Laurel, NJ
Philadelphia, PA
Ziemba, Elizabeth A. ....Boston, MA
Ziemba, Henry J. ....New Hartford, NY
Ziemba, Mark A. ....Costa Mesa, CA
Ziemba, Mark V. ....Brooklyn, NY
Ziemba, Paul E. ....Omaha, NE
Ziemba, Peter M. ....New York, NY
Ziemba, Thomas M. ....Houston, TX
Ziemelis, H. Scott ....Middletown, NY
Ziemer, David ....Milwaukee, WI
Ziemer, Kristen A. ....Minneapolis, MN
Ziemer, Stayman, Weitzel & Shoulders, LLP
Evansville, IN
Henderson, KY
Ziemer, Ted C., Jr. ....Evansville, IN
Ziemianski, Joseph A. ....Houston, TX
Ziemke, Eileen Anstandig ....Pittsburgh, PA
Ziemke, Eileen G. ....Battle Creek, MI
Ziemke, William H. ....Ada, MI
Ziemnicki, Aida Kennedy ....Houston, TX
Ziems, Robert F. ....Washington, DC
Zientek, Diane L. ....Buffalo, NY
Zientek, Steve M. ....San Jose, CA
Zients, Michael R. ....New York, NY
Zienty, Jerome A. ....Des Plaines, IL
Zientz, Mark L. ....Miami, FL
Zientz, Michael Wayne ....Addison, TX
Zieper, David Todd ....Boca Raton, FL
Zieper, Laurence E. ....Miami, FL
Zier, Douglas F. ....Salem, OR
Zier, Jill H. ....New York, NY
Zier, Kelly F. ....North Augusta, SC
Zier, Larry A. ....Woodland Hills, CA
Zier Law Offices ....Fort Collins, CO
Zier, Paul D. ....Denver, CO
Zier, Richard F. ....Fort Collins, CO
Zier, Stephen M. ....Midland, MI
Ziercher & Hocker, P.C. ....St. Louis, MO
Ziercher, Mark C. ....Marion, OH
Zierdt, Alyson K. ....Oshkosh, WI
Zierdt, Candace M. ....Grand Forks, ND
Zieren, Leslie ....Tulsa, OK
Zierhut, Jay A. ....New Berlin, WI
Ziering, Diane Delpit ....Pacific Palisades, CA
Ziering, Jeanne ....Santa Monica, CA
Ziering, Peter Tod ....West Orange, NJ
Zieringer, Mathew P. ....Denver, CO

Zierk, George W., III ....Aurora, CO
Zierk, Gregory J. ....Bay City, MI
Zierk, Marsha K. ....Boston, MA
Zierk, Thomas A. ....Larchmont, NY
Zierke, Charles R. ....Hot Springs Village, AR
Zierler, Philip ....Brooklyn, NY
Ziermaier, Klaus M. ....Cincinnati, OH
Zieroth, Lee W. ....Englewood, CO
Zierott, Rex R. ....Buena Park, CA
Zies, Peter J. ....Sanford, FL
Ziese, Robert J. ....Rockaway, NJ
Ziesel, Stephanie R. ....San Francisco, CA
Zieselman, Jerold ....New York, NY
Ziesenheim, Frederick B. ....Pittsburgh, PA
Zieser, John S. ....Des Moines, IA
Zieser & Rothschadl ....Tyndall, SD
Ziesing, Marcy E. ....Tiburon, CA
Ziesing, Sinclair A. ....Philadelphia, PA
Zieske, Lewis H., Jr. ....Chehalis, WA
Zieske, William F. ....Chicago, IL
Ziesman, Jeffrey A. ....Kansas City, MO
Ziesmann, Steven J. ....Milwaukee, WI
Ziessler, Martin ....New York, NY
Zietlow, Mark H. ....Holland, MI
Ziety, James P. ....Dearborn, MI
Zietz, Mortyn K. ....Fort Lauderdale, FL
Zietz, Sam M. ....New York, NY
Zietz, Sheila S. ....New York, NY
Ziev, Joel H. ....Easton, PA
Zieve, Allison M. ....Washington, DC
Zieve, Andrew Sherman ....Brookfield, WI
Zieve, Les ....Los Angeles, CA
Ontario, CA
Zievers, Frederick L. ....Kenosha, WI
Ziewacz, Elizabeth K. ....Columbus, OH
Zieziula, Timothy M. ....Erie, PA
Zifchak, William C. ....New York, NY
Zifchak, William N.
Upper Marlboro, MD
Ziff, Barry D. ....Worcester, MA
Ziff, Bertram A. ....Elmira, NY
Ziff, Brian M. ....Detroit, MI
Ziff, David F. ....New York, NY
Ziff, Elaine D. ....New York, NY
Ziff, Hali E. ....Manhattan Beach, CA
Ziff, Harvey L. ....Palo Alto, CA
Ziff, Herbert ....Jersey City, NJ
Ziff, Howard G. ....Armonk, NY
Ziff, Julian H. ....Decatur, GA
Ziff, Norman D. ....Los Angeles, CA
Ziff, Richard Newton ....Providence, RI
Ziff, Ronald K. ....Pasadena, CA
Ziff, Sheila N. ....Washington, DC
Ziff, Sheldon M. ....North Hollywood, CA
Ziff, Weiermiller, Hayden & Mustico, LLP
Elmira, NY
Ziffer, Adam S. ....New York, NY
Ziffer, Deborah W. ....Washington, DC
Ziffer, Felix C. ....New York, NY
Ziffer, Matthew ....New York, NY
Ziffra, Allan L. ....Port Orange, FL
Ziffren, Brittenham, Branca & Fischer LLP
Los Angeles, CA
Ziffren, Kenneth ....Los Angeles, CA
Ziffren, Leo G. ....Los Angeles, CA
Ziffren, Lester ....Los Angeles, CA
Ziffren, Paul ....Los Angeles, CA
Zifkin, Walter ....Beverly Hills, CA
Zifrony, Matthew ....Fort Lauderdale, FL
Zifzider, Tova Eugenia ....Brooklyn, NY
Ziga, Kathleen ....Philadelphia, PA
Zigel, James M. ....Buffalo, NY
Ziglar, James W., Sr. ....United States Senate,
Senatorial Assistants, GV
Zigler, Greg A. ....Guymon, OK
Zigler, Robert A. ....Fortuna, CA
Zigman, Andrea K. ....Cincinnati, OH
Zigman, Anita J. ....New York, NY
Zigman, David B. ....New York, NY
Zigman, Edward D. ....Chicago, IL
Zigman, Louis ....Los Angeles, CA
Zigman, Lynette M. ....Milwaukee, WI
Zigmund, Edmund W. J. ....Wilkes-Barre, PA
Zigmund, Robert A. ....Jenkintown, PA
Zigmund, Rudolph E. ....Pasadena, CA
Zignego, Julie R. ....Silver Spring, MD
Zigray, Daniel F. ....Toledo, OH
Zigrino, Kenneth D. ....St. Paul, MN
Zigterman, Bonnie L. ....Lombard, IL
Zigterman, Kent A. ....Chicago, IL
Zigterman, Paul ....Northbrook, IL
Zigun, Stuart B. ....Oceanport, NJ
Ziherl, Stanley G. ....Mentor, OH
Ziifle, Marcella M. ....Gretna, LA
Ziino, Joseph J. ....Milwaukee, WI
Ziino, Joseph J., Jr. ....Milwaukee, WI
Ziino, Pulito and Germanotta
Milwaukee, WI
Zika, Patrick John ....Oakland, CA
Zikakis, Salome J. ....Fort Lauderdale, FL
Zikan, Karel John ....Monterey, CA
Ziker, Barry G., (P.S.) ....Seattle, WA
Zikes, Denny Z. ....Beaverton, OR
Ziki, Marcia ....Warren, PA
Zikic, Gordon ....Berkeley, IL
Ziko, Thomas J. ....Raleigh, NC
Zikos, Gregory Antonios
Palos Verdes Estates, CA
Zilaff, Denis J. ....Sacramento, CA
Zilaff, Francis W. ....Sacramento, CA
Zilaff, Gary F. ....Sacramento, CA
Zilahy, Myra V. ....Suncook, NH
Zilar, Dean H. ....Elgin, IL
Zilavy, Thomas D. ....Madison, WI
Zilber, J. J. ....Milwaukee, WI
Zilber, Martin G. ....Miami, FL
Zilber, Maurice L., (P.C.) ....Boston, MA
Zilber, Norman A. ....San Francisco, CA

Zilberberg, Benjamin ....Miami, FL
Zilberberg, David A. ....New York, NY
Zilberfein, Paul S. ....Denville, NJ
New York, NY
Zilberg, Michael A. ....New York, NY
Zilberstein, Arthur ....Argonne, IL
Zilberstein, Seymour R. ....Chicago, IL
Zilberstein, Seymour R., P.C. ....Chicago, IL
Zilbert, Beth Janssen ....Portland, OR
Zilbert, Todd A. ....Portland, OR
Zile, Zigurds L. ....Madison, WI
Zilgme, Arnis ....Newtonville, NY
Zilin, Sadye J. ....Albany, NY
Zilinskas & Jacobs ....Santa Barbara, CA
Zilinskas, Victor G. ....Santa Barbara, CA
Zilinski, Jeffery S. ....Burton, MI
Zilinsky, John C. ....Conway, SC
Zilis, Paul J. ....Boulder, CO
Zilka, Diane T. ....New York, NY
Zilka, Paul P. ....Stone Mountain, GA
Zilko, Mildred J. ....Hempstead, NY
Zill, David A. ....Daytona Beach, FL
Zill, David A., P.A. ....Daytona Beach, FL
Zill, Stacey L. ....Los Angeles, CA
Ziller, Arthur J. ....Buffalo, NY
Ziller, Marsh & Lang, LLP ....Buffalo, NY
Zillgitt, George E. ....Pasadena, CA
Zillgitt, Karl A. ....Jacksonville, FL
Zillgitt, Raynor D., Jr. ....East Lansing, MI
Zilli, Marilyn C. ....Harrisburg, PA
Zillig, Molly J. ....Milwaukee, WI
Zillmann, Harold A. ....Ellenton, FL
Oswego, IL
Zillmer, John R. ....Milwaukee, WI
Zillmer, Robert W., Jr. ....Racine, WI
Zillo, Joseph A. ....Washington, DC
Zilly, Thomas S. ....Seattle, WA
Zilske Law Firm, S.C. ....Milwaukee, WI
Zilske, Robert H. ....Milwaukee, WI
Zilton, La'Sean M. ....Atlanta, GA
Ziluck, Scott Alan ....New York, NY
Zilz, Douglas R. ....Hudson, WI
Zilz, Estreen and Ogland ....Hudson, WI
Zilz, Hillary S. ....New York, NY
Zim, Craig D. ....Carle Place, NY
Zim, Valerie G. ....Williamsport, PA
Zima, Bryan F. ....Columbus, OH
Zima, Gary D. ....Chicago, IL
Zima, John Paul ....Greenwood, IN
Zima, Joseph W. ....Topeka, KS
Ziman, Allan W. ....San Diego, CA
Ziman, Kenneth S. ....New York, NY
Ziman, Richard S. ....Los Angeles, CA
Ziman, Roger J. ....New York, NY
Zimand, Harvey Folks ....New York, NY
Zimarowski, James B. ....Morgantown, WV
Zimba, Pamela ....Benicia, CA
Zimbalist, Chaim H. ....St. Louis, MO
Zimbalist, Lisa B. ....Mamaroneck, NY
Zimbalist, Stuart H. ....St. Louis, MO
Zimbalist, Toby ....Phoenix, AZ
Zimbel, Barbara R. ....Lowell, MA
Zimbel, Seymore ....Buffalo, NY
Zimbelman, Eric ....Bellevue, WA
Zimberg, Goldie S. ....Richmond, VA
Zimberg, Joyce S. ....New York, NY
Zimberg, Leslie C. ....Washington, DC
Zimberg, Stephanie L. ....Bronx, NY
Zimberlin, Winona ....Hartford, CT
Zimberoff, David M. ....Van Nuys, CA
Zimbert, Michael B. ....Sherman Oaks, CA
Zimbert, Richard ....Los Angeles, CA
Zimble & Brettler, LLP ....Boston, MA
Zimble, Kenneth H., (P.C.) ....Boston, MA
Zimbler, Jay H. ....Chicago, IL
Zimbrakos, Dorothy B. ....Chicago, IL
Zimbrick, Thomas J. ....Madison, WI
Zimecki, Michael W. ....Pittsburgh, PA
Zimel, Jeffrey M. ....Riverside, CA
Zimelis, Robert D. ....Chicago, IL
Zimelman, Eric Mark ....Miami, FL
Zimelman, Robin L. ....Baltimore, MD
Zimet, Anne E. ....West Palm Beach, FL
Zimet, Barbara T. ....Chappaqua, NY
Zimet, Bruce A. ....Fort Lauderdale, FL
Zimet, Bruce A., P.A.
Fort Lauderdale, FL
Miami, FL
Palm Beach, FL
Zimet, Deborah Ohman ....Fort Lauderdale, FL
Zimet, Haines, Friedman & Kaplan
New York, NY
Zimet, Jonathan D. ....Princeton, NJ
Zimet, Laurel Lesser ....Downingtown, PA
Zimet, Lee G. ....New York, NY
Zimet, Millard J. ....Aspen, CO
Zimet, Robert D. ....Arlington, VA
Zimet, Robert E. ....New York, NY
Zimet, Sidney ....Brooklyn, NY
Zimic, Deborah Lee ....Baltimore, MD
Zimiles, Jonah D. ....Maplewood, NJ
Zimlich, Mark Stephen ....Mobile, AL
Zimm, Laura A. ....Duluth, MN
Zimm, Melvin R. ....Norfolk, VA
Zimman, Jeffrey S. ....San Francisco, CA
Zimmar, David G. ....Seattle, WA
Zimmar, Michael John ....Seattle, WA
Zimmer, Aaron W. ....Encino, CA
Zimmer, A. L. ....Chicago, IL
Zimmer, Andrew P. ....Arlington, VA
Zimmer, Ann Lawrence ....Frankfort, KY
Zimmer, Bradley A. ....Merrillville, IN
Zimmer, Christine M. ....Cincinnati, OH
Zimmer, Clifford ....Escondido, CA
Zimmer, Curtis M. ....Wilbraham, MA
Zimmer, Daryl L. ....Hopkins, MN
Zimmer, David O. ....Cleveland, OH
Zimmer, Donald E. ....Charlotte, MI

Zimmerman, William Martin
Sherman Oaks, CA
Zimmerman, William P. ....**Philadelphia, PA**
Zimmerman, William R.
Newport Beach, CA
Zimmerman, William R. ....Sidney, OH
Zimmerman, William R., Co., L.P.A.
Sidney, OH
Zimmerman, Zimmerman & McGregor, Law Offices of, A Professional Corporation
Waco, TX
Zimmerman, Zimmerman and Miceli, P.A.
Pompano Beach, FL
Zimmerman & Zimmerman, P.C.
San Antonio, TX
Zimmermann, A. Christopher
Carson City, NV
Zimmermann, Albert W. ....Indianapolis, IN
Zimmermann, Ann Marie ....**El Centro, CA**
Zimmermann, Barbara A. ....Los Angeles, CA
Zimmermann, Clark J., Jr. ....Rochester, NY
Zimmermann, Cynthia Ann Brewer
Charlotte, NC
Zimmermann, Daniel R. ....**Los Angeles, CA**
Zimmermann, Daniel R.
Cold Spring, MN
Zimmermann, David C. ....Alexandria, VA
Zimmermann, David Conrad
Albuquerque, NM
Zimmermann, E. Neal ....**Secaucus, NJ**
Zimmermann, George M. ....**Buffalo, NY**
Zimmermann, George Michael ....Buffalo, NY
Zimmermann, H. Fredrick ....Old Hickory, TN
Zimmermann, Hansel F.
Minneapolis, MN
Zimmermann, Harry L. ....Dallas, TX
Zimmermann, Harry L., P.C. ....Dallas, TX
Zimmermann, Helen W. ....Buffalo, NY
Zimmermann, Jack B. ....**Houston, TX**
Zimmermann, James B. ....McKinney, TX
Zimmermann, Jeremy G. ....**New Haven, CT**
Zimmermann, John C. ....Nashville, TN
Zimmermann, John E. ....Missoula, MT
Zimmermann, John J.
Mount Prospect, IL
Zimmermann, Karl J. ....**New Orleans, LA**
Zimmermann, Kent M. ....**Chicago, IL**
Zimmermann, Koomer, Connolly & Finkel LLP ....**Los Angeles, CA**
Zimmermann, Kurt F. ....**New Haven, CT**
Zimmermann, Lauren L.
New Orleans, LA
Zimmermann and Lavine, P.C.
Houston, TX
Zimmermann, Linda M. ....Denver, CO
Zimmermann, M. Josef ....Mequon, WI
Milwaukee, WI
Racine, WI
Zimmermann, Mark J. ....**Hartford, CT**
Zimmermann, Mark J. ....**Dallas, TX**
Zimmermann, Michael F.
Mount Prospect, IL
Zimmermann, Molly C. ....Syracuse, NY
Zimmermann, Patricia J. ....Riverside, CA
Zimmermann, Raymond A. ....Lubbock, TX
Zimmermann, Richard H. ....Iowa City, IA
Zimmermann, Robert ....Tamworth, NH
Zimmermann, Robert ....West Ossipee, NH
Zimmermann, Scott Z. ....**Los Angeles, CA**
Zimmermann, Stephen S. ....Greenbelt, MD
Zimmermann, Susan ....Denver, CO
Zimmermann, Theodore A. ....East Alton, IL
Zimmermann, Victor L., Jr.
Stamford, CT
Zimmern, Kenneth A. ....Houston, TX
Zimmern, Michael R. ....Round Rock, TX
Zimmers, George L. ....Laramie, WY
Zimmers and Lopez, P.C. ....Laramie, WY
Zimmers, Neal F., Jr. ....Columbus, OH
Zimmet, Alan S. ....**Clearwater, FL**
Zimmet, Brian J. ....New York, NY
Zimmet, Keith Todd ....**Encino, CA**
Zimmet, Raymond M.
Federal Energy Regulatory Commission, Office of the Administrative Law Judges, GV
Zimmet, Sheila Cohen ....Washington, DC
Zimmett, Blair I. ....**Miami, FL**
Zimmett, Craig A. ....**Miami, FL**
Zimmett, Mark P., Law Offices of
New York, NY
Zimmett & Zimmett, A Prof. Assn., Law Offices ....**Miami, FL**
Zimmitti, Andrew ....**Washington, DC**
Zimmitti, Laura Cohen ....**Washington, DC**
Zimney, Thomas L. ....**Grand Forks, ND**
Zimny, Max ....New York, NY
Zimolzak, Joanne L. ....**Washington, DC**
Zimon, Jeffrey D. ....**Cleveland, OH**
Zimostrad, Stanley, (P.C.) ....Bay City, MI
Zimpfer, George F. ....Lancaster, OH
Zimpfer, Matthew J. ....Carmel, IN
Zimpritch, James B. ....**Portland, ME**
Zimring, Franklin E. ....Berkeley, CA
Zimring, Frederic E. ....Dallas, TX
Zimring, Jon ....**Chicago, IL**
Zimring, Jonathan A. ....**Atlanta, GA**
Zimring, Joseph N. ....Los Angeles, CA
Zimring, Michael ....Deerfield, IL
Zimring Smith & Billips, P.C.
Atlanta, GA
Zimring, Stuart D. ....**Los Angeles, CA**
Zimring, Stuart D. ....**North Hollywood, CA**
Zimroth, Peter L. ....**New York, NY**
Zimski, Patrick D. ....**Oakland, CA**
Zimskind, Jeffrey M. ....**Lehigh Valley, PA**
Zimsky, William E. ....**Durango, CO**
Zimtbaum, Lorence M. ....**Scottsdale, AZ**
Zimtbaum, Lorence M., P.C. ....**Phoenix, AZ**
Scottsdale, AZ
Zinaman, Edward M. ....Boston, MA
Zinbarg, Eugene D. ....New York, NY
Zinberg, Arthur D. ....New York, NY
Zinberg, David J. ....New York, NY
Zinberg, Helene ....Madison, WI
Zinberg, Joel M. ....New York, NY
Zinberg, Lynette Remen ....**New York, NY**
Zincani, John ....**New York, NY**
Zincke, Mary E. ....Bronx, NY
Zincke, Patricia ....New York, NY
Zinda, Craig J. ....**St. Petersburg, FL**
Zindel, Timothy L. ....Sacramento, CA
Zinder, Blackburn, Park, Clements & Keenan, A Professional Corporation
Los Angeles, CA
Orange, CA
San Diego, CA
Ventura, CA
Walnut Creek, CA
Zinder, David M. ....Chicago, IL
Zinder, Jeffrey E. ....Orange, CA
Walnut Creek, CA
Zinder, Lawrence A. ....Chicago, IL
Zinder, Michael I. ....**New York, NY**
Zinder, Samuel B. ....Sands Point, NY
Zinder, Stanley H. ....New York, NY
Zinder, Susan F. ....Manhasset, NY
Zindle, Charles W. ....Akron, OH
Zindler, Michael A. ....**Lawrenceville, NJ**
Zindrick, Thomas D. ....**Thousand Oaks, CA**
Zingale, Anthony G. ....New York, NY
Zingale, Douglas A. ....**Boston, MA**
Zingale, Mary Rose ....Elko, NV
Zingale, Roland P. ....Colorado Springs, CO
Zingale, Sam A. ....Cleveland, OH
Zingales, Ann Marie ....**Secaucus, NJ**
Zingales, Joseph A. ....Bedford, OH
Zingali, Catherine A. ....**San Diego, CA**
Zingarelli, John ....Decatur, AL
Zingarelli, Larry R. ....Columbus, OH
Zinger, Charles ....Los Angeles, CA
Zinger, David F. ....**Denver, CO**
Zinger, Simon G. ....San Francisco, CA
Zinger, Theodore B. ....Downey, CA
Zinger, Wm. F. ....Chatham, NJ
Zingerman, Scott R. ....**Tulsa, OK**
Zingg, Elaine Oser ....Columbus, OH
Zingg, Paul ....**Ottumwa, IA**
Zingheim, Francis E. ....San Jose, CA
Zinghini, Kenneth J. ....New York, NY
Zingler, Leonard W. M. ....Buffalo, NY
Zingman, Edgar A. ....**Louisville, KY**
Zingman, Mitchell S. ....New York, NY
Zingone, Gerald ....**Washington, DC**
Zini, Gregory ....**Washington, DC**
Zinicola, Frank J. ....King Of Prussia, PA
Zinicola, Michael D. ....Euclid, OH
Zinis, Lisa A. ....Houston, TX
Zink, Brown, Baumgartner & Cutts
Moorestown, NJ
Zink, Charles T. ....**Atlanta, GA**
Zink, Christopher Russell ....**Chicago, IL**
Zink, Colleen G. ....Corning, NY
Zink, Darla S. ....**Wichita, KS**
Zink, Deborah B. ....Atlanta, GA
Zink, Diane K. ....La Place, LA
Zink, Ed E. ....Billings, MT
Zink, James M. ....Palisade, CO
Zink, Jeffrey E. ....Cleveland, OH
Zink, John A. ....Louisville, KY
Zink, John F. ....Louisville, KY
Zink, John H., III ....**Towson, MD**
Zink, Joseph D. "J.D.", (Inc.) ....**Chico, CA**
Zink, Larry A. ....**Canton, OH**
Zink & Lenzi ....**Chico, CA**
Zink, N. Theodore, Jr. ....**New York, NY**
Zink, R.D. ....**Indianapolis, IN**
Zink, Robert L. ....Tulsa, OK
Zink, Ronald O. ....**Redmond, WA**
Zink, Sharon Anne ....Rockville, MD
Zink, Sherwood K. ....Madison, WI
Zink, Timothy K. ....St. Louis, MO
Zink, Walter E., II ....**Lincoln, NE**
Zink, Zink & Zink Co., L.P.A.
Canton, OH
Zinkan, Lisa A. ....San Francisco, CA
Zinkan, Stephen P. ....Indianapolis, IN
Zinkand, John L. ....**Fremont, OH**
Zinke, Dudley A. ....San Francisco, CA
Zinke, John R., Jr. ....Chicago, IL
Zinkel, Robert J., Jr. ....Birmingham, MI
Zinker, Edward ....Smithtown, NY
Zinkgraf, Gary M. ....**Washington, DC**
Zinkham, Robert ....**Baltimore, MD**
Zinkhan, Lydia S. ....**Houston, TX**
Zinkin, Anne F. ....**San Francisco, CA**
Zinkin, Benjamin ....**New York, NY**
Zinkin, Ephraim Z. ....**Princeton, NJ**
Zinkin, Robert ....**Portland, OR**
Zinkow, Jack H. ....Hawthorne, FL
Zinkula, Thomas R. ....Dubuque, IA
Zinman, Daniel C. ....**New York, NY**
Zinman, Daniel N. ....**New York, NY**
Zinman, Edwin J. ....**San Francisco, CA**
Zinman, Herbert ....Woodland Hills, CA
Zinman, Ira B. ....Bloomington, IN
Zinman, Jack S., Jr.
Federal Communications Commission, Common Carrier Bureau, GV
Zinman, James C. ....Bethesda, MD
Zinman, Jon D. ....New York, NY
Zinman, Lance A. ....**Chicago, IL**
Zinman, Lauren Bauer ....**New York, NY**
Zinman, Marvin ....Los Angeles, CA
Zinman, Peter E. ....**New York, NY**
Zinman, Robert M. ....**New York, NY**
Zinman, Roberta Scharlin ....Los Angeles, CA
Zinman, Scott L ....**Blue Bell, PA**
Zinman, Seth D. ....Department of Labor, Office of the Solicitor, GV
Zinn & Associates ....Nashville, TN
Zinn, Brian D. ....**Saddle Brook, NJ**
Zinn, Carter M. ....**San Francisco, CA**
Zinn, Charles A. ....Temple Terrace, FL
Zinn, David M. ....**Washington, DC**
Zinn, David S. ....Nashville, TN
Zinn, Donald E. ....**Washington, DC**
Zinn, Donald S. ....Berkeley, CA
Zinn, Eric Jon ....**Denver, CO**
Zinn, Eugene R. ....Ironwood, MI
Zinn, Frank B. ....Albuquerque, NM
Zinn, Frank K. ....**Detroit, MI**
Zinn, Frederic M. ....Rhinebeck, NY
Zinn, George H., Jr. ....**Detroit, MI**
Zinn, Gregory A. ....**Minneapolis, MN**
Zinn, H. Jackson ....Stockton, CA
Zinn, Harold M. ....Newport Beach, CA
Zinn, Harry A. ....Santa Monica, CA
Zinn, Jeffery N. ....**Sparks, MD**
Zinn, Jennifer A. ....Detroit, MI
Zinn, Karen Lanster ....Miami, FL
Zinn, Katherine ....Santa Fe, NM
Zinn, L. Pahl ....**Detroit, MI**
Zinn, Larry ....San Antonio, TX
Zinn, Lisa M. ....**Cherry Hill, NJ**
Jersey City, NJ
Philadelphia, PA
Zinn & Lorand ....Anaheim, CA
Zinn, Marci S. ....**Garden City, NY**
Zinn, Mark David ....Prairie Village, KS
Zinn, Matthew J. ....**Washington, DC**
Zinn, Matthew P. ....**Englewood, CO**
Zinn, Philip M. ....Philadelphia, PA
Zinn, Richard ....Miami, FL
Zinn, Richard A. ....Mineola, NY
Zinn, Richard C. ....New York, NY
Zinn, Richard L. ....**Lawrence, KS**
Zinn, Robert A. ....**Miami, FL**
Zinn, Robert K. ....Clawson, MI
Zinn, Robert P. ....**Pittsburgh, PA**
Zinn, Robert S. ....**Englewood, CO**
Zinn, Steven R. ....Topeka, KS
Zinn, Susan Finkelstein ....San Antonio, TX
Zinn, Sylvia Ivey ....**St. Paul, MN**
Zinn, Thomas R. ....Lexington, KY
Zinn, Wayne Michael ....Anaheim, CA
Zinna, Frank J. ....Nutley, NJ
Zinna, Randy P. ....**Baton Rouge, LA**
Zinnecker, Rhe E. ....**Seattle, WA**
Zinnecker, Timothy R. ....Houston, TX
Zinnemann, Paula Reddish
Beverly Hills, CA
Zinner, Richard M. ....**Boston, MA**
Zinner, Stanley S. ....**White Plains, NY**
Zinner, Thelma S. ....Ocean Springs, MS
Zinner, Theodore L., Jr. ....St. Paul, MN
Zinnershine, Robert C. ....**Boston, MA**
Zinni, Frank V. ....Batavia, NY
Zinni, Michael W. ....Newton, MA
Zinni, Nicholas ....Batavia, NY
Zino, Dona Rita ....**Garden City, NY**
Zinober, Fredric S. ....**Clearwater, FL**
Zinober & McCrea, P.A. ....**Clearwater, FL**
Orlando, FL
St. Petersburg, FL
Tampa, FL
Zinober, Peter W. ....**Tampa, FL**
Zins, Jacqueline E. ....**Washington, DC**
Zinser, Kelly H. ....**Los Angeles, CA**
Zinser, L. Michael ....**Nashville, TN**
Zinser, Linda ....**Denver, CO**
Zinser, Michelle R. ....Madison, NJ
Zinser and Patterson, P.L.L.C.
Nashville, TN
Zinski, Christopher J. ....**Chicago, IL**
Zinski, Kevin R. ....Pittsburgh, PA
Zinsner, Mary C. Hohman
Tysons Corner, VA
Zinsser, August, III ....Washington, DC
Zinsser, Barbara L. ....**New York, NY**
Zinter, Edward ....Holtville, CA
Zinter, Leah M. ....La Mesa, CA
Zinter, Steven L. ....Pierre, SD
Zintgraff, Teresa K. ....**Santa Monica, CA**
Zintsmaster, John A. ....Flushing, MI
Ziober, Emily Phillips ....Baton Rouge, LA
Ziober, John David ....**Baton Rouge, LA**
Ziobro, Catherine L. ....**Washington, DC**
Ziobro, Lucy M. ....Bridgeport, CT
Ziobrowski, Stephen ....**Boston, MA**
Ziogas, James, Jr. ....**Bristol, CT**
Ziogas, Mark ....Bristol, CT
Ziogas, Robert A. ....**Roanoke, VA**
Ziol, Gwen Glenn ....**Rosemead, CA**
Ziolko, Lynn T. ....**Phoenix, AZ**
Ziolkowski, Leon A. ....Homewood, IL
Ziolkowski, Rachel D. ....**Houston, TX**
Ziolkowski, Robert L. ....Detroit, MI
Ziolkowski, Steven M. ....**Princeton, NJ**
Ziolkowski, Thomas A ....**Detroit, MI**
Ziolkowski, Timothy J. ....**Milwaukee, WI**
Ziomek, Megin Z. ....Amherst, MA
Ziomek, S. Peter, Jr. ....Amherst, MA
Ziomek, Thomas J. ....**Philadelphia, PA**
Ziomek & Ziomek ....Amherst, MA
Zion, Adina ....**New York, NY**
Zion, Benson ....Philadelphia, PA
Zion, Benson, & Associates
Philadelphia, PA
Zion, Cory B. ....Portland, OR
Zion, Fran E. ....Miami, FL
Zion, Isaac ....**New York, NY**
Zion, Jacqueline ....**New York, NY**
Zion, Jacqueline ....**White Plains, NY**
Zion, James W., Jr. ....Window Rock, AZ
Zion, Marvin H. ....Tucker, GA
Zion, Paul B. ....**Spartanburg, SC**
Zion, Peter P., II ....Malvern, PA
Zion, Tarleton & Siskin, P.C. ....**Atlanta, GA**
Tucker, GA
Zionts, Berkley ....Allentown, PA
Zionts, Harriette A. ....Buffalo, NY
Zionts, Leon S. ....Indianapolis, IN
Ziontz, Alvin J. ....**Seattle, WA**
Ziontz, Chestnut, Varnell, Berley & Slonim
Seattle, WA
Ziontz, Martin L. ....**Seattle, WA**
Ziontz, Mel ....**Santa Monica, CA**
Ziontz, Mitch C. ....**Santa Monica, CA**
Ziontz, Natalie C. ....Santa Monica, CA
Ziotas, Angelo A. ....**Stamford, CT**
Ziouras, Michael J. ....**Salt Lake City, UT**
Zioze, Dean G. ....**Boston, MA**
Ziparo, Peter M. ....**New York, NY**
Zipay, James M. ....Scranton, PA
Ziperman, Philip D. ....Washington, DC
Ziperski, James R. ....Milwaukee, WI
Ziperski, Joseph A. ....Milwaukee, WI
Zipes, Jeffrey S. ....**Carmel, IN**
Zipf, Edwin A. ....**Florham Park, NJ**
Zipf, Henry G. ....Tucson, AZ
Zipfel, David A. ....East Hartford, CT
Zipfel, Michael P. ....**Philadelphia, PA**
Zipfel, Thomas C. ....**Elkins Park, PA**
Zipin, Janet M. ....**Boston, MA**
Zipin, Philip B. ....Silver Spring, MD
Zipkin, Adam H. ....Newark, NJ
Zipkin, Fink & Whiting ....Cleveland, OH
Zipkin, Gary A. ....**Anchorage, AK**
Zipkin, Judith A. ....**Los Angeles, CA**
Zipkin, Lewis A. ....Cleveland, OH
Zipkin, Neil M. ....**New York, NY**
Zipkowitz, Eric M. ....**New York, NY**
Zipoli, Richard P. ....Waterbury, CT
Ziporin, Eric M. ....**Denver, CO**
Ziporyn, Charlotte W. ....Skokie, IL
Zipp, Alan S. ....Rockville, MD
Zipp, Joel F. ....**Washington, DC**
Zipp, Peter J. ....Jamesburg, NJ
Zipp, Robert V. W. ....Menlo Park, CA
Zipp, Ronald D. ....New Braunfels, TX
Zipp, Ronald D., P.C. ....New Braunfels, TX
Zippay, Catherine W. ....**Coral Springs, FL**
Zippe, Kent D. ....Irvine, CA
Zippel, Barbara A. ....Phoenix, AZ
Zippel, Wilma L ....**Minneapolis, MN**
Zipper, Arnold M. ....**Fort Lauderdale, FL**
Zipper, Deborah McKenna ....Madison, NJ
Zipper, Michael E. ....**New York, NY**
Zipper, Sheila ....New York, NY
Zipperer, Alex L. ....**Savannah, GA**
Zipperer & Lorberbaum, P.C.
Savannah, GA
Zipperer, Robert E. ....Crescent City, CA
Zipperer, Robert H. ....Savannah, GA
Zipperian & Chediak, Law Corporation
Sacramento, CA
Zipperian, LenArd S. ....**Sacramento, CA**
Zipperle, Gene F., Jr. ....**Louisville, KY**
Zipperman, Barbara Irshay
Beverly Hills, CA
Zipperman, Barbara J. ....Los Angeles, CA
Zipperman, Barry L., (P.C.) ....**Atlanta, GA**
Zipperman, Steven J. ....Newport Beach, CA
Zipperstein, Diane Flanagan ....Irwindale, CA
Zipperstein, Irvin J. ....Dayton, OH
Zipperstein, Steven E. ....Los Angeles, CA
Zippin, Robert Stewart ....**Tamarac, FL**
Zippin, Robert Stewart, P.A.
Tamarac, FL
Zipprich, John L., II ....Houston, TX
Zipps, David R. ....**Boston, MA**
Ziprick, Robert H. ....**Redlands, CA**
Ziprick, Schilt, Heinrich & Cramer
Redlands, CA
Ziprick, William F. ....**Redlands, CA**
Ziprin, Jordan ....Phoenix, AZ
Zips, Craig D. ....**Dallas, TX**
Zipse, Mark L. ....Portland, OR
Zipse, Randy ....Boston, MA
Zipser, Dean J. ....**Irvine, CA**
Zipser, Eleanor B. ....Lauderhill, FL
Zipser, Geraldine M. ....**Westborough, MA**
Zipser, Herman B. ....Lauderhill, FL
Zipser, Howard Alan ....**New York, NY**
Zipser, Michael F. ....Traverse City, MI
Zipser, Richard P. ....**Bloomfield Hills, MI**
Zipser, Stanley ....Carlsbad, CA
Zipursky, Benjamin C. ....New York, NY
Zipursky, Diane R. ....**Washington, DC**
Zirafi, Nan ....**Los Angeles, CA**
Zirbel, Mark A. ....**Oxnard, CA**
Zirbes, Peter M. ....Queens Village, NY
Zirille, Anthony M. ....Fort Wayne, IN
Zirin, James D. ....**New York, NY**
Zirin-Hyman, Judith Amy ....New York, NY
Zirinis, Basil P., III ....**New York, NY**
Zirinsky, Bruce R. ....**New York, NY**
Zirinsky, John ....New York, NY
Zirinsky, Robert A. ....New York, NY
Zirkel, Alexandra ....**Los Angeles, CA**
Zirkel, Perry A. ....Bethlehem, PA
Zirkelbach, Andrew E. ....**Broomfield, CO**
Zirkelbach, Brian K. ....Belleville, IL
Zirkelbach, Gail D. ....**Denver, CO**
Zirkelbach, Gail Frulla ....Denver, CO
Zirkelback, Anne Marie ....Port Lavaca, TX
Zirker, Daniel R. ....Department of Commerce, Patent and Trademark Office, GV
Zirkin, Stanley R.
National Labor Relations Board, Office of the General Counsel, GV
Zirkle, Charles B., Jr. ....**Atlanta, GA**

Zirkle, Christopher John ... Sacramento, CA
Zirkle and Hoffman ... Atlanta, GA
Zirkle, Jo Ann ... Tucson, AZ
Zirkle, Lori A. ... Phoenix, AZ
Zirkle, R. Douglas ... Tucson, AZ
Zirkle, R. Kent ... Tulsa, OK
Zirkle, Richard M. ... San Angelo, TX
Zirkle, Ronald S. ... Yakima, WA
Zirkle, Warren E. ... Richmond, VA
Zirkman, Joseph A. ... Syracuse, NY
Zirkman, Kenneth L. ... Atlanta, GA
Zirlin, Harry ... New York, NY
Zirm, Kenneth A. ... Cleveland, OH
Zirn, Alison N. ... Chicago, IL
Zirnhelt, Peter J. ... Traverse City, MI
Zirnhelt, Peter J., P.C. ... Traverse City, MI
Zirogiannis, Marc A. ... Westbury, NY
Ziropoulos, Kimberly D. ... Washington, DC
Zirpoli, Dominic A. ... Norristown, PA
Zirpoli, Robert ... Hackensack, NJ
Zirpolo, Michael P. ... Canton, OH
Zirrith, Daniel J. ... Livingston, NJ
Zirulnik, Barry S. ... Jackson, MS
Zirulnik, Mark B. ... Roseland, NJ
Zisa, Charles R. ... Wyckoff, NJ
Zisa, Joseph C. ... Hackensack, NJ
Zisa, Joseph C., Jr. ... Hackensack, NJ
Zisa and McArdle ... Hackensack, NJ
Zisa, Thomas M. ... Rochelle Park, NJ
Zisblatt, Efrat B. ... Los Angeles, CA
Zisch, Heidi M. ... Boston, MA
Zischkau, Herbert S., III ... Sanford, FL
Zischkau, Jonathan D. ... Washington, DC
Zischke, Jacqueline M. ... Salinas, CA
Zischke, Michael H. ... San Francisco, CA
Ziser, Andrew J. ... Fayetteville, AR
Ziser, Boris ... New York, NY
Ziser, George J. ... San Francisco, CA
Zisgen, Robert P. ... Mahwah, NJ
Suffern, NY
Zisholtz, Gerald ... Mineola, NY
Zisholtz, Jennifer A. ... Boca Raton, FL
Zisholtz, Stuart Shalom ... Mineola, NY
Zisholtz & Zisholtz, LLP ... Mineola, NY
Zisholz, Murray ... San Francisco, CA
Zisimopoulos, Georgia ... Boston, MA
Zisk, Matthew B. ... New York, NY
Zisk, Robert L. ... Washington, DC
Ziskey, Michael ... Humboldt, NE
Ziskin, Daniel I. ... Phoenix, AZ
Ziskin, Daniel I., P.C. ... Phoenix, AZ
Ziskin, Donald A. ... Santa Rosa, CA
Ziskin, Jay H. ... Los Angeles, CA
Ziskin, Kenneth A. ... Studio City, CA
Ziskin, Linda S. ... Sacramento, CA
Ziskin, Richard Barry ... Commack, NY
Ziskin, Robert M. ... Commack, NY
Ziskin, Sara R. ... Phoenix, AZ
Ziskin, Stacey Ellen ... Commack, NY
Ziskin, Suzanne Harmon ... Commack, NY
Ziskind & Arvin, P.A. ... Miami, FL
Ziskind, Charles G. ... Norwalk, CT
Ziskind, Gerald N. ... Pittsburgh, PA
Ziskind, Gregg M. ... Los Angeles, CA
Ziskind, Jay A. ... Miami, FL
Ziskind, Karen L. ... Sacramento, CA
Ziskind, Martha Andes ... Louisville, KY
Ziskinder, Steven ... Fort Pierce, FL
Zisko, Gwynne G. ... Pembroke, MA
Zisko, William E. ... Palo Alto, CA
Ziskrout, David A. ... Los Angeles, CA
Zisla, Paul B. ... Minneapolis, MN
Zisman, Barry S. ... Dallas, TX
Zisman and Ingraham, P.C. ... Denver, CO
Zisman Law Firm, The, A Professional Corporation ... Dallas, TX
Zisman, Sanford ... Denver, CO
Zisman, Stuart R. ... Houston, TX
Zisook, Phillip J. ... Chicago, IL
Zisook, Sheldon P. ... Memphis, TN
Zisowitz, Terry Sue ... Westbury, NY
Ziss, Jonathan S. ... Westmont, NJ
Philadelphia, PA
Ziss, Judith Seplowitz ... Boston, MA
Zissa, Jeffrey J. ... Alice, TX
Zisselman, Isaac W. ... New York, NY
Zisser, Barry L. ... Jacksonville, FL
Zisser, Bruce R. ... Los Angeles, CA
Zisser, Carolyn S., (P.A.)
Neptune Beach, FL
Zisser, David A. ... Denver, CO
Zisser, David H. ... Sausalito, CA
Zisser, Elliot ... Jacksonville, FL
Zisser, Peter Alan ... New York, NY
Zisser, Robison, Brown, Nowlis & Maciejewski, P.A. ... Jacksonville, FL
Zisser, Roy L. ... New York, NY
Zisser, Steven B. ... San Diego, CA
Zisser, Steven L. ... Columbus, OH
Zissimos, Maria M. ... Philadelphia, PA
Zissis, Kristina ... Washington, DC
Zissler, James ... New York, NY
Zissman, Marshall L. ... Wilmette, IL
Zissman, Michael C. ... Chicago, IL
Zissman, Sharon D.
Federal Deposit Insurance Corporation, Professional Liability Section, GV
Zisson, Richard L. ... Dennis, MA
Wellesley, MA
Zisson and Veara ... Dennis, MA
Wellesley, MA
Zissou, Steve ... Bayside, NY
Zissu, Frederick ... New York, NY
Zissu Gumbinger Stolzar & Wasserman
New York, NY
Zissu, Michael J. ... New York, NY
Zissu, Roger L. ... New York, NY
Zissu, Stein & Mosher ... New York, NY

Zitani, Genius A ... La Jolla, CA
Zitani, Gregory A. ... Sarasota, FL
Zitano, Elisa R. ... Sacramento, CA
Zitek, Judith A. ... Omaha, NE
Zitelli, David V. ... Park Ridge, NJ
Zitelli, William E. ... Richfield, OH
Zitelli, William E., Jr. ... Princeton, NJ
Ziter, Jill K. ... Springfield, MA
Ziter, Michael P. ... Westfield, MA
Zitko, John R. ... Washington, DC
Zitko, Robert D. ... Columbus, OH
Zitko, Robert R. ... Chicago, IL
Zitkovsky, Ivan David ... Boston, MA
Zitlau, Warren A. ... Washington, DC
Zitler, Justin Asher ... New Orleans, LA
Zitner, Robert J. ... Jamaica, NY
Zitnik, Edwin J. ... Berwyn, IL
Zitny, John J. ... Buena Park, CA
Zito, Anthony S., Jr. ... Chicago, IL
Zito, Bruce E. ... Eau Claire, WI
Zito, Christopher J. ... Frankfort, NY
Zito, Dominic J. ... Utica, NY
Zito, Donald L. ... Chicago, IL
Zito, Donna R. ... Hartford, CT
Zito, Edward A. ... Wethersfield, CT
Zito, Frank W. ... Malverne, NY
Zito, James V. ... Atlanta, GA
Zito, Jennifer L. ... Meriden, CT
Zito, Joseph J. ... Washington, DC
Zito, Joseph J. ... Damascus, MD
Zito, Leonard N. ... Bangor, PA
Zito, Louise R. ... New Haven, CT
Zito, Martino & Karasek ... Bangor, PA
Zito, Mary Ann ... Huntington Woods, MI
Zito, Maureen Fiorilli ... Cleveland, OH
Zito, Michael C. ... Miami, FL
Zito, Nicholas E. ... Houston, TX
Zito, Robert J. A. ... New York, NY
Zitoli, Gerard A. ... Waltham, MA
Zitomer, Alan ... Hartford, CT
Zitomer, Burton ... Florham Park, NJ
Zitomer, Deborah G.
Plymouth Meeting, PA
Zitomer, Marc H. ... Florham Park, NJ
Zitomer, Michael ... Palm Springs, CA
Zito-Nash, Judith Amy ... Channahon, IL
Zitowitz, Leon R. ... Worcester, MA
Zitrin, Anthony ... New York, NY
Zitrin, Deborah J. ... Ormond Beach, FL
Zitrin, Elizabeth A. ... San Francisco, CA
Zitrin & Mastromonaco, LLP
San Francisco, CA
Zitrin, Richard A. ... San Francisco, CA
Zitron, Anne E. ... New York, NY
Zitron, Jeffrey Martin ... Atlanta, GA
Zitser, Barry S. ... Hartford, CT
Zitser, Diana P. ... Pasadena, CA
Zitsman, James A. ... Columbus, OH
Zitta, Michael J. ... Minneapolis, MN
Zitta, Robert J. ... Grand Haven, MI
Zittel, Matthew Charles ... Belleville, IL
Zittell, Arthur ... Thousand Oaks, CA
Zittell, Warren E. ... Hudson, NY
Zittenfield, Lee M. ... Portland, OR
Zitter, Hillary Esbit ... Stamford, CT
Zitter, Kenneth A. ... New York, NY
Zitter, Mary Pat ... Celina, OH
Zitterkopf, Jack ... Grand Island, NE
Zitterman, Susan Healy ... Detroit, MI
Zittlau, Ewald ... Philadelphia, PA
Zitto, Donald A. ... Cherry Hill, NJ
Zittrain, Jonathan L. ... Cambridge, MA
Zittrain, Lester E. ... Pittsburgh, PA
Zittrain, Ruth A. ... Pittsburgh, PA
Zittrain and Zittrain ... Pittsburgh, PA
Zitver, Leon ... Washington, DC
New York, NY
Zitver, Murray A. ... Beltsville, MD
Zitzelsberger, G. H. ... Bradenton, FL
Zitzer, Daniel L. ... Milwaukee, WI
Zitzer, Dennis M. ... Chicago, IL
Zitzewitz, Mark H. ... Minneapolis, MN
Zitzka, Kathleen I. ... Willowbrook, IL
Zitzkat, W. David ... Hartford, CT
Zitzman, Timothy F. ... Knoxville, TN
Zitzmann, Kelly C. ... New Milford, CT
Zitzmann, Oliver A. ... Danbury, CT
Ziv, Alvin R. ... Redford, MI
Ziv, Barbara J. ... New Orleans, LA
Ziv, Roberta ... Philadelphia, PA
Zivanovic, Crista ... Valparaiso, IN
Zive, David L. ... Philadelphia, PA
Zive, Gregg W. ... Reno, NV
Ziven, Steven L. ... Los Angeles, CA
Zivian, Bruce A. ... Chicago, IL
Zivian, Etta B. ... Bingham Farms, MI
Zivian, Michael T. ... Telluride, CO
Zivian & Zwickl ... Bingham Farms, MI
Zivic, Jerrold S. ... Chicago, IL
Zivic, Stephen J. ... Pittsburgh, PA
Zivin, Lee R. ... Northbrook, IL
Zivin, Norman H. ... New York, NY
Zivitz, Andrew L. ... Philadelphia, PA
Zivitz, Ellen Prince ... Chicago, IL
Zivitz, Eric M. ... Miami, FL
Zivitz, Stephen C. ... Philadelphia, PA
Zivkovich, George ... Parkersburg, WV
Zivley, Walter P. ... Houston, TX
Zivot, Louis J. ... Plano, TX
Zivotov, Boris ... Brooklyn, NY
Zivyak, Jeffrey L. ... New York, NY
Ziwisky, Ronald W. ... Watertown, WI
Zix, Timothy L. ... Cleveland, OH
Zizelman, Frederick W. ... Sun City Center, FL
Zizelman, Frederick W., Jr., P.C.
Sun City Center, FL
Zizik, David W. ... Wellesley, MA
Providence, RI

Zizik, LaSalle & Powers, A Professional Corporation ... Boston, MA
Falmouth, MA
Wellesley, MA
Providence, RI
Zizila, Frances ... Department of Justice, Environment and Natural Resources Division, GV
Zizka, Michael A. ... Hartford, CT
Zizmor, Andrew S. ... New York, NY
Zizmor, Edward S. ... Hackensack, NJ
Ziznewski, Jay J. ... Woodbridge, NJ
Ziznewski, Joseph W. ... Metuchen, NJ
Zizza, Michael M. ... Boston, MA
Zizzi, Perry V. ... New York, NY
Zizzo, John M. ... New York, NY
Zizzo, Joyce A. ... El Segundo, CA
Zlahn, Johannes Zogbay ... Boston, MA
Zlaket, Eugene ... Tucson, AZ
Zlaket, Thomas A. ... Phoenix, AZ
Zlatkin, Lawrence J. ... Stamford, CT
Zlatkoff, Michael ... Los Angeles, CA
Zlatos, Elizabeth Ann ... Indianapolis, IN
Zlatos, Stephen E. ... Indianapolis, IN
Zlatow, Jeffrey ... San Francisco, CA
Zlimen, Allan J. ... Minneapolis, MN
Zlobinsky, Vladimir ... New York, NY
Zloch, James E. ... Fort Lauderdale, FL
Zloch, William J. ... Fort Lauderdale, FL
Zlock, C. Gilbert ... Newtown, PA
Zlock, Tracy N. ... Washington, DC
Zlocki, Stanley J. ... Mount Carmel, PA
Zlokas, Eli A. ... Pittsburgh, PA
Zlotchew, David M. ... New York, NY
Zlotchew, Ethan G. ... New York, NY
Zlotkin and Bentley ... Freehold, NJ
Hightstown, NJ
Zlotkin, Isadore I. ... Freehold, NJ
Zlotkin, Jacob ... Freehold, NJ
Zlotkin, Jean M. ... San Juan Bautista, CA
Zlotky, Jeffrey A. ... Dallas, TX
Zlotnick & Castleman ... Springfield, MA
Zlotnick, Craig D. ... New York, NY
Zlotnick, Gary Alan ... Philadelphia, PA
Zlotnick, Julius A. ... Youngstown, OH
Zlotnick, Norman L. ... Atlantic City, NJ
Zlotnick, Peter B. ... New York, NY
Zlotnick, Robt. V. ... Springfield, MA
Zlotnick, S. S. ... Washington, DC
Zlotnik, Arna H. ... Los Angeles, CA
Zlotnik, Gerald ... Houston, TX
Zlotnik, Jack V. ... Riverwoods, IL
Zlotocha, Edward J. ... Milwaukee, WI
Zlotoff, Mara G. ... San Jose, CA
Zlotogura, Barry ... Edmond, OK
Zlotogura, Carol K. ... Edmond, OK
Zlotogura, Mindy R. ... Spring Valley, NY
Zlotogura and Zlotogura ... Edmond, OK
Zlotolow, Louis ... New York, NY
Zlotucha, Frederick R. ... San Antonio, TX
Zmaila, Anthony A. ... Las Vegas, NV
Zmigrocki, James J. ... Chicago, IL
Zmigrocki, James J., Chartered ... Chicago, IL
Zmistowski, Sarah S. ... Old Town, ME
Zmistowski, Thad B. ... Bangor, ME
Zmrzel, Laurie E. ... Auburn, CA
Zmuda, Gene A. ... Toledo, OH
Zmuda, James S. ... Moline, IL
Zmuda, Paul F. ... Bethesda, MD
Zmudzinski, Spring M. ... Mishawaka, IN
Zmurkiewicz, A. P. ... San Diego, CA
Znaniecki, Jay E. ... Urbana, IL
Znidarsic, Joseph R. ... Chardon, OH
Znosko, Gerald F. ... Maitland, FL
Znoy-Rapalski, Michelle ... Falls Church, VA
Zoarski, Howard F. ... New Haven, CT
Zoba, C. David ... Columbus, OH
Zobair, Talha A., (Mr.) ... Washington, DC
Zobal, Arthur F. ... Fort Worth, TX
Zobbi, Joanne B. ... Boston, MA
Zobec, Frank T. ... Cleveland, OH
Zobel, Craig R. ... West Palm Beach, FL
Zobel, David M. ... Virginia Beach, VA
Zobel, Hallie L. ... Orlando, FL
Zobel, Hiller B. ... Boston, MA
Zobel, John H. ... Seattle, WA
Zobel, Lawrence J. ... Mayville, NY
Zobel, Mark R. ... Irving, TX
Zobel, Patricia L. ... Anchorage, AK
Zobel, Rya W.
Federal Judicial Center, GV
ZoBell, Karen M. ... San Diego, CA
Zobell, Karl ... La Jolla, CA
Zobenica, Tracey ... Tucson, AZ
Zoberg, David H., (P.A.) ... Miami, FL
Zoberman, Solomon B. ... Boca Raton, FL
Zoberman, Wendy Hope
West Palm Beach, FL
Zoberst, William R. ... Seattle, WA
Zobkiw, David J. ... Syracuse, NY
Zobler, Marian L.
Nuclear Regulatory Commission, Office of the General Counsel, GV
Zobrist, Karl ... Kansas City, MO
Zobrist, Markham L. ... New Haven, MO
Zobrosky, Ann E. ... Marion, IN
Zoby & Broccoletti ... Norfolk, VA
Zoby, J. Gerard ... Norfolk, VA
Zocca, Robert L. ... New Brunswick, NJ
Zoccola, Christine B. ... Indianapolis, IN
Zoccola, James E. ... Indianapolis, IN
Zoccola, William L. ... Memphis, TN
Zoch, Susan Aldrich ... Washington, DC
Zochowski, Christopher M.
Washington, DC
Zochowski, Scott P. ... Livonia, MI
Zochowski, T. Robert ... Jupiter, FL
Princeton Junction, NJ

Zochowski, T. Robert, Jr. ... New York, NY
Zocolo, Lori A. ... Cleveland, OH
Zoda, Frederick A. ... Trenton, NJ
Zodda, Richard V ... Sayville, NY
Zodicoff, Elissa Sue ... Queens Village, NY
Zodrow, Charles F. ... Uniontown, OH
Zodrow, Christopher N. ... West Point, GA
Zodrow, Donald T. ... Milwaukee, WI
Zodrow Et Al, P.C. ... San Diego, CA
Zodrow Et Al, P.C. ... Denver, CO
Zodrow, John J. ... San Diego, CA
Denver, CO
Zody, Brenda Wheeler ... Kalamazoo, MI
Zody, Michael A. ... Salt Lake City, UT
Zoeckler, Robert L. ... Conyers, GA
Zoeller, Ann Marie ... New York, NY
Zoeller, Brian K. ... Indianapolis, IN
Zoeller, Christopher C. ... Indianapolis, IN
Zoeller, D. Bryce ... Indianapolis, IN
Zoeller, David L. ... Cleveland, OH
Zoeller, Donald J. ... New York, NY
Zoeller, Gregory F. ... Indianapolis, IN
Zoeller, Jean E. ... Los Angeles, CA
Zoeller, Lee A. ... Philadelphia, PA
Zoeller, Mark L. ... Englewood, CO
Zoeller, Paul J. ... Dallas, TX
Zoeller, Susan M. ... Indianapolis, IN
Zoeller, William D. ... Vero Beach, FL
Zoellers, Charles H. ... London, KY
Zoellick, Robert B. ... Washington, DC
Zoellner, Alison C.M. ... New York, NY
Zoellner, Don V. ... San Diego, CA
Zoercher Huber McEntarfer & Goffinet
Tell City, IN
Zoercher, Ralph P. ... Tell City, IN
Zoes, Caroline S. ... Woodstock, IL
Zoes, Frederick E. ... Montgomery, AL
Zoes, Nick H. ... Dallas, TX
Zoesch, Thomas J. ... Appleton, WI
Zofchak, Linda M. ... Atlanta, GA
Zoffer, David B. ... Chapel Hill, NC
Chapel Hill, NC
Zoffer, Joseph M. ... Pittsburgh, PA
Zoffer, Steven W. ... Pittsburgh, PA
Zoffer & Wedner ... Pittsburgh, PA
Zoffer, William M.
Research Triangle Park, NC
Zogas, Paul M. ... Bridgeview, IL
Zogas, Peter N. ... Brooklyn, NY
Melville, NY
Zogas, Robert F. ... Rochester, NY
Zogby, Joseph R. ... Washington, DC
Zogby, Peter S. ... Utica, NY
Zogel, Leslie J. ... Coral Gables, FL
Zogg, Paul A. ... Boulder, CO
Zoghby, Alex W., P.C. ... Mobile, AL
Zoghby, George M. ... Mobile, AL
Zoghby, Guy A. ... Niceville, FL
Pittsburgh, PA
Zoghlin, Mindy Lee ... Rochester, NY
Zogleman, Nancy G. ... Topeka, KS
Zoglio, David L. ... Lansing, MI
Zoglio, Eugene M. ... Bowie, MD
Zografos, Dean T. ... Lake Oswego, OR
Zogran, Gregory H. ... Stuart, FL
Zogry, Eric Jay ... Raleigh, NC
Zohar, Dan ... Tampa, FL
Zohar, Daniel Y. ... Los Angeles, CA
Zohar, Lior Z. ... Los Angeles, CA
Zohar Lynton, Stephanie
Birmingham, AL
Zohdy, Hany ... Baton Rouge, LA
Zohlman, John A., III ... Cherry Hill, NJ
Zohn, Edward J. ... Somerville, NJ
Zohn, Eric Scott ... New York, NY
Zohn, Jack ... Des Moines, IA
Zohn, Martin S. ... Los Angeles, CA
Zohn, Patricia Mullon ... Newark, NJ
Zoia, Rose M. ... Glen Ellen, CA
Zokan, Tammy A. ... Coeur d'Alene, ID
Zoken, Mollee Sue O. ... Mountain View, CA
Zokoff, Karen A. ... Rainbow City, AL
Zokvic, Charles F. ... Vero Beach, FL
Zola, George E. ... Columbus, OH
Zola, Joseph ... Wilkes-Barre, PA
Zola, Michael S. ... Kailua-Kona, HI
Zola, Neil L. ... New York, NY
Zola, Paul ... New York, NY
Zolan, Craig ... New York, NY
Zolan, Paul B. ... Hartford, CT
Zoland, Deborah L. ... New York, NY
Zolbert, William A. ... Dearborn, MI
Zolbrod Law Offices ... Everett, WA
Zolbrod, Morilun ... Everett, WA
Zoldak, Joyce A. ... Department of Justice, Bureau of Prisons, GV
Zoldan, Alex M. ... Scarsdale, NY
Zoldan, Kenneth J. ... Philadelphia, PA
Zoldan, Melissa B. ... New York, NY
Zoldessy, Adam ... Princeton, NJ
Zoler, Amelia J. ... New York, NY
Zolet, Theresa I. ... Washington, DC
Zolezzi, Carl K. ... Palatka, FL
Zolezzi, Jeanne Marie ... Stockton, CA
Zolezzi, Richard V. ... San Francisco, CA
Zolezzi, Thomas P. ... Albany, NY
Zolfaghari, Alexander ... New York, NY
Zolfaghari, Paul N. ... Department of Justice, Civil Division, GV
Zolfo, Anthony P. ... Parsippany, NJ
Zoli, Elise N. ... Boston, MA
Zolin, Donald M. ... New York, NY
Zoline, Joseph T. ... Beverly Hills, CA
Zolke, Scott B. ... Beverly Hills, CA
Zolkin, Claude ... Encino, CA
Zolkin, Claude, Inc., A.P.C. ... Encino, CA
Zolkin, David B. ... Los Angeles, CA
Zolkowski, Dan J. ... East Lansing, MI

Zoll, B. Ray ..... Draper, UT
Zoll, David ..... Chestnut Hill, MA
Zoll, David Forsyth ..... Arlington, VA
Zoll, David W. ..... Toledo, OH
Zoll, Donafaye Wilson ..... Haddonfield, NJ
Zoll, Jeffery M. ..... Chicago, IL
Zoll & Kranz, LLC ..... Toledo, OH
Zoll, Otto Kip ..... Boston, MA
Zoll, Samuel E. ..... Boston, MA
Zolla, Carol Elias ..... San Jose, CA
Zolla, Marshall S., (A P.C.)
Los Angeles, CA
Zolla and Meyer ..... Los Angeles, CA
Zolla, William A. ..... Chicago, IL
Zolla, William A., II ..... New York, NY
Zollar, Carolyn C. ..... Arlington, VA
Zollar, Nikki M. ..... Chicago, IL
Zoller, Barry ..... San Francisco, CA
Zoller, Daniel B. ..... Chicago, IL
Zoller, Deborah L. ..... Fallbrook, CA
Zoller, Howard L. ..... Southfield, MI
Zoller, John J. ..... Little Falls, NY
Zoller, Lewis W. ..... Longwood, FL
Zoller, Nicholas ..... San Francisco, CA
Zoller, Norman E. ..... Atlanta, GA
Zoller, Robert Paul ..... Trenton, NJ
Zoller, Thomas M. ..... Wooster, OH
Zoller, William G. ..... Nevada City, CA
Zollicker, Samuel S., Law Office of
Kansas City, MO
Zollicoffer, John H., Jr. ..... Henderson, NC
Zollicoffer & Long ..... Henderson, NC
Zollicoffer, Thurman W., Jr.
Baltimore, MD
Zollinger, Brian P. ..... Dallas, TX
Zollinger, Clayne S., Jr. ..... Rupert, ID
Zollinger, Fred H., Jr. ..... North Canton, OH
Zollinger, Frederick H., III ..... Canton, OH
Zollinger, Jay A. ..... Portland, OR
Zollinger, Jeremy Scott ..... New Orleans, LA
Zollinger, Keith A. ..... Pocatello, ID
Zollinger, Lewis P. ..... San Diego, CA
Zollinger, Stephen Porter ..... Rexburg, ID
Zollinger, Thomas T. ..... Gillette, WY
Zollinger, Timothy B. ..... Sterling, IL
Zollman, Ron S. ..... San Diego, CA
Zollmann, William J., III ..... Wentzville, MO
Zollner, Daniel J. ..... Chicago, IL
Zollner, Max E. ..... Joliet, IL
Zollner, Robert S. ..... Andover, MA
Zollner, Stephen R. ..... Louisville, KY
Zollo, Nina M. ..... Tallahassee, FL
Zollo, Shannon S. ..... Waltham, MA
Zollo, Thomas M. ..... New York, NY
Zolman, Carla J. ..... St. Louis, MO
Zolna, Bruce A. ..... Chicago, IL
Zolna, Fredrick ..... Syracuse, NY
Zolna, Leonard A., Jr.
Spring Lake Park, MN
Zolner, Michael Derek ..... Chicago, IL
Zolno, Mark S. ..... Chicago, IL
Zolonz, Jeffrey A. ..... Culver City, CA
Zolot, Barbara ..... New York, NY
Zolot, Lawrence P. ..... Hollywood, FL
Zolot, Norman ..... Woodbridge, CT
Zolot, Saul ..... Hollis, NY
Zolotar, Barry ..... Sacramento, CA
Zoloto, Allan L. ..... Chicago, IL
Zolotor, Ronald P. ..... Excelsior Springs, MO
Zolotorofe, David B. ..... Clifton, NJ
Zolper, Peter C. ..... Department of the Army, U.S. Army Legal Services Agency, GV
Zolt, Edmond L. ..... Washington, DC
Zolt, Eric M. ..... Los Angeles, CA
Zoltak, John P. ..... New York, NY
Zoltan, Carol B. ..... Brooklyn, NY
Zoltanski, Edward F. ..... Monclova, OH
Zoltanski, Teresa A. ..... Denver, CO
Zoltick, Martin M. ..... Reston, VA
Zolton, Darrell R. ..... Saginaw, MI
Zoltowski, Scott Michael ..... Washington, DC
Zombek, Andrew ..... New York, NY
Zomber, Peter J. ..... Los Angeles, CA
Zomcik, Michael J. ..... Houston, TX
Zometa, Rebecca Hamilton ..... Tampa, FL
Zomick, Nomi N. ..... Cedarhurst, NY
Zommick, Kenneth ..... Long Beach, CA
Zomnir, Richard M. ..... Pittsburgh, PA
Zomparelli, Gino ..... Middleburg Heights, OH
Zomper, Dianne ..... Houston, TX
Zomper, Jeffrey B. ..... New York, NY
Zomper, Susan ..... New York, NY
Zona, Dean J. ..... Walla Walla, WA
Zona, Heather Martinez ..... New York, NY
Zonakis, Steven B. ..... Fort Wayne, IN
Zonana, David A. ..... Palo Alto, CA
Zonana, Katherine A. ..... Sunnyvale, CA
Zonana, Victor ..... New York, NY
Zonarich, John R. ..... Harrisburg, PA
Steelton, PA
Zonay, Thomas A. ..... Woodstock, VT
Zonder, Scott D. ..... Pasadena, CA
Zonderman, Hershel ..... Boston, MA
Zonderman, Lauren J. ..... Nantucket, MA
Zonderman, Paul S. ..... Schenectady, NY
Zondorak, Valerie A. ..... New York, NY
Zone & Bernstein ..... Stamford, CT
Zone, Joseph J. ..... Cleveland, OH
Zonen, Ronald J. ..... Santa Barbara, CA
Zoneraich, Davy E. ..... New York, NY
Zonetti, Alicia A. ..... Trenton, NJ
Zonghetti, Gino A. ..... Newark, NJ
New York, NY
Zongker, James B. ..... Wichita, KS
Zonies, Daniel B. ..... Cherry Hill, NJ
Zonies, Deborah R. ..... Boston, MA
Zonies, Joseph J. ..... Denver, CO
Zonis, Jonathan ..... New York, NY

Zonn, Sidney ..... Pittsburgh, PA
Zonna, Craig A. ..... Erie, PA
Zonnenberg, Patricia K. ..... Marblehead, MA
Zonni, Ginocchio and Taylor, Professional Corporation ..... Glendale, CA
San Diego, CA
Santa Ana, CA
Ventura, CA
Zonni, Marco J. ..... Glendale, CA
Zonon, Barry I. ..... New York, NY
Zontini, J. Michael ..... Cleveland, OH
Zoob, Theo. O. ..... Long Island City, NY
Zoochie, William R. ..... Playa Del Rey, CA
Zoogman, Nicholas J. ..... New York, NY
Zook, Albert L. ..... Torrance, CA
Zook, Bill ..... Mesquite, TX
Zook, David H. ..... Colorado Springs, CO
Zook, David R. ..... Washington, DC
Zook, Keith H. ..... Boulder, CO
Zook, Kerry E. ..... Indianapolis, IN
Zook, R. Brent ..... Goshen, IN
Zook, Richard J. ..... Houston, TX
Zook, Ted H. ..... Chicago, IL
Zook, Tom W. ..... St. Louis, MO
Zoolalian, Britt David ..... Orange, CA
Zoole, Mark H. ..... St. Louis, MO
Zooper, Joan Goodwin ..... Garden City, NY
Zopatti, Christopher J. ..... Tustin, CA
Zopf, George E. ..... Claremont, NH
Zopf, Gerard J. ..... Hawthorne, NY
Zopf, Michael J. ..... Champaign, IL
Zopf, M. J., P.C. ..... Champaign, IL
Zopff, John S. ..... Mason, OH
Zopfi, Gerard D. ..... Stamford, CT
Zophres, Theo G. ..... Plantation, FL
Zopp, Andrea L. ..... Chicago, IL
Zopp, E. Frederick ..... Louisville, KY
Zopp, Gerald Martin, Jr. ..... Woodstock, IL
Zoppi, Anthony M. ..... Avenel, NJ
Zoppo, Darien J. ..... White Plains, NY
Zoppo, Joseph P. ..... Bridgeport, CT
Zoppoth, Scott P. ..... Louisville, KY
Zoppoth Valenti & Hanley, PLLC
Louisville, KY
Zorabedian, Katherine Ann ..... Swansea, MA
Zorach, Jonathan ..... Lancaster, PA
Zorb, George A. ..... Temecula, CA
Zorbas, Alexis J. ..... New York, NY
Zorc, Joseph M. ..... Washington, DC
Zordani, Jan M. ..... Chicago, IL
Zordani, Jennifer L. ..... Chicago, IL
Zore, Ernest F. ..... Cleveland, OH
Zore, Gerald S. ..... Indianapolis, IN
Zorea, Lior ..... Palo Alto, CA
Zorea, Moshe Calberg ..... Anchorage, AK
Zorea, Robyn ..... Palo Alto, CA
Zorensky, David F. ..... Ross, CA
Zorensky, Louis I. ..... St. Louis, MO
Zoretic, Michael T. ..... Seattle, WA
Zorfas, Jason M. ..... Boston, MA
Zoric, Steven ..... Chicago, IL
New York, NY
Zorich, Carolyn R. ..... Spokane, WA
Zorie, Stephanie M. ..... Satellite Beach, FL
Zorie, Stephanie M., P.A.
Satellite Beach, FL
Zorigian, James ..... Los Angeles, CA
Zorin, David N. ..... Lexington, KY
Zork, Lesley S. ..... Washington, DC
Zorman, Jack ..... Sacramento, CA
Zorn, Brian M. ..... Rochester, NY
Zorn & Caldwell ..... Jesup, GA
Zorn, Catherine ..... St. Paul, OR
Zorn, Daniel K. ..... Oklahoma City, OK
Zorn, Edward J. ..... Anaheim, CA
Zorn, Edward L. ..... Fort Morgan, CO
Zorn & Girardeau ..... Baytown, TX
Zorn, James E. ..... Odanah, WI
Zorn, Jean G. ..... New York, NY
Zorn, Jonathan M. ..... Boston, MA
Zorn, Joseph R. ..... Baytown, TX
Zorn, Judith Lynn ..... Troy, MI
Zorn, Karen Johnson ..... Corvallis, OR
Zorn, Kenneth M. ..... Troy, MI
Zorn & Mandlebaum, P.C. ..... Troy, MI
Zorn, Nicholas D., Jr. ..... Bartow, FL
Zorn, Peter A. ..... Winston-Salem, NC
Zorn, Philip L., Jr. ..... Cincinnati, OH
Zorn, Richard L.
Federal Labor Relations Authority, Office of the General Counsel, GV
Zorn, Stephanie O. ..... St. Louis, MO
Zorn, Stephen A. ..... New York, NY
Zorn, William T. ..... St. Louis, MO
Zorn, William V. A. ..... Manchester, NH
Zornada, George J.
Securities and Exchange Commission, Division of Investment Management, GV
Zorne, Lee, Law Offices of
Beverly Hills, CA
Zornes, James D. ..... Columbia, KY
Zornes, Walter W. ..... Riverhead, NY
Zornow, David M. ..... New York, NY
Zornow, Harry B. ..... Hamilton, OH
Zornoza, Simon ..... North Quincy, MA
Zoro, Gregory Serge ..... Renton, WA
Zorpette, Tracy ..... Washington, DC
Zorrilla, Jose, Jr. ..... Costa Mesa, CA
Zorrilla, Juan C. ..... Miami, FL
Zorthian, Barry ..... Washington, DC
Zorza, John L., II ..... Troy, MI
Zorzi, Mary Elizabeth ..... Owings Mills, MD
Zosa, Marie Denyse ..... Washington, DC
Zosel, K. Paul ..... Bloomfield Hills, MI
Zosel, Marit Westman ..... Minneapolis, MN
Zoslov, Amy J.
Federal Communications Commission, Wireless Telecommunications Bureau, GV

Zoss, David L. ..... St. Paul, MN
Zoss, Paul A. ..... Des Moines, IA
Zoss, Robert E., Sr. ..... Evansville, IN
Zotian, Edward V. ..... Greensboro, NC
Zoto, Jason S. ..... New York, NY
Zotos, Andrew P. ..... New Hyde Park, NY
Zotos, Nicholas G. ..... Detroit, MI
Zotos, Nick A. ..... St. Louis, MO
Zotos, Thomas A. ..... Clayton, MO
Zott, Amy J. Lamerand ..... Burlington, WI
Zott, David J. ..... Chicago, IL
Zott, Elizabeth J. ..... Hinsdale, IL
Zotter, Bruce C. ..... Washington, DC
Zotter, Jean M. ..... Boston, MA
Zotter, John W. ..... Pittsburgh, PA
Zotter, Walter J. ..... Detroit, MI
Zotti, Robert J. ..... Oakbrook Terrace, IL
Zottola, Armand J. ..... Washington, DC
Zottola, John A. ..... Pittsburgh, PA
Zou, Ji ..... New York, NY
Zou, Philip S. ..... Chicago, IL
Zouaoui, Jamil ..... Washington, DC
Zoub, Burton I. ..... Chicago, IL
Zoub, Jeffrey R. ..... Tucson, AZ
Zoubek, Nancy A. ..... New York, NY
Zoubek, Paul H. ..... Camden, NJ
Zoucha, Joseph R. ..... Redwood City, CA
Zouck, Robert L., Jr. ..... Baltimore, MD
Zoufal, Donald R. ..... Chicago, IL
Zougras, Elizabeth Rizos ..... Munster, IN
Zouhary, Jack ..... Toledo, OH
Zouhary, Kathleen Maher ..... Maumee, OH
Zoumberis, Nikitis ..... Warner Robins, GA
Zouras, James B. ..... Chicago, IL
Zouros, Maria ..... Melville, NY
Zouski, Ruth ..... Wautoma, WI
Zousmer, Michael I. ..... Bloomfield Hills, MI
Zousmer, William J. ..... Detroit, MI
Zovas, Anne Kelly ..... Glastonbury, CT
Zovich, Thomas M. ..... Los Angeles, CA
Zovickian, Stephen A. ..... San Francisco, CA
Zovod, Shawn Jennifer
Walnut Creek, CA
Zowine, Louis C. ..... Bridgeport, CT
Zox, Benjamin L. ..... Columbus, OH
Zox, Melissa L. ..... Columbus, OH
Zox, William P. ..... Columbus, OH
Zozula, Robert B. ..... Boston, MA
Zpevak, Michael J. ..... Dallas, TX
Zraick, Edw. A. ..... New York, NY
Zraick, Nahas & Rich ..... New York, NY
Zraik, T. Joseph ..... Toledo, OH
Zraik, Thomas G. ..... Toledo, OH
Zrake, Virginia A. ..... Baltimore, MD
Zralek, Stephen J. ..... Nashville, TN
Zreczny, Alan I. ..... Rosemont, IL
Zrenda, Stephen A., Jr.
Oklahoma City, OK
Zrenda, Stephen A., Jr., P.C., A Prof. Corp.
Oklahoma City, OK
Zrnich, John A. ..... Los Angeles, CA
Zromkoski, Randall J. ..... Fort Wayne, IN
Valparaiso, IN
Zrust, Frank J. ..... Pittsburgh, PA
Zsalman, Robert D. ..... Department of the Navy, Office of the Judge Advocate General, GV
Zschau, Julius J. ..... Clearwater, FL
Zschiesche, Ray E. ..... Oklahoma City, OK
Zschunke, William E. ..... Atlanta, GA
Zseleczky, E. Peter, Jr. ..... Anchorage, AK
Zuanich, Robert P. ..... Seattle, WA
Zuares, Elena B. ..... Marlton, NJ
Zuba, James T. ..... Rockford, IL
Zuba, Kathryn A. ..... Treasury Department, Internal Revenue Service, GV
Zubalsky, Harry ..... Lodi, NJ
Zubalsky, Harry, P.A. ..... Lodi, NJ
Zubatch, Brian D. ..... Marlton, NJ
Zube, George Christopher
San Rafael, CA
Zube, L. David ..... Binghamton, NY
Zubek, Matthew F. ..... Oak Lawn, IL
Zubek, S. Gregory ..... Indianapolis, IN
Zubel, Eric ..... Las Vegas, NV
Zubel, Eric, Chartered ..... Las Vegas, NV
Zubel, Stanley F. ..... San Diego, CA
Zubel, Thomas F. ..... Grand Rapids, MI
Zuber, Arvid V. ..... Kansas City, MO
Zuber, Bradford C. ..... Iowa City, IA
Zuber, David ..... Houston, TX
Zuber, Donald S. ..... Baton Rouge, LA
Zuber, Heather A. ..... New York, NY
Zuber, Henry Bernard, III
Ocean Springs, MS
Zuber, J. Gordon ..... Houston, TX
Zuber, Jeffrey M. ..... New Brunswick, NJ
Zuber, Joan E. ..... Columbus, OH
Zuber, Nicholas J. ..... Duluth, MN
Zuber, Nicholas J., Ltd. ..... Duluth, MN
Zuber, Phillip R. ..... Upper Marlboro, MD
Zuber, R. Blake ..... San Antonio, TX
Zuber, Regine N. ..... Atlanta, GA
Zuber, Richard I. ..... Denver, CO
Zuber, Richard I., P.C. ..... Denver, CO
Zuber, Robert M. ..... Omaha, NE
Zuber, Scott A. ..... Morristown, NJ
Zuber, Stephen R. ..... Superior, WI
Zuber, Teresa L. ..... Sacramento, CA
Zuber, Thomas J. ..... Columbus, OH
Zuber, William L. ..... Arroyo Grande, CA
Zuberbier, Timothy L. ..... Milwaukee, WI
Zuberman, Marlene ..... Trenton, NJ
Zubi, Marwan S. ..... Springfield, MA
Zubiago, Stephen D. ..... Providence, RI
Zubieta, Charles A. ..... Los Angeles, CA
Zubizarreta, April M. ..... Houston, TX
Zubke, David J. ..... Minneapolis, MN
Zubkoff, Daniel J. ..... New York, NY

Zubkoff, David J. ..... San Diego, CA
Zubkus, Margarita ..... New York, NY
Zubkus, Robert A. ..... Exeter, NH
Zublatt, Alan B. ..... Monmouth Junction, NJ
Zubler, Jill M. ..... Buffalo, NY
Zubler, Monica L. ..... Washington, DC
Zubler, Todd ..... Washington, DC
Zuboff, Steven D. ..... Manchester, CT
Zubok, James ..... New York, NY
Zubras, Joan A. ..... Philadelphia, PA
Zubrensky, Leonard S. ..... Milwaukee, WI
Zubrensky, Michael A.
Department of Justice, Civil Rights Division, GV
Zubrensky, Padden, Horwitz & Weir
Milwaukee, WI
Zubres, Merton L. ..... Albany, NY
Zubrin, Douglas B. ..... Encino, CA
Zubrin, Peter M. ..... Detroit, MI
Zubrinic, Anne T. ..... Golden, CO
Zubrod, Tracy L. ..... Cheyenne, WY
Zubrow, Barry L. ..... New Vernon, NJ
Zubrow, Luize ..... Washington, DC
Zubrow, Stephen S. ..... Pittsburgh, PA
Zubrzycki, Charles R. ..... New York, NY
Zubyk, Charles B. ..... Niles, OH
Zucaro, Alfred, Jr. ..... West Palm Beach, FL
Zucca, David F. ..... Burlingame, CA
Zucca, George R. ..... Bayonne, NJ
Zuccardy, Jill M. ..... New York, NY
Zuccarini, John P. ..... Birmingham, MI
Zuccarini, Michael J. ..... Bellevue, WA
Zuccaro, Edward R. ..... St. Johnsbury, VT
Zuccaro, Emil A. ..... San Diego, CA
Zuccaro, Emil A., A Professional Corporation ..... San Diego, CA
Zuccaro, Joseph S. ..... Natchez, MS
Zuccaro, Louis J. ..... Scottsdale, AZ
Zuccaro, Robert A. ..... New York, NY
Zuccaro, Sharon M. ..... Naples, FL
Zuccaro, Willis & Bent, A Professional Corporation ..... St. Johnsbury, VT
Zucchi, Jeffrey J. ..... Rockford, IL
Zucchi, John A. ..... Framingham, MA
Zucco, Chris M. ..... Kew Gardens, NY
Zucco, George C. ..... Cleveland, OH
Zucco, Jeff T. ..... Cleveland, OH
Zucco, Richard I. ..... Niagara Falls, NY
Zucco, William C. ..... Minneapolis, MN
Zucconi, John C. ..... San Diego, CA
Zucconi, Robert E. ..... Jersey City, NJ
Zuccotti, Andrew H. ..... Seattle, WA
Zuch, Frederic L. ..... Akron, OH
Zuch, Jennifer L. ..... New York, NY
Zuch, Lynette Gerland ..... St. Louis, MO
Zuch, Sharyn B. ..... Hartford, CT
Zuchlewski, Pearl ..... New York, NY
Zuchowski, Bruce Edward ..... San Jose, CA
Zucker, Adam D. ..... Norristown, PA
Zucker, Ann Hedges ..... New Haven, CT
Zucker, Arthur P. ..... Hackensack, NJ
Zucker, Audrey ..... Boston, MA
Zucker & Ballen ..... Brooklyn, NY
Zucker, Bernard ..... Basking Ridge, NJ
Zucker, Bruce Alan ..... Northridge, CA
Zucker, Carol Davis ..... Las Vegas, NV
Zucker, Charles S. ..... West Orange, NJ
Zucker, Claudia J. ..... Arlington, VA
Zucker, Craig E. ..... Southfield, MI
Zucker, Dale P. ..... Cleveland, OH
Zucker, Dale P., Co., L.P.A. ..... Cleveland, OH
Zucker, Dana W. ..... Laconia, NH
Zucker, Daniel A. ..... Roslyn, NY
Zucker, Daniel Baron ..... New York, NY
Zucker, Daniel N. ..... Chicago, IL
Zucker, David C. ..... Los Angeles, CA
Zucker, David G. ..... Kew Gardens, NY
Zucker, David M. ..... Brooklyn, NY
Zucker, Del ..... New York, NY
Zucker, Donna G. ..... Philadelphia, PA
Zucker, Douglas S. ..... Morristown, NJ
Zucker, Ellen J. ..... Boston, MA
Zucker, Elliott J. ..... New York, NY
Zucker, Eric I. ..... Boston, MA
Zucker, Eric J. ..... Pasadena, CA
Zucker, Erika A. ..... Los Angeles, CA
Zucker, Evan H. ..... San Diego, CA
Zucker, Facher and Zucker, A Professional Corporation ..... West Orange, NJ
Zucker, Gary A. ..... Brooklyn, NY
Zucker, Goldberg & Ackerman
Mountainside, NJ
Zucker, Greg ..... Mineola, NY
Zucker, Gregg ..... Los Angeles, CA
Zucker, Howard ..... New York, NY
Zucker, Howard B. ..... Denver, CO
Zucker, Irwin D. ..... San Antonio, TX
Zucker, Isaac M. ..... New York, NY
Zucker, James S. ..... New York, NY
Zucker, Jeffrey ..... Voorhees, NJ
Philadelphia, PA
Zucker, Jeffrey C. ..... Fort Lauderdale, FL
Camden, NJ
Zucker, Jeffrey P. ..... Las Vegas, NV
Zucker, Jennifer ..... Houston, TX
Zucker, Jill M. ..... Washington, DC
Zucker, Jody C. ..... Hollywood, CA
Zucker, John W. ..... New York, NY
Zucker, Jonathan S. ..... Washington, DC
Zucker, Judith B. ..... Wilton, CT
Zucker, Karen Eisner ..... Berwyn, PA
Zucker, Karen Lee ..... Washington, DC
Zucker, Kenneth H. ..... Berwyn, PA
Zucker, Krauss & Borchardt
White Plains, NY
Zucker, Lary I. ..... Moorestown, NJ
Philadelphia, PA
Zucker, Laura E. ..... Moorestown, NJ

Zucker, Lawrence ... New York, NY
Zucker, Leo ... West Palm Beach, FL
White Plains, NY
Zucker, Leo C. ... Livingston, NJ
Zucker, Leonard B. ... Mountainside, NJ
Zucker, Linda ... Portland, OR
Zucker, Lisa B. ... Philadelphia, PA
Zucker, Marc J. ... Philadelphia, PA
Zucker, Marjorie Roth ... New York, NY
Zucker, Mark Jay ... Newark, NJ
Zucker, Martin A. ... Princeton, NJ
Zucker, Martin A. ... Chappaqua, NY
Zucker, Martin P. ... St. Louis, MO
Zucker, Michael S. ... Burbank, CA
Zucker, Michele Ludwig ... Philadelphia, PA
Zucker, Morris R. ... West Orange, NJ
Zucker, Morton H. ... White Plains, NY
Zucker, Patricia Carey ... Harrisburg, PA
Zucker, Peggy Mara ... Hauppauge, NY
Zucker, Ralph H. ... Mohegan Lake, NY
Zucker, Rebecca L. ... Chicago, IL
Zucker, Richard L. ... Roseland, NJ
Zucker, Richard Mark ... Englewood, CO
Zucker, Richard Mark ... Philadelphia, PA
Zucker, Rick E. ... Overland Park, KS
Zucker, Scott D. ... New York, NY
Zucker, Scott I. ... Atlanta, GA
Zucker, Stanley ... New York, NY
Zucker, Stephen W. ... Chicago, IL
Zucker, Stephen Wade, Ltd. ... Chicago, IL
Zucker, Susan M. ... Northbrook, IL
Zucker, Todd J. ... Houston, TX
Zucker, William A. ... Boston, MA
Zuckerberg, Harry J. ... Hicksville, NY
Zuckerberg, Joshua ... New York, NY
Zuckerberg, Mark S. ... Indianapolis, IN
Zuckerbraun, David ... New London, CT
Zuckerbrod, Alan D. ... New York, NY
Zuckerbrod, Martin ... Cedarhurst, NY
Zuckerbrod & Taubenfeld ... Cedarhurst, NY
Zuckerbrot, Kenneth ... New York, NY
Zuckerman, Adrian ... New York, NY
Zuckerman, Alan H. ... Cherry Hill, NJ
Zuckerman, Alan J. ... San Diego, CA
Zuckerman, Alan R. ... Los Angeles, CA
Zuckerman, Alan S.
General Accounting Office,
Office of the General Counsel, GV
Zuckerman, Allan C. ... Chicago, IL
Zuckerman, Andrew J. ... Newark, NJ
Zuckerman, Anne D. ... Boca Raton, FL
Zuckerman, Barbara J. ... Burbank, CA
Zuckerman, Barbara J. ... New York, NY
Zuckerman, Barbara L. ... New York, NY
Zuckerman, Bart B. ... St. Louis, MO
Zuckerman, Benjamin E.
Philadelphia, PA
Zuckerman & Braunstein ... White Plains, NY
Zuckerman, Brian D. ... Philadelphia, PA
Zuckerman, Carol A. ... Baltimore, MD
Zuckerman, Charles J. ... Baltimore, MD
Zuckerman, Claudia J. ... Baltimore, MD
Zuckerman, David B. ... Seattle, WA
Zuckerman, David G. ... Goshen, NY
Zuckerman, David M. ... San Francisco, CA
Zuckerman, David S. ... San Francisco, CA
Zuckerman, David S. ... Mount Kisco, NY
Zuckerman & Devine ... Gray, ME
Zuckerman, Diane I. ... Tampa, FL
Zuckerman, Elias M. ... New York, NY
Zuckerman, Eliot H. ... New York, NY
Zuckerman, Elizabeth ... Princeton, NJ
Zuckerman, Ellen M. ... Thousand Oaks, CA
Zuckerman, Emily ... New York, NY
Zuckerman, Emily B. ... New York, NY
Zuckerman & Fisher, LLC
Lawrenceville, NJ
Princeton, NJ
Trenton, NJ
Zuckerman, Gary J. ... New York, NY
Zuckerman, George D. ... New York, NY
Zuckerman, George R. ... Bay Shore, NY
Zuckerman, Gerald ... Ossining, NY
Zuckerman, Gerald M. ... Washington, DC
Zuckerman, Glenda ... White Plains, NY
Zuckerman, Glenn ... New York, NY
Zuckerman, Harold C. ... Tulsa, OK
Zuckerman, Heather P. ... New York, NY
Zuckerman, Herbert L. ... Newark, NJ
New York, NY
Zuckerman, Ira H. ... New York, NY
Zuckerman, Ira L. ... Fort Lauderdale, FL
Weston, FL
Zuckerman, Ira L., P.A.
Fort Lauderdale, FL
Weston, FL
Zuckerman, Ira S. ... Atlanta, GA
Zuckerman, James R. ... Lake Success, NY
Zuckerman, Janet A. ... Rockville, MD
Zuckerman, Jay D. ... Dallas, TX
Zuckerman, Jeffrey I. ... Washington, DC
Zuckerman, Jeffrey R. ... New York, NY
Zuckerman, Joseph ... New York, NY
Zuckerman, Karen M. ... Houston, TX
Zuckerman, Lanny M. ... Pittsfield, MA
Zuckerman, Laura A. ... New York, NY
Zuckerman, Laura J. ... San Francisco, CA
Zuckerman, Lawrence J. ... Gray, ME
Zuckerman, Leo T. ... Englewood, CO
Zuckerman, Leo T., P.C. ... Englewood, CO
Zuckerman, Leslie H. ... Hollywood, FL
Zuckerman, Lois R. ... Department of Labor,
Office of the Solicitor, GV
Zuckerman, Lyle S. ... New York, NY
Zuckerman, M. Michael ... Radnor, PA
Zuckerman, M. Michael ... Wayne, PA
Zuckerman, Marilyn H. ... Boston, MA
Zuckerman, Marjorie E. ... Bay Shore, NY
Zuckerman, Mark S. ... Concord, NH
Zuckerman, Martin H. ... New York, NY
Zuckerman & McQuiller
San Francisco, CA
Zuckerman, Michael ... New York, NY
Zuckerman, Michael ... Philadelphia, PA
Zuckerman, Michael H. ... Binghamton, NY
Zuckerman, Michael J. ... Glendale, CA
Zuckerman, Mitchell ... New York, NY
Zuckerman, Neal H. ... New York, NY
Zuckerman, P. Benjamin ... Boca Raton, FL
Zuckerman, Paul A. ... New York, NY
Zuckerman, Paul H. ... New York, NY
Zuckerman, Paul S. ... Los Angeles, CA
Zuckerman, Peter J. ... New York, NY
Zuckerman, Richard E. ... Detroit, MI
Zuckerman, Richard K. ... Mineola, NY
New York, NY
Zuckerman, Richard M. ... New York, NY
Zuckerman, Richard S. ... San Francisco, CA
Zuckerman, Richard W. ... Peoria, IL
Zuckerman, Robert
Department of Transportation,
Federal Aviation Administration, GV
Zuckerman, Roger E. ... Washington, DC
Zuckerman, Rosalie G. ... New York, NY
Zuckerman, Russell I. ... Rochester, NY
Zuckerman, Seth E. ... Millburn, NJ
Zuckerman, Spaeder, Goldstein, Taylor & Better, L.L.P. ... Baltimore, MD
Zuckerman, Spaeder, Goldstein, Taylor & Kolker, L.L.P. ... Washington, DC
New York, NY
Vienna, VA
Zuckerman, Spaeder, Taylor & Evans, L.L.P.
Fort Lauderdale, FL
Miami, FL
Tampa, FL
Zuckerman, Stephen D. ... Los Angeles, CA
Zuckerman, Steven M. ... Northbrook, IL
Zuckerman, Terry R. ... Kenilworth, NJ
Zuckerman, Thomas M. ... Stockton, CA
Zuckerman, Tod I. ... Los Angeles, CA
San Francisco, CA
Zuckerman, William ... Department of Labor,
Office of the Solicitor, GV
Zuckerman, William E. ... New York, NY
Zuckerman & Zuckerman ... Bay Shore, NY
Zuckermann, Steven M. ... Uniondale, NY
Zuckernik, James B. ... Boston, MA
Zuckert, Donald M. ... New York, NY
Zuckert, Eugene M. ... Washington, DC
Zuckert, Judith F. ... Irvine, CA
Zuckert, Laura D. ... Chicago, IL
Zuckert, Michael S. ... New York, NY
Zuckert, Owen M. ... Stamford, CT
New York, NY
Zuckert, Robert B. ... Walpole, NH
Zuckert, Scoutt & Rasenberger, L.L.P.
Washington, DC
Zuckman, Harvey L. ... Washington, DC
Zuckman, Mark ... Los Angeles, CA
Zuckoff, Eugene V. ... Catskill, NY
Zudekoff, Shimen B. ... North Haven, CT
Zuech, Melinda S. ... Menlo Park, CA
Zuefle, Howard M., Jr. ... Horn Lake, MS
Zuege, Judith R. ... Elkhorn, WI
Zuehl, James J. ... Chicago, IL
Zuelch, Kirk C. ... Key West, FL
Zuengler, Matthew C. ... Manitowoc, WI
Zuercher, Brian K. ... Cary, NC
Zuercher, Bruce W. ... Wichita, KS
Zuercher, H. M. ... San Antonio, TX
Zuercher, JoAnn L. ... Bethesda, MD
Zuerker, R. Scott ... Fort Smith, AR
Zuetel, Kenneth R., Jr. ... Pasadena, CA
Zuetel & Tomlinson ... Los Angeles, CA
Pasadena, CA
Santa Ana, CA
Zufall, Rachael M. ... Washington, DC
Zufelt, Weldon V. ... Sheboygan, WI
Zuffante, Mark ... New York, NY
Zuffranieri, Benjamin M., Jr. ... Buffalo, NY
New York, NY
Zuffranieri, Martin J. ... Buffalo, NY
Zuflacht, Adrienne ... San Antonio, TX
Zuflacht, Harold C. ... San Antonio, TX
Zuflacht, Robert A. ... Carle Place, NY
Zug, Jon Robert ... Charlottesville, VA
Zugay, Anthony A., Jr. ... Toledo, OH
Zugelder, Mark A. ... Dayton, OH
Zugelder, Michael T. ... Norfolk, VA
Zugelter, Frank L. ... North Hollywood, CA
Zuger, John A., P.C. ... Bismarck, ND
Zuger Kirmis & Smith ... Bismarck, ND
Zuger, William P. ... Bismarck, ND
Zughaft, Sharon M. ... West Orange, NJ
Zughaib, Edward E. ... Washington, DC
Zughaib, Karen A. ... Washington, DC
Zugibe, Mary E. ... Garnerville, NY
Zugibe, Patricia ... Bardonia, NY
Zugibe, Thomas P. ... Garnerville, NY
Zugrave, George V., Jr. ... Akron, OH
Zugravu, Leroy V. ... Canton, OH
Zugsmith, George S., A Professional Law Corporation ... Long Beach, CA
Zugsmith, George S., Jr. ... Long Beach, CA
Zuhdi, Leyla Nazette ... Oklahoma City, OK
Zuhdi, Nabil (Bill) ... Oklahoma City, OK
Zuhl, Gary E. ... Troy, OH
Zuhlke, James R. ... Schaumburg, IL
Zuhowski, Susan ... Severna Park, MD
Zuhusky, Judy Krikalo ... New York, NY
Zuidmulder, Appel & Gammeltoft, S.C.
Green Bay, WI
Zuidmulder, Donald R. ... Green Bay, WI
Zuiker, Sharon Sobczak ... Chicago, IL
Zujkowski, Edward P. ... New York, NY
Zujkowski, Frances ... New York, NY
Zujkowski, Marie L. ... Boston, MA
Zuk, Brandon W. ... Lansing, MI
Zuk, Caroline ... Los Angeles, CA
Zuk, Michael A. ... Los Angeles, CA
Newport Beach, CA
Zuk, Nicholas W. ... Columbus, OH
Zuk, Peter M. ... Boston, MA
Zuk, W. Kenneth ... Amelia, OH
Zukaitis, Thomas P. ... Louisville, CO
Zukauckas, Bill ... Austin, TX
Zuke, Randall D. ... Omaha, NE
Zukel, Lawrence G. ... Kansas City, KS
Zuker, Ronald J. ... Knoxville, TN
Zukeran, Guy C. ... Honolulu, HI
Zukerberg, Paul H. ... Washington, DC
Zukerman, Barbara ... Chicago, IL
Zukerman & Daiker Co., L.P.A.
Cleveland, OH
Zukerman, David R. ... Bronx, NY
Zukerman Gore & Brandeis, LLP
New York, NY
Zukerman, Jeffrey D. ... New York, NY
Zukerman, Larry William ... Cleveland, OH
Zukerman, Michael ... New York, NY
Zukerman, Michael J. ... Oakland, CA
Zukerman, Rosaline L., Law Offices of
Los Angeles, CA
Zukerman, Roy C. ... Los Angeles, CA
Zukernick, Harry ... Miami Beach, FL
Zukernick, Michael ... San Francisco, CA
Zukin, Deborah E. ... West Bloomfield, MI
Zukin, Helen E., The Law Offices of
Los Angeles, CA
Zukin, Robin ... Santa Monica, CA
Zukin, Wayne J. ... Chadds Ford, PA
Zuklie, Mitchell Stanton ... Menlo Park, CA
Zukoff, Seth D. ... New York, NY
Zukor, Abram C. ... Beverly Hills, CA
Zukor & Nelson, A Professional Law Corporation ... Beverly Hills, CA
Zukoski, Eric A. ... Dallas, TX
Zukosky, Edward ... Wenona, IL
Zukowski & Bresenhan, L.L.P.
Houston, TX
Zukowski, Christine A. ... New York, NY
Zukowski, Edwin F. ... Crystal Lake, IL
Zukowski, Janet M. ... Northbrook, IL
Zukowski, John ... Park Ridge, IL
Zukowski, John A. ... Garden City, NY
Zukowski, John M. ... Houston, TX
Zukowski, Mark D. ... Phoenix, AZ
Zukowski, Michael C. ... Phoenix, AZ
Zukowski, Paul A. ... Crystal Lake, IL
Zukowski, Rogers, Flood & McArdle
Crystal Lake, IL
Woodstock, IL
Zukowski, Rogers, Flood, McArdle & Orr
Chicago, IL
Zukowski, Walter J. ... Peru, IL
Zukowsky, Philip A. ... Dayton, OH
Zulack, John F. ... New York, NY
Zulakis, George ... Okemos, MI
Zulanas, Christopher J. ... Birmingham, AL
Zulanas, Summer H. ... Birmingham, AL
Zulandt, Robert E. ... Chardon, OH
Zulauf, Jay H. ... Seattle, WA
Zulauf, Karen M. ... Denver, CO
Zulch, Thelma Hogevoll ... Palo Alto, CA
Zulch, Thomas R. ... Farmington Hills, MI
Zulch, William F. ... Irvine, CA
Zuleski, Rebecca J. ... Fairmont, WV
Morgantown, WV
Zulian, David A. ... Naples, FL
Zulick, Arthur L. ... Stroudsburg, PA
Zulick, Barbara B. ... Norristown, PA
Zulick, James L. ... Nazareth, PA
Zulick, P. Alan ... Norristown, PA
Zulick & Zulick ... Norristown, PA
Zulieve, Andrew Jeffrey ... Portland, ME
Zulkey, Edward J. ... Chicago, IL
Zulkey, Richard E. ... Chicago, IL
Zulkey, Richard E., and Associates, Chartered ... Chicago, IL
Zulkie, Paul L. ... Chicago, IL
Zulkoski, Walter P. ... White Plains, NY
Zulkowski, Susan D. ... El Paso, TX
Zull, Peggy Ann ... Detroit, MI
Zullas, Michael F. ... Boston, MA
Zullas, Robert J. ... Brockton, MA
Zuller & Bondy ... New York, NY
Zuller, Michael E. ... New York, NY
Zulli, Francis A. ... Harrisburg, PA
Zulli, Joseph D. ... Philadelphia, PA
Zulli, Philip L. ... Harrisburg, PA
Zullig, Walter E., Jr. ... New York, NY
Zullinger, Joel R. ... Chambersburg, PA
Shippensburg, PA
Zullo, Alfred J. ... East Haven, CT
Zullo, Alfred J., & Associates, LLC, Law Offices of ... East Haven, CT
Zullo, Frank N. ... Norwalk, CT
Zullo, John M. ... North Haven, CT
Zullo, Judith L. ... Burlington, VT
Zullo, Laura Naclerio ... Cheshire, CT
Zullo, Matthew D. ... Raleigh, NC
Zullo, Matthew J. ... Melville, NY
Zullo, Peter F. ... Chicago, IL
Zullo, Peter F. ... Kew Gardens, NY
Zullo, Robert J., Jr. ... New Brunswick, NJ
Zullo, Thomas P. ... Ledgewood, NJ
Zullow, Fredrick M. ... New York, NY
Zullow, Keith A. ... New York, NY
Zultowsky, Heidi ... New Britain, CT
Zulty, Wesley J. ... Madison, WI
Zulu, Zadinga N. ... Washington, DC
Zulueta, Ignacio G. ... Miami, FL
Zumas, Nicholas H. ... Washington, DC
Zumas, Nicholas M. ... Bethlehem, PA
Zumbach, Steven E. ... Des Moines, IA
Zumbado, Hector E. ... Boston, MA
Newburyport, MA
Hampton Falls, NH
Zumbakis, S. Paul ... Chicago, IL
Zumbano, George C. ... West Chester, PA
Zumbar, Andrew L. ... Alliance, OH
Hartville, OH
Zumbehl, Cathy ... Overland Park, KS
Zumberge, Paul A. ... Pomona, CA
Zumbiel, Edward A. ... Cincinnati, OH
Zumbro, Claudia D.P. ... New York, NY
Zumbrun, Ronald A. ... Sacramento, CA
Zumbrunn, Gregory L. ... Victorville, CA
Zumbrunn & Hand ... Babylon, NY
Zumbrunn, Lynn E., A Law Corporation
Barstow, CA
Big Bear Lake, CA
Victorville, CA
Zumbrunn, Lynn Edward ... Victorville, CA
Zumbrunn, Werner J. ... Babylon, NY
zumBrunnen, Kathryn ... Spooner, WI
Zumdahl, Mark E. ... Milledgeville, IL
Sterling, IL
Zumeta, Zena D. ... Ann Arbor, MI
Zumkehr, Charles E. ... Akron, OH
Zummer, Anthony S. ... Chicago, IL
Zummo, Jos. L. ... Chicago, IL
Zummo, Lisa Gerling ... Houston, TX
Zummo, Mark J. ... Cincinnati, OH
Zummo, Mitchell & Perry ... Houston, TX
Zummo, Patrick A. ... Houston, TX
Zummo, Peter G. ... Williamsville, NY
Zummo, Valerie Brown
Highland Heights, KY
Zumoff, Robert A. ... Phoenix, AZ
Zumout, Nabil E. ... Fresno, CA
Zumout, Samia M. ... Sacramento, CA
Zumpano, Carlos A. ... Miami, FL
Zumpano, David J. ... New Hartford, NY
Zumpano, Joseph I. ... Miami, FL
Zumpft, Charles Scott ... Minden, NV
Zumstein, Bruce L. ... Joliet, IL
Zumstein, R. William ... Columbus, OH
Zumwalt, Almon & Hayes ... Nashville, TN
Zumwalt, Debra L. ... Palo Alto, CA
Zumwalt, Frank T. ... Modesto, CA
Zumwalt, James G. ... Nashville, TN
Zumwalt, William J. ... Encino, CA
Zun, Selwyn ... Chicago, IL
Zundel, Craig E. ... Palm Desert, CA
Zundel, Frederick G. ... Pocatello, ID
Zundel, J. Scott ... Palm Desert, CA
Zundel, J. Scott, A Prof. Law Corp.
Palm Desert, CA
Zundel, Jurg ... Peoria, IL
Zundel, Michael N. ... Salt Lake City, UT
Zundel, Robert C., Jr. ... Naples, FL
Zundel, Susan Powell ... Fairhope, AL
Zundell, Donald ... Miami, FL
Zung, Richard Y. K. ... Silver Spring, MD
Zunica, Richard A. ... Lowell, IN
Zunich, Jeanne Ellen ... White Plains, NY
Zunich, Robert A. ... Pittsburgh, PA
Zúñiga, Antonio R. ... Phoenix, AZ
Zuniga, Augustin M. ... Los Angeles, CA
Zúñiga, Juan E. ... San Diego, CA
Zuniga, Pablo ... Beltsville, MD
Zuniga, Richard S. ... Los Angeles, CA
Zúñiga López, Guillermo ... San Juan, PR
Zunino, E. Mark ... Oakland, CA
Zunka, John W. ... Charlottesville, VA
Zunker, Butler, Estes & Crane ... Austin, TX
Zunker, George A. ... Cheyenne, WY
Zunker, George A., P.C. ... Cheyenne, WY
Zunker, Jerry L. ... Austin, TX
Zunk-Ovadia, Stephanie G.
Garden City, NY
Zunno, Harriet L. ... Hilton, NY
Zunshine, Zach ... Columbus, OH
Zunz, Edward A., Jr. ... Morristown, NJ
Zunz, Lyonel E. ... Hackensack, NJ
New York, NY
Zupan, Katharine ... Worcester, MA
Zupan, Michael L. ... Falls Church, VA
Zupanc, Thomas ... St. Cloud, MN
Zupancic, James D. ... Portland, OR
Zupancic, Joseph M. ... Charleroi, PA
Washington, PA
Zupancic, Joyce E. ... Chicago, IL
Zupanski, Sandra M. ... Seattle, WA
Zupcic, Anthony M. ... New York, NY
Zupcofska, Peter F. ... Boston, MA
Zupke, Steven H. ... St. Paul, MN
Zupkus & Angell, P.C. ... Denver, CO
Zupkus, Robert A. ... Denver, CO
Zupo, Antone L. ... Lodi, CA
Zupon, Nanette C. ... Torrance, CA
Zupp, Robert R. ... Fresno, CA
Zuppke, David F. ... Bingham Farms, MI
Zuppke, David F., P.C. ... Bingham Farms, MI
Zuppone, Michael L. ... New York, NY
Zur, Ben-Tzion H. ... Newark, NJ
Zur, Grace L. ... Westport, CT
Zur, Ilan ... Pittsburgh, PA
Zurada, Martin J. ... Cleveland, OH
Zurakowski, Scott M. ... Alliance, OH
Zurasky, Jamie K. ... Pittsburgh, PA
Zurav, David B. ... Union, NJ
Zurav, Edward H. ... Union, NJ
Zuravel, David Lee ... Fayetteville, NC
Zuravin, Charles B. ... Columbia, MD
Zuravsky, Marvin A. ... Pickerington, OH
Zurawic, Nicholas A. ... Ann Arbor, MI
Zurawik, Jack G. ... Tulsa, OK
Zurawsky, Lawrence G. ... Pittsburgh, PA
Zurborg, J. David ... Springdale, AR

Zurborg & Spaulding, P.A. ....Springdale, AR
Zurbriggen, Jeff M., P.C. ....Tempe, AZ
Zurbriggen, Jeffrey M. ....Tempe, AZ
Zurbuch, Corey T. ....Charleston, WV
Zurbuch, Jeffrey S. ....Elkins, WV
Zurbuch, Peter G. ....Elkins, WV
Zurcher, Arnold J., Jr. ....New York, NY
Zurcher, Jackie A. ....Cincinnati, OH
Zurcher, Susan E. S. ....Decatur, IN
Zurek, Barbara A. ....Minneapolis, MN
Zurek, James W. ....Vernon Hills, IL
Zurek, Kenneth P. ....Franklin Park, IL
Zurek, Ronald ....Los Angeles, CA
Zurek, Thomas M. ....Houston, TX
Zurer, Burt M. ....Kensington, MD
Zurhellen, J. Owen, III ....New York, NY
Zurhellen & La Rue ....New York, NY
Zurich, John R. ....Williamsport, PA
Zurick, James A. ....Shamokin, PA
Zurier, Lauren Sandler ....Providence, RI
Zurier, Melvin L. ....Providence, RI
Zurier, Samuel D. ....Providence, RI
Zuriff, Eugene I. ....New York, NY
Zurik, Sam, III ....New Orleans, LA
Zuris, Stanley P. ....Albuquerque, NM
Zurkuhlen, Paul R. ....Louisville, KY
Zurlini, Jack G., Jr. ....Santa Barbara, CA
Zurlo, George J. ....Glens Falls, NY
Zurn, David M. ....Erie, PA
Zurn, Marianne G. ....Northampton, MA
Zurndorfer, M. David ....New York, NY
Zuroff, Bernard L. ....Englewood, CO
Zuroff, Mark G. ....Wellesley, MA
Zurofsky, Adam ....New York, NY
Zurofsky, Bennet D. ....Newark, NJ
Zurosky, Kirk S. ....Charlotte, NC
Zurvalec, Dana L. ....White Lake, MI
Zurvalec, David S. ....Lansing, MI
Zurvalec, Lori Ann ....Grosse Pointe, MI
Zury, James C. ....Columbus, OH
Zurz, Richard V. ....Akron, OH
Zurz, Richard V., Jr. ....Akron, OH
Zurzolo, Barbara H. ....Philadelphia, PA
Zurzolo, Vincent P. ....Los Angeles, CA
Zuschek, Mark A. ....Fairfax, VA
Zuschlag, Dirk F. ....Southfield, MI
Zuschlag, Noble R. ....Pittsburgh, PA
Zuschlag, Rebecca A. ....Roswell, NM
Zuschlag, Steven T. ....Syosset, NY
Zusman, Anita Sacks ....Beverly Hills, CA
Zusman, Edward S. ....San Francisco, CA
Zusman, Lynne K. ....Washington, DC
Zusman, Lynne K., & Associates, P.C.
Washington, DC
Zusman, Marina ....Beverly Hills, CA
Zusman, Michael C. ....Portland, OR
Zusman, Ronit ....Rochester, NY
Zusmann, Samuel J., Jr. ....Orlando, FL
Zuspann, Eugene P. ....Denver, CO
Goodland, KS
Zuspann, Eugene P., II ....Denver, CO
Goodland, KS
Zuspann & Zuspann ....Denver, CO
Goodland, KS
Zussman, Arthur D. ....Evanston, IL
Zussman, Gary T. ....Chicago, IL
Zussman, Marc I. ....Los Angeles, CA
Zussman, Marilyn ....Pacific Palisades, CA
Zussman, Milton Y. ....Birmingham, MI
Zussman, Richard A. ....Detroit, MI
Zussman & Sklar ....Birmingham, MI
Zussman, Susan B. ....Birmingham, MI
Zust, Sheryl S. ....Daytona Beach, FL
Zusy, F. Jonathan ....Indianapolis, IN
Zutell, Raymond ....Bronx, NY
Zutz, Lawrence I. ....Wilmington, DE
Zutz, Robert J. ....Washington, DC
Zuvekas, Ann West ....Washington, DC
Zuydhoek, Paul B. ....Buffalo, NY
Zuzelo, Emily A. ....Philadelphia, PA
Zuzga, Cynthia A. ....Los Angeles, CA
Zuzik, Denis P. ....Greensburg, PA
Zuzolo, Ralph A. ....Niles, OH
Zuzovsky, Guy ....Washington, DC
Zuzuarregui, Rene F. ....Fresno, CA
Zvara, David M. ....Dallas, TX
Zvara, John S. ....Houston, TX
Zvara, William L. ....Birmingham, AL
Jacksonville, FL
Zvara, William L., P.A. ....Jacksonville, FL
Zverina, George F. ....La Plata, MD
Zverinova, Margaret M.
Minneapolis, MN
Zverins, Debra M. ....Brooklyn, NY
Zvetina, Raymond F. ....San Diego, CA
Zvi, Miles A. ....Chicago, IL
Zvibleman, Alan N. ....St. Louis, MO
Zvibleman, Mark A. ....Chesterfield, MO
Zvoleff, Vernon I. ....San Francisco, CA
Zvonek, John J. ....New Orleans, LA
Zvonkovic, Mark ....New York, NY
Zwaan, Susan Garnett ....Lawton, OK
Zwaanstra, James E. ....Hillsboro, OR
Zwack, Henry F. ....Stephentown, NY
Zwack, Joseph P. ....Dubuque, IA
Zwaig, Michael A. ....Towson, MD
Zwaig, Michael A., P.A. ....Towson, MD
Zwaig, Ricardo D. ....Baltimore, MD
Zwaik, Mitchell C. ....Blue Point, NY
Zwaik, Stanley N. ....New York, NY
Zwain, Gary M. ....Metairie, LA
Zwak, Joseph D. ....Minneapolis, MN
Zwakman, John C. ....Minneapolis, MN
Zwald, Duff D. ....Honolulu, HI
Zwally, Charles B. ....Harrisburg, PA
Zwang, Glenn P. ....San Francisco, CA
Zwany, Deborah B. ....Brooklyn, NY
Zwanzig, John D. ....Ottawa, IL
Zwart, Cheryl R. ....Lincoln, NE
Zwart, David D. ....Lincoln, NE
Zwart, David L. ....St. Louis, MO
Zwas, Marla Gottlieb
Bloomfield Hills, MI
Zwaschka, Susan R. ....Minneapolis, MN
Zwayer, Ted ....Blytheville, AR
Zweben, Andrew P. ....Kingston, NY
Zweben, Gene R. ....Stuart, FL
Zweben, Marc S. ....Rydal, PA
Zweben, Murray ....Washington, DC
Zweben, Robert J. ....Berkeley, CA
Zweber, John W. ....Roseville, MN
Zweber, Julian J. ....St. Paul, MN
Zweber, Michael C. ....El Paso, TX
Zwecker, Samuel W. ....Fairfield, CT
Zweiacher, Brian D. ....Harrisburg, PA
Zweiback, Hotz & Lamberty ....Omaha, NE
Zweiban, Neil S. ....Buffalo Grove, IL
Zweibel, Emily J. ....New York, NY
Zweibel, Joel B. ....New York, NY
Zweibel, Morris ....Garden City, NY
Zweibel, Robert J. ....Bethesda, MD
Zweifach, Gerson A. ....Washington, DC
Zweifach, Lawrence J. ....New York, NY
Zweifel, Gary D. ....Atlanta, GA
Zweifel Law Firm, The ....Atlanta, GA
Zweifel, William R. ....Houston, TX
Zweifel, William R., P.C. ....Houston, TX
Zweifler, Adam F. ....Hartford, CT
Zweifler, David ....New York, NY
Zweifler, Mark J. ....New York, NY
Zweig, Bertram R. ....Los Angeles, CA
Zweig, David S. ....San Diego, CA
Zweig, David S., Law Firm of
San Diego, CA
Zweig, Henry L. ....Far Rockaway, NY
Zweig, Howard P., (P.C.) ....Chicago, IL
Zweig, Jason A. ....New York, NY
Zweig, Jay A. ....Phoenix, AZ
Zweig, Jonathan E. ....Burbank, CA
Zweig, Karen L. ....Boston, MA
Zweig, Marie L. ....Uniondale, NY
Zweig, Meryl Sugar ....Bronx, NY
Zweig, Michael K. ....Santa Monica, CA
Zweig, Michael L. ....Gurnee, IL
Zweig, Michael P. ....New York, NY
Zweig, Richard H. ....New York, NY
Zweig, Sally Franklin ....Indianapolis, IN
Zweig, Shelby L. ....Chicago, IL
Zweig, Stephen E., (P.C.) ....New York, NY
Zweig, Steven ....Trenton, NJ
Zweig, Steven M. ....Buffalo, NY
Zweigart, Robert G. ....Maysville, KY
Zweigart, Steven R. ....Maysville, KY
Zweigbaum, Barry E. ....New York, NY
Zweighaft, Peter K. ....Los Angeles, CA
Zweighaft, Rachel Mead ....New York, NY
Zweiman, Beverly H. ....Newton, MA
Zweiman, Robert M. ....Fort Lee, NJ
Zweizig, Jonathan ....Dayton, OH
Zwelling, Howard S. ....Zanesville, OH
Zwerner, Joel C. ....Fort Pierce, FL
Zwerdling & Crowley ....Eureka, CA
Zwerdling, Jeffrey M. ....Richmond, VA
Zwerdling and Oppleman ....Richmond, VA
Zwerdling, Paul, Leibig, Kahn, Thompson & Driesen, P.C. ....Washington, DC
Zwerdling, Zachary E. ....Eureka, CA
Zwerling & Altemus ....Hackensack, NJ
Zwerling, Andrew Leslie ....Kew Gardens, NY
Zwerling, David James ....Hackensack, NJ
Zwerling, Irving ....New York, NY
Zwerling, Jay S. ....New York, NY
Zwerling, Jeffrey C. ....New York, NY
Westbury, NY
Zwerling, John Kenneth ....Alexandria, VA
Zwerling & Kemler, P.C. ....Washington, DC
Alexandria, VA
Zwerling, Robin F. ....New York, NY
Zwerling, Schachter & Zwerling, LLP
New York, NY
Westbury, NY
Seattle, WA
Zwerling, Susanna M.
Federal Communications Commission, Mass Media Bureau, GV
Zwerling & Zwerling ....New York, NY
Zwernemann, Donald H. ....Bellaire, TX
Zwernemann, Gerald R. ....San Antonio, TX
Zwerner, Daniel P. ....Somers, NY
Zwerner, David F. ....Dallas, TX
Zweroff, Arthur I. ....Central Islip, NY
Zwetchkenbaum, Marc P. ....Boston, MA
Zwetsch, Kevin D. ....Tampa, FL
Zwibel, Elizabeth A. ....Fairfax, VA
Zwibel, Jonathan A. ....Miami, FL
Zwibel, Ketta Katherine ....Charleston, SC
Zwibelman, Irvin R. ....Clayton, MO
Sullivan, MO
Zwibelman, Myron S. ....St. Louis, MO
Zwick, Ann M. ....Chicago, IL
Springfield, IL
Zwick, Charles M. ....Charlotte, MI
Zwick, Coleman D. ....Cleveland, OH
Zwick, Edward F. ....Boca Raton, FL
Zwick, Gary A. ....Cleveland, OH
Zwick, Kenneth L. ....Department of Justice, Civil Division, GV
Zwick, Kenneth T. ....Huntington Beach, CA
Zwick Law Offices ....Sarasota, FL
Zwick Law Offices Co., L.P.A. ....Canton, OH
Zwick, Leander P., III ....Canton, OH
Zwick, Marc E. ....Birmingham, MI
Zwick, Mary ....Ada, MI
Zwick, Mary Lou ....Chicago, IL
Zwick, Michael E. ....Grand Rapids, MI
Zwick, Michael J. ....Southfield, MI
Zwick, Shelly C. ....San Marcos, CA
Zwick & Sigler ....Decatur, IN
Zwick, Steven ....Santa Ana, CA
Zwick, Susan ....Chicago, IL
Zwick, Tracy ....New York, NY
Zwick, William S. ....Sarasota, FL
Zwick, Zane R. ....Decatur, IN
Zwickel, Arthur L. ....Los Angeles, CA
Zwickel, Charles ....Catskill, NY
Zwickel, James E. ....Nashville, TN
Zwickel, Sandra N. ....Whippany, NJ
Zwicker, David E. ....Aledo, IL
Zwicker, Glen M. ....Washington, DC
Zwicker, Joseph H. ....Boston, MA
Zwicker, Kenneth D. ....Woodland Hills, CA
Zwicker, Laura A. ....Los Angeles, CA
Zwicker, Mark L. ....Brattleboro, VT
Zwicker, Mark L., P.C. ....Brattleboro, VT
Zwickl, Michael D. ....Casper, WY
Zwickl, Sara Zivian ....Bingham Farms, MI
Zwicklbauer, Liesl K. ....Albany, NY
Zwicky, Bob ....Fort Lauderdale, FL
Zwicky, Steven J. ....Rutland, VT
Zwiebach, Burton M. ....Flushing, NY
Zwiebach, Peter ....New York, NY
Zwiebel, Alan S. ....Kingston, NY
Zwiebel, Brody & Gold, P.C. ....Kingston, NY
Zwiebel, David ....New York, NY
Zwiebel, Eric B. ....Plantation, FL
Zwiebel, Eric B., P.A. ....Plantation, FL
Zwiefelhofer, Peter J. ....Milwaukee, WI
Zwiefler, Mark J. ....New York, NY
Zwieg, Darwin L. ....Neillsville, WI
Zwieg, John R. ....Madison, WI
Zwiener, Lonny F. ....Austin, TX
Zwier, Paul J. ....Philadelphia, PA
Zwierlein, Robert F. ....Coto De Caza, CA
Zwierzynski, Steven ....Portland, OR
Zwillenberg, Bernard E. ....Dallas, TX
Zwilling, Arlene S. ....Hauppauge, NY
Zwilling, Edward I. ....Pelham, AL
Zwilling, Thomas M. ....Pittsburgh, PA
Zwillinger, Gary R. ....Phoenix, AZ
Zwillinger, Keith E. ....Solana Beach, CA
Zwillinger, Marc J. ....Department of Justice, Criminal Division, GV
Zwillinger, Stanley ....New City, NY
Zwillman, Blair R. ....Maplewood, NJ
Zwillman, Evan W. ....Maplewood, NJ
Zwillman & Zwillman ....Irvington, NJ
Maplewood, NJ
Newark, NJ
Zwingli, Laurie H. ....Lake Oswego, OR
Zwirb, Robert S.
Commodity Futures Trading Commission, Office of the General Counsel, GV
Zwirblis, W. Alan ....New Bedford, MA
Zwirecki, Angela M. ....Buffalo, NY
Zwirn, Benjamin L. ....Port Washington, NY
Zwirn, Daniel K. ....Los Angeles, CA
Zwirn, Gerard ....Long Island City, NY
Zwirn, Irving ....Moravia, NY
Zwirn, Richard J. ....Moravia, NY
Zwirn, Sherwood M. ....Northbrook, IL
Zwirn, Sherwood M., & Associates, Ltd.
Northbrook, IL
Zwirn & Zwirn ....Moravia, NY
Zwirner, Richard T. ....Chicago, IL
Zwisler, Carl E., III ....Washington, DC
Zwisler, Margaret M. ....Washington, DC
Zwisohn, Van ....Clifton Park, NY
Zwissler, Diedolf, Feuer & Volkmann, L.L.P.
Patchogue, NY
Zwissler, H. Alan ....Venice, FL
Zwit, Joan Zaworski ....Chicago, IL
Zwyer, Arlyne R. ....New York, NY
Zwygart, Christopher C. ....West Bend, WI
Zybach, Judy F. ....Los Angeles, CA
Zybala, David A. ....Baltimore, MD
Zybala, Michael G. ....San Diego, CA
Zybert, Ann P. ....Syosset, NY
Zyble, David A. ....DeWitt, MI
Zyblut, Chester A. ....Washington, DC
Zyburski, Paul F. ....Mount Clemens, MI
Zych, Edward J. ....Danville, PA
Zych, Eleonora M. ....Pittsburgh, PA
Zych, Thomas F. ....Cleveland, OH
Zychal, Marianne K. ....New York, NY
Zychick, Joel D. ....Westbury, NY
Zychick, Joel D. ....Westbury, NY
Zychowicz, Ralph C. ....Toledo, OH
Zyckowski, Thomas S. ....Seaville, NJ
Zydeck, Jacqueline M. ....Chicago, IL
Zydor, Ava A. ....Pelham Manor, NY
Zydron, John E. ....Virginia Beach, VA
Zygaj, David S. ....Buffalo, NY
Zygela, Frank I. ....Phoenix, AZ
Zygelman, Corine ....Los Angeles, CA
Zygmunt, Jay A. ....Los Angeles, CA
Zygmuntowicz, Joseph A. ....Chicago, IL
Zykorie, Henry M. ....Arlington, VA
Zyla, Albert J. ....Clifton, NJ
Zyla and Schuetz ....Clifton, NJ
Zylberberg, Abraham L. ....New York, NY
Zylberberg, Marc P. ....Albany, NY
Zylberberg, Renée S. ....New York, NY
Zylberberg, Samuel M. ....New York, NY
Zylstra, Alexandria ....Kansas City, MO
Zylstra Beeksma and Waller, P.L.L.C.
Oak Harbor, WA
Zylstra, David ....Kansas City, MO
Zylstra, Gina L. ....Nashville, TN
Zylstra, James E. ....Madison, WI
Zylstra, Kendall S. ....Philadelphia, PA
Zylstra, Michael J. ....Lebanon, TN
Zylstra, Paul J. ....Denver, CO
Zylstra, Paul J., P.C. ....Denver, CO
Zylstra, Sarah A. ....Madison, WI
Zylstra, Ted D. ....Oak Harbor, WA
Zymelman, Ari S. ....Washington, DC
Zynda, Stephen R. ....Williamston, MI
Zynda, Thomas H. ....Fresno, CA
Zynda, Thomas R. ....Anadarko, OK
Zyndorf, Sol ....Toledo, OH
Zyne, Philip M. ....Miami, FL
Zyne, Saleeby & Saleh, P.A. ....Miami, FL
Zyne, Yasmine B. ....Delray Beach, FL
Zyra, Deborah A. ....Colonia, NJ
Zyra, Lawrence J. ....Schenectady, NY
Zyromski, Michelle V. ....Santa Rosa, CA
Zysik, Jeffrey C. ....Fort Lauderdale, FL
Zysk, Robert J. ....Patchogue, NY
Zyskind, Morris ....Los Angeles, CA
Zyskind, Neil W. ....Suffern, NY
Zyskowski, James C. ....Midland, MI
Zyskowski, Lori Iannotti ....Stamford, CT
Zysman, Zev B. ....Los Angeles, CA
Zysow, Aron ....Seattle, WA
Zytnick, Joel H. ....Pittsburgh, PA
Zyvoloski, Hubert J. ....St. Cloud, MN
Zywan, Darin A. ....Washington, DC
Zywiak, Louis J. ....Utica, NY
Zywica, Rebecca Leynaud ....Peru, IL
Zywiciel, Philip A. ....Yorba Linda, CA
Zywicki, Kimberly M. ....Washington, DC
Zywicki, Todd J. ....Jackson, MS
Zywicz, Margaret A. ....Oakland, CA
Zyzda, Christine A. ....Chicago, IL

SERVICES, SUPPLIERS, CONSULTANTS NATIONAL ALPHABETICAL INDEX

The Services, Suppliers, Consultants Section provides information on businesses and professionals serving the legal community. This index is listed alphabetically by category then within each category alphabetically by service name. Whether you are looking for a court reporter in your own jurisdiction or an expert witness in another state, the Services, Suppliers, Consultants Section is your direct link to legal support services.

SERVICES, SUPPLIERS, CONSULTANTS

List of Categories

Abogado - World Nations League Corporate Code
Abstractors
Accident Investigation & Reconstruction Services
Accident Investigation, Safety-Training-Environmental
Accountants
Accounting
Acoustics Consultants
Actuaries
Admiralty & Maritime Expert & Consultant
Advertising & Public Relations Firms
Aerial Photography
Affirmative Action Plan Development
Alternative Dispute Resolution
(See Arbitration & Mediation)
Americans With Disabilities Act (ADA)
Ancillary Financial/Trust Services
Appearance by Phone/Court Conferencing
Appellate Consultant
Appraisal & Valuation Services
Appraisal Services
Appraisal Services - Books
Appraisal Services - Estate & Gift Taxes
Appraisal Services - Health Care Property
Appraisal Services - Jewelry & Gems
Appraisal Services - Mines & Quarries
Appraisal Services - Personal Property
Arbitration & Mediation Services
Arbitrators - World Nations League Corporate Code
Asset Locators
Asset Management
Association Management
Attorney - Lobbyist
Attorney - World Nations League Corporate Code
Attorney Referral Services
Attorney Services
Auctioneers & Appraisers
Auctioneers & Appraisers Of Autographs, Rare Books
Audio Tape Analysis/Authentication/Voice ID
Audio/Video Services
Audiology/Hearing & Sound
Autographs, Rare Books
(See Process Servers))
Automated Records Management Software
Automobile & Office Equipment Leasing
Autopsy Service
Aviation Consultants
Aviation Medicine
Aviation-Investigation

Bail Bonds
Bank Associations & Societies
Banking - On Line Internet Access
Bankruptcy Software
Bankruptcy/Turnaround/Insolvency
Banks & Trust Companies
Bar Associations
Barter & Reciprocal Trade
Bilingual Staffing
Bodyguards
Bonds - Surety & Fidelity
Bowling Centers - Valuation & Financial Analysis
Brain Injury - Rehabilitation Services
Briefs
(See Legal Brief Printers)
Building Evaluation - Due Diligence
Building/Home Inspection
Business & Financial Information Providers
Business & Trade Organizations
Business Finance & Purchase of Receivables
Business Valuations
Business Valuations - Marine

CD-ROM Products
Captioning
Career Services
Case Management Services
Case Management Systems
Civil Rights Under Color of Law
Class Action Locators
Class Action Notice
Closed Captioning
Coins and Currency
Collection Agencies
Commercial Real Estate Services/Brokerage
Computer - Programming & Consulting
Computer Animation, Graphics & Simulation
Computer Consultants
Computer Evidence Investigation
Computer Hardware & Software
Computer Security Data & Hardware
Computer Systems Integration
Computer Software - Text Search
Computer Training
Conference/Seminar Center
Conferencing
Construction & Engineering Litigation
Construction Accidents, Safety
Construction Consultants
Construction Consultants-Construction Defects
Construction Consultants-Structural Damage
Consultant Referral Services
Contact Management
Continuing Legal Education
Copier Services
Corporate Services Companies
Corporate Supplies
Corporation Companies
Cost Recovery
Courier Services
Court House Research
Court Recording Systems
Court Reporters
Courtroom Sketching
Credit Bureaus
Crime Scene Reconstruction
Criminal Background Checks
Criminal Investigations
Criminal Records Research

DNA Forensic Testing
Debt Collection Software
Debugging
Delivery Services
Demonstrative Evidence
Demonstrative Exhibits
Deposition Summaries
Depositions - Video & Audio
Depositions on Written Questions
Dictating Equipment & Supplies
Directory/On-Line
Disability Assessment - Learning and/or Behavioral
Discovery and Document Reproduction Services
Dispute Analysis & Investigation
Diversity/Teambuilding
Divorce Financial Software
Document Delivery Systems
(See Process Servers)
Document Imaging
Document Management Services
Document Research, Retrieval & Filing
Document Scanning
Document/Data Conversion
Drug Detection

E-Business
Economic and Statistical Consulting Services
Economic and Statistical Consulting Services - Automobiles
Educational Consultant
Elder Care
Electronic Billing
Electronic Countermeasures
Electronic Packaging & Production
Employment Agencies - Permanent/Temporary
Employment Screening
Engineering & Scientific Consulting Services
Engineering - Mechanical Design & Safety
Engineering - Metallurgy/Reconstruction/Forensic Consulting

Notary Services
Nursing Consultants

Offender Monitoring Services
Office Management Services
Offshore Financial Services
Oil & Gas Engineering
Online Network/Internet Provider
Online Public Records Service
Office Products & Services

Pain Management
Paralegal Services
Parliamentarian
Patent, Trademark & Copyright Search Services
Patent/Trademark Illustrators
Personal Injury
  (See Medical Malpractice)
Personality Profiling
Personnel Consultants
Petrochemical, Refining, Gas Plant, Pipeline Engineers
Petroleum Source Identification
Photographs, Video & Map Analysis
Photography
Polygraph Examination Services
Press Releases
Printing & Reprographics
Process Servers & Document Delivery Services
Process Servers & Document Retrieval
Product Liability
Product Liability - Ergonomics
Product Safety
Project Attorney Services
Property Management
Psychological Injury - File Review & Analysis
Purchases of Medical Receivables/Probates & Trusts
Purchases of Mortgages/Trust Deeds
Purchases of Structured Settlements & Annuities

Real Estate Consultants
Real Estate Reporting
Receiverships
Record Services
Repossession

Secretarial Support
Secured Email
Securities Litigation Consulting Services
Security Consultants
Security Equipment
Security; Expert Witness
  (See also Expert Witness - Police/Security)
Seminars
Sexual Harassment - Training & Testing Programs
Skip Tracers
Solar Energy Consultants
Sports Accidents/Serious Slips & Falls
Stock & Bond Brokers Associations
Stock & Bond Brokers Internet Access
Stock Brokers - International Stock Exchange
Stock Exchanges - Direct Internet Access
Storage/Record Services
Strategic Planning
Subpoena Preparation Services
Surveying - Land
Surveys & Opinion Research

TV News Research
Technical Publications - Electrical Handbooks
Technical Service Companies
Technical, Management and Financial Experts
Teleconferencing
Temporary Attorney Services
Time Billing Software/Systems
Title & Abstract Companies
Title Insurance
Toxicology
Trademark Investigation
Training Seminars & Retreats
Transcription Services

Translation Services
  (See also Interpreters; Interpreters & Translators)
Transportation Engineering - Consulting & Forensic Services
Trial Consultants
Trial Exhibits
Trial Preparation
Trial Presentation Systems
Trust & Fiduciary Services
Trust Companies

Unemployment Hearings & Appeals Consultants
UCC Filing - Publications
UCC Search Services

Valuation Services
Video Conferencing
Video Production, Editing & Graphics
Video Tape Services
Video Teleconferencing
Video Trial Presentations
Video, Computer, Audio Equipment for Court/Trials
Violence in the Workplace
Vocational Disability Assessment
Vocational Evaluations/Life Care Planning
Vocational Rehabilitation

Weather & Climate
Web Design - Internet Consulting
White Collar Criminal/Fraud Investigation
Witness Locator
World Nations League Corporate Code - Practitioners

SERVICES, SUPPLIERS, CONSULTANTS NATIONAL ALPHABETICAL INDEX

ACCIDENT INVESTIGATION & RECONSTRUCTION SERVICES

ACCOUNTANTS

ACCOUNTING

ACOUSTICS CONSULTANTS

ADMIRALTY & MARITIME EXPERT & CONSULTANT

ADVERTISING & PUBLIC RELATIONS FIRMS

AERIAL PHOTOGRAPHY

AFFIRMATIVE ACTION PLAN DEVELOPMENT

AMERICANS WITH DISABILITIES ACT (ADA)

Name	Location	Volume
RHETA BARON KING, CRC, CDMS	Pasadena, California	(Volume 3)
CARNOW, CONIBEAR & ASSOC. LTD.	Chicago, Illinois	(Volume 8)

APPELLATE CONSULTANT

Name	Location	Volume
COUNSEL PRESS LLC	New York, New York	(Volume 13)
STEPHEN R. FELSON	Cincinnati, Ohio	(Volume 14)

APPRAISAL & VALUATION SERVICES

Name	Location	Volume
A.R.E. REAL ESTATE SERVICES	New Orleans, Louisiana	(Volume 9)
AMERICAN APPRAISAL ASSOCIATES, INC.	Milwaukee, Wisconsin	(Volume 18)
ASSET CONTROL SERVICES	Jacksonville, Florida	(Volume 6)
CALIFORNIA MARKET VALUES, INC.	Los Angeles, California	(Volume 2)
LECG, A SUBSIDIARY OF NAVIGANT CONSULTING, INC.	Berkeley, California	(Volume 2)
LOVEMAN-CURTISS, INC.	Cleveland, Ohio	(Volume 14)
NAVIGANT CONSULTING, INC.	Washington, District of Columbia	(Volume 5)
VALUATION CONSULTING GROUP A KANE REECE ASSOCIATES, INC. PRACTICE GROUP	New York, New York	(Volume 13)
VALUATION RESEARCH CORPORATION	Milwaukee, Wisconsin	(Volume 18)

APPRAISAL SERVICES

Name	Location	Volume
AMERICAN SOCIETY OF APPRAISERS	New York, New York	(Volume 13)
AUTO APPRAISAL GROUP, INC.	Charlottesville, Virginia	(Volume 18)
BRADBURY'S APPRAISALS, INC.	Phoenix, Arizona	(Volume 1)
BURGOYNE & O'NEILL REAL PROPERTY APPRAISAL COMPANY	Charlotte, North Carolina	(Volume 14)
INTEGRATED LOAN SERVICES	Hartford, Connecticut	(Volume 4)
LECG, A SUBSIDIARY OF NAVIGANT CONSULTING, INC.	Berkeley, California	(Volume 2)

APPRAISAL SERVICES - JEWELRY & GEMS

Name	Location	Volume
INTERNATIONAL GEMMOLOGICAL INSTITUTE	New York, New York	(Volume 13)

APPRAISAL SERVICES - MINES & QUARRIES

Name	Location	Volume
TREVOR R. ELLIS, CPG, CMA	Denver, Colorado	(Volume 4)
MINERAL BUSINESS APPRAISAL	Reno, Nevada	(Volume 11)

APPRAISAL SERVICES - PERSONAL PROPERTY

Name	Location	Volume
O'TOOLE-EWALD ART ASSOCIATES, INC.	New York, New York	(Volume 13)

ARBITRATION & MEDIATION SERVICES

Name	Location	Volume
ANDREOLI, JOHANSON & WOOD	Los Angeles, California	(Volume 2)
ATTORNEY MEDIATION	Los Angeles, California	(Volume 2)
	San Diego, California	(Volume 3)
	San Jose, California	(Volume 3)
	Colorado Springs, Colorado	(Volume 4)
	Denver, Colorado	(Volume 4)
	Washington, District of Columbia	(Volume 5)
	Miami, Florida	(Volume 6)
	Boston, Massachusetts	(Volume 10)
	Detroit, Michigan	(Volume 10)
	New York, New York	(Volume 13)
	Philadelphia, Pennsylvania	(Volume 15)
	Dallas, Texas	(Volume 17)
	Houston, Texas	(Volume 17)
	San Antonio, Texas	(Volume 17)
	Seattle, Washington	(Volume 18)
CYBERSETTLE.COM	New York, New York	(Volume 13)
ELLIOTT MEDIATION	Dallas, Texas	(Volume 17)
ERNEST BROWN & COMPANY	San Francisco, California	(Volume 3)
LUCAS, HORSFALL, MURPHY & PINDROH, LLP	Los Angeles, California	(Volume 2)
RESOLUTE SYSTEMS, INC.	Atlanta, Georgia	(Volume 7)
	Chicago, Illinois	(Volume 8)
	Des Moines, Iowa	(Volume 8)
	Garden City, New York	(Volume 12)
	New York, New York	(Volume 13)
	Memphis, Tennessee	(Volume 16)
	Houston, Texas	(Volume 17)
	Milwaukee, Wisconsin	(Volume 18)
ROBERT D. LEMBKE & ASSOCIATES, INC.	San Francisco, California	(Volume 3)

ASSET LOCATORS

ASSET MANAGEMENT

ATTORNEY REFERRAL SERVICES

ATTORNEY SERVICES

ATTORNEY SERVICES - Continued

Company	Location	Volume
A & E, INC. - Continued	Las Vegas, Nevada	(Volume 11)
	Manchester, New Hampshire	(Volume 11)
	New York, New York	(Volume 13)
	Cincinnati, Ohio	(Volume 14)
	Cleveland, Ohio	(Volume 14)
	Columbus, Ohio	(Volume 14)
	Tulsa, Oklahoma	(Volume 14)
	Philadelphia, Pennsylvania	(Volume 15)
	Nashville, Tennessee	(Volume 16)
	Houston, Texas	(Volume 17)
	San Antonio, Texas	(Volume 17)
	Rutland, Vermont	(Volume 18)
	Alexandria, Virginia	(Volume 18)
	Arlington, Virginia	(Volume 18)
	Milwaukee, Wisconsin	(Volume 18)
A-1 ATTORNEY SERVICE	Fresno, California	(Volume 2)
A.S.K. SERVICES, INC.	Detroit, Michigan	(Volume 10)
AAA LEGAL SERVICES	Phoenix, Arizona	(Volume 1)
AMERICAN INVESTIGATIVE SERVICES, INC.	Boston, Massachusetts	(Volume 10)
ASHENOFF AND ASSOCIATES, INC.	Miami, Florida	(Volume 6)
BORG PROCESS SERVERS INC.	Phoenix, Arizona	(Volume 1)
	Los Angeles, California	(Volume 2)
	San Francisco, California	(Volume 3)
	Washington, District of Columbia	(Volume 5)
	Miami, Florida	(Volume 6)
	Orlando, Florida	(Volume 6)
	Tampa, Florida	(Volume 6)
	Atlanta, Georgia	(Volume 7)
	Chicago, Illinois	(Volume 8)
	Baltimore, Maryland	(Volume 9)
	Boston, Massachusetts	(Volume 10)
	Detroit, Michigan	(Volume 10)
	New York, New York	(Volume 13)
	Philadelphia, Pennsylvania	(Volume 15)
	Dallas, Texas	(Volume 17)
	Houston, Texas	(Volume 17)
BRADFORD ASSOCIATES	Washington, District of Columbia	(Volume 5)
COURTFAX	New York, New York	(Volume 13)
DANTE INVESTIGATORS	Newark, New Jersey	(Volume 12)
	New York, New York	(Volume 13)
EAST END LEGAL SERVICE, INC.	New York, New York	(Volume 13)
ERDMAN ATTORNEY SERVICE	Oakland, California	(Volume 2)
EVEREADY PROCESS SERVICE, INC.	White Plains, New York	(Volume 13)
EXCALIBUR ATTORNEY SERVICE™	Santa Rosa, California	(Volume 3)
GKL CORPORATE/SEARCH, INC.	Sacramento, California	(Volume 3)
GIETZEN & ASSOCIATES, INC.	Tampa, Florida	(Volume 6)
GOODWIN ATTORNEY SERVICES, INC.	Seattle, Washington	(Volume 18)
	Spokane, Washington	(Volume 18)
	Tacoma, Washington	(Volume 18)
	Vancouver, Washington	(Volume 18)
GOTCHA LEGAL PROCESS SERVICE, INC.	Mineola, New York	(Volume 12)
	New York, New York	(Volume 13)
HANRAHAN INVESTIGATIONS	Chicago, Illinois	(Volume 8)
INTERBORO ATTORNEY SERVICE CORP.	New York, New York	(Volume 13)
JOE SOLO FILINGS	Los Angeles, California	(Volume 2)
KEATING & WALKER ATTORNEY SERVICE, INC.	New York, New York	(Volume 13)
LA SALLE PROCESS SERVERS, L.P.	Los Angeles, California	(Volume 2)
	Miami, Florida	(Volume 6)
	Chicago, Illinois	(Volume 8)
	New York, New York	(Volume 13)
	Dallas, Texas	(Volume 17)
LAWYER SUPPORT SERVICES	Brownsville, Texas	(Volume 17)
LEGAL LANGUAGE SERVICES	San Francisco, California	(Volume 3)
	Washington, District of Columbia	(Volume 5)
	Kansas City, Kansas	(Volume 9)
	Baltimore, Maryland	(Volume 9)
	Minneapolis, Minnesota	(Volume 11)
	Kansas City, Missouri	(Volume 11)
	St. Louis, Missouri	(Volume 11)
	Las Vegas, Nevada	(Volume 11)
	Mineola, New York	(Volume 12)

AUCTIONEERS & APPRAISERS

AUCTIONEERS & APPRAISERS OF AUTOGRAPHS, RARE BOOKS

AUDIO TAPE ANALYSIS/AUTHENTICATION/VOICE ID

AUDIO/VIDEO SERVICES

AUDIOLOGY/HEARING & SOUND

AUTOMATED RECORDS MANAGEMENT SOFTWARE

AVIATION CONSULTANTS

BAIL BONDS

BANKRUPTCY/TURNAROUND/INSOLVENCY

BANKS & TRUST COMPANIES

BODYGUARDS

BONDS - SURETY & FIDELITY

BOWLING CENTERS - VALUATION & FINANCIAL ANALYSIS

SANDY HANSELL & ASSOCIATES, INC.	Detroit, Michigan	(Volume 10)

BRAIN INJURY - REHABILITATION SERVICES

BEECHWOOD REHABILITATION SERVICES	Langhorne, Pennsylvania	(Volume 15)
THE BROWN SCHOOLS REHABILITATION CENTER	Austin, Texas	(Volume 17)
LAKEVIEW NEUROREHABILITATION CENTER	Concord, New Hampshire	(Volume 11)

BUILDING EVALUATION - DUE DILIGENCE

WISS, JANNEY, ELSTNER ASSOCIATES, INC.	Chicago, Illinois	(Volume 8)

BUILDING/HOME INSPECTION

KENNETH J. STOYACK, AIA, PP	Nutley, New Jersey	(Volume 12)

BUSINESS & FINANCIAL INFORMATION PROVIDERS

GLOBAL SECURITIES INFORMATION, INC. (GSI)	Washington, District of Columbia	(Volume 5)

BUSINESS FINANCE & PURCHASE OF RECEIVABLES

PALMTREE FUNDING	Seattle, Washington	(Volume 18)

BUSINESS VALUATIONS

ADAMS CAPITAL, INC.	Atlanta, Georgia	(Volume 7)
ADVANCED VALUATION ANALYTICS, LTD. BUSINESS VALUATION CONSULTANTS	Washington, District of Columbia	(Volume 5)
MIRTHA GUERRA AGUIRRE, CPA*, ABV, AM, BVAL	Miami, Florida	(Volume 6)
AMERICAN BUSINESS APPRAISERS A DIVISION OF HELM & MCCULLAR, INC.	Los Angeles, California	(Volume 2)
BIA FINANCIAL NETWORK	Washington, District of Columbia	(Volume 5)
BLACKMAN KALLICK BARTELSTEIN, LLP	Chicago, Illinois	(Volume 8)
BROWN SMITH WALLACE, LLC	St. Louis, Missouri	(Volume 11)
BUSINESS VALUATION SERVICES	San Diego, California	(Volume 3)
	San Francisco, California	(Volume 3)
	New York, New York	(Volume 13)
	Dallas, Texas	(Volume 17)
CALIFORNIA MARKET VALUES, INC.	Los Angeles, California	(Volume 2)
AMANDA CAPO'-ROSSELLO', CPA, CVA, CFE	San Juan, Puerto Rico	(Volume 18)
CENTENNIAL VALUATION GROUP, PLLC	Nashville, Tennessee	(Volume 16)
CLIFTON GUNDERSON L.L.C.	Denver, Colorado	(Volume 4)
COOPER NORMAN & CO.	Boise, Idaho	(Volume 7)
CORNERSTONE FINANCIAL MANAGEMENT, INC.	Richmond, Virginia	(Volume 18)
D.L. HEISEY & CO INCORPORATED	New York, New York	(Volume 13)
EIDE BAILLY LLP	Fargo, North Dakota	(Volume 14)
G. R. BILL COMPANY APPRAISERS	San Diego, California	(Volume 3)
HEMMING MORSE, INC.	San Francisco, California	(Volume 3)
ISRAELOFF, TRATTNER & CO. CPAS	New York, New York	(Volume 13)
HENRY L. JANUS, CPA/ABV	Boca Raton, Florida	(Volume 6)
JEROME H. LIPMAN & CO. LTD.	Chicago, Illinois	(Volume 8)
KLARIS, THOMSON & SCHROEDER, INC.	Los Angeles, California	(Volume 2)
LECG, A SUBSIDIARY OF NAVIGANT CONSULTING, INC.	Berkeley, California	(Volume 2)
LAPORTE, SEHRT, ROMIG & HAND	Metairie, Louisiana	(Volume 9)
LATTIMORE BLACK MORGAN & CAIN, P.C.	Nashville, Tennessee	(Volume 16)
LEGIER & MATERNE	New Orleans, Louisiana	(Volume 9)
LEWIS B. FREEMAN & PARTNERS, INC.	Miami, Florida	(Volume 6)
LOVEMAN-CURTISS, INC.	Cleveland, Ohio	(Volume 14)
MANAGEMENT PLANNING, INC.	Princeton, New Jersey	(Volume 12)
	New York, New York	(Volume 13)
MEARA, KING & CO.	Kansas City, Missouri	(Volume 11)
MAURICE MITCHELL, CPA/ABV, MAI	Birmingham, Alabama	(Volume 1)
MOORE STEPHENS FROST	Little Rock, Arkansas	(Volume 1)
NAVIGANT CONSULTING, INC.	Washington, District of Columbia	(Volume 5)
OFFUTT CHILDERS & PUTMAN, P.C.	Vienna, Virginia	(Volume 18)
OSTROVE, KRANTZ & OSTROVE, A P.C.	Los Angeles, California	(Volume 2)
ROBERT M. POWER, JR. CPA, CVA, ABV	Meadville, Pennsylvania	(Volume 15)
REGENT PACIFIC ®	Los Angeles, California	(Volume 2)
	San Francisco, California	(Volume 3)
	Boston, Massachusetts	(Volume 10)
	New York, New York	(Volume 13)
RICHMAN ASSOCIATES	Fairfax, Virginia	(Volume 18)
ROGOFF ERICKSON DIAMOND & WALKER, LLP	Albuquerque, New Mexico	(Volume 12)

Company	Location	Volume
SANLI PASTORE & HILL, INC.	Los Angeles, California	(Volume 2)
	Sacramento, California	(Volume 3)
	San Diego, California	(Volume 3)
	San Francisco, California	(Volume 3)
	Boca Raton, Florida	(Volume 6)
	West Palm Beach, Florida	(Volume 6)
	Chicago, Illinois	(Volume 8)
SKORHEIM & ASSOCIATES	Irvine, California	(Volume 2)
STERN STEWART & CO.	Los Angeles, California	(Volume 2)
	Washington, District of Columbia	(Volume 5)
	New York, New York	(Volume 13)
	Houston, Texas	(Volume 17)
SYNERGY VALUATIONS, LLC	New York, New York	(Volume 13)
VALUATION CONSULTING GROUP A KANE REECE ASSOCIATES, INC. PRACTICE GROUP	New York, New York	(Volume 13)
WALTER & SHUFFAIN, P.C.	Boston, Massachusetts	(Volume 10)
WHITE, ZUCKERMAN, WARSAVSKY, LUNA & WOLF	Los Angeles, California	(Volume 2)
WITHUM, SMITH & BROWN	Newark, New Jersey	(Volume 12)

CAPTIONING

Company	Location	Volume
PARADIGM REPORTING & CAPTIONING INC.	Minneapolis, Minnesota	(Volume 11)
STARKOVICH REPORTING SERVICES	Seattle, Washington	(Volume 18)
	Tacoma, Washington	(Volume 18)

CAREER SERVICES

Company	Location	Volume
LEE HECHT HARRISON, INC.	New York, New York	(Volume 13)

CASE MANAGEMENT SERVICES

Company	Location	Volume
CARE MANAGERS, INC.	Lansing, Michigan	(Volume 10)
CASE MANAGEMENT, INC.	Birmingham, Alabama	(Volume 1)
CATASTROPHIC & REHABILITATION MANAGEMENT, INC.	Grand Rapids, Michigan	(Volume 10)

CASE MANAGEMENT SYSTEMS

Company	Location	Volume
ADC LEGAL SYSTEMS, INC.	Orlando, Florida	(Volume 6)
	Raleigh, North Carolina	(Volume 14)
COMPUTER PACKAGES INC.	Washington, District of Columbia	(Volume 5)
SAGA, INC.	New York, New York	(Volume 13)

CLASS ACTION LOCATORS

Company	Location	Volume
CLASS ACTION LOCATOR SERVICE	Los Angeles, California	(Volume 2)
	San Francisco, California	(Volume 3)

CLASS ACTION NOTICE

Company	Location	Volume
HILSOFT NOTIFICATIONS ™	Philadelphia, Pennsylvania	(Volume 15)
KINSELLA COMMUNICATIONS, LTD.	Washington, District of Columbia	(Volume 5)

COLLECTION AGENCIES

Company	Location	Volume
COMMERCIAL RECOVERY ASSOCIATES, INC. DBA ASHTON, LASSITTER & SINCLAIR	New York, New York	(Volume 13)
GILLERY & COMPANY INVESTIGATIONS, INC.	Houston, Texas	(Volume 17)

COMMERCIAL REAL ESTATE SERVICES/BROKERAGE

Company	Location	Volume
JULIEN J. STUDLEY, INC.	Los Angeles, California	(Volume 2)
	Washington, District of Columbia	(Volume 5)
	Newark, New Jersey	(Volume 12)
	New York, New York	(Volume 13)

COMPUTER - PROGRAMMING & CONSULTING

Company	Location	Volume
Z-TECH CONSULTING LLC	New York, New York	(Volume 13)

COMPUTER ANIMATION, GRAPHICS & SIMULATION

Company	Location	Volume
24 HOUR COMPANY	Washington, District of Columbia	(Volume 5)
	Arlington, Virginia	(Volume 18)
BENEDICT ENGINEERING COMPANY, INC.	Tallahassee, Florida	(Volume 6)
ELEVENTH HOUR ANIMATION	Chicago, Illinois	(Volume 8)
FORDYN DIGITAL PRODUCTIONS, INC.	Phoenix, Arizona	(Volume 1)

COMPUTER ANIMATION, GRAPHICS & SIMULATION - Continued

Company	Location	Volume
FORENSIC ANALYSIS & ENGINEERING CORPORATION	Raleigh, North Carolina	(Volume 14)
GEN-TEK COMPUTER GRAPHIC COMPANY, INC.	New York, New York	(Volume 13)
LMC - A LITIGATION MEDIA CENTER	Houston, Texas	(Volume 17)
REC ENGINEERING	Murfreesboro, Tennessee	(Volume 16)
STARR LITIGATION SERVICES, INC	Phoenix, Arizona	(Volume 1)
	Los Angeles, California	(Volume 2)
	Chicago, Illinois	(Volume 8)
VIDEO COURT REPORTING, INC.	Miami, Florida	(Volume 6)
WENDELL HULL & ASSOCIATES, INC.	Las Cruces, New Mexico	(Volume 12)

COMPUTER CONSULTANTS

Company	Location	Volume
ADVANTAGELAW, INC.	Los Angeles, California	(Volume 2)
ARRIBA CONNECT	San Francisco, California	(Volume 3)
COURSE DESIGN INTERNATIONAL, INC.	New York, New York	(Volume 13)
FB&B CONSULTING GROUP, INC.	Los Angeles, California	(Volume 2)
GOODHAND COMPUTING SOLUTIONS	Rochester, New York	(Volume 12)
I.S. WORKSTATIONS	Los Angeles, California	(Volume 2)
	Oakland, California	(Volume 2)
	Sacramento, California	(Volume 3)
	San Diego, California	(Volume 3)
	San Francisco, California	(Volume 3)
	San Jose, California	(Volume 3)

COMPUTER EVIDENCE INVESTIGATION

Company	Location	Volume
INVESTIGATIVE SOLUTIONS, INC.	Atlanta, Georgia	(Volume 7)
ONTRACK DATA INTERNATIONAL, INC.	Minneapolis, Minnesota	(Volume 11)

COMPUTER HARDWARE & SOFTWARE

Company	Location	Volume
FIRST E COMMERCE	Santa Clara, California	(Volume 3)
GOLDEN OMEGA SOFTWARE	Santa Clara, California	(Volume 3)
GOODHAND COMPUTING SOLUTIONS	Rochester, New York	(Volume 12)
HOTDOCS ®	Los Angeles, California	(Volume 2)
	New York, New York	(Volume 13)
I.S. WORKSTATIONS	Los Angeles, California	(Volume 2)
	Oakland, California	(Volume 2)
	Sacramento, California	(Volume 3)
	San Diego, California	(Volume 3)
	San Francisco, California	(Volume 3)
	San Jose, California	(Volume 3)

COMPUTER SECURITY DATA & HARDWARE

Company	Location	Volume
ID-GARD ™	San Francisco, California	(Volume 3)

COMPUTER SOFTWARE - TEXT SEARCH

Company	Location	Volume
DT SOFTWARE, INC.	Washington, District of Columbia	(Volume 5)

COMPUTER SYSTEMS INTEGRATION

Company	Location	Volume
ARRIBA CONNECT	San Francisco, California	(Volume 3)
I.S. WORKSTATIONS	Los Angeles, California	(Volume 2)
	Oakland, California	(Volume 2)
	Sacramento, California	(Volume 3)
	San Diego, California	(Volume 3)
	San Francisco, California	(Volume 3)
	San Jose, California	(Volume 3)
LAN SOLUTIONS, INC.	Fairfax, Virginia	(Volume 18)

COMPUTER TRAINING

Company	Location	Volume
GOODHAND COMPUTING SOLUTIONS	Rochester, New York	(Volume 12)
SOFTWORKS CORPORATE TRAINING, LLC	Los Angeles, California	(Volume 2)

CONFERENCING

Company	Location	Volume
LYN RUBENSTEIN & ASSOCIATES	Media, Pennsylvania	(Volume 15)
	Norristown, Pennsylvania	(Volume 15)
	Philadelphia, Pennsylvania	(Volume 15)

CONSTRUCTION & ENGINEERING LITIGATION

Company	Location	Volume
ERNEST BROWN & COMPANY	San Francisco, California	(Volume 3)

CONSTRUCTION ACCIDENTS, SAFETY

CONSTRUCTION CONSULTANTS

CONSTRUCTION CONSULTANTS-CONSTRUCTION DEFECTS

CONSTRUCTION CONSULTANTS-STRUCTURAL DAMAGE

CONSULTANT REFERRAL SERVICES

CONTACT MANAGEMENT

CONTINUING LEGAL EDUCATION

COPIER SERVICES

CORPORATE SERVICES COMPANIES

CORPORATE SUPPLIES

Company	Location	Volume
CAPITAL CONNECTION, INC.	Tallahassee, Florida	(Volume 6)
TCS - LIBERTY LEGAL	Houston, Texas	(Volume 17)

CORPORATION COMPANIES

Company	Location	Volume
ACCESS INCORPORATION SERVICES, INC.	Los Angeles, California	(Volume 2)
CAPITAL CONNECTION, INC.	Tallahassee, Florida	(Volume 6)
CORPAMERICA, INC.	Dover, Delaware	(Volume 4)
CSC THE UNITED STATES CORPORATION COMPANY	Los Angeles, California	(Volume 2)
	Wilmington, Delaware	(Volume 4)
	Tallahassee, Florida	(Volume 6)
	Chicago, Illinois	(Volume 8)
	New York, New York	(Volume 13)
	Dallas, Texas	(Volume 17)
GKL CORPORATE/SEARCH, INC.	Sacramento, California	(Volume 3)
INTERCOUNTY CLEARANCE CORPORATION	New York, New York	(Volume 13)
NATIONAL DATA ACCESS CORPORATION	Columbia, South Carolina	(Volume 16)
NEVADA & OFFSHORE BUSINESS FORMATION, INC.	Carson City, Nevada	(Volume 11)
RESIDENT AGENTS OF NEVADA, INC.	Carson City, Nevada	(Volume 11)
STATE AGENT AND TRANSFER SYNDICATE, INC.	Carson City, Nevada	(Volume 11)

COST RECOVERY

Company	Location	Volume
THE INFORTEXT GROUP	Chicago, Illinois	(Volume 8)

COURIER SERVICES

Company	Location	Volume
CALIFORNIA OVERNIGHT	Los Angeles, California	(Volume 2)
	Oakland, California	(Volume 2)
	San Diego, California	(Volume 3)
	San Francisco, California	(Volume 3)
CAPITAL CONNECTION, INC.	Tallahassee, Florida	(Volume 6)
LEGAL COURIER SERVICE	Orlando, Florida	(Volume 6)
NEW JERSEY LAWYERS SERVICE	Atlantic City, New Jersey	(Volume 12)
	Cherry Hill, New Jersey	(Volume 12)
	Morristown, New Jersey	(Volume 12)
	Newark, New Jersey	(Volume 12)
	Princeton, New Jersey	(Volume 12)
	Trenton, New Jersey	(Volume 12)
SUREWAY LEGAL SERVICES	New York, New York	(Volume 13)

COURT HOUSE RESEARCH

Company	Location	Volume
PROFILE INFORMATION SERVICES	Austin, Texas	(Volume 17)

COURT REPORTERS

Company	Location	Volume
1-2-3 REPORTING SERVICE A DIVISION OF CERTIFIED REPORTING COMPANY	Los Angeles, California	(Volume 2)
	San Jose, California	(Volume 3)
	Denver, Colorado	(Volume 4)
	Chicago, Illinois	(Volume 8)
	Baltimore, Maryland	(Volume 9)
	Boston, Massachusetts	(Volume 10)
	New York, New York	(Volume 13)
	Columbus, Ohio	(Volume 14)
	Oklahoma City, Oklahoma	(Volume 14)
	Houston, Texas	(Volume 17)
1-800-FOR-DEPO-ALDERSONREPORTING	Los Angeles, California	(Volume 2)
	Palo Alto, California	(Volume 3)
	Sacramento, California	(Volume 3)
	San Diego, California	(Volume 3)
	San Francisco, California	(Volume 3)
	Denver, Colorado	(Volume 4)
	Washington, District of Columbia	(Volume 5)
	Jacksonville, Florida	(Volume 6)
	Miami, Florida	(Volume 6)
	Tampa, Florida	(Volume 6)
	Atlanta, Georgia	(Volume 7)
	Chicago, Illinois	(Volume 8)
	Annapolis, Maryland	(Volume 9)
	Baltimore, Maryland	(Volume 9)
	Bethesda, Maryland	(Volume 9)
	Columbia, Maryland	(Volume 9)

COURT REPORTERS - Continued

AA1 PARLIAMENTARY REPORTING	Los Angeles, California	(Volume 2)
	San Diego, California	(Volume 3)
	San Francisco, California	(Volume 3)
	Newark, New Jersey	(Volume 12)
	New York, New York	(Volume 13)
	Dallas, Texas	(Volume 17)
	Houston, Texas	(Volume 17)
AA1 PARLIAMENTARY REPORTING, INC.	Washington, District of Columbia	(Volume 5)
	Jacksonville, Florida	(Volume 6)
	Miami, Florida	(Volume 6)
	Orlando, Florida	(Volume 6)
	Tampa, Florida	(Volume 6)
AAA-D & D REPORTING SERVICE, INC.	St. Petersburg, Florida	(Volume 6)
	Tampa, Florida	(Volume 6)
AAAA GENE DOLGINOFF ASSOCIATES, LTD.	Kansas City, Kansas	(Volume 9)
	Overland Park, Kansas	(Volume 9)
	Kansas City, Missouri	(Volume 11)
AABBEY-WHITMAN REPORTING SERVICE	Washington, District of Columbia	(Volume 5)
	Rockville, Maryland	(Volume 9)
	Pittsburgh, Pennsylvania	(Volume 15)
AATABAY DEPOSITION REPORTING	Washington, District of Columbia	(Volume 5)
	Rockville, Maryland	(Volume 9)
ABBOTT LEGAL VIDEO SERVICES	Los Angeles, California	(Volume 2)
ABOUND VIDEO SERVICES	Orlando, Florida	(Volume 6)
ABRAMS, MAH & KAHN	Beverly Hills, California	(Volume 2)
	Irvine, California	(Volume 2)
	Long Beach, California	(Volume 2)
	Los Angeles, California	(Volume 2)
	Newport Beach, California	(Volume 2)
	Oakland, California	(Volume 2)
	Riverside, California	(Volume 3)
	San Francisco, California	(Volume 3)
	Santa Ana, California	(Volume 3)
	Torrance, California	(Volume 3)
ABSOLUTELY VERBATIM SERVICES	Bardstown, Kentucky	(Volume 9)
ACCU-BETA COURT REPORTERS & VIDEOGRAPHERS, INC.	Richmond, Virginia	(Volume 18)
ACCURATE COURT REPORTING	Nashville, Tennessee	(Volume 16)
ACCURATE COURT REPORTING SERVICES	San Antonio, Texas	(Volume 17)
ACCURATE REPORTERS, INC.	New Orleans, Louisiana	(Volume 9)
	Austin, Texas	(Volume 17)
	Dallas, Texas	(Volume 17)
	Houston, Texas	(Volume 17)
	San Antonio, Texas	(Volume 17)
ACCURATE REPORTING SERVICE OF JACKSONVILLE, INC.	Jacksonville, Florida	(Volume 6)
ACCURATE REPORTING SERVICES, L.L.C.	Colorado Springs, Colorado	(Volume 4)
	Denver, Colorado	(Volume 4)
ACCURATE REPORTING OF SHREVEPORT, INC.	Shreveport, Louisiana	(Volume 9)
ACCURATE STENOTYPE REPORTERS, INC.	Tallahassee, Florida	(Volume 6)
ACCUSCRIBE COURT REPORTING	Atlanta, Georgia	(Volume 7)
	Chattanooga, Tennessee	(Volume 16)
ACCUTRON REPORTING SERVICE, INC.	Lexington, Kentucky	(Volume 9)
ACE COURT REPORTING, INC.	Hazleton, Pennsylvania	(Volume 15)
ACE REPORTERS	Tulsa, Oklahoma	(Volume 14)
ACE REPORTING SERVICES	Cincinnati, Ohio	(Volume 14)
ACE-FEDERAL REPORTERS, INC.	Washington, District of Columbia	(Volume 5)
	Alexandria, Virginia	(Volume 18)
	Arlington, Virginia	(Volume 18)
	Fairfax, Virginia	(Volume 18)
ACEHOSTETLER & ASSOCIATES	Kansas City, Kansas	(Volume 9)
	Overland Park, Kansas	(Volume 9)
	Kansas City, Missouri	(Volume 11)
ACR ACCREDITED COURT REPORTERS	Columbus, Georgia	(Volume 7)
ACTION COURT REPORTERS	Lexington, Kentucky	(Volume 9)
ACTION REPORTING SERVICE, LLC	Syracuse, New York	(Volume 13)
ACUSCRIBE COURT REPORTERS	Austin, Texas	(Volume 17)
AD HOC REPORTING & VIDEO	Springfield, Illinois	(Volume 8)
	Louisville, Kentucky	(Volume 9)
	St. Louis, Missouri	(Volume 11)

COURT REPORTERS - Continued

Name	Location	Volume
AREA WIDE REPORTING SERVICE	Champaign, Illinois	(Volume 8)
ARIZONA REPORTING SERVICE, INC.	Phoenix, Arizona	(Volume 1)
ARKANSAS LITIGATION SUPPORT SERVICES, INC.	Little Rock, Arkansas	(Volume 1)
ARLINGTON COURT REPORTING, INC.	Arlington, Texas	(Volume 17)
	Austin, Texas	(Volume 17)
	Dallas, Texas	(Volume 17)
	Fort Worth, Texas	(Volume 17)
	San Antonio, Texas	(Volume 17)
	Tyler, Texas	(Volume 17)
ARMSTRONG & OKEY, INC.	Columbus, Ohio	(Volume 14)
ASAP COURT REPORTING, INC.	San Diego, California	(Volume 3)
ASAP COURT REPORTING / STEN-TEL, INC.	Altoona, Pennsylvania	(Volume 15)
ASK, ZENDER & TRONDSON	Minneapolis, Minnesota	(Volume 11)
	St. Paul, Minnesota	(Volume 11)
ASSOCIATE REPORTING AGENCY, INC.	Greenville, South Carolina	(Volume 16)
ASSOCIATED COURT REPORTERS	Milton, Florida	(Volume 6)
	Charlotte, North Carolina	(Volume 14)
ASSOCIATED COURT REPORTERS JUDY COMP & ASSOCIATES, INC.	Greenville, South Carolina	(Volume 16)
ASSOCIATED COURT REPORTERS, INC.	Ocala, Florida	(Volume 6)
ASSOCIATED PROFESSIONAL REPORTERS	Ogden, Utah	(Volume 17)
	Provo, Utah	(Volume 17)
	Salt Lake City, Utah	(Volume 17)
ASSOCIATED REPORTERS	Minneapolis, Minnesota	(Volume 11)
	Kennewick, Washington	(Volume 18)
ASSOCIATED REPORTERS INT'L, INC.	Albany, New York	(Volume 12)
ASSOCIATED REPORTERS OF NEVADA	Los Angeles, California	(Volume 2)
	Las Vegas, Nevada	(Volume 11)
ASSOCIATED REPORTERS, INC.	Fort Myers, Florida	(Volume 6)
ASSOCIATED REPORTING SERVICES, INC.	Lexington, Kentucky	(Volume 9)
ASSOCIATED REPORTING, INC.	Indianapolis, Indiana	(Volume 8)
ASSOCIATED STENOTYPE REPORTERS	Jacksonville, Florida	(Volume 6)
ASSOCIATED/TRI-STATE REPORTING	Lake Havasu City, Arizona	(Volume 1)
AT LAW LITIGATION SUPPORT, INC.	Irvine, California	(Volume 2)
	Long Beach, California	(Volume 2)
	Los Angeles, California	(Volume 2)
	Palm Springs, California	(Volume 3)
	San Diego, California	(Volume 3)
	Ventura, California	(Volume 3)
ATLANTIC CITY COURT REPORTING, LLC	Atlantic City, New Jersey	(Volume 12)
ATLANTIC REPORTING	Fort Pierce, Florida	(Volume 6)
	Okeechobee, Florida	(Volume 6)
	Port St. Lucie, Florida	(Volume 6)
	Stuart, Florida	(Volume 6)
	Vero Beach, Florida	(Volume 6)
ATTLESON REPORTING	Seattle, Washington	(Volume 18)
ATWOOD, JENNINGS & ASSOCIATES	El Centro, California	(Volume 2)
AUDIO-VISUAL REPORTING SERVICES, INC.	Richmond, Virginia	(Volume 18)
AUDREY PATRICK REPORTING SERVICE	San Bernardino, California	(Volume 3)
AURELIA RUFFIN & ASSOCIATES, INC.	Wilmington, North Carolina	(Volume 14)
BABER FREELANCE REPORTERS	Bradenton, Florida	(Volume 6)
BALDWIN COURT REPORTING AND LEGAL-VISUAL SERVICES	Springfield, Illinois	(Volume 8)
BALLERINI COURT REPORTERS	Los Angeles, California	(Volume 2)
	San Diego, California	(Volume 3)
BARBARA PERRY & COMPANY	Orlando, Florida	(Volume 6)
BARKLEY REPORTING SERVICE - MICAL BARKLEY	Janesville, Wisconsin	(Volume 18)
BARNES REPORTING SERVICE, INC.	Omaha, Nebraska	(Volume 11)
BARNETT & ASSOCIATES	Bloomfield Hills, Michigan	(Volume 10)
BARRISTERS' REPORTING SERVICE	Santa Ana, California	(Volume 3)
BARRON & RICH	Sacramento, California	(Volume 3)
BEACON HILL COURT REPORTING	Boston, Massachusetts	(Volume 10)
BEAN & ASSOCIATES, INC.	Albuquerque, New Mexico	(Volume 12)
	Farmington, New Mexico	(Volume 12)
	Las Cruces, New Mexico	(Volume 12)
	Santa Fe, New Mexico	(Volume 12)
BEHMKE REPORTING & VIDEO SERVICES	Oakland, California	(Volume 2)
	Palo Alto, California	(Volume 3)
	San Francisco, California	(Volume 3)
	San Jose, California	(Volume 3)
	San Mateo, California	(Volume 3)

Reporter	Location	Volume
BELL & MYERS CERTIFIED SHORTHAND REPORTER, INC.	Menlo Park, California	(Volume 2)
	Monterey, California	(Volume 2)
	Palo Alto, California	(Volume 3)
	San Francisco, California	(Volume 3)
	San Jose, California	(Volume 3)
BEMA REPORTING	San Francisco, California	(Volume 3)
BEN HYATT CERTIFIED DEPOSITION REPORTERS	Los Angeles, California	(Volume 2)
BENJAMIN REPORTING SERVICE AN ALR REPORTING COMPANY	New York, New York	(Volume 13)
BENTONVILLE COURT REPORTING	Bentonville, Arkansas	(Volume 1)
BEOVICH WALTER & FRIEND	Portland, Oregon	(Volume 15)
BERRYHILL & ASSOCIATES, INC.	St. Petersburg, Florida	(Volume 6)
	Tampa, Florida	(Volume 6)
BIGGS & FLEET, LTD.	Norfolk, Virginia	(Volume 18)
BISH & ASSOCIATES, INC.	Akron, Ohio	(Volume 14)
BLANDO REPORTING & VIDEO SERVICE, INC.	Boulder, Colorado	(Volume 4)
BLASING COURT REPORTERS, INC.	Albuquerque, New Mexico	(Volume 12)
BLAYNE & DUGAN COURT REPORTERS	Medford, Oregon	(Volume 15)
BLUE RIDGE COURT REPORTING, INC	Hillsville, Virginia	(Volume 18)
BLUM-MOORE REPORTING SERVICES, INC.	Doylestown, Pennsylvania	(Volume 15)
	Philadelphia, Pennsylvania	(Volume 15)
BOB MCCANN & ASSOCIATES	Van Nuys, California	(Volume 2)
BODENHEIMER VERBATIM REPORTING	Chapel Hill, North Carolina	(Volume 14)
	Durham, North Carolina	(Volume 14)
BOGGS & ASSOCIATES	Montgomery, Alabama	(Volume 1)
BONANZA REPORTING - RENO	Reno, Nevada	(Volume 11)
BONANZA REPORTING-LAS VEGAS	Las Vegas, Nevada	(Volume 11)
BORAK REPORTING SERVICE AN ALR REPORTING COMPANY	New York, New York	(Volume 13)
BOSTON COURT REPORTING	Boston, Massachusetts	(Volume 10)
BOWLAND REPORTING SERVICE	Fort Wayne, Indiana	(Volume 8)
BRADFORD ASSOCIATES	Washington, District of Columbia	(Volume 5)
BRAGAN REPORTING ASSOCIATES, INC.	Manchester, New Hampshire	(Volume 11)
BRANDON REPORTING SERVICE	Hartford, Connecticut	(Volume 4)
BRANNON RASPBERRY & ASSOCIATES, INC.	El Paso, Texas	(Volume 17)
BREDEMAN & ASSOCIATES, INC.	Jefferson City, Missouri	(Volume 11)
BRITTON & ASSOCIATES, INC.	Cincinnati, Ohio	(Volume 14)
	Dayton, Ohio	(Volume 14)
BROWN & TOLEU, LTD. COURT REPORTERS	Phoenix, Arizona	(Volume 1)
BROWN & WINGO COURT REPORTING	Knoxville, Tennessee	(Volume 16)
BROWN REPORTING AGENCY	Beckley, West Virginia	(Volume 18)
BROWN REPORTING, INC.	Atlanta, Georgia	(Volume 7)
	Augusta, Georgia	(Volume 7)
BRUSILOW & ASSOCIATES	Philadelphia, Pennsylvania	(Volume 15)
BRYANT & STINGLEY, INC.	Harlingen, Texas	(Volume 17)
	McAllen, Texas	(Volume 17)
BUCHANAN REPORTING SERVICE	Pocatello, Idaho	(Volume 7)
BULL & ASSOCIATES, INC.	Atlanta, Georgia	(Volume 7)
BURNHAM, HABEL & ASSOCIATES, INC.	Boise, Idaho	(Volume 7)
BUSHMAN COURT REPORTING	Little Rock, Arkansas	(Volume 1)
BUTLER & ASSOCIATES REPORTING SERVICE, INC.	Tulsa, Oklahoma	(Volume 14)
BUTTERFIELD & BUTTERFIELD	Las Vegas, Nevada	(Volume 11)
BYERS & ANDERSON, INC.	Olympia, Washington	(Volume 18)
	Seattle, Washington	(Volume 18)
	Tacoma, Washington	(Volume 18)
C & C COURT REPORTING	Eugene, Oregon	(Volume 15)
C & G	Cleveland, Ohio	(Volume 14)
CADY REPORTING SERVICE	Douglas, Georgia	(Volume 7)
CALNORTH REPORTING SERVICE	Santa Rosa, California	(Volume 3)
CALABRO REPORTING SERVICES, L.L.C.	Tucson, Arizona	(Volume 1)
CALIFORNIA SHORTHAND REPORTING	San Rafael, California	(Volume 3)
CALVERT REPORTING SERVICE	Corpus Christi, Texas	(Volume 17)
CANTON COURT REPORTES	Canton, Ohio	(Volume 14)
CAPITAL CITY REPORTING SERVICE	Harrisburg, Pennsylvania	(Volume 15)
CAPITAL REPORTING SERVICE, INC.	Fort Lauderdale, Florida	(Volume 6)
CAPITOL COURT REPORTERS, INC.	Burlington, Vermont	(Volume 18)
CAPITOL REPORTERS	Salt Lake City, Utah	(Volume 17)
CAPITOL REPORTING SERVICE, INC.	Springfield, Illinois	(Volume 8)
CARLSON & GATES, INC.	Austin, Texas	(Volume 17)
	Corpus Christi, Texas	(Volume 17)
	Dallas, Texas	(Volume 17)
	Houston, Texas	(Volume 17)
	San Antonio, Texas	(Volume 17)
MARGIE L. CARLSON, CCR #287	Las Vegas, Nevada	(Volume 11)

COURT REPORTERS - Continued

Name	Location	Volume
CARNAZZO COURT REPORTING COMPANY LTD.	Honolulu, Hawaii	(Volume 7)
CAROL D. HILL & ASSOCIATES	Cleveland, Ohio	(Volume 14)
CAROL J. THOMAS STENOTYPE REPORTING SERVICES, INC.	Washington, District of Columbia	(Volume 5)
	Baltimore, Maryland	(Volume 9)
	Bethesda, Maryland	(Volume 9)
	Chevy Chase, Maryland	(Volume 9)
	Rockville, Maryland	(Volume 9)
	Silver Spring, Maryland	(Volume 9)
	Alexandria, Virginia	(Volume 18)
	Arlington, Virginia	(Volume 18)
	Fairfax, Virginia	(Volume 18)
	Falls Church, Virginia	(Volume 18)
	Fredericksburg, Virginia	(Volume 18)
	Manassas, Virginia	(Volume 18)
	McLean, Virginia	(Volume 18)
	Reston, Virginia	(Volume 18)
	Richmond, Virginia	(Volume 18)
	Springfield, Virginia	(Volume 18)
	Tysons Corner, Virginia	(Volume 18)
	Vienna, Virginia	(Volume 18)
CAROLYN F. ENGEL & ASSOCIATES	Brooksville, Florida	(Volume 6)
CASCADE COURT REPORTERS	Bend, Oregon	(Volume 15)
CASPER COURT REPORTING	Green Bay, Wisconsin	(Volume 18)
CASSEL MEYER COURT REPORTING	Sioux City, Iowa	(Volume 8)
	Vermillion, South Dakota	(Volume 16)
CASTILLO & CASTILLO	Miami, Florida	(Volume 6)
CATHERINE TEACH REPORTING	San Francisco, California	(Volume 3)
	Washington, District of Columbia	(Volume 5)
	New York, New York	(Volume 13)
	Eugene, Oregon	(Volume 15)
	Portland, Oregon	(Volume 15)
	Salem, Oregon	(Volume 15)
	Vancouver, Washington	(Volume 18)
CATUOGNO COURT REPORTING SERVICE, INC.	Boston, Massachusetts	(Volume 10)
	Springfield, Massachusetts	(Volume 10)
	Worcester, Massachusetts	(Volume 10)
CEFARATTI GROUP	Akron, Ohio	(Volume 14)
	Cleveland, Ohio	(Volume 14)
CEN-TEX REPORTING SERVICE	Waco, Texas	(Volume 17)
CENTER CITY REPORTING, INC.	Philadelphia, Pennsylvania	(Volume 15)
CENTRAL FLORIDA REPORTERS, INC.	Orlando, Florida	(Volume 6)
	Tampa, Florida	(Volume 6)
CENTRAL REPORTERS ASSOCIATED	Chicago, Illinois	(Volume 8)
CENTRAL VALLEY REPORTERS	Fresno, California	(Volume 2)
CERTIFIED COURT REPORTERS, INC.	Jacksonville, Florida	(Volume 6)
	Miami, Florida	(Volume 6)
	Orlando, Florida	(Volume 6)
	Tampa, Florida	(Volume 6)
CERTIFIED REPORTING & VIDEO SERVICE	Corpus Christi, Texas	(Volume 17)
CHANDLER AND HALASZ, INC.	Richmond, Virginia	(Volume 18)
CHARLOTTE COURT REPORTING, INC.	Charlotte, North Carolina	(Volume 14)
CHILDERS & SHELNUTT, INC.	Atlanta, Georgia	(Volume 7)
CHISHOLM TRAIL REPORTERS	Enid, Oklahoma	(Volume 14)
CHRISTINE FELTS & ASSOCIATES	Ann Arbor, Michigan	(Volume 10)
	Detroit, Michigan	(Volume 10)
	Flint, Michigan	(Volume 10)
	Kalamazoo, Michigan	(Volume 10)
	Lansing, Michigan	(Volume 10)
	Troy, Michigan	(Volume 10)
CHRISTINE HAWTHORNE COURT REPORTING	Dade City, Florida	(Volume 6)
CIN-TEL CORPORATION	Cincinnati, Ohio	(Volume 14)
CIPOLLONI & ASSOCIATES	Atlantic City, New Jersey	(Volume 12)
	Camden, New Jersey	(Volume 12)
CITY REPORTERS	Oklahoma City, Oklahoma	(Volume 14)
CLARK CERTIFIED COURT REPORTERS	Phoenix, Arizona	(Volume 1)
CLARK REPORTING	Berkeley, California	(Volume 2)
CLARK REPORTING SERVICE, INC.	St. Petersburg, Florida	(Volume 6)
	Tampa, Florida	(Volume 6)
CLASSIC REPORTING SERVICE	Toledo, Ohio	(Volume 14)
CLAUDE JOINER REPORTING SERVICE, INC.	Macon, Georgia	(Volume 7)
CLAY LEMASTER, INC.	Amarillo, Texas	(Volume 17)

COURT REPORTERS - Continued

Name	Location	Volume
COURT REPORTING ASSOCIATES	Dothan, Alabama	(Volume 1)
	Jacksonville, Florida	(Volume 6)
COURT REPORTING ASSOCIATES, INC.	Macon, Georgia	(Volume 7)
COURT REPORTING CONCEPTS, INC.	Baltimore, Maryland	(Volume 9)
A COURT REPORTING SERVICE	Seattle, Washington	(Volume 18)
	Spokane, Washington	(Volume 18)
COURT REPORTING SERVICES	Durham, North Carolina	(Volume 14)
	Raleigh, North Carolina	(Volume 14)
	Winston-Salem, North Carolina	(Volume 14)
COURT REPORTING SERVICES OF CHARLOTTE, INC.	Charlotte, North Carolina	(Volume 14)
COURT REPORTING SERVICES, INC.	Newark, New Jersey	(Volume 12)
CRANE-SNEAD & ASSOCIATES, INC.	Charlottesville, Virginia	(Volume 18)
	Fredericksburg, Virginia	(Volume 18)
	Richmond, Virginia	(Volume 18)
CREEL COURT REPORTING, INC.	Columbia, South Carolina	(Volume 16)
TOM CRITES & ASSOCIATES INTERNATIONAL, INC.	Savannah, Georgia	(Volume 7)
	Hilton Head Island, South Carolina	(Volume 16)
CROPPER & ASSOCIATES, LTD.	Phoenix, Arizona	(Volume 1)
CSR ASSOCIATES OF NEVADA	Los Angeles, California	(Volume 2)
CUMBRE COURT REPORTING, INC.	Santa Fe, New Mexico	(Volume 12)
THE CUNNINGHAM GROUP, INC.	Hartford, Connecticut	(Volume 4)
	Stamford, Connecticut	(Volume 4)
CURREN & LANDRIEU, INC.	Baton Rouge, Louisiana	(Volume 9)
	Lafayette, Louisiana	(Volume 9)
	New Orleans, Louisiana	(Volume 9)
	Gulfport, Mississippi	(Volume 11)
CURTIS D. RUFF AND ASSOCIATES	Lubbock, Texas	(Volume 17)
CZERENDA COURT REPORTING	Binghamton, New York	(Volume 12)
D & D REPORTING SERVICE, INC.	Clearwater, Florida	(Volume 6)
DALCO REPORTING, INC.	White Plains, New York	(Volume 13)
JAMES A. DALE, JR.	Bowling Green, Kentucky	(Volume 9)
DALLAS REPORTING CERTIFIED COURT REPORTERS	Charlotte, North Carolina	(Volume 14)
DE SCRIBE REPORTING, INC.	Southfield, Michigan	(Volume 10)
DEMICHELLE DEPOSITION REPORTERS	Fairfield, California	(Volume 2)
	Napa, California	(Volume 2)
	Sacramento, California	(Volume 3)
	Santa Rosa, California	(Volume 3)
DEPAOLO - CROSBY REPORTING SERVICES, INC.	Buffalo, New York	(Volume 12)
DEBORAH TODD COURT REPORTING	Kingsport, Tennessee	(Volume 16)
DENNIS A. PARISE & ASSOCIATES	Cleveland, Ohio	(Volume 14)
DENSLOW, GRYCZ & ASSOCIATES	Dayton, Ohio	(Volume 14)
DEPOMAX REPORTING SERVICES, INC	Provo, Utah	(Volume 17)
	Salt Lake City, Utah	(Volume 17)
DEPOSITION SERVICES, INC.	Washington, District of Columbia	(Volume 5)
	Bethesda, Maryland	(Volume 9)
	Frederick, Maryland	(Volume 9)
	Rockville, Maryland	(Volume 9)
DEPOSITION SERVICES, LTD	Anchorage, Alaska	(Volume 1)
	Kodiak, Alaska	(Volume 1)
DEPOSITIONS BY THE BUNCH	Kokomo, Indiana	(Volume 8)
DEPOSITIONS PLUS	San Antonio, Texas	(Volume 17)
DEPOSITIONS UNLIMITED	Galveston, Texas	(Volume 17)
DICHARIA & ASSOCIATES COURT REPORTING, INC.	Fort Myers, Florida	(Volume 6)
	Naples, Florida	(Volume 6)
	Port Charlotte, Florida	(Volume 6)
DIANE HROMEK'S COURT REPORTERS, INC.	Chicago, Illinois	(Volume 8)
DISCOVERY REPORTING, INC.	Annapolis, Maryland	(Volume 9)
DOERNER & GOLDBERG	Washington, District of Columbia	(Volume 5)
	Cherry Hill, New Jersey	(Volume 12)
	Morristown, New Jersey	(Volume 12)
	New Brunswick, New Jersey	(Volume 12)
	Newark, New Jersey	(Volume 12)
	Princeton, New Jersey	(Volume 12)
	Red Bank, New Jersey	(Volume 12)
	Roseland, New Jersey	(Volume 12)
	Trenton, New Jersey	(Volume 12)
	Philadelphia, Pennsylvania	(Volume 15)
DOLORES STEWART & ASSOCIATES, INC.	Fort Worth, Texas	(Volume 17)
DONALD COURT REPORTING, INC.	Fayetteville, Arkansas	(Volume 1)
DONOVAN COURT REPORTING, INC.	Fort Myers, Florida	(Volume 6)
	Naples, Florida	(Volume 6)
DONOVAN REPORTING, P.C.	Atlanta, Georgia	(Volume 7)
	Marietta, Georgia	(Volume 7)

COURT REPORTERS - Continued

Name	Location	Volume
FIVECOAT AND WITH	San Diego, California	(Volume 3)
DONNA JEAN FLOOK	Dayton, Ohio	(Volume 14)
FLYNN REPORTING ASSOCIATES	Worcester, Massachusetts	(Volume 10)
FOR THE RECORD, INC.	Washington, District of Columbia	(Volume 5)
	Baltimore, Maryland	(Volume 9)
	Waldorf, Maryland	(Volume 9)
FOSHEE & TURNER	Birmingham, Alabama	(Volume 1)
FREELANCE REPORTERS, INC.	Oklahoma City, Oklahoma	(Volume 14)
FULTON-BELANGER & ASSOCIATES	Louisville, Kentucky	(Volume 9)
GABRIEL & SWEENEY COURT REPORTING	Boston, Massachusetts	(Volume 10)
GAF LEGAL SERVICES, INC.	Atlantic City, New Jersey	(Volume 12)
	Cherry Hill, New Jersey	(Volume 12)
	Newark, New Jersey	(Volume 12)
	Roseland, New Jersey	(Volume 12)
GAINESVILLE REPORTERS	Gainesville, Florida	(Volume 6)
GAROUTTE'S	Stockton, California	(Volume 3)
GARRETT REPORTING SERVICE	Charleston, West Virginia	(Volume 18)
GAUDET, KAISER & PEPPER, L.L.C.	New Orleans, Louisiana	(Volume 9)
GEIGER & LORIA REPORTING SERVICE	Harrisburg, Pennsylvania	(Volume 15)
GEORGIA WINEGEART & ASSOCIATES	Jacksonville, Florida	(Volume 6)
GERALDINE KERR & ASSOCIATES	Sanford, Florida	(Volume 6)
GERGER-MORETTI REPORTING	Kalamazoo, Michigan	(Volume 10)
GIBSON COURT REPORTING	Knoxville, Tennessee	(Volume 16)
GLENDA FULLER & ASSOCIATES	Austin, Texas	(Volume 17)
GOLDING COURT REPORTERS	Los Angeles, California	(Volume 2)
GORE & PERRY REPORTING COMPANY	Alton, Illinois	(Volume 8)
	Belleville, Illinois	(Volume 8)
	Edwardsville, Illinois	(Volume 8)
	Clayton, Missouri	(Volume 11)
	St. Charles, Missouri	(Volume 11)
	St. Louis, Missouri	(Volume 11)
GORE BROTHERS REPORTING & VIDEO COMPANY, INC.	Baltimore, Maryland	(Volume 9)
GORE REPORTING COMPANY	Washington, District of Columbia	(Volume 5)
GRAMANN REPORTING, LTD.	Milwaukee, Wisconsin	(Volume 18)
GRANT & MAYBRIER, LLC	Louisville, Kentucky	(Volume 9)
GREAT LAKES SHORTHAND	Washington, District of Columbia	(Volume 5)
	Chicago, Illinois	(Volume 8)
	Ann Arbor, Michigan	(Volume 10)
	Benton Harbor, Michigan	(Volume 10)
	Detroit, Michigan	(Volume 10)
	Grand Rapids, Michigan	(Volume 10)
	Kalamazoo, Michigan	(Volume 10)
	Lansing, Michigan	(Volume 10)
	Muskegon, Michigan	(Volume 10)
	St. Joseph, Michigan	(Volume 10)
	Traverse City, Michigan	(Volume 10)
GREENHOUSE REPORTING INC.	New York, New York	(Volume 13)
GROSHONG-QUAINTANCE	Tacoma, Washington	(Volume 18)
GULF BAY REPORTING	Panama City, Florida	(Volume 6)
GULFCOAST REPORTING INC.	Clearwater, Florida	(Volume 6)
HABEAS VIDEAS	Los Angeles, California	(Volume 2)
HAHN AND BOWERSOCK	Irvine, California	(Volume 2)
	Long Beach, California	(Volume 2)
	Los Angeles, California	(Volume 2)
	San Bernardino, California	(Volume 3)
	San Diego, California	(Volume 3)
	Ventura, California	(Volume 3)
ALICE N. HALBERT, CSR, RPR	San Francisco, California	(Volume 3)
HALLOCK REPORTING SERVICES	Lutherville, Maryland	(Volume 9)
HANDY, CHUPPE & SOERGEL LLC	Louisville, Kentucky	(Volume 9)
HANSEN REPORTING SERVICE	Sebring, Florida	(Volume 6)
HANSON/RENAISSANCE COURT REPORTERS	Dearborn, Michigan	(Volume 10)
	Detroit, Michigan	(Volume 10)
	Southfield, Michigan	(Volume 10)
HARBORTOWN COURT REPORTERS	Southfield, Michigan	(Volume 10)
HARRY A. CANNON, INC.	San Francisco, California	(Volume 3)
HARTSOCK & CERVONE	St. Petersburg, Florida	(Volume 6)
	Tampa, Florida	(Volume 6)
HEARTLAND COURT REPORTERS	Fairbanks, Alaska	(Volume 1)
HENDERSON & ASSOCIATES COURT REPORTERS, INC.	Mobile, Alabama	(Volume 1)
HENDRIX REPORTING SERVICE	Little Rock, Arkansas	(Volume 1)

COURT REPORTERS - Continued

Reporter	Location	Volume
JAY E. SUDDRETH & ASSOCIATES, INC.	Overland Park, Kansas	(Volume 9)
	Clayton, Missouri	(Volume 11)
	Jefferson City, Missouri	(Volume 11)
	Kansas City, Missouri	(Volume 11)
	Springfield, Missouri	(Volume 11)
	St. Charles, Missouri	(Volume 11)
	St. Louis, Missouri	(Volume 11)
JEFFRIES COURT REPORTING, INC.	Missoula, Montana	(Volume 11)
JOHN E. CONNOR & ASSOCIATES, INC.	Indianapolis, Indiana	(Volume 8)
JOHN J. PROUT & ASSOCIATES, INC.	Florham Park, New Jersey	(Volume 12)
	Morristown, New Jersey	(Volume 12)
JOHNS, STEPHENSON & DUNNE ADVANTAGE COURT REPORTERS	Gainesville, Florida	(Volume 6)
JOHNSON & ASSOCIATES	Tampa, Florida	(Volume 6)
JOHNSON, MOORE, HENDERSON & KONSTEN	Denver, Colorado	(Volume 4)
	Portland, Oregon	(Volume 15)
RONALD E. JOHNSON, RMR	Washington, District of Columbia	(Volume 5)
JONES FRITZ & SHEEHAN	Boston, Massachusetts	(Volume 10)
J.V. KILLINGSWORTH & ASSOCIATES	Redding, California	(Volume 3)
KANABAY COURT REPORTERS	Bradenton, Florida	(Volume 6)
	Clearwater, Florida	(Volume 6)
	Orlando, Florida	(Volume 6)
	Sarasota, Florida	(Volume 6)
	St. Petersburg, Florida	(Volume 6)
	Tampa, Florida	(Volume 6)
KARASCH & ASSOCIATES	Norristown, Pennsylvania	(Volume 15)
KARYN ABBOTT & ASSOCIATES	Beverly Hills, California	(Volume 2)
	Los Angeles, California	(Volume 2)
	Santa Ana, California	(Volume 3)
KATHY TOWNSEND COURT REPORTERS	Albuquerque, New Mexico	(Volume 12)
KAY MCGOVERN & ASSOCIATES	Raleigh, North Carolina	(Volume 14)
KEMPFER REPORTING COMPANY, INC.	Milwaukee, Wisconsin	(Volume 18)
KEN OWEN & ASSOCIATES	Austin, Texas	(Volume 17)
KING REPORTING SERVICE, INC.	Melbourne, Florida	(Volume 6)
KINSELLA, HARTIGAN & KELZER, INC.	Minneapolis, Minnesota	(Volume 11)
KNIPES-COHEN ASSOCIATES, INC.	Cherry Hill, New Jersey	(Volume 12)
	Norristown, Pennsylvania	(Volume 15)
	Philadelphia, Pennsylvania	(Volume 15)
KOOL & NYGREN, INC.	Cedar Rapids, Iowa	(Volume 8)
KRON ASSOCIATES	Anchorage, Alaska	(Volume 1)
K-VIDEO, INC.	Phoenix, Arizona	(Volume 1)
LACEY SHORTHAND REPORTING CORPORATION AND LACEY VIDEO SERVICES	Los Angeles, California	(Volume 2)
LANDI COURT REPORTERS	San Jose, California	(Volume 3)
LANGSTAFF REPORTING SERVICE	Fairfield, California	(Volume 2)
LATIMER REPORTING	Lincoln, Nebraska	(Volume 11)
LAUNIUS REPORTING SERVICE	Rockford, Illinois	(Volume 8)
LAUREN BIENENSTOCK & ASSOCIATES	Ann Arbor, Michigan	(Volume 10)
	Detroit, Michigan	(Volume 10)
	Flint, Michigan	(Volume 10)
	Lansing, Michigan	(Volume 10)
	Southfield, Michigan	(Volume 10)
	Troy, Michigan	(Volume 10)
LAURIE WEBB & ASSOCIATES	Las Vegas, Nevada	(Volume 11)
LAWS REPORTING, INC.	Fort Lauderdale, Florida	(Volume 6)
	Jacksonville, Florida	(Volume 6)
	Miami, Florida	(Volume 6)
	Orlando, Florida	(Volume 6)
	West Palm Beach, Florida	(Volume 6)
LEE BERGER & ASSOCIATES, INC.	Portland, Oregon	(Volume 15)
LEGAL REPORTING SERVICES	Greensboro, North Carolina	(Volume 14)
LEITCH, TAYLOR & BAKER, INC.	Pensacola, Florida	(Volume 6)
LITICORP	Chicago, Illinois	(Volume 8)
LNS COURT REPORTING	Portland, Oregon	(Volume 15)
	Salem, Oregon	(Volume 15)
	Vancouver, Washington	(Volume 18)
LOCKLEAR REPORTING SERVICE, INC.	Philadelphia, Pennsylvania	(Volume 15)
LOUINE M. PERNICE & ASSOCIATES	West Palm Beach, Florida	(Volume 6)
LOWER ALABAMA COURT REPORTING	Mobile, Alabama	(Volume 1)
LUFKIN COURT REPORTING SERVICE	Lufkin, Texas	(Volume 17)
LYN RUBENSTEIN & ASSOCIATES	Media, Pennsylvania	(Volume 15)
	Norristown, Pennsylvania	(Volume 15)
	Philadelphia, Pennsylvania	(Volume 15)

COURT REPORTERS - Continued

Firm	Location	Volume
MERRILL & ASSOCIATES, INC.	Detroit, Michigan	(Volume 10)
	Southfield, Michigan	(Volume 10)
METRO COURT REPORTING, INC.	St. Louis, Missouri	(Volume 11)
METRO REPORTERS INC.	Washington, District of Columbia	(Volume 5)
	Alexandria, Virginia	(Volume 18)
	Fairfax, Virginia	(Volume 18)
METROPOLITAN REPORTING, INC.	Lansing, Michigan	(Volume 10)
METZGER COURT REPORTING, INC.	Punta Gorda, Florida	(Volume 6)
MIDWEST PROFESSIONAL REPORTING, INC.	Rockford, Illinois	(Volume 8)
MIDWEST REPORTING	South Bend, Indiana	(Volume 8)
MIKE MOBLEY REPORTING	Cincinnati, Ohio	(Volume 14)
	Cleveland, Ohio	(Volume 14)
	Dayton, Ohio	(Volume 14)
MILLER REPORTING SERVICES	Charlotte, North Carolina	(Volume 14)
MILLERPARKER	Dallas, Texas	(Volume 17)
MILLS & LESSARD, INC.	Seattle, Washington	(Volume 18)
MJW COURT REPORTING SERVICES	Burlington, Iowa	(Volume 8)
M.O.A. DEPOSITION REPORTERS	Sacramento, California	(Volume 3)
	Yuba City, California	(Volume 3)
MONTANA REPORTING SERVICE, INC.	Clearwater, Florida	(Volume 6)
	Fort Myers, Florida	(Volume 6)
	Orlando, Florida	(Volume 6)
	Sarasota, Florida	(Volume 6)
	Tampa, Florida	(Volume 6)
MONTEREY PENINSULA COURT REPORTERS INC.	Monterey, California	(Volume 2)
NAGY-BAKER COURT REPORTING, INC.	Warren, Ohio	(Volume 14)
	Youngstown, Ohio	(Volume 14)
NARUP, VOUVAKIS, INC.	Daytona Beach, Florida	(Volume 6)
	Orlando, Florida	(Volume 6)
NATIONAL COURT REPORTING INC.	Southfield, Michigan	(Volume 10)
NATIONAL COURT REPORTING SERVICES	Birmingham, Alabama	(Volume 1)
NATIONAL REPORTING SERVICE	Asheville, North Carolina	(Volume 14)
NEAL R. GROSS AND CO. INC.	Washington, District of Columbia	(Volume 5)
NETWORK REPORTING CORPORATION	Detroit, Michigan	(Volume 10)
NEW YORK LEGAL VIDEO SERVICES	Washington, District of Columbia	(Volume 5)
NEWBERRY & COMPANY	Atlanta, Georgia	(Volume 7)
NICOLE CARTER & ASSOCIATES/BEVERLY HILLS DEPOSITION REPORTERS	Beverly Hills, California	(Volume 2)
	Los Angeles, California	(Volume 2)
	New York, New York	(Volume 13)
NIZIANKIEWICZ & MILLER REPORTING SERVICES	Bridgeport, Connecticut	(Volume 4)
	Hartford, Connecticut	(Volume 4)
	New Haven, Connecticut	(Volume 4)
	Stamford, Connecticut	(Volume 4)
	Waterbury, Connecticut	(Volume 4)
NOLEN-MARTINA REPORTING SERVICES	Fort Myers, Florida	(Volume 6)
NORTH SUBURBAN REPORTING & LEGAL MEDIA, INC.	Chicago, Illinois	(Volume 8)
NORTHERN CALIFORNIA COURT REPORTERS	Sacramento, California	(Volume 3)
NORTHWESTERN COURT REPORTERS	Eau Claire, Wisconsin	(Volume 18)
O'BRIEN & BAILS	Battle Creek, Michigan	(Volume 10)
	Detroit, Michigan	(Volume 10)
	Grand Rapids, Michigan	(Volume 10)
	Kalamazoo, Michigan	(Volume 10)
	Lansing, Michigan	(Volume 10)
O'BRIEN REPORTING SERVICES, INC.	Rutland, Vermont	(Volume 18)
O'HARA COURT REPORTING	Boston, Massachusetts	(Volume 10)
O'HARE REPORTING SERVICE, INC.	Chicago, Illinois	(Volume 8)
	Des Plaines, Illinois	(Volume 8)
	Northbrook, Illinois	(Volume 8)
	Park Ridge, Illinois	(Volume 8)
	Schaumburg, Illinois	(Volume 8)
OAKLAND COURT REPORTING & LEGAL VIDEO	Bloomfield Hills, Michigan	(Volume 10)
OBUJEN & MCCUTCHEON	Palo Alto, California	(Volume 3)
OHIO VALLEY REPORTING SERVICE	Owensboro, Kentucky	(Volume 9)
ON THE RECORD REPORTING & VIDEO	Birmingham, Michigan	(Volume 10)
	Dearborn, Michigan	(Volume 10)
	Southfield, Michigan	(Volume 10)
OPPENHEIMER REPORTING SERVICES	Austin, Texas	(Volume 17)
ORANGE REPORTING, INC.	Orlando, Florida	(Volume 6)
AN OVERNITE COURT REPORTING SERVICE	Washington, District of Columbia	(Volume 5)
PACE REPORTING SERVICE	Raleigh, North Carolina	(Volume 14)
PACIFIC REPORTING SERVICES UNLIMITED, INC.	Honolulu, Hawaii	(Volume 7)

COURT REPORTERS - Continued

Reporter	Location	Volume
RELIABLE REPORTING, INC.	Lakeland, Florida	(Volume 6)
RENNILLO REPORTING SERVICES	Akron, Ohio	(Volume 14)
	Cleveland, Ohio	(Volume 14)
REPORTERS COOPERATIVE, INC.	Phoenix, Arizona	(Volume 1)
	Tucson, Arizona	(Volume 1)
	Anaheim, California	(Volume 2)
	Bakersfield, California	(Volume 2)
	Los Angeles, California	(Volume 2)
	Riverside, California	(Volume 3)
	Sacramento, California	(Volume 3)
	San Bernardino, California	(Volume 3)
	San Diego, California	(Volume 3)
	San Francisco, California	(Volume 3)
	San Jose, California	(Volume 3)
	Aurora, Colorado	(Volume 4)
	Boulder, Colorado	(Volume 4)
	Colorado Springs, Colorado	(Volume 4)
	Denver, Colorado	(Volume 4)
	Hartford, Connecticut	(Volume 4)
	Norwalk, Connecticut	(Volume 4)
	Stamford, Connecticut	(Volume 4)
	Wilmington, Delaware	(Volume 4)
	Washington, District of Columbia	(Volume 5)
	Boca Raton, Florida	(Volume 6)
	Fort Lauderdale, Florida	(Volume 6)
	Lakeland, Florida	(Volume 6)
	Melbourne, Florida	(Volume 6)
	Miami, Florida	(Volume 6)
	Orlando, Florida	(Volume 6)
	Sarasota, Florida	(Volume 6)
	Tampa, Florida	(Volume 6)
	Winter Haven, Florida	(Volume 6)
	Atlanta, Georgia	(Volume 7)
	Brunswick, Georgia	(Volume 7)
	Savannah, Georgia	(Volume 7)
	Boise, Idaho	(Volume 7)
	Idaho Falls, Idaho	(Volume 7)
	Chicago, Illinois	(Volume 8)
	Peoria, Illinois	(Volume 8)
	Rockford, Illinois	(Volume 8)
	Kansas City, Kansas	(Volume 9)
	Wichita, Kansas	(Volume 9)
	Lexington, Kentucky	(Volume 9)
	Louisville, Kentucky	(Volume 9)
	Annapolis, Maryland	(Volume 9)
	Baltimore, Maryland	(Volume 9)
	Rockville, Maryland	(Volume 9)
	Boston, Massachusetts	(Volume 10)
	Cambridge, Massachusetts	(Volume 10)
	Detroit, Michigan	(Volume 10)
	East Lansing, Michigan	(Volume 10)
	Grand Rapids, Michigan	(Volume 10)
	Kalamazoo, Michigan	(Volume 10)
	Minneapolis, Minnesota	(Volume 11)
	St. Paul, Minnesota	(Volume 11)
	St. Louis, Missouri	(Volume 11)
	Billings, Montana	(Volume 11)
	Omaha, Nebraska	(Volume 11)
	Las Vegas, Nevada	(Volume 11)
	Reno, Nevada	(Volume 11)
	Manchester, New Hampshire	(Volume 11)
	Elizabeth, New Jersey	(Volume 12)
	Newark, New Jersey	(Volume 12)
	Roseland, New Jersey	(Volume 12)
	Albuquerque, New Mexico	(Volume 12)
	Santa Fe, New Mexico	(Volume 12)
	Buffalo, New York	(Volume 12)
	Mineola, New York	(Volume 12)
	New York, New York	(Volume 13)
	Rochester, New York	(Volume 12)
	Charlotte, North Carolina	(Volume 14)
	Durham, North Carolina	(Volume 14)
	Bismarck, North Dakota	(Volume 14)

Firm	Location	Volume
REPORTERS COOPERATIVE, INC. - Continued	Akron, Ohio	(Volume 14)
	Cincinnati, Ohio	(Volume 14)
	Cleveland, Ohio	(Volume 14)
	Columbus, Ohio	(Volume 14)
	Dayton, Ohio	(Volume 14)
	Oklahoma City, Oklahoma	(Volume 14)
	Portland, Oregon	(Volume 15)
	Salem, Oregon	(Volume 15)
	Philadelphia, Pennsylvania	(Volume 15)
	Pittsburgh, Pennsylvania	(Volume 15)
	Providence, Rhode Island	(Volume 16)
	Charleston, South Carolina	(Volume 16)
	Memphis, Tennessee	(Volume 16)
	Nashville, Tennessee	(Volume 16)
	Austin, Texas	(Volume 17)
	Dallas, Texas	(Volume 17)
	Fort Worth, Texas	(Volume 17)
	Galveston, Texas	(Volume 17)
	Houston, Texas	(Volume 17)
	San Antonio, Texas	(Volume 17)
	Provo, Utah	(Volume 17)
	Salt Lake City, Utah	(Volume 17)
	Norfolk, Virginia	(Volume 18)
	Richmond, Virginia	(Volume 18)
	Seattle, Washington	(Volume 18)
	Spokane, Washington	(Volume 18)
	Tacoma, Washington	(Volume 18)
	Vancouver, Washington	(Volume 18)
	Charleston, West Virginia	(Volume 18)
	Madison, Wisconsin	(Volume 18)
	Milwaukee, Wisconsin	(Volume 18)
	Jackson, Wyoming	(Volume 18)
THE REPORTERS GROUP, INC.	Tampa, Florida	(Volume 6)
RICE REPORTING AGENCY	Rochester, Minnesota	(Volume 11)
RICHARD E. PEPPEY REPORTING CO. INC.	Milwaukee, Wisconsin	(Volume 18)
RICHARD LEE REPORTING	Tampa, Florida	(Volume 6)
RICHARDSON REPORTING SERVICE	Denver, Colorado	(Volume 4)
RIDENOUR REPORTING	Sarasota, Florida	(Volume 6)
RIGLER & O'NEILL COURT REPORTERS, INC.	Washington, District of Columbia	(Volume 5)
	Annapolis, Maryland	(Volume 9)
	Baltimore, Maryland	(Volume 9)
	Towson, Maryland	(Volume 9)
	Philadelphia, Pennsylvania	(Volume 15)
RIPKA, BOROSKI & ASSOCIATES	Flint, Michigan	(Volume 10)
	Saginaw, Michigan	(Volume 10)
ROBERT A. DEMPSTER & ASSOCIATES	Clearwater, Florida	(Volume 6)
	St. Petersburg, Florida	(Volume 6)
	Tampa, Florida	(Volume 6)
ROBERT BARNES ASSOCIATES	San Francisco, California	(Volume 3)
ROBERT H. LANGE CO. INC.	Boston, Massachusetts	(Volume 10)
ROBERTS & ASSOCIATES	Kansas City, Missouri	(Volume 11)
ROBERTS & KIDWELL	Charlotte, North Carolina	(Volume 14)
ROCKLAND & ORANGE REPORTING	New City, New York	(Volume 12)
RON FLEMING VIDEO	Orlando, Florida	(Volume 6)
ROSENBERG & ASSOCIATES	Jersey City, New Jersey	(Volume 12)
	Newark, New Jersey	(Volume 12)
	Princeton, New Jersey	(Volume 12)
	Roseland, New Jersey	(Volume 12)
	Trenton, New Jersey	(Volume 12)
ROSS REPORTING SERVICES, INC.	Houston, Texas	(Volume 17)
ROYAL COURT REPORTING SERVICE, INC.	Philadelphia, Pennsylvania	(Volume 15)
RUTH ANN JOHNSON COURT REPORTER SERVICE	Grand Forks, North Dakota	(Volume 14)
RYAN REPORTING	Melbourne, Florida	(Volume 6)
SALOMON REPORTING SERVICE, INC.	Washington, District of Columbia	(Volume 5)
	Annapolis, Maryland	(Volume 9)
	Baltimore, Maryland	(Volume 9)
	Columbia, Maryland	(Volume 9)
	Frederick, Maryland	(Volume 9)
	Towson, Maryland	(Volume 9)
SANDY SATTERWHITE REPORTING	Spartanburg, South Carolina	(Volume 16)

COURT REPORTERS - Continued

Firm	Location	Volume
SARGENT'S COURT REPORTING SERVICE, INC.	Harrisburg, Pennsylvania	(Volume 15)
	Johnstown, Pennsylvania	(Volume 15)
	Philadelphia, Pennsylvania	(Volume 15)
	Pittsburgh, Pennsylvania	(Volume 15)
	Wilkes-Barre, Pennsylvania	(Volume 15)
	Charleston, West Virginia	(Volume 18)
SAWYER COURT REPORTING	Kansas City, Missouri	(Volume 11)
SCHINDHELM & ASSOCIATES, INC.	Milwaukee, Wisconsin	(Volume 18)
SCLAFANI WILLIAMS COURT REPORTERS, INC.	Bradenton, Florida	(Volume 6)
	Clearwater, Florida	(Volume 6)
	Fort Lauderdale, Florida	(Volume 6)
	Lakeland, Florida	(Volume 6)
	Orlando, Florida	(Volume 6)
	Sarasota, Florida	(Volume 6)
	Sebring, Florida	(Volume 6)
	St. Petersburg, Florida	(Volume 6)
	Tampa, Florida	(Volume 6)
	Winter Haven, Florida	(Volume 6)
	Chicago, Illinois	(Volume 8)
SCRIBE ASSOCIATES, INC.	Gainesville, Florida	(Volume 6)
SEATTLE DEPOSITION REPORTERS	Portland, Oregon	(Volume 15)
	Seattle, Washington	(Volume 18)
	Spokane, Washington	(Volume 18)
SHARP HOLLAND INTERNATIONAL COURT REPORTING, INC.	Dallas, Texas	(Volume 17)
	Fort Worth, Texas	(Volume 17)
	Houston, Texas	(Volume 17)
SHOEMAKER & ASSOCIATES	Huntsville, Alabama	(Volume 1)
SIERRA NEVADA REPORTERS	Reno, Nevada	(Volume 11)
SILVERMAN & GARWOOD COURT REPORTING SERVICE	Tucson, Arizona	(Volume 1)
SOUTH TEXAS COURT REPORTERS, INC.	San Antonio, Texas	(Volume 17)
SOUTHEAST REPORTING	Mobile, Alabama	(Volume 1)
SOUTHERN COURT REPORTERS, INC.	Jacksonville, Florida	(Volume 6)
	Melbourne, Florida	(Volume 6)
	Miami, Florida	(Volume 6)
	Orlando, Florida	(Volume 6)
	Tampa, Florida	(Volume 6)
SOUTHERN INDIANA REPORTING	Evansville, Indiana	(Volume 8)
SOUTHWEST REPORTING & VIDEO SERVICE, INC.	Houston, Texas	(Volume 17)
SPANGLER REPORTING SERVICES, INC.	Cincinnati, Ohio	(Volume 14)
SPECTRUM REPORTING, INC.	Columbus, Ohio	(Volume 14)
STANLEY, RICE AND ASSOCIATES A LEGALINK COMPANY	Dallas, Texas	(Volume 17)
STAR REPORTING SERVICE, INC.	Oakland, California	(Volume 2)
	Sacramento, California	(Volume 3)
	San Francisco, California	(Volume 3)
	San Mateo, California	(Volume 3)
	San Rafael, California	(Volume 3)
STARKOVICH REPORTING SERVICES	Seattle, Washington	(Volume 18)
	Tacoma, Washington	(Volume 18)
STATEWIDE COURT REPORTERS	Charlottesville, Virginia	(Volume 18)
STATEWIDE REPORTING SERVICE	Jacksonville, Florida	(Volume 6)
STEFFAN & STAUFFER LTD.	Altoona, Pennsylvania	(Volume 15)
	Erie, Pennsylvania	(Volume 15)
	Greensburg, Pennsylvania	(Volume 15)
	Johnstown, Pennsylvania	(Volume 15)
	Pittsburgh, Pennsylvania	(Volume 15)
	Washington, Pennsylvania	(Volume 15)
STERLING REPORTING SERVICE, INC.	Los Angeles, California	(Volume 2)
	San Francisco, California	(Volume 3)
	Miami, Florida	(Volume 6)
	New York, New York	(Volume 13)
	Houston, Texas	(Volume 17)
STEVE GENTRY & ASSOCIATES, INC.	Dallas, Texas	(Volume 17)
STEVENSON REPORTING SERVICE, INC.	Cleveland, Ohio	(Volume 14)
STIREWALT & ASSOCIATES	Minneapolis, Minnesota	(Volume 11)
STONER & SCHLENKER CERTIFIED SHORTHAND REPORTERS	Bakersfield, California	(Volume 2)

COURT REPORTERS - Continued

Name	Location	Volume
VERBATIM REPORTING SERVICE, LLC	Madison, Wisconsin	(Volume 18)
VERBATIM SERVICES	Morristown, New Jersey	(Volume 12)
	Newark, New Jersey	(Volume 12)
VERITEXT L.L.C.	Boca Raton, Florida	(Volume 6)
	Fort Lauderdale, Florida	(Volume 6)
	Miami, Florida	(Volume 6)
	West Palm Beach, Florida	(Volume 6)
VIDEO COURT REPORTING, INC.	Miami, Florida	(Volume 6)
VIDEO SOLUTIONS	San Francisco, California	(Volume 3)
VIGNATI REPORTING	Oakland, California	(Volume 2)
	San Francisco, California	(Volume 3)
VINCENT M. LUCENTE & ASSOCIATES, INC.	St. Petersburg, Florida	(Volume 6)
VOICE PRINT, INC. COURT REPORTING & LEGAL VIDEO SERVICES	Philadelphia, Pennsylvania	(Volume 15)
WALLS REPORTING, INC.	Baltimore, Maryland	(Volume 9)
WAYRYNEN & LIVELY REPORTING SERVICE	Butte, Montana	(Volume 11)
WE DO DEPOSITIONS, INC.	Baltimore, Maryland	(Volume 9)
WEATHERS & ASSOCIATES, INC.	West Palm Beach, Florida	(Volume 6)
WHEELER COURT REPORTING	Rapid City, South Dakota	(Volume 16)
WICHMANN REPORTING SERVICE	Chicago, Illinois	(Volume 8)
WIERZBICKI & STEPHENSON COURT REPORTING SERVICE	Pensacola, Florida	(Volume 6)
PAULINE E. WILLIMAN	Albany, New York	(Volume 12)
WILSON GEORGE COURT REPORTERS, INC.	Fort Collins, Colorado	(Volume 4)
WINTERS O. HOPE & ASSOCIATES	Birmingham, Alabama	(Volume 1)
	Montgomery, Alabama	(Volume 1)
WORTH COURT REPORTING	Fond du Lac, Wisconsin	(Volume 18)
WRIGHT WATSON STEN-TEL	Austin, Texas	(Volume 17)
ZACCO & ASSOCIATES REPORTING SERVICES	Daytona Beach, Florida	(Volume 6)
	Fort Lauderdale, Florida	(Volume 6)
	Gainesville, Florida	(Volume 6)
	Jacksonville, Florida	(Volume 6)
	Lakeland, Florida	(Volume 6)
	Miami, Florida	(Volume 6)
	Orlando, Florida	(Volume 6)
	Sanford, Florida	(Volume 6)
	Sarasota, Florida	(Volume 6)
	St. Petersburg, Florida	(Volume 6)
	Tallahassee, Florida	(Volume 6)
	Tampa, Florida	(Volume 6)
	Tavares, Florida	(Volume 6)
	West Palm Beach, Florida	(Volume 6)
ZANDONELLA REPORTING SERVICE, INC.	Walnut Creek, California	(Volume 3)

COURTROOM SKETCHING

Name	Location	Volume
ART OF EVE	Houston, Texas	(Volume 17)

CRIME SCENE RECONSTRUCTION

Name	Location	Volume
WAYNE N. HILL, SR.	East Moline, Illinois	(Volume 8)
JAMES AND ASSOCIATES FORENSIC CONSULTANTS, INC.	Fort Lauderdale, Florida	(Volume 6)

CRIMINAL BACKGROUND CHECKS

Name	Location	Volume
THE CHAPMAN CORPORATION	Charlotte, North Carolina	(Volume 14)
OHIO PARALEGAL SERVICES, INC.	Akron, Ohio	(Volume 14)
VANCE INTERNATIONAL, INC.	Washington, District of Columbia	(Volume 5)

CRIMINAL INVESTIGATIONS

Name	Location	Volume
INVESTIGATIVE GROUP INTERNATIONAL, INC. (IGI)	Los Angeles, California	(Volume 2)
VANCE INTERNATIONAL, INC.	Washington, District of Columbia	(Volume 5)

CRIMINAL RECORDS RESEARCH

Name	Location	Volume
COURT DATA RESEARCH SERVICES	Tulsa, Oklahoma	(Volume 14)
G.A. PUBLIC RECORD SERVICES, INC.	Dallas, Texas	(Volume 17)
OHIO PARALEGAL SERVICES, INC.	Akron, Ohio	(Volume 14)

DNA FORENSIC TESTING

Name	Location	Volume
IDENTITY GENETICS, INC.	Brookings, South Dakota	(Volume 16)

DEBUGGING

ACIS ELECTRONIC COUNTERMEASURES CORP. .... Seattle, Washington .... (Volume 18)

DELIVERY SERVICES

OHIO PARALEGAL SERVICES, INC. .... Akron, Ohio .... (Volume 14)

DEMONSTRATIVE EVIDENCE

24 HOUR COMPANY .... Washington, District of Columbia .... (Volume 5)
Arlington, Virginia .... (Volume 18)
AERIALS, INC. .... Miami, Florida .... (Volume 6)
BEST EVIDENCE, INC. .... St. Petersburg, Florida .... (Volume 6)
Tampa, Florida .... (Volume 6)
ELEVENTH HOUR ANIMATION .... Chicago, Illinois .... (Volume 8)
ENGINEERING ANIMATION, INC. .... Ames, Iowa .... (Volume 8)
EVIDENCE EXPRESS .... Detroit, Michigan .... (Volume 10)
FORDYN DIGITAL PRODUCTIONS, INC. .... Phoenix, Arizona .... (Volume 1)
GEN-TEK COMPUTER GRAPHIC COMPANY, INC. .... New York, New York .... (Volume 13)
LMC - A LITIGATION MEDIA CENTER .... Houston, Texas .... (Volume 17)
SMP DIGITAL GRAPHICS .... New York, New York .... (Volume 13)
STARR LITIGATION SERVICES, INC .... Phoenix, Arizona .... (Volume 1)
Los Angeles, California .... (Volume 2)
Chicago, Illinois .... (Volume 8)
TRIAL GRAPHICS & MODELS .... Dallas, Texas .... (Volume 17)
TWGRAPHICS .... Milwaukee, Wisconsin .... (Volume 18)
VISUAL EVIDENCE CO. .... Cleveland, Ohio .... (Volume 14)

DEMONSTRATIVE EXHIBITS

CH COMMUNCIATIONS, INC. .... New Orleans, Louisiana .... (Volume 9)
Houston, Texas .... (Volume 17)
LITIGATION MULTIMEDIA .... Los Angeles, California .... (Volume 2)
LITIGRAPHICS, INC. .... Denver, Colorado .... (Volume 4)
ZAGNOLI MCEVOY FOLEY LTD. .... Chicago, Illinois .... (Volume 8)

DEPOSITION SUMMARIES

RANDY BLACK & ASSOCIATES, INC. .... San Francisco, California .... (Volume 3)

DEPOSITIONS - VIDEO & AUDIO

GEOMATRIX PRODUCTIONS .... New Haven, Connecticut .... (Volume 4)

DEPOSITIONS ON WRITTEN QUESTIONS

QUALITY RECORD SERVICES .... Houston, Texas .... (Volume 17)

DICTATING EQUIPMENT & SUPPLIES

F&C AUDIO, COMPUTER MANUFACTURING AND SUPPLY, INC. .... Los Angeles, California .... (Volume 2)
New York, New York .... (Volume 13)

DIRECTORY/ON-LINE

LEGALOPINION.COM .... Seattle, Washington .... (Volume 18)

DISABILITY ASSESSMENT - LEARNING AND/OR BEHAVIORAL

STEVE C. IMBER, PH.D. .... Providence, Rhode Island .... (Volume 16)

DISCOVERY AND DOCUMENT REPRODUCTION SERVICES

LEGAL COPY, INC. .... Seattle, Washington .... (Volume 18)
LEGAL EAGLE ®, INC. .... Greenville, South Carolina .... (Volume 16)

DISPUTE ANALYSIS & INVESTIGATION

ERNEST BROWN & COMPANY .... San Francisco, California .... (Volume 3)
PRICEWATERHOUSECOOPERS LLP .... Los Angeles, California .... (Volume 2)
New York, New York .... (Volume 13)

DOCUMENT IMAGING

CATHERINE TEACH REPORTING .... Portland, Oregon .... (Volume 15)
DOCUMENT SCANNING SYSTEMS INCORPORATED .... Los Angeles, California .... (Volume 2)
San Diego, California .... (Volume 3)
HORIZON MICROGRAPHICS, INC. .... Dallas, Texas .... (Volume 17)

DOCUMENT IMAGING - Continued

IMAGEMAX	New York, New York	(Volume 13)
LAURIE WEBB & ASSOCIATES	Las Vegas, Nevada	(Volume 11)
LEGAL COPY, INC.	Seattle, Washington	(Volume 18)
LEGAL EAGLE ®, INC.	Greenville, South Carolina	(Volume 16)
LEGAL IMAGING, INC.	Atlanta, Georgia	(Volume 7)
LEGALSOURCE	Los Angeles, California	(Volume 2)
LITIGATION SYSTEMS, INC.	Washington, District of Columbia	(Volume 5)
PC&A LITIGATION SUPPORT SERVICES	Minneapolis, Minnesota	(Volume 11)

DOCUMENT MANAGEMENT SERVICES

CHESAPEAKE PAPER TRAIL	Havre de Grace, Maryland	(Volume 9)
INTERLINGUA.COM, INC.	Los Angeles, California	(Volume 2)
LEGAL EAGLE ®, INC.	Greenville, South Carolina	(Volume 16)
LITIGATION SYSTEMS, INC.	Washington, District of Columbia	(Volume 5)
LMC - A LITIGATION MEDIA CENTER	Houston, Texas	(Volume 17)
WORLDOX/WORLD SOFTWARE	New York, New York	(Volume 13)

DOCUMENT RESEARCH, RETRIEVAL & FILING

1ST AMERICAN PROCESS SERVICE, INC.	San Diego, California	(Volume 3)
	San Francisco, California	(Volume 3)
	San Jose, California	(Volume 3)
	Jacksonville, Florida	(Volume 6)
	Miami, Florida	(Volume 6)
	Orlando, Florida	(Volume 6)
	Tampa, Florida	(Volume 6)
	Boston, Massachusetts	(Volume 10)
	Detroit, Michigan	(Volume 10)
	Newark, New Jersey	(Volume 12)
	Trenton, New Jersey	(Volume 12)
	Portland, Oregon	(Volume 15)
	Philadelphia, Pennsylvania	(Volume 15)
	Pittsburgh, Pennsylvania	(Volume 15)
	Austin, Texas	(Volume 17)
	Dallas, Texas	(Volume 17)
	Houston, Texas	(Volume 17)
	San Antonio, Texas	(Volume 17)
	Seattle, Washington	(Volume 18)
	Milwaukee, Wisconsin	(Volume 18)
A & E, INC.	Washington, District of Columbia	(Volume 5)
	Baltimore, Maryland	(Volume 9)
AAA PROCESS SERVERS, INC.	Denver, Colorado	(Volume 4)
ACCESS INFORMATION SERVICES, INC.	Albany, New York	(Volume 12)
ACCU-FAX SERVICES, A DIVISION OF CEO CORPORATE SECURITY GROUP, INC.	Washington, District of Columbia	(Volume 5)
	Miami, Florida	(Volume 6)
	Newark, New Jersey	(Volume 12)
	New York, New York	(Volume 13)
	Philadelphia, Pennsylvania	(Volume 15)
	Richmond, Virginia	(Volume 18)
ALASKA PUBLIC RECORDS SEARCH, LLC	Anchorage, Alaska	(Volume 1)
ALL-SEARCH & INSPECTION, INC.	Los Angeles, California	(Volume 2)
	San Francisco, California	(Volume 3)
	Chicago, Illinois	(Volume 8)
	New York, New York	(Volume 13)
	Dallas, Texas	(Volume 17)
	Houston, Texas	(Volume 17)
	Salt Lake City, Utah	(Volume 17)
ALLSTATE PROCESS SERVERS	Boston, Massachusetts	(Volume 10)
THE ALPHA AND OMEGA AGENCY	Corpus Christi, Texas	(Volume 17)
AMERICAN INFORMATION NETWORK	Detroit, Michigan	(Volume 10)
APEX DOCUMENT MANAGEMENT, INC.	McAllen, Texas	(Volume 17)
ARKANSAS LITIGATION SUPPORT SERVICES, INC.	Little Rock, Arkansas	(Volume 1)
A.S.A. INFORMATION SERVICES	Dallas, Texas	(Volume 17)
A.S.K. SERVICES, INC.	Detroit, Michigan	(Volume 10)
ATLANTA ATTORNEY SERVICES	Atlanta, Georgia	(Volume 7)
BLACKWELL LAND & TITLE RESEARCH	Huntsville, Alabama	(Volume 1)
CAPITAL CONNECTION, INC.	Tallahassee, Florida	(Volume 6)
CAPITOL COMMERCE REPORTER, INC.	Austin, Texas	(Volume 17)
THE CHATTEL MORTGAGE REPORTER, INC.	Chicago, Illinois	(Volume 8)
COASTAL OFFICE DIMENSIONS	Pensacola, Florida	(Volume 6)
COLBY ATTORNEYS SERVICE CO. INC.	Albany, New York	(Volume 13)
COLORADO RECORDS SEARCH, INC.	Denver, Colorado	(Volume 4)
COURT DATA RESEARCH SERVICES	Tulsa, Oklahoma	(Volume 14)

DOCUMENT RESEARCH, RETRIEVAL & FILING - Continued

TYLER-MCLENNON CORP.	Chicago, Illinois	(Volume 8)
UNISEARCH INC.	Seattle, Washington	(Volume 18)
WRIGHT WATSON STEN-TEL	Austin, Texas	(Volume 17)

DOCUMENT SCANNING

AMERICAN LEGALTECH DALLAS, INC.	Dallas, Texas	(Volume 17)
DOCUMENT SCANNING SYSTEMS INCORPORATED	Los Angeles, California	(Volume 2)
	San Diego, California	(Volume 3)
IMAGEMAX	New York, New York	(Volume 13)
LEGAL EAGLE ®, INC.	Greenville, South Carolina	(Volume 16)

DOCUMENT/DATA CONVERSION

LITIGATION SYSTEMS, INC.	Washington, District of Columbia	(Volume 5)

E-BUSINESS

COMPUTER AND COMMUNICATIONS LAW CONSULTANTS	Washington, District of Columbia	(Volume 5)
FIRST E COMMERCE	Santa Clara, California	(Volume 3)
EVELOCITY CORPORATION	Boston, Massachusetts	(Volume 10)

ECONOMIC AND STATISTICAL CONSULTING SERVICES

ANALYSIS GROUP/ECONOMICS	Los Angeles, California	(Volume 2)
	Menlo Park, California	(Volume 2)
	San Francisco, California	(Volume 3)
	Washington, District of Columbia	(Volume 5)
	Boston, Massachusetts	(Volume 10)
ANALYSIS AND INFERENCE, INC.	Washington, District of Columbia	(Volume 5)
	New York, New York	(Volume 13)
THE BRATTLE GROUP	Washington, District of Columbia	(Volume 5)
	Boston, Massachusetts	(Volume 10)
BUSINESS VALUATION SERVICES	San Diego, California	(Volume 3)
	San Francisco, California	(Volume 3)
	New York, New York	(Volume 13)
	Dallas, Texas	(Volume 17)
CHARLES R. MANN ASSOCIATES, INC.	Washington, District of Columbia	(Volume 5)
CHARLES RIVER ASSOCIATES INCORPORATED	Los Angeles, California	(Volume 2)
	San Francisco, California	(Volume 3)
	Washington, District of Columbia	(Volume 5)
	Chicago, Illinois	(Volume 8)
	Boston, Massachusetts	(Volume 10)
	New York, New York	(Volume 13)
	Dallas, Texas	(Volume 17)
ECON ONE RESEARCH, INC.	Los Angeles, California	(Volume 2)
FTI/KAHN	New York, New York	(Volume 13)
LEXECON INC.	Chicago, Illinois	(Volume 8)
	Boston, Massachusetts	(Volume 10)
MICRONOMICS, INC.	Los Angeles, California	(Volume 2)
NATHAN ASSOCIATES INC.	Washington, District of Columbia	(Volume 5)
NATIONAL ECONOMIC RESEARCH ASSOCIATES, INC.	Los Angeles, California	(Volume 2)
	San Francisco, California	(Volume 3)
	Washington, District of Columbia	(Volume 5)
	Chicago, Illinois	(Volume 8)
	Boston, Massachusetts	(Volume 10)
	New York, New York	(Volume 13)
RESOLUTION ECONOMICS LLC	Los Angeles, California	(Volume 2)
	San Francisco, California	(Volume 3)
TECHNICAL ASSOCIATES, INC.	Richmond, Virginia	(Volume 18)
WATTS & ASSOCIATES, INC.	Billings, Montana	(Volume 11)

ECONOMIC AND STATISTICAL CONSULTING SERVICES - AUTOMOBILES

THE FONTANA GROUP, INC.	Los Angeles, California	(Volume 2)
FROST & SULLIVAN	Los Angeles, California	(Volume 2)
	San Francisco, California	(Volume 3)
	Newark, New Jersey	(Volume 12)
	New York, New York	(Volume 13)
	Austin, Texas	(Volume 17)
	San Antonio, Texas	(Volume 17)

ENVIRONMENTAL ENGINEERING & REMEDIATION SERVICES

ADVENT ENVIRONMENTAL, INC. .... Louisville, Kentucky .... (Volume 9)
St. Louis, Missouri .... (Volume 11)
Charlotte, North Carolina .... (Volume 14)
Raleigh, North Carolina .... (Volume 14)
Charleston, South Carolina .... (Volume 16)
ALPINE ENVIRONMENTAL, INC. .... Denver, Colorado .... (Volume 4)
OMNI TECH INTERNATIONAL, LTD. .... Chicago, Illinois .... (Volume 8)
Houston, Texas .... (Volume 17)

ENVIRONMENTAL INVESTIGATIONS

ADVENT ENVIRONMENTAL, INC. .... Louisville, Kentucky .... (Volume 9)
St. Louis, Missouri .... (Volume 11)
Charlotte, North Carolina .... (Volume 14)
Raleigh, North Carolina .... (Volume 14)
Charleston, South Carolina .... (Volume 16)
INVESTIGATIVE GROUP INTERNATIONAL, INC. (IGI) .... Los Angeles, California .... (Volume 2)
ZYMAX FORENSICS .... Los Angeles, California .... (Volume 2)

ENVIRONMENTAL RISK ASSESSMENT AND CONSULTING

ADVENT ENVIRONMENTAL, INC. .... Louisville, Kentucky .... (Volume 9)
St. Louis, Missouri .... (Volume 11)
Charlotte, North Carolina .... (Volume 14)
Raleigh, North Carolina .... (Volume 14)
Charleston, South Carolina .... (Volume 16)

ENVIRONMENTAL RISK MANAGEMENT & COMPLIANCE INFORMATION

ENVIRONMENTAL DATA RESOURCES, INC. (EDR) .... Washington, District of Columbia .... (Volume 5)

EQUINE - APPRAISERS & CONSULTANTS

EXPERT EQUINE RESEARCH CENTER .... Los Angeles, California .... (Volume 2)

ESCROW SERVICES

ARIZONA ESCROW & FINANCIAL CORPORATION .... Phoenix, Arizona .... (Volume 1)
THE ESCROW SOURCE, INC. .... Palm Desert, California .... (Volume 3)

ESTATE PLANNING & PERSONAL BENEFITS

COMMONWEALTH TRUST COMPANY .... Wilmington, Delaware .... (Volume 4)
FRANK A. FERRARO, CPA, PA .... Stuart, Florida .... (Volume 6)
BOBBY E. JELKS, CPA, PFS .... Shreveport, Louisiana .... (Volume 9)
WORSHAM & SAMMONS, LLC .... Atlanta, Georgia .... (Volume 7)

ESTATE VALUATIONS

LECG, A SUBSIDIARY OF NAVIGANT CONSULTING, INC. .... Berkeley, California .... (Volume 2)

EXAMINERS OF QUESTIONED DOCUMENTS (HANDWRITING EXPERTS)

ADVANCED DOCUMENT & HANDWRITING EXAMINATION SERVICES .... Fort Worth, Texas .... (Volume 17)
ALAMO AREA FORENSIC LABS .... San Antonio, Texas .... (Volume 17)
JAMES A. BLACK .... Los Angeles, California .... (Volume 2)
JAMES BLANCO .... Sacramento, California .... (Volume 3)
FISHER FORENSIC DOCUMENT LABORATORY, INC. .... San Francisco, California .... (Volume 3)
FORENSIC DOCUMENT EXAMINERS .... Baltimore, Maryland .... (Volume 9)
FORGERY FORENSICS© A DIVISION OF QUESTIONED DOCUMENTS, INCORPORATED .... Princeton, New Jersey .... (Volume 12)
ANN B. HOOTEN .... Minneapolis, Minnesota .... (Volume 11)
JAMES A. GREEN - FORENSIC DOCUMENT EXAMINER .... Eugene, Oregon .... (Volume 15)
GUS R. LESNEVICH .... Philadelphia, Pennsylvania .... (Volume 15)
F. AURELIUS MCKANZE, PH.D. .... Cleveland, Ohio .... (Volume 14)
PATRICIA SIEGEL ENTERPRISES, INC. .... Great Neck, New York .... (Volume 12)
PAUL A. OSBORN & SON .... New York, New York .... (Volume 13)
MARTY PEARCE, CDE, CGA .... Nashville, Tennessee .... (Volume 16)
THE PECORARO GROUP .... Schenectady, New York .... (Volume 13)
CHARLES E. PERROTTA .... Charlotte, North Carolina .... (Volume 14)
SEIFER HANDWRITING CONSULTANTS .... Providence, Rhode Island .... (Volume 16)
SHIVER & NELSON DOCUMENT INVESTIGATION LABORATORY, INC. .... Tallahassee, Florida .... (Volume 6)
ANDREW SULNER, M.S. J.D. .... New York, New York .... (Volume 13)
VICTORIA MERTES-DOCUMENT EXAMINER .... Beverly Hills, California .... (Volume 2)

EXECUTIVE PROTECTIVE SERVICES

EXPERT WITNESS

ACCIDENT INVESTIGATION & RECONSTRUCTION

ACCIDENT RECONSTRUCTION

ACCIDENTS/FIRES/PRODUCT LIABILITY

ACCOUNTING

EXPERT WITNESS - Continued

ACCOUNTING - Continued

BUSINESS DAMAGES

MIRTHA GUERRA AGUIRRE, CPA*, ABV, AM, BVAL	Miami, Florida	(Volume 6)
BROWN SMITH WALLACE, LLC	St. Louis, Missouri	(Volume 11)
AMANDA CAPO'-ROSSELLO', CPA, CVA, CFE	San Juan, Puerto Rico	(Volume 18)
CLIFTON GUNDERSON L.L.C.	Denver, Colorado	(Volume 4)
FROST & SULLIVAN	Los Angeles, California	(Volume 2)
	San Francisco, California	(Volume 3)
	Newark, New Jersey	(Volume 12)
	New York, New York	(Volume 13)
	Austin, Texas	(Volume 17)
	San Antonio, Texas	(Volume 17)
HEMMING MORSE, INC.	San Francisco, California	(Volume 3)
HENRY L. JANUS, CPA/ABV	Boca Raton, Florida	(Volume 6)
MEARA, KING & CO.	Kansas City, Missouri	(Volume 11)
SUGARMAN & COMPANY LLP	San Francisco, California	(Volume 3)
WHITE, ZUCKERMAN, WARSAVSKY, LUNA & WOLF	Los Angeles, California	(Volume 2)

MALPRACTICE

FRANK, RIMERMAN & CO. CPA'S	San Jose, California	(Volume 3)
FRIEDMAN, DUQUE & CO.	Fort Lauderdale, Florida	(Volume 6)
WILLIAM L. RABY, CPA	Phoenix, Arizona	(Volume 1)

ACOUSTICS

SOUND, NOISE & VIBRATION

ACOUSTICS SPECIALISTS GROUP	New York, New York	(Volume 13)
BROOKS ACOUSTICS CORPORATION	Hartford, Connecticut	(Volume 4)

ADMIRALTY

KENAI NAVIGATION INTERNATIONAL	San Francisco, California	(Volume 3)
THOMAS ELECTRIC CONTROL, INC.	New York, New York	(Volume 13)

AGRI-HORTICULTURAL

A.L.I.S. -AGRICULTURAL LITIGATION & INFORMATION SPECIALISTS	Fort Collins, Colorado	(Volume 4)
TRANSAGRO	Salinas, California	(Volume 3)

AIR POLLUTION

WALTER SMITH & ASSOCIATES	Raleigh, North Carolina	(Volume 14)

AIR SAFETY

AIRSAFETY EXPERTS, INC.	Denver, Colorado	(Volume 4)

APPRAISAL SERVICES

A.R.E. REAL ESTATE SERVICES	New Orleans, Louisiana	(Volume 9)
LECG, A SUBSIDIARY OF NAVIGANT CONSULTING, INC.	Berkeley, California	(Volume 2)

AQUATICS

CARNEY & ASSOCIATES, INC.	Somerset, New Jersey	(Volume 12)
PATRICK L. DURKIN	San Diego, California	(Volume 3)
NATIONAL SAFETY CONSULTANTS	West Orange, New Jersey	(Volume 12)

ARBORICULTURE & FORESTRY

PAUL M. DAVIS, ASLA	Orlando, Florida	(Volume 6)
SOUTHERN URBAN FORESTRY ASSOCIATES	Tuscaloosa, Alabama	(Volume 1)

ARCHITECTS

WISS, JANNEY, ELSTNER ASSOCIATES, INC.	Chicago, Illinois	(Volume 8)

AUDIO-TAPE ANALYSIS/AUTHENTICATION/VOICE ID

PROFESSIONAL AUDIO LABORATORIES, INC.	New York, New York	(Volume 13)
W. S. ATARAS ENGINEERING, INC.	Washington, District of Columbia	(Volume 5)

AUDIOLOGY

ACOUSTIC ASSOCIATES, LTD.	Chicago, Illinois	(Volume 8)
THE ROBINSON GROUP, LTD.	Bloomfield Hills, Michigan	(Volume 10)

EXPERT WITNESS - Continued

CONSTRUCTION - Continued

Name	Location	Volume
	San Francisco, California	(Volume 3)
PROJECT SUPPORT GROUP	Ann Arbor, Michigan	(Volume 10)
DAVID A. STERN	Santa Monica, California	(Volume 3)
SUMMIT PROFESSIONAL RESOURCES LLC	Hackettstown, New Jersey	(Volume 12)
WAGNER . HOHNS . INGLIS, INC.	Mount Holly, New Jersey	(Volume 12)

BUILDING CODES

Name	Location	Volume
JOSEPH D. BELCHER, CBO	Orlando, Florida	(Volume 6)
DAVID A. STERN	Santa Monica, California	(Volume 3)
KENNETH J. STOYACK, AIA, PP	Nutley, New Jersey	(Volume 12)

DEFECTS

Name	Location	Volume
AQUATECH CONSULTANCY, INC.	San Rafael, California	(Volume 3)
GREGORY I. MOWAT FORENSIC TILE CONSULTANTS	San Diego, California	(Volume 3)
DAVID A. STERN	Santa Monica, California	(Volume 3)

COOLING TOWERS

Name	Location	Volume
BURGER COOLING TOWER COMPANY, INC.	Arlington, Virginia	(Volume 18)

CORRECTIONS

JAIL/PRISON/LOCKUP

Name	Location	Volume
ERNEST C. WEBER, CJM	New York, New York	(Volume 13)

CRANES

Name	Location	Volume
BARTH CRANE INSPECTIONS	Charleston, South Carolina	(Volume 16)
THOMAS ELECTRIC CONTROL, INC.	New York, New York	(Volume 13)

CRIMINALISTICS & FIREARMS

Name	Location	Volume
JOHN H. DILLON, JR.	Manassas, Virginia	(Volume 18)
JAMES AND ASSOCIATES FORENSIC CONSULTANTS, INC.	Fort Lauderdale, Florida	(Volume 6)

CURRENCY TRADING

Name	Location	Volume
MARKET CONSULTING CORPORATION	New York, New York	(Volume 13)

DUI

Name	Location	Volume
ALI Z. HAMELI, M.D. P.A.	New York, New York	(Volume 13)

DAMAGE VALUATION

Name	Location	Volume
ADAMS CAPITAL, INC.	Atlanta, Georgia	(Volume 7)
BLACKMAN KALLICK BARTELSTEIN, LLP	Chicago, Illinois	(Volume 8)
CLIFTON GUNDERSON L.L.C.	Denver, Colorado	(Volume 4)
G. R. BILL COMPANY APPRAISERS	San Diego, California	(Volume 3)
LECG, A SUBSIDIARY OF NAVIGANT CONSULTING, INC.	Berkeley, California	(Volume 2)
MAURICE MITCHELL, CPA/ABV, MAI	Birmingham, Alabama	(Volume 1)
SUGARMAN & COMPANY LLP	San Francisco, California	(Volume 3)
TECHNICAL ASSOCIATES, INC.	Richmond, Virginia	(Volume 18)

DEMOLITION

Name	Location	Volume
DEMOLITION CONSULTANTS	Houston, Texas	(Volume 17)

DOCUMENT EXAMINATION/COMPREHENSION

Name	Location	Volume
VICTORIA MERTES-DOCUMENT EXAMINER	Beverly Hills, California	(Volume 2)

DRUGS/ALCOHOL/TOXICOLOGY

Name	Location	Volume
NATIONAL TOXICOLOGY SPECIALISTS, INC.	Chicago, Illinois	(Volume 8)
STEPHEN M. PITTEL, PH.D.	Los Angeles, California	(Volume 2)
VINA R. SPIEHLER, PH.D. DABFT	Los Angeles, California	(Volume 2)

ECONOMICS/ECONOMISTS

Name	Location	Volume
BUSINESS VALUATION SERVICES	San Diego, California	(Volume 3)
	San Francisco, California	(Volume 3)
	New York, New York	(Volume 13)
CHARLES RIVER ASSOCIATES INCORPORATED	San Francisco, California	(Volume 3)
	Washington, District of Columbia	(Volume 5)
	New York, New York	(Volume 13)

EXPERT WITNESS

EMPLOYEE/EMPLOYMENT - Continued

OSHA REGULATIONS/PROCEDURES

AEGIS CORP.	Philadelphia, Pennsylvania	(Volume 15)
CARNOW, CONIBEAR & ASSOC. LTD.	Chicago, Illinois	(Volume 8)
NATIONAL SAFE WORKPLACE INSTITUTE	Miami, Florida	(Volume 6)

PRACTICES

RESOLUTION ECONOMICS LLC	Los Angeles, California	(Volume 2)

WRONGFUL TERMINATION/HARASSMENT

WILLIAM P. ANTHONY, PH.D.	Tallahassee, Florida	(Volume 6)
G. GOVINE CONSULTING	Pasadena, California	(Volume 3)
BRIAN H. KLEINER, PH.D.	Los Angeles, California	(Volume 2)
SARJEANT & SARJEANT, INC.	Orlando, Florida	(Volume 6)

EMPLOYMENT PRACTICES

HR ASSOCIATES	Miami, Florida	(Volume 6)

ENGINEERS/ENGINEERING

ADVENT ENVIRONMENTAL, INC.	Louisville, Kentucky	(Volume 9)
	St. Louis, Missouri	(Volume 11)
	Charlotte, North Carolina	(Volume 14)
	Raleigh, North Carolina	(Volume 14)
	Charleston, South Carolina	(Volume 16)
KAIGLER CONSULTING SERVICE, INC.	Lafayette, Louisiana	(Volume 9)
MANX RESEARCH	Los Angeles, California	(Volume 2)
STRESS ENGINEERING SERVICES, INC.	Houston, Texas	(Volume 17)
SUMMIT PROFESSIONAL RESOURCES LLC	Hackettstown, New Jersey	(Volume 12)
TETRA ENGINEERING GROUP, INC.	Hartford, Connecticut	(Volume 4)
WISS, JANNEY, ELSTNER ASSOCIATES, INC.	Chicago, Illinois	(Volume 8)
W. S. ATARAS ENGINEERING, INC.	Washington, District of Columbia	(Volume 5)

ACOUSTICS

BROOKS ACOUSTICS CORPORATION	Hartford, Connecticut	(Volume 4)

ARCHITECTURE

ERNEST BROWN & COMPANY	San Francisco, California	(Volume 3)
KENNETH J. STOYACK, AIA, PP	Nutley, New Jersey	(Volume 12)

AUTOMOTIVE

CAIRD & ASSOCIATES CONSULTANTS INC. TRUCK TRAILER MANAGEMENT SERVICES DIVISION	San Francisco, California	(Volume 3)
THOMAS J. FEAHENY	Detroit, Michigan	(Volume 10)
PARC ENGINEERING ASSOCIATES	Asheville, North Carolina	(Volume 14)

CHEMICAL

CHEMTECH CONSULTANTS, INC.	New York, New York	(Volume 13)
	Pittsburgh, Pennsylvania	(Volume 15)
CREATIVE PROCESS ENGINEERING	Pocatello, Idaho	(Volume 7)

CIVIL/MECHANICAL/STRUCTURAL

AEGIS CORP.	Philadelphia, Pennsylvania	(Volume 15)
CHEMTECH CONSULTANTS, INC.	Pittsburgh, Pennsylvania	(Volume 15)
ERNEST BROWN & COMPANY	San Francisco, California	(Volume 3)
LAWRENCE G. SPIELVOGEL, INC. CONSULTING ENGINEERS	Philadelphia, Pennsylvania	(Volume 15)
WISS, JANNEY, ELSTNER ASSOCIATES, INC.	Chicago, Illinois	(Volume 8)

ELECTRICAL

YALE BARKAN (YBI)	Los Angeles, California	(Volume 2)

FIRE PROTECTION

FISHER RESEARCH & DEVELOPMENT, INC.	Los Angeles, California	(Volume 2)
KLINKER & ASSOCIATES, INC.	Washington, District of Columbia	(Volume 5)

FORENSIC ENGINEERING

CTL, INC.	Chicago, Illinois	(Volume 8)
EMERALD ENGINEERING LABORATORIES, LLC	Seattle, Washington	(Volume 18)
HUTTON ENGINEERING SERVICES	Little Falls, New York	(Volume 13)
JAMES SAMUEL MCKNIGHT, PH.D.	Raleigh, North Carolina	(Volume 14)
PFS CORPORATION	Madison, Wisconsin	(Volume 18)
LLOYD M. SONENTHAL, P.E.	Chicago, Illinois	(Volume 8)
SUMMIT PROFESSIONAL RESOURCES LLC	Hackettstown, New Jersey	(Volume 12)
WISS, JANNEY, ELSTNER ASSOCIATES, INC.	Chicago, Illinois	(Volume 8)

GEOSCIENCE

OBONI ASSOCIATES, INC.	San Francisco, California	(Volume 3)

GEOTECHNICAL

EXPERT TECHNOLOGIES INTERNATIONAL	Los Angeles, California	(Volume 2)

INDUSTRIAL REFRIGERATION

MDK ENGINEERING CORP.	Harrisburg, Pennsylvania	(Volume 15)

LIFTING EQUIPMENT

HEATH AND ASSOCIATES	Louisville, Kentucky	(Volume 9)

MECHANICAL/MACHINE DESIGN

ERIK K. ANTONSSON, PH.D. P.E.	Los Angeles, California	(Volume 2)

PLANT MANAGEMENT

JAMES J. "JIM" GADWOOD	Chicago, Illinois	(Volume 8)

SAFETY

ADVENT ENVIRONMENTAL, INC.	Louisville, Kentucky	(Volume 9)
	St. Louis, Missouri	(Volume 11)
	Charlotte, North Carolina	(Volume 14)
	Raleigh, North Carolina	(Volume 14)
	Charleston, South Carolina	(Volume 16)
AEGIS CORP.	Philadelphia, Pennsylvania	(Volume 15)
PROFESSIONAL SAFETY CONSULTANT SERVICE, INC.	Orlando, Florida	(Volume 6)
PROFESSIONAL SAFETY INCORPORATED	West Palm Beach, Florida	(Volume 6)
SAFETY MANAGEMENT ASSOCIATES	Fairfax, Virginia	(Volume 18)

TRANSPORTATION & HEAVY EQUIPMENT

CAIRD & ASSOCIATES CONSULTANTS INC. TRUCK TRAILER MANAGEMENT SERVICES DIVISION	San Francisco, California	(Volume 3)

ENVIRONMENTAL

ADVENT ENVIRONMENTAL, INC.	Louisville, Kentucky	(Volume 9)
	St. Louis, Missouri	(Volume 11)
	Charlotte, North Carolina	(Volume 14)
	Raleigh, North Carolina	(Volume 14)
	Charleston, South Carolina	(Volume 16)
ALPHA GEOLOGICAL SERVICES, INC.	Albany, New York	(Volume 12)
THE BRATTLE GROUP	Washington, District of Columbia	(Volume 5)
	Boston, Massachusetts	(Volume 10)

BUILDINGS & BUILDING SYSTEMS

LAURENCE B. MOLLOY	New York, New York	(Volume 13)

ENVIRONMENTAL CONSULTANT

ADVENT ENVIRONMENTAL, INC.	Louisville, Kentucky	(Volume 9)
	St. Louis, Missouri	(Volume 11)
	Charlotte, North Carolina	(Volume 14)
	Raleigh, North Carolina	(Volume 14)
	Charleston, South Carolina	(Volume 16)
REALTY ECONOMICS GROUP	Lawrenceville, New Jersey	(Volume 12)
TRINITY CONSULTANTS INCORPORATED	Dallas, Texas	(Volume 17)

ENVIRONMENTAL CONTAMINATION/SPILLS

ZYMAX FORENSICS	Los Angeles, California	(Volume 2)

ENVIRONMENTAL HEALTH & SAFETY

BARER ENGINEERING, P.A.	Newark, New Jersey	(Volume 12)
CARNOW, CONIBEAR & ASSOC. LTD.	Chicago, Illinois	(Volume 8)
ENVIRONMENTAL HEALTH ASSOCIATES, LTD.	New York, New York	(Volume 13)
GRANBERRY & ASSOCIATES, INC.	Washington, District of Columbia	(Volume 5)
	Orlando, Florida	(Volume 6)
	Dallas, Texas	(Volume 17)
REALTY ECONOMICS GROUP	Lawrenceville, New Jersey	(Volume 12)

ERGONOMICS

ERGONOMICS INC.	Seattle, Washington	(Volume 18)

EVIDENCE PROCUREMENT & ANALYSIS

SECONDWAVE INFORMATION SYSTEMS	Los Angeles, California	(Volume 2)

EXPLOSIVES

POST BLAST & PYROTECHNICS

SGT. DAVE AUDSLEY (RET.)	Pinedale, Arizona	(Volume 1)

EXPERT WITNESS - Continued

FAILURE ANALYSIS

CC TECHNOLOGIES SERVICES, INC. .... Columbus, Ohio .... (Volume 14)
VERSITECH CORPORATION .... Atlanta, Georgia .... (Volume 7)
WISS, JANNEY, ELSTNER ASSOCIATES, INC. .... Chicago, Illinois .... (Volume 8)

FIRE

FIRE SCIENCE AND TECHNOLOGY INC. .... Seattle, Washington .... (Volume 18)
M.A. STRINGER & ASSOCIATES, INC. .... New Orleans, Louisiana .... (Volume 9)

PROTECTION, INVESTIGATION

LFW, INC. .... Charleston, South Carolina .... (Volume 16)

FIRE CAUSE & ORIGIN

SUMMIT PROFESSIONAL RESOURCES LLC .... Hackettstown, New Jersey .... (Volume 12)

FIREARMS DESIGN

G&G FIREARMS EXPERTS .... Lowell, Massachusetts .... (Volume 10)
HUTTON ENGINEERING SERVICES .... Little Falls, New York .... (Volume 12)

FIREARMS/GUN EXPLOSIONS

G&G FIREARMS EXPERTS .... Lowell, Massachusetts .... (Volume 10)
HUTTON ENGINEERING SERVICES .... Little Falls, New York .... (Volume 12)

FIREARMS/TRAINING/SAFETY/POLICE PROCEDURES

THE PEREGRINE CORPORATION .... New York, New York .... (Volume 13)

FORENSIC PATHOLOGIST

ALI Z. HAMELI, M.D. P.A. .... New York, New York .... (Volume 13)

FORENSIC PSYCHOLOGIST

MOSS AUBREY, PH.D. .... Albuquerque, New Mexico .... (Volume 12)

FORENSIC PSYCHOLOGY

SEXUAL OFFENDERS

MOSS AUBREY, PH.D. .... Albuquerque, New Mexico .... (Volume 12)

FORENSIC VOCATIONAL/MEDICAL CONSULTANT

CENTER FOR HEAD AND FACIAL PAIN .... South Amboy, New Jersey .... (Volume 12)

FRANCHISING

EDWARD KUSHELL .... Los Angeles, California .... (Volume 2)

FRAUD

CLIFTON GUNDERSON L.L.C. .... Denver, Colorado .... (Volume 4)
EMERALD GROUP .... Los Angeles, California .... (Volume 2)
THE HALPIN GROUP, INC. .... Iselin, New Jersey .... (Volume 12)
EDMUND J. PANKAU, CLI, CPP .... Houston, Texas .... (Volume 17)
VONA & ASSOCIATES .... New York, New York .... (Volume 13)
M.D. WILLIAMSON, SR. CPA, CFE .... Dallas, Texas .... (Volume 17)

FUTURES AND OPTIONS

MARKET CONSULTING CORPORATION .... New York, New York .... (Volume 13)

GLASS

GLASS FRACTURE ANALYTICAL .... Watkins Glen, New York .... (Volume 13)
LINGNELL CONSULTING SERVICES .... Dallas, Texas .... (Volume 17)
DR. R. C. ROPP, F.R.S.C. F.A.I.C. B.C.F.E. .... Warren, New Jersey .... (Volume 12)

GRAPHICS

ORIGIN POINT, INCORPORATED .... Los Angeles, California .... (Volume 2)

HEALTH CARE FRAUD

MCSWANE & ASSOCIATES .... Houston, Texas .... (Volume 17)

HEARING LOSS

THE ROBINSON GROUP, LTD. .... Bloomfield Hills, Michigan .... (Volume 10)

HEATING/VENTILATION/AIR CONDITIONING

HOTEL/RESTAURANT INDUSTRY

HUMAN FACTORS & SAFETY

INFECTIOUS DISEASES

INSURANCE

AGENCY CONDUCT

BAD FAITH

CASUALTY/PROFESSIONAL LIABILITY

LIFE, DISABILITY & LONG TERM CARE

MARINE

INSURANCE FRAUD

INTELLECTUAL PROPERTY/INFRINGEMENT DAMAGES

EXPERT WITNESS - Continued

LAW ENFORCEMENT
DENNIS WALLER & ASSOCIATES, INC. .... Milwaukee, Wisconsin .... (Volume 18)

LEGAL ETHICS/MALPRACTICE
RHETTA M. DANIEL, ESQUIRE .... Richmond, Virginia .... (Volume 18)
BOYD S. LEMON, ESQ. .... Los Angeles, California .... (Volume 2)
CHRISTOPHER ROLIN, J.D. .... Los Angeles, California .... (Volume 2)

LEGAL FEES
ACCOUNTABILITY SERVICES .... New York, New York .... (Volume 13)
LEGAL MANAGEMENT & AUDIT GROUP, INC. .... Morristown, New Jersey .... (Volume 12)

LEGAL MALPRACTICE CASES
LITIGATION MALPRACTICE EXPERT
GARY M. WEISS .... Jupiter, Florida .... (Volume 6)

LIBEL/LINGUISTIC ANALYSIS
MEDIA ANALYSIS & COMMUNICATIONS RESEARCH .... Philadelphia, Pennsylvania .... (Volume 15)

MAGAZINE PUBLISHING
BAY SHERMAN CRAIG & GOLDSTEIN, LLP .... Los Angeles, California .... (Volume 2)

MARINE
ARTHUR B. CAMPBELL AND ASSOCIATES .... Fort Lauderdale, Florida .... (Volume 6)
B & K MARINE ENGINEERING INC. .... Trenton, New Jersey .... (Volume 12)
SUMMIT PROFESSIONAL RESOURCES LLC .... Hackettstown, New Jersey .... (Volume 12)
THOMAS ELECTRIC CONTROL, INC. .... New York, New York .... (Volume 13)
THOMAS W. BELL & ASSOCIATES .... Santa Monica, California .... (Volume 3)

MEDICARE & MEDICAID FRAUD & ABUSE
MCSWANE & ASSOCIATES .... Houston, Texas .... (Volume 17)

MENTAL HEALTH
MICHAEL H. FLYNN, PH.D. .... Dallas, Texas .... (Volume 17)
PSYCHIATRY AND MEDICINE .... Boston, Massachusetts .... (Volume 10)

METALLURGY/FAILURE ANALYSIS
AMERICAN METALLURGICAL CONSULTANTS .... Pensacola, Florida .... (Volume 6)

METEOROLOGY/CLIMATOLOGY
ALLIED WEATHER CONSULTANTS .... Los Angeles, California .... (Volume 2)
CLIMATOLOGICAL CONSULTING CORPORATION .... San Francisco, California .... (Volume 3)
Miami, Florida .... (Volume 6)
Kansas City, Kansas .... (Volume 9)
Asheville, North Carolina .... (Volume 14)
CONTINENTAL WEATHER & EARTH SCIENCES, INC. .... Los Angeles, California .... (Volume 2)
WEATHER WORKS, INC. .... Hackettstown, New Jersey .... (Volume 12)

MINING
ALPHA GEOLOGICAL SERVICES, INC. .... Albany, New York .... (Volume 12)
TREVOR R. ELLIS, CPG, CMA .... Denver, Colorado .... (Volume 4)
JOYCE ASSOCIATES, INC. .... Fairfax, Virginia .... (Volume 18)

MOTORCYCLE ACCIDENT RECONSTRUCTION
DENNIS A. TOASPERN, BCFE .... Binghamton, New York .... (Volume 12)

OIL & GAS
DON BECK & ASSOCIATES, INC. .... Richardson, Texas .... (Volume 17)
R.S.E. INC. .... Houston, Texas .... (Volume 17)
WILLIS, GRAVES & ASSOCIATES, INC. .... Austin, Texas .... (Volume 17)
ZYMAX FORENSICS .... Los Angeles, California .... (Volume 2)

PATENT LAW
JULIAN CAPLAN .... San Francisco, California .... (Volume 3)

EXPERT WITNESS - Continued

SECURITY NEGLIGENCE

SLIP, TRIP AND FALL

SPORTS, LEISURE, RECREATION

TELECOMMUNICATIONS

TELEPHONE POLES

THIRD PARTY LIABILITY ISSUES

TOXICOLOGY

TRAFFIC ENGINEERING

TRANSPORTATION

AVIATION

RAILROADS

TRAFFIC ENGINEERING & SAFETY

UNCLAIMED PROPERTY

VOCATIONAL EVALUATION

LIFE CARE PLANS

WEATHER & CLIMATE

WHEELCHAIRS

FAILURE ANALYSIS/TESTING SERVICES

CHEMIR/POLYTECH LABORATORIES, INC.	St. Louis, Missouri	(Volume 11)
FORENSIC SCIENCES INC.	Philadelphia, Pennsylvania	(Volume 15)
HAUSER LABORATORIES	Boulder, Colorado	(Volume 4)
WISS, JANNEY, ELSTNER ASSOCIATES, INC.	Chicago, Illinois	(Volume 8)

FAIRNESS OPINIONS

BUSINESS VALUATION SERVICES	San Diego, California	(Volume 3)
	San Francisco, California	(Volume 3)
	New York, New York	(Volume 13)
	Dallas, Texas	(Volume 17)
FROST & SULLIVAN	Los Angeles, California	(Volume 2)
	San Francisco, California	(Volume 3)
	Newark, New Jersey	(Volume 12)
	New York, New York	(Volume 13)
	Austin, Texas	(Volume 17)
	San Antonio, Texas	(Volume 17)

FILING COURT DOCUMENTS BY FAX

FAX & FILE LEGAL SERVICES, INC.	Los Angeles, California	(Volume 2)
	San Francisco, California	(Volume 3)

FINANCIAL DOCUMENT SERVICES

MERRILL CORPORATION	New York, New York	(Volume 13)

FINANCIAL INVESTIGATION/FORENSIC ACCOUNTING

BRACKIN & CROOKS PROFESSIONAL INVESTIGATIONS, INC.	Baton Rouge, Louisiana	(Volume 9)
LECG, A SUBSIDIARY OF NAVIGANT CONSULTING, INC.	Berkeley, California	(Volume 2)
VANCE INTERNATIONAL, INC.	Washington, District of Columbia	(Volume 5)
VONA & ASSOCIATES	New York, New York	(Volume 13)

FIRE INVESTIGATORS

CASALINOVA INVESTIGATIONS	Cleveland, Ohio	(Volume 14)
CONTINENTAL WEATHER & EARTH SCIENCES, INC.	Los Angeles, California	(Volume 2)
FIRE ENGINEERING CONSULTANTS, INC.	Panama City, Florida	(Volume 6)
FIRE SCIENCE AND TECHNOLOGY INC.	Seattle, Washington	(Volume 18)
M.A. STRINGER & ASSOCIATES, INC.	New Orleans, Louisiana	(Volume 9)

FIRE LOSS EXPERTS

KODIAK ENTERPRISES, INC.	Fort Wayne, Indiana	(Volume 8)
M.A. STRINGER & ASSOCIATES, INC.	New Orleans, Louisiana	(Volume 9)

FORENSIC DOCUMENTATION - DEMONSTRATIVE EVIDENCE

FORGERY FORENSICS© A DIVISION OF QUESTIONED DOCUMENTS, INCORPORATED	Princeton, New Jersey	(Volume 12)

FORENSIC ENGINEERING METALLURGY/FAILURE ANALYSIS

BODYCOTE TAUSSIG, INC.	Chicago, Illinois	(Volume 8)
FIBERGLASS STRUCTURAL ENGINEERING, INC.	Bellingham, Washington	(Volume 18)

FORENSIC ENGINEERS

BARER ENGINEERING, P.A.	Newark, New Jersey	(Volume 12)
BENEDICT ENGINEERING COMPANY, INC.	Tallahassee, Florida	(Volume 6)
CTL, INC.	Chicago, Illinois	(Volume 8)
ENGINEERING DATA SERVICES, INC.	Houston, Texas	(Volume 17)
FIRE & ACCIDENT RECONSTRUCTION	Los Angeles, California	(Volume 2)
FORENSIC ANALYSIS & ENGINEERING CORPORATION	Raleigh, North Carolina	(Volume 14)
FORENSIC SCIENCES INC.	Philadelphia, Pennsylvania	(Volume 15)
OMNI TECH INTERNATIONAL, LTD.	Chicago, Illinois	(Volume 8)
	Houston, Texas	(Volume 17)
ROTHFUSS ENGINEERING COMPANY	Baltimore, Maryland	(Volume 9)
WISS, JANNEY, ELSTNER ASSOCIATES, INC.	Chicago, Illinois	(Volume 8)

FORENSIC FINANCIAL ANALYSIS

FORENSIC GEOCHEMISTRY

FORENSIC MEDICINE

FORENSIC PSYCHIATRY

FORENSIC PSYCHOLOGY

FORENSIC SERVICES

GEMOLOGY

GENEALOGICAL SERVICES

GEOLOGY

HANDWRITING EXPERTS

Name	Location	Volume
ADVANCED DOCUMENT & HANDWRITING EXAMINATION SERVICES	Dallas, Texas	(Volume 17)
JAMES A. GREEN - FORENSIC DOCUMENT EXAMINER	Eugene, Oregon	(Volume 15)
PATRICIA SIEGEL ENTERPRISES, INC.	Great Neck, New York	(Volume 12)
THE SCRIPTORIUM	Los Angeles, California	(Volume 2)

HEIR TRACERS

Name	Location	Volume
AMERICAN RESEARCH BUREAU, INC.	Los Angeles, California	(Volume 2)
	Fort Lauderdale, Florida	(Volume 6)
ASSOCIATION OF PROFESSIONAL GENEALOGISTS NEW YORK METRO CHAPTER	New York, New York	(Volume 13)
HOERNER BANK	Los Angeles, California	(Volume 2)
	San Francisco, California	(Volume 3)
	Washington, District of Columbia	(Volume 5)
	Miami, Florida	(Volume 6)
	Tampa, Florida	(Volume 6)
	Chicago, Illinois	(Volume 8)
	Boston, Massachusetts	(Volume 10)
	Minneapolis, Minnesota	(Volume 11)
	Newark, New Jersey	(Volume 12)
	New York, New York	(Volume 13)
	Philadelphia, Pennsylvania	(Volume 15)
	Houston, Texas	(Volume 17)
	Seattle, Washington	(Volume 18)
	Milwaukee, Wisconsin	(Volume 18)
INTERNATIONAL GENEALOGICAL SEARCH INC.	Montgomery, Alabama	(Volume 1)
	Miami, Florida	(Volume 6)
	Seattle, Washington	(Volume 18)
LOCATORS, INC.	Anchorage, Alaska	(Volume 1)
	San Francisco, California	(Volume 3)
	Denver, Colorado	(Volume 4)
	Tampa, Florida	(Volume 6)
	New York, New York	(Volume 13)
	Redmond, Oregon	(Volume 15)
SEARCH INTERNATIONAL, LLC	Los Angeles, California	(Volume 2)
	San Francisco, California	(Volume 3)
	Hartford, Connecticut	(Volume 4)
	Miami, Florida	(Volume 6)
	Philadelphia, Pennsylvania	(Volume 15)
	Dallas, Texas	(Volume 17)
TITLE RESEARCH	New York, New York	(Volume 13)
W.C. COX AND COMPANY	Los Angeles, California	(Volume 2)
	San Francisco, California	(Volume 3)
	Chicago, Illinois	(Volume 8)
	Detroit, Michigan	(Volume 10)
	St. Louis, Missouri	(Volume 11)
	Austin, Texas	(Volume 17)
	Seattle, Washington	(Volume 18)
	Milwaukee, Wisconsin	(Volume 18)

HUMAN FACTORS & ERGONOMICS CONSULTING

Name	Location	Volume
JOY M. EBBEN, PH.D.	Los Angeles, California	(Volume 2)

IMMIGRATION & CUSTOMS CONSULTING

Name	Location	Volume
VANCE INTERNATIONAL, INC.	Washington, District of Columbia	(Volume 5)

INCORPORATION SERVICES

Name	Location	Volume
CAPITAL CONNECTION, INC.	Tallahassee, Florida	(Volume 6)
CSC THE UNITED STATES CORPORATION COMPANY	Los Angeles, California	(Volume 2)
	Wilmington, Delaware	(Volume 4)
	Tallahassee, Florida	(Volume 6)
	Chicago, Illinois	(Volume 8)
	New York, New York	(Volume 13)
	Dallas, Texas	(Volume 17)
INTERCOUNTY CLEARANCE CORPORATION	New York, New York	(Volume 13)
INTERSTATE DOCUMENT FILINGS	New York, New York	(Volume 13)
NEVADA & OFFSHORE BUSINESS FORMATION, INC.	Carson City, Nevada	(Volume 11)
RESIDENT AGENTS OF NEVADA, INC.	Carson City, Nevada	(Volume 11)
SERVICO	Albany, New York	(Volume 12)

INFORMATION CLEARING HOUSE

Name	Location	Volume
TAXPAYERS AGAINST FRAUD THE FALSE CLAIMS ACT LEGAL CENTER	Washington, District of Columbia	(Volume 5)

INSURANCE

Name	Location	Volume
AMERICAN BAR INSURANCE PLANS CONSULTANTS, INC.	Chicago, Illinois	(Volume 8)
JOHN S. MURPHY	Los Angeles, California	(Volume 2)

INSURANCE - EMPLOYMENT PRACTICES

Name	Location	Volume
ATLA MUTUAL	Chicago, Illinois	(Volume 8)
BERTHOLON-ROWLAND CORP.	New York, New York	(Volume 13)

INSURANCE - PROFESSIONAL LIABILITY

Name	Location	Volume
ATLA MUTUAL	Chicago, Illinois	(Volume 8)
BERTHOLON-ROWLAND CORP.	New York, New York	(Volume 13)
INSURANCE LITIGATION EXPERTS/CONSULTANTS	Los Angeles, California	(Volume 2)
KERNAN ASSOCIATES, INC.	New York, New York	(Volume 13)
PROQUEST INSURANCE AGENCY	Birmingham, Michigan	(Volume 10)

INSURANCE - PROPERTY/CASUALTY

Name	Location	Volume
KERNAN ASSOCIATES, INC.	New York, New York	(Volume 13)

INSURANCE - RISK MANAGEMENT CONSULTING

Name	Location	Volume
JAS ADVANCED STRATEGIES, INC. [D.B.A.] INTERNATIONAL RISK MANAGEMENT CONSULTANTS	Phoenix, Arizona	(Volume 1)
LECG, A SUBSIDIARY OF NAVIGANT CONSULTING, INC.	Berkeley, California	(Volume 2)

INSURANCE/REINSURANCE AUDITING SERVICES

Name	Location	Volume
ROBERT D. LEMBKE & ASSOCIATES, INC.	San Francisco, California	(Volume 3)

INTELLECTUAL PROPERTY DOCUMENT SERVICES

Name	Location	Volume
US-JAPAN TRANSLATIONS	Austin, Texas	(Volume 17)

INTERNATIONAL PERSONAL TAX CONSULTANT

Name	Location	Volume
ROGER B. HODGEMAN	New York, New York	(Volume 13)

INTERNET SERVICES

Name	Location	Volume
CT CORPORATION SYSTEM	New York, New York	(Volume 13)
LAWINFO.COM	San Diego, California	(Volume 3)

INTERNET/INTRANET SERVICES

Name	Location	Volume
FIRST E COMMERCE	Santa Clara, California	(Volume 3)

INTERPRETERS

Name	Location	Volume
800-TRANSLATE	New York, New York	(Volume 13)
AMERICAN LINGUISTS INTERPRETERS & TRANSLATORS, INC.	New York, New York	(Volume 13)
JEAN-MARIE BANATTE, PH.D. C.P.A	Miami, Florida	(Volume 6)
BERLITZ INTERPRETATION AND TRANSLATION SERVICES	Los Angeles, California	(Volume 2)
	San Francisco, California	(Volume 3)
	Denver, Colorado	(Volume 4)
	Hartford, Connecticut	(Volume 4)
	Washington, District of Columbia	(Volume 5)
	Miami, Florida	(Volume 6)
	Chicago, Illinois	(Volume 8)
	Boston, Massachusetts	(Volume 10)
	Detroit, Michigan	(Volume 10)
	New York, New York	(Volume 13)
	Philadelphia, Pennsylvania	(Volume 15)
	Dallas, Texas	(Volume 17)
	Houston, Texas	(Volume 17)
	Seattle, Washington	(Volume 18)
GINETTE CESAR	New York, New York	(Volume 13)
CRISTINA HELMERICHS D.	Austin, Texas	(Volume 17)
CZAR COMMUNICATIONS, INC.	Atlanta, Georgia	(Volume 7)
INTERNATIONAL LIAISON, LTD.	New York, New York	(Volume 13)
THE JURIDICAL IT, INC.	New York, New York	(Volume 13)
LANGUAGE PROS, LLC	New York, New York	(Volume 13)

INTERPRETERS & TRANSLATORS

INTERPRETERS & TRANSLATORS- Continued

Name	Location	Volume
JLS LANGUAGE CORPORATION	Los Angeles, California	(Volume 2)
	San Francisco, California	(Volume 3)
	Washington, District of Columbia	(Volume 5)
	New York, New York	(Volume 13)
THE JURIDICAL IT, INC.	New York, New York	(Volume 13)
LANGUAGE AT WORK, INC.	Naples, Florida	(Volume 6)
L.\NGUAGE PROS, LLC	New York, New York	(Volume 13)
THE LANGUAGE WORKS, INC.	Los Angeles, California	(Volume 2)
	San Francisco, California	(Volume 3)
	Washington, District of Columbia	(Volume 5)
	Princeton, New Jersey	(Volume 12)
	New York, New York	(Volume 13)
LANGUAGES INCORPORATED	Falls Church, Virginia	(Volume 18)
LANGUAGES UNLIMITED	Washington, District of Columbia	(Volume 5)
LEGAL LANGUAGE SERVICES	Los Angeles, California	(Volume 2)
	Oakland, California	(Volume 2)
	Sacramento, California	(Volume 3)
	San Diego, California	(Volume 3)
	San Francisco, California	(Volume 3)
	San Jose, California	(Volume 3)
	Denver, Colorado	(Volume 4)
	Hartford, Connecticut	(Volume 4)
	Washington, District of Columbia	(Volume 5)
	Fort Lauderdale, Florida	(Volume 6)
	Miami, Florida	(Volume 6)
	Atlanta, Georgia	(Volume 7)
	Honolulu, Hawaii	(Volume 7)
	Chicago, Illinois	(Volume 8)
	Indianapolis, Indiana	(Volume 8)
	Kansas City, Kansas	(Volume 9)
	New Orleans, Louisiana	(Volume 9)
	Baltimore, Maryland	(Volume 9)
	Boston, Massachusetts	(Volume 10)
	Detroit, Michigan	(Volume 10)
	Minneapolis, Minnesota	(Volume 11)
	Kansas City, Missouri	(Volume 11)
	St. Louis, Missouri	(Volume 11)
	Las Vegas, Nevada	(Volume 11)
	Camden, New Jersey	(Volume 12)
	Jersey City, New Jersey	(Volume 12)
	Newark, New Jersey	(Volume 12)
	Princeton, New Jersey	(Volume 12)
	Trenton, New Jersey	(Volume 12)
	Albuquerque, New Mexico	(Volume 12)
	Albany, New York	(Volume 12)
	Buffalo, New York	(Volume 12)
	Mineola, New York	(Volume 12)
	New York, New York	(Volume 13)
	Syracuse, New York	(Volume 13)
	Raleigh, North Carolina	(Volume 14)
	Cleveland, Ohio	(Volume 14)
	Portland, Oregon	(Volume 15)
	Philadelphia, Pennsylvania	(Volume 15)
	Austin, Texas	(Volume 17)
	Dallas, Texas	(Volume 17)
	El Paso, Texas	(Volume 17)
	Fort Worth, Texas	(Volume 17)
	Houston, Texas	(Volume 17)
	San Antonio, Texas	(Volume 17)
	Richmond, Virginia	(Volume 18)
	Seattle, Washington	(Volume 18)
	San Juan, Puerto Rico	(Volume 18)
THE LEGAL TRANSLATORS.COM	Washington, District of Columbia	(Volume 5)
	New York, New York	(Volume 13)
LEXIT	New York, New York	(Volume 13)
LAWRENCE LOCKWOOD	Boston, Massachusetts	(Volume 10)
NTEXT TRANSLATIONS	New York, New York	(Volume 13)
OLIVIA JOHNSTON & ASSOCIATES	Riverside, California	(Volume 3)
ONE WORLD LANGUAGE SERVICES	Albany, New York	(Volume 12)
PRINCETON TECHNICAL TRANSLATION CENTER	New Brunswick, New Jersey	(Volume 12)

INTERPRETING - DEAF/SIGN LANGUAGE

INVESTIGATIVE CONSULTANTS

INVESTIGATORS

INVESTIGATORS - Continued

Name	Location	Volume
BELTRANTE & ASSOCIATES	Washington, District of Columbia	(Volume 5)
	Chevy Chase, Maryland	(Volume 9)
	Alexandria, Virginia	(Volume 18)
BENCO ENTERPRISES, INC.	Muskegon, Michigan	(Volume 10)
BENEFICIAL INVESTIGATION SERVICES, INC.	Hartford, Connecticut	(Volume 4)
	Norwalk, Connecticut	(Volume 4)
	Stamford, Connecticut	(Volume 4)
BLACKHAWK INVESTIGATIONS	Colorado Springs, Colorado	(Volume 4)
BLAKE AND ASSOCIATES, INC.	Denver, Colorado	(Volume 4)
BLAKELEY INVESTIGATIVE SERVICES	Lexington, Kentucky	(Volume 9)
BLAZER INVESTIGATIVE	Charleston, South Carolina	(Volume 16)
BLI ™	Mobile, Alabama	(Volume 1)
BLUE MOON INVESTIGATIONS	Houston, Texas	(Volume 17)
BOB WILSON, INVESTIGATIONS	Phoenix, Arizona	(Volume 1)
BOSCH CONSULTING INVESTIGATIONS, L.L.C.	New Orleans, Louisiana	(Volume 9)
BRADLEY G. MILLER INVESTIGATORS, INC.	Beverly Hills, California	(Volume 2)
BRADSHAW INVESTIGATIVE & SECURITY CONSULTANTS	Wilkes-Barre, Pennsylvania	(Volume 15)
BRYDGES INVESTIGATIONS	Tucson, Arizona	(Volume 1)
BUSINESS CONTROLS, INC.	Denver, Colorado	(Volume 4)
CAPE FEAR INVESTIGATIONS, LTD.	Wilmington, North Carolina	(Volume 14)
CARDINAL SECURITY RESEARCHERS	Chicago, Illinois	(Volume 8)
CASALINOVA INVESTIGATIONS	Cleveland, Ohio	(Volume 14)
CENTURION PROFESSIONAL SERVICES, INC.	Charlotte, North Carolina	(Volume 14)
CHARLES R. SEAL & ASSOCIATES, INC.	Alexandria, Virginia	(Volume 18)
CITYWIDE INVESTIGATORS AND SECURITY, INC.	New York, New York	(Volume 13)
C.J. SECURITY SERVICES, INC.	White Plains, New York	(Volume 13)
CLARK INVESTIGATIVE ASSOCIATES, INC.	Boston, Massachusetts	(Volume 10)
COASTAL SECURITY SERVICE, INC.	Miami, Florida	(Volume 6)
	Virginia Beach, Virginia	(Volume 18)
CONFIDENTIAL ADVISORY SERVICES, INC.	Houston, Texas	(Volume 17)
CONFIDENTIAL SECURITY AGENCY, INC.	Columbus, Ohio	(Volume 14)
CONWAY & HENNESSY ASSOCIATES, INC.	New York, New York	(Volume 13)
COOK'S INVESTIGATION AGENCY, L.L.C.	Cedar Rapids, Iowa	(Volume 8)
COPS, INC.	Baltimore, Maryland	(Volume 9)
CORPORATE INVESTIGATIVE SERVICES, INC.	Cleveland, Ohio	(Volume 14)
CORPORATE RESOLUTIONS INC.	New York, New York	(Volume 13)
CORWIN RESEARCH & INVESTIGATIONS, LLC	Albuquerque, New Mexico	(Volume 12)
C.R. COCHRAN & ASSOCIATES	San Diego, California	(Volume 3)
CRUMBAUGH & ASSOCIATES	Chattanooga, Tennessee	(Volume 16)
DANTE INVESTIGATORS	Newark, New Jersey	(Volume 12)
	New York, New York	(Volume 13)
DATATRACE INVESTIGATIONS, INC.	Salt Lake City, Utah	(Volume 17)
DAY'S INVESTIGATIONS	New Orleans, Louisiana	(Volume 9)
DELTA AGENCY	San Francisco, California	(Volume 3)
THE DELTA COMPANY	Colorado Springs, Colorado	(Volume 4)
DENNIS R. SHERAW & ASSOCIATES, INC.	Christiansted, St. Croix, Virgin Islands	(Volume 18)
DESVERNINE ASSOCIATES	San Francisco, California	(Volume 3)
DIG DIRT INC. ™	Los Angeles, California	(Volume 2)
	Washington, District of Columbia	(Volume 5)
	Miami, Florida	(Volume 6)
	Trenton, New Jersey	(Volume 12)
	New York, New York	(Volume 13)
	Dallas, Texas	(Volume 17)
DISCOVERY DETECTIVE GROUP	Phoenix, Arizona	(Volume 1)
DOUGLAS BALDWIN & ASSOCIATES, INC.	Los Angeles, California	(Volume 2)
EAGLE INVESTIGATIONS	San Diego, California	(Volume 3)
ECONOMIC RESEARCH GROUP, INC.	Fort Lauderdale, Florida	(Volume 6)
ED GERUSA INVESTIGATIONS SERVICES CO.	Brownsville, Texas	(Volume 17)
EMERALD GROUP	Los Angeles, California	(Volume 2)
ET AL WORLD WIDE LITIGATION SUPPORT SERVICES	Austin, Texas	(Volume 17)
	Dallas, Texas	(Volume 17)
	Houston, Texas	(Volume 17)
	San Antonio, Texas	(Volume 17)
EYEWITNESS INVESTIGATIONS, INC.	Hackensack, New Jersey	(Volume 12)
FABER INVESTIGATIONS	Springfield, Missouri	(Volume 11)
FAST-TRACK INFORMATION SERVICES INC.	Ridgefield, New Jersey	(Volume 12)
FEDERATED INVESTIGATIONS	Fort Lauderdale, Florida	(Volume 6)
FIDELIFACTS/METROPOLITAN NEW YORK, INC.	New York, New York	(Volume 13)
FOCI, INCORPORATED	Lansing, Michigan	(Volume 10)
FORT ENTERPRISES PROCESS SERVERS & INVESTIGATORS	Fairbanks, Alaska	(Volume 1)

INVESTIGATORS - Continued

Name	Location	Volume
ON WATCH ™, LTD.	Los Angeles, California	(Volume 2)
	Miami, Florida	(Volume 6)
	Central Islip, New York	(Volume 12)
	Freeport, New York	(Volume 12)
	Mineola, New York	(Volume 12)
	New York, New York	(Volume 13)
OSI INVESTIGATIONS	Philadelphia, Pennsylvania	(Volume 15)
EDMUND J. PANKAU, CLI, CPP	Houston, Texas	(Volume 17)
PAPER CHASERS	Farmington, New Mexico	(Volume 12)
PARAMOUNT DETECTIVE AGENCY, INC.	Salt Lake City, Utah	(Volume 17)
PARISH LITIGATION SERVICES & INVESTIGATIONS, INC.	Tyler, Texas	(Volume 17)
PARKER INVESTIGATIONS/SECURITY	Albany, Georgia	(Volume 7)
PARKER, MADISON & LINDQUIST, INC.	Salt Lake City, Utah	(Volume 17)
PAULA DRAKE INVESTIGATIONS	Palo Alto, California	(Volume 3)
THE PECORARO GROUP	Schenectady, New York	(Volume 13)
PHOENIX RESEARCH CORPORATION	New York, New York	(Volume 13)
PINNACLE INVESTIGATIONS, INC.	Red Bank, New Jersey	(Volume 12)
PLI INC.	Sacramento, California	(Volume 3)
PREMIER INVESTIGATIONS, INC.	Memphis, Tennessee	(Volume 16)
PRICON INVESTIGATIONS	White Plains, New York	(Volume 13)
PRIMESOURCE INTELLIGENCE GROUP	Jefferson City, Missouri	(Volume 11)
	Kansas City, Missouri	(Volume 11)
	Springfield, Missouri	(Volume 11)
	St. Louis, Missouri	(Volume 11)
PRIORITY INVESTIGATIONS	Columbus, Ohio	(Volume 14)
PROFESSIONAL LEGAL INQUIRIES	Woburn, Massachusetts	(Volume 10)
	Manchester, New Hampshire	(Volume 11)
RAETHER INVESTIGATIONS	Appleton, Wisconsin	(Volume 18)
RICHARD A. MARTINEZ INVESTIGATIVE SERVICES	Santa Fe, New Mexico	(Volume 12)
THE RICHMOND GROUP INTERNATIONAL	Washington, District of Columbia	(Volume 5)
R.J. MONTGOMERY ASSOCIATES	Hackensack, New Jersey	(Volume 12)
R. L. HUNT ENTERPRISES	Santa Barbara, California	(Volume 3)
ROBERT CLARK INVESTIGATIONS	Hamilton, New Jersey	(Volume 12)
ROBERT J. CASTELLI ASSOCIATES, INC.	New York, New York	(Volume 13)
RON SCHEIDERER & ASSOCIATES	Marion, Ohio	(Volume 14)
ROSS SECURITY CONSULTANTS, INC.	Newark, New Jersey	(Volume 12)
	New York, New York	(Volume 13)
ROWELL & ASSOCIATES	Little Rock, Arkansas	(Volume 1)
SARAO & ASSOCIATES ™	Atlantic City, New Jersey	(Volume 12)
	Hackensack, New Jersey	(Volume 12)
	Newark, New Jersey	(Volume 12)
SCHNEIDER SECURITY & INVESTIGATIVE SERVICES	Pensacola, Florida	(Volume 6)
SECURITY INTELLIGENCE AGENCY	Washington, District of Columbia	(Volume 5)
SEWELL INVESTIGATIONS	Flagstaff, Arizona	(Volume 1)
SHADOW WARRIOR INVESTIGATIONS	New York, New York	(Volume 13)
SHOALS INVESTIGATIVE SERVICES	Birmingham, Alabama	(Volume 1)
	New York, New York	(Volume 13)
SIERRA INVESTIGATIONS	Knoxville, Tennessee	(Volume 16)
SIGHTHOUND INC.	Washington, District of Columbia	(Volume 5)
SIMMONS AGENCY, INC.	Boston, Massachusetts	(Volume 10)
SMITH INVESTIGATIONS & ENTERPRISES	Shreveport, Louisiana	(Volume 9)
SOUTHWEST SECURITY AND INVESTIGATIONS	Dallas, Texas	(Volume 17)
SPECIAL INVESTIGATIONS, INC.	Indianapolis, Indiana	(Volume 8)
SPECIALIZED INVESTIGATIONS	Los Angeles, California	(Volume 2)
SPYGLASS INVESTIGATIONS	Sacramento, California	(Volume 3)
S.S. INVESTIGATIONS, INC.	El Paso, Texas	(Volume 17)
STATE INFORMATION BUREAU	Tallahassee, Florida	(Volume 6)
STEPHENS INVESTIGATIONS, INC.	Alexandria, Louisiana	(Volume 9)
SUPER SEARCH, INC.	Dallas, Texas	(Volume 17)
SURVEILLANCE TECHNOLOGIES, INC.	Birmingham, Alabama	(Volume 1)
SUTHERLIN ASSOCIATED SERVICES	San Diego, California	(Volume 3)
SUTTON & KISER INTERNATIONAL INVESTIGATIVE SERVICE, INC.	Greenville, South Carolina	(Volume 16)
TALONE & ASSOCIATES, INC.	Philadelphia, Pennsylvania	(Volume 15)
T.A.M.A. INVESTIGATIONS, INC.	Atlanta, Georgia	(Volume 7)
TECHNICAL SECURITY ANALYSTS, INC.	Detroit, Michigan	(Volume 10)
TELESIS INFORMATION SYSTEMS, INC.	Dallas, Texas	(Volume 17)
THIRD EYE INVESTIGATIONS	Houston, Texas	(Volume 17)
TRIAD INVESTIGATIONS, INC.	Rogers, Arkansas	(Volume 1)
TRIAD PROTECTIVE & INVESTIGATIVE SERVICES, LLC	Morristown, New Jersey	(Volume 12)
TSCHIRGI INVESTIGATIONS, INC.	Orlando, Florida	(Volume 6)
U.S. INTELL®	Chicago, Illinois	(Volume 8)

JAIL MAIL

JURY CONSULTANTS

LABORATORIES - GEOCHEMICAL/PETROLEUM/SOURCE ID

LABORATORIES - PARENTAGE TESTING

LAW OFFICE AUTOMATION SERVICES

LAWYER REFERRAL SERVICE

Name	Location	Volume
ALL NATIONAL LAWYER REFERRAL SERVICE	Denver, Colorado	(Volume 4)
	Honolulu, Hawaii	(Volume 7)
	Portland, Oregon	(Volume 15)
	Seattle, Washington	(Volume 18)

LAWYER SEARCH & PLACEMENT CONSULTANTS

Name	Location	Volume
A V SEARCH CONSULTANTS	Bridgewater, New Jersey	(Volume 12)
ASSOCIATED COUNSEL OF AMERICA ®	Houston, Texas	(Volume 17)
AUDREY GOLDEN ASSOCIATES, LTD.	New York, New York	(Volume 13)
BARRY GOLDBERG & ASSOCIATES, INC.	Los Angeles, California	(Volume 2)
BAUM, STEVENS, INC.	New York, New York	(Volume 13)
BELLON & ASSOCIATES, INC.	Atlanta, Georgia	(Volume 7)
CALDWELL & ASSOCIATES, INC.	Dallas, Texas	(Volume 17)
CALDWELL LEGAL RECRUITING CONSULTANTS	Chicago, Illinois	(Volume 8)
CHARLES V. SNIDER & ASSOCIATES	Cleveland, Ohio	(Volume 14)
CHEMONICS INTERNATIONAL	Washington, District of Columbia	(Volume 5)
CHICAGO LEGAL SEARCH, LTD	Chicago, Illinois	(Volume 8)
COUNSEL SEARCH	Atlanta, Georgia	(Volume 7)
DFM & ASSOCIATES	Dallas, Texas	(Volume 17)
DOUG SEARS & ASSOCIATES	Charlotte, North Carolina	(Volume 14)
	Philadelphia, Pennsylvania	(Volume 15)
ECG RESOURCES	New York, New York	(Volume 13)
ELAINE P. DINE INC.	New York, New York	(Volume 13)
ELAINE P. DINE TEMPORARY ATTORNEYS & PARALEGALS LLC	New York, New York	(Volume 13)
EMPLAWYERNET	San Francisco, California	(Volume 3)
THE ESTRIN ORGANIZATION	Los Angeles, California	(Volume 2)
F-O-R-T-U-N-E PERSONNEL CONSULTANTS OF DETROIT, INC.	Detroit, Michigan	(Volume 10)
FERGUS LEGAL SEARCH & CONSULTING INC./FERGUS PARTNERSHIP CONSULTING INC.	New York, New York	(Volume 13)
H. HERTNER ASSOCIATES, INC.	Miami, Florida	(Volume 6)
HAYSTACK CONSULTING	Grand Rapids, Michigan	(Volume 10)
HOUSER MARTIN MORRIS	Seattle, Washington	(Volume 18)
JM ASSOCIATES	Los Angeles, California	(Volume 2)
JURIS PLACEMENT INTERNATIONAL	New York, New York	(Volume 13)
KAPLAN & JASS	Boston, Massachusetts	(Volume 10)
LANDMARK LEGAL PROFESSIONALS	San Jose, California	(Volume 3)
LEGEND LEGAL STAFFING, INC.	Newark, New Jersey	(Volume 12)
	New York, New York	(Volume 13)
MAJOR LEGAL SERVICES, INC.	Cleveland, Ohio	(Volume 14)
MATTESON PARTNERS LTD.	Atlanta, Georgia	(Volume 7)
MCCORMACK SCHREIBER LEGAL SEARCH	Chicago, Illinois	(Volume 8)
THE MCCORMICK GROUP, INC.	Washington, District of Columbia	(Volume 5)
MCMORROW ASSOCIATES, INC.	Los Angeles, California	(Volume 2)
MILLER & ASSOCIATES	Tampa, Florida	(Volume 6)
MYRA BINSTOCK LEGAL SEARCH	New York, New York	(Volume 13)
NEW ENGLAND LEGAL SEARCH	Boston, Massachusetts	(Volume 10)
ODELL LEGAL SEARCH	Dallas, Texas	(Volume 17)
PERSONNEL RESOURCES ORGANIZATION, INC.	Wilmington, Delaware	(Volume 4)
	Washington, District of Columbia	(Volume 5)
	Baltimore, Maryland	(Volume 9)
	Princeton, New Jersey	(Volume 12)
	New York, New York	(Volume 13)
	Philadelphia, Pennsylvania	(Volume 15)
THE PETERSAN GROUP, INC.	New York, New York	(Volume 13)
PITTLEMAN & ASSOCIATES	New York, New York	(Volume 13)
PREFERRED PLACEMENT, INC.	New York, New York	(Volume 13)
RAND THOMPSON CONSULTANTS, INC	New York, New York	(Volume 13)
S.R. CLARKE, INC.	Fairfax, Virginia	(Volume 18)
SOUTHSEARCH, INC. LEGAL RECRUITERS	Miami, Florida	(Volume 6)
	Atlanta, Georgia	(Volume 7)
SOUTHERN ASSOCIATES	Chicago, Illinois	(Volume 8)
SUTHERLAND HERMANN ASSOCIATES	Washington, District of Columbia	(Volume 5)
TOPAZ ATTORNEY SEARCH	West Orange, New Jersey	(Volume 12)
UPDATE LEGAL STAFFING	Boston, Massachusetts	(Volume 10)
	Newark, New Jersey	(Volume 12)
	New York, New York	(Volume 13)
	Philadelphia, Pennsylvania	(Volume 15)
	Houston, Texas	(Volume 17)
WILLIAM K. MCLAUGHLIN ASSOCIATES	New York, New York	(Volume 13)
ZISKIND GREENE CONTRACT ATTORNEYS & PARALEGALS	Los Angeles, California	(Volume 2)

LEGAL RESEARCH

CHARLES JONES, LLC	Newark, New Jersey	(Volume 12)
	Trenton, New Jersey	(Volume 12)
GREENE-COHEN & WINSTON, INC.	New York, New York	(Volume 13)
IDEX ™	Shawnee Mission, Kansas	(Volume 9)
LEXIS PUBLISHING ™	Los Angeles, California	(Volume 2)
	San Francisco, California	(Volume 3)
	Miami, Florida	(Volume 6)
	Newark, New Jersey	(Volume 12)
	New York, New York	(Volume 13)
	Dallas, Texas	(Volume 17)
THE NATIONAL CRIME VICTIM BAR ASSOCIATION	Arlington, Virginia	(Volume 18)
NEW YORK LEGISLATIVE SERVICE, INC.	New York, New York	(Volume 13)
TENNESSEE ATTORNEYS MEMO	Nashville, Tennessee	(Volume 16)

LEGAL SOFTWARE

ADC LEGAL SYSTEMS, INC.	Orlando, Florida	(Volume 6)
	Raleigh, North Carolina	(Volume 14)
ARMSTRONG DISTRIBUTORS, INC.	Seattle, Washington	(Volume 18)
CIT	Los Angeles, California	(Volume 2)
	San Diego, California	(Volume 3)
	San Francisco, California	(Volume 3)
	Miami, Florida	(Volume 6)
	Tampa, Florida	(Volume 6)
	New York, New York	(Volume 13)
	Dallas, Texas	(Volume 17)
	Houston, Texas	(Volume 17)
COMPUTER LAW SYSTEMS, INC. (CLS)	Minneapolis, Minnesota	(Volume 11)
COMPUTER PACKAGES INC.	Washington, District of Columbia	(Volume 5)
FIRST E COMMERCE	Santa Clara, California	(Volume 3)
GOLDEN OMEGA SOFTWARE	Santa Clara, California	(Volume 3)
GOODHAND COMPUTING SOLUTIONS	Rochester, New York	(Volume 12)
HOTDOCS ®	Los Angeles, California	(Volume 2)
	New York, New York	(Volume 13)
JURIS, INC.	Los Angeles, California	(Volume 2)
KAHUNA SOFTWARE, INC.	New York, New York	(Volume 13)
LACKNER GROUP, INC.	Pittsburgh, Pennsylvania	(Volume 15)
LAWGIC PUBLISHING COMPANY	Novato, California	(Volume 2)
LEGAL+PLUS SOFTWARE GROUP, INC.	Seattle, Washington	(Volume 18)
NORTH AMERICAN SOFTWARE, INC.	Cincinnati, Ohio	(Volume 14)
SAGA, INC.	New York, New York	(Volume 13)
SAGE U.S. INCORPORATED	Dallas, Texas	(Volume 17)
TIMEBILLS.COM	Los Angeles, California	(Volume 2)
WORLDOX/WORLD SOFTWARE	New York, New York	(Volume 13)

LEGAL SUPPORT PERSONNEL - TEMPORARY & PERMANENT

ELAINE P. DINE TEMPORARY ATTORNEYS & PARALEGALS LLC	New York, New York	(Volume 13)
INITIAL LEGAL STAFFING	Los Angeles, California	(Volume 2)
MAJOR LEGAL SERVICES, INC.	Cleveland, Ohio	(Volume 14)
NRI LEGAL STAFFING	Washington, District of Columbia	(Volume 5)
PATRICIA CARROLL PERSONNEL CONSULTANTS	Philadelphia, Pennsylvania	(Volume 15)
TRUEX LEGAL	San Francisco, California	(Volume 3)
UPDATE LEGAL STAFFING	Boston, Massachusetts	(Volume 10)
	Newark, New Jersey	(Volume 12)
	New York, New York	(Volume 13)
	Philadelphia, Pennsylvania	(Volume 15)
	Houston, Texas	(Volume 17)
ZISKIND GREENE CONTRACT ATTORNEYS & PARALEGALS	Los Angeles, California	(Volume 2)

LIBRARY MANAGEMENT SERVICES

AXELROTH & ASSOCIATES	Los Angeles, California	(Volume 2)
LAW LIBRARY MANAGEMENT, INCORPORATED	New York, New York	(Volume 13)

LIFE CARE PLANNING

BEACON REHABILITATION SERVICES, INC.	Ann Arbor, Michigan	(Volume 10)
CARE MANAGERS, INC.	Lansing, Michigan	(Volume 10)
CASE MANAGEMENT, INC.	Birmingham, Alabama	(Volume 1)
CMS HEALTH MANAGEMENT SERVICES	Huntsville, Alabama	(Volume 1)

LINGUISTICS

LITIGATION CONSULTING

LITIGATION SUPPORT - ENVIRONMENTAL

LITIGATION SUPPORT - INTERNATIONAL

LITIGATION SUPPORT SERVICES

LITIGATION SUPPORT SERVICES - Continued

LITIGATION SUPPORT SOFTWARE

LOBBYIST

MALPRACTICE LEGAL DEFENSE

MANAGEMENT CONSULTANTS

MARINE CONSULTANTS

MARKETING

MEDICAL CASE REVIEW & PREPARATION/TRIAL CONSULTING

MEDICAL EVALUATION - BRAIN INJURIES

MEDICAL EXPERT WITNESS

MEDICAL EXPERT WITNESS - Continued

ANESTHESIOLOGY

MEDIAMEDICA .... Philadelphia, Pennsylvania .... (Volume 15)

CARDIOLOGY

THOMAS J. BERGER M.D. F.A.C.S. F.C.C.P. F.A.C.F.E. .... Los Angeles, California .... (Volume 2)
New York, New York .... (Volume 13)

MEDIAMEDICA .... Philadelphia, Pennsylvania .... (Volume 15)

CARDIOLOGY, INTERNAL MEDICINE & GERIATRIC

CCC CONSOLIDATED CONSULTANTS CO. .... New York, New York .... (Volume 13)

DENTAL

J. CRYSTAL BAXTER, DMD, MDS .... Chicago, Illinois .... (Volume 8)
MELVYN A. BLAKE, D.D.S. J.D. - DENTAL CONSULTANT .... Cherry Hill, New Jersey .... (Volume 12)
WILLEAM A. CHOBY BS RDH DMD MAGD FICCMO MPA .... Johnstown, Pennsylvania .... (Volume 15)
HUGH R. HUNSINGER, D.M.D. F.A.G.D. L.L.C. .... New York, New York .... (Volume 13)

TMJ

CENTER FOR HEAD AND FACIAL PAIN .... South Amboy, New Jersey .... (Volume 12)
THE CENTER OF MYOFACIAL PAIN/TMJ THERAPY .... New York, New York .... (Volume 13)
RONALD L. NEER, D.D.S. .... Chicago, Illinois .... (Volume 8)

EMERGENCY MEDICAL SERVICES - E.M.S.

RONALD CROWELL, M.D. A PROFESSIONAL CORPORATION .... Santa Fe Springs, California .... (Volume 3)

FAMILY PRACTICE

DAVID A. LIBERT, M.D. F.A.A.F.P. .... Orlando, Florida .... (Volume 6)

FOOT SURGERY/CARE

JEFFREY L. ADLER, D.P.M. .... Eastchester, New York .... (Volume 13)

FORENSIC PATHOLOGY

ALI Z. HAMELI, M.D. P.A. .... New York, New York .... (Volume 13)

GASTROENTEROLOGY

GASTROINTESTINAL MEDICAL EXPERTS .... New York, New York .... (Volume 13)

INTERNAL MEDICINE

GASTROINTESTINAL MEDICAL EXPERTS .... New York, New York .... (Volume 13)
MEDIAMEDICA .... Philadelphia, Pennsylvania .... (Volume 15)

MEDICAL CASE REVIEW

MALPRACTICE & PERS. INJ.

AMERICAN MEDICAL FORENSIC SPECIALISTS, INC. .... Los Angeles, California .... (Volume 2)
San Francisco, California .... (Volume 3)
Miami, Florida .... (Volume 6)
New York, New York .... (Volume 13)
Philadelphia, Pennsylvania .... (Volume 15)
Houston, Texas .... (Volume 17)

MEDICALLY SPEAKING ® .... Los Angeles, California .... (Volume 2)

MEDICAL DEVICES

AINSLIE .... New York, New York .... (Volume 13)

MEDICAL INFORMATION SPECIALIST

MEDISYS MEDICAL INFORMATION SYSTEMS .... Kingston, New York .... (Volume 12)

NEPHROLOGY

CONSULTANT NEPHROLOGIST .... Cooperstown, New York .... (Volume 12)

NEUROLOGY

ARTHUR TAUB, M.D. PH.D. P.C. .... New York, New York .... (Volume 13)
CALIFORNIA NEUROLOGICAL SPECIALISTS .... Los Angeles, California .... (Volume 2)
MEDIAMEDICA .... Philadelphia, Pennsylvania .... (Volume 15)
JOHN STIRLING MEYER, M.D. .... Houston, Texas .... (Volume 17)

MEDICAL EXPERT WITNESS - Continued

PSYCHOLOGY

FORENSIC

BARRINGTON PSYCHIATRIC CENTER .... Los Angeles, California .... (Volume 2)
NEUROLEGAL SCIENCES, INC. .... Albuquerque, New Mexico .... (Volume 12)
NEW ENGLAND FORENSIC ASSOCIATES .... Arlington, Massachusetts .... (Volume 10)
THE NEW YORK CENTER FOR NEUROPSYCHOLOGY & FORENSIC BEHAVIORAL SCIENCE .... New York, New York .... (Volume 13)
RICHARD M. SAMUELS, PH.D. FCLINP, FAACS. .... New York, New York .... (Volume 13)
SHEALY, HOLT AND JACOBS .... Birmingham, Alabama .... (Volume 1)
RICHARD UGLAND, EDD, L.P. .... Minneapolis, Minnesota .... (Volume 11)

NEUROPSYCHOLOGY

ARTHUR TAUB, M.D. PH.D. P.C. .... New York, New York .... (Volume 13)
BOB L. GANT, PH.D. .... Dallas, Texas .... (Volume 17)
THE NEW YORK CENTER FOR NEUROPSYCHOLOGY & FORENSIC BEHAVIORAL SCIENCE .... New York, New York .... (Volume 13)
ROLLAND S. PARKER, PH.D. .... New York, New York .... (Volume 13)

RADIOLOGY

BARRY B. CAMPBELL, M.D. .... Carlsbad, California .... (Volume 2)
CONSULTANTS IN MEDICAL IMAGING .... Philadelphia, Pennsylvania .... (Volume 15)
DARWOOD B. HANCE, M.D. .... Los Angeles, California .... (Volume 2)

MRI/MUSCULOSKELETAL IMAGING

CONSULTANTS IN MEDICAL IMAGING .... Philadelphia, Pennsylvania .... (Volume 15)

SURGERY

CARDIOVASCULAR THORACIC

THOMAS J. BERGER M.D. F.A.C.S. F.C.C.P. F.A.C.F.E. .... Los Angeles, California .... (Volume 2)
New York, New York .... (Volume 13)
MICHAEL J. O'SULLIVAN, M.D. J.D. INC. .... San Diego, California .... (Volume 3)

HAND SURGERY

JONATHAN A. LEWIS, MD, FACS .... Houston, Texas .... (Volume 17)
JOHN J. O'HARA, M.D. .... Los Angeles, California .... (Volume 2)

ORTHOPEDIC

ROBERT ANTHONY BAIRD, M.D. .... Irvine, California .... (Volume 2)
JONATHAN A. LEWIS, MD, FACS .... Houston, Texas .... (Volume 17)

TOXICOLOGY

ALAN BUCHWALD, M.D. FAAEM, ACMT, ABEM (TOX.) .... Santa Cruz, California .... (Volume 3)
THERESA HOFFMAN-TILL, PH.D. .... Washington, District of Columbia .... (Volume 5)
NATIONAL MEDICAL SERVICES, INC. .... Philadelphia, Pennsylvania .... (Volume 15)
RICHARD J. SCHLESINGER, PH.D. DABFT .... Los Angeles, California .... (Volume 2)
NORMAN M. TRIEFF, PH.D. .... Houston, Texas .... (Volume 17)

UROLOGY

GEORGE KLEIN, M.D. .... New York, New York .... (Volume 13)

VOCATIONAL REHABILITATION

RICHARD UGLAND, EDD, L.P. .... Minneapolis, Minnesota .... (Volume 11)

MEDICAL EXPERT WITNESS REFERRAL SERVICES

CCC CONSOLIDATED CONSULTANTS CO. .... San Francisco, California .... (Volume 3)
CERA, INC. .... Pensacola, Florida .... (Volume 6)
GISELLE T. LETOURNEAU .... Butte, Montana .... (Volume 11)
MEDIAMEDICA .... Philadelphia, Pennsylvania .... (Volume 15)
MEDICAL RESEARCH CONSULTANTS, INC. .... Houston, Texas .... (Volume 17)

MEDICAL ILLUSTRATORS

THE MEDICAL ILLUSTRATION STUDIO .... Nashville, Tennessee .... (Volume 16)
MEDICAL RENDERINGS & IMAGES .... Philadelphia, Pennsylvania .... (Volume 15)

MEDICAL MALPRACTICE CONSULTING/PERSONAL INJURY

MEDICAL - LEGAL CONSULTING .... Charleston, West Virginia .... (Volume 18)
PALM BEACH MEDICAL CONSULTANTS .... Miami, Florida .... (Volume 6)
PSYCHIATRY AND MEDICINE .... Boston, Massachusetts .... (Volume 10)

PARALEGAL SERVICES - Continued

Name	Location	Volume
COLTEN & CO. TRANSLATORS; AND BIOMEDICAL TRANSLATION CO.	Arlington, Virginia	(Volume 18)
COMPLETE OFFICE SUPPORT, INC.	Tucson, Arizona	(Volume 1)
COURTFAX	New York, New York	(Volume 13)
ELAINE P. DINE TEMPORARY ATTORNEYS & PARALEGALS LLC	New York, New York	(Volume 13)
EXPERT DOCUMENTS, INC.	Tucson, Arizona	(Volume 1)
GREAT BASIN PARALEGALS	Elko, Nevada	(Volume 11)
INTEGRATED LEGAL SERVICE & ASSOCIATES	Phoenix, Arizona	(Volume 1)
INTERCOUNTY CLEARANCE CORPORATION	New York, New York	(Volume 13)
GISELLE T. LETOURNEAU	Butte, Montana	(Volume 11)
MAJOR LEGAL SERVICES, INC.	Cleveland, Ohio	(Volume 14)
MIDWEST PARALEGAL SERVICES, INC.	Milwaukee, Wisconsin	(Volume 18)
NRI LEGAL STAFFING	Washington, District of Columbia	(Volume 5)
OCALA PARALEGAL SERVICES, INC.	Ocala, Florida	(Volume 6)
OHIO PARALEGAL SERVICES, INC.	Akron, Ohio	(Volume 14)
PARALEGAL RESOURCE CENTER, INC.	Boston, Massachusetts	(Volume 10)
PARALEGAL RESOURCES	Atlanta, Georgia	(Volume 7)
PARALEGAL SERVICES	Washington, District of Columbia	(Volume 5)
PARALEGAL SERVICES OF NORTH CAROLINA, INC.	Raleigh, North Carolina	(Volume 14)
SEATTLE DETECTIVE BUREAU	Seattle, Washington	(Volume 18)
W.H. COUCH & COMPANY	Baltimore, Maryland	(Volume 9)
ZISKIND GREENE CONTRACT ATTORNEYS & PARALEGALS	Los Angeles, California	(Volume 2)

PATENT, TRADEMARK & COPYRIGHT SEARCH SERVICES

Name	Location	Volume
1-800-4-TRADEMARK, INC.	Miami, Florida	(Volume 6)
COMPUTER PACKAGES INC.	Washington, District of Columbia	(Volume 5)
GOVERNMENT LIAISON SERVICES, INC.	Arlington, Virginia	(Volume 18)
INTELLECTUAL PROPERTY MANAGEMENT	Los Angeles, California	(Volume 2)
SPECIALIZED PATENT SERVICES	Arlington, Virginia	(Volume 18)
THOMSON & THOMSON	Los Angeles, California	(Volume 2)
	Boston, Massachusetts	(Volume 10)
TM INVESTIGATIONS GROUP, INC.	New York, New York	(Volume 13)
TRADEMARKS CORPORATE SERVICE BUREAU	Albany, New York	(Volume 12)
US-JAPAN TRANSLATIONS	Austin, Texas	(Volume 17)

PERSONNEL CONSULTANTS

Name	Location	Volume
LAW FIRM MANAGEMENT CONSULTING, INC.	Dallas, Texas	(Volume 17)

PETROCHEMICAL, REFINING, GAS PLANT, PIPELINE ENGINEERS

Name	Location	Volume
GREENE & ASSOCIATES, INC.	Dallas, Texas	(Volume 17)
	Houston, Texas	(Volume 17)

PETROLEUM SOURCE IDENTIFICATION

Name	Location	Volume
ZYMAX FORENSICS	Los Angeles, California	(Volume 2)

PHOTOGRAPHY

Name	Location	Volume
SUMMIT PROFESSIONAL RESOURCES LLC	Hackettstown, New Jersey	(Volume 12)

POLYGRAPH EXAMINATION SERVICES

Name	Location	Volume
ARGUS INVESTIGATIVE SERVICES, INC.	Newark, New Jersey	(Volume 12)
BOB FERRER, INC.	Miami, Florida	(Volume 6)
FEDERAL POLYGRAPH ASSOCIATES, L.L.C.	Atlanta, Georgia	(Volume 7)
INVESTIGATIVE SOLUTIONS, INC.	Atlanta, Georgia	(Volume 7)
IQM, INC: BUSINESS INVESTIGATIONS	Dallas, Texas	(Volume 17)
IVEY INVESTIGATIVE SERVICES	Peoria, Illinois	(Volume 8)
JACK TRIMARCO & ASSOCIATES POLYGRAPH/INVESTIGATIONS, INC.	Los Angeles, California	(Volume 2)
JOHN E. REID AND ASSOCIATES, INC.	Chicago, Illinois	(Volume 8)
MARYLAND INSTITUTE OF CRIMINAL JUSTICE	Baltimore, Maryland	(Volume 9)
SCIENTIFIC LIE DETECTION, INC.	New York, New York	(Volume 13)
SHAFFER & ASSOCIATES FORENSIC TECHNOLOGIES	Orlando, Florida	(Volume 6)
SUTTON & KISER INTERNATIONAL INVESTIGATIVE SERVICE, INC.	Greenville, South Carolina	(Volume 16)

PRESS RELEASES

Name	Location	Volume
LAW & MEDIA GROUP, INC.	Atlanta, Georgia	(Volume 7)

PROCESS SERVERS & DOCUMENT DELIVERY SERVICES

PROCESS SERVERS & DOCUMENT DELIVERY SERVICES - Continued

A-1 RELIABLE COURIER SERVICE, INC.	Alachua, Florida	(Volume 6)
	Miami, Florida	(Volume 6)
AA RIVER CITY REPORTERS & VIDEO	Jacksonville, Florida	(Volume 6)
AAA LEGAL SERVICES	Phoenix, Arizona	(Volume 1)
AAA PROCESS SERVERS, INC.	Denver, Colorado	(Volume 4)
AAA WORLDWIDE PROCESS & DETECTIVE AGENCY, INC.	Fort Lauderdale, Florida	(Volume 6)
	Jacksonville, Florida	(Volume 6)
	Miami, Florida	(Volume 6)
	Orlando, Florida	(Volume 6)
	St. Petersburg, Florida	(Volume 6)
	Tampa, Florida	(Volume 6)
ACCURATE PROCESS SERVICE	Milwaukee, Wisconsin	(Volume 18)
ACE PROCESS SERVICE	Los Angeles, California	(Volume 2)
ACE REPORTING SERVICES	Cincinnati, Ohio	(Volume 14)
ALLSTATE PROCESS SERVERS	Boston, Massachusetts	(Volume 10)
THE ALPHA AND OMEGA AGENCY	Corpus Christi, Texas	(Volume 17)
AMERICAN CIVIL PROCESS SERVICES, INC.	Houston, Texas	(Volume 17)
AMERICAN CLERICAL SERVICE	New York, New York	(Volume 13)
AMERICAN INVESTIGATIVE SERVICES, INC.	Boston, Massachusetts	(Volume 10)
APR INTERNATIONAL	Schenectady, New York	(Volume 13)
A.S.A. INFORMATION SERVICES	Dallas, Texas	(Volume 17)
A.S.A.P. ATTORNEY SERVICES	Dayton, Ohio	(Volume 14)
ASSOCIATED INVESTIGATORS, INC.	Washington, District of Columbia	(Volume 5)
ATLANTA ATTORNEY SERVICES	Atlanta, Georgia	(Volume 7)
ATLANTA LEGAL SERVICES, INC.	Atlanta, Georgia	(Volume 7)
ATTORNEY SERVICES OF NORTHEAST OHIO	Cleveland, Ohio	(Volume 14)
ATTORNEY'S MEDICAL RECORDS	San Antonio, Texas	(Volume 17)
ATTORNEYS' PERSONAL SERVICES, INC.	Atlanta, Georgia	(Volume 7)
AUTHORIZED PROCESS SERVERS BY P.S. IVAN	Albuquerque, New Mexico	(Volume 12)
BEXAR PROFESSIONAL CIVIL PROCESS SERVICE INC.	San Antonio, Texas	(Volume 17)
BIG APPLE PROCESS SERVICE	New York, New York	(Volume 13)
BLAKELEY INVESTIGATIVE SERVICES	Lexington, Kentucky	(Volume 9)
BLAZER INVESTIGATIVE	Charleston, South Carolina	(Volume 16)
BLI ™	Mobile, Alabama	(Volume 1)
BORG PROCESS SERVERS INC.	Phoenix, Arizona	(Volume 1)
	Los Angeles, California	(Volume 2)
	San Francisco, California	(Volume 3)
	Washington, District of Columbia	(Volume 5)
	Miami, Florida	(Volume 6)
	Orlando, Florida	(Volume 6)
	Tampa, Florida	(Volume 6)
	Atlanta, Georgia	(Volume 7)
	Chicago, Illinois	(Volume 8)
	Baltimore, Maryland	(Volume 9)
	Boston, Massachusetts	(Volume 10)
	Detroit, Michigan	(Volume 10)
	New York, New York	(Volume 13)
	Philadelphia, Pennsylvania	(Volume 15)
	Dallas, Texas	(Volume 17)
	Houston, Texas	(Volume 17)
BRIEF ENCOUNTERS, INC.	Nashville, Tennessee	(Volume 16)
BUTLER AND ASSOCIATES CONSTABLES, INC.	Boston, Massachusetts	(Volume 10)
C & G	Cleveland, Ohio	(Volume 14)
CAGEY BEE SERVICES	Sacramento, California	(Volume 3)
CAPITOL PROCESS SERVICES AND CAPITOL INVESTIGATOR SERVICES	Washington, District of Columbia	(Volume 5)
CHICAGO METRO LEGAL PROCESS	Arlington Heights, Illinois	(Volume 8)
C.J. SECURITY SERVICES, INC.	White Plains, New York	(Volume 13)
CONNECTICUT PROCESS SERVICE	Bridgeport, Connecticut	(Volume 4)
	Hartford, Connecticut	(Volume 4)
	New Haven, Connecticut	(Volume 4)
	Stamford, Connecticut	(Volume 4)
	Waterbury, Connecticut	(Volume 4)
COPS, INC.	Baltimore, Maryland	(Volume 9)
CRUMBAUGH & ASSOCIATES	Chattanooga, Tennessee	(Volume 16)
CURTIS D. RUFF AND ASSOCIATES	Lubbock, Texas	(Volume 17)
DATATRACE INVESTIGATIONS, INC.	Salt Lake City, Utah	(Volume 17)
DAVID SCOTT BUSCH LEGAL SUPPORT SERVICES	San Antonio, Texas	(Volume 17)
DHR & ASSOCIATES	Boston, Massachusetts	(Volume 10)

PROCESS SERVERS & DOCUMENT DELIVERY SERVICES - Continued

Company	Location	Volume
LEGALEASE INC.	St. Petersburg, Florida	(Volume 6)
	Baton Rouge, Louisiana	(Volume 9)
	Las Vegas, Nevada	(Volume 11)
	New York, New York	(Volume 13)
LONE STAR ATTORNEY SERVICE, INC.	Houston, Texas	(Volume 17)
MARYLAND PROCESS SERVERS, INC.	Baltimore, Maryland	(Volume 9)
MCDANIEL & ASSOCIATES	Montgomery, Alabama	(Volume 1)
MERCURY MESSENGERS, INC.	Topeka, Kansas	(Volume 9)
METRO LEGAL SERVICES, INC.	Minneapolis, Minnesota	(Volume 11)
	St. Paul, Minnesota	(Volume 11)
MID-SOUTH LEGAL SERVICES	Birmingham, Alabama	(Volume 1)
NATIONAL DATA ACCESS CORPORATION	Charlotte, North Carolina	(Volume 14)
	Greensboro, North Carolina	(Volume 14)
	Raleigh, North Carolina	(Volume 14)
	Columbia, South Carolina	(Volume 16)
	Greenville, South Carolina	(Volume 16)
	Spartanburg, South Carolina	(Volume 16)
NATIONWIDE LEGAL SERVICES, LLC	Sacramento, California	(Volume 3)
NEW JERSEY LAWYERS SERVICE	Atlantic City, New Jersey	(Volume 12)
	Cherry Hill, New Jersey	(Volume 12)
	Morristown, New Jersey	(Volume 12)
	Newark, New Jersey	(Volume 12)
	Princeton, New Jersey	(Volume 12)
	Trenton, New Jersey	(Volume 12)
NIZIANKIEWICZ & MILLER REPORTING SERVICES	Stamford, Connecticut	(Volume 4)
NORCAL ATTORNEY SERVICE	Sacramento, California	(Volume 3)
NORTHWEST PROCESS & INVESTIGATIONS, INC.	Tacoma, Washington	(Volume 18)
NUMARK INVESTIGATIONS	Las Vegas, Nevada	(Volume 11)
OKLAHOMA LEGAL PROCESS SERVICE, INC.	Lawton, Oklahoma	(Volume 14)
ON WATCH ™, LTD.	Los Angeles, California	(Volume 2)
	Miami, Florida	(Volume 6)
	Central Islip, New York	(Volume 12)
	Freeport, New York	(Volume 12)
	Mineola, New York	(Volume 12)
	New York, New York	(Volume 13)
PACIFIC PROCESS SERVICE	Spokane, Washington	(Volume 18)
PAPER CHASERS	Farmington, New Mexico	(Volume 12)
PAPER HANGERS	Charlotte, North Carolina	(Volume 14)
PARALEGAL SERVICES	Washington, District of Columbia	(Volume 5)
PARALEGAL SERVICES OF NORTH CAROLINA, INC.	Raleigh, North Carolina	(Volume 14)
PARAMOUNT DETECTIVE AGENCY, INC.	Salt Lake City, Utah	(Volume 17)
PARKER, MADISON & LINDQUIST, INC.	Salt Lake City, Utah	(Volume 17)
PRO-VEST, INC.	Fort Lauderdale, Florida	(Volume 6)
PROFESSIONAL PROCESS SERVICE OF ATLANTA, INC.	Atlanta, Georgia	(Volume 7)
PROFESSIONAL PROCESS SERVING, INC.	Rockville, Maryland	(Volume 9)
THE RICHMOND GROUP INTERNATIONAL	Washington, District of Columbia	(Volume 5)
RONDOUT LEGAL SERVICES, INC.	Kingston, New York	(Volume 12)
	Poughkeepsie, New York	(Volume 12)
SARAO & ASSOCIATES ™	Atlantic City, New Jersey	(Volume 12)
	Hackensack, New Jersey	(Volume 12)
SECURITY INTELLIGENCE AGENCY	Washington, District of Columbia	(Volume 5)
SHAMROCK LEGAL SUPPORT	Seattle, Washington	(Volume 18)
SHELBY COUNTY PROCESS SERVERS, INC. TENNESSEE INVESTIGATIONS & PARALEGAL SERVICE, INC.	Memphis, Tennessee	(Volume 16)
SHERMAN, ALEXANDER & ASSOCIATES LLC	Los Angeles, California	(Volume 2)
SUPER SEARCH, INC.	Dallas, Texas	(Volume 17)
T.A.M.A. INVESTIGATIONS, INC.	Atlanta, Georgia	(Volume 7)
TALONE & ASSOCIATES, INC.	Philadelphia, Pennsylvania	(Volume 15)
TECHNICAL SECURITY ANALYSTS, INC.	Detroit, Michigan	(Volume 10)
TEXAS CIVIL PROCESS, INCORPORATED	Corpus Christi, Texas	(Volume 17)
THOMAS G. KEANE & ASSOC. LTD.	Chicago, Illinois	(Volume 8)
TRACK DOWN, INC.	Phoenix, Arizona	(Volume 1)
UNITED PROCESS SERVICE	Phoenix, Arizona	(Volume 1)
UNITED PROCESS SERVICE, INC.	New York, New York	(Volume 13)
UPSTATE PROCESS SERVICES	Greenville, South Carolina	(Volume 16)
UPTOWN LEGAL SERVICES, INC.	San Diego, California	(Volume 3)
VAUSE'S PROCESS SERVICE	Tallahassee, Florida	(Volume 6)
WASHINGTON PRE-TRIAL SERVICES, INC.	Washington, District of Columbia	(Volume 5)
WEEKS AND ASSOCIATES L.L.C.	Austin, Texas	(Volume 17)
WORLD CLASS INVESTIGATIONS, INC. D/B/A PROCESS EXPRESS	Melbourne, Florida	(Volume 6)

SECURITY CONSULTANTS

INVESTIGATIVE SOLUTIONS, INC.	Atlanta, Georgia	(Volume 7)
PROFESSIONAL SAFETY INCORPORATED	West Palm Beach, Florida	(Volume 6)
ROBERT J. CASTELLI ASSOCIATES, INC.	New York, New York	(Volume 13)
VANCE INTERNATIONAL, INC.	Washington, District of Columbia	(Volume 5)

SECURITY; EXPERT WITNESS

INVESTIGATIVE SOLUTIONS, INC.	Atlanta, Georgia	(Volume 7)

SEXUAL HARASSMENT - TRAINING & TESTING PROGRAMS

G. GOVINE CONSULTING	Pasadena, California	(Volume 3)

SKIP TRACERS

AUTHORIZED PROCESS SERVERS BY P.S. IVAN	Albuquerque, New Mexico	(Volume 12)
CAGEY BEE SERVICES	Sacramento, California	(Volume 3)
COLLEXX, INC.	Long Valley, New Jersey	(Volume 12)
DATALAND INVESTIGATIVE & FINANCIAL INFORMATION RESOURCES	Beverly Hills, California	(Volume 2)
DAY'S INVESTIGATIONS	New Orleans, Louisiana	(Volume 9)
PEOPLE LOCATOR	Fort Lauderdale, Florida	(Volume 6)
TRAK AMERICA, INC.	Huntington, New York	(Volume 12)

STRATEGIC PLANNING

FROST & SULLIVAN	Los Angeles, California	(Volume 2)
	San Francisco, California	(Volume 3)
	Newark, New Jersey	(Volume 12)
	New York, New York	(Volume 13)
	Austin, Texas	(Volume 17)
	San Antonio, Texas	(Volume 17)
RACKEMANN STRATEGIC CONSULTING, INC.	Boston, Massachusetts	(Volume 10)

SURVEYING - LAND

BOCK & CLARK	Akron, Ohio	(Volume 14)

SURVEYS & OPINION RESEARCH

BEHAVIORAL SCIENCE RESEARCH	Miami, Florida	(Volume 6)
COGAN RESEARCH GROUP	Los Angeles, California	(Volume 2)

TECHNICAL SERVICE COMPANIES

AMERICAN STANDARDS TESTING BUREAU, INC.	New York, New York	(Volume 13)

TECHNICAL, MANAGEMENT AND FINANCIAL EXPERTS

LAW FIRM MANAGEMENT CONSULTING, INC.	Dallas, Texas	(Volume 17)

TELECONFERENCING

MIVNET	Miami, Florida	(Volume 6)

TEMPORARY ATTORNEY SERVICES

ADJUNCTLEGAL	Washington, District of Columbia	(Volume 5)
BELLON & ASSOCIATES, INC.	Atlanta, Georgia	(Volume 7)
ELAINE P. DINE TEMPORARY ATTORNEYS & PARALEGALS LLC	New York, New York	(Volume 13)
LAWCORPS® LEGAL STAFFING SERVICES	Chicago, Illinois	(Volume 8)
ZISKIND GREENE CONTRACT ATTORNEYS & PARALEGALS	Los Angeles, California	(Volume 2)

TIME BILLING SOFTWARE/SYSTEMS

ADC LEGAL SYSTEMS, INC.	Orlando, Florida	(Volume 6)
	Raleigh, North Carolina	(Volume 14)
CMS/DATA CORPORATION ®	Tallahassee, Florida	(Volume 6)
GOODHAND COMPUTING SOLUTIONS	Rochester, New York	(Volume 12)
JURIS, INC.	Los Angeles, California	(Volume 2)
SAGE U.S. INCORPORATED	Dallas, Texas	(Volume 17)
TIMEBILLS.COM	Los Angeles, California	(Volume 2)
EVELOCITY CORPORATION	Boston, Massachusetts	(Volume 10)

TITLE & ABSTRACT COMPANIES

TITLE INSURANCE

TOXICOLOGY

TRAINING SEMINARS & RETREATS

TRANSCRIPTION SERVICES

TRANSCRIPTION SERVICES - Continued

LNS COURT REPORTING	Portland, Oregon	(Volume 15)
	Salem, Oregon	(Volume 15)
	Vancouver, Washington	(Volume 18)
MARSHALL GOLDBERG ASSOCIATES	Newark, New Jersey	(Volume 12)
	Trenton, New Jersey	(Volume 12)
MONTANA REPORTING SERVICE, INC.	Tampa, Florida	(Volume 6)
PRIDE TRANSCRIPTION	Albany, New York	(Volume 12)
RANDY BLACK & ASSOCIATES, INC.	San Francisco, California	(Volume 3)
ROBERT H. LANGE CO. INC.	Boston, Massachusetts	(Volume 10)
STEN-TEL	Phoenix, Arizona	(Volume 1)
	Los Angeles, California	(Volume 2)
	San Diego, California	(Volume 3)
	San Francisco, California	(Volume 3)
	Washington, District of Columbia	(Volume 5)
	Jacksonville, Florida	(Volume 6)
	Miami, Florida	(Volume 6)
	Orlando, Florida	(Volume 6)
	Atlanta, Georgia	(Volume 7)
	Chicago, Illinois	(Volume 8)
	Baltimore, Maryland	(Volume 9)
	Boston, Massachusetts	(Volume 10)
	Newark, New Jersey	(Volume 12)
	Buffalo, New York	(Volume 12)
	New York, New York	(Volume 13)
	Philadelphia, Pennsylvania	(Volume 15)
	Dallas, Texas	(Volume 17)
	Houston, Texas	(Volume 17)
TACOMA MEDICAL TRANSCRIPTION	Tacoma, Washington	(Volume 18)
WORDCENTER, INC.	Albuquerque, New Mexico	(Volume 12)
WORDS ON THE GO, ETC.	Oakland, California	(Volume 2)
YOUR PROFESSIONAL SECRETARY	Austin, Texas	(Volume 17)

TRANSLATION SERVICES

3I COMPANY	Philadelphia, Pennsylvania	(Volume 15)
800-TRANSLATE	New York, New York	(Volume 13)
ACCENT ON LANGUAGE	New York, New York	(Volume 13)
AD-EX WORLDWIDE	Menlo Park, California	(Volume 2)
ADVANCED LINGUISTIC SERVICES	San Francisco, California	(Volume 3)
ALBORS & ASSOCIATES, INC.	Miami, Florida	(Volume 6)
ALL LANGUAGES BY MENTANI, INC.	Tampa, Florida	(Volume 6)
ALL-LANGUAGE SERVICES, INC.	Trenton, New Jersey	(Volume 12)
	New York, New York	(Volume 13)
ALLIANCE LANGUAGE SERVICES	Dallas, Texas	(Volume 17)
AMERICAN LINGUISTS INTERPRETERS & TRANSLATORS, INC.	New York, New York	(Volume 13)
JEAN-MARIE BANATTE, PH.D. C.P.A	Miami, Florida	(Volume 6)
BERKELEY SCIENTIFIC TRANSLATION SERVICE, INC.	Berkeley, California	(Volume 2)
BERLITZ INTERPRETATION AND TRANSLATION SERVICES	Los Angeles, California	(Volume 2)
	San Francisco, California	(Volume 3)
	Denver, Colorado	(Volume 4)
	Hartford, Connecticut	(Volume 4)
	Washington, District of Columbia	(Volume 5)
	Miami, Florida	(Volume 6)
	Chicago, Illinois	(Volume 8)
	Boston, Massachusetts	(Volume 10)
	Detroit, Michigan	(Volume 10)
	New York, New York	(Volume 13)
	Philadelphia, Pennsylvania	(Volume 15)
	Dallas, Texas	(Volume 17)
	Houston, Texas	(Volume 17)
	Seattle, Washington	(Volume 18)
GINETTE CESAR	New York, New York	(Volume 13)
RALITSA R. COMBS	New York, New York	(Volume 13)
CZAR COMMUNICATIONS, INC.	Atlanta, Georgia	(Volume 7)
EURONET LANGUAGE SERVICES, INC.	New York, New York	(Volume 13)
CRISTINA HELMERICHS D.	Austin, Texas	(Volume 17)
ROBERT O. HESS, J.D.	San Francisco, California	(Volume 3)
INTERLINGUA.COM, INC.	Los Angeles, California	(Volume 2)
INTERLINGUA EXPRESS	Los Angeles, California	(Volume 2)
INTERNATIONAL LIAISON, LTD.	New York, New York	(Volume 13)

Name	Location	Volume
JAPAN COMMUNICATION CONSULTANTS, LLC	New York, New York	(Volume 13)
JLS LANGUAGE CORPORATION	Los Angeles, California	(Volume 2)
	San Francisco, California	(Volume 3)
	San Jose, California	(Volume 3)
	Washington, District of Columbia	(Volume 5)
	New York, New York	(Volume 13)
THE JURIDICAL IT, INC.	New York, New York	(Volume 13)
LANGUAGE AT WORK, INC.	Naples, Florida	(Volume 6)
LANGUAGE LEARNING ENTERPRISES INC.	Washington, District of Columbia	(Volume 5)
LANGUAGE PROS, LLC	New York, New York	(Volume 13)
THE LANGUAGE WORKS, INC.	Los Angeles, California	(Volume 2)
	San Francisco, California	(Volume 3)
	Washington, District of Columbia	(Volume 5)
	Princeton, New Jersey	(Volume 12)
	New York, New York	(Volume 13)
LANGUAGES INCORPORATED	Falls Church, Virginia	(Volume 18)
LCS LANGUAGE & CULTURAL SERVICES	New York, New York	(Volume 13)
LEGAL LANGUAGE SERVICES	Los Angeles, California	(Volume 2)
	Oakland, California	(Volume 2)
	Sacramento, California	(Volume 3)
	San Francisco, California	(Volume 3)
	San Jose, California	(Volume 3)
	Denver, Colorado	(Volume 4)
	Hartford, Connecticut	(Volume 4)
	Washington, District of Columbia	(Volume 5)
	Miami, Florida	(Volume 6)
	Atlanta, Georgia	(Volume 7)
	Chicago, Illinois	(Volume 8)
	Baltimore, Maryland	(Volume 9)
	Boston, Massachusetts	(Volume 10)
	Detroit, Michigan	(Volume 10)
	Kansas City, Missouri	(Volume 11)
	St. Louis, Missouri	(Volume 11)
	Las Vegas, Nevada	(Volume 11)
	Camden, New Jersey	(Volume 12)
	Jersey City, New Jersey	(Volume 12)
	Newark, New Jersey	(Volume 12)
	Princeton, New Jersey	(Volume 12)
	Trenton, New Jersey	(Volume 12)
	Albany, New York	(Volume 12)
	Buffalo, New York	(Volume 12)
	Mineola, New York	(Volume 12)
	New York, New York	(Volume 13)
	Cincinnati, Ohio	(Volume 14)
	Cleveland, Ohio	(Volume 14)
	Philadelphia, Pennsylvania	(Volume 15)
	Dallas, Texas	(Volume 17)
	Houston, Texas	(Volume 17)
	San Antonio, Texas	(Volume 17)
	Richmond, Virginia	(Volume 18)
	Seattle, Washington	(Volume 18)
THE LEGAL TRANSLATORS.COM	Los Angeles, California	(Volume 2)
	Washington, District of Columbia	(Volume 5)
	Miami, Florida	(Volume 6)
	New York, New York	(Volume 13)
	Dallas, Texas	(Volume 17)
	Houston, Texas	(Volume 17)
LEO KANNER ASSOCIATES	San Jose, California	(Volume 3)
LEXIT	New York, New York	(Volume 13)
LAWRENCE LOCKWOOD	Boston, Massachusetts	(Volume 10)
DAVID N. MARINELLI	New York, New York	(Volume 13)
NTEXT TRANSLATIONS	New York, New York	(Volume 13)
ONE WORLD LANGUAGE SERVICES	Albany, New York	(Volume 12)
ANNA MARIA PALMISANO	New York, New York	(Volume 13)
PRINCETON TECHNICAL TRANSLATION CENTER	New Brunswick, New Jersey	(Volume 12)
PROFESSIONAL GERMAN TRANSLATIONS	New York, New York	(Volume 13)
AMY RUSSELL, M.A.	San Francisco, California	(Volume 3)
NICOLE THIBAUD	New York, New York	(Volume 13)
TRANSLATION & INTERPRETING GROUP	Providence, Rhode Island	(Volume 16)
WORLD LANGUAGE SERVICES	Newark, New Jersey	(Volume 12)

TRANSLATION SERVICES - Continued

Company	Location	Volume
WORLDWIDE TRANSLATIONS, INC.	Miami, Florida	(Volume 6)
	Boston, Massachusetts	(Volume 10)
	Newark, New Jersey	(Volume 12)
	New York, New York	(Volume 13)
	Houston, Texas	(Volume 17)

TRANSPORTATION ENGINEERING - CONSULTING & FORENSIC SERVICES

Company	Location	Volume
R.H. DUNN & ASSOCIATES, INC.	Jacksonville, Florida	(Volume 6)
	Norfolk, Virginia	(Volume 18)
	Richmond, Virginia	(Volume 18)
TRANSPORTATION RESEARCH CORPORATION	Alexandria, Virginia	(Volume 18)

TRIAL CONSULTANTS

Company	Location	Volume
ADVOCACY RESEARCH INSTITUTE, INC.	Kansas City, Missouri	(Volume 11)
BEHAVIORAL SCIENCE RESEARCH	Miami, Florida	(Volume 6)
BEST EVIDENCE, INC.	St. Petersburg, Florida	(Volume 6)
	Tampa, Florida	(Volume 6)
COURTROOM SCIENCES, INC.	Dallas, Texas	(Volume 17)
KARLA FISCHER, PH.D. J.D.	New York, New York	(Volume 13)
HBH SERVICES	Los Angeles, California	(Volume 2)
HENNINGTON & ASSOCIATES	Los Angeles, California	(Volume 2)
	New York, New York	(Volume 13)
JURY DYNAMICS, INC.	Woodcliff Lake, New Jersey	(Volume 12)
JURY RESEARCH INSTITUTE	Los Angeles, California	(Volume 2)
	San Francisco, California	(Volume 3)
LAURIE WEBB & ASSOCIATES	Las Vegas, Nevada	(Volume 11)
LMC - A LITIGATION MEDIA CENTER	Houston, Texas	(Volume 17)
NATIONAL JURY PROJECT/EAST	New York, New York	(Volume 13)
NATIONAL JURY PROJECT/MIDWEST	Chicago, Illinois	(Volume 8)
	Columbus, Ohio	(Volume 14)
NATIONAL JURY PROJECT/WEST	Los Angeles, California	(Volume 2)
	San Francisco, California	(Volume 3)
	Seattle, Washington	(Volume 18)
ON TRIAL ASSOCIATES, INC.	Washington, District of Columbia	(Volume 5)
PC&A LITIGATION SUPPORT SERVICES	Minneapolis, Minnesota	(Volume 11)
SCHLESINGER ASSOCIATES, INC.	New York, New York	(Volume 13)
TRIAL CONSULTING ASSOCIATES	Newton, Massachusetts	(Volume 10)
ZAGNOLI MCEVOY FOLEY LTD.	Chicago, Illinois	(Volume 8)

TRIAL EXHIBITS

Company	Location	Volume
BEST EVIDENCE, INC.	St. Petersburg, Florida	(Volume 6)
	Tampa, Florida	(Volume 6)
ZAGNOLI MCEVOY FOLEY LTD.	Chicago, Illinois	(Volume 8)

TRUST & FIDUCIARY SERVICES

Company	Location	Volume
COMMONWEALTH TRUST COMPANY	Wilmington, Delaware	(Volume 4)
GISELLE T. LETOURNEAU	Butte, Montana	(Volume 11)

TRUST COMPANIES

Company	Location	Volume
ANDREOLI, JOHANSON & WOOD	Los Angeles, California	(Volume 2)
COMMONWEALTH TRUST COMPANY	Wilmington, Delaware	(Volume 4)

UCC FILING - PUBLICATIONS

Company	Location	Volume
INTERCOUNTY CLEARANCE CORPORATION	New York, New York	(Volume 13)
OHIO PARALEGAL SERVICES, INC.	Akron, Ohio	(Volume 14)

UCC SEARCH SERVICES

Company	Location	Volume
ACCESS INFORMATION SERVICES, INC.	Albany, New York	(Volume 12)
COASTAL OFFICE DIMENSIONS	Pensacola, Florida	(Volume 6)
COLORADO RECORDS SEARCH, INC.	Denver, Colorado	(Volume 4)
DILIGENZ	Seattle, Washington	(Volume 18)
INTERCOUNTY CLEARANCE CORPORATION	New York, New York	(Volume 13)
IQ DATA SYSTEMS	Sacramento, California	(Volume 3)
LAURA A. LIVINGSTON D/B/A EQUISEARCH	Lexington, Kentucky	(Volume 9)

UNEMPLOYMENT HEARINGS & APPEALS CONSULTANTS

VALUATION SERVICES

VIDEO CONFERENCING

VIDEO PRODUCTION, EDITING & GRAPHICS

VIDEO TAPE SERVICES

VIDEO TAPE SERVICES - Continued

Firm	Location	Volume
CATUOGNO COURT REPORTING SERVICE, INC.	Boston, Massachusetts	(Volume 10)
	Springfield, Massachusetts	(Volume 10)
CERTIFIED COURT REPORTERS, INC.	Jacksonville, Florida	(Volume 6)
	Miami, Florida	(Volume 6)
	Orlando, Florida	(Volume 6)
	Tampa, Florida	(Volume 6)
CERTIFIED REPORTING & VIDEO SERVICE	Corpus Christi, Texas	(Volume 17)
CHRISTINE FELTS & ASSOCIATES	Ann Arbor, Michigan	(Volume 10)
	Detroit, Michigan	(Volume 10)
	Flint, Michigan	(Volume 10)
	Kalamazoo, Michigan	(Volume 10)
	Lansing, Michigan	(Volume 10)
	Troy, Michigan	(Volume 10)
CONNELL REPORTING	Moline, Illinois	(Volume 8)
CORPOLONGO & QUELCH, INC.	Seattle, Washington	(Volume 18)
COURT REPORTING SERVICES, INC.	Newark, New Jersey	(Volume 12)
DE SCRIBE REPORTING, INC.	Southfield, Michigan	(Volume 10)
DESKTOP VIDEO PRODUCTIONS, INC.	Atlanta, Georgia	(Volume 7)
EMPIRE LEGAL VIDEO	Santa Ana, California	(Volume 3)
FULTON-BELANGER & ASSOCIATES	Louisville, Kentucky	(Volume 9)
GEOMATRIX PRODUCTIONS	New Haven, Connecticut	(Volume 4)
GORE & PERRY REPORTING COMPANY	St. Louis, Missouri	(Volume 11)
GREEN LEGAL VIDEO, LLC.	Tucson, Arizona	(Volume 1)
HABEAS VIDEAS	Los Angeles, California	(Volume 2)
HANSON/RENAISSANCE COURT REPORTERS	Detroit, Michigan	(Volume 10)
HOUSTON REPORTING & VIDEO SERVICES	Houston, Texas	(Volume 17)
INTERIM COURT REPORTING	Seattle, Washington	(Volume 18)
	Tacoma, Washington	(Volume 18)
JONES FRITZ & SHEEHAN	Boston, Massachusetts	(Volume 10)
JUPITER LEGAL VIDEO SERVICES	New York, New York	(Volume 13)
KNIPES-COHEN ASSOCIATES, INC.	Philadelphia, Pennsylvania	(Volume 15)
LACEY SHORTHAND REPORTING CORPORATION AND LACEY VIDEO SERVICES	Los Angeles, California	(Volume 2)
LAURIE WEBB & ASSOCIATES	Las Vegas, Nevada	(Volume 11)
LAWS REPORTING, INC.	Miami, Florida	(Volume 6)
LEGAL MEDIA INCORPORATED	Houston, Texas	(Volume 17)
LEGAL VIDEO SERVICE	Nashville, Tennessee	(Volume 16)
LEGAL VIDEO SERVICES, INC.	Indianapolis, Indiana	(Volume 8)
LEGAL VIDEO SPECIALISTS, INC.	Seattle, Washington	(Volume 18)
LEGAL VIDEO, INC.	St. Paul, Minnesota	(Volume 11)
LEWIS LEGAL VIDEO	Houston, Texas	(Volume 17)
LITICORP	Chicago, Illinois	(Volume 8)
LITIGATION VIDEO SERVICES (LITVID)	Los Angeles, California	(Volume 2)
MAES & SIMSON, INC.	Los Angeles, California	(Volume 2)
	Oakland, California	(Volume 2)
	Sacramento, California	(Volume 3)
	San Diego, California	(Volume 3)
	San Francisco, California	(Volume 3)
	Santa Rosa, California	(Volume 3)
MCGINNIS & ASSOCIATES, INC.	Columbus, Ohio	(Volume 14)
METRO COURT REPORTING, INC.	St. Louis, Missouri	(Volume 11)
N.T.V. PRODUCTIONS LEGAL SERVICES	Las Vegas, Nevada	(Volume 11)
NATIONWIDE VIDEO PRODUCTIONS	Newark, New Jersey	(Volume 12)
	Roseland, New Jersey	(Volume 12)
NEW YORK LEGAL VIDEO SERVICES	New York, New York	(Volume 13)
NORTH SUBURBAN REPORTING & LEGAL MEDIA, INC.	Chicago, Illinois	(Volume 8)
PC&A LITIGATION SUPPORT SERVICES	Minneapolis, Minnesota	(Volume 11)
PARALEGAL SERVICES	Washington, District of Columbia	(Volume 5)
PATTERSON REPORTING & VIDEO SERVICE, INC.	Denver, Colorado	(Volume 4)
PRO-SYSTEMS COURT REPORTING & VIDEO SERVICES	Minneapolis, Minnesota	(Volume 11)
RAY EGGEBRAATEN CSR, INC.	Fresno, California	(Volume 2)
ROBERT A. DEMPSTER & ASSOCIATES	St. Petersburg, Florida	(Volume 6)
	Tampa, Florida	(Volume 6)
RON FLEMING VIDEO	Orlando, Florida	(Volume 6)
SCLAFANI WILLIAMS COURT REPORTERS, INC.	Sarasota, Florida	(Volume 6)
	St. Petersburg, Florida	(Volume 6)
	Tampa, Florida	(Volume 6)

VIDEO TELECONFERENCING

VIDEO TRIAL PRESENTATIONS

VIOLENCE IN THE WORKPLACE

VOCATIONAL DISABILITY ASSESSMENT

VOCATIONAL EVALUATIONS/LIFE CARE PLANNING

VOCATIONAL REHABILITATION

WEATHER & CLIMATE

CONTINENTAL WEATHER & EARTH SCIENCES, INC. .... Los Angeles, California .... (Volume 2)

WEB DESIGN - INTERNET CONSULTING

FB&B CONSULTING GROUP, INC. .... Los Angeles, California .... (Volume 2)
FIRST E COMMERCE .... Santa Clara, California .... (Volume 3)

WHITE COLLAR CRIMINAL/FRAUD INVESTIGATION

BCA PROTECTIVE & INVESTIGATIVE SERVICES .... Los Angeles, California .... (Volume 2)
INVESTIGATIVE SOLUTIONS, INC. .... Atlanta, Georgia .... (Volume 7)
LAPORTE, SEHRT, ROMIG & HAND .... Metairie, Louisiana .... (Volume 9)
THE PECORARO GROUP .... Schenectady, New York .... (Volume 13)
PROFILE INFORMATION SERVICES .... Austin, Texas .... (Volume 17)
SARAO & ASSOCIATES ™ .... Atlantic City, New Jersey .... (Volume 12)
Hackensack, New Jersey .... (Volume 12)
VANCE INTERNATIONAL, INC. .... Washington, District of Columbia .... (Volume 5)

SERVICES, SUPPLIERS, CONSULTANTS NATIONAL GEOGRAPHICAL INDEX

The Services, Suppliers, Consultants Section provides information on businesses and professionals serving the legal community. This index is listed alphabetically by category then within each category alphabetically by state, city and service name. Whether you are looking for a court reporter in your own jurisdiction or an expert witness in another state, the Services, Suppliers, Consultants Section is your direct link to legal support services.

SERVICES, SUPPLIERS, CONSULTANTS

List of Categories

- Engineers/Engineering
- Engineers/Engineering - Architectural
- Environmental & Ecological Services
- Environmental Consultants
- Environmental Engineering & Remediation Services
- Environmental Health & Safety
- Environmental Investigations
- Environmental Risk Assessment and Consulting
- Environmental Risk Management & Compliance Information
- Equine - Appraisers & Consultants
- Escrow Services
- Estate Planning & Personal Benefits
- Estate Valuations
- Examiners Of Questioned Documents (Handwriting Experts)
- Executive Protective Services
- Expert Witness
  - Arboriculture & Forestry
  - Accident Investigation & Reconstruction
  - Accident Reconstruction
  - Accidents/Fires/Product Liability
  - Accounting
    - Business Damages
    - Malpractice
  - Acoustics
    - Sound, Noise & Vibration
  - Admiralty
  - Agri-Horticultural
  - Agronomy
  - Air Pollution
  - Air Safety
  - Animal Behavior
  - Antiquity & Art Conservation
  - Appraisal Services
    - Gems & Jewelry
  - Aquatics
  - Architects
  - Audio-Tape Analysis/Authentication/Voice ID
  - Audiology
  - Automobile
    - Appraiser & Consultant
    - Forensic
    - Occupant Biomechanics
  - Banking
    - Finance
    - Trusts & Investments
  - Biomechanical Engineering
  - Biomedical Engineering
  - Blasting Damage
  - Bunk Bed Safety
  - Burglar & Fire Alarm
  - Bus Operations
    - School/Transit/Highway
  - Carpal Tunnel Syndrome
  - Chemical Process
    - Safety
  - Class Action Notice
  - Coatings/Paint
  - Commercial Law
  - Commodity Futures
  - Communications
  - Computer & Business Information Systems
  - Computer Forensics/Data Recovery
  - Computer Programming & Consulting
  - Computer Science/Intellectual Property
  - Computer Technology Industry
  - Construction
    - Building Codes
    - Chimney & Fireplace
    - Defects
    - Scaffolding
  - Conveyor Safety
  - Cooling Towers
  - Corporate Whistle Blowers/Former Employees
  - Corrections
    - Jail/Prison/Lockup
  - Corrections (Adult & Juvenile)/Use of Force/Wrongful Death
  - Cranes
  - Criminalistics & Firearms
  - Currency Trading
  - DUI
  - Damage Valuation
  - Demolition
  - Document Examination/Comprehension
  - Drugs/Alcohol/Toxicology
  - Economics/Economists
    - Agricultural/Environmental
    - Financial Valuation
    - Statistics
  - Economics/Statistics
  - Education/Schools
  - Electrical
    - Electrical Utility Problems
    - Electrocution, Explosion & Fire
    - Electronics
  - Electronic Countermeasures
  - Electronic Devices& Systems
  - Electrostatic & Radiation
  - Elevators
  - Eminent Domain/Planning & Engineering
  - Employee/Employment
    - Discrimination
    - Negligence Hiring/Retention
    - OSHA Regulations/Procedures
    - Practices
    - Wrongful Termination/Harassment
  - Employment Discrimination & Disparate Impact
  - Employment Practices
  - Engineers/Engineering
    - Acoustics
    - Agricultural/Mechanical
    - Architecture
    - Automotive
    - Chemical
    - Civil/Mechanical/Structural
    - Corrosion
    - Electrical
    - Electrical Project Management
    - Electrical/Accidents/Utilities
    - Fire Protection
    - Forensic Engineering
    - GeoScience
    - Geotechnical
    - Industrial Refrigeration
    - Lifting Equipment
    - Materials
    - Mechanical/Machine Design
    - Plant Management
    - Refrigeration
    - Safety
    - Scientific
    - Transportation & Heavy Equipment
  - Entertainment & Music
  - Entertainment, Leisure, Recreation
    - Theme Parks
  - Environmental
    - Buildings & Building Systems
  - Environmental Consultant
  - Environmental Containment/Spills
  - Environmental Health & Safety
  - Ergonomics
  - Evidence Procurement & Analysis
  - Explosives
    - Post Blast & Pyrotechnics
  - Failure Analysis
  - Federal Taxation and Tax Accounting
  - Fire
    - Protection, Investigation
    - Reconstruction
    - Wildland/Urban Interface
  - Fire Cause & Origin
  - Firearms Design
  - Firearms/Gun Explosions
  - Firearms/Training/Safety/Police Procedures
  - Forensic Pathologist
  - Forensic Psychologist
  - Forensic Psychology
    - Sexual Offenders
  - Forensic Vocational/Medical Consultant
  - Franchising
  - Fraud
  - Futures and Options
  - Gas Engineering
  - Glass
  - Government Contract Claims
  - Graphics
  - Health Care Fraud
  - Hearing Loss
  - Heating/Ventilation/Air Conditioning
  - Horses (Equine)

Expert Witness (continued)
- Hotel/Restaurant Industry
- Human Factors & Safety
- Infectious Diseases
- Insurance
  - Agency Conduct
  - Bad Faith
  - Casualty/Professional Liability
  - Life, Disability & Long Term Care
  - Life, Disability & Medical Expense
  - Marine
- Insurance Fraud
- Intellectual Property/Infringement Damages
- Ladders
- Law Enforcement
- Lead Based Paint
- Legal Ethics/Malpractice
- Legal Fees
- Legal Malpractice
  - Litigation Malpractice Expert
- Legislative Intent
- Libel/Linguistic Analysis
- Magazine Publishing
- Marine
- Marketing
  - Specializing in Direct Mail
- Medicare & Medicaid Fraud & Abuse
- Medicare Fraud & Abuse
- Mental Health
- Metallurgy/Failure Analysis
- Meteorology/Climatology
- Mining
- Mortality/Longevity Analysis
- Motion Pictures
- Motorcycle Accident Reconstruction
- Motorcycle/ATV Accident/Invest/Reconstruction
- Oil & Gas
- Packaging
- Patent Law
- Personal Injury
- Photographic Analysis
  - Environmental Site Assessment
- Planning/Zoning/Land Planning
- Playground Equipment Accidents
- Plumbing & Electric
- Police Misconduct
- Police/Security
  - Hotel/Resort/Casino
  - Negligence
    - (See also Security; Expert Witness)
  - Negligence/Security Misconduct
- Use of Force
- Premises Security & Liability
  - (See also Expert Witness - Slip, Trip and Fall)
- Product Liability
- Public Utilities
- Railroad Accidents
- Real Estate
  - Appraisal & Valuation
- Recreation
- Repossession Standards of Conduct
- Research
- Retail Bankruptcies
- Roofing & Waterproofing
- Safety
- Securities Law
- Securities/Litigation Support
- Security Negligence
- Slip, Trip and Fall
  - (See also Expert Witness - Premises Security & Liability)
- Sports, Leisure, Recreation
- Telecommunications
- Telephone Poles
- Testimony Retrieval
- Third Party Liability Issues
- Tire Identification
- Toxicology
  - Respiratory
- Traffic Engineering
- Transportation
  - Aviation
  - Aviation/Aircraft/Airports
  - Railroads
  - Tire & Wheel
  - Traffic Engineering & Safety
- Trees
- Unclaimed Property
- Underground Tanks
- Vocational Evaluation
  - Life Care Plans
- Water Accidents
- Weather & Climate
- Wheelchairs
- Windows & Doors
- Wood Products (Adhesive-Bonded)
- Wood Science & Technology
- Wood Utility Poles

Expert Witness Referral Service - Environmental
Expert Witness Referral Services
Expert Witness Testimony Retrieval

Facilities Management
Failure Analysis/Testing Services
Fairness Opinions
Family Business Consultants
Filing Court Documents By Fax
Financial Case Prosecution
Financial Document Services
Financial Investigation/Forensic Accounting
Fingerprint Analysis
Fire Investigators
Fire Loss Experts
Foreign Embassy Services
Forensic Documentation - Demonstrative Evidence
Forensic Engineering Metallurgy/Failure Analysis
Forensic Engineers
Forensic Financial Analysis
Forensic Geochemistry
Forensic Medicine
Forensic Psychiatry
Forensic Psychology
Forensic Services

Gemology
Genealogical Services
Geology
Government - Foreign Government Incorporating Offices
Government - Foreign Government Philatelic Bureaus
Government Contract Claims Consultant
Government Regulatory Research Specialists
Graphics Design & Production
Groupware

Handwriting Experts
Hedonic Damages/Loss of Enjoyment of Life
Heir Tracers
Heir/Probate Research
Home Detection Monitoring
Homicide Events
Hotel/Apartment Consultants & Experts
Human Factors & Ergonomics Consulting

Independent Medical Examiners - Neurology
Imaging Services
Immigration & Customs Consulting
Immigration Investment
Importer Associations
Incorporating Companies - Overseas Corporations
Incorporation Services
Independent Medical Examiner Referral Services
Independent Medical Examiners
Independent Medical Examiners - Chiropractic
Independent Medical Examiners - National Referral Service
Independent Medical Examiners - Neurosurgery
Independent Medical Examiners - Orthopaedics
Independent Medical Examiners - Physiatry
Independent Medical Examiners - Psychiatry
Information Brokers
Information Brokers - Medical
Information Clearing House
Information Security Specialists
Insurance
Insurance - Corporate Owned Life Insurance
Insurance - Employment Practices
Insurance - Expert Witness Referral Service
Insurance - Health
Insurance - Intellectual Property
Insurance - Professional Liability

Insurance - Property/Casualty
Insurance - Risk Management Consulting
Insurance/Reinsurance Auditing Services
Intellectual Property Document Services
International Finance/Venture Capital
International Personal Tax Consultant
International Trade Consultants
Internet On Line Stock Exchange
Internet Services
Internet/Intranet Services
Interpreters
(See also Interpreters & Translators; Translation Services)
Interpreters & Translators
(See also Translation Services)
Interpreting - Deaf/Sign Language
Investigative Consultants
Investigators
Investment Clubs

Jury Consultants
Jury Verdict Reporting Services

Labor Relations, Products & Services
Laboratories - Geochemical/Petroleum/Source ID
Laboratories - Parentage Testing
Law Books - New/Used
Law Office Automation Consulting
Law Office Automation Services
Lawyer Referral Service
Lawyer Search & Placement Consultants
Lease Auditors
Leasing & Financing
Legal Advertising
Legal Associations
Legal Auditors
Legal Brief Printers
Legal Copying
Legal Editor
Legal Forms - Computerized
Legal Publications
Legal Research
Legal Research/Appellate Practice
Legal Software
Legal Support Personnel - Temporary & Permanent
Legislative Intent Research
Letters of Credit
Libraries/Books Purchased
Library Management Services
Library Management Software
Lie Detectors
Life Care Planning
Linguistics
Liquidators
Litigation Consulting
Litigation Support - Detecting Deception
Litigation Support - Environmental
Litigation Support - International
Litigation Support Services
Litigation Support Software
Lobbyist

Mail Order Consultants
Mail Room Services
Malpractice Legal Defense
Malpractice Prevention Consultants
Management Consultants
Marine Consultants
Marketing
Medi-Cal Planning
Medical Case Review & Preparation/Trial Consulting
Medical Evaluation - Brain Injuries
Medical Evaluation - Orthopedics
Medical Expert Testimony
Medical Expert Witness
- Anesthesiology
- Asbestos Related Diseases
- Breast Implants
- Cardiology
- Cardiology, Internal Medicine & Geriatric
- Chiropractic Medicine
- Class Action Litigation
- Dental
  - TMJ
- Electric Shock/Injury
- Emergency Medical Services - E.M.S.
- Emergency Medicine/Malpractice
- Epilepsy/Seizure Disorder
- Eye/Eye Surgery
- Family Practice
- Foot Surgery/Care
- Forensic Pathology
- Gastroenterology
- Genetics
- Head Injury
  - Forensic Neuropsychology
  - Forensic Psychiatry
- Hospital/Healthcare Administration
- Internal Medicine
- Medical Case Review
  - Malpractice & Pers. Inj.
- Medical Devices
- Medical Information Specialist
- Neonatology/Pediatrics
- Nephrology
- Neurology
  - Neurosurgery
- Nursing
- Nursing Homes/Assisted Living
- Obstetrics & Gynecology
- Oncology
  - Breast Cancer Delayed Diagnosis
  - Gynecology
- Ophthalmology
  - Eye Injuries/Safety
  - Retina
- Ophthalmology/Eyelid Plastic Surgery
- Pain Management
- Pathology
- Pathology/Dermatopathology
- Pediatrics
  - Endocrinology
- Pharmacy
- Pharmacy & Pharmacology
- Physical Medicine & Rehabilitation
- Physician Assistant
- Podiatry
- Product Injury
- Psychiatry
  - (See also Medical Expert Witness - Neurology)
  - Forensic
  - Neuropsychiatry
  - Psychopharmacology
- Psychology
  - Educational Matters
  - Forensic
  - Neuropsychology
  - Trauma
- Radiology
  - MRI/Musculoskeletal Imaging
- Rehab.
  - Catastrophic Inj./Life Care Planning
- Sleeping Disorders
- Surgery
  - Cardiovascular Thoracic
  - Hand Surgery
  - Orthopedic
  - Orthopedic/Sports Medicine
  - Pedicle
  - Plastic Reconstructive/Burns
  - Vascular
- Toxicology
- Urology
- Vocational Rehabilitation

Medical Expert Witness Referral Services
Medical Illustrators
Medical Literature Research
Medical Malpractice Consulting/Personal Injury
Medical Records
Medical Services
Medical-Legal Education
Mergers & Acquisitions
Messenger Services
Meteorology
Microfilming Services
Mining
Missing Persons

Network - CD-ROM
News Services On Line Internet Access
News/Media Services

SERVICES, SUPPLIERS, CONSULTANTS
NATIONAL GEOGRAPHICAL INDEX

ACCIDENT INVESTIGATION & RECONSTRUCTION SERVICES

ALABAMA
BIRMINGHAM .... WILLIAM J. (JIM) GRIFFIN .... (Volume 1)

ARIZONA
FLAGSTAFF .... SEWELL INVESTIGATIONS .... (Volume 1)

ARKANSAS
LITTLE ROCK .... ACCIDENT ANALYSIS ASSOCIATES .... (Volume 1)

CALIFORNIA
LOS ANGELES .... CRASH FACTS .... (Volume 2)
KAUDERER & ASSOCIATES .... (Volume 2)
SACRAMENTO .... KAUDERER & ASSOCIATES .... (Volume 3)
SAN FRANCISCO .... CAIRD & ASSOCIATES CONSULTANTS INC. TRUCK TRAILER MANAGEMENT SERVICES DIVISION .... (Volume 3)

FLORIDA
MIAMI .... AERIALS, INC. .... (Volume 6)
TALLAHASSEE .... BENEDICT ENGINEERING COMPANY, INC. .... (Volume 6)

GEORGIA
ATLANTA .... INVESTIGATIVE SOLUTIONS, INC. .... (Volume 7)
PETER S. PARSONSON, PH.D. P.E. .... (Volume 7)
VERSITECH CORPORATION .... (Volume 7)

ILLINOIS
CHICAGO .... NORTHBROOK ENGINEERING .... (Volume 8)
PACKER ENGINEERING, INC. .... (Volume 8)
PAUL C. BOX AND ASSOCIATES, INC. .... (Volume 8)
PEORIA .... CENTRAL ILLINOIS CONSULTING SERVICES .... (Volume 8)

NEVADA
LAS VEGAS .... JOHN R. HOWELL & ASSOCIATES .... (Volume 11)

NEW JERSEY
ATLANTIC CITY .... SARAO & ASSOCIATES ™ .... (Volume 12)
HACKENSACK .... SARAO & ASSOCIATES ™ .... (Volume 12)
NEWARK .... BARER ENGINEERING, P.A. .... (Volume 12)

NEW MEXICO
LAS CRUCES .... WENDELL HULL & ASSOCIATES, INC. .... (Volume 12)

NORTH CAROLINA
ASHEVILLE .... PARC ENGINEERING ASSOCIATES .... (Volume 14)
RALEIGH .... FORENSIC ANALYSIS & ENGINEERING CORPORATION .... (Volume 14)

PENNSYLVANIA
PHILADELPHIA .... ACA ACCIDENT CAUSE & ANALYSIS .... (Volume 15)
PITTSBURGH .... ROMUALDI, DAVIDSON & ASSOCIATES, INC. .... (Volume 15)

TENNESSEE
MURFREESBORO .... REC ENGINEERING .... (Volume 16)

TEXAS
AUSTIN .... STEVEN J. OLSON, P.E. AN ASSOCIATE OF REED ENGINEERING .... (Volume 17)
DALLAS .... TARAS, INC. .... (Volume 17)
HOUSTON .... COLLISION RESEARCH ASSOCIATES .... (Volume 17)

ACCOUNTANTS

CALIFORNIA
LOS ANGELES .... ANDREOLI, JOHANSON & WOOD .... (Volume 2)
KINSEL ACCOUNTANCY CORPORATION .... (Volume 2)
SACRAMENTO .... JOHN WADDELL & CO. CPAS .... (Volume 3)

FLORIDA
MIAMI .... STANLEY I. FOODMAN, B.B.A. M.S. CPA, CFE .... (Volume 6)
STUART .... FRANK A. FERRARO, CPA, PA .... (Volume 6)
TAMPA .... VALIENTEHERNANDEZ P.A. .... (Volume 6)

LOUISIANA
SHREVEPORT .... BOBBY E. JELKS, CPA, PFS .... (Volume 9)

ACCOUNTANTS - Continued

NEW MEXICO

ALBUQUERQUE .... ROGOFF ERICKSON DIAMOND & WALKER, LLP .... (Volume 12)

NORTH DAKOTA

FARGO .... EIDE BAILLY LLP .... (Volume 14)

WASHINGTON

TACOMA .... SMITH CARR & MCLANE .... (Volume 18)

ACCOUNTING

CALIFORNIA

IRVINE .... SKORHEIM & ASSOCIATES .... (Volume 2)

FLORIDA

FORT LAUDERDALE .... FRIEDMAN, DUQUE & CO. .... (Volume 6)

ACOUSTICS CONSULTANTS

MASSACHUSETTS

BOSTON .... ACENTECH INCORPORATED .... (Volume 10)

ADMIRALTY & MARITIME EXPERT & CONSULTANT

NEW YORK

NEW YORK .... THOMAS ELECTRIC CONTROL, INC. .... (Volume 13)

ADVERTISING & PUBLIC RELATIONS FIRMS

GEORGIA

ATLANTA .... LAW & MEDIA GROUP, INC. .... (Volume 7)

AERIAL PHOTOGRAPHY

FLORIDA

MIAMI .... AERIALS, INC. .... (Volume 6)

AFFIRMATIVE ACTION PLAN DEVELOPMENT

DISTRICT OF COLUMBIA

WASHINGTON .... CHARLES R. MANN ASSOCIATES, INC. .... (Volume 5)

AMERICANS WITH DISABILITIES ACT (ADA)

CALIFORNIA

PASADENA .... RHETA BARON KING, CRC, CDMS .... (Volume 3)

ILLINOIS

CHICAGO .... CARNOW, CONIBEAR & ASSOC. LTD. .... (Volume 8)

APPELLATE CONSULTANT

NEW YORK

NEW YORK .... COUNSEL PRESS LLC .... (Volume 13)

OHIO

CINCINNATI .... STEPHEN R. FELSON .... (Volume 14)

APPRAISAL & VALUATION SERVICES

CALIFORNIA

BERKELEY .... LECG, A SUBSIDIARY OF NAVIGANT CONSULTING, INC. .... (Volume 2)

LOS ANGELES .... CALIFORNIA MARKET VALUES, INC. .... (Volume 2)

DISTRICT OF COLUMBIA

WASHINGTON .... NAVIGANT CONSULTING, INC. .... (Volume 5)

FLORIDA

JACKSONVILLE .... ASSET CONTROL SERVICES .... (Volume 6)

LOUISIANA

NEW ORLEANS .... A.R.E. REAL ESTATE SERVICES .... (Volume 9)

NEW YORK

NEW YORK .... VALUATION CONSULTING GROUP A KANE REECE ASSOCIATES, INC. PRACTICE GROUP .... (Volume 13)

OHIO

CLEVELAND .... LOVEMAN-CURTISS, INC. .... (Volume 14)

ARBITRATION & MEDIATION SERVICES - Continued

NEW YORK, NEW YORK - Continued

CYBERSETTLE.COM .... (Volume 13)
RESOLUTE SYSTEMS, INC. .... (Volume 13)

PENNSYLVANIA

PHILADELPHIA .... ATTORNEY MEDIATION .... (Volume 15)

TENNESSEE

MEMPHIS .... RESOLUTE SYSTEMS, INC. .... (Volume 16)

TEXAS

DALLAS .... ATTORNEY MEDIATION .... (Volume 17)
ELLIOTT MEDIATION .... (Volume 17)
HOUSTON .... ATTORNEY MEDIATION .... (Volume 17)
RESOLUTE SYSTEMS, INC. .... (Volume 17)
SAN ANTONIO .... ATTORNEY MEDIATION .... (Volume 17)

WASHINGTON

SEATTLE .... ATTORNEY MEDIATION .... (Volume 18)

WISCONSIN

MILWAUKEE .... RESOLUTE SYSTEMS, INC. .... (Volume 18)

ASSET LOCATORS

CALIFORNIA

SACRAMENTO .... CAGEY BEE SERVICES .... (Volume 3)

DISTRICT OF COLUMBIA

WASHINGTON .... WASHINGTON PRE-TRIAL SERVICES, INC. .... (Volume 5)

GEORGIA

ATLANTA .... INVESTIGATIVE SOLUTIONS, INC. .... (Volume 7)

NEW JERSEY

LONG VALLEY .... COLLEXX, INC. .... (Volume 12)

NEW YORK

NEW YORK .... BCA PROTECTIVE & INVESTIGATIVE SERVICES .... (Volume 13)
SCHENECTADY .... TRACERS INTERNATIONAL .... (Volume 13)

TEXAS

AUSTIN .... PROFILE INFORMATION SERVICES .... (Volume 17)

ASSET MANAGEMENT

MASSACHUSETTS

BOSTON .... MELLON PRIVATE ASSET MANAGEMENT ® .... (Volume 10)

ATTORNEY REFERRAL SERVICES

FLORIDA

BOCA RATON .... A-A-A ATTORNEY REFERRAL SERVICE, INC. ℠ .... (Volume 6)

GEORGIA

ATLANTA .... A-A-A ATTORNEY REFERRAL SERVICE, INC. ℠ .... (Volume 7)

ATTORNEY SERVICES

ARIZONA

PHOENIX .... 007 ATTORNEY SERVICES, INC. .... (Volume 1)
A & E, INC. .... (Volume 1)
AAA LEGAL SERVICES .... (Volume 1)
BORG PROCESS SERVERS INC. .... (Volume 1)

CALIFORNIA

FRESNO .... A-1 ATTORNEY SERVICE .... (Volume 2)
LOS ANGELES .... 1ST AMERICAN PROCESS SERVICE, INC. .... (Volume 2)
A & E, INC. .... (Volume 2)
BORG PROCESS SERVERS INC. .... (Volume 2)
JOE SOLO FILINGS .... (Volume 2)
LA SALLE PROCESS SERVERS, L.P. .... (Volume 2)
LEGAL SUPPORT SERVICES, INC. .... (Volume 2)
SHERMAN, ALEXANDER & ASSOCIATES LLC .... (Volume 2)
OAKLAND .... ERDMAN ATTORNEY SERVICE .... (Volume 2)
SACRAMENTO .... GKL CORPORATE/SEARCH, INC. .... (Volume 3)
SAN DIEGO .... 1ST AMERICAN PROCESS SERVICE, INC. .... (Volume 3)
A & E, INC. .... (Volume 3)

ATTORNEY SERVICES - Continued

MICHIGAN

DETROIT	1ST AMERICAN PROCESS SERVICE, INC.	(Volume 10)
	A & E, INC.	(Volume 10)
	A.S.K. SERVICES, INC.	(Volume 10)
	BORG PROCESS SERVERS INC.	(Volume 10)

MINNESOTA

MINNEAPOLIS	A & E, INC.	(Volume 11)
	LEGAL LANGUAGE SERVICES	(Volume 11)
	LEGALEASE INC.	(Volume 11)
	METRO LEGAL SERVICES, INC.	(Volume 11)

MISSOURI

KANSAS CITY	A & E, INC.	(Volume 11)
	LEGAL LANGUAGE SERVICES	(Volume 11)
ST. LOUIS	A & E, INC.	(Volume 11)
	LEGAL LANGUAGE SERVICES	(Volume 11)

NEVADA

LAS VEGAS	A & E, INC.	(Volume 11)
	LEGAL LANGUAGE SERVICES	(Volume 11)

NEW HAMPSHIRE

MANCHESTER	A & E, INC.	(Volume 11)

NEW JERSEY

NEWARK	1ST AMERICAN PROCESS SERVICE, INC.	(Volume 12)
	DANTE INVESTIGATORS	(Volume 12)
TRENTON	1ST AMERICAN PROCESS SERVICE, INC.	(Volume 12)

NEW YORK

MINEOLA	GOTCHA LEGAL PROCESS SERVICE, INC.	(Volume 12)
	LEGAL LANGUAGE SERVICES	(Volume 12)
NEW YORK	1ST AMERICAN PROCESS SERVICE, INC.	(Volume 13)
	A & E, INC.	(Volume 13)
	BORG PROCESS SERVERS INC.	(Volume 13)
	COURTFAX	(Volume 13)
	DANTE INVESTIGATORS	(Volume 13)
	EAST END LEGAL SERVICE, INC.	(Volume 13)
	GOTCHA LEGAL PROCESS SERVICE, INC.	(Volume 13)
	INTERBORO ATTORNEY SERVICE CORP.	(Volume 13)
	KEATING & WALKER ATTORNEY SERVICE, INC.	(Volume 13)
	LA SALLE PROCESS SERVERS, L.P.	(Volume 13)
	LEGAL LANGUAGE SERVICES	(Volume 13)
	LEGALEASE INC.	(Volume 13)
	NEWCO CORPORATE SERVICES, INC.	(Volume 13)
WHITE PLAINS	EVEREADY PROCESS SERVICE, INC.	(Volume 13)

OHIO

CINCINNATI	A & E, INC.	(Volume 14)
CLEVELAND	A & E, INC.	(Volume 14)
COLUMBUS	A & E, INC.	(Volume 14)

OKLAHOMA

TULSA	A & E, INC.	(Volume 14)

OREGON

PORTLAND	1ST AMERICAN PROCESS SERVICE, INC.	(Volume 15)

PENNSYLVANIA

PHILADELPHIA	1ST AMERICAN PROCESS SERVICE, INC.	(Volume 15)
	A & E, INC.	(Volume 15)
	BORG PROCESS SERVERS INC.	(Volume 15)
	LEGAL LANGUAGE SERVICES	(Volume 15)
PITTSBURGH	1ST AMERICAN PROCESS SERVICE, INC.	(Volume 15)

TENNESSEE

NASHVILLE	A & E, INC.	(Volume 16)

TEXAS

AUSTIN	1ST AMERICAN PROCESS SERVICE, INC.	(Volume 17)
BROWNSVILLE	LAWYER SUPPORT SERVICES	(Volume 17)
DALLAS	1ST AMERICAN PROCESS SERVICE, INC.	(Volume 17)
	BORG PROCESS SERVERS INC.	(Volume 17)
	LA SALLE PROCESS SERVERS, L.P.	(Volume 17)
HOUSTON	1ST AMERICAN PROCESS SERVICE, INC.	(Volume 17)

BANKRUPTCY/TURNAROUND/INSOLVENCY

CALIFORNIA

SAN FRANCISCO .... CHARLES RIVER ASSOCIATES INCORPORATED .... (Volume 3)

DISTRICT OF COLUMBIA

WASHINGTON .... CHARLES RIVER ASSOCIATES INCORPORATED .... (Volume 5)

FLORIDA

FORT LAUDERDALE .... FRIEDMAN, DUQUE & CO. .... (Volume 6)

NEW YORK

NEW YORK .... CHARLES RIVER ASSOCIATES INCORPORATED .... (Volume 13)
FTI/KAHN .... (Volume 13)

BANKS & TRUST COMPANIES

CALIFORNIA

SAN FRANCISCO .... CALIFORNIA BANK & TRUST .... (Volume 3)

DELAWARE

WILMINGTON .... WILMINGTON TRUST COMPANY .... (Volume 4)

ILLINOIS

CHICAGO .... THE NORTHERN TRUST COMPANY .... (Volume 8)

MASSACHUSETTS

BOSTON .... MELLON PRIVATE ASSET MANAGEMENT ® .... (Volume 10)

NEW YORK

NEW YORK .... LEGIS GROUP .... (Volume 13)
SARATOGA SPRINGS .... THE ADIRONDACK TRUST COMPANY .... (Volume 13)

BODYGUARDS

MARYLAND

BALTIMORE .... N.R. COCHRAN & ASSOCIATES .... (Volume 9)

BONDS - SURETY & FIDELITY

NEW JERSEY

JERSEY CITY .... TONY FERRARA & ASSOCIATES .... (Volume 12)

NEW YORK

NEW YORK .... THE BLAIKIE GROUP .... (Volume 13)
OFFENHARTZ & PEDERSEN, LTD. .... (Volume 13)

TEXAS

DALLAS .... GALLAGHER CONSTRUCTION MANAGEMENT SERVICES .... (Volume 17)

BOWLING CENTERS - VALUATION & FINANCIAL ANALYSIS

MICHIGAN

DETROIT .... SANDY HANSELL & ASSOCIATES, INC. .... (Volume 10)

BRAIN INJURY - REHABILITATION SERVICES

NEW HAMPSHIRE

CONCORD .... LAKEVIEW NEUROREHABILITATION CENTER .... (Volume 11)

PENNSYLVANIA

LANGHORNE .... BEECHWOOD REHABILITATION SERVICES .... (Volume 15)

TEXAS

AUSTIN .... THE BROWN SCHOOLS REHABILITATION CENTER .... (Volume 17)

BUILDING EVALUATION - DUE DILIGENCE

ILLINOIS

CHICAGO .... WISS, JANNEY, ELSTNER ASSOCIATES, INC. .... (Volume 8)

BUILDING/HOME INSPECTION

NEW JERSEY

NUTLEY .... KENNETH J. STOYACK, AIA, PP .... (Volume 12)

BUSINESS & FINANCIAL INFORMATION PROVIDERS

DISTRICT OF COLUMBIA

WASHINGTON .... GLOBAL SECURITIES INFORMATION, INC. (GSI) .... (Volume 5)

BUSINESS FINANCE & PURCHASE OF RECEIVABLES

WASHINGTON

BUSINESS VALUATIONS

ALABAMA

ARKANSAS

CALIFORNIA

COLORADO

DISTRICT OF COLUMBIA

FLORIDA

GEORGIA

IDAHO

ILLINOIS

LOUISIANA

MASSACHUSETTS

MISSOURI

NEW JERSEY

NEW MEXICO

BUSINESS VALUATIONS - Continued

NEW YORK

NEW YORK .... BUSINESS VALUATION SERVICES .... (Volume 13)
D.L. HEISEY & CO INCORPORATED .... (Volume 13)
ISRAELOFF, TRATTNER & CO. CPAS .... (Volume 13)
MANAGEMENT PLANNING, INC. .... (Volume 13)
REGENT PACIFIC ® .... (Volume 13)
STERN STEWART & CO. .... (Volume 13)
SYNERGY VALUATIONS, LLC .... (Volume 13)
VALUATION CONSULTING GROUP A KANE REECE ASSOCIATES, INC. PRACTICE GROUP .... (Volume 13)

NORTH DAKOTA

FARGO .... EIDE BAILLY LLP .... (Volume 14)

OHIO

CLEVELAND .... LOVEMAN-CURTISS, INC. .... (Volume 14)

PENNSYLVANIA

MEADVILLE .... ROBERT M. POWER, JR. CPA, CVA, ABV .... (Volume 15)

TENNESSEE

NASHVILLE .... CENTENNIAL VALUATION GROUP, PLLC .... (Volume 16)
LATTIMORE BLACK MORGAN & CAIN, P.C. .... (Volume 16)

TEXAS

DALLAS .... BUSINESS VALUATION SERVICES .... (Volume 17)
HOUSTON .... STERN STEWART & CO. .... (Volume 17)

VIRGINIA

FAIRFAX .... RICHMAN ASSOCIATES .... (Volume 18)
RICHMOND .... CORNERSTONE FINANCIAL MANAGEMENT, INC. .... (Volume 18)
VIENNA .... OFFUTT CHILDERS & PUTMAN, P.C. .... (Volume 18)

PUERTO RICO

SAN JUAN .... AMANDA CAPO'-ROSSELLO', CPA, CVA, CFE .... (Volume 18)

CAPTIONING

MINNESOTA

MINNEAPOLIS .... PARADIGM REPORTING & CAPTIONING INC. .... (Volume 11)

WASHINGTON

SEATTLE .... STARKOVICH REPORTING SERVICES .... (Volume 18)
TACOMA .... STARKOVICH REPORTING SERVICES .... (Volume 18)

CAREER SERVICES

NEW YORK

NEW YORK .... LEE HECHT HARRISON, INC. .... (Volume 13)

CASE MANAGEMENT SERVICES

ALABAMA

BIRMINGHAM .... CASE MANAGEMENT, INC. .... (Volume 1)

MICHIGAN

GRAND RAPIDS .... CATASTROPHIC & REHABILITATION MANAGEMENT, INC. .... (Volume 10)
LANSING .... CARE MANAGERS, INC. .... (Volume 10)

CASE MANAGEMENT SYSTEMS

DISTRICT OF COLUMBIA

WASHINGTON .... COMPUTER PACKAGES INC. .... (Volume 5)

FLORIDA

ORLANDO .... ADC LEGAL SYSTEMS, INC. .... (Volume 6)

NEW YORK

NEW YORK .... SAGA, INC. .... (Volume 13)

NORTH CAROLINA

RALEIGH .... ADC LEGAL SYSTEMS, INC. .... (Volume 14)

CLASS ACTION LOCATORS

CALIFORNIA

LOS ANGELES .... CLASS ACTION LOCATOR SERVICE .... (Volume 2)
SAN FRANCISCO .... CLASS ACTION LOCATOR SERVICE .... (Volume 3)

CONSTRUCTION & ENGINEERING LITIGATION

CALIFORNIA

CONSTRUCTION ACCIDENTS, SAFETY

MICHIGAN

PENNSYLVANIA

CONSTRUCTION CONSULTANTS

CALIFORNIA

DISTRICT OF COLUMBIA

FLORIDA

GEORGIA

ILLINOIS

IOWA

MICHIGAN

NEW JERSEY

NEW MEXICO

NEW YORK

PENNSYLVANIA

TEXAS

WASHINGTON

CONSTRUCTION CONSULTANTS-CONSTRUCTION DEFECTS

ILLINOIS

NEW JERSEY

CONSTRUCTION CONSULTANTS-STRUCTURAL DAMAGE

ILLINOIS

NEW JERSEY

CONSULTANT REFERRAL SERVICES

MASSACHUSETTS

BOSTON .... THE CONSULTING EXCHANGE .... (Volume 10)

CONTACT MANAGEMENT

CALIFORNIA

SAN FRANCISCO .... COLE VALLEY SOFTWARE .... (Volume 3)

CONTINUING LEGAL EDUCATION

NEW YORK

NEW YORK .... PRACTISING LAW INSTITUTE ® .... (Volume 13)

TEXAS

AUSTIN .... CLEONLINE.COM .... (Volume 17)

SAN ANTONIO .... LITIGATION STRATEGIES ™ GROUP .... (Volume 17)

VIRGINIA

ARLINGTON .... THE NATIONAL CRIME VICTIM BAR ASSOCIATION .... (Volume 18)

COPIER SERVICES

CALIFORNIA

SAN FRANCISCO .... PANDA LEGAL COPY .... (Volume 3)

NEW YORK

NEW YORK .... A.D.S. COPYING, INC. .... (Volume 13)

POOLED OFFICE SERVICES .... (Volume 13)

SOUTH CAROLINA

GREENVILLE .... LEGAL EAGLE ®, INC. .... (Volume 16)

WASHINGTON

SEATTLE .... LEGAL COPY, INC. .... (Volume 18)

CORPORATE SERVICES COMPANIES

ALASKA

JUNEAU .... COMPLETE CORPORATE SERVICES OF ALASKA, INC. .... (Volume 1)

FLORIDA

TALLAHASSEE .... CAPITAL CONNECTION, INC. .... (Volume 6)

GEORGIA

ATLANTA .... PARANET CORPORATION SERVICES, INC. .... (Volume 7)

MARYLAND

BALTIMORE .... HYLIND SEARCH COMPANY, INC. .... (Volume 9)

NEW YORK

NEW YORK .... INTERCOUNTY CLEARANCE CORPORATION .... (Volume 13)

NORTH CAROLINA

RALEIGH .... NATIONAL DATA ACCESS CORPORATION .... (Volume 14)

SOUTH CAROLINA

COLUMBIA .... NATIONAL DATA ACCESS CORPORATION .... (Volume 16)

CORPORATE SUPPLIES

FLORIDA

TALLAHASSEE .... CAPITAL CONNECTION, INC. .... (Volume 6)

TEXAS

HOUSTON .... TCS - LIBERTY LEGAL .... (Volume 17)

CORPORATION COMPANIES

CALIFORNIA

LOS ANGELES .... ACCESS INCORPORATION SERVICES, INC. .... (Volume 2)

CSC THE UNITED STATES CORPORATION COMPANY .... (Volume 2)

SACRAMENTO .... GKL CORPORATE/SEARCH, INC. .... (Volume 3)

DELAWARE

DOVER .... CORPAMERICA, INC. .... (Volume 4)

WILMINGTON .... CSC THE UNITED STATES CORPORATION COMPANY .... (Volume 4)

FLORIDA

TALLAHASSEE .... CAPITAL CONNECTION, INC. .... (Volume 6)

CSC THE UNITED STATES CORPORATION COMPANY .... (Volume 6)

COURT REPORTERS - Continued

ALASKA - Continued

FAIRBANKS	HEARTLAND COURT REPORTERS	(Volume 1)
	R & R COURT REPORTERS, INC.	(Volume 1)
KODIAK	DEPOSITION SERVICES, LTD	(Volume 1)

ARIZONA

GLENDALE	COASH & COASH, INC.	(Volume 1)
	COURT REPORTERS	(Volume 1)
LAKE HAVASU CITY	ASSOCIATED/TRI-STATE REPORTING	(Volume 1)
	FAYETTE & ASSOCIATES	(Volume 1)
MESA	A.A. NICHOLS, INC.	(Volume 1)
	COASH & COASH, INC.	(Volume 1)
PHOENIX	A.A. NICHOLS, INC.	(Volume 1)
	ARIZONA REPORTING SERVICE, INC.	(Volume 1)
	BROWN & TOLEU, LTD. COURT REPORTERS	(Volume 1)
	CLARK CERTIFIED COURT REPORTERS	(Volume 1)
	COASH & COASH, INC.	(Volume 1)
	CROPPER & ASSOCIATES, LTD.	(Volume 1)
	DRIVER AND NIX COURT REPORTERS	(Volume 1)
	K-VIDEO, INC.	(Volume 1)
	REPORTERS COOPERATIVE, INC.	(Volume 1)
	THACKER & THACKER, INC.	(Volume 1)
SCOTTSDALE	A.A. NICHOLS, INC.	(Volume 1)
	COASH & COASH, INC.	(Volume 1)
SUN CITY	COASH & COASH, INC.	(Volume 1)
TEMPE	COASH & COASH, INC.	(Volume 1)
TUCSON	A.A. NICHOLS, INC.	(Volume 1)
	CALABRO REPORTING SERVICES, L.L.C.	(Volume 1)
	EATON, GREEN & WILLIAMS, INC.	(Volume 1)
	HUNT REPORTING	(Volume 1)
	REPORTERS COOPERATIVE, INC.	(Volume 1)
	SILVERMAN & GARWOOD COURT REPORTING SERVICE	(Volume 1)

ARKANSAS

BENTONVILLE	BENTONVILLE COURT REPORTING	(Volume 1)
FAYETTEVILLE	DONALD COURT REPORTING, INC.	(Volume 1)
LITTLE ROCK	A/M REPORTERS, INC.	(Volume 1)
	ARKANSAS LITIGATION SUPPORT SERVICES, INC.	(Volume 1)
	BUSHMAN COURT REPORTING	(Volume 1)
	HENDRIX REPORTING SERVICE	(Volume 1)

CALIFORNIA

ANAHEIM	REPORTERS COOPERATIVE, INC.	(Volume 2)
BAKERSFIELD	ESQUIRE™ DEPOSITION SERVICES	(Volume 2)
	REPORTERS COOPERATIVE, INC.	(Volume 2)
	STONER & SCHLENKER CERTIFIED SHORTHAND REPORTERS	(Volume 2)
BERKELEY	CLARK REPORTING	(Volume 2)
BEVERLY HILLS	A.A. NICHOLS, INC.	(Volume 2)
	ABRAMS, MAH & KAHN	(Volume 2)
	INTERIM COURT REPORTING	(Volume 2)
	KARYN ABBOTT & ASSOCIATES	(Volume 2)
	NICOLE CARTER & ASSOCIATES/BEVERLY HILLS DEPOSITION REPORTERS	(Volume 2)
CARLSBAD	A.A. NICHOLS, INC.	(Volume 2)
CENTURY CITY	INTERIM COURT REPORTING	(Volume 2)
DEL MAR	A.A. NICHOLS, INC.	(Volume 2)
EL CENTRO	ATWOOD, JENNINGS & ASSOCIATES	(Volume 2)
FAIRFIELD	DEMICHELLE DEPOSITION REPORTERS	(Volume 2)
	LANGSTAFF REPORTING SERVICE	(Volume 2)
FORT BRAGG	ADAIR, POTSWALD & HENNESSEY	(Volume 2)
FREMONT	PULONE & STROMBERG	(Volume 2)
FRESNO	CENTRAL VALLEY REPORTERS	(Volume 2)
	ESQUIRE™ DEPOSITION SERVICES	(Volume 2)
	INTERIM COURT REPORTING	(Volume 2)
	RAY EGGEBRAATEN CSR, INC.	(Volume 2)
GILROY	PULONE & STROMBERG	(Volume 2)
IRVINE	A.A. NICHOLS, INC.	(Volume 2)
	ABRAMS, MAH & KAHN	(Volume 2)
	AT LAW LITIGATION SUPPORT, INC.	(Volume 2)
	HAHN AND BOWERSOCK	(Volume 2)

City	Reporter	Volume
	LYNDEN J. AND ASSOCIATES, INC.	(Volume 2)
LA JOLLA	A.A. NICHOLS, INC.	(Volume 2)
LAKEPORT	ADAIR, POTSWALD & HENNESSEY	(Volume 2)
LONG BEACH	ABRAMS, MAH & KAHN	(Volume 2)
	AT LAW LITIGATION SUPPORT, INC.	(Volume 2)
	HAHN AND BOWERSOCK	(Volume 2)
	INTERIM COURT REPORTING	(Volume 2)
	LYNDEN J. AND ASSOCIATES, INC.	(Volume 2)
LOS ANGELES	1-2-3 REPORTING SERVICE A DIVISION OF CERTIFIED REPORTING COMPANY	(Volume 2)
	1-800-FOR-DEPO-ALDERSONREPORTING	(Volume 2)
	A. EDELIST DEPOSITION SERVICE, INC.	(Volume 2)
	A.A. NICHOLS, INC.	(Volume 2)
	AA1 PARLIAMENTARY REPORTING	(Volume 2)
	ABBOTT LEGAL VIDEO SERVICES	(Volume 2)
	ABRAMS, MAH & KAHN	(Volume 2)
	ASSOCIATED REPORTERS OF NEVADA	(Volume 2)
	AT LAW LITIGATION SUPPORT, INC.	(Volume 2)
	BALLERINI COURT REPORTERS	(Volume 2)
	BEN HYATT CERTIFIED DEPOSITION REPORTERS	(Volume 2)
	CSR ASSOCIATES OF NEVADA	(Volume 2)
	DORIS O. WONG ASSOCIATES, INC.	(Volume 2)
	DOYLE REPORTING, INC. AN ALR REPORTING COMPANY	(Volume 2)
	ELLEN GRAUER COURT REPORTING CO.	(Volume 2)
	ESQUIRE™ DEPOSITION SERVICES	(Volume 2)
	GOLDING COURT REPORTERS	(Volume 2)
	HABEAS VIDEAS	(Volume 2)
	HAHN AND BOWERSOCK	(Volume 2)
	HUTCHINGS COURT REPORTERS, LLC ℠	(Volume 2)
	INTERIM COURT REPORTING	(Volume 2)
	KARYN ABBOTT & ASSOCIATES	(Volume 2)
	LACEY SHORTHAND REPORTING CORPORATION AND LACEY VIDEO SERVICES	(Volume 2)
	LYNDEN J. AND ASSOCIATES, INC.	(Volume 2)
	LYON REPORTING, INC.	(Volume 2)
	MAES & SIMSON, INC.	(Volume 2)
	MARY BARDELLINI & ASSOCIATES	(Volume 2)
	MC CORKLE COURT REPORTERS, INC.	(Volume 2)
	NICOLE CARTER & ASSOCIATES/BEVERLY HILLS DEPOSITION REPORTERS	(Volume 2)
	PARKER REPORTING, INC.	(Volume 2)
	PETERSON & ASSOCIATES COURT REPORTING, INC.	(Volume 2)
	REASON REPORTING	(Volume 2)
	REPORTERS COOPERATIVE, INC.	(Volume 2)
	STERLING REPORTING SERVICE, INC.	(Volume 2)
	VENTURA COUNTY REPORTING SERVICE	(Volume 2)
MENLO PARK	BELL & MYERS CERTIFIED SHORTHAND REPORTER, INC.	(Volume 2)
	COMBS & GREENLEY	(Volume 2)
MODESTO	AL CALA & ASSOCIATES	(Volume 2)
MONTEREY	BELL & MYERS CERTIFIED SHORTHAND REPORTER, INC.	(Volume 2)
	MONTEREY PENINSULA COURT REPORTERS INC.	(Volume 2)
	PULONE & STROMBERG	(Volume 2)
MORGAN HILL	PULONE & STROMBERG	(Volume 2)
NAPA	DEMICHELLE DEPOSITION REPORTERS	(Volume 2)
NEWPORT BEACH	ABRAMS, MAH & KAHN	(Volume 2)
	LYNDEN J. AND ASSOCIATES, INC.	(Volume 2)
OAKLAND	ABRAMS, MAH & KAHN	(Volume 2)
	BEHMKE REPORTING & VIDEO SERVICES	(Volume 2)
	INTERIM COURT REPORTING	(Volume 2)
	MAES & SIMSON, INC.	(Volume 2)
	PULONE & STROMBERG	(Volume 2)
	STAR REPORTING SERVICE, INC.	(Volume 2)
	VIGNATI REPORTING	(Volume 2)
PALM DESERT	ALL-IN-ONE DEPOSITION REPORTING	(Volume 3)
PALM SPRINGS	ALL-IN-ONE DEPOSITION REPORTING	(Volume 3)
	AT LAW LITIGATION SUPPORT, INC.	(Volume 3)
PALO ALTO	1-800-FOR-DEPO-ALDERSONREPORTING	(Volume 3)
	BEHMKE REPORTING & VIDEO SERVICES	(Volume 3)
	BELL & MYERS CERTIFIED SHORTHAND REPORTER, INC.	(Volume 3)

COURT REPORTERS - Continued

CALIFORNIA, PALO ALTO - Continued

City	Reporter	Volume
	COMBS & GREENLEY	(Volume 3)
	INTERIM COURT REPORTING	(Volume 3)
	OBUJEN & MCCUTCHEON	(Volume 3)
	PULONE & STROMBERG	(Volume 3)
PASADENA	INTERIM COURT REPORTING	(Volume 3)
RED BLUFF	RED BLUFF REPORTERS, INC.	(Volume 3)
REDDING	ADVANCED COURT REPORTING & VIDEO SERVICE	(Volume 3)
	J.V. KILLINGSWORTH & ASSOCIATES	(Volume 3)
RIVERSIDE	ABRAMS, MAH & KAHN	(Volume 3)
	HUTCHINGS COURT REPORTERS, LLC SM	(Volume 3)
	LYNDEN J. AND ASSOCIATES, INC.	(Volume 3)
	REPORTERS COOPERATIVE, INC.	(Volume 3)
SACRAMENTO	1-800-FOR-DEPO-ALDERSONREPORTING	(Volume 3)
	BARRON & RICH	(Volume 3)
	COMBS & GREENLEY	(Volume 3)
	DEMICHELLE DEPOSITION REPORTERS	(Volume 3)
	ESQUIRE™ DEPOSITION SERVICES	(Volume 3)
	INTERIM COURT REPORTING	(Volume 3)
	M.O.A. DEPOSITION REPORTERS	(Volume 3)
	MAES & SIMSON, INC.	(Volume 3)
	NORTHERN CALIFORNIA COURT REPORTERS	(Volume 3)
	PULONE & STROMBERG	(Volume 3)
	REPORTERS COOPERATIVE, INC.	(Volume 3)
	STAR REPORTING SERVICE, INC.	(Volume 3)
SAN BERNARDINO	AUDREY PATRICK REPORTING SERVICE	(Volume 3)
	HAHN AND BOWERSOCK	(Volume 3)
	PETERSON & ASSOCIATES COURT REPORTING, INC.	(Volume 3)
	REPORTERS COOPERATIVE, INC.	(Volume 3)
SAN CLEMENTE	HUTCHINGS COURT REPORTERS, LLC SM	(Volume 3)
SAN DIEGO	1-800-FOR-DEPO-ALDERSONREPORTING	(Volume 3)
	A.A. NICHOLS, INC.	(Volume 3)
	AA1 PARLIAMENTARY REPORTING	(Volume 3)
	ASAP COURT REPORTING, INC.	(Volume 3)
	AT LAW LITIGATION SUPPORT, INC.	(Volume 3)
	BALLERINI COURT REPORTERS	(Volume 3)
	ESQUIRE™ DEPOSITION SERVICES	(Volume 3)
	FIVECOAT AND WITH	(Volume 3)
	HAHN AND BOWERSOCK	(Volume 3)
	HUTCHINGS COURT REPORTERS, LLC SM	(Volume 3)
	INTERIM COURT REPORTING	(Volume 3)
	LYNDEN J. AND ASSOCIATES, INC.	(Volume 3)
	MAES & SIMSON, INC.	(Volume 3)
	PETERSON & ASSOCIATES COURT REPORTING, INC.	(Volume 3)
	PROVANCHA SHELBURNE SHERR COURT REPORTERS, INC.	(Volume 3)
	REPORTERS COOPERATIVE, INC.	(Volume 3)
	VAIL, CHRISTIANS & ASSOCIATES	(Volume 3)
SAN FRANCISCO	1-800-FOR-DEPO-ALDERSONREPORTING	(Volume 3)
	A.A. NICHOLS, INC.	(Volume 3)
	AA1 PARLIAMENTARY REPORTING	(Volume 3)
	ABRAMS, MAH & KAHN	(Volume 3)
	ADVANTAGE REPORTING SERVICES	(Volume 3)
	BEHMKE REPORTING & VIDEO SERVICES	(Volume 3)
	BELL & MYERS CERTIFIED SHORTHAND REPORTER, INC.	(Volume 3)
	BEMA REPORTING	(Volume 3)
	CATHERINE TEACH REPORTING	(Volume 3)
	COMBS & GREENLEY	(Volume 3)
	ESQUIRE™ DEPOSITION SERVICES	(Volume 3)
	FINK & CARNEY REPORTING AND VIDEO/RALPH FINK & ASSOCIATES, INC.	(Volume 3)
	ALICE N. HALBERT, CSR, RPR	(Volume 3)
	HARRY A. CANNON, INC.	(Volume 3)
	HILL REPORTING SERVICE	(Volume 3)
	HUTCHINGS COURT REPORTERS, LLC SM	(Volume 3)
	INTERIM COURT REPORTING	(Volume 3)
	LYON REPORTING, INC.	(Volume 3)
	MAES & SIMSON, INC.	(Volume 3)

City	Reporter	Volume
	MARY HILLABRAND INC.	(Volume 3)
	REPORTERS COOPERATIVE, INC.	(Volume 3)
	ROBERT BARNES ASSOCIATES	(Volume 3)
	STAR REPORTING SERVICE, INC.	(Volume 3)
	STERLING REPORTING SERVICE, INC.	(Volume 3)
	VIGNATI REPORTING	(Volume 3)
SAN JOSE	1-2-3 REPORTING SERVICE A DIVISION OF CERTIFIED REPORTING COMPANY	(Volume 3)
	ADVANTAGE REPORTING SERVICES	(Volume 3)
	BEHMKE REPORTING & VIDEO SERVICES	(Volume 3)
	BELL & MYERS CERTIFIED SHORTHAND REPORTER, INC.	(Volume 3)
	COMPUTER REPORTING SERVICE	(Volume 3)
	INTERIM COURT REPORTING	(Volume 3)
	LANDI COURT REPORTERS	(Volume 3)
	MARCIA HUNTER COURT REPORTING SERVICES	(Volume 3)
	MARY HILLABRAND INC.	(Volume 3)
	PULONE & STROMBERG	(Volume 3)
	REPORTERS COOPERATIVE, INC.	(Volume 3)
	TALTY COURT REPORTERS, INC.	(Volume 3)
SAN LUIS OBISPO	MERIT REPORTING AND VIDEO	(Volume 3)
SAN MATEO	BEHMKE REPORTING & VIDEO SERVICES	(Volume 3)
	PULONE & STROMBERG	(Volume 3)
	STAR REPORTING SERVICE, INC.	(Volume 3)
	TALTY COURT REPORTERS, INC.	(Volume 3)
SAN RAFAEL	CALIFORNIA SHORTHAND REPORTING	(Volume 3)
	STAR REPORTING SERVICE, INC.	(Volume 3)
SANTA ANA	ABRAMS, MAH & KAHN	(Volume 3)
	BARRISTERS' REPORTING SERVICE	(Volume 3)
	ESQUIRE™ DEPOSITION SERVICES	(Volume 3)
	HUTCHINGS COURT REPORTERS, LLC ℠	(Volume 3)
	KARYN ABBOTT & ASSOCIATES	(Volume 3)
	LYNDEN J. AND ASSOCIATES, INC.	(Volume 3)
	PETERSON & ASSOCIATES COURT REPORTING, INC.	(Volume 3)
SANTA BARBARA	AHLSTRAND AND ASSOCIATES	(Volume 3)
	MERIT REPORTING AND VIDEO	(Volume 3)
	REHWOLDT PROFESSIONAL REPORTING	(Volume 3)
	VENTURA COUNTY REPORTING SERVICE	(Volume 3)
SANTA CLARA	PULONE & STROMBERG	(Volume 3)
SANTA CRUZ	PULONE & STROMBERG	(Volume 3)
SANTA MONICA	A.A. NICHOLS, INC.	(Volume 3)
SANTA ROSA	ADAIR, POTSWALD & HENNESSEY	(Volume 3)
	CALNORTH REPORTING SERVICE	(Volume 3)
	COASTAL REPORTING SERVICES	(Volume 3)
	DEMICHELLE DEPOSITION REPORTERS	(Volume 3)
	MAES & SIMSON, INC.	(Volume 3)
STOCKTON	GAROUTTE'S	(Volume 3)
	INTERIM COURT REPORTING	(Volume 3)
TORRANCE	ABRAMS, MAH & KAHN	(Volume 3)
TRUCKEE	HILL REPORTING SERVICE	(Volume 3)
UKIAH	ADAIR, POTSWALD & HENNESSEY	(Volume 3)
VALLEJO	DOUCETTE LEGAL SERVICES	(Volume 3)
VAN NUYS	BOB MCCANN & ASSOCIATES	(Volume 3)
VENTURA	AT LAW LITIGATION SUPPORT, INC.	(Volume 3)
	HAHN AND BOWERSOCK	(Volume 3)
	VENTURA COUNTY REPORTING SERVICE	(Volume 3)
VISTA	A.A. NICHOLS, INC.	(Volume 3)
WALNUT CREEK	PULONE & STROMBERG	(Volume 3)
	ZANDONELLA REPORTING SERVICE, INC.	(Volume 3)
YUBA CITY	M.O.A. DEPOSITION REPORTERS	(Volume 3)

COLORADO

City	Reporter	Volume
AURORA	REPORTERS COOPERATIVE, INC.	(Volume 4)
BOULDER	BLANDO REPORTING & VIDEO SERVICE, INC.	(Volume 4)
	REPORTERS COOPERATIVE, INC.	(Volume 4)
COLORADO SPRINGS	ACCURATE REPORTING SERVICES, L.L.C.	(Volume 4)
	PAMP REPORTING AGENCY	(Volume 4)
	REPORTERS COOPERATIVE, INC.	(Volume 4)
DENVER	1-2-3 REPORTING SERVICE A DIVISION OF CERTIFIED REPORTING COMPANY	(Volume 4)
	1-800-FOR-DEPO-ALDERSONREPORTING	(Volume 4)
	ACCURATE REPORTING SERVICES, L.L.C.	(Volume 4)

COURT REPORTERS - Continued

COLORADO, DENVER - Continued

City	Reporter	Volume
	AGREN REPORTING & VIDEO, INC.	(Volume 4)
	JOHNSON, MOORE, HENDERSON & KONSTEN	(Volume 4)
	PATTERSON REPORTING & VIDEO SERVICE, INC.	(Volume 4)
	REPORTERS COOPERATIVE, INC.	(Volume 4)
	RICHARDSON REPORTING SERVICE	(Volume 4)
FORT COLLINS	MEADORS COURT REPORTING, LLC	(Volume 4)
	WILSON GEORGE COURT REPORTERS, INC.	(Volume 4)
GRAND JUNCTION	COLORADO WEST REPORTERS	(Volume 4)

CONNECTICUT

City	Reporter	Volume
BRIDGEPORT	NIZIANKIEWICZ & MILLER REPORTING SERVICES	(Volume 4)
	POST REPORTING SERVICE, INC.	(Volume 4)
HARTFORD	BRANDON REPORTING SERVICE	(Volume 4)
	THE CUNNINGHAM GROUP, INC.	(Volume 4)
	DOYLE REPORTING, INC. AN ALR REPORTING COMPANY	(Volume 4)
	NIZIANKIEWICZ & MILLER REPORTING SERVICES	(Volume 4)
	REPORTERS COOPERATIVE, INC.	(Volume 4)
NEW HAVEN	NIZIANKIEWICZ & MILLER REPORTING SERVICES	(Volume 4)
	POST REPORTING SERVICE, INC.	(Volume 4)
NORWALK	REPORTERS COOPERATIVE, INC.	(Volume 4)
STAMFORD	THE CUNNINGHAM GROUP, INC.	(Volume 4)
	NIZIANKIEWICZ & MILLER REPORTING SERVICES	(Volume 4)
	REPORTERS COOPERATIVE, INC.	(Volume 4)
WATERBURY	NIZIANKIEWICZ & MILLER REPORTING SERVICES	(Volume 4)

DELAWARE

City	Reporter	Volume
WILMINGTON	CORBETT & ASSOCIATES	(Volume 4)
	REPORTERS COOPERATIVE, INC.	(Volume 4)
	STRESKI REPORTING & VIDEO SERVICE	(Volume 4)

DISTRICT OF COLUMBIA

City	Reporter	Volume
WASHINGTON	1-800-FOR-DEPO-ALDERSONREPORTING	(Volume 5)
	AA BETA REPORTING	(Volume 5)
	AA1 PARLIAMENTARY REPORTING, INC.	(Volume 5)
	AABBEY-WHITMAN REPORTING SERVICE	(Volume 5)
	AATABAY DEPOSITION REPORTING	(Volume 5)
	ACE-FEDERAL REPORTERS, INC.	(Volume 5)
	ANN RILEY & ASSOCIATES, LTD.	(Volume 5)
	BRADFORD ASSOCIATES	(Volume 5)
	CAROL J. THOMAS STENOTYPE REPORTING SERVICES, INC.	(Volume 5)
	CATHERINE TEACH REPORTING	(Volume 5)
	DEPOSITION SERVICES, INC.	(Volume 5)
	DOERNER & GOLDBERG	(Volume 5)
	EVANS REPORTING SERVICE, INC.	(Volume 5)
	FINK & CARNEY REPORTING AND VIDEO/RALPH FINK & ASSOCIATES, INC.	(Volume 5)
	FOR THE RECORD, INC.	(Volume 5)
	GORE REPORTING COMPANY	(Volume 5)
	GREAT LAKES SHORTHAND	(Volume 5)
	HUTCHINGS COURT REPORTERS, LLC ℠	(Volume 5)
	RONALD E. JOHNSON, RMR	(Volume 5)
	LYON REPORTING, INC.	(Volume 5)
	METRO REPORTERS INC.	(Volume 5)
	NEAL R. GROSS AND CO. INC.	(Volume 5)
	NEW YORK LEGAL VIDEO SERVICES	(Volume 5)
	AN OVERNITE COURT REPORTING SERVICE	(Volume 5)
	PAGES INK COURT AND CONFERENCE REPORTERS	(Volume 5)
	REPORTERS COOPERATIVE, INC.	(Volume 5)
	RIGLER & O'NEILL COURT REPORTERS, INC.	(Volume 5)
	SALOMON REPORTING SERVICE, INC.	(Volume 5)
	STRESKI REPORTING & VIDEO SERVICE	(Volume 5)

FLORIDA

City	Reporter	Volume
ALACHUA	A COURT REPORTER REGISTRY	(Volume 6)
	THE COURT REPORTER REGISTRY	(Volume 6)

COURT REPORTERS - Continued

FLORIDA, MELBOURNE - Continued

	REPORTERS COOPERATIVE, INC.	(Volume 6)
	RYAN REPORTING	(Volume 6)
	SOUTHERN COURT REPORTERS, INC.	(Volume 6)
MIAMI	1-800-FOR-DEPO-ALDERSONREPORTING	(Volume 6)
	AA1 PARLIAMENTARY REPORTING, INC.	(Volume 6)
	CASTILLO & CASTILLO	(Volume 6)
	CERTIFIED COURT REPORTERS, INC.	(Volume 6)
	A COURT REPORTER REGISTRY	(Volume 6)
	DORIS O. WONG ASSOCIATES, INC.	(Volume 6)
	FINK & CARNEY REPORTING AND VIDEO/RALPH FINK & ASSOCIATES, INC.	(Volume 6)
	LAWS REPORTING, INC.	(Volume 6)
	MEDICAL COURT REPORTERS REGISTRY	(Volume 6)
	REPORTERS COOPERATIVE, INC.	(Volume 6)
	SOUTHERN COURT REPORTERS, INC.	(Volume 6)
	STERLING REPORTING SERVICE, INC.	(Volume 6)
	VERITEXT L.L.C.	(Volume 6)
	VIDEO COURT REPORTING, INC.	(Volume 6)
	ZACCO & ASSOCIATES REPORTING SERVICES	(Volume 6)
MILTON	ASSOCIATED COURT REPORTERS	(Volume 6)
NAPLES	DICHARIA & ASSOCIATES COURT REPORTING, INC.	(Volume 6)
	DONOVAN COURT REPORTING, INC.	(Volume 6)
	MEDICAL COURT REPORTERS REGISTRY	(Volume 6)
NEW PORT RICHEY	THE COURT REPORTER REGISTRY	(Volume 6)
	EXECUTIVE REPORTING SERVICE	(Volume 6)
OCALA	ASSOCIATED COURT REPORTERS, INC.	(Volume 6)
	THE COURT REPORTER REGISTRY	(Volume 6)
	MEDICAL COURT REPORTERS REGISTRY	(Volume 6)
OKEECHOBEE	ATLANTIC REPORTING	(Volume 6)
OLDSMAR	THE COURT REPORTER REGISTRY	(Volume 6)
ORLANDO	AA1 PARLIAMENTARY REPORTING, INC.	(Volume 6)
	ABOUND VIDEO SERVICES	(Volume 6)
	BARBARA PERRY & COMPANY	(Volume 6)
	CENTRAL FLORIDA REPORTERS, INC.	(Volume 6)
	CERTIFIED COURT REPORTERS, INC.	(Volume 6)
	A COURT REPORTER REGISTRY	(Volume 6)
	KANABAY COURT REPORTERS	(Volume 6)
	LAWS REPORTING, INC.	(Volume 6)
	MEDICAL COURT REPORTERS REGISTRY	(Volume 6)
	MONTANA REPORTING SERVICE, INC.	(Volume 6)
	NARUP, VOUVAKIS, INC.	(Volume 6)
	ORANGE REPORTING, INC.	(Volume 6)
	REPORTERS COOPERATIVE, INC.	(Volume 6)
	RON FLEMING VIDEO	(Volume 6)
	SCLAFANI WILLIAMS COURT REPORTERS, INC.	(Volume 6)
	SOUTHERN COURT REPORTERS, INC.	(Volume 6)
	ZACCO & ASSOCIATES REPORTING SERVICES	(Volume 6)
PALATKA	ELLIOTT & ASSOCIATES	(Volume 6)
PALM HARBOR	THE COURT REPORTER REGISTRY	(Volume 6)
PANAMA CITY	GULF BAY REPORTING	(Volume 6)
PENSACOLA	ANCHOR COURT REPORTING	(Volume 6)
	LEITCH, TAYLOR & BAKER, INC.	(Volume 6)
	WIERZBICKI & STEPHENSON COURT REPORTING SERVICE	(Volume 6)
PORT CHARLOTTE	DICHARIA & ASSOCIATES COURT REPORTING, INC.	(Volume 6)
PORT ST. LUCIE	ATLANTIC REPORTING	(Volume 6)
PUNTA GORDA	METZGER COURT REPORTING, INC.	(Volume 6)
SANFORD	GERALDINE KERR & ASSOCIATES	(Volume 6)
	ZACCO & ASSOCIATES REPORTING SERVICES	(Volume 6)
SARASOTA	THE COURT REPORTER REGISTRY	(Volume 6)

City	Court Reporter	Volume
	THE COURT REPORTERS	(Volume 6)
	KANABAY COURT REPORTERS	(Volume 6)
	MEDICAL COURT REPORTERS REGISTRY	(Volume 6)
	MONTANA REPORTING SERVICE, INC.	(Volume 6)
	REPORTERS COOPERATIVE, INC.	(Volume 6)
	RIDENOUR REPORTING	(Volume 6)
	SCLAFANI WILLIAMS COURT REPORTERS, INC.	(Volume 6)
	VERBATIM COURT REPORTING	(Volume 6)
	ZACCO & ASSOCIATES REPORTING SERVICES	(Volume 6)
SEBRING	HANSEN REPORTING SERVICE	(Volume 6)
	SCLAFANI WILLIAMS COURT REPORTERS, INC.	(Volume 6)
ST. AUGUSTINE	ELLIOTT & ASSOCIATES	(Volume 6)
ST. PETERSBURG	AAA-D & D REPORTING SERVICE, INC.	(Volume 6)
	BERRYHILL & ASSOCIATES, INC.	(Volume 6)
	CLARK REPORTING SERVICE, INC.	(Volume 6)
	THE COURT REPORTER REGISTRY	(Volume 6)
	EXECUTIVE REPORTING SERVICE	(Volume 6)
	HARTSOCK & CERVONE	(Volume 6)
	KANABAY COURT REPORTERS	(Volume 6)
	MEDICAL COURT REPORTERS REGISTRY	(Volume 6)
	ROBERT A. DEMPSTER & ASSOCIATES	(Volume 6)
	SCLAFANI WILLIAMS COURT REPORTERS, INC.	(Volume 6)
	VINCENT M. LUCENTE & ASSOCIATES, INC.	(Volume 6)
	ZACCO & ASSOCIATES REPORTING SERVICES	(Volume 6)
STUART	ATLANTIC REPORTING	(Volume 6)
	ESQUIRE REPORTING, INC.	(Volume 6)
TALLAHASSEE	A-1 STENOTYPE REPORTERS	(Volume 6)
	ACCURATE STENOTYPE REPORTERS, INC.	(Volume 6)
	A COURT REPORTER REGISTRY	(Volume 6)
	ZACCO & ASSOCIATES REPORTING SERVICES	(Volume 6)
TAMPA	1-800-FOR-DEPO-ALDERSONREPORTING	(Volume 6)
	AA1 PARLIAMENTARY REPORTING, INC.	(Volume 6)
	AAA-D & D REPORTING SERVICE, INC.	(Volume 6)
	AMERICAN HIGH-TECH TRANSCRIPTION	(Volume 6)
	BERRYHILL & ASSOCIATES, INC.	(Volume 6)
	CENTRAL FLORIDA REPORTERS, INC.	(Volume 6)
	CERTIFIED COURT REPORTERS, INC.	(Volume 6)
	CLARK REPORTING SERVICE, INC.	(Volume 6)
	THE COURT REPORTER REGISTRY	(Volume 6)
	A COURT REPORTER REGISTRY	(Volume 6)
	DREYER & ASSOCIATES	(Volume 6)
	EXECUTIVE REPORTING SERVICE	(Volume 6)
	HARTSOCK & CERVONE	(Volume 6)
	INDEPENDENT REPORTING SERVICE	(Volume 6)
	JOHNSON & ASSOCIATES	(Volume 6)
	KANABAY COURT REPORTERS	(Volume 6)
	MEDICAL COURT REPORTERS REGISTRY	(Volume 6)
	MONTANA REPORTING SERVICE, INC.	(Volume 6)
	REPORTERS COOPERATIVE, INC.	(Volume 6)
	THE REPORTERS GROUP, INC.	(Volume 6)
	RICHARD LEE REPORTING	(Volume 6)
	ROBERT A. DEMPSTER & ASSOCIATES	(Volume 6)
	SCLAFANI WILLIAMS COURT REPORTERS, INC.	(Volume 6)
	SOUTHERN COURT REPORTERS, INC.	(Volume 6)
	ZACCO & ASSOCIATES REPORTING SERVICES	(Volume 6)
TAVARES	ZACCO & ASSOCIATES REPORTING SERVICES	(Volume 6)
VERO BEACH	AMERICAN REPORTING	(Volume 6)
	ATLANTIC REPORTING	(Volume 6)
WEST PALM BEACH	EVERMAN & ASSOCIATES, INC.	(Volume 6)
	LAWS REPORTING, INC.	(Volume 6)
	LOUINE M. PERNICE & ASSOCIATES	(Volume 6)
	MEDICAL COURT REPORTERS REGISTRY	(Volume 6)
	VERITEXT L.L.C.	(Volume 6)
	WEATHERS & ASSOCIATES, INC.	(Volume 6)
	ZACCO & ASSOCIATES REPORTING SERVICES	(Volume 6)

COURT REPORTERS - Continued

FLORIDA - Continued

WINTER HAVEN	REPORTERS COOPERATIVE, INC.	(Volume 6)
	SCLAFANI WILLIAMS COURT REPORTERS, INC.	(Volume 6)

GEORGIA

ATLANTA	1-800-FOR-DEPO-ALDERSONREPORTING	(Volume 7)
	ACCUSCRIBE COURT REPORTING	(Volume 7)
	AMERICAN COURT REPORTING COMPANY	(Volume 7)
	BROWN REPORTING, INC.	(Volume 7)
	BULL & ASSOCIATES, INC.	(Volume 7)
	CHILDERS & SHELNUTT, INC.	(Volume 7)
	COMBS COURT REPORTING	(Volume 7)
	DONOVAN REPORTING, P.C.	(Volume 7)
	ESQUIRE™ DEPOSITION SERVICES	(Volume 7)
	ESTEB & ASSOCIATES, LLC	(Volume 7)
	HUSEBY & ASSOCIATES	(Volume 7)
	LYON REPORTING, INC.	(Volume 7)
	NEWBERRY & COMPANY	(Volume 7)
	PARNELL REPORTING	(Volume 7)
	REGENCY REPORTING, INC.	(Volume 7)
	REPORTERS COOPERATIVE, INC.	(Volume 7)
AUGUSTA	BROWN REPORTING, INC.	(Volume 7)
BRUNSWICK	REPORTERS COOPERATIVE, INC.	(Volume 7)
COLUMBUS	ACR ACCREDITED COURT REPORTERS	(Volume 7)
DOUGLAS	CADY REPORTING SERVICE	(Volume 7)
GAINESVILLE	HUSEBY & ASSOCIATES	(Volume 7)
	TDL COURT REPORTING	(Volume 7)
LA GRANGE	ESTEB & ASSOCIATES, LLC	(Volume 7)
MACON	CLAUDE JOINER REPORTING SERVICE, INC.	(Volume 7)
	COURT REPORTING ASSOCIATES, INC.	(Volume 7)
MARIETTA	DONOVAN REPORTING, P.C.	(Volume 7)
NEWNAN	ESTEB & ASSOCIATES, LLC	(Volume 7)
SAVANNAH	TOM CRITES & ASSOCIATES INTERNATIONAL, INC.	(Volume 7)
	REPORTERS COOPERATIVE, INC.	(Volume 7)

HAWAII

HONOLULU	CARNAZZO COURT REPORTING COMPANY LTD.	(Volume 7)
	PACIFIC REPORTING SERVICES UNLIMITED, INC.	(Volume 7)
	POWERS & ASSOCIATES	(Volume 7)
	RALPH ROSENBERG COURT REPORTERS, INC.	(Volume 7)

IDAHO

BOISE	BURNHAM, HABEL & ASSOCIATES, INC.	(Volume 7)
	REPORTERS COOPERATIVE, INC.	(Volume 7)
IDAHO FALLS	REPORTERS COOPERATIVE, INC.	(Volume 7)
POCATELLO	BUCHANAN REPORTING SERVICE	(Volume 7)

ILLINOIS

ALTON	GORE & PERRY REPORTING COMPANY	(Volume 8)
ASHTON	IN TOTIDEM VERBIS (ITV)	(Volume 8)
BELLEVILLE	GORE & PERRY REPORTING COMPANY	(Volume 8)
	RANKIN REPORTING & LEGAL VIDEO, INC.	(Volume 8)
CHAMPAIGN	AREA WIDE REPORTING SERVICE	(Volume 8)
CHICAGO	1-2-3 REPORTING SERVICE A DIVISION OF CERTIFIED REPORTING COMPANY	(Volume 8)
	1-800-FOR-DEPO-ALDERSONREPORTING	(Volume 8)
	A 1 REPORTING SERVICE	(Volume 8)
	A-1 LEGAL VIDEO	(Volume 8)
	ADVANTAGE REPORTING SERVICE	(Volume 8)
	AREA COURT REPORTERS	(Volume 8)
	CENTRAL REPORTERS ASSOCIATED	(Volume 8)
	DIANE HROMEK'S COURT REPORTERS, INC.	(Volume 8)
	ESPIRITU & ASSOCIATES	(Volume 8)
	ESQUIRE™ DEPOSITION SERVICES	(Volume 8)
	GREAT LAKES SHORTHAND	(Volume 8)
	HUTCHINGS COURT REPORTERS, LLC ℠	(Volume 8)
	INTERIM COURT REPORTING	(Volume 8)
	LITICORP	(Volume 8)
	LYON REPORTING, INC.	(Volume 8)
	MC CORKLE COURT REPORTERS, INC.	(Volume 8)
	NORTH SUBURBAN REPORTING & LEGAL MEDIA, INC.	(Volume 8)

	O'HARE REPORTING SERVICE, INC.	(Volume 8)
	PATTI BLAIR COURT REPORTERS, P.C.	(Volume 8)
	REPORTERS COOPERATIVE, INC.	(Volume 8)
	SCLAFANI WILLIAMS COURT REPORTERS, INC.	(Volume 8)
	SULLIVAN REPORTING COMPANY	(Volume 8)
	WICHMANN REPORTING SERVICE	(Volume 8)
DES PLAINES	O'HARE REPORTING SERVICE, INC.	(Volume 8)
EDWARDSVILLE	GORE & PERRY REPORTING COMPANY	(Volume 8)
	RANKIN REPORTING & LEGAL VIDEO, INC.	(Volume 8)
JOLIET	ADVANTAGE REPORTING SERVICE	(Volume 8)
MOLINE	CONNELL REPORTING	(Volume 8)
NAPERVILLE	AREA COURT REPORTERS	(Volume 8)
NASHVILLE	RANKIN REPORTING & LEGAL VIDEO, INC.	(Volume 8)
NORTHBROOK	AREA COURT REPORTERS	(Volume 8)
	INTERIM COURT REPORTING	(Volume 8)
	O'HARE REPORTING SERVICE, INC.	(Volume 8)
PARK RIDGE	O'HARE REPORTING SERVICE, INC.	(Volume 8)
PEORIA	ADVANTAGE REPORTING SERVICE	(Volume 8)
	REPORTERS COOPERATIVE, INC.	(Volume 8)
ROCKFORD	AREA COURT REPORTERS	(Volume 8)
	ELITE REPORTING SERVICES, LTD.	(Volume 8)
	LAUNIUS REPORTING SERVICE	(Volume 8)
	MIDWEST PROFESSIONAL REPORTING, INC.	(Volume 8)
	REPORTERS COOPERATIVE, INC.	(Volume 8)
SCHAUMBURG	AREA COURT REPORTERS	(Volume 8)
	ESPIRITU & ASSOCIATES	(Volume 8)
	O'HARE REPORTING SERVICE, INC.	(Volume 8)
SPRINGFIELD	AD HOC REPORTING & VIDEO	(Volume 8)
	ADVANTAGE REPORTING SERVICE	(Volume 8)
	BALDWIN COURT REPORTING AND LEGAL-VISUAL SERVICES	(Volume 8)
	CAPITOL REPORTING SERVICE, INC.	(Volume 8)

INDIANA

EVANSVILLE	SOUTHERN INDIANA REPORTING	(Volume 8)
FORT WAYNE	BOWLAND REPORTING SERVICE	(Volume 8)
HAMMOND	FISSINGER & KNIGHT, INC.	(Volume 8)
INDIANAPOLIS	ASSOCIATED REPORTING, INC.	(Volume 8)
	JOHN E. CONNOR & ASSOCIATES, INC.	(Volume 8)
KOKOMO	DEPOSITIONS BY THE BUNCH	(Volume 8)
MICHIGAN CITY	MARILYN M. JONES & ASSOCIATES LTD.	(Volume 8)
NOBLESVILLE	AMERICAN REPORTING SERVICE	(Volume 8)
SOUTH BEND	EDISON LAKES - OLMSTED & ASSOCIATES LTD	(Volume 8)
	MIDWEST REPORTING	(Volume 8)

IOWA

BURLINGTON	MJW COURT REPORTING SERVICES	(Volume 8)
CEDAR RAPIDS	KOOL & NYGREN, INC.	(Volume 8)
DES MOINES	HUNEY - VAUGHN COURT REPORTERS, LTD.	(Volume 8)
	SWEENEY COURT REPORTING SERVICE	(Volume 8)
SIOUX CITY	CASSEL MEYER COURT REPORTING	(Volume 8)
WATERLOO	VAN WYNGARDEN & ABRAHAMSON, INC.	(Volume 8)

KANSAS

KANSAS CITY	AAAA GENE DOLGINOFF ASSOCIATES, LTD.	(Volume 9)
	ACEHOSTETLER & ASSOCIATES	(Volume 9)
	REPORTERS COOPERATIVE, INC.	(Volume 9)
OVERLAND PARK	AAAA GENE DOLGINOFF ASSOCIATES, LTD.	(Volume 9)
	ACEHOSTETLER & ASSOCIATES	(Volume 9)
	JAY E. SUDDRETH & ASSOCIATES, INC.	(Volume 9)
TOPEKA	APPINO & BIGGS REPORTING SERVICE	(Volume 9)
WICHITA	REPORTERS COOPERATIVE, INC.	(Volume 9)

KENTUCKY

BARDSTOWN	ABSOLUTELY VERBATIM SERVICES	(Volume 9)
BOWLING GREEN	JAMES A. DALE, JR.	(Volume 9)
FLORENCE	VERBATIM REPORTING	(Volume 9)
LEXINGTON	ACCUTRON REPORTING SERVICE, INC.	(Volume 9)
	ACTION COURT REPORTERS	(Volume 9)
	AN/DOR REPORTING SERVICE, INC.	(Volume 9)
	ASSOCIATED REPORTING SERVICES, INC.	(Volume 9)
	COLLINS & HUGHES REPORTING AND VIDEO SERVICE	(Volume 9)
	REPORTERS COOPERATIVE, INC.	(Volume 9)
LOUISVILLE	AD HOC REPORTING & VIDEO	(Volume 9)
	FULTON-BELANGER & ASSOCIATES	(Volume 9)

COURT REPORTERS - Continued

KENTUCKY, LOUISVILLE - Continued

	GRANT & MAYBRIER, LLC	(Volume 9)
	HANDY, CHUPPE & SOERGEL LLC	(Volume 9)
	REPORTERS COOPERATIVE, INC.	(Volume 9)
OWENSBORO	OHIO VALLEY REPORTING SERVICE	(Volume 9)

LOUISIANA

BATON ROUGE	A R I - ASSOCIATED REPORTERS, INC.	(Volume 9)
	CURREN & LANDRIEU, INC.	(Volume 9)
LAFAYETTE	A R I - ASSOCIATED REPORTERS, INC.	(Volume 9)
	CURREN & LANDRIEU, INC.	(Volume 9)
NEW ORLEANS	A R I - ASSOCIATED REPORTERS, INC.	(Volume 9)
	A-LEGAL VIDEO SERVICE	(Volume 9)
	ACCURATE REPORTERS, INC.	(Volume 9)
	CURREN & LANDRIEU, INC.	(Volume 9)
	GAUDET, KAISER & PEPPER, L.L.C.	(Volume 9)
	HUFFMAN & ROBINSON, INC.	(Volume 9)
SHREVEPORT	ACCURATE REPORTING OF SHREVEPORT, INC.	(Volume 9)
	ALLIED COURT REPORTING SERVICE	(Volume 9)
	PREMIER REPORTING, LLC	(Volume 9)

MAINE

PORTLAND	DOWNING & PETERS REPORTING ASSOCIATES	(Volume 9)

MARYLAND

ANNAPOLIS	1-800-FOR-DEPO-ALDERSONREPORTING	(Volume 9)
	DISCOVERY REPORTING, INC.	(Volume 9)
	REPORTERS COOPERATIVE, INC.	(Volume 9)
	RIGLER & O'NEILL COURT REPORTERS, INC.	(Volume 9)
	SALOMON REPORTING SERVICE, INC.	(Volume 9)
BALTIMORE	1-2-3 REPORTING SERVICE A DIVISION OF CERTIFIED REPORTING COMPANY	(Volume 9)
	1-800-FOR-DEPO-ALDERSONREPORTING	(Volume 9)
	AA BETA REPORTING	(Volume 9)
	CAROL J. THOMAS STENOTYPE REPORTING SERVICES, INC.	(Volume 9)
	COURT REPORTING CONCEPTS, INC.	(Volume 9)
	ELITE REPORTING	(Volume 9)
	EVANS REPORTING SERVICE, INC.	(Volume 9)
	FINK & CARNEY REPORTING AND VIDEO/RALPH FINK & ASSOCIATES, INC.	(Volume 9)
	FOR THE RECORD, INC.	(Volume 9)
	GORE BROTHERS REPORTING & VIDEO COMPANY, INC.	(Volume 9)
	HUNT REPORTING COMPANY	(Volume 9)
	REPORTERS COOPERATIVE, INC.	(Volume 9)
	RIGLER & O'NEILL COURT REPORTERS, INC.	(Volume 9)
	SALOMON REPORTING SERVICE, INC.	(Volume 9)
	WALLS REPORTING, INC.	(Volume 9)
	WE DO DEPOSITIONS, INC.	(Volume 9)
BETHESDA	1-800-FOR-DEPO-ALDERSONREPORTING	(Volume 9)
	AA BETA REPORTING	(Volume 9)
	CAROL J. THOMAS STENOTYPE REPORTING SERVICES, INC.	(Volume 9)
	DEPOSITION SERVICES, INC.	(Volume 9)
CHEVY CHASE	AA BETA REPORTING	(Volume 9)
	CAROL J. THOMAS STENOTYPE REPORTING SERVICES, INC.	(Volume 9)
COLUMBIA	1-800-FOR-DEPO-ALDERSONREPORTING	(Volume 9)
	SALOMON REPORTING SERVICE, INC.	(Volume 9)
FREDERICK	DEPOSITION SERVICES, INC.	(Volume 9)
	SALOMON REPORTING SERVICE, INC.	(Volume 9)
GAITHERSBURG	AA BETA REPORTING	(Volume 9)
GREENBELT	1-800-FOR-DEPO-ALDERSONREPORTING	(Volume 9)
LUTHERVILLE	HALLOCK REPORTING SERVICES	(Volume 9)
ROCKVILLE	1-800-FOR-DEPO-ALDERSONREPORTING	(Volume 9)
	AA BETA REPORTING	(Volume 9)
	AABBEY-WHITMAN REPORTING SERVICE	(Volume 9)
	AATABAY DEPOSITION REPORTING	(Volume 9)
	CAROL J. THOMAS STENOTYPE REPORTING SERVICES, INC.	(Volume 9)
	DEPOSITION SERVICES, INC.	(Volume 9)
	REPORTERS COOPERATIVE, INC.	(Volume 9)
SILVER SPRING	AA BETA REPORTING	(Volume 9)
	CAROL J. THOMAS STENOTYPE REPORTING SERVICES, INC.	(Volume 9)
TOWSON	RIGLER & O'NEILL COURT REPORTERS, INC.	(Volume 9)

City	Court Reporter	Volume
	SALOMON REPORTING SERVICE, INC.	(Volume 9)
WALDORF	FOR THE RECORD, INC.	(Volume 9)

MASSACHUSETTS

City	Court Reporter	Volume
BOSTON	1-2-3 REPORTING SERVICE A DIVISION OF CERTIFIED REPORTING COMPANY	(Volume 10)
	BEACON HILL COURT REPORTING	(Volume 10)
	BOSTON COURT REPORTING	(Volume 10)
	CATUOGNO COURT REPORTING SERVICE, INC.	(Volume 10)
	COPLEY COURT REPORTING	(Volume 10)
	DORIS O. WONG ASSOCIATES, INC.	(Volume 10)
	DUNN & GOUDREAU COURT REPORTING SERVICE, INC.	(Volume 10)
	EYAL COURT REPORTING, INC.	(Volume 10)
	GABRIEL & SWEENEY COURT REPORTING	(Volume 10)
	JONES FRITZ & SHEEHAN	(Volume 10)
	MAHANEY REPORTING SERVICES	(Volume 10)
	MC CORKLE COURT REPORTERS, INC.	(Volume 10)
	O'HARA COURT REPORTING	(Volume 10)
	REPORTERS COOPERATIVE, INC.	(Volume 10)
	ROBERT H. LANGE CO. INC.	(Volume 10)
BROOKLINE	COPLEY COURT REPORTING	(Volume 10)
CAMBRIDGE	COPLEY COURT REPORTING	(Volume 10)
	REPORTERS COOPERATIVE, INC.	(Volume 10)
NEWTON	COPLEY COURT REPORTING	(Volume 10)
QUINCY	COPLEY COURT REPORTING	(Volume 10)
SALEM	COPLEY COURT REPORTING	(Volume 10)
SPRINGFIELD	CATUOGNO COURT REPORTING SERVICE, INC.	(Volume 10)
	PERLIK AND COYLE REPORTING	(Volume 10)
WORCESTER	CATUOGNO COURT REPORTING SERVICE, INC.	(Volume 10)
	FLYNN REPORTING ASSOCIATES	(Volume 10)
	MCCARTHY REPORTING SERVICE AND MCCARTHY LEGAL VIDEO SERVICES	(Volume 10)

MICHIGAN

City	Court Reporter	Volume
ANN ARBOR	CHRISTINE FELTS & ASSOCIATES	(Volume 10)
	GREAT LAKES SHORTHAND	(Volume 10)
	HURON REPORTING SERVICE, INC.	(Volume 10)
	LAUREN BIENENSTOCK & ASSOCIATES	(Volume 10)
BATTLE CREEK	O'BRIEN & BAILS	(Volume 10)
BENTON HARBOR	GREAT LAKES SHORTHAND	(Volume 10)
BIRMINGHAM	ON THE RECORD REPORTING & VIDEO	(Volume 10)
BLOOMFIELD HILLS	BARNETT & ASSOCIATES	(Volume 10)
	OAKLAND COURT REPORTING & LEGAL VIDEO	(Volume 10)
DEARBORN	HANSON/RENAISSANCE COURT REPORTERS	(Volume 10)
	ON THE RECORD REPORTING & VIDEO	(Volume 10)
DETROIT	AIMCO SERVICES	(Volume 10)
	CHRISTINE FELTS & ASSOCIATES	(Volume 10)
	ESQUIRE™ DEPOSITION SERVICES	(Volume 10)
	FINK & CARNEY REPORTING AND VIDEO/RALPH FINK & ASSOCIATES, INC.	(Volume 10)
	GREAT LAKES SHORTHAND	(Volume 10)
	HANSON/RENAISSANCE COURT REPORTERS	(Volume 10)
	HURON REPORTING SERVICE, INC.	(Volume 10)
	LAUREN BIENENSTOCK & ASSOCIATES	(Volume 10)
	MC CORKLE COURT REPORTERS, INC.	(Volume 10)
	MERRILL & ASSOCIATES, INC.	(Volume 10)
	NETWORK REPORTING CORPORATION	(Volume 10)
	O'BRIEN & BAILS	(Volume 10)
	REPORTERS COOPERATIVE, INC.	(Volume 10)
EAST LANSING	REPORTERS COOPERATIVE, INC.	(Volume 10)
FLINT	CHRISTINE FELTS & ASSOCIATES	(Volume 10)
	LAUREN BIENENSTOCK & ASSOCIATES	(Volume 10)
	RIPKA, BOROSKI & ASSOCIATES	(Volume 10)
GRAND RAPIDS	GREAT LAKES SHORTHAND	(Volume 10)
	O'BRIEN & BAILS	(Volume 10)
	Q & A REPORTING, INC.	(Volume 10)
	REPORTERS COOPERATIVE, INC.	(Volume 10)
KALAMAZOO	CHRISTINE FELTS & ASSOCIATES	(Volume 10)
	GERGER-MORETTI REPORTING	(Volume 10)
	GREAT LAKES SHORTHAND	(Volume 10)
	O'BRIEN & BAILS	(Volume 10)
	REPORTERS COOPERATIVE, INC.	(Volume 10)

COURT REPORTERS - Continued

MICHIGAN - Continued

LANSING	CHRISTINE FELTS & ASSOCIATES	(Volume 10)
	GREAT LAKES SHORTHAND	(Volume 10)
	LAUREN BIENENSTOCK & ASSOCIATES	(Volume 10)
	METROPOLITAN REPORTING, INC.	(Volume 10)
	O'BRIEN & BAILS	(Volume 10)
MOUNT CLEMENS	MACOMB COURT REPORTERS, INC.	(Volume 10)
MUSKEGON	GREAT LAKES SHORTHAND	(Volume 10)
SAGINAW	RIPKA, BOROSKI & ASSOCIATES	(Volume 10)
SOUTHFIELD	DE SCRIBE REPORTING, INC.	(Volume 10)
	HANSON/RENAISSANCE COURT REPORTERS	(Volume 10)
	HARBORTOWN COURT REPORTERS	(Volume 10)
	LAUREN BIENENSTOCK & ASSOCIATES	(Volume 10)
	MERRILL & ASSOCIATES, INC.	(Volume 10)
	NATIONAL COURT REPORTING INC.	(Volume 10)
	ON THE RECORD REPORTING & VIDEO	(Volume 10)
ST. JOSEPH	GREAT LAKES SHORTHAND	(Volume 10)
TRAVERSE CITY	GREAT LAKES SHORTHAND	(Volume 10)
TROY	CHRISTINE FELTS & ASSOCIATES	(Volume 10)
	LAUREN BIENENSTOCK & ASSOCIATES	(Volume 10)

MINNESOTA

BLOOMINGTON	JANET SHADDIX & ASSOCIATES	(Volume 11)
MINNEAPOLIS	1-800-FOR-DEPO-ALDERSONREPORTING	(Volume 11)
	1400 RIVERVIEW TOWER REPORTERS	(Volume 11)
	AFFILIATED COURT REPORTERS	(Volume 11)
	ASK, ZENDER & TRONDSON	(Volume 11)
	ASSOCIATED REPORTERS	(Volume 11)
	HERBERT L. PETERSON & ASSOCIATES, INC.	(Volume 11)
	KINSELLA, HARTIGAN & KELZER, INC.	(Volume 11)
	PARADIGM REPORTING & CAPTIONING INC.	(Volume 11)
	PC&A LITIGATION SUPPORT SERVICES	(Volume 11)
	PRO-SYSTEMS COURT REPORTING & VIDEO SERVICES	(Volume 11)
	REPORTERS COOPERATIVE, INC.	(Volume 11)
	STIREWALT & ASSOCIATES	(Volume 11)
ROCHESTER	RICE REPORTING AGENCY	(Volume 11)
ST. PAUL	1400 RIVERVIEW TOWER REPORTERS	(Volume 11)
	ASK, ZENDER & TRONDSON	(Volume 11)
	PC&A LITIGATION SUPPORT SERVICES	(Volume 11)
	REPORTERS COOPERATIVE, INC.	(Volume 11)

MISSISSIPPI

BILOXI	COAST-WIDE REPORTERS	(Volume 11)
GULFPORT	CURREN & LANDRIEU, INC.	(Volume 11)
TUPELO	RAKESTRAW COURT REPORTING	(Volume 11)

MISSOURI

CLAYTON	GORE & PERRY REPORTING COMPANY	(Volume 11)
	JAY E. SUDDRETH & ASSOCIATES, INC.	(Volume 11)
	RANKIN REPORTING & LEGAL VIDEO, INC.	(Volume 11)
COLUMBIA	POE & COMPANY ELECTRONIC REPORTING	(Volume 11)
	VERB8M COURT REPORTERS	(Volume 11)
JEFFERSON CITY	BREDEMAN & ASSOCIATES, INC.	(Volume 11)
	JAY E. SUDDRETH & ASSOCIATES, INC.	(Volume 11)
KANSAS CITY	1-800-FOR-DEPO-ALDERSONREPORTING	(Volume 11)
	AAAA GENE DOLGINOFF ASSOCIATES, LTD.	(Volume 11)
	ACEHOSTETLER & ASSOCIATES	(Volume 11)
	JAY E. SUDDRETH & ASSOCIATES, INC.	(Volume 11)
	ROBERTS & ASSOCIATES	(Volume 11)
	SAWYER COURT REPORTING	(Volume 11)
SPRINGFIELD	COURT REPORTERS OF THE MIDWEST	(Volume 11)
	JAY E. SUDDRETH & ASSOCIATES, INC.	(Volume 11)
ST. CHARLES	GORE & PERRY REPORTING COMPANY	(Volume 11)
	JAY E. SUDDRETH & ASSOCIATES, INC.	(Volume 11)
	RANKIN REPORTING & LEGAL VIDEO, INC.	(Volume 11)
ST. LOUIS	1-800-FOR-DEPO-ALDERSONREPORTING	(Volume 11)
	AD HOC REPORTING & VIDEO	(Volume 11)
	GORE & PERRY REPORTING COMPANY	(Volume 11)
	INTERIM COURT REPORTING	(Volume 11)
	JAY E. SUDDRETH & ASSOCIATES, INC.	(Volume 11)

COURT REPORTERS - Continued

NEW JERSEY, NEWARK - Continued

City	Reporter	Volume
	REPORTERS COOPERATIVE, INC.	(Volume 12)
	ROSENBERG & ASSOCIATES	(Volume 12)
	VERBATIM SERVICES	(Volume 12)
PRINCETON	DOERNER & GOLDBERG	(Volume 12)
	ROSENBERG & ASSOCIATES	(Volume 12)
RED BANK	DOERNER & GOLDBERG	(Volume 12)
ROSELAND	DOERNER & GOLDBERG	(Volume 12)
	GAF LEGAL SERVICES, INC.	(Volume 12)
	REPORTERS COOPERATIVE, INC.	(Volume 12)
	ROSENBERG & ASSOCIATES	(Volume 12)
TRENTON	DOERNER & GOLDBERG	(Volume 12)
	MEL WEINER & ASSOCIATES	(Volume 12)
	ROSENBERG & ASSOCIATES	(Volume 12)
WOODBRIDGE	ESQUIRE™ DEPOSITION SERVICES	(Volume 12)

NEW MEXICO

City	Reporter	Volume
ALBUQUERQUE	ADVANCED COURT REPORTING	(Volume 12)
	AMERICAN REPORTING	(Volume 12)
	BEAN & ASSOCIATES, INC.	(Volume 12)
	BLASING COURT REPORTERS, INC.	(Volume 12)
	KATHY TOWNSEND COURT REPORTERS	(Volume 12)
	REPORTERS COOPERATIVE, INC.	(Volume 12)
FARMINGTON	BEAN & ASSOCIATES, INC.	(Volume 12)
LAS CRUCES	BEAN & ASSOCIATES, INC.	(Volume 12)
SANTA FE	BEAN & ASSOCIATES, INC.	(Volume 12)
	CUMBRE COURT REPORTING, INC.	(Volume 12)
	REPORTERS COOPERATIVE, INC.	(Volume 12)

NEW YORK

City	Reporter	Volume
ALBANY	A.S.E. REPORTING SERVICE	(Volume 12)
	ALLIANCE REPORTING SERVICE	(Volume 12)
	ASSOCIATED REPORTERS INT'L, INC.	(Volume 12)
	PAULINE E. WILLIMAN	(Volume 12)
BINGHAMTON	CZERENDA COURT REPORTING	(Volume 12)
	VERBATIM COURT REPORTING SERVICE, INC.	(Volume 12)
BRONX	PRECISE COURT REPORTING SERVICE, INC.	(Volume 13)
BROOKLYN	PRECISE COURT REPORTING SERVICE, INC.	(Volume 13)
BUFFALO	DEPAOLO - CROSBY REPORTING SERVICES, INC.	(Volume 12)
	REPORTERS COOPERATIVE, INC.	(Volume 12)
GARDEN CITY	TANKOOS REPORTING COMPANY, INC.	(Volume 12)
	TOMMER REPORTING, INC.	(Volume 12)
GREAT NECK	TANKOOS REPORTING COMPANY, INC.	(Volume 12)
HAUPPAUGE	ENRIGHT COURT REPORTING, INC.	(Volume 12)
	TANKOOS REPORTING COMPANY, INC.	(Volume 12)
	TOMMER REPORTING, INC.	(Volume 12)
HUNTINGTON	TANKOOS REPORTING COMPANY, INC.	(Volume 12)
ITHACA	PAIGE REPORTING	(Volume 12)
	VERBATIM COURT REPORTING SERVICE, INC.	(Volume 12)
JAMAICA	PRECISE COURT REPORTING SERVICE, INC.	(Volume 13)
MELVILLE	SUZANNE HAND & ASSOCIATES, INC.	(Volume 12)
	TOMMER REPORTING, INC.	(Volume 12)
MINEOLA	PRECISE COURT REPORTING SERVICE, INC.	(Volume 12)
	REPORTERS COOPERATIVE, INC.	(Volume 12)
	TANKOOS REPORTING COMPANY, INC.	(Volume 12)
	TOMMER REPORTING, INC.	(Volume 12)
NEW CITY	ROCKLAND & ORANGE REPORTING	(Volume 12)
NEW YORK	1-2-3 REPORTING SERVICE A DIVISION OF CERTIFIED REPORTING COMPANY	(Volume 13)
	1-800-FOR-DEPO-ALDERSONREPORTING	(Volume 13)
	A.S.A.P. REPORTING CO. INC.	(Volume 13)
	AA1 PARLIAMENTARY REPORTING	(Volume 13)
	BENJAMIN REPORTING SERVICE AN ALR REPORTING COMPANY	(Volume 13)
	BORAK REPORTING SERVICE AN ALR REPORTING COMPANY	(Volume 13)
	CATHERINE TEACH REPORTING	(Volume 13)
	COMPUTER REPORTING, INC.	(Volume 13)
	DORIS O. WONG ASSOCIATES, INC.	(Volume 13)
	DOYLE REPORTING, INC. AN ALR REPORTING COMPANY	(Volume 13)
	ELLEN GRAUER COURT REPORTING CO.	(Volume 13)

COURT REPORTERS - Continued

OHIO, AKRON - Continued

City	Reporter	Volume
	MERIT REPORTING SERVICES	(Volume 14)
	RENNILLO REPORTING SERVICES	(Volume 14)
	REPORTERS COOPERATIVE, INC.	(Volume 14)
CANTON	CANTON COURT REPORTES	(Volume 14)
CINCINNATI	ACE REPORTING SERVICES	(Volume 14)
	ANDERSON REPORTING SERVICES, INC.	(Volume 14)
	BRITTON & ASSOCIATES, INC.	(Volume 14)
	CIN-TEL CORPORATION	(Volume 14)
	MERIT® LITIGATION SUPPORT SERVICES	(Volume 14)
	MIKE MOBLEY REPORTING	(Volume 14)
	REPORTERS COOPERATIVE, INC.	(Volume 14)
	SPANGLER REPORTING SERVICES, INC.	(Volume 14)
	VERBATIM REPORTING	(Volume 14)
CLEVELAND	ANDERSON REPORTING SERVICES, INC.	(Volume 14)
	C & G	(Volume 14)
	CAROL D. HILL & ASSOCIATES	(Volume 14)
	CEFARATTI GROUP	(Volume 14)
	CLEVELAND COURT REPORTERS	(Volume 14)
	DENNIS A. PARISE & ASSOCIATES	(Volume 14)
	FINCUN-MANCINI, INC.	(Volume 14)
	HOLLAND & ASSOCIATES, INC.	(Volume 14)
	MEHLER & HAGESTROM	(Volume 14)
	MERIT REPORTING SERVICES	(Volume 14)
	MIKE MOBLEY REPORTING	(Volume 14)
	RENNILLO REPORTING SERVICES	(Volume 14)
	REPORTERS COOPERATIVE, INC.	(Volume 14)
	STEVENSON REPORTING SERVICE, INC.	(Volume 14)
	STRESKI REPORTING & VIDEO SERVICE	(Volume 14)
COLUMBUS	1-2-3 REPORTING SERVICE A DIVISION OF CERTIFIED REPORTING COMPANY	(Volume 14)
	ANDERSON REPORTING SERVICES, INC.	(Volume 14)
	ARMSTRONG & OKEY, INC.	(Volume 14)
	MCGINNIS & ASSOCIATES, INC.	(Volume 14)
	PROFESSIONAL REPORTERS, INC.	(Volume 14)
	REPORTERS COOPERATIVE, INC.	(Volume 14)
	SPECTRUM REPORTING, INC.	(Volume 14)
	STRESKI REPORTING & VIDEO SERVICE	(Volume 14)
DAYTON	ANDERSON REPORTING SERVICES, INC.	(Volume 14)
	BRITTON & ASSOCIATES, INC.	(Volume 14)
	DENSLOW, GRYCZ & ASSOCIATES	(Volume 14)
	DONNA JEAN FLOOK	(Volume 14)
	MIKE MOBLEY REPORTING	(Volume 14)
	REPORTERS COOPERATIVE, INC.	(Volume 14)
	VERBATIM REPORTING	(Volume 14)
ST. CLAIRSVILLE	STRESKI REPORTING & VIDEO SERVICE	(Volume 14)
STEUBENVILLE	STRESKI REPORTING & VIDEO SERVICE	(Volume 14)
TOLEDO	ANDERSON REPORTING SERVICES, INC.	(Volume 14)
	CLASSIC REPORTING SERVICE	(Volume 14)
	COLLINS REPORTING SERVICE, INC.	(Volume 14)
	POWERS & HERTZFELD REPORTING SERVICE, INC.	(Volume 14)
WARREN	NAGY-BAKER COURT REPORTING, INC.	(Volume 14)
YOUNGSTOWN	NAGY-BAKER COURT REPORTING, INC.	(Volume 14)

OKLAHOMA

City	Reporter	Volume
ENID	CHISHOLM TRAIL REPORTERS	(Volume 14)
OKLAHOMA CITY	1-2-3 REPORTING SERVICE A DIVISION OF CERTIFIED REPORTING COMPANY	(Volume 14)
	CITY REPORTERS	(Volume 14)
	FREELANCE REPORTERS, INC.	(Volume 14)
	INDEPENDENT REPORTING SERVICE, INC.	(Volume 14)
	REPORTERS COOPERATIVE, INC.	(Volume 14)
TULSA	ACE REPORTERS	(Volume 14)
	ADVANCED REPORTING SERVICES, INC.	(Volume 14)
	BUTLER & ASSOCIATES REPORTING SERVICE, INC.	(Volume 14)

	ERWIN-ROPER REPORTING	(Volume 14)

OREGON

City	Reporter	Volume
BEND	CASCADE COURT REPORTERS	(Volume 15)
EUGENE	C & C COURT REPORTING	(Volume 15)
	CATHERINE TEACH REPORTING	(Volume 15)
KLAMATH FALLS	ADVANCED COURT REPORTING & VIDEO SERVICE	(Volume 15)
MEDFORD	ADVANCED COURT REPORTING & VIDEO SERVICE	(Volume 15)
	BLAYNE & DUGAN COURT REPORTERS	(Volume 15)
PORTLAND	BEOVICH WALTER & FRIEND	(Volume 15)
	CATHERINE TEACH REPORTING	(Volume 15)
	JOHNSON, MOORE, HENDERSON & KONSTEN	(Volume 15)
	LEE BERGER & ASSOCIATES, INC.	(Volume 15)
	LNS COURT REPORTING	(Volume 15)
	REPORTERS COOPERATIVE, INC.	(Volume 15)
	SEATTLE DEPOSITION REPORTERS	(Volume 15)
SALEM	CATHERINE TEACH REPORTING	(Volume 15)
	LNS COURT REPORTING	(Volume 15)
	REPORTERS COOPERATIVE, INC.	(Volume 15)

PENNSYLVANIA

City	Reporter	Volume
ALTOONA	ASAP COURT REPORTING / STEN-TEL, INC.	(Volume 15)
	STEFFAN & STAUFFER LTD.	(Volume 15)
DOYLESTOWN	BLUM-MOORE REPORTING SERVICES, INC.	(Volume 15)
ERIE	AKF REPORTERS, INC.	(Volume 15)
	STEFFAN & STAUFFER LTD.	(Volume 15)
GREENSBURG	STEFFAN & STAUFFER LTD.	(Volume 15)
HARRISBURG	CAPITAL CITY REPORTING SERVICE	(Volume 15)
	GEIGER & LORIA REPORTING SERVICE	(Volume 15)
	SARGENT'S COURT REPORTING SERVICE, INC.	(Volume 15)
	STRESKI REPORTING & VIDEO SERVICE	(Volume 15)
HAZLETON	ACE COURT REPORTING, INC.	(Volume 15)
JOHNSTOWN	SARGENT'S COURT REPORTING SERVICE, INC.	(Volume 15)
	STEFFAN & STAUFFER LTD.	(Volume 15)
LANCASTER	ANDERSON COURT REPORTING AGENCY	(Volume 15)
MEDIA	LYN RUBENSTEIN & ASSOCIATES	(Volume 15)
NORRISTOWN	KARASCH & ASSOCIATES	(Volume 15)
	KNIPES-COHEN ASSOCIATES, INC.	(Volume 15)
	LYN RUBENSTEIN & ASSOCIATES	(Volume 15)
PHILADELPHIA	1-800-FOR-DEPO-ALDERSONREPORTING	(Volume 15)
	A & A COURT REPORTING & ASSOCIATES	(Volume 15)
	ADVOCATE COURT REPORTING SERVICE, INC.	(Volume 15)
	ARCHIVE REPORTING, LLC	(Volume 15)
	BLUM-MOORE REPORTING SERVICES, INC.	(Volume 15)
	BRUSILOW & ASSOCIATES	(Volume 15)
	CENTER CITY REPORTING, INC.	(Volume 15)
	DOERNER & GOLDBERG	(Volume 15)
	ESQUIRE™ DEPOSITION SERVICES	(Volume 15)
	HUDSON REPORTING & VIDEO, INC.	(Volume 15)
	IRVING L. STARKMAN ASSOCIATES	(Volume 15)
	KNIPES-COHEN ASSOCIATES, INC.	(Volume 15)
	LOCKLEAR REPORTING SERVICE, INC.	(Volume 15)
	LYN RUBENSTEIN & ASSOCIATES	(Volume 15)
	REPORTERS COOPERATIVE, INC.	(Volume 15)
	RIGLER & O'NEILL COURT REPORTERS, INC.	(Volume 15)
	ROYAL COURT REPORTING SERVICE, INC.	(Volume 15)
	SARGENT'S COURT REPORTING SERVICE, INC.	(Volume 15)
	STRESKI REPORTING & VIDEO SERVICE	(Volume 15)
	VOICE PRINT, INC. COURT REPORTING & LEGAL VIDEO SERVICES	(Volume 15)
PITTSBURGH	1-800-FOR-DEPO-ALDERSONREPORTING	(Volume 15)
	AKF REPORTERS, INC.	(Volume 15)
	MAXINE JACOBY & ASSOCIATES	(Volume 15)
	PAPPAS REPORTING SERVICE, INC.	(Volume 15)
	POWERS GARRISON & HUGHES	(Volume 15)
	REPORTERS COOPERATIVE, INC.	(Volume 15)
	SARGENT'S COURT REPORTING SERVICE, INC.	(Volume 15)
	STEFFAN & STAUFFER LTD.	(Volume 15)
	STRESKI REPORTING & VIDEO SERVICE	(Volume 15)
SCRANTON	DRAKE REPORTING AGENCY	(Volume 15)
WASHINGTON	STEFFAN & STAUFFER LTD.	(Volume 15)
	STRESKI REPORTING & VIDEO SERVICE	(Volume 15)

COURT REPORTERS - Continued

PENNSYLVANIA - Continued

WILKES-BARRE	SARGENT'S COURT REPORTING SERVICE, INC.	(Volume 15)

RHODE ISLAND

PROVIDENCE	ALLIED COURT REPORTERS, INC.	(Volume 16)
	REPORTERS COOPERATIVE, INC.	(Volume 16)

SOUTH CAROLINA

CHARLESTON	A. WILLIAM ROBERTS, JR. & ASSOCIATES	(Volume 16)
	HUSEBY & ASSOCIATES	(Volume 16)
	REPORTERS COOPERATIVE, INC.	(Volume 16)
COLUMBIA	A. WILLIAM ROBERTS, JR. & ASSOCIATES	(Volume 16)
	COMPUSCRIPTS, INC.	(Volume 16)
	CREEL COURT REPORTING, INC.	(Volume 16)
	HUSEBY & ASSOCIATES	(Volume 16)
FLORENCE	HUSEBY & ASSOCIATES	(Volume 16)
GREENVILLE	A. WILLIAM ROBERTS, JR. & ASSOCIATES	(Volume 16)
	ASSOCIATE REPORTING AGENCY, INC.	(Volume 16)
	ASSOCIATED COURT REPORTERS JUDY COMP & ASSOCIATES, INC.	(Volume 16)
	HUSEBY & ASSOCIATES	(Volume 16)
HILTON HEAD ISLAND	A. WILLIAM ROBERTS, JR. & ASSOCIATES	(Volume 16)
	TOM CRITES & ASSOCIATES INTERNATIONAL, INC.	(Volume 16)
SPARTANBURG	SANDY SATTERWHITE REPORTING	(Volume 16)

SOUTH DAKOTA

RAPID CITY	THOMPSON & THOMPSON REPORTING, INC.	(Volume 16)
	WHEELER COURT REPORTING	(Volume 16)
VERMILLION	CASSEL MEYER COURT REPORTING	(Volume 16)

TENNESSEE

CHATTANOOGA	ACCUSCRIBE COURT REPORTING	(Volume 16)
	ANGEL & ASSOCIATES COURT REPORTING	(Volume 16)
	HUSEBY & ASSOCIATES	(Volume 16)
KINGSPORT	DEBORAH TODD COURT REPORTING	(Volume 16)
KNOXVILLE	A BETTER COURT REPORTING FIRM	(Volume 16)
	BROWN & WINGO COURT REPORTING	(Volume 16)
	GIBSON COURT REPORTING	(Volume 16)
	TRUESDEL & RUSK	(Volume 16)
MEMPHIS	ALPHA REPORTING CORPORATION	(Volume 16)
	REPORTERS COOPERATIVE, INC.	(Volume 16)
MURFREESBORO	MENCK, BUCHANAN & ASSOCIATES	(Volume 16)
NASHVILLE	ACCURATE COURT REPORTING	(Volume 16)
	CLEETON, DAVIS & SMITH	(Volume 16)
	COOPER COURT REPORTING	(Volume 16)
	HUGHES, MARKHAM & JESKE, LLC	(Volume 16)
	MENCK, BUCHANAN & ASSOCIATES	(Volume 16)
	REPORTERS COOPERATIVE, INC.	(Volume 16)

TEXAS

AMARILLO	AMARILLO COURT REPORTING, INC.	(Volume 17)
	CLAY LEMASTER, INC.	(Volume 17)
ARLINGTON	ARLINGTON COURT REPORTING, INC.	(Volume 17)
AUSTIN	ACCURATE REPORTERS, INC.	(Volume 17)
	ACUSCRIBE COURT REPORTERS	(Volume 17)
	AFFILIATED REPORTERS & VIDEO	(Volume 17)
	ARLINGTON COURT REPORTING, INC.	(Volume 17)
	CARLSON & GATES, INC.	(Volume 17)
	CONTINENTAL COURT REPORTERS, INC.	(Volume 17)
	GLENDA FULLER & ASSOCIATES	(Volume 17)
	KEN OWEN & ASSOCIATES	(Volume 17)
	OPPENHEIMER REPORTING SERVICES	(Volume 17)
	REPORTERS COOPERATIVE, INC.	(Volume 17)
	TEXAS VERBATIM REPORTERS	(Volume 17)
	WRIGHT WATSON STEN-TEL	(Volume 17)
BEAUMONT	JAN GIROUARD & ASSOCIATES	(Volume 17)
BROWNSVILLE	POCKRUS COURT REPORTING SERVICE	(Volume 17)
CORPUS CHRISTI	CALVERT REPORTING SERVICE	(Volume 17)
	CARLSON & GATES, INC.	(Volume 17)
	CERTIFIED REPORTING & VIDEO SERVICE	(Volume 17)

City	Firm	Volume
DALLAS	1-800-FOR-DEPO-ALDERSONREPORTING	(Volume 17)
	AA1 PARLIAMENTARY REPORTING	(Volume 17)
	ACCURATE REPORTERS, INC.	(Volume 17)
	AFFILIATED REPORTERS	(Volume 17)
	ALLEGRO REPORTING SERVICE, INC.	(Volume 17)
	ARLINGTON COURT REPORTING, INC.	(Volume 17)
	CARLSON & GATES, INC.	(Volume 17)
	CONTINENTAL COURT REPORTERS, INC.	(Volume 17)
	COURT REPORTERS ASSOCIATED	(Volume 17)
	DONOVAN REPORTING, P.C.	(Volume 17)
	ESQUIRE™ DEPOSITION SERVICES	(Volume 17)
	MARION WARD & ASSOCIATES, LLC	(Volume 17)
	MILLERPARKER	(Volume 17)
	REPORTERS COOPERATIVE, INC.	(Volume 17)
	SHARP HOLLAND INTERNATIONAL COURT REPORTING, INC.	(Volume 17)
	STANLEY, RICE AND ASSOCIATES A LEGALINK COMPANY	(Volume 17)
	STEVE GENTRY & ASSOCIATES, INC.	(Volume 17)
	UNITED AMERICAN REPORTING SERVICES, INC.	(Volume 17)
EL PASO	BRANNON RASPBERRY & ASSOCIATES, INC.	(Volume 17)
FORT WORTH	ALLIED STENOTYPE REPORTERS, A PARTNERSHIP	(Volume 17)
	ARLINGTON COURT REPORTING, INC.	(Volume 17)
	DOLORES STEWART & ASSOCIATES, INC.	(Volume 17)
	MERIT COURT REPORTERS	(Volume 17)
	REPORTERS COOPERATIVE, INC.	(Volume 17)
	SHARP HOLLAND INTERNATIONAL COURT REPORTING, INC.	(Volume 17)
GALVESTON	CONTINENTAL COURT REPORTERS, INC.	(Volume 17)
	DEPOSITIONS UNLIMITED	(Volume 17)
	REPORTERS COOPERATIVE, INC.	(Volume 17)
HARLINGEN	BRYANT & STINGLEY, INC.	(Volume 17)
	POCKRUS COURT REPORTING SERVICE	(Volume 17)
HOUSTON	1-2-3 REPORTING SERVICE A DIVISION OF CERTIFIED REPORTING COMPANY	(Volume 17)
	1-800-FOR-DEPO-ALDERSONREPORTING	(Volume 17)
	A-AMES COURT REPORTING & VIDEO	(Volume 17)
	AA1 PARLIAMENTARY REPORTING	(Volume 17)
	ACCURATE REPORTERS, INC.	(Volume 17)
	ALLEGRO REPORTING SERVICE, INC.	(Volume 17)
	ALLIED ADVANCED REPORTING, INC.	(Volume 17)
	CARLSON & GATES, INC.	(Volume 17)
	CONTINENTAL COURT REPORTERS, INC.	(Volume 17)
	ESQUIRE™ DEPOSITION SERVICES	(Volume 17)
	FINK & CARNEY REPORTING AND VIDEO/RALPH FINK & ASSOCIATES, INC.	(Volume 17)
	HOUSTON REPORTING & VIDEO SERVICES	(Volume 17)
	REPORTERS COOPERATIVE, INC.	(Volume 17)
	ROSS REPORTING SERVICES, INC.	(Volume 17)
	SHARP HOLLAND INTERNATIONAL COURT REPORTING, INC.	(Volume 17)
	SOUTHWEST REPORTING & VIDEO SERVICE, INC.	(Volume 17)
	STERLING REPORTING SERVICE, INC.	(Volume 17)
	UNITED-WOMACK REPORTING A LEGALINK COMPANY	(Volume 17)
LUBBOCK	CURTIS D. RUFF AND ASSOCIATES	(Volume 17)
LUFKIN	LUFKIN COURT REPORTING SERVICE	(Volume 17)
MCALLEN	BRYANT & STINGLEY, INC.	(Volume 17)
	POCKRUS COURT REPORTING SERVICE	(Volume 17)
MIDLAND	PERMIAN COURT REPORTERS, INC.	(Volume 17)
SAN ANTONIO	ACCURATE COURT REPORTING SERVICES	(Volume 17)
	ACCURATE REPORTERS, INC.	(Volume 17)
	ARLINGTON COURT REPORTING, INC.	(Volume 17)
	CARLSON & GATES, INC.	(Volume 17)
	DEPOSITIONS PLUS	(Volume 17)
	FEDERAL COURT REPORTERS OF SAN ANTONIO	(Volume 17)
	REPORTERS COOPERATIVE, INC.	(Volume 17)
	SOUTH TEXAS COURT REPORTERS, INC.	(Volume 17)
TYLER	ANN CURRY COURT REPORTING	(Volume 17)
	ARLINGTON COURT REPORTING, INC.	(Volume 17)
WACO	CEN-TEX REPORTING SERVICE	(Volume 17)

UTAH

City	Firm	Volume
CEDAR CITY	TEMPEST REPORTING, INC.	(Volume 17)

COURT REPORTERS - Continued

UTAH - Continued

City	Reporter	Volume
LOGAN	TEMPEST REPORTING, INC.	(Volume 17)
OGDEN	ASSOCIATED PROFESSIONAL REPORTERS	(Volume 17)
	TEMPEST REPORTING, INC.	(Volume 17)
PROVO	ASSOCIATED PROFESSIONAL REPORTERS	(Volume 17)
	DEPOMAX REPORTING SERVICES, INC	(Volume 17)
	REPORTERS COOPERATIVE, INC.	(Volume 17)
	TEMPEST REPORTING, INC.	(Volume 17)
SALT LAKE CITY	ASSOCIATED PROFESSIONAL REPORTERS	(Volume 17)
	CAPITOL REPORTERS	(Volume 17)
	DEPOMAX REPORTING SERVICES, INC	(Volume 17)
	HORIZON REPORTING & VIDEO, INC.	(Volume 17)
	INDEPENDENT REPORTING & VIDEOGRAPHY	(Volume 17)
	REPORTERS COOPERATIVE, INC.	(Volume 17)
	TEMPEST REPORTING, INC.	(Volume 17)
ST. GEORGE	TEMPEST REPORTING, INC.	(Volume 17)

VERMONT

City	Reporter	Volume
BURLINGTON	CAPITOL COURT REPORTERS, INC.	(Volume 18)
	COURT REPORTERS ASSOCIATES	(Volume 18)
RUTLAND	O'BRIEN REPORTING SERVICES, INC.	(Volume 18)

VIRGINIA

City	Reporter	Volume
ALEXANDRIA	AA BETA REPORTING	(Volume 18)
	ACE-FEDERAL REPORTERS, INC.	(Volume 18)
	CAROL J. THOMAS STENOTYPE REPORTING SERVICES, INC.	(Volume 18)
	METRO REPORTERS INC.	(Volume 18)
ARLINGTON	AA BETA REPORTING	(Volume 18)
	ACE-FEDERAL REPORTERS, INC.	(Volume 18)
	CAROL J. THOMAS STENOTYPE REPORTING SERVICES, INC.	(Volume 18)
	M.A.R. REPORTING GROUP, LLC	(Volume 18)
CHANTILLY	AA BETA REPORTING	(Volume 18)
CHARLOTTESVILLE	CRANE-SNEAD & ASSOCIATES, INC.	(Volume 18)
	STATEWIDE COURT REPORTERS	(Volume 18)
CHESAPEAKE	ALVIS & CHEESEBREW COURT REPORTING SERVICES	(Volume 18)
FAIRFAX	AA BETA REPORTING	(Volume 18)
	ACE-FEDERAL REPORTERS, INC.	(Volume 18)
	ANITA B. GLOVER & ASSOCIATES, LTD.	(Volume 18)
	CAROL J. THOMAS STENOTYPE REPORTING SERVICES, INC.	(Volume 18)
	METRO REPORTERS INC.	(Volume 18)
	PLATT & DAWSON, INC.	(Volume 18)
	TURNER REPORTING SERVICES	(Volume 18)
FALLS CHURCH	AA BETA REPORTING	(Volume 18)
	CAROL J. THOMAS STENOTYPE REPORTING SERVICES, INC.	(Volume 18)
FREDERICKSBURG	CAROL J. THOMAS STENOTYPE REPORTING SERVICES, INC.	(Volume 18)
	CRANE-SNEAD & ASSOCIATES, INC.	(Volume 18)
	MADDOX REPORTING SERVICE, INC.	(Volume 18)
HERNDON	AA BETA REPORTING	(Volume 18)
HILLSVILLE	BLUE RIDGE COURT REPORTING, INC	(Volume 18)
MANASSAS	AA BETA REPORTING	(Volume 18)
	CAROL J. THOMAS STENOTYPE REPORTING SERVICES, INC.	(Volume 18)
MCLEAN	AA BETA REPORTING	(Volume 18)
	CAROL J. THOMAS STENOTYPE REPORTING SERVICES, INC.	(Volume 18)
NORFOLK	BIGGS & FLEET, LTD.	(Volume 18)
	REPORTERS COOPERATIVE, INC.	(Volume 18)
	TAYLOE ASSOCIATES, INC.	(Volume 18)
RESTON	AA BETA REPORTING	(Volume 18)
	CAROL J. THOMAS STENOTYPE REPORTING SERVICES, INC.	(Volume 18)
RICHMOND	1-800-FOR-DEPO-ALDERSONREPORTING	(Volume 18)
	AA BETA REPORTING	(Volume 18)
	ACCU-BETA COURT REPORTERS & VIDEOGRAPHERS, INC.	(Volume 18)
	AUDIO-VISUAL REPORTING SERVICES, INC.	(Volume 18)
	CAROL J. THOMAS STENOTYPE REPORTING SERVICES, INC.	(Volume 18)
	CHANDLER AND HALASZ, INC.	(Volume 18)
	CRANE-SNEAD & ASSOCIATES, INC.	(Volume 18)
	REPORTERS COOPERATIVE, INC.	(Volume 18)
SPRINGFIELD	CAROL J. THOMAS STENOTYPE REPORTING SERVICES, INC.	(Volume 18)
TYSONS CORNER	CAROL J. THOMAS STENOTYPE REPORTING SERVICES, INC.	(Volume 18)
VIENNA	1-800-FOR-DEPO-ALDERSONREPORTING	(Volume 18)
	AA BETA REPORTING	(Volume 18)
	CAROL J. THOMAS STENOTYPE REPORTING SERVICES, INC.	(Volume 18)

COURT REPORTERS - Continued

WISCONSIN - Continued

OSHKOSH .... THE COURT REPORTER REGISTRY .... (Volume 18)
RACINE .... THE COURT REPORTER REGISTRY .... (Volume 18)
WAUKESHA .... THE COURT REPORTER REGISTRY .... (Volume 18)

WYOMING

JACKSON .... REPORTERS COOPERATIVE, INC. .... (Volume 18)

PUERTO RICO

SAN JUAN .... TRIAL TRANSCRIBERS .... (Volume 18)

COURTROOM SKETCHING

TEXAS

HOUSTON .... ART OF EVE .... (Volume 17)

CRIME SCENE RECONSTRUCTION

FLORIDA

FORT LAUDERDALE .... JAMES AND ASSOCIATES FORENSIC CONSULTANTS, INC. .... (Volume 6)

ILLINOIS

EAST MOLINE .... WAYNE N. HILL, SR. .... (Volume 8)

CRIMINAL BACKGROUND CHECKS

DISTRICT OF COLUMBIA

WASHINGTON .... VANCE INTERNATIONAL, INC. .... (Volume 5)

NORTH CAROLINA

CHARLOTTE .... THE CHAPMAN CORPORATION .... (Volume 14)

OHIO

AKRON .... OHIO PARALEGAL SERVICES, INC. .... (Volume 14)

CRIMINAL INVESTIGATIONS

CALIFORNIA

LOS ANGELES .... INVESTIGATIVE GROUP INTERNATIONAL, INC. (IGI) .... (Volume 2)

DISTRICT OF COLUMBIA

WASHINGTON .... VANCE INTERNATIONAL, INC. .... (Volume 5)

CRIMINAL RECORDS RESEARCH

OHIO

AKRON .... OHIO PARALEGAL SERVICES, INC. .... (Volume 14)

OKLAHOMA

TULSA .... COURT DATA RESEARCH SERVICES .... (Volume 14)

TEXAS

DALLAS .... G.A. PUBLIC RECORD SERVICES, INC. .... (Volume 17)

DNA FORENSIC TESTING

SOUTH DAKOTA

BROOKINGS .... IDENTITY GENETICS, INC. .... (Volume 16)

DEBUGGING

WASHINGTON

SEATTLE .... ACIS ELECTRONIC COUNTERMEASURES CORP. .... (Volume 18)

DELIVERY SERVICES

OHIO

AKRON .... OHIO PARALEGAL SERVICES, INC. .... (Volume 14)

DEMONSTRATIVE EVIDENCE

ARIZONA

PHOENIX .... FORDYN DIGITAL PRODUCTIONS, INC. .... (Volume 1)
STARR LITIGATION SERVICES, INC .... (Volume 1)

CALIFORNIA

LOS ANGELES .... STARR LITIGATION SERVICES, INC .... (Volume 2)

DISTRICT OF COLUMBIA

WASHINGTON .... 24 HOUR COMPANY .... (Volume 5)

DISCOVERY AND DOCUMENT REPRODUCTION SERVICES

SOUTH CAROLINA

GREENVILLE .... LEGAL EAGLE ®, INC. .... (Volume 16)

WASHINGTON

SEATTLE .... LEGAL COPY, INC. .... (Volume 18)

DISPUTE ANALYSIS & INVESTIGATION

CALIFORNIA

LOS ANGELES .... PRICEWATERHOUSECOOPERS LLP .... (Volume 2)
SAN FRANCISCO .... ERNEST BROWN & COMPANY .... (Volume 3)

NEW YORK

NEW YORK .... PRICEWATERHOUSECOOPERS LLP .... (Volume 13)

DOCUMENT IMAGING

CALIFORNIA

LOS ANGELES .... DOCUMENT SCANNING SYSTEMS INCORPORATED .... (Volume 2)
LEGALSOURCE .... (Volume 2)
SAN DIEGO .... DOCUMENT SCANNING SYSTEMS INCORPORATED .... (Volume 3)

DISTRICT OF COLUMBIA

WASHINGTON .... LITIGATION SYSTEMS, INC. .... (Volume 5)

GEORGIA

ATLANTA .... LEGAL IMAGING, INC. .... (Volume 7)

MINNESOTA

MINNEAPOLIS .... PC&A LITIGATION SUPPORT SERVICES .... (Volume 11)

NEVADA

LAS VEGAS .... LAURIE WEBB & ASSOCIATES .... (Volume 11)

NEW YORK

NEW YORK .... IMAGEMAX .... (Volume 13)

OREGON

PORTLAND .... CATHERINE TEACH REPORTING .... (Volume 15)

SOUTH CAROLINA

GREENVILLE .... LEGAL EAGLE ®, INC. .... (Volume 16)

TEXAS

DALLAS .... HORIZON MICROGRAPHICS, INC. .... (Volume 17)

WASHINGTON

SEATTLE .... LEGAL COPY, INC. .... (Volume 18)

DOCUMENT MANAGEMENT SERVICES

CALIFORNIA

LOS ANGELES .... INTERLINGUA.COM, INC. .... (Volume 2)

DISTRICT OF COLUMBIA

WASHINGTON .... LITIGATION SYSTEMS, INC. .... (Volume 5)

MARYLAND

HAVRE DE GRACE .... CHESAPEAKE PAPER TRAIL .... (Volume 9)

NEW YORK

NEW YORK .... WORLDOX/WORLD SOFTWARE .... (Volume 13)

SOUTH CAROLINA

GREENVILLE .... LEGAL EAGLE ®, INC. .... (Volume 16)

TEXAS

HOUSTON .... LMC - A LITIGATION MEDIA CENTER .... (Volume 17)

DOCUMENT RESEARCH, RETRIEVAL & FILING

ALABAMA

BIRMINGHAM .... DOCUMENT SOLUTION CENTER .... (Volume 1)
HUNTSVILLE .... BLACKWELL LAND & TITLE RESEARCH .... (Volume 1)

ALASKA

ANCHORAGE .... ALASKA PUBLIC RECORDS SEARCH, LLC .... (Volume 1)
INFORMALASKA .... (Volume 1)

ARKANSAS

LITTLE ROCK .... ARKANSAS LITIGATION SUPPORT SERVICES, INC. .... (Volume 1)
QUEST RESEARCH .... (Volume 1)

DOCUMENT RESEARCH, RETRIEVAL & FILING - Continued

NEW JERSEY

City	Service	Volume
NEWARK	1ST AMERICAN PROCESS SERVICE, INC.	(Volume 12)
	ACCU-FAX SERVICES, A DIVISION OF CEO CORPORATE SECURITY GROUP, INC.	(Volume 12)
TRENTON	1ST AMERICAN PROCESS SERVICE, INC.	(Volume 12)
	INTERCOUNTY CLEARANCE CORPORATION	(Volume 12)
	INTERSTATE DOCUMENT FILINGS	(Volume 12)
	KAUFMAN INFORMATION RESOURCES, INC.	(Volume 12)

NEW YORK

City	Service	Volume
ALBANY	ACCESS INFORMATION SERVICES, INC.	(Volume 12)
	COLBY ATTORNEYS SERVICE CO. INC.	(Volume 12)
	NATIONWIDE INFORMATION SERVICES, INC.	(Volume 12)
MINEOLA	GOTCHA LEGAL PROCESS SERVICE, INC.	(Volume 12)
NEW YORK	ACCU-FAX SERVICES, A DIVISION OF CEO CORPORATE SECURITY GROUP, INC.	(Volume 13)
	ALL-SEARCH & INSPECTION, INC.	(Volume 13)
	COURTFAX	(Volume 13)
	CSC THE UNITED STATES CORPORATION COMPANY	(Volume 13)
	CT CORPORATION SYSTEM	(Volume 13)
	D.L.S. INC. (DEMOVSKY LAWYER SERVICE)	(Volume 13)
	INTERCOUNTY CLEARANCE CORPORATION	(Volume 13)
	INTERSTATE DOCUMENT FILINGS	(Volume 13)
	KEATING & WALKER ATTORNEY SERVICE, INC.	(Volume 13)
	LEXIS® DOCUMENT SERVICES	(Volume 13)
	ORIGIN INFORMATION & SERVICES, INC.	(Volume 13)
	PARASEC	(Volume 13)
WHITE PLAINS	EVEREADY PROCESS SERVICE, INC.	(Volume 13)

NORTH CAROLINA

City	Service	Volume
CHARLOTTE	NATIONAL DATA ACCESS CORPORATION	(Volume 14)
GREENSBORO	NATIONAL DATA ACCESS CORPORATION	(Volume 14)
RALEIGH	NATIONAL DATA ACCESS CORPORATION	(Volume 14)

OHIO

City	Service	Volume
AKRON	OHIO PARALEGAL SERVICES, INC.	(Volume 14)
CLEVELAND	INVESTIGATIVE SOLUTIONS, INC.	(Volume 14)
COLUMBUS	INFINITY INFORMATION NETWORK, INC.	(Volume 14)
MARION	NATIONAL SERVICE INFORMATION, INC.	(Volume 14)

OKLAHOMA

City	Service	Volume
TULSA	COURT DATA RESEARCH SERVICES	(Volume 14)

OREGON

City	Service	Volume
PORTLAND	1ST AMERICAN PROCESS SERVICE, INC.	(Volume 15)
	DATA RESEARCH, INC.	(Volume 15)

PENNSYLVANIA

City	Service	Volume
PHILADELPHIA	1ST AMERICAN PROCESS SERVICE, INC.	(Volume 15)
	ACCU-FAX SERVICES, A DIVISION OF CEO CORPORATE SECURITY GROUP, INC.	(Volume 15)
	NATIONWIDE RESEARCH SERVICES	(Volume 15)
PITTSBURGH	1ST AMERICAN PROCESS SERVICE, INC.	(Volume 15)
	PENNCORP SERVICEGROUP INC.	(Volume 15)

SOUTH CAROLINA

City	Service	Volume
COLUMBIA	NATIONAL DATA ACCESS CORPORATION	(Volume 16)
GREENVILLE	NATIONAL DATA ACCESS CORPORATION	(Volume 16)
SPARTANBURG	NATIONAL DATA ACCESS CORPORATION	(Volume 16)

TENNESSEE

City	Service	Volume
MEMPHIS	RECORD-CHECK SERVICES, INC.	(Volume 16)

TEXAS

City	Service	Volume
AUSTIN	1ST AMERICAN PROCESS SERVICE, INC.	(Volume 17)
	CAPITOL COMMERCE REPORTER, INC.	(Volume 17)
	RESEARCH NETWORK	(Volume 17)
	SUPER SEARCH, INC.	(Volume 17)
	WRIGHT WATSON STEN-TEL	(Volume 17)
CORPUS CHRISTI	THE ALPHA AND OMEGA AGENCY	(Volume 17)
DALLAS	1ST AMERICAN PROCESS SERVICE, INC.	(Volume 17)
	A.S.A. INFORMATION SERVICES	(Volume 17)
	ALL-SEARCH & INSPECTION, INC.	(Volume 17)
	CSC THE UNITED STATES CORPORATION COMPANY	(Volume 17)
	SUPER SEARCH, INC.	(Volume 17)
FORTH WORTH	SUPER SEARCH, INC.	(Volume 17)

ECONOMIC AND STATISTICAL CONSULTING SERVICES - Continued

DISTRICT OF COLUMBIA, WASHINGTON - Continued

THE BRATTLE GROUP .... (Volume 5)
CHARLES R. MANN ASSOCIATES, INC. .... (Volume 5)
CHARLES RIVER ASSOCIATES INCORPORATED .... (Volume 5)
NATHAN ASSOCIATES INC. .... (Volume 5)
NATIONAL ECONOMIC RESEARCH ASSOCIATES, INC. .... (Volume 5)

ILLINOIS

CHICAGO .... CHARLES RIVER ASSOCIATES INCORPORATED .... (Volume 8)
LEXECON INC. .... (Volume 8)
NATIONAL ECONOMIC RESEARCH ASSOCIATES, INC. .... (Volume 8)

MASSACHUSETTS

BOSTON .... ANALYSIS GROUP/ECONOMICS .... (Volume 10)
THE BRATTLE GROUP .... (Volume 10)
CHARLES RIVER ASSOCIATES INCORPORATED .... (Volume 10)
LEXECON INC. .... (Volume 10)
NATIONAL ECONOMIC RESEARCH ASSOCIATES, INC. .... (Volume 10)

MONTANA

BILLINGS .... WATTS & ASSOCIATES, INC. .... (Volume 11)

NEW YORK

NEW YORK .... ANALYSIS AND INFERENCE, INC. .... (Volume 13)
BUSINESS VALUATION SERVICES .... (Volume 13)
CHARLES RIVER ASSOCIATES INCORPORATED .... (Volume 13)
FTI/KAHN .... (Volume 13)
NATIONAL ECONOMIC RESEARCH ASSOCIATES, INC. .... (Volume 13)

TEXAS

DALLAS .... BUSINESS VALUATION SERVICES .... (Volume 17)
CHARLES RIVER ASSOCIATES INCORPORATED .... (Volume 17)

VIRGINIA

RICHMOND .... TECHNICAL ASSOCIATES, INC. .... (Volume 18)

ECONOMIC AND STATISTICAL CONSULTING SERVICES - AUTOMOBILES

CALIFORNIA

LOS ANGELES .... THE FONTANA GROUP, INC. .... (Volume 2)
FROST & SULLIVAN .... (Volume 2)
SAN FRANCISCO .... FROST & SULLIVAN .... (Volume 3)

NEW JERSEY

NEWARK .... FROST & SULLIVAN .... (Volume 12)

NEW YORK

NEW YORK .... FROST & SULLIVAN .... (Volume 13)

TEXAS

AUSTIN .... FROST & SULLIVAN .... (Volume 17)
SAN ANTONIO .... FROST & SULLIVAN .... (Volume 17)

EMPLOYMENT AGENCIES - PERMANENT/TEMPORARY

CALIFORNIA

LOS ANGELES .... ZISKIND GREENE CONTRACT ATTORNEYS & PARALEGALS .... (Volume 2)
SAN FRANCISCO .... EMPLAWYERNET .... (Volume 3)

NEW JERSEY

NEWARK .... LEGEND LEGAL STAFFING, INC. .... (Volume 12)

NEW YORK

NEW YORK .... ELAINE P. DINE TEMPORARY ATTORNEYS & PARALEGALS LLC .... (Volume 13)
LEGEND LEGAL STAFFING, INC. .... (Volume 13)

OHIO

CLEVELAND .... MAJOR LEGAL SERVICES, INC. .... (Volume 14)

EMPLOYMENT DISCRIMINATION & DISPARATE IMPACT

CALIFORNIA

LOS ANGELES .... FRIEDLAND ASSOCIATES .... (Volume 2)

ENVIRONMENTAL & ECOLOGICAL SERVICES - Continued

KENTUCKY
LOUISVILLE .... ADVENT ENVIRONMENTAL, INC. .... (Volume 9)

MISSOURI
ST. LOUIS .... ADVENT ENVIRONMENTAL, INC. .... (Volume 11)

NEW JERSEY
SOMERVILLE .... PRINCETON-SOMERSET GROUP, INC. .... (Volume 12)

NORTH CAROLINA
CHARLOTTE .... ADVENT ENVIRONMENTAL, INC. .... (Volume 14)
RALEIGH .... ADVENT ENVIRONMENTAL, INC. .... (Volume 14)

SOUTH CAROLINA
CHARLESTON .... ADVENT ENVIRONMENTAL, INC. .... (Volume 16)

ENVIRONMENTAL CONSULTANTS

GEORGIA
ATLANTA .... ADVENT ENVIRONMENTAL, INC. .... (Volume 7)

ILLINOIS
CHICAGO .... CARNOW, CONIBEAR & ASSOC. LTD. .... (Volume 8)

KENTUCKY
LOUISVILLE .... ADVENT ENVIRONMENTAL, INC. .... (Volume 9)

MISSOURI
SPRINGFIELD .... THE FORRESTER GROUP .... (Volume 11)
ST. LOUIS .... ADVENT ENVIRONMENTAL, INC. .... (Volume 11)

NEW JERSEY
EAST BRUNSWICK .... THE WHITMAN COMPANIES, INC. .... (Volume 12)
PRINCETON .... TOXILOGICS, INC. .... (Volume 12)
SOMERVILLE .... PRINCETON-SOMERSET GROUP, INC. .... (Volume 12)

NEW YORK
NEW YORK .... LAURENCE B. MOLLOY .... (Volume 13)

NORTH CAROLINA
CHARLOTTE .... ADVENT ENVIRONMENTAL, INC. .... (Volume 14)
RALEIGH .... ADVENT ENVIRONMENTAL, INC. .... (Volume 14)

SOUTH CAROLINA
CHARLESTON .... ADVENT ENVIRONMENTAL, INC. .... (Volume 16)

TEXAS
DALLAS .... TRINITY CONSULTANTS INCORPORATED .... (Volume 17)

ENVIRONMENTAL ENGINEERING & REMEDIATION SERVICES

COLORADO
DENVER .... ALPINE ENVIRONMENTAL, INC. .... (Volume 4)

ILLINOIS
CHICAGO .... OMNI TECH INTERNATIONAL, LTD. .... (Volume 8)

KENTUCKY
LOUISVILLE .... ADVENT ENVIRONMENTAL, INC. .... (Volume 9)

MISSOURI
ST. LOUIS .... ADVENT ENVIRONMENTAL, INC. .... (Volume 11)

NORTH CAROLINA
CHARLOTTE .... ADVENT ENVIRONMENTAL, INC. .... (Volume 14)
RALEIGH .... ADVENT ENVIRONMENTAL, INC. .... (Volume 14)

SOUTH CAROLINA
CHARLESTON .... ADVENT ENVIRONMENTAL, INC. .... (Volume 16)

TEXAS
HOUSTON .... OMNI TECH INTERNATIONAL, LTD. .... (Volume 17)

ENVIRONMENTAL INVESTIGATIONS

CALIFORNIA
LOS ANGELES .... INVESTIGATIVE GROUP INTERNATIONAL, INC. (IGI) .... (Volume 2)
ZYMAX FORENSICS .... (Volume 2)

KENTUCKY
LOUISVILLE .... ADVENT ENVIRONMENTAL, INC. .... (Volume 9)

MISSOURI
ST. LOUIS .... ADVENT ENVIRONMENTAL, INC. .... (Volume 11)

EXAMINERS OF QUESTIONED DOCUMENTS (HANDWRITING EXPERTS) - Continued

NEW YORK

GREAT NECK	PATRICIA SIEGEL ENTERPRISES, INC.	(Volume 12)
NEW YORK	PAUL A. OSBORN & SON	(Volume 13)
	ANDREW SULNER, M.S. J.D.	(Volume 13)
SCHENECTADY	THE PECORARO GROUP	(Volume 13)

NORTH CAROLINA

CHARLOTTE	CHARLES E. PERROTTA	(Volume 14)

OHIO

CLEVELAND	F. AURELIUS MCKANZE, PH.D.	(Volume 14)

OREGON

EUGENE	JAMES A. GREEN - FORENSIC DOCUMENT EXAMINER	(Volume 15)

PENNSYLVANIA

PHILADELPHIA	GUS R. LESNEVICH	(Volume 15)

RHODE ISLAND

PROVIDENCE	SEIFER HANDWRITING CONSULTANTS	(Volume 16)

TENNESSEE

NASHVILLE	MARTY PEARCE, CDE, CGA	(Volume 16)

TEXAS

FORT WORTH	ADVANCED DOCUMENT & HANDWRITING EXAMINATION SERVICES	(Volume 17)
SAN ANTONIO	ALAMO AREA FORENSIC LABS	(Volume 17)

EXECUTIVE PROTECTIVE SERVICES

CALIFORNIA

LOS ANGELES	BCA PROTECTIVE & INVESTIGATIVE SERVICES	(Volume 2)

DISTRICT OF COLUMBIA

WASHINGTON	VANCE INTERNATIONAL, INC.	(Volume 5)

NORTH CAROLINA

CHARLOTTE	PRO DETECTIVE SERVICES	(Volume 14)

EXPERT WITNESS

CALIFORNIA

LOS ANGELES	ANDREOLI, JOHANSON & WOOD	(Volume 2)
	APPRAISERS WEST	(Volume 2)
	CONSULTLEAGUE AT KILZER & ASSOCIATES	(Volume 2)
	FAINSBERT MASE & SNYDER, LLP	(Volume 2)
	FROST & SULLIVAN	(Volume 2)
SAN FRANCISCO	CCC CONSOLIDATED CONSULTANTS CO.	(Volume 3)
	FROST & SULLIVAN	(Volume 3)

NEW JERSEY

NEWARK	FROST & SULLIVAN	(Volume 12)

NEW YORK

NEW YORK	FROST & SULLIVAN	(Volume 13)

TEXAS

AUSTIN	FROST & SULLIVAN	(Volume 17)
SAN ANTONIO	FROST & SULLIVAN	(Volume 17)

ACCIDENT INVESTIGATION & RECONSTRUCTION

ALABAMA

BIRMINGHAM	WILLIAM J. (JIM) GRIFFIN	(Volume 1)

ARIZONA

PHOENIX	MICHAEL S. BROUGHTON ACCIDENT RECONSTRUCTION ASSOCIATES, INC.	(Volume 1)

ARKANSAS

LITTLE ROCK	ACCIDENT ANALYSIS ASSOCIATES	(Volume 1)

CALIFORNIA

LOS ANGELES	DONALD C. BERMAN, P.E.	(Volume 2)
	EXPERT TECHNOLOGIES INTERNATIONAL	(Volume 2)
	KAUDERER & ASSOCIATES	(Volume 2)
	SOTTER ENGINEERING CORPORATION	(Volume 2)
SACRAMENTO	KAUDERER & ASSOCIATES	(Volume 3)

FLORIDA

MIAMI	AERIALS, INC.	(Volume 6)

EXPERT WITNESS

ACCOUNTING - BUSINESS DAMAGES - Continued

CALIFORNIA, SAN FRANCISCO - Continued

SUGARMAN & COMPANY LLP .... (Volume 3)

COLORADO

DENVER .... CLIFTON GUNDERSON L.L.C. .... (Volume 4)

FLORIDA

BOCA RATON .... HENRY L. JANUS, CPA/ABV .... (Volume 6)
MIAMI .... MIRTHA GUERRA, AGUIRRE, CPA*, ABV, AM, BVAL .... (Volume 6)

MISSOURI

KANSAS CITY .... MEARA, KING & CO. .... (Volume 11)
ST. LOUIS .... BROWN SMITH WALLACE, LLC .... (Volume 11)

NEW JERSEY

NEWARK .... FROST & SULLIVAN .... (Volume 12)

NEW YORK

NEW YORK .... FROST & SULLIVAN .... (Volume 13)

TEXAS

AUSTIN .... FROST & SULLIVAN .... (Volume 17)
SAN ANTONIO .... FROST & SULLIVAN .... (Volume 17)

PUERTO RICO

SAN JUAN .... AMANDA CAPO'-ROSSELLO', CPA, CVA, CFE .... (Volume 18)

MALPRACTICE

ARIZONA

PHOENIX .... WILLIAM L. RABY, CPA .... (Volume 1)

CALIFORNIA

SAN JOSE .... FRANK RIMERMAN & CO. CPA'S .... (Volume 3)

FLORIDA

FORT LAUDERDALE .... FRIEDMAN, DUQUE & CO. .... (Volume 6)

ACOUSTICS

SOUND, NOISE & VIBRATION

CONNECTICUT

HARTFORD .... BROOKS ACOUSTICS CORPORATION .... (Volume 4)

NEW YORK

NEW YORK .... ACOUSTICS SPECIALISTS GROUP .... (Volume 13)

ADMIRALTY

CALIFORNIA

SAN FRANCISCO .... KENAI NAVIGATION INTERNATIONAL .... (Volume 3)

NEW YORK

NEW YORK .... THOMAS ELECTRIC CONTROL, INC. .... (Volume 13)

AGRI-HORTICULTURAL

CALIFORNIA

SALINAS .... TRANSAGRO .... (Volume 3)

COLORADO

FORT COLLINS .... A.L.I.S. -AGRICULTURAL LITIGATION & INFORMATION SPECIALISTS .... (Volume 4)

AIR POLLUTION

NORTH CAROLINA

RALEIGH .... WALTER SMITH & ASSOCIATES .... (Volume 14)

AIR SAFETY

COLORADO

DENVER .... AIRSAFETY EXPERTS, INC. .... (Volume 4)

APPRAISAL SERVICES

CALIFORNIA

BERKELEY .... LECG, A SUBSIDIARY OF NAVIGANT CONSULTING, INC. .... (Volume 2)

LOUISIANA

NEW ORLEANS .... A.R.E. REAL ESTATE SERVICES .... (Volume 9)

EXPERT WITNESS

CHEMICAL PROCESS - SAFETY - Continued

PENNSYLVANIA

PITTSBURGH .... CHEMTECH CONSULTANTS, INC. .... (Volume 15)

TEXAS

DALLAS .... GRANBERRY & ASSOCIATES, INC. .... (Volume 17)
HOUSTON .... OMNI TECH INTERNATIONAL, LTD. .... (Volume 17)

CLASS ACTION NOTICE

PENNSYLVANIA

PHILADELPHIA .... HILSOFT NOTIFICATIONS ™ .... (Volume 15)

COATINGS/PAINT

ILLINOIS

CHICAGO .... WISS, JANNEY, ELSTNER ASSOCIATES, INC. .... (Volume 8)

TEXAS

HOUSTON .... GEORGE MILLS & ASSOCIATES INTERNATIONAL, INC. .... (Volume 17)

COMMERCIAL LAW

CALIFORNIA

IRVINE .... SKORHEIM & ASSOCIATES .... (Volume 2)

COMMODITY FUTURES

NEW YORK

NEW YORK .... MARKET CONSULTING CORPORATION .... (Volume 13)

COMMUNICATIONS

DISTRICT OF COLUMBIA

WASHINGTON .... COMPUTER AND COMMUNICATIONS LAW CONSULTANTS .... (Volume 5)

NEW YORK

NEW YORK .... COMPUTER AND COMMUNICATIONS LAW CONSULTANTS .... (Volume 13)

COMPUTER & BUSINESS INFORMATION SYSTEMS

DISTRICT OF COLUMBIA

WASHINGTON .... COMPUTER AND COMMUNICATIONS LAW CONSULTANTS .... (Volume 5)

NEW YORK

NEW YORK .... COMPUTER AND COMMUNICATIONS LAW CONSULTANTS .... (Volume 13)

NORTH CAROLINA

RALEIGH .... EAGLE VISION SOFTWARE TECHNOLOGIES, INC. .... (Volume 14)

COMPUTER FORENSICS/DATA RECOVERY

CALIFORNIA

LOS ANGELES .... JUDD ROBBINS .... (Volume 2)

COMPUTER SCIENCE/INTELLECTUAL PROPERTY

CALIFORNIA

SAN FRANCISCO .... MARGARET L. JOHNSON, PH.D. .... (Volume 3)
DR. JOHN P.J. KELLY .... (Volume 3)

DISTRICT OF COLUMBIA

WASHINGTON .... COMPUTER AND COMMUNICATIONS LAW CONSULTANTS .... (Volume 5)

NEW YORK

NEW YORK .... COMPUTER AND COMMUNICATIONS LAW CONSULTANTS .... (Volume 13)

CONSTRUCTION

CALIFORNIA

IRVINE .... CCL CONSTRUCTION CONSULTANTS, INC. .... (Volume 2)
LOS ANGELES .... JAX KNEPPERS ASSOCIATES, INC. .... (Volume 2)
SAN FRANCISCO .... JAX KNEPPERS ASSOCIATES, INC. .... (Volume 3)
SANTA MONICA .... DAVID A. STERN .... (Volume 3)

FLORIDA

MIAMI .... GENE FARMER, ARA, CCPM, CCI .... (Volume 6)

EXPERT WITNESS - DAMAGE VALUATION - Continued

CALIFORNIA - Continued

SAN DIEGO .... G. R. BILL COMPANY APPRAISERS .... (Volume 3)
SAN FRANCISCO .... SUGARMAN & COMPANY LLP .... (Volume 3)

COLORADO

DENVER .... CLIFTON GUNDERSON L.L.C. .... (Volume 4)

GEORGIA

ATLANTA .... ADAMS CAPITAL, INC. .... (Volume 7)

ILLINOIS

CHICAGO .... BLACKMAN KALLICK BARTELSTEIN, LLP .... (Volume 8)

VIRGINIA

RICHMOND .... TECHNICAL ASSOCIATES, INC. .... (Volume 18)

DEMOLITION

TEXAS

HOUSTON .... DEMOLITION CONSULTANTS .... (Volume 17)

DOCUMENT EXAMINATION/COMPREHENSION

CALIFORNIA

BEVERLY HILLS .... VICTORIA MERTES-DOCUMENT EXAMINER .... (Volume 2)

DRUGS/ALCOHOL/TOXICOLOGY

CALIFORNIA

LOS ANGELES .... STEPHEN M. PITTEL, PH.D. .... (Volume 2)
VINA R. SPIEHLER, PH.D. DABFT .... (Volume 2)

ILLINOIS

CHICAGO .... NATIONAL TOXICOLOGY SPECIALISTS, INC. .... (Volume 8)

ECONOMICS/ECONOMISTS

CALIFORNIA

BERKELEY .... LECG, A SUBSIDIARY OF NAVIGANT CONSULTING, INC. .... (Volume 2)
LOS ANGELES .... FROST & SULLIVAN .... (Volume 2)
WHITE, ZUCKERMAN, WARSAVSKY, LUNA & WOLF .... (Volume 2)
SAN DIEGO .... BUSINESS VALUATION SERVICES .... (Volume 3)
SAN FRANCISCO .... BUSINESS VALUATION SERVICES .... (Volume 3)
CHARLES RIVER ASSOCIATES INCORPORATED .... (Volume 3)
FROST & SULLIVAN .... (Volume 3)

DISTRICT OF COLUMBIA

WASHINGTON .... CHARLES RIVER ASSOCIATES INCORPORATED .... (Volume 5)
NAVIGANT CONSULTING, INC. .... (Volume 5)

FLORIDA

MIAMI .... REHABILITATION SERVICES, INC. .... (Volume 6)

ILLINOIS

SPRINGFIELD .... LANGFORD AND ASSOCIATES .... (Volume 8)

NEW JERSEY

NEWARK .... FROST & SULLIVAN .... (Volume 12)

NEW YORK

NEW YORK .... BUSINESS VALUATION SERVICES .... (Volume 13)
CHARLES RIVER ASSOCIATES INCORPORATED .... (Volume 13)
FROST & SULLIVAN .... (Volume 13)
EDMUND H. MANTELL, PH.D. .... (Volume 13)

TEXAS

AUSTIN .... FROST & SULLIVAN .... (Volume 17)
SAN ANTONIO .... FROST & SULLIVAN .... (Volume 17)

AGRICULTURAL/ENVIRONMENTAL

VERMONT

BURLINGTON .... ROBERT L. BANCROFT, PH.D. .... (Volume 18)

FINANCIAL VALUATION

CALIFORNIA

BERKELEY .... LECG, A SUBSIDIARY OF NAVIGANT CONSULTING, INC. .... (Volume 2)
LOS ANGELES .... FROST & SULLIVAN .... (Volume 2)
SAN FRANCISCO .... FROST & SULLIVAN .... (Volume 3)

DISTRICT OF COLUMBIA

WASHINGTON .... THE BRATTLE GROUP .... (Volume 5)

EXPERT WITNESS
EMPLOYEE/EMPLOYMENT - DISCRIMINATION - Continued

FLORIDA
ORLANDO .... SARJEANT & SARJEANT, INC. .... (Volume 6)

MASSACHUSETTS
BOSTON .... PSYCHIATRY AND MEDICINE .... (Volume 10)

OSHA REGULATIONS/PROCEDURES

FLORIDA
MIAMI .... NATIONAL SAFE WORKPLACE INSTITUTE .... (Volume 6)

ILLINOIS
CHICAGO .... CARNOW, CONIBEAR & ASSOC. LTD. .... (Volume 8)

PENNSYLVANIA
PHILADELPHIA .... AEGIS CORP. .... (Volume 15)

PRACTICES

CALIFORNIA
LOS ANGELES .... RESOLUTION ECONOMICS LLC .... (Volume 2)

WRONGFUL TERMINATION/HARASSMENT

CALIFORNIA
LOS ANGELES .... BRIAN H. KLEINER, PH.D. .... (Volume 2)
PASADENA .... G. GOVINE CONSULTING .... (Volume 3)

FLORIDA
ORLANDO .... SARJEANT & SARJEANT, INC. .... (Volume 6)
TALLAHASSEE .... WILLIAM P. ANTHONY, PH.D. .... (Volume 6)

EMPLOYMENT PRACTICES

FLORIDA
MIAMI .... HR ASSOCIATES .... (Volume 6)

ENGINEERS/ENGINEERING

CALIFORNIA
LOS ANGELES .... MANX RESEARCH .... (Volume 2)

CONNECTICUT
HARTFORD .... TETRA ENGINEERING GROUP, INC. .... (Volume 4)

DISTRICT OF COLUMBIA
WASHINGTON .... W. S. ATARAS ENGINEERING, INC. .... (Volume 5)

ILLINOIS
CHICAGO .... WISS, JANNEY, ELSTNER ASSOCIATES, INC. .... (Volume 8)

KENTUCKY
LOUISVILLE .... ADVENT ENVIRONMENTAL, INC. .... (Volume 9)

LOUISIANA
LAFAYETTE .... KAIGLER CONSULTING SERVICE, INC. .... (Volume 9)

MISSOURI
ST. LOUIS .... ADVENT ENVIRONMENTAL, INC. .... (Volume 11)

NEW JERSEY
HACKETTSTOWN .... SUMMIT PROFESSIONAL RESOURCES LLC .... (Volume 12)

NORTH CAROLINA
CHARLOTTE .... ADVENT ENVIRONMENTAL, INC. .... (Volume 14)
RALEIGH .... ADVENT ENVIRONMENTAL, INC. .... (Volume 14)

SOUTH CAROLINA
CHARLESTON .... ADVENT ENVIRONMENTAL, INC. .... (Volume 16)

TEXAS
HOUSTON .... STRESS ENGINEERING SERVICES, INC. .... (Volume 17)

ACOUSTICS

CONNECTICUT
HARTFORD .... BROOKS ACOUSTICS CORPORATION .... (Volume 4)

ARCHITECTURE

CALIFORNIA
SAN FRANCISCO .... ERNEST BROWN & COMPANY .... (Volume 3)

NEW JERSEY
NUTLEY .... KENNETH J. STOYACK, AIA, PP .... (Volume 12)

EXPERT WITNESS - ENGINEERS/ENGINEERING - Continued

MECHANICAL/MACHINE DESIGN

CALIFORNIA

LOS ANGELES .... ERIK K. ANTONSSON, PH.D. P.E. .... (Volume 2)

PLANT MANAGEMENT

ILLINOIS

CHICAGO .... JAMES J. "JIM" GADWOOD .... (Volume 8)

SAFETY

FLORIDA

ORLANDO .... PROFESSIONAL SAFETY CONSULTANT SERVICE, INC. .... (Volume 6)
WEST PALM BEACH .... PROFESSIONAL SAFETY INCORPORATED .... (Volume 6)

KENTUCKY

LOUISVILLE .... ADVENT ENVIRONMENTAL, INC. .... (Volume 9)

MISSOURI

ST. LOUIS .... ADVENT ENVIRONMENTAL, INC. .... (Volume 11)

NORTH CAROLINA

CHARLOTTE .... ADVENT ENVIRONMENTAL, INC. .... (Volume 14)
RALEIGH .... ADVENT ENVIRONMENTAL, INC. .... (Volume 14)

PENNSYLVANIA

PHILADELPHIA .... AEGIS CORP. .... (Volume 15)

SOUTH CAROLINA

CHARLESTON .... ADVENT ENVIRONMENTAL, INC. .... (Volume 16)

VIRGINIA

FAIRFAX .... SAFETY MANAGEMENT ASSOCIATES .... (Volume 18)

TRANSPORTATION & HEAVY EQUIPMENT

CALIFORNIA

SAN FRANCISCO .... CAIRD & ASSOCIATES CONSULTANTS INC. TRUCK TRAILER MANAGEMENT SERVICES DIVISION .... (Volume 3)

ENVIRONMENTAL

DISTRICT OF COLUMBIA

WASHINGTON .... THE BRATTLE GROUP .... (Volume 5)

KENTUCKY

LOUISVILLE .... ADVENT ENVIRONMENTAL, INC. .... (Volume 9)

MASSACHUSETTS

BOSTON .... THE BRATTLE GROUP .... (Volume 10)

MISSOURI

ST. LOUIS .... ADVENT ENVIRONMENTAL, INC. .... (Volume 11)

NEW YORK

ALBANY .... ALPHA GEOLOGICAL SERVICES, INC. .... (Volume 12)

NORTH CAROLINA

CHARLOTTE .... ADVENT ENVIRONMENTAL, INC. .... (Volume 14)
RALEIGH .... ADVENT ENVIRONMENTAL, INC. .... (Volume 14)

SOUTH CAROLINA

CHARLESTON .... ADVENT ENVIRONMENTAL, INC. .... (Volume 16)

BUILDINGS & BUILDING SYSTEMS

NEW YORK

NEW YORK .... LAURENCE B. MOLLOY .... (Volume 13)

ENVIRONMENTAL CONSULTANT

KENTUCKY

LOUISVILLE .... ADVENT ENVIRONMENTAL, INC. .... (Volume 9)

MISSOURI

ST. LOUIS .... ADVENT ENVIRONMENTAL, INC. .... (Volume 11)

NEW JERSEY

LAWRENCEVILLE .... REALTY ECONOMICS GROUP .... (Volume 12)

NORTH CAROLINA

CHARLOTTE .... ADVENT ENVIRONMENTAL, INC. .... (Volume 14)
RALEIGH .... ADVENT ENVIRONMENTAL, INC. .... (Volume 14)

SOUTH CAROLINA

CHARLESTON .... ADVENT ENVIRONMENTAL, INC. .... (Volume 16)

EXPERT WITNESS - Continued

FIREARMS/GUN EXPLOSIONS

MASSACHUSETTS

LOWELL .... G&G FIREARMS EXPERTS .... (Volume 10)

NEW YORK

LITTLE FALLS .... HUTTON ENGINEERING SERVICES .... (Volume 12)

FIREARMS/TRAINING/SAFETY/POLICE PROCEDURES

NEW YORK

NEW YORK .... THE PEREGRINE CORPORATION .... (Volume 13)

FORENSIC PATHOLOGIST

NEW YORK

NEW YORK .... ALI Z. HAMELI, M.D. P.A. .... (Volume 13)

FORENSIC PSYCHOLOGIST

NEW MEXICO

ALBUQUERQUE .... MOSS AUBREY, PH.D. .... (Volume 12)

FORENSIC PSYCHOLOGY

SEXUAL OFFENDERS

NEW MEXICO

ALBUQUERQUE .... MOSS AUBREY, PH.D. .... (Volume 12)

FORENSIC VOCATIONAL/MEDICAL CONSULTANT

NEW JERSEY

SOUTH AMBOY .... CENTER FOR HEAD AND FACIAL PAIN .... (Volume 12)

FRANCHISING

CALIFORNIA

LOS ANGELES .... EDWARD KUSHELL .... (Volume 2)

FRAUD

CALIFORNIA

LOS ANGELES .... EMERALD GROUP .... (Volume 2)

COLORADO

DENVER .... CLIFTON GUNDERSON L.L.C. .... (Volume 4)

NEW JERSEY

ISELIN .... THE HALPIN GROUP, INC. .... (Volume 12)

NEW YORK

NEW YORK .... VONA & ASSOCIATES .... (Volume 13)

TEXAS

DALLAS .... M.D. WILLIAMSON, SR. CPA, CFE .... (Volume 17)

HOUSTON .... EDMUND J. PANKAU, CLI, CPP .... (Volume 17)

FUTURES AND OPTIONS

NEW YORK

NEW YORK .... MARKET CONSULTING CORPORATION .... (Volume 13)

GLASS

NEW JERSEY

WARREN .... DR. R. C. ROPP, F.R.S.C. F.A.I.C. B.C.F.E. .... (Volume 12)

NEW YORK

WATKINS GLEN .... GLASS FRACTURE ANALYTICAL .... (Volume 13)

TEXAS

DALLAS .... LINGNELL CONSULTING SERVICES .... (Volume 17)

GRAPHICS

CALIFORNIA

LOS ANGELES .... ORIGIN POINT, INCORPORATED .... (Volume 2)

EXPERT WITNESS

INSURANCE - BAD FAITH - Continued

CONNECTICUT

FAIRFIELD .... GUY C. HATFIELD, CPCU, CIC .... (Volume 4)

DISTRICT OF COLUMBIA

WASHINGTON .... ROBERT L. HOLBROOK, CPCU, SCLA .... (Volume 5)

NEW JERSEY

DENVILLE .... CASTELLINI INSURANCE SERVICES .... (Volume 12)

NEW YORK

NEW YORK .... KERNAN ASSOCIATES, INC. .... (Volume 13)

CASUALTY/PROFESSIONAL LIABILITY

ILLINOIS

CHICAGO .... DONALD J. BRAYER AND ASSOC. LTD. .... (Volume 8)

NEW JERSEY

DENVILLE .... CASTELLINI INSURANCE SERVICES .... (Volume 12)

NEW YORK

NEW YORK .... KERNAN ASSOCIATES, INC. .... (Volume 13)

LIFE, DISABILITY & LONG TERM CARE

GEORGIA

ATLANTA .... LITTELL CONSULTING SERVICES AND SECOND OPINION INSURANCE SERVICES, LLP .... (Volume 7)

MARINE

CALIFORNIA

SAN FRANCISCO .... BERNARD S. RICHARDSON .... (Volume 3)

INSURANCE FRAUD

OHIO

CLEVELAND .... CASALINOVA INVESTIGATIONS .... (Volume 14)

INTELLECTUAL PROPERTY/INFRINGEMENT DAMAGES

CALIFORNIA

BERKELEY .... LECG, A SUBSIDIARY OF NAVIGANT CONSULTING, INC. .... (Volume 2)
LOS ANGELES .... FROST & SULLIVAN .... (Volume 2)
SAN FRANCISCO .... CHARLES RIVER ASSOCIATES INCORPORATED .... (Volume 3)
FROST & SULLIVAN .... (Volume 3)

DISTRICT OF COLUMBIA

WASHINGTON .... THE BRATTLE GROUP .... (Volume 5)
CHARLES RIVER ASSOCIATES INCORPORATED .... (Volume 5)
COMPUTER AND COMMUNICATIONS LAW CONSULTANTS .... (Volume 5)

MASSACHUSETTS

BOSTON .... THE BRATTLE GROUP .... (Volume 10)

NEW JERSEY

NEWARK .... FROST & SULLIVAN .... (Volume 12)

NEW YORK

NEW YORK .... CHARLES RIVER ASSOCIATES INCORPORATED .... (Volume 13)
COMPUTER AND COMMUNICATIONS LAW CONSULTANTS .... (Volume 13)
FROST & SULLIVAN .... (Volume 13)

TEXAS

AUSTIN .... FROST & SULLIVAN .... (Volume 17)
SAN ANTONIO .... FROST & SULLIVAN .... (Volume 17)

LAW ENFORCEMENT

WISCONSIN

MILWAUKEE .... DENNIS WALLER & ASSOCIATES, INC. .... (Volume 18)

LEGAL ETHICS/MALPRACTICE

CALIFORNIA

LOS ANGELES .... BOYD S. LEMON, ESQ. .... (Volume 2)
CHRISTOPHER ROLIN, J.D. .... (Volume 2)

VIRGINIA

RICHMOND .... RHETTA M. DANIEL, ESQUIRE .... (Volume 18)

EXPERT WITNESS

MINING - Continued

NEW YORK

ALBANY .... ALPHA GEOLOGICAL SERVICES, INC. .... (Volume 12)

VIRGINIA

FAIRFAX .... JOYCE ASSOCIATES, INC. .... (Volume 18)

MOTORCYCLE ACCIDENT RECONSTRUCTION

NEW YORK

BINGHAMTON .... DENNIS A. TOASPERN, BCFE .... (Volume 12)

OIL & GAS

CALIFORNIA

LOS ANGELES .... ZYMAX FORENSICS .... (Volume 2)

TEXAS

AUSTIN .... WILLIS, GRAVES & ASSOCIATES, INC. .... (Volume 17)
HOUSTON .... R.S.E., INC. .... (Volume 17)
RICHARDSON .... DON BECK & ASSOCIATES, INC. .... (Volume 17)

PATENT LAW

CALIFORNIA

SAN FRANCISCO .... JULIAN CAPLAN .... (Volume 3)

PERSONAL INJURY

ILLINOIS

CHICAGO .... RONALD L. NEER, D.D.S. .... (Volume 8)

PHOTOGRAPHIC ANALYSIS

FLORIDA

MIAMI .... AERIALS, INC. .... (Volume 6)

NEW YORK

NEW YORK .... NATIONAL AERIAL RESOURCES .... (Volume 13)

ENVIRONMENTAL SITE ASSESSMENT

NEW YORK

ALBANY .... ALPHA GEOLOGICAL SERVICES, INC. .... (Volume 12)

PLAYGROUND EQUIPMENT ACCIDENTS

MICHIGAN

EAST LANSING .... LOUIS F. TWARDZIK .... (Volume 10)

POLICE MISCONDUCT

TEXAS

DALLAS .... IMWALLE, POWERS & ASSOCIATES, INC. .... (Volume 17)

POLICE/SECURITY

CALIFORNIA

LOS ANGELES .... EMERALD GROUP .... (Volume 2)

COLORADO

DENVER .... BLAKE AND ASSOCIATES, INC. .... (Volume 4)

NEVADA

LAS VEGAS .... JOHN L. SULLIVAN .... (Volume 11)

NEW YORK

NEW YORK .... ROBERT J. CASTELLI ASSOCIATES, INC. .... (Volume 13)

NEGLIGENCE

WASHINGTON

SEATTLE .... ALAN H. BAXTER .... (Volume 18)

USE OF FORCE

TEXAS

DALLAS .... IMWALLE, POWERS & ASSOCIATES, INC. .... (Volume 17)

PREMISES SECURITY & LIABILITY

FLORIDA

MIAMI .... NATIONAL SAFE WORKPLACE INSTITUTE .... (Volume 6)

EXPERT WITNESS - Continued

SECURITY NEGLIGENCE

FLORIDA

WEST PALM BEACH .... PROFESSIONAL SAFETY INCORPORATED .... (Volume 6)

SOUTH CAROLINA

CHARLESTON .... LFW, INC. .... (Volume 16)

SLIP, TRIP AND FALL

CALIFORNIA

LOS ANGELES .... SOTTER ENGINEERING CORPORATION .... (Volume 2)
SAN FRANCISCO .... J2 ENGINEERING, INC. .... (Volume 3)

NEW JERSEY

HACKETTSTOWN .... SUMMIT PROFESSIONAL RESOURCES LLC .... (Volume 12)
NUTLEY .... KENNETH J. STOYACK, AIA, PP .... (Volume 12)

SPORTS, LEISURE, RECREATION

MICHIGAN

EAST LANSING .... LOUIS F. TWARDZIK .... (Volume 10)

NEW JERSEY

HACKETTSTOWN .... SUMMIT PROFESSIONAL RESOURCES LLC .... (Volume 12)
WEST ORANGE .... NATIONAL SAFETY CONSULTANTS .... (Volume 12)

NEW YORK

NEW YORK .... REINER ASSOCIATES, INC. .... (Volume 13)
SPORTS AND RECREATION CONSULTANTS, INC. .... (Volume 13)

TELECOMMUNICATIONS

DISTRICT OF COLUMBIA

WASHINGTON .... THE BRATTLE GROUP .... (Volume 5)

MASSACHUSETTS

BOSTON .... THE BRATTLE GROUP .... (Volume 10)

TELEPHONE POLES

VIRGINIA

FAIRFAX .... JAMES A. TAYLOR .... (Volume 18)

THIRD PARTY LIABILITY ISSUES

CALIFORNIA

LOS ANGELES .... JAMES F. BRODER, CFE, CPP, FACFE .... (Volume 2)

TOXICOLOGY

CALIFORNIA

LOS ANGELES .... GAMAL E. IBRAHIM .... (Volume 2)
RICHARD J. SCHLESINGER, PH.D. DABFT .... (Volume 2)
SAN FRANCISCO .... ENTOX & ASSOCIATES .... (Volume 3)
THOMAS H. MILBY, M.D. .... (Volume 3)

DISTRICT OF COLUMBIA

WASHINGTON .... THERESA HOFFMAN-TILL, PH.D. .... (Volume 5)

NEW JERSEY

PRINCETON .... TOXILOGICS, INC. .... (Volume 12)
SOMERVILLE .... PRINCETON-SOMERSET GROUP, INC. .... (Volume 12)

PENNSYLVANIA

PHILADELPHIA .... NATIONAL MEDICAL SERVICES, INC. .... (Volume 15)

TEXAS

HOUSTON .... NORMAN M. TRIEFF, PH.D. .... (Volume 17)

TRAFFIC ENGINEERING

VIRGINIA

ALEXANDRIA .... TRANSPORTATION RESEARCH CORPORATION .... (Volume 18)

EXPERT WITNESS REFERRAL SERVICES - Continued

CALIFORNIA - Continued

SAN DIEGO .... EXPERT RESOURCES, INC. .... (Volume 3)
TASA .... (Volume 3)
SAN FRANCISCO .... EXPERT RESOURCES, INC. .... (Volume 3)
TASA .... (Volume 3)

COLORADO

DENVER .... EXPERT RESOURCES, INC. .... (Volume 4)
TASA .... (Volume 4)

CONNECTICUT

BRIDGEPORT .... RESOURCE CONNECTOR, INC. .... (Volume 4)

DELAWARE

WILMINGTON .... THE CECON GROUP INC. .... (Volume 4)

DISTRICT OF COLUMBIA

WASHINGTON .... EXPERT RESOURCES, INC. .... (Volume 5)
TASA .... (Volume 5)

FLORIDA

MIAMI .... EXPERT RESOURCES, INC. .... (Volume 6)
TASA .... (Volume 6)
WEST PALM BEACH .... PROFESSIONAL SAFETY INCORPORATED .... (Volume 6)

GEORGIA

ATLANTA .... EXPERT RESOURCES, INC. .... (Volume 7)
TASA .... (Volume 7)

HAWAII

HONOLULU .... EXPERT RESOURCES, INC. .... (Volume 7)

ILLINOIS

CHICAGO .... EXPERT RESOURCES, INC. .... (Volume 8)
OMNI TECH INTERNATIONAL, LTD. .... (Volume 8)
TASA .... (Volume 8)
PEORIA .... EXPERT RESOURCES, INC. .... (Volume 8)

LOUISIANA

NEW ORLEANS .... EXPERT RESOURCES, INC. .... (Volume 9)

MASSACHUSETTS

BOSTON .... THE CONSULTING EXCHANGE .... (Volume 10)
EXPERT RESOURCES, INC. .... (Volume 10)
TASA .... (Volume 10)

MICHIGAN

DETROIT .... EXPERT RESOURCES, INC. .... (Volume 10)
TASA .... (Volume 10)

MINNESOTA

MINNEAPOLIS .... EXPERT RESOURCES, INC. .... (Volume 11)
TASA .... (Volume 11)

MISSOURI

ST. LOUIS .... EXPERT RESOURCES, INC. .... (Volume 11)
TASA .... (Volume 11)

NEW YORK

NEW YORK .... EXPERT RESOURCES, INC. .... (Volume 13)
TASA .... (Volume 13)
TRIAL SEARCH, INC. .... (Volume 13)

OHIO

CINCINNATI .... EXPERT RESOURCES, INC. .... (Volume 14)
TASA .... (Volume 14)

PENNSYLVANIA

BLUE BELL .... MEDICAL ADVISORS, INC. .... (Volume 15)
PHILADELPHIA .... EXPERT RESOURCES, INC. .... (Volume 15)
TASA .... (Volume 15)

TEXAS

DALLAS .... EXPERT RESOURCES, INC. .... (Volume 17)
TASA .... (Volume 17)
HOUSTON .... EXPERT RESOURCES, INC. .... (Volume 17)
OMNI TECH INTERNATIONAL, LTD. .... (Volume 17)
TASA .... (Volume 17)

WASHINGTON

SEATTLE .... EXPERT RESOURCES, INC. .... (Volume 18)
TASA .... (Volume 18)

FIRE LOSS EXPERTS

INDIANA

FORT WAYNE .... KODIAK ENTERPRISES, INC. .... (Volume 8)

LOUISIANA

NEW ORLEANS .... M.A. STRINGER & ASSOCIATES, INC. .... (Volume 9)

FORENSIC DOCUMENTATION - DEMONSTRATIVE EVIDENCE

NEW JERSEY

PRINCETON .... FORGERY FORENSICS© A DIVISION OF QUESTIONED DOCUMENTS, INCORPORATED .... (Volume 12)

FORENSIC ENGINEERING METALLURGY/FAILURE ANALYSIS

ILLINOIS

CHICAGO .... BODYCOTE TAUSSIG, INC. .... (Volume 8)

WASHINGTON

BELLINGHAM .... FIBERGLASS STRUCTURAL ENGINEERING, INC. .... (Volume 18)

FORENSIC ENGINEERS

CALIFORNIA

LOS ANGELES .... FIRE & ACCIDENT RECONSTRUCTION .... (Volume 2)

FLORIDA

TALLAHASSEE .... BENEDICT ENGINEERING COMPANY, INC. .... (Volume 6)

ILLINOIS

CHICAGO .... CTL, INC. .... (Volume 8)
OMNI TECH INTERNATIONAL, LTD. .... (Volume 8)
WISS, JANNEY, ELSTNER ASSOCIATES, INC. .... (Volume 8)

MARYLAND

BALTIMORE .... ROTHFUSS ENGINEERING COMPANY .... (Volume 9)

NEW JERSEY

NEWARK .... BARER ENGINEERING, P.A. .... (Volume 12)

NORTH CAROLINA

RALEIGH .... FORENSIC ANALYSIS & ENGINEERING CORPORATION .... (Volume 14)

PENNSYLVANIA

PHILADELPHIA .... FORENSIC SCIENCES INC. .... (Volume 15)

TEXAS

HOUSTON .... ENGINEERING DATA SERVICES, INC. .... (Volume 17)
OMNI TECH INTERNATIONAL, LTD. .... (Volume 17)

FORENSIC FINANCIAL ANALYSIS

CALIFORNIA

BERKELEY .... LECG, A SUBSIDIARY OF NAVIGANT CONSULTING, INC. .... (Volume 2)
LOS ANGELES .... OSTROVE, KRANTZ & OSTROVE, A P.C. .... (Volume 2)
VOCATIONAL ECONOMIC ANALYSTS .... (Volume 2)

FLORIDA

MIAMI .... LEWIS B. FREEMAN & PARTNERS, INC. .... (Volume 6)

PENNSYLVANIA

PHILADELPHIA .... PARENTE RANDOLPH ORLANDO CAREY & ASSOCIATES, LLC .... (Volume 15)

FORENSIC GEOCHEMISTRY

CALIFORNIA

LOS ANGELES .... ZYMAX FORENSICS .... (Volume 2)

FORENSIC MEDICINE

NEW YORK

NEW YORK .... ALI Z. HAMELI, M.D. P.A. .... (Volume 13)

FORENSIC PSYCHIATRY

CALIFORNIA

LOS ANGELES .... ALFRED COODLEY, M.D. PH.D. .... (Volume 2)
SAN DIEGO .... ALLAN J. ADLER, M.D. F.A.P.A. .... (Volume 3)

MASSACHUSETTS

BOSTON .... PSYCHIATRY AND MEDICINE .... (Volume 10)

GEOLOGY - Continued

KENTUCKY
LOUISVILLE .... ADVENT ENVIRONMENTAL, INC. .... (Volume 9)

MISSOURI
ST. LOUIS .... ADVENT ENVIRONMENTAL, INC. .... (Volume 11)

NORTH CAROLINA
CHARLOTTE .... ADVENT ENVIRONMENTAL, INC. .... (Volume 14)
RALEIGH .... ADVENT ENVIRONMENTAL, INC. .... (Volume 14)

SOUTH CAROLINA
CHARLESTON .... ADVENT ENVIRONMENTAL, INC. .... (Volume 16)

HANDWRITING EXPERTS

CALIFORNIA
LOS ANGELES .... THE SCRIPTORIUM .... (Volume 2)

NEW YORK
GREAT NECK .... PATRICIA SIEGEL ENTERPRISES, INC. .... (Volume 12)

OREGON
EUGENE .... JAMES A. GREEN - FORENSIC DOCUMENT EXAMINER .... (Volume 15)

TEXAS
DALLAS .... ADVANCED DOCUMENT & HANDWRITING EXAMINATION SERVICES .... (Volume 17)

HEIR TRACERS

ALABAMA
MONTGOMERY .... INTERNATIONAL GENEALOGICAL SEARCH INC. .... (Volume 1)

ALASKA
ANCHORAGE .... LOCATORS, INC. .... (Volume 1)

CALIFORNIA
LOS ANGELES .... AMERICAN RESEARCH BUREAU, INC. .... (Volume 2)
HOERNER BANK .... (Volume 2)
SEARCH INTERNATIONAL, LLC .... (Volume 2)
W.C. COX AND COMPANY .... (Volume 2)
SAN FRANCISCO .... HOERNER BANK .... (Volume 3)
LOCATORS, INC. .... (Volume 3)
SEARCH INTERNATIONAL, LLC .... (Volume 3)
W.C. COX AND COMPANY .... (Volume 3)

COLORADO
DENVER .... LOCATORS, INC. .... (Volume 4)

CONNECTICUT
HARTFORD .... SEARCH INTERNATIONAL, LLC .... (Volume 4)

DISTRICT OF COLUMBIA
WASHINGTON .... HOERNER BANK .... (Volume 5)

FLORIDA
FORT LAUDERDALE .... AMERICAN RESEARCH BUREAU, INC. .... (Volume 6)
MIAMI .... HOERNER BANK .... (Volume 6)
INTERNATIONAL GENEALOGICAL SEARCH INC. .... (Volume 6)
SEARCH INTERNATIONAL, LLC .... (Volume 6)
TAMPA .... HOERNER BANK .... (Volume 6)
LOCATORS, INC. .... (Volume 6)

ILLINOIS
CHICAGO .... HOERNER BANK .... (Volume 8)
W.C. COX AND COMPANY .... (Volume 8)

MASSACHUSETTS
BOSTON .... HOERNER BANK .... (Volume 10)

MICHIGAN
DETROIT .... W.C. COX AND COMPANY .... (Volume 10)

MINNESOTA
MINNEAPOLIS .... HOERNER BANK .... (Volume 11)

MISSOURI
ST. LOUIS .... W.C. COX AND COMPANY .... (Volume 11)

NEW JERSEY
NEWARK .... HOERNER BANK .... (Volume 12)

NEW YORK
NEW YORK .... ASSOCIATION OF PROFESSIONAL GENEALOGISTS NEW YORK METRO CHAPTER .... (Volume 13)

HUMAN FACTORS & ERGONOMICS CONSULTING

IMMIGRATION & CUSTOMS CONSULTING

INCORPORATION SERVICES

INDEPENDENT MEDICAL EXAMINER REFERRAL SERVICES

INDEPENDENT MEDICAL EXAMINERS

INDEPENDENT MEDICAL EXAMINERS - Continued

CALIFORNIA - Continued

SACRAMENTO .... ALLEN C. HASSAN, M.D. J.D. .... (Volume 3)

FLORIDA

MELBOURNE .... HEALTH FIRST OCCUPATIONAL MEDICINE .... (Volume 6)

ILLINOIS

CHICAGO .... CARNOW, CONIBEAR & ASSOC. LTD. .... (Volume 8)
JAMES P. ELMES, M.D. F.A.C.S. .... (Volume 8)

INDIANA

FORT WAYNE .... FORT WAYNE ORTHOPAEDICS .... (Volume 8)
INDIANAPOLIS .... SAMUEL L. GOODLOE, M.D. .... (Volume 8)
HEALTHWORKS-OCCUPATIONAL HEALTH CLINIC .... (Volume 8)

IOWA

WATERLOO .... ARNOLD E. DELBRIDGE, M.D. .... (Volume 8)

MICHIGAN

DETROIT .... DENNIS W. DOBRITT, D.O. BCFE, BCFM, FAADEP .... (Volume 10)
MEDICOLEGAL SERVICES, INC. .... (Volume 10)
FLINT .... HENRY HAGENSTEIN, D.O. P.C. .... (Volume 10)

NEW JERSEY

JERSEY CITY .... MONICA MEHTA, M.D. .... (Volume 12)

NEW YORK

ALBANY .... ORTHOPAEDIC AND WELLNESS CENTER .... (Volume 12)
NEW YORK .... JOHN H. BUCKNER, MD .... (Volume 13)
SEAPORT ORTHOPAEDIC ASSOCIATES .... (Volume 13)

OHIO

CLEVELAND .... REGIONAL SPINE CLINIC, INC. .... (Volume 14)

PENNSYLVANIA

PHILADELPHIA .... PERSPECTIVE CONSULTING, INC. .... (Volume 15)
PITTSBURGH .... SELIM EL-ATTRACHE, M.D. F.A.C.S. AAOS, AADEP .... (Volume 15)

WEST VIRGINIA

HUNTINGTON .... OCCUPATIONAL MEDICINE INCORPORATED .... (Volume 18)
MORGANTOWN .... NORTHERN WEST VIRGINIA PAIN MANAGEMENT CENTER .... (Volume 18)

PUERTO RICO

SAN JUAN .... BORIS ROJAS, M.D. .... (Volume 18)

INDEPENDENT MEDICAL EXAMINERS - CHIROPRACTIC

FLORIDA

PALM BEACH .... ROCCO J. PELLEGRINO, DC, CICE, CCSP .... (Volume 6)

NEVADA

RENO .... JOHN H. DUDLEY, D.C. .... (Volume 11)

INDEPENDENT MEDICAL EXAMINERS - NEUROLOGY

FLORIDA

FORT LAUDERDALE .... THOMAS J. GOLDSCHMIDT, M.D. .... (Volume 6)

NORTH CAROLINA

RALEIGH .... ATLANTIC NEUROSCIENCE ASSOCIATES .... (Volume 14)

SOUTH CAROLINA

MYRTLE BEACH .... ATLANTIC COASTAL NEUROSCIENCE ASSOCIATES .... (Volume 16)

INDEPENDENT MEDICAL EXAMINERS - ORTHOPAEDICS

WASHINGTON

SEATTLE .... INSTITUTE OF MUSCULORSKELETAL MEDICINE OF WASHINGTON .... (Volume 18)

INDEPENDENT MEDICAL EXAMINERS - PHYSIATRY

FLORIDA

FORT LAUDERDALE .... ALAN K. GRUSKIN, D.O. P.A. F.A.A.P.M. & R. F.A.O.C.R.M. .... (Volume 6)

INDEPENDENT MEDICAL EXAMINERS - PSYCHIATRY

FLORIDA

FORT LAUDERDALE .... THOMAS J. GOLDSCHMIDT, M.D. .... (Volume 6)

INFORMATION BROKERS

ALASKA
ANCHORAGE .... INFORMALASKA .... (Volume 1)

CALIFORNIA
SACRAMENTO .... CAGEY BEE SERVICES .... (Volume 3)

COLORADO
DENVER .... ACCESS/INFORMATION, INC. .... (Volume 4)

MICHIGAN
DETROIT .... A.S.K. SERVICES, INC. .... (Volume 10)

MISSOURI
JEFFERSON CITY .... PRIMESOURCE INTELLIGENCE GROUP .... (Volume 11)
KANSAS CITY .... PRIMESOURCE INTELLIGENCE GROUP .... (Volume 11)
SPRINGFIELD .... PRIMESOURCE INTELLIGENCE GROUP .... (Volume 11)
ST. LOUIS .... PRIMESOURCE INTELLIGENCE GROUP .... (Volume 11)

OHIO
COLUMBUS .... INFINITY INFORMATION NETWORK, INC. .... (Volume 14)

INFORMATION BROKERS - MEDICAL

MARYLAND
BETHESDA .... RESEARCH ASSOCIATES .... (Volume 9)

INFORMATION CLEARING HOUSE

DISTRICT OF COLUMBIA
WASHINGTON .... TAXPAYERS AGAINST FRAUD THE FALSE CLAIMS ACT LEGAL CENTER .... (Volume 5)

INSURANCE

CALIFORNIA
LOS ANGELES .... JOHN S. MURPHY .... (Volume 2)

ILLINOIS
CHICAGO .... AMERICAN BAR INSURANCE PLANS CONSULTANTS, INC. .... (Volume 8)

INSURANCE - EMPLOYMENT PRACTICES

ILLINOIS
CHICAGO .... ATLA MUTUAL .... (Volume 8)

NEW YORK
NEW YORK .... BERTHOLON-ROWLAND CORP. .... (Volume 13)

INSURANCE - PROFESSIONAL LIABILITY

CALIFORNIA
LOS ANGELES .... INSURANCE LITIGATION EXPERTS/CONSULTANTS .... (Volume 2)

ILLINOIS
CHICAGO .... ATLA MUTUAL .... (Volume 8)

MICHIGAN
BIRMINGHAM .... PROQUEST INSURANCE AGENCY .... (Volume 10)

NEW YORK
NEW YORK .... BERTHOLON-ROWLAND CORP. .... (Volume 13)
KERNAN ASSOCIATES, INC. .... (Volume 13)

INSURANCE - PROPERTY/CASUALTY

NEW YORK
NEW YORK .... KERNAN ASSOCIATES, INC. .... (Volume 13)

INSURANCE - RISK MANAGEMENT CONSULTING

ARIZONA
PHOENIX .... JAS ADVANCED STRATEGIES, INC. [D.B.A.] INTERNATIONAL RISK MANAGEMENT CONSULTANTS .... (Volume 1)

CALIFORNIA
BERKELEY .... LECG, A SUBSIDIARY OF NAVIGANT CONSULTING, INC. .... (Volume 2)

INSURANCE/REINSURANCE AUDITING SERVICES

CALIFORNIA

SAN FRANCISCO .... ROBERT D. LEMBKE & ASSOCIATES, INC. .... (Volume 3)

INTELLECTUAL PROPERTY DOCUMENT SERVICES

TEXAS

AUSTIN .... US-JAPAN TRANSLATIONS .... (Volume 17)

INTERNATIONAL PERSONAL TAX CONSULTANT

NEW YORK

NEW YORK .... ROGER B. HODGEMAN .... (Volume 13)

INTERNET SERVICES

CALIFORNIA

SAN DIEGO .... LAWINFO.COM .... (Volume 3)

NEW YORK

NEW YORK .... CT CORPORATION SYSTEM .... (Volume 13)

INTERNET/INTRANET SERVICES

CALIFORNIA

SANTA CLARA .... FIRST E COMMERCE .... (Volume 3)

INTERPRETERS

CALIFORNIA

LOS ANGELES .... BERLITZ INTERPRETATION AND TRANSLATION SERVICES .... (Volume 2)
THE LANGUAGE WORKS, INC. .... (Volume 2)
LEGAL LANGUAGE SERVICES .... (Volume 2)

SAN FRANCISCO .... BERLITZ INTERPRETATION AND TRANSLATION SERVICES .... (Volume 3)
THE LANGUAGE WORKS, INC. .... (Volume 3)
LEGAL LANGUAGE SERVICES .... (Volume 3)

COLORADO

DENVER .... BERLITZ INTERPRETATION AND TRANSLATION SERVICES .... (Volume 4)

CONNECTICUT

HARTFORD .... BERLITZ INTERPRETATION AND TRANSLATION SERVICES .... (Volume 4)

DISTRICT OF COLUMBIA

WASHINGTON .... BERLITZ INTERPRETATION AND TRANSLATION SERVICES .... (Volume 5)
THE LANGUAGE WORKS, INC. .... (Volume 5)
LEGAL LANGUAGE SERVICES .... (Volume 5)
THE LEGAL TRANSLATORS.COM .... (Volume 5)

FLORIDA

MIAMI .... JEAN-MARIE BANATTE, PH.D. C.P.A .... (Volume 6)
BERLITZ INTERPRETATION AND TRANSLATION SERVICES .... (Volume 6)

NAPLES .... LANGUAGE AT WORK, INC. .... (Volume 6)

GEORGIA

ATLANTA .... CZAR COMMUNICATIONS, INC. .... (Volume 7)

ILLINOIS

CHICAGO .... BERLITZ INTERPRETATION AND TRANSLATION SERVICES .... (Volume 8)
LEGAL LANGUAGE SERVICES .... (Volume 8)

MASSACHUSETTS

BOSTON .... BERLITZ INTERPRETATION AND TRANSLATION SERVICES .... (Volume 10)
LAWRENCE LOCKWOOD .... (Volume 10)

MICHIGAN

DETROIT .... BERLITZ INTERPRETATION AND TRANSLATION SERVICES .... (Volume 10)

NEW JERSEY

NEWARK .... LEGAL LANGUAGE SERVICES .... (Volume 12)
WORLD LANGUAGE SERVICES .... (Volume 12)

PRINCETON .... THE LANGUAGE WORKS, INC. .... (Volume 12)

NEW YORK

ALBANY .... ONE WORLD LANGUAGE SERVICES .... (Volume 12)

NEW YORK .... 800-TRANSLATE .... (Volume 13)
AMERICAN LINGUISTS INTERPRETERS & TRANSLATORS, INC. .... (Volume 13)
BERLITZ INTERPRETATION AND TRANSLATION SERVICES .... (Volume 13)
GINETTE CESAR .... (Volume 13)
INTERNATIONAL LIAISON, LTD. .... (Volume 13)

INTERPRETERS & TRANSLATORS

INTERPRETERS & TRANSLATORS - Continued

FLORIDA, MIAMI - Continued

City	Name	Volume
	BERLITZ INTERPRETATION AND TRANSLATION SERVICES	(Volume 6)
	LEGAL LANGUAGE SERVICES	(Volume 6)
	SVETLANA S. ROMANOV, PH.D.	(Volume 6)
	WORLDWIDE TRANSLATIONS, INC.	(Volume 6)
NAPLES	LANGUAGE AT WORK, INC.	(Volume 6)
ORLANDO	ALBORS & ASSOCIATES, INC.	(Volume 6)
TAMPA	ALL LANGUAGES BY MENTANI, INC.	(Volume 6)

GEORGIA

City	Name	Volume
ATLANTA	CZAR COMMUNICATIONS, INC.	(Volume 7)
	LEGAL LANGUAGE SERVICES	(Volume 7)

HAWAII

City	Name	Volume
HONOLULU	LEGAL LANGUAGE SERVICES	(Volume 7)

ILLINOIS

City	Name	Volume
CHICAGO	BERLITZ INTERPRETATION AND TRANSLATION SERVICES	(Volume 8)
	LEGAL LANGUAGE SERVICES	(Volume 8)

INDIANA

City	Name	Volume
INDIANAPOLIS	LEGAL LANGUAGE SERVICES	(Volume 8)

KANSAS

City	Name	Volume
KANSAS CITY	LEGAL LANGUAGE SERVICES	(Volume 9)

LOUISIANA

City	Name	Volume
NEW ORLEANS	LEGAL LANGUAGE SERVICES	(Volume 9)

MARYLAND

City	Name	Volume
BALTIMORE	LEGAL LANGUAGE SERVICES	(Volume 9)

MASSACHUSETTS

City	Name	Volume
BOSTON	BERLITZ INTERPRETATION AND TRANSLATION SERVICES	(Volume 10)
	LEGAL LANGUAGE SERVICES	(Volume 10)
	LAWRENCE LOCKWOOD	(Volume 10)

MICHIGAN

City	Name	Volume
DETROIT	BERLITZ INTERPRETATION AND TRANSLATION SERVICES	(Volume 10)
	LEGAL LANGUAGE SERVICES	(Volume 10)

MINNESOTA

City	Name	Volume
MINNEAPOLIS	LEGAL LANGUAGE SERVICES	(Volume 11)

MISSOURI

City	Name	Volume
KANSAS CITY	LEGAL LANGUAGE SERVICES	(Volume 11)
ST. LOUIS	LEGAL LANGUAGE SERVICES	(Volume 11)

NEVADA

City	Name	Volume
ELKO	GREAT BASIN PARALEGALS	(Volume 11)
LAS VEGAS	LEGAL LANGUAGE SERVICES	(Volume 11)

NEW JERSEY

City	Name	Volume
CAMDEN	LEGAL LANGUAGE SERVICES	(Volume 12)
JERSEY CITY	LEGAL LANGUAGE SERVICES	(Volume 12)
NEW BRUNSWICK	PRINCETON TECHNICAL TRANSLATION CENTER	(Volume 12)
NEWARK	LEGAL LANGUAGE SERVICES	(Volume 12)
	WORLD LANGUAGE SERVICES	(Volume 12)
	WORLDWIDE TRANSLATIONS, INC.	(Volume 12)
PRINCETON	THE LANGUAGE WORKS, INC.	(Volume 12)
	LEGAL LANGUAGE SERVICES	(Volume 12)
TRENTON	LEGAL LANGUAGE SERVICES	(Volume 12)
WEST ORANGE	ABC INTERPRETING, INC.	(Volume 12)

NEW MEXICO

City	Name	Volume
ALBUQUERQUE	LEGAL LANGUAGE SERVICES	(Volume 12)

NEW YORK

City	Name	Volume
ALBANY	LEGAL LANGUAGE SERVICES	(Volume 12)
	ONE WORLD LANGUAGE SERVICES	(Volume 12)
BUFFALO	LEGAL LANGUAGE SERVICES	(Volume 12)
MINEOLA	LEGAL LANGUAGE SERVICES	(Volume 12)
NEW YORK	800-TRANSLATE	(Volume 13)
	AMERICAN LINGUISTS INTERPRETERS & TRANSLATORS, INC.	(Volume 13)
	ATG LANGUAGE SOLUTIONS	(Volume 13)
	BERLITZ INTERPRETATION AND TRANSLATION SERVICES	(Volume 13)
	GINETTE CESAR	(Volume 13)
	EURONET LANGUAGE SERVICES, INC.	(Volume 13)
	INTERNATIONAL LIAISON, LTD.	(Volume 13)
	JAPAN COMMUNICATION CONSULTANTS, LLC	(Volume 13)

INVESTIGATORS - Continued

ALABAMA, BIRMINGHAM - Continued

City	Firm	Volume
	SURVEILLANCE TECHNOLOGIES, INC.	(Volume 1)
MOBILE	BLI ™	(Volume 1)
MONTGOMERY	MCDANIEL & ASSOCIATES	(Volume 1)

ALASKA

City	Firm	Volume
FAIRBANKS	FORT ENTERPRISES PROCESS SERVERS & INVESTIGATORS	(Volume 1)

ARIZONA

City	Firm	Volume
FLAGSTAFF	SEWELL INVESTIGATIONS	(Volume 1)
MESA	NORTH AMERICA LOCATORS	(Volume 1)
PHOENIX	ALPHA INVESTIGATIONS INC.	(Volume 1)
	BOB WILSON, INVESTIGATIONS	(Volume 1)
	DISCOVERY DETECTIVE GROUP	(Volume 1)
SCOTTSDALE	ALPHA INVESTIGATIONS INC.	(Volume 1)
TUCSON	BRYDGES INVESTIGATIONS	(Volume 1)

ARKANSAS

City	Firm	Volume
FAYETTEVILLE	AG INVESTIGATIONS	(Volume 1)
LITTLE ROCK	ARKANSAS INVESTIGATIVE SERVICES	(Volume 1)
	LANDS INVESTIGATIONS COMPANY	(Volume 1)
	ROWELL & ASSOCIATES	(Volume 1)
ROGERS	TRIAD INVESTIGATIONS, INC.	(Volume 1)

CALIFORNIA

City	Firm	Volume
BEVERLY HILLS	BRADLEY G. MILLER INVESTIGATORS, INC.	(Volume 2)
ENCINO	ALPHA DETECTIVE AGENCY, INC.	(Volume 2)
HIGHLAND	WILLETTE'S INVESTIGATIVE SERVICE	(Volume 2)
LOS ANGELES	#1 WORLDWIDE PERSON & INFORMATION LOCATORS	(Volume 2)
	BARNES & ASSOCIATES PROFESSIONAL SERVICES, INC.	(Volume 2)
	BCA PROTECTIVE & INVESTIGATIVE SERVICES	(Volume 2)
	DIG DIRT INC. ™	(Volume 2)
	DOUGLAS BALDWIN & ASSOCIATES, INC.	(Volume 2)
	EMERALD GROUP	(Volume 2)
	THOMAS GLEIM	(Volume 2)
	HBH SERVICES	(Volume 2)
	HOLLENBECK INVESTIGATIONS	(Volume 2)
	INVESTIGATIVE GROUP INTERNATIONAL, INC. (IGI)	(Volume 2)
	L.A. CONFIDENTIAL INVESTIGATIONS	(Volume 2)
	MANGANARO, WEITZMAN & ASSOCIATES	(Volume 2)
	MICHAEL G. KESSLER & ASSOCIATES, LTD.	(Volume 2)
	ON WATCH ™, LTD.	(Volume 2)
	SPECIALIZED INVESTIGATIONS	(Volume 2)
	US INVESTIGATIONS SERVICES	(Volume 2)
NEWPORT BEACH	GREAT WEST INVESTIGATIONS	(Volume 2)
PALO ALTO	PAULA DRAKE INVESTIGATIONS	(Volume 3)
SACRAMENTO	PLI INC.	(Volume 3)
	SPYGLASS INVESTIGATIONS	(Volume 3)
SAN DIEGO	C.R. COCHRAN & ASSOCIATES	(Volume 3)
	EAGLE INVESTIGATIONS	(Volume 3)
	GLOBAL INVESTIGATIVE GROUP	(Volume 3)
	SUTHERLIN ASSOCIATED SERVICES	(Volume 3)
SAN FRANCISCO	DELTA AGENCY	(Volume 3)
	DESVERNINE ASSOCIATES	(Volume 3)
SAN JOSE	AVANTGUARD SECURITY CONSULTING	(Volume 3)
SANTA BARBARA	R. L. HUNT ENTERPRISES	(Volume 3)
VENTURA	LEN NEWCOMB INVESTIGATIVE SERVICES	(Volume 3)

COLORADO

City	Firm	Volume
COLORADO SPRINGS	BLACKHAWK INVESTIGATIONS	(Volume 4)
	THE DELTA COMPANY	(Volume 4)
DENVER	A.C.E. RESEARCH INC.	(Volume 4)
	AAA PROCESS SERVERS, INC.	(Volume 4)
	BLAKE AND ASSOCIATES, INC.	(Volume 4)
	BUSINESS CONTROLS, INC.	(Volume 4)

CONNECTICUT

City	Firm	Volume
HARTFORD	BENEFICIAL INVESTIGATION SERVICES, INC.	(Volume 4)
	JENNINGS SMITH INVESTIGATIONS	(Volume 4)
NORWALK	BENEFICIAL INVESTIGATION SERVICES, INC.	(Volume 4)
STAMFORD	BENEFICIAL INVESTIGATION SERVICES, INC.	(Volume 4)

DISTRICT OF COLUMBIA

City	Firm	Volume
WASHINGTON	A.C.E. RESEARCH INC.	(Volume 5)

INVESTIGATORS - Continued

LOUISIANA

City	Firm	Volume
ALEXANDRIA	STEPHENS INVESTIGATIONS, INC.	(Volume 9)
NEW ORLEANS	ARA DETECTIVE AGENCY	(Volume 9)
	BOSCH CONSULTING INVESTIGATIONS, L.L.C.	(Volume 9)
	DAY'S INVESTIGATIONS	(Volume 9)
	M.G. BUSH & ASSOCIATES, INC.	(Volume 9)
	VINSON DETECTIVE AGENCY	(Volume 9)
SHREVEPORT	SMITH INVESTIGATIONS & ENTERPRISES	(Volume 9)

MARYLAND

City	Firm	Volume
BALTIMORE	COPS, INC.	(Volume 9)
	N.R. COCHRAN & ASSOCIATES	(Volume 9)
BETHESDA	ADVANCED PRIVATE INVESTIGATIONS GROUP	(Volume 9)
CHEVY CHASE	BELTRANTE & ASSOCIATES	(Volume 9)

MASSACHUSETTS

City	Firm	Volume
BOSTON	AMERICAN INVESTIGATIVE SERVICES, INC.	(Volume 10)
	CLARK INVESTIGATIVE ASSOCIATES, INC.	(Volume 10)
	SIMMONS AGENCY, INC.	(Volume 10)
WOBURN	PROFESSIONAL LEGAL INQUIRIES	(Volume 10)

MICHIGAN

City	Firm	Volume
DETROIT	HARRIS INVESTIGATIONS, INC.	(Volume 10)
	L.S.S. CONSULTING, INC.	(Volume 10)
	TECHNICAL SECURITY ANALYSTS, INC.	(Volume 10)
LANSING	FOCI, INCORPORATED	(Volume 10)
MUSKEGON	BENCO ENTERPRISES, INC.	(Volume 10)

MISSISSIPPI

City	Firm	Volume
JACKSON	MCALLISTER & ASSOCIATES, INC.	(Volume 11)

MISSOURI

City	Firm	Volume
COLUMBIA	KIMBLE DETECTIVE SERVICES, L.L.C.	(Volume 11)
JEFFERSON CITY	PRIMESOURCE INTELLIGENCE GROUP	(Volume 11)
KANSAS CITY	PRIMESOURCE INTELLIGENCE GROUP	(Volume 11)
SPRINGFIELD	FABER INVESTIGATIONS	(Volume 11)
	PRIMESOURCE INTELLIGENCE GROUP	(Volume 11)
ST. LOUIS	PRIMESOURCE INTELLIGENCE GROUP	(Volume 11)

NEBRASKA

City	Firm	Volume
OMAHA	HORNE INVESTIGATIVE AND SECURITY AGENCY SERVICE, INC.	(Volume 11)

NEVADA

City	Firm	Volume
LAS VEGAS	NUMARK INVESTIGATIONS	(Volume 11)

NEW HAMPSHIRE

City	Firm	Volume
MANCHESTER	PROFESSIONAL LEGAL INQUIRIES	(Volume 11)

NEW JERSEY

City	Firm	Volume
ATLANTIC CITY	SARAO & ASSOCIATES ™	(Volume 12)
HACKENSACK	EYEWITNESS INVESTIGATIONS, INC.	(Volume 12)
	R.J. MONTGOMERY ASSOCIATES	(Volume 12)
	SARAO & ASSOCIATES ™	(Volume 12)
HAMILTON	ROBERT CLARK INVESTIGATIONS	(Volume 12)
ISELIN	THE HALPIN GROUP, INC.	(Volume 12)
MARLTON	METRO SOUTH INC.	(Volume 12)
MORRISTOWN	TRIAD PROTECTIVE & INVESTIGATIVE SERVICES, LLC	(Volume 12)
NEWARK	#1 WORLDWIDE PERSON & INFORMATION LOCATORS	(Volume 12)
	ARGUS INVESTIGATIVE SERVICES, INC.	(Volume 12)
	DANTE INVESTIGATORS	(Volume 12)
	MICHAEL G. KESSLER & ASSOCIATES, LTD.	(Volume 12)
	ROSS SECURITY CONSULTANTS, INC.	(Volume 12)
	SARAO & ASSOCIATES ™	(Volume 12)
RED BANK	PINNACLE INVESTIGATIONS, INC.	(Volume 12)
RIDGEFIELD	FAST-TRACK INFORMATION SERVICES INC.	(Volume 12)
SOMERVILLE	J & K ASSOCIATES, INC.	(Volume 12)
TRENTON	DIG DIRT INC. ™	(Volume 12)

NEW MEXICO

City	Firm	Volume
ALBUQUERQUE	CORWIN RESEARCH & INVESTIGATIONS, LLC	(Volume 12)
FARMINGTON	PAPER CHASERS	(Volume 12)
SANTA FE	RICHARD A. MARTINEZ INVESTIGATIVE SERVICES	(Volume 12)

NEW YORK

City	Firm	Volume
BRONX	I.G. DETECTIVE SECURITY, INC.	(Volume 13)
BROOKLYN	NOEL RODRIGUEZ INVESTIGATIONS	(Volume 13)
CENTRAL ISLIP	ON WATCH ™, LTD.	(Volume 12)

FREEPORT	ON WATCH ™, LTD.	(Volume 12)
MINEOLA	ON WATCH ™, LTD.	(Volume 12)
NEW YORK	#1 WORLDWIDE PERSON & INFORMATION LOCATORS	(Volume 13)
	A.C.E. RESEARCH INC.	(Volume 13)
	A.J. STERLING & ASSOCIATES LTD	(Volume 13)
	BACKGROUND INVESTIGATIVE SERVICES, INC.	(Volume 13)
	BARRY SECURITY INC.	(Volume 13)
	BCA PROTECTIVE & INVESTIGATIVE SERVICES	(Volume 13)
	CITYWIDE INVESTIGATORS AND SECURITY, INC.	(Volume 13)
	CONWAY & HENNESSY ASSOCIATES, INC.	(Volume 13)
	CORPORATE RESOLUTIONS INC.	(Volume 13)
	DANTE INVESTIGATORS	(Volume 13)
	DIG DIRT INC. ™	(Volume 13)
	FIDELIFACTS/METROPOLITAN NEW YORK, INC.	(Volume 13)
	INTERFOR, INC.	(Volume 13)
	JJH INVESTIGATION, INC.	(Volume 13)
	MICHAEL G. KESSLER & ASSOCIATES, LTD.	(Volume 13)
	ON WATCH ™, LTD.	(Volume 13)
	PHOENIX RESEARCH CORPORATION	(Volume 13)
	ROBERT J. CASTELLI ASSOCIATES, INC.	(Volume 13)
	ROSS SECURITY CONSULTANTS, INC.	(Volume 13)
	SHADOW WARRIOR INVESTIGATIONS	(Volume 13)
	SHOALS INVESTIGATIVE SERVICES	(Volume 13)
	US INVESTIGATIONS SERVICES	(Volume 13)
	WORLDLINK INVESTIGATIVE SERVICES, INC.	(Volume 13)
PLATTSBURGH	MCKEE & ASSOCIATES, INC.	(Volume 12)
SCHENECTADY	THE PECORARO GROUP	(Volume 13)
WHITE PLAINS	C.J. SECURITY SERVICES, INC.	(Volume 13)
	PRICON INVESTIGATIONS	(Volume 13)

NORTH CAROLINA

CHARLOTTE	CENTURION PROFESSIONAL SERVICES, INC.	(Volume 14)
	J.L. FRY RESEARCH & INVESTIGATIONS	(Volume 14)
WILMINGTON	CAPE FEAR INVESTIGATIONS, LTD.	(Volume 14)

OHIO

CINCINNATI	G.C.I./GENERAL CORPORATE INVESTIGATION/GREATER CINCINNATI INVESTIGATION	(Volume 14)
CLEVELAND	ARGUS INVESTIGATIONS	(Volume 14)
	CASALINOVA INVESTIGATIONS	(Volume 14)
	CORPORATE INVESTIGATIVE SERVICES, INC.	(Volume 14)
COLUMBUS	CONFIDENTIAL SECURITY AGENCY, INC.	(Volume 14)
	INSIGHT CONSULTANTS, INC.	(Volume 14)
	PRIORITY INVESTIGATIONS	(Volume 14)
MARION	RON SCHEIDERER & ASSOCIATES	(Volume 14)

OKLAHOMA

OKLAHOMA CITY	MID-WEST INVESTIGATIONS & PROCESS SERVING INC.	(Volume 14)

PENNSYLVANIA

PHILADELPHIA	NATIONWIDE RESEARCH SERVICES	(Volume 15)
	OSI INVESTIGATIONS	(Volume 15)
	TALONE & ASSOCIATES, INC.	(Volume 15)
PITTSBURGH	ALLIED SECURITY INC.	(Volume 15)
WILKES-BARRE	BRADSHAW INVESTIGATIVE & SECURITY CONSULTANTS	(Volume 15)

SOUTH CAROLINA

CHARLESTON	BLAZER INVESTIGATIVE	(Volume 16)
	VIP SERVICES	(Volume 16)
COLUMBIA	INVESTIGATIVE RESEARCH GROUP, INC.	(Volume 16)
GREENVILLE	SUTTON & KISER INTERNATIONAL INVESTIGATIVE SERVICE, INC.	(Volume 16)
	WESTERN CAROLINA INVESTIGATION	(Volume 16)
HILTON HEAD ISLAND	THE GEREN AGENCY	(Volume 16)

TENNESSEE

CHATTANOOGA	CRUMBAUGH & ASSOCIATES	(Volume 16)
KNOXVILLE	SIERRA INVESTIGATIONS	(Volume 16)
MEMPHIS	PREMIER INVESTIGATIONS, INC.	(Volume 16)

TEXAS

AUSTIN	ET AL WORLD WIDE LITIGATION SUPPORT SERVICES	(Volume 17)
	THE INFORMATION BANK OF TEXAS, INC.	(Volume 17)
	WEEKS AND ASSOCIATES L.L.C.	(Volume 17)
BROWNSVILLE	ED GERUSA INVESTIGATIONS SERVICES CO.	(Volume 17)
DALLAS	#1 WORLDWIDE PERSON & INFORMATION LOCATORS	(Volume 17)

INVESTIGATORS - Continued

TEXAS, DALLAS - Continued

City	Firm	Volume
	ALL THE FACTS INVESTIGATIONS	(Volume 17)
	DIG DIRT INC. ™	(Volume 17)
	ET AL WORLD WIDE LITIGATION SUPPORT SERVICES	(Volume 17)
	INTELQUEST, INC.	(Volume 17)
	INTERFOR, INC.	(Volume 17)
	IRA INVESTIGATIVE RESEARCH ASSOCIATES	(Volume 17)
	SOUTHWEST SECURITY AND INVESTIGATIONS	(Volume 17)
	SUPER SEARCH, INC.	(Volume 17)
	TELESIS INFORMATION SYSTEMS, INC.	(Volume 17)
EL PASO	S.S. INVESTIGATIONS, INC.	(Volume 17)
HOUSTON	BLUE MOON INVESTIGATIONS	(Volume 17)
	CONFIDENTIAL ADVISORY SERVICES, INC.	(Volume 17)
	ET AL WORLD WIDE LITIGATION SUPPORT SERVICES	(Volume 17)
	THE INFORMATION BANK OF TEXAS, INC.	(Volume 17)
	MORITZ & ASSOCIATES, INC.	(Volume 17)
	EDMUND J. PANKAU, CLI, CPP	(Volume 17)
	THIRD EYE INVESTIGATIONS	(Volume 17)
SAN ANTONIO	ET AL WORLD WIDE LITIGATION SUPPORT SERVICES	(Volume 17)
TYLER	PARISH LITIGATION SERVICES & INVESTIGATIONS, INC.	(Volume 17)

UTAH

City	Firm	Volume
SALT LAKE CITY	DATATRACE INVESTIGATIONS, INC.	(Volume 17)
	PARAMOUNT DETECTIVE AGENCY, INC.	(Volume 17)
	PARKER, MADISON & LINDQUIST, INC.	(Volume 17)

VERMONT

City	Firm	Volume
BURLINGTON	BARTON AGENCY	(Volume 18)

VIRGINIA

City	Firm	Volume
ALEXANDRIA	ADVANCED PRIVATE INVESTIGATIONS GROUP	(Volume 18)
	BELTRANTE & ASSOCIATES	(Volume 18)
	CHARLES R. SEAL & ASSOCIATES, INC.	(Volume 18)
FAIRFAX	LEGAL INVESTIGATIONS, INC.	(Volume 18)
VIRGINIA BEACH	COASTAL SECURITY SERVICE, INC.	(Volume 18)

WASHINGTON

City	Firm	Volume
SEATTLE	ACIS ELECTRONIC COUNTERMEASURES CORP.	(Volume 18)
	BAYSIDE INVESTIGATIONS	(Volume 18)
	INVESTIGATORS DETECTIVE AGENCY	(Volume 18)
TACOMA	NORTHWEST PROCESS & INVESTIGATIONS, INC.	(Volume 18)

WISCONSIN

City	Firm	Volume
APPLETON	RAETHER INVESTIGATIONS	(Volume 18)

VIRGIN ISLANDS

City	Firm	Volume
CHRISTIANSTED, ST. CROIX	DENNIS R. SHERAW & ASSOCIATES, INC.	(Volume 18)

JAIL MAIL

CALIFORNIA

City	Firm	Volume
SACRAMENTO	SPECIAL PROTECTION & INVESTIGATIVE SERVICES	(Volume 3)

JURY CONSULTANTS

ARIZONA

City	Firm	Volume
PHOENIX	STARR LITIGATION SERVICES, INC	(Volume 1)

CALIFORNIA

City	Firm	Volume
LOS ANGELES	HENNINGTON & ASSOCIATES	(Volume 2)
	JURY RESEARCH INSTITUTE	(Volume 2)
	NATIONAL JURY PROJECT/WEST	(Volume 2)
	STARR LITIGATION SERVICES, INC	(Volume 2)
	TUNNO & ASSOCIATES	(Volume 2)
SAN FRANCISCO	JURY RESEARCH INSTITUTE	(Volume 3)
	NATIONAL JURY PROJECT/WEST	(Volume 3)
	TRIAL BEHAVIOR CONSULTING, INC.	(Volume 3)

COLORADO

City	Firm	Volume
DENVER	ANN COLE OPINION RESEARCH AND ANALYSIS	(Volume 4)

DISTRICT OF COLUMBIA

City	Firm	Volume
WASHINGTON	ON TRIAL ASSOCIATES, INC.	(Volume 5)

FLORIDA

City	Firm	Volume
MIAMI	BEHAVIORAL SCIENCE RESEARCH	(Volume 6)
ST. PETERSBURG	BEST EVIDENCE, INC.	(Volume 6)

LAWYER SEARCH & PLACEMENT CONSULTANTS - Continued

CALIFORNIA, LOS ANGELES - Continued

LEGAL PUBLICATIONS - Continued

COLORADO

DENVER .... CCH INCORPORATED .... (Volume 4)

DISTRICT OF COLUMBIA

WASHINGTON .... THE BUREAU OF NATIONAL AFFAIRS, INC. .... (Volume 5)
CCH INCORPORATED .... (Volume 5)

FLORIDA

MIAMI .... CCH INCORPORATED .... (Volume 6)

GEORGIA

ATLANTA .... CCH INCORPORATED .... (Volume 7)

ILLINOIS

CHICAGO .... ASSOCIATION OF LEGAL ADMINISTRATORS .... (Volume 8)
CCH INCORPORATED .... (Volume 8)

MARYLAND

BALTIMORE .... CCH INCORPORATED .... (Volume 9)
GAITHERSBURG .... ASPEN LAW & BUSINESS .... (Volume 9)

MASSACHUSETTS

BOSTON .... CCH INCORPORATED .... (Volume 10)

MINNESOTA

MINNEAPOLIS .... CCH INCORPORATED .... (Volume 11)

NEW JERSEY

NEWARK .... CCH INCORPORATED .... (Volume 12)

NEW YORK

NEW YORK .... AMERICAN LAWYER MEDIA .... (Volume 13)
ASPEN LAW & BUSINESS .... (Volume 13)
CCH INCORPORATED .... (Volume 13)
THE DAILY DEAL .... (Volume 13)
PRACTISING LAW INSTITUTE ® .... (Volume 13)

OHIO

CINCINNATI .... CCH INCORPORATED .... (Volume 14)

PENNSYLVANIA

PHILADELPHIA .... ANDREWS PUBLICATIONS .... (Volume 15)
CCH INCORPORATED .... (Volume 15)
MEALEY'S LITIGATION REPORTS AND CONFERENCES .... (Volume 15)

TENNESSEE

MEMPHIS .... CCH INCORPORATED .... (Volume 16)
NASHVILLE .... TENNESSEE ATTORNEYS MEMO .... (Volume 16)

TEXAS

HOUSTON .... CCH INCORPORATED .... (Volume 17)

VIRGINIA

ARLINGTON .... THE NATIONAL CRIME VICTIM BAR ASSOCIATION .... (Volume 18)

WASHINGTON

SEATTLE .... CCH INCORPORATED .... (Volume 18)

LEGAL RESEARCH

CALIFORNIA

LOS ANGELES .... LEXIS PUBLISHING ™ .... (Volume 2)
SAN FRANCISCO .... LEXIS PUBLISHING ™ .... (Volume 3)

FLORIDA

MIAMI .... LEXIS PUBLISHING ™ .... (Volume 6)

KANSAS

SHAWNEE MISSION .... IDEX ™ .... (Volume 9)

NEW JERSEY

NEWARK .... CHARLES JONES, LLC .... (Volume 12)
LEXIS PUBLISHING ™ .... (Volume 12)
TRENTON .... CHARLES JONES, LLC .... (Volume 12)

NEW YORK

NEW YORK .... GREENE-COHEN & WINSTON, INC. .... (Volume 13)
LEXIS PUBLISHING ™ .... (Volume 13)
NEW YORK LEGISLATIVE SERVICE, INC. .... (Volume 13)

TENNESSEE

NASHVILLE .... TENNESSEE ATTORNEYS MEMO .... (Volume 16)

TEXAS

DALLAS .... LEXIS PUBLISHING ™ .... (Volume 17)

LIBRARY MANAGEMENT SERVICES

CALIFORNIA

LOS ANGELES .... AXELROTH & ASSOCIATES .... (Volume 2)

NEW YORK

NEW YORK .... LAW LIBRARY MANAGEMENT, INCORPORATED .... (Volume 13)

LIFE CARE PLANNING

ALABAMA

BIRMINGHAM .... CASE MANAGEMENT, INC. .... (Volume 1)
MARY HOUSE KESSLER, PH.D. .... (Volume 1)
HUNTSVILLE .... CMS HEALTH MANAGEMENT SERVICES .... (Volume 1)

FLORIDA

TAMPA .... LIFE CARE SOLUTIONS, INC. .... (Volume 6)

MICHIGAN

ANN ARBOR .... BEACON REHABILITATION SERVICES, INC. .... (Volume 10)
LANSING .... CARE MANAGERS, INC. .... (Volume 10)

NEW JERSEY

WYCKOFF .... LINDA LAJTERMAN, RN, CCM,CDMS, ABDA, CLCP .... (Volume 12)

PENNSYLVANIA

PHILADELPHIA .... PERSPECTIVE CONSULTING, INC. .... (Volume 15)
REHAB ADVANTAGE .... (Volume 15)

LINGUISTICS

TENNESSEE

KNOXVILLE .... BETHANY K. DUMAS, J.D. PH.D. .... (Volume 16)

LITIGATION CONSULTING

CALIFORNIA

BERKELEY .... LECG, A SUBSIDIARY OF NAVIGANT CONSULTING, INC. .... (Volume 2)
PASADENA .... G. GOVINE CONSULTING .... (Volume 3)

DISTRICT OF COLUMBIA

WASHINGTON .... PROFESSIONAL BANK SERVICES .... (Volume 5)

ILLINOIS

CHICAGO .... ARTHUR ANDERSEN .... (Volume 8)
ZAGNOLI MCEVOY FOLEY LTD. .... (Volume 8)

NEW YORK

NEW YORK .... G. GOVINE CONSULTING .... (Volume 13)

TEXAS

HOUSTON .... LMC - A LITIGATION MEDIA CENTER .... (Volume 17)

LITIGATION SUPPORT - ENVIRONMENTAL

CALIFORNIA

IRVINE .... MCLAREN/HART, INC. .... (Volume 2)

LITIGATION SUPPORT - INTERNATIONAL

CALIFORNIA

LOS ANGELES .... MANX RESEARCH .... (Volume 2)
SAN FRANCISCO .... LEGAL LANGUAGE SERVICES .... (Volume 3)

DISTRICT OF COLUMBIA

WASHINGTON .... LEGAL LANGUAGE SERVICES .... (Volume 5)
VANCE INTERNATIONAL, INC. .... (Volume 5)

ILLINOIS

CHICAGO .... LEGAL LANGUAGE SERVICES .... (Volume 8)

NEW YORK

NEW YORK .... LEGAL LANGUAGE SERVICES .... (Volume 13)

WASHINGTON

SEATTLE .... LEGAL LANGUAGE SERVICES .... (Volume 18)

LITIGATION SUPPORT SERVICES

ARIZONA

MESA .... COASH & COASH, INC. .... (Volume 1)
PHOENIX .... COASH & COASH, INC. .... (Volume 1)

LITIGATION SUPPORT SERVICES - Continued

MINNESOTA, MINNEAPOLIS - Continued

	QUORUM/LANIER	(Volume 11)
	SCHECHTER DOKKEN KANTER ANDREWS & SELCER LTD	(Volume 11)
MISSOURI		
ST. LOUIS	GORE & PERRY REPORTING COMPANY	(Volume 11)
NEW JERSEY		
NEWARK	WITHUM, SMITH & BROWN	(Volume 12)
NEW MEXICO		
ALBUQUERQUE	BEAN & ASSOCIATES, INC.	(Volume 12)
	ROGOFF ERICKSON DIAMOND & WALKER, LLP	(Volume 12)
SANTA FE	BEAN & ASSOCIATES, INC.	(Volume 12)
NEW YORK		
NEW YORK	1ST AMERICAN PROCESS SERVICE, INC.	(Volume 13)
	ANALYSIS AND INFERENCE, INC.	(Volume 13)
	IMAGEMAX	(Volume 13)
	KERNAN ASSOCIATES, INC.	(Volume 13)
	LEGAL LANGUAGE SERVICES	(Volume 13)
	PANETH, HABER & ZIMMERMAN, LLP	(Volume 13)
	REGENT PACIFIC ®	(Volume 13)
	SMP DIGITAL GRAPHICS	(Volume 13)
	STERLING REPORTING SERVICE, INC.	(Volume 13)
OHIO		
CINCINNATI	ACE REPORTING SERVICES	(Volume 14)
PENNSYLVANIA		
MEADVILLE	ROBERT M. POWER, JR. CPA, CVA, ABV	(Volume 15)
PHILADELPHIA	1ST AMERICAN PROCESS SERVICE, INC.	(Volume 15)
	PATRICIA CARROLL PERSONNEL CONSULTANTS	(Volume 15)
SOUTH CAROLINA		
GREENVILLE	LEGAL EAGLE ®, INC.	(Volume 16)
TENNESSEE		
NASHVILLE	KRAFT BROS. ESSTMAN, PATTON & HARRELL, PLLC (KRAFTCPAS)	(Volume 16)
	LATTIMORE BLACK MORGAN & CAIN, P.C.	(Volume 16)
TEXAS		
ARLINGTON	ARLINGTON COURT REPORTING, INC.	(Volume 17)
AUSTIN	1ST AMERICAN PROCESS SERVICE, INC.	(Volume 17)
DALLAS	1ST AMERICAN PROCESS SERVICE, INC.	(Volume 17)
	ARLINGTON COURT REPORTING, INC.	(Volume 17)
	SHARP HOLLAND INTERNATIONAL COURT REPORTING, INC.	(Volume 17)
FORT WORTH	ARLINGTON COURT REPORTING, INC.	(Volume 17)
	SHARP HOLLAND INTERNATIONAL COURT REPORTING, INC.	(Volume 17)
HOUSTON	1ST AMERICAN PROCESS SERVICE, INC.	(Volume 17)
	ACCURATE REPORTERS, INC.	(Volume 17)
	BAKER ROBBINS & COMPANY	(Volume 17)
	LMC - A LITIGATION MEDIA CENTER	(Volume 17)
	PILKO & ASSOCIATES, INC.	(Volume 17)
MCALLEN	APEX DOCUMENT MANAGEMENT, INC.	(Volume 17)
VIRGINIA		
FAIRFAX	RICHMAN ASSOCIATES	(Volume 18)
WASHINGTON		
SEATTLE	LITIGATION ABSTRACT, INC.	(Volume 18)
	STARKOVICH REPORTING SERVICES	(Volume 18)
TACOMA	STARKOVICH REPORTING SERVICES	(Volume 18)
PUERTO RICO		
SAN JUAN	AMANDA CAPO'-ROSSELLO', CPA, CVA, CFE	(Volume 18)

LITIGATION SUPPORT SOFTWARE

CALIFORNIA		
SAN FRANCISCO	SUMMATION LEGAL TECHNOLOGIES, INC.	(Volume 3)
MASSACHUSETTS		
BOSTON	STEELPOINT TECHNOLOGIES, INC.	(Volume 10)

LOBBYIST

CALIFORNIA

SACRAMENTO	LUCAS ADVOCATES	(Volume 3)

DISTRICT OF COLUMBIA

WASHINGTON	FRENCH & COMPANY	(Volume 5)
	MARLOWE & COMPANY	(Volume 5)

FLORIDA

TALLAHASSEE	ADG BUSINESS AND GOVERNMENTAL CONSULTANTS	(Volume 6)

NEW YORK

ALBANY	CAPITOL GROUP, LLC	(Volume 12)

MALPRACTICE LEGAL DEFENSE

CALIFORNIA

LOS ANGELES	OSTROVE, KRANTZ & OSTROVE, A P.C.	(Volume 2)

MANAGEMENT CONSULTANTS

CALIFORNIA

LOS ANGELES	ALTMAN WEIL, INC.	(Volume 2)
SAN FRANCISCO	THE CULTUREPIECE	(Volume 3)

NEW YORK

NEW YORK	ALTMAN WEIL, INC.	(Volume 13)

PENNSYLVANIA

PHILADELPHIA	ALTMAN WEIL, INC.	(Volume 15)

TEXAS

DALLAS	LAW FIRM MANAGEMENT CONSULTING, INC.	(Volume 17)

MARINE CONSULTANTS

NEW YORK

NEW YORK	THOMAS ELECTRIC CONTROL, INC.	(Volume 13)

TEXAS

HOUSTON	KDON CONSULTANTS	(Volume 17)

MARKETING

CALIFORNIA

LOS ANGELES	JM ASSOCIATES	(Volume 2)
SAN FRANCISCO	COLE VALLEY SOFTWARE	(Volume 3)

GEORGIA

ATLANTA	LAW & MEDIA GROUP, INC.	(Volume 7)

MEDICAL CASE REVIEW & PREPARATION/TRIAL CONSULTING

CALIFORNIA

LOS ANGELES	LOS ANGELES LEGAL NURSE CONSULTING INSTITUTE	(Volume 2)
	MEDICALLY SPEAKING ®	(Volume 2)
SAN DIEGO	CHRIS COCHRAN TRELEASE, MSN, RN, C. CWCN	(Volume 3)

FLORIDA

ORLANDO	DAVID A. LIBERT, M.D. F.A.A.F.P.	(Volume 6)

GEORGIA

ATLANTA	LEGAL NURSE CONSULTANTS, LLC	(Volume 7)
MACON	RIDLEY MEDICAL-LEGAL CONSULTING	(Volume 7)

ILLINOIS

CHICAGO	KIMBERLY M. PAGE, R.N. B.S.N. J.D.	(Volume 8)

KANSAS

WICHITA	DON R. HIRSCHMAN, C.R.N.A. M.H.A.	(Volume 9)

MARYLAND

HAVRE DE GRACE	LBS ASSOCIATES, INC.	(Volume 9)

MASSACHUSETTS

BOSTON	NEUROADVANCE, INC.	(Volume 10)

MICHIGAN

GRAND RAPIDS	CATASTROPHIC & REHABILITATION MANAGEMENT, INC.	(Volume 10)
MUSKEGON	BENCO ENTERPRISES, INC.	(Volume 10)

NEW YORK

KINGSTON	MEDISYS MEDICAL INFORMATION SYSTEMS	(Volume 12)

MEDICAL CASE REVIEW & PREPARATION/TRIAL CONSULTING - Continued

OHIO
CLEVELAND .... LITIGATION MANAGEMENT, INC. .... (Volume 14)

PENNSYLVANIA
PHILADELPHIA .... CONSULTANTS IN MEDICAL IMAGING .... (Volume 15)
PERSPECTIVE CONSULTING, INC. .... (Volume 15)
PITTSBURGH .... CONORALEXANDRA .... (Volume 15)

TEXAS
CORPUS CHRISTI .... C & E ASSOCIATES .... (Volume 17)
HOUSTON .... CLINICAL FORENSICS CONSORTIUM .... (Volume 17)
MEDICAL RESEARCH CONSULTANTS, INC. .... (Volume 17)
SAN ANTONIO .... LITIGATION STRATEGIES ™ GROUP .... (Volume 17)

WEST VIRGINIA
CHARLESTON .... MEDICAL - LEGAL CONSULTING .... (Volume 18)
MORGANTOWN .... NORTHERN WEST VIRGINIA PAIN MANAGEMENT CENTER .... (Volume 18)

MEDICAL EVALUATION - BRAIN INJURIES

MASSACHUSETTS
BOSTON .... NEUROADVANCE, INC. .... (Volume 10)

MEDICAL EXPERT WITNESS

CALIFORNIA
LOS ANGELES .... AMERICAN MEDICAL FORENSIC SPECIALISTS, INC. .... (Volume 2)
CCC CONSOLIDATED CONSULTANTS CO. .... (Volume 2)
SAN FRANCISCO .... AMERICAN MEDICAL FORENSIC SPECIALISTS, INC. .... (Volume 3)

FLORIDA
MIAMI .... AMERICAN MEDICAL FORENSIC SPECIALISTS, INC. .... (Volume 6)

MARYLAND
POTOMAC .... PERRY HOOKMAN, M.D. P.A. PROFESSIONAL ASSOCIATES .... (Volume 9)

NEW YORK
NEW YORK .... AMERICAN MEDICAL FORENSIC SPECIALISTS, INC. .... (Volume 13)
CCC CONSOLIDATED CONSULTANTS CO. .... (Volume 13)
MEDQUEST, LTD. .... (Volume 13)

PENNSYLVANIA
PHILADELPHIA .... AMERICAN MEDICAL FORENSIC SPECIALISTS, INC. .... (Volume 15)
CONSULTANTS IN MEDICAL IMAGING .... (Volume 15)

TEXAS
HOUSTON .... AMERICAN MEDICAL FORENSIC SPECIALISTS, INC. .... (Volume 17)

ANESTHESIOLOGY

PENNSYLVANIA
PHILADELPHIA .... MEDIAMEDICA .... (Volume 15)

CARDIOLOGY

CALIFORNIA
LOS ANGELES .... THOMAS J. BERGER M.D. F.A.C.S. F.C.C.P. F.A.C.F.E. .... (Volume 2)

NEW YORK
NEW YORK .... THOMAS J. BERGER M.D. F.A.C.S. F.C.C.P. F.A.C.F.E. .... (Volume 13)

PENNSYLVANIA
PHILADELPHIA .... MEDIAMEDICA .... (Volume 15)

CARDIOLOGY, INTERNAL MEDICINE & GERIATRIC

NEW YORK
NEW YORK .... CCC CONSOLIDATED CONSULTANTS CO. .... (Volume 13)

DENTAL

ILLINOIS
CHICAGO .... J. CRYSTAL BAXTER, DMD, MDS .... (Volume 8)

NEW JERSEY
CHERRY HILL .... MELVYN A. BLAKE, D.D.S. J.D. - DENTAL CONSULTANT .... (Volume 12)

NEW YORK
NEW YORK .... HUGH R. HUNSINGER, D.M.D. F.A.G.D. L.L.C. .... (Volume 13)

MEDICAL EXPERT WITNESS - Continued

NEUROLOGY

CALIFORNIA

LOS ANGELES ... CALIFORNIA NEUROLOGICAL SPECIALISTS ... (Volume 2)
SAN FRANCISCO ... RICHARD A. RUBENSTEIN, M.D. ... (Volume 3)
MARK H. STRASSBERG, MD ... (Volume 3)

NEW YORK

NEW YORK ... ARTHUR TAUB, M.D. PH.D. P.C. ... (Volume 13)

PENNSYLVANIA

PHILADELPHIA ... MEDIAMEDICA ... (Volume 15)

TEXAS

HOUSTON ... JOHN STIRLING MEYER, M.D. ... (Volume 17)

NEUROSURGERY

CALIFORNIA

SANTA MARIA ... EDWARD A. SMITH, M.D. INC. ... (Volume 3)

NURSING

PENNSYLVANIA

PHILADELPHIA ... AUDREY STEPHAN, ED.D. R.N. CCRN ... (Volume 15)

NURSING HOMES/ASSISTED LIVING

FLORIDA

FORT LAUDERDALE ... JOANN ALDERMAN R.N. M.S.N. C.C.M. ... (Volume 6)

OKLAHOMA

OKLAHOMA CITY ... ANDREA M. WEST, R.N. PH.D. ... (Volume 14)

OBSTETRICS & GYNECOLOGY

CONNECTICUT

BRIDGEPORT ... RESOURCE CONNECTOR, INC. ... (Volume 4)

ONCOLOGY

BREAST CANCER DELAYED DIAGNOSIS

NEW YORK

NEW YORK ... MICHAEL W. RETSKY, PH.D. ... (Volume 13)

OPHTHALMOLOGY

NEW YORK

SYRACUSE ... WILLIAM M. TUCKER, MD ... (Volume 13)

EYE INJURIES/SAFETY

MASSACHUSETTS

BOSTON ... PAUL F. VINGER, M.D. ... (Volume 10)

RETINA

CALIFORNIA

SANTA ANA ... JOHN M. MAGGIANO, M..D., INC.. ... (Volume 3)

PAIN MANAGEMENT

WEST VIRGINIA

MORGANTOWN ... NORTHERN WEST VIRGINIA PAIN MANAGEMENT CENTER ... (Volume 18)

PATHOLOGY

NEW YORK

NEW YORK ... ALI Z. HAMELI, M.D. P.A. ... (Volume 13)

PEDIATRICS

CALIFORNIA

SAN FRANCISCO ... STEPHEN L. KAUFMAN, M.D. ... (Volume 3)

ENDOCRINOLOGY

CALIFORNIA

SAN FRANCISCO ... STEPHEN L. KAUFMAN, M.D. ... (Volume 3)

PHARMACY & PHARMACOLOGY

ILLINOIS

CHICAGO ... PHARMACONSULTANTS INC. ... (Volume 8)

MEDICAL EXPERT WITNESS

PSYCHOLOGY - FORENSIC - Continued

NEW YORK, NEW YORK - Continued

RICHARD M. SAMUELS, PH.D. FCLINP, FAACS. (Volume 13)

NEUROPSYCHOLOGY

NEW YORK

NEW YORK ... ARTHUR TAUB, M.D. PH.D. P.C. ... (Volume 13)
THE NEW YORK CENTER FOR NEUROPSYCHOLOGY & FORENSIC BEHAVIORAL SCIENCE ... (Volume 13)
ROLLAND S. PARKER, PH.D. ... (Volume 13)

TEXAS

DALLAS ... BOB L. GANT, PH.D. ... (Volume 17)

RADIOLOGY

CALIFORNIA

CARLSBAD ... BARRY B. CAMPBELL, M.D. ... (Volume 2)
LOS ANGELES ... DARWOOD B. HANCE, M.D. ... (Volume 2)

PENNSYLVANIA

PHILADELPHIA ... CONSULTANTS IN MEDICAL IMAGING ... (Volume 15)

MRI/MUSCULOSKELETAL IMAGING

PENNSYLVANIA

PHILADELPHIA ... CONSULTANTS IN MEDICAL IMAGING ... (Volume 15)

SURGERY

CARDIOVASCULAR THORACIC

CALIFORNIA

LOS ANGELES ... THOMAS J. BERGER M.D. F.A.C.S. F.C.C.P. F.A.C.F.E. ... (Volume 2)
SAN DIEGO ... MICHAEL J. O'SULLIVAN, M.D. J.D. INC. ... (Volume 3)

NEW YORK

NEW YORK ... THOMAS J. BERGER M.D. F.A.C.S. F.C.C.P. F.A.C.F.E. ... (Volume 13)

HAND SURGERY

CALIFORNIA

LOS ANGELES ... JOHN J. O'HARA, M.D. ... (Volume 2)

TEXAS

HOUSTON ... JONATHAN A. LEWIS, MD, FACS ... (Volume 17)

ORTHOPEDIC

CALIFORNIA

IRVINE ... ROBERT ANTHONY, BAIRD, M.D. ... (Volume 2)

TEXAS

HOUSTON ... JONATHAN A. LEWIS, MD, FACS ... (Volume 17)

TOXICOLOGY

CALIFORNIA

LOS ANGELES ... RICHARD J. SCHLESINGER, PH.D. DABFT ... (Volume 2)
SANTA CRUZ ... ALAN BUCHWALD, M.D. FAAEM, ACMT, ABEM (TOX.) ... (Volume 3)

DISTRICT OF COLUMBIA

WASHINGTON ... THERESA HOFFMAN-TILL, PH.D. ... (Volume 5)

PENNSYLVANIA

PHILADELPHIA ... NATIONAL MEDICAL SERVICES, INC. ... (Volume 15)

TEXAS

HOUSTON ... NORMAN M. TRIEFF, PH.D. ... (Volume 17)

UROLOGY

NEW YORK

NEW YORK ... GEORGE KLEIN, M.D. ... (Volume 13)

VOCATIONAL REHABILITATION

MINNESOTA

MINNEAPOLIS ... RICHARD UGLAND, EDD, L.P. ... (Volume 11)

NETWORK - CD-ROM

NEW YORK

NEW YORK .... DIGI-COM GROUP, INC. .... (Volume 13)

NEWS/MEDIA SERVICES

DISTRICT OF COLUMBIA

WASHINGTON .... U.S. NEWSWIRE .... (Volume 5)

NURSING CONSULTANTS

ALABAMA

FAIRHOPE .... ELIZABETH CHAPMAN, R.N. M.S. CCRN .... (Volume 1)

CALIFORNIA

BURLINGAME .... JO MARIE UPLAND, R.N. BSN, PHN .... (Volume 2)

LOS ANGELES .... FYLER ASSOCIATES .... (Volume 2)

LOS ANGELES LEGAL NURSE CONSULTING INSTITUTE .... (Volume 2)

ILLINOIS

SPRINGFIELD .... ANNE ROOT, RN, RA, CNOR .... (Volume 8)

TEXAS

FORTH WORTH .... GLENNA RICHARDS ALLBRITTON, RN, MSN, CFNP .... (Volume 17)

WISCONSIN

MILWAUKEE .... GAIL ROBISON CONSULTANTS .... (Volume 18)

OFFENDER MONITORING SERVICES

INDIANA

EVANSVILLE .... THE HANNA BLACKFORD MONITORING AGENCY .... (Volume 8)

OFFICE PRODUCTS & SERVICES

NEW YORK

NEW YORK .... @VANTAGE .... (Volume 13)

OIL & GAS ENGINEERING

CALIFORNIA

LOS ANGELES .... DUKE ENGINEERING & SERVICES .... (Volume 2)

ONLINE PUBLIC RECORDS SERVICE

ALASKA

ANCHORAGE .... INFORMALASKA .... (Volume 1)

CALIFORNIA

SACRAMENTO .... IQ DATA SYSTEMS .... (Volume 3)

NEW JERSEY

NEWARK .... SUPERIOR INFORMATION SERVICES, L.L.C. .... (Volume 12)

TRENTON .... SUPERIOR INFORMATION SERVICES, L.L.C. .... (Volume 12)

NEW YORK

NEW YORK .... INTERCOUNTY CLEARANCE CORPORATION .... (Volume 13)

SUPERIOR INFORMATION SERVICES, L.L.C. .... (Volume 13)

WASHINGTON

SEATTLE .... DILIGENZ .... (Volume 18)

UNISEARCH INC. .... (Volume 18)

PARALEGAL SERVICES

ALASKA

ANCHORAGE .... ALASKA COURT REPORTING AND TRANSCRIBING SERVICES .... (Volume 1)

ARIZONA

PHOENIX .... INTEGRATED LEGAL SERVICE & ASSOCIATES .... (Volume 1)

TUCSON .... COMPLETE OFFICE SUPPORT, INC. .... (Volume 1)

EXPERT DOCUMENTS, INC. .... (Volume 1)

CALIFORNIA

LOS ANGELES .... ZISKIND GREENE CONTRACT ATTORNEYS & PARALEGALS .... (Volume 2)

DISTRICT OF COLUMBIA

WASHINGTON .... NRI LEGAL STAFFING .... (Volume 5)

PARALEGAL SERVICES .... (Volume 5)

PHOTOGRAPHY

NEW JERSEY

HACKETTSTOWN .... SUMMIT PROFESSIONAL RESOURCES LLC .... (Volume 12)

POLYGRAPH EXAMINATION SERVICES

CALIFORNIA

LOS ANGELES .... JACK TRIMARCO & ASSOCIATES POLYGRAPH/INVESTIGATIONS, INC. .... (Volume 2)

FLORIDA

MIAMI .... BOB FERRER, INC. .... (Volume 6)
ORLANDO .... SHAFFER & ASSOCIATES FORENSIC TECHNOLOGIES .... (Volume 6)

GEORGIA

ATLANTA .... FEDERAL POLYGRAPH ASSOCIATES, L.L.C. .... (Volume 7)
INVESTIGATIVE SOLUTIONS, INC. .... (Volume 7)

ILLINOIS

CHICAGO .... JOHN E. REID AND ASSOCIATES, INC. .... (Volume 8)
PEORIA .... IVEY INVESTIGATIVE SERVICES .... (Volume 8)

MARYLAND

BALTIMORE .... MARYLAND INSTITUTE OF CRIMINAL JUSTICE .... (Volume 9)

NEW JERSEY

NEWARK .... ARGUS INVESTIGATIVE SERVICES, INC. .... (Volume 12)

NEW YORK

NEW YORK .... SCIENTIFIC LIE DETECTION, INC. .... (Volume 13)

SOUTH CAROLINA

GREENVILLE .... SUTTON & KISER INTERNATIONAL INVESTIGATIVE SERVICE, INC. .... (Volume 16)

TEXAS

DALLAS .... IQM, INC: BUSINESS INVESTIGATIONS .... (Volume 17)

PRESS RELEASES

GEORGIA

ATLANTA .... LAW & MEDIA GROUP, INC. .... (Volume 7)

PROCESS SERVERS & DOCUMENT DELIVERY SERVICES

ALABAMA

BIRMINGHAM .... MID-SOUTH LEGAL SERVICES .... (Volume 1)
MOBILE .... 007 ATTORNEY SERVICES, INC. .... (Volume 1)
BLI ™ .... (Volume 1)
MONTGOMERY .... 007 ATTORNEY SERVICES, INC. .... (Volume 1)
MCDANIEL & ASSOCIATES .... (Volume 1)

ALASKA

FAIRBANKS .... FORT ENTERPRISES PROCESS SERVERS & INVESTIGATORS .... (Volume 1)

ARIZONA

PHOENIX .... 007 ATTORNEY SERVICES, INC. .... (Volume 1)
A & E, INC. .... (Volume 1)
AAA LEGAL SERVICES .... (Volume 1)
BORG PROCESS SERVERS INC. .... (Volume 1)
HAWKINS AND CAMPBELL INCORPORATED .... (Volume 1)
TRACK DOWN, INC. .... (Volume 1)
UNITED PROCESS SERVICE .... (Volume 1)

ARKANSAS

LITTLE ROCK .... LANDS INVESTIGATIONS COMPANY .... (Volume 1)

CALIFORNIA

FRESNO .... A-1 ATTORNEY SERVICE .... (Volume 2)
LOS ANGELES .... 1ST AMERICAN PROCESS SERVICE, INC. .... (Volume 2)
A & E, INC. .... (Volume 2)
ACE PROCESS SERVICE .... (Volume 2)
BORG PROCESS SERVERS INC. .... (Volume 2)
D.L.S. INC. (DEMOVSKY LAWYER SERVICE) .... (Volume 2)
FAX & FILE LEGAL SERVICES, INC. .... (Volume 2)
LA SALLE PROCESS SERVERS, L.P. .... (Volume 2)
LEGAL SUPPORT SERVICES, INC. .... (Volume 2)
ON WATCH ™, LTD. .... (Volume 2)
SHERMAN, ALEXANDER & ASSOCIATES LLC .... (Volume 2)
OAKLAND .... ERDMAN ATTORNEY SERVICE .... (Volume 2)

PROCESS SERVERS & DOCUMENT DELIVERY SERVICES - Continued

FLORIDA, ORLANDO - Continued

	AAA WORLDWIDE PROCESS & DETECTIVE AGENCY, INC.	(Volume 6)
	BORG PROCESS SERVERS INC.	(Volume 6)
ST. PETERSBURG	AAA WORLDWIDE PROCESS & DETECTIVE AGENCY, INC.	(Volume 6)
	GIETZEN & ASSOCIATES, INC.	(Volume 6)
	LEGALEASE INC.	(Volume 6)
TALLAHASSEE	A & E, INC.	(Volume 6)
	VAUSE'S PROCESS SERVICE	(Volume 6)
TAMPA	1ST AMERICAN PROCESS SERVICE, INC.	(Volume 6)
	A & E, INC.	(Volume 6)
	AAA WORLDWIDE PROCESS & DETECTIVE AGENCY, INC.	(Volume 6)
	BORG PROCESS SERVERS INC.	(Volume 6)
	GIETZEN & ASSOCIATES, INC.	(Volume 6)
GEORGIA		
ATLANTA	A & E, INC.	(Volume 7)
	ATLANTA ATTORNEY SERVICES	(Volume 7)
	ATLANTA LEGAL SERVICES, INC.	(Volume 7)
	ATTORNEYS' PERSONAL SERVICES, INC.	(Volume 7)
	BORG PROCESS SERVERS INC.	(Volume 7)
	PROFESSIONAL PROCESS SERVICE OF ATLANTA, INC.	(Volume 7)
	T.A.M.A. INVESTIGATIONS, INC.	(Volume 7)
IDAHO		
LEWISTON	H&H LEGAL MESSENGERS	(Volume 7)
ILLINOIS		
ARLINGTON HEIGHTS	CHICAGO METRO LEGAL PROCESS	(Volume 8)
CHICAGO	A & E, INC.	(Volume 8)
	BORG PROCESS SERVERS INC.	(Volume 8)
	IT'S YOUR SERVE	(Volume 8)
	LA SALLE PROCESS SERVERS, L.P.	(Volume 8)
	LEGAL LANGUAGE SERVICES	(Volume 8)
	THOMAS G. KEANE & ASSOC. LTD.	(Volume 8)
KANSAS		
KANSAS CITY	LEGAL LANGUAGE SERVICES	(Volume 9)
TOPEKA	MERCURY MESSENGERS, INC.	(Volume 9)
KENTUCKY		
LEXINGTON	BLAKELEY INVESTIGATIVE SERVICES	(Volume 9)
LOUISVILLE	20/20 INVESTIGATIVE SERVICES, INC.	(Volume 9)
LOUISIANA		
BATON ROUGE	A & E, INC.	(Volume 9)
	LEGALEASE INC.	(Volume 9)
NEW ORLEANS	A & E, INC.	(Volume 9)
MARYLAND		
ANNAPOLIS	A & E, INC.	(Volume 9)
BALTIMORE	A & E, INC.	(Volume 9)
	BORG PROCESS SERVERS INC.	(Volume 9)
	COPS, INC.	(Volume 9)
	MARYLAND PROCESS SERVERS, INC.	(Volume 9)
BETHESDA	A & E, INC.	(Volume 9)
ROCKVILLE	A & E, INC.	(Volume 9)
	PROFESSIONAL PROCESS SERVING, INC.	(Volume 9)
MASSACHUSETTS		
BOSTON	1ST AMERICAN PROCESS SERVICE, INC.	(Volume 10)
	A & E, INC.	(Volume 10)
	ALLSTATE PROCESS SERVERS	(Volume 10)
	AMERICAN INVESTIGATIVE SERVICES, INC.	(Volume 10)
	BORG PROCESS SERVERS INC.	(Volume 10)
	BUTLER AND ASSOCIATES CONSTABLES, INC.	(Volume 10)
	DHR & ASSOCIATES	(Volume 10)
MICHIGAN		
DETROIT	1ST AMERICAN PROCESS SERVICE, INC.	(Volume 10)
	A & E, INC.	(Volume 10)
	BORG PROCESS SERVERS INC.	(Volume 10)
	EXPRESS PROCESS SERVICE	(Volume 10)
	TECHNICAL SECURITY ANALYSTS, INC.	(Volume 10)

PROCESS SERVERS & DOCUMENT DELIVERY SERVICES - Continued

NORTH CAROLINA

City	Service	Volume
CHARLOTTE	NATIONAL DATA ACCESS CORPORATION	(Volume 14)
	PAPER HANGERS	(Volume 14)
GREENSBORO	NATIONAL DATA ACCESS CORPORATION	(Volume 14)
RALEIGH	NATIONAL DATA ACCESS CORPORATION	(Volume 14)
	PARALEGAL SERVICES OF NORTH CAROLINA, INC.	(Volume 14)

OHIO

City	Service	Volume
CINCINNATI	A & E, INC.	(Volume 14)
	ACE REPORTING SERVICES	(Volume 14)
	HOLZBERGER & ASSOCIATES, INC.	(Volume 14)
CLEVELAND	A & E, INC.	(Volume 14)
	ATTORNEY SERVICES OF NORTHEAST OHIO	(Volume 14)
	C & G	(Volume 14)
COLUMBUS	A & E, INC.	(Volume 14)
DAYTON	A.S.A.P. ATTORNEY SERVICES	(Volume 14)

OKLAHOMA

City	Service	Volume
LAWTON	OKLAHOMA LEGAL PROCESS SERVICE, INC.	(Volume 14)
TULSA	A & E, INC.	(Volume 14)

OREGON

City	Service	Volume
PORTLAND	1ST AMERICAN PROCESS SERVICE, INC.	(Volume 15)

PENNSYLVANIA

City	Service	Volume
PHILADELPHIA	1ST AMERICAN PROCESS SERVICE, INC.	(Volume 15)
	A & E, INC.	(Volume 15)
	BORG PROCESS SERVERS INC.	(Volume 15)
	FIRST CLASS SUBPOENA SERVICES, INC.	(Volume 15)
	LEGAL LANGUAGE SERVICES	(Volume 15)
	TALONE & ASSOCIATES, INC.	(Volume 15)
PITTSBURGH	1ST AMERICAN PROCESS SERVICE, INC.	(Volume 15)
	FIRST CLASS SUBPOENA SERVICES, INC.	(Volume 15)

SOUTH CAROLINA

City	Service	Volume
CHARLESTON	BLAZER INVESTIGATIVE	(Volume 16)
	EWERS INVESTIGATIONS	(Volume 16)
COLUMBIA	NATIONAL DATA ACCESS CORPORATION	(Volume 16)
GREENVILLE	NATIONAL DATA ACCESS CORPORATION	(Volume 16)
	UPSTATE PROCESS SERVICES	(Volume 16)
HILTON HEAD ISLAND	THE GEREN AGENCY	(Volume 16)
SPARTANBURG	NATIONAL DATA ACCESS CORPORATION	(Volume 16)

TENNESSEE

City	Service	Volume
CHATTANOOGA	CRUMBAUGH & ASSOCIATES	(Volume 16)
MEMPHIS	SHELBY COUNTY PROCESS SERVERS, INC. TENNESSEE INVESTIGATIONS & PARALEGAL SERVICE, INC.	(Volume 16)
NASHVILLE	A & E, INC.	(Volume 16)
	BRIEF ENCOUNTERS, INC.	(Volume 16)

TEXAS

City	Service	Volume
AUSTIN	1ST AMERICAN PROCESS SERVICE, INC.	(Volume 17)
	ET AL WORLD WIDE LITIGATION SUPPORT SERVICES	(Volume 17)
	WEEKS AND ASSOCIATES L.L.C.	(Volume 17)
BROWNSVILLE	LAWYER SUPPORT SERVICES	(Volume 17)
CORPUS CHRISTI	THE ALPHA AND OMEGA AGENCY	(Volume 17)
	TEXAS CIVIL PROCESS, INCORPORATED	(Volume 17)
DALLAS	1ST AMERICAN PROCESS SERVICE, INC.	(Volume 17)
	A.S.A. INFORMATION SERVICES	(Volume 17)
	BORG PROCESS SERVERS INC.	(Volume 17)
	ET AL WORLD WIDE LITIGATION SUPPORT SERVICES	(Volume 17)
	LA SALLE PROCESS SERVERS, L.P.	(Volume 17)
	SUPER SEARCH, INC.	(Volume 17)
HOUSTON	1ST AMERICAN PROCESS SERVICE, INC.	(Volume 17)
	A & E, INC.	(Volume 17)
	AMERICAN CIVIL PROCESS SERVICES, INC.	(Volume 17)
	BORG PROCESS SERVERS INC.	(Volume 17)
	ET AL WORLD WIDE LITIGATION SUPPORT SERVICES	(Volume 17)
	LONE STAR ATTORNEY SERVICE, INC.	(Volume 17)
LUBBOCK	CURTIS D. RUFF AND ASSOCIATES	(Volume 17)
SAN ANTONIO	1ST AMERICAN PROCESS SERVICE, INC.	(Volume 17)
	A & E, INC.	(Volume 17)
	ATTORNEY'S MEDICAL RECORDS	(Volume 17)

PURCHASES OF MORTGAGES/TRUST DEEDS

CALIFORNIA
LOS ANGELES .... CREATIVE INVESTMENT GROUP .... (Volume 2)

COLORADO
COLORADO SPRINGS .... NATIONWIDE FINANCIAL SERVICES (NFSC, INC.) .... (Volume 4)

FLORIDA
TALLAHASSEE .... SELLERS FUNDING .... (Volume 6)

NEW YORK
NEW YORK .... R&P CAPITAL RESOURCES, INC. .... (Volume 13)

NORTH CAROLINA
RALEIGH .... KG FUNDING .... (Volume 14)

OHIO
TOLEDO .... LAFE E. TOLLIVER .... (Volume 14)

TEXAS
DALLAS .... NORA E. CARAMBOT .... (Volume 17)
HOUSTON .... UNITED MORTGAGE & INVESTMENT GROUP .... (Volume 17)

PURCHASES OF STRUCTURED SETTLEMENTS & ANNUITIES

CALIFORNIA
LONG BEACH .... SWEEZER'S CONSULTANTS .... (Volume 2)
LOS ANGELES .... CREATIVE INVESTMENT GROUP .... (Volume 2)
SAN FRANCISCO .... ANDERSON CAPITAL FUNDING .... (Volume 3)

COLORADO
COLORADO SPRINGS .... NATIONWIDE FINANCIAL SERVICES (NFSC, INC.) .... (Volume 4)

FLORIDA
TALLAHASSEE .... H&H CAPITAL RESOURCES, INC. .... (Volume 6)
SELLERS FUNDING .... (Volume 6)

NEW YORK
NEW YORK .... R&P CAPITAL RESOURCES, INC. .... (Volume 13)

NORTH CAROLINA
RALEIGH .... KG FUNDING .... (Volume 14)

OREGON
PORTLAND .... INTEGRITY FUNDING SOURCES .... (Volume 15)

RECEIVERSHIPS

CALIFORNIA
LOS ANGELES .... ALDEN MANAGEMENT GROUP .... (Volume 2)

RECORD SERVICES

OHIO
AKRON .... OHIO PARALEGAL SERVICES, INC. .... (Volume 14)

TEXAS
HOUSTON .... COURT RECORD RESEARCH, INC. .... (Volume 17)

SECRETARIAL SUPPORT

CALIFORNIA
SAN FRANCISCO .... LASERGIRL .... (Volume 3)

DISTRICT OF COLUMBIA
WASHINGTON .... NRI LEGAL STAFFING .... (Volume 5)

TEXAS
AUSTIN .... YOUR PROFESSIONAL SECRETARY .... (Volume 17)

SECURED EMAIL

DISTRICT OF COLUMBIA
WASHINGTON .... TENFOUR US, INC. .... (Volume 5)

SECURITIES LITIGATION CONSULTING SERVICES

CALIFORNIA
LOS ANGELES .... SECURITIES RECEIVABLE ARBITRATION, INC. .... (Volume 2)

NEW JERSEY
NEWARK .... S.D. KRASNER ASSOCIATES .... (Volume 12)

TECHNICAL, MANAGEMENT AND FINANCIAL EXPERTS

TEXAS

DALLAS .... LAW FIRM MANAGEMENT CONSULTING, INC. .... (Volume 17)

TELECONFERENCING

FLORIDA

MIAMI .... MIVNET .... (Volume 6)

TEMPORARY ATTORNEY SERVICES

CALIFORNIA

LOS ANGELES .... ZISKIND GREENE CONTRACT ATTORNEYS & PARALEGALS .... (Volume 2)

DISTRICT OF COLUMBIA

WASHINGTON .... ADJUNCTLEGAL .... (Volume 5)

GEORGIA

ATLANTA .... BELLON & ASSOCIATES, INC. .... (Volume 7)

ILLINOIS

CHICAGO .... LAWCORPS® LEGAL STAFFING SERVICES .... (Volume 8)

NEW YORK

NEW YORK .... ELAINE P. DINE TEMPORARY ATTORNEYS & PARALEGALS LLC .... (Volume 13)

TIME BILLING SOFTWARE/SYSTEMS

CALIFORNIA

LOS ANGELES .... JURIS, INC. .... (Volume 2)
TIMEBILLS.COM .... (Volume 2)

FLORIDA

ORLANDO .... ADC LEGAL SYSTEMS, INC. .... (Volume 6)
TALLAHASSEE .... CMS/DATA CORPORATION ® .... (Volume 6)

MASSACHUSETTS

BOSTON .... EVELOCITY CORPORATION .... (Volume 10)

NEW YORK

ROCHESTER .... GOODHAND COMPUTING SOLUTIONS .... (Volume 12)

NORTH CAROLINA

RALEIGH .... ADC LEGAL SYSTEMS, INC. .... (Volume 14)

TEXAS

DALLAS .... SAGE U.S. INCORPORATED .... (Volume 17)

TITLE & ABSTRACT COMPANIES

ARKANSAS

FORREST CITY .... FORREST CITY/ST. FRANCIS COUNTY ABSTRACT CO. INC. .... (Volume 1)

CONNECTICUT

HARTFORD .... INTEGRATED LOAN SERVICES .... (Volume 4)

GEORGIA

ATLANTA .... PARALEGAL RESOURCES .... (Volume 7)

MASSACHUSETTS

WORCESTER .... TAYLOR ABSTRACT COMPANY .... (Volume 10)

NEW JERSEY

MILLBURN .... ACRES LAND TITLE AGENCY, INC. .... (Volume 12)
MORRISTOWN .... PROGRESSIVE TITLE AGENCY, INC. .... (Volume 12)

OHIO

CLEVELAND .... ATTORNEY SERVICES OF NORTHEAST OHIO .... (Volume 14)

OKLAHOMA

MUSKOGEE .... PIONEER ABSTRACT & TITLE .... (Volume 14)

TENNESSEE

CHATTANOOGA .... MILLIGAN-REYNOLDS GUARANTY TITLE AGENCY, INC. .... (Volume 16)

TEXAS

LAREDO .... NEEL TITLE CORPORATION .... (Volume 17)

TITLE INSURANCE

GEORGIA

ATLANTA .... SOUTHLAND TITLE COMPANY .... (Volume 7)

ILLINOIS

CHICAGO .... CHICAGO TITLE INSURANCE COMPANY .... (Volume 8)

TRANSCRIPTION SERVICES - Continued

KANSAS

KANSAS CITY .... LEGAL LANGUAGE SERVICES .... (Volume 9)

MARYLAND

BALTIMORE .... LEGAL LANGUAGE SERVICES .... (Volume 9)
STEN-TEL .... (Volume 9)

MASSACHUSETTS

BOSTON .... ROBERT H. LANGE CO. INC. .... (Volume 10)
STEN-TEL .... (Volume 10)

MICHIGAN

DETROIT .... HANSON/RENAISSANCE COURT REPORTERS .... (Volume 10)
KALAMAZOO .... GERGER-MORETTI REPORTING .... (Volume 10)

MISSOURI

KANSAS CITY .... LEGAL LANGUAGE SERVICES .... (Volume 11)
ST. LOUIS .... LEGAL LANGUAGE SERVICES .... (Volume 11)

NEVADA

LAS VEGAS .... BUTTERFIELD & BUTTERFIELD .... (Volume 11)
LAURIE WEBB & ASSOCIATES .... (Volume 11)
LEGAL LANGUAGE SERVICES .... (Volume 11)

NEW JERSEY

NEWARK .... LEGAL LANGUAGE SERVICES .... (Volume 12)
MARSHALL GOLDBERG ASSOCIATES .... (Volume 12)
STEN-TEL .... (Volume 12)
TOMS RIVER .... COLE TRANSCRIPTION AND RECORDING SERVICE .... (Volume 12)
TRENTON .... MARSHALL GOLDBERG ASSOCIATES .... (Volume 12)

NEW MEXICO

ALBUQUERQUE .... WORDCENTER, INC. .... (Volume 12)

NEW YORK

ALBANY .... PRIDE TRANSCRIPTION .... (Volume 12)
BUFFALO .... STEN-TEL .... (Volume 12)
NEW YORK .... COMPU-CRAFT BUSINESS SERVICE .... (Volume 13)
EXECUTIVE OFFICE SERVICES .... (Volume 13)
LEGAL LANGUAGE SERVICES .... (Volume 13)
STEN-TEL .... (Volume 13)

OREGON

PORTLAND .... LNS COURT REPORTING .... (Volume 15)
SALEM .... LNS COURT REPORTING .... (Volume 15)

PENNSYLVANIA

ALTOONA .... ASAP COURT REPORTING / STEN-TEL, INC. .... (Volume 15)
PHILADELPHIA .... STEN-TEL .... (Volume 15)

TEXAS

AUSTIN .... YOUR PROFESSIONAL SECRETARY .... (Volume 17)
DALLAS .... ARLINGTON COURT REPORTING, INC. .... (Volume 17)
STEN-TEL .... (Volume 17)
FORT WORTH .... ARLINGTON COURT REPORTING, INC. .... (Volume 17)
HOUSTON .... LEGAL LANGUAGE SERVICES .... (Volume 17)
STEN-TEL .... (Volume 17)
SAN ANTONIO .... LEGAL LANGUAGE SERVICES .... (Volume 17)

VIRGINIA

RICHMOND .... LEGAL LANGUAGE SERVICES .... (Volume 18)

WASHINGTON

SEATTLE .... BYERS & ANDERSON, INC. .... (Volume 18)
LEGAL LANGUAGE SERVICES .... (Volume 18)
TACOMA .... TACOMA MEDICAL TRANSCRIPTION .... (Volume 18)
VANCOUVER .... LNS COURT REPORTING .... (Volume 18)

TRANSLATION SERVICES

CALIFORNIA

BERKELEY .... BERKELEY SCIENTIFIC TRANSLATION SERVICE, INC. .... (Volume 2)
LOS ANGELES .... BERLITZ INTERPRETATION AND TRANSLATION SERVICES .... (Volume 2)
INTERLINGUA.COM, INC. .... (Volume 2)
INTERLINGUA EXPRESS .... (Volume 2)
JLS LANGUAGE CORPORATION .... (Volume 2)
THE LANGUAGE WORKS, INC. .... (Volume 2)
LEGAL LANGUAGE SERVICES .... (Volume 2)
THE LEGAL TRANSLATORS.COM .... (Volume 2)

TRANSLATION SERVICES - Continued

NEW YORK

City	Firm	Volume
ALBANY	LEGAL LANGUAGE SERVICES	(Volume 12)
	ONE WORLD LANGUAGE SERVICES	(Volume 12)
BUFFALO	LEGAL LANGUAGE SERVICES	(Volume 12)
MINEOLA	LEGAL LANGUAGE SERVICES	(Volume 12)
NEW YORK	800-TRANSLATE	(Volume 13)
	ACCENT ON LANGUAGE	(Volume 13)
	ALL-LANGUAGE SERVICES, INC.	(Volume 13)
	AMERICAN LINGUISTS INTERPRETERS & TRANSLATORS, INC.	(Volume 13)
	BERLITZ INTERPRETATION AND TRANSLATION SERVICES	(Volume 13)
	GINETTE CESAR	(Volume 13)
	RALITSA R. COMBS	(Volume 13)
	EURONET LANGUAGE SERVICES, INC.	(Volume 13)
	INTERNATIONAL LIAISON, LTD.	(Volume 13)
	JAPAN COMMUNICATION CONSULTANTS, LLC	(Volume 13)
	JLS LANGUAGE CORPORATION	(Volume 13)
	THE JURIDICAL IT, INC.	(Volume 13)
	LANGUAGE PROS, LLC	(Volume 13)
	THE LANGUAGE WORKS, INC.	(Volume 13)
	LCS LANGUAGE & CULTURAL SERVICES	(Volume 13)
	LEGAL LANGUAGE SERVICES	(Volume 13)
	THE LEGAL TRANSLATORS.COM	(Volume 13)
	LEXIT	(Volume 13)
	DAVID N. MARINELLI	(Volume 13)
	NTEXT TRANSLATIONS	(Volume 13)
	ANNA MARIA PALMISANO	(Volume 13)
	PROFESSIONAL GERMAN TRANSLATIONS	(Volume 13)
	NICOLE THIBAUD	(Volume 13)
	WORLDWIDE TRANSLATIONS, INC.	(Volume 13)

OHIO

City	Firm	Volume
CINCINNATI	LEGAL LANGUAGE SERVICES	(Volume 14)
CLEVELAND	LEGAL LANGUAGE SERVICES	(Volume 14)

PENNSYLVANIA

City	Firm	Volume
PHILADELPHIA	3I COMPANY	(Volume 15)
	BERLITZ INTERPRETATION AND TRANSLATION SERVICES	(Volume 15)
	LEGAL LANGUAGE SERVICES	(Volume 15)

RHODE ISLAND

City	Firm	Volume
PROVIDENCE	TRANSLATION & INTERPRETING GROUP	(Volume 16)

TEXAS

City	Firm	Volume
AUSTIN	CRISTINA HELMERICHS D.	(Volume 17)
DALLAS	ALLIANCE LANGUAGE SERVICES	(Volume 17)
	BERLITZ INTERPRETATION AND TRANSLATION SERVICES	(Volume 17)
	LEGAL LANGUAGE SERVICES	(Volume 17)
	THE LEGAL TRANSLATORS.COM	(Volume 17)
HOUSTON	BERLITZ INTERPRETATION AND TRANSLATION SERVICES	(Volume 17)
	LEGAL LANGUAGE SERVICES	(Volume 17)
	THE LEGAL TRANSLATORS.COM	(Volume 17)
	WORLDWIDE TRANSLATIONS, INC.	(Volume 17)
SAN ANTONIO	LEGAL LANGUAGE SERVICES	(Volume 17)

VIRGINIA

City	Firm	Volume
FALLS CHURCH	LANGUAGES INCORPORATED	(Volume 18)
RICHMOND	LEGAL LANGUAGE SERVICES	(Volume 18)

WASHINGTON

City	Firm	Volume
SEATTLE	BERLITZ INTERPRETATION AND TRANSLATION SERVICES	(Volume 18)
	LEGAL LANGUAGE SERVICES	(Volume 18)

TRANSPORTATION ENGINEERING - CONSULTING & FORENSIC SERVICES

FLORIDA

City	Firm	Volume
JACKSONVILLE	R.H. DUNN & ASSOCIATES, INC.	(Volume 6)

VIRGINIA

City	Firm	Volume
ALEXANDRIA	TRANSPORTATION RESEARCH CORPORATION	(Volume 18)
NORFOLK	R.H. DUNN & ASSOCIATES, INC.	(Volume 18)
RICHMOND	R.H. DUNN & ASSOCIATES, INC.	(Volume 18)

UCC FILING - PUBLICATIONS - Continued

OHIO

AKRON .... OHIO PARALEGAL SERVICES, INC. .... (Volume 14)

UCC SEARCH SERVICES

ARKANSAS

LITTLE ROCK .... QUEST RESEARCH .... (Volume 1)

CALIFORNIA

SACRAMENTO .... IQ DATA SYSTEMS .... (Volume 3)

COLORADO

DENVER .... COLORADO RECORDS SEARCH, INC. .... (Volume 4)

FLORIDA

PENSACOLA .... COASTAL OFFICE DIMENSIONS .... (Volume 6)

KENTUCKY

LEXINGTON .... LAURA A. LIVINGSTON D/B/A EQUISEARCH .... (Volume 9)

NEW YORK

ALBANY .... ACCESS INFORMATION SERVICES, INC. .... (Volume 12)
NEW YORK .... INTERCOUNTY CLEARANCE CORPORATION .... (Volume 13)

NORTH CAROLINA

CHARLOTTE .... NATIONAL DATA ACCESS CORPORATION .... (Volume 14)
GREENSBORO .... NATIONAL DATA ACCESS CORPORATION .... (Volume 14)
RALEIGH .... NATIONAL DATA ACCESS CORPORATION .... (Volume 14)

OHIO

AKRON .... OHIO PARALEGAL SERVICES, INC. .... (Volume 14)

PENNSYLVANIA

PITTSBURGH .... PENNCORP SERVICEGROUP INC. .... (Volume 15)

SOUTH CAROLINA

COLUMBIA .... NATIONAL DATA ACCESS CORPORATION .... (Volume 16)
GREENVILLE .... NATIONAL DATA ACCESS CORPORATION .... (Volume 16)
SPARTANBURG .... NATIONAL DATA ACCESS CORPORATION .... (Volume 16)

WASHINGTON

SEATTLE .... DILIGENZ .... (Volume 18)

UNEMPLOYMENT HEARINGS & APPEALS CONSULTANTS

FLORIDA

POMPANO BEACH .... NORMAN B. SELLINGER .... (Volume 6)

VALUATION SERVICES

NEW YORK

NEW YORK .... ECO-STAT CORPORATION .... (Volume 13)

VIDEO CONFERENCING

CALIFORNIA

LOS ANGELES .... ENLIGHTEN ™ TECHNOLOGIES INCORPORATED BY LAWCHECK ® .... (Volume 2)

FLORIDA

MIAMI .... ENLIGHTEN ™ TECHNOLOGIES INCORPORATED BY LAWCHECK ® .... (Volume 6)

NEW YORK

NEW YORK .... ENLIGHTEN ™ TECHNOLOGIES INCORPORATED BY LAWCHECK ® ...... (Volume 13)

TEXAS

DALLAS .... ENLIGHTEN ™ TECHNOLOGIES INCORPORATED BY LAWCHECK ® ...... (Volume 17)

VIDEO PRODUCTION, EDITING & GRAPHICS

COLORADO

DENVER .... WREN VIDEO SERVICES .... (Volume 4)

CONNECTICUT

NEW HAVEN .... GEOMATRIX PRODUCTIONS .... (Volume 4)

ILLINOIS

CHICAGO .... IMAGE RESOURCES, INC. .... (Volume 8)
LITICORP .... (Volume 8)

VIDEO TAPE SERVICES

VIDEO TAPE SERVICES - Continued

FLORIDA - Continued

City	Firm	Volume
TAMPA	CERTIFIED COURT REPORTERS, INC.	(Volume 6)
	ROBERT A. DEMPSTER & ASSOCIATES	(Volume 6)
	SCLAFANI WILLIAMS COURT REPORTERS, INC.	(Volume 6)

GEORGIA

City	Firm	Volume
ATLANTA	AMERICAN COURT REPORTING COMPANY	(Volume 7)
	DESKTOP VIDEO PRODUCTIONS, INC.	(Volume 7)

ILLINOIS

City	Firm	Volume
CHICAGO	A-1 LEGAL VIDEO	(Volume 8)
	LITICORP	(Volume 8)
	NORTH SUBURBAN REPORTING & LEGAL MEDIA, INC.	(Volume 8)
	WICHMANN REPORTING SERVICE	(Volume 8)
MOLINE	CONNELL REPORTING	(Volume 8)
SPRINGFIELD	BALDWIN COURT REPORTING AND LEGAL-VISUAL SERVICES	(Volume 8)

INDIANA

City	Firm	Volume
INDIANAPOLIS	LEGAL VIDEO SERVICES, INC.	(Volume 8)

KENTUCKY

City	Firm	Volume
LOUISVILLE	FULTON-BELANGER & ASSOCIATES	(Volume 9)

LOUISIANA

City	Firm	Volume
NEW ORLEANS	A-LEGAL VIDEO SERVICE	(Volume 9)
SHREVEPORT	ALLIED COURT REPORTING SERVICE	(Volume 9)

MASSACHUSETTS

City	Firm	Volume
BOSTON	BOSTON COURT REPORTING	(Volume 10)
	CATUOGNO COURT REPORTING SERVICE, INC.	(Volume 10)
	JONES FRITZ & SHEEHAN	(Volume 10)
SPRINGFIELD	CATUOGNO COURT REPORTING SERVICE, INC.	(Volume 10)

MICHIGAN

City	Firm	Volume
ANN ARBOR	CHRISTINE FELTS & ASSOCIATES	(Volume 10)
DETROIT	CHRISTINE FELTS & ASSOCIATES	(Volume 10)
	HANSON/RENAISSANCE COURT REPORTERS	(Volume 10)
FLINT	CHRISTINE FELTS & ASSOCIATES	(Volume 10)
KALAMAZOO	CHRISTINE FELTS & ASSOCIATES	(Volume 10)
LANSING	CHRISTINE FELTS & ASSOCIATES	(Volume 10)
SOUTHFIELD	DE SCRIBE REPORTING, INC.	(Volume 10)
TROY	CHRISTINE FELTS & ASSOCIATES	(Volume 10)

MINNESOTA

City	Firm	Volume
MINNEAPOLIS	PC&A LITIGATION SUPPORT SERVICES	(Volume 11)
	PRO-SYSTEMS COURT REPORTING & VIDEO SERVICES	(Volume 11)
ST. PAUL	LEGAL VIDEO, INC.	(Volume 11)

MISSOURI

City	Firm	Volume
ST. LOUIS	GORE & PERRY REPORTING COMPANY	(Volume 11)
	METRO COURT REPORTING, INC.	(Volume 11)

NEBRASKA

City	Firm	Volume
OMAHA	THINK VIDEO	(Volume 11)
	THOMAS & THOMAS COURT REPORTERS & CERTIFIED LEGAL VIDEO	(Volume 11)

NEVADA

City	Firm	Volume
LAS VEGAS	LAURIE WEBB & ASSOCIATES	(Volume 11)
	N.T.V. PRODUCTIONS LEGAL SERVICES	(Volume 11)

NEW JERSEY

City	Firm	Volume
NEWARK	COURT REPORTING SERVICES, INC.	(Volume 12)
	NATIONWIDE VIDEO PRODUCTIONS	(Volume 12)
ROSELAND	NATIONWIDE VIDEO PRODUCTIONS	(Volume 12)

NEW YORK

City	Firm	Volume
MINEOLA	TANKOOS REPORTING COMPANY, INC.	(Volume 12)
NEW YORK	ACTION LEGAL VIDEO, INC.	(Volume 13)
	JUPITER LEGAL VIDEO SERVICES	(Volume 13)
	NEW YORK LEGAL VIDEO SERVICES	(Volume 13)
	TANKOOS REPORTING COMPANY, INC.	(Volume 13)

NORTH CAROLINA

City	Firm	Volume
CHAPEL HILL	BODENHEIMER VERBATIM REPORTING	(Volume 14)
DURHAM	BODENHEIMER VERBATIM REPORTING	(Volume 14)

OHIO

City	Firm	Volume
CINCINNATI	ACE REPORTING SERVICES	(Volume 14)
CLEVELAND	C & G	(Volume 14)

VIDEO TELECONFERENCING

VIDEO TRIAL PRESENTATIONS

VIOLENCE IN THE WORKPLACE

COLORADO

DENVER .... BUSINESS CONTROLS, INC. .... (Volume 4)

VOCATIONAL DISABILITY ASSESSMENT

TENNESSEE

JOHNSON CITY .... SPANGLER & ASSOCIATES, LLC .... (Volume 16)

VOCATIONAL EVALUATIONS/LIFE CARE PLANNING

ALABAMA

BIRMINGHAM .... MARY HOUSE KESSLER, PH.D. .... (Volume 1)

ALASKA

ANCHORAGE .... MTL SERVICES .... (Volume 1)

ARIZONA

PHOENIX .... VOCATIONAL DIAGNOSTICS, INC. .... (Volume 1)

CONNECTICUT

HARTFORD .... RONALD FREEDMAN, M.ED. CRC, LPC .... (Volume 4)

FLORIDA

MIAMI .... REHABILITATION SERVICES, INC. .... (Volume 6)

MICHIGAN

LANSING .... CARE MANAGERS, INC. .... (Volume 10)

VOCATIONAL REHABILITATION

PENNSYLVANIA

PHILADELPHIA .... KCS CONSULTING SERVICES, INC. .... (Volume 15)

WEATHER & CLIMATE

CALIFORNIA

LOS ANGELES .... CONTINENTAL WEATHER & EARTH SCIENCES, INC. .... (Volume 2)

WEB DESIGN - INTERNET CONSULTING

CALIFORNIA

LOS ANGELES .... FB&B CONSULTING GROUP, INC. .... (Volume 2)
SANTA CLARA .... FIRST E COMMERCE .... (Volume 3)

WHITE COLLAR CRIMINAL/FRAUD INVESTIGATION

CALIFORNIA

LOS ANGELES .... BCA PROTECTIVE & INVESTIGATIVE SERVICES .... (Volume 2)

DISTRICT OF COLUMBIA

WASHINGTON .... VANCE INTERNATIONAL, INC. .... (Volume 5)

GEORGIA

ATLANTA .... INVESTIGATIVE SOLUTIONS, INC. .... (Volume 7)

LOUISIANA

METAIRIE .... LAPORTE, SEHRT, ROMIG & HAND .... (Volume 9)

NEW JERSEY

ATLANTIC CITY .... SARAO & ASSOCIATES ™ .... (Volume 12)
HACKENSACK .... SARAO & ASSOCIATES ™ .... (Volume 12)

NEW YORK

SCHENECTADY .... THE PECORARO GROUP .... (Volume 13)

TEXAS

AUSTIN .... PROFILE INFORMATION SERVICES .... (Volume 17)